The Princeton Review®

PrincetonReview.com

THE COMPLETE BOOK OF COLLEGES

2016 EDITION

Penguin
Random
House

The Princeton Review
24 Prime Parkway, Suite 201
Natick, MA 01760
editorialsupport@review.com

Published in the United States by Penguin Random
House LLC, New York, and in Canada by Random
House of Canada, a division of Penguin Random
House Ltd.,Toronto. This is a revised edition of a
book first published in 1989.

ISBN: 978-0-8041-2631-1
ISSN: 1088-8594

Production: Best Content Solutions, LLC
Production Editor: Melissa Duclos-Yourdon

Printed in the United States of America.

9 8 7 6 5 4 3 2 1

2016 Edition

The Princeton Review is not affiliated with Princeton
University.

Editorial

Robert Franek, Publisher
David Soto, Director of Content Development
Kristen O'Toole, Editorial Director
Stephen Koch, Student Survey Manager
Pia Aliperti, Editor

Random House Publishing Team

Tom Russell, Publisher
Alison Stoltzfus, Publishing Manager
Ellen L. Reed, Production Manager
Melinda Ackell, Managing Editor
Kristin Lindner, Production Supervisor
Andrea Lau, Designer

ACKNOWLEDGMENTS

Each year we assemble an awe-inspiringly talented group of colleagues who work together to produce our guidebooks; this year is no exception. Everyone involved in this effort—authors, editors, data collectors, production specialists, and designers—gives so much more than is required to make *The Complete Book of Colleges* an exceptional student resource guide.

My sincere thanks go to the many who contributed to this tremendous project. Very special thanks go to Kristen O'Toole for her editorial commitment and vision. A warm and special thank you goes to our Student Survey expert, Stephen Koch, who continues to work in partnership with school administrators and students alike. My continued thanks go to our data collection pro, David Soto, for his successful efforts in collecting and accurately representing the statistical data that appear with each college profile and to Melissa Duclos-Yourdon for her dedication to reading through the massive amounts of data. The enormousness of this project and its deadline constraints could not have been realized without the calm presence of our production partner, Scott Harris. Scott's many years of dedication and focus continue to delight and remind me of what a pleasure it is to work together on this project each year. Special thanks also go to Jeanne Krier, our Random House publicist, for the dedicated work she continues to do on this book and the overall series since its inception. Jeanne continues to be my trusted colleague, media advisor, and friend. I would also like to make special mention of Tom Russell and Alison Stoltzfus, our Random House publishing team, for their continuous investment and faith in our ideas. Last, I thank my Princeton Review Partner Team, Mandy Ginsberg, Sharon Van Wyck, Jennifer Kohn, Casey Cornelius, Vincent Jungels, Shar Dubey, and Clark Rothrock, for their confidence in me and my content team and for their commitment to providing students the resources they need to find the right fit school for them. Again, to all who contributed so much to this publication, thank you for your efforts; they do not go unnoticed.

Robert Franek
SVP—Publisher

CONTENTS

CONTENTS

FOREWORD

Welcome. You have found the best place to begin, fine-tune, and execute the search for your perfect college. With the understanding that choosing a school wisely is a top priority for each prospective student, we have provided a significant breadth of information in this text to help you navigate the exciting, amazing, and sometimes confusing process of choosing the right college.

The design of this guidebook will allow you to narrow your search of colleges from 1,573 to a few dozen. Here you'll find all the individual college statistics you'll need to make informed choices about the competitiveness, size, location, and academic offerings of the schools available to you. In addition, you can find even more information about individual schools at The Princeton Review's website, PrincetonReview. com. The site includes college search features, college profiles, college discussion boards, a college majors search engine, and much more.

By using this book, you can search for, choose, and apply to colleges with the confidence of a pro—or at the very least a well-informed undergraduate hopeful! We supply the information and guidance, and you ultimately make your own decision.

The college selection, application, and interview processes can be overwhelming at times. They can also be rewarding experiences. For most, choosing a college is the first major life decision. I know it was mine. Remember that your college decision is yours alone, so arm yourself with the best available information. Badger teachers, friends, high school and college admissions counselors, brothers, sisters, and parents; ask them how they chose their colleges and why. The more you know when beginning the process, the more in control of the situation you'll feel.

Whatever it is that you choose as your path in life, your college selection will forever be your first step in that direction. The friends you make, the professors you meet, and the classes you take are all springboards to the next phase of your life.

I wish you much luck and success at whichever college you decide to attend. My sincere hope is that this publication and other Princeton Review tools will be helpful in the process.

Robert Franek
SVP, Publisher

INTRODUCTION

Before you dive into *The Complete Book of Colleges*, we want to give you some tips for your college search—especially on how to get the most out of this book and what to do once you've made your choices and are ready to apply. Since the most important thing for you to do now is to start your search, we want to start right off by revealing the secret to getting admitted to the college of your choice.

It's almost never the focus of talk about college admissions in the media, and parents and students discuss the subject all the time without even realizing that it's the crucial element to getting admitted. We're talking about matchmaking: that is, finding colleges that have the educational and social environments you're looking for, where you are well-suited academically and have something the college is looking for in return. You have a lot more control over where you end up going to college than you might think.

Matchmaking is a two-step process. You should begin with a thorough self-examination or personal inventory. Your personal inventory is best structured in the form of a chart, so that when you begin to consider your options, you can check off those colleges that satisfy the various needs or wants you've identified. In this way, your best college choices will gradually begin to identify themselves.

Divide your inventory into two sections. One section should be biographical, including your high school course selection, GPA, SAT or ACT scores, class rank, and personal information like extracurricular activities—especially those you plan to continue in college. This will help you to assess how you stack up against each college's admissions standards and student body. The second section is a listing of the characteristics you need or want in the college you'll choose to attend. This list should include anything and everything you consider important, such as location, size of the student body, availability of scholarships, dormitory options, clubs and activities, even school colors if you want. This part of your inventory should grow continuously as you become more and more aware of what is important to you in your choice of colleges.

Armed with your personal inventory, you can begin to take advantage of the numerous resources available to help you narrow your choices of where to apply. There are five sources for information and advice that have become standard for most college-bound students:

1. College admissions brochures, websites, videos, and catalogs

If you are a junior or senior in high school, you probably know more about the kinds of information these materials should include than the people who are responsible for designing and writing them. No college that spends half a million dollars on glossy literature is going to be objective about its content. In the best of this material, you can probably get a decent idea of the academic offerings and the basic admissions requirements. In all of it, you will never see anything but the most appealing architecture and the best-looking students on campus, nor will you hear about the recent tuition increases that were greater than the rate of inflation. Look these materials over, but don't make any decisions based solely on what you read or see.

2. Your friends

No one knows colleges and universities better than the students who currently attend them. Seek out any and all of your friends, sons and daughters of family friends, and recent graduates of your high school who attend colleges that you are considering. Talk to them when they come home. Arrange to stay with them when you visit their colleges. Pick their brains for everything they know. It doesn't get any more direct and honest than this.

3. Books and college guides

There are two types of books that can be helpful to you in your search: those that discuss specific aspects of going to college and college guides. A great narrative guide that stresses students' own opinions of colleges is our own *The Best 380 Colleges*. In addition, look at other guides for good second opinions. As for comprehensive guides—those that emphasize data over narrative content—you're holding the most up-to-date and useful one in your hands.

4. Computers

There's a lot of help out there. Using our site, PrincetonReview.com, is the best way to find the right school for you and prepare for college.

5. Your counselor

Since it's *critically* important, we'll say it again: Once you've developed some ideas about your personal inventory and college options, schedule a meeting with your guidance counselor. The more research you've done before you get together, the more help you're likely to get. Good advice comes out of thoughtful discussion, not from the expectation that your counselor will do your work. When it comes time to file applications, look over the materials and requirements together, and allow plenty of time to put forth your best.

USING COLLEGE INFORMATION IN THE COMPLETE BOOK OF COLLEGES AND ELSEWHERE

Throughout the course of your college search, you'll confront an amazing array of statistics and other data related to every college you consider. In order for all of this information to be helpful, you need to have some sense of how to interpret it. We've included a detailed key to the college entries in this book a few pages deeper into this introduction. Almost all the statistics we've compiled are self-explanatory, but there are a few that will be more useful with some elaboration.

Let's start with student/teacher ratio. Don't use it to assess average class size; they are not interchangeable terms. At almost every college, the average class size is larger than its student/teacher ratio. At many big universities, it is considerably larger. What is useful about the ratio is that it can give you an idea of how accessible your professors will be outside of the classroom. Once you are in college, you'll grow to realize just how important this is.

In the same way, the percentage of faculty who hold PhDs is useful information. When you're paying thousands of dollars in tuition each year, there's something comforting about knowing that your professors have a considerably broader and deeper grasp of what you're studying than you do. In contrast, teaching assistants (TAs) may often be just one or two steps ahead of you.

Another interesting group of statistics deals with the percentage of students who go on to graduate or professional school. Never allow yourself to be swayed by such statistics, unless you've taken the time to ponder their meaning and visited the college in question. High percentages almost always mean one of two things: that the college is an intellectual enclave that inspires students onward to further their education, or that it is a pre-professional bastion of aggressive careerists. There isn't anything inherently wrong with either scenario, but neither has universal appeal to prospective students. Colleges that are exceptions to this rule are rare and precious. The most misleading figures provided to prospective students are those for medical school acceptance rates. Virtually every college in the country can boast of high acceptance rates to medical school for its graduates; pre-med programs are designed to weed out those who will not be strong candidates before they even get to apply! If you're thinking about medical school, ask colleges how many of their students apply to medical school each year. Also, try to get a sense of the attrition rate within the pre-med program.

One final piece of advice about statistics relates to the college's acceptance rate. Simply knowing the percentage of applicants who are admitted each year is helpful, but it is even more helpful if you also know how many applied. When you compare these figures to the freshman profile, you have the most accurate picture of just how tough it is to get in. An 80 percent acceptance rate doesn't mean there's an open door if you don't match up well to the academic achievements of the college's typical freshman. Beyond this, keep an eye out for colleges that have relatively self-selecting applicant pools. In these cases, high acceptance rates may be misleading. When evaluating highly selective public colleges as an out-of-state applicant, remember that you will likely face a more selective evaluation than state residents.

A Few Final Thoughts

Once you've narrowed down your options and decided where to apply, find the applications on PrincetonReview.com and get to work filling them out. The admissions process is stressful enough without putting extra pressure on yourself by waiting until the last minute. The first thing you should do when you receive the necessary forms is go over them with your guidance counselor. Immediately remove the recommendation forms (if they are required) and give them to the teachers and counselor(s) who will be completing them for you. They'll have a better opportunity to write a thorough and supportive recommendation if you give them enough time to complete them. This is also the time to make your request for official transcripts. Again, it takes time to do these things. Plan ahead.

As for completing the applications, organize yourself and all the materials. Keep everything in folders and accessible in case you need to speak with an admissions officer over the telephone. When essays and information on your extracurricular activities are required, do some outlining and rough draft-writing before you commit yourself to the actual forms or online tools.

Paying for college requires some of your attention too. Though we don't have nearly enough space to go into such a complicated and stressful subject now, it's very important that you get to work on your financial circumstances right away. Keep in mind that while college is costly, few people pay the "sticker price." Regardless, you have to have your finances in order before you can get the most financial aid possible. We've developed a financial center on PrincetonReview.com to help demystify the sometimes bewildering task of financing your education. You can also find the most exhaustive strategies for financing your education in our book *Paying for College Without Going Broke*.

Last but not least, **don't take it easy during your senior year!** Colleges routinely request mid-year grades, and they expect you to continue taking challenging academic courses and keep your grades up throughout your high school career. Doing so takes you one step closer to getting good news. On behalf of The Princeton Review, have a good time, and good luck. See you on campus!

Nota Bene

The data reported in this book, unless otherwise noted, was collected from the profiled colleges from the fall of 2013 through the spring of 2014. In some cases, we were unable to publish the most recent data because schools did not report the necessary statistics to us in time, despite our repeated outreach efforts. Because enrollment and financial statistics as well as application and financial aid deadlines fluctuate from one year to another, we recommend that you check to make sure you have the most current information before applying. Best of luck!

HOW THE COMPLETE BOOK OF COLLEGES IS ORGANIZED

There are two types of profiles in this book. Not every school listed will have both. All of the 1,573 colleges and universities included in this book have their own informational profiles, and each entry follows the same basic format. Many of the institutions also have special two-page portraits located at the back of the book. These are written by the colleges and universities that wanted to present detailed descriptions of their campuses and programs.

Unless noted in the descriptions below, the Admissions Services Division of The Princeton Review collected all of the data presented in the informational profiles. As is customary with college guides, all data reflect figures for the academic year prior to publication, unless otherwise indicated. Since college offerings and demographics vary significantly from one institution to another and some colleges report data more thoroughly than others, few entries will include all of the individual data points described below.

The Heading

This section includes school name, address, telephone number, fax number, e-mail address, website, financial aid telephone number, and college code numbers for both the College Board (CEEB) and the American College Testing Program (ACT) when applicable. All website addresses were accurate and functioning at the time of publication. Check PrincetonReview.com for the most up-to-date links to colleges.

The Icons

The icons are a feature we hope will make using *The Complete Book of Colleges* easier. Icons appear under the school name for schools that are profiled in *The Best 380 Colleges*.

The Blurb

Describes the college or university. Includes all available data that relate to the date of founding of the school, religious affiliation, whether the school is public or private, and campus size.

Ratings

This section includes the school's Fire Safety Rating, its Admissions Selectivity Rating, and its Green Rating.

Admissions Selectivity Rating

The number listed for each college is The Princeton Review's exclusive rating of admissions competitiveness. It is a very general assessment determined by several factors, among which are the school's acceptance rate, and the class rank and average test scores of entering first-year students. By incorporating all these factors, the rating adjusts for "self-selecting" applicant pools. *Note:* The Selectivity Rating for visual and performing arts schools are approximations only. Estimated Selectivity Ratings are included to give you a general idea of where they fit in the selectivity scale, but auditions and portfolios carry the greatest weight in admissions decisions.

Schools that received an Admissions Selectivity rating of 60* did not supply sufficient data for proper calculation of this rating. By default, these schools are given this rating, although their rating may have been significantly higher had they supplied sufficient data.

Fire Safety

We asked all the schools from which we collect data annually to answer several questions about their efforts to ensure fire safety for campus residents. Each school's responses to nine of those questions were considered when calculating its Fire Safety Rating. The questions were developed in consultation with the Center for Campus Fire Safety (www.campusfire.org), and they cover: 1) The percentage of student housing sleeping rooms protected by an automatic fire sprinkler system with a fire sprinkler head located in the individual sleeping rooms; 2) The percentage of student housing sleeping rooms equipped with a smoke detector connected to a supervised fire alarm system; 3) The number of malicious fire alarms that occur in student housing per year; 4) The number of unwanted fire alarms that occur in student housing per year; 5) The banning of certain hazardous items and activities in residence halls, like candles, smoking, halogen lamps, etc.; 6) The percentage of student housing building fire alarm systems that, if activated, result in a signal being transmitted to a monitored location on campus or the fire department.

Schools that did not report answers to any of the above questions receive a Fire Safety Rating of 60*. The schools have an opportunity to update their fire safety data every year and will have their fire safety ratings re-calculated and published annually.

Each individual rating places a college on a continuum for purposes of comparing all colleges within this academic year only. Though similar, these ratings are not intended to be compared directly to those that appeared on PrincetonReview. com in any prior academic year or within any Princeton Review print publication, except for *The Best 380 Colleges, 2016 Edition*. Our ratings computations are refined and change annually.

Students & Faculty

Enrollment
The total number of full-time undergraduates.

Student Body
The percentage of male, female, out-of-state, and international students, and the number of foreign countries represented.

Ethnic Representation
By percentage according to ethnic group. Figures may not add up to 100 percent, as student reporting of ethnicity is voluntary by law.

Retention and Graduation
The percentage of freshmen who return for sophomore year. The percentage of last year's seniors who entered as freshmen and graduated in four years. The percentage of graduates who pursue further study within one year. The percentage of graduates who pursue further study at law school. The percentage of graduates who pursue further study at business school. The percentage of graduates who pursue further study at medical school.

Faculty
The ratio of undergraduates to full-time faculty. The number of full-time instructional faculty. The percentage of faculty who hold PhDs. The percentage of faculty members who teach undergraduates.

Academics

Degrees
The types of degrees awarded to students.

Academic Requirements
Areas in which all or most students are required to complete some course work prior to graduation. Can include general education (nonspecific), arts / fine arts, computer literacy, philosophy, foreign languages, history, humanities, mathematics, English (including composition), sciences (biological or physical), social sciences, and other requirements as specified by each school.

Classes

Number of students in an average regular class and an average lab/discussion section.

Majors with Highest Enrollment

The most popular majors.

Special Study Options

May include accelerated programs, cross registration, cooperative (work-study) program, distance learning, double majors, dual enrollment, English as a Second Language, student exchange programs (domestic), external degree programs, honors programs, independent study, internships, liberal arts/career combinations, student-designed majors, study abroad, teacher certification programs, weekend college, and other options as specified by each school.

Facilities

Housing

Types of school-owned or affiliated housing available. May include coed dorms, women's dorms, men's dorms, apartments for married students, apartments for single students, special housing for disabled students, special housing for international students, fraternity/sorority housing, cooperative housing, and other options as specified by the school. The availability of assistance in finding off-campus housing. Any housing requirements that may exist, such as required on-campus residence for freshmen.

Special Academic Facilities/Equipment

Other facilities and equipment of note (e.g., nuclear reactor, on-campus elementary school for student teachers, scanning electron microscopes, and so forth).

Campus Life

Activities

Standard activities available. May include campus ministries, choral groups, concert band, dance, drama/theater, international student organization, jazz band, literary magazine, Model UN, musical ensembles, musical theater, opera, pep band, radio station, student film society, student government, student newspaper, symphony orchestra, television station, and yearbook.

Organizations
Total number of registered organizations, honor societies, religious organizations, fraternities, sororities.

Athletics
Intercollegiate athletics available, listed by sex.

Admissions

Freshman Academic Profile
Average high school GPA. Class rank distribution. The percentage from public high schools. Average SAT (Math, Critical Reading, and Writing sections) and/or ACT composite scores. Median range of SAT (Math, Critical Reading, and Writing sections) and/or ACT composite scores. Test of English as a Foreign Language (TOEFL) requirements for international students.

Basis for Candidate Selection
The criteria considered by the admissions committee in evaluating candidates. May include secondary school record, class rank, recommendations, standardized test scores, essay, interview, extracurricular activities, talent/ability, character/personal qualities, alumni/-ae relations, geographic residence, state residency, religious affiliation/commitment, minority status, volunteer work, work experience.

Freshman Admission Requirements
High school diploma/GED requirements. The number of academic units required or recommended in total and by academic subject. (Individual subject totals may not equal the complete sum of academic units required; in most cases, the difference is made up with electives. Check with the admissions office for any additional requirements.)

Freshman Admissions Statistics
The number of students who applied, the percentage of applicants who were accepted, and the percentage of those accepted who ultimately enrolled.

Transfer Admissions Requirements
Application requirements (may include high school transcript, college transcript, essay, interview, standardized tests, statement of good standing from prior school). Minimum high school GPA required. Minimum college GPA required. Lowest course grade transferable.

General Admissions Information

Application fee. Application deadlines. Admission notification date. "Rolling" indicates that decisions are sent to candidates as they are made, rather than held for a common notification date. Registration policy for terms other than the fall term. Common Application participation. Credit policies for College Entrance Examination Board Advanced Placement tests. Deferred admission policy.

Costs and Financial Aid

Tuition, room & board, fees, and books.

Required Forms and Deadlines

Forms that applicants for financial aid must file and their respective deadlines. May include FAFSA, institution's own financial aid form, CSS/Financial Aid PROFILE, business/farm supplement, state aid form, noncustodial (divorced/separated) parent statement, and other forms specified by the school. Deadlines for filing financial aid forms.

Notification of Awards

The date that notification of financial aid awards occurs. "Rolling" indicates that notification is ongoing—the sooner you complete all of your required financial aid paperwork, the sooner you'll hear about your package.

Types of Aid

Need-based scholarships and grants may include Federal Pell, SEOG, state scholarships/grants, private scholarships, college/university gift aid from institutional funds, United Negro College Fund, Federal Nursing Scholarship, and other resources as specified by the school. Loans may include Direct Subsidized Stafford Loans, Direct Unsubsidized Stafford Loans, Direct PLUS Loans, Federal Perkins Loans, Federal Nursing Loans, state loans, college/university loans from institutional funds, and other resources as specified by the school.

Student Employment

Availability of Federal Work-Study, a federal program that is need-based and part of most financial aid packages. Availability of part-time jobs direct from the college that are not based on need. The college's own assessment of part-time employment opportunities off campus.

Financial Aid Statistics

The percentage of freshmen who received some form of need-based financial aid. The percentage of undergraduates who received some form of need-based financial aid. The number of freshmen and undergrads who received an athletic scholarship or grant. The average amount of freshman scholarships and grants. The average amount of freshman loans. The average income from an on-campus job.

The Best 380 Colleges Icon

 Indicates whether the school can be found in our book, *The Best 380 Colleges*. In that book, each school has a detailed profile that includes the results of our surveys regarding student opinion, about many aspects of their schools and their educations.

COLLEGE DIRECTORY

ABILENE CHRISTIAN UNIVERSITY

ACU Box 29000, Abilene, TX 79699
Phone: 325-674-2650 · **Financial Aid Phone:** 325-674-2300
E-mail: info@admissions.acu.edu · **CEEB Code:** 6001
Fax: 325-674-2130 · **Website:** www.acu.edu · **ACT Code:** 4050

This private school, affiliated with the Church of Christ Church, was founded in 1906. It has a 208-acre campus.

RATINGS

Admissions Selectivity Rating: 88   **Fire Safety Rating:** 70

STUDENTS AND FACULTY

Enrollment: 3,572. **Student Body:** 58% female, 42% male, 14% out-of-state, 4% international (37 countries represented). Asian 1%, African American 8%, Caucasian 66%, Hispanic 14%, Native American <1%
Retention and Graduation: 45% freshmen graduate within 4 years. 62% freshmen graduate within 6 years. 36% grads go on to further study within 1 year. 20% grads pursue arts and sciences degrees. 1% grads pursue law degrees. 7% grads pursue business degrees. 6% grads pursue medical degrees. **Faculty:** 251 full-time faculty, 76% hold PhDs, 34% are members of minority groups, 10% are women. 1% of classes are taught by teaching assistants.

ACADEMICS

Degrees: associate, bachelor's, master's, post-bachelor's certificate, post-master's certificate. **Classes:** Most classes have 20–29 students. Most lab/discussion sessions have 10–19 students. **Majors with Highest Enrollment:** Business Administration and Management; Psychology; Accounting. **Special Study Options:** cross-registration, distance learning, double major, dual enrollment, English as a Second Language (ESL), honors program, independent study, internships, student-designed major, study abroad, teacher certification program. **Honors programs:** The Honors College offers highly motivated students extra stimulation and recognition in their course work, opportunities to work with selected faculty members and the chance to do independent projects in their major field. Ten percent of the ACU students participate. To graduate with University Honors requires 30 hours of Honors Courses. **Disability Services:** Special programs offered to physically disabled students include note-taking services, reader services, tape recorders. **Career services:** Alumni network, alumni services, career/job search classes, career assessment, internships. Career services highlights include the Body and Soul Pre-med program, College of Business Administration Leadership Deveopment.

FACILITIES

Housing: special housing for disabled students, men's dorms, special housing for international students, women's dorms. 95% of campus accessible to physically disabled. **Special Academic Facilities/Equipment:** Museum of university's history, biblical restoration studies center, voice institute, demonstration farm and ranch, observatory. **Computers:** 100% of classrooms, 100% of dorms, 100% of libraries, 100% of dining areas, 100% of student union, 87% of common outdoor areas have wireless network access. Students can register for classes online. Administrative functions (other than registration) can be performed online.

CAMPUS LIFE

Environment: City. **Activities:** Choral groups, concert band, drama/theater, jazz band, literary magazine, marching band, music ensembles, musical theater, opera, radio station, student government, student newspaper, symphony orchestra, television station, yearbook, Campus Ministries, International Student Organization. 108 registered organizations, 14 honor societies, 16 religious organizations. 4 fraternities, 7 sororities. **Athletics (Intercollegiate):** *Men:* baseball, basketball, cross-country, football, tennis, track/field (outdoor), track/field (indoor). *Women:* basketball, cross-country, soccer, softball, tennis, track/field (outdoor), track/field (indoor), volleyball. **On-Campus Highlights:** Learning Commons in Brown Library, Jacob's Dream Sculpture, World Famous Bean in McGlothlin Campus Cntr., Hunter Welcome Center, Williams Performing Arts Building, Abilene Christian University remains proud to be one of the first to catch the vision of the learning commons nationwide. The Learning Commons combines group work space with computers and Starbucks coffee inside the Library. **Environmental Initiatives:** Student initiatives including Recycle Mania, Campus Sustainability Day, Blue Bag Paper Recycling; Use of recycled paper products, stocked by ACU Central Stores'; Shredding for Offices; Facilities: light fixture retrofit, HVAC; Energy saving initiatives; Use of effluent water for irrigation.

ADMISSIONS

Freshman Academic Profile: Average high school GPA 3.7. 29% in top 10% of high school class, 64% in top 25% of high school class, 90% in top 50% of high school class. 68% from public high schools. SAT Math middle 50% range 490-600. SAT Critical Reading middle 50% range 470-590. SAT Writing middle 50% range 520-610. ACT middle 50% range 21-27. Minimum internet-based TOEFL 80. Minimum paper TOEFL 525. **Basis for Candidate Selection:** *Very important factors considered include:* Class rank, application essay, rigor of secondary school record, standardized test scores. *Important factors considered include:* academic GPA, character/personal qualities, talent/ability. *Other factors considered include:* recommendation(s), alumni/ae relation, extracurricular activities, first generation, level of applicant's interest, volunteer work, work experience. **Freshman Admission Requirements:** High school diploma is required and GED is accepted. **Freshman Admission Statistics:** 9,384 applied, 50% admitted, 21% enrolled. **Transfer Admission Requirements:** High school transcript, college transcript(s), interview, Minimum college GPA of 2.0 required. Lowest grade transferable 2. **General Admission Information:** Application Fee $50. Regular application deadline 2/15. Regular notification 2/15. Nonfall registration accepted. Credit offered for CEEB Advanced Placement tests.

COSTS AND FINANCIAL AID

Annual tuition $29,450. Room and board $9,000. Required fees $0. Average book expense $1,250. **Required Forms and Deadlines:** FAFSA. **Notification of Awards:** Applicants will be notified of awards on a rolling basis beginning 4/1. **Types of Aid:** *Need-based scholarships/grants:* Federal Pell, SEOG, state scholarships/grants, private scholarships, the school's own gift aid, United Negro College Fund. *Loans:* Subsidized Stafford, Unsubsidized Stafford, PLUS, Federal Perkins, state loans, college/university loans from institutional funds. *Student Employment:* Federal Work-Study Program available. Institutional employment available. Highest amount earned per year from on-campus jobs $1,500. Off-campus job opportunities are good. **Financial Aid Statistics:** 100% freshmen, 99% undergrads receive need-based scholarship or grant aid. 100% freshmen, 95% undergrads receive non-need-based scholarship or grant aid. 76% freshmen, 73% undergrads receive need-based self-help aid. 6% freshmen, 6% undergrads receive athletic scholarships. 100% freshmen, 94% undergrads receive any aid. 66% undergrads borrow to pay for school. Average cumulative indebtedness $32,252. **Criteria for awarding institutional aid:** *Non-need-based:* academics, art, athletics, leadership, minority status, music/drama, religious affiliation, state/district residency.

ACADEMY OF ART UNIVERSITY

79 New Montgomery St, San Francisco, CA 94105
Phone: 415-274-2222 · **Financial Aid Phone:** 800-544-2787
E-mail: info@academyart.edu
Fax: 415-618-6287 · **Website:** www.academyart.edu · **ACT Code:** 155

This proprietary school was founded in 1929. It has a 20-acre campus.

RATINGS

Admissions Selectivity Rating: 60*   **Fire Safety Rating:** 85

STUDENTS AND FACULTY

Enrollment: 9,885. **Student Body:** 57% female, 43% male, 40% out-of-state, 25% international (103 countries represented). Asian 8%, African American 7%, Caucasian 24%, Hispanic 11%, Native American 1%
Retention and Graduation: 75% freshmen return for sophomore year. 5% freshmen graduate within 4 years. 31% freshmen graduate within 6 years. **Faculty:** 283 full-time faculty, 16% hold PhDs, 38% are members of minority groups, 12% are women. 0% of classes are taught by teaching assistants.

ACADEMICS

Degrees: associate, bachelor's, certificate, master's. **Classes:** Most classes have 10–19 students. **Majors with Highest Enrollment:** Fashion/Apparel Design; Animation, Interactive Technology, Video Graphics and Special Effects; Photography. **Special Study Options:** Accelerated program, cooperative education program, distance learning, English as a Second Language (ESL), independent study, internships, weekend college, Portfolio Development, Personal Enrichment program. **Disability Services:** Special programs offered to physically disabled students include note-taking services, reader services, tape recorders, tutors. **Career services:** Alumni network

FACILITIES

Housing: Coed dorms, men's dorms, women's dorms, apartments for married students, apartments for single students. 80% of campus accessible to physically disabled. **Special Academic Facilities/Equipment:** 3 Art galleries (public) for display of student work **Computers:** Students can register for classes online. Administrative functions (other than registration) can be performed online.

CAMPUS LIFE

Environment: Metropolis. **Activities:** dance, drama/theater, musical theater, student newspaper, student-run film society, International Student Organization. 27 registered organizations. **Athletics (Intercollegiate):** *Men:* baseball, basketball, cross-country, golf, soccer, tennis, track/field (outdoor). *Women:* basketball, cross-country, golf, soccer, softball, tennis, track/field (outdoor), volleyball.

ADMISSIONS

Freshman Admission Requirements: High school diploma is required and GED is accepted. **Freshman Admission Statistics:** 2,852 applied, 41% enrolled. **Transfer Admission Requirements:** High school transcript, college transcript(s), Minimum college GPA of 2.0 required. Lowest grade transferable C. **General Admission Information:** Application Fee $100. Nonfall registration accepted. Admission may be deferred for a maximum of 24 months.

COSTS AND FINANCIAL AID

Annual tuition $25,050. Room and board $14,160. Required fees $300. Average book expense $1,746. **Required Forms and Deadlines:** FAFSA, Institution's own financial aid form. **Types of Aid:** *Need-based scholarships/grants:* Federal Pell, SEOG, state scholarships/grants. *Loans:* Direct Subsidized Stafford, Direct Unsubsidized Stafford, Direct PLUS, Subsidized Stafford, Unsubsidized Stafford, PLUS. *Student Employment:* Federal Work-Study Program available. Off-campus job opportunities are good. **Financial Aid Statistics:** 73% freshmen, 71% undergrads receive need-based scholarship or grant aid. 5% freshmen, 5% undergrads receive non-need-based scholarship or grant aid. 85% freshmen, 86% undergrads receive need-based self-help aid. 2% freshmen, 2% undergrads receive athletic scholarships. 60% freshmen, 64% undergrads receive any aid. 62% undergrads borrow to pay for school. Average cumulative indebtedness $23,858. **Criteria for awarding institutional aid:** *Non-need-based:* academics, art, athletics.

ACADIA UNIVERSITY

Admissions Office, Wolfville, NS B4P 2R6, Canada
Phone: 1-902-585-1446 · **Financial Aid Phone:** 902-585-1016
E-mail: pam.dimock@acadiau.ca
Fax: 902-585-1092 · **Website:** www.acadiau.ca

This public school was founded in 1838. It has a 200-acre campus.

RATINGS

Admissions Selectivity Rating: 65   **Fire Safety Rating:** 60*

STUDENTS AND FACULTY

Enrollment: 2,928. **Student Body:** 55% female, 45% male, 42% out-of-state. **Retention and Graduation:** 83% freshmen return for sophomore year. **Faculty:** 243 full-time faculty, 36% are members of minority groups. 0% of classes are taught by teaching assistants.

ACADEMICS

Degrees: bachelor's, certificate, diploma, master's. **Special Study Options:** cooperative education program, distance learning, double major, English as a Second Language (ESL), exchange student program (domestic), honors program, independent study, internships, study abroad. **Career services:** career/job search classes, career assessment, internships.

FACILITIES

Housing: Coed dorms, special housing for disabled students, men's dorms, women's dorms, apartments for single students. **Computers:** Students can register for classes online. Administrative functions (other than registration) can be performed online.

CAMPUS LIFE

Environment: Rural. **Activities:** Choral groups, concert band, dance, drama/theater, jazz band, literary magazine, music ensembles, musical theater, opera, pep band, radio station, student government, student newspaper, symphony orchestra, yearbook, Campus Ministries, International Student Organization. 60 registered organizations, 3 religious organizations. **Athletics (Intercollegiate):** *Men:* basketball, cheerleading, cross-country, football, ice hockey, rugby, soccer, track/field (outdoor), volleyball. *Women:* basketball, cheerleading, cross-country, ice hockey, rugby, soccer, track/field (outdoor), volleyball. **On-Campus Highlights:** KC Irving Environmental Science Centre, The Sheldon L. Fountain Learning Commons.

ADMISSIONS

Freshman Academic Profile: 80% from public high schools. Minimum paper TOEFL 550. **Basis for Candidate Selection:** *Very important factors considered include:* academic GPA, rigor of secondary school record. *Important factors considered include:* recommendation(s), talent/ability. *Other factors considered include:* Class rank, standardized test scores, character/personal qualities, extracurricular activities, geographical residence, volunteer work, work experience. **Freshman Admission Requirements:** High school diploma

is required and GED is not accepted. *Academic units required:* 1 English, 1 mathematics. **Freshman Admission Statistics:** 1,600 applied, 49% admitted, 68% enrolled. **Transfer Admission Requirements:** college transcript(s). **General Admission Information:** Application Fee $25. Notification on a rolling basis, beginning on or about 11/1. Nonfall registration accepted. Admission may be deferred for a maximum of 1. Credit and/or placement offered for CEEB Advanced Placement tests.

COSTS AND FINANCIAL AID

Average book expense $1,200. **Notification of Awards:** Applicants will be notified of awards on or about 4/15. **Types of Aid:** *Loans:* Direct Subsidized Stafford, Direct Unsubsidized Stafford, Direct PLUS. *Student Employment:* Off-campus job opportunities are excellent. **Criteria for awarding institutional aid:** *Non-need-based:* academics, leadership, music/drama, state/district residency.

ADAMS STATE UNIVERSITY

208 Edgemont Blvd, Alamosa, CO 81102
Phone: 719-587-7712 · **Financial Aid Phone:** 719-587-7306
E-mail: ascadmit@adams.edu · **CEEB Code:** 4001
Fax: 719-587-7522 · **ACT Code:** 496

This public school was founded in 1921. It has a 90-acre campus.

RATINGS

Admissions Selectivity Rating: 76   **Fire Safety Rating:** 68

STUDENTS AND FACULTY

Enrollment: 2,334. **Student Body:** 53% female, 47% male, 20% out-of-state, 0% international (10 countries represented). Asian 1%, African American 6%, Caucasian 51%, Hispanic 31%, Native American 1%
Retention and Graduation: 55% freshmen return for sophomore year. 8% freshmen graduate within 4 years. 24% freshmen graduate within 6 years.
Faculty: 112 full-time faculty, 66% hold PhDs, 46% are members of minority groups, 20% are women. 0% of classes are taught by teaching assistants.

ACADEMICS

Degrees: associate, bachelor's, master's. **Classes:** Most classes have fewer than 10 students. Most lab/discussion sessions have 10–19 students. **Majors with Highest Enrollment:** Teacher Education, Multiple Levels; Business Administration and Management; Kinesiology and Exercise Science. **Special Study Options:** Accelerated program, distance learning, double major, independent study, internships, study abroad, teacher certification program, weekend college, High School dual enrollment. **Disability Services:** Special programs offered to physically disabled students include note-taking services, reader services, tutors. **Career services:** Alumni network, career/job search classes, career assessment, internships. Career services highlights include On-Campus Interviews, Career Fair, Career Counseling Services.

FACILITIES

Housing: Coed dorms, men's dorms, women's dorms, apartments for married students, apartments for single students, Learning Community. 95% of campus accessible to physically disabled. **Special Academic Facilities/Equipment:** Luther Bean Museum, Hatfield Gallery, Gallery 114, Leon Memorial Music Hall, Zacheis Planetarium, Ryan Geology Museum. **Computers:** 10% of classrooms, 100% of dorms, 100% of libraries, 100% of dining areas, 99% of student union, have wireless network access. Students can register for classes online. Administrative functions (other than registration) can be performed online.

CAMPUS LIFE

Environment: Village. **Activities:** Choral groups, concert band, dance, drama/theater, jazz band, literary magazine, marching band, music ensembles, musical theater, pep band, radio station, student government, student newspaper, Campus Ministries, Model UN. 23 registered organizations, 2 religious organizations. **Athletics (Intercollegiate):** *Men:* basketball, cross-country, football, golf, soccer, track/field (outdoor), track/field (indoor), wrestling. *Women:* basketball, cross-country, golf, soccer, softball, swimming, track/field (outdoor), track/field (indoor), volleyball. **On-Campus Highlights:** Leon Memorial Concert Hall, Zacheis Planetarium, Nielson Library, Plachy Hall, Rex Activity Center, Student Union Building (SUB). **Environmental Initiatives:** Establishment of EARTH (Environmental Action for Resources, Transportation, & Health) group on campus. Partnering with the City of Alamosa and Habitat for Humanity to increase recycling opportunities on our campus. Water Project: Phase 1—convert supply to non-potable water; Phase 2—update inefficient system with one with a weather station Note that phase 2 has not been implemented yet, and may not be for a few years.

ADMISSIONS

Freshman Academic Profile: Average high school GPA 3.02. 9% in top 10% of high school class, 23% in top 25% of high school class, 53% in top 50% of high school class. SAT Math middle 50% range 435-550. SAT Critical Reading middle 50% range 410-530. SAT Writing middle 50% range 402.5-500. ACT middle 50% range 18-23. Minimum internet-based TOEFL 79. Minimum paper TOEFL 550. **Basis for Candidate Selection:** *Very important factors considered include:* rigor of secondary school record, standardized test scores. *Important factors considered include:* academic GPA. *Other factors considered include:* Class rank, recommendation(s), character/personal qualities, extracurricular activities, geographical residence, interview, state residency. **Freshman Admission Requirements:** High school diploma is required and GED is accepted. **Freshman Admission Statistics:** 2,569 applied, 66% admitted, 31% enrolled. **Transfer Admission Requirements:** college transcript(s), Minimum college GPA of 2.0 required. Lowest grade transferable D. **General Admission Information:** Application Fee $30. Nonfall registration accepted. Admission may be deferred for a maximum of 2 years. Credit offered for CEEB Advanced Placement tests.

COSTS AND FINANCIAL AID

Required Forms and Deadlines: FAFSA. **Notification of Awards:** Applicants will be notified of awards on a rolling basis beginning 3/1. **Types of Aid:** *Need-based scholarships/grants:* Federal Pell, SEOG, state scholarships/grants, private scholarships, the school's own gift aid. *Loans:* Subsidized Stafford, Unsubsidized Stafford, PLUS, Federal Perkins, Alternative Loans. *Student Employment:* Federal Work-Study Program available. Institutional employment available. Highest amount earned per year from on-campus jobs $1,854. Off-campus job opportunities are good. **Financial Aid Statistics:** 94% freshmen, 92% undergrads receive need-based scholarship or grant aid. 0% freshmen, 0% undergrads receive non-need-based scholarship or grant aid. 67% freshmen, 77% undergrads receive need-based self-help aid. 0% freshmen, 0% undergrads receive athletic scholarships. 95% freshmen, 94% undergrads receive any aid. 75% undergrads borrow to pay for school. Average cumulative indebtedness $27,687. **Criteria for awarding institutional aid:** *Non-need-based:* academics, alumni affiliation, art, athletics, leadership, minority status, music/drama, state/district residency.

ADELPHI UNIVERSITY

Levermore Hall 114, Garden City, NY 11530
Phone: 516-877-3050 · **Financial Aid Phone:** 516-877-3080
E-mail: admissions@adelphi.edu · **CEEB Code:** 2003
Fax: 516-877-3039 · **Website:** www.adelphi.edu · **ACT Code:** 2664

This private school was founded in 1896. It has a 75-acre campus.

RATINGS

Admissions Selectivity Rating: 86   **Fire Safety Rating:** 98

STUDENTS AND FACULTY

Enrollment: 5,036. **Student Body:** 70% female, 30% male, 7% out-of-state, 4% international (43 countries represented). Asian 8%, African American 10%, Caucasian 54%, Hispanic 14%, Native American <1%
Retention and Graduation: 83% freshmen return for sophomore year. 54% freshmen graduate within 4 years. 64% freshmen graduate within 6 years. 37% grads go on to further study within 1 year. 2% grads pursue law degrees. 5% grads pursue business degrees. 3% grads pursue medical degrees. **Faculty:** 314 full-time faculty, 87% hold PhDs, 55% are members of minority groups, 22% are women. 0% of classes are taught by teaching assistants.

ACADEMICS

Degrees: associate, bachelor's, master's, post-bachelor's certificate, post-master's certificate. **Classes:** Most classes have 10–19 students. Most lab/discussion sessions have 10–19 students. **Majors with Highest Enrollment:** Education; Business/Commerce. **Special Study Options:** Accelerated program, cross-registration, distance learning, double major, dual enrollment, English as a Second Language (ESL), honors program, independent study, internships, liberal arts/career combination, student-designed major, study abroad, teacher certification program, weekend college, Joint Degrees; Learning Disabilities Program; Distance Learning Program is being restructured. **Honors programs:** The Honors College seeks to prepare highly talented and motivated students to face the 21st century by providing them with the intellectual perspectives and critical skills necessary to exercise responsible leadership. It involves an intense curricular and extracurricular program that asks students to view themselves and their work with integrity, passion, and seriousness. Combined degree programs: BA/JD, BA/MA, BA/DDS, BA/MEng, Optometry, Dentistry, Physical therapy, Law, Environment Stud, Osteopathic. **Disability Services:** Special programs offered to physically disabled students include note-taking services, reader services,

tape recorders, tutors. **Career services:** Alumni network, alumni services, career/job search classes, career assessment, internships, regional alumni.

FACILITIES

Housing: Coed dorms, special housing for disabled students, Theme Housing, Honors students live in the same residence hall; EXCEL mentoring program. 95% of campus accessible to physically disabled. **Special Academic Facilities/Equipment:** Art gallery, sculpture and ceramics studios, bronze-casting foundry, theatre, language labs. **Computers:** 90% of dorms, 99% of libraries, 99% of dining areas, 90% of student union, 75% of common outdoor areas have wireless network access. Students can register for classes online. Administrative functions (other than registration) can be performed online.

CAMPUS LIFE

Environment: Metropolis. **Activities:** Choral groups, concert band, dance, drama/theater, jazz band, literary magazine, music ensembles, musical theater, opera, radio station, student government, student newspaper, student-run film society, symphony orchestra, yearbook, Campus Ministries, International Student Organization, Model UN. 80 registered organizations, 21 honor society, 5 religious organizations. 3 fraternities, 7 sororities. **Athletics (Intercollegiate):** *Men:* baseball, basketball, cross-country, golf, lacrosse, soccer, swimming, tennis, track/field (outdoor), track/field (indoor). *Women:* basketball, bowling, cross-country, field hockey, lacrosse, soccer, softball, swimming, tennis, track/field (outdoor), track/field (indoor), volleyball. **On-Campus Highlights:** Ruth S. Harley University Center, UnderGround Café, Swirbul Library, New Fine Arts Building, New Recreational Center. **Environmental Initiatives:** LEED silver rating for the CSPA project; 100% green electrical; Use of Geo-thermal heating and cooling systems in the newly constructed and proposed residence halls.

ADMISSIONS

Freshman Academic Profile: Average high school GPA 3.45. 29% in top 10% of high school class, 62% in top 25% of high school class, 88% in top 50% of high school class. 74% from public high schools. SAT Math middle 50% range 510-620. SAT Critical Reading middle 50% range 500-600. SAT Writing middle 50% range 510-610. ACT middle 50% range 19-24. Minimum paper TOEFL 550. **Basis for Candidate Selection:** *Very important factors considered include:* rigor of secondary school record. *Important factors considered include:* Class rank, application essay, academic GPA, standardized test scores, character/personal qualities, extracurricular activities, talent/ability, volunteer work. *Other factors considered include:* alumni/ae relation, first generation, interview, level of applicant's interest, work experience. **Freshman Admission Requirements:** High school diploma is required and GED is accepted. **Freshman Admission Statistics:** 8,806 applied, 72% admitted, 15% enrolled. **Transfer Admission Requirements:** college transcript(s), essay or personal statement, Minimum college GPA of 2.3 required. **General Admission Information:** Application Fee $35. Notification on a rolling basis, beginning on or about 10/1. Nonfall registration accepted. Credit and/or placement offered for CEEB Advanced Placement tests.

COSTS AND FINANCIAL AID

Annual tuition $30,840. Room and board $13,620. Required fees $1,500. Average book expense $1,400. **Required Forms and Deadlines:** FAFSA, State aid form. **Notification of Awards:** Applicants will be notified of awards on a rolling basis beginning 2/15. **Types of Aid:** *Need-based scholarships/grants:* Federal Pell, SEOG, state scholarships/grants, private scholarships, the school's own gift aid, United Negro College Fund. *Loans:* Subsidized Stafford, Unsubsidized Stafford, PLUS, Federal Perkins, Federal Nursing, New York HELP Program (private alternative). *Student Employment:* Federal Work-Study Program available. Institutional employment available. Highest amount earned per year from on-campus jobs $20,594. Off-campus job opportunities are good. **Financial Aid Statistics:** 69% freshmen, 63% undergrads receive need-based scholarship or grant aid. 84% freshmen, 80% undergrads receive non-need-based scholarship or grant aid. 85% freshmen, 81% undergrads receive need-based self-help aid. 1% freshmen, 2% undergrads receive athletic scholarships. 98% freshmen, 94% undergrads receive any aid. 75% undergrads borrow to pay for school. Average cumulative indebtedness $24,968. **Criteria for awarding institutional aid:** *Non-need-based:* academics, alumni affiliation, art, athletics, leadership, minority status, music/drama, religious affiliation.

ADRIAN COLLEGE

110 South Madison Street, Adrian, MI 49221
Phone: 517-265-5161 · **Financial Aid Phone:** 517-265-5161
E-mail: admissions@adrian.edu · **CEEB Code:** 1001
Fax: 517-264-3331 · **Website:** www.adrian.edu · **ACT Code:** 1954

This private school, affiliated with the Methodist Church, was founded in 1859. It has a 100-acre campus.

RATINGS

Admissions Selectivity Rating: 82 · **Fire Safety Rating:** 65

STUDENTS AND FACULTY

Enrollment: 1,308. **Student Body:** 47% female, 53% male, 24% out-of-state, 4% international (6 countries represented). Asian 1%, African American 4%, Caucasian 77%, Hispanic 2%, Native American <1%
Retention and Graduation: 73% freshmen return for sophomore year. 40% freshmen graduate within 4 years. 50% freshmen graduate within 6 years. 25% grads go on to further study within 1 year. 51% grads pursue arts and sciences degrees. 9% grads pursue law degrees. 9% grads pursue business degrees. 22% grads pursue medical degrees. **Faculty:** 78 full-time faculty, 82% hold PhDs, 41% are members of minority groups, 9% are women. 0% of classes are taught by teaching assistants.

ACADEMICS

Degrees: associate, bachelor's, transfer associate. **Classes:** Most classes have 10–19 students. Most lab/discussion sessions have 10–19 students. **Majors with Highest Enrollment:** Business/Commerce; English Language and Literature; Kinesiology and Exercise Science. **Special Study Options:** double major, dual enrollment, honors program, independent study, internships, student-designed major, study abroad, teacher certification program. Combined degree programs: BA/MEng. **Disability Services:** Special programs offered to physically disabled students include note-taking services, reader services, tape recorders, tutors. **Career services:** Alumni network, alumni services, career assessment, internships, regional alumni. Career services highlights include internships.

FACILITIES

Housing: Coed dorms, men's dorms, women's dorms, fraternity/sorority housing, apartments for single students, special-interest houses. 50% of campus accessible to physically disabled. **Special Academic Facilities/Equipment:** Art gallery, studio theatre, arboretum, education resource center, language lab, observatory, planetarium, solar greenhouse, nuclear magnetic resonance spectrometer, differential scanning calorimeter. **Computers:** 100% of classrooms, 100% of dorms, 100% of libraries, 100% of dining areas, 100% of student union, 100% of common outdoor areas have wireless network access. Students can register for classes online. Administrative functions (other than registration) can be performed online.

CAMPUS LIFE

Environment: Town. **Activities:** Choral groups, concert band, dance, drama/theater, jazz band, literary magazine, marching band, music ensembles, musical theater, pep band, radio station, student government, student newspaper, symphony orchestra, yearbook, Campus Ministries, International Student Organization. 68 registered organizations, 13 honor societies, 8 religious organizations. 4 fraternities, 3 sororities. **Athletics (Intercollegiate):** *Men:* baseball, basketball, cross-country, football, golf, ice hockey, lacrosse, soccer, tennis, track/field (outdoor). *Women:* basketball, bowling, cross-country, golf, ice hockey, lacrosse, soccer, softball, tennis, track/field (outdoor), volleyball. **On-Campus Highlights:** Caine Student Center, Shipman Library, Merillat Sport and Fitness Center.

ADMISSIONS

Freshman Academic Profile: Average high school GPA 3.3. 17% in top 10% of high school class, 46% in top 25% of high school class, 81% in top 50% of high school class. SAT Math middle 50% range 410-535. SAT Critical Reading middle 50% range 430-515. ACT middle 50% range 20-25. Minimum paper TOEFL 500. **Basis for Candidate Selection:** *Very important factors considered include:* Class rank, rigor of secondary school record. *Important factors considered include:* academic GPA, standardized test scores, talent/ability. *Other factors considered include:* alumni/ae relation, character/personal qualities, extracurricular activities, interview, level of applicant's interest, volunteer work, work experience. **Freshman Admission Requirements:** High school diploma is required and GED is accepted. **Freshman Admission Statistics:** 3,709 applied, 64% admitted, 21% enrolled. **Transfer Admission Requirements:** High school transcript, college transcript(s), Minimum college GPA of 2.7 required. Lowest grade transferable C. **General Admission Information:** Notification on a rolling basis, beginning on or about 9/1. Nonfall registration not accepted. Admission may be deferred for a maximum of 1 year. Credit and/or placement offered for CEEB Advanced Placement tests.

COSTS AND FINANCIAL AID

Annual tuition $23,090. Room and board $7,600. Required fees $300. Average book expense $400. **Required Forms and Deadlines:** FAFSA. **Notification of Awards:** Applicants will be notified of awards on a rolling basis beginning 3/15. **Types of Aid:** *Need-based scholarships/grants:* Federal Pell, SEOG, state scholarships/grants, private scholarships, the school's own gift aid. *Loans:* Subsidized Stafford, Unsubsidized Stafford, PLUS, Federal Perkins. *Student Employment:* Federal Work-Study Program available. Institutional employment available. Highest amount earned per year from on-campus jobs $1,700. Off-campus job opportunities are good. **Financial Aid Statistics:** 87% freshmen, 86% undergrads receive need-based scholarship or grant aid. 88% freshmen, 86% undergrads receive non-need-based scholarship or grant aid. 89% freshmen, 88% undergrads receive need-based self-help aid. 0% freshmen, 0% undergrads receive athletic scholarships. 98% freshmen, 92% undergrads receive any aid. 81% undergrads borrow to pay for school. Average cumulative indebtedness $17,160. **Criteria for awarding institutional aid:** *Non-need-based:* academics, alumni affiliation, art, leadership, music/drama, religious affiliation.

AGNES SCOTT COLLEGE

141 E. College Ave., Decatur, GA 30030-3770
Phone: 404-471-6285 · **Financial Aid Phone:** 404-471-6395
E-mail: admission@agnesscott.edu · **CEEB Code:** 5002
Fax: 404-471-6414 · **Website:** www.agnesscott.edu · **ACT Code:** 780

This private school, affiliated with the Presbyterian Church, was founded in 1889. It has a 100-acre campus.

RATINGS

Admissions Selectivity Rating: 88 · **Fire Safety Rating:** 93

STUDENTS AND FACULTY

Enrollment: 802. **Student Body:** 100% female, 0% male, 42% out-of-state, 9% international (32 countries represented). Asian 5%, African American 35%, Caucasian 32%, Hispanic 9%, Native American <1%
Retention and Graduation: 82% freshmen return for sophomore year. 73% freshmen graduate within 4 years. 21% grads go on to further study within 1 year. **Faculty:** 73 full-time faculty, 100% hold PhDs, 64% are members of minority groups, 16% are women. 0% of classes are taught by teaching assistants.

ACADEMICS

Degrees: bachelor's, master's, post-bachelor's certificate. **Classes:** Most classes have 10–19 students. Most lab/discussion sessions have 10–19 students. **Majors with Highest Enrollment:** Psychology; Creative Writing; Business Administration and Management. **Special Study Options:** Accelerated program, cross-registration, double major, dual enrollment, exchange student program (domestic), external degree program, independent study, internships, student-designed major, study abroad, teacher certification program, Woodruff Scholars program for women beyond traditional college age; exchange program with Mills College; Atlanta Semester. Combined degree programs: BA/MA, BA/MA Arch. w/Wash. U., BA/BS Eng, BA/BSN w/Emory. **Disability Services:** Special programs offered to physically disabled students include note-taking services, reader services, tape recorders, tutors. **Career services:** Alumni network, alumni services, career/job search classes, career assessment, internships, regional alumni. Career services highlights include internships.

FACILITIES

Housing: women's dorms, apartments for single students, Theme Housing. 90% of campus accessible to physically disabled. **Special Academic Facilities/Equipment:** Art galleries, state-of the art science building opened in January 2003, collaborative learning centers, language lab, electron microscope, observatory, 30-inch Beck telescope, planetarium, interactive learning center, multimedia presentation classrooms, instructional technology center, multimedia production facility. **Computers:** 50% of classrooms, 100% of libraries, 100% of student union, 10% of common outdoor areas have wireless network access. Students can register for classes online. Administrative functions (other than registration) can be performed online.

CAMPUS LIFE

Environment: Metropolis. **Activities:** Choral groups, dance, drama/theater, literary magazine, marching band, music ensembles, musical theater, pep band, student government, student newspaper, symphony orchestra, television station, yearbook, Campus Ministries, International Student Organization, Model

UN. 80 registered organizations, 12 honor societies, 12 religious organizations. **Athletics (Intercollegiate):** *Women:* basketball, lacrosse, soccer, softball, tennis, volleyball. **On-Campus Highlights:** New $36.5 million Science Center, Alston Campus Center, Newly renovated Bradley Observatory, McCain Library, Several residence halls are on the National Regist. **Environmental Initiatives:** Converted to campus-wide single stream recycling and composting. Agnes Scott is committed to Zero Waste, and has already achived a 62% waste diversion rate. Implementing a climate action plan with major efficiency and renewable energy commitments. Continued guidance and leadership from an inclusive sustainability steering committee with active Board and alumnae representatives as well as students, faculty, staff, and all management.

ADMISSIONS

Freshman Academic Profile: Average high school GPA 3.66. 36.9% in top 10% of high school class, 70.3% in top 25% of high school class, 93.7% in top 50% of high school class. 72% from public high schools. SAT Math middle 50% range 520-600. SAT Critical Reading middle 50% range 540-660. SAT Writing middle 50% range 530-640. ACT middle 50% range 23-27. **Basis for Candidate Selection:** *Very important factors considered include:* Class rank, application essay, academic GPA, recommendation(s), rigor of secondary school record, standardized test scores, character/personal qualities, talent/ability. *Important factors considered include:* extracurricular activities, volunteer work, work experience. *Other factors considered include:* alumni/ae relation, first generation, geographical residence, interview, level of applicant's interest, racial/ethnic status, state residency. **Freshman Admission Requirements:** High school diploma is required and GED is accepted. **Freshman Admission Statistics:** 1,394 applied, 68% admitted, 24% enrolled. **Transfer Admission Requirements:** High school transcript, college transcript(s), essay or personal statement, statement of good standing from prior institution(s). Minimum college GPA of 3.0 required. Lowest grade transferable C. **General Admission Information:** Application Fee $35. Nonfall registration accepted. Admission may be deferred for a maximum of 1 year. Credit and/or placement offered for CEEB Advanced Placement tests.

COSTS AND FINANCIAL AID

Average book expense $1,000. **Required Forms and Deadlines:** FAFSA. **Notification of Awards:** Applicants will be notified of awards on a rolling basis beginning 3/1. **Types of Aid:** *Need-based scholarships/grants:* Federal Pell, SEOG, state scholarships/grants, private scholarships, the school's own gift aid. *Loans:* Subsidized Stafford, Unsubsidized Stafford, PLUS. *Student Employment:* Federal Work-Study Program available. Institutional employment available. Off-campus job opportunities are excellent. **Financial Aid Statistics:** 100% freshmen, 100% undergrads receive need-based scholarship or grant aid. 29% freshmen, 20% undergrads receive non-need-based scholarship or grant aid. 80% freshmen, 87% undergrads receive need-based self-help aid. 0% freshmen, 0% undergrads receive athletic scholarships. 100% freshmen, 99% undergrads receive any aid. 71% undergrads borrow to pay for school. Average cumulative indebtedness $25,393. **Criteria for awarding institutional aid:** *Non-need-based:* academics, leadership, minority status, music/drama, religious affiliation, state/district residency.

ALABAMA A&M UNIVERSITY

P.O. Box 908, Normal, AL 35762
Phone: 256-851-5245
E-mail: juan.alexander@aamu.edu • **CEEB Code:** 1003
Fax: 256-851-5249 • **ACT Code:** 2

This public school was founded in 1875. It has a 880-acre campus.

RATINGS

Admissions Selectivity Rating: 75   **Fire Safety Rating:** 60*

STUDENTS AND FACULTY

Enrollment: 4,489. **Student Body:** 52% female, 48% male, 31% out-of-state, 1% international (42 countries represented). Asian 0%, African American 70%, Caucasian 2%, Hispanic 0%, Native American <1%
Retention and Graduation: 77% grads go on to further study within 1 year. 40% grads pursue arts and sciences degrees. 2% grads pursue law degrees. 45% grads pursue business degrees. 11% grads pursue medical degrees. **Faculty:** 314 full-time faculty, 45% hold PhDs, 39% are members of minority groups, 55% are women. 1% of classes are taught by teaching assistants.

ACADEMICS

Degrees: bachelor's, master's, post-master's certificate. **Classes:** Most classes have fewer than 10 students. Most lab/discussion sessions have 20–29 students. **Majors with Highest Enrollment:** Elementary Education and Teaching; Mechanical Engineering Related Technologies/Technicians; Biology/Biological

Sciences. **Special Study Options:** Accelerated program, cooperative education program, distance learning, double major, dual enrollment, exchange student program (domestic), honors program, independent study, internships, study abroad, teacher certification program, weekend college. **Disability Services:** Special programs offered to physically disabled students include note-taking services, reader services, tape recorders, tutors. **Career services:** career/job search classes, career assessment, internships, regional alumni.

FACILITIES

Housing: men's dorms, women's dorms, apartments for single students. 65% of campus accessible to physically disabled. **Special Academic Facilities/Equipment:** State Black Archives. **Computers:** Students can register for classes online.

CAMPUS LIFE

Environment: City. **Activities:** Choral groups, concert band, dance, drama/theater, jazz band, literary magazine, marching band, music ensembles, pep band, radio station, student government, student newspaper, symphony orchestra, television station, yearbook, Campus Ministries, International Student Organization. 76 registered organizations, 14 honor societies, 3 religious organizations. 4 fraternities, 4 sororities. **Athletics (Intercollegiate):** *Men:* baseball, basketball, cross-country, football, golf, soccer, track/field (outdoor). *Women:* basketball, cross-country, soccer, softball, track/field (outdoor), volleyball. **On-Campus Highlights:** Engineering Building, Cafeteria, Gym, Business School, Dawson Building.

ADMISSIONS

Freshman Academic Profile: 90% from public high schools. SAT Math middle 50% range 380-470. SAT Critical Reading middle 50% range 400-470. SAT Writing middle 50% range 380-460. ACT middle 50% range 16-19. Minimum paper TOEFL 550. **Basis for Candidate Selection:** *Very important factors considered include:* standardized test scores, alumni/ae relation, geographical residence, state residency. *Important factors considered include:* racial/ethnic status. *Other factors considered include:* Class rank, recommendation(s). **Freshman Admission Requirements:** High school diploma is required and GED is accepted. *Academic units required:* 4 English, 4 mathematics, 4 science, (2 science labs), 4 social studies, 4 history. **Freshman Admission Statistics:** 5,697 applied, 47% admitted, 39% enrolled. **Transfer Admission Requirements:** High school transcript, college transcript(s), standardized test scores, statement of good standing from prior institution(s). Minimum college GPA of 2.5 required. Lowest grade transferable C. **General Admission Information:** Application Fee $10. Regular application deadline 7/1. Notification on a rolling basis, beginning on or about 4/15. Nonfall registration accepted. Admission may be deferred for a maximum of 12 months. Neither credit nor placement offered for CEEB Advanced Placement tests.

COSTS AND FINANCIAL AID

Annual out-of-state tuition $7,896. Room and board $5,350. Required fees $744. **Required Forms and Deadlines:** FAFSA, Institution's own financial aid form. **Types of Aid:** *Need-based scholarships/grants:* Federal Pell, SEOG, state scholarships/grants, private scholarships, the school's own gift aid, United Negro College Fund. *Loans:* Direct Subsidized Stafford, Direct Unsubsidized Stafford, Direct PLUS, Federal Perkins, state loans, college/university loans from institutional funds. *Student Employment:* Highest amount earned per year from on-campus jobs $5,400.

ALABAMA STATE UNIVERSITY

915 South Jackson Street, Montgomery, AL 36104
Phone: 334-229-4291
E-mail: dlamar@asunet.alasu.edu
Fax: 334-229-4984 • **Website:** www.alasu.edu • **ACT Code:** 8

This public school was founded in 1867.

RATINGS

Admissions Selectivity Rating: 66   **Fire Safety Rating:** 60*

STUDENTS AND FACULTY

Enrollment: 5,125. **Student Body:** 59% female, 41% male, 35% out-of-state, 0% international. Asian 0%, African American 95%, Caucasian 4%, Hispanic 0%, Native American <1%
Retention and Graduation: 68% freshmen return for sophomore year. 50% grads go on to further study within 1 year. **Faculty:** 229 full-time faculty, 59% hold PhDs, 54% are members of minority groups, 67% are women. 0% of classes are taught by teaching assistants.

ACADEMICS

Degrees: bachelor's, master's. **Majors with Highest Enrollment:** Computer and Information Sciences; Elementary Education and Teaching; Criminal Justice/Safety Studies. **Special Study Options:** cooperative education program, cross-registration, double major, honors program, internships, teacher certification program. **Disability Services:** Special programs offered to physically disabled students include note-taking services, tape recorders. **Career services:** career/job search classes, internships.

FACILITIES

Housing: men's dorms, women's dorms, apartments for single students, Honor dorms. 90% of campus accessible to physically disabled. **Special Academic Facilities/Equipment:** Levi Watkins Learning Center Special Collections. **Computers:** Students can register for classes online. Administrative functions (other than registration) can be performed online.

CAMPUS LIFE

Activities: Choral groups, concert band, dance, drama/theater, jazz band, marching band, music ensembles, musical theater, pep band, radio station, student government, student newspaper, symphony orchestra, yearbook. 64 registered organizations, 17 honor societies, 5 fraternities, 4 sororities. **Athletics (Intercollegiate):** *Men:* baseball, basketball, cheerleading, cross-country, football, golf, tennis, track/field (outdoor), track/field (indoor). *Women:* basketball, cheerleading, cross-country, golf, softball, tennis, track/field (outdoor), track/field (indoor), volleyball.

ADMISSIONS

Freshman Academic Profile: Average high school GPA 2.67. SAT Math middle 50% range 340-444. SAT Critical Reading middle 50% range 350-457. ACT middle 50% range 14-18. Minimum paper TOEFL 500. **Basis for Candidate Selection:** *Very important factors considered include:* rigor of secondary school record. *Important factors considered include:* Class rank, standardized test scores. *Other factors considered include:* recommendation(s). **Freshman Admission Requirements:** High school diploma is required and GED is accepted. **Transfer Admission Requirements:** college transcript(s), Minimum college GPA of 2.0 required. Lowest grade transferable C. **General Admission Information:** Regular application deadline 7/30. Notification on a rolling basis, beginning on or about 8/30. Nonfall registration accepted. Admission may be deferred for a maximum of semester. Credit and/or placement offered for CEEB Advanced Placement tests.

COSTS AND FINANCIAL AID

Annual in-state tuition $2,904. Annual out-of-state tuition $5,808. Room and board $3,700. Average book expense $800. **Required Forms and Deadlines:** FAFSA, State aid form. **Notification of Awards:** Applicants will be notified of awards on a rolling basis beginning 5/15. **Types of Aid:** *Need-based scholarships/grants:* Federal Pell, SEOG, state scholarships/grants, private scholarships, the school's own gift aid. *Loans:* Subsidized Stafford, Unsubsidized Stafford, PLUS, Federal Perkins. *Student Employment:* Federal Work-Study Program available. Institutional employment available. Highest amount earned per year from on-campus jobs $2,400. Off-campus job opportunities are good. **Financial Aid Statistics:** 82% freshmen, 79% undergrads receive need-based scholarship or grant aid. 20% freshmen, 23% undergrads receive non-need-based scholarship or grant aid. 87% freshmen, 84% undergrads receive need-based self-help aid. 3% freshmen, 5% undergrads receive athletic scholarships. 72% undergrads borrow to pay for school. **Criteria for awarding institutional aid:** *Non-need-based:* academics, athletics.

ALASKA BIBLE COLLEGE

P.O. Box 289, Glennallen, AK 99588
Phone: 907-822-3201
E-mail: info@akbible.edu
Fax: 907-822-5027 • **Website:** www.akbible.edu

This private school, affiliated with the Christian (Nondenominational) Church, was founded in 1966. It has a 90-acre campus.

RATINGS

Admissions Selectivity Rating: 60*   **Fire Safety Rating:** 60*

STUDENTS AND FACULTY

Enrollment: 42. **Student Body:** 60% out-of-state, (0 countries represented). **Retention and Graduation:** 67% freshmen return for sophomore year. **Faculty:** 4 full-time faculty, 25% hold PhDs.

ACADEMICS

Degrees: associate, bachelor's, certificate, terminal associate, transfer associate. **Special Study Options:** cooperative education program, double major, independent study, internships.

FACILITIES

Housing: men's dorms, women's dorms, apartments for married students, apartments for single students.

CAMPUS LIFE

Environment: Rural. **On-Campus Highlights:** Annette Ball Memorial Library, Food Cache, Murdock Campus Center, Vince Joy Hall, Firebreak.

ADMISSIONS

Freshman Academic Profile: Minimum paper TOEFL 500. **Basis for Candidate Selection:** *Very important factors considered include:* application essay, recommendation(s), rigor of secondary school record, standardized test scores, character/personal qualities, interview, religious affiliation/commitment. *Important factors considered include:* volunteer work, work experience. *Other factors considered include:* extracurricular activities, racial/ethnic status, talent/ability. **Freshman Admission Requirements:** High school diploma is required and GED is accepted. **Freshman Admission Statistics:** 11 applied, 100% admitted, 100% enrolled. **Transfer Admission Requirements:** High school transcript, college transcript(s), essay or personal statement, interview, standardized test scores, statement of good standing from prior institution(s). Minimum college GPA of 2.0 required. Lowest grade transferable C. **General Admission Information:** Application Fee $35. Regular application deadline 7/1. Nonfall registration accepted. Admission may be deferred for a maximum of 1 year.

COSTS AND FINANCIAL AID

Annual tuition $5,720. Room and board $4,570. Required fees $185. Average book expense $400.

ALASKA PACIFIC UNIVERSITY

4101 University Drive, Anchorage, AK 99508-4625
Phone: 907-564-8248 • **Financial Aid Phone:** 907-564-8341
E-mail: admissions@alaskapacific.edu • **CEEB Code:** 4201
Fax: 907-564-8317 • **Website:** http://www.alaskapacific.edu • **ACT Code:** 62

This private school was founded in 1957. It has a 170-acre campus.

RATINGS

Admissions Selectivity Rating: 85   **Fire Safety Rating:** 84

STUDENTS AND FACULTY

Enrollment: 455. **Student Body:** 65% female, 35% male, 32% out-of-state, 0% international (3 countries represented). Asian 2%, African American 3%, Caucasian 58%, Hispanic 3%, Native American 15%
Retention and Graduation: 67% freshmen return for sophomore year. 20% freshmen graduate within 4 years. 27% freshmen graduate within 6 years. **Faculty:** 50 full-time faculty, 64% hold PhDs, 58% are members of minority groups, 4% are women. 0% of classes are taught by teaching assistants.

ACADEMICS

Degrees: associate, bachelor's, certificate, master's, post-bachelor's certificate, terminal associate. **Classes:** Most classes have fewer than 10 students. Most lab/discussion sessions have fewer than 10 students. **Majors with Highest Enrollment:** Marine Biology and Biological Oceanography; Elementary Education and Teaching; Business Administration and Management. **Special Study Options:** distance learning, double major, exchange student program (domestic), independent study, internships, student-designed major, study abroad, teacher certification program, Degree Completion program for adult students and a distance education program for Rural Alaskan Native Adults. **Disability Services:** Special programs offered to physically disabled students include note-taking services, tape recorders, tutors. **Career services:** career/job search classes, career assessment, internships.

FACILITIES

Housing: Coed dorms, cooperative housing, several theme houses, for example the "Nordic Skiers House" for ski team members. 75% of campus accessible to physically disabled. **Special Academic Facilities/Equipment:** Alaskana collection; GIS lab; gym with pool; Student Center with weight room and indoor climbing wall; Outdoor recreation center with classes and rental equipment; Lake for canoeing and kayaking trails for running, skiing, hiking, biking, etc. connected to city's trail system. **Computers:** 100% of classrooms, 100% of dorms, 100% of libraries, 100% of dining areas, 100% of student union, 100% of common outdoor areas have wireless network access. Students can register for classes online. Administrative functions (other than registration) can be performed online.

CAMPUS LIFE

Environment: City. **Activities:** drama/theater, literary magazine, music ensembles, student government, student newspaper, yearbook. 15 registered organizations, 1 religious organization. **On-Campus Highlights:** Student Center, Climbing wall and weight room, Pool, lounges in Grant Hall and in Carr Gottst. **Environmental Initiatives:** Kellogg Farm dedicated to organic and sustainable enterprises. APU does not use paper plates, plastic silverware, etc. Also paperless initiative. Committed to building a LEEDs level student center.

ADMISSIONS

Freshman Academic Profile: Average high school GPA 3.34. 17% in top 10% of high school class, 31% in top 25% of high school class, 72% in top 50% of high school class. 95% from public high schools. SAT Math middle 50% range 470-560. SAT Critical Reading middle 50% range 490-600. SAT Writing middle 50% range 460-610. ACT middle 50% range 21-27. Minimum internet-based TOEFL 79. Minimum paper TOEFL 550. **Basis for Candidate Selection:** *Very important factors considered include:* application essay, academic GPA, rigor of secondary school record. *Important factors considered include:* recommendation(s), standardized test scores, alumni/ae relation, level of applicant's interest. *Other factors considered include:* extracurricular activities, talent/ability, volunteer work, work experience. **Freshman Admission Requirements:** High school diploma is required and GED is accepted. **Freshman Admission Statistics:** 245 applied, 48% admitted, 43% enrolled. **Transfer Admission Requirements:** college transcript(s), essay or personal statement, statement of good standing from prior institution(s). Minimum college GPA of 2.0 required. Lowest grade transferable C. **General Admission Information:** Application Fee $25. Regular application deadline 8/15. Notification on a rolling basis, beginning on or about 1/15. Nonfall registration accepted. Admission may be deferred for a maximum of 12 months. Credit offered for CEEB Advanced Placement tests.

COSTS AND FINANCIAL AID

Annual tuition $26,250. Room and board $9,300. Required fees $110. Average book expense $1,000. **Required Forms and Deadlines:** FAFSA. **Notification of Awards:** Applicants will be notified of awards on a rolling basis beginning 2/1. **Types of Aid:** *Need-based scholarships/grants:* Federal Pell, SEOG, state scholarships/grants, private scholarships, the school's own gift aid. *Loans:* Subsidized Stafford, Unsubsidized Stafford, PLUS, state loans, college/university loans from institutional funds. *Student Employment:* Federal Work-Study Program available. Institutional employment available. Off-campus job opportunities are good. **Financial Aid Statistics:** 47% freshmen, 55% undergrads receive need-based scholarship or grant aid. 100% freshmen, 48% undergrads receive non-need-based scholarship or grant aid. 68% freshmen, 42% undergrads receive need-based self-help aid. 0% freshmen, 0% undergrads receive athletic scholarships. 88% freshmen, 92% undergrads receive any aid. 93% undergrads borrow to pay for school. Average cumulative indebtedness $22,783. **Criteria for awarding institutional aid:** *Non-need-based:* academics, alumni affiliation, leadership, religious affiliation, state/district residency.

ALBANY COLLEGE OF PHARMACY

106 New Scotland Avenue, Albany, NY 12208
Phone: 518-694-7221 · **Financial Aid Phone:** 518-694-7256
E-mail: admissions@acp.edu · **CEEB Code:** 2013
Fax: 518-694-7322 · **Website:** www.acp.edu · **ACT Code:** 2672

This private school was founded in 1881. It has a 21-acre campus.

RATINGS

Admissions Selectivity Rating: 90   Fire Safety Rating: 66

STUDENTS AND FACULTY

Enrollment: 1,015. **Student Body:** 58% female, 42% male, 10% out-of-state, 8% international (6 countries represented). Asian 13%, African American 2%, Caucasian 73%, Hispanic 1%, Native American <1%
Retention and Graduation: 79% freshmen return for sophomore year. **Faculty:** 82 full-time faculty, 74% hold PhDs, 49% are members of minority groups, 12% are women. 0% of classes are taught by teaching assistants.

ACADEMICS

Degrees: bachelor's, certificate, first professional. **Classes:** Most classes have 20–29 students. Most lab/discussion sessions have 20–29 students. **Majors with Highest Enrollment:** Pharmacy. **Special Study Options:** Accelerated program, cross-registration. Combined degree programs: BA/JD, Pharm.D./MS, Pharm.D./MBA, BS/Phy Asst. **Disability Services:** Special programs offered to physically disabled students include tutors. **Career services:** career/job search classes, career assessment.

FACILITIES

Housing: Coed dorms, apartments for single students. 100% of campus accessible to physically disabled. **Special Academic Facilities/Equipment:** Throop

Pharmaceutical Museum. **Computers:** Students can register for classes online. Administrative functions (other than registration) can be performed online. Undergraduates are required to own a computer.

CAMPUS LIFE

Environment: City. **Activities:** Choral groups, concert band, dance, literary magazine, student government, student newspaper, yearbook, International Student Organization. 2 honor societies, 1 religious organization. **Athletics (Intercollegiate):** *Men:* basketball, soccer. *Women:* basketball, soccer. **On-Campus Highlights:** NEW ACP Student Center.

ADMISSIONS

Freshman Academic Profile: Average high school GPA 92. 47% in top 10% of high school class, 86% in top 25% of high school class, 99% in top 50% of high school class. SAT Math middle 50% range 570-650. SAT Critical Reading middle 50% range 530-620. SAT Writing middle 50% range 510-600. ACT middle 50% range 23-28. Minimum paper TOEFL 600. **Basis for Candidate Selection:** *Very important factors considered include:* academic GPA, standardized test scores. *Important factors considered include:* Class rank, rigor of secondary school record. *Other factors considered include:* application essay, recommendation(s), alumni/ae relation, character/personal qualities, extracurricular activities, geographical residence, level of applicant's interest, talent/ability, volunteer work, work experience. **Freshman Admission Requirements:** High school diploma is required and GED is accepted. *Academic units required:* 4 English, 4 mathematics, 3 science, (3 science labs), 0 foreign language, 4 social studies. **Freshman Admission Statistics:** 1,050 applied, 54% admitted, 43% enrolled. **Transfer Admission Requirements:** college transcript(s), essay or personal statement, statement of good standing from prior institution(s). Minimum college GPA of 3.2 required. Lowest grade transferable B. **General Admission Information:** Application Fee $75. Early decision application deadline 11/1. Regular application deadline 3/1. Regular notification 3/15. Nonfall registration not accepted. Admission may be deferred for a maximum of 1 year. Credit offered for CEEB Advanced Placement tests.

COSTS AND FINANCIAL AID

Required Forms and Deadlines: FAFSA. **Notification of Awards:** Applicants will be notified of awards on a rolling basis beginning 3/25. **Types of Aid:** *Need-based scholarships/grants:* Federal Pell, SEOG, state scholarships/grants, private scholarships, the school's own gift aid. *Loans:* Subsidized Stafford, Unsubsidized Stafford, PLUS, Federal Perkins. **Financial Aid Statistics:** 92% freshmen, 80% undergrads receive need-based scholarship or grant aid. 12% freshmen, 6% undergrads receive non-need-based scholarship or grant aid. 84% freshmen, 90% undergrads receive need-based self-help aid. 0% freshmen, 0% undergrads receive athletic scholarships. 92% undergrads borrow to pay for school. Average cumulative indebtedness $9,520. **Criteria for awarding institutional aid:** *Non-need-based:* academics, alumni affiliation, leadership.

ALBANY STATE UNIVERSITY

504 College Drive, Albany, GA 31705
Phone: 229-430-4646 · **Financial Aid Phone:** 229-430-4650
E-mail: enrollmentservices@asurams.edu · **CEEB Code:** 5004
Fax: 229-430-4105 · **Website:** http://www.asurams.edu · **ACT Code:** 782

This public school was founded in 1903. It has a 232-acre campus.

RATINGS

Admissions Selectivity Rating: 83   Fire Safety Rating: 84

STUDENTS AND FACULTY

Enrollment: 4,173. **Student Body:** 66% female, 34% male, 4% out-of-state, 0% international (22 countries represented). Asian 0%, African American 83%, Caucasian 4%, Hispanic 1%, Native American <1%
Retention and Graduation: 41% freshmen graduate within 6 years. **Faculty:** 164 full-time faculty, 77% hold PhDs, 45% are members of minority groups, 78% are women. 0% of classes are taught by teaching assistants.

ACADEMICS

Degrees: associate, bachelor's, master's, post-master's certificate. **Classes:** Most classes have 20–29 students. **Majors with Highest Enrollment:** Business Administration and Management; Early Childhood Education and Teaching; Criminal Justice/Safety Studies. **Special Study Options:** cooperative education program, cross-registration, distance learning, double major, dual enrollment, honors program, independent study, internships, liberal arts/career combination, study abroad, teacher certification program, weekend college, 3+2 & 2+2 engineering program with GA Tech. Pre-med, pre-med technology, pre-pharmacy study options. Online degree programs. **Honors programs:** The Velma Fudge Grant Honors Program represents a commitment made by Albany

State University (ASU) to broaden and enrich educational experiences of bright, highly motivated and creative students. Honors Program students are provided opportunities for scholarships, access to special extracurricular programs, a chance to pursue independent projects and research interests, professional experience through internship programs and special service options. Through its specially designed curriculum, the University provides the opportunity for faculty to teach academically talented students in inventive, interdisciplinary, small class settings designed to fulfill core curriculum requirements, as well as in advanced or intensive classes in particular disciplines. The Honors Program is specifically designed for academic scholarship recipients, academically talented students and entering freshman and transfer students with a proven dedication to academic excellence and scholarship. The Honors Program student must reach beyond good grades for success and have the courage to demonstrate superior ethical leadership in his/her chosen field of study. **Disability Services:** Special programs offered to physically disabled students include note-taking services, reader services, tape recorders, tutors. **Career services:** Alumni network, alumni services, career assessment, internships, regional alumni. All opportunities are welcomed to provide experiential learning experiences for ASU students, especially those that result in employment opportunities.

FACILITIES

Housing: Coed dorms, men's dorms, women's dorms, apartments for single students, Upper classmen and graduate halls. 50% of campus accessible to physically disabled. **Computers:** 67% of dorms, have wireless network access.

CAMPUS LIFE

Environment: City. **Activities:** Choral groups, concert band, dance, drama/theater, jazz band, marching band, opera, radio station, student government, student newspaper, television station, Campus Ministries, International Student Organization, Model UN. 70 registered organizations, 10 honor societies, 6 fraternities, 4 sororities. **Athletics (Intercollegiate):** *Men:* baseball, basketball, cross-country, football, track/field (outdoor). *Women:* basketball, cross-country, softball, tennis, track/field (outdoor), volleyball. **On-Campus Highlights:** Student Affairs Building, Gymnasium, Housing, Stadium **Environmental Initiatives:** Hazardous Waste Labe, Paint shops and carpentry, Universal Waste, Recycling Toner Cartridges, Paper and Paper products, Used Motor Oil, Used cooking oil, Automotive operation, Pesticide application, Containment for elevator reservirs.

ADMISSIONS

Freshman Academic Profile: 10% in top 10% of high school class, 30% in top 25% of high school class, 67% in top 50% of high school class. SAT Math middle 50% range 390-460. SAT Critical Reading middle 50% range 390-450. ACT middle 50% range 16-19. Minimum paper TOEFL 523. **Basis for Candidate Selection:** *Very important factors considered include:* academic GPA, standardized test scores. *Other factors considered include:* interview. **Freshman Admission Requirements:** *Academic units required:* 4 English, 4 mathematics, 3 science, (2 science labs), 2 foreign language, 3 social studies. **Freshman Admission Statistics:** 6,554 applied, 29% admitted, 57% enrolled. **Transfer Admission Requirements:** college transcript(s), Minimum college GPA of 2.0 required. Lowest grade transferable D. **General Admission Information:** Application Fee $20. Regular application deadline 7/1. Nonfall registration accepted. Admission may be deferred for a maximum of one year.

COSTS AND FINANCIAL AID

Required Forms and Deadlines: FAFSA, State aid form. *Student Employment:* Federal Work-Study Program available. Institutional employment available. Off-campus job opportunities are poor.

ALBERTA COLLEGE OF ART + DESIGN

1407 14 Avenue NW, Calgary, AB T2N 4R3
Phone: 403-284-7617 · **Financial Aid Phone:** 403-284-7600
E-mail: admissions@acad.ca
Fax: 403-284-7644 · **Website:** www.acad.ca

This public school was founded in 1926.

RATINGS

Admissions Selectivity Rating: 62   **Fire Safety Rating:** 60*

STUDENTS AND FACULTY

Enrollment: 1,112. **Student Body:** 73% female, 27% male, 11% out-of-state, 5% international (49 countries represented). Asian 0%, African American 0%, Caucasian 0%, Hispanic 0%, Native American <1%
Retention and Graduation: 64% freshmen return for sophomore year. 38% freshmen graduate within 4 years. 1% freshmen graduate within 6 years. **Faculty:** 46 full-time faculty.

ACADEMICS

Degrees: bachelor's. **Majors with Highest Enrollment:** Drawing; Painting; Sculpture. **Special Study Options:** cross-registration, exchange student program (domestic), internships, study abroad, Mobility and Exchange. **Disability Services:** Special programs offered to physically disabled students include reader services, tutors.

FACILITIES

Housing: Coed dorms, Assisted off-campus housing search. 100% of campus accessible to physically disabled. **Special Academic Facilities/Equipment:** 2 Art Galleries **Computers:** 100% of classrooms, have wireless network access. Students can register for classes online. Administrative functions (other than registration) can be performed online.

CAMPUS LIFE

Environment: Metropolis. **Activities:** student government. **Athletics (Intercollegiate):** *Men:* basketball, ice hockey, volleyball. *Women:* basketball, volleyball. **On-Campus Highlights:** Facilities, Glass Department, Graffitt Stairwell, Residence.

ADMISSIONS

Freshman Academic Profile: Minimum internet-based TOEFL 83. Minimum paper TOEFL 560. **Basis for Candidate Selection:** *Very important factors considered include:* application essay, academic GPA, level of applicant's interest, talent/ability. *Other factors considered include:* recommendation(s), standardized test scores, character/personal qualities, extracurricular activities, work experience. **Freshman Admission Requirements:** High school diploma is required and GED is not accepted. *Academic units required:* 4 English. **Freshman Admission Statistics:** 576 applied, 65% admitted, 73% enrolled. **Transfer Admission Requirements:** college transcript(s), essay or personal statement. **General Admission Information:** Application Fee $85. Early decision application deadline 2/1. Regular application deadline 4/1. Regular notification 5/15. Nonfall registration accepted. Credit and/or placement offered for CEEB Advanced Placement tests.

COSTS AND FINANCIAL AID

Average book expense $3,150. **Required Forms and Deadlines:** FAFSA. *Student Employment:* Off-campus job opportunities are good. **Criteria for awarding institutional aid:** *Non-need-based:* academics, art.

ALBERTUS MAGNUS COLLEGE

700 Prospect Street, New Haven, CT 6511
Phone: 203-773-8501 · **Financial Aid Phone:** 203-773-8508
E-mail: admissions@albertus.edu · **CEEB Code:** 3001
Fax: 203-773-5248 · **Website:** www.albertus.edu · **ACT Code:** 549

This private school, affiliated with the Roman Catholic Church, was founded in 1925. It has a 50-acre campus.

RATINGS

Admissions Selectivity Rating: 73   **Fire Safety Rating:** 77

STUDENTS AND FACULTY

Enrollment: 1,682. **Student Body:** 68% female, 32% male, 15% out-of-state, 0% international. Asian 1%, African American 27%, Caucasian 55%, Hispanic 10%, Native American <1%
Retention and Graduation: 78% freshmen return for sophomore year. 49% freshmen graduate within 4 years. 62% freshmen graduate within 6 years. **Faculty:** 42 full-time faculty, 79% hold PhDs, 43% are members of minority groups. 0% of classes are taught by teaching assistants.

ACADEMICS

Degrees: associate, bachelor's, certificate, master's. **Classes:** Most classes have 10–19 students. **Majors with Highest Enrollment:** Psychology; Business/Commerce; Education. **Special Study Options:** Accelerated program, double major, honors program, independent study, internships, student-designed major, teacher certification program. **Honors programs:** Students may apply to follow the Honors Program, which involves work in special courses designated each semester as honors courses and the development of individual projects designed in consultation with faculty mentors. Entering qualified students are assigned to special honors courses and returning students interested in such a program should consult, by the spring of their sophomore year or earlier, with their advisor and the Director of the Honors Program. **Disability Services:** Special programs offered to physically disabled students include note-taking services, reader services, tape recorders, tutors. **Career services:** Alumni network, career/job search classes, career assessment, internships.

FACILITIES

Housing: Coed dorms, women's dorms, Mansion style residence halls. Substance free and quiet halls. 70% of campus accessible to physically disabled. **Special Academic Facilities/Equipment:** Margart McDonough Art Gallery.

CAMPUS LIFE

Environment: City. **Activities:** Choral groups, dance, drama/theater, literary magazine, musical theater, student government, yearbook, Campus Ministries 1 honor society, 1 religious organization. **Athletics (Intercollegiate):** *Men:* baseball, basketball, cross-country, lacrosse, soccer, tennis, volleyball. *Women:* basketball, cross-country, lacrosse, soccer, softball, tennis, volleyball. **On-Campus Highlights:** Center for Science, Art and Technology, Athletic Center, Library, Campus Center, Art Gallery.

ADMISSIONS

Freshman Academic Profile: Average high school GPA 3. 10% in top 10% of high school class, 29% in top 25% of high school class, 68% in top 50% of high school class. 70% from public high schools. SAT Math middle 50% range 470-500. SAT Critical Reading middle 50% range 490-560. SAT Writing middle 50% range 430-560. Minimum paper TOEFL 550. **Basis for Candidate Selection:** *Very important factors considered include:* academic GPA, rigor of secondary school record. *Important factors considered include:* recommendation(s), standardized test scores. *Other factors considered include:* Class rank, application essay, alumni/ae relation, character/personal qualities, extracurricular activities, first generation, interview, level of applicant's interest, talent/ability, volunteer work, work experience. **Freshman Admission Requirements:** High school diploma is required and GED is accepted. *Academic units required:* 4 English, 2 mathematics, 2 science, 2 foreign language, 2 social studies, 2 history, 2 academic electives. **Freshman Admission Statistics:** 587 applied, 82% admitted, 21% enrolled. **Transfer Admission Requirements:** college transcript(s), Minimum college GPA of 2.0 required. Lowest grade transferable C. **General Admission Information:** Application Fee $35. Notification on a rolling basis, beginning on or about 12/1. Nonfall registration accepted. Admission may be deferred for a maximum of 12. Credit offered for CEEB Advanced Placement tests.

COSTS AND FINANCIAL AID

Annual tuition $20,166. Room and board $8,907. Required fees $908. Average book expense $920. **Required Forms and Deadlines:** FAFSA, Institution's own financial aid form. **Notification of Awards:** Applicants will be notified of awards on a rolling basis beginning 3/1. **Types of Aid:** *Need-based scholarships/grants:* Federal Pell, SEOG, state scholarships/grants, the school's own gift aid. *Loans:* Direct Subsidized Stafford, Direct Unsubsidized Stafford, Direct PLUS, Subsidized Stafford, Unsubsidized Stafford, PLUS, Federal Perkins. *Student Employment:* Federal Work-Study Program available. **Financial Aid Statistics:** 89% freshmen, 93% undergrads receive need-based scholarship or grant aid. 60% freshmen, 65% undergrads receive non-need-based scholarship or grant aid. 37% freshmen, 39% undergrads receive need-based self-help aid. 87% freshmen, 75% undergrads receive any aid. **Criteria for awarding institutional aid:** *Non-need-based:* academics, leadership, religious affiliation.

ALBION COLLEGE

611 East Porter, Albion, MI 49224
Phone: 517-629-0321 · **Financial Aid Phone:** 517-629-0440
E-mail: admission@albion.edu · **CEEB Code:** 1007
Fax: 517-629-0569 · **Website:** www.albion.edu · **ACT Code:** 1956

This private school, affiliated with the Methodist Church, was founded in 1835. It has a 585-acre campus.

RATINGS

Admissions Selectivity Rating: 78   **Fire Safety Rating:** 82

STUDENTS AND FACULTY

Enrollment: 1,249. **Student Body:** 49% female, 51% male, 8% out-of-state, 2% international (14 countries represented). Asian 2%, African American 4%, Caucasian 80%, Hispanic 4%, Native American <1%.
Retention and Graduation: 61% freshmen graduate within 4 years. 72% freshmen graduate within 6 years. 42% grads go on to further study within 1 year. 26% grads pursue arts and sciences degrees. 4% grads pursue law degrees. 1% grads pursue business degrees. 8% grads pursue medical degrees. **Faculty:** 98 full-time faculty, 95% hold PhDs, 50% are members of minority groups, 13% are women. 0% of classes are taught by teaching assistants.

ACADEMICS

Degrees: bachelor's. **Classes:** Most classes have 10–19 students. Most lab/discussion sessions have 10–19 students. **Majors with Highest Enrollment:** Biology/Biological Sciences; Economics; Psychology. **Special Study Options:** double major, dual enrollment, honors program, independent study, internships, liberal arts/career combination, student-designed major, study abroad, teacher certification program, Environmental Institute, Ford Institute for Public Service, Gerstacker Liberal Arts Program in Professional Management. **Honors programs:** The Honors Program at Albion was founded in 1976, and in August of 2004 it was renamed The Prentiss M. Brown Honors Institute. We provide an exciting and unique variety of academic experiences for highly motivated and talented students. The Institute's mix of small discussion classes, independent research, academic rigor, and personal attention provides Honors students with special challenges and opportunities for growth. Many of the College's finest teachers and scholars regularly contribute to the Institute's curriculum. Combined degree programs: BA/MEng. **Disability Services:** Special programs offered to physically disabled students include note-taking services, reader services, tape recorders, tutors. **Career services:** Alumni network, alumni services, career assessment, internships, regional alumni. Career services highlights include our six academic institutes: Professional Management, Environmental, Education, Public Policy & Service, Honors and Pre-Health. All incorporate internships or experiential learning into the curriculum.

FACILITIES

Housing: Coed dorms, special housing for disabled students, women's dorms, fraternity/sorority housing, apartments for married students, cooperative housing, apartments for single students, Special interest annexes available. 90% of campus accessible to physically disabled. **Special Academic Facilities/Equipment:** Visual arts museum, nature center, science complex museum, shark aquarium, greenhouse, geographic information systems/computer-aided mapping lab, observatory. **Computers:** 95% of classrooms, 100% of dorms, 100% of libraries, 100% of dining areas, 100% of student union, 25% of common outdoor areas have wireless network access. Students can register for classes online. Administrative functions (other than registration) can be performed online.

CAMPUS LIFE

Environment: Village. **Activities:** Choral groups, concert band, dance, drama/theater, jazz band, literary magazine, marching band, music ensembles, musical theater, pep band, radio station, student government, symphony orchestra, yearbook, Campus Ministries, International Student Organization, Model UN. 122 registered organizations, 17 honor societies, 11 religious organization. 6 fraternities, 7 sororities. **Athletics (Intercollegiate):** *Men:* baseball, basketball, cross-country, diving, equestrian sports, football, golf, soccer, swimming, tennis, track/field (outdoor), track/field (indoor). *Women:* basketball, cross-country, diving, equestrian sports, golf, soccer, softball, swimming, tennis, track/field (outdoor), track/field (indoor), volleyball. **On-Campus Highlights:** Kellogg Center—Student Center, Dow Recreation Center—Athletic Facility, Quad—Lawn in the center of campus, Baldwin—Dining Hall, Science Center Atrium, Albion is often lauded for the amount of student space available. Whether it's lounge areas, computer classrooms, meeting spaces, or the myriad rooms in the Kellogg Center, Albion students find many areas to congregate socially and academically. **Environmental Initiatives:** Sustainability was chosen as a key theme in Albion's new strategic plan. Sustainability was showcased in the inaugural edition of our Theme Year initiative in 2010–11. The Sustainability Theme Year encompassed facilities management and a variety of campus activities including a common reading, named lectures, a film series, career fairs, dining hall meals, and an ongoing lifestyle challenge. We are currently in our second year (2013-14) of this initiative. Development of Center for Sustainability and the Environment, which fosters involvement and projects by students. Examples include establishment of residential E-House (2006-present), E.P.A. P3 grant (2006-07), two National Wildlife Federation Sustainability Fellows (2008), active "Focus the Nation" and "Step it Up" participation (2007-08), and starting a student organic farm (2010). Development of an environmental "category requirement" as a graduation requirement for all students. This has fostered development of over 20 environmental courses spread over the Arts, Humanities, Natural Sciences, and Social Sciences.

ADMISSIONS

Freshman Academic Profile: Average high school GPA 3.49. SAT Math middle 50% range 520-640. SAT Critical Reading middle 50% range 490-570. ACT middle 50% range 22-27. Minimum internet-based TOEFL 79. Minimum paper TOEFL 550. **Basis for Candidate Selection:** *Very important factors considered include:* application essay, academic GPA, recommendation(s), rigor of secondary school record, standardized test scores, alumni/ae relation, character/personal qualities, extracurricular activities, first generation, geographical residence, level of applicant's interest, state residency, talent/ability, volunteer work, work experience. **Freshman Admission Requirements:** High school diploma is required and GED is accepted. *Academic units required:* 4 English, 3 mathematics, 3 science, (2 science labs), 2 foreign language, 3 social studies, 1 history. **Freshman Admission Statistics:** 4,886 applied, 61% admitted, 12%

enrolled. **Transfer Admission Requirements:** High school transcript, college transcript(s), essay or personal statement, interview, standardized test scores, statement of good standing from prior institution(s). Minimum college GPA of 2.5 required. Lowest grade transferable C. **General Admission Information:** Application Fee $40. Notification on a rolling basis, beginning on or about 11/1. Nonfall registration accepted. Admission may be deferred for a maximum of 1 year. Credit and/or placement offered for CEEB Advanced Placement tests.

COSTS AND FINANCIAL AID
Annual tuition $36,872. Room and board $10,550. Required fees $613. Average book expense $800. **Required Forms and Deadlines:** FAFSA. **Notification of Awards:** Applicants will be notified of awards on a rolling basis beginning 3/15. **Types of Aid:** *Need-based scholarships/grants:* Federal Pell, SEOG, state scholarships/grants, private scholarships, the school's own gift aid. *Loans:* Direct Subsidized Stafford, Direct Unsubsidized Stafford, Direct PLUS, Subsidized Stafford, Unsubsidized Stafford, PLUS, Federal Perkins. *Student Employment:* Federal Work-Study Program available. Institutional employment available. Highest amount earned per year from on-campus jobs $5,330. Off-campus job opportunities are fair. **Financial Aid Statistics:** 100% freshmen, 100% undergrads receive need-based scholarship or grant aid. 99% freshmen, 95% undergrads receive non-need-based scholarship or grant aid. 81% freshmen, 85% undergrads receive need-based self-help aid. 0% freshmen, 0% undergrads receive athletic scholarships. 98% freshmen, 98% undergrads receive any aid. 65% undergrads borrow to pay for school. Average cumulative indebtedness $27,001. **Criteria for awarding institutional aid:** *Non-need-based:* academics, alumni affiliation, art, leadership, music/drama.

ALBRIGHT COLLEGE

PO Box 15234, Reading, PA 19612-5234
Phone: 610-921-7799 · **Financial Aid Phone:** 610-921-7515
E-mail: admission@albright.edu · **CEEB Code:** 2004
Fax: 610-921-7729 · **Website:** www.albright.edu · **ACT Code:** 2004

This private school, affiliated with the Methodist Church, was founded in 1856. It has a 118-acre campus.

RATINGS
Admissions Selectivity Rating: 86   Fire Safety Rating: 61

STUDENTS AND FACULTY
Enrollment: 1,755. **Student Body:** 57% female, 43% male, 3% international (26 countries represented). Asian 4%, African American 18%, Caucasian 60%, Hispanic 10%, Native American 1%
Retention and Graduation: 76% freshmen return for sophomore year. 44% freshmen graduate within 4 years. 52% freshmen graduate within 6 years.
Faculty: 109 full-time faculty, 79% hold PhDs, 50% are members of minority groups, 15% are women.

ACADEMICS
Degrees: bachelor's, certificate, master's. **Classes:** Most classes have 10–19 students. Most lab/discussion sessions have 10–19 students. **Majors with Highest Enrollment:** Sociology; Business/Commerce. **Special Study Options:** Accelerated program, cross-registration, dual enrollment, English as a Second Language (ESL), exchange student program (domestic), honors program, independent study, internships, liberal arts/career combination, student-designed major, study abroad, teacher certification program, Interdisciplinary.

FACILITIES
Housing: Coed dorms, men's dorms, women's dorms, apartments for single students, Honors, Special Interest, Freshmen Floors vs Dorms. **Special Academic Facilities/Equipment:** Freedman Art Gallery.

CAMPUS LIFE
Environment: City. **Activities:** Choral groups, concert band, dance, drama/theater, jazz band, literary magazine, music ensembles, musical theater, pep band, radio station, student government, student newspaper, television station, yearbook. 84 registered organizations, 10 honor societies, 3 religious organizations. 4 fraternities, 3 sororities. **Athletics (Intercollegiate):** *Men:* baseball, basketball, cheerleading, cross-country, football, golf, soccer, swimming, tennis, track/field (outdoor), track/field (indoor), wrestling. *Women:* badminton, basketball, cheerleading, cross-country, field hockey, soccer, softball, swimming, tennis, track/field (outdoor), track/field (indoor), volleyball. **On-Campus Highlights:** Student Center, Jake's Place, Wachovia Theatre, Sports Center, Natatorium.

ADMISSIONS
Freshman Academic Profile: Average high school GPA 3.4. 23% in top 10% of high school class, 49% in top 25% of high school class, 78% in top 50% of

high school class. 77% from public high schools. SAT Math middle 50% range 480-570. SAT Critical Reading middle 50% range 480-580. ACT middle 50% range 20-25. **Basis for Candidate Selection:** *Very important factors considered include:* rigor of secondary school record. *Important factors considered include:* Class rank, application essay, academic GPA, recommendation(s), standardized test scores, character/personal qualities. *Other factors considered include:* alumni/ae relation, extracurricular activities, talent/ability, volunteer work, work experience. **Freshman Admission Requirements:** High school diploma is required and GED is accepted. *Academic units required:* 4 English, 2 mathematics, 3 science, (1 science labs), 2 foreign language, 2 social studies, 1 history, 2 academic electives. **Freshman Admission Statistics:** 7,604 applied, 50% admitted, 14% enrolled. **Transfer Admission Requirements:** college transcript(s), essay or personal statement, statement of good standing from prior institution(s). Minimum college GPA of 2.0 required. Lowest grade transferable C-. **General Admission Information:** Application Fee $25. Notification on a rolling basis, beginning on or about 10/1. Nonfall registration accepted. Admission may be deferred for a maximum of 12 months. Credit and/or placement offered for CEEB Advanced Placement tests.

COSTS AND FINANCIAL AID
Annual tuition $37,320. Room and board $10,400. Required fees $900. **Notification of Awards:** Applicants will be notified of awards on a rolling basis beginning 2/14. **Types of Aid:** *Need-based scholarships/grants:* Federal Pell, SEOG, state scholarships/grants, private scholarships, the school's own gift aid. *Loans:* Subsidized Stafford, Unsubsidized Stafford, PLUS, Federal Perkins, private educational loans. *Student Employment:* Federal Work-Study Program available. Institutional employment available. Highest amount earned per year from on-campus jobs $1,100. Off-campus job opportunities are good. **Financial Aid Statistics:** 100% freshmen, 100% undergrads receive need-based scholarship or grant aid. 7% freshmen, 7% undergrads receive non-need-based scholarship or grant aid. 91% freshmen, 91% undergrads receive need-based self-help aid. 0% freshmen, 0% undergrads receive athletic scholarships. Average cumulative indebtedness $26,252. **Criteria for awarding institutional aid:** *Non-need-based:* academics, alumni affiliation, art, leadership, minority status, music/drama, religious affiliation, state/district residency.

ALCORN STATE UNIVERSITY

1000 ASU Drive #300, Lorman, MS 39096
Phone: 601-877-6147
E-mail: ksampson@alcorn.edu · **CEEB Code:** 1008
Fax: 601-877-6347 · **Website:** www.alcorn.edu · **ACT Code:** 2176

This public school was founded in 1871. It has a 1756-acre campus.

RATINGS
Admissions Selectivity Rating: 70   Fire Safety Rating: 60*

STUDENTS AND FACULTY
Enrollment: 3,006. **Student Body:** 64% female, 36% male, 13% out-of-state, 1% international (14 countries represented). Asian 0%, African American 94%, Caucasian 2%, Hispanic 0%, Native American <1%
Retention and Graduation: 76% freshmen return for sophomore year. 20% freshmen graduate within 4 years. 40% freshmen graduate within 6 years. 38% grads go on to further study within 1 year. **Faculty:** 163 full-time faculty, 66% hold PhDs, 45% are members of minority groups, 80% are women.

ACADEMICS
Degrees: associate, bachelor's, master's, post-master's certificate. **Classes:** Most classes have 20–29 students. Most lab/discussion sessions have fewer than 10 students. **Majors with Highest Enrollment:** Elementary Education and Teaching; Liberal Arts and Sciences/Liberal Studies; Biology. **Special Study Options:** Accelerated program, cooperative education program, distance learning, double major, dual enrollment, honors program, independent study, internships, liberal arts/career combination, study abroad, teacher certification program, Undergrads may take grad level classes (restrictions apply). Combined degree programs: Cooperative physics program with Howard U. **Career services:** internships.

FACILITIES
Housing: men's dorms, women's dorms, Honor's Dorm. **Special Academic Facilities/Equipment:** Honor's Resident Hall **Computers:** Students can register for classes online. Administrative functions (other than registration) can be performed online.

CAMPUS LIFE
Environment: Rural. **Activities:** Choral groups, concert band, dance, drama/theater, jazz band, marching band, music ensembles, radio station, student government, student newspaper, television station, yearbook. 120 registered organi-

zations, 10 honor societies, 8 religious organizations. 8 fraternities, 7 sororities. **Athletics (Intercollegiate):** *Men:* baseball, basketball, cross-country, football, golf, tennis, track/field (outdoor). *Women:* basketball, cross-country, golf, soccer, softball, tennis, track/field (outdoor), volleyball.

ADMISSIONS
Freshman Academic Profile: Average high school GPA 2.99. 68% in top 50% of high school class. 99% from public high schools. SAT Math middle 50% range 405-500. SAT Critical Reading middle 50% range 390-485. ACT middle 50% range 16-20. Minimum paper TOEFL 525. **Basis for Candidate Selection:** *Very important factors considered include:* Class rank, academic GPA, rigor of secondary school record. *Important factors considered include:* standardized test scores. *Other factors considered include:* recommendation(s), interview. **Freshman Admission Requirements:** High school diploma is required and GED is accepted. *Academic units required:* 4 English, 3 mathematics, 3 science, (2 science labs), 3 social studies, 2 academic electives. **Freshman Admission Statistics:** 2,078 applied, 78% admitted, 32% enrolled. **Transfer Admission Requirements:** college transcript(s), statement of good standing from prior institution(s). Minimum college GPA of 2.0 required. Lowest grade transferable C. **General Admission Information:** Nonfall registration accepted. Credit and/or placement offered for CEEB Advanced Placement tests.

COSTS AND FINANCIAL AID
Required Forms and Deadlines: FAFSA, Institution's own financial aid form. **Notification of Awards:** Applicants will be notified of awards on a rolling basis beginning 4/1. **Types of Aid:** *Need-based scholarships/grants:* Federal Pell, SEOG, state scholarships/grants, private scholarships, the school's own gift aid. *Loans:* Direct Subsidized Stafford, Direct Unsubsidized Stafford, Direct PLUS. *Student Employment:* Federal Work-Study Program available. Institutional employment available. Highest amount earned per year from on-campus jobs $500. Off-campus job opportunities are poor. **Financial Aid Statistics:** 95% freshmen, 93% undergrads receive need-based scholarship or grant aid. 33% freshmen, 24% undergrads receive non-need-based scholarship or grant aid. 75% freshmen, 84% undergrads receive need-based self-help aid. 10% freshmen, 8% undergrads receive athletic scholarships. 90% undergrads borrow to pay for school. Average cumulative indebtedness $34,117. **Criteria for awarding institutional aid:** *Non-need-based:* academics, athletics.

ALDERSON BROADDUS UNIVERSITY

101 College Hill Drive, Philippi, WV 26416
Phone: 800-263-1549 · **Financial Aid Phone:** 304-457-6354
E-mail: admissions@ab.edu · **CEEB Code:** 5005
Fax: 304-457-6239 · **Website:** www.ab.edu · **ACT Code:** 4508

This private school, affiliated with the American Baptist Church, was founded in 1871. It has a 170-acre campus.

RATINGS
Admissions Selectivity Rating: 85   Fire Safety Rating: 74

STUDENTS AND FACULTY
Enrollment: 1,024. **Student Body:** 48% female, 52% male, 59% out-of-state, 3% international (11 countries represented). Asian 1%, African American 16%, Caucasian 74%, Hispanic 4%, Native American <1%
Retention and Graduation: 56% freshmen return for sophomore year. 30% freshmen graduate within 4 years. 43% freshmen graduate within 6 years. 15% grads go on to further study within 1 year. 19% grads pursue arts and sciences degrees. 4% grads pursue law degrees. 7% grads pursue business degrees. 11% grads pursue medical degrees. **Faculty:** 61 full-time faculty, 52% hold PhDs, 56% are members of minority groups, 13% are women. 0% of classes are taught by teaching assistants.

ACADEMICS
Degrees: associate, bachelor's, certificate, master's, post-bachelor's certificate. **Classes:** Most classes have fewer than 10 students. Most lab/discussion sessions have 10–19 students. **Majors with Highest Enrollment:** Registered Nursing/Registered Nurse; Biology/Biological Sciences; Athletic Training/Trainer. **Special Study Options:** double major, honors program, independent study, internships, liberal arts/career combination, study abroad, teacher certification program, Business Department offers on-line certificate program. **Disability Services:** Special programs offered to physically disabled students include note-taking services, reader services, tape recorders, tutors. **Career services:** Alumni network, career/job search classes, career assessment, internships.

FACILITIES
Housing: Coed dorms, special housing for disabled students, women's dorms, apartments for married students, apartments for single students, Wellness Housing. 70% of campus accessible to physically disabled. **Special Academic Facilities/Equipment:** Art Gallery in Burbick Hall. Campbell School House

Computers: 75% of classrooms, 100% of dorms, 90% of libraries, 100% of dining areas, 100% of student union, have wireless network access. Administrative functions (other than registration) can be performed online.

CAMPUS LIFE
Environment: Rural. **Activities:** Choral groups, concert band, drama/theater, jazz band, literary magazine, music ensembles, musical theater, radio station, student government, student newspaper, television station, yearbook, Campus Ministries. 49 registered organizations, 2 honor societies, 2 religious organizations. 2 fraternities, 3 sororities. **Athletics (Intercollegiate):** *Men:* baseball, basketball, cross-country, soccer, track/field (outdoor), track/field (indoor). *Women:* basketball, cross-country, soccer, softball, track/field (outdoor), track/field (indoor), volleyball. **On-Campus Highlights:** Cave, Burbick Hall, Rex Pyles Arena, Wilcox Chapel **Environmental Initiatives:** recycling efforts electric maintenance vehicles sustainability survey

ADMISSIONS
Freshman Academic Profile: Average high school GPA 3.2. 11% in top 10% of high school class, 32% in top 25% of high school class, 68% in top 50% of high school class. 97% from public high schools. SAT Math middle 50% range 420-530. SAT Critical Reading middle 50% range 430-520. SAT Writing middle 50% range 420-500. ACT middle 50% range 19-24. Minimum paper TOEFL 500. **Basis for Candidate Selection:** *Very important factors considered include:* academic GPA, rigor of secondary school record, standardized test scores. *Important factors considered include:* application essay. *Other factors considered include:* recommendation(s), alumni/ae relation, first generation, interview, level of applicant's interest, talent/ability. **Freshman Admission Requirements:** High school diploma is required and GED is accepted. *Academic units required:* 4 English, 3 mathematics, 3 science, (1 science labs), 0 foreign language, 1 social studies, 0 history. **Freshman Admission Statistics:** 3,880 applied, 43% admitted, 21% enrolled. **Transfer Admission Requirements:** High school transcript, college transcript(s), statement of good standing from prior institution(s). Minimum college GPA of 2.0 required. Lowest grade transferable C. **General Admission Information:** Application Fee $25. Nonfall registration accepted. Admission may be deferred for a maximum of 1 year. Placement offered for CEEB Advanced Placement tests.

COSTS AND FINANCIAL AID
Annual tuition $22,530. Room and board $7,236. Required fees $210. Average book expense $800. **Required Forms and Deadlines:** FAFSA, State aid form. **Notification of Awards:** Applicants will be notified of awards on a rolling basis beginning 2/15. **Types of Aid:** *Need-based scholarships/grants:* Federal Pell, SEOG, state scholarships/grants, private scholarships, the school's own gift aid, Federal Nursing Scholarships., National Health Service Corp, Scholarship for disadvantaged students. *Loans:* Subsidized Stafford, Unsubsidized Stafford, PLUS, Federal Perkins, Federal Nursing, college/university loans from institutional funds. *Student Employment:* Federal Work-Study Program available. Highest amount earned per year from on-campus jobs $1,400. Off-campus job opportunities are fair. **Financial Aid Statistics:** 100% freshmen, 100% undergrads receive need-based scholarship or grant aid. 12% freshmen, 23% undergrads receive non-need-based scholarship or grant aid. 82% freshmen, 80% undergrads receive need-based self-help aid. 5% freshmen, 7% undergrads receive athletic scholarships. 100% freshmen, 99% undergrads receive any aid. 90% undergrads borrow to pay for school. Average cumulative indebtedness $24,957. **Criteria for awarding institutional aid:** *Non-need-based:* academics, athletics, music/drama.

ALFRED UNIVERSITY

Best 380

Alumni Hall, Alfred, NY 14802-1205
Phone: 607-871-2115 · **Financial Aid Phone:** 607-871-2159
E-mail: admissions@alfred.edu · **CEEB Code:** 2005
Fax: 607-871-2198 · **Website:** www.alfred.edu · **ACT Code:** 2666

This private school was founded in 1836. It has a 600-acre campus.

RATINGS
Admissions Selectivity Rating: 82   Fire Safety Rating: 80

STUDENTS AND FACULTY
Enrollment: 1,929. **Student Body:** 51% female, 49% male, 24% out-of-state, 3% international (4 countries represented). Asian 2%, African American 8%, Caucasian 67%, Hispanic 7%, Native American <1%

Retention and Graduation: 44% freshmen graduate within 4 years. 62% freshmen graduate within 6 years. 30% grads go on to further study within 1 year. **Faculty:** 159 full-time faculty. 45% are members of minority groups. 0% of classes are taught by teaching assistants.

ACADEMICS

Degrees: bachelor's, master's, post-master's certificate. **Classes:** Most classes have 10–19 students. Most lab/discussion sessions have fewer than 10 students. **Majors with Highest Enrollment:** Business/Commerce; Ceramic Arts and Ceramics; Psychology. **Special Study Options:** cooperative education program, cross-registration, double major, English as a Second Language (ESL), exchange student program (domestic), honors program, independent study, internships, liberal arts/career combination, student-designed major, study abroad, teacher certification program. **Honors programs:** The Alfred University Honors Program is designed to enrich the lives of exceptional students. It has two components: an honors seminar - meets one evening a week and the senior thesis. Combined degree programs: 4+1 MBA program for bus, liberal arts and sciences. **Disability Services:** Special programs offered to physically disabled students include note-taking services, tape recorders, tutors. **Career services:** Alumni network, career assessment, internships. We are extremely proud of all of the services offered by the staff at the Robert R. McComsey Career Development Center.

FACILITIES

Housing: Coed dorms, apartments for single students, Theme housing (i.e. Environmental Studies House, Language House, etc.). 50% of campus accessible to physically disabled. **Special Academic Facilities/Equipment:** Art museums, carillon, language labs, electron microscope, observatory, extensive engineering equipment, performing arts center. **Computers:** 90% of classrooms, 100% of dorms, 100% of libraries, 100% of student union, have wireless network access. Students can register for classes online. Administrative functions (other than registration) can be performed online.

CAMPUS LIFE

Environment: Rural. **Activities:** Choral groups, concert band, dance, drama/theater, literary magazine, music ensembles, musical theater, pep band, radio station, student government, student newspaper, student-run film society, television station, yearbook, Campus Ministries, International Student Organization. 90 registered organizations, 13 honor societies, 3 religious organizations. **Athletics (Intercollegiate):** *Men:* basketball, cross-country, diving, equestrian sports, football, lacrosse, skiing (downhill/alpine), soccer, swimming, tennis, track/field (outdoor), track/field (indoor). *Women:* basketball, cross-country, diving, equestrian sports, lacrosse, skiing (downhill/alpine), soccer, softball, swimming, tennis, track/field (outdoor), track/field (indoor), volleyball. **On-Campus Highlights:** Powell Campus Center, Binns Merrill Hall, Schein-Joseph International Museum of Ceramic Art, John L. Stull Observatory, Robert Turner Student Art Gallery. **Environmental Initiatives:** Campus-wide recycling program (paper, glass, plastic, electronics, printer/toner cartridges); Re-usable material exchange (REPO); Tray-less dining.

ADMISSIONS

Freshman Academic Profile: Average high school GPA 3.18. 16.4% in top 10% of high school class, 43.1% in top 25% of high school class, 83.6% in top 50% of high school class. SAT Math middle 50% range 510-610. SAT Critical Reading middle 50% range 490-590. SAT Writing middle 50% range 460-570. ACT middle 50% range 22-27. Minimum internet-based TOEFL 80. Minimum paper TOEFL 550. **Basis for Candidate Selection:** *Very important factors considered include:* Class rank, recommendation(s), rigor of secondary school record, character/personal qualities, extracurricular activities. *Important factors considered include:* application essay, standardized test scores, volunteer work, work experience. *Other factors considered include:* interview, racial/ethnic status, talent/ability. **Freshman Admission Requirements:** High school diploma is required and GED is accepted. *Academic units required:* 4 English, 2 mathematics, 2 science, (2 science labs), 2 social studies. **Freshman Admission Statistics:** 3,417 applied, 70% admitted, 22% enrolled. **Transfer Admission Requirements:** college transcript(s), statement of good standing from prior institution(s). Minimum college GPA of 2.5 required. Lowest grade transferable C. **General Admission Information:** Application Fee $40. Early decision application deadline 12/1. Notification on a rolling basis, beginning on or about 2/15. Nonfall registration accepted. Admission may be deferred for a maximum of 2 years. Credit offered for CEEB Advanced Placement tests.

COSTS AND FINANCIAL AID

Annual tuition $27,824. Room and board $11,618. Required fees $950. Average book expense $1,150. **Required Forms and Deadlines:** FAFSA, Institution's own financial aid form, State aid form, Noncustodial PROFILE, Business/Farm Supplement. **Notification of Awards:** Applicants will be notified of awards on a rolling basis beginning 2/15. **Types of Aid:** *Need-based scholarships/grants:* Federal Pell, SEOG, state scholarships/grants, private scholarships, the school's own gift aid. *Loans:* Subsidized Stafford, Unsubsidized Stafford, PLUS, Federal Perkins, college/university loans from institutional funds, Private alternative loans. *Student Employment:* Federal Work-Study Program available. Institu-

tional employment available. Off-campus job opportunities are poor. **Financial Aid Statistics:** 100% freshmen, 99% undergrads receive need-based scholarship or grant aid. 78% freshmen, 62% undergrads receive non-need-based scholarship or grant aid. 90% freshmen, 89% undergrads receive need-based self-help aid. 0% freshmen, 0% undergrads receive athletic scholarships. 96% freshmen, 92% undergrads receive any aid. 82% undergrads borrow to pay for school. **Criteria for awarding institutional aid:** *Non-need-based:* academics, art, leadership, music/drama.

ALICE LLOYD COLLEGE

100 Purpose Road, Pippa Passes, KY 41844
Phone: 606-368-6036
E-mail: admissions@alc.edu • **CEEB Code:** 1098
Fax: 606-368-6215 • **Website:** www.alc.edu • **ACT Code:** 1502

This private school was founded in 1923. It has a 225-acre campus.

RATINGS

Admissions Selectivity Rating: 87   Fire Safety Rating: 89

STUDENTS AND FACULTY

Enrollment: 607. **Student Body:** 51% female, 49% male, 13% out-of-state, 0% international (1 countries represented). Asian 0%, African American 1%, Caucasian 99%, Hispanic 0%, Native American <1%
Retention and Graduation: 63% freshmen return for sophomore year. 25% freshmen graduate within 4 years. 33% freshmen graduate within 6 years. 55% grads go on to further study within 1 year. 35% grads pursue arts and sciences degrees. 5% grads pursue law degrees. 10% grads pursue business degrees. 5% grads pursue medical degrees. **Faculty:** 29 full-time faculty, 59% hold PhDs, 41% are members of minority groups, 10% are women. 0% of classes are taught by teaching assistants.

ACADEMICS

Degrees: bachelor's. **Classes:** Most classes have 20–29 students. **Majors with Highest Enrollment:** Business/Commerce; Education; Biology/Biological Sciences. **Special Study Options:** cooperative education program, double major, honors program, independent study, internships, liberal arts/career combination, study abroad, teacher certification program. **Disability Services:** Special programs offered to physically disabled students include reader services, tutors. **Career services:** Alumni network, alumni services, career assessment, internships, regional alumni.

FACILITIES

Housing: men's dorms, women's dorms. 90% of campus accessible to physically disabled. **Special Academic Facilities/Equipment:** Photographic archives, oral history museum, Appalachian collection, on-campus day care center, kindergarten, elementary, and secondary school. **Computers:** 100% of classrooms, 50% of dorms, 100% of libraries, 100% of dining areas, 75% of common outdoor areas have wireless network access.

CAMPUS LIFE

Environment: Rural. **Activities:** Choral groups, drama/theater, music ensembles, musical theater, pep band, radio station, student government, student newspaper, yearbook. 19 registered organizations, 2 honor societies, 1 religious organization. **Athletics (Intercollegiate):** *Men:* baseball, basketball, cheerleading, cross-country, golf, tennis. *Women:* basketball, cheerleading, cross-country, golf, softball, tennis. **On-Campus Highlights:** Jerry Davis Student Center, Historical Tour, Grady Nutt Athletic Center, Campbell Arts Center, Cushing Hall.

ADMISSIONS

Freshman Academic Profile: Average high school GPA 3.39. 30% in top 10% of high school class, 58% in top 25% of high school class, 86% in top 50% of high school class. 90% from public high schools. SAT Math middle 50% range 480-570. SAT Critical Reading middle 50% range 440-590. SAT Writing middle 50% range 430-520. ACT middle 50% range 17-23. Minimum paper TOEFL 550. **Basis for Candidate Selection:** *Very important factors considered include:* rigor of secondary school record, standardized test scores, character/personal qualities, geographical residence. *Important factors considered include:* Class rank, recommendation(s), alumni/ae relation, state residency. *Other factors considered include:* application essay, extracurricular activities, interview, talent/ability, volunteer work, work experience. **Freshman Admission Requirements:** High school diploma is required and GED is accepted. *Academic units required:* 4 English, 3 mathematics, 2 science, 2 social studies, 1 history. **Freshman Admission Statistics:** 994 applied, 56% admitted, 32% enrolled. **Transfer Admission Requirements:** High school transcript, college transcript(s), standardized test scores, statement of good standing from prior institution(s). Minimum college GPA of 2.0 required. Lowest grade transferable C. **General Admission Information:** Regular application deadline 5/1. Nonfall registration accepted. Credit and/or placement offered for CEEB Advanced Placement tests.

COSTS AND FINANCIAL AID

Room and board $4,250. Required fees $1,300. Average book expense $850. **Required Forms and Deadlines:** FAFSA. **Notification of Awards:** Applicants will be notified of awards on a rolling basis beginning 4/1. **Types of Aid:** *Need-based scholarships/grants:* Federal Pell, SEOG, state scholarships/grants, private scholarships, the school's own gift aid. *Loans:* Subsidized Stafford, Unsubsidized Stafford, PLUS, college/university loans from institutional funds. *Student Employment:* Federal Work-Study Program available. Institutional employment available. Off-campus job opportunities are fair. **Financial Aid Statistics:** 99% freshmen, 99% undergrads receive need-based scholarship or grant aid. 11% freshmen, 16% undergrads receive non-need-based scholarship or grant aid. 89% freshmen, 84% undergrads receive need-based self-help aid. 7% freshmen, 5% undergrads receive athletic scholarships. 100% freshmen, 100% undergrads receive any aid. 33% undergrads borrow to pay for school. Average cumulative indebtedness $5,216. **Criteria for awarding institutional aid:** *Non-need-based:* athletics, minority status, state/district residency.

ALLEGHENY COLLEGE

Best 380

Allegheny College, Meadville, PA 16335
Phone: 814-332-4351 · **Financial Aid Phone:** 800-835-7780
E-mail: admissions@allegheny.edu · **CEEB Code:** 2006
Fax: 814-337-0431 · **Website:** www.allegheny.edu · **ACT Code:** 3520

This private school was founded in 1815. It has a 565-acre campus.

RATINGS

Admissions Selectivity Rating: 88   **Fire Safety Rating:** 79

STUDENTS AND FACULTY

Enrollment: 1,968. **Student Body:** 55% female, 45% male, 46% out-of-state, 2% international (47 countries represented). Asian 2%, African American 5%, Caucasian 79%, Hispanic 6%, Native American <1%
Retention and Graduation: 83% freshmen return for sophomore year. 73% freshmen graduate within 4 years. 78% freshmen graduate within 6 years. 28% grads go on to further study within 1 year. 8% grads pursue arts and sciences degrees. 4% grads pursue law degrees. 1% grads pursue business degrees. 6% grads pursue medical degrees. **Faculty:** 171 full-time faculty, 92% hold PhDs, 47% are members of minority groups, 16% are women. 0% of classes are taught by teaching assistants.

ACADEMICS

Degrees: bachelor's. **Classes:** Most classes have 10–19 students. Most lab/discussion sessions have 10–19 students. **Majors with Highest Enrollment:** Biology/Biological Sciences; Psychology; English Language and Literature. **Special Study Options:** double major, dual enrollment, English as a Second Language (ESL), exchange student program (domestic), independent study, internships, student-designed major, study abroad, Pre-professional programs, teacher preparation partnerships, combined degree programs, experiential learning terms (summer study program), marine biology study program, Washington Semester, medical school partnerships, graduate school partnerships, double minor, domestic off campus semester away study programs, accelerated masters and doctorate degree programs. Combined degree programs: BA/MA, BA/MEng, Mangmnt,Public Policy,Teachng,Nursing,Occ&Phy Therapy,osteo. med.,phys. asst. **Disability Services:** Special programs offered to physically disabled students include note-taking services, tape recorders, tutors. **Career services:** Alumni network, alumni services, career/job search classes, career assessment, internships, regional alumni. Career services highlights include experiential learning that connects classroom learning to the wider world, including social issues, international relations, key concepts in leadership development, and ultimately career and life goals. Through internships, community service programs and service learning, off-campus study, and other leadership opportunities students become active participants in the learning process by adapting academic skills and knowledge to meet new challenges. ACCEL, Allegheny College Center for Experiential Learning, unites resources, personnel, and funding sources to create experiential learning initiatives for Allegheny students.

FACILITIES

Housing: Coed dorms, special housing for disabled students, men's dorms, women's dorms, fraternity/sorority housing, apartments for single students, Wellness Housing, Theme Housing, quiet study floors, townhouses-environmentally-sensitive, low fume material, LEED certified. 35% of campus accessible to physically disabled. **Special Academic Facilities/Equipment:** New Center For Communication Arts with a trap stage and green and blue screen room; radio and television stations; state-of-the-art, nationally acclaimed science complex; videoconference facilities; planetarium; observatory; GIS lab; state-of-the-art language-learning center; smart classrooms; renovated dance and art studios and performance spaces; art galleries; world's largest solid-volume glass sculpture grouping; 283-acre Environmental Research Reserve; 80-acre protected forest; new alumni center; comprehensive sports and fitness center, seismographic network station, Center for Political Participation, Center for Economic and Environmental Development, environmental roof garden. **Computers:** 50% of classrooms, 100% of dorms, 100% of libraries, 100% of dining areas, 100% of student union, 100% of common outdoor areas have wireless network access. Students can register for classes online. Administrative functions (other than registration) can be performed online.

CAMPUS LIFE

Environment: Town. **Activities:** Choral groups, concert band, dance, drama/theater, jazz band, literary magazine, music ensembles, musical theater, radio station, student government, student newspaper, symphony orchestra, television station, yearbook, Campus Ministries, International Student Organization, Model UN. 113 registered organizations, 15 honor societies, 8 religious organizations. 5 fraternities, 5 sororities. **Athletics (Intercollegiate):** *Men:* baseball, basketball, cross-country, diving, football, golf, soccer, swimming, tennis, track/field (outdoor), track/field (indoor). *Women:* basketball, cross-country, diving, golf, lacrosse, soccer, softball, swimming, tennis, track/field (outdoor), track/field (indoor), volleyball. **On-Campus Highlights:** Rustic Bridge, Wise Sport and Fitness Center, Henderson Campus Center, Pelletier Library, World's largest solid-volume glass sculpture group, State-of-the-art, nationally acclaimed science complex dedicated to biology, chemistry and environmental science; Patricia Bush Tippie Alumni Center; seismographic network station; Center for Political Participation; Center for Economic & Environmental Development; radio and TV stations, Grounds For Change Coffeehouse, Vukovich Communication Arts Building Environmental Roof Garden; Robertson athletic fields and recreation area. **Environmental Initiatives:** Climate action plan; Energy efficiency through energy audit, retrofits, geothermal wells, education, green building, submetering, dorm competitions, wind energy; Composting.

ADMISSIONS

Freshman Academic Profile: Average high school GPA 3.75. 43% in top 10% of high school class, 73% in top 25% of high school class, 95% in top 50% of high school class. 80% from public high schools. SAT Math middle 50% range 520-630. SAT Critical Reading middle 50% range 530-640. SAT Writing middle 50% range 510-640. ACT middle 50% range 23-29. Minimum internet-based TOEFL 80. Minimum paper TOEFL 550. **Basis for Candidate Selection:** *Very important factors considered include:* Class rank, academic GPA, rigor of secondary school record. *Important factors considered include:* recommendation(s), standardized test scores, character/personal qualities, extracurricular activities, interview, level of applicant's interest. *Other factors considered include:* application essay, alumni/ae relation, first generation, geographical residence, racial/ethnic status, talent/ability, volunteer work, work experience. **Freshman Admission Requirements:** High school diploma is required and GED is accepted. *Academic units required:* 4 English, 3 mathematics, 3 science, 2 foreign language, 3 social studies, 1 academic electives. **Freshman Admission Statistics:** 3,857 applied, 72% admitted, 17% enrolled. **Transfer Admission Requirements:** High school transcript, college transcript(s), essay or personal statement, standardized test scores, Minimum college GPA of 2.5 required. Lowest grade transferable C. **General Admission Information:** Application Fee $35. Early decision application deadline 11/15. Regular application deadline 2/15. Regular notification 4/1. Nonfall registration accepted. Admission may be deferred for a maximum of 1 year. Credit and/or placement offered for CEEB Advanced Placement tests.

COSTS AND FINANCIAL AID

Annual tuition $41,970. Room and board $10,740. Required fees $500. Average book expense $1,000. **Required Forms and Deadlines:** FAFSA. **Notification of Awards:** Applicants will be notified of awards on a rolling basis beginning 3/1. **Types of Aid:** *Need-based scholarships/grants:* Federal Pell, SEOG, state scholarships/grants, private scholarships, the school's own gift aid, Federal Academic Competitiveness Grant, National SMART Grant, Veterans Educational Benefits, Yellow Ribbon Program. *Loans:* Direct Subsidized Stafford, Direct Unsubsidized Stafford, Direct PLUS, Federal Perkins, Private loans from commercial lenders. *Student Employment:* Federal Work-Study Program available. Institutional employment available. Highest amount earned per year from on-campus jobs $8,350. Off-campus job opportunities are excellent. **Financial Aid Statistics:** 100% freshmen, 100% undergrads receive need-based scholarship or grant aid. 25% freshmen, 18% undergrads receive non-need-based scholarship or grant aid. 82% freshmen, 85% undergrads receive need-based self-help aid. 0% freshmen, 0% undergrads receive athletic scholarships. 100% freshmen, 99% undergrads receive any aid. Average cumulative indebtedness $28,174. **Criteria for awarding institutional aid:** *Non-need-based:* academics, leadership, minority status, state/district residency.

ALLEN COLLEGE

1825 Logan Avenue, Waterloo, IA 50703
Phone: 319-226-2000 · **Financial Aid Phone:** 319-226-2000
E-mail: Admissions@AllenCollege.edu
Fax: 319-226-2051 · **Website:** www.allencollege.edu · **ACT Code:** 30691

This private school was founded in 1989.

RATINGS

Admissions Selectivity Rating: 64   **Fire Safety Rating:** 89

STUDENTS AND FACULTY

Enrollment: 397. **Student Body:** 93% female, 7% male, 5% out-of-state, 1% international (2 countries represented). Asian 1%, African American 2%, Caucasian 90%, Hispanic 1%, Native American <1%
Retention and Graduation: 64% freshmen graduate within 4 years. 64% freshmen graduate within 6 years. 10% grads go on to further study within 1 year. **Faculty:** 28 full-time faculty, 36% hold PhDs, 96% are members of minority groups, 4% are women. 0% of classes are taught by teaching assistants.

ACADEMICS

Degrees: associate, bachelor's, certificate, master's, post-master's certificate. **Classes:** Most classes have fewer than 10 students. Most lab/discussion sessions have fewer than 10 students. **Majors with Highest Enrollment:** Health Services/Allied Health/Health Sciences. **Special Study Options:** Accelerated program, cooperative education program, distance learning, honors program, independent study, internships. **Disability Services:** Special programs offered to physically disabled students include tutors.

FACILITIES

Housing: Coed dorms, Housing also available at a cooperating institution. 100% of campus accessible to physically disabled. **Computers:** 100% of classrooms, 100% of dorms, 100% of libraries, 100% of student union, 100% of common outdoor areas have wireless network access. Administrative functions (other than registration) can be performed online.

CAMPUS LIFE

Environment: City. **Activities:** Choral groups, student government, student newspaper, yearbook. 4 registered organizations, 1 honor society, 1 religious organization.

ADMISSIONS

Freshman Academic Profile: Minimum paper TOEFL 550. **Basis for Candidate Selection:** *Very important factors considered include:* Class rank, academic GPA, rigor of secondary school record, standardized test scores. *Important factors considered include:* application essay, recommendation(s). *Other factors considered include:* character/personal qualities, extracurricular activities, first generation, interview, talent/ability. **Freshman Admission Requirements:** High school diploma is required and GED is accepted. *Academic units required:* 8 English, 6 mathematics, 6 science, 6 social studies. **Freshman Admission Statistics:** 4 applied, 50% admitted, 100% enrolled. **Transfer Admission Requirements:** High school transcript, college transcript(s), essay or personal statement, standardized test scores, Minimum college GPA of 2.7 required. Lowest grade transferable C. **General Admission Information:** Application Fee $50. Regular application deadline 3/1. Notification on a rolling basis, beginning on or about 3/15. Nonfall registration accepted. Credit offered for CEEB Advanced Placement tests.

COSTS AND FINANCIAL AID

Annual tuition $13,650. Room and board $7,281. Required fees $953. Average book expense $1,200. **Required Forms and Deadlines:** FAFSA, Institution's own financial aid form. **Notification of Awards:** Applicants will be notified of awards on a rolling basis beginning 4/1. **Types of Aid:** *Need-based scholarships/grants:* Federal Pell, SEOG, state scholarships/grants, private scholarships, the school's own gift aid, Federal Nursing Scholarships. Various funds from HRSA (SDS- Scholarship for Disadvantaged Students, NSP, Nursing Scholarship Program, AENT—Advanced Education Nurse Traineeship. *Loans:* Direct Subsidized Stafford, Direct Unsubsidized Stafford, Direct PLUS, Federal Perkins, Federal Nursing, college/university loans from institutional funds, Alternative Loans. *Student Employment:* Federal Work-Study Program available. Off-campus job opportunities are excellent. **Financial Aid Statistics:** 100% freshmen,

88% undergrads receive need-based scholarship or grant aid. 0% freshmen, 0% undergrads receive non-need-based scholarship or grant aid. 50% freshmen, 93% undergrads receive need-based self-help aid. 0% freshmen, 0% undergrads receive athletic scholarships. 100% freshmen, 97% undergrads receive any aid. 0% undergrads borrow to pay for school. Average cumulative indebtedness $0. **Criteria for awarding institutional aid:** *Non-need-based:* academics, alumni affiliation, leadership, minority status, state/district residency.

ALMA COLLEGE

614 West Superior Street, Alma, MI 48801-1599
Phone: 989-463-7139 · **Financial Aid Phone:** 989-463-7347
E-mail: admissions@alma.edu · **CEEB Code:** 1010
Fax: 989-463-7057 · **Website:** www.alma.edu · **ACT Code:** 1958

This private school, affiliated with the Presbyterian Church, was founded in 1886. It has a 125-acre campus.

RATINGS

Admissions Selectivity Rating: 79   **Fire Safety Rating:** 65

STUDENTS AND FACULTY

Enrollment: 1,362. **Student Body:** 55% female, 45% male, 9% out-of-state, 1% international (13 countries represented). Asian 1%, African American 3%, Caucasian 84%, Hispanic 4%, Native American 1%
Retention and Graduation: 78% freshmen return for sophomore year. 48% freshmen graduate within 4 years. 61% freshmen graduate within 6 years. 22% grads go on to further study within 1 year. **Faculty:** 92 full-time faculty, 84% hold PhDs, 39% are members of minority groups, 13% are women. 0% of classes are taught by teaching assistants.

ACADEMICS

Degrees: bachelor's. **Classes:** Most classes have 10–19 students. Most lab/discussion sessions have 10–19 students. **Majors with Highest Enrollment:** Business Administration and Management; Health and Physical Education/Fitness; Psychology. **Special Study Options:** double major, dual enrollment, exchange student program (domestic), honors program, independent study, internships, student-designed major, study abroad, teacher certification program. **Honors programs:** Students in the Honors Program participate in special seminar opportunities and enroll in courses designed for honors scholars. Combined degree programs: 3-2 occupational therapy. **Disability Services:** Special programs offered to physically disabled students include note-taking services, reader services, tape recorders, tutors. **Career services:** alumni services, career assessment, internships.

FACILITIES

Housing: Coed dorms, fraternity/sorority housing, Theme Housing. 75% of campus accessible to physically disabled. **Special Academic Facilities/Equipment:** Music and arts centers, science lab, planetarium, a DNA synthesizer and sequencer, and a multinuclear magnetic resonance spectrometer. **Computers:** 60% of classrooms, 100% of libraries, 100% of dining areas, 100% of student union, have wireless network access. Students can register for classes online.

CAMPUS LIFE

Environment: Village. **Activities:** Choral groups, concert band, dance, drama/theater, jazz band, marching band, music ensembles, radio station, student government, student newspaper, symphony orchestra, yearbook, Campus Ministries, International Student Organization, Model UN. 75 registered organizations, 20 honor societies, 4 religious organizations. 6 fraternities, 5 sororities. **Athletics (Intercollegiate):** *Men:* baseball, basketball, cross-country, diving, football, golf, soccer, swimming, tennis, track/field (outdoor). *Women:* basketball, cross-country, diving, golf, soccer, softball, swimming, tennis, track/field (outdoor), volleyball. **On-Campus Highlights:** Joe's Place, Stone Center for Recreation, Library, Remick Heritage Center, Wright Hall (residence hall). **Environmental Initiatives:** Alma's green residence hall, Wright Hall, was completed in January 2005. The modern, 60-bed apartment-style hall features a number of environmentally friendly features, including geothermal heating and cooling, recycled-content ceiling tiles and carpeting, energy-efficient windows, rooftop solar heating panels, energy-efficient showers and washing machines, and a computerized energy monitoring system. The Hogan Center is the first official LEED-certified building for green construction at Alma College and Gratiot County. The renovated Hogan Center and new Art Smith Arena were awarded LEED certification at the Silver level by the U.S. Green Building Council (USGBC) and verified by the Green Building Certification Institute (GBCI). LEED is the nations preeminent program for the design, construction and operation of high performance green buildings. The arena serves as the primary venue for commencement, convocations, major speakers, concerts, athletics and other major events, Alma College and the Pine River Superfund Task Force organized an international conference that examined the impact of DDT on human health and the environment. The Eugene Kenaga International DDT Conference on Environment and Health took place March 14, 2008 at Alma College. It brought together international experts to frame and lead discussions of current knowledge of DDT and other persistent organic pollutants (POPs).

ADMISSIONS
Freshman Academic Profile: Average high school GPA 3.53. 18% in top 10% of high school class, 21% in top 25% of high school class, 57.5% in top 50% of high school class. 91% from public high schools. SAT Math middle 50% range 453-555. SAT Critical Reading middle 50% range 470-568. SAT Writing middle 50% range 453-555. ACT middle 50% range 21-27. Minimum internet-based TOEFL 79. Minimum paper TOEFL 550. **Basis for Candidate Selection:** *Very important factors considered include:* academic GPA, standardized test scores. *Important factors considered include:* application essay. *Other factors considered include:* Class rank, recommendation(s), rigor of secondary school record, alumni/ae relation, character/personal qualities, extracurricular activities, geographical residence, interview, level of applicant's interest, state residency, talent/ability, volunteer work, work experience. **Freshman Admission Requirements:** High school diploma is required and GED is accepted. *Academic units required:* 4 English, 3 mathematics, 3 science, 3 social studies. **Freshman Admission Statistics:** 2,338 applied, 72% admitted, 21% enrolled. **Transfer Admission Requirements:** High school transcript, college transcript(s), statement of good standing from prior institution(s). Minimum college GPA of 3.0 required. Lowest grade transferable C. **General Admission Information:** Application Fee $25. Notification on a rolling basis, beginning on or about 9/1. Nonfall registration accepted. Admission may be deferred for a maximum of 1 year. Credit and/or placement offered for CEEB Advanced Placement tests.

COSTS AND FINANCIAL AID
Annual tuition $34,190. Room and board $9,490. Required fees $395. Average book expense $1,100. **Required Forms and Deadlines:** FAFSA. **Notification of Awards:** Applicants will be notified of awards on a rolling basis beginning 3/1. **Types of Aid:** *Need-based scholarships/grants:* Federal Pell, SEOG, state scholarships/grants, the school's own gift aid. *Loans:* Subsidized Stafford, Unsubsidized Stafford, PLUS, Federal Perkins, college/university loans from institutional funds, Alternative loans. *Student Employment:* Federal Work-Study Program available. Institutional employment available. Off-campus job opportunities are good. **Financial Aid Statistics:** 100% freshmen, 100% undergrads receive need-based scholarship or grant aid. 15% freshmen, 12% undergrads receive non-need-based scholarship or grant aid. 86% freshmen, 88% undergrads receive need-based self-help aid. 0% freshmen, 0% undergrads receive athletic scholarships. 99% freshmen, 99% undergrads receive any aid. 78% undergrads borrow to pay for school. Average cumulative indebtedness $27,458. **Criteria for awarding institutional aid:** *Non-need-based:* academics, alumni affiliation, art, minority status, music/drama.

ALVERNIA COLLEGE

400 St. Bernardine Street, Reading, PA 19607
Phone: 610-796-8220 · **Financial Aid Phone:** 610-796-8356
E-mail: admissions@alvernia.edu
Fax: 610-796-8336

This private school, affiliated with the Roman Catholic Church, was founded in 1958. It has a 80-acre campus.

RATINGS
Admissions Selectivity Rating: 74   **Fire Safety Rating:** 73

STUDENTS AND FACULTY
Enrollment: 2,019. **Student Body:** 71% female, 29% male, 14% out-of-state, 0% international (9 countries represented). Asian 1%, African American 11%, Caucasian 74%, Hispanic 6%, Native American <1%
Retention and Graduation: 77% freshmen return for sophomore year. 40% freshmen graduate within 4 years. 46% freshmen graduate within 6 years.
Faculty: 74 full-time faculty, 68% hold PhDs, 57% are members of minority groups, 7% are women. 0% of classes are taught by teaching assistants.

ACADEMICS
Degrees: associate, bachelor's, certificate, master's, post-bachelor's certificate, post-master's certificate. **Classes:** Most classes have 10–19 students. Most lab/discussion sessions have 10–19 students. **Majors with Highest Enrollment:** Elementary Education and Teaching; Criminal Justice/Law Enforcement Administration; Substance Abuse/Addiction Counseling. **Special Study Options:** Accelerated program, cross-registration, double major, dual enrollment, English as a Second Language (ESL), honors program, independent study, internships, student-designed major, study abroad, teacher certification program. **Honors**

programs: Alvernia College Honors Program Combined degree programs: BA/MA, BS/MS Occupational Therapy. **Disability Services:** Special programs offered to physically disabled students include note-taking services, tape recorders, tutors. **Career services:** career/job search classes, career assessment, internships. Career services highlights include The Washington Center and many local internship opportunities.

FACILITIES
Housing: Coed dorms, special housing for disabled students, women's dorms, Single-sex suites in townhouses. Single-sex floors in dorms. 90% of campus accessible to physically disabled. **Computers:** Students can register for classes online. Administrative functions (other than registration) can be performed online.

CAMPUS LIFE
Environment: Village. **Activities:** Choral groups, dance, drama/theater, literary magazine, music ensembles, student government, student newspaper, yearbook. 35 registered organizations, 5 honor societies, 5 religious organizations. **Athletics (Intercollegiate):** *Men:* baseball, basketball, cross-country, golf, lacrosse, soccer, tennis. *Women:* basketball, cheerleading, cross-country, field hockey, lacrosse, soccer, softball, tennis, volleyball. **On-Campus Highlights:** Student Center, Crusader Café, Library, Gym, Residence Hall Lounge.

ADMISSIONS
Freshman Academic Profile: Average high school GPA 2.88. 8% in top 10% of high school class, 27% in top 25% of high school class, 53% in top 50% of high school class. 74% from public high schools. SAT Math middle 50% range 420-530. SAT Critical Reading middle 50% range 420-520. Minimum paper TOEFL 550. **Basis for Candidate Selection:** *Very important factors considered include:* academic GPA, standardized test scores. *Important factors considered include:* Class rank, application essay, recommendation(s), rigor of secondary school record, character/personal qualities, extracurricular activities, interview, level of applicant's interest, talent/ability, volunteer work, work experience. *Other factors considered include:* religious affiliation/commitment. **Freshman Admission Requirements:** High school diploma is required and GED is accepted. **Freshman Admission Statistics:** 922 applied, 76% admitted, 41% enrolled. **Transfer Admission Requirements:** High school transcript, college transcript(s), essay or personal statement, Minimum college GPA of 2.0 required. Lowest grade transferable C. **General Admission Information:** Application Fee $25. Nonfall registration accepted. Admission may be deferred for a maximum of 12 months. Credit and/or placement offered for CEEB Advanced Placement tests.

COSTS AND FINANCIAL AID
Annual tuition $20,220. Room and board $8,220. Required fees $202. Average book expense $1,200. **Required Forms and Deadlines:** FAFSA. **Notification of Awards:** Applicants will be notified of awards on a rolling basis beginning 2/10. **Types of Aid:** *Need-based scholarships/grants:* Federal Pell, SEOG, state scholarships/grants, private scholarships. *Loans:* Subsidized Stafford, Unsubsidized Stafford, PLUS. *Student Employment:* Highest amount earned per year from on-campus jobs $3,886. **Financial Aid Statistics:** 100% freshmen, 100% undergrads receive need-based scholarship or grant aid. 1% freshmen, 12% undergrads receive non-need-based scholarship or grant aid. 95% freshmen, 95% undergrads receive need-based self-help aid. 0% freshmen, 0% undergrads receive athletic scholarships. 94% freshmen, 98% undergrads receive any aid. 91% undergrads borrow to pay for school. **Criteria for awarding institutional aid:** *Non-need-based:* academics, alumni affiliation.

See page 998.

ALVERNO COLLEGE

3400 South 43rd Street, Milwaukee, WI 53234-3922
Phone: 414-382-6101 · **Financial Aid Phone:** 414-382-6046
E-mail: admissions@alverno.edu · **CEEB Code:** 1012
Fax: 414-382-6055 · **Website:** www.alverno.edu · **ACT Code:** 4558

This private school, affiliated with the Roman Catholic Church, was founded in 1887. It has a 47-acre campus.

RATINGS
Admissions Selectivity Rating: 70   **Fire Safety Rating:** 76

STUDENTS AND FACULTY
Enrollment: 1,680. **Student Body:** 100% female, 0% male, 5% out-of-state, 1% international (13 countries represented). Asian 5%, African American 16%, Caucasian 53%, Hispanic 21%, Native American 1%
Retention and Graduation: 74% freshmen return for sophomore year. 11% freshmen graduate within 4 years. **Faculty:** 108 full-time faculty, 94% hold

PhDs, 77% are members of minority groups, 7% are women. 0% of classes are taught by teaching assistants.

ACADEMICS

Degrees: associate, bachelor's, master's, post-bachelor's certificate, post-master's certificate. **Classes:** Most classes have 20–29 students. Most lab/discussion sessions have 20–29 students. **Majors with Highest Enrollment:** Business Administration and Management; Registered Nursing/Registered Nurse; Education. **Special Study Options:** double major, independent study, internships, student-designed major, study abroad, teacher certification program, weekend college. **Disability Services:** Special programs offered to physically disabled students include note-taking services, reader services, tape recorders, tutors. **Career services:** alumni services, career/job search classes, career assessment. We are proudest of our integration into the Alverno curriculum. Counselors design and teach 3 courses that are required by various disciplines (one at the first-year level and two at the senior level), as well as teach segments in several additional courses. The result is that virtually every student has done in-class work with a career counselor prior to graduation.

FACILITIES

Housing: women's dorms. 95% of campus accessible to physically disabled. **Special Academic Facilities/Equipment:** Art & Culture Gallery, Career Center, Fitness center, Reiman Gymnasium, Nursing Skills Lab, Student centered multi-media production facility, Diagnostic Digital Portfolio, computer center, science labs, theatre venue. **Computers:** 35% of classrooms, 100% of dorms, 100% of libraries, 100% of dining areas, 100% of student union, have wireless network access. Students can register for classes online. Administrative functions (other than registration) can be performed online.

CAMPUS LIFE

Environment: Metropolis. **Activities:** Choral groups, dance, drama/theater, literary magazine, music ensembles, student government, student newspaper, Campus Ministries, International Student Organization. 37 registered organizations, 1 honor society, 1 religious organization, 2 sororities. **Athletics (Intercollegiate):** *Women:* basketball, cross-country, soccer, softball, tennis, volleyball. **On-Campus Highlights:** Teaching, Learning and Technology Center, The Mug Coffee House, Fitness Center, The Pipeline—Activity Center, Reiman Gymnasium. **Environmental Initiatives:** Created sustainability guidelines for construction and renovation (2011). Converting to energy efficient lighting as feasible (i.e., 2011-12 replaced incandescent lighting in chapel with compact fluorescent-88% savings; metal halide in gym with hi-bay fluorescent-66% savings; stairwell lights to T8 fixtures controlled by automatic sensors) Installed new domestic 92% energy-efficient hot water system, replacing 75-80% system.

ADMISSIONS

Freshman Academic Profile: Average high school GPA 3.03. 93% from public high schools. ACT middle 50% range 17-22. Minimum internet-based TOEFL 68. Minimum paper TOEFL 520. **Basis for Candidate Selection:** *Very important factors considered include:* academic GPA, standardized test scores. *Important factors considered include:* application essay, rigor of secondary school record. *Other factors considered include:* recommendation(s), character/personal qualities, extracurricular activities, interview, level of applicant's interest, talent/ability, volunteer work, work experience. **Freshman Admission Requirements:** High school diploma is required and GED is accepted. *Academic units required:* 4 English, 3 mathematics, 3 science, 3 social studies, 4 academic electives. **Freshman Admission Statistics:** 655 applied, 77% admitted, 39% enrolled. **Transfer Admission Requirements:** High school transcript, college transcript(s), essay or personal statement, Minimum college GPA of 2.0 required. Lowest grade transferable C. **General Admission Information:** Application Fee $20. Notification on a rolling basis, beginning on or about 9/1. Nonfall registration accepted. Admission may be deferred for a maximum of 1 year. Credit and/or placement offered for CEEB Advanced Placement tests.

COSTS AND FINANCIAL AID

Average book expense $1,056. **Required Forms and Deadlines:** FAFSA, Institution's own financial aid form. **Notification of Awards:** Applicants will be notified of awards on a rolling basis beginning 3/15. **Types of Aid:** *Need-based scholarships/grants:* Federal Pell, SEOG, state scholarships/grants, private scholarships, the school's own gift aid, Federal Nursing Scholarships. *Loans:* Subsidized Stafford, Unsubsidized Stafford, PLUS, Federal Perkins, state loans. *Student Employment:* Federal Work-Study Program available. Institutional employment available. Highest amount earned per year from on-campus jobs $8,830. Off-campus job opportunities are good. **Financial Aid Statistics:** 100% freshmen, 99% undergrads receive need-based scholarship or grant aid. 96% freshmen, 87% undergrads receive non-need-based scholarship or grant aid. 100% freshmen, 88% undergrads receive need-based self-help aid. 0% freshmen, 0% undergrads receive athletic scholarships. 99% freshmen, 94% undergrads receive any aid. 93% undergrads borrow to pay for school. Average cumulative indebtedness $34,744. **Criteria for awarding institutional aid:** *Non-need-based:* academics, alumni affiliation.

AMERICAN CONSERVATORY OF MUSIC

252 Wildwood Road, Hammond, IN 46324
Phone: 219-931-6000
E-mail: registrar@americanconservatory.edu
Fax: 219-931-6089 • **Website:** 252 Wildwood Road •

This private school, affiliated with the Greek Orthodox Church, was founded in 1886.

RATINGS

Admissions Selectivity Rating: 60*   Fire Safety Rating: 60*

ACADEMICS

Degrees: associate, bachelor's, certificate, diploma, master's. **Special Study Options:** Accelerated program, distance learning, double major, English as a Second Language (ESL).

FACILITIES

Housing: apartments for married students, apartments for single students **Computers:** Undergraduates are required to own a computer.

CAMPUS LIFE

Environment: Metropolis. **Activities:** Choral groups, jazz band, music ensembles, opera, symphony orchestra.

ADMISSIONS

Transfer Admission Requirements: High school transcript, college transcript(s), essay or personal statement, interview, statement of good standing from prior institution(s). Minimum college GPA of 2.0 required. Lowest grade transferable C.

COSTS AND FINANCIAL AID

Average book expense $2,400. **Criteria for awarding institutional aid:** *Non-need-based:* music/drama.

AMERICAN INDIAN COLLEGE
OF THE ASSEMBLIES OF GOD, INC.

, Phoenix, AZ 85021
Phone: 602-944-3335
E-mail: aicadm@aicag.edu
Fax: 602-943-8299 • **Website:** www.aicag.edu • **ACT Code:** 6005

This private school, affiliated with the Assemblies of God Church, was founded in 1957. It has a 10-acre campus.

RATINGS

Admissions Selectivity Rating: 66   Fire Safety Rating: 60*

STUDENTS AND FACULTY

Enrollment: 70. **Student Body:** 44% female, 56% male, 69% out-of-state, 1% international (2 countries represented). Asian 6%, African American 4%, Caucasian 14%, Hispanic 6%, Native American 69%
Faculty: 8 full-time faculty, 88% hold PhDs, 38% are members of minority groups, 0% are women. 0% of classes are taught by teaching assistants.

ACADEMICS

Degrees: associate, bachelor's. **Classes:** Most classes have fewer than 10 students. Most lab/discussion sessions have fewer than 10 students. **Special Study Options:** double major.

FACILITIES

Housing: special housing for disabled students, men's dorms, women's dorms, apartments for married students.

CAMPUS LIFE

Environment: Metropolis. **Activities:** Choral groups, drama/theater, literary magazine, music ensembles, musical theater, student government, student newspaper, yearbook, Campus Ministries. **On-Campus Highlights:** Gymnasium, Cree Student Union, Ramsey Cafeteria, Chapel, Prayer Mountain Trail.

ADMISSIONS

Freshman Academic Profile: Average high school GPA 2.5. 0% in top 10% of high school class, 0% in top 25% of high school class, 60% in top 50% of high school class. SAT Math middle 50% range 500-. SAT Critical Reading middle 50% range 540-. ACT middle 50% range 15-. Minimum paper TOEFL 500.

Basis for Candidate Selection: *Very important factors considered include:* Class rank, recommendation(s), rigor of secondary school record, standardized test scores, character/personal qualities, religious affiliation/commitment. *Important factors considered include:* application essay. *Other factors considered include:* extracurricular activities, interview, talent/ability, volunteer work, work experience. **Freshman Admission Requirements:** High school diploma is required and GED is accepted. **Freshman Admission Statistics:** 18 applied, 44% admitted. **Transfer Admission Requirements:** High school transcript, college transcript(s), standardized test scores, Minimum college GPA of 2.0 required. Lowest grade transferable C. **General Admission Information:** Nonfall registration accepted.

COSTS AND FINANCIAL AID

Annual tuition $4,950. Room and board $3,850. Required fees $605. Average book expense $500. **Required Forms and Deadlines:** FAFSA, Institution's own financial aid form, CSS/Financial Aid PROFILE, State aid form, Noncustodial PROFILE, Business/Farm Supplement. **Types of Aid:** *Need-based scholarships/grants:* Federal Pell, SEOG, state scholarships/grants, private scholarships, the school's own gift aid. *Loans:* Subsidized Stafford, Unsubsidized Stafford, PLUS. *Student Employment:* Off-campus job opportunities are fair. **Financial Aid Statistics:** 46% undergrads receive any aid.

AMERICAN INTERNATIONAL COLLEGE

1000 State Street, Springfield, MA 01109-3184
Phone: 413-205-3201 · **Financial Aid Phone:** 413-205-3259
E-mail: inquiry@aic.edu · **CEEB Code:** 3002
Fax: 413-205-3051 · **Website:** www.aic.edu · **ACT Code:** 1772

This private school was founded in 1885. It has a 58-acre campus.

RATINGS

Admissions Selectivity Rating: 71   **Fire Safety Rating:** 89

STUDENTS AND FACULTY

Enrollment: 1,492. **Student Body:** 56% female, 44% male, 37% out-of-state, 2% international (30 countries represented). Asian 1%, African American 24%, Caucasian 41%, Hispanic 9%, Native American <1%
Retention and Graduation: 61% freshmen return for sophomore year. 20% grads go on to further study within 1 year. 9% grads pursue arts and sciences degrees. 5% grads pursue law degrees. 15% grads pursue business degrees. 2% grads pursue medical degrees. **Faculty:** 74 full-time faculty, 51% hold PhDs, 61% are members of minority groups, 12% are women. 0% of classes are taught by teaching assistants.

ACADEMICS

Degrees: associate, bachelor's, master's, post-master's certificate, terminal associate. **Classes:** Most classes have 10–19 students. Most lab/discussion sessions have 10–19 students. **Majors with Highest Enrollment:** Psychology; Registered Nursing/Registered Nurse; Criminal Justice and Corrections. **Special Study Options:** Accelerated program, cross-registration, distance learning, double major, dual enrollment, English as a Second Language (ESL), honors program, independent study, internships, liberal arts/career combination, study abroad, teacher certification program, weekend college, Off-campus study in Washington, DC; upper division undergrads may take grad level courses. **Honors programs:** Four Year Honors program open to students in any major with appropriate credentials. Combined degree programs: BA/MA, 4-1 bachelor's/M.B.A. program. **Disability Services:** Special programs offered to physically disabled students include note-taking services, reader services, tape recorders, tutors. **Career services:** alumni services, career/job search classes, career assessment, internships.

FACILITIES

Housing: Coed dorms, women's dorms, Wellness Housing. 75% of campus accessible to physically disabled. **Special Academic Facilities/Equipment:** Centers for child development, cultural arts, and human technology. **Computers:** 100% of classrooms, 90% of dorms, 100% of libraries, 100% of dining areas, 100% of student union, 100% of common outdoor areas have wireless network access. Students can register for classes online. Administrative functions (other than registration) can be performed online.

CAMPUS LIFE

Environment: City. **Activities:** Choral groups, dance, drama/theater, literary magazine, musical theater, pep band, radio station, student government, student newspaper, yearbook, Campus Ministries, International Student Organization. 45 registered organizations, 5 honor societies, 3 religious organizations. 4 fraternities, 5 sororities. **Athletics (Intercollegiate):** *Men:* baseball, basketball, cheerleading, cross-country, football, golf, ice hockey, lacrosse, soccer, tennis,

track/field (outdoor), track/field (indoor), wrestling. *Women:* basketball, cheerleading, cross-country, field hockey, lacrosse, soccer, softball, tennis, track/field (outdoor), track/field (indoor), volleyball. **On-Campus Highlights:** Courniotes Hall - Health Sciences, Karen Sprague Cultural Arts Center, Butova & Metcalf Gymnasiums, WAIC-FM (Radio Station)

ADMISSIONS

Freshman Academic Profile: Average high school GPA 2.59. SAT Math middle 50% range 355-565. SAT Critical Reading middle 50% range 340-530. SAT Writing middle 50% range 315-525. ACT middle 50% range 16-22. Minimum internet-based TOEFL 80. Minimum paper TOEFL 550. **Basis for Candidate Selection:** *Important factors considered include:* Class rank, academic GPA, rigor of secondary school record, standardized test scores. *Other factors considered include:* application essay, recommendation(s), alumni/ae relation, character/personal qualities, extracurricular activities, first generation, interview, level of applicant's interest, racial/ethnic status, volunteer work, work experience. **Freshman Admission Requirements:** High school diploma is required and GED is accepted. *Academic units required:* 4 English, 3 mathematics, 2 science, (2 science labs), 1 foreign language, 1 social studies, 2 history, 4 academic electives. **Freshman Admission Statistics:** 1,522 applied, 74% admitted, 27% enrolled. **Transfer Admission Requirements:** High school transcript, college transcript(s), Minimum college GPA of 2.0 required. Lowest grade transferable C. **General Admission Information:** Application Fee $25. Notification on a rolling basis, beginning on or about 12/15. Nonfall registration accepted. Admission may be deferred for a maximum of 2 years. Credit and/or placement offered for CEEB Advanced Placement tests.

COSTS AND FINANCIAL AID

Annual tuition $29,015. Room and board $11,710. Required fees $0. Average book expense $1,200. **Required Forms and Deadlines:** FAFSA. **Notification of Awards:** Applicants will be notified of awards on a rolling basis beginning 3/15. **Types of Aid:** *Need-based scholarships/grants:* Federal Pell, SEOG, state scholarships/grants, private scholarships, the school's own gift aid, Federal Nursing Scholarships. *Loans:* Subsidized Stafford, Unsubsidized Stafford, PLUS, Federal Perkins, college/university loans from institutional funds. *Student Employment:* Federal Work-Study Program available. Institutional employment available. Highest amount earned per year from on-campus jobs $2,200. Off-campus job opportunities are good. **Financial Aid Statistics:** 100% freshmen, 99% undergrads receive need-based scholarship or grant aid. 12% freshmen, 12% undergrads receive non-need-based scholarship or grant aid. 89% freshmen, 88% undergrads receive need-based self-help aid. 12% freshmen, 8% undergrads receive athletic scholarships. 100% freshmen, 85% undergrads receive any aid. 86% undergrads borrow to pay for school. Average cumulative indebtedness $30,524. **Criteria for awarding institutional aid:** *Non-need-based:* academics, alumni affiliation, athletics, leadership.

AMERICAN JEWISH UNIVERSITY

15600 Mulholland Drive, Familian Campus, Bel Air, CA 90077
Phone: 310-440-1247 · **Financial Aid Phone:** 310-440-1252
E-mail: admissions@ajula.edu · **CEEB Code:** 4876
Fax: 310-471-3657 · **Website:** www.ajula.edu · **ACT Code:** 462

This private school, affiliated with the Jewish Church, was founded in 1947. It has a 28-acre campus.

RATINGS

Admissions Selectivity Rating: 71   **Fire Safety Rating:** 70

STUDENTS AND FACULTY

Enrollment: 120. **Student Body:** 49% female, 51% male, 15% out-of-state, 6% international (6 countries represented). Asian 3%, African American 3%, Caucasian 51%, Hispanic 3%, Native American 3%
Retention and Graduation: 58% freshmen return for sophomore year. 36% freshmen graduate within 6 years. **Faculty:** 8 full-time faculty, 88% hold PhDs, 38% are members of minority groups. 0% of classes are taught by teaching assistants.

ACADEMICS

Degrees: bachelor's, master's. **Classes:** Most classes have fewer than 10 students. Most lab/discussion sessions have fewer than 10 students. **Majors with Highest Enrollment:** Political Science and Government; Business/Commerce; Bioethics/Medical Ethics. **Special Study Options:** cross-registration, double major, independent study, internships, student-designed major, study abroad. Combined degree programs: BA/MA, BA/MBA, BA/MAEd. **Career services:** career assessment, internships. Our students have had internships with American Jewish Joint Distribution Committee, Anti-Defamation League, Cedars-Sinai Medical Center, Jewish Federation of Greater Los Angeles, Jewish Telegraphic Agency, Jewish Television Network, Los Angeles Holocaust Museum, Museum of Tolerance, New Line Cinema, and the Simon Wiesenthal Center.

FACILITIES
Housing: Coed dorms, special housing for disabled students, apartments for married students, apartments for single students. 90% of campus accessible to physically disabled. **Special Academic Facilities/Equipment:** Art Gallery, Ostrow Library **Computers:** 100% of dorms, 100% of libraries, 100% of student union, 50% of common outdoor areas have wireless network access. Administrative functions (other than registration) can be performed online.

CAMPUS LIFE
Environment: Metropolis. **Activities:** Choral groups, drama/theater, literary magazine, student government, student newspaper, Model UN. 17 registered organizations, 1 religious organization. **On-Campus Highlights:** Residence Halls, Auerbach Student Union, The Berg, our kosher dining hall, Sculpture Garden, Ostrow Library. **Environmental Initiatives:** Energy Management Conserving Water Recycling

ADMISSIONS
Freshman Academic Profile: Average high school GPA 3.11. 0% in top 10% of high school class, 33% in top 25% of high school class, 67% in top 50% of high school class. 36% from public high schools. SAT Math middle 50% range 500-570. SAT Critical Reading middle 50% range 490-520. SAT Writing middle 50% range 500-560. ACT middle 50% range 17-22. Minimum internet-based TOEFL 75. Minimum paper TOEFL 530. **Basis for Candidate Selection:** *Very important factors considered include:* application essay, recommendation(s), character/personal qualities, extracurricular activities, interview, talent/ability, volunteer work. *Important factors considered include:* academic GPA, standardized test scores, level of applicant's interest. *Other factors considered include:* Class rank, rigor of secondary school record, alumni/ae relation, geographical residence, religious affiliation/commitment, state residency, work experience. **Freshman Admission Requirements:** High school diploma is required and GED is accepted. **Freshman Admission Statistics:** 28 applied, 96% admitted, 48% enrolled. **Transfer Admission Requirements:** college transcript(s), essay or personal statement, Minimum college GPA of N/A required. Lowest grade transferable C. **General Admission Information:** Application Fee $35. Regular application deadline 5/31. Notification on a rolling basis, beginning on or about 9/15. Nonfall registration accepted. Admission may be deferred for a maximum of 1 year. Credit offered for CEEB Advanced Placement tests.

COSTS AND FINANCIAL AID
Annual tuition $26,784. Room and board $14,082. Required fees $1,712. Average book expense $1,710. **Required Forms and Deadlines:** FAFSA, Institution's own financial aid form. **Notification of Awards:** Applicants will be notified of awards on a rolling basis beginning 1/1. **Types of Aid:** *Need-based scholarships/grants:* Federal Pell, SEOG, state scholarships/grants, private scholarships, the school's own gift aid. *Loans:* Subsidized Stafford, Unsubsidized Stafford, PLUS. *Student Employment:* Federal Work-Study Program available. Institutional employment available. Highest amount earned per year from on-campus jobs $1,000. Off-campus job opportunities are good. **Financial Aid Statistics:** 27% freshmen, 51% undergrads receive need-based scholarship or grant aid. 100% freshmen, 86% undergrads receive non-need-based scholarship or grant aid. 36% freshmen, 54% undergrads receive need-based self-help aid. 0% freshmen, 0% undergrads receive athletic scholarships. 100% undergrads borrow to pay for school. Average cumulative indebtedness $3,964. **Criteria for awarding institutional aid:** *Non-need-based:* leadership, minority status, music/drama, state/district residency.

AMERICAN UNIVERSITY

4400 Massachusetts Ave, NW, Washington, DC 20016-8001
Phone: 202-885-6000 · **Financial Aid Phone:** 202-885-6500
E-mail: admissions@american.edu · **CEEB Code:** 5007
Fax: 202-885-1025 · **Website:** www.american.edu · **ACT Code:** 648

This private school, affiliated with the Methodist Church, was founded in 1893. It has a 84-acre campus.

RATINGS
Admissions Selectivity Rating: 92   **Fire Safety Rating:** 74

STUDENTS AND FACULTY
Enrollment: 7,094. **Student Body:** 62% female, 38% male, 81% out-of-state, 7% international (115 countries represented). Asian 7%, African American 6%, Caucasian 58%, Hispanic 11%, Native American <1%
Retention and Graduation: 76% freshmen graduate within 4 years. **Faculty:** 776 full-time faculty, 86% hold PhDs, 47% are members of minority groups, 18% are women. 0% of classes are taught by teaching assistants.

ACADEMICS
Degrees: associate, bachelor's, certificate, first professional, master's, post-bachelor's certificate. **Majors with Highest Enrollment:** International Relations and Affairs; Business/Commerce; Political Science and Government. **Special Study Options:** Accelerated program, cooperative education program, cross-registration, double major, exchange student program (domestic), honors program, independent study, internships, student-designed major, study abroad, teacher certification program, weekend college, AU Abroad offers more than 100 study Abroad programs in 33 geographic locations around the world. Earn college credit, learn a foreign language, pursue and internship and gain international experience and contacts. One-semester, full year, alternative spring break, and language immersion options are available. With AU Abroad partner universities in Canada, Mexico, England, Scotland, Ireland, Argentina, Australia, Egypt,the United Arab Emirates and numerous other countries around the world, you have the ability to go almost anywhere. **Honors programs:** The University Honors Program is designed to promote a continuous learning environment, making optimum use of AU"s outstanding faculty, campus facilities and the numerous resources available in the Washington, D.C. area and abroad. Students enjoy small classes, proven instructors, cultural events, a wide range of social activities and the option of living in Honors housing. Members of the University Honors Program can major in any discipline at the university and can also participate in multidisciplinary Honors Colloquia. Combined degree programs: BA/MA, BS/MS, BA/MPA, BA/MS. **Disability Services:** Special programs offered to physically disabled students include note-taking services, reader services, tape recorders, tutors. **Career services:** Alumni network, alumni services, career/job search classes, career assessment, internships, regional alumni. Career services highlights can be found at: http://www.american.edu/careercenter/SuccessStories/internvideo.html.

FACILITIES
Housing: Coed dorms, special housing for disabled students, special housing for international students, apartments for married students, apartments for single students. 94% of campus accessible to physically disabled. **Special Academic Facilities/Equipment:** Student-run Radio and TV Facilities; Watkins Art Gallery; Katzen Arts Center; Experimental Theatre; Greenberg Theatre; Friedheim Journalism Center; William I Jacobs Fitness Center; Language Resource Center; Multimedia Center; Audiotechnology Lab; UNIX and Oracle Labs; Kay Spiritual Life Center(interdenominational). **Computers:** 100% of classrooms, 100% of dorms, 100% of libraries, 100% of dining areas, 100% of student union, 100% of common outdoor areas have wireless network access. Students can register for classes online. Administrative functions (other than registration) can be performed online.

CAMPUS LIFE
Environment: Metropolis. **Activities:** Choral groups, dance, drama/theater, jazz band, literary magazine, music ensembles, musical theater, opera, pep band, radio station, student government, student newspaper, student-run film society, symphony orchestra, television station, yearbook, International Student Organization. 180 registered organizations, 15 honor societies, 15 religious organizations. 11 fraternity, 12 sororities. **Athletics (Intercollegiate):** *Men:* basketball, cross-country, diving, soccer, swimming, track/field (outdoor), track/field (indoor), wrestling. *Women:* basketball, cross-country, diving, field hockey, lacrosse, soccer, swimming, track/field (outdoor), track/field (indoor), volleyball. **On-Campus Highlights:** Mary Graydon Center, Sports Center Complex and Jacobs Fitness, Katzen Arts Center, The Quad, Terrace Dining Room. **Environmental Initiatives:** A Climate Action Plan which calls for achieving carbon neutrality by 2020. The certification of 65% of campus buildings to LEED for Existing Buildings, and new buildings to LEED for New Construction. The development of a Zero Waste Policy through which a team has been created to develop a plan for reducing and diverting 100% of the university's waste stream.

ADMISSIONS
Freshman Academic Profile: Average high school GPA 3.71. 39% in top 10% of high school class, 75% in top 25% of high school class, 96% in top 50% of high school class. SAT Math middle 50% range 560-660. SAT Critical Reading middle 50% range 590-680. SAT Writing middle 50% range 580-670. ACT middle 50% range 26-30. Minimum internet-based TOEFL 80. Minimum paper TOEFL 550. **Basis for Candidate Selection:** *Very important factors considered include:* academic GPA, rigor of secondary school record, standardized test scores, level of applicant's interest. *Important factors considered include:* application essay, recommendation(s), extracurricular activities, volunteer work. *Other factors considered include:* alumni/ae relation, character/personal qualities, first generation, geographical residence, racial/ethnic status, talent/ability, work experience. **Freshman Admission Requirements:** High

school diploma is required and GED is accepted. *Academic units required:* 4 English, 3 mathematics, 3 science, (2 science labs), 2 foreign language, 2 social studies, 3 academic electives. **Freshman Admission Statistics:** 15,119 applied, 46% admitted, 26% enrolled. **Transfer Admission Requirements:** college transcript(s), essay or personal statement, Minimum college GPA of 2.5 required. Lowest grade transferable C. **General Admission Information:** Application Fee $60. Early decision application deadline 11/15. Regular application deadline 1/15. Regular notification 4/1. Nonfall registration accepted. Admission may be deferred for a maximum of 12 months. Credit and/or placement offered for CEEB Advanced Placement tests.

COSTS AND FINANCIAL AID
Annual tuition $41,316. Room and board $14,408. Required fees $517. Average book expense $800. **Required Forms and Deadlines:** FAFSA, CSS/Financial Aid PROFILE. **Notification of Awards:** Applicants will be notified of awards on or about 4/1. **Types of Aid:** *Need-based scholarships/grants:* Federal Pell, SEOG, state scholarships/grants, private scholarships, the school's own gift aid, Academic merit scholarships: Presidential Scholarships, Dean's Scholarships, Leadership Scholarships, Phi Theta Kappa Scholarships (transfers only), Tuition Exchange Scholarships, United Methodist Scholarships, and other private/restricted scholarships are awarded by the Undergraduate Admissions Office. Most scholarships do not require a separate application and are renewable for up to three years if certain criteria are met. *Loans:* Direct Subsidized Stafford, Direct Unsubsidized Stafford, Direct PLUS, PLUS, Federal Perkins, college/university loans from institutional funds. *Student Employment:* Federal Work-Study Program available. Institutional employment available. Off-campus job opportunities are excellent. **Financial Aid Statistics:** 89% freshmen, 82% undergrads receive need-based scholarship or grant aid. 36% freshmen, 33% undergrads receive non-need-based scholarship or grant aid. 92% freshmen, 92% undergrads receive need-based self-help aid. 2% freshmen, 2% undergrads receive athletic scholarships. 87% freshmen, 72% undergrads receive any aid. **Criteria for awarding institutional aid:** *Non-need-based:* academics, alumni affiliation, athletics, leadership, minority status, music/drama, religious affiliation, state/district residency.

AMERICAN UNIVERSITY IN CAIRO

AUC Avenue, P.O. Box 74 New Cairo 11835,
Phone: 2-02-2615-1459 • **Financial Aid Phone:** 2-02-2615-3865
E-mail: enrolauc@aucegypt.edu
Website: www.aucegypt.edu

This private school was founded in 1919. It has a 260-acre campus.

RATINGS
Admissions Selectivity Rating: 87   **Fire Safety Rating:** 78

STUDENTS AND FACULTY
Enrollment: 5,627. **Student Body:** 53% female, 47% male, (38 countries represented).
Retention and Graduation: 94% freshmen return for sophomore year. 22% freshmen graduate within 4 years. 80% freshmen graduate within 6 years.
Faculty: 451 full-time faculty, 71% hold PhDs, 48% are members of minority groups. 0% of classes are taught by teaching assistants.

ACADEMICS
Degrees: bachelor's, diploma, master's. **Classes:** Most classes have 10–19 students. Most lab/discussion sessions have 10–19 students. **Majors with Highest Enrollment:** Mechanical Engineering; Business Administration, Management and Operations; Construction Engineering. **Special Study Options:** double major, English as a Second Language (ESL), independent study, internships, liberal arts/career combination, study abroad. **Career services:** Alumni network, alumni services, career/job search classes, career assessment, internships. Career services highlights include job shadowing and internships to help students explore career options. Online recruitment and Employment Fairs generate employment opportunities.

FACILITIES
Housing: men's dorms, women's dorms, apartments for married students, apartments for single students. 100% of campus accessible to physically disabled. **Computers:** 100% of classrooms, 100% of dorms, 100% of libraries, 100% of dining areas, 100% of student union, 100% of common outdoor areas have wireless network access. Students can register for classes online. Administrative functions (other than registration) can be performed online.

CAMPUS LIFE
Environment: Metropolis. **Activities:** Choral groups, dance, drama/theater, literary magazine, music ensembles, radio station, student government, student newspaper, student-run film society, yearbook, International Student Organiza-

tion, Model UN. 62 registered organizations. **Athletics (Intercollegiate):** *Men:* basketball, boxing, fencing, football, gymnastics, handball, rugby, soccer, squash, swimming, table tennis, tennis, track/field (outdoor), volleyball, water polo, wrestling. *Women:* basketball, fencing, football, gymnastics, handball, soccer, squash, swimming, table tennis, tennis, track/field (outdoor), volleyball. **On-Campus Highlights:** Athletic Facility, Food Court, Library, Student Center **Environmental Initiatives:** Campus sustainability effort; Carbon Footprint; Recycling; Bus/Transportation System.

ADMISSIONS
Freshman Academic Profile: SAT Math middle 50% range 540-650. SAT Critical Reading middle 50% range 430-520. SAT Writing middle 50% range 520-610. Minimum internet-based TOEFL 48. Minimum paper TOEFL 460. **Basis for Candidate Selection:** *Very important factors considered include:* academic GPA, recommendation(s), character/personal qualities, level of applicant's interest, religious affiliation/commitment. *Important factors considered include:* application essay, rigor of secondary school record. *Other factors considered include:* Class rank, standardized test scores, alumni/ae relation, extracurricular activities, first generation, talent/ability, volunteer work, work experience. **Freshman Admission Requirements:** High school diploma is required and GED is accepted. **Freshman Admission Statistics:** 3,042 applied, 51% admitted, 97% enrolled. **Transfer Admission Requirements:** High school transcript, college transcript(s), essay or personal statement, standardized test scores, statement of good standing from prior institution(s). Minimum college GPA of 2.0 required. Lowest grade transferable C. **General Admission Information:** Application Fee $45. Regular application deadline 8/1. Nonfall registration accepted. Admission may be deferred for a maximum of One year. Credit offered for CEEB Advanced Placement tests.

COSTS AND FINANCIAL AID
Required Forms and Deadlines: Institution's own financial aid form. **Types of Aid:** *Need-based scholarships/grants:* Federal Pell, SEOG, state scholarships/grants, private scholarships, the school's own gift aid, United Negro College Fund. *Loans:* Subsidized Stafford, Unsubsidized Stafford, PLUS, college/university loans from institutional funds. *Student Employment:* Federal Work-Study Program available. Institutional employment available. Highest amount earned per year from on-campus jobs $5,000. Off-campus job opportunities are good. **Financial Aid Statistics:** 3% freshmen, 2% undergrads receive athletic scholarships. 61% freshmen, 63% undergrads receive any aid. **Criteria for awarding institutional aid:** *Non-need-based:* alumni affiliation.

THE AMERICAN UNIVERSITY OF PARIS (CO)

US Admissions Office, Denver, CO 80246
Phone: 303-757-6333 • **Financial Aid Phone:** +1 4-062-0720
E-mail: usoffice@aup.edu • **CEEB Code:** 866
Fax: 303-757-6444 • **ACT Code:** 5295

This private school was founded in 1962.

RATINGS
Admissions Selectivity Rating: 80   **Fire Safety Rating:** 60*

STUDENTS AND FACULTY
Enrollment: 925. **Student Body:** 67% female, 33% male, (100 countries represented).
Retention and Graduation: 64% freshmen return for sophomore year. 32% freshmen graduate within 4 years. 45% freshmen graduate within 6 years.
Faculty: 56 full-time faculty, 80% hold PhDs, 46% are members of minority groups. 0% of classes are taught by teaching assistants.

ACADEMICS
Degrees: bachelor's, master's. **Classes:** Most classes have 10–19 students. Most lab/discussion sessions have 10–19 students. **Special Study Options:** double major, exchange student program (domestic), independent study, internships, study abroad. Combined degree programs: BA/MA, BA/MA. **Career services:** Alumni network, alumni services, career assessment, internships.

FACILITIES
Housing: Students are housed in independent rooms or with French families. 60% of campus accessible to physically disabled. **Computers:** Administrative functions (other than registration) can be performed online.

CAMPUS LIFE
Environment: Metropolis. **Activities:** drama/theater, literary magazine, musical theater, student government, student newspaper, yearbook. 20 registered organizations. **Athletics (Intercollegiate):** *Men:* basketball, football, rugby, soccer, swimming, volleyball. *Women:* basketball, football, soccer, swimming, volleyball.

ADMISSIONS

Freshman Academic Profile: SAT Math middle 50% range 520-640. SAT Critical Reading middle 50% range 550-660. Minimum paper TOEFL 600. **Basis for Candidate Selection:** *Very important factors considered include:* Class rank, application essay, recommendation(s), rigor of secondary school record. *Important factors considered include:* academic GPA, standardized test scores, character/personal qualities, extracurricular activities, level of applicant's interest. *Other factors considered include:* alumni/ae relation, interview, talent/ability, volunteer work, work experience. **Freshman Admission Requirements:** High school diploma is required and GED is accepted. **Freshman Admission Statistics:** 541 applied, 71% admitted, 41% enrolled. **Transfer Admission Requirements:** college transcript(s), essay or personal statement, statement of good standing from prior institution(s). Minimum college GPA of 3.0 required. Lowest grade transferable C. **General Admission Information:** Application Fee $50. Nonfall registration accepted. Admission may be deferred for a maximum of 1 year. Credit and/or placement offered for CEEB Advanced Placement tests.

COSTS AND FINANCIAL AID

Average book expense $1,200. **Required Forms and Deadlines:** FAFSA, Institution's own financial aid form. **Types of Aid:** *Need-based scholarships/grants:* the school's own gift aid. *Loans:* Subsidized Stafford, Unsubsidized Stafford, PLUS. *Student Employment:* Highest amount earned per year from on-campus jobs $2,500. **Financial Aid Statistics:** 0% freshmen, 0% undergrads receive athletic scholarships. **Criteria for awarding institutional aid:** *Non-need-based:* academics, alumni affiliation.

AMERICAN UNIVERSITY OF PUERTO RICO

PO Box 2037, Bayamon, PR 00960-2037
Phone: 787-740-6410
E-mail: mcruz@aupr.edu
Fax: 787-785-7377 • **Website:** www.aupr.edu

This private school was founded in 1963.

RATINGS

Admissions Selectivity Rating: 60*   **Fire Safety Rating:** 60*

STUDENTS AND FACULTY

Enrollment: 4,060. **Student Body:** 59% female, 41% male.

ACADEMICS

Degrees: associate, bachelor's, master's. **Special Study Options:** cooperative education program, distance learning, English as a Second Language (ESL), honors program, independent study, liberal arts/career combination, student-designed major. **Career services:** career/job search classes.

CAMPUS LIFE

Activities: dance, drama/theater, literary magazine. **Athletics (Intercollegiate):** *Men:* baseball, basketball, soccer, tennis, volleyball. *Women:* baseball, basketball, soccer, tennis, volleyball.

ADMISSIONS

Freshman Academic Profile: Average high school GPA 2.49. 66% from public high schools. **Basis for Candidate Selection:** *Very important factors considered include:* rigor of secondary school record, standardized test scores. *Other factors considered include:* character/personal qualities, interview, talent/ability. **Freshman Admission Requirements:** High school diploma is required and GED is accepted. **Freshman Admission Statistics:** 1,131 applied, 100% admitted, 71% enrolled. **General Admission Information:** Application Fee $15. Nonfall registration accepted. Admission may be deferred for a maximum of info. not avail.

COSTS AND FINANCIAL AID

Average book expense $160. **Types of Aid:** *Need-based scholarships/grants:* Federal Pell, SEOG, state scholarships/grants. *Loans:* Direct Subsidized Stafford, state loans. *Student Employment:* Federal Work-Study Program available. Off-campus job opportunities are good. **Financial Aid Statistics:** 100% freshmen, 98% undergrads receive need-based scholarship or grant aid. 0% freshmen, 0% undergrads receive non-need-based scholarship or grant aid. 92% freshmen, 52% undergrads receive need-based self-help aid. 4% freshmen, 3% undergrads receive athletic scholarships. **Criteria for awarding institutional aid:** *Non-need-based:* academics, alumni affiliation, art, athletics, job skills, leadership, minority status, music/drama, religious affiliation, state/district residency.

AMHERST COLLEGE

220 South Pleasant Street, Amherst, MA 1002
Phone: 413-542-2328 • **Financial Aid Phone:** 413-542-2296
E-mail: admission@amherst.edu • **CEEB Code:** 3003
Fax: 413-542-2040 • **Website:** www.amherst.edu • **ACT Code:** 1774

This private school was founded in 1821. It has a 999-acre campus.

RATINGS

Admissions Selectivity Rating: 98   **Fire Safety Rating:** 75

STUDENTS AND FACULTY

Enrollment: 1,792. **Student Body:** 48% female, 52% male, 88% out-of-state, 10% international (54 countries represented). Asian 13%, African American 12%, Caucasian 42%, Hispanic 13%, Native American <1%
Retention and Graduation: 98% freshmen return for sophomore year. 87% freshmen graduate within 4 years. **Faculty:** 220 full-time faculty, 97% hold PhDs, 50% are members of minority groups, 2110% are women. 0% of classes are taught by teaching assistants.

ACADEMICS

Degrees: bachelor's. **Classes:** Most classes have 10–19 students. Most lab/discussion sessions have fewer than 10 students. **Majors with Highest Enrollment:** Economics; Psychology; History. **Special Study Options:** cross-registration, double major, exchange student program (domestic), honors program, independent study, student-designed major, study abroad, teacher certification program. **Honors programs:** Senior Honors Thesis-an opportunity to engage in extensive research with a professor as the student's advisor. **Disability Services:** Special programs offered to physically disabled students include note-taking services, reader services, tape recorders, tutors. **Career services:** Alumni network, alumni services, career/job search classes, career assessment, internships, regional alumni.

FACILITIES

Housing: Coed dorms, cooperative housing, French/Spanish language house, German/Russian language house, Latino culture house, African American culture house, Health and Wellness house, Arts house, Food Cooperative house and single sex floors for men and women within specific dorms. **Special Academic Facilities/Equipment:** Art, natural history, geology museums, language labs, observatory, planetarium, The Amherst Center for Russian Culture, The Dickinson Homestead. **Computers:** Administrative functions (other than registration) can be performed online.

CAMPUS LIFE

Environment: Town. **Activities:** Choral groups, concert band, dance, drama/theater, jazz band, literary magazine, music ensembles, musical theater, opera, radio station, student government, student newspaper, student-run film society, symphony orchestra, yearbook, International Student Organization, Model UN. 100 registered organizations, 2 honor societies, 7 religious organizations. **Athletics (Intercollegiate):** *Men:* baseball, basketball, cross-country, diving, football, golf, ice hockey, lacrosse, soccer, squash, swimming, tennis, track/field (outdoor), track/field (indoor). *Women:* basketball, cross-country, diving, field hockey, golf, ice hockey, lacrosse, soccer, softball, squash, swimming, tennis, track/field (outdoor), track/field (indoor), volleyball. **On-Campus Highlights:** Mead Art Museum, Pratt Museum of Natural History, Russian Cultural Center, Japanese Peace Garden, Observatory.

ADMISSIONS

Freshman Academic Profile: 84% in top 10% of high school class, 97% in top 25% of high school class, 99.42% in top 50% of high school class. 58% from public high schools. SAT Math middle 50% range 680-770. SAT Critical Reading middle 50% range 670-780. SAT Writing middle 50% range 670-770. ACT middle 50% range 30-34. Minimum internet-based TOEFL 100. Minimum paper TOEFL 600. **Basis for Candidate Selection:** *Very important factors considered include:* application essay, academic GPA, recommendation(s), rigor of secondary school record, standardized test scores, character/personal qualities, extracurricular activities, first generation, talent/ability. *Important factors considered include:* Class rank, alumni/ae relation, volunteer work. *Other factors considered include:* geographical residence, state residency, work experience. **Freshman Admission Requirements:** High school diploma or equivalent is not required. **Freshman Admission Statistics:** 8,478 applied, 14% admitted, 40% enrolled. **Transfer Admission Requirements:** High school transcript, college transcript(s), essay or personal statement, statement of good standing from prior institution(s). Minimum college GPA of 3.5 required. Lowest grade transferable C. **General Admission Information:** Application Fee $60. Early decision application deadline 11/15. Regular application deadline 1/1. Regular notification 4/5. Nonfall registration not accepted. Admission may be deferred for a maximum of 2 years. Neither credit nor placement offered for CEEB Advanced Placement tests.

COSTS AND FINANCIAL AID
Annual tuition $47,720. Room and board $12,680. Required fees $806. Average book expense $1,000. **Required Forms and Deadlines:** FAFSA, CSS/Financial Aid PROFILE, State aid form, Noncustodial PROFILE, Business/Farm Supplement. **Notification of Awards:** Applicants will be notified of awards on or about 4/1. **Types of Aid:** *Need-based scholarships/grants:* Federal Pell, SEOG, state scholarships/grants, private scholarships, the school's own gift aid. *Loans:* Direct Subsidized Stafford, Direct Unsubsidized Stafford, Direct PLUS, Federal Perkins, college/university loans from institutional funds. *Student Employment:* Federal Work-Study Program available. Institutional employment available. Off-campus job opportunities are excellent. **Financial Aid Statistics:** 100% freshmen, 100% undergrads receive need-based scholarship or grant aid. 0% freshmen, 0% undergrads receive non-need-based scholarship or grant aid. 100% freshmen, 100% undergrads receive need-based self-help aid. 0% freshmen, 0% undergrads receive athletic scholarships. 61% freshmen, 58% undergrads receive any aid. 31% undergrads borrow to pay for school. Average cumulative indebtedness $13,411.

ANDERSON UNIVERSITY (IN)

1100 East Fifth Street, Anderson, IN 46012-3495
Phone: 765-641-4080 · **Financial Aid Phone:** 765-641-4180
E-mail: info@anderson.edu · **CEEB Code:** 1016
Fax: 765-641-4091 · **Website:** www.anderson.edu · **ACT Code:** 1174

This private school, affiliated with the Church of God Church, was founded in 1917. It has a 100-acre campus.

RATINGS
Admissions Selectivity Rating: 86   **Fire Safety Rating:** 77

STUDENTS AND FACULTY
Enrollment: 1,831. **Student Body:** 60% female, 40% male, 26% out-of-state, 3% international (17 countries represented). Asian 1%, African American 6%, Caucasian 80%, Hispanic 3%, Native American <1%
Retention and Graduation: 75% freshmen return for sophomore year. 48% freshmen graduate within 4 years. 63% freshmen graduate within 6 years. 20% grads go on to further study within 1 year. **Faculty:** 127 full-time faculty, 67% hold PhDs, 40% are members of minority groups, 8% are women. 0% of classes are taught by teaching assistants.

ACADEMICS
Degrees: associate, bachelor's, first professional, master's. **Classes:** Most classes have 10–19 students. Most lab/discussion sessions have 10–19 students. **Majors with Highest Enrollment:** Registered Nursing/Registered Nurse; Marketing/Marketing Management; Psychology. **Special Study Options:** Accelerated program, cross-registration, double major, honors program, independent study, internships, student-designed major, study abroad, teacher certification program, Summer over seas service program. **Honors programs:** The Honors Program at Anderson University is devoted to fostering within its honors scholars a passionate dedication to intellectual inquiry and spiritual development so that they may serve as vibrant leaders in their professions and in their communities. **Disability Services:** Special programs offered to physically disabled students include note-taking services, reader services, tape recorders, tutors.

FACILITIES
Housing: Coed dorms, men's dorms, women's dorms, apartments for married students, apartments for single students, one house. 95% of campus accessible to physically disabled. **Special Academic Facilities/Equipment:** Gustav Jeeninga Museum of Bible and Near Eastern Studies, Wilson Galleries, Archives of the Church of God **Computers:** Students can register for classes online. Administrative functions (other than registration) can be performed online.

CAMPUS LIFE
Environment: Town. **Activities:** Choral groups, concert band, dance, drama/theater, jazz band, literary magazine, music ensembles, musical theater, opera, pep band, radio station, student government, student newspaper, symphony orchestra, yearbook. 33 registered organizations, 12 honor societies, 15 religious organizations. **Athletics (Intercollegiate):** *Men:* baseball, basketball, cheerleading, cross-country, football, golf, soccer, tennis, track/field (outdoor). *Women:* basketball, cheerleading, cross-country, golf, soccer, softball, tennis,

track/field (outdoor), volleyball. **On-Campus Highlights:** Kardatzke Wellness Center, Mocha Joe's in the Olt Student Center, Decker Commons and Café Ole, Reardon Auditorium. **Environmental Initiatives:** recycling, teaching awareness.

ADMISSIONS
Freshman Academic Profile: Average high school GPA 3.452. 23% in top 10% of high school class, 52% in top 25% of high school class, 82% in top 50% of high school class. 95% from public high schools. SAT Math middle 50% range 460-570. SAT Critical Reading middle 50% range 460-570. ACT middle 50% range 21-25. Minimum internet-based TOEFL 78. Minimum paper TOEFL 547. **Basis for Candidate Selection:** *Very important factors considered include:* recommendation(s), rigor of secondary school record, religious affiliation/commitment. *Important factors considered include:* Class rank, standardized test scores, character/personal qualities, extracurricular activities, interview, volunteer work. *Other factors considered include:* application essay, alumni/ae relation, first generation, level of applicant's interest, racial/ethnic status, talent/ability. **Freshman Admission Requirements:** High school diploma is required and GED is not accepted. *Academic units required:* 4 English, 3 mathematics, 3 science, (3 science labs), 2 foreign language, 1 social studies, 1 history. **Freshman Admission Statistics:** 2,659 applied, 55% admitted, 30% enrolled. **Transfer Admission Requirements:** High school transcript, college transcript(s), standardized test scores, statement of good standing from prior institution(s). Minimum college GPA of 2.0 required. Lowest grade transferable C-. **General Admission Information:** Application Fee $25. Regular application deadline 7/1. Notification on a rolling basis, beginning on or about 9/1. Nonfall registration accepted. Admission may be deferred for a maximum of 1 year. Credit and/or placement offered for CEEB Advanced Placement tests.

COSTS AND FINANCIAL AID
Annual tuition $26,770. Room and board $9,250. Required fees $80. Average book expense $1,200. **Required Forms and Deadlines:** FAFSA. **Notification of Awards:** Applicants will be notified of awards on a rolling basis beginning 2/15. **Types of Aid:** *Need-based scholarships/grants:* Federal Pell, SEOG, state scholarships/grants, private scholarships, the school's own gift aid. *Loans:* Subsidized Stafford, Unsubsidized Stafford, PLUS, Federal Perkins, college/university loans from institutional funds. *Student Employment:* Federal Work-Study Program available. **Financial Aid Statistics:** 100% freshmen, 100% undergrads receive need-based scholarship or grant aid. 73% freshmen, 63% undergrads receive non-need-based scholarship or grant aid. 98% freshmen, 99% undergrads receive need-based self-help aid. 0% freshmen, 0% undergrads receive athletic scholarships76% undergrads borrow to pay for school. **Criteria for awarding institutional aid:** *Non-need-based:* academics.

ANDERSON UNIVERSITY (SC)

316 Boulevard, Anderson, SC 29621
Phone: 864-231-2030 · **Financial Aid Phone:** 864-231-2070
E-mail: admission@andersonuniversity.edu · **CEEB Code:** 5008
Fax: 864-231-2033 · **Website:** www.andersonuniversity.edu · **ACT Code:** 3832

This private school, affiliated with the Southern Baptist Church was founded in 1911. It has a 56-acre campus.

RATINGS
Admissions Selectivity Rating: 86   **Fire Safety Rating:** 75

STUDENTS AND FACULTY
Enrollment: 2,499. **Student Body:** 66% female, 34% male, 1% international (29 countries represented). Asian 1%, African American 7%, Caucasian 60%, Hispanic 2%, Native American <1%
Retention and Graduation: 77% freshmen return for sophomore year. 45% freshmen graduate within 4 years. 40% grads go on to further study within 1 year. 13% grads pursue arts and sciences degrees. 1% grads pursue law degrees. 9% grads pursue business degrees. 3% grads pursue medical degrees. **Faculty:** 128 full-time faculty, 63% hold PhDs, 54% are members of minority groups, 5% are women. 0% of classes are taught by teaching assistants.

ACADEMICS
Degrees: bachelor's, master's. **Classes:** Most classes have 20–29 students. Most lab/discussion sessions have 20–29 students. **Majors with Highest Enrollment:** Kinesiology and Exercise Science; Business Administration and Management; Elementary Education and Teaching. **Special Study Options:** Accelerated program, cooperative education program, distance learning, double major, dual enrollment, honors program, independent study, internships, liberal arts/career combination, study abroad, teacher certification program, Washington Semester. **Disability Services:** Special programs offered to physically disabled students include note-taking services, reader services, tape recorders, tutors. **Career services:** career/job search classes, career assessment, internships.

FACILITIES

Housing: men's dorms, women's dorms. **Special Academic Facilities/Equipment:** Electronic classroom, Art galleries, Recording studio. **Computers:** Students can register for classes online. Administrative functions (other than registration) can be performed online.

CAMPUS LIFE

Environment: Town. **Activities:** Choral groups, concert band, dance, drama/theater, jazz band, literary magazine, music ensembles, musical theater, student government, student newspaper, symphony orchestra, yearbook, Campus Ministries. 27 registered organizations, 1 honor society, 6 religious organizations. **Athletics (Intercollegiate):** *Men:* baseball, basketball, cross-country, equestrian sports, golf, soccer, tennis, track/field (outdoor), wrestling. *Women:* basketball, cheerleading, cross-country, equestrian sports, golf, soccer, softball, tennis, track/field (outdoor), volleyball. **On-Campus Highlights:** Java City, Student Center, Bunton Computer Lab, Thrift Libary, Fitness Center.

ADMISSIONS

Freshman Academic Profile: Average high school GPA 3.52. 42% in top 10% of high school class, 63% in top 25% of high school class, 89% in top 50% of high school class. SAT Math middle 50% range 460-590. SAT Critical Reading middle 50% range 460-580. SAT Writing middle 50% range 460-578. ACT middle 50% range 20-26. Minimum paper TOEFL 550. **Basis for Candidate Selection:** *Very important factors considered include:* academic GPA, standardized test scores. *Important factors considered include:* Class rank, rigor of secondary school record. *Other factors considered include:* application essay, recommendation(s), alumni/ae relation, character/personal qualities, first generation, interview, racial/ethnic status, religious affiliation/commitment, talent/ability, volunteer work. **Freshman Admission Requirements:** High school diploma is required and GED is accepted. *Academic units required:* 4 English, 3 mathematics, 3 science, (2 science labs), 2 foreign language, 2 social studies, 2 history, 4 academic electives. **Freshman Admission Statistics:** 2,142 applied, 72% admitted, 40% enrolled. **Transfer Admission Requirements:** college transcript(s), Minimum college GPA of 2.0 required. Lowest grade transferable C. **General Admission Information:** Application Fee $25. Notification on a rolling basis, beginning on or about 9/2. Nonfall registration accepted. Admission may be deferred for a maximum of 1 year. Credit and/or placement offered for CEEB Advanced Placement tests.

COSTS AND FINANCIAL AID

Annual tuition $21,660. Room and board $8,674. Required fees $2,090. Average book expense $2,000. **Required Forms and Deadlines:** FAFSA, State aid form. **Notification of Awards:** Applicants will be notified of awards on a rolling basis beginning 3/15. **Types of Aid:** *Need-based scholarships/grants:* Federal Pell, SEOG, state scholarships/grants, the school's own gift aid. *Loans:* Subsidized Stafford, Unsubsidized Stafford, PLUS, Federal Perkins. **Financial Aid Statistics:** 63% freshmen, 71% undergrads receive need-based scholarship or grant aid. 100% freshmen, 100% undergrads receive non-need-based scholarship or grant aid. 73% freshmen, 71% undergrads receive need-based self-help aid. 5% freshmen, 4% undergrads receive athletic scholarships. **Criteria for awarding institutional aid:** *Non-need-based:* academics, alumni affiliation, art, athletics, leadership, minority status, music/drama, religious affiliation, state/district residency.

ANDREWS UNIVERSITY

Office of Admissions, Berrien Springs, MI 49104
Phone: 269-471-6343
E-mail: enroll@andrews.edu • **CEEB Code:** 1030
Fax: 269-471-2670 • **Website:** www.andrews.edu • **ACT Code:** 1992

This private school, affiliated with the Seventh Day Adventist Church, was founded in 1874. It has a 1600-acre campus.

RATINGS

Admissions Selectivity Rating: 70   **Fire Safety Rating:** 60*

STUDENTS AND FACULTY

Enrollment: 1,746. **Student Body:** 56% female, 44% male, 42% out-of-state, 15% international. Asian 10%, African American 21%, Caucasian 52%, Hispanic 8%, Native American <1%

Retention and Graduation: 69% freshmen return for sophomore year. 24% grads go on to further study within 1 year. 24% grads pursue arts and sciences degrees. **Faculty:** 10% of classes are taught by teaching assistants.

ACADEMICS

Degrees: associate, bachelor's, diploma, first professional, master's. **Special Study Options:** study abroad, Undergrads may take grad level classes.

Combined degree programs: BA/MD, BA/DDS, BA/MEng, Co-op in dental assisting, hygiene; med record admi. **Career services:** internships.

FACILITIES

Housing: men's dorms, women's dorms, apartments for married students, apartments for single students. **Special Academic Facilities/Equipment:** Audio-visual center, lab school, natural history and archaeological museums, observatory, physical therapy facilities.

CAMPUS LIFE

Environment: Rural. **Activities:** Choral groups, concert band, radio station, student government, student newspaper, yearbook 2 religious organizations.

ADMISSIONS

Freshman Academic Profile: 23% from public high schools. SAT Math middle 50% range 420-600. SAT Critical Reading middle 50% range 440-610. ACT middle 50% range 19-27. **Freshman Admission Requirements:** High school diploma is required and GED is accepted. **Freshman Admission Statistics:** Minimum college GPA of 2.0 required. Lowest grade transferable C. **General Admission Information:** Application Fee $30. Early decision application deadline 1/1. Nonfall registration accepted. Credit offered for CEEB Advanced Placement tests.

COSTS AND FINANCIAL AID

Average book expense $1,128. **Required Forms and Deadlines:** FAFSA, Institution's own financial aid form, State aid form. **Types of Aid:** *Need-based scholarships/grants:* state scholarships/grants. *Loans:* Subsidized Stafford, PLUS. *Student Employment:* Federal Work-Study Program available. Institutional employment available. Highest amount earned per year from on-campus jobs $1,200. Off-campus job opportunities are good.

ANGELO STATE UNIVERSITY

ASU Station #11014, San Angelo, TX 76909-1014
Phone: 325-942-2041 • **Financial Aid Phone:** 325-942-2246
E-mail: admissions@angelo.edu • **CEEB Code:** 6644
Fax: 325-942-2078 • **Website:** www.angelo.edu • **ACT Code:** 4164

This public school was founded in 1928. It has a 268-acre campus.

RATINGS

Admissions Selectivity Rating: 74   **Fire Safety Rating:** 95

STUDENTS AND FACULTY

Enrollment: 5,503. **Student Body:** 54% female, 46% male, 3% out-of-state, 3% international (24 countries represented). Asian 1%, African American 8%, Caucasian 55%, Hispanic 30%, Native American <1%

Retention and Graduation: 12% freshmen graduate within 4 years. 28% freshmen graduate within 6 years. 15% grads go on to further study within 1 year. **Faculty:** 281 full-time faculty, 75% hold PhDs, 44% are members of minority groups, 17% are women. 3% of classes are taught by teaching assistants.

ACADEMICS

Degrees: associate, bachelor's, master's. **Classes:** Most classes have 20–29 students. Most lab/discussion sessions have 20–29 students. **Majors with Highest Enrollment:** Multi-/Interdisciplinary Studies; Business Administration and Management. **Special Study Options:** distance learning, double major, dual enrollment, honors program, independent study, internships, study abroad, teacher certification program, 4+1 programs in various disciplines allowing students to complete a bachelor's degree in four years and a master's degree in a related field in one year at Texas Tech University. Also, 3+2 physics/pre-engineering program allowing three years of study in applied physics and two years at an affiliated university for an engineering degree. **Honors programs:** http://www.angelo.edu/dept/honors/index.htm. Combined degree programs: BBA/MBA. **Disability Services:** Special programs offered to physically disabled students include note-taking services, tutors. **Career services:** Alumni network, alumni services, career/job search classes, career assessment, internships. ASU's multiple internship programs have provided exceptional worklife experiences for undergraduates with students interning in positions ranging from the Los Alamos National Labs to Washington, D.C., news services. Additionally, the Career Development Office Career Exploration and Planning classes, which help broaden student understanding of career possibilities and the value of internships.

FACILITIES

Housing: Coed dorms, women's dorms, apartments for single students, Theme Housing, Rooms for disabled and Honors students. 99% of campus accessible to physically disabled. **Special Academic Facilities/Equipment:** Planetarium; West Texas Collection; Management, Instruction, and Research (Agricultural) Center; Food Safety and Product Development Lab. **Computers:** 100% of classrooms, 100% of dorms, 100% of libraries, 100% of dining areas, 100% of student union, 100% of common outdoor areas have wireless network access. Students can register for classes online. Administrative functions (other than registration) can be performed online.

CAMPUS LIFE

Environment: City. **Activities:** Choral groups, concert band, dance, drama/theater, jazz band, literary magazine, marching band, music ensembles, musical theater, pep band, radio station, student government, student newspaper, student-run film society, television station, Campus Ministries, International Student Organization. 76 registered organizations, 11 honor society, 9 religious organizations. 4 fraternities, 2 sororities. **Athletics (Intercollegiate):** *Men:* baseball, basketball, cross-country, football, track/field (outdoor). *Women:* basketball, cross-country, golf, soccer, softball, track/field (outdoor), volleyball. **On-Campus Highlights:** Houston Harte University Center, Junell Center/Stephens Arena, ASU Planetarium, ASU Lake House, West Texas Collection, ASU Mall and Student Gathering Areas Porter Henderson Library. **Environmental Initiatives:** LEED Certification initiataives in all new buildings; Recycling programs; Utilizing green cleaning products.

ADMISSIONS

Freshman Academic Profile: 10.8% in top 10% of high school class, 35% in top 25% of high school class, 72.5% in top 50% of high school class. 96% from public high schools. SAT Math middle 50% range 440-540. SAT Critical Reading middle 50% range 420-520. ACT middle 50% range 18-23. Minimum internet-based TOEFL 79. Minimum paper TOEFL 550. **Basis for Candidate Selection:** *Very important factors considered include:* Class rank, rigor of secondary school record, standardized test scores. **Freshman Admission Requirements:** High school diploma is required and GED is accepted. **Freshman Admission Statistics:** 2,599 applied, 80% admitted, 58% enrolled. **Transfer Admission Requirements:** college transcript(s), statement of good standing from prior institution(s). Minimum college GPA of 2.0 required. Lowest grade transferable D. **General Admission Information:** Application Fee $25. Nonfall registration accepted. Credit offered for CEEB Advanced Placement tests.

COSTS AND FINANCIAL AID

Annual in-state tuition $4,700. Annual out-of-state tuition $15,560. Room and board $7,602. Required fees $2,942. Average book expense $1,200. **Required Forms and Deadlines:** FAFSA. **Notification of Awards:** Applicants will be notified of awards on a rolling basis beginning 4/1. **Types of Aid:** *Need-based scholarships/grants:* Federal Pell, SEOG, state scholarships/grants, private scholarships, the school's own gift aid, Federal Nursing Scholarships. *Loans:* Subsidized Stafford, Unsubsidized Stafford, PLUS, Federal Perkins, Federal Nursing, state loans, college/university loans from institutional funds. *Student Employment:* Federal Work-Study Program available. Institutional employment available. Off-campus job opportunities are good. **Financial Aid Statistics:** 77% freshmen, 85% undergrads receive need-based scholarship or grant aid. 61% freshmen, 38% undergrads receive non-need-based scholarship or grant aid. 74% freshmen, 77% undergrads receive need-based self-help aid. 5% freshmen, 5% undergrads receive athletic scholarships. 87% freshmen, 81% undergrads receive any aid. 58% undergrads borrow to pay for school. Average cumulative indebtedness $24,360. **Criteria for awarding institutional aid:** *Non-need-based:* academics, art, athletics, leadership, music/drama, state/district residency.

ANNA MARIA COLLEGE

50 Sunset Lane, Paxton, MA 01612-1198
Phone: 508-849-3360 · **Financial Aid Phone:** 508-849-3366
E-mail: admission@annamaria.edu · **CEEB Code:** 3005
Fax: 508-849-3362 · **Website:** www.annamaria.edu · **ACT Code:** 3232

This private school, affiliated with the Roman Catholic Church, was founded in 1946. It has a 190-acre campus.

RATINGS

Admissions Selectivity Rating: 69   Fire Safety Rating: 75

STUDENTS AND FACULTY

Enrollment: 978. **Student Body:** 56% female, 44% male, 12% out-of-state, 1% international. Asian 1%, African American 6%, Caucasian 73%, Hispanic

5%, Native American <1%

Retention and Graduation: 70% freshmen return for sophomore year. 50% freshmen graduate within 4 years. 59% freshmen graduate within 6 years. 47% grads go on to further study within 1 year. 19% grads pursue arts and sciences degrees. 2% grads pursue law degrees. 1% grads pursue business degrees. **Faculty:** 50 full-time faculty, 72% hold PhDs, 66% are members of minority groups. 0% of classes are taught by teaching assistants.

ACADEMICS

Degrees: associate, bachelor's, certificate, master's, post-bachelor's certificate, post-master's certificate. **Classes:** Most classes have 10–19 students. Most lab/discussion sessions have fewer than 10 students. **Majors with Highest Enrollment:** Fire Science/Fire-fighting; Criminal Justice/Safety Studies; Business Administration and Management. **Special Study Options:** Accelerated program, cooperative education program, cross-registration, double major, independent study, internships, liberal arts/career combination, student-designed major, study abroad, teacher certification program. **Honors programs:** The Honors Program at Anna Maria College is designed to intellectually challenge highly motivated scholastic achievers. The Program is now a member of "National Collegiate Honors Programs," the national association of Honors Programs. Each Honors Program participant will have the opportunity to engage directly in foreign culture through interesting study abroad programs, such as a semester abroad experience,or a focused Urban Seminar that meets in a city like Paris, Vienna, Rome or Berlin that is sponsored by the College and supervised by a professor who oversees the program. Combined degree programs: BA/MA. **Disability Services:** Special programs offered to physically disabled students include note-taking services, reader services, tape recorders, tutors. **Career services:** alumni services, career assessment, internships.

FACILITIES

Housing: Coed dorms, special housing for disabled students, Wellness Housing. **Special Academic Facilities/Equipment:** The Mondor-Eagan Library houses Anna Maria College's volumes, stacks, periodicals, study rooms, computer center, resource centers, and language laboratory. Classrooms are located in Trinity Hall, Cardinal Cushing Hall, and Foundress Hall. Foundress Hall houses the Zecco Performing Arts Center. Trinity Hall also houses the learning center. Among the other buildings are Madore Chapel, St. Joseph's Hall for sciences and Miriam Hall for music, performance, and art. **Computers:** 100% of classrooms, 100% of dorms, 100% of libraries, 100% of dining areas, 100% of student union, 100% of common outdoor areas have wireless network access. Administrative functions (other than registration) can be performed online.

CAMPUS LIFE

Environment: Rural. **Activities:** Choral groups, dance, drama/theater, jazz band, pep band, student government, student newspaper, yearbook, Campus Ministries. 17 registered organizations, 5 honor societies, 1 religious organization. **Athletics (Intercollegiate):** *Men:* baseball, basketball, cross-country, football, golf, lacrosse, soccer, tennis. *Women:* basketball, field hockey, lacrosse, soccer, softball, tennis, volleyball. **On-Campus Highlights:** NEW: Residence Hall, NEW: Exercise / Weight Room, New Art Building w/ art gallery, Snack bar / Lounge, Student Center. **Environmental Initiatives:** There is a "Green Committee" that meets regularly to discuss environmental issues and ways that the college can be be more sustainable. Efforts are ongoing in moving to a paperless environment. We have made significant progress in this area.

ADMISSIONS

Freshman Academic Profile: Average high school GPA 2.62. 2% in top 10% of high school class, 13% in top 25% of high school class, 41% in top 50% of high school class. SAT Math middle 50% range 378-480. SAT Critical Reading middle 50% range 378-490. ACT middle 50% range 18-21. Minimum paper TOEFL 500. **Basis for Candidate Selection:** *Very important factors considered include:* academic GPA, standardized test scores. *Other factors considered include:* application essay, recommendation(s), rigor of secondary school record, extracurricular activities, level of applicant's interest, volunteer work, work experience. **Freshman Admission Requirements:** High school diploma is required and GED is accepted. *Academic units required:* 4 English, 3 mathematics, 3 science, (1 science labs), 2 foreign language, 2 social studies, 2 history, 4 academic electives. **Freshman Admission Statistics:** 935 applied, 89% admitted, 30% enrolled. **Transfer Admission Requirements:** High school transcript, college transcript(s), essay or personal statement, statement of good standing from prior institution(s). Minimum college GPA of 2.0 required. Lowest grade transferable C. **General Admission Information:** Application Fee $40. Notification on a rolling basis, beginning on or about 12/1. Nonfall registration accepted. Admission may be deferred for a maximum of 1 year. Credit and/or placement offered for CEEB Advanced Placement tests.

COSTS AND FINANCIAL AID

Annual tuition $23,500. Room and board $9,350. Required fees $2,350. Average book expense $800. **Required Forms and Deadlines:** FAFSA, State aid form. **Notification of Awards:** Applicants will be notified of awards on a rolling basis beginning 4/1. **Types of Aid:** *Need-based scholarships/grants:* Federal Pell,

SEOG, state scholarships/grants, private scholarships, the school's own gift aid, United Negro College Fund. *Loans:* Subsidized Stafford, Unsubsidized Stafford, PLUS, Federal Perkins, college/university loans from institutional funds. *Student Employment:* Federal Work-Study Program available. Off-campus job opportunities are good. **Financial Aid Statistics:** 99% freshmen, 98% undergrads receive need-based scholarship or grant aid. 99% freshmen, 98% undergrads receive non-need-based scholarship or grant aid. 92% freshmen, 92% undergrads receive need-based self-help aid. 0% freshmen, 0% undergrads receive athletic scholarships. 98% freshmen, 95% undergrads receive any aid. 92% undergrads borrow to pay for school. Average cumulative indebtedness $17,926. **Criteria for awarding institutional aid:** *Non-need-based:* academics, alumni affiliation, music/drama, religious affiliation, state/district residency.

ANTIOCH COLLEGE

1 Morgan Place, Yellow Springs, OH 45387
Phone: 937-319-6082 · **Financial Aid Phone:** 937-319-6016
E-mail: mcanal@antiochcollege.org
Fax: 937-319-6085 · **Website:** www.antiochcollege.org · **ACT Code:** 3232

This private school was founded in 1852. It has a 100-acre campus.

RATINGS

Admissions Selectivity Rating: 83   **Fire Safety Rating:** 86

STUDENTS AND FACULTY

Enrollment: 236. **Student Body:** 67% female, 33% male, 70% out-of-state, 0% international (13 countries represented). Asian 3%, African American 7%, Caucasian 72%, Hispanic 1%, Native American 1%
Retention and Graduation: 91% freshmen return for sophomore year. **Faculty:** 31 full-time faculty, 100% hold PhDs, 58% are members of minority groups, 35% are women. 0% of classes are taught by teaching assistants.

ACADEMICS

Degrees: bachelor's. **Classes:** Most classes have fewer than 10 students. **Special Study Options:** cooperative education program, cross-registration, dual enrollment, independent study, internships, liberal arts/career combination, student-designed major, study abroad. **Disability Services:** Special programs offered to physically disabled students include note-taking services, reader services, tape recorders, tutors. **Career services:** alumni services, career/job search classes, career assessment, internships.

FACILITIES

Housing: Coed dorms, special housing for disabled students, special housing for international students, Gender specific floors. 25% of campus accessible to physically disabled. **Special Academic Facilities/Equipment:** 1,000-acre nature preserve.

CAMPUS LIFE

Environment: Rural. **Activities:** Choral groups, dance, drama/theater, literary magazine, music ensembles, musical theater, radio station, student government, student newspaper. 16 registered organizations. **On-Campus Highlights:** Herndon Gallery, Glen Hellen Nature Preserve, Japanese Tea Garden, Community Bike Shop, Alternative Library.

ADMISSIONS

Freshman Academic Profile: Average high school GPA 3.01. SAT Math middle 50% range 493-607. SAT Critical Reading middle 50% range 558-720. ACT middle 50% range 25-31. **Basis for Candidate Selection:** *Very important factors considered include:* application essay, academic GPA, recommendation(s), rigor of secondary school record, character/personal qualities, interview, level of applicant's interest. *Important factors considered include:* Class rank, volunteer work, work experience. *Other factors considered include:* standardized test scores, alumni/ae relation, extracurricular activities, first generation, talent/ability. **Freshman Admission Requirements:** High school diploma is required and GED is accepted. *Academic units required:* 4 English. **Transfer Admission Requirements:** High school transcript, college transcript(s), essay or personal statement, statement of good standing from prior institution(s). **General Admission Information:** Notification on a rolling basis, beginning on or about 1/1. Nonfall registration not accepted. Admission may be deferred for a maximum of 1 year. Credit and/or placement offered for CEEB Advanced Placement tests.

COSTS AND FINANCIAL AID

Annual tuition $30,250. Room and board $9,720. Required fees $700. Average book expense $750. **Required Forms and Deadlines:** Institution's own financial aid form. **Notification of Awards:** Applicants will be notified of awards on a rolling basis beginning 3/15. **Types of Aid:** *Need-based scholarships/grants:* Federal Pell, SEOG, state scholarships/grants, private scholarships, the school's

own gift aid. *Loans:* Direct Subsidized Stafford, Direct Unsubsidized Stafford, Direct PLUS, Subsidized Stafford, Unsubsidized Stafford, PLUS, Federal Perkins. *Student Employment:* Federal Work-Study Program available. Institutional employment available. Off-campus job opportunities are fair. **Financial Aid Statistics:** 100% freshmen, 100% undergrads receive need-based scholarship or grant aid. 112% freshmen. 92% freshmen, 94% undergrads receive need-based self-help aid. 100% freshmen, 100% undergrads receive athletic scholarships. 100% freshmen, 100% undergrads receive any aid. 0% undergrads borrow to pay for school. Average cumulative indebtedness $0. **Criteria for awarding institutional aid:** *Non-need-based:* academics.

ANTIOCH SOUTHERN CALIFORNIA/ LOS ANGELES

Office of Admissions, Culver City, CA 90230
Phone: 310-578-1090
E-mail: admissions@atiochla.edu · **CEEB Code:** 1862
Fax: 310-822-4824 · **Website:** www.antiochla.edu

This private school was founded in 1852. It has a 800-acre campus.

RATINGS

Admissions Selectivity Rating: 60*   **Fire Safety Rating:** 60*

STUDENTS AND FACULTY

Enrollment: 188. **Student Body:** 100% female, 0% male, 9% out-of-state, 0% international (20 countries represented). Asian 5%, African American 24%, Caucasian 80%, Hispanic 11%, Native American 2%
Retention and Graduation: 73% grads go on to further study within 1 year. 82% grads pursue arts and sciences degrees. 4% grads pursue law degrees. 12% grads pursue business degrees. **Faculty:** 21 full-time faculty, 81% hold PhDs, 71% are members of minority groups, 24% are women. 0% of classes are taught by teaching assistants.

ACADEMICS

Degrees: bachelor's, certificate, diploma, master's, post-bachelor's certificate, post-master's certificate. **Classes:** Most classes have 10–19 students. **Special Study Options:** cross-registration, double major, independent study, internships, teacher certification program, weekend college. Combined degree programs: BA/MA. **Disability Services:** Special programs offered to physically disabled students include note-taking services, tape recorders. **Career services:** internships.

FACILITIES

Housing: Coed dorms. 100% of campus accessible to physically disabled.

CAMPUS LIFE

Environment: City. **Activities:** radio station, student government, Campus Ministries. 1 registered organization. **On-Campus Highlights:** Student Lounge, Campus Services, Classrooms, Computer lab, Faculty and Student Services Offices.

ADMISSIONS

Freshman Academic Profile: Minimum paper TOEFL 600. **Transfer Admission Requirements:** college transcript(s), essay or personal statement, Lowest grade transferable C. **General Admission Information:** Application Fee $60. Regular application deadline 8/1. Notification on a rolling basis, beginning on or about 9/1. Nonfall registration not accepted. Admission may be deferred for a maximum of 1 yr. Credit and/or placement offered for CEEB Advanced Placement tests.

COSTS AND FINANCIAL AID

Average book expense $0. **Required Forms and Deadlines:** FAFSA, Institution's own financial aid form. **Notification of Awards:** Applicants will be notified of awards on a rolling basis beginning 4/15. **Types of Aid:** *Need-based scholarships/grants:* Federal Pell, SEOG, state scholarships/grants, private scholarships, the school's own gift aid. *Loans:* Subsidized Stafford, Unsubsidized Stafford, PLUS, Federal Perkins. *Student Employment:* Federal Work-Study Program available. Institutional employment available. Off-campus job opportunities are excellent. **Financial Aid Statistics:** 91% undergrads receive need-based scholarship or grant aid. 0% undergrads receive non-need-based scholarship or grant aid. 100% undergrads receive need-based self-help aid. 0% undergrads receive athletic scholarships. **Criteria for awarding institutional aid:** *Non-need-based:* academics, leadership.

ANTIOCH UNIVERSITY SANTA BARBARA

801 Garden Street, Santa Barbara, CA 93101
Phone: 805-962-8179 • **Financial Aid Phone:** 805-962-8179
E-mail: admissions@antiochsb.edu
Fax: 805-962-4786 • **Website:** www.antiochsb.edu

This private school was founded in 1852.

RATINGS

Admissions Selectivity Rating: 60*   **Fire Safety Rating:** 60*

STUDENTS AND FACULTY

Enrollment: 105. **Student Body:** 75% female, 25% male, (11 countries represented).
Faculty: 16 full-time faculty.

ACADEMICS

Degrees: bachelor's, master's. **Special Study Options:** cross-registration, double major, independent study, internships, liberal arts/career combination, study abroad, teacher certification program, weekend college.

FACILITIES

Computers: Students can register for classes online. Administrative functions (other than registration) can be performed online.

CAMPUS LIFE

Environment: City.

ADMISSIONS

Freshman Admission Requirements: High school diploma is required and GED is accepted. **Transfer Admission Requirements:** High school transcript, college transcript(s), essay or personal statement, interview, statement of good standing from prior institution(s). Minimum college GPA of 2.0 required. Lowest grade transferable C. **General Admission Information:** Application Fee $60. Nonfall registration not accepted.

COSTS AND FINANCIAL AID

Required Forms and Deadlines: FAFSA, Institution's own financial aid form. **Types of Aid:** *Need-based scholarships/grants:* Federal Pell, SEOG, state scholarships/grants, private scholarships, the school's own gift aid. *Loans:* Subsidized Stafford, Unsubsidized Stafford, PLUS, Federal Perkins. **Financial Aid Statistics:** 54% undergrads receive need-based scholarship or grant aid. 0% undergrads receive non-need-based scholarship or grant aid. 54% undergrads receive need-based self-help aid. 75% undergrads borrow to pay for school. Average cumulative indebtedness $25,000.

APPALACHIAN STATE UNIVERSITY

Office of Admissions, Boone, NC 28608-2004
Phone: 828-262-2120 • **Financial Aid Phone:** 828-262-2190
E-mail: admissions@appstate.edu • **CEEB Code:** 5010
Fax: 828-262-3296 • **Website:** www.appstate.edu • **ACT Code:** 3062

This public school was founded in 1899. It has a 1300-acre campus.

RATINGS

Admissions Selectivity Rating: 87   **Fire Safety Rating:** 91

STUDENTS AND FACULTY

Enrollment: 16,116. **Student Body:** 54% female, 46% male, 8% out-of-state, 1% international (61 countries represented). Asian 2%, African American 3%, Caucasian 86%, Hispanic 4%, Native American <1%
Retention and Graduation: 88% freshmen return for sophomore year. 44% freshmen graduate within 4 years. 70% freshmen graduate within 6 years.
Faculty: 920 full-time faculty, 99% hold PhDs, 48% are members of minority groups, 5% are women. 1% of classes are taught by teaching assistants.

ACADEMICS

Degrees: bachelor's, certificate, master's, post-bachelor's certificate, post-master's certificate. **Classes:** Most classes have 20–29 students. Most lab/discussion sessions have 20–29 students. **Majors with Highest Enrollment:** Psychology; Kinesiology and Exercise Science; Business Administration and Management. **Special Study Options:** distance learning, double major, dual enrollment, English as a Second Language (ESL), exchange student program (domestic), honors program, independent study, internships, liberal arts/career combination, student-designed major, study abroad, teacher certification program. **Hon-**

ors programs: Heltzer Honors Program offers promising and highly motivated students opportunities by providing honors classes in many fields. **Disability Services:** Special programs offered to physically disabled students include note-taking services, reader services, tape recorders, tutors. **Career services:** Alumni network, alumni services, career/job search classes, career assessment, internships, regional alumni.

FACILITIES

Housing: Coed dorms, special housing for disabled students, men's dorms, special housing for international students, women's dorms, apartments for married students, apartments for single students, Wellness Housing, Theme Housing, Sorority housing. 100% of campus accessible to physically disabled. **Special Academic Facilities/Equipment:** Language lab, Dark Sky Observatory http://www.dancaton.physics.appstate.edu/Observatories/DSO/index.htm, meteorological reporting station, art gallery, Living Learning Center, geology museum and rock garden http://www.geology.appstate.edu/museum/museum. htm, wind research site http://www.wind.appstate.edu/swiwind/smallwindrdsite. php, library Special Collections http://www.library.appstate.edu/collections/sc/ index.html. **Computers:** 95% of classrooms, 70% of dorms, 90% of libraries, 90% of dining areas, 85% of student union, 5% of common outdoor areas have wireless network access. Students can register for classes online. Administrative functions (other than registration) can be performed online.

CAMPUS LIFE

Environment: Village. **Activities:** Choral groups, concert band, dance, drama/theater, jazz band, literary magazine, marching band, music ensembles, musical theater, opera, pep band, radio station, student government, student newspaper, student-run film society, symphony orchestra, Campus Ministries, International Student Organization, Model UN. 270 registered organizations, 20 honor societies, 25 religious organizations. 18 fraternities, 11 sorority. **Athletics (Intercollegiate):** *Men:* baseball, basketball, cross-country, football, golf, soccer, tennis, track/field (outdoor), track/field (indoor), wrestling. *Women:* basketball, cross-country, field hockey, golf, soccer, softball, tennis, track/field (outdoor), track/field (indoor), volleyball. **On-Campus Highlights:** Student Union, Central Dining Hall, Belk Library, Student Recreation Center, Holmes Convocation Center. **Environmental Initiatives:** Signatory of the American College and University Presidents Climate Commitment. On track with the target requirements. Climate Action Plan completed 2010. Climate neutrality date of 2050. Appalachian Energy Summit to help chart strategic path for sustainable energy future. The three-day Appalachian Energy Summit, hosted by Appalachian State University, in partnership with Rocky Mountain Institute, convened representatives from all 17 campuses in the UNC system, including the North Carolina School of Science and Mathematics, plus five private colleges: Catawba College, Davidson College, Duke University, Warren Wilson College and Wake Forest University. The event is designed to aid in the creation of actionable energy plans that benefit students, the environment and the local economy and help advance the work toward carbon neutrality by. http://sustain.appstate.edu/ participants-2012-energysummit. ASU has a commitment of zero waste and intends to divert at least 90% of waste. A target date of 2022 is set for this goal.

ADMISSIONS

Freshman Academic Profile: Average high school GPA 4.06. 19% in top 10% of high school class, 56% in top 25% of high school class, 91% in top 50% of high school class. 91% from public high schools. SAT Math middle 50% range 530-620. SAT Critical Reading middle 50% range 530-620. SAT Writing middle 50% range 500-600. ACT middle 50% range 23-27. Minimum internet-based TOEFL 75. **Basis for Candidate Selection:** *Very important factors considered include:* Class rank, academic GPA, rigor of secondary school record, standardized test scores. *Other factors considered include:* application essay, recommendation(s), character/personal qualities, extracurricular activities, first generation, racial/ethnic status, talent/ability, volunteer work, work experience. **Freshman Admission Requirements:** High school diploma is required and GED is not accepted. *Academic units required:* 4 English, 4 mathematics, 3 science, (1 science labs), 2 foreign language, 1 social studies, 1 history. **Freshman Admission Statistics:** 13,506 applied, 63% admitted, 36% enrolled. **Transfer Admission Requirements:** High school transcript, college transcript(s), Minimum college GPA of 2.0 required. Lowest grade transferable C. **General Admission Information:** Application Fee $50. Nonfall registration accepted. Admission may be deferred for a maximum of 1 yr. Credit and/or placement offered for CEEB Advanced Placement tests.

COSTS AND FINANCIAL AID

Annual in-state tuition $3,772. Annual out-of-state tuition $16,939. Room and board $7,675. Required fees $2,781. Average book expense $700. **Required Forms and Deadlines:** FAFSA. **Notification of Awards:** Applicants will be notified of awards on a rolling basis beginning 4/1. **Types of Aid:** *Need-based scholarships/grants:* Federal Pell, SEOG, state scholarships/grants, private scholarships, the school's own gift aid. *Loans:* Subsidized Stafford, Unsubsidized Stafford, PLUS, Federal Perkins. **Financial Aid Statistics:** 76% freshmen, 75% undergrads receive need-based scholarship or grant aid. 35% freshmen, 34% undergrads receive non-need-based scholarship or grant aid. 71%

freshmen, 77% undergrads receive need-based self-help aid. 2% freshmen, 1% undergrads receive athletic scholarships. 66% freshmen, 71% undergrads receive any aid. 56% undergrads borrow to pay for school. Average cumulative indebtedness $19,705. **Criteria for awarding institutional aid:** *Non-need-based:* academics, alumni affiliation, art, athletics, job skills, leadership, minority status, music/drama, religious affiliation, state/district residency.

AQUINAS COLLEGE

1607 Robinson Road SE, Grand Rapids, MI 49506-1799
Phone: 616-632-2900 · **Financial Aid Phone:** 616-632-2893
E-mail: admissions@aquinas.edu · **CEEB Code:** 1018
Fax: 616-732-4469 · **Website:** www.aquinas.edu · **ACT Code:** 1962

This private school was founded in 1886. It has a 107-acre campus.

RATINGS

Admissions Selectivity Rating: 81   **Fire Safety Rating:** 96

STUDENTS AND FACULTY

Enrollment: 1,851. **Student Body:** 62% female, 38% male, 6% out-of-state, 1% international (8 countries represented). Asian 1%, African American 3%, Caucasian 85%, Hispanic 5%, Native American <1%
Retention and Graduation: 33% freshmen graduate within 4 years. 17% grads go on to further study within 1 year. 7% grads pursue arts and sciences degrees. 3% grads pursue law degrees. 3% grads pursue business degrees. 2% grads pursue medical degrees. **Faculty:** 86 full-time faculty, 78% hold PhDs, 44% are members of minority groups, 9% are women.

ACADEMICS

Degrees: associate, bachelor's, master's. **Classes:** Most classes have 20–29 students. **Majors with Highest Enrollment:** Liberal Arts and Sciences/Liberal Studies. **Special Study Options:** Accelerated program, cooperative education program, cross-registration, distance learning, double major, dual enrollment, exchange student program (domestic), honors program, independent study, internships, liberal arts/career combination, student-designed major, study abroad, teacher certification program, Service learning experiences in Peru, Haiti, Mexico. Semester abroad in Costa Rica, France, Germany, Spain,Italy, Japan and Ireland. Domestic exchange in California, Florida and Chicago. **Honors programs:** Insignis Honors Program. **Disability Services:** Special programs offered to physically disabled students include note-taking services, reader services, tape recorders, tutors. **Career services:** alumni services, career/job search classes, career assessment, internships.

FACILITIES

Housing: Coed dorms, women's dorms, apartments for single students, Theme Housing. 95% of campus accessible to physically disabled. **Special Academic Facilities/Equipment:** Observatory and Jarecki Center for Advanced Learning featuring high-speed, two-way interactive video conferencing for courses and a virtual connection for external experts to interact with classes (sound, video, graphics) using a laptop computer equipped with a camera that is housed in a self-contained briefcase. The package includes all the technology needed to accomplish the connection through a standard phone jack. This "virtual faculty briefcase" can be shipped to a guest lecturer at another location anywhere in the world and they are able to conduct an interactive lecture or discussion with an Aquinas classroom. **Computers:** 100% of classrooms, 100% of dorms, 100% of libraries, 100% of dining areas, 100% of student union, 80% of common outdoor areas have wireless network access. Administrative functions (other than registration) can be performed online.

CAMPUS LIFE

Environment: Metropolis. **Activities:** Choral groups, concert band, dance, drama/theater, jazz band, literary magazine, music ensembles, radio station, student government, student newspaper, Campus Ministries, Model UN. 71 registered organizations, 4 honor societies, 2 religious organizations. **Athletics (Intercollegiate):** *Men:* baseball, basketball, cheerleading, cross-country, golf, lacrosse, soccer, tennis, track/field (outdoor), track/field (indoor). *Women:* basketball, cheerleading, cross-country, golf, lacrosse, soccer, softball, tennis, track/field (outdoor), track/field (indoor), volleyball. **On-Campus Highlights:** Physical Education Building, Jarecki Center, Moose Café, Wege Student Center, Performing Arts Center, The new, state-of-the-art, Grace Hauenstein Library located in the Jarecki Center opened in August 2006. With ample parking, many meeting rooms, and the latest technology, it is now the most popular meeting place on the campus. **Environmental Initiatives:** Sustainable Business practices restore environmental quality, promote stable and healthy communities, and increase long-term profitability. The Aquinas Sustainable Business Degree program fosters ecological and social intelligence in all business decisions and is

the only undergraduate program of its kind in Michigan and possibly the United States. Aquinas also offers a Master of Sustainable Business. Aquinas has a formal sustainability initiative process for addressing college redesign, consisting of sustainability committees built into the governing document of the college. The Faculty Assembly, the Staff Assembly, and the Student Senate all have such standing sustainability committees, each of which send representatives to a joint committee on sustainability. A number of outcomes have emerged, including increased awareness and utilization of the principles of sustainability by students, staff and faculty. Multiple projects generated from proposed sustainability initiatives are also being implemented. In 2008, Aquinas became a signatory of the American College and University Presidents Climate Commitment, and set a future goal of carbon neutrality by 2040. A recent update to the carbon footprint report revealed a 10.5% decrease in carbon emissions since the 2009 baseline. The Center for Sustainability at Aquinas College is working diligently to meet our first, short term goals laid out in the Climate Action Plan, and develop a system to better track directly financed outsourced travel.

ADMISSIONS

Freshman Academic Profile: Average high school GPA 3.46. 19% in top 10% of high school class, 44.8% in top 25% of high school class, 77% in top 50% of high school class. 80% from public high schools. ACT middle 50% range 21-26. Minimum paper TOEFL 550. **Basis for Candidate Selection:** *Very important factors considered include:* academic GPA, rigor of secondary school record, standardized test scores. *Other factors considered include:* character/personal qualities, extracurricular activities, first generation, talent/ability, volunteer work, work experience. **Freshman Admission Requirements:** High school diploma is required and GED is not accepted. *Academic units required:* 4 English, 4 mathematics, 3 science, 4 social studies. **Freshman Admission Statistics:** 2,602 applied, 71% admitted, 21% enrolled. **Transfer Admission Requirements:** High school transcript, college transcript(s), Minimum college GPA of 2.0 required. Lowest grade transferable D. **General Admission Information:** Notification on a rolling basis, beginning on or about 9/15. Nonfall registration accepted. Admission may be deferred for a maximum of one year. Credit offered for CEEB Advanced Placement tests.

COSTS AND FINANCIAL AID

Annual tuition $27,332. Room and board $8,350. Required fees $394. Average book expense $800. **Required Forms and Deadlines:** FAFSA. **Notification of Awards:** Applicants will be notified of awards on a rolling basis beginning 3/1. **Types of Aid:** *Need-based scholarships/grants:* Federal Pell, SEOG, state scholarships/grants, private scholarships, the school's own gift aid. *Loans:* Direct Subsidized Stafford, Direct Unsubsidized Stafford, Direct PLUS, Federal Perkins. *Student Employment:* Federal Work-Study Program available. Institutional employment available. Highest amount earned per year from on-campus jobs $13,040. Off-campus job opportunities are good. **Financial Aid Statistics:** 100% freshmen, 100% undergrads receive need-based scholarship or grant aid. 74% freshmen, 69% undergrads receive non-need-based scholarship or grant aid. 100% freshmen, 100% undergrads receive need-based self-help aid. 2% freshmen, 6% undergrads receive athletic scholarships. 95% freshmen, 90% undergrads receive any aid. 76% undergrads borrow to pay for school. Average cumulative indebtedness $21,969. **Criteria for awarding institutional aid:** *Non-need-based:* academics, alumni affiliation, art, athletics, leadership, music/drama.

AQUINAS COLLEGE (TN)

4210 Harding Road, Nashville, TN 37205
Phone: 615-297-7545
E-mail: admissions@aquinas-tn.edu
Fax: 615-297-7970 · **Website:** www.aquinas-tn.edu · **ACT Code:** 3942

This private school, affiliated with the Roman Catholic Church, was founded in 1961. It has a 80-acre campus.

RATINGS

Admissions Selectivity Rating: 61   **Fire Safety Rating:** 60*

STUDENTS AND FACULTY

Enrollment: 329. **Student Body:** 77% female, 23% male, 12% out-of-state. **Faculty:** 21 full-time faculty, 43% hold PhDs, 67% are members of minority groups, 5% are women. 0% of classes are taught by teaching assistants.

ACADEMICS

Degrees: associate, bachelor's, post-bachelor's certificate, terminal associate, transfer associate. **Special Study Options:** liberal arts/career combination, teacher certification program, weekend college. **Career services:** career/job search classes, career assessment.

FACILITIES

Housing: 70% of campus accessible to physically disabled.

CAMPUS LIFE

Activities: student government, student newspaper. 5 registered organizations. **Athletics (Intercollegiate):** *Men:* baseball, basketball. *Women:* cheerleading.

ADMISSIONS

Freshman Academic Profile: 80% from public high schools. Minimum paper TOEFL 525. **Basis for Candidate Selection:** *Very important factors considered include:* rigor of secondary school record, standardized test scores. *Other factors considered include:* recommendation(s), alumni/ae relation, character/personal qualities, extracurricular activities, interview, work experience. **Freshman Admission Requirements:** High school diploma is required and GED is accepted. **Freshman Admission Statistics:** 329 applied, 73% admitted, 28% enrolled. **Transfer Admission Requirements:** college transcript(s), Minimum college GPA of 2.0 required. Lowest grade transferable c. **General Admission Information:** Application Fee $10. Notification on a rolling basis, beginning on or about 10/1. Nonfall registration accepted. Admission may be deferred for a maximum of 1 yr. Credit offered for CEEB Advanced Placement tests.

COSTS AND FINANCIAL AID

Required Forms and Deadlines: FAFSA, Institution's own financial aid form. **Notification of Awards:** Applicants will be notified of awards on a rolling basis beginning 3/1. **Types of Aid:** *Need-based scholarships/grants:* Federal Pell, SEOG, state scholarships/grants, private scholarships, the school's own gift aid. *Loans:* Subsidized Stafford, Unsubsidized Stafford, PLUS. *Student Employment:* Federal Work-Study Program available. Off-campus job opportunities are excellent. **Financial Aid Statistics:** 51% freshmen, 38% undergrads receive need-based scholarship or grant aid. 0% freshmen, 0% undergrads receive non-need-based scholarship or grant aid. 82% freshmen, 59% undergrads receive need-based self-help aid. 2% undergrads receive athletic scholarships. **Criteria for awarding institutional aid:** *Non-need-based:* academics, athletics, leadership, religious affiliation.

ARCADIA UNIVERSITY

450 South Easton Road, Glenside, PA 19038
Phone: 215-572-2910 · **Financial Aid Phone:** 215-572-2980
E-mail: admiss@arcadia.edu · **CEEB Code:** 2039
Fax: 215-572-4049 · **Website:** www.arcadia.edu

This private school, affiliated with the Presbyterian Church, was founded in 1853. It has a 60-acre campus.

RATINGS

Admissions Selectivity Rating: 88   **Fire Safety Rating:** 60*

STUDENTS AND FACULTY

Enrollment: 2,151. **Student Body:** 71% female, 29% male, 38% out-of-state, 1% international (28 countries represented). Asian 4%, African American 7%, Caucasian 67%, Hispanic 5%, Native American <1%
Retention and Graduation: 78% freshmen return for sophomore year. 52% freshmen graduate within 4 years. 61% freshmen graduate within 6 years. 28% grads go on to further study within 1 year. 24% grads pursue arts and sciences degrees. 2% grads pursue law degrees. 2% grads pursue business degrees. 2% grads pursue medical degrees. **Faculty:** 161 full-time faculty. 0% of classes are taught by teaching assistants.

ACADEMICS

Degrees: bachelor's, master's, post-bachelor's certificate, post-master's certificate. **Classes:** Most classes have 10–19 students. Most lab/discussion sessions have 10–19 students. **Majors with Highest Enrollment:** Biology/Biological Sciences; Psychology; English Language and Literature. **Special Study Options:** cooperative education program, cross-registration, double major, exchange student program (domestic), honors program, independent study, internships, liberal arts/career combination, student-designed major, study abroad, teacher certification program, Arcadia also offers programs in Washington DC and a Philadelphia Urban Semester. Undergraduate students may also take gradutate courses. The university also offers evening and some weekend classes. **Honors programs:** Honors program for invited students. Combined degree programs: BA/MA, 4-2 1/2 PT;4+2 PA, 4+2, FS, 7-yr optometry. **Disability Services:** Special programs offered to physically disabled students include reader services, tape recorders, tutors. **Career services:** Alumni network, alumni services, career assessment, internships.

FACILITIES

Housing: Coed dorms, special housing for disabled students, women's dorms, apartments for single students, Living Learning Communities. 99% of campus accessible to physically disabled. **Special Academic Facilities/Equipment:** Art gallery, language lab, observatory. **Computers:** Students can register for classes online. Administrative functions (other than registration) can be performed online.

CAMPUS LIFE

Environment: Town. **Activities:** Choral groups, dance, drama/theater, literary magazine, music ensembles, musical theater, radio station, student government, student newspaper, television station, yearbook. 40 registered organizations, 8 honor societies, 3 religious organizations. **Athletics (Intercollegiate):** *Men:* baseball, basketball, cheerleading, golf, soccer, swimming, tennis. *Women:* basketball, cheerleading, field hockey, lacrosse, soccer, softball, swimming, tennis, volleyball. **On-Campus Highlights:** Grey Towers Castle, Kuch Center, The Chat, Walk of Pride, Landman Library.

ADMISSIONS

Freshman Academic Profile: Average high school GPA 3.63. 30% in top 10% of high school class, 62% in top 25% of high school class, 90% in top 50% of high school class. 72% from public high schools. SAT Math middle 50% range 510-600. SAT Critical Reading middle 50% range 510-600. SAT Writing middle 50% range 500-600. ACT middle 50% range 22-27. Minimum internet-based TOEFL 90. Minimum paper TOEFL 530. **Basis for Candidate Selection:** *Very important factors considered include:* academic GPA, rigor of secondary school record. *Important factors considered include:* Class rank, application essay, recommendation(s), standardized test scores, extracurricular activities. *Other factors considered include:* alumni/ae relation, character/personal qualities, interview, talent/ability, volunteer work, work experience. **Freshman Admission Requirements:** High school diploma is required and GED is accepted. **Freshman Admission Statistics:** 7,673 applied, 54% admitted, 12% enrolled. **Transfer Admission Requirements:** college transcript(s), essay or personal statement, Minimum college GPA of 2.5 required. Lowest grade transferable C-. **General Admission Information:** Application Fee $30. Early decision application deadline 10/15. Regular application deadline 8/1. Notification on a rolling basis, beginning on or about 11/1. Nonfall registration accepted. Admission may be deferred for a maximum of 12 months. Credit and/or placement offered for CEEB Advanced Placement tests.

COSTS AND FINANCIAL AID

Average book expense $1,400. **Required Forms and Deadlines:** FAFSA, Institution's own financial aid form. *Student Employment:* Off-campus job opportunities are good. **Financial Aid Statistics:** 90% freshmen, 99% undergrads receive need-based scholarship or grant aid. 11% freshmen, 10% undergrads receive non-need-based scholarship or grant aid. 78% freshmen, 87% undergrads receive need-based self-help aid. 0% freshmen, 0% undergrads receive athletic scholarships. 97% freshmen receive any aid. 100% undergrads borrow to pay for school. Average cumulative indebtedness $28,750.

ARIZONA CHRISTIAN UNIVERSITY

2625 East Cactus Road, Phoenix, AZ 85032
Phone: 602-386-4100 · **Financial Aid Phone:** 602-386-4106
E-mail: admissions@arizonachristian.edu
Fax: 602-404-2159 · **Website:** www.arizonachristian.edu ·

This private school, affiliated with the Baptist Church, was founded in 1960. It has a 17-acre campus.

RATINGS

Admissions Selectivity Rating: 69   **Fire Safety Rating:** 76

STUDENTS AND FACULTY

Enrollment: 175. **Student Body:** 57% female, 43% male, 27% out-of-state, 4% international. Asian 4%, African American 13%, Caucasian 131%, Hispanic 13%, Native American 1%
Retention and Graduation: 56% freshmen return for sophomore year. 70% freshmen graduate within 4 years. 70% freshmen graduate within 6 years. **Faculty:** 13 full-time faculty, 69% hold PhDs.

ACADEMICS

Degrees: associate, bachelor's, certificate.

FACILITIES

Housing: men's dorms, women's dorms, apartments for single students.

CAMPUS LIFE

Environment: Village. **Activities:** Choral groups, drama/theater, music ensembles, student government, student newspaper, yearbook. **Athletics (Intercollegiate):** *Men:* basketball. *Women:* basketball, volleyball.

ADMISSIONS

Freshman Academic Profile: 72% from public high schools. SAT Math middle 50% range 450-560. SAT Critical Reading middle 50% range 460-570. ACT middle 50% range 19-24. Minimum internet-based TOEFL 61. Minimum paper TOEFL 500. **Basis for Candidate Selection:** *Very important factors considered include:* application essay, recommendation(s), rigor of secondary school record, standardized test scores, religious affiliation/commitment. *Important factors considered include:* character/personal qualities. *Other factors considered include:* extracurricular activities, interview. **Freshman Admission Requirements:** High school diploma is required and GED is accepted. **Transfer Admission Requirements:** High school transcript, college transcript(s), essay or personal statement, statement of good standing from prior institution(s). Minimum college GPA of 2.0 required. Lowest grade transferable C. **General Admission Information:** Application Fee $25. Nonfall registration accepted. Admission may be deferred for a maximum of 1 semester.

COSTS AND FINANCIAL AID

Average book expense $1,600. **Required Forms and Deadlines:** FAFSA, Institution's own financial aid form. **Notification of Awards:** Applicants will be notified of awards on a rolling basis beginning 5/1. **Types of Aid:** *Need-based scholarships/grants:* Federal Pell, SEOG, state scholarships/grants. *Loans:* Subsidized Stafford, Unsubsidized Stafford, PLUS, Federal Perkins. *Student Employment:* Federal Work-Study Program available. Institutional employment available. **Financial Aid Statistics:** 0% freshmen, 0% undergrads receive athletic scholarships. **Criteria for awarding institutional aid:** *Non-need-based:* academics, alumni affiliation, leadership, music/drama, religious affiliation.

ARIZONA STATE UNIVERSITY AT THE POLYTECHNIC CAMPUS

Admissions Services, Tempe, AZ 85287-0112
Phone: 480-965-7788 · **Financial Aid Phone:** 480-965-1127
E-mail: admissions@asu.edu · **CEEB Code:** 4007
Fax: 480-965-3610 · **Website:** https://campus.asu.edu/polytechnic · **ACT Code:** 88

RATINGS

Admissions Selectivity Rating: 78   **Fire Safety Rating:** 87

STUDENTS AND FACULTY

Enrollment: 3,312. **Student Body:** 20% out-of-state, (39 countries represented).
Retention and Graduation: 82% freshmen return for sophomore year. 36% freshmen graduate within 4 years. 60% freshmen graduate within 6 years. **Faculty:** 189 full-time faculty, 75% hold PhDs, 41% are members of minority groups, 20% are women.

ACADEMICS

Majors with Highest Enrollment: Engineering; Biology/Biological Sciences; Business, Management, Marketing, and Related Support Services.

ADMISSIONS

Freshman Academic Profile: Average high school GPA 3.4. 22% in top 10% of high school class, 54% in top 25% of high school class, 86% in top 50% of high school class. SAT Math middle 50% range 513-640. SAT Critical Reading middle 50% range 490-620. ACT middle 50% range 22-28. Minimum internet-based TOEFL 61. Minimum paper TOEFL 500.

COSTS AND FINANCIAL AID

Annual in-state tuition $9,010. Annual out-of-state tuition $22,639. Room and board $10,720. Required fees $673. Average book expense $1,060. **Required Forms and Deadlines:** FAFSA. **Financial Aid Statistics:** 98% freshmen, 90% undergrads receive need-based scholarship or grant aid. 12% freshmen, 6% undergrads receive non-need-based scholarship or grant aid. 62% freshmen, 77% undergrads receive need-based self-help aid. 0% freshmen, 0% undergrads receive athletic scholarships. 92% freshmen, 86% undergrads receive any aid. 63% undergrads borrow to pay for school. Average cumulative indebtedness $21,830.

ARIZONA STATE UNIVERSITY AT THE TEMPE CAMPUS

PO Box 870112, Tempe, AZ 85287-0112
Phone: 480-965-7788 · **Financial Aid Phone:** 480-965-1127
E-mail: admissions@asu.edu · **CEEB Code:** 4007
Fax: 480-965-3610 · **Website:** www.asu.edu · **ACT Code:** 88

This public school was founded in 1885. It has a 1963. 73-acre campus.

RATINGS

Admissions Selectivity Rating: 84   **Fire Safety Rating:** 87

STUDENTS AND FACULTY

Enrollment: 39,323. **Student Body:** 44% female, 56% male, 24% out-of-state, 9% international (97 countries represented). Asian 7%, African American 4%, Caucasian 55%, Hispanic 19%, Native American 1%
Retention and Graduation: 86% freshmen return for sophomore year. 43% freshmen graduate within 4 years. 63% freshmen graduate within 6 years. **Faculty:** 2,033 full-time faculty, 87% hold PhDs, 41% are members of minority groups, 24% are women.

ACADEMICS

Degrees: bachelor's, master's, post-bachelor's certificate, post-master's certificate. **Classes:** Most classes have 10–19 students. Most lab/discussion sessions have 20–29 students. **Majors with Highest Enrollment:** Business, Management, Marketing, and Related Support Services; Multi-/Interdisciplinary Studies; Biology/Biological Sciences. **Special Study Options:** Accelerated program, cooperative education program, distance learning, double major, exchange student program (domestic), honors program, independent study, internships, study abroad, teacher certification program, ASU offers internships in many disciplines, study abroad in 60 countries, work-study programs, accelerated degree programs and a variety of interdisciplinary undergraduate programs. Students may participate in educational programs supported by several institutes and centers. Also available are continuing education programs and a summer programs for high school students. **Honors programs:** The Honors College at ASU, Barrett, is a selective, residential college that educates academically outstanding undergraduates from across the nation. Students enrolled in Barrett are part of both the honors college community and an ASU disciplinary college of their choice. They may major in any field offered at any one of ASU's four campuses. Honors courses are taught by honors faculty within the college and within a variety of departments and programs. Combined degree programs: BA/MA, MBA/MSE EE; MBA/MHSM; MArch/MBS; MAIS/MBA; JD/MBA; JD/MHSM; MPA/MSW. **Disability Services:** Special programs offered to physically disabled students include note-taking services, reader services, tape recorders, tutors. **Career services:** Alumni network, alumni services, career/job search classes, career assessment, internships. ASU Career Services worked with APPLE during the Spring 2009 semester to educate the campus community on a new Summer Customer Support program that is full-time during the Summer and then continues on a part-time basis for the following academic year. ASU was one of only 5 schools selected for this program, and attracted the most students of any of the 5 schools (about 80 students were hired). APPLE will continue recruiting for the 2010 year at ASU because of the coordination support from ASU and the positive results of this program.

FACILITIES

Housing: Coed dorms, fraternity/sorority housing, apartments for married students, apartments for single students, Freshmen Housing. Please visit - http://www.asu.edu/housing. 99% of campus accessible to physically disabled. **Special Academic Facilities/Equipment:** Art, anthropology, geology, history, and sports museums, early childhood development lab, herbarium, robotics lab, semiconductor clean room, high-resolution electron microscope facility, gamma cell irradiation chamber, solar research facilities, nuclear reactor, biodesign institute, thermal emission imaging system, melikian center, KAET (public television station), KASR 1260 AM, Phoenix urban research laboratory, Arizona biomedical collaborative, altitude chamber, simulator building, planetarium. **Computers:** 100% of classrooms, 100% of dorms, 100% of libraries, 100% of dining areas, 100% of student union, 70% of common outdoor areas have wireless network access. Students can register for classes online. Administrative functions (other than registration) can be performed online.

CAMPUS LIFE

Environment: Metropolis. **Activities:** Choral groups, concert band, dance, drama/theater, jazz band, literary magazine, marching band, music ensembles, musical theater, opera, pep band, radio station, student government, student newspaper, student-run film society, symphony orchestra, television station, Campus Ministries, International Student Organization, Model UN. 675 registered organizations, 16 honor societies, 51 religious organization. 32 fraternities, 22 sororities. **Athletics (Intercollegiate):** *Men:* baseball, basketball, cross-country, diving, football, golf, swimming, track/field (outdoor), wrestling. *Women:* basketball, cross-country, diving, golf, gymnastics, soccer, softball, swimming, tennis, track/field (outdoor), volleyball, water polo. **On-Campus Highlights:** ASU Memorial Union—Tempe campus, Grady Gammage Auditorium—Tempe campus, Barrett Honors Complex—Tempe campus, Fletcher Library—West campus, Union—Polytechnic campus, Hayden Library—Tempe campus, Walter Cronkite School of Journalism and Mass Communication—Downtown Phoenix campus, Academic Complex—Polytechnic campus, Las Casas Residence Hall—West campus, Taylor Place—Downtown Phoenix campus.

ADMISSIONS

Freshman Academic Profile: Average high school GPA 3.46. 30% in top 10% of high school class, 60% in top 25% of high school class, 89% in top 50% of high school class. SAT Math middle 50% range 520-640. SAT Critical Reading middle 50% range 500-630. ACT middle 50% range 22-28. Minimum internet-based TOEFL 61. Minimum paper TOEFL 500. **Basis for Candidate Selection:** *Very important factors considered include:* Class rank, academic GPA, standardized test scores. *Important factors considered include:* state residency. **Freshman Admission Requirements:** High school diploma is required and GED is accepted. *Academic units required:* 4 English, 4 mathematics, 3 science, (3 science labs), 2 foreign language, 1 social studies, 1 history, 1 Fine Arts. **Freshman Admission Statistics:** 22,581 applied, 84% admitted, 40% enrolled. **Transfer Admission Requirements:** college transcript(s), standardized test scores, Minimum college GPA of 2.0 required. Lowest grade transferable C. **General Admission Information:** Application Fee $50. Regular application deadline 2/1. Nonfall registration accepted. Credit and/or placement offered for CEEB Advanced Placement tests.

COSTS AND FINANCIAL AID

Annual in-state tuition $9,484. Annual out-of-state tuition $23,830. Room and board $10,010. Required fees $673. Average book expense $1,060. **Required Forms and Deadlines:** FAFSA. **Types of Aid:** *Need-based scholarships/grants:* Federal Pell, SEOG, state scholarships/grants, private scholarships, the school's own gift aid, Federal Nursing Scholarships. *Loans:* Direct Subsidized Stafford, Direct Unsubsidized Stafford, Direct PLUS, PLUS, Federal Perkins. *Student Employment:* Federal Work-Study Program available. Institutional employment available. Off-campus job opportunities are good. **Financial Aid Statistics:** 99% freshmen, 93% undergrads receive need-based scholarship or grant aid. 15% freshmen, 9% undergrads receive non-need-based scholarship or grant aid. 58% freshmen, 71% undergrads receive need-based self-help aid. 0% freshmen, 1% undergrads receive athletic scholarships. 91% freshmen, 83% undergrads receive any aid. 54% undergrads borrow to pay for school. Average cumulative indebtedness $19,524.

ARIZONA STATE UNIVERSITY AT THE WEST CAMPUS

Admissions Services, Tempe, AZ 85287-0112
Phone: 480-965-7788 · **Financial Aid Phone:** 480-965-1127
E-mail: admissions@asu.edu · **CEEB Code:** 4007
Fax: 480-965-3610 · **Website:** www.asu.edu · **ACT Code:** 880

RATINGS

Admissions Selectivity Rating: 81   Fire Safety Rating: 87

STUDENTS AND FACULTY

Enrollment: 3,250. **Student Body:** 13% out-of-state, (17 countries represented).
Retention and Graduation: 86% freshmen return for sophomore year. 42% freshmen graduate within 4 years. 59% freshmen graduate within 6 years.
Faculty: 227 full-time faculty, 82% hold PhDs, 57% are members of minority groups, 22% are women.

ACADEMICS

Majors with Highest Enrollment: Psychology; Business, Management, Marketing, and Related Support Services; Biology/Biological Sciences.

ADMISSIONS

Freshman Academic Profile: Average high school GPA 3.53. 35% in top 10% of high school class, 66% in top 25% of high school class, 91% in top 50% of high school class. SAT Math middle 50% range 490-590. SAT Critical Reading middle 50% range 490-600. ACT middle 50% range 21-27. Minimum internet-based TOEFL 61. Minimum paper TOEFL 500.

COSTS AND FINANCIAL AID

Annual in-state tuition $9,010. Annual out-of-state tuition $22,639. Room and board $9,440. Required fees $673. Average book expense $1,060. **Required Forms and Deadlines:** FAFSA. **Financial Aid Statistics:** 99% freshmen, 90% undergrads receive need-based scholarship or grant aid. 13% freshmen, 5% undergrads receive non-need-based scholarship or grant aid. 59% freshmen, 76% undergrads receive need-based self-help aid. 0% freshmen, 0% undergrads receive athletic scholarships. 96% freshmen, 87% undergrads receive any aid. 65% undergrads borrow to pay for school. Average cumulative indebtedness $17,376.

ARKANSAS STATE UNIVERSITY

PO Box 1630, State University, AR 72467
Phone: 870-972-3024
E-mail: admissions@astate.edu · **CEEB Code:** 6011
Fax: 870-910-8094 · **Website:** www.astate.edu · **ACT Code:** 116

This public school was founded in 1909. It has a 941-acre campus.

RATINGS

Admissions Selectivity Rating: 72   Fire Safety Rating: 60*

STUDENTS AND FACULTY

Enrollment: 9,000. **Student Body:** 59% female, 41% male, 10% out-of-state, 1% international (56 countries represented). Asian 1%, African American 15%, Caucasian 82%, Hispanic 1%, Native American <1%
Retention and Graduation: 70% freshmen return for sophomore year. 15% freshmen graduate within 4 years. 37% freshmen graduate within 6 years. 3% grads go on to further study within 1 year. 1% grads pursue arts and sciences degrees. 1% grads pursue law degrees. 2% grads pursue business degrees. 1% grads pursue medical degrees. **Faculty:** 446 full-time faculty, 62% hold PhDs, 43% are members of minority groups, 11% are women. 3% of classes are taught by teaching assistants.

ACADEMICS

Degrees: associate, bachelor's, certificate, master's, post-bachelor's certificate, post-master's certificate. **Classes:** Most classes have 20–29 students. Most lab/discussion sessions have fewer than 10 students. **Majors with Highest Enrollment:** Data Processing and Data Processing Technology/Technician; Early Childhood Education; Business/Commerce. **Special Study Options:** Accelerated program, cooperative education program, distance learning, double major, dual enrollment, English as a Second Language (ESL), exchange student program (domestic), honors program, independent study, internships, study abroad, teacher certification program. **Disability Services:** Special programs offered to physically disabled students include note-taking services, reader services, tape recorders, tutors. **Career services:** alumni services, career/job search classes, career assessment, internships.

FACILITIES

Housing: men's dorms, women's dorms, fraternity/sorority housing, apartments for married students, apartments for single students, Married and graduate student housing. 95% of campus accessible to physically disabled. **Special Academic Facilities/Equipment:** Art gallery, museum of Native American cultures and Arkansas artifacts, Ecotoxicology research facility, electron microscope facility, geographic information system facility, Equine center. **Computers:** Students can register for classes online. Administrative functions (other than registration) can be performed online.

CAMPUS LIFE

Environment: Town. **Activities:** Choral groups, concert band, dance, drama/theater, jazz band, marching band, music ensembles, musical theater, opera, pep band, radio station, student government, student newspaper, symphony orchestra, television station, yearbook. 192 registered organizations, 42 honor societies, 16 religious organizations. 12 fraternities, 9 sororities. **Athletics (Intercollegiate):** *Men:* baseball, basketball, cross-country, football, golf, track/field (outdoor), track/field (indoor). *Women:* basketball, cross-country, golf, soccer, tennis, track/field (outdoor), track/field (indoor), volleyball. **On-Campus Highlights:** New Student Union, Fowler Center for Performing Arts, ASU Convocation Center, Outdoor theatre, ASU Museum.

ADMISSIONS

Freshman Academic Profile: Average high school GPA 3.2. 0% in top 25% of high school class, 0% in top 50% of high school class. 93% from public high schools. ACT middle 50% range 18-25. Minimum paper TOEFL 500. **Basis for Candidate Selection:** *Very important factors considered include:* rigor of secondary school record, standardized test scores. *Other factors considered include:* Class rank, recommendation(s), talent/ability. **Freshman Admission**

Requirements: High school diploma is required and GED is accepted. **Freshman Admission Statistics:** 3,088 applied, 66% admitted, 75% enrolled. **Transfer Admission Requirements:** college transcript(s), Minimum college GPA of 2.0 required. Lowest grade transferable C. **General Admission Information:** Application Fee $15. Regular application deadline 8/23. Nonfall registration accepted. Admission may be deferred for a maximum of no maximum. Credit offered for CEEB Advanced Placement tests.

COSTS AND FINANCIAL AID

Annual in-state tuition $3,750. Annual out-of-state tuition $9,660. Room and board $3,640. Required fees $1,060. Average book expense $1,000. **Required Forms and Deadlines:** FAFSA, Institution's own financial aid form. **Notification of Awards:** Applicants will be notified of awards on a rolling basis beginning 6/1. **Types of Aid:** *Need-based scholarships/grants:* Federal Pell, SEOG, state scholarships/grants, private scholarships, the school's own gift aid. *Loans:* Subsidized Stafford, Unsubsidized Stafford, PLUS, Federal Perkins. *Student Employment:* Federal Work-Study Program available. Institutional employment available. Highest amount earned per year from on-campus jobs $3,600. Off-campus job opportunities are good. **Financial Aid Statistics:** 90% freshmen, 85% undergrads receive need-based scholarship or grant aid. 23% freshmen, 39% undergrads receive non-need-based scholarship or grant aid. 39% freshmen, 60% undergrads receive need-based self-help aid. 3% freshmen, 3% undergrads receive athletic scholarships. 76% freshmen, 67% undergrads receive any aid. 63% undergrads borrow to pay for school. **Criteria for awarding institutional aid:** *Non-need-based:* academics, alumni affiliation, art, athletics, leadership, minority status, music/drama, state/district residency.

ARKANSAS TECH UNIVERSITY

Doc Bryan; 1605 Coliseum Dr, Russellville, AR 72801
Phone: 479-968-0343 · **Financial Aid Phone:** 479-968-0399
E-mail: tech.enroll@atu.edu · **CEEB Code:** 6010
Fax: 479-964-0522 · **Website:** http://www.atu.edu/ · **ACT Code:** 114

This public school was founded in 1909. It has a 541-acre campus.

RATINGS

Admissions Selectivity Rating: 75   **Fire Safety Rating:** 82

STUDENTS AND FACULTY

Enrollment: 8,845. **Student Body:** 56% female, 44% male, 5% out-of-state, 4% international (35 countries represented). Asian 1%, African American 9%, Caucasian 78%, Hispanic 5%, Native American 1%
Retention and Graduation: 27% freshmen graduate within 4 years. 45% freshmen graduate within 6 years. **Faculty:** 346 full-time faculty, 60% hold PhDs, 50% are members of minority groups, 8% are women. 1.34% of classes are taught by teaching assistants.

ACADEMICS

Degrees: associate, bachelor's, certificate, master's, post-master's certificate, terminal associate. **Classes:** Most classes have 20–29 students. Most lab/discussion sessions have 10–19 students. **Special Study Options:** distance learning, double major, dual enrollment, English as a Second Language (ESL), honors program, independent study, internships, study abroad, teacher certification program. **Disability Services:** Special programs offered to physically disabled students include note-taking services, reader services, tape recorders, tutors. **Career services:** career assessment, internships.

FACILITIES

Housing: Coed dorms, special housing for disabled students, men's dorms, women's dorms, fraternity/sorority housing, apartments for single students. 100% of campus accessible to physically disabled. **Special Academic Facilities/Equipment:** 1. Arkansas Center for Energy, Natural Resources, and Environmental Studies. 2. Crabaugh Communications Center. 3. Museum of Prehistory and History. 4. Technology Center. **Computers:** Students can register for classes online. Administrative functions (other than registration) can be performed online.

CAMPUS LIFE

Environment: Town. **Activities:** Choral groups, concert band, dance, drama/theater, jazz band, literary magazine, marching band, music ensembles, musical theater, pep band, radio station, student government, student newspaper, television station, Campus Ministries, International Student Organization. 130 registered organizations, 14 honor societies, 13 religious organizations. 6 fraternities, 4 sororities. **Athletics (Intercollegiate):** *Men:* baseball, basketball, cheerleading, football, golf. *Women:* basketball, cheerleading, cross-country, golf, softball, tennis, volleyball. **On-Campus Highlights:** Ross Pendergraft Library and Technology Center, Tech Fit, Doc's Place, Summit Hall, Tucker Coliseum.

ADMISSIONS

Freshman Academic Profile: Average high school GPA 3.18. 13% in top 10% of high school class, 34% in top 25% of high school class, 64% in top 50% of high school class. SAT Math middle 50% range 460-630. SAT Critical Reading middle 50% range 455-570. ACT middle 50% range 18-25. Minimum internet-based TOEFL 61. Minimum paper TOEFL 500. **Basis for Candidate Selection:** *Very important factors considered include:* academic GPA, standardized test scores. *Important factors considered include:* rigor of secondary school record. **Freshman Admission Requirements:** High school diploma is required and GED is accepted. *Academic units required:* 4 mathematics. **Freshman Admission Statistics:** 4,162 applied, 86% admitted, 54% enrolled. **Transfer Admission Requirements:** college transcript(s), Minimum college GPA of 2.0 required. Lowest grade transferable D. **General Admission Information:** Nonfall registration accepted. Admission may be deferred for a maximum of 1 semester. Credit and/or placement offered for CEEB Advanced Placement tests.

COSTS AND FINANCIAL AID

Annual in-state tuition $6,270. Annual out-of-state tuition $12,540. Room and board $6,734. Required fees $978. Average book expense $1,410. **Required Forms and Deadlines:** FAFSA, Institution's own financial aid form. **Notification of Awards:** Applicants will be notified of awards on a rolling basis beginning 5/1. **Types of Aid:** *Need-based scholarships/grants:* Federal Pell, SEOG, state scholarships/grants, private scholarships. *Loans:* Subsidized Stafford, Unsubsidized Stafford, PLUS, Federal Perkins. *Student Employment:* Federal Work-Study Program available. Institutional employment available. Off-campus job opportunities are excellent. **Financial Aid Statistics:** 83% freshmen, 82% undergrads receive need-based scholarship or grant aid. 64% freshmen, 45% undergrads receive non-need-based scholarship or grant aid. 61% freshmen, 69% undergrads receive need-based self-help aid. 5% freshmen, 3% undergrads receive athletic scholarships. 62% undergrads borrow to pay for school. Average cumulative indebtedness $28,935. **Criteria for awarding institutional aid:** *Non-need-based:* academics, athletics, leadership, music/drama, state/district residency.

ARLINGTON BAPTIST COLLEGE

Admissions Office, Arlington, TX 76012
Phone: 817-461-8741 · **Financial Aid Phone:** 817-461-8741, ext 110
E-mail: jtaylor@arlingtonbaptistcollege.edu
Fax: 817-274-1138 · **Website:** www.arlingtonbaptistcollege.edu · **ACT Code:** 4163

This private school, affiliated with the Baptist Church, was founded in 1939. It has a 35-acre campus.

RATINGS

Admissions Selectivity Rating: 60*   **Fire Safety Rating:** 90

STUDENTS AND FACULTY

Enrollment: 220. **Student Body:** 45% female, 55% male, 17% out-of-state, 1% international (1 countries represented). Asian 0%, African American 18%, Caucasian 71%, Hispanic 8%, Native American 2%
Retention and Graduation: 51% freshmen return for sophomore year. 19% freshmen graduate within 4 years. 41% freshmen graduate within 6 years. 15% grads go on to further study within 1 year. **Faculty:** 12 full-time faculty, 17% hold PhDs, 25% are members of minority groups.

ACADEMICS

Degrees: bachelor's, certificate, diploma, master's. **Classes:** Most classes have fewer than 10 students. Most lab/discussion sessions have 10–19 students. **Majors with Highest Enrollment:** Religious Education; Theological and Ministerial Studies; Pastoral Studies/Counseling. **Special Study Options:** distance learning, double major, dual enrollment, external degree program, teacher certification program.

FACILITIES

Housing: men's dorms, women's dorms, Wellness Housing. **Special Academic Facilities/Equipment:** Heritage Collection. **Computers:** 100% of classrooms, 100% of dorms, 100% of libraries, have wireless network access.

CAMPUS LIFE

Environment: Metropolis. **Activities:** Choral groups, student government, yearbook, Campus Ministries 5 religious organizations. **Athletics (Intercollegiate):** *Men:* baseball, basketball. *Women:* basketball, cheerleading, volleyball. **On-Campus Highlights:** Student Union Building, Library, Heritage Collection.

ADMISSIONS

Freshman Academic Profile: Average high school GPA 2.88. 2% in top 10% of high school class, 21% in top 25% of high school class, 47% in top 50% of high school class. 80% from public high schools. Minimum paper TOEFL 550. **Basis for Candidate Selection:** *Very important factors considered include:* application essay, recommendation(s), religious affiliation/commitment. *Important factors considered include:* interview, level of applicant's interest. *Other factors considered include:* character/personal qualities, extracurricular activities. **Freshman Admission Requirements:** High school diploma is required and GED is accepted. *Academic units required:* 3 English, 2 mathematics, 1 science, 2 social studies. **Freshman Admission Statistics:** 86 applied, 100% admitted, 63% enrolled. **Transfer Admission Requirements:** High school transcript, college transcript(s), essay or personal statement, Lowest grade transferable C. **General Admission Information:** Application Fee $15. Nonfall registration accepted. Admission may be deferred for a maximum of three semesters. Neither credit nor placement offered for CEEB Advanced Placement tests.

COSTS AND FINANCIAL AID

Annual tuition $7,100. Room and board $4,800. Required fees $740. Average book expense $750. **Required Forms and Deadlines:** FAFSA. **Notification of Awards:** Applicants will be notified of awards on a rolling basis beginning 6/1. **Types of Aid:** *Need-based scholarships/grants:* Federal Pell, SEOG, private scholarships, the school's own gift aid. *Loans:* Subsidized Stafford, Unsubsidized Stafford, PLUS. *Student Employment:* Institutional employment available. Highest amount earned per year from on-campus jobs $5,600. Off-campus job opportunities are excellent. **Financial Aid Statistics:** 100% freshmen, 100% undergrads receive need-based scholarship or grant aid. 0% freshmen, 0% undergrads receive non-need-based scholarship or grant aid. 0% freshmen, 0% undergrads receive need-based self-help aid. 0% freshmen, 0% undergrads receive athletic scholarships. 80% freshmen, 80% undergrads receive any aid. 88% undergrads borrow to pay for school. Average cumulative indebtedness $6,750.

ARMSTRONG ATLANTIC STATE UNIVERSITY

11935 Abercorn Street, Savannah, GA 31419-1997
Phone: 912-927-5277
E-mail: adm-info@mail.armstrong.edu · **CEEB Code:** 5012
Fax: 912-927-5462 · **Website:** www.armstrong.edu · **ACT Code:** 786

This public school was founded in 1935. It has a 250-acre campus.

RATINGS

Admissions Selectivity Rating: 72   **Fire Safety Rating:** 69

STUDENTS AND FACULTY

Enrollment: 5,281. **Student Body:** 68% female, 32% male, 8% out-of-state, 2% international (71 countries represented). Asian 3%, African American 22%, Caucasian 65%, Hispanic 3%, Native American <1%
Faculty: 229 full-time faculty, 70% hold PhDs, 51% are members of minority groups, 16% are women. 0% of classes are taught by teaching assistants.

ACADEMICS

Degrees: associate, bachelor's, master's, post-bachelor's certificate, post-master's certificate. **Classes:** Most classes have 20–29 students. Most lab/discussion sessions have fewer than 10 students. **Majors with Highest Enrollment:** Registered Nursing/Registered Nurse; Liberal Arts and Sciences/Liberal Studies; Early Childhood Education. **Special Study Options:** cooperative education program, cross-registration, distance learning, double major, dual enrollment, honors program, independent study, internships, study abroad, teacher certification program, weekend college. Combined degree programs: BSPT/MSPT, BSN/MSN. **Disability Services:** Special programs offered to physically disabled students include note-taking services, reader services, tape recorders, tutors. **Career services:** alumni services, career/job search classes, career assessment, internships.

FACILITIES

Housing: apartments for single students. 80% of campus accessible to physically disabled. **Special Academic Facilities/Equipment:** Language lab, Criminal justice training center, Sports medicine clinic, Speech/lang. pathology lab. **Computers:** Students can register for classes online. Administrative functions (other than registration) can be performed online.

CAMPUS LIFE

Environment: City. **Activities:** Choral groups, concert band, drama/theater, jazz band, literary magazine, music ensembles, musical theater, pep band, student government, student newspaper, symphony orchestra. 55 registered organizations, 7 honor societies, 3 religious organizations. 1 fraternity, 1 sorority. **Athletics (Intercollegiate):** *Men:* baseball, basketball, golf, tennis. *Women:* basketball, softball, tennis, volleyball. **On-Campus Highlights:** Library, Main computer lab, Compass Point (on-campus apartments), Gym, Cafeteria.

ADMISSIONS

Freshman Academic Profile: Average high school GPA 3.05. SAT Math middle 50% range 450-550. SAT Critical Reading middle 50% range 470-570. ACT middle 50% range 18-23. Minimum paper TOEFL 523. **Basis for Candidate Selection:** *Important factors considered include:* rigor of secondary school record, standardized test scores. *Other factors considered include:* extracurricular activities, volunteer work. **Freshman Admission Requirements:** High school diploma is required and GED is accepted. *Academic units required:* 4 English, 4 mathematics, 3 science, (2 science labs), 2 foreign language, 3 social studies. 4 English, 4 mathematics, 3 science, (2 science labs), 2 foreign language, 3 social studies. **Freshman Admission Statistics:** 1,685 applied, 65% admitted, 75% enrolled. **Transfer Admission Requirements:** college transcript(s), Minimum college GPA of 2.0 required. Lowest grade transferable D. **General Admission Information:** Application Fee $20. Regular application deadline 7/1. Notification on a rolling basis, beginning on or about 1/1. Nonfall registration accepted. Admission may be deferred for a maximum of 1 year. Credit and/or placement offered for CEEB Advanced Placement tests.

COSTS AND FINANCIAL AID

Annual in-state tuition $2,212. Annual out-of-state tuition $8,848. Room and board $4,500. Required fees $390. Average book expense $800. **Required Forms and Deadlines:** FAFSA. **Notification of Awards:** Applicants will be notified of awards on or about 2/1. **Types of Aid:** *Need-based scholarships/grants:* Federal Pell, SEOG, state scholarships/grants, private scholarships, the school's own gift aid, Federal Nursing Scholarships. *Loans:* Subsidized Stafford, Unsubsidized Stafford, PLUS, state loans. *Student Employment:* Federal Work-Study Program available. Institutional employment available. Off-campus job opportunities are excellent. **Financial Aid Statistics:** 34% freshmen, 50% undergrads receive need-based scholarship or grant aid. 40% freshmen, 30% undergrads receive non-need-based scholarship or grant aid. 29% freshmen, 73% undergrads receive need-based self-help aid. 6% freshmen, 3% undergrads receive athletic scholarships. 90% freshmen, 90% undergrads receive any aid. 55% undergrads borrow to pay for school. **Criteria for awarding institutional aid:** *Non-need-based:* academics, athletics, leadership, minority status, religious affiliation, state/district residency.

ARNOLD AND MARIE SCHWARTZ COLLEGE OF PHARMACY AND HEALTH SCIENCE

Long Island University, Brooklyn, NY 11201
Phone: 718-403-1011
E-mail: admissions@brooklyn.liu.edu
Fax: 718-797-2399 · **Website:** www.liu.edu

This is a private school.

RATINGS

Admissions Selectivity Rating: 60*   **Fire Safety Rating:** 60*

ACADEMICS

Degrees: first professional, master's. **Special Study Options:** honors program.

FACILITIES

Housing: Coed dorms, women's dorms, apartments for single students.

CAMPUS LIFE

Activities: 3 honor societies, 2 religious organizations. **Athletics (Intercollegiate):** *Men:* basketball, cross-country, softball, tennis, track/field (outdoor), track/field (indoor).

ADMISSIONS

Freshman Academic Profile: Minimum paper TOEFL 500. **Basis for Candidate Selection:** *Very important factors considered include:* rigor of secondary school record, standardized test scores. *Important factors considered include:* character/personal qualities, extracurricular activities, talent/ability. *Other factors considered include:* Class rank, recommendation(s), interview, volunteer work, work experience. **Freshman Admission Requirements:** High school diploma is required and GED is accepted. *Academic units required:* 2 mathematics, 1 science, (1 science labs). **Transfer Admission Requirements:** college transcript(s), Minimum college GPA of 3.0 required. Lowest grade transferable C. **General Admission Information:** Application Fee $30. Nonfall registration not accepted.

COSTS AND FINANCIAL AID

Required Forms and Deadlines: FAFSA. **Types of Aid:** *Need-based scholarships/grants:* Federal Pell, SEOG, state scholarships/grants, private scholarships, the school's own gift aid. *Loans:* Direct Subsidized Stafford, Direct Unsubsidized Stafford, Direct PLUS, Federal Perkins, Health Professions Student Loan (HPSL). *Student Employment:* Federal Work-Study Program available. **Criteria for awarding institutional aid:** *Non-need-based:* academics.

ART ACADEMY OF CINCINNATI

1212 Jackson Street, Cincinnati, OH 45202
Phone: 513-562-8740 • **Financial Aid Phone:** 513-562-8751
E-mail: admissions@artacademy.edu
Fax: 513-562-8778 • **Website:** www.artacademy.edu • **ACT Code:** 3011

This private school was founded in 1887.

RATINGS

Admissions Selectivity Rating: 83   **Fire Safety Rating:** 61

STUDENTS AND FACULTY

Enrollment: 159. **Student Body:** 64% female, 36% male, 1% international (2 countries represented). Asian 1%, African American 4%, Caucasian 90%, Hispanic 1%, Native American <1% **Faculty:** 14 full-time faculty, 100% hold PhDs, 57% are members of minority groups, 7% are women. 0% of classes are taught by teaching assistants.

ACADEMICS

Degrees: associate, bachelor's, master's. **Majors with Highest Enrollment:** Graphic Design; Illustration; Painting. **Special Study Options:** cooperative education program, cross-registration, double major, internships. **Disability Services:** Special programs offered to physically disabled students include note-taking services, tape recorders, tutors.

FACILITIES

Housing: Coed dorms.

CAMPUS LIFE

Environment: Metropolis. **Activities:** literary magazine, student government, student-run film society, yearbook. **On-Campus Highlights:** New Building, Dorms, Student Studios, Student Commons, Three Art Galleries. **Environmental Initiatives:** Received Leadership in Energy and Environmental Design (LEED) Green Building certification by the United States Green Building Council. On-going recycling program.

ADMISSIONS

Freshman Academic Profile: SAT Math middle 50% range 420-570. SAT Critical Reading middle 50% range 480-600. ACT middle 50% range 18-24. Minimum internet-based TOEFL 80. Minimum paper TOEFL 550. **Basis for Candidate Selection:** *Very important factors considered include:* rigor of secondary school record, interview, talent/ability. *Important factors considered include:* application essay, academic GPA. *Other factors considered include:* recommendation(s), standardized test scores, character/personal qualities, extracurricular activities. **Freshman Admission Requirements:** High school diploma is required and GED is accepted. **Transfer Admission Requirements:** High school transcript, college transcript(s), essay or personal statement, interview, Minimum college GPA of 2.0 required. Lowest grade transferable C. **General Admission Information:** Regular application deadline 6/30. Notification on a rolling basis, beginning on or about 9/1. Nonfall registration accepted. Admission may be deferred for a maximum of one year.

COSTS AND FINANCIAL AID

Annual tuition $21,500. Room and board $6,000. Required fees $380. Average book expense $1,200. **Required Forms and Deadlines:** FAFSA, State aid form. **Notification of Awards:** Applicants will be notified of awards on a rolling basis beginning 3/1. **Types of Aid:** *Need-based scholarships/grants:* Federal Pell, SEOG, state scholarships/grants, private scholarships, the school's own gift aid. *Loans:* Direct Subsidized Stafford, Direct Unsubsidized Stafford, Direct PLUS, Subsidized Stafford, Unsubsidized Stafford, PLUS, Federal Perkins. *Student Employment:* Federal Work-Study Program available. Institutional employment available. Off-campus job opportunities are good. **Financial Aid Statistics:** 95% undergrads receive any aid. **Criteria for awarding institutional aid:** *Non-need-based:* academics, art.

ART CENTER COLLEGE OF DESIGN

1700 Lida Street, Pasadena, CA 91103-1999
Phone: 626-396-2373 • **Financial Aid Phone:** 626-396-2215
E-mail: admissions@artcenter.edu • **CEEB Code:** 4009
Fax: 626-795-0578 • **Website:** www.artcenter.edu • **ACT Code:** 164

This private school was founded in 1930. It has a 175-acre campus.

RATINGS

Admissions Selectivity Rating: 60*   **Fire Safety Rating:** 60*

STUDENTS AND FACULTY

Enrollment: 1,814. **Student Body:** 50% female, 50% male, 27% international (43 countries represented). Asian 35%, African American 1%, Caucasian 20%, Hispanic 11%, Native American <1% **Retention and Graduation:** 31% freshmen graduate within 4 years. **Faculty:** 0% of classes are taught by teaching assistants.

ACADEMICS

Degrees: bachelor's, master's. **Classes:** Most classes have 10–19 students. **Majors with Highest Enrollment:** Industrial and Product Design; Graphic Design; Illustration. **Special Study Options:** cooperative education program, independent study, internships. **Disability Services:** Special programs offered to physically disabled students include note-taking services, tape recorders, tutors. **Career services:** Alumni network, alumni services, internships

FACILITIES

Housing: 100% of campus accessible to physically disabled. **Special Academic Facilities/Equipment:** 2 art galleries. **Computers:** Administrative functions (other than registration) can be performed online.

CAMPUS LIFE

Environment: City. **Activities:** student government. 12 registered organizations. **On-Campus Highlights:** Student Gallery **Environmental Initiatives:** Replaced all non-recyclable disposables in cafeteria with compostable items and established recycling area in cafeteria. Established community garden Added filtered water units to all drinking fountains dispensing hot and cold water.

ADMISSIONS

Freshman Academic Profile: Minimum internet-based TOEFL 80. **Basis for Candidate Selection:** *Very important factors considered include:* application essay, academic GPA, rigor of secondary school record, talent/ability. *Important factors considered include:* Class rank, standardized test scores. *Other factors considered include:* recommendation(s), character/personal qualities, extracurricular activities, interview, racial/ethnic status, volunteer work, work experience. **Freshman Admission Requirements:** High school diploma is required and GED is accepted. **Freshman Admission Statistics:** 534 applied, 81% admitted, 40% enrolled. **Transfer Admission Requirements:** college transcript(s), essay or personal statement, Lowest grade transferable c. **General Admission Information:** Application Fee $50. Notification on a rolling basis, beginning on or about 1/1. Nonfall registration accepted. Admission may be deferred for a maximum of 1 consecutive semest. Credit offered for CEEB Advanced Placement tests.

COSTS AND FINANCIAL AID

Required Forms and Deadlines: FAFSA. **Types of Aid:** *Need-based scholarships/grants:* Federal Pell, SEOG, state scholarships/grants, private scholarships, the school's own gift aid. *Loans:* Direct Subsidized Stafford, Direct Unsubsidized Stafford, Direct PLUS. *Student Employment:* Federal Work-Study Program available. Institutional employment available.

THE ART INSTITUTE OF ATLANTA

6600 Peachtree Dunwoody Road, Atlanta, GA 30328
Phone: 770-394-8300 • **Financial Aid Phone:** 770-689-4824
E-mail: aia-admis@aii.edu
Fax: 770-394-0008 • **Website:** http://www.artinstitutes.edu/atlanta/ • **ACT Code:** 859

This proprietary school was founded in 1949. It has a 7-acre campus.

RATINGS

Admissions Selectivity Rating: 60*   **Fire Safety Rating:** 60*

STUDENTS AND FACULTY

Enrollment: 3,839. **Student Body:** 44% female, 56% male, 0% international (33 countries represented). Asian 0%, African American 22%, Caucasian 19%, Hispanic 2%, Native American <1%

Faculty: 131 full-time faculty, 48% hold PhDs, 45% are members of minority groups, 21% are women.

ACADEMICS

Degrees: associate, bachelor's, certificate, diploma. **Classes:** Most classes have 10–19 students. **Majors with Highest Enrollment:** Culinary Arts/Chef Training; Commercial and Advertising Art; Interior Design. **Special Study Options:** Accelerated program, distance learning, dual enrollment, honors program, independent study, internships, study abroad, weekend college. **Honors programs:** Design Honors Studio for graphic design students: students work with clients in the community. **Disability Services:** Special programs offered to physically disabled students include note-taking services, reader services, tape recorders, tutors. **Career services:** Alumni network, alumni services, career/job search classes, internships.

FACILITIES

Housing: Coed dorms. 100% of campus accessible to physically disabled. **Special Academic Facilities/Equipment:** Art gallery, multi-camera video studio with digital and non-linear video editing suites, and an audio studio and control room featuring Protools stations. Professional photography studios with traditional and digital darkroom facilities containing high-end professional equipment such as the Imacon scanner, Cone Piezograph BandW printers, Epson 5500 printer, and Epson 10000 printer. Photographic video editing stations consist of Dual Processor G4s with cinema displays that are color managed with Greytag MacBeth equipment. Culinary facilities with five teaching kitchens and a dining lab. **Computers:** Students can register for classes online.

CAMPUS LIFE

Environment: Metropolis. **Activities:** student government, International Student Organization. 16 registered organizations. **On-Campus Highlights:** Gallery, Supply Store, Coffee Bar, Snack Bar, Creations Dining Lab, Entertainers perform in the coffee bar and reduced-price tickets are often available for events in Atlanta. The student affairs department also coordinates college community service programs and quarterly blood drives. Besides being enjoyable, student activities provide opportunities for making new friends and trying new experiences, as well as offering a great way to gain leadership experience.

ADMISSIONS

Freshman Academic Profile: Minimum paper TOEFL 550. **Basis for Candidate Selection:** *Very important factors considered include:* application essay, academic GPA, recommendation(s), standardized test scores. *Important factors considered include:* interview. **Freshman Admission Requirements:** High school diploma is required and GED is accepted. **Transfer Admission Requirements:** High school transcript, college transcript(s), essay or personal statement, interview, standardized test scores, statement of good standing from prior institution(s). Lowest grade transferable C. **General Admission Information:** Application Fee $50. Nonfall registration accepted. Admission may be deferred for a maximum of 4 quarters. Credit and/or placement offered for CEEB Advanced Placement tests.

COSTS AND FINANCIAL AID

Annual tuition $23,535. Room and board $9,984. Average book expense $1,700. **Required Forms and Deadlines:** FAFSA, State aid form. **Notification of Awards:** Applicants will be notified of awards on a rolling basis beginning 3/15. **Types of Aid:** *Need-based scholarships/grants:* Federal Pell, SEOG, state scholarships/grants, private scholarships, the school's own gift aid. *Loans:* Direct Subsidized Stafford, Direct Unsubsidized Stafford, Direct PLUS, Subsidized Stafford, Unsubsidized Stafford, PLUS, Federal Perkins. *Student Employment:* Federal Work-Study Program available. Institutional employment available. Off-campus job opportunities are good. **Financial Aid Statistics:** 52% freshmen, 72% undergrads receive need-based scholarship or grant aid. 39% freshmen, 8% undergrads receive non-need-based scholarship or grant aid. 100% freshmen, 100% undergrads receive need-based self-help aid. 0% freshmen, 0% undergrads receive athletic scholarships. 19% freshmen, 81% undergrads receive any aid. 90% undergrads borrow to pay for school. **Criteria for awarding institutional aid:** *Non-need-based:* academics, art, state/district residency.

THE ART INSTITUTE OF BOSTON
AT LESLEY UNIVERSITY

700 Beacon Street, Boston, MA 02215-2598
Phone: 617-585-6710 · **Financial Aid Phone:** 617-349-8710
E-mail: admissions@aiboston.edu · **CEEB Code:** 3777
Fax: 617-585-6720 · **Website:** aiboston.edu · **ACT Code:** 1850

This private school was founded in 1912. It has a 1-acre campus.

RATINGS

Admissions Selectivity Rating: 81   Fire Safety Rating: 80

STUDENTS AND FACULTY

Enrollment: 1,261. **Student Body:** 75% female, 25% male, 44% out-of-state, 3% international (15 countries represented). Asian 3%, African American 4%, Caucasian 63%, Hispanic 5%, Native American <1%
Retention and Graduation: 66% freshmen return for sophomore year. 37% freshmen graduate within 4 years. 49% freshmen graduate within 6 years.
Faculty: 73 full-time faculty, 68% hold PhDs, 55% are members of minority groups, 12% are women. 0% of classes are taught by teaching assistants.

ACADEMICS

Degrees: associate, bachelor's, master's, post-master's certificate. **Classes:** Most classes have 10–19 students. **Majors with Highest Enrollment:** Graphic Design; Illustration; Photography. **Special Study Options:** Accelerated program, cross-registration, distance learning, double major, dual enrollment, exchange student program (domestic), honors program, independent study, internships, liberal arts/career combination, student-designed major, study abroad, teacher certification program, Studio Courses. **Honors programs:** First year foundation students are eligible for advanced placement, foundation studio exemptions, and enrolling in Honors Studio and Honors English. Combined degree programs: BFA/M.Ed. **Disability Services:** Special programs offered to physically disabled students include note-taking services, reader services, tape recorders, tutors. **Career services:** Alumni network, alumni services, career/job search classes, career assessment, internships, regional alumni. We are proud of the wide range of services available to our students and alumni through our new online system, Lesley Career Connection, which includes job listings, internships. Career fairs, career center workshops, employer directory and more.

FACILITIES

Housing: Coed dorms, women's dorms, Special Interest and themed housing. 90% of campus accessible to physically disabled. **Special Academic Facilities/Equipment:** Art Gallery with regular shows of prominant artists; art library; applied art facilities, including state of the art photo and computer labs, annimation studio, ceramics studio, wood shop, metals studio, and printmaking studio **Computers:** 100% of classrooms, 10% of dorms, 100% of libraries, 100% of dining areas, 100% of student union, 25% of common outdoor areas have wireless network access. Students can register for classes online. Administrative functions (other than registration) can be performed online.

CAMPUS LIFE

Environment: Metropolis. **Activities:** Choral groups, dance, drama/theater, literary magazine, musical theater, student government, student newspaper, Campus Ministries, International Student Organization. 25 registered organizations, 2 honor societies, 2 religious organizations. **Athletics (Intercollegiate):** *Men:* basketball, cross-country, soccer, tennis, volleyball. *Women:* basketball, crew/rowing, cross-country, soccer, softball, tennis, volleyball. **On-Campus Highlights:** Gallery, Computer Labs, Animation Studio, Photo Labs, Student Lounge. **Environmental Initiatives:** Continual enhancement of recycling, waste management and composting programs on campus. The formation of sustainability recommendations for faculty, staff and students. Student groups on campus are involved with and sponsor sustainability events.

ADMISSIONS

Freshman Academic Profile: Average high school GPA 3. 12% in top 10% of high school class, 38% in top 25% of high school class, 70% in top 50% of high school class. 84% from public high schools. SAT Math middle 50% range 460-560. SAT Critical Reading middle 50% range 490-600. SAT Writing middle 50% range 490-590. ACT middle 50% range 19-26. Minimum internet-based TOEFL 61. Minimum paper TOEFL 500. **Basis for Candidate Selection:** *Very important factors considered include:* academic GPA, rigor of secondary school record. *Important factors considered include:* Class rank, application essay, recommendation(s), standardized test scores, character/personal qualities, extracurricular activities, interview, talent/ability. *Other factors considered include:* alumni/ae relation, first generation, geographical residence, level of applicant's interest, racial/ethnic status, volunteer work, work experience. **Freshman Admission Requirements:** High school diploma is required and GED is accepted. *Academic units required:* 4 English. **Freshman Admission Statistics:** 2,523 applied, 65% admitted, 20% enrolled. **Transfer Admission Requirements:** High school transcript, college transcript(s), essay or personal statement, interview, statement of good standing from prior institution(s). Minimum college GPA of 2.0 required. Lowest grade transferable C. **General Admission Information:** Application Fee $50. Notification on a rolling basis, beginning on or about 1/15. Nonfall registration accepted. Admission may be deferred for a maximum of 1 year. Credit and/or placement offered for CEEB Advanced Placement tests.

COSTS AND FINANCIAL AID

Annual tuition $28,000. Room and board $13,250. Required fees $750. Average book expense $1,575. **Required Forms and Deadlines:** FAFSA. **Notification of Awards:** Applicants will be notified of awards on a rolling basis beginning 2/15. **Types of Aid:** *Need-based scholarships/grants:* Federal Pell, SEOG, state scholarships/grants, private scholarships, the school's own gift aid. *Loans:* Direct

Subsidized Stafford, Direct Unsubsidized Stafford, Direct PLUS, Subsidized Stafford, Unsubsidized Stafford, PLUS, Federal Perkins, state loans. *Student Employment:* Federal Work-Study Program available. Institutional employment available. Highest amount earned per year from on-campus jobs $1,200. Off-campus job opportunities are excellent. **Financial Aid Statistics:** 98% freshmen, 96% undergrads receive need-based scholarship or grant aid. 24% freshmen, 64% undergrads receive non-need-based scholarship or grant aid. 93% freshmen, 118% undergrads receive need-based self-help aid. 0% freshmen, 0% undergrads receive athletic scholarships. 70% freshmen, 70% undergrads receive any aid. 93% undergrads borrow to pay for school. Average cumulative indebtedness $18,000. **Criteria for awarding institutional aid:** *Non-need-based:* academics, art, leadership, minority status, state/district residency.

ART INSTITUTE OF COLORADO

1200 Lincoln St., Denver, CO 80203
Phone: 303-837-0825
E-mail: aicinfo@artinstitutes.edu • **CEEB Code:**
Fax: 303-860-8520 • **Website:** www.aic.artinstitutes.edu • **ACT Code:** 495

This proprietary school was founded in 1952.

RATINGS

Admissions Selectivity Rating: 64   Fire Safety Rating: 60*

STUDENTS AND FACULTY

Enrollment: 2,320. **Student Body:** 48% female, 52% male, 0% international. Asian 2%, African American 1%, Caucasian 43%, Hispanic 6%, Native American 1%
Faculty: 64 full-time faculty, 17% hold PhDs, 38% are members of minority groups, 11% are women.

ACADEMICS

Degrees: associate, bachelor's, certificate, diploma. **Majors with Highest Enrollment:** Missions/Missionary Studies and Missiology; Pre-Theology/Pre-Ministerial Studies; Pastoral Studies/Counseling. **Special Study Options:** independent study, internships, study abroad. **Career services:** alumni services, career/job search classes, internships.

FACILITIES

Housing: apartments for single students. **Computers:** Administrative functions (other than registration) can be performed online.

CAMPUS LIFE

Activities: 3 honor societies.

ADMISSIONS

Freshman Academic Profile: Minimum paper TOEFL 480. **Basis for Candidate Selection:** *Important factors considered include:* application essay, standardized test scores, interview. *Other factors considered include:* rigor of secondary school record. **Freshman Admission Requirements:** High school diploma is required and GED is accepted. **Freshman Admission Statistics:** 748 applied, 52% admitted, 96% enrolled. **Transfer Admission Requirements:** High school transcript, essay or personal statement, interview, Lowest grade transferable C. **General Admission Information:** Application Fee $50. Nonfall registration accepted. Admission may be deferred for a maximum of 1 yr. Credit offered for CEEB Advanced Placement tests.

COSTS AND FINANCIAL AID

Average book expense $2,250. **Required Forms and Deadlines:** FAFSA, Institution's own financial aid form. **Types of Aid:** *Need-based scholarships/ grants:* Federal Pell, SEOG, state scholarships/grants, private scholarships, the school's own gift aid. *Loans:* Subsidized Stafford, Unsubsidized Stafford, PLUS, Federal Perkins, state loans. *Student Employment:* Federal Work-Study Program available. Institutional employment available. Off-campus job opportunities are excellent. **Financial Aid Statistics:** 5% undergrads receive non-need-based scholarship or grant aid. 100% undergrads receive need-based self-help aid. 97% undergrads borrow to pay for school.

THE ART INSTITUTE OF LAS VEGAS

2350 Corporate Cir, Henderson, NV 89074
Phone: 702-369-9944
E-mail: ailvadm@aii.edu
Fax: 702-992-8458 • **Website:** http://www.artinstitutes.edu/lasvegas/

This is a proprietary school. It has a 1.5-acre campus.

RATINGS

Admissions Selectivity Rating: 61   Fire Safety Rating: 66

STUDENTS AND FACULTY

Enrollment: 1,301. **Student Body:** 48% female, 52% male, 0% international. Asian 12%, African American 9%, Caucasian 35%, Hispanic 14%, Native American 1%
Retention and Graduation: 54% freshmen return for sophomore year. **Faculty:** 27 full-time faculty, 7% hold PhDs, 22% are members of minority groups. 0% of classes are taught by teaching assistants.

ACADEMICS

Degrees: associate, bachelor's. **Classes:** Most classes have 10–19 students. **Majors with Highest Enrollment:** Digital Communication and Media/Multi-media; Culinary Arts/Chef Training. **Special Study Options:** distance learning, independent study, internships, study abroad. **Disability Services:** Special programs offered to physically disabled students include note-taking services, reader services, tape recorders, tutors. **Career services:** Alumni network, alumni services, career/job search classes, career assessment, internships, regional alumni.

FACILITIES

Housing: apartments for single students, Wellness Housing.

CAMPUS LIFE

Environment: City. **Activities:** student-run film society. **On-Campus Highlights:** Student Lounge

ADMISSIONS

Freshman Academic Profile: Average high school GPA 2.61. Minimum paper TOEFL 500. **Basis for Candidate Selection:** *Very important factors considered include:* application essay, interview. *Important factors considered include:* level of applicant's interest, talent/ability. *Other factors considered include:* academic GPA, standardized test scores, character/personal qualities. **Freshman Admission Requirements:** High school diploma is required and GED is accepted. **Freshman Admission Statistics:** 436 applied, 68% admitted, 78% enrolled. **Transfer Admission Requirements:** High school transcript, college transcript(s), essay or personal statement, interview, statement of good standing from prior institution(s). Minimum college GPA of 2.0 required. Lowest grade transferable 2. **General Admission Information:** Application Fee $150. Non-fall registration accepted. Admission may be deferred for a maximum of None.

COSTS AND FINANCIAL AID

Student Employment: Federal Work-Study Program available.

THE ART INSTITUTE OF PITTSBURGH

420 Blvd. of The Allies, Pittsburgh, PA 15219
Phone: 412-263-6600 • **Financial Aid Phone:** 412-291-6376
E-mail: aip_admissions@aii.edu
Fax: 412-263-6667 • **Website:** www.aip.aii.edu

This proprietary school was founded in 1921.

RATINGS

Admissions Selectivity Rating: 65   Fire Safety Rating: 64

STUDENTS AND FACULTY

Enrollment: 4,864. **Student Body:** 55% female, 45% male, 1% out-of-state, 0% international (20 countries represented). Asian 0%, African American 2%, Caucasian 30%, Hispanic 0%, Native American <1%
Faculty: 44 full-time faculty, 50% hold PhDs, 70% are members of minority groups, 102% are women. 0% of classes are taught by teaching assistants.

ACADEMICS

Degrees: associate, bachelor's, diploma, transfer associate. **Special Study Options:** distance learning, English as a Second Language (ESL), internships.

Disability Services: Special programs offered to physically disabled students include note-taking services, tape recorders, tutors. **Career services:** alumni services, career/job search classes, internships, regional alumni.

FACILITIES
Housing: 100% of campus accessible to physically disabled.

CAMPUS LIFE
Activities: student government, student newspaper, student-run film society 21 registered organizations, 2 honor societies, 1 religious organization.

ADMISSIONS
Basis for Candidate Selection: *Very important factors considered include:* application essay, rigor of secondary school record. *Important factors considered include:* talent/ability. *Other factors considered include:* recommendation(s), extracurricular activities. **Freshman Admission Requirements:** High school diploma is required and GED is accepted. **Freshman Admission Statistics:** 2,177 applied, 46% admitted, 100% enrolled. **Transfer Admission Requirements:** High school transcript, essay or personal statement, interview, Lowest grade transferable C. **General Admission Information:** Application Fee $150. Nonfall registration accepted. Admission may be deferred for a maximum of 1 year. Neither credit nor placement offered for CEEB Advanced Placement tests.

COSTS AND FINANCIAL AID
Annual tuition $16,740. Room and board $6,525. Required fees $150. Average book expense $900. **Required Forms and Deadlines:** FAFSA, Institution's own financial aid form, State aid form. **Types of Aid:** *Need-based scholarships/grants:* Federal Pell, SEOG, state scholarships/grants, private scholarships, the school's own gift aid. *Loans:* Subsidized Stafford, Unsubsidized Stafford, PLUS, Federal Perkins, state loans, college/university loans from institutional funds. *Student Employment:* Federal Work-Study Program available. Institutional employment available. Off-campus job opportunities are excellent. **Financial Aid Statistics:** 0% undergrads receive athletic scholarships. 88% undergrads receive any aid.

THE ART INSTITUTES INTERNATIONAL MINNESOTA

15 South 9th Street, Minneapolis, mn 55402
Phone: 612-332-3361 • **Financial Aid Phone:** 612-332-3361
E-mail: aimadm@aii.edu
Fax: 612-332-3934 • **Website:** www.artinstitutes.edu/minneapolis

This proprietary school was founded in 1997.

RATINGS
Admissions Selectivity Rating: 60*   **Fire Safety Rating:** 76

STUDENTS AND FACULTY
Enrollment: 1,974. **Student Body:** 61% female, 39% male, 20% out-of-state. **Retention and Graduation:** 60% freshmen return for sophomore year. **Faculty:** 56 full-time faculty, 36% are members of minority groups.

ACADEMICS
Degrees: associate, bachelor's, certificate. **Special Study Options:** distance learning, independent study, internships, study abroad, Evening & Weekend. **Disability Services:** Special programs offered to physically disabled students include note-taking services, tape recorders, tutors. **Career services:** Alumni network, alumni services, career/job search classes, internships, regional alumni.

FACILITIES
Housing: apartments for single students. 100% of campus accessible to physically disabled. **Computers:** 100% of classrooms, 100% of dorms, 100% of libraries, 100% of dining areas, 100% of student union, have wireless network access. Students can register for classes online. Administrative functions (other than registration) can be performed online.

CAMPUS LIFE
Environment: Metropolis. **Activities:** literary magazine, student newspaper, Campus Ministries, International Student Organization. 16 registered organizations, 1 honor society. **On-Campus Highlights:** School dining lab, Art galleries, Connection to the city's skyway system, New second campus.

ADMISSIONS
Basis for Candidate Selection: *Other factors considered include:* state residency. **Transfer Admission Requirements:** High school transcript, college transcript(s). **General Admission Information:** Application Fee $20. Nonfall registration accepted. Admission may be deferred for a maximum of none.

COSTS AND FINANCIAL AID
Required Forms and Deadlines: FAFSA.

ASBURY COLLEGE

1 Macklem Drive, Wilmore, KY 40390
Phone: 859-858-3511
E-mail: admissions@asbury.edu • **CEEB Code:** 1019
Fax: 859-858-3921 • **Website:** www.asbury.edu • **ACT Code:** 1486

This private school was founded in 1890. It has a 400-acre campus.

RATINGS
Admissions Selectivity Rating: 86   **Fire Safety Rating:** 60*

STUDENTS AND FACULTY
Enrollment: 1,167. **Student Body:** 58% female, 42% male, 70% out-of-state, 1% international (10 countries represented). Asian 1%, African American 1%, Caucasian 96%, Hispanic 1%, Native American <1%. **Retention and Graduation:** 82% freshmen return for sophomore year. 49% freshmen graduate within 4 years. 63% freshmen graduate within 6 years. **Faculty:** 90 full-time faculty, 78% hold PhDs, 27% are members of minority groups, 0% are women. 0% of classes are taught by teaching assistants.

ACADEMICS
Degrees: bachelor's, master's. **Classes:** Most classes have 10–19 students. **Majors with Highest Enrollment:** Communications Technologies/Technicians and Support Services; Elementary Education and Teaching; Psychology. **Special Study Options:** double major, internships, teacher certification program, 3-2 programs in engineering and computer science with the University of Kentucky. **Disability Services:** Special programs offered to physically disabled students include tape recorders, tutors. **Career services:** alumni services, career/job search classes, career assessment, internships.

FACILITIES
Housing: special housing for disabled students, men's dorms, women's dorms, apartments for married students, apartments for single students, Spanish House. 70% of campus accessible to physically disabled. **Special Academic Facilities/Equipment:** Art gallery, Art Annex, practice rooms, theatre building, Luce Physical Activities Center, TV/radio studios and Mac lab. **Computers:** Administrative functions (other than registration) can be performed online.

CAMPUS LIFE
Environment: Rural. **Activities:** Choral groups, concert band, drama/theater, jazz band, literary magazine, music ensembles, opera, radio station, student government, student newspaper, symphony orchestra, television station, yearbook. 41 registered organizations, 6 honor societies, 8 religious organizations. **Athletics (Intercollegiate):** *Men:* baseball, basketball, cross-country, diving, soccer, swimming, tennis, track/field (outdoor). *Women:* basketball, cross-country, diving, soccer, softball, swimming, tennis, track/field (outdoor), volleyball.

ADMISSIONS
Freshman Academic Profile: Average high school GPA 3.55. 30% in top 10% of high school class, 60% in top 25% of high school class, 86% in top 50% of high school class. 65% from public high schools. SAT Math middle 50% range 490-620. SAT Critical Reading middle 50% range 530-650. ACT middle 50% range 21-28. Minimum paper TOEFL 550. **Basis for Candidate Selection:** *Very important factors considered include:* recommendation(s), rigor of secondary school record, standardized test scores, character/personal qualities, racial/ethnic status, religious affiliation/commitment. *Important factors considered include:* Class rank, application essay, volunteer work, work experience. *Other factors considered include:* alumni/ae relation, extracurricular activities, geographical residence, state residency, talent/ability. **Freshman Admission Requirements:** High school diploma is required and GED is accepted. **Freshman Admission Statistics:** 820 applied, 73% admitted, 49% enrolled. **Transfer Admission Requirements:** High school transcript, college transcript(s), essay or personal statement, standardized test scores, Minimum college GPA of 2.5 required. Lowest grade transferable C-. **General Admission Information:** Application Fee $30. Nonfall registration accepted. Admission may be deferred for a maximum of 1 year. Neither credit nor placement offered for CEEB Advanced Placement tests.

COSTS AND FINANCIAL AID
Annual tuition $17,660. Room and board $4,498. Required fees $148. Average book expense $600. **Required Forms and Deadlines:** FAFSA, Institution's own financial aid form. **Notification of Awards:** Applicants will be notified of awards on a rolling basis beginning 3/1. **Types of Aid:** *Need-based scholarships/grants:* Federal Pell, SEOG, state scholarships/grants, the school's own gift aid.

Loans: Subsidized Stafford, Unsubsidized Stafford, PLUS, Federal Perkins, college/university loans from institutional funds, Private alternative loans. *Student Employment:* Federal Work-Study Program available. Institutional employment available. Highest amount earned per year from on-campus jobs $1,200. Off-campus job opportunities are good. **Financial Aid Statistics:** 99% freshmen, 99% undergrads receive need-based scholarship or grant aid. 35% freshmen, 3% undergrads receive non-need-based scholarship or grant aid. 93% freshmen, 88% undergrads receive need-based self-help aid. 1% freshmen, 0% undergrads receive athletic scholarships. 68% undergrads borrow to pay for school. **Criteria for awarding institutional aid:** *Non-need-based:* academics, alumni affiliation, athletics, leadership, music/drama.

ASHLAND UNIVERSITY

401 College Ave, Ashland, OH 44805
Phone: 419-289-5052 · **Financial Aid Phone:** 419-289-5002
E-mail: enrollme@ashland.edu · **CEEB Code:** 1021
Fax: 419-289-5999 · **Website:** www.ashland.edu · **ACT Code:** 3234

This private school, affiliated with the Church of Brethren Church, was founded in 1878. It has a 12-acre campus.

RATINGS

Admissions Selectivity Rating: 81   Fire Safety Rating: 68

STUDENTS AND FACULTY

Enrollment: 2,701. **Student Body:** 62% female, 38% male, 8% out-of-state, 2% international (16 countries represented). Asian 1%, African American 4%, Caucasian 85%, Hispanic 2%, Native American 1%
Retention and Graduation: 69% freshmen return for sophomore year. 43% freshmen graduate within 4 years. 59% freshmen graduate within 6 years. 13% grads go on to further study within 1 year. 2% grads pursue arts and sciences degrees. 1% grads pursue law degrees. 1% grads pursue business degrees. 1% grads pursue medical degrees. **Faculty:** 272 full-time faculty, 82% hold PhDs, 46% are members of minority groups, 7% are women. 0% of classes are taught by teaching assistants.

ACADEMICS

Degrees: associate, bachelor's, certificate, diploma, doctoral, master's, terminal associate, transfer associate. **Classes:** Most classes have 10–19 students. Most lab/discussion sessions have 10–19 students. **Majors with Highest Enrollment:** Education; Business/Commerce. **Special Study Options:** double major, English as a Second Language (ESL), honors program, independent study, internships, student-designed major, study abroad, teacher certification program, weekend college, Ashbrook Center for Public Affairs. **Honors programs:** Ashland University Honors Program. **Disability Services:** Special programs offered to physically disabled students include note-taking services, reader services, tape recorders, tutors. **Career services:** Alumni network, alumni services, career/job search classes, career assessment, internships.

FACILITIES

Housing: Coed dorms, special housing for disabled students, men's dorms, women's dorms, fraternity/sorority housing, apartments for single students, Theme Housing. 70% of campus accessible to physically disabled. **Special Academic Facilities/Equipment:** Neumismatic Center, Patterson Technology Center, Coburn Art Gallery, Hugo Young Theatre, Studio Theatre, 33 room Radio/Television Condex, Media Center, Pre-Columbian Art Exhibit, Ashbrook Center. **Computers:** 90% of classrooms, 50% of dorms, 100% of libraries, 50% of dining areas, 100% of student union, 50% of common outdoor areas have wireless network access. Students can register for classes online. Administrative functions (other than registration) can be performed online.

CAMPUS LIFE

Environment: Town. **Activities:** Choral groups, concert band, dance, drama/theater, jazz band, literary magazine, marching band, music ensembles, musical theater, pep band, radio station, student government, student newspaper, symphony orchestra, television station, yearbook, Campus Ministries, International Student Organization. 102 registered organizations, 18 honor societies, 9 religious organizations. 4 fraternities, 5 sororities. **Athletics (Intercollegiate):** *Men:* baseball, basketball, cross-country, diving, football, golf, soccer, swimming, track/field (outdoor), track/field (indoor), wrestling. *Women:* basketball, cheerleading, cross-country, diving, golf, soccer, softball, swimming, tennis, track/field (outdoor), track/field (indoor), volleyball. **On-Campus Highlights:** Kettering Science Center, Recreation and Sport Sciences Center, Schar College of Education, Dauch College of Business and Economics, National ranked food service, NCAA Division II Athletics, New football stadium as of 2009-2010, new soccer complex, new track and field complex.

ADMISSIONS

Freshman Academic Profile: Average high school GPA 3.37. 22.2% in top 10% of high school class, 48.9% in top 25% of high school class, 80.1% in top 50% of high school class. 89% from public high schools. SAT Math middle 50% range 490-580. SAT Critical Reading middle 50% range 460-560. ACT middle 50% range 20-25. Minimum internet-based TOEFL 65. Minimum paper TOEFL 500. **Basis for Candidate Selection:** *Very important factors considered include:* rigor of secondary school record, standardized test scores. *Important factors considered include:* Class rank, academic GPA, alumni/ae relation, character/personal qualities, extracurricular activities, interview, level of applicant's interest. *Other factors considered include:* application essay, recommendation(s), geographical residence, religious affiliation/commitment, state residency, talent/ability, volunteer work, work experience. **Freshman Admission Requirements:** High school diploma is required and GED is accepted. *Academic units required:* 3 English, 2 mathematics, 2 science, 0 foreign language, 2 social studies, 1 history. **Freshman Admission Statistics:** 3,530 applied, 77% admitted, 25% enrolled. **Transfer Admission Requirements:** college transcript(s), essay or personal statement, Minimum college GPA of 2.5 required. Lowest grade transferable C-. **General Admission Information:** Regular application deadline 8/15. Notification on a rolling basis, beginning on or about 10/15. Nonfall registration accepted. Admission may be deferred for a maximum of 1 Semester. Credit and/or placement offered for CEEB Advanced Placement tests.

COSTS AND FINANCIAL AID

Annual tuition $26,566. Room and board $9,352. Required fees $846. Average book expense $900. **Required Forms and Deadlines:** FAFSA. **Notification of Awards:** Applicants will be notified of awards on a rolling basis beginning 3/1. **Types of Aid:** *Need-based scholarships/grants:* Federal Pell, SEOG, state scholarships/grants, private scholarships, the school's own gift aid. *Loans:* Direct Subsidized Stafford, Direct Unsubsidized Stafford, Direct PLUS, Subsidized Stafford, Unsubsidized Stafford, PLUS, Federal Perkins, Federal Nursing, state loans, college/university loans from institutional funds. *Student Employment:* Federal Work-Study Program available. Institutional employment available. Highest amount earned per year from on-campus jobs $2,800. Off-campus job opportunities are good. **Financial Aid Statistics:** 100% freshmen, 100% undergrads receive need-based scholarship or grant aid. 106% freshmen, 95% undergrads receive non-need-based scholarship or grant aid. 93% freshmen, 93% undergrads receive need-based self-help aid. 3% freshmen, 3% undergrads receive athletic scholarships. 99% freshmen, 98% undergrads receive any aid. 79% undergrads borrow to pay for school. Average cumulative indebtedness $21,926. **Criteria for awarding institutional aid:** *Non-need-based:* academics, alumni affiliation, art, athletics, job skills, leadership, minority status, music/drama, religious affiliation.

ASSUMPTION COLLEGE

500 Salisbury Street, Worcester, MA 01609-1296
Phone: 508-767-7285 · **Financial Aid Phone:** 508-767-7158
E-mail: admiss@assumption.edu · **CEEB Code:** 3009
Fax: 508-799-4412 · **Website:** www.assumption.edu · **ACT Code:** 1782

This private school, affiliated with the Roman Catholic Church, was founded in 1904. It has a 180-acre campus.

RATINGS

Admissions Selectivity Rating: 80   Fire Safety Rating: 74

STUDENTS AND FACULTY

Enrollment: 2,002. **Student Body:** 60% female, 40% male, 36% out-of-state, 1% international (23 countries represented). Asian 2%, African American 4%, Caucasian 74%, Hispanic 7%, Native American <1%
Retention and Graduation: 70% freshmen graduate within 4 years. 25% grads go on to further study within 1 year. 15% grads pursue arts and sciences degrees. 2% grads pursue law degrees. 3% grads pursue business degrees. 1% grads pursue medical degrees. **Faculty:** 146 full-time faculty, 94% hold PhDs, 42% are members of minority groups, 5% are women. 0% of classes are taught by teaching assistants.

ACADEMICS

Degrees: bachelor's, master's, post-master's certificate. **Classes:** Most classes have 20–29 students. Most lab/discussion sessions have 10–19 students. **Majors with Highest Enrollment:** Rehabilitation and Therapeutic Professions; Psychology; Accounting. **Special Study Options:** cross-registration, double major, honors program, independent study, internships, student-designed major, study abroad, teacher certification program. **Honors programs:** The Assumption College Honors Program is a selective program designed to foster academic engagement inside and outside the classroom. The program promotes intellectual friendship and discourse while providing a common, intensive learning experience in small seminar classes. Combined degree programs: BA/MA, BA/MAs SP ED, Rehab Couns, School Couns; BA/MBA. **Disability Services:** Special programs offered to physically disabled students include note-taking services, reader services, tape recorders, tutors. **Career services:** Alumni network, career/job search classes, career assessment, internships, regional alumni.

FACILITIES
Housing: Coed dorms, special housing for disabled students, women's dorms, Wellness Housing, Theme Housing, Freshmen dorms. 71% of campus accessible to physically disabled. **Special Academic Facilities/Equipment:** French Institute museum, Institute for Social and Rehabilitation Services, language lab, media center Living/Learning Center Testa Science Center Information Technology Center **Computers:** 100% of classrooms, 100% of libraries, 50% of dining areas, 100% of student union, 25% of common outdoor areas have wireless network access. Students can register for classes online. Administrative functions (other than registration) can be performed online.

CAMPUS LIFE
Environment: City. **Activities:** Choral groups, concert band, drama/theater, literary magazine, musical theater, pep band, student government, student newspaper, student-run film society, television station, yearbook, Campus Ministries. 50 registered organizations, 12 honor societies, 1 religious organization. **Athletics (Intercollegiate):** *Men:* baseball, basketball, cross-country, football, golf, ice hockey, lacrosse, soccer, tennis, track/field (outdoor), track/field (indoor). *Women:* basketball, crew/rowing, cross-country, field hockey, lacrosse, soccer, softball, swimming, tennis, track/field (outdoor), track/field (indoor), volleyball. **On-Campus Highlights:** Testa Science Center, Living Learning Center, Plourde Recreation Center, Charlie's Café, D'Alzon Library.

ADMISSIONS
Freshman Academic Profile: Average high school GPA 3.32. 10% in top 10% of high school class, 40% in top 25% of high school class, 79% in top 50% of high school class. 68% from public high schools. SAT Math middle 50% range 510-620. SAT Critical Reading middle 50% range 510-595. ACT middle 50% range 23-27. Minimum internet-based TOEFL 80. Minimum paper TOEFL 550. **Basis for Candidate Selection:** *Very important factors considered include:* application essay, academic GPA. *Important factors considered include:* recommendation(s), rigor of secondary school record, interview, level of applicant's interest, volunteer work. *Other factors considered include:* Class rank, standardized test scores, alumni/ae relation, character/personal qualities, extracurricular activities, first generation, racial/ethnic status, talent/ability. **Freshman Admission Requirements:** High school diploma is required and GED is accepted. *Academic units required:* 4 English, 3 mathematics, 2 science, 2 foreign language, 2 history, 5 academic electives. 4 English, 3 mathematics, 2 science, 2 foreign language, 2 history, 5 academic electives, **Freshman Admission Statistics:** 4,659 applied, 74% admitted, 15% enrolled. **Transfer Admission Requirements:** High school transcript, college transcript(s), essay or personal statement, statement of good standing from prior institution(s). Minimum college GPA of 2.5 required. Lowest grade transferable C. **General Admission Information:** Application Fee $50. Regular application deadline 2/15. Nonfall registration accepted. Admission may be deferred for a maximum of 1 year. Credit and/or placement offered for CEEB Advanced Placement tests.

COSTS AND FINANCIAL AID
Annual tuition $35,510. Room and board $10,962. Required fees $650. Average book expense $1,000. **Required Forms and Deadlines:** FAFSA. **Notification of Awards:** Applicants will be notified of awards on a rolling basis beginning 2/16. **Types of Aid:** *Need-based scholarships/grants:* Federal Pell, SEOG, state scholarships/grants, private scholarships, the school's own gift aid. *Loans:* Direct Subsidized Stafford, Direct Unsubsidized Stafford, Direct PLUS, Unsubsidized Stafford, PLUS. *Student Employment:* Federal Work-Study Program available. Institutional employment available. Highest amount earned per year from on-campus jobs $2,948. Off-campus job opportunities are good. **Financial Aid Statistics:** 100% freshmen, 100% undergrads receive need-based scholarship or grant aid. 11% freshmen, 12% undergrads receive non-need-based scholarship or grant aid. 83% freshmen, 84% undergrads receive need-based self-help aid. 4% freshmen, 3% undergrads receive athletic scholarships. 98% freshmen, 98% undergrads receive any aid. 79% undergrads borrow to pay for school. Average cumulative indebtedness $25,309. **Criteria for awarding institutional aid:** *Non-need-based:* academics, athletics.

See page 1000.

ATHABASCA UNIVERSITY

1 University Drive, Athabasca, AB T9S 3A3
Phone: 800-788-9041 • **Financial Aid Phone:** 780-675-6147
Fax: 780-675-6145 • **Website:** www.athabascau.ca

This public school was founded in 1970.

RATINGS
Admissions Selectivity Rating: 60*   Fire Safety Rating: 60*

STUDENTS AND FACULTY
Student Body: 61% out-of-state, (90 countries represented).

ACADEMICS
Degrees: bachelor's, certificate, diploma, master's, post-bachelor's certificate, post-master's certificate. **Majors with Highest Enrollment:** Elementary Education and Teaching; Criminal Justice/Safety Studies. **Special Study Options:** Accelerated program, cross-registration, distance learning, English as a Second Language (ESL), external degree program. **Disability Services:** Special programs offered to physically disabled students include tape recorders, tutors.

FACILITIES
Housing: Coed dorms. **Computers:** Students can register for classes online. Administrative functions (other than registration) can be performed online.

CAMPUS LIFE
Environment: Rural. **Activities:** student government, yearbook.

ADMISSIONS
Transfer Admission Requirements: High school transcript, college transcript(s). **General Admission Information:** Application Fee $56. Nonfall registration accepted. Admission may be deferred for a maximum of 1 year.

AUBURN UNIVERSITY

Best 380

108 Mary Martin Hall, Auburn, AL 36849-5149
Phone: 334-844-4080 • **Financial Aid Phone:** 334-844-4634
E-mail: admissions@auburn.edu • **CEEB Code:** 1005
Fax: 334-844-6436 • **Website:** www.auburn.edu • **ACT Code:** 11

This public school was founded in 1856. It has a 1875-acre campus.

RATINGS
Admissions Selectivity Rating: 86   Fire Safety Rating: 82

STUDENTS AND FACULTY
Enrollment: 20,514. **Student Body:** 49% female, 51% male, 38% out-of-state, 1% international (85 countries represented). Asian 2%, African American 7%, Caucasian 85%, Hispanic 2%, Native American 1%
Retention and Graduation: 90% freshmen return for sophomore year. 42% freshmen graduate within 4 years. 71% freshmen graduate within 6 years. 41% grads go on to further study within 1 year. 6% grads pursue arts and sciences degrees. 7% grads pursue law degrees. 19% grads pursue business degrees. 30% grads pursue medical degrees. **Faculty:** 1,209 full-time faculty, 93% hold PhDs, 37% are members of minority groups, 17% are women.

ACADEMICS
Degrees: bachelor's, doctoral, master's, post-master's certificate. **Classes:** Most classes have 20–29 students. Most lab/discussion sessions have 20–29 students. **Majors with Highest Enrollment:** Mechanical Engineering; Business Administration and Management; Secondary Education and Teaching. **Special Study Options:** Accelerated program, cooperative education program, distance learning, double major, dual enrollment, English as a Second Language (ESL), honors program, independent study, internships, liberal arts/career combination, study abroad, teacher certification program. **Honors programs:** The Auburn University's Honors College offers qualified students a unique academic experience, designed to provide many of the advantages of a small college in the midst of the many diverse opportunities available at a large university. It is designed for students capable of academic excellence. The program selects 200 entering freshmen each year, who may be enrolled in any College or School of the University which has undergraduate programs or offerings. Students

already enrolled at Auburn can also qualify for the Honors College. Combined degree programs: w/ Liberal Arts or Agriculture. **Disability Services:** Special programs offered to physically disabled students include note-taking services, reader services, tape recorders, tutors. **Career services:** Alumni network, alumni services, career/job search classes, career assessment, internships.

FACILITIES

Housing: Coed dorms, special housing for disabled students, men's dorms, women's dorms, fraternity/sorority housing, apartments for married students, apartments for single students, Housing for students enrolled in Honors College and academic-themed learning communities (i.e. Agriculture Pre-Vet, AT&T Minority Engineering Program, Conservation Biology). 95% of campus accessible to physically disabled. **Special Academic Facilities/Equipment:** Nuclear Science Center; Hybridoma Facility; Freeman Herbarium; Jule Collins Smith Art Museum; Hypervelocity Impact Facility; Advanced Microscopy & Imaging Laboratory; Alabama Microelectronics Science & Technology Center; Alabama Water Resources Research Institute; AU Airport with single/multi-engine aircraft and flight simulators; Center for Forest Sustainability; Center for Governmental Services; Center for Pharmacy Operations & Designs; Drug Information & Learning Resources Center; Economic & Community Development Institute; Fish Molecular Genetics & Biotechnology Laboratory; Forest Policy Center; Forest Products Development Center; Fusion Lab; Harris Early Learning Center; Dept of Psychology Health Behavior Assessment Center; Highway Research Center; Marriage & Family Therapy Center; Microfibrous Materials Manufacturing Center; Dept of Kinesiology Biomechanics Lab, and Motor Behavior Center; Plasma Sciences Lab; Veterinary Medicine Radiology Clinic, Scott-Ritchey Research Center, Southeastern Raptor Rehabilitation Center, Small & Large Animal Health Clinics. **Computers:** 35% of classrooms, 100% of dorms, 95% of libraries, 50% of dining areas, 100% of student union, 30% of common outdoor areas have wireless network access. Students can register for classes online. Administrative functions (other than registration) can be performed online.

CAMPUS LIFE

Environment: Town. **Activities:** Choral groups, concert band, dance, drama/theater, jazz band, literary magazine, marching band, music ensembles, musical theater, opera, pep band, radio station, student government, student newspaper, student-run film society, symphony orchestra, television station, yearbook, International Student Organization. 300 registered organizations, 56 honor societies, 15 religious organizations. 30 fraternities, 19 sororities. **Athletics (Intercollegiate):** *Men:* baseball, basketball, cheerleading, cross-country, diving, football, golf, swimming, tennis, track/field (outdoor), track/field (indoor). *Women:* basketball, cheerleading, cross-country, diving, equestrian sports, golf, gymnastics, soccer, softball, swimming, tennis, track/field (outdoor), track/field (indoor), volleyball. **On-Campus Highlights:** Telfair B. Peet Theatre, Student Activity Center, Haley Center Concourse, Library Coffee Shop, War Eagle Dining, Student Center; Arboretum; Agricultural Heritage Park; Forest Ecology Preserve. **Environmental Initiatives:** Incorporation of sustainability initiatives into university curricula, including one of the first truly interdisciplinary sustainability minors in the country. Establishment of campus-wide sustainability policy in December, 2011. 2008 University Strategic Plan incorporating commitment to sustainability as guiding concept: "We recognize the importance of sustainability as crucial for this century, and we are integrating this theme into our work."

ADMISSIONS

Freshman Academic Profile: Average high school GPA 3.77. 29% in top 10% of high school class, 61% in top 25% of high school class, 88% in top 50% of high school class. 86% from public high schools. SAT Math middle 50% range 530-645. SAT Critical Reading middle 50% range 520-630. SAT Writing middle 50% range 520-610. ACT middle 50% range 24-30. Minimum internet-based TOEFL 79. Minimum paper TOEFL 550. **Basis for Candidate Selection:** *Very important factors considered include:* application essay, academic GPA, standardized test scores. *Important factors considered include:* rigor of secondary school record, alumni/ae relation, character/personal qualities, extracurricular activities, first generation, geographical residence, level of applicant's interest, state residency, talent/ability, volunteer work, work experience. *Other factors considered include:* recommendation(s). **Freshman Admission Requirements:** High school diploma is required and GED is accepted. *Academic units required:* 4 English, 3 mathematics, 2 science, (1 science labs), 3 social studies. **Freshman Admission Statistics:** 16,958 applied, 83% admitted, 32% enrolled. **Transfer Admission Requirements:** college transcript(s), Minimum college GPA of 2.5 required. Lowest grade transferable C. **General Admission Information:** Application Fee $40. Regular application deadline 6/1. Regular notification 2/15. Notification on a rolling basis, beginning on or about 10/15. Nonfall registration accepted. Admission may be deferred for a maximum of 1 year. Credit and/or placement offered for CEEB Advanced Placement tests.

COSTS AND FINANCIAL AID

Annual in-state tuition $8,592. Annual out-of-state tuition $25,776. Room and board $12,178. Required fees $1,608. Average book expense $1,200. **Required**

Forms and Deadlines: FAFSA. **Notification of Awards:** Applicants will be notified of awards on a rolling basis beginning 10/2. **Types of Aid:** *Need-based scholarships/grants:* Federal Pell, SEOG, state scholarships/grants, private scholarships, the school's own gift aid. *Loans:* Direct Subsidized Stafford, Direct Unsubsidized Stafford, Direct PLUS, Federal Perkins, Federal Nursing, college/university loans from institutional funds. *Student Employment:* Federal Work-Study Program available. Institutional employment available. Highest amount earned per year from on-campus jobs $10,920. Off-campus job opportunities are good. **Financial Aid Statistics:** 86% freshmen, 74% undergrads receive need-based scholarship or grant aid. 13% freshmen, 9% undergrads receive non-need-based scholarship or grant aid. 65% freshmen, 78% undergrads receive need-based self-help aid. 2% freshmen, 2% undergrads receive athletic scholarships. 51% freshmen, 45% undergrads receive any aid. 41% undergrads borrow to pay for school. Average cumulative indebtedness $22,133.

AUBURN UNIVERSITY AT MONTGOMERY

P.O. Box 244023, Montgomery, AL 36124-4023
Phone: 334-244-3615 • **Financial Aid Phone:** 334-244-3571
E-mail: admissions@aum.edu
Fax: 334-244-3795 • **Website:** www.aum.edu • **ACT Code:** 57

This public school was founded in 1967. It has a 500-acre campus.

RATINGS

Admissions Selectivity Rating: 78   **Fire Safety Rating:** 83

STUDENTS AND FACULTY

Enrollment: 4,230. **Student Body:** 63% female, 37% male, 4% out-of-state, 4% international (33 countries represented). Asian 2%, African American 34%, Caucasian 54%, Hispanic 1%, Native American <1%
Retention and Graduation: 8% freshmen graduate within 4 years. 22% freshmen graduate within 6 years. **Faculty:** 215 full-time faculty, 47% are members of minority groups, 20% are women. 2.5% of classes are taught by teaching assistants.

ACADEMICS

Degrees: bachelor's, master's, post-master's certificate. **Classes:** Most classes have 20–29 students. Most lab/discussion sessions have 20–29 students. **Majors with Highest Enrollment:** Elementary Education and Teaching; Business/Commerce; Registered Nursing/Registered Nurse. **Special Study Options:** Accelerated program, cooperative education program, cross-registration, distance learning, double major, dual enrollment, English as a Second Language (ESL), honors program, independent study, internships, liberal arts/career combination, study abroad, teacher certification program, weekend college, Joint Ph.D.in public administration with Auburn University; Ed.D. in cooperation with Auburn University. **Disability Services:** Special programs offered to physically disabled students include note-taking services, reader services, tape recorders, tutors. **Career services:** Alumni network, alumni services, career/job search classes, career assessment, internships.

FACILITIES

Housing: Coed dorms, special housing for disabled students, apartments for married students, apartments for single students. 100% of campus accessible to physically disabled. **Computers:** Students can register for classes online. Administrative functions (other than registration) can be performed online.

CAMPUS LIFE

Environment: City. **Activities:** Choral groups, dance, drama/theater, musical theater, student government, student newspaper, student-run film society, Campus Ministries, International Student Organization. 50 registered organizations, 10 honor societies, 7 religious organizations. 3 fraternities, 6 sororities. **Athletics (Intercollegiate):** *Men:* baseball, basketball, cheerleading, soccer, tennis. *Women:* basketball, cheerleading, soccer, softball, tennis. **On-Campus Highlights:** Senator's Café, Computer Labs, Taylor Center/Student Union, Residence Hall, Athletic Facility. **Environmental Initiatives:** Recycling, Campus Beautification—Plant Trees, Educating the Campus on Sustainability Initiative.

ADMISSIONS

Freshman Academic Profile: Average high school GPA 3.3. 18.1% in top 10% of high school class, 46.2% in top 25% of high school class, 78.7% in top 50% of high school class. SAT Math middle 50% range 468-550. SAT Critical Reading middle 50% range 433-538. ACT middle 50% range 19-24. Minimum internet-based TOEFL 61. Minimum paper TOEFL 500. **Basis for Candidate Selection:** *Very important factors considered include:* Class rank, academic GPA, rigor of secondary school record, standardized test scores. *Other factors considered include:* recommendation(s), alumni/ae relation, extracurricular activities, geographical residence, state residency. **Freshman Admission**

Requirements: High school diploma is required and GED is accepted. **Freshman Admission Statistics:** 2,123 applied, 80% admitted, 36% enrolled. **Transfer Admission Requirements:** college transcript(s), Minimum college GPA of 2.0 required. Lowest grade transferable D. **General Admission Information:** Application Fee $25. Nonfall registration accepted. Admission may be deferred for a maximum of 1 year. Credit offered for CEEB Advanced Placement tests.

COSTS AND FINANCIAL AID
Annual. Annual out-of-state tuition $18,990. Room and board $5,390. Required fees $650. Average book expense $1,000. **Required Forms and Deadlines:** FAFSA. **Notification of Awards:** Applicants will be notified of awards on a rolling basis beginning 6/1. **Types of Aid:** *Need-based scholarships/grants:* Federal Pell. *Loans:* Subsidized Stafford, Unsubsidized Stafford, PLUS, Federal Perkins. *Student Employment:* Federal Work-Study Program available. Institutional employment available. **Financial Aid Statistics:** 80% freshmen, 75% undergrads receive need-based scholarship or grant aid. 27% freshmen, 23% undergrads receive non-need-based scholarship or grant aid. 83% freshmen, 83% undergrads receive need-based self-help aid. 0% freshmen, 0% undergrads receive athletic scholarships. 85% freshmen, 50% undergrads receive any aid. **Criteria for awarding institutional aid:** *Non-need-based:* academics, alumni affiliation, art, athletics, job skills, leadership, minority status, music/drama.

AUGSBURG COLLEGE

2211 Riverside Avenue South, Minneapolis, MN 55454
Phone: 612-330-1001 · **Financial Aid Phone:** 612-330-1046
E-mail: admissions@augsburg.edu · **CEEB Code:** 6014
Fax: 612-330-1590 · **Website:** www.augsburg.edu · **ACT Code:** 2080

This private school, affiliated with the Lutheran Church, was founded in 1869. It has a 23-acre campus.

RATINGS
Admissions Selectivity Rating: 84   **Fire Safety Rating:** 75

STUDENTS AND FACULTY
Enrollment: 3,014. **Student Body:** 55% female, 45% male, 13% out-of-state, 2% international (24 countries represented). Asian 7%, African American 9%, Caucasian 68%, Hispanic 3%, Native American 2%
Retention and Graduation: 83% freshmen return for sophomore year. 41% freshmen graduate within 4 years. 62% freshmen graduate within 6 years. 27% grads go on to further study within 1 year. 15% grads pursue arts and sciences degrees. 2% grads pursue law degrees. 4% grads pursue business degrees. 5% grads pursue medical degrees. **Faculty:** 195 full-time faculty, 75% hold PhDs, 51% are members of minority groups, 8% are women. 0% of classes are taught by teaching assistants.

ACADEMICS
Degrees: bachelor's, certificate, master's. **Classes:** Most classes have 10–19 students. Most lab/discussion sessions have 10–19 students. **Majors with Highest Enrollment:** Education; Business/Commerce. **Special Study Options:** cooperative education program, cross-registration, double major, dual enrollment, honors program, independent study, internships, liberal arts/career combination, student-designed major, study abroad, teacher certification program, weekend college. **Honors programs:** First, the Honors Signature Courses, based on the medieval divisions of knowledge, automatically satisfy all of the College's general education requirements (except health/physical education and modern language) in a simple sequence of challenging courses, created just for Honors students. Second, Student-Created Courses allow students to design their own courses as either a replacement or supplement to the established Honors courses. Students can learn through one-on-one tutoring, small reading groups, or out-of-classroom experiences. Third, Honors Leadership Activities give Honors students access to the The Augsburg Review, Honors Debate League, Faculty/Student Research Collaboration, and the Honors Houses. Through these activities, students can engage in travel abroad, service-learning, social justice activities, political activism, leadership, research, and social gatherings with their friends. Combined degree programs: BA/MEng. **Disability Services:** Special programs offered to physically disabled students include note-taking services, reader services, tape recorders, tutors. **Career services:** career/job search classes, internships.

FACILITIES
Housing: Coed dorms, special housing for disabled students, Special housing for Step-Up program students (i.e. Sober student program). 99% of campus accessible to physically disabled. **Special Academic Facilities/Equipment:** Electron microscope, center for atmospheric science research, theatre, pipe organ. **Computers:** Students can register for classes online. Administrative functions (other than registration) can be performed online.

CAMPUS LIFE
Environment: Metropolis. **Activities:** Choral groups, concert band, dance, drama/theater, jazz band, literary magazine, music ensembles, opera, radio station, student government, student newspaper, yearbook, Campus Ministries, International Student Organization. 35 registered organizations, 1 honor society, 1 religious organization. **Athletics (Intercollegiate):** *Men:* baseball, basketball, cross-country, football, golf, ice hockey, soccer, tennis, track/field (outdoor), track/field (indoor), wrestling. *Women:* basketball, cheerleading, cross-country, golf, ice hockey, soccer, softball, swimming, tennis, track/field (outdoor), track/field (indoor), volleyball. **On-Campus Highlights:** Christensen Center/Starbucks Coffee Shop, Si Melby Athletic Fieldhouse, Lindell Library, Foss Center/Atrium, Gateway Center.

ADMISSIONS
Freshman Academic Profile: Average high school GPA 3.27. 11% in top 10% of high school class, 37% in top 25% of high school class, 69% in top 50% of high school class. SAT Math middle 50% range 500-640. SAT Critical Reading middle 50% range 510-640. SAT Writing middle 50% range 480-600. ACT middle 50% range 19-25. Minimum paper TOEFL 550. **Basis for Candidate Selection:** *Very important factors considered include:* Class rank, application essay, academic GPA, recommendation(s), rigor of secondary school record. *Important factors considered include:* standardized test scores, alumni/ae relation, extracurricular activities, level of applicant's interest. *Other factors considered include:* first generation, interview, talent/ability, volunteer work, work experience. **Freshman Admission Requirements:** High school diploma is required and GED is accepted. *Academic units required:* 4 English, 3 mathematics, 3 science, 2 foreign language, 2 social studies. **Freshman Admission Statistics:** 2,192 applied, 54% admitted, 35% enrolled. **Transfer Admission Requirements:** college transcript(s), statement of good standing from prior institution(s). Minimum college GPA of 2.5 required. Lowest grade transferable B. **General Admission Information:** Application Fee $25. Regular application deadline 8/15. Notification on a rolling basis, beginning on or about 11/1. Nonfall registration accepted. Admission may be deferred for a maximum of 24 mos. Neither credit nor placement offered for CEEB Advanced Placement tests.

COSTS AND FINANCIAL AID
Annual tuition $29,794. Room and board $8,072. Required fees $624. Average book expense $1,000. **Required Forms and Deadlines:** FAFSA. **Notification of Awards:** Applicants will be notified of awards on a rolling basis beginning 3/1. **Types of Aid:** *Need-based scholarships/grants:* Federal Pell, SEOG, state scholarships/grants, private scholarships, the school's own gift aid. *Loans:* Subsidized Stafford, Unsubsidized Stafford, PLUS, Federal Perkins, Federal Nursing, state loans, Supplemental Loans from Private Lenders. *Student Employment:* Institutional employment available. Highest amount earned per year from on-campus jobs $3,000. Off-campus job opportunities are good. **Financial Aid Statistics:** 99% freshmen, 91% undergrads receive need-based scholarship or grant aid. 19% freshmen, 17% undergrads receive non-need-based scholarship or grant aid. 94% freshmen, 92% undergrads receive need-based self-help aid. 0% freshmen, 0% undergrads receive athletic scholarships. 93% freshmen, 86% undergrads receive any aid. 83% undergrads borrow to pay for school. Average cumulative indebtedness $20,378. **Criteria for awarding institutional aid:** *Non-need-based:* academics, alumni affiliation, art, leadership, minority status, music/drama, religious affiliation.

AUGUSTA STATE UNIVERSITY

2500 Walton Way, Augusta, GA 30904-2200
Phone: 706-737-1632 · **Financial Aid Phone:** 706-737-1431
E-mail: admissio@aug.edu · **CEEB Code:** 5336
Fax: 706-667-4355 · **ACT Code:** 796

This public school was founded in 1925. It has a 76-acre campus.

RATINGS
Admissions Selectivity Rating: 76   **Fire Safety Rating:** 68

STUDENTS AND FACULTY
Enrollment: 5,394. **Student Body:** 64% female, 36% male, 9% out-of-state, 1% international (60 countries represented). Asian 3%, African American 28%, Caucasian 59%, Hispanic 3%, Native American <1%
Retention and Graduation: 69% freshmen return for sophomore year. 4% freshmen graduate within 4 years. 21% freshmen graduate within 6 years. **Faculty:** 236 full-time faculty, 64% hold PhDs, 51% are members of minority groups, 16% are women. 0% of classes are taught by teaching assistants.

ACADEMICS

Degrees: associate, bachelor's, master's, post-master's certificate, terminal associate, transfer associate. **Classes:** Most classes have 20–29 students. Most lab/discussion sessions have 20–29 students. **Majors with Highest Enrollment:** Elementary Education and Teaching; Biology/Biological Sciences; Psychology. **Special Study Options:** cooperative education program, cross-registration, distance learning, double major, dual enrollment, English as a Second Language (ESL), honors program, independent study, internships, study abroad, teacher certification program, Paralegal Certification. **Honors programs:** Augusta State University's Honors Program provides about 100 of our best students with special sections of classes in the core curriculum. Those classes are usually smaller, involve much closer interaction with the professor, and encourage more independent and collaborative work than non-honors sections of these courses. In their Junior and Senior years, Honors students take two interdisciplinary courses, prepare, write, and defend a thesis, and conclude their undergraduate program with a Capstone course. **Disability Services:** Special programs offered to physically disabled students include note-taking services, reader services, tape recorders, tutors. **Career services:** alumni services. Career services highlights include our outreach to students via the classrooms and appointments for individualized help.

FACILITIES

Housing: apartments for single students. 90% of campus accessible to physically disabled. **Special Academic Facilities/Equipment:** Performing Arts Theatre, Christenberry Field House, Forest Hill Golf Course. **Computers:** 95% of classrooms, 5% of dorms, 100% of libraries, 100% of dining areas, 100% of student union, have wireless network access. Students can register for classes online. Administrative functions (other than registration) can be performed online.

CAMPUS LIFE

Environment: City. **Activities:** Choral groups, concert band, drama/theater, jazz band, literary magazine, pep band, radio station, student government, student newspaper. 60 registered organizations, 5 honor societies, 5 religious organizations. 3 fraternities, 3 sororities. **Athletics (Intercollegiate):** *Men:* baseball, basketball, golf, tennis. *Women:* basketball, golf, softball, tennis, volleyball. **On-Campus Highlights:** Allgood Hall, Christenberry Field House, University Hall, Jaguar Student Activities Center, Maxwell Performing Arts Theater.

ADMISSIONS

Freshman Academic Profile: Average high school GPA 2.93. 95% from public high schools. SAT Math middle 50% range 430-540. SAT Critical Reading middle 50% range 440-540. ACT middle 50% range 17-21. Minimum paper TOEFL 500. **Basis for Candidate Selection:** *Important factors considered include:* academic GPA, rigor of secondary school record, standardized test scores. **Freshman Admission Requirements:** High school diploma is required and GED is accepted. *Academic units required:* 4 English, 4 mathematics, 3 science, 2 foreign language, 3 social studies. **Freshman Admission Statistics:** 2,418 applied, 57% admitted, 68% enrolled. **Transfer Admission Requirements:** college transcript(s), Minimum college GPA of 2.0 required. Lowest grade transferable D. **General Admission Information:** Application Fee $20. Nonfall registration accepted. Admission may be deferred for a maximum of Period is not limite. Credit and/or placement offered for CEEB Advanced Placement tests.

COSTS AND FINANCIAL AID

Average book expense $1,000. **Required Forms and Deadlines:** FAFSA, State aid form. **Notification of Awards:** Applicants will be notified of awards on or about 6/1. **Types of Aid:** *Need-based scholarships/grants:* Federal Pell, SEOG, state scholarships/grants, private scholarships, the school's own gift aid. *Loans:* Subsidized Stafford, Unsubsidized Stafford, PLUS, Federal Perkins, state loans, college/university loans from institutional funds, Alternative loans. *Student Employment:* Highest amount earned per year from on-campus jobs $10,637. **Financial Aid Statistics:** 73% freshmen, 67% undergrads receive need-based scholarship or grant aid. 25% freshmen, 29% undergrads receive non-need-based scholarship or grant aid. 67% freshmen, 65% undergrads receive need-based self-help aid. 0% freshmen, 2% undergrads receive athletic scholarships. 36% undergrads borrow to pay for school. Average cumulative indebtedness $5,914. **Criteria for awarding institutional aid:** *Non-need-based:* academics, alumni affiliation, art, athletics, job skills, leadership, minority status, music/drama, state/district residency.

AUGUSTANA COLLEGE (IL)

639 38th Street, Rock Island, IL 61201-2296
Phone: 309-794-7341 • **Financial Aid Phone:** 309-794-7207
E-mail: admissions@augustana.edu • **CEEB Code:** 1025
Fax: 309-794-7422 • **Website:** www.augustana.edu • **ACT Code:** 946

This private school, affiliated with the Lutheran Church, was founded in 1860. It has a 115-acre campus.

RATINGS

Admissions Selectivity Rating: 88   **Fire Safety Rating:** 88

STUDENTS AND FACULTY

Enrollment: 2,473. **Student Body:** 58% female, 42% male, 16% out-of-state, 2% international (29 countries represented). Asian 2%, African American 4%, Caucasian 76%, Hispanic 10%, Native American <1%
Retention and Graduation: 71% freshmen graduate within 4 years. 30% grads go on to further study within 1 year. 12% grads pursue arts and sciences degrees. 1% grads pursue law degrees. 6% grads pursue business degrees. 9% grads pursue medical degrees. **Faculty:** 195 full-time faculty, 91% hold PhDs, 44% are members of minority groups, 11% are women. 0% of classes are taught by teaching assistants.

ACADEMICS

Degrees: bachelor's. **Classes:** Most classes have 10–19 students. **Majors with Highest Enrollment:** Biology/Biological Sciences; Business Administration and Management; Psychology. **Special Study Options:** Accelerated program, double major, honors program, independent study, internships, liberal arts/career combination, student-designed major, study abroad, teacher certification program. **Honors programs:** Augustana has two tracks in first-year honors studies, Foundations and Logos. The Foundations program is a challenging interdisciplinary honors curriculum offering an intensive examination of the basic questions that have perplexed humans for centuries, and focuses on integrated learning and the development of critical thinking and writing skills. Logos is a challenging interdisciplinary honors curriculum with a special focus on how science has evolved across the centuries, how science has been used and viewed at particular historical moments, and how we live with the fruits of science today. Combined degree programs: Env. Mgt., Forestry, Occ. Therapy, Landscape Arch. **Disability Services:** Special programs offered to physically disabled students include reader services, tape recorders, tutors. **Career services:** Alumni network, alumni services, career/job search classes, career assessment, internships.

FACILITIES

Housing: Coed dorms, men's dorms, women's dorms, apartments for single students. 80% of campus accessible to physically disabled. **Special Academic Facilities/Equipment:** Educational technology building, art gallery, black culture house, Hispanic culture house, geology museum, on-campus preschool, immigration research center, scanning and transmission electron microscopes, nuclear magnetic resonance, atomic absorption, and diode array mass spectrophotometers, planetarium, observatory with celestron telescope, environmental field stations. **Computers:** 50% of classrooms, 30% of dorms, 100% of libraries, 100% of dining areas, 90% of student union, 25% of common outdoor areas have wireless network access. Students can register for classes online. Administrative functions (other than registration) can be performed online.

CAMPUS LIFE

Environment: City. **Activities:** Choral groups, concert band, dance, drama/theater, jazz band, literary magazine, music ensembles, musical theater, opera, pep band, radio station, student government, student newspaper, symphony orchestra, yearbook, Campus Ministries, International Student Organization, Model UN. 128 registered organizations, 15 honor societies, 5 religious organizations. 7 fraternities, 6 sororities. **Athletics (Intercollegiate):** *Men:* baseball, basketball, cross-country, diving, football, golf, soccer, swimming, tennis, track/field (outdoor), track/field (indoor), wrestling. *Women:* basketball, cross-country, diving, golf, lacrosse, soccer, softball, swimming, tennis, track/field (outdoor), track/field (indoor), volleyball. **On-Campus Highlights:** Thomas Tredway Libarary, Pepsico Recreation Center, Java 101-Coffee shop, F.W. Olin Center for Educational Technology, College Center. **Environmental Initiatives:** Recycling Program, LEEDS certification for new construction, including geothermal heating for newest housing, Farm to Fork Program - Food services practices with partnerships involving local agriculture producers, keeping small-scale and family businesses profitable.

ADMISSIONS

Freshman Academic Profile: Average high school GPA 3.29. 29% in top 10% of high school class, 66% in top 25% of high school class, 91% in top 50% of high school class. SAT Math middle 50% range 532.5-670. SAT Critical Reading middle 50% range 530-590. SAT Writing middle 50% range 490-600.

ACT middle 50% range 23-29. Minimum internet-based TOEFL 80. Minimum paper TOEFL 550. **Basis for Candidate Selection:** *Very important factors considered include:* Class rank, academic GPA, rigor of secondary school record. *Important factors considered include:* application essay, recommendation(s), standardized test scores, character/personal qualities, extracurricular activities, interview, level of applicant's interest, talent/ability. *Other factors considered include:* alumni/ae relation, geographical residence, racial/ethnic status, religious affiliation/commitment, volunteer work, work experience. **Freshman Admission Requirements:** High school diploma is required and GED is accepted. *Academic units required:* 3 English, 3 mathematics, 3 science, (2 science labs), 1 foreign language, 1 social studies, 1 history. **Freshman Admission Statistics:** 6,053 applied, 54% admitted, 22% enrolled. **Transfer Admission Requirements:** High school transcript, college transcript(s), statement of good standing from prior institution(s). Minimum college GPA of 2.0 required. Lowest grade transferable D. **General Admission Information:** Application Fee $35. Non-fall registration accepted. Credit and/or placement offered for CEEB Advanced Placement tests.

COSTS AND FINANCIAL AID

Required Forms and Deadlines: FAFSA, Institution's own financial aid form. **Types of Aid:** *Need-based scholarships/grants:* Federal Pell, SEOG, state scholarships/grants, private scholarships, the school's own gift aid. *Loans:* Subsidized Stafford, Unsubsidized Stafford, PLUS, Federal Perkins. *Student Employment:* Federal Work-Study Program available. Institutional employment available. Highest amount earned per year from on-campus jobs $900. Off-campus job opportunities are excellent. **Financial Aid Statistics:** 98% freshmen, 98% undergrads receive need-based scholarship or grant aid. 15% freshmen, 14% undergrads receive non-need-based scholarship or grant aid. 80% freshmen, 79% undergrads receive need-based self-help aid. 0% freshmen, 0% undergrads receive athletic scholarships. 99% freshmen, 99% undergrads receive any aid. 77% undergrads borrow to pay for school. Average cumulative indebtedness $25,483. **Criteria for awarding institutional aid:** *Non-need-based:* academics, alumni affiliation, art, leadership, music/drama, religious affiliation.

AUGUSTANA COLLEGE (SD)

2001 South Summit Avenue, Sioux Falls, SD 57197
Phone: 605-274-5516 • **Financial Aid Phone:** 605-274-5216
E-mail: admission@augie.edu • **CEEB Code:** 6015
Fax: 605-274-5518 • **Website:** www.augie.edu • **ACT Code:** 3902

This private school, affiliated with the Lutheran Church, was founded in 1860. It has a 100-acre campus.

RATINGS

Admissions Selectivity Rating: 88   **Fire Safety Rating:** 90

STUDENTS AND FACULTY

Enrollment: 1,608. **Student Body:** 60% female, 40% male, 52% out-of-state, 7% international (39 countries represented). Asian 1%, African American 2%, Caucasian 87%, Hispanic 2%, Native American <1%
Retention and Graduation: 81% freshmen return for sophomore year. 49% freshmen graduate within 4 years. 21% grads go on to further study within 1 year. 10% grads pursue arts and sciences degrees. 2% grads pursue law degrees. 10% grads pursue business degrees. 6% grads pursue medical degrees. **Faculty:** 127 full-time faculty, 83% hold PhDs, 45% are members of minority groups, 8% are women. 0% of classes are taught by teaching assistants.

ACADEMICS

Degrees: bachelor's, master's. **Classes:** Most classes have 10–19 students. Most lab/discussion sessions have fewer than 10 students. **Majors with Highest Enrollment:** Business Administration, Management and Operations; Registered Nursing/Registered Nurse; Education. **Special Study Options:** cooperative education program, cross-registration, double major, dual enrollment, exchange student program (domestic), external degree program, honors program, independent study, internships, liberal arts/career combination, study abroad, teacher certification program, Metro-Urban Studies through HECUA. January Abroad program through UMAIE. Washington, D.C. Semesters. Study Austrailia through EAN. Dual Degree Program in Engineering. Service-Learning Spring Breaks trips; Faculty-led Spring Breaks Abroad; Honors Courses in Western Civilization, Chemistry, and Religion. Civitas honors program for students with 27 ACT and 3.5 GPA. **Honors programs:** Our campus-wide, interdisciplinary Honors program is called Civitas (citizenship). Specific majors also offer departmental honors programs for students willing to accept academic challenges that go well beyond those required for graduation. **Disability Services:** Special programs offered to physically disabled students

include note-taking services, reader services, tape recorders, tutors. **Career services:** Alumni network, alumni services, career/job search classes, career assessment, internships, regional alumni. The city of Sioux Falls (151,000), along with Augustana alumni and connections, provides excellent opportunities for internships and research opportunities. It is the best laboratory for our students to apply their knowledge.

FACILITIES

Housing: Coed dorms, special housing for disabled students, apartments for married students, apartments for single students, Theme HousingHousing is available for students with children. 80% of campus accessible to physically disabled. **Special Academic Facilities/Equipment:** Center for Western Studies, Archeology Lab, Eide/Dalrymple Gallery, Center for Liturgical Art. **Computers:** 25% of classrooms, 25% of dorms, 100% of libraries, 100% of dining areas, 75% of student union, have wireless network access. Students can register for classes online. Administrative functions (other than registration) can be performed online.

CAMPUS LIFE

Environment: City. **Activities:** Choral groups, concert band, dance, drama/theater, jazz band, literary magazine, music ensembles, musical theater, opera, pep band, student government, student newspaper, student-run film society, symphony orchestra, yearbook, Campus Ministries, International Student Organization. 92 registered organizations, 13 honor societies, 9 religious organizations. **Athletics (Intercollegiate):** *Men:* baseball, basketball, cross-country, football, golf, tennis, track/field (outdoor), track/field (indoor), wrestling. *Women:* basketball, cheerleading, cross-country, golf, soccer, softball, tennis, track/field (outdoor), track/field (indoor), volleyball. **On-Campus Highlights:** Morrison Commons, The Huddle, Mikkelson Library, Elmen Center, Center for Visual Arts, The Madsen Center, home to our social science programs, is also a popular place for students to gather and study, or use the computer lab. With newly renovated and refurbished lounges, our resident halls also serve as gathering areas for students to converse, watch TV, play ping pong or pool. **Environmental Initiatives:** Examples include: Additional recycle bins placed in all campus buildings; Dining Services has decreased food and beverage waste by 50% through redesigning of trays and cups. They have also cut back on paper waste by installing high-definition televisions to post announcements and by substituting post-recycled cups and napkins for students on-the-go. Green bike program offers students the chance to use bikes for free transportation on and around campus. Student group, Augie Green, has started an Augustana garden and a program called "trash talkers".

ADMISSIONS

Freshman Academic Profile: Average high school GPA 3.7. 31% in top 10% of high school class, 65% in top 25% of high school class, 89% in top 50% of high school class. 85% from public high schools. ACT middle 50% range 23-28. Minimum internet-based TOEFL 79. Minimum paper TOEFL 550. **Basis for Candidate Selection:** *Very important factors considered include:* academic GPA, standardized test scores. *Important factors considered include:* Class rank, application essay, recommendation(s), rigor of secondary school record, extracurricular activities. *Other factors considered include:* interview, volunteer work, work experience. **Freshman Admission Requirements:** High school diploma is required and GED is accepted. **Freshman Admission Statistics:** 1,545 applied, 61% admitted, 42% enrolled. **Transfer Admission Requirements:** High school transcript, college transcript(s), essay or personal statement, Minimum college GPA of 2.2 required. Lowest grade transferable C-. **General Admission Information:** Notification on a rolling basis, beginning on or about 10/1. Nonfall registration not accepted. Admission may be deferred for a maximum of 1 year. Credit offered for CEEB Advanced Placement tests.

COSTS AND FINANCIAL AID

Annual tuition $28,764. Room and board $7,286. Required fees $450. Average book expense $1,000. **Required Forms and Deadlines:** FAFSA. **Notification of Awards:** Applicants will be notified of awards on a rolling basis beginning 4/1. **Types of Aid:** *Need-based scholarships/grants:* Federal Pell, SEOG, state scholarships/grants, private scholarships, the school's own gift aid. *Loans:* Direct Subsidized Stafford, Direct Unsubsidized Stafford, Direct PLUS, Subsidized Stafford, Unsubsidized Stafford, PLUS, Federal Perkins, Federal Nursing, college/university loans from institutional funds. *Student Employment:* Federal Work-Study Program available. Institutional employment available. Highest amount earned per year from on-campus jobs $1,794. Off-campus job opportunities are excellent. **Financial Aid Statistics:** 100% freshmen, 100% undergrads receive need-based scholarship or grant aid. 98% freshmen, 98% undergrads receive non-need-based scholarship or grant aid. 68% freshmen, 76% undergrads receive need-based self-help aid. 15% freshmen, 12% undergrads receive athletic scholarships. 99% freshmen, 99% undergrads receive any aid. 74% undergrads borrow to pay for school. Average cumulative indebtedness $26,428. **Criteria for awarding institutional aid:** *Non-need-based:* academics, alumni affiliation, art, athletics, leadership, minority status, music/drama, religious affiliation, state/district residency.

AURORA UNIVERSITY

347 South Gladstone Ave, Aurora, IL 60506
Phone: 630-844-5533 · **Financial Aid Phone:** 630-844-6190
E-mail: admission@aurora.edu · **CEEB Code:** 1027
Fax: 630-844-5535 · **Website:** www.aurora.edu · **ACT Code:** 950

This private school was founded in 1893. It has a 30-acre campus.

RATINGS

Admissions Selectivity Rating: 77   **Fire Safety Rating:** 80

STUDENTS AND FACULTY

Enrollment: 2,614. **Student Body:** 65% female, 35% male, 8% out-of-state, 0% international (2 countries represented). Asian 3%, African American 8%, Caucasian 71%, Hispanic 14%, Native American <1%
Retention and Graduation: 74% freshmen return for sophomore year. 42% freshmen graduate within 4 years. 54% freshmen graduate within 6 years.
Faculty: 116 full-time faculty, 86% hold PhDs, 49% are members of minority groups, 9% are women. 0% of classes are taught by teaching assistants.

ACADEMICS

Degrees: bachelor's, master's, post-bachelor's certificate, post-master's certificate. **Classes:** Most classes have 10–19 students. Most lab/discussion sessions have 10–19 students. **Majors with Highest Enrollment:** Elementary Education and Teaching; Registered Nursing/Registered Nurse; Business Administration and Management. **Special Study Options:** Accelerated program, cross-registration, double major, honors program, independent study, internships, liberal arts/career combination, student-designed major, study abroad, teacher certification program. **Honors programs:** Honors Program including honors seminars, honors section of some general education courses and a senior honors project. **Disability Services:** Special programs offered to physically disabled students include note-taking services, reader services, tape recorders, tutors. **Career services:** Alumni network, alumni services, career/job search classes, career assessment, internships.

FACILITIES

Housing: Coed dorms. 95% of campus accessible to physically disabled. **Special Academic Facilities/Equipment:** Schingoethe Center for Native American Culture Downstairs Dunham Gallery Center For Faith And Action Perry Theatre in the Aurora Foundation Center for Community Education **Computers:** 100% of classrooms, 80% of dorms, 100% of libraries, 100% of dining areas, 100% of student union, 90% of common outdoor areas have wireless network access. Administrative functions (other than registration) can be performed online.

CAMPUS LIFE

Environment: City. **Activities:** Choral groups, drama/theater, literary magazine, pep band, radio station, student government, student newspaper, Campus Ministries, Model UN. 49 registered organizations, 2 honor societies, 1 religious organization. 1 fraternity, 4 sororities. **Athletics (Intercollegiate):** *Men:* baseball, basketball, cross-country, football, golf, soccer, tennis, track/field (outdoor), track/field (indoor). *Women:* basketball, cross-country, golf, soccer, softball, tennis, track/field (outdoor), track/field (indoor), volleyball. **On-Campus Highlights:** The Spartan Spot, Fitness Center, The Learning Center, Computer Labs, Vago Stadium. **Environmental Initiatives:** Campus-wide recycling Use of green chemicals for cleaning. Energy conservation audit for campus-wide lighting.

ADMISSIONS

Freshman Academic Profile: Average high school GPA 3.3. 12% in top 10% of high school class, 38% in top 25% of high school class, 73% in top 50% of high school class. 92% from public high schools. SAT Math middle 50% range 440-510. SAT Critical Reading middle 50% range 450-520. ACT middle 50% range 20-24. Minimum internet-based TOEFL 79. Minimum paper TOEFL 550. **Basis for Candidate Selection:** *Very important factors considered include:* Class rank, academic GPA, rigor of secondary school record, standardized test scores, interview. *Important factors considered include:* alumni/ae relation, character/personal qualities, extracurricular activities. *Other factors considered include:* application essay, recommendation(s), first generation, level of applicant's interest, talent/ability, volunteer work, work experience. **Freshman Admission Requirements:** High school diploma is required and GED is accepted. *Academic units required:* 4 English, 3 mathematics, 3 science, 3 social studies, 3 academic electives. **Freshman Admission Statistics:** 1,872 applied, 73% admitted, 37% enrolled. **Transfer Admission Requirements:** college transcript(s), statement of good standing from prior institution(s). Minimum college GPA of 2.0 required. Lowest grade transferable C. **General Admission Information:** Application Fee $25. Regular application deadline 5/1. Notification on a rolling basis, beginning on or about 9/1. Nonfall registration accepted.

Admission may be deferred for a maximum of two years. Credit and/or placement offered for CEEB Advanced Placement tests.

COSTS AND FINANCIAL AID

Annual tuition $19,250. Room and board $9,100. Required fees $200. Average book expense $1,000. **Required Forms and Deadlines:** FAFSA. **Notification of Awards:** Applicants will be notified of awards on a rolling basis beginning 3/1. **Types of Aid:** *Need-based scholarships/grants:* Federal Pell, SEOG, state scholarships/grants, private scholarships, the school's own gift aid. *Loans:* Subsidized Stafford, Unsubsidized Stafford, PLUS, Federal Perkins, college/university loans from institutional funds. *Student Employment:* Federal Work-Study Program available. Institutional employment available. Highest amount earned per year from on-campus jobs $4,960. Off-campus job opportunities are excellent. **Financial Aid Statistics:** 78% freshmen, 81% undergrads receive need-based scholarship or grant aid. 100% freshmen, 93% undergrads receive non-need-based scholarship or grant aid. 84% freshmen, 86% undergrads receive need-based self-help aid. 0% freshmen, 0% undergrads receive athletic scholarships. 100% freshmen, 98% undergrads receive any aid. 80% undergrads borrow to pay for school. Average cumulative indebtedness $20,382. **Criteria for awarding institutional aid:** *Non-need-based:* academics, alumni affiliation, art, music/drama, religious affiliation, state/district residency.

AUSTIN COLLEGE

900 North Grand Ave, Suite 6N, Sherman, TX 75090-4400
Phone: 903-813-3000 · **Financial Aid Phone:** 903-813-2900
E-mail: admission@austincollege.edu · **CEEB Code:** 6016
Fax: 903-813-3198 · **Website:** www.austincollege.edu · **ACT Code:** 4058

This private school, affiliated with the Presbyterian Church, was founded in 1849. It has a 70-acre campus.

RATINGS

Admissions Selectivity Rating: 88   **Fire Safety Rating:** 76

STUDENTS AND FACULTY

Enrollment: 1,272. **Student Body:** 52% female, 48% male, 10% out-of-state, 3% international (15 countries represented). Asian 14%, African American 7%, Caucasian 56%, Hispanic 19%, Native American 1%
Retention and Graduation: 86% freshmen return for sophomore year. 72% freshmen graduate within 4 years. 35% grads go on to further study within 1 year. 3% grads pursue law degrees. 9% grads pursue medical degrees. **Faculty:** 91 full-time faculty, 98% hold PhDs, 32% are members of minority groups, 11% are women. 0% of classes are taught by teaching assistants.

ACADEMICS

Degrees: bachelor's, master's. **Classes:** Most classes have 10–19 students. Most lab/discussion sessions have fewer than 10 students. **Majors with Highest Enrollment:** Biology/Biological Sciences; Business/Commerce; Psychology. **Special Study Options:** double major, exchange student program (domestic), honors program, independent study, internships, student-designed major, study abroad, teacher certification program, Phi Beta Kappa. Combined degree programs: 3-2 Program in Engineeri with UT, Dal and Wash Univ. **Disability Services:** Special programs offered to physically disabled students include tutors. **Career services:** Alumni network, alumni services, career/job search classes, career assessment, internships

FACILITIES

Housing: Coed dorms, special housing for disabled students, men's dorms, women's dorms, apartments for single students, Jordan Family Language House. 99% of campus accessible to physically disabled. **Special Academic Facilities/Equipment:** Tissue culture facility, high-performance numerics and graphics computing facility. **Computers:** 30% of classrooms, 100% of dorms, 100% of libraries, 100% of dining areas, 100% of student union, 30% of common outdoor areas have wireless network access. Students can register for classes online. Administrative functions (other than registration) can be performed online.

CAMPUS LIFE

Environment: Town. **Activities:** Choral groups, dance, drama/theater, jazz band, literary magazine, music ensembles, musical theater, pep band, student government, student newspaper, symphony orchestra, yearbook, Campus Ministries, International Student Organization, Model UN. 52 registered organizations, 15 honor societies, 6 religious organizations. 6 fraternities, 6 sororities. **Athletics (Intercollegiate):** *Men:* baseball, basketball, football, soccer, swimming, tennis. *Women:* basketball, soccer, softball, swimming, tennis, volleyball. **On-Campus Highlights:** Wright Campus Center, Jordan Family Language House, Verde Dickey Fitness Pavilion, Abell Library, Residence hall facilities, Roo Suites, a suite-style residence facility for upperclass students is the favored residential experience. **Environmental Initiatives:** Board approval of Climate Action Plan to reduce emissions to 0 by 2020. Month-long student dorm energy saving competition Construct a new science building to be LEED silver certified.

ADMISSIONS

Freshman Academic Profile: Average high school GPA 3.45. 24% in top 10% of high school class, 55% in top 25% of high school class, 87% in top 50% of high school class. 77% from public high schools. SAT Math middle 50% range 540-650. SAT Critical Reading middle 50% range 530-670. SAT Writing middle 50% range 520-640. ACT middle 50% range 22-27. Minimum paper TOEFL 550. **Basis for Candidate Selection:** *Very important factors considered include:* academic GPA, rigor of secondary school record. *Important factors considered include:* Class rank, application essay, recommendation(s), standardized test scores, character/personal qualities, extracurricular activities, talent/ability. *Other factors considered include:* alumni/ae relation, first generation, geographical residence, interview, racial/ethnic status, religious affiliation/commitment, state residency, volunteer work, work experience. **Freshman Admission Requirements:** High school diploma is required and GED is accepted. *Academic units required:* 4 English, 3 mathematics, 3 science, (2 science labs), 2 foreign language, 2 social studies, 1 visual/performing arts, 1 academic electives. **Freshman Admission Statistics:** 3,038 applied, 54% admitted, 22% enrolled. **Transfer Admission Requirements:** college transcript(s), essay or personal statement, statement of good standing from prior institution(s). Minimum college GPA of 3.0 required. Lowest grade transferable C. **General Admission Information:** Application Fee $35. Regular application deadline 5/1. Notification on a rolling basis, beginning on or about 12/15. Nonfall registration accepted. Admission may be deferred for a maximum of 1 year. Credit and/or placement offered for CEEB Advanced Placement tests.

COSTS AND FINANCIAL AID

Required Forms and Deadlines: FAFSA. **Notification of Awards:** Applicants will be notified of awards on a rolling basis beginning 3/1. **Types of Aid:** *Need-based scholarships/grants:* Federal Pell, SEOG, state scholarships/grants, private scholarships, the school's own gift aid. *Loans:* Subsidized Stafford, Unsubsidized Stafford, PLUS, Federal Perkins, state loans, college/university loans from institutional funds, Alternative loans through various sources. *Student Employment:* Federal Work-Study Program available. Institutional employment available. Highest amount earned per year from on-campus jobs $1,164. Off-campus job opportunities are good. **Financial Aid Statistics:** 100% freshmen, 99% undergrads receive need-based scholarship or grant aid. 28% freshmen, 16% undergrads receive non-need-based scholarship or grant aid. 71% freshmen, 66% undergrads receive need-based self-help aid. 0% freshmen, 0% undergrads receive athletic scholarships. 97% freshmen, 98% undergrads receive any aid. **Criteria for awarding institutional aid:** *Non-need-based:* academics, alumni affiliation, art, leadership, music/drama, religious affiliation, state/district residency.

AUSTIN PEAY STATE UNIVERSITY

P.O. Box 4548, Clarksville, TN 37044
Phone: (931) 221-7661
E-mail: admissions@apsu.edu · **CEEB Code:** 1028
Fax: (931) 221-6168 · **Website:** www.apsu.edu · **ACT Code:** 3944

This public school was founded in 1927. It has a 210-acre campus.

RATINGS

Admissions Selectivity Rating: 74   Fire Safety Rating: 60*

STUDENTS AND FACULTY

Enrollment: 9,003. **Student Body:** 59% female, 41% male, 11% out-of-state, 0% international (13 countries represented). Asian 2%, African American 20%, Caucasian 65%, Hispanic 6%, Native American <1%
Retention and Graduation: 72% freshmen return for sophomore year. 17% freshmen graduate within 4 years. 39% freshmen graduate within 6 years. **Faculty:** 359 full-time faculty, 49% are members of minority groups, 12% are women. 0% of classes are taught by teaching assistants.

ACADEMICS

Degrees: associate, bachelor's, certificate, master's, post-bachelor's certificate, post-master's certificate, terminal associate, transfer associate. **Classes:** Most classes have 20–29 students. Most lab/discussion sessions have 20–29 students.

Special Study Options: Accelerated program, cooperative education program, distance learning, double major, dual enrollment, English as a Second Language (ESL), honors program, independent study, internships, study abroad, teacher certification program, Servicemembers Opportunity College (SOC) for associate and bachelor's degrees. **Disability Services:** Special programs offered to physically disabled students include note-taking services, reader services, tutors. **Career services:** career/job search classes, career assessment, internships.

FACILITIES

Housing: Coed dorms, special housing for disabled students, men's dorms, women's dorms, fraternity/sorority housing, apartments for married students, apartments for single students, For faculty/staff. 100% of campus accessible to physically disabled. **Special Academic Facilities/Equipment:** Art museum, biology museum, language lab, demonstration farm, 21st century classroom.

CAMPUS LIFE

Environment: Village. **Activities:** Choral groups, concert band, dance, drama/theater, jazz band, literary magazine, marching band, music ensembles, musical theater, opera, pep band, radio station, student government, student newspaper, student-run film society, symphony orchestra, television station, yearbook, Campus Ministries, International Student Organization. 50 registered organizations, 13 honor societies, 10 religious organizations. 8 fraternities, 6 sororities. **Athletics (Intercollegiate):** *Men:* baseball, basketball, cheerleading, cross-country, football, golf, tennis. *Women:* basketball, cheerleading, cross-country, golf, riflery, soccer, softball, tennis, track/field (outdoor), volleyball. **On-Campus Highlights:** University Center, Sundquist Science Complex, Hand Village, Dunn Center.

ADMISSIONS

Freshman Academic Profile: Average high school GPA 3.23. 13% in top 10% of high school class, 36% in top 25% of high school class, 73% in top 50% of high school class. 95% from public high schools. SAT Math middle 50% range 390-605. SAT Critical Reading middle 50% range 375-540. ACT middle 50% range 19-24. Minimum paper TOEFL 500. **Basis for Candidate Selection:** *Very important factors considered include:* academic GPA, standardized test scores. *Other factors considered include:* rigor of secondary school record. **Freshman Admission Requirements:** High school diploma is required and GED is accepted. *Academic units required:* 4 English, 3 mathematics, 2 science, (1 science labs), 2 foreign language, 1 social studies, 1 history, 1 Visual/Performing Arts. **Freshman Admission Statistics:** 3,307 applied, 89% admitted, 51% enrolled. **Transfer Admission Requirements:** college transcript(s), Lowest grade transferable D. **General Admission Information:** Application Fee $15. Regular application deadline 7/29. Nonfall registration accepted. Admission may be deferred for a maximum of 12 months. Credit offered for CEEB Advanced Placement tests.

COSTS AND FINANCIAL AID

Average book expense $1,550. **Required Forms and Deadlines:** FAFSA. **Notification of Awards:** Applicants will be notified of awards on a rolling basis beginning 5/1. **Types of Aid:** *Need-based scholarships/grants:* Federal Pell, SEOG, state scholarships/grants, private scholarships, the school's own gift aid, Corporate. *Loans:* Subsidized Stafford, Unsubsidized Stafford, PLUS, Federal Perkins. *Student Employment:* Federal Work-Study Program available. Institutional employment available. Off-campus job opportunities are good. **Financial Aid Statistics:** 81% freshmen, 86% undergrads receive need-based scholarship or grant aid. 82% freshmen, 54% undergrads receive non-need-based scholarship or grant aid. 58% freshmen, 68% undergrads receive need-based self-help aid. 1% freshmen, 1% undergrads receive athletic scholarships. 60% undergrads borrow to pay for school. Average cumulative indebtedness $28,800. **Criteria for awarding institutional aid:** *Non-need-based:* academics, alumni affiliation, art, athletics, leadership, music/drama, state/district residency.

AVERETT UNIVERSITY

420 West Main Street, Danville, VA 24541
Phone: 434-791-5600 · **Financial Aid Phone:** 434-791-5890 · **CEEB Code:** 5017
Fax: 434-797-2784 · **Website:** www.averett.edu · **ACT Code:** 4338

This private school was founded in 1859. It has a 19-acre campus.

RATINGS

Admissions Selectivity Rating: 79   Fire Safety Rating: 94

STUDENTS AND FACULTY

Enrollment: 840. **Student Body:** 52% female, 48% male, 31% out-of-state, 5% international (11 countries represented). Asian 1%, African American 28%, Caucasian 61%, Hispanic 4%, Native American 1%
Retention and Graduation: 22% freshmen graduate within 4 years. **Faculty:** 56 full-time faculty, 73% hold PhDs, 54% are members of minority groups, 5% are women. 0% of classes are taught by teaching assistants.

The Princeton Review's Complete Book of Colleges

ACADEMICS

Degrees: associate, bachelor's, master's, transfer associate. **Classes:** Most classes have 10–19 students. Most lab/discussion sessions have 10–19 students. **Majors with Highest Enrollment:** Pre-Medicine/Pre-Medical Studies; Nursing Science; Criminal Justice/Law Enforcement Administration. **Special Study Options:** Accelerated program, cooperative education program, cross-registration, distance learning, double major, dual enrollment, exchange student program (domestic), honors program, independent study, internships, student-designed major, study abroad, teacher certification program, Also offered: Interdisciplinary studies and Leadership studies. Undergraduates may take grad level classes. Some online courses available. **Honors programs:** Averett's Honors Program gives students the opportunity to go a step beyond regular classroom study. Honors students explore, in-depth, selected areas of academics. Participation in the Honors Program demonstrates a commitment to scholarship and will give students an edge in graduate study or in the job market. To earn the honors distinction, approximately 20% of all coursework completed must carry honors credit. The program culminates with a senior honors project. Honors Program students may also participate in the Honors Association and attend conferences, social activities and cultural performances. **Disability Services:** Special programs offered to physically disabled students include note-taking services, reader services, tape recorders, tutors. **Career services:** Alumni network, alumni services, career/job search classes, career assessment, internships, regional alumni.

FACILITIES

Housing: Coed dorms, men's dorms, women's dorms, apartments for single students. 73% of campus accessible to physically disabled. **Special Academic Facilities/Equipment:** Averett's Flight Center located 4 miles from the main campus at Danville Regional Airport has two runways (one with ILS approach), automated weather system, and UNICOM service. Averett's facility houses aircraft, areas for ground instruction, simulator rooms, technology center. Averett's 100-acre Equestrian Center is a 15-minute drive from the main campus. It houses an indoor ring, 40 stalls with removable partitions, 3 tack rooms, wash room for horses and equipment, breeding area, offices, and a laboratory. The outdoor facilities include a round pen, riding ring, jumping area, pastures, and cross-country trails. **Computers:** 100% of libraries, 100% of dining areas, 100% of student union, have wireless network access. Students can register for classes online. Administrative functions (other than registration) can be performed online.

CAMPUS LIFE

Environment: Town. **Activities:** Choral groups, drama/theater, literary magazine, musical theater, student government, student newspaper, International Student Organization. 30 registered organizations, 4 honor societies, 4 religious organizations. 1 fraternity, 1 sorority. **Athletics (Intercollegiate):** *Men:* baseball, basketball, cheerleading, cross-country, equestrian sports, football, golf, soccer, tennis. *Women:* basketball, cheerleading, cross-country, equestrian sports, soccer, softball, tennis, volleyball. **On-Campus Highlights:** Student Center, Grant Athletic Center (North Campus), Equestrian Center, Airport Facilities, Jut's Café.

ADMISSIONS

Freshman Academic Profile: Average high school GPA 3.23. 11% in top 10% of high school class, 30% in top 25% of high school class, 58% in top 50% of high school class. SAT Math middle 50% range 420-518. SAT Critical Reading middle 50% range 410-510. ACT middle 50% range 16-22. Minimum internet-based TOEFL 61. Minimum paper TOEFL 500. **Basis for Candidate Selection:** *Very important factors considered include:* academic GPA, rigor of secondary school record. *Important factors considered include:* Class rank, standardized test scores. *Other factors considered include:* application essay, recommendation(s), alumni/ae relation, character/personal qualities, extracurricular activities, interview, level of applicant's interest, talent/ability, volunteer work, work experience. **Freshman Admission Requirements:** High school diploma is required and GED is accepted. *Academic units required:* 4 English, 3 mathematics, 3 science, (3 science labs), 0 foreign language, 3 social studies, 0 history, 0 visual/performing arts, 0 computer science, 3 academic electives. **Freshman Admission Statistics:** 1,878 applied, 60% admitted, 19% enrolled. **Transfer Admission Requirements:** college transcript(s), statement of good standing from prior institution(s). Minimum college GPA of 2.0 required. Lowest grade transferable C. **General Admission Information:** Regular application deadline 7/15. Nonfall registration accepted. Admission may be deferred for a maximum of 1 year. Credit and/or placement offered for CEEB Advanced Placement tests.

COSTS AND FINANCIAL AID

Annual tuition $29,150. Room and board $8,600. Average book expense $1,000. **Required Forms and Deadlines:** FAFSA, State aid form. **Notification of Awards:** Applicants will be notified of awards on a rolling basis beginning 2/15. **Types of Aid:** *Need-based scholarships/grants:* Federal Pell, SEOG, state scholarships/grants, private scholarships, the school's own gift aid. *Loans:* Subsidized Stafford, Unsubsidized Stafford, PLUS, Federal Perkins, state loans,

college/university loans from institutional funds, Private. *Student Employment:* Federal Work-Study Program available. Institutional employment available. Highest amount earned per year from on-campus jobs $2,000. Off-campus job opportunities are fair. **Financial Aid Statistics:** 100% freshmen, 100% undergrads receive need-based scholarship or grant aid. 10% freshmen, 8% undergrads receive non-need-based scholarship or grant aid. 82% freshmen, 83% undergrads receive need-based self-help aid. 0% freshmen, 0% undergrads receive athletic scholarships. 99% freshmen, 99% undergrads receive any aid. 73% undergrads borrow to pay for school. Average cumulative indebtedness $31,876. **Criteria for awarding institutional aid:** *Non-need-based:* academics, alumni affiliation, art, leadership, minority status, music/drama, state/district residency.

AVILA UNIVERSITY

11901 Wornall Road, Kansas City, MO 64145-1698
Phone: 816-942-8400
E-mail: admissions@mail.avila.edu • **CEEB Code:** 6109
Fax: 816-942-3362 • **Website:** www.avila.edu • **ACT Code:** 2278

This private school, affiliated with the Roman Catholic Church, was founded in 1916. It has a 48-acre campus.

RATINGS

Admissions Selectivity Rating: 84 **Fire Safety Rating:** 60*

STUDENTS AND FACULTY

Enrollment: 1,096. **Student Body:** 64% female, 36% male, 34% out-of-state, 3% international. Asian 1%, African American 18%, Caucasian 70%, Hispanic 4%, Native American 1%
Retention and Graduation: 69% freshmen return for sophomore year. 30% freshmen graduate within 4 years. 36% freshmen graduate within 6 years. 40% grads go on to further study within 1 year. 20% grads pursue arts and sciences degrees. 2% grads pursue law degrees. 15% grads pursue business degrees. 3% grads pursue medical degrees. **Faculty:** 63 full-time faculty, 71% hold PhDs, 63% are members of minority groups, 3% are women. 0% of classes are taught by teaching assistants.

ACADEMICS

Degrees: bachelor's, certificate, master's. **Classes:** Most classes have fewer than 10 students. **Majors with Highest Enrollment:** Psychology Business/Commerce. **Special Study Options:** Accelerated program, double major, dual enrollment, English as a Second Language (ESL), independent study, internships, study abroad, teacher certification program.

FACILITIES

Housing: Coed dorms.

CAMPUS LIFE

Environment: Metropolis. **Activities:** Choral groups, drama/theater, literary magazine, student government, student newspaper, television station 12 religious organizations. **Athletics (Intercollegiate):** *Men:* baseball, basketball, football, soccer, volleyball. *Women:* basketball, cheerleading, golf, soccer, softball, volleyball.

ADMISSIONS

Freshman Academic Profile: Average high school GPA 3.2. 17% in top 10% of high school class, 39% in top 25% of high school class, 74% in top 50% of high school class. 92% from public high schools. ACT middle 50% range 18-25. Minimum paper TOEFL 550. **Basis for Candidate Selection:** *Very important factors considered include:* rigor of secondary school record, standardized test scores. *Other factors considered include:* Class rank, application essay, recommendation(s), character/personal qualities, extracurricular activities, interview, talent/ability. **Freshman Admission Requirements:** High school diploma is required and GED is accepted. **Freshman Admission Statistics:** 936 applied, 42% admitted, 38% enrolled. **Transfer Admission Requirements:** college transcript(s), Minimum college GPA of 2.0 required. Lowest grade transferable C. **General Admission Information:** Notification on a rolling basis, beginning on or about 9/4. Nonfall registration accepted. Admission may be deferred for a maximum of 12 months. Credit and/or placement offered for CEEB Advanced Placement tests.

COSTS AND FINANCIAL AID

Annual tuition $14,700. Room and board $5,300. Required fees $187. Average book expense $800. **Required Forms and Deadlines:** FAFSA, Institution's own financial aid form. **Notification of Awards:** Applicants will be notified of awards on a rolling basis beginning 2/15. **Types of Aid:** *Need-based scholarships/grants:* Federal Pell, SEOG, state scholarships/grants. *Loans:* Subsidized Stafford, Unsubsidized Stafford, PLUS, Federal Perkins. *Student Employment:*

Federal Work-Study Program available. Institutional employment available. Highest amount earned per year from on-campus jobs $1,500. **Financial Aid Statistics:** 66% freshmen, 70% undergrads receive need-based scholarship or grant aid. 100% freshmen, 80% undergrads receive non-need-based scholarship or grant aid. 100% freshmen, 90% undergrads receive need-based self-help aid. 100% freshmen, 70% undergrads receive athletic scholarships. 75% undergrads borrow to pay for school. **Criteria for awarding institutional aid:** *Non-need-based:* academics, alumni affiliation, art, athletics, music/drama, religious affiliation, state/district residency.

AZUSA PACIFIC UNIVERSITY

PO Box 7000, Azusa, CA 91702-7000
Phone: 626-812-3016 · **Financial Aid Phone:** 626-812-3009
E-mail: admissions@apu.edu · **CEEB Code:** 4596
Fax: 626-812-3096 · **Website:** www.apu.edu

This private school, affiliated with the Christian (Nondenominational) Church, was founded in 1899. It has a 103-acre campus.

RATINGS

Admissions Selectivity Rating: 82   **Fire Safety Rating:** 61

STUDENTS AND FACULTY

Enrollment: 6,160. **Student Body:** 64% female, 36% male, 18% out-of-state, 2% international (41 countries represented). Asian 9%, African American 5%, Caucasian 47%, Hispanic 26%, Native American <1% **Retention and Graduation:** 85% freshmen return for sophomore year. 47% freshmen graduate within 4 years. **Faculty:** 447 full-time faculty, 67% hold PhDs, 53% are members of minority groups, 27% are women. 0% of classes are taught by teaching assistants.

ACADEMICS

Degrees: bachelor's, master's. **Classes:** Most classes have 10–19 students. Most lab/discussion sessions have 10–19 students. **Majors with Highest Enrollment:** Business, Management, Marketing, and Related Support Services Psychology. **Special Study Options:** Accelerated program, cooperative education program, distance learning, double major, English as a Second Language (ESL), exchange student program (domestic), honors program, independent study, internships, study abroad, teacher certification program. Combined degree programs: BA/MA. **Career services:** career/job search classes, career assessment, internships.

FACILITIES

Housing: Coed dorms, men's dorms, women's dorms, apartments for single students. 100% of campus accessible to physically disabled. **Special Academic Facilities/Equipment:** Electron microscope. **Computers:** 100% of classrooms, 100% of dorms, 100% of libraries, 100% of dining areas, 100% of student union, 100% of common outdoor areas have wireless network access. Students can register for classes online. Administrative functions (other than registration) can be performed online.

CAMPUS LIFE

Environment: Town. **Activities:** Choral groups, concert band, drama/theater, jazz band, marching band, music ensembles, musical theater, opera, pep band, radio station, student government, student newspaper, symphony orchestra, television station, yearbook. 30 registered organizations, 7 honor societies. **Athletics (Intercollegiate):** *Men:* baseball, basketball, cross-country, football, soccer, tennis, track/field (outdoor), volleyball. *Women:* basketball, cheerleading, cross-country, diving, soccer, softball, swimming, tennis, track/field (outdoor), volleyball, water polo. **On-Campus Highlights:** Coffee Shops, Cougars' Den (Dining Facility), An Athletic Facility, Darling Library, Cougar Dome.

ADMISSIONS

Freshman Academic Profile: Average high school GPA 3.64. 25% in top 10% of high school class, 55% in top 25% of high school class, 86% in top 50% of high school class. SAT Math middle 50% range 490-540. SAT Critical Reading middle 50% range 490-540. SAT Writing middle 50% range 490-530. ACT middle 50% range 21-24. Minimum paper TOEFL 500. **Basis for Candidate Selection:** *Very important factors considered include:* Class rank, application essay, academic GPA, recommendation(s), standardized test scores. *Important factors considered include:* character/personal qualities, state residency. *Other factors considered include:* rigor of secondary school record, alumni/ae relation, extracurricular activities, first generation, interview, level of applicant's interest, racial/ethnic status, talent/ability, volunteer work, work experience. **Freshman Admission Requirements:** High school diploma is required and GED is accepted. **Freshman Admission Statistics:** 5,202 applied, 82% admitted, 33% enrolled. **Transfer Admission Requirements:** college transcript(s), essay or personal statement, statement of good standing from prior institution(s).

Minimum college GPA of 2.2 required. Lowest grade transferable C. **General Admission Information:** Application Fee $45. Regular application deadline 6/1. Regular notification 4/1. Nonfall registration accepted. Credit offered for CEEB Advanced Placement tests.

COSTS AND FINANCIAL AID

Annual tuition $32,516. Room and board $8,990. Required fees $580. Average book expense $1,746. **Notification of Awards:** Applicants will be notified of awards on a rolling basis beginning 3/1. **Types of Aid:** *Need-based scholarships/grants:* Federal Pell, SEOG, state scholarships/grants, private scholarships, the school's own gift aid, Federal Nursing Scholarships. *Loans:* Subsidized Stafford, Unsubsidized Stafford, PLUS, Federal Perkins, Federal Nursing. *Student Employment:* Federal Work-Study Program available. Institutional employment available. Highest amount earned per year from on-campus jobs $8,000. Off-campus job opportunities are good. **Financial Aid Statistics:** 86% freshmen, 87% undergrads receive need-based scholarship or grant aid. 80% freshmen, 76% undergrads receive non-need-based scholarship or grant aid. 59% freshmen, 67% undergrads receive need-based self-help aid. 4% freshmen, 3% undergrads receive athletic scholarships. 90% undergrads receive any aid. 74% undergrads borrow to pay for school. Average cumulative indebtedness $17,037. **Criteria for awarding institutional aid:** *Non-need-based:* academics, athletics, leadership, minority status, music/drama, religious affiliation.

BABSON COLLEGE

Best 380

Lunder Hall, Babson Park, MA 2457
Phone: 781-239-5522 · **Financial Aid Phone:** 781-239-4015
E-mail: ugradadmission@babson.edu · **CEEB Code:** 2121
Fax: 781-239-4006 · **Website:** www.babson.edu · **ACT Code:** 1780

This private school was founded in 1919. It has a 370-acre campus.

RATINGS

Admissions Selectivity Rating: 93   **Fire Safety Rating:** 90

STUDENTS AND FACULTY

Enrollment: 2,107. **Student Body:** 47% female, 53% male, 72% out-of-state, 27% international (72 countries represented). Asian 11%, African American 5%, Caucasian 39%, Hispanic 10%, Native American <1% **Retention and Graduation:** 94% freshmen return for sophomore year. 82% freshmen graduate within 4 years. 5% grads go on to further study within 1 year. **Faculty:** 169 full-time faculty, 88% hold PhDs, 38% are members of minority groups, 17% are women. 0% of classes are taught by teaching assistants.

ACADEMICS

Degrees: bachelor's, master's, post-master's certificate. **Classes:** Most classes have 30-39 students. **Majors with Highest Enrollment:** Business Administration and Management. **Special Study Options:** cross-registration, exchange student program (domestic), honors program, independent study, internships, liberal arts/career combination, study abroad, We offer 26 concentrations which provide groupings of courses that help students choose a coherent set of courses for academic and external recognition. **Honors programs:** The Honors Program consists of three components in which participants add to their academic and cocurricular development. These include honors courses, an honors project and an international experience. Combined degree programs: BS/MS In Accounting. **Disability Services:** Special programs offered to physically disabled students include note-taking services, reader services, tape recorders. **Career services:** Alumni network, alumni services, career/job search classes, career assessment, internships, regional alumni. Career services highlights include Coaching for Leadership and Teamwork.

FACILITIES

Housing: Coed dorms, special housing for disabled students, fraternity/sorority housing, substance free, special interest housing. 50% of campus accessible to physically disabled. **Special Academic Facilities/Equipment:** The Babson World Globe, Roger Babson Museum, Isaac Newton Museum, Arthur M. Blank Center for Entrepreneurship. **Computers:** 100% of classrooms, 100% of dorms, 100% of libraries, 100% of dining areas, 100% of student union, 100% of common outdoor areas have wireless network access. Students can register for classes online. Administrative functions (other than registration) can be performed online. Undergraduates are required to own a computer.

CAMPUS LIFE

Environment: Village. **Activities:** dance, drama/theater, jazz band, literary magazine, musical theater, radio station, student government, student newspaper, yearbook. 78 registered organizations, 3 religious organizations. 4 fraternities, 3 sororities. **Athletics (Intercollegiate):** *Men:* baseball, basketball, cross-country, diving, golf, ice hockey, lacrosse, skiing (downhill/alpine), soccer, swimming, tennis, track/field (outdoor), track/field (indoor). *Women:* basketball, cross-country, diving, field hockey, lacrosse, skiing (downhill/alpine), soccer, softball, swimming, tennis, track/field (outdoor), track/field (indoor), volleyball. **On-Campus Highlights:** Sorenson Arts Center, Blank Center for Entrepeneurship, Glavin Family Chapel, Reynolds Student Center, Webster Athletic Center. **Environmental Initiatives:** Babson joined the American College & University Presidents Climate Commitment and wrote a Sustainability and Climate Action Plan. To implement its commitments, Babson engages GreenerU, Inc.—an innovative, higher education-focused energy and sustainability services company—to operate our dedicated Sustainability Office. Babson has invested heavily in energy efficiency, and has reduced its emissions by approximately 40% in the past decade. Savings from energy efficiency have been reinvested in renewable energy purchases. Babson offers both a concentration in environmental sustainability, and (jointly) offers a certificate in sustainability. The Sustainability Certificate program is a collaborate effort between Babson College (business) Olin College (engineering) and Wellesley College (liberal arts).

ADMISSIONS

Freshman Academic Profile: SAT Math middle 50% range 610-710. SAT Critical Reading middle 50% range 570-660. SAT Writing middle 50% range 570-670. ACT middle 50% range 26-30. Minimum internet-based TOEFL 100. Minimum paper TOEFL 600. **Basis for Candidate Selection:** *Very important factors considered include:* application essay, academic GPA, recommendation(s), rigor of secondary school record, standardized test scores, character/personal qualities. *Important factors considered include:* Class rank, extracurricular activities. *Other factors considered include:* alumni/ae relation, first generation, geographical residence, interview, level of applicant's interest, racial/ethnic status, state residency, talent/ability, volunteer work, work experience. **Freshman Admission Requirements:** High school diploma is required and GED is accepted. **Freshman Admission Statistics:** 6,199 applied, 26% admitted, 31% enrolled. **Transfer Admission Requirements:** High school transcript, college transcript(s), essay or personal statement, statement of good standing from prior institution(s). Lowest grade transferable C. **General Admission Information:** Application Fee $65. Early decision application deadline 11/1. Regular application deadline 1/15. Regular notification 4/1. Nonfall registration not accepted. Admission may be deferred for a maximum of 1 year. Credit and/or placement offered for CEEB Advanced Placement tests.

COSTS AND FINANCIAL AID

Annual tuition $46,784. Room and board $14,928. Required fees $0. Average book expense $1,050. **Required Forms and Deadlines:** FAFSA, CSS/Financial Aid PROFILE, Noncustodial PROFILE. **Notification of Awards:** Applicants will be notified of awards on or about 4/1. **Types of Aid:** *Need-based scholarships/grants:* Federal Pell, SEOG, state scholarships/grants, the school's own gift aid. *Loans:* Subsidized Stafford, Unsubsidized Stafford, PLUS, Federal Perkins, state loans. *Student Employment:* Federal Work-Study Program available. Institutional employment available. Highest amount earned per year from on-campus jobs $5,400. Off-campus job opportunities are good. **Financial Aid Statistics:** 91% freshmen, 94% undergrads receive need-based scholarship or grant aid. 14% freshmen, 15% undergrads receive non-need-based scholarship or grant aid. 86% freshmen, 89% undergrads receive need-based self-help aid. 0% freshmen, 0% undergrads receive athletic scholarships. 50% freshmen, 50% undergrads receive any aid. 43% undergrads borrow to pay for school. Average cumulative indebtedness $24,823. **Criteria for awarding institutional aid:** *Non-need-based:* academics, leadership.

See page 1002.

BAKER UNIVERSITY

P.O. Box 65, Baldwin City, KS 66006
Phone: 785-594-8307 · **Financial Aid Phone:** 785-594-4595
E-mail: admissions@bakeru.edu · **CEEB Code:** 6031
Fax: 785-594-8372 · **Website:** www.bakerU.edu · **ACT Code:** 1386

This private school, affiliated with the Methodist Church, was founded in 1858. It has a 36-acre campus.

RATINGS

Admissions Selectivity Rating: 79   **Fire Safety Rating:** 75

STUDENTS AND FACULTY

Enrollment: 822. **Student Body:** 45% female, 55% male, 32% out-of-state, 3% international (13 countries represented). Asian 0%, African American 9%, Caucasian 73%, Hispanic 6%, Native American 3% **Retention and Graduation:** 80% freshmen return for sophomore year. 42% freshmen graduate within 4 years. 58% freshmen graduate within 6 years. 30% grads go on to further study within 1 year. 17% grads pursue arts and sciences degrees. 2% grads pursue law degrees. 4% grads pursue business degrees. 1% grads pursue medical degrees. **Faculty:** 64 full-time faculty, 78% hold PhDs, 48% are members of minority groups, 5% are women. 0% of classes are taught by teaching assistants.

ACADEMICS

Degrees: bachelor's. **Classes:** Most classes have 10–19 students. Most lab/discussion sessions have fewer than 10 students. **Majors with Highest Enrollment:** Biology/Biological Sciences; Business/Commerce; Kinesiology and Exercise Science. **Special Study Options:** Accelerated program, double major, honors program, independent study, internships, liberal arts/career combination, student-designed major, study abroad, teacher certification program, Students can transfer to the School of Nursing (located in a clinical setting in Topeka, KS) after completing their first two years of general education and pre-nursing course work. Baker also offers an Interterm program (3 weeks in January), during which students can take classes on campus, pursue travel courses, or work in internships. **Honors programs:** Honors Program, Bronston Fellows Program Combined degree programs: 3-2 forestry program with Duke U. **Disability Services:** Special programs offered to physically disabled students include note-taking services, reader services, tape recorders, tutors. **Career services:** alumni services, career/job search classes, career assessment, internships. Career services highlights include professional project-based practicum experiences sponsored by local businesses and organizations (facilitated by faculty within the Business and Economics Department).

FACILITIES

Housing: Coed dorms, special housing for disabled students, men's dorms, women's dorms, fraternity/sorority housing, apartments for single students. 85% of campus accessible to physically disabled. **Special Academic Facilities/Equipment:** Old Castle Museum, Quayle Bible Collection **Computers:** 95% of classrooms, 100% of dorms, 100% of libraries, 100% of dining areas, 100% of student union, have wireless network access. Students can register for classes online. Administrative functions (other than registration) can be performed online.

CAMPUS LIFE

Environment: Rural. **Activities:** Choral groups, concert band, dance, drama/theater, jazz band, literary magazine, music ensembles, pep band, radio station, student government, student newspaper, television station, yearbook, International Student Organization. 60 registered organizations, 18 honor societies, 2 religious organizations. 5 fraternities, 5 sororities. **Athletics (Intercollegiate):** *Men:* baseball, basketball, cheerleading, cross-country, football, golf, soccer, tennis, track/field (outdoor), track/field (indoor), wrestling. *Women:* basketball, bowling, cheerleading, cross-country, golf, soccer, softball, tennis, track/field (outdoor), track/field (indoor), volleyball. **On-Campus Highlights:** Library, Wildcat Café, Osborne Chapel, Fitness Center, Living Learning Center.

ADMISSIONS

Freshman Academic Profile: Average high school GPA 3.4. 15% in top 10% of high school class, 42% in top 25% of high school class, 78% in top 50% of high school class. 90% from public high schools. SAT Math middle 50% range 430-580. SAT Critical Reading middle 50% range 430-525. ACT middle 50% range 20-26. Minimum internet-based TOEFL 69. Minimum paper TOEFL 525. **Basis for Candidate Selection:** *Very important factors considered include:* academic GPA, recommendation(s), rigor of secondary school record, standardized test scores, level of applicant's interest. *Important factors considered include:* Class rank. *Other factors considered include:* application essay, alumni/ae relation, character/personal qualities, extracurricular activities, geographical residence, interview, talent/ability, volunteer work, work experience. **Freshman Admission Requirements:** High school diploma is required and GED is accepted. **Freshman Admission Statistics:** 971 applied, 76% admitted, 30% enrolled. **Transfer Admission Requirements:** High school transcript, college transcript(s), standardized test scores, Minimum college GPA of 2.3 required. Lowest grade transferable C. **General Admission Information:** Nonfall registration accepted. Admission may be deferred for a maximum of 1 year. Credit and/or placement offered for CEEB Advanced Placement tests.

COSTS AND FINANCIAL AID

Annual tuition $25,950. Room and board $8,040. Required fees $340. Average book expense $1,200. **Required Forms and Deadlines:** FAFSA. **Notification of Awards:** Applicants will be notified of awards on a rolling basis beginning 3/1. **Types of Aid:** *Need-based scholarships/grants:* Federal Pell, SEOG, state scholarships/grants, private scholarships, the school's own gift aid. *Loans:* Subsidized Stafford, Unsubsidized Stafford, PLUS, Federal Perkins. *Student Employment:* Federal Work-Study Program available. Institutional employment available. Off-campus job opportunities are good. **Criteria for awarding institutional aid:** *Non-need-based:* academics, alumni affiliation, art, athletics, leadership, music/drama, religious affiliation.

BALDWIN WALLACE UNIVERSITY

275 Eastland Rd, Berea, OH 44017
Phone: 440-826-2222 · **Financial Aid Phone:** 440-826-2108
E-mail: admission@bw.edu · **CEEB Code:** 1050
Fax: 440-826-3830 · **Website:** www.bw.edu · **ACT Code:** 3236

This private school was founded in 1845. It has a 100-acre campus.

RATINGS

Admissions Selectivity Rating: 84   **Fire Safety Rating:** 73

STUDENTS AND FACULTY

Enrollment: 3,272. **Student Body:** 55% female, 45% male, 19% out-of-state, 1% international (26 countries represented). Asian 1%, African American 9%, Caucasian 79%, Hispanic 5%, Native American <1%
Retention and Graduation: 81% freshmen return for sophomore year. 51% freshmen graduate within 4 years. 68% freshmen graduate within 6 years. 9% grads go on to further study within 1 year. 6% grads pursue arts and sciences degrees. 1% grads pursue law degrees. 1% grads pursue business degrees. **Faculty:** 187 full-time faculty, 75% hold PhDs, 44% are members of minority groups, 9% are women. 0% of classes are taught by teaching assistants.

ACADEMICS

Degrees: bachelor's, certificate, master's. **Classes:** Most classes have 10–19 students. Most lab/discussion sessions have 20–29 students. **Majors with Highest Enrollment:** Business Administration and Management; Accounting; Psychology. **Special Study Options:** Accelerated program, cross-registration, distance learning, double major, dual enrollment, English as a Second Language (ESL), exchange student program (domestic), honors program, independent study, internships, liberal arts/career combination, student-designed major, study abroad, teacher certification program, weekend college, 3-2 in Engineering with Case Western Reserve University and Columbia University; 3-2 in Social Work with Case Western Reserve University; 3/2 Accounting MBA, 3/2 Human Resources MBA and 3/2 Computer Science/Info. Systems MBA Programs. **Honors programs:** Liberal Arts Program Combined degree programs: BA/MBA Acct,BA/MBA HR, BS-CompSci/MBA,BS-CompInfoSyst/MBA,BA/MSSASocialWork. **Disability Services:** Special programs offered to physically disabled students include note-taking services, reader services, tutors. **Career services:** Alumni network, alumni services, career assessment, internships. Career services highlights include: On Campus Recruiting Services, Employer Meet and Greets, Career and Internship Expo (annual job fair) and Career Connections (alumni network and mentor program), Fall Career Week and Spring Career Week that coincide with job fairs.

FACILITIES

Housing: Coed dorms, special housing for disabled students, special housing for international students, women's dorms, fraternity/sorority housing, apartments for single students, Theme HousingCarmel Living Learning Center (Education-based), Student-Directed Learning Communities (Sustainability, Art, Women's Christian, Men's Christian), Themed Housing (STEM, Language, Conservatory, SPROUT-for single mothers and children). 80% of campus accessible to physically disabled. **Special Academic Facilities/Equipment:** Art gallery, electron microscope, observatory. **Computers:** 100% of classrooms, 100% of dorms, 100% of libraries, 100% of dining areas, 100% of student union, 100% of common outdoor areas have wireless network access. Students can register for classes online. Administrative functions (other than registration) can be performed online.

CAMPUS LIFE

Environment: Village. **Activities:** Choral groups, concert band, dance, drama/theater, jazz band, literary magazine, marching band, music ensembles, musical theater, opera, pep band, radio station, student government, student newspaper, student-run film society, symphony orchestra, television station, yearbook, Campus Ministries, International Student Organization, Model UN. 136 registered organizations, 25 honor societies, 7 religious organizations. 5 fraternities, 5 sororities. **Athletics (Intercollegiate):** *Men:* baseball, basketball, cross-country, diving, football, golf, soccer, swimming, tennis, track/field (outdoor), track/field (indoor), wrestling. *Women:* basketball, cross-country, diving, golf, soccer, softball, swimming, tennis, track/field (outdoor), track/field (indoor), volleyball. **On-Campus Highlights:** CyberCafe, The Hive, The S.A.C. (Student Activities Center), Conservatory/Theatre performances, Recreation Center, The new Lou Higgins Recreation Center features a Fitness Center, Weight Room, Dance Studio, multipurpose basketball, volleyball, badminton courts and racquetball

courts, swimming pool, indoor batting cage and second-floor computer lab. The Student Activities Center provides a club-like atmosphere for entertainment programming on campus. It features a pulsating sound and dance light system, a 10' x 12' video screen, neon lights and snack bar. Comedians, live bands, disc jockeys, multi-media capabilities and special snack foods attracting students to all-campus events. **Environmental Initiatives:** Commitment to geo-thermal energy with all new buildings and major renovations; Creation of Ohio's first undergraduate major in Sustainability and MBA in Sustainability; Considerable investments in electricity energy conservation and renewable energy sources.

ADMISSIONS

Freshman Academic Profile: Average high school GPA 3.43. 22% in top 10% of high school class, 46% in top 25% of high school class, 77% in top 50% of high school class. 81% from public high schools. SAT Math middle 50% range 480-590. SAT Critical Reading middle 50% range 480-590. SAT Writing middle 50% range 470-590. ACT middle 50% range 20-25. Minimum internet-based TOEFL 79. Minimum paper TOEFL 550. **Basis for Candidate Selection:** *Very important factors considered include:* academic GPA, rigor of secondary school record. *Important factors considered include:* Class rank, application essay, character/personal qualities, extracurricular activities, talent/ability. *Other factors considered include:* recommendation(s), standardized test scores, alumni/ae relation, first generation, geographical residence, interview, level of applicant's interest, racial/ethnic status, state residency, volunteer work, work experience. **Freshman Admission Requirements:** High school diploma is required and GED is accepted. *Academic units required:* 4 English, 3 mathematics, 3 science, (2 science labs), 1 foreign language, 2 social studies, 1 history. **Freshman Admission Statistics:** 4,224 applied, 64% admitted, 27% enrolled. **Transfer Admission Requirements:** High school transcript, college transcript(s), statement of good standing from prior institution(s). Minimum college GPA of 2.5 required. Lowest grade transferable C. **General Admission Information:** Application Fee $25. Notification on a rolling basis, beginning on or about 11/1. Nonfall registration accepted. Admission may be deferred for a maximum of 1 year. Credit and/or placement offered for CEEB Advanced Placement tests.

COSTS AND FINANCIAL AID

Annual tuition $28,814. Room and board $8,048. Average book expense $1,456. **Required Forms and Deadlines:** FAFSA. **Notification of Awards:** Applicants will be notified of awards on a rolling basis beginning 2/14. **Types of Aid:** *Need-based scholarships/grants:* Federal Pell, SEOG, state scholarships/grants, private scholarships, the school's own gift aid. *Loans:* Subsidized Stafford, Unsubsidized Stafford, PLUS, Federal Perkins, college/university loans from institutional funds. *Student Employment:* Federal Work-Study Program available. Institutional employment available. Highest amount earned per year from on-campus jobs $2,400. Off-campus job opportunities are excellent. **Financial Aid Statistics:** 100% freshmen, 100% undergrads receive need-based scholarship or grant aid. 15% freshmen, 18% undergrads receive non-need-based scholarship or grant aid. 85% freshmen, 80% undergrads receive need-based self-help aid. 0% freshmen, 0% undergrads receive athletic scholarships. 100% freshmen, 97% undergrads receive any aid. 80% undergrads borrow to pay for school. Average cumulative indebtedness $27,593. **Criteria for awarding institutional aid:** *Non-need-based:* academics, alumni affiliation, minority status, music/drama, religious affiliation, state/district residency.

BALL STATE UNIVERSITY

Office of Admissions, Muncie, IN 47306
Phone: 765-285-8300 · **Financial Aid Phone:** 765-285-5600
E-mail: askus@bsu.edu · **CEEB Code:** 1051
Fax: 765-285-1632 · **Website:** www.bsu.edu · **ACT Code:** 1176

This public school was founded in 1918. It has a 1035-acre campus.

RATINGS

Admissions Selectivity Rating: 83   **Fire Safety Rating:** 83

STUDENTS AND FACULTY

Enrollment: 16,323. **Student Body:** 57% female, 43% male, 10% out-of-state, 2% international (44 countries represented). Asian 1%, African American 6%, Caucasian 85%, Hispanic 3%, Native American <1%
Retention and Graduation: 77% freshmen return for sophomore year.
Faculty: 959 full-time faculty, 74% hold PhDs, 45% are members of minority groups, 13% are women.

ACADEMICS

Degrees: associate, bachelor's, doctoral, master's, post-bachelor's certificate, post-master's certificate. **Classes:** Most classes have 20–29 students. **Majors with Highest Enrollment:** General Studies; Elementary Education and

Teaching; Radio and Television. **Special Study Options:** Accelerated program, distance learning, double major, dual enrollment, English as a Second Language (ESL), exchange student program (domestic), external degree program, honors program, independent study, internships, student-designed major, study abroad, teacher certification program. **Honors programs:** BSU offers an Honors College which has its own curriculum, undergraduate research fellowships and study abroad programs. **Disability Services:** Special programs offered to physically disabled students include note-taking services, reader services, tape recorders, tutors. **Career services:** alumni services, career assessment, internships, regional alumni. Career services highlights include the professional skills development programs and services provided by the career center, which offer the highest level of staff expertise and training methods. Student use of these services has grown an average of 86% over the past three years. Students and alumni use the online resume review program, professional etiquette dinners, and individual appointments for job coaching including video-taped practice interviews to prepare for internships and job searches.

FACILITIES

Housing: Coed dorms, special housing for disabled students, men's dorms, special housing for international students, women's dorms, fraternity/sorority housing, apartments for married students, apartments for single students, Wellness Housing, Theme HousingLiving/Learning Communities. 95% of campus accessible to physically disabled. **Special Academic Facilities/Equipment:** Art gallery, museum, on-campus school (K-12), learning center, weather station, physical therapy lab, human performance lab, planetarium/observatory, wildlife and nature preserve. **Computers:** 100% of classrooms, 100% of dorms, 100% of libraries, 100% of dining areas, 100% of student union, 100% of common outdoor areas have wireless network access. Students can register for classes online. Administrative functions (other than registration) can be performed online. Undergraduates are required to own a computer.

CAMPUS LIFE

Environment: City. **Activities:** Choral groups, concert band, dance, drama/theater, jazz band, literary magazine, marching band, music ensembles, musical theater, opera, pep band, radio station, student government, student newspaper, student-run film society, symphony orchestra, television station, Campus Ministries. 355 registered organizations, 31 honor society, 32 religious organizations. 15 fraternities, 12 sororities. **Athletics (Intercollegiate):** *Men:* baseball, basketball, cheerleading, cross-country, diving, football, golf, swimming, tennis, volleyball. *Women:* basketball, cheerleading, cross-country, diving, field hockey, golf, gymnastics, soccer, softball, swimming, tennis, track/field (outdoor), volleyball. **On-Campus Highlights:** Museum of Art, Worthen Arena, Emens Auditorium, Atrium, Letterman Communication & Media Bldg, Emens Auditorium, Music Building/Sursa Hall, Bracken Library. **Environmental Initiatives:** Installing a district-scale ground-source heating and cooling system to serve all 45 campus buildings and eliminate four coal-fired boilers and reduce our GHG emissions by nearly 50%. Creating in 2001 a Council on the environment which represents every constituency group on campus and in the surrounding community whoich in turn has shepherded creation of unit-level sustainability plans for 102 administrative units on campus. Requiring that all new construction be LEED Silver Certified at minimum and that all renovation and remodeling seek the same performance levels.

ADMISSIONS

Freshman Academic Profile: Average high school GPA 3.35. 18% in top 10% of high school class, 48% in top 25% of high school class, 88% in top 50% of high school class. 93% from public high schools. SAT Math middle 50% range 480-580. SAT Critical Reading middle 50% range 480-580. SAT Writing middle 50% range 470-560. ACT middle 50% range 19-23. Minimum internet-based TOEFL 79. Minimum paper TOEFL 550. **Basis for Candidate Selection:** *Very important factors considered include:* academic GPA, rigor of secondary school record, standardized test scores. *Other factors considered include:* Class rank, application essay, recommendation(s), character/personal qualities, extracurricular activities, talent/ability, volunteer work, work experience. **Freshman Admission Requirements:** High school diploma is required and GED is accepted. *Academic units required:* 4 English, 3 mathematics, 3 science, (2 science labs), 3 social studies. **Freshman Admission Statistics:** 16,896 applied, 61% admitted, 34% enrolled. **Transfer Admission Requirements:** college transcript(s), Minimum college GPA of 2.0 required. Lowest grade transferable C. **General Admission Information:** Application Fee $25. Regular application deadline 8/15. Nonfall registration accepted. Admission may be deferred for a maximum of one year. Credit and/or placement offered for CEEB Advanced Placement tests.

COSTS AND FINANCIAL AID

Annual in-state tuition $8,318. Annual out-of-state tuition $22,988. Room and board $8,870. Required fees $662. Average book expense $1,020. **Required Forms and Deadlines:** FAFSA. **Notification of Awards:** Applicants will be notified of awards on a rolling basis beginning 4/1. **Types of Aid:** *Need-based scholarships/grants:* Federal Pell, SEOG, state scholarships/grants, private scholarships, the school's own gift aid. *Loans:* Direct Subsidized Stafford, Direct Unsubsidized Stafford, Direct PLUS, Federal Perkins. *Student Employment:* Federal Work-Study Program available. Institutional employment available. Off-campus job opportunities are good. **Financial Aid Statistics:** 63% freshmen, 59% undergrads receive need-based scholarship or grant aid. 40% freshmen, 35% undergrads receive non-need-based scholarship or grant aid. 94% freshmen, 92% undergrads receive need-based self-help aid. 2% freshmen, 2% undergrads receive athletic scholarships. 82% freshmen, 78% undergrads receive any aid. 72% undergrads borrow to pay for school. Average cumulative indebtedness $23,716. **Criteria for awarding institutional aid:** *Non-need-based:* academics, athletics, leadership, minority status, music/drama, state/district residency.

BALTIMORE HEBREW UNIVERSITY

5800 Park Heights, Baltimore, MD 21215
Phone: 410-578-6967
E-mail: bhu@bhu.edu · **CEEB Code:** 5035
Fax: 410-578-6940 · **Website:** www.bhu.edu · **ACT Code:** 20093

This private school was founded in 1919.

RATINGS

Admissions Selectivity Rating: 60*   **Fire Safety Rating:** 60*

STUDENTS AND FACULTY

Enrollment: 75. **Student Body:** 63% female, 37% male, 0% international (4 countries represented). Asian 0%, African American 3%, Caucasian 139%, Hispanic 0%, Native American <1%
Retention and Graduation: 67% freshmen return for sophomore year. 33% freshmen graduate within 4 years. 34% freshmen graduate within 6 years.

ACADEMICS

Degrees: associate, bachelor's, certificate, master's. **Special Study Options:** cross-registration, double major, dual enrollment, independent study, internships, study abroad, teacher certification program, English language skills program for non-native speakers. **Disability Services:** Special programs offered to physically disabled students include tape recorders.

FACILITIES

Housing: 65% of campus accessible to physically disabled. **Special Academic Facilities/Equipment:** Joseph Meyerhoff Library Cohen Auditorium.

CAMPUS LIFE

Activities: 2 registered organizations.

ADMISSIONS

Freshman Academic Profile: Minimum paper TOEFL 250. **Basis for Candidate Selection:** *Very important factors considered include:* recommendation(s), interview. *Other factors considered include:* Class rank, rigor of secondary school record, standardized test scores, character/personal qualities. **Freshman Admission Requirements:** High school diploma is required and GED is accepted. **Freshman Admission Statistics:** 6 applied, 100% admitted, 67% enrolled. **Transfer Admission Requirements:** college transcript(s), Minimum college GPA of 2.0 required. Lowest grade transferable C. **General Admission Information:** Application Fee $20. Nonfall registration accepted. Admission may be deferred for a maximum of one year.

COSTS AND FINANCIAL AID

Required fees $30. Average book expense $600. **Required Forms and Deadlines:** FAFSA. **Types of Aid:** *Need-based scholarships/grants:* Federal Pell, state scholarships/grants, private scholarships, the school's own gift aid. *Loans:* Subsidized Stafford, Unsubsidized Stafford, PLUS. *Student Employment:* Off-campus job opportunities are excellent. **Financial Aid Statistics:** 0% freshmen, 2% undergrads receive need-based scholarship or grant aid. 0% freshmen, 0% undergrads receive non-need-based scholarship or grant aid. 0% freshmen, 2% undergrads receive need-based self-help aid. 0% freshmen, 0% undergrads receive athletic scholarships. 0% undergrads borrow to pay for school. **Criteria for awarding institutional aid:** *Non-need-based:* academics.

BAPTIST BIBLE COLLEGE AND SEMINARY

538 Venard Rd, Clarks Summit, PA 18411
Phone: 570-586-2400 · **Financial Aid Phone:** 570-585-9206
E-mail: admissions@bbc.edu · **CEEB Code:** 2036
Fax: 570-585-9299 · **Website:** www/bbc/edu · **ACT Code:** 3523

This private school, affiliated with the Baptist Church, was founded in 1932. It has a 121-acre campus.

RATINGS

Admissions Selectivity Rating: 74   **Fire Safety Rating:** 64

STUDENTS AND FACULTY

Enrollment: 668. **Student Body:** 59% female, 41% male, 68% out-of-state, 2% international (13 countries represented). Asian 1%, African American 1%, Caucasian 94%, Hispanic 2%, Native American <1%
Retention and Graduation: 69% freshmen return for sophomore year.
Faculty: 35 full-time faculty, 57% hold PhDs, 29% are members of minority groups, 3% are women. 0% of classes are taught by teaching assistants.

ACADEMICS

Degrees: associate, bachelor's, certificate, master's. **Classes:** Most classes have fewer than 10 students. **Majors with Highest Enrollment:** Elementary Education and Teaching; Theology and Religious Vocations. **Special Study Options:** distance learning, double major, dual enrollment, independent study, internships, study abroad, teacher certification program. **Career services:** alumni services, internships.

FACILITIES

Housing: men's dorms, women's dorms **Computers:** 100% of classrooms, 100% of libraries, 100% of dining areas, 100% of student union, 100% of common outdoor areas have wireless network access. Students can register for classes online. Administrative functions (other than registration) can be performed online.

CAMPUS LIFE

Environment: Town. **Activities:** Choral groups, concert band, drama/theater, music ensembles, student government, yearbook, Campus Ministries. **Athletics (Intercollegiate):** *Men:* baseball, basketball, cross-country, golf, soccer. *Women:* basketball, cross-country, soccer, softball, tennis, volleyball. **On-Campus Highlights:** Underground Café, Dorm, Student Center, Classroom building.

ADMISSIONS

Freshman Academic Profile: 40% from public high schools. SAT Math middle 50% range 430-560. SAT Critical Reading middle 50% range 460-570. ACT middle 50% range 20-24. Minimum paper TOEFL 500. **Basis for Candidate Selection:** *Very important factors considered include:* application essay, recommendation(s), rigor of secondary school record, standardized test scores, character/personal qualities, religious affiliation/commitment. *Important factors considered include:* academic GPA. *Other factors considered include:* extracurricular activities, interview, level of applicant's interest, talent/ability, volunteer work, work experience. **Freshman Admission Requirements:** High school diploma is required and GED is accepted. **Freshman Admission Statistics:** 452 applied, 76% admitted, 48% enrolled. **Transfer Admission Requirements:** High school transcript, college transcript(s), essay or personal statement, Minimum college GPA of 2 required. Lowest grade transferable 2. **General Admission Information:** Application Fee $30. Regular application deadline 8/15. Nonfall registration accepted. Credit offered for CEEB Advanced Placement tests.

COSTS AND FINANCIAL AID

Annual tuition $6,840. Room and board $5,900. Required fees $468. **Required Forms and Deadlines:** FAFSA, Institution's own financial aid form. **Notification of Awards:** Applicants will be notified of awards on a rolling basis beginning 10/1. **Types of Aid:** *Need-based scholarships/grants:* Federal Pell, state scholarships/grants, the school's own gift aid. *Loans:* Direct Unsubsidized Stafford, Subsidized Stafford, Unsubsidized Stafford, PLUS, state loans. *Student Employment:* Federal Work-Study Program available. Institutional employment available. Off-campus job opportunities are excellent. **Financial Aid Statistics:** 100% freshmen, 96% undergrads receive any aid. **Criteria for awarding institutional aid:** *Non-need-based:* academics, leadership.

BAPTIST COLLEGE OF FLORIDA

5400 College Drive, Graceville, FL 32440-1898
Phone: 850-263-3261 · **Financial Aid Phone:** 1-800-328-2660 ext. 461
E-mail: admissions@baptistcollege.edu
Fax: 850-263-9026 · **Website:** www.baptistcollege.edu · **ACT Code:** 6870

This private school, affiliated with the Southern Baptist Church, was founded in 1943. It has a 217-acre campus.

RATINGS

Admissions Selectivity Rating: 88   **Fire Safety Rating:** 73

STUDENTS AND FACULTY

Enrollment: 458. **Student Body:** 38% female, 62% male, 26% out-of-state, 0% international (1 countries represented). Asian 0%, African American 7%, Caucasian 73%, Hispanic 4%, Native American 1%
Retention and Graduation: 63% freshmen return for sophomore year. 27% freshmen graduate within 4 years. 47% freshmen graduate within 6 years. 51% grads go on to further study within 1 year. 84% grads pursue arts and sciences degrees. 2% grads pursue law degrees. 4% grads pursue business degrees. **Faculty:** 26 full-time faculty, 65% hold PhDs, 23% are members of minority groups, 0% are women. 0% of classes are taught by teaching assistants.

ACADEMICS

Degrees: associate, bachelor's, certificate, terminal associate. **Classes:** Most classes have fewer than 10 students. Most lab/discussion sessions have 10–19 students. **Majors with Highest Enrollment:** Religious Education; Theology/Theological Studies; Pastoral Studies/Counseling. **Special Study Options:** distance learning, double major, independent study, internships, teacher certification program, Academic Remediation, Advanced Placement Credit, Learning Disabilities Services. **Disability Services:** Special programs offered to physically disabled students include note-taking services, reader services, tape recorders, tutors. **Career services:** alumni services, internships.

FACILITIES

Housing: special housing for disabled students, men's dorms, women's dorms, apartments for married students. 100% of campus accessible to physically disabled. **Special Academic Facilities/Equipment:** Florida Baptist Historical Society; Heritage Village; Weight Rooms in Assembly Center. **Computers:** 100% of classrooms, 100% of dorms, 100% of libraries, 100% of dining areas, 100% of student union, 100% of common outdoor areas have wireless network access. Students can register for classes online. Administrative functions (other than registration) can be performed online.

CAMPUS LIFE

Environment: Rural. **Activities:** Choral groups, concert band, drama/theater, jazz band, music ensembles, radio station, Campus Ministries. 3 registered organizations, 2 religious organizations. **Athletics (Intercollegiate):** *Men:* golf. *Women:* volleyball. **On-Campus Highlights:** Athletic Center, Coffee Shop, Courtyard, Student Center, Chapel.

ADMISSIONS

Freshman Academic Profile: 90% from public high schools. SAT Math middle 50% range 390-540. SAT Critical Reading middle 50% range 450-640. ACT middle 50% range 17-22. Minimum paper TOEFL 500. **Basis for Candidate Selection:** *Very important factors considered include:* recommendation(s), character/personal qualities, level of applicant's interest, religious affiliation/commitment. *Important factors considered include:* academic GPA, alumni/ae relation, talent/ability. *Other factors considered include:* Class rank, rigor of secondary school record, standardized test scores, extracurricular activities, interview, volunteer work. **Freshman Admission Requirements:** High school diploma is required and GED is accepted. **Freshman Admission Statistics:** 144 applied, 56% admitted, 41% enrolled. **Transfer Admission Requirements:** High school transcript, college transcript(s), essay or personal statement, Minimum college GPA of 2.0 required. Lowest grade transferable C. **General Admission Information:** Application Fee $25. Regular application deadline 8/15. Notification on a rolling basis, beginning on or about 9/1. Nonfall registration accepted. Admission may be deferred for a maximum of 2 semesters. Neither credit nor placement offered for CEEB Advanced Placement tests.

COSTS AND FINANCIAL AID

Annual tuition $9,300. Room and board $4,888. Required fees $400. Average book expense $900. **Required Forms and Deadlines:** FAFSA, Institution's own financial aid form, State aid form, Business/Farm Supplement. **Notification of Awards:** Applicants will be notified of awards on a rolling basis beginning 6/15. **Types of Aid:** *Need-based scholarships/grants:* Federal Pell, SEOG, state scholarships/grants, private scholarships, the school's own gift aid. *Loans:* Subsidized Stafford, Unsubsidized Stafford, PLUS, college/university loans from institutional funds, Alternative Loans. *Student Employment:* Federal

Work-Study Program available. Institutional employment available. Highest amount earned per year from on-campus jobs $7,600. Off-campus job opportunities are good. **Financial Aid Statistics:** 61% freshmen, 73% undergrads receive need-based scholarship or grant aid. 4% freshmen, 3% undergrads receive non-need-based scholarship or grant aid. 45% freshmen, 53% undergrads receive need-based self-help aid. 0% freshmen, 0% undergrads receive athletic scholarships. 86% freshmen, 97% undergrads receive any aid. 85% undergrads borrow to pay for school. Average cumulative indebtedness $504,704. **Criteria for awarding institutional aid:** *Non-need-based:* academics, minority status, music/drama, religious affiliation.

BARBER SCOTIA COLLEGE

145 Cabarrus Avenue, Concord, NC 28025
Phone: 704-789-2901
E-mail: wwhite@b-sc.edu • **CEEB Code:**
Fax: 704-789-2624 • **Website:** www.barber-scotia.edu • **ACT Code:** 3060

This private school, affiliated with the Presbyterian Church, was founded in 1867. It has a 40-acre campus.

RATINGS

Admissions Selectivity Rating: 63   Fire Safety Rating: 60*

STUDENTS AND FACULTY

Enrollment: 475. **Student Body:** 45% female, 55% male, 45% out-of-state, 0% international (2 countries represented). Asian 0%, African American 101%, Caucasian 1%, Hispanic 0%, Native American <1%
Retention and Graduation: 61% freshmen return for sophomore year. 9% grads go on to further study within 1 year. 7% grads pursue arts and sciences degrees. 2% grads pursue business degrees.

ACADEMICS

Degrees: bachelor's. **Special Study Options:** cooperative education program, double major, dual enrollment, honors program, internships, student-designed major, teacher certification program. Combined degree programs: BA/JD, BA/BSN. **Disability Services:** Special programs offered to physically disabled students include note-taking services, reader services, tape recorders, tutors. **Career services:** alumni services, career/job search classes, career assessment, internships.

FACILITIES

Housing: special housing for disabled students, men's dorms, women's dorms, apartments for married students. 50% of campus accessible to physically disabled. **Special Academic Facilities/Equipment:** Barber-Scotia's African-American Women's History Collection: This Collection houses one of the largest bodies of documents related to African-American women in the United States. Major areas of interest are the Reconstruction-Jim Crow Era. **Computers:**

CAMPUS LIFE

Environment: Village. **Activities:** Choral groups, dance, pep band, student government, student newspaper, yearbook. 18 registered organizations, 2 honor societies, 2 religious organizations. 4 fraternities, 4 sororities. **Athletics (Intercollegiate): Men:** basketball, cross-country, track/field (outdoor). *Women:* basketball, cheerleading, cross-country, softball, track/field (outdoor), volleyball.

ADMISSIONS

Freshman Academic Profile: 98% from public high schools. **Basis for Candidate Selection:** *Very important factors considered include:* Class rank, application essay, recommendation(s), interview. *Important factors considered include:* rigor of secondary school record, extracurricular activities, talent/ability, volunteer work. *Other factors considered include:* alumni/ae relation, character/personal qualities, state residency. **Freshman Admission Requirements:** High school diploma is required and GED is accepted. *Academic units required:* 4 English, 3 mathematics, 3 science, 2 social studies, 1 history. 4 English, 3 mathematics, 3 science, 2 social studies, 1 history, **Freshman Admission Statistics:** 840 applied, 64% admitted, 32% enrolled. **Transfer Admission Requirements:** college transcript(s), Minimum college GPA of 2.0 required. Lowest grade transferable C. **General Admission Information:** Application Fee $15. Regular application deadline 7/1. Nonfall registration accepted. Credit and/or placement offered for CEEB Advanced Placement tests.

COSTS AND FINANCIAL AID

Annual tuition $7,400. Room and board $3,500. Required fees $466. Average book expense $250. **Required Forms and Deadlines:** FAFSA. **Notification of Awards:** Applicants will be notified of awards on or about 6/15. **Types of Aid:** *Need-based scholarships/grants:* Federal Pell, SEOG, state scholarships/grants, private scholarships, the school's own gift aid, United Negro College Fund. *Loans:* Direct Subsidized Stafford, Direct Unsubsidized Stafford, Direct

PLUS, Subsidized Stafford, Unsubsidized Stafford, PLUS. *Student Employment:* Federal Work-Study Program available. Institutional employment available. Off-campus job opportunities are excellent. **Financial Aid Statistics:** 94% freshmen, 98% undergrads receive need-based scholarship or grant aid. 8% freshmen, 29% undergrads receive non-need-based scholarship or grant aid. 86% freshmen, 70% undergrads receive need-based self-help aid. 8% freshmen, 10% undergrads receive athletic scholarships. 84% undergrads borrow to pay for school. **Criteria for awarding institutional aid:** *Non-need-based:* academics, alumni affiliation, athletics, leadership, minority status, music/drama, religious affiliation, state/district residency.

BARD COLLEGE

Office of Admissions, Annandale-on-Hudson, NY 12504
Phone: 845-758-7472 • **Financial Aid Phone:** 845-758-7526
E-mail: admission@bard.edu • **CEEB Code:** 2037
Fax: 845-758-5208 • **Website:** www.bard.edu • **ACT Code:** 2674

This private school was founded in 1860. It has a 600-acre campus.

RATINGS

Admissions Selectivity Rating: 93   Fire Safety Rating: 95

STUDENTS AND FACULTY

Enrollment: 1,999. **Student Body:** 55% female, 45% male, 67% out-of-state, 11% international (54 countries represented). Asian 6%, African American 7%, Caucasian 63%, Hispanic 1%, Native American 1%
Retention and Graduation: 66% freshmen graduate within 4 years. 75% freshmen graduate within 6 years. **Faculty:** 152 full-time faculty, 96% hold PhDs, 43% are members of minority groups, 14% are women. 0% of classes are taught by teaching assistants.

ACADEMICS

Degrees: associate, bachelor's, doctoral, master's. **Majors with Highest Enrollment:** English Language and Literature; Social Sciences; Visual and Performing Arts. **Special Study Options:** cross-registration, double major, dual enrollment, English as a Second Language (ESL), independent study, internships, student-designed major, study abroad, Intensive language studies in Italy, Germany, France, Mexico, Russia, China, program in International Education (Central and Eastern Europe and Southern Africa). Combined degree programs: BA/MA, BA/MEng, See catalog, pp. 244. **Disability Services:** Special programs offered to physically disabled students include note-taking services, reader services, tape recorders, tutors. **Career services:** Alumni network, alumni services, career/job search classes, career assessment, internships, regional alumni. Career services highlights include over 30 career information workshops a year.

FACILITIES

Housing: Coed dorms, women's dorms, cooperative housing, Wellness Housing, Theme Housing. 70% of campus accessible to physically disabled. **Special Academic Facilities/Equipment:** Performing arts center, gallery, art museum, collection of contemporary art, center for curatorial studies, language lab, nursery school, ecology field station, archaeology field school, economics institute. **Computers:** 5% of classrooms, 50% of dorms, 100% of libraries, 100% of dining areas, 100% of student union, have wireless network access. Students can register for classes online. Administrative functions (other than registration) can be performed online.

CAMPUS LIFE

Environment: Rural. **Activities:** Choral groups, concert band, dance, drama/theater, jazz band, literary magazine, music ensembles, musical theater, opera, radio station, student government, student newspaper, student-run film society, symphony orchestra, Campus Ministries, International Student Organization, Model UN. 120 registered organizations, 5 religious organizations. **Athletics (Intercollegiate): Men:** basketball, cross-country, soccer, squash, tennis, track/field (outdoor), volleyball. *Women:* basketball, cross-country, soccer, tennis, track/field (outdoor), volleyball. **On-Campus Highlights:** Richard B Fisher Center for the Performing Arts, Stevenson Library, Bertelsmann Campus Center, Museum @ Center for Curatorial Studies, Levy Economics Institute - Blithewood Mansion, A new Center for Science and Computation designed by the renowned firm Rafael Vinoly Architects opened in the fall of 2007. **Environmental Initiatives:** Renewable energy (geothermal) installed in new buildings and currently in place in 20 existing buildings. 100% food composting onsite. (#1 in "Food Scrap" category in 2009 Recyclemania). Sustainability literacy of first-year students.

ADMISSIONS

Freshman Academic Profile: Average high school GPA 3.5. 60% in top 10% of high school class, 95% in top 25% of high school class, 99% in top 50% of high school class. 59% from public high schools. SAT Math middle 50% range 570-680. SAT Critical Reading middle 50% range 600-710. Minimum internet-based TOEFL 100. Minimum paper TOEFL 600. **Basis for Candidate Selection:** *Very important factors considered include:* application essay, academic GPA, recommendation(s), rigor of secondary school record, character/personal qualities, extracurricular activities, talent/ability. *Important factors considered include:* volunteer work, work experience. *Other factors considered include:* Class rank, standardized test scores, alumni/ae relation, first generation, geographical residence, interview, level of applicant's interest, racial/ethnic status, religious affiliation/commitment, state residency. **Freshman Admission Requirements:** High school diploma is required and GED is accepted. **Freshman Admission Statistics:** 6,960 applied, 45% admitted, 18% enrolled. **Transfer Admission Requirements:** college transcript(s), essay or personal statement, statement of good standing from prior institution(s). Minimum college GPA of 3.0 required. Lowest grade transferable C. **General Admission Information:** Application Fee $50. Regular application deadline 1/15. Regular notification 4/1. Nonfall registration not accepted. Admission may be deferred for a maximum of 12 months. Credit offered for CEEB Advanced Placement tests.

COSTS AND FINANCIAL AID

Annual tuition $47,560. Room and board $13,772. Required fees $680. Average book expense $950. **Required Forms and Deadlines:** FAFSA, CSS/Financial Aid PROFILE, State aid form, Noncustodial PROFILE. **Notification of Awards:** Applicants will be notified of awards on or about 4/1. **Types of Aid:** *Need-based scholarships/grants:* Federal Pell, SEOG, state scholarships/grants, private scholarships, the school's own gift aid. *Loans:* Subsidized Stafford, Unsubsidized Stafford, PLUS, Federal Perkins, Loans from institutional funds (for international students only). *Student Employment:* Federal Work-Study Program available. Institutional employment available. Highest amount earned per year from on-campus jobs $1,800. Off-campus job opportunities are good. **Financial Aid Statistics:** 97% freshmen, 96% undergrads receive need-based scholarship or grant aid. 0% freshmen, 0% undergrads receive non-need-based scholarship or grant aid. 85% freshmen, 78% undergrads receive need-based self-help aid. 0% freshmen, 0% undergrads receive athletic scholarships. 72% freshmen, 72% undergrads receive any aid. 52% undergrads borrow to pay for school. Average cumulative indebtedness $24,039. **Criteria for awarding institutional aid:** *Non-need-based:* academics.

BARD COLLEGE AT SIMON'S ROCK

Best 380

84 Alford Road, Great Barrington, MA 1230
Financial Aid Phone: 413-528-7297
E-mail: admit@simons-rock.edu • **CEEB Code:** 3795
Fax: 413-541-0081 • **Website:** www.simons-rock.edu • **ACT Code:** 1893

This private school was founded in 1964. It has a 275-acre campus.

RATINGS

Admissions Selectivity Rating: 89   **Fire Safety Rating:** 91

STUDENTS AND FACULTY

Enrollment: 344. **Student Body:** 58% female, 42% male, 88% out-of-state, 10% international (15 countries represented). Asian 6%, African American 7%, Caucasian 57%, Hispanic 2%, Native American <1%
Retention and Graduation: 21% freshmen graduate within 4 years. **Faculty:** 48 full-time faculty, 90% hold PhDs, 44% are members of minority groups, 15% are women. 0% of classes are taught by teaching assistants.

ACADEMICS

Degrees: associate, bachelor's. **Classes:** Most classes have 10–19 students. Most lab/discussion sessions have 10–19 students. **Majors with Highest Enrollment:** Visual and Performing Arts; Multi-/Interdisciplinary Studies; Social Sciences. **Special Study Options:** Accelerated program, cooperative education program, cross-registration, dual enrollment, exchange student program (domestic), independent study, internships, student-designed major, study abroad,

Study Abroad Program(s)within in the last two years: In Hondorus, Spain, England, Germany, Thailand, South Africa, Japan, China. Combined degree programs: BS Eng) from Dartmouth/Washington U/or Columbia. **Disability Services:** Special programs offered to physically disabled students include tape recorders, tutors. **Career services:** Alumni network, career/job search classes, internships, regional alumni.

FACILITIES

Housing: Coed dorms, men's dorms, women's dorms, apartments for single students, If students propose a plan for cooperative housing it will be considered by Dean of Student Life. 75% of campus accessible to physically disabled. **Special Academic Facilities/Equipment:** Daniel Arts Center, Fisher Science and Academic Center. **Computers:** Administrative functions (other than registration) can be performed online.

CAMPUS LIFE

Environment: Village. **Activities:** Choral groups, dance, drama/theater, jazz band, literary magazine, music ensembles, radio station, student government, student newspaper, student-run film society, yearbook. 21 registered organizations, 3 religious organizations. **Athletics (Intercollegiate):** *Men:* basketball, soccer, swimming, tennis. *Women:* basketball, soccer, swimming, tennis. **On-Campus Highlights:** Fisher Science and Academic Center, Daniel Arts Center, Alumni Library, Kellogg Music Center, Kilpatrick Athletic Center, New building coming on line in 2005: Livingston Hall Student Union.

ADMISSIONS

Freshman Academic Profile: Average high school GPA 3.71. 46% in top 10% of high school class, 67% in top 25% of high school class, 89% in top 50% of high school class. 71% from public high schools. SAT Math middle 50% range 600-710. SAT Critical Reading middle 50% range 690-750. SAT Writing middle 50% range 620-710. ACT middle 50% range 24-27. Minimum internet-based TOEFL 100. Minimum paper TOEFL 600. **Basis for Candidate Selection:** *Very important factors considered include:* application essay, recommendation(s), rigor of secondary school record, character/personal qualities, interview, talent/ability. *Important factors considered include:* Class rank, academic GPA, level of applicant's interest. *Other factors considered include:* standardized test scores, alumni/ae relation, extracurricular activities, first generation, racial/ethnic status, volunteer work, work experience. **Freshman Admission Requirements:** High school diploma or equivalent is not required. **Freshman Admission Statistics:** 218 applied, 92% admitted, 72% enrolled. **Transfer Admission Requirements:** college transcript(s), essay or personal statement, interview, Minimum college GPA of 2.0 required. Lowest grade transferable C. **General Admission Information:** Application Fee $50. Regular application deadline 5/31. Notification on a rolling basis, beginning on or about 9/1. Nonfall registration accepted. Admission may be deferred for a maximum of 12 months. Credit and/or placement offered for CEEB Advanced Placement tests.

COSTS AND FINANCIAL AID

Annual tuition $45,618. Room and board $12,690. Required fees $1,695. Average book expense $1,000. **Required Forms and Deadlines:** FAFSA, CSS/Financial Aid PROFILE, State aid form, Noncustodial PROFILE. **Notification of Awards:** Applicants will be notified of awards on a rolling basis beginning 4/15. **Types of Aid:** *Need-based scholarships/grants:* Federal Pell, SEOG, state scholarships/grants, private scholarships, the school's own gift aid. *Loans:* Subsidized Stafford, Unsubsidized Stafford, PLUS, Federal Perkins, state loans, Alternative Educational Loans. *Student Employment:* Federal Work-Study Program available. Institutional employment available. Highest amount earned per year from on-campus jobs $1,300. Off-campus job opportunities are good. **Financial Aid Statistics:** 97% freshmen, 88% undergrads receive need-based scholarship or grant aid. 0% freshmen, 0% undergrads receive non-need-based scholarship or grant aid. 76% freshmen, 71% undergrads receive need-based self-help aid. 0% freshmen, 0% undergrads receive athletic scholarships. 90% freshmen, 86% undergrads receive any aid. 56% undergrads borrow to pay for school. Average cumulative indebtedness $24,053. **Criteria for awarding institutional aid:** *Non-need-based:* academics, alumni affiliation, leadership, state/district residency.

BARNARD COLLEGE

Best 380

3009 Broadway, New York, NY 10027
Phone: 212-854-2014 · **Financial Aid Phone:** 212-854-2154
E-mail: admissions@barnard.edu · **CEEB Code:** 2038
Fax: 212-854-6220 · **Website:** www.barnard.edu · **ACT Code:** 2718

This private school was founded in 1889. It has a 4-acre campus.

RATINGS

Admissions Selectivity Rating: 97   **Fire Safety Rating:** 72

STUDENTS AND FACULTY

Enrollment: 2,561. **Student Body:** 100% female, 0% male, 63% out-of-state, 7% international (47 countries represented). Asian 14%, African American 6%, Caucasian 55%, Hispanic 11%, Native American <1% **Retention and Graduation:** 97% freshmen return for sophomore year. 82% freshmen graduate within 4 years. 29% grads go on to further study within 1 year. 15% grads pursue law degrees. 17% grads pursue medical degrees. **Faculty:** 210 full-time faculty, 93% hold PhDs, 61% are members of minority groups, 20% are women. 0% of classes are taught by teaching assistants.

ACADEMICS

Degrees: bachelor's. **Classes:** Most classes have 10–19 students. Most lab/discussion sessions have 10–19 students. **Majors with Highest Enrollment:** Psychology; English Language and Literature; Economics. **Special Study Options:** Accelerated program, cross-registration, double major, dual enrollment, exchange student program (domestic), honors program, independent study, internships, liberal arts/career combination, student-designed major, study abroad, teacher certification program, independant scholars program, BA/BS in engineering and applied science. **Honors programs:** The Barnard Centennial Scholars Program, established in 1984, offers selected students the opportunity to pursue courses of independent study early in their college careers. Working closely with mentors of their choice over a period of several semesters, these young women undertake investigations in areas of personal interest that culminate in projects presented to faculty and peers. The Athena Center for Leadership Studies was launched in September of 2009 and offers a range of academic courses that examines all aspects of women's leadership, sponsored lectures, mentoring and leadership opportunities and a lab which offers a wide range of workshops designed to teach practical elements of leadership to students, alums and other leaders in New York. Combined degree programs: BA/JD, BA/DDS, BA/MIA or BA/MBA Col. Schl. of Intern. and Public Af. **Disability Services:** Special programs offered to physically disabled students include note-taking services, reader services, tape recorders, tutors. **Career services:** Alumni network, alumni services, career/job search classes, career assessment, internships, regional alumni. Because of our urban setting, our students are exposed to extremely wide range of internship opportunities. Barnard also offers funding for some unpaid internships.

FACILITIES

Housing: Coed dorms, special housing for disabled students, women's dorms, apartments for single students. 100% of campus accessible to physically disabled. **Special Academic Facilities/Equipment:** Black Box theater, infant-toddler center, greenhouse, academic computer center, advanced architecture labs. **Computers:** 60% of classrooms, 80% of dorms, 80% of libraries, 100% of dining areas, 100% of student union, 100% of common outdoor areas have wireless network access. Students can register for classes online. Administrative functions (other than registration) can be performed online.

CAMPUS LIFE

Environment: Metropolis. **Activities:** Choral groups, concert band, dance, drama/theater, jazz band, literary magazine, marching band, music ensembles, musical theater, opera, pep band, radio station, student government, student newspaper, student-run film society, symphony orchestra, television station, yearbook, Campus Ministries. 100 registered organizations, 1 honor society. **Athletics (Intercollegiate):** *Women:* archery, basketball, crew/rowing, cross-country, diving, fencing, field hockey, golf, lacrosse, soccer, softball, swimming, tennis, track/field (outdoor), volleyball. **On-Campus Highlights:** Diana Center, Arthur Ross Greenhouse, Held Auditorium, Smart Media Classrooms, Liz's Place Café. **Environmental Initiatives:** Barnard has mandated LEED certification for new buildings. The newest addition to Barnard's campus, The Diana Center, is a LEED Gold building. Barnard is partnered with other New York City organizations as part of Mayor Bloomberg's "PlanNYC 2030 Challenge" to reduce the City's greenhouse gas footprint and improve the urban infrastructure and environment. In 2008, Barnard purchased and installed LabStats, a program that tracks the hourly activity of the computers in the student labs. Barnard is keeping logs of the use of these computers to help optimize power management in the labs.

ADMISSIONS

Freshman Academic Profile: Average high school GPA 3.9. 82% in top 10% of high school class, 97% in top 25% of high school class, 100% in top 50% of high school class. 48% from public high schools. SAT Math middle 50% range 620-710. SAT Critical Reading middle 50% range 630-730. SAT Writing middle 50% range 650-730. ACT middle 50% range 28-32. Minimum internet-based TOEFL 100. Minimum paper TOEFL 600. **Basis for Candidate Selection:** *Very important factors considered include:* academic GPA, recommendation(s), rigor of secondary school record, standardized test scores, character/personal qualities, extracurricular activities. *Important factors considered include:* application essay, talent/ability, volunteer work. *Other factors considered include:* Class rank, alumni/ae relation, first generation, geographical residence, interview, level of applicant's interest, racial/ethnic status, work experience. **Freshman Admission Requirements:** High school diploma or equivalent is not required. **Freshman Admission Statistics:** 5,676 applied, 24% admitted, 46% enrolled. **Transfer Admission Requirements:** High school transcript, college transcript(s), essay or personal statement, standardized test scores, statement of good standing from prior institution(s). Lowest grade transferable C-. **General Admission Information:** Application Fee $55. Early decision application deadline 11/15. Regular application deadline 1/1. Regular notification 4/1. Non-fall registration not accepted. Admission may be deferred for a maximum of 12 months. Credit and/or placement offered for CEEB Advanced Placement tests.

COSTS AND FINANCIAL AID

Annual tuition $44,300. Room and board $14,660. Required fees $1,740. Average book expense $1,150. **Required Forms and Deadlines:** FAFSA, CSS/Financial Aid PROFILE, State aid form, Noncustodial PROFILE. **Notification of Awards:** Applicants will be notified of awards on or about 3/31. **Types of Aid:** *Need-based scholarships/grants:* Federal Pell, SEOG, state scholarships/grants, private scholarships, the school's own gift aid. *Loans:* Subsidized Stafford, Unsubsidized Stafford, PLUS, Federal Perkins, state loans, college/university loans from institutional funds. *Student Employment:* Federal Work-Study Program available. Institutional employment available. Highest amount earned per year from on-campus jobs $8,325. Off-campus job opportunities are excellent. **Financial Aid Statistics:** 97% freshmen, 98% undergrads receive need-based scholarship or grant aid. 0% freshmen, 0% undergrads receive non-need-based scholarship or grant aid. 100% freshmen, 100% undergrads receive need-based self-help aid. 0% freshmen, 0% undergrads receive athletic scholarships. 53% freshmen, 48% undergrads receive any aid. 49% undergrads borrow to pay for school. Average cumulative indebtedness $16,213.

See page 1004.

BARRY UNIVERSITY

11300 North East Second Avenue, Miami Shores, FL 33161-6695
Phone: 305-899-3100 · **Financial Aid Phone:** 305-899-3673
E-mail: Des-forms@mail.barry.edu · **CEEB Code:** 5053
Fax: 305-899-2971 · **Website:** www.barry.edu · **ACT Code:** 718

This private school, affiliated with the Roman Catholic Church, was founded in 1940. It has a 122-acre campus.

RATINGS

Admissions Selectivity Rating: 78   **Fire Safety Rating:** 60*

STUDENTS AND FACULTY

Enrollment: 4,551. **Student Body:** 63% female, 37% male, 26% out-of-state, 7% international (101 countries represented). Asian 1%, African American 19%, Caucasian 13%, Hispanic 17%, Native American <1% **Retention and Graduation:** 62% freshmen return for sophomore year. **Faculty:** 340 full-time faculty, 84% hold PhDs, 53% are members of minority groups, 26% are women.

ACADEMICS

Degrees: bachelor's, first professional, master's, post-bachelor's certificate, post-master's certificate. **Classes:** Most classes have 10–19 students. **Majors with Highest Enrollment:** Information Science/Studies; Elementary Education and Teaching; Business/Commerce. **Special Study Options:** Accelerated program, double major, English as a Second Language (ESL), honors program, internships, study abroad, teacher certification program. Combined degree programs: DPM/MBA; JD/MBA; MSN/MBA. **Disability Services:** Special programs offered to physically disabled students include note-taking services, reader services, tape recorders, tutors. **Career services:** alumni services.

FACILITIES

Housing: Coed dorms, special housing for disabled students, men's dorms, women's dorms. 82% of campus accessible to physically disabled. **Special Academic Facilities/Equipment:** Human performance lab, broadcasting studio, radio station, athletic training room, cell biology/biotechnology labs, Classroom of Tomorrow, Biomechanics lab, Photogrpahy lab, darkroom, and studio, Language lab, athletic training room. **Computers:** Students can register for classes online. Administrative functions (other than registration) can be performed online.

CAMPUS LIFE

Environment: Village. **Activities:** Choral groups, dance, drama/theater, literary magazine, music ensembles, musical theater, radio station, student government, student newspaper, television station, Campus Ministries, International Student Organization. 67 registered organizations, 20 honor societies, 5 religious organizations. 2 fraternities, 2 sororities. **Athletics (Intercollegiate):** *Men:* baseball, basketball, golf, soccer, tennis. *Women:* basketball, crew/rowing, golf, soccer, softball, tennis, volleyball. **On-Campus Highlights:** Thompson Hall-Student Center, Human Performance Leisure Sciences-Athletic Complex, Penaport Pool, Residence Halls, Library.

ADMISSIONS

Freshman Academic Profile: Average high school GPA 3.14. 100% in top 50% of high school class. SAT Math middle 50% range 420-520. SAT Critical Reading middle 50% range 440-520. ACT middle 50% range 18-21. Minimum internet-based TOEFL 61. **Basis for Candidate Selection:** *Very important factors considered include:* academic GPA, standardized test scores. *Important factors considered include:* character/personal qualities, interview, talent/ability. *Other factors considered include:* Class rank, application essay, recommendation(s), rigor of secondary school record, extracurricular activities, volunteer work, work experience. **Freshman Admission Requirements:** High school diploma is required and GED is accepted. **Freshman Admission Statistics:** 7,645 applied, 52% admitted, 16% enrolled. **Transfer Admission Requirements:** college transcript(s), Minimum college GPA of 2.0 required. Lowest grade transferable C. **General Admission Information:** Application Fee $30. Notification on a rolling basis, beginning on or about 9/8. Nonfall registration accepted. Admission may be deferred for a maximum of 1 year. Credit offered for CEEB Advanced Placement tests.

COSTS AND FINANCIAL AID

Annual tuition $28,160. Room and board $9,300. Average book expense $1,200. **Required Forms and Deadlines:** FAFSA. **Notification of Awards:** Applicants will be notified of awards on a rolling basis beginning 1/25. **Types of Aid:** *Need-based scholarships/grants:* Federal Pell, SEOG, state scholarships/grants, private scholarships, the school's own gift aid, Federal Nursing Scholarships. *Loans:* Subsidized Stafford, Unsubsidized Stafford, PLUS, Federal Perkins, Federal Nursing, college/university loans from institutional funds, Alternative Loans. *Student Employment:* Federal Work-Study Program available. Institutional employment available. Highest amount earned per year from on-campus jobs $7,400. Off-campus job opportunities are good. **Financial Aid Statistics:** 83% freshmen, 71% undergrads receive need-based scholarship or grant aid. 99% freshmen, 98% undergrads receive non-need-based scholarship or grant aid. 95% freshmen, 93% undergrads receive need-based self-help aid. 4% freshmen, 4% undergrads receive athletic scholarships. 98% freshmen, 85% undergrads receive any aid. **Criteria for awarding institutional aid:** *Non-need-based:* academics, art, athletics, music/drama.

BARTON COLLEGE

Box 5000, Wilson, NC 27893-7000
Phone: 252-399-6317 · **Financial Aid Phone:** 252-399-6316
E-mail: enroll@barton.edu · **CEEB Code:** 5016
Fax: 252-399-6572 · **Website:** www.barton.edu · **ACT Code:** 3066

This private school, affiliated with the Disciples of Christ Church, was founded in 1902. It has a 76-acre campus.

RATINGS

Admissions Selectivity Rating: 83   **Fire Safety Rating:** 80

STUDENTS AND FACULTY

Enrollment: 1,076. **Student Body:** 69% female, 31% male, 11% out-of-state, 3% international (8 countries represented). Asian 1%, African American 27%, Caucasian 58%, Hispanic 3%, Native American 1%

Retention and Graduation: 71% freshmen return for sophomore year. 35% freshmen graduate within 4 years. 47% freshmen graduate within 6 years.

Faculty: 69 full-time faculty, 68% hold PhDs, 49% are members of minority groups, 13% are women. 0% of classes are taught by teaching assistants.

ACADEMICS

Degrees: bachelor's. **Classes:** Most classes have 10–19 students. Most lab/discussion sessions have fewer than 10 students. **Majors with Highest Enrollment:** Elementary Education and Teaching; Registered Nursing/Registered Nurse; Business Administration and Management. **Special Study Options:** cooperative education program, double major, honors program, independent study, internships, liberal arts/career combination, study abroad, teacher certification program, weekend college. **Honors programs:** Three competitive international travel scholarships awarded to entering honors students. **Disability Services:** Special programs offered to physically disabled students include note-taking services, reader services, tape recorders, tutors. **Career services:** alumni services, career/job search classes, career assessment, internships.

FACILITIES

Housing: Coed dorms, special housing for disabled students, women's dorms, fraternity/sorority housing. 90% of campus accessible to physically disabled. **Special Academic Facilities/Equipment:** tv station, art museum, music recording studio, greenhouse. **Computers:** 90% of libraries, 90% of dining areas, have wireless network access. Administrative functions (other than registration) can be performed online.

CAMPUS LIFE

Environment: Town. **Activities:** Choral groups, dance, drama/theater, musical theater, pep band, student government, student newspaper, symphony orchestra, Campus Ministries 51 registered organizations, 7 honor societies, 4 religious organizations. 3 fraternities, 3 sororities. **Athletics (Intercollegiate):** *Men:* baseball, basketball, cross-country, golf, soccer, tennis. *Women:* basketball, cross-country, soccer, softball, tennis, volleyball. **On-Campus Highlights:** Hamlin Student Center, Sam and Marjorie Ragan Writing Center, Kennedy Recreation and Intramural Center, Hackney Library, Barton Art Museum.

ADMISSIONS

Freshman Academic Profile: Average high school GPA 3.04. 12% in top 10% of high school class, 35% in top 25% of high school class, 73% in top 50% of high school class. 87% from public high schools. SAT Math middle 50% range 430-540. SAT Critical Reading middle 50% range 420-520. Minimum paper TOEFL 525. **Basis for Candidate Selection:** *Very important factors considered include:* academic GPA, standardized test scores. *Other factors considered include:* Class rank, recommendation(s), rigor of secondary school record, extracurricular activities, interview, volunteer work, work experience. **Freshman Admission Requirements:** High school diploma is required and GED is accepted. *Academic units required:* 4 English, 3 mathematics, 2 science, (1 science labs), 1 academic electives. **Freshman Admission Statistics:** 3,017 applied, 44% admitted, 15% enrolled. **Transfer Admission Requirements:** college transcript(s), statement of good standing from prior institution(s). Minimum college GPA of 2.0 required. Lowest grade transferable C. **General Admission Information:** Application Fee $25. Notification on a rolling basis, beginning on or about 8/15. Nonfall registration accepted. Admission may be deferred for a maximum of 1 year. Credit and/or placement offered for CEEB Advanced Placement tests.

COSTS AND FINANCIAL AID

Annual tuition $22,278. Room and board $7,940. Required fees $1,902. Average book expense $1,200. **Required Forms and Deadlines:** FAFSA. **Types of Aid:** *Need-based scholarships/grants:* Federal Pell, SEOG, state scholarships/grants, private scholarships, the school's own gift aid. *Loans:* Subsidized Stafford, Unsubsidized Stafford, PLUS, Federal Perkins. *Student Employment:* Federal Work-Study Program available. Institutional employment available. Highest amount earned per year from on-campus jobs $1,500. Off-campus job opportunities are good. **Financial Aid Statistics:** 99% freshmen, 96% undergrads receive need-based scholarship or grant aid. 10% freshmen, 6% undergrads receive non-need-based scholarship or grant aid. 86% freshmen, 85% undergrads receive need-based self-help aid. 9% freshmen, 6% undergrads receive athletic scholarships. 98% freshmen, 93% undergrads receive any aid. **Criteria for awarding institutional aid:** *Non-need-based:* academics, alumni affiliation, art, athletics, leadership, minority status, music/drama, religious affiliation, state/district residency.

BASTYR UNIVERSITY

14500 Juanita Drive NE, Kenmore, WA 98028
Phone: 425-602-3330 · **Financial Aid Phone:** 425-602-3083
E-mail: admissions@bastyr.edu
Fax: 4256023090 · **Website:** www.bastyr.edu

This private school was founded in 1978. It has a 51-acre campus.

RATINGS

Admissions Selectivity Rating: 60*   **Fire Safety Rating:** 79

STUDENTS AND FACULTY

Enrollment: 249. **Student Body:** 85% female, 15% male, 27% out-of-state, 4% international (31 countries represented). Asian 8%, African American 5%, Caucasian 72%, Hispanic 4%, Native American <1%
Faculty: 43 full-time faculty, 63% are members of minority groups, 19% are women. 0% of classes are taught by teaching assistants.

ACADEMICS

Degrees: bachelor's, certificate, master's, post-master's certificate. **Majors with Highest Enrollment:** Acupuncture and Oriental Medicine; Nutrition Sciences; Herbalism/Herbalist. **Special Study Options:** double major, internships, selected tracks within major. Combined degree programs: naturopathic medicine and acupuncture. **Career services:** career/job search classes, career assessment, internships.

FACILITIES

Housing: Coed dorms, Wellness Housing.

CAMPUS LIFE

Environment: Town. **Activities:** Choral groups, student government. **On-Campus Highlights:** Vegetarian cafeteria, Medicinal herb garden, Spacious campus grounds and playfields, Adjacent state park, Bookstore. **Environmental Initiatives:** Our 11-building Student Village has earned LEED Platinum-certification (the first student housing project on the West Coast to receive this honor) and the U.S. Green Building Council's (USGBC) Outstanding Multifamily Project in the 2010 LEED for Homes Awards. The buildings feature "butterfly" roofs to capture rainwater, high efficiency water heaters and gas boilers, energy-efficient appliances and light fixtures, low-flow plumbing, natural ventilation, radiant-heat flooring made of finished concrete, sustainable landscaping, and bicycle storage. Our campus features a rigorous composting and recycling program that allows us to divert 65 percent of waste from landfills. All disposable dishware, cups, silverware and paper towels are compostable. We offer bins for recycling paper, styrofoam, batteries, and light bulbs. A paperless office policy further allows us to reduce paper usage. Our buildings also include automatic lighting and other lighting efficiency, resulting in 14 percent reduced wattage consumption based on 2010 levels. Our dining services and our nutrition curriculum follow a distinctive whole-food philosophy that emphasizes a plant-focused diet and eating a wide variety of foods in unprocessed form. Local, organic, and responsibly-sourced food (both vegetarian and meat) comprise 75 percent of our food expenditures. Our cafeteria is known in the neighboring community for offering restaurant-quality, healthy food, and is frequently mentioned by students as a highlight of the school.

ADMISSIONS

Freshman Academic Profile: Minimum internet-based TOEFL 79. Minimum paper TOEFL 550. **Transfer Admission Requirements:** college transcript(s), essay or personal statement, Minimum college GPA of 2.25 required. Lowest grade transferable 2. **General Admission Information:** Application Fee $60. Notification on a rolling basis, beginning on or about 4/15.

COSTS AND FINANCIAL AID

Average book expense $2,250. **Required Forms and Deadlines:** FAFSA, Institution's own financial aid form. **Notification of Awards:** Applicants will be notified of awards on a rolling basis beginning 5/15. **Types of Aid:** *Need-based scholarships/grants:* Federal Pell, SEOG, state scholarships/grants, private scholarships, the school's own gift aid. *Loans:* Direct Subsidized Stafford, Direct Unsubsidized Stafford, Direct PLUS, Subsidized Stafford, Unsubsidized Stafford, PLUS, Federal Perkins. *Student Employment:* Federal Work-Study Program available. **Financial Aid Statistics:** 91% undergrads receive need-based scholarship or grant aid. 2% undergrads receive non-need-based scholarship or grant aid. 0% undergrads receive athletic scholarships. 87% undergrads receive any aid. 0% undergrads borrow to pay for school. Average cumulative indebtedness $0. **Criteria for awarding institutional aid:** *Non-need-based:* academics, alumni affiliation.

BATES COLLEGE

23 Campus Avenue, Lewiston, ME 4240
Phone: 207-786-6000 · **Financial Aid Phone:** 207-786-6096
E-mail: admission@bates.edu · **CEEB Code:** 3076
Fax: 207-786-6025 · **Website:** www.bates.edu · **ACT Code:** 1634

This private school was founded in 1855. It has a 109-acre campus.

RATINGS

Admissions Selectivity Rating: 96   **Fire Safety Rating:** 97

STUDENTS AND FACULTY

Enrollment: 1,773. **Student Body:** 50% female, 50% male, 89% out-of-state, 7% international (71 countries represented). Asian 5%, African American 5%, Caucasian 72%, Hispanic 7%, Native American <1%
Retention and Graduation: 83% freshmen graduate within 4 years. **Faculty:** 163 full-time faculty, 93% hold PhDs, 50% are members of minority groups, 17% are women. 0% of classes are taught by teaching assistants.

ACADEMICS

Degrees: bachelor's. **Classes:** Most classes have 10–19 students. Most lab/discussion sessions have 10–19 students. **Majors with Highest Enrollment:** Political Science and Government; Psychology; History. **Special Study Options:** Accelerated program, cooperative education program, double major, honors program, independent study, internships, liberal arts/career combination, student-designed major, study abroad, teacher certification program. **Honors programs:** The Honors Program. **Disability Services:** Special programs offered to physically disabled students include note-taking services, reader services, tape recorders, tutors. **Career services:** Alumni network, alumni services, career/job search classes, career assessment, internships, regional alumni. Career services highlights include Finance Boot Camp: a day long introductory workshop presented by alumni working in all facets of the industry. The day provides a soup to nuts look at the industry with class specific small group options and networking opportunities.

FACILITIES

Housing: Coed dorms, men's dorms, women's dorms, Theme houses, quiet/study houses and halls, chem-free and low chem houses and halls. 65% of campus accessible to physically disabled. **Special Academic Facilities/Equipment:** Art gallery, Edmund S. Muskie Archives, language labs, planetarium, 600-acre conservation area on seacoast for environmental studies, scanning electron microscope, Imaging Center. **Computers:** 40% of classrooms, 100% of dorms, 100% of libraries, 100% of dining areas, 100% of student union, 10% of common outdoor areas have wireless network access. Students can register for classes online. Administrative functions (other than registration) can be performed online.

CAMPUS LIFE

Environment: Town. **Activities:** Choral groups, dance, drama/theater, jazz band, literary magazine, music ensembles, pep band, radio station, student government, student newspaper, student-run film society, symphony orchestra, yearbook, Campus Ministries, International Student Organization. 99 registered organizations, 3 honor societies, 9 religious organizations. **Athletics (Intercollegiate):** *Men:* baseball, basketball, crew/rowing, cross-country, diving, football, golf, lacrosse, skiing (downhill/alpine), skiing (nordic/cross-country), soccer, squash, swimming, tennis, track/field (outdoor), track/field (indoor). *Women:* basketball, crew/rowing, cross-country, diving, field hockey, golf, lacrosse, skiing (downhill/alpine), skiing (nordic/cross-country), soccer, softball, squash, swimming, tennis, track/field (outdoor), track/field (indoor), volleyball. **On-Campus Highlights:** Pettengill Hall, Bates College Museum of Art, Dining Commons, The George and Helen Ladd Library, Merrill Gymnasium/Underhill Arena. **Environmental Initiatives:** Developing sustainable building guidelines and campus energy goals. Developing an environmental leadership course for students. Adopting metrics to measure progress in campus sustainability.

ADMISSIONS

Freshman Academic Profile: 69% in top 10% of high school class, 95% in top 25% of high school class, 100% in top 50% of high school class. 53% from public high schools. SAT Math middle 50% range 640-710. SAT Critical Reading middle 50% range 640-720. SAT Writing middle 50% range 640-710. ACT middle 50% range 29-32. **Basis for Candidate Selection:** *Very important factors considered include:* Class rank, application essay, academic GPA, recommendation(s), rigor of secondary school record, character/personal qualities, extracurricular activities, interview, level of applicant's interest, talent/ability. *Other factors considered include:* standardized test scores, alumni/

ae relation, first generation, geographical residence, racial/ethnic status, state residency, volunteer work, work experience. **Freshman Admission Requirements:** High school diploma is required and GED is not accepted. *Academic units required:* 4 English, 3 mathematics, 3 science, (2 science labs), 2 foreign language, 3 social studies. **Freshman Admission Statistics:** 5,044 applied, 25% admitted, 38% enrolled. **Transfer Admission Requirements:** High school transcript, college transcript(s), essay or personal statement, statement of good standing from prior institution(s). Lowest grade transferable C. **General Admission Information:** Application Fee $60. Early decision application deadline 11/15. Regular application deadline 1/1. Regular notification 3/31. Nonfall registration accepted. Admission may be deferred for a maximum of 1 year. Credit and/or placement offered for CEEB Advanced Placement tests.

COSTS AND FINANCIAL AID

Average book expense $800. **Required Forms and Deadlines:** FAFSA, CSS/Financial Aid PROFILE, Noncustodial PROFILE. **Notification of Awards:** Applicants will be notified of awards on or about 4/1. **Types of Aid:** *Need-based scholarships/grants:* Federal Pell, SEOG, state scholarships/grants, private scholarships, the school's own gift aid. *Loans:* Subsidized Stafford, Unsubsidized Stafford, PLUS, Federal Perkins, state loans. *Student Employment:* Federal Work-Study Program available. Institutional employment available. Off-campus job opportunities are good. **Financial Aid Statistics:** 100% freshmen, 36% undergrads receive need-based scholarship or grant aid. 0% freshmen, 0% undergrads receive non-need-based scholarship or grant aid. 99% freshmen, 98% undergrads receive need-based self-help aid. 0% freshmen, 0% undergrads receive athletic scholarships. 42% freshmen, 42% undergrads receive any aid. 40% undergrads borrow to pay for school. Average cumulative indebtedness $15,435.

BAYLOR UNIVERSITY

One Bear Place #97056, Waco, TX 76798-7056
Phone: 254-710-3435 • **Financial Aid Phone:** 254-710-2611
E-mail: admissions@baylor.edu • **CEEB Code:** 6032
Fax: 254-710-3436 • **Website:** www.baylor.edu • **ACT Code:** 4062

This private school was founded in 1845. It has a 508-acre campus.

RATINGS

Admissions Selectivity Rating: 89	Fire Safety Rating: 98

STUDENTS AND FACULTY

Enrollment: 13,801. **Student Body:** 58% female, 42% male, 24% out-of-state, 3% international (73 countries represented). Asian 6%, African American 7%, Caucasian 64%, Hispanic 14%, Native American <1%
Retention and Graduation: 89% freshmen return for sophomore year. 55% freshmen graduate within 4 years. 72% freshmen graduate within 6 years. **Faculty:** 957 full-time faculty, 82% hold PhDs, 39% are members of minority groups, 13% are women.

ACADEMICS

Degrees: bachelor's, master's, post-master's certificate. **Classes:** Most classes have 10–19 students. Most lab/discussion sessions have 10–19 students. **Majors with Highest Enrollment:** Biology/Biological Sciences; Psychology; Registered Nursing/Registered Nurse. **Special Study Options:** Accelerated program, double major, honors program, internships, student-designed major, study abroad, teacher certification program. **Honors programs:** Honors Program, University Scholars Program, Great Texts Program Combined degree programs: BBA/MAccounting, BBA/MTax, BSN/MSNursing, BBA/MBA, BSE/MSBE, BSE/ME, ETC. **Disability Services:** Special programs offered to physically disabled students include note-taking services, reader services. **Career services:** Alumni network, alumni services, career/job search classes, career assessment, internships

FACILITIES

Housing: special housing for disabled students, men's dorms, special housing for international students, women's dorms, apartments for married students, apartments for single students, Theme HousingLiving-Learning centers. **Special Academic Facilities/Equipment:** Language and environmental studies labs, natural science museum, high definition television, Armstrong Browning library, Texas Collection Library, Strecker Museum/Bill and Vara Daniel Historical Village, TV Station, Radio Station **Computers:** 98% of classrooms,

10% of dorms, 95% of libraries, 95% of dining areas, 95% of student union, 50% of common outdoor areas have wireless network access. Students can register for classes online. Administrative functions (other than registration) can be performed online.

CAMPUS LIFE

Environment: City. **Activities:** Choral groups, concert band, dance, drama/theater, jazz band, literary magazine, marching band, music ensembles, musical theater, opera, pep band, radio station, student government, student newspaper, student-run film society, symphony orchestra, television station, yearbook, Campus Ministries, International Student Organization, Model UN. 222 registered organizations, 32 honor societies, 11 religious organization. 22 fraternities, 20 sororities. **Athletics (Intercollegiate):** *Men:* baseball, basketball, cheerleading, cross-country, football, golf, tennis, track/field (outdoor), track/field (indoor). *Women:* basketball, cheerleading, cross-country, equestrian sports, golf, soccer, softball, tennis, track/field (outdoor), track/field (indoor), volleyball. **On-Campus Highlights:** Mayborn Museum Complex, Armstrong Browning Library, Baylor Sciences Building, Student Life Center, Chili's Too—1st on a University Campus. **Environmental Initiatives:** Campus wide recycling, with over 700 locations on campus to recycle in which to recycle and collaboration with Athletics Department to recycle at all university sporting events. Financing wind power generation facilities through our contract for the next 10 years to finance the construction of wind turbines. 3. Campus wide commitment to energy conservation through campaigns such as Last Out, Lights Out.

ADMISSIONS

Freshman Academic Profile: 39% in top 10% of high school class, 74% in top 25% of high school class, 96% in top 50% of high school class. SAT Math middle 50% range 570-670. SAT Critical Reading middle 50% range 560-660. SAT Writing middle 50% range 530-640. ACT middle 50% range 24-30. Minimum internet-based TOEFL 76. Minimum paper TOEFL 540. **Basis for Candidate Selection:** *Very important factors considered include:* Class rank, rigor of secondary school record, standardized test scores. *Important factors considered include:* academic GPA. *Other factors considered include:* application essay, recommendation(s), alumni/ae relation, character/personal qualities, extracurricular activities, first generation, interview, level of applicant's interest, religious affiliation/commitment, talent/ability, volunteer work. **Freshman Admission Requirements:** High school diploma is required and GED is accepted. *Academic units required:* 4 English, 3 mathematics, 3 science, (2 science labs), 2 foreign language, 1 social studies, 1 history. **Freshman Admission Statistics:** 33,898 applied, 55% admitted, 19% enrolled. **Transfer Admission Requirements:** college transcript(s), Minimum college GPA of 2.5 required. Lowest grade transferable C. **General Admission Information:** Application Fee $50. Nonfall registration accepted. Credit and/or placement offered for CEEB Advanced Placement tests.

COSTS AND FINANCIAL AID

Annual tuition $36,360. Room and board $11,360. Required fees $3,838. Average book expense $1,276. **Required Forms and Deadlines:** FAFSA. **Notification of Awards:** Applicants will be notified of awards on a rolling basis beginning 3/1. **Types of Aid:** *Need-based scholarships/grants:* Federal Pell, SEOG, state scholarships/grants, the school's own gift aid. *Loans:* Subsidized Stafford, Unsubsidized Stafford, PLUS, Federal Perkins, Federal Nursing, state loans. *Student Employment:* Federal Work-Study Program available. Institutional employment available. Highest amount earned per year from on-campus jobs $9,325. Off-campus job opportunities are good. **Financial Aid Statistics:** 100% freshmen, 97% undergrads receive need-based scholarship or grant aid. 98% freshmen, 92% undergrads receive non-need-based scholarship or grant aid. 83% freshmen, 82% undergrads receive need-based self-help aid. 2% freshmen, 3% undergrads receive athletic scholarships. 97% freshmen, 92% undergrads receive any aid. **Criteria for awarding institutional aid:** *Non-need-based:* academics, art, athletics, job skills, leadership, music/drama.

BAY PATH UNIVERSITY

588 Longmeadow Street, Longmeadow, MA 01106-2292
Phone: 413-565-1331 • **Financial Aid Phone:** 413-565-1345
E-mail: admiss@baypath.edu • **CEEB Code:** 2122
Fax: 413-565-1105 • **Website:** www.baypath.edu • **ACT Code:** 1785

This private school was founded in 1897. It has a 48-acre campus.

RATINGS

Admissions Selectivity Rating: 81	Fire Safety Rating: 99

STUDENTS AND FACULTY

Enrollment: 1,578. **Student Body:** 100% female, 0% male, 43% out-of-state, 0% international (7 countries represented). Asian 1%, African American 14%,

Caucasian 57%, Hispanic 16%, Native American <1%
Retention and Graduation: 77% freshmen return for sophomore year. 54% freshmen graduate within 4 years. **Faculty:** 55 full-time faculty, 71% hold PhDs, 69% are members of minority groups, 7% are women. 0% of classes are taught by teaching assistants.

ACADEMICS

Degrees: associate, bachelor's, certificate, master's, post-bachelor's certificate. **Classes:** Most classes have 10–19 students. Most lab/discussion sessions have 10–19 students. **Majors with Highest Enrollment:** Pre-Occupational Therapy Studies; Psychology; Biomedical Sciences. **Special Study Options:** Accelerated program, cooperative education program, cross-registration, distance learning, double major, English as a Second Language (ESL), exchange student program (domestic), honors program, independent study, internships, student-designed major, study abroad, teacher certification program, weekend college, Directed study program. **Honors programs:** The Bay Path Honors Program offers unique learning experiences to the most qualified undergraduate students through honors courses, service projects, on and off campus events and participation in and development of the Bay Path College Honors Program community. The Honors Program at Bay Path provides academically talented and motivated students with uniquely challenging and intellectually stimulating educational opportunities. In the first two years, Honors students take team-taught, interdisciplinary seminars on specific topics, such as Darwin Across the Disciplines. This innovative approach broadens exposure to areas outside the major and provides connections with other Honors students. In the last two years, under the guidance of a faculty mentor, students are immersed in their field of study, and are urged to explore new areas of knowledge with an Honors thesis or creative project. **Disability Services:** Special programs offered to physically disabled students include tutors. **Career services:** Alumni network, alumni services, career/job search classes, career assessment, internships, regional alumni. We have a very strong internship program, with all students required in each respective major to perform fieldwork, an internship, student teaching, or experiential learning. Internships are listed in the top 3 important experiences employers wish to see on a college student's resume, aside from major and degree achieved.

FACILITIES

Housing: women's dorms. 50% of campus accessible to physically disabled. **Special Academic Facilities/Equipment:** Blake Student Commons, Bashevkin Academic Development Center, Breck Fitness Center, occupational therapy laboratory, and D'Amour Hall for Business, Communications and Technology. **Computers:** 100% of libraries, 100% of dining areas, 100% of student union, 25% of common outdoor areas have wireless network access. Students can register for classes online. Administrative functions (other than registration) can be performed online.

CAMPUS LIFE

Environment: Village. **Activities:** Choral groups, dance, drama/theater, literary magazine, musical theater, student government, student newspaper, International Student Organization, Model UN. 42 registered organizations, 3 honor societies, 1 religious organization. **Athletics (Intercollegiate):** *Women:* basketball, cross-country, field hockey, soccer, softball, tennis, volleyball. **On-Campus Highlights:** Carpe Diem Café, Toner/Helliwell Hearth and Lounge, Game Room, Breck Fitness Center, D'Amour Hall for Business, Communications and Tech. **Environmental Initiatives:** Recycling program; Energy Conservation Efforts; conversion of electric heat in student residence hall to gas heat.

ADMISSIONS

Freshman Academic Profile: Average high school GPA 3.28. 10.23% in top 10% of high school class, 38.64% in top 25% of high school class, 78.41% in top 50% of high school class. SAT Math middle 50% range 420-520. SAT Critical Reading middle 50% range 420-543. SAT Writing middle 50% range 430-520. ACT middle 50% range 17-23. Minimum internet-based TOEFL 71. **Basis for Candidate Selection:** *Very important factors considered include:* academic GPA, rigor of secondary school record. *Important factors considered include:* standardized test scores. *Other factors considered include:* Class rank, application essay, recommendation(s), alumni/ae relation, character/personal qualities, extracurricular activities, first generation, geographical residence, interview, level of applicant's interest, state residency, talent/ability, volunteer work, work experience. **Freshman Admission Requirements:** High school diploma is required and GED is accepted. *Academic units required:* 4 English, 3 mathematics, 2 science, (2 science labs), 0 foreign language, 2 social studies, 1 history. **Freshman Admission Statistics:** 893 applied, 63% admitted, 23% enrolled. **Transfer Admission Requirements:** college transcript(s), Minimum college GPA of 2.0 required. Lowest grade transferable C-. **General Admission Information:** Application Fee $25. Notification on a rolling basis, beginning on or about 9/15. Nonfall registration accepted. Placement offered for CEEB Advanced Placement tests.

COSTS AND FINANCIAL AID

Annual tuition $30,859. Room and board $12,852. Average book expense $975. **Required Forms and Deadlines:** FAFSA. **Notification of Awards:** Appli-

cants will be notified of awards on a rolling basis beginning 3/1. **Types of Aid:** *Need-based scholarships/grants:* Federal Pell, SEOG, state scholarships/grants, private scholarships, the school's own gift aid. *Loans:* Subsidized Stafford, Unsubsidized Stafford, PLUS, Federal Perkins, state loans. *Student Employment:* Federal Work-Study Program available. Institutional employment available. Highest amount earned per year from on-campus jobs $2,000. **Financial Aid Statistics:** 100% freshmen, 100% undergrads receive need-based scholarship or grant aid. 5% freshmen, 6% undergrads receive non-need-based scholarship or grant aid. 91% freshmen, 90% undergrads receive need-based self-help aid. 0% freshmen, 0% undergrads receive athletic scholarships. 98% freshmen, 90% undergrads receive any aid. 91% undergrads borrow to pay for school. Average cumulative indebtedness $30,449. **Criteria for awarding institutional aid:** *Non-need-based:* academics, state/district residency.

BEACON COLLEGE

105 E. Main Street, Leesburg, FL 34748
Phone: 352-638-9731 • **Financial Aid Phone:** 352-787-6306
E-mail: admissions@beaconcollege.edu
Fax: 352-787-0721 • **Website:** www.beaconcollege.edu • **ACT Code:** 704

This private school was founded in 1989.

RATINGS

Admissions Selectivity Rating: 61   Fire Safety Rating: 88

STUDENTS AND FACULTY

Enrollment: 128. **Student Body:** 38% female, 63% male, 80% out-of-state, 0% international (2 countries represented). Asian 2%, African American 10%, Caucasian 85%, Hispanic 3%, Native American <1%
Retention and Graduation: 73% freshmen return for sophomore year. 50% freshmen graduate within 4 years. **Faculty:** 17 full-time faculty, 65% hold PhDs, 59% are members of minority groups, 6% are women. 0% of classes are taught by teaching assistants.

ACADEMICS

Degrees: associate, bachelor's. **Classes:** Most classes have 10–19 students. **Special Study Options:** cooperative education program, independent study, internships, study abroad. **Honors programs:** Psi Tau Omega is the academic honor society at Beacon College. **Disability Services:** Special programs offered to physically disabled students include note-taking services, reader services, tape recorders, tutors.

FACILITIES

Housing: special housing for disabled students, apartments for single students, Students enjoy 1, 2, and 3 bedroom apartment style living accommodations. **Computers:** 100% of classrooms, have wireless network access.

CAMPUS LIFE

Environment: Village. **Activities:** Choral groups, drama/theater, literary magazine, student government, student newspaper, yearbook. 13 registered organizations, 1 honor society, 1 fraternity, 1 sorority. **On-Campus Highlights:** New Resident Apartment Complex, Student Center, Stoer Building - Office of Student Services, Beacon College Library, Administration Building.

ADMISSIONS

Freshman Academic Profile: Average high school GPA 2.8. Minimum paper TOEFL 525. **Basis for Candidate Selection:** *Very important factors considered include:* recommendation(s). *Important factors considered include:* application essay, rigor of secondary school record, standardized test scores, character/personal qualities, talent/ability. *Other factors considered include:* Class rank, academic GPA, extracurricular activities, interview, volunteer work, work experience. **Freshman Admission Requirements:** High school diploma is required and GED is accepted. *Academic units required:* 4 English, 1 mathematics, 1 science, 1 social studies, 2 history, 3 academic electives. **Freshman Admission Statistics:** 53 applied, 92% admitted, 59% enrolled. **Transfer Admission Requirements:** High school transcript, college transcript(s), essay or personal statement, interview, Lowest grade transferable C. **General Admission Information:** Application Fee $50. Regular application deadline 8/1. Notification on a rolling basis, beginning on or about 9/1. Nonfall registration accepted. Credit offered for CEEB Advanced Placement tests.

COSTS AND FINANCIAL AID

Annual tuition $27,000. Room and board $8,150. Required fees $700. Average book expense $900. **Required Forms and Deadlines:** FAFSA, Institution's own financial aid form, State aid form. **Notification of Awards:** Applicants will be notified of awards on or about 2/1. **Types of Aid:** *Need-based scholarships/grants:* Federal Pell, SEOG, state scholarships/grants, private scholarships, the school's own gift aid. *Loans: Student Employment:* Federal Work-Study Program available. Highest amount earned per year from on-campus jobs $6,000. Off-campus job opportunities are good. **Financial Aid Statistics:** 60% freshmen, 22% undergrads receive need-based scholarship or grant aid. 0% freshmen, 0% undergrads receive non-need-based scholarship or grant aid. 60% freshmen, 22% undergrads receive need-based self-help aid. 0% freshmen, 0% undergrads receive athletic scholarships. 67% undergrads borrow to pay for school. Average cumulative indebtedness $28,000.

BECKER COLLEGE

61 Sever Street, Worcester, MA 1609
Phone: 508-373-9400 • **Financial Aid Phone:** 508-373-9440
E-mail: admissions@becker.edu • **CEEB Code:** 3079
Fax: 508-890-1500 • **Website:** www.becker.edu • **ACT Code:** 1784

RATINGS
Admissions Selectivity Rating: 76   **Fire Safety Rating:** 79

STUDENTS AND FACULTY
Enrollment: 2,021. **Student Body:** 59% female, 41% male, 34% out-of-state, 1% international (19 countries represented). Asian 2%, African American 6%, Caucasian 55%, Hispanic 6%, Native American <1%
Retention and Graduation: 67% freshmen return for sophomore year. 16% freshmen graduate within 4 years. 28% freshmen graduate within 6 years.
Faculty: 45 full-time faculty, 64% hold PhDs, 67% are members of minority groups, 9% are women. 0% of classes are taught by teaching assistants.

ACADEMICS
Degrees: Majors with Highest Enrollment: Registered Nursing/Registered Nurse; Game and Interactive Media Design; Veterinary Sciences/Veterinary Clinical Sciences.

ADMISSIONS
Freshman Academic Profile: Average high school GPA 3.2. 4% in top 10% of high school class, 27% in top 25% of high school class, 62% in top 50% of high school class. 65% from public high schools. SAT Math middle 50% range 440-560. SAT Critical Reading middle 50% range 430-550. SAT Writing middle 50% range 430-520. ACT middle 50% range 18-24. Minimum paper TOEFL 550. **Basis for Candidate Selection:** *Very important factors considered include:* Class rank, academic GPA, standardized test scores. *Important factors considered include:* recommendation(s). *Other factors considered include:* application essay, rigor of secondary school record, alumni/ae relation, character/personal qualities, extracurricular activities, interview, level of applicant's interest, volunteer work, work experience. **Freshman Admission Requirements:** High school diploma is required and GED is accepted. *Academic units required:* 4 English, 3 mathematics, 2 science, (2 science labs), 0 foreign language, 2 social studies, 1 history, 4 academic electives. **Freshman Admission Statistics:** 3,040 applied, 65% admitted, 21% enrolled. **Transfer Admission Requirements:** college transcript(s), Minimum college GPA of 2.00 required. Lowest grade transferable C. **General Admission Information:** Application Fee $50. Notification on a rolling basis, beginning on or about 11/1. Nonfall registration accepted. Admission may be deferred for a maximum of 1 year. Credit and/or placement offered for CEEB Advanced Placement tests.

COSTS AND FINANCIAL AID
Annual tuition $31,320. Room and board $12,000. Required fees $1,550. Average book expense $960. **Required Forms and Deadlines:** FAFSA, Institution's own financial aid form. **Types of Aid:** *Need-based scholarships/grants:* Federal Pell, SEOG, state scholarships/grants, private scholarships, the school's own gift aid. *Loans:* Subsidized Stafford, Unsubsidized Stafford, PLUS, Federal Perkins. *Student Employment:* Federal Work-Study Program available. Institutional employment available. Off-campus job opportunities are good. **Financial Aid Statistics:** 79% freshmen, 68% undergrads receive need-based scholarship or grant aid. 101% freshmen, 100% undergrads receive non-need-based scholarship or grant aid. 96% freshmen, 94% undergrads receive need-based self-help aid. 0% freshmen, 0% undergrads receive athletic scholarships. 100% freshmen, 93% undergrads receive any aid. 94% undergrads borrow to pay for school. Average cumulative indebtedness $28,273. **Criteria for awarding institutional aid:** *Non-need-based:* academics, alumni affiliation, athletics, leadership.

BELHAVEN UNIVERSITY

1500 Peachtree Street, Jackson, MS 39202
Phone: 601-968-5940 • **Financial Aid Phone:** 601-968-5933
E-mail: admission@belhaven.edu • **CEEB Code:** 1055
Fax: 601-968-8946 • **Website:** www.belhaven.edu • **ACT Code:** 2180

This private school, affiliated with the Presbyterian Church, was founded in 1883. It has a 42-acre campus.

RATINGS
Admissions Selectivity Rating: 85   **Fire Safety Rating:** 60*

STUDENTS AND FACULTY
Enrollment: 2,443. **Student Body:** 66% female, 34% male, 45% out-of-state, (20 countries represented).
Retention and Graduation: 73% freshmen return for sophomore year. 43% freshmen graduate within 4 years. 54% freshmen graduate within 6 years.
Faculty: 60 full-time faculty, 72% hold PhDs, 38% are members of minority groups. 0% of classes are taught by teaching assistants.

ACADEMICS
Degrees: associate, bachelor's, certificate, master's. **Classes:** Most classes have fewer than 10 students. Most lab/discussion sessions have fewer than 10 students. **Majors with Highest Enrollment:** Elementary Education and Teaching; Social Sciences; Dance. **Special Study Options:** Accelerated program, distance learning, double major, dual enrollment, English as a Second Language (ESL), honors program, independent study, internships, student-designed major, study abroad, teacher certification program. **Honors programs:** Honors Program: The Honors College at Belhaven College gives academically advanced, highly motivated students a forum in which to deepen and expand their college education, both intellectually and spiritually. Enrollment in the Honors College is limited to students who demonstrate a past record of academic achievement, seriousness about their calling, and enthusiasm for challenging dialogue with students and scholars from a variety of fields. Combined degree programs: BA/MEng. **Career services:** internships.

FACILITIES
Housing: men's dorms, women's dorms. **Special Academic Facilities/Equipment:** Bitsy Irby art gallery. **Computers:** 100% of dorms, 100% of libraries, 100% of student union, have wireless network access. Students can register for classes online. Administrative functions (other than registration) can be performed online.

CAMPUS LIFE
Environment: City. **Activities:** Choral groups, dance, drama/theater, jazz band, literary magazine, marching band, music ensembles, pep band, student government, student newspaper, yearbook, International Student Organization. 29 registered organizations, 5 religious organizations. **Athletics (Intercollegiate):** *Men:* baseball, basketball, cheerleading, cross-country, football, golf, soccer, tennis. *Women:* basketball, cheerleading, cross-country, golf, soccer, softball, tennis, volleyball.

ADMISSIONS
Freshman Academic Profile: Average high school GPA 3.22. 14% in top 10% of high school class, 29% in top 25% of high school class, 64% in top 50% of high school class. SAT Math middle 50% range 440-560. SAT Critical Reading middle 50% range 450-600. ACT middle 50% range 20-25. Minimum internet-based TOEFL 61. Minimum paper TOEFL 500. **Basis for Candidate Selection:** *Very important factors considered include:* academic GPA, standardized test scores. *Other factors considered include:* application essay, recommendation(s), interview. **Freshman Admission Requirements:** High school diploma is required and GED is accepted. *Academic units required:* 4 English, 2 mathematics, 1 science, (0 science labs), 0 foreign language, 0 social studies, 1 history, 8 academic electives. **Freshman Admission Statistics:** 1,568 applied, 46% admitted, 26% enrolled. **Transfer Admission Requirements:** college transcript(s), Minimum college GPA of 2.0 required. Lowest grade transferable D. **General Admission Information:** Application Fee $25. Nonfall registration accepted. Admission may be deferred for a maximum of 12. Credit and/or placement offered for CEEB Advanced Placement tests.

COSTS AND FINANCIAL AID
Annual tuition $17,700. Room and board $6,500. Average book expense $1,400. **Required Forms and Deadlines:** FAFSA, State aid form. **Notification of Awards:** Applicants will be notified of awards on a rolling basis beginning 2/1. **Types of Aid:** *Need-based scholarships/grants:* Federal Pell, SEOG, state scholarships/grants, private scholarships, the school's own gift aid. *Loans:* Subsidized Stafford, Unsubsidized Stafford, PLUS, Federal Perkins. *Student Employment:* Federal Work-Study Program available. **Financial Aid Statistics:** 99% freshmen, 98% undergrads receive need-based scholarship or grant aid.

9% freshmen, 7% undergrads receive non-need-based scholarship or grant aid. 81% freshmen, 82% undergrads receive need-based self-help aid. 15% freshmen, 9% undergrads receive athletic scholarships. 100% undergrads borrow to pay for school. Average cumulative indebtedness $28,516. **Criteria for awarding institutional aid:** *Non-need-based:* academics, alumni affiliation, art, athletics, music/drama.

BELLARMINE UNIVERSITY

2001 Newburg Road, Louisville, KY 40205
Phone: 502-272-8131 · **Financial Aid Phone:** 502-272-8124
E-mail: admissions@bellarmine.edu · **CEEB Code:** 1056
Fax: 502-272-8002 · **Website:** www.bellarmine.edu · **ACT Code:** 1490

This private school, affiliated with the Roman Catholic Church, was founded in 1950. It has a 135-acre campus.

RATINGS

Admissions Selectivity Rating: 82 **Fire Safety Rating:** 93

STUDENTS AND FACULTY

Enrollment: 2,499. **Student Body:** 65% female, 35% male, 32% out-of-state, 1% international (20 countries represented). Asian 2%, African American 4%, Caucasian 84%, Hispanic 3%, Native American <1%
Retention and Graduation: 80% freshmen return for sophomore year. 53% freshmen graduate within 4 years. 67% freshmen graduate within 6 years. 20% grads go on to further study within 1 year. **Faculty:** 163 full-time faculty, 81% hold PhDs, 58% are members of minority groups, 10% are women. 0% of classes are taught by teaching assistants.

ACADEMICS

Degrees: bachelor's, master's, post-bachelor's certificate. **Classes:** Most classes have 10–19 students. Most lab/discussion sessions have 10–19 students. **Majors with Highest Enrollment:** Psychology; Registered Nursing/Registered Nurse; Kinesiology and Exercise Science. **Special Study Options:** Accelerated program, cross-registration, double major, dual enrollment, honors program, independent study, internships, liberal arts/career combination, student-designed major, study abroad, teacher certification program. **Honors programs:** Bellarmine Honors Program Bellarmine Brown Scholars Program Combined degree programs: Accounting BA and MBA. **Disability Services:** Special programs offered to physically disabled students include note-taking services, reader services, tutors. **Career services:** Alumni network, alumni services, career/job search classes, career assessment, internships. 80% of Bellarmine undergraduates will complete an internship or another form of experiential learning before graduating (Source NSSE 2007 BU Seniors).

FACILITIES

Housing: Coed dorms, special housing for disabled students, men's dorms, women's dorms, 4 bedroom or 2 bedroom suites. 85% of campus accessible to physically disabled. **Special Academic Facilities/Equipment:** McGrath Art Gallery; Thomas Merton Center. **Computers:** 50% of classrooms, 100% of dorms, 100% of libraries, 25% of dining areas, 100% of student union, 25% of common outdoor areas have wireless network access. Students can register for classes online. Administrative functions (other than registration) can be performed online.

CAMPUS LIFE

Environment: Metropolis. **Activities:** Choral groups, concert band, dance, drama/theater, jazz band, literary magazine, music ensembles, musical theater, pep band, radio station, student government, student newspaper, yearbook, Campus Ministries, International Student Organization. 70 registered organizations, 3 honor societies, 6 religious organizations. 1 fraternity, 1 sorority. **Athletics (Intercollegiate):** *Men:* baseball, basketball, bowling, cross-country, golf, lacrosse, soccer, tennis, track/field (outdoor). *Women:* basketball, bowling, cheerleading, cross-country, field hockey, golf, soccer, softball, tennis, track/field (outdoor), volleyball. **On-Campus Highlights:** Norton Health Science Center, Our Lady of the Woods Chapel, Siena Halls, Owsley B. Frazier Stadium, The Thomas Merton Center, The $5.1 million Owsley B. Frazier Stadium has taken approximately 18 months to build and will be the new home for Bellarmine's soccer, field hockey, lacrosse, and track teams. The new facility has several outstanding features which are outlined below: Artificial Turf—The artificial turf product, called "24/7," was produced and installed by the Motz Group. It has permanent markings for soccer, field hockey, and lacrosse and has an exception-

al drainage system to allow for extensive play in all weather conditions. Lighting—Lighting has been installed at the field to allow for night play. The Musco Lighting system features redirected lighting which bends spill lighting back on to the field, drastically reducing the amount of light which will fall outside the stadium's perimeter. Track Surface—The track is an eight-lane, 400-meter track, featuring three long jump pits, two pole vault areas, a high jump pit, and a steeplechase water jump pit. The surface is a dual-durometer, polyurethane poured surface provided by Beynon Sport Surfaces, the same company which has installed tracks at other top college facilities over the past three years including Illinois, Maryland, and Purdue. Capacity—Chairback bench seating is available for 2,000 spectators. Scoreboard—A Daktronics scoreboard featuring a 17' x 3' scrolling message board is installed on the three-story clock tower at the south end of the stadium. Press Box—The fully enclosed press box features seating for 14 people and wireless internet access. The stadium also has a concession stand, public address system, officials' locker rooms, storage areas, and public restrooms. **Environmental Initiatives:** Development of an on-campus fruit/vegetable garden. Our major geothermal heating/cooling project and improved energy efficiency in new dormitory construction. Establishment of the Center for Regional Environmental Studies in July 2009.

ADMISSIONS

Freshman Academic Profile: Average high school GPA 3.48. 21% in top 10% of high school class, 53% in top 25% of high school class, 87.2% in top 50% of high school class. 67% from public high schools. SAT Math middle 50% range 500-590. SAT Critical Reading middle 50% range 510-590. ACT middle 50% range 22-27. Minimum internet-based TOEFL 80. Minimum paper TOEFL 550. **Basis for Candidate Selection:** *Very important factors considered include:* academic GPA, recommendation(s), rigor of secondary school record, standardized test scores, character/personal qualities, level of applicant's interest. *Important factors considered include:* Class rank, extracurricular activities. *Other factors considered include:* application essay, alumni/ae relation, first generation, geographical residence, interview, racial/ethnic status, state residency, talent/ability, volunteer work, work experience. **Freshman Admission Requirements:** High school diploma is required and GED is accepted. *Academic units required:* 4 English, 3 mathematics, 3 science, (2 science labs), 2 foreign language, 2 social studies, 1 history, 0 visual/performing arts, 0 computer science, 5 academic electives. **Freshman Admission Statistics:** 5,631 applied, 83% admitted, 14% enrolled. **Transfer Admission Requirements:** college transcript(s), Minimum college GPA of 2.0 required. Lowest grade transferable D. **General Admission Information:** Application Fee $25. Regular application deadline 8/15. Notification on a rolling basis, beginning on or about 10/1. Nonfall registration accepted. Admission may be deferred for a maximum of 12 months. Credit offered for CEEB Advanced Placement tests.

COSTS AND FINANCIAL AID

Annual tuition $36,210. Room and board $10,990. Required fees $1,440. Average book expense $788. **Required Forms and Deadlines:** FAFSA. **Notification of Awards:** Applicants will be notified of awards on a rolling basis beginning 4/1. **Types of Aid:** *Need-based scholarships/grants:* Federal Pell, SEOG, state scholarships/grants, private scholarships, the school's own gift aid. *Loans:* Subsidized Stafford, Unsubsidized Stafford, PLUS, Federal Perkins, state loans, college/university loans from institutional funds. *Student Employment:* Federal Work-Study Program available. Institutional employment available. Highest amount earned per year from on-campus jobs $2,500. Off-campus job opportunities are excellent. **Financial Aid Statistics:** 100% freshmen, 97% undergrads receive need-based scholarship or grant aid. 32% freshmen, 31% undergrads receive non-need-based scholarship or grant aid. 73% freshmen, 66% undergrads receive need-based self-help aid. 6% freshmen, 7% undergrads receive athletic scholarships. 100% freshmen, 90% undergrads receive any aid. 71% undergrads borrow to pay for school. Average cumulative indebtedness $25,758. **Criteria for awarding institutional aid:** *Non-need-based:* academics, alumni affiliation, art, athletics, leadership, minority status, music/drama, religious affiliation, state/district residency.

BELMONT ABBEY COLLEGE

100 Belmont-Mount Holly Road, Belmont, NC 28012
Financial Aid Phone: 704-461-6718
E-mail: admissions@bac.edu · **CEEB Code:** 5055
Website: www.belmontabbeycollege.edu · **ACT Code:** 3070

This private school, affiliated with the Roman Catholic Church, was founded in 1876. It has a 650-acre campus.

RATINGS

Admissions Selectivity Rating: 77 **Fire Safety Rating:** 75

STUDENTS AND FACULTY

Enrollment: 1,545. **Student Body:** 57% female, 43% male, 28% out-of-state, 1% international (13 countries represented). Asian 1%, African American 25%, Caucasian 41%, Hispanic 1%, Native American <1%
Retention and Graduation: 63% freshmen return for sophomore year. 33% freshmen graduate within 4 years. 38% freshmen graduate within 6 years. **Faculty:** 75 full-time faculty, 69% hold PhDs, 47% are members of minority groups, 5% are women. 0% of classes are taught by teaching assistants.

ACADEMICS

Degrees: bachelor's. **Classes:** Most classes have 10–19 students. **Majors with Highest Enrollment:** Education; Business Administration and Management; Elementary Education and Teaching. **Special Study Options:** Accelerated program, cooperative education program, double major, dual enrollment, external degree program, honors program, independent study, internships, liberal arts/career combination, study abroad, teacher certification program, weekend college. **Honors programs:** Anne Horne Little Honors Program Hintemeyer Scholars Program. **Disability Services:** Special programs offered to physically disabled students include tutors. **Career services:** Alumni network, alumni services, career/job search classes, career assessment, internships, regional alumni. Career services highlights include internships.

FACILITIES

Housing: Coed dorms, men's dorms, women's dorms, apartments for single students. **Special Academic Facilities/Equipment:** Museum with rare book collection. **Computers:** 10% of classrooms, 100% of libraries, 100% of dining areas, 100% of student union, have wireless network access.

CAMPUS LIFE

Environment: Village. **Activities:** Choral groups, drama/theater, literary magazine, musical theater, student government, student newspaper; Campus Ministries, International Student Organization. 21 registered organizations, 5 honor societies, 3 religious organizations. 5 fraternities, 4 sororities. **Athletics (Intercollegiate):** *Men:* baseball, basketball, cross-country, golf, soccer, tennis, wrestling. *Women:* basketball, cross-country, soccer, softball, tennis, volleyball. **On-Campus Highlights:** Church/Basillica, Weeler Center Athletic Center, Dining hall, Holy Grounds Coffee Shop.

ADMISSIONS

Freshman Academic Profile: Average high school GPA 3.13. 8% in top 10% of high school class, 26% in top 25% of high school class, 60% in top 50% of high school class. SAT Math middle 50% range 440-530. SAT Critical Reading middle 50% range 428-540. ACT middle 50% range 18-24. Minimum internet-based TOEFL 79. Minimum paper TOEFL 550. **Basis for Candidate Selection:** *Very important factors considered include:* rigor of secondary school record, standardized test scores, character/personal qualities. *Important factors considered include:* Class rank, alumni/ae relation, extracurricular activities, interview, volunteer work. *Other factors considered include:* application essay, recommendation(s), talent/ability, work experience. **Freshman Admission Requirements:** High school diploma is required and GED is accepted. *Academic units required:* 4 English, 3 mathematics, 2 science, (0 science labs), 2 foreign language, 1 social studies, 1 history, 3 academic electives. **Freshman Admission Statistics:** 1,981 applied, 68% admitted, 21% enrolled. **Transfer Admission Requirements:** college transcript(s), Minimum college GPA of 2.0 required. Lowest grade transferable C. **General Admission Information:** Application Fee $35. Regular application deadline 8/2. Notification on a rolling basis, beginning on or about 9/15. Nonfall registration accepted. Admission may be deferred for a maximum of 1 yr. Credit offered for CEEB Advanced Placement tests.

COSTS AND FINANCIAL AID

Annual tuition $18,500. Room and board $10,094. Average book expense $1,200. **Required Forms and Deadlines:** FAFSA. **Notification of Awards:** Applicants will be notified of awards on a rolling basis beginning 3/10. **Types of Aid:** *Need-based scholarships/grants:* Federal Pell, SEOG, state scholarships/grants, private scholarships, the school's own gift aid. *Loans:* Direct Subsidized Stafford, Direct Unsubsidized Stafford, Direct PLUS, Federal Perkins. *Student Employment:* Federal Work-Study Program available. Institutional employment available. Highest amount earned per year from on-campus jobs $1,800. Off-campus job opportunities are fair. **Financial Aid Statistics:** 93% freshmen, 95% undergrads receive need-based scholarship or grant aid. 11% freshmen, 9% undergrads receive non-need-based scholarship or grant aid. 7% freshmen, 4% undergrads receive need-based self-help aid. 8% freshmen, 6% undergrads receive athletic scholarships. 98% freshmen, 90% undergrads receive any aid. 84% undergrads borrow to pay for school. Average cumulative indebtedness $26,542. **Criteria for awarding institutional aid:** *Non-need-based:* academics, athletics, leadership, religious affiliation, state/district residency.

BELMONT UNIVERSITY

1900 Belmont Blvd, Tennessee, TN Tennessee
Phone: 615-460-6785 • **Financial Aid Phone:** 615-460-6403
E-mail: mary.lucus@belmont.edu • **CEEB Code:** 1058
Fax: 615-460-5434 • **ACT Code:** 3946

This private school, affiliated with the Christian (Nondenominational) Church, was founded in 1860. It has a 66-acre campus.

RATINGS

Admissions Selectivity Rating: 86 **Fire Safety Rating:** 98

STUDENTS AND FACULTY

Enrollment: 5,778. **Student Body:** 61% female, 39% male, 66% out-of-state, 1% international (30 countries represented). Asian 2%, African American 4%, Caucasian 80%, Hispanic 5%, Native American <1%
Retention and Graduation: 83% freshmen return for sophomore year. 56% freshmen graduate within 4 years. 70% freshmen graduate within 6 years. 17% grads go on to further study within 1 year. **Faculty:** 332 full-time faculty, 85% hold PhDs, 51% are members of minority groups, 11% are women.

ACADEMICS

Degrees: bachelor's, master's, post-bachelor's certificate, post-master's certificate. **Classes:** Most classes have 10–19 students. Most lab/discussion sessions have 10–19 students. **Majors with Highest Enrollment:** Music Management; Registered Nursing/Registered Nurse; Music. **Special Study Options:** Accelerated program, cooperative education program, distance learning, double major, honors program, independent study, internships, liberal arts/career combination, student-designed major, study abroad, teacher certification program. **Career services:** Alumni network, alumni services, career/job search classes, career assessment, internships. Career services highlights include the campus-based business program. Our undergraduate students run five campus-based businesses that are collaborations with other programs on campus. This offers experiential learning for students who do not have a business of their own. Three of these businesses are retail oriented—located in 3,400 square feet of prime retail space in our student life building facing the edge of campus—and the other two are service business. These programs involve as many as 60 students at any given time.

FACILITIES

Housing: men's dorms, women's dorms, apartments for single students. 98% of campus accessible to physically disabled. **Special Academic Facilities/Equipment:** Language lab, recording studio, the Belmont Mansion, Little Theatre. **Computers:** 100% of classrooms, 100% of dorms, 100% of libraries, 100% of dining areas, 100% of student union, 100% of common outdoor areas have wireless network access. Students can register for classes online. Administrative functions (other than registration) can be performed online.

CAMPUS LIFE

Environment: Metropolis. **Activities:** Choral groups, concert band, dance, drama/theater, jazz band, literary magazine, marching band, music ensembles, musical theater, opera, pep band, radio station, student government, student newspaper, symphony orchestra, television station, Campus Ministries, International Student Organization. 80 registered organizations, 17 honor societies, 12 religious organizations. 3 fraternities, 4 sororities. **Athletics (Intercollegiate):** *Men:* baseball, basketball, cross-country, golf, soccer, tennis, track/field (outdoor). *Women:* basketball, cross-country, golf, soccer, softball, tennis, track/field (outdoor), volleyball. **On-Campus Highlights:** Beaman Student Life Center, Curb Event Center, Belmont Mansion, Center for Music Business Recording Studios, Massey Courtyard. **Environmental Initiatives:** Recycling; Composting of all leaves; Conservation.

ADMISSIONS

Freshman Academic Profile: Average high school GPA 3.52. 32% in top 10% of high school class, 60% in top 25% of high school class, 89% in top 50% of high school class. SAT Math middle 50% range 530-630. SAT Critical Reading middle 50% range 530-630. ACT middle 50% range 23-29. Minimum paper TOEFL 550. **Basis for Candidate Selection:** *Very important factors considered include:* Class rank, academic GPA, rigor of secondary school record, standardized test scores. *Important factors considered include:* application essay, recommendation(s). *Other factors considered include:* alumni/ae relation, character/personal qualities, extracurricular activities, first generation, racial/ethnic status, talent/ability, volunteer work, work experience. **Freshman Admission Requirements:** High school diploma is required and GED is accepted. *Academic units required:* 4 English, 3 mathematics, 3 science, 2 foreign language, 3 social studies, 3 academic electives. **Freshman Admission Statistics:** 5,665 applied, 83% admitted, 30% enrolled. **Transfer Admission Requirements:** High school transcript, college transcript(s), essay or personal statement, standardized test scores, Minimum college GPA of 2.0 required. Lowest grade transferable C. **General Admission Information:** Application Fee $50. Regular application deadline 8/1. Notification on a rolling basis, beginning on or about 9/1. Nonfall registration accepted. Admission may be deferred for a maximum of 1 YEAR. Credit and/or placement offered for CEEB Advanced Placement tests.

COSTS AND FINANCIAL AID
Required Forms and Deadlines: FAFSA. **Notification of Awards:** Applicants will be notified of awards on a rolling basis beginning 3/15. **Types of Aid:** *Need-based scholarships/grants:* Federal Pell, SEOG, state scholarships/grants, private scholarships, the school's own gift aid. *Loans:* Direct PLUS, Subsidized Stafford, Unsubsidized Stafford, PLUS, Federal Perkins, college/university loans from institutional funds. *Student Employment:* Federal Work-Study Program available. Highest amount earned per year from on-campus jobs $4,000. Off-campus job opportunities are excellent. **Financial Aid Statistics:** 85% freshmen, 81% undergrads receive need-based scholarship or grant aid. 10% freshmen, 8% undergrads receive non-need-based scholarship or grant aid. 80% freshmen, 85% undergrads receive need-based self-help aid. 2% freshmen, 2% undergrads receive athletic scholarships. 56% undergrads borrow to pay for school. Average cumulative indebtedness $23,285. **Criteria for awarding institutional aid:** *Non-need-based:* academics, art, athletics, leadership, music/drama, religious affiliation, state/district residency.

See page 1006.

BELOIT COLLEGE

700 College Street, Beloit, WI 53511
Phone: 608-363-2500 • **Financial Aid Phone:** 608-363-2663
E-mail: admiss@beloit.edu • **CEEB Code:** 1059
Fax: 608-363-2075 • **Website:** www.beloit.edu • **ACT Code:** 4564

This private school was founded in 1846. It has a 75-acre campus.

RATINGS
Admissions Selectivity Rating: 89   **Fire Safety Rating:** 75

STUDENTS AND FACULTY
Enrollment: 1,225. **Student Body:** 58% female, 42% male, 81% out-of-state, 9% international (38 countries represented). Asian 3%, African American 5%, Caucasian 70%, Hispanic 9%, Native American <1%
Retention and Graduation: 85% freshmen return for sophomore year. 71% freshmen graduate within 4 years. **Faculty:** 110 full-time faculty, 97% hold PhDs, 55% are members of minority groups, 15% are women. 0% of classes are taught by teaching assistants.

ACADEMICS
Degrees: bachelor's. **Classes:** Most classes have 10–19 students. **Majors with Highest Enrollment:** Psychology; Science, Technology and Society; Anthropology. **Special Study Options:** double major, English as a Second Language (ESL), exchange student program (domestic), independent study, internships, liberal arts/career combination, student-designed major, study abroad, teacher certification program, 3-2 Programs in Engineering and Forestry. Over half of our graduates earn credit off-campus for at least a semester through our comprehensive study abroad and "field term" programs. Combined degree programs: BA/MEng, Rush University—Nursing and Med. Tech. **Disability Services:** Special programs offered to physically disabled students include note-taking services, tape recorders, tutors. **Career services:** Alumni network, alumni services, career assessment, internships, regional alumni. Beloit offers career exploration programs and services that connect students with alumni and other professionals for job shadowing, informational interviews and internships. Programs can be reviewed at http://www.beloit.edu/facs/.

FACILITIES
Housing: Coed dorms, women's dorms, fraternity/sorority housing, cooperative housing, apartments for single students, Theme HousingWide variety of special-interest housing, particularly for languages. See Beloit College's web site for a current list of special-interest housing. 35% of campus accessible to physically disabled. **Special Academic Facilities/Equipment:** Wright Museum of Art Logan Museum of Anthropology Center for Language Study Student Run Market Research Company (BELMARK) Alfred S. Thompson Observatory Center for Entrepreneurial Leadership (CELEB) **Computers:** 80% of classrooms,

10% of dorms, 100% of libraries, 100% of dining areas, 80% of student union, 4% of common outdoor areas have wireless network access. Administrative functions (other than registration) can be performed online.

CAMPUS LIFE
Environment: Town. **Activities:** Choral groups, dance, drama/theater, jazz band, literary magazine, music ensembles, musical theater, radio station, student government, student newspaper, student-run film society, symphony orchestra, television station, yearbook, International Student Organization. 95 registered organizations, 6 honor societies, 3 religious organizations. 3 fraternities, 3 sororities. **Athletics (Intercollegiate):** *Men:* baseball, basketball, cross-country, football, golf, soccer, swimming, tennis, track/field (outdoor), track/field (indoor). *Women:* basketball, cross-country, soccer, softball, swimming, tennis, track/field (outdoor), track/field (indoor), volleyball. **On-Campus Highlights:** Logan Museum of Anthropology, Wright Museum of Art, Center for the Sciences, Alfred S. Thompson Observatory, Laura H. Idrich Neese Theatre Complex, Other popular spaces include the Poetry Garden, the Java Joint, Morse Library, Sports Center, and Pearsons Hall. **Environmental Initiatives:** New Science Center has been platinum-level LEED certified, one of only three such buildings in the state Established institutional framework for sustainability through the formation of a Steering Committee and hiring a full time Sustainability Coordinator. Green meal plan for food service is under continuous discussion and development. The introduction of tray-less dining in 2008 has reduced waste by 35%, locally sourced food and produce from the campus vegetable garden are used whenever possible, and two campus dining options have switched to biodegradable utensils and plates.

ADMISSIONS
Freshman Academic Profile: Average high school GPA 3.34. 42% in top 10% of high school class, 75% in top 25% of high school class, 95% in top 50% of high school class. 64% from public high schools. SAT Math middle 50% range 560-680. SAT Critical Reading middle 50% range 540-690. ACT middle 50% range 24-30. Minimum internet-based TOEFL 80. Minimum paper TOEFL 550. **Basis for Candidate Selection:** *Very important factors considered include:* application essay, academic GPA, recommendation(s), rigor of secondary school record. *Important factors considered include:* Class rank, standardized test scores, interview. *Other factors considered include:* alumni/ae relation, character/personal qualities, extracurricular activities, first generation, level of applicant's interest, talent/ability, volunteer work, work experience. **Freshman Admission Requirements:** High school diploma is required and GED is accepted. **Freshman Admission Statistics:** 2,281 applied, 69% admitted, 19% enrolled. **Transfer Admission Requirements:** college transcript(s), essay or personal statement, statement of good standing from prior institution(s). Minimum college GPA of 3.00 required. Lowest grade transferable C. **General Admission Information:** Application Fee $35. Notification on a rolling basis, beginning on or about 2/15. Nonfall registration accepted. Admission may be deferred for a maximum of 12 months. Credit and/or placement offered for CEEB Advanced Placement tests.

COSTS AND FINANCIAL AID
Annual tuition $42,220. Room and board $7,470. Required fees $280. Average book expense $1,000. **Required Forms and Deadlines:** Institution's own financial aid form, CSS/Financial Aid PROFILE. **Notification of Awards:** Applicants will be notified of awards on a rolling basis beginning 4/1. **Types of Aid:** *Need-based scholarships/grants:* Federal Pell, SEOG, state scholarships/grants, private scholarships, the school's own gift aid. *Loans:* Subsidized Stafford, Unsubsidized Stafford, PLUS, Federal Perkins, college/university loans from institutional funds. *Student Employment:* Federal Work-Study Program available. Institutional employment available. Highest amount earned per year from on-campus jobs $3,000. Off-campus job opportunities are good. **Financial Aid Statistics:** 100% freshmen, 99% undergrads receive need-based scholarship or grant aid. 55% freshmen, 51% undergrads receive non-need-based scholarship or grant aid. 78% freshmen, 82% undergrads receive need-based self-help aid. 0% freshmen, 0% undergrads receive athletic scholarships. 99% freshmen, 93% undergrads receive any aid. 65% undergrads borrow to pay for school. Average cumulative indebtedness $25,406. **Criteria for awarding institutional aid:** *Non-need-based:* academics, leadership, minority status, music/drama.

See page 1008.

BEMIDJI STATE UNIVERSITY

1500 Birchmont Dr. NE, Bemidji, MN 56601
Phone: 218-755-2040 · **Financial Aid Phone:** 218-755-4143
E-mail: admissions@bemidjistate.edu · **CEEB Code:** 6676
Fax: 218-755-2074 · **Website:** www.bemidjistate.edu · **ACT Code:** 2084

This public school was founded in 1919. It has a 90-acre campus.

RATINGS

Admissions Selectivity Rating: 72   **Fire Safety Rating:** 67

STUDENTS AND FACULTY

Enrollment: 4,362. **Student Body:** 52% female, 48% male, 9% out-of-state, (35 countries represented).
Retention and Graduation: 33% freshmen graduate within 4 years. 49% freshmen graduate within 6 years. 34% grads go on to further study within 1 year. 27% grads pursue arts and sciences degrees. 1% grads pursue law degrees. 5% grads pursue business degrees. 1% grads pursue medical degrees. **Faculty:** 192 full-time faculty, 60% hold PhDs, 40% are members of minority groups, 6% are women. 5% of classes are taught by teaching assistants.

ACADEMICS

Degrees: associate, bachelor's, master's. **Classes:** Most classes have 10–19 students. Most lab/discussion sessions have 20–29 students. **Majors with Highest Enrollment:** Education; Industrial Production Technologies/Technicians; Business/Commerce. **Special Study Options:** Accelerated program, cooperative education program, distance learning, double major, dual enrollment, English as a Second Language (ESL), exchange student program (domestic), external degree program, honors program, independent study, internships, liberal arts/career combination, study abroad, teacher certification program, Eurospring Semester, Sino-Summer, Exchange program with other Minnesota state universities; other study-travel. **Disability Services:** Special programs offered to physically disabled students include note-taking services, reader services, tutors. **Career services:** Alumni network, career/job search classes, career assessment, regional alumni.

FACILITIES

Housing: Coed dorms, men's dorms, special housing for international students, women's dorms, apartments for married students, cooperative housing, apartments for single students, Two floors for SOTA (Students Older Than Average age.)Cooperative housing for international students. 95% of campus accessible to physically disabled. **Special Academic Facilities/Equipment:** Aquatics lab. Waterfront. C.V. Hobson Forest. Center for Research and Innovation (CRI). **Computers:** 90% of classrooms, 90% of dorms, 100% of libraries, 100% of student union, have wireless network access. Students can register for classes online. Administrative functions (other than registration) can be performed online.

CAMPUS LIFE

Environment: Village. **Activities:** Choral groups, concert band, dance, drama/theater, jazz band, literary magazine, music ensembles, musical theater, opera, pep band, radio station, student government, student newspaper, student-run film society, symphony orchestra, television station, Campus Ministries, International Student Organization, Model UN. 83 registered organizations, 1 honor society, 8 religious organizations. 2 fraternities, 1 sorority. **Athletics (Intercollegiate): Men:** baseball, basketball, cross-country, football, golf, ice hockey, soccer, softball, tennis, track/field (outdoor), track/field (indoor), volleyball. *Women:* basketball, cross-country, golf, ice hockey, soccer, softball, tennis, track/field (outdoor), track/field (indoor), volleyball. **On-Campus Highlights:** Recreation Center, Student Union, Library, Dormitories, Computer labs. **Environmental Initiatives:** Signature theme of Environmental Stewardship; ACUPCC signatory; Talloires Declaration Signatory.

ADMISSIONS

Freshman Academic Profile: Average high school GPA 3.33. 4% in top 10% of high school class, 27% in top 25% of high school class, 62% in top 50% of high school class. 95% from public high schools. ACT middle 50% range 19-24. Minimum paper TOEFL 550. **Basis for Candidate Selection:** *Very important factors considered include:* Class rank, standardized test scores. *Important factors considered include:* rigor of secondary school record. *Other factors considered include:* application essay, recommendation(s). **Freshman Admission Requirements:** High school diploma is required and GED is accepted. *Academic units required:* 4 English, 3 mathematics, 3 science, (1 science labs), 2 foreign language, 3 social studies, 1 history, 1 Art/Music/World Culture. **Freshman Admission Statistics:** 2,062 applied, 83% admitted, 45% enrolled. Minimum college GPA of 2.0 required. Lowest grade transferable C. **General Admission Information:** Application Fee $20. Regular application deadline 8/15. Nonfall registration accepted. Admission may be deferred for a maximum of 1 year. Placement offered for CEEB Advanced Placement tests.

COSTS AND FINANCIAL AID

Annual in-state tuition $6,410. Annual out-of-state tuition $6,410. Room and board $6,325. Required fees $950. Average book expense $800. **Required Forms and Deadlines:** Institution's own financial aid form. **Notification of Awards:** Applicants will be notified of awards on a rolling basis beginning 5/15. **Types of Aid:** *Need-based scholarships/grants:* Federal Pell, SEOG, state scholarships/grants, private scholarships, the school's own gift aid. *Loans:* Direct Subsidized Stafford, Direct Unsubsidized Stafford, Direct PLUS, Federal Perkins, state loans. *Student Employment:* Federal Work-Study Program available. Institutional employment available. Highest amount earned per year from on-campus jobs $2,700. Off-campus job opportunities are good. **Financial Aid Statistics:** 69% freshmen, 75% undergrads receive need-based scholarship or grant aid. 74% freshmen, 71% undergrads receive non-need-based scholarship or grant aid. 88% freshmen, 88% undergrads receive need-based self-help aid. 13% freshmen, 4% undergrads receive athletic scholarships. 77% freshmen, 77% undergrads receive any aid. 67% undergrads borrow to pay for school. **Criteria for awarding institutional aid:** *Non-need-based:* academics, alumni affiliation, art, athletics, music/drama.

BENEDICT COLLEGE

1600 Harden St, Columbia, SC 29204
Phone: 803-705-4491
E-mail: thompso@benedict.edu
Fax: 803-253-5167 · **Website:** www.benedict.edu

This private school, affiliated with the Baptist Church, was founded in 1870. It has a 110-acre campus.

RATINGS

Admissions Selectivity Rating: 70   **Fire Safety Rating:** 60*

STUDENTS AND FACULTY

Enrollment: 2,641. **Student Body:** 51% female, 49% male, 40% out-of-state. Asian 0%, African American 99%, Caucasian 0%, Hispanic 1%, Native American <1%
Retention and Graduation: 53% freshmen return for sophomore year. 11% freshmen graduate within 4 years. 26% freshmen graduate within 6 years. **Faculty:** 117 full-time faculty, 65% hold PhDs, 58% are members of minority groups, 95% are women.

ACADEMICS

Degrees: bachelor's. **Classes:** Most classes have fewer than 10 students. Most lab/discussion sessions have fewer than 10 students. **Special Study Options:** Accelerated program, double major, dual enrollment, external degree program, honors program, internships, teacher certification program, weekend college.

FACILITIES

Housing: men's dorms, women's dorms.

CAMPUS LIFE

Environment: City. **Activities:** Choral groups, concert band, marching band, student government, student newspaper, Campus Ministries, International Student Organization.

ADMISSIONS

Freshman Academic Profile: Average high school GPA 2.54. 5% in top 10% of high school class, 15% in top 25% of high school class, 39% in top 50% of high school class. 67% from public high schools. SAT Math middle 50% range 320-430. SAT Critical Reading middle 50% range 320-430. ACT middle 50% range 13-17. Minimum internet-based TOEFL 80. Minimum paper TOEFL 550. **Freshman Admission Requirements:** High school diploma is required and GED is accepted. **Freshman Admission Statistics:** 4,624 applied, 83% admitted, 17% enrolled. **Transfer Admission Requirements:** High school transcript, college transcript(s), statement of good standing from prior institution(s). Minimum college GPA of 2.0 required. Lowest grade transferable C. **General Admission Information:** Application Fee $25. Nonfall registration accepted. Credit offered for CEEB Advanced Placement tests.

COSTS AND FINANCIAL AID

Average book expense $1,000. **Required Forms and Deadlines:** FAFSA. **Types of Aid:** *Need-based scholarships/grants:* Federal Pell, SEOG, state scholarships/grants, private scholarships, the school's own gift aid, United Negro College Fund. *Loans:* Direct Subsidized Stafford, Direct Unsubsidized Stafford, Direct PLUS.

BENEDICTINE COLLEGE

1020 North Second Street, Atchison, KS 66002
Phone: 913-360-7476 · **Financial Aid Phone:** 913-360-7480
E-mail: bcadmiss@benedictine.edu · **CEEB Code:** 6056
Fax: 913-367-5462 · **Website:** www.benedictine.edu · **ACT Code:** 1444

This private school, affiliated with the Roman Catholic Church, was founded in 1859. It has a 225-acre campus.

RATINGS
Admissions Selectivity Rating: 80   **Fire Safety Rating:** 60*

STUDENTS AND FACULTY
Enrollment: 1,836. **Student Body:** 52% female, 48% male, 74% out-of-state, 3% international (13 countries represented). Asian 1%, African American 4%, Caucasian 79%, Hispanic 6%, Native American <1%
Retention and Graduation: 44% freshmen graduate within 4 years. 60% freshmen graduate within 6 years. **Faculty:** 105 full-time faculty, 68% hold PhDs, 32% are members of minority groups, 5% are women. 0% of classes are taught by teaching assistants.

ACADEMICS
Degrees: associate, bachelor's, master's. **Classes:** Most classes have 20–29 students. Most lab/discussion sessions have 10–19 students. **Majors with Highest Enrollment:** Elementary Education and Teaching; Business/Commerce. **Special Study Options:** cooperative education program, double major, dual enrollment, English as a Second Language (ESL), independent study, internships, liberal arts/career combination, student-designed major, study abroad, teacher certification program. Combined degree programs: BA/MA, BA/MEng, 3-2 occupational therapy with Washington U. **Disability Services:** Special programs offered to physically disabled students include tutors. **Career services:** alumni services, career/job search classes, career assessment, internships.

FACILITIES
Housing: Coed dorms, men's dorms, women's dorms, Off-campus college-owned housing. 80% of campus accessible to physically disabled. **Special Academic Facilities/Equipment:** Language and special education labs, high tech classroom, stadium, student union. **Computers:** 60% of classrooms, 100% of dorms, 100% of libraries, 100% of dining areas, 100% of student union, 75% of common outdoor areas have wireless network access. Administrative functions (other than registration) can be performed online.

CAMPUS LIFE
Environment: Town. **Activities:** Choral groups, concert band, dance, drama/theater, jazz band, literary magazine, music ensembles, musical theater, pep band, student government, student newspaper, symphony orchestra, yearbook. 38 registered organizations, 14 honor societies, 4 religious organizations. **Athletics (Intercollegiate):** *Men:* baseball, basketball, cheerleading, cross-country, football, golf, soccer, tennis, track/field (outdoor), track/field (indoor). *Women:* basketball, cheerleading, cross-country, golf, soccer, softball, tennis, track/field (outdoor), track/field (indoor), volleyball. **On-Campus Highlights:** Raven Roost, Ferrell Hall, Student Union, Abbey Church, River Lookout.

ADMISSIONS
Freshman Academic Profile: Average high school GPA 3.52. 24% in top 10% of high school class, 44% in top 25% of high school class, 72% in top 50% of high school class. SAT Math middle 50% range 460-600. SAT Critical Reading middle 50% range 485-645. ACT middle 50% range 22-27. **Basis for Candidate Selection:** *Very important factors considered include:* Class rank, rigor of secondary school record, standardized test scores. *Other factors considered include:* application essay, recommendation(s), alumni/ae relation, character/personal qualities, extracurricular activities, interview, racial/ethnic status, talent/ability, volunteer work, work experience. **Freshman Admission Requirements:** High school diploma is required and GED is accepted. *Academic units required:* 4 English, 3 mathematics, 2 science, 2 foreign language, 2 social studies, 2 history, 1 academic electives. **Freshman Admission Statistics:** 2,249 applied, 98% admitted, 22% enrolled. **Transfer Admission Requirements:** college transcript(s), Minimum college GPA of 2.0 required. Lowest grade transferable C. **General Admission Information:** Application Fee $25. Notification on a rolling basis, beginning on or about 3/1. Nonfall registration accepted. Admission may be deferred for a maximum of 1 year. Credit and/or placement offered for CEEB Advanced Placement tests.

COSTS AND FINANCIAL AID
Required Forms and Deadlines: FAFSA. **Notification of Awards:** Applicants will be notified of awards on a rolling basis beginning 2/1. **Types of Aid:** *Need-based scholarships/grants:* Federal Pell, SEOG, state scholarships/grants, private scholarships, the school's own gift aid. *Loans:* Subsidized Stafford, Unsubsidized Stafford, PLUS, Federal Perkins, Alternative Loans. *Student Employment:* Federal Work-Study Program available. Institutional employment available. Off-campus job opportunities are good. **Financial Aid Statistics:** 52% freshmen, 58% undergrads receive need-based scholarship or grant aid. 100% freshmen, 100% undergrads receive non-need-based scholarship or grant aid. 71% freshmen, 75% undergrads receive need-based self-help aid. 7% freshmen, 8% undergrads receive athletic scholarships. 73% undergrads borrow to pay for school. Average cumulative indebtedness $25,561. **Criteria for awarding institutional aid:** *Non-need-based:* academics, alumni affiliation, art, athletics, job skills, leadership, minority status, music/drama, religious affiliation.

BENEDICTINE UNIVERSITY

5700 College Road, Lisle, IL 60532-0900
Phone: 630-829-6300 · **Financial Aid Phone:** 630-829-6100
E-mail: admissions@ben.edu · **CEEB Code:** 1707
Fax: 630-829-6301 · **Website:** www.ben.edu · **ACT Code:** 1132

This private school, affiliated with the Roman Catholic Church, was founded in 1887. It has a 108-acre campus.

RATINGS
Admissions Selectivity Rating: 82   **Fire Safety Rating:** 94

STUDENTS AND FACULTY
Enrollment: 2,903. **Student Body:** 58% female, 42% male, 8% out-of-state, 1% international (17 countries represented). Asian 18%, African American 8%, Caucasian 44%, Hispanic 10%, Native American <1%
Retention and Graduation: 74% freshmen return for sophomore year. 38% freshmen graduate within 4 years. 52% freshmen graduate within 6 years. **Faculty:** 128 full-time faculty, 88% hold PhDs, 48% are members of minority groups, 16% are women. 0% of classes are taught by teaching assistants.

ACADEMICS
Degrees: associate, bachelor's, certificate, master's, post-bachelor's certificate, transfer associate. **Classes:** Most classes have 10–19 students. **Majors with Highest Enrollment:** Psychology; Biology/Biological Sciences; Organizational Behavior Studies. **Special Study Options:** Accelerated program, cross-registration, distance learning, double major, dual enrollment, English as a Second Language (ESL), honors program, independent study, internships, study abroad, teacher certification program, weekend college, Engineering degree program with Illinois Institute of Technology. **Honors programs:** University Scholars Program. **Disability Services:** Special programs offered to physically disabled students include note-taking services, reader services, tape recorders, tutors. **Career services:** Alumni network, alumni services, career/job search classes, career assessment, internships. Career services highlights include an internship program.

FACILITIES
Housing: Coed dorms, men's dorms, women's dorms, apartments for married students, apartments for single students, Wellness Housing. 100% of campus accessible to physically disabled. **Special Academic Facilities/Equipment:** Natural science and history museums,http://www.ben.edu/museum/ Exercise physiology lab. **Computers:** 100% of dorms, 100% of libraries, 100% of student union, have wireless network access. Students can register for classes online. Administrative functions (other than registration) can be performed online.

CAMPUS LIFE
Environment: Town. **Activities:** Choral groups, concert band, dance, drama/theater, jazz band, literary magazine, music ensembles, pep band, student government, student newspaper, student-run film society, symphony orchestra, television station, Campus Ministries, International Student Organization, Model UN. 40 registered organizations, 3 religious organizations. **Athletics (Intercollegiate):** *Men:* baseball, basketball, cross-country, football, golf, soccer, track/field (outdoor), track/field (indoor). *Women:* basketball, cross-country, golf, soccer, softball, tennis, track/field (outdoor), track/field (indoor), volleyball. **On-Campus Highlights:** Jurica Nature Museum, Kindlon Hall and Benedictine Library, Birck Hall of Science, Krasa Center: Chapel, cafeteria, snack bar, The Sports Complex, Coal Ben. **Environmental Initiatives:** Energy reduction Education Recycling

ADMISSIONS
Freshman Academic Profile: Average high school GPA 3.39. 21% in top 10% of high school class, 48% in top 25% of high school class, 79% in top 50% of high school class. 85% from public high schools. ACT middle 50% range 20-26. Minimum internet-based TOEFL 79. Minimum paper TOEFL 550. **Basis for Candidate Selection:** *Very important factors considered include:* Class rank, academic GPA, rigor of secondary school record, standardized test scores. *Other factors considered include:* application essay, recommendation(s), extracurricu-

lar activities, interview. **Freshman Admission Requirements:** High school diploma is required and GED is accepted. *Academic units required:* 4 English, 3 mathematics, 2 science, (1 science labs), 2 foreign language, 3 social studies, 1 history. **Freshman Admission Statistics:** 2,108 applied, 69% admitted, 32% enrolled. **Transfer Admission Requirements:** college transcript(s), statement of good standing from prior institution(s). Minimum college GPA of 2.0 required. Lowest grade transferable D. **General Admission Information:** Application Fee $40. Regular application deadline 8/30. Nonfall registration accepted. Admission may be deferred for a maximum of 4. Credit offered for CEEB Advanced Placement tests.

COSTS AND FINANCIAL AID
Average book expense $1,450. **Required Forms and Deadlines:** FAFSA. **Notification of Awards:** Applicants will be notified of awards on a rolling basis beginning 2/15. **Types of Aid:** *Need-based scholarships/grants:* Federal Pell, SEOG, state scholarships/grants, private scholarships, the school's own gift aid. *Loans:* Subsidized Stafford, Unsubsidized Stafford, PLUS, Federal Perkins. *Student Employment:* Federal Work-Study Program available. Institutional employment available. Highest amount earned per year from on-campus jobs $11,506. Off-campus job opportunities are excellent. **Financial Aid Statistics:** 63% freshmen, 62% undergrads receive need-based scholarship or grant aid. 98% freshmen, 84% undergrads receive non-need-based scholarship or grant aid. 76% freshmen, 89% undergrads receive need-based self-help aid. 0% freshmen, 0% undergrads receive athletic scholarships. 98% freshmen, 89% undergrads receive any aid. 65% undergrads borrow to pay for school. Average cumulative indebtedness $18,250. **Criteria for awarding institutional aid:** *Non-need-based:* academics, alumni affiliation, leadership, music/drama, religious affiliation, state/district residency.

BENNETT COLLEGE

900 East Washington Street, Greensboro, NC 27401
Phone: 336-370-8624 • **Financial Aid Phone:** 336-517-2220
E-mail: admiss@bennett.edu • **CEEB Code:** 5058
Fax: 336-370-8653 • **Website:** www.bennett.edu • **ACT Code:** 3072

This private school, affiliated with the Methodist Church, was founded in 1873. It has a 55-acre campus.

RATINGS
Admissions Selectivity Rating: 74   Fire Safety Rating: 72

STUDENTS AND FACULTY
Enrollment: 651. **Student Body:** 100% female, 0% male, 62% out-of-state, 0% international (2 countries represented). African American 94%, Caucasian 0%, Hispanic 2%, Native American <1%
Retention and Graduation: 20% freshmen graduate within 4 years. 34% freshmen graduate within 6 years. **Faculty:** 61 full-time faculty, 64% hold PhDs, 77% are members of minority groups, 70% are women. 0% of classes are taught by teaching assistants.

ACADEMICS
Degrees: bachelor's. **Classes:** Most classes have fewer than 10 students. Most lab/discussion sessions have 30-39 students. **Majors with Highest Enrollment:** Communication and Media Studies; Psychology; Biological and Physical Sciences. **Special Study Options:** Accelerated program, cooperative education program, cross-registration, double major, dual enrollment, honors program, independent study, internships, student-designed major, study abroad, teacher certification program, Collaborative degree program with Howard University in Nursing (2x2). **Disability Services:** Special programs offered to physically disabled students include tape recorders, tutors. **Career services:** alumni services, career/job search classes.

FACILITIES
Housing: women's dorms, Wellness Housing. 21% of campus accessible to physically disabled. **Special Academic Facilities/Equipment:** Children's House, Constance Maiteena collection, college archives, telecommunications satellite dish. **Computers:** Students can register for classes online.

CAMPUS LIFE
Environment: City. **Activities:** Choral groups, dance, drama/theater, literary magazine, music ensembles, student government, student newspaper, Campus Ministries, International Student Organization. 34 registered organizations, 5 honor societies, 1 religious organization. 4 sororities. **Athletics (Intercollegiate):** *Women:* basketball, cheerleading, cross-country, softball, swimming, tennis, track/field (outdoor), volleyball. **On-Campus Highlights:** Student Union, Chapel, Little Theatre, Holgate Library, Lda Goode Gym.

ADMISSIONS
Freshman Academic Profile: 8.1% in top 10% of high school class, 12.1% in top 25% of high school class, 49.5% in top 50% of high school class. SAT Math middle 50% range 350-420. SAT Critical Reading middle 50% range 350-430. **Basis for Candidate Selection:** *Very important factors considered include:* academic GPA, rigor of secondary school record, standardized test scores. *Important factors considered include:* Class rank, application essay, recommendation(s), alumni/ae relation, talent/ability. *Other factors considered include:* character/personal qualities, extracurricular activities, first generation, geographical residence, interview, level of applicant's interest, racial/ethnic status, religious affiliation/commitment, state residency, volunteer work, work experience. **Freshman Admission Requirements:** High school diploma is required and GED is accepted. *Academic units required:* 4 English, 3 mathematics, 2 science, 2 foreign language, 2 social studies, 5 academic electives. **Freshman Admission Statistics:** 1,433 applied, 63% admitted, 18% enrolled. **Transfer Admission Requirements:** college transcript(s), essay or personal statement, Minimum college GPA of 2.0 required. Lowest grade transferable C. **General Admission Information:** Application Fee $30. Nonfall registration accepted. Credit offered for CEEB Advanced Placement tests.

COSTS AND FINANCIAL AID
Annual tuition $14,614. Room and board $7,428. Required fees $2,180. Average book expense $1,500. **Required Forms and Deadlines:** FAFSA, Institution's own financial aid form. **Notification of Awards:** Applicants will be notified of awards on or about 7/15. **Types of Aid:** *Need-based scholarships/grants:* Federal Pell, SEOG, state scholarships/grants, private scholarships, the school's own gift aid, United Negro College Fund, Federal Nursing Scholarships. *Loans:* Subsidized Stafford, Unsubsidized Stafford, PLUS, Federal Perkins, The College has emergency funds available. *Student Employment:* Federal Work-Study Program available. Institutional employment available. Highest amount earned per year from on-campus jobs $1,500. Off-campus job opportunities are good. **Financial Aid Statistics:** 96% freshmen, 93% undergrads receive need-based scholarship or grant aid. 1% freshmen, 2% undergrads receive non-need-based scholarship or grant aid. 96% freshmen, 94% undergrads receive need-based self-help aid. 0% freshmen, 0% undergrads receive athletic scholarships. 94% undergrads borrow to pay for school. Average cumulative indebtedness $33,491. **Criteria for awarding institutional aid:** *Non-need-based:* academics, alumni affiliation, leadership, minority status, religious affiliation, state/district residency.

BENNINGTON COLLEGE

One College Drive, Bennington, VT 5201
Phone: 802-440-4312 • **Financial Aid Phone:** 800-833-6845
E-mail: admissions@bennington.edu • **CEEB Code:** 3080
Fax: 802-440-4320 • **Website:** www.bennington.edu • **ACT Code:** 4296

This private school was founded in 1932. It has a 470-acre campus.

RATINGS
Admissions Selectivity Rating: 89   Fire Safety Rating: 94

STUDENTS AND FACULTY
Enrollment: 631. **Student Body:** 67% female, 33% male, 97% out-of-state, 13% international (35 countries represented). Asian 3%, African American 1%, Caucasian 69%, Hispanic 5%, Native American 2%
Retention and Graduation: 58% freshmen graduate within 4 years. 10% grads go on to further study within 1 year. 10% grads pursue arts and sciences degrees. **Faculty:** 57 full-time faculty, 75% hold PhDs, 49% are members of minority groups, 11% are women. 1% of classes are taught by teaching assistants.

ACADEMICS
Degrees: bachelor's, master's, post-bachelor's certificate. **Classes:** Most classes have 10–19 students. Most lab/discussion sessions have 10–19 students. **Majors with Highest Enrollment:** English Language and Literature; Visual and Performing Arts; Social Sciences. **Special Study Options:** Accelerated program, cross-registration, double major, English as a Second Language (ESL), independent study, internships, student-designed major, study abroad, teacher certification program, Postbaccalaureate program in preparation for Medical or Allied Health School Grad Programs. Combined degree programs: BA/MAT. **Disability Services:** Special programs offered to physically disabled students include note-taking services, reader services, tape recorders. **Career services:**

Alumni network, alumni services, career/job search classes, career assessment, internships. Each academic year at Bennington College includes a seven-week winter term of field work off campus. During Field Work Term, students take their interests to the world beyond the College, where they work at jobs or internships in fields that complement their studies, clarify their interests, and open possibilities for their future.

FACILITIES

Housing: Coed dorms, cooperative housing, Theme Housing, Off-campus. 78% of campus accessible to physically disabled. **Special Academic Facilities/ Equipment:** Observatory; greenhouse; digital arts lab; architecture, drawing, painting, printmaking, and sculpture studios; ceramics studio and kilns; color and black-and-white photography darkrooms; film and video editing studio; fully equipped professional theaters; scripts library; dance studios and archives; electronic music and sound recording studios; music practice rooms and music library. **Computers:** 100% of classrooms, 100% of dorms, 100% of libraries, 100% of dining areas, 100% of student union, 75% of common outdoor areas have wireless network access. Administrative functions (other than registration) can be performed online.

CAMPUS LIFE

Environment: Town. **Activities:** Choral groups, dance, drama/theater, literary magazine, music ensembles, musical theater, radio station, student government, student newspaper, International Student Organization 21 registered organizations. **On-Campus Highlights:** Edward Clark Crossett Library, Visual and Performing Arts Center, Student Center, Commons Dining Hall and Lounge, Meyer Recreation Barn, Opening in 2011, the Center for the Advancement of Public Action (CAPA), is a $20-million, state-of-the-art, green, academic facility for Bennington's new citizenship curriculum. It morphs the studio of the artist, the laboratory of a scientist, the workshop of a craftsman, and the think tank of policy work. **Environmental Initiatives:** Converting to a campus-wide bio-mass heating system New green construction Energy conservation program.

ADMISSIONS

Freshman Academic Profile: 42% from public high schools. SAT Math middle 50% range 560-670. SAT Critical Reading middle 50% range 610-730. SAT Writing middle 50% range 580-700. ACT middle 50% range 27-32. Minimum paper TOEFL 577. **Basis for Candidate Selection:** *Very important factors considered include:* Class rank, application essay, academic GPA, recommendation(s), rigor of secondary school record, character/personal qualities, extracurricular activities, interview, talent/ability. *Other factors considered include:* standardized test scores, alumni/ae relation, first generation, geographical residence, level of applicant's interest, racial/ethnic status, volunteer work, work experience. **Freshman Admission Requirements:** High school diploma is required and GED is accepted. **Freshman Admission Statistics:** 1,032 applied, 72% admitted, 26% enrolled. **Transfer Admission Requirements:** High school transcript, college transcript(s), essay or personal statement, statement of good standing from prior institution(s). Lowest grade transferable C. **General Admission Information:** Application Fee $60. Regular application deadline 1/3. Regular notification 4/1. Nonfall registration accepted. Admission may be deferred for a maximum of one year. Neither credit nor placement offered for CEEB Advanced Placement tests.

COSTS AND FINANCIAL AID

Required Forms and Deadlines: FAFSA, Institution's own financial aid form, CSS/Financial Aid PROFILE, Noncustodial PROFILE. **Notification of Awards:** Applicants will be notified of awards on or about 4/1. **Types of Aid:** *Need-based scholarships/grants:* Federal Pell, SEOG, state scholarships/grants, private scholarships, the school's own gift aid. *Loans:* Direct Subsidized Stafford, Direct Unsubsidized Stafford, Direct PLUS, college/university loans from institutional funds NOTE: College/university loans from institutional funds for International students only. *Student Employment:* Federal Work-Study Program available. Institutional employment available. Highest amount earned per year from on-campus jobs $1,900. Off-campus job opportunities are good. **Financial Aid Statistics:** 59% undergrads borrow to pay for school. Average cumulative indebtedness $24,617. **Criteria for awarding institutional aid:** *Non-need-based:* academics.

BENTLEY UNIVERSITY

Best 380

175 Forest Street, Waltham, MA 2452
Phone: 781-891-2244 · **Financial Aid Phone:** 781-891-3441
E-mail: ugadmission@bentley.edu · **CEEB Code:** 3096
Fax: 781-891-3414 · **Website:** www.bentley.edu · **ACT Code:** 1783

This private school was founded in 1917. It has a 163-acre campus.

RATINGS

Admissions Selectivity Rating: 90   **Fire Safety Rating:** 99

STUDENTS AND FACULTY

Enrollment: 4,190. **Student Body:** 40% female, 60% male, 54% out-of-state, 15% international (93 countries represented). Asian 8%, African American 3%, Caucasian 60%, Hispanic 7%, Native American <1%
Retention and Graduation: 94% freshmen return for sophomore year. 83% freshmen graduate within 4 years. 88% freshmen graduate within 6 years.
Faculty: 282 full-time faculty, 77% hold PhDs, 38% are members of minority groups, 13% are women.

ACADEMICS

Degrees: associate, bachelor's, doctoral, master's, post-bachelor's certificate, post-master's certificate, terminal associate, transfer associate. **Classes:** Most classes have 30-39 students. **Majors with Highest Enrollment:** Marketing/ Marketing Management; Finance; Accounting. **Special Study Options:** Accelerated program, cross-registration, double major, honors program, independent study, internships, liberal arts/career combination, student-designed major, study abroad, 5 year Bachelors/Masters program in Business Administration, Accountancy, Finance, Marketing, Analytics, Info Technology, Financial Planning, Taxation. **Honors programs:** The Honors Program is a four-year journey that provides special challenge and fulfillment to select Bentley students. Students in approximately the top ten percent of the entering class are invited to participate in this four-year program. Combined degree programs: BA-MS, BS-MS, BA-MBA, BS-MBA. **Disability Services:** Special programs offered to physically disabled students include note-taking services, reader services, tape recorders, tutors. **Career services:** Alumni network, alumni services, career/ job search classes, career assessment, internships, regional alumni. For the past several years, Bentley students have journeyed to Ghana, West Africa, to work on a long-term economic development partnership focused on helping an orphanage become self-sustaining. This effort has expanded to include students who now implement and train Ghanian NGOs in the use of accounting software to allow them to apply for an receive USAID funding.

FACILITIES

Housing: Coed dorms, special housing for disabled students, apartments for single students, Wellness Housing, Theme HousingThree Wellness Houses with an overall health and wellness theme are available. Global living floors with a focus on connecting international and US students are available to residents. 70% of campus accessible to physically disabled. **Special Academic Facilities/ Equipment:** Academic Technology Center, Alliance for Ethics and Social Responsibility, Center for Business Ethics, Center for International Students and Scholars, Center for Quantitative Analysis, Art Gallery, Center for Marketing Technology, Center for Languages and International Collaboration, ESOL Center, Math Learning Center, Writing Center, Financial Trading Room, Design and Usability Center, Service Learning Center, Cronin International Center, Cyberlaw Center, Enterprise Risk Management Program, Hughey Center for Financial Services, Library, Media & Culture labs and studio, Valente Center for Arts and Sciences, Winer Accounting Center, Women's Leadership Institute, Academic Technology Center, Spiritual Life Center. **Computers:** 100% of classrooms, 100% of dorms, 100% of libraries, 100% of dining areas, 100% of student union, 100% of common outdoor areas have wireless network access. Students can register for classes online. Administrative functions (other than registration) can be performed online. Undergraduates are required to own a computer.

CAMPUS LIFE

Environment: Town. **Activities:** Choral groups, dance, drama/theater, jazz band, literary magazine, music ensembles, pep band, radio station, student government, student newspaper, television station, Campus Ministries, International Student Organization, Model UN 101 registered organizations, 3 honor societies, 4 religious organizations. 5 fraternities, 4 sororities. **Athletics (Intercollegiate):** *Men:* baseball, basketball, cross-country, diving, football, golf, ice hockey, lacrosse, soccer, swimming, tennis, track/field (outdoor), track/field (indoor). *Women:* basketball, cross-country, diving, field hockey, lacrosse, soccer, softball, swimming, tennis, track/field (outdoor), track/field (indoor), volleyball. **On-Campus Highlights:** Student Center, Dana Athletic Center, Currito Burrito, Einstein's Coffee Shop, Library. **Environmental Initiatives:** Bentley University is committed to the following carbon footprint reduction targets (compared to a 2008 baseline): 50% by 2015, 70% by 2020 and 100% by 2030. As of January 1, 2014 we have achieved a 42% reduction in our carbon footprint. Bentley University is committed to an increase in recycling and overall waste deduction. As of January 1, 2014 we have increased our waste diversion rate from 13% in 2012 to 35%. Bentley University is committed to an increase in faculty, student and staff understanding and engagement in sustainability issues. Outreach on various topics is achieved via: social media, a sustainability film series, a monthly newsletter, training offered during new student, faculty and staff orientation, a faculty and staff Eco-Rep program, a student Eco-Rep program, a student-led Green Society (group), a Green (campus) Department Certification Program, a Green (student) Groups certification program, student residential electricity-saving competition, among other projects.

ADMISSIONS

Freshman Academic Profile: 38% in top 10% of high school class, 75% in top 25% of high school class, 97% in top 50% of high school class. 70% from public high schools. SAT Math middle 50% range 610-690. SAT Critical Reading middle 50% range 540-640. SAT Writing middle 50% range 550-650. ACT middle 50% range 26-30. Minimum internet-based TOEFL 90. Minimum paper TOEFL 577. **Basis for Candidate Selection:** *Very important factors considered include:* academic GPA, rigor of secondary school record, standardized test scores. *Important factors considered include:* application essay, recommendation(s), character/personal qualities, extracurricular activities, level of applicant's interest, volunteer work. *Other factors considered include:* Class rank, alumni/ae relation, first generation, geographical residence, interview, racial/ethnic status, state residency, talent/ability, work experience. **Freshman Admission Requirements:** High school diploma is required and GED is accepted. **Freshman Admission Statistics:** 7,477 applied, 46% admitted, 28% enrolled. **Transfer Admission Requirements:** High school transcript, college transcript(s), essay or personal statement, statement of good standing from prior institution(s). Lowest grade transferable C. **General Admission Information:** Application Fee $50. Early decision application deadline 11/1. Regular application deadline 1/15. Regular notification 4/1. Nonfall registration accepted. Admission may be deferred for a maximum of 1 year. Credit and/or placement offered for CEEB Advanced Placement tests.

COSTS AND FINANCIAL AID

Annual tuition $40,990. Room and board $13,949. Required fees $1,521. Average book expense $1,200. **Required Forms and Deadlines:** FAFSA, CSS/Financial Aid PROFILE, Noncustodial PROFILE, Business/Farm Supplement. **Notification of Awards:** Applicants will be notified of awards on a rolling basis beginning 3/25. **Types of Aid:** *Need-based scholarships/grants:* Federal Pell, SEOG, state scholarships/grants, private scholarships, the school's own gift aid. *Loans:* Subsidized Stafford, Unsubsidized Stafford, PLUS, Federal Perkins, state loans. *Student Employment:* Federal Work-Study Program available. Institutional employment available. Off-campus job opportunities are good. **Financial Aid Statistics:** 98% freshmen, 97% undergrads receive need-based scholarship or grant aid. 20% freshmen, 13% undergrads receive non-need-based scholarship or grant aid. 96% freshmen, 96% undergrads receive need-based self-help aid. 1% freshmen, 1% undergrads receive athletic scholarships. 68% freshmen, 66% undergrads receive any aid. 57% undergrads borrow to pay for school. Average cumulative indebtedness $25,739. **Criteria for awarding institutional aid:** *Non-need-based:* academics, athletics, leadership, minority status.

See page 1010.

BEREA COLLEGE

CPO 2220, Berea, KY 40404
Phone: 859-985-3500 · **Financial Aid Phone:** 859-985-3310
E-mail: askadmissions@berea.edu · **CEEB Code:** 1060
Fax: 859-985-3512 · **Website:** www.berea.edu · **ACT Code:** 1492

This private school was founded in 1855. It has a 140-acre campus.

RATINGS

Admissions Selectivity Rating: 90   **Fire Safety Rating:** 91

STUDENTS AND FACULTY

Enrollment: 1,587. **Student Body:** 57% female, 43% male, 54% out-of-state, 8% international (58 countries represented). Asian 2%, African American 15%, Caucasian 64%, Hispanic 4%, Native American <1%
Retention and Graduation: 47% freshmen graduate within 4 years. 62% freshmen graduate within 6 years. **Faculty:** 133 full-time faculty, 89% hold PhDs, 45% are members of minority groups, 17% are women. 0% of classes are taught by teaching assistants.

ACADEMICS

Degrees: bachelor's. **Classes:** Most classes have 10-19 students. **Majors with Highest Enrollment:** Business/Commerce; Family and Consumer Sciences/Human Sciences; Biology/Biological Sciences. **Special Study Options:** double major, English as a Second Language (ESL), exchange student program (domestic), honors program, independent study, internships, student-designed major, study abroad, teacher certification program, 3-2 engineering program with Washington University, St. Louis, and University of Kentucky. Combined degree programs: at UK or Washington Univ (MO) resulting in BS. **Disability Services:** Special programs offered to physically disabled students include note-taking services, reader services, tape recorders. **Career services:** Alumni network, alumni services, career/job search classes, career assessment, internships.

FACILITIES

Housing: men's dorms, women's dorms, apartments for married students, Apartments for single parents and married students at our Ecovillage (see the following site for more information: http://www.berea.edu/sens/ecovillage/). 75% of campus accessible to physically disabled. **Special Academic Facilities/Equipment:** Appalachian Gallery, Special Collections and Sound Archives in the Hutchins Library, Planetarium and Observatory, Geology Museum, The Ecovillage, the Child Development Laboratory, extensive acreage of farmland and forestland, and the Monty Saulmon Early Technology Lab. **Computers:** 33% of classrooms, 100% of libraries, 100% of dining areas, 100% of student union, 33% of common outdoor areas have wireless network access. Students can register for classes online. Administrative functions (other than registration) can be performed online. Undergraduates are required to own a computer.

CAMPUS LIFE

Environment: Village. **Activities:** Choral groups, dance, drama/theater, jazz band, literary magazine, music ensembles, pep band, student government, student newspaper, yearbook, Campus Ministries, International Student Organization. 75 registered organizations, 14 honor societies, 5 religious organizations. **Athletics (Intercollegiate):** *Men:* baseball, basketball, cross-country, golf, soccer, swimming, tennis, track/field (outdoor). *Women:* basketball, cross-country, soccer, softball, swimming, tennis, track/field (outdoor), volleyball. **On-Campus Highlights:** Carillon (in Draper building tower), EcoVillage (married and single parent housing), Alumni Building (cafeteria, lounge, gameroom), Woods-Penn Complex (post office, café, etc), Seabury Center (gym).

ADMISSIONS

Freshman Academic Profile: Average high school GPA 3.42. 24.8% in top 10% of high school class, 72.5% in top 25% of high school class, 95.2% in top 50% of high school class. SAT Math middle 50% range 513-610. SAT Critical Reading middle 50% range 510-630. SAT Writing middle 50% range 483-610. ACT middle 50% range 22-26. Minimum internet-based TOEFL 61. Minimum paper TOEFL 500. **Basis for Candidate Selection:** *Very important factors considered include:* Class rank, academic GPA, rigor of secondary school record, standardized test scores, interview. *Important factors considered include:* application essay, character/personal qualities. *Other factors considered include:* recommendation(s), extracurricular activities, first generation, geographical residence, level of applicant's interest, racial/ethnic status, state residency, talent/ability, volunteer work, work experience. **Freshman Admission Requirements:** High school diploma is required and GED is accepted. **Freshman Admission Statistics:** 1,606 applied, 34% admitted, 72% enrolled. **Transfer Admission Requirements:** High school transcript, college transcript(s), interview, Minimum college GPA of 2.0 required. Lowest grade transferable C. **General Admission Information:** Regular application deadline 4/30. Notification on a rolling basis, beginning on or about 11/1. Nonfall registration accepted. Credit offered for CEEB Advanced Placement tests.

COSTS AND FINANCIAL AID

Room and board $6,322. Required fees $870. Average book expense $700. **Required Forms and Deadlines:** FAFSA. **Notification of Awards:** Applicants will be notified of awards on a rolling basis beginning 4/1. **Types of Aid:** *Need-based scholarships/grants:* Federal Pell, SEOG, state scholarships/grants, private scholarships, the school's own gift aid. *Loans:* Subsidized Stafford, Unsubsidized Stafford, PLUS, Federal Perkins, college/university loans from institutional funds. *Student Employment:* Federal Work-Study Program available. **Financial Aid Statistics:** 100% freshmen, 100% undergrads receive need-based scholarship or grant aid. 0% freshmen, 0% undergrads receive non-need-based scholarship or grant aid. 100% freshmen, 100% undergrads receive need-based self-help aid. 0% freshmen, 0% undergrads receive athletic scholarships. 100% freshmen, 100% undergrads receive any aid. 67% undergrads borrow to pay for school. Average cumulative indebtedness $7,403.

BERKELEY COLLEGE

44 Rifle Camp Road, Woodland Park, NJ 7424
Phone: 1-800-446-5400 xG26
E-mail: info@berkeleycollege.edu · **CEEB Code:** 2061
ACT Code: 2576

This proprietary school was founded in 1931. It has a 25-acre campus.

RATINGS

Admissions Selectivity Rating: 60*   Fire Safety Rating: 69

STUDENTS AND FACULTY

Enrollment: 2,709. **Student Body:** 72% female, 28% male, 4% out-of-state, 1% international. Asian 5%, African American 20%, Caucasian 35%, Hispanic 35%, Native American <1%
Retention and Graduation: 53% freshmen return for sophomore year.
Faculty: 54 full-time faculty, 54% are members of minority groups, 15% are women.

ACADEMICS

Degrees: associate, bachelor's, certificate, terminal associate, transfer associate. **Majors with Highest Enrollment:** Business Administration and Management; Accounting; Fashion Merchandising. **Special Study Options:** Accelerated program, distance learning, internships, study abroad, Academic remediation, Off-campus study at Berkeley College, New York City; Berkeley College, White Plains. **Disability Services:** Special programs offered to physically disabled students include tutors.

FACILITIES

Housing: Coed dorms **Computers:** Administrative functions (other than registration) can be performed online.

CAMPUS LIFE

Environment: City. **Activities:** Choral groups, literary magazine, student government, student newspaper. 8 registered organizations, 1 honor society.

ADMISSIONS

Freshman Academic Profile: Minimum paper TOEFL 500. **Basis for Candidate Selection:** *Very important factors considered include:* rigor of secondary school record. *Important factors considered include:* standardized test scores. *Other factors considered include:* Class rank, academic GPA, recommendation(s), character/personal qualities, extracurricular activities, talent/ability, volunteer work, work experience. **Freshman Admission Requirements:** High school diploma is required and GED is accepted. **Transfer Admission Requirements:** college transcript(s), Lowest grade transferable C. **General Admission Information:** Application Fee $50. Nonfall registration accepted. Admission may be deferred for a maximum of no time limi. Credit and/or placement offered for CEEB Advanced Placement tests.

COSTS AND FINANCIAL AID

Annual tuition $17,400. Room and board $12,500. Required fees $750. Average book expense $1,200. **Required Forms and Deadlines:** FAFSA. **Notification of Awards:** Applicants will be notified of awards on or about 3/1. **Types of Aid:** *Need-based scholarships/grants:* Federal Pell, SEOG, state scholarships/grants, private scholarships, the school's own gift aid. *Loans:* Subsidized Stafford, Unsubsidized Stafford, PLUS. *Student Employment:* Federal Work-Study Program available. Institutional employment available. Off-campus job opportunities are excellent. **Financial Aid Statistics:** 85% freshmen receive any aid. 88% undergrads borrow to pay for school. **Criteria for awarding institutional aid:** *Non-need-based:* academics, alumni affiliation.

BERKLEE COLLEGE OF MUSIC

1140 Boylston Street, Boston, MA 02215-3693
Phone: 617-747-2222 · **Financial Aid Phone:** 617-747-2274
E-mail: admissions@berklee.edu · **CEEB Code:** 3107
Fax: 617-747-2047 · **Website:** www.berklee.edu · **ACT Code:** 1789

This private school was founded in 1945.

RATINGS

Admissions Selectivity Rating: 71   Fire Safety Rating: 60*

STUDENTS AND FACULTY

Enrollment: 3,846. **Student Body:** 31% female, 69% male, 84% out-of-state, 25% international (70 countries represented). Asian 3%, African American 6%, Caucasian 45%, Hispanic 10%, Native American <1%
Faculty: 240 full-time faculty, 15% hold PhDs, 23% are members of minority groups.

ACADEMICS

Degrees: bachelor's, diploma. **Classes:** Most classes have fewer than 10 students. **Majors with Highest Enrollment:** Music Performance; Music. **Special Study Options:** cooperative education program, cross-registration, distance learning, double major, dual enrollment, English as a Second Language (ESL), independent study, internships, student-designed major, study abroad, teacher certification program, Berkleemusic.com is the online continuing education division of Berklee College of Music. Study is online with Berklee's renowned faculty in areas that include Music Business, Music Production, Guitar, Theory, Harmony & Ear Training, and Songwriting. **Disability Services:** Special programs offered to physically disabled students include reader services, tape recorders, tutors. **Career services:** alumni services, career/job search classes, internships.

FACILITIES

Housing: Coed dorms. 80% of campus accessible to physically disabled. **Special Academic Facilities/Equipment:** Ensemble library, 10 professional recording studios, film scoring and editing studio, analog and digital music synthesis labs, 1,200-seat performance center, learning center.

CAMPUS LIFE

Environment: Metropolis. **Activities:** Choral groups, concert band, dance, jazz band, literary magazine, music ensembles, musical theater, radio station, student government, student newspaper, student-run film society, International Student Organization. 47 registered organizations, 2 honor societies, 4 religious organizations. **On-Campus Highlights:** Student Activities Center, Berklee Performance Center, Practice Rooms, Stan Getz Media Center.

ADMISSIONS

Freshman Academic Profile: Minimum paper TOEFL 500. **Basis for Candidate Selection:** *Very important factors considered include:* character/personal qualities, interview, talent/ability. *Important factors considered include:* application essay, academic GPA, rigor of secondary school record. *Other factors considered include:* Class rank, recommendation(s), standardized test scores, alumni/ae relation, extracurricular activities, first generation, level of applicant's interest, volunteer work, work experience. **Freshman Admission Requirements:** High school diploma is required and GED is accepted. **Freshman Admission Statistics:** 5,538 applied, 19% admitted, 84% enrolled. **Transfer Admission Requirements:** High school transcript, college transcript(s), essay or personal statement, interview, Lowest grade transferable C. **General Admission Information:** Application Fee $150. Regular application deadline 1/15. Regular notification 3/31. Nonfall registration accepted. Admission may be deferred for a maximum of 1 year. Credit offered for CEEB Advanced Placement tests.

COSTS AND FINANCIAL AID

Room and board $17,200. Required fees $5,132. Average book expense $474. *Student Employment:* Federal Work-Study Program available. Highest amount earned per year from on-campus jobs $2,000. Off-campus job opportunities are good. **Financial Aid Statistics:** 50% freshmen, 50% undergrads receive need-based scholarship or grant aid. 48% freshmen, 49% undergrads receive non-need-based scholarship or grant aid. 97% freshmen, 97% undergrads receive need-based self-help aid. 0% freshmen, 0% undergrads receive athletic scholarships. 57% freshmen, 38% undergrads receive any aid.

BERRY COLLEGE

P.O. Box 490159, Mount Berry, GA 30149-0159
Phone: 706-236-2215 · **Financial Aid Phone:** 706-236-1714
E-mail: admissions@berry.edu · **CEEB Code:** 5059
Fax: 706-290-2178 · **Website:** www.berry.edu · **ACT Code:** 798

This private school was founded in 1902. It has a 26000-acre campus.

RATINGS

Admissions Selectivity Rating: 88   Fire Safety Rating: 90

STUDENTS AND FACULTY

Enrollment: 2,065. **Student Body:** 61% female, 39% male, 29% out-of-state, 1% international (13 countries represented). Asian 1%, African American 4%, Caucasian 83%, Hispanic 6%, Native American <1%

Retention and Graduation: 79% freshmen return for sophomore year. 54% freshmen graduate within 4 years. 62% freshmen graduate within 6 years. **Faculty:** 165 full-time faculty, 88% hold PhDs, 43% are members of minority groups, 7% are women.

ACADEMICS

Degrees: bachelor's, master's, post-master's certificate. **Classes:** Most classes have 10–19 students. Most lab/discussion sessions have 20–29 students. **Majors with Highest Enrollment:** Animal Sciences; Biology/Biological Sciences; Psychology. **Special Study Options:** cooperative education program, cross-registration, double major, dual enrollment, honors program, independent study, internships, student-designed major, study abroad, teacher certification program, 3-2 nursing with Emory University, 3-2 engineering with Georgia Institute of Technology. **Honors programs:** The Berry College Honors Program provides students with an opportunity to learn within an intellectually challenging community of peers and instructors. Honors courses familiarize students with works that have been central to our past and contemporary intellectual traditions, while encouraging them to examine issues or themes from multiple and conflicting perspectives. All Honors courses are taught as seminars that provide an ideal environment for the development of effective communication and critical-thinking skills. As part of the Honors program the Oxbridge Lecture Series uses the English model of instruction with public lectures and private tutorials. Students enrolled benefit from small group, intensive student-faculty interaction, and exploratory assignments that stimulate inquiry and intellectual growth. Additionally, the Berry College Honors Program now offers a unique education abroad opportunity in conjunction with the University of Glasgow in Scotland and Berry College International Programs. Combined degree programs: 3-2 Nursing with Emory University. **Disability Services:** Special programs offered to physically disabled students include note-taking services, reader services, tape recorders, tutors. **Career services:** Alumni network, alumni services, career/job search classes, career assessment, internships, regional alumni.

FACILITIES

Housing: Coed dorms, men's dorms, women's dorms, apartments for single students, Wellness HousingTraditional residence halls are single sex; apartments and townhouses are co-ed by site or apartment. Special-interest houses for Women in Math and Science (primarily first-year students). 80% of campus accessible to physically disabled. **Special Academic Facilities/Equipment:** The 131,000-square-foot Steven J. Cage Athletic and Recreation Center, National Historic Site containing Oak Hill and The Martha Berry Museum, 34-foot overshot waterwheel, Georgia wildlife management area and refuge, equine center, dairy and beef cattle research center, on-campus elementary and middle schools, child development center, science center featuring 60-foot Foucault pendulum. **Computers:** 100% of classrooms, 100% of dorms, 100% of libraries, 100% of dining areas, 100% of student union, 10% of common outdoor areas have wireless network access. Students can register for classes online. Administrative functions (other than registration) can be performed online.

CAMPUS LIFE

Environment: Town. **Activities:** Choral groups, concert band, dance, drama/theater, jazz band, literary magazine, music ensembles, musical theater, student government, student newspaper, symphony orchestra, television station, yearbook, Campus Ministries, International Student Organization, Model UN. 75 registered organizations, 15 honor societies, 11 religious organization. **Athletics (Intercollegiate):** *Men:* baseball, basketball, cross-country, diving, golf, lacrosse, soccer, swimming, tennis. *Women:* basketball, cross-country, diving, equestrian sports, golf, lacrosse, soccer, softball, swimming, tennis, volleyball. **On-Campus Highlights:** Steven J. Cage Athletic & Recreation Ctr, Ford Complex, Science Center, Gunby Equestrian Center (Mountain Campus), The Old Mill (Mountain Campus), The 131,000 square foot Steven J. Cage Athletic and Recreation Center houses an indoor swimming pool, three basketball courts, two racquetball courts, one multi-purpose court and a jogging track. Berry Beanery (Starbucks) in Krannert Student Center. **Environmental Initiatives:** President's Climate Commitment: Sustainability office formed. Energy Star Policy, Recyclemania Environmental Land Management: Carbon Reserve, wetland banking, and EPA Compliance-Peer Audit Berry has an environmental science major.

ADMISSIONS

Freshman Academic Profile: Average high school GPA 3.73. 34% in top 10% of high school class, 66% in top 25% of high school class, 93% in top 50% of high school class. 70% from public high schools. SAT Math middle 50% range 530-630. SAT Critical Reading middle 50% range 530-630. SAT Writing middle 50% range 520-620. ACT middle 50% range 24-29. Minimum internet-based TOEFL 80. Minimum paper TOEFL 550. **Basis for Candidate Selection:** *Very important factors considered include:* academic GPA, rigor of secondary school record, standardized test scores. *Important factors considered include:* extracurricular activities. *Other factors considered include:* Class rank, application essay, recommendation(s), interview, volunteer work, work experience. **Freshman Admission Requirements:** High school diploma is required and GED is accepted. *Academic units required:* 4 English, 4 mathematics, 3 science, 2 foreign language, 3 social studies. **Freshman Admission**

Statistics: 3,801 applied, 61% admitted, 25% enrolled. **Transfer Admission Requirements:** college transcript(s), statement of good standing from prior institution(s). Minimum college GPA of 2.5 required. Lowest grade transferable C. **General Admission Information:** Application Fee $50. Regular application deadline 7/23. Notification on a rolling basis, beginning on or about 11/1. Nonfall registration accepted. Admission may be deferred for a maximum of Up to one year. Credit and/or placement offered for CEEB Advanced Placement tests.

COSTS AND FINANCIAL AID

Annual tuition $30,330. Room and board $10,660. Required fees $200. Average book expense $1,000. **Required Forms and Deadlines:** FAFSA, State aid form. **Notification of Awards:** Applicants will be notified of awards on a rolling basis beginning 2/1. **Types of Aid:** *Need-based scholarships/grants:* Federal Pell, SEOG, state scholarships/grants, private scholarships, the school's own gift aid. *Loans:* Subsidized Stafford, Unsubsidized Stafford, PLUS, Federal Perkins, college/university loans from institutional funds. *Student Employment:* Federal Work-Study Program available. Institutional employment available. Highest amount earned per year from on-campus jobs $5,873. Off-campus job opportunities are good. **Financial Aid Statistics:** 100% freshmen, 100% undergrads receive need-based scholarship or grant aid. 24% freshmen, 22% undergrads receive non-need-based scholarship or grant aid. 79% freshmen, 80% undergrads receive need-based self-help aid. 0% freshmen, 0% undergrads receive athletic scholarships. 100% freshmen, 99% undergrads receive any aid. 65% undergrads borrow to pay for school. Average cumulative indebtedness $21,898. **Criteria for awarding institutional aid:** *Non-need-based:* academics, art, job skills, leadership, minority status, music/drama, state/district residency.

BETHANY COLLEGE (KS)

335 E Swensson, Lindsborg, KS 67456-1897
Phone: 785-227-3311 · **Financial Aid Phone:** 785-227-3311
E-mail: admissions@bethanylb.edu · **CEEB Code:** 6034
Fax: 785-227-8993 · **Website:** www.bethanylb.edu · **ACT Code:** 1388

This private school, affiliated with the Lutheran Church, was founded in 1881. It has a 62-acre campus.

RATINGS

Admissions Selectivity Rating: 82   **Fire Safety Rating:** 94

STUDENTS AND FACULTY

Enrollment: 569. **Student Body:** 48% female, 52% male, 49% out-of-state, 6% international (29 countries represented). Asian 1%, African American 11%, Caucasian 71%, Hispanic 7%, Native American 1%
Retention and Graduation: 61% freshmen return for sophomore year. 32% freshmen graduate within 4 years. 40% freshmen graduate within 6 years. 20% grads go on to further study within 1 year. 1% grads pursue law degrees. 3% grads pursue medical degrees. **Faculty:** 44 full-time faculty, 57% hold PhDs, 36% are members of minority groups, 5% are women. 0% of classes are taught by teaching assistants.

ACADEMICS

Degrees: bachelor's. **Classes:** Most classes have fewer than 10 students. Most lab/discussion sessions have fewer than 10 students. **Majors with Highest Enrollment:** Elementary Education and Teaching; Biology/Biological Sciences; Business Administration and Management. **Special Study Options:** Accelerated program, cross-registration, double major, dual enrollment, exchange student program (domestic), honors program, independent study, internships, liberal arts/career combination, student-designed major, study abroad, teacher certification program. **Honors programs:** Honors program offered Combined degree programs: BA/MEng. **Disability Services:** Special programs offered to physically disabled students include note-taking services, reader services, tape recorders, tutors. **Career services:** Alumni network, alumni services, career/job search classes, career assessment, internships, regional alumni. Career services highlights include Experienced Based Education.

FACILITIES

Housing: Coed dorms, women's dorms, apartments for single students, special interest housing- bid on by student groups, community service and house improvements. 80% of campus accessible to physically disabled. **Special Academic Facilities/Equipment:** Mingenback Gallery,Bethany College Archives,Plym Gallery, Sandzen Gallery.

CAMPUS LIFE

Environment: Rural. **Activities:** Choral groups, concert band, dance, drama/theater, jazz band, music ensembles, musical theater, pep band, student government, student newspaper, symphony orchestra, yearbook, Campus Ministries, International Student Organization. 49 registered organizations, 8 honor societies, 9 religious organizations. 3 fraternities, 3 sororities. **Athletics (Intercollegiate): Men:** baseball, basketball, cheerleading, cross-country, football, golf, soccer, tennis, track/field (outdoor), track/field (indoor). *Women:* basketball, cheerleading, cross-country, golf, soccer, softball, tennis, track/field (outdoor), track/field (indoor), volleyball. **On-Campus Highlights:** Student Union, Walderstadt Library, Mingenback Art Gallery, Residence Halls, Athletic Fields.

ADMISSIONS

Freshman Academic Profile: Average high school GPA 3.33. 15% in top 10% of high school class, 42% in top 25% of high school class, 76% in top 50% of high school class. 97% from public high schools. SAT Math middle 50% range 420-560. SAT Critical Reading middle 50% range 370-500. SAT Writing middle 50% range 380-490. ACT middle 50% range 19-24. Minimum internet-based TOEFL 71. Minimum paper TOEFL 525. **Basis for Candidate Selection:** *Very important factors considered include:* academic GPA, rigor of secondary school record, standardized test scores. *Other factors considered include:* application essay, recommendation(s), character/personal qualities, extracurricular activities, racial/ethnic status, talent/ability, volunteer work. **Freshman Admission Requirements:** High school diploma is required and GED is accepted. **Freshman Admission Statistics:** 811 applied, 65% admitted, 34% enrolled. **Transfer Admission Requirements:** college transcript(s), statement of good standing from prior institution(s). Minimum college GPA of 2.3 required. Lowest grade transferable D. **General Admission Information:** Application Fee $20. Regular application deadline 7/1. Notification on a rolling basis, beginning on or about 10/1. Nonfall registration accepted. Neither credit nor placement offered for CEEB Advanced Placement tests.

COSTS AND FINANCIAL AID

Annual tuition $17,824. Room and board $5,650. Required fees $300. Average book expense $1,000. **Required Forms and Deadlines:** FAFSA. **Notification of Awards:** Applicants will be notified of awards on a rolling basis beginning 3/1. **Types of Aid:** *Need-based scholarships/grants:* Federal Pell, SEOG, state scholarships/grants, private scholarships, the school's own gift aid, Federal ACG and Federal SMART and TEACH Grant. *Loans:* Subsidized Stafford, Unsubsidized Stafford, PLUS, Federal Perkins. *Student Employment:* Federal Work-Study Program available. Institutional employment available. Highest amount earned per year from on-campus jobs $1,500. Off-campus job opportunities are good. **Financial Aid Statistics:** 85% freshmen, 84% undergrads receive need-based scholarship or grant aid. 40% freshmen, 32% undergrads receive non-need-based scholarship or grant aid. 76% freshmen, 78% undergrads receive need-based self-help aid. 0% freshmen, 7% undergrads receive athletic scholarships. 100% freshmen, 98% undergrads receive any aid. 82% undergrads borrow to pay for school. Average cumulative indebtedness $16,161. **Criteria for awarding institutional aid:** *Non-need-based:* academics, alumni affiliation, art, athletics, leadership, music/drama, religious affiliation.

BETHANY COLLEGE (WV)

31 E Campus Dr, Bethany, WV 26032
Phone: 304-829-7611 · **Financial Aid Phone:** 304-829-7611
E-mail: enrollment@bethanywv.edu · **CEEB Code:** 5060
Fax: 304-829-7142 · **Website:** www.bethanywv.edu · **ACT Code:** 4512

This private school, affiliated with the Disciples of Christ Church, was founded in 1840. It has a 400-acre campus.

RATINGS

Admissions Selectivity Rating: 77   **Fire Safety Rating:** 81

STUDENTS AND FACULTY

Enrollment: 716. **Student Body:** 41% female, 59% male, 68% out-of-state, 2% international (11 countries represented). Asian 0%, African American 20%, Caucasian 54%, Hispanic 4%, Native American 1%
Retention and Graduation: 70% freshmen return for sophomore year.
Faculty: 48 full-time faculty, 79% hold PhDs, 44% are members of minority groups, 4% are women. 0% of classes are taught by teaching assistants.

ACADEMICS

Degrees: bachelor's. **Classes:** Most classes have 10–19 students. Most lab/discussion sessions have 10–19 students. **Majors with Highest Enrollment:** Psychology; Speech Communication and Rhetoric; Elementary Education and Teaching. **Special Study Options:** double major, exchange student program (domestic), independent study, internships, liberal arts/career combination, student-designed major, study abroad, teacher certification program, Off Campus Study: Washington, DC. Combined degree programs: BA/JD, BA/MEng, BA/JD with Duquesne University. **Disability Services:** Special programs offered to physically disabled students include note-taking services, reader services, tape recorders, tutors.

FACILITIES

Housing: Coed dorms, special housing for disabled students, men's dorms, women's dorms, fraternity/sorority housing, apartments for married students, apartments for single students. **Computers:** Administrative functions (other than registration) can be performed online.

CAMPUS LIFE

Environment: Rural. **Activities:** Choral groups, concert band, drama/theater, jazz band, literary magazine, music ensembles, musical theater, pep band, radio station, student government, student newspaper, student-run film society, television station, yearbook. 38 registered organizations, 16 honor societies, 3 religious organizations. 6 fraternities, 3 sororities. **Athletics (Intercollegiate):** *Men:* baseball, basketball, cross-country, diving, football, golf, soccer, swimming, tennis, track/field (outdoor), track/field (indoor). *Women:* basketball, cross-country, diving, golf, soccer, softball, swimming, tennis, track/field (outdoor), track/field (indoor), volleyball. **On-Campus Highlights:** Old Main, Bethany House, Athletic Facilities, Campbell Village, Campbell Mansion.

ADMISSIONS

Freshman Academic Profile: Average high school GPA 2.94. 6% in top 10% of high school class, 20% in top 25% of high school class, 49% in top 50% of high school class. 90% from public high schools. SAT Math middle 50% range 390-490. SAT Critical Reading middle 50% range 370-500. SAT Writing middle 50% range 360-470. ACT middle 50% range 17-23. Minimum internet-based TOEFL 90. Minimum paper TOEFL 500. **Basis for Candidate Selection:** *Very important factors considered include:* Class rank, application essay, recommendation(s), rigor of secondary school record, standardized test scores. *Important factors considered include:* interview. *Other factors considered include:* alumni/ae relation, character/personal qualities, extracurricular activities, talent/ability, volunteer work, work experience. **Freshman Admission Requirements:** High school diploma is required and GED is accepted. *Academic units required:* 4 English, 3 mathematics, 3 science, 2 foreign language, 3 social studies. **Freshman Admission Statistics:** 1,394 applied, 62% admitted, 28% enrolled. **Transfer Admission Requirements:** college transcript(s), essay or personal statement, statement of good standing from prior institution(s). Minimum college GPA of 2.0 required. Lowest grade transferable D°. **General Admission Information:** Application Fee $25. Notification on a rolling basis, beginning on or about 10/1. Nonfall registration accepted. Admission may be deferred for a maximum of 1 year. Credit and/or placement offered for CEEB Advanced Placement tests.

COSTS AND FINANCIAL AID

Annual tuition $24,836. Room and board $9,636. Required fees $900. Average book expense $1,200. **Required Forms and Deadlines:** FAFSA. **Notification of Awards:** Applicants will be notified of awards on a rolling basis beginning 3/1. **Types of Aid:** *Need-based scholarships/grants:* Federal Pell, SEOG, state scholarships/grants, private scholarships, the school's own gift aid. *Loans:* Direct Subsidized Stafford, Direct Unsubsidized Stafford, Direct PLUS, Federal Perkins. *Student Employment:* Federal Work-Study Program available. Institutional employment available. Highest amount earned per year from on-campus jobs $1,000. Off-campus job opportunities are fair. **Financial Aid Statistics:** 80% freshmen, 79% undergrads receive need-based scholarship or grant aid. 100% freshmen, 99% undergrads receive non-need-based scholarship or grant aid. 77% freshmen, 79% undergrads receive need-based self-help aid. 0% freshmen, 0% undergrads receive athletic scholarships. 99% freshmen, 99% undergrads receive any aid. **Criteria for awarding institutional aid:** *Non-need-based:* academics, alumni affiliation, leadership, music/drama, religious affiliation.

See page 1012.

BETHANY UNIVERSITY

800 Bethany Drive, Scotts Valley, CA 95066
Phone: 831-438-3800
E-mail: info@bethany.edu · **CEEB Code:** 4021
Fax: 831-438-6104

This is a private school.

RATINGS

Admissions Selectivity Rating: 70   **Fire Safety Rating:** 60*

STUDENTS AND FACULTY

Enrollment: 504. **Student Body:** 60% female, 40% male, 19% out-of-state, 2% international. Asian 5%, African American 10%, Caucasian 62%, Hispanic 18%, Native American 1%
Retention and Graduation: 59% freshmen return for sophomore year. 6% grads go on to further study within 1 year. 6% grads pursue arts and sciences degrees. **Faculty:** 25 full-time faculty, 84% hold PhDs, 40% are members of minority groups.

ACADEMICS

Degrees: associate, bachelor's, certificate, master's, post-bachelor's certificate. **Classes:** Most classes have 10–19 students. Most lab/discussion sessions have fewer than 10 students. **Special Study Options:** Accelerated program, distance learning, double major, external degree program, independent study, internships, teacher certification program, weekend college.

FACILITIES

Housing: Coed dorms, special housing for disabled students, men's dorms, women's dorms, fraternity/sorority housing, apartments for married students, apartments for single students, Theme Housing.

CAMPUS LIFE

Activities: Choral groups, concert band, dance, drama/theater, jazz band, literary magazine, marching band, music ensembles, musical theater, opera, pep band, radio station, student government, student newspaper, student-run film society, symphony orchestra, television station, yearbook, Campus Ministries, International Student Organization. 1 honor society, 1 religious organization. **Athletics (Intercollegiate):** *Men:* basketball, cheerleading, golf. *Women:* basketball, cheerleading, softball, volleyball.

ADMISSIONS

Freshman Academic Profile: 16% in top 10% of high school class, 59% in top 25% of high school class, 75% in top 50% of high school class. Minimum paper TOEFL 500. **Basis for Candidate Selection:** *Very important factors considered include:* application essay, academic GPA, recommendation(s), standardized test scores, religious affiliation/commitment. *Other factors considered include:* Class rank, rigor of secondary school record, character/personal qualities, extracurricular activities, level of applicant's interest. **Freshman Admission Statistics:** 228 applied, 55% admitted, 67% enrolled. **Transfer Admission Requirements:** college transcript(s), essay or personal statement, Minimum college GPA of 2.0 required. **General Admission Information:** Application Fee $35. Regular application deadline 7/1. Nonfall registration accepted. Admission may be deferred for a maximum of 2 years.

COSTS AND FINANCIAL AID

Average book expense $500. **Required Forms and Deadlines:** FAFSA, Institution's own financial aid form. **Types of Aid:** *Need-based scholarships/grants:* Federal Pell, SEOG, state scholarships/grants, private scholarships, the school's own gift aid. *Loans:* Subsidized Stafford, Unsubsidized Stafford, PLUS, Federal Perkins, college/university loans from institutional funds. *Student Employment:* Federal Work-Study Program available.

BETHEL COLLEGE (IN)

1001 W McKinley Avenue, Mishawaka, IN 46545
Phone: 574-257-3339 · **Financial Aid Phone:** 574-257-3316
E-mail: admissions@bethelcollege.edu · **CEEB Code:** 1079
Fax: 574-257-3335 · **Website:** www.bethelcollege.edu · **ACT Code:** 1178

This private school was founded in 1947. It has a 75-acre campus.

RATINGS

Admissions Selectivity Rating: 60*   **Fire Safety Rating:** 60*

STUDENTS AND FACULTY

Enrollment: 1,974. **Student Body:** 34% female, 66% male, 27% out-of-state, 2% international (18 countries represented). Asian 2%, African American 10%, Caucasian 80%, Hispanic 3%, Native American <1%
Retention and Graduation: 79% freshmen return for sophomore year. 37% freshmen graduate within 4 years. 59% freshmen graduate within 6 years. **Faculty:** 97 full-time faculty, 43% are members of minority groups, 10% are women. 0% of classes are taught by teaching assistants.

ACADEMICS

Degrees: associate, bachelor's, master's. **Classes:** Most classes have 10–19 students. Most lab/discussion sessions have fewer than 10 students. **Majors with Highest Enrollment:** Elementary Education and Teaching; Registered Nursing/Registered Nurse; Business/Commerce. **Special Study Options:** Accelerated program, cross-registration, double major, English as a Second Language (ESL), exchange student program (domestic), independent study, internships, student-designed major, study abroad, teacher certification program. **Disability Services:** Special programs offered to physically disabled students include note-taking services, reader services, tape recorders, tutors. **Career services:** alumni services, career/job search classes, career assessment, internships. Reputation of Career Service Office Usership is up.

FACILITIES

Housing: special housing for disabled students, men's dorms, women's dorms. 90% of campus accessible to physically disabled. **Special Academic Facilities/**

Equipment: Bowen Museum Weaver Gallery **Computers:** 25% of classrooms, 100% of dorms, 100% of libraries, 100% of dining areas, 100% of student union, 25% of common outdoor areas have wireless network access. Administrative functions (other than registration) can be performed online.

CAMPUS LIFE

Environment: City. **Activities:** Choral groups, concert band, dance, drama/theater, jazz band, literary magazine, music ensembles, musical theater, pep band, radio station, student government, student newspaper, yearbook. 18 registered organizations, 1 honor society, 5 religious organizations. **Athletics (Intercollegiate):** *Men:* baseball, basketball, cheerleading, cross-country, golf, soccer, tennis, track/field (outdoor), track/field (indoor). *Women:* basketball, cheerleading, cross-country, golf, soccer, softball, tennis, track/field (outdoor), track/field (indoor), volleyball. **On-Campus Highlights:** Acorn Student Center, Everst Rohrer Chapel, Sufficient Grounds Coffee House, Wiekamp Athletic Center, Dining Commons, workout and weight rooms. **Environmental Initiatives:** Recycle trash; Working with local community on MS4 program; Recycle leaves.

ADMISSIONS

Freshman Academic Profile: Average high school GPA 3. 15% in top 10% of high school class, 39% in top 25% of high school class, 74% in top 50% of high school class. 70% from public high schools. SAT Math middle 50% range 460-590. SAT Critical Reading middle 50% range 450-570. SAT Writing middle 50% range 435-560. ACT middle 50% range 19-25. Minimum internet-based TOEFL 76. Minimum paper TOEFL 540. **Basis for Candidate Selection:** *Important factors considered include:* Class rank, application essay, academic GPA, recommendation(s), rigor of secondary school record, standardized test scores, character/personal qualities, extracurricular activities. *Other factors considered include:* interview, racial/ethnic status, volunteer work. **Freshman Admission Requirements:** High school diploma is required and GED is accepted. **Freshman Admission Statistics:** 645 applied, 91% admitted, 53% enrolled. **Transfer Admission Requirements:** High school transcript, college transcript(s), essay or personal statement, standardized test scores, statement of good standing from prior institution(s). Minimum college GPA of 2.0 required. Lowest grade transferable C-. **General Admission Information:** Application Fee $25. Regular application deadline 8/15. Notification on a rolling basis, beginning on or about 10/1. Nonfall registration accepted. Admission may be deferred for a maximum of 1 year. Credit and/or placement offered for CEEB Advanced Placement tests.

COSTS AND FINANCIAL AID

Annual tuition $17,450. Room and board $5,380. Required fees $600. Average book expense $1,600. **Required Forms and Deadlines:** FAFSA. **Notification of Awards:** Applicants will be notified of awards on a rolling basis beginning 4/15. **Types of Aid:** *Need-based scholarships/grants:* Federal Pell, SEOG, state scholarships/grants, private scholarships, the school's own gift aid, Federal Nursing Scholarships. *Loans:* Subsidized Stafford, Unsubsidized Stafford, PLUS, Federal Perkins, college/university loans from institutional funds. *Student Employment:* Federal Work-Study Program available. Institutional employment available. Highest amount earned per year from on-campus jobs $2,500. Off-campus job opportunities are excellent. **Financial Aid Statistics:** 79% freshmen, 73% undergrads receive need-based scholarship or grant aid. 96% freshmen, 88% undergrads receive non-need-based scholarship or grant aid. 96% freshmen, 92% undergrads receive need-based self-help aid. 25% freshmen, 17% undergrads receive athletic scholarships. 76% freshmen, 73% undergrads receive any aid. 83% undergrads borrow to pay for school. Average cumulative indebtedness $14,378. **Criteria for awarding institutional aid:** *Non-need-based:* academics, art, athletics, job skills, leadership, minority status, music/drama, religious affiliation, state/district residency.

BETHEL COLLEGE (KS)

300 E 27th Street, North Newton, KS 67117
Phone: 316-284-5230 · **Financial Aid Phone:** 316-284-5232
E-mail: admissions@bethelks.edu · **CEEB Code:** 6037
Fax: 316-284-5870 · **Website:** www.bethelks.edu · **ACT Code:** 1390

This private school was founded in 1887. It has a 60-acre campus.

RATINGS

Admissions Selectivity Rating: 60*   **Fire Safety Rating:** 60*

STUDENTS AND FACULTY

Enrollment: 484. **Student Body:** 51% female, 49% male, 38% out-of-state, 2% international (13 countries represented). Asian 0%, African American 15%, Caucasian 70%, Hispanic 10%, Native American <1%

Retention and Graduation: 63% freshmen return for sophomore year. 42% freshmen graduate within 4 years. **Faculty:** 38 full-time faculty, 66% hold PhDs, 55% are members of minority groups, 5% are women. 0% of classes are taught by teaching assistants.

ACADEMICS

Degrees: bachelor's, certificate. **Classes:** Most classes have 10–19 students. Most lab/discussion sessions have 10–19 students. **Majors with Highest Enrollment:** Business/Commerce; Registered Nursing/Registered Nurse; Biology/Biological Sciences. **Special Study Options:** cross-registration, double major, dual enrollment, independent study, internships, liberal arts/career combination, study abroad, teacher certification program. Combined degree programs: BA/MEng. **Disability Services:** Special programs offered to physically disabled students include note-taking services, reader services, tape recorders, tutors. **Career services:** Alumni network, career/job search classes, career assessment. The liberal arts program provides students with a foundational, broad understanding of the social and natural world. Focused study in a major field equips students with the intellectual achievement vital to vocational success. Internships are thus an additional, integrated component of a larger academic program that fosters in students a powerful sense of purpose. The skills developed in a liberal education—the ability to speak, read and write correctly, clearly and cogently—are the skills needed in employment. Internship experiences help students understand the relationship of their educational experience to potential careers.

FACILITIES

Housing: Coed dorms, special housing for disabled students, apartments for married students, apartments for single students. 75% of campus accessible to physically disabled. **Special Academic Facilities/Equipment:** Art gallery, natural history and midwestern/Kansas history museums, 80 acre natural history field laboratory for biological studies, Mennonite Historical Library and Archives, Institute for Peace and Conflict Resolution, observatory. **Computers:** 25% of classrooms, 75% of libraries, 100% of dining areas, 100% of student union, 50% of common outdoor areas have wireless network access. Administrative functions (other than registration) can be performed online.

CAMPUS LIFE

Environment: Village. **Activities:** Choral groups, concert band, dance, drama/theater, jazz band, literary magazine, music ensembles, musical theater, opera, radio station, student government, student newspaper, symphony orchestra, television station, yearbook, Campus Ministries, International Student Organization. 50 registered organizations, 2 religious organizations. **Athletics (Intercollegiate):** *Men:* basketball, cross-country, football, golf, soccer, tennis, track/field (outdoor), track/field (indoor). *Women:* basketball, cross-country, golf, soccer, tennis, track/field (outdoor), track/field (indoor), volleyball. **On-Campus Highlights:** Student Center, Krehbiel Science Center, Athletic Complex, The Green, Warkentine Court.

ADMISSIONS

Freshman Academic Profile: Average high school GPA 3.38. 17% in top 10% of high school class, 38% in top 25% of high school class, 73% in top 50% of high school class. 97% from public high schools. SAT Math middle 50% range 425-475. SAT Critical Reading middle 50% range 380-435. SAT Writing middle 50% range 340-440. ACT middle 50% range 19-25. Minimum internet-based TOEFL 76. Minimum paper TOEFL 540. **Basis for Candidate Selection:** *Very important factors considered include:* academic GPA, standardized test scores, level of applicant's interest. *Important factors considered include:* Class rank, alumni/ae relation, character/personal qualities, extracurricular activities. *Other factors considered include:* recommendation(s), rigor of secondary school record. **Freshman Admission Requirements:** High school diploma is required and GED is accepted. **Freshman Admission Statistics:** 833 applied, 49% admitted, 27% enrolled. **Transfer Admission Requirements:** High school transcript, college transcript(s), statement of good standing from prior institution(s). Lowest grade transferable D-. **General Admission Information:** Application Fee $20. Notification on a rolling basis, beginning on or about 9/1. Nonfall registration accepted. Admission may be deferred for a maximum of 1 yr. Credit and/or placement offered for CEEB Advanced Placement tests.

COSTS AND FINANCIAL AID

Annual tuition $23,500. Room and board $7,980. Average book expense $900. **Required Forms and Deadlines:** FAFSA. **Notification of Awards:** Applicants will be notified of awards on a rolling basis beginning 2/1. **Types of Aid:** *Need-based scholarships/grants:* Federal Pell, SEOG, state scholarships/grants, private scholarships, the school's own gift aid. *Loans:* Direct Subsidized Stafford, Direct Unsubsidized Stafford, Direct PLUS, Subsidized Stafford, Unsubsidized Stafford, PLUS, Federal Perkins. *Student Employment:* Federal Work-Study Program available. Institutional employment available. Highest amount earned per year from on-campus jobs $9,278. Off-campus job opportunities are good. **Financial Aid Statistics:** 88% freshmen, 85% undergrads receive need-based scholarship or grant aid. 100% freshmen, 100% undergrads receive non-need-based scholarship or grant aid. 89% freshmen, 90% undergrads receive need-based self-help aid. 66% freshmen, 48% undergrads receive athletic scholarships. 100% freshmen, 94% undergrads receive any aid. 82%

undergrads borrow to pay for school. Average cumulative indebtedness $22,553. **Criteria for awarding institutional aid:** *Non-need-based:* academics, alumni affiliation, art, athletics, minority status, music/drama, religious affiliation, state/district residency.

BETHEL UNIVERSITY

Office of Admissions - CAS, Saint Paul, MN 55112
Phone: 651-638-6242 · **Financial Aid Phone:** 651-638-6241
E-mail: BUadmissions-cas@bethel.edu · **CEEB Code:** 6038
Fax: 651-635-1490 · **Website:** www.bethel.edu · **ACT Code:** 2088

This private school was founded in 1871. It has a 247-acre campus.

RATINGS

Admissions Selectivity Rating: 60*   **Fire Safety Rating:** 60*

STUDENTS AND FACULTY

Enrollment: 2,943. **Student Body:** 62% female, 38% male, 22% out-of-state, 0% international (11 countries represented). Asian 3%, African American 5%, Caucasian 85%, Hispanic 3%, Native American <1%
Retention and Graduation: 83% freshmen return for sophomore year. 63% freshmen graduate within 4 years. 73% freshmen graduate within 6 years. 28% grads go on to further study within 1 year. 6% grads pursue arts and sciences degrees. 1% grads pursue law degrees. 2% grads pursue business degrees. 5% grads pursue medical degrees. **Faculty:** 177 full-time faculty, 81% hold PhDs, 44% are members of minority groups, 7% are women. 0% of classes are taught by teaching assistants.

ACADEMICS

Degrees: associate, bachelor's, master's, post-bachelor's certificate, post-master's certificate. **Classes:** Most classes have 10–19 students. Most lab/discussion sessions have 10–19 students. **Majors with Highest Enrollment:** Business Administration and Management; Education; Registered Nursing/Registered Nurse. **Special Study Options:** double major, exchange student program (domestic), honors program, independent study, internships, student-designed major, study abroad, teacher certification program. **Honors programs:** The program consists of two honors courses in the freshman year, one in the sophomore year and one in the junior year. In their senior year the student will complete an Honors Senior Project. The two courses in the sophomore year and junior year, as well as the Honors Senior Project are geared toward a discipline of the students choosing. This program also consists of other Honors classes and Honors Forums throughout all four years. Combined degree programs: Dual degree B.A./B.S. Program in Engineering. **Disability Services:** Special programs offered to physically disabled students include note-taking services, reader services, tape recorders, tutors. **Career services:** alumni services, career/job search classes, career assessment, internships. We have a very collaborative network of colleagues around the state and provide high quality job fairs through our joint effort.

FACILITIES

Housing: Coed dorms, special housing for disabled students, apartments for single students. 99% of campus accessible to physically disabled. **Special Academic Facilities/Equipment:** Two Art galleries, media center, closed circuit TV, television studio, and radio station, cadaver lab **Computers:** 100% of classrooms, 50% of dorms, 100% of libraries, 100% of dining areas, 100% of student union, 50% of common outdoor areas have wireless network access. Students can register for classes online. Administrative functions (other than registration) can be performed online.

CAMPUS LIFE

Environment: Metropolis. **Activities:** Choral groups, concert band, dance, drama/theater, jazz band, literary magazine, music ensembles, musical theater, radio station, student government, student newspaper, student-run film society, symphony orchestra, Campus Ministries, International Student Organization. 55 registered organizations, 5 honor societies, 20 religious organizations. **Athletics (Intercollegiate):** *Men:* baseball, basketball, cross-country, football, golf, ice hockey, soccer, tennis, track/field (outdoor), track/field (indoor). *Women:* basketball, cross-country, golf, ice hockey, soccer, softball, tennis, track/field (outdoor), track/field (indoor), volleyball. **On-Campus Highlights:** Brushaber Commons (new student facility), SRC-Student Recreation Center, Market Square/Dining Center, Lissner Hall-New Dorm/ Lounges, Ona Orth Athletic Complex, Brushaber Commons: all new student facility. Great Hall: seats 1600 people; location of Chapel services, Vespers, concerts, musicals and large on-campus events. **Environmental Initiatives:** Green Roof and Permeable Pavers for Brushaber Commons; Day Lighting Control for Monson Dining Center; North Village Composting.

ADMISSIONS

Freshman Academic Profile: Average high school GPA 3.5. 29% in top 10% of high school class, 57% in top 25% of high school class, 83% in top 50% of high school class. 80% from public high schools. ACT middle 50% range 22-28. Minimum internet-based TOEFL 70. Minimum paper TOEFL 525. **Basis for Candidate Selection:** *Very important factors considered include:* academic GPA, rigor of secondary school record, standardized test scores, character/personal qualities, religious affiliation/commitment. *Important factors considered include:* Class rank, application essay, extracurricular activities. *Other factors considered include:* recommendation(s), alumni/ae relation, first generation, geographical residence, interview, level of applicant's interest, racial/ethnic status, state residency, talent/ability, volunteer work. **Freshman Admission Requirements:** High school diploma is required and GED is accepted. *Academic units required:* 4 English, 3 mathematics, 3 science, (3 science labs), 4 social studies. **Freshman Admission Statistics:** 2,059 applied, 95% admitted, 31% enrolled. **Transfer Admission Requirements:** college transcript(s), essay or personal statement, Minimum college GPA of 2.5 required. Lowest grade transferable C. **General Admission Information:** Notification on a rolling basis, beginning on or about 10/1. Nonfall registration accepted. Admission may be deferred for a maximum of 1 term. Credit and/or placement offered for CEEB Advanced Placement tests.

COSTS AND FINANCIAL AID

Annual tuition $31,620. Room and board $9,200. Required fees $140. Average book expense $1,080. **Required Forms and Deadlines:** FAFSA, Institution's own financial aid form. **Notification of Awards:** Applicants will be notified of awards on a rolling basis beginning 3/1. **Types of Aid:** *Need-based scholarships/grants:* Federal Pell, SEOG, state scholarships/grants, private scholarships, the school's own gift aid. *Loans:* Direct Subsidized Stafford, Direct Unsubsidized Stafford, Direct PLUS, Federal Perkins, state loans. *Student Employment:* Federal Work-Study Program available. Institutional employment available. Highest amount earned per year from on-campus jobs $6,500. Off-campus job opportunities are excellent. **Financial Aid Statistics:** 100% freshmen, 100% undergrads receive need-based scholarship or grant aid. 13% freshmen, 11% undergrads receive non-need-based scholarship or grant aid. 86% freshmen, 86% undergrads receive need-based self-help aid. 0% freshmen, 0% undergrads receive athletic scholarships. 99% freshmen, 99% undergrads receive any aid. 80% undergrads borrow to pay for school. Average cumulative indebtedness $23,774. **Criteria for awarding institutional aid:** *Non-need-based:* academics, alumni affiliation, art, leadership, music/drama, state/district residency.

BETHUNE-COOKMAN COLLEGE

640 Dr. Mary McLeod Bethune Boulevard, Daytona Beach, FL 32114-3099
Phone: 386-481-2600 · **Financial Aid Phone:** 386-481-2626
E-mail: admissions@cookman.edu · **CEEB Code:** 5061
Fax: 386-481-2601 · **Website:** www.bethune.cookman.edu · **ACT Code:** 720

This private school, affiliated with the Methodist Church, was founded in 1904. It has a 78-acre campus.

RATINGS

Admissions Selectivity Rating: 70   **Fire Safety Rating:** 71

STUDENTS AND FACULTY

Enrollment: 3,093. **Student Body:** 58% female, 42% male, 30% out-of-state, 3% international (25 countries represented). Asian 0%, African American 91%, Caucasian 1%, Hispanic 2%, Native American <1%
Retention and Graduation: 69% freshmen return for sophomore year. 13% freshmen graduate within 4 years. 33% freshmen graduate within 6 years. 28% grads go on to further study within 1 year. 12% grads pursue arts and sciences degrees. 1% grads pursue law degrees. 14% grads pursue business degrees. 1% grads pursue medical degrees. **Faculty:** 161 full-time faculty, 57% hold PhDs, 50% are members of minority groups, 58% are women. 0% of classes are taught by teaching assistants.

ACADEMICS

Degrees: bachelor's, master's. **Classes:** Most classes have 20–29 students. Most lab/discussion sessions have fewer than 10 students. **Majors with Highest Enrollment:** Elementary Education and Teaching; Corrections and Criminal Justice; Business/Commerce. **Special Study Options:** Accelerated program, distance learning, double major, honors program, independent study, internships, study abroad, teacher certification program, weekend college. **Honors programs:** The Honors program is designed to provide expanded study opportunities for highly motivated and exceptionally qualified students, broaden their intellectual horizons, integrate various areas of knowledge, and explore intensively major fields of study through innovative techniques of individualized learning and independent research, preparing students more adequately for

graduate school. **Disability Services:** Special programs offered to physically disabled students include tutors. **Career services:** internships. Career services highlights include opportunities in the Teacher Education Internships.

FACILITIES

Housing: men's dorms, women's dorms, Scholarship Housing. 70% of campus accessible to physically disabled. **Special Academic Facilities/Equipment:** Historic archives, founder's home and gravesite (historic landmark), outreach center, telecommunications satellite network, art gallery/studio, audiologic recording studio, observatory. **Computers:** Students can register for classes online. Administrative functions (other than registration) can be performed online.

CAMPUS LIFE

Environment: Town. **Activities:** Choral groups, concert band, drama/theater, jazz band, marching band, music ensembles, radio station, student government, student newspaper, yearbook. 40 registered organizations, 9 honor societies, 2 religious organizations. 5 fraternities, 4 sororities. **Athletics (Intercollegiate):** *Men:* baseball, basketball, cross-country, football, golf, tennis, track/field (outdoor), track/field (indoor). *Women:* basketball, cross-country, golf, softball, tennis, track/field (outdoor), track/field (indoor), volleyball. **On-Campus Highlights:** Bethune Foundation (the Founder's Home), Bethune Performing Arts Center, Bethune Fine Arts studio and Gallery, Swisher Library Archives and Exhibit Rooms, Heyn Memorial Chapel (White Hall).

ADMISSIONS

Freshman Academic Profile: Average high school GPA 2.75. 5% in top 10% of high school class, 15% in top 25% of high school class, 48% in top 50% of high school class. 90% from public high schools. SAT Math middle 50% range 360-460. SAT Critical Reading middle 50% range 360-460. ACT middle 50% range 14-18. Minimum paper TOEFL 550. **Basis for Candidate Selection:** *Very important factors considered include:* academic GPA, rigor of secondary school record, standardized test scores. *Important factors considered include:* recommendation(s), character/personal qualities. *Other factors considered include:* Class rank, application essay, alumni/ae relation, extracurricular activities, first generation, interview, level of applicant's interest, talent/ability, volunteer work, work experience. **Freshman Admission Requirements:** High school diploma is required and GED is accepted. *Academic units required:* 4 English, 3 mathematics, 3 science, (1 science labs), 1 social studies, 2 history, 6 academic electives. **Freshman Admission Statistics:** 4,129 applied, 78% admitted, 28% enrolled. **Transfer Admission Requirements:** college transcript(s), essay or personal statement, statement of good standing from prior institution(s). Minimum college GPA of 2.2 required. Lowest grade transferable C. **General Admission Information:** Application Fee $25. Nonfall registration accepted. Admission may be deferred for a maximum of 1 year. Credit offered for CEEB Advanced Placement tests.

COSTS AND FINANCIAL AID

Annual tuition $11,792. Room and board $7,206. Average book expense $850. **Required Forms and Deadlines:** FAFSA. **Notification of Awards:** Applicants will be notified of awards on a rolling basis beginning 4/1. **Types of Aid:** *Need-based scholarships/grants:* Federal Pell, SEOG, state scholarships/grants, private scholarships, the school's own gift aid, United Negro College Fund, Federal Nursing Scholarships. *Loans:* Direct Subsidized Stafford, Direct Unsubsidized Stafford, Direct PLUS, Subsidized Stafford, Unsubsidized Stafford, PLUS. *Student Employment:* Federal Work-Study Program available. Institutional employment available. Highest amount earned per year from on-campus jobs $2,500. Off-campus job opportunities are good. **Financial Aid Statistics:** 78% freshmen, 79% undergrads receive need-based scholarship or grant aid. 11% freshmen, 13% undergrads receive non-need-based scholarship or grant aid. 86% freshmen, 89% undergrads receive need-based self-help aid. 8% freshmen, 9% undergrads receive athletic scholarships. 94% freshmen, 93% undergrads receive any aid. 85% undergrads borrow to pay for school. Average cumulative indebtedness $26,298. **Criteria for awarding institutional aid:** *Non-need-based:* academics, athletics, leadership, music/drama, religious affiliation, state/district residency.

BIOLA UNIVERSITY

13800 Biola Avenue, La Mirada, CA 90639
Phone: 1-800-OK-BIOLA · **Financial Aid Phone:** 562-903-4752
E-mail: admissions@biola.edu · **CEEB Code:** 4017
Fax: 562-903-4709 · **Website:** www.biola.edu · **ACT Code:** 172

This private school, affiliated with the Christian (Nondenominational) Church, was founded in 1908. It has a 95-acre campus.

RATINGS

Admissions Selectivity Rating: 85   **Fire Safety Rating:** 77

STUDENTS AND FACULTY

Enrollment: 4,370. **Student Body:** 63% female, 37% male, 22% out-of-state, 3% international (40 countries represented). Asian 16%, African American 2%, Caucasian 52%, Hispanic 18%, Native American <1%
Retention and Graduation: 87% freshmen return for sophomore year. 53% freshmen graduate within 4 years. **Faculty:** 259 full-time faculty, 82% hold PhDs, 34% are members of minority groups, 19% are women. 0% of classes are taught by teaching assistants.

ACADEMICS

Degrees: bachelor's, first professional, master's, post-master's certificate. **Classes:** Most classes have 10–19 students. Most lab/discussion sessions have 10–19 students. **Majors with Highest Enrollment:** Elementary Education and Teaching; Psychology; Business/Commerce. **Special Study Options:** double major, English as a Second Language (ESL), exchange student program (domestic), honors program, internships, study abroad, teacher certification program. **Disability Services:** Special programs offered to physically disabled students include note-taking services, reader services, tape recorders, tutors. **Career services:** Alumni network, alumni services, career/job search classes, career assessment, internships, regional alumni. Biola University provides internships applicable to a student's major allowing them to gain academic credit and career development.

FACILITIES

Housing: Coed dorms, special housing for disabled students, men's dorms, women's dorms, apartments for married students, apartments for single students, Flex style dorms—separate floors and wings for specific genders, Off Campus Apartments, On Campus Apartments. 70% of campus accessible to physically disabled. **Special Academic Facilities/Equipment:** Art gallery, electron microscope, TV production facility, film editing facility, media center, writing center, Student Ministry Union and tutoring services. **Computers:** 100% of dorms, 100% of libraries, 100% of student union, 75% of common outdoor areas have wireless network access. Students can register for classes online. Administrative functions (other than registration) can be performed online.

CAMPUS LIFE

Environment: Town. **Activities:** Choral groups, concert band, drama/theater, jazz band, music ensembles, musical theater, opera, radio station, student government, student newspaper, student-run film society, symphony orchestra, television station, yearbook. 33 registered organizations, 2 honor societies. **Athletics (Intercollegiate):** *Men:* baseball, basketball, cross-country, golf, soccer, swimming, tennis, track/field (outdoor). *Women:* basketball, cross-country, golf, soccer, softball, swimming, tennis, track/field (outdoor), volleyball. **On-Campus Highlights:** Common Grounds, The Eagle's Nest, Art Gallery, McNally Field, The Sub (Student Union Building). **Environmental Initiatives:** Cogen—We produce clean power on campus and use clean waste heat. A certain percentage of this is also used towards cooling purposes. We use 85% all green cleaning chemicals for janitorial purposes. Recycling—We have an intense recycling system on campus where we can divert a great amount of waste by use of our cardboard baler on campus as well as other recycling stations.

ADMISSIONS

Freshman Academic Profile: Average high school GPA 3.51. 30% in top 10% of high school class, 58% in top 25% of high school class, 88% in top 50% of high school class. 59% from public high schools. SAT Math middle 50% range 490-610. SAT Critical Reading middle 50% range 490-620. SAT Writing middle 50% range 490-610. ACT middle 50% range 22-28. Minimum internet-based TOEFL 100. Minimum paper TOEFL 600. **Basis for Candidate Selection:** *Very important factors considered include:* application essay, academic GPA, recommendation(s), standardized test scores, character/personal qualities, religious affiliation/commitment. *Important factors considered include:* rigor of secondary school record, extracurricular activities, interview. *Other factors considered include:* Class rank, alumni/ae relation, first generation, geographical residence, level of applicant's interest, state residency, volunteer work, work experience. **Freshman Admission Requirements:** High school diploma is required and GED is accepted. **Freshman Admission Statistics:** 3,874 applied, 75% admitted, 32% enrolled. **Transfer Admission Requirements:** High school transcript, college transcript(s), essay or personal statement, statement of good standing from prior institution(s). Minimum college GPA of 2.0 required. Lowest grade transferable C. **General Admission Information:** Application Fee $45. Regular application deadline 3/1. Regular notification 4/1. Nonfall registration not accepted. Admission may be deferred for a maximum of 2 years. Credit offered for CEEB Advanced Placement tests.

COSTS AND FINANCIAL AID

Annual tuition $33,322. Room and board $9,316. Required fees $0. Average book expense $1,746. **Required Forms and Deadlines:** FAFSA, Institution's own financial aid form, State aid form. **Notification of Awards:** Applicants will be notified of awards on a rolling basis beginning 3/1. **Types of Aid:** *Need-based scholarships/grants:* Federal Pell, SEOG, state scholarships/grants, private scholarships, the school's own gift aid. *Loans:* Subsidized Stafford, Unsubsidized Stafford, PLUS, Federal Perkins, Federal Nursing, college/university loans from institutional funds. *Student Employment:* Highest amount earned

per year from on-campus jobs $2,000. Off-campus job opportunities are good. **Financial Aid Statistics:** 98% freshmen, 97% undergrads receive need-based scholarship or grant aid. 6% freshmen, 3% undergrads receive non-need-based scholarship or grant aid. 76% freshmen, 81% undergrads receive need-based self-help aid. 2% freshmen, 2% undergrads receive athletic scholarships. 87% freshmen, 91% undergrads receive any aid. 68% undergrads borrow to pay for school. Average cumulative indebtedness $25,197. **Criteria for awarding institutional aid:** *Non-need-based:* academics, alumni affiliation, art, athletics, leadership, minority status, music/drama.

BIRMINGHAM-SOUTHERN COLLEGE

Box 549008, Birmingham, AL 35254
Phone: 205-226-4696 · **Financial Aid Phone:** 205-226-4688
E-mail: admission@bsc.edu · **CEEB Code:** 1064
Fax: 205-226-3074 · **Website:** www.bsc.edu · **ACT Code:** 1012

This private school, affiliated with the Methodist Church, was founded in 1856. It has a 196-acre campus.

RATINGS

Admissions Selectivity Rating: 87   **Fire Safety Rating:** 78

STUDENTS AND FACULTY

Enrollment: 1,226. **Student Body:** 47% female, 53% male, 41% out-of-state, 0% international (12 countries represented). Asian 4%, African American 8%, Caucasian 83%, Hispanic 3%, Native American 1%
Retention and Graduation: 81% freshmen return for sophomore year. 65% freshmen graduate within 6 years. 42% grads go on to further study within 1 year. 27% grads pursue arts and sciences degrees. 17% grads pursue law degrees. 13% grads pursue business degrees. 24% grads pursue medical degrees. **Faculty:** 86 full-time faculty, 97% hold PhDs, 38% are members of minority groups, 3% are women. 0% of classes are taught by teaching assistants.

ACADEMICS

Degrees: bachelor's, master's. **Classes:** Most classes have 10–19 students. Most lab/discussion sessions have 10–19 students. **Majors with Highest Enrollment:** Business/Commerce; Psychology; Biology/Biological Sciences. **Special Study Options:** cooperative education program, cross-registration, double major, dual enrollment, exchange student program (domestic), honors program, independent study, internships, liberal arts/career combination, student-designed major, study abroad, teacher certification program. **Honors programs:** The Honors Program at Birmingham-Southern is designed to engage students' intellectual curiosity, enhance their oral and written communications skills, and further develop their ability to think and study independently. The importance of viewing issues from interdisciplinary perspectives and of integrating—as well as analyzing—knowledge is a special focus of the program's courses and requirements. The program addresses its mission through small, interdisciplinary seminars developed specifically for Honors students and through upper-level courses with an interdisciplinary focus. The Honors Program serves as a complementary approach to fulfilling the requirements of the College's Foundations Plan for General Education. "Honors students are open to new ideas, aware of expanding horizons, and willing to change their own ideas to make room for the knowledge that they gain. They incorporate, embrace, and encourage differences. 'Honors' is not synonymous with straight A's and valedictorians. Ideal Honors students would participate in the program even if it did not appear on their transcripts."—Excerpted from "The Ideal Student in the Honors Program" as adopted by the Honors Committee 2002. The Honors Program component of Honors student's general education consists of five units of Honors seminars and one unit of independent study, known as the Honors Project. The specific general education requirements met by Honors courses and those met by regular courses will vary from student to student, depending on which Honors courses the student elects to take. Students may take one January Interim Term Honors project which will count toward the five units of Honors seminars. Students who participate in study abroad programs that include interdisciplinary courses also may petition to count one such course toward their Honors requirements. Honors students' remaining general education coursework is completed in the regular curriculum of the College. The student's sixth unit in independent study is typically taken over two terms. One-half unit is taken while the project is being designed by the student, the program director, and a faculty sponsor. The project must be interdisciplinary in nature and outside the student's major. Once approved by the Honors Program Committee, the independent study is completed the next term, giving the second half-unit of credit. All Honors Senior, or independent study, projects are presented publicly as part of the program's requirements. Combined degree programs: BA/MEng, BS/MSN (with Vanderbilt University; BS/MF or BS/MEM (with Duke Univ.). **Career services:** Alumni network, alumni services, career/job search classes, career assessment, internships, regional alumni. Career services highlights include The Mentor Program, a unique job shadowing program that matches students with local successful professionals in the student's field of interest.

FACILITIES

Housing: special housing for disabled students, men's dorms, special housing for international students, women's dorms, fraternity/sorority housing, apartments for married students, apartments for single students, Wellness Housing, Theme Housing, "Honors" floors in residence halls. 90% of campus accessible to physically disabled. **Special Academic Facilities/Equipment:** Theatre planetarium Environmental Center Urban Environmental Park Kennedy Art Center Ropes Course for Leadership Training. **Computers:** 100% of classrooms, 100% of dorms, 100% of libraries, 100% of dining areas, 100% of student union, 90% of common outdoor areas have wireless network access. Students can register for classes online. Administrative functions (other than registration) can be performed online.

CAMPUS LIFE

Environment: Metropolis. **Activities:** Choral groups, dance, drama/theater, jazz band, literary magazine, musical theater, opera, pep band, student government, student newspaper, yearbook, Campus Ministries, International Student Organization. 70 registered organizations, 18 honor societies, 5 religious organizations. 6 fraternities, 6 sororities. **Athletics (Intercollegiate):** *Men:* baseball, basketball, cheerleading, cross-country, football, golf, lacrosse, soccer, tennis, track/field (outdoor), track/field (indoor). *Women:* basketball, cheerleading, cross-country, golf, lacrosse, riflery, soccer, softball, tennis, track/field (outdoor), track/field (indoor), volleyball. **On-Campus Highlights:** Urban Environmental Park, Striplin Physical Fitness Center, The Cellar - Coffee House, The Court. **Environmental Initiatives:** 10 compressed natural gas operations vehicles will come on line this spring. Campus police vehicles are hybrids. The Southern Environmental Center (SEC) is the largest educational facility of its kind in Alabama. In addition to its award winning interactive museum and Ecoscape Gardens, the SEC is also active in the community. Annually, 15,000 school children visit the center. See www.myecoscapes.org An Urban Environmental Park, which opened in the fall of 2009, serves as both a place of recreation for students, as well as an academic laboratory for the study of environmental issues.

ADMISSIONS

Freshman Academic Profile: Average high school GPA 3.48. 29% in top 10% of high school class, 61% in top 25% of high school class, 82% in top 50% of high school class. 65% from public high schools. SAT Math middle 50% range 510-610. SAT Critical Reading middle 50% range 500-610. SAT Writing middle 50% range 490-583. ACT middle 50% range 23-29. Minimum internet-based TOEFL 61. Minimum paper TOEFL 500. **Basis for Candidate Selection:** *Very important factors considered include:* application essay, academic GPA, recommendation(s), rigor of secondary school record, standardized test scores. *Important factors considered include:* character/personal qualities. *Other factors considered include:* extracurricular activities, interview, level of applicant's interest, talent/ability, work experience. **Freshman Admission Requirements:** High school diploma is required and GED is accepted. *Academic units required:* 4 English. **Freshman Admission Statistics:** 1,846 applied, 65% admitted, 27% enrolled. **Transfer Admission Requirements:** High school transcript, college transcript(s), essay or personal statement, standardized test scores, statement of good standing from prior institution(s). Minimum college GPA of 2.0 required. Lowest grade transferable D. **General Admission Information:** Application Fee $40. Notification on a rolling basis, beginning on or about 7/1. Nonfall registration accepted. Admission may be deferred for a maximum of 1 year. Credit and/or placement offered for CEEB Advanced Placement tests.

COSTS AND FINANCIAL AID

Average book expense $1,300. **Required Forms and Deadlines:** FAFSA, State aid form. **Notification of Awards:** Applicants will be notified of awards on a rolling basis beginning 3/1. **Types of Aid:** *Need-based scholarships/grants:* Federal Pell, SEOG, state scholarships/grants, private scholarships, the school's own gift aid, United Negro College Fund. *Loans:* Subsidized Stafford, Unsubsidized Stafford, PLUS, Federal Perkins. *Student Employment:* Federal Work-Study Program available. Institutional employment available. Highest amount earned per year from on-campus jobs $1,800. Off-campus job opportunities are excellent. **Financial Aid Statistics:** 76% freshmen, 82% undergrads receive need-based scholarship or grant aid. 92% freshmen, 89% undergrads receive non-need-based scholarship or grant aid. 99% freshmen, 82% undergrads receive need-based self-help aid. 0% freshmen, 0% undergrads receive athletic scholarships. 99% freshmen, 98% undergrads receive any aid. 50% undergrads borrow to pay for school. Average cumulative indebtedness $23,883. **Criteria for awarding institutional aid:** *Non-need-based:* academics, alumni affiliation, art, leadership, minority status, music/drama, religious affiliation.

BISHOP'S UNIVERSITY

2600 College Street, Sherbrooke, QC J1M0C8
Phone: 819-822-9600
E-mail: admissio@ubishops.ca
Fax: 819-822-9616 • **Website:** www.ubishops.ca

This public school was founded in 1843. It has a 550-acre campus.

RATINGS

Admissions Selectivity Rating: 60*   **Fire Safety Rating:** 60*

STUDENTS AND FACULTY

Enrollment: 2,408.
Retention and Graduation: 78% freshmen return for sophomore year. 57% freshmen graduate within 4 years. 69% freshmen graduate within 6 years. 50% grads go on to further study within 1 year. **Faculty:** 120 full-time faculty, 68% hold PhDs, 30% are members of minority groups. 0% of classes are taught by teaching assistants.

ACADEMICS

Degrees: bachelor's, certificate, master's. **Classes:** Most classes have 10–19 students. Most lab/discussion sessions have 10–19 students. **Majors with Highest Enrollment:** Education; Biology; Business/Commerce. **Special Study Options:** double major, English as a Second Language (ESL), exchange student program (domestic), honors program, independent study, liberal arts/career combination, student-designed major, study abroad, teacher certification program. **Disability Services:** Special programs offered to physically disabled students include note-taking services, reader services, tape recorders, tutors. **Career services:** alumni services, career/job search classes, career assessment.

FACILITIES

Housing: Coed dorms, special housing for disabled students, women's dorms. 75% of campus accessible to physically disabled. **Special Academic Facilities/Equipment:** Eastern Townships Research Centre, Cormier Economics Centre, Dobson-Lagasse Entreprenneurship Centre, Molson Fine Arts Building, Art Gallery.

CAMPUS LIFE

Environment: Rural. **Activities:** Choral groups, concert band, dance, drama/theater, jazz band, literary magazine, music ensembles, musical theater, radio station, student government, student newspaper, yearbook. 60 registered organizations, 2 religious organizations. **Athletics (Intercollegiate):** *Men:* basketball, football, golf, rugby, skiing (downhill/alpine). *Women:* basketball, rugby, skiing (downhill/alpine), soccer.

ADMISSIONS

Freshman Academic Profile: Minimum paper TOEFL 550. **Basis for Candidate Selection:** *Very important factors considered include:* rigor of secondary school record. *Important factors considered include:* standardized test scores. *Other factors considered include:* Class rank, application essay, recommendation(s), character/personal qualities, extracurricular activities, talent/ability, volunteer work. **Freshman Admission Requirements:** High school diploma is required and GED is accepted. **Transfer Admission Requirements:** college transcript(s). **General Admission Information:** Application Fee $55. Notification on a rolling basis, beginning on or about 2/1. Nonfall registration accepted. Admission may be deferred for a maximum of 1 year. Credit offered for CEEB Advanced Placement tests.

COSTS AND FINANCIAL AID

Annual out-of-state tuition $3,438. Room and board $4,000. Required fees $525. Average book expense $625. **Required Forms and Deadlines:** State aid form. **Types of Aid:** *Loans:* Direct Subsidized Stafford, Direct Unsubsidized Stafford, Subsidized Stafford, Unsubsidized Stafford, state loans. *Student Employment:* Off-campus job opportunities are good. **Financial Aid Statistics:** 0% freshmen, 0% undergrads receive athletic scholarships. 33% undergrads borrow to pay for school.

BLACKBURN COLLEGE

700 College Ave., Carlinville, IL 62626
Phone: 217-854-3231
E-mail: admit@blackburn.edu • **CEEB Code:**
Fax: 217-854-3713 • **Website:** www.blackburn.edu • **ACT Code:** 958

This private school, affiliated with the Presbyterian Church, was founded in 1837. It has a 80-acre campus.

RATINGS

Admissions Selectivity Rating: 66   **Fire Safety Rating:** 60*

STUDENTS AND FACULTY

Enrollment: 603. **Student Body:** 59% female, 41% male.
Faculty: 31 full-time faculty, 35% are members of minority groups, 6% are women.

ACADEMICS

Degrees: bachelor's. **Special Study Options:** double major, exchange student program (domestic), honors program, independent study, internships, liberal arts/career combination, student-designed major, study abroad, teacher certification program.

FACILITIES

Housing: Coed dorms, men's dorms, women's dorms, Theme Housing.

CAMPUS LIFE

Environment: Village. **Activities:** Choral groups, dance, drama/theater, jazz band, literary magazine, music ensembles, musical theater, radio station, student government, student newspaper, student-run film society, yearbook, Campus Ministries, International Student Organization.

ADMISSIONS

Freshman Academic Profile: Average high school GPA 3.45. 16% in top 10% of high school class, 22% in top 25% of high school class, 37% in top 50% of high school class. 80% from public high schools. Minimum internet-based TOEFL 70. Minimum paper TOEFL 525. **Basis for Candidate Selection:** *Very important factors considered include:* academic GPA, rigor of secondary school record, standardized test scores. *Important factors considered include:* Class rank, level of applicant's interest. *Other factors considered include:* application essay, recommendation(s), alumni/ae relation, character/personal qualities, extracurricular activities, talent/ability, volunteer work, work experience. **Freshman Admission Requirements:** High school diploma is required and GED is accepted. **Freshman Admission Statistics:** 893 applied, 64% admitted, 26% enrolled. **Transfer Admission Requirements:** High school transcript, college transcript(s), standardized test scores, Minimum college GPA of 2.0 required. Lowest grade transferable C. **General Admission Information:** Nonfall registration accepted. Credit and/or placement offered for CEEB Advanced Placement tests.

COSTS AND FINANCIAL AID

Annual tuition $14,176. Room and board $4,581. Required fees $110. Average book expense $1,000.

BLACK HILLS STATE UNIVERSITY

1200 University Street Unit 9502, Spearfish, SD 57799-9502
Phone: 605-642-6343
E-mail: admissions@bhsu.edu • **CEEB Code:** 6042
Fax: 605-642-6254 • **ACT Code:** 3904

This public school was founded in 1883. It has a 123-acre campus.

RATINGS

Admissions Selectivity Rating: 70   **Fire Safety Rating:** 62

STUDENTS AND FACULTY

Enrollment: 3,138. **Student Body:** 63% female, 37% male, 21% out-of-state, 1% international (6 countries represented). Asian 1%, African American 1%, Caucasian 87%, Hispanic 2%, Native American 4%
Retention and Graduation: 55% freshmen return for sophomore year. 10% freshmen graduate within 4 years. 22% freshmen graduate within 6 years. 20% grads go on to further study within 1 year. 1% grads pursue arts and sciences degrees. 2% grads pursue law degrees. 2% grads pursue business degrees. 2% grads pursue medical degrees. **Faculty:** 117 full-time faculty, 71% hold PhDs, 39% are members of minority groups, 8% are women. 0% of classes are taught by teaching assistants.

ACADEMICS

Degrees: associate, bachelor's, master's, post-bachelor's certificate. **Classes:** Most classes have 20–29 students. Most lab/discussion sessions have 20–29 students. **Special Study Options:** cooperative education program, distance learning, double major, dual enrollment, honors program, independent study, internships, study abroad, teacher certification program. **Disability Services:** Special programs offered to physically disabled students include note-taking services, reader services, tape recorders, tutors.

FACILITIES

Housing: Coed dorms, men's dorms, women's dorms, apartments for married students, apartments for single students **Special Academic Facilities/Equipment:** Art galleries, museum collections, western historical studies library, center for Indian studies, center for advancement and study of tourism, small business institute, center of excellence for math and science education. **Computers:** Students can register for classes online.

CAMPUS LIFE

Environment: Village. **Activities:** Choral groups, concert band, drama/theater, jazz band, music ensembles, pep band, radio station, student government, student newspaper, television station. 60 registered organizations, 5 honor societies, 3 religious organizations. 1 fraternity, 1 sorority. **Athletics (Intercollegiate):** *Men:* basketball, cross-country, football, track/field (outdoor), track/field (indoor). *Women:* basketball, cross-country, track/field (outdoor), track/field (indoor), volleyball. **On-Campus Highlights:** Clare and Josef Meier Hall, Donald E. Young Sports and Fitness Center, David B. Miller Yellow Jacket Student Union, Woodburn Hall, Jonas Hall.

ADMISSIONS

Freshman Academic Profile: Average high school GPA 3.09. 6% in top 10% of high school class, 24% in top 25% of high school class, 60% in top 50% of high school class. ACT middle 50% range 18-23. Minimum paper TOEFL 520. **Basis for Candidate Selection:** *Very important factors considered include:* Class rank, rigor of secondary school record, standardized test scores. *Other factors considered include:* character/personal qualities, extracurricular activities, talent/ability. **Freshman Admission Requirements:** High school diploma is required and GED is accepted. *Academic units required:* 4 English, 3 mathematics, 3 science, (3 science labs), 3 social studies, 1 Fine Arts. **Freshman Admission Statistics:** 1,341 applied, 93% admitted, 52% enrolled. **Transfer Admission Requirements:** High school transcript, college transcript(s), Minimum college GPA of 2.0 required. Lowest grade transferable D. **General Admission Information:** Application Fee $20. Nonfall registration accepted. Credit and/or placement offered for CEEB Advanced Placement tests.

COSTS AND FINANCIAL AID

Annual in-state tuition $2,382. Annual out-of-state tuition $8,074. Room and board $4,667. Required fees $2,619. Average book expense $800. **Required Forms and Deadlines:** FAFSA. **Notification of Awards:** Applicants will be notified of awards on or about 5/15. **Types of Aid:** *Need-based scholarships/grants:* Federal Pell, SEOG, state scholarships/grants, private scholarships, the school's own gift aid. *Loans:* Subsidized Stafford, Unsubsidized Stafford, PLUS, Federal Perkins. *Student Employment:* Highest amount earned per year from on-campus jobs $1,700. **Financial Aid Statistics:** 0% freshmen, 0% undergrads receive athletic scholarships. 75% undergrads borrow to pay for school. **Criteria for awarding institutional aid:** *Non-need-based:* academics, art, athletics.

BLESSING-RIEMAN COLLEGE OF NURSING

Broadway at 11th Street, Quincy, IL 62305-7005
Phone: 217-228-5520
E-mail: hmutter@blessinghospital.com
Fax: 217-223-4661 • **Website:** www.brcn.edu • **ACT Code:** 956

This private school was founded in 1891. It has a 1-acre campus.

RATINGS

Admissions Selectivity Rating: 88   **Fire Safety Rating:** 60*

STUDENTS AND FACULTY

Enrollment: 177. **Student Body:** 97% female, 3% male, 28% out-of-state, 0% international. Asian 0%, African American 2%, Caucasian 84%, Hispanic 1%, Native American 1%
Retention and Graduation: 76% freshmen return for sophomore year. 47% freshmen graduate within 4 years. 53% freshmen graduate within 6 years.
Faculty: 13 full-time faculty, 31% hold PhDs, 100% are members of minority groups, 0% are women.

ACADEMICS
Degrees: bachelor's. **Classes:** Most classes have 10–19 students. Most lab/discussion sessions have fewer than 10 students. **Special Study Options:** double major.

FACILITIES
Housing: apartments for single students, Men's and Women's dormitories available at Culver-Stockton College and Quincy University. 100% of campus accessible to physically disabled. **Computers:** Students can register for classes online. Administrative functions (other than registration) can be performed online.

CAMPUS LIFE
Activities: student government. 1 registered organization, 1 honor society.

ADMISSIONS
Freshman Academic Profile: Average high school GPA 3.63. 20% in top 10% of high school class, 97% in top 25% of high school class, 100% in top 50% of high school class. 89% from public high schools. ACT middle 50% range 22-27. Minimum paper TOEFL 550. **Basis for Candidate Selection:** *Very important factors considered include:* Class rank, rigor of secondary school record, standardized test scores. **Freshman Admission Requirements:** High school diploma is required and GED is accepted. *Academic units required:* 4 English, 2 mathematics, 3 science, (2 science labs), 3 social studies. **Freshman Admission Statistics:** 153 applied, 50% admitted, 34% enrolled. **Transfer Admission Requirements:** High school transcript, college transcript(s), Minimum college GPA of 2.0 required. Lowest grade transferable C. **General Admission Information:** Notification on a rolling basis, beginning on or about 9/1. Nonfall registration accepted.

COSTS AND FINANCIAL AID
Average book expense $800. **Required Forms and Deadlines:** FAFSA. **Notification of Awards:** Applicants will be notified of awards on a rolling basis beginning 9/1. **Types of Aid:** *Need-based scholarships/grants:* Federal Pell, state scholarships/grants, Federal Nursing Scholarships. *Loans:* Subsidized Stafford, Unsubsidized Stafford, PLUS, Federal Nursing, college/university loans from institutional funds. *Student Employment:* Institutional employment available. Off-campus job opportunities are excellent. **Financial Aid Statistics:** 100% undergrads receive need-based scholarship or grant aid. 0% undergrads receive non-need-based scholarship or grant aid. 43% undergrads receive need-based self-help aid. 0% undergrads receive athletic scholarships. 75% undergrads borrow to pay for school.

BLOOMFIELD COLLEGE

One Park Place, Bloomfield, NJ 7003
Phone: 973-748-9000 x1230 · **Financial Aid Phone:** 973-748-9000 x1213
E-mail: admission@bloomfield.edu · **CEEB Code:** 2044
Fax: 973-748-0916 · **Website:** www.bloomfield.edu · **ACT Code:** 2540

This private school, affiliated with the Presbyterian Church, was founded in 1868. It has a 12.5-acre campus.

RATINGS

Admissions Selectivity Rating: 74   **Fire Safety Rating:** 98

STUDENTS AND FACULTY
Enrollment: 1,963. **Student Body:** 65% female, 35% male, 6% out-of-state, 3% international (22 countries represented). Asian 4%, African American 50%, Caucasian 13%, Hispanic 22%, Native American <1%
Retention and Graduation: 63% freshmen return for sophomore year. 20% freshmen graduate within 4 years. 14% grads go on to further study within 1 year. **Faculty:** 72 full-time faculty, 72% hold PhDs, 60% are members of minority groups, 26% are women. 0% of classes are taught by teaching assistants.

ACADEMICS
Degrees: bachelor's, certificate, post-bachelor's certificate. **Classes:** Most classes have 10–19 students. Most lab/discussion sessions have 10–19 students. **Majors with Highest Enrollment:** Visual and Performing Arts; Sociology; Registered Nursing/Registered Nurse. **Special Study Options:** Accelerated program, distance learning, double major, dual enrollment, English as a Second Language (ESL), honors program, independent study, internships, liberal arts/career combination, student-designed major, study abroad, teacher certification program, Four-year clinical laboratory science program and allied health technologies major offered in conjunction with University of Medicine and Dentistry of New Jersey. Joint BS/MS in computer information systems program offered with NJIT. Special programs offered by the Institute of Technology and Professional Studies. **Honors programs:** Honors program open to new

and enrolled students consisting of interdisciplinary courses, honors seminars in the arts and sciences, special courses, and honors projects. Combined degree programs: BA/MA, Joint BS/MS Comp Inform Sys Dgr with NJ Inst Tech.
Disability Services: Special programs offered to physically disabled students include note-taking services, reader services, tape recorders, tutors. **Career services:** Alumni network, alumni services, career/job search classes, career assessment, internships, regional alumni. Personalized career counseling to indentify individual skills and abilities as the relate to career options and internship opportunities.

FACILITIES
Housing: Coed dorms, Theme Housing. 55% of campus accessible to physically disabled. **Special Academic Facilities/Equipment:** Westminster Theatre, Art Gallery, State-of-the-Art Library. **Computers:** 20% of classrooms, 100% of dorms, 100% of libraries, 100% of dining areas, 100% of student union, have wireless network access. Administrative functions (other than registration) can be performed online.

CAMPUS LIFE
Environment: Town. **Activities:** dance, drama/theater, radio station, student government, Campus Ministries, International Student Organization. 40 registered organizations, 4 honor societies, 1 religious organization. 6 fraternities, 6 sororities. **Athletics (Intercollegiate):** *Men:* baseball, basketball, cross-country, soccer, tennis. *Women:* basketball, cross-country, soccer, softball, volleyball. **On-Campus Highlights:** Library, Art Gallery, College Center, Deacons Den, Gymnasium, Quad. **Environmental Initiatives:** Campus-wide recycling program; E-waste recycling; Continued upgrading of newer, more efficient heating systems.

ADMISSIONS
Freshman Academic Profile: Average high school GPA 2.65. 6% in top 10% of high school class, 24% in top 25% of high school class, 55% in top 50% of high school class. 80% from public high schools. SAT Math middle 50% range 390-470. SAT Critical Reading middle 50% range 380-460. Minimum internet-based TOEFL 79. Minimum paper TOEFL 550. **Basis for Candidate Selection:** *Very important factors considered include:* application essay, academic GPA, recommendation(s), rigor of secondary school record, standardized test scores. *Important factors considered include:* Class rank, extracurricular activities, interview, talent/ability, volunteer work. *Other factors considered include:* alumni/ae relation, work experience. **Freshman Admission Statistics:** 2,987 applied, 59% admitted, 24% enrolled. **Transfer Admission Requirements:** college transcript(s), Minimum college GPA of 2.0 required. Lowest grade transferable 2. **General Admission Information:** Application Fee $40. Regular application deadline 8/1. Notification on a rolling basis, beginning on or about 10/1. Nonfall registration accepted. Admission may be deferred for a maximum of 1 Year. Credit and/or placement offered for CEEB Advanced Placement tests.

COSTS AND FINANCIAL AID
Annual tuition $25,550. Room and board $11,100. Required fees $1,200. Average book expense $1,200. **Required Forms and Deadlines:** FAFSA. **Notification of Awards:** Applicants will be notified of awards on a rolling basis beginning 3/15. **Types of Aid:** *Need-based scholarships/grants:* Federal Pell, SEOG, state scholarships/grants, private scholarships, the school's own gift aid. *Loans:* Subsidized Stafford, Unsubsidized Stafford, PLUS. *Student Employment:* Federal Work-Study Program available. Institutional employment available. Highest amount earned per year from on-campus jobs $2,400. Off-campus job opportunities are good. **Financial Aid Statistics:** 100% freshmen, 97% undergrads receive need-based scholarship or grant aid. 38% freshmen, 31% undergrads receive non-need-based scholarship or grant aid. 49% freshmen, 31% undergrads receive need-based self-help aid. 1% freshmen, 1% undergrads receive athletic scholarships. 98% freshmen, 95% undergrads receive any aid. 89% undergrads borrow to pay for school. Average cumulative indebtedness $29,199. **Criteria for awarding institutional aid:** *Non-need-based:* academics, alumni affiliation, athletics, music/drama, religious affiliation.

BLOOMSBURG UNIVERSITY OF PENNSYLVANIA

104 Student Services Center, Bloomsburg, PA 17815
Phone: 570-389-4316 · **Financial Aid Phone:** 570-389-4279
E-mail: www.bloomu.edu/admissions · **CEEB Code:** 2646
Fax: 570-389-4741 · **Website:** www.bloomu.edu · **ACT Code:** 3692

This public school was founded in 1839. It has a 282-acre campus.

RATINGS

Admissions Selectivity Rating: 72   **Fire Safety Rating:** 96

STUDENTS AND FACULTY

Enrollment: 9,109. **Student Body:** 57% female, 43% male, 10% out-of-state, 1% international (31 countries represented). Asian 1%, African American 8%, Caucasian 81%, Hispanic 5%, Native American <1%
Retention and Graduation: 43% freshmen graduate within 4 years. 65% freshmen graduate within 6 years. 24% grads go on to further study within 1 year. **Faculty:** 419 full-time faculty, 86% hold PhDs, 41% are members of minority groups, 11% are women. 0% of classes are taught by teaching assistants.

ACADEMICS

Degrees: bachelor's, certificate, master's, post-bachelor's certificate, post-master's certificate. **Classes:** Most classes have 20–29 students. Most lab/discussion sessions have 10–19 students. **Majors with Highest Enrollment:** Business Administration and Management; Organizational Communication; Teacher Education and Professional Development, Specific Levels and Methods. **Special Study Options:** cooperative education program, cross-registration, distance learning, double major, dual enrollment, English as a Second Language (ESL), exchange student program (domestic), honors program, independent study, internships, liberal arts/career combination, study abroad, teacher certification program. **Honors programs:** The Honors Program's goals are: to challenge students to perform at the highest level of excellence to encourage independent thinking and learning; to create a supportive environment that encourages the aspirations and achievements of students and fosters their dignity, self esteem and sense of initiative; to encourage creativity, intellectual independence, analytical thinking and problem solving and the growth of communication skills through a strong emphasis on reading, writing and research; to provide opportunities for students to develop a broader perspective on national and global issues; to provide forums for symposia, experiential learning and independent study; to create a meaningful learning community; to develop students' leadership potential; to enable students to engage in a rigorous, coherent, integrated academic experience with a high degree of student-faculty interaction. **Disability Services:** Special programs offered to physically disabled students include note-taking services, reader services, tape recorders, tutors. **Career services:** career/job search classes, career assessment Career services highlights include http://internships.bloomu.edu/.

FACILITIES

Housing: Coed dorms, apartments for single students, Affiliated off-campus apartments operated by the Community Government Association. 100% of campus accessible to physically disabled. **Special Academic Facilities/Equipment:** Art gallery, language lab, TV studio, radio station. **Computers:** 100% of classrooms, 100% of libraries, 100% of student union, 50% of common outdoor areas have wireless network access. Students can register for classes online. Administrative functions (other than registration) can be performed online.

CAMPUS LIFE

Environment: Village. **Activities:** Choral groups, concert band, dance, drama/theater, literary magazine, marching band, music ensembles, pep band, radio station, student government, student newspaper, television station, yearbook, Campus Ministries, International Student Organization, Model UN. 195 registered organizations, 19 honor societies, 8 religious organizations. 15 fraternities, 13 sororities. **Athletics (Intercollegiate):** *Men:* baseball, basketball, cheerleading, cross-country, football, soccer, swimming, tennis, track/field (outdoor), track/field (indoor), wrestling. *Women:* basketball, cheerleading, cross-country, field hockey, lacrosse, soccer, softball, swimming, tennis, track/field (outdoor), track/field (indoor). **On-Campus Highlights:** Kehr Student Union, Dining Hall/Food Court, Climbing Wall, Recreation Center, Redman Stadium, Starbucks. **Environmental Initiatives:** Biofuel bus One of Bloomsburg's shuttle buses uses carbon neutral B100 fuel processed from dining services used cooking oil during fall and spring. Two 1951 vintage coal boilers have been replaced with a biomass (wood chip) boiler and a natural gas boiler to reduce emissions at Bloomsburg's heating plant. 1,500 gallons of water are saved by going trayless each Tuesday at the campus dining hall. Food waste is reduced as well. Possibly completely trayless in near future.

ADMISSIONS

Freshman Academic Profile: Average high school GPA 3.28. 9% in top 10% of high school class, 27% in top 25% of high school class, 64% in top 50% of high school class. 88% from public high schools. SAT Math middle 50% range 440-540. SAT Critical Reading middle 50% range 440-530. SAT Writing middle 50% range 420-510. ACT middle 50% range 17-22. Minimum paper TOEFL 550. **Basis for Candidate Selection:** *Very important factors considered include:* Class rank, academic GPA, rigor of secondary school record, standardized test scores. *Other factors considered include:* application essay, recommendation(s), character/personal qualities, extracurricular activities, geographical residence, interview, state residency, talent/ability, volunteer work, work experience. **Freshman Admission Requirements:** High school diploma is required and GED is accepted. *Academic units required:* 4 English, 3 mathematics, 3 science, 2 social studies, 2 history, 2 academic electives. **Freshman Admission Statistics:** 10,043 applied, 88% admitted, 25% enrolled. **Transfer Admission Requirements:** High school transcript, college transcript(s),

Minimum college GPA of 2.0 required. Lowest grade transferable C. **General Admission Information:** Application Fee $30. Notification on a rolling basis, beginning on or about 9/18. Nonfall registration accepted. Admission may be deferred for a maximum of 1 year. Credit and/or placement offered for CEEB Advanced Placement tests.

COSTS AND FINANCIAL AID

Annual. Annual out-of-state tuition $17,050. Room and board $8,168. Required fees $2,094. Average book expense $1,200. **Required Forms and Deadlines:** FAFSA. **Notification of Awards:** Applicants will be notified of awards on a rolling basis beginning 4/1. *Types of Aid: Need-based scholarships/grants:* Federal Pell, SEOG, state scholarships/grants, private scholarships, the school's own gift aid, Federal ACG and Federal Smart Grants. *Loans:* Subsidized Stafford, Unsubsidized Stafford, PLUS, Federal Perkins, state loans, Alternative Loans. *Student Employment:* Federal Work-Study Program available. Institutional employment available. Highest amount earned per year from on-campus jobs $4,640. **Financial Aid Statistics:** 63% freshmen, 62% undergrads receive need-based scholarship or grant aid. 23% freshmen, 16% undergrads receive non-need-based scholarship or grant aid. 89% freshmen, 91% undergrads receive need-based self-help aid. 2% freshmen, 2% undergrads receive athletic scholarships. 84% undergrads receive any aid. 75% undergrads borrow to pay for school. Average cumulative indebtedness $24,737. **Criteria for awarding institutional aid:** *Non-need-based:* academics, art, athletics, job skills, leadership, minority status, music/drama, state/district residency.

BLUE MOUNTAIN COLLEGE

PO Box 160, Blue Mountain, MS 38610
Phone: 662-685-4771 · **Financial Aid Phone:** 662-685-4771
E-mail: admissions@bmc.edu
Fax: 662-685-4776 · **Website:** bmc.edu

This private school, affiliated with the Baptist Church, was founded in 1873. It has a 44-acre campus.

RATINGS

Admissions Selectivity Rating: 84   **Fire Safety Rating:** 66

STUDENTS AND FACULTY

Enrollment: 406. **Student Body:** 64% female, 36% male, 12% out-of-state, 0% international (1 countries represented). Asian 0%, African American 12%, Caucasian 87%, Hispanic 0%, Native American <1%
Retention and Graduation: 72% freshmen return for sophomore year. 31% freshmen graduate within 4 years. 58% freshmen graduate within 6 years. 14% grads go on to further study within 1 year. 14% grads pursue arts and sciences degrees. 1% grads pursue business degrees. 2% grads pursue medical degrees. **Faculty:** 24 full-time faculty, 67% hold PhDs, 54% are members of minority groups, 0% are women. 0% of classes are taught by teaching assistants.

ACADEMICS

Degrees: bachelor's, master's. **Classes:** Most classes have 10–19 students. Most lab/discussion sessions have 10–19 students. **Majors with Highest Enrollment:** Elementary Education and Teaching; Bible/Biblical Studies; Psychology. **Special Study Options:** double major, honors program, internships, teacher certification program. **Honors programs:** Academic Honors Program. **Disability Services:** Special programs offered to physically disabled students include note-taking services, tutors.

FACILITIES

Housing: men's dorms, women's dorms. 50% of campus accessible to physically disabled.

CAMPUS LIFE

Environment: Rural. **Activities:** Choral groups, drama/theater, literary magazine, musical theater, student government, yearbook. 28 registered organizations, 4 honor societies, 2 religious organizations. **Athletics (Intercollegiate):** *Women:* basketball, tennis. **On-Campus Highlights:** Johnnie Armstrong Galry, Student Union Building, Tyler Gymnasium, Broach Hall, Fisher-Washburn Hall.

ADMISSIONS

Freshman Academic Profile: Average high school GPA 3.3. 19% in top 10% of high school class, 50% in top 25% of high school class, 86% in top 50% of high school class. 73% from public high schools. ACT middle 50% range 18-23. Minimum paper TOEFL 500. **Basis for Candidate Selection:** *Important factors considered include:* Class rank, academic GPA, rigor of secondary school record, standardized test scores. *Other factors considered include:* recommendation(s), alumni/ae relation, character/personal qualities. **Freshman Admission Requirements:** High school diploma is required and GED is accepted. *Academic units required:* 4 English, 3 mathematics, 3 science, (2 science labs), 2 foreign language, 1 social studies, 2 history. **Freshman Admission Statistics:** 197 applied, 50% admitted, 60% enrolled. **Transfer Admission Requirements:** college transcript(s), Lowest grade transferable C. **General Admission Information:** Application Fee $10. Notification on a rolling basis, beginning on or about 10/1. Nonfall registration accepted. Admission may be deferred for a maximum of semester. Credit offered for CEEB Advanced Placement tests.

COSTS AND FINANCIAL AID

Average book expense $650. **Required Forms and Deadlines:** FAFSA, Institution's own financial aid form. **Notification of Awards:** Applicants will be notified of awards on a rolling basis beginning 4/1. **Types of Aid:** *Need-based scholarships/grants:* Federal Pell, SEOG, state scholarships/grants, private scholarships. *Loans:* Subsidized Stafford, Unsubsidized Stafford, PLUS, Federal Perkins. *Student Employment:* Federal Work-Study Program available. Institutional employment available. Highest amount earned per year from on-campus jobs $1,400. Off-campus job opportunities are good. **Financial Aid Statistics:** 81% freshmen, 64% undergrads receive need-based scholarship or grant aid. 81% freshmen, 100% undergrads receive non-need-based scholarship or grant aid. 62% freshmen, 18% undergrads receive need-based self-help aid. 8% freshmen, 6% undergrads receive athletic scholarships. 95% freshmen, 96% undergrads receive any aid. 83% undergrads borrow to pay for school. **Criteria for awarding institutional aid:** *Non-need-based:* academics, alumni affiliation, athletics, religious affiliation, state/district residency.

BLUEFIELD COLLEGE

3000 College Drive, Bluefield, VA 24605
Phone: 540-326-4214 • **Financial Aid Phone:** 800-872-0175
E-mail: thavens@mail.bluefield.edu • **CEEB Code:** 5063
Fax: 540-326-4288 • **Website:** www.bluefield.edu • **ACT Code:** 4340

This private school, affiliated with the Baptist Church, was founded in 1922.

RATINGS

Admissions Selectivity Rating: 85   Fire Safety Rating: 60*

STUDENTS AND FACULTY

Enrollment: 776. **Student Body:** 60% female, 40% male, 22% out-of-state, 0% international. Asian 1%, African American 18%, Caucasian 78%, Hispanic 1%, Native American <1%
Retention and Graduation: 66% freshmen return for sophomore year. 36% freshmen graduate within 4 years. 47% freshmen graduate within 6 years. 23% grads go on to further study within 1 year. 10% grads pursue arts and sciences degrees. 3% grads pursue law degrees. 8% grads pursue business degrees. 2% grads pursue medical degrees. **Faculty:** 33 full-time faculty, 64% hold PhDs, 30% are members of minority groups, 0% are women. 0% of classes are taught by teaching assistants.

ACADEMICS

Degrees: bachelor's. **Classes:** Most classes have fewer than 10 students. Most lab/discussion sessions have 10–19 students. **Majors with Highest Enrollment:** Christian Studies; Criminal Justice/Law Enforcement Administration; Business/Commerce. **Special Study Options:** Accelerated program, double major, dual enrollment, honors program, internships, student-designed major, study abroad, teacher certification program, weekend college. **Disability Services:** Special programs offered to physically disabled students include tape recorders, tutors. **Career services:** Alumni network, alumni services, career/job search classes, internships,

FACILITIES

Housing: Coed dorms, men's dorms, women's dorms. 50% of campus accessible to physically disabled. **Special Academic Facilities/Equipment:** Art center.

CAMPUS LIFE

Environment: Rural. **Activities:** Choral groups, drama/theater, literary magazine, music ensembles, student government, student newspaper, yearbook. 18 registered organizations, 7 honor societies, 6 religious organizations, 2 fraternities, 2 sororities. **Athletics (Intercollegiate):** *Men:* baseball, basketball, golf, soccer, tennis. *Women:* basketball, soccer, softball, tennis, volleyball.

ADMISSIONS

Freshman Academic Profile: Average high school GPA 3.2. 23% in top 10% of high school class, 44% in top 25% of high school class, 83% in top 50% of high school class. 95% from public high schools. SAT Math middle 50% range 420-520. SAT Critical Reading middle 50% range 440-530. ACT middle 50% range 19-24. **Basis for Candidate Selection:** *Very important factors considered include:* rigor of secondary school record, standardized test

scores, character/personal qualities. *Important factors considered include:* Class rank, interview. *Other factors considered include:* application essay, recommendation(s), alumni/ae relation, extracurricular activities, talent/ability, volunteer work, work experience. **Freshman Admission Requirements:** High school diploma is required and GED is accepted. *Academic units required:* 4 English, 3 mathematics, 3 science, (1 science labs), 3 social studies, 6 academic electives. **Freshman Admission Statistics:** 537 applied, 50% admitted, 40% enrolled. **Transfer Admission Requirements:** college transcript(s), Minimum college GPA of 2.0 required. Lowest grade transferable D. **General Admission Information:** Application Fee $30. Notification on a rolling basis, beginning on or about 9/1. Nonfall registration accepted. Admission may be deferred for a maximum of semester.

COSTS AND FINANCIAL AID

Average book expense $900. **Required Forms and Deadlines:** FAFSA, Institution's own financial aid form, State aid form. **Notification of Awards:** Applicants will be notified of awards on a rolling basis beginning 3/10. **Types of Aid:** *Need-based scholarships/grants:* Federal Pell, SEOG, state scholarships/grants, private scholarships, the school's own gift aid. *Loans:* Subsidized Stafford, Unsubsidized Stafford, PLUS, Keesee Foundation. *Student Employment:* Highest amount earned per year from on-campus jobs $700. Off-campus job opportunities are good. **Financial Aid Statistics:** 99% freshmen, 95% undergrads receive need-based scholarship or grant aid. 16% freshmen, 12% undergrads receive non-need-based scholarship or grant aid. 73% freshmen, 82% undergrads receive need-based self-help aid. 0% freshmen, 0% undergrads receive athletic scholarships. 80% undergrads borrow to pay for school. **Criteria for awarding institutional aid:** *Non-need-based:* academics, art, athletics, leadership, minority status, music/drama, religious affiliation, state/district residency.

BLUEFIELD STATE COLLEGE

219 Rock Street, Bluefield, WV 24701
Phone: 304-327-4065
E-mail: bscadmit@bluefieldstate.edu • **CEEB Code:** 5064
Fax: 304-325-7747 • **Website:** www.bluefieldstate.edu • **ACT Code:** 4514

This public school was founded in 1895. It has a 40-acre campus.

RATINGS

Admissions Selectivity Rating: 68   Fire Safety Rating: 60*

STUDENTS AND FACULTY

Enrollment: 3,092. **Student Body:** 65% female, 35% male, 5% out-of-state, 0% international (15 countries represented). Asian 0%, African American 11%, Caucasian 100%, Hispanic 1%, Native American <1%
Retention and Graduation: 76% freshmen return for sophomore year. 24% freshmen graduate within 4 years. 45% freshmen graduate within 6 years. 9% grads go on to further study within 1 year. 4% grads pursue arts and sciences degrees. 1% grads pursue law degrees. 3% grads pursue business degrees. 1% grads pursue medical degrees. **Faculty:** 92 full-time faculty, 40% hold PhDs, 55% are members of minority groups, 9% are women. 0% of classes are taught by teaching assistants.

ACADEMICS

Degrees: associate, bachelor's, certificate, terminal associate, transfer associate. **Classes:** Most classes have 10–19 students. Most lab/discussion sessions have 10–19 students. **Majors with Highest Enrollment:** Elementary Education and Teaching; Registered Nursing/Registered Nurse; Business/Commerce. **Special Study Options:** distance learning, dual enrollment, honors program, internships, student-designed major, teacher certification program. **Honors programs:** Bluefield State College Honors Program. **Disability Services:** Special programs offered to physically disabled students include note-taking services, reader services, tape recorders, tutors. **Career services:** career/job search classes

FACILITIES

Housing: Off-campus housing services provided, including referrals and resources. 100% of campus accessible to physically disabled. **Computers:** Students can register for classes online. Administrative functions (other than registration) can be performed online.

CAMPUS LIFE

Environment: Village. **Activities:** Choral groups, student government, student newspaper, yearbook. 28 registered organizations, 6 honor societies, 1 religious organization. 3 fraternities, 4 sororities. **Athletics (Intercollegiate):** *Men:* baseball, basketball, cross-country, golf, tennis. *Women:* basketball, cheerleading, cross-country, softball, tennis, volleyball.

ADMISSIONS

Freshman Academic Profile: Average high school GPA 3.15. 10% in top 10% of high school class, 27% in top 25% of high school class, 73% in top 50% of high school class. 98% from public high schools. ACT middle 50% range 21-16. Minimum paper TOEFL 550. **Basis for Candidate Selection:** *Important factors considered include:* rigor of secondary school record, standardized test scores. **Freshman Admission Requirements:** High school diploma is required and GED is accepted. *Academic units required:* 4 English, 3 mathematics, 3 science, (2 science labs), 0 foreign language, 3 social studies, 1 history, 1 academic electives. **Freshman Admission Statistics:** 1,135 applied, 98% admitted, 53% enrolled. **Transfer Admission Requirements:** college transcript(s), Lowest grade transferable D. **General Admission Information:** Nonfall registration accepted. Admission may be deferred for a maximum of 1 semester. Credit and/or placement offered for CEEB Advanced Placement tests.

COSTS AND FINANCIAL AID

Annual in-state tuition $3,114. Annual out-of-state tuition $6,894. Average book expense $1,200. **Required Forms and Deadlines:** FAFSA, Institution's own financial aid form, State aid form. **Notification of Awards:** Applicants will be notified of awards on a rolling basis beginning 6/1. **Types of Aid:** *Need-based scholarships/grants:* Federal Pell, SEOG, state scholarships/grants, private scholarships, the school's own gift aid. *Loans:* Direct Subsidized Stafford, Direct Unsubsidized Stafford, Direct PLUS, Federal Perkins. *Student Employment:* Highest amount earned per year from on-campus jobs $1,500. **Financial Aid Statistics:** 100% freshmen, 100% undergrads receive need-based scholarship or grant aid. 16% freshmen, 18% undergrads receive non-need-based scholarship or grant aid. 80% freshmen, 78% undergrads receive need-based self-help aid. 5% freshmen, 5% undergrads receive athletic scholarships. 50% undergrads borrow to pay for school. **Criteria for awarding institutional aid:** *Non-need-based:* academics, alumni affiliation, athletics, leadership, minority status, state/district residency.

BLUFFTON UNIVERSITY

Office of Admissions, Bluffton, OH 45817
Phone: 419-358-3257
E-mail: admissions@bluffton.edu • **CEEB Code:** 1067
Fax: 419-358-3081 • **Website:** www.bluffton.edu • **ACT Code:** 3238

This private school, affiliated with the Mennonite Church, was founded in 1899. It has a 65-acre campus.

RATINGS

Admissions Selectivity Rating: 78   Fire Safety Rating: 60*

STUDENTS AND FACULTY

Enrollment: 943. **Student Body:** 51% female, 49% male, 12% out-of-state, 2% international. Asian 1%, African American 7%, Caucasian 85%, Hispanic 2%, Native American <1%
Retention and Graduation: 75% freshmen return for sophomore year. 56% freshmen graduate within 4 years. 64% freshmen graduate within 6 years. 9% grads go on to further study within 1 year. 9% grads pursue arts and sciences degrees. 1% grads pursue law degrees. 1% grads pursue medical degrees. **Faculty:** 62 full-time faculty, 73% hold PhDs, 34% are members of minority groups, 2% are women. 0% of classes are taught by teaching assistants.

ACADEMICS

Degrees: bachelor's, master's. **Classes:** Most classes have 10–19 students. Most lab/discussion sessions have 10–19 students. **Special Study Options:** distance learning, double major, dual enrollment, English as a Second Language (ESL), honors program, independent study, internships, student-designed major, study abroad, teacher certification program. **Disability Services:** Special programs offered to physically disabled students include reader services, tape recorders, tutors. **Career services:** alumni services, career/job search classes.

FACILITIES

Housing: Coed dorms, men's dorms, women's dorms, Theme Housing. 99% of campus accessible to physically disabled. **Special Academic Facilities/Equipment:** Mennonite historical library, peace arts center, nature preserve.

CAMPUS LIFE

Environment: Rural. **Activities:** Choral groups, concert band, dance, drama/theater, jazz band, literary magazine, music ensembles, musical theater, pep band, radio station, student government, Campus Ministries, International Student Organization. 50 registered organizations, 19 honor societies, 10 religious organizations. **Athletics (Intercollegiate):** *Men:* baseball, basketball, cheerleading, cross-country, football, golf, soccer, tennis, track/field (outdoor),

track/field (indoor). *Women:* basketball, cheerleading, cross-country, golf, soccer, softball, tennis, track/field (outdoor), track/field (indoor), volleyball.
On-Campus Highlights: Centennial Hall—academic center, Marbeck Center—student union, College Hall—administrative/classroom building, Salzman Stadium—Football Stadium, Founders Hall—gymnasium.

ADMISSIONS

Freshman Academic Profile: Average high school GPA 3.18. 14% in top 10% of high school class, 33% in top 25% of high school class, 67% in top 50% of high school class. 98% from public high schools. SAT Math middle 50% range 450-600. SAT Critical Reading middle 50% range 420-570. ACT middle 50% range 19-24. Minimum paper TOEFL 500. **Basis for Candidate Selection:** *Very important factors considered include:* Class rank, academic GPA, standardized test scores. *Important factors considered include:* recommendation(s). *Other factors considered include:* application essay, rigor of secondary school record, character/personal qualities, religious affiliation/commitment, talent/ability, volunteer work. **Freshman Admission Requirements:** High school diploma is required and GED is accepted. **Freshman Admission Statistics:** 1,674 applied, 66% admitted, 23% enrolled. **Transfer Admission Requirements:** High school transcript, college transcript(s), statement of good standing from prior institution(s). Minimum college GPA of 2.0 required. Lowest grade transferable C-. **General Admission Information:** Application Fee $20. Regular application deadline 8/15. Nonfall registration accepted. Admission may be deferred for a maximum of two years. Credit and/or placement offered for CEEB Advanced Placement tests.

COSTS AND FINANCIAL AID

Annual tuition $23,594. Room and board $8,170. Required fees $450. Average book expense $1,400. **Required Forms and Deadlines:** FAFSA. **Notification of Awards:** Applicants will be notified of awards on a rolling basis beginning 3/1. **Types of Aid:** *Need-based scholarships/grants:* Federal Pell, SEOG, state scholarships/grants, private scholarships, the school's own gift aid. *Loans:* Subsidized Stafford, Unsubsidized Stafford, PLUS, Federal Perkins. *Student Employment:* Federal Work-Study Program available. Institutional employment available. Highest amount earned per year from on-campus jobs $1,350. Off-campus job opportunities are good. **Financial Aid Statistics:** 100% freshmen, 98% undergrads receive need-based scholarship or grant aid. 1% freshmen, 5% undergrads receive non-need-based scholarship or grant aid. 94% freshmen, 93% undergrads receive need-based self-help aid. 0% freshmen, 0% undergrads receive athletic scholarships. 88% undergrads borrow to pay for school. Average cumulative indebtedness $19,684. **Criteria for awarding institutional aid:** *Non-need-based:* academics, art, job skills, leadership, minority status, music/drama, religious affiliation, state/district residency.

BOB JONES UNIVERSITY

1700 Wade Hampton Blvd, Greenville, SC 29614
Phone: 800-252-6363 • **Financial Aid Phone:** 864-242-5100 Ext 3040
E-mail: admission@bju.edu • **CEEB Code:** 5065
Fax: 800-232-9258 • **Website:** www.bju.edu • **ACT Code:** 3836

This proprietary school was founded in 1927. It has a 225-acre campus.

RATINGS

Admissions Selectivity Rating: 78   Fire Safety Rating: 79

STUDENTS AND FACULTY

Enrollment: 2,552. **Student Body:** 56% female, 44% male, 67% out-of-state, 6% international (47 countries represented). Asian 2%, African American 1%, Caucasian 77%, Hispanic 6%, Native American <1%
Retention and Graduation: 59% freshmen graduate within 4 years. 72% freshmen graduate within 6 years. 18% grads go on to further study within 1 year. 1% grads pursue arts and sciences degrees. 1% grads pursue law degrees. 2% grads pursue business degrees. 3% grads pursue medical degrees. **Faculty:** 190 full-time faculty, 56% hold PhDs, 38% are members of minority groups, 3% are women.

ACADEMICS

Degrees: associate, bachelor's, certificate, doctoral, master's, transfer associate. **Classes:** Most classes have fewer than 10 students. Most lab/discussion sessions have fewer than 10 students. **Majors with Highest Enrollment:** Registered Nursing/Registered Nurse; Accounting; Business Administration and Management. **Special Study Options:** Accelerated program, distance learning, English as a Second Language (ESL), internships, teacher certification program. **Disability Services:** Special programs offered to physically disabled students include note-taking services, reader services, tape recorders, tutors. **Career services:** alumni services, career/job search classes, career assessment.

FACILITIES

Housing: special housing for disabled students, men's dorms, women's dorms, apartments for married students, apartments for single students. 90% of campus accessible to physically disabled. **Special Academic Facilities/Equipment:** Museum & Gallery Davis Field House Rodeheaver Auditorium Bob Jones Jr. Memorial Seminary & Evangelism Center **Computers:** 85% of classrooms, 100% of dorms, 100% of libraries, 20% of dining areas, 100% of student union, 70% of common outdoor areas have wireless network access. Students can register for classes online. Administrative functions (other than registration) can be performed online.

CAMPUS LIFE

Environment: City. **Activities:** Choral groups, concert band, drama/theater, music ensembles, opera, radio station, student government, student newspaper, symphony orchestra, television station, yearbook, Campus Ministries 31 registered organizations, 18 religious organizations. **On-Campus Highlights:** University Student Center, Davis Field House, Cuppa Jones coffee shop, Fast Break lunch area, BJU Museum & Gallery.

ADMISSIONS

Freshman Academic Profile: Average high school GPA 3.39. 12% in top 10% of high school class, 35% in top 25% of high school class, 62% in top 50% of high school class. 5% from public high schools. ACT middle 50% range 20-26. Minimum internet-based TOEFL 61. Minimum paper TOEFL 500. **Basis for Candidate Selection:** *Important factors considered include:* academic GPA, rigor of secondary school record, standardized test scores. *Other factors considered include:* recommendation(s), state residency. **Freshman Admission Requirements:** High school diploma is required and GED is accepted. *Academic units required:* 4 English, 3 mathematics, 2 science, (2 science labs), 2 foreign language, 1 social studies, 1 history, 1 visual/performing arts, 0 computer science, 1 academic electives. **Freshman Admission Statistics:** 1,048 applied, 81% admitted, 72% enrolled. **Transfer Admission Requirements:** college transcript(s), Minimum college GPA of 2.0 required. Lowest grade transferable D-. **General Admission Information:** Application Fee $55. Regular application deadline 11/30. Notification on a rolling basis, beginning on or about 10/2. Nonfall registration accepted. Admission may be deferred for a maximum of 1 semester. Credit and/or placement offered for CEEB Advanced Placement tests.

COSTS AND FINANCIAL AID

Annual tuition $13,570. Room and board $6,090. Required fees $650. Average book expense $1,200. **Required Forms and Deadlines:** FAFSA. **Notification of Awards:** Applicants will be notified of awards on or about 3/1. **Types of Aid:** *Need-based scholarships/grants:* Federal Pell, SEOG, state scholarships/grants, private scholarships, the school's own gift aid. *Loans:* Direct Subsidized Stafford, Direct Unsubsidized Stafford, Direct PLUS, Subsidized Stafford, Unsubsidized Stafford, PLUS, Federal Perkins. *Student Employment:* Federal Work-Study Program available. Institutional employment available. Highest amount earned per year from on-campus jobs $12,914. Off-campus job opportunities are good. **Financial Aid Statistics:** 100% undergrads receive need-based scholarship or grant aid. 39% undergrads receive non-need-based scholarship or grant aid. 58% undergrads receive need-based self-help aid. 0% undergrads receive athletic scholarships. 60% freshmen, 61% undergrads receive any aid. **Criteria for awarding institutional aid:** *Non-need-based:* academics, alumni affiliation, athletics, leadership, state/district residency.

BOISE BIBLE COLLEGE

8695 W Marigold Street, Boise, ID 83714-1220
Phone: 208-376-7731
E-mail: boisebible@boisebible.edu · **CEEB Code:** 891
Fax: 208-376-7743 · **ACT Code:** 917

This private school, affiliated with the Christian (Nondenominational) Church, was founded in 1945. It has a 16-acre campus.

RATINGS

Admissions Selectivity Rating: 73   **Fire Safety Rating:** 60*

STUDENTS AND FACULTY

Enrollment: 175. **Student Body:** 50% female, 50% male, 55% out-of-state, 2% international (3 countries represented). Asian 2%, African American 1%, Caucasian 89%, Hispanic 3%, Native American 1%
Retention and Graduation: 60% freshmen return for sophomore year. **Faculty:** 8 full-time faculty, 13% hold PhDs, 13% are members of minority groups, 0% are women.

ACADEMICS

Degrees: associate, bachelor's, certificate. **Majors with Highest Enrollment:** Religious Education; Theological and Ministerial Studies; Pastoral Studies/Counseling. **Special Study Options:** double major, internships, teacher certification program.

FACILITIES

Housing: men's dorms, women's dorms.

CAMPUS LIFE

Environment: Village. **Activities:** Choral groups, music ensembles, student government.

ADMISSIONS

Freshman Academic Profile: Average high school GPA 3.22. 8% in top 10% of high school class, 40% in top 25% of high school class, 70% in top 50% of high school class. SAT Math middle 50% range 410-540. SAT Critical Reading middle 50% range 460-550. ACT middle 50% range 16-21. Minimum paper TOEFL 500. **Basis for Candidate Selection:** *Important factors considered include:* Class rank, application essay, academic GPA, recommendation(s), standardized test scores, character/personal qualities, religious affiliation/commitment. *Other factors considered include:* interview, level of applicant's interest. **Freshman Admission Requirements:** High school diploma is required and GED is accepted. **Freshman Admission Statistics:** 80 applied, 99% admitted, 75% enrolled. **Transfer Admission Requirements:** college transcript(s), essay or personal statement, statement of good standing from prior institution(s). Minimum college GPA of 2.0 required. Lowest grade transferable C. **General Admission Information:** Application Fee $25. Regular application deadline 8/15. Notification on a rolling basis, beginning on or about 2/15. Nonfall registration accepted. Admission may be deferred for a maximum of 1 year. Credit offered for CEEB Advanced Placement tests.

COSTS AND FINANCIAL AID

Annual tuition $6,840. Room and board $4,800. Required fees $99. Average book expense $450. **Required Forms and Deadlines:** FAFSA, Institution's own financial aid form. **Types of Aid:** *Need-based scholarships/grants:* Federal Pell, SEOG, private scholarships. *Loans:* Direct Subsidized Stafford, Direct Unsubsidized Stafford, Direct PLUS. *Student Employment:* Federal Work-Study Program available. **Criteria for awarding institutional aid:** *Non-need-based:* academics, leadership, music/drama.

BOISE STATE UNIVERSITY

1910 University Drive, Boise, ID 83725
Phone: 208-426-1156 · **Financial Aid Phone:** 208-426-1664
E-mail: bsuinfo@boisestate.edu · **CEEB Code:** 4018
Fax: 208-426-3765 · **ACT Code:** 914

This public school was founded in 1932. It has a 150-acre campus.

RATINGS

Admissions Selectivity Rating: 77   **Fire Safety Rating:** 73

STUDENTS AND FACULTY

Enrollment: 17,069. **Student Body:** 53% female, 47% male, 20% out-of-state, 3% international (73 countries represented). Asian 2%, African American 2%, Caucasian 77%, Hispanic 8%, Native American 1%
Retention and Graduation: 72% freshmen return for sophomore year. 7% freshmen graduate within 4 years. 30% freshmen graduate within 6 years. 15% grads go on to further study within 1 year. 4% grads pursue arts and sciences degrees. 1% grads pursue law degrees. 2% grads pursue business degrees. 1% grads pursue medical degrees. **Faculty:** 615 full-time faculty, 67% hold PhDs, 47% are members of minority groups, 8% are women. 1% of classes are taught by teaching assistants.

ACADEMICS

Degrees: associate, bachelor's, doctoral, master's, post-bachelor's certificate. **Classes:** Most classes have 20-29 students. Most lab/discussion sessions have 20-29 students. **Majors with Highest Enrollment:** Speech Communication and Rhetoric; Registered Nursing/Registered Nurse; Business/Commerce. **Special Study Options:** cooperative education program, distance learning, double major, dual enrollment, English as a Second Language (ESL), exchange student program (domestic), honors program, independent study, internships, liberal arts/career combination, study abroad, teacher certification program, weekend college. **Disability Services:** Special programs offered to physically disabled students include note-taking services, reader services, tape recorders, tutors. **Career services:** Alumni network, alumni services, career assessment, internships. Career services highlights include one of the larger intrnship programs in the Northwest.

FACILITIES

Housing: Coed dorms, special housing for disabled students, men's dorms, women's dorms, fraternity/sorority housing, apartments for married students, apartments for single students. 95% of campus accessible to physically disabled. **Computers:** Students can register for classes online. Administrative functions (other than registration) can be performed online.

CAMPUS LIFE

Environment: City. **Activities:** Choral groups, drama/theater, literary magazine, marching band, music ensembles, musical theater, pep band, radio station, student government, student newspaper, student-run film society, International Student Organization. 180 registered organizations, 4 fraternities, 3 sororities. **Athletics (Intercollegiate):** *Men:* basketball, cheerleading, cross-country, football, golf, tennis, track/field (outdoor), track/field (indoor), wrestling. *Women:* basketball, cheerleading, cross-country, golf, gymnastics, skiing (downhill/alpine), soccer, tennis, track/field (outdoor), track/field (indoor), volleyball.

ADMISSIONS

Freshman Academic Profile: Average high school GPA 3.43. 14% in top 10% of high school class, 38% in top 25% of high school class, 73% in top 50% of high school class. 89% from public high schools. SAT Math middle 50% range 480-600. SAT Critical Reading middle 50% range 470-580. SAT Writing middle 50% range 450-560. ACT middle 50% range 20-25. Minimum paper TOEFL 500. **Basis for Candidate Selection:** *Very important factors considered include:* academic GPA, rigor of secondary school record, standardized test scores. *Other factors considered include:* Class rank, extracurricular activities, first generation, racial/ethnic status, talent/ability. **Freshman Admission Requirements:** High school diploma is required and GED is accepted. *Academic units required:* 4 English, 3 mathematics, 3 science, 1 foreign language, 2 social studies, 1 academic elective. **Freshman Admission Statistics:** 5,184 applied, 85% admitted, 54% enrolled. **Transfer Admission Requirements:** college transcript(s), Minimum college GPA of 2.0 required. Lowest grade transferable c. **General Admission Information:** Application Fee $50. Regular application deadline 6/30. Notification on a rolling basis, beginning on or about 4/1. Nonfall registration accepted. Credit offered for CEEB Advanced Placement tests.

COSTS AND FINANCIAL AID

Annual in-state tuition $3,991. Annual out-of-state tuition $15,431. Required fees $1,893. Average book expense $1,200. **Required Forms and Deadlines:** FAFSA. **Notification of Awards:** Applicants will be notified of awards on a rolling basis beginning 4/1. **Types of Aid:** *Need-based scholarships/grants:* Federal Pell, SEOG, state scholarships/grants, private scholarships, the school's own gift aid. *Loans:* Direct Subsidized Stafford, Direct Unsubsidized Stafford, Direct PLUS, Federal Perkins, college/university loans from institutional funds. *Student Employment:* Federal Work-Study Program available. Institutional employment available. Highest amount earned per year from on-campus jobs $10,000. Off-campus job opportunities are excellent. **Financial Aid Statistics:** 81% freshmen, 77% undergrads receive need-based scholarship or grant aid. 15% freshmen, 6% undergrads receive non-need-based scholarship or grant aid. 84% freshmen, 92% undergrads receive need-based self-help aid. 0% freshmen, 1% undergrads receive athletic scholarships. 70% freshmen, 80% undergrads receive any aid. 64% undergrads borrow to pay for school. Average cumulative indebtedness $26,496. **Criteria for awarding institutional aid:** *Non-need-based:* academics, art, athletics, music/drama.

BOSTON ARCHITECTURAL COLLEGE

320 Newbury Street, Boston, MA 02115-2703
Phone: 617-585-0123
E-mail: admissions@the-bac.edu • **CEEB Code:** 1168
Fax: 617-585-0121 • **Website:** www.the-bac.edu

This private school was founded in 1889.

RATINGS

Admissions Selectivity Rating: 60* **Fire Safety Rating:** 60*

STUDENTS AND FACULTY

Enrollment: 365.

ACADEMICS

Degrees: bachelor's, certificate, first professional, master's. **Majors with Highest Enrollment:** Computer and Information Sciences; Elementary Education and Teaching; Psychology. **Special Study Options:** cross-registration, distance learning, study abroad, Concurrent academic and practice-based learning. **Career services:** career/job search classes, internships.

FACILITIES

Housing: 100% of campus accessible to physically disabled. **Special Academic Facilities/Equipment:** McCormick Gallery.

CAMPUS LIFE

Activities: student newspaper. 2 registered organizations.

ADMISSIONS

Freshman Academic Profile: Minimum paper TOEFL 550. **Freshman Admission Requirements:** High school diploma is required and GED is accepted. **Freshman Admission Statistics:** 368 applied, 94% admitted, 32% enrolled. **Transfer Admission Requirements:** High school transcript, college transcript(s), Lowest grade transferable C. **General Admission Information:** Application Fee $50. Nonfall registration accepted. Admission may be deferred for a maximum of 1 Semester. Credit and/or placement offered for CEEB Advanced Placement tests.

COSTS AND FINANCIAL AID

Annual tuition $7,438. Required fees $150. Average book expense $1,105. **Required Forms and Deadlines:** FAFSA, Institution's own financial aid form. **Notification of Awards:** Applicants will be notified of awards on a rolling basis beginning 4/30. **Types of Aid:** *Need-based scholarships/grants:* Federal Pell, state scholarships/grants, private scholarships. *Loans:* Subsidized Stafford, Unsubsidized Stafford, PLUS, state loans. *Student Employment:* Off-campus job opportunities are excellent. **Financial Aid Statistics:** 0% freshmen, 0% undergrads receive need-based scholarship or grant aid. 0% freshmen, 0% undergrads receive non-need-based scholarship or grant aid. 0% freshmen, 0% undergrads receive need-based self-help aid. 50% undergrads borrow to pay for school. **Criteria for awarding institutional aid:** *Non-need-based:* academics, job skills.

BOSTON COLLEGE

Best 380

140 Commonwealth Avenue, Chestnut Hill, MA 02467-3809
Phone: 617-552-3100 • **Financial Aid Phone:** 617-552-3300 • **CEEB Code:** 3083
Fax: 617-552-0798 • **Website:** www.bc.edu • **ACT Code:** 1788

This private school, affiliated with the Roman Catholic Church, was founded in 1863. It has a 386.1-acre campus.

RATINGS

Admissions Selectivity Rating: 96 **Fire Safety Rating:** 97

STUDENTS AND FACULTY

Enrollment: 9,154. **Student Body:** 54% female, 46% male, 75% out-of-state, 6% international (95 countries represented). Asian 10%, African American 4%, Caucasian 62%, Hispanic 10%, Native American <1%
Retention and Graduation: 96% freshmen return for sophomore year. 88% freshmen graduate within 4 years. 91% freshmen graduate within 6 years. 21% grads go on to further study within 1 year. 8% grads pursue arts and sciences degrees. 5% grads pursue law degrees. 1% grads pursue business degrees. 3% grads pursue medical degrees. **Faculty:** 758 full-time faculty, 94% hold PhDs, 40% are members of minority groups, 18% are women.

ACADEMICS

Degrees: bachelor's, doctoral, master's, post-master's certificate. **Classes:** Most classes have 10–19 students. **Majors with Highest Enrollment:** Communication and Media Studies; Finance; Economics. **Special Study Options:** Accelerated program, cross-registration, distance learning, double major, English as a Second Language (ESL), exchange student program (domestic), honors program, independent study, internships, liberal arts/career combination, student-designed major, study abroad, teacher certification program. **Honors programs:** Multiple Honors Programs in various Schools and Departments, along with a Presidential Scholars Program Combined degree programs: BA/MD, BA/MA, MD with Tufts Medical School. **Disability Services:** Special programs offered to physically disabled students include note-taking services, reader services, tape recorders, tutors. **Career services:** Alumni network, alumni services, career/job search classes, career assessment, internships, regional alumni. Career services highlights include internships.

FACILITIES

Housing: Coed dorms, special housing for disabled students, women's dorms, Greycliff Honors House, multicultural and intercultural floors, a quiet floor, social justice floor, a community living floor, and a leadership house. Also apartment style housing and Townhouse apartments. 95% of campus accessible to physically disabled. **Special Academic Facilities/Equipment:** Art museum, theatre arts center, on-campus school for multihandicapped students, athletic facility, state-of-the-art science facilities. **Computers:** 100% of classrooms, 100% of dorms, 100% of libraries, 100% of dining areas, 100% of student union, 100% of common outdoor areas have wireless network access. Students can register for classes online. Administrative functions (other than registration) can be performed online.

CAMPUS LIFE

Environment: City. **Activities:** Choral groups, concert band, dance, drama/theater, jazz band, literary magazine, marching band, music ensembles, musical theater, pep band, radio station, student government, student newspaper, student-run film society, symphony orchestra, television station, yearbook, Campus Ministries, International Student Organization. 225 registered organizations, 12 honor societies, 14 religious organizations. **Athletics (Intercollegiate):** *Men:* baseball, basketball, cross-country, diving, fencing, football, golf, ice hockey, lacrosse, sailing, skiing (downhill/alpine), soccer, swimming, tennis, track/field (outdoor), track/field (indoor). *Women:* basketball, crew/rowing, cross-country, diving, fencing, field hockey, golf, ice hockey, lacrosse, sailing, skiing (downhill/alpine), soccer, softball, swimming, tennis, track/field (outdoor), track/field (indoor), volleyball. **On-Campus Highlights:** McMullen Museum of Art, Alumni Stadium/Conte Forum, Robsham Theater, Bapst Library, McElroy Commons/Bookstore. **Environmental Initiatives:** 180K SF Building Registered for LEED Silver; 4 Buildings—LEED Certified Platinum; 1 Building—Anticipate LEED Gold; Energery Conservation program metering 75% of buildings. Carbon footprint is completed. Setting new goals.

ADMISSIONS

Freshman Academic Profile: 81% in top 10% of high school class, 95% in top 25% of high school class, 99% in top 50% of high school class. 47% from public high schools. SAT Math middle 50% range 640-740. SAT Critical Reading middle 50% range 630-720. SAT Writing middle 50% range 640-730. ACT middle 50% range 30-33. Minimum internet-based TOEFL 100. Minimum paper TOEFL 600. **Basis for Candidate Selection:** *Very important factors considered include:* academic GPA, rigor of secondary school record, standardized test scores. *Important factors considered include:* Class rank, application essay, recommendation(s), alumni/ae relation, character/personal qualities, extracurricular activities, religious affiliation/commitment, talent/ability, volunteer work. *Other factors considered include:* first generation, racial/ethnic status, work experience. **Freshman Admission Requirements:** High school diploma is required and GED is accepted. **Freshman Admission Statistics:** 23,223 applied, 34% admitted, 29% enrolled. **Transfer Admission Requirements:** High school transcript, college transcript(s), essay or personal statement, standardized test scores, statement of good standing from prior institution(s). Minimum college GPA of 3.0 required. Lowest grade transferable C. **General Admission Information:** Application Fee $70. Regular application deadline 1/1. Regular notification 4/15. Nonfall registration accepted. Admission may be deferred for a maximum of 2 years. Placement offered for CEEB Advanced Placement tests.

COSTS AND FINANCIAL AID

Annual tuition $46,670. Room and board $13,186. Required fees $766. Average book expense $1,000. **Required Forms and Deadlines:** FAFSA, CSS/Financial Aid PROFILE, Noncustodial PROFILE, Business/Farm Supplement. **Notification of Awards:** Applicants will be notified of awards on or about 4/1. **Types of Aid:** *Need-based scholarships/grants:* Federal Pell, SEOG, state scholarships/grants, private scholarships, the school's own gift aid. *Loans:* Subsidized Stafford, Unsubsidized Stafford, PLUS, Federal Perkins, Federal Nursing, state loans. *Student Employment:* Federal Work-Study Program available. Institutional employment available. Highest amount earned per year from on-campus jobs $2,400. Off-campus job opportunities are good. **Financial Aid Statistics:** 87% freshmen, 87% undergrads receive need-based scholarship or grant aid. 2% freshmen, 2% undergrads receive non-need-based scholarship or grant aid. 93% freshmen, 93% undergrads receive need-based self-help aid. 3% freshmen, 3% undergrads receive athletic scholarships. 63% freshmen, 68% undergrads receive any aid. 51% undergrads borrow to pay for school. Average cumulative indebtedness $18,978. **Criteria for awarding institutional aid:** *Non-need-based:* academics, athletics, leadership.

BOSTON CONSERVATORY

8 The Fenway, Boston, MA 2215
Phone: 617-912-9153
E-mail: admissions@bostonconservatory.edu • **CEEB Code:** 3084
Fax: 617-247-3159 • **Website:** www.bostonconservatory.edu • **ACT Code:** 1790

This private school was founded in 1867.

RATINGS

Admissions Selectivity Rating: 66   **Fire Safety Rating:** 60*

STUDENTS AND FACULTY

Enrollment: 450. **Student Body:** 63% female, 37% male, 60% out-of-state, (26 countries represented).
Retention and Graduation: 68% freshmen return for sophomore year. 35% freshmen graduate within 4 years. 72% freshmen graduate within 6 years. **Faculty:** 44 full-time faculty, 59% are members of minority groups, 0% are women. 0% of classes are taught by teaching assistants.

ACADEMICS

Degrees: bachelor's, diploma, master's, post-bachelor's certificate, post-master's certificate. **Classes:** Most classes have fewer than 10 students. **Special Study Options:** cross-registration, double major, English as a Second Language (ESL), independent study, teacher certification program. **Career services:** alumni services, career/job search classes, career assessment, internships.

FACILITIES

Housing: Coed dorms, women's dorms, Graduate house.

CAMPUS LIFE

Activities: literary magazine, student government, student newspaper 11 registered organizations, 1 honor society, 1 religious organization.

ADMISSIONS

Freshman Academic Profile: 90% from public high schools. **Basis for Candidate Selection:** *Very important factors considered include:* recommendation(s), character/personal qualities, talent/ability. *Important factors considered include:* Class rank, application essay, rigor of secondary school record, interview. *Other factors considered include:* extracurricular activities. **Freshman Admission Requirements:** High school diploma is required and GED is accepted. *Academic units required:* 4 English, 3 mathematics, 2 science, 2 foreign language, 2 social studies, 2 history. **Freshman Admission Statistics:** 989 applied, 43% admitted, 28% enrolled. **Transfer Admission Requirements:** High school transcript, college transcript(s), essay or personal statement, Minimum college GPA of 2.5 required. Lowest grade transferable C. **General Admission Information:** Application Fee $100. Regular notification 4/1. Nonfall registration accepted. Admission may be deferred for a maximum of 12. Credit offered for CEEB Advanced Placement tests.

COSTS AND FINANCIAL AID

Average book expense $0. **Required Forms and Deadlines:** FAFSA, Institution's own financial aid form. **Notification of Awards:** Applicants will be notified of awards on or about 4/1. **Types of Aid:** *Need-based scholarships/grants:* Federal Pell, SEOG, state scholarships/grants, private scholarships, the school's own gift aid. *Loans:* Subsidized Stafford, Unsubsidized Stafford, PLUS, college/university loans from institutional funds, Private Educational Loans. *Student Employment:* Federal Work-Study Program available. Institutional employment available. Highest amount earned per year from on-campus jobs $830. Off-campus job opportunities are excellent. **Financial Aid Statistics:** 22% freshmen, 25% undergrads receive need-based scholarship or grant aid. 55% freshmen, 72% undergrads receive non-need-based scholarship or grant aid. 71% freshmen, 81% undergrads receive need-based self-help aid. 0% freshmen, 0% undergrads receive athletic scholarships. 76% undergrads borrow to pay for school. **Criteria for awarding institutional aid:** *Non-need-based:* music/drama.

BOSTON UNIVERSITY

233 Bay State Road, Boston, MA 2215
Phone: 617-353-2300 · **Financial Aid Phone:** 617-353-4176
E-mail: admissions@bu.edu · **CEEB Code:** 3087
Fax: 617-353-9695 · **Website:** www.bu.edu · **ACT Code:** 1794

This private school was founded in 1839. It has a 132-acre campus.

RATINGS

Admissions Selectivity Rating: 95   **Fire Safety Rating:** 63

STUDENTS AND FACULTY

Enrollment: 16,457. **Student Body:** 61% female, 39% male, 74% out-of-state, 19% international (134 countries represented). Asian 13%, African American 3%, Caucasian 46%, Hispanic 10%, Native American <1% **Retention and Graduation:** 80% freshmen graduate within 4 years. 85% freshmen graduate within 6 years. **Faculty:** 1,673 full-time faculty, 88% hold PhDs, 40% are members of minority groups, 14% are women. 6% of classes are taught by teaching assistants.

ACADEMICS

Degrees: bachelor's, first professional, first professional certificate, master's, post-bachelor's certificate, post-master's certificate. **Classes:** Most classes have 10–19 students. Most lab/discussion sessions have 20–29 students. **Majors with Highest Enrollment:** Communication; Communication; Engineering. **Special Study Options:** Accelerated program, cooperative education program, cross-registration, distance learning, double major, dual enrollment, English as a Second Language (ESL), honors program, independent study, internships, liberal arts/career combination, student-designed major, study abroad, teacher certification program, weekend college, Field study in Marine Science at the Woods Hole Institute and in Environmental/Ecological Science in Ecuador at the Biodiversity Station in the tropical rain forest. The Photonics Center. **Honors programs:** Honors Programs are offered in the College of Arts and Sciences and the School of Management Combined degree programs: BA/MD, BA/MA, BA/DMD, BS/MS, BA/MD,BS/MSOT,BS/DPT. **Disability Services:** Special programs offered to physically disabled students include note-taking services, reader services, tape recorders, tutors. **Career services:** Alumni network, alumni services, career/job search classes, career assessment, internships, regional alumni. Career services highlights include our internship program, which provides opportunities for student to work with early stage companies at the BU incubators, as well as in the community. One particularly unusual aspect of the program is that we provide opportunities for non-business students to "intern" with startups our business students are creating. One such program this year had Graphic Design students working with MBA student entrepreneurs to develop corporate identity programs for them.

FACILITIES

Housing: Coed dorms, special housing for disabled students, women's dorms, apartments for married students, cooperative housing, apartments for single students, Specialty dorms/floors for groups of students with a common interest or academic major. 90% of campus accessible to physically disabled. **Special Academic Facilities/Equipment:** Center for Computational Science, Center for Advanced Biotechnology, Center for Photonics Research, art galleries, planetarium, commercial TV station, National Public Radio station, 20th century archives, professional theatre and theatre company, Center for Remote Sensing, Geddes Language Labratory, speech, language and hearing clinic, Culinary Center, Metcalf Center for Science and Engineering, Tsai Performance Center, and College of Communication Multimedia Lab. **Computers:** Students can register for classes online. Administrative functions (other than registration) can be performed online.

CAMPUS LIFE

Environment: Metropolis. **Activities:** Choral groups, concert band, dance, drama/theater, jazz band, literary magazine, marching band, music ensembles, musical theater, opera, radio station, student government, student newspaper, student-run film society, symphony orchestra, yearbook, International Student Organization. 400 registered organizations, 11 honor society, 26 religious organizations. 9 fraternities, 9 sororities. **Athletics (Intercollegiate):** *Men:* basketball, crew/rowing, cross-country, diving, golf, ice hockey, soccer, swimming, tennis, track/field (outdoor), track/field (indoor), wrestling. *Women:* basketball, crew/rowing, cross-country, diving, field hockey, golf, ice hockey, lacrosse, soccer, softball, swimming, tennis, track/field (outdoor), track/field (indoor). **On-Campus Highlights:** Marsh Chapel Plaza, Mugar Memorial Library, special collections, DeWolfe Boathouse, George Sherman Student Union, The

Photonics Center. **Environmental Initiatives:** Energy Efficiency Retrofits http://www.bu.edu/facilities/what-we-do/energy/ Recycling Program http://www.bu.edu/sustainability/what-were-doing/waste-reduction/ Green building practices heep://www.bu.edu/sustainability/what-were-doing/green-buildings

ADMISSIONS

Freshman Academic Profile: Average high school GPA 3.6. 59% in top 10% of high school class, 89% in top 25% of high school class, 99% in top 50% of high school class. 65% from public high schools. SAT Math middle 50% range 620-730. SAT Critical Reading middle 50% range 570-680. SAT Writing middle 50% range 600-690. ACT middle 50% range 27-31. **Basis for Candidate Selection:** *Very important factors considered include:* rigor of secondary school record. *Important factors considered include:* Class rank, application essay, academic GPA, recommendation(s), standardized test scores. *Other factors considered include:* alumni/ae relation, character/personal qualities, extracurricular activities, first generation, geographical residence, level of applicant's interest, racial/ethnic status, state residency, volunteer work, work experience. **Freshman Admission Requirements:** High school diploma is required and GED is accepted. *Academic units required:* 4 English, 3 mathematics, 3 science, (3 science labs), 2 foreign language, 3 social studies, 0 academic electives. **Freshman Admission Statistics:** 54,190 applied, 35% admitted, 42% enrolled. **Transfer Admission Requirements:** High school transcript, college transcript(s), essay or personal statement, standardized test scores, statement of good standing from prior institution(s). Minimum college GPA of 3.5 required. Lowest grade transferable C. **General Admission Information:** Application Fee $75. Early decision application deadline 11/1. Regular application deadline 1/1. Nonfall registration accepted. Admission may be deferred for a maximum of 1 year. Credit and/or placement offered for CEEB Advanced Placement tests.

COSTS AND FINANCIAL AID

Annual tuition $45,686. Room and board $14,030. Required fees $978. Average book expense $1,000. **Required Forms and Deadlines:** FAFSA, CSS/Financial Aid PROFILE, Noncustodial PROFILE. **Notification of Awards:** Applicants will be notified of awards on a rolling basis beginning 3/15. **Types of Aid:** *Need-based scholarships/grants:* Federal Pell, SEOG, state scholarships/grants, private scholarships, the school's own gift aid. *Loans:* Direct Subsidized Stafford, Direct Unsubsidized Stafford, Direct PLUS, Federal Perkins, state loans. *Student Employment:* Federal Work-Study Program available. Institutional employment available. Off-campus job opportunities are excellent. **Financial Aid Statistics:** 98% freshmen, 98% undergrads receive need-based scholarship or grant aid. 9% freshmen, 5% undergrads receive non-need-based scholarship or grant aid. 86% freshmen, 88% undergrads receive need-based self-help aid. 2% freshmen, 2% undergrads receive athletic scholarships. 56% freshmen, 57% undergrads receive any aid. 57% undergrads borrow to pay for school. Average cumulative indebtedness $25,879. **Criteria for awarding institutional aid:** *Non-need-based:* academics, alumni affiliation, art, athletics, leadership, music/drama, religious affiliation, state/district residency.

See page 1014.

BOWDOIN COLLEGE

5000 College Station, Brunswick, ME 04011-8441
Phone: 207-725-3100 · **Financial Aid Phone:** 207-725-3146
E-mail: admissions@bowdoin.edu · **CEEB Code:** 3089
Fax: 207-725-3101 · **Website:** www.bowdoin.edu · **ACT Code:** 1636

This private school was founded in 1794. It has a 205-acre campus.

RATINGS

Admissions Selectivity Rating: 98   **Fire Safety Rating:** 93

STUDENTS AND FACULTY

Enrollment: 1,797. **Student Body:** 50% female, 50% male, 89% out-of-state, 5% international (28 countries represented). Asian 6%, African American 5%, Caucasian 64%, Hispanic 13%, Native American <1% **Retention and Graduation:** 98% freshmen return for sophomore year. 86% freshmen graduate within 4 years. 93% freshmen graduate within 6 years. 20% grads go on to further study within 1 year. 15% grads pursue arts and sciences degrees. 1% grads pursue law degrees. 1% grads pursue business degrees. 3% grads pursue medical degrees. **Faculty:** 189 full-time faculty, 99% hold PhDs, 48% are members of minority groups, 15% are women. 0% of classes are taught by teaching assistants.

ACADEMICS

Degrees: bachelor's. **Classes:** Most classes have 10–19 students. Most lab/discussion sessions have 10–19 students. **Majors with Highest Enrollment:** Political Science and Government; Economics; Mathematics. **Special Study Options:** Accelerated program, double major, exchange student program (domestic), independent study, liberal arts/career combination, student-designed major, study abroad, teacher certification program, 3-2 or 4-2 Engineering Degree Programs with Dartmouth College, California Institute of Technology, Columbia University and the University of Maine; and 3-3 Legal Studies Degree Program with Columbia University Law School. Pass/Fail grading options are available. Combined degree programs: BA/JD, BA/MEng, 3-3 Law - Columbia University Law. **Disability Services:** Special programs offered to physically disabled students include note-taking services, reader services, tape recorders, tutors. **Career services:** Alumni network, alumni services, career/job search classes, career assessment, internships, regional alumni. Career services highlights include paid internship opportunities through the generosity of donors. Many of these internships serve the needs of underserved and disadvantaged populations.

FACILITIES

Housing: Coed dorms, special housing for disabled students, apartments for single students, Wellness Housing, Three small college houses and 8 college house system houses. 70% of campus accessible to physically disabled. **Special Academic Facilities/Equipment:** Art Museum; Arctic Museum; Arctic Studies Center; coastal marine biology and ornithology research facility on Orr's Island; scientific station on Kent Island; black box theater; Pickard Theater; Baldwin Center for Learning and Teaching; Outdoor Leadership Center; Visual Arts Center; Crafts Center; 8 specialized libraries, including the Language Media Center; Coleman Farm; Quantitative Skills Program; The Writing Project; Gibson Hall of Music; Recital Hall; Educational Technology Center; Environmental Studies Center; Russwurm African-American Center; Women's Resource Center; Off-Campus Study Office; Office of Health Professions Advising; Pre-Law Advising Office; Career Planning Center; Community Service Resource Center; Electronic Classroom; Recording Studio; and a state-of-the-art science facility. **Computers:** 100% of classrooms, 100% of dorms, 100% of libraries, 100% of dining areas, 100% of student union, 100% of common outdoor areas have wireless network access. Administrative functions (other than registration) can be performed online.

CAMPUS LIFE

Environment: Village. **Activities:** Choral groups, concert band, dance, drama/theater, jazz band, literary magazine, music ensembles, musical theater, radio station, student government, student newspaper, student-run film society, symphony orchestra, television station, yearbook, International Student Organization. 109 registered organizations, 1 honor society, 4 religious organizations. **Athletics (Intercollegiate):** *Men:* baseball, basketball, cross-country, diving, football, golf, ice hockey, lacrosse, sailing, skiing (nordic/cross-country), soccer, squash, swimming, tennis, track/field (outdoor), track/field (indoor). *Women:* basketball, cross-country, diving, field hockey, golf, ice hockey, lacrosse, rugby, sailing, skiing (nordic/cross-country), soccer, softball, squash, swimming, tennis, track/field (outdoor), track/field (indoor), volleyball. **On-Campus Highlights:** Bowdoin College Museum of Art, Druckenmiller Science Building, Studzinski Recital Hall, Schwartz Outdoor Leadership Center, Wish / Pickard Theater, Peary MacMillan Arctic Museum; Visual Arts Center and McLellan art studios; Hawthorne-Longfellow Library; Smith Student Union; Thorne Dining Hall; top of Coles Tower (for birds-eye view); athletic facilities and playing fields/trails; walk the Bowdoin Quad and the Bowdoin Pines. **Environmental Initiatives:** Bowdoin has committed to becoming a carbon-neutral campus by 2020 and provided a detailed Climate Action Plan to help achieve the goal. As part of this plan, Bowdoin installed a co-generation system at its campus steam plant, along with a 1,920-square-foot solar hot water system, and is preparing to break ground in the spring of 2014 on a 1,300 kilowatt solar photovoltaic system. The Co-Gen system produced 1,076,000 kWhs or roughly 6% of Bowdoin's electricity in FY12-13, its first full year of operation. It is anticipated that the new solar PV system will produce roughly 8% of Bowdoins annual electricity usage once on line. Bowdoin Dining has a strong commitment to local food. Bowdoin works with dozens of local farms to supply 34% of total purchases from local sources. This includes fresh meats, cheeses, dairy, maple syrup, and produce. As part of this effort, Bowdoin Dining operates a certified organic garden that provides produce to the dining halls as well as offering academic and co-curricular opportunities for students. Bowdoin maintains a comprehensive approach to alternative transportation. Bowdoin's comprehensive transportation program includes a bike sharing program, Zipcars, a free campus shuttle for students, as well as reserved parking for carpoolers and increased emphasis on biking infrastructure on campus. Bowdoin's vehicle fleet includes both hybrid and plug-in hybrid vehicles, as well as mini-trucks that get up to 45 mpg. Bowdoin's efforts to promote biking on campus have garnered Bowdoin a silver designation from the League of American Bicyclists Bicycle Friendly University program.

ADMISSIONS

Freshman Academic Profile: 86% in top 10% of high school class, 97% in top 25% of high school class, 100% in top 50% of high school class. 53% from pub-

lic high schools. SAT Math middle 50% range 680-760. SAT Critical Reading middle 50% range 690-760. SAT Writing middle 50% range 680-770. ACT middle 50% range 31-34. Minimum internet-based TOEFL 100. Minimum paper TOEFL 600. **Basis for Candidate Selection:** *Very important factors considered include:* Class rank, application essay, academic GPA, recommendation(s), rigor of secondary school record, character/personal qualities, extracurricular activities, talent/ability. *Important factors considered include:* standardized test scores, alumni/ae relation, first generation. *Other factors considered include:* geographical residence, interview, racial/ethnic status, state residency. **Freshman Admission Requirements:** High school diploma is required and GED is not accepted. **Freshman Admission Statistics:** 6,935 applied, 15% admitted, 49% enrolled. **Transfer Admission Requirements:** High school transcript, college transcript(s), essay or personal statement, statement of good standing from prior institution(s). Minimum college GPA of 3.0 required. Lowest grade transferable C-. **General Admission Information:** Application Fee $60. Early decision application deadline 11/15. Regular application deadline 1/1. Regular notification 4/5. Nonfall registration not accepted. Admission may be deferred for a maximum of 12 months. Credit and/or placement offered for CEEB Advanced Placement tests.

COSTS AND FINANCIAL AID

Annual tuition $46,354. Room and board $12,760. Required fees $454. Average book expense $832. **Required Forms and Deadlines:** FAFSA, CSS/Financial Aid PROFILE, Noncustodial PROFILE, Business/Farm Supplement. **Notification of Awards:** Applicants will be notified of awards on or about 4/5. **Types of Aid:** *Need-based scholarships/grants:* Federal Pell, SEOG, state scholarships/grants, private scholarships, the school's own gift aid. *Loans:* Subsidized Stafford, Unsubsidized Stafford, PLUS, Federal Perkins, state loans. *Student Employment:* Federal Work-Study Program available. Institutional employment available. Highest amount earned per year from on-campus jobs $2,000. Off-campus job opportunities are good. **Financial Aid Statistics:** 100% freshmen, 100% undergrads receive need-based scholarship or grant aid. 0% freshmen, 0% undergrads receive non-need-based scholarship or grant aid. 90% freshmen, 91% undergrads receive need-based self-help aid. 0% freshmen, 0% undergrads receive athletic scholarships. 51% freshmen, 49% undergrads receive any aid. 32% undergrads borrow to pay for school. Average cumulative indebtedness $19,289. **Criteria for awarding institutional aid:** *Non-need-based:* academics, leadership.

BOWIE STATE UNIVERSITY

14000 Jericho Park Road, Bowie, MD 20715
Phone: 301-860-3415 · **Financial Aid Phone:** 301-860-3543
E-mail: dkiah@bowiestate.edu · **CEEB Code:** 5401
Fax: 301-860-3438 · **Website:** www.bowiestate.edu

This public school was founded in 1865. It has a 312-acre campus.

RATINGS

Admissions Selectivity Rating: 73   **Fire Safety Rating:** 70

STUDENTS AND FACULTY

Enrollment: 3,953. **Student Body:** 64% female, 36% male, 8% out-of-state, 1% international (48 countries represented). Asian 1%, African American 74%, Caucasian 5%, Hispanic 1%, Native American <1%
Retention and Graduation: 72% freshmen return for sophomore year. 11% freshmen graduate within 4 years. 36% freshmen graduate within 6 years. 30% grads go on to further study within 1 year. **Faculty:** 191 full-time faculty, 68% hold PhDs, 45% are members of minority groups, 73% are women. 0% of classes are taught by teaching assistants.

ACADEMICS

Degrees: bachelor's, certificate, master's, post-bachelor's certificate, post-master's certificate. **Classes:** Most classes have 20–29 students. **Special Study Options:** cooperative education program, cross-registration, distance learning, double major, dual enrollment, exchange student program (domestic), honors program, independent study, internships, liberal arts/career combination, study abroad, teacher certification program, Dual degree Mathematics/Engineering Program. Combined degree programs: BA/MEng. **Disability Services:** Special programs offered to physically disabled students include note-taking services, reader services, tape recorders, tutors. **Career services:** career/job search classes, internships.

FACILITIES

Housing: Coed dorms, men's dorms, women's dorms, apartments for single students, Honors' Residence available; Special interest floors. 100% of campus accessible to physically disabled. **Special Academic Facilities/Equipment:**

Science and math labs, computer academy, art galleries. **Computers:** Students can register for classes online. Administrative functions (other than registration) can be performed online.

CAMPUS LIFE

Environment: Town. **Activities:** Choral groups, concert band, dance, drama/theater, jazz band, literary magazine, marching band, music ensembles, musical theater, pep band, radio station, student government, student newspaper, television station, yearbook 71 registered organizations, 17 honor societies, 2 religious organizations. 4 fraternities, 4 sororities. **Athletics (Intercollegiate):** *Men:* basketball, cross-country, football, track/field (outdoor). *Women:* basketball, cross-country, softball, tennis, track/field (outdoor), volleyball. **On-Campus Highlights:** New Science Bldg, The Jazz man Coffee Shop.

ADMISSIONS

Freshman Academic Profile: Average high school GPA 3.11. 88% from public high schools. SAT Math middle 50% range 400-480. SAT Critical Reading middle 50% range 400-490. Minimum paper TOEFL 500. **Basis for Candidate Selection:** *Very important factors considered include:* rigor of secondary school record, standardized test scores. *Other factors considered include:* application essay, recommendation(s), extracurricular activities, interview. **Freshman Admission Requirements:** High school diploma is required and GED is accepted. *Academic units required:* 4 English, 3 mathematics, 3 science, 2 foreign language, 1 social studies, 2 history. **Freshman Admission Statistics:** 2,826 applied, 52% admitted, 44% enrolled. **Transfer Admission Requirements:** college transcript(s), Minimum college GPA of 2.0 required. Lowest grade transferable C. **General Admission Information:** Application Fee $40. Notification on a rolling basis, beginning on or about 4/3. Nonfall registration accepted. Admission may be deferred for a maximum of 1 year. Credit and/or placement offered for CEEB Advanced Placement tests.

COSTS AND FINANCIAL AID

Average book expense $1,388. **Required Forms and Deadlines:** FAFSA. **Types of Aid:** *Need-based scholarships/grants:* Federal Pell, SEOG, state scholarships/grants, private scholarships, the school's own gift aid. *Loans:* Direct Subsidized Stafford, Direct Unsubsidized Stafford, Direct PLUS, Federal Perkins. *Student Employment:* Federal Work-Study Program available. **Financial Aid Statistics:** 71% freshmen, 73% undergrads receive need-based scholarship or grant aid. 50% freshmen, 55% undergrads receive non-need-based scholarship or grant aid. 59% freshmen, 74% undergrads receive need-based self-help aid. 7% freshmen, 8% undergrads receive athletic scholarships. 34% undergrads borrow to pay for school. **Criteria for awarding institutional aid:** *Non-need-based:* academics, art, athletics, music/drama, state/district residency.

BOWLING GREEN STATE UNIVERSITY

110 McFall Center, Bowling Green, OH 43403-0085
Phone: 419-372-BGSU • **Financial Aid Phone:** 419-372-2651
E-mail: choosebgsu@bgsu.edu • **CEEB Code:** 1069
Fax: 419-372-6955 • **Website:** http://www.bgsu.edu • **ACT Code:** 3240

This public school was founded in 1910. It has a 1250-acre campus.

RATINGS

Admissions Selectivity Rating: 83   **Fire Safety Rating:** 85

STUDENTS AND FACULTY

Enrollment: 13,697. **Student Body:** 56% female, 44% male, 12% out-of-state, 2% international (31 countries represented). Asian 1%, African American 10%, Caucasian 77%, Hispanic 4%, Native American <1%
Retention and Graduation: 76% freshmen return for sophomore year. 32% freshmen graduate within 4 years. **Faculty:** 696 full-time faculty, 82% hold PhDs, 48% are members of minority groups, 13% are women.

ACADEMICS

Degrees: bachelor's, doctoral, master's, post-master's certificate. **Classes:** Most classes have 20–29 students. **Majors with Highest Enrollment:** Biology/Biological Sciences; Special Education and Teaching; Psychology. **Special Study Options:** Accelerated program, cooperative education program, cross-registration, distance learning, double major, dual enrollment, English as a Second Language (ESL), exchange student program (domestic), honors program, independent study, internships, liberal arts/career combination, student-designed major, study abroad, teacher certification program. **Honors programs:** http://www.bgsu.edu/offices/honors/. **Disability Services:** Special programs offered to physically disabled students include note-taking services, reader services, tape recorders, tutors. **Career services:** Alumni network, alumni services, career/job search classes, career assessment, internships, regional alumni. Career services highlights include http://www.bgsu.edu/offices/sa/career/.

FACILITIES

Housing: Coed dorms, fraternity/sorority housing, Wellness Housing, Theme Housing, residental learning communities (including Wellness Community), no-alcohol wings. **Special Academic Facilities/Equipment:** http://go2.bgsu.edu/choose/campus/tour/ http://www.bgsu.edu/map/buildings/ **Computers:** 99% of classrooms, 64% of dorms, 100% of libraries, 100% of dining areas, 100% of student union, 40% of common outdoor areas have wireless network access. Students can register for classes online. Administrative functions (other than registration) can be performed online.

CAMPUS LIFE

Environment: Town. **Activities:** Choral groups, concert band, dance, drama/theater, jazz band, literary magazine, marching band, music ensembles, musical theater, radio station, student government, student newspaper, student-run film society, symphony orchestra, television station, yearbook, International Student Organization 20 honor societies, 24 fraternities, 19 sororities. **Athletics (Intercollegiate):** *Men:* baseball, basketball, cross-country, football, golf, ice hockey, soccer. *Women:* basketball, cross-country, golf, gymnastics, soccer, softball, swimming, tennis, track/field (outdoor), track/field (indoor), volleyball. **On-Campus Highlights:** Bowen Thompson Student Union, Jerome Library, McFall Center, College of Business Administration, Residence Halls: http://go2.bgsu.edu/choose/campus/tour/. **Environmental Initiatives:** Recent completion and current certification process for 4 new minimum LEED certified buildings (Current points indicate one gold; two silver, and one LEED certified) Moving forward on becoming a part of the ACUPCC with formation of University-wide committee Funding of a dozen sustainability projects with student fee monies procured through Student Green Initiatives Fund, approved by student body which projects were conceived by and submitted by students, and the approval of which was provided by a committee composed of students

ADMISSIONS

Freshman Academic Profile: Average high school GPA 3.3. 13% in top 10% of high school class, 35% in top 25% of high school class, 70% in top 50% of high school class. 89% from public high schools. SAT Math middle 50% range 470-580. SAT Critical Reading middle 50% range 460-580. SAT Writing middle 50% range 440-550. ACT middle 50% range 20-25. Minimum internet-based TOEFL 71. Minimum paper TOEFL 500. **Basis for Candidate Selection:** *Very important factors considered include:* academic GPA, rigor of secondary school record, standardized test scores. *Important factors considered include:* Class rank, talent/ability. *Other factors considered include:* application essay, recommendation(s), alumni/ae relation, character/personal qualities, extracurricular activities, first generation, interview, level of applicant's interest, racial/ethnic status, volunteer work, work experience. **Freshman Admission Requirements:** High school diploma is required and GED is accepted. *Academic units required:* 4 English, 3 mathematics, 3 science, (2 science labs), 2 foreign language, 3 social studies, 0 history, 0 academic electives, 1 visual/performing arts. **Freshman Admission Statistics:** 14,509 applied, 53% admitted, 39% enrolled. Minimum college GPA of 2.5 required. Lowest grade transferable C. **General Admission Information:** Application Fee $40. Regular application deadline 7/15. Notification on a rolling basis, beginning on or about 10/1. Nonfall registration accepted. Admission may be deferred for a maximum of 12 months. Credit and/or placement offered for CEEB Advanced Placement tests.

COSTS AND FINANCIAL AID

Average book expense $1,050. **Required Forms and Deadlines:** FAFSA. **Notification of Awards:** Applicants will be notified of awards on a rolling basis beginning 4/15. **Types of Aid:** *Need-based scholarships/grants:* Federal Pell, SEOG, state scholarships/grants, private scholarships, the school's own gift aid. *Loans:* Direct Subsidized Stafford, Direct Unsubsidized Stafford, Direct PLUS, Federal Perkins, Federal Nursing, state loans, college/university loans from institutional funds. *Student Employment:* Federal Work-Study Program available. Institutional employment available. Highest amount earned per year from on-campus jobs $13,544. Off-campus job opportunities are good. **Financial Aid Statistics:** 96% freshmen, 88% undergrads receive any aid. **Criteria for awarding institutional aid:** *Non-need-based:* academics, alumni affiliation, art, athletics, leadership, minority status, music/drama, state/district residency.

BRADLEY UNIVERSITY

1501 West Bradley Avenue, Peoria, IL 61625
Phone: 309-677-1000 · **Financial Aid Phone:** 309-677-3089
E-mail: admissions@bradley.edu · **CEEB Code:** 1070
Fax: 309-677-2797 · **Website:** www.bradley.edu · **ACT Code:** 960

This private school was founded in 1897. It has a 85-acre campus.

RATINGS
Admissions Selectivity Rating: 88   **Fire Safety Rating:** 86

STUDENTS AND FACULTY
Enrollment: 4,872. **Student Body:** 53% female, 47% male, 12% out-of-state, 1% international (34 countries represented). Asian 4%, African American 7%, Caucasian 80%, Hispanic 6%, Native American <1%
Retention and Graduation: 10% grads go on to further study within 1 year. 6% grads pursue arts and sciences degrees. 1% grads pursue law degrees. 1% grads pursue business degrees. 1% grads pursue medical degrees. **Faculty:** 352 full-time faculty, 84% hold PhDs, 61% are members of minority groups, 17% are women. 0% of classes are taught by teaching assistants.

ACADEMICS
Degrees: bachelor's, master's. **Classes:** Most classes have 20–29 students. **Majors with Highest Enrollment:** Mechanical Engineering; Family Practice Nurse/Nursing; Communication. **Special Study Options:** Accelerated program, cooperative education program, distance learning, double major, honors program, independent study, internships, liberal arts/career combination, student-designed major, study abroad, teacher certification program, Limited distance learning courses available. Collaborative classes with other institutions taught through Internet2. **Honors programs:** The Honors Program is structured so that students majoring in any department are eligible to participate. The programs builds progressively through a student's four years, beginning with special honors sections of General Education courses and leading to interdisciplinary seminars and possibilities for independent research. Combined degree programs: BA/MSA. **Disability Services:** Special programs offered to physically disabled students include tutors. **Career services:** Alumni network, alumni services, career/job search classes, career assessment, internships, regional alumni. Bradley recently established the Marjorie and Bill Springer Center for Excellence in Internships. The Center will focus on five areas: expanding opportunities for students to gain career-related experience; generating more student participation in the cooperative education and internship program; increasing awareness of international internship opportunities; enhancing activities that assist students in conducting their job searches and preparing them for on-the-job success; and providing continuous evaluation and improvement of the cooperative education and internship program policies, procedures, and data collected.

FACILITIES
Housing: Coed dorms, fraternity/sorority housing, apartments for single students, Wellness HousingService and leadership floor. 75% of campus accessible to physically disabled. **Special Academic Facilities/Equipment:** Caterpillar Global Communication Center, two art galleries on campus. **Computers:** 95% of classrooms, 5% of dorms, 100% of libraries, 80% of dining areas, 100% of student union, 30% of common outdoor areas have wireless network access. Students can register for classes online. Administrative functions (other than registration) can be performed online.

CAMPUS LIFE
Environment: City. **Activities:** Choral groups, concert band, dance, drama/theater, jazz band, literary magazine, music ensembles, musical theater, pep band, radio station, student government, student newspaper, student-run film society, symphony orchestra, television station, yearbook, Campus Ministries, International Student Organization, Model UN. 220 registered organizations, 31 honor society, 17 religious organizations. 16 fraternities, 11 sororities. **Athletics (Intercollegiate):** *Men:* baseball, basketball, cross-country, golf, soccer, tennis. *Women:* basketball, cross-country, golf, softball, tennis, track/field (outdoor), track/field (indoor), volleyball. **On-Campus Highlights:** Markin Family Student Recreation Center, Caterpillar Global Communications Center, Olin Hall of Science, Michel Student Center, Cullom-Davis Library, Bradley's 85 acre campus, is the heart of a residential neighborhood just 1 mile from downtown. Peoria is the largest metropolitan area in Illinois south of Chicago.

ADMISSIONS
Freshman Academic Profile: Average high school GPA 3.69. 34.6% in top 10% of high school class, 69.1% in top 25% of high school class, 94.1% in top 50% of high school class. 82% from public high schools. SAT Math middle 50% range 510-650. SAT Critical Reading middle 50% range 520-660. SAT Writing middle 50% range 520-620. ACT middle 50% range 23-28. Minimum internet-based TOEFL 79. Minimum paper TOEFL 550. **Basis for Candidate Selection:** *Very important factors considered include:* academic GPA, rigor of secondary school record. *Important factors considered include:* Class rank, standardized test scores. *Other factors considered include:* application essay, recommendation(s), alumni/ae relation, character/personal qualities, extracurricular activities, geographical residence, interview, level of applicant's interest, racial/ethnic status, talent/ability, volunteer work, work experience. **Freshman Admission Requirements:** High school diploma is required and GED is accepted. *Academic units required:* 4 English, 3 mathematics, 2 science, (2 science labs), 2 social studies. **Freshman Admission Statistics:** 7,562 applied, 63% admitted, 21% enrolled. **Transfer Admission Requirements:** college transcript(s), statement of good standing from prior institution(s). Minimum college GPA of 2.0 required. Lowest grade transferable C. **General Admission Information:** Application Fee $35. Notification on a rolling basis, beginning on or about 9/15. Nonfall registration accepted. Admission may be deferred for a maximum of 12 months. Credit and/or placement offered for CEEB Advanced Placement tests.

COSTS AND FINANCIAL AID
Annual tuition $30,500. Room and board $9,420. Required fees $344. Average book expense $1,200. **Required Forms and Deadlines:** FAFSA. **Types of Aid:** *Need-based scholarships/grants:* Federal Pell, SEOG, state scholarships/grants, private scholarships, the school's own gift aid. *Loans:* Direct Subsidized Stafford, Direct Unsubsidized Stafford, Direct PLUS, PLUS, Federal Perkins, Federal Nursing. *Student Employment:* Federal Work-Study Program available. Institutional employment available. **Financial Aid Statistics:** 99% freshmen, 96% undergrads receive need-based scholarship or grant aid. 11% freshmen, 10% undergrads receive non-need-based scholarship or grant aid. 76% freshmen, 82% undergrads receive need-based self-help aid. 5% freshmen, 3% undergrads receive athletic scholarships. 97% freshmen, 94% undergrads receive any aid. Average cumulative indebtedness $18,887. **Criteria for awarding institutional aid:** *Non-need-based:* academics, alumni affiliation, art, athletics, leadership, music/drama, state/district residency.

BRANDEIS UNIVERSITY

415 South St., Waltham, MA 02454-9110
Phone: 781-736-3500 · **Financial Aid Phone:** 781-736-3700
E-mail: admissions@brandeis.edu · **CEEB Code:** 3092
Fax: 781-736-3536 · **Website:** http://www.brandeis.edu/ · **ACT Code:** 1802

This private school was founded in 1948. It has a 235-acre campus.

RATINGS
Admissions Selectivity Rating: 97   **Fire Safety Rating:** 96

STUDENTS AND FACULTY
Enrollment: 3,715. **Student Body:** 57% female, 43% male, 72% out-of-state, 18% international. Asian 13%, African American 5%, Caucasian 49%, Hispanic 7%, Native American <1%
Retention and Graduation: 93% freshmen return for sophomore year. 85% freshmen graduate within 4 years. **Faculty:** 362 full-time faculty, 95% hold PhDs, 40% are members of minority groups, 13% are women.

ACADEMICS
Degrees: bachelor's, doctoral, master's, post-bachelor's certificate. **Classes:** Most classes have 10–19 students. **Majors with Highest Enrollment:** Biology/Biological Sciences; Economics; Business Administration, Management and Operations. **Special Study Options:** cross-registration, double major, independent study, internships, student-designed major, study abroad. Combined degree programs: BA/MA, Early admission to Mt. Sinai; Tufts medical schools. **Disability Services:** Special programs offered to physically disabled students include note-taking services, tape recorders. **Career services:** Alumni network, alumni services, career/job search classes, career assessment, internships, regional alumni.

FACILITIES

Housing: Coed dorms, men's dorms, women's dorms, apartments for single students, Thematic Learning Communities. 78% of campus accessible to physically disabled. **Special Academic Facilities/Equipment:** Art museum, multicultural library, intercultural center, theater arts complex, language lab, spatial orientation lab, research centers on aging, basic medical sciences, complex systems, family/children's policy, health policy, mental retardation, public policy, study of European Jewry, student leadership Development Room. **Computers:** 100% of classrooms, 100% of dorms, 100% of libraries, 100% of dining areas, 100% of student union, 100% of common outdoor areas have wireless network access. Students can register for classes online. Administrative functions (other than registration) can be performed online.

CAMPUS LIFE

Environment: City. **Activities:** Choral groups, concert band, dance, drama/theater, jazz band, literary magazine, music ensembles, musical theater, radio station, student government, student newspaper, student-run film society, symphony orchestra, television station, yearbook, Campus Ministries, International Student Organization. 253 registered organizations, 4 honor societies, 19 religious organizations. **Athletics (Intercollegiate):** *Men:* baseball, basketball, cross-country, diving, fencing, soccer, tennis, track/field (outdoor), track/field (indoor), wrestling. *Women:* basketball, cheerleading, cross-country, diving, fencing, soccer, softball, tennis, track/field (outdoor), track/field (indoor), volleyball, wrestling. **On-Campus Highlights:** Shapiro Science Center, Spingold Theater, Usen Castle, Shapiro Campus Center, Rapaporte Treasure Hall. **Environmental Initiatives:** The Brandeis University Climate Action Plan was completed in Fall of 2009. This plan sets aggressive goals for future energy and climate impact reductions. Brandeis has invested significantly since 2005 in energy reduction efforts—realizing an over 10% drop in campus energy use. The Climate Action Plan builds on these past successes to further reduce cost and environmental impact A 277 kW sized Solar Photovolatic Array, was installed on the Gosman Sports Center. The solar array is one of the larges in Massachusetts. This system is owned by a for profit business, while Brandeis essentially rents the power affordably. This innovative financing structure has allowed Brandeis to support the renewable energy industry, educate students about a growing technology, and reduce world wide carbon impact. To be clear, as the array is not currently owned by the University we can not claim the percent of solar energy generated in other questions on this survey because of federal marketing regulations. However, the solar generated at Brandeis is improving air quality for the region. Brandeis is proud of the active student engagement in activism and education on environmental issues. Students are involved in Eco-Reps, where each residential building as a environmental peer educator. Many other accomplishments for sustainability have been brought about through student innovation and education. Brandeis Students voted to create the Brandeis Sustainability Fund creating $50,000 of funded projects for sustainability.

ADMISSIONS

Freshman Academic Profile: Average high school GPA 3.84. 70.55% in top 10% of high school class, 92.4% in top 25% of high school class, 97.45% in top 50% of high school class. 62% from public high schools. SAT Math middle 50% range 660-770. SAT Critical Reading middle 50% range 590-710. SAT Writing middle 50% range 640-710. ACT middle 50% range 29-33. Minimum internet-based TOEFL 100. Minimum paper TOEFL 600. **Basis for Candidate Selection:** *Very important factors considered include:* Class rank, academic GPA, rigor of secondary school record, standardized test scores, character/personal qualities. *Important factors considered include:* application essay, recommendation(s), extracurricular activities, level of applicant's interest, talent/ability, volunteer work, work experience. *Other factors considered include:* alumni/ae relation, first generation, geographical residence, interview, racial/ethnic status. **Freshman Admission Requirements:** High school diploma is required and GED is accepted. **Freshman Admission Statistics:** 10,004 applied, 23% admitted, 37% enrolled. **Transfer Admission Requirements:** High school transcript, college transcript(s), essay or personal statement, standardized test scores, statement of good standing from prior institution(s). Minimum college GPA of 3.20 required. Lowest grade transferable C-. **General Admission Information:** Application Fee $55. Early decision application deadline 11/15. Regular application deadline 1/15. Regular notification 4/1. Nonfall registration accepted. Admission may be deferred for a maximum of 1 year. Credit and/or placement offered for CEEB Advanced Placement tests.

COSTS AND FINANCIAL AID

Annual tuition $46,022. Room and board $13,192. Required fees $1,811. Average book expense $1,000. **Required Forms and Deadlines:** FAFSA, CSS/Financial Aid PROFILE, State aid form, Noncustodial PROFILE. **Types of Aid:** *Need-based scholarships/grants:* Federal Pell, SEOG, state scholarships/grants, private scholarships, the school's own gift aid. *Loans:* Direct Subsidized Stafford, Direct Unsubsidized Stafford, Direct PLUS, Federal Perkins, state loans, college/university loans from institutional funds. *Student Employment:* Federal Work-Study Program available. Institutional employment available. Off-campus job opportunities are fair. **Financial Aid Statistics:** 97% freshmen,

95% undergrads receive need-based scholarship or grant aid. 9% freshmen, 6% undergrads receive non-need-based scholarship or grant aid. 87% freshmen, 91% undergrads receive need-based self-help aid. 0% freshmen, 0% undergrads receive athletic scholarships. 65% freshmen, 65% undergrads receive any aid. 60% undergrads borrow to pay for school. Average cumulative indebtedness $24,407. **Criteria for awarding institutional aid:** *Non-need-based:* academics.

BRANDON UNIVERSITY

270-18TH Street, Brandon, MB R7A 6A9
Phone: 204-727-9784
E-mail: admission@brandonu.ca
Fax: 204-728-3221 · **Website:** www.brandonu.ca

This public school was founded in 1899. It has a 3-acre campus.

RATINGS

Admissions Selectivity Rating: 60*   **Fire Safety Rating:** 60*

STUDENTS AND FACULTY

Enrollment: 3,097. **Student Body:** 68% female, 32% male, 55% out-of-state, 0% international (30 countries represented). Asian 0%, African American 0%, Caucasian 0%, Hispanic 0%, Native American <1%
Retention and Graduation: 65% freshmen return for sophomore year. **Faculty:** 215 full-time faculty.

ACADEMICS

Degrees: bachelor's, certificate, master's. **Classes:** Most classes have fewer than 10 students. **Majors with Highest Enrollment:** Pharmacy. **Special Study Options:** distance learning, double major, English as a Second Language (ESL), teacher certification program. Combined degree programs: BMus/BEd (AD). **Disability Services:** Special programs offered to physically disabled students include note-taking services, reader services, tape recorders, tutors.

FACILITIES

Housing: men's dorms, women's dorms. 80% of campus accessible to physically disabled. **Special Academic Facilities/Equipment:** B.J. Hales Museum **Computers:** Administrative functions (other than registration) can be performed online.

CAMPUS LIFE

Environment: Town. **Activities:** Choral groups, music ensembles, student government. **Athletics (Intercollegiate):** *Men:* basketball, volleyball. *Women:* basketball, volleyball.

ADMISSIONS

Freshman Academic Profile: Minimum paper TOEFL 550. **Basis for Candidate Selection:** *Very important factors considered include:* academic GPA, rigor of secondary school record. **Freshman Admission Requirements:** High school diploma is required and GED is accepted. **Transfer Admission Requirements:** college transcript(s), statement of good standing from prior institution(s). **General Admission Information:** Application Fee $125. Notification on a rolling basis, beginning on or about 11/1. Nonfall registration accepted. Admission may be deferred for a maximum of nil.

COSTS AND FINANCIAL AID

Average book expense $1,000. **Required Forms and Deadlines:** Institution's own financial aid form.

BRENAU UNIVERSITY

500 Washington St SE, Gainesville, GA 30501
Phone: 770-534-6100 · **Financial Aid Phone:** 770-534-6152
E-mail: admissions@brenau.edu · **CEEB Code:** 5066
Fax: 770-538-4306 · **Website:** www.brenau.edu · **ACT Code:** 800

This private school was founded in 1878. It has a 56-acre campus.

RATINGS

Admissions Selectivity Rating: 70   **Fire Safety Rating:** 87

STUDENTS AND FACULTY

Enrollment: 1,683. **Student Body:** 89% female, 11% male, 5% out-of-state, 3% international. Asian 2%, African American 31%, Caucasian 51%, Hispanic 6%, Native American <1%

Retention and Graduation: 67% freshmen return for sophomore year. 33% freshmen graduate within 4 years. **Faculty:** 108 full-time faculty, 73% hold PhDs, 73% are members of minority groups, 13% are women. 0% of classes are taught by teaching assistants.

ACADEMICS

Degrees: bachelor's, master's. **Classes:** Most classes have 10–19 students. Most lab/discussion sessions have 10–19 students. **Majors with Highest Enrollment:** Occupational Therapy/Therapist; Nursing Practice; Biology/Biological Sciences. **Special Study Options:** cross-registration, distance learning, double major, dual enrollment, English as a Second Language (ESL), honors program, independent study, internships, student-designed major, study abroad, teacher certification program, weekend college. **Honors programs:** The Honors Program at the Women's College of Brenau University begins in the freshman year and is followed throughout the student's entire college career at Brenau. Special classes reserved for honors students are taught in an enriched manner, affording these students an approach to their general education courses which enables them to study these subjects at an advanced level. Combined degree programs: B.S/MS in Occupational Therapy. **Disability Services:** Special programs offered to physically disabled students include note-taking services, tape recorders, tutors.

FACILITIES

Housing: special housing for disabled students, special housing for international students, women's dorms, fraternity/sorority housing, cooperative housing, apartments for single students 90% of campus accessible to physically disabled. **Special Academic Facilities/Equipment:** Simmons Art Gallery, Wages House, Whitepath House, Natatorium Physical Fitness Center, Leo Castelli Art Gallery **Computers:** Students can register for classes online. Administrative functions (other than registration) can be performed online.

CAMPUS LIFE

Environment: Town. **Activities:** Choral groups, dance, drama/theater, literary magazine, music ensembles, musical theater, radio station, student government, student newspaper, television station, yearbook, Campus Ministries, International Student Organization. 54 registered organizations, 12 honor societies, 2 religious organizations. 8 sororities. **Athletics (Intercollegiate):** *Women:* basketball, cross-country, soccer, softball, swimming, tennis, volleyball. **On-Campus Highlights:** Pearce Auditorium, Burd Center for Performing Arts, Fitness Center, Dining Hall and Tea Room, Northeast Georgia History Center.

ADMISSIONS

Freshman Academic Profile: SAT Math middle 50% range 440-510. SAT Critical Reading middle 50% range 450-560. SAT Writing middle 50% range 440-530. ACT middle 50% range 19-22. Minimum internet-based TOEFL 61. Minimum paper TOEFL 500. **Basis for Candidate Selection:** *Important factors considered include:* academic GPA, rigor of secondary school record, standardized test scores. *Other factors considered include:* Class rank, character/personal qualities, extracurricular activities, first generation, interview, level of applicant's interest, talent/ability, volunteer work, work experience. **Freshman Admission Requirements:** High school diploma is required and GED is accepted. **Freshman Admission Statistics:** 2,160 applied, 78% admitted, 12% enrolled. **Transfer Admission Requirements:** college transcript(s), Minimum college GPA of 2.0 required. Lowest grade transferable C. **General Admission Information:** Application Fee $35. Notification on a rolling basis, beginning on or about 10/1. Nonfall registration accepted. Credit and/or placement offered for CEEB Advanced Placement tests.

COSTS AND FINANCIAL AID

Annual tuition $24,380. Room and board $11,998. Required fees $400. Average book expense $1,250. **Required Forms and Deadlines:** FAFSA. **Notification of Awards:** Applicants will be notified of awards on a rolling basis beginning 3/1. **Types of Aid:** *Need-based scholarships/grants:* Federal Pell, SEOG, state scholarships/grants, private scholarships, the school's own gift aid, National Smart Grant. *Loans:* Subsidized Stafford, Unsubsidized Stafford, PLUS, Federal Perkins, state loans, Private Alternative Loans. *Student Employment:* Off-campus job opportunities are excellent. **Financial Aid Statistics:** 99% freshmen, 79% undergrads receive need-based scholarship or grant aid. 8% freshmen, 7% undergrads receive non-need-based scholarship or grant aid. 87% freshmen, 81% undergrads receive need-based self-help aid. 4% freshmen, 3% undergrads receive athletic scholarships. 72% undergrads borrow to pay for school. Average cumulative indebtedness $30,901. **Criteria for awarding institutional aid:** *Non-need-based:* academics, art, athletics, leadership, minority status, music/drama.

BRESCIA UNIVERSITY

717 Frederica Street, Owensboro, KY 42301-3023
Phone: 270-686-4241 · **Financial Aid Phone:** 1-877-BRESCIA
E-mail: admissions@brescia.edu · **CEEB Code:** 1071
Fax: 270-686-4314 · **Website:** www.brescia.edu · **ACT Code:** 14980

This private school, affiliated with the Roman Catholic Church, was founded in 1950. It has a 9-acre campus.

RATINGS

Admissions Selectivity Rating: 82   **Fire Safety Rating:** 90

STUDENTS AND FACULTY

Enrollment: 1,007. **Student Body:** 74% female, 26% male, 29% out-of-state, 0% international (17 countries represented). Asian 0%, African American 13%, Caucasian 66%, Hispanic 3%, Native American 1%
Retention and Graduation: 64% freshmen return for sophomore year. **Faculty:** 37 full-time faculty, 70% hold PhDs, 51% are members of minority groups, 16% are women. 0% of classes are taught by teaching assistants.

ACADEMICS

Degrees: associate, bachelor's, master's, post-bachelor's certificate. **Classes:** Most classes have fewer than 10 students. Most lab/discussion sessions have fewer than 10 students. **Majors with Highest Enrollment:** Elementary Education and Teaching; General Studies; Social Work. **Special Study Options:** Accelerated program, cross-registration, distance learning, double major, English as a Second Language (ESL), exchange student program (domestic), honors program, independent study, internships, liberal arts/career combination, student-designed major, teacher certification program, weekend college. **Disability Services:** Special programs offered to physically disabled students include note-taking services, tape recorders, tutors. **Career services:** alumni services, career/job search classes, career assessment, internships.

FACILITIES

Housing: Coed dorms, special housing for disabled students, men's dorms, women's dorms, apartments for single students, Theme Housing **Special Academic Facilities/Equipment:** Art Gallery, computer labs, campus center, greenhouse, observatory, science building. **Computers:** 100% of classrooms, 100% of dorms, 100% of libraries, 100% of dining areas, 100% of common outdoor areas have wireless network access. Administrative functions (other than registration) can be performed online.

CAMPUS LIFE

Environment: City. **Activities:** Choral groups, dance, drama/theater, literary magazine, pep band, student government, student newspaper, Campus Ministries, International Student Organization. 22 registered organizations, 3 honor societies, 2 religious organizations. **Athletics (Intercollegiate):** *Men:* baseball, basketball, cross-country, golf, soccer, tennis, track/field (outdoor). *Women:* basketball, cross-country, golf, soccer, softball, tennis, track/field (outdoor), volleyball. **Environmental Initiatives:** Recycling Purchasing more energy efficient windows Purchasing more energy efficient equipment when needed.

ADMISSIONS

Freshman Academic Profile: Average high school GPA 3.25. 61% from public high schools. SAT Math middle 50% range 400-580. SAT Critical Reading middle 50% range 440-480. ACT middle 50% range 20-25. Minimum paper TOEFL 550. **Basis for Candidate Selection:** *Very important factors considered include:* academic GPA, standardized test scores. **Freshman Admission Requirements:** High school diploma is required and GED is accepted. **Freshman Admission Statistics:** 3,748 applied, 49% admitted, 9% enrolled. **Transfer Admission Requirements:** High school transcript, college transcript(s), Minimum college GPA of 2.0 required. Lowest grade transferable C. **General Admission Information:** Application Fee $25. Notification on a rolling basis, beginning on or about 9/1. Nonfall registration accepted. Admission may be deferred for a maximum of 1 year. Credit and/or placement offered for CEEB Advanced Placement tests.

COSTS AND FINANCIAL AID

Annual tuition $19,500. Room and board $8,000. Required fees $490. **Required Forms and Deadlines:** FAFSA. **Notification of Awards:** Applicants will be notified of awards on a rolling basis beginning 3/1. **Types of Aid:** *Need-based scholarships/grants:* Federal Pell, SEOG, state scholarships/grants, private scholarships, the school's own gift aid. *Loans:* Direct Subsidized Stafford, Direct Unsubsidized Stafford, Direct PLUS, Subsidized Stafford, Unsubsidized Stafford, PLUS, Federal Perkins, college/university loans from institutional funds. *Student Employment:* Federal Work-Study Program available. Institutional employment available. Highest amount earned per year from on-campus jobs $1,236. Off-campus job opportunities are excellent. **Financial Aid Statistics:** 0% freshmen, 0% undergrads receive athletic scholarships. 99% freshmen, 98% undergrads receive any aid. **Criteria for awarding institu-**

tional aid: *Non-need-based:* academics, alumni affiliation, art, athletics, minority status, music/drama, religious affiliation, state/district residency.

BREVARD COLLEGE

One Brevard College Drive, Brevard, NC 28712
Phone: 828-884-8300 · **Financial Aid Phone:** 828-884-8261
E-mail: admissions@brevard.edu · **CEEB Code:** 5067
Fax: 828-884-3790 · **ACT Code:** 3074

This private school, affiliated with the Methodist Church, was founded in 1853. It has a 120-acre campus.

RATINGS

Admissions Selectivity Rating: 82   **Fire Safety Rating:** 73

STUDENTS AND FACULTY

Enrollment: 696. **Student Body:** 42% female, 58% male, 42% out-of-state, 6% international (17 countries represented). Asian 1%, African American 10%, Caucasian 71%, Hispanic 2%, Native American 1%
Retention and Graduation: 59% freshmen return for sophomore year. 36% freshmen graduate within 4 years. 43% freshmen graduate within 6 years.
Faculty: 51 full-time faculty, 84% hold PhDs, 47% are members of minority groups, 0% are women. 0% of classes are taught by teaching assistants.

ACADEMICS

Degrees: bachelor's. **Classes:** Most classes have 10–19 students. Most lab/discussion sessions have 10–19 students. **Majors with Highest Enrollment:** Business Administration and Management; Parks, Recreation and Leisure Studies; Multi-/Interdisciplinary Studies. **Special Study Options:** double major, dual enrollment, honors program, independent study, internships, student-designed major, study abroad, teacher certification program. **Honors programs:** To complete the Honors Program, students must take a minimum of 19 s.h. in honors courses during the typical 4-year period of their enrollment at Brevard College. These hours include honors enrichment seminar courses, honors-designated sections of courses, and a senior project. The only coursework of these 19 hours that is not directly attributable to core or major requirements is 4 s.h. of Enrichment seminars. **Disability Services:** Special programs offered to physically disabled students include note-taking services, reader services, tape recorders, tutors. **Career services:** career/job search classes, career assessment, internships.

FACILITIES

Housing: Coed dorms, special housing for disabled students, men's dorms, women's dorms, Coed upper classperson dorm. 100% of campus accessible to physically disabled. **Special Academic Facilities/Equipment:** Porter Center for Performing Arts; Sims Art Center; Morrison Playhouse; Fitness Appraisal Laboratory; Academic Enrichment Center; Center for Career, Service, and Learning; Medical Services Building; Stamey Counseling Center; 24-hour computer lab; Library with wireless connection; Moore Science Annex Building **Computers:** 25% of dorms, 100% of libraries, 100% of dining areas, 100% of student union, have wireless network access. Administrative functions (other than registration) can be performed online.

CAMPUS LIFE

Environment: Village. **Activities:** Choral groups, concert band, dance, drama/theater, jazz band, literary magazine, music ensembles, musical theater, opera, pep band, student government, student newspaper, yearbook, Campus Ministries. 32 registered organizations, 3 honor societies, 1 religious organization. **Athletics (Intercollegiate):** *Men:* baseball, basketball, cheerleading, cross-country, cycling, football, golf, soccer, tennis, track/field (outdoor). *Women:* basketball, cheerleading, cross-country, cycling, golf, soccer, softball, tennis, track/field (outdoor), volleyball. **On-Campus Highlights:** Food Court & Dining Hall, Porter Center for Performing Arts, The Village, MG Super Lab, Moore Science Annex Building, Academic Enrichment Center. **Environmental Initiatives:** Campus-wide recycling program; Ongoing HVAC renovations to increase energy efficiency; Ongoing master landscaping plan that focuses on native vegetation.

ADMISSIONS

Freshman Academic Profile: Average high school GPA 3.07. 6% in top 10% of high school class, 24% in top 25% of high school class, 62% in top 50% of high school class. 82% from public high schools. SAT Math middle 50% range 420-530. SAT Critical Reading middle 50% range 420-520. ACT middle 50% range 17-22. Minimum paper TOEFL 537. **Basis for Candidate Selection:** *Very important factors considered include:* academic GPA, rigor of secondary school record, standardized test scores, level of applicant's interest. *Important factors considered include:* Class rank, application essay, character/personal

qualities, extracurricular activities, interview, talent/ability, volunteer work. *Other factors considered include:* recommendation(s), alumni/ae relation, work experience. **Freshman Admission Requirements:** High school diploma is required and GED is accepted. **Freshman Admission Statistics:** 2,858 applied, 43% admitted, 18% enrolled. **Transfer Admission Requirements:** High school transcript, college transcript(s), essay or personal statement, standardized test scores, statement of good standing from prior institution(s). Minimum college GPA of 2.0 required. Lowest grade transferable C-. **General Admission Information:** Application Fee $30. Notification on a rolling basis, beginning on or about 7/1. Nonfall registration accepted. Admission may be deferred for a maximum of one semester. Credit and/or placement offered for CEEB Advanced Placement tests.

COSTS AND FINANCIAL AID

Required Forms and Deadlines: FAFSA. **Notification of Awards:** Applicants will be notified of awards on a rolling basis beginning 2/1. **Types of Aid:** *Need-based scholarships/grants:* Federal Pell, SEOG, state scholarships/grants, private scholarships, the school's own gift aid. *Loans:* Direct Subsidized Stafford, Direct Unsubsidized Stafford, Direct PLUS, Subsidized Stafford, Unsubsidized Stafford, PLUS, Federal Perkins, state loans. *Student Employment:* Federal Work-Study Program available. Institutional employment available. Highest amount earned per year from on-campus jobs $1,860. Off-campus job opportunities are fair. **Financial Aid Statistics:** 82% freshmen, 80% undergrads receive need-based scholarship or grant aid. 100% freshmen, 60% undergrads receive non-need-based scholarship or grant aid. 82% freshmen, 80% undergrads receive need-based self-help aid. 7% freshmen, 7% undergrads receive athletic scholarships. 76% undergrads borrow to pay for school. Average cumulative indebtedness $24,392. **Criteria for awarding institutional aid:** *Non-need-based:* academics, art, athletics, job skills, leadership, minority status, music/drama, religious affiliation, state/district residency.

BREWTON-PARKER COLLEGE

P.O. Box 2011, Mt. Vernon, GA 30445
Phone: 912-583-3265
E-mail: admissions@bpc.edu
Fax: 912-583-3598 · **Website:** www.bpc.edu

This private school, affiliated with the Baptist Church, was founded in 1904. It has a 270-acre campus.

RATINGS

Admissions Selectivity Rating: 78   **Fire Safety Rating:** 65

STUDENTS AND FACULTY

Enrollment: 1,124. **Student Body:** 64% female, 36% male, 5% out-of-state, 2% international (19 countries represented). Asian 0%, African American 20%, Caucasian 65%, Hispanic 2%, Native American <1%
Retention and Graduation: 59% freshmen return for sophomore year. 8% freshmen graduate within 4 years. 18% freshmen graduate within 6 years. 10% grads go on to further study within 1 year. **Faculty:** 52 full-time faculty, 73% hold PhDs, 38% are members of minority groups. 0% of classes are taught by teaching assistants.

ACADEMICS

Degrees: associate, bachelor's. **Classes:** Most classes have fewer than 10 students. **Majors with Highest Enrollment:** Education; Psychology; Business/Commerce. **Special Study Options:** double major, dual enrollment, exchange student program (domestic), honors program, independent study, internships, teacher certification program, weekend college. **Disability Services:** Special programs offered to physically disabled students include note-taking services, reader services, tape recorders, tutors. **Career services:** alumni services, career assessment, internships,

FACILITIES

Housing: men's dorms, women's dorms. 80% of campus accessible to physically disabled. **Special Academic Facilities/Equipment:** Library **Computers:** Students can register for classes online.

CAMPUS LIFE

Environment: Rural. **Activities:** Choral groups, concert band, drama/theater, jazz band, literary magazine, music ensembles, musical theater, student government, student newspaper, yearbook. 24 registered organizations, 1 honor society, 5 religious organizations. 3 fraternities, 3 sororities. **Athletics (Intercollegiate):** *Men:* baseball, basketball, cheerleading, soccer. *Women:* basketball, cheerleading, soccer, softball, volleyball. **On-Campus Highlights:** New Student Activities Center, Upstairs Café, Phillips Student Center Lobby, McAllister Lobby, Baseball/Softball Field.

ADMISSIONS

Freshman Academic Profile: 12% in top 10% of high school class, 26% in top 25% of high school class, 62% in top 50% of high school class. 80% from public high schools. SAT Math middle 50% range 400-500. SAT Critical Reading middle 50% range 390-510. ACT middle 50% range 17-21. **Basis for Candidate Selection:** *Very important factors considered include:* standardized test scores. *Important factors considered include:* Class rank, rigor of secondary school record. **Freshman Admission Requirements:** High school diploma is required and GED is accepted. *Academic units required:* 4 English, 3 mathematics, 3 science, 3 social studies. **Freshman Admission Statistics:** 498 applied, 48% admitted, 49% enrolled. **Transfer Admission Requirements:** college transcript(s), statement of good standing from prior institution(s). Minimum college GPA of 2.0 required. Lowest grade transferable D. **General Admission Information:** Application Fee $25. Regular notification 1/1. Nonfall registration accepted. Admission may be deferred for a maximum of 1 year.

COSTS AND FINANCIAL AID

Annual tuition $11,500. Room and board $5,200. Required fees $1,100. Average book expense $1,000. **Required Forms and Deadlines:** FAFSA, State aid form. **Notification of Awards:** Applicants will be notified of awards on a rolling basis beginning 2/1. **Types of Aid:** *Need-based scholarships/grants:* Federal Pell, SEOG, state scholarships/grants, private scholarships, the school's own gift aid, Georgia Baptist Funds. *Loans:* Subsidized Stafford, Unsubsidized Stafford, PLUS, Federal Perkins, state loans, college/university loans from institutional funds. *Student Employment:* Federal Work-Study Program available. Institutional employment available. Highest amount earned per year from on-campus jobs $1,235. Off-campus job opportunities are fair. **Financial Aid Statistics:** 100% freshmen, 100% undergrads receive need-based scholarship or grant aid. 9% freshmen, 8% undergrads receive non-need-based scholarship or grant aid. 70% freshmen, 75% undergrads receive need-based self-help aid. 6% freshmen, 6% undergrads receive athletic scholarships. 82% undergrads borrow to pay for school. **Criteria for awarding institutional aid:** *Non-need-based:* academics, art, athletics, leadership, music/drama, religious affiliation, state/district residency.

BRIAR CLIFF UNIVERSITY

Admissions Office, Sioux City, IA 51104-0100
Phone: 712-279-5200 · **Financial Aid Phone:** 712-279-5239
E-mail: admissions@briarcliff.edu · **CEEB Code:** 1846
Fax: 712-279-1632 · **Website:** www.briarcliff.edu · **ACT Code:** 1276

This private school, affiliated with the Roman Catholic Church, was founded in 1930. It has a 70-acre campus.

RATINGS

Admissions Selectivity Rating: 80   **Fire Safety Rating:** 81

STUDENTS AND FACULTY

Enrollment: 978. **Student Body:** 54% female, 46% male, 42% out-of-state, 1% international (11 countries represented). Asian 2%, African American 7%, Caucasian 78%, Hispanic 9%, Native American 2%
Retention and Graduation: 68% freshmen return for sophomore year. 43% freshmen graduate within 4 years. 55% freshmen graduate within 6 years. 37% grads go on to further study within 1 year. 3% grads pursue arts and sciences degrees. 3% grads pursue law degrees. 4% grads pursue business degrees. 11% grads pursue medical degrees. **Faculty:** 61 full-time faculty, 75% hold PhDs, 54% are members of minority groups, 2% are women. 0% of classes are taught by teaching assistants.

ACADEMICS

Degrees: associate, bachelor's, master's, post-bachelor's certificate, post-master's certificate. **Classes:** Most classes have 10–19 students. Most lab/discussion sessions have fewer than 10 students. **Majors with Highest Enrollment:** Business/Commerce; Elementary Education and Teaching. **Special Study Options:** Accelerated program, cross-registration, distance learning, double major, dual enrollment, honors program, independent study, internships, liberal arts/career combination, student-designed major, study abroad, teacher certification program, weekend college. **Honors programs:** Briar Cliffs Honor Program involves elements of leadership, service and character as well as academics, and is led by the Student Honors Executive Board. In addition to talking Honors courses with small enrollments, Honors students perform individual research work with faculty at the upper levels. **Disability Services:** Special programs offered to physically disabled students include note-taking services, reader services, tape recorders, tutors. **Career services:** alumni services, career/job search classes, career assessment, internships. Career services highlights include the Chicago Semester, which allows students from any major field of study to work, study, and live in Chicago for a semester.

FACILITIES

Housing: Coed dorms, men's dorms, women's dorms, apartments for single students. 90% of campus accessible to physically disabled. **Special Academic Facilities/Equipment:** Nursing Simulation Lab Integrated Multimedia Center Human Anatomy Lab Clausen Art Gallery **Computers:** 100% of classrooms, 100% of libraries, 100% of dining areas, 100% of student union, have wireless network access. Administrative functions (other than registration) can be performed online.

CAMPUS LIFE

Environment: City. **Activities:** Choral groups, drama/theater, jazz band, literary magazine, music ensembles, musical theater, opera, radio station, student government, student newspaper, Campus Ministries. 36 registered organizations, 2 honor societies, 3 religious organizations. **Athletics (Intercollegiate):** *Men:* baseball, basketball, cross-country, football, golf, soccer, tennis, track/field (outdoor), track/field (indoor), wrestling. *Women:* basketball, cross-country, golf, soccer, softball, tennis, track/field (outdoor), track/field (indoor), volleyball. **On-Campus Highlights:** Java City, Stark Student Center, Newman Flanagan Athletic Center, Game Room, tunnels, The McCoy Arnold Athletic Facility was completed in 2004. This multi-use athletic facility provides additional facilities for students to work on personal training and fitness. **Environmental Initiatives:** Recycling; Prairie Restoration; Trayless dining.

ADMISSIONS

Freshman Academic Profile: Average high school GPA 3.13. 11% in top 10% of high school class, 32% in top 25% of high school class, 68% in top 50% of high school class. 82% from public high schools. ACT middle 50% range 18-23. Minimum internet-based TOEFL 70. Minimum paper TOEFL 525. **Basis for Candidate Selection:** *Very important factors considered include:* academic GPA, rigor of secondary school record, standardized test scores. *Other factors considered include:* Class rank, application essay, recommendation(s), alumni/ae relation, character/personal qualities, extracurricular activities, first generation, interview, talent/ability. **Freshman Admission Requirements:** High school diploma is required and GED is accepted. **Freshman Admission Statistics:** 1,774 applied, 58% admitted, 23% enrolled. **Transfer Admission Requirements:** High school transcript, college transcript(s), statement of good standing from prior institution(s). Minimum college GPA of 2.0 required. Lowest grade transferable D. **General Admission Information:** Application Fee $20. Nonfall registration accepted. Admission may be deferred for a maximum of One year. Credit offered for CEEB Advanced Placement tests.

COSTS AND FINANCIAL AID

Average book expense $1,050. **Required Forms and Deadlines:** FAFSA. **Types of Aid:** *Need-based scholarships/grants:* Federal Pell, SEOG, state scholarships/grants, private scholarships, the school's own gift aid. *Loans:* Subsidized Stafford, Unsubsidized Stafford, PLUS, Federal Perkins, state loans. *Student Employment:* Federal Work-Study Program available. Institutional employment available. Highest amount earned per year from on-campus jobs $2,500. Off-campus job opportunities are excellent. **Financial Aid Statistics:** 100% freshmen, 100% undergrads receive need-based scholarship or grant aid. 100% freshmen, 100% undergrads receive non-need-based scholarship or grant aid. 100% freshmen, 100% undergrads receive need-based self-help aid. 61% freshmen, 47% undergrads receive athletic scholarships. 100% freshmen, 97% undergrads receive any aid. 89% undergrads borrow to pay for school. Average cumulative indebtedness $19,145. **Criteria for awarding institutional aid:** *Non-need-based:* academics, alumni affiliation, art, athletics, leadership, music/drama, religious affiliation, state/district residency.

BRIDGEWATER COLLEGE

402 East College Street, Bridgewater, VA 22812-1599
Phone: 540-828-5375 · **Financial Aid Phone:** 540-828-5376
E-mail: admissions@bridgewater.edu · **CEEB Code:** 5069
Fax: 540-828-5481 · **Website:** www.bridgewater.edu · **ACT Code:** 4342

This private school, affiliated with the Church of Brethren Church, was founded in 1880. It has a 190-acre campus.

RATINGS

Admissions Selectivity Rating: 87   **Fire Safety Rating:** 77

STUDENTS AND FACULTY

Enrollment: 1,768. **Student Body:** 54% female, 46% male, 24% out-of-state, 1% international (9 countries represented). Asian 1%, African American 10%, Caucasian 76%, Hispanic 4%, Native American <1%
Retention and Graduation: 74% freshmen return for sophomore year. 56% freshmen graduate within 4 years. 61% freshmen graduate within 6 years. 22%

grads go on to further study within 1 year. **Faculty:** 111 full-time faculty, 80% hold PhDs, 57% are members of minority groups, 5% are women. 0% of classes are taught by teaching assistants.

ACADEMICS

Degrees: bachelor's. **Classes:** Most classes have 10–19 students. Most lab/discussion sessions have 10–19 students. **Majors with Highest Enrollment:** Business Administration and Management; Biology/Biological Sciences; Health and Physical Education/Fitness. **Special Study Options:** double major, honors program, independent study, internships, liberal arts/career combination, study abroad, teacher certification program, Dual Degree Programs: 3-2 Engineering Program with George Washington University(BA/BA) 3-2 Engineering Program with Virginia Tech (BA/BA) 3-2 Nursing Program with Vanderbilt University (BA/MN) 3-4 Veterinary Science Program with Virginia Tech (BA/DVM) 3-4 Physical Therapy Program with Shenandoah University (BA/DPT) Pre Professional Programs in Dentistry, Engineering, Law, Medicine, Ministry, Nursing, Occupational Therapy, Pharmacy, Physical Therapy, and Veterinary Science. **Honors programs:** The Honors Program is designed to provide additional challenges and opportunities for outstanding students. Honors courses are taught as smaller classes and provide opportunities for different types of student learning and faculty teaching--greater independence, research, and discussion formats. An Honors Project is one in which a student researches a subject, by examination of relevant literature or by experimentation or both; the student reports the results in an accurately documented and well-written paper or appropriate representation of the work. Combined degree programs: BA/MA, Vet. Science, Physical Therapy, Nursing. **Disability Services:** Special programs offered to physically disabled students include note-taking services, reader services, tape recorders, tutors. **Career services:** alumni services, career/job search classes, career assessment, internships. Career services highlights include the internship program, which promotes student participation and establishes new opportunities/sites for internships within the local, regional, and distant communities.

FACILITIES

Housing: Coed dorms, special housing for disabled students, men's dorms, women's dorms, apartments for single students, Wellness Housing, Theme Housing, Honor Housing. 95% of campus accessible to physically disabled. **Special Academic Facilities/Equipment:** Museum of Shenandoah region and Brethren history. **Computers:** 5% of classrooms, 10% of dorms, 75% of libraries, 100% of dining areas, 100% of student union, have wireless network access. Students can register for classes online. Administrative functions (other than registration) can be performed online.

CAMPUS LIFE

Environment: Village. **Activities:** Choral groups, concert band, dance, drama/theater, jazz band, literary magazine, music ensembles, musical theater, pep band, radio station, student government, student newspaper, yearbook, Campus Ministries, International Student Organization. 74 registered organizations, 8 honor societies, 9 religious organizations. **Athletics (Intercollegiate):** Men: baseball, basketball, cross-country, equestrian sports, football, golf, soccer, tennis, track/field (outdoor), track/field (indoor). Women: basketball, cross-country, equestrian sports, field hockey, lacrosse, soccer, softball, swimming, tennis, track/field (outdoor), track/field (indoor), volleyball. **On-Campus Highlights:** McKinney Center for Science and Mathematics, Kline Campus Center, Funkhouser Center for Health and Wellness, Carter Center for Worship and Music, Eagle's Nest (snack shop). **Environmental Initiatives:** Energy and water conservation 3R's - Reduce, Reuse and Recycle Food Services: trayless operation, use of local produce, and project clean plate

ADMISSIONS

Freshman Academic Profile: Average high school GPA 3.61. 20.9% in top 10% of high school class, 50.9% in top 25% of high school class, 83.2% in top 50% of high school class. 93% from public high schools. SAT Math middle 50% range 480-570. SAT Critical Reading middle 50% range 470-570. SAT Writing middle 50% range 440-540. ACT middle 50% range 21-27. Minimum internet-based TOEFL 79. Minimum paper TOEFL 550. **Basis for Candidate Selection:** Very important factors considered include: academic GPA, rigor of secondary school record, standardized test scores. Important factors considered include: Class rank, recommendation(s), character/personal qualities, extracurricular activities, interview, talent/ability. Other factors considered include: geographical residence, level of applicant's interest, state residency, volunteer work, work experience. **Freshman Admission Requirements:** High school diploma is required and GED is accepted. Academic units required: 4 English, 3 mathematics, 2 science, (2 science labs), 0 foreign language, 4 academic electives, 2 Social Studies and History. **Freshman Admission Statistics:** 6,169 applied, 48% admitted, 17% enrolled. **Transfer Admission Requirements:** High school transcript, college transcript(s), standardized test scores, statement of good standing from prior institution(s). Minimum college GPA of 2.2 required. Lowest grade transferable C. **General Admission Information:** Application Fee $30. Notification on a rolling basis, beginning on or about 9/1. Nonfall registration accepted. Admission may be deferred for a maximum of 1 year. Credit and/or placement offered for CEEB Advanced Placement tests.

COSTS AND FINANCIAL AID

Annual tuition $30,800. Room and board $11,520. Required fees $680. Average book expense $1,150. **Required Forms and Deadlines:** FAFSA, State aid form. **Notification of Awards:** Applicants will be notified of awards on a rolling basis beginning 3/16. **Types of Aid:** Need-based scholarships/grants: Federal Pell, SEOG, state scholarships/grants, private scholarships, the school's own gift aid. Loans: Subsidized Stafford, Unsubsidized Stafford, PLUS, Federal Perkins. Student Employment: Federal Work-Study Program available. Institutional employment available. Highest amount earned per year from on-campus jobs $1,947. Off-campus job opportunities are good. **Financial Aid Statistics:** 100% freshmen, 100% undergrads receive need-based scholarship or grant aid. 100% freshmen, 100% undergrads receive non-need-based scholarship or grant aid. 65% freshmen, 70% undergrads receive need-based self-help aid. 0% freshmen, 0% undergrads receive athletic scholarships. 99% freshmen, 99% undergrads receive any aid. 79% undergrads borrow to pay for school. Average cumulative indebtedness $27,316. **Criteria for awarding institutional aid:** Non-need-based: academics, music/drama, religious affiliation.

BRIDGEWATER STATE COLLEGE

Gates House, Bridgewater State College, Bridgewater, MA 2325
Phone: 508-531-1237 · **Financial Aid Phone:** 508-531-1341
E-mail: admission@bridgew.edu · **CEEB Code:** 3517
Fax: 508-531-1746 · **Website:** www.bridgew.edu · **ACT Code:** 1900

This public school was founded in 1840. It has a 235-acre campus.

RATINGS

Admissions Selectivity Rating: 76   Fire Safety Rating: 60*

STUDENTS AND FACULTY

Enrollment: 8,310. **Student Body:** 60% female, 40% male, 5% out-of-state, 1% international (52 countries represented). Asian 2%, African American 6%, Caucasian 81%, Hispanic 2%, Native American <1%
Retention and Graduation: 80% freshmen return for sophomore year. 22% freshmen graduate within 4 years. 51% freshmen graduate within 6 years. 16% grads go on to further study within 1 year. 2% grads pursue law degrees. 1% grads pursue business degrees. **Faculty:** 306 full-time faculty, 90% hold PhDs, 48% are members of minority groups, 11% are women. 0% of classes are taught by teaching assistants.

ACADEMICS

Degrees: bachelor's, master's, post-bachelor's certificate, post-master's certificate. **Classes:** Most classes have 20–29 students. Most lab/discussion sessions have 10–19 students. **Majors with Highest Enrollment:** Elementary Education and Teaching; Psychology; Business/Commerce. **Special Study Options:** Accelerated program, cross-registration, distance learning, double major, dual enrollment, English as a Second Language (ESL), exchange student program (domestic), honors program, independent study, internships, study abroad, teacher certification program. Combined degree programs: BS/MSM in Management, BSE/M.Ed in Elem/Spec. Ed. **Disability Services:** Special programs offered to physically disabled students include note-taking services, reader services, tape recorders, tutors. **Career services:** alumni services, career/job search classes, career assessment, internships.

FACILITIES

Housing: Coed dorms, special housing for disabled students, apartments for single students, break housing for athletes, student teachers, international students, visiting lecturers. 95% of campus accessible to physically disabled. **Special Academic Facilities/Equipment:** On-campus school, children's physical development clinic, human performance lab, TV studio, observatory, flight simulators, electron microscope, Moakley Technology Center **Computers:** Students can register for classes online. Administrative functions (other than registration) can be performed online. Undergraduates are required to own a computer.

CAMPUS LIFE

Environment: Village. **Activities:** Choral groups, concert band, dance, drama/theater, jazz band, literary magazine, marching band, music ensembles, musical theater, radio station, student government, student newspaper, yearbook, Campus Ministries, International Student Organization. 67 registered organizations, 11 honor society, 1 religious organization. **Athletics (Intercollegiate):** Men: baseball, basketball, cross-country, football, soccer, swimming, tennis, track/field (outdoor), wrestling. Women: basketball, cross-country, field hockey, lacrosse, soccer, softball, swimming, tennis, track/field (outdoor), volleyball.

ADMISSIONS

Freshman Academic Profile: Average high school GPA 3.01. 8% in top 10% of high school class, 32% in top 25% of high school class, 77% in top 50% of high school class. SAT Math middle 50% range 470-560. SAT Critical Reading middle 50% range 460-560. ACT middle 50% range 19-23. Minimum paper TOEFL 500. **Basis for Candidate Selection:** *Very important factors considered include:* academic GPA, rigor of secondary school record. *Important factors considered include:* Class rank, standardized test scores. *Other factors considered include:* application essay, recommendation(s), alumni/ae relation, character/personal qualities, extracurricular activities, racial/ethnic status, talent/ability, volunteer work, work experience. **Freshman Admission Requirements:** High school diploma is required and GED is accepted. *Academic units required:* 4 English, 3 mathematics, 3 science, (2 science labs), 2 foreign language, 1 social studies, 1 history, 2 academic electives. **Freshman Admission Statistics:** 6,226 applied, 72% admitted, 33% enrolled. **Transfer Admission Requirements:** college transcript(s), essay or personal statement, Minimum college GPA of 2.0 required. Lowest grade transferable C-. **General Admission Information:** Notification on a rolling basis, beginning on or about 12/15. Nonfall registration accepted. Credit and/or placement offered for CEEB Advanced Placement tests.

COSTS AND FINANCIAL AID

Annual in-state tuition $910. Annual out-of-state tuition $7,050. Room and board $6,852. Average book expense $1,000. **Required Forms and Deadlines:** FAFSA. **Types of Aid:** *Need-based scholarships/grants:* Federal Pell, SEOG, state scholarships/grants, private scholarships, the school's own gift aid. *Loans:* Direct Subsidized Stafford, Direct Unsubsidized Stafford, Direct PLUS, Federal Perkins, state loans. *Student Employment:* Federal Work-Study Program available. Institutional employment available. Highest amount earned per year from on-campus jobs $4,000. Off-campus job opportunities are good. **Financial Aid Statistics:** 83% freshmen, 83% undergrads receive need-based scholarship or grant aid. 24% freshmen, 10% undergrads receive non-need-based scholarship or grant aid. 96% freshmen, 100% undergrads receive need-based self-help aid. Average cumulative indebtedness $16,971. **Criteria for awarding institutional aid:** *Non-need-based:* academics, leadership, minority status, state/district residency.

BRIERCREST COLLEGE AND SEMINARY

510 College Drive, Caronport, SK S0H 0S0
Phone: 1-800-667-5199
E-mail: admissions@briercrest.ca
Fax: 800-667-5500 · **Website:** www.briercrest.ca

This private school was founded in 1935. It has a 160-acre campus.

RATINGS

Admissions Selectivity Rating: 60*   Fire Safety Rating: 60*

STUDENTS AND FACULTY

Enrollment: 632. **Student Body:** 6% out-of-state.
Faculty: 31 full-time faculty.

ACADEMICS

Degrees: associate, bachelor's, certificate, master's, post-bachelor's certificate. **Special Study Options:** distance learning, double major, English as a Second Language (ESL), independent study, internships, study abroad. **Career services:** alumni services, career assessment.

FACILITIES

Housing: Coed dorms, special housing for disabled students, Suite, corridor, singles, smoke-free, over 21 yrs, over 24 yrs, wellness living, quiet study, same curriculum housing, baccalaureate, single room options, and computer life style New upperclassmen apartment suite complex. **Computers:** Students can register for classes online.

CAMPUS LIFE

Environment: Rural. **Activities:** Choral groups, concert band, drama/theater, jazz band, literary magazine, music ensembles, musical theater, radio station, student government, student newspaper, symphony orchestra, yearbook. **Athletics (Intercollegiate):** *Men:* basketball, ice hockey, volleyball. *Women:* basketball, volleyball.

ADMISSIONS

Transfer Admission Requirements: High school transcript, college transcript(s), essay or personal statement. **General Admission Information:** Nonfall registration accepted.

COSTS AND FINANCIAL AID

Annual tuition $7,470. Room and board $2,515. Required fees $250. Average book expense $500. **Required Forms and Deadlines:** Institution's own financial aid form, State aid form.

BRIGHAM YOUNG UNIVERSITY (UT)

A-153 ASB, Provo, UT 84602-1110
Phone: 801-422-2507 · **Financial Aid Phone:** 801-378-4104
E-mail: admissions@byu.edu · **CEEB Code:** 4019
Fax: 801-422-0005 · **Website:** www.byu.edu · **ACT Code:** 4266

This private school, affiliated with the Church of Jesus Christ of Latt Church, was founded in 1875. It has a 557-acre campus.

RATINGS

Admissions Selectivity Rating: 94   Fire Safety Rating: 70

STUDENTS AND FACULTY

Enrollment: 27,163. **Student Body:** 45% female, 55% male, 67% out-of-state, 3% international (121 countries represented). Asian 2%, African American 1%, Caucasian 83%, Hispanic 6%, Native American <1%
Retention and Graduation: 87% freshmen return for sophomore year. 29% freshmen graduate within 4 years. **Faculty:** 1,247 full-time faculty, 92% hold PhDs, 21% are members of minority groups, 5% are women.

ACADEMICS

Degrees: bachelor's, master's. **Classes:** Most classes have 10–19 students. **Majors with Highest Enrollment:** Business/Commerce; Exercise Physiology; Elementary Education and Teaching. **Special Study Options:** Accelerated program, cooperative education program, cross-registration, distance learning, double major, English as a Second Language (ESL), external degree program, honors program, independent study, internships, liberal arts/career combination, study abroad, teacher certification program. **Honors programs:** The Honors Program, participation in which is open to all BYU students, complements the university's expansive educational agenda by providing the benefits of a small liberal arts learning community. These benefits include offering small classes with high-quality teaching and learning that challenge students to reach their highest potential; fostering a spirit of ongoing inquiry that includes undergraduate research in a mentored environment; and underscoring the importance of combining personal excellence, faithful discipleship, and meaningful service. Combined degree programs: BA/JD, BA/MA, BA/Macc, BS/MS. **Disability Services:** Special programs offered to physically disabled students include note-taking services, reader services, tape recorders, tutors.

FACILITIES

Housing: special housing for disabled students, men's dorms, women's dorms, apartments for married students, apartments for single students, Language houses are available. 97% of campus accessible to physically disabled. **Special Academic Facilities/Equipment:** Art, peoples/cultures, life science, and earth science museums, film studio, on-campus nursery school, language research center, seismography equipment, electron microscope. **Computers:** 10% of classrooms, 100% of libraries, 100% of dining areas, 100% of student union, have wireless network access. Students can register for classes online. Administrative functions (other than registration) can be performed online.

CAMPUS LIFE

Environment: City. **Activities:** Choral groups, concert band, dance, drama/theater, jazz band, literary magazine, marching band, music ensembles, musical theater, opera, pep band, radio station, student government, student newspaper, student-run film society, symphony orchestra, television station. 390 registered organizations, 22 honor societies, 25 religious organizations. **Athletics (Intercollegiate):** *Men:* baseball, basketball, cheerleading, cross-country, diving, football, golf, swimming, tennis, track/field (outdoor), track/field (indoor), volleyball. *Women:* basketball, cheerleading, cross-country, diving, golf, gymnastics, soccer, softball, swimming, tennis, track/field (outdoor), track/field (indoor), volleyball. **On-Campus Highlights:** Monte L. Bean Life Science Museum, The Museum of Art, Gordon B. Hinckley Alumni & Visitors Cen, Harold B. Lee Library, Wilkinson Student Center, Some of the popular places on campus are the HFAC theatres and music halls, the Creamery on 9th, and the Marriott Center (where weekly devotionals and forums as well as sports events are held). Campus highlights also include BYU's new Student Athlete Building houses the impressive Legacy Hall (BYU sports Hall of Fame) and the popular Legends Grille, the very large (athletic teams')Indoor Practice Facility is completed, the newly remodeled Brimhall Building is housing the Communications Department, and the new Joseph F. Smith Building (which replaced the Smith Family Living Center) has been completed and now houses the College of Family, Home and Social Sciences.

ADMISSIONS

Freshman Academic Profile: Average high school GPA 3.81. 55% in top 10% of high school class, 87% in top 25% of high school class, 98% in top 50% of high school class. SAT Math middle 50% range 580-680. SAT Critical Reading middle 50% range 570-690. ACT middle 50% range 27-31. Minimum paper TOEFL 500. **Basis for Candidate Selection:** *Very important factors considered include:* academic GPA, rigor of secondary school record, standardized test scores, character/personal qualities, interview, religious affiliation/commitment. *Important factors considered include:* application essay, recommendation(s), extracurricular activities, racial/ethnic status, volunteer work. *Other factors considered include:* first generation, talent/ability, work experience. **Freshman Admission Requirements:** High school diploma is required and GED is accepted. *Academic units required:* 4 English, 3 mathematics, 2 science, (2 science labs), 2 foreign language, 2 history, 2 Literature or Writing. **Freshman Admission Statistics:** 11,078 applied, 47% admitted, 78% enrolled. **Transfer Admission Requirements:** college transcript(s), essay or personal statement, interview, Minimum college GPA of 3.0 required. Lowest grade transferable C-. **General Admission Information:** Application Fee $30. Regular application deadline 2/1. Nonfall registration accepted. Admission may be deferred for a maximum of 2 years. Credit and/or placement offered for CEEB Advanced Placement tests.

COSTS AND FINANCIAL AID

Annual tuition $10,000. Room and board $7,330. Required fees $0. Average book expense $992. **Required Forms and Deadlines:** FAFSA. **Notification of Awards:** Applicants will be notified of awards on a rolling basis beginning 5/1. **Types of Aid:** *Need-based scholarships/grants:* Federal Pell, state scholarships/grants, private scholarships, the school's own gift aid. *Loans:* Subsidized Stafford, Unsubsidized Stafford, PLUS. **Financial Aid Statistics:** 51% freshmen, 78% undergrads receive need-based scholarship or grant aid. 96% freshmen, 51% undergrads receive non-need-based scholarship or grant aid. 26% freshmen, 31% undergrads receive need-based self-help aid. 3% freshmen, 2% undergrads receive athletic scholarships. 53% freshmen, 64% undergrads receive any aid. 26% undergrads borrow to pay for school. Average cumulative indebtedness $14,021. **Criteria for awarding institutional aid:** *Non-need-based:* academics, art, athletics, leadership, minority status, music/drama, religious affiliation, state/district residency.

BRIGHAM YOUNG UNIVERSITY—HAWAII

BYU- Hawaii # 1973, Laie, HI 96762
Phone: 808-675-3738 · **Financial Aid Phone:** 808-293-3530
E-mail: admissions@byuh.edu · **CEEB Code:** 4106
Fax: 808-675-3741 · **ACT Code:** 899

This private school, affiliated with the Church of Jesus Christ of Latt Church, was founded in 1955. It has a 60-acre campus.

RATINGS

Admissions Selectivity Rating: 84   **Fire Safety Rating:** 67

STUDENTS AND FACULTY

Enrollment: 2,312. **Student Body:** 56% female, 44% male, 68% out-of-state, 44% international (67 countries represented). Asian 22%, African American 1%, Caucasian 29%, Hispanic 2%, Native American 1%
Retention and Graduation: 57% freshmen return for sophomore year. 25% freshmen graduate within 4 years. 39% freshmen graduate within 6 years. **Faculty:** 122 full-time faculty, 80% hold PhDs, 21% are members of minority groups, 23% are women. 0% of classes are taught by teaching assistants.

ACADEMICS

Degrees: bachelor's. **Classes:** Most classes have 10–19 students. Most lab/discussion sessions have 10–19 students. **Majors with Highest Enrollment:** Information Science/Studies; Intercultural/Multicultural and Diversity Studies; International Business/Trade/Commerce. **Special Study Options:** Accelerated program, cooperative education program, distance learning, English as a Second Language (ESL), exchange student program (domestic), honors program, independent study, internships, student-designed major, teacher certification program. **Honors programs:** The University Honors Program is open to all interested students who feel they are capable of accepting the challenge of an Honors Education. You will have the opportunity to participate in a stimulating class environment with other top students and the best professors. **Disability Services:** Special programs offered to physically disabled students include note-taking services, reader services, tape recorders, tutors.

FACILITIES

Housing: men's dorms, women's dorms, apartments for married students. 90% of campus accessible to physically disabled. **Special Academic Facilities/Equipment:** Museum of Natural History Media Lab **Computers:** 100% of classrooms, 100% of libraries, 100% of dining areas, 100% of student union, 100% of common outdoor areas have wireless network access. Students can register for classes online. Administrative functions (other than registration) can be performed online.

CAMPUS LIFE

Environment: Village. **Activities:** Choral groups, concert band, dance, jazz band, literary magazine, music ensembles, pep band, student government, student newspaper, student-run film society. 52 registered organizations, 3 honor societies. **Athletics (Intercollegiate):** *Men:* basketball, cross-country, golf, soccer, tennis. *Women:* basketball, cross-country, soccer, softball, tennis, volleyball. **On-Campus Highlights:** Joseph F. Smith Library, Cannon Activities Center, The Club Café, The Seasider Snackbar, Aloha Center.

ADMISSIONS

Freshman Academic Profile: Average high school GPA 3.42 SAT Math middle 50% range 480-600. SAT Critical Reading middle 50% range 460-580. ACT middle 50% range 20-27. Minimum paper TOEFL 475. **Basis for Candidate Selection:** *Very important factors considered include:* application essay, recommendation(s), rigor of secondary school record, standardized test scores, character/personal qualities, extracurricular activities, geographical residence, interview, religious affiliation/commitment. *Important factors considered include:* Class rank, alumni/ae relation, talent/ability, volunteer work, work experience. *Other factors considered include:* state residency. **Freshman Admission Requirements:** High school diploma is required and GED is not accepted. **Freshman Admission Statistics:** 1,268 applied, 48% admitted, 49% enrolled. **Transfer Admission Requirements:** college transcript(s), essay or personal statement, statement of good standing from prior institution(s). Minimum college GPA of 3.0 required. Lowest grade transferable C-. **General Admission Information:** Application Fee $30. Regular application deadline 2/15. Regular notification 4/1. Nonfall registration accepted. Admission may be deferred for a maximum of 1 semester. Credit offered for CEEB Advanced Placement tests.

COSTS AND FINANCIAL AID

Annual tuition $3,600. Room and board $5,568. Required fees $0. Average book expense $900. **Required Forms and Deadlines:** FAFSA, Institution's own financial aid form. **Notification of Awards:** Applicants will be notified of awards on or about 6/30. **Types of Aid:** *Need-based scholarships/grants:* Federal Pell, private scholarships, the school's own gift aid. *Loans:* Subsidized Stafford, Unsubsidized Stafford, PLUS, college/university loans from institutional funds. *Student Employment:* Institutional employment available. Highest amount earned per year from on-campus jobs $4,500. Off-campus job opportunities are fair. **Financial Aid Statistics:** 88% freshmen, 64% undergrads receive need-based scholarship or grant aid. 23% freshmen, 41% undergrads receive non-need-based scholarship or grant aid. 70% freshmen, 41% undergrads receive need-based self-help aid. 13% freshmen, 7% undergrads receive athletic scholarships. 70% freshmen, 72% undergrads receive any aid. 36% undergrads borrow to pay for school. Average cumulative indebtedness $12,300. **Criteria for awarding institutional aid:** *Non-need-based:* academics, art, athletics, leadership, music/drama, state/district residency.

BROCK UNIVERSITY

500 Glenridge Avenue, St. Catharines, ON L2S 3A1
Phone: 905-688-5550
E-mail: admissns@brocku.ca
Fax: 905-988-5488 · **Website:** www.brocku.ca

This public school was founded in 1964. It has a 457-acre campus.

RATINGS

Admissions Selectivity Rating: 60*   **Fire Safety Rating:** 77

STUDENTS AND FACULTY

Enrollment: 16,284. **Student Body:** 8% out-of-state, (80 countries represented).
Retention and Graduation: 52% freshmen graduate within 4 years. **Faculty:** 577 full-time faculty, 43% are members of minority groups. 0% of classes are taught by teaching assistants.

ACADEMICS

Degrees: bachelor's, certificate, master's. **Majors with Highest Enrollment:** Education; Health Professions and Related Clinical Sciences; Business/Commerce. **Special Study Options:** cooperative education program, double major, English as a Second Language (ESL), exchange student program (domestic), honors program, internships, liberal arts/career combination, student-designed major, study abroad, teacher certification program, Liberal arts/career combination: Students may choose from 7 Concurrent Education programs, combining their undergraduate degree and Bachelor of Education degree. Combined degree programs: BA/BEd; BSc/BEd; BPHEd/BEd. **Disability Services:** Special programs offered to physically disabled students include note-taking services, reader services, tape recorders, tutors. **Career services:** career/job search classes, internships. Brock offers the third largest selection of Co-op programs in Ontario. A variety of additional experiential learning opportunities are built into virtually all of our programs.

FACILITIES

Housing: Coed dorms, special housing for disabled students, women's dorms, Village Residence and Quarry View Residence (Townhouses). 100% of campus accessible to physically disabled. **Special Academic Facilities/Equipment:** Cool Climate Oenology and Viticulture Institute Map Library Intructional Resource Centre Rodman Hall Arts Centre Cypriote Museum **Computers:** 100% of classrooms, 100% of libraries, 100% of student union, have wireless network access. Students can register for classes online. Administrative functions (other than registration) can be performed online.

CAMPUS LIFE

Environment: City. **Activities:** Choral groups, concert band, dance, drama/theater, literary magazine, music ensembles, musical theater, radio station, student government, student newspaper, student-run film society, symphony orchestra, television station, yearbook, Campus Ministries. 40 registered organizations, 6 religious organizations. **Athletics (Intercollegiate):** *Men:* baseball, basketball, cheerleading, crew/rowing, cross-country, curling, fencing, ice hockey, lacrosse, rugby, soccer, squash, swimming, wrestling. *Women:* basketball, cheerleading, crew/rowing, cross-country, curling, fencing, ice hockey, rugby, soccer, swimming, volleyball, wrestling. **On-Campus Highlights:** Residences, Walker Complex—athletic facility, Computer Commons, Isaacs, Plaza Building. **Environmental Initiatives:** Our newest building earned LEED Silver Certification. The energy cost performance is almost 43 per cent better than the Model National Energy Code. Brock's campus has been designated as a UNESCO Biosphere Reserve.

ADMISSIONS

Freshman Academic Profile: Minimum internet-based TOEFL 88. **Basis for Candidate Selection:** *Very important factors considered include:* academic GPA, rigor of secondary school record. *Important factors considered include:* standardized test scores. *Other factors considered include:* Class rank, recommendation(s), talent/ability. **Freshman Admission Requirements:** High school diploma is required and GED is accepted. **Transfer Admission Requirements:** High school transcript, college transcript(s). **General Admission Information:** Application Fee $155. Regular application deadline 4/1. Notification on a rolling basis, beginning on or about 1/1. Nonfall registration not accepted. Neither credit nor placement offered for CEEB Advanced Placement tests.

COSTS AND FINANCIAL AID

Room and board $8,215. Average book expense $900. **Required Forms and Deadlines:** Institution's own financial aid form. **Types of Aid:** *Need-based scholarships/grants:* the school's own gift aid. *Loans:* Ontario Student Assistance Program. *Student Employment:* Federal Work-Study Program available. Institutional employment available. Off-campus job opportunities are good. **Financial Aid Statistics:** 29% undergrads receive need-based scholarship or grant aid. 0% undergrads receive non-need-based scholarship or grant aid. 0% undergrads receive need-based self-help aid. 0% undergrads receive athletic scholarships. 39% undergrads receive any aid. **Criteria for awarding institutional aid:** *Non-need-based:* academics, athletics, leadership.

BROWN UNIVERSITY

Best 380

Box 1876, Providence, RI 2912
Phone: 401-863-2378 · **Financial Aid Phone:** 401-863-2721
E-mail: admission@brown.edu · **CEEB Code:** 3094
Fax: 401-863-9300 · **Website:** www.brown.edu · **ACT Code:** 3800

This private school was founded in 1764. It has a 146-acre campus.

RATINGS

Admissions Selectivity Rating: 99   **Fire Safety Rating:** 87

STUDENTS AND FACULTY

Enrollment: 6,264. **Student Body:** 51% female, 49% male, 95% out-of-state, 12% international (109 countries represented). Asian 13%, African American 7%, Caucasian 44%, Hispanic 11%, Native American <1%
Retention and Graduation: 98% freshmen return for sophomore year. 84% freshmen graduate within 4 years. 96% freshmen graduate within 6 years. 22% grads go on to further study within 1 year. 11% grads pursue arts and sciences degrees. 2% grads pursue law degrees. 6% grads pursue medical degrees.
Faculty: 871 full-time faculty, 93% hold PhDs, 36% are members of minority groups, 18% are women.

ACADEMICS

Degrees: bachelor's, master's. **Classes:** Most classes have 10–19 students. **Majors with Highest Enrollment:** Economics; Biology/Biological Sciences; History. **Special Study Options:** cross-registration, double major, exchange student program (domestic), honors program, independent study, internships, student-designed major, study abroad, teacher certification program, 8-Year medical program (AB or SCB plus MD) 5-year degree program (AB and SCB). Combined degree programs: BA/MD, BA/MA, BS/MD, BS/MS, BA/BS. **Disability Services:** Special programs offered to physically disabled students include note-taking services, reader services, tape recorders, tutors. **Career services:** Alumni network, career/job search classes, career assessment, internships, regional alumni. Each year, hundreds of Brown students receive funding to pursue independent research, internships, projects, or faculty collaborations to deepen and connect their learning and experience. The Brown Internship Award Program provides funding on a competitive basis for students pursuing unpaid or low-paying summer internships. The program has two components, a living stipend and, for students on financial aid, the opportunity to have their summer earnings requirement waived. The Royce Fellowship is one of several Brown fellowships which invite proposals for summer projects of students' own design. They Royce provides not only a financial award for research projects but ongoing seminars and programs for fellows in the academic year following their award. Each of the fellowships has a particular focus: research, international service, social entrepreneurship, public interest law, sports and human rights, etc. The Undergraduate Teaching and Research Award supports nearly 300 students each year to collaborate with a Brown faculty member on course development or research. More information on these programs can be found at http://www.brown.edu/Administration/Dean_of_the_College/fellowships/.

FACILITIES

Housing: Coed dorms, special housing for disabled students, fraternity/sorority housing, cooperative housing, apartments for single students, Wellness Housing, Theme Housing. **Special Academic Facilities/Equipment:** Art gallery, anthropology museum, language lab, information technology center, NASA research center, center for modern culture/media. **Computers:** 50% of classrooms, 100% of dorms, 100% of libraries, 100% of dining areas, 100% of student union, 50% of common outdoor areas have wireless network access. Students can register for classes online. Administrative functions (other than registration) can be performed online.

CAMPUS LIFE

Environment: City. **Activities:** Choral groups, concert band, dance, drama/theater, jazz band, literary magazine, marching band, music ensembles, musical theater, opera, pep band, radio station, student government, student newspaper, student-run film society, symphony orchestra, television station, yearbook, Campus Ministries, International Student Organization, Model UN. 400 registered organizations, 3 honor societies, 20 religious organizations. 8 fraternities, 2 sororities. **Athletics (Intercollegiate):** *Men:* baseball, basketball, crew/rowing, cross-country, diving, fencing, football, golf, ice hockey, lacrosse, soccer, squash, swimming, tennis, track/field (outdoor), track/field (indoor), water polo, wrestling. *Women:* basketball, crew/rowing, cross-country, diving, equestrian sports, fencing, field hockey, golf, gymnastics, ice hockey, lacrosse, skiing (downhill/alpine), soccer, softball, squash, swimming, tennis, track/field (outdoor), track/field (indoor), volleyball, water polo. **On-Campus Highlights:** The College Green, Bell Gallery, Libraries - Jon Hay, John Carter Brown, Watson Institute, Lyman Hall & Dill Center. **Environmental Initiatives:** Reduce GHG emissions to 42% (15% below 1990) below 2007 for existing buildings by 2020; Reduce GHG emissions for all newly constructed facilities between 25% and 50% below code requirements; Reduce GHG emissions for all newly acquired facilities by a minimum of 15% and as much as 30%.

ADMISSIONS

Freshman Academic Profile: 92% in top 10% of high school class, 98% in top 25% of high school class, 100% in top 50% of high school class. 59% from public high schools. SAT Math middle 50% range 670-780. SAT Critical Reading middle 50% range 660-770. SAT Writing middle 50% range 670-780. ACT middle 50% range 30-34. Minimum internet-based TOEFL 100. Minimum paper TOEFL 600. **Basis for Candidate Selection:** *Very important factors considered include:* rigor of secondary school record, character/personal qualities, level of applicant's interest, talent/ability. *Important factors considered include:* Class rank, application essay, academic GPA, recommendation(s), standardized test scores, extracurricular activities. *Other factors considered include:* alumni/ae relation, first generation, geographical residence, interview, racial/ethnic status, state residency, volunteer work, work experience. **Freshman Admission Requirements:** High school diploma is required and GED is not accepted. *Academic units required:* 4 English, 3 mathematics, 3 science, (2 science labs), 3 foreign language, 0 social studies, 2 history, 0 visual/performing arts, 0 computer science, 1 academic electives. **Freshman Admission Statistics:** 30,431 applied, 9% admitted, 59% enrolled. **Transfer Admission Requirements:** High school transcript, college transcript(s), essay or personal statement, standardized test scores, statement of good standing from prior institution(s). Lowest grade transferable C. **General Admission Information:** Application Fee $75. Early decision application deadline 11/1. Regular application deadline 1/1. Regular notification 4/1. Nonfall registration not accepted. Admission may be deferred for a maximum of 1 year. Placement offered for CEEB Advanced Placement tests.

COSTS AND FINANCIAL AID

Annual tuition $46,408. Room and board $11,994. Required fees $1,026. Average book expense $1,420. **Required Forms and Deadlines:** FAFSA, CSS/Financial Aid PROFILE, Noncustodial PROFILE. **Notification of Awards:** Applicants will be notified of awards on or about 4/1. **Types of Aid:** *Need-based scholarships/grants:* Federal Pell, SEOG, state scholarships/grants, private scholarships, the school's own gift aid. *Loans:* Direct Subsidized Stafford, Direct Unsubsidized Stafford, Direct PLUS, Federal Perkins, college/university loans from institutional funds. *Student Employment:* Federal Work-Study Program available. Institutional employment available. Off-campus job opportunities are excellent. **Financial Aid Statistics:** 96% freshmen, 99% undergrads receive need-based scholarship or grant aid. 0% freshmen, 0% undergrads receive non-need-based scholarship or grant aid. 84% freshmen, 89% undergrads receive need-based self-help aid. 0% freshmen, 0% undergrads receive athletic scholarships. 65% freshmen, 57% undergrads receive any aid. 35% undergrads borrow to pay for school. Average cumulative indebtedness $19,758.

BRYAN COLLEGE

Bryan College Office of Admissions, Dayton, TN 37321
Phone: 423-775-7158 • **Financial Aid Phone:** 423-775-7339
E-mail: admissions@bryan.edu • **CEEB Code:** 1908
Fax: 423-775-7199 • **Website:** www.bryan.edu • **ACT Code:** 4038

This private school was founded in 1930. It has a 125-acre campus.

RATINGS

Admissions Selectivity Rating: 87   **Fire Safety Rating:** 96

STUDENTS AND FACULTY

Enrollment: 605. **Student Body:** 53% female, 47% male, 66% out-of-state, 5% international (22 countries represented). Asian 0%, African American 3%, Caucasian 87%, Hispanic 3%, Native American <1%
Retention and Graduation: 60% freshmen return for sophomore year. 45% freshmen graduate within 4 years. 54% freshmen graduate within 6 years. **Faculty:** 36 full-time faculty, 64% hold PhDs, 28% are members of minority groups. 0% of classes are taught by teaching assistants.

ACADEMICS

Degrees: associate, bachelor's, master's. **Classes:** Most classes have 10–19 students. **Majors with Highest Enrollment:** Business Administration and Management; Health and Physical Education/Fitness; Communication, Journalism, and Related Programs. **Special Study Options:** distance learning, dual enrollment, honors program, independent study, internships, study abroad. **Disability Services:** Special programs offered to physically disabled students include note-taking services, reader services, tape recorders, tutors. **Career services:** Alumni network, alumni services, career/job search classes, career assessment, internships.

FACILITIES

Housing: men's dorms, women's dorms, apartments for married students, apartments for single students. **Special Academic Facilities/Equipment:** Willard Henning Natural History Museum **Computers:** 100% of classrooms, 100% of dorms, 100% of libraries, 100% of dining areas, 100% of student union, 80% of common outdoor areas have wireless network access. Administrative functions (other than registration) can be performed online.

CAMPUS LIFE

Environment: Town. **Activities:** Choral groups, drama/theater, musical theater, radio station, student government, student newspaper, yearbook, Campus Ministries. **Athletics (Intercollegiate):** *Men:* baseball, basketball, cross-country, golf, soccer, track/field (outdoor), track/field (indoor). *Women:* basketball, cross-country, golf, soccer, softball, track/field (outdoor), track/field (indoor).

On-Campus Highlights: Student Center, Library, The "Grassy Bowl", The Commons.

ADMISSIONS

Freshman Academic Profile: Average high school GPA 3.55. 16% in top 10% of high school class, 48% in top 25% of high school class, 76% in top 50% of high school class. 55% from public high schools. SAT Math middle 50% range 450-580. SAT Critical Reading middle 50% range 450-600. SAT Writing middle 50% range 440-590. ACT middle 50% range 20-26. Minimum internet-based TOEFL 75. **Basis for Candidate Selection:** *Very important factors considered include:* application essay, academic GPA, rigor of secondary school record, standardized test scores. *Important factors considered include:* character/personal qualities, level of applicant's interest, religious affiliation/commitment. *Other factors considered include:* Class rank, recommendation(s), alumni/ae relation, extracurricular activities, interview, talent/ability, volunteer work. **Freshman Admission Requirements:** High school diploma is required and GED is accepted. *Academic units required:* 4 English, 3 mathematics, 3 science, 2 foreign language, 3 social studies. **Freshman Admission Statistics:** 760 applied, 48% admitted, 50% enrolled. **Transfer Admission Requirements:** college transcript(s), essay or personal statement, standardized test scores, Minimum college GPA of 2.75 required. Lowest grade transferable 2. **General Admission Information:** Application Fee $35. Nonfall registration accepted. Credit offered for CEEB Advanced Placement tests.

COSTS AND FINANCIAL AID

Annual tuition $22,200. Room and board $6,550. Average book expense $1,250. **Required Forms and Deadlines:** FAFSA. **Notification of Awards:** Applicants will be notified of awards on a rolling basis beginning 2/15. **Types of Aid:** *Need-based scholarships/grants:* Federal Pell, SEOG, state scholarships/grants, private scholarships, the school's own gift aid. *Loans:* Direct Subsidized Stafford, Direct Unsubsidized Stafford, Direct PLUS, Subsidized Stafford, Unsubsidized Stafford, PLUS, Federal Perkins, college/university loans from institutional funds. *Student Employment:* Federal Work-Study Program available. Institutional employment available. Off-campus job opportunities are fair. **Financial Aid Statistics:** 0% freshmen, 2% undergrads receive athletic scholarships. 100% freshmen, 98% undergrads receive any aid. 96% undergrads borrow to pay for school. Average cumulative indebtedness $11,935. **Criteria for awarding institutional aid:** *Non-need-based:* academics, alumni affiliation, athletics, leadership, minority status, music/drama, state/district residency.

BRYANT UNIVERSITY

Office of Admission; 1150 Douglas Pike, Smithfield, RI 02917-1291
Phone: 401-232-6000 • **Financial Aid Phone:** 401-232-6020
E-mail: admission@bryant.edu • **CEEB Code:** 3095
Fax: 401-232-6731 • **Website:** www.bryant.edu • **ACT Code:** 3802

This private school was founded in 1863. It has a 420-acre campus.

RATINGS

Admissions Selectivity Rating: 84   **Fire Safety Rating:** 94

STUDENTS AND FACULTY

Enrollment: 3,263. **Student Body:** 41% female, 59% male, 87% out-of-state, 7% international (72 countries represented). Asian 4%, African American 4%, Caucasian 74%, Hispanic 6%, Native American <1%
Retention and Graduation: 90% freshmen return for sophomore year. 78% freshmen graduate within 4 years. 23% grads go on to further study within 1 year. 2% grads pursue arts and sciences degrees. 2% grads pursue law degrees. 17% grads pursue business degrees. **Faculty:** 165 full-time faculty, 81% hold PhDs, 41% are members of minority groups, 18% are women. 0% of classes are taught by teaching assistants.

ACADEMICS

Degrees: bachelor's, master's. **Classes:** Most classes have 30-39 students. Most lab/discussion sessions have fewer than 10 students. **Majors with Highest Enrollment:** Finance; Accounting; Marketing/Marketing Management. **Special Study Options:** double major, English as a Second Language (ESL), honors program, independent study, internships, study abroad. **Honors programs:** The Bryant University Honors Program offers its members a personalized, distinctive experience that enriches their academic, social, cultural and professional talents in a mentor-oriented environment. The Program offers its members a different experience to develop the unique talents of exceptionally prepared and focused individuals. Designated courses in the Honors Program are organized to encourage in-depth classroom discussions and application of business and liberal arts disciplines with reduced class sizes. **Disability Services:** Special programs offered to physically disabled students include note-taking services, tape recorders, tutors. **Career services:** Alumni network, alumni services, career/job search classes, career assessment, internships, regional alumni. In 2008, 343 companies participated in the Corporate Recruiting Program.

FACILITIES

Housing: Coed dorms, special housing for disabled students, women's dorms, apartments for single students, Honors, International Business. 90% of campus accessible to physically disabled. **Special Academic Facilities/Equipment:** George E. Bello Center for Information and Technology, Koffler Technology Center and Communications Complex, John H. Chafee Center for International Business, Koffler Television Studio, C.V. Starr Financial Markets Center, Learning and Language Lab. **Computers:** 100% of classrooms, 100% of dorms, 100% of libraries, 100% of dining areas, 100% of student union, 100% of common outdoor areas have wireless network access. Students can register for classes online. Administrative functions (other than registration) can be performed online. Undergraduates are required to own a computer.

CAMPUS LIFE

Environment: Village. **Activities:** Choral groups, dance, drama/theater, jazz band, literary magazine, music ensembles, musical theater, pep band, radio station, student government, student newspaper, television station, yearbook, Campus Ministries, International Student Organization. 87 registered organizations, 6 honor societies, 5 religious organizations. 6 fraternities, 2 sororities. **Athletics (Intercollegiate):** *Men:* baseball, basketball, cross-country, football, golf, lacrosse, soccer, swimming, tennis, track/field (outdoor), track/field (indoor). *Women:* basketball, cross-country, field hockey, lacrosse, soccer, softball, swimming, tennis, track/field (outdoor), track/field (indoor), volleyball. **On-Campus Highlights:** Bello Center for Information andTechnolo, Chase Athletics and Wellness Center, Unistructure Rotunda, Koffler Technology and Communications Co, Bryant Center, The Bello Center for Information & Technology houses the Douglas & Judith Krupp Library, the Stepan Grand Hall, and the C.V. Starr Financial Markets Center (FMC) featuring real-time stock market data and Reuters 3000. The Wellness Center features a fitness center modeled after private health clubs and a six-lane, 25-yard swimming pool. The Bryant Center houses offices for student organizations around campus including The Archway, the student newspaper, as well as dining options including Subway, South Side Deli, the Scoop, South Café, and the Sky Ranch Grill. The Rotunda is a hub of student activity located in the main classroom building, the Unistructure. The Communication Complex houses the all-digital television studio and radio station, WJMF, as well as advanced multimedia editing rooms for use with AVID software. WJMF streams live over the internet and offers podcasts on its website, http://www.wjmf887.com. **Environmental Initiatives:** Recycling Program; Green Data Center; Purchasing renewable energy credits.

ADMISSIONS

Freshman Academic Profile: Average high school GPA 3.32. 18% in top 10% of high school class, 50% in top 25% of high school class, 88% in top 50% of high school class. 69% from public high schools. SAT Math middle 50% range 540-630. SAT Critical Reading middle 50% range 510-590. SAT Writing middle 50% range 500-590. ACT middle 50% range 23-27. Minimum internet-based TOEFL 80. Minimum paper TOEFL 550. **Basis for Candidate Selection:** *Very important factors considered include:* academic GPA, rigor of secondary school record. *Important factors considered include:* Class rank, application essay, recommendation(s), standardized test scores. *Other factors considered include:* alumni/ae relation, character/personal qualities, extracurricular activities, first generation, geographical residence, interview, level of applicant's interest, racial/ethnic status, state residency, talent/ability, volunteer work, work experience. **Freshman Admission Requirements:** High school diploma is required and GED is accepted. *Academic units required:* 4 English, 4 mathematics, 2 science, (2 science labs), 2 foreign language, 2 history. **Freshman Admission Statistics:** 6,013 applied, 77% admitted, 19% enrolled. **Transfer Admission Requirements:** High school transcript, college transcript(s), essay or personal statement, Minimum college GPA of 2.5 required. Lowest grade transferable C. **General Admission Information:** Application Fee $50. Early decision application deadline 11/16. Regular application deadline 2/1. Regular notification 3/21. Nonfall registration accepted. Admission may be deferred for a maximum of 1 year. Credit and/or placement offered for CEEB Advanced Placement tests.

COSTS AND FINANCIAL AID

Annual tuition $38,199. Room and board $14,102. Required fees $375. Average book expense $1,300. **Required Forms and Deadlines:** FAFSA. **Notification of Awards:** Applicants will be notified of awards on or about 3/24. **Types of Aid:** *Need-based scholarships/grants:* Federal Pell, SEOG, state scholarships/grants, private scholarships, the school's own gift aid. *Loans:* Direct Subsidized Stafford, Direct Unsubsidized Stafford, PLUS, Federal Perkins, privately funded education loans. *Student Employment:* Federal Work-Study Program

available. Institutional employment available. Highest amount earned per year from on-campus jobs $7,378. Off-campus job opportunities are fair. **Financial Aid Statistics:** 76% freshmen, 82% undergrads receive need-based scholarship or grant aid. 73% freshmen, 59% undergrads receive non-need-based scholarship or grant aid. 83% freshmen, 86% undergrads receive need-based self-help aid. 4% freshmen, 4% undergrads receive athletic scholarships. 79% freshmen, 87% undergrads receive any aid. 81% undergrads borrow to pay for school. Average cumulative indebtedness $27,418. **Criteria for awarding institutional aid:** *Non-need-based:* academics, athletics, minority status.

See page 1016.

BRYN ATHYN COLLEGE OF THE NEW CHURCH

P.O. Box 462, Bryn Athyn, PA 19009
Phone: 267-502-6000 · **Financial Aid Phone:** 267-502-2493
E-mail: admissions@brynathyn.edu · **CEEB Code:** 2002
Fax: 267-502-2593 · **Website:** www.brynathyn.edu · **ACT Code:** 3228

This private school was founded in 1877. It has a 130-acre campus.

RATINGS

Admissions Selectivity Rating: 82   **Fire Safety Rating:** 79

STUDENTS AND FACULTY

Enrollment: 271. **Student Body:** 51% female, 49% male, 41% out-of-state, 6% international (12 countries represented). Asian 1%, African American 20%, Caucasian 64%, Hispanic 7%, Native American <1% **Retention and Graduation:** 76% freshmen return for sophomore year. 45% freshmen graduate within 4 years. **Faculty:** 30 full-time faculty, 57% hold PhDs, 43% are members of minority groups, 7% are women. 0% of classes are taught by teaching assistants.

ACADEMICS

Degrees: associate, bachelor's, master's. **Classes:** Most classes have 10–19 students. **Majors with Highest Enrollment:** Multi-/Interdisciplinary Studies; English Language and Literature; History. **Special Study Options:** Accelerated program, cooperative education program, cross-registration, distance learning, English as a Second Language (ESL), independent study, internships, student-designed major, study abroad, teacher certification program. **Disability Services:** Special programs offered to physically disabled students include tape recorders, tutors. **Career services:** Alumni network, internships. Internships at Bryn Athyn College are developed on an individual basis, and occur in places around the world. Opportunities can be arranged as early as the first year, founded on the belief that this applied learning can help new first-year students chart their academic programs of study.

FACILITIES

Housing: men's dorms, women's dorms, On-campus cottages for upperclassmen. 65% of campus accessible to physically disabled. **Special Academic Facilities/Equipment:** Glencairn Museum, Swedenborg Library, Swedenborgiana Academy of the New Church. Archives: John Pitcairn Archives, Raymond and Mildred Pitcairn Archives. **Computers:** 100% of classrooms, 100% of dorms, 100% of libraries, 75% of common outdoor areas have wireless network access.

CAMPUS LIFE

Environment: Village. **Activities:** Choral groups, concert band, dance, drama/theater, music ensembles, student government, student newspaper, International Student Organization. 15 registered organizations. **On-Campus Highlights:** College Grounds Café, Swedenborg Library, Brickman Center for Student Life, Asplundh Field House, Glencairn Museum. **Environmental Initiatives:** Chemical purchase, storage and disposal plan, Recycling program for glass and paper in all buildings. LEED certified construction. Bryn Athyn College Garden, and recycled bike program

ADMISSIONS

Freshman Academic Profile: Average high school GPA 3.06. SAT Math middle 50% range 390-510. SAT Critical Reading middle 50% range 390-500. SAT Writing middle 50% range 380-480. ACT middle 50% range 15-24. Minimum internet-based TOEFL 70. Minimum paper TOEFL 520. **Basis for Candidate Selection:** *Very important factors considered include:* application essay, academic GPA, recommendation(s), rigor of secondary school record, standardized test scores, level of applicant's interest. *Important factors considered include:* character/personal qualities, religious affiliation/commitment, talent/ability. *Other factors considered include:* Class rank, alumni/ae relation, extracurricular activities, interview, volunteer work, work experience. **Freshman Admission Requirements:** High school diploma is required and GED is accepted. *Aca-*

demic units required: 4 English, 3 mathematics, 3 science, 2 foreign language, 3 Social Studies or History. **Freshman Admission Statistics:** 374 applied, 58% admitted, 48% enrolled. **Transfer Admission Requirements:** High school transcript, college transcript(s), essay or personal statement, Minimum college GPA of 2.0 required. Lowest grade transferable C. **General Admission Information:** Regular application deadline 7/1. Notification on a rolling basis, beginning on or about 12/1. Nonfall registration accepted. Credit and/or placement offered for CEEB Advanced Placement tests.

COSTS AND FINANCIAL AID

Annual tuition $17,235. Room and board $10,773. Required fees $1,284. Average book expense $750. **Required Forms and Deadlines:** FAFSA, State aid form. **Notification of Awards:** Applicants will be notified of awards on a rolling basis beginning 4/1. **Types of Aid:** *Need-based scholarships/grants:* Federal Pell, SEOG, state scholarships/grants, private scholarships, the school's own gift aid. *Loans:* Direct Subsidized Stafford, Direct Unsubsidized Stafford, Direct PLUS, Subsidized Stafford, Unsubsidized Stafford, PLUS, college/university loans from institutional funds. *Student Employment:* Institutional employment available. Highest amount earned per year from on-campus jobs $13,780. Off-campus job opportunities are good. **Financial Aid Statistics:** 89% freshmen, 87% undergrads receive need-based scholarship or grant aid. 32% freshmen, 43% undergrads receive non-need-based scholarship or grant aid. 92% freshmen, 87% undergrads receive need-based self-help aid. 0% freshmen, 0% undergrads receive athletic scholarships. 71% freshmen, 65% undergrads receive any aid. 59% undergrads borrow to pay for school. Average cumulative indebtedness $19,032. **Criteria for awarding institutional aid:** *Non-need-based:* academics, leadership, religious affiliation.

BRYN MAWR COLLEGE

Best 380

101 North Merion Avenue, Bryn Mawr, PA 19010-2859
Phone: 610-526-5152 · **Financial Aid Phone:** 610-526-5245
E-mail: admissions@brynmawr.edu · **CEEB Code:** 2049
Fax: 610-526-7471 · **Website:** www.brynmawr.edu · **ACT Code:** 3526

This private school was founded in 1885. It has a 135-acre campus.

RATINGS

Admissions Selectivity Rating: 94   Fire Safety Rating: 77

STUDENTS AND FACULTY

Enrollment: 1,303. **Student Body:** 100% female, 0% male, 81% out-of-state, 24% international (57 countries represented). Asian 12%, African American 5%, Caucasian 36%, Hispanic 9%, Native American <1%
Retention and Graduation: 91% freshmen return for sophomore year. 76% freshmen graduate within 4 years. 14% grads go on to further study within 1 year. 7% grads pursue arts and sciences degrees. 2% grads pursue law degrees. 1% grads pursue medical degrees. **Faculty:** 149 full-time faculty, 97% hold PhDs, 53% are members of minority groups, 18% are women. 0% of classes are taught by teaching assistants.

ACADEMICS

Degrees: bachelor's, master's, post-bachelor's certificate. **Classes:** Most classes have 10–19 students. **Majors with Highest Enrollment:** Mathematics; English Language and Literature; Psychology. **Special Study Options:** Accelerated program, cross-registration, double major, dual enrollment, exchange student program (domestic), independent study, internships, liberal arts/career combination, student-designed major, study abroad, teacher certification program, A.B./M.A. City Planning 3-2 Program in City and Regional Planning offered with the University of Pennsylvania. A.B./B.S. 3-2 engineering programs with Cal Tech. Combined degree programs: BA/MA, 3-2 progam in city planning w/U Penn. **Disability Services:** Special programs offered to physically disabled students include note-taking services, reader services, tape recorders, tutors. **Career services:** Alumni network, alumni services, career/job search classes, career assessment, internships, regional alumni. Career services highlights include Praxis I for 3 hours per week, Praxis II for 6-8 hours per week and Praxis III as a supervised independent study involving 10-12 hours per week in the field. These are courses for full credit.

FACILITIES

Housing: Coed dorms, women's dorms, cooperative housing, apartments for single students, Students may live at Haverford. Foreign language houses available to students studying Chinese, French, German, Hebrew, Italian, Russsian or Spanish. Coed housing is available. Special housing available for non-traditional-aged students. Co-ops, such as Vegan House, are available as well. **Special Academic Facilities/Equipment:** Museum of classical and Near Eastern archaeology, mineral collection, Child Study Institute, on-campus nursery school, Newfeld Collection of African Art, Language Learning Center. **Computers:** 60% of classrooms, 10% of dorms, 25% of libraries, 10% of dining areas, 100% of student union, 10% of common outdoor areas have wireless network access. Students can register for classes online. Administrative functions (other than registration) can be performed online.

CAMPUS LIFE

Environment: Metropolis. **Activities:** Choral groups, dance, drama/theater, jazz band, literary magazine, marching band, music ensembles, musical theater, radio station, student government, student newspaper, student-run film society, yearbook. 94 registered organizations, 10 religious organizations. **Athletics (Intercollegiate):** *Women:* badminton, basketball, crew/rowing, cross-country, field hockey, lacrosse, soccer, swimming, tennis, track/field (outdoor), track/field (indoor), volleyball. **On-Campus Highlights:** Thomas Hall (on National Historic Landma, Erdman Hall (designed by famed architect, The Cloister and Great Hall, Taft Garden, Rhys Carpenter Library, Goodhart Theater. **Environmental Initiatives:** We have received two Pennsylvania Growing Greener Grants for watershed improvements under the Environmental improvement and Watershed Protection Act. We are committed to being good steward's of the waterway that pass through our campus. We currently removing all incandescent light bulbs from Campus. We are committed to reducing our consumption of electricity through the use of technology. All capital projects are required to be designed using the appropriate LEED checklist archiving a minimum of 26 points. We are committed to designing sustainability into the renovations of our buildings.

ADMISSIONS

Freshman Academic Profile: 65% in top 10% of high school class, 88% in top 25% of high school class, 99% in top 50% of high school class. 62% from public high schools. SAT Math middle 50% range 600-730. SAT Critical Reading middle 50% range 600-710. SAT Writing middle 50% range 630-720. ACT middle 50% range 27-32. Minimum internet-based TOEFL 100. Minimum paper TOEFL 600. **Basis for Candidate Selection:** *Very important factors considered include:* recommendation(s), rigor of secondary school record. *Important factors considered include:* application essay, academic GPA, character/personal qualities, extracurricular activities. *Other factors considered include:* Class rank, standardized test scores, alumni/ae relation, first generation, geographical residence, interview, racial/ethnic status, talent/ability, volunteer work, work experience. **Freshman Admission Requirements:** High school diploma is required and GED is accepted. *Academic units required:* 2 academic electives. **Freshman Admission Statistics:** 2,706 applied, 40% admitted, 32% enrolled. **Transfer Admission Requirements:** High school transcript, college transcript(s), essay or personal statement, standardized test scores, statement of good standing from prior institution(s). Lowest grade transferable C. **General Admission Information:** Application Fee $50. Early decision application deadline 11/15. Regular application deadline 1/15. Regular notification 4/1. Nonfall registration not accepted. Admission may be deferred for a maximum of 12 months. Credit and/or placement offered for CEEB Advanced Placement tests.

COSTS AND FINANCIAL AID

Annual tuition $46,030. Room and board $14,850. Required fees $1,110. Average book expense $1,000. **Required Forms and Deadlines:** FAFSA, CSS/Financial Aid PROFILE. **Notification of Awards:** Applicants will be notified of awards on or about 3/23. **Types of Aid:** *Need-based scholarships/grants:* Federal Pell, SEOG, state scholarships/grants, the school's own gift aid, Federal Academic Competitiveness Grant (ACG), Federal National Science and Mathematics to Retain Talent Grant (SMART). *Loans:* Subsidized Stafford, Unsubsidized Stafford, PLUS, Federal Perkins. *Student Employment:* Highest amount earned per year from on-campus jobs $2,000. **Financial Aid Statistics:** 100% freshmen, 98% undergrads receive need-based scholarship or grant aid. 7% freshmen, 4% undergrads receive non-need-based scholarship or grant aid. 93% freshmen, 94% undergrads receive need-based self-help aid. 0% freshmen, 0% undergrads receive athletic scholarships. 75% freshmen, 75% undergrads receive any aid. 64% undergrads borrow to pay for school. Average cumulative indebtedness $24,956. **Criteria for awarding institutional aid:** *Non-need-based:* academics, leadership.

BUCKNELL UNIVERSITY

Office of Admissions, 1 Dent Drive, Lewisburg, PA 17837
Phone: 570-577-3000 · **Financial Aid Phone:** 570-577-1331
E-mail: admissions@bucknell.edu · **CEEB Code:** 2050
Fax: 570-577-3538 · **Website:** www.bucknell.edu · **ACT Code:** 3528

This private school was founded in 1846. It has a 446-acre campus.

RATINGS
Admissions Selectivity Rating: 96   **Fire Safety Rating:** 89

STUDENTS AND FACULTY
Enrollment: 3,528. **Student Body:** 52% female, 48% male, 77% out-of-state, 5% international (45 countries represented). Asian 4%, African American 3%, Caucasian 79%, Hispanic 5%, Native American <1%
Retention and Graduation: 93% freshmen return for sophomore year. 85% freshmen graduate within 4 years. 21% grads go on to further study within 1 year. 7% grads pursue arts and sciences degrees. 1% grads pursue law degrees. 1% grads pursue business degrees. 5% grads pursue medical degrees. **Faculty:** 372 full-time faculty, 97% hold PhDs, 41% are members of minority groups, 15% are women. 0% of classes are taught by teaching assistants.

ACADEMICS
Degrees: bachelor's, master's. **Classes:** Most classes have 10–19 students. Most lab/discussion sessions have 10–19 students. **Majors with Highest Enrollment:** Economics; Biology; Marketing/Marketing Management. **Special Study Options:** double major, dual enrollment, honors program, independent study, internships, liberal arts/career combination, student-designed major, study abroad, teacher certification program. Combined degree programs: BS/MS 5-yr. program in biology, chem, math, eng. **Disability Services:** Special programs offered to physically disabled students include tape recorders, tutors. **Career services:** Alumni network, alumni services, career/job search classes, career assessment, internships, regional alumni. Career services highlights include Bucknell's Institute for Leadership in Technology and Management (ILTM), founded in 1993 to offer Bucknell students a unique learning experience that bridges the disciplines of engineering and management. Consisting of a two-summer sequence of programs, the ILTM brings together in the first summer 18 of the best and most highly motivated rising juniors in engineering and management to engage in an extremely intensive, six-week, on-campus program that focuses on globalization, ethics, communication skills, critical thinking, teamwork, and leadership.

FACILITIES
Housing: Coed dorms, special housing for disabled students, men's dorms, special housing for international students, women's dorms, fraternity/sorority housing, cooperative housing, apartments for single students, Wellness Housing, Theme Housing. 70% of campus accessible to physically disabled. **Special Academic Facilities/Equipment:** Art gallery, center for performing arts, poetry center, photography lab, observatory, 63-acre nature site, greenhouse, primate facility, gas chromatograph/mass spectrometer, electron microscope, herbarium, crafts center, engineering structural test lab, nuclear magnetic resonance spectrometer, 18-hole golf course, conference center, high ropes course **Computers:** 100% of classrooms, 100% of dorms, 100% of libraries, 100% of dining areas, 100% of student union, 95% of common outdoor areas have wireless network access. Students can register for classes online. Administrative functions (other than registration) can be performed online.

CAMPUS LIFE
Environment: Village. **Activities:** Choral groups, concert band, dance, drama/theater, jazz band, literary magazine, music ensembles, musical theater, opera, pep band, radio station, student government, student newspaper, student-run film society, symphony orchestra, yearbook, Campus Ministries, International Student Organization, Model UN. 150 registered organizations, 23 honor societies, 13 religious organizations. 12 fraternities, 8 sororities. **Athletics (Intercollegiate):** *Men:* baseball, basketball, cross-country, diving, football, golf, lacrosse, soccer, swimming, tennis, track/field (outdoor), track/field (indoor), water polo, wrestling. *Women:* basketball, crew/rowing, cross-country, diving, field hockey, golf, lacrosse, soccer, softball, swimming, tennis, track/field (outdoor), track/field (indoor), volleyball, water polo. **On-Campus Highlights:** Weis Center for the Performing Arts, Outdoor Primate Facilities, Uptown Night Club, Stadler Poetry Center, Library with Technology and Media Commons, Bertrand Library, Seventh Street Café, Elaine Langone Center (student center), Bucknell Observatory, Environmental Center, Samek Art Gallery. **Environmental Initiatives:** In May 2009, the Bucknell University Environmental Center (BUEC) completed a campus-wide environmental assessment of the university's operations, involving over 70 faculty, students, staff, and community members in a highly educational and collaborative project. Teams conducted research on ten indicators of sustainability, including administration/policy, education, energy, water, solid waste, hazardous materials, purchasing, dining, built environment, and landscape. The full report is available at http:www.bucknell.edu/x45647.xml. Environmental Connections Requirement: In 2009 the faculty overwhelmingly passed an ammendment to the curriculum that requires all Arts and Sciences students to complete an environmental course before graduating. Energy conservation initiatives: In 1998 Bucknell University transitioned from a conventional coal-burning power plant to a highly efficient co-generation power plant fueled by cleaner-burning natural gas. The new power plant has allowed Bucknell to reduce its greenhouse gas emissions by 40% compared to pre-1998 levels, a fact that was established through the completion of the universitys first greenhouse gas inventory in 2006. In 2011 Bucknell hired a full-time energy manager dedicated to indentifying and implementing energy conservation measures on campus.

ADMISSIONS
Freshman Academic Profile: Average high school GPA 3.56. 68% in top 10% of high school class, 91% in top 25% of high school class, 99% in top 50% of high school class. 63% from public high schools. SAT Math middle 50% range 620-720. SAT Critical Reading middle 50% range 590-680. SAT Writing middle 50% range 610-700. ACT middle 50% range 28-32. Minimum internet-based TOEFL 100. Minimum paper TOEFL 600. **Basis for Candidate Selection:** *Very important factors considered include:* Class rank, application essay, academic GPA, rigor of secondary school record, standardized test scores, character/personal qualities, talent/ability. *Important factors considered include:* recommendation(s), extracurricular activities, level of applicant's interest, volunteer work, work experience. *Other factors considered include:* alumni/ae relation, first generation, geographical residence, racial/ethnic status, religious affiliation/commitment. **Freshman Admission Requirements:** High school diploma is required and GED is accepted. *Academic units required:* 4 English, 3 mathematics, 2 science, 2 foreign language, 2 social studies, 2 history, 1 academic electives. **Freshman Admission Statistics:** 7,864 applied, 31% admitted, 39% enrolled. **Transfer Admission Requirements:** High school transcript, college transcript(s), essay or personal statement, standardized test scores, statement of good standing from prior institution(s). Minimum college GPA of 2.5 required. Lowest grade transferable C. **General Admission Information:** Application Fee $60. Early decision application deadline 11/15. Regular application deadline 1/15. Regular notification 4/1. Nonfall registration not accepted. Admission may be deferred for a maximum of 2 years. Credit and/or placement offered for CEEB Advanced Placement tests.

COSTS AND FINANCIAL AID
Annual tuition $48,234. Room and board $11,642. Required fees $264. Average book expense $900. **Required Forms and Deadlines:** FAFSA, CSS/Financial Aid PROFILE, Noncustodial PROFILE. **Notification of Awards:** Applicants will be notified of awards on or about 4/1. **Types of Aid:** *Need-based scholarships/grants:* Federal Pell, SEOG, state scholarships/grants, private scholarships, the school's own gift aid, Federal ACG Grant, Federal SMART. *Loans:* Subsidized Stafford, Unsubsidized Stafford, PLUS, Federal Perkins. *Student Employment:* Federal Work-Study Program available. Institutional employment available. Highest amount earned per year from on-campus jobs $1,500. Off-campus job opportunities are poor. **Financial Aid Statistics:** 94% freshmen, 94% undergrads receive need-based scholarship or grant aid. 27% freshmen, 19% undergrads receive non-need-based scholarship or grant aid. 100% freshmen, 100% undergrads receive need-based self-help aid. 3% freshmen, 3% undergrads receive athletic scholarships. 62% freshmen, 61% undergrads receive any aid. 55% undergrads borrow to pay for school. Average cumulative indebtedness $22,500. **Criteria for awarding institutional aid:** *Non-need-based:* academics, art, athletics, leadership, music/drama.

See page 1018.

BUENA VISTA UNIVERSITY

610 West Fourth Street, Storm Lake, IA 50588-1798
Phone: 712-749-2235 · **Financial Aid Phone:** 712-749-2164
E-mail: admissions@bvu.edu · **CEEB Code:** 6047
Fax: 712-749-1459 · **Website:** www.bvu.edu · **ACT Code:** 1278

This private school, affiliated with the Presbyterian Church, was founded in 1891. It has a 60-acre campus.

RATINGS
Admissions Selectivity Rating: 83   **Fire Safety Rating:** 62

STUDENTS AND FACULTY

Enrollment: 837. **Student Body:** 51% female, 49% male, 23% out-of-state, 6% international (11 countries represented). Asian 3%, African American 2%, Caucasian 76%, Hispanic 8%, Native American <1%

Retention and Graduation: 73% freshmen return for sophomore year. 35% freshmen graduate within 4 years. 46% freshmen graduate within 6 years. 29% grads go on to further study within 1 year. **Faculty:** 84 full-time faculty, 74% hold PhDs, 46% are members of minority groups, 12% are women. 0% of classes are taught by teaching assistants.

ACADEMICS

Degrees: bachelor's, master's. **Classes:** Most classes have 10–19 students. Most lab/discussion sessions have 10–19 students. **Majors with Highest Enrollment:** Elementary Education and Teaching; Biology/Biological Sciences; Management Science. **Special Study Options:** distance learning, double major, dual enrollment, English as a Second Language (ESL), external degree program, honors program, independent study, internships, student-designed major, study abroad, teacher certification program, **Off-Campus Study:** Other semester-away programs available. Academic and cultural events series brings national and world leaders and performers to campus; students earn credits for attendance. Combined degree programs: BA/MEng. **Disability Services:** Special programs offered to physically disabled students include note-taking services, reader services, tape recorders, tutors. **Career services:** Alumni network, alumni services, career/job search classes, career assessment, internships.

FACILITIES

Housing: Coed dorms, men's dorms, women's dorms **Special Academic Facilities/Equipment:** Art gallery, language lab, television station, radio station, satellite telecommunications system, computer labs/centers, electron microscope. **Computers:** 100% of classrooms, 100% of dorms, 100% of libraries, 100% of dining areas, 100% of common outdoor areas have wireless network access. Students can register for classes online. Administrative functions (other than registration) can be performed online.

CAMPUS LIFE

Environment: Village. **Activities:** Choral groups, concert band, dance, drama/theater, jazz band, music ensembles, musical theater, pep band, radio station, student government, student newspaper, television station, Campus Ministries, International Student Organization. 65 registered organizations, 5 honor societies, 3 religious organizations. **Athletics (Intercollegiate):** *Men:* baseball, basketball, cross-country, football, golf, soccer, tennis, track/field (outdoor), track/field (indoor), wrestling. *Women:* basketball, cross-country, golf, soccer, softball, tennis, track/field (outdoor), track/field (indoor), volleyball. **On-Campus Highlights:** Recreation Center, Harold Walter Siebens Forum, Centennial Room, a Suites are the biggest dorms on campus.

ADMISSIONS

Freshman Academic Profile: Average high school GPA 3.46. 20% in top 10% of high school class, 49% in top 25% of high school class, 82% in top 50% of high school class. 85% from public high schools. ACT middle 50% range 20-25. Minimum internet-based TOEFL 52. Minimum paper TOEFL 500. **Basis for Candidate Selection:** *Very important factors considered include:* Class rank, academic GPA, recommendation(s), rigor of secondary school record, standardized test scores. *Other factors considered include:* application essay, alumni/ae relation, character/personal qualities, extracurricular activities, first generation, interview, talent/ability, volunteer work, work experience. **Freshman Admission Requirements:** High school diploma is required and GED is accepted. *Academic units required:* 4 English, 2 science, 2 social studies. **Freshman Admission Statistics:** 1,227 applied, 68% admitted, 24% enrolled. **Transfer Admission Requirements:** college transcript(s), statement of good standing from prior institution(s). Minimum college GPA of 2.0 required. Lowest grade transferable D. **General Admission Information:** Nonfall registration accepted. Admission may be deferred for a maximum of 1 year. Credit and/or placement offered for CEEB Advanced Placement tests.

COSTS AND FINANCIAL AID

Annual tuition $29,448. Room and board $8,506. Average book expense $885. **Required Forms and Deadlines:** FAFSA. **Notification of Awards:** Applicants will be notified of awards on a rolling basis beginning 2/15. **Types of Aid:** *Need-based scholarships/grants:* Federal Pell, SEOG, state scholarships/grants, private scholarships, the school's own gift aid. *Loans:* Subsidized Stafford, Unsubsidized Stafford, PLUS, Federal Perkins, college/university loans from institutional funds. *Student Employment:* Federal Work-Study Program available. Institutional employment available. Off-campus job opportunities are excellent. **Financial Aid Statistics:** 88% freshmen, 88% undergrads receive need-based scholarship or grant aid. 100% freshmen, 97% undergrads receive non-need-based scholarship or grant aid. 83% freshmen, 81% undergrads receive need-based self-help aid. 0% freshmen, 0% undergrads receive athletic scholarships. 99% freshmen, 98% undergrads receive any aid. 80% undergrads borrow to pay for school. Average cumulative indebtedness $27,230. **Criteria for awarding institutional aid:** *Non-need-based:* academics, art, minority status, music/drama, religious affiliation.

BURLINGTON COLLEGE

351 North Ave, Burlington, VT 5401
Phone: 802-862-9616 x104 · **Financial Aid Phone:** 802-862-9616 ext 110
E-mail: admissions@burlington.edu · **CEEB Code:** 1119
Fax: 802/660-4331 · **Website:** www.burlington.edu · **ACT Code:** 4329

This private school was founded in 1972. It has a 1-acre campus.

RATINGS

Admissions Selectivity Rating: 72   **Fire Safety Rating:** 66

STUDENTS AND FACULTY

Enrollment: 178. **Student Body:** 48% female, 52% male, 46% out-of-state, 2% international (5 countries represented). Asian 1%, African American 1%, Caucasian 83%, Hispanic 2%, Native American 1%

Retention and Graduation: 40% freshmen return for sophomore year. 16% grads go on to further study within 1 year. 10% grads pursue arts and sciences degrees. 5% grads pursue law degrees. **Faculty:** 5 full-time faculty, 60% hold PhDs, 60% are members of minority groups. 0% of classes are taught by teaching assistants.

ACADEMICS

Degrees: associate, bachelor's, certificate. **Classes:** Most classes have fewer than 10 students. **Majors with Highest Enrollment:** Multi-/Interdisciplinary Studies; Cinematography and Film/Video Production; English Language and Literature/Letters. **Special Study Options:** cross-registration, distance learning, double major, dual enrollment, external degree program, independent study, internships, liberal arts/career combination, student-designed major, study abroad, Flexible, self-designed degree program, independent study option. **Honors programs:** A capstone Degree Project, equivalent to a graduate thesis, is required of all BA candidates. **Disability Services:** Special programs offered to physically disabled students include note-taking services, reader services, tape recorders, tutors. **Career services:** career/job search classes, internships. Career services highlights include the Action Learning/Internship. There is an internship requirement for each major carrying a minimum of 3 academic credits (96 on-site hours). For each credit, the student must complete 32 hrs of field-supervised, hands-on experience and attend a concurrent seminar which provides guidance and support.

FACILITIES

Housing: cooperative housing, apartments for single students. 100% of campus accessible to physically disabled. **Special Academic Facilities/Equipment:** The main campus houses classrooms, film and video editing labs, a photography darkroom, a college-operated gallery and a community garden. We are within walking distance from the ECHO lake aquarium and science center, the Waterfront Blackbox Theatre and Cinema, the Community Sailing Center, the YMCA, and the Flynn Theatre. As Burlington's College, our downtown location also allows us to utilize multiple local art galleries and music venues for showcasing students arts and talents. **Computers:** 100% of classrooms, 100% of dorms, 100% of libraries, 100% of student union, have wireless network access.

CAMPUS LIFE

Environment: Town. **Activities:** literary magazine, student government, student-run film society, 1 registered organization. **On-Campus Highlights:** Burlington College Community Gallery, Miller Studio, Photography Darkroom. **Environmental Initiatives:** New lighting with motion sensors; New air handling system; New pump system.

ADMISSIONS

Freshman Academic Profile: Average high school GPA 2.89. 5% in top 10% of high school class, 19% in top 25% of high school class, 38% in top 50% of high school class. 72% from public high schools. SAT Math middle 50% range 425-530. SAT Critical Reading middle 50% range 440-575. SAT Writing middle 50% range 420-565. ACT middle 50% range 18-26. Minimum internet-based TOEFL 79. Minimum paper TOEFL 550. **Basis for Candidate Selection:** *Very important factors considered include:* application essay, character/personal qualities, interview, level of applicant's interest. *Important factors considered include:* recommendation(s), talent/ability, volunteer work. *Other factors considered include:* academic GPA, rigor of secondary school record, standardized test scores, alumni/ae relation, extracurricular activities, first generation, work experience. **Freshman Admission Requirements:** High school diploma is required and GED is accepted. *Academic units required:* 0 English, 0 mathematics, 0 science, (0 science labs), 0 foreign language, 0 social studies, 0 history, 0 visual/performing arts, 0 computer science, 0 academic electives. **Freshman Admission Statistics:** 180 applied, 86% admitted, 25% enrolled. **Transfer Admission Requirements:** High school transcript, college transcript(s), essay or personal statement, Lowest grade transferable C. **General Admission Information:** Application Fee $50. Regular application deadline 8/15. Nonfall registration accepted. Admission may be deferred for a maximum of 2 semesters. Credit and/or placement offered for CEEB Advanced Placement tests.

COSTS AND FINANCIAL AID

Annual tuition $22,410. Room and board $6,670. Required fees $135. Average book expense $1,064. **Required Forms and Deadlines:** FAFSA. **Notification of Awards:** Applicants will be notified of awards on a rolling basis beginning 3/15. **Types of Aid:** *Need-based scholarships/grants:* Federal Pell, SEOG, state scholarships/grants, private scholarships, the school's own gift aid. *Loans:* Subsidized Stafford, Unsubsidized Stafford, PLUS, Federal Perkins. *Student Employment:* Federal Work-Study Program available. Off-campus job opportunities are good. **Financial Aid Statistics:** 100% freshmen, 95% undergrads receive need-based scholarship or grant aid. 0% freshmen, 0% undergrads receive non-need-based scholarship or grant aid. 93% freshmen, 95% undergrads receive need-based self-help aid. 0% freshmen, 0% undergrads receive athletic scholarships. 75% freshmen, 76% undergrads receive any aid. 90% undergrads borrow to pay for school. Average cumulative indebtedness $27,910. **Criteria for awarding institutional aid:** *Non-need-based:* academics, leadership.

BUTLER UNIVERSITY

4600 Sunset Avenue, Indianapolis, IN 46208
Phone: 317-940-8100 • **Financial Aid Phone:** 317-940-8200
E-mail: admission@butler.edu • **CEEB Code:** 1073
Fax: 317-940-8150 • **Website:** www.butler.edu • **ACT Code:** 1180

This private school was founded in 1855. It has a 290-acre campus.

RATINGS

Admissions Selectivity Rating: 89   Fire Safety Rating: 66

STUDENTS AND FACULTY

Enrollment: 4,013. **Student Body:** 60% female, 40% male, 51% out-of-state, 2% international (56 countries represented). Asian 3%, African American 4%, Caucasian 83%, Hispanic 3%, Native American <1%
Retention and Graduation: 90% freshmen return for sophomore year. 62% freshmen graduate within 4 years. 19% grads go on to further study within 1 year. 9% grads pursue arts and sciences degrees. 14% grads pursue law degrees. 13% grads pursue business degrees. 9% grads pursue medical degrees. **Faculty:** 351 full-time faculty, 78% hold PhDs, 46% are members of minority groups, 10% are women. 0% of classes are taught by teaching assistants.

ACADEMICS

Degrees: associate, bachelor's, master's. **Classes:** Most classes have 10–19 students. Most lab/discussion sessions have 20–29 students. **Majors with Highest Enrollment:** Marketing/Marketing Management; Pharmacy; Biology/Biological Sciences. **Special Study Options:** cross-registration, double major, dual enrollment, exchange student program (domestic), honors program, independent study, internships, student-designed major, study abroad, teacher certification program, Cooperative program in Business only. **Honors programs:** The Butler University Honors Program exists to meet the expectations of academically outstanding students in all colleges and majors who wish to develop their talents and potential to the fullest. Through a combination of honors courses, cultural events, independent study, creative activity and research, it is designed to foster a diverse and challenging intellectual environment for honors students and to enhance our academic community by adding a distinctive note of innovative thinking and interdisciplinary dialogue. Combined degree programs: BA/MEng. **Disability Services:** Special programs offered to physically disabled students include note-taking services, reader services. **Career services:** Alumni network, alumni services, career/job search classes, career assessment, internships, regional alumni. The College of Business assigns each student a career mentor and requires two internships for each of their majors; 75% of Butler undergraduates participate in some form of experiential learning.

FACILITIES

Housing: Coed dorms, women's dorms, fraternity/sorority housing, apartments for single students. 90% of campus accessible to physically disabled. **Special Academic Facilities/Equipment:** Holcomb Observatory, Clowes Memorial Hall (performing arts theatre). **Computers:** 100% of classrooms, 100% of dorms, 100% of libraries, 100% of dining areas, 100% of student union, have wireless network access. Students can register for classes online. Administrative functions (other than registration) can be performed online.

CAMPUS LIFE

Environment: Metropolis. **Activities:** Choral groups, concert band, dance, drama/theater, jazz band, literary magazine, marching band, music ensembles, musical theater, opera, pep band, student government, student newspaper, symphony orchestra, television station, yearbook, Campus Ministries, International Student Organization, Model UN. 135 registered organizations, 8 honor societies, 6 religious organizations. 7 fraternities, 9 sororities. **Athletics (Intercol-**

legiate): *Men:* baseball, basketball, cross-country, football, golf, soccer, tennis, track/field (outdoor), track/field (indoor). *Women:* basketball, cross-country, golf, soccer, softball, swimming, tennis, track/field (outdoor), track/field (indoor), volleyball. **On-Campus Highlights:** Starbucks in the Union, Carillon on Lake Road, Holcomb Gardens, Fairbanks Center, Lilly Music Hall (newly renovated). **Environmental Initiatives:** College of Pharmacy and Health Sciences building will be "Leed Certified-Silver." IDEM grant for campus recycling, $25,000. Completely Green cleaning operations for our custodial operation.

ADMISSIONS

Freshman Academic Profile: Average high school GPA 3.81. 49% in top 10% of high school class, 79% in top 25% of high school class, 97% in top 50% of high school class. SAT Math middle 50% range 530-650. SAT Critical Reading middle 50% range 530-630. SAT Writing middle 50% range 520-610. ACT middle 50% range 25-30. Minimum internet-based TOEFL 79. Minimum paper TOEFL 550. **Basis for Candidate Selection:** *Very important factors considered include:* application essay, academic GPA, rigor of secondary school record, standardized test scores. *Important factors considered include:* Class rank, extracurricular activities, talent/ability. *Other factors considered include:* recommendation(s), alumni/ae relation, character/personal qualities, volunteer work, work experience. **Freshman Admission Requirements:** High school diploma is required and GED is accepted. *Academic units required:* 4 English, 3 mathematics, 3 science, (2 science labs), 2 foreign language, 2 social studies, 2 history. **Freshman Admission Statistics:** 10,103 applied, 68% admitted, 14% enrolled. **Transfer Admission Requirements:** college transcript(s), essay or personal statement, statement of good standing from prior institution(s). Minimum college GPA of 2.0 required. Lowest grade transferable C. **General Admission Information:** Application Fee $35. Regular application deadline 8/1. Notification on a rolling basis, beginning on or about 3/6. Nonfall registration accepted. Admission may be deferred for a maximum of 1 year. Credit offered for CEEB Advanced Placement tests.

COSTS AND FINANCIAL AID

Average book expense $1,000. **Required Forms and Deadlines:** FAFSA. **Notification of Awards:** Applicants will be notified of awards on a rolling basis beginning 3/15. **Types of Aid:** *Need-based scholarships/grants:* Federal Pell, SEOG, state scholarships/grants, the school's own gift aid. *Loans:* Subsidized Stafford, Unsubsidized Stafford, PLUS, Federal Perkins. *Student Employment:* Federal Work-Study Program available. Institutional employment available. Highest amount earned per year from on-campus jobs $3,000. Off-campus job opportunities are excellent. **Financial Aid Statistics:** 99% freshmen, 97% undergrads receive need-based scholarship or grant aid. 16% freshmen, 14% undergrads receive non-need-based scholarship or grant aid. 75% freshmen, 76% undergrads receive need-based self-help aid. 1% freshmen, 2% undergrads receive athletic scholarships. 68% undergrads borrow to pay for school. Average cumulative indebtedness $25,502. **Criteria for awarding institutional aid:** *Non-need-based:* academics, athletics, music/drama.

CABRINI COLLEGE

610 King of Prussia Road, Radnor, PA 19087-3698
Phone: 610-902-8552 • **Financial Aid Phone:** 610-902-8420
E-mail: admit@cabrini.edu • **CEEB Code:** 2071
Fax: 610-902-8508 • **Website:** www.cabrini.edu • **ACT Code:** 3532

This private school, affiliated with the Roman Catholic Church, was founded in 1957. It has a 112-acre campus.

RATINGS

Admissions Selectivity Rating: 74   Fire Safety Rating: 93

STUDENTS AND FACULTY

Enrollment: 1,820. **Student Body:** 66% female, 34% male, 34% out-of-state, 1% international (34 countries represented). Asian 2%, African American 6%, Caucasian 83%, Hispanic 3%, Native American <1%
Retention and Graduation: 66% freshmen return for sophomore year. 46% freshmen graduate within 4 years. 59% freshmen graduate within 6 years. 21% grads go on to further study within 1 year. 16% grads pursue arts and sciences degrees. 1% grads pursue law degrees. 3% grads pursue business degrees. 1% grads pursue medical degrees. **Faculty:** 64 full-time faculty, 80% hold PhDs, 55% are members of minority groups, 5% are women. 0% of classes are taught by teaching assistants.

ACADEMICS

Degrees: bachelor's, certificate, master's, post-bachelor's certificate. **Classes:** Most classes have 20–29 students. Most lab/discussion sessions have 10–19 students. **Majors with Highest Enrollment:** Elementary Education and Teaching; Business, Management, Marketing, and Related Support Services.

Special Study Options: Accelerated program, cooperative education program, cross-registration, double major, honors program, independent study, internships, liberal arts/career combination, student-designed major, study abroad, teacher certification program. **Honors programs:** Cabrini College Honors Program; Honors in the major. **Disability Services:** Special programs offered to physically disabled students include note-taking services, reader services, tape recorders, tutors. **Career services:** Alumni network, alumni services, career/job search classes, career assessment, internships. Career services highlights include the Parallel cooperative education program semester to semester.

FACILITIES

Housing: Coed dorms, special housing for disabled students, women's dorms, Special Interest Housing is available. 97% of campus accessible to physically disabled. **Special Academic Facilities/Equipment:** Exercise Science Lab; Communications center (includes a graphic design lab, radio station, newsroom, and television studio); Science Education and Technology building with state-of-the-art biology, chemistry, and physics labs; Instructional Technology labs; and research space. **Computers:** 100% of classrooms, 95% of dorms, 100% of libraries, 100% of dining areas, 100% of student union, 95% of common outdoor areas have wireless network access. Students can register for classes online. Administrative functions (other than registration) can be performed online.

CAMPUS LIFE

Environment: Town. **Activities:** Choral groups, dance, drama/theater, literary magazine, radio station, student government, student newspaper, student-run film society, television station, yearbook, Campus Ministries, International Student Organization. 32 registered organizations, 18 honor societies, 1 religious organization. **Athletics (Intercollegiate):** *Men:* basketball, cross-country, golf, lacrosse, soccer, swimming, tennis, track/field (outdoor). *Women:* basketball, cross-country, field hockey, lacrosse, soccer, softball, swimming, tennis, track/field (outdoor), volleyball. **On-Campus Highlights:** Dixon Center- Athletic/Recreation facility, Jazzman's Café, Holy Spirit Library, Mansion, Science Technology Education Building, The College also has a Communications Center with a radio station, newsroom, graphic design lab, and a television studio.

ADMISSIONS

Freshman Academic Profile: Average high school GPA 3.06. 6% in top 10% of high school class, 20% in top 25% of high school class, 49% in top 50% of high school class. 56% from public high schools. SAT Math middle 50% range 430-520. SAT Critical Reading middle 50% range 440-530. Minimum paper TOEFL 500. **Basis for Candidate Selection:** *Very important factors considered include:* academic GPA, standardized test scores. *Important factors considered include:* level of applicant's interest. *Other factors considered include:* Class rank, application essay, recommendation(s), rigor of secondary school record, alumni/ae relation, character/personal qualities, extracurricular activities, interview, talent/ability, volunteer work, work experience. **Freshman Admission Requirements:** High school diploma is required and GED is accepted. *Academic units required:* 4 English, 3 mathematics, 3 science, 2 foreign language, 3 social studies, 3 history, 0 academic electives. **Freshman Admission Statistics:** 4,015 applied, 75% admitted, 17% enrolled. **Transfer Admission Requirements:** college transcript(s), Minimum college GPA of 2.2 required. Lowest grade transferable C-. **General Admission Information:** Application Fee $35. Notification on a rolling basis, beginning on or about 8/1. Nonfall registration accepted. Admission may be deferred for a maximum of One year. Credit and/or placement offered for CEEB Advanced Placement tests.

COSTS AND FINANCIAL AID

Average book expense $960. **Required Forms and Deadlines:** FAFSA. **Notification of Awards:** Applicants will be notified of awards on a rolling basis beginning 2/20. **Types of Aid:** *Need-based scholarships/grants:* Federal Pell, SEOG, state scholarships/grants, private scholarships, the school's own gift aid. *Loans:* Subsidized Stafford, Unsubsidized Stafford, PLUS, Federal Perkins. *Student Employment:* Highest amount earned per year from on-campus jobs $4,160. Off-campus job opportunities are good. **Financial Aid Statistics:** 81% freshmen, 78% undergrads receive need-based scholarship or grant aid. 92% freshmen, 94% undergrads receive non-need-based scholarship or grant aid. 80% freshmen, 84% undergrads receive need-based self-help aid. 0% freshmen, 0% undergrads receive athletic scholarships. 98% freshmen, 97% undergrads receive any aid. 77% undergrads borrow to pay for school. Average cumulative indebtedness $12,261. **Criteria for awarding institutional aid:** *Non-need-based:* academics, alumni affiliation.

CAIRN UNIVERSITY

200 Manor Avenue, Langhorne, PA 19047
Phone: 215-702-4235 • **Financial Aid Phone:** 215-702-4246
E-mail: admissions@cairn.edu
Fax: 215-702-4248 • **Website:** www.cairn.edu • **ACT Code:** 3658

This private school, affiliated with the Protestant Church, was founded in 1913. It has a 114-acre campus.

RATINGS

Admissions Selectivity Rating: 82   **Fire Safety Rating:** 74

STUDENTS AND FACULTY

Enrollment: 937. **Student Body:** 53% female, 47% male, 44% out-of-state, 2% international (31 countries represented). Asian 4%, African American 14%, Caucasian 72%, Hispanic 5%, Native American 1%
Retention and Graduation: 78% freshmen return for sophomore year. 20% freshmen graduate within 4 years. 40% grads go on to further study within 1 year. **Faculty:** 50 full-time faculty, 70% hold PhDs, 30% are members of minority groups, 18% are women. 0% of classes are taught by teaching assistants.

ACADEMICS

Degrees: bachelor's, certificate, master's. **Classes:** Most classes have 10–19 students. **Majors with Highest Enrollment:** Elementary Education and Teaching; Bible/Biblical Studies; Social Work. **Special Study Options:** Accelerated program, double major, honors program, internships, study abroad, teacher certification program. Combined degree programs: BS in Bible+ MS in Chr Counseling or MS in Education or MS in Org. Leader. **Disability Services:** Special programs offered to physically disabled students include reader services, tutors. **Career services:** alumni services, career/job search classes, career assessment.

FACILITIES

Housing: special housing for disabled students, men's dorms, special housing for international students, women's dorms, apartments for married students, apartments for single students. 99% of campus accessible to physically disabled. **Special Academic Facilities/Equipment:** Biblical Learning Center Museum area **Computers:** 59% of classrooms, 62% of dorms, 90% of libraries, 100% of dining areas, 100% of student union, 15% of common outdoor areas have wireless network access. Students can register for classes online. Administrative functions (other than registration) can be performed online.

CAMPUS LIFE

Environment: Village. **Activities:** Choral groups, concert band, drama/theater, music ensembles, musical theater, opera, student government, student newspaper, symphony orchestra, yearbook, Campus Ministries, International Student Organization. 25 registered organizations, 4 honor societies, 3 religious organizations. **Athletics (Intercollegiate):** *Men:* baseball, basketball, cross-country, golf, soccer, volleyball. *Women:* basketball, cross-country, soccer, softball, tennis, volleyball. **On-Campus Highlights:** Eagle's Nest grill & café, Student Lounge, Campus Walkway, Sports Fields, Heritage Hall Lounge.

ADMISSIONS

Freshman Academic Profile: Average high school GPA 3.3. 18% in top 10% of high school class, 39% in top 25% of high school class, 17% in top 50% of high school class. 60% from public high schools. SAT Math middle 50% range 450-580. SAT Critical Reading middle 50% range 470-590. ACT middle 50% range 17-24.3. Minimum paper TOEFL 520. **Basis for Candidate Selection:** *Very important factors considered include:* academic GPA, standardized test scores, religious affiliation/commitment. *Important factors considered include:* application essay, rigor of secondary school record, character/personal qualities, interview. *Other factors considered include:* Class rank, recommendation(s), extracurricular activities, level of applicant's interest. **Freshman Admission Requirements:** High school diploma is required and GED is accepted. **Freshman Admission Statistics:** 482 applied, 74% admitted, 41% enrolled. **Transfer Admission Requirements:** college transcript(s), essay or personal statement, interview, Minimum college GPA of 2.2 required. Lowest grade transferable C. **General Admission Information:** Application Fee $25. Notification on a rolling basis, beginning on or about 7/1. Nonfall registration accepted. Admission may be deferred for a maximum of 1 year. Credit and/or placement offered for CEEB Advanced Placement tests.

COSTS AND FINANCIAL AID

Annual tuition $21,500. Room and board $8,525. Required fees $205. Average book expense $1,200. **Required Forms and Deadlines:** FAFSA. **Notification of Awards:** Applicants will be notified of awards on a rolling basis beginning 2/15. **Types of Aid:** *Need-based scholarships/grants:* Federal Pell, SEOG, state scholarships/grants, private scholarships, the school's own gift aid. *Loans:* Direct Subsidized Stafford, Direct Unsubsidized Stafford, Direct PLUS, Subsidized Stafford, Unsubsidized Stafford, PLUS, state loans. *Student Employment:*

Federal Work-Study Program available. Institutional employment available. Off-campus job opportunities are excellent. **Financial Aid Statistics:** 99% freshmen, 96% undergrads receive need-based scholarship or grant aid. 6% freshmen, 6% undergrads receive non-need-based scholarship or grant aid. 98% freshmen, 96% undergrads receive need-based self-help aid. 0% freshmen, 0% undergrads receive athletic scholarships. 84% freshmen, 82% undergrads receive any aid. 82% undergrads borrow to pay for school. Average cumulative indebtedness $22,541. **Criteria for awarding institutional aid:** *Non-need-based:* academics, leadership, minority status.

CALDWELL COLLEGE

9 Ryerson Avenue, Caldwell, NJ 07006-6195
Phone: 973-618-3500 · **Financial Aid Phone:** 973-618-3221
E-mail: admissions@caldwell.edu · **CEEB Code:** 2072
Fax: 973-618-3600 · **Website:** www.caldwell.edu · **ACT Code:** 2542

This private school, affiliated with the Roman Catholic Church, was founded in 1939. It has a 80-acre campus.

RATINGS

Admissions Selectivity Rating: 74   **Fire Safety Rating:** 71

STUDENTS AND FACULTY

Enrollment: 1,563. **Student Body:** 67% female, 33% male, 14% out-of-state, 5% international (26 countries represented). Asian 2%, African American 16%, Caucasian 61%, Hispanic 12%, Native American <1%
Retention and Graduation: 73% freshmen return for sophomore year. 45% freshmen graduate within 4 years. 52% freshmen graduate within 6 years. **Faculty:** 80 full-time faculty, 83% hold PhDs, 63% are members of minority groups. 0% of classes are taught by teaching assistants.

ACADEMICS

Degrees: bachelor's, certificate, master's, post-bachelor's certificate, post-master's certificate. **Majors with Highest Enrollment:** Elementary Education and Teaching; Psychology; Business Administration and Management. **Special Study Options:** Accelerated program, cooperative education program, distance learning, double major, English as a Second Language (ESL), external degree program, honors program, independent study, internships, liberal arts/career combination, student-designed major, study abroad, teacher certification program, weekend college. **Disability Services:** Special programs offered to physically disabled students include note-taking services, reader services, tape recorders, tutors. **Career services:** alumni services, career/job search classes, career assessment, internships.

FACILITIES

Housing: Coed dorms. 85% of campus accessible to physically disabled. **Special Academic Facilities/Equipment:** Art gallery, theatre, library with media center, TV studio, state of the art technology building with Interactive Television Classroom, new student center. **Computers:** Students can register for classes online. Administrative functions (other than registration) can be performed online.

CAMPUS LIFE

Environment: Village. **Activities:** Choral groups, drama/theater, jazz band, literary magazine, music ensembles, musical theater, pep band, student government, student newspaper, yearbook. 20 registered organizations, 15 honor societies, 1 religious organization. **Athletics (Intercollegiate):** *Men:* baseball, basketball, golf, soccer, tennis. *Women:* basketball, golf, soccer, softball, tennis. **On-Campus Highlights:** Newly opened 60,000 square-foot Recreation Center, Renovated Science Labs, Brand new Fitness Center, Radio and TV Studios, Art Department Galleries.

ADMISSIONS

Freshman Academic Profile: Average high school GPA 3.03. 7% in top 10% of high school class, 14% in top 25% of high school class, 47% in top 50% of high school class. 81% from public high schools. SAT Math middle 50% range 430-530. SAT Critical Reading middle 50% range 440-520. Minimum internet-based TOEFL 70. Minimum paper TOEFL 550. **Basis for Candidate Selection:** *Very important factors considered include:* rigor of secondary school record, extracurricular activities. *Important factors considered include:* Class rank, academic GPA, standardized test scores, talent/ability. *Other factors considered include:* application essay, recommendation(s), alumni/ae relation, character/personal qualities, interview, volunteer work, work experience. **Freshman Admission Requirements:** High school diploma is required and GED is accepted. *Academic units required:* 4 English, 2 mathematics, 2 science, (1 science labs), 2 foreign language, 1 history, 5 academic electives. **Freshman Admission Statistics:** 1,442 applied, 66% admitted, 30% enrolled. **Transfer Admission Requirements:** High school transcript, college

transcript(s), Minimum college GPA of 2.0 required. Lowest grade transferable c. **General Admission Information:** Application Fee $40. Regular application deadline 4/1. Nonfall registration accepted. Admission may be deferred for a maximum of 1 semester. Credit and/or placement offered for CEEB Advanced Placement tests.

COSTS AND FINANCIAL AID

Room and board $7,000. Required fees $100. Average book expense $800. **Required Forms and Deadlines:** FAFSA, Institution's own financial aid form. **Notification of Awards:** Applicants will be notified of awards on a rolling basis beginning 3/1. **Types of Aid:** *Need-based scholarships/grants:* Federal Pell, SEOG, state scholarships/grants, private scholarships, the school's own gift aid. *Loans:* Subsidized Stafford, Unsubsidized Stafford, PLUS, state loans, Alternative Loans, such as Key, TERL, Signature. *Student Employment:* Federal Work-Study Program available. Institutional employment available. Highest amount earned per year from on-campus jobs $1,000. Off-campus job opportunities are excellent. **Financial Aid Statistics:** 83% freshmen, 83% undergrads receive need-based scholarship or grant aid. 0% freshmen, 0% undergrads receive non-need-based scholarship or grant aid. 73% freshmen, 63% undergrads receive need-based self-help aid. 0% freshmen, 0% undergrads receive athletic scholarships. 79% undergrads borrow to pay for school. **Criteria for awarding institutional aid:** *Non-need-based:* academics, alumni affiliation, art, athletics, leadership, music/drama, religious affiliation.

CALIFORNIA BAPTIST UNIVERSITY

8432 Magnolia Ave, Riverside, CA 92504
Phone: 951-343-4212 · **Financial Aid Phone:** 951-343-4236
E-mail: admissions@calbaptist.edu · **CEEB Code:** 4094
Fax: 951-343-4525 · **Website:** www.calbaptist.edu · **ACT Code:** 4094

This private school, affiliated with the Southern Baptist Church, was founded in 1950. It has a 103-acre campus.

RATINGS

Admissions Selectivity Rating: 76   **Fire Safety Rating:** 63

STUDENTS AND FACULTY

Enrollment: 6,435. **Student Body:** 63% female, 37% male, 5% out-of-state, 2% international (27 countries represented). Asian 5%, African American 8%, Caucasian 41%, Hispanic 32%, Native American 1%
Retention and Graduation: 83% freshmen return for sophomore year. 40% freshmen graduate within 4 years. 55% freshmen graduate within 6 years. **Faculty:** 278 full-time faculty, 75% hold PhDs, 45% are members of minority groups, 23% are women. 0% of classes are taught by teaching assistants.

ACADEMICS

Degrees: bachelor's, master's. **Classes:** Most classes have 10–19 students. Most lab/discussion sessions have 10–19 students. **Majors with Highest Enrollment:** Registered Nursing/Registered Nurse; Psychology; Business/Commerce. **Special Study Options:** Accelerated program, distance learning, double major, English as a Second Language (ESL), exchange student program (domestic), honors program, internships, liberal arts/career combination, study abroad, teacher certification program, weekend college. **Honors programs:** The Honors program offers students from all major areas of study the opportunity to participate in rigorous study, requiring diligence in reading primary sources and writing original essays thorough 8 intensive seminars. Honors students progressively investigate a single generative idea using primary texts, drawing upon the expertise of leading faculty. These seminars may be used to fulfill elective unit requirements and specially selected general education requirements. Successful completion of the Honors Program will be posted on the academic transcript and students will be designated as Honors Program graduates at commencement. **Disability Services:** Special programs offered to physically disabled students include note-taking services, tutors. **Career services:** alumni services, career/job search classes, internships. Internship elective credit is available for students in all academic disciplines. In addition, a RE-FOCUS program is available which seeks to prepare students in their transition from the academic culture of the university to a professional culture. The program is designed for Juniors and Seniors and offers interactive workshops such as mock interviews hosted by a national employer, business etiquette dinners, resume and interview skills workshops and graduate school information sessions.

FACILITIES

Housing: men's dorms, women's dorms, cooperative housing, apartments for single students. 95% of campus accessible to physically disabled. **Special Academic Facilities/Equipment:** Metcalf Art Gallery, Annie Gabriel Library, Wallace Theater, P. Boyd Smith Hymnology Collection, School of Music Performance and Recording Studios, Nie Wieder! Collection, Lancer Sports Complex and Aquatic Center **Computers:** 40% of classrooms, 10% of dorms, 100% of libraries, 100% of dining areas, 100% of student union, 25% of common outdoor areas have wireless network access. Students can register for classes online. Administrative functions (other than registration) can be performed online.

CAMPUS LIFE

Environment: City. **Activities:** Choral groups, concert band, drama/theater, jazz band, music ensembles, musical theater, pep band, student government, student newspaper, symphony orchestra, yearbook, Campus Ministries, International Student Organization. 30 registered organizations, 2 honor societies, 6 religious organizations. **Athletics (Intercollegiate):** *Men:* baseball, basketball, cheerleading, cross-country, diving, golf, soccer, swimming, volleyball, water polo, wrestling. *Women:* basketball, cheerleading, cross-country, diving, golf, soccer, softball, swimming, volleyball, water polo. **On-Campus Highlights:** Alumni Dining Commons, Student Activity Center, Wanda's (Coffee Shop), Van Dyne Gymnasium, Aquatic Center. **Environmental Initiatives:** Energy Efficient Lighting; HVAC Regulators; Strategic Landscaping Considerations.

ADMISSIONS

Freshman Academic Profile: Average high school GPA 3.35. 13% in top 10% of high school class, 40% in top 25% of high school class, 77% in top 50% of high school class. 88% from public high schools. SAT Math middle 50% range 420-550. SAT Critical Reading middle 50% range 420-550. SAT Writing middle 50% range 420-530. ACT middle 50% range 18-24. Minimum internet-based TOEFL 71. Minimum paper TOEFL 527. **Basis for Candidate Selection:** *Very important factors considered include:* application essay, academic GPA, recommendation(s), rigor of secondary school record, standardized test scores, character/personal qualities. *Important factors considered include:* level of applicant's interest. *Other factors considered include:* Class rank, extracurricular activities, talent/ability, volunteer work. **Freshman Admission Requirements:** High school diploma is required and GED is accepted. *Academic units required:* 4 English, 3 mathematics, 1 science, (1 science labs), 2 foreign language, 2 social studies, 2 history. **Freshman Admission Statistics:** 4,211 applied, 80% admitted, 33% enrolled. **Transfer Admission Requirements:** college transcript(s), essay or personal statement, statement of good standing from prior institution(s). Minimum college GPA of 2.0 required. Lowest grade transferable C. **General Admission Information:** Application Fee $45. Notification on a rolling basis, beginning on or about 11/9. Nonfall registration accepted. Admission may be deferred for a maximum of 1 year. Credit and/or placement offered for CEEB Advanced Placement tests.

COSTS AND FINANCIAL AID

Annual tuition $27,612. Room and board $9,370. Required fees $1,810. Average book expense $1,746. **Required Forms and Deadlines:** FAFSA, State aid form. **Notification of Awards:** Applicants will be notified of awards on a rolling basis beginning 3/2. **Types of Aid:** *Need-based scholarships/grants:* Federal Pell, SEOG, state scholarships/grants, private scholarships, the school's own gift aid, Federal Nursing Scholarships. *Loans:* Subsidized Stafford, Unsubsidized Stafford, PLUS, Federal Perkins, Federal Nursing, Alternative Loans. *Student Employment:* Federal Work-Study Program available. Institutional employment available. Highest amount earned per year from on-campus jobs $1,900. Off-campus job opportunities are good. **Financial Aid Statistics:** 72% freshmen, 68% undergrads receive need-based scholarship or grant aid. 67% freshmen, 52% undergrads receive non-need-based scholarship or grant aid. 74% freshmen, 75% undergrads receive need-based self-help aid. 8% freshmen, 6% undergrads receive athletic scholarships. 90% freshmen, 90% undergrads receive any aid. 80% undergrads borrow to pay for school. Average cumulative indebtedness $26,132. **Criteria for awarding institutional aid:** *Non-need-based:* academics, art, athletics, music/drama, religious affiliation.

CALIFORNIA COLLEGE OF THE ARTS

1111 Eighth Street, San Francisco, CA 94107
Phone: 415-703-9523 · **Financial Aid Phone:** 415-703-9528
E-mail: enroll@cca.edu · **CEEB Code:** 4031
Fax: 415-703-9539 · **Website:** www.cca.edu · **ACT Code:** 176

This private school was founded in 1907. It has a 4-acre campus.

RATINGS

Admissions Selectivity Rating: 73   Fire Safety Rating: 83

STUDENTS AND FACULTY

Enrollment: 1,512. **Student Body:** 62% female, 38% male, 34% out-of-state, 27% international (54 countries represented). Asian 16%, African American 4%, Caucasian 29%, Hispanic 13%, Native American <1%.
Retention and Graduation: 81% freshmen return for sophomore year. 29% freshmen graduate within 4 years. 54% freshmen graduate within 6 years.

Faculty: 91 full-time faculty, 76% hold PhDs, 44% are members of minority groups, 26% are women. 0% of classes are taught by teaching assistants.

ACADEMICS

Degrees: bachelor's, master's. **Classes:** Most classes have 10–19 students. **Majors with Highest Enrollment:** Graphic Design; Illustration; Architecture. **Special Study Options:** cross-registration, double major, English as a Second Language (ESL), exchange student program (domestic), independent study, internships, student-designed major, study abroad, Sponsored studios and project-based learning with community engagement courses integrated in the curriculum. Learning disability services also offered. Combined degree programs: MFA/MA, MFA/MBA. **Disability Services:** Special programs offered to physically disabled students include note-taking services, reader services, tape recorders, tutors. **Career services:** Alumni network, alumni services, career/job search classes, career assessment, internships. Career services highlights include Engage at CCA combines project-based learning with community engagement throughout the curriculum of CCA's diverse programs. An example of an Engage course includes a furniture design class working with Lighthouse Community Charter School to create tables for the school's courtyard atrium.

FACILITIES

Housing: Coed dorms, special housing for disabled students, apartments for single students, Theme Housing Themed communities and living-learning communities. 80% of campus accessible to physically disabled. **Special Academic Facilities/Equipment:** Logan Gallery on the San Francisco Campus, Wattis Institute for Contemporary Art **Computers:** 100% of classrooms, 60% of dorms, 100% of libraries, 100% of dining areas, 90% of common outdoor areas have wireless network access. Students can register for classes online. Administrative functions (other than registration) can be performed online.

CAMPUS LIFE

Environment: Metropolis. **Activities:** literary magazine, student government, student-run film society, International Student Organization. 10 registered organizations, 1 fraternity. **On-Campus Highlights:** The Nave—San Francisco campus, The Foundry—Oakland campus, Individualized Painting Studios—SF, North/South Student Galleries—Oakland, Wattis Institute for Contemporary Art. Students learn from individuals, the inter-cultural community, and the myriad events and activities sponsored by the Center for Art and Public Life, the CCA Wattis Institute, and the Student Affairs Office. Activities range from social events, yoga classes, exhibition receptions, workshops, and topical forums to programs designed to engage the public and the academic community in a dialogue about the nature of arts and culture. Readings, lectures, performances, issue-based symposia, and panel discussions on the arts, architecture, design, and humanities are offered throughout the year. **Environmental Initiatives:** Largest solar heated facility in San Francisco, named Top Ten Green Building on Earth Day 2001. Curricular content commitment to sustainability with national experts teaching. Ongoing partnerships with Pacific Energy Center, Sustainable Cotton Project, IDSA's Okala curriculum standards, etc.

ADMISSIONS

Freshman Academic Profile: Average high school GPA 3.27. 55% from public high schools. SAT Math middle 50% range 490-630. SAT Critical Reading middle 50% range 460-600. SAT Writing middle 50% range 470-600. ACT middle 50% range 20-26. Minimum internet-based TOEFL 79. Minimum paper TOEFL 550. **Basis for Candidate Selection:** *Very important factors considered include:* application essay, academic GPA, talent/ability. *Important factors considered include:* recommendation(s). *Other factors considered include:* rigor of secondary school record, standardized test scores, alumni/ae relation, character/personal qualities, extracurricular activities, first generation, interview, level of applicant's interest, racial/ethnic status, volunteer work, work experience. **Freshman Admission Requirements:** High school diploma is required and GED is accepted. **Freshman Admission Statistics:** 1,547 applied, 83% admitted, 21% enrolled. **Transfer Admission Requirements:** college transcript(s), essay or personal statement, Minimum college GPA of 2.0 required. Lowest grade transferable C. **General Admission Information:** Application Fee $60. Notification on a rolling basis, beginning on or about 1/15. Nonfall registration accepted. Admission may be deferred for a maximum of one semester. Credit and/or placement offered for CEEB Advanced Placement tests.

COSTS AND FINANCIAL AID

Annual tuition $41,592. Room and board $8,400. Required fees $350. Average book expense $1,500. **Required Forms and Deadlines:** FAFSA, State aid form. **Notification of Awards:** Applicants will be notified of awards on a rolling basis beginning 3/15. **Types of Aid:** *Need-based scholarships/grants:* Federal Pell, SEOG, state scholarships/grants, private scholarships, the school's own gift aid. *Loans:* Subsidized Stafford, Unsubsidized Stafford, PLUS, Federal Perkins, state loans. *Student Employment:* Federal Work-Study Program available. Institutional employment available. Highest amount earned per year from on-campus jobs $1,800. Off-campus job opportunities are good. **Financial Aid Statistics:** 100% freshmen, 100% undergrads receive need-based scholarship or grant aid. 89% freshmen, 59% undergrads receive non-need-based scholarship or grant aid. 91% freshmen, 97% undergrads receive need-based self-help aid.

0% freshmen, 0% undergrads receive athletic scholarships. 60% freshmen, 60% undergrads receive any aid. 63% undergrads borrow to pay for school. Average cumulative indebtedness $27,425. **Criteria for awarding institutional aid:** *Non-need-based:* academics, art.

See page 1020.

CALIFORNIA COLLEGE FOR HEALTH SCIENCES

2423 Hoover Avenue, National City, CA 91950
Phone: 619-477-4800
E-mail: admissns@cchs.edu
Fax: 619-477-4360 • **Website:** www.cchs.edu

This proprietary school was founded in 1978. It has a 1-acre campus.

RATINGS

Admissions Selectivity Rating: 60*   **Fire Safety Rating:** 60*

STUDENTS AND FACULTY

Enrollment: 4,517. **Student Body:**
Faculty: 5 full-time faculty.

ACADEMICS

Degrees: associate, bachelor's, master's. **Special Study Options:** distance learning.

CAMPUS LIFE

Environment: Metropolis. **Activities:** 2 honor societies.

ADMISSIONS

Freshman Admission Requirements: High school diploma is required and GED is accepted. **Transfer Admission Requirements:** college transcript(s), Lowest grade transferable C. **General Admission Information:** Application Fee $35. Notification on a rolling basis, beginning on or about 11/11. Nonfall registration accepted. Admission may be deferred for a maximum of 11 months. Neither credit nor placement offered for CEEB Advanced Placement tests.

COSTS AND FINANCIAL AID

Annual in-state tuition $5,098. Annual out-of-state tuition $17,994. Room and board $8,532. Required fees $1,858. Average book expense $1,500.

CALIFORNIA INSTITUTE OF THE ARTS

24700 McBean Parkway, Valencia, CA 91355
Phone: 661-255-1050 • **Financial Aid Phone:** 661-253-7869
E-mail: admissions@calarts.edu • **CEEB Code:** 4049
Fax: 661-253-7710 • **Website:** www.calarts.edu • **ACT Code:** 121

This private school was founded in 1961. It has a 60-acre campus.

RATINGS

Admissions Selectivity Rating: 68   **Fire Safety Rating:** 70

STUDENTS AND FACULTY

Enrollment: 888. **Student Body:** 49% female, 51% male, 49% out-of-state, 8% international (34 countries represented). Asian 12%, African American 8%, Caucasian 58%, Hispanic 12%, Native American 1%
Retention and Graduation: 75% freshmen return for sophomore year. 57% freshmen graduate within 6 years. **Faculty:** 160 full-time faculty, 100% hold PhDs, 44% are members of minority groups, 18% are women. 0% of classes are taught by teaching assistants.

ACADEMICS

Degrees: bachelor's, certificate, doctoral, master's, post-bachelor's certificate. **Classes:** Most classes have fewer than 10 students. **Majors with Highest Enrollment:** Music Performance. **Special Study Options:** independent study, internships, student-designed major, study abroad. **Disability Services:** Special programs offered to physically disabled students include note-taking services, reader services, tape recorders, tutors. **Career services:** career/job search classes, career assessment, internships. Career services highlights include the new career mentoship program, "Arts In The world Coaching."

FACILITIES

Housing: Coed dorms, special housing for disabled students, apartments for single students. 98% of campus accessible to physically disabled. **Special Academic Facilities/Equipment:** 7 Art galleries, TV studio, Walt Disney

Theater, Roy Disney Music Hall, Sharon Disney Lund Dance Theater, Bijou Film Theater **Computers:** 20% of classrooms, 100% of libraries, 100% of dining areas, 20% of common outdoor areas have wireless network access. Students can register for classes online. Administrative functions (other than registration) can be performed online.

CAMPUS LIFE

Environment: City. **Activities:** Choral groups, dance, drama/theater, jazz band, literary magazine, music ensembles, opera, radio station, student government, student newspaper, student-run film society, symphony orchestra, television station. 5 registered organizations. **On-Campus Highlights:** Modular Theater, Permanent Set, Gamelan Room, Main Gallery, Lund Dance Theater, Roy O. Disney Music Hall, Bijou Theater. **Environmental Initiatives:** Recycling Program; Boiler Modernization; White Energy Efficient Roofing in Ahmanson Building.

ADMISSIONS

Freshman Academic Profile: Minimum internet-based TOEFL 80. Minimum paper TOEFL 550. **Basis for Candidate Selection:** *Very important factors considered include:* application essay, talent/ability. *Important factors considered include:* recommendation(s), extracurricular activities. *Other factors considered include:* academic GPA, rigor of secondary school record, character/personal qualities, interview, level of applicant's interest. **Freshman Admission Requirements:** High school diploma is required and GED is accepted. **Freshman Admission Statistics:** 1,186 applied, 33% admitted, 40% enrolled. **Transfer Admission Requirements:** High school transcript, college transcript(s), essay or personal statement, Lowest grade transferable C. **General Admission Information:** Application Fee $70. Regular application deadline 1/5. Notification on a rolling basis, beginning on or about 4/1. Nonfall registration accepted. Credit offered for CEEB Advanced Placement tests.

COSTS AND FINANCIAL AID

Annual tuition $36,166. Room and board $9,293. Required fees $576. Average book expense $1,500. **Required Forms and Deadlines:** FAFSA. **Notification of Awards:** Applicants will be notified of awards on a rolling basis beginning 4/1. **Types of Aid:** *Need-based scholarships/grants:* Federal Pell, SEOG, state scholarships/grants, private scholarships, the school's own gift aid. *Loans:* Subsidized Stafford, Unsubsidized Stafford, PLUS, Federal Perkins, college/university loans from institutional funds, Private/Alternative Loans. *Student Employment:* Federal Work-Study Program available. Institutional employment available. Highest amount earned per year from on-campus jobs $3,222. Off-campus job opportunities are good. **Financial Aid Statistics:** 92% freshmen, 93% undergrads receive need-based scholarship or grant aid. 0% freshmen, 0% undergrads receive non-need-based scholarship or grant aid. 85% freshmen, 89% undergrads receive need-based self-help aid. 0% freshmen, 0% undergrads receive athletic scholarships. 71% freshmen, 77% undergrads receive any aid. 67% undergrads borrow to pay for school. Average cumulative indebtedness $22,943. **Criteria for awarding institutional aid:** *Non-need-based:* art, minority status, music/drama.

CALIFORNIA INSTITUTE OF INTEGRAL STUDIES

1453 Mission St., San Francisco, CA 94103
Phone: 415-575-6154 • **Financial Aid Phone:** 415-575-6122
E-mail: admissions@ciis.edu
Fax: 415-575-1268 • **Website:** www.ciis.edu

This private school was founded in 1968. It has a 1-acre campus.

RATINGS

Admissions Selectivity Rating: 60*   **Fire Safety Rating:** 60*

STUDENTS AND FACULTY

Student Body: 10% out-of-state, (42 countries represented).
Faculty: 62 full-time faculty, 48% are members of minority groups, 19% are women. 0% of classes are taught by teaching assistants.

ACADEMICS

Degrees: bachelor's, certificate, master's. **Majors with Highest Enrollment:** Dance Therapy/Therapist Marriage and Family Therapy/Counseling. **Special Study Options:** distance learning, dual enrollment, student-designed major, weekend college. Combined degree programs: BA/MA. **Disability Services:** Special programs offered to physically disabled students include note-taking services, reader services, tape recorders.

FACILITIES

Housing: 100% of campus accessible to physically disabled. **Computers:** 100% of classrooms, 100% of libraries, 100% of dining areas, 100% of student union,

100% of common outdoor areas have wireless network access. Students can register for classes online. Administrative functions (other than registration) can be performed online.

CAMPUS LIFE

Environment: Metropolis. **Activities:** student government, International Student Organization. **On-Campus Highlights:** CIIS Café, Meditation Room, Roof Top Garden, Library, Bookstore.

ADMISSIONS

Freshman Academic Profile: Minimum internet-based TOEFL 80. Minimum paper TOEFL 550. **Transfer Admission Requirements:** college transcript(s), essay or personal statement, Minimum college GPA of 3.0 required. Lowest grade transferable C.

COSTS AND FINANCIAL AID

Annual tuition $21,285. Required fees $21,285.

CALIFORNIA INSTITUTE OF TECHNOLOGY

Best 380

1200 East California Boulevard, Pasadena, CA 91125
Phone: 626-395-6341 · **Financial Aid Phone:** 626-395-6280
E-mail: ugadmissions@caltech.edu · **CEEB Code:** 4034
Fax: 626-683-3026 · **Website:** admissions.caltech.edu · **ACT Code:** 182

This private school was founded in 1891. It has a 124-acre campus.

RATINGS

Admissions Selectivity Rating: 99   **Fire Safety Rating:** 67

STUDENTS AND FACULTY

Enrollment: 977. **Student Body:** 37% female, 63% male, 63% out-of-state, 9% international (32 countries represented). Asian 42%, African American 2%, Caucasian 30%, Hispanic 10%, Native American <1%
Retention and Graduation: 97% freshmen return for sophomore year. 82% freshmen graduate within 4 years. 53% grads go on to further study within 1 year. 40% grads pursue arts and sciences degrees. 1% grads pursue law degrees. 3% grads pursue medical degrees. **Faculty:** 318 full-time faculty, 98% hold PhDs, 20% are members of minority groups, 19% are women. 0% of classes are taught by teaching assistants.

ACADEMICS

Degrees: bachelor's, master's, post-master's certificate. **Classes:** Most classes have fewer than 10 students. Most lab/discussion sessions have 20–29 students. **Majors with Highest Enrollment:** Mechanical Engineering; Physics; Mathematics. **Special Study Options:** cooperative education program, cross-registration, double major, English as a Second Language (ESL), exchange student program (domestic), independent study, liberal arts/career combination, student-designed major, study abroad, "Remedial services" are not formally offered. However, remediation is available for students who are deficient in basic scientific knowledge or technical skills. Combined degree programs: Caltech-UCSD Medical Scholars Program. **Disability Services:** Special programs offered to physically disabled students include note-taking services, reader services, tape recorders, tutors.

FACILITIES

Housing: Coed dorms, special housing for disabled students, apartments for married students, single-unit houses. 95% of campus accessible to physically disabled. **Special Academic Facilities/Equipment:** Jet Propulsion Laboratory, Palomar Observatory, Seismological Laboratory, Beckman Institute for Fundamental Research in Biology and Chemistry, Mead Chemistry Laboratory, Moore Laboratory. **Computers:** 50% of classrooms, 50% of dorms, 100% of libraries, 50% of dining areas, 100% of student union, 50% of common outdoor areas have wireless network access. Students can register for classes online. Administrative functions (other than registration) can be performed online.

CAMPUS LIFE

Environment: Metropolis. **Activities:** Choral groups, concert band, dance, drama/theater, jazz band, literary magazine, music ensembles, musical theater, opera, pep band, student government, student newspaper, student-run film society, symphony orchestra, yearbook. 148 registered organizations, 2 honor societies, 6 religious organizations. **Athletics (Intercollegiate):** *Men:* baseball, basketball, cross-country, diving, fencing, soccer, swimming, tennis, track/field (outdoor), water polo. *Women:* basketball, cross-country, diving, fencing,

swimming, tennis, track/field (outdoor), volleyball, water polo. **On-Campus Highlights:** Caltech Bookstore, Moore Laboratory, Mead Chemistry Laboratory, Broad Center for the Biological Sciences, Red Door Café. **Environmental Initiatives:** Energy efficiency and retro-commissioning programs finances through the use of a green revolving loan fund (http://sustainability.caltech.edu/energy/CECIP) Greenhouse gas mitigation program and AB 32 cap-and-trade compliance (http://sustainability.caltech.edu/climate) Sustainability focused research: Joint Center for Artificial Photosynthesis, Linde Center for Global Environmental Science, Resnick Institute (http://sustainability.caltech.edu/research).

ADMISSIONS

Freshman Academic Profile: 99% in top 10% of high school class, 100% in top 25% of high school class, 100% in top 50% of high school class. 70% from public high schools. SAT Math middle 50% range 770-800. SAT Critical Reading middle 50% range 720-800. SAT Writing middle 50% range 720-790. ACT middle 50% range 33-35. **Basis for Candidate Selection:** *Very important factors considered include:* rigor of secondary school record. *Important factors considered include:* Class rank, application essay, academic GPA, recommendation(s), standardized test scores, character/personal qualities, extracurricular activities. *Other factors considered include:* alumni/ae relation, first generation, racial/ethnic status, talent/ability, volunteer work, work experience. **Freshman Admission Requirements:** High school diploma or equivalent is not required. *Academic units required:* 3 English, 4 mathematics, 2 science, (1 science labs), 1 social studies, 1 history. **Freshman Admission Statistics:** 5,535 applied, 11% admitted, 42% enrolled. **Transfer Admission Requirements:** High school transcript, college transcript(s), essay or personal statement, statement of good standing from prior institution(s). **General Admission Information:** Application Fee $60. Regular application deadline 1/1. Regular notification 4/1. Nonfall registration not accepted. Admission may be deferred for a maximum of 1 year. Neither credit nor placement offered for CEEB Advanced Placement tests.

COSTS AND FINANCIAL AID

Annual tuition $41,790. Room and board $12,918. Required fees $1,572. Average book expense $1,323. **Required Forms and Deadlines:** FAFSA, Institution's own financial aid form, CSS/Financial Aid PROFILE, Noncustodial PROFILE, Business/Farm Supplement. **Notification of Awards:** Applicants will be notified of awards on or about 4/15. **Types of Aid:** *Need-based scholarships/grants:* Federal Pell, SEOG, state scholarships/grants, private scholarships. *Loans:* Direct Subsidized Stafford, Direct Unsubsidized Stafford, Direct PLUS, Federal Perkins, college/university loans from institutional funds. *Student Employment:* Federal Work-Study Program available. Institutional employment available. **Financial Aid Statistics:** 100% freshmen, 100% undergrads receive need-based scholarship or grant aid. 1% freshmen, 2% undergrads receive non-need-based scholarship or grant aid. 63% freshmen, 70% undergrads receive need-based self-help aid. 0% freshmen, 0% undergrads receive athletic scholarships. 60% freshmen, 60% undergrads receive any aid. 40% undergrads borrow to pay for school. Average cumulative indebtedness $13,723. **Criteria for awarding institutional aid:** *Non-need-based:* academics.

CALIFORNIA LUTHERAN UNIVERSITY

60 West Olsen Road, Thousand Oaks, CA 91360
Phone: 805-493-3135 · **Financial Aid Phone:** 805-493-3115
E-mail: admissions@callutheran.edu · **CEEB Code:** 4088
Fax: 805-493-3645 · **Website:** www.callutheran.edu · **ACT Code:** 183

This private school, affiliated with the Lutheran Church, was founded in 1959. It has a 290-acre campus.

RATINGS

Admissions Selectivity Rating: 87   **Fire Safety Rating:** 82

STUDENTS AND FACULTY

Enrollment: 2,799. **Student Body:** 56% female, 44% male, 19% out-of-state, 4% international (52 countries represented). Asian 7%, African American 4%, Caucasian 51%, Hispanic 25%, Native American 1%
Retention and Graduation: 83% freshmen return for sophomore year. 58% freshmen graduate within 4 years. 28% grads go on to further study within 1 year. 35% grads pursue arts and sciences degrees. 3% grads pursue law degrees. 7% grads pursue business degrees. 4% grads pursue medical degrees. **Faculty:** 190 full-time faculty, 85% hold PhDs, 46% are members of minority groups, 17% are women. 0% of classes are taught by teaching assistants.

ACADEMICS

Degrees: bachelor's, master's, post-bachelor's certificate, post-master's certificate. **Classes:** Most classes have 20–29 students. Most lab/discussion sessions have 10–19 students. **Majors with Highest Enrollment:** Liberal

Arts and Sciences/Liberal Studies; Business/Commerce; Psychology. **Special Study Options:** Accelerated program, cooperative education program, double major, dual enrollment, exchange student program (domestic), honors program, independent study, internships, student-designed major, study abroad, teacher certification program. **Honors programs:** Honors Program Combined degree programs: 3-2 with Washington University. **Disability Services:** Special programs offered to physically disabled students include note-taking services, reader services, tape recorders, tutors. **Career services:** career/job search classes, career assessment, internships.

FACILITIES

Housing: Coed dorms, special housing for disabled students, apartments for single students. 90% of campus accessible to physically disabled. **Special Academic Facilities/Equipment:** On-campus pre-school, hypermedia lab, multimedia center and program,film studio, Kwan Fong Art Gallary, Scandinavian Center, Educational Technology Center. **Computers:** Students can register for classes online. Administrative functions (other than registration) can be performed online.

CAMPUS LIFE

Environment: Town. **Activities:** Choral groups, concert band, dance, drama/theater, jazz band, literary magazine, music ensembles, musical theater, pep band, radio station, student government, student newspaper, symphony orchestra, television station, yearbook. 75 registered organizations, 11 honor society, 3 religious organizations. **Athletics (Intercollegiate):** *Men:* baseball, basketball, cheerleading, cross-country, diving, football, golf, soccer, swimming, tennis, track/field (outdoor), water polo. *Women:* basketball, cheerleading, cross-country, diving, soccer, softball, swimming, tennis, track/field (outdoor), volleyball, water polo. **On-Campus Highlights:** Education and Technology Building, Soland Humanities Center, The Apartments, Kingsmen Park, Samuelson Chapel, Will begin construction on a new athletics complex and lab facilities for sports medicine in January 2004.

ADMISSIONS

Freshman Academic Profile: Average high school GPA 3.7. 28% in top 10% of high school class, 63% in top 25% of high school class, 92% in top 50% of high school class. 75% from public high schools. SAT Math middle 50% range 500-600. SAT Critical Reading middle 50% range 500-600. ACT middle 50% range 22-27. Minimum internet-based TOEFL 79. Minimum paper TOEFL 550. **Basis for Candidate Selection:** *Very important factors considered include:* recommendation(s), rigor of secondary school record, standardized test scores. *Important factors considered include:* application essay, extracurricular activities, talent/ability, volunteer work, work experience. *Other factors considered include:* Class rank, alumni/ae relation, character/personal qualities, geographical residence, interview, racial/ethnic status, religious affiliation/commitment, state residency. **Freshman Admission Requirements:** High school diploma is required and GED is accepted. *Academic units required:* 4 English, 3 mathematics, 3 science, 2 foreign language, 2 social studies, 1 history, 2 Humanities. **Freshman Admission Statistics:** 6,490 applied, 61% admitted, 14% enrolled. **Transfer Admission Requirements:** college transcript(s), essay or personal statement, statement of good standing from prior institution(s). Minimum college GPA of 2.8 required. Lowest grade transferable D. **General Admission Information:** Application Fee $45. Notification on a rolling basis, beginning on or about 12/1. Nonfall registration accepted. Admission may be deferred for a maximum of 1 year. Credit and/or placement offered for CEEB Advanced Placement tests.

COSTS AND FINANCIAL AID

Annual tuition $36,690. Room and board $12,400. Required fees $450. Average book expense $1,746. **Required Forms and Deadlines:** FAFSA, State aid form. **Notification of Awards:** Applicants will be notified of awards on a rolling basis beginning 4/1. *Types of Aid: Need-based scholarships/grants:* Federal Pell, SEOG, state scholarships/grants, private scholarships, the school's own gift aid. *Loans:* Subsidized Stafford, Unsubsidized Stafford, PLUS, Federal Perkins, Opportunity Loans From Loan Servicer. *Student Employment:* Federal Work-Study Program available. Institutional employment available. Highest amount earned per year from on-campus jobs $1,200. Off-campus job opportunities are good. **Financial Aid Statistics:** 100% freshmen, 95% undergrads receive need-based scholarship or grant aid. 87% freshmen, 88% undergrads receive non-need-based scholarship or grant aid. 79% freshmen, 76% undergrads receive need-based self-help aid. 0% freshmen, 0% undergrads receive athletic scholarships. 96% freshmen, 95% undergrads receive any aid. 74% undergrads borrow to pay for school. Average cumulative indebtedness $24,148. **Criteria for awarding institutional aid:** *Non-need-based:* academics, art, leadership, music/drama, religious affiliation.

CALIFORNIA MARITIME ACADEMY OF CALIFORNIA STATE UNIVERSITY

200 Maritime Academy, Vallejo, CA 94590-0644
Phone: 707-654-1330 · **Financial Aid Phone:** 707-654-1276
E-mail: admission@csum.edu · **CEEB Code:** 4035
Fax: 707-654-1336 · **Website:** www.csum.edu · **ACT Code:** 184

This public school was founded in 1929. It has a 67-acre campus.

RATINGS

Admissions Selectivity Rating: 61   **Fire Safety Rating:** 60*

STUDENTS AND FACULTY

Enrollment: 974. **Student Body:** 13% female, 87% male, 15% out-of-state. Asian 0%, African American 1%, Caucasian 4%, Hispanic 15%.
Retention and Graduation: 82% freshmen return for sophomore year. **Faculty:** 0% of classes are taught by teaching assistants.

ACADEMICS

Degrees: bachelor's. **Majors with Highest Enrollment:** Mechanical Engineering; Marine Science/Merchant Marine Officer; International Relations and Affairs. **Special Study Options:** cooperative education program, distance learning, double major, internships, all students participate in at least one 2-month training cruise around the pacific rim over the summer on The GOLDEN BEAR. **Disability Services:** Special programs offered to physically disabled students include tutors. **Career services:** alumni services, career/job search classes, internships.

FACILITIES

Housing: Coed dorms. 70% of campus accessible to physically disabled. **Special Academic Facilities/Equipment:** Bookstore, Library, Gym, Swimming Pool.

CAMPUS LIFE

Activities: student government. 16 registered organizations. **Athletics (Intercollegiate):** *Men:* basketball, crew/rowing, golf, sailing, soccer, water polo. *Women:* crew/rowing, sailing, volleyball.

ADMISSIONS

Freshman Academic Profile: Average high school GPA 3.1. 80% from public high schools. Minimum paper TOEFL 550. **Basis for Candidate Selection:** *Very important factors considered include:* rigor of secondary school record, standardized test scores. *Other factors considered include:* application essay, recommendation(s), alumni/ae relation, character/personal qualities, extracurricular activities, geographical residence, interview, state residency, talent/ability, volunteer work, work experience. **Freshman Admission Requirements:** High school diploma is required and GED is accepted. *Academic units required:* 4 English, 3 mathematics, 2 science, (2 science labs), 2 foreign language, 1 social studies, 1 history, 1 visual/performing arts, 1 academic electives. **Freshman Admission Statistics:** 893 applied, 75% admitted, 30% enrolled. **Transfer Admission Requirements:** college transcript(s), statement of good standing from prior institution(s). Minimum college GPA of 2.0 required. Lowest grade transferable C. **General Admission Information:** Application Fee $55. Regular application deadline 5/1. Regular notification 5/1. Notification on a rolling basis, beginning on or about 11/30. Nonfall registration not accepted.

COSTS AND FINANCIAL AID

Annual in-state tuition $5,472. Room and board $10,694. Required fees $2,620. Average book expense $1,262. **Required Forms and Deadlines:** FAFSA. **Notification of Awards:** Applicants will be notified of awards on a rolling basis beginning 4/15. **Types of Aid:** *Need-based scholarships/grants:* Federal Pell, SEOG, state scholarships/grants, private scholarships, the school's own gift aid. *Loans:* Subsidized Stafford, Unsubsidized Stafford, PLUS, Federal Perkins. *Student Employment:* Federal Work-Study Program available. Highest amount earned per year from on-campus jobs $750. Off-campus job opportunities are fair.

CALIFORNIA POLYTECHNIC STATE UNIVERSITY, SAN LUIS OBISPO

Admissions Office, San Luis Obispo, CA 93407-0031
Phone: 805-756-2311 · **Financial Aid Phone:** 805-756-2927
E-mail: admissions@calpoly.edu · **CEEB Code:** 4038
Fax: 805-756-5400 · **Website:** www.calpoly.edu · **ACT Code:** 188

This public school was founded in 1901. It has a 9678-acre campus.

RATINGS

Admissions Selectivity Rating: 93   **Fire Safety Rating:** 63

STUDENTS AND FACULTY

Enrollment: 19,176. **Student Body:** 46% female, 54% male, 12% out-of-state, 1% international. Asian 12%, African American 1%, Caucasian 59%, Hispanic 15%, Native American <1%
Retention and Graduation: 37% freshmen graduate within 4 years. 78% freshmen graduate within 6 years. **Faculty:** 823 full-time faculty, 76% hold PhDs, 34% are members of minority groups.

ACADEMICS

Degrees: bachelor's, master's. **Classes:** Most classes have 20–29 students. Most lab/discussion sessions have 20–29 students. **Special Study Options:** cooperative education program, distance learning, double major, English as a Second Language (ESL), exchange student program (domestic), honors program, internships, liberal arts/career combination, study abroad, teacher certification program. Combined degree programs: BS/MS. **Disability Services:** Special programs offered to physically disabled students include note-taking services, reader services, tape recorders, tutors. **Career services:** Alumni network, alumni services, career/job search classes, career assessment, internships, regional alumni. Career services highlights include the Cooperative Education Program.

FACILITIES

Housing: Coed dorms, special housing for disabled students, special housing for international students, apartments for single students, Theme Housing. **Special Academic Facilities/Equipment:** Dairy, veterinary clinic, printing museum, art gallery. **Computers:** 100% of classrooms, 5% of dorms, 100% of libraries, 100% of dining areas, 100% of student union, 5% of common outdoor areas have wireless network access. Students can register for classes online. Administrative functions (other than registration) can be performed online.

CAMPUS LIFE

Environment: Town. **Activities:** Choral groups, concert band, dance, drama/theater, jazz band, literary magazine, marching band, music ensembles, musical theater, opera, pep band, radio station, student government, student newspaper, symphony orchestra, television station, Campus Ministries, International Student Organization, Model UN. 400 registered organizations, 14 religious organizations. 25 fraternities, 14 sororities. **Athletics (Intercollegiate):** *Men:* baseball, basketball, cross-country, football, golf, soccer, swimming, tennis, track/field (outdoor), wrestling. *Women:* basketball, cross-country, golf, soccer, softball, swimming, tennis, track/field (outdoor), track/field (indoor), volleyball. **On-Campus Highlights:** Performing Arts Center, Recreation Center, Julian's Coffee Shop, Spanos Stadium, University Union, El Corral Bookstore.

ADMISSIONS

Freshman Academic Profile: Average high school GPA 3.88. 52% in top 10% of high school class, 85% in top 25% of high school class, 98% in top 50% of high school class. SAT Math middle 50% range 580-680. SAT Critical Reading middle 50% range 550-640. ACT middle 50% range 25-30. Minimum internet-based TOEFL 80. Minimum paper TOEFL 550. **Basis for Candidate Selection:** *Very important factors considered include:* academic GPA, rigor of secondary school record, standardized test scores. *Other factors considered include:* extracurricular activities, first generation, geographical residence, talent/ability, volunteer work, work experience. **Freshman Admission Requirements:** High school diploma is required and GED is accepted. *Academic units required:* 4 English, 3 mathematics, 3 science, (1 science labs), 2 foreign language, 2 social studies, 1 history, 1 visual/performing arts, 1 academic elective. **Freshman Admission Statistics:** 43,812 applied, 31% admitted, 34% enrolled. **Transfer Admission Requirements:** college transcript(s), Minimum college GPA of 2.0 required. Lowest grade transferable D. **General Admission Information:** Application Fee $55. Early decision application deadline 10/31. Regular application deadline 11/30. Regular notification 4/1. Nonfall registration not accepted. Credit offered for CEEB Advanced Placement tests.

COSTS AND FINANCIAL AID

Annual in-state tuition $5,472. Room and board $11,123. Required fees $3,252. Average book expense $1,776. **Required Forms and Deadlines:** FAFSA.

Notification of Awards: Applicants will be notified of awards on a rolling basis beginning 4/1. **Types of Aid:** *Need-based scholarships/grants:* Federal Pell, SEOG, state scholarships/grants, private scholarships, the school's own gift aid, Federal TEACH Grant. *Loans:* Direct Subsidized Stafford, Direct Unsubsidized Stafford, Direct PLUS, Federal Perkins, college/university loans from institutional funds, Alternative loans. *Student Employment:* Federal Work-Study Program available. Institutional employment available. Off-campus job opportunities are fair. **Financial Aid Statistics:** 74% freshmen, 71% undergrads receive need-based scholarship or grant aid. 3% freshmen, 1% undergrads receive non-need-based scholarship or grant aid. 66% freshmen, 66% undergrads receive need-based self-help aid. 2% freshmen, 2% undergrads receive athletic scholarships. **Criteria for awarding institutional aid:** *Non-need-based:* academics, alumni affiliation, art, athletics, job skills, leadership, music/drama, state/district residency.

CALIFORNIA STATE POLYTECHNIC UNIVERSITY, POMONA

3801 West Temple Avenue, Pomona, CA 91768
Phone: 909-869-3210 · **Financial Aid Phone:** 909-869-3700
E-mail: admissions@cpp.edu · **CEEB Code:** 4082
Fax: 909-869-4529 · **Website:** www.cpp.edu · **ACT Code:** 4048

This public school was founded in 1938. It has a 1437-acre campus.

RATINGS

Admissions Selectivity Rating: 82   **Fire Safety Rating:** 87

STUDENTS AND FACULTY

Enrollment: 22,269. **Student Body:** 44% female, 56% male, 1% out-of-state, 5% international (99 countries represented). Asian 25%, African American 3%, Caucasian 20%, Hispanic 39%, Native American <1%
Retention and Graduation: 88% freshmen return for sophomore year. 12% freshmen graduate within 4 years. 57% freshmen graduate within 6 years. **Faculty:** 565 full-time faculty, 81% hold PhDs, 42% are members of minority groups, 39% are women. 3% of classes are taught by teaching assistants.

ACADEMICS

Degrees: bachelor's, master's. **Classes:** Most classes have 30-39 students. Most lab/discussion sessions have 20–29 students. **Majors with Highest Enrollment:** Business Administration and Management; Hospitality Administration/Management; Mechanical Engineering. **Special Study Options:** cooperative education program, cross-registration, distance learning, double major, dual enrollment, English as a Second Language (ESL), exchange student program (domestic), external degree program, honors program, internships, study abroad, teacher certification program, Ocean Studies Institute Desert Studies Consortium. **Honors programs:** See web site for complete information about The Kellogg Honors College: http://www.csupomona.edu/~honorscollege/. **Disability Services:** Special programs offered to physically disabled students include note-taking services, reader services, tutors. **Career services:** Alumni network, alumni services, career/job search classes, career assessment, internships, regional alumni. Career services highlights include Career Development/Counseling: The Career Center assists all students in selecting or changing their major, as well as, what students can do with their major. Students are offered a number of career assessment inventories to assist with career development. The Career Center at Cal Poly Pomona has one of the largest number of organizations recruiting Cal Poly Pomona students in the State of California.

FACILITIES

Housing: Coed dorms, apartments for single students. 95% of campus accessible to physically disabled. **Special Academic Facilities/Equipment:** Center for hospitality management, art gallery, center for regenerative studies, citrus-packing house, meat-processing building, poultry plant, feed mill, beef, sheep, swine, Arabian horse units, horse show arena, and aerospace wind tunnel. **Computers:** 10% of classrooms, 10% of dorms, 100% of libraries, 100% of dining areas, 100% of student union, 60% of common outdoor areas have wireless network access. Students can register for classes online. Administrative functions (other than registration) can be performed online.

CAMPUS LIFE

Environment: City. **Activities:** Choral groups, concert band, dance, drama/theater, jazz band, literary magazine, music ensembles, musical theater, opera, pep band, student government, student newspaper, symphony orchestra, yearbook, Campus Ministries, International Student Organization. 280 registered organizations, 26 honor societies, 10 religious organizations. 12 fraternities, 8 sororities. **Athletics (Intercollegiate):** *Men:* baseball, basketball, cheerleading, cross-country, soccer, tennis, track/field (outdoor). *Women:* basketball, cheerleading, cross-country, soccer, tennis, track/field (outdoor), volleyball. **On-Campus Highlights:** The Farmstore at Kellogg Ranch, The Rain Bird Aquatic, Ethnobotany & Rainforest Learning Centers, W.K. Kellogg Arabian Horse Center, Kellogg House Pomona, John T. Lyle Center for Regenerative Studies. Cal Poly Pomona is located on the eastern edge of Southern California's San Gabriel Valley. The University's 1,400-acre campus features lush rolling hills; flowers, plants and trees from all seven continents; a rose garden personally built by W.K. Kellogg; and a beautifully landscaped Japanese garden. The university's aesthetic qualities are one of its best kept secrets. Some of the world's finest architects and landscape architects designed and built the ranch— a hybrid of architecture, which combined the formal courtyards, gardens and elements of Spanish, Italian and Islamic architecture with the informality of a growing nouveau-riche society. Pasadena architect Myron Hunt (Rose Bowl, Huntington Library) designed W.K. Kellogg's main house. Charles Gibbs Adams whose work included the Hearst Castle Gardens in San Simeon, California was selected to landscape the grounds. Later, the landscape was completed by Florence Yoch and Lucile Council, widely recognized as two of the finest garden designers and landscape architects in California. More recently, Antoine Predock designed the University's administration building with a desert theme. **Environmental Initiatives:** Completed baseline inventory and updated GHG inventory for 2009. Established LEED Silver Standard or Equivalent on all new buildings. Established Energy Star Policy on Purchase of Office Equipment and Appliances.

ADMISSIONS

Freshman Academic Profile: Average high school GPA 3.42. 88% from public high schools. SAT Math middle 50% range 470-620. SAT Critical Reading middle 50% range 450-570. ACT middle 50% range 20-26. Minimum paper TOEFL 525. **Basis for Candidate Selection:** *Very important factors considered include:* academic GPA, rigor of secondary school record, standardized test scores. **Freshman Admission Requirements:** High school diploma is required and GED is accepted. *Academic units required:* 4 English, 3 mathematics, 2 science, (2 science labs), 2 foreign language, 1 social studies, 1 history, 1 visual/performing arts, 1 academic electives. **Freshman Admission Statistics:** 32,801 applied, 52% admitted, 21% enrolled. **Transfer Admission Requirements:** college transcript(s), statement of good standing from prior institution(s). Minimum college GPA of 2.0 required. **General Admission Information:** Application Fee $55. Regular application deadline 11/30. Notification on a rolling basis, beginning on or about 10/2. Nonfall registration not accepted. Credit and/or placement offered for CEEB Advanced Placement tests.

COSTS AND FINANCIAL AID

Annual in-state tuition $5,472. Annual out-of-state tuition $16,632. Room and board $13,284. Required fees $1,400. Average book expense $1,500. **Required Forms and Deadlines:** FAFSA. **Notification of Awards:** Applicants will be notified of awards on a rolling basis beginning 4/1. **Types of Aid:** *Need-based scholarships/grants:* Federal Pell, SEOG, state scholarships/grants, private scholarships, the school's own gift aid. *Loans:* Subsidized Stafford, Unsubsidized Stafford, PLUS, Federal Perkins, college/university loans from institutional funds. *Student Employment:* Federal Work-Study Program available. Institutional employment available. Off-campus job opportunities are good. **Financial Aid Statistics:** 88% freshmen, 89% undergrads receive need-based scholarship or grant aid. 9% freshmen, 6% undergrads receive non-need-based scholarship or grant aid. 54% freshmen, 51% undergrads receive need-based self-help aid. 0% freshmen, 0% undergrads receive athletic scholarships. 78% freshmen, 72% undergrads receive any aid. 50% undergrads borrow to pay for school. Average cumulative indebtedness $20,795. **Criteria for awarding institutional aid:** *Non-need-based:* academics, alumni affiliation, athletics, leadership, state/district residency.

CALIFORNIA STATE UNIVERSITY, BAKERSFIELD

9001 Stockdale Highway, Bakersfield, CA 93311
Phone: 661-664-3036
E-mail: swatkin@csub.edu · **CEEB Code:** 4110
Fax: 661-664-3389 · **Website:** www.csub.edu

This public school was founded in 1970. It has a 375-acre campus.

RATINGS

Admissions Selectivity Rating: 60*   **Fire Safety Rating:** 60*

STUDENTS AND FACULTY

Enrollment: 4,309. **Student Body:** 10% out-of-state.
Retention and Graduation: 20% grads go on to further study within 1 year. 10% grads pursue arts and sciences degrees. 10% grads pursue business degrees.

ACADEMICS

Degrees: bachelor's, master's. **Majors with Highest Enrollment:** Liberal Arts and Sciences/Liberal Studies; Psychology; Business, Management, Marketing, and Related Support Services. **Special Study Options:** Accelerated program, cooperative education program, cross-registration, distance learning, double major, dual enrollment, English as a Second Language (ESL), exchange student program (domestic), external degree program, honors program, independent study, internships, liberal arts/career combination, student-designed major, study abroad, teacher certification program. **Disability Services:** Special programs offered to physically disabled students include note-taking services, reader services, tape recorders, tutors. **Career services:** alumni services, career/job search classes, career assessment, internships.

FACILITIES

Housing: Coed dorms, women's dorms. 100% of campus accessible to physically disabled. **Special Academic Facilities/Equipment:** Todd Madigan Art Gallery; Frances Dor Theater; Calif. Well Sample Repository; Geotechnology Training Center; Family Business Institute. **Computers:** Students can register for classes online.

CAMPUS LIFE

Environment: Village. **Activities:** Choral groups, concert band, drama/theater, jazz band, literary magazine, music ensembles, musical theater, opera, pep band, student government, student newspaper. 71 registered organizations, 1 honor society, 2 religious organizations. 2 fraternities, 2 sororities. **Athletics (Intercollegiate):** *Men:* basketball, diving, golf, soccer, swimming, track/field (outdoor), wrestling. *Women:* basketball, cross-country, diving, soccer, softball, swimming, tennis, track/field (outdoor), volleyball, water polo.

ADMISSIONS

Freshman Academic Profile: 99% from public high schools. Minimum paper TOEFL 550. **Freshman Admission Requirements:** High school diploma is required and GED is accepted. *Academic units required:* 4 English, 3 mathematics, 1 science, (2 science labs), 2 foreign language, 2 history, 1 academic electives, 1 Visual/Performing Arts. **Transfer Admission Requirements:** college transcript(s), Minimum college GPA of 2.0 required. Lowest grade transferable D. **General Admission Information:** Application Fee $55. Nonfall registration accepted. Admission may be deferred for a maximum of N/A. Credit and/or placement offered for CEEB Advanced Placement tests.

COSTS AND FINANCIAL AID

Required Forms and Deadlines: FAFSA, State aid form. **Types of Aid:** *Need-based scholarships/grants:* Federal Pell, SEOG, state scholarships/grants, private scholarships, the school's own gift aid, United Negro College Fund, Federal Nursing Scholarships. *Loans:* Direct Subsidized Stafford, Subsidized Stafford, Federal Perkins, Federal Nursing, state loans, college/university loans from institutional funds. *Student Employment:* Federal Work-Study Program available. Institutional employment available. Highest amount earned per year from on-campus jobs $3,916. Off-campus job opportunities are good. **Financial Aid Statistics:** 85% freshmen, 83% undergrads receive need-based scholarship or grant aid. 23% freshmen, 8% undergrads receive non-need-based scholarship or grant aid. 48% freshmen, 68% undergrads receive need-based self-help aid. 0% freshmen, 0% undergrads receive athletic scholarships. 72% undergrads borrow to pay for school.

CALIFORNIA STATE UNIVERSITY, CHICO

400 West First Street, Chico, CA 95929-0722
Phone: 530-898-4428 · **Financial Aid Phone:** 530-898-6451
E-mail: info@csuchico.edu · **CEEB Code:** 4048
Fax: 530-898-6456 · **Website:** www.csuchico.edu · **ACT Code:** 212

This public school was founded in 1887. It has a 130-acre campus.

RATINGS

Admissions Selectivity Rating: 83   **Fire Safety Rating:** 68

STUDENTS AND FACULTY

Enrollment: 16,255. **Student Body:** 52% female, 48% male, 1% out-of-state, 4% international (46 countries represented). Asian 6%, African American 2%, Caucasian 49%, Hispanic 26%, Native American 1%.
Retention and Graduation: 87% freshmen return for sophomore year.
Faculty: 459 full-time faculty, 82% hold PhDs, 44% are members of minority groups, 15% are women. 1% of classes are taught by teaching assistants.

ACADEMICS

Degrees: bachelor's, certificate, master's, post-bachelor's certificate, post-master's certificate. **Classes:** Most classes have 20–29 students. Most lab/discussion sessions have 20–29 students. **Majors with Highest Enrollment:** Liberal Arts and Sciences/Liberal Studies; Business Administration and Management; Art/Art Studies. **Special Study Options:** cooperative education program, cross-registration, distance learning, double major, dual enrollment, English as a Second Language (ESL), exchange student program (domestic), external degree program, honors program, independent study, internships, student-designed major, study abroad, teacher certification program. **Honors programs:** Honors in General Education (HGE) Honors in the Major (HIM) Combined degree programs: We currently offer BA or BS combined with a post-bac credential. **Disability Services:** Special programs offered to physically disabled students include note-taking services, reader services, tape recorders, tutors. **Career services:** Alumni network, career assessment, internships. We are most proud of the experiential learning that we afford our students. Typical of the types of projects our entrepreneurship students engage in is the collaboration between teams of students associated with our Center for Entrepreneurship (CFE) and teams of students enrolled in the College of Engineering's Manufacturing Technology Program. This collaboration takes these student teams out of the classroom and into the middle of one of the most important industries (rice) in the University's service region. In March 2007, Chico State Manufacturing Technology Program (MFP) students won the Grand Prize in the prestigious WESTEC (Western Tool Exposition and Conference) Manufacturing Challenge for building a bio-diesel reactor unit that they redesigned from an existing manually operated home bio-diesel kit. The bio diesel reactor unit was originally designed to reduce, reuse and recycle the used vegetable oil and animal fat from Chico State's residence hall kitchen. The project team also considered use of animal renderings from the university farm as a potential feedstock for bio-diesel fuel. While the Chico State bio-diesel reactor unit was built more for research than for commercial production, conversations between our CFE Director and the MFP Director led to a CFE-initiated assessment of the feasibility of alternative feed stock products from which bio-diesel could be produced. A study conducted by the interdisciplinary team of students led to the discovery that rice processing provides an effective feedstock for the production of bio-diesel. The study demonstrated that rice producing areas in Butte and Glenn counties may be capable of producing sufficient bio diesel from rice bran to substantially impact the amount of petroleum-based diesel fuel needed for the industry's production processes. The study concluded that feedstock within the university's 12-county service region would be plentiful, thereby creating new revenue sources for the local agricultural business community and facilitating new opportunities in the area of sustainable farming. This and other types of experiential learning projects that we make available for our students aligns perfectly with the college's vision for a world-class Center for Entrepreneurship at California State University, Chico. It also supports the University's strong commitment and unique competencies in the area of sustainability, it furthers our commitment to provide students with experiential learning opportunities, and it helps us mobilize campus resources that can contribute to the vibrancy of the local economy.

FACILITIES

Housing: Coed dorms, special housing for disabled students, special housing for international students, fraternity/sorority housing, apartments for single students, Thematic housing for honors, engineering, minorities in engineering and science, business, and math. Theme floors include community service, recreational sports, leadership, and Adventure Outings. 95% of campus accessible to physically disabled. **Special Academic Facilities/Equipment:** Anthropology museum, center for intercultural studies, satellite communication dishes, biological field station, university farm, electron microscope. **Computers:** 100% of classrooms, 100% of dorms, 100% of libraries, 100% of dining areas, 100% of student union, 25% of common outdoor areas have wireless network access. Students can register for classes online. Administrative functions (other than registration) can be performed online.

CAMPUS LIFE

Environment: City. **Activities:** Choral groups, concert band, dance, drama/theater, jazz band, literary magazine, music ensembles, musical theater, opera, pep band, radio station, student government, student newspaper, student-run film society, symphony orchestra, yearbook. 192 registered organizations, 18 honor societies, 12 religious organizations. 15 fraternities, 14 sororities. **Athletics (Intercollegiate):** *Men:* baseball, basketball, cross-country, golf, soccer, track/field (outdoor). *Women:* basketball, cross-country, golf, soccer, softball, track/field (outdoor), volleyball. **On-Campus Highlights:** Bell Memorial Union, Meriam Library, Turner Print Museum, Humanities Gallery/University Gallery, Wildcat Recreation Center, Nettleton Stadium; on-campus housing facilities; athletic facilities; recording arts studio. **Environmental Initiatives:** This Way to Sustainability Conference; AASHE STARS; Pilot Project; ACUPCC.

ADMISSIONS

Freshman Academic Profile: 35% in top 10% of high school class, 76% in top 25% of high school class, 100% in top 50% of high school class. 91% from public high schools. SAT Math middle 50% range 440-5550. SAT Critical Reading middle 50% range 440-550. ACT middle 50% range 19-24. Minimum internet-based TOEFL 79. Minimum paper TOEFL 500. **Basis for Candi-**

date Selection: *Very important factors considered include:* academic GPA, standardized test scores. *Important factors considered include:* geographical residence, state residency. **Freshman Admission Requirements:** High school diploma is required and GED is accepted. *Academic units required:* 4 English, 3 mathematics, 2 science, (2 science labs), 2 foreign language, 2 social studies, 1 visual/performing arts, 1 academic electives. **Freshman Admission Statistics:** 20,360 applied, 75% admitted, 19% enrolled. **Transfer Admission Requirements:** college transcript(s), statement of good standing from prior institution(s). Minimum college GPA of 2.0 required. Lowest grade transferable D. **General Admission Information:** Application Fee $55. Regular application deadline 11/30. Regular notification 3/1. Nonfall registration accepted. Admission may be deferred for a maximum of 1 year. Credit offered for CEEB Advanced Placement tests.

COSTS AND FINANCIAL AID

Annual in-state tuition $7,002. Annual out-of-state tuition $18,162. Room and board $11,626. Required fees $1,530. Average book expense $1,746. **Required Forms and Deadlines:** FAFSA. **Notification of Awards:** Applicants will be notified of awards on a rolling basis beginning 3/2. **Types of Aid:** *Need-based scholarships/grants:* Federal Pell, SEOG, state scholarships/grants, private scholarships, the school's own gift aid. *Loans:* Direct Subsidized Stafford, Direct Unsubsidized Stafford, Direct PLUS, Federal Perkins, college/university loans from institutional funds. *Student Employment:* Federal Work-Study Program available. Institutional employment available. Off-campus job opportunities are fair. **Financial Aid Statistics:** 75% freshmen, 77% undergrads receive need-based scholarship or grant aid. 23% freshmen, 13% undergrads receive non-need-based scholarship or grant aid. 64% freshmen, 67% undergrads receive need-based self-help aid. 2% freshmen, 1% undergrads receive athletic scholarships. 66% freshmen, 63% undergrads receive any aid. 83% undergrads borrow to pay for school. Average cumulative indebtedness $18,480. **Criteria for awarding institutional aid:** *Non-need-based:* academics, art, athletics, leadership, minority status, music/drama, religious affiliation.

CALIFORNIA STATE UNIVERSITY, DOMINGUEZ HILLS

100 East Victoria Street, Carson, CA 90747
Phone: 310-243-3645 • **Financial Aid Phone:** 310-243-3691
E-mail: info@csudh.edu • **CEEB Code:** 4098
Fax: 310-516-3609 • **Website:** www.csudh.edu • **ACT Code:** 203

This public school was founded in 1960. It has a 346-acre campus.

RATiNGS

Admissions Selectivity Rating: 69   **Fire Safety Rating:** 67

STUDENTS AND FACULTY

Enrollment: 12,134. **Student Body:** 64% female, 36% male, 0% out-of-state, 3% international (37 countries represented). Asian 9%, African American 15%, Caucasian 8%, Hispanic 58%, Native American <1%
Retention and Graduation: 80% freshmen return for sophomore year. 5% freshmen graduate within 4 years. **Faculty:** 254 full-time faculty, 85% hold PhDs, 55% are members of minority groups, 38% are women. 0% of classes are taught by teaching assistants.

ACADEMICS

Degrees: bachelor's, certificate, master's, post-bachelor's certificate. **Classes:** Most classes have 20–29 students. Most lab/discussion sessions have 20–29 students. **Majors with Highest Enrollment:** Psychology; Registered Nursing/Registered Nurse; Business Administration and Management. **Special Study Options:** cooperative education program, cross-registration, distance learning, double major, dual enrollment, external degree program, honors program, independent study, internships, study abroad, teacher certification program, weekend college. **Disability Services:** Special programs offered to physically disabled students include note-taking services, reader services, tape recorders, tutors.

FACILITIES

Housing: apartments for married students, apartments for single students. 100% of campus accessible to physically disabled. **Special Academic Facilities/Equipment:** University Art Gallery. Olympic Velodrome University Theater.

CAMPUS LIFE

Environment: City. **Activities:** Choral groups, concert band, dance, drama/theater, jazz band, music ensembles, student government, student newspaper, symphony orchestra. 65 registered organizations, 6 honor societies, 3 religious organizations. 4 fraternities, 4 sororities. **Athletics (Intercollegiate):** *Men:* baseball, basketball, golf, soccer. *Women:* basketball, cross-country, soccer, softball, tennis, track/field (outdoor), volleyball. **On-Campus Highlights:** Welch Hall, Student Union, Library, Athletic Fields/Home Depot Center, Sculpture Garden.

ADMISSIONS

Freshman Academic Profile: Average high school GPA 3.12. 93% from public high schools. SAT Math middle 50% range 380-470. SAT Critical Reading middle 50% range 380-470. SAT Writing middle 50% range 380-470. ACT middle 50% range 15-20. Minimum internet-based TOEFL 61. Minimum paper TOEFL 500. **Basis for Candidate Selection:** *Other factors considered include:* recommendation(s), geographical residence, state residency. **Freshman Admission Requirements:** High school diploma is required and GED is accepted. *Academic units required:* 4 English, 3 mathematics, 2 science, (2 science labs), 2 foreign language, 2 social studies, 1 history, 1 academic electives, 1 Visual/Performing Arts. **Freshman Admission Statistics:** 8,257 applied, 81% admitted, 20% enrolled. **Transfer Admission Requirements:** High school transcript, college transcript(s), Minimum college GPA of 2.0 required. Lowest grade transferable c. **General Admission Information:** Application Fee $55. Regular application deadline 6/1. Nonfall registration accepted. Credit offered for CEEB Advanced Placement tests.

COSTS AND FINANCIAL AID

Average book expense $1,746. **Required Forms and Deadlines:** FAFSA. **Notification of Awards:** Applicants will be notified of awards on a rolling basis beginning 2/28. **Types of Aid:** *Need-based scholarships/grants:* Federal Pell, state scholarships/grants. *Loans:* Direct Subsidized Stafford, Direct Unsubsidized Stafford, PLUS, Federal Perkins. *Student Employment:* Highest amount earned per year from on-campus jobs $3,000. **Financial Aid Statistics:** 89% freshmen, 84% undergrads receive need-based scholarship or grant aid. 16% freshmen, 30% undergrads receive non-need-based scholarship or grant aid. 1% freshmen, 3% undergrads receive need-based self-help aid. 0% freshmen, 0% undergrads receive athletic scholarships. 87% freshmen, 81% undergrads receive any aid. 60% undergrads borrow to pay for school. Average cumulative indebtedness $16,979.

CALIFORNIA STATE UNIVERSITY, EAST BAY

25800 Carlos Bee Blvd., Hayward, CA 94542-3035
Phone: 510-885-2784 · **Financial Aid Phone:** 510-885-2784
E-mail: admissions@csueastbay.edu · **CEEB Code:** 4011
Fax: 510-885-3505 · **Website:** www.csueastbay.edu · **ACT Code:** 154

This public school was founded in 1957. It has a 342-acre campus.

RATINGS

Admissions Selectivity Rating: 83   **Fire Safety Rating:** 69

STUDENTS AND FACULTY

Enrollment: 9,788. **Student Body:** 60% female, 40% male, 1% out-of-state, 8% international (86 countries represented). Asian 20%, African American 10%, Caucasian 22%, Hispanic 19%, Native American <1%
Retention and Graduation: 16% freshmen graduate within 4 years. 43% freshmen graduate within 6 years. **Faculty:** 322 full-time faculty, 49% are members of minority groups, 34% are women. 5% of classes are taught by teaching assistants.

ACADEMICS

Degrees: bachelor's, certificate, master's, post-bachelor's certificate, post-master's certificate. **Special Study Options:** cooperative education program, cross-registration, distance learning, double major, dual enrollment, English as a Second Language (ESL), exchange student program (domestic), external degree program, honors program, independent study, internships, liberal arts/career combination, student-designed major, study abroad, teacher certification program, weekend college, Year round operation with state supported summer quarter. Joint Master's Degree in Marine Science offered at Moss Landing Marine Lab. Joint MFA in Creative Writing in summer. Overseas MBA programs in Hong Kong, Moscow, Singapore, and Vienna. **Disability Services:** Special programs offered to physically disabled students include note-taking services, reader services, tape recorders, tutors. **Career services:** alumni services, career/job search classes, career assessment, internships.

FACILITIES

Housing: apartments for single students. 95% of campus accessible to physically disabled. **Special Academic Facilities/Equipment:** Anthropology museum, art gallery, scanning electron microsope facility, marine lab, ecological field station, geology summer camp. **Computers:** Students can register for classes online. Administrative functions (other than registration) can be performed online.

118

CAMPUS LIFE

Environment: City. **Activities:** Choral groups, concert band, dance, drama/theater, jazz band, literary magazine, music ensembles, musical theater, opera, pep band, radio station, student government, student newspaper, symphony orchestra, television station. 100 registered organizations, 2 honor societies, 2 religious organizations. 7 fraternities, 7 sororities. **Athletics (Intercollegiate):** *Men:* baseball, basketball, cross-country, golf, soccer. *Women:* basketball, cross-country, golf, soccer, softball, swimming, volleyball, water polo. **On-Campus Highlights:** University Union, Gymnasium/Pools, Warren Hall /Administration, University Theatre, University Art Gallery.

ADMISSIONS

Freshman Academic Profile: Average high school GPA 3.08. SAT Math middle 50% range 400-510. SAT Critical Reading middle 50% range 400-500. SAT Writing middle 50% range 410-500. ACT middle 50% range 16-21. Minimum paper TOEFL 525. **Basis for Candidate Selection:** *Very important factors considered:* academic GPA, rigor of secondary school record, standardized test scores. *Other factors considered include:* recommendation(s), state residency. **Freshman Admission Requirements:** High school diploma is required and GED is accepted. *Academic units required:* 4 English, 3 mathematics, 2 science, (2 science labs), 2 foreign language, 1 social studies, 1 history, 1 academic electives, 1 Visual/Performing Arts. **Freshman Admission Statistics:** 10,749 applied, 36% admitted, 32% enrolled. **Transfer Admission Requirements:** college transcript(s), statement of good standing from prior institution(s). Minimum college GPA of 2.0 required. Lowest grade transferable D. **General Admission Information:** Application Fee $55. Early decision application deadline 3/15. Regular application deadline 6/30. Notification on a rolling basis, beginning on or about 3/15. Nonfall registration accepted. Admission may be deferred for a maximum of 2 quarters. Credit and/or placement offered for CEEB Advanced Placement tests.

COSTS AND FINANCIAL AID

Annual in-state tuition $5,091. Annual out-of-state tuition $14,019. Room and board $11,042. Average book expense $1,734. **Required Forms and Deadlines:** FAFSA. **Notification of Awards:** Applicants will be notified of awards on a rolling basis beginning 3/15. **Types of Aid:** *Need-based scholarships/grants:* Federal Pell, SEOG, state scholarships/grants, private scholarships, the school's own gift aid. *Loans:* Subsidized Stafford, Unsubsidized Stafford, PLUS, Federal Perkins. *Student Employment:* Federal Work-Study Program available. Institutional employment available. Off-campus job opportunities are excellent. **Financial Aid Statistics:** 83% freshmen, 83% undergrads receive need-based scholarship or grant aid. 0% freshmen, 0% undergrads receive non-need-based scholarship or grant aid. 61% freshmen, 61% undergrads receive need-based self-help aid. 0% freshmen, 0% undergrads receive athletic scholarships. 43% freshmen, 42% undergrads receive any aid. 34% undergrads borrow to pay for school. **Criteria for awarding institutional aid:** *Non-need-based:* academics.

CALIFORNIA STATE UNIVERSITY, FRESNO

5150 North Maple Ave. M/S JA 57, Fresno, CA 93740-8026
Phone: 559-278-2261 · **Financial Aid Phone:** 559-278-2182
E-mail: admissions@csufresno.edu · **CEEB Code:** 4312
Fax: 559-278-4812 · **Website:** www.csufresno.edu · **ACT Code:** 266

This public school was founded in 1911. It has a 388-acre campus.

RATINGS

Admissions Selectivity Rating: 84   **Fire Safety Rating:** 71

STUDENTS AND FACULTY

Enrollment: 18,784. **Student Body:** 57% female, 43% male, 0% out-of-state, 3% international (116 countries represented). Asian 15%, African American 5%, Caucasian 30%, Hispanic 38%, Native American 1%
Retention and Graduation: 14% freshmen graduate within 4 years. 49% freshmen graduate within 6 years. **Faculty:** 624 full-time faculty, 95% hold PhDs, 42% are members of minority groups, 29% are women. 8% of classes are taught by teaching assistants.

ACADEMICS

Degrees: bachelor's, master's. **Classes:** Most classes have 20–29 students. Most lab/discussion sessions have 20–29 students. **Majors with Highest Enrollment:** Liberal Arts and Sciences/Liberal Studies; Psychology; Health Services/Allied Health/Health Sciences. **Special Study Options:** Accelerated program, cooperative education program, cross-registration, distance learning, double major, dual enrollment, English as a Second Language (ESL), exchange student program (domestic), honors program, independent study, internships, student-designed major, study abroad, teacher certification program. **Disability Services:** Special programs offered to physically disabled students include note-taking services, reader services, tape recorders, tutors.

FACILITIES

Housing: Coed dorms, men's dorms, women's dorms, fraternity/sorority housing. 100% of campus accessible to physically disabled. **Special Academic Facilities/Equipment:** Marine lab, Downing Planeterium. **Computers:** 100% of classrooms, 100% of dorms, 100% of libraries, 100% of dining areas, 100% of student union, 20% of common outdoor areas have wireless network access. Students can register for classes online. Administrative functions (other than registration) can be performed online. Undergraduates are required to own a computer.

CAMPUS LIFE

Environment: Metropolis. **Activities:** Choral groups, concert band, dance, drama/theater, jazz band, marching band, music ensembles, musical theater, radio station, student government, student newspaper, symphony orchestra, television station, International Student Organization. 250 registered organizations, 21 honor society, 11 religious organization. 19 fraternities, 13 sororities. **Athletics (Intercollegiate):** *Men:* baseball, basketball, cheerleading, cross-country, football, golf, tennis, track/field (outdoor). *Women:* basketball, cheerleading, cross-country, diving, equestrian sports, golf, lacrosse, light weight football, soccer, softball, swimming, tennis, track/field (outdoor), volleyball. **On-Campus Highlights:** Savemart Events Center, Downing Planetarium, Kennel Bookstore, New Ciminology Center, Henry Madden Library, Please check out our website for more inforamtion: www.gotofresnostate.com. **Environmental Initiatives:** Solar Photovoltaic Canopy Parking Structure (Lot V) This structure is a 1.1 megawatt solar system, making it the largest photovoltaic paneled parting installation at a U.S. university. Completed in the fall of 2007, the structure was estimated to provide 20% of the core campus power. The system offsets approximately 950 metric tons of carbon monoxide emissions ?û that is equivalent to planting over 24,300 trees or eliminating from our road systems over 200 vehicles a year! On February 20, 2009, students, faculty and members of the community were in attendance of the long-awaited opening of the new Henry Madden Library. With the wide range of attractive features such as electronic compact bookshelves, hi-definition flat screens, comfortably furnished study rooms, and of course the ever-popular Starbucks café, its no wonder why the library has become the new focal point of Fresno State. However, many people are still unaware of the sustainable features of the Henry Madden Library that, despite the structure's size, make it the most environmentally friendly building on campus. These features include: One of the largest collections of movable stacks in the country, which helps to minimize the overall carbon footprint of the library; Highest standards of energy efficient insulation; Centralized HVAC which controls air handling areas of the library; Thermal comfort managed using fresh, outdoor air rather than conditioned air when appropriate; Ubiquitous compact fluorescent lighting; Motion sensor activated lighting system in conference and private study rooms; North side made entirely of class providing year-round natural lighting, thus lowering energy usage and costs; Recycling of the old building materials during demolition; Furniture made from recycled materials; Carpet tiles designed, produced and disposed of in a cradle-to-cradle process; Building materials that were sourced from local manufacturers (i.e. granite and wood used to furnish the library); Newly renovated Peace Garden, which contains native species that require no irrigation and help to manage storm water, thus maximizing efficiency of water use! The University understands the importance of water as a finite resource and has been taking a leadership role in developing ways to utilize water more efficiently by establishing the International Center for Water Technology (ICWT). In 2007, the campus reduced the amount of water used to irrigate the 380-acre academic core of campus by an estimated 33%. This was done through alternative watering schedules, repairs to failing irrigation lines and the installation of better controls. Phase II of the planned Campus Utility Infrastructure Replacement will include new water mains that will provide non-potable water to campus irrigation systems.

ADMISSIONS

Freshman Academic Profile: Average high school GPA 3.33. 15% in top 10% of high school class, 80% in top 25% of high school class, 100% in top 50% of high school class. 99% from public high schools. SAT Math middle 50% range 410-530. SAT Critical Reading middle 50% range 400-510. SAT Writing middle 50% range 400-510. ACT middle 50% range 16-22. Minimum internet-based TOEFL 61. Minimum paper TOEFL 500. **Basis for Candidate Selection:** *Very important factors considered include:* academic GPA, rigor of secondary school record, standardized test scores. **Freshman Admission Requirements:** High school diploma is required and GED is accepted. *Academic units required:* 4 English, 3 mathematics, 1 science, (1 science labs), 2 foreign language, 1 social studies, 1 history, 1 visual/performing arts, 0 computer science, 1 academic electives. **Freshman Admission Statistics:** 15,482 applied, 60% admitted, 31% enrolled. **Transfer Admission Requirements:** college transcript(s). Minimum college GPA of 2.4 required. Lowest grade transferable D. **General Admission Information:** Application Fee $55. Regular application deadline 11/30. Notification on a rolling basis, beginning on or about 8/1. Nonfall registration accepted. Credit offered for CEEB Advanced Placement tests.

COSTS AND FINANCIAL AID

Annual out-of-state tuition $11,160. Room and board $10,550. Required fees $790. Average book expense $1,256. **Required Forms and Deadlines:**

FAFSA. **Notification of Awards:** Applicants will be notified of awards on a rolling basis beginning 4/1. **Types of Aid:** *Need-based scholarships/grants:* Federal Pell, SEOG, state scholarships/grants, private scholarships, the school's own gift aid. *Loans:* Subsidized Stafford, Unsubsidized Stafford, PLUS, Federal Perkins, Federal Nursing, college/university loans from institutional funds. *Student Employment:* Federal Work-Study Program available. Institutional employment available. Off-campus job opportunities are good. **Financial Aid Statistics:** 83% freshmen, 80% undergrads receive need-based scholarship or grant aid. 2% freshmen, 9% undergrads receive non-need-based scholarship or grant aid. 67% freshmen, 79% undergrads receive need-based self-help aid. 3% freshmen, 2% undergrads receive athletic scholarships. 76% freshmen, 78% undergrads receive any aid. 79% undergrads borrow to pay for school. Average cumulative indebtedness $11,349. **Criteria for awarding institutional aid:** *Non-need-based:* academics, art, athletics, leadership, music/drama, state/district residency.

CALIFORNIA STATE UNIVERSITY, FULLERTON

P.O.Box 6900, Fullerton, CA 92834-6900
Phone: 657-278-7788 · **Financial Aid Phone:** 657-278-3125
E-mail: admissions@fullerton.edu · **CEEB Code:** 4589
Fax: 657-278-7699 · **Website:** www.fullerton.edu · **ACT Code:** 355

This public school was founded in 1957. It has a 225-acre campus.

RATINGS

Admissions Selectivity Rating: 87   **Fire Safety Rating:** 75

STUDENTS AND FACULTY

Enrollment: 32,610. **Student Body:** 55% female, 45% male, 1% out-of-state, 5% international (75 countries represented). Asian 22%, African American 2%, Caucasian 24%, Hispanic 39%, Native American <1%
Retention and Graduation: 89% freshmen return for sophomore year. 14% freshmen graduate within 4 years. **Faculty:** 944 full-time faculty, 49% are members of minority groups, 29% are women. 0% of classes are taught by teaching assistants.

ACADEMICS

Degrees: bachelor's, master's. **Classes:** Most classes have 20–29 students. Most lab/discussion sessions have 20–29 students. **Majors with Highest Enrollment:** Psychology; Finance; Early Childhood Education and Teaching. **Special Study Options:** cooperative education program, double major, honors program, independent study, internships, student-designed major, study abroad. **Disability Services:** Special programs offered to physically disabled students include note-taking services, reader services, tape recorders. **Career services:** alumni services, career/job search classes, career assessment, internships.

FACILITIES

Housing: fraternity/sorority housing, apartments for single students. 90% of campus accessible to physically disabled. **Computers:** Students can register for classes online. Administrative functions (other than registration) can be performed online.

CAMPUS LIFE

Activities: Choral groups, concert band, dance, drama/theater, jazz band, music ensembles, musical theater, radio station, student government, student newspaper. **Athletics (Intercollegiate):** *Men:* baseball, basketball, cross-country, fencing, soccer, track/field (outdoor), wrestling. *Women:* basketball, cross-country, fencing, gymnastics, soccer, softball, tennis, track/field (outdoor), volleyball. **On-Campus Highlights:** Fullerton Arboretum, 5 Starbucks Coffee shops, Titan Student Union Underground.

ADMISSIONS

Freshman Academic Profile: Average high school GPA 3.53. 24% in top 10% of high school class, 66% in top 25% of high school class, 96% in top 50% of high school class. 88% from public high schools. SAT Math middle 50% range 470-580. SAT Critical Reading middle 50% range 450-550. ACT middle 50% range 19-24. Minimum internet-based TOEFL 61. Minimum paper TOEFL 500. **Basis for Candidate Selection:** *Very important factors considered include:* rigor of secondary school record, standardized test scores. *Other factors considered include:* state residency. **Freshman Admission Requirements:** High school diploma is required and GED is accepted. *Academic units required:* 2 science, (2 science labs), 2 history, 1 academic electives, 1 Visual/Performing Arts. **Freshman Admission Statistics:** 40,955 applied, 24% admitted, 24% enrolled. **Transfer Admission Requirements:** college transcript(s), statement of good standing from prior institution(s). Minimum college GPA of 2.0 required. Lowest grade transferable C. **General Admission Information:** Application Fee $55. Regular application deadline 4/15. Notification on a rolling basis, beginning on or about 1/1. Nonfall registration accepted. Credit and/or placement offered for CEEB Advanced Placement tests.

COSTS AND FINANCIAL AID

Annual in-state tuition $5,472. Annual out-of-state tuition $16,632. Room and board $13,510. Required fees $844. Average book expense $1,806. **Required Forms and Deadlines:** FAFSA. **Notification of Awards:** Applicants will be notified of awards on a rolling basis beginning 3/1. **Types of Aid:** *Need-based scholarships/grants:* Federal Pell, SEOG, state scholarships/grants, private scholarships, the school's own gift aid. *Loans:* Subsidized Stafford, Unsubsidized Stafford, PLUS, Federal Perkins, college/university loans from institutional funds. *Student Employment:* Federal Work-Study Program available. Institutional employment available. Off-campus job opportunities are good. **Financial Aid Statistics:** 80% freshmen, 78% undergrads receive need-based scholarship or grant aid. 14% freshmen, 9% undergrads receive non-need-based scholarship or grant aid. 52% freshmen, 53% undergrads receive need-based self-help aid. 1% freshmen, 1% undergrads receive athletic scholarships. 66% freshmen, 45% undergrads receive any aid. 42% undergrads borrow to pay for school. Average cumulative indebtedness $14,983. **Criteria for awarding institutional aid:** *Non-need-based:* academics.

CALIFORNIA STATE UNIVERSITY, LONG BEACH

1250 Bellflower Boulevard, Long Beach, CA 90840
Phone: 562-985-5471
E-mail: eslb@csulb.edu • **CEEB Code:** 4389
Fax: 562-985-4973 • **Website:** www.csulb.edu

This public school was founded in 1949. It has a 322-acre campus.

RATINGS

Admissions Selectivity Rating: 89   **Fire Safety Rating:** 64

STUDENTS AND FACULTY

Enrollment: 31,523. **Student Body:** 56% female, 44% male, 1% out-of-state, 6% international. Asian 23%, African American 4%, Caucasian 20%, Hispanic 38%, Native American <1%
Retention and Graduation: 90% freshmen return for sophomore year. 14% freshmen graduate within 4 years. 65% freshmen graduate within 6 years.
Faculty: 941 full-time faculty, 86% hold PhDs, 46% are members of minority groups, 33% are women. 8% of classes are taught by teaching assistants.

ACADEMICS

Degrees: bachelor's, master's, post-bachelor's certificate. **Classes:** Most classes have 20–29 students. Most lab/discussion sessions have 20–29 students. **Majors with Highest Enrollment:** Psychology; Corrections and Criminal Justice; Management Information Systems. **Special Study Options:** Accelerated program, cross-registration, distance learning, double major, dual enrollment, English as a Second Language (ESL), honors program, independent study, internships, student-designed major, study abroad, teacher certification program. **Disability Services:** Special programs offered to physically disabled students include note-taking services, reader services. **Career services:** alumni services, career assessment, internships

FACILITIES

Housing: Coed dorms, special housing for international students. 98% of campus accessible to physically disabled. **Special Academic Facilities/Equipment:** Art and science museums, Japanese garden, special events arena with meeting facilities.

CAMPUS LIFE

Activities: Choral groups, concert band, dance, drama/theater, jazz band, literary magazine, music ensembles, musical theater, opera, radio station, student government, student newspaper, student-run film society, symphony orchestra, television station, yearbook. 300 registered organizations, 25 honor societies, 20 religious organizations. 16 fraternities, 15 sororities. **Athletics (Intercollegiate):** *Men:* baseball, basketball, cross-country, golf, track/field (outdoor), volleyball, water polo. *Women:* basketball, cross-country, golf, soccer, softball, tennis, track/field (outdoor), volleyball, water polo.

ADMISSIONS

Freshman Academic Profile: Average high school GPA 3.52. 0% in top 25% of high school class, 0% in top 50% of high school class. 82% from public high schools. SAT Math middle 50% range 480-600. SAT Critical Reading middle 50% range 460-570. ACT middle 50% range 20-25. Minimum paper TOEFL 525. **Basis for Candidate Selection:** *Very important factors considered include:* academic GPA, standardized test scores, geographical residence, state residency. *Important factors considered include:* talent/ability. *Other factors considered include:* application essay, recommendation(s), rigor of secondary school record, character/personal qualities, extracurricular activities, volunteer work, work experience. **Freshman Admission Requirements:** High school diploma is required and GED is accepted. *Academic units required:* 4 English,

3 mathematics, 2 science, (2 science labs), 2 foreign language, 1 social studies, 1 history, 1 academic electives, 1 Fine Arts. **Freshman Admission Statistics:** 56,357 applied, 36% admitted, 21% enrolled. **Transfer Admission Requirements:** college transcript(s), Minimum college GPA of 2.0 required. Lowest grade transferable C. **General Admission Information:** Application Fee $55. Regular application deadline 11/30. Notification on a rolling basis, beginning on or about 12/1. Nonfall registration accepted. Credit offered for CEEB Advanced Placement tests.

COSTS AND FINANCIAL AID

Annual in-state tuition $5,440. Annual out-of-state tuition $11,160. Room and board $11,688. Required fees $980. Average book expense $1,828. **Required Forms and Deadlines:** FAFSA. **Notification of Awards:** Applicants will be notified of awards on a rolling basis beginning 3/30. **Types of Aid:** *Need-based scholarships/grants:* Federal Pell, SEOG, state scholarships/grants, private scholarships, the school's own gift aid. *Loans:* Direct Subsidized Stafford, Direct Unsubsidized Stafford, Direct PLUS, Federal Perkins. *Student Employment:* Federal Work-Study Program available. Institutional employment available. Highest amount earned per year from on-campus jobs $3,000. Off-campus job opportunities are good. **Financial Aid Statistics:** 80% freshmen, 80% undergrads receive need-based scholarship or grant aid. 24% freshmen, 24% undergrads receive non-need-based scholarship or grant aid. 71% freshmen, 79% undergrads receive need-based self-help aid. 2% freshmen, 1% undergrads receive athletic scholarships. 43% undergrads borrow to pay for school. Average cumulative indebtedness $15,680. **Criteria for awarding institutional aid:** *Non-need-based:* academics, art, athletics, music/drama.

CALIFORNIA STATE UNIVERSITY, LOS ANGELES

5151 State University Drive, Los Angeles, CA 90032
Phone: 323-343-3901 • **Financial Aid Phone:** 323-343-6260
E-mail: admission@calstatela.edu • **CEEB Code:** 4399
Fax: 323-343-6306 • **ACT Code:** 320

This public school was founded in 1947. It has a 175-acre campus.

RATINGS

Admissions Selectivity Rating: 76   **Fire Safety Rating:** 70

STUDENTS AND FACULTY

Enrollment: 18,074. **Student Body:** 59% female, 41% male, 0% out-of-state, 4% international (121 countries represented). Asian 17%, African American 5%, Caucasian 8%, Hispanic 58%, Native American <1%
Retention and Graduation: 81% freshmen return for sophomore year. 7% freshmen graduate within 4 years. 37% freshmen graduate within 6 years.
Faculty: 533 full-time faculty, 46% hold PhDs, 47% are members of minority groups, 44% are women. 14% of classes are taught by teaching assistants.

ACADEMICS

Degrees: bachelor's, certificate, master's, post-bachelor's certificate. **Classes:** Most classes have 20–29 students. **Majors with Highest Enrollment:** Psychology; Criminal Justice/Law Enforcement Administration; Business Administration and Management. **Special Study Options:** Accelerated program, cooperative education program, cross-registration, distance learning, double major, dual enrollment, English as a Second Language (ESL), exchange student program (domestic), honors program, independent study, internships, student-designed major, study abroad, teacher certification program. **Disability Services:** Special programs offered to physically disabled students include note-taking services, reader services. **Career services:** career/job search classes, internships.

FACILITIES

Housing: Coed dorms, special housing for international students, fraternity/sorority housing, apartments for single students, Wellness Housing, Theme Housing (Special Interest Housing): First Year House; Quiet House; ACLP/International House; The Neighborhood Wellness/Substance Free House; The Village Quiet House. **Special Academic Facilities/Equipment:** Baroque pipe organ, bilingual center, entrepreneurship and small business institutes, center for study of armament and disarmament, Van de Graaff accelerator. **Computers:** Administrative functions (other than registration) can be performed online.

CAMPUS LIFE

Environment: Metropolis. **Activities:** Choral groups, dance, drama/theater, jazz band, literary magazine, music ensembles, musical theater, opera, radio station, student government, student newspaper, symphony orchestra, yearbook. 130 registered organizations, 3 religious organizations. 7 fraternities, 4 sororities. **Athletics (Intercollegiate):** *Men:* baseball, basketball, cross-country, soccer, track/field (outdoor). *Women:* basketball, cross-country, soccer, tennis, track/field (outdoor), volleyball.

ADMISSIONS

Freshman Academic Profile: Average high school GPA 3.16. SAT Math middle 50% range 390-510. SAT Critical Reading middle 50% range 380-480. SAT Writing middle 50% range 930-480. ACT middle 50% range 15-20. Minimum paper TOEFL 550. **Basis for Candidate Selection:** *Very important factors considered include:* academic GPA, rigor of secondary school record, standardized test scores. *Other factors considered include:* state residency. **Freshman Admission Requirements:** High school diploma is required and GED is accepted. *Academic units required:* 4 English, 3 mathematics, 2 science, (2 science labs), 2 foreign language, 1 social studies, 1 history, 1 academic electives, 1 Visual and Performing Arts. **Freshman Admission Statistics:** 27,321 applied, 65% admitted, 16% enrolled. **Transfer Admission Requirements:** college transcript(s), Minimum college GPA of 2.0 required. Lowest grade transferable C. **General Admission Information:** Application Fee $55. Regular application deadline 6/15. Nonfall registration accepted. Credit and/or placement offered for CEEB Advanced Placement tests.

COSTS AND FINANCIAL AID

Annual in-state tuition $6,101. Annual out-of-state tuition $17,759. Room and board $9,728. Average book expense $1,665. **Required Forms and Deadlines:** FAFSA. **Types of Aid:** *Need-based scholarships/grants:* Federal Pell, SEOG, state scholarships/grants, private scholarships, the school's own gift aid, Federal and State Work Study. *Loans:* Direct Subsidized Stafford, Direct Unsubsidized Stafford, PLUS, Federal Perkins, Federal Nursing. *Student Employment:* Federal Work-Study Program available. Institutional employment available. Off-campus job opportunities are good. **Financial Aid Statistics:** 88% freshmen, 88% undergrads receive need-based scholarship or grant aid. 0% freshmen, 0% undergrads receive non-need-based scholarship or grant aid. 65% freshmen, 79% undergrads receive need-based self-help aid. 0% freshmen, 0% undergrads receive athletic scholarships. 76% freshmen, 77% undergrads receive any aid.

CALIFORNIA STATE UNIVERSITY, MONTEREY BAY

100 Campus Center, Seaside, CA 93955
Phone: 831-582-3738 • **Financial Aid Phone:** 831-582-5100
E-mail: admissions@csumb.edu • **CEEB Code:** 1945
Fax: 831-582-3783 • **Website:** http://www.csumb.edu • **ACT Code:** 321

This public school was founded in 1994. It has a 1387-acre campus.

RATINGS

Admissions Selectivity Rating: 78   **Fire Safety Rating:** 79

STUDENTS AND FACULTY

Enrollment: 6,234. **Student Body:** 62% female, 38% male, 2% out-of-state, 5% international (20 countries represented). Asian 6%, African American 7%, Caucasian 35%, Hispanic 35%, Native American 1%
Retention and Graduation: 84% freshmen return for sophomore year. 17% freshmen graduate within 4 years. **Faculty:** 123 full-time faculty, 90% hold PhDs, 50% are members of minority groups, 44% are women. 0% of classes are taught by teaching assistants.

ACADEMICS

Degrees: bachelor's, master's. **Classes:** Most classes have 20–29 students. Most lab/discussion sessions have 20–29 students. **Majors with Highest Enrollment:** Business Administration and Management; Psychology; Health and Physical Education/Fitness. **Special Study Options:** cross-registration, distance learning, double major, exchange student program (domestic), independent study, internships, student-designed major, study abroad, teacher certification program, service learning. **Disability Services:** Special programs offered to physically disabled students include note-taking services, reader services, tape recorders. **Career services:** alumni services, career/job search classes, career assessment, internships. Career services highlights include annual career conference that brings together students, alumni and other working professionals together for a day of networking and learning was featured in the "Good Ideas" section of Campus Career Counselor magazine.

FACILITIES

Housing: Coed dorms, special housing for disabled students, special housing for international students, apartments for married students, apartments for single students, Wellness Housing, Theme Housing, six-person suite-style living with living areas and kitchenette, substance-free residence hall. 75% of campus accessible to physically disabled. **Special Academic Facilities/Equipment:** Panetta Institute, Tanimura & Antle Family Memorial Library. **Computers:** 100% of classrooms, 100% of dorms, 100% of libraries, 100% of dining areas,

100% of student union, 25% of common outdoor areas have wireless network access. Students can register for classes online. Administrative functions (other than registration) can be performed online.

CAMPUS LIFE

Environment: Village. **Activities:** Choral groups, concert band, dance, drama/theater, jazz band, music ensembles, radio station, student government, student newspaper, Campus Ministries, International Student Organization, Model UN. 71 registered organizations, 4 religious organizations. 5 fraternities, 8 sororities. **Athletics (Intercollegiate): Men:** baseball, basketball, cross-country, golf, sailing, soccer. *Women:* basketball, cross-country, golf, sailing, soccer, softball, volleyball, water polo. **On-Campus Highlights:** Black Box Cabaret, University Center, Student Center, Tanimura & Antle Library, Chapman Science Academic Center. **Environmental Initiatives:** We are an early signatory to the Presidents Climate Commitment We have completed a one megawatt PV Solar Array that provides 16% of our electrical load. Our Food Service operations has a high commitment to organic foods, compostable packaging and serving products, and new programming, such as meatless Mondays.

ADMISSIONS

Freshman Academic Profile: Average high school GPA 3.23. 12% in top 10% of high school class, 43% in top 25% of high school class, 82% in top 50% of high school class. 89% from public high schools. SAT Math middle 50% range 430-540. SAT Critical Reading middle 50% range 430-540. SAT Writing middle 50% range 430-530. ACT middle 50% range 18-24. Minimum internet-based TOEFL 61. Minimum paper TOEFL 500. **Basis for Candidate Selection:** *Very important factors considered include:* academic GPA, standardized test scores. *Important factors considered include:* application essay, recommendation(s), interview, level of applicant's interest, work experience. *Other factors considered include:* Class rank, rigor of secondary school record, character/personal qualities, extracurricular activities, talent/ability, volunteer work. **Freshman Admission Requirements:** High school diploma is required and GED is accepted. **Freshman Admission Statistics:** 14,684 applied, 69% admitted, 13% enrolled. **Transfer Admission Requirements:** High school transcript, essay or personal statement, standardized test scores, Minimum college GPA of 2.5 required. Lowest grade transferable C. **General Admission Information:** Application Fee $35. Nonfall registration accepted. Admission may be deferred for a maximum of 1 year.

COSTS AND FINANCIAL AID

Annual. Annual out-of-state tuition $11,160. Room and board $9,748. Required fees $5,963. Average book expense $1,261. **Required Forms and Deadlines:** FAFSA, State aid form. **Types of Aid:** *Need-based scholarships/grants:* Federal Pell, SEOG, private scholarships, the school's own gift aid. *Loans:* Subsidized Stafford, Unsubsidized Stafford, PLUS, college/university loans from institutional funds. **Financial Aid Statistics:** 77% freshmen, 78% undergrads receive need-based scholarship or grant aid. 14% freshmen, 8% undergrads receive non-need-based scholarship or grant aid. 63% freshmen, 59% undergrads receive need-based self-help aid. 2% freshmen, 3% undergrads receive athletic scholarships. 49% freshmen, 59% undergrads receive any aid. 73% undergrads borrow to pay for school. Average cumulative indebtedness $18,825. **Criteria for awarding institutional aid:** *Non-need-based:* academics.

CALIFORNIA STATE UNIVERSITY, NORTHRIDGE

Admissions and Records, CSU Northridge, Northridge, CA 91330-8207
Phone: 818-677-3700
E-mail: admissions.records@csun.edu • **CEEB Code:** 4707
Fax: 818-677-3766 • **Website:** www.csun.edu • **ACT Code:** 400

This public school was founded in 1956. It has a 350-acre campus.

RATINGS

Admissions Selectivity Rating: 61   **Fire Safety Rating:** 60*

STUDENTS AND FACULTY

Enrollment: 31,119. **Student Body:** 55% female, 45% male, 1% out-of-state, 7% international. Asian 11%, African American 7%, Caucasian 28%, Hispanic 38%, Native American <1%
Retention and Graduation: 4% freshmen graduate within 4 years. 28% freshmen graduate within 6 years.

ACADEMICS

Degrees: bachelor's, master's. **Majors with Highest Enrollment:** Psychology. **Special Study Options:** Accelerated program, English as a Second Language (ESL), honors program, student-designed major, study abroad. **Disability Services:** Special programs offered to physically disabled students include note-taking services, reader services, tape recorders, tutors. **Career services:** alumni services, career/job search classes.

FACILITIES

Housing: Coed dorms, special housing for international students, fraternity/sorority housing, apartments for married students, apartments for single students. **Special Academic Facilities/Equipment:** Anthropology museum, art galleries, deafness center, urban archives, map library, cancer research/developmental biology center, planetarium, observatory.

CAMPUS LIFE

Activities: Choral groups, concert band, drama/theater, jazz band, literary magazine, marching band, music ensembles, musical theater, radio station, student government, student newspaper, yearbook. 267 registered organizations, 18 honor societies, 13 religious organizations. 24 fraternities, 12 sororities. **Athletics (Intercollegiate):** *Men:* baseball, basketball, cross-country, diving, football, golf, soccer, swimming, track/field (outdoor), track/field (indoor), volleyball. *Women:* basketball, cross-country, diving, football, golf, soccer, softball, swimming, tennis, track/field (outdoor), track/field (indoor), volleyball.

ADMISSIONS

Freshman Academic Profile: 81% from public high schools. Minimum paper TOEFL 500. **Basis for Candidate Selection:** *Very important factors considered include:* standardized test scores. **Freshman Admission Requirements:** High school diploma is required and GED is accepted. High school diploma is required and GED is not accepted. *Academic units required:* 4 English, 3 mathematics, 1 science, (2 science labs), 2 foreign language, 2 history, 1 academic electives, 1 Visual/Performing Arts. **Freshman Admission Statistics:** 7,931 applied, 78% admitted, 38% enrolled. Lowest grade transferable D. **General Admission Information:** Application Fee $55. Notification on a rolling basis, beginning on or about 11/30. Nonfall registration accepted. Credit and/or placement offered for CEEB Advanced Placement tests.

COSTS AND FINANCIAL AID

Average book expense $1,754. **Required Forms and Deadlines:** Institution's own financial aid form. **Types of Aid:** *Need-based scholarships/grants:* Federal Pell, SEOG, state scholarships/grants, private scholarships, the school's own gift aid, Federal Nursing Scholarships. *Loans:* Subsidized Stafford, Unsubsidized Stafford, PLUS, Federal Perkins, Federal Nursing, college/university loans from institutional funds. *Student Employment:* Federal Work-Study Program available. Institutional employment available. Highest amount earned per year from on-campus jobs $3,000. Off-campus job opportunities are good.

CALIFORNIA STATE UNIVERSITY, SACRAMENTO

6000 J Street, Sacramento, CA 95819-2694
Phone: 916-278-7766 · **Financial Aid Phone:** 916-278-6554
E-mail: outreach@csus.edu · **CEEB Code:** 4671
Fax: 916-278-5603 · **Website:** www.csus.edu · **ACT Code:** 382

This public school was founded in 1947. It has a 300-acre campus.

RATINGS

Admissions Selectivity Rating: 72 **Fire Safety Rating:** 68

STUDENTS AND FACULTY

Enrollment: 25,457. **Student Body:** 57% female, 43% male, 1% out-of-state, 1% international (122 countries represented). Asian 21%, African American 6%, Caucasian 39%, Hispanic 19%, Native American 1%
Retention and Graduation: 10% freshmen graduate within 4 years. 41% freshmen graduate within 6 years. **Faculty:** 558 full-time faculty, 87% hold PhDs, 47% are members of minority groups, 31% are women. 0% of classes are taught by teaching assistants.

ACADEMICS

Degrees: bachelor's, master's. **Classes:** Most classes have 20–29 students. Most lab/discussion sessions have 10–19 students. **Majors with Highest Enrollment:** Criminal Justice/Law Enforcement Administration; Registered Nursing/Registered Nurse; Business/Commerce. **Special Study Options:** Accelerated program, cooperative education program, cross-registration, distance learning, double major, dual enrollment, English as a Second Language (ESL), honors program, independent study, internships, student-designed major, study abroad, teacher certification program. Combined degree programs: BA/MA. **Disability Services:** Special programs offered to physically disabled students include note-taking services, reader services, tape recorders, tutors. **Career services:** Alumni network, alumni services, career assessment, internships, regional alumni.

FACILITIES

Housing: Coed dorms. 95% of campus accessible to physically disabled. **Special Academic Facilities/Equipment:** CSUS Museum of Anthropology;

University Library Gallery (Art); Else Gallery (Art); Witt Gallery (Art). **Computers:** Students can register for classes online. Administrative functions (other than registration) can be performed online.

CAMPUS LIFE

Environment: Metropolis. **Activities:** Choral groups, concert band, dance, drama/theater, jazz band, marching band, music ensembles, musical theater, opera, pep band, radio station, student government, student newspaper, symphony orchestra. 222 registered organizations, 7 honor societies, 13 religious organizations. 19 fraternities, 20 sororities. **Athletics (Intercollegiate):** *Men:* baseball, basketball, cheerleading, cross-country, football, golf, soccer, tennis, track/field (outdoor). *Women:* basketball, cheerleading, crew/rowing, cross-country, golf, gymnastics, soccer, softball, tennis, track/field (outdoor), volleyball. **On-Campus Highlights:** University Union, River Front Center, Guy West Bridge, Mariposa Hall, Hornet Stadium.

ADMISSIONS

Freshman Academic Profile: Average high school GPA 3.26. 100% in top 50% of high school class. 89% from public high schools. SAT Math middle 50% range 430-540. SAT Critical Reading middle 50% range 410-520. ACT middle 50% range 17-22. Minimum paper TOEFL 510. **Basis for Candidate Selection:** *Very important factors considered include:* rigor of secondary school record, standardized test scores. *Important factors considered include:* state residency. *Other factors considered include:* recommendation(s), extracurricular activities, geographical residence, interview, talent/ability. **Freshman Admission Requirements:** High school diploma is required and GED is accepted. *Academic units required:* 4 English, 3 mathematics, 2 science, (2 science labs), 2 foreign language, 1 social studies, 1 history, 1 academic electives, 1 visual/performing arts. **Freshman Admission Statistics:** 19,702 applied, 70% admitted, 23% enrolled. **Transfer Admission Requirements:** college transcript(s), statement of good standing from prior institution(s). Minimum college GPA of 2.0 required. Lowest grade transferable D. **General Admission Information:** Application Fee $55. Regular application deadline 11/30. Notification on a rolling basis, beginning on or about 11/1. Nonfall registration accepted. Admission may be deferred for a maximum of one semester. Credit and/or placement offered for CEEB Advanced Placement tests.

COSTS AND FINANCIAL AID

Annual in-state tuition $5,472. Annual out-of-state tuition $16,632. Room and board $10,370. Required fees $1,130. Average book expense $1,754. **Required Forms and Deadlines:** FAFSA. **Notification of Awards:** Applicants will be notified of awards on a rolling basis beginning 4/1. **Types of Aid:** *Need-based scholarships/grants:* Federal Pell, SEOG, state scholarships/grants, private scholarships, Federal Nursing Scholarships. *Loans:* Direct Subsidized Stafford, Direct Unsubsidized Stafford, Direct PLUS, Federal Perkins, Federal Nursing. *Student Employment:* Federal Work-Study Program available. Institutional employment available. Off-campus job opportunities are fair. **Financial Aid Statistics:** 77% freshmen, 78% undergrads receive need-based scholarship or grant aid. 15% freshmen, 7% undergrads receive non-need-based scholarship or grant aid. 92% freshmen, 93% undergrads receive need-based self-help aid. 0% freshmen, 0% undergrads receive athletic scholarships. 50% undergrads receive any aid. 43% undergrads borrow to pay for school.

CALIFORNIA STATE UNIVERSITY, SAN BERNARDINO

5500 University Parkway, San Bernardino, CA 92407-2397
Phone: 909-537-5188 · **Financial Aid Phone:** 909-537-5227
E-mail: moreinfo@mail.csusb.edu · **CEEB Code:** 4099
Fax: 909-537-7034 · **Website:** www.csusb.edu · **ACT Code:** 205

This public school was founded in 1965. It has a 430-acre campus.

RATINGS

Admissions Selectivity Rating: 70 **Fire Safety Rating:** 60*

STUDENTS AND FACULTY

Enrollment: 16,676. **Student Body:** 61% female, 39% male, 1% out-of-state, 7% international (81 countries represented). Asian 6%, African American 6%, Caucasian 16%, Hispanic 58%, Native American <1%
Retention and Graduation: 88% freshmen return for sophomore year. 11% freshmen graduate within 4 years. 47% freshmen graduate within 6 years. **Faculty:** 437 full-time faculty, 78% hold PhDs, 50% are members of minority groups, 31% are women.

ACADEMICS

Degrees: bachelor's, doctoral, master's. **Classes:** Most classes have 20–29 students. Most lab/discussion sessions have 20–29 students. **Majors with High-**

est **Enrollment:** Business Administration and Management; Psychology; Social Sciences. **Special Study Options:** Accelerated program, cooperative education program, cross-registration, distance learning, double major, dual enrollment, exchange student program (domestic), honors program, independent study, internships, study abroad, teacher certification program, School of Social and Behavioral Sciences offers Master's in National Security Studies. **Disability Services:** Special programs offered to physically disabled students include note-taking services, reader services, tape recorders.

FACILITIES

Housing: Coed dorms, women's dorms, apartments for single students, Wellness Housing **Special Academic Facilities/Equipment:** Simulation labs, electronic music studios, language lab, desert studies center. Robert V. Fullerton Art Museum. Anthropology Museum **Computers:** Students can register for classes online. Administrative functions (other than registration) can be performed online.

CAMPUS LIFE

Environment: City. **Activities:** Choral groups, dance, drama/theater, jazz band, music ensembles, musical theater, radio station, student government, student newspaper, television station, Campus Ministries, International Student Organization, Model UN. 97 registered organizations, 3 religious organizations. 9 fraternities, 6 sororities. **Athletics (Intercollegiate):** *Men:* baseball, basketball, golf, soccer, swimming, water polo. *Women:* basketball, cross-country, soccer, softball, swimming, tennis, volleyball, water polo. **On-Campus Highlights:** Coussoulis Arena, Robert V. Fullerton Art Museum, Social and Behavorial Sciences Building, Santos Manuel Student Union, Pfau Library.

ADMISSIONS

Freshman Academic Profile: Average high school GPA 3.23. 95% from public high schools. SAT Math middle 50% range 400-500. SAT Critical Reading middle 50% range 390-490. SAT Writing middle 50% range 392-480. ACT middle 50% range 16-20. Minimum internet-based TOEFL 61. Minimum paper TOEFL 500. **Basis for Candidate Selection:** *Very important factors considered include:* academic GPA, recommendation(s), standardized test scores. *Other factors considered include:* geographical residence. **Freshman Admission Requirements:** High school diploma is required and GED is accepted. *Academic units required:* 4 English, 3 mathematics, 2 science, (2 science labs), 2 foreign language, 1 social studies, 1 history, 1 visual/performing arts. **Freshman Admission Statistics:** 12,951 applied, 84% admitted, 25% enrolled. **Transfer Admission Requirements:** college transcript(s), Minimum college GPA of 2.0 required. Lowest grade transferable C. **General Admission Information:** Application Fee $55. Nonfall registration accepted. Credit and/or placement offered for CEEB Advanced Placement tests.

COSTS AND FINANCIAL AID

Annual out-of-state tuition $11,160. Room and board $9,933. Required fees $1,086. Average book expense $1,557. **Required Forms and Deadlines:** FAFSA, State aid form. **Notification of Awards:** Applicants will be notified of awards on a rolling basis beginning 4/1. **Types of Aid:** *Need-based scholarships/grants:* Federal Pell, SEOG, state scholarships/grants, private scholarships, the school's own gift aid. *Loans:* Direct Subsidized Stafford, Direct Unsubsidized Stafford, Direct PLUS, Federal Perkins. *Student Employment:* Federal Work-Study Program available. Institutional employment available. Off-campus job opportunities are fair. **Financial Aid Statistics:** 94% freshmen, 95% undergrads receive need-based scholarship or grant aid. 23% freshmen, 13% undergrads receive non-need-based scholarship or grant aid. 39% freshmen, 45% undergrads receive need-based self-help aid. 0% freshmen, 0% undergrads receive athletic scholarships. 66% undergrads borrow to pay for school. Average cumulative indebtedness $19,262. **Criteria for awarding institutional aid:** *Non-need-based:* academics, alumni affiliation, art, athletics, leadership, music/drama, state/district residency.

CALIFORNIA STATE UNIVERSITY, SAN MARCOS

333 S. Twin Oaks Valley Rd., San Marcos, CA 92078
Phone: 760-750-4848 • **Financial Aid Phone:** 760-750-4850
E-mail: apply@csusm.edu • **CEEB Code:** 5677
Fax: 760-750-3248 • **Website:** www.csusm.edu

This public school was founded in 1989. It has a 304-acre campus.

RATINGS

Admissions Selectivity Rating: 68   **Fire Safety Rating:** 60*

STUDENTS AND FACULTY

Enrollment: 8,686. **Student Body:** 61% female, 39% male, 1% out-of-state.
Retention and Graduation: 74% freshmen return for sophomore year. 14% freshmen graduate within 4 years. 46% freshmen graduate within 6 years.
Faculty: 202 full-time faculty.

ACADEMICS

Degrees: bachelor's, master's. **Classes:** Most classes have 30-39 students. **Special Study Options:** Accelerated program, cross-registration, distance learning, double major, dual enrollment, English as a Second Language (ESL), independent study, internships, student-designed major, study abroad, teacher certification program, weekend college, Evening degree program, Program for Adult College Education (PACE), Saturday classes, Air Force ROTC, extended studies, open university, special sessions, including winter. **Disability Services:** Special programs offered to physically disabled students include note-taking services, reader services, tape recorders, tutors. **Career services:** alumni services, career assessment, internships.

FACILITIES

Housing: special housing for disabled students, special housing for international students, apartments for single students, Our housing is privatized and operated by Allen and O'Hara. **Computers:** Students can register for classes online.

CAMPUS LIFE

Environment: Town. **Activities:** Choral groups, drama/theater, music ensembles, student newspaper. 70 registered organizations, 5 honor societies, 2 religious organizations. 2 fraternities, 2 sororities. **Athletics (Intercollegiate):** *Men:* baseball, cross-country, golf, soccer, track/field (outdoor). *Women:* cross-country, golf, soccer, softball, track/field (outdoor).

ADMISSIONS

Freshman Academic Profile: Average high school GPA 3.15. SAT Math middle 50% range 430-540. SAT Critical Reading middle 50% range 430-530. Minimum paper TOEFL 550. **Basis for Candidate Selection:** *Very important factors considered include:* rigor of secondary school record, standardized test scores. *Other factors considered include:* geographical residence, state residency. **Freshman Admission Requirements:** High school diploma is required and GED is accepted. *Academic units required:* 4 English, 3 mathematics, 2 science, (2 science labs), 2 foreign language, 2 social studies, 0 history, 1 academic electives, 1 Visual Performing Arts. **Transfer Admission Requirements:** college transcript(s), Minimum college GPA of 2.0 required. Lowest grade transferable C. **General Admission Information:** Application Fee $55. Notification on a rolling basis, beginning on or about 12/1. Nonfall registration not accepted. Credit and/or placement offered for CEEB Advanced Placement tests.

COSTS AND FINANCIAL AID

Annual out-of-state tuition $8,136. Room and board $6,250. Required fees $3,650. Average book expense $1,386. **Required Forms and Deadlines:** FAFSA. **Notification of Awards:** Applicants will be notified of awards on or about 4/15. **Types of Aid:** *Need-based scholarships/grants:* Federal Pell, SEOG, state scholarships/grants, private scholarships, the school's own gift aid. *Loans:* Direct Subsidized Stafford, Direct Unsubsidized Stafford, Direct PLUS, PLUS, Federal Perkins, college/university loans from institutional funds. **Criteria for awarding institutional aid:** *Non-need-based:* academics, athletics, leadership, state/district residency.

CALIFORNIA STATE UNIVERSITY, STANISLAUS

One University Circle, Turlock, CA 95382
Phone: 209-667-3070 • **Financial Aid Phone:** 209-667-3336
E-mail: Outreach_Help_Desk@csustan.edu • **CEEB Code:** 4713
Fax: 209-667-3788 • **Website:** www.csustan.edu • **ACT Code:** 435

This public school was founded in 1957. It has a 228-acre campus.

RATINGS

Admissions Selectivity Rating: 71   **Fire Safety Rating:** 83

STUDENTS AND FACULTY

Enrollment: 7,844. **Student Body:** 64% female, 36% male, 3% international (22 countries represented). Asian 11%, African American 2%, Caucasian 26%, Hispanic 48%, Native American <1%
Retention and Graduation: 15% freshmen graduate within 4 years. **Faculty:** 263 full-time faculty, 89% hold PhDs, 48% are members of minority groups, 29% are women.

ACADEMICS

Degrees: bachelor's, master's, post-bachelor's certificate, post-master's certificate. **Classes:** Most classes have 20–29 students. Most lab/discussion sessions have 20–29 students. **Majors with Highest Enrollment:** Business/Commerce; Psychology; Criminal Justice/Safety Studies. **Special Study Options:** cooperative education program, distance learning, double major, dual enrollment, English as a Second Language (ESL), exchange student program (domestic), honors program, independent study, internships, liberal arts/career combination, student-designed major, study abroad, teacher certification program. **Honors programs:** University Honors Program. **Disability Services:** Special programs offered to physically disabled students include note-taking services, reader services, tape recorders, tutors. **Career services:** Alumni network, alumni services, career/job search classes, career assessment, internships, regional alumni. Our Internship Program is exceptional. We work with employers to develop internship and coop opportunities, post information online for students to help them connect with their college department internship coordinator for course credit, and post internship information in the Career Services Center to help students identify appropriate opportunities related to their major course of study.

FACILITIES

Housing: Coed dorms, apartments for single students, Housing available in the summer months. ADA compliant units available. 99% of campus accessible to physically disabled. **Special Academic Facilities/Equipment:** Marine sciences station, laser lab, greenhouse, art gallery, mainstage theatre, recital hall, observatory, science building, art complex, distance learning studios, BioAg Eco building. **Computers:** 100% of classrooms, 100% of dorms, 100% of libraries, 100% of dining areas, 100% of student union, 10% of common outdoor areas have wireless network access. Students can register for classes online. Administrative functions (other than registration) can be performed online.

CAMPUS LIFE

Environment: Town. **Activities:** Choral groups, concert band, dance, drama/theater, jazz band, music ensembles, musical theater, opera, radio station, student government, student newspaper, symphony orchestra, television station, International Student Organization. 76 registered organizations, 11 honor society, 4 religious organizations. 7 fraternities, 9 sororities. **Athletics (Intercollegiate):** *Men:* baseball, basketball, cross-country, golf, soccer, track/field (outdoor), track/field (indoor). *Women:* basketball, cross-country, soccer, softball, tennis, track/field (outdoor), track/field (indoor), volleyball. **On-Campus Highlights:** Naraghi Hall of Science, MSR Educational Services Gateway Buildin, JFR Faculty Development Center, CSU Stanislaus University Art Gallery, Cafeteria and adjoining room, Student Union recently renovated; game room. **Environmental Initiatives:** The campus has replaced ten building air handler units in three major buildings. These new air handler units are more energy efficient and have also improved the air quality of the conditioned spaces. Project cost $1.6 million. Scheduled to have solar-generating (photovoltaic) equipment installed that will deliver zero-emission energy directly to the campus at economical costs. Installation date TBD. The campus, in fiscal year 2009/10, reset building thermostats to 78 degrees during the summer months to conserve energy. During this time, Science Building I was shutdown completely to conserve energy.

ADMISSIONS

Freshman Academic Profile: Average high school GPA 3.26. 96% from public high schools. SAT Math middle 50% range 400-510. SAT Critical Reading middle 50% range 400-500. SAT Writing middle 50% range 400-500. ACT middle 50% range 16-21. Minimum internet-based TOEFL 61. Minimum paper TOEFL 500. **Basis for Candidate Selection:** *Very important factors considered include:* academic GPA, rigor of secondary school record, standardized test scores. *Important factors considered include:* Class rank. **Freshman Admission Requirements:** High school diploma is required and GED is accepted. *Academic units required:* 4 English, 3 mathematics, 2 science, (2 science labs), 2 foreign language, 1 social studies, 1 history, 1 visual/performing arts, 1 academic electives. **Freshman Admission Statistics:** 6,265 applied, 73% admitted, 27% enrolled. **Transfer Admission Requirements:** college transcript(s), statement of good standing from prior institution(s). Minimum college GPA of 2.0 required. Lowest grade transferable D. **General Admission Information:** Application Fee $55. Regular application deadline 3/1. Notification on a rolling basis, beginning on or about 10/1. Nonfall registration accepted. Credit offered for CEEB Advanced Placement tests.

COSTS AND FINANCIAL AID

Required Forms and Deadlines: FAFSA, State aid form. **Notification of Awards:** Applicants will be notified of awards on a rolling basis beginning 3/15. **Types of Aid:** *Need-based scholarships/grants:* Federal Pell, SEOG, state scholarships/grants, private scholarships, the school's own gift aid, Federal Nursing Scholarships. *Loans:* Subsidized Stafford, Unsubsidized Stafford, PLUS, Federal Perkins, college/university loans from institutional funds. *Student Employment:* Federal Work-Study Program available. Institutional employment available. Highest amount earned per year from on-campus jobs $17,680. Off-campus job opportunities are good. **Financial Aid Statistics:** 83% freshmen receive any aid. **Criteria for awarding institutional aid:** *Non-need-based:* academics, alumni affiliation, art, athletics, leadership, minority status, music/drama, state/district residency.

CALIFORNIA UNIVERSITY OF PENNSYLVANIA

250 University Avenue, California, PA 15419
Phone: 724-938-4404 · **Financial Aid Phone:** 724-938-4415
E-mail: inquiry@cup.edu · **CEEB Code:** 2647
Fax: 724-938-4564 · **Website:** www.calu.edu · **ACT Code:** 3694

This public school was founded in 1852. It has a 188-acre campus.

RATINGS

Admissions Selectivity Rating: 73   **Fire Safety Rating:** 96

STUDENTS AND FACULTY

Enrollment: 6,031. **Student Body:** 52% female, 48% male, 10% out-of-state, 1% international (29 countries represented). Asian 1%, African American 11%, Caucasian 78%, Hispanic 3%, Native American <1%. **Retention and Graduation:** 76% freshmen return for sophomore year. 36% freshmen graduate within 4 years. 13% grads go on to further study within 1 year. **Faculty:** 264 full-time faculty, 68% hold PhDs, 48% are members of minority groups, 15% are women. 0% of classes are taught by teaching assistants.

ACADEMICS

Degrees: associate, bachelor's, certificate, master's, post-bachelor's certificate, post-master's certificate, terminal associate. **Classes:** Most classes have 20–29 students. Most lab/discussion sessions have 20–29 students. **Majors with Highest Enrollment:** Business Administration and Management; Sport and Fitness Administration/Management; Criminal Justice/Safety Studies. **Special Study Options:** Accelerated program, cooperative education program, distance learning, double major, dual enrollment, exchange student program (domestic), honors program, independent study, internships, liberal arts/career combination, student-designed major, study abroad, teacher certification program, weekend college, Undergrads may take grad classes. **Disability Services:** Special programs offered to physically disabled students include note-taking services, reader services, tape recorders, tutors. **Career services:** Alumni network, alumni services, career/job search classes, career assessment, internships, regional alumni. Career services highlights include extensive programs in internships and training.

FACILITIES

Housing: Coed dorms, special housing for disabled students, men's dorms, special housing for international students, women's dorms, fraternity/sorority housing, cooperative housing, Wellness Housing, Theme Housing, Jefferson Apartments, Garden style with outdoor pool/sandlot volleyball court and extensive gym. 90% of campus accessible to physically disabled. **Special Academic Facilities/Equipment:** Manderino Gallery of Fine Arts, hosts top 40 corporate art collection sin the world. **Computers:** Students can register for classes online. Administrative functions (other than registration) can be performed online.

CAMPUS LIFE

Environment: Village. **Activities:** Choral groups, concert band, dance, drama/theater, jazz band, literary magazine, marching band, music ensembles, musical theater, opera, pep band, radio station, student government, student newspaper, symphony orchestra, television station, yearbook, Campus Ministries, International Student Organization, 25 honor societies, 1 religious organization. 6 fraternities, 7 sororities. **Athletics (Intercollegiate):** *Men:* baseball, basketball, cheerleading, cross-country, football, golf, rugby, soccer, softball, track/field (outdoor), track/field (indoor), volleyball. *Women:* basketball, cheerleading, cross-country, diving, golf, rugby, soccer, softball, swimming, tennis, track/field (outdoor), track/field (indoor), volleyball. **On-Campus Highlights:** Residence Halls, Student Union, Classrooms, Herron Rec Center, Library. **Environmental Initiatives:** Multimillion Dollar Geothermal project plus replacing ALL residence halls in less than 5 years with Green buildings. Massive implementation of Johnson Controls systems to reduce our carbon footprint and energy usage. Campus wide sustainability awareness programs. Since 2011, California University of PA has participated in Recyclemania. In addition, the university is committed to developing a regional environmental center of excellence in Southwestern Pennsylvania to educate and collaborate with people via research and training.

ADMISSIONS

Freshman Academic Profile: Average high school GPA 3.1. 6% in top 10% of high school class, 24% in top 25% of high school class, 58% in top 50% of high school class. 80% from public high schools. SAT Math middle 50% range 420-510. SAT Critical Reading middle 50% range 420-520. SAT Writing middle 50% range 400-490. ACT middle 50% range 17-22. Minimum paper TOEFL 450. **Basis for Candidate Selection:** *Very important factors considered include:* Class rank, rigor of secondary school record, standardized test scores. *Other factors considered include:* application essay, recommendation(s), extracurricular activities, interview, talent/ability, work experience. **Freshman Admis-**

sion Requirements: High school diploma is required and GED is accepted. *Academic units required:* 4 English, 3 mathematics, 1 science, (1 science labs), 2 social studies, 2 history, 6 academic electives, 1 Arts and Humanities. **Freshman Admission Statistics:** 3,714 applied, 74% admitted, 37% enrolled. **Transfer Admission Requirements:** High school transcript, college transcript(s), statement of good standing from prior institution(s). Minimum college GPA of 2.3 required. Lowest grade transferable C. **General Admission Information:** Application Fee $25. Nonfall registration accepted. Admission may be deferred for a maximum of one semester. Credit offered for CEEB Advanced Placement tests.

COSTS AND FINANCIAL AID
Annual in-state tuition $6,820. Annual out-of-state tuition $10,230. Room and board $10,086. Required fees $2,736. Average book expense $1,000. **Required Forms and Deadlines:** FAFSA. **Notification of Awards:** Applicants will be notified of awards on a rolling basis beginning 4/1. **Types of Aid:** *Need-based scholarships/grants:* Federal Pell, SEOG, state scholarships/grants, private scholarships, the school's own gift aid. *Loans:* Subsidized Stafford, Unsubsidized Stafford, PLUS, Federal Perkins. *Student Employment:* Federal Work-Study Program available. Institutional employment available. Off-campus job opportunities are good. **Financial Aid Statistics:** 86% freshmen, 74% undergrads receive need-based scholarship or grant aid. 33% freshmen, 20% undergrads receive non-need-based scholarship or grant aid. 98% freshmen, 97% undergrads receive need-based self-help aid. 2% freshmen, 2% undergrads receive athletic scholarships. 80% freshmen, 77% undergrads receive any aid. 88% undergrads borrow to pay for school. Average cumulative indebtedness $18,342. **Criteria for awarding institutional aid:** *Non-need-based:* academics, athletics, leadership, minority status, music/drama, state/district residency.

CALVARY BIBLE COLLEGE AND THEOLOGICAL SEMINARY

15800 Calvary Rd., Kansas City, MO 64147
Phone: 816-322-3960 · **Financial Aid Phone:** 816-322-0110
E-mail: admissions@calvary.edu
Fax: 816-331-4474 · **Website:** http://www.college.calvary.edu/ · **ACT Code:** 2312

This private school was founded in 1961. It has a 55-acre campus.

RATINGS
Admissions Selectivity Rating: 70   **Fire Safety Rating:** 83

STUDENTS AND FACULTY
Enrollment: 225. **Student Body:** 49% female, 51% male, 46% out-of-state, 0% international (2 countries represented). Asian 1%, African American 11%, Caucasian 80%, Hispanic 3%, Native American 1%
Retention and Graduation: 54% freshmen return for sophomore year. 30% freshmen graduate within 4 years. **Faculty:** 16 full-time faculty, 50% hold PhDs, 38% are members of minority groups, 13% are women. 0% of classes are taught by teaching assistants.

ACADEMICS
Degrees: associate, bachelor's, certificate, first professional, master's, terminal associate, transfer associate. **Majors with Highest Enrollment:** Bible/Biblical Studies; Pastoral Studies/Counseling; Music. **Special Study Options:** cooperative education program, double major, independent study, internships, student-designed major, teacher certification program.

FACILITIES
Housing: men's dorms, women's dorms, apartments for married students, apartments for single students, Single students required to live in college housing unless living with parents or at least 23 years of age. Duplexes available for married students. **Computers:** 100% of dorms, 100% of libraries, 100% of student union, have wireless network access. Students can register for classes online.

CAMPUS LIFE
Environment: Village. **Activities:** Choral groups, drama/theater, music ensembles, musical theater, pep band, radio station, student government, yearbook. **Athletics (Intercollegiate):** *Men:* basketball, soccer. *Women:* basketball, volleyball. **On-Campus Highlights:** Student Lounge, The Point, Gymnasium

ADMISSIONS
Freshman Academic Profile: Average high school GPA 3.398. SAT Math middle 50% range 502.5-522.5. SAT Critical Reading middle 50% range 480-595. SAT Writing middle 50% range 516.67-565.83. ACT middle 50% range 19-24.25. Minimum paper TOEFL 525. **Basis for Candidate Selection:** *Very*

important factors considered include: academic GPA, recommendation(s), standardized test scores, religious affiliation/commitment. *Important factors considered include:* character/personal qualities. *Other factors considered include:* application essay. **Freshman Admission Requirements:** High school diploma is required and GED is accepted. **Freshman Admission Statistics:** 48 applied, 100% admitted, 79% enrolled. **Transfer Admission Requirements:** college transcript(s), essay or personal statement, Minimum college GPA of 2.0 required. Lowest grade transferable C-. **General Admission Information:** Application Fee $25. Regular application deadline 7/15. Nonfall registration accepted. Admission may be deferred for a maximum of 2 Semesters.

COSTS AND FINANCIAL AID
Required Forms and Deadlines: FAFSA. **Notification of Awards:** Applicants will be notified of awards on a rolling basis beginning 5/1. **Types of Aid:** *Need-based scholarships/grants:* Federal Pell, SEOG, private scholarships, the school's own gift aid. *Loans:* Subsidized Stafford, Unsubsidized Stafford, PLUS. *Student Employment:* Federal Work-Study Program available. Institutional employment available. Off-campus job opportunities are good. **Financial Aid Statistics:** 63% freshmen, 59% undergrads receive need-based scholarship or grant aid. 67% freshmen, 54% undergrads receive non-need-based scholarship or grant aid. 41% freshmen, 48% undergrads receive need-based self-help aid. 0% freshmen, 0% undergrads receive athletic scholarships. 42% undergrads borrow to pay for school. Average cumulative indebtedness $9,343. **Criteria for awarding institutional aid:** *Non-need-based:* academics, alumni affiliation, job skills, music/drama, religious affiliation.

CALVIN COLLEGE

Best 380

3201 Burton Street S.E., Grand Rapids, MI 49546
Phone: 616-526-6106 · **Financial Aid Phone:** 800-688-0122
E-mail: admissions@calvin.edu · **CEEB Code:** 1095
Fax: 616-526-6777 · **Website:** www.calvin.edu · **ACT Code:** 1968

This private school, affiliated with the Christian Reformed Church, was founded in 1876. It has a 400-acre campus.

RATINGS
Admissions Selectivity Rating: 87   **Fire Safety Rating:** 73

STUDENTS AND FACULTY
Enrollment: 3,825. **Student Body:** 55% female, 45% male, 44% out-of-state, 10% international (57 countries represented). Asian 4%, African American 2%, Caucasian 75%, Hispanic 3%, Native American <1%
Retention and Graduation: 58% freshmen graduate within 4 years. 26% grads go on to further study within 1 year. 21% grads pursue arts and sciences degrees. 1% grads pursue law degrees. 1% grads pursue business degrees. 2% grads pursue medical degrees. **Faculty:** 275 full-time faculty, 85% hold PhDs, 35% are members of minority groups, 10% are women. 0% of classes are taught by teaching assistants.

ACADEMICS
Degrees: bachelor's, master's, post-bachelor's certificate. **Classes:** Most classes have 20–29 students. Most lab/discussion sessions have 10–19 students. **Majors with Highest Enrollment:** Business/Commerce; Engineering; Registered Nursing/Registered Nurse. **Special Study Options:** Accelerated program, double major, dual enrollment, honors program, independent study, internships, student-designed major, study abroad, teacher certification program, Academically-based Service-learning. **Honors programs:** For almost forty years Calvin College has challenged its best students with a campus-wide Honors Program--part of our overall mission to encourage academic excellence in a Christ-centered environment. The McGregor Sophomore Scholars Program develops targeted programming for sophomores in the Honors Program, such as one-on-one mentoring with faculty and program leaders and special events. **Disability Services:** Special programs offered to physically disabled students include note-taking services, reader services, tape recorders, tutors. **Career services:** Alumni network, alumni services, career/job search classes, career assessment, internships, regional alumni.

FACILITIES
Housing: men's dorms, women's dorms, apartments for single students, Theme Housing, Project Neighborhood Houses. 95% of campus accessible to physically disabled. **Special Academic Facilities/Equipment:** Art gallery, observatory, ecosystem preserve, electron microscope, seismograph lab. **Computers:** 40% of classrooms, 100% of dorms, 100% of libraries, 75% of dining areas, 20% of student union, 10% of common outdoor areas have wireless network access.

Students can register for classes online. Administrative functions (other than registration) can be performed online.

CAMPUS LIFE
Environment: City. **Activities:** Choral groups, concert band, dance, drama/theater, jazz band, literary magazine, music ensembles, musical theater, pep band, student government, student newspaper, student-run film society, symphony orchestra, yearbook, Campus Ministries, International Student Organization, Model UN. 60 registered organizations, 6 honor societies, 5 religious organizations. **Athletics (Intercollegiate):** *Men:* baseball, basketball, cross-country, diving, golf, soccer, swimming, tennis, track/field (outdoor). *Women:* basketball, cross-country, diving, golf, soccer, softball, swimming, tennis, track/field (outdoor), volleyball. **On-Campus Highlights:** Field House, Johnny's Café, Heckman Library, DeVos Communications Building, Engineering Projects and Design Building. **Environmental Initiatives:** The Calvin Energy Recovery Fund, a green revolving fund(http://www.calvin.edu/admin/development/cerf) The Calvin College Ecosystem Preserve and the Bunker Interpretive Center (http://www.calvin.edu/academic/eco-preserve/bunker) The Calvin Sustainability Summit in 2011(http://www.calvin.edu/admin/provost/documents/2011-SustainabilityReport.pdf).

ADMISSIONS
Freshman Academic Profile: Average high school GPA 3.69. 32% in top 10% of high school class, 58% in top 25% of high school class, 85% in top 50% of high school class. 45% from public high schools. SAT Math middle 50% range 530-660. SAT Critical Reading middle 50% range 520-640. ACT middle 50% range 23-29. Minimum internet-based TOEFL 80. Minimum paper TOEFL 550. **Basis for Candidate Selection:** *Very important factors considered include:* academic GPA, rigor of secondary school record, standardized test scores, religious affiliation/commitment. *Important factors considered include:* application essay, recommendation(s), character/personal qualities, extracurricular activities. *Other factors considered include:* Class rank, level of applicant's interest, volunteer work, work experience. **Freshman Admission Requirements:** High school diploma is required and GED is accepted. *Academic units required:* 3 English, 3 mathematics, 2 science, 0 foreign language, 2 social studies, 3 academic electives. **Freshman Admission Statistics:** 3,679 applied, 73% admitted, 35% enrolled. **Transfer Admission Requirements:** High school transcript, college transcript(s), essay or personal statement, statement of good standing from prior institution(s). Minimum college GPA of 2.5 required. Lowest grade transferable C. **General Admission Information:** Application Fee $35. Regular application deadline 8/15. Notification on a rolling basis, beginning on or about 11/1. Nonfall registration accepted. Admission may be deferred for a maximum of 1 year. Credit and/or placement offered for CEEB Advanced Placement tests.

COSTS AND FINANCIAL AID
Annual tuition $29,400. Room and board $9,485. Required fees $235. Average book expense $1,000. **Required Forms and Deadlines:** FAFSA. **Notification of Awards:** Applicants will be notified of awards on a rolling basis beginning 3/15. **Types of Aid:** *Need-based scholarships/grants:* Federal Pell, SEOG, state scholarships/grants, private scholarships, the school's own gift aid. *Loans:* Direct Subsidized Stafford, Direct Unsubsidized Stafford, Direct PLUS, Federal Perkins, state loans, college/university loans from institutional funds, Alternative Educational Loans. *Student Employment:* Federal Work-Study Program available. Institutional employment available. Highest amount earned per year from on-campus jobs $5,000. Off-campus job opportunities are excellent. **Financial Aid Statistics:** 100% freshmen, 99% undergrads receive need-based scholarship or grant aid. 12% freshmen, 9% undergrads receive non-need-based scholarship or grant aid. 89% freshmen, 92% undergrads receive need-based self-help aid. 0% freshmen, 0% undergrads receive athletic scholarships. 97% freshmen, 95% undergrads receive any aid. 67% undergrads borrow to pay for school. Average cumulative indebtedness $23,581. **Criteria for awarding institutional aid:** *Non-need-based:* academics, alumni affiliation, art, leadership, minority status, music/drama, religious affiliation, state/district residency.

CAMBRIDGE COLLEGE

1000 Massachusetts Avenue, Cambridge, MA 02138-5304
Phone: 617-868-1000 • **Financial Aid Phone:** 800-877-4723 ext. 1440
E-mail: admit@cambridgecollege.edu
Fax: 617-349-3561 • **Website:** www.cambridgecollege.edu

This is a private school.

RATINGS
Admissions Selectivity Rating: 60*   **Fire Safety Rating:** 60*

STUDENTS AND FACULTY
Enrollment: 1,002. **Student Body:** 75% female, 25% male, 18% out-of-state, 9% international. Asian 3%, African American 30%, Caucasian 18%, Hispanic 22%, Native American <1%
Retention and Graduation: 21% freshmen return for sophomore year.
Faculty: 19 full-time faculty, 68% hold PhDs, 47% are members of minority groups, 26% are women.

ACADEMICS
Degrees: bachelor's, certificate, master's, post-master's certificate.

ADMISSIONS
Freshman Academic Profile: Minimum paper TOEFL 550.

COSTS AND FINANCIAL AID
Annual tuition $13,140. Required fees $140. **Required Forms and Deadlines:** FAFSA, Institution's own financial aid form. **Financial Aid Statistics:** 0% freshmen, 1% undergrads receive need-based scholarship or grant aid. 0% freshmen, 0% undergrads receive non-need-based scholarship or grant aid. 0% freshmen, 0% undergrads receive need-based self-help aid. 0% freshmen, 0% undergrads receive athletic scholarships.

CAMERON UNIVERSITY

2800 West Gore Boulevard, Lawton, OK 73505
Phone: 580-581-2230 • **Financial Aid Phone:** 580-581-2293
E-mail: admiss@cua.cameron.edu • **CEEB Code:** 6080
Fax: 580-581-5514 • **ACT Code:** 3386

This public school was founded in 1908. It has a 369-acre campus.

RATINGS
Admissions Selectivity Rating: 70   **Fire Safety Rating:** 86

STUDENTS AND FACULTY
Enrollment: 5,076. **Student Body:** 60% female, 40% male, 1% out-of-state, 3% international (50 countries represented). Asian 3%, African American 19%, Caucasian 58%, Hispanic 9%, Native American 8%
Retention and Graduation: 56% freshmen return for sophomore year. 24% freshmen graduate within 4 years. 29% freshmen graduate within 6 years.
Faculty: 180 full-time faculty, 69% hold PhDs, 36% are members of minority groups, 14% are women. 0% of classes are taught by teaching assistants.

ACADEMICS
Degrees: associate, bachelor's, master's. **Classes:** Most classes have 20–29 students. Most lab/discussion sessions have 10–19 students. **Special Study Options:** Accelerated program, distance learning, double major, dual enrollment, honors program, independent study, internships, liberal arts/career combination, teacher certification program, Undergrads may take grad classes. Evening and saturday classes offered; extension study possible. **Honors programs:** Honors programs have been created for exceptional scholors. This includes studies in Europe and travel to scholarly programs in the U.S.A. Courses and programs providechallenging multidisciplinary activities. Combined degree programs: BA/MD. **Disability Services:** Special programs offered to physically disabled students include note-taking services, reader services, tape recorders, tutors.

FACILITIES
Housing: men's dorms, women's dorms, quiet and wellness (non-smoking) areas available. 88% of campus accessible to physically disabled. **Special Academic Facilities/Equipment:** Satellite labs **Computers:** Administrative functions (other than registration) can be performed online.

CAMPUS LIFE
Environment: City. **Activities:** Choral groups, concert band, dance, drama/theater, jazz band, literary magazine, music ensembles, musical theater, pep band, radio station, student government, student newspaper, symphony orchestra, television station, yearbook. 66 registered organizations, 19 honor societies, 4 religious organizations. 2 fraternities, 3 sororities. **Athletics (Intercollegiate):** *Men:* baseball, basketball, cross-country, golf, tennis. *Women:* basketball, golf, softball, tennis, volleyball. **On-Campus Highlights:** Student Union, Cameron Village, Moody Blue, Student Activities Building, Fitness Center.

ADMISSIONS
Freshman Academic Profile: 8% in top 10% of high school class, 28% in top 25% of high school class, 62% in top 50% of high school class. 99% from public high schools. ACT middle 50% range 16-22. Minimum paper TOEFL 500. **Basis for Candidate Selection:** *Important factors considered include:* Class rank, academic GPA, standardized test scores, geographical residence, state residency. **Freshman Admission Requirements:** High school diploma

is required and GED is accepted. *Academic units required:* 4 English, 3 mathematics, 2 science, (2 science labs), 2 history, 3 academic electives. **Freshman Admission Statistics:** 1,357 applied, 100% admitted, 70% enrolled. **Transfer Admission Requirements:** college transcript(s), Minimum college GPA of 2.0 required. Lowest grade transferable D. **General Admission Information:** Application Fee $15. Nonfall registration accepted. Admission may be deferred for a maximum of 12. Credit and/or placement offered for CEEB Advanced Placement tests.

COSTS AND FINANCIAL AID

Annual. Annual out-of-state tuition $7,830. Room and board $3,014. Required fees $200. Average book expense $1,050. **Required Forms and Deadlines:** FAFSA. **Notification of Awards:** Applicants will be notified of awards on a rolling basis beginning 4/1. **Types of Aid:** *Need-based scholarships/grants:* Federal Pell, SEOG, state scholarships/grants, private scholarships, the school's own gift aid. *Loans:* Subsidized Stafford, Unsubsidized Stafford, PLUS. **Financial Aid Statistics:** 94% freshmen, 75% undergrads receive need-based scholarship or grant aid. 60% freshmen, 41% undergrads receive non-need-based scholarship or grant aid. 76% freshmen, 53% undergrads receive need-based self-help aid. 0% freshmen, 1% undergrads receive athletic scholarships. 36% freshmen, 26% undergrads receive any aid. 30% undergrads borrow to pay for school. **Criteria for awarding institutional aid:** *Non-need-based:* academics, alumni affiliation, art, athletics, leadership, music/drama.

CAMPBELL UNIVERSITY

Post Office Box 546, Buies Creek, NC 27506
Phone: 910-893-1200
E-mail: admissions@campbell.edu • **CEEB Code:** 5100
Website: www.campbell.edu • **ACT Code:** 3076

This private school, affiliated with the Southern Baptist Church, was founded in 1887. It has a 850-acre campus.

RATINGS

Admissions Selectivity Rating: 75	Fire Safety Rating: 69

STUDENTS AND FACULTY

Enrollment: 4,236. **Student Body:** 52% female, 48% male, 22% out-of-state, 2% international. Asian 2%, African American 18%, Caucasian 57%, Hispanic 7%, Native American 1%
Retention and Graduation: 37% freshmen graduate within 4 years. 23% grads go on to further study within 1 year. 5% grads pursue arts and sciences degrees. 4% grads pursue law degrees. 7% grads pursue business degrees. **Faculty:** 196 full-time faculty, 91% hold PhDs, 33% are members of minority groups. 0% of classes are taught by teaching assistants.

ACADEMICS

Degrees: associate, bachelor's, first professional, master's. **Classes:** Most classes have fewer than 10 students. **Special Study Options:** Accelerated program, cooperative education program, distance learning, double major, dual enrollment, exchange student program (domestic), honors program, independent study, internships, liberal arts/career combination, study abroad, teacher certification program. Combined degree programs: BA/JD, BA/MA, BA/MBA PHD/MBA. **Disability Services:** Special programs offered to physically disabled students include note-taking services, tape recorders. **Career services:** career/job search classes, career assessment, internships.

FACILITIES

Housing: special housing for disabled students, men's dorms, women's dorms, apartments for married students, apartments for single students, Student apartments and suites for sophomores, juniors and seniors; also graduate apartments. All off-campus housing must be approved by the Office of Residence Life. 75% of campus accessible to physically disabled. **Special Academic Facilities/ Equipment:** Taylor Bott-Rogers Fine Arts Bldg. Lundy-Fetterman School of Business museum and exhibit hall School of Pharmacy Clinical Research Facility.

CAMPUS LIFE

Environment: Rural. **Activities:** Choral groups, concert band, drama/theater, jazz band, literary magazine, music ensembles, musical theater, pep band, radio station, student government, student newspaper, yearbook, Campus Ministries, International Student Organization. 44 registered organizations, 14 honor societies, 20 religious organizations. **Athletics (Intercollegiate):** *Men:* baseball, basketball, cross-country, golf, soccer, tennis, track/field (outdoor), wrestling. *Women:* basketball, cheerleading, cross-country, golf, soccer, softball, swimming, tennis, track/field (outdoor), volleyball. **On-Campus Highlights:** Lundy-Fetterman School of Business, Wallace Student Center/Oasis Grill/ Starbucks, Keith Hills Country Club and Golf Course, Eakes Sports Complex, D. Rich Memorial Hall, Saylor Park.

ADMISSIONS

Freshman Academic Profile: Average high school GPA 3.4. 38% in top 10% of high school class, 80% in top 25% of high school class, 92% in top 50% of high school class. 85% from public high schools. Minimum paper TOEFL 500. **Basis for Candidate Selection:** *Very important factors considered include:* academic GPA, rigor of secondary school record, standardized test scores. *Important factors considered include:* Class rank, interview, talent/ability. *Other factors considered include:* application essay, recommendation(s), alumni/ae relation, character/personal qualities, extracurricular activities, level of applicant's interest, volunteer work, work experience. **Freshman Admission Requirements:** High school diploma is required and GED is accepted. *Academic units required:* 4 English, 3 mathematics, 2 science, (1 science labs), 2 foreign language, 2 social science. **Freshman Admission Statistics:** 3,348 applied, 60% admitted, 45% enrolled. **Transfer Admission Requirements:** High school transcript, college transcript(s), standardized test scores, statement of good standing from prior institution(s). Minimum college GPA of 2.5 required. Lowest grade transferable C. **General Admission Information:** Application Fee $35. Regular application deadline 8/19. Notification on a rolling basis, beginning on or about 9/1. Nonfall registration accepted. Admission may be deferred for a maximum of 12. Credit and/or placement offered for CEEB Advanced Placement tests.

COSTS AND FINANCIAL AID

Annual tuition $19,650. Room and board $6,830. Required fees $700. Average book expense $1,100. **Required Forms and Deadlines:** FAFSA. **Notification of Awards:** Applicants will be notified of awards on a rolling basis beginning 3/1. **Types of Aid:** *Need-based scholarships/grants:* Federal Pell, SEOG, state scholarships/grants, private scholarships, the school's own gift aid. *Loans:* Subsidized Stafford, Unsubsidized Stafford, PLUS, Federal Perkins, state loans, college/university loans from institutional funds. *Student Employment:* Federal Work-Study Program available. Institutional employment available. Highest amount earned per year from on-campus jobs $600. Off-campus job opportunities are good. **Financial Aid Statistics:** 69% freshmen, 73% undergrads receive need-based scholarship or grant aid. 95% freshmen, 77% undergrads receive non-need-based scholarship or grant aid. 87% freshmen, 88% undergrads receive need-based self-help aid. 4% freshmen, 3% undergrads receive athletic scholarships. 97% freshmen, 92% undergrads receive any aid. 74% undergrads borrow to pay for school. Average cumulative indebtedness $27,046. **Criteria for awarding institutional aid:** *Non-need-based:* academics, athletics, music/ drama, religious affiliation, state/district residency.

CAMPBELLSVILLE UNIVERSITY

1 University Drive, Campbellsville, KY 42718-2799
Phone: 270-789-5220 • **Financial Aid Phone:** 270-789-5013
E-mail: admissions@campbellsville.edu • **CEEB Code:** 1097
Fax: 270-789-5071 • **ACT Code:** 1500

This private school, affiliated with the Baptist Church, was founded in 1906. It has a 90-acre campus.

RATINGS

Admissions Selectivity Rating: 80	Fire Safety Rating: 70

STUDENTS AND FACULTY

Enrollment: 2,250. **Student Body:** 58% female, 42% male, 12% out-of-state, 7% international. Asian 0%, African American 15%, Caucasian 74%, Hispanic 1%, Native American <1%
Retention and Graduation: 65% freshmen return for sophomore year. 26% freshmen graduate within 4 years. 41% freshmen graduate within 6 years. 20% grads go on to further study within 1 year. 25% grads pursue arts and sciences degrees. 1% grads pursue law degrees. 15% grads pursue business degrees. 1% grads pursue medical degrees. **Faculty:** 146 full-time faculty, 62% hold PhDs, 49% are members of minority groups, 10% are women. 0% of classes are taught by teaching assistants.

ACADEMICS

Degrees: associate, bachelor's, master's. **Classes:** Most classes have fewer than 10 students. **Majors with Highest Enrollment:** Business, Management, Marketing, and Related Support Services; Junior High/Intermediate/Middle School Education and Teaching; Registered Nursing/Registered Nurse. **Special Study Options:** cooperative education program, distance learning, double major, dual enrollment, English as a Second Language (ESL), honors program, independent study, internships, liberal arts/career combination, study abroad, teacher certification program, weekend college. **Disability Services:** Special programs offered to physically disabled students include tutors. **Career services:** alumni services, career assessment, internships.

FACILITIES

Housing: men's dorms, women's dorms, apartments for married students, apartments for single students. 70% of campus accessible to physically disabled. **Special Academic Facilities/Equipment:** Computer labs: Technology lab **Computers:** Students can register for classes online. Administrative functions (other than registration) can be performed online.

CAMPUS LIFE

Environment: Rural. **Activities:** Choral groups, concert band, dance, drama/theater, jazz band, literary magazine, marching band, music ensembles, musical theater, pep band, radio station, student government, student newspaper, television station, yearbook, Campus Ministries, International Student Organization. 49 registered organizations, 1 honor society, 7 religious organizations. **Athletics (Intercollegiate):** *Men:* baseball, basketball, bowling, cheerleading, cross-country, football, golf, soccer, tennis, track/field (outdoor), wrestling. *Women:* basketball, bowling, cheerleading, cross-country, golf, soccer, softball, swimming, tennis, track/field (outdoor), volleyball. **On-Campus Highlights:** Technology Center, Athletic Center, New Resident Village, Library, Fine Arts Center.

ADMISSIONS

Freshman Academic Profile: Average high school GPA 3.18. 17% in top 10% of high school class, 38% in top 25% of high school class, 69% in top 50% of high school class. 90% from public high schools. SAT Math middle 50% range 430-580. SAT Critical Reading middle 50% range 420-590. SAT Writing middle 50% range 410-540. ACT middle 50% range 18-23. Minimum paper TOEFL 500. **Basis for Candidate Selection:** *Very important factors considered include:* rigor of secondary school record. *Important factors considered include:* Class rank, recommendation(s), standardized test scores, character/personal qualities, interview. *Other factors considered include:* application essay, alumni/ae relation, extracurricular activities, religious affiliation/commitment, talent/ability, volunteer work, work experience. **Freshman Admission Requirements:** High school diploma is required and GED is accepted. **Freshman Admission Statistics:** 2,477 applied, 67% admitted, 35% enrolled. **Transfer Admission Requirements:** college transcript(s), Lowest grade transferable C. **General Admission Information:** Application Fee $20. Regular application deadline 8/15. Notification on a rolling basis, beginning on or about 9/1. Nonfall registration accepted. Admission may be deferred for a maximum of 12. Credit and/or placement offered for CEEB Advanced Placement tests.

COSTS AND FINANCIAL AID

Annual tuition $21,100. Room and board $7,120. Required fees $500. Average book expense $1,000. **Required Forms and Deadlines:** FAFSA. **Notification of Awards:** Applicants will be notified of awards on a rolling basis beginning 2/15. **Types of Aid:** *Need-based scholarships/grants:* Federal Pell, SEOG, state scholarships/grants, private scholarships, the school's own gift aid. *Loans:* Subsidized Stafford, Unsubsidized Stafford, PLUS, Federal Perkins, college/university loans from institutional funds. *Student Employment:* Federal Work-Study Program available. Institutional employment available. Highest amount earned per year from on-campus jobs $2,000. Off-campus job opportunities are good. **Financial Aid Statistics:** 100% freshmen, 97% undergrads receive need-based scholarship or grant aid. 14% freshmen, 10% undergrads receive non-need-based scholarship or grant aid. 74% freshmen, 77% undergrads receive need-based self-help aid. 5% freshmen, 6% undergrads receive athletic scholarships. 95% freshmen, 92% undergrads receive any aid. 90% undergrads borrow to pay for school. Average cumulative indebtedness $19,400. **Criteria for awarding institutional aid:** *Non-need-based:* academics, art, athletics, leadership, minority status, music/drama, religious affiliation, state/district residency.

CANISIUS COLLEGE

2001 Main Street, Buffalo, NY 14208
Phone: 716-888-2200 · **Financial Aid Phone:** 716-888-2300
E-mail: admissions@canisius.edu · **CEEB Code:** 2073
Fax: 716-888-3230 · **Website:** http://www.canisius.edu · **ACT Code:** 2690

This private school, affiliated with the Roman Catholic-Jesuit Church, was founded in 1870. It has a 32-acre campus.

RATINGS

Admissions Selectivity Rating: 81   **Fire Safety Rating:** 81

STUDENTS AND FACULTY

Enrollment: 2,736. **Student Body:** 54% female, 46% male, 9% out-of-state, 4% international (31 countries represented). Asian 2%, African American 7%, Caucasian 74%, Hispanic 5%, Native American <1%.
Retention and Graduation: 86% freshmen return for sophomore year. 57% freshmen graduate within 4 years. 68% freshmen graduate within 6 years.

Faculty: 195 full-time faculty, 97% hold PhDs, 61% are members of minority groups, 9% are women. 0% of classes are taught by teaching assistants.

ACADEMICS

Degrees: associate, bachelor's, master's, post-bachelor's certificate, post-master's certificate. **Classes:** Most classes have 20–29 students. Most lab/discussion sessions have 20–29 students. **Majors with Highest Enrollment:** Biology/Biological Sciences; Psychology; Business Administration and Management. **Special Study Options:** cooperative education program, cross-registration, distance learning, double major, dual enrollment, English as a Second Language (ESL), exchange student program (domestic), honors program, independent study, internships, study abroad, teacher certification program, 4 + 1 BS/MBA 3 + 4 BS/DD (Bio and Dentistry)-Early Assurance guaranteed Medical School Admission). **Honors programs:** The All College Honors Program offers outstanding students the opportunity for a highly demanding and rewarding experience of the core curriculum. Students study under the college's most distinguished faculty, participate in educational travel, write a senior thesis and compete for special awards and honors. Combined degree programs: BA/DDS, BA/BS-MBA, BA/BS-MBAPA. **Disability Services:** Special programs offered to physically disabled students include note-taking services, reader services, tape recorders, tutors. **Career services:** Alumni network, alumni services, career/job search classes, career assessment, internships, regional alumni.

FACILITIES

Housing: Coed dorms, special housing for disabled students, special housing for international students, apartments for single students, Honors Student Housing. All college owned housing is handicapped accessible. 95% of campus accessible to physically disabled. **Special Academic Facilities/Equipment:** TV studio, electron microscope, seismograph, language lab, digital lab, human performance lab, molecular biology and physics labs, mini-planetarium. **Computers:** 100% of classrooms, 100% of dorms, 100% of libraries, 100% of dining areas, 100% of student union, 100% of common outdoor areas have wireless network access. Students can register for classes online. Administrative functions (other than registration) can be performed online.

CAMPUS LIFE

Environment: Metropolis. **Activities:** Choral groups, concert band, dance, drama/theater, jazz band, literary magazine, music ensembles, musical theater, pep band, radio station, student government, student newspaper, student-run film society, television station, yearbook, Campus Ministries, International Student Organization, Model UN. 102 registered organizations, 16 honor societies, 2 religious organizations. 1 fraternity, 1 sorority. **Athletics (Intercollegiate):** *Men:* baseball, basketball, cross-country, diving, golf, ice hockey, lacrosse, soccer, swimming. *Women:* basketball, cross-country, diving, lacrosse, soccer, softball, swimming, synchronized swimming, volleyball. **On-Campus Highlights:** Montante Cultural Center, Delavan Townhouses, Palisano Pavillion, Koessler Athletic Center, Richard E. Winter Student Center, Canisius College sponsors a variety of on-campus entertainment to keep students busy throughout the year. Our highly popular Java Jams is a weekly coffee-style event offering entertainment in the Palisano Pavilion. **Environmental Initiatives:** Canisius College is deeply committed to utility conservation and the sustainability of our natural resources. This is accomplished in part through our development of policies and practices which are designed to promote sound energy management, and the economic, social and environmental well-being of our students and staff. Canisius College is working with Ecology and Environment, Inc. (E & E) to develop and implement an energy conservation program. The overall goal of the program is to reduce the colleges annual electric consumption by five percent, based on historical consumption during the last three academic years. A web page is being designed to explain how Canisius College conserves and supports sustainable use of our natural resources Canisius College has made major strides towards decreasing our environmental footprint by changing the way we operate, maintain, and construct our facilities. Future design and construction will be weighed against environmentally friendly LEED° recommended practices to ensure the responsible use of our natural resources. Canisius has also made a significant investment in energy conservation measures and software that reduces our consumption of utilities. Topics such as Sustainability, Carbon inventory, Ongoing Conservation Efforts, Green Building Design Strategies, Green Computing, Heating and Cooling Standards, Recycling, Renewable Energy, Smart Energy Behaviors and Awareness and Promotional Campaigns will be introduced and explained in future web issues.

ADMISSIONS

Freshman Academic Profile: Average high school GPA 89.5. 20.28% in top 10% of high school class, 51.83% in top 25% of high school class, 83.95% in top 50% of high school class. 71% from public high schools. SAT Math middle 50% range 490-600. SAT Critical Reading middle 50% range 480-580. ACT middle 50% range 21-27. Minimum internet-based TOEFL 65. Minimum paper TOEFL 500. **Basis for Candidate Selection:** *Very important factors considered include:* academic GPA, rigor of secondary school record. *Important factors considered include:* application essay, recommendation(s), standardized test scores. *Other factors considered include:* Class rank, alumni/ae relation, character/personal qualities, extracurricular activities, first generation, interview, talent/ability, volunteer work, work experience. **Freshman Admission Requirements:** High school diploma is required and GED is accepted. *Academic units required:* 4 English, 3 mathematics, 2 science, (2 science labs), 2 foreign language, 4 social studies. **Freshman Admission Statistics:** 3,667 applied, 80% admitted, 21% enrolled. **Transfer Admission Requirements:** college transcript(s), statement of good standing from prior institution(s). Minimum college GPA of 2.0 required. Lowest grade transferable C. **General Admission Information:** Application Fee $40. Regular application deadline 5/1. Notification on a rolling basis, beginning on or about 12/15. Nonfall registration accepted. Admission may be deferred for a maximum of 1 year. Credit and/or placement offered for CEEB Advanced Placement tests.

COSTS AND FINANCIAL AID
Annual tuition $32,630. Room and board $12,516. Required fees $1,370. Average book expense $1,000. **Required Forms and Deadlines:** FAFSA, State aid form. **Notification of Awards:** Applicants will be notified of awards on a rolling basis beginning 3/1. **Types of Aid:** *Need-based scholarships/grants:* Federal Pell, SEOG, state scholarships/grants, private scholarships, the school's own gift aid. *Loans:* Subsidized Stafford, Unsubsidized Stafford, PLUS, Federal Perkins. *Student Employment:* Federal Work-Study Program available. Institutional employment available. Highest amount earned per year from on-campus jobs $2,175. Off-campus job opportunities are excellent. **Financial Aid Statistics:** 100% freshmen, 99% undergrads receive need-based scholarship or grant aid. 25% freshmen, 21% undergrads receive non-need-based scholarship or grant aid. 82% freshmen, 80% undergrads receive need-based self-help aid. 4% freshmen, 4% undergrads receive athletic scholarships. 98% freshmen, 97% undergrads receive any aid. 70% undergrads borrow to pay for school. Average cumulative indebtedness $24,091. **Criteria for awarding institutional aid:** *Non-need-based:* academics, alumni affiliation, art, athletics, job skills, music/drama, religious affiliation.

CAPE BRETON UNIVERSITY

PO Box 5300, Sydney, NS B1P 6L2
Phone: 902-563-1117 · **Financial Aid Phone:** 902-563-1420
E-mail: registrar@uccb.ns.ca
Fax: 902-563-1371 · **Website:** www.cbu.ca

This public school was founded in 1974. It has a 140-acre campus.

RATINGS
Admissions Selectivity Rating: 60*   Fire Safety Rating: 60*

STUDENTS AND FACULTY
Enrollment: 2,702. **Student Body:** 58% female, 42% male, (40 countries represented).
Retention and Graduation: 55% freshmen return for sophomore year. 54% freshmen graduate within 4 years. 96% freshmen graduate within 6 years. **Faculty:** 189 full-time faculty, 41% hold PhDs, 25% are members of minority groups. 0% of classes are taught by teaching assistants.

ACADEMICS
Degrees: bachelor's, certificate, diploma, master's, post-bachelor's certificate. **Classes:** Most classes have fewer than 10 students. **Majors with Highest Enrollment:** Education; Early Childhood Education and Teaching; Mathematics and Computer Science. **Special Study Options:** cooperative education program, distance learning, double major, honors program, independent study, internships, liberal arts/career combination, study abroad. Combined degree programs: BBA/BACS. **Disability Services:** Special programs offered to physically disabled students include note-taking services, reader services, tape recorders, tutors.

FACILITIES
Housing: Coed dorms. 100% of campus accessible to physically disabled. **Special Academic Facilities/Equipment:** Art Gallery Boardmore Playhouse CAPR Radio. **Computers:** Students can register for classes online. Administrative functions (other than registration) can be performed online.

CAMPUS LIFE
Environment: Town. **Activities:** drama/theater, literary magazine, radio station, student government, student newspaper, yearbook. 72 registered organizations, 1 honor society. **Athletics (Intercollegiate):** *Men:* basketball, soccer. *Women:* basketball, soccer, volleyball. **On-Campus Highlights:** Pit Lounge, Sullivan Field House Athletic Centre, Great Hall, Boardmore Playhouse, Centre for Cape Breton Studies.

ADMISSIONS
Freshman Academic Profile: 80% from public high schools. Minimum paper TOEFL 550. **Basis for Candidate Selection:** *Important factors considered*

include: rigor of secondary school record. **Freshman Admission Requirements:** High school diploma is required and GED is not accepted. *Academic units required:* 3 English, 2 mathematics. **Freshman Admission Statistics:** 1,679 applied, 89% admitted, 85% enrolled. **Transfer Admission Requirements:** college transcript(s). **General Admission Information:** Application Fee $20. Regular application deadline 8/1. Notification on a rolling basis, beginning on or about 3/1. Nonfall registration accepted. Admission may be deferred for a maximum of 1 year.

COSTS AND FINANCIAL AID
Student Employment: Institutional employment available. Off-campus job opportunities are good.

CAPITAL UNIVERSITY

Admission Office, Columbus, OH 43209
Phone: 614-236-6101 · **Financial Aid Phone:** 614-236-6511
E-mail: admission@capital.edu · **CEEB Code:** 1099
Fax: 614-236-6926 · **Website:** www.capital.edu · **ACT Code:** 3242

This private school, affiliated with the Lutheran Church, was founded in 1830. It has a 48-acre campus.

RATINGS
Admissions Selectivity Rating: 80   Fire Safety Rating: 63

STUDENTS AND FACULTY
Enrollment: 2,647. **Student Body:** 57% female, 43% male, 9% out-of-state, 1% international (16 countries represented). Asian 1%, African American 9%, Caucasian 80%, Hispanic 3%, Native American <1%
Retention and Graduation: 74% freshmen return for sophomore year. 52% freshmen graduate within 4 years. 58% freshmen graduate within 6 years. **Faculty:** 175 full-time faculty, 78% hold PhDs, 47% are members of minority groups, 10% are women. 0% of classes are taught by teaching assistants.

ACADEMICS
Degrees: bachelor's, first professional, master's. **Classes:** Most classes have 10–19 students. Most lab/discussion sessions have 20–29 students. **Majors with Highest Enrollment:** Education; Registered Nursing/Registered Nurse; Business Administration and Management. **Special Study Options:** Accelerated program, cooperative education program, cross-registration, double major, English as a Second Language (ESL), exchange student program (domestic), honors program, independent study, internships, liberal arts/career combination, student-designed major, study abroad, teacher certification program. **Honors programs:** Capital University Honors Program. Combined degree programs: MSN/JD, MSN/MBA, MSN/Master's of Lay Ministry. **Disability Services:** Special programs offered to physically disabled students include tape recorders, tutors. **Career services:** Alumni network, alumni services, career/job search classes, career assessment, internships.

FACILITIES
Housing: Coed dorms, special housing for disabled students, special housing for international students, fraternity/sorority housing, apartments for single students, Student organization and special interest housing. 100% of campus accessible to physically disabled. **Special Academic Facilities/Equipment:** Art gallery, Conservatory of Music. **Computers:** Students can register for classes online. Administrative functions (other than registration) can be performed online.

CAMPUS LIFE
Environment: Metropolis. **Activities:** Choral groups, concert band, dance, drama/theater, jazz band, literary magazine, music ensembles, musical theater, radio station, student government, student newspaper, symphony orchestra, television station, yearbook, Campus Ministries, International Student Organization. 63 registered organizations, 16 honor societies, 5 religious organizations. 5 fraternities, 5 sororities. **Athletics (Intercollegiate):** *Men:* baseball, basketball, cross-country, football, golf, soccer, tennis, track/field (outdoor), track/field (indoor). *Women:* basketball, cross-country, golf, soccer, softball, tennis, track/field (outdoor), track/field (indoor), volleyball. **On-Campus Highlights:** Capital Center, College Avenue Residence Hall, Schumacher Gallery **Environmental Initiatives:** Energy management; Solid waste recycling; Behavior modification.

ADMISSIONS
Freshman Academic Profile: Average high school GPA 3.44. 16% in top 10% of high school class, 45% in top 25% of high school class, 78% in top 50% of high school class. 92% from public high schools. SAT Math middle 50% range 490-610. SAT Critical Reading middle 50% range 470-600. SAT Writing middle

50% range 440-580. ACT middle 50% range 21-27. Minimum paper TOEFL 500. **Basis for Candidate Selection:** *Very important factors considered include:* academic GPA, rigor of secondary school record, standardized test scores. *Important factors considered include:* Class rank, extracurricular activities, interview. *Other factors considered include:* recommendation(s), alumni/ae relation, character/personal qualities, level of applicant's interest, racial/ethnic status, religious affiliation/commitment, talent/ability. **Freshman Admission Requirements:** High school diploma is required and GED is accepted. *Academic units required:* 4 English, 3 mathematics, 3 science, (2 science labs), 2 foreign language, 3 social studies, 1 academic electives. **Freshman Admission Statistics:** 3,640 applied, 76% admitted, 25% enrolled. **Transfer Admission Requirements:** college transcript(s), Minimum college GPA of 2.5 required. Lowest grade transferable C-. **General Admission Information:** Application Fee $25. Notification on a rolling basis, beginning on or about 9/15. Nonfall registration accepted. Admission may be deferred for a maximum of 1 year. Credit and/or placement offered for CEEB Advanced Placement tests.

COSTS AND FINANCIAL AID
Annual tuition $31,990. Room and board $8,710. Average book expense $1,500. **Required Forms and Deadlines:** FAFSA. **Notification of Awards:** Applicants will be notified of awards on a rolling basis beginning 3/1. **Types of Aid:** *Need-based scholarships/grants:* Federal Pell, SEOG, state scholarships/grants, private scholarships, the school's own gift aid. *Loans:* Subsidized Stafford, Unsubsidized Stafford, PLUS, Federal Perkins, Federal Nursing, state loans, college/university loans from institutional funds. *Student Employment:* Federal Work-Study Program available. Institutional employment available. Off-campus job opportunities are good. **Financial Aid Statistics:** 98% freshmen, 95% undergrads receive need-based scholarship or grant aid. 98% freshmen, 92% undergrads receive non-need-based scholarship or grant aid. 78% freshmen, 81% undergrads receive need-based self-help aid. 0% freshmen, 0% undergrads receive athletic scholarships. 99 86% undergrads borrow to pay for school. Average cumulative indebtedness $26,725.

CAPITOL COLLEGE

11301 Springfield Road, Laurel, MD 20708
Phone: 800-950-1992
E-mail: admissions@capitol-college.edu
Fax: 301-953-1442 • **Website:** www.capitol-college.edu

This is a private school.

RATINGS
Admissions Selectivity Rating: 70   **Fire Safety Rating:** 60*

STUDENTS AND FACULTY
Enrollment: 452. **Student Body:** 22% female, 78% male, 14% out-of-state, 4% international. Asian 7%, African American 36%, Caucasian 48%, Hispanic 2%, Native American <1%
Retention and Graduation: 60% freshmen return for sophomore year. 5% freshmen graduate within 4 years. 36% freshmen graduate within 6 years. 10% grads go on to further study within 1 year. 10% grads pursue arts and sciences degrees. **Faculty:** 21 full-time faculty, 33% hold PhDs, 29% are members of minority groups, 14% are women.

ACADEMICS
Degrees: associate, bachelor's, certificate, master's, post-bachelor's certificate, transfer associate. **Classes:** Most classes have 10–19 students. Most lab/discussion sessions have fewer than 10 students. **Majors with Highest Enrollment:** Aerospace, Aeronautical and Astronautical/Space Engineering; Computer Engineering; Electrical and Electronics Engineering. **Special Study Options:** cooperative education program, distance learning, double major, independent study, internships, weekend college. **Disability Services:** Special programs offered to physically disabled students include note-taking services, tape recorders, tutors. **Career services:** alumni services, career/job search classes, career assessment, internships.

FACILITIES
Housing: men's dorms, women's dorms, apartments for single students. 99% of campus accessible to physically disabled.

CAMPUS LIFE
Activities: dance, drama/theater, literary magazine, radio station, student government, student newspaper. 10 registered organizations, 3 honor societies.

ADMISSIONS
Freshman Academic Profile: 85% from public high schools. SAT Math middle 50% range 350-590. SAT Critical Reading middle 50% range 400-520. Minimum paper TOEFL 500. **Basis for Candidate Selection:** *Very important*

factors considered include: rigor of secondary school record. *Important factors considered include:* application essay, standardized test scores. *Other factors considered include:* recommendation(s), alumni/ae relation, character/personal qualities, extracurricular activities, interview, talent/ability, volunteer work, work experience. **Freshman Admission Requirements:** High school diploma is required and GED is accepted. *Academic units required:* 4 English, 3 mathematics, 3 science, (2 science labs), 0 foreign language, 0 social studies, 0 history. **Freshman Admission Statistics:** 190 applied, 86% admitted, 21% enrolled. **Transfer Admission Requirements:** college transcript(s), essay or personal statement, Minimum college GPA of 2.0 required. Lowest grade transferable c. **General Admission Information:** Application Fee $25. Notification on a rolling basis, beginning on or about 11/15. Nonfall registration accepted. Admission may be deferred for a maximum of 1. Credit and/or placement offered for CEEB Advanced Placement tests.

COSTS AND FINANCIAL AID
Annual tuition $16,500. Room and board $3,710. Required fees $600. Average book expense $800. **Required Forms and Deadlines:** FAFSA, Institution's own financial aid form. **Notification of Awards:** Applicants will be notified of awards on a rolling basis beginning 6/30. **Types of Aid:** *Need-based scholarships/grants:* Federal Pell, SEOG, state scholarships/grants, private scholarships, the school's own gift aid. *Loans:* Subsidized Stafford, Unsubsidized Stafford, PLUS, Federal Perkins. *Student Employment:* Federal Work-Study Program available. Institutional employment available. Highest amount earned per year from on-campus jobs $2,000. Off-campus job opportunities are excellent. **Financial Aid Statistics:** 114% freshmen, 83% undergrads receive need-based scholarship or grant aid. 0% freshmen, 3% undergrads receive non-need-based scholarship or grant aid. 47% freshmen, 69% undergrads receive need-based self-help aid. 0% freshmen, 0% undergrads receive athletic scholarships. 89% undergrads borrow to pay for school. **Criteria for awarding institutional aid:** *Non-need-based:* academics, alumni affiliation, leadership, minority status.

CARLETON COLLEGE

Best 380

100 South College Street, Northfield, MN 55057
Phone: 507-222-4190 • **Financial Aid Phone:** 507-222-4138
E-mail: admissions@carleton.edu • **CEEB Code:** 6081
Fax: 507-222-4526 • **Website:** www.carleton.edu • **ACT Code:** 2092

This private school was founded in 1866. It has a 955-acre campus.

RATINGS
Admissions Selectivity Rating: 96   **Fire Safety Rating:** 72

STUDENTS AND FACULTY
Enrollment: 2,023. **Student Body:** 53% female, 47% male, 81% out-of-state, 9% international (37 countries represented). Asian 9%, African American 4%, Caucasian 66%, Hispanic 6%, Native American <1%
Retention and Graduation: 96% freshmen return for sophomore year. 90% freshmen graduate within 4 years. 92% freshmen graduate within 6 years. 33% grads go on to further study within 1 year. **Faculty:** 211 full-time faculty, 97% hold PhDs, 47% are members of minority groups, 25% are women. 0% of classes are taught by teaching assistants.

ACADEMICS
Degrees: bachelor's. **Classes:** Most classes have 10–19 students. Most lab/discussion sessions have 10–19 students. **Majors with Highest Enrollment:** Biology/Biological Sciences; Economics; Computer and Information Sciences. **Special Study Options:** Accelerated program, cross-registration, double major, dual enrollment, independent study, internships, student-designed major, study abroad, teacher certification program. Combined degree programs: BA/JD, 3-2 Nursing, Elementary Education. **Disability Services:** Special programs offered to physically disabled students include note-taking services, reader services, tape recorders, tutors. **Career services:** Alumni network, regional alumni.

FACILITIES
Housing: Coed dorms, special housing for disabled students, apartments for single students, 25 college-owned houses within 2 blocks of campus with varying meal plan options. Some are designated as special interest houses (ex: Green House, Culinary House). 28% of campus accessible to physically disabled. **Special Academic Facilities/Equipment:** Arboretum, greenhouse, observatory, scanning and transmission electron microscopes, refractor and reflector telescopes, nuclear magnetic resonance spectrometer, art gallery. **Computers:**

45% of classrooms, 15% of dorms, 85% of libraries, 50% of dining areas, 100% of student union, 15% of common outdoor areas have wireless network access. Students can register for classes online.

CAMPUS LIFE

Environment: Village. **Activities:** Choral groups, concert band, dance, drama/theater, jazz band, literary magazine, music ensembles, musical theater, radio station, student government, student newspaper, student-run film society, symphony orchestra, yearbook, Campus Ministries, International Student Organization, Model UN. 132 registered organizations, 3 honor societies, 17 religious organizations. **Athletics (Intercollegiate):** *Men:* baseball, basketball, cross-country, diving, football, golf, soccer, swimming, tennis, track/field (outdoor), track/field (indoor). *Women:* basketball, cross-country, diving, golf, soccer, softball, swimming, synchronized swimming, tennis, track/field (outdoor), track/field (indoor), volleyball. **On-Campus Highlights:** Cowling Arboretum, Art Gallery, Historic Goodsell Observatory, Japanese Garden, Recreation Center, Sayles Campus Center, Library. **Environmental Initiatives:** 2nd Wind Turbine provided power directly to the campus grid; Completed climate action plan; Hiring a manager of Campus Energy and Sustainability and five student sustainability assistants (STA's).

ADMISSIONS

Freshman Academic Profile: 70% in top 10% of high school class, 94% in top 25% of high school class, 99% in top 50% of high school class. 60% from public high schools. SAT Math middle 50% range 660-760. SAT Critical Reading middle 50% range 650-750. SAT Writing middle 50% range 650-750. ACT middle 50% range 30-33. Minimum paper TOEFL 600. **Basis for Candidate Selection:** *Very important factors considered include:* Class rank, academic GPA, rigor of secondary school record. *Important factors considered include:* application essay, recommendation(s), standardized test scores, alumni/ae relation, character/personal qualities, extracurricular activities, racial/ethnic status, talent/ability, volunteer work, work experience. *Other factors considered include:* first generation, geographical residence, interview, state residency. **Freshman Admission Requirements:** High school diploma is required and GED is accepted. **Freshman Admission Statistics:** 6,297 applied, 23% admitted, 36% enrolled. **Transfer Admission Requirements:** High school transcript, college transcript(s), essay or personal statement, standardized test scores, statement of good standing from prior institution(s). Minimum college GPA of 2.0 required. Lowest grade transferable C-. **General Admission Information:** Application Fee $30. Early decision application deadline 11/15. Regular application deadline 1/15. Regular notification 4/15. Nonfall registration not accepted. Admission may be deferred for a maximum of 1 year. Credit and/or placement offered for CEEB Advanced Placement tests.

COSTS AND FINANCIAL AID

Required Forms and Deadlines: FAFSA, CSS/Financial Aid PROFILE, Noncustodial PROFILE. **Notification of Awards:** Applicants will be notified of awards on or about 4/1. **Types of Aid:** *Need-based scholarships/grants:* Federal Pell, SEOG, state scholarships/grants, private scholarships, the school's own gift aid. *Loans:* Subsidized Stafford, Unsubsidized Stafford, PLUS, Federal Perkins, state loans, college/university loans from institutional funds, Minnesota SELF Loan program. *Student Employment:* Federal Work-Study Program available. **Financial Aid Statistics:** 100% freshmen, 100% undergrads receive need-based scholarship or grant aid. 13% freshmen, 16% undergrads receive non-need-based scholarship or grant aid. 97% freshmen, 98% undergrads receive need-based self-help aid. 0% freshmen, 0% undergrads receive athletic scholarships. 53% freshmen, 55% undergrads receive any aid. 39% undergrads borrow to pay for school. Average cumulative indebtedness $15,772. **Criteria for awarding institutional aid:** *Non-need-based:* academics.

CARLOS ALBIZU UNIVERSITY—CAU

2173 NW 99 Ave, Miami, FL 33172
Phone: 800-672-3246
E-mail: admissions@albizu.edu
Fax: 305-593-1854 • **Website:** www.mia.albizu.edu

This private school was founded in 1966. It has a 18-acre campus.

RATINGS

Admissions Selectivity Rating: 62   **Fire Safety Rating:** 60*

STUDENTS AND FACULTY

Enrollment: 563. **Student Body:** 74% female, 26% male, 2% international. Asian 0%, African American 17%, Caucasian 6%, Hispanic 137%, Native American <1%

Retention and Graduation: 60% grads go on to further study within 1 year. 85% grads pursue arts and sciences degrees. **Faculty:** 4 full-time faculty, 100% hold PhDs, 50% are members of minority groups, 25% are women.

ACADEMICS

Degrees: bachelor's, diploma, master's. **Special Study Options:** Accelerated program, cooperative education program, cross-registration, double major, dual enrollment, English as a Second Language (ESL), independent study, internships, teacher certification program, weekend college.

CAMPUS LIFE

Activities: student government, student newspaper. 3 registered organizations, 1 honor society.

ADMISSIONS

Basis for Candidate Selection: *Very important factors considered include:* rigor of secondary school record. **Freshman Admission Requirements:** High school diploma is required and GED is accepted. **Freshman Admission Statistics:** 185 applied, 64% admitted, 54% enrolled. Minimum college GPA of 2.0 required. Lowest grade transferable C. **General Admission Information:** Application Fee $25. Nonfall registration accepted. Admission may be deferred for a maximum of 1 year.

COSTS AND FINANCIAL AID

Average book expense $690. **Required Forms and Deadlines:** FAFSA, Institution's own financial aid form. **Notification of Awards:** Applicants will be notified of awards on a rolling basis beginning 2/1. *Student Employment:* Off-campus job opportunities are good. **Financial Aid Statistics:** 83% freshmen, 90% undergrads receive need-based scholarship or grant aid. 0% freshmen, 3% undergrads receive non-need-based scholarship or grant aid. 96% freshmen, 97% undergrads receive need-based self-help aid. 0% freshmen, 0% undergrads receive athletic scholarships. 85% undergrads borrow to pay for school. **Criteria for awarding institutional aid:** *Non-need-based:* academics.

CARLOW UNIVERSITY

3333 Fifth Avenue, Pittsburgh, PA 15213-3165
Phone: 412-578-6059
E-mail: admissions@carlow.edu • **CEEB Code:** 2421
Fax: 412-578-6321 • **Website:** www.carlow.edu • **ACT Code:** 2421

This private school, affiliated with the Roman Catholic Church, was founded in 1929. It has a 15-acre campus.

RATINGS

Admissions Selectivity Rating: 73   **Fire Safety Rating:** 67

STUDENTS AND FACULTY

Enrollment: 1,323. **Student Body:** 90% female, 10% male, 5% out-of-state, 0% international (2 countries represented). Asian 1%, African American 23%, Caucasian 59%, Hispanic 2%, Native American <1%
Retention and Graduation: 44% freshmen graduate within 4 years. **Faculty:** 101 full-time faculty, 71% hold PhDs, 73% are members of minority groups, 4% are women. 0% of classes are taught by teaching assistants.

ACADEMICS

Degrees: bachelor's, master's, post-bachelor's certificate, post-master's certificate. **Classes:** Most classes have 10–19 students. **Majors with Highest Enrollment:** Registered Nursing/Registered Nurse; Biology/Biological Sciences; Psychology. **Special Study Options:** Accelerated program, cross-registration, distance learning, double major, dual enrollment, honors program, independent study, internships, liberal arts/career combination, student-designed major, study abroad, teacher certification program, weekend college, 3/2 programs with Carnegie Mellon for Chem. Engineering, Environmental Engineering, Mechanical Engineering. Other programs with Duquesne U. in Environmental Science and Mgt.(3/2), several programs with Art Institute of Pittsburgh. **Career services:** Alumni network, career/job search classes.

FACILITIES

Housing: women's dorms **Special Academic Facilities/Equipment:** The A.J. Palumbo Hall of Science and Technology. features research labs, as well as a greenhouse, darkroom, biochamber, an on-site reference library and specially designed study and work zones on every floor to encourage team research. The building incorporates more than 1000 outlets for internet access. Also,on-campus preschool and elementary school. **Computers:** 100% of classrooms, 100% of dorms, 100% of libraries, 100% of dining areas, 100% of student union, have wireless network access. Students can register for classes online.

CAMPUS LIFE

Environment: City. **Activities:** Choral groups, drama/theater, literary magazine, student government, student newspaper, yearbook, Campus Ministries, International Student Organization. 28 registered organizations, 5 honor societies, 1 religious organization. **Athletics (Intercollegiate):** *Women:* basketball, soccer, softball, tennis, volleyball.

ADMISSIONS

Freshman Academic Profile: Average high school GPA 3.37. 13.8% in top 10% of high school class, 36.6% in top 25% of high school class, 73.8% in top 50% of high school class. SAT Math middle 50% range 420-520. SAT Critical Reading middle 50% range 420-528. SAT Writing middle 50% range 400-510. ACT middle 50% range 17-22. **Basis for Candidate Selection:** *Very important factors considered include:* academic GPA, rigor of secondary school record, standardized test scores. *Important factors considered include:* Class rank. *Other factors considered include:* application essay, recommendation(s), alumni/ae relation, character/personal qualities, extracurricular activities, first generation, interview, level of applicant's interest, talent/ability, volunteer work, work experience. **Freshman Admission Requirements:** High school diploma is required and GED is accepted. *Academic units required:* 4 English, 3 mathematics, 3 science, 2 social studies, 2 history, 4 academic electives. **Freshman Admission Statistics:** 663 applied, 91% admitted, 34% enrolled. **Transfer Admission Requirements:** college transcript(s), Minimum college GPA of 2.0 required. Lowest grade transferable C. **General Admission Information:** Application Fee $20. Nonfall registration accepted. Credit and/or placement offered for CEEB Advanced Placement tests.

COSTS AND FINANCIAL AID

Annual tuition $25,956. Room and board $10,314. Required fees $222. Average book expense $1,020. **Required Forms and Deadlines:** FAFSA, State aid form. **Notification of Awards:** Applicants will be notified of awards on a rolling basis beginning 2/15. **Types of Aid:** *Need-based scholarships/grants:* Federal Pell, SEOG, state scholarships/grants, private scholarships, the school's own gift aid. *Loans:* Subsidized Stafford, Unsubsidized Stafford, PLUS, Federal Perkins, Federal Nursing. **Financial Aid Statistics:** 100% freshmen, 100% undergrads receive need-based scholarship or grant aid. 39% freshmen, 36% undergrads receive non-need-based scholarship or grant aid. 97% freshmen, 95% undergrads receive need-based self-help aid. 0% freshmen, 1% undergrads receive athletic scholarships. 97% undergrads borrow to pay for school. Average cumulative indebtedness $30,670. **Criteria for awarding institutional aid:** *Non-need-based:* academics, athletics, leadership.

CARNEGIE MELLON UNIVERSITY

5000 Forbes Avenue, Pittsburgh, PA 15213
Phone: 412-268-2082 • **Financial Aid Phone:** 412-268-8186
E-mail: undergraduate-admissions@andrew.cmu.edu • **CEEB Code:** 2074
Fax: 412-268-7838 • **Website:** www.cmu.edu • **ACT Code:** 3534

This private school was founded in 1900. It has a 136-acre campus.

RATINGS

Admissions Selectivity Rating: 98   **Fire Safety Rating:** 95

STUDENTS AND FACULTY

Enrollment: 6,237. **Student Body:** 44% female, 56% male, 84% out-of-state, 21% international (70 countries represented). Asian 25%, African American 5%, Caucasian 33%, Hispanic 7%, Native American <1%
Retention and Graduation: 96% freshmen return for sophomore year. 72% freshmen graduate within 4 years. 88% freshmen graduate within 6 years. 27% grads go on to further study within 1 year. 7% grads pursue arts and sciences degrees. 1% grads pursue law degrees. 1% grads pursue business degrees. 1% grads pursue medical degrees. **Faculty:** 944 full-time faculty, 92% hold PhDs, 27% are members of minority groups, 20% are women.

ACADEMICS

Degrees: bachelor's, master's, post-master's certificate. **Classes:** Most classes have fewer than 10 students. Most lab/discussion sessions have 20–29 students. **Majors with Highest Enrollment:** Computer Science; Electrical and Electronics Engineering; Mechanical Engineering. **Special Study Options:** cooperative education program, cross-registration, distance learning, double major, dual enrollment, exchange student program (domestic), independent study, internships, liberal arts/career combination, student-designed major,

study abroad, teacher certification program. Combined degree programs: BA/MA, BA/MEng, BS/MBA Industrial Admin; BS/MPM Public Management. **Disability Services:** Special programs offered to physically disabled students include note-taking services, reader services, tape recorders, tutors. **Career services:** Alumni network, alumni services, career/job search classes, career assessment, internships, regional alumni. Career services highlights include internships. Our mission: Students who value experiential learning and who have participated in internships; campus, summer, part-time employment; and/or community service opportunities. An energized and expanding employer base (artistic, corporate, public, service, campus) committed to long term relationships with Carnegie Mellon (and the Career Center) founded on the continual enhancement and development of employer relationships. Internship Development and Placement Programs: Student Employment-Experiential and Professional Development; Pittsburgh Funded Internships (provide funds for students to stay in Pittsburgh for a summer position); Employment Opportunities Conference (Job Fair); On-Campus Recruiting; Networking Events-New York, DC, Boston, Chicago, Silicon Valley, Pittsburgh, Baltimore; Internship Search Workshop Series.

FACILITIES

Housing: Coed dorms, special housing for disabled students, men's dorms, women's dorms, fraternity/sorority housing, apartments for single students, Special interest housing. 95% of campus accessible to physically disabled. **Special Academic Facilities/Equipment:** Rare books collection, Entertainment Technology Center, Art galleries, Theatres, Botanical Institute, Extensive lab facilities and equipment, Recording studio, Robotics Institute, Design studios, Photo shoot studio and darkrooms, Radio station, Collaborative Innovation Center, LEED-certified green residence hall, Campo Garden, Observatory, Wood shops. **Computers:** 100% of classrooms, 100% of dorms, 100% of libraries, 100% of dining areas, 100% of student union, 100% of common outdoor areas have wireless network access. Students can register for classes online. Administrative functions (other than registration) can be performed online.

CAMPUS LIFE

Environment: Metropolis. **Activities:** Choral groups, concert band, dance, drama/theater, literary magazine, marching band, music ensembles, musical theater, pep band, radio station, student government, student newspaper, student-run film society, symphony orchestra, television station, yearbook, Campus Ministries, International Student Organization. 225 registered organizations, 18 religious organizations. 16 fraternities, 7 sororities. **Athletics (Intercollegiate):** *Men:* basketball, cheerleading, cross-country, diving, football, golf, soccer, swimming, tennis, track/field (outdoor). *Women:* basketball, cheerleading, cross-country, diving, soccer, swimming, tennis, track/field (outdoor), volleyball. **On-Campus Highlights:** Hunt Library, Skibo Coffee House, The Cut, The Underground, University Center Building - Student Center. **Environmental Initiatives:** Practice: Bellfield Boiler Plant now using Natural Gas instead of Coal as fuel to produce steam, the purchase of 100% renewable electricity for campus electricity needs and, at minimum, USGBC LEED Silver guidelines required for all building projects and most renovations. Education: We strive to make every student a steward of the environment through both formal and informal education. Carnegie Mellon offers many courses in the realm of environment and sustainability, including a weekend long immersion course, Environment Today, which is a student driven course focusing on a different sustainability topic each year. CMU offers graduate programs in Civil and Environmental Enginnering, Sustainable Design Engineering and Public Policy and Energy, Science, Technology and Policy. Undergraduate majors are available in Civil and Environmental Enginerering and Environmental Policy, with minors available in Environmental Studies and Environmental Science. Informal education is delivered through our campus operations and promoted by our Green Practices Committee as well as our many student groups. http://cmu.edu/environment. Research: At Carnegie Mellon we are building a path to an environmentally sustainable society by promoting a culture of interdisciplinary, collaborative research in the realm of science, technology, policy, culture and community. The Steinbrenner Institute for Environmental Education and Research, formed in 2004 to promote Carnegie Mellon's strategic goal of "transitioning towards an environmentally sustainable society" coordinates and advances the research done by 20 centers that are spread among all seven colleges at the Univesity. Research Centers include; Climate Decision Making Center, The Green Design Institute, WaterQUEST, and the STUDIO for Creative Inquiry. A full list of centers and links to their research can be found at: http://cmu.edu/environment.

ADMISSIONS

Freshman Academic Profile: Average high school GPA 3.72. 79% in top 10% of high school class, 94% in top 25% of high school class, 99% in top 50% of high school class. SAT Math middle 50% range 700-800. SAT Critical Reading middle 50% range 640-740. SAT Writing middle 50% range 660-760. ACT middle 50% range 30-34. Minimum internet-based TOEFL 102. Minimum paper TOEFL 600. **Basis for Candidate Selection:** *Very important factors considered include:* Class rank, academic GPA, rigor of secondary school record, standardized test scores. *Important factors considered include:* application essay, recommendation(s), alumni/ae relation, character/personal qualities, extracurricular activities, first generation, interview, level of applicant's interest, racial/ethnic status, talent/ability, volunteer work, work experience. **Freshman Admission Requirements:** High school diploma is required and GED is accepted. *Academic units required:* 4 English, 4 mathematics, 3 science, (3 science labs), 2 foreign language, 0 social studies, 0 history, 3 academic electives. **Freshman Admission Statistics:** 19,812 applied, 25% admitted, 30% enrolled. **Transfer Admission Requirements:** High school transcript, college transcript(s), essay or personal statement, standardized test scores, statement of good standing from prior institution(s). **General Admission Information:** Application Fee $70. Early decision application deadline 11/1. Regular application deadline 1/1. Regular notification 4/15. Nonfall registration not accepted. Admission may be deferred for a maximum of 1 year. Credit offered for CEEB Advanced Placement tests.

COSTS AND FINANCIAL AID

Annual tuition $49,610. Room and board $12,830. Required fees $1,055. Average book expense $2,400. **Required Forms and Deadlines:** FAFSA, Institution's own financial aid form, CSS/Financial Aid PROFILE, Noncustodial PROFILE. **Notification of Awards:** Applicants will be notified of awards on or about 3/15. **Types of Aid:** *Need-based scholarships/grants:* Federal Pell, SEOG, state scholarships/grants, private scholarships, the school's own gift aid. *Loans:* Subsidized Stafford, Unsubsidized Stafford, PLUS, Federal Perkins. *Student Employment:* Federal Work-Study Program available. Institutional employment available. Off-campus job opportunities are good. **Financial Aid Statistics:** 94% freshmen, 95% undergrads receive need-based scholarship or grant aid. 18% freshmen, 10% undergrads receive non-need-based scholarship or grant aid. 82% freshmen, 86% undergrads receive need-based self-help aid. 0% freshmen, 0% undergrads receive athletic scholarships. 46% freshmen, 45% undergrads receive any aid. 45% undergrads borrow to pay for school. Average cumulative indebtedness $25,430. **Criteria for awarding institutional aid:** *Non-need-based:* academics, art, leadership, minority status, music/drama, state/district residency.

CARROLL COLLEGE (MT)

1601 North Benton Avenue, Helena, MT 59625
Phone: 406-447-4384 • **Financial Aid Phone:** 406-447-5423
E-mail: admission@carroll.edu • **CEEB Code:** 4041
Fax: 406-447-4533 • **Website:** www.carroll.edu • **ACT Code:** 2408

This private school, affiliated with the Roman Catholic Church, was founded in 1909. It has a 63-acre campus.

RATINGS

Admissions Selectivity Rating: 88   **Fire Safety Rating:** 64

STUDENTS AND FACULTY

Enrollment: 1,376. **Student Body:** 58% female, 42% male, 54% out-of-state, 1% international (15 countries represented). Asian 1%, African American 1%, Caucasian 81%, Hispanic 4%, Native American 1%
Retention and Graduation: 81% freshmen return for sophomore year. 50% freshmen graduate within 4 years. 67% freshmen graduate within 6 years. 22% grads go on to further study within 1 year. **Faculty:** 80 full-time faculty, 70% hold PhDs, 36% are members of minority groups, 3% are women. 0% of classes are taught by teaching assistants.

ACADEMICS

Degrees: associate, bachelor's, certificate, transfer associate. **Classes:** Most classes have 10–19 students. Most lab/discussion sessions have 20–29 students. **Majors with Highest Enrollment:** Registered Nursing, Nursing Administration, Nursing Research and Clinical Nursing; Biology/Biological Sciences; Psychology. **Special Study Options:** Accelerated program, cooperative education program, double major, dual enrollment, English as a Second Language (ESL), exchange student program (domestic), honors program, independent study, internships, liberal arts/career combination, student-designed major, study abroad, teacher certification program. **Disability Services:** Special programs offered to physically disabled students include tutors. **Career services:** career/job search classes, career assessment, internships.

FACILITIES

Housing: Coed dorms, apartments for single students, Theme Housing. 75% of campus accessible to physically disabled. **Special Academic Facilities/Equipment:** Arts lab, observatory, seismograph station, engineering lab.

CAMPUS LIFE

Environment: Village. **Activities:** Choral groups, dance, drama/theater, literary magazine, music ensembles, musical theater, pep band, radio station, student government, student newspaper, student-run film society, yearbook,

Campus Ministries, International Student Organization. 34 registered organizations, 10 honor societies, 4 religious organizations. **Athletics (Intercollegiate):** *Men:* basketball, cheerleading, football, golf. *Women:* basketball, cheerleading, golf, soccer, volleyball. **On-Campus Highlights:** Science and Technology Center, Nelson Stadium, Campus Center, St. Charles Chapel, Fitness Center.

ADMISSIONS

Freshman Academic Profile: Average high school GPA 3.47. 25% in top 10% of high school class, 61% in top 25% of high school class, 90% in top 50% of high school class. 75% from public high schools. SAT Math middle 50% range 510-610. SAT Critical Reading middle 50% range 490-620. SAT Writing middle 50% range 490-590. ACT middle 50% range 22-27. **Basis for Candidate Selection:** *Very important factors considered include:* rigor of secondary school record, standardized test scores. *Important factors considered include:* Class rank, application essay, academic GPA, recommendation(s), character/personal qualities. *Other factors considered include:* alumni/ae relation, extracurricular activities, interview, level of applicant's interest, religious affiliation/commitment, talent/ability, volunteer work, work experience. **Freshman Admission Requirements:** High school diploma is required and GED is accepted. **Freshman Admission Statistics:** 3,279 applied, 53% admitted, 18% enrolled. **Transfer Admission Requirements:** college transcript(s), essay or personal statement, statement of good standing from prior institution(s). Minimum college GPA of 2.5 required. Lowest grade transferable C. **General Admission Information:** Application Fee $35. Regular application deadline 6/1. Notification on a rolling basis, beginning on or about 9/10. Nonfall registration accepted. Admission may be deferred for a maximum of 1 year. Credit and/or placement offered for CEEB Advanced Placement tests.

COSTS AND FINANCIAL AID

Annual tuition $27,304. Room and board $8,668. Required fees $610. Average book expense $1,000. **Required Forms and Deadlines:** FAFSA. **Notification of Awards:** Applicants will be notified of awards on a rolling basis beginning 3/1. **Types of Aid:** *Need-based scholarships/grants:* Federal Pell, SEOG, state scholarships/grants, private scholarships, the school's own gift aid. *Loans:* Subsidized Stafford, Unsubsidized Stafford, PLUS, Federal Perkins, private loans. *Student Employment:* Federal Work-Study Program available. Institutional employment available. Off-campus job opportunities are good. **Financial Aid Statistics:** 99% freshmen, 99% undergrads receive need-based scholarship or grant aid. 17% freshmen, 14% undergrads receive non-need-based scholarship or grant aid. 81% freshmen, 85% undergrads receive need-based self-help aid. 20% freshmen, 19% undergrads receive athletic scholarships. 98% freshmen, 98% undergrads receive any aid. 65% undergrads borrow to pay for school. Average cumulative indebtedness $23,429. **Criteria for awarding institutional aid:** *Non-need-based:* academics, art, athletics, leadership, minority status, music/drama, religious affiliation.

CARROLL UNIVERSITY

100 North East Avenue, Waukesha, WI 53186
Phone: 262-524-7220 • **Financial Aid Phone:** 262-524-7297 • **CEEB Code:** 1101
Fax: 262-951-3037 • **Website:** www.carrollu.edu • **ACT Code:** 4570

This private school, affiliated with the Presbyterian Church, was founded in 1846. It has a 52-acre campus.

RATINGS

Admissions Selectivity Rating: 84   **Fire Safety Rating:** 68

STUDENTS AND FACULTY

Enrollment: 3,124. **Student Body:** 31% out-of-state, (39 countries represented).
Retention and Graduation: 41% freshmen graduate within 4 years. 53% freshmen graduate within 6 years. 13% grads go on to further study within 1 year. **Faculty:** 139 full-time faculty. 0% of classes are taught by teaching assistants.

ACADEMICS

Degrees: bachelor's, master's, post-bachelor's certificate. **Classes:** Most classes have 10–19 students. Most lab/discussion sessions have 10–19 students. **Majors with Highest Enrollment:** Business Administration and Management; Psychology; Biology/Biological Sciences. **Special Study Options:** distance learning, double major, exchange student program (domestic), honors program, independent study, internships, liberal arts/career combination, student-designed major, study abroad, teacher certification program. **Disability Services:** Special programs offered to physically disabled students include note-taking services, tape recorders, tutors. **Career services:** Alumni network, career/job search classes, career assessment, internships.

FACILITIES

Housing: Coed dorms, women's dorms, apartments for single students. 50% of campus accessible to physically disabled. **Special Academic Facilities/Equipment:** A 60 acre scientific study and conservancy area with a class 1 trout stream and associated wetland and upland habitats. **Computers:** 80% of classrooms, 100% of dorms, 100% of libraries, 100% of dining areas, 100% of student union, 90% of common outdoor areas have wireless network access. Students can register for classes online. Administrative functions (other than registration) can be performed online.

CAMPUS LIFE

Environment: Town. **Activities:** Choral groups, concert band, dance, drama/theater, jazz band, literary magazine, music ensembles, pep band, radio station, student government, student newspaper, International Student Organization. 40 registered organizations, 2 religious organizations. 2 fraternities, 4 sororities. **Athletics (Intercollegiate):** *Men:* baseball, basketball, cross-country, football, golf, soccer, swimming, tennis, track/field (outdoor), track/field (indoor). *Women:* basketball, cross-country, golf, soccer, softball, swimming, tennis, track/field (outdoor), track/field (indoor), volleyball. **On-Campus Highlights:** Main Hall, Van Male Fieldhouse, Campus Center, Shattuck, Physical Therapy Building.

ADMISSIONS

Freshman Academic Profile: 38% in top 10% of high school class, 62% in top 25% of high school class, 83% in top 50% of high school class. 87% from public high schools. ACT middle 50% range 21-26. Minimum paper TOEFL 550. **Basis for Candidate Selection:** *Very important factors considered include:* Class rank, academic GPA, rigor of secondary school record. *Important factors considered include:* standardized test scores. *Other factors considered include:* application essay, recommendation(s), alumni/ae relation, character/personal qualities, extracurricular activities, geographical residence, interview, racial/ethnic status, state residency, talent/ability, work experience. **Freshman Admission Requirements:** High school diploma is required and GED is accepted. **Freshman Admission Statistics:** 2,868 applied, 83% admitted, 0% enrolled. **Transfer Admission Requirements:** High school transcript, college transcript(s), Minimum college GPA of 2.0 required. Lowest grade transferable C. **General Admission Information:** Nonfall registration accepted. Credit and/or placement offered for CEEB Advanced Placement tests.

COSTS AND FINANCIAL AID

Required Forms and Deadlines: FAFSA. **Notification of Awards:** Applicants will be notified of awards on a rolling basis beginning 2/15. **Types of Aid:** *Need-based scholarships/grants:* Federal Pell, SEOG, state scholarships/grants, private scholarships, the school's own gift aid, Federal Nursing Scholarships. *Loans:* Unsubsidized Stafford, PLUS, Federal Perkins, state loans. *Student Employment:* Federal Work-Study Program available. Institutional employment available. Highest amount earned per year from on-campus jobs $4,270. **Financial Aid Statistics:** 100% freshmen, 100% undergrads receive need-based scholarship or grant aid. 91% freshmen, 91% undergrads receive non-need-based scholarship or grant aid. 73% freshmen, 79% undergrads receive need-based self-help aid. 0% freshmen, 0% undergrads receive athletic scholarships. 98% freshmen, 98% undergrads receive any aid. 73% undergrads borrow to pay for school. Average cumulative indebtedness $16,681. **Criteria for awarding institutional aid:** *Non-need-based:* academics, alumni affiliation, art, leadership, minority status, religious affiliation.

CARSON-NEWMAN UNIVERSITY

1646 Russell Avenue, Jefferson City, TN 37760
Phone: 865-471-3223
E-mail: admitme@cn.edu · **CEEB Code:** 1102
Fax: 865-471-4817 · **Website:** www.cn.edu · **ACT Code:** 3950

This private school, affiliated with the Baptist Church, was founded in 1851. It has a 90-acre campus.

RATINGS

Admissions Selectivity Rating: 77   **Fire Safety Rating:** 60*

STUDENTS AND FACULTY

Enrollment: 1,711. **Student Body:** 57% female, 43% male, 24% out-of-state, 2% international. Asian 1%, African American 8%, Caucasian 84%, Hispanic 2%, Native American <1%
Retention and Graduation: 71% freshmen return for sophomore year. 36% freshmen graduate within 4 years. 25% grads go on to further study within 1 year. 20% grads pursue arts and sciences degrees. 3% grads pursue law degrees. 1% grads pursue business degrees. 2% grads pursue medical degrees. **Faculty:** 129 full-time faculty, 77% hold PhDs, 52% are members of minority groups, 6% are women. 0% of classes are taught by teaching assistants.

ACADEMICS

Degrees: associate, bachelor's, master's. **Classes:** Most classes have 10–19 students. Most lab/discussion sessions have 10–19 students. **Special Study Options:** cooperative education program, double major, dual enrollment, English as a Second Language (ESL), honors program, independent study, internships, student-designed major, study abroad, teacher certification program. **Disability Services:** Special programs offered to physically disabled students include note-taking services, reader services, tape recorders, tutors. **Career services:** alumni services, career/job search classes, career assessment.

FACILITIES

Housing: men's dorms, women's dorms, apartments for married students, apartments for single students. 80% of campus accessible to physically disabled. **Special Academic Facilities/Equipment:** Art galleries, Appalachian history museum, home management house, language lab.

CAMPUS LIFE

Environment: Rural. **Activities:** Choral groups, concert band, dance, drama/theater, jazz band, literary magazine, marching band, music ensembles, musical theater, opera, pep band, student government, student newspaper, television station, yearbook. 45 registered organizations, 10 honor societies, 5 religious organizations. 2 fraternities, 2 sororities. **Athletics (Intercollegiate):** *Men:* baseball, basketball, cheerleading, cross-country, football, golf, soccer, tennis, track/field (outdoor), wrestling. *Women:* basketball, cheerleading, cross-country, soccer, softball, tennis, track/field (outdoor), volleyball. **On-Campus Highlights:** Maddox Student Activities Center, Coffee House (in MSAC) and TV lounge, Workout/Weight Rooms (in MSAC), Cafeteria, Swann Field (Intramurals).

ADMISSIONS

Freshman Academic Profile: Average high school GPA 3.51. 87% from public high schools. SAT Math middle 50% range 440-583. SAT Critical Reading middle 50% range 458-570. ACT middle 50% range 21-26. Minimum paper TOEFL 550. **Basis for Candidate Selection:** *Very important factors considered include:* rigor of secondary school record, standardized test scores. *Important factors considered include:* Class rank. *Other factors considered include:* application essay, recommendation(s), alumni/ae relation, character/personal qualities, extracurricular activities, interview, religious affiliation/commitment, talent/ability, volunteer work, work experience. **Freshman Admission Requirements:** High school diploma is required and GED is accepted. *Academic units required:* 4 English, 2 mathematics, 2 science, (1 science labs), 1 social studies, 1 history, 4 academic electives. **Freshman Admission Statistics:** 4,880 applied, 62% admitted, 16% enrolled. **Transfer Admission Requirements:** college transcript(s), Minimum college GPA of 2.0 required. Lowest grade transferable d. **General Admission Information:** Application Fee $25. Notification on a rolling basis, beginning on or about 6/1. Nonfall registration accepted. Admission may be deferred for a maximum of 2 years. Credit and/or placement offered for CEEB Advanced Placement tests.

COSTS AND FINANCIAL AID

Annual tuition $24,200. Room and board $8,270. Required fees $1,160. Average book expense $1,600. **Required Forms and Deadlines:** FAFSA. **Types of Aid:** *Need-based scholarships/grants:* Federal Pell, SEOG, state scholarships/grants, private scholarships, the school's own gift aid. *Loans:* Direct Subsidized Stafford, Direct Unsubsidized Stafford, Direct PLUS, Federal Perkins, Federal Nursing. *Student Employment:* Federal Work-Study Program available. Institutional employment available. Highest amount earned per year from on-campus jobs $900. Off-campus job opportunities are good. **Financial Aid Statistics:** 100% freshmen, 99% undergrads receive need-based scholarship or grant aid. 13% freshmen, 18% undergrads receive non-need-based scholarship or grant aid. 79% freshmen, 80% undergrads receive need-based self-help aid. 3% freshmen, 5% undergrads receive athletic scholarships. 70% undergrads borrow to pay for school. Average cumulative indebtedness $25,555. **Criteria for awarding institutional aid:** *Non-need-based:* academics, art, athletics, leadership, minority status, music/drama, religious affiliation.

CARTHAGE COLLEGE

2001 Alford Park Drive, Kenosha, WI 53140
Phone: 262-551-6000 · **Financial Aid Phone:** 262-551-6001
E-mail: admissions@carthage.edu · **CEEB Code:** 1103
Fax: 262-551-5762 · **Website:** www.carthage.edu · **ACT Code:** 4571

This private school, affiliated with the Lutheran Church, was founded in 1847. It has a 95-acre campus.

RATINGS

Admissions Selectivity Rating: 85   **Fire Safety Rating:** 73

STUDENTS AND FACULTY

Enrollment: 2,874. **Student Body:** 54% female, 46% male, 68% out-of-state, 0% international (16 countries represented). Asian 1%, African American 5%, Caucasian 76%, Hispanic 4%, Native American <1%. **Retention and Graduation:** 78% freshmen return for sophomore year. 54% freshmen graduate within 4 years. 16% grads go on to further study within 1 year. 4% grads pursue arts and sciences degrees. 2% grads pursue law degrees. 1% grads pursue business degrees. 1% grads pursue medical degrees. **Faculty:** 149 full-time faculty, 91% hold PhDs, 40% are members of minority groups, 7% are women. 0% of classes are taught by teaching assistants.

ACADEMICS

Degrees: bachelor's, certificate, master's. **Classes:** Most classes have 20–29 students. **Majors with Highest Enrollment:** Elementary Education and Teaching; Biology/Biological Sciences; Business Administration and Management. **Special Study Options:** Accelerated program, cross-registration, double major, honors program, independent study, internships, student-designed major, study abroad, teacher certification program. **Honors programs:** We offer All College Honors as well as Honors in the Major. Combined degree programs: BA/MA, Occupational Therapy at Wash Univ. in St. Louis. **Disability Services:** Special programs offered to physically disabled students include note-taking services, reader services, tape recorders, tutors. **Career services:** career/job search classes, career assessment, internships.

FACILITIES

Housing: Coed dorms, men's dorms, women's dorms, fraternity/sorority housing, Best Western Harborside through Carthage. 99% of campus accessible to physically disabled. **Special Academic Facilities/Equipment:** H.F. Johnson Art Gallery, Center for CHildren's Literature, planetarium, undergraduate science research lab, graphic design lab, greenhouse, computer/math research lab, physics research lab, ScienceWorks lab, A.W. Clausen Center Boardroom. **Computers:** Students can register for classes online. Administrative functions (other than registration) can be performed online.

CAMPUS LIFE

Environment: City. **Activities:** Choral groups, concert band, dance, drama/theater, jazz band, literary magazine, music ensembles, musical theater, opera, pep band, radio station, student government, student newspaper, student-run film society, symphony orchestra, yearbook. 90 registered organizations, 20 honor societies, 7 religious organizations. 8 fraternities, 7 sororities. **Athletics (Intercollegiate):** *Men:* baseball, basketball, cross-country, football, golf, soccer, swimming, tennis, track/field (outdoor), track/field (indoor), volleyball. *Women:* basketball, cross-country, golf, soccer, softball, swimming, tennis, track/field (outdoor), track/field (indoor), volleyball, water polo. **On-Campus Highlights:** Tarble Athletic and Recreation Center, Hedberg Library, A.W. Clausen Center for World Business, Oaks Residence Halls, Lake Michigan. Located midway between Chicago and Milwaukee, Carthage is easily accessible by car, airplane and train. Our 95 acre, park-like campus is on the shore of Lake Michigan.

ADMISSIONS

Freshman Academic Profile: Average high school GPA 3.31. 21% in top 10% of high school class, 44% in top 25% of high school class, 75% in top 50% of high school class. 91% from public high schools. SAT Math middle 50% range 490-620. SAT Critical Reading middle 50% range 480-610. ACT middle 50% range 21-27. Minimum paper TOEFL 500. **Basis for Candidate Selection:** *Very important factors considered include:* academic GPA, rigor of secondary school record, standardized test scores. *Other factors considered include:* Class rank, application essay, recommendation(s), character/personal qualities, extracurricular activities, interview, talent/ability, volunteer work, work experience. **Freshman Admission Requirements:** High school diploma is required and GED is accepted. *Academic units required:* 0 English, 0 mathematics, 0 science, (0 science labs), 0 foreign language, 0 social studies, 0 history, 0 academic electives. **Freshman Admission Statistics:** 7,174 applied, 70% admitted, 14% enrolled. **Transfer Admission Requirements:** college transcript(s), statement of good standing from prior institution(s). Minimum college GPA of 2.0 required. Lowest grade transferable C-. **General Admission Information:** Application Fee $25. Notification on a rolling basis, beginning on or about 9/15. Nonfall registration accepted. Admission may be deferred for a maximum of one year. Credit and/or placement offered for CEEB Advanced Placement tests.

COSTS AND FINANCIAL AID

Annual tuition $36,570. Room and board $9,970. Required fees $0. Average book expense $1,600. **Required Forms and Deadlines:** FAFSA. **Notification of Awards:** Applicants will be notified of awards on a rolling basis beginning 3/1. *Types of Aid:* Need-based scholarships/grants: Federal Pell, SEOG, state scholarships/grants, private scholarships, the school's own gift aid. *Loans:* Subsidized Stafford, Unsubsidized Stafford, PLUS, Federal Perkins, state loans, college/university loans from institutional funds. *Student Employment:* Highest amount earned per year from on-campus jobs $1,000. **Financial Aid Statistics:** 100% freshmen, 100% undergrads receive need-based scholarship or

grant aid. 13% freshmen, 11% undergrads receive non-need-based scholarship or grant aid. 83% freshmen, 84% undergrads receive need-based self-help aid. 0% freshmen, 0% undergrads receive athletic scholarships. 97% freshmen, 97% undergrads receive any aid. 79% undergrads borrow to pay for school. Average cumulative indebtedness $17,938. **Criteria for awarding institutional aid:** *Non-need-based:* academics, alumni affiliation, art, leadership, minority status, music/drama, religious affiliation.

CASCADE COLLEGE

9101 East Burnside Street, Portland, OR 97216-1515
Phone: 503-257-1202 · **Financial Aid Phone:** 503-257-1241
E-mail: admissions@cascade.edu · **CEEB Code:**
Fax: 503-257-1222 · **Website:** www.cascade.edu · **ACT Code:** 3459

This private school, affiliated with the Church of Christ Church, was founded in 1993. It has a 12-acre campus.

RATINGS

Admissions Selectivity Rating: 60*   **Fire Safety Rating:** 65

STUDENTS AND FACULTY

Enrollment: 262. **Student Body:** 59% female, 41% male, 64% out-of-state, 1% international (8 countries represented). Asian 3%, African American 5%, Caucasian 26%, Hispanic 5%, Native American <1%. **Retention and Graduation:** 46% freshmen return for sophomore year. 23% freshmen graduate within 4 years. 30% freshmen graduate within 6 years. 15% grads go on to further study within 1 year. 10% grads pursue arts and sciences degrees. 2% grads pursue law degrees. 1% grads pursue business degrees. **Faculty:** 15 full-time faculty, 60% hold PhDs, 27% are members of minority groups, 13% are women. 0% of classes are taught by teaching assistants.

ACADEMICS

Degrees: bachelor's. **Classes:** Most classes have 10–19 students. Most lab/discussion sessions have fewer than 10 students. **Majors with Highest Enrollment:** Teacher Education, Multiple Levels; Psychology; Business/Commerce. **Special Study Options:** double major, dual enrollment, independent study, internships, student-designed major, study abroad, teacher certification program. **Disability Services:** Special programs offered to physically disabled students include note-taking services, reader services, tutors. Most majors provide an opportunity for students to participate in an internship or practicum in the area of the major giving most graduates hand-on experience and an opportunity to experience a career in the major.

FACILITIES

Housing: special housing for disabled students, men's dorms, women's dorms, apartments for married students. 70% of campus accessible to physically disabled. **Computers:** 100% of classrooms, 100% of dorms, 100% of libraries, 100% of dining areas, 100% of student union, 100% of common outdoor areas have wireless network access. Administrative functions (other than registration) can be performed online.

CAMPUS LIFE

Environment: Metropolis. **Activities:** Choral groups, drama/theater, jazz band, literary magazine, music ensembles, musical theater, student government, yearbook. 16 registered organizations, 2 honor societies. **Athletics (Intercollegiate):** *Men:* basketball, cross-country, soccer, track/field (outdoor), track/field (indoor). *Women:* basketball, cross-country, soccer, track/field (outdoor), track/field (indoor), volleyball. **On-Campus Highlights:** Classrooms, Student Center, The Cabin (coffee shop), Weight room, Womack and Hamstreet Fountains.

ADMISSIONS

Freshman Academic Profile: Average high school GPA 3. 85% from public high schools. Minimum paper TOEFL 500. **Basis for Candidate Selection:** *Other factors considered include:* academic GPA, recommendation(s), standardized test scores. **Freshman Admission Requirements:** High school diploma is required and GED is accepted. **Transfer Admission Requirements:** High school transcript, college transcript(s), Minimum college GPA of 2.0 required. Lowest grade transferable D. **General Admission Information:** Application Fee $25. Nonfall registration accepted. Admission may be deferred for a maximum of 1 year. Credit offered for CEEB Advanced Placement tests.

COSTS AND FINANCIAL AID

Average book expense $900. **Required Forms and Deadlines:** FAFSA, Institution's own financial aid form. **Notification of Awards:** Applicants will be notified of awards on a rolling basis beginning 2/15. **Types of Aid:** *Need-based scholarships/grants:* Federal Pell, SEOG, private scholarships, the school's own gift aid. *Loans:* Subsidized Stafford, Unsubsidized Stafford, PLUS, Private Loans. *Student Employment:* Federal Work-Study Program available.

Institutional employment available. Highest amount earned per year from on-campus jobs $2,000. Off-campus job opportunities are excellent. **Financial Aid Statistics:** 100% freshmen, 63% undergrads receive need-based scholarship or grant aid. 19% freshmen, 92% undergrads receive non-need-based scholarship or grant aid. 87% freshmen, 84% undergrads receive need-based self-help aid. 48% freshmen, 36% undergrads receive athletic scholarships. 100% freshmen, 99% undergrads receive any aid. 84% undergrads borrow to pay for school. **Criteria for awarding institutional aid:** *Non-need-based:* academics, athletics, leadership, music/drama, religious affiliation, state/district residency.

CASE WESTERN RESERVE UNIVERSITY

Wolstein Hall, Cleveland, OH 44106-7055
Phone: 216-368-4450 • **Financial Aid Phone:** 216-368-4530
E-mail: admission@case.edu • **CEEB Code:** 1105
Fax: 216-368-5111 • **Website:** www.case.edu • **ACT Code:** 3244

This private school was founded in 1826. It has a 155-acre campus.

RATINGS

Admissions Selectivity Rating: 94   Fire Safety Rating: 79

STUDENTS AND FACULTY

Enrollment: 4,807. **Student Body:** 46% female, 54% male, 67% out-of-state, 9% international (37 countries represented). Asian 19%, African American 4%, Caucasian 53%, Hispanic 6%, Native American <1%
Retention and Graduation: 64% freshmen graduate within 4 years. 81% freshmen graduate within 6 years. 38% grads go on to further study within 1 year. 17% grads pursue arts and sciences degrees. 2% grads pursue law degrees. 3% grads pursue business degrees. 8% grads pursue medical degrees. **Faculty:** 763 full-time faculty, 91% hold PhDs, 43% are members of minority groups, 17% are women. 6% of classes are taught by teaching assistants.

ACADEMICS

Degrees: bachelor's, doctoral, master's, post-bachelor's certificate. **Classes:** Most classes have 10–19 students. Most lab/discussion sessions have 20–29 students. **Majors with Highest Enrollment:** Bioengineering and Biomedical Engineering; Psychology. **Special Study Options:** Accelerated program, cooperative education program, cross-registration, double major, dual enrollment, English as a Second Language (ESL), exchange student program (domestic), honors program, independent study, internships, liberal arts/career combination, student-designed major, study abroad, teacher certification program, Washington Semester. **Honors programs:** The College Scholars Program is a three-year honors program for a small group of students interested in exploring how academic learning can address larger world concerns. Combined degree programs: BA/MA, BA/DDS, BA/MEng, BS/MS, BS/MBA, BS/MAcc, BA/MPH, Sr Yr Prof Studies. **Disability Services:** Special programs offered to physically disabled students include note-taking services, reader services, tape recorders, tutors. **Career services:** Alumni network, alumni services, career/job search classes, career assessment, internships, regional alumni. Case's experiential learning options come in many forms. More than 83% of our undergraduate students participate in opportunities for research, cultural immersion through study abroad programs, clinical work in nursing, and internship and co-op programs, or garner valuable leadership experiences through campus, club, and community interactions.

FACILITIES

Housing: Coed dorms, fraternity/sorority housing, apartments for single students, Wellness HousingSecured women-only floor available. Special-interest housing available. Residential Colleges for first-year students. 90% of campus accessible to physically disabled. **Special Academic Facilities/Equipment:** Art, natural history, and auto-aviation museums, historical society, botanical garden, biology field stations, observatory. **Computers:** 100% of classrooms, 100% of dorms, 100% of libraries, 100% of dining areas, 100% of student union, 100% of common outdoor areas have wireless network access. Students can register for classes online. Administrative functions (other than registration) can be performed online.

CAMPUS LIFE

Environment: Metropolis. **Activities:** Choral groups, concert band, dance, drama/theater, jazz band, literary magazine, marching band, music ensembles, musical theater, pep band, radio station, student government, student newspaper, student-run film society, symphony orchestra, yearbook, Campus Ministries, International Student Organization, Model UN. 150 registered

organizations, 8 honor societies, 4 religious organizations. 16 fraternities, 8 sororities. **Athletics (Intercollegiate):** *Men:* baseball, basketball, cross-country, football, soccer, swimming, tennis, track/field (outdoor), track/field (indoor), wrestling. *Women:* basketball, cross-country, soccer, softball, swimming, tennis, track/field (outdoor), track/field (indoor), volleyball. **On-Campus Highlights:** North Residential Village, Peter B. Lewis Building, Kelvin Smith Library, Veale Convocation and Athletic Center, Turning Point Sculpture Garden. **Environmental Initiatives:** 2008 Signatory to the American College and University President's Climate Commitment, which includes an ongoing comprehensive energy reduction program and a Climate Action Plan published in 2011. This effort continues to net cultural change and drive innovation of business practices. The University's district, non-profit utility provider created a new green, revolving loan fund to help member institutions implement energy efficiency projects. CWRU applied for and was awarded $998,000.00 to implement energy efficiency upgrades in nine buildings in a one-year period of time. This is a significant leap in the University's investment in energy usage reduction. A new University Center is under construction and a major addition to the Dental School is in design and will break ground in FY13, both will apply for LEED Silver with the U.S. Green Building Council. The University Center will house new dining options, event spaces, student group offices and more, will include a 100% live, green roof, a solar array and will strive to operate as a zero to landfill facility.

ADMISSIONS

Freshman Academic Profile: 68% in top 10% of high school class, 92% in top 25% of high school class, 99% in top 50% of high school class. 70% from public high schools. SAT Math middle 50% range 660-760. SAT Critical Reading middle 50% range 610-710. SAT Writing middle 50% range 610-710. ACT middle 50% range 29-33. Minimum internet-based TOEFL 90. Minimum paper TOEFL 577. **Basis for Candidate Selection:** *Very important factors considered include:* Class rank, academic GPA, rigor of secondary school record, standardized test scores, extracurricular activities. *Important factors considered include:* application essay, recommendation(s), character/personal qualities, interview, level of applicant's interest, talent/ability, volunteer work, work experience. *Other factors considered include:* alumni/ae relation, first generation, racial/ethnic status. **Freshman Admission Requirements:** High school diploma is required and GED is accepted. *Academic units required:* 4 English, 3 mathematics, 3 science, (2 science labs), 2 foreign language, 3 social studies. **Freshman Admission Statistics:** 21,733 applied, 38% admitted, 15% enrolled. **Transfer Admission Requirements:** High school transcript, college transcript(s), essay or personal statement, statement of good standing from prior institution(s). Minimum college GPA of 3.2 required. Lowest grade transferable C. **General Admission Information:** Regular application deadline 1/15. Regular notification 4/1. Nonfall registration accepted. Admission may be deferred for a maximum of 1 year. Credit and/or placement offered for CEEB Advanced Placement tests.

COSTS AND FINANCIAL AID

Required Forms and Deadlines: FAFSA, Institution's own financial aid form, CSS/Financial Aid PROFILE. **Notification of Awards:** Applicants will be notified of awards on a rolling basis beginning 3/15. **Types of Aid:** *Need-based scholarships/grants:* Federal Pell, SEOG, state scholarships/grants, private scholarships, the school's own gift aid. *Loans:* Subsidized Stafford, Unsubsidized Stafford, PLUS, Federal Perkins, Federal Nursing, state loans, college/university loans from institutional funds, Alternative loans. *Student Employment:* Federal Work-Study Program available. Institutional employment available. Highest amount earned per year from on-campus jobs $3,200. Off-campus job opportunities are excellent. **Financial Aid Statistics:** 80% freshmen, 84% undergrads receive need-based scholarship or grant aid. 18% freshmen, 12% undergrads receive non-need-based scholarship or grant aid. 79% freshmen, 84% undergrads receive need-based self-help aid. 0% freshmen, 0% undergrads receive athletic scholarships. 87% freshmen, 90% undergrads receive any aid. 60% undergrads borrow to pay for school. Average cumulative indebtedness $24,313. **Criteria for awarding institutional aid:** *Non-need-based:* academics, art, leadership, music/drama.

CASTLETON STATE COLLEGE

Office of Admissions, Castleton, VT 5735
Phone: 802-468-1213 • **Financial Aid Phone:** 802-468-6070
E-mail: info@castleton.edu • **CEEB Code:** 3765
Fax: 802-468-1476 • **Website:** www.castleton.edu • **ACT Code:** 4314

This public school was founded in 1787. It has a 165-acre campus.

RATINGS

Admissions Selectivity Rating: 75   Fire Safety Rating: 78

STUDENTS AND FACULTY

Enrollment: 1,890. **Student Body:** 52% female, 48% male, 30% out-of-state, 2% international (16 countries represented). Asian 1%, African American 2%, Caucasian 85%, Hispanic 2%, Native American <1% **Retention and Graduation:** 37% freshmen graduate within 4 years. 50% freshmen graduate within 6 years. **Faculty:** 102 full-time faculty, 93% hold PhDs, 51% are members of minority groups, 6% are women. 0% of classes are taught by teaching assistants.

ACADEMICS

Degrees: associate, bachelor's, master's, post-bachelor's certificate, post-master's certificate. **Classes:** Most classes have 10–19 students. Most lab/discussion sessions have 10–19 students. **Majors with Highest Enrollment:** Psychology; Business/Commerce. **Special Study Options:** cooperative education program, double major, dual enrollment, honors program, independent study, internships, liberal arts/career combination, student-designed major, study abroad, teacher certification program. Combined degree programs: BA/MA, 4-1 M.B.A.; 4 + 3 Phys. Therapy; 4 + 2. **Disability Services:** Special programs offered to physically disabled students include note-taking services, reader services, tape recorders, tutors.

FACILITIES

Housing: Coed dorms. 100% of campus accessible to physically disabled. **Special Academic Facilities/Equipment:** Historical/medical museum **Computers:** 25% of classrooms, 100% of dorms, 100% of libraries, 100% of dining areas, 100% of student union, have wireless network access.

CAMPUS LIFE

Environment: Rural. **Activities:** Choral groups, dance, drama/theater, jazz band, literary magazine, music ensembles, musical theater, radio station, student government, student newspaper, student-run film society, television station, yearbook. 40 registered organizations, 7 honor societies, 1 religious organization. **Athletics (Intercollegiate):** *Men:* baseball, basketball, cross-country, football, ice hockey, lacrosse, skiing (downhill/alpine), soccer, tennis. *Women:* basketball, cross-country, field hockey, ice hockey, lacrosse, skiing (downhill/alpine), soccer, softball, tennis. **On-Campus Highlights:** Fireside Café, Coffee Cottage, Fitness center, Library **Environmental Initiatives:** Student-driven recycling effort; New construction is significantly green; Purchasing is significantly green.

ADMISSIONS

Freshman Academic Profile: Average high school GPA 3. 6% in top 10% of high school class, 29% in top 25% of high school class, 61% in top 50% of high school class. SAT Math middle 50% range 430-540. SAT Critical Reading middle 50% range 420-530. SAT Writing middle 50% range 420-520. ACT middle 50% range 18-22. Minimum internet-based TOEFL 80. Minimum paper TOEFL 500. **Basis for Candidate Selection:** *Very important factors considered include:* Class rank, application essay, academic GPA, recommendation(s), rigor of secondary school record, character/personal qualities. *Important factors considered include:* standardized test scores. *Other factors considered include:* extracurricular activities, interview, level of applicant's interest, volunteer work, work experience. **Freshman Admission Requirements:** High school diploma is required and GED is accepted. *Academic units required:* 4 English, 3 mathematics, 2 science, (2 science labs), 3 social studies, 3 history. **Freshman Admission Statistics:** 2,397 applied, 78% admitted, 20% enrolled. **Transfer Admission Requirements:** college transcript(s), essay or personal statement, Minimum college GPA of 2.0 required. Lowest grade transferable C-. **General Admission Information:** Application Fee $35. Notification on a rolling basis, beginning on or about 12/15. Nonfall registration accepted. Admission may be deferred for a maximum of 1 year. Credit and/or placement offered for CEEB Advanced Placement tests.

COSTS AND FINANCIAL AID

Annual in-state tuition $9,768. Annual out-of-state tuition $24,432. Room and board $9,414. Required fees $1,224. Average book expense $1,000. **Required Forms and Deadlines:** FAFSA. **Notification of Awards:** Applicants will be notified of awards on a rolling basis beginning 2/15. **Types of Aid:** *Need-based scholarships/grants:* Federal Pell, SEOG, state scholarships/grants, private scholarships, the school's own gift aid. *Loans:* Subsidized Stafford, Unsubsidized Stafford, PLUS, Federal Perkins, Federal Nursing. *Student Employment:* Federal Work-Study Program available. Institutional employment available. Off-campus job opportunities are good. **Criteria for awarding institutional aid:** *Non-need-based:* academics, alumni affiliation, art, leadership, music/drama, state/district residency.

CATAWBA COLLEGE

2300 West Innes Street, Salisbury, NC 28144
Phone: 704-637-4402 • **Financial Aid Phone:** 704-637-4416
E-mail: admission@catawba.edu • **CEEB Code:** 5103
Fax: 704-637-4222 • **Website:** www.catawba.edu • **ACT Code:** 3080

This private school, affiliated with the United Church of Christ Church, was founded in 1851. It has a 276-acre campus.

RATINGS

Admissions Selectivity Rating: 84   **Fire Safety Rating:** 83

STUDENTS AND FACULTY

Enrollment: 1,309. **Student Body:** 53% female, 47% male, 20% out-of-state, 3% international (16 countries represented). Asian 1%, African American 20%, Caucasian 69%, Hispanic 4%, Native American 1% **Retention and Graduation:** 46% freshmen graduate within 4 years. 37% grads go on to further study within 1 year. 33% grads pursue arts and sciences degrees. 7% grads pursue law degrees. 10% grads pursue business degrees. 5% grads pursue medical degrees. **Faculty:** 72 full-time faculty, 86% hold PhDs, 47% are members of minority groups, 10% are women. 0% of classes are taught by teaching assistants.

ACADEMICS

Degrees: bachelor's, master's. **Classes:** Most classes have 10–19 students. Most lab/discussion sessions have 20–29 students. **Majors with Highest Enrollment:** Business Administration and Management; Sport and Fitness Administration/Management; Drama and Dramatics/Theatre Arts. **Special Study Options:** cross-registration, double major, dual enrollment, honors program, independent study, internships, liberal arts/career combination, student-designed major, study abroad, teacher certification program. **Disability Services:** Special programs offered to physically disabled students include note-taking services, tape recorders, tutors. **Career services:** career/job search classes, career assessment Career services highlights include limited internships in Brussels, Belgium offered by Food Lion (Delhaize Group).

FACILITIES

Housing: Coed dorms, men's dorms, women's dorms, Substance free housing. 90% of campus accessible to physically disabled. **Special Academic Facilities/Equipment:** Ecology preserve (183 acres). Wildlife preserve (300 acres) **Computers:** 90% of classrooms, 95% of dorms, 100% of libraries, 25% of dining areas, 80% of student union, 10% of common outdoor areas have wireless network access. Administrative functions (other than registration) can be performed online.

CAMPUS LIFE

Environment: Town. **Activities:** Choral groups, concert band, dance, drama/theater, jazz band, literary magazine, music ensembles, musical theater, pep band, student government, student newspaper, symphony orchestra, yearbook, Campus Ministries. 38 registered organizations, 9 honor societies, 4 religious organizations. **Athletics (Intercollegiate):** *Men:* baseball, basketball, cheerleading, cross-country, football, golf, lacrosse, soccer, swimming, tennis. *Women:* basketball, cheerleading, cross-country, golf, soccer, softball, swimming, tennis, volleyball. **On-Campus Highlights:** Center for the Environment, Cannon Field House, Robertson College Community Center, Ketner Hall, Cannon Student Center. **Environmental Initiatives:** Center for the Environment, along with its national, regional, and community environmental outreach; Office of Waste & Recycling and its various efforts on campus; LEED certified residence halls, and LEED certification-pending; Center for the Environment building.

ADMISSIONS

Freshman Academic Profile: Average high school GPA 2.82. 10% in top 10% of high school class, 36% in top 25% of high school class, 73% in top 50% of high school class. 90% from public high schools. SAT Math middle 50% range 430-550. SAT Critical Reading middle 50% range 430-540. ACT middle 50% range 18-24. Minimum internet-based TOEFL 69. **Basis for Candidate Selection:** *Very important factors considered include:* Class rank, application essay, academic GPA, recommendation(s), standardized test scores. *Important factors considered include:* rigor of secondary school record, character/personal qualities, extracurricular activities, interview, level of applicant's interest, talent/ability. *Other factors considered include:* volunteer work. **Freshman Admission Requirements:** High school diploma is required and GED is accepted. **Freshman Admission Statistics:** 3,694 applied, 36% admitted, 26% enrolled. **Transfer Admission Requirements:** High school transcript, college transcript(s), essay or personal statement, statement of good standing from prior institution(s). Minimum college GPA of 2.0 required. Lowest grade transferable C. **General Admission Information:** Application Fee $25. Notification on a rolling basis, beginning on or about 10/1. Nonfall registration accepted. Admission may be deferred for a maximum of 1 Year. Credit and/or placement offered for CEEB Advanced Placement tests.

COSTS AND FINANCIAL AID

Annual tuition $28,730. Room and board $10,080. Average book expense $1,400. **Required Forms and Deadlines:** FAFSA, State aid form. **Notification of Awards:** Applicants will be notified of awards on a rolling basis beginning 2/15. **Types of Aid:** *Need-based scholarships/grants:* Federal Pell, SEOG, state scholarships/grants, private scholarships, the school's own gift aid. *Loans:* Unsubsidized Stafford, PLUS, Federal Perkins, college/university loans from institutional funds, TERI Loans, Nellie Mae Loans, Advantage Loans, Alternative Loans. *Student Employment:* Federal Work-Study Program available. Institutional employment available. Highest amount earned per year from on-campus jobs $2,000. Off-campus job opportunities are good. **Financial Aid Statistics:** 81% freshmen, 82% undergrads receive need-based scholarship or grant aid. 100% freshmen, 83% undergrads receive non-need-based scholarship or grant aid. 83% freshmen, 81% undergrads receive need-based self-help aid. 23% freshmen, 25% undergrads receive athletic scholarships. 99% freshmen, 99% undergrads receive any aid. 72% undergrads borrow to pay for school. Average cumulative indebtedness $25,565. **Criteria for awarding institutional aid:** *Non-need-based:* academics, athletics, leadership, music/drama, state/district residency.

THE CATHOLIC UNIVERSITY OF AMERICA

Office of Undergraduate Admissions, Washington, DC 20064
Phone: 202-319-5305 • **Financial Aid Phone:** 202-319-5307
E-mail: cua-admissions@cua.edu • **CEEB Code:** 5104
Fax: 202-319-6533 • **Website:** www.cua.edu • **ACT Code:** 654

This private school, affiliated with the Roman Catholic Church, was founded in 1887. It has a 193-acre campus.

RATINGS

Admissions Selectivity Rating: 78   **Fire Safety Rating:** 89

STUDENTS AND FACULTY

Enrollment: 3,499. **Student Body:** 53% female, 47% male, 96% out-of-state, 5% international (82 countries represented). Asian 3%, African American 6%, Caucasian 64%, Hispanic 12%, Native American <1%
Retention and Graduation: 82% freshmen return for sophomore year. 60% freshmen graduate within 4 years. 32% grads go on to further study within 1 year. 15% grads pursue law degrees. 5% grads pursue medical degrees. **Faculty:** 404 full-time faculty, 96% hold PhDs, 38% are members of minority groups, 12% are women. 12% of classes are taught by teaching assistants.

ACADEMICS

Degrees: associate, bachelor's, doctoral, master's, post-bachelor's certificate, post-master's certificate. **Classes:** Most classes have 10–19 students. Most lab/discussion sessions have 10–19 students. **Majors with Highest Enrollment:** Architecture; Political Science and Government; Registered Nursing/Registered Nurse. **Special Study Options:** Accelerated program, cross-registration, distance learning, double major, dual enrollment, English as a Second Language (ESL), honors program, independent study, internships, study abroad, teacher certification program. **Honors programs:** The University Honors Program offers classes in the classical liberal arts and contemporary social and environmental sciences to compliment students" major studies. Students take small, rigorous, discussion-based courses from offerings in philosophy, theology, history and literature, social science, environmental science, and media studies. Students completing any of these six tracks receive distinction at graduation; students completing three tracks and a senior seminar are designated University Scholars. Special lectures, symposia, social events, and trips are organized for students in the program. Combined degree programs: BA/MA, BS/MS, BSN/MSN. **Disability Services:** Special programs offered to physically disabled students include note-taking services, reader services, tape recorders, tutors. **Career services:** Alumni network, alumni services, career assessment, internships, regional alumni. Through Cardinal Connection (Jobs and Internships Online), we share with students the amazing variety and quality of experiential opportunities available to them. Each year hundreds of organizations in the

Washington, D.C. area and nationwide list internships that give students a chance to become involved in a range of responsibilities in politics, research, marketing, accounting, finance, public relations, computer science, engineering, architecture and arts management, to name a few. These experiences not only complement students' classroom education, they often lead to offers of full-time employment upon graduation from CUA.

FACILITIES

Housing: Coed dorms, special housing for disabled students, men's dorms, women's dorms, apartments for single students, Wellness Housing, Theme Housing, Residential college, honors community, politics and current events community, living as leaders community and social justice community. 85% of campus accessible to physically disabled. **Special Academic Facilities/Equipment:** Facilities available on the university campus include an art department gallery; the John K. Mullen of Denver Memorial Library, which features a rare book collection containing 65,000 volumes that range from medieval documents to first editions of 20th-century authors; the university archives, which has nearly 9,000 feet of records and manuscripts; the Vitreous State Laboratory, which engages some of the world"s leading glass scientists to help research and develop methods for safe containment of disposed radioactive materials, primarily by converting nuclear waste into solid glass using vitrification techniques. In 2008, the university dedicated Opus Hall, the first LEED (Leadership in Energy and Environmental Design)-compliant residence hall among colleges and universities in Washington, D.C. The Edward J. Pryzbyla University Center includes nine meeting spaces, two separate dining facilities, a convenience store, the campus bookstore, offices, various atrium and lounge spaces and a 7,500-square-foot great room, where Pope Benedict XVI delivered a speech in April 2008. Adjacent to the campus is the Roman Catholic Basilica of the National Shrine of the Immaculate Conception, the largest church in the Western hemisphere. University Masses and commencement are held every year at the National Shrine. Directly across the street from the university is the Pope John Paul II Cultural Center, a major Catholic museum. **Computers:** 40% of classrooms, 90% of dorms, 100% of libraries, 100% of dining areas, 100% of student union, 20% of common outdoor areas have wireless network access. Students can register for classes online. Administrative functions (other than registration) can be performed online.

CAMPUS LIFE

Environment: Metropolis. **Activities:** Choral groups, dance, drama/theater, jazz band, literary magazine, music ensembles, musical theater, opera, radio station, student government, student newspaper, student-run film society, symphony orchestra, yearbook, Campus Ministries, International Student Organization. 87 registered organizations, 16 honor societies, 4 religious organizations. 1 fraternity, 1 sorority. **Athletics (Intercollegiate):** *Men:* baseball, basketball, cross-country, football, lacrosse, soccer, swimming, tennis, track/field (outdoor), track/field (indoor). *Women:* basketball, cross-country, field hockey, lacrosse, soccer, softball, swimming, tennis, track/field (outdoor), track/field (indoor), volleyball. **On-Campus Highlights:** Edward J. Pryzbyla University Center, Eugene I. Kane Fitness Center, St. Vincent de Paul Chapel, Raymond A. Dufour (athletic) Center, John K. Mullen of Denver Memorial Library, Catholic University's 193 acre campus is the largest among universities in Washington, D.C. Its spacious campus setting is adjacent to a Washington Metrorail and has several campus malls for frisbee, football, softball, picnicking and sunning. **Environmental Initiatives:** LEED-NC Certified, 402 Bed Student Dormitory; LEED-Silver (anticipated) Administrative Building—major renovation; Alternative energy purchasing at 100% of electricity consumption. The University just installed 1505 solar panels on 4 campus buildings. These solar panels will produce 720,000 kwh of clean electrical energy on an annual basis. This is the largest solar installation in DC. CUA Beautification Day—On campus planting of trees (large canopy type) in collaberaton with The Casey Tree Foundation, Washington DC. This has been a continued collaboration over past four years.

ADMISSIONS

Freshman Academic Profile: Average high school GPA 3.37. 57% from public high schools. SAT Math middle 50% range 510-610. SAT Critical Reading middle 50% range 510-620. ACT middle 50% range 22-28. Minimum internet-based TOEFL 80. Minimum paper TOEFL 550. **Basis for Candidate Selection:** *Very important factors considered include:* academic GPA, recommendation(s), rigor of secondary school record, standardized test scores, character/personal qualities, level of applicant's interest, volunteer work. *Important factors considered include:* application essay, extracurricular activities, first generation, interview, talent/ability. *Other factors considered include:* Class rank, alumni/ae relation, racial/ethnic status, work experience. **Freshman Admission Requirements:** High school diploma is required and GED is accepted. **Freshman Admission Statistics:** 6,363 applied, 74% admitted, 18% enrolled. **Transfer Admission Requirements:** High school transcript, college transcript(s), essay or personal statement, standardized test scores, Minimum college GPA of 2.8 required. Lowest grade transferable C. **General Admission Information:** Application Fee $55. Regular application deadline 2/15. Notification on a rolling basis, beginning on or about 3/15. Nonfall registration accepted. Admission may be deferred for a maximum of 1 year. Credit and/or placement offered for CEEB Advanced Placement tests.

COSTS AND FINANCIAL AID

Annual tuition $39,200. Room and board $14,518. Required fees $526. Average book expense $1,000. **Required Forms and Deadlines:** FAFSA, CSS/Financial Aid PROFILE. **Notification of Awards:** Applicants will be notified of awards on a rolling basis beginning 4/1. **Types of Aid:** *Need-based scholarships/grants:* Federal Pell, SEOG, state scholarships/grants, private scholarships, the school's own gift aid. *Loans:* Direct Subsidized Stafford, Direct Unsubsidized Stafford, Direct PLUS, Commericial Loans. *Student Employment:* Federal Work-Study Program available. Institutional employment available. Off-campus job opportunities are good. **Financial Aid Statistics:** 98% freshmen, 97% undergrads receive need-based scholarship or grant aid. 0% freshmen, 0% undergrads receive non-need-based scholarship or grant aid. 87% freshmen, 88% undergrads receive need-based self-help aid. 0% freshmen, 0% undergrads receive athletic scholarships. 95% freshmen, 90% undergrads receive any aid. **Criteria for awarding institutional aid:** *Non-need-based:* academics, alumni affiliation, music/drama, religious affiliation.

CAZENOVIA COLLEGE

3 Sullivan Street, Cazenovia, NY 13035
Phone: 315-655-7208 • **Financial Aid Phone:** 315-655-7887
E-mail: admission@cazenovia.edu
Fax: 315-655-4860 • **Website:** www.cazenovia.edu

This private school was founded in 1824.

RATINGS

Admissions Selectivity Rating: 77   **Fire Safety Rating:** 99

STUDENTS AND FACULTY

Enrollment: 1,031. **Student Body:** 73% female, 27% male, 12% out-of-state, 0% international (3 countries represented). Asian 1%, African American 8%, Caucasian 75%, Hispanic 7%, Native American 1%
Retention and Graduation: 72% freshmen return for sophomore year. 53% freshmen graduate within 4 years. 59% freshmen graduate within 6 years. 20% grads go on to further study within 1 year. **Faculty:** 58 full-time faculty, 79% hold PhDs, 69% are members of minority groups, 3% are women. 0% of classes are taught by teaching assistants.

ACADEMICS

Degrees: associate, bachelor's, certificate. **Classes:** Most classes have 10–19 students. **Majors with Highest Enrollment:** Interior Design; Fine/Studio Arts; Business Administration, Management and Operations. **Special Study Options:** Accelerated program, double major, exchange student program (domestic), honors program, independent study, internships, student-designed major, study abroad, teacher certification program. **Honors programs:** The All-College Honors Program at Cazenovia College offers to outstanding students in all majors (in the liberal arts and in the professional studies) a stimulating learning environment beyond that found in standard classroom coursework, and fosters their exceptional academic talents and intellectual curiosity. Demanding curriculum, independent research opportunities and co-curricular activities challenge students to achieve their full educational potential not only through encouraging academic excellence but also through promoting social responsibilities in the global community. An honors degree certifies that students have produced academic work that meets the highest standards of academic rigor in both general education and in their career field. **Disability Services:** Special programs offered to physically disabled students include note-taking services, reader services, tape recorders, tutors. **Career services:** Alumni network, alumni services, career/job search classes, career assessment, internships, regional alumni. The College's academic programs provide students the opportunity to participate in off-campus internships, often as a graduation requirement. Internships generally provide students with one of three types of experience: A continuation of work in a familiar field to increase student knowledge by performing tasks beyond those already mastered in this career area; An experience intended to broaden student expertise within a career area by working in an area of that profession not previously experienced; and A shadowing or observational experience of a professional in a specific career field as a means of exploring a possible new career interest. Regardless of the type of experience, internships make valuable connections between the world of work and the student's academic study. Each academic program has specific eligibility requirements for internships that can be checked in the College Catalog or by contacting either the Program Director or the Director of Career Services.

FACILITIES

Housing: Coed dorms, special housing for disabled students, women's dorms, Single room suites. **Special Academic Facilities/Equipment:** Reisman Hall is a state-of-the-art Art and Design facility and gallery; 243-acre Equine Educa-

tion Center; historic Catherine Cummings Theatre. **Computers:** Administrative functions (other than registration) can be performed online.

CAMPUS LIFE

Environment: Rural. **Activities:** Choral groups, dance, drama/theater, jazz band, musical theater, radio station, student government, student newspaper, student-run film society, yearbook, Campus Ministries. 54 registered organizations, 5 honor societies, 1 religious organization. **Athletics (Intercollegiate):** *Men:* baseball, basketball, cheerleading, crew/rowing, cross-country, equestrian sports, golf, horseback riding, lacrosse, soccer, swimming. *Women:* basketball, cheerleading, crew/rowing, cross-country, equestrian sports, horseback riding, lacrosse, soccer, softball, swimming, volleyball. **On-Campus Highlights:** Residence Halls, Academic Facilities; Art and Design Building, Equestrian Center, Athletic Facilities / Pool, Dining Hall. **Environmental Initiatives:** Environmental Studies education programs; Look Again program—sustainability in fashion. Sustainability is a goal in the institution's Strategic Plan and a study of our institutional carbon footprint is underway, use all biodegradable corn based products in place of foam and paper products in dining halls and kitchens, all green chemicals used in dining halls and kitchens, Apex system in use, and solar panels in use in two buildings on campus; contract with gas and electric energy providers that guarantee a minimum of 5% of energy comes from renewable sources. Cazenovia College hosts the Annual Symposium on Energy in the 21st Century: Seeking Environmental Solutions Through Partnerships. http://www.cazenovia.edu/energy

ADMISSIONS

Freshman Academic Profile: Average high school GPA 3.3. 14% in top 10% of high school class, 40% in top 25% of high school class, 78% in top 50% of high school class. 90% from public high schools. SAT Math middle 50% range 430-530. SAT Critical Reading middle 50% range 430-540. ACT middle 50% range 19-24. Minimum paper TOEFL 550. **Basis for Candidate Selection:** *Very important factors considered include:* rigor of secondary school record, extracurricular activities. *Important factors considered include:* Class rank, academic GPA, recommendation(s), standardized test scores, character/personal qualities, interview, talent/ability. *Other factors considered include:* application essay, level of applicant's interest, volunteer work, work experience. **Freshman Admission Requirements:** High school diploma is required and GED is accepted. **Freshman Admission Statistics:** 2,440 applied, 78% admitted, 18% enrolled. **Transfer Admission Requirements:** High school transcript, college transcript(s), Minimum college GPA of 2.0 required. Lowest grade transferable C. **General Admission Information:** Application Fee $30. Notification on a rolling basis, beginning on or about 11/1. Nonfall registration accepted. Admission may be deferred for a maximum of 1 year. Credit and/or placement offered for CEEB Advanced Placement tests.

COSTS AND FINANCIAL AID

Annual tuition $28,900. Room and board $11,880. Required fees $510. Average book expense $1,000. **Required Forms and Deadlines:** FAFSA, State aid form. **Notification of Awards:** Applicants will be notified of awards on a rolling basis beginning 11/1. **Types of Aid:** *Need-based scholarships/grants:* Federal Pell, SEOG, state scholarships/grants, private scholarships, the school's own gift aid. *Loans:* Direct Subsidized Stafford, Direct Unsubsidized Stafford, Direct PLUS. *Student Employment:* Federal Work-Study Program available. **Financial Aid Statistics:** 100% freshmen, 100% undergrads receive need-based scholarship or grant aid. 8% freshmen, 10% undergrads receive non-need-based scholarship or grant aid. 92% freshmen, 100% undergrads receive need-based self-help aid. 0% freshmen, 0% undergrads receive athletic scholarships. 92% freshmen, 91% undergrads receive any aid. 82% undergrads borrow to pay for school. Average cumulative indebtedness $21,521. **Criteria for awarding institutional aid:** *Non-need-based:* academics.

CEDAR CREST COLLEGE

100 College Drive, Allentown, PA 18104
Phone: 610-740-3780 • **Financial Aid Phone:** 610-606-4602
E-mail: admissions@cedarcrest.edu • **CEEB Code:** 2079
Fax: 610-606-4647 • **Website:** http://www.cedarcrest.edu • **ACT Code:** 3536

This private school was founded in 1867. It has a 84-acre campus.

RATINGS

Admissions Selectivity Rating: 85   **Fire Safety Rating:** 73

STUDENTS AND FACULTY

Enrollment: 1,310. **Student Body:** 93% female, 7% male, 13% out-of-state, 2% international (29 countries represented). Asian 3%, African American 10%, Caucasian 67%, Hispanic 13%, Native American <1%
Retention and Graduation: 69% freshmen return for sophomore year. 59% freshmen graduate within 4 years. 69% freshmen graduate within 6 years. 65%

grads go on to further study within 1 year. 55% grads pursue arts and sciences degrees. 1% grads pursue law degrees. 2% grads pursue business degrees. 3% grads pursue medical degrees. **Faculty:** 73 full-time faculty, 70% hold PhDs, 74% are members of minority groups, 5% are women. 0% of classes are taught by teaching assistants.

ACADEMICS
Degrees: bachelor's, master's, post-bachelor's certificate, post-master's certificate. **Classes:** Most classes have 10–19 students. Most lab/discussion sessions have 10–19 students. **Majors with Highest Enrollment:** Registered Nursing/Registered Nurse; Psychology; Business Administration and Management. **Special Study Options:** cross-registration, distance learning, double major, honors program, independent study, internships, liberal arts/career combination, student-designed major, study abroad, teacher certification program, Ethics. **Honors programs:** Special courses reserved for Honors Students, undergraduate research opportunities, including Honors Thesis. **Disability Services:** Special programs offered to physically disabled students include note-taking services, reader services, tape recorders, tutors. **Career services:** Alumni network, alumni services, career/job search classes, career assessment, internships, regional alumni. Career services highlights include our Marketing Practicum course, which has worked with employers such as Just Born, Crayola and the PA Liquor Control Board to provide internship opportunities for students and hands-on experience.

FACILITIES
Housing: special housing for disabled students, women's dorms. 90% of campus accessible to physically disabled. **Special Academic Facilities/Equipment:** Alumnae Museum. **Computers:** 75% of classrooms, 85% of dorms, 100% of libraries, 85% of dining areas, 85% of student union, 50% of common outdoor areas have wireless network access. Students can register for classes online. Administrative functions (other than registration) can be performed online.

CAMPUS LIFE
Environment: City. **Activities:** Choral groups, dance, drama/theater, literary magazine, music ensembles, musical theater, radio station, student government, student newspaper, yearbook, Campus Ministries, International Student Organization. 18 honor societies, 4 religious organizations. **Athletics (Intercollegiate):** *Women:* basketball, cross-country, field hockey, lacrosse, soccer, softball, tennis, volleyball. **On-Campus Highlights:** Bistro, College Center, Fitness Center, Rodale Aquatic Center **Environmental Initiatives:** Recycling: participating in national Recyclemania Decentralized heat plant Install CFL'S & electronic ballasts & started upgrading exterior lighting to LED's

ADMISSIONS
Freshman Academic Profile: Average high school GPA 3.37. 22% in top 10% of high school class, 44% in top 25% of high school class, 86% in top 50% of high school class. 92% from public high schools. SAT Math middle 50% range 450-550. SAT Critical Reading middle 50% range 437.5-570. SAT Writing middle 50% range 440-550. ACT middle 50% range 20-23.25. Minimum internet-based TOEFL 61. Minimum paper TOEFL 500. **Basis for Candidate Selection:** *Very important factors considered include:* Class rank, application essay, academic GPA, recommendation(s), rigor of secondary school record, standardized test scores. *Other factors considered include:* alumni/ae relation, extracurricular activities, interview, volunteer work, work experience. **Freshman Admission Requirements:** High school diploma is required and GED is accepted. *Academic units required:* 4 English, 3 mathematics, 2 science, (2 science labs), 2 foreign language, 3 social studies, 0 history, 0 visual/performing arts, 0 computer science. **Freshman Admission Statistics:** 1,246 applied, 52% admitted, 26% enrolled. **Transfer Admission Requirements:** High school transcript, college transcript(s), Minimum college GPA of 2.00 required. Lowest grade transferable C. **General Admission Information:** Application Fee $30. Notification on a rolling basis, beginning on or about 9/15. Nonfall registration accepted. Credit and/or placement offered for CEEB Advanced Placement tests.

COSTS AND FINANCIAL AID
Required Forms and Deadlines: FAFSA. **Notification of Awards:** Applicants will be notified of awards on a rolling basis beginning 1/1. **Types of Aid:** *Need-based scholarships/grants:* Federal Pell, SEOG, state scholarships/grants, private scholarships, the school's own gift aid, Federal Nursing Scholarships. *Loans:* Direct Subsidized Stafford, Direct Unsubsidized Stafford, Direct PLUS, Federal Perkins, Federal Nursing. *Student Employment:* Federal Work-Study Program available. Institutional employment available. Highest amount earned per year from on-campus jobs $2,200. Off-campus job opportunities are fair. **Financial Aid Statistics:** 100% freshmen, 100% undergrads receive need-based scholarship or grant aid. 11% freshmen, 9% undergrads receive non-need-based scholarship or grant aid. 85% freshmen, 87% undergrads receive need-based self-help aid. 0% freshmen, 0% undergrads receive athletic scholarships. 97% freshmen, 99% undergrads receive any aid. 92% undergrads borrow to pay for school. Average cumulative indebtedness $28,402. **Criteria for awarding institutional aid:** *Non-need-based:* academics, alumni affiliation, art, leadership, music/drama.

CEDARVILLE UNIVERSITY

251 N.Main Street, Cedarville, OH 45314
Phone: 937-766-7700 · **Financial Aid Phone:** 937-766-7866
E-mail: admissions@cedarville.edu
Fax: 937-766-7575 · **Website:** www.cedarville.edu · **ACT Code:** 3245

This private school, affiliated with the Baptist Church, was founded in 1887. It has a 400-acre campus.

RATINGS
Admissions Selectivity Rating: 88   **Fire Safety Rating:** 91 ·

STUDENTS AND FACULTY
Enrollment: 3,082. **Student Body:** 52% female, 48% male, 62% out-of-state, 2% international (33 countries represented). Asian 2%, African American 2%, Caucasian 87%, Hispanic 2%, Native American <1%
Retention and Graduation: 88% freshmen return for sophomore year. 57% freshmen graduate within 4 years. 70% freshmen graduate within 6 years. 23% grads go on to further study within 1 year. 14% grads pursue arts and sciences degrees. 1% grads pursue law degrees. 5% grads pursue medical degrees. **Faculty:** 216 full-time faculty, 67% hold PhDs, 38% are members of minority groups, 11% are women. 0% of classes are taught by teaching assistants.

ACADEMICS
Degrees: bachelor's, certificate, master's. **Classes:** Most classes have 10–19 students. Most lab/discussion sessions have 10–19 students. **Majors with Highest Enrollment:** Registered Nursing/Registered Nurse; Mechanical Engineering; Early Childhood Education and Teaching. **Special Study Options:** Accelerated program, distance learning, double major, dual enrollment, honors program, independent study, internships, student-designed major, study abroad, teacher certification program. **Disability Services:** Special programs offered to physically disabled students include reader services, tape recorders, tutors. **Career services:** Alumni network, alumni services, career/job search classes, internships, regional alumni.

FACILITIES
Housing: men's dorms, women's dorms, apartments for married students **Computers:** 100% of classrooms, 100% of dorms, 100% of libraries, 100% of dining areas, 100% of student union, 80% of common outdoor areas have wireless network access. Students can register for classes online. Administrative functions (other than registration) can be performed online.

CAMPUS LIFE
Environment: Rural. **Activities:** Choral groups, concert band, drama/theater, jazz band, music ensembles, musical theater, pep band, radio station, student government, student newspaper, symphony orchestra, yearbook. 74 registered organizations, 4 honor societies. **Athletics (Intercollegiate):** *Men:* baseball, basketball, cheerleading, cross-country, golf, soccer, tennis, track/field (outdoor), track/field (indoor). *Women:* basketball, cheerleading, cross-country, soccer, softball, tennis, track/field (outdoor), track/field (indoor), volleyball. **On-Campus Highlights:** Fitness and Recreation Center, The Hive - student snack shop, Dixon Ministry Center—daily chapel and concerts, Chucks—student cafeteria (popular hangout), Callan Athletic Center.

ADMISSIONS
Freshman Academic Profile: Average high school GPA 3.65. 35% in top 10% of high school class, 65% in top 25% of high school class, 89% in top 50% of high school class. 52% from public high schools. SAT Math middle 50% range 540-650. SAT Critical Reading middle 50% range 540-650. SAT Writing middle 50% range 510-630. ACT middle 50% range 23-29. Minimum internet-based TOEFL 80. Minimum paper TOEFL 550. **Basis for Candidate Selection:** *Very important factors considered include:* application essay, academic GPA, rigor of secondary school record, standardized test scores, character/personal qualities, religious affiliation/commitment. *Important factors considered include:* recommendation(s), racial/ethnic status. *Other factors considered include:* Class rank, alumni/ae relation, extracurricular activities, interview, talent/ability, volunteer work. **Freshman Admission Requirements:** High school diploma is required and GED is accepted. **Freshman Admission Statistics:** 3,003 applied, 74% admitted, 35% enrolled. **Transfer Admission Requirements:** High school transcript, college transcript(s), essay or personal statement, statement of good standing from prior institution(s). Minimum college GPA of 3.0 required. Lowest grade transferable C-. **General Admission Information:** Application Fee $30. Notification on a rolling basis, beginning on or about 8/1. Nonfall registration accepted. Admission may be deferred for a maximum of 12 months/1 year. Credit and/or placement offered for CEEB Advanced Placement tests.

COSTS AND FINANCIAL AID
Annual tuition $27,006. Room and board $6,542. Required fees $200. Average book expense $1,200. **Required Forms and Deadlines:** FAFSA. **Notification**

of Awards: Applicants will be notified of awards on a rolling basis beginning 3/1. **Types of Aid:** *Need-based scholarships/grants:* Federal Pell, SEOG, state scholarships/grants, private scholarships, the school's own gift aid. *Loans:* Subsidized Stafford, Unsubsidized Stafford, PLUS, Federal Perkins, Federal Nursing, state loans, college/university loans from institutional funds. *Student Employment:* Highest amount earned per year from on-campus jobs $5,238. **Financial Aid Statistics:** 82% freshmen, 84% undergrads receive need-based scholarship or grant aid. 74% freshmen, 78% undergrads receive non-need-based scholarship or grant aid. 75% freshmen, 80% undergrads receive need-based self-help aid. 0% freshmen, 0% undergrads receive athletic scholarships. 96% freshmen, 88% undergrads receive any aid. 65% undergrads borrow to pay for school. Average cumulative indebtedness $22,444. **Criteria for awarding institutional aid:** *Non-need-based:* academics, alumni affiliation, athletics, leadership, minority status, music/drama, state/district residency.

CENTENARY COLLEGE

400 Jefferson Street, Hackettstown, NJ 7840
Phone: 800-236-8679 · **Financial Aid Phone:** 800-236-8679
E-mail: admissions@centenarycollege.edu · **CEEB Code:** 2080
Fax: 908-852-3454 · **Website:** www.centenarycollege.edu · **ACT Code:** 2544

This private school, affiliated with the Methodist Church, was founded in 1867. It has a 42-acre campus.

RATINGS

Admissions Selectivity Rating: 74   **Fire Safety Rating:** 60*

STUDENTS AND FACULTY

Enrollment: 1,708. **Student Body:** 60% female, 40% male, 20% out-of-state, 4% international (17 countries represented). Asian 1%, African American 7%, Caucasian 42%, Hispanic 6%, Native American <1%
Retention and Graduation: 71% freshmen return for sophomore year. 56% freshmen graduate within 4 years. 57% freshmen graduate within 6 years. 18% grads go on to further study within 1 year. 8% grads pursue arts and sciences degrees. 8% grads pursue business degrees. **Faculty:** 79 full-time faculty, 62% hold PhDs, 54% are members of minority groups, 8% are women. 0% of classes are taught by teaching assistants.

ACADEMICS

Degrees: associate, bachelor's, master's, post-bachelor's certificate, terminal associate, transfer associate. **Classes:** Most classes have 10–19 students. Most lab/discussion sessions have 10–19 students. **Majors with Highest Enrollment:** Elementary Education and Teaching; Business Administration and Management; Criminal Justice/Police Science. **Special Study Options:** Accelerated program, cross-registration, distance learning, double major, dual enrollment, English as a Second Language (ESL), exchange student program (domestic), honors program, independent study, internships, liberal arts/career combination, student-designed major, study abroad, teacher certification program, weekend college. **Disability Services:** Special programs offered to physically disabled students include note-taking services, reader services, tutors. **Career services:** Alumni network, alumni services, career/job search classes, career assessment, internships, regional alumni.

FACILITIES

Housing: Coed dorms, apartments for single students. 60% of campus accessible to physically disabled. **Special Academic Facilities/Equipment:** Art gallery, radio station WNTI 91.9FM, equity-status theater, equestrian center. **Computers:** 100% of classrooms, 100% of dorms, 100% of libraries, 100% of dining areas, 100% of student union, 100% of common outdoor areas have wireless network access. Students can register for classes online. Administrative functions (other than registration) can be performed online. Undergraduates are required to own a computer.

CAMPUS LIFE

Environment: Town. **Activities:** Choral groups, dance, drama/theater, literary magazine, music ensembles, musical theater, radio station, student government, student newspaper, student-run film society, television station, yearbook, Campus Ministries, International Student Organization, Model UN. 30 registered organizations, 2 honor societies, 2 fraternities, 3 sororities. **Athletics (Intercollegiate):** *Men:* baseball, basketball, cross-country, golf, lacrosse, soccer, wrestling. *Women:* basketball, cross-country, golf, lacrosse, soccer, softball, volleyball. **On-Campus Highlights:** Reeves Athletic Facility, Bennett Smith Dormitory, Tilly's Café, Library Cyber Café.

ADMISSIONS

Freshman Academic Profile: Average high school GPA 3.04. 11% in top 10% of high school class, 28% in top 25% of high school class, 55% in top 50% of high school class. 85% from public high schools. SAT Math middle 50% range

410-550. SAT Critical Reading middle 50% range 410-540. SAT Writing middle 50% range 400-540. ACT middle 50% range 18-23. Minimum paper TOEFL 450. **Basis for Candidate Selection:** *Very important factors considered include:* application essay, academic GPA, standardized test scores, interview. *Important factors considered include:* recommendation(s), rigor of secondary school record, character/personal qualities, extracurricular activities, talent/ability, volunteer work. *Other factors considered include:* Class rank, alumni/ae relation, level of applicant's interest, religious affiliation/commitment, work experience. **Freshman Admission Requirements:** High school diploma is required and GED is accepted. *Academic units required:* 4 English, 3 mathematics, 2 science, (1 science labs), 0 foreign language, 0 social studies, 0 history, 0 visual/performing arts, 0 computer science, 0 academic electives. **Freshman Admission Statistics:** 1,038 applied, 81% admitted, 25% enrolled. **Transfer Admission Requirements:** High school transcript, college transcript(s), essay or personal statement, Minimum college GPA of 2.0 required. Lowest grade transferable C-. **General Admission Information:** Application Fee $30. Notification on a rolling basis, beginning on or about 12/15. Nonfall registration accepted. Admission may be deferred for a maximum of 1 semester. Credit offered for CEEB Advanced Placement tests.

COSTS AND FINANCIAL AID

Annual tuition $15,700. Room and board $6,850. Required fees $1,100. Average book expense $666. **Required Forms and Deadlines:** FAFSA. **Notification of Awards:** Applicants will be notified of awards on a rolling basis beginning 3/15. **Types of Aid:** *Need-based scholarships/grants:* Federal Pell, SEOG, state scholarships/grants, private scholarships, the school's own gift aid. *Loans:* Subsidized Stafford, Unsubsidized Stafford, PLUS, Federal Perkins, state loans, Alternative. *Student Employment:* Off-campus job opportunities are excellent. **Financial Aid Statistics:** 100% freshmen, 99% undergrads receive need-based scholarship or grant aid. 10% freshmen, 7% undergrads receive non-need-based scholarship or grant aid. 90% freshmen, 92% undergrads receive need-based self-help aid. 0% freshmen, 0% undergrads receive athletic scholarships. 98 79% undergrads borrow to pay for school. Average cumulative indebtedness $26,065. **Criteria for awarding institutional aid:** *Non-need-based:* academics, alumni affiliation, art, leadership, minority status, music/drama, religious affiliation, state/district residency.

CENTENARY COLLEGE OF LOUISIANA

Best 380

P.O. Box 41188, Shreveport, LA 71134-1188
Phone: 318-869-5131 · **Financial Aid Phone:** 318-869-5137
E-mail: admissions@centenary.edu
Fax: 318-869-5005 · **Website:** www.centenary.edu · **ACT Code:** 1576

This private school, affiliated with the Methodist Church, was founded in 1825. It has a 68-acre campus.

RATINGS

Admissions Selectivity Rating: 86   **Fire Safety Rating:** 71

STUDENTS AND FACULTY

Enrollment: 579. **Student Body:** 56% female, 44% male, 36% out-of-state, 2% international (7 countries represented). Asian 3%, African American 15%, Caucasian 70%, Hispanic 6%, Native American 1%
Retention and Graduation: 76% freshmen return for sophomore year. 49% freshmen graduate within 4 years. 59% freshmen graduate within 6 years. **Faculty:** 57 full-time faculty, 98% hold PhDs, 33% are members of minority groups. 0% of classes are taught by teaching assistants.

ACADEMICS

Degrees: bachelor's, master's. **Classes:** Most classes have 10–19 students. **Special Study Options:** cross-registration, double major, dual enrollment, exchange student program (domestic), honors program, independent study, internships, liberal arts/career combination, student-designed major, study abroad, teacher certification program, weekend college, 3/2 Dual Degree (Liberal Arts/Engineering) program in cooperation with Case Western Reserve University, Columbia University, Texas A and M University, University of Southern California, and Washington University in St. Louis; Mathematics/Computer Science double degree program with Southern Methodist University; Semester in Washington D.C.; British Studies at Oxford summer program. **Disability Services:** Special programs offered to physically disabled students include note-taking services, reader services, tape recorders, tutors. **Career services:** alumni services, career/job search classes, career assessment, internships.

Career services highlights include both Service Learning and Intercultural Experience that expose students to people and places quite different from their own and help them appreciate and understand human diversity.

FACILITIES

Housing: Coed dorms, women's dorms, fraternity/sorority housing. 95% of campus accessible to physically disabled. **Special Academic Facilities/Equipment:** Art museum, Art Center, art studios, theatre, performance and practice organs, piano lab, language lab, School of Music recording studio, Science Hall multimedia auditorium. **Computers:** 50% of classrooms, 25% of dorms, 50% of libraries, 100% of dining areas, 50% of student union, 10% of common outdoor areas have wireless network access. Students can register for classes online. Administrative functions (other than registration) can be performed online.

CAMPUS LIFE

Environment: Metropolis. **Activities:** Choral groups, concert band, dance, drama/theater, jazz band, literary magazine, music ensembles, musical theater, opera, radio station, student government, student newspaper, student-run film society, yearbook, Campus Ministries, International Student Organization. 58 registered organizations, 15 honor societies, 8 religious organizations. 5 fraternities, 2 sororities. **Athletics (Intercollegiate):** *Men:* baseball, basketball, cross-country, golf, soccer, swimming, tennis. *Women:* basketball, cross-country, golf, gymnastics, soccer, softball, swimming, tennis, volleyball. **On-Campus Highlights:** Fitness Center, Jones-Rice Field, Student Union Building, Anderson Choral Building, Gold Dome, Peavy Climbing Tower Anderson Choral Building Crumley Gardens Aboretum Feazel Instrumental Hall.

ADMISSIONS

Freshman Academic Profile: Average high school GPA 3.52. 25% in top 10% of high school class, 58% in top 25% of high school class, 86% in top 50% of high school class. SAT Math middle 50% range 495-600. SAT Critical Reading middle 50% range 480-585. ACT middle 50% range 22-28. Minimum paper TOEFL 550. **Basis for Candidate Selection:** *Very important factors considered include:* academic GPA, rigor of secondary school record. *Important factors considered include:* Class rank, application essay, recommendation(s), standardized test scores, alumni/ae relation, character/personal qualities, extracurricular activities, interview, level of applicant's interest, talent/ability, volunteer work, work experience. *Other factors considered include:* first generation, geographical residence, racial/ethnic status, religious affiliation/commitment. **Freshman Admission Requirements:** High school diploma is required and GED is accepted. **Freshman Admission Statistics:** 670 applied, 66% admitted, 29% enrolled. **Transfer Admission Requirements:** High school transcript, college transcript(s), essay or personal statement, statement of good standing from prior institution(s). Minimum college GPA of 2.0 required. Lowest grade transferable C. **General Admission Information:** Application Fee $30. Regular application deadline 8/1. Notification on a rolling basis, beginning on or about 10/1. Nonfall registration accepted. Admission may be deferred for a maximum of 1 year. Credit and/or placement offered for CEEB Advanced Placement tests.

COSTS AND FINANCIAL AID

Annual tuition $33,500. Room and board $12,150. Required fees $0. **Required Forms and Deadlines:** FAFSA. **Notification of Awards:** Applicants will be notified of awards on or about 3/15. **Types of Aid:** *Need-based scholarships/grants:* Federal Pell, SEOG, state scholarships/grants, private scholarships, the school's own gift aid. *Loans:* Subsidized Stafford, Unsubsidized Stafford, PLUS, Federal Perkins. *Student Employment:* Federal Work-Study Program available. Institutional employment available. Highest amount earned per year from on-campus jobs $4,000. Off-campus job opportunities are good. **Financial Aid Statistics:** 97% freshmen, 100% undergrads receive need-based scholarship or grant aid. 15% freshmen, 15% undergrads receive non-need-based scholarship or grant aid. 73% freshmen, 72% undergrads receive need-based self-help aid. 0% freshmen, 0% undergrads receive athletic scholarships. 62% undergrads borrow to pay for school. Average cumulative indebtedness $23,760. **Criteria for awarding institutional aid:** *Non-need-based:* academics, art, athletics, music/drama, religious affiliation, state/district residency.

CENTRAL BAPTIST COLLEGE

1501 College Avenue, Conway, AR 72034
Phone: 501-329-6872 E-mail: ccalhoun@cbc.edu and lwatson@cbc.edu
Fax: 501-329-2941 • **Website:** www.cbc.edu • **ACT Code:** 119

This private school, affiliated with the Baptist Church, was founded in 1952. It has a 13-acre campus.

RATINGS

Admissions Selectivity Rating: 62   **Fire Safety Rating:** 60*

STUDENTS AND FACULTY

Enrollment: 394. **Student Body:** 46% female, 54% male, 11% out-of-state, 1% international. Asian 1%, African American 9%, Caucasian 92%, Hispanic 2%, Native American 1%
Faculty: 16 full-time faculty, 44% hold PhDs, 38% are members of minority groups. 0% of classes are taught by teaching assistants.

ACADEMICS

Degrees: associate, bachelor's. **Majors with Highest Enrollment:** Elementary Education and Teaching; Theology and Religious Vocations; Psychology.

FACILITIES

Housing: men's dorms, women's dorms.

CAMPUS LIFE

Environment: Rural. **Activities:** Choral groups, music ensembles, musical theater, student government, yearbook. **Athletics (Intercollegiate):** *Men:* baseball, basketball. *Women:* basketball, volleyball.

ADMISSIONS

Freshman Academic Profile: Average high school GPA 3.08. 11% in top 10% of high school class, 29% in top 25% of high school class, 66% in top 50% of high school class. Minimum paper TOEFL 500. **Basis for Candidate Selection:** *Very important factors considered include:* Class rank, recommendation(s), rigor of secondary school record, standardized test scores, character/personal qualities. *Important factors considered include:* religious affiliation/commitment. *Other factors considered include:* extracurricular activities, talent/ability. **Freshman Admission Requirements:** High school diploma is required and GED is accepted. **Freshman Admission Statistics:** 164 applied, 84% admitted, 75% enrolled. **Transfer Admission Requirements:** college transcript(s), essay or personal statement, standardized test scores, Minimum college GPA of 2.0 required. Lowest grade transferable c. **General Admission Information:** Application Fee $25. Regular application deadline 8/15. Nonfall registration accepted. Admission may be deferred for a maximum of 12.

COSTS AND FINANCIAL AID

Average book expense $700. **Required Forms and Deadlines:** FAFSA. **Types of Aid:** *Need-based scholarships/grants:* Federal Pell, SEOG, state scholarships/grants, private scholarships. *Loans:* Subsidized Stafford, Unsubsidized Stafford, PLUS. *Student Employment:* Federal Work-Study Program available. Off-campus job opportunities are good. Financial Aid **Criteria for awarding institutional aid:** *Non-need-based:* academics, alumni affiliation, leadership, music/drama, religious affiliation.

CENTRAL COLLEGE

812 University Street, Pella, IA 50219-1999
Phone: 641-628-5286 • **Financial Aid Phone:** 641-628-5336
E-mail: admission@central.edu • **CEEB Code:** 6087
Fax: 641-628-5983 • **Website:** www.central.edu • **ACT Code:** 1284

This private school, affiliated with the Reformed Church Church, was founded in 1853. It has a 133-acre campus.

RATINGS

Admissions Selectivity Rating: 86   **Fire Safety Rating:** 81

STUDENTS AND FACULTY

Enrollment: 1,417. **Student Body:** 53% female, 47% male, 19% out-of-state, 0% international (12 countries represented). Asian 1%, African American 2%, Caucasian 89%, Hispanic 3%, Native American <1%
Retention and Graduation: 83% freshmen return for sophomore year. 62% freshmen graduate within 4 years. 19% grads go on to further study within 1 year. 5% grads pursue arts and sciences degrees. 1% grads pursue law degrees. 1% grads pursue business degrees. 2% grads pursue medical degrees. **Faculty:** 98 full-time faculty, 84% hold PhDs, 42% are members of minority groups, 9% are women. 0% of classes are taught by teaching assistants.

ACADEMICS

Degrees: bachelor's. **Classes:** Most classes have 10–19 students. Most lab/discussion sessions have 10–19 students. **Majors with Highest Enrollment:** Kinesiology and Exercise Science; Business/Commerce; Spanish Language and Literature. **Special Study Options:** double major, English as a Second Language (ESL), honors program, independent study, internships, liberal arts/career combination, student-designed major, study abroad, teacher certification program, **Off-Campus Study:** Washington, DC, Chicago Metro Program. Study abroad in nine countries. Exploring Student Program encourages two years of multidisciplinary study before selecting a major. **Honors programs:** The entire 4-year Honors program is outstanding Combined degree programs: BA/MEng, 3-4 architecture program with Washington U. **Disability Services:** Special programs offered to physically disabled students include note-taking services, reader services, tape recorders, tutors.

FACILITIES

Housing: Coed dorms, special housing for disabled students, men's dorms, special housing for international students, women's dorms, fraternity/sorority housing, apartments for married students, apartments for single students. 95% of campus accessible to physically disabled. **Special Academic Facilities/Equipment:** Art gallery, center for communication and theatre, music center, language lab, glass-blowing studio. **Computers:** Students can register for classes online. Administrative functions (other than registration) can be performed online.

CAMPUS LIFE

Environment: Village. **Activities:** Choral groups, concert band, drama/theater, jazz band, literary magazine, music ensembles, musical theater, radio station, student government, student newspaper, symphony orchestra, yearbook. 50 registered organizations, 4 religious organizations. 4 fraternities, 2 sororities. **Athletics (Intercollegiate):** *Men:* baseball, basketball, football, golf, soccer, tennis, track/field (outdoor), track/field (indoor), wrestling. *Women:* basketball, cross-country, golf, softball, tennis, track/field (outdoor), track/field (indoor), volleyball.

ADMISSIONS

Freshman Academic Profile: Average high school GPA 3.61. 25% in top 10% of high school class, 58% in top 25% of high school class, 89% in top 50% of high school class. 95% from public high schools. SAT Math middle 50% range 470-570. SAT Critical Reading middle 50% range 460-550. ACT middle 50% range 21-26. Minimum internet-based TOEFL 71. Minimum paper TOEFL 530. **Basis for Candidate Selection:** *Very important factors considered include:* academic GPA, rigor of secondary school record, standardized test scores. *Important factors considered include:* Class rank. *Other factors considered include:* application essay, recommendation(s), alumni/ae relation, character/personal qualities, extracurricular activities, first generation, interview, talent/ability, volunteer work, work experience. **Freshman Admission Requirements:** High school diploma is required and GED is accepted. *Academic units required:* 4 English, 2 mathematics, 2 science, (2 science labs), 3 social studies, 2 history. **Freshman Admission Statistics:** 2,471 applied, 65% admitted, 20% enrolled. **Transfer Admission Requirements:** High school transcript, college transcript(s), standardized test scores, statement of good standing from prior institution(s). Minimum college GPA of 2.5 required. Lowest grade transferable C-. **General Admission Information:** Application Fee $25. Notification on a rolling basis, beginning on or about 9/15. Nonfall registration accepted. Admission may be deferred for a maximum of 1 yr. Credit and/or placement offered for CEEB Advanced Placement tests.

COSTS AND FINANCIAL AID

Required Forms and Deadlines: FAFSA. **Notification of Awards:** Applicants will be notified of awards on a rolling basis beginning 3/15. **Types of Aid:** *Need-based scholarships/grants:* Federal Pell, SEOG, state scholarships/grants, private scholarships, the school's own gift aid. *Loans:* Direct Subsidized Stafford, Direct Unsubsidized Stafford, Direct PLUS, Federal Perkins, college/university loans from institutional funds, Private Alternative Loans. *Student Employment:* Highest amount earned per year from on-campus jobs $2,600. **Financial Aid Statistics:** 100% freshmen, 100% undergrads receive need-based scholarship or grant aid. 25% freshmen, 10% undergrads receive non-need-based scholarship or grant aid. 83% freshmen, 86% undergrads receive need-based self-help aid. 0% freshmen, 0% undergrads receive athletic scholarships. 100% freshmen, 99% undergrads receive any aid. 85% undergrads borrow to pay for school. Average cumulative indebtedness $22,406. **Criteria for awarding institutional aid:** *Non-need-based:* academics, alumni affiliation, art, minority status, music/drama, religious affiliation, state/district residency.

CENTRAL CONNECTICUT STATE UNIVERSITY

1615 Stanley Street, New Britain, CT 6050
Phone: 860-832-2278 · **Financial Aid Phone:** 860-832-2200
E-mail: admissions@ccsu.edu · **CEEB Code:** 3898
Fax: 862-832-2295 · **Website:** www.ccsu.edu · **ACT Code:** 596

This public school was founded in 1849. It has a 294-acre campus.

RATINGS

Admissions Selectivity Rating: 77   **Fire Safety Rating:** 84

STUDENTS AND FACULTY

Enrollment: 9,600. **Student Body:** 47% female, 53% male, 3% out-of-state, 1% international (28 countries represented). Asian 4%, African American 11%, Caucasian 66%, Hispanic 13%, Native American <1%
Retention and Graduation: 80% freshmen return for sophomore year. 22% freshmen graduate within 4 years. 52% freshmen graduate within 6 years. **Faculty:** 451 full-time faculty, 84% hold PhDs, 43% are members of minority groups, 20% are women. 0% of classes are taught by teaching assistants.

ACADEMICS

Degrees: bachelor's, master's, post-bachelor's certificate, post-master's certificate. **Classes:** Most classes have 20–29 students. Most lab/discussion sessions have fewer than 10 students. **Majors with Highest Enrollment:** Accounting; Psychology; Criminology. **Special Study Options:** cooperative education program, cross-registration, distance learning, double major, dual enrollment, English as a Second Language (ESL), exchange student program (domestic), honors program, independent study, internships, student-designed major, study abroad, teacher certification program, Undergrads may take grad classes. Co-Op programs: Arts, Business, Computer Science, Education, Humanities, Natural Science, Social/Behavioral Science, Technologies. **Honors programs:** Interdisciplinary writing/reading program for undergraduates with strong academic skills. Areas of study: Western Culture, Science and Society, and World Culture, capstone honors thesis in junior year, Scholarship available. Combined degree programs: BA/MEng. **Disability Services:** Special programs offered to physically disabled students include note-taking services, reader services, tape recorders, tutors. **Career services:** alumni services, career/job search classes, career assessment, internships. Career services highlights include cooperative learning in the form of cooperative education.

FACILITIES

Housing: Coed dorms, women's dorms. 95% of campus accessible to physically disabled. **Special Academic Facilities/Equipment:** Art gallery, language lab, childhood center, planetarium and space science center, center for economic education, TV studio. **Computers:** 50% of classrooms, 100% of libraries, 100% of dining areas, 100% of student union, 50% of common outdoor areas have wireless network access. Students can register for classes online. Administrative functions (other than registration) can be performed online.

CAMPUS LIFE

Environment: Town. **Activities:** Choral groups, concert band, dance, drama/theater, jazz band, literary magazine, music ensembles, musical theater, radio station, student government, student newspaper, student-run film society, television station, yearbook, International Student Organization 101 registered organizations, 18 honor societies, 5 religious organizations. 1 sorority. **Athletics (Intercollegiate):** *Men:* baseball, basketball, cross-country, football, golf, soccer, track/field (outdoor), track/field (indoor). *Women:* basketball, cross-country, diving, golf, lacrosse, soccer, softball, swimming, track/field (outdoor), track/field (indoor), volleyball. **On-Campus Highlights:** Student Center, Cafeteria, Memorial Hall, Torp Theatre, Davidson Hall, Vance Academic Center, Vance Hall, James Hall (Residence Hall), Semesters, Student Center. **Environmental Initiatives:** Fuel cell Class schedule for carpool ease Building use in summer On-campus education and programs for more sustainable practices providing non-fosill fuel programs for campus stakeholders to change practices Reducing solid waste production and promoting recycling.

ADMISSIONS

Freshman Academic Profile: Average high school GPA 3. 9.2% in top 10% of high school class, 19.2% in top 25% of high school class, 68.3% in top 50% of high school class. 95% from public high schools. SAT Math middle 50% range 460-560. SAT Critical Reading middle 50% range 460-550. SAT Writing middle 50% range 450-540. ACT middle 50% range 20-23. Minimum paper TOEFL 500. **Basis for Candidate Selection:** *Very important factors considered include:* rigor of secondary school record. *Important factors considered include:* Class rank, academic GPA, standardized test scores. *Other factors considered include:* application essay, recommendation(s), extracurricular activities, geographical residence, interview, racial/ethnic status, talent/ability. **Freshman Admission Requirements:** High school diploma is required and GED is accepted. *Academic units required:* 4 English, 3 mathematics, 2 science, (1 science labs), 2 social studies, 1 history. **Freshman Admission Statistics:** 8,173 applied, 60% admitted, 28% enrolled. **Transfer Admission Requirements:** High school transcript, college transcript(s), statement of good standing from prior institution(s). Minimum college GPA of 2.0 required. Lowest grade transferable C. **General Admission Information:** Application Fee $50. Regular application deadline 6/1. Notification on a rolling basis, beginning on or about 12/1. Nonfall registration accepted. Credit offered for CEEB Advanced Placement tests.

COSTS AND FINANCIAL AID

Annual out-of-state tuition $14,886. Room and board $10,872. Required fees $4,277. Average book expense $1,200. **Required Forms and Deadlines:** FAFSA. **Notification of Awards:** Applicants will be notified of awards on a rolling basis beginning 3/15. **Types of Aid:** *Need-based scholarships/grants:* Federal Pell, SEOG, state scholarships/grants, the school's own gift aid. *Loans:* Direct Subsidized Stafford, Direct Unsubsidized Stafford, Direct PLUS, PLUS, Federal Perkins. *Student Employment:* Federal Work-Study Program available. Institutional employment available. Highest amount earned per year from on-campus jobs $5,000. Off-campus job opportunities are good. **Financial Aid Statistics:** 88% freshmen, 78% undergrads receive need-based scholarship or grant aid. 13% freshmen, 13% undergrads receive non-need-based scholarship or grant aid. 76% freshmen, 72% undergrads receive need-based self-help aid. 1% freshmen, 3% undergrads receive athletic scholarships. 69% freshmen, 61% undergrads receive any aid. 53% undergrads borrow to pay for school. Average cumulative indebtedness $21,200. **Criteria for awarding institutional aid:** *Non-need-based:* academics, athletics, minority status.

See page 1022.

CENTRAL METHODIST UNIVERSITY

411 Central Methodist Square, Fayette, MO 65248
Phone: 660-248-6251
E-mail: admissions@centralmethodist.edu • **CEEB Code:** 6089
Fax: 660-248-1872 • **Website:** www.centralmethodist.edu • **ACT Code:** 2270

This private school, affiliated with the Methodist Church, was founded in 1854. It has a 90-acre campus.

RATINGS
Admissions Selectivity Rating: 74   **Fire Safety Rating:** 60*

STUDENTS AND FACULTY
Enrollment: 1,143. **Student Body:** 50% female, 50% male, 10% out-of-state, 2% international (15 countries represented). Asian 0%, African American 5%, Caucasian 62%, Hispanic 1%, Native American <1%
Retention and Graduation: 57% freshmen return for sophomore year. 30% freshmen graduate within 4 years. 41% freshmen graduate within 6 years. 15% grads go on to further study within 1 year. 15% grads pursue arts and sciences degrees. 5% grads pursue law degrees. 5% grads pursue business degrees. 4% grads pursue medical degrees. **Faculty:** 54 full-time faculty, 65% hold PhDs, 43% are members of minority groups, 4% are women. 0% of classes are taught by teaching assistants.

ACADEMICS
Degrees: associate, bachelor's, master's. **Classes:** Most classes have fewer than 10 students. **Majors with Highest Enrollment:** Elementary Education and Teaching; Early Childhood Education; Business/Commerce. **Special Study Options:** Accelerated program, distance learning, double major, dual enrollment, honors program, independent study, internships, liberal arts/career combination, student-designed major, study abroad, teacher certification program. **Career services:** career/job search classes, career assessment, internships.

FACILITIES
Housing: Coed dorms, men's dorms, women's dorms, apartments for married students, apartments for single students. 39% of campus accessible to physically disabled. **Special Academic Facilities/Equipment:** 2 museums. Telecommunity Technology Center, computer lab in Residence halls.

CAMPUS LIFE
Environment: Rural. **Activities:** Choral groups, concert band, drama/theater, jazz band, literary magazine, marching band, music ensembles, musical theater, radio station, student government, student newspaper, symphony orchestra, television station, yearbook. 41 registered organizations, 13 honor societies, 2 religious organizations. 6 fraternities, 4 sororities. **Athletics (Intercollegiate):** *Men:* baseball, basketball, cheerleading, cross-country, football, golf, soccer, track/field (outdoor). *Women:* basketball, cheerleading, cross-country, golf, soccer, softball, track/field (outdoor), volleyball.

ADMISSIONS
Freshman Academic Profile: Average high school GPA 3.21. 7% in top 10% of high school class, 34% in top 25% of high school class, 70% in top 50% of high school class. ACT middle 50% range 19-23. Minimum paper TOEFL 500. **Basis for Candidate Selection:** *Very important factors considered include:* Class rank, rigor of secondary school record, standardized test scores, extracurricular activities. *Important factors considered include:* alumni/ae relation, character/personal qualities, racial/ethnic status, religious affiliation/commitment, talent/ability, volunteer work, work experience. *Other factors considered include:* recommendation(s), geographical residence, interview, state residency. **Freshman Admission Requirements:** High school diploma is required and GED is accepted. **Freshman Admission Statistics:** 1,033 applied, 73% admitted, 30% enrolled. **Transfer Admission Requirements:** High school transcript, college transcript(s), standardized test scores, statement of good

standing from prior institution(s). Minimum college GPA of 2.0 required. Lowest grade transferable D. **General Admission Information:** Regular application deadline 8/1. Nonfall registration accepted. Admission may be deferred for a maximum of None. Credit offered for CEEB Advanced Placement tests.

COSTS AND FINANCIAL AID
 equired Forms and Deadlines: FAFSA. **Notification of Awards:** Applicants will be notified of awards on a rolling basis beginning 1/30. **Types of Aid:** *Need-based scholarships/grants:* Federal Pell, SEOG, state scholarships/grants, private scholarships, the school's own gift aid. *Loans:* Subsidized Stafford, Unsubsidized Stafford, PLUS, Federal Perkins, college/university loans from institutional funds. *Student Employment:* Federal Work-Study Program available. Off-campus job opportunities are good. **Financial Aid Statistics:** 100% freshmen, 100% undergrads receive need-based scholarship or grant aid. 100% freshmen, 99% undergrads receive non-need-based scholarship or grant aid. 89% freshmen, 81% undergrads receive need-based self-help aid. 2% freshmen, 1% undergrads receive athletic scholarships. 66% undergrads borrow to pay for school. **Criteria for awarding institutional aid:** *Non-need-based:* academics, alumni affiliation, athletics, leadership, music/drama, religious affiliation.

CENTRAL MICHIGAN UNIVERSITY

102 Warriner Hall, Mount Pleasant, MI 48859
Phone: 989-774-3076 • **Financial Aid Phone:** 888-392-0007
E-mail: cmuadmit@cmich.edu • **CEEB Code:** 1106
Fax: 989-774-7267 • **Website:** www.cmich.edu • **ACT Code:** 1972

This public school was founded in 1892. It has a 854-acre campus.

RATINGS
Admissions Selectivity Rating: 80   **Fire Safety Rating:** 88

STUDENTS AND FACULTY
Enrollment: 20,837. **Student Body:** 57% female, 43% male, 4% out-of-state, 2% international (56 countries represented). Asian 1%, African American 8%, Caucasian 77%, Hispanic 3%, Native American 1%
Retention and Graduation: 76% freshmen return for sophomore year. 20% freshmen graduate within 4 years. 18% grads go on to further study within 1 year. 26% grads pursue arts and sciences degrees. 5% grads pursue business degrees. **Faculty:** 798 full-time faculty, 82% hold PhDs, 42% are members of minority groups, 19% are women. 5% of classes are taught by teaching assistants.

ACADEMICS
Degrees: bachelor's, doctoral, master's, post-bachelor's certificate, post-master's certificate. **Classes:** Most classes have 20–29 students. Most lab/discussion sessions have 10–19 students. **Majors with Highest Enrollment:** Kinesiology and Exercise Science; Psychology; Marketing/Marketing Management. **Special Study Options:** Accelerated program, distance learning, double major, dual enrollment, English as a Second Language (ESL), honors program, independent study, internships, student-designed major, study abroad, teacher certification program, Leadership Institute: The Central Michigan University Leadership Institute, which features a four-year leadership development program, an academic minor, and a scholarship cohort that includes a residential experience, s the premier center for leadership education, training, and development in the Midwest. **Honors programs:** The Honors Program, Centralis Program Combined degree programs: BA/MA, 8 Accelerated Masters Degree Programs. **Disability Services:** Special programs offered to physically disabled students include note-taking services, reader services, tape recorders, tutors. **Career services:** Alumni network, alumni services, career/job search classes, career assessment, internships, regional alumni. 100% of undergraduates complete internships.

FACILITIES
Housing: Coed dorms, special housing for disabled students, men's dorms, special housing for international students, women's dorms, fraternity/sorority housing, apartments for married students, apartments for single students, Theme Housing, Residential Colleges: areas of residence halls designated for students with the same majors or academic interests. 95% of campus accessible to physically disabled. **Special Academic Facilities/Equipment:** Clarke Historical Library, Central Michigan University Museum of Cultural and Natural History, Gerald L. Poor School Museum, Brooks Astronomical Observatory, University Art Gallery, University Theater, Public Broadcasting, Student Activity Center, Charles V. Park Library, body scanner **Computers:** 100% of classrooms, 100% of dorms, 100% of libraries, 100% of dining areas, 100% of student union, have wireless network access. Students can register for classes online. Administrative functions (other than registration) can be performed online.

CAMPUS LIFE

Environment: Town. **Activities:** Choral groups, concert band, dance, drama/theater, jazz band, literary magazine, marching band, music ensembles, musical theater, pep band, radio station, student government, student newspaper, student-run film society, television station, yearbook, Campus Ministries, International Student Organization. 150 registered organizations, 6 honor societies, 12 religious organizations. 15 fraternities, 15 sororities. **Athletics (Intercollegiate):** *Men:* baseball, basketball, cross-country, football, track/field (outdoor), track/field (indoor), wrestling. *Women:* basketball, cross-country, field hockey, gymnastics, soccer, softball, track/field (outdoor), track/field (indoor), volleyball. **On-Campus Highlights:** Education Building (2009), Student Activity Center, Bovee University Center, Park Library, Academic Buildings. **Environmental Initiatives:** Campus Sustainability Advisory Committee; FTE Energy Optimization; FTE Retro-Commissioning Achieving LEED certification on all new buildings, additions and major renovations.

ADMISSIONS

Freshman Academic Profile: Average high school GPA 3.34. 15% in top 10% of high school class, 39% in top 25% of high school class, 73% in top 50% of high school class. 88% from public high schools. SAT Math middle 50% range 470-592. SAT Critical Reading middle 50% range 450-587. SAT Writing middle 50% range 425-520. ACT middle 50% range 20-25. **Basis for Candidate Selection:** *Very important factors considered include:* academic GPA, rigor of secondary school record, standardized test scores. *Important factors considered include:* Class rank, talent/ability. *Other factors considered include:* application essay, recommendation(s), alumni/ae relation, character/personal qualities, extracurricular activities, geographical residence, interview, level of applicant's interest, volunteer work, work experience. **Freshman Admission Requirements:** High school diploma is required and GED is accepted. **Freshman Admission Statistics:** 17,999 applied, 70% admitted, 30% enrolled. **Transfer Admission Requirements:** college transcript(s), statement of good standing from prior institution(s). Minimum college GPA of 2.00 required. Lowest grade transferable C-. **General Admission Information:** Application Fee $35. Regular application deadline 7/1. Nonfall registration accepted. Admission may be deferred for a maximum of 1 semester. Credit and/or placement offered for CEEB Advanced Placement tests.

COSTS AND FINANCIAL AID

Annual in-state tuition $11,550. Annual out-of-state tuition $23,670. Room and board $8,780. Required fees $0. Average book expense $1,000. **Required Forms and Deadlines:** FAFSA. **Notification of Awards:** Applicants will be notified of awards on a rolling basis beginning 4/1. **Types of Aid:** *Need-based scholarships/grants:* Federal Pell, SEOG, state scholarships/grants, private scholarships, the school's own gift aid. *Loans:* Direct Subsidized Stafford, Direct Unsubsidized Stafford, Direct PLUS, Federal Perkins, state loans, alternative loans. *Student Employment:* Federal Work-Study Program available. Institutional employment available. Highest amount earned per year from on-campus jobs $3,500. Off-campus job opportunities are good. **Financial Aid Statistics:** 82% freshmen, 74% undergrads receive need-based scholarship or grant aid. 5% freshmen, 3% undergrads receive non-need-based scholarship or grant aid. 82% freshmen, 88% undergrads receive need-based self-help aid. 5% freshmen, 1% undergrads receive athletic scholarships. 89% freshmen, 84% undergrads receive any aid. 74% undergrads borrow to pay for school. Average cumulative indebtedness $28,961. **Criteria for awarding institutional aid:** *Non-need-based:* academics, alumni affiliation, art, athletics, leadership, minority status, music/drama, state/district residency.

CENTRAL STATE UNIVERSITY

PO Box 1004, Wilberforce, OH 45384
Phone: 937-376-6348
E-mail: admissions@centralstate.edu • **CEEB Code:** 1107
Fax: 937-376-6648 • **Website:** www.centralstate.edu • **ACT Code:** 3246

This public school was founded in 1887. It has a 60-acre campus.

RATINGS

Admissions Selectivity Rating: 78   **Fire Safety Rating:** 60*

STUDENTS AND FACULTY

Enrollment: 2,090. **Student Body:** 53% female, 47% male, 42% out-of-state, 0% international. Asian 0%, African American 79%, Caucasian 1%, Hispanic 1%, Native American <1%
Retention and Graduation: 51% freshmen return for sophomore year. 11% freshmen graduate within 4 years. 22% freshmen graduate within 6 years. 32% grads go on to further study within 1 year. 50% grads pursue arts and sciences degrees. 7% grads pursue law degrees. 29% grads pursue business degrees.

Faculty: 94 full-time faculty, 76% hold PhDs, 43% are members of minority groups, 78% are women.

ACADEMICS

Degrees: bachelor's, master's. **Classes:** Most classes have 20–29 students. Most lab/discussion sessions have 10–19 students. **Majors with Highest Enrollment:** Early Childhood Education; Biology; Business/Commerce. **Special Study Options:** cooperative education program, cross-registration, double major, honors program, independent study, internships, study abroad, teacher certification program. **Disability Services:** Special programs offered to physically disabled students include note-taking services, reader services, tape recorders, tutors. **Career services:** alumni services, career/job search classes, career assessment, internships, regional alumni.

FACILITIES

Housing: Coed dorms, men's dorms, women's dorms. 1% of campus accessible to physically disabled. **Special Academic Facilities/Equipment:** National Afro-American Museum and Cultural Center; CJ McLin International Center for Water Resources Management; Center for Integrated Manufacturing Protocols Architectures and Logistics Laboratory; Biology Technique Laboratory; Electrochemistry Research Laboratory; Cosby Mass Communication Center; Paul Robeson Cultural and Performing Arts Center. **Computers:** Administrative functions (other than registration) can be performed online.

CAMPUS LIFE

Environment: Rural. **Activities:** Choral groups, concert band, dance, drama/theater, jazz band, marching band, music ensembles, pep band, radio station, student government, student newspaper, television station, Campus Ministries. 30 registered organizations, 3 honor societies, 4 religious organizations. 1 fraternity, 3 sororities. **Athletics (Intercollegiate):** *Men:* basketball, cheerleading, cross-country, golf, track/field (outdoor). *Women:* basketball, cheerleading, cross-country, golf, track/field (outdoor), volleyball.

ADMISSIONS

Freshman Academic Profile: Average high school GPA 2.6. SAT Math middle 50% range 340-460. SAT Critical Reading middle 50% range 350-450. ACT middle 50% range 15-18. Minimum paper TOEFL 500. **Basis for Candidate Selection:** *Very important factors considered include:* academic GPA, rigor of secondary school record, standardized test scores. *Important factors considered include:* Class rank, application essay, character/personal qualities, geographical residence, state residency. *Other factors considered include:* recommendation(s), extracurricular activities, interview, talent/ability. **Freshman Admission Requirements:** High school diploma is required and GED is accepted. **Freshman Admission Statistics:** 5,944 applied, 38% admitted, 18% enrolled. **Transfer Admission Requirements:** college transcript(s), statement of good standing from prior institution(s). Minimum college GPA of 2.0 required. Lowest grade transferable D. **General Admission Information:** Application Fee $20. Nonfall registration accepted. Admission may be deferred for a maximum of none. Credit and/or placement offered for CEEB Advanced Placement tests.

COSTS AND FINANCIAL AID

Average book expense $1,200. **Required Forms and Deadlines:** FAFSA. **Notification of Awards:** Applicants will be notified of awards on a rolling basis beginning 5/1. **Types of Aid:** *Need-based scholarships/grants:* Federal Pell, SEOG, state scholarships/grants, private scholarships, the school's own gift aid, United Negro College Fund. *Loans:* Direct Subsidized Stafford, Direct Unsubsidized Stafford, Direct PLUS, college/university loans from institutional funds. *Student Employment:* Federal Work-Study Program available. Institutional employment available. Off-campus job opportunities are fair. **Financial Aid Statistics:** 100% freshmen, 100% undergrads receive need-based scholarship or grant aid. 96% freshmen, 100% undergrads receive non-need-based scholarship or grant aid. 100% freshmen, 100% undergrads receive need-based self-help aid. 0% freshmen, 0% undergrads receive athletic scholarships. **Criteria for awarding institutional aid:** *Non-need-based:* academics, alumni affiliation, art, athletics, leadership, music/drama, religious affiliation, state/district residency.

CENTRAL WASHINGTON UNIVERSITY

Admissions Office, Ellensburg, WA 98926-7463
Phone: 509-963-1211 • **Financial Aid Phone:** 509-963-1611
E-mail: cwuadmis@cwu.edu • **CEEB Code:** 4044
Fax: 509-963-3022 • **Website:** www.cwu.edu • **ACT Code:** 4444

This public school was founded in 1891. It has a 350-acre campus.

RATINGS

Admissions Selectivity Rating: 72   **Fire Safety Rating:** 70

STUDENTS AND FACULTY

Enrollment: 9,688. **Student Body:** 51% female, 49% male, 2% out-of-state, 2% international (60 countries represented). Asian 7%, African American 3%, Caucasian 75%, Hispanic 8%, Native American 3%

Retention and Graduation: 26% freshmen graduate within 4 years. 55% freshmen graduate within 6 years. **Faculty:** 432 full-time faculty, 39% are members of minority groups, 12% are women. 3% of classes are taught by teaching assistants.

ACADEMICS

Degrees: bachelor's, master's, post-bachelor's certificate. **Classes:** Most classes have 20–29 students. Most lab/discussion sessions have 10–19 students. **Majors with Highest Enrollment:** Business/Commerce; Elementary Education and Teaching; Social Sciences. **Special Study Options:** cooperative education program, distance learning, double major, dual enrollment, English as a Second Language (ESL), exchange student program (domestic), honors program, independent study, internships, liberal arts/career combination, student-designed major, study abroad, teacher certification program. **Honors programs:** The Douglas Honors College student is expected to maintain a grade point average above 3.0. A student will be placed on probation if the grade point average falls below 3.0, and will be dismissed from the Douglas Honors College if the cumulative grade point average is below 3.0 for two consecutive quarters. This policy does not affect academic standing as a student of Central Washington University. **Disability Services:** Special programs offered to physically disabled students include note-taking services, reader services, tape recorders, tutors. **Career services:** Alumni network, alumni services, career/job search classes, career assessment, internships, regional alumni.

FACILITIES

Housing: Coed dorms, special housing for disabled students, special housing for international students, women's dorms, apartments for married students, apartments for single students, Theme **Housing:** Upperclassmen and 21 years and older. 100% of campus accessible to physically disabled. **Special Academic Facilities/Equipment:** Chimpanzee and Human Communication Institute; Geodesy Laboratory, a data analysis facility of the Pacific Northwest Geodetic Array; Educational Technology Center; Museum collection of NW Native American and Circum-Pacific artifacts for teaching and research; regional site of the National Consortium for Rural Geospatial Innovations; Sarah Spugeon Art Gallery; Science Facility Building. **Computers:** 100% of libraries, 100% of dining areas, 100% of student union, 100% of common outdoor areas have wireless network access. Students can register for classes online. Administrative functions (other than registration) can be performed online.

CAMPUS LIFE

Environment: Village. **Activities:** Choral groups, concert band, dance, drama/theater, jazz band, literary magazine, marching band, music ensembles, musical theater, opera, pep band, radio station, student government, student newspaper, student-run film society, symphony orchestra, television station, Campus Ministries, International Student Organization. 96 registered organizations, 3 honor societies, 9 religious organizations. **Athletics (Intercollegiate):** *Men:* baseball, basketball, cheerleading, cross-country, football, track/field (outdoor), track/field (indoor). *Women:* basketball, cheerleading, cross-country, soccer, softball, track/field (outdoor), track/field (indoor), volleyball. **On-Campus Highlights:** Award-winning Student Union Recreation Center, Japanese Garden, Nicholson Pavilion Athletic Facilities, Chimpanzee and Human Communication Institute, Performing Arts Center, Presidential Speaker Series. **Environmental Initiatives:** Carbon Reduction; Sustainability as defined by our "Sphere of Distinction"; Energy Conservation.

ADMISSIONS

Freshman Academic Profile: Average high school GPA 3.2. 4% in top 10% of high school class, 23% in top 25% of high school class, 65% in top 50% of high school class. SAT Math middle 50% range 440-550. SAT Critical Reading middle 50% range 440-540. ACT middle 50% range 18-23. Minimum paper TOEFL 525. **Basis for Candidate Selection:** *Very important factors considered include:* academic GPA, rigor of secondary school record. *Important factors considered include:* application essay, standardized test scores. *Other factors considered include:* Class rank, recommendation(s), character/personal qualities, extracurricular activities, first generation, interview, level of applicant's interest, talent/ability, volunteer work, work experience. **Freshman Admission Requirements:** High school diploma is required and GED is accepted. *Academic units required:* 4 English, 3 mathematics, 2 science, (1 science labs), 2 foreign language, 3 social studies. **Freshman Admission Statistics:** 5,013 applied, 79% admitted, 40% enrolled. **Transfer Admission Requirements:** college transcript(s), statement of good standing from prior institution(s). Minimum college GPA of 2.5 required. Lowest grade transferable D-. **General Admission Information:** Application Fee $55. Regular application deadline 4/1. Notification on a rolling basis, beginning on or about 11/1. Nonfall registration accepted. Credit and/or placement offered for CEEB Advanced Placement tests.

COSTS AND FINANCIAL AID

Annual in-state tuition $4,842. Annual out-of-state tuition $14,013. Room and board $8,052. Required fees $882. Average book expense $924. **Required Forms and Deadlines:** FAFSA. **Notification of Awards:** Applicants will be notified of awards on a rolling basis beginning 4/15. **Types of Aid:** *Need-based scholarships/grants:* Federal Pell, SEOG, state scholarships/grants, private scholarships, the school's own gift aid. *Loans:* Direct Subsidized Stafford, Direct Unsubsidized Stafford, Direct PLUS, Federal Perkins, state loans, college/university loans from institutional funds. *Student Employment:* Highest amount earned per year from on-campus jobs $10,166. **Financial Aid Statistics:** 68% freshmen, 68% undergrads receive any aid. **Criteria for awarding institutional aid:** *Non-need-based:* academics, alumni affiliation, art, athletics, job skills, leadership, minority status, music/drama, religious affiliation, state/district residency.

CENTRAL WYOMING COLLEGE

2660 Peck Avenue, Riverton, WY 82501
Phone: 307-855-2000 · **Financial Aid Phone:** 307-855-2150
E-mail: admit@cwc.edu · **CEEB Code:** 4115
Fax: 307-855-2065 · **Website:** www.cwc.edu · **ACT Code:** 514999

This public school was founded in 1966. It has a 200-acre campus.

RATINGS

Admissions Selectivity Rating: 70   **Fire Safety Rating:** 75

STUDENTS AND FACULTY

Enrollment: 1,095. **Student Body:** 60% female, 40% male, 11% out-of-state, 1% international (6 countries represented). Asian 1%, African American 1%, Caucasian 71%, Hispanic 8%, Native American 13%

Retention and Graduation: 48% freshmen return for sophomore year. **Faculty:** 81 full-time faculty, 53% hold PhDs, 46% are members of minority groups, 9% are women. 0% of classes are taught by teaching assistants.

ACADEMICS

Degrees: associate, certificate, diploma, terminal associate, transfer associate. **Classes:** Most classes have fewer than 10 students. **Majors with Highest Enrollment:** General Studies; Parks, Recreation and Leisure Facilities Management. **Special Study Options:** cooperative education program, cross-registration, distance learning, double major, dual enrollment, external degree program, honors program, independent study, student-designed major, teacher certification program. **Disability Services:** Special programs offered to physically disabled students include note-taking services, reader services, tape recorders, tutors. **Career services:** career/job search classes, career assessment, internships. Career services highlights include experiential learning.

FACILITIES

Housing: Coed dorms, apartments for married students, apartments for single students 100% of campus accessible to physically disabled. **Special Academic Facilities/Equipment:** Fine Arts Center, Microsoft training lab, Cisco training lab, Wyoming Public Television Station and Radio station, Stewart Collection (Native American Artifacts), Sinks Canyon Center, Rodeo Arena, Library, Arts Gallery. **Computers:** Students can register for classes online. Administrative functions (other than registration) can be performed online.

CAMPUS LIFE

Environment: Village. **Activities:** Choral groups, concert band, dance, drama/theater, jazz band, music ensembles, musical theater, radio station, student government, television station, International Student Organization. 16 registered organizations, 2 honor societies, 2 religious organizations. **Athletics (Intercollegiate):** *Men:* basketball, rodeo. *Women:* basketball, rodeo, volleyball. **On-Campus Highlights:** Arts Center, Stewart Collection, Student Center, Food Court, The Underground, Others depend on the students interests. For instance, if they are interested in our equine program we would take them to our equine facilities.

ADMISSIONS

Freshman Academic Profile: Average high school GPA 3.01. 6% in top 10% of high school class, 24% in top 25% of high school class, 57% in top 50% of high school class. 89% from public high schools. SAT Math middle 50% range 440-580. SAT Critical Reading middle 50% range 400-560. ACT middle 50% range 17-22. Minimum internet-based TOEFL 60. Minimum paper TOEFL 500. **Freshman Admission Requirements:** High school diploma is required and GED is accepted. **Freshman Admission Statistics:** 527 applied, 100% admitted, 51% enrolled. **General Admission Information:** Application Fee $20.

COSTS AND FINANCIAL AID

Annual in-state tuition $1,992. Annual out-of-state tuition $5,976. Room and board $5,105. Required fees $720. Average book expense $1,200. **Required Forms and Deadlines:** FAFSA, Institution's own financial aid form. **Financial Aid Statistics:** 78% freshmen, 79% undergrads receive need-based scholarship or grant aid. 80% freshmen, 77% undergrads receive non-need-based scholarship or grant aid. 28% freshmen, 35% undergrads receive need-based self-help aid. 0% freshmen, 0% undergrads receive athletic scholarships. 38% freshmen, 48% undergrads receive any aid.

CENTRE COLLEGE

600 West Walnut Street, Danville, KY 40422
Phone: 859-238-5350 · **Financial Aid Phone:** 800-423-6236
E-mail: admission@centre.edu · **CEEB Code:** 1109
Fax: 859-238-5373 · **Website:** www.centre.edu · **ACT Code:** 1506

This private school, affiliated with the Presbyterian Church, was founded in 1819. It has a 115-acre campus.

RATINGS

Admissions Selectivity Rating: 89 **Fire Safety Rating:** 70

STUDENTS AND FACULTY

Enrollment: 1,379. **Student Body:** 52% female, 48% male, 44% out-of-state, 6% international (8 countries represented), Asian 3%, African American 5%, Caucasian 80%, Hispanic 2%, Native American <1%
Retention and Graduation: 90% freshmen return for sophomore year. 80% freshmen graduate within 4 years. 82% freshmen graduate within 6 years. 41% grads go on to further study within 1 year. 35% grads pursue arts and sciences degrees. 21% grads pursue law degrees. 3% grads pursue business degrees. 13% grads pursue medical degrees. **Faculty:** 123 full-time faculty, 97% hold PhDs, 39% are members of minority groups, 7% are women. 0% of classes are taught by teaching assistants.

ACADEMICS

Degrees: bachelor's. **Classes:** Most classes have 10–19 students. Most lab/discussion sessions have 10–19 students. **Majors with Highest Enrollment:** Economics; History; Psychology. **Special Study Options:** cross-registration, double major, honors program, independent study, internships, student-designed major, study abroad, teacher certification program. **Disability Services:** Special programs offered to physically disabled students include note-taking services, reader services, tape recorders, tutors. **Career services:** Alumni network, alumni services, career/job search classes, career assessment, internships, regional alumni. We provide a college-wide comprehensive internship program. We also provide a unique program of career counseling called "Centre Futures."

FACILITIES

Housing: Coed dorms, special housing for disabled students, men's dorms, fraternity/sorority housing, apartments for single students, Wellness Housing, Theme Housing. 80% of campus accessible to physically disabled. **Special Academic Facilities/Equipment:** Arts center, physical science and math facility, electron microscope, visible and infrared mass spectroscopy equipment, visual arts center. **Computers:** Administrative functions (other than registration) can be performed online.

CAMPUS LIFE

Environment: Village. **Activities:** Choral groups, dance, drama/theater, jazz band, literary magazine, music ensembles, musical theater, opera, pep band, radio station, student government, student newspaper, symphony orchestra, television station, Campus Ministries, International Student Organization. 70 registered organizations, 12 honor societies, 6 religious organizations. 4 fraternities, 4 sororities. **Athletics (Intercollegiate):** *Men:* baseball, basketball, cheerleading, cross-country, diving, football, golf, soccer, swimming, tennis, track/field (outdoor). *Women:* basketball, cheerleading, cross-country, diving, field hockey, golf, soccer, softball, swimming, tennis, track/field (outdoor), volleyball. **On-Campus Highlights:** Norton Center for the Arts, College Centre, athletic and library, Combs Center, student center, 21 campus buildings on National Register, Jazzman's Café. **Environmental Initiatives:** All new buildings and major renovations will be designed and built to conserve energy and enhance the human environment as evaluated by LEED silver standards or equivalent. Certification through U.S.G.B.C. will be pursued as appropriate. Energy consumption and life-cycle costs will be considered in purchases of all equipment

and appliances. The intention will be to purchase E.P.A. Energy Star products in all areas for which such ratings exist. Waste minimization will be promoted and pursued by policy and practice. Specific activities will depend upon technical and economic opportunities. Current efforts include participation in the Waste minimization component of the Recyclemania competition.

ADMISSIONS

Freshman Academic Profile: Average high school GPA 3.71. 53% in top 10% of high school class, 79% in top 25% of high school class, 96% in top 50% of high school class. 79% from public high schools. SAT Math middle 50% range 560-680. SAT Critical Reading middle 50% range 550-660. SAT Writing middle 50% range 550-680. ACT middle 50% range 26-31. Minimum paper TOEFL 580. **Basis for Candidate Selection:** *Very important factors considered include:* academic GPA, rigor of secondary school record. *Important factors considered include:* Class rank, application essay, recommendation(s), standardized test scores. *Other factors considered include:* alumni/ae relation, character/personal qualities, extracurricular activities, first generation, geographical residence, interview, racial/ethnic status, talent/ability, volunteer work, work experience. **Freshman Admission Requirements:** High school diploma or equivalent is not required. *Academic units required:* 4 English, 3 mathematics, 2 science, (2 science labs), 2 foreign language, 1 social studies, 1 history. **Freshman Admission Statistics:** 2,494 applied, 72% admitted, 22% enrolled. **Transfer Admission Requirements:** High school transcript, college transcript(s), essay or personal statement, standardized test scores, statement of good standing from prior institution(s). Lowest grade transferable C. **General Admission Information:** Application Fee $40. Regular application deadline 2/1. Regular notification 3/15. Nonfall registration not accepted. Admission may be deferred for a maximum of 1 year. Credit and/or placement offered for CEEB Advanced Placement tests.

COSTS AND FINANCIAL AID

Annual tuition $37,100. Room and board $9,340. Average book expense $1,500. **Required Forms and Deadlines:** FAFSA, Institution's own financial aid form. **Notification of Awards:** Applicants will be notified of awards on or about 4/1. **Types of Aid:** *Need-based scholarships/grants:* Federal Pell, SEOG, state scholarships/grants, private scholarships, the school's own gift aid, Federal ACG Federal SMART + Federal TEACH. *Loans:* Subsidized Stafford, Unsubsidized Stafford, PLUS, Federal Perkins, college/university loans from institutional funds. *Student Employment:* Federal Work-Study Program available. Institutional employment available. Off-campus job opportunities are fair. **Financial Aid Statistics:** 99% freshmen, 100% undergrads receive need-based scholarship or grant aid. 0% freshmen, 0% undergrads receive non-need-based scholarship or grant aid. 64% freshmen, 68% undergrads receive need-based self-help aid. 0% freshmen, 0% undergrads receive athletic scholarships. 97% freshmen, 96% undergrads receive any aid. 54% undergrads borrow to pay for school. Average cumulative indebtedness $22,376. **Criteria for awarding institutional aid:** *Non-need-based:* academics, alumni affiliation, music/drama.

CHADRON STATE COLLEGE

1000 Main Street, Chadron, NE 69337
Phone: 308-432-6263 · **Financial Aid Phone:** 308-432-6230
E-mail: inquire@csc.edu · **CEEB Code:** 6466
Fax: 308-432-6229 · **Website:** www.csc.edu · **ACT Code:** 2466

This public school was founded in 1911. It has a 281-acre campus.

RATINGS

Admissions Selectivity Rating: 62 **Fire Safety Rating:** 68

STUDENTS AND FACULTY

Enrollment: 2,152. **Student Body:** 57% female, 43% male, 32% out-of-state, 1% international (16 countries represented). Asian 1%, African American 1%, Caucasian 73%, Hispanic 2%, Native American 2%
Retention and Graduation: 70% freshmen return for sophomore year. 17% freshmen graduate within 4 years. 43% freshmen graduate within 6 years. 41% grads go on to further study within 1 year. 25% grads pursue arts and sciences degrees. 3% grads pursue law degrees. 10% grads pursue business degrees. 3% grads pursue medical degrees. **Faculty:** 101 full-time faculty, 57% hold PhDs, 36% are members of minority groups, 4% are women. 0% of classes are taught by teaching assistants.

ACADEMICS

Degrees: bachelor's, master's, post-master's certificate. **Classes:** Most classes have fewer than 10 students. **Majors with Highest Enrollment:** Elementary Education and Teaching; Criminal Justice/Law Enforcement Administration; Business/Commerce. **Special Study Options:** Accelerated program, cooperative education program, cross-registration, distance learning, double major, dual enrollment, honors program, independent study, internships, student-designed major, study abroad, teacher certification program. **Disability Services:** Special programs offered to physically disabled students include note-taking services, tape recorders, tutors. **Career services:** career/job search classes.

FACILITIES
Housing: Coed dorms, men's dorms, women's dorms, apartments for married students, apartments for single students. 100% of campus accessible to physically disabled. **Special Academic Facilities/Equipment:** Planetarium, herbarium, geology museum, Mari Sandoz Center. **Computers:** Students can register for classes online. Administrative functions (other than registration) can be performed online.

CAMPUS LIFE
Environment: Rural. **Activities:** Choral groups, concert band, dance, drama/theater, jazz band, literary magazine, music ensembles, musical theater, pep band, radio station, student government, student newspaper, yearbook. 65 registered organizations, 14 honor societies, 5 religious organizations. **Athletics (Intercollegiate):** *Men:* basketball, football, track/field (outdoor), track/field (indoor), wrestling. *Women:* basketball, golf, track/field (outdoor), track/field (indoor), volleyball. **On-Campus Highlights:** Mari Sandoz Heritage Center, Educatiional Facility, Laboratories, Student Center.

ADMISSIONS
Freshman Academic Profile: Average high school GPA 3.13. 11% in top 10% of high school class, 33% in top 25% of high school class, 65% in top 50% of high school class. 83% from public high schools. Minimum paper TOEFL 550. **Basis for Candidate Selection:** *Other factors considered include:* academic GPA. **Freshman Admission Requirements:** High school diploma is required and GED is accepted **Transfer Admission Requirements:** college transcript(s), Minimum college GPA of 2.0 required. Lowest grade transferable D. **General Admission Information:** Application Fee $15. Nonfall registration accepted. Credit and/or placement offered for CEEB Advanced Placement tests.

COSTS AND FINANCIAL AID
Annual in-state tuition $2,933. Annual out-of-state tuition $5,865. Room and board $4,074. Required fees $730. **Required Forms and Deadlines:** FAFSA, Institution's own financial aid form. **Notification of Awards:** Applicants will be notified of awards on a rolling basis beginning 4/1. **Types of Aid:** *Need-based scholarships/grants:* Federal Pell, SEOG, state scholarships/grants, private scholarships, the school's own gift aid. *Loans:* Direct Subsidized Stafford, Direct Unsubsidized Stafford, Direct PLUS, Subsidized Stafford, Unsubsidized Stafford, PLUS, Federal Perkins. *Student Employment:* Federal Work-Study Program available. Institutional employment available. **Financial Aid Statistics:** 91% freshmen, 81% undergrads receive need-based scholarship or grant aid. 0% freshmen, 0% undergrads receive non-need-based scholarship or grant aid. 64% freshmen, 71% undergrads receive need-based self-help aid. 0% freshmen, 0% undergrads receive athletic scholarships. **Criteria for awarding institutional aid:** *Non-need-based:* academics, alumni affiliation, art, athletics, leadership, minority status, music/drama, state/district residency.

CHAMINADE UNIVERSITY OF HONOLULU

3140 Waialae Avenue, Honolulu, HI 96816-1578
Phone: 808-739-8340 · **Financial Aid Phone:** 808-735-4780
E-mail: admissions@chaminade.edu · **CEEB Code:** 4105
Fax: 808-739-4647 · **Website:** www.chaminade.edu · **ACT Code:** 898

This private school, affiliated with the Roman Catholic Church, was founded in 1955. It has a 67-acre campus.

RATINGS
Admissions Selectivity Rating: 71   **Fire Safety Rating:** 62

STUDENTS AND FACULTY
Enrollment: 1,298. **Student Body:** 68% female, 32% male, 32% out-of-state, 2% international (18 countries represented). Asian 37%, African American 3%, Caucasian 14%, Hispanic 5%, Native American <1%
Retention and Graduation: 29% freshmen graduate within 4 years. **Faculty:** 88 full-time faculty, 43% are members of minority groups, 30% are women. 0% of classes are taught by teaching assistants.

ACADEMICS
Degrees: associate, bachelor's, master's, post-bachelor's certificate, post-master's certificate. **Classes:** Most classes have 10–19 students. Most lab/discussion sessions have 10–19 students. **Majors with Highest Enrollment:** Criminal Justice/Safety Studies; Psychology; Registered Nursing, Nursing Administration, Nursing Research and Clinical Nursing. **Special Study Options:** Accelerated program, distance learning, double major, exchange student program (domes-

---

tic), independent study, internships, student-designed major, study abroad, teacher certification program. **Disability Services:** Special programs offered to physically disabled students include note-taking services, reader services, tape recorders. **Career services:** career/job search classes, career assessment, internships.

FACILITIES
Housing: Coed dorms, women's dorms, apartments for single students. 75% of campus accessible to physically disabled. **Special Academic Facilities/Equipment:** Montessori lab school, observatory, black box theatre. **Computers:** Students can register for classes online. Administrative functions (other than registration) can be performed online.

CAMPUS LIFE
Environment: Metropolis. **Activities:** Choral groups, drama/theater, literary magazine, musical theater, student government, student newspaper, symphony orchestra, yearbook, Campus Ministries. 38 registered organizations, 7 honor societies, 1 religious organization. **Athletics (Intercollegiate):** *Men:* basketball, cross-country, golf, tennis, water polo. *Women:* cross-country, golf, softball, tennis, volleyball. **On-Campus Highlights:** Jean E. Rolles Sculoture Center, Henry Hall Courtyard Café, Brother's Brew Café, Weigand Observatory, Vi and Paul Loo Student Center.

ADMISSIONS
Freshman Academic Profile: Average high school GPA 3.38. 3% in top 10% of high school class, 5% in top 25% of high school class, 18% in top 50% of high school class. SAT Math middle 50% range 430-530. SAT Critical Reading middle 50% range 430-510. ACT middle 50% range 19-22. Minimum internet-based TOEFL 79. Minimum paper TOEFL 550. **Basis for Candidate Selection:** *Very important factors considered include:* academic GPA, standardized test scores. *Important factors considered include:* application essay, character/personal qualities, extracurricular activities, interview, talent/ability, volunteer work. *Other factors considered include:* recommendation(s), rigor of secondary school record, work experience. **Freshman Admission Requirements:** High school diploma is required and GED is accepted. **Freshman Admission Statistics:** 918 applied, 85% admitted, 30% enrolled. **Transfer Admission Requirements:** college transcript(s), essay or personal statement, statement of good standing from prior institution(s). Minimum college GPA of 2.0 required. Lowest grade transferable C. **General Admission Information:** Application Fee $50. Nonfall registration accepted. Admission may be deferred for a maximum of 1 year. Credit and/or placement offered for CEEB Advanced Placement tests.

COSTS AND FINANCIAL AID
Annual tuition $20,810. Room and board $11,640. Required fees $144. Average book expense $1,600. **Required Forms and Deadlines:** FAFSA. **Notification of Awards:** Applicants will be notified of awards on a rolling basis beginning 3/1. **Types of Aid:** *Need-based scholarships/grants:* Federal Pell, SEOG, private scholarships, the school's own gift aid, LEAP, ASG, SMART, TEACH. *Loans:* Subsidized Stafford, Unsubsidized Stafford, PLUS, Federal Perkins, CitiAssist Loans, Sallie Mae Signature Education Loan Program. *Student Employment:* Federal Work-Study Program available. Institutional employment available. Highest amount earned per year from on-campus jobs $8,056. Off-campus job opportunities are fair. **Financial Aid Statistics:** 97% freshmen, 90% undergrads receive need-based scholarship or grant aid. 99% freshmen, 96% undergrads receive non-need-based scholarship or grant aid. 85% freshmen, 89% undergrads receive need-based self-help aid. 8% freshmen, 8% undergrads receive athletic scholarships. 99% freshmen, 96% undergrads receive any aid. 64% undergrads borrow to pay for school. Average cumulative indebtedness $23,846. **Criteria for awarding institutional aid:** *Non-need-based:* academics, art, athletics, leadership, religious affiliation.

CHAMPLAIN COLLEGE

163 South Willard Street Box 670, Burlington, VT 05402-0670
Phone: 802-860-2727 · **Financial Aid Phone:** 802-860-2730
E-mail: admission@champlain.edu · **CEEB Code:** 3291
Fax: 802-860-2767 · **Website:** www.champlain.edu/ · **ACT Code:** 3291

This private school was founded in 1878. It has a 19-acre campus.

RATINGS
Admissions Selectivity Rating: 78   **Fire Safety Rating:** 98

STUDENTS AND FACULTY

Enrollment: 2,067. **Student Body:** 39% female, 61% male, 70% out-of-state, 0% international (23 countries represented). Asian 2%, African American 1%, Caucasian 69%, Hispanic 2%, Native American <1% **Retention and Graduation:** 76% freshmen return for sophomore year. 52% freshmen graduate within 4 years. 10% grads go on to further study within 1 year. 3% grads pursue arts and sciences degrees. 1% grads pursue law degrees. 6% grads pursue business degrees. **Faculty:** 96 full-time faculty, 56% hold PhDs, 30% are members of minority groups, 7% are women. 0% of classes are taught by teaching assistants.

ACADEMICS

Degrees: associate, bachelor's, certificate, master's, terminal associate, transfer associate. **Classes:** Most classes have 10–19 students. Most lab/discussion sessions have fewer than 10 students. **Majors with Highest Enrollment:** Business/Commerce; Intermedia/Multimedia; Game and Interactive Media Design. **Special Study Options:** Accelerated program, cross-registration, distance learning, double major, honors program, independent study, internships, liberal arts/career combination, study abroad, teacher certification program. **Honors programs:** Honors Program invitation based on high school gpa and SAT/ACT scores. Combined degree programs: 4+1 MBA offered with Clarkson and SNHU. **Disability Services:** Special programs offered to physically disabled students include note-taking services, reader services, tape recorders, tutors. **Career services:** career/job search classes, internships.

FACILITIES

Housing: Coed dorms, special housing for international students, women's dorms, Wellness, Performing Arts, International dorm. Suites style singles with common living room and kitchenette (for selected sophomores, juniors and seniors. 50% of campus accessible to physically disabled. **Computers:** Students can register for classes online. Administrative functions (other than registration) can be performed online.

CAMPUS LIFE

Environment: Town. **Activities:** Choral groups, dance, drama/theater, literary magazine, musical theater, radio station, student government, student newspaper, television station. 40 registered organizations, 2 honor societies, 1 religious organization. **On-Campus Highlights:** Center for Global Technology, The View, Hauke Family Center, Student Life Center, Main Street Suites, Miller Information Commons. **Environmental Initiatives:** Green Buildings (Master Plan); Waste Reduction (Recycling & Composting); New Environmental Policy; Academic Program.

ADMISSIONS

Freshman Academic Profile: 11% in top 10% of high school class, 35% in top 25% of high school class, 70% in top 50% of high school class. 85% from public high schools. SAT Math middle 50% range 490-590. SAT Critical Reading middle 50% range 500-610. ACT middle 50% range 20-25. Minimum internet-based TOEFL 61. Minimum paper TOEFL 500. **Basis for Candidate Selection:** *Very important factors considered include:* application essay, academic GPA, rigor of secondary school record. *Important factors considered include:* Class rank, recommendation(s), standardized test scores, first generation, interview. *Other factors considered include:* alumni/ae relation, character/personal qualities, extracurricular activities, level of applicant's interest, talent/ability, volunteer work, work experience. **Freshman Admission Requirements:** High school diploma is required and GED is accepted. *Academic units required:* 4 English, 3 mathematics, 3 science, (2 science labs), 4 history, 4 academic electives. **Freshman Admission Statistics:** 3,077 applied, 85% admitted, 25% enrolled. **Transfer Admission Requirements:** High school transcript, college transcript(s), essay or personal statement, Minimum college GPA of 2.0 required. Lowest grade transferable C. **General Admission Information:** Application Fee $40. Early decision application deadline 11/15. Regular application deadline 1/31. Regular notification 3/25. Nonfall registration accepted. Admission may be deferred for a maximum of 1 yr w no tr. Credit offered for CEEB Advanced Placement tests.

COSTS AND FINANCIAL AID

Annual tuition $31,250. Room and board $13,500. Required fees $140. Average book expense $1,000. **Required Forms and Deadlines:** FAFSA, Institution's own financial aid form, State aid form, Noncustodial PROFILE. **Notification of Awards:** Applicants will be notified of awards on a rolling basis beginning 3/1. **Types of Aid:** *Need-based scholarships/grants:* Federal Pell, SEOG, state scholarships/grants, private scholarships, the school's own gift aid. *Loans:* Subsidized Stafford, Unsubsidized Stafford, PLUS, Federal Perkins. *Student Employment:* Highest amount earned per year from on-campus jobs $2,211. **Financial Aid Statistics:** 74% freshmen, 74% undergrads receive need-based scholarship or grant aid. 2% freshmen, 2% undergrads receive non-need-based scholarship or grant aid. 92% freshmen, 92% undergrads receive need-based self-help aid. 0% freshmen, 0% undergrads receive athletic scholarships. 90% freshmen, 83% undergrads receive any aid. **Criteria for awarding institutional aid:** *Non-need-based:* academics, leadership.

CHAPMAN UNIVERSITY

Best 380

One University Drive, Orange, CA 92866
Phone: 714-997-6711 · **Financial Aid Phone:** 714-997-6741
E-mail: admit@chapman.edu · **CEEB Code:** 4047
Fax: 714-997-6713 · **Website:** www.chapman.edu · **ACT Code:** 210

This private school, affiliated with the Disciples of Christ Church, was founded in 1861. It has a 75-acre campus.

RATINGS

Admissions Selectivity Rating: 92   **Fire Safety Rating:** 78

STUDENTS AND FACULTY

Enrollment: 5,940. **Student Body:** 59% female, 41% male, 26% out-of-state, 4% international (67 countries represented). Asian 10%, African American 2%, Caucasian 60%, Hispanic 14%, Native American <1% **Retention and Graduation:** 91% freshmen return for sophomore year. 59% freshmen graduate within 4 years. 76% freshmen graduate within 6 years. **Faculty:** 392 full-time faculty, 86% hold PhDs, 42% are members of minority groups, 14% are women. 0% of classes are taught by teaching assistants.

ACADEMICS

Degrees: bachelor's, master's, post-bachelor's certificate. **Classes:** Most classes have 20–29 students. Most lab/discussion sessions have 10–19 students. **Majors with Highest Enrollment:** Business Administration and Management; Cinematography and Film/Video Production; Public Relations/Image Management. **Special Study Options:** distance learning, double major, English as a Second Language (ESL), honors program, independent study, internships, liberal arts/career combination, student-designed major, study abroad, teacher certification program. **Honors programs:** University Honors Program Combined degree programs: BS/MBA. **Disability Services:** Special programs offered to physically disabled students include note-taking services, reader services, tape recorders, tutors. **Career services:** alumni services, career/job search classes, career assessment, internships. We are particularly proud of our Internship Program, which strengthens the link between classroom learning and the work world. Chapman's Program allows students to earn academic credit through faculty and site supervisor advisement. Internships offer students the opportunity to increase their understanding of career fields, gain hands-on work experience and learn job skills, build self-confidence, and gain a new perspective. This "real world" experience gives our graduates an edge when they join the work force.

FACILITIES

Housing: Coed dorms, special housing for disabled students, apartments for married students, apartments for single students, Houses for married, single, and students with dependents. **Special Academic Facilities/Equipment:** Anderson Center for Economic Research, Leatherby Center for Entrepreneurship and Business Ethics, Schmid Center for International Business, Law and organizational Economics Center, Center for Cold War Studies, Henley Social Science Research Laboratory, Guggenhiem Art gallery, TV studio, film and television production and digital editing studios, Waltmer Theatre, Albert Schweitzer Collection. **Computers:** 100% of classrooms, 100% of dorms, 100% of libraries, 100% of dining areas, 100% of common outdoor areas have wireless network access. Students can register for classes online. Administrative functions (other than registration) can be performed online.

CAMPUS LIFE

Environment: Metropolis. **Activities:** Choral groups, concert band, dance, drama/theater, jazz band, literary magazine, music ensembles, musical theater, opera, pep band, radio station, student government, student newspaper, student-run film society, symphony orchestra, yearbook, Campus Ministries, International Student Organization, Model UN. 84 registered organizations, 8 honor societies, 8 religious organizations. 6 fraternities, 6 sororities. **Athletics (Intercollegiate):** *Men:* baseball, basketball, cross-country, football, golf, soccer, tennis, water polo. *Women:* basketball, crew/rowing, cross-country, soccer, softball, swimming, tennis, track/field (outdoor), volleyball, water polo. **On-Campus Highlights:** Marion Knott Film Studios, Leatherby Libraries, Liberty Plaza, Beckman Hall, All-Faiths Chapel. **Environmental Initiatives:** Adoption of LEED standards in new building projects. Expanded commitment to reduce use and increase recycling of paper. Investment in energy-saving devices and new requirement of energy-star rating on newly purchased electronic devices and appliances.

ADMISSIONS

Freshman Academic Profile: Average high school GPA 3.68. 48% in top 10% of high school class, 93% in top 25% of high school class, 98% in top 50% of

high school class. 70% from public high schools. SAT Math middle 50% range 570-660. SAT Critical Reading middle 50% range 550-640. SAT Writing middle 50% range 560-650. ACT middle 50% range 24-29. Minimum paper TOEFL 550. **Basis for Candidate Selection:** *Very important factors considered include:* Class rank, application essay, academic GPA, rigor of secondary school record, standardized test scores, character/personal qualities. *Important factors considered include:* extracurricular activities, talent/ability, volunteer work. *Other factors considered include:* recommendation(s), alumni/ae relation, first generation, geographical residence, racial/ethnic status, state residency, work experience. **Freshman Admission Requirements:** High school diploma is required and GED is accepted. *Academic units required:* 2 English, 2 mathematics, 2 science, (1 science labs), 2 foreign language, 3 social studies. **Freshman Admission Statistics:** 11,750 applied, 45% admitted, 25% enrolled. **Transfer Admission Requirements:** college transcript(s), essay or personal statement. Minimum college GPA of 2.5 required. Lowest grade transferable C-. **General Admission Information:** Application Fee $55. Regular application deadline 1/15. Notification on a rolling basis, beginning on or about 3/15. Nonfall registration accepted. Credit and/or placement offered for CEEB Advanced Placement tests.

COSTS AND FINANCIAL AID

Annual tuition $44,710. Room and board $12,954. Required fees $683. Average book expense $1,560. **Required Forms and Deadlines:** FAFSA, State aid form. **Notification of Awards:** Applicants will be notified of awards on a rolling basis beginning 3/15. **Types of Aid:** *Need-based scholarships/grants:* Federal Pell, SEOG, state scholarships/grants, private scholarships, the school's own gift aid, Academic Competitiveness Grants. *Loans:* Subsidized Stafford, Unsubsidized Stafford, PLUS, Federal Perkins. *Student Employment:* Federal Work-Study Program available. Institutional employment available. Off-campus job opportunities are excellent. **Financial Aid Statistics:** 90% freshmen, 88% undergrads receive need-based scholarship or grant aid. 74% freshmen, 62% undergrads receive non-need-based scholarship or grant aid. 88% freshmen, 91% undergrads receive need-based self-help aid. 0% freshmen, 0% undergrads receive athletic scholarships. 63% undergrads borrow to pay for school. Average cumulative indebtedness $21,813. **Criteria for awarding institutional aid:** *Non-need-based:* academics, alumni affiliation, art, music/drama, religious affiliation.

See page 1024.

CHARLESTON SOUTHERN UNIVERSITY

Enrollment Services, Charleston, SC 29423
Phone: 843-863-7050 · **Financial Aid Phone:** 843-863-7050
E-mail: enroll@csuniv.edu · **CEEB Code:** 5079
Fax: 843-863-7070 · **Website:** www.charlestonsouthern.edu · **ACT Code:** 3833

This private school, affiliated with the Southern Baptist Church, was founded in 1964. It has a 300-acre campus.

RATINGS
Admissions Selectivity Rating: 80   Fire Safety Rating: 60*

STUDENTS AND FACULTY
Enrollment: 2,473. **Student Body:** 61% female, 39% male, 18% out-of-state, 2% international (30 countries represented). Asian 2%, African American 27%, Caucasian 55%, Hispanic 1%, Native American 1%
Retention and Graduation: 60% freshmen return for sophomore year. 22% freshmen graduate within 4 years. 36% freshmen graduate within 6 years. 14% grads go on to further study within 1 year. **Faculty:** 107 full-time faculty, 63% hold PhDs, 45% are members of minority groups, 2% are women. 0% of classes are taught by teaching assistants.

ACADEMICS
Degrees: bachelor's, master's. **Classes:** Most classes have 20–29 students. Most lab/discussion sessions have 20–29 students. **Majors with Highest Enrollment:** Elementary Education and Teaching; Psychology; Business/Commerce. **Special Study Options:** Accelerated program, cooperative education program, cross-registration, distance learning, double major, dual enrollment, honors program, internships, study abroad, teacher certification program, Other Special Programs: Evening Division. **Honors programs:** SAT 1200 or higher or ACT 27 or higher and High School GPA of 3.50 or higher. Combined degree programs: BA/MD, Allied health tech with Medical U of S. Carolina. **Disability Services:** Special programs offered to physically disabled students include note-taking services, reader services, tape recorders, tutors. **Career services:** career assessment, internships. Career services highlights include applied learning internships for credit.

FACILITIES
Housing: men's dorms, women's dorms. 80% of campus accessible to physically disabled. **Special Academic Facilities/Equipment:** Earthquake Education Center; computer labs w/ wireless internet; nursing clinical lab, specialized music rehearsal modules and advanced music keyboard technology. **Computers:** Students can register for classes online. Administrative functions (other than registration) can be performed online.

CAMPUS LIFE
Environment: Metropolis. **Activities:** Choral groups, concert band, dance, drama/theater, jazz band, literary magazine, marching band, music ensembles, musical theater, pep band, student government, student newspaper, yearbook. 22 registered organizations, 3 honor societies, 4 religious organizations. **Athletics (Intercollegiate):** *Men:* baseball, basketball, cross-country, football, golf, tennis, track/field (outdoor), track/field (indoor). *Women:* basketball, cross-country, golf, soccer, softball, tennis, track/field (outdoor), track/field (indoor), volleyball.

ADMISSIONS
Freshman Academic Profile: Average high school GPA 3.3. 18% in top 10% of high school class, 47% in top 25% of high school class, 80% in top 50% of high school class. 81% from public high schools. SAT Math middle 50% range 480-570. SAT Critical Reading middle 50% range 490-570. ACT middle 50% range 20-24. Minimum paper TOEFL 550. **Basis for Candidate Selection:** *Very important factors considered include:* rigor of secondary school record, standardized test scores. *Important factors considered include:* Class rank. *Other factors considered include:* application essay, recommendation(s), character/personal qualities, extracurricular activities, interview, religious affiliation/commitment, talent/ability, work experience. **Freshman Admission Requirements:** High school diploma is required and GED is accepted. *Academic units required:* 4 English, 3 mathematics, 3 science, (2 science labs), 0 foreign language, 3 history, 3 academic electives. **Freshman Admission Statistics:** 2,283 applied, 72% admitted, 47% enrolled. **Transfer Admission Requirements:** college transcript(s), statement of good standing from prior institution(s). Minimum college GPA of 2.0 required. Lowest grade transferable C. **General Admission Information:** Application Fee $30. Nonfall registration accepted. Credit and/or placement offered for CEEB Advanced Placement tests.

COSTS AND FINANCIAL AID
Average book expense $1,000. **Required Forms and Deadlines:** FAFSA. **Notification of Awards:** Applicants will be notified of awards on a rolling basis beginning 2/1. **Types of Aid:** *Need-based scholarships/grants:* Federal Pell, SEOG, state scholarships/grants, private scholarships, the school's own gift aid. *Loans:* Direct Subsidized Stafford, Direct Unsubsidized Stafford, Direct PLUS, Subsidized Stafford, PLUS, Federal Perkins, state loans. *Student Employment:* Highest amount earned per year from on-campus jobs $2,000. **Financial Aid Statistics:** 100% freshmen, 99% undergrads receive need-based scholarship or grant aid. 15% freshmen, 14% undergrads receive non-need-based scholarship or grant aid. 81% freshmen, 79% undergrads receive need-based self-help aid. 4% freshmen, 4% undergrads receive athletic scholarships. **Criteria for awarding institutional aid:** *Non-need-based:* academics, alumni affiliation, art, athletics, leadership, music/drama, religious affiliation, state/district residency.

CHARTER OAK STATE COLLEGE

55 Paul Manafort Drive, New Britain, CT 6053
Phone: 860-515-3701 · **Financial Aid Phone:** 860-515-3703
E-mail: admissions@charteroak.edu
Website: www.charteroak.edu

This public school was founded in 1973.

RATINGS
Admissions Selectivity Rating: 60*   Fire Safety Rating: 60*

STUDENTS AND FACULTY
Enrollment: 1,799. **Student Body:** 67% female, 33% male, 22% out-of-state, 1% international. Asian 1%, African American 18%, Caucasian 61%, Hispanic 13%, Native American <1%

ACADEMICS
Degrees: associate, bachelor's, transfer associate. **Special Study Options:** distance learning, external degree program, independent study, liberal arts/career combination, student-designed major.

FACILITIES
Housing: 100% of campus accessible to physically disabled. **Computers:** Students can register for classes online. Administrative functions (other than registration) can be performed online.

CAMPUS LIFE

Environment: Village.

ADMISSIONS

Freshman Admission Requirements: High school diploma is required and GED is accepted. **Transfer Admission Requirements:** college transcript(s), Lowest grade transferable D. **General Admission Information:** Application Fee $75. Nonfall registration not accepted. Admission may be deferred for a maximum of 12 months. Credit offered for CEEB Advanced Placement tests.

COSTS AND FINANCIAL AID

Required Forms and Deadlines: FAFSA. **Notification of Awards:** Applicants will be notified of awards on a rolling basis beginning 8/15. **Types of Aid:** *Need-based scholarships/grants:* Federal Pell, state scholarships/grants, private scholarships, the school's own gift aid. *Loans:* Subsidized Stafford, Unsubsidized Stafford, PLUS. **Financial Aid Statistics:** 81% undergrads receive need-based scholarship or grant aid. 0% undergrads receive non-need-based scholarship or grant aid. 88% undergrads receive need-based self-help aid. 0% undergrads receive athletic scholarships.

CHATHAM UNIVERSITY

Woodland Road, Pittsburgh, PA 15232
Phone: 412-365-1825 · **Financial Aid Phone:** 412-365-2797
E-mail: admission@chatham.edu · **CEEB Code:** 2081
Fax: 412-365-1609 · **Website:** www.chatham.edu · **ACT Code:** 3538

This private school was founded in 1869. It has a 39388-acre campus.

RATINGS

Admissions Selectivity Rating: 87   **Fire Safety Rating:** 73

STUDENTS AND FACULTY

Enrollment: 599. **Student Body:** 97% female, 3% male, 19% out-of-state, 5% international (19 countries represented). Asian 3%, African American 12%, Caucasian 69%, Hispanic 4%, Native American <1%
Retention and Graduation: 47% freshmen graduate within 4 years. 56% freshmen graduate within 6 years. 15% grads go on to further study within 1 year. 9% grads pursue arts and sciences degrees. 3% grads pursue law degrees. 3% grads pursue business degrees. 9% grads pursue medical degrees. **Faculty:** 110 full-time faculty, 88% hold PhDs, 67% are members of minority groups, 8% are women. 0% of classes are taught by teaching assistants.

ACADEMICS

Degrees: bachelor's, master's, post-bachelor's certificate, post-master's certificate. **Classes:** Most classes have 10–19 students. Most lab/discussion sessions have 10–19 students. **Majors with Highest Enrollment:** Biology/Biological Sciences; Psychology; Registered Nursing, Nursing Administration, Nursing Research and Clinical Nursing. **Special Study Options:** Accelerated program, cooperative education program, cross-registration, distance learning, double major, dual enrollment, English as a Second Language (ESL), exchange student program (domestic), honors program, independent study, internships, liberal arts/career combination, student-designed major, study abroad, teacher certification program, Five-year bachelors/masters programs; five-year bachelors/masters programs also available with Carnegie Mellon (e.g. engineering, public policy) and other institutions. **Honors programs:** The Chatham Scholars Program offers students a challenging, integrated curriculum with special opportunities for enrichment, mentoring, and networking. Combined degree programs: BA/MA, 3-2 b/m in 9 fields and 4-2 b/doctorate in Phys Ther. **Disability Services:** Special programs offered to physically disabled students include note-taking services, reader services, tape recorders, tutors. **Career services:** Alumni network, alumni services, career/job search classes, career assessment, internships.

FACILITIES

Housing: women's dorms, apartments for married students, apartments for single students, Theme Housing. 75% of campus accessible to physically disabled. **Special Academic Facilities/Equipment:** Athletic and Fitness Center; Art and Design Center; broadcast studio; art gallery, classroom space, and coffee shop; campus arboretum and greenhouse; proscenium theater. **Computers:** 100% of classrooms, 20% of dorms, 100% of libraries, 100% of dining areas, 100% of student union, 75% of common outdoor areas have wireless network access. Students can register for classes online. Administrative functions (other than registration) can be performed online. Undergraduates are required to own a computer.

CAMPUS LIFE

Environment: Metropolis. **Activities:** Choral groups, dance, drama/theater, literary magazine, music ensembles, musical theater, student government,

student newspaper, yearbook. 25 registered organizations, 10 honor societies, 6 religious organizations. **Athletics (Intercollegiate):** *Women:* basketball, cross-country, ice hockey, soccer, softball, swimming, tennis, volleyball, water polo. **On-Campus Highlights:** New coffee shop and art gallery (2005), Athletic and Fitness Center (2004), Art and Design Center (2004), Science Complex (2001), Campus Arboretum, Many of the campus residence halls are renovated historic mansions. The campus also features an outdoor meditation labyrinth, the largest in Pittsburgh. The Shadyside Campus on Woodland Road is a registered arboretum, with over 120 distinct tree species. **Environmental Initiatives:** The creation of the School of Sustainability and the Environment, and the hiring of the founding Dean. The new School will provide innovative, interdisciplinary education and research opportunities for undergraduate, graduate and professional students to better prepare them to identify and solve challenges related to the environment and sustainability. The school will be located at Eden Hall Campus, on a 300-acre farm with forest. The campus is in the master planning stage, and is intended as a net-zero energy campus. Installation of cutting-edge micro-channel solar hot water systems on our two largest residence halls, in use year-round. An interactive demonstration and teaching unit has been installed on our research greenhouse. The systems provide approximately 75% of total hot water use for the buildings over a year, and during the sunnier months, it is able to provide 100% of hot water needs with no combustion required. Our environmentally-friendly transportation initiatives continue. Chatham Bike-Works, a bike repair shop, is open and teaching bike repair and maintenance, as well as providing a bike rental program. Our regular transportation programs continue, including Zipcars on campus, public transit pass full subsidy, biofuel shuttle fleet for inter-campus travel.

ADMISSIONS

Freshman Academic Profile: Average high school GPA 3.63. 26% in top 10% of high school class, 54% in top 25% of high school class, 85% in top 50% of high school class. SAT Math middle 50% range 445-570. SAT Critical Reading middle 50% range 470-590. SAT Writing middle 50% range 450-560. ACT middle 50% range 19-27. Minimum internet-based TOEFL 60. Minimum paper TOEFL 500. **Basis for Candidate Selection:** *Very important factors considered include:* rigor of secondary school record. *Important factors considered include:* application essay, academic GPA. *Other factors considered include:* Class rank, recommendation(s), standardized test scores, alumni/ae relation, character/personal qualities, extracurricular activities, interview, level of applicant's interest, talent/ability, volunteer work, work experience. **Freshman Admission Requirements:** High school diploma is required and GED is accepted. *Academic units required:* 4 English, 2 mathematics, 2 science, 0 foreign language, 3 Social Science. **Freshman Admission Statistics:** 619 applied, 53% admitted, 32% enrolled. **Transfer Admission Requirements:** college transcript(s), essay or personal statement, Minimum college GPA of 2.0 required. Lowest grade transferable C-. **General Admission Information:** Application Fee $35. Regular application deadline 8/1. Notification on a rolling basis, beginning on or about 10/15. Nonfall registration accepted. Admission may be deferred for a maximum of 1 year. Credit offered for CEEB Advanced Placement tests.

COSTS AND FINANCIAL AID

Annual tuition $33,200. Room and board $10,720. Required fees $1,240. Average book expense $860. **Required Forms and Deadlines:** FAFSA. **Notification of Awards:** Applicants will be notified of awards on a rolling basis beginning 2/15. **Types of Aid:** *Need-based scholarships/grants:* Federal Pell, SEOG, state scholarships/grants, private scholarships, the school's own gift aid, United Negro College Fund. *Loans:* Subsidized Stafford, Unsubsidized Stafford, PLUS, Federal Perkins. *Student Employment:* Federal Work-Study Program available. Institutional employment available. Highest amount earned per year from on-campus jobs $2,200. Off-campus job opportunities are good. **Financial Aid Statistics:** 81% freshmen, 79% undergrads receive need-based scholarship or grant aid. 87% freshmen, 77% undergrads receive non-need-based scholarship or grant aid. 92% freshmen, 79% undergrads receive need-based self-help aid. 0% freshmen, 0% undergrads receive athletic scholarships. 100% freshmen, 95% undergrads receive any aid. 74% undergrads borrow to pay for school. Average cumulative indebtedness $25,009. **Criteria for awarding institutional aid:** *Non-need-based:* academics, alumni affiliation, leadership, minority status.

CHESTNUT HILL COLLEGE

9601 Germantown Avenue, Philadelphia, PA 19118-2693
Phone: 215-248-7100 • **Financial Aid Phone:** 215-248-7182
E-mail: chcapply@chc.edu • **CEEB Code:** 2082
Fax: 215-248-7082 • **Website:** www.chc.edu • **ACT Code:** 3540

This private school, affiliated with the Roman Catholic Church, was founded in 1924. It has a 75-acre campus.

RATINGS

Admissions Selectivity Rating: 78   **Fire Safety Rating:** 80

STUDENTS AND FACULTY

Enrollment: 1,455. **Student Body:** 67% female, 33% male, 24% out-of-state, 2% international (40 countries represented). Asian 2%, African American 36%, Caucasian 41%, Hispanic 9%, Native American <1%
Retention and Graduation: 37% freshmen graduate within 4 years. 47% freshmen graduate within 6 years. 20% grads go on to further study within 1 year. 8% grads pursue arts and sciences degrees. 1% grads pursue law degrees. 5% grads pursue business degrees. 1% grads pursue medical degrees. **Faculty:** 88 full-time faculty, 84% hold PhDs, 66% are members of minority groups, 6% are women. 0% of classes are taught by teaching assistants.

ACADEMICS

Degrees: associate, bachelor's, certificate, master's, post-bachelor's certificate, post-master's certificate, transfer associate. **Classes:** Most classes have 10–19 students. Most lab/discussion sessions have 10–19 students. **Majors with Highest Enrollment:** Human Services; Criminal Justice/Law Enforcement Administration; Psychology. **Special Study Options:** cooperative education program, cross-registration, double major, dual enrollment, English as a Second Language (ESL), exchange student program (domestic), honors program, independent study, internships, student-designed major, study abroad, teacher certification program, Upperclass undergraduates may take graduate classes. **Honors programs:** Interdisciplinary Honors Program for outstanding incoming first year students offers team-taught interdisciplinary seminars emphasizing discussion and writing which satisfy general education requirements. Departmental Honors challenges students in the junior and senior year to complete an independent research project in their major field. Combined degree programs: BA/MA, BS/MEd, MA/PsyD, BS/DPM, BS/BS med tech, BS/MS Human Services. **Disability Services:** Special programs offered to physically disabled students include reader services, tutors. **Career services:** Alumni network, career/job search classes, career assessment, internships. Chestnut Hill College encourages all students to participate in some form of experiential learning. Internships are available in a large number of majors and work areas.

FACILITIES

Housing: Coed dormsOn-campus housing includes singles, doubles, suites, and apartment-like units. A new main campus residence hall opened in Fall 2006 and a renovated building opened as a residence hall on the SugarLoaf Hill campus in 2008. 80% of campus accessible to physically disabled. **Special Academic Facilities/Equipment:** Rare book collection, Irish literature collection, observatory, planetarium. **Computers:** 40% of classrooms, 100% of dorms, 100% of libraries, have wireless network access. Students can register for classes online. Undergraduates are required to own a computer.

CAMPUS LIFE

Environment: Metropolis. **Activities:** Choral groups, drama/theater, jazz band, literary magazine, music ensembles, musical theater, opera, student government, student newspaper, symphony orchestra, television station, yearbook, Campus Ministries, International Student Organization. 19 registered organizations, 14 honor societies, 1 religious organization. **Athletics (Intercollegiate):** *Men:* baseball, basketball, cross-country, golf, lacrosse, soccer, tennis. *Women:* basketball, cross-country, golf, lacrosse, soccer, softball, tennis, volleyball. **On-Campus Highlights:** Martino Hall (smart classrooms, gym), Griffin's Den, Fitzsimmons Hall (new residence hall), Dining Hall, Rotunda of Saint Joseph Hall, SugarLoaf Hill, a 32-acre recent addition to campus, will soon provide additional space for many campus activities. **Environmental Initiatives:** Recycling program Go Green Committee

ADMISSIONS

Freshman Academic Profile: Average high school GPA 3.15. 8% in top 10% of high school class, 28% in top 25% of high school class, 59% in top 50% of high school class. 60% from public high schools. SAT Math middle 50% range 420-550. SAT Critical Reading middle 50% range 430-530. SAT Writing middle 50% range 420-520. ACT middle 50% range 19-23. Minimum internet-based TOEFL 79. Minimum paper TOEFL 550. **Basis for Candidate Selection:** *Very important factors considered include:* application essay, rigor of secondary school record. *Important factors considered include:* academic GPA,

recommendation(s), standardized test scores, character/personal qualities, extracurricular activities, interview. *Other factors considered include:* Class rank, alumni/ae relation, level of applicant's interest, talent/ability, volunteer work, work experience. **Freshman Admission Requirements:** High school diploma is required and GED is accepted. **Freshman Admission Statistics:** 1,916 applied, 62% admitted, 16% enrolled. **Transfer Admission Requirements:** college transcript(s), essay or personal statement, Minimum college GPA of 2.0 required. Lowest grade transferable C. **General Admission Information:** Application Fee $35. Early decision application deadline 12/10. Notification on a rolling basis, beginning on or about 9/1. Nonfall registration accepted. Admission may be deferred for a maximum of 1 year. Credit and/or placement offered for CEEB Advanced Placement tests.

COSTS AND FINANCIAL AID

Annual tuition $32,930. Room and board $10,200. Required fees $190. Average book expense $1,200. **Required Forms and Deadlines:** FAFSA. **Notification of Awards:** Applicants will be notified of awards on a rolling basis beginning 1/31. **Types of Aid:** *Need-based scholarships/grants:* Federal Pell, SEOG, state scholarships/grants, private scholarships, the school's own gift aid. *Loans:* Subsidized Stafford, Unsubsidized Stafford, PLUS, Federal Perkins. *Student Employment:* Federal Work-Study Program available. Highest amount earned per year from on-campus jobs $1,500. Off-campus job opportunities are good. **Financial Aid Statistics:** 72% freshmen, 87% undergrads receive any aid. **Criteria for awarding institutional aid:** *Non-need-based:* academics, alumni affiliation, athletics, leadership, religious affiliation.

See page 1026.

CHEYNEY UNIVERSITY OF PENNSYLVANIA

1837 University Circle, Cheyney, PA 19319
Phone: 610-399-2275 • **Financial Aid Phone:** 610-399-2302
E-mail: abrown@cheyney.edu • **CEEB Code:** 2648
Fax: 610-399-2099 • **Website:** www.cheyney.edu

This public school was founded in 1837. It has a 275-acre campus.

RATINGS

Admissions Selectivity Rating: 74   **Fire Safety Rating:** 97

STUDENTS AND FACULTY

Enrollment: 1,339. **Student Body:** 53% female, 47% male, 22% out-of-state, 0% international (4 countries represented). Asian 0%, African American 92%, Caucasian 1%, Hispanic 1%, Native American <1%
Retention and Graduation: 60% freshmen return for sophomore year. **Faculty:** 75 full-time faculty, 48% are members of minority groups, 79% are women. 0% of classes are taught by teaching assistants.

ACADEMICS

Degrees: associate, bachelor's, master's, post-bachelor's certificate. **Majors with Highest Enrollment:** Speech Communication and Rhetoric; Social Sciences; Business Administration and Management. **Special Study Options:** cooperative education program, cross-registration, distance learning, double major, honors program, independent study, internships, study abroad, teacher certification program. **Honors programs:** Keystone Honors Program. **Disability Services:** Special programs offered to physically disabled students include note-taking services, tape recorders, tutors. **Career services:** alumni services, career/job search classes, internships.

FACILITIES

Housing: Coed dorms, men's dorms, women's dorms, Honors dorm. 60% of campus accessible to physically disabled. **Special Academic Facilities/Equipment:** Afro-American history/culture collection, planetarium, weather station, satellite communication network. **Computers:** 60% of classrooms, 100% of libraries, 100% of student union, 20% of common outdoor areas have wireless network access. Students can register for classes online. Administrative functions (other than registration) can be performed online.

CAMPUS LIFE

Environment: Village. **Activities:** Choral groups, drama/theater, jazz band, marching band, music ensembles, radio station, student government, student newspaper, student-run film society, television station, yearbook. 30 registered organizations, 12 honor societies, 1 religious organization. 5 fraternities, 4 sororities. **Athletics (Intercollegiate):** *Men:* basketball, cross-country, football, tennis, track/field (outdoor), wrestling. *Women:* basketball, bowling, cross-country, tennis, track/field (outdoor), volleyball. **On-Campus Highlights:** Athletics, Culinary Arts, Communication Arts, Dorms, Bookstore. **Environmental Initiatives:** Re-cycling, Oils Conversion-Biofuels, Energy Consonvation-Electric Power.

ADMISSIONS

Freshman Academic Profile: Average high school GPA 2.4. 6% in top 10% of high school class, 15% in top 25% of high school class, 46% in top 50% of high school class. SAT Math middle 50% range 320-410. SAT Critical Reading middle 50% range 330-420. SAT Writing middle 50% range 320-405. ACT middle 50% range 14-21. Minimum paper TOEFL 500. **Basis for Candidate Selection:** *Very important factors considered include:* recommendation(s), rigor of secondary school record. *Important factors considered include:* Class rank, application essay, standardized test scores, extracurricular activities, interview, state residency. *Other factors considered include:* racial/ethnic status, talent/ability. **Freshman Admission Requirements:** High school diploma is required and GED is accepted. *Academic units required:* 4 English, 3 mathematics, 2 science, 2 foreign language, 2 history. 4 English, 3 mathematics, 2 science, 2 foreign language, 2 history, **Freshman Admission Statistics:** 3,298 applied, 50% admitted, 37% enrolled. **Transfer Admission Requirements:** college transcript(s), interview, statement of good standing from prior institution(s). Minimum college GPA of 2.0 required. Lowest grade transferable C. **General Admission Information:** Application Fee $20. Regular application deadline 3/31. Nonfall registration accepted. Admission may be deferred for a maximum of 1 year. Placement offered for CEEB Advanced Placement tests.

COSTS AND FINANCIAL AID

Required Forms and Deadlines: FAFSA. **Notification of Awards:** Applicants will be notified of awards on a rolling basis beginning 3/15. **Types of Aid:** *Need-based scholarships/grants:* Federal Pell, SEOG, state scholarships/grants, private scholarships, the school's own gift aid. *Loans:* Subsidized Stafford, Unsubsidized Stafford, PLUS, Federal Perkins. *Student Employment:* Federal Work-Study Program available. Institutional employment available. Off-campus job opportunities are good. **Financial Aid Statistics:** 82% freshmen, 94% undergrads receive need-based scholarship or grant aid. 30% freshmen, 37% undergrads receive non-need-based scholarship or grant aid. 79% freshmen, 95% undergrads receive need-based self-help aid. 0% freshmen, 0% undergrads receive athletic scholarships. 96% undergrads borrow to pay for school. **Criteria for awarding institutional aid:** *Non-need-based:* academics, alumni affiliation, athletics, minority status.

CHICAGO STATE UNIVERSITY

9501 South Street King Drive, Chicago, IL 60628
Phone: 773-995-2513
E-mail: ug-Admissions@csu.edu
Fax: 773-995-3820 • **Website:** www.csu.edu • **ACT Code:** 1694

This public school was founded in 1867. It has a 161-acre campus.

RATINGS

Admissions Selectivity Rating: 76   **Fire Safety Rating:** 60*

STUDENTS AND FACULTY

Enrollment: 4,818. **Student Body:** 73% female, 27% male, 2% out-of-state, 0% international. Asian 1%, African American 87%, Caucasian 3%, Hispanic 6%, Native American <1%
Faculty: 322 full-time faculty, 51% are members of minority groups, 61% are women.

ACADEMICS

Degrees: bachelor's, master's, post-bachelor's certificate. **Classes:** Most classes have 20–29 students. **Majors with Highest Enrollment:** Elementary Education and Teaching; Liberal Arts and Sciences/Liberal Studies; Registered Nursing/Registered Nurse. **Special Study Options:** cooperative education program, distance learning, double major, English as a Second Language (ESL), honors program, independent study, internships, student-designed major, study abroad, teacher certification program, Programs for mature adults (University Without Walls, Individual Curriculum, and Board of Governors degree program). **Disability Services:** Special programs offered to physically disabled students include note-taking services, reader services, tape recorders, tutors. **Career services:** alumni services, career/job search classes, career assessment, internships.

FACILITIES

Housing: Coed dorms. 51% of campus accessible to physically disabled. **Special Academic Facilities/Equipment:** Art Gallery; Electron microscopes; Greenhouse. **Computers:** Students can register for classes online.

CAMPUS LIFE

Activities: Choral groups, concert band, dance, drama/theater, jazz band, literary magazine, music ensembles, radio station, student government, student newspaper, television station. 47 registered organizations, 30 honor societies, 4 religious organizations. 4 fraternities, 4 sororities. **Athletics (Intercollegiate):**

Men: baseball, basketball, cross-country, golf, tennis, track/field (outdoor), track/field (indoor). *Women:* basketball, cross-country, golf, tennis, track/field (outdoor), track/field (indoor), volleyball.

ADMISSIONS

Freshman Academic Profile: Average high school GPA 2.69. 13% in top 10% of high school class, 35% in top 25% of high school class, 64% in top 50% of high school class. 80% from public high schools. ACT middle 50% range 16-19. Minimum paper TOEFL 500. **Basis for Candidate Selection:** *Very important factors considered include:* rigor of secondary school record, standardized test scores. **Freshman Admission Requirements:** High school diploma is required and GED is accepted. *Academic units required:* 4 English, 3 mathematics, 3 science, 3 social studies, 2 academic electives. 4 English, 3 mathematics, 3 science, 3 social studies, 2 academic electives, **Freshman Admission Statistics:** 3,949 applied, 56% admitted, 25% enrolled. **Transfer Admission Requirements:** college transcript(s), Minimum college GPA of 2.0 required. Lowest grade transferable D. **General Admission Information:** Application Fee $25. Regular application deadline 7/15. Nonfall registration accepted. Admission may be deferred for a maximum of 1 Semester. Credit and/or placement offered for CEEB Advanced Placement tests.

COSTS AND FINANCIAL AID

Annual in-state tuition $3,762. Annual out-of-state tuition $8,448. Room and board $5,700. Required fees $1,060. Average book expense $1,400. **Required Forms and Deadlines:** FAFSA, Institution's own financial aid form. **Notification of Awards:** Applicants will be notified of awards on a rolling basis beginning 3/1. **Types of Aid:** *Need-based scholarships/grants:* Federal Pell, SEOG, state scholarships/grants, private scholarships, the school's own gift aid. *Loans:* Subsidized Stafford, Unsubsidized Stafford, PLUS, Federal Perkins. *Student Employment:* Federal Work-Study Program available. Institutional employment available. Highest amount earned per year from on-campus jobs $2,000. Off-campus job opportunities are good. **Financial Aid Statistics:** 82% freshmen, 93% undergrads receive need-based scholarship or grant aid. 0% freshmen, 2% undergrads receive non-need-based scholarship or grant aid. 29% freshmen, 51% undergrads receive need-based self-help aid. 0% freshmen, 0% undergrads receive athletic scholarships. Criteriafor awarding institutional aid: *Non-need-based:* academics, athletics, state/district residency.

CHOWAN UNIVERSITY

One University Place, Murfreesboro, NC 27855
Phone: 252-398-1236 • **Financial Aid Phone:** 252-398-6513
E-mail: admissions@chowan.edu
Fax: 252-398-1190 • **Website:** www.chowan.edu

This is a private school.

RATINGS

Admissions Selectivity Rating: 73   **Fire Safety Rating:** 70

STUDENTS AND FACULTY

Enrollment: 886. **Student Body:** 46% female, 54% male, 48% out-of-state. **Retention and Graduation:** 54% freshmen return for sophomore year. 18% freshmen graduate within 4 years. 26% freshmen graduate within 6 years. 5% grads go on to further study within 1 year. 2% grads pursue arts and sciences degrees. 1% grads pursue law degrees. 1% grads pursue business degrees. 1% grads pursue medical degrees. **Faculty:** 47 full-time faculty, 64% hold PhDs, 43% are members of minority groups, 11% are women. 0% of classes are taught by teaching assistants.

ACADEMICS

Degrees: associate, bachelor's, terminal associate. **Classes:** Most classes have fewer than 10 students. **Majors with Highest Enrollment:** Graphic Communications; Health Services/Allied Health/Health Sciences; Business/Commerce. **Special Study Options:** distance learning, double major, dual enrollment, honors program, independent study, internships, liberal arts/career combination, study abroad, teacher certification program. **Honors programs:** Honors College. **Disability Services:** Special programs offered to physically disabled students include note-taking services, reader services, tape recorders, tutors. **Career services:** internships. Career services highlights include Business Administration internships.

FACILITIES

Housing: special housing for disabled students, men's dorms, women's dorms. 80% of campus accessible to physically disabled. **Special Academic Facilities/Equipment:** Antiquities Room in Whitaker Library Ward Parlor in McDowell Columns Building Green Hall Art Gallery Daniel Hall Recital Hall **Computers:** Students can register for classes online. Administrative functions (other than registration) can be performed online.

CAMPUS LIFE

Activities: Choral groups, concert band, drama/theater, jazz band, literary magazine, music ensembles, pep band, student government, yearbook. 52 registered organizations, 5 honor societies, 2 religious organizations. 2 fraternities, 2 sororities. **Athletics (Intercollegiate):** *Men:* baseball, basketball, cheerleading, football, golf, soccer, tennis. *Women:* basketball, cheerleading, cross-country, golf, soccer, softball, tennis, volleyball. **On-Campus Highlights:** McDowell Columns Building (historic landmark), Jesse Helms Athletic Center, Jenkins Center for Health, Whitaker Library, McSweeney Computer Center.

ADMISSIONS

Freshman Academic Profile: Average high school GPA 2.6. 4% in top 10% of high school class, 35% in top 50% of high school class. 95% from public high schools. SAT Math middle 50% range 380-490. SAT Critical Reading middle 50% range 380-480. ACT middle 50% range 15-19. Minimum paper TOEFL 450. **Basis for Candidate Selection:** *Very important factors considered include:* academic GPA, rigor of secondary school record, standardized test scores. *Other factors considered include:* Class rank, application essay, recommendation(s), alumni/ae relation, character/personal qualities, extracurricular activities, interview, level of applicant's interest, talent/ability, volunteer work, work experience. **Freshman Admission Requirements:** High school diploma is required and GED is accepted. **Freshman Admission Statistics:** 2,385 applied, 61% admitted, 24% enrolled. **Transfer Admission Requirements:** High school transcript, college transcript(s), statement of good standing from prior institution(s). Minimum college GPA of 2.0 required. Lowest grade transferable C. **General Admission Information:** Application Fee $20. Notification on a rolling basis, beginning on or about 3/1. Nonfall registration accepted. Admission may be deferred for a maximum of 1 year. Credit and/or placement offered for CEEB Advanced Placement tests.

COSTS AND FINANCIAL AID

Annual tuition $15,800. Room and board $6,800. Required fees $240. Average book expense $885. **Required Forms and Deadlines:** FAFSA. **Notification of Awards:** Applicants will be notified of awards on a rolling basis beginning 3/1. **Types of Aid:** *Need-based scholarships/grants:* SEOG, state scholarships/grants, private scholarships, the school's own gift aid. *Loans:* Unsubsidized Stafford, PLUS, college/university loans from institutional funds, Alternative Loans. *Student Employment:* Federal Work-Study Program available. Institutional employment available. Highest amount earned per year from on-campus jobs $700. Off-campus job opportunities are fair. **Financial Aid Statistics:** 95% freshmen, 97% undergrads receive need-based scholarship or grant aid. 7% freshmen, 8% undergrads receive non-need-based scholarship or grant aid. 90% freshmen, 88% undergrads receive need-based self-help aid. 0% freshmen, 0% undergrads receive athletic scholarships. 86% freshmen, 86% undergrads receive any aid. 80% undergrads borrow to pay for school. **Criteria for awarding institutional aid:** *Non-need-based:* academics, leadership, music/drama, religious affiliation, state/district residency.

FACILITIES

Housing: men's dorms, women's dorms.

CAMPUS LIFE

Environment: Rural. **Activities:** Choral groups, dance, drama/theater, literary magazine, musical theater, student government, student newspaper, student-run film society, yearbook. 5 registered organizations, 4 religious organizations. **Athletics (Intercollegiate):** *Men:* baseball, basketball, soccer. *Women:* basketball, soccer, softball, volleyball. **On-Campus Highlights:** St. John the Evangelist Library, Chapel of Christ the King, Regina Coeli Building, John Paul II Student Center.

ADMISSIONS

Freshman Academic Profile: Average high school GPA 3.5. 40% in top 10% of high school class, 63% in top 25% of high school class, 100% in top 50% of high school class. 20% from public high schools. SAT Math middle 50% range 520-630. SAT Critical Reading middle 50% range 570-700. SAT Writing middle 50% range 560-690. ACT middle 50% range 23-28. Minimum paper TOEFL 550. **Basis for Candidate Selection:** *Very important factors considered include:* application essay, standardized test scores, character/personal qualities, level of applicant's interest, religious affiliation/commitment. *Important factors considered include:* recommendation(s), rigor of secondary school record, interview. *Other factors considered include:* Class rank, academic GPA, alumni/ae relation, extracurricular activities, first generation, talent/ability, volunteer work, work experience. **Freshman Admission Requirements:** High school diploma or equivalent is not required. **Freshman Admission Statistics:** 271 applied, 88% admitted, 52% enrolled. **Transfer Admission Requirements:** college transcript(s), essay or personal statement, Minimum college GPA of 2.8 required. Lowest grade transferable C. **General Admission Information:** Application Fee $25. Regular application deadline 3/1. Regular notification 4/1. Nonfall registration not accepted. Credit offered for CEEB Advanced Placement tests.

COSTS AND FINANCIAL AID

Annual tuition $16,290. Room and board $6,066. Required fees $450. Average book expense $450. **Required Forms and Deadlines:** Institution's own financial aid form. **Notification of Awards:** Applicants will be notified of awards on a rolling basis beginning 2/1. **Types of Aid:** *Need-based scholarships/grants:* private scholarships, the school's own gift aid. *Loans:* college/university loans from institutional funds. *Student Employment:* Institutional employment available. Highest amount earned per year from on-campus jobs $1,850. Off-campus job opportunities are fair. **Financial Aid Statistics:** 95% freshmen, 97% undergrads receive need-based scholarship or grant aid. 30% freshmen, 25% undergrads receive non-need-based scholarship or grant aid. 100% freshmen, 100% undergrads receive need-based self-help aid. 0% freshmen, 0% undergrads receive athletic scholarships. 80% freshmen, 65% undergrads receive any aid. 60% undergrads borrow to pay for school. **Criteria for awarding institutional aid:** *Non-need-based:* academics.

CHRISTENDOM COLLEGE

134 Christendom Drive, Front Royal, VA 22630
Phone: 540-636-2900 · **Financial Aid Phone:** 800-877-5456
E-mail: admissions@christendom.edu · **CEEB Code:** 5691
Fax: 540-636-1655 · **Website:** www.christendom.edu · **ACT Code:** 4339

This private school, affiliated with the Roman Catholic Church, was founded in 1977. It has a 100-acre campus.

RATINGS

Admissions Selectivity Rating: 87   **Fire Safety Rating:** 62

STUDENTS AND FACULTY

Enrollment: 421. **Student Body:** 54% female, 46% male, 78% out-of-state, 4% international (3 countries represented). Asian 2%, African American 0%, Caucasian 92%, Hispanic 2%, Native American <1%
Retention and Graduation: 91% freshmen return for sophomore year. 74% freshmen graduate within 4 years. 77% freshmen graduate within 6 years. 25% grads go on to further study within 1 year. 15% grads pursue arts and sciences degrees. 5% grads pursue law degrees. 5% grads pursue business degrees. **Faculty:** 23 full-time faculty, 78% hold PhDs, 9% are members of minority groups, 0% are women. 0% of classes are taught by teaching assistants.

ACADEMICS

Degrees: associate, bachelor's, master's. **Classes:** Most classes have 10–19 students. **Majors with Highest Enrollment:** Philosophy; Political Science and Government; History. **Special Study Options:** double major, honors program, independent study, internships, study abroad, Semester in Rome.

CHRISTIAN BROTHERS UNIVERSITY

Admissions, Box T-6, Memphis, TN 38104-5519
Phone: 901-321-3205 · **Financial Aid Phone:** 901-321-3306
E-mail: admissions@cbu.edu · **CEEB Code:** 1121
Fax: 901-321-3202 · **Website:** www.cbu.edu · **ACT Code:** 3952

This private school, affiliated with the Roman Catholic Church, was founded in 1871. It has a 75-acre campus.

RATINGS

Admissions Selectivity Rating: 88   **Fire Safety Rating:** 66

STUDENTS AND FACULTY

Enrollment: 1,295. **Student Body:** 55% female, 45% male, 20% out-of-state, 3% international (24 countries represented). Asian 5%, African American 32%, Caucasian 45%, Hispanic 7%, Native American <1%
Retention and Graduation: 83% freshmen return for sophomore year. 33% freshmen graduate within 4 years. 55% freshmen graduate within 6 years. **Faculty:** 100 full-time faculty, 81% hold PhDs, 41% are members of minority groups, 12% are women. 0% of classes are taught by teaching assistants.

ACADEMICS

Degrees: bachelor's, master's, post-bachelor's certificate. **Classes:** Most classes have 10–19 students. **Majors with Highest Enrollment:** Business Administration and Management; Psychology; Accounting. **Special Study Options:** Accelerated program, distance learning, double major, dual enrollment, honors program, independent study, internships, liberal arts/career combination, study abroad, teacher certification program. **Honors programs:** The Honors Program at Christian Brothers University is designed to serve the capacities and needs of students with proven academic abilities who seek a more intensive and challenging educational experience. Students accepted into the Honors Program will be allowed each semester to take at least one special-topics course offered only to a limited number of Honors students by an instructor carefully chosen for his or her teaching expertise. These Honors courses will explore important topics in depth, often through a multi-disciplinary approach, and while the pace and the workload will demand self-motivated students, the small size of each Honors class will insure ample group discussion and individual interaction with the instructor. Besides taking honors classes, members of the Honors Program will participate in various extra-curricular activities, including outings to cultural events and regional honors conferences. **Disability Services:** Special programs offered to physically disabled students include note-taking services, reader services, tape recorders, tutors. **Career services:** alumni services, career assessment, internships.

FACILITIES

Housing: men's dorms, women's dorms, apartments for single students, Theme HousingJuniors and seniors may live in on-campus apartments. All freshmen and sophomores whose permanent address is beyond a 30 mile radius are required to to live on campus. Some houses are available. A private quiet study facility is available. **Special Academic Facilities/Equipment:** Art exhibits, audiovisual lab, MAC graphics lab, engineering graphics lab, Ghandi institute for nonviolence, Facing History. **Computers:** 90% of classrooms, 100% of libraries, 100% of dining areas, 25% of common outdoor areas have wireless network access. Students can register for classes online. Administrative functions (other than registration) can be performed online.

CAMPUS LIFE

Environment: Metropolis. **Activities:** Choral groups, drama/theater, literary magazine, radio station, student government, yearbook, Campus Ministries. 37 registered organizations, 10 honor societies, 3 religious organizations. 5 fraternities, 6 sororities. **Athletics (Intercollegiate):** *Men:* baseball, basketball, cross-country, golf, soccer, tennis. *Women:* basketball, cross-country, golf, soccer, softball, tennis, volleyball. **On-Campus Highlights:** Thomas Center (cafeteria, coffee shop/grill gather, Canale Arena Gymnasium, Computer Center, Canale Outdoor Pool, Art Gallery in library. **Environmental Initiatives:** Building a new "green" dorm that has 90+ beds; Joining AASHE.

ADMISSIONS

Freshman Academic Profile: Average high school GPA 3.73. 28% in top 10% of high school class, 60% in top 25% of high school class, 93% in top 50% of high school class. 69% from public high schools. ACT middle 50% range 21-27. Minimum paper TOEFL 500. **Basis for Candidate Selection:** *Very important factors considered include:* academic GPA, rigor of secondary school record, standardized test scores. *Important factors considered include:* Class rank, application essay, recommendation(s), alumni/ae relation, extracurricular activities, interview, talent/ability, volunteer work, work experience. **Freshman Admission Requirements:** High school diploma is required and GED is accepted. **Freshman Admission Statistics:** 2,229 applied, 50% admitted, 32% enrolled. **Transfer Admission Requirements:** college transcript(s), Minimum college GPA of 2.5 required. Lowest grade transferable C. **General Admission Information:** Application Fee $25. Regular application deadline 8/1. Notification on a rolling basis, beginning on or about 12/1. Nonfall registration accepted. Admission may be deferred for a maximum of 1 year. Credit and/or placement offered for CEEB Advanced Placement tests.

COSTS AND FINANCIAL AID

Annual tuition $27,620. Room and board $6,520. Required fees $590. Average book expense $1,146. **Required Forms and Deadlines:** FAFSA. **Notification of Awards:** Applicants will be notified of awards on a rolling basis beginning 3/1. **Types of Aid:** *Need-based scholarships/grants:* Federal Pell, SEOG, state scholarships/grants, private scholarships, the school's own gift aid. *Loans:* Subsidized Stafford, Unsubsidized Stafford, PLUS, Federal Perkins, state loans. *Student Employment:* Federal Work-Study Program available. Off-campus job opportunities are good. **Financial Aid Statistics:** 99% freshmen, 98% undergrads receive need-based scholarship or grant aid. 49% freshmen, 52% undergrads receive non-need-based scholarship or grant aid. 71% freshmen, 72% undergrads receive need-based self-help aid. 8% freshmen, 7% undergrads receive athletic scholarships. 100% freshmen, 100% undergrads receive any aid. 64% undergrads borrow to pay for school. **Criteria for awarding institutional aid:** *Non-need-based:* academics, alumni affiliation, athletics, leadership, music/drama, religious affiliation, state/district residency.

CHRISTOPHER NEWPORT UNIVERSITY

1 Avenue of the Arts, Newport News, VA 23606-3072
Phone: 757-594-7015 • **Financial Aid Phone:** 757-594-7170
E-mail: admit@cnu.edu • **CEEB Code:** 5128
Fax: 757-594-7333 • **Website:** www.cnu.edu • **ACT Code:** 4345

This public school was founded in 1960. It has a 260-acre campus.

RATINGS

Admissions Selectivity Rating: 87   **Fire Safety Rating:** 95

STUDENTS AND FACULTY

Enrollment: 5,084. **Student Body:** 57% female, 43% male, 7% out-of-state, 0% international (31 countries represented). Asian 2%, African American 8%, Caucasian 75%, Hispanic 5%, Native American <1%
Retention and Graduation: 87% freshmen return for sophomore year. 55% freshmen graduate within 4 years. 68% freshmen graduate within 6 years. 27% grads go on to further study within 1 year. 13% grads pursue arts and sciences degrees. 7% grads pursue law degrees. 6% grads pursue business degrees. 3% grads pursue medical degrees. **Faculty:** 274 full-time faculty, 87% hold PhDs, 45% are members of minority groups, 12% are women. 0% of classes are taught by teaching assistants.

ACADEMICS

Degrees: bachelor's, master's. **Classes:** Most classes have 20–29 students. **Majors with Highest Enrollment:** Psychology; Biology/Biological Sciences; Speech Communication and Rhetoric. **Special Study Options:** cross-registration, double major, dual enrollment, honors program, independent study, internships, student-designed major, study abroad, Member of the Virginia Tidewater Consortium, Freshman Learning Communities. **Honors programs:** CNU Honors Program provides enriched educational experience for academically talented students motivated to participate in challenging courses and cultural and intellectual activities. **Disability Services:** Special programs offered to physically disabled students include note-taking services, tape recorders. **Career services:** career/job search classes, career assessment, internships. Career services highlights include a new initiative called the Freshman Academic Success Program (incorporation of study skills, major choices, and career opportunities).

FACILITIES

Housing: Coed dorms, fraternity/sorority housing, apartments for single students, Theme Housing 96% of campus accessible to physically disabled. **Special Academic Facilities/Equipment:** Falk Art Gallery, The Freeman Center, The Ferguson Center for the Arts, Trible Library houses the Mariners Museum Collection. **Computers:** 10% of classrooms, 10% of dorms, 100% of libraries, 100% of dining areas, 100% of student union, 100% of common outdoor areas have wireless network access. Students can register for classes online. Administrative functions (other than registration) can be performed online.

CAMPUS LIFE

Environment: City. **Activities:** Choral groups, concert band, dance, drama/theater, jazz band, literary magazine, marching band, music ensembles, musical theater, opera, pep band, radio station, student government, student newspaper, student-run film society, symphony orchestra, television station, Campus Ministries, International Student Organization, Model UN. 139 registered organizations, 23 honor societies, 12 religious organizations. 7 fraternities, 7 sororities. **Athletics (Intercollegiate):** *Men:* baseball, basketball, cheerleading, cross-country, football, golf, lacrosse, sailing, soccer, tennis, track/field (outdoor), track/field (indoor). *Women:* basketball, cheerleading, cross-country, field hockey, lacrosse, sailing, soccer, softball, tennis, track/field (outdoor), track/field (indoor), volleyball. **On-Campus Highlights:** Trible Library, Freeman Athletic Center, Ferguson Center for the Arts, McMurran Classroom Building, David Student Union, CNU Village for upper class students.

ADMISSIONS

Freshman Academic Profile: Average high school GPA 3.76. 18% in top 10% of high school class, 54% in top 25% of high school class, 91% in top 50% of high school class. SAT Math middle 50% range 530-620. SAT Critical Reading middle 50% range 530-630. SAT Writing middle 50% range 510-610. ACT middle 50% range 23-27. Minimum internet-based TOEFL 71. Minimum paper TOEFL 530. **Basis for Candidate Selection:** *Very important factors considered include:* academic GPA, rigor of secondary school record. *Important factors considered include:* recommendation(s), alumni/ae relation, first generation. *Other factors considered include:* application essay, standardized test scores, character/personal qualities, extracurricular activities, level of applicant's interest, talent/ability, volunteer work, work experience. **Freshman Admission Requirements:** High school diploma is required and GED is accepted. *Academic units required:* 4 English, 4 mathematics, 3 science, 3 foreign language, 3 history. **Freshman Admission Statistics:** 7,366 applied, 56% admitted, 30% enrolled. **Transfer Admission Requirements:** High school transcript, college transcript(s), statement of good standing from prior institution(s). Minimum college GPA of 3.0 required. Lowest grade transferable C. **General Admission Information:** Application Fee $45. Regular application deadline 3/1. Notification on a rolling basis, beginning on or about 12/1. Nonfall registration accepted. Admission may be deferred for a maximum of 12 Months. Credit and/or placement offered for CEEB Advanced Placement tests.

COSTS AND FINANCIAL AID

Required Forms and Deadlines: FAFSA. **Notification of Awards:** Applicants will be notified of awards on a rolling basis beginning 2/21. **Types of Aid:** *Need-based scholarships/grants:* Federal Pell, SEOG, state scholarships/grants, private scholarships, the school's own gift aid. *Loans:* Subsidized Stafford, Unsubsidized Stafford, PLUS. *Student Employment:* Federal Work-Study Program available. Institutional employment available. Off-campus job opportunities are good. **Financial Aid Statistics:** 64% freshmen, 63% undergrads receive need-based scholarship or grant aid. 42% freshmen, 29% undergrads receive non-need-based scholarship or grant aid. 77% freshmen, 83% undergrads receive need-based self-help aid. 0% freshmen, 0% undergrads receive athletic scholarships. 74% freshmen, 70% undergrads receive any aid. 63% undergrads borrow to pay for school. Average cumulative indebtedness $23,118. **Criteria for awarding institutional aid:** *Non-need-based:* academics, art, leadership, music/drama, state/district residency.

CIRCLEVILLE BIBLE COLLEGE

1476 Lancaster Pike, Circleville, OH 43113-9487
Phone: 740-477-7701
E-mail: enroll@biblecollege.edu
Fax: 740-477-7755 · **Website:** www.biblecollege.edu · **ACT Code:** 3030

This private school was founded in 1948.

RATINGS

Admissions Selectivity Rating: 75   **Fire Safety Rating:** 60*

STUDENTS AND FACULTY

Enrollment: 349. **Student Body:** 51% female, 49% male, 24% out-of-state, 0% international. Asian 1%, African American 6%, Caucasian 91%, Hispanic 2%, Native American 1%
Retention and Graduation: 58% freshmen return for sophomore year. 20% freshmen graduate within 6 years. **Faculty:** 14 full-time faculty, 64% hold PhDs, 14% are members of minority groups.

ACADEMICS

Degrees: associate, bachelor's, terminal associate, transfer associate. **Classes:** Most classes have 10–19 students. **Special Study Options:** double major, independent study, internships, liberal arts/career combination, student-designed major. **Disability Services:** Special programs offered to physically disabled students include note-taking services, reader services, tape recorders, tutors. **Career services:**

FACILITIES

Housing: men's dorms, special housing for international students, women's dorms, apartments for married students.

CAMPUS LIFE

Environment: Rural. **Activities:** Choral groups, drama/theater, music ensembles, student government, yearbook. **Athletics (Intercollegiate):** *Men:* baseball, basketball. *Women:* basketball, volleyball.

ADMISSIONS

Freshman Academic Profile: Average high school GPA 2.93. 21% in top 10% of high school class, 24% in top 25% of high school class, 32% in top 50% of high school class. ACT middle 50% range 17–23. **Basis for Candidate Selection:** *Very important factors considered include:* Class rank, recommendation(s), rigor of secondary school record, standardized test scores, religious affiliation/commitment. *Important factors considered include:* application essay, character/personal qualities. *Other factors considered include:* interview. **Freshman Admission Requirements:** High school diploma is required and GED is accepted. **Freshman Admission Statistics:** 138 applied, 69% admitted, 75% enrolled. **Transfer Admission Requirements:** High school transcript, college transcript(s), essay or personal statement, standardized test scores, statement of good standing from prior institution(s). Minimum college GPA of 2.0 required. Lowest grade transferable C. **General Admission Information:** Application Fee $25. Nonfall registration accepted. Admission may be deferred for a maximum of one year.

COSTS AND FINANCIAL AID

Average book expense $500. **Required Forms and Deadlines:** FAFSA, Institution's own financial aid form, CSS/Financial Aid PROFILE. **Notification of Awards:** Applicants will be notified of awards on or about 6/1. *Student Employment:* Federal Work-Study Program available. Off-campus job opportunities are excellent. **Financial Aid Statistics:** 28% freshmen, 32% undergrads receive need-based scholarship or grant aid. 28% freshmen, 32% undergrads receive non-need-based scholarship or grant aid. 28% freshmen, 32% undergrads receive need-based self-help aid. 0% freshmen, 0% undergrads receive athletic scholarships.

THE CITADEL, THE MILITARY COLLEGE OF SOUTH CAROLINA

171 Moultrie Street, Charleston, SC 29409
Phone: 843-953-5230 · **Financial Aid Phone:** 843-953-5187
E-mail: admissions@citadel.edu
Fax: 843-953-7036 · **Website:** www.citadel.edu · **ACT Code:** 3838

This public school was founded in 1842. It has a 300-acre campus.

RATINGS

Admissions Selectivity Rating: 80   **Fire Safety Rating:** 99

STUDENTS AND FACULTY

Enrollment: 2,688. **Student Body:** 8% female, 92% male, 42% out-of-state, 1% international (12 countries represented). Asian 2%, African American 8%, Caucasian 77%, Hispanic 7%, Native American 1%
Retention and Graduation: 86% freshmen return for sophomore year. **Faculty:** 188 full-time faculty, 94% hold PhDs, 34% are members of minority groups, 15% are women. 0% of classes are taught by teaching assistants.

ACADEMICS

Degrees: bachelor's, master's, post-master's certificate. **Classes:** Most classes have 20–29 students. Most lab/discussion sessions have 10–19 students. **Majors with Highest Enrollment:** Business Administration and Management; Criminal Justice/Law Enforcement Administration; Political Science and Government. **Special Study Options:** cooperative education program, distance learning, double major, English as a Second Language (ESL), honors program, independent study, internships, study abroad, teacher certification program. **Honors programs:** The Citadel's Honors Program is a specially designed educational experience meeting the needs of students with an outstanding record of academic achievement and a sense of intellectual adventure. While pursuing any one of seventeen degree programs offered by The Citadel, Honors Students take a series of Core Curriculum Honors courses—for example, studies based in literature and writing, history, and mathematics—concentrated in their first two years, and an occasional Honors Seminar in their third and fourth years. For the qualified student, advantages of the Honors Program are clear: special program of pre-professional counseling, small classes, discussion-style teaching, tutorial session, special curriculum, fellow honors students, student advisory committee, honors faculty, special diploma seal and transcript, and emphasis on leadership. **Career services:** Alumni network, alumni services, career/job search classes, career assessment, internships.

FACILITIES

Housing: Coed dorms. **Special Academic Facilities/Equipment:** Archives and Museum **Computers:** 5% of classrooms, 20% of dorms, 100% of libraries, 75% of student union, 10% of common outdoor areas have wireless network access. Students can register for classes online. Administrative functions (other than registration) can be performed online.

CAMPUS LIFE

Environment: City. **Activities:** Choral groups, concert band, jazz band, literary magazine, marching band, pep band, student government, student newspaper, yearbook, Campus Ministries. 79 registered organizations, 12 honor societies, 16 religious organizations. **Athletics (Intercollegiate):** *Men:* baseball, basketball, cross-country, football, riflery, tennis, track/field (outdoor), track/field (indoor), wrestling. *Women:* cross-country, golf, riflery, soccer, track/field (outdoor), track/field (indoor), volleyball. **On-Campus Highlights:** Summerall Chapel, Mark Clark Hall, Daniel Library, Citadel Museum, McAlister Field House. **Environmental Initiatives:** $5 Million Energy Performance Contract Expanding Energy Management System to nearly 100% of campus. Expanding recycling and waste reduction to 100% of campus.

ADMISSIONS

Freshman Academic Profile: Average high school GPA 3.59. 12% in top 10% of high school class, 33% in top 25% of high school class, 74% in top 50% of

high school class. SAT Math middle 50% range 500-600. SAT Critical Reading middle 50% range 490-590. ACT middle 50% range 20-25. Minimum internet-based TOEFL 79. Minimum paper TOEFL 550. **Basis for Candidate Selection:** *Very important factors considered include:* academic GPA, standardized test scores, level of applicant's interest. *Important factors considered include:* rigor of secondary school record, character/personal qualities, extracurricular activities, state residency, talent/ability. *Other factors considered include:* Class rank, recommendation(s), alumni/ae relation, first generation, geographical residence, interview, volunteer work. **Freshman Admission Requirements:** High school diploma is required and GED is accepted. *Academic units required:* 4 English, 3 mathematics, 3 science, (3 science labs), 2 foreign language, 2 social studies, 1 history, 4 academic electives, 1 PE or ROTC. **Freshman Admission Statistics:** 2,625 applied, 76% admitted, 31% enrolled. **Transfer Admission Requirements:** High school transcript, college transcript(s), standardized test scores, statement of good standing from prior institution(s). Minimum college GPA of 2.0 required. Lowest grade transferable C. **General Admission Information:** Application Fee $40. Early decision application deadline 10/26. Notification on a rolling basis, beginning on or about 7/15. Nonfall registration not accepted. Credit and/or placement offered for CEEB Advanced Placement tests.

COSTS AND FINANCIAL AID
Annual. Annual out-of-state tuition $30,706. Room and board $6,381. Required fees $1,470. Average book expense $7,425. **Required Forms and Deadlines:** FAFSA. **Notification of Awards:** Applicants will be notified of awards on a rolling basis beginning 4/1. **Types of Aid:** *Need-based scholarships/grants:* Federal Pell, SEOG, state scholarships/grants, the school's own gift aid. *Loans:* Direct Subsidized Stafford, Direct Unsubsidized Stafford, Direct PLUS, Federal Perkins. *Student Employment:* Federal Work-Study Program available. **Financial Aid Statistics:** 79% freshmen, 78% undergrads receive need-based scholarship or grant aid. 14% freshmen, 15% undergrads receive non-need-based scholarship or grant aid. 68% freshmen, 71% undergrads receive need-based self-help aid. 12% freshmen, 11% undergrads receive athletic scholarships. 83% freshmen, 85% undergrads receive any aid. 65% undergrads borrow to pay for school. Average cumulative indebtedness $22,759. **Criteria for awarding institutional aid:** *Non-need-based:* academics, alumni affiliation, athletics, leadership, state/district residency.

CITY UNIVERSITY

11900 NE First Street, Bellevue, WA 98005
Phone: 425-637-1010 · **Financial Aid Phone:** 425-709-5251
E-mail: info@cityu.edu
Fax: 425-709-5361 · **Website:** www.cityu.edu

This private school was founded in 1973. It has a 5-acre campus.

RATINGS
Admissions Selectivity Rating: 60*   **Fire Safety Rating:** 60*

STUDENTS AND FACULTY
Enrollment: 1,848. **Student Body:** 55% female, 45% male, 0% out-of-state, 5% international. Asian 6%, African American 5%, Caucasian 66%, Hispanic 3%, Native American 1%. **Faculty:** 36 full-time faculty, 25% hold PhDs, 47% are members of minority groups, 19% are women.

ACADEMICS
Degrees: associate, bachelor's, certificate, master's, transfer associate. **Majors with Highest Enrollment:** Computer and Information Sciences and Support Services; Elementary Education and Teaching; Business Administration and Management. **Special Study Options:** Accelerated program, distance learning, double major, dual enrollment, English as a Second Language (ESL), internships, student-designed major, teacher certification program, weekend college. **Career services:**

FACILITIES
Housing: Computers: Students can register for classes online. Administrative functions (other than registration) can be performed online.

CAMPUS LIFE
Environment: Metropolis. **Activities:** Choral groups, drama/theater, music ensembles, student government, student newspaper.

ADMISSIONS
Freshman Academic Profile: Minimum paper TOEFL 540. **Freshman Admission Requirements:** High school diploma is required and GED is accepted. **Freshman Admission Statistics:** 15 applied, 100% admitted, 307% enrolled. **Transfer Admission Requirements:** High school transcript, college transcript(s), Lowest grade transferable C. **General Admission Information:**

Application Fee $80. Nonfall registration accepted. Admission may be deferred for a maximum of Undetermined.

COSTS AND FINANCIAL AID
Annual tuition $9,320. Required fees $120. Average book expense $500. *Student Employment:* Federal Work-Study Program available. **Financial Aid Statistics:** 27% freshmen, 29% undergrads receive any aid.

CITY UNIVERSITY OF NEW YORK— BARUCH COLLEGE

Best 380

One Bernard Baruch Way, New York, NY 10010
Phone: 646-312-1400 · **Financial Aid Phone:** 646-312-1390
E-mail: admissions@baruch.cuny.edu · **CEEB Code:** 2034
Fax: 646-312-1361 · **Website:** www.baruch.cuny.edu

This public school was founded in 1968.

RATINGS
Admissions Selectivity Rating: 92   **Fire Safety Rating:** 60*

STUDENTS AND FACULTY
Enrollment: 14,420. **Student Body:** 48% female, 52% male, 4% out-of-state, 12% international (168 countries represented). Asian 33%, African American 9%, Caucasian 25%, Hispanic 19%, Native American <1% **Retention and Graduation:** 35% freshmen graduate within 4 years. **Faculty:** 516 full-time faculty, 89% hold PhDs, 39% are members of minority groups, 29% are women. 1% of classes are taught by teaching assistants.

ACADEMICS
Degrees: bachelor's, master's, post-master's certificate. **Classes:** Most classes have 20–29 students. Most lab/discussion sessions have 20–29 students. **Majors with Highest Enrollment:** Accounting; Finance. **Special Study Options:** Accelerated program, cross-registration, distance learning, double major, English as a Second Language (ESL), exchange student program (domestic), honors program, independent study, internships, liberal arts/career combination, student-designed major, study abroad. **Honors programs:** CUNY Honors Program Combined degree programs: BA/MA. **Disability Services:** Special programs offered to physically disabled students include note-taking services, reader services, tape recorders, tutors. **Career services:** Alumni network, alumni services, career/job search classes, career assessment, internships. Career services highlights include The Lawrence N. Field Center for Entrepreneurship, the jewel of our programs. The Field Center is a model of entrepreneurship education built around the collaboration of an institution of higher education, government, and the private sector. Faculty and students from Baruch's Zicklin School of Business, Baruch's Small Business Development Center (SBDC) Business Advisors, alumni and volunteers are brought together to support the entrepreneurial endeavors of start-up and established businesses and the college's constituents. The Center's vision reflects the College's overarching principles of research, teaching, and service. Specifically, are founding vision was to: Develop a strong, research-based, academic program; Build a strong program at the BBA and MBA level; Create an outreach program that made the College''s expertise available to operating small businesses and aspiring entrepreneurs. Accomplishing these goals requires that we serve our constituencies via various **Activities:** Faculty—through research opportunities, interfacing and learning from real-world entrepreneurs, and course instruction; Students—through courses, internship opportunities, exposure to networks, and other programs such as the business plan competition; Entrepreneurs—through training, counseling, access to capital, and exposure to networks. The Field Center recently celebrated its 15 year anniversary which comes at the heel of the continuing generosity of Lawrence N. Field ('52) and his family. In 2008 the Eris and Larry Field Foundation endowed the Field Center with a $10 million gift (previously Larry Field endowed the Center with a $3 million gift). In 2008 and worldwide, approximately 2,300 out of 3,000 institutions of higher education teach entrepreneurship. Of these institutions, only 100 institutions have significant endowments devoted to Entrepreneurship. Therefore, our recent $10 million gift from Lawrence N. Field garners us an elite national presence within this select group of institutions with endowed programs. Among these 100 institutions, there are only a few which have a $50 million or greater endowment and about a dozen which have endowments at $30 million. This Lawrence N. Field gift places us among the top 5 percent of institutions globally with significant endowments devoted to Entrepreneurship.

FACILITIES

Housing: 100% of campus accessible to physically disabled. **Special Academic Facilities/Equipment:** Art gallery, Subotnik Financial Services Center and Wasserman Trading Floor. **Computers:** 25% of classrooms, 100% of libraries, 100% of dining areas, 100% of student union, 100% of common outdoor areas have wireless network access. Students can register for classes online. Administrative functions (other than registration) can be performed online.

CAMPUS LIFE

Environment: Metropolis. **Activities:** Choral groups, dance, drama/theater, literary magazine, musical theater, radio station, student government, student newspaper, yearbook, Campus Ministries, Model UN 172 registered organizations, 9 honor societies, 7 religious organizations, 9 fraternities, 7 sororities. **Athletics (Intercollegiate):** *Men:* baseball, basketball, cross-country, soccer, swimming, tennis, volleyball. *Women:* basketball, cheerleading, cross-country, softball, swimming, tennis, volleyball. **On-Campus Highlights:** Student Club Area- Vertical Campus Build, NewMan Library, Lobby- 23 St. Building, Food Court- Vertical Campus Building, College Fitness Center-Vertical Campus.

ADMISSIONS

Freshman Academic Profile: Average high school GPA 3.3. 48% in top 10% of high school class, 78% in top 25% of high school class, 95% in top 50% of high school class. 90% from public high schools. SAT Math middle 50% range 590-690. SAT Critical Reading middle 50% range 530-640. Minimum internet-based TOEFL 80. Minimum paper TOEFL 550. **Basis for Candidate Selection:** *Very important factors considered include:* academic GPA, rigor of secondary school record, standardized test scores. *Important factors considered include:* application essay, recommendation(s). *Other factors considered include:* Class rank, alumni/ae relation, character/personal qualities, extracurricular activities, interview, talent/ability, work experience. **Freshman Admission Requirements:** High school diploma is required and GED is accepted. *Academic units required:* 4 English, 3 mathematics, 2 science, (2 science labs), 2 foreign language, 4 social studies, 0 history, 0 academic electives, 0 Fine Arts. **Freshman Admission Statistics:** 19,768 applied, 28% admitted, 23% enrolled. **Transfer Admission Requirements:** High school transcript, college transcript(s), statement of good standing from prior institution(s). Minimum college GPA of 2.7 required. Lowest grade transferable C. **General Admission Information:** Application Fee $65. Early decision application deadline 12/13. Regular application deadline 2/1. Regular notification 5/15. Notification on a rolling basis, beginning on or about 2/1. Nonfall registration accepted. Admission may be deferred for a maximum of Six months. Credit and/or placement offered for CEEB Advanced Placement tests.

COSTS AND FINANCIAL AID

Annual in-state tuition $6,330. Annual out-of-state tuition $16,800. Average book expense $1,304. **Required Forms and Deadlines:** FAFSA, State aid form. **Notification of Awards:** Applicants will be notified of awards on a rolling basis beginning 4/1. **Types of Aid:** *Need-based scholarships/grants:* Federal Pell, SEOG, state scholarships/grants, the school's own gift aid, City merit scholarships. *Loans:* Direct Subsidized Stafford, Direct Unsubsidized Stafford, Direct PLUS, Federal Perkins. *Student Employment:* Federal Work-Study Program available. Institutional employment available. Off-campus job opportunities are excellent. **Financial Aid Statistics:** 100% freshmen, 99% undergrads receive need-based scholarship or grant aid. 6% freshmen, 3% undergrads receive non-need-based scholarship or grant aid. 22% freshmen, 34% undergrads receive need-based self-help aid. 0% freshmen, 0% undergrads receive athletic scholarships. 67% freshmen, 53% undergrads receive any aid. 20% undergrads borrow to pay for school. Average cumulative indebtedness $8,871. **Criteria for awarding institutional aid:** *Non-need-based:* academics, alumni affiliation, state/district residency.

CITY UNIVERSITY OF NEW YORK—BOROUGH OF MANHATTAN COMMUNITY COLLEGE

199 Chambers Street, New York, NY 10007-1097
Phone: 212-220-1265
E-mail: ebarrios@bmcc.cuny.edu
Fax: 212-346-8110

This public school was founded in 1964. It has a 5-acre campus.

RATINGS

Admissions Selectivity Rating: 60*   **Fire Safety Rating:** 60*

STUDENTS AND FACULTY

Enrollment: 16,732. **Student Body:** 64% female, 36% male, 12% international. Asian 10%, African American 37%, Caucasian 11%, Hispanic 30%, Native American <1%

Retention and Graduation: 40% grads go on to further study within 1 year. **Faculty:** 315 full-time faculty.

ACADEMICS

Degrees: associate, certificate, terminal associate, transfer associate. **Special Study Options:** cooperative education program, distance learning, English as a Second Language (ESL), honors program, independent study, internships, study abroad, weekend college. **Disability Services:** Special programs offered to physically disabled students include note-taking services, reader services, tape recorders, tutors. **Career services:** alumni services, career/job search classes, career assessment, internships.

FACILITIES

Housing: special housing for disabled students, men's dorms, special housing for international students, women's dorms, apartments for single students. 100% of campus accessible to physically disabled. **Computers:** Students can register for classes online.

CAMPUS LIFE

Activities: Choral groups, concert band, dance, drama/theater, jazz band, music ensembles, pep band, student government, student newspaper, yearbook.

ADMISSIONS

Freshman Admission Requirements: High school diploma is required and GED is accepted. **Freshman Admission Statistics:** 6,374 applied, 85% admitted, 60% enrolled. **Transfer Admission Requirements:** college transcript(s). **General Admission Information:** Application Fee $40. Nonfall registration not accepted.

COSTS AND FINANCIAL AID

Annual in-state tuition $2,500. Annual out-of-state tuition $3,076. Required fees $80. Average book expense $350. *Student Employment:* Federal Work-Study Program available. Institutional employment available. Off-campus job opportunities are good.

CITY UNIVERSITY OF NEW YORK— BROOKLYN COLLEGE

Best 380

2900 Bedford Avenue, Brooklyn, NY 11210
Phone: 718-951-5001 · **Financial Aid Phone:** 718-951-51 · **CEEB Code:**
Fax: 718-951-4506 · **Website:** www.brooklyn.cuny.edu · **ACT Code:** 20169

This public school was founded in 1930. It has a 26-acre campus.

RATINGS

Admissions Selectivity Rating: 87   **Fire Safety Rating:** 60*

STUDENTS AND FACULTY

Enrollment: 12,922. **Student Body:** 58% female, 42% male, 2% out-of-state, 3% international. Asian 18%, African American 22%, Caucasian 35%, Hispanic 20%, Native American <1%
Retention and Graduation: 24% freshmen graduate within 4 years. 50% freshmen graduate within 6 years. **Faculty:** 556 full-time faculty, 94% hold PhDs, 46% are members of minority groups, 23% are women.

ACADEMICS

Degrees: bachelor's, certificate, master's, post-bachelor's certificate, post-master's certificate. **Classes:** Most classes have 20–29 students. **Majors with Highest Enrollment:** Business Administration and Management; Psychology; Accounting. **Special Study Options:** distance learning, double major, dual enrollment, English as a Second Language (ESL), honors program, independent study, internships, study abroad, teacher certification program, weekend college. **Honors programs:** See the URL below for more information: http://www.brooklyn.cuny.edu/pub/1654.htm Combined degree programs: BA/MD. **Disability Services:** Special programs offered to physically disabled students include note-taking services, reader services, tutors. **Career services:** Alumni network, alumni services, career/job search classes, career assessment, internships.

FACILITIES

Housing: 100% of campus accessible to physically disabled. **Special Academic Facilities/Equipment:** Art museum. language lab, TV studios, speech clinic, research centers and institutes, paricle accelerator. **Computers:** 2% of classrooms, 90% of libraries, 100% of dining areas, 75% of student union, 75% of common outdoor areas have wireless network access. Students can register for classes online. Administrative functions (other than registration) can be performed online.

CAMPUS LIFE

Environment: Metropolis. **Activities:** dance, drama/theater, literary magazine, music ensembles, musical theater, radio station, student government, student newspaper, television station, yearbook, International Student Organization 171 registered organizations, 7 honor societies, 7 fraternities, 9 sororities. **Athletics (Intercollegiate):** *Men:* basketball, cross-country, soccer, tennis, track/field (outdoor), track/field (indoor), volleyball. *Women:* basketball, cross-country, softball, tennis, track/field (outdoor), track/field (indoor), volleyball. **On-Campus Highlights:** Library, Student Center, Lily Pond, Library Café, Cafeteria, Dining Hall, Magner Center, James Hall. **Environmental Initiatives:** Reduce material consumption/waste; Increase awareness/education; Reduce energy use.

ADMISSIONS

Freshman Academic Profile: Average high school GPA 3.28. 18% in top 10% of high school class, 49% in top 25% of high school class, 76% in top 50% of high school class. SAT Math 50% range 500-600. SAT Critical Reading middle 50% range 470-560. Minimum paper TOEFL 500. **Basis for Candidate Selection:** *Very important factors considered include:* academic GPA, rigor of secondary school record, standardized test scores. **Freshman Admission Requirements:** High school diploma is required and GED is accepted. **Freshman Admission Statistics:** 20,260 applied, 35% admitted, 19% enrolled. **Transfer Admission Requirements:** college transcript(s), Minimum college GPA of 2.3 required. Lowest grade transferable C-. **General Admission Information:** Application Fee $65. Notification on a rolling basis, beginning on or about 2/1. Nonfall registration accepted. Credit and/or placement offered for CEEB Advanced Placement tests.

COSTS AND FINANCIAL AID

Annual in-state tuition $6,330. Required fees $505. **Required Forms and Deadlines:** FAFSA. **Notification of Awards:** Applicants will be notified of awards on a rolling basis beginning 5/1. **Types of Aid:** *Need-based scholarships/grants:* Federal Pell, SEOG, state scholarships/grants, private scholarships, the school's own gift aid. *Loans:* Direct Subsidized Stafford, Direct Unsubsidized Stafford, Direct PLUS, Federal Perkins. *Student Employment:* Federal Work-Study Program available. Institutional employment available. Off-campus job opportunities are excellent. **Financial Aid Statistics:** 70% freshmen, 81% undergrads receive need-based scholarship or grant aid. 24% freshmen, 23% undergrads receive non-need-based scholarship or grant aid. 68% freshmen, 75% undergrads receive need-based self-help aid. 0% freshmen, 0% undergrads receive athletic scholarships. 45% undergrads borrow to pay for school. Average cumulative indebtedness $9,100. **Criteria for awarding institutional aid:** *Non-need-based:* academics, art, leadership, music/drama, state/district residency.

CITY UNIVERSITY OF NEW YORK— CITY COLLEGE

160 Convent Avenue, Wille Admin. Bldg., New York, NY 10031
Phone: 212 650 6977 · **Financial Aid Phone:** 212 650 5824
E-mail: admissions@ccny.cuny.edu · **CEEB Code:** 2083
Fax: 212 650 6417 · **Website:** www.ccny.cuny.edu · **ACT Code:** 2950

This public school was founded in 1847. It has a 36-acre campus.

RATINGS

Admissions Selectivity Rating: 82   **Fire Safety Rating:** 96

STUDENTS AND FACULTY

Enrollment: 12,171. **Student Body:** 51% female, 49% male, 1% out-of-state, 7% international (100 countries represented). Asian 25%, African American 19%, Caucasian 19%, Hispanic 30%, Native American <1%
Retention and Graduation: 86% freshmen return for sophomore year. 10% freshmen graduate within 4 years. 42% freshmen graduate within 6 years. 18% grads go on to further study within 1 year. 1% grads pursue law degrees. 2% grads pursue business degrees. 27% grads pursue medical degrees. **Faculty:** 527 full-time faculty, 81% hold PhDs, 42% are members of minority groups, 19% are women.

ACADEMICS

Degrees: bachelor's, master's, post-master's certificate. **Classes:** Most classes have 20–29 students. **Majors with Highest Enrollment:** Communication and Media Studies; Mechanical Engineering/Mechanical Technology/Technician; Psychology. **Special Study Options:** Accelerated program, cross-registration, double major, English as a Second Language (ESL), honors program, independent study, internships, study abroad, teacher certification program, Adult program called The Center for Worker Education which offers a evening and weekend program in liberal arts. **Honors programs:** CUNY Macauley College and City College Honors Program. Combined degree programs: BA/MD, BA/MA. **Disability Services:** Special programs offered to physically disabled students include note-taking services, reader services, tape recorders, tutors. **Career services:** Alumni network, alumni services, career/job search classes, career assessment, internships.

FACILITIES

Housing: The Towers new residence hall with apartment style quarter. **Special Academic Facilities/Equipment:** Planetarium, NYC Structural Biological Center, Aaron Davis Hall/Harlem Stage Gatehouse, Landmarked Gothic orignaial campus buildings. **Computers:** 100% of classrooms, 100% of libraries, 100% of dining areas, 100% of common outdoor areas have wireless network access. Students can register for classes online. Administrative functions (other than registration) can be performed online.

CAMPUS LIFE

Environment: Metropolis. **Activities:** Choral groups, concert band, dance, drama/theater, jazz band, literary magazine, radio station, student government, student newspaper, student-run film society, yearbook, International Student Organization, Model UN. 145 registered organizations, 8 religious organizations. 2 fraternities, 1 sorority. **Athletics (Intercollegiate):** *Men:* baseball, basketball, cross-country, soccer, tennis, track/field (outdoor), track/field (indoor), volleyball. *Women:* basketball, fencing, soccer, tennis, track/field (outdoor), track/field (indoor), volleyball. **On-Campus Highlights:** NAC Rotunda and Plaza, Spitzer School of Archtiecture, Wingate Hall Athletic Center, North Campus Quad in warm weather, The Towers—Residence Hall. **Environmental Initiatives:** Signed on to ACUPCC and NYC Mayor's Campus 30in10 Challenge to reduce GHG emissions; Task Force to place sustainability at forefront in all operations, outreach and educational mission; Undergraduate and Graduate programs in sustainability, interdisciplinary with Science, Engineering, Architecture and Economics.

ADMISSIONS

Freshman Academic Profile: 85% from public high schools. SAT Math middle 50% range 520-640. SAT Critical Reading middle 50% range 460-580. SAT Writing middle 50% range 450-580. Minimum internet-based TOEFL 61. Minimum paper TOEFL 500. **Basis for Candidate Selection:** *Very important factors considered include:* academic GPA, rigor of secondary school record. *Important factors considered include:* standardized test scores. *Other factors considered include:* application essay, recommendation(s). **Freshman Admission Requirements:** High school diploma is required and GED is accepted. **Freshman Admission Statistics:** 25,445 applied, 38% admitted, 15% enrolled. **Transfer Admission Requirements:** college transcript(s), Minimum college GPA of 2.0 required. Lowest grade transferable c. **General Admission Information:** Application Fee $65. Notification on a rolling basis, beginning on or about 2/1. Nonfall registration accepted. Credit offered for CEEB Advanced Placement tests.

COSTS AND FINANCIAL AID

Annual in-state tuition $6,030. Annual out-of-state tuition $16,050. Room and board $13,848. Required fees $442. Average book expense $1,404. **Required Forms and Deadlines:** FAFSA, State aid form. **Notification of Awards:** Applicants will be notified of awards on a rolling basis beginning 4/1. **Types of Aid:** *Need-based scholarships/grants:* Federal Pell, SEOG, state scholarships/grants, the school's own gift aid. *Loans:* Direct Subsidized Stafford, Direct Unsubsidized Stafford, Direct PLUS. *Student Employment:* Federal Work-Study Program available. Institutional employment available. Highest amount earned per year from on-campus jobs $7,200. Off-campus job opportunities are fair. **Financial Aid Statistics:** 91% freshmen, 97% undergrads receive need-based scholarship or grant aid. 52% freshmen, 12% undergrads receive non-need-based scholarship or grant aid. 44% freshmen, 61% undergrads receive need-based self-help aid. 0% freshmen, 0% undergrads receive athletic scholarships. 80% freshmen, 79% undergrads receive any aid. 21% undergrads borrow to pay for school. Average cumulative indebtedness $16,635. **Criteria for awarding institutional aid:** *Non-need-based:* academics, alumni affiliation, art, leadership, minority status, music/drama.

See page 1028.

CITY UNIVERSITY OF NEW YORK— THE COLLEGE OF STATEN ISLAND

2800 Victory Boulevard, Staten Island, NY 10314
Phone: 718-982-2010 · **Financial Aid Phone:** 718-982-2030
E-mail: admissions@csi.cuny.edu · **CEEB Code:** 2778
Fax: 718-982-2500 · **Website:** www.csi.cuny.edu · **ACT Code:** 2950

This public school was founded in 1955. It has a 204-acre campus.

RATINGS
Admissions Selectivity Rating: 68   **Fire Safety Rating:** 83

STUDENTS AND FACULTY
Enrollment: 12,942. **Student Body:** 56% female, 44% male, 1% out-of-state, 2% international (99 countries represented). Asian 12%, African American 15%, Caucasian 54%, Hispanic 17%, Native American <1%
Retention and Graduation: 80% freshmen return for sophomore year. 21% freshmen graduate within 4 years. 41% freshmen graduate within 6 years.
Faculty: 352 full-time faculty, 89% hold PhDs, 46% are members of minority groups, 27% are women.

ACADEMICS
Degrees: associate, bachelor's, certificate, master's, post-master's certificate, terminal associate. **Classes:** Most classes have 30-39 students. Most lab/discussion sessions have 30-39 students. **Majors with Highest Enrollment:** Psychology; Business/Commerce; Registered Nursing/Registered Nurse.
Special Study Options: Accelerated program, cooperative education program, cross-registration, distance learning, double major, dual enrollment, English as a Second Language (ESL), exchange student program (domestic), honors program, independent study, internships, liberal arts/career combination, study abroad, teacher certification program, weekend college. **Honors programs:** CSI is one of seven campuses within CUNY that participates in the William E. Macaulay Honors College. **Disability Services:** Special programs offered to physically disabled students include note-taking services, reader services, tape recorders, tutors. **Career services:** alumni services, career/job search classes, career assessment, internships. Career services highlights include internships and the On Campus Recruitment Program.

FACILITIES
Housing: 95% of campus accessible to physically disabled. **Special Academic Facilities/Equipment:** Astrophysical Observatory, Archives and Special Collections, Center for the Arts, Center for Engineered Polymeric Materials, Center for Environmental Science, Center for Developmental Neuroscience and Developmental Disabilities, and the CSI Art Gallery **Computers:** 97% of classrooms, 100% of libraries, 100% of dining areas, 100% of student union, 100% of common outdoor areas have wireless network access. Students can register for classes online. Administrative functions (other than registration) can be performed online.

CAMPUS LIFE
Environment: Metropolis. **Activities:** Choral groups, dance, drama/theater, jazz band, literary magazine, music ensembles, radio station, student government, student newspaper, student-run film society, yearbook, Campus Ministries, International Student Organization. 47 registered organizations, 2 honor societies, 4 religious organizations. **Athletics (Intercollegiate):** Men: baseball, basketball, cross-country, diving, soccer, swimming, tennis. Women: basketball, cross-country, diving, soccer, softball, swimming, tennis, volleyball.
On-Campus Highlights: Campus Center Rotunda, Center for the Performing Arts, Library, Sports and Recreation Center, Campus Center Game Room, The Student Lounges are also a popular site on campus for students.

ADMISSIONS
Freshman Academic Profile: Average high school GPA 3.02. 79% from public high schools. SAT Math middle 50% range 470-570. SAT Critical Reading middle 50% range 440-530. SAT Writing middle 50% range 430-530. Minimum internet-based TOEFL 45. Minimum paper TOEFL 450. **Basis for Candidate Selection:** *Very important factors considered include:* rigor of secondary school record. *Important factors considered include:* academic GPA, standardized test scores. **Freshman Admission Requirements:** High school diploma is required and GED is accepted. *Academic units required:* 4 English, 2 mathematics, 2 science, 2 foreign language, 4 social studies. **Freshman Admission Statistics:** 13,084 applied, 100% admitted, 19% enrolled. **Transfer Admission Requirements:** college transcript(s), Minimum college GPA of 2.0 required. Lowest grade transferable C. **General Admission Information:** Application Fee $65. Notification on a rolling basis, beginning on or about 12/15. Nonfall registration accepted. Admission may be deferred for a maximum of 1 semester. Credit and/or placement offered for CEEB Advanced Placement tests.

COSTS AND FINANCIAL AID
Required Forms and Deadlines: FAFSA, State aid form. **Types of Aid:** *Need-based scholarships/grants:* Federal Pell, SEOG, state scholarships/grants, private scholarships, the school's own gift aid. *Loans:* Direct Subsidized Stafford, Direct Unsubsidized Stafford, Direct PLUS, Federal Perkins, Alternative Proprietary Loans. *Student Employment:* Federal Work-Study Program available. Institutional employment available. Off-campus job opportunities are good. **Financial Aid Statistics:** 92% freshmen, 91% undergrads receive need-based scholarship or grant aid. 82% freshmen, 79% undergrads receive non-need-based scholarship or grant aid. 38% freshmen, 35% undergrads receive need-based self-help aid. 0% freshmen, 0% undergrads receive athletic scholarships. Criteriafor awarding institutional aid: *Non-need-based:* academics, art, leadership, minority status, music/drama, state/district residency.

CITY UNIVERSITY OF NEW YORK— HUNTER COLLEGE

Best 380

695 Park Ave, Room N203, New York, NY 10065
Phone: 212-772-4490 · **Financial Aid Phone:** 212-772-4820
E-mail: admissions@hunter.cuny.edu · **CEEB Code:** 2301
Fax: 212-650-3472 · **Website:** www.hunter.cuny.edu

This public school was founded in 1870.

RATINGS
Admissions Selectivity Rating: 83   **Fire Safety Rating:** 96

STUDENTS AND FACULTY
Enrollment: 15,776. **Student Body:** 65% female, 35% male, 3% out-of-state, 6% international (151 countries represented). Asian 27%, African American 11%, Caucasian 36%, Hispanic 20%, Native American <1%
Retention and Graduation: 22% freshmen graduate within 4 years. 52% freshmen graduate within 6 years. **Faculty:** 728 full-time faculty, 80% hold PhDs, 52% are members of minority groups, 18% are women.

ACADEMICS
Degrees: bachelor's, master's, post-master's certificate. **Classes:** Most classes have 20–29 students. **Majors with Highest Enrollment:** Psychology; English Language and Literature; Chemistry. **Special Study Options:** Accelerated program, cross-registration, distance learning, double major, dual enrollment, exchange student program (domestic), honors program, independent study, internships, liberal arts/career combination, student-designed major, study abroad, teacher certification program. Combined degree programs: BA/MA, BA/MS. **Disability Services:** Special programs offered to physically disabled students include note-taking services, reader services, tape recorders, tutors. **Career services:** Alumni network, alumni services, career/job search classes, internships

FACILITIES
Housing: Coed dorms. 100% of campus accessible to physically disabled. **Special Academic Facilities/Equipment:** Art Gallery, theatre, geology club, on-campus elementary and secondary schools. **Computers:** 70% of classrooms, have wireless network access. Students can register for classes online.

CAMPUS LIFE
Environment: Metropolis. **Activities:** Choral groups, concert band, dance, drama/theater, jazz band, literary magazine, music ensembles, musical theater, radio station, student government, student newspaper, student-run film society, symphony orchestra, television station, yearbook. 150 registered organizations, 20 honor societies, 2 fraternities, 2 sororities. **Athletics (Intercollegiate):** Men: basketball, cross-country, fencing, soccer, tennis, track/field (outdoor), track/field (indoor), volleyball, wrestling. Women: basketball, cross-country, diving, fencing, softball, swimming, tennis, track/field (outdoor), track/field (indoor), volleyball. **On-Campus Highlights:** Over 100 Campus Clubs, CARSI Geography Lab, Television Studio, Learning Center and Computer Lab, Sports Complex. **Environmental Initiatives:** Hunter has an extensive program for recycling paper, metal, glass, plastic, e-waste, and household batteries. This program is continuously being expanded. A major library renovation of approximately 15,000 GSF at Hunters main Upper East Side campus is incorporating sustainable elements, such as window glazing and an efficient HVAC system, and Phase I of the project will seek LEED certification. Other projects include

white roofs that reduce building heat load and urban heat island effects and a 3-kW photovoltaic rooftop installation that serves as a teaching tool. Under CUNY leadership, the college examines energy data to develop solutions that manage usage more efficiently. Such measures include a pilot program for convection heating, extensive building HVAC retrocommissioning, and timers for air handling units and lab compressors.

ADMISSIONS
Freshman Academic Profile: 70% from public high schools. SAT Math middle 50% range 540-640. SAT Critical Reading middle 50% range 520-610. Minimum paper TOEFL 500. **Basis for Candidate Selection:** *Very important factors considered include:* application essay, academic GPA, rigor of secondary school record, standardized test scores. **Freshman Admission Requirements:** High school diploma is required and GED is accepted. *Academic units required:* 2 English, 2 mathematics, 1 science, (1 science labs). **Freshman Admission Statistics:** 31,100 applied, 35% admitted, 19% enrolled. **Transfer Admission Requirements:** college transcript(s), Minimum college GPA of 2.3 required. Lowest grade transferable C. **General Admission Information:** Application Fee $65. Regular application deadline 3/15. Notification on a rolling basis, beginning on or about 1/15. Nonfall registration accepted. Credit and/or placement offered for CEEB Advanced Placement tests.

COSTS AND FINANCIAL AID
Annual in-state tuition $6,330. Annual out-of-state tuition $13,440. Room and board $8,655. Required fees $450. **Required Forms and Deadlines:** FAFSA, State aid form. **Notification of Awards:** Applicants will be notified of awards on a rolling basis beginning 5/15. **Types of Aid:** *Need-based scholarships/grants:* Federal Pell, state scholarships/grants, the school's own gift aid. *Loans:* Direct Subsidized Stafford, Direct Unsubsidized Stafford, Direct PLUS, Federal Perkins, state loans, college/university loans from institutional fundsCUNY Student Assistance Program(CUSTA), Aide for Part-Time-Study (APTS), SEEK. *Student Employment:* Federal Work-Study Program available. Institutional employment available. Off-campus job opportunities are fair. **Financial Aid Statistics:** 89% freshmen, 82% undergrads receive need-based scholarship or grant aid. 82% freshmen, 13% undergrads receive non-need-based scholarship or grant aid. 21% freshmen, 22% undergrads receive need-based self-help aid. 0% freshmen, 0% undergrads receive athletic scholarships. 91% freshmen, 94% undergrads receive any aid. 71% undergrads borrow to pay for school. Average cumulative indebtedness $7,500. **Criteria for awarding institutional aid:** *Non-need-based:* academics.

CITY UNIVERSITY OF NEW YORK— JOHN JAY COLLEGE OF CRIMINAL JUSTICE

899 Tenth Avenue, New York, NY 10019
Phone: 212-237-8869
E-mail: admissions@jjay.cuny.edu • **CEEB Code:** 2115
Fax: 212-237-8777 • **Website:** www.jjay.cuny.edu

This public school was founded in 1964.

RATINGS
Admissions Selectivity Rating: 60*   **Fire Safety Rating:** 60*

STUDENTS AND FACULTY
Enrollment: 12,224. **Student Body:** 150 countries represented.

ACADEMICS
Degrees: associate, bachelor's, certificate, master's, transfer associate. **Special Study Options:** cooperative education program, distance learning, English as a Second Language (ESL), exchange student program (domestic), study abroad, weekend college, Undergrads may take grad level classes. **Off-Campus Study:** Albany Internship Program. Co-Op Programs: Public Service. Combined degree programs: BA/MA. **Disability Services:** Special programs offered to physically disabled students include note-taking services, reader services, tape recorders, tutors. **Career services:** alumni services, career/job search classes, career assessment

FACILITIES
Housing: List of possible housing arrangements can be obtained from Student Activities at 212-237-8698. **Special Academic Facilities/Equipment:** Criminal justice center, center for violence/human survival, toxicology research/training center, fire science institute, institute for criminal justice ethics, institute for the study of genocide, and institute on alcohol/substance abuse. **Computers:** Students can register for classes online.

CAMPUS LIFE
Environment: Metropolis. **Activities:** Choral groups, dance, drama/theater, musical theater, radio station, student government, student newspaper, yearbook. **Athletics (Intercollegiate):** *Men:* basketball, cross-country, riflery, soccer. *Women:* cross-country, riflery, softball, tennis, volleyball.

ADMISSIONS
Freshman Academic Profile: 63% from public high schools. Minimum paper TOEFL 500. **Freshman Admission Requirements:** High school diploma is required and GED is accepted.High school diploma is required and GED is not accepted. Minimum college GPA of 2.0 required. Lowest grade transferable C. **General Admission Information:** Application Fee $50. Regular application deadline 3/15. Nonfall registration accepted. Credit offered for CEEB Advanced Placement tests.

COSTS AND FINANCIAL AID
Average book expense $500. **Required Forms and Deadlines:** FAFSA. **Types of Aid:** *Need-based scholarships/grants:* Federal Pell, SEOG, state scholarships/grants, private scholarships, the school's own gift aid. *Loans:* Subsidized Stafford, Unsubsidized Stafford, PLUS, Federal Perkins, college/university loans from institutional funds. *Student Employment:* Federal Work-Study Program available. Institutional employment available. Highest amount earned per year from on-campus jobs $2,500. Off-campus job opportunities are good.

CITY UNIVERSITY OF NEW YORK— KINGSBOROUGH COMMUNITY COLLEGE

2001 Oriental Blvd., Brooklyn, NY 11235
Phone: 718-368-4600 • **Financial Aid Phone:** 718-368-4644
E-mail: info@kbcc.cuny.edu
Fax: 718-368-5356

This is a public school.

RATINGS
Admissions Selectivity Rating: 60*   **Fire Safety Rating:** 60*

STUDENTS AND FACULTY
Enrollment: 14,997. **Student Body:** 56% female, 44% male, 4% international (137 countries represented). Asian 12%, African American 35%, Caucasian 33%, Hispanic 16%, Native American <1%
Faculty: 354 full-time faculty, 54% hold PhDs, 52% are members of minority groups, 26% are women. 0% of classes are taught by teaching assistants.

ACADEMICS
Degrees: associate, certificate, terminal associate, transfer associate. **Classes:** Most classes have 20–29 students. **Majors with Highest Enrollment:** Liberal Arts and Sciences/Liberal Studies; Business/Commerce; Biology/Biological Sciences. **Special Study Options:** Accelerated program, cross-registration, dual enrollment, English as a Second Language (ESL), honors program, independent study, internships, My Turn Program for senior citizens. New Start Program for students academically dismissed from 4-year institutions.

ADMISSIONS
Freshman Academic Profile: Minimum paper TOEFL 475. **Basis for Candidate Selection:** *Very important factors considered include:* interview. *Important factors considered include:* application essay. *Other factors considered include:* Class rank, recommendation(s), rigor of secondary school record, standardized test scores, alumni/ae relation, character/personal qualities, extracurricular activities, geographical residence, racial/ethnic status, religious affiliation/commitment, state residency, talent/ability, volunteer work, work experience. **Freshman Admission Requirements:** High school diploma or equivalent is not required. **Transfer Admission Requirements:** college transcript(s), essay or personal statement, interview, Lowest grade transferable C. **General Admission Information:** Application Fee $35. Nonfall registration accepted.

COSTS AND FINANCIAL AID
Annual in-state tuition $3,610. Annual out-of-state tuition $7,200. Required fees $350. **Notification of Awards:** Applicants will be notified of awards on or about 7/1. **Types of Aid:** *Need-based scholarships/grants:* Federal Pell, the school's own gift aid. *Loans:* Direct Subsidized Stafford, Direct Unsubsidized Stafford, Direct PLUS.

CITY UNIVERSITY OF NEW YORK— LEHMAN COLLEGE

250 Bedford Park Boulevard West, Bronx, NY 10468
Phone: 718-960-8000 · **Financial Aid Phone:** 718-960-8545
E-mail: wilkes@alpha.lehman.cuny.edu · **CEEB Code:** 2950
Fax: 718-960-8712

This public school was founded in 1968. It has a 38-acre campus.

RATINGS

Admissions Selectivity Rating: 84   **Fire Safety Rating:** 60*

STUDENTS AND FACULTY

Enrollment: 8,236. **Student Body:** 71% female, 29% male, 1% out-of-state, 5% international (123 countries represented). Asian 4%, African American 32%, Caucasian 10%, Hispanic 49%, Native American <1%
Retention and Graduation: 77% freshmen return for sophomore year. 12% freshmen graduate within 4 years. 33% freshmen graduate within 6 years. **Faculty:** 368 full-time faculty, 75% hold PhDs, 52% are members of minority groups, 27% are women.

ACADEMICS

Degrees: bachelor's, certificate, diploma, master's. **Classes:** Most classes have 20–29 students. **Majors with Highest Enrollment:** Social Work; Sociology; Registered Nursing/Registered Nurse. **Special Study Options:** Accelerated program, cooperative education program, cross-registration, distance learning, double major, dual enrollment, English as a Second Language (ESL), exchange student program (domestic), honors program, independent study, internships, student-designed major, study abroad, teacher certification program, weekend college, bilingual liberal arts (first 2 years may be taken in Spanish), professional writing concentration, 3-2 engineering program with City College. **Honors programs:** Lehman Scholars Program. Students receive full tuition, stipends, an expense account to use for academically enriching experiences and a laptop computer. Combined degree programs: BA/MA. **Disability Services:** Special programs offered to physically disabled students include note-taking services, reader services, tape recorders, tutors.

FACILITIES

Housing: 80% of campus accessible to physically disabled. **Special Academic Facilities/Equipment:** Art gallery, concert hall, sports complex. **Computers:** Students can register for classes online. Administrative functions (other than registration) can be performed online.

CAMPUS LIFE

Environment: Metropolis. **Activities:** Choral groups, concert band, dance, drama/theater, jazz band, literary magazine, music ensembles, musical theater, opera, radio station, student government, student newspaper, student-run film society, symphony orchestra, television station, yearbook, International Student Organization 3 honor societies, 1 religious organization. 1 fraternity, 1 sorority. **Athletics (Intercollegiate):** *Men:* badminton, baseball, basketball, cross-country, diving, swimming, tennis, track/field (outdoor), volleyball. *Women:* badminton, basketball, cross-country, diving, softball, swimming, tennis, track/field (outdoor), volleyball. **On-Campus Highlights:** APEX athletic facility, Cyber Café, Art Gallery, Concert Hall, Information Technology Center.

ADMISSIONS

Freshman Academic Profile: Average high school GPA 2.7. 74% from public high schools. SAT Math middle 50% range 400-500. SAT Critical Reading middle 50% range 400-490. Minimum paper TOEFL 500. **Basis for Candidate Selection:** *Very important factors considered include:* rigor of secondary school record, standardized test scores. *Important factors considered include:* academic GPA. *Other factors considered include:* application essay, recommendation(s), extracurricular activities, interview, talent/ability. **Freshman Admission Requirements:** High school diploma is required and GED is accepted. *Academic units required:* 4 English, 2 mathematics, 2 science, (1 science labs), 2 foreign language, 1 social studies, 1 history. **Freshman Admission Statistics:** 14,155 applied, 32% admitted, 58% enrolled. **Transfer Admission Requirements:** college transcript(s), Minimum college GPA of 2 required. Lowest grade transferable C. **General Admission Information:** Application Fee $65. Regular registration deadline 8/15. Nonfall registration accepted. Admission may be deferred for a maximum of 1 semester. Credit offered for CEEB Advanced Placement tests.

COSTS AND FINANCIAL AID

Annual in-state tuition $4,000. Annual out-of-state tuition $10,800. Required fees $290. Average book expense $938. **Required Forms and Deadlines:** FAFSA, State aid form. **Notification of Awards:** Applicants will be notified of awards on a rolling basis beginning 3/1. **Types of Aid:** *Need-based scholarships/ grants:* Federal Pell, SEOG, state scholarships/grants, private scholarships, the school's own gift aid, MARC,NBRS. *Loans:* Direct Subsidized Stafford, Direct Unsubsidized Stafford, Direct PLUS, Federal Perkins, state loans, college/ university loans from institutional funds. *Student Employment:* Federal Work-Study Program available. Institutional employment available. Off-campus job opportunities are excellent. **Financial Aid Statistics:** 88% freshmen, 90% undergrads receive need-based scholarship or grant aid. 42% freshmen, 15% undergrads receive non-need-based scholarship or grant aid. 19% freshmen, 44% undergrads receive need-based self-help aid. 0% freshmen, 0% undergrads receive athletic scholarships. 83% freshmen, 80% undergrads receive any aid. 34% undergrads borrow to pay for school. Average cumulative indebtedness $13,700. **Criteria for awarding institutional aid:** *Non-need-based:* academics.

CITY UNIVERSITY OF NEW YORK— MEDGAR EVERS COLLEGE

1665 Bedford Avenue, Brooklyn, NY 11225
Phone: 718-270-6024 · **Financial Aid Phone:** 718-270-6139
E-mail: applytomec@mec.cuny.edu
Fax: 718-270-6411

This public school was founded in 1969. It has a 7-acre campus.

RATINGS

Admissions Selectivity Rating: 65   **Fire Safety Rating:** 60*

STUDENTS AND FACULTY

Enrollment: 6,582. **Student Body:** 74% female, 26% male, 0% out-of-state, 1% international. Asian 2%, African American 85%, Caucasian 1%, Hispanic 9%, Native American <1%
Retention and Graduation: 20% freshmen graduate within 6 years. **Faculty:** 177 full-time faculty, 59% hold PhDs, 47% are members of minority groups, 81% are women. 0% of classes are taught by teaching assistants.

ACADEMICS

Degrees: associate, bachelor's, certificate. **Classes:** Most classes have 30-39 students. Most lab/discussion sessions have 10–19 students. **Majors with Highest Enrollment:** Liberal Arts and Sciences/Liberal Studies; Business Administration and Management; Biology/Biological Sciences. **Special Study Options:** cross-registration, distance learning, English as a Second Language (ESL), honors program, independent study, internships, study abroad, teacher certification program. **Disability Services:** Special programs offered to physically disabled students include note-taking services, reader services, tape recorders, tutors. **Career services:** alumni services, career/job search classes, career assessment, internships. Career services highlights include Career Job Search classes, Business Etiquette Series, Interviewing Skills.

FACILITIES

Housing: 100% of campus accessible to physically disabled. **Computers:** 90% of classrooms, 100% of libraries, have wireless network access. Students can register for classes online. Administrative functions (other than registration) can be performed online.

CAMPUS LIFE

Environment: Metropolis. **Activities:** Choral groups, dance, drama/theater, jazz band, literary magazine, musical theater, radio station, student government, student newspaper, television station, yearbook, International Student Organization. 32 registered organizations, 4 honor societies, 2 religious organizations. **Athletics (Intercollegiate):** *Men:* basketball, cross-country, soccer, swimming, track/field (outdoor), track/field (indoor), volleyball. *Women:* basketball, cheerleading, cross-country, soccer, softball, swimming, tennis, track/field (outdoor), track/field (indoor), volleyball. **On-Campus Highlights:** Amphitheater, NASA Space Center Lab, Library, Departments, New Building.

ADMISSIONS

Freshman Academic Profile: SAT Math middle 50% range 340-440. SAT Critical Reading middle 50% range 350-430. SAT Writing middle 50% range 340-430. Minimum paper TOEFL 475. **Basis for Candidate Selection:** *Other factors considered include:* academic GPA, rigor of secondary school record, standardized test scores. **Freshman Admission Requirements:** High school diploma is required and GED is accepted. **Freshman Admission Statistics:** 8,042 applied, 100% admitted, 15% enrolled. **Transfer Admission Requirements:** college transcript(s), Minimum college GPA of 2.0 required. Lowest grade transferable C. **General Admission Information:** Application Fee $65. Nonfall registration accepted. Admission may be deferred for a maximum of one semester.

COSTS AND FINANCIAL AID
Annual out-of-state tuition $13,800. Required fees $302. Average book expense $1,179. **Required Forms and Deadlines:** FAFSA, State aid form. **Notification of Awards:** Applicants will be notified of awards on a rolling basis beginning 5/1. **Types of Aid:** *Need-based scholarships/grants:* Federal Pell, SEOG, state scholarships/grants. *Loans:* Direct Subsidized Stafford, Direct Unsubsidized Stafford, Direct PLUS, Federal Perkins. *Student Employment:* Federal Work-Study Program available. Institutional employment available. Highest amount earned per year from on-campus jobs $1,300. Off-campus job opportunities are good. **Financial Aid Statistics:** 0% freshmen, 0% undergrads receive athletic scholarships. Criteria for awarding institutional aid: *Non-need-based:* academics, leadership.

CITY UNIVERSITY OF NEW YORK— NEW YORK CITY COLLEGE OF TECHNOLOGY

300 Jay Street, Brooklyn, NY 11201
Phone: 718-260-5500 · **Financial Aid Phone:** 718-260-5700
E-mail: admissions@citytech.cuny.edu · **CEEB Code:** 2550
Fax: 718-260-5504 · **Website:** http://www.citytech.cuny.edu/ · **ACT Code:** 2950

This public school was founded in 1946. It has a 3-acre campus.

RATINGS
Admissions Selectivity Rating: 61   **Fire Safety Rating:** 60*

STUDENTS AND FACULTY
Enrollment: 15,917. **Student Body:** 44% female, 56% male, 1% out-of-state, 5% international (106 countries represented). Asian 18%, African American 32%, Caucasian 13%, Hispanic 31%, Native American <1%
Retention and Graduation: 77% freshmen return for sophomore year. 3% freshmen graduate within 4 years. 24% freshmen graduate within 6 years.
Faculty: 433 full-time faculty, 63% hold PhDs, 48% are members of minority groups, 45% are women. 0% of classes are taught by teaching assistants.

ACADEMICS
Degrees: associate, bachelor's, certificate. **Classes:** Most classes have 20–29 students. Most lab/discussion sessions have 20–29 students. **Majors with Highest Enrollment:** Information Science/Studies; Design and Visual Communications; Hospitality Administration/Management. **Special Study Options:** distance learning, dual enrollment, English as a Second Language (ESL), honors program, independent study, internships, study abroad, teacher certification program, Bridge programs to higher education or careers in engineering technology, alternate format program for those out of high school 5 years with or without diploma. **Disability Services:** Special programs offered to physically disabled students include note-taking services, reader services, tape recorders, tutors. **Career services:** career assessment, internships.

FACILITIES
Housing: Some housing avilable at nearby university. 100% of campus accessible to physically disabled. **Computers:** Students can register for classes online. Administrative functions (other than registration) can be performed online.

CAMPUS LIFE
Environment: Metropolis. **Activities:** dance, drama/theater, musical theater, student government, student newspaper. 60 registered organizations. **Athletics (Intercollegiate):** *Men:* basketball, tennis, track/field (outdoor). *Women:* basketball, tennis, track/field (outdoor). **Environmental Initiatives:** reducing the amount of waste produced by our purchasing and procurement system.

ADMISSIONS
Freshman Academic Profile: Minimum internet-based TOEFL 61. Minimum paper TOEFL 500. **Basis for Candidate Selection:** *Important factors considered include:* academic GPA, rigor of secondary school record. *Other factors considered include:* Class rank, application essay, recommendation(s), standardized test scores. **Freshman Admission Requirements:** High school diploma is required and GED is accepted. *Academic units required:* 4 English, 3 mathematics, 2 science, (2 science labs), 2 foreign language, 3 social studies, 1 academic electives, 1 Fine Arts. **Freshman Admission Statistics:** 17,465 applied, 71% admitted, 27% enrolled. **Transfer Admission Requirements:** High school transcript, college transcript(s), statement of good standing from prior institution(s). Minimum college GPA of 2.0 required. Lowest grade transferable C. **General Admission Information:** Application Fee $65. Notification on a rolling basis, beginning on or about 1/15. Nonfall registration accepted. Admission may be deferred for a maximum of 1 semester. Credit and/or placement offered for CEEB Advanced Placement tests.

COSTS AND FINANCIAL AID
Annual in-state tuition $5,730. Annual out-of-state tuition $15,300. Required fees $339. **Required Forms and Deadlines:** FAFSA, State aid form. **Types of Aid:** *Need-based scholarships/grants:* Federal Pell, SEOG, state scholarships/grants, Federal Nursing Scholarships. *Loans:* Direct Subsidized Stafford, Direct Unsubsidized Stafford, Direct PLUS, Federal Perkins. *Student Employment:* Federal Work-Study Program available. Institutional employment available. Off-campus job opportunities are fair. **Criteria for awarding institutional aid:** *Non-need-based:* state/district residency.

CITY UNIVERSITY OF NEW YORK— QUEENSBOROUGH COMMUNITY COLLEGE

222-05 56th Ave, A-210, Queens, NY 11364
Phone: 718-631-6236
E-mail: wyarde@qcc.cuny.edu · **CEEB Code:** 2751
Fax: 718-281-5208

This public school was founded in 1967. It has a 34-acre campus.

RATINGS
Admissions Selectivity Rating: 60*   **Fire Safety Rating:** 60*

STUDENTS AND FACULTY
Enrollment: 10,955. **Student Body:** 57% female, 43% male, 1% out-of-state, 12% international (132 countries represented). Asian 18%, African American 25%, Caucasian 24%, Hispanic 21%, Native American <1%
Faculty: 289 full-time faculty. 0% of classes are taught by teaching assistants.

ACADEMICS
Degrees: associate, certificate, terminal associate, transfer associate. **Special Study Options:** cooperative education program, distance learning, double major, dual enrollment, English as a Second Language (ESL), honors program, independent study, internships, liberal arts/career combination, study abroad, weekend college, external education for homebound students, honors program for high school seniors. **Honors programs:** Honors program that has smaller class size and enriched course material and activities. **Disability Services:** Special programs offered to physically disabled students include note-taking services, reader services, tape recorders, tutors. **Career services:** alumni services, career/job search classes, career assessment, internships.

FACILITIES
Housing: Coed dorms, special housing for disabled students, men's dorms, special housing for international students, women's dorms, fraternity/sorority housing, apartments for married students, cooperative housing, apartments for single students. 85% of campus accessible to physically disabled. **Special Academic Facilities/Equipment:** Oakland Art Gallery, Performing Arts Center, The Holocaust Center. **Computers:** Students can register for classes online. Administrative functions (other than registration) can be performed online.

CAMPUS LIFE
Environment: Metropolis. **Activities:** 37 registered organizations, 3 honor societies. **Athletics (Intercollegiate):** *Men:* baseball, basketball, cross-country, soccer, swimming, tennis, track/field (indoor), volleyball. *Women:* basketball, cross-country, softball, swimming, tennis, volleyball. **On-Campus Highlights:** Holecaust Resources Center and Archives, Student Union, Instructional Support Services Center, Registration Center, Library.

ADMISSIONS
Freshman Academic Profile:10% in top 50% of high school class. 80% from public high schools. Minimum paper TOEFL 475. **Basis for Candidate Selection:** *Other factors considered include:* academic GPA, standardized test scores. **Freshman Admission Requirements:** High school diploma is required and GED is accepted. **Freshman Admission Statistics:** 7,471 applied, 99% admitted, 35% enrolled. **Transfer Admission Requirements:** High school transcript, college transcript(s), Minimum college GPA of 2.0 required. Lowest grade transferable D. **General Admission Information:** Application Fee $50. Notification on a rolling basis, beginning on or about 12/1. Nonfall registration accepted. Credit offered for CEEB Advanced Placement tests.

COSTS AND FINANCIAL AID
Required Forms and Deadlines: FAFSA, Institution's own financial aid form. **Notification of Awards:** Applicants will be notified of awards on a rolling basis beginning 7/15. **Types of Aid:** *Need-based scholarships/grants:* Federal Pell, SEOG, state scholarships/grants, the school's own gift aid. *Loans:* Direct Subsidized Stafford, Direct Unsubsidized Stafford, Direct PLUS. *Student Employment:* Federal Work-Study Program available. Institutional employment available. Off-campus job opportunities are good. **Financial Aid Statistics:**

CITY UNIVERSITY OF NEW YORK— QUEENS COLLEGE

Best 380

6530 Kissena Blvd, Flushing, NY 11367
Phone: 718-997-5600 · **Financial Aid Phone:** 718-997-5123
E-mail: vincent.angrisani@qc.cuny.edu · **CEEB Code:** 2750
Fax: 718-997-5617 · **Website:** www.qc.cuny.edu · **ACT Code:** 20173

This public school was founded in 1937. It has a 76-acre campus.

RATINGS

Admissions Selectivity Rating: 82   **Fire Safety Rating:** 96

STUDENTS AND FACULTY

Enrollment: 14,842. **Student Body:** 55% female, 45% male, 1% out-of-state, 5% international (176 countries represented). Asian 28%, African American 9%, Caucasian 39%, Hispanic 20%, Native American <1%
Retention and Graduation: 27% freshmen graduate within 4 years. 56% freshmen graduate within 6 years. 35% grads go on to further study within 1 year. 10% grads pursue arts and sciences degrees. 2% grads pursue law degrees. 1% grads pursue business degrees. 1% grads pursue medical degrees. **Faculty:** 606 full-time faculty, 89% hold PhDs, 44% are are members of minority groups, 22% are women. 0.5% of classes are taught by teaching assistants.

ACADEMICS

Degrees: bachelor's, master's, post-bachelor's certificate, post-master's certificate. **Classes:** Most classes have 20-29 students. **Majors with Highest Enrollment:** Accounting; Psychology; Economics. **Special Study Options:** Accelerated program, cross-registration, double major, dual enrollment, English as a Second Language (ESL), honors program, independent study, internships, liberal arts/career combination, student-designed major, study abroad, teacher certification program, weekend college, Courses offered through Blackboard. **Honors programs:** Queens College participates in the CUNY Honors College—a highly selective program that offers a challenging curriculum and a full tuition scholarship plus other financial support. The program accepts first-time freshmen in the fall semester only. Combined degree programs: BA/MA. **Disability Services:** Special programs offered to physically disabled students include note-taking services, reader services, tape recorders, tutors. **Career services:** career/job search classes, career assessment, internships Career services highlights include Career Fair—over 70 employers from various fields (Accounting, Banking, Finance, Human Services, Publishing, Media, Government, Technology, etc) come to the campus to interview and meet with students.

FACILITIES

Housing: Coed dorms 100% of campus accessible to physically diasbled. **Special Academic Facilities/Equipment:** Godwin-Ternbach Museum, Louis Armstrong House Museum & Archieves, Colden Auditorium, Kupferberg Center for the Performing Arts, Art Library **Computers:** 100% of classrooms, 100% of dorms, 100% of libraries, 100% of dining areas, 100% of student union, 100% of common outdoor areas have wireless network access. Students can register for classes online. Administrative functions (other than registration) can be performed online.

CAMPUS LIFE

Environment: Metropolis. **Activities:** Choral groups, concert band, dance, drama/theater, jazz band, literary magazine, music ensembles, musical theater, radio station, student government, student newspaper, student-run film society, symphony orchestra, television station, yearbook, International Student Organization 114. registered organizations, 5 honor societies, 12 religious organizations. 4 fraternities, 3 sororities. **Athletics (Intercollegiate):** *Men:* baseball, basketball, cross-country, diving, soccer, swimming, tennis, track/field (outdoor), water polo. *Women:* basketball, cross-country, diving, fencing, lacrosse, soccer, softball, swimming, tennis, track/field (outdoor), volleyball, water polo.
On-Campus Highlights: Rosenthal Library, Student Union, Athletic Center, Dining Hall, Classrooms and Laboratory Facilities, Cafes around campus. **Environmental Initiatives:** Mechanical upgrade 27M for the new Science Building that will signfically reduce the energy consumption Facade and windows replacement of 13 floor tower plus the mechanical system replacement/rehab/upgrade that will tremendously reduce the energy consumption The design and construction of a Central chiller plant for the the 87 Acre Campus that will initially supply HVAC to 3 of the science buildings to be expanded to cover the entire 87 acres, 47 buildings that will reduce the campus energy consumption.

ADMISSIONS

Freshman Academic Profile: 75% from public high schools. SAT Math middle 50% range 540-610. SAT Critical Reading middle 50% range 480-570. SAT Writing middle 50% range 460-570. Minimum internet-based TOEFL 62. Minimum paper TOEFL 500. **Basis for Candidate Selection:** *Very important factors considered include:* academic GPA, rigor of secondary school record, standardized test scores. **Freshman Admission Requirements:** High school diploma is required and GED is accepted. *Academic units required:* 4 English, 3 mathematics, 2 science, (2 science labs), 3 foreign language, 4 social studies. **Freshman Admission Statistics:** 18,289 applied, 40% admitted, 21% enrolled. **Transfer Admission Requirements:** High school transcript, college transcript(s), standardized test scores, Minimum college GPA of 2.25 required. Lowest grade transferable 2. **General Admission Information:** Application Fee $65. Notification on a rolling basis, beginning on or about 1/15. Nonfall registration accepted. Admission may be deferred for a maximum of 1 semester. Credit offered for CEEB Advanced Placement tests.

COSTS AND FINANCIAL AID

Annual in-state tuition $6,030. Annual out-of-state tuition $16,050. Room and board $14,168. Required fees $608. Average book expense $1,304. **Required Forms and Deadlines:** FAFSA, Institution's own financial aid form, State aid form. **Notification of Awards:** Applicants will be notified of awards on a rolling basis beginning 3/1. **Types of Aid:** *Need-based scholarships/grants:* Federal Pell, SEOG, state scholarships/grants, private scholarships, the school's own gift aid. *Loans:* Direct Subsidized Stafford, Direct Unsubsidized Stafford, Direct PLUS, Federal Perkins. *Student Employment:* Federal Work-Study Program available. Institutional employment available. Off-campus job opportunities are good. **Financial Aid Statistics:** 86% freshmen, 85% undergrads receive need-based scholarship or grant aid. 4% freshmen, 3% undergrads receive non-need-based scholarship or grant aid. 13% freshmen, 23% undergrads receive need-based self-help aid. 2% freshmen, 1% undergrads receive athletic scholarships. 62% freshmen, 48% undergrads receive any aid. 15% undergrads borrow to pay for school. Average cumulative indebtedness $11,000. **Criteria for awarding institutional aid:** *Non-need-based:* academics, athletics.

CITY UNIVERSITY OF NEW YORK— YORK COLLEGE

94-20 Guy R Brewer Boulevard, Jamaica, NY 11451
Phone: 718-262-2165
E-mail: admissions@york.cuny.edu · **CEEB Code:** 2992
Fax: 718-262-2601 · **Website:** www.york.cuny.edu · **ACT Code:** 20175

This public school was founded in 1968. It has a 50-acre campus.

RATINGS

Admissions Selectivity Rating: 83   **Fire Safety Rating:** 60*

STUDENTS AND FACULTY

Enrollment: 5,311. **Student Body:** 71% female, 29% male, 0% out-of-state, 7% international (113 countries represented). Asian 8%, African American 44%, Caucasian 4%, Hispanic 14%, Native American <1%
Retention and Graduation: 77% freshmen return for sophomore year. 9% freshmen graduate within 4 years. 28% freshmen graduate within 6 years. **Faculty:** 166 full-time faculty, 73% hold PhDs, 46% are members of minority groups, 39% are women. 0% of classes are taught by teaching assistants.

ACADEMICS

Degrees: bachelor's. **Majors with Highest Enrollment:** Psychology; Sociology; Accounting. **Special Study Options:** cooperative education program, double major, dual enrollment, English as a Second Language (ESL), honors program, independent study, internships, teacher certification program, Co-Op programs: Business, Computer Science, Health Professions. **Disability Services:** Special programs offered to physically disabled students include note-taking services, reader services, tape recorders, tutors. **Career services:** alumni services, career/job search classes, internships.

FACILITIES

Housing: 100% of campus accessible to physically disabled. **Special Academic Facilities/Equipment:** Center for educational technology. State-of-the-art cardio-pneumo-simulator **Computers:** Students can register for classes online. Administrative functions (other than registration) can be performed online.

CAMPUS LIFE

Activities: Choral groups, drama/theater, jazz band, literary magazine, student government, student newspaper, student-run film society, television station, yearbook. 50 registered organizations, 1 honor society, 2 religious organizations. **Athletics (Intercollegiate):** *Men:* basketball, cheerleading, cross-country, soccer, swimming, tennis, track/field (outdoor), volleyball. *Women:* basketball, cheerleading, cross-country, softball, swimming, track/field (outdoor), volleyball.

ADMISSIONS

Freshman Academic Profile: 68% from public high schools. SAT Math middle 50% range 390-470. SAT Critical Reading middle 50% range 363-460. Minimum paper TOEFL 470. **Basis for Candidate Selection:** *Very important factors considered include:* rigor of secondary school record, standardized test scores. **Freshman Admission Requirements:** High school diploma is required and GED is accepted. *Academic units required:* 3 English, 2 mathematics, 10 academic electives. **Freshman Admission Statistics:** 2,389 applied, 31% admitted, 80% enrolled. **Transfer Admission Requirements:** High school transcript, college transcript(s), standardized test scores, Minimum college GPA of 2.0 required. Lowest grade transferable C. **General Admission Information:** Application Fee $40. Notification on a rolling basis, beginning on or about 2/16. Nonfall registration accepted. Admission may be deferred for a maximum of 1 semester. Placement offered for CEEB Advanced Placement tests.

COSTS AND FINANCIAL AID

Annual in-state tuition $3,200. Annual out-of-state tuition $6,800. Required fees $242. Average book expense $692. **Required Forms and Deadlines:** FAFSA, State aid form. **Notification of Awards:** Applicants will be notified of awards on a rolling basis beginning 3/1. **Types of Aid:** *Need-based scholarships/grants:* Federal Pell, SEOG, state scholarships/grants, private scholarships. *Loans:* Direct Subsidized Stafford, Direct Unsubsidized Stafford, Direct PLUS, Federal Perkins, college/university loans from institutional funds. *Student Employment:* Federal Work-Study Program available.

CLAFLIN UNIVERSITY

400 Magnolia Street, Orangeburg, SC 29115
Phone: 803-535-5340 · **Financial Aid Phone:** 803-535-5720
E-mail: admissions@claflin.edu · **CEEB Code:** 5109
Fax: 803-535-5387 · **ACT Code:** 3840

This private school, affiliated with the Methodist Church, was founded in 1869. It has a 43-acre campus.

RATINGS

Admissions Selectivity Rating: 78   **Fire Safety Rating:** 80

STUDENTS AND FACULTY

Enrollment: 1,784. **Student Body:** 65% female, 35% male, 19% out-of-state, 3% international (15 countries represented). Asian 1%, African American 93%, Caucasian 2%, Hispanic 2%, Native American 1%
Retention and Graduation: 73% freshmen return for sophomore year. 32% freshmen graduate within 4 years. 49% freshmen graduate within 6 years. **Faculty:** 119 full-time faculty, 84% hold PhDs, 43% are members of minority groups, 76% are women.

ACADEMICS

Degrees: bachelor's, master's. **Classes:** Most classes have 20–29 students. Most lab/discussion sessions have 10–19 students. **Majors with Highest Enrollment:** Business Administration and Management; Sociology; Biology/ Biological Sciences. **Special Study Options:** Accelerated program, cooperative education program, cross-registration, double major, dual enrollment, English as a Second Language (ESL), honors program, independent study, internships, study abroad, teacher certification program, weekend college, (3+2) BS Mathematics(Applied Mathematics Track)/Claflin + BS Engineering/Clemson (3+2) BS Mathematics(Applied Mathematics Track)/Claflin + BS Engineering Technology/South Carolina State University (2+2) Associates Degree/ Orangeburg-Calhoun Technical College + BS Biotechnology/Claflin University. **Honors programs:** The Alice Carson Tisdale Honors College. Combined degree programs: Dual-degree(2+2) in Biotechnology. **Disability Services:** Special programs offered to physically disabled students include note-taking services. **Career services:** career/job search classes, career assessment, internships.

FACILITIES

Housing: men's dorms, women's dorms. 90% of campus accessible to physically disabled. **Special Academic Facilities/Equipment:** T.V. studio, NMR Wilbur R. Gregg collection, Aruther Rose Museum. **Computers:** 33% of classrooms, 100% of libraries, 100% of dining areas, have wireless network access. Students can register for classes online. Administrative functions (other than registration) can be performed online.

CAMPUS LIFE

Environment: Village. **Activities:** Choral groups, concert band, dance, drama/ theater, jazz band, literary magazine, music ensembles, radio station, student government, student newspaper, student-run film society, television station, yearbook, International Student Organization 3 honor societies, 4 fraternities, 4 sororities. **Athletics (Intercollegiate):** *Men:* baseball, basketball, cross-country, track/field (outdoor), track/field (indoor). *Women:* basketball, cross-country, softball, track/field (outdoor), track/field (indoor), volleyball. **On-Campus Highlights:** Student Life Center, Computer Labs, SOAR Center, Center for Vocational Reflections, Arthur Rose Museum, Jonas T. Kennedy Health and Physical Education Center. **Environmental Initiatives:** Recycling Program.

ADMISSIONS

Freshman Academic Profile: Average high school GPA 2.73. 10% in top 10% of high school class, 26% in top 25% of high school class, 63% in top 50% of high school class. SAT Math middle 50% range 350-440. SAT Critical Reading middle 50% range 350-440. ACT middle 50% range 15-19. **Basis for Candidate Selection:** *Very important factors considered include:* Class rank, academic GPA, rigor of secondary school record, standardized test scores, character/ personal qualities, first generation. *Important factors considered include:* application essay, alumni/ae relation, extracurricular activities, level of applicant's interest, talent/ability. *Other factors considered include:* recommendation(s), state residency, volunteer work, work experience. **Freshman Admission Requirements:** High school diploma is required and GED is accepted. *Academic units required:* 4 English, 3 mathematics, 2 science, (1 science labs), 0 foreign language, 2 social studies, 1 history, 7 academic electives, 0 social studies unit includes history. **Freshman Admission Statistics:** 5,237 applied, 44% admitted, 17% enrolled. **Transfer Admission Requirements:** college transcript(s), statement of good standing from prior institution(s). Minimum college GPA of 2.0 required. Lowest grade transferable C. **General Admission Information:** Application Fee $20. Regular application deadline 7/15. Notification on a rolling basis, beginning on or about 10/1. Nonfall registration accepted. Admission may be deferred for a maximum of 12. Credit and/or placement offered for CEEB Advanced Placement tests.

COSTS AND FINANCIAL AID

Annual tuition $14,640. Room and board $8,420. Required fees $370. Average book expense $1,750. **Required Forms and Deadlines:** FAFSA, Institution's own financial aid form. **Notification of Awards:** Applicants will be notified of awards on a rolling basis beginning 5/15. **Types of Aid:** *Need-based scholarships/grants:* Federal Pell, SEOG, state scholarships/grants, private scholarships, the school's own gift aid, United Negro College Fund. *Loans:* Subsidized Stafford, Unsubsidized Stafford, PLUS, Federal Perkins. *Student Employment:* Federal Work-Study Program available. Institutional employment available. Highest amount earned per year from on-campus jobs $1,600. **Financial Aid Statistics:** 88% freshmen, 95% undergrads receive need-based scholarship or grant aid. 6% freshmen, 6% undergrads receive non-need-based scholarship or grant aid, 67% freshmen, 105% undergrads receive need-based self-help aid. 0% freshmen, 0% undergrads receive athletic scholarships. 90% undergrads borrow to pay for school. Average cumulative indebtedness $29,476.

CLAREMONT MCKENNA COLLEGE

Best 380

888 Columbia Avenue, Claremont, CA 91711
Phone: (909) 621-8088 · **Financial Aid Phone:** 909-621-8356
E-mail: admission@cmc.edu · **CEEB Code:** 4054
Fax: (909) 621-8516 · **Website:** www.claremontmckenna.edu · **ACT Code:** 224

This private school was founded in 1946. It has a 56-acre campus.

RATINGS

Admissions Selectivity Rating: 97   **Fire Safety Rating:** 80

STUDENTS AND FACULTY

Enrollment: 1,293. **Student Body:** 48% female, 52% male, 56% out-of-state, 17% international (31 countries represented). Asian 10%, African American 4%, Caucasian 43%, Hispanic 12%, Native American <1%
Retention and Graduation: 96% freshmen return for sophomore year. 80% freshmen graduate within 4 years. **Faculty:** 145 full-time faculty, 99% hold PhDs, 32% are members of minority groups, 18% are women.

ACADEMICS

Degrees: bachelor's, master's. **Classes:** Most classes have 10–19 students. **Majors with Highest Enrollment:** Economics; Political Science and Government; Psychology. **Special Study Options:** cross-registration, double major,

English as a Second Language (ESL), exchange student program (domestic), independent study, internships, student-designed major, study abroad. Combined degree programs: BA/JD, BA/MA, BA/MEng, BA/MBA. **Disability Services:** Special programs offered to physically disabled students include note-taking services, reader services, tape recorders, tutors. **Career services:** Alumni network, alumni services, career/job search classes, career assessment, internships, regional alumni. Career services highlights include school sponsored grants to cover political, community service, and international-based internships.

FACILITIES

Housing: Coed dorms, special housing for disabled students, apartments for single students. 95% of campus accessible to physically disabled. **Special Academic Facilities/Equipment:** Art galleries, athenaeum complex, centers for Black and Chicano studies, computer lab, leadership lab, science center. **Computers:** 100% of classrooms, 100% of dorms, 100% of libraries, 100% of dining areas, 100% of student union, 100% of common outdoor areas have wireless network access. Administrative functions (other than registration) can be performed online.

CAMPUS LIFE

Environment: Town. **Activities:** Choral groups, dance, drama/theater, music ensembles, pep band, radio station, student government, student newspaper, symphony orchestra, yearbook, Campus Ministries, International Student Organization, Model UN. 280 registered organizations, 7 honor societies, 5 religious organizations. **Athletics (Intercollegiate):** *Men:* baseball, basketball, cross-country, diving, football, golf, soccer, swimming, tennis, track/field (outdoor), water polo. *Women:* basketball, cross-country, diving, golf, lacrosse, soccer, softball, swimming, tennis, track/field (outdoor), volleyball, water polo. **On-Campus Highlights:** Marian Miner Cook Athenaeum, Athletic/Aquatics Center, Emett Student Center/The Hub, The Research Institutes, Keck Science Center, 11 of our 13 dorms have either been recently built or remodelled. Our newest dorm, Claremont Hall, finished construction last summer and is LEED certified Silver.

ADMISSIONS

Freshman Academic Profile: 78% in top 10% of high school class, 97% in top 25% of high school class, 100% in top 50% of high school class. SAT Math middle 50% range 690-770. SAT Critical Reading middle 50% range 660-750. SAT Writing middle 50% range 680-760. ACT middle 50% range 30-33. Minimum internet-based TOEFL 100. Minimum paper TOEFL 600. **Basis for Candidate Selection:** *Very important factors considered include:* rigor of secondary school record, standardized test scores, extracurricular activities. *Important factors considered include:* application essay, recommendation(s). *Other factors considered include:* academic GPA, alumni/ae relation, character/personal qualities, first generation, geographical residence, interview, racial/ethnic status, talent/ability, volunteer work, work experience. **Freshman Admission Requirements:** High school diploma is required and GED is accepted. *Academic units required:* 4 English, 3 mathematics, 2 science, (2 science labs), 3 foreign language, 1 social studies, 1 history. **Freshman Admission Statistics:** 6,043 applied, 11% admitted, 50% enrolled. **Transfer Admission Requirements:** High school transcript, college transcript(s), essay or personal statement, statement of good standing from prior institution(s). Lowest grade transferable C. **General Admission Information:** Application Fee $60. Early decision application deadline 11/15. Regular application deadline 1/2. Regular notification 4/1. Nonfall registration not accepted. Admission may be deferred for a maximum of 1 year. Credit and/or placement offered for CEEB Advanced Placement tests.

COSTS AND FINANCIAL AID

Required Forms and Deadlines: FAFSA, CSS/Financial Aid PROFILE, State aid form, Noncustodial PROFILE, Business/Farm Supplement. **Types of Aid:** *Need-based scholarships/grants:* Federal Pell, SEOG, state scholarships/grants, private scholarships, the school's own gift aid, United Negro College Fund. *Loans:* Direct Subsidized Stafford, Direct Unsubsidized Stafford, Direct PLUS, Subsidized Stafford, Unsubsidized Stafford, PLUS, Federal Perkins, college/university loans from institutional funds. *Student Employment:* Federal Work-Study Program available. Institutional employment available. Off-campus job opportunities are excellent. **Financial Aid Statistics:** 97% freshmen, 98% undergrads receive need-based scholarship or grant aid. 58% freshmen, 45% undergrads receive non-need-based scholarship or grant aid. 88% freshmen, 91% undergrads receive need-based self-help aid. 0% freshmen, 0% undergrads receive athletic scholarships. 43% freshmen, 45% undergrads receive any aid. 31% undergrads borrow to pay for school. Average cumulative indebtedness $13,123. **Criteria for awarding institutional aid:** *Non-need-based:* academics, leadership.

Admissions Office, Clarion, PA 16214
Phone: 814-393-2306 • **Financial Aid Phone:** 814-393-2315
E-mail: admissions@clarion.edu • **CEEB Code:** 2649
Fax: 814-393-2030 • **Website:** www.clarion.edu • **ACT Code:** 3698

This public school was founded in 1867. It has a 192-acre campus.

RATINGS

Admissions Selectivity Rating: 70   **Fire Safety Rating:** 88

STUDENTS AND FACULTY

Enrollment: 5,046. **Student Body:** 62% female, 38% male, 10% out-of-state, 1% international (35 countries represented). Asian 0%, African American 7%, Caucasian 88%, Hispanic 1%, Native American <1%
Retention and Graduation: 33% freshmen graduate within 4 years. **Faculty:** 222 full-time faculty, 87% hold PhDs, 49% are members of minority groups, 14% are women. 0% of classes are taught by teaching assistants.

ACADEMICS

Degrees: associate, bachelor's, certificate, master's, post-bachelor's certificate, post-master's certificate. **Classes:** Most classes have 20–29 students. Most lab/discussion sessions have 10–19 students. **Majors with Highest Enrollment:** Elementary Education and Teaching; Business Administration and Management. **Special Study Options:** Accelerated program, cooperative education program, distance learning, double major, dual enrollment, honors program, independent study, internships, liberal arts/career combination, student-designed major, study abroad, teacher certification program, weekend college. **Honors programs:** Clarion University's Honors Program is a close-knit group of talented students preparing for the future. Honors courses satisfy general educational requirements and include field experiences. The 21-credit curriculum promotes development of essential life skills targeted for successful career outcomes. The Honors experience extends beyond the walls of the traditional classroom. Students may spend time with archaeologists in Italy, with anthropologists at a primate center, with large corporate firms and in small businesses, and with molecular biologists in laboratories. Studies have included 20th-century music, learning the art of problem solving, and pondered the ethical implications of research. Co-curricular themes prepare Honors Program students to assume leadership roles. The Honors Program is not for all students—only those individuals who desire professional success, demand academic excellence, and expect to create the future. Each year 50 freshmen are selected for the Honors Program. Courses are taught as special topics and faculty instructors are recruited for their scholarly expertise. Honors students major in every department within the university and receive pre-professional advisement. Students take a six-credit linked English and Speech class and a three-credit Humanities course in the Freshman year. In the sophomore year, students take a three-credit mathematics or science class and a three-credit social sciences course. As juniors, students take a Junior Seminar that culminates in a project prospectus for the capstone experience. Honors 450 is the Senior Presentation delivered in a university-wide presentation. The following program standards must be maintained at the end of each academic year: Freshman Year—3.0 QPA, 9 program credits; Sophomore Year—3.25 QPA, 15 program credits; Junior Year—3.4 QPA, 18 program credits; Senior Year—3.4 QPA, 21 program credits. To be considered for Honors Program admission, entering freshman must have a minimum SAT score of 1150 or equivalent ACT scores, graduate in the top 15 percent of high school class, and successful completion of an interview. Undergraduate students already enrolled or transfer students may also apply. Candidates for graduation with an associate degree must complete a minimum of 30 credit hours in residence at the Venango Campus in Oil City, Pennsylvania. If a student should fail to residence at Clarion University, maintain the required QPA and course progression, the student will be placed on probation and have one semester to meet the requirements. A student who fails to achieve the required QPA and course progression by the end of the probationary semester will not be allowed to continue in the Honors Program or to continue to receive an Honors scholarship. **Disability Services:** Special programs offered to physically disabled students include note-taking services, reader services, tape recorders, tutors. **Career services:** career/job search classes, career assessment, internships.

FACILITIES

Housing: Coed dorms, men's dorms, women's dorms, fraternity/sorority housing, apartments for single students, Sororities occupy floors of residence halls. 98% of campus accessible to physically disabled. **Special Academic Facilities/Equipment:** Planetarium. Art Gallery. **Computers:** 40% of classrooms, 100% of libraries, 50% of dining areas, 90% of student union, 10% of common outdoor areas have wireless network access. Students can register for classes online. Administrative functions (other than registration) can be performed online.

CAMPUS LIFE

Environment: Village. **Activities:** Choral groups, concert band, dance, drama/theater, jazz band, literary magazine, marching band, music ensembles, musical theater, pep band, radio station, student government, student newspaper, television station, Campus Ministries, International Student Organization. 150 registered organizations, 17 honor societies, 4 religious organizations. 5 fraternities, 8 sororities. **Athletics (Intercollegiate):** *Men:* baseball, basketball, diving, football, golf, swimming, wrestling. *Women:* basketball, cross-country, diving, soccer, softball, swimming, tennis, track/field (outdoor), volleyball. **On-Campus Highlights:** Recreation Center, Carlson Library/Art Gallery, Student Center, Athletic Field, Tippin Gymnasium.

ADMISSIONS

Freshman Academic Profile: Average high school GPA 3.15. 2% in top 10% of high school class, 9% in top 25% of high school class, 39% in top 50% of high school class. 87% from public high schools. SAT Math middle 50% range 420-520. SAT Critical Reading middle 50% range 420-510. SAT Writing middle 50% range 400-490. ACT middle 50% range 17-22. Minimum paper TOEFL 500. **Basis for Candidate Selection:** *Very important factors considered include:* Class rank, academic GPA, rigor of secondary school record, standardized test scores. *Important factors considered include:* application essay, recommendation(s). *Other factors considered include:* character/personal qualities, extracurricular activities, interview, level of applicant's interest, talent/ability, volunteer work, work experience. **Freshman Admission Requirements:** High school diploma is required and GED is accepted. *Academic units required:* 4 English, 3 mathematics, 3 science, (0 science labs), 0 foreign language, 3 social studies, 0 history, 0 visual/performing arts, 0 computer science, 0 academic electives. **Freshman Admission Statistics:** 2,071 applied, 93% admitted, 55% enrolled. **Transfer Admission Requirements:** High school transcript, college transcript(s), statement of good standing from prior institution(s). Minimum college GPA of 2.0 required. Lowest grade transferable C. **General Admission Information:** Notification on a rolling basis, beginning on or about 9/1. Nonfall registration accepted. Credit offered for CEEB Advanced Placement tests.

COSTS AND FINANCIAL AID

Annual in-state tuition $5,554. Annual out-of-state tuition $11,108. Room and board $6,390. Required fees $1,826. Average book expense $900. **Required Forms and Deadlines:** FAFSA, State aid form. **Notification of Awards:** Applicants will be notified of awards on a rolling basis beginning 3/1. **Types of Aid:** *Need-based scholarships/grants:* Federal Pell, SEOG, state scholarships/grants, private scholarships, the school's own gift aid, United Negro College Fund, Federal Nursing Scholarships. *Loans:* Direct Subsidized Stafford, Direct Unsubsidized Stafford, Direct PLUS, PLUS. *Student Employment:* Federal Work-Study Program available. Institutional employment available. Highest amount earned per year from on-campus jobs $12,000. Off-campus job opportunities are fair. **Financial Aid Statistics:** 78% freshmen, 75% undergrads receive need-based scholarship or grant aid. 38% freshmen, 25% undergrads receive non-need-based scholarship or grant aid. 87% freshmen, 60% undergrads receive need-based self-help aid. 4% freshmen, 3% undergrads receive athletic scholarships. 78% freshmen, 75% undergrads receive any aid. 79% undergrads borrow to pay for school. Average cumulative indebtedness $23,277. **Criteria for awarding institutional aid:** *Non-need-based:* academics, art, athletics, leadership, minority status, music/drama, state/district residency.

CLARK ATLANTA UNIVERSITY

223 James P. Brawley Dr., SW, Atlanta, GA 30314-4391
Phone: 404-880-8784 · **Financial Aid Phone:** 404-880-8992
E-mail: cauadmissions@cau.edu · **CEEB Code:** 5110
Fax: 404-880-6605 · **Website:** www.cau.edu · **ACT Code:** 804

This private school, affiliated with the Methodist Church, was founded in 1988. It has a 126-acre campus.

RATINGS

Admissions Selectivity Rating: 72   **Fire Safety Rating:** 95

STUDENTS AND FACULTY

Enrollment: 2,567. **Student Body:** 75% female, 25% male, 63% out-of-state, 1% international (10 countries represented). Asian 0%, African American 87%, Caucasian 0%, Hispanic 0%, Native American <1%.
Retention and Graduation: 60% freshmen return for sophomore year. 24% freshmen graduate within 4 years. 41% freshmen graduate within 6 years. 26% grads go on to further study within 1 year. 19% grads pursue arts and sciences degrees. 1% grads pursue law degrees. 3% grads pursue business degrees. 1% grads pursue medical degrees. **Faculty:** 170 full-time faculty, 81% hold PhDs.

41% are members of minority groups, 90% are women. 0% of classes are taught by teaching assistants.

ACADEMICS

Degrees: bachelor's, master's, post-bachelor's certificate, post-master's certificate. **Classes:** Most classes have 20–29 students. Most lab/discussion sessions have fewer than 10 students. **Majors with Highest Enrollment:** Business Administration and Management; Radio, Television, and Digital Communication; Biology/Biological Sciences. **Special Study Options:** Accelerated program, cooperative education program, cross-registration, double major, dual enrollment, exchange student program (domestic), honors program, independent study, internships, study abroad, teacher certification program, weekend college. Combined degree programs: BA/MA, BA/MEng. **Disability Services:** Special programs offered to physically disabled students include note-taking services, reader services, tape recorders, tutors. **Career services:** career/job search classes, career assessment, internships,

FACILITIES

Housing: Coed dorms, men's dorms, women's dorms, apartments for single students. 80% of campus accessible to physically disabled. **Computers:** 100% of classrooms, 5% of dorms, 100% of libraries, 100% of dining areas, 100% of student union, 80% of common outdoor areas have wireless network access. Students can register for classes online. Administrative functions (other than registration) can be performed online.

CAMPUS LIFE

Environment: Metropolis. **Activities:** Choral groups, concert band, dance, drama/theater, marching band, music ensembles, musical theater, opera, pep band, radio station, student government, student newspaper, student-run film society, symphony orchestra, television station, yearbook, Campus Ministries, International Student Organization. 80 registered organizations, 12 honor societies, 5 religious organizations. 4 fraternities, 4 sororities. **Athletics (Intercollegiate):** *Men:* baseball, basketball, cross-country, football, track/field (outdoor). *Women:* basketball, cross-country, softball, tennis, track/field (outdoor), volleyball. **On-Campus Highlights:** Robert W. Woodruff Library, CAU Radio & Television Station, CAU Art Galleries, Heritage Commons Residence Hall, Henderson Student Center.

ADMISSIONS

Freshman Academic Profile: Average high school GPA 3.01. 7% in top 10% of high school class, 26% in top 25% of high school class, 68% in top 50% of high school class. 90% from public high schools. SAT Math middle 50% range 380-460. SAT Critical Reading middle 50% range 390-470. ACT middle 50% range 16-20. Minimum paper TOEFL 500. **Basis for Candidate Selection:** *Very important factors considered include:* academic GPA, rigor of secondary school record, standardized test scores, character/personal qualities. *Important factors considered include:* application essay, recommendation(s), talent/ability. *Other factors considered include:* alumni/ae relation, level of applicant's interest, work experience. **Freshman Admission Requirements:** High school diploma is required and GED is accepted. *Academic units required:* 4 English, 3 mathematics, 3 science, (1 science labs), 2 foreign language, 3 social studies, 3 academic electives. **Freshman Admission Statistics:** 5,140 applied, 85% admitted, 16% enrolled. **Transfer Admission Requirements:** college transcript(s), statement of good standing from prior institution(s). Minimum college GPA of 2.5 required. Lowest grade transferable C. **General Admission Information:** Application Fee $35. Regular application deadline 6/1. Notification on a rolling basis, beginning on or about 1/1. Nonfall registration accepted. Admission may be deferred for a maximum of One Year. Credit and/or placement offered for CEEB Advanced Placement tests.

COSTS AND FINANCIAL AID

Annual tuition $19,682. Room and board $10,262. Required fees $1,652. Average book expense $2,000. **Required Forms and Deadlines:** FAFSA, State aid form. **Notification of Awards:** Applicants will be notified of awards on a rolling basis beginning 4/1. **Types of Aid:** *Need-based scholarships/grants:* Federal Pell, SEOG, state scholarships/grants, private scholarships, the school's own gift aid, United Negro College Fund. *Loans:* Subsidized Stafford, Unsubsidized Stafford, PLUS, Federal Perkins, state loans, Private Loans. *Student Employment:* Federal Work-Study Program available. Institutional employment available. Highest amount earned per year from on-campus jobs $8,500. Off-campus job opportunities are fair. **Financial Aid Statistics:** 89% freshmen, 88% undergrads receive need-based scholarship or grant aid. 15% freshmen, 20% undergrads receive non-need-based scholarship or grant aid. 93% freshmen, 93% undergrads receive need-based self-help aid. 0% freshmen, 0% undergrads receive athletic scholarships. 96% freshmen, 96% undergrads receive any aid. 97% undergrads borrow to pay for school. Average cumulative indebtedness $25,878. **Criteria for awarding institutional aid:** *Non-need-based:* academics, art, athletics, leadership, minority status, music/drama, religious affiliation, state/district residency.

CLARK UNIVERSITY

Best 380

950 Main Street, Worcester, MA 01610-1477
Phone: 508-793-7431 · **Financial Aid Phone:** 508-793-7478
E-mail: admissions@clarku.edu · **CEEB Code:** 3279
Fax: 508-793-8821 · **Website:** www.clarku.edu · **ACT Code:** 1808

This private school was founded in 1887. It has a 50-acre campus.

RATINGS

Admissions Selectivity Rating: 90   **Fire Safety Rating:** 97

STUDENTS AND FACULTY

Enrollment: 2,236. **Student Body:** 59% female, 41% male, 62% out-of-state, 14% international (64 countries represented). Asian 7%, African American 4%, Caucasian 60%, Hispanic 6%, Native American <1%
Retention and Graduation: 88% freshmen return for sophomore year. 72% freshmen graduate within 4 years. 45% grads go on to further study within 1 year. 25% grads pursue arts and sciences degrees. 2% grads pursue law degrees. 6% grads pursue business degrees. 2% grads pursue medical degrees. **Faculty:** 198 full-time faculty, 95% hold PhDs, 43% are members of minority groups, 21% are women. 1% of classes are taught by teaching assistants.

ACADEMICS

Degrees: bachelor's, master's, post-bachelor's certificate, post-master's certificate. **Classes:** Most classes have 10–19 students. Most lab/discussion sessions have 10–19 students. **Majors with Highest Enrollment:** Biology/Biological Sciences; Political Science and Government; Psychology. **Special Study Options:** cross-registration, double major, English as a Second Language (ESL), independent study, internships, liberal arts/career combination, student-designed major, study abroad, teacher certification program. Combined degree programs: BA/MA, BA/MA BAMAT BA/MBA BA/MSF BA/MSPC. **Disability Services:** Special programs offered to physically disabled students include note-taking services, tutors. **Career services:** Alumni network, alumni services, career/job search classes, career assessment, internships, regional alumni.

FACILITIES

Housing: Coed dorms, special housing for disabled students, women's dorms, apartments for single students, Wellness Housing. 95% of campus accessible to physically disabled. **Special Academic Facilities/Equipment:** Galleries, theatres, Robert H. Goddard historical exhibition, rare book room, craft center, music center, map library, arboretum, herbarium, extensive darkroom facilities, satellite dish for international program reception, electron microscope, nuclear magnetic resonance spectrometer. **Computers:** 100% of classrooms, 15% of dorms, 100% of libraries, 100% of dining areas, 100% of student union, 15% of common outdoor areas have wireless network access. Students can register for classes online. Administrative functions (other than registration) can be performed online.

CAMPUS LIFE

Environment: City. **Activities:** Choral groups, concert band, dance, drama/theater, jazz band, literary magazine, marching band, music ensembles, musical theater, pep band, radio station, student government, student newspaper, student-run film society, symphony orchestra, television station, yearbook, Campus Ministries, International Student Organization, Model UN. 110 registered organizations, 10 honor societies, 7 religious organizations. **Athletics (Intercollegiate):** *Men:* baseball, basketball, crew/rowing, cross-country, diving, lacrosse, soccer, swimming, tennis. *Women:* basketball, crew/rowing, cross-country, diving, field hockey, soccer, softball, swimming, tennis, volleyball. **On-Campus Highlights:** Larger than life statue of Freud, Rare book room, Goddard Library, Traina Center for the Arts, New: Dolan Field House and updated fields, The Green on a warm spring day. **Environmental Initiatives:** Becoming Climate Neutral—Zero Emissions—by 2030. Clark University has operated an on-campus cogeneration facility since 1982, but recently invested in a more efficient engine with new steam distribution lines, a more extensive energy metering system, and updated management practices. Clark University Sustainability Task Force.

ADMISSIONS

Freshman Academic Profile: Average high school GPA 3.6. 37% in top 10% of high school class, 73% in top 25% of high school class, 96% in top 50% of high school class. 70% from public high schools. SAT Math middle 50% range 558-670. SAT Critical Reading middle 50% range 550-663. SAT Writing middle 50% range 560-660. ACT middle 50% range 25-31. Minimum paper TOEFL

550. Basis for Candidate Selection: *Very important factors considered include:* academic GPA, recommendation(s), rigor of secondary school record, standardized test scores, character/personal qualities. *Important factors considered include:* application essay, extracurricular activities, talent/ability, volunteer work. *Other factors considered include:* Class rank, alumni/ae relation, first generation, geographical residence, interview, level of applicant's interest, racial/ethnic status, work experience. **Freshman Admission Requirements:** High school diploma is required and GED is accepted. **Freshman Admission Statistics:** 7,304 applied, 54% admitted, 14% enrolled. **Transfer Admission Requirements:** High school transcript, college transcript(s), essay or personal statement, standardized test scores, statement of good standing from prior institution(s). Minimum college GPA of 2.8 required. **General Admission Information:** Application Fee $55. Early decision application deadline 11/15. Regular application deadline 1/15. Regular notification 4/1. Nonfall registration accepted. Admission may be deferred for a maximum of 1 year. Credit and/or placement offered for CEEB Advanced Placement tests.

COSTS AND FINANCIAL AID

Annual tuition $41,590. Room and board $8,200. Required fees $350. Average book expense $800. **Required Forms and Deadlines:** FAFSA, CSS/Financial Aid PROFILE, Noncustodial PROFILE. **Notification of Awards:** Applicants will be notified of awards on or about 3/31. **Types of Aid:** *Need-based scholarships/grants:* Federal Pell, SEOG, state scholarships/grants, the school's own gift aid. *Loans:* Direct Subsidized Stafford, Direct Unsubsidized Stafford, Direct PLUS, Federal Perkins, state loans. *Student Employment:* Federal Work-Study Program available. Institutional employment available. Highest amount earned per year from on-campus jobs $2,500. Off-campus job opportunities are good. **Financial Aid Statistics:** 98% freshmen, 99% undergrads receive need-based scholarship or grant aid. 44% freshmen, 39% undergrads receive non-need-based scholarship or grant aid. 84% freshmen, 84% undergrads receive need-based self-help aid. 0% freshmen, 0% undergrads receive athletic scholarships. 90% freshmen, 88% undergrads receive any aid. 91% undergrads borrow to pay for school. Average cumulative indebtedness $23,125. **Criteria for awarding institutional aid:** *Non-need-based:* academics, leadership.

CLARKE UNIVERSITY

1550 Clarke Drive, Dubuque, IA 52001-3198
Phone: 563-588-6316
E-mail: admissions@clarke.edu · **CEEB Code:** 6099
Fax: 563-588-6789 · **Website:** www.clarke.edu · **ACT Code:** 1290

This private school, affiliated with the Roman Catholic Church, was founded in 1843. It has a 55-acre campus.

RATINGS

Admissions Selectivity Rating: 83   **Fire Safety Rating:** 60*

STUDENTS AND FACULTY

Enrollment: 933. **Student Body:** 69% female, 31% male, 38% out-of-state, 1% international (8 countries represented). Asian 1%, African American 4%, Caucasian 89%, Hispanic 5%, Native American <1%
Retention and Graduation: 73% freshmen return for sophomore year. 49% freshmen graduate within 4 years. 68% freshmen graduate within 6 years. 25% grads go on to further study within 1 year. 23% grads pursue arts and sciences degrees. 2% grads pursue business degrees. **Faculty:** 89 full-time faculty, 67% hold PhDs, 67% are members of minority groups, 3% are women. 0% of classes are taught by teaching assistants.

ACADEMICS

Degrees: associate, bachelor's, master's, terminal associate. **Classes:** Most classes have fewer than 10 students. Most lab/discussion sessions have fewer than 10 students. **Majors with Highest Enrollment:** Psychology; Registered Nursing/Registered Nurse; Business/Commerce. **Special Study Options:** Accelerated program, cross-registration, distance learning, double major, honors program, independent study, internships, student-designed major, study abroad, teacher certification program. Combined degree programs: BS/MS in Physical Therapy. **Disability Services:** Special programs offered to physically disabled students include note-taking services, reader services, tape recorders, tutors. **Career services:** alumni services, career/job search classes, career assessment, internships.

FACILITIES

Housing: Coed dorms, men's dorms, women's dorms, apartments for single students. 90% of campus accessible to physically disabled. **Special Academic Facilities/Equipment:** Art gallery, computer classrooms for math, biology, and computer science, computer-interfaced chemistry lab, human gross anatomy and nursing labs, electron microscope, music performance hall, foreign language lab, distance learning classroom **Computers:** Students can register for classes online. Administrative functions (other than registration) can be performed online.

CAMPUS LIFE

Environment: Town. **Activities:** Choral groups, concert band, dance, drama/ theater, jazz band, literary magazine, music ensembles, musical theater, radio station, student government, student newspaper, yearbook, 48 registered organizations, 5 honor societies, 1 religious organization. **Athletics (Intercollegiate):** *Men:* baseball, basketball, cheerleading, cross-country, golf, soccer, tennis, volleyball. *Women:* basketball, cheerleading, cross-country, golf, soccer, softball, tennis, volleyball.

ADMISSIONS

Freshman Academic Profile: Average high school GPA 3.51. 13% in top 10% of high school class, 55% in top 25% of high school class, 84% in top 50% of high school class. 81% from public high schools. SAT Math middle 50% range 475-550. SAT Critical Reading middle 50% range 470-530. ACT middle 50% range 20-24. Minimum paper TOEFL 527. **Basis for Candidate Selection:** *Very important factors considered include:* academic GPA, rigor of secondary school record, standardized test scores, talent/ability. *Important factors considered include:* Class rank. *Other factors considered include:* extracurricular activities, interview, racial/ethnic status, volunteer work. **Freshman Admission Requirements:** High school diploma is required and GED is accepted. *Academic units required:* 4 English, 3 mathematics, 3 science, (2 science labs), 2 foreign language, 2 social studies, 4 academic electives. **Freshman Admission Statistics:** 1,359 applied, 70% admitted, 19% enrolled. **Transfer Admission Requirements:** High school transcript, college transcript(s), standardized test scores, statement of good standing from prior institution(s). Minimum college GPA of 2.0 required. Lowest grade transferable C. **General Admission Information:** Application Fee $25. Notification on a rolling basis, beginning on or about 1/15. Nonfall registration accepted. Admission may be deferred for a maximum of 12 months. Credit and/or placement offered for CEEB Advanced Placement tests.

COSTS AND FINANCIAL AID

Average book expense $1,160. **Notification of Awards:** Applicants will be notified of awards on a rolling basis beginning 3/1. **Types of Aid:** *Need-based scholarships/grants:* Federal Pell, SEOG, state scholarships/grants, private scholarships, the school's own gift aid. *Loans:* Subsidized Stafford, Unsubsidized Stafford, PLUS, Federal Perkins, Federal Nursing, state loans, college/ university loans from institutional funds, alternative and private loans. *Student Employment:* Federal Work-Study Program available. Institutional employment available. Highest amount earned per year from on-campus jobs $1,422. Off-campus job opportunities are excellent. **Financial Aid Statistics:** 100% freshmen, 100% undergrads receive need-based scholarship or grant aid. 99% freshmen, 95% undergrads receive non-need-based scholarship or grant aid. 90% freshmen, 89% undergrads receive need-based self-help aid. 41% freshmen, 33% undergrads receive athletic scholarships. 90% undergrads borrow to pay for school. Average cumulative indebtedness $26,141. **Criteria for awarding institutional aid:** *Non-need-based:* academics, alumni affiliation, art, athletics, leadership, minority status, music/drama, religious affiliation, state/ district residency.

CLARKSON UNIVERSITY

Best 380

8 Clarkson Ave, Box 5605, Potsdam, NY 13699
Phone: 315-268-6480 · **Financial Aid Phone:** 315-268-6480
E-mail: admission@clarkson.edu · **CEEB Code:** 2084·
Fax: 315-268-7647 · **Website:** www.clarkson.edu

This private school was founded in 1896. It has a 640-acre campus.

RATINGS

Admissions Selectivity Rating: 89   **Fire Safety Rating:** 93

STUDENTS AND FACULTY

Enrollment: 3,130. **Student Body:** 30% female, 70% male, 25% out-of-state, 2% international (45 countries represented). Asian 3%, African American 2%, Caucasian 83%, Hispanic 5%, Native American <1%
Retention and Graduation: 58% freshmen graduate within 4 years. 73%

freshmen graduate within 6 years. 13% grads go on to further study within 1 year. 5% grads pursue arts and sciences degrees. 1% grads pursue business degrees. **Faculty:** 239 full-time faculty, 88% hold PhDs, 27% are members of minority groups, 19% are women. 0% of classes are taught by teaching assistants.

ACADEMICS

Degrees: bachelor's, master's. **Classes:** Most classes have 10–19 students. Most lab/discussion sessions have 20–29 students. **Majors with Highest Enrollment:** Mechanical Engineering; Civil Engineering; Business Administration and Management. **Special Study Options:** Accelerated program, cooperative education program, cross-registration, distance learning, double major, dual enrollment, English as a Second Language (ESL), honors program, independent study, liberal arts/career combination, student-designed major, study abroad, Women In Science and Engineering (WISE) Living/Learning Community; interdisciplinary degree programs that combine Engineering and Business, Business and Liberal Arts, and Environmental Science and Policy; a large number of 3+2 and 2+2 articulation agreements that facilitate transfer to Clarkson from community colleges and other baccalaureate institutions; business students experience a unique introduction to entrepreneurship through working with the Shipley Center for Innovation, the Clarkson Entrepreneurs Organization (CEO) and the Clarkson Center for Global Competitiveness. **Honors programs:** Built upon current and emerging problems in science, technology and society, the Clarkson University Honors Program offers unique academic challenges and opportunities for Clarkson's most promising students. The program is a gateway to a multitude of opportunities that include internships, research experience, fellowships, graduate schools, study abroad, and jobs. Combined degree programs: Business/Liberal Studies. **Disability Services:** Special programs offered to physically disabled students include note-taking services, reader services, tape recorders, tutors. **Career services:** Alumni network, alumni services, career/job search classes, career assessment, internships, regional alumni. The Clarkson University School of Business requires that all students complete an internship as part of their degree requirements. The commitment form the University to coordinate and facilitate placement of all students has resulted in tremendous placement outcomes a well as increased experiential application in the classroom.

FACILITIES

Housing: Coed dorms, special housing for disabled students, men's dorms, special housing for international students, women's dorms, fraternity/sorority housing, apartments for single students, Wellness Housing, Theme Housing. 85% of campus accessible to physically disabled. **Special Academic Facilities/Equipment:** The Center for Advanced Materials Processing (CAMP) is dedicated to developing innovations in advanced materials processing and to transfer this technology to business and industry, and is built on Clarkson's recognized expertise in colloid and surface science and fine particle technology. The Center for the Environment facilitates the development, promotion and operation of environmental activities within the University and among its partners. The Center for Rehabilitative Science and Technology (CREST) **Computers:** 100% of classrooms, 100% of libraries, 100% of dining areas, 100% of student union, 20% of common outdoor areas have wireless network access. Students can register for classes online. Administrative functions (other than registration) can be performed online.

CAMPUS LIFE

Environment: Village. **Activities:** Choral groups, drama/theater, jazz band, literary magazine, musical theater, pep band, radio station, student government, student newspaper, symphony orchestra, television station, yearbook, International Student Organization. 117 registered organizations, 7 honor societies, 3 religious organizations. 11 fraternity, 3 sororities. **Athletics (Intercollegiate):** *Men:* baseball, basketball, cross-country, diving, golf, ice hockey, lacrosse, skiing (downhill/alpine), skiing (nordic/cross-country), soccer, swimming. *Women:* basketball, cross-country, diving, ice hockey, lacrosse, skiing (downhill/alpine), skiing (nordic/cross-country), soccer, swimming, volleyball. **On-Campus Highlights:** Snell Hall Shipley Center for Innovation, Adirondack Lodge, Cheel Campus Center Club 99, CAMP Building SPEED Labs, Java City/Library, Fitness Center. **Environmental Initiatives:** All new construction is designed to meet at least Silver LEED certification. Significant heat and lighting upgrades are included in all renovations. Clarkson offers a wide breadth of environmentally-related academic majors and minors. Recent introductions include a green track within the MBA program, a Master's of Science in Environmental Policy & Governance, and minors for undergraduate students in Sustainable Energy Systems Engineering and Sustainable Solutions for the Developing World. Clarkson students have designed, constructed and are now operating a greenhouse to test the feasibility of year-round vegetable production in cold climates. The greenhouse is integrated with an anaerobic digester that converts some of the campus's food waste into biogas, electricity and heat, and an energy cabin that generates solar thermal and wood pellet heat for the greenhouse and digester.

ADMISSIONS

Freshman Academic Profile: Average high school GPA 3.7. 41% in top 10% of high school class, 76% in top 25% of high school class, 96% in top 50% of

high school class. 82% from public high schools. SAT Math middle 50% range 570-670. SAT Critical Reading middle 50% range 520-620. SAT Writing middle 50% range 500-600. ACT middle 50% range 24-29. Minimum internet-based TOEFL 80. Minimum paper TOEFL 550. **Basis for Candidate Selection:** *Very important factors considered include:* academic GPA, rigor of secondary school record. *Important factors considered include:* Class rank, recommendation(s), standardized test scores, extracurricular activities, volunteer work. *Other factors considered include:* application essay, alumni/ae relation, character/personal qualities, first generation, level of applicant's interest, talent/ability, work experience. **Freshman Admission Requirements:** High school diploma is required and GED is accepted. *Academic units required:* 4 English, 3 mathematics, 3 science. **Freshman Admission Statistics:** 7,401 applied, 62% admitted, 17% enrolled. **Transfer Admission Requirements:** college transcript(s), Minimum college GPA of 2.75 required. Lowest grade transferable 2. **General Admission Information:** Application Fee $50. Early decision application deadline 12/1. Regular application deadline 1/15. Notification on a rolling basis, beginning on or about 2/1. Nonfall registration accepted. Admission may be deferred for a maximum of 12 months. Credit offered for CEEB Advanced Placement tests.

COSTS AND FINANCIAL AID
Required Forms and Deadlines: FAFSA, State aid form. **Notification of Awards:** Applicants will be notified of awards on a rolling basis beginning 3/19. **Types of Aid:** *Need-based scholarships/grants:* Federal Pell, SEOG, state scholarships/grants, private scholarships, the school's own gift aid, HEOP. *Loans:* Direct Subsidized Stafford, Direct Unsubsidized Stafford, Direct PLUS, Subsidized Stafford, Unsubsidized Stafford, PLUS, Federal Perkins, college/university loans from institutional funds, Private/alternative loans. *Student Employment:* Federal Work-Study Program available. Institutional employment available. Off-campus job opportunities are excellent. **Financial Aid Statistics:** 100% freshmen, 99% undergrads receive need-based scholarship or grant aid. 17% freshmen, 12% undergrads receive non-need-based scholarship or grant aid. 80% freshmen, 84% undergrads receive need-based self-help aid. 2% freshmen, 1% undergrads receive athletic scholarships. 98% freshmen, 98% undergrads receive any aid. 85% undergrads borrow to pay for school. Average cumulative indebtedness $27,000. **Criteria for awarding institutional aid:** *Non-need-based:* academics, alumni affiliation, leadership, minority status.

CLAYTON STATE UNIVERSITY

2000 Clayton State Blvd., Morrow, GA 30206-0285
Phone: 678-466-4115
E-mail: ccsu-info@mail.clayton.edu
Fax: 678-466-4149 · **Website:** www.clayton.edu

This is a public school.

RATINGS
Admissions Selectivity Rating: 71   Fire Safety Rating: 60*

STUDENTS AND FACULTY
Enrollment: 5,661. **Student Body:** 69% female, 31% male, 5% out-of-state, 2% international. Asian 4%, African American 48%, Caucasian 43%, Hispanic 3%, Native American 1%.
Retention and Graduation: 61% freshmen return for sophomore year. **Faculty:** 157 full-time faculty, 57% hold PhDs, 59% are members of minority groups, 15% are women.

ACADEMICS
Degrees: associate, bachelor's, certificate, master's, terminal associate, transfer associate. **Classes:** Most classes have 20-29 students. Most lab/discussion sessions have fewer than 10 students. **Special Study Options:** cooperative education program, cross-registration, distance learning, double major, dual enrollment, exchange student program (domestic), honors program, independent study, internships, liberal arts/career combination, study abroad, teacher certification program.

FACILITIES
Housing: apartments for single studentsLocal Private Apartment Living.

CAMPUS LIFE
Activities: Choral groups, drama/theater, jazz band, literary magazine, music ensembles, musical theater, opera, pep band, student government, student newspaper.

ADMISSIONS
Freshman Academic Profile: Average high school GPA 2.88. SAT Math middle 50% range 440-550. SAT Critical Reading middle 50% range 450-550. ACT middle 50% range 17-21. **Basis for Candidate Selection:** *Very important factors considered include:* academic GPA, rigor of secondary school

record, standardized test scores. *Other factors considered include:* Class rank, extracurricular activities, talent/ability. **Freshman Admission Requirements:** High school diploma is required and GED is not accepted. *Academic units required:* 4 English, 4 mathematics, 3 science, 2 foreign language, 3 social studies. **Freshman Admission Statistics:** 2,920 applied, 71% admitted, 63% enrolled. **Transfer Admission Requirements:** college transcript(s), statement of good standing from prior institution(s). Minimum college GPA of 2.0 required. Lowest grade transferable D. **General Admission Information:** Application Fee $40. Regular application deadline 7/1. Notification on a rolling basis, beginning on or about 1/1. Nonfall registration accepted.

COSTS AND FINANCIAL AID
Average book expense $1,000. **Required Forms and Deadlines:** FAFSA, State aid form. **Types of Aid:** *Need-based scholarships/grants:* Federal Pell, SEOG, state scholarships/grants, private scholarships, the school's own gift aid, Federal Nursing Scholarships. *Loans:* Subsidized Stafford, Unsubsidized Stafford, PLUS, state loans. **Financial Aid Statistics:** 65% freshmen, 67% undergrads receive need-based scholarship or grant aid. 75% freshmen, 43% undergrads receive non-need-based scholarship or grant aid. 45% freshmen, 62% undergrads receive need-based self-help aid. 1% freshmen, 3% undergrads receive athletic scholarships. Criteriafor awarding institutional aid: *Non-need-based:* academics.

CLEAR CREEK BAPTIST BIBLE COLLEGE

300 Clear Creek Road, Pineville, KY 40977-9754
Phone: 606-337-3196 · **Financial Aid Phone:** 606-337-1457
E-mail: ccbbc@ccbbc.edu
Fax: 606-337-2372 · **Website:** www.ccbbc.edu

This private school, affiliated with the Southern Baptist Church, was founded in 1926. It has a 700-acre campus.

RATINGS
Admissions Selectivity Rating: 60*   Fire Safety Rating: 67

STUDENTS AND FACULTY
Enrollment: 160. **Student Body:** 22% female, 78% male, 60% out-of-state, 0% international (0 countries represented). Asian 1%, African American 1%, Caucasian 103%, Hispanic 3%, Native American <1%.
Retention and Graduation: 93% freshmen return for sophomore year. 25% freshmen graduate within 4 years. 30% grads go on to further study within 1 year. **Faculty:** 6 full-time faculty, 83% hold PhDs, 0% are members of minority groups, 0% are women.

ACADEMICS
Degrees: associate, bachelor's, certificate, diploma. **Classes:** Most classes have 10-19 students. Most lab/discussion sessions have 10-19 students. **Majors with Highest Enrollment:** Bible/Biblical Studies. **Special Study Options:** distance learning, double major, independent study, internships. **Career services:** Alumni network.

FACILITIES
Housing: men's dorms, women's dorms, apartments for married students, apartments for single students, Wellness Housing. 95% of campus accessible to physically disabled. **Special Academic Facilities/Equipment:** Jerusalem model **Computers:** 10% of dorms, 100% of libraries, 5% of common outdoor areas have wireless network access. Students can register for classes online.

CAMPUS LIFE
Environment: Rural. **Activities:** Choral groups, music ensembles, radio station, student government, student newspaper, Campus Ministries. **On-Campus Highlights:** Kelly Hall, Jerusalem model, Family Life Center, Creek and walking trails, Carolyn Boatman Brooks Memorial Library.

ADMISSIONS
Freshman Academic Profile: 95% from public high schools. Minimum paper TOEFL 550. **Basis for Candidate Selection:** *Very important factors considered include:* application essay, recommendation(s), character/personal qualities, religious affiliation/commitment. *Other factors considered include:* alumni/ae relation, interview, level of applicant's interest, talent/ability. **Freshman Admission Requirements:** High school diploma is required and GED is accepted. **Freshman Admission Statistics:** 14 applied, 93% admitted, 85% enrolled. **Transfer Admission Requirements:** High school transcript, college transcript(s), essay or personal statement, interview, Minimum college GPA of 2.0 required. Lowest grade transferable C. **General Admission Information:** Application Fee $40. Regular application deadline 8/2. Notification on a rolling basis, beginning on or about 4/1. Nonfall registration accepted. Admission may be deferred for a maximum of 2 years. Neither credit nor placement offered for CEEB Advanced Placement tests.

COSTS AND FINANCIAL AID

Annual tuition $5,482. Room and board $3,470. Required fees $400. Average book expense $1,200. **Required Forms and Deadlines:** FAFSA, Institution's own financial aid form. **Notification of Awards:** Applicants will be notified of awards on a rolling basis beginning 5/1. **Types of Aid:** *Need-based scholarships/grants:* Federal Pell, SEOG, private scholarships, the school's own gift aid. *Student Employment:* Federal Work-Study Program available. Institutional employment available. Highest amount earned per year from on-campus jobs $7,000. Off-campus job opportunities are fair. **Financial Aid Statistics:** 100% freshmen, 100% undergrads receive need-based scholarship or grant aid. 22% freshmen, 42% undergrads receive non-need-based scholarship or grant aid. 33% freshmen, 37% undergrads receive need-based self-help aid. 0% freshmen, 0% undergrads receive athletic scholarships. 81% freshmen, 75% undergrads receive any aid. 0% undergrads borrow to pay for school. Average cumulative indebtedness $0. **Criteria for awarding institutional aid:** *Non-need-based:* academics, leadership, religious affiliation, state/district residency.

CLEARWATER CHRISTIAN COLLEGE

3400 Gulf-to-Bay Boulevard, Clearwater, FL 33759-4595
Phone: 727-726-1153 · **Financial Aid Phone:** 727-726-1153
E-mail: admissions@clearwater.edu
Fax: 727-726-8597 · **Website:** www.clearwater.edu · **ACT Code:** 715

This private school, affiliated with the Christian (Nondenominational) Church, was founded in 1966. It has a 138-acre campus.

RATINGS

Admissions Selectivity Rating: 70 **Fire Safety Rating:** 94

STUDENTS AND FACULTY

Enrollment: 546. **Student Body:** 50% female, 50% male, 52% out-of-state, 0% international (2 countries represented). Asian 1%, African American 5%, Caucasian 82%, Hispanic 4%, Native American <1%
Retention and Graduation: 70% freshmen return for sophomore year. 34% freshmen graduate within 4 years. 42% freshmen graduate within 6 years. 26% grads go on to further study within 1 year. 16% grads pursue arts and sciences degrees. 1% grads pursue law degrees. 2% grads pursue business degrees. 4% grads pursue medical degrees. **Faculty:** 28 full-time faculty, 68% hold PhDs, 32% are members of minority groups, 4% are women. 0% of classes are taught by teaching assistants.

ACADEMICS

Degrees: associate, bachelor's, certificate, master's. **Classes:** Most classes have fewer than 10 students. **Majors with Highest Enrollment:** Business Administration and Management; Elementary Education and Teaching; Kinesiology and Exercise Science. **Special Study Options:** cooperative education program, distance learning, double major, dual enrollment, honors program, independent study, internships, liberal arts/career combination, student-designed major, study abroad, teacher certification program, Semester in Washington, DC. **Honors programs:** Interdisciplinary Studies, a self-designed multidisciplinary program for students with exceptional ability and focus. **Disability Services:** Special programs offered to physically disabled students include tape recorders, tutors. **Career services:** alumni services, career/job search classes, internships. During an education student's last semester, the director of clinical field experiences places the student in Hillsborough and Pinellas County public and private schools for a 14-week teaching internship.

FACILITIES

Housing: men's dorms, women's dorms. **Computers:** 100% of classrooms, 100% of dorms, 100% of libraries, 100% of dining areas, have wireless network access. Administrative functions (other than registration) can be performed online.

CAMPUS LIFE

Environment: City. **Activities:** Choral groups, concert band, drama/theater, music ensembles, pep band, student government, student newspaper, student-run film society, symphony orchestra, yearbook, Campus Ministries. 17 registered organizations, 1 honor society, 1 religious organization. 5 fraternities, 6 sororities. **Athletics (Intercollegiate):** *Men:* baseball, basketball, golf, soccer. *Women:* basketball, golf, soccer, softball, volleyball. **On-Campus Highlights:** Centre Court Café, Gymnasium, Cathcart Hall Cafeteria, Easter Library.

ADMISSIONS

Freshman Academic Profile: 30% from public high schools. SAT Math middle 50% range 450-530. SAT Critical Reading middle 50% range 470-560. ACT middle 50% range 21-23. Minimum internet-based TOEFL 84. Minimum paper TOEFL 500. **Basis for Candidate Selection:** *Very important factors considered include:* application essay, recommendation(s), standardized test

scores, character/personal qualities, religious affiliation/commitment. *Important factors considered include:* academic GPA, rigor of secondary school record, interview. *Other factors considered include:* alumni/ae relation, level of applicant's interest, volunteer work. **Freshman Admission Requirements:** High school diploma is required and GED is accepted. *Academic units required:* 4 English, 3 mathematics, 3 science, 2 foreign language, 3 social studies. **Transfer Admission Requirements:** High school transcript, college transcript(s), essay or personal statement, standardized test scores, statement of good standing from prior institution(s). Minimum college GPA of 2.0 required. Lowest grade transferable C-. **General Admission Information:** Application Fee $35. Regular application deadline 8/1. Nonfall registration not accepted. Admission may be deferred for a maximum of 1 year. Credit offered for CEEB Advanced Placement tests.

COSTS AND FINANCIAL AID

Annual tuition $16,250. Room and board $7,470. Required fees $95. Average book expense $1,000. **Required Forms and Deadlines:** FAFSA, Institution's own financial aid form, State aid form. **Types of Aid:** *Need-based scholarships/grants:* Federal Pell, SEOG, state scholarships/grants, private scholarships, the school's own gift aid, Additional scholarships available for students who are considered first generation, international, or whose parents are involved in Christian ministry. *Loans:* Direct Subsidized Stafford, Direct Unsubsidized Stafford, Direct PLUS, Subsidized Stafford, Unsubsidized Stafford, PLUS, state loans. *Student Employment:* Federal Work-Study Program available. Institutional employment available. Off-campus job opportunities are excellent. **Financial Aid Statistics:** 100% freshmen, 99% undergrads receive need-based scholarship or grant aid. 9% freshmen, 9% undergrads receive non-need-based scholarship or grant aid. 63% freshmen, 63% undergrads receive need-based self-help aid. 0% freshmen, 0% undergrads receive athletic scholarships. 97% freshmen, 94% undergrads receive any aid. 51% undergrads borrow to pay for school. Average cumulative indebtedness $6,364. **Criteria for awarding institutional aid:** *Non-need-based:* academics, alumni affiliation, leadership, music/drama, religious affiliation.

CLEARY UNIVERSITY

3750 Cleary Drive, Howell, MI 48843
Phone: 517-548-3670
E-mail: admissions@cleary.edu · **CEEB Code:** 1123
Fax: 517-552-7805 · **Website:** www.cleary.edu · **ACT Code:** 1974

This private school was founded in 1883. It has a 32-acre campus.

RATINGS

Admissions Selectivity Rating: 60* **Fire Safety Rating:** 60*

STUDENTS AND FACULTY

Enrollment: 626. **Student Body:** 54% female, 46% male, 0% out-of-state, 1% international (5 countries represented). Asian 1%, African American 6%, Caucasian 77%, Hispanic 1%, Native American 1%
Retention and Graduation: 75% freshmen return for sophomore year. **Faculty:** 8 full-time faculty, 25% hold PhDs, 63% are members of minority groups, 13% are women. 0% of classes are taught by teaching assistants.

ACADEMICS

Degrees: associate, bachelor's, certificate, master's, terminal associate, transfer associate. **Classes:** Most classes have 10-19 students. Most lab/discussion sessions have 10-19 students. **Majors with Highest Enrollment:** Business/Commerce; Accounting; Management Information Systems. **Special Study Options:** Accelerated program, cooperative education program, distance learning, dual enrollment, independent study, internships. **Disability Services:** Special programs offered to physically disabled students include tutors. **Career services:** Alumni network, alumni services, career/job search classes, internships.

FACILITIES

Housing: 90% of campus accessible to physically disabled. **Special Academic Facilities/Equipment:** Center for Quality, Quality Resource Collection, Center for Business Ethics and Leadership **Computers:** Administrative functions (other than registration) can be performed online. Undergraduates are required to own a computer.

CAMPUS LIFE

Environment: Town. **Activities:** 1 registered organization. **On-Campus Highlights:** Internet Café, Nature Trail, Computer Lab.

ADMISSIONS

Freshman Academic Profile: Average high school GPA 2.97. 85% from public high schools. Minimum paper TOEFL 600. **Basis for Candidate Selection:** *Very important factors considered include:* rigor of secondary school record. *Important factors considered include:* standardized test scores, interview. *Other factors considered include:* application essay, recommendation(s). **Fresh-**

man **Admission Requirements:** High school diploma is required and GED is accepted. **Transfer Admission Requirements:** High school transcript, college transcript(s), statement of good standing from prior institution(s). Minimum college GPA of 2.5 required. Lowest grade transferable D. **General Admission Information:** Application Fee $25. Regular application deadline 8/15. Nonfall registration not accepted. Admission may be deferred for a maximum of 1 year. Credit and/or placement offered for CEEB Advanced Placement tests.

COSTS AND FINANCIAL AID

Annual tuition $13,680. Required fees $0. Average book expense $0. **Required Forms and Deadlines:** FAFSA, Institution's own financial aid form. **Types of Aid:** *Need-based scholarships/grants:* Federal Pell, SEOG, state scholarships/grants, private scholarships, the school's own gift aid. *Loans:* Subsidized Stafford, Unsubsidized Stafford, PLUS. **Financial Aid Statistics:** 79% freshmen, 67% undergrads receive need-based scholarship or grant aid. 15% freshmen, 4% undergrads receive non-need-based scholarship or grant aid. 79% freshmen, 92% undergrads receive need-based self-help aid. 0% freshmen, 0% undergrads receive athletic scholarships. 75% freshmen, 48% undergrads receive any aid. 36% undergrads borrow to pay for school. **Criteria for awarding institutional aid:** *Non-need-based:* academics.

CLEMSON UNIVERSITY

Best 380

105 Sikes Hall, Clemson, SC 29634-5124
Phone: 864-656-2287 · **Financial Aid Phone:** 864-656-2280
E-mail: cuadmissions@clemson.edu · **CEEB Code:** 5111
Fax: 864-656-2464 · **Website:** www.clemson.edu · **ACT Code:** 3842

This public school was founded in 1889.

RATINGS

Admissions Selectivity Rating: 90   **Fire Safety Rating:** 95

STUDENTS AND FACULTY

Enrollment: 16,801. **Student Body:** 46% female, 54% male, 35% out-of-state, 1% international (84 countries represented). Asian 2%, African American 6%, Caucasian 84%, Hispanic 3%, Native American <1%
Retention and Graduation: 92% freshmen return for sophomore year. 59% freshmen graduate within 4 years. 83% freshmen graduate within 6 years. 28% grads go on to further study within 1 year. 25% grads pursue arts and sciences degrees. 5% grads pursue law degrees. 21% grads pursue business degrees. 8% grads pursue medical degrees. **Faculty:** 1,101 full-time faculty, 88% hold PhDs, 35% are members of minority groups, 18% are women. 7% of classes are taught by teaching assistants.

ACADEMICS

Degrees: bachelor's, master's, post-master's certificate. **Classes:** Most classes have 10–19 students. Most lab/discussion sessions have 20–29 students. **Majors with Highest Enrollment:** Engineering; Business/Commerce; Biology/Biological Sciences. **Special Study Options:** cooperative education program, distance learning, double major, exchange student program (domestic), honors program, independent study, internships, study abroad, teacher certification program, We have an RN to BSN program located in Greenville, SC. This is an off-campus degree program for students that have a 2 year degree in Nursing and an RN. **Honors programs:** The National Scholars Program. Please visit: http://www.clemson.edu/national_scholars/ Combined degree programs: BA/MEng, Rn to BSN program. **Disability Services:** Special programs offered to physically disabled students include note-taking services, reader services, tape recorders, tutors. **Career services:** Alumni network, alumni services, career/job search classes, career assessment, internships. Career services highlights include our alumni network, which has grown in both strength and number over the past few years. Current alumni recognize that today's Clemson graduates are significantly better prepared to enter the job market, if they choose to delay graduate school. Assisting other members of the "Clemson Family" is a natural bond ingrained as one prepares to leave the campus—as hard as that may be!.

FACILITIES

Housing: Coed dorms, men's dorms, special housing for international students, women's dorms, fraternity/sorority housing, apartments for single students, Wellness Housing, Theme Housing, Learning-living communities. **Special Academic Facilities/Equipment:** The South Carolina Botanical Gardens, the Campbell Geology Museum, the Brooks Center for the Performing Arts, the Rudolph Lee Art Gallery, The Garrison Livestock Arena, The John C. Calhoun

Home. **Computers:** 75% of classrooms, 25% of dorms, 100% of libraries, 100% of dining areas, 100% of student union, 40% of common outdoor areas have wireless network access. Students can register for classes online. Administrative functions (other than registration) can be performed online. Undergraduates are required to own a computer.

CAMPUS LIFE

Environment: Village. **Activities:** Choral groups, concert band, dance, drama/theater, jazz band, literary magazine, marching band, music ensembles, pep band, radio station, student government, student newspaper, television station, yearbook. 292 registered organizations, 23 honor societies, 24 religious organizations. 26 fraternities, 17 sororities. **Athletics (Intercollegiate):** *Men:* baseball, basketball, cheerleading, cross-country, diving, football, golf, soccer, swimming, tennis, track/field (outdoor), track/field (indoor). *Women:* basketball, cheerleading, crew/rowing, cross-country, diving, soccer, swimming, tennis, track/field (outdoor), track/field (indoor), volleyball. **On-Campus Highlights:** SC Botanical Garden/ Discovery Center/Geology Muse, Hendrix Student Center, Clemson Ice Cream, Conference Center and Inn at Clemson/Walker Golf C, Fort Hill, John C. Calhoun House, Lee Art Gallery, Please visit: http://www.clemson.edu/visitors/index.html. **Environmental Initiatives:** LEED Energy Conservation policy; President's Commission on Sustainability.

ADMISSIONS

Freshman Academic Profile: 89% from public high schools. ACT middle 50% range 26-31. Minimum paper TOEFL 550. **Basis for Candidate Selection:** *Very important factors considered include:* Class rank, academic GPA, rigor of secondary school record, standardized test scores, state residency. *Important factors considered include:* alumni/ae relation. *Other factors considered include:* application essay, recommendation(s), extracurricular activities, talent/ability. **Freshman Admission Requirements:** High school diploma is required and GED is accepted. *Academic units required:* 4 English, 3 mathematics, 3 science, (3 science labs), 3 foreign language, 3 social studies, 1 history, 2 academic electives, 1 PE or ROTC. **Freshman Admission Statistics:** 18,604 applied, 57% admitted, 31% enrolled. **Transfer Admission Requirements:** college transcript(s), Minimum college GPA of 2.5 required. Lowest grade transferable C. **General Admission Information:** Application Fee $60. Regular application deadline 5/1. Notification on a rolling basis, beginning on or about 2/15. Nonfall registration accepted. Credit and/or placement offered for CEEB Advanced Placement tests.

COSTS AND FINANCIAL AID

Annual in-state tuition $13,382. Annual out-of-state tuition $30,826. Room and board $8,142. Average book expense $1,112. **Required Forms and Deadlines:** FAFSA. **Notification of Awards:** Applicants will be notified of awards on a rolling basis beginning 4/1. **Types of Aid:** *Need-based scholarships/grants:* Federal Pell, SEOG, state scholarships/grants, private scholarships, the school's own gift aid, Federal Nursing Scholarships. *Loans:* Direct Subsidized Stafford, Direct Unsubsidized Stafford, Direct PLUS, Subsidized Stafford, Unsubsidized Stafford, PLUS, Federal Perkins, state loans, college/university loans from institutional funds. *Student Employment:* Federal Work-Study Program available. Institutional employment available. Highest amount earned per year from on-campus jobs $3,500. Off-campus job opportunities are fair. **Financial Aid Statistics:** 44% freshmen, 44% undergrads receive need-based scholarship or grant aid. 64% freshmen, 42% undergrads receive non-need-based scholarship or grant aid. 61% freshmen, 70% undergrads receive need-based self-help aid. 4% freshmen, 3% undergrads receive athletic scholarships. 87% freshmen, 71% undergrads receive any aid. 49% undergrads borrow to pay for school. Average cumulative indebtedness $26,934. **Criteria for awarding institutional aid:** *Non-need-based:* academics, art, athletics, leadership, minority status, music/drama, state/district residency.

See page 1030.

THE CLEVELAND INSTITUTE OF ART

11141 East Boulevard, Cleveland, OH 44106
Phone: 216-421-7418 · **Financial Aid Phone:** 216-421-7425
E-mail: admissions@cia.edu · **CEEB Code:** 1152
Fax: 216-754-3634 · **Website:** www.cia.edu · **ACT Code:** 3243

This private school was founded in 1882. It has a 488-acre campus.

RATINGS

Admissions Selectivity Rating: 82   **Fire Safety Rating:** 91

STUDENTS AND FACULTY

Enrollment: 551. **Student Body:** 55% female, 45% male, 31% out-of-state, 7% international (9 countries represented). Asian 3%, African American 10%,

Caucasian 70%, Hispanic 6%, Native American <1%
Retention and Graduation: 81% freshmen return for sophomore year. 60% freshmen graduate within 4 years. 64% freshmen graduate within 6 years. 3% grads go on to further study within 1 year. 2% grads pursue arts and sciences degrees. **Faculty:** 45 full-time faculty, 62% hold PhDs, 38% are members of minority groups, 11% are women. 0% of classes are taught by teaching assistants.

ACADEMICS
Degrees: bachelor's. **Classes:** Most classes have 10–19 students. Most lab/discussion sessions have 10–19 students. **Majors with Highest Enrollment:** Illustration; Industrial and Product Design; Painting. **Special Study Options:** cooperative education program, cross-registration, exchange student program (domestic), honors program, independent study, internships, study abroad, Study for up to 2 semesters at an Alliance of Independent Colleges of Art and Design. **Disability Services:** Special programs offered to physically disabled students include note-taking services, tape recorders, tutors. **Career services:** Alumni network, alumni services, career/job search classes, career assessment, internships.

FACILITIES
Housing: Coed dorms, fraternity/sorority housing, apartments for single students **Special Academic Facilities/Equipment:** The Reinberger Galleries **Computers:** 40% of classrooms, 100% of dorms, 100% of libraries, have wireless network access. Students can register for classes online. Administrative functions (other than registration) can be performed online.

CAMPUS LIFE
Environment: Metropolis. **Activities:** marching band, student government, student newspaper, student-run film society, Campus Ministries. 7 registered organizations, 2 religious organizations. **On-Campus Highlights:** Arabica Coffee Shop, Frank Gehry and Peter B. Lewis Building, Live music at Barking Spider, Cleveland Museum of Art, Reinberger Galleries. **Environmental Initiatives:** Recycling Energy Management Purchase of High Efficiency Boilers and other Equipment

ADMISSIONS
Freshman Academic Profile: Average high school GPA 3.06. 15% in top 10% of high school class, 36% in top 25% of high school class, 64% in top 50% of high school class. SAT Math middle 50% range 440-560. SAT Critical Reading middle 50% range 470-620. SAT Writing middle 50% range 440-570. ACT middle 50% range 19-26. Minimum internet-based TOEFL 79. Minimum paper TOEFL 550. **Basis for Candidate Selection:** *Very important factors considered include:* rigor of secondary school record, talent/ability. *Important factors considered include:* application essay, academic GPA, recommendation(s), standardized test scores, character/personal qualities, interview. *Other factors considered include:* extracurricular activities, level of applicant's interest. **Freshman Admission Requirements:** High school diploma is required and GED is accepted. **Freshman Admission Statistics:** 715 applied, 67% admitted, 29% enrolled. **Transfer Admission Requirements:** college transcript(s), essay or personal statement, Minimum college GPA of 2.0 required. Lowest grade transferable C. **General Admission Information:** Application Fee $30. Notification on a rolling basis, beginning on or about 10/1. Nonfall registration not accepted. Admission may be deferred for a maximum of 1 year. Credit offered for CEEB Advanced Placement tests.

COSTS AND FINANCIAL AID
Annual tuition $35,270. Room and board $11,120. Required fees $2,304. Average book expense $2,150. **Required Forms and Deadlines:** FAFSA, Institution's own financial aid form. **Notification of Awards:** Applicants will be notified of awards on a rolling basis beginning 3/15. **Types of Aid:** *Need-based scholarships/grants:* Federal Pell, SEOG, state scholarships/grants, private scholarships, the school's own gift aid, Academic Merit scholarships/grants (institutional funds). *Loans:* Subsidized Stafford, Unsubsidized Stafford, PLUS, Federal Perkins. *Student Employment:* Federal Work-Study Program available. Off-campus job opportunities are good. **Financial Aid Statistics:** 100% freshmen, 100% undergrads receive need-based scholarship or grant aid. 3% freshmen, 4% undergrads receive non-need-based scholarship or grant aid. 92% freshmen, 94% undergrads receive need-based self-help aid. 0% freshmen, 0% undergrads receive athletic scholarships. 99% freshmen, 99% undergrads receive any aid. 91% undergrads borrow to pay for school. Average cumulative indebtedness $30,163. **Criteria for awarding institutional aid:** *Non-need-based:* academics, art.

CLEVELAND STATE UNIVERSITY

2121 Euclid Avenue, Cleveland, OH 44115-2214
Phone: 216-523-7416 · **Financial Aid Phone:** 216-687-5411
E-mail: admissions@csuohio.edu · **CEEB Code:** 3032
Fax: 216-687-5501 · **Website:** www.csuohio.edu · **ACT Code:** 1221

This public school was founded in 1964. It has a 82-acre campus.

RATINGS
Admissions Selectivity Rating: 80   **Fire Safety Rating:** 60*

STUDENTS AND FACULTY
Enrollment: 11,170. **Student Body:** 55% female, 45% male, 3% out-of-state, 4% international (85 countries represented). Asian 2%, African American 21%, Caucasian 62%, Hispanic 4%, Native American <1%
Retention and Graduation: 65% freshmen return for sophomore year.
Faculty: 520 full-time faculty, 89% hold PhDs, 40% are members of minority groups, 24% are women. 1% of classes are taught by teaching assistants.

ACADEMICS
Degrees: bachelor's, doctoral, master's, post-bachelor's certificate, post-master's certificate. **Classes:** Most classes have 20–29 students. **Majors with Highest Enrollment:** Psychology; Accounting; Business Administration, Management and Operations. **Special Study Options:** Accelerated program, cooperative education program, cross-registration, distance learning, double major, dual enrollment, English as a Second Language (ESL), exchange student program (domestic), honors program, independent study, internships, liberal arts/career combination, student-designed major, study abroad, teacher certification program, weekend college. **Honors programs:** CSU's Honors Program was established in 2004 to serve the needs of academically talented students. Each year, it accepts approximately 40 first-year students and 20-25 juniors who have demonstrated superior academic achievement through their coursework and results on tests such as the ACT and SAT. Honors students at CSU receive a scholarship that covers full tuition as well as all academic fees and the cost of books required for their classes. Honors students in good standing receive this support throughout their four-year undergraduate academic career. Combined degree programs: JD/MBA. **Disability Services:** Special programs offered to physically disabled students include note-taking services, reader services, tape recorders, tutors. **Career services:** alumni services, career/job search classes, career assessment, internships.

FACILITIES
Housing: Coed dorms, special housing for disabled students, fraternity/sorority housing. 90% of campus accessible to physically disabled. **Computers:** Students can register for classes online. Administrative functions (other than registration) can be performed online.

CAMPUS LIFE
Environment: Metropolis. **Activities:** Choral groups, concert band, dance, drama/theater, jazz band, literary magazine, musical theater, opera, pep band, radio station, student government, student newspaper, student-run film society, symphony orchestra, International Student Organization 10 religious organizations. 8 fraternities, 7 sororities. **Athletics (Intercollegiate):** *Men:* baseball, basketball, fencing, golf, soccer, swimming, wrestling. *Women:* basketball, cross-country, fencing, softball, swimming, tennis, track/field (outdoor), track/field (indoor), volleyball. **On-Campus Highlights:** Recreation Center, Main Classroom Atrium, Michael Schwartz Library, The Green Room, Farmer's Market.

ADMISSIONS
Freshman Academic Profile: Average high school GPA 3.19. 12% in top 10% of high school class, 38% in top 25% of high school class, 74% in top 50% of high school class. SAT Math middle 50% range 450-580. SAT Critical Reading middle 50% range 440-570. ACT middle 50% range 19-24. Minimum paper TOEFL 525. **Basis for Candidate Selection:** *Very important factors considered include:* academic GPA, rigor of secondary school record, standardized test scores. *Important factors considered include:* Class rank. **Freshman Admission Requirements:** High school diploma is required and GED is accepted. *Academic units required:* 4 English, 3 mathematics, 3 science, 3 social studies. **Freshman Admission Statistics:** 5,938 applied, 63% admitted, 42% enrolled. **Transfer Admission Requirements:** college transcript(s), Minimum college GPA of 2.0 required. Lowest grade transferable D. **General Admission Information:** Application Fee $30. Regular application deadline 8/15. Notification on a rolling basis, beginning on or about 9/1. Nonfall registration accepted. Admission may be deferred for a maximum of 1 year. Credit and/or placement offered for CEEB Advanced Placement tests.

COSTS AND FINANCIAL AID
Annual in-state tuition $9,264. Annual out-of-state tuition $12,386. Room and board $11,662. Average book expense $800. **Required Forms and Deadlines:** FAFSA. **Notification of Awards:** Applicants will be notified of awards on a

rolling basis beginning 3/15. **Types of Aid:** *Need-based scholarships/grants:* Federal Pell, SEOG, state scholarships/grants, private scholarships, the school's own gift aid. *Loans:* Subsidized Stafford, Unsubsidized Stafford, PLUS, Federal Perkins, state loans, Alternative. *Student Employment:* Federal Work-Study Program available. Institutional employment available. Off-campus job opportunities are excellent. **Financial Aid Statistics:** 86% freshmen, 78% undergrads receive need-based scholarship or grant aid. 4% freshmen, 3% undergrads receive non-need-based scholarship or grant aid. 83% freshmen, 84% undergrads receive need-based self-help aid. 1% freshmen, 2% undergrads receive athletic scholarships. 57% undergrads borrow to pay for school. Average cumulative indebtedness $21,974. **Criteria for awarding institutional aid:** *Non-need-based:* academics, alumni affiliation, art, athletics, leadership, minority status, music/drama, religious affiliation.

COASTAL CAROLINA UNIVERSITY

PO Box 261954, Conway, SC 29528-6054
Phone: 843-349-2170 · **Financial Aid Phone:** 843-349-2313
E-mail: admissions@coastal.edu · **CEEB Code:** 5837
Fax: 843-349-2127 · **Website:** www.coastal.edu · **ACT Code:** 3843

This public school was founded in 1954. It has a 302-acre campus.

RATINGS

Admissions Selectivity Rating: 80   Fire Safety Rating: 83

STUDENTS AND FACULTY

Enrollment: 9,058. **Student Body:** 54% female, 46% male, 50% out-of-state, 1% international (51 countries represented). Asian 1%, African American 20%, Caucasian 70%, Hispanic 4%, Native American <1%
Retention and Graduation: 67% freshmen return for sophomore year. 26% freshmen graduate within 4 years. 45% freshmen graduate within 6 years.
Faculty: 416 full-time faculty, 81% hold PhDs, 42% are members of minority groups, 11% are women. 0% of classes are taught by teaching assistants.

ACADEMICS

Degrees: bachelor's, master's, post-bachelor's certificate. **Classes:** Most classes have 20–29 students. Most lab/discussion sessions have 10–19 students. **Majors with Highest Enrollment:** Marine Biology and Biological Oceanography; Business Administration and Management; Kinesiology and Exercise Science. **Special Study Options:** Accelerated program, cooperative education program, distance learning, double major, dual enrollment, honors program, independent study, internships, student-designed major, study abroad, teacher certification program. **Disability Services:** Special programs offered to physically disabled students include note-taking services, reader services, tape recorders, tutors. **Career services:** Alumni network, alumni services, career/job search classes, career assessment, internships. Career services highlights include our Career Assessment Program which is an integral part of University 110 and is required of all freshmen.

FACILITIES

Housing: Coed dorms, special housing for disabled students. 98% of campus accessible to physically disabled. **Computers:** 100% of classrooms, 100% of libraries, 100% of dining areas, 100% of student union, 83% of common outdoor areas have wireless network access. Students can register for classes online. Administrative functions (other than registration) can be performed online.

CAMPUS LIFE

Environment: Town. **Activities:** Choral groups, concert band, dance, drama/theater, jazz band, literary magazine, marching band, music ensembles, musical theater, pep band, radio station, student government, student newspaper, Campus Ministries, International Student Organization. 91 registered organizations, 32 honor societies, 13 religious organizations. 9 fraternities, 7 sororities. **Athletics (Intercollegiate):** *Men:* baseball, basketball, cheerleading, cross-country, football, golf, soccer, tennis, track/field (outdoor). *Women:* basketball, cheerleading, cross-country, golf, soccer, softball, tennis, track/field (outdoor), volleyball. **On-Campus Highlights:** Humanities and Fine Arts Building, Brooks Stadium, CINO Grille / Student Center, Recreation Center, Java City Café. **Environmental Initiatives:** Sustainable Transportation including: Zip Car, 120 in the bike sharing fleet, bike fix stations, shuttles and EV stations; Green Power, including on-site solar and electric vehicle charging stations with 43 water refill station.

ADMISSIONS

Freshman Academic Profile: Average high school GPA 3.37. 8% in top 10% of high school class, 29% in top 25% of high school class, 67% in top 50% of high school class. 88% from public high schools. SAT Math middle 50% range 460-550. SAT Critical Reading middle 50% range 450-540. ACT middle 50% range 19-23. Minimum internet-based TOEFL 71. Minimum paper TOEFL

527. **Basis for Candidate Selection:** *Very important factors considered include:* academic GPA, rigor of secondary school record, standardized test scores. *Important factors considered include:* Class rank. *Other factors considered include:* application essay, recommendation(s), character/personal qualities, extracurricular activities, first generation, geographical residence, interview, level of applicant's interest, state residency, talent/ability, work experience. **Freshman Admission Requirements:** High school diploma is required and GED is accepted. *Academic units required:* 4 English, 3 mathematics, 3 science, (3 science labs), 2 foreign language, 2 social studies, 1 history, 4 academic electives, 1 PE or ROTC. **Freshman Admission Statistics:** 14,799 applied, 64% admitted, 25% enrolled. **Transfer Admission Requirements:** college transcript(s), statement of good standing from prior institution(s). Minimum college GPA of 2.0 required. Lowest grade transferable C-. **General Admission Information:** Application Fee $45. Regular application deadline 8/15. Notification on a rolling basis, beginning on or about 9/15. Nonfall registration accepted. Admission may be deferred for a maximum of 1 year. Credit and/or placement offered for CEEB Advanced Placement tests.

COSTS AND FINANCIAL AID

Annual in-state tuition $9,960. Annual out-of-state tuition $23,300. Room and board $8,440. Required fees $180. Average book expense $1,142. **Required Forms and Deadlines:** FAFSA. **Notification of Awards:** Applicants will be notified of awards on a rolling basis beginning 3/1. **Types of Aid:** *Need-based scholarships/grants:* Federal Pell, SEOG, state scholarships/grants, private scholarships, the school's own gift aid, ACG/SMART. *Loans:* Subsidized Stafford, Unsubsidized Stafford, PLUS, Federal Perkins, state loans. *Student Employment:* Federal Work-Study Program available. Institutional employment available. Highest amount earned per year from on-campus jobs $20,030. Off-campus job opportunities are excellent. **Financial Aid Statistics:** 51% freshmen, 55% undergrads receive need-based scholarship or grant aid. 45% freshmen, 29% undergrads receive non-need-based scholarship or grant aid. 92% freshmen, 91% undergrads receive need-based self-help aid. 4% freshmen, 5% undergrads receive athletic scholarships. 89% freshmen, 95% undergrads receive any aid. 77% undergrads borrow to pay for school. Average cumulative indebtedness $27,114. **Criteria for awarding institutional aid:** *Non-need-based:* academics, art, athletics, leadership, music/drama, state/district residency.

COE COLLEGE

Best 380

1220 First Avenue NE, Cedar Rapids, IA 52402
Phone: 319-399-8500 · **Financial Aid Phone:** 319-399-8540
E-mail: admission@coe.edu · **CEEB Code:** 6101
Fax: 319-399-8816 · **Website:** www.coe.edu · **ACT Code:** 1294

This private school, affiliated with the Presbyterian Church, was founded in 1851. It has a 53-acre campus.

RATINGS

Admissions Selectivity Rating: 89   Fire Safety Rating: 79

STUDENTS AND FACULTY

Enrollment: 1,350. **Student Body:** 56% female, 44% male, 51% out-of-state, 2% international (17 countries represented). Asian 2%, African American 5%, Caucasian 76%, Hispanic 8%, Native American <1%
Retention and Graduation: 78% freshmen return for sophomore year. 61% freshmen graduate within 4 years. 71% freshmen graduate within 6 years. 17% grads go on to further study within 1 year. 3% grads pursue arts and sciences degrees. 3% grads pursue law degrees. 2% grads pursue business degrees. 4% grads pursue medical degrees. **Faculty:** 95 full-time faculty, 91% hold PhDs, 40% are members of minority groups, 8% are women. 0% of classes are taught by teaching assistants.

ACADEMICS

Degrees: bachelor's, master's. **Classes:** Most classes have 10–19 students. Most lab/discussion sessions have 10–19 students. **Majors with Highest Enrollment:** Biology/Biological Sciences; Business Administration and Management; Psychology. **Special Study Options:** Accelerated program, cross-registration, double major, dual enrollment, English as a Second Language (ESL), exchange student program (domestic), honors program, independent study, internships, student-designed major, study abroad, teacher certification program. **Honors programs:** College honors program consisting of five honors seminars and an honors project or thesis. Combined degree programs: BA/MArch Washington University. **Disability Services:** Special programs offered to physically disabled students include note-taking services, tape recorders, tutors. **Career services:** Alumni network, career/job search classes, career assessment, internships, regional alumni. Career services highlights include The Coe Plan, which requires all students to complete an internship, research, study abroad, or other "out of the classroom" experience during their junior year.

FACILITIES
Housing: Coed dorms, men's dorms, women's dorms, fraternity/sorority housing, apartments for single students, Wellness Housing, Theme Housing. 70% of campus accessible to physically disabled. **Special Academic Facilities/Equipment:** Ornithological museum, writing lab, theatre. **Computers:** 70% of classrooms, 10% of dorms, 100% of libraries, 100% of dining areas, 100% of student union, 80% of common outdoor areas have wireless network access. Students can register for classes online.

CAMPUS LIFE
Environment: City. **Activities:** Choral groups, concert band, dance, drama/theater, jazz band, literary magazine, music ensembles, musical theater, pep band, radio station, student government, student newspaper, symphony orchestra, television station, yearbook, Campus Ministries, International Student Organization. 60 registered organizations, 8 honor societies, 4 religious organizations. 5 fraternities, 3 sororities. **Athletics (Intercollegiate):** *Men:* baseball, basketball, cross-country, diving, football, golf, soccer, swimming, tennis, track/field (outdoor), track/field (indoor), wrestling. *Women:* basketball, cheerleading, cross-country, diving, golf, soccer, softball, swimming, tennis, track/field (outdoor), track/field (indoor), volleyball. **On-Campus Highlights:** Student Union/Coffee Shop, Dows Theatre, Library/Art Galleries, Fitness Center, Racquet Center. **Environmental Initiatives:** Wilderness Field Station; Peterson Hall renovation; Steam Plant.

ADMISSIONS
Freshman Academic Profile: Average high school GPA 3.65. 34% in top 10% of high school class, 67% in top 25% of high school class, 91% in top 50% of high school class. SAT Math middle 50% range 530-630. SAT Critical Reading middle 50% range 500-645. SAT Writing middle 50% range 480-605. ACT middle 50% range 22-28. Minimum internet-based TOEFL 68. Minimum paper TOEFL 520. **Basis for Candidate Selection:** *Very important factors considered include:* academic GPA, standardized test scores. *Important factors considered include:* Class rank, application essay, recommendation(s). *Other factors considered include:* rigor of secondary school record, alumni/ae relation, character/personal qualities, extracurricular activities, first generation, interview, level of applicant's interest, racial/ethnic status, talent/ability, volunteer work. **Freshman Admission Requirements:** High school diploma is required and GED is accepted. **Freshman Admission Statistics:** 3,403 applied, 55% admitted, 20% enrolled. **Transfer Admission Requirements:** High school transcript, college transcript(s), essay or personal statement, statement of good standing from prior institution(s). Minimum college GPA of 2.5 required. Lowest grade transferable C. **General Admission Information:** Application Fee $30. Regular application deadline 3/1. Regular notification 3/15. Notification on a rolling basis, beginning on or about 10/1. Nonfall registration accepted. Admission may be deferred for a maximum of 2 years. Credit and/or placement offered for CEEB Advanced Placement tests.

COSTS AND FINANCIAL AID
Required Forms and Deadlines: FAFSA. **Notification of Awards:** Applicants will be notified of awards on a rolling basis beginning 3/15. **Types of Aid:** *Need-based scholarships/grants:* Federal Pell, SEOG, state scholarships/grants, private scholarships, the school's own gift aid. *Loans:* Direct Subsidized Stafford, Direct Unsubsidized Stafford, Direct PLUS, Federal Perkins, college/university loans from institutional funds. *Student Employment:* Federal Work-Study Program available. Institutional employment available. Highest amount earned per year from on-campus jobs $500. Off-campus job opportunities are excellent. **Financial Aid Statistics:** 100% freshmen, 100% undergrads receive need-based scholarship or grant aid. 16% freshmen, 15% undergrads receive non-need-based scholarship or grant aid. 81% freshmen, 82% undergrads receive need-based self-help aid. 0% freshmen, 0% undergrads receive athletic scholarships. 99% freshmen, 99% undergrads receive any aid. 77% undergrads borrow to pay for school. Average cumulative indebtedness $27,024. **Criteria for awarding institutional aid:** *Non-need-based:* academics, alumni affiliation, art, music/drama.

COGSWELL COLLEGE

1175 Bordeaux Drive, Sunnyvale, CA 94089-1299
Phone: 408-498-5160 • **Financial Aid Phone:** 408-498-5107
E-mail: admissions@cogswell.edu • **CEEB Code:** 1177
Fax: 408-747-0764 • **ACT Code:** 1177

This private school was founded in 1887. It has a 5-acre campus.

RATINGS
Admissions Selectivity Rating: 75   **Fire Safety Rating:** 92

STUDENTS AND FACULTY
Enrollment: 457. **Student Body:** 24% female, 76% male, 11% out-of-state, 1% international (13 countries represented). Asian 12%, African American 4%, Caucasian 42%, Hispanic 15%, Native American <1%
Retention and Graduation: 80% freshmen return for sophomore year. 19% freshmen graduate within 4 years. 31% freshmen graduate within 6 years. 1% grads pursue business degrees. **Faculty:** 18 full-time faculty, 61% hold PhDs, 17% are members of minority groups, 0% are women. 0% of classes are taught by teaching assistants.

ACADEMICS
Degrees: bachelor's. **Classes:** Most classes have fewer than 10 students. **Majors with Highest Enrollment:** Recording Arts Technology/Technician, Animation, Interactive Technology, Video Graphics and Special Effects. **Special Study Options:** cooperative education program, distance learning, double major, exchange student program (domestic), internships, student-designed major, study abroad. Combined degree programs: Digital art and animation, Digital Audio Technology. **Career services:** Alumni network, career/job search classes,

FACILITIES
Housing: apartments for single students. 100% of campus accessible to physically disabled. **Special Academic Facilities/Equipment:** The Gallery at Cogswell **Computers:** 100% of classrooms, 100% of libraries, 100% of dining areas, 100% of student union, have wireless network access. Students can register for classes online. Administrative functions (other than registration) can be performed online. Undergraduates are required to own a computer.

CAMPUS LIFE
Environment: Village. **Activities:** drama/theater, radio station, student government. 5 registered organizations. **On-Campus Highlights:** Gallery, Library, Smart Lab, Dragon's Den, Audio Recording Studio. **Environmental Initiatives:** saving energy, recycling, saving water.

ADMISSIONS
Freshman Academic Profile: SAT Math middle 50% range 500-700. SAT Critical Reading middle 50% range 500-660. SAT Writing middle 50% range 490-660. ACT middle 50% range 23-25. Minimum paper TOEFL 525. **Basis for Candidate Selection:** *Very important factors considered include:* academic GPA, talent/ability. *Important factors considered include:* application essay, recommendation(s). *Other factors considered include:* extracurricular activities, interview, level of applicant's interest, volunteer work. **Freshman Admission Requirements:** High school diploma is required and GED is accepted. *Academic units required:* 3 English, 3 mathematics, 1 science, (1 science labs). **Freshman Admission Statistics:** 194 applied, 78% admitted, 68% enrolled. **Transfer Admission Requirements:** High school transcript, college transcript(s), essay or personal statement, Minimum college GPA of 2.5 required. Lowest grade transferable C. **General Admission Information:** Application Fee $55. Regular application deadline 3/1. Nonfall registration accepted. Admission may be deferred for a maximum of 1 year. Credit and/or placement offered for CEEB Advanced Placement tests.

COSTS AND FINANCIAL AID
Annual tuition $15,980. Room and board $7,200. Required fees $180. Average book expense $1,710. **Required Forms and Deadlines:** FAFSA, State aid form. **Notification of Awards:** Applicants will be notified of awards on a rolling basis beginning 3/15. **Types of Aid:** *Need-based scholarships/grants:* Federal Pell, SEOG, state scholarships/grants, private scholarships, the school's own gift aid. *Loans:* Subsidized Stafford, Unsubsidized Stafford, PLUS. *Student Employment:* Federal Work-Study Program available. Institutional employment available. Off-campus job opportunities are good. **Criteria for awarding institutional aid:** *Non-need-based:* academics, art, music/drama.

COKER COLLEGE

300 East College Avenue, Hartsville, SC 29550
Phone: 843-383-8050
E-mail: admissions@coker.edu • **CEEB Code:**
Fax: 843-383-8056 • **Website:** www.coker.edu

This is a private school.

RATINGS

Admissions Selectivity Rating: 80   Fire Safety Rating: 60*

STUDENTS AND FACULTY

Enrollment: 674. **Student Body:** 63% female, 37% male, 19% out-of-state, 3% international. Asian 0%, African American 27%, Caucasian 67%, Hispanic 2%, Native American 1%
Retention and Graduation: 71% freshmen return for sophomore year. 48% freshmen graduate within 4 years. 60% freshmen graduate within 6 years. **Faculty:** 58 full-time faculty, 81% hold PhDs, 47% are members of minority groups, 12% are women. 0% of classes are taught by teaching assistants.

ACADEMICS

Degrees: bachelor's. **Classes:** Most classes have 10–19 students. Most lab/discussion sessions have 10–19 students. **Majors with Highest Enrollment:** Psychology; Graphic Design; Business/Commerce. **Special Study Options:** double major, dual enrollment, honors program, independent study, internships, student-designed major, study abroad, teacher certification program. **Disability Services:** Special programs offered to physically disabled students include tape recorders, tutors. **Career services:** career/job search classes, career assessment, internships. With our internships students have the opportunity to receive hands-on experience in their field, which gives them a competitive edge in today's job market.

FACILITIES

Housing: Coed dorms, special housing for international students. 80% of campus accessible to physically disabled. **Special Academic Facilities/Equipment:** Art gallery, state-of-the-art performing arts center, dark rooms, botanical gardens, graduate-level science equipment. **Computers:** Administrative functions (other than registration) can be performed online.

CAMPUS LIFE

Activities: Choral groups, dance, drama/theater, literary magazine, music ensembles, musical theater, student government, student newspaper, Campus Ministries, International Student Organization. 27 registered organizations, 4 honor societies, 2 religious organizations. **Athletics (Intercollegiate):** *Men:* baseball, basketball, cheerleading, cross-country, golf, soccer, tennis. *Women:* basketball, cheerleading, cross-country, soccer, softball, tennis, volleyball. **On-Campus Highlights:** The Cobra Den, The Cobra Caf, The Student Center, The Performing Arts Center, Outdoor Volleyball Courts, The Cobra Den includes a coffee area, dance floor, and a game room.

ADMISSIONS

Freshman Academic Profile: Average high school GPA 3.37. 1% in top 10% of high school class, 28% in top 25% of high school class, 70% in top 50% of high school class. SAT Math middle 50% range 440-570. SAT Critical Reading middle 50% range 420-570. ACT middle 50% range 17-22. Minimum paper TOEFL 500. **Basis for Candidate Selection:** *Very important factors considered include:* academic GPA, standardized test scores. *Important factors considered include:* Class rank, rigor of secondary school record, level of applicant's interest. *Other factors considered include:* application essay, recommendation(s), alumni/ae relation, character/personal qualities, extracurricular activities, interview, talent/ability, volunteer work, work experience. **Freshman Admission Requirements:** High school diploma is required and GED is accepted. *Academic units required:* 4 English, 3 mathematics, 3 science, (1 science labs), 2 foreign language, 3 social studies. **Freshman Admission Statistics:** 1,112 applied, 56% admitted, 25% enrolled. **Transfer Admission Requirements:** High school transcript, college transcript(s), statement of good standing from prior institution(s). Minimum college GPA of 2.0 required. Lowest grade transferable C. **General Admission Information:** Application Fee $15. Regular application deadline 8/1. Notification on a rolling basis, beginning on or about 9/1. Nonfall registration accepted. Admission may be deferred for a maximum of 1 year. Credit and/or placement offered for CEEB Advanced Placement tests.

COSTS AND FINANCIAL AID

Annual tuition $22,200. Room and board $6,950. Average book expense $1,500. **Required Forms and Deadlines:** FAFSA. **Notification of Awards:** Applicants will be notified of awards on a rolling basis beginning 3/1. **Types of Aid:** *Need-based scholarships/grants:* Federal Pell, SEOG, state scholarships/grants, private scholarships, the school's own gift aid. *Loans:* Subsidized Stafford, Un-subsidized Stafford, PLUS, Federal Perkins, state loans, Private Source Loans. *Student Employment:* Federal Work-Study Program available. Institutional employment available. Highest amount earned per year from on-campus jobs $1,072. Off-campus job opportunities are good. **Financial Aid Statistics:** 96% freshmen, 96% undergrads receive need-based scholarship or grant aid. 100% freshmen, 93% undergrads receive non-need-based scholarship or grant aid. 78% freshmen, 80% undergrads receive need-based self-help aid. 5% freshmen, 6% undergrads receive athletic scholarships. 100% freshmen, 100% undergrads receive any aid. 81% undergrads borrow to pay for school. Average cumulative indebtedness $23,222. **Criteria for awarding institutional aid:** *Non-need-based:* academics, alumni affiliation, art, athletics, job skills, leadership, minority status, music/drama, religious affiliation, state/district residency.

COLBY COLLEGE

4800 Mayflower Hill, Waterville, ME 4901
Phone: 207-859-4828 • **Financial Aid Phone:** 207-859-4832
E-mail: admissions@colby.edu • **CEEB Code:** 3280
Fax: 207-859-4828 • **Website:** www.colby.edu • **ACT Code:** 1638

This private school was founded in 1813. It has a 714-acre campus.

RATINGS

Admissions Selectivity Rating: 94   Fire Safety Rating: 97

STUDENTS AND FACULTY

Enrollment: 1,847. **Student Body:** 53% female, 47% male, 86% out-of-state, 11% international (74 countries represented). Asian 6%, African American 3%, Caucasian 60%, Hispanic 6%, Native American <1%
Retention and Graduation: 85% freshmen graduate within 4 years. 29% grads go on to further study within 1 year. 20% grads pursue arts and sciences degrees. 3% grads pursue law degrees. 3% grads pursue medical degrees. **Faculty:** 171 full-time faculty, 97% hold PhDs, 43% are members of minority groups, 14% are women. 0% of classes are taught by teaching assistants.

ACADEMICS

Degrees: bachelor's. **Classes:** Most classes have 10–19 students. Most lab/discussion sessions have 10–19 students. **Majors with Highest Enrollment:** Biology/Biological Sciences; Economics; English Language and Literature. **Special Study Options:** cross-registration, double major, exchange student program (domestic), honors program, independent study, internships, student-designed major, study abroad, teacher certification program, Summer research assistantships; Colby has coordinated 3-2 engineering programs with Dartmouth; Colby offers junior-year abroad programs in France, Spain, and Russia. **Disability Services:** Special programs offered to physically disabled students include note-taking services, reader services, tape recorders, tutors. **Career services:** Alumni network, alumni services, career/job search classes, career assessment, internships, regional alumni. Career services highlights include Colby Connect (see website for details) http://www.colby.edu/academics_cs/resources/offices/careerservices/index.cfm.

FACILITIES

Housing: Coed dorms, Wellness Housing, Theme Housing, Quiet halls, chem-free halls, apartments for seniors only, student interest halls. 92% of campus accessible to physically disabled. **Special Academic Facilities/Equipment:** 28,000 square foot art museum, completely renovated student center (Pulver Pavilion), arboretum, electronic microscopes, greenhouse, astronomical observatory, writer's center, cross-country ski trails, Goldfarb Center for Public Affairs and Civic Engagement, multicultural center, rare books and archives library, computer research classroom, language lab. **Computers:** 100% of classrooms, 100% of dorms, 100% of libraries, 100% of dining areas, 100% of student union, 10% of common outdoor areas have wireless network access. Students can register for classes online. Administrative functions (other than registration) can be performed online.

CAMPUS LIFE

Environment: Village. **Activities:** Choral groups, concert band, dance, drama/theater, jazz band, literary magazine, music ensembles, musical theater, radio station, student government, student newspaper, student-run film society, symphony orchestra, yearbook, International Student Organization. 91 registered organizations, 9 honor societies, 6 religious organizations. **Athletics (Intercollegiate):** *Men:* baseball, basketball, crew/rowing, cross-country, diving, football, golf, ice hockey, lacrosse, skiing (downhill/alpine), skiing (nordic/cross-country), soccer, squash, swimming, tennis, track/field (outdoor), track/field (indoor). *Women:* basketball, crew/rowing, cross-country, diving, field hockey, golf, ice hockey, lacrosse, skiing (downhill/alpine), skiing (nordic/cross-country), soccer, softball, squash, swimming, tennis, track/field (outdoor), track/field (indoor), volleyball. **On-Campus Highlights:** Pulver Pavillion, Colby College Museum of Art, Johnson Pond, Perkins Arboretum trails (running, cross country). **Environmental Initiatives:** Since October 2003 Colby used electricity only from 100-percent renewable sources. A biomass plant heating plant—burning fuel certified by the Sustainable Forestry Initiative was completed in early 2012, replacing 90 percent (about 1 millon gallons) of heating oil annually. It is a major component of the commitment to carbon-neutrality by 2015. Colby seeks LEED certification for new construction and renovation projects. At the end of 2011 Colby had six LEED-certified buildings, including three certified at the gold level.

ADMISSIONS

Freshman Academic Profile: 61% in top 10% of high school class, 86% in top 25% of high school class, 96% in top 50% of high school class. 48% from public high schools. SAT Math middle 50% range 620-720. SAT Critical Reading middle 50% range 610-710. SAT Writing middle 50% range 630-710. ACT middle 50% range 28-32. Minimum internet-based TOEFL 100. **Basis for Candidate Selection:** *Very important factors considered include:* rigor of secondary school record, character/personal qualities. *Important factors considered include:* Class rank, application essay, academic GPA, recommendation(s), standardized test scores, extracurricular activities, racial/ethnic status, talent/ability. *Other factors considered include:* alumni/ae relation, first generation, geographical residence, interview, level of applicant's interest, state residency, volunteer work, work experience. **Freshman Admission Requirements:** High school diploma or equivalent is not required. **Freshman Admission Statistics:** 5,148 applied, 28% admitted, 33% enrolled. **Transfer Admission Requirements:** High school transcript, college transcript(s), essay or personal statement, standardized test scores, statement of good standing from prior institution(s). Minimum college GPA of 3.0 required. Lowest grade transferable C. **General Admission Information:** Application Fee $65. Early decision application deadline 11/15. Regular application deadline 1/1. Regular notification 4/1. Nonfall registration accepted. Admission may be deferred for a maximum of 1 year. Credit and/or placement offered for CEEB Advanced Placement tests.

COSTS AND FINANCIAL AID

Annual tuition $45,360. Room and board $12,150. Required fees $1,990. Average book expense $700. **Required Forms and Deadlines:** FAFSA, CSS/Financial Aid PROFILE, Business/Farm Supplement. **Notification of Awards:** Applicants will be notified of awards on or about 4/1. **Types of Aid:** *Need-based scholarships/grants:* Federal Pell, SEOG, state scholarships/grants, private scholarships, the school's own gift aid. *Loans:* Direct Subsidized Stafford, Direct Unsubsidized Stafford, Direct PLUS, Subsidized Stafford, Unsubsidized Stafford, PLUS, Federal Perkins, state loans, college/university loans from institutional funds, Alternative Loans. *Student Employment:* Federal Work-Study Program available. Institutional employment available. Highest amount earned per year from on-campus jobs $5,600. Off-campus job opportunities are poor. **Financial Aid Statistics:** 100% freshmen, 100% undergrads receive need-based scholarship or grant aid. 2% freshmen, 2% undergrads receive non-need-based scholarship or grant aid. 68% freshmen, 74% undergrads receive need-based self-help aid. 0% freshmen, 0% undergrads receive athletic scholarships. 41% freshmen, 43% undergrads receive any aid. 33% undergrads borrow to pay for school. Average cumulative indebtedness $16,374.

COLBY-SAWYER COLLEGE

541 Main Street, New London, NH 03257-7835
Phone: 603-526-3700 · **Financial Aid Phone:** 603-526-3717
E-mail: admissions@colbysawyer.edu · **CEEB Code:** 3281
Fax: 603-526-3452 · **Website:** www.colby-sawyer.edu · **ACT Code:** 2506

This private school was founded in 1837. It has a 200-acre campus.

RATINGS

Admissions Selectivity Rating: 71   **Fire Safety Rating:** 69

STUDENTS AND FACULTY

Enrollment: 942. **Student Body:** 65% female, 35% male, 68% out-of-state, 1% international (11 countries represented). Asian 1%, African American 1%, Caucasian 90%, Hispanic 1%, Native American <1%
Retention and Graduation: 51% freshmen graduate within 4 years. 60% freshmen graduate within 6 years. **Faculty:** 60 full-time faculty, 73% hold PhDs, 52% are members of minority groups, 2% are women. 0% of classes are taught by teaching assistants.

ACADEMICS

Degrees: associate, bachelor's, transfer associate. **Classes:** Most classes have 10–19 students. Most lab/discussion sessions have 10–19 students. **Majors with Highest Enrollment:** Business Administration and Management; Registered Nursing/Registered Nurse; Sport and Fitness Administration/Management. **Special Study Options:** Accelerated program, cross-registration, double major, dual enrollment, English as a Second Language (ESL), exchange student program (domestic), honors program, independent study, internships, student-designed major, study abroad, teacher certification program. **Honors programs:** The Wesson Honors Program is designed to provide highly motivated students with an optional intensive experience in the liberal arts. By creating academic, cultural, and social opportunities for integrative and interdisciplinary intellectual discovery, the program challenges students not only to widen their own avenues of intellectual exploration, but to take leadership in a community of scholars and participate as catalysts for inquiry and discussion across the college. **Disability Services:** Special programs offered to physically disabled students include tape recorders, tutors.

FACILITIES

Housing: Coed dorms, special housing for disabled students, women's dorms, Substance-free Residence Hall. 50% of campus accessible to physically disabled. **Special Academic Facilities/Equipment:** Sawyer Fine Arts Center, Windy Hill School (pre-school—grade 3 laboratory school), Ivey Science Center, Hogan Sports Center, Video Studio and Editing Room, Radio Station (WSCS 90.9 FM).

CAMPUS LIFE

Environment: Rural. **Activities:** Choral groups, dance, drama/theater, literary magazine, musical theater, radio station, student government, student newspaper, yearbook. 40 registered organizations, 5 honor societies, 1 religious organization. **Athletics (Intercollegiate):** *Men:* baseball, basketball, diving, equestrian sports, skiing (downhill/alpine), soccer, swimming, tennis, track/field (outdoor). *Women:* basketball, diving, equestrian sports, lacrosse, skiing (downhill/alpine), soccer, swimming, tennis, track/field (outdoor), volleyball. **On-Campus Highlights:** Dan and Kathleen Hogan Sports Center, Susan Colgate Cleveland Library/Learning Center, Lethbridge Lodge, Thornton Livingroom, Rooke Hall.

ADMISSIONS

Freshman Academic Profile: Average high school GPA 3. 83% from public high schools. SAT Math middle 50% range 440-530. SAT Critical Reading middle 50% range 440-540. ACT middle 50% range 18-22. Minimum paper TOEFL 500. **Basis for Candidate Selection:** *Very important factors considered include:* academic GPA, rigor of secondary school record, interview. *Important factors considered include:* Class rank, application essay, recommendation(s), standardized test scores, alumni/ae relation, extracurricular activities, level of applicant's interest, talent/ability, volunteer work, work experience. *Other factors considered include:* first generation, geographical residence, state residency. **Freshman Admission Requirements:** High school diploma is required and GED is accepted. **Freshman Admission Statistics:** 1,672 applied, 87% admitted, 24% enrolled. **Transfer Admission Requirements:** college transcript(s), essay or personal statement, Minimum college GPA of 2.0 required. Lowest grade transferable C. **General Admission Information:** Application Fee $45. Early decision application deadline 12/1. Regular application deadline 4/1. Notification on a rolling basis, beginning on or about 1/1. Nonfall registration accepted. Admission may be deferred for a maximum of 1 YEAR. Credit and/or placement offered for CEEB Advanced Placement tests.

COSTS AND FINANCIAL AID

Annual tuition $29,620. Room and board $10,340. Required fees $0. Average book expense $750. **Required Forms and Deadlines:** FAFSA. **Notification of Awards:** Applicants will be notified of awards on a rolling basis beginning 3/1. **Types of Aid:** *Need-based scholarships/grants:* Federal Pell, SEOG, state scholarships/grants, private scholarships, the school's own gift aid. *Loans:* Subsidized Stafford, Unsubsidized Stafford, PLUS, Federal Perkins, state loans, college/university loans from institutional funds. *Student Employment:* Federal Work-Study Program available. Institutional employment available. Off-campus job opportunities are good. **Financial Aid Statistics:** 100% freshmen, 95% undergrads receive need-based scholarship or grant aid. 4% freshmen, 5% undergrads receive non-need-based scholarship or grant aid. 93% freshmen, 96% undergrads receive need-based self-help aid. 0% freshmen, 0% undergrads receive athletic scholarships. 83% freshmen, 83% undergrads receive any aid. 77% undergrads borrow to pay for school. Average cumulative indebtedness $18,306. **Criteria for awarding institutional aid:** *Non-need-based:* academics, alumni affiliation, art, leadership, music/drama.

COLGATE UNIVERSITY

13 Oak Drive, Hamilton, NY 13346
Phone: 315-228-7401 · **Financial Aid Phone:** 315-228-7431
E-mail: admission@colgate.edu · **CEEB Code:** 2086
Fax: 315-228-7544 · **Website:** www.colgate.edu · **ACT Code:** 2702

This private school was founded in 1819. It has a 515-acre campus.

RATINGS

Admissions Selectivity Rating: 97   **Fire Safety Rating:** 92

STUDENTS AND FACULTY

Enrollment: 2,872. **Student Body:** 55% female, 45% male, 73% out-of-state, 8% international (47 countries represented). Asian 3%, African American 4%, Caucasian 68%, Hispanic 8%, Native American <1%
Retention and Graduation: 87% freshmen graduate within 4 years. 18% grads go on to further study within 1 year. 10% grads pursue arts and sciences degrees. 4% grads pursue law degrees. 1% grads pursue business degrees. 3% grads pursue medical degrees. **Faculty:** 296 full-time faculty, 99% hold PhDs, 42% are members of minority groups, 22% are women.

ACADEMICS

Degrees: bachelor's, master's. **Classes:** Most classes have 10–19 students. Most lab/discussion sessions have 10–19 students. **Majors with Highest Enrollment:** English Language and Literature; Economics; History. **Special Study Options:** cross-registration, double major, honors program, independent study, internships, liberal arts/career combination, student-designed major, study abroad, teacher certification program, Extended study program allows students to further academic work with a 3-5 week off campus experience during the winter or summer break. Recent trips have travelled to 13 locations around the world including South Africa, Ireland, and China. **Honors programs:** Each year, Colgate honors its top (approximately) 200 accepted students as Alumni Memorial Scholars. This recognition is the highest honor within the admission process, and an indication of an excellent match, both academically and personally, with Colgate. Combined degree programs: Pre-Engineering: BA/MS in Architecture. **Disability Services:** Special programs offered to physically disabled students include note-taking services, reader services, tape recorders, tutors. **Career services:** Alumni network, alumni services, career assessment, internships. Career services highlights include Colgate alumni, who are a valuable resource for students who are exploring their career options. Recently, more than 350 alumni helped currenst students in career exploration. Approximately 4,000 alumni are registered with Career Services to aid students in internship and job searches.

FACILITIES

Housing: Coed dorms, special housing for disabled students, fraternity/sorority housing, cooperative housing, apartments for single students, Wellness Housing, Theme Housing: Peace Studies, La Casa Pan Latina, Harlem Reniassance Center, French-Italian House, etc. Accomodations for students with special needs. Townhouses for small groups of students. 20% of campus accessible to physically disabled. **Special Academic Facilities/Equipment:** Art galleries, anthropology museum, language lab, cable TV station, life sciences complex, geology/fossil collection, observatory, electron microscopes, laser lab, weather lab. **Computers:** Students can register for classes online. Administrative functions (other than registration) can be performed online.

CAMPUS LIFE

Environment: Rural. **Activities:** Choral groups, concert band, dance, drama/theater, jazz band, literary magazine, music ensembles, musical theater, pep band, radio station, student government, student newspaper, student-run film society, symphony orchestra, television station, yearbook, Campus Ministries, International Student Organization, Model UN. 160 registered organizations, 4 honor societies, 8 religious organizations. 6 fraternities, 3 sororities. **Athletics (Intercollegiate):** *Men:* basketball, crew/rowing, cross-country, diving, football, golf, ice hockey, lacrosse, soccer, swimming, tennis, track/field (outdoor). *Women:* basketball, crew/rowing, cross-country, diving, field hockey, ice hockey, lacrosse, soccer, softball, swimming, tennis, track/field (outdoor), volleyball. **On-Campus Highlights:** Picker Art Gallery, Case-Geyer Library, ALANA Culture Center, Ho Science Center, O'Connor Campus Center (The Coop), Two recently completed building projects: $52 million renovation to the Case Library and The Robert H.N. Ho Science Center. **Environmental Initiatives:** All electricity used on campus is hydroelectric, with some supplemental nuclear power. Colgates wood-chip-burning heating plant utilizes a renewable energy source to provide about 70 percent of our total requirement. Colgate signed an agreement with Clean Air-Cool Planet in 2004, agreeing to complete a campuswide greenhouse gas emissions inventory, raise awareness about the importance of addressing climate change within the campus community, adopt a greenhouse gas emissions reduction target, and develop and implement a strategic plan to meet established targets and monitor progress over time. Colgate routinely builds and renovates to LEED silver standards. Architectural consultants are required to be LEED certified and to provide a rigorous analysis of sustainable features for each major design and construction project.

ADMISSIONS

Freshman Academic Profile: Average high school GPA 3.66. 76% in top 10% of high school class, 93% in top 25% of high school class, 99% in top 50% of high school class. 57% from public high schools. SAT Math middle 50% range 650-730. SAT Critical Reading middle 50% range 620-720. ACT middle 50% range 30-32. **Basis for Candidate Selection:** *Very important factors considered include:* Class rank, academic GPA, rigor of secondary school record. *Important factors considered include:* application essay, recommendation(s), standardized test scores, character/personal qualities, extracurricular activities, talent/ability. *Other factors considered include:* alumni/ae relation, first generation, geographical residence, racial/ethnic status, volunteer work, work experience. **Freshman Admission Requirements:** High school diploma is required and GED is accepted. *Academic units required:* 4 English, 3 mathematics, 3 science, (2 science labs), 3 foreign language, 3 social studies. **Freshman Admission Statistics:** 8,375 applied, 27% admitted, 34% enrolled. **Transfer Admission Requirements:** High school transcript, college transcript(s), essay or personal statement, standardized test scores, statement of good standing from prior institution(s). Minimum college GPA of 3.00 required. Lowest grade transferable C. **General Admission Information:** Application Fee $55. Early decision application deadline 11/15. Regular application deadline 1/15. Regular notification 4/1. Nonfall registration not accepted. Admission may be deferred for a maximum of 1 year. Credit and/or placement offered for CEEB Advanced Placement tests.

COSTS AND FINANCIAL AID

Annual tuition $47,855. Room and board $11,510. Required fees $320. Average book expense $1,100. **Required Forms and Deadlines:** CSS/Financial Aid PROFILE, Noncustodial PROFILE. **Notification of Awards:** Applicants will be notified of awards on or about 4/1. **Types of Aid:** *Need-based scholarships/grants:* Federal Pell, SEOG, state scholarships/grants, private scholarships, the school's own gift aid. *Loans:* Subsidized Stafford, Unsubsidized Stafford, PLUS, Federal Perkins. *Student Employment:* Federal Work-Study Program available. Institutional employment available. Highest amount earned per year from on-campus jobs $1,600. Off-campus job opportunities are fair. **Financial Aid Statistics:** 100% freshmen, 98% undergrads receive need-based scholarship or grant aid. 100% freshmen, 100% undergrads receive non-need-based scholarship or grant aid. 82% freshmen, 80% undergrads receive need-based self-help aid. 8% freshmen, 7% undergrads receive athletic scholarships. 41% freshmen, 42% undergrads receive any aid. 34% undergrads borrow to pay for school. Average cumulative indebtedness $15,995. **Criteria for awarding institutional aid:** *Non-need-based:* athletics.

COLLEGE OF THE ATLANTIC

105 Eden Street, Bar Harbor, ME 4609
Phone: 207-288-5015 · **Financial Aid Phone:** 207-801-5645
E-mail: inquiry@coa.edu · **CEEB Code:** 3305
Fax: 207-288-4126 · **Website:** www.coa.edu · **ACT Code:** 1637

This private school was founded in 1969. It has a 35-acre campus.

RATINGS

Admissions Selectivity Rating: 91   **Fire Safety Rating:** 95

STUDENTS AND FACULTY

Enrollment: 365. **Student Body:** 70% female, 30% male, 79% out-of-state, 16% international (40 countries represented). Asian 2%, African American 1%, Caucasian 70%, Hispanic 6%, Native American 1%
Retention and Graduation: 81% freshmen return for sophomore year. 57% freshmen graduate within 4 years. 71% freshmen graduate within 6 years. 16% grads go on to further study within 1 year. 8% grads pursue arts and sciences degrees. 4% grads pursue law degrees. 2% grads pursue medical degrees. **Faculty:** 29 full-time faculty, 86% hold PhDs, 38% are members of minority groups, 7% are women. 0% of classes are taught by teaching assistants.

ACADEMICS

Degrees: bachelor's, master's. **Classes:** Most classes have 10–19 students. Most lab/discussion sessions have 10–19 students. **Majors with Highest Enrollment:** Ecology; Humanities/Humanistic Studies; Multi-/Interdisciplinary Studies. **Special Study Options:** cross-registration, exchange student program (domestic), independent study, internships, liberal arts/career combination, student-designed major, study abroad, teacher certification program, Winter term program in Yucatan, Mexico. EcoLeague - consortium agreement with five other colleges for student exchanges (Alaska Pacific University, Antioch College, Green Mountain College, Northland College, Prescott College. Exchange program with Olin College of Engineering and University of Maine at Orono. **Honors programs:** We consider all our students to be capable of honors work, which is why all students finish their time at COA with a term-long capstone, or senior project. Combined degree programs: n/a. **Disability Services:** Special programs offered to physically disabled students include note-taking services, reader services, tape recorders, tutors. **Career services:** Alumni network, alumni services, career assessment, internships, regional alumni. Career services highlights include internships, which are required for graduation and allow students to apply their classroom knowledge to the world of work over ten weeks and 400 hours.

FACILITIES

Housing: Coed dorms, special housing for disabled students, Substance-free housing; green (environmentally conscious)housing. 70% of campus accessible to physically disabled. **Special Academic Facilities/Equipment:** Natural history museum, pottery studio, greenhouse, Geographic Information Systems lab, Green Graphics Studio Deering Common Campus Center, organic community garden, Blum Gallery, outdoor equipment, two boats: Indigo and Borealis, off-site organic farm and two island research stations. **Computers:** 100% of classrooms, 100% of dorms, 100% of libraries, 100% of dining areas, 100% of student union, 25% of common outdoor areas have wireless network access. Students can register for classes online. Administrative functions (other than registration) can be performed online.

CAMPUS LIFE

Environment: Rural. **Activities:** Choral groups, dance, drama/theater, jazz band, literary magazine, music ensembles, student government, student newspaper, yearbook. **On-Campus Highlights:** George B. Dorr Museum of Natural History, Blum Art Gallery, The pier, Turrets, Take-A-Break, College of the Atlantic has recently completed state-of-the-art sustainable dorms and a creative restoration of an historic building into a similarly sustainable campus center. These are also very popular places to visit. **Environmental Initiatives:** Energy Framework: In March of 2013 the college adopted an Energy Framework that seeks to make the college fossil fuel-free by 2050. The framework includes interim goals for 2015 and 2020 that the college is working on now to achieve. The framework focuses on reducing fossil fuel use and pursuing renewable sources of energy on campus and at our two nearby farms. Integral to the policy is the requirement that our students be involved in creating a fossil fuel-free campus through our hands-on curriculum. We have purchased an electric van and lease an electric Ford Focus for student transportation and have established three solar/electric charging stations for them on campus and at our two farms. These will also be used for additional electric vehicles we expect to bring into service. Energy conservation through constructing energy efficiency buildings and improvements to existing buildings: COA's newest student residences (2008)have space heating and hot water provided by a wood pellet boiler, the buildings are super-insulated, have triple-pane windows and composting toilets. Three of the roofs, one on each duplex, have solar pv arrays—totaling 25kW—providing approximately 30,000 kWh a year. An old ocean front cottage was renovated to serve as the campus center and received numerous energy efficient improvements. It too is heated by the same wood pellet boiler system. During 2013, the main administration building, known as Turrets, an 1895 granite "cottage" on the National Register of Historic Places, was retrofitted with 99 new energy efficient windows. Local and organic food: COA has two organic farms and hosts an organic community garden on its campus. One farm and the community garden supply the college cafeteria with organic produce when possible given the northern growing season. Another farm raised its first flock of broiler chickens for the college cafeteria in the fall of 2012 and winter 2013. A good percentage of what the farms can't supply is still local and organic. All food waste is composted, with food waste bins in all residences as well as the cafeteria. The college has now initiated a Sustainable Food Systems Program to tie together its work in organic agriculture and larger food systems issues. Additionally, the cafeteria is tray-less to reduce food waste and we have had a policy of no bottled water on campus, or even for off-campus college-related activities for more then two years.

ADMISSIONS

Freshman Academic Profile: Average high school GPA 3.68. 55% in top 10% of high school class, 79% in top 25% of high school class, 100% in top 50% of high school class. 67% from public high schools. SAT Math middle 50% range 530-650. SAT Critical Reading middle 50% range 570-690. SAT

Writing middle 50% range 550-640. ACT middle 50% range 26-30. Minimum internet-based TOEFL 86. Minimum paper TOEFL 567. **Basis for Candidate Selection:** *Very important factors considered include:* application essay, recommendation(s), rigor of secondary school record. *Important factors considered include:* Class rank, academic GPA, character/personal qualities, extracurricular activities, interview, talent/ability, volunteer work, work experience. *Other factors considered include:* standardized test scores, alumni/ae relation, first generation, geographical residence, level of applicant's interest, racial/ethnic status, state residency. **Freshman Admission Requirements:** High school diploma is required and GED is accepted. *Academic units required:* 4 English, 3 mathematics, 2 science, (2 science labs), 0 foreign language, 2 social studies, 0 academic electives. **Freshman Admission Statistics:** 429 applied, 71% admitted, 26% enrolled. **Transfer Admission Requirements:** High school transcript, college transcript(s), essay or personal statement, Minimum college GPA of 3.0 required. Lowest grade transferable C. **General Admission Information:** Application Fee $45. Early decision application deadline 12/1. Regular application deadline 2/15. Regular notification 4/1. Nonfall registration accepted. Admission may be deferred for a maximum of 1 year. Credit and/or placement offered for CEEB Advanced Placement tests.

COSTS AND FINANCIAL AID

Annual tuition $41,535. Room and board $9,432. Required fees $549. Average book expense $600. **Required Forms and Deadlines:** FAFSA, Institution's own financial aid form, Noncustodial PROFILE, Business/Farm Supplement. **Notification of Awards:** Applicants will be notified of awards on or about 4/1. **Types of Aid:** *Need-based scholarships/grants:* Federal Pell, SEOG, state scholarships/grants, private scholarships, the school's own gift aid. *Loans:* Subsidized Stafford, Unsubsidized Stafford, PLUS, Federal Perkins. *Student Employment:* Federal Work-Study Program available. Off-campus job opportunities are good. **Financial Aid Statistics:** 100% freshmen, 100% undergrads receive need-based scholarship or grant aid. 0% freshmen, 1% undergrads receive non-need-based scholarship or grant aid. 99% freshmen, 98% undergrads receive need-based self-help aid. 0% freshmen, 0% undergrads receive athletic scholarships. 98% freshmen, 97% undergrads receive any aid. 67% undergrads borrow to pay for school. Average cumulative indebtedness $20,713. **Criteria for awarding institutional aid:** *Non-need-based:* academics.

COLLEGE OF CHARLESTON

66 George Street, Charleston, SC 29424
Phone: 843-953-5670 · **Financial Aid Phone:** 843-953-5540
E-mail: admissions@cofc.edu · **CEEB Code:** 5113
Fax: 843-953-6322 · **Website:** www.cofc.edu · **ACT Code:** 3846

This public school was founded in 1770. It has a 52-acre campus.

RATINGS

Admissions Selectivity Rating: 85   **Fire Safety Rating:** 94

STUDENTS AND FACULTY

Enrollment: 10,069. **Student Body:** 63% female, 37% male, 36% out-of-state, 1% international (55 countries represented). Asian 2%, African American 7%, Caucasian 81%, Hispanic 4%, Native American <1%
Retention and Graduation: 79% freshmen return for sophomore year. 55% freshmen graduate within 4 years. 66% freshmen graduate within 6 years. 48% grads go on to further study within 1 year. 3% grads pursue law degrees. 3% grads pursue medical degrees. **Faculty:** 569 full-time faculty, 90% hold PhDs, 44% are members of minority groups, 13% are women. 0.2% of classes are taught by teaching assistants.

ACADEMICS

Degrees: bachelor's, master's, post-bachelor's certificate. **Classes:** Most classes have 20–29 students. Most lab/discussion sessions have 20–29 students. **Majors with Highest Enrollment:** Business Administration and Management; Biology/Biological Sciences; Psychology. **Special Study Options:** Accelerated program, cooperative education program, cross-registration, distance learning, double major, dual enrollment, English as a Second Language (ESL), exchange student program (domestic), honors program, independent study, internships, liberal arts/career combination, study abroad, teacher certification program, Semester at Sea. **Honors programs:** The Honors College at the College of Charleston began as an Honors Program in 1978 to provide a program and a community for talented and motivated students who enjoy active participation in small stimulating classes and want to be involved in a meaningful way in undergraduate research. In order to better serve the needs of the students, it became an Honors College in 2005, with new positions to provide academic advising and assistance in applying for postgraduate fellowships and additional funding to support its mission. The Honors College is dedicated to providing these students with a place where they can flourish and grow, a true learning community of teachers and students. In addition to receiving exciting and unique educational experiences, students can participate with their fellow Honors students in social, cultural, and intellectual events on the campus and in historic Charleston, SC. The Honors College challenges intellectually talented students to make the most of the opportunities available to them, to become actively involved in their own education, and to prepare themselves to excel in graduate programs, medical or law school, or in whatever comes after they complete their undergraduate education. In Honors classes, students take responsibility for their own learning through class discussions, through interaction with faculty and fellow students, and through independent research. Honors students are advised by a full time Honors academic advisor and specially chosen faculty mentors, receive priority registration, and have the opportunity to room with other Honors students in special Honors residence halls. Classes, seminars, and student gatherings are held in the Honors Center, the historic William Aiken House built by Governor William Aiken in 1839. **Disability Services:** Special programs offered to physically disabled students include note-taking services, reader services, tape recorders, tutors. **Career services:** Alumni network, alumni services, career/job search classes, career assessment, internships, regional alumni. Career services highlights include internships. Most academic departments offer internships for credit and the career center offers a certificate/no-credit option. A large number of students do these each year.

FACILITIES
Housing: Coed dorms, men's dorms, women's dorms, fraternity/sorority housing, apartments for single students, Theme HousingRestored old Charleston houses used as residence halls, some with kitchen facilities in suites. 80% of campus accessible to physically disabled. **Special Academic Facilities/Equipment:** Halsey Institute of Contemporary Art, sculpture facility, Rivers Communications Museum, Miles Early Childhood Development Center, Avery Institute for African-American History and Culture, physics and astronomy observatory, Grice Marine Laboratory, Patriots Point Athletics Complex (includes softball, baseball, tennis, soccer and sailing). **Computers:** 75% of classrooms, 100% of dorms, 100% of libraries, 100% of dining areas, 100% of student union, 80% of common outdoor areas have wireless network access. Students can register for classes online. Administrative functions (other than registration) can be performed online.

CAMPUS LIFE
Environment: City. **Activities:** Choral groups, dance, drama/theater, jazz band, literary magazine, music ensembles, musical theater, pep band, radio station, student government, student newspaper, symphony orchestra, yearbook, Campus Ministries, International Student Organization. 120 registered organizations, 19 honor societies, 16 religious organizations. 13 fraternities, 12 sororities. **Athletics (Intercollegiate):** *Men:* baseball, basketball, cross-country, diving, golf, sailing, soccer, swimming, tennis. *Women:* basketball, cross-country, diving, equestrian sports, golf, sailing, soccer, softball, swimming, tennis, track/field (outdoor), track/field (indoor), volleyball. **On-Campus Highlights:** The Cistern Yard, Carolina First Arena, Fresh Food Company, Addleston Library, Cougar Plaza, The College opened two new facilities in January 2010: The The Marion and Wayland H. Cato Jr. Center for the Arts and a second building for the School of Sciences and Mathematics. Their completion is part of a significant transformation of the College's facilities, providing students with the best and most effective learning and recreational opportunities. Six new facilities were completed in 2007, and several others were finished in 2008. Patriots Point Athletics Complex is located just across the Ravenel Bridge in Mt. Pleasant. Recently renovated, this 35-acre complex is home to baseball, soccer, softball, sailing and tennis. **Environmental Initiatives:** Completed the campus' first GHG Inventory 2011. Created formally the "Office of Sustainability" and hired a Director. Building a decentralized network of governance on sustainability issues that builds on relationships and connections as foundation for campus sustainability.

ADMISSIONS
Freshman Academic Profile: Average high school GPA 3.86. 21.1% in top 10% of high school class, 54.5% in top 25% of high school class, 89.5% in top 50% of high school class. 76% from public high schools. SAT Math middle 50% range 510-610. SAT Critical Reading middle 50% range 520-620. ACT middle 50% range 23-27. Minimum internet-based TOEFL 80. **Basis for Candidate Selection:** *Very important factors considered include:* academic GPA, rigor of secondary school record, standardized test scores, state residency. *Important factors considered include:* Class rank, character/personal qualities, first generation, talent/ability. *Other factors considered include:* application essay, recommendation(s), extracurricular activities, racial/ethnic status, volunteer

work, work experience. **Freshman Admission Requirements:** High school diploma is required and GED is accepted. *Academic units required:* 4 English, 3 mathematics, 3 science, (3 science labs), 3 foreign language, 3 social studies, 4 academic electives. **Freshman Admission Statistics:** 11,179 applied, 78% admitted, 25% enrolled. **Transfer Admission Requirements:** college transcript(s), Minimum college GPA of 2.6 required. Lowest grade transferable C. **General Admission Information:** Application Fee $50. Regular application deadline 2/1. Nonfall registration accepted. Admission may be deferred for a maximum of 1or2semester. Credit and/or placement offered for CEEB Advanced Placement tests.

COSTS AND FINANCIAL AID
Required Forms and Deadlines: FAFSA. **Notification of Awards:** Applicants will be notified of awards on a rolling basis beginning 4/10. **Types of Aid:** *Need-based scholarships/grants:* Federal Pell, SEOG, state scholarships/grants, private scholarships, the school's own gift aid. *Loans:* Direct Subsidized Stafford, Direct Unsubsidized Stafford, Direct PLUS, Federal Perkins. *Student Employment:* Federal Work-Study Program available. Institutional employment available. Highest amount earned per year from on-campus jobs $9,400. Off-campus job opportunities are fair. **Financial Aid Statistics:** 71% freshmen, 68% undergrads receive need-based scholarship or grant aid. 75% freshmen, 45% undergrads receive non-need-based scholarship or grant aid. 69% freshmen, 75% undergrads receive need-based self-help aid. 1% freshmen, 2% undergrads receive athletic scholarships. 47% freshmen, 46% undergrads receive any aid. 52% undergrads borrow to pay for school. Average cumulative indebtedness $22,589. **Criteria for awarding institutional aid:** *Non-need-based:* academics, alumni affiliation, art, athletics, music/drama.

COLLEGE FOR CREATIVE STUDIES

201 East Kirby, Detroit, MI 48202
Phone: 313-664-7425 · **Financial Aid Phone:** 313-664-7495
E-mail: admissions@ccscad.edu
Fax: 313-872-2739 · **Website:** www.ccscad.edu

This private school was founded in 1906. It has a 11-acre campus.

RATINGS
Admissions Selectivity Rating: 82   **Fire Safety Rating:** 78

STUDENTS AND FACULTY
Enrollment: 0. **Student Body:** 17% out-of-state.
Retention and Graduation: 73% freshmen return for sophomore year.
Faculty: 51 full-time faculty, 61% hold PhDs, 31% are members of minority groups, 14% are women. 0% of classes are taught by teaching assistants.

ACADEMICS
Degrees: bachelor's, post-bachelor's certificate. **Majors with Highest Enrollment:** Commercial and Advertising Art; Industrial and Product Design; Film/Video and Photographic Arts. **Special Study Options:** cooperative education program, double major, dual enrollment, English as a Second Language (ESL), exchange student program (domestic), independent study, internships, study abroad, teacher certification program. **Disability Services:** Special programs offered to physically disabled students include reader services, tape recorders, tutors. **Career services:** Alumni network, alumni services, career/job search classes, career assessment, internships, regional alumni. Career services highlights include a practicum class that all seniors take part in that allows students to work with and for outside companies, such as Ford Motor Company, Pixar, DaimlerChrysler and various companies.

FACILITIES
Housing: Coed dorms. 95% of campus accessible to physically disabled. **Special Academic Facilities/Equipment:** Top-of-the-line technology for design, animation and audiovisual editing. Wood and Metal shops, hot glass studio, gallery, private studios.

CAMPUS LIFE
Environment: Metropolis. **Activities:** student government. 5 registered organizations. **On-Campus Highlights:** Center Galleries, U245 Student Art Gallery, Jazzman's Café.

ADMISSIONS
Freshman Academic Profile: ACT middle 50% range 18-23. Minimum paper TOEFL 525. **Basis for Candidate Selection:** *Very important factors considered include:* talent/ability. *Important factors considered include:* academic GPA, standardized test scores. *Other factors considered include:* level of applicant's interest. **Freshman Admission Requirements:** High school diploma is required and GED is accepted. **Freshman Admission Statistics:**

1,260 applied, 39% admitted, 51% enrolled. **Transfer Admission Requirements:** High school transcript, college transcript(s), Minimum college GPA of 2.0 required. Lowest grade transferable C. **General Admission Information:** Application Fee $35. Regular application deadline 8/1. Notification on a rolling basis, beginning on or about 9/15. Nonfall registration accepted. Admission may be deferred for a maximum of 4 semesters. Credit offered for CEEB Advanced Placement tests.

COSTS AND FINANCIAL AID
Annual tuition $27,090. Room and board $4,300. Required fees $1,185. Average book expense $2,500. **Required Forms and Deadlines:** FAFSA. **Notification of Awards:** Applicants will be notified of awards on a rolling basis beginning 3/15. **Types of Aid:** *Need-based scholarships/grants:* Federal Pell, SEOG, state scholarships/grants, private scholarships, the school's own gift aid. *Loans:* Subsidized Stafford, Unsubsidized Stafford, PLUS, Alternative loans. *Student Employment:* Highest amount earned per year from on-campus jobs $1,000. **Financial Aid Statistics:** 74% undergrads borrow to pay for school. Average cumulative indebtedness $22,922. **Criteria for awarding institutional aid:** *Non-need-based:* academics, art, minority status.

COLLEGE OF THE HOLY CROSS

1 College Street, Worcester, MA 01610-2395
Phone: 508-793-2443 · **Financial Aid Phone:** 508-793-2265
E-mail: admissions@holycross.edu · **CEEB Code:** 3282
Fax: 508-793-3888 · **Website:** www.holycross.edu · **ACT Code:** 1810

This private school, affiliated with the Roman Catholic Church, was founded in 1843. It has a 174-acre campus.

RATINGS
Admissions Selectivity Rating: 93   **Fire Safety Rating:** 96

STUDENTS AND FACULTY
Enrollment: 2,904. **Student Body:** 49% female, 51% male, 63% out-of-state, 1% international (16 countries represented). Asian 5%, African American 4%, Caucasian 70%, Hispanic 11%, Native American <1%
Retention and Graduation: 94% freshmen return for sophomore year. 90% freshmen graduate within 4 years. 92% freshmen graduate within 6 years. 18% grads go on to further study within 1 year. 11% grads pursue arts and sciences degrees. 3% grads pursue law degrees. 1% grads pursue business degrees. 2% grads pursue medical degrees. **Faculty:** 287 full-time faculty, 96% hold PhDs, 46% are members of minority groups, 13% are women. 0% of classes are taught by teaching assistants.

ACADEMICS
Degrees: bachelor's. **Classes:** Most classes have 10–19 students. Most lab/discussion sessions have 10–19 students. **Majors with Highest Enrollment:** Economics; Political Science and Government; English Language and Literature. **Special Study Options:** Accelerated program, cross-registration, double major, dual enrollment, exchange student program (domestic), honors program, independent study, internships, liberal arts/career combination, student-designed major, study abroad, teacher certification program, First-year integrated living and learning program ("Montserrat"). **Honors programs:** Fenwick Scholar Program. **Disability Services:** Special programs offered to physically disabled students include note-taking services, reader services, tutors. **Career services:** Alumni network, career/job search classes, internships, regional alumni. Career services highlights include the Summer Internship Program.

FACILITIES
Housing: Coed dorms, special housing for disabled students, apartments for single students, Suites on campus available for juniors and seniors. Substance-free housing also available. 85% of campus accessible to physically disabled. **Special Academic Facilities/Equipment:** Art gallery, Concert Hall, Taylor and Boody tracker organ, O'Callahan Science Library, Rehm Library, Multimedia Resource Center, Wellness Center; scientific equipment on par with the best research universities **Computers:** 100% of classrooms, 100% of dorms, 100% of libraries, 100% of dining areas, 100% of student union, 60% of common outdoor areas have wireless network access. Students can register for classes online. Administrative functions (other than registration) can be performed online.

CAMPUS LIFE
Environment: City. **Activities:** Choral groups, concert band, dance, drama/theater, jazz band, literary magazine, marching band, music ensembles, musical theater, pep band, radio station, student government, student newspaper, yearbook, Campus Ministries, International Student Organization. 105 registered organizations, 20 honor societies, 4 religious organizations. **Athletics (Intercollegiate):** *Men:* baseball, basketball, crew/rowing, cross-country, diving, football, golf, ice hockey, lacrosse, soccer, swimming, tennis, track/field (outdoor), track/field (indoor). *Women:* basketball, crew/rowing, cross-country, diving, field hockey, golf, ice hockey, lacrosse, soccer, softball, swimming, tennis, track/field (outdoor), track/field (indoor), volleyball. **On-Campus Highlights:** Library, Smith Hall, St. Joseph Chapel, Hart Recreation Center, Hogan Campus Center. **Environmental Initiatives:** College committed to a 20% carbon reduction by 2015 and Carbon Neutrality however the College has already achieved a 41% reduction in carbon emissions. The College achieved LEED Gold for a science complex addition and renovation project as well as LEED Gold for a new residence, Figge Hall. College is continuously investing in energy efficient equipment and fixtures. This includes solar lighting, LED lighting, HVAC systems & controls and underground steam lines.

ADMISSIONS
Freshman Academic Profile: 56% in top 10% of high school class, 83% in top 25% of high school class, 98% in top 50% of high school class. 49% from public high schools. SAT Math middle 50% range 620-690. SAT Critical Reading middle 50% range 610-690. SAT Writing middle 50% range 610-710. ACT middle 50% range 28-31. Minimum internet-based TOEFL 100. Minimum paper TOEFL 600. **Basis for Candidate Selection:** *Very important factors considered include:* Class rank, academic GPA, recommendation(s), rigor of secondary school record, interview. *Important factors considered include:* application essay, character/personal qualities, extracurricular activities, level of applicant's interest. *Other factors considered include:* standardized test scores, alumni/ae relation, first generation, geographical residence, racial/ethnic status, talent/ability, volunteer work, work experience. **Freshman Admission Requirements:** High school diploma is required and GED is accepted. **Freshman Admission Statistics:** 5,302 applied, 43% admitted, 34% enrolled. **Transfer Admission Requirements:** High school transcript, college transcript(s), essay or personal statement, statement of good standing from prior institution(s). Lowest grade transferable C. **General Admission Information:** Application Fee $60. Early decision application deadline 12/15. Regular application deadline 1/15. Nonfall registration not accepted. Admission may be deferred for a maximum of 12 months. Credit offered for CEEB Advanced Placement tests.

COSTS AND FINANCIAL AID
Annual tuition $46,550. Room and board $12,748. Required fees $626. Average book expense $700. **Required Forms and Deadlines:** FAFSA, CSS/Financial Aid PROFILE, Noncustodial PROFILE, Business/Farm Supplement. **Notification of Awards:** Applicants will be notified of awards on or about 4/1. **Types of Aid:** *Need-based scholarships/grants:* Federal Pell, SEOG, state scholarships/grants, private scholarships, the school's own gift aid. *Loans:* Direct Subsidized Stafford, Direct Unsubsidized Stafford, Direct PLUS, Federal Perkins, MEFA. *Student Employment:* Federal Work-Study Program available. Institutional employment available. Highest amount earned per year from on-campus jobs $1,604. Off-campus job opportunities are fair. **Financial Aid Statistics:** 84% freshmen, 83% undergrads receive need-based scholarship or grant aid. 3% freshmen, 3% undergrads receive non-need-based scholarship or grant aid. 81% freshmen, 83% undergrads receive need-based self-help aid. 4% freshmen, 3% undergrads receive athletic scholarships. 61% freshmen, 60% undergrads receive any aid. 59% undergrads borrow to pay for school. Average cumulative indebtedness $25,061. **Criteria for awarding institutional aid:** *Non-need-based:* academics, athletics.

THE COLLEGE OF IDAHO

2112 Cleveland Blvd, Caldwell, ID 83605-4432
Phone: 208-459-5305 · **Financial Aid Phone:** 208-459-5307
E-mail: admissions@collegeofidaho.edu · **CEEB Code:** 4060
Fax: 208-459-5757 · **Website:** www.collegeofidaho.edu · **ACT Code:** 916

This private school was founded in 1891. It has a 50-acre campus.

RATINGS
Admissions Selectivity Rating: 74   **Fire Safety Rating:** 81

STUDENTS AND FACULTY

Enrollment: 1,113. **Student Body:** 52% female, 48% male, 17% out-of-state, 7% international (46 countries represented). Asian 3%, African American 2%, Caucasian 65%, Hispanic 16%, Native American 1%

Retention and Graduation: 45% freshmen graduate within 4 years. **Faculty:** 87 full-time faculty, 78% hold PhDs, 40% are members of minority groups, 7% are women. 0% of classes are taught by teaching assistants.

ACADEMICS

Degrees: bachelor's, master's. **Classes:** Most classes have fewer than 10 students. **Majors with Highest Enrollment:** Biology/Biological Sciences; Business Administration and Management; Psychology. **Special Study Options:** cross-registration, double major, dual enrollment, exchange student program (domestic), honors program, independent study, internships, liberal arts/career combination, student-designed major, study abroad, teacher certification program. **Honors programs:** Heritage Scholars Program, Gipson Honors Program; Kathryn Albertson Scholars Program; Davis United World Scholars Combined degree programs: BA/JD, MBA (Gonzaga, BSU), MNR (U of ID), Nursing (ISU). **Disability Services:** Special programs offered to physically disabled students include note-taking services, reader services, tape recorders. **Career services:** Alumni network, alumni services, career assessment, internships, regional alumni. Career services highlights include our internship program through which students are required to connect their internship with the academic coursework though writing.

FACILITIES

Housing: Coed dorms, special housing for disabled students, fraternity/sorority housing, apartments for single students, College owned houses; dorms for Healthy/Quiet Lifestyle, Academic Honor, First Year Community, Honor Code. 80% of campus accessible to physically disabled. **Special Academic Facilities/ Equipment:** Art and natural history museums, gem and mineral collections, observatory, planetarium, nuclear magnetic resonance spectrometer, gas chromatograph, gamma camera, graphic computer, art gallery, Robert E. Smylie Archives. **Computers:** 100% of classrooms, 100% of dorms, 100% of libraries, 100% of dining areas, 100% of student union, 100% of common outdoor areas have wireless network access. Administrative functions (other than registration) can be performed online.

CAMPUS LIFE

Environment: Town. **Activities:** Choral groups, concert band, dance, drama/ theater, jazz band, literary magazine, music ensembles, musical theater, opera, pep band, radio station, student government, student newspaper, student-run film society, symphony orchestra, yearbook, Campus Ministries, International Student Organization, Model UN. 55 registered organizations, 4 honor societies, 3 religious organizations. 3 fraternities, 4 sororities. **Athletics (Intercollegiate):** *Men:* baseball, cheerleading, cross-country, golf, skiing (downhill/alpine), skiing (nordic/cross-country), snowboarding, soccer, swimming, tennis, track/ field (outdoor). *Women:* basketball, cheerleading, cross-country, golf, skiing (downhill/alpine), skiing (nordic/cross-country), snowboarding, soccer, softball, swimming, tennis, track/field (outdoor), volleyball. **On-Campus Highlights:** J.A. Albertson Activity Center, McCain Student Center, Langroise Center for Performing and Fine Arts, Centennial Amphitheater, Dorms. **Environmental Initiatives:** Student Sustainability Steward Position; College Garden; Campus Sustainability council.

ADMISSIONS

Freshman Academic Profile: Average high school GPA 3.51. 18% in top 10% of high school class, 23% in top 25% of high school class, 71% in top 50% of high school class. SAT Math middle 50% range 470-590. SAT Critical Reading middle 50% range 450-600. SAT Writing middle 50% range 440-570. ACT middle 50% range 21-27. Minimum internet-based TOEFL 79. Minimum paper TOEFL 550. **Basis for Candidate Selection:** *Very important factors considered include:* application essay, academic GPA, recommendation(s), rigor of secondary school record, standardized test scores, character/personal qualities, extracurricular activities, level of applicant's interest. *Important factors considered include:* Class rank, interview. *Other factors considered include:* alumni/ ae relation, first generation, geographical residence, talent/ability, volunteer work. **Freshman Admission Requirements:** High school diploma is required and GED is accepted. *Academic units required:* 3 English, 2 mathematics, 0 science, (0 science labs), 0 foreign language, 3 social studies, 3 history, 0 visual/performing arts, 0 computer science, 3 academic electives. **Freshman Admission Statistics:** 944 applied, 93% admitted, 31% enrolled. **Transfer Admission Requirements:** college transcript(s), essay or personal statement, Minimum college GPA of 2.2 required. Lowest grade transferable D-. **General Admission Information:** Regular application deadline 8/1. Notification on a rolling basis, beginning on or about 10/15. Nonfall registration accepted. Admission may be deferred for a maximum of one year. Credit and/or placement offered for CEEB Advanced Placement tests.

COSTS AND FINANCIAL AID

Annual tuition $25,410. Room and board $8,990. Required fees $755. Average book expense $1,200. **Required Forms and Deadlines:** FAFSA, Institution's own financial aid form. **Notification of Awards:** Applicants will be notified of awards on a rolling basis beginning 2/1. **Types of Aid:** *Need-based scholarships/ grants:* Federal Pell, SEOG, state scholarships/grants, private scholarships, the school's own gift aid. *Loans:* Subsidized Stafford, Unsubsidized Stafford, PLUS, Federal Perkins, Alternative Education Loans. *Student Employment:* Federal Work-Study Program available. Highest amount earned per year from on-campus jobs $77,073. Off-campus job opportunities are good. **Financial Aid Statistics:** 100% freshmen, 100% undergrads receive need-based scholarship or grant aid. 100% freshmen, 100% undergrads receive non-need-based scholarship or grant aid. 85% freshmen, 84% undergrads receive need-based self-help aid. 21% freshmen, 7% undergrads receive athletic scholarships. 99% freshmen, 100% undergrads receive any aid. 63% undergrads borrow to pay for school. Average cumulative indebtedness $26,130. **Criteria for awarding institutional aid:** *Non-need-based:* academics, alumni affiliation, art, athletics, leadership, minority status, music/drama, religious affiliation, state/district residency.

COLLEGE OF MOUNT SAINT VINCENT

6301 Riverdale Avenue, Riverdale, NY 10471
Phone: 718-405-3267 · **Financial Aid Phone:** 718-405-3349
E-mail: admissions@mountsaintvincent.edu · **CEEB Code:** 2088
Fax: 718-549-7945 · **Website:** www.mountsaintvincent.edu

This private school, affiliated with the Roman Catholic Church, was founded in 1847. It has a 70-acre campus.

RATINGS

Admissions Selectivity Rating: 70   **Fire Safety Rating:** 71

STUDENTS AND FACULTY

Enrollment: 1,655. **Student Body:** 72% female, 28% male, 9% out-of-state, 1% international (6 countries represented). Asian 8%, African American 16%, Caucasian 27%, Hispanic 36%, Native American <1%

Retention and Graduation: 71% freshmen return for sophomore year. 41% freshmen graduate within 4 years. 57% freshmen graduate within 6 years. 39% grads go on to further study within 1 year. 9% grads pursue arts and sciences degrees. 1% grads pursue law degrees. 1% grads pursue business degrees. **Faculty:** 0% of classes are taught by teaching assistants.

ACADEMICS

Degrees: associate, bachelor's, master's, post-master's certificate. **Classes:** Most classes have 20–29 students. Most lab/discussion sessions have 10–19 students. **Majors with Highest Enrollment:** Business/Commerce; Registered Nursing/Registered Nurse; Communication and Media Studies. **Special Study Options:** Accelerated program, double major, honors program, independent study, internships, liberal arts/career combination, study abroad, teacher certification program. **Honors programs:** At present, the Honors Program reflects several distinctive dimensions and provides gifted students with the opportunity to develop critical thinking skills, an affirmative acknowledgement of the human dignity of self and others, and a commitment to realize one's intellectual potential, through participation in enhanced learning experiences both in and out of the classroom. Freshman and sophomore honors students are required to complete six of eight paired Honors Sections of the college's Core Curriculum courses. Specifically, in freshman year, literature is paired with psychology and fine arts with history; sociology is paired with economics and philosophy with religious studies in sophomore year. Juniors and seniors are challenged to enrich themselves through involvement in research projects that are faculty-mentored and through engaging themselves in reflective extra-curricular events (e.g., attending lectures, conferences, or cultural event) with faculty assistance and support. At the same time, the college has initiated a process to further develop and restructure the honors experience by the development of courses that are more inter-disciplinary in nature, utilize more diversified pedagogical styles, and, consistent with the college's mission, provide the opportunity for community service and learning. Through its honors program, the college seeks to develop informed, critically reflective, and value-oriented young men and women who will successfully pursue higher educational opportunities and make meaningful contributions to society both professionally and in their personal lives. **Disability Services:** Special programs offered to physically disabled students include note-taking services, tape recorders, tutors. **Career services:** career/job search classes, career assessment, internships, regional alumni.

FACILITIES

Housing: Coed dorms, special housing for disabled students, women's dorms. 90% of campus accessible to physically disabled. **Special Academic Facilities/ Equipment:** Newly renovated Maryvale Hall, with newly constructed wing, for Communications and Fine Arts Departments; Nursing lab, TV studio, radio station, Elizabeth Seton Travelling Museum, Forensic Laboratory equipment. **Computers:** Students can register for classes online. Administrative functions (other than registration) can be performed online.

CAMPUS LIFE

Environment: Metropolis. **Activities:** dance, drama/theater, literary magazine, musical theater, radio station, student government, student newspaper, television station, yearbook, Campus Ministries. 30 registered organizations, 15 honor societies, 2 religious organizations. **Athletics (Intercollegiate):** *Men:* baseball, basketball, cross-country, lacrosse, soccer, swimming, tennis, volleyball. *Women:* basketball, cross-country, lacrosse, soccer, softball, swimming, tennis, track/field (outdoor), volleyball. **On-Campus Highlights:** Crossroads (Student Lounge), Maryvale (new Communication/Art building), Fitness Center (includes swimming pool), Benedict's Café **Environmental Initiatives:** Recycling; Green cleaning products; Green construction.

ADMISSIONS

Freshman Academic Profile: Average high school GPA 3.3. 3% in top 10% of high school class, 17% in top 25% of high school class, 44% in top 50% of high school class. 46% from public high schools. SAT Math middle 50% range 400-490. SAT Critical Reading middle 50% range 410-500. SAT Writing middle 50% range 410-490. ACT middle 50% range 16-21. Minimum paper TOEFL 550. **Basis for Candidate Selection:** *Very important factors considered include:* academic GPA, rigor of secondary school record. *Important factors considered include:* application essay, recommendation(s), standardized test scores, character/personal qualities, extracurricular activities, interview. *Other factors considered include:* Class rank, alumni/ae relation, first generation, geographical residence, religious affiliation/commitment, state residency, volunteer work, work experience. **Freshman Admission Requirements:** High school diploma is required and GED is accepted. *Academic units required:* 4 English, 2 mathematics, 2 science, 2 foreign language, 3 social studies, 3 academic electives. **Freshman Admission Statistics:** 2,637 applied, 92% admitted, 20% enrolled. **Transfer Admission Requirements:** college transcript(s), essay or personal statement, Minimum college GPA of 2.0 required. Lowest grade transferable C. **General Admission Information:** Application Fee $35. Notification on a rolling basis, beginning on or about 2/1. Nonfall registration accepted. Admission may be deferred for a maximum of 1 year. Credit and/or placement offered for CEEB Advanced Placement tests.

COSTS AND FINANCIAL AID

Annual tuition $28,980. Room and board $12,060. Required fees $1,310. Average book expense $1,185. **Required Forms and Deadlines:** FAFSA, State aid form. **Notification of Awards:** Applicants will be notified of awards on a rolling basis beginning 3/1. **Types of Aid:** *Need-based scholarships/grants:* Federal Pell, SEOG, state scholarships/grants, private scholarships, the school's own gift aid. *Loans:* Subsidized Stafford, Unsubsidized Stafford, PLUS, Federal Perkins. *Student Employment:* Federal Work-Study Program available. Institutional employment available. Off-campus job opportunities are good. **Financial Aid Statistics:** 100% freshmen, 100% undergrads receive need-based scholarship or grant aid. 0% freshmen, 0% undergrads receive non-need-based scholarship or grant aid. 100% freshmen, 100% undergrads receive need-based self-help aid. 0% freshmen, 0% undergrads receive athletic scholarships. 87% freshmen, 86% undergrads receive any aid. 80% undergrads borrow to pay for school. **Criteria for awarding institutional aid:** *Non-need-based:* academics, alumni affiliation, leadership.

THE COLLEGE OF NEW JERSEY

PO Box 7718, Ewing, NJ 08628-0718
Phone: 609-771-2131 · **Financial Aid Phone:** 609-771-2211
E-mail: tcnjinfo@tcnj.edu · **CEEB Code:** 2519
Fax: 609-637-5174 · **Website:** www.tcnj.edu · **ACT Code:** 2614

This public school was founded in 1855. It has a 289-acre campus.

RATINGS

Admissions Selectivity Rating: 91   **Fire Safety Rating:** 98

STUDENTS AND FACULTY

Enrollment: 6,536. **Student Body:** 57% female, 43% male, 7% out-of-state, 0% international (32 countries represented). Asian 10%, African American 5%, Caucasian 66%, Hispanic 12%, Native American <1%
Retention and Graduation: 73% freshmen graduate within 4 years. 86% freshmen graduate within 6 years. 25% grads go on to further study within 1 year. 16% grads pursue arts and sciences degrees. 3% grads pursue law degrees. 3% grads pursue medical degrees. **Faculty:** 356 full-time faculty, 90% hold PhDs, 51% are members of minority groups, 22% are women. 0% of classes are taught by teaching assistants.

ACADEMICS

Degrees: bachelor's, master's, post-bachelor's certificate, post-master's certificate. **Classes:** Most classes have 20–29 students. Most lab/discussion sessions have 10–19 students. **Majors with Highest Enrollment:** Biology/Biological Sciences; Psychology; Business Administration and Management. **Special Study Options:** Accelerated program, double major, dual enrollment, exchange student program (domestic), honors program, independent study, internships, liberal arts/career combination, student-designed major, study abroad, teacher certification program, 7 year medical program with UMDNJ, 7 year BS/OD program with SUNY, Mentored undergraduate summer research program. Combined degree programs: BA/MD, BS/MD, BS/OD, BS/MAT. **Disability Services:** Special programs offered to physically disabled students include note-taking services, reader services, tape recorders, tutors. **Career services:** alumni services, career/job search classes, career assessment, internships. Career services highlights include Education Interview Days; each Spring TCNJ hosts up to 150 school district interview visits. The districts send administrators to conduct 30 minute interviews on-campus. Over the four days the visits are scheduled more than 1500 first-round interviews are conducted. Though the school districts are primarily from New Jersey and the surrounding area, we attract school districts from throughout the nation, including as far away as Hawaii. Students and employers both report that this is a highly successful program for meeting their recruitment needs.

FACILITIES

Housing: Coed dorms, special housing for disabled students, special housing for international students, women's dorms, apartments for single students, Wellness Housing. Faculty and students have the opportunity to develop their own special interest learning communities on campus. 90% of campus accessible to physically disabled. **Special Academic Facilities/Equipment:** Art gallery, concert hall, greenhouse, observatory, planetarium, nuclear magnetic resonance lab, optical spectroscopy lab, scanning and transmission electron microscopes. **Computers:** 22% of classrooms, 5% of dorms, 100% of libraries, 85% of dining areas, 70% of student union, 5% of common outdoor areas have wireless network access. Students can register for classes online. Administrative functions (other than registration) can be performed online.

CAMPUS LIFE

Environment: Village. **Activities:** Choral groups, concert band, dance, drama/theater, jazz band, literary magazine, music ensembles, musical theater, opera, pep band, radio station, student government, student newspaper, symphony orchestra, television station, yearbook, Campus Ministries, International Student Organization, Model UN. 205 registered organizations, 16 honor societies, 11 religious organization. 12 fraternities, 16 sororities. **Athletics (Intercollegiate):** *Men:* baseball, basketball, cross-country, diving, football, soccer, swimming, tennis, track/field (outdoor), track/field (indoor). *Women:* basketball, cross-country, diving, field hockey, lacrosse, soccer, softball, swimming, tennis, track/field (outdoor), track/field (indoor). **On-Campus Highlights:** New Library, New Science Complex, New Arts and Multimedia Building, Student Center, Athletic Center. **Environmental Initiatives:** Commitment to sustainability being incorporated into the curriculum at TCNJ. This may include Freshman seminars, liberal learning programs, research and possible new minor or major degrees. The College's Municipal Land Use Center is authoring the State's sustainabilty and climate neutrality plans. Development of a plan to achieve climate neutrality. Consultant was hired to prepare a comprehensive sustainability and climate neutrality plan for the College. That plan outlines potential projects and initiatives to bring the College to neutrality by 2040. The College has committed to offsetting greenhouse gas produced by faculty and staff travel on an annual basis through the purchase of carbon offsets.

ADMISSIONS

Freshman Academic Profile: 49% in top 10% of high school class, 85% in top 25% of high school class, 99% in top 50% of high school class. 70% from public high schools. SAT Math middle 50% range 570-670. SAT Critical Reading middle 50% range 550-640. SAT Writing middle 50% range 550-660. ACT middle 50% range 24-29. Minimum internet-based TOEFL 90. Minimum paper TOEFL 550. **Basis for Candidate Selection:** *Very important factors considered include:* Class rank, rigor of secondary school record, standardized test scores, extracurricular activities, volunteer work. *Important factors considered include:* application essay, recommendation(s), character/personal qualities, geographical residence, state residency, talent/ability. *Other factors considered include:* academic GPA, alumni/ae relation, first generation, level of applicant's interest, racial/ethnic status, work experience. **Freshman Admission Requirements:** High school diploma is required and GED is accepted. *Academic units required:* 4 English, 3 mathematics, 3 science, (2 science labs), 2 foreign language, 2 social studies. **Freshman Admission Statistics:** 10,937 applied, 49% admitted, 26% enrolled. **Transfer Admission Requirements:** High school transcript, college transcript(s), essay or personal statement, standardized test scores, statement of good standing from prior institution(s). Minimum college GPA of 2.5 required. Lowest grade transferable C. **General Admission Information:** Application Fee $70. Early decision application deadline 11/15.

Regular application deadline 1/15. Notification on a rolling basis, beginning on or about 1/15. Nonfall registration accepted. Admission may be deferred for a maximum of 2 semesters. Credit and/or placement offered for CEEB Advanced Placement tests.

COSTS AND FINANCIAL AID

Annual in-state tuition $10,562. Annual out-of-state tuition $21,175. Room and board $11,677. Required fees $4,462. Average book expense $1,200. **Required Forms and Deadlines:** FAFSA, CSS/Financial Aid PROFILE. **Notification of Awards:** Applicants will be notified of awards on a rolling basis beginning 6/1. **Types of Aid:** *Need-based scholarships/grants:* Federal Pell, SEOG, state scholarships/grants, private scholarships, the school's own gift aid. *Loans:* Subsidized Stafford, Unsubsidized Stafford, PLUS, Federal Perkins, Federal Nursing. *Student Employment:* Federal Work-Study Program available. Institutional employment available. Highest amount earned per year from on-campus jobs $9,329. Off-campus job opportunities are excellent. **Financial Aid Statistics:** 36% freshmen, 39% undergrads receive need-based scholarship or grant aid. 40% freshmen, 32% undergrads receive non-need-based scholarship or grant aid. 63% freshmen, 74% undergrads receive need-based self-help aid. 0% freshmen, 0% undergrads receive athletic scholarships. 70% freshmen, 62% undergrads receive any aid. 60% undergrads borrow to pay for school. Average cumulative indebtedness $21,907. **Criteria for awarding institutional aid:** *Non-need-based:* academics.

See page 1032.

THE COLLEGE OF NEW ROCHELLE

29 Castle Place, New Rochelle, NY 10805-2339
Phone: 914-654-5452
E-mail: admission@cnr.edu · **CEEB Code:** 2089
Fax: 914-654-5464 · **ACT Code:** 2712

This private school, affiliated with the Roman Catholic Church, was founded in 1904. It has a 20-acre campus.

RATINGS

Admissions Selectivity Rating: 71   Fire Safety Rating: 60*

STUDENTS AND FACULTY

Enrollment: 1,003. **Student Body:** 95% female, 5% male, 10% out-of-state, 1% international (6 countries represented). Asian 6%, African American 39%, Caucasian 14%, Hispanic 13%, Native American <1%. **Retention and Graduation:** 70% freshmen return for sophomore year. 41% freshmen graduate within 4 years. 15% grads go on to further study within 1 year. **Faculty:** 85 full-time faculty, 84% hold PhDs, 71% are members of minority groups, 12% are women. 0% of classes are taught by teaching assistants.

ACADEMICS

Degrees: bachelor's, master's, post-bachelor's certificate, post-master's certificate. **Classes:** Most classes have 10–19 students. Most lab/discussion sessions have fewer than 10 students. **Majors with Highest Enrollment:** Mass Communication/Media Studies; Psychology; Registered Nursing/Registered Nurse. **Special Study Options:** Accelerated program, cooperative education program, cross-registration, double major, exchange student program (domestic), honors program, independent study, internships, liberal arts/career combination, student-designed major, study abroad, teacher certification program. Combined degree programs: BA/MA. **Disability Services:** Special programs offered to physically disabled students include tape recorders, tutors. **Career services:** alumni services, career/job search classes, career assessment, internships.

FACILITIES

Housing: women's dorms. 25% of campus accessible to physically disabled. **Special Academic Facilities/Equipment:** Art gallery, multimedia theatre/teleconference center, language lab, centers for media, computer studies, TV studio, Learning Center for Women, Learning Center for Nursing. **Computers:** Students can register for classes online. Administrative functions (other than registration) can be performed online.

CAMPUS LIFE

Environment: Village. **Activities:** Choral groups, dance, drama/theater, literary magazine, musical theater, student government, student newspaper, yearbook. 26 registered organizations, 2 honor societies, 1 religious organization. **Athletics (Intercollegiate):** *Women:* basketball, cross-country, softball, swimming, tennis, volleyball.

ADMISSIONS

Freshman Academic Profile: 15% in top 10% of high school class, 46% in top 25% of high school class, 82% in top 50% of high school class. 76% from public high schools. SAT Math middle 50% range 440-530. SAT Critical Read-

ing middle 50% range 440-530. ACT middle 50% range 16-22. Minimum paper TOEFL 550. **Basis for Candidate Selection:** *Very important factors considered include:* rigor of secondary school record. *Important factors considered include:* Class rank, application essay, standardized test scores. *Other factors considered include:* recommendation(s), alumni/ae relation, character/personal qualities, extracurricular activities, interview, talent/ability, volunteer work, work experience. **Freshman Admission Requirements:** High school diploma is required and GED is accepted. **Transfer Admission Requirements:** High school transcript, college transcript(s), Lowest grade transferable C-. **General Admission Information:** Application Fee $20. Early decision application deadline 11/1. Notification on a rolling basis, beginning on or about 11/1. Nonfall registration accepted. Admission may be deferred for a maximum of 1 year. Credit and/or placement offered for CEEB Advanced Placement tests.

COSTS AND FINANCIAL AID

Annual tuition $23,200. Room and board $9,700. Required fees $500. Average book expense $600. **Required Forms and Deadlines:** FAFSA, Institution's own financial aid form. **Notification of Awards:** Applicants will be notified of awards on a rolling basis beginning 1/1. **Types of Aid:** *Need-based scholarships/grants:* Federal Pell, SEOG, state scholarships/grants, private scholarships, the school's own gift aid. *Loans:* Direct Subsidized Stafford, Direct Unsubsidized Stafford, PLUS, Federal Perkins, Federal Nursing. *Student Employment:* Federal Work-Study Program available. Institutional employment available. Highest amount earned per year from on-campus jobs $1,500. Off-campus job opportunities are excellent. **Financial Aid Statistics:** 97% freshmen, 93% undergrads receive need-based scholarship or grant aid. 55% freshmen, 57% undergrads receive non-need-based scholarship or grant aid. 84% freshmen, 85% undergrads receive need-based self-help aid. 0% freshmen, 0% undergrads receive athletic scholarships. Criteria for awarding institutional aid: *Non-need-based:* academics, art, leadership.

COLLEGE OF NOTRE DAME OF MARYLAND

4701 North Charles Street, Baltimore, MD 21210
Phone: 410-532-5330 · **Financial Aid Phone:** 410-532-5369
E-mail: admiss@ndm.edu · **CEEB Code:** 5114
Fax: 410-532-6287 · **Website:** www.ndm.edu · **ACT Code:** 1727

This private school, affiliated with the Roman Catholic Church, was founded in 1896. It has a 58-acre campus.

RATINGS

Admissions Selectivity Rating: 78   Fire Safety Rating: 60*

STUDENTS AND FACULTY

Enrollment: 1,686. **Student Body:** 94% female, 6% male, 2% international. Asian 3%, African American 26%, Caucasian 66%, Hispanic 3%, Native American <1%
Retention and Graduation: 87% freshmen return for sophomore year. 49% freshmen graduate within 4 years. 66% freshmen graduate within 6 years. **Faculty:** 83 full-time faculty, 78% hold PhDs, 65% are members of minority groups, 4% are women. 0% of classes are taught by teaching assistants.

ACADEMICS

Degrees: bachelor's, master's, post-master's certificate. **Classes:** Most classes have 20–29 students. **Majors with Highest Enrollment:** Liberal Arts and Sciences/Liberal Studies; Registered Nursing/Registered Nurse; Business, Management, Marketing, and Related Support Services. **Special Study Options:** Accelerated program, cross-registration, double major, dual enrollment, English as a Second Language (ESL), exchange student program (domestic), honors program, independent study, internships, liberal arts/career combination, student-designed major, study abroad, teacher certification program, weekend college, Orientation program for all new students to college which includes a first semester seminar course for entering freshman. Also a Career Action Plan for all students and an academic consortium with seven local colleges and universities. **Honors programs:** Exceptionally motivated students with outstanding academic ability may be invited to become a Morrissy Scholar. Students take selected interdisciplinary courses throughout their academic program and must complete 18 credits in the program to graduate as a Morrissy Scholar. The students are engaged in various activities on campus, off campus - nationally and internationally. The group selected each year to join the program is approximatly 10-12% of the entering class. Combined degree programs: BA/MA, BA/MAT; dual degree BA/BS; BA/MA in Business. **Disability Services:** Special programs offered to physically disabled students include note-taking services, reader services, tutors. **Career services:** Alumni network, alumni services, career/job search classes, career assessment, internships, regional alumni. Approximately 90% or more of all graduating students from the Women's College have at least on internship experience upon graduating. This takes the liberal arts in-classroom learning and ties it directly to practical experience—the best of all worlds.

FACILITIES

Housing: women's dorms **Special Academic Facilities/Equipment:** Art gallery, photo labs, language labs, child care center, fitness center, television and radio studios, music practice labs, planetarium. **Computers:** Administrative functions (other than registration) can be performed online.

CAMPUS LIFE

Environment: Metropolis. **Activities:** Choral groups, dance, drama/theater, literary magazine, music ensembles, radio station, student government, student newspaper, student-run film society, television station, yearbook. 24 registered organizations, 7 honor societies. **Athletics (Intercollegiate):** *Women:* basketball, field hockey, lacrosse, soccer, swimming, tennis, volleyball. **On-Campus Highlights:** Gator Alley—pub-like eatery, MBK Sports and Activities center (fitness center), Loyola/Notre Dame library, Doyle Hall—residence hall, student activity area, Marikle Chapel.

ADMISSIONS

Freshman Academic Profile: Average high school GPA 3.35. 15% in top 10% of high school class, 43% in top 25% of high school class, 80% in top 50% of high school class. 71% from public high schools. SAT Math middle 50% range 450-560. SAT Critical Reading middle 50% range 490-580. **Basis for Candidate Selection:** *Very important factors considered include:* application essay, recommendation(s), rigor of secondary school record, standardized test scores, interview. *Important factors considered include:* extracurricular activities, volunteer work. *Other factors considered include:* Class rank, alumni/ae relation, character/personal qualities, talent/ability, work experience. **Freshman Admission Requirements:** High school diploma is required and GED is accepted. *Academic units required:* 4 English, 3 mathematics, 2 science, (2 science labs), 3 foreign language, 2 history, 4 academic electives. **Freshman Admission Statistics:** 450 applied, 72% admitted, 46% enrolled. **Transfer Admission Requirements:** college transcript(s), essay or personal statement, Minimum college GPA of 2.5 required. Lowest grade transferable C. **General Admission Information:** Application Fee $40. Notification on a rolling basis, beginning on or about 10/1. Nonfall registration accepted. Admission may be deferred for a maximum of 12 months. Credit and/or placement offered for CEEB Advanced Placement tests.

COSTS AND FINANCIAL AID

Annual tuition $19,900. Room and board $7,800. Required fees $400. Average book expense $800. **Required Forms and Deadlines:** FAFSA. **Notification of Awards:** Applicants will be notified of awards on a rolling basis beginning 3/1. **Types of Aid:** *Need-based scholarships/grants:* Federal Pell, SEOG, state scholarships/grants. *Loans:* Direct Subsidized Stafford, Direct Unsubsidized Stafford, Direct PLUS, Federal Perkins. *Student Employment:* Federal Work-Study Program available. Institutional employment available. Off-campus job opportunities are good. **Financial Aid Statistics:** 97% freshmen, 86% undergrads receive need-based scholarship or grant aid. 88% freshmen, 87% undergrads receive non-need-based scholarship or grant aid. 74% freshmen, 80% undergrads receive need-based self-help aid. 0% freshmen, 0% undergrads receive athletic scholarships. Criteria for awarding institutional aid: *Non-need-based:* academics, alumni affiliation, art, leadership, music/drama.

COLLEGE OF THE OZARKS

Office of Admissions, Point Lookout, MO 65726
Phone: 417-690-2636 • **Financial Aid Phone:** 417-690-3292
E-mail: admiss4@cofo.edu • **CEEB Code:** 6713
Fax: 417-335-2618 • **Website:** www.cofo.edu • **ACT Code:** 2364

This private school was founded in 1906. It has a 1000-acre campus.

RATINGS

Admissions Selectivity Rating: 92   **Fire Safety Rating:** 80

STUDENTS AND FACULTY

Enrollment: 1,433. **Student Body:** 51% female, 49% male, 22% out-of-state, 2% international (16 countries represented). Asian 0%, African American 1%, Caucasian 73%, Hispanic 2%, Native American <1%.
Retention and Graduation: 87% freshmen return for sophomore year. 60% freshmen graduate within 4 years. 63% freshmen graduate within 6 years. 9%

grads go on to further study within 1 year. 6% grads pursue arts and sciences degrees. 1% grads pursue business degrees. **Faculty:** 83 full-time faculty, 54% hold PhDs, 45% are members of minority groups, 1% are women. 0% of classes are taught by teaching assistants.

ACADEMICS

Degrees: bachelor's. **Classes:** Most classes have 10–19 students. Most lab/discussion sessions have 10–19 students. **Majors with Highest Enrollment:** Elementary Education and Teaching; Business Administration and Management; Agricultural Business and Management. **Special Study Options:** Accelerated program, double major, dual enrollment, independent study, internships, student-designed major, teacher certification program. Combined degree programs: BA/JD, BA/MEng. **Disability Services:** Special programs offered to physically disabled students include note-taking services, reader services, tape recorders, tutors. **Career services:** Alumni network, alumni services, career/job search classes, career assessment, internships. Career services highlights include outstanding internships that offer graduates opportunities for phenomenal careers.

FACILITIES

Housing: men's dorms, women's dorms, Wellness Housing. All full-time students must live in residence halls unless they meet one of the following criteria: 21 years of age or older, married, living with parents, or veteran of the armed forces. 75% of campus accessible to physically disabled. **Special Academic Facilities/Equipment:** Ralph Foster Museum; Edwards Mill; The Keeter Center; Fruitcake and Jelly Kitchen; Greenhouses. **Computers:** 100% of dorms, 100% of libraries, 100% of dining areas, 100% of student union, have wireless network access. Students can register for classes online. Administrative functions (other than registration) can be performed online.

CAMPUS LIFE

Environment: Rural. **Activities:** Choral groups, concert band, drama/theater, jazz band, literary magazine, music ensembles, musical theater, pep band, radio station, student government, student newspaper, student-run film society, yearbook, Campus Ministries. 45 registered organizations, 6 honor societies, 10 religious organizations. **Athletics (Intercollegiate):** *Men:* baseball, basketball, cheerleading. *Women:* basketball, cheerleading, volleyball. **On-Campus Highlights:** Memorial Fieldhouse and Keeter Gymnasium, Ralph Foster Museum, Williams Memorial Chapel, The Keeter Center, Agriculture, Edwards Mill, Fruitcake and Jelly Kitchen. **Environmental Initiatives:** The College ensures proper management of hazardous, special and universal waste. There is campus-wide recycling: plastic bottles, corrugated cardboard, aluminum cans, tin cans, batteries, tires, light bulbs and electronic products. Light bulb reclamation (recycle of bulbs) and energy efficient lights. Agricultural Livestock Waste Containment program (protects area lakes). Many campus buildings have cooling systems that utilize 48 degree lake water and save energy. Ground source heating and cooling pumps.

ADMISSIONS

Freshman Academic Profile: Average high school GPA 3.59. 22% in top 10% of high school class, 52% in top 25% of high school class, 92% in top 50% of high school class. 76% from public high schools. SAT Math middle 50% range 540-640. SAT Critical Reading middle 50% range 560-620. SAT Writing middle 50% range 540-620. ACT middle 50% range 21-25. Minimum internet-based TOEFL 79. Minimum paper TOEFL 550. **Basis for Candidate Selection:** *Very important factors considered include:* Class rank, rigor of secondary school record, character/personal qualities, interview. *Important factors considered include:* academic GPA, recommendation(s), standardized test scores, geographical residence, level of applicant's interest, volunteer work, work experience. *Other factors considered include:* alumni/ae relation, extracurricular activities, first generation, religious affiliation/commitment, state residency, talent/ability. **Freshman Admission Requirements:** High school diploma is required and GED is accepted. **Freshman Admission Statistics:** 3,407 applied, 8% admitted, 90% enrolled. **Transfer Admission Requirements:** college transcript(s), interview, statement of good standing from prior institution(s). Minimum college GPA of 3.0 required. Lowest grade transferable D-. **General Admission Information:** Regular application deadline 2/15. Notification on a rolling basis, beginning on or about 3/1. Nonfall registration accepted. Credit offered for CEEB Advanced Placement tests.

COSTS AND FINANCIAL AID

Room and board $6,200. Required fees $430. Average book expense $1,000. **Required Forms and Deadlines:** FAFSA. **Notification of Awards:** Applicants will be notified of awards on or about 7/1. **Types of Aid:** *Need-based scholarships/grants:* Federal Pell, SEOG, state scholarships/grants, private scholarships, the school's own gift aid. *Loans: Student Employment:* Federal Work-Study Program available. Off-campus job opportunities are excellent. **Financial Aid Statistics:** 100% freshmen, 100% undergrads receive need-based scholarship or grant aid. 12% freshmen, 13% undergrads receive non-need-based scholarship or grant aid. 88% freshmen, 87% undergrads receive need-based self-help aid. 3% freshmen, 2% undergrads receive athletic scholarships.

100% freshmen, 100% undergrads receive any aid. 8% undergrads borrow to pay for school. Average cumulative indebtedness $0. **Criteria for awarding institutional aid:** *Non-need-based:* academics, art, athletics, leadership, minority status, music/drama, state/district residency.

COLLEGE OF SAINT BENEDICT/ SAINT JOHN'S UNIVERSITY

Best 380

PO Box 7155, Collegeville, MN 56321-7155
Phone: 320-363-5060 · **Financial Aid Phone:** 320-363-5388
E-mail: admissions@csbsju.edu · **CEEB Code:** 6624
Fax: 320-363-5650 · **Website:** www.csbsju.edu · **ACT Code:** 2140

This private school, affiliated with the Roman Catholic Church, was founded in 1857. It has a 2400-acre campus.

RATINGS

Admissions Selectivity Rating: 84   **Fire Safety Rating:** 94

STUDENTS AND FACULTY

Enrollment: 3,809. **Student Body:** 53% female, 47% male, 18% out-of-state, 5% international (28 countries represented). Asian 4%, African American 3%, Caucasian 81%, Hispanic 5%, Native American 1%
Retention and Graduation: 88% freshmen return for sophomore year. 73% freshmen graduate within 4 years. 81% freshmen graduate within 6 years. 16% grads go on to further study within 1 year. **Faculty:** 283 full-time faculty, 90% hold PhDs, 51% are members of minority groups, 10% are women. 0% of classes are taught by teaching assistants.

ACADEMICS

Degrees: bachelor's, first professional, master's. **Classes:** Most classes have 20–29 students. Most lab/discussion sessions have 10–19 students. **Majors with Highest Enrollment:** Business Administration and Management; Biology/Biological Sciences; Rhetoric and Composition. **Special Study Options:** cross-registration, double major, dual enrollment, English as a Second Language (ESL), exchange student program (domestic), honors program, independent study, internships, student-designed major, study abroad, teacher certification program. **Honors programs:** All departments may contribute courses to our honors program. Students in all majors may participate in the Honors Program and receive honors distinction inside the major. Combined degree programs: 3/2 program in engineering with U of MN-TC. **Disability Services:** Special programs offered to physically disabled students include note-taking services, tape recorders, tutors. **Career services:** Alumni network, alumni services, career/job search classes, career assessment, internships, regional alumni. At CSB/SJU academic internships have tripled in the last decade. Currently 8% of our total student body engage in internships with a credit requirement attached. In any given semester students in 20 different majors receive individual guidance from faculty, so that intentional learning and reflection are integrated into the experience. Internship opportunities exist, not only for business-related majors in the private sector, but also for a variety of humanities and social science majors (Communication, Psychology, Political Science, Environmental Studies, Peace Studies to name a few) in government, education and the non profit sector. Within the last three years 53% of the total internships at CSB/SJU were completed in the private sector by business majors while 47% were service-related internships completed by non business majors.

FACILITIES

Housing: special housing for disabled students, men's dorms, special housing for international students, women's dorms, apartments for single students, Health and Wellness floor, Global Initiative Group house, ROTC housing. 90% of campus accessible to physically disabled. **Special Academic Facilities/Equipment:** Hill Museum and Manuscript Library, art galleries, natural science museum, arboretum, Benedicta Arts Center, Sommers Digital Lab. **Computers:** 100% of classrooms, 20% of dorms, 100% of libraries, 100% of dining areas, 100% of student union, 100% of common outdoor areas have wireless network access. Students can register for classes online. Administrative functions (other than registration) can be performed online.

CAMPUS LIFE

Environment: Village. **Activities:** Choral groups, concert band, dance, drama/theater, jazz band, literary magazine, music ensembles, musical theater, opera, pep band, radio station, student government, student newspaper, symphony orchestra, Campus Ministries, International Student Organization, Model UN. 85 registered organizations, 3 honor societies, 4 religious organizations. **Athletics (Intercollegiate):** *Men:* baseball, basketball, cross-country, diving, football, golf, ice hockey, skiing (nordic/cross-country), soccer, swimming, tennis, track/field (outdoor), track/field (indoor), wrestling. *Women:* basketball, cross-country, diving, golf, ice hockey, skiing (nordic/cross-country), soccer, softball, swimming, tennis, track/field (outdoor), track/field (indoor), volleyball. **On-Campus Highlights:** Gorecki Dining Center, Benedicta Ars Center, Warner Palaestra/Clemens Field House, Lake Sagatagan/Stell Maris Chapel, Brother Willie's Pub/O'Connell's Coffee, Abbey Church/Sacred Heart Chapel; Hill Museum and Manuscript Library; 15 KM hiking trails. **Environmental Initiatives:** Renewable Energy/Carbon neutrality; Student programming: increase recycling/move out initiative.

ADMISSIONS

Freshman Academic Profile: Average high school GPA 3.57. 30% in top 10% of high school class, 62% in top 25% of high school class, 90% in top 50% of high school class. 73% from public high schools. SAT Math middle 50% range 490-600. SAT Critical Reading middle 50% range 490-610. SAT Writing middle 50% range 480-590. ACT middle 50% range 23-28. Minimum internet-based TOEFL 80. Minimum paper TOEFL 550. **Basis for Candidate Selection:** *Very important factors considered include:* application essay, academic GPA, rigor of secondary school record, standardized test scores. *Important factors considered include:* recommendation(s), extracurricular activities. *Other factors considered include:* Class rank, alumni/ae relation, character/personal qualities, first generation, geographical residence, interview, racial/ethnic status, talent/ability, volunteer work, work experience. **Freshman Admission Requirements:** High school diploma is required and GED is accepted. *Academic units required:* 4 English, 3 mathematics, 2 science, (2 science labs), 2 social studies, 4 academic electives. **Freshman Admission Statistics:** 3,237 applied, 81% admitted, 38% enrolled. **Transfer Admission Requirements:** High school transcript, college transcript(s), essay or personal statement, statement of good standing from prior institution(s). Minimum college GPA of 2.75 required. Lowest grade transferable C. **General Admission Information:** Nonfall registration accepted. Admission may be deferred for a maximum of one year. Credit and/or placement offered for CEEB Advanced Placement tests.

COSTS AND FINANCIAL AID

Annual tuition $38,428. Room and board $9,957. Required fees $974. Average book expense $1,000. **Required Forms and Deadlines:** FAFSA, Institution's own financial aid form. **Notification of Awards:** Applicants will be notified of awards on a rolling basis beginning 3/15. **Types of Aid:** *Need-based scholarships/grants:* Federal Pell, SEOG, state scholarships/grants, private scholarships, the school's own gift aid. *Loans:* Subsidized Stafford, Unsubsidized Stafford, PLUS, Federal Perkins, state loans, Various private education loans. *Student Employment:* Federal Work-Study Program available. Institutional employment available. Highest amount earned per year from on-campus jobs $6,870. Off-campus job opportunities are fair. **Financial Aid Statistics:** 99% freshmen, 98% undergrads receive need-based scholarship or grant aid. 96% freshmen, 95% undergrads receive non-need-based scholarship or grant aid. 90% freshmen, 92% undergrads receive need-based self-help aid. 0% freshmen, 0% undergrads receive athletic scholarships. 96% freshmen, 94% undergrads receive any aid. 72% undergrads borrow to pay for school. Average cumulative indebtedness $24,289. **Criteria for awarding institutional aid:** *Non-need-based:* academics, art, leadership, music/drama.

COLLEGE OF SAINT ELIZABETH

Admissions Office, Morristown, NJ 07960-6989
Phone: 973-290-4700 · **Financial Aid Phone:** 973-290-4432
E-mail: apply@cse.edu · **CEEB Code:** 2090
Fax: 973-290-4710

This private school, affiliated with the Roman Catholic Church, was founded in 1899. It has a 200-acre campus.

RATINGS

Admissions Selectivity Rating: 75   **Fire Safety Rating:** 94

STUDENTS AND FACULTY

Enrollment: 852. **Student Body:** 94% female, 6% male, 4% out-of-state, 2% international (8 countries represented). Asian 1%, African American 22%, Caucasian 14%, Hispanic 11%, Native American <1%
Retention and Graduation: 69% freshmen return for sophomore year. 39% freshmen graduate within 4 years. 50% freshmen graduate within 6 years. **Faculty:** 52 full-time faculty, 83% hold PhDs, 65% are members of minority groups, 8% are women. 0% of classes are taught by teaching assistants.

ACADEMICS

Degrees: bachelor's, certificate, master's, post-bachelor's certificate, post-master's certificate. **Classes:** Most classes have 10–19 students. **Majors with Highest Enrollment:** Registered Nursing/Registered Nurse; Psychology; Criminal Justice/Safety Studies. **Special Study Options:** Accelerated program, cross-registration, distance learning, double major, dual enrollment, English as a Second Language (ESL), exchange student program (domestic), honors program, independent study, internships, student-designed major, study abroad, teacher certification program, weekend college. Combined degree programs: BA/MA, BS/MS. **Disability Services:** Special programs offered to physically disabled students include note-taking services, reader services, tape recorders, tutors. **Career services:** Alumni network, career/job search classes, career assessment, internships. Career services highlights include partnerships with employers such as American Red Cross, MEDCO Solutions, Verizon Wireless & the Department of Human Services, which have fortified our students with practical opportunities for development. An example of this is a collaborative venture between Career Services, the Communications and Business departments and the Business Club. Students are scheduled to spend a half day at Verizon, experiencing corporate culture and attend workshops lead by Verizon Human Resources staff on topics such as "Group Interviewing."

FACILITIES

Housing: women's dorms. 85% of campus accessible to physically disabled. **Computers:** 100% of classrooms, 100% of dorms, 100% of libraries, 100% of dining areas, 100% of student union, 5% of common outdoor areas have wireless network access.

CAMPUS LIFE

Environment: Village. **Activities:** Choral groups, dance, drama/theater, literary magazine, music ensembles, student government, student newspaper, yearbook, Campus Ministries, International Student Organization. 28 registered organizations, 9 honor societies, 1 religious organization. **Athletics (Intercollegiate):** *Women:* basketball, equestrian sports, soccer, softball, swimming, tennis. **On-Campus Highlights:** St. Joesph's Hall-Student Center, Henderson Hall-Classroom Building, O'Connor Hall-Residence Hall, Santa Rita Hall-Administration Building, Mahoney Library. **Environmental Initiatives:** Hazardous Waste Management process exists. Training of faculty and staff completed. Environmental Policy Statement exists and Environmental Management System (EMS) being implemented.

ADMISSIONS

Freshman Academic Profile: 81% from public high schools. SAT Math middle 50% range 370-465. SAT Critical Reading middle 50% range 380-470. SAT Writing middle 50% range 380-488. Minimum internet-based TOEFL 61. Minimum paper TOEFL 500. **Basis for Candidate Selection:** *Very important factors considered include:* Class rank, academic GPA, recommendation(s), rigor of secondary school record, standardized test scores. *Important factors considered include:* application essay, character/personal qualities. *Other factors considered include:* alumni/ae relation, extracurricular activities, first generation, geographical residence, interview, level of applicant's interest, talent/ability, volunteer work, work experience. **Freshman Admission Requirements:** High school diploma is required and GED is accepted. *Academic units required:* 3 English, 2 mathematics, 1 science, (1 science labs), 2 foreign language, 1 history, 7 academic electives. **Freshman Admission Statistics:** 2,496 applied, 48% admitted, 10% enrolled. **Transfer Admission Requirements:** college transcript(s), essay or personal statement, Minimum college GPA of 2.0 required. Lowest grade transferable C. **General Admission Information:** Application Fee $35. Regular application deadline 8/15. Notification on a rolling basis, beginning on or about 11/15. Nonfall registration accepted. Admission may be deferred for a maximum of 1 year. Credit and/or placement offered for CEEB Advanced Placement tests.

COSTS AND FINANCIAL AID

Annual tuition $29,148. Room and board $12,744. Required fees $1,947. Average book expense $1,300. **Required Forms and Deadlines:** FAFSA. **Notification of Awards:** Applicants will be notified of awards on a rolling basis beginning 11/15. **Types of Aid:** *Need-based scholarships/grants:* Federal Pell, SEOG, state scholarships/grants, private scholarships, the school's own gift aid. *Loans:* Subsidized Stafford, Unsubsidized Stafford, PLUS, Federal Perkins, state loans. *Student Employment:* Federal Work-Study Program available. Institutional employment available. Highest amount earned per year from on-campus jobs $4,350. Off-campus job opportunities are good. **Financial Aid Statistics:** 89% freshmen, 81% undergrads receive need-based scholarship or grant aid. 100% freshmen, 88% undergrads receive non-need-based scholarship or grant aid. 93% freshmen, 91% undergrads receive need-based self-help aid. 0% freshmen, 0% undergrads receive athletic scholarships. 87% freshmen, 98% undergrads receive any aid. 42% undergrads borrow to pay for school. Average cumulative indebtedness $8,189. **Criteria for awarding institutional aid:** *Non-need-based:* academics, alumni affiliation, art, leadership, religious affiliation, state/district residency.

COLLEGE OF SAINT JOSEPH IN VERMONT

71 Clement Road, Rutland, VT 5701
Phone: 802-776-5286 • **Financial Aid Phone:** 802-776-5218
E-mail: admissions@csj.edu • **CEEB Code:** 3297
Fax: 802-776-5258 • **Website:** www.csj.edu

This private school, affiliated with the Roman Catholic Church, was founded in 1956. It has a 116-acre campus.

RATINGS

Admissions Selectivity Rating: 70   **Fire Safety Rating:** 70

STUDENTS AND FACULTY

Enrollment: 208. **Student Body:** 55% female, 45% male, 42% out-of-state, 0% international (6 countries represented). Asian 1%, African American 4%, Caucasian 89%, Hispanic 5%, Native American 1%
Retention and Graduation: 83% freshmen return for sophomore year. 40% freshmen graduate within 4 years. 45% freshmen graduate within 6 years. **Faculty:** 15 full-time faculty, 47% hold PhDs, 40% are members of minority groups, 0% are women. 0% of classes are taught by teaching assistants.

ACADEMICS

Degrees: associate, bachelor's, master's. **Classes:** Most classes have fewer than 10 students. **Majors with Highest Enrollment:** Business, Management, Marketing, and Related Support Services; Psychology; Elementary Education and Teaching. **Special Study Options:** Accelerated program, double major, dual enrollment, independent study, internships, liberal arts/career combination, teacher certification program. **Disability Services:** Special programs offered to physically disabled students include note-taking services, reader services, tape recorders, tutors. **Career services:** alumni services, career/job search classes, career assessment, internships. Career services highlights include a variety of available internships.

FACILITIES

Housing: men's dorms, women's dorms. 100% of campus accessible to physically disabled. **Special Academic Facilities/Equipment:** Theater and Athletic Center. **Computers:** 100% of libraries, have wireless network access.

CAMPUS LIFE

Environment: Village. **Activities:** Choral groups, drama/theater, literary magazine, student government, Campus Ministries 20 registered organizations, 6 honor societies, 1 religious organization. **Athletics (Intercollegiate):** *Men:* baseball, basketball, soccer. *Women:* basketball, soccer, softball. **On-Campus Highlights:** Tuttle Hall-Student Center, Athletic Center, Theater, Giorgetti Library, St. Joseph Hall.

ADMISSIONS

Freshman Academic Profile: Average high school GPA 2.63. 0% in top 10% of high school class, 3% in top 25% of high school class, 36% in top 50% of high school class. 75% from public high schools. SAT Math middle 50% range 390-490. SAT Critical Reading middle 50% range 410-530. ACT middle 50% range 17-23. Minimum internet-based TOEFL 79. Minimum paper TOEFL 550. **Basis for Candidate Selection:** *Very important factors considered include:* academic GPA, recommendation(s), rigor of secondary school record. *Important factors considered include:* application essay, standardized test scores, character/personal qualities, interview. *Other factors considered include:* Class rank, alumni/ae relation, extracurricular activities, level of applicant's interest, talent/ability, volunteer work. **Freshman Admission Requirements:** High school diploma is required and GED is not accepted. *Academic units required:* 4 English, 3 mathematics, 2 science, 2 social studies, 2 history, 5 academic electives. **Freshman Admission Statistics:** 101 applied, 88% admitted, 37% enrolled. **Transfer Admission Requirements:** High school transcript, college transcript(s), essay or personal statement, Minimum college GPA of 2.0 required. Lowest grade transferable C. **General Admission Information:** Application Fee $25. Notification on a rolling basis, beginning on or about 10/1. Nonfall registration accepted. Admission may be deferred for a maximum of 1 year. Credit and/or placement offered for CEEB Advanced Placement tests.

COSTS AND FINANCIAL AID

Annual tuition $15,500. Room and board $7,600. Required fees $260. Average book expense $1,000. **Required Forms and Deadlines:** FAFSA, Institution's own financial aid form. **Notification of Awards:** Applicants will be notified of awards on a rolling basis beginning 3/15. **Types of Aid:** *Need-based scholarships/grants:* Federal Pell, SEOG, state scholarships/grants, private scholarships, the school's own gift aid. *Loans:* Subsidized Stafford, Unsubsidized Stafford, PLUS, Federal Perkins. *Student Employment:* Federal Work-Study Program available. Institutional employment available. Highest amount earned per year from on-campus jobs $1,317. Off-campus job opportunities are good. **Financial Aid Statistics:** 100% freshmen, 98% undergrads receive need-based scholarship or grant aid. 0% freshmen, 3% undergrads receive non-need-based scholarship or grant aid. 96% freshmen, 94% undergrads receive need-based self-help aid. 0% freshmen, 0% undergrads receive athletic scholarships. 91% freshmen, 88% undergrads receive any aid. 100% undergrads borrow to pay for school. Average cumulative indebtedness $18,726. **Criteria for awarding institutional aid:** *Non-need-based:* academics, music/drama.

COLLEGE OF SAINT MARY

7000 Mercy Rd., Omaha, NE 68106
Phone: 402-399-2355 · **Financial Aid Phone:** 402-399-2415
E-mail: enroll@csm.edu · **CEEB Code:** 6106
Fax: 402-399-2412 · **Website:** www.csm.edu · **ACT Code:** 2440

This private school, affiliated with the Roman Catholic Church, was founded in 1923. It has a 25-acre campus.

RATINGS
Admissions Selectivity Rating: 86   **Fire Safety Rating:** 94

STUDENTS AND FACULTY
Enrollment: 691. **Student Body:** 100% female, 0% male, 20% out-of-state, 1% international (7 countries represented). Asian 1%, African American 6%, Caucasian 78%, Hispanic 11%, Native American <1%
Retention and Graduation: 79% freshmen return for sophomore year. 28% freshmen graduate within 4 years. 40% freshmen graduate within 6 years. 51% grads go on to further study within 1 year. **Faculty:** 61 full-time faculty, 66% hold PhDs, 77% are members of minority groups, 11% are women. 0% of classes are taught by teaching assistants.

ACADEMICS
Degrees: associate, bachelor's, certificate, doctoral, master's, post-bachelor's certificate, terminal associate. **Classes:** Most classes have fewer than 10 students. Most lab/discussion sessions have fewer than 10 students. **Majors with Highest Enrollment:** Registered Nursing/Registered Nurse; Biology; Business Administration and Management. **Special Study Options:** Accelerated program, cooperative education program, distance learning, double major, dual enrollment, honors program, independent study, internships, study abroad, teacher certification program, weekend college. **Honors programs:** Honors Program Combined degree programs: BS/Eng. **Disability Services:** Special programs offered to physically disabled students include note-taking services, reader services, tape recorders, tutors. **Career services:** alumni services, career/job search classes, career assessment, internships. Career services highlights include service learning projects that are an integral part of classes.

FACILITIES
Housing: special housing for disabled students, women's dorms, women with children housing. 100% of campus accessible to physically disabled. **Special Academic Facilities/Equipment:** Hillmer Art Gallery Gross Auditorium **Computers:** 100% of classrooms, 100% of dorms, 100% of libraries, 100% of dining areas, 100% of student union, 100% of common outdoor areas have wireless network access. Students can register for classes online. Administrative functions (other than registration) can be performed online.

CAMPUS LIFE
Environment: Metropolis. **Activities:** Choral groups, music ensembles, student government, Campus Ministries. 20 registered organizations, 2 honor societies, 1 religious organization. **Athletics (Intercollegiate):** *Women:* basketball, cross-country, soccer, softball, swimming, volleyball. **On-Campus Highlights:** Hillmer Art Gallery—Year round exhibits, Gross Theater, Hixson-Lied Commons—Student Center, Library, Lied Fitness Center—gym, weight room, pool, tennis, Our Lady of Mercy Chapel—Daily Mass offered, Our residence halls include computer labs, lounge areas, a prayer and reflection room, and study area/small group meeting rooms. **Environmental Initiatives:** Reuseable to-go containers in dining hall. Going tray-less in the dining hall. Recycle receptacles located across campus.

ADMISSIONS
Freshman Academic Profile: Average high school GPA 3.6. 28% in top 10% of high school class, 51% in top 25% of high school class, 87% in top 50% of high school class. 80% from public high schools. ACT middle 50% range 20-26. Minimum internet-based TOEFL 80. **Basis for Candidate Selection:** *Very important factors considered include:* Class rank, academic GPA, standardized test scores. *Other factors considered include:* application essay, recommendation(s), rigor of secondary school record, alumni/ae relation, character/personal qualities, extracurricular activities, interview, level of applicant's interest, talent/ability. **Freshman Admission Requirements:** High school diploma is required and GED is accepted. *Academic units required:* 4 English, 2 mathematics, 2 science, 2 social studies. **Freshman Admission Statistics:**

347 applied, 54% admitted, 47% enrolled. **Transfer Admission Requirements:** High school transcript, college transcript(s), Minimum college GPA of 2.0 required. Lowest grade transferable C. **General Admission Information:** Application Fee $30. Nonfall registration accepted. Admission may be deferred for a maximum of 12 months. Credit and/or placement offered for CEEB Advanced Placement tests.

COSTS AND FINANCIAL AID
Annual tuition $24,830. Room and board $6,800. Required fees $480. Average book expense $1,280. **Required Forms and Deadlines:** FAFSA. **Notification of Awards:** Applicants will be notified of awards on a rolling basis beginning 3/15. **Types of Aid:** *Need-based scholarships/grants:* Federal Pell, SEOG, state scholarships/grants, private scholarships, the school's own gift aid, Federal Nursing Scholarships. *Loans:* Direct Subsidized Stafford, Direct Unsubsidized Stafford, Direct PLUS, Federal Perkins, Federal Nursing. *Student Employment:* Federal Work-Study Program available. Highest amount earned per year from on-campus jobs $1,800. Off-campus job opportunities are fair. **Financial Aid Statistics:** 100% freshmen, 97% undergrads receive need-based scholarship or grant aid. 26% freshmen, 8% undergrads receive non-need-based scholarship or grant aid. 69% freshmen, 89% undergrads receive need-based self-help aid. 15% freshmen, 7% undergrads receive athletic scholarships. 94% freshmen, 92% undergrads receive any aid. 79% undergrads borrow to pay for school. Average cumulative indebtedness $32,264. **Criteria for awarding institutional aid:** *Non-need-based:* academics, art, athletics, leadership, music/drama.

THE COLLEGE OF SAINT ROSE

432 Western Avenue, Albany, NY 12203
Phone: 518-454-5150
E-mail: admit@strose.edu · **CEEB Code:** 2091
Fax: 518-454-2013 · **Website:** www.strose.edu · **ACT Code:** 2714

This private school, affiliated with the Roman Catholic Church, was founded in 1920. It has a 28-acre campus.

RATINGS
Admissions Selectivity Rating: 78   **Fire Safety Rating:** 91

STUDENTS AND FACULTY
Enrollment: 2,614. **Student Body:** 66% female, 34% male, 12% out-of-state, 1% international (20 countries represented). Asian 2%, African American 8%, Caucasian 72%, Hispanic 6%, Native American <1%
Retention and Graduation: 54% freshmen graduate within 4 years. **Faculty:** 207 full-time faculty, 94% hold PhDs, 56% are members of minority groups, 12% are women. 0% of classes are taught by teaching assistants.

ACADEMICS
Degrees: bachelor's, master's, post-bachelor's certificate, post-master's certificate. **Classes:** Most classes have 20–29 students. Most lab/discussion sessions have 10–19 students. **Special Study Options:** Accelerated program, cross-registration, double major, exchange student program (domestic), independent study, internships, liberal arts/career combination, student-designed major, study abroad, teacher certification program. Combined degree programs: BA/JD, BA/MA, MBA/JD graduate degree. **Disability Services:** Special programs offered to physically disabled students include note-taking services, reader services, tape recorders, tutors.

FACILITIES
Housing: Coed dorms, men's dorms, women's dorms, apartments for single students. 90% of campus accessible to physically disabled. **Special Academic Facilities/Equipment:** The Center for Art and Design houses the Saint Rose Art Gallery, the venue for student art shows and exhibits by acclaimed visiting artists, in addition to one of the largest screen printing facilities in the state of New York. The College's full-scale television studio is where communications students produce three 30-minute weekly television shows aired on Time Warner Cable. The Music Center features the Saints and Sinners Sound Studio, a 16-track professional recording studio, in addition to a music library. Athletic Facilities include the College's new Fitness Center, competition-size pool, weight room, and regulation NCAA basketball court. The Hubbard Interfaith Sanctuary is home to Campus Ministry and hosts a variety of interfaith lectures, concerts and poetry readings. With private meditation rooms and an indoor garden, this interreligious space provides a place to escape for a few minutes of quiet prayer. The Center for Cultural Diversity provides academic, social, and cultural support in an effort to enhance the quality of experiences for our diverse student population. **Computers:** 98% of classrooms, 90% of dorms, 100% of libraries, 100% of dining areas, 100% of student union, 80% of common outdoor areas have wireless network access. Students can register for classes online. Administrative functions (other than registration) can be performed online.

CAMPUS LIFE

Environment: City. **Activities:** Choral groups, concert band, dance, drama/theater, jazz band, literary magazine, music ensembles, musical theater, radio station, student government, student newspaper, symphony orchestra, television station, yearbook, Campus Ministries, International Student Organization. 38 registered organizations, 6 honor societies, 2 religious organizations. **Athletics (Intercollegiate):** *Men:* baseball, basketball, cross-country, golf, soccer, swimming, track/field (outdoor). *Women:* basketball, cross-country, soccer, softball, swimming, tennis, track/field (outdoor), volleyball. **On-Campus Highlights:** Lally School of Education, Massry Center for the Fine Arts/Center for Art and D, Events and Athletic Center, Quiznos and Starbucks, Student Solution Center, Completely renovated (all) classrooms.

ADMISSIONS

Freshman Academic Profile: Average high school GPA 3.39. 11% in top 10% of high school class, 34% in top 25% of high school class, 73% in top 50% of high school class. 82% from public high schools. SAT Math middle 50% range 470-580. SAT Critical Reading middle 50% range 470-570. ACT middle 50% range 20-26. Minimum internet-based TOEFL 83. Minimum paper TOEFL 500. **Basis for Candidate Selection:** *Very important factors considered include:* academic GPA, rigor of secondary school record, interview, level of applicant's interest, talent/ability, work experience. *Important factors considered include:* standardized test scores, extracurricular activities, geographical residence, volunteer work. *Other factors considered include:* Class rank, application essay, alumni/ae relation, racial/ethnic status, state residency. **Freshman Admission Requirements:** High school diploma is required and GED is accepted. *Academic units required:* 4 English, 4 mathematics, 4 science, (2 science labs), 3 foreign language, 4 social studies, 4 history. **Freshman Admission Statistics:** 5,525 applied, 76% admitted, 13% enrolled. **Transfer Admission Requirements:** High school transcript, college transcript(s), statement of good standing from prior institution(s). Minimum college GPA of 2.5 required. Lowest grade transferable C-. **General Admission Information:** Application Fee $35. Regular application deadline 2/1. Notification on a rolling basis, beginning on or about 12/1. Nonfall registration accepted. Admission may be deferred for a maximum of 1 year. Credit and/or placement offered for CEEB Advanced Placement tests.

COSTS AND FINANCIAL AID

Required Forms and Deadlines: FAFSA, State aid form. **Notification of Awards:** Applicants will be notified of awards on a rolling basis beginning 3/15. **Types of Aid:** *Need-based scholarships/grants:* Federal Pell, SEOG, state scholarships/grants, private scholarships, the school's own gift aid. *Loans:* Subsidized Stafford, Unsubsidized Stafford, PLUS, Federal Perkins. **Financial Aid Statistics:** 90% freshmen, 90% undergrads receive need-based scholarship or grant aid. 85% freshmen, 76% undergrads receive non-need-based scholarship or grant aid. 81% freshmen, 81% undergrads receive need-based self-help aid. 2% freshmen, 2% undergrads receive athletic scholarships. 87% undergrads borrow to pay for school. Average cumulative indebtedness $25,326. **Criteria for awarding institutional aid:** *Non-need-based:* academics, alumni affiliation, art, athletics, minority status, music/drama.

THE COLLEGE OF SAINT SCHOLASTICA

1200 Kenwood Avenue, Duluth, MN 55811-4199
Phone: 218-723-6046 • **Financial Aid Phone:** 218-723-6047
E-mail: admissions@css.edu • **CEEB Code:** 6107
Fax: 218-723-5991 • **Website:** www.css.edu • **ACT Code:** 2098

This private school, affiliated with the Roman Catholic Church, was founded in 1912. It has a 186-acre campus.

RATINGS

Admissions Selectivity Rating: 86   **Fire Safety Rating:** 72

STUDENTS AND FACULTY

Enrollment: 2,816. **Student Body:** 70% female, 30% male, 60% out-of-state, 4% international (34 countries represented). Asian 2%, African American 3%, Caucasian 83%, Hispanic 2%, Native American 2%
Retention and Graduation: 55% freshmen graduate within 4 years. 61% freshmen graduate within 6 years. 29% grads go on to further study within 1 year. **Faculty:** 181 full-time faculty, 56% hold PhDs, 61% are members of minority groups, 12% are women. 0% of classes are taught by teaching assistants.

ACADEMICS

Degrees: bachelor's, certificate, master's, post-bachelor's certificate, post-master's certificate. **Classes:** Most classes have 20–29 students. Most lab/discussion sessions have 20–29 students. **Majors with Highest Enrollment:** Com-

puter and Information Sciences; Business Administration and Management; Registered Nursing/Registered Nurse. **Special Study Options:** Accelerated program, cross-registration, distance learning, double major, dual enrollment, external degree program, honors program, independent study, internships, liberal arts/career combination, student-designed major, study abroad, teacher certification program. **Honors programs:** The Honors Program at The College of St. Scholastica was created to give honors students enriched learning experiences and to provide a community of support for learners devoted to a vigorous life of the mind. Combined degree programs: BA/MA, BA/Doctor of Physical Therapy. **Disability Services:** Special programs offered to physically disabled students include note-taking services, reader services, tape recorders, tutors. **Career services:** Alumni network, alumni services, career/job search classes, career assessment, internships. Career services highlights include Semester abroad in Mexico: an international service learning program devoted to educating students about social justice issues and the life of the poor in Mexico.

FACILITIES

Housing: Coed dorms, special housing for disabled students, special housing for international students, apartments for single students, Wellness Housing, Apartments for students with dependent children. Quiet or study wings available. 95% of campus accessible to physically disabled. **Computers:** Students can register for classes online. Administrative functions (other than registration) can be performed online.

CAMPUS LIFE

Environment: City. **Activities:** Choral groups, concert band, dance, drama/theater, jazz band, literary magazine, music ensembles, pep band, student government, student newspaper, television station, Campus Ministries, International Student Organization. 67 registered organizations, 2 honor societies, 7 religious organizations. **Athletics (Intercollegiate):** *Men:* baseball, basketball, cross-country, ice hockey, skiing (nordic/cross-country), soccer, tennis, track/field (outdoor), track/field (indoor). *Women:* basketball, cross-country, skiing (nordic/cross-country), soccer, softball, tennis, track/field (outdoor), track/field (indoor), volleyball. **On-Campus Highlights:** Wellness Center, Student Union, Storm's Den, Cedar Hall.

ADMISSIONS

Freshman Academic Profile: Average high school GPA 3.51. 19% in top 10% of high school class, 50% in top 25% of high school class, 85% in top 50% of high school class. SAT Math middle 50% range 490-630. SAT Critical Reading middle 50% range 540-590. SAT Writing middle 50% range 490-540. ACT middle 50% range 21-27. Minimum internet-based TOEFL 79. Minimum paper TOEFL 550. **Basis for Candidate Selection:** *Very important factors considered include:* academic GPA, standardized test scores. *Important factors considered include:* Class rank, rigor of secondary school record. *Other factors considered include:* application essay, recommendation(s), interview. **Freshman Admission Requirements:** High school diploma is required and GED is accepted. **Freshman Admission Statistics:** 3,368 applied, 66% admitted, 21% enrolled. **Transfer Admission Requirements:** college transcript(s), Minimum college GPA of 1.5 required. Lowest grade transferable C. **General Admission Information:** Application Fee $25. Notification on a rolling basis, beginning on or about 9/1. Nonfall registration accepted. Admission may be deferred for a maximum of 1 year. Credit and/or placement offered for CEEB Advanced Placement tests.

COSTS AND FINANCIAL AID

Annual tuition $32,642. Room and board $8,598. Required fees $200. Average book expense $1,150. **Required Forms and Deadlines:** FAFSA. **Notification of Awards:** Applicants will be notified of awards on a rolling basis beginning 3/1. **Types of Aid:** *Need-based scholarships/grants:* Federal Pell, SEOG, state scholarships/grants, private scholarships, the school's own gift aid. *Loans:* Direct Subsidized Stafford, Direct Unsubsidized Stafford, Direct PLUS, Federal Perkins, Federal Nursing, state loans, Private supplemental loans. *Student Employment:* Federal Work-Study Program available. Institutional employment available. Highest amount earned per year from on-campus jobs $4,688. Off-campus job opportunities are good. **Financial Aid Statistics:** 80% freshmen, 80% undergrads receive need-based scholarship or grant aid. 100% freshmen, 82% undergrads receive non-need-based scholarship or grant aid. 72% freshmen, 77% undergrads receive need-based self-help aid. 0% freshmen, 0% undergrads receive athletic scholarships. 75% freshmen, 98% undergrads receive any aid. 77% undergrads borrow to pay for school. Average cumulative indebtedness $26,176. **Criteria for awarding institutional aid:** *Non-need-based:* academics, alumni affiliation, music/drama, religious affiliation, state/district residency.

THE COLLEGE OF WILLIAM AND MARY

Office of Admissions, P.O. Box 8795, Williamsburg, VA 23187-8795
Phone: 757-221-4223 · **Financial Aid Phone:** 757-221-2420
E-mail: admission@wm.edu · **CEEB Code:** 5115
Fax: 757-221-1242 · **Website:** www.wm.edu · **ACT Code:** 4344

This public school was founded in 1693. It has a 1200-acre campus.

RATINGS
Admissions Selectivity Rating: 96   **Fire Safety Rating:** 93

STUDENTS AND FACULTY
Enrollment: 6,256. **Student Body:** 56% female, 44% male, 30% out-of-state, 5% international (37 countries represented). Asian 8%, African American 7%, Caucasian 59%, Hispanic 9%, Native American <1%
Retention and Graduation: 83% freshmen graduate within 4 years. 90% freshmen graduate within 6 years.

ACADEMICS
Degrees: bachelor's, doctoral, master's, post-master's certificate. **Classes:** Most classes have 10–19 students. Most lab/discussion sessions have 10–19 students. **Special Study Options:** Accelerated program, double major, dual enrollment, honors program, independent study, internships, student-designed major, study abroad, teacher certification program. **Honors programs:** Monroe Scholars; Sharpe Scholars; Murray Scholars; William and Mary Scholar Award; Alpha Lambda Delta and Phi Eta Sigma Honor Societies for Freshman **Combined degree programs:** BA/MEng, Bachelor's/Master of Forestry or Master of Env. Management from Duke Univ. **Disability Services:** Special programs offered to physically disabled students include note-taking services, reader services, tape recorders, tutors. **Career services:** Alumni network, alumni services, career/job search classes, career assessment, internships. Career services highlights include The Alumni Mentoring Program, which provides valuable and searchable information for students and alumni alike to connect for the purposes of seeking career advice, support, and referral. The synergy of this networking program simultaneously strengthens the College community.

FACILITIES
Housing: Coed dorms, special housing for disabled students, special housing for international students, fraternity/sorority housing, apartments for single students, Wellness Housing, Theme **Housing:** International Studies hall, Eco-House, Community Scholars House, Africana House, Multicultural Unit, and 8 language houses (Arabic, Chinese, French, German, Italian, Japanese, Russian, Spanish). 80% of campus accessible to physically disabled. **Special Academic Facilities/Equipment:** observatory, continuous beam accelerator, 3 interdisciplinary centers in humanities, international studies, writing resources, marine science institute, materials processes research center, public policy research center. **Computers:** 100% of classrooms, 100% of dorms, 100% of libraries, 100% of dining areas, 100% of student union, 33% of common outdoor areas have wireless network access. Students can register for classes online. Administrative functions (other than registration) can be performed online. Undergraduates are required to own a computer.

CAMPUS LIFE
Environment: Village. **Activities:** Choral groups, concert band, dance, drama/theater, jazz band, literary magazine, music ensembles, musical theater, opera, pep band, radio station, student government, student newspaper, student-run film society, symphony orchestra, television station, yearbook, Campus Ministries, International Student Organization, Model UN. 375 registered organizations, 32 honor societies, 32 religious organizations. 18 fraternities, 11 sorority. **Athletics (Intercollegiate):** *Men:* baseball, basketball, cheerleading, cross-country, diving, football, golf, gymnastics, soccer, swimming, tennis, track/field (outdoor), track/field (indoor). *Women:* basketball, cheerleading, cross-country, diving, field hockey, golf, gymnastics, lacrosse, soccer, swimming, tennis, track/field (outdoor), track/field (indoor), volleyball. **On-Campus Highlights:** Wren Building (oldest academic building), Muscarelle Museum of Art, Lake Matoaka/College Woods, Crim Dell Bridge, Sunken Garden. **Environmental Initiatives:** Adhere to LEED construction guidelines in all new construction and renovations. Three buildings have been LEED certified to date and two are in progress. Retrofit of systems to improve energy consumption and reduce consumption. Participated in major ESCO contract for Athletic Center. Purchase of environmentally sustainable materials. Develop a sustainable procurement manual. Provide leadership in providing state-wide sustainable procurement guidelines in higher education.

ADMISSIONS
Freshman Academic Profile: Average high school GPA 4.16. 81% in top 10% of high school class, 96% in top 25% of high school class, 99% in top 50% of high school class. 75% from public high schools. SAT Math middle 50% range 630-740. SAT Critical Reading middle 50% range 640-730. SAT Writing middle 50% range 620-720. ACT middle 50% range 29-33. Minimum internet-based TOEFL 100. Minimum paper TOEFL 600. **Basis for Candidate Selection:** *Very important factors considered include:* Class rank, application essay, academic GPA, recommendation(s), rigor of secondary school record, standardized test scores, character/personal qualities, extracurricular activities, state residency, talent/ability, volunteer work, work experience. *Other factors considered include:* alumni/ae relation, first generation, geographical residence, interview, racial/ethnic status. **Freshman Admission Requirements:** High school diploma or equivalent is not required. **Freshman Admission Statistics:** 14,552 applied, 33% admitted, 31% enrolled. **Transfer Admission Requirements:** High school transcript, college transcript(s), essay or personal statement, statement of good standing from prior institution(s). Minimum college GPA of 3.00 required. Lowest grade transferable C. **General Admission Information:** Application Fee $60. Early decision application deadline 11/1. Regular application deadline 1/1. Regular notification 4/1. Nonfall registration not accepted. Admission may be deferred for a maximum of 1 year. Credit and/or placement offered for CEEB Advanced Placement tests.

COSTS AND FINANCIAL AID
Notification of Awards: Applicants will be notified of awards on a rolling basis beginning 3/15. **Types of Aid:** *Need-based scholarships/grants:* Federal Pell, SEOG, state scholarships/grants, private scholarships, the school's own gift aid. *Loans:* Subsidized Stafford, Unsubsidized Stafford, PLUS, Federal Perkins. *Student Employment:* Federal Work-Study Program available. Institutional employment available. Highest amount earned per year from on-campus jobs $1,400. Off-campus job opportunities are excellent. **Financial Aid Statistics:** 53% freshmen, 52% undergrads receive any aid. **Criteria for awarding institutional aid:** *Non-need-based:* academics, art, athletics, leadership, music/drama, state/district residency.

THE COLLEGE OF WOOSTER

847 College Avenue, Wooster, OH 44691
Phone: 330-263-2322 · **Financial Aid Phone:** 800-877-3688
E-mail: admissions@wooster.edu · **CEEB Code:** 1134
Fax: 330-263-2621 · **Website:** www.wooster.edu · **ACT Code:** 3260

This private school was founded in 1866. It has a 240-acre campus.

RATINGS
Admissions Selectivity Rating: 89   **Fire Safety Rating:** 77

STUDENTS AND FACULTY
Enrollment: 2,029. **Student Body:** 55% female, 45% male, 61% out-of-state, 8% international (39 countries represented). Asian 4%, African American 8%, Caucasian 70%, Hispanic 5%, Native American 1%
Retention and Graduation: 70% freshmen graduate within 4 years. 76% freshmen graduate within 6 years. 27% grads go on to further study within 1 year. 20% grads pursue arts and sciences degrees. 3% grads pursue law degrees. 1% grads pursue business degrees. 3% grads pursue medical degrees. **Faculty:** 171 full-time faculty, 96% hold PhDs, 50% are members of minority groups, 17% are women. 0% of classes are taught by teaching assistants.

ACADEMICS
Degrees: bachelor's. **Classes:** Most classes have 10–19 students. Most lab/discussion sessions have 10–19 students. **Majors with Highest Enrollment:** History; Psychology; English Language and Literature. **Special Study Options:** cooperative education program, double major, dual enrollment, exchange student program (domestic), independent study, internships, student-designed major, study abroad, teacher certification program. Combined degree programs: BA/MA, BA/DDS, BA/MEng, many combined programs with other institutions. **Disability Services:** Special programs offered to physically disabled students include note-taking services, reader services, tape recorders, tutors. **Career services:** Alumni network, alumni services, career/job search classes, career assessment, internships, regional alumni.

FACILITIES

Housing: Coed dorms, special housing for international students, women's dorms, fraternity/sorority housing, apartments for single students, Theme HousingSpecial housing for students participating in volunteer programs. 95% of campus accessible to physically disabled. **Special Academic Facilities/Equipment:** Art museum, language lab, on-campus nursery school, science library. **Computers:** 100% of classrooms, 95% of dorms, 100% of libraries, 100% of dining areas, 100% of student union, 50% of common outdoor areas have wireless network access. Students can register for classes online. Administrative functions (other than registration) can be performed online.

CAMPUS LIFE

Environment: Town. **Activities:** Choral groups, concert band, dance, drama/theater, jazz band, literary magazine, marching band, music ensembles, musical theater, pep band, radio station, student government, student newspaper, student-run film society, symphony orchestra, yearbook, Campus Ministries, International Student Organization, Model UN. 100 registered organizations, 6 honor societies, 9 religious organizations. 5 fraternities, 6 sororities. **Athletics (Intercollegiate):** *Men:* baseball, basketball, cross-country, diving, football, golf, lacrosse, soccer, swimming, tennis, track/field (outdoor), track/field (indoor). *Women:* basketball, cross-country, diving, field hockey, lacrosse, soccer, softball, swimming, tennis, track/field (outdoor), track/field (indoor), volleyball. **On-Campus Highlights:** Kauke Hall, Severance Hall Chemistry Bldg., Timken Science Library, Ebert Art Center, Burton D. Morgan Hall, Gault Manor (residence hall). **Environmental Initiatives:** Completing $5M Energy Performance Contract that reduced the College's carbon footprint by 36% through lighting and water conservation, building automation system upgrades, and the installation of two new electric chillers and a steam condensor at the Power Plant. Installation of a 20,000 square foot solar array. This is the largest solar roof on any College or University campus in the United States and is estimated to generate 284,000 kWh annually. Construction of the College's first LEED building. The Scot Center is on pace for a LEED Gold rating.

ADMISSIONS

Freshman Academic Profile: Average high school GPA 3.6. 41% in top 10% of high school class, 71% in top 25% of high school class, 92% in top 50% of high school class. 66% from public high schools. SAT Math middle 50% range 560-670. SAT Critical Reading middle 50% range 540-650. SAT Writing middle 50% range 540-650. ACT middle 50% range 25-30. Minimum internet-based TOEFL 81. **Basis for Candidate Selection:** *Very important factors considered include:* Class rank, academic GPA, rigor of secondary school record. *Important factors considered include:* application essay, recommendation(s), standardized test scores, character/personal qualities, talent/ability. *Other factors considered include:* alumni/ae relation, extracurricular activities, geographical residence, interview, racial/ethnic status, state residency, volunteer work, work experience. **Freshman Admission Requirements:** High school diploma is required and GED is accepted. *Academic units required:* 4 English, 3 mathematics, 3 science, 2 foreign language, 3 social studies, 2 academic electives. **Freshman Admission Statistics:** 5,497 applied, 59% admitted, 17% enrolled. **Transfer Admission Requirements:** High school transcript, college transcript(s), essay or personal statement, standardized test scores, statement of good standing from prior institution(s). Minimum college GPA of 2.5 required. Lowest grade transferable C. **General Admission Information:** Application Fee $40. Early decision application deadline 12/1. Regular application deadline 2/15. Nonfall registration accepted. Admission may be deferred for a maximum of 1 year. Credit and/or placement offered for CEEB Advanced Placement tests.

COSTS AND FINANCIAL AID

Annual tuition $42,920. Room and board $10,250. Required fees $430. Average book expense $1,000. **Required Forms and Deadlines:** FAFSA, Institution's own financial aid form, CSS/Financial Aid PROFILE. **Notification of Awards:** Applicants will be notified of awards on or about 4/1. **Types of Aid:** *Need-based scholarships/grants:* Federal Pell, SEOG, state scholarships/grants, private scholarships, the school's own gift aid. *Loans:* Direct Subsidized Stafford, Direct Unsubsidized Stafford, Direct PLUS, Federal Perkins, college/university loans from institutional funds. *Student Employment:* Federal Work-Study Program available. Institutional employment available. Off-campus job opportunities are good. **Financial Aid Statistics:** 99% freshmen, 98% undergrads receive need-based scholarship or grant aid. 15% freshmen, 11% undergrads receive non-need-based scholarship or grant aid. 83% freshmen, 86% undergrads receive need-based self-help aid. 0% freshmen, 0% undergrads receive athletic scholarships. 99% freshmen, 99% undergrads receive any aid. 56% undergrads borrow to pay for school. Average cumulative indebtedness $22,436. **Criteria for awarding institutional aid:** *Non-need-based:* academics, leadership, minority status, music/drama, religious affiliation, state/district residency.

COLORADO CHRISTIAN UNIVERSITY

8787 W. Alameda Ave., Lakewood, CO 80226
Phone: 303-963-3200 · **Financial Aid Phone:** 303-963-3233
E-mail: ccuadmissions@ccu.edu · **CEEB Code:** 4659
Fax: 303-963-3201 · **Website:** www.ccu.edu · **ACT Code:** 523

This private school, affiliated with the Christian (Nondenominational) Church, was founded in 1914. It has a 26-acre campus.

RATINGS

Admissions Selectivity Rating: 83   **Fire Safety Rating:** 61

STUDENTS AND FACULTY

Enrollment: 1,849. **Student Body:** 60% female, 40% male, 56% out-of-state, 0% international. Asian 1%, African American 3%, Caucasian 69%, Hispanic 8%, Native American 1%
Retention and Graduation: 86% freshmen return for sophomore year. 34% freshmen graduate within 4 years. 44% freshmen graduate within 6 years. **Faculty:** 41 full-time faculty, 68% hold PhDs, 46% are members of minority groups, 5% are women. 0% of classes are taught by teaching assistants.

ACADEMICS

Degrees: associate, bachelor's, master's. **Classes:** Most classes have fewer than 10 students. Most lab/discussion sessions have 10–19 students. **Majors with Highest Enrollment:** Computer/Information Technology Services Administration and Management; Liberal Arts and Sciences/Liberal Studies; Management Information Systems. **Special Study Options:** Accelerated program, cooperative education program, distance learning, double major, honors program, independent study, internships, student-designed major, study abroad, teacher certification program, weekend college, American Studies Program (Washington DC); Host University for Institute for Family Studies; China Studies Program (various sites in China); Latin American Studies Program (Costa Rica); Los Angeles Film Studies Center; Middle East Studies (Cairo, Egypt); Oxford Honors Program (University of Oxford, England); Russian Studies Program (various sites in Russia); Summer Institute of Journalism (Washington DC). **Disability Services:** Special programs offered to physically disabled students include tutors. **Career services:** alumni services, career/job search classes, career assessment, internships.

FACILITIES

Housing: Coed dorms, special housing for disabled students, men's dorms, women's dorms, apartments for single students, Theme Housing. 85% of campus accessible to physically disabled. **Special Academic Facilities/Equipment:** Music recording studio, electron microscope. **Computers:** 100% of classrooms, 100% of dorms, 100% of student union, have wireless network access. Students can register for classes online. Administrative functions (other than registration) can be performed online.

CAMPUS LIFE

Activities: Choral groups, concert band, drama/theater, jazz band, literary magazine, music ensembles, musical theater, student government, student newspaper, symphony orchestra 21 registered organizations, 3 honor societies, 14 religious organizations. **Athletics (Intercollegiate):** *Men:* basketball, cross-country, golf, soccer, tennis. *Women:* basketball, cross-country, soccer, tennis, volleyball.

ADMISSIONS

Freshman Academic Profile: Average high school GPA 3.44. 22% in top 10% of high school class, 46% in top 25% of high school class, 79% in top 50% of high school class. SAT Math middle 50% range 480-590. SAT Critical Reading middle 50% range 510-630. ACT middle 50% range 20-26. Minimum paper TOEFL 500. **Basis for Candidate Selection:** *Very important factors considered include:* application essay, rigor of secondary school record, standardized test scores, character/personal qualities, first generation, religious affiliation/commitment, talent/ability. *Important factors considered include:* Class rank, academic GPA, recommendation(s), extracurricular activities, level of applicant's interest, racial/ethnic status, volunteer work. *Other factors considered include:* alumni/ae relation, interview, work experience. **Freshman Admission Requirements:** High school diploma is required and GED is accepted. **Freshman Admission Statistics:** 946 applied, 77% admitted, 33% enrolled. **Transfer Admission Requirements:** college transcript(s), essay or personal statement, statement of good standing from prior institution(s). Minimum college GPA of 2.0 required. Lowest grade transferable C. **General Admission Information:** Application Fee $50. Regular application deadline 8/21. Notification on a rolling basis, beginning on or about 11/1. Nonfall registration accepted. Admission may be deferred for a maximum of 1 YEAR. Credit and/or placement offered for CEEB Advanced Placement tests.

COSTS AND FINANCIAL AID

Annual tuition $18,850. Room and board $6,682. Required fees $150. Average book expense $1,188. **Required Forms and Deadlines:** FAFSA. **Notification of Awards:** Applicants will be notified of awards on a rolling basis beginning 4/1. **Types of Aid:** *Need-based scholarships/grants:* Federal Pell, SEOG, private scholarships, the school's own gift aid. *Loans:* Subsidized Stafford, Unsubsidized Stafford, PLUS, Federal Perkins. *Student Employment:* Federal Work-Study Program available. Institutional employment available. Off-campus job opportunities are good. **Financial Aid Statistics:** 97% freshmen, 88% undergrads receive need-based scholarship or grant aid. 85% freshmen, 72% undergrads receive non-need-based scholarship or grant aid. 97% freshmen, 88% undergrads receive need-based self-help aid. 14% freshmen, 7% undergrads receive athletic scholarships. 61% undergrads borrow to pay for school. **Criteria for awarding institutional aid:** *Non-need-based:* academics, athletics, leadership, minority status.

COLORADO COLLEGE

14 East Cache la Poudre Street, Colorado Springs, CO 80903
Phone: 719-389-6344 • **Financial Aid Phone:** 719-389-6651
E-mail: admission@coloradocollege.edu • **CEEB Code:** 4072
Fax: 719-389-6816 • **Website:** www.coloradocollege.edu • **ACT Code:** 498

This private school was founded in 1874. It has a 90-acre campus.

RATINGS

Admissions Selectivity Rating: 96   Fire Safety Rating: 93

STUDENTS AND FACULTY

Enrollment: 2,036. **Student Body:** 53% female, 47% male, 82% out-of-state, 6% international (57 countries represented). Asian 5%, African American 2%, Caucasian 66%, Hispanic 9%, Native American <1%
Retention and Graduation: 94% freshmen return for sophomore year. 81% freshmen graduate within 4 years. 86% freshmen graduate within 6 years. **Faculty:** 170 full-time faculty, 99% hold PhDs, 43% are members of minority groups, 21% are women. 0% of classes are taught by teaching assistants.

ACADEMICS

Degrees: bachelor's, master's. **Classes:** Most classes have 20–29 students. **Majors with Highest Enrollment:** Economics; Ecology and Evolutionary Biology; Fine/Studio Arts. **Special Study Options:** double major, English as a Second Language (ESL), independent study, internships, liberal arts/career combination, student-designed major, study abroad, Teacher licensure program; Cooperative 3/2 program. Combined degree programs: BA/JD, BA/MEng, Columbia University School of Law. **Disability Services:** Special programs offered to physically disabled students include note-taking services, tutors. **Career services:** Alumni network, alumni services, career assessment, internships.

FACILITIES

Housing: Coed dorms, men's dorms, women's dorms, fraternity/sorority housing, apartments for single students, Theme Housing. **Special Academic Facilities/Equipment:** Electronic music studio, telescope dome, multimedia computer laboratory, Balinese orchestras, The Colorado Electronic music studio, Observatory, Extensive herbarium collection, 4 greenhouses, Environmental Science van equipped for field research, Fourier transform nuclear magnetic resonance spectrometer, Packard Hall, 300 seat concert/lecture hall, Photography darkrooms. Drama/Dance: Armstrong Theatre, 740 seat proscenium theatre Armstrong 32, 100 seat experimental theatre, 4 dance studios w/ Marley, variable speed cd players, Drama computer lab. Geology: Petrographic microscopes X-ray diffractometer, Sedimentology lab. El Pomar Sports Center: Metabolic Equipment (COSMED Quark PFT Ergo), Hydrostatic Weighing Equipment, Cadaver study in Sports Science. Biology: Scanning electron microscope, Transmission electron microscope. **Computers:** 100% of classrooms, 100% of dorms, 100% of libraries, 100% of dining areas, 100% of student union, 80% of common outdoor areas have wireless network access. Students can register for classes online. Administrative functions (other than registration) can be performed online.

CAMPUS LIFE

Environment: Metropolis. **Activities:** Choral groups, concert band, dance, drama/theater, jazz band, literary magazine, music ensembles, musical theater, radio station, student government, student newspaper, student-run film society, yearbook, Campus Ministries, International Student Organization. 147 registered organizations, 13 honor societies, 20 religious organizations. 1 fraternity, 3 sororities. **Athletics (Intercollegiate):** *Men:* basketball, cross-country, ice hockey, lacrosse, soccer, swimming, tennis, track/field (outdoor). *Women:* basketball, cross-country, lacrosse, soccer, swimming, tennis, track/field (outdoor), track/field (indoor), volleyball. **On-Campus Highlights:** Worner Student Center, Palmer Hall, Shove Chapel, Cutler Hall - Admission, View of Pikes Peak. **Environmental Initiatives:** The College is committed to achieving carbon neutrality by 2020. The plan includes an efficiency target in all campus buildings that will reduce energy intensity by 30%, along with a 20% reduction target through behavior change and conservation, and a strategy to derive 100% of electricity from renewable sources. The College has a comprehensive waste minimization plan that includes single stream recycling, composting in all major dining halls, and the phase-out of single use plastic bags and bottled water. Colorado College President Richard Celeste has joined local government, business and non-profit leaders in signing a statement of commitment to pursue a cooperative approach to sustainability in the Pikes Peak region. This commitment will initiate a regional sustainability planning process.

ADMISSIONS

Freshman Academic Profile: 69.2% in top 10% of high school class, 90.2% in top 25% of high school class, 99.3% in top 50% of high school class. SAT Math middle 50% range 630-730. SAT Critical Reading middle 50% range 620-730. SAT Writing middle 50% range 620-710. ACT middle 50% range 28-32. **Basis for Candidate Selection:** *Very important factors considered include:* rigor of secondary school record. *Important factors considered include:* Class rank, application essay, academic GPA, recommendation(s), standardized test scores, extracurricular activities, interview. *Other factors considered include:* alumni/ae relation, character/personal qualities, first generation, level of applicant's interest, racial/ethnic status, religious affiliation/commitment, talent/ability, volunteer work, work experience. **Freshman Admission Requirements:** High school diploma or equivalent is not required. *Academic units required:* 4 English. **Freshman Admission Statistics:** 40% enrolled. **Transfer Admission Requirements:** High school transcript, college transcript(s), essay or personal statement, standardized test scores, statement of good standing from prior institution(s). Lowest grade transferable C. **General Admission Information:** Application Fee $50. Early decision application deadline 11/15. Regular application deadline 1/15. Regular notification 4/1. Nonfall registration accepted. Admission may be deferred for a maximum of 1 year. Credit and/or placement offered for CEEB Advanced Placement tests.

COSTS AND FINANCIAL AID

Annual tuition $43,812. Room and board $10,312. Required fees $410. Average book expense $1,244. **Required Forms and Deadlines:** FAFSA, CSS/Financial Aid PROFILE, Noncustodial PROFILE. **Notification of Awards:** Applicants will be notified of awards on or about 3/20. **Types of Aid:** *Need-based scholarships/grants:* Federal Pell, SEOG, state scholarships/grants, private scholarships, Federal ACG and SMART grants. *Loans:* Direct Subsidized Stafford, Direct Unsubsidized Stafford, Direct PLUS, Federal Perkins. *Student Employment:* Federal Work-Study Program available. Institutional employment available. Off-campus job opportunities are good. **Financial Aid Statistics:** 95% freshmen, 94% undergrads receive need-based scholarship or grant aid. 58% freshmen, 55% undergrads receive non-need-based scholarship or grant aid. 90% freshmen, 89% undergrads receive need-based self-help aid. 1% freshmen, 2% undergrads receive athletic scholarships. 53% freshmen, 52% undergrads receive any aid. 30% undergrads borrow to pay for school. Average cumulative indebtedness $16,444. **Criteria for awarding institutional aid:** *Non-need-based:* academics, athletics.

COLORADO SCHOOL OF MINES

1600 Maple Street, Golden, CO 80401
Phone: 303-273-3220 • **Financial Aid Phone:** 303-273-3220
E-mail: admit@mines.edu • **CEEB Code:** 4073
Fax: 303-273-3509 • **Website:** www.mines.edu • **ACT Code:** 500

This public school was founded in 1874. It has a 373-acre campus.

RATINGS

Admissions Selectivity Rating: 95   Fire Safety Rating: 70

STUDENTS AND FACULTY

Enrollment: 4,199. **Student Body:** 27% female, 73% male, 32% out-of-state, 4% international (79 countries represented). Asian 5%, African American 1%, Caucasian 75%, Hispanic 8%, Native American <1%
Retention and Graduation: 92% freshmen return for sophomore year. 38% freshmen graduate within 4 years. 70% freshmen graduate within 6 years. 14%

grads go on to further study within 1 year. 4% grads pursue arts and sciences degrees. 1% grads pursue law degrees. 2% grads pursue business degrees. 1% grads pursue medical degrees. **Faculty:** 263 full-time faculty, 91% hold PhDs, 27% are members of minority groups, 16% are women. 3% of classes are taught by teaching assistants.

ACADEMICS

Degrees: bachelor's, master's, post-master's certificate. **Classes:** Most classes have 10–19 students. Most lab/discussion sessions have 20–29 students. **Majors with Highest Enrollment:** Mechanical Engineering; Chemical Engineering; Petroleum Engineering. **Special Study Options:** Accelerated program, cooperative education program, double major, dual enrollment, English as a Second Language (ESL), exchange student program (domestic), honors program, independent study, internships, study abroad. **Honors programs:** The McBride Honors Program, instituted in 1978 through a grant from the National Endowment for the Humanities, is a 24 semester-hour program of seminars and off-campus activities that has as its primary goal: To provide a select community of CSM students the enhanced opportunity to explore the interfaces between their areas of technical expertise and the humanities and social sciences; to gain the sensitivity to project and test the moral and social implications of their future professional judgments and activities; and to foster their leadership abilities in preparation for managing change and promoting the general welfare in an evolving technological and global context. To achieve this goal, the program seeks to bring themes from the humanities and the social sciences into the engineering curriculum that will encourage in students the habits of thought necessary for effective management and enlightened leadership. Combined degree programs: BS/MS. **Disability Services:** Special programs offered to physically disabled students include note-taking services, reader services, tape recorders, tutors. **Career services:** alumni services, career/job search classes, career assessment, internships. One of the newest opportunities is through the Renewable Energy Materials Research Science and Engineering Center: The Center focuses on preparing undergraduate and graduate students to embark on careers in renewable fields by providing a multitude of research and classroom experiences in renewable energy. REMRSEC offers a coordinated approach from K to gray in renewable energy education, outreach, and work force development founded on research proven best practices. National Renewable Energy Laboratory (NREL) will be a principle partner in the Colorado School of Mines (CSM) Renewable Energy Materials Research Science and Engineering Center (REMRSEC), building upon and strengthening the existing relationship between CSM and NREL. The goals of this partnership are to provide a convenient avenue to transition basic research and engineering discoveries into more applied projects and ultimately into the market place using NREL's strengths, to facilitate the training of future scientists and engineers by providing access to world class researchers and equipment at NREL, and to greatly augment the outreach efforts of the Center by coupling with the superb outreach efforts at NREL. http://remrsec.mines.edu/educationoutreach.htm.

FACILITIES

Housing: Coed dorms, fraternity/sorority housing, apartments for married students, apartments for single students. 100% of campus accessible to physically disabled. **Special Academic Facilities/Equipment:** Geology Museum, US Geological Survey & Earthquake Center, Edgar Experimental Mine, Graduate Research Laboratory (GRL), Center for Technology & Learning Media which houses supercomputer "Ra,"—a high performance computing (HPC) cluster that aims to be a national hub for computational inquiries aimed at the discovery of new ways to meet the world's energy demands. Estimated peak performance will be approximately 20 teraflops. This places the machine well within the top-100 fastest computers in the world. The new facility, administered by the Golden Energy Computing Organization (GECO), is dedicated to advancing energy-related science. **Computers:** 100% of classrooms, 100% of dorms, 100% of libraries, 100% of dining areas, 100% of student union, 80% of common outdoor areas have wireless network access. Students can register for classes online. Administrative functions (other than registration) can be performed online.

CAMPUS LIFE

Environment: Metropolis. **Activities:** Choral groups, concert band, dance, drama/theater, jazz band, literary magazine, marching band, music ensembles, musical theater, pep band, radio station, student government, student newspaper, symphony orchestra, yearbook, Campus Ministries, International Student Organization. 148 registered organizations, 9 honor societies, 7 religious organizations. 7 fraternities, 3 sororities. **Athletics (Intercollegiate):** *Men:* baseball, basketball, cross-country, diving, football, golf, soccer, swimming, track/field (outdoor), track/field (indoor), wrestling. *Women:* basketball, cross-country, diving, soccer, softball, swimming, track/field (outdoor), track/field (indoor), volleyball. **On-Campus Highlights:** Student Recreation Center, Outdoor Recreation Center, Geology Museum, National Earthquake Center, Computer Commons at the CTLM.

ADMISSIONS

Freshman Academic Profile: Average high school GPA 3.8. 66% in top 10% of high school class, 93% in top 25% of high school class, 100% in top 50% of

high school class. 90% from public high schools. SAT Math middle 50% range 640-740. SAT Critical Reading middle 50% range 590-690. SAT Writing middle 50% range 560-670. ACT middle 50% range 28-32. Minimum internet-based TOEFL 79. Minimum paper TOEFL 550. **Basis for Candidate Selection:** *Very important factors considered include:* Class rank, academic GPA, rigor of secondary school record. *Important factors considered include:* standardized test scores. *Other factors considered include:* application essay, recommendation(s), alumni/ae relation, character/personal qualities, extracurricular activities, geographical residence, interview, level of applicant's interest, state residency, talent/ability. **Freshman Admission Requirements:** High school diploma is required and GED is accepted. *Academic units required:* 4 English, 4 mathematics, 3 science, (3 science labs), 3 social studies, 2 academic electives. **Freshman Admission Statistics:** 12,169 applied, 36% admitted, 22% enrolled. **Transfer Admission Requirements:** High school transcript, college transcript(s), statement of good standing from prior institution(s). Minimum college GPA of 2.75 required. Lowest grade transferable C. **General Admission Information:** Application Fee $45. Regular application deadline 5/1. Notification on a rolling basis, beginning on or about 10/1. Nonfall registration accepted. Admission may be deferred for a maximum of 12 months. Credit and/or placement offered for CEEB Advanced Placement tests.

COSTS AND FINANCIAL AID

Annual in-state tuition $14,400. Annual out-of-state tuition $30,330. Room and board $10,103. Required fees $2,085. Average book expense $1,500. **Required Forms and Deadlines:** FAFSA. **Notification of Awards:** Applicants will be notified of awards on a rolling basis beginning 3/15. **Types of Aid:** *Need-based scholarships/grants:* Federal Pell, SEOG, state scholarships/grants, private scholarships, the school's own gift aid. *Loans:* Subsidized Stafford, Unsubsidized Stafford, PLUS, Federal Perkins, college/university loans from institutional funds. *Student Employment:* Federal Work-Study Program available. Institutional employment available. Highest amount earned per year from on-campus jobs $3,000. Off-campus job opportunities are good. **Financial Aid Statistics:** 52% freshmen, 53% undergrads receive need-based scholarship or grant aid. 74% freshmen, 61% undergrads receive non-need-based scholarship or grant aid. 91% freshmen, 91% undergrads receive need-based self-help aid. 3% freshmen, 4% undergrads receive athletic scholarships. 85% freshmen, 85% undergrads receive any aid. 68% undergrads borrow to pay for school. Average cumulative indebtedness $17,699. **Criteria for awarding institutional aid:** *Non-need-based:* academics, athletics, music/drama.

COLORADO STATE UNIVERSITY

1062 Campus Delivery, Fort Collins, CO 80523-1062
Phone: 970-491-6909 • **Financial Aid Phone:** 970-491-6321
E-mail: admissions@colostate.edu • **CEEB Code:** 4075
Fax: 970-491-7799 • **Website:** www.colostate.edu/ • **ACT Code:** 504

This public school was founded in 1870. It has a 582-acre campus.

RATINGS

Admissions Selectivity Rating: 82   **Fire Safety Rating:** 80

STUDENTS AND FACULTY

Enrollment: 22,506. **Student Body:** 51% female, 49% male, 20% out-of-state, 4% international (72 countries represented). Asian 2%, African American 2%, Caucasian 74%, Hispanic 10%, Native American 1%
Retention and Graduation: 86% freshmen return for sophomore year. 39% freshmen graduate within 4 years. 67% freshmen graduate within 6 years. 23% grads go on to further study within 1 year. 6% grads pursue arts and sciences degrees. 1% grads pursue business degrees. 1% grads pursue medical degrees. **Faculty:** 1,004 full-time faculty, 99% hold PhDs, 37% are members of minority groups, 18% are women. 9.5% of classes are taught by teaching assistants.

ACADEMICS

Degrees: bachelor's, doctoral, master's. **Classes:** Most classes have 10–19 students. Most lab/discussion sessions have 20–29 students. **Majors with Highest Enrollment:** Business Administration and Management; Biology/Biological Sciences; Mechanical Engineering. **Special Study Options:** Accelerated program, cooperative education program, cross-registration, distance learning, double major, dual enrollment, English as a Second Language (ESL), exchange student program (domestic), honors program, independent study, internships, liberal arts/career combination, study abroad, teacher certification program. **Honors programs:** University Honors Program. Combined degree programs:

MS/DVM. MBA/DVM, PhD/DVM, MS of Public Health/DVM, BS/MS. **Disability Services:** Special programs offered to physically disabled students include note-taking services, reader services, tape recorders, tutors. **Career services:** Alumni network, alumni services, career/job search classes, career assessment, internships.

FACILITIES

Housing: Coed dorms, special housing for disabled students, apartments for married students, apartments for single students, Wellness Housing, Theme HousingNon college-owned fraternity/sorority housing is available. Also available are Living-Learning Communities, and special interest floors. 97% of campus accessible to physically disabled. **Special Academic Facilities/Equipment:** International Poster collection, Gustafson Gallery—historic clothing, Curfman Gallery—Art, Student Recreation Center, Ropes Course, University Center for the Arts (performance hall, thrust theater, art museum), Avenir Museum of Design and Merchandising (Costumes, Textiles, Interior Artifacts). **Computers:** 100% of classrooms, 100% of dorms, 100% of libraries, 100% of dining areas, 100% of student union, 60% of common outdoor areas have wireless network access. Students can register for classes online. Administrative functions (other than registration) can be performed online.

CAMPUS LIFE

Environment: City. **Activities:** Choral groups, concert band, dance, drama/theater, jazz band, literary magazine, marching band, music ensembles, musical theater, opera, pep band, radio station, student government, student newspaper, symphony orchestra, television station, Campus Ministries, International Student Organization. 350 registered organizations, 35 honor societies, 28 religious organizations. 21 fraternity, 14 sororities. **Athletics (Intercollegiate):** *Men:* basketball, cross-country, football, golf, track/field (outdoor), track/field (indoor). *Women:* basketball, cross-country, diving, golf, softball, swimming, tennis, track/field (outdoor), track/field (indoor), volleyball, water polo. **On-Campus Highlights:** Lory Student Center, Student Recreation Center, Library, University Center For the Arts, Moby Arena. The University Center for the Arts is complete, featuring the newly-constructed University Art Museum. Also housed at the UCA is the Griffin Concert Hall, Bohemian Complex with 317 seat thrust theatre, Casavant Organ Recital Hall, and other world-class student resources. **Environmental Initiatives:** Several renewable energy sources went live in the year 2010 including: a second phase of a large solar array that now totals 5,300 kilowatts on the Foothills Campus, an 18.9 kW solar array on the roof of the Engineering building, and a 12.6 kW solar array at the Academic Village residence hall, 133 kW solar array on the roof of the Lake Street Parking Garage, a 15.8 kW on the Behavioral Sciences Building and a 54 kW solar array at the Research Innovation Center. The five smaller arrays are owned and operated by the University, the larger array is owned by a third party and Colorado State serves as a site host and purchases the power produced by the panels. In addition to solar power, CSUs Foothills Campus is also home to a biomass heating plant on the Foothills Campus. This plant burns wood chips to produce hot water for building heat and displaces natural gas use. Campaigns to engage campus faculty staff and students have launched in 2009 to advance sustainability efforts on campus. The faculty campaign, Green is Gold is intended to encourage environmentally friendly habits in the workplace. More information can be found at http://www.green.colostate.edu/gold/. The "Green Warrior Campaign" aims to engage students in creating a climate of sustainability at CSU. The student campaign provides incentives for students to live more sustainably. More information can be found at http://www.green.colostate.edu/greenwarrior/ Colorado State has constructed eleven new buildings on campus. All of these buildings have achieved LEED Gold certification. The university has embraced the green building concept and is getting creative on how to build and renovate buildings more sustainably. Some of the green features on these buildings involve collaboration with researchers on campus in order to further the value of the green buildings. For example, a greywater research project at the new residence hall will study the effects and feasibility of using greywater for irrigation on campus.

ADMISSIONS

Freshman Academic Profile: Average high school GPA 3.61. 20.5% in top 10% of high school class, 49.6% in top 25% of high school class, 84.7% in top 50% of high school class. SAT Math middle 50% range 520-630. SAT Critical Reading middle 50% range 510-620. ACT middle 50% range 22-27. Minimum internet-based TOEFL 45. Minimum paper TOEFL 450. **Basis for Candidate Selection:** *Very important factors considered include:* Class rank, academic GPA, rigor of secondary school record. *Important factors considered include:* application essay, recommendation(s), standardized test scores, character/personal qualities, extracurricular activities, talent/ability, volunteer work. *Other factors considered include:* alumni/ae relation, first generation, geographical residence, interview, level of applicant's interest, state residency, work experience. **Freshman Admission Requirements:** High school diploma is required and GED is accepted. *Academic units required:* 4 English, 4 mathematics, 3 science, (2 science labs), 1 foreign language, 2 social studies, 1 history, 2 academic electives. **Freshman Admission Statistics:** 16,655 applied, 80% admitted, 32% enrolled. **Transfer Admission Requirements:** college transcript(s), essay or personal statement, Minimum college GPA of 2.0 required. Lowest

grade transferable C-. **General Admission Information:** Application Fee $50. Regular application deadline 2/1. Notification on a rolling basis, beginning on or about 10/1. Nonfall registration accepted. Admission may be deferred for a maximum of 1 year. Credit and/or placement offered for CEEB Advanced Placement tests.

COSTS AND FINANCIAL AID

Annual in-state tuition $7,868. Annual out-of-state tuition $24,048. Room and board $10,488. Required fees $2,029. Average book expense $1,140. **Required Forms and Deadlines:** FAFSA. **Notification of Awards:** Applicants will be notified of awards on a rolling basis beginning 3/1. **Types of Aid:** *Need-based scholarships/grants:* Federal Pell, SEOG, state scholarships/grants, private scholarships, the school's own gift aid. *Loans:* Direct Subsidized Stafford, Direct Unsubsidized Stafford, Direct PLUS, Federal Perkins, college/university loans from institutional funds, Alternative Loans. *Student Employment:* Federal Work-Study Program available. Institutional employment available. Highest amount earned per year from on-campus jobs $2,500. Off-campus job opportunities are excellent. **Financial Aid Statistics:** 72% freshmen, 65% undergrads receive need-based scholarship or grant aid. 1% freshmen, 1% undergrads receive non-need-based scholarship or grant aid. 69% freshmen, 75% undergrads receive need-based self-help aid. 1% freshmen, 1% undergrads receive athletic scholarships. 67% freshmen, 73% undergrads receive any aid. 56% undergrads borrow to pay for school. Average cumulative indebtedness $21,240. **Criteria for awarding institutional aid:** *Non-need-based:* academics, art, athletics, leadership, music/drama, state/district residency.

COLORADO STATE UNIVERSITY—PUEBLO

Admissions, Pueblo, CO 81001
Phone: 719-549-2461 · **Financial Aid Phone:** 719-549-2178
E-mail: info@colostate-pueblo.edu · **CEEB Code:** 4611
Fax: 719-549-2419 · **Website:** www.colostate-pueblo.edu · **ACT Code:** 524

This public school was founded in 1933. It has a 275-acre campus.

RATINGS

Admissions Selectivity Rating: 70   **Fire Safety Rating:** 72

STUDENTS AND FACULTY

Enrollment: 3,947. **Student Body:** 57% female, 43% male, 7% out-of-state, 2% international (27 countries represented). Asian 3%, African American 6%, Caucasian 55%, Hispanic 25%, Native American 2%
Retention and Graduation: 63% freshmen return for sophomore year.
Faculty: 155 full-time faculty, 47% are members of minority groups, 17% are women. 0% of classes are taught by teaching assistants.

ACADEMICS

Degrees: bachelor's, master's. **Classes:** Most classes have 10–19 students. Most lab/discussion sessions have 10–19 students. **Majors with Highest Enrollment:** Mass Communication/Media Studies; Liberal Arts and Sciences/Liberal Studies; Biology/Biological Sciences. **Special Study Options:** Accelerated program, cooperative education program, distance learning, double major, dual enrollment, English as a Second Language (ESL), external degree program, independent study, internships, liberal arts/career combination, study abroad, teacher certification program, weekend college. **Honors programs:** We do not have an Honor Program, however, we offer several undergraduate honor courses. Combined degree programs: BSBA/MBA, BS/MS. **Disability Services:** Special programs offered to physically disabled students include note-taking services, reader services, tape recorders, tutors.

FACILITIES

Housing: Coed dorms, special housing for disabled students, apartments for single students. 100% of campus accessible to physically disabled. **Special Academic Facilities/Equipment:** Recital hall, public television and radio station. **Computers:** Students can register for classes online. Administrative functions (other than registration) can be performed online.

CAMPUS LIFE

Environment: City. **Activities:** Choral groups, concert band, dance, jazz band, literary magazine, music ensembles, pep band, student government, student newspaper, symphony orchestra, television station. 24 registered organizations, 6 honor societies, 4 religious organizations. 2 fraternities, 1 sorority. **Athletics (Intercollegiate):** *Men:* baseball, basketball, golf, soccer, tennis. *Women:* basketball, cross-country, golf, soccer, softball, tennis, volleyball. **On-Campus Highlights:** University Library, Occhiato University Center, La Cantina, The Underground, The Pavillion, The Wall.

ADMISSIONS .

Freshman Academic Profile: Average high school GPA 3.1. 2% in top 10% of high school class, 8% in top 25% of high school class, 36% in top 50% of high school class. 85% from public high schools. SAT Math middle 50% range 420-550. SAT Critical Reading middle 50% range 420-530. ACT middle 50% range 18-22. Minimum paper TOEFL 500. **Basis for Candidate Selection:** *Very important factors considered include:* academic GPA, rigor of secondary school record, standardized test scores. *Important factors considered include:* Class rank. *Other factors considered include:* application essay, recommendation(s), character/personal qualities, interview, level of applicant's interest, talent/ability, volunteer work, work experience. **Freshman Admission Requirements:** High school diploma is required and GED is accepted. *Academic units required:* 4 English, 3 mathematics, 3 science, (2 science labs), 2 foreign language, 2 social studies, 1 history. **Freshman Admission Statistics:** 1,485 applied, 94% admitted, 46% enrolled. **Transfer Admission Requirements:** college transcript(s), Minimum college GPA of 2.3 required. Lowest grade transferable C-. **General Admission Information:** Application Fee $25. Regular application deadline 8/1. Notification on a rolling basis, beginning on or about 8/1. Nonfall registration accepted. Admission may be deferred for a maximum of 1 semester. Credit offered for CEEB Advanced Placement tests.

COSTS AND FINANCIAL AID
Annual out-of-state tuition $13,543. Room and board $6,300. Required fees $996. Average book expense $1,698. **Required Forms and Deadlines:** FAFSA, Institution's own financial aid form. **Notification of Awards:** Applicants will be notified of awards on a rolling basis beginning 3/15. **Types of Aid:** *Need-based scholarships/grants:* Federal Pell, SEOG, state scholarships/grants, private scholarships, the school's own gift aid, Academic Competitiveness Grant and National SMART Grant. *Loans:* Subsidized Stafford, Unsubsidized Stafford, PLUS, Federal Perkins. *Student Employment:* Highest amount earned per year from on-campus jobs $8,000. **Financial Aid Statistics:** 81% freshmen, 80% undergrads receive need-based scholarship or grant aid. 7% freshmen, 4% undergrads receive non-need-based scholarship or grant aid. 78% freshmen, 86% undergrads receive need-based self-help aid. 3% freshmen, 4% undergrads receive athletic scholarships. 81% freshmen, 86% undergrads receive any aid. 54% undergrads borrow to pay for school. Average cumulative indebtedness $16,176. **Criteria for awarding institutional aid:** *Non-need-based:* academics, alumni affiliation, art, athletics, leadership, minority status, music/drama, state/district residency.

COLORADO TECHNICAL UNIVERSITY

4435 North Chestnut Street, Colorado Springs, CO 80907-3740
Phone: 719-598-0200
E-mail: cosadmissions@coloradotech.edu
Website: http://www.coloradotech.edu/

This is a proprietary school.

RATINGS
Admissions Selectivity Rating: 60*   **Fire Safety Rating:** 60*

STUDENTS AND FACULTY
Enrollment: 1,297.
Faculty: 31 full-time faculty, 52% hold PhDs, 35% are members of minority groups, 13% are women.

ACADEMICS
Degrees: associate, bachelor's, certificate, master's, transfer associate. **Classes:** Most classes have 10-19 students. **Special Study Options:** Accelerated program, double major, independent study, internships, weekend college, Sixteen and 1/2 month M.S. degree programs and 2-year doctoral programs.

CAMPUS LIFE
Activities: student government.

ADMISSIONS
Basis for Candidate Selection: *Other factors considered include:* Class rank, recommendation(s), rigor of secondary school record, standardized test scores, alumni/ae relation, character/personal qualities, interview, work experience. **Freshman Admission Requirements:** *Academic units required:* 1 English, 1 mathematics, 1 science, (1 science labs). **Transfer Admission Requirements:** college transcript(s), statement of good standing from prior institution(s). Lowest grade transferable C. **General Admission Information:** Application Fee $50. Regular application deadline 10/2. Nonfall registration accepted.

COSTS AND FINANCIAL AID
Average book expense $1,000. **Required Forms and Deadlines:** FAFSA, Institution's own financial aid form, State aid form. **Notification of Awards:** Applicants will be notified of awards on a rolling basis beginning 2/1. **Types of Aid:** *Loans:* Subsidized Stafford, Unsubsidized Stafford, PLUS, Federal Perkins.

COLUMBIA COLLEGE (MO)

1001 Rogers St., Columbia, MO 65216
Phone: 573-875-7352 • **Financial Aid Phone:** 573-875-7390
E-mail: admissions@ccis.edu • **CEEB Code:** 6095
Fax: 573-875-7506 • **Website:** http://www.ccis.edu • **ACT Code:** 2276

This private school, affiliated with the Disciples of Christ Church, was founded in 1851. It has a 33-acre campus.

RATINGS
Admissions Selectivity Rating: 89   **Fire Safety Rating:** 83

STUDENTS AND FACULTY
Enrollment: 873. **Student Body:** 55% female, 45% male, 13% out-of-state, 9% international (36 countries represented). Asian 1%, African American 4%, Caucasian 71%, Hispanic 2%, Native American 1%
Retention and Graduation: 76% freshmen return for sophomore year. 29% freshmen graduate within 4 years. 21% grads go on to further study within 1 year. 2% grads pursue arts and sciences degrees. 26% grads pursue law degrees. 2% grads pursue business degrees. 2% grads pursue medical degrees. **Faculty:** 69 full-time faculty, 90% hold PhDs, 46% are members of minority groups, 10% are women. 0% of classes are taught by teaching assistants.

ACADEMICS
Degrees: associate, bachelor's, certificate, master's, post-bachelor's certificate. **Classes:** Most classes have 10-19 students. Most lab/discussion sessions have 10-19 students. **Majors with Highest Enrollment:** Business Administration and Management; Psychology; Criminal Justice/Law Enforcement Administration. **Special Study Options:** cross-registration, distance learning, double major, dual enrollment, English as a Second Language (ESL), honors program, independent study, internships, student-designed major, study abroad, teacher certification program. **Honors programs:** The Honors Program is designed for high achieving students who are philosophers in the literal sense, i.e., lovers of wisdom. The goal of the program is to promote genuine inquiry and collaborative learning, emphasizing the dialogic nature of academic work and intellectual discovery. **Disability Services:** Special programs offered to physically disabled students include note-taking services, tutors. **Career services:** Alumni network, alumni services, career/job search classes, internships, regional alumni. All of our Career Services that are offered to our regular students are offered to Alumni and free.

FACILITIES
Housing: Coed dorms, special housing for disabled students, special housing for international students, women's dorms, apartments for single students, Wellness Housing. 97% of campus accessible to physically disabled. **Special Academic Facilities/Equipment:** Most classrooms are multimedia with SmartBoards, new student commons building, arts center, Larson Gallery, Jane Froman Archive. **Computers:** 100% of classrooms, 100% of dorms, 100% of libraries, 100% of dining areas, 100% of student union, have wireless network access. Students can register for classes online. Administrative functions (other than registration) can be performed online.

CAMPUS LIFE
Environment: City. **Activities:** Choral groups, dance, drama/theater, literary magazine, music ensembles, musical theater, student government, student newspaper, Campus Ministries, International Student Organization, Model UN. 42 registered organizations, 16 honor societies, 2 religious organizations. **Athletics (Intercollegiate):** *Men:* basketball, soccer. *Women:* basketball, softball, volleyball. **On-Campus Highlights:** Larson Art Gallery, The newly expanded Southwell Athletic Complex, New Atkins-Holman Student Commons building, Stafford Library **Environmental Initiatives:** 77% of campus building square footage is on highly efficient ground source water heat pump system. We have in place a fairly substantial recycling program. We have in place a lighting retrofit program replacing ineffient lights with more efficient ones.

ADMISSIONS
Freshman Academic Profile: Average high school GPA 3.47. 15% in top 10% of high school class, 35% in top 25% of high school class, 77% in top 50% of high school class. SAT Math middle 50% range 490-635. SAT Critical Reading middle 50% range 970-1243. SAT Writing middle 50% range 423-588. ACT middle 50% range 21-26. Minimum internet-based TOEFL 61. Minimum paper TOEFL 500. **Basis for Candidate Selection:** *Very important factors considered include:* Class rank, academic GPA, standardized test scores. *Other factors considered include:* rigor of secondary school record, character/personal qualities. **Freshman Admission Requirements:** High school diploma is required and GED is accepted. **Freshman Admission Statistics:** 616 applied, 19% admitted, 97% enrolled. **Transfer Admission Requirements:** college transcript(s), statement of good standing from prior institution(s). Minimum college GPA of 2.0 required. Lowest grade transferable 2. **General Admission Information:** Regular application deadline 8/14. Notification on a rolling basis,

beginning on or about 9/15. Nonfall registration accepted. Admission may be deferred for a maximum of 1 year. Credit and/or placement offered for CEEB Advanced Placement tests.

COSTS AND FINANCIAL AID

Annual tuition $19,386. Room and board $8,240. Average book expense $1,315. **Required Forms and Deadlines:** FAFSA. **Notification of Awards:** Applicants will be notified of awards on a rolling basis beginning 3/1. **Types of Aid:** *Need-based scholarships/grants:* Federal Pell, SEOG, state scholarships/grants, private scholarships. *Loans:* Direct Subsidized Stafford, Direct Unsubsidized Stafford, Direct PLUS. *Student Employment:* Federal Work-Study Program available. Institutional employment available. Highest amount earned per year from on-campus jobs $5,982. Off-campus job opportunities are excellent. **Financial Aid Statistics:** 66% freshmen, 71% undergrads receive need-based scholarship or grant aid. 90% freshmen, 77% undergrads receive non-need-based scholarship or grant aid. 69% freshmen, 70% undergrads receive need-based self-help aid. 16% freshmen, 17% undergrads receive athletic scholarships. 62% freshmen, 56% undergrads receive any aid. 55% undergrads borrow to pay for school. Average cumulative indebtedness $13,870. **Criteria for awarding institutional aid:** *Non-need-based:* academics, alumni affiliation, art, athletics, job skills, leadership, music/drama, religious affiliation, state/district residency.

See page 1034.

COLUMBIA COLLEGE (SC)

1301 Columbia College Drive, Columbia, SC 29203
Phone: 803-786-3871 · **Financial Aid Phone:** 803-786-3612
E-mail: admissions@columbiasc.edu · **CEEB Code:** 5117
Fax: 803-786-3674 · **Website:** www.columbiacollegesc.edu · **ACT Code:** 3850

This private school, affiliated with the Methodist Church, was founded in 1854. It has a 33-acre campus.

RATINGS

Admissions Selectivity Rating: 79   **Fire Safety Rating:** 78

STUDENTS AND FACULTY

Enrollment: 1,225. **Student Body:** 97% female, 3% male, 6% out-of-state, 0% international (14 countries represented). Asian 1%, African American 44%, Caucasian 47%, Hispanic 2%, Native American 2%
Retention and Graduation: 62% freshmen return for sophomore year. 39% freshmen graduate within 4 years. 47% freshmen graduate within 6 years. **Faculty:** 87 full-time faculty, 75% hold PhDs, 68% are members of minority groups, 11% are women. 0% of classes are taught by teaching assistants.

ACADEMICS

Degrees: bachelor's, master's, post-bachelor's certificate. **Classes:** Most classes have 10–19 students. **Majors with Highest Enrollment:** Business Administration and Management; Human Development, Family Studies, and Related Services; Elementary Education and Teaching. **Special Study Options:** distance learning, double major, dual enrollment, honors program, independent study, internships, student-designed major, study abroad, teacher certification program. **Honors programs:** The Columbia College Honors Program provides enriched academic and co-curricular experiences for outstanding, motivated students committed to excellence. Offering a variety of opportunities for superior, engaged learning both within and outside the classroom, honors challenges students to reach their highest potential as scholars, individual thinkers, and leaders by emphasizing rigorous intellectual standards, risk, creativity, integrity, and dedication to service and leadership. The program is deeply active in the National Collegiate Honors Council and its regional association, regularly sponsoring numerous faculty and students at annual conferences and in executive leadership positions; honors has also earned special recognition through national and regional awards for honors faculty and students. To complete honors, students take 24 semester hours across disciplines in honors courses, including the 3 hour interdisciplinary senior seminar and the 3–4 hour mentored independent project. Students must maintain at least a 3.4 cumulative GPA to remain in honors. **Career services:** career/job search classes, career assessment, internships.

FACILITIES

Housing: women's dorms, Special programs: Leadership; Honors Program. 75% of campus accessible to physically disabled. **Special Academic Facilities/Equipment:** Language lab, Alumnae Hall, Barbara Bush Center for Science and Technology, Breed Leadership Center for Women. **Computers:** 50% of libraries, 100% of dining areas, 100% of student union, 30% of common outdoor areas have wireless network access. Students can register for classes online. Administrative functions (other than registration) can be performed online.

CAMPUS LIFE

Environment: Metropolis. **Activities:** Choral groups, concert band, dance, drama/theater, literary magazine, music ensembles, musical theater, opera, student government, student newspaper, yearbook, Campus Ministries, International Student Organization. 53 registered organizations, 10 honor societies, 7 religious organizations. **Athletics (Intercollegiate):** *Women:* basketball, soccer, softball, tennis, volleyball. **On-Campus Highlights:** Leadership Center, Terrace Café, Student Union, Cottingham Performance Theatre, Bush Science Center. **Environmental Initiatives:** Student-sponsored and initiated recycling program.

ADMISSIONS

Freshman Academic Profile: Average high school GPA 3.47. 19% in top 10% of high school class, 45% in top 25% of high school class, 78% in top 50% of high school class. SAT Math middle 50% range 450-550. SAT Critical Reading middle 50% range 450-570. SAT Writing middle 50% range 440-560. ACT middle 50% range 18-24. Minimum paper TOEFL 550. **Basis for Candidate Selection:** *Very important factors considered include:* recommendation(s), rigor of secondary school record, standardized test scores. *Important factors considered include:* Class rank, character/personal qualities. *Other factors considered include:* application essay, alumni/ae relation, extracurricular activities, talent/ability, volunteer work. **Freshman Admission Requirements:** High school diploma is required and GED is accepted. **Freshman Admission Statistics:** 1,078 applied, 76% admitted, 34% enrolled. **Transfer Admission Requirements:** High school transcript, college transcript(s), standardized test scores, statement of good standing from prior institution(s). Minimum college GPA of 2.0 required. Lowest grade transferable C. **General Admission Information:** Application Fee $25. Regular application deadline 8/1. Notification on a rolling basis, beginning on or about 10/1. Nonfall registration accepted. Admission may be deferred for a maximum of 1 year. Credit offered for CEEB Advanced Placement tests.

COSTS AND FINANCIAL AID

Annual tuition $22,580. Room and board $6,450. Required fees $450. **Required Forms and Deadlines:** FAFSA. **Notification of Awards:** Applicants will be notified of awards on a rolling basis beginning 3/1. **Types of Aid:** *Need-based scholarships/grants:* Federal Pell, SEOG, state scholarships/grants, private scholarships, the school's own gift aid, United Negro College Fund. *Loans:* Subsidized Stafford, Unsubsidized Stafford, PLUS, Federal Perkins, state loans, signature student loan. *Student Employment:* Federal Work-Study Program available. Institutional employment available. Highest amount earned per year from on-campus jobs $1,000. Off-campus job opportunities are excellent. **Financial Aid Statistics:** 98% freshmen, 95% undergrads receive need-based scholarship or grant aid. 85% freshmen, 76% undergrads receive non-need-based scholarship or grant aid. 83% freshmen, 85% undergrads receive need-based self-help aid. 2% freshmen, 3% undergrads receive athletic scholarships. 99% freshmen, 92% undergrads receive any aid. 94% undergrads borrow to pay for school. Average cumulative indebtedness $13,740. **Criteria for awarding institutional aid:** *Non-need-based:* academics, alumni affiliation, art, athletics, leadership, music/drama.

COLUMBIA COLLEGE CHICAGO (IL)

600 South Michigan Avenue, Chicago, IL 60605-1996
Phone: 1-312-369-7130 · **Financial Aid Phone:** 312-369-7831
E-mail: admissions@colum.edu · **CEEB Code:** 1135
Fax: 312-369-8024 · **Website:** www.colum.edu · **ACT Code:** 1002

This private school was founded in 1890.

RATINGS

Admissions Selectivity Rating: 76   **Fire Safety Rating:** 73

STUDENTS AND FACULTY

Enrollment: 8,929. **Student Body:** 56% female, 44% male, 40% out-of-state, 3% international (48 countries represented). Asian 3%, African American 16%, Caucasian 57%, Hispanic 10%, Native American <1%
Retention and Graduation: 71% freshmen return for sophomore year. 30% freshmen graduate within 4 years. 9% grads go on to further study within 1 year. 10% grads pursue arts and sciences degrees. **Faculty:** 374 full-time faculty, 51% hold PhDs, 47% are members of minority groups, 17% are women. 0% of classes are taught by teaching assistants.

ACADEMICS

Degrees: bachelor's, master's, post-bachelor's certificate, post-master's certificate. **Classes:** Most classes have 10–19 students. **Majors with Highest Enrollment:** Cinematography and Film/Video Production; Drama and Dramatics/Theatre Arts; Photography. **Special Study Options:** cross-registration, exchange student program (domestic), honors program, independent study, internships, student-designed major, study abroad, teacher certification program. **Disability Services:** Special programs offered to physically disabled students include note-taking services, reader services, tape recorders, tutors.

FACILITIES

Housing: Coed dorms, apartments for single students. 90% of campus accessible to physically disabled. **Special Academic Facilities/Equipment:** Art galleries, center for black music research, contemporary photography museum, dance center. **Computers:** Students can register for classes online. Administrative functions (other than registration) can be performed online.

CAMPUS LIFE

Environment: Metropolis. **Activities:** Choral groups, concert band, dance, drama/theater, jazz band, literary magazine, music ensembles, musical theater, opera, radio station, student government, student newspaper, student-run film society, television station, Campus Ministries, International Student Organization. 64 registered organizations. **On-Campus Highlights:** Museum of Contemporary Photography, Center for Black Music Research, Hokin Annex and Gallery **Environmental Initiatives:** Campus-wide recycling of paper, plastic, glass, techno; Sustainable materials in capital construction projects; LEED cerfitication in capital construction projects.

ADMISSIONS

Freshman Academic Profile: Average high school GPA 3.25. 8% in top 10% of high school class, 29% in top 25% of high school class, 63% in top 50% of high school class. SAT Math middle 50% range 440-570. SAT Critical Reading middle 50% range 485-605. SAT Writing middle 50% range 470-590. ACT middle 50% range 19-25. Minimum internet-based TOEFL 80. Minimum paper TOEFL 533. **Basis for Candidate Selection:** *Important factors considered include:* application essay, academic GPA, recommendation(s), character/personal qualities, talent/ability. *Other factors considered include:* rigor of secondary school record, standardized test scores, extracurricular activities, interview, volunteer work, work experience. **Freshman Admission Requirements:** High school diploma is required and GED is accepted. **Freshman Admission Statistics:** 8,953 applied, 82% admitted, 25% enrolled. **Transfer Admission Requirements:** High school transcript, college transcript(s), essay or personal statement, Lowest grade transferable C. **General Admission Information:** Application Fee $35. Nonfall registration accepted. Admission may be deferred for a maximum of 1 year. Credit and/or placement offered for CEEB Advanced Placement tests.

COSTS AND FINANCIAL AID

Annual tuition $22,884. Room and board $12,450. Required fees $660. Average book expense $1,708. **Required Forms and Deadlines:** FAFSA, Institution's own financial aid form. **Types of Aid:** *Need-based scholarships/grants:* Federal Pell, SEOG, state scholarships/grants, private scholarships, the school's own gift aid. *Loans:* Direct Subsidized Stafford, Direct Unsubsidized Stafford, Direct PLUS. *Student Employment:* Federal Work-Study Program available. **Financial Aid Statistics:** 90% freshmen, 82% undergrads receive need-based scholarship or grant aid. 0% freshmen, 0% undergrads receive non-need-based scholarship or grant aid. 0% freshmen, 1% undergrads receive need-based self-help aid. 0% freshmen, 0% undergrads receive athletic scholarships. 73% freshmen, 71% undergrads receive any aid.

COLUMBIA COLLEGE—HOLLYWOOD

18618 Oxnard St., Tarzana, CA 91356
Phone: 818-345-8414
E-mail: admissions@columbiacollege.edu · **CEEB Code:** 7213
Fax: 818-345-9053 · **Website:** www.columbiacollege.edu

This private school was founded in 1952.

RATINGS

Admissions Selectivity Rating: 61   **Fire Safety Rating:** 60*

STUDENTS AND FACULTY

Enrollment: 150. **Student Body:** 31% female, 69% male, 10% international (24 countries represented). Asian 5%, African American 9%, Caucasian 60%, Hispanic 14%, Native American 1%
Retention and Graduation: 47% freshmen return for sophomore year. 36% freshmen graduate within 4 years. 5% grads go on to further study within 1 year. **Faculty:** 0% of classes are taught by teaching assistants.

ACADEMICS

Degrees: associate, bachelor's. **Majors with Highest Enrollment:** Film/Cinema/Video Studies; Cinematography and Film/Video Production. **Special Study Options:** Accelerated program, double major, internships, liberal arts/

career combination. Combined degree programs: Combined BA degree in Cinema and Video/TV. **Career services:** Alumni network, career assessment, internships. All students are strongly encouraged to meet with the Placement Advisor upon enrollment. Employment is not guaranteed but CCH offers career counseling and guidance that prepares students to meet the challenges of the highly competitive entertainment industry. For-pay and for-college credit internships at entertainment production companies are available year round. The Placement Advisor assists students in selecting internships, drafting resumes, and preparing for interviews. In addition, the Faculty Association mentors students with senior status. Each student is matched with a faculty advisor in his or her chosen field of study. The advisor offers one-on-one counseling. Many faculty members are industry insiders with invaluable insight into the craft and the business of movie and television production.

FACILITIES

Housing: CCH does not offer housing, but our staff does assist students in trying to find apartments and potential roommates.

CAMPUS LIFE

Environment: Metropolis. **Activities:** student government. 1 registered organization, 3 honor societies.

ADMISSIONS

Freshman Academic Profile: Average high school GPA 3.3. 50% from public high schools. Minimum paper TOEFL 550. **Basis for Candidate Selection:** *Very important factors considered include:* application essay, recommendation(s), rigor of secondary school record. *Other factors considered include:* standardized test scores, character/personal qualities, extracurricular activities, interview, talent/ability. **Freshman Admission Requirements:** High school diploma is required and GED is accepted. **Freshman Admission Statistics:** 87 applied, 77% admitted, 90% enrolled. **Transfer Admission Requirements:** High school transcript, college transcript(s), essay or personal statement, Minimum college GPA of 2.0 required. Lowest grade transferable C. **General Admission Information:** Application Fee $50. Nonfall registration accepted. Admission may be deferred for a maximum of 12 months. Neither credit nor placement offered for CEEB Advanced Placement tests.

COSTS AND FINANCIAL AID

Annual tuition $11,400. Required fees $300. Average book expense $400. **Required Forms and Deadlines:** FAFSA, Institution's own financial aid form. **Types of Aid:** *Need-based scholarships/grants:* Federal Pell, SEOG, state scholarships/grants. *Loans:* Subsidized Stafford, Unsubsidized Stafford, PLUS. *Student Employment:* Federal Work-Study Program available. Off-campus job opportunities are excellent. **Financial Aid Statistics:** 63% freshmen, 74% undergrads receive need-based scholarship or grant aid. 0% freshmen, 0% undergrads receive non-need-based scholarship or grant aid. 0% freshmen, 0% undergrads receive need-based self-help aid. 0% freshmen, 0% undergrads receive athletic scholarships. 78% freshmen, 75% undergrads receive any aid. 95% undergrads borrow to pay for school.

COLUMBIA INTERNATIONAL UNIVERSITY

PO Box 3122, Columbia, SC 29230-3122
Phone: 803-754-4100
E-mail: yesciu@ciu.edu
Fax: 803-786-4041 · **Website:** www.ciu.edu · **ACT Code:** 5016

This private school was founded in 1923. It has a 400-acre campus.

RATINGS

Admissions Selectivity Rating: 81   **Fire Safety Rating:** 60*

STUDENTS AND FACULTY

Enrollment: 568. **Student Body:** 54% female, 46% male, 56% out-of-state, 0% international. Asian 0%, African American 0%, Caucasian 0%, Hispanic 0%, Native American <1%
Retention and Graduation: 77% freshmen return for sophomore year. 35% freshmen graduate within 4 years. **Faculty:** 19 full-time faculty, 58% hold PhDs, 21% are members of minority groups, 11% are women.

ACADEMICS

Degrees: associate, bachelor's, certificate, first professional, master's, post-bachelor's certificate, terminal associate, transfer associate. **Special Study Options:** cross-registration, distance learning, double major, dual enrollment, English as a Second Language (ESL), independent study, internships, liberal arts/career combination, study abroad, Cooperative studies with Midlands Technical College. **Disability Services:** Special programs offered to physically disabled students include note-taking services, reader services, tape recorders, tutors. **Career services:** alumni services.

FACILITIES

Housing: men's dorms, women's dorms, apartments for single students, mobile home park for married students.

CAMPUS LIFE

Environment: Village. **Activities:** Choral groups, concert band, drama/theater, music ensembles, student government, symphony orchestra, yearbook. 4 religious organizations.

ADMISSIONS

Freshman Academic Profile: Average high school GPA 3.85. 27% in top 10% of high school class, 47% in top 25% of high school class, 75% in top 50% of high school class. SAT Math middle 50% range 490-580. SAT Critical Reading middle 50% range 530-630. SAT Writing middle 50% range 490-600. ACT middle 50% range 20-26. Minimum paper TOEFL 525. **Basis for Candidate Selection:** *Very important factors considered include:* rigor of secondary school record, character/personal qualities, religious affiliation/commitment. *Important factors considered include:* application essay, recommendation(s), standardized test scores, volunteer work. *Other factors considered include:* Class rank, extracurricular activities, interview, talent/ability. **Freshman Admission Requirements:** High school diploma is required and GED is accepted. **Freshman Admission Statistics:** 163 applied, 99% admitted, 52% enrolled. **Transfer Admission Requirements:** college transcript(s), essay or personal statement, statement of good standing from prior institution(s). Minimum college GPA of 2.0 required. Lowest grade transferable C. **General Admission Information:** Application Fee $25. Notification on a rolling basis, beginning on or about 9/1. Nonfall registration accepted. Admission may be deferred for a maximum of n/a.

COSTS AND FINANCIAL AID

Annual tuition $8,980. Room and board $4,520. Average book expense $800. **Required Forms and Deadlines:** FAFSA. **Types of Aid:** *Need-based scholarships/grants:* Federal Pell, SEOG, state scholarships/grants, private scholarships, the school's own gift aid. *Loans:* Subsidized Stafford, Unsubsidized Stafford, PLUS, college/university loans from institutional funds. *Student Employment:* Federal Work-Study Program available. Highest amount earned per year from on-campus jobs $1,200. Off-campus job opportunities are good. **Financial Aid Statistics:** 75% freshmen, 78% undergrads receive need-based scholarship or grant aid. 18% freshmen, 23% undergrads receive non-need-based scholarship or grant aid. 99% freshmen, 97% undergrads receive need-based self-help aid. 0% freshmen, 0% undergrads receive athletic scholarships. 58% undergrads borrow to pay for school.

COLUMBIA UNIVERSITY

212 Hamilton Hall MC 2807, New York, NY 10027
Phone: 212-854-2522 • **CEEB Code:** 2116
Fax: 212-894-1209 • **Website:** http://undergrad.admissions.columbia.edu
ACT Code: 2717

This private school was founded in 1754. It has a 36-acre campus.

RATINGS

Admissions Selectivity Rating: 98   Fire Safety Rating: 62

STUDENTS AND FACULTY

Enrollment: 6,170. **Student Body:** 48% female, 52% male, 76% out-of-state, 13% international (87 countries represented). Asian 22%, African American 12%, Caucasian 35%, Hispanic 12%, Native American 2% **Retention and Graduation:** 99% freshmen return for sophomore year. 90% freshmen graduate within 4 years. 96% freshmen graduate within 6 years. **Faculty:** 0% of classes are taught by teaching assistants.

ACADEMICS

Degrees: bachelor's, master's. **Classes:** Most classes have 10–19 students. **Majors with Highest Enrollment:** Political Science and Government; English Language and Literature; Engineering. **Special Study Options:** Accelerated program, cooperative education program, cross-registration, double major, dual enrollment, English as a Second Language (ESL), exchange student program (domestic), independent study, internships, liberal arts/career combination, student-designed major, study abroad, teacher certification program, Combined 3-2 program. Combined degree programs: BA/JD, BA/MIA and BA/MPA (programs with SIPA). **Disability Services:** Special programs offered to physically

disabled students include note-taking services, reader services, tape recorders, tutors. **Career services:** Alumni network, alumni services, career/job search classes, career assessment, internships.

FACILITIES

Housing: Coed dorms, special housing for disabled students, fraternity/sorority housing, Special Interest **Housing:** Single-Sex First-Year Floor available. 95% of campus accessible to physically disabled. **Special Academic Facilities/Equipment:** Art and Architecture Galleries; Theatres, Cinema, Observatory **Computers:** Students can register for classes online. Administrative functions (other than registration) can be performed online.

CAMPUS LIFE

Environment: Metropolis. **Activities:** Choral groups, concert band, dance, drama/theater, jazz band, literary magazine, marching band, music ensembles, musical theater, opera, pep band, radio station, student government, student newspaper, student-run film society, symphony orchestra, television station, yearbook, Campus Ministries, International Student Organization, Model UN. 300 registered organizations, 17 religious organizations. 17 fraternities, 11 sorority. **Athletics (Intercollegiate):** *Men:* baseball, basketball, crew/rowing, cross-country, diving, fencing, football, golf, soccer, swimming, tennis, track/field (outdoor), track/field (indoor), wrestling. *Women:* archery, basketball, crew/rowing, cross-country, diving, fencing, field hockey, golf, lacrosse, soccer, softball, swimming, tennis, track/field (outdoor), track/field (indoor), volleyball. **On-Campus Highlights:** Low Library and Plaza, Butler Library, Postcrypt Coffee House, Ferris Booth Commons, Levian Gym, www.studentaffairs. columbia.edu/admissions/virtualvisit/. **Environmental Initiatives:** Greenhouse gas reduction program targeted to meet a 30% reduction by 2017 and clean heat initiative to improve air quality and asthma rates by phasing out the use of heavy heating oils to cleaner fuels like natural gas and low-sulfur #2 oil. Columbia has also converted its entire 14 car public safety fleet to hybrid vehicles. As part of our energy efficiency initiatives, 45% of all food purchased is local and/ororganic. All honey and apples are purchased through vendors at the on-campus green market from NY farmers. Annually Dining Services contracts with a local NY farmer and canner to make all the salsa and strawberry jam for the year. In addition all milk is local and hormone free. Liquid eggs are certified humane. All coffee is roasted locally and is fair-trade, organic, shade grown and bird friendly. Tomatoes are also fair trade. All bakery items and grab and go sandwiches are purchased from local vendors. 50% of daily meals served in the dining halls are vegetarian and Meatless Mondays are run every Monday. Green building and construction commitment: LEED Silver baseline commitment for all new construction that includes 4 LEED Gold Buildings; LEED for Neighborhood Development pilot program for 17 acre campus expansion. Columbia's robust surplus reuse program diverts furniture and equipment from landfill as well as achieves a 90% construction recycling rate for recent LEED projects. The model clean construction program has significantly reduced particulates and other pollutants that are a contributor to Harlem's high asthma rates. http://news.columbia.edu/newyorkstories/2477 http://www.environment.columbia.edu/reuse Columbia is the leading U.S. research and educational institution on the environment and climate change. Twenty-four environmental degree granting programs including a sustainable development major; 33 environmental research centers, home of the Earth Institute and the Lamont Doherty Earth Observatory, also NASA/GISS -- Columbia University is one of the worlds leading research institutions on climate and earth systems; The term global warming was coined at Columbia and the phenomanom of El Nino was discovered here.

ADMISSIONS

Freshman Academic Profile: 57% from public high schools. SAT Math middle 50% range 700-790. SAT Critical Reading middle 50% range 690-780. SAT Writing middle 50% range 700-780. ACT middle 50% range 31-34. Minimum paper TOEFL 600. **Basis for Candidate Selection:** *Very important factors considered include:* Class rank, application essay, academic GPA, recommendation(s), rigor of secondary school record, standardized test scores, character/personal qualities. *Important factors considered include:* extracurricular activities, talent/ability. *Other factors considered include:* alumni/ae relation, geographical residence, interview, racial/ethnic status, volunteer work, work experience. **Freshman Admission Requirements:** High school diploma is required and GED is accepted. **Freshman Admission Statistics:** 32,967 applied, 7% admitted, 62% enrolled. **Transfer Admission Requirements:** High school transcript, college transcript(s), essay or personal statement, standardized test scores, statement of good standing from prior institution(s). Lowest grade transferable C. **General Admission Information:** Application Fee $70. Early decision application deadline 11/1. Regular application deadline 1/2. Regular notification 4/1. Nonfall registration not accepted. Admission may be deferred for a maximum of 2 years. Credit and/or placement offered for CEEB Advanced Placement tests.

COSTS AND FINANCIAL AID

Annual tuition $46,846. Room and board $11,978. Required fees $2,813. Average book expense $1,170. **Required Forms and Deadlines:** FAFSA, CSS/Financial Aid PROFILE, Noncustodial PROFILE. **Notification of Awards:**

Applicants will be notified of awards on or about 4/1. **Types of Aid:** *Need-based scholarships/grants:* Federal Pell, SEOG, state scholarships/grants, private scholarships, the school's own gift aid. *Loans:* Subsidized Stafford, Unsubsidized Stafford, PLUS, Federal Perkins, Alternative loans. *Student Employment:* Federal Work-Study Program available. Institutional employment available. Off-campus job opportunities are excellent. **Financial Aid Statistics:** 95% freshmen, 96% undergrads receive need-based scholarship or grant aid. 1% freshmen, 1% undergrads receive non-need-based scholarship or grant aid. 76% freshmen, 85% undergrads receive need-based self-help aid. 0% freshmen, 0% undergrads receive athletic scholarships. 55% freshmen, 60% undergrads receive any aid.Average cumulative indebtedness $15,269.

COLUMBIA UNIVERSITY SCHOOL OF GENERAL STUDIES

408 Lewisohn Hall, Mail Code 4101, New York, NY 10027
Phone: 212-854-2772 · **Financial Aid Phone:** 212-854-5410
E-mail: gsdegree@columbia.edu · **CEEB Code:** 2095
Fax: 212-854-6316 · **Website:** www.gs.columbia.edu · **ACT Code:** 2716

This private school was founded in 1947. It has a 36-acre campus.

RATINGS
Admissions Selectivity Rating: 95   Fire Safety Rating: 80

STUDENTS AND FACULTY
Enrollment: 1,898. **Student Body:** 42% female, 58% male, 55% out-of-state, 14% international (62 countries represented). Asian 7%, African American 5%, Caucasian 48%, Hispanic 10%, Native American <1%
Faculty:

ACADEMICS
Degrees: bachelor's, post-bachelor's certificate. **Majors with Highest Enrollment:** Economics; Political Science and Government; English Language and Literature. **Special Study Options:** Accelerated program, cross-registration, double major, dual enrollment, exchange student program (domestic), honors program, independent study, internships, student-designed major, study abroad, teacher certification program. **Honors programs:** Honor Society of School of General Studies Combined degree programs: BA/JD, BA/MA, BA/DDS, BA/MEng, Joint Programs. **Disability Services:** Special programs offered to physically disabled students include note-taking services, reader services, tape recorders, tutors. **Career services:** Alumni network, alumni services, career/job search classes, career assessment, internships, regional alumni.

FACILITIES
Housing: Coed dorms, special housing for international students, fraternity/sorority housing, apartments for married students, cooperative housing, apartments for single students, Theme Housing. 100% of campus accessible to physically disabled. **Special Academic Facilities/Equipment:** Earth Institute, Lamont-Doherty Earth Observatory University Art Collection Miller Theatre Low Memorial Library Rotunda LeRoy Neiman Center for Print Studies Music at St. Paul's Postcrypt Coffeehouse Miriam and Ira D. Wallach Art Gallery Language Houses **Computers:** 50% of classrooms, 10% of dorms, 64% of libraries, 50% of dining areas, 90% of student union, 25% of common outdoor areas have wireless network access. Students can register for classes online. Administrative functions (other than registration) can be performed online.

CAMPUS LIFE
Environment: Metropolis. **Activities:** Choral groups, concert band, dance, drama/theater, jazz band, literary magazine, marching band, music ensembles, musical theater, opera, radio station, student government, student newspaper, student-run film society, symphony orchestra, television station, yearbook, Campus Ministries, International Student Organization, Model UN. 250 registered organizations, 2 honor societies, 21 religious organization. **Athletics (Intercollegiate):** *Men:* baseball, basketball, crew/rowing, cross-country, diving, fencing, football, golf, soccer, swimming, track/field (outdoor), track/field (indoor). *Women:* archery, basketball, crew/rowing, cross-country, diving, fencing, field hockey, golf, lacrosse, soccer, softball, swimming, track/field (outdoor), track/field (indoor), volleyball. **On-Campus Highlights:** Low Library, Lerner Hall, Butler Library, Miller Theater, College Walk, Low Plaza. **Environmental Initiatives:** Greenhouse gas reduction program targeted to meet a 30% reduction by 2017 and clean heat initiative to improve air quality and asthma rates by phasing out the use of heavy heating oils to cleaner fuels like natural gas and low-sulfur #2 oil. Columbia has also converted its entire 14 car public safety fleet to hybrid vehicles. As part of our energy efficiency initiatives, 45% of all food purchased is local and/ororganic. All honey and apples are purchased through vendors at the on-campus green market from NY farmers. Annually Dining Services contracts with a local NY farmer and canner to make all the salsa and strawberry jam for the year. In addition all milk is local and hormone free. Liquid eggs are certified humane. All coffee is roasted locally and is fair-trade, organic, shade grown and bird friendly. Tomatoes are also fair trade. All bakery items and grab and go sandwiches are purchased from local vendors. 50% of daily meals served in the dining halls are vegetarian and Meatless Mondays are run every Monday. Green building and construction commitment: LEED Silver baseline commitment for all new construction that includes 4 LEED Gold Buildings; LEED for Neighborhood Development pilot program for 17 acre campus expansion. Columbia's robust surplus reuse program diverts furniture and equipment from landfill as well as achieves a 90% construction recycling rate for recent LEED projects. The model clean construction program has significantly reduced particulates and other pollutants that are a contributor to Harlem's high asthma rates. http://news.columbia.edu/newyorkstories/2477 http://www.environment.columbia.edu/reuse Columbia is the leading U.S. research and educational institution on the environment and climate change. Twenty-four environmental degree granting programs including a sustainable development major; 33 environmental research centers, home of the Earth Institute and the Lamont Doherty Earth Observatory, also NASA/GISS—Columbia University is one of the worlds leading research institutions on climate and earth systems; The term global warming was coined at Columbia and the phenomanom of El Nino was discovered here.

ADMISSIONS
Freshman Academic Profile: Average high school GPA 3.89. SAT Math middle 50% range 670-760. SAT Critical Reading middle 50% range 650-760. SAT Writing middle 50% range 665-760. ACT middle 50% range 29.5-34. Minimum paper TOEFL 600. **Basis for Candidate Selection:** *Very important factors considered include:* Class rank, academic GPA, rigor of secondary school record, standardized test scores. *Important factors considered include:* application essay, recommendation(s). *Other factors considered include:* alumni/ae relation, extracurricular activities, talent/ability. **Freshman Admission Requirements:** High school diploma is required and GED is accepted. *Academic units required:* 4 English, 3 mathematics, 2 science, (2 science labs), 2 foreign language, 2 history, 1 academic electives. **Freshman Admission Statistics:** 602 applied, 34% admitted, 59% enrolled. **Transfer Admission Requirements:** High school transcript, college transcript(s), Lowest grade transferable C. **General Admission Information:** Application Fee $20. Nonfall registration accepted.

COSTS AND FINANCIAL AID
Required Forms and Deadlines: FAFSA, Institution's own financial aid form. **Notification of Awards:** Applicants will be notified of awards on a rolling basis beginning 5/1. **Types of Aid:** *Need-based scholarships/grants:* Federal Pell, SEOG, state scholarships/grants, private scholarships. *Loans:* Direct Subsidized Stafford, Direct Unsubsidized Stafford, Direct PLUS, Subsidized Stafford, Unsubsidized Stafford, PLUS, Federal Perkins. **Financial Aid Statistics:** 70% undergrads receive any aid. **Criteria for awarding institutional aid:** *Non-need-based:* academics, alumni affiliation, art, athletics, leadership, music/drama, state/district residency.

See page 1036.

COLUMBUS COLLEGE OF ART AND DESIGN

Admissions, Columbus, OH 43215-3875
Phone: 614-222-3261 · **Financial Aid Phone:** 614-222-3295
E-mail: admissions@ccad.edu · **CEEB Code:** 1085
Fax: 614-232-8344 · **Website:** www.ccad.edu · **ACT Code:** 3281

This private school was founded in 1879. It has a 17-acre campus.

RATINGS
Admissions Selectivity Rating: 73   Fire Safety Rating: 86

STUDENTS AND FACULTY
Enrollment: 1,261. **Student Body:** 62% female, 38% male, 27% out-of-state, 8% international (35 countries represented). Asian 3%, African American 8%, Caucasian 69%, Hispanic 5%, Native American <1%
Retention and Graduation: 78% freshmen return for sophomore year. 47% freshmen graduate within 4 years. 8% grads go on to further study within 1 year. 7% grads pursue arts and sciences degrees. 1% grads pursue medical degrees. **Faculty:** 72 full-time faculty, 69% hold PhDs, 38% are members of minority groups, 7% are women. 0% of classes are taught by teaching assistants.

ACADEMICS
Degrees: bachelor's. **Majors with Highest Enrollment:** Graphic Design; Illustration. **Special Study Options:** cooperative education program, cross-registration, internships, study abroad, Undergrads may take grad level classes.

Other Special Programs: Evening classes for credit. Saturday School (ages 6-18). **Career services:** career/job search classes, internships.

FACILITIES
Housing: Coed dorms **Special Academic Facilities/Equipment:** Student art exhibition hall, gallery, auditorium, recreation center.

CAMPUS LIFE
Activities: literary magazine, student government, student newspaper. 2 registered organizations, 1 religious organization.

ADMISSIONS
Freshman Academic Profile: Average high school GPA 3.15. 6% in top 10% of high school class, 18% in top 25% of high school class, 59% in top 50% of high school class. SAT Math middle 50% range 450-570. SAT Critical Reading middle 50% range 470-610. SAT Writing middle 50% range 460-580. ACT middle 50% range 19-25. Minimum internet-based TOEFL 173. Minimum paper TOEFL 500. **Basis for Candidate Selection:** *Very important factors considered include:* rigor of secondary school record, talent/ability. *Important factors considered include:* application essay, recommendation(s), standardized test scores, character/personal qualities, interview. *Other factors considered include:* Class rank, extracurricular activities. **Freshman Admission Requirements:** High school diploma is required and GED is accepted. **Freshman Admission Statistics:** 666 applied, 87% admitted, 40% enrolled. **Transfer Admission Requirements:** High school transcript, college transcript(s), essay or personal statement, Minimum college GPA of 2.0 required. Lowest grade transferable C. **General Admission Information:** Application Fee $25. Nonfall registration accepted. Admission may be deferred for a maximum of 1 year. Credit and/or placement offered for CEEB Advanced Placement tests.

COSTS AND FINANCIAL AID
Average book expense $4,000. **Required Forms and Deadlines:** FAFSA. **Notification of Awards:** Applicants will be notified of awards on or about 6/15. **Types of Aid:** *Need-based scholarships/grants:* Federal Pell, SEOG, state scholarships/grants, private scholarships, the school's own gift aid. *Loans:* Subsidized Stafford, Unsubsidized Stafford, PLUS, Federal Perkins, state loans. *Student Employment:* Federal Work-Study Program available. Institutional employment available. Highest amount earned per year from on-campus jobs $2,500. Off-campus job opportunities are excellent. **Financial Aid Statistics:** 100% freshmen, 98% undergrads receive need-based scholarship or grant aid. 4% freshmen, 3% undergrads receive non-need-based scholarship or grant aid. 84% freshmen, 83% undergrads receive need-based self-help aid. 0% freshmen, 0% undergrads receive athletic scholarships. 74% freshmen, 81% undergrads receive any aid. 94% undergrads borrow to pay for school. Average cumulative indebtedness $22,050. **Criteria for awarding institutional aid:** *Non-need-based:* academics, art.

COLUMBUS STATE UNIVERSITY

4225 University Avenue, Columbus, GA 31907-5645
Phone: 706-568-2035 · **Financial Aid Phone:** 706-507-8800
E-mail: admissions@colstate.edu
Fax: 706-568-5091 · **Website:** www.columbusstate.edu

This public school was founded in 1958. It has a 150-acre campus.

RATINGS
Admissions Selectivity Rating: 74   **Fire Safety Rating:** 78

STUDENTS AND FACULTY
Enrollment: 6,890. **Student Body:** 60% female, 40% male, 14% out-of-state, 1% international (67 countries represented). Asian 2%, African American 35%, Caucasian 55%, Hispanic 4%, Native American 1%
Retention and Graduation: 69% freshmen return for sophomore year. 12% freshmen graduate within 4 years. **Faculty:** 279 full-time faculty, 78% hold PhDs, 43% are members of minority groups, 23% are women. 0% of classes are taught by teaching assistants.

ACADEMICS
Degrees: bachelor's, certificate, doctoral, master's, post-master's certificate, terminal associate, transfer associate. **Classes:** Most classes have 20–29 students. Most lab/discussion sessions have 10–19 students. **Majors with Highest Enrollment:** Registered Nursing/Registered Nurse; Early Childhood Education and Teaching; Business/Commerce. **Special Study Options:** Accelerated program, cooperative education program, distance learning, double major, dual enrollment, English as a Second Language (ESL), honors program, independent study, internships, liberal arts/career combination, study abroad, teacher certification program. **Honors programs:** Honors Program Servant Leadership

Program. **Disability Services:** Special programs offered to physically disabled students include note-taking services, reader services, tape recorders, tutors. **Career services:** Alumni network, alumni services, career/job search classes, career assessment, internships, regional alumni. Career services highlights include internships and experiential learning via volunteer placements in the community.

FACILITIES
Housing: special housing for disabled students, special housing for international students, apartments for married students, apartments for single students, Theme Housing. 100% of campus accessible to physically disabled. **Computers:** 80% of classrooms, 100% of libraries, 100% of dining areas, 100% of student union, 25% of common outdoor areas have wireless network access. Students can register for classes online. Administrative functions (other than registration) can be performed online.

CAMPUS LIFE
Environment: City. **Activities:** Choral groups, concert band, dance, drama/theater, jazz band, literary magazine, music ensembles, musical theater, pep band, student government, student newspaper, symphony orchestra, Campus Ministries, International Student Organization, Model UN. 90 registered organizations, 22 honor societies, 10 religious organizations. 7 fraternities, 6 sororities. **Athletics (Intercollegiate):** *Men:* baseball, basketball, cheerleading, cross-country, golf, riflery, tennis. *Women:* basketball, cheerleading, cross-country, golf, riflery, soccer, softball, tennis. **On-Campus Highlights:** Einstein Bos. Bagels, RiverPark Campus, Davidson Student Center, Lumpkin Center, Coca Cola Space Science Center. **Environmental Initiatives:** Green Seal Cleaning Products Recycling of paper, plastic, & aluminum cans Energy efficient equipment upgrades throughout campus.

ADMISSIONS
Freshman Academic Profile: Average high school GPA 2.96. SAT Math middle 50% range 420-540. SAT Critical Reading middle 50% range 430-550. SAT Writing middle 50% range 420-530. ACT middle 50% range 17-22. Minimum internet-based TOEFL 79. Minimum paper TOEFL 550. **Basis for Candidate Selection:** *Very important factors considered include:* rigor of secondary school record. *Important factors considered include:* academic GPA, standardized test scores. *Other factors considered include:* extracurricular activities, geographical residence, interview, talent/ability. **Freshman Admission Requirements:** High school diploma is required and GED is not accepted. *Academic units required:* 4 English, 4 mathematics, 3 science, (2 science labs), 2 foreign language, 3 social studies. **Freshman Admission Statistics:** 3,454 applied, 60% admitted, 60% enrolled. **Transfer Admission Requirements:** college transcript(s), statement of good standing from prior institution(s). Minimum college GPA of 2.00 required. Lowest grade transferable D. **General Admission Information:** Application Fee $30. Regular application deadline 6/30. Notification on a rolling basis, beginning on or about 9/1. Nonfall registration accepted. Admission may be deferred for a maximum of One year. Credit and/or placement offered for CEEB Advanced Placement tests.

COSTS AND FINANCIAL AID
Annual in-state tuition $4,596. Annual out-of-state tuition $16,572. Room and board $7,280. Required fees $1,300. Average book expense $1,072. **Required Forms and Deadlines:** FAFSA. **Notification of Awards:** Applicants will be notified of awards on a rolling basis beginning 5/15. **Types of Aid:** *Need-based scholarships/grants:* Federal Pell, SEOG, state scholarships/grants, private scholarships, the school's own gift aid. *Loans:* Direct Subsidized Stafford, Direct Unsubsidized Stafford, Direct PLUS, Federal Perkins, Federal Nursing, state loans, college/university loans from institutional funds. *Student Employment:* Federal Work-Study Program available. Institutional employment available. Off-campus job opportunities are good. **Financial Aid Statistics:** 71% freshmen, 72% undergrads receive need-based scholarship or grant aid. 50% freshmen, 33% undergrads receive non-need-based scholarship or grant aid. 66% freshmen, 72% undergrads receive need-based self-help aid. 4% freshmen, 4% undergrads receive athletic scholarships. 87% freshmen, 78% undergrads receive any aid. 63% undergrads borrow to pay for school. Average cumulative indebtedness $21,595. **Criteria for awarding institutional aid:** *Non-need-based:* academics, alumni affiliation, art, athletics, job skills, leadership, minority status, music/drama.

CONCEPTION SEMINARY COLLEGE

P.O. Box 502, Conception, MO 64433
Phone: 660-944-2886
E-mail: vocations@conception.edu
Fax: 660-944-2829 • **Website:** www.conception.edu • **ACT Code:** 2280

This private school, affiliated with the Roman Catholic Church, was founded in 1886. It has a 30-acre campus.

RATINGS

Admissions Selectivity Rating: 69   **Fire Safety Rating:** 60*

STUDENTS AND FACULTY

Enrollment: 96. **Student Body:** 0% female, 100% male, 73% out-of-state, 5% international. Asian 10%, African American 0%, Caucasian 56%, Hispanic 2%, Native American <1%
Retention and Graduation: 50% freshmen return for sophomore year. 60% grads go on to further study within 1 year. **Faculty:** 20 full-time faculty, 85% hold PhDs, 15% are members of minority groups, 10% are women. 0% of classes are taught by teaching assistants.

ACADEMICS

Degrees: bachelor's, certificate. **Special Study Options:** double major, English as a Second Language (ESL), independent study.

FACILITIES

Housing: men's dorms. **Computers:** Administrative functions (other than registration) can be performed online.

CAMPUS LIFE

Environment: Rural. **Activities:** drama/theater, music ensembles, student government, student newspaper, yearbook. 12 registered organizations. **Athletics (Intercollegiate):** *Men:* soccer, volleyball.

ADMISSIONS

Freshman Academic Profile: ACT middle 50% range 12-29. **Basis for Candidate Selection:** *Very important factors considered include:* application essay, recommendation(s), religious affiliation/commitment. *Important factors considered include:* rigor of secondary school record, standardized test scores, character/personal qualities, talent/ability. *Other factors considered include:* Class rank, extracurricular activities, interview, volunteer work, work experience. **Freshman Admission Requirements:** High school diploma is required and GED is accepted. *Academic units required:* 4 English, 4 science, 4 social studies. **Freshman Admission Statistics:** 17 applied, 100% admitted, 100% enrolled. **Transfer Admission Requirements:** college transcript(s), essay or personal statement, Minimum college GPA of 2.0 required. Lowest grade transferable C. **General Admission Information:** Regular application deadline 8/15. Notification on a rolling basis, beginning on or about 1/1. Nonfall registration accepted. Admission may be deferred for a maximum of 1 year.

COSTS AND FINANCIAL AID

Required Forms and Deadlines: FAFSA. **Financial Aid Statistics:** 73% freshmen, 81% undergrads receive need-based scholarship or grant aid. 27% freshmen, 47% undergrads receive non-need-based scholarship or grant aid. 27% freshmen, 49% undergrads receive need-based self-help aid. 0% freshmen, 0% undergrads receive athletic scholarships. 33% undergrads borrow to pay for school. **Criteria for awarding institutional aid:** *Non-need-based:* academics.

CONCORD UNIVERSITY

1000 Vermillion Street, Athens, WV 24712
Phone: 304-384-5248 • **Financial Aid Phone:** 304-384-6069
E-mail: admissions@concord.edu • **CEEB Code:** 5120
Fax: 304-384-9044 • **Website:** www.concord.edu • **ACT Code:** 3810

This public school was founded in 1872. It has a 123-acre campus.

RATINGS

Admissions Selectivity Rating: 82   **Fire Safety Rating:** 86

STUDENTS AND FACULTY

Enrollment: 2,611. **Student Body:** 55% female, 45% male, 18% out-of-state, 0% international (16 countries represented). Asian 2%, African American 7%, Caucasian 100%, Hispanic 1%, Native American <1%
Retention and Graduation: 65% freshmen return for sophomore year. 15% freshmen graduate within 4 years. 39% freshmen graduate within 6 years. 33%

grads go on to further study within 1 year. 8% grads pursue arts and sciences degrees. 2% grads pursue law degrees. 10% grads pursue business degrees. 3% grads pursue medical degrees. **Faculty:** 121 full-time faculty, 64% hold PhDs, 41% are members of minority groups, 3% are women.

ACADEMICS

Degrees: associate, bachelor's, master's, terminal associate. **Classes:** Most classes have fewer than 10 students. Most lab/discussion sessions have 10–19 students. **Majors with Highest Enrollment:** Education; Business Administration and Management; Social Sciences. **Special Study Options:** cooperative education program, double major, dual enrollment, English as a Second Language (ESL), honors program, student-designed major, teacher certification program. **Career services:** alumni services, career/job search classes, career assessment, internships.

FACILITIES

Housing: Coed dorms, special housing for disabled students, men's dorms, special housing for international students, women's dorms, apartments for married students. 100% of campus accessible to physically disabled. **Computers:** 50% of classrooms, 20% of dorms, 100% of libraries, 100% of dining areas, 100% of student union, 50% of common outdoor areas have wireless network access. Students can register for classes online. Administrative functions (other than registration) can be performed online.

CAMPUS LIFE

Environment: Rural. **Activities:** Choral groups, concert band, drama/theater, jazz band, pep band, radio station, student government, student newspaper, student-run film society, television station, yearbook. 57 registered organizations, 1 honor society, 2 religious organizations. 6 fraternities, 4 sororities. **Athletics (Intercollegiate):** *Men:* baseball, basketball, cheerleading, cross-country, football, golf, soccer, tennis, track/field (outdoor). *Women:* basketball, cheerleading, cross-country, golf, soccer, softball, tennis, track/field (outdoor), volleyball. **On-Campus Highlights:** Rahall Technology Ctr, 48 Bell Carillon, University Point, Beasley Student Ctr., Callaghan Stadium.

ADMISSIONS

Freshman Academic Profile: Average high school GPA 3.2. 18% in top 10% of high school class, 45% in top 25% of high school class, 73% in top 50% of high school class. 95% from public high schools. SAT Math middle 50% range 420-520. SAT Critical Reading middle 50% range 420-540. ACT middle 50% range 17-25. Minimum paper TOEFL 500. **Basis for Candidate Selection:** *Very important factors considered include:* rigor of secondary school record. *Important factors considered include:* Class rank, standardized test scores, extracurricular activities. *Other factors considered include:* application essay, recommendation(s), alumni/ae relation, character/personal qualities, geographical residence, interview, racial/ethnic status, talent/ability, volunteer work, work experience. **Freshman Admission Requirements:** High school diploma is required and GED is accepted. *Academic units required:* 4 English, 2 mathematics, 2 science, (2 science labs), 2 social studies, 1 history, 6 academic electives. **Freshman Admission Statistics:** 2,290 applied, 61% admitted, 41% enrolled. **Transfer Admission Requirements:** college transcript(s), Lowest grade transferable D. **General Admission Information:** Notification on a rolling basis, beginning on or about 9/1. Nonfall registration accepted. Admission may be deferred for a maximum of 1 YEAR. Credit and/or placement offered for CEEB Advanced Placement tests.

COSTS AND FINANCIAL AID

Annual out-of-state tuition $11,050. Room and board $6,962. Required fees $85. Average book expense $1,100. **Required Forms and Deadlines:** FAFSA, Institution's own financial aid form. **Notification of Awards:** Applicants will be notified of awards on a rolling basis beginning 3/1. **Types of Aid:** *Need-based scholarships/grants:* Federal Pell, SEOG, state scholarships/grants, the school's own gift aid. *Loans:* Subsidized Stafford, Unsubsidized Stafford, PLUS, Federal Perkins. *Student Employment:* Federal Work-Study Program available. Institutional employment available. Highest amount earned per year from on-campus jobs $1,343. Off-campus job opportunities are excellent. **Financial Aid Statistics:** 84% freshmen, 83% undergrads receive need-based scholarship or grant aid. 52% freshmen, 36% undergrads receive non-need-based scholarship or grant aid. 73% freshmen, 74% undergrads receive need-based self-help aid. 5% freshmen, 4% undergrads receive athletic scholarships. 90% freshmen, 77% undergrads receive any aid. 85% undergrads borrow to pay for school. Average cumulative indebtedness $14,760. **Criteria for awarding institutional aid:** *Non-need-based:* academics, alumni affiliation, art, athletics, job skills, leadership, minority status, music/drama, state/district residency.

CONCORDIA COLLEGE (MOORHEAD, MN)

901 Eighth Street South, Moorhead, MN 56562
Phone: 218-299-3004
E-mail: admissions@cord.edu · **CEEB Code:** 6113
Fax: 218-299-4720 · **Website:** www.goconcordia.com · **ACT Code:** 2104

This private school, affiliated with the Lutheran Church, was founded in 1891. It has a 120-acre campus.

RATINGS

Admissions Selectivity Rating: 83   **Fire Safety Rating:** 63

STUDENTS AND FACULTY

Enrollment: 2,793. **Student Body:** 63% female, 37% male, 33% out-of-state, 6% international (42 countries represented). Asian 2%, African American 1%, Caucasian 92%, Hispanic 1%, Native American <1%
Retention and Graduation: 80% freshmen return for sophomore year. 57% freshmen graduate within 4 years. 66% freshmen graduate within 6 years. 20% grads go on to further study within 1 year. 9% grads pursue arts and sciences degrees. 4% grads pursue law degrees. 3% grads pursue business degrees. 4% grads pursue medical degrees. **Faculty:** 175 full-time faculty, 78% hold PhDs, 45% are members of minority groups, 3% are women. 0% of classes are taught by teaching assistants.

ACADEMICS

Degrees: bachelor's, master's. **Classes:** Most classes have 20–29 students. **Special Study Options:** cooperative education program, double major, exchange student program (domestic), honors program, independent study, internships, liberal arts/career combination, study abroad, teacher certification program. Combined degree programs: BA/BS Engineering NOSU, U of Minnesota Institute o. **Disability Services:** Special programs offered to physically disabled students include note-taking services, reader services, tape recorders, tutors. **Career services:** Alumni network, alumni services, career/job search classes, career assessment, internships.

FACILITIES

Housing: Coed dorms, special housing for disabled students, men's dorms, women's dorms, apartments for single students, French, German, and Spanish language houses. 95% of campus accessible to physically disabled. **Special Academic Facilities/Equipment:** Cyrus M. Running Gallery. **Computers:** Administrative functions (other than registration) can be performed online.

CAMPUS LIFE

Environment: City. **Activities:** Choral groups, concert band, dance, drama/theater, jazz band, literary magazine, music ensembles, musical theater, pep band, radio station, student government, student newspaper, symphony orchestra, television station, yearbook. 80 registered organizations, 22 honor societies, 12 religious organizations. 2 fraternities, 2 sororities. **Athletics (Intercollegiate):** *Men:* baseball, basketball, cross-country, football, golf, ice hockey, soccer, tennis, track/field (outdoor), track/field (indoor), wrestling. *Women:* basketball, cross-country, diving, golf, ice hockey, soccer, softball, swimming, tennis, track/field (outdoor), track/field (indoor), volleyball.

ADMISSIONS

Freshman Academic Profile: 31% in top 10% of high school class, 62% in top 25% of high school class, 89% in top 50% of high school class. SAT Math middle 50% range 520-630. SAT Critical Reading middle 50% range 530-650. ACT middle 50% range 21-27. Minimum paper TOEFL 550. **Basis for Candidate Selection:** *Very important factors considered include:* rigor of secondary school record. *Important factors considered include:* Class rank, recommendation(s). *Other factors considered include:* standardized test scores, alumni/ae relation, character/personal qualities, extracurricular activities, racial/ethnic status, talent/ability, volunteer work. **Freshman Admission Requirements:** High school diploma is required and GED is accepted. **Freshman Admission Statistics:** 2,444 applied, 86% admitted, 37% enrolled. **Transfer Admission Requirements:** college transcript(s), Minimum college GPA of 2.0 required. Lowest grade transferable C-. **General Admission Information:** Application Fee $20. Nonfall registration accepted. Admission may be deferred for a maximum of 1. Credit and/or placement offered for CEEB Advanced Placement tests.

COSTS AND FINANCIAL AID

Average book expense $700. *Student Employment:* Federal Work-Study Program available. Institutional employment available. Off-campus job opportunities are excellent. **Financial Aid Statistics:** 97% freshmen, 94% undergrads receive any aid.

CONCORDIA COLLEGE (NY)

171 White Plains Road, Bronxville, NY 10708
Phone: 914-337-9300
E-mail: admission@concordia-ny.edu · **CEEB Code:** 2096
Fax: 914-395-4636 · **Website:** www.concordia-ny.edu · **ACT Code:** 2722

This private school, affiliated with the Lutheran Church, was founded in 1881. It has a 33-acre campus.

RATINGS

Admissions Selectivity Rating: 67   **Fire Safety Rating:** 60*

STUDENTS AND FACULTY

Enrollment: 0. **Student Body:** 27% out-of-state, (36 countries represented). **Retention and Graduation:** 69% freshmen return for sophomore year. 40% grads go on to further study within 1 year. 30% grads pursue arts and sciences degrees. 2% grads pursue law degrees. 30% grads pursue business degrees. 10% grads pursue medical degrees. **Faculty:** 54 full-time faculty. 0% of classes are taught by teaching assistants.

ACADEMICS

Degrees: associate, bachelor's. **Classes:** Most classes have 10–19 students. Most lab/discussion sessions have 10–19 students. **Majors with Highest Enrollment:** Education; Social Sciences; Business/Commerce. **Special Study Options:** Accelerated program, cooperative education program, cross-registration, double major, English as a Second Language (ESL), exchange student program (domestic), honors program, independent study, internships, liberal arts/career combination, student-designed major, study abroad, teacher certification program. **Disability Services:** Special programs offered to physically disabled students include reader services, tutors. **Career services:** career/job search classes, career assessment, internships.

FACILITIES

Housing: men's dorms, women's dorms. 50% of campus accessible to physically disabled. **Special Academic Facilities/Equipment:** Art gallery, center for worship and performing arts, English language center, distance learning classroom.

CAMPUS LIFE

Environment: Village. **Activities:** Choral groups, concert band, drama/theater, jazz band, literary magazine, music ensembles, musical theater, student government, student newspaper, yearbook. 35 registered organizations, 1 honor society, 3 religious organizations. **Athletics (Intercollegiate):** *Men:* baseball, basketball, soccer, tennis, volleyball. *Women:* basketball, soccer, softball, tennis, volleyball.

ADMISSIONS

Freshman Academic Profile: Average high school GPA 2.7. 60% from public high schools. SAT Math middle 50% range 415-505. SAT Critical Reading middle 50% range 420-500. SAT Writing middle 50% range 415-480. ACT middle 50% range 16-20. Minimum paper TOEFL 550. **Basis for Candidate Selection:** *Very important factors considered include:* rigor of secondary school record. *Important factors considered include:* Class rank, standardized test scores, character/personal qualities, interview. *Other factors considered include:* application essay, recommendation(s), alumni/ae relation, extracurricular activities, religious affiliation/commitment, talent/ability, volunteer work, work experience. **Freshman Admission Requirements:** High school diploma is required and GED is accepted. *Academic units required:* 4 English, 3 mathematics, 2 science, (2 science labs), 2 foreign language, 2 social studies, 2 history. **Transfer Admission Requirements:** High school transcript, college transcript(s), statement of good standing from prior institution(s). Minimum college GPA of 2.0 required. Lowest grade transferable C. **General Admission Information:** Application Fee $40. Regular application deadline 3/15. Notification on a rolling basis, beginning on or about 1/15. Nonfall registration accepted. Admission may be deferred for a maximum of 12. Credit and/or placement offered for CEEB Advanced Placement tests.

COSTS AND FINANCIAL AID

Annual tuition $27,740. Room and board $10,265. Required fees $1,030. Average book expense $1,000. *Student Employment:* Federal Work-Study Program available. Institutional employment available. Highest amount earned per year from on-campus jobs $2,000. Off-campus job opportunities are excellent.

CONCORDIA UNIVERSITY (OR)

2811 NE Holman St, Portland, OR 97211-6099
Phone: 503-280-8501 · **Financial Aid Phone:** 800-321-9371
E-mail: admissions@cu-portland.edu · **CEEB Code:** 4078
Fax: 503-280-8531 · **Website:** www.cu-portland.edu · **ACT Code:** 3458

This private school, affiliated with the Lutheran Church, was founded in 1905. It has a 12-acre campus.

RATINGS

Admissions Selectivity Rating: 84   **Fire Safety Rating:** 60*

STUDENTS AND FACULTY

Enrollment: 1,073. **Student Body:** 64% female, 36% male, 41% out-of-state, 1% international. Asian 6%, African American 7%, Caucasian 65%, Hispanic 6%, Native American 1%
Retention and Graduation: 74% freshmen return for sophomore year. 41% freshmen graduate within 6 years. **Faculty:** 52 full-time faculty, 67% hold PhDs, 48% are members of minority groups, 4% are women. 0% of classes are taught by teaching assistants.

ACADEMICS

Degrees: bachelor's, certificate, master's, post-bachelor's certificate, terminal associate. **Classes:** Most classes have 10–19 students. **Special Study Options:** Accelerated program, cross-registration, distance learning, dual enrollment, English as a Second Language (ESL), honors program, independent study, internships, study abroad, teacher certification program. **Honors programs:** Honors program features limited enrollment to 25 students create greater intellectual opportunity. **Career services:** alumni services, career assessment, internships, regional alumni. Career services highlights include the Concordia Commitment, which offers students who complete the 4-year program partial tuition reimbursement if they are not employed in the field of their choice 6 months after graduation.

FACILITIES

Housing: Coed dorms, apartments for single students. **Computers:** Administrative functions (other than registration) can be performed online.

CAMPUS LIFE

Environment: Metropolis. **Activities:** Choral groups, drama/theater, literary magazine, music ensembles, student government, student newspaper, Campus Ministries, International Student Organization. 10 registered organizations, 2 honor societies, 1 religious organization. **Athletics (Intercollegiate):** *Men:* baseball, basketball, cross-country, golf, soccer, track/field (outdoor), track/field (indoor). *Women:* basketball, cross-country, golf, soccer, softball, track/field (outdoor), track/field (indoor), volleyball.

ADMISSIONS

Freshman Academic Profile: Average high school GPA 3.4. 19% in top 10% of high school class, 45% in top 25% of high school class, 76% in top 50% of high school class. SAT Math middle 50% range 460-560. SAT Critical Reading middle 50% range 450-570. ACT middle 50% range 18-24. Minimum paper TOEFL 500. **Basis for Candidate Selection:** *Very important factors considered include:* recommendation(s), rigor of secondary school record, standardized test scores. *Other factors considered include:* Class rank, application essay, academic GPA, character/personal qualities, interview. **Freshman Admission Requirements:** High school diploma is required and GED is accepted. **Freshman Admission Statistics:** 1,002 applied, 59% admitted, 32% enrolled. **Transfer Admission Requirements:** college transcript(s), statement of good standing from prior institution(s). Minimum college GPA of 2.0 required. Lowest grade transferable D. **General Admission Information:** Application Fee $20. Regular application deadline 7/1. Notification on a rolling basis, beginning on or about 1/1. Nonfall registration accepted. Admission may be deferred for a maximum of 1.

COSTS AND FINANCIAL AID

Annual tuition $20,900. Room and board $6,270. Required fees $210. Average book expense $800. **Required Forms and Deadlines:** FAFSA. **Notification of Awards:** Applicants will be notified of awards on a rolling basis beginning 3/15. **Types of Aid:** *Need-based scholarships/grants:* Federal Pell, SEOG, state scholarships/grants, the school's own gift aid. *Loans:* Subsidized Stafford, Unsubsidized Stafford, PLUS, Federal Perkins. *Student Employment:* Federal Work-Study Program available. Institutional employment available. Off-campus job opportunities are good. **Financial Aid Statistics:** 83% freshmen, 81% undergrads receive need-based scholarship or grant aid. 91% freshmen, 88% undergrads receive non-need-based scholarship or grant aid. 77% freshmen, 78% undergrads receive need-based self-help aid. 28% freshmen, 27% undergrads receive athletic scholarships. 95 78% undergrads borrow to pay for school. Average cumulative indebtedness $18,328. **Criteria for awarding institu-**

CONCORDIA UNIVERSITY AT AUSTIN

tional aid: *Non-need-based:* academics, athletics, leadership, music/drama, religious affiliation.

3400 I-35 N, Austin, TX 78705
Phone: 512-486-1106 · **Financial Aid Phone:** 512-486-2000
E-mail: admissions@concordia.edu · **CEEB Code:** 6127
Fax: 512-486-1350 · **Website:** www.concordia.edu · **ACT Code:** 4124

This private school, affiliated with the Lutheran Church, was founded in 1926. It has a 23-acre campus.

RATINGS

Admissions Selectivity Rating: 73   **Fire Safety Rating:** 61

STUDENTS AND FACULTY

Enrollment: 966. **Student Body:** 56% female, 44% male, 7% out-of-state, 1% international (10 countries represented). Asian 2%, African American 9%, Caucasian 67%, Hispanic 14%, Native American 1%
Retention and Graduation: 56% freshmen return for sophomore year. 12% freshmen graduate within 4 years. 22% freshmen graduate within 6 years. 12% grads go on to further study within 1 year. 9% grads pursue arts and sciences degrees. 1% grads pursue law degrees. 2% grads pursue business degrees. **Faculty:** 33 full-time faculty, 70% hold PhDs, 36% are members of minority groups, 6% are women. 0% of classes are taught by teaching assistants.

ACADEMICS

Degrees: associate, bachelor's, certificate, diploma, master's, post-bachelor's certificate. **Classes:** Most classes have 10–19 students. Most lab/discussion sessions have 20–29 students. **Majors with Highest Enrollment:** Elementary Education and Teaching; Biology; Business/Commerce. **Special Study Options:** Accelerated program, cooperative education program, cross-registration, distance learning, double major, dual enrollment, exchange student program (domestic), external degree program, honors program, independent study, internships, study abroad, teacher certification program. **Honors programs:** Honors Program.

FACILITIES

Housing: Coed dorms, men's dorms, women's dorms. 95% of campus accessible to physically disabled.

CAMPUS LIFE

Environment: Metropolis. **Activities:** Choral groups, drama/theater, jazz band, literary magazine, music ensembles, student government, yearbook. 20 registered organizations, 4 honor societies, 5 religious organizations. **Athletics (Intercollegiate):** *Men:* baseball, basketball, cross-country, golf, rugby, soccer, tennis. *Women:* basketball, cross-country, golf, soccer, softball, tennis, volleyball. **On-Campus Highlights:** Oliver R. Harms Residential Suites (opened in 2001), Bokenkamp Student Center, Louise T Peter Center-communication and Fine Arts, Woltman Activity Center-Gymnasium, Texas Hall-Dining Facility.

ADMISSIONS

Freshman Academic Profile: Average high school GPA 3.14. 8% in top 10% of high school class, 26% in top 25% of high school class, 60% in top 50% of high school class. 86% from public high schools. SAT Math middle 50% range 450-550. SAT Critical Reading middle 50% range 430-500. ACT middle 50% range 18-24. **Basis for Candidate Selection:** *Very important factors considered include:* rigor of secondary school record, standardized test scores. *Other factors considered include:* Class rank, application essay, recommendation(s). **Freshman Admission Requirements:** High school diploma is required and GED is accepted. **Freshman Admission Statistics:** 523 applied, 76% admitted, 40% enrolled. **Transfer Admission Requirements:** college transcript(s), Minimum college GPA of 2.0 required. Lowest grade transferable C. **General Admission Information:** Application Fee $25. Nonfall registration accepted. Credit offered for CEEB Advanced Placement tests.

COSTS AND FINANCIAL AID

Required Forms and Deadlines: FAFSA, Institution's own financial aid form. **Notification of Awards:** Applicants will be notified of awards on a rolling basis beginning 2/1. **Types of Aid:** *Need-based scholarships/grants:* Federal Pell, SEOG, state scholarships/grants, the school's own gift aid. *Loans:* Subsidized Stafford, Unsubsidized Stafford, PLUS, state loans. *Student Employment:* Federal Work-Study Program available. Highest amount earned per year from on-campus jobs $1,000. Off-campus job opportunities are excellent. **Financial Aid Statistics:** 83% freshmen, 83% undergrads receive need-based scholarship or grant aid. 81% freshmen, 57% undergrads receive non-need-based scholarship or grant aid. 75% freshmen, 74% undergrads receive need-based self-help aid. 0% freshmen, 0% undergrads receive athletic scholarships.85% undergrads receive any aid. 54% undergrads borrow to pay for school. **Criteria for awarding institutional aid:** *Non-need-based:* academics, leadership, music/drama, religious affiliation.

CONCORDIA UNIVERSITY CHICAGO

7400 Augusta Street, River Forest, IL 60305-1499
Phone: 708-209-3100 · **Financial Aid Phone:** 708-209-3113
E-mail: admission@cuchicago.edu · **CEEB Code:** 1140
Fax: 708-209-3473 · **Website:** www.CUChicago.edu · **ACT Code:** 1004

This private school, affiliated with the Lutheran Church, was founded in 1864. It has a 40-acre campus.

RATINGS

Admissions Selectivity Rating: 80   **Fire Safety Rating:** 72

STUDENTS AND FACULTY

Enrollment: 1,011. **Student Body:** 62% female, 38% male, 0% international (1 countries represented). Asian 1%, African American 13%, Caucasian 70%, Hispanic 9%, Native American <1%
Retention and Graduation: 79% freshmen return for sophomore year. 23% grads go on to further study within 1 year. **Faculty:** 99 full-time faculty. 0% of classes are taught by teaching assistants.

ACADEMICS

Degrees: bachelor's, master's, post-master's certificate. **Classes:** Most classes have 10–19 students. **Majors with Highest Enrollment:** Elementary Education and Teaching; Kinesiology and Exercise Science; Business/Commerce. **Special Study Options:** double major, exchange student program (domestic), honors program, independent study, internships, study abroad, teacher certification program. **Honors programs:** Honors Program. **Disability Services:** Special programs offered to physically disabled students include note-taking services, reader services, tape recorders, tutors. **Career services:** alumni services, career/job search classes, career assessment, internships.

FACILITIES

Housing: Coed dorms, special housing for disabled students, men's dorms, women's dorms. 74% of campus accessible to physically disabled. **Special Academic Facilities/Equipment:** Art museum, zoology exhibit, human performance lab, early childhood education lab school, TV studio, weather station, radio station. **Computers:** Students can register for classes online. Administrative functions (other than registration) can be performed online.

CAMPUS LIFE

Environment: Metropolis. **Activities:** Choral groups, concert band, dance, drama/theater, jazz band, literary magazine, music ensembles, musical theater, pep band, radio station, student government, student newspaper, television station, yearbook. 15 registered organizations, 3 honor societies, 5 religious organizations. **Athletics (Intercollegiate):** *Men:* baseball, basketball, cheerleading, cross-country, football, soccer, tennis, track/field (outdoor). *Women:* basketball, cheerleading, cross-country, soccer, softball, tennis, track/field (outdoor), volleyball. **On-Campus Highlights:** Fitness center, Soccer, football and track stadium, Library Café, Triangle, Chapel of our Lord.

ADMISSIONS

Freshman Academic Profile: Average high school GPA 3.12. 18% in top 10% of high school class, 41% in top 25% of high school class, 67% in top 50% of high school class. ACT middle 50% range 19-26. Minimum paper TOEFL 500. **Basis for Candidate Selection:** *Important factors considered include:* Class rank, academic GPA, rigor of secondary school record, standardized test scores. *Other factors considered include:* application essay, recommendation(s), character/personal qualities, extracurricular activities, interview. **Freshman Admission Requirements:** High school diploma is required and GED is accepted. *Academic units required:* 4 English, 3 mathematics, 2 science, (1 science labs), 2 social studies. **Freshman Admission Statistics:** 1,092 applied, 65% admitted, 30% enrolled. **Transfer Admission Requirements:** college transcript(s), statement of good standing from prior institution(s). Minimum college GPA of 2.0 required. Lowest grade transferable C. **General Admission Information:** Notification on a rolling basis, beginning on or about 9/4. Nonfall registration accepted. Admission may be deferred for a maximum of 1. Credit and/or placement offered for CEEB Advanced Placement tests.

COSTS AND FINANCIAL AID

Average book expense $600. *Student Employment:* Federal Work-Study Program available. Institutional employment available. Highest amount earned per year from on-campus jobs $17,000. Off-campus job opportunities are good. **Financial Aid Statistics:** 81% freshmen, 77% undergrads receive any aid.

CONCORDIA UNIVERSITY IRVINE

1530 Concordia West, Irvine, CA 92612-3299
Phone: 949-854-8002 · **Financial Aid Phone:** 949-854-8002
E-mail: admission@cui.edu
Fax: 949-854-6894 · **Website:** www.cui.edu · **ACT Code:** 227

This private school, affiliated with the Lutheran Church, was founded in 1976. It has a 70-acre campus.

RATINGS

Admissions Selectivity Rating: 83   **Fire Safety Rating:** 82

STUDENTS AND FACULTY

Enrollment: 1,203. **Student Body:** 61% female, 39% male, 17% out-of-state, 2% international (18 countries represented). Asian 4%, African American 4%, Caucasian 68%, Hispanic 13%, Native American 1%
Retention and Graduation: 73% freshmen return for sophomore year. 56% freshmen graduate within 4 years. 62% freshmen graduate within 6 years. **Faculty:** 91 full-time faculty, 67% hold PhDs, 37% are members of minority groups. 0% of classes are taught by teaching assistants.

ACADEMICS

Degrees: associate, bachelor's, master's, post-bachelor's certificate. **Classes:** Most classes have 10–19 students. **Majors with Highest Enrollment:** Liberal Arts and Sciences/Liberal Studies; Psychology; Business/Commerce. **Special Study Options:** Accelerated program, cross-registration, distance learning, double major, dual enrollment, English as a Second Language (ESL), exchange student program (domestic), honors program, independent study, internships, liberal arts/career combination, student-designed major, study abroad, teacher certification program. **Honors programs:** General Education Honor Programs Combined degree programs: BA/MA. **Disability Services:** Special programs offered to physically disabled students include tutors. **Career services:** We are proud of all the programs offered by Concordia University.

FACILITIES

Housing: special housing for disabled students, men's dorms, women's dorms. 75% of campus accessible to physically disabled. **Special Academic Facilities/Equipment:** A hi-tech Educational/Business/Technology building, which was recently completed, houses also an art gallery. **Computers:** 60% of classrooms, 100% of dorms, 95% of libraries, 70% of dining areas, 100% of student union, 10% of common outdoor areas have wireless network access. Students can register for classes online.

CAMPUS LIFE

Environment: City. **Activities:** Choral groups, concert band, dance, drama/theater, literary magazine, music ensembles, musical theater, pep band, radio station, student government, student newspaper, student-run film society, yearbook, Campus Ministries. 18 registered organizations, 5 honor societies, 8 religious organizations. **Athletics (Intercollegiate):** *Men:* baseball, basketball, cross-country, golf, soccer, swimming, tennis, track/field (outdoor), water polo. *Women:* basketball, cross-country, golf, soccer, softball, swimming, tennis, track/field (outdoor), volleyball, water polo. **On-Campus Highlights:** The Gym, Student Life Center (Lounge and computer resource), Library, CU Center (Worship Center), Student Union (cafeteria).

ADMISSIONS

Freshman Academic Profile: Average high school GPA 3.51. 20% in top 10% of high school class, 54% in top 25% of high school class, 84% in top 50% of high school class. SAT Math middle 50% range 450-570. SAT Critical Reading middle 50% range 450-570. ACT middle 50% range 20-24. Minimum paper TOEFL 550. **Basis for Candidate Selection:** *Very important factors considered include:* Class rank, academic GPA, rigor of secondary school record, standardized test scores, character/personal qualities. *Important factors considered include:* recommendation(s), religious affiliation/commitment. *Other factors considered include:* application essay, alumni/ae relation, extracurricular activities, interview, level of applicant's interest, racial/ethnic status, talent/ability, volunteer work, work experience. **Freshman Admission Requirements:** High school diploma is required and GED is accepted. *Academic units required:* 4 English, 3 mathematics, 3 science, 2 foreign language, 2 social studies. **Freshman Admission Statistics:** 827 applied, 67% admitted, 41% enrolled. **Transfer Admission Requirements:** High school transcript, college transcript(s), statement of good standing from prior institution(s). Minimum college GPA of 2.3 required. Lowest grade transferable D. **General Admission Information:** Application Fee $50. Nonfall registration accepted. Admission may be deferred for a maximum of 12 months. Credit and/or placement offered for CEEB Advanced Placement tests.

COSTS AND FINANCIAL AID

Annual tuition $23,400. Room and board $7,650. Required fees $300. **Required Forms and Deadlines:** FAFSA, Institution's own financial aid form,

State aid form. **Notification of Awards:** Applicants will be notified of awards on a rolling basis beginning 2/1. **Types of Aid:** *Need-based scholarships/grants:* Federal Pell, SEOG, state scholarships/grants, private scholarships, the school's own gift aid. *Loans:* Subsidized Stafford, Unsubsidized Stafford, PLUS. *Student Employment:* Highest amount earned per year from on-campus jobs $2,000. Off-campus job opportunities are good. **Financial Aid Statistics:** 95% freshmen, 92% undergrads receive need-based scholarship or grant aid. 18% freshmen, 13% undergrads receive non-need-based scholarship or grant aid. 71% freshmen, 76% undergrads receive need-based self-help aid. 10% freshmen, 7% undergrads receive athletic scholarships. 74% freshmen, 71% undergrads receive any aid. 67% undergrads borrow to pay for school. Average cumulative indebtedness $15,440. **Criteria for awarding institutional aid:** *Non-need-based:* academics, art, athletics, leadership, music/drama, religious affiliation.

CONCORDIA UNIVERSITY, NEBRASKA

800 North Columbia Avenue, Seward, NE 68434-1556
Phone: 800-535-5494 • **Financial Aid Phone:** 800-535-5494
E-mail: admiss@cune.edu • **CEEB Code:** 6116
Fax: 402-643-4073 • **Website:** www.cune.edu • **ACT Code:** 2442

This private school, affiliated with the Lutheran Church, was founded in 1894. It has a 120-acre campus.

RATINGS

Admissions Selectivity Rating: 82   **Fire Safety Rating:** 83

STUDENTS AND FACULTY

Enrollment: 1,232. **Student Body:** 51% female, 49% male, 54% out-of-state, 3% international (10 countries represented). Asian 2%, African American 4%, Caucasian 104%, Hispanic 1%, Native American <1%
Retention and Graduation: 80% freshmen return for sophomore year. 46% freshmen graduate within 4 years. 66% freshmen graduate within 6 years. 24% grads go on to further study within 1 year. 47% grads pursue arts and sciences degrees. 8% grads pursue business degrees. 20% grads pursue medical degrees. **Faculty:** 66 full-time faculty, 74% hold PhDs, 33% are members of minority groups, 2% are women. 0% of classes are taught by teaching assistants.

ACADEMICS

Degrees: bachelor's, master's, post-bachelor's certificate. **Classes:** Most classes have 20–29 students. Most lab/discussion sessions have 10–19 students. **Majors with Highest Enrollment:** Education; Biology/Biological Sciences; Business/Commerce. **Special Study Options:** Accelerated program, distance learning, double major, dual enrollment, English as a Second Language (ESL), exchange student program (domestic), independent study, internships, study abroad, teacher certification program, Undergradate students may take graduate level classes. **Disability Services:** Special programs offered to physically disabled students include note-taking services, reader services, tape recorders, tutors. **Career services:** Alumni network, alumni services, career/job search classes, career assessment, internships, regional alumni. Career services highlights include an intentional "4 year plan" to serve students prior to graduation.

FACILITIES

Housing: special housing for disabled students, men's dorms, women's dorms, apartments for married students, apartments for single students. 60% of campus accessible to physically disabled. **Special Academic Facilities/Equipment:** Art gallery, Bartels rock museum, observatory, arboretum **Computers:** 40% of classrooms, 100% of dorms, 100% of libraries, 100% of student union, have wireless network access. Students can register for classes online. Administrative functions (other than registration) can be performed online.

CAMPUS LIFE

Environment: Village. **Activities:** Choral groups, concert band, dance, drama/theater, jazz band, literary magazine, music ensembles, musical theater, pep band, student government, student newspaper, symphony orchestra, yearbook, Campus Ministries. 33 registered organizations, 1 honor society, 5 religious organizations. **Athletics (Intercollegiate):** *Men:* baseball, basketball, cross-country, football, golf, soccer, tennis, track/field (outdoor), track/field (indoor), wrestling. *Women:* basketball, cross-country, golf, soccer, softball, tennis, track/field (outdoor), track/field (indoor), volleyball. **On-Campus Highlights:** Student Center / Game Room, Coffee Shop, Marxhausen Art Gallery, Osten Observatory, Physical Education Building. **Environmental Initiatives:** The committee is charged with outlining short-term and long-term plans that will render the university carbon neutral as soon as is feasible and to report progress periodically. Specific plans have not yet been formulated. Purchasing "Energy Star" equipment. Incorporating sustainability in new construction and renovation projects.

ADMISSIONS

Freshman Academic Profile: Average high school GPA 3.5. 17% in top 10% of high school class, 43% in top 25% of high school class, 75% in top 50% of high school class. SAT Math middle 50% range 440-520. SAT Critical Reading middle 50% range 440-540. ACT middle 50% range 20-27. Minimum paper TOEFL 500. **Basis for Candidate Selection:** *Very important factors considered include:* academic GPA, standardized test scores. *Important factors considered include:* Class rank, rigor of secondary school record, character/personal qualities. *Other factors considered include:* recommendation(s), alumni/ae relation, extracurricular activities, interview, religious affiliation/commitment. **Freshman Admission Requirements:** High school diploma is required and GED is accepted. **Freshman Admission Statistics:** 1,428 applied, 77% admitted, 30% enrolled. **Transfer Admission Requirements:** High school transcript, college transcript(s), Minimum college GPA of 2.0 required. Lowest grade transferable D. **General Admission Information:** Regular application deadline 8/1. Notification on a rolling basis, beginning on or about 9/1. Nonfall registration accepted. Admission may be deferred for a maximum of 1 year. Credit and/or placement offered for CEEB Advanced Placement tests.

COSTS AND FINANCIAL AID

Annual tuition $26,810. Room and board $7,260. Required fees $300. Average book expense $1,000. **Required Forms and Deadlines:** FAFSA. **Notification of Awards:** Applicants will be notified of awards on a rolling basis beginning 3/1. **Types of Aid:** *Need-based scholarships/grants:* Federal Pell, SEOG, state scholarships/grants, private scholarships, the school's own gift aid. *Loans:* Subsidized Stafford, Unsubsidized Stafford, PLUS, Federal Perkins. *Student Employment:* Federal Work-Study Program available. Institutional employment available. Highest amount earned per year from on-campus jobs $3,500. Off-campus job opportunities are good. **Financial Aid Statistics:** 100% freshmen, 100% undergrads receive need-based scholarship or grant aid. 21% freshmen, 17% undergrads receive non-need-based scholarship or grant aid. 69% freshmen, 68% undergrads receive need-based self-help aid. 14% freshmen, 14% undergrads receive athletic scholarships. 100% freshmen, 99% undergrads receive any aid. 73% undergrads borrow to pay for school. Average cumulative indebtedness $26,739. **Criteria for awarding institutional aid:** *Non-need-based:* academics, alumni affiliation, art, athletics, leadership, music/drama, religious affiliation.

CONCORDIA UNIVERSITY—ST. PAUL

1282 Concordia Avenue, Saint Paul, MN 55104-5494
Phone: 651-641-8230 • **Financial Aid Phone:** 651-603-6300
E-mail: admission@csp.edu • **CEEB Code:** 6114
Fax: 651-603-6320 • **ACT Code:** 2106

This private school, affiliated with the Lutheran Church, was founded in 1893. It has a 37-acre campus.

RATINGS

Admissions Selectivity Rating: 81   **Fire Safety Rating:** 73

STUDENTS AND FACULTY

Enrollment: 2,147. **Student Body:** 58% female, 42% male, 26% out-of-state, 5% international (11 countries represented). Asian 6%, African American 13%, Caucasian 64%, Hispanic 4%, Native American 1%
Retention and Graduation: 71% freshmen return for sophomore year. 27% freshmen graduate within 4 years. 46% freshmen graduate within 6 years. **Faculty:** 88 full-time faculty, 73% hold PhDs, 45% are members of minority groups, 8% are women. 0% of classes are taught by teaching assistants.

ACADEMICS

Degrees: associate, bachelor's, certificate, master's, post-bachelor's certificate. **Classes:** Most classes have 10–19 students. **Majors with Highest Enrollment:** Criminal Justice/Safety Studies; Business/Commerce; Education. **Special Study Options:** Accelerated program, cross-registration, distance learning, double major, dual enrollment, exchange student program (domestic), honors program, independent study, internships, student-designed major, study abroad, teacher certification program. **Disability Services:** Special programs offered to physically disabled students include note-taking services, reader services, tape recorders, tutors. **Career services:** career assessment, internships.

FACILITIES

Housing: Coed dorms, men's dorms, women's dorms, apartments for married students, apartments for single students. 75% of campus accessible to physically disabled. **Computers:** Students can register for classes online. Administrative functions (other than registration) can be performed online.

CAMPUS LIFE

Environment: Metropolis. **Activities:** Choral groups, concert band, drama/theater, jazz band, music ensembles, musical theater, student government, student newspaper, television station, Campus Ministries. **Athletics (Intercollegiate):** *Men:* baseball, basketball, cross-country, football, golf, track/field (outdoor), track/field (indoor). *Women:* basketball, cross-country, golf, soccer, softball, track/field (outdoor), track/field (indoor), volleyball. **On-Campus Highlights:** Residence Life Center, Library Technology Center, Graebner Memorial Chapel, Gangelhoff Athletic Center, Pearson Theater.

ADMISSIONS

Freshman Academic Profile: Average high school GPA 3.12. 12% in top 10% of high school class, 31% in top 25% of high school class, 66% in top 50% of high school class. 90% from public high schools. ACT middle 50% range 18-24. Minimum internet-based TOEFL 65. **Basis for Candidate Selection:** *Very important factors considered include:* academic GPA, recommendation(s), standardized test scores. *Important factors considered include:* rigor of secondary school record, character/personal qualities, talent/ability. *Other factors considered include:* application essay, extracurricular activities, level of applicant's interest. **Freshman Admission Requirements:** High school diploma is required and GED is accepted. *Academic units required:* 4 English, 2 mathematics, 2 science, (2 science labs), 1 social studies, 1 history, 3 fine arts and 1 health/P.E. **Freshman Admission Statistics:** 1,435 applied, 53% admitted, 32% enrolled. **Transfer Admission Requirements:** college transcript(s), statement of good standing from prior institution(s). Minimum college GPA of 2.0 required. Lowest grade transferable D. **General Admission Information:** Application Fee $30. Regular application deadline 8/1. Nonfall registration accepted. Admission may be deferred for a maximum of 1 year. Credit and/or placement offered for CEEB Advanced Placement tests.

COSTS AND FINANCIAL AID

Annual tuition $20,750. Room and board $8,300. Required fees $0. Average book expense $2,000. **Required Forms and Deadlines:** FAFSA, State aid form. **Notification of Awards:** Applicants will be notified of awards on a rolling basis beginning 3/15. **Types of Aid:** *Need-based scholarships/grants:* Federal Pell, SEOG, state scholarships/grants, private scholarships, the school's own gift aid. *Loans:* Subsidized Stafford, Unsubsidized Stafford, PLUS, Federal Perkins, state loans. *Student Employment:* Federal Work-Study Program available. Institutional employment available. Off-campus job opportunities are fair. **Financial Aid Statistics:** 99% freshmen, 95% undergrads receive need-based scholarship or grant aid. 9% freshmen, 6% undergrads receive non-need-based scholarship or grant aid. 74% freshmen, 76% undergrads receive need-based self-help aid. 5% freshmen, 2% undergrads receive athletic scholarships. 92% freshmen, 73% undergrads receive any aid. 82% undergrads borrow to pay for school. Average cumulative indebtedness $29,890. **Criteria for awarding institutional aid:** *Non-need-based:* academics, art, athletics, minority status, music/drama, religious affiliation.

CONCORDIA UNIVERSITY WISCONSIN

12800 North Lake Shore Drive, Mequon, WI 53097-2418
Phone: 262-243-5700 · **Financial Aid Phone:** 262-243-4392
E-mail: admissions@cuw.edu · **CEEB Code:** 1139
Fax: 262-243-4545 · **Website:** www.cuw.edu · **ACT Code:** 4574

This private school, affiliated with the Lutheran Church, was founded in 1881. It has a 192-acre campus.

RATINGS

Admissions Selectivity Rating: 80   Fire Safety Rating: 60*

STUDENTS AND FACULTY

Enrollment: 4,326. **Student Body:** 65% female, 35% male, 20% out-of-state, 1% international (23 countries represented). Asian 2%, African American 18%, Caucasian 67%, Hispanic 2%, Native American 1%
Retention and Graduation: 74% freshmen return for sophomore year. 35% freshmen graduate within 4 years. 28% grads go on to further study within 1 year. **Faculty:** 162 full-time faculty, 77% hold PhDs, 49% are members of minority groups, 6% are women. 0% of classes are taught by teaching assistants.

ACADEMICS

Degrees: associate, bachelor's, certificate, master's, post-bachelor's certificate. **Classes:** Most classes have 10–19 students. Most lab/discussion sessions have 10–19 students. **Majors with Highest Enrollment:** Education; Health Services/Allied Health/Health Sciences; Business/Commerce. **Special Study Options:** Accelerated program, cross-registration, distance learning, double major, dual enrollment, English as a Second Language (ESL), exchange

student program (domestic), independent study, internships, liberal arts/career combination, student-designed major, study abroad, teacher certification program, CUW offers cooperative programs with Cardinal Stritch University, Marquette University, Milwaukee Institute of Art and Design and Alverno College. Combined degree programs: 2-2 interior design program. **Disability Services:** Special programs offered to physically disabled students include note-taking services, reader services, tape recorders, tutors. **Career services:** Alumni network, alumni services, career/job search classes, career assessment, internships, regional alumni.

FACILITIES

Housing: men's dorms, women's dorms.

CAMPUS LIFE

Environment: Village. **Activities:** Choral groups, concert band, dance, drama/theater, jazz band, music ensembles, musical theater, pep band, radio station, student government, student newspaper, Campus Ministries, International Student Organization. **Athletics (Intercollegiate):** *Men:* baseball, basketball, cross-country, football, ice hockey, soccer, tennis, track/field (outdoor), volleyball, wrestling. *Women:* basketball, cross-country, ice hockey, soccer, softball, tennis, track/field (outdoor), volleyball. **On-Campus Highlights:** Coberg Residence Hall—new, Sports and Fitness Center, Field House **Environmental Initiatives:** Construction of environmental education center with LEED status.

ADMISSIONS

Freshman Academic Profile: Average high school GPA 3.34. 16% in top 10% of high school class, 40% in top 25% of high school class, 75% in top 50% of high school class. SAT Math middle 50% range 453-600. SAT Critical Reading middle 50% range 450-530. SAT Writing middle 50% range 437-520. ACT middle 50% range 20-25. Minimum paper TOEFL 500. **Basis for Candidate Selection:** *Very important factors considered include:* application essay, academic GPA, rigor of secondary school record. *Important factors considered include:* character/personal qualities, work experience. *Other factors considered include:* Class rank, recommendation(s), standardized test scores, alumni/ae relation, extracurricular activities, interview, racial/ethnic status, religious affiliation/commitment, state residency, talent/ability, volunteer work. **Freshman Admission Requirements:** High school diploma is required and GED is accepted. *Academic units required:* 3 English, 2 mathematics, 2 science, 2 social studies, 5 academic electives. **Freshman Admission Statistics:** 2,517 applied, 70% admitted, 35% enrolled. **Transfer Admission Requirements:** college transcript(s), statement of good standing from prior institution(s). Minimum college GPA of 2.0 required. Lowest grade transferable C. **General Admission Information:** Application Fee $35. Regular application deadline 8/15. Notification on a rolling basis, beginning on or about 10/15. Nonfall registration accepted.

COSTS AND FINANCIAL AID

Required Forms and Deadlines: FAFSA. **Notification of Awards:** Applicants will be notified of awards on a rolling basis beginning 2/1. **Types of Aid:** *Need-based scholarships/grants:* Federal Pell, SEOG, state scholarships/grants, private scholarships, the school's own gift aid. *Loans:* Direct Subsidized Stafford, Direct Unsubsidized Stafford, Direct PLUS. *Student Employment:* Off-campus job opportunities are excellent. **Financial Aid Statistics:** 97% freshmen, 93% undergrads receive need-based scholarship or grant aid. 22% freshmen, 16% undergrads receive non-need-based scholarship or grant aid. 82% freshmen, 83% undergrads receive need-based self-help aid. 0% freshmen, 0% undergrads receive athletic scholarships. 95 80% undergrads borrow to pay for school. Average cumulative indebtedness $28,077.

CONNECTICUT COLLEGE

270 Mohegan Avenue, New London, CT 6320
Phone: 860-439-2200 · **Financial Aid Phone:** 860-439-2058
E-mail: admission@conncoll.edu · **CEEB Code:** 3284
Fax: 860-439-4301 · **Website:** www.connecticutcollege.edu · **ACT Code:** 556

This private school was founded in 1911. It has a 750-acre campus.

RATINGS

Admissions Selectivity Rating: 94   Fire Safety Rating: 82

STUDENTS AND FACULTY

Enrollment: 1,816. **Student Body:** 59% female, 41% male, 83% out-of-state, 4% international (74 countries represented). Asian 3%, African American 4%, Caucasian 74%, Hispanic 8%, Native American <1%

Retention and Graduation: 84% freshmen graduate within 4 years. 85% freshmen graduate within 6 years. 25% grads go on to further study within 1 year. **Faculty:** 179 full-time faculty, 91% hold PhDs, 50% are members of minority groups, 16% are women. 0% of classes are taught by teaching assistants.

ACADEMICS

Degrees: bachelor's, master's. **Classes:** Most classes have 10–19 students. Most lab/discussion sessions have 10–19 students. **Majors with Highest Enrollment:** Political Science and Government; Economics; Psychology. **Special Study Options:** cross-registration, double major, exchange student program (domestic), independent study, internships, student-designed major, study abroad, teacher certification program, Cross-registration with the U.S. Coast Guard Academy, Trinity College, and Wesleyan University; 3-2 Program with Washington University or Boston University for a five-year BA/BS degree; Exchange Student Program; 12 Exchanges. Combined degree programs: BA/MA. **Disability Services:** Special programs offered to physically disabled students include note-taking services, reader services, tape recorders, tutors. **Career services:** Alumni network, alumni services, career/job search classes, career assessment, internships, regional alumni. Career services highlights include our Career-Enhancing Life Skills (CELS) office, which administers a program that facilitates College-funded internships for students who complete a series of preparatory seminars and workshops.

FACILITIES

Housing: Coed dorms, special housing for disabled students, Wellness Housing, Theme HousingThematic housing (environmentalism, foreign language, substance-free housing, etc.), men's floors, women's floors; living and learning arrangements. **Special Academic Facilities/Equipment:** Children's Program used as "lab school" for human development program, language lab, 750-acre arboretum, botanic garden, greenhouse, environment control labs, transmission and scanning electron microscope, ion accelerator, GIS lab, refracting telescope, observatory. **Computers:** 75% of classrooms, 100% of dorms, 100% of libraries, 100% of dining areas, 100% of student union, 70% of common outdoor areas have wireless network access. Students can register for classes online. Administrative functions (other than registration) can be performed online.

CAMPUS LIFE

Environment: Town. **Activities:** Choral groups, concert band, dance, drama/theater, jazz band, literary magazine, music ensembles, radio station, student government, student newspaper, student-run film society, symphony orchestra, yearbook, Campus Ministries, International Student Organization. 60 registered organizations, 5 honor societies, 6 religious organizations. **Athletics (Intercollegiate):** *Men:* basketball, crew/rowing, cross-country, diving, ice hockey, lacrosse, sailing, soccer, squash, swimming, tennis, track/field (outdoor), track/field (indoor), water polo. *Women:* basketball, crew/rowing, cross-country, diving, field hockey, ice hockey, lacrosse, sailing, soccer, squash, swimming, tennis, track/field (outdoor), track/field (indoor), volleyball, water polo. **On-Campus Highlights:** College Center (Crozier-Williams), Connecticut College Arboretum, Blue Camel Café (in library), Athletics Center, Coffee Grounds. **Environmental Initiatives:** Signatory of the American College and University President's Climate Commitment Signatory of the Talloires Declaration U.S. Environmental Protection Agency Green Power Partner

ADMISSIONS

Freshman Academic Profile: 56% in top 10% of high school class, 95% in top 25% of high school class, 100% in top 50% of high school class. 52% from public high schools. SAT Math middle 50% range 615-700. SAT Critical Reading middle 50% range 620-710. SAT Writing middle 50% range 640-725. ACT middle 50% range 28-31. Minimum internet-based TOEFL 100. Minimum paper TOEFL 600. **Basis for Candidate Selection:** *Very important factors considered include:* Class rank, academic GPA, rigor of secondary school record, character/personal qualities. *Important factors considered include:* application essay, recommendation(s), extracurricular activities, interview, racial/ethnic status, talent/ability, volunteer work, work experience. *Other factors considered include:* standardized test scores, alumni/ae relation, first generation, geographical residence, level of applicant's interest, religious affiliation/commitment, state residency. **Freshman Admission Requirements:** High school diploma is required and GED is accepted. **Freshman Admission Statistics:** 4,837 applied, 36% admitted, 29% enrolled. **Transfer Admission Requirements:** High school transcript, college transcript(s), essay or personal statement, statement of good standing from prior institution(s). Lowest grade transferable C. **General Admission Information:** Application Fee $60. Early decision application deadline 11/15. Regular application deadline 1/1. Regular notification 3/31. Nonfall registration not accepted. Admission may be deferred for a maximum of 1 year. Credit and/or placement offered for CEEB Advanced Placement tests.

COSTS AND FINANCIAL AID

Annual tuition $45,765. Room and board $12,695. Required fees $320. Average book expense $1,000. **Required Forms and Deadlines:** FAFSA, CSS/Financial Aid PROFILE, Noncustodial PROFILE, Business/Farm Supplement. **Notification of Awards:** Applicants will be notified of awards on or about

4/1. **Types of Aid:** *Need-based scholarships/grants:* Federal Pell, SEOG, state scholarships/grants, the school's own gift aid. *Loans:* Direct Subsidized Stafford, Direct Unsubsidized Stafford, Direct PLUS, Subsidized Stafford, Unsubsidized Stafford, PLUS, Federal Perkins. *Student Employment:* Federal Work-Study Program available. Institutional employment available. Off-campus job opportunities are good. **Financial Aid Statistics:** 93% freshmen, 94% undergrads receive need-based scholarship or grant aid. 0% freshmen, 0% undergrads receive non-need-based scholarship or grant aid. 90% freshmen, 89% undergrads receive need-based self-help aid. 0% freshmen, 0% undergrads receive athletic scholarships. 48% freshmen, 50% undergrads receive any aid. 50% undergrads borrow to pay for school. Average cumulative indebtedness $17,780.

See page 1038.

CONVERSE COLLEGE

580 East Main Street, Spartanburg, SC 29302
Phone: 864-596-9040 · **Financial Aid Phone:** 864-596-9019
E-mail: admissions@converse.edu · **CEEB Code:** 5121
Fax: 864-596-9225 · **Website:** www.converse.edu · **ACT Code:** 3852

This private school was founded in 1889. It has a 70-acre campus.

RATINGS

Admissions Selectivity Rating: 86   **Fire Safety Rating:** 71

STUDENTS AND FACULTY

Enrollment: 687. **Student Body:** 100% female, 0% male, 23% out-of-state, 1% international. Asian 1%, African American 8%, Caucasian 46%, Hispanic 3%, Native American <1%

Retention and Graduation: 76% freshmen return for sophomore year. 56% freshmen graduate within 4 years. 57% freshmen graduate within 6 years. 37% grads go on to further study within 1 year. **Faculty:** 76 full-time faculty, 91% hold PhDs, 59% are members of minority groups, 7% are women. 0% of classes are taught by teaching assistants.

ACADEMICS

Degrees: bachelor's, master's, post-master's certificate. **Classes:** Most classes have fewer than 10 students. Most lab/discussion sessions have fewer than 10 students. **Majors with Highest Enrollment:** Education; Psychology; Biology. **Special Study Options:** cross-registration, double major, English as a Second Language (ESL), honors program, independent study, internships, liberal arts/career combination, student-designed major, study abroad, teacher certification program, Undergrads may take grad level classes. **Honors programs:** Nisbet Honors Program. **Disability Services:** Special programs offered to physically disabled students include note-taking services, tape recorders, tutors. **Career services:** Alumni network, alumni services, career/job search classes, career assessment, internships, regional alumni. Career services highlights include a program that guarantees every undergraduate student at Converse an internship.

FACILITIES

Housing: women's dorms. **Special Academic Facilities/Equipment:** Language lab. Phifer Science Building, Blackman Auditorium (Music), DNA sequencer and lab. **Computers:** Students can register for classes online. Administrative functions (other than registration) can be performed online.

CAMPUS LIFE

Environment: City. **Activities:** Choral groups, concert band, dance, drama/theater, literary magazine, music ensembles, musical theater, opera, student government, student newspaper, symphony orchestra, yearbook. 60 registered organizations, 16 honor societies, 7 religious organizations. **Athletics (Intercollegiate):** *Women:* basketball, cross-country, lacrosse, soccer, swimming, tennis, volleyball. **On-Campus Highlights:** Montgomery Student Life Center, Weisiger Physical Activity Complex, Phifer Science Complex, Petrie School of Music- Twichell Auditorium, Outdoor Quad area for studying and relaxing. **Environmental Initiatives:** LEED Certified new construction; Sustainable foodstuffs bought and used by Dining Services; Student Environmental Group—WISE.

ADMISSIONS

Freshman Academic Profile: 18% in top 10% of high school class, 43% in top 25% of high school class, 80% in top 50% of high school class. 80% from public high schools. SAT Math middle 50% range 460-570. SAT Critical Reading middle 50% range 470-600. ACT middle 50% range 20-26. Minimum internet-based TOEFL 79. Minimum paper TOEFL 550. **Basis for Candidate Selection:** *Very important factors considered include:* academic GPA, rigor of secondary school record. *Important factors considered include:* Class rank, application essay, recommendation(s), standardized test scores, character/personal qualities, extracurricular activities, talent/ability. *Other factors considered include:* alumni/ae relation, first generation, interview, level of applicant's interest, racial/ethnic status, volunteer work, work experience. **Freshman Admission Requirements:** High school diploma is required and GED is accepted. **Freshman Admission Statistics:** 1,383 applied, 51% admitted, 26% enrolled. **Transfer Admission Requirements:** college transcript(s), statement of good standing from prior institution(s). Minimum college GPA of 2.0 required. Lowest grade transferable C. **General Admission Information:** Notification on a rolling basis, beginning on or about 10/1. Nonfall registration accepted. Admission may be deferred for a maximum of 1 year. Credit offered for CEEB Advanced Placement tests.

COSTS AND FINANCIAL AID

Annual tuition $27,276. Room and board $8,854. Required fees $1,000. Average book expense $1,000. **Required Forms and Deadlines:** FAFSA. **Notification of Awards:** Applicants will be notified of awards on a rolling basis beginning 3/1. **Types of Aid:** *Need-based scholarships/grants:* Federal Pell, SEOG, state scholarships/grants, private scholarships, the school's own gift aid. *Loans:* Subsidized Stafford, Unsubsidized Stafford, PLUS, Federal Perkins, state loans. *Student Employment:* Federal Work-Study Program available. Institutional employment available. Off-campus job opportunities are good. **Financial Aid Statistics:** 100% freshmen, 98% undergrads receive need-based scholarship or grant aid. 18% freshmen, 17% undergrads receive non-need-based scholarship or grant aid. 79% freshmen, 76% undergrads receive need-based self-help aid. 14% freshmen, 8% undergrads receive athletic scholarships. 95% freshmen, 93% undergrads receive any aid. Average cumulative indebtedness $27,916. **Criteria for awarding institutional aid:** *Non-need-based:* academics, alumni affiliation, art, athletics, leadership, music/drama, state/district residency.

THE COOPER UNION FOR THE ADVANCEMENT OF SCIENCE AND ART

30 Cooper Square, New York, NY 10003
Phone: 212-353-4120 • **Financial Aid Phone:** 212-353-4130
E-mail: admissions@cooper.edu • **CEEB Code:** 2097
Fax: 212-353-4342 • **Website:** cooper.edu • **ACT Code:** 2724

This private school was founded in 1859.

RATINGS

Admissions Selectivity Rating: 97   **Fire Safety Rating:** 96

STUDENTS AND FACULTY

Enrollment: 855. **Student Body:** 34% female, 66% male, 48% out-of-state, 14% international. Asian 20%, African American 5%, Caucasian 33%, Hispanic 10%, Native American 1%
Retention and Graduation: 97% freshmen return for sophomore year. 65% freshmen graduate within 4 years. 82% freshmen graduate within 6 years. 60% grads go on to further study within 1 year. 15% grads pursue arts and sciences degrees. 6% grads pursue law degrees. 10% grads pursue business degrees. 3% grads pursue medical degrees. **Faculty:** 52 full-time faculty, 87% hold PhDs, 29% are members of minority groups, 8% are women. 0% of classes are taught by teaching assistants.

ACADEMICS

Degrees: bachelor's, certificate, master's. **Classes:** Most classes have 10–19 students. Most lab/discussion sessions have greater than 100 students. **Majors with Highest Enrollment:** Electrical and Electronics Engineering; Mechanical Engineering; Fine and Studio Arts. **Special Study Options:** cross-registration, exchange student program (domestic), independent study, internships, student-designed major, study abroad, Cooper Union is indeed an all-honors college. Research opportunities available. Students may take up to one year off during their studies with us to pursue other interests. **Honors programs:** Cooper Union is an all-honors college Combined degree programs: MEng/MD. **Disability Services:** Special programs offered to physically disabled students include reader services, tape recorders, tutors. **Career services:** Alumni network, alumni services, career/job search classes, career assessment, internships, regional alumni. Career services highlights include Cooper Union Professional Internship Program, which provides funding for students to learn through internships that normally don't pay.

FACILITIES

Housing: Coed dorms. 75% of campus accessible to physically disabled. **Special Academic Facilities/Equipment:** The Great Hall; Houghton Gallery; The Brooks Lab; Prototyping Lab; Bio-Medical Engineering Lab; Tissue Engineering Lab; Center for Sustainable Design; Center for Infrastructure and Urban Systems; Center for Signal Processing Communications and Computer Engineering Research, **Computers:** 85% of classrooms, have wireless network access. Administrative functions (other than registration) can be performed online.

CAMPUS LIFE

Environment: Metropolis. **Activities:** Choral groups, concert band, dance, drama/theater, jazz band, literary magazine, music ensembles, student government, student newspaper, student-run film society, symphony orchestra, yearbook. 90 registered organizations, 18 honor societies, 8 religious organizations. 2 fraternities, 1 sorority. **Athletics (Intercollegiate):** *Men:* baseball, basketball, cross-country, soccer, tennis, volleyball. *Women:* basketball, cross-country, soccer, tennis, volleyball. **On-Campus Highlights:** Great Hall, 41 Cooper Square, Foundation Building, Houghton Gallery, 41 Cooper Square Gallery, 41 Cooper Square-our newest building, Opened in September of 2009 to critical acclaim. Designed by Pritzker Prize winning architect, Thom Mayne, this building has many green features and is targeted to earn Platinum LEED certification. **Environmental Initiatives:** 41 Cooper Square Building please see: cooper.edu

ADMISSIONS

Freshman Academic Profile: Average high school GPA 3.5. 88% in top 10% of high school class, 90% in top 25% of high school class, 95% in top 50% of high school class. 65% from public high schools. SAT Math middle 50% range 650-770. SAT Critical Reading middle 50% range 600-730. SAT Writing middle 50% range 610-710. ACT middle 50% range 30-34. Minimum internet-based TOEFL 100. Minimum paper TOEFL 600. **Basis for Candidate Selection:** *Very important factors considered include:* academic GPA, rigor of secondary school record, standardized test scores, level of applicant's interest, talent/ability. *Important factors considered include:* application essay, character/personal qualities, extracurricular activities. *Other factors considered include:* Class rank, recommendation(s), first generation, interview, racial/ethnic status, volunteer work, work experience. **Freshman Admission Requirements:** High school diploma is required and GED is accepted. *Academic units required:* 4 English, 1 mathematics, 1 science, 0 foreign language, 1 social studies, 1 history, 8 academic electives. **Freshman Admission Statistics:** 2,536 applied, 15% admitted, 60% enrolled. **Transfer Admission Requirements:** High school transcript, college transcript(s), essay or personal statement, standardized test scores, statement of good standing from prior institution(s). Minimum college GPA of 3.0 required. Lowest grade transferable B. **General Admission Information:** Application Fee $65. Early decision application deadline 12/1. Regular application deadline 1/1. Regular notification 4/1. Nonfall registration not accepted. Admission may be deferred for a maximum of 1 year. Credit and/ or placement offered for CEEB Advanced Placement tests.

COSTS AND FINANCIAL AID

Annual tuition $39,600. Room and board $15,220. Required fees $1,850. Average book expense $1,600. **Required Forms and Deadlines:** FAFSA, CSS/Financial Aid PROFILE. **Notification of Awards:** Applicants will be notified of awards on or about 6/1. **Types of Aid:** *Need-based scholarships/grants:* Federal Pell, SEOG, state scholarships/grants, private scholarships, the school's own gift aid. *Loans:* Subsidized Stafford, Unsubsidized Stafford, PLUS, Federal Perkins, college/university loans from institutional funds. *Student Employment:* Federal Work-Study Program available. Institutional employment available. Off-campus job opportunities are excellent. **Financial Aid Statistics:** 100% freshmen, 100% undergrads receive need-based scholarship or grant aid. 100% freshmen, 100% undergrads receive non-need-based scholarship or grant aid. 80% freshmen, 60% undergrads receive need-based self-help aid. 0% freshmen, 0% undergrads receive athletic scholarships. 100% freshmen, 100% undergrads receive any aid. 26% undergrads borrow to pay for school. Average cumulative indebtedness $18,813. **Criteria for awarding institutional aid:** *Non-need-based:* academics.

COPPIN STATE UNIVERSITY

2500 West North Avenue, Baltimore, MD 21216
Phone: 410-951-3600 • **Financial Aid Phone:** 410-951-3636
E-mail: admissions@coppin.edu • **CEEB Code:** 5122
Fax: 410-523-7351 • **Website:** www.coppin.edu • **ACT Code:** 1688

This public school was founded in 1900. It has a 52-acre campus.

RATINGS

Admissions Selectivity Rating: 75   **Fire Safety Rating:** 74

STUDENTS AND FACULTY

Enrollment: 3,185. **Student Body:** 77% female, 23% male, 8% out-of-state, 3% international. Asian 0%, African American 95%, Caucasian 2%, Hispanic 0%, Native American <1%

Retention and Graduation: 65% freshmen return for sophomore year. 7% freshmen graduate within 4 years. 53% freshmen graduate within 6 years. **Faculty:** 130 full-time faculty, 59% hold PhDs, 49% are members of minority groups, 82% are women. 0% of classes are taught by teaching assistants.

ACADEMICS

Degrees: bachelor's, master's, post-master's certificate. **Majors with Highest Enrollment:** Criminal Justice/Law Enforcement Administration; Registered Nursing/Registered Nurse; Management Science. **Special Study Options:** Accelerated program, cooperative education program, distance learning, double major, dual enrollment, external degree program, honors program, independent study, internships, liberal arts/career combination, study abroad, teacher certification program, weekend college, 3-2 programs in Engineering; Pharmacy; Denistry; Physical Therapy. **Honors programs:** Honors Program and McNair Program Combined degree programs: BA/MA, Dental and Pharmacy. **Disability Services:** Special programs offered to physically disabled students include reader services, tutors. **Career services:** alumni services, career/job search classes, career assessment, internships. Career services highlights include our Cooperative Education Program.

FACILITIES

Housing: Coed dorms, special housing for disabled students. 75% of campus accessible to physically disabled. **Special Academic Facilities/Equipment:** Language lab, school of special education, TV studio. **Computers:** Students can register for classes online. Administrative functions (other than registration) can be performed online.

CAMPUS LIFE

Environment: City. **Activities:** Choral groups, concert band, dance, drama/theater, music ensembles, radio station, student government, student newspaper, student-run film society, television station, yearbook. 28 registered organizations, 1 honor society, 1 religious organization. 3 fraternities, 4 sororities. **Athletics (Intercollegiate):** *Men:* baseball, basketball, cross-country, tennis, track/field (outdoor), track/field (indoor). *Women:* basketball, bowling, cheerleading, cross-country, golf, softball, tennis, track/field (outdoor), track/field (indoor), volleyball. **On-Campus Highlights:** New Dining Facility (no official naming), Tawes Building (Student Building), Greek Row (located in front of Dorms), Coppin Center (Athletic Facility).

ADMISSIONS

Freshman Academic Profile: Average high school GPA 2.83. SAT Math middle 50% range 370-450. SAT Critical Reading middle 50% range 380-460. Minimum paper TOEFL 500. **Basis for Candidate Selection:** *Very important factors considered include:* rigor of secondary school record. *Important factors considered include:* recommendation(s), standardized test scores, talent/ability. *Other factors considered include:* Class rank, application essay, alumni/ae relation, character/personal qualities, extracurricular activities, geographical residence, interview, racial/ethnic status, state residency, volunteer work, work experience. **Freshman Admission Requirements:** High school diploma is required and GED is accepted. *Academic units required:* 4 English, 3 mathematics, 2 science, (2 science labs), 2 foreign language, 3 social studies, 2 Advanced Tech Prep (alternative to Foreign language requirement **Freshman Admission Statistics:** 3,075 applied, 46% admitted, 44% enrolled. **Transfer Admission Requirements:** college transcript(s), Minimum college GPA of 2.0 required. Lowest grade transferable C. **General Admission Information:** Application Fee $35. Regular application deadline 7/15. Notification on a rolling basis, beginning on or about 3/15. Nonfall registration accepted. Admission may be deferred for a maximum of 1 semester. Credit and/or placement offered for CEEB Advanced Placement tests.

COSTS AND FINANCIAL AID

Required Forms and Deadlines: FAFSA. **Notification of Awards:** Applicants will be notified of awards on a rolling basis beginning 4/15. **Types of Aid:** *Need-based scholarships/grants:* Federal Pell, SEOG, state scholarships/grants, private scholarships, the school's own gift aid, United Negro College Fund, Federal Nursing Scholarships. *Loans:* Direct Subsidized Stafford, Direct Unsubsidized Stafford, Direct PLUS, PLUS, Federal Perkins, college/university loans from institutional funds, Sallie Mae's Signature Loans and Key Alternative Loan. *Student Employment:* Federal Work-Study Program available. Institutional employment available. Off-campus job opportunities are excellent. **Financial Aid Statistics:** 61% freshmen, 86% undergrads receive need-based scholarship or grant aid. 13% freshmen, 20% undergrads receive non-need-based scholarship or grant aid. 68% freshmen, 85% undergrads receive need-based self-help aid. 5% freshmen, 5% undergrads receive athletic scholarships. 90% undergrads borrow to pay for school. **Criteria for awarding institutional aid:** *Non-need-based:* academics, alumni affiliation, athletics, state/district residency.

CORBAN UNIVERSITY

5000 Deer Park Drive SE, Salem, OR 97317
Phone: 503-375-7005 • **Financial Aid Phone:** 503-375-7007
E-mail: admissions@corban.edu
Fax: 503-585-4316 • **Website:** www.corban.edu • **ACT Code:** 477

This private school, affiliated with the Baptist Church, was founded in 1935. It has a 145-acre campus.

RATINGS

Admissions Selectivity Rating: 89   **Fire Safety Rating:** 77

STUDENTS AND FACULTY

Enrollment: 855. **Student Body:** 60% female, 40% male, 47% out-of-state, 1% international (6 countries represented). Asian 2%, African American 1%, Caucasian 84%, Hispanic 4%, Native American 1%

Retention and Graduation: 77% freshmen return for sophomore year. 47% freshmen graduate within 4 years. **Faculty:** 50 full-time faculty, 74% hold PhDs, 26% are members of minority groups, 4% are women. 0% of classes are taught by teaching assistants.

ACADEMICS

Degrees: associate, bachelor's, master's. **Classes:** Most classes have 10–19 students. Most lab/discussion sessions have 10–19 students. **Majors with Highest Enrollment:** Psychology; Education; Business Administration and Management. **Special Study Options:** Accelerated program, cross-registration, distance learning, double major, dual enrollment, honors program, independent study, internships, liberal arts/career combination, study abroad, teacher certification program, weekend college. Combined degree programs: BA/MA, Education. **Disability Services:** Special programs offered to physically disabled students include note-taking services, reader services, tape recorders, tutors. **Career services:** Career services highlights include a program in which students in business program work with local business and agencies on various projects beneficial to both.

FACILITIES

Housing: men's dorms, women's dorms, apartments for married students, apartments for single students. 80% of campus accessible to physically disabled. **Special Academic Facilities/Equipment:** Prewitt-Allen Archeological Museum. Psalms Performing Arts Center. **Computers:** Students can register for classes online.

CAMPUS LIFE

Environment: City. **Activities:** Choral groups, concert band, drama/theater, jazz band, music ensembles, student government, student newspaper, yearbook, Campus Ministries 1 honor society, 10 religious organizations. **Athletics (Intercollegiate):** *Men:* baseball, basketball, cross-country, golf, soccer, track/field (outdoor). *Women:* basketball, cross-country, golf, soccer, softball, track/field (outdoor), volleyball. **On-Campus Highlights:** Common Grounds Coffee Shop, Dining Hall, Gymnasium and Athletic Fields, Computer Lab, Book Store, 6. Archaeological Museum, 7. Psalms Performing Arts Center.

ADMISSIONS

Freshman Academic Profile: Average high school GPA 3.5. 33% in top 10% of high school class, 63% in top 25% of high school class, 89% in top 50% of high school class. 60% from public high schools. SAT Math middle 50% range 470-590. SAT Critical Reading middle 50% range 480-590. SAT Writing middle 50% range 450-568. ACT middle 50% range 20-26. Minimum paper TOEFL 500. **Basis for Candidate Selection:** *Very important factors considered include:* application essay, academic GPA, recommendation(s), religious affiliation/commitment. *Important factors considered include:* rigor of secondary school record, standardized test scores, character/personal qualities, level of applicant's interest. *Other factors considered include:* Class rank, alumni/ae relation, extracurricular activities, interview. **Freshman Admission Requirements:** High school diploma is required and GED is accepted. **Freshman Admission Statistics:** 2,711 applied, 34% admitted, 24% enrolled. **Transfer Admission Requirements:** High school transcript, college transcript(s), essay or personal statement, Minimum college GPA of 2.00 required. Lowest grade transferable C-. **General Admission Information:** Application Fee $40. Regular application deadline 8/1. Notification on a rolling basis, beginning on or about 12/1. Nonfall registration accepted. Credit offered for CEEB Advanced Placement tests.

COSTS AND FINANCIAL AID

Annual tuition $26,976. Room and board $8,876. Required fees $510. Average book expense $900. **Required Forms and Deadlines:** FAFSA. **Notification of Awards:** Applicants will be notified of awards on a rolling basis beginning 3/1. **Types of Aid:** *Need-based scholarships/grants:* Federal Pell, SEOG, state scholarships/grants, private scholarships, the school's own gift aid. *Loans:* Direct

Subsidized Stafford, Direct Unsubsidized Stafford, Direct PLUS, Federal Perkins, state loans. *Student Employment:* Federal Work-Study Program available. Institutional employment available. Highest amount earned per year from on-campus jobs $1,000. Off-campus job opportunities are fair. **Financial Aid Statistics:** 100% freshmen, 100% undergrads receive need-based scholarship or grant aid. 15% freshmen, 10% undergrads receive non-need-based scholarship or grant aid. 71% freshmen, 74% undergrads receive need-based self-help aid. 14% freshmen, 10% undergrads receive athletic scholarships. 97% freshmen, 97% undergrads receive any aid. 82% undergrads borrow to pay for school. Average cumulative indebtedness $22,912. **Criteria for awarding institutional aid:** *Non-need-based:* academics, alumni affiliation, athletics, leadership, music/drama.

CORCORAN COLLEGE OF ART + DESIGN

500 17th Street NW, Washington, DC 20006-4804
Phone: 202-639-1814 · **Financial Aid Phone:** 202-639-1851
E-mail: admissions@corcoran.org
Fax: 202-639-1830 · **Website:** www.corcoran.edu

This private school was founded in 1890. It has a 7-acre campus.

RATINGS
Admissions Selectivity Rating: 60*   **Fire Safety Rating:** 64

STUDENTS AND FACULTY
Faculty: 0% of classes are taught by teaching assistants.

ACADEMICS
Degrees: associate, bachelor's, certificate, master's. **Classes:** Most classes have fewer than 10 students. **Majors with Highest Enrollment:** Graphic Design; Photography; Fine/Studio Arts. **Special Study Options:** cross-registration, exchange student program (domestic), internships, study abroad. Combined degree programs: BA/MA. **Disability Services:** Special programs offered to physically disabled students include note-taking services, reader services, tape recorders, tutors. **Career services:** Alumni network, alumni services, career/job search classes, internships.

FACILITIES
Housing: Corcoran Leased Apartments and assistance in finding area housing. 70% of campus accessible to physically disabled. **Special Academic Facilities/Equipment:** Art gallery, Student exhibition spaces. **Computers:** Administrative functions (other than registration) can be performed online. Undergraduates are required to own a computer.

CAMPUS LIFE
Environment: Metropolis. **Activities:** student government, student-run film society. **On-Campus Highlights:** Corcoran Gallery, Corcoran Studios, Corcoran Café des Artistes.

ADMISSIONS
Freshman Academic Profile: Minimum internet-based TOEFL 80. **Basis for Candidate Selection:** *Very important factors considered include:* academic GPA, rigor of secondary school record, interview, talent/ability. *Important factors considered include:* Class rank, application essay, recommendation(s), standardized test scores. *Other factors considered include:* alumni/ae relation, character/personal qualities, extracurricular activities, volunteer work, work experience. **Freshman Admission Requirements:** High school diploma is required and GED is accepted. **Transfer Admission Requirements:** High school transcript, college transcript(s), Minimum college GPA of 2.5 required. Lowest grade transferable C. **General Admission Information:** Application Fee $40. Notification on a rolling basis, beginning on or about 1/1. Nonfall registration accepted. Admission may be deferred for a maximum of 1 year. Credit and/or placement offered for CEEB Advanced Placement tests.

COSTS AND FINANCIAL AID
Notification of Awards: Applicants will be notified of awards on a rolling basis beginning 4/1. **Types of Aid:** *Need-based scholarships/grants:* Federal Pell, SEOG, state scholarships/grants, the school's own gift aid. *Loans:* Direct Subsidized Stafford, Direct Unsubsidized Stafford, Direct PLUS, Subsidized Stafford, Unsubsidized Stafford, PLUS, Federal Perkins, Alternative loans, ie: PLATO, Signature Loans. *Student Employment:* Federal Work-Study Program available. Institutional employment available. Off-campus job opportunities are excellent. **Criteria for awarding institutional aid:** *Non-need-based:* academics, art.

CORNELL COLLEGE

600 First Street South West, Mount Vernon, IA 52314-1098
Phone: 319-895-4161 · **Financial Aid Phone:** 319-895-4216
E-mail: admissions@cornellcollege.edu · **CEEB Code:** 6119
Fax: 319-895-4451 · **Website:** www.cornellcollege.edu · **ACT Code:** 1296

This private school, affiliated with the Methodist Church, was founded in 1853. It has a 129-acre campus.

RATINGS
Admissions Selectivity Rating: 85   **Fire Safety Rating:** 73

STUDENTS AND FACULTY
Enrollment: 1,075. **Student Body:** 54% female, 46% male, 82% out-of-state, 4% international (15 countries represented). Asian 2%, African American 5%, Caucasian 66%, Hispanic 13%, Native American <1%
Retention and Graduation: 83% freshmen return for sophomore year. 64% freshmen graduate within 4 years. 68% freshmen graduate within 6 years. **Faculty:** 86 full-time faculty, 97% hold PhDs, 58% are members of minority groups, 9% are women. 0% of classes are taught by teaching assistants.

ACADEMICS
Degrees: bachelor's. **Classes:** Most classes have 10–19 students. **Majors with Highest Enrollment:** Economics; Psychology; Biochemistry. **Special Study Options:** Accelerated program, double major, English as a Second Language (ESL), exchange student program (domestic), independent study, internships, liberal arts/career combination, student-designed major, study abroad, teacher certification program. Combined degree programs: BA/MA, Engineering; Forestry and Environmental Management, Duke Universi. **Disability Services:** Special programs offered to physically disabled students include tape recorders, tutors. **Career services:** Alumni network, alumni services, career/job search classes, career assessment, internships, regional alumni. Career services highlights include fellowships with premier internship programs, externship Program, 3-5 day job shadowing opportunites.

FACILITIES
Housing: Coed dorms, men's dorms, women's dorms, apartments for single students, Our first year students live on first- year only floors and/or in first-year only residence halls. 47% of campus accessible to physically disabled. **Special Academic Facilities/Equipment:** Geology center and museum, MNR machine in West Sc. Building, Luce Art Gallery. **Computers:** 100% of classrooms, 20% of dorms, 100% of libraries, 100% of dining areas, 100% of student union, 10% of common outdoor areas have wireless network access. Administrative functions (other than registration) can be performed online.

CAMPUS LIFE
Environment: Rural. **Activities:** Choral groups, concert band, dance, drama/theater, jazz band, literary magazine, music ensembles, musical theater, opera, radio station, student government, student newspaper, symphony orchestra, yearbook, Campus Ministries, International Student Organization. 90 registered organizations, 11 honor society, 11 religious organization. 8 fraternities, 7 sororities. **Athletics (Intercollegiate):** *Men:* baseball, basketball, cross-country, football, golf, soccer, tennis, track/field (outdoor), track/field (indoor), wrestling. *Women:* basketball, cross-country, golf, soccer, softball, tennis, track/field (outdoor), track/field (indoor), volleyball. **On-Campus Highlights:** Commons - Orange Carpet - student center, Cole Library, Small Multi-Sports Center, Kimmel Theatre - new state of the art theatre, McWethy Hall - newly renovated art building, Most prodominant features on campus are our beautiful King Chapel. A newly renovated Armstrong Hall of Fine Arts. A new pedestrian mall [with outdoor ampitheatre]that connects the entire campus. **Environmental Initiatives:** Engineering study on costs of replacing current campus-side steam heat network, including specific costs and energy savings payback times for each building. Implementation of plan in two building remodels and designed into two upcoming remodel projects. Wrote and received grant for recycling facility construction and negotiating contract with cleaning service for nightly collection of recyclable categories possible in our area. Currently spec'ing biodiesel refinery to convert food service discarded oils into fuel for college equipment

ADMISSIONS
Freshman Academic Profile: Average high school GPA 3.42. 17% in top 10% of high school class, 45% in top 25% of high school class, 76% in top 50% of high school class. SAT Math middle 50% range 520-650. SAT Critical Reading middle 50% range 520-680. SAT Writing middle 50% range 490-640. ACT

middle 50% range 23-30. Minimum internet-based TOEFL 79. Minimum paper TOEFL 550. **Basis for Candidate Selection:** *Very important factors considered include:* application essay, academic GPA, recommendation(s), rigor of secondary school record. *Important factors considered include:* Class rank, standardized test scores, character/personal qualities, extracurricular activities, first generation, interview, level of applicant's interest, talent/ability, volunteer work, work experience. *Other factors considered include:* alumni/ae relation, geographical residence, racial/ethnic status, state residency. **Freshman Admission Requirements:** High school diploma is required and GED is accepted. **Freshman Admission Statistics:** 1,915 applied, 74% admitted, 19% enrolled. **Transfer Admission Requirements:** college transcript(s), essay or personal statement, statement of good standing from prior institution(s). Lowest grade transferable C. **General Admission Information:** Application Fee $30. Regular application deadline 2/1. Regular notification 3/20. Nonfall registration accepted. Admission may be deferred for a maximum of 1 year. Credit and/or placement offered for CEEB Advanced Placement tests.

COSTS AND FINANCIAL AID

Annual tuition $37,500. Room and board $8,500. Required fees $225. Average book expense $1,164. **Required Forms and Deadlines:** FAFSA. **Notification of Awards:** Applicants will be notified of awards on a rolling basis beginning 3/1. **Types of Aid:** *Need-based scholarships/grants:* Federal Pell, SEOG, state scholarships/grants, private scholarships, the school's own gift aid, AC, SMART, and TEACH Grants. *Loans:* Direct Subsidized Stafford, Direct Unsubsidized Stafford, Direct PLUS, Sherman Loan, United Methodist Loan. *Student Employment:* Federal Work-Study Program available. Institutional employment available. Highest amount earned per year from on-campus jobs $350. Off-campus job opportunities are fair. **Financial Aid Statistics:** 100% freshmen, 100% undergrads receive need-based scholarship or grant aid. 99% freshmen, 92% undergrads receive non-need-based scholarship or grant aid. 77% freshmen, 86% undergrads receive need-based self-help aid. 0% freshmen, 0% undergrads receive athletic scholarships. 99% freshmen, 98% undergrads receive any aid. 79% undergrads borrow to pay for school. Average cumulative indebtedness $21,401. **Criteria for awarding institutional aid:** *Non-need-based:* academics, art, leadership, minority status, music/drama, religious affiliation, state/district residency.

CORNELL UNIVERSITY

Ithaca, NY 14850
Phone: 607-255-5241 · **Financial Aid Phone:** 607-255-5145
E-mail: admissions@cornell.edu · **CEEB Code:** 2098
Fax: 607-255-0659 · **Website:** www.cornell.edu · **ACT Code:** 2726

This private school was founded in 1865. It has a 745-acre campus.

RATINGS

Admissions Selectivity Rating: 97   **Fire Safety Rating:** 82

STUDENTS AND FACULTY

Enrollment: 14,366. **Student Body:** 51% female, 49% male, 64% out-of-state, 10% international (85 countries represented). Asian 17%, African American 6%, Caucasian 42%, Hispanic 12%, Native American <1%
Retention and Graduation: 87% freshmen graduate within 4 years. 93% freshmen graduate within 6 years. **Faculty:** 1,702 full-time faculty, 93% hold PhDs, 34% are members of minority groups, 18% are women.

ACADEMICS

Degrees: bachelor's, master's. **Classes:** Most classes have 10–19 students. Most lab/discussion sessions have 10–19 students. **Majors with Highest Enrollment:** Biology/Biological Sciences; Hotel/Motel Administration/Management; Labor and Industrial Relations. **Special Study Options:** Accelerated program, cooperative education program, cross-registration, distance learning, double major, English as a Second Language (ESL), exchange student program (domestic), honors program, independent study, internships, liberal arts/career combination, student-designed major, study abroad, teacher certification program. **Disability Services:** Special programs offered to physically disabled students include note-taking services, reader services, tape recorders, tutors. **Career services:** Alumni network, alumni services, career/job search classes, career assessment, internships, regional alumni. Career services highlights include two of our stellar programs, the Extern Program and FRESH, which provide students the opportunity to shadow and work with alumni. This gives

students a chance to broaden their horizons by exploring unfamiliar career fields or to deepen their knowledge of a career field through hands-on exposure. Either way, the programs build networking skills in students and foster positive alumni connections with the University.

FACILITIES

Housing: Coed dorms, special housing for disabled students, men's dorms, special housing for international students, women's dorms, fraternity/sorority housing, apartments for married students, cooperative housing, apartments for single students, Theme Housing, See http://www.campuslife.cornell.edu/campuslife/housing. **Special Academic Facilities/Equipment:** Biotechnology institute, a woods sanctuary, 4 designated national resource centers, 2 local optical observatories, Africana studies and research center, arboretum, particle accelerator, supercomputer, national research centers, performing arts center, art museum, lab of ornithology, vertebrates museum, living and learning communities, campus orchard, dairy pilot plant, mineralogical museum, animal teaching hospital, 2 agricultural experiment stations, and marine laboratory. **Computers:** 20% of classrooms, 100% of dorms, 100% of libraries, 100% of dining areas, 75% of student union, 20% of common outdoor areas have wireless network access. Students can register for classes online. Administrative functions (other than registration) can be performed online.

CAMPUS LIFE

Environment: Town. **Activities:** Choral groups, concert band, dance, drama/theater, jazz band, literary magazine, marching band, music ensembles, musical theater, pep band, radio station, student government, student newspaper, student-run film society, symphony orchestra, television station, yearbook, Campus Ministries, International Student Organization, Model UN. 841 registered organizations, 22 honor societies, 61 religious organization. 50 fraternities, 19 sororities. **Athletics (Intercollegiate):** *Men:* baseball, basketball, crew/rowing, cross-country, diving, football, golf, ice hockey, lacrosse, polo, soccer, squash, swimming, tennis, track/field (outdoor), track/field (indoor), wrestling. *Women:* basketball, crew/rowing, cross-country, diving, equestrian sports, fencing, field hockey, gymnastics, ice hockey, lacrosse, polo, soccer, softball, squash, swimming, tennis, track/field (outdoor), track/field (indoor), volleyball. **On-Campus Highlights:** Johnson Art Museum, Gorges and waterfalls bordering campus, Center for Theater Arts, Cornell Plantations, including Beebe Lak, Willard Straight Hall, http://explore.cornell.edu/. **Environmental Initiatives:** Cornell has one LEED Platinum and eight GOLD buildings and a policy for all new major construction to obtain LEED Silver and 30 percent more energy-efficient than national standards. Cornell is also constructing a net-zero energy building on New York City's Roosevelt Island. http://tech.cornell.edu/future-campus/ Cornell is implementing a plan to be carbon neutral by 2050 and achieved a 32 percent carbon emissions reduction since 2008. Another critical part of Cornells carbon reduction strategy is a $46 million investment in energy conservation. Transportation Services provides free bus passes to freshman and staff, and offers incentives to use Ithaca Carshare, vanpools, public transportation, and the student-run Big Red Bikes, bike-share program At Cornell University, students can choose from more than 400 courses and twenty-eight majors to study sustainability in every college, including minors in climate change and sustainable energy and majors in environmental science and sustainabiity and global sustainable enterprise. The Atkinson Center for a Sustainable Future brings together students, faculty and staff to help advance multidisciplinary research and cultivate innovative collaborations within and beyond Cornell to foster a sustainable future for all. The Center provides seed grants for cutting-edge interdisciplinary research advances the local and national conversation on sustainability through activities that engage government agencies and officials, foundations, businesses, NGOs, and others.

ADMISSIONS

Freshman Academic Profile: 87% in top 10% of high school class, 98% in top 25% of high school class, 99% in top 50% of high school class. SAT Math middle 50% range 680-770. SAT Critical Reading middle 50% range 650-740. ACT middle 50% range 30-34. Minimum internet-based TOEFL 100. Minimum paper TOEFL 600. **Basis for Candidate Selection:** *Very important factors considered include:* application essay, academic GPA, recommendation(s), rigor of secondary school record, standardized test scores, extracurricular activities, talent/ability. *Important factors considered include:* Class rank. *Other factors considered include:* alumni/ae relation, character/personal qualities, first generation, geographical residence, interview, racial/ethnic status, state residency, volunteer work, work experience. **Freshman Admission Requirements:** High school diploma or equivalent is not required. *Academic units required:* 4 English, 3 mathematics. **Freshman Admission Statistics:** 43,037 applied, 14% admitted, 53% enrolled. **Transfer Admission Requirements:** High school transcript, college transcript(s), essay or personal statement, statement of good standing from prior institution(s). Lowest grade transferable C. **General Admission Information:** Application Fee $70. Early decision application deadline 11/1. Regular application deadline 1/2. Regular notification 4/1. Nonfall registration not accepted. Credit and/or placement offered for CEEB Advanced Placement tests.

COSTS AND FINANCIAL AID

Required Forms and Deadlines: FAFSA, CSS/Financial Aid PROFILE, Noncustodial PROFILE. **Notification of Awards:** Applicants will be notified of awards on or about 4/1. **Types of Aid:** *Need-based scholarships/grants:* Federal Pell, SEOG, state scholarships/grants, private scholarships, the school's own gift aid. *Loans:* Direct Subsidized Stafford, Direct Unsubsidized Stafford, Direct PLUS, Subsidized Stafford, Unsubsidized Stafford, PLUS, Federal Perkins, college/university loans from institutional funds. *Student Employment:* Federal Work-Study Program available. Institutional employment available. Highest amount earned per year from on-campus jobs $2,500. Off-campus job opportunities are fair. **Financial Aid Statistics:** 98% freshmen, 98% undergrads receive need-based scholarship or grant aid. 0% freshmen, 0% undergrads receive non-need-based scholarship or grant aid. 87% freshmen, 92% undergrads receive need-based self-help aid. 0% freshmen, 0% undergrads receive athletic scholarships. 60% freshmen, 57% undergrads receive any aid. 45% undergrads borrow to pay for school. Average cumulative indebtedness $14,415.

CORNERSTONE UNIVERSITY

1001 East Beltline Avenue, NE, Grand Rapids, MI 49525-5897
Phone: 616-222-1418 · **Financial Aid Phone:** 616-949-5300
E-mail: admissions@cornerstone.edu
Fax: 616-222-1418 · **Website:** www.cornerstone.edu · **ACT Code:** 2002

This private school, affiliated with the Christian (Nondenominational) Church, was founded in 1941. It has a 130-acre campus.

RATINGS

Admissions Selectivity Rating: 73   **Fire Safety Rating:** 94

STUDENTS AND FACULTY

Enrollment: 1,741. **Student Body:** 59% female, 41% male, 16% out-of-state, 1% international (15 countries represented). Asian 1%, African American 11%, Caucasian 83%, Hispanic 4%, Native American <1%
Retention and Graduation: 69% freshmen return for sophomore year. 15% grads go on to further study within 1 year. 10% grads pursue arts and sciences degrees. 1% grads pursue law degrees. 3% grads pursue business degrees. 1% grads pursue medical degrees. **Faculty:** 62 full-time faculty, 50% hold PhDs, 32% are members of minority groups, 5% are women. 0% of classes are taught by teaching assistants.

ACADEMICS

Degrees: associate, bachelor's, certificate, diploma, first professional, master's, terminal associate. **Classes:** Most classes have 10–19 students. **Majors with Highest Enrollment:** Youth Ministry; Elementary Education and Teaching; Mass Communication/Media Studies. **Special Study Options:** Accelerated program, distance learning, double major, dual enrollment, English as a Second Language (ESL), honors program, independent study, internships, liberal arts/career combination, study abroad, teacher certification program, weekend college. **Honors programs:** Honors Program based on a "great books" curriculum. **Disability Services:** Special programs offered to physically disabled students include note-taking services, reader services, tape recorders, tutors. **Career services:** career/job search classes, career assessment, internships. Career services highlights include the required internship of all students as part of the graduation requirements.

FACILITIES

Housing: special housing for disabled students, men's dorms, women's dorms, apartments for married students, apartments for single students, Theme Housing. 100% of campus accessible to physically disabled. **Computers:** 100% of classrooms, 100% of dorms, 100% of libraries, 100% of dining areas, 100% of student union, 100% of common outdoor areas have wireless network access. Students can register for classes online. Administrative functions (other than registration) can be performed online.

CAMPUS LIFE

Environment: City. **Activities:** Choral groups, concert band, dance, drama/theater, jazz band, literary magazine, music ensembles, musical theater, opera, pep band, radio station, student government, student newspaper, student-run film society, Campus Ministries, International Student Organization 11 registered organizations, 2 honor societies, 1 religious organization. **Athletics (Intercollegiate):** *Men:* basketball, cross-country, golf, soccer, track/field (outdoor), track/field (indoor). *Women:* basketball, cross-country, golf, soccer, softball, track/field (outdoor), track/field (indoor), volleyball. **On-Campus Highlights:** Corum Student Union, Bernice Hansen Athletic Center, Campus Bookstore Atrium, Faber Hall Seating Area, Gordon Music Hall. **Environmental Initiatives:** On campus dialogue and focus on sustainability issues. Joining a community organization.

ADMISSIONS

Freshman Academic Profile: Average high school GPA 3.3. 60% from public high schools. SAT Math middle 50% range 440-540. SAT Critical Reading middle 50% range 360-580. SAT Writing middle 50% range 480-500. ACT middle 50% range 20-25. Minimum paper TOEFL 500. **Basis for Candidate Selection:** *Very important factors considered include:* application essay, academic GPA, recommendation(s), standardized test scores, character/personal qualities, religious affiliation/commitment. *Important factors considered include:* Class rank, rigor of secondary school record. *Other factors considered include:* level of applicant's interest. **Freshman Admission Requirements:** High school diploma is required and GED is accepted. **Freshman Admission Statistics:** 939 applied, 75% admitted, 31% enrolled. **Transfer Admission Requirements:** High school transcript, college transcript(s), essay or personal statement, Minimum college GPA of 2.0 required. Lowest grade transferable C-. **General Admission Information:** Application Fee $25. Nonfall registration accepted. Credit and/or placement offered for CEEB Advanced Placement tests.

COSTS AND FINANCIAL AID

Annual tuition $19,190. Room and board $6,500. Required fees $340. Average book expense $1,000. **Required Forms and Deadlines:** FAFSA. **Notification of Awards:** Applicants will be notified of awards on a rolling basis beginning 2/15. **Types of Aid:** *Need-based scholarships/grants:* Federal Pell, SEOG, state scholarships/grants, private scholarships, the school's own gift aid. *Loans:* Subsidized Stafford, Unsubsidized Stafford, PLUS, Federal Perkins. *Student Employment:* Federal Work-Study Program available. Highest amount earned per year from on-campus jobs $5,500. Off-campus job opportunities are good. **Financial Aid Statistics:** 100% freshmen, 99% undergrads receive need-based scholarship or grant aid. 100% freshmen, 94% undergrads receive non-need-based scholarship or grant aid. 81% freshmen, 79% undergrads receive need-based self-help aid. 23% freshmen, 15% undergrads receive athletic scholarships. 100% freshmen, 98% undergrads receive any aid. 77% undergrads borrow to pay for school. Average cumulative indebtedness $17,438. **Criteria for awarding institutional aid:** *Non-need-based:* academics, athletics, leadership, music/drama, state/district residency.

CORNISH COLLEGE OF THE ARTS

1000 Lenora Street, Seattle, WA 98121
Phone: 206-726-5016 · **Financial Aid Phone:** 206-726-5013
E-mail: admissions@cornish.edu · **CEEB Code:** 58
Fax: 206-720-1011 · **Website:** www.cornish.edu · **ACT Code:** 4801

This private school was founded in 1914. It has a 4-acre campus.

RATINGS

Admissions Selectivity Rating: 61   **Fire Safety Rating:** 60*

STUDENTS AND FACULTY

Enrollment: 765. **Student Body:** 64% female, 36% male, 52% out-of-state, 3% international (25 countries represented). Asian 5%, African American 3%, Caucasian 50%, Hispanic 7%, Native American 1%
Retention and Graduation: 12% grads go on to further study within 1 year. 5% grads pursue arts and sciences degrees. **Faculty:**

ACADEMICS

Degrees: bachelor's. **Classes:** Most classes have 10–19 students. **Majors with Highest Enrollment:** Design and Visual Communications; Drama and Dramatics/Theatre Arts; Music Performance. **Special Study Options:** cooperative education program, independent study, internships, study abroad. **Disability Services:** Special programs offered to physically disabled students include note-taking services, tape recorders. **Career services:** internships.

FACILITIES

Housing: 50% of campus accessible to physically disabled. **Special Academic Facilities/Equipment:** Art galleries, extensive art studio space, theatres, electronic music studio, dance studio, concert hall.

CAMPUS LIFE

Environment: Metropolis. **Activities:** Choral groups, concert band, dance, drama/theater, jazz band, literary magazine, music ensembles, musical theater, opera, student government, student newspaper, student-run film society 18 registered organizations, 6 honor societies, 1 religious organization. **On-Campus Highlights:** Raisbeck Performance Hall, Cornsh Gallery, Nellie's Café.

ADMISSIONS

Freshman Academic Profile: Average high school GPA 3.15. 75% from public high schools. Minimum paper TOEFL 525. **Basis for Candidate Selection:** *Very important factors considered include:* talent/ability. *Important* *factors considered include:* application essay, rigor of secondary school record. *Other factors considered include:* recommendation(s), standardized test scores, extracurricular activities, interview. **Freshman Admission Requirements:** High school diploma is required and GED is accepted. **Freshman Admission Statistics:** 1,134 applied, 86% admitted, 17% enrolled. **Transfer Admission Requirements:** High school transcript, college transcript(s), essay or personal statement, interview, Minimum college GPA of 2.0 required. Lowest grade transferable C. **General Admission Information:** Application Fee $35. Regular application deadline 2/15. Notification on a rolling basis, beginning on or about 1/1. Nonfall registration not accepted. Admission may be deferred for a maximum of 12 months. Credit offered for CEEB Advanced Placement tests.

COSTS AND FINANCIAL AID

Required Forms and Deadlines: FAFSA, Institution's own financial aid form. **Notification of Awards:** Applicants will be notified of awards on or about 5/15. **Types of Aid:** *Need-based scholarships/grants:* Federal Pell, SEOG, state scholarships/grants, Merit scholarships based on artistic merit and merit w/need scholarships Both are insitutional money. *Loans:* Subsidized Stafford, Unsubsidized Stafford, PLUS, Federal Perkins. *Student Employment:* Federal Work-Study Program available. Highest amount earned per year from on-campus jobs $3,000. Off-campus job opportunities are excellent. **Financial Aid Statistics:**84% undergrads receive need-based scholarship or grant aid.100% undergrads receive non-need-based scholarship or grant aid.84% undergrads receive need-based self-help aid.0% undergrads receive athletic scholarships. Criteriafor awarding institutional aid: *Non-need-based:* academics, art, music/drama.

COVENANT COLLEGE

14049 Scenic Highway, Lookout Mtn., GA 30750
Phone: 706-820-2398 · **Financial Aid Phone:** 706-419-1126
E-mail: admissions@covenant.edu · **CEEB Code:** 6124
Fax: 706-820-0893 · **Website:** www.covenant.edu · **ACT Code:** 3951

This private school was founded in 1955. It has a 300-acre campus.

RATINGS

Admissions Selectivity Rating: 83   **Fire Safety Rating:** 80

STUDENTS AND FACULTY

Enrollment: 1,066. **Student Body:** 58% female, 42% male, 78% out-of-state, 2% international (21 countries represented). Asian 2%, African American 3%, Caucasian 87%, Hispanic 3%, Native American <1%
Retention and Graduation: 85% freshmen return for sophomore year. 48% freshmen graduate within 4 years. 57% freshmen graduate within 6 years. 28% grads go on to further study within 1 year. 10% grads pursue arts and sciences degrees. 1% grads pursue law degrees. 2% grads pursue business degrees. 1% grads pursue medical degrees. **Faculty:** 66 full-time faculty, 91% hold PhDs, 23% are members of minority groups, 9% are women. 0% of classes are taught by teaching assistants.

ACADEMICS

Degrees: associate, bachelor's, master's. **Classes:** Most classes have 10–19 students. Most lab/discussion sessions have 20–29 students. **Majors with Highest Enrollment:** Sociology; English Language and Literature; Elementary Education and Teaching. **Special Study Options:** double major, dual enrollment, exchange student program (domestic), independent study, internships, student-designed major, study abroad, teacher certification program, Dual-engineering degree with Georgia Tech; cooperative nursing program with Emory University and Chattanooga State; bridge program for MSN with Vanderbilt University. **Disability Services:** Special programs offered to physically disabled students include note-taking services, tape recorders. **Career services:** Alumni network, alumni services, career assessment, internships. Career services highlights include our internship program.

FACILITIES

Housing: men's dorms, women's dorms, apartments for single students. 95% of campus accessible to physically disabled. **Computers:** 100% of classrooms, 100% of dorms, 100% of libraries, 100% of dining areas, NA% of student union, 100% of common outdoor areas have wireless network access. Students can register for classes online. Administrative functions (other than registration) can be performed online.

CAMPUS LIFE

Environment: City. **Activities:** Choral groups, concert band, drama/theater, jazz band, literary magazine, music ensembles, radio station, student government, student newspaper, yearbook. 40 registered organizations, 4 honor societies, 1 religious organization. **Athletics (Intercollegiate):** *Men:* baseball, basketball, cross-country, golf, soccer, tennis. *Women:* basketball, cross-country, golf, soccer, softball, tennis, volleyball. **On-Campus Highlights:** Probasco Visitor's Center, Carter Hall, The Overlook, The Chapel, Ashe Gym, The campus is located on top of Lookout Mountain in Georgia, providing a backdrop of scenic beauty.

ADMISSIONS

Freshman Academic Profile: Average high school GPA 3.6. 25.5% in top 10% of high school class, 50% in top 25% of high school class, 75.5% in top 50% of high school class. 55% from public high schools. SAT Math middle 50% range 510-620. SAT Critical Reading middle 50% range 540-660. SAT Writing middle 50% range 530-650. ACT middle 50% range 23-29. Minimum internet-based TOEFL 75. **Basis for Candidate Selection:** *Very important factors considered include:* application essay, academic GPA, recommendation(s), rigor of secondary school record, standardized test scores, character/personal qualities. *Important factors considered include:* interview. *Other factors considered include:* Class rank, alumni/ae relation, extracurricular activities, first generation, level of applicant's interest, racial/ethnic status, religious affiliation/commitment, volunteer work. **Freshman Admission Requirements:** High school diploma is required and GED is accepted. *Academic units required:* 4 English, 3 mathematics, 2 science, 2 social studies, 3 academic electives. **Freshman Admission Statistics:** 655 applied, 97% admitted, 42% enrolled. **Transfer Admission Requirements:** High school transcript, college transcript(s), essay or personal statement, interview, standardized test scores, statement of good standing from prior institution(s). Minimum college GPA of 2.0 required. Lowest grade transferable C-. **General Admission Information:** Application Fee $35. Notification on a rolling basis, beginning on or about 8/1. Nonfall registration accepted. Admission may be deferred for a maximum of 1 year. Credit offered for CEEB Advanced Placement tests.

COSTS AND FINANCIAL AID

Annual tuition $29,300. Room and board $8,830. Required fees $860. Average book expense $1,100. **Required Forms and Deadlines:** FAFSA, State aid form. **Notification of Awards:** Applicants will be notified of awards on a rolling basis beginning 2/1. **Types of Aid:** *Need-based scholarships/grants:* Federal Pell, SEOG, state scholarships/grants, private scholarships, the school's own gift aid. *Loans:* Subsidized Stafford, Unsubsidized Stafford, PLUS, Federal Perkins, state loans, college/university loans from institutional funds. *Student Employment:* Federal Work-Study Program available. Institutional employment available. Highest amount earned per year from on-campus jobs $3,840. Off-campus job opportunities are good. **Financial Aid Statistics:** 100% freshmen, 99% undergrads receive need-based scholarship or grant aid. 18% freshmen, 15% undergrads receive non-need-based scholarship or grant aid. 91% freshmen, 90% undergrads receive need-based self-help aid. 0% freshmen, 0% undergrads receive athletic scholarships. 100% freshmen, 99% undergrads receive any aid. 69% undergrads borrow to pay for school. Average cumulative indebtedness $22,208. **Criteria for awarding institutional aid:** *Non-need-based:* academics, alumni affiliation, art, athletics, job skills, leadership, minority status, music/drama, religious affiliation, state/district residency.

CRANDALL UNIVERSITY

Crandall Admissions Office, Moncton, NB E1C 9L7
Phone: 506-858-8970
E-mail: admissions@crandallu.ca
Fax: 506-858-9694 · **Website:** www.crandallu.ca

This is a private school.

RATINGS

Admissions Selectivity Rating: 60*   **Fire Safety Rating:** 60*

STUDENTS AND FACULTY

Enrollment: 0. **Student Body:** 11% out-of-state.
Retention and Graduation: 48% freshmen return for sophomore year. 33% freshmen graduate within 4 years. **Faculty:** 26 full-time faculty, 81% hold PhDs, 35% are members of minority groups, 15% are women.

ACADEMICS

Degrees: bachelor's, certificate, post-bachelor's certificate. **Special Study Options:** cooperative education program, double major, dual enrollment, English as a Second Language (ESL), honors program, independent study, internships, liberal arts/career combination, study abroad, teacher certification program.

FACILITIES

Housing: men's dorms, women's dorms.

CAMPUS LIFE

Activities: drama/theater, student government, student newspaper, yearbook, Campus Ministries, International Student Organization.

ADMISSIONS

Freshman Admission Statistics: 149 applied, 93% admitted, 71% enrolled. **Transfer Admission Requirements:** college transcript(s), Lowest grade transferable C-.

COSTS AND FINANCIAL AID

Average book expense $1,600.

CREIGHTON UNIVERSITY

2500 California Plaza, Omaha, NE 68178
Phone: 402-280-2703 · **Financial Aid Phone:** 402-280-2731
E-mail: admissions@creighton.edu · **CEEB Code:** 6121
Fax: 402-280-2685 · **Website:** www.creighton.edu · **ACT Code:** 2444

This private school, affiliated with the Roman Catholic Church, was founded in 1878. It has a 130-acre campus.

RATINGS

Admissions Selectivity Rating: 89   **Fire Safety Rating:** 89

STUDENTS AND FACULTY

Enrollment: 3,977. **Student Body:** 58% female, 42% male, 72% out-of-state, 3% international (33 countries represented). Asian 9%, African American 3%, Caucasian 73%, Hispanic 7%, Native American <1%
Retention and Graduation: 91% freshmen return for sophomore year. 71% freshmen graduate within 4 years. 78% freshmen graduate within 6 years. 33% grads go on to further study within 1 year. 11% grads pursue arts and sciences degrees. 4% grads pursue law degrees. 6% grads pursue medical degrees.
Faculty: 553 full-time faculty, 92% hold PhDs, 43% are members of minority groups, 10% are women. 0% of classes are taught by teaching assistants.

ACADEMICS

Degrees: associate, bachelor's, certificate, master's. **Classes:** Most classes have 20–29 students. Most lab/discussion sessions have 10–19 students. **Majors with Highest Enrollment:** Registered Nursing/Registered Nurse; Biology/Biological Sciences; Psychology. **Special Study Options:** Accelerated program, cross-registration, distance learning, double major, dual enrollment, English as a Second Language (ESL), exchange student program (domestic), honors program, independent study, internships, liberal arts/career combination, study abroad, teacher certification program, 3-3 Engineering Program with University of Detroit Mercy; 3-3 Law Program within Creighton University. **Honors programs:** Designed for talented, imaginative students desirous of participation in small, iscussion-oriented classes and in courses on interdisciplinary and topical issues. Combined degree programs: BA/JD, BA/DDS, BA/MEng. **Disability Services:** Special programs offered to physically disabled students include note-taking services, reader services, tape recorders, tutors. **Career services:** Alumni network, alumni services, career/job search classes, career assessment, internships, regional alumni. Career services highlights include interships. For more information see: http://www2.creighton.edu/careercenter/internships/internshipsearchsites/index.php.

FACILITIES

Housing: Coed dorms, special housing for disabled students, women's dorms, apartments for married students, apartments for single students, Honors, Freshman Leadership. 97% of campus accessible to physically disabled. **Special Academic Facilities/Equipment:** Fine arts/performing center, health science and research complex, hospital. **Computers:** 100% of classrooms, 100% of dorms, 100% of libraries, 100% of dining areas, 100% of student union, 100% of common outdoor areas have wireless network access. Students can register for classes online. Administrative functions (other than registration) can be performed online.

CAMPUS LIFE

Environment: Metropolis. **Activities:** Choral groups, concert band, dance, drama/theater, jazz band, literary magazine, music ensembles, musical theater, pep band, student government, student newspaper, symphony orchestra, television station, yearbook, Campus Ministries, International Student Organization, Model UN. 182 registered organizations, 11 honor society, 6 religious organizations. 5 fraternities, 8 sororities. **Athletics (Intercollegiate):** *Men:* baseball, basketball, cross-country, golf, soccer, tennis. *Women:* basketball, crew/rowing, cross-country, golf, soccer, softball, tennis, volleyball. **On-Campus Highlights:** Harper Living Learning Center, Campus Mall and green in front of Studen,

Hixson-Lied Science Building, Morrison Soccer stadium, Jesuit Gardens, Ryan Athletics Center and D.J. Sokol Auditorium completed Fall 2009. **Environmental Initiatives:** Stewardship of the environment has become central to the mission of Creighton University and the wider Jesuit community. The Energy Technology Program has allowed the university to become more sustainable, with 120 kW of renewable energy generated on site, including the largest solar photovoltaic array in Nebraska. Not only have these technologies reduced Creightons environmental footprint, but they have also become the foundation for a hands-on educational platform, allowing students to work and conduct research on professional systems. The University has continued to expand renewable energy sources including solar photovoltaic and solar thermal panels, four wind turbines designed for urban environments, geothermal hearing, low voltage lighting, solar hot water, and a ground source heat pump. The presence of these technologies at Creighton exposes everyone in the community to them and concretely conveys Creightons commitment to environmental responsibility. In 2013, Father Lannon,the president of Creighton University, signed the St. Francis Pledge to Care for Creation and the Poor on behalf of the university. The St. Francis Pledge is a commitment that families, schools, individuals, businesses, and organizations can sign that promotes sustainable living and encourages anyone and everyone to take action on behalf of protecting the environment. In 2009, Father Schlegel signed the American College and University Presidents Climate Commitment (ACUPCC). The Climate Action Plan, finalized in 2013, contains plans for reducing the universitys greenhouse gas emissions to zero by 2050.

ADMISSIONS

Freshman Academic Profile: Average high school GPA 3.75. 38% in top 10% of high school class, 72% in top 25% of high school class, 93% in top 50% of high school class. 49% from public high schools. SAT Math middle 50% range 550-665. SAT Critical Reading middle 50% range 520-630. SAT Writing middle 50% range 520-640. ACT middle 50% range 24-29. Minimum internet-based TOEFL 80. Minimum paper TOEFL 550. **Basis for Candidate Selection:** *Very important factors considered include:* academic GPA, rigor of secondary school record. *Important factors considered include:* application essay, standardized test scores. *Other factors considered include:* Class rank, recommendation(s), character/personal qualities, extracurricular activities, first generation, level of applicant's interest, racial/ethnic status, talent/ability, volunteer work. **Freshman Admission Requirements:** High school diploma is required and GED is accepted. *Academic units required:* 4 English, 3 mathematics, 2 science, (0 science labs), 2 foreign language, 2 social studies, 0 history, 3 academic electives. **Freshman Admission Statistics:** 8,398 applied, 73% admitted, 26% enrolled. **Transfer Admission Requirements:** High school transcript, college transcript(s), statement of good standing from prior institution(s). Minimum college GPA of 2.50 required. Lowest grade transferable C. **General Admission Information:** Application Fee $40. Regular application deadline 2/15. Notification on a rolling basis, beginning on or about 12/15. Nonfall registration accepted. Admission may be deferred for a maximum of 12 months. Credit and/or placement offered for CEEB Advanced Placement tests.

COSTS AND FINANCIAL AID

Annual tuition $33,796. Room and board $9,996. Required fees $1,564. Average book expense $1,200. **Required Forms and Deadlines:** FAFSA, Institution's own financial aid form. **Notification of Awards:** Applicants will be notified of awards on a rolling basis beginning 3/15. **Types of Aid:** *Need-based scholarships/grants:* Federal Pell, SEOG, state scholarships/grants, private scholarships, the school's own gift aid. *Loans:* Subsidized Stafford, Unsubsidized Stafford, PLUS, Federal Perkins, Federal Nursing. *Student Employment:* Federal Work-Study Program available. Institutional employment available. Highest amount earned per year from on-campus jobs $1,400. Off-campus job opportunities are excellent. **Financial Aid Statistics:** 100% freshmen, 99% undergrads receive need-based scholarship or grant aid. 94% freshmen, 91% undergrads receive non-need-based scholarship or grant aid. 80% freshmen, 83% undergrads receive need-based self-help aid. 4% freshmen, 6% undergrads receive athletic scholarships. 100% freshmen, 89% undergrads receive any aid. 64% undergrads borrow to pay for school. Average cumulative indebtedness $27,507. **Criteria for awarding institutional aid:** *Non-need-based:* academics, alumni affiliation, art, athletics, leadership, minority status, music/drama.

CROWN COLLEGE

8700 College View Drive, St. Bonifacius, MN 55375-9001
Phone: 952-446-4142 • **Financial Aid Phone:** 952-446-4175
E-mail: info@crown.edu
Fax: 952-446-4149 • **Website:** www.crown.edu • **ACT Code:** 2152

This private school, affiliated with the Christian & Missionary Alliance Church, was founded in 1916. It has a 215-acre campus.

RATINGS

Admissions Selectivity Rating: 81 **Fire Safety Rating:** 68

STUDENTS AND FACULTY

Enrollment: 1,017. **Student Body:** 57% female, 43% male, 31% out-of-state, 1% international (21 countries represented). Asian 7%, African American 4%, Caucasian 78%, Hispanic 2%, Native American 1%
Retention and Graduation: 63% freshmen return for sophomore year. 40% freshmen graduate within 4 years. 52% freshmen graduate within 6 years. **Faculty:** 34 full-time faculty, 47% hold PhDs, 26% are members of minority groups, 6% are women. 0% of classes are taught by teaching assistants.

ACADEMICS

Degrees: associate, bachelor's, certificate, master's, post-bachelor's certificate. **Classes:** Most classes have 10–19 students. Most lab/discussion sessions have 20–29 students. **Majors with Highest Enrollment:** Theology and Religious Vocations; Elementary Education and Teaching; Business Administration and Management. **Special Study Options:** Accelerated program, distance learning, double major, dual enrollment, English as a Second Language (ESL), honors program, independent study, internships, study abroad, teacher certification program, weekend college, 2-2 with non-accredited Bible colleges. **Honors programs:** The Honors Program. **Disability Services:** Special programs offered to physically disabled students include note-taking services, reader services, tape recorders, tutors. **Career services:** alumni services, career/job search classes, career assessment, internships. We are very excited about the number of opportunities that students have to engage in practical hands-on learning activities through the SIFE and practicum programs.

FACILITIES

Housing: special housing for disabled students, men's dorms, women's dorms, apartments for married students, apartments for single studentsApartments for students with dependent children. 95% of campus accessible to physically disabled. **Special Academic Facilities/Equipment:** Peter Watne Memorial Library **Computers:** 100% of classrooms, 20% of dorms, 100% of libraries, 100% of dining areas, 100% of student union, 10% of common outdoor areas have wireless network access. Administrative functions (other than registration) can be performed online.

CAMPUS LIFE

Environment: Rural. **Activities:** Choral groups, concert band, drama/theater, jazz band, literary magazine, music ensembles, musical theater, pep band, radio station, student government, student newspaper, student-run film society, yearbook, Campus Ministries, International Student Organization. 19 registered organizations, 1 honor society, 6 religious organizations. **Athletics (Intercollegiate):** *Men:* baseball, basketball, cross-country, football, golf, soccer. *Women:* basketball, cross-country, golf, soccer, softball, volleyball. **On-Campus Highlights:** Student Center, Coffee Shoppe and Climbing Wall, Storm Café/student union, Wild Athletic Center/Weight Room, Life Fitness Center. **Environmental Initiatives:** The College recycles all cardboard and provides co-mingled recycling containers in all common areas, each classroom, and in each office. We post recycling program notes on our website from time to time and also posters throughout the building quarterly. Large amounts of metals, plastics, light bulbs, electronics, etc. are recycled each month by facilities mgmt. Low flow toilets are used to replace older units as needed and all water fixtures are being replaced with low flow units. All water heaters and HVAC components are being replaced (both planned and unplanned) with high-efficiency units Appliance replacement cycles utilize high-efficiency appliances (stoves, refrigerators, etc). We are working to integrate all campus building systems to one central control system in order to decrease our energy footprint.

ADMISSIONS

Freshman Academic Profile: Average high school GPA 3.36. 13% in top 10% of high school class, 38% in top 25% of high school class, 79% in top 50% of high school class. SAT Math middle 50% range 475-598. SAT Critical Reading middle 50% range 508-600. SAT Writing middle 50% range 533-618. ACT middle 50% range 21-25. Minimum internet-based TOEFL 75. Minimum paper TOEFL 500. **Basis for Candidate Selection:** *Very important factors considered include:* application essay, academic GPA, recommendation(s), rigor of secondary school record, standardized test scores, religious affiliation/

commitment. *Important factors considered include:* Class rank, character/personal qualities. *Other factors considered include:* extracurricular activities, interview, level of applicant's interest, talent/ability, volunteer work, work experience. **Freshman Admission Requirements:** High school diploma is required and GED is accepted. **Freshman Admission Statistics:** 453 applied, 78% admitted, 42% enrolled. **Transfer Admission Requirements:** High school transcript, college transcript(s), essay or personal statement, Minimum college GPA of 2.0 required. Lowest grade transferable C. **General Admission Information:** Application Fee $35. Regular application deadline 8/20. Nonfall registration accepted. Admission may be deferred for a maximum of 1 year. Credit offered for CEEB Advanced Placement tests.

COSTS AND FINANCIAL AID

Annual tuition $22,100. Room and board $7,480. Average book expense $1,140. **Required Forms and Deadlines:** FAFSA, Institution's own financial aid form. **Notification of Awards:** Applicants will be notified of awards on a rolling basis beginning 4/1. **Types of Aid:** *Need-based scholarships/grants:* Federal Pell, SEOG, state scholarships/grants, private scholarships, the school's own gift aid. *Loans:* Subsidized Stafford, Unsubsidized Stafford, PLUS, Federal Perkins, state loans, US Bank No Fee Education loans, CitiAssist loans, Signature loans, Wells Fargo Collegiate Loan. *Student Employment:* Federal Work-Study Program available. Off-campus job opportunities are good. **Financial Aid Statistics:** 84% freshmen, 83% undergrads receive any aid. 82% undergrads borrow to pay for school. Average cumulative indebtedness $19,249. **Criteria for awarding institutional aid:** *Non-need-based:* academics, alumni affiliation, leadership, minority status, music/drama, religious affiliation.

CULVER-STOCKTON COLLEGE

One College Hill, Canton, MO 63435
Phone: 573-288-6331 • **Financial Aid Phone:** 573-288-6307
E-mail: admissions@culver.edu • **CEEB Code:** 6123
Fax: 573-288-6618 • **ACT Code:** 2290

This private school, affiliated with the Disciples of Christ Church, was founded in 1853. It has a 139-acre campus.

RATINGS

Admissions Selectivity Rating: 82 **Fire Safety Rating:** 68

STUDENTS AND FACULTY

Enrollment: 931. **Student Body:** 47% female, 53% male, 45% out-of-state, 5% international (11 countries represented). Asian 0%, African American 13%, Caucasian 74%, Hispanic 5%, Native American <1%
Retention and Graduation: 76% freshmen return for sophomore year. 34% freshmen graduate within 4 years. 41% freshmen graduate within 6 years. **Faculty:** 49 full-time faculty, 65% hold PhDs, 47% are members of minority groups, 4% are women. 0% of classes are taught by teaching assistants.

ACADEMICS

Degrees: bachelor's. **Classes:** Most classes have 10–19 students. Most lab/discussion sessions have 10–19 students. **Majors with Highest Enrollment:** Registered Nursing/Registered Nurse; Business Administration and Management; Psychology. **Special Study Options:** Accelerated program, distance learning, double major, dual enrollment, honors program, independent study, internships, liberal arts/career combination, student-designed major, study abroad, teacher certification program. **Honors programs:** Honors Scholars are expected to complete both an academic and enrichment requirement. Combined degree programs: BA/MA, Washington University-OT program. **Disability Services:** Special programs offered to physically disabled students include note-taking services, reader services, tape recorders, tutors. **Career services:** Alumni network, alumni services, career/job search classes, career assessment, internships, regional alumni. Career services highlights include experiential learning which all students have participated in since fall 2008 as part of the new CSC@EXP curriculum.

FACILITIES

Housing: Coed dorms, fraternity/sorority housing. 40% of campus accessible to physically disabled. **Special Academic Facilities/Equipment:** Art gallery, performing arts center. **Computers:** 100% of classrooms, 100% of dorms, 100% of libraries, 100% of dining areas, 100% of student union, 100% of common outdoor areas have wireless network access. Students can register for classes online. Administrative functions (other than registration) can be performed online.

CAMPUS LIFE

Environment: Rural. **Activities:** Choral groups, concert band, dance, drama/theater, jazz band, literary magazine, music ensembles, musical theater, pep band, radio station, student government, student newspaper, Campus

Ministries, International Student Organization, Model UN. 44 registered organizations, 11 honor society, 4 religious organizations. 4 fraternities, 3 sororities. **Athletics (Intercollegiate):** *Men:* baseball, basketball, cheerleading, cross-country, football, golf, soccer, track/field (outdoor), track/field (indoor). *Women:* basketball, cheerleading, cross-country, golf, soccer, softball, track/field (outdoor), track/field (indoor), volleyball. **On-Campus Highlights:** Computer labs, Cat's 'Pause', Cafeteria, Joe Charles Field House, Activity & Recreation Center. **Environmental Initiatives:** Thermostat control; Sustainability focus group; Limited use of disposable containers and removal of cafeteria trays.

ADMISSIONS

Freshman Academic Profile: Average high school GPA 3.19. 11% in top 10% of high school class, 32% in top 25% of high school class, 64% in top 50% of high school class. 95% from public high schools. SAT Math middle 50% range 440-540. SAT Critical Reading middle 50% range 420-520. ACT middle 50% range 19-23. Minimum internet-based TOEFL 79. Minimum paper TOEFL 550. **Basis for Candidate Selection:** *Very important factors considered include:* academic GPA, standardized test scores. *Important factors considered include:* rigor of secondary school record. *Other factors considered include:* application essay, recommendation(s), alumni/ae relation. **Freshman Admission Requirements:** High school diploma is required and GED is accepted. **Freshman Admission Statistics:** 2,372 applied, 58% admitted, 21% enrolled. **Transfer Admission Requirements:** college transcript(s), Minimum college GPA of 2.0 required. Lowest grade transferable C-. **General Admission Information:** Notification on a rolling basis, beginning on or about 10/15. Nonfall registration accepted. Admission may be deferred for a maximum of 1 year. Credit and/or placement offered for CEEB Advanced Placement tests.

COSTS AND FINANCIAL AID

Annual tuition $23,750. Room and board $7,780. Required fees $300. Average book expense $1,200. **Required Forms and Deadlines:** FAFSA. **Notification of Awards:** Applicants will be notified of awards on a rolling basis beginning 2/15. **Types of Aid:** *Need-based scholarships/grants:* Federal Pell, SEOG, state scholarships/grants, private scholarships, the school's own gift aid. *Loans:* Direct Subsidized Stafford, Direct Unsubsidized Stafford, Direct PLUS, PLUS, Federal Perkins, state loans, college/university loans from institutional funds. *Student Employment:* Federal Work-Study Program available. Institutional employment available. Highest amount earned per year from on-campus jobs $4,954. Off-campus job opportunities are fair. **Financial Aid Statistics:** 100% freshmen, 100% undergrads receive need-based scholarship or grant aid. 14% freshmen, 12% undergrads receive non-need-based scholarship or grant aid. 84% freshmen, 87% undergrads receive need-based self-help aid. 20% freshmen, 15% undergrads receive athletic scholarships. 96% freshmen, 98% undergrads receive any aid. 85% undergrads borrow to pay for school. Average cumulative indebtedness $22,449. **Criteria for awarding institutional aid:** *Non-need-based:* academics, alumni affiliation, art, athletics, job skills, leadership, music/drama, religious affiliation, state/district residency.

CUMBERLAND UNIVERSITY

Cumberland University, Lebanon, TN 37087-3408
Phone: 615-444-2562
E-mail: admissions@cumberland.edu • **CEEB Code:** 1146
Fax: 615-444-2569 • **Website:** www.cumberland.edu • **ACT Code:** 3954

This private school was founded in 1842. It has a 40-acre campus.

RATINGS

Admissions Selectivity Rating: 75   Fire Safety Rating: 65

STUDENTS AND FACULTY

Enrollment: 921. **Student Body:** 57% female, 43% male, 15% out-of-state, 3% international (27 countries represented). Asian 2%, African American 14%, Caucasian 77%, Hispanic 1%, Native American <1%
Retention and Graduation: 69% freshmen return for sophomore year. 23% freshmen graduate within 4 years. 37% freshmen graduate within 6 years. 15% grads go on to further study within 1 year. 5% grads pursue arts and sciences degrees. 3% grads pursue law degrees. 5% grads pursue business degrees. 1% grads pursue medical degrees. **Faculty:** 79 full-time faculty, 57% hold PhDs, 38% are members of minority groups, 5% are women. 0% of classes are taught by teaching assistants.

ACADEMICS

Degrees: associate, bachelor's, master's. **Classes:** Most classes have fewer than 10 students. Most lab/discussion sessions have fewer than 10 students. **Majors with Highest Enrollment:** Elementary Education and Teaching; Registered Nursing/Registered Nurse; Business/Commerce. **Special Study Options:**

Accelerated program, distance learning, double major, dual enrollment, honors program, independent study, internships, teacher certification program. **Disability Services:** Special programs offered to physically disabled students include tutors. **Career services:** career/job search classes, career assessment.

FACILITIES

Housing: special housing for disabled students, men's dorms, women's dorms 100% of campus accessible to physically disabled. **Special Academic Facilities/Equipment:** Cavett Wild Game Collection.

CAMPUS LIFE

Environment: Town. **Activities:** Choral groups, dance, drama/theater, jazz band, marching band, music ensembles, musical theater, radio station, student government, student newspaper, yearbook. 15 registered organizations, 13 honor societies, 2 religious organizations. 3 fraternities, 2 sororities. **Athletics (Intercollegiate):** *Men:* baseball, basketball, cheerleading, cross-country, football, golf, soccer, tennis, wrestling. *Women:* basketball, cheerleading, cross-country, golf, soccer, softball, tennis, volleyball. **On-Campus Highlights:** Labry Hall Atrium, Memorial Hall Student Lounge, Mitchell Student Center, Phillips Dining Hall Patio.

ADMISSIONS

Freshman Academic Profile: Average high school GPA 3.03. 12% in top 10% of high school class, 32% in top 25% of high school class, 70% in top 50% of high school class. 89% from public high schools. SAT Math middle 50% range 380-510. SAT Critical Reading middle 50% range 410-530. ACT middle 50% range 17-22. Minimum paper TOEFL 500. **Basis for Candidate Selection:** *Very important factors considered include:* Class rank, rigor of secondary school record, standardized test scores. *Other factors considered include:* application essay, recommendation(s), alumni/ae relation. **Freshman Admission Requirements:** High school diploma is required and GED is accepted. **Freshman Admission Statistics:** 532 applied, 66% admitted, 59% enrolled. **Transfer Admission Requirements:** college transcript(s), Minimum college GPA of 2.0 required. Lowest grade transferable C. **General Admission Information:** Application Fee $25. Nonfall registration accepted. Admission may be deferred for a maximum of one year. Credit offered for CEEB Advanced Placement tests.

COSTS AND FINANCIAL AID

Annual tuition $12,130. Room and board $4,680. Required fees $100. Average book expense $1,040. **Required Forms and Deadlines:** FAFSA, Institution's own financial aid form. **Notification of Awards:** Applicants will be notified of awards on or about 5/1. **Types of Aid:** *Need-based scholarships/grants:* Federal Pell, SEOG, state scholarships/grants, private scholarships, the school's own gift aid. *Loans:* Subsidized Stafford, Unsubsidized Stafford, PLUS, Federal Perkins, state loans. *Student Employment:* Federal Work-Study Program available. Off-campus job opportunities are excellent. **Financial Aid Statistics:** 56% freshmen, 59% undergrads receive need-based scholarship or grant aid. 107% freshmen, 104% undergrads receive non-need-based scholarship or grant aid. 68% freshmen, 70% undergrads receive need-based self-help aid. 85% freshmen, 96% undergrads receive athletic scholarships. 85% freshmen, 85% undergrads receive any aid. 70% undergrads borrow to pay for school.

CURRY COLLEGE

1071 Blue Hill Avenue, Milton, MA 2186
Phone: 617-333-2210
E-mail: curryadm@curry.edu • **CEEB Code:** 3285
Fax: 617-333-2114 • **Website:** www.curry.edu • **ACT Code:** 1814

This private school was founded in 1879. It has a 137-acre campus.

RATINGS

Admissions Selectivity Rating: 64   Fire Safety Rating: 60*

STUDENTS AND FACULTY

Enrollment: 1,709. **Student Body:** 53% female, 47% male, 40% out-of-state, 1% international (20 countries represented). Asian 1%, African American 4%, Caucasian 48%, Hispanic 2%, Native American <1%
Retention and Graduation: 68% freshmen return for sophomore year. 44% freshmen graduate within 4 years. 53% freshmen graduate within 6 years. 17% grads go on to further study within 1 year. 10% grads pursue arts and sciences degrees. 1% grads pursue law degrees. 2% grads pursue business degrees. **Faculty:** 0% of classes are taught by teaching assistants.

ACADEMICS

Degrees: bachelor's, master's. **Special Study Options:** Accelerated program, double major, honors program, independent study, internships, liberal arts/career combination, student-designed major, study abroad, teacher certification program, weekend college. **Disability Services:** Special programs offered to physically disabled students include tape recorders, tutors.

FACILITIES

Housing: Coed dorms, special housing for international students, women's dorms **Special Academic Facilities/Equipment:** On-campus preschool, nursing lab, psychology lab. **Computers:** Students can register for classes online.

CAMPUS LIFE

Environment: Village. **Activities:** Choral groups, dance, drama/theater, literary magazine, music ensembles, radio station, student government, student newspaper, television station, yearbook 1 honor society, 2 religious organizations. **Athletics (Intercollegiate):** *Men:* baseball, basketball, cheerleading, football, ice hockey, lacrosse, soccer, tennis. *Women:* basketball, cheerleading, cross-country, lacrosse, soccer, softball, tennis. **On-Campus Highlights:** Drapkin Student Center, Levin Library, WMLN Campus Radio Station, The Suites- New Residence Hall, Hafer Academic Center.

ADMISSIONS

Freshman Academic Profile: Average high school GPA 2.3. 5% in top 10% of high school class, 22% in top 25% of high school class, 65% in top 50% of high school class. 76% from public high schools. Minimum paper TOEFL 500. **Basis for Candidate Selection:** *Important factors considered include:* Class rank, academic GPA, recommendation(s), rigor of secondary school record. *Other factors considered include:* application essay, standardized test scores, alumni/ae relation, character/personal qualities, extracurricular activities, interview, volunteer work, work experience. **Freshman Admission Requirements:** High school diploma is required and GED is accepted. *Academic units required:* 4 English, 3 mathematics, 2 science, (2 science labs), 0 foreign language, 1 social studies, 1 history, 5 academic electives. **Freshman Admission Statistics:** 3,509 applied, 66% admitted, 30% enrolled. **Transfer Admission Requirements:** college transcript(s), essay or personal statement, Minimum college GPA of 2.0 required. Lowest grade transferable C-. **General Admission Information:** Application Fee $40. Early decision application deadline 12/1. Regular application deadline 4/1. Notification on a rolling basis, beginning on or about 1/15. Nonfall registration accepted. Admission may be deferred for a maximum of 12. Credit and/or placement offered for CEEB Advanced Placement tests.

COSTS AND FINANCIAL AID

Annual tuition $17,160. Room and board $6,870. Required fees $755. Average book expense $700. **Required Forms and Deadlines:** FAFSA, Institution's own financial aid form. **Notification of Awards:** Applicants will be notified of awards on a rolling basis beginning 3/1. **Types of Aid:** *Need-based scholarships/grants:* Federal Pell, SEOG, state scholarships/grants, private scholarships, the school's own gift aid. *Loans:* Subsidized Stafford, Unsubsidized Stafford, PLUS, Federal Perkins, state loans. **Financial Aid Statistics:** 90% freshmen, 81% undergrads receive need-based scholarship or grant aid. 0% freshmen, 0% undergrads receive non-need-based scholarship or grant aid. 100% freshmen, 100% undergrads receive need-based self-help aid. 0% freshmen, 0% undergrads receive athletic scholarships. 65% undergrads borrow to pay for school.

See page 1040.

DAEMEN COLLEGE

4380 Main Street, Amherst, NY 14226-3592
Phone: 716-839-8225 · **Financial Aid Phone:** 716-839-8254
E-mail: admissions@daemen.edu · **CEEB Code:** 2762
Fax: 716-839-8229 · **Website:** www.daemen.edu · **ACT Code:** 2874

This private school was founded in 1947. It has a 35-acre campus.

RATINGS

Admissions Selectivity Rating: 81   **Fire Safety Rating:** 83

STUDENTS AND FACULTY

Enrollment: 1,894. **Student Body:** 73% female, 27% male, 5% out-of-state, 1% international (6 countries represented). Asian 2%, African American 11%, Caucasian 77%, Hispanic 5%, Native American <1%. **Retention and Graduation:** 29% freshmen graduate within 4 years. 49% freshmen graduate within 6 years. **Faculty:** 122 full-time faculty, 76% hold PhDs, 59% are members of minority groups, 6% are women. 0% of classes are taught by teaching assistants.

ACADEMICS

Degrees: bachelor's, certificate, master's, post-master's certificate. **Classes:** Most classes have 10–19 students. Most lab/discussion sessions have 10–19 students. **Majors with Highest Enrollment:** Registered Nursing/Registered Nurse; Elementary Education and Teaching; Natural Sciences. **Special Study**

Options: Accelerated program, cross-registration, distance learning, double major, dual enrollment, English as a Second Language (ESL), exchange student program (domestic), honors program, independent study, internships, liberal arts/career combination, student-designed major, study abroad, teacher certification program, weekend college, Washington semester through the Washington Internship Institute. Dual degree (BS/MS) awarded at the completion of the program in physician assistant studies and professional accountancy. **Honors programs:** The Honors Program provides an enriched curriculum relying upon multiple perspectives and using primary sources rather than textbooks. Honors program students enjoy special residential accommodations, priority registration by class rank, opportunities for domestic and international travel, and unique offerings such as field trips, access to campus speakers, and research and publication opportunities. Combined degree programs: BS/MS Health Sci/Phys. Asst.; BS/MS Accountancy; BS Nursing 1-2-1. **Disability Services:** Special programs offered to physically disabled students include note-taking services, tape recorders, tutors. **Career services:** Alumni network, alumni services, career/job search classes, career assessment, internships, regional alumni.

FACILITIES

Housing: Coed dorms, Coed apartment-style residence halls for single students; some apartments are handicapped accessible. 92% of campus accessible to physically disabled. **Special Academic Facilities/Equipment:** Teaching Resource Center; Franette Goldman/Carolyn Greenfield Art Gallery; Natural and Health Sciences Research Center; video conferencing center; Research & Information Commons (new). **Computers:** 60% of classrooms, 100% of dorms, 100% of libraries, 75% of dining areas, 50% of student union, 10% of common outdoor areas have wireless network access. Students can register for classes online. Administrative functions (other than registration) can be performed online.

CAMPUS LIFE

Environment: City. **Activities:** Choral groups, dance, drama/theater, literary magazine, student government, student newspaper, yearbook, Campus Ministries. 45 registered organizations, 8 honor societies, 1 fraternity, 4 sororities. **Athletics (Intercollegiate):** *Men:* basketball, cross-country, golf, soccer. *Women:* basketball, cross-country, soccer, volleyball. **On-Campus Highlights:** Research and Information Commons, Modern Apartment-Style Residence Halls, Wick Student Center, Academic Computing Facilities, Athletic Facilities. **Environmental Initiatives:** College has hosted conferences and symposia on campus: Annual Environmental Summit; Green Jobs Workshop; World on Your Plate Symposium, Focus the Nation Teach-In. College offers sustainability-focused courses and majors http://www.daemen.edu/ACADEMICS/INTER-DISCIPLINARYPROGRAMS/Pages/EnvironmentalStudies.aspx. On 1/27/2009 opened new building on campus and received Gold LEED certification from U.S. Green Building Council.

ADMISSIONS

Freshman Academic Profile: Average high school GPA 3.59. SAT Math middle 50% range 460-580. SAT Critical Reading middle 50% range 440-550. SAT Writing middle 50% range 440-540. ACT middle 50% range 21-26. Minimum internet-based TOEFL 61. Minimum paper TOEFL 500. **Basis for Candidate Selection:** *Very important factors considered include:* academic GPA, rigor of secondary school record. *Important factors considered include:* Class rank, application essay, recommendation(s), interview. *Other factors considered include:* standardized test scores, alumni/ae relation, character/personal qualities, extracurricular activities, level of applicant's interest, talent/ability, volunteer work, work experience. **Freshman Admission Requirements:** High school diploma is required and GED is accepted. **Freshman Admission Statistics:** 2,938 applied, 50% admitted, 30% enrolled. **Transfer Admission Requirements:** college transcript(s), statement of good standing from prior institution(s). Minimum college GPA of 2.0 required. Lowest grade transferable C. **General Admission Information:** Application Fee $25. Notification on a rolling basis, beginning on or about 10/15. Nonfall registration accepted. Admission may be deferred for a maximum of 12 months. Credit offered for CEEB Advanced Placement tests.

COSTS AND FINANCIAL AID

Annual tuition $21,800. Room and board $10,300. Required fees $510. Average book expense $800. **Required Forms and Deadlines:** FAFSA, State aid form. **Notification of Awards:** Applicants will be notified of awards on a rolling basis beginning 2/15. **Types of Aid:** *Need-based scholarships/grants:* Federal Pell, SEOG, state scholarships/grants, private scholarships, the school's own gift aid. *Loans:* Subsidized Stafford, Unsubsidized Stafford, PLUS, Federal Perkins, college/university loans from institutional funds, Alternative Loans through private lenders. *Student Employment:* Federal Work-Study Program available. Institutional employment available. Highest amount earned per year from on-campus jobs $800. Off-campus job opportunities are fair. **Financial Aid Statistics:** 92% freshmen, 94% undergrads receive need-based scholarship or grant aid. 96% freshmen, 96% undergrads receive non-need-based scholarship or grant aid. 91% freshmen, 92% undergrads receive need-based self-help aid. 5% freshmen, 5% undergrads receive athletic scholarships. 99% freshmen, 84% undergrads receive any aid. 87% undergrads borrow to pay for school. Average cumulative indebtedness $19,409. **Criteria for awarding institutional aid:** *Non-need-based:* academics, art, athletics.

See page 1042.

DAKOTA STATE UNIVERSITY

820 North Washington Ave., Madison, SD 57042
Phone: 605-256-5139 · **Financial Aid Phone:** 605-256-5152
E-mail: admissions@dsu.edu · **CEEB Code:** 6247
Fax: 605-256-5020 · **Website:** www.dsu.edu · **ACT Code:** 3910

This public school was founded in 1881. It has a 20-acre campus.

RATINGS

Admissions Selectivity Rating: 73   **Fire Safety Rating:** 76

STUDENTS AND FACULTY

Enrollment: 1,770. **Student Body:** 38% female, 62% male, 31% out-of-state, 1% international (12 countries represented). Asian 1%, African American 4%, Caucasian 84%, Hispanic 4%, Native American 1%
Retention and Graduation: 18% freshmen graduate within 4 years. 41% freshmen graduate within 6 years. **Faculty:** 97 full-time faculty, 70% hold PhDs, 36% are members of minority groups, 8% are women. 1% of classes are taught by teaching assistants.

ACADEMICS

Degrees: associate, bachelor's, certificate, master's. **Classes:** Most classes have 20–29 students. Most lab/discussion sessions have 10–19 students. **Majors with Highest Enrollment:** Computer Graphics; Computer and Information Systems Security/Information Assurance; Computer and Information Sciences. **Special Study Options:** cooperative education program, cross-registration, distance learning, double major, dual enrollment, English as a Second Language (ESL), honors program, independent study, internships, teacher certification program. **Honors programs:** Center of Excellence(CEX), Honors. **Disability Services:** Special programs offered to physically disabled students include note-taking services, reader services, tape recorders, tutors. **Career services:** alumni services, career/job search classes, career assessment, internships. Career services highlights include on-campus interviews.

FACILITIES

Housing: Coed dorms, men's dorms, special housing for international students, women's dorms, apartments for single students. 80% of campus accessible to physically disabled. **Special Academic Facilities/Equipment:** Smith Zimmerman Museum. **Computers:** 100% of classrooms, 100% of dorms, 100% of libraries, 100% of dining areas, 100% of student union, 100% of common outdoor areas have wireless network access. Students can register for classes online. Administrative functions (other than registration) can be performed online. Undergraduates are required to own a computer.

CAMPUS LIFE

Environment: Rural. **Activities:** Choral groups, dance, drama/theater, literary magazine, music ensembles, musical theater, pep band, radio station, student government, student newspaper, International Student Organization. 33 registered organizations, 3 honor societies, 2 religious organizations. **Athletics (Intercollegiate):** *Men:* baseball, basketball, cheerleading, cross-country, football, track/field (outdoor), track/field (indoor). *Women:* basketball, cheerleading, cross-country, softball, track/field (outdoor), track/field (indoor), volleyball.
On-Campus Highlights: Tunhiem Classroom Building, Community Center, Trojan Center, Myxers Coffee Shop, The Marketplace. **Environmental Initiatives:** LEED Silver project in progress; Designated smoking areas on campus; Lighting retrofits.

ADMISSIONS

Freshman Academic Profile: Average high school GPA 3.1. 6.5% in top 10% of high school class, 20.4% in top 25% of high school class, 48.9% in top 50% of high school class. SAT Math middle 50% range 415-575. SAT Critical Reading middle 50% range 435-560. ACT middle 50% range 19-25. Minimum internet-based TOEFL 79. Minimum paper TOEFL 550. **Basis for Candidate Selection:** *Important factors considered include:* Class rank, academic GPA, rigor of secondary school record, standardized test scores, level of applicant's interest. **Freshman Admission Requirements:** High school diploma is required and GED is accepted. **Freshman Admission Statistics:** 772 applied, 84% admitted, 45% enrolled. **Transfer Admission Requirements:** High school transcript, college transcript(s), Minimum college GPA of 2.0 required. Lowest grade transferable D. **General Admission Information:** Application Fee $20. Nonfall registration accepted. Credit and/or placement offered for CEEB Advanced Placement tests.

COSTS AND FINANCIAL AID

Annual in-state tuition $3,993. Annual out-of-state tuition $5,993. Room and board $5,941. Required fees $4,293. Average book expense $1,000. **Required Forms and Deadlines:** FAFSA. **Notification of Awards:** Applicants will be notified of awards on a rolling basis beginning 4/1. **Types of Aid:** *Need-based scholarships/grants:* Federal Pell, SEOG, state scholarships/grants, private scholarships, the school's own gift aid, Agency Assistance (Veteran Benefits/ Department of Labor). *Loans:* Subsidized Stafford, Unsubsidized Stafford, PLUS, Federal Perkins, alternative commercial loans. *Student Employment:* Federal Work-Study Program available. Institutional employment available. Highest amount earned per year from on-campus jobs $5,637. Off-campus job opportunities are good. **Financial Aid Statistics:** 56% freshmen, 57% undergrads receive need-based scholarship or grant aid. 69% freshmen, 44% undergrads receive non-need-based scholarship or grant aid. 91% freshmen, 93% undergrads receive need-based self-help aid. 17% freshmen, 11% undergrads receive athletic scholarships. 79% freshmen, 79% undergrads receive any aid. 79% undergrads borrow to pay for school. Average cumulative indebtedness $22,854. **Criteria for awarding institutional aid:** *Non-need-based:* academics, alumni affiliation, art, athletics, leadership, minority status, music/drama, state/district residency.

DAKOTA WESLEYAN UNIVERSITY

1200 West University Avenue, Mitchell, SD 57301-4398
Phone: 605-995-2650 · **Financial Aid Phone:** 605-995-2656
E-mail: admissions@dwu.edu · **CEEB Code:** 6155
Fax: 605-995-2699 · **Website:** www.dwu.edu · **ACT Code:** 3906

This private school, affiliated with the Methodist Church, was founded in 1885. It has a 50-acre campus.

RATINGS

Admissions Selectivity Rating: 76   **Fire Safety Rating:** 68

STUDENTS AND FACULTY

Enrollment: 654. **Student Body:** 59% female, 41% male, 24% out-of-state, 1% international (5 countries represented). Asian 1%, African American 4%, Caucasian 90%, Hispanic 2%, Native American 2%
Retention and Graduation: 58% freshmen return for sophomore year. 23% freshmen graduate within 4 years. 35% freshmen graduate within 6 years. 10% grads go on to further study within 1 year. **Faculty:** 45 full-time faculty, 64% hold PhDs, 47% are members of minority groups, 2% are women. 0% of classes are taught by teaching assistants.

ACADEMICS

Degrees: associate, bachelor's, master's, terminal associate. **Classes:** Most classes have 10–19 students. Most lab/discussion sessions have 10–19 students. **Majors with Highest Enrollment:** Elementary Education and Teaching; Human Services; Business/Commerce. **Special Study Options:** distance learning, double major, dual enrollment, honors program, independent study, internships, liberal arts/career combination, student-designed major, study abroad, teacher certification program. **Honors programs:** University Scholars Program, students take at least three USP courses, have a 3.5 GPA, and present original scholarship at the USP Symposium Combined degree programs: BA, M.Div. **Disability Services:** Special programs offered to physically disabled students include note-taking services, reader services, tape recorders, tutors.

FACILITIES

Housing: Coed dorms, men's dorms, women's dorms, apartments for married students, apartments for single students, Koka "honor housing" for upper class women; ADA rooms, apartments available. 100% of campus accessible to physically disabled. **Special Academic Facilities/Equipment:** Friends of the Middle Border Museum and Grounds. **Computers:** Administrative functions (other than registration) can be performed online. Undergraduates are required to own a computer.

CAMPUS LIFE

Environment: Village. **Activities:** Choral groups, concert band, drama/theater, literary magazine, music ensembles, student government, student newspaper, yearbook. 5 registered organizations, 6 honor societies, 3 religious organizations. **Athletics (Intercollegiate):** *Men:* baseball, basketball, cheerleading, cross-country, football, golf, track/field (outdoor), track/field (indoor), wrestling. *Women:* basketball, cheerleading, cross-country, golf, softball, track/field (outdoor), track/field (indoor), volleyball. **On-Campus Highlights:** Athletic Department/gym/wellness center, cafeteria/coffee shop, student lounge, residence halls common lounge, residence hall computer labs.

ADMISSIONS

Freshman Academic Profile: Average high school GPA 3.01. 10% in top 10% of high school class, 35% in top 25% of high school class, 75% in top 50% of high school class. 98% from public high schools. ACT middle 50% range 22-28. Minimum paper TOEFL 500. **Basis for Candidate Selection:** *Very important factors considered include:* Class rank, rigor of secondary school record, standardized test scores. *Important factors considered include:* application essay. *Other factors considered include:* recommendation(s). **Freshman Admission Requirements:** High school diploma is required and GED is accepted. **Freshman Admission Statistics:** 423 applied, 79% admitted, 41% enrolled. **Transfer Admission Requirements:** college transcript(s), Minimum college GPA of 2.0 required. Lowest grade transferable D-. **General Admission Information:** Application Fee $25. Regular application deadline 8/29. Notification on a rolling basis, beginning on or about 9/1. Nonfall registration accepted. Admission may be deferred for a maximum of no set date. Credit and/or placement offered for CEEB Advanced Placement tests.

COSTS AND FINANCIAL AID

Annual tuition $15,600. Room and board $4,744. Required fees $0. Average book expense $900. **Required Forms and Deadlines:** FAFSA. **Notification of Awards:** Applicants will be notified of awards on a rolling basis beginning 3/1. **Types of Aid:** *Need-based scholarships/grants:* Federal Pell, SEOG, private scholarships, the school's own gift aid, Federal Nursing Scholarships, South Dakota Board of Nursing Scholarships/Loans. *Loans:* Subsidized Stafford, Unsubsidized Stafford, PLUS, Federal Perkins, Methodist Loans, and Private Alternative Student Loans. *Student Employment:* Highest amount earned per year from on-campus jobs $3,300. **Financial Aid Statistics:** 100% freshmen, 100% undergrads receive need-based scholarship or grant aid. 68% freshmen, 41% undergrads receive non-need-based scholarship or grant aid. 100% freshmen, 97% undergrads receive need-based self-help aid. 65% freshmen, 41% undergrads receive athletic scholarships. 98% freshmen, 98% undergrads receive any aid. 98% undergrads borrow to pay for school. **Criteria for awarding institutional aid:** *Non-need-based:* academics, alumni affiliation, art, athletics, leadership, minority status, music/drama, religious affiliation.

DALLAS BAPTIST UNIVERSITY

3000 Mountain Creek Parkway, Dallas, TX 75211-9299
Phone: 214-333-5360 · **Financial Aid Phone:** 214-333-5363
E-mail: admiss@dbu.edu · **CEEB Code:** 6159
Fax: 214-333-5447 · **Website:** http://www.dbu.edu/ · **ACT Code:** 4080

This private school, affiliated with the Baptist Church, was founded in 1898. It has a 293-acre campus.

RATINGS

Admissions Selectivity Rating: 87   **Fire Safety Rating:** 83

STUDENTS AND FACULTY

Enrollment: 3,357. **Student Body:** 58% female, 42% male, 8% out-of-state, 6% international (64 countries represented). Asian 2%, African American 15%, Caucasian 61%, Hispanic 14%, Native American 1%
Retention and Graduation: 72% freshmen return for sophomore year. 38% freshmen graduate within 4 years. **Faculty:** 129 full-time faculty, 80% hold PhDs, 42% are members of minority groups, 12% are women. 0% of classes are taught by teaching assistants.

ACADEMICS

Degrees: associate, bachelor's, certificate, master's, post-bachelor's certificate, post-master's certificate, transfer associate. **Classes:** Most classes have 10–19 students. Most lab/discussion sessions have 10–19 students. **Majors with Highest Enrollment:** Multi-/Interdisciplinary Studies; Business Administration and Management; Psychology. **Special Study Options:** Accelerated program, distance learning, double major, dual enrollment, English as a Second Language (ESL), honors program, independent study, internships, study abroad, teacher certification program, weekend college. **Honors programs:** www.dbu.edu/honors/. **Disability Services:** Special programs offered to physically disabled students include note-taking services, reader services, tape recorders, tutors. **Career services:** alumni services, career/job search classes, career assessment, internships. Career services highlights include an online job serach engine called CareerBridge.

FACILITIES

Housing: special housing for disabled students, men's dorms, women's dorms, apartments for married students, apartments for single students, Wellness HousingTownhomes. 75% of campus accessible to physically disabled. **Special Academic Facilities/Equipment:** Corrie ten Boom Collection. **Computers:** Students can register for classes online.

CAMPUS LIFE

Environment: Metropolis. **Activities:** Choral groups, dance, drama/theater, music ensembles, musical theater, opera, student government, yearbook, Campus Ministries, International Student Organization. 36 registered organizations, 4 honor societies, 3 religious organizations. **Athletics (Intercollegiate):** *Men:* baseball, cross-country, golf, soccer, tennis, track/field (outdoor). *Women:* cross-country, golf, soccer, tennis, track/field (outdoor), volleyball. **On-Campus Highlights:** Mahler Student Center, Burg Center, Coffee House, Collins Learning Center, Crowley Co-Ed.

ADMISSIONS

Freshman Academic Profile: Average high school GPA 3.5. 18% in top 10% of high school class, 46% in top 25% of high school class, 74% in top 50% of high school class. 76% from public high schools. SAT Math middle 50% range 462-640. SAT Critical Reading middle 50% range 466-649. ACT middle 50% range 18-27. Minimum internet-based TOEFL 71. Minimum paper TOEFL 525. **Basis for Candidate Selection:** *Very important factors considered include:* Class rank, application essay, academic GPA, rigor of secondary school record, standardized test scores, character/personal qualities, religious affiliation/commitment, talent/ability. *Important factors considered include:* extracurricular activities, first generation, interview. *Other factors considered include:* recommendation(s), alumni/ae relation, volunteer work, work experience. **Freshman Admission Requirements:** High school diploma is required and GED is accepted. **Freshman Admission Statistics:** 2,787 applied, 46% admitted, 38% enrolled. **Transfer Admission Requirements:** college transcript(s), essay or personal statement, Minimum college GPA of 2.5 required. Lowest grade transferable C. **General Admission Information:** Application Fee $25. Nonfall registration accepted. Credit offered for CEEB Advanced Placement tests.

COSTS AND FINANCIAL AID

Annual tuition $23,250. Room and board $6,930. Required fees $400. Average book expense $2,280. **Required Forms and Deadlines:** FAFSA, Institution's own financial aid form. **Types of Aid:** *Need-based scholarships/grants:* Federal Pell, SEOG, state scholarships/grants, private scholarships, the school's own gift aid. *Loans:* Subsidized Stafford, Unsubsidized Stafford, PLUS, Federal Perkins, state loans, college/university loans from institutional funds. *Student Employment:* Federal Work-Study Program available. Institutional employment available. Highest amount earned per year from on-campus jobs $2,880. Off-campus job opportunities are good. **Financial Aid Statistics:** 60% freshmen, 62% undergrads receive need-based scholarship or grant aid. 91% freshmen, 85% undergrads receive non-need-based scholarship or grant aid. 82% freshmen, 77% undergrads receive need-based self-help aid. 5% freshmen, 5% undergrads receive athletic scholarships. 96% freshmen, 90% undergrads receive any aid. 80% undergrads borrow to pay for school. Average cumulative indebtedness $20,153. **Criteria for awarding institutional aid:** *Non-need-based:* academics, athletics, job skills, leadership, music/drama, religious affiliation.

DANA COLLEGE

2848 College Drive, Blair, NE 68008-1099
Phone: 402-426-7222 · **Financial Aid Phone:** 402-426-7226
E-mail: admissions@dana.edu
Fax: 402-426-7386 · **Website:** http://www.dana.edu/ · **ACT Code:** 2446

This private school, affiliated with the Lutheran Church, was founded in 1884. It has a 150-acre campus.

RATINGS

Admissions Selectivity Rating: 80   **Fire Safety Rating:** 82

STUDENTS AND FACULTY

Enrollment: 595. **Student Body:** 47% female, 53% male, 42% out-of-state, 1% international (3 countries represented). Asian 1%, African American 3%, Caucasian 91%, Hispanic 4%, Native American 1%
Retention and Graduation: 60% freshmen return for sophomore year. 33% freshmen graduate within 4 years. 49% freshmen graduate within 6 years. 13% grads go on to further study within 1 year. 5% grads pursue arts and sciences degrees. 1% grads pursue law degrees. 1% grads pursue business degrees. 1% grads pursue medical degrees. **Faculty:** 31 full-time faculty, 81% hold PhDs, 58% are members of minority groups, 3% are women. 0% of classes are taught by teaching assistants.

ACADEMICS

Degrees: bachelor's. **Classes:** Most classes have fewer than 10 students. Most lab/discussion sessions have fewer than 10 students. **Majors with Highest Enrollment:** Education; Criminal Justice/Law Enforcement Administration;

Business/Commerce. **Special Study Options:** Accelerated program, cross-registration, double major, dual enrollment, English as a Second Language (ESL), honors program, independent study, internships, liberal arts/career combination, student-designed major, study abroad, teacher certification program. **Disability Services:** Special programs offered to physically disabled students include note-taking services, reader services, tutors. **Career services:** career/job search classes, career assessment, internships.

FACILITIES

Housing: Coed dorms, women's dorms, apartments for married students, apartments for single students. 80% of campus accessible to physically disabled. **Special Academic Facilities/Equipment:** Danish Archives. **Computers:** Administrative functions (other than registration) can be performed online.

CAMPUS LIFE

Environment: Rural. **Activities:** Choral groups, concert band, dance, drama/theater, jazz band, literary magazine, music ensembles, musical theater, radio station, student government, student newspaper, television station, yearbook. 25 registered organizations, 3 honor societies, 3 religious organizations. **Athletics (Intercollegiate):** *Men:* baseball, basketball, cross-country, football, soccer, track/field (outdoor), wrestling. *Women:* basketball, cheerleading, cross-country, golf, soccer, softball, track/field (outdoor), volleyball. **On-Campus Highlights:** Gardner-Hawks Center, Dragon's Head.

ADMISSIONS

Freshman Academic Profile: Average high school GPA 3.24. 16% in top 10% of high school class, 37% in top 25% of high school class, 62% in top 50% of high school class. SAT Math middle 50% range 420-550. SAT Critical Reading middle 50% range 480-560. ACT middle 50% range 20-25. Minimum paper TOEFL 500. **Basis for Candidate Selection:** *Very important factors considered include:* academic GPA, rigor of secondary school record, standardized test scores. *Other factors considered include:* application essay, recommendation(s), extracurricular activities, interview, level of applicant's interest, volunteer work, work experience. **Freshman Admission Requirements:** High school diploma is required and GED is accepted. **Freshman Admission Statistics:** 830 applied, 72% admitted, 24% enrolled. **Transfer Admission Requirements:** college transcript(s), Minimum college GPA of 2.0 required. Lowest grade transferable C. **General Admission Information:** Notification on a rolling basis, beginning on or about 9/1. Nonfall registration accepted. Admission may be deferred for a maximum of 2 Years. Credit offered for CEEB Advanced Placement tests.

COSTS AND FINANCIAL AID

Average book expense $900. **Required Forms and Deadlines:** FAFSA, Institution's own financial aid form. **Notification of Awards:** Applicants will be notified of awards on a rolling basis beginning 3/4. **Types of Aid:** *Need-based scholarships/grants:* Federal Pell, SEOG, state scholarships/grants, private scholarships, the school's own gift aid. *Loans:* Subsidized Stafford, Unsubsidized Stafford, PLUS, Federal Perkins. *Student Employment:* Federal Work-Study Program available. Institutional employment available. Highest amount earned per year from on-campus jobs $1,500. Off-campus job opportunities are good. **Financial Aid Statistics:** 46% freshmen, 59% undergrads receive need-based scholarship or grant aid. 74% freshmen, 72% undergrads receive non-need-based scholarship or grant aid. 77% freshmen, 79% undergrads receive need-based self-help aid. 68% freshmen, 59% undergrads receive athletic scholarships. 86% undergrads borrow to pay for school. Average cumulative indebtedness $16,656. **Criteria for awarding institutional aid:** *Non-need-based:* academics, alumni affiliation, art, athletics, leadership, music/drama, religious affiliation, state/district residency.

DANIEL WEBSTER COLLEGE

20 University Drive, Nashua, NH 03063-1300
Phone: 603-577-6600
E-mail: admissions@dwc.edu • **CEEB Code:** 3648
Fax: 603-577-6001 • **Website:** http://www.dwc.edu/ • **ACT Code:** 2525

This private school was founded in 1965. It has a 50-acre campus.

RATINGS

Admissions Selectivity Rating: 72   **Fire Safety Rating:** 60*

STUDENTS AND FACULTY

Enrollment: 785. **Student Body:** 25% female, 75% male, 72% out-of-state, (11 countries represented). Asian 1%, African American 4%, Hispanic 3%, Native American <1%
Retention and Graduation: 64% freshmen return for sophomore year. 40% freshmen graduate within 4 years. 53% freshmen graduate within 6 years. 8%

grads go on to further study within 1 year. 8% grads pursue arts and sciences degrees. **Faculty:** 39 full-time faculty, 54% hold PhDs, 23% are members of minority groups. 0% of classes are taught by teaching assistants.

ACADEMICS

Degrees: associate, bachelor's, master's, transfer associate. **Classes:** Most classes have 10–19 students. Most lab/discussion sessions have fewer than 10 students. **Majors with Highest Enrollment:** Computer and Information Sciences; Airline/Commercial/Professional Pilot and Flight Crew; Business/Commerce. **Special Study Options:** Accelerated program, cooperative education program, cross-registration, distance learning, double major, dual enrollment, independent study, internships, study abroad. Combined degree programs: 2-2 aeronautical enginering and engineering scienc. **Disability Services:** Special programs offered to physically disabled students include tutors. **Career services:** Alumni network, alumni services, career/job search classes, career assessment, internships.

FACILITIES

Housing: Coed dorms, men's dorms, women's dorms, Men's Townhouses Women's Townhouses Suites. 80% of campus accessible to physically disabled. **Special Academic Facilities/Equipment:** Campus is adjacent to municipal airport; over 35 aircraft are available for flight training. Three flight simulators, aviation center.

CAMPUS LIFE

Environment: Village. **Activities:** Choral groups, drama/theater, jazz band, musical theater, student government, student newspaper, student-run film society, yearbook. 17 registered organizations, 2 honor societies, 1 religious organization. **Athletics (Intercollegiate):** *Men:* baseball, basketball, cross-country, lacrosse, soccer. *Women:* basketball, cross-country, soccer, softball, volleyball.

ADMISSIONS

Freshman Academic Profile: Average high school GPA 3.06. 7% in top 10% of high school class, 21% in top 25% of high school class, 52% in top 50% of high school class. 83% from public high schools. SAT Math middle 50% range 480-610. SAT Critical Reading middle 50% range 470-570. ACT middle 50% range 19-24. Minimum paper TOEFL 520. **Basis for Candidate Selection:** *Very important factors considered include:* rigor of secondary school record. *Important factors considered include:* Class rank, recommendation(s), standardized test scores, extracurricular activities, interview. *Other factors considered include:* application essay, character/personal qualities, level of applicant's interest, talent/ability, volunteer work, work experience. **Freshman Admission Requirements:** High school diploma is required and GED is accepted. *Academic units required:* 4 English, 3 mathematics, 3 science, (2 science labs), 2 social studies, 2 history, 2 academic electives. **Freshman Admission Statistics:** 823 applied. **Transfer Admission Requirements:** High school transcript, college transcript(s), Minimum college GPA of 2.5 required. Lowest grade transferable C. **General Admission Information:** Application Fee $35. Nonfall registration accepted. Admission may be deferred for a maximum of 1 year. Credit and/or placement offered for CEEB Advanced Placement tests.

COSTS AND FINANCIAL AID

Average book expense $750. **Required Forms and Deadlines:** FAFSA, Institution's own financial aid form. **Notification of Awards:** Applicants will be notified of awards on a rolling basis beginning 3/15. **Types of Aid:** *Need-based scholarships/grants:* Federal Pell, SEOG, state scholarships/grants, the school's own gift aid. *Loans:* Direct Subsidized Stafford, Direct Unsubsidized Stafford, Direct PLUS, Federal Perkins. *Student Employment:* Federal Work-Study Program available. Institutional employment available. Highest amount earned per year from on-campus jobs $2,000. Off-campus job opportunities are excellent. **Financial Aid Statistics:** 93% freshmen, 79% undergrads receive need-based scholarship or grant aid. 83% freshmen, 78% undergrads receive non-need-based scholarship or grant aid. 100% freshmen, 81% undergrads receive need-based self-help aid. 0% freshmen, 0% undergrads receive athletic scholarships. 83% undergrads borrow to pay for school. **Criteria for awarding institutional aid:** *Non-need-based:* academics, leadership.

DARTMOUTH COLLEGE

6016 McNutt Hall, Hanover, NH 3755
Phone: 603-646-2875 · **Financial Aid Phone:** 800-443-3605
E-mail: admissions.reply@dartmouth.edu · **CEEB Code:** 3351
Fax: 603-646-1216 · **Website:** www.dartmouth.edu · **ACT Code:** 2508

This private school was founded in 1769. It has a 265-acre campus.

RATINGS
Admissions Selectivity Rating: 99   **Fire Safety Rating:** 81

STUDENTS AND FACULTY
Enrollment: 4,098. **Student Body:** 50% female, 50% male, 96% out-of-state, 8% international (70 countries represented). Asian 14%, African American 7%, Caucasian 48%, Hispanic 8%, Native American 2%
Retention and Graduation: 98% freshmen return for sophomore year. 88% freshmen graduate within 4 years. 21% grads go on to further study within 1 year. **Faculty:** 542 full-time faculty, 95% hold PhDs, 37% are members of minority groups, 18% are women. 0% of classes are taught by teaching assistants.

ACADEMICS
Degrees: bachelor's, doctoral, master's. **Classes:** Most classes have 10–19 students. **Majors with Highest Enrollment:** Economics; Psychology; Political Science and Government. **Special Study Options:** double major, exchange student program (domestic), honors program, independent study, internships, student-designed major, study abroad, teacher certification program. **Honors programs:** Presidential Scholarship Research Program; Senior Honors Thesis; Senior Fellowship Combined degree programs: BA/BENG- 5 year program.
Disability Services: Special programs offered to physically disabled students include note-taking services, tape recorders, tutors. **Career services:** Alumni network, alumni services, career/job search classes, career assessment, internships, regional alumni. Career services highlights include financial support for unpaid internships through the Rockefeller Center (public policy or political internships), the Dickey Center for International Understanding (overseas opportunities), the Tucker Foundation (religious or community service organizations), and through other sources on campus.

FACILITIES
Housing: Coed dorms, special housing for international students, fraternity/sorority housing, apartments for married students, cooperative housing, apartments for single students, Theme Housing, Academic Affinity Housing, Faculty-In-Residence Programs, Sustainable Living Center, Interfaith Living, Special Interest Housing. 75% of campus accessible to physically disabled. **Special Academic Facilities/Equipment:** Hood Museum of Art, Hopkins Center for Performing Arts, Tucker Foundation for volunteer services, observatory, centers for humanities, social science, and science. **Computers:** 100% of classrooms, 100% of dorms, 100% of libraries, 100% of dining areas, 100% of student union, 100% of common outdoor areas have wireless network access. Students can register for classes online. Administrative functions (other than registration) can be performed online. Undergraduates are required to own a computer.

CAMPUS LIFE
Environment: Village. **Activities:** Choral groups, concert band, dance, drama/theater, jazz band, literary magazine, marching band, music ensembles, musical theater, opera, pep band, radio station, student government, student newspaper, student-run film society, symphony orchestra, television station, yearbook, Campus Ministries, International Student Organization, Model UN. 330 registered organizations, 26 religious organizations. 14 fraternities, 6 sororities. **Athletics (Intercollegiate):** *Men:* baseball, basketball, crew/rowing, cross-country, diving, equestrian sports, fencing, football, golf, ice hockey, lacrosse, sailing, skiing (downhill/alpine), skiing (nordic/cross-country), soccer, squash, swimming, tennis, track/field (outdoor), track/field (indoor). *Women:* basketball, crew/rowing, cross-country, diving, equestrian sports, fencing, field hockey, golf, ice hockey, lacrosse, sailing, skiing (downhill/alpine), skiing (nordic/cross-country), soccer, softball, squash, swimming, tennis, track/field (outdoor), track/field (indoor), volleyball. **On-Campus Highlights:** Hopkins Center for Creative and Performing Arts, Hood Museum of Art, Murals by Jose Clemente Orozco, Ten library system, all open to visitors, Ledyard Canoe Club, oldest in the country.
Environmental Initiatives: As part of our commitment to reduce greenhouse gas emissions, Dartmouth commissioned an energy audit for the buildings that collectively use 75% of the energy on campus. Based on the results of this audit, the Trustees invested $12.5 million in 250 energy conservation and efficiency projects in existing buildings, which are now underway. Dartmouth established

a Sustainable Living Center and is working with students to develop it as a model green dormitory and center. As part of this effort we are working on plans to push the building toward zero net energy and developing a sustainable food system for the students who live there. (See www.dartmouth.edu/~slc). Building energy metering equipment has been upgraded and the innovative Green Lite Dartmouth feedback displays will be used to provide occupants with real-time resource use information. (See greenlite.dartmouth.edu). In the first term of operation, the students reduced electricity use by 58% below past years through behavioral change alone. Dartmouth established a new tenured faculty position in Sustainability Sciences. The position has been filled and new courses in sustainability will be added in fall of 2009.

ADMISSIONS
Freshman Academic Profile: 90% in top 10% of high school class, 97% in top 25% of high school class, 100% in top 50% of high school class. 55% from public high schools. SAT Math middle 50% range 680-780. SAT Critical Reading middle 50% range 670-780. SAT Writing middle 50% range 680-790. ACT middle 50% range 30-34. Minimum internet-based TOEFL 250. Minimum paper TOEFL 600. **Basis for Candidate Selection:** *Very important factors considered include:* Class rank, application essay, academic GPA, recommendation(s), rigor of secondary school record, standardized test scores, character/personal qualities, extracurricular activities. *Important factors considered include:* talent/ability, volunteer work. *Other factors considered include:* alumni/ae relation, first generation, geographical residence, interview, racial/ethnic status. **Freshman Admission Requirements:** High school diploma or equivalent is not required. **Freshman Admission Statistics:** 23,110 applied, 10% admitted, 49% enrolled. **Transfer Admission Requirements:** High school transcript, college transcript(s), essay or personal statement, standardized test scores, statement of good standing from prior institution(s). Lowest grade transferable B. **General Admission Information:** Application Fee $70. Early decision application deadline 11/1. Regular application deadline 1/1. Regular notification 4/1. Nonfall registration not accepted. Admission may be deferred for a maximum of 2 years. Credit and/or placement offered for CEEB Advanced Placement tests.

COSTS AND FINANCIAL AID
Annual tuition $46,764. Room and board $13,829. Required fees $1,514. Average book expense $1,176. **Required Forms and Deadlines:** FAFSA, CSS/Financial Aid PROFILE, Noncustodial PROFILE, Business/Farm Supplement. **Notification of Awards:** Applicants will be notified of awards on or about 4/2. **Types of Aid:** *Need-based scholarships/grants:* Federal Pell, SEOG, state scholarships/grants, private scholarships, the school's own gift aid. *Loans:* Subsidized Stafford, Unsubsidized Stafford, PLUS, Federal Perkins, college/university loans from institutional funds. *Student Employment:* Federal Work-Study Program available. Institutional employment available. Off-campus job opportunities are excellent. **Financial Aid Statistics:** 96% freshmen, 94% undergrads receive need-based scholarship or grant aid. 0% freshmen, 0% undergrads receive non-need-based scholarship or grant aid. 92% freshmen, 94% undergrads receive need-based self-help aid. 0% freshmen, 0% undergrads receive athletic scholarships. 58% freshmen, 54% undergrads receive any aid. 56% undergrads borrow to pay for school. Average cumulative indebtedness $14,279.

DAVENPORT UNIVERSITY

6191 Kraft Avenue S.E., Grand Rapids, MI 49512
Phone: 616-698-7111 · **Financial Aid Phone:** 313-581-4400
E-mail: gradmiss@davenport.edu
Fax: 616-698-0333 · **Website:** http://www.davenport.edu/

This private school was founded in 1866. It has a 43-acre campus.

RATINGS
Admissions Selectivity Rating: 60*   **Fire Safety Rating:** 71

STUDENTS AND FACULTY
Enrollment: 11,736. **Student Body:** 76% female, 24% male, 2% out-of-state, 0% international (29 countries represented). Asian 1%, African American 24%, Caucasian 58%, Hispanic 4%, Native American <1%
Retention and Graduation: 61% freshmen return for sophomore year.
Faculty: 130 full-time faculty, 24% hold PhDs, 54% are members of minority groups. 0% of classes are taught by teaching assistants.

ACADEMICS
Degrees: associate, bachelor's, diploma, master's, post-bachelor's certificate.
Classes: Most classes have fewer than 10 students. **Special Study Options:** Accelerated program, distance learning, dual enrollment, English as a Second

Language (ESL), independent study, internships, student-designed major, study abroad. Combined degree programs: BA/MA. **Disability Services:** Special programs offered to physically disabled students include tutors.

FACILITIES
Housing: Coed dorms.

CAMPUS LIFE
Environment: City.

ADMISSIONS
Freshman Academic Profile: Minimum paper TOEFL 500. **Freshman Admission Requirements:** High school diploma is required and GED is accepted. *Academic units required:* 6 English, 6 mathematics, 9 social studies, 31 academic electives, 10 Interdisciplinary. *Academic units recommended:* 6 English, 6 mathematics, 9 social studies, 31 academic electives, 10 Interdisciplinary. **Freshman Admission Statistics:** 1,231 applied, 100% admitted, 100% enrolled. **Transfer Admission Requirements:** High school transcript, college transcript(s), Minimum college GPA of 2 required. Lowest grade transferable C. **General Admission Information:** Application Fee $25. Notification on a rolling basis, beginning on or about 9/1. Nonfall registration accepted. Admission may be deferred for a maximum of ongoing. Neither credit nor placement offered for CEEB Advanced Placement tests.

COSTS AND FINANCIAL AID
Annual tuition $8,760. Room and board $4,200. Required fees $120. Average book expense $1,000. **Required Forms and Deadlines:** FAFSA. **Notification of Awards:** Applicants will be notified of awards on a rolling basis beginning 3/1. **Types of Aid:** *Need-based scholarships/grants:* Federal Pell, SEOG, state scholarships/grants, private scholarships, the school's own gift aid, State of MI Nursing Scholarships. *Loans:* Subsidized Stafford, Unsubsidized Stafford, PLUS, state loans. **Financial Aid Statistics:** 88% freshmen, 88% undergrads receive need-based scholarship or grant aid. 61% freshmen, 34% undergrads receive non-need-based scholarship or grant aid. 80% freshmen, 91% undergrads receive need-based self-help aid. 2% freshmen, 2% undergrads receive athletic scholarships. 75% undergrads borrow to pay for school. **Criteria for awarding institutional aid:** *Non-need-based:* academics, alumni affiliation, athletics, leadership.

DAVIDSON COLLEGE

Best 380

PO Box 7156, Davidson, NC 28035-7156
Phone: 704-894-2230
E-mail: admission@davidson.edu • **CEEB Code:** 5150
Fax: 704-894-2016 • **Website:** www.davidson.edu • **ACT Code:** 3086

This private school, affiliated with the Presbyterian Church, was founded in 1837. It has a 556-acre campus.

RATINGS
Admissions Selectivity Rating: 96   **Fire Safety Rating:** 60*

STUDENTS AND FACULTY
Enrollment: 1,782. **Student Body:** 50% female, 50% male, 77% out-of-state, 5% international (42 countries represented). Asian 5%, African American 7%, Caucasian 69%, Hispanic 6%, Native American 1%
Retention and Graduation: 96% freshmen return for sophomore year. 92% freshmen graduate within 4 years. 95% freshmen graduate within 6 years. 21% grads go on to further study within 1 year. **Faculty:** 174 full-time faculty, 97% hold PhDs, 41% are members of minority groups, 20% are women. 0% of classes are taught by teaching assistants.

ACADEMICS
Degrees: bachelor's. **Classes:** Most classes have 10–19 students. Most lab/discussion sessions have 10–19 students. **Majors with Highest Enrollment:** Biology/Biological Sciences; Political Science and Government; Psychology. **Special Study Options:** cross-registration, double major, exchange student program (domestic), honors program, independent study, student-designed major, study abroad, teacher certification program. **Disability Services:** Special programs offered to physically disabled students include note-taking services, reader services, tape recorders, tutors. **Career services:** Alumni network, alumni services, career/job search classes, career assessment, internships

FACILITIES
Housing: Coed dorms, cooperative housing, apartments for single students, Wellness Housing, Theme Housing. 90% of campus accessible to physically

disabled. **Special Academic Facilities/Equipment:** Art gallery, scanning electron microscopes, UV-visible spectrometer, laser systems, Baker sports complex, Visual Arts building. **Computers:** Students can register for classes online.

CAMPUS LIFE
Environment: Village. **Activities:** Choral groups, concert band, dance, drama/theater, jazz band, literary magazine, music ensembles, musical theater, pep band, radio station, student government, student newspaper, symphony orchestra, yearbook, Campus Ministries, International Student Organization 151 registered organizations, 15 honor societies, 16 religious organizations. 8 fraternities. **Athletics (Intercollegiate):** *Men:* baseball, basketball, cross-country, diving, football, golf, soccer, swimming, tennis, track/field (outdoor), wrestling. *Women:* basketball, cross-country, diving, field hockey, lacrosse, soccer, swimming, tennis, track/field (outdoor), volleyball. **On-Campus Highlights:** Belk Visual Arts Center, Baker-Watt Science Complex, Baker Sports Complex, Campus Center, Lake Campus. **Environmental Initiatives:** Solar PV and solar thermal array on Baker Sports Complex; Rigorous co-curricular programs, workshops, internships, student clubs, and leadership opportunities; Ecological co-op—where ten students live comunally and practice sustainable living.

ADMISSIONS
Freshman Academic Profile: Average high school GPA 3.98. 64% in top 10% of high school class, 91% in top 25% of high school class, 100% in top 50% of high school class. 44% from public high schools. SAT Math middle 50% range 600-710. SAT Critical Reading middle 50% range 630-730. SAT Writing middle 50% range 610-710. ACT middle 50% range 29-33. Minimum internet-based TOEFL 100. Minimum paper TOEFL 600. **Basis for Candidate Selection:** *Very important factors considered include:* recommendation(s), rigor of secondary school record, character/personal qualities, volunteer work. *Important factors considered include:* application essay, standardized test scores, extracurricular activities, interview, talent/ability. *Other factors considered include:* Class rank, alumni/ae relation. **Freshman Admission Requirements:** High school diploma is required and GED is not accepted. *Academic units required:* 4 English, 3 mathematics, 2 science, 2 foreign language, 2 Social Studies or History. **Freshman Admission Statistics:** 4,745 applied, 26% admitted, 40% enrolled. **Transfer Admission Requirements:** High school transcript, college transcript(s), essay or personal statement, standardized test scores, statement of good standing from prior institution(s). Minimum college GPA of 3.0 required. Lowest grade transferable C. **General Admission Information:** Application Fee $50. Early decision application deadline 11/15. Regular application deadline 1/2. Regular notification 4/1. Nonfall registration not accepted. Admission may be deferred for a maximum of 1 year. Credit and/or placement offered for CEEB Advanced Placement tests.

COSTS AND FINANCIAL AID
Annual tuition $44,928. Room and board $12,769. Required fees $449. Average book expense $1,000. **Required Forms and Deadlines:** FAFSA, CSS/Financial Aid PROFILE, Noncustodial PROFILE, Business/Farm Supplement. **Notification of Awards:** Applicants will be notified of awards on or about 4/1. **Types of Aid:** *Need-based scholarships/grants:* Federal Pell, SEOG, state scholarships/grants, private scholarships, the school's own gift aid. *Loans:* Subsidized Stafford, Unsubsidized Stafford, PLUS, Federal Perkins, alternative loans. *Student Employment:* Federal Work-Study Program available. Institutional employment available. Off-campus job opportunities are excellent. **Financial Aid Statistics:** 98% freshmen, 99% undergrads receive need-based scholarship or grant aid. 17% freshmen, 14% undergrads receive non-need-based scholarship or grant aid. 60% freshmen, 68% undergrads receive need-based self-help aid. 8% freshmen, 10% undergrads receive athletic scholarships. 45% freshmen, 46% undergrads receive any aid. 22% undergrads borrow to pay for school. Average cumulative indebtedness $20,176. **Criteria for awarding institutional aid:** *Non-need-based:* academics, art, athletics, leadership, minority status, music/drama.

DAVIS AND ELKINS COLLEGE

100 Campus Drive, Elkins, WV 26241
Phone: 304-637-1230 • **Financial Aid Phone:** 304-637-1373
E-mail: admiss@davisandelkins.edu • **CEEB Code:** 5151
Fax: 304-637-1800 • **Website:** www.davisandelkins.edu • **ACT Code:** 4518

This private school, affiliated with the Presbyterian Church, was founded in 1904. It has a 170-acre campus.

RATINGS
Admissions Selectivity Rating: 80   **Fire Safety Rating:** 64

STUDENTS AND FACULTY
Enrollment: 624. **Student Body:** 63% female, 37% male, 23% out-of-state, 0% international (15 countries represented). Asian 4%, African American 2%, Caucasian 98%, Hispanic 1%, Native American <1%

The Princeton Review's Complete Book of Colleges

Retention and Graduation: 64% freshmen return for sophomore year. 29% freshmen graduate within 4 years. 50% freshmen graduate within 6 years. 13% grads go on to further study within 1 year. 2% grads pursue law degrees. 11% grads pursue business degrees. **Faculty:** 44 full-time faculty, 84% hold PhDs, 50% are members of minority groups, 11% are women. 0% of classes are taught by teaching assistants.

ACADEMICS

Degrees: associate, bachelor's, terminal associate, transfer associate. **Classes:** Most classes have fewer than 10 students. Most lab/discussion sessions have 20–29 students. **Majors with Highest Enrollment:** Registered Nursing/Registered Nurse; Business Administration and Management; Marketing/Marketing Management. **Special Study Options:** cooperative education program, cross-registration, double major, dual enrollment, external degree program, honors program, independent study, internships, student-designed major, study abroad, teacher certification program. **Disability Services:** Special programs offered to physically disabled students include note-taking services, reader services, tape recorders, tutors. **Career services:** alumni services, career assessment, internships, regional alumni.

FACILITIES

Housing: Coed dorms, men's dorms, women's dorms. 80% of campus accessible to physically disabled. **Special Academic Facilities/Equipment:** planetarium, Graceland Inn and Conference Center(19th century Victorian mansion)-now used as training center for the Hospitality Program, Darby Collection-Civil War collection, Comstock collection, Pearl S. Buck collection **Computers:** Administrative functions (other than registration) can be performed online.

CAMPUS LIFE

Environment: Village. **Activities:** Choral groups, concert band, drama/theater, jazz band, literary magazine, music ensembles, musical theater, radio station, student government, student newspaper, yearbook. 39 registered organizations, 7 honor societies, 1 religious organization. 2 fraternities, 2 sororities. **Athletics (Intercollegiate):** *Men:* baseball, basketball, cross-country, golf, skiing (downhill/alpine), soccer. *Women:* basketball, cross-country, skiing (downhill/alpine), soccer, softball, volleyball. **On-Campus Highlights:** Mansions/ Halliehurst and Graceland, Icehouse, Chapel, Madden Student Center, Library, The 170 acre campus offers an historic district and newly renovated student center.

ADMISSIONS

Freshman Academic Profile: Average high school GPA 3.06. 12% in top 10% of high school class, 33% in top 25% of high school class, 71% in top 50% of high school class. 91% from public high schools. SAT Math middle 50% range 420-510. SAT Critical Reading middle 50% range 420-510. ACT middle 50% range 18-22. Minimum paper TOEFL 450. **Basis for Candidate Selection:** *Very important factors considered include:* rigor of secondary school record, level of applicant's interest. *Important factors considered include:* Class rank, academic GPA, recommendation(s), standardized test scores, character/personal qualities, extracurricular activities, talent/ability. *Other factors considered include:* application essay, alumni/ae relation, first generation, interview, volunteer work, work experience. **Freshman Admission Requirements:** High school diploma is required and GED is accepted. *Academic units required:* 4 English, 1 mathematics, 3 science, (1 science labs), 1 foreign language, 3 social studies, 2 Mathematics units must include algebra I or II and geometry. **Freshman Admission Statistics:** 563 applied, 55% admitted, 34% enrolled. **Transfer Admission Requirements:** High school transcript, college transcript(s), Minimum college GPA of 2.0 required. Lowest grade transferable D. **General Admission Information:** Application Fee $35. Notification on a rolling basis, beginning on or about 9/30. Nonfall registration accepted. Admission may be deferred for a maximum of 1 yr. Credit and/or placement offered for CEEB Advanced Placement tests.

COSTS AND FINANCIAL AID

Average book expense $800. **Required Forms and Deadlines:** FAFSA. **Notification of Awards:** Applicants will be notified of awards on or about 5/1. **Types of Aid:** *Need-based scholarships/grants:* Federal Pell, SEOG, state scholarships/grants, private scholarships, the school's own gift aid. *Loans:* Subsidized Stafford, Unsubsidized Stafford, PLUS, Federal Perkins, state loans. *Student Employment:* Federal Work-Study Program available. Institutional employment available. Highest amount earned per year from on-campus jobs $1,000. Off-campus job opportunities are good. **Financial Aid Statistics:** 45% freshmen, 62% undergrads receive need-based scholarship or grant aid. 100% freshmen, 100% undergrads receive non-need-based scholarship or grant aid. 65% freshmen, 81% undergrads receive need-based self-help aid. 44% freshmen, 24% undergrads receive athletic scholarships. 98% freshmen, 98% undergrads receive any aid. 76% undergrads borrow to pay for school. **Criteria for awarding institutional aid:** *Non-need-based:* academics, alumni affiliation, art, athletics, leadership, minority status, music/drama, religious affiliation.

DE SALES UNIVERSITY

3001 Emrick Blvd, Bethlehem, PA 18020
Phone: 610-282-4443 • **Financial Aid Phone:** 610-282-4443
E-mail: admiss@desales.edu • **CEEB Code:** 2021
Fax: 610-282-0131 • **Website:** www.desales.edu

This private school, affiliated with the Roman Catholic Church, was founded in 1964. It has a 400-acre campus.

RATINGS

Admissions Selectivity Rating: 79   **Fire Safety Rating:** 86

STUDENTS AND FACULTY

Enrollment: 2,381. **Student Body:** 60% female, 40% male, 23% out-of-state, 0% international (4 countries represented). Asian 3%, African American 4%, Caucasian 76%, Hispanic 10%, Native American 1%
Retention and Graduation: 84% freshmen return for sophomore year. 64% freshmen graduate within 4 years. 70% freshmen graduate within 6 years. **Faculty:** 118 full-time faculty, 84% hold PhDs, 53% are members of minority groups, 9% are women. 0% of classes are taught by teaching assistants.

ACADEMICS

Degrees: bachelor's, certificate, master's, post-bachelor's certificate, post-master's certificate. **Classes:** Most classes have 20–29 students. Most lab/discussion sessions have fewer than 10 students. **Majors with Highest Enrollment:** Drama and Dramatics/Theatre Arts; Physician Assistant. **Special Study Options:** Accelerated program, cross-registration, distance learning, double major, dual enrollment, English as a Second Language (ESL), exchange student program (domestic), honors program, independent study, internships, liberal arts/career combination, student-designed major, study abroad, teacher certification program, weekend college, Online degrees. **Honors programs:** Faith and Reason Honors Program is competive and is limited to fifteen (15) students in each academic class. Studnets can find a description of the program at: www4.desales.edu/SCFC/FRseminars. Combined degree programs: BS/MSPAS; BSN/MSN; MBA/MNS. **Disability Services:** Special programs offered to physically disabled students include note-taking services, reader services, tape recorders, tutors. **Career services:** Alumni network, alumni services, career/job search classes, career assessment, internships.

FACILITIES

Housing: men's dorms, women's dorms, cooperative housing, Theme Housing. 98% of campus accessible to physically disabled. **Computers:** 100% of classrooms, 5% of dorms, 100% of libraries, 100% of dining areas, 5% of student union, 20% of common outdoor areas have wireless network access. Students can register for classes online. Administrative functions (other than registration) can be performed online.

CAMPUS LIFE

Environment: Town. **Activities:** Choral groups, dance, drama/theater, musical theater, pep band, radio station, student government, student newspaper, television station, yearbook, Campus Ministries, International Student Organization, Model UN. 42 registered organizations, 12 honor societies, 1 religious organization. **Athletics (Intercollegiate):** *Men:* baseball, basketball, cross-country, golf, lacrosse, soccer, tennis, track/field (outdoor), track/field (indoor). *Women:* basketball, cross-country, field hockey, soccer, softball, tennis, track/field (outdoor), track/field (indoor), volleyball. **On-Campus Highlights:** Billera Athletics and Recreation Center, Hurd Science Center, Dog Pound in McShea Student Center, University Center, Labuda Center for the Performing Arts, Summer brings the Pennsylvania Shakespeare Festival to campus at the Labuda Center for the Performing Arts. **Environmental Initiatives:** Water reduction program - after adding one new residence hall we still reduced our water usage by 10% from 2008 to 2009. Open Space Land preservation recently obtained over 80 acres for campus open space and for land preservation. DeSales Dining Services Sustainability Program.

ADMISSIONS

Freshman Academic Profile: Average high school GPA 3.2. 13% in top 10% of high school class, 44% in top 25% of high school class, 71% in top 50% of high school class. 60% from public high schools. SAT Math middle 50% range 440-570. SAT Critical Reading middle 50% range 450-580. SAT Writing middle 50% range 440-560. ACT middle 50% range 21-27. Minimum paper TOEFL 550. **Basis for Candidate Selection:** *Very important factors considered include:* Class rank, academic GPA, recommendation(s), rigor of secondary school record. *Important factors considered include:* standardized test scores, extracurricular activities, interview, talent/ability. *Other factors considered include:* application essay, geographical residence, racial/ethnic status, state residency, volunteer work, work experience. **Freshman Admission Requirements:** High school diploma is required and GED is accepted. *Academic units required:* 4

English, 3 mathematics, 2 science, (2 science labs), 2 foreign language, 3 social studies, 9 history, 19 academic electives. **Freshman Admission Statistics:** 2,658 applied, 80% admitted, 19% enrolled. **Transfer Admission Requirements:** High school transcript, college transcript(s), statement of good standing from prior institution(s). Minimum college GPA of 2.00 required. Lowest grade transferable 2. **General Admission Information:** Regular application deadline 8/1. Notification on a rolling basis, beginning on or about 11/1. Nonfall registration accepted. Credit offered for CEEB Advanced Placement tests.

COSTS AND FINANCIAL AID
Annual tuition $31,000. Room and board $11,620. Required fees $1,550. Average book expense $1,198. **Required Forms and Deadlines:** FAFSA, Noncustodial PROFILE. **Notification of Awards:** Applicants will be notified of awards on a rolling basis beginning 2/15. **Types of Aid:** *Need-based scholarships/grants:* Federal Pell, SEOG, state scholarships/grants, private scholarships, the school's own gift aid, Federal Nursing Scholarships. *Loans:* Subsidized Stafford, Unsubsidized Stafford, PLUS, Federal Perkins, Federal Nursing, state loans. *Student Employment:* Federal Work-Study Program available. Institutional employment available. Off-campus job opportunities are good. **Financial Aid Statistics:** 100% freshmen, 94% undergrads receive need-based scholarship or grant aid. 95% freshmen, 78% undergrads receive non-need-based scholarship or grant aid. 84% freshmen, 84% undergrads receive need-based self-help aid. 0% freshmen, 0% undergrads receive athletic scholarships. 82% undergrads borrow to pay for school. Average cumulative indebtedness $25,875. **Criteria for awarding institutional aid:** *Non-need-based:* academics, leadership, music/drama.

See page 1044.

DEAN COLLEGE

Office of Admission, Franklin, MA 02038-1994
Phone: 508-541-1508
E-mail: admission@dean.edu
Fax: 508-541-8726 · **Website:** www.dean.edu

This is a private school.

RATINGS
Admissions Selectivity Rating: 71   **Fire Safety Rating:** 60*

STUDENTS AND FACULTY
Enrollment: 1,106. **Student Body:** 48% female, 52% male, 53% out-of-state, 10% international. Asian 1%, African American 7%, Caucasian 50%, Hispanic 3%, Native American 1%
Retention and Graduation: 62% freshmen return for sophomore year. **Faculty:** 33 full-time faculty, 36% hold PhDs, 55% are members of minority groups, 9% are women.

ACADEMICS
Degrees: associate, bachelor's, certificate. **Classes:** Most classes have 10–19 students. Most lab/discussion sessions have fewer than 10 students. **Special Study Options:** Accelerated program, double major, English as a Second Language (ESL), honors program, independent study, internships, liberal arts/career combination, study abroad.

FACILITIES
Housing: Coed dorms, women's dorms.

CAMPUS LIFE
Activities: dance, drama/theater, literary magazine, musical theater, radio station, student government, yearbook.

ADMISSIONS
Freshman Academic Profile: Average high school GPA 2.2. SAT Math middle 50% range 380-490. SAT Critical Reading middle 50% range 390-490. ACT middle 50% range 15-20. **Basis for Candidate Selection:** *Other factors considered include:* Class rank, application essay, academic GPA, recommendation(s), rigor of secondary school record, standardized test scores, alumni/ae relation, character/personal qualities, extracurricular activities, interview, level of applicant's interest, talent/ability, volunteer work, work experience. **Freshman Admission Requirements:** High school diploma is required and GED is accepted. *Academic units required:* 3 English, 1 mathematics, 1 science, (1 science labs), 0 foreign language, 1 social studies, 1 history, 0 academic electives. **Freshman Admission Statistics:** 1,910 applied, 73% admitted, 39% enrolled. **Transfer Admission Requirements:** High school transcript, college transcript(s), essay or personal statement, Lowest grade transferable C-. **General Admission Information:** Application Fee $35. Notification on a rolling basis, beginning on or about 12/1. Nonfall registration accepted. Admission may be deferred for a maximum of 1 year.

COSTS AND FINANCIAL AID
Required Forms and Deadlines: FAFSA. **Notification of Awards:** Applicants will be notified of awards on a rolling basis beginning 3/1. **Types of Aid:** *Need-based scholarships/grants:* Federal Pell, SEOG, state scholarships/grants, private scholarships, the school's own gift aid. *Loans:* Subsidized Stafford, Unsubsidized Stafford, PLUS, Federal Perkins. **Financial Aid Statistics:** 100% freshmen, 99% undergrads receive need-based scholarship or grant aid. 13% freshmen, 13% undergrads receive non-need-based scholarship or grant aid. 93% freshmen, 94% undergrads receive need-based self-help aid. 2% freshmen, 3% undergrads receive athletic scholarships. 73% undergrads borrow to pay for school. **Criteria for awarding institutional aid:** *Non-need-based:* academics, athletics, leadership, music/drama.

DEEP SPRINGS COLLEGE

Applications Committee, Dyer, NV 89010
Phone: 760-872-2000 · **Financial Aid Phone:** 760-872-2000
E-mail: apcom@deepsprings.edu · **CEEB Code:** 4281
Fax: 760-872-4466 · **Website:** www.deepsprings.edu

This private school was founded in 1917. It has a 30000-acre campus.

RATINGS
Admissions Selectivity Rating: 99   **Fire Safety Rating:** 79

STUDENTS AND FACULTY
Enrollment: 28. **Student Body:** 0% female, 100% male, 82% out-of-state, 14% international (3 countries represented). Asian 14%, African American 0%, Caucasian 64%, Hispanic 4%, Native American <1%
Retention and Graduation: 92% freshmen return for sophomore year. 96% grads go on to further study within 1 year. **Faculty:** 3 full-time faculty, 100% hold PhDs, 67% are members of minority groups, 0% are women. 0% of classes are taught by teaching assistants.

ACADEMICS
Degrees: associate. **Classes:** Most classes have fewer than 10 students. **Majors with Highest Enrollment:** Liberal Arts and Sciences Studies and Humanities. **Special Study Options:** independent study, internships.

FACILITIES
Housing: men's dorms. 100% of campus accessible to physically disabled. **Special Academic Facilities/Equipment:** Ranch- 300 cattle, 20 horses, organic farm growing hay and produce; thousands of acres of wilderness surround the college.

CAMPUS LIFE
Environment: Rural. **Activities:** student government. 1 registered organization. **On-Campus Highlights:** Boarding House, Dairy Barn, Horse Stables, The Upper Reservoir, The Druid.

ADMISSIONS
Freshman Academic Profile: 100% in top 10% of high school class, 100% in top 25% of high school class, 100% in top 50% of high school class. 64% from public high schools. SAT Math middle 50% range 670-740. SAT Critical Reading middle 50% range 740-800. **Basis for Candidate Selection:** *Very important factors considered include:* application essay, character/personal qualities, interview, level of applicant's interest. *Important factors considered include:* academic GPA, rigor of secondary school record, extracurricular activities, volunteer work, work experience. *Other factors considered include:* Class rank, recommendation(s), standardized test scores, racial/ethnic status, talent/ability. **Freshman Admission Requirements:** High school diploma or equivalent is not required. **Freshman Admission Statistics:** 200 applied, 10% admitted, 84% enrolled. **Transfer Admission Requirements:** High school transcript, college transcript(s), essay or personal statement, interview, standardized test scores. **General Admission Information:** Regular application deadline 11/15. Regular notification 4/15. Nonfall registration not accepted. Neither credit nor placement offered for CEEB Advanced Placement tests.

COSTS AND FINANCIAL AID
Average book expense $1,200. **Notification of Awards:** Applicants will be notified of awards on or about 4/15. **Financial Aid Statistics:** 0% freshmen, 0% undergrads receive athletic scholarships. 100% freshmen, 100% undergrads receive any aid. 0% undergrads borrow to pay for school. Average cumulative indebtedness $0.

DEFIANCE COLLEGE

701 North Clinton Street, Defiance, OH 43512-1695
Phone: 419-783-2359 · **Financial Aid Phone:** 419-783-2458
E-mail: admissions@defiance.edu · **CEEB Code:** 1162
Fax: 419-783-2468 · **Website:** www.defiance.edu · **ACT Code:** 3264

This private school, affiliated with the United Church of Christ Church, was founded in 1850. It has a 150-acre campus.

RATINGS
Admissions Selectivity Rating: 77   **Fire Safety Rating:** 84

STUDENTS AND FACULTY
Enrollment: 340. **Student Body:** 49% female, 51% male, 28% out-of-state, 4% international (2 countries represented). Asian 2%, African American 29%, Caucasian 182%, Hispanic 12%, Native American 3%
Retention and Graduation: 42% freshmen graduate within 4 years. 49% freshmen graduate within 6 years. **Faculty:** 39 full-time faculty, 67% hold PhDs, 46% are members of minority groups, 13% are women. 0% of classes are taught by teaching assistants.

ACADEMICS
Degrees: associate, bachelor's, certificate, master's. **Classes:** Most classes have 10–19 students. Most lab/discussion sessions have 10–19 students. **Majors with Highest Enrollment:** Education; Forensic Science and Technology; Criminal Justice and Corrections. **Special Study Options:** cooperative education program, distance learning, double major, dual enrollment, honors program, independent study, internships, student-designed major, study abroad, teacher certification program, weekend college. **Career services:** Alumni network, alumni services, career/job search classes, career assessment, internships. Career services highlights include Cooperative Learning.

FACILITIES
Housing: Coed dorms, apartments for single students. 100% of campus accessible to physically disabled. **Special Academic Facilities/Equipment:** Art gallery, media center, Eisenhower archives room, curriculum resource center, Cultural Arts Center, Indian wars collection. **Computers:** 100% of classrooms, 30% of dorms, 100% of libraries, 100% of dining areas, 100% of student union, 100% of common outdoor areas have wireless network access.

CAMPUS LIFE
Environment: Rural. **Activities:** Choral groups, concert band, drama/theater, literary magazine, musical theater, pep band, student government, student newspaper, yearbook, Campus Ministries. 30 registered organizations, 1 honor society, 2 religious organizations. 1 fraternity, 2 sororities. **Athletics (Intercollegiate):** *Men:* baseball, basketball, cross-country, football, golf, soccer, tennis, track/field (outdoor), track/field (indoor). *Women:* basketball, cross-country, golf, soccer, softball, tennis, track/field (outdoor), track/field (indoor), volleyball. **On-Campus Highlights:** Smart Fitness Center, Tenzer Hall, Serrick Center, Hubbard Hall, Weaner/McMaster Center. **Environmental Initiatives:** Lowering Electrical, Gas, and Water Usage.

ADMISSIONS
Freshman Academic Profile: Average high school GPA 3.08. 12% in top 10% of high school class, 29% in top 25% of high school class, 57% in top 50% of high school class. 97% from public high schools. SAT Math middle 50% range 390-500. SAT Critical Reading middle 50% range 400-500. SAT Writing middle 50% range 350-480. ACT middle 50% range 18-23. Minimum internet-based TOEFL 79. Minimum paper TOEFL 550. **Basis for Candidate Selection:** *Very important factors considered include:* academic GPA, rigor of secondary school record, standardized test scores. *Other factors considered include:* Class rank, character/personal qualities, extracurricular activities, interview, volunteer work. **Freshman Admission Requirements:** High school diploma is required and GED is accepted. **Freshman Admission Statistics:** 1,671 applied, 65% admitted, 22% enrolled. **Transfer Admission Requirements:** High school transcript, college transcript(s), essay or personal statement, statement of good standing from prior institution(s). Minimum college GPA of 2.0 required. Lowest grade transferable C. **General Admission Information:** Application Fee $25. Notification on a rolling basis, beginning on or about 9/1. Nonfall registration accepted. Admission may be deferred for a maximum of one year. Credit and/or placement offered for CEEB Advanced Placement tests.

COSTS AND FINANCIAL AID
Annual tuition $29,256. Room and board $9,522. Required fees $719. Average book expense $1,350. **Required Forms and Deadlines:** FAFSA. **Types of Aid:** *Need-based scholarships/grants:* Federal Pell, SEOG, state scholarships/grants, private scholarships, the school's own gift aid. *Loans:* Subsidized Stafford, Unsubsidized Stafford, PLUS, Federal Perkins, ALTERNATIVE LOANS. *Student Employment:* Federal Work-Study Program available. Institutional employment available. Off-campus job opportunities are good. **Financial Aid Statistics:** 86% freshmen, 83% undergrads receive need-based scholarship or grant aid. 100% freshmen, 97% undergrads receive non-need-based scholarship or grant aid. 93% freshmen, 92% undergrads receive need-based self-help aid. 0% freshmen, 0% undergrads receive athletic scholarships. 100% freshmen, 99% undergrads receive any aid. 90% undergrads borrow to pay for school. Average cumulative indebtedness $22,630. **Criteria for awarding institutional aid:** *Non-need-based:* academics, leadership.

DELAWARE VALLEY COLLEGE

700 East Butler Avenue, Doylestown, PA 18901-2697
Phone: 215-489-2211 · **Financial Aid Phone:** 215-489-2272
E-mail: ADMITME@delval.edu · **CEEB Code:** 2510
Fax: 215-230-2968 · **Website:** www.delval.edu · **ACT Code:** 3551

This private school was founded in 1896. It has a 600-acre campus.

RATINGS
Admissions Selectivity Rating: 84   **Fire Safety Rating:** 78

STUDENTS AND FACULTY
Enrollment: 1,877. **Student Body:** 58% female, 42% male, 39% out-of-state, 0% international (4 countries represented). Asian 1%, African American 4%, Caucasian 84%, Hispanic 2%, Native American <1%
Retention and Graduation: 76% freshmen return for sophomore year. 37% freshmen graduate within 4 years. 50% freshmen graduate within 6 years. 51% grads go on to further study within 1 year. 1% grads pursue law degrees. 9% grads pursue business degrees. 10% grads pursue medical degrees. **Faculty:** 82 full-time faculty, 57% hold PhDs, 41% are members of minority groups, 10% are women. 0% of classes are taught by teaching assistants.

ACADEMICS
Degrees: associate, bachelor's, certificate, master's, terminal associate, transfer associate. **Classes:** Most classes have 10–19 students. Most lab/discussion sessions have 10–19 students. **Majors with Highest Enrollment:** Animal Sciences; Animal Sciences; Business Administration and Management. **Special Study Options:** Accelerated program, cross-registration, distance learning, double major, honors program, independent study, internships, study abroad, teacher certification program, weekend college. **Honors programs:** The DVC Honors Program is an educational enrichment program designed to enhance the eductional opportunities and experiences of students admitted to the program. The programs consists of an Honors Colloquium followed by independent study programs in the 3rd and 4th years. It features guest lecturers, field trips and both faculty and student-led discussions. **Disability Services:** Special programs offered to physically disabled students include note-taking services, reader services, tape recorders. **Career services:** alumni services, career/job search classes, career assessment, internships. Career services highlights include our required employment program, which requires students to work 500 hours in their field before they graduate. Delaware Valley College's Employment Program, an experience-based graduation requirement, fosters the integration of theory and practice throughout the educational continuum, and helps students develop linkages with professionals in their fields of study. The Employment Program empowers students by equipping them with the skills and abilities necessary for success as they transition from college to career. Because of the college's commitment to career-oriented education, students graduate with a level of skill and experience that far exceeds that of the average entry-level candidate. Delaware Valley College is one of only 3% of colleges nationwide with a mandatory experiential-learning requirement, making it one of the most important and unique aspects of the DelVal educational experience.

FACILITIES
Housing: Coed dorms, women's dorms. **Special Academic Facilities/Equipment:** Dairy processing plant, greenhouse and nursery lab complex, small animal science labs, poultry diagnostic lab, arboretum, equine facilities, 500+-acre farm, tissue culture lab. **Computers:** 25% of classrooms, 100% of dorms, 100% of libraries, 80% of student union, 20% of common outdoor areas have wireless network access. Students can register for classes online. Administrative functions (other than registration) can be performed online.

CAMPUS LIFE
Environment: Village. **Activities:** Choral groups, concert band, drama/theater, literary magazine, music ensembles, radio station, student government, student newspaper, yearbook. 62 registered organizations, 2 honor societies, 2 religious organizations. 5 fraternities, 3 sororities. **Athletics (Intercollegiate):** *Men:* baseball, basketball, cross-country, football, golf, soccer, track/field (outdoor), track/field (indoor), wrestling. *Women:* basketball, cheerleading, cross-country,

field hockey, soccer, softball, track/field (outdoor), track/field (indoor), volleyball. **On-Campus Highlights:** Smart Classroom, Small Animal Facility, Athletic Complex, Student Center, Equine center, The campus has many unique areas that are are of specific interest depending on a student's major field of study (i.e. dairy barn, equine center, etc.). **Environmental Initiatives:** Recycling, Wind Energy, Bio-Diesel Fuel.

ADMISSIONS

Freshman Academic Profile: Average high school GPA 3.47. 13% in top 10% of high school class, 73% in top 25% of high school class, 27% in top 50% of high school class. 85% from public high schools. SAT Math middle 50% range 460-560. SAT Critical Reading middle 50% range 450-550. SAT Writing middle 50% range 430-550. ACT middle 50% range 20-25. Minimum paper TOEFL 500. **Basis for Candidate Selection:** *Very important factors considered include:* academic GPA, standardized test scores. *Important factors considered include:* Class rank, rigor of secondary school record, interview. *Other factors considered include:* application essay, recommendation(s), alumni/ae relation, character/personal qualities, extracurricular activities, level of applicant's interest, talent/ability, volunteer work, work experience. **Freshman Admission Requirements:** High school diploma is required and GED is accepted. *Academic units required:* 3 English, 2 mathematics, 2 science, (1 science labs), 2 social studies, 6 academic electives. **Freshman Admission Statistics:** 1,770 applied, 72% admitted, 36% enrolled. **Transfer Admission Requirements:** High school transcript, college transcript(s), statement of good standing from prior institution(s). Minimum college GPA of 2.0 required. Lowest grade transferable C. **General Admission Information:** Application Fee $35. Notification on a rolling basis, beginning on or about 10/31. Nonfall registration accepted. Admission may be deferred for a maximum of 12 months. Credit and/or placement offered for CEEB Advanced Placement tests.

COSTS AND FINANCIAL AID

Annual tuition $28,596. Room and board $10,842. Required fees $2,050. **Required Forms and Deadlines:** FAFSA, State aid form. **Notification of Awards:** Applicants will be notified of awards on a rolling basis beginning 2/1. **Types of Aid:** *Need-based scholarships/grants:* Federal Pell, SEOG, state scholarships/grants, private scholarships, the school's own gift aid. *Loans:* Subsidized Stafford, Unsubsidized Stafford, PLUS, Federal Perkins, Alternative Loans. *Student Employment:* Federal Work-Study Program available. Institutional employment available. Highest amount earned per year from on-campus jobs $2,200. **Financial Aid Statistics:** 99% freshmen, 99% undergrads receive need-based scholarship or grant aid. 9% freshmen, 8% undergrads receive non-need-based scholarship or grant aid. 82% freshmen, 80% undergrads receive need-based self-help aid. 0% freshmen, 0% undergrads receive athletic scholarships. 98% freshmen, 91% undergrads receive any aid. 73% undergrads borrow to pay for school. Average cumulative indebtedness $19,488. **Criteria for awarding institutional aid:** *Non-need-based:* academics, alumni affiliation, music/drama.

DELTA STATE UNIVERSITY

Highway 8 West, Cleveland, MS 38733
Phone: 662-846-4018
E-mail: dheslep@deltastate.edu
Fax: 662-846-4683 • **Website:** www.deltastate.edu • **ACT Code:** 2190

This public school was founded in 1924. It has a 332-acre campus.

RATINGS

Admissions Selectivity Rating: 82   **Fire Safety Rating:** 69

STUDENTS AND FACULTY

Enrollment: 3,156. **Student Body:** 62% female, 38% male, 10% out-of-state, 0% international (3 countries represented). Asian 1%, African American 33%, Caucasian 66%, Hispanic 1%, Native American <1%
Retention and Graduation: 68% freshmen return for sophomore year. 24% freshmen graduate within 4 years. 48% freshmen graduate within 6 years. **Faculty:** 162 full-time faculty, 60% hold PhDs, 49% are members of minority groups, 7% are women. 0% of classes are taught by teaching assistants.

ACADEMICS

Degrees: bachelor's, master's, post-master's certificate. **Majors with Highest Enrollment:** Elementary Education and Teaching; Business/Commerce; Management Information Systems. **Special Study Options:** cooperative education program, distance learning, double major, dual enrollment, honors program, independent study, internships, teacher certification program, weekend college. **Disability Services:** Special programs offered to physically disabled students include note-taking services, reader services, tape recorders, tutors.

FACILITIES

Housing: men's dorms, women's dorms, apartments for married students, Apartments for students with dependent children. 65% of campus accessible to physically disabled. **Special Academic Facilities/Equipment:** Art museum, performing arts center, natural history museum, language lab, airport facility with 12 airplanes, flight simulator, planetarium, Art museum, Performing Arts Center, Natural History Museum, Language Lab, Airport facility, flight simulation, planetarium **Computers:** Students can register for classes online. Administrative functions (other than registration) can be performed online.

CAMPUS LIFE

Environment: Village. **Activities:** Choral groups, concert band, drama/theater, jazz band, literary magazine, marching band, music ensembles, musical theater, opera, student government, student newspaper, symphony orchestra, yearbook. 46 registered organizations, 27 honor societies, 11 religious organization. 8 fraternities, 6 sororities. **Athletics (Intercollegiate):** *Men:* baseball, basketball, diving, football, golf, soccer, swimming, tennis. *Women:* basketball, cross-country, diving, soccer, softball, swimming, tennis.

ADMISSIONS

Freshman Academic Profile: 4% in top 25% of high school class, 57% in top 50% of high school class. ACT middle 50% range 17-21. Minimum paper TOEFL 525. **Basis for Candidate Selection:** *Very important factors considered include:* Class rank, rigor of secondary school record, standardized test scores. *Other factors considered include:* recommendation(s), interview. **Freshman Admission Requirements:** High school diploma is required and GED is accepted. *Academic units required:* 4 English, 3 mathematics, 3 science, (2 science labs), 1 foreign language, 3 social studies, 1 academic electives. **Freshman Admission Statistics:** 1,289 applied, 32% admitted, 79% enrolled. **Transfer Admission Requirements:** college transcript(s), Minimum college GPA of 2.0 required. Lowest grade transferable D. **General Admission Information:** Application Fee $15. Regular application deadline 8/1. Notification on a rolling basis, beginning on or about 5/15. Nonfall registration accepted. Admission may be deferred for a maximum of N/A. Credit and/or placement offered for CEEB Advanced Placement tests.

COSTS AND FINANCIAL AID

Average book expense $700. **Required Forms and Deadlines:** FAFSA, Institution's own financial aid form. **Notification of Awards:** Applicants will be notified of awards on a rolling basis beginning 5/1. **Types of Aid:** *Need-based scholarships/grants:* Federal Pell, SEOG, private scholarships, the school's own gift aid. *Loans:* Subsidized Stafford, Unsubsidized Stafford, PLUS, Federal Perkins, college/university loans from institutional funds. *Student Employment:* Federal Work-Study Program available. Institutional employment available. Highest amount earned per year from on-campus jobs $1,200. Off-campus job opportunities are fair. **Financial Aid Statistics:** 0% freshmen, 0% undergrads receive athletic scholarships. Criteriafor awarding institutional aid: *Non-need-based:* academics, alumni affiliation, art, athletics, leadership, music/drama, religious affiliation, state/district residency.

DENISON UNIVERSITY

Best 380

Box H, Granville, OH 43023
Phone: 740-587-6276 • **Financial Aid Phone:** 800-336-4766
E-mail: admissions@denison.edu • **CEEB Code:** 1164
Fax: 740-587-6306 • **Website:** www.denison.edu • **ACT Code:** 3266

This private school was founded in 1831. It has a 900-acre campus.

RATINGS

Admissions Selectivity Rating: 90   **Fire Safety Rating:** 93

STUDENTS AND FACULTY

Enrollment: 2,304. **Student Body:** 58% female, 42% male, 71% out-of-state, 7% international (27 countries represented). Asian 3%, African American 6%, Caucasian 71%, Hispanic 8%, Native American <1%
Retention and Graduation: 92% freshmen return for sophomore year. 84% freshmen graduate within 4 years. 86% freshmen graduate within 6 years. 25% grads go on to further study within 1 year. 15% grads pursue arts and sciences degrees. 3% grads pursue law degrees. 3% grads pursue business degrees. 3% grads pursue medical degrees. **Faculty:** 211 full-time faculty, 99% hold PhDs, 45% are members of minority groups, 18% are women. 0% of classes are taught by teaching assistants.

ACADEMICS

Degrees: bachelor's. **Classes:** Most classes have 10–19 students. **Majors with Highest Enrollment:** Economics; Psychology; Biology. **Special Study Options:** double major, honors program, independent study, internships, student-designed major, study abroad, teacher certification program, 3-2 Duke U Environmental Management; 3-2 U. of Michigan Natural Resources, 3-4 Case Western Reserve Dental; 3-2 Rensselaer Poly., Washington U. (St. Louis), Case Western Reserve, Columbia U. Engineering; Washington U. (St. Louis) Occupational Therapy. **Disability Services:** Special programs offered to physically disabled students include note-taking services, reader services, tape recorders, tutors. **Career services:** Alumni network, alumni services, career assessment, internships, regional alumni. We are proud of all of our programs.

FACILITIES

Housing: Coed dorms, men's dorms, women's dorms, cooperative housing, apartments for single students, Wellness Housing, Theme Housing. 66% of campus accessible to physically disabled. **Special Academic Facilities/Equipment:** Burmese art collection in the Dension Museum, language lab, research station in 350-acre biological reserve, observatory, high resolution spectrometer lab, nuclear magnetic resonance spectrometer, planetarium, Economics computer laboratories. **Computers:** 100% of classrooms, 100% of dorms, 100% of libraries, 100% of dining areas, 100% of student union, 100% of common outdoor areas have wireless network access. Administrative functions (other than registration) can be performed online.

CAMPUS LIFE

Environment: Village. **Activities:** Choral groups, dance, drama/theater, jazz band, music ensembles, musical theater, radio station, student government, student newspaper, student-run film society, television station, yearbook, Campus Ministries, International Student Organization. 160 registered organizations, 15 honor societies, 7 religious organizations. 8 fraternities, 6 sororities. **Athletics (Intercollegiate):** *Men:* baseball, basketball, cross-country, diving, football, golf, lacrosse, soccer, swimming, tennis, track/field (outdoor), track/field (indoor). *Women:* basketball, cross-country, diving, field hockey, golf, lacrosse, soccer, softball, swimming, tennis, track/field (outdoor), track/field (indoor), volleyball. **On-Campus Highlights:** Samson Talbot Hall of Biological Science, Mitchell Recreation and Athletics Center, Swasey Chapel, Biological Reserve and Polly Anderson Fi, Burke Hall Art Gallery, Burton D. Morgan Center. **Environmental Initiatives:** The signing of the ACUPCC and the development of a standing Campus Sustainability Committee as part of the campus governance system. Completion of a comprehensive greenhouse gas inventory and campus sustainability assessment using the STARS program. Development of a Policy to build and renovate to LEED Silver or better standards.

ADMISSIONS

Freshman Academic Profile: Average high school GPA 3.5. 49% in top 10% of high school class, 39% in top 25% of high school class, 12% in top 50% of high school class. 70% from public high schools. SAT Math middle 50% range 600-680. SAT Critical Reading middle 50% range 600-720. ACT middle 50% range 27-31. Minimum paper TOEFL 599. **Basis for Candidate Selection:** *Very important factors considered include:* application essay, academic GPA, recommendation(s), rigor of secondary school record. *Important factors considered include:* extracurricular activities, interview, level of applicant's interest, talent/ability. *Other factors considered include:* Class rank, standardized test scores, alumni/ae relation, character/personal qualities, first generation, geographical residence, racial/ethnic status, state residency, volunteer work, work experience. **Freshman Admission Requirements:** High school diploma is required and GED is accepted. *Academic units required:* 4 English, 4 mathematics, 4 science, 3 foreign language, 2 social studies, 1 history, 1 academic electives. **Freshman Admission Statistics:** 4,757 applied, 50% admitted, 27% enrolled. **Transfer Admission Requirements:** High school transcript, college transcript(s), essay or personal statement, statement of good standing from prior institution(s). Minimum college GPA of 3.0 required. Lowest grade transferable C-. **General Admission Information:** Application Fee $40. Early decision application deadline 11/15. Regular application deadline 1/15. Regular notification 4/1. Nonfall registration not accepted. Admission may be deferred for a maximum of 1 year. Credit and/or placement offered for CEEB Advanced Placement tests.

COSTS AND FINANCIAL AID

Annual tuition $42,990. Room and board $10,760. Required fees $920. **Required Forms and Deadlines:** FAFSA. **Notification of Awards:** Applicants will be notified of awards on or about 3/28. **Types of Aid:** *Need-based scholarships/grants:* Federal Pell, SEOG, state scholarships/grants, private scholarships, the school's own gift aid. *Loans:* Direct Subsidized Stafford, Direct Unsubsidized Stafford, Direct PLUS, Federal Perkins, college/university loans from institutional funds. *Student Employment:* Federal Work-Study Program available. Institutional employment available. Highest amount earned per year from on-campus jobs $2,530. Off-campus job opportunities are fair. **Financial Aid Statistics:** 100% freshmen, 100% undergrads receive need-based scholarship or grant aid. 93% freshmen, 90% undergrads receive non-need-based

scholarship or grant aid. 73% freshmen, 77% undergrads receive need-based self-help aid. 0% freshmen, 0% undergrads receive athletic scholarships. 97% freshmen, 96% undergrads receive any aid. Average cumulative indebtedness $20,162. **Criteria for awarding institutional aid:** *Non-need-based:* academics, alumni affiliation, art, leadership, minority status, music/drama, state/district residency.

DEPAUL UNIVERSITY

1 East Jackson Boulevard, Chicago, IL 60604-2287
Phone: 312-362-8300 • **Financial Aid Phone:** 312-362-8091
E-mail: admission@depaul.edu • **CEEB Code:** 001671-00
Fax: 312-362-5749 • **Website:** www.depaul.edu • **ACT Code:** 1012

This private school, affiliated with the Roman Catholic Church, was founded in 1898. It has a 36-acre campus.

RATINGS

Admissions Selectivity Rating: 85   **Fire Safety Rating:** 99

STUDENTS AND FACULTY

Enrollment: 15,858. **Student Body:** 53% female, 47% male, 21% out-of-state, 3% international (84 countries represented). Asian 8%, African American 8%, Caucasian 55%, Hispanic 18%, Native American <1%
Retention and Graduation: 56% freshmen graduate within 4 years. 71% freshmen graduate within 6 years. 27% grads go on to further study within 1 year. **Faculty:** 919 full-time faculty, 86% hold PhDs, 46% are members of minority groups, 19% are women. 3% of classes are taught by teaching assistants.

ACADEMICS

Degrees: bachelor's, certificate, master's, post-bachelor's certificate, post-master's certificate. **Classes:** Most classes have 20–29 students. Most lab/discussion sessions have 10–19 students. **Majors with Highest Enrollment:** Accounting; Public Relations, Advertising, and Applied Communication; Psychology. **Special Study Options:** Accelerated program, cooperative education program, distance learning, double major, dual enrollment, English as a Second Language (ESL), honors program, independent study, internships, student-designed major, study abroad, teacher certification program, weekend college. **Honors programs:** DePaul's honors program offers small classes organized in a seminar format and taught by faculty committed to academic excellence and the attainment of lifelong learning strategies. Benefits of our scholarly community include academic advising, an Honors Lounge, a student government, peer mentoring, student-faculty dinners, newsletters, cultural outings, service activities, and many other experiences that enrich the Honors community while extending the Honors experience beyond the classroom. Combined degree programs: BA/MA, BS/MS. **Disability Services:** Special programs offered to physically disabled students include note-taking services, reader services, tape recorders, tutors. **Career services:** Alumni network, alumni services, career/job search classes, career assessment, internships, regional alumni. In response to a mandated experiential learning requirement, we set up an university wide internship program that places 1,020 students a year in internships that meet the requirements.

FACILITIES

Housing: Coed dorms, special housing for disabled students, special housing for international students, apartments for single students, Theme Housing. 95% of campus accessible to physically disabled. **Special Academic Facilities/Equipment:** Monsignor Andrew J. McGowan Environmental Science & Chemistry building (gold LEED-certified, 2009), Digital Cinema laboratory with motion-capture system, Green-screen studio, converged newsroom, Merle Reskin Theatre, Art Museum, William G. McGowan Biological & Environmental Science Building (1998), Ray Meyer Fitness & Recreational Center (1999), and Three-level student center (2002). **Computers:** 60% of classrooms, 100% of dorms, 100% of libraries, 100% of dining areas, 75% of student union, 25% of common outdoor areas have wireless network access. Students can register for classes online. Administrative functions (other than registration) can be performed online.

CAMPUS LIFE

Environment: Metropolis. **Activities:** Choral groups, concert band, dance, drama/theater, jazz band, literary magazine, marching band, music ensembles, musical theater, opera, pep band, radio station, student government, student newspaper, student-run film society, symphony orchestra, yearbook, Campus Ministries, International Student Organization, Model UN. 311 registered organizations, 9 honor societies, 19 religious organizations. 9 fraternities, 13 sororities. **Athletics (Intercollegiate):** *Men:* basketball, cross-country, golf, soccer, tennis, track/field (outdoor), track/field (indoor). *Women:* basketball, cross-country, soccer, softball, tennis, track/field (outdoor), track/field (indoor), volleyball. **On-Campus Highlights:** Quad (outside center of campus), Ray Meyer Fitness Center, Student Center, Student Lounge in DePaul Center, The Bean Café in the Schmitt Acad. Cntr. **Environmental Initiatives:** 1. The Sustainability Initiative Task Force (SITF) created an Institutional Sustainability Plan, which can be accessed at http://mission.depaul.edu/Programs/Sustainability/Documents/SUSTAINABILITYPLANFINAL.pdf. This plan is derived from the results of a comprehensive sustainability audit conducted by five SITF Working Groups Curriculum, Operations, Administration and Planning, Research, and Engagement—and builds on SITF Report #4 (Sustainability at DePaul University: Recommendations to the Strategic Planning Task Force) which describes the Working Groups recommendations and attendant actionable goals for making environmental, social and economic sustainability clearly articulated strategic priorities of the next University Strategic Plan. Each Working Group was responsible for conducting the wide-ranging Sustainability Tracking, Assessment, and Rating System TM (STARS) audit. This report also influenced Vision 2018, DePauls strategic plan, which can be accessed at the following link: http://offices.depaul.edu/president/strategic-directions/vision-2018/Pages/default.aspx. 2. DePaul University has pledged to secure LEED certification for all new campus buildings and is undertaking a program to retrofit existing facilities. In addition, 80 percent of the landscaping outside those buildings is managed organically. The university will be installing building automation systems in all new buildings that will help to improve efficiencies of operation and therefore save on energy expended. DePauls Monsignor Andrew J. McGowan Science Building was awarded a Gold Leadership in Energy and Environmental Design (LEED) certificate by the U.S. Green Building Council. 3. DePaul's students, faculty, and administration have all made contributions to make the University a more environmentally friendly campus. The administration has made its support for environmentalism clear by donating funds to the Student Government Association for sustainable initiatives. Students participate in classes and school community organizations to help promote environmental awareness and action.

ADMISSIONS

Freshman Academic Profile: Average high school GPA 3.56. 21% in top 10% of high school class, 53% in top 25% of high school class, 86% in top 50% of high school class. 78% from public high schools. SAT Math middle 50% range 510-630. SAT Critical Reading middle 50% range 520-640. ACT middle 50% range 23-28. Minimum internet-based TOEFL 80. Minimum paper TOEFL 550. **Basis for Candidate Selection:** *Very important factors considered include:* application essay, academic GPA, rigor of secondary school record, standardized test scores. *Important factors considered include:* Class rank, recommendation(s), character/personal qualities, extracurricular activities, level of applicant's interest, talent/ability, volunteer work, work experience. *Other factors considered include:* alumni/ae relation, first generation, geographical residence, interview, racial/ethnic status, religious affiliation/commitment, state residency. **Freshman Admission Requirements:** High school diploma is required and GED is accepted. *Academic units required:* 4 English, 3 mathematics, 3 science, (2 science labs), 0 foreign language, 0 history, 2 Social Science/History. **Freshman Admission Statistics:** 19,533 applied, 70% admitted, 19% enrolled. **Transfer Admission Requirements:** college transcript(s), Minimum college GPA of 2.0 required. Lowest grade transferable D. **General Admission Information:** Application Fee $40. Regular application deadline 2/1. Regular notification 3/15. Nonfall registration accepted. Admission may be deferred for a maximum of 1 year. Credit and/or placement offered for CEEB Advanced Placement tests.

COSTS AND FINANCIAL AID

Annual tuition $34,390. Room and board $12,552. Required fees $681. Average book expense $1,104. **Required Forms and Deadlines:** FAFSA. **Notification of Awards:** Applicants will be notified of awards on a rolling basis beginning 3/15. **Types of Aid:** *Need-based scholarships/grants:* Federal Pell, SEOG, state scholarships/grants, private scholarships, the school's own gift aid, Federal Academic Competitiveness Grant, Federal SMART Grant, and Federal TEACH Grant. *Loans:* Direct Subsidized Stafford, Direct Unsubsidized Stafford, Direct PLUS, Federal Perkins, Private Loans. *Student Employment:* Federal Work-Study Program available. Institutional employment available. Highest amount earned per year from on-campus jobs $14,000. Off-campus job opportunities are excellent. **Financial Aid Statistics:** 85% freshmen, 85% undergrads receive need-based scholarship or grant aid. 91% freshmen, 59% undergrads receive non-need-based scholarship or grant aid. 70% freshmen, 77% undergrads receive need-based self-help aid. 2% freshmen, 2% undergrads receive athletic scholarships. 98% freshmen, 87% undergrads receive any aid. 60% undergrads borrow to pay for school. Average cumulative indebtedness $24,292. **Criteria for awarding institutional aid:** *Non-need-based:* academics, art, athletics, leadership, music/drama, state/district residency.

DEPAUW UNIVERSITY

101 E. Seminary Street, Greencastle, IN 46135
Phone: 765-658-4006 · **Financial Aid Phone:** 765-658-4030
E-mail: admission@depauw.edu · **CEEB Code:** 1166
Fax: 765-658-4007 · **Website:** www.depauw.edu · **ACT Code:** 1184

This private school, affiliated with the Methodist Church, was founded in 1837. It has a 1100-acre campus.

RATINGS

Admissions Selectivity Rating: 91   **Fire Safety Rating:** 68

STUDENTS AND FACULTY

Enrollment: 2,187. **Student Body:** 54% female, 46% male, 63% out-of-state, 9% international (34 countries represented). Asian 3%, African American 6%, Caucasian 69%, Hispanic 3%, Native American <1%
Retention and Graduation: 75% freshmen graduate within 4 years. 23% grads go on to further study within 1 year. 15% grads pursue arts and sciences degrees. 5% grads pursue law degrees. 1% grads pursue business degrees. 2% grads pursue medical degrees. **Faculty:** 207 full-time faculty, 97% hold PhDs, 42% are members of minority groups, 20% are women. 0% of classes are taught by teaching assistants.

ACADEMICS

Degrees: bachelor's. **Classes:** Most classes have 10–19 students. Most lab/discussion sessions have 10–19 students. **Majors with Highest Enrollment:** Economics; Speech Communication and Rhetoric. **Special Study Options:** double major, dual enrollment, exchange student program (domestic), honors program, independent study, internships, student-designed major, study abroad, teacher certification program. **Honors programs:** Please visit the following website for information about DePauw's **Honors programs:** http://www.depauw.edu/honors/index.asp. **Disability Services:** Special programs offered to physically disabled students include note-taking services, reader services, tape recorders, tutors. **Career services:** Alumni network, alumni services, career/job search classes, career assessment, internships, regional alumni. Career services highlights include http://www.depauw.edu/admin/acadaffairs/student-programs/internship.asp.

FACILITIES

Housing: Coed dorms, special housing for disabled students, special housing for international students, fraternity/sorority housing, apartments for single students. 85% of campus accessible to physically disabled. **Special Academic Facilities/Equipment:** Recently opened Peeler Art Center housing gallery and studio space; Center for Contemporary Media; Performing Arts Center; Anthropology Museum; Shidzuo Iikudo Museum **Computers:** Students can register for classes online. Administrative functions (other than registration) can be performed online. Undergraduates are required to own a computer.

CAMPUS LIFE

Environment: Village. **Activities:** Choral groups, concert band, dance, drama/theater, jazz band, literary magazine, music ensembles, musical theater, opera, pep band, radio station, student government, student newspaper, student-run film society, symphony orchestra, television station, Campus Ministries, International Student Organization. 119 registered organizations, 13 honor societies, 10 religious organizations. 13 fraternities, 11 sorority. **Athletics (Intercollegiate):** *Men:* baseball, basketball, cross-country, diving, football, golf, soccer, swimming, tennis, track/field (outdoor), track/field (indoor). *Women:* basketball, cross-country, diving, field hockey, golf, soccer, softball, swimming, tennis, track/field (outdoor), track/field (indoor), volleyball. **On-Campus Highlights:** DePauw University School of Music, Roy O. West Library, Music Library, and the Prevo Science Library, Café Roy coffee shop, Memorial Student Union, Bowman Park. **Environmental Initiatives:** LEED certified construction of the Janet Prindle Institute for Ethics. 2007-08 full year of campus programming, speakers, and colloquia on sustainability: Boswell Symposium on environmental justice, featuring Majora Carter (http://www.depauw.edu/admin/acadaffairs/Boswell/Symposium_2007.asp) Ubben Lecture by Ralph Nader (http://www.depauw.edu/news/index.asp?id=20101) Arts Fest 2007 on Art and the Environment (http://www.depauw.edu/arts/artsfest/) DePauw Discourse on Sustainability and Global Citizenship, featuring Bill McKibben and Robert Kennedy, Jr. (http://www.depauw.edu/discourse/) Focus the Nation teach-in on global warming (http://www.depauw.edu/univ/sustain/ftn/index.asp) DePauw Colloquium on the Liberal Arts: Liberal Education in a Time of Climate Crisis (http://www.depauw.edu/admin/acadaffairs/facdev/Events/DePauwColloquium2008.

asp) Earth Week events currently in planning stages. Significant investment in/upgrades to campus utilities/infrastructure, including an HVAC audit, upgraded steam pipes, chiller planet water system replacement, lightbulb replacement, and a bike-share program, among other changes.

ADMISSIONS

Freshman Academic Profile: Average high school GPA 3.86. 48% in top 10% of high school class, 83% in top 25% of high school class, 97% in top 50% of high school class. 83% from public high schools. SAT Math middle 50% range 560-660. SAT Critical Reading middle 50% range 530-640. SAT Writing middle 50% range 520-630. ACT middle 50% range 25-29. Minimum paper TOEFL 560. **Basis for Candidate Selection:** *Very important factors considered include:* academic GPA, rigor of secondary school record, standardized test scores. *Important factors considered include:* Class rank, application essay, recommendation(s). *Other factors considered include:* alumni/ae relation, character/personal qualities, extracurricular activities, first generation, geographical residence, interview, level of applicant's interest, state residency, talent/ability, volunteer work, work experience. **Freshman Admission Requirements:** High school diploma is required and GED is accepted. **Freshman Admission Statistics:** 5,282 applied, 57% admitted, 17% enrolled. **Transfer Admission Requirements:** High school transcript, college transcript(s), essay or personal statement, statement of good standing from prior institution(s). Minimum college GPA of 3.0 required. Lowest grade transferable C. **General Admission Information:** Application Fee $40. Early decision application deadline 11/1. Regular application deadline 2/1. Regular notification 4/1. Nonfall registration accepted. Admission may be deferred for a maximum of 1 year. Credit and/or placement offered for CEEB Advanced Placement tests.

COSTS AND FINANCIAL AID

Annual tuition $42,050. Room and board $11,200. Required fees $696. Average book expense $900. **Required Forms and Deadlines:** FAFSA, CSS/Financial Aid PROFILE. **Notification of Awards:** Applicants will be notified of awards on or about 4/1. **Types of Aid:** *Need-based scholarships/grants:* Federal Pell, SEOG, state scholarships/grants, private scholarships, the school's own gift aid, United Negro College Fund. *Loans:* Direct Subsidized Stafford, Direct Unsubsidized Stafford, Direct PLUS, Subsidized Stafford, Unsubsidized Stafford, PLUS, Federal Perkins, state loans, college/university loans from institutional funds. *Student Employment:* Federal Work-Study Program available. Institutional employment available. Off-campus job opportunities are fair. **Financial Aid Statistics:** 100% freshmen, 100% undergrads receive need-based scholarship or grant aid. 22% freshmen, 19% undergrads receive non-need-based scholarship or grant aid. 77% freshmen, 81% undergrads receive need-based self-help aid. 0% freshmen, 0% undergrads receive athletic scholarships. 54% undergrads borrow to pay for school. Average cumulative indebtedness $21,111. **Criteria for awarding institutional aid:** *Non-need-based:* academics, alumni affiliation, art, leadership, minority status, music/drama, religious affiliation, state/district residency.

DEVRY INSTITUTE OF TECHNOLOGY (LONG ISLAND CITY, NY)

3020 Thomson Avenue, Long Island City, NY 11101-3051
Phone: 718-472-2728
E-mail: nyemailleads@ny.devry.edu
Fax: 718-361-0004 • **Website:** www.devry.edu

This proprietary school was founded in 1931. It has a 4-acre campus.

RATINGS

Admissions Selectivity Rating: 60*   Fire Safety Rating: 60*

STUDENTS AND FACULTY

Enrollment: 1,839. **Student Body:** 24% female, 76% male, 3% international (17 countries represented). Asian 8%, African American 40%, Caucasian 10%, Hispanic 23%, Native American 1%
Retention and Graduation: 36% freshmen return for sophomore year. **Faculty:** 60 full-time faculty.

ACADEMICS

Degrees: associate, bachelor's, master's, post-bachelor's certificate, terminal associate. **Majors with Highest Enrollment:** Electrical, Electronic and Communications Engineering Technology/Technician. **Special Study Options:** Accelerated program, cooperative education program, distance learning, double major, weekend college. **Disability Services:** Special programs offered to physically disabled students include note-taking services, reader services, tape recorders, tutors. **Career services:** alumni services, career/job search classes.

FACILITIES

Housing: Private apartments;student plan housing, private rooms. 100% of campus accessible to physically disabled. **Computers:** Administrative functions (other than registration) can be performed online.

CAMPUS LIFE

Activities: 4 registered organizations, 1 honor society.

ADMISSIONS

Freshman Academic Profile: Minimum paper TOEFL 500. **Basis for Candidate Selection:** *Important factors considered include:* interview. *Other factors considered include:* standardized test scores. **Freshman Admission Requirements:** High school diploma is required and GED is accepted. *Academic units required:* 1 mathematics. 1 mathematics, **Transfer Admission Requirements:** college transcript(s), standardized test scores, Minimum college GPA of 2.0 required. Lowest grade transferable C. **General Admission Information:** Application Fee $50. Notification on a rolling basis, beginning on or about 11/2. Nonfall registration accepted. Admission may be deferred for a maximum of 12 months. Credit offered for CEEB Advanced Placement tests.

COSTS AND FINANCIAL AID

Annual tuition $12,450. Required fees $340. Average book expense $1,200. **Required Forms and Deadlines:** FAFSA. **Types of Aid:** *Need-based scholarships/grants:* Federal Pell, SEOG, private scholarships, the school's own gift aid. *Loans:* Subsidized Stafford, Unsubsidized Stafford, PLUS, Federal Perkins, college/university loans from institutional funds. *Student Employment:* Federal Work-Study Program available. Institutional employment available. Highest amount earned per year from on-campus jobs $5,994. Off-campus job opportunities are good. **Financial Aid Statistics:** 92% freshmen, 87% undergrads receive need-based scholarship or grant aid. 0% freshmen, 0% undergrads receive non-need-based scholarship or grant aid. 97% freshmen, 98% undergrads receive need-based self-help aid. 0% freshmen, 0% undergrads receive athletic scholarships.

DEVRY UNIVERSITY (ADDISON, IL)

1221 North Swift Road, Addison, IL 60101
Phone: 630-953-2000
E-mail: info@devry.edu
Fax: 630-953-1236 • **Website:** www.devry.edu

This proprietary school was founded in 1931. It has a 13-acre campus.

RATINGS

Admissions Selectivity Rating: 60*   Fire Safety Rating: 60*

STUDENTS AND FACULTY

Enrollment: 4,827. **Student Body:** 34% female, 66% male, 1% international (23 countries represented). Asian 8%, African American 13%, Caucasian 52%, Hispanic 8%, Native American 1%
Retention and Graduation: 51% freshmen return for sophomore year. 33% freshmen graduate within 6 years. **Faculty:** 69 full-time faculty.

ACADEMICS

Degrees: associate, bachelor's, terminal associate. **Majors with Highest Enrollment:** Electrical, Electronic and Communications Engineering Technology/Technician. **Special Study Options:** Accelerated program, cooperative education program, distance learning, double major, weekend college. **Disability Services:** Special programs offered to physically disabled students include note-taking services, reader services, tape recorders, tutors. **Career services:** alumni services, career/job search classes,

FACILITIES

Housing: Concord Residence. 100% of campus accessible to physically disabled. **Computers:** Students can register for classes online. Administrative functions (other than registration) can be performed online.

CAMPUS LIFE

Environment: Village. **Activities:** student government 11 registered organizations, 3 honor societies, 1 religious organization.

ADMISSIONS

Freshman Academic Profile: Minimum paper TOEFL 500. **Basis for Candidate Selection:** *Important factors considered include:* interview. *Other factors considered include:* standardized test scores. **Freshman Admission Requirements:** High school diploma is required and GED is accepted. *Academic units required:* 1 mathematics. 1 mathematics, **Transfer Admission Requirements:** college transcript(s), standardized test scores, Minimum college GPA of 2.0 required. Lowest grade transferable C. **General Admission Information:**

Application Fee $50. Notification on a rolling basis, beginning on or about 11/2. Nonfall registration accepted. Admission may be deferred for a maximum of 12 months. Credit offered for CEEB Advanced Placement tests.

COSTS AND FINANCIAL AID

Annual tuition $11,330. Required fees $340. Average book expense $1,200. **Required Forms and Deadlines:** FAFSA. *Types of Aid: Need-based scholarships/grants:* Federal Pell, SEOG, private scholarships, the school's own gift aid. *Loans:* Subsidized Stafford, Unsubsidized Stafford, PLUS, Federal Perkins, college/university loans from institutional funds. *Student Employment:* Federal Work-Study Program available. Institutional employment available. Highest amount earned per year from on-campus jobs $6,750. Off-campus job opportunities are excellent. **Financial Aid Statistics:** 64% freshmen, 60% undergrads receive need-based scholarship or grant aid. 1% freshmen, 0% undergrads receive non-need-based scholarship or grant aid. 98% freshmen, 98% undergrads receive need-based self-help aid. 0% freshmen, 0% undergrads receive athletic scholarships.

DEVRY UNIVERSITY (ALPHARETTA, GA)

2555 Northwinds Parkway, Alpharetta, GA 30004
Phone: 770-664-9520
E-mail: admissions@devry.com • **CEEB Code:**
Fax: 770-664-8824 • **Website:** www.devry.edu

This proprietary school was founded in 1931. It has a 21-acre campus.

RATINGS

Admissions Selectivity Rating: 60*   **Fire Safety Rating:** 60*

STUDENTS AND FACULTY

Enrollment: 1,286. **Student Body:** 34% female, 66% male, 2% international (17 countries represented). Asian 3%, African American 32%, Caucasian 28%, Hispanic 3%, Native American 1%
Retention and Graduation: 40% freshmen return for sophomore year. **Faculty:** 38 full-time faculty.

ACADEMICS

Degrees: associate, bachelor's, master's, post-bachelor's certificate, terminal associate. **Special Study Options:** Accelerated program, cooperative education program, distance learning, double major, weekend college. **Disability Services:** Special programs offered to physically disabled students include note-taking services, reader services, tape recorders, tutors. **Career services:** alumni services, career/job search classes,

FACILITIES

Housing: Private apartments. Student plan housing and private rooms. 98% of campus accessible to physically disabled. **Computers:** Students can register for classes online. Administrative functions (other than registration) can be performed online.

CAMPUS LIFE

Environment: City. **Activities:** student government. 12 registered organizations, 4 honor societies.

ADMISSIONS

Freshman Academic Profile: Minimum paper TOEFL 500. **Basis for Candidate Selection:** *Important factors considered include:* interview. *Other factors considered include:* standardized test scores. **Freshman Admission Requirements:** High school diploma is required and GED is accepted. *Academic units required:* 1 mathematics. 1 mathematics, **Transfer Admission Requirements:** college transcript(s), standardized test scores, Minimum college GPA of 2.0 required. Lowest grade transferable C. **General Admission Information:** Application Fee $50. Nonfall registration accepted. Admission may be deferred for a maximum of 12. Credit offered for CEEB Advanced Placement tests.

COSTS AND FINANCIAL AID

Annual tuition $11,240. Required fees $340. Average book expense $1,200. **Required Forms and Deadlines:** FAFSA. *Types of Aid: Need-based scholarships/grants:* Federal Pell, SEOG, private scholarships, the school's own gift aid. *Loans:* Subsidized Stafford, Unsubsidized Stafford, PLUS, Federal Perkins, college/university loans from institutional funds. **Financial Aid Statistics:** 95% freshmen, 93% undergrads receive need-based scholarship or grant aid. 0% freshmen, 2% undergrads receive non-need-based scholarship or grant aid. 97% freshmen, 96% undergrads receive need-based self-help aid. 0% freshmen, 0% undergrads receive athletic scholarships.

DEVRY UNIVERSITY (CHICAGO, IL)

3300 North Cambell Avenue, Chicago, IL 60618
Phone: 773-697-2155
E-mail: keaster@chi.devry.edu
Fax: 773-697-2710 • **Website:** www.devry.edu

This proprietary school was founded in 1931. It has a 16-acre campus.

RATINGS

Admissions Selectivity Rating: 60*   **Fire Safety Rating:** 60*

STUDENTS AND FACULTY

Enrollment: 2,896. **Student Body:** 36% female, 64% male, 2% international (26 countries represented). Asian 11%, African American 69%, Caucasian 22%, Hispanic 31%, Native American <1%
Retention and Graduation: 46% freshmen return for sophomore year. **Faculty:** 74 full-time faculty.

ACADEMICS

Degrees: associate, bachelor's, terminal associate. **Majors with Highest Enrollment:** Electrical, Electronic and Communications Engineering Technology/Technician. **Special Study Options:** Accelerated program, cooperative education program, distance learning, double major, dual enrollment, English as a Second Language (ESL), weekend college. **Disability Services:** Special programs offered to physically disabled students include note-taking services, reader services, tape recorders, tutors. **Career services:** alumni services, career/job search classes.

FACILITIES

Housing: men's dorms, women's dorms, apartments for married students, apartments for single students. 100% of campus accessible to physically disabled. **Computers:** Students can register for classes online. Administrative functions (other than registration) can be performed online.

CAMPUS LIFE

Environment: Metropolis. **Activities:** Choral groups, drama/theater, music ensembles, yearbook. 16 registered organizations, 3 honor societies, 2 religious organizations.

ADMISSIONS

Freshman Academic Profile: Minimum paper TOEFL 500. **Basis for Candidate Selection:** *Important factors considered include:* interview. *Other factors considered include:* standardized test scores. **Freshman Admission Requirements:** High school diploma is required and GED is accepted. *Academic units required:* 1 mathematics. 1 mathematics, **Transfer Admission Requirements:** college transcript(s), standardized test scores, Minimum college GPA of 2.0 required. Lowest grade transferable C. **General Admission Information:** Application Fee $50. Notification on a rolling basis, beginning on or about 11/2. Nonfall registration accepted. Admission may be deferred for a maximum of 12 months. Credit offered for CEEB Advanced Placement tests.

COSTS AND FINANCIAL AID

Annual tuition $11,330. Required fees $340. Average book expense $1,200. **Required Forms and Deadlines:** FAFSA. **Types of Aid:** *Need-based scholarships/grants:* Federal Pell, SEOG, private scholarships, the school's own gift aid. *Loans:* Subsidized Stafford, Unsubsidized Stafford, PLUS, Federal Perkins, college/university loans from institutional funds. *Student Employment:* Federal Work-Study Program available. Institutional employment available. Highest amount earned per year from on-campus jobs $9,000. Off-campus job opportunities are good. **Financial Aid Statistics:** 84% freshmen, 81% undergrads receive need-based scholarship or grant aid. 0% freshmen, 0% undergrads receive non-need-based scholarship or grant aid. 96% freshmen, 98% undergrads receive need-based self-help aid. 0% freshmen, 0% undergrads receive athletic scholarships.

DEVRY UNIVERSITY (COLUMBUS, OH)

1350 Alum Creek Drive, Columbus, OH 43209-2705
Phone: 614-253-1525
E-mail: admissions@devry.edu
Fax: 614-253-0843 • **Website:** www.devry.edu

This proprietary school was founded in 1931. It has a 13-acre campus.

RATINGS

Admissions Selectivity Rating: 60*   **Fire Safety Rating:** 60*

STUDENTS AND FACULTY

Enrollment: 3,145. **Student Body:** 25% female, 75% male, 12% out-of-state, 1% international (3 countries represented). Asian 3%, African American 20%, Caucasian 73%, Hispanic 1%, Native American <1%
Retention and Graduation: 40% freshmen return for sophomore year. **Faculty:** 83 full-time faculty.

ACADEMICS

Degrees: associate, bachelor's, master's, post-bachelor's certificate, terminal associate. **Majors with Highest Enrollment:** Electrical, Electronic and Communications Engineering Technology/Technician. **Special Study Options:** Accelerated program, cooperative education program, distance learning, double major, weekend college. **Disability Services:** Special programs offered to physically disabled students include note-taking services, reader services, tape recorders, tutors. **Career services:** alumni services, career/job search classes.

FACILITIES

Housing: Private apartments Student plan housing and private rooms. 90% of campus accessible to physically disabled. **Computers:** Students can register for classes online. Administrative functions (other than registration) can be performed online.

CAMPUS LIFE

Environment: Metropolis. **Activities:** student government, student newspaper. 13 registered organizations, 2 honor societies.

ADMISSIONS

Freshman Academic Profile: Minimum paper TOEFL 500. **Basis for Candidate Selection:** *Important factors considered include:* interview. *Other factors considered include:* standardized test scores. **Freshman Admission Requirements:** High school diploma is required and GED is accepted. *Academic units required:* 1 mathematics. **Transfer Admission Requirements:** college transcript(s), standardized test scores, Minimum college GPA of 2.0 required. Lowest grade transferable C. **General Admission Information:** Application Fee $50. Notification on a rolling basis, beginning on or about 11/2. Nonfall registration accepted. Admission may be deferred for a maximum of 12 months. Credit offered for CEEB Advanced Placement tests.

COSTS AND FINANCIAL AID

Annual tuition $11,240. Required fees $340. Average book expense $1,200. **Required Forms and Deadlines:** FAFSA. **Types of Aid:** *Need-based scholarships/grants:* Federal Pell, SEOG, private scholarships, the school's own gift aid. *Loans:* Subsidized Stafford, Unsubsidized Stafford, PLUS, Federal Perkins, college/university loans from institutional funds. *Student Employment:* Federal Work-Study Program available. Institutional employment available. Highest amount earned per year from on-campus jobs $12,000. Off-campus job opportunities are excellent. **Financial Aid Statistics:** 88% freshmen, 74% undergrads receive need-based scholarship or grant aid. 1% freshmen, 1% undergrads receive non-need-based scholarship or grant aid. 96% freshmen, 98% undergrads receive need-based self-help aid. 0% freshmen, 0% undergrads receive athletic scholarships.

DEVRY UNIVERSITY (DECATUR, GA)

250 N. Arcadia Avenue, Decatur, GA 30030
Phone: 404-292-2645
E-mail: dsilva@admin.atl.devry.edu
Fax: 404-292-7011 · **Website:** www.atl.devry.edu

This proprietary school was founded in 1931. It has a 23-acre campus.

RATINGS

Admissions Selectivity Rating: 60*   **Fire Safety Rating:** 60*

STUDENTS AND FACULTY

Enrollment: 1,550. **Student Body:** 44% female, 56% male, 17% out-of-state, 3% international (8 countries represented). Asian 3%, African American 84%, Caucasian 15%, Hispanic 3%, Native American <1%
Retention and Graduation: 41% freshmen return for sophomore year. **Faculty:** 63 full-time faculty.

ACADEMICS

Degrees: associate, bachelor's, master's, post-bachelor's certificate, terminal associate. **Majors with Highest Enrollment:** Business Administration, Management and Operations. **Special Study Options:** Accelerated program, cooperative education program, distance learning, double major, weekend college. **Disability Services:** Special programs offered to physically disabled students include note-taking services, reader services, tape recorders, tutors. **Career services:** alumni services, career/job search classes,

FACILITIES

Housing: Private apartments, student palm housing, private rooms. 100% of campus accessible to physically disabled. **Computers:** Students can register for classes online. Administrative functions (other than registration) can be performed online.

CAMPUS LIFE

Environment: City. **Activities:** 10 registered organizations, 4 honor societies.

ADMISSIONS

Freshman Academic Profile: Minimum paper TOEFL 500. **Basis for Candidate Selection:** *Important factors considered include:* interview. *Other factors considered include:* standardized test scores. **Freshman Admission Requirements:** High school diploma is required and GED is accepted. *Academic units required:* 1 mathematics. 1 mathematics, **Transfer Admission Requirements:** college transcript(s), standardized test scores, Minimum college GPA of 2.0 required. Lowest grade transferable C. **General Admission Information:** Application Fee $50. Notification on a rolling basis, beginning on or about 11/2. Nonfall registration accepted. Admission may be deferred for a maximum of 12 months. Credit offered for CEEB Advanced Placement tests.

COSTS AND FINANCIAL AID

Annual tuition $17,104. Room and board $12,018. Required fees $340. Average book expense $1,346. **Required Forms and Deadlines:** FAFSA. **Types of Aid:** *Need-based scholarships/grants:* Federal Pell, SEOG, private scholarships, the school's own gift aid. *Loans:* Subsidized Stafford, Unsubsidized Stafford, PLUS, Federal Perkins, college/university loans from institutional funds. *Student Employment:* Federal Work-Study Program available. Institutional employment available. Highest amount earned per year from on-campus jobs $6,743. Off-campus job opportunities are good. **Financial Aid Statistics:** 94% freshmen, 93% undergrads receive need-based scholarship or grant aid. 1% freshmen, 1% undergrads receive non-need-based scholarship or grant aid. 97% freshmen, 97% undergrads receive need-based self-help aid. 0% freshmen, 0% undergrads receive athletic scholarships.

DEVRY UNIVERSITY (DENVER)

Office of Admissions, Denver, CO 80234-2010
Phone: 303-280-7400
E-mail: info@devry.edu
Fax: 303-280-7606 · **Website:** www.devry.edu/denver

This proprietary school was founded in 1931. It has a 13-acre campus.

RATINGS

Admissions Selectivity Rating: 60*   **Fire Safety Rating:** 60*

ACADEMICS

Degrees: associate, bachelor's, terminal associate. **Special Study Options:** Accelerated program, cooperative education program, distance learning, double major, dual enrollment, weekend college. **Disability Services:** Special programs offered to physically disabled students include note-taking services, reader services, tape recorders, tutors. **Career services:** alumni services, career/job search classes,

FACILITIES

Housing: 100% of campus accessible to physically disabled. **Computers:** Students can register for classes online. Administrative functions (other than registration) can be performed online.

CAMPUS LIFE

Environment: City. **Activities:** 3 registered organizations.

ADMISSIONS

Freshman Academic Profile: Minimum paper TOEFL 500. **General Admission Information:** Credit offered for CEEB Advanced Placement tests.

COSTS AND FINANCIAL AID

Annual tuition $11,870. Required fees $340. Average book expense $1,200. *Student Employment:* Federal Work-Study Program available. Institutional employment available. Off-campus job opportunities are good.

DEVRY UNIVERSITY (FREMONT, CA)

6600 Dumbarton Circle, Fremont, CA 94555
Phone: 510-574-1200
E-mail: info@devry.edu
Fax: 510-742-0868 • **Website:** www.fre.devry.edu

This proprietary school was founded in 1931. It has a 17-acre campus.

RATINGS
Admissions Selectivity Rating: 60*   Fire Safety Rating: 60*

STUDENTS AND FACULTY
Enrollment: 1,477. **Student Body:** 26% female, 74% male, 1% international (9 countries represented). Asian 28%, African American 4%, Caucasian 15%, Hispanic 15%, Native American 1%
Faculty: 51 full-time faculty.

ACADEMICS
Degrees: associate, bachelor's, master's, post-bachelor's certificate, terminal associate. **Special Study Options:** Accelerated program, cooperative education program, distance learning, double major, weekend college. **Disability Services:** Special programs offered to physically disabled students include note-taking services, reader services, tape recorders, tutors. **Career services:** alumni services, career/job search classes.

FACILITIES
Housing: There is no on campus housing. 90% of campus accessible to physically disabled. **Computers:** Students can register for classes online. Administrative functions (other than registration) can be performed online.

CAMPUS LIFE
Environment: City. **Activities:** student government. 10 registered organizations, 2 honor societies.

ADMISSIONS
Freshman Academic Profile: Minimum paper TOEFL 500. **Basis for Candidate Selection:** *Important factors considered include:* interview. *Other factors considered include:* standardized test scores. **Freshman Admission Requirements:** High school diploma is required and GED is accepted. *Academic units required:* 1 mathematics. **Transfer Admission Requirements:** college transcript(s), standardized test scores, Minimum college GPA of 2.0 required. Lowest grade transferable C. **General Admission Information:** Application Fee $50. Notification on a rolling basis, beginning on or about 11/2. Nonfall registration accepted. Admission may be deferred for a maximum of 12 months. Credit offered for CEEB Advanced Placement tests.

COSTS AND FINANCIAL AID
Annual tuition $12,450. Required fees $340. Average book expense $1,200.
Required Forms and Deadlines: FAFSA. **Types of Aid:** *Need-based scholarships/grants:* Federal Pell, SEOG, state scholarships/grants, private scholarships, the school's own gift aid. *Loans:* Subsidized Stafford, Unsubsidized Stafford, PLUS, Federal Perkins, college/university loans from institutional funds. *Student Employment:* Federal Work-Study Program available. Institutional employment available. Highest amount earned per year from on-campus jobs $2,700. Off-campus job opportunities are good. **Financial Aid Statistics:** 64% freshmen, 65% undergrads receive need-based scholarship or grant aid. 1% freshmen, 1% undergrads receive non-need-based scholarship or grant aid. 85% freshmen, 94% undergrads receive need-based self-help aid. 0% freshmen, 0% undergrads receive athletic scholarships. 91% undergrads borrow to pay for school. **Criteria for awarding institutional aid:** *Non-need-based:* academics.

DEVRY UNIVERSITY (IRVING, TX)

4800 Regent Boulevard, Irving, TX 75063-2439
Phone: 972-929-5777
E-mail: cwilliams@mail.dal.devry.edu
Fax: 972-929-2860 • **Website:** www.devry.edu

This proprietary school was founded in 1931. It has a 9-acre campus.

RATINGS
Admissions Selectivity Rating: 60*   Fire Safety Rating: 60*

STUDENTS AND FACULTY
Enrollment: 2,500. **Student Body:** 29% female, 71% male, 0% out-of-state, 1% international (5 countries represented). Asian 5%, African American 32%, Caucasian 42%, Hispanic 19%, Native American <1%

Retention and Graduation: 36% freshmen return for sophomore year. **Faculty:** 77 full-time faculty.

ACADEMICS
Degrees: associate, bachelor's, master's, post-bachelor's certificate, terminal associate. **Majors with Highest Enrollment:** Computer Systems Networking and Telecommunications; Electrical, Electronic and Communications Engineering Technology/Technician. **Special Study Options:** Accelerated program, cooperative education program, distance learning, double major, weekend college. **Disability Services:** Special programs offered to physically disabled students include note-taking services, reader services, tape recorders, tutors. **Career services:** alumni services, career/job search classes.

FACILITIES
Housing: Private apartments, student plan housing, private rooms. 100% of campus accessible to physically disabled. **Computers:** Students can register for classes online. Administrative functions (other than registration) can be performed online.

CAMPUS LIFE
Environment: Metropolis. **Activities:** student newspaper. 15 registered organizations.

ADMISSIONS
Freshman Academic Profile: Minimum paper TOEFL 500. **Basis for Candidate Selection:** *Important factors considered include:* interview. *Other factors considered include:* standardized test scores. **Freshman Admission Requirements:** High school diploma is required and GED is accepted. *Academic units required:* 1 mathematics. **Transfer Admission Requirements:** college transcript(s), standardized test scores, statement of good standing from prior institution(s). Minimum college GPA of 2.0 required. Lowest grade transferable C. **General Admission Information:** Application Fee $50. Notification on a rolling basis, beginning on or about 11/2. Nonfall registration accepted. Admission may be deferred for a maximum of 12 months. Credit offered for CEEB Advanced Placement tests.

COSTS AND FINANCIAL AID
Annual tuition $11,240. Required fees $340. Average book expense $1,200.
Required Forms and Deadlines: FAFSA. **Types of Aid:** *Need-based scholarships/grants:* Federal Pell, SEOG, private scholarships, the school's own gift aid. *Loans:* Subsidized Stafford, Unsubsidized Stafford, PLUS, Federal Perkins, college/university loans from institutional funds. *Student Employment:* Federal Work-Study Program available. Institutional employment available. Highest amount earned per year from on-campus jobs $7,500. Off-campus job opportunities are good. **Financial Aid Statistics:** 64% freshmen, 59% undergrads receive need-based scholarship or grant aid. 0% freshmen, 0% undergrads receive non-need-based scholarship or grant aid. 98% freshmen, 99% undergrads receive need-based self-help aid. 0% freshmen, 0% undergrads receive athletic scholarships.

DEVRY UNIVERSITY (KANSAS CITY, MO)

11224 Holmes Street, Kansas City, MO 64131
Phone: 816-941-2810
E-mail: ssmeed@kc.devry.edu
Fax: 816-941-0896 • **Website:** www.devry.edu

This proprietary school was founded in 1931. It has a 8-acre campus.

RATINGS
Admissions Selectivity Rating: 60*   Fire Safety Rating: 60*

STUDENTS AND FACULTY
Enrollment: 1,927. **Student Body:** 26% female, 74% male, 1% international (8 countries represented). Asian 3%, African American 16%, Caucasian 76%, Hispanic 4%, Native American 1%
Retention and Graduation: 51% freshmen return for sophomore year. **Faculty:** 69 full-time faculty.

ACADEMICS
Degrees: associate, bachelor's, master's, post-bachelor's certificate, terminal associate. **Majors with Highest Enrollment:** Computer Systems Networking and Telecommunications; Electrical, Electronic and Communications Engineering Technology/Technician. **Special Study Options:** Accelerated program, cooperative education program, distance learning, double major, weekend college. **Disability Services:** Special programs offered to physically disabled students include note-taking services, reader services, tape recorders, tutors. **Career services:** alumni services, career/job search classes.

FACILITIES

Housing: Private apartments, student plan housing, private rooms. 100% of campus accessible to physically disabled. **Computers:** Students can register for classes online. Administrative functions (other than registration) can be performed online.

CAMPUS LIFE

Environment: Metropolis. **Activities:** student newspaper 8 registered organizations, 1 honor society.

ADMISSIONS

Freshman Academic Profile: Minimum paper TOEFL 500. **Basis for Candidate Selection:** *Important factors considered include:* interview. *Other factors considered include:* standardized test scores. **Freshman Admission Requirements:** High school diploma is required and GED is accepted. *Academic units required:* 1 mathematics. **Transfer Admission Requirements:** college transcript(s), standardized test scores, Minimum college GPA of 2.0 required. Lowest grade transferable C. **General Admission Information:** Application Fee $50. Notification on a rolling basis, beginning on or about 11/2. Nonfall registration accepted. Admission may be deferred for a maximum of 12 months. Credit offered for CEEB Advanced Placement tests.

COSTS AND FINANCIAL AID

Annual tuition $11,240. Required fees $340. Average book expense $1,200. **Required Forms and Deadlines:** FAFSA. **Types of Aid:** *Need-based scholarships/grants:* Federal Pell, SEOG, private scholarships, the school's own gift aid. *Loans:* Subsidized Stafford, Unsubsidized Stafford, PLUS. *Student Employment:* Federal Work-Study Program available. Institutional employment available. Highest amount earned per year from on-campus jobs $5,625. Off-campus job opportunities are excellent. **Financial Aid Statistics:** 65% freshmen, 57% undergrads receive need-based scholarship or grant aid. 1% freshmen, 1% undergrads receive non-need-based scholarship or grant aid. 98% freshmen, 98% undergrads receive need-based self-help aid. 0% freshmen, 0% undergrads receive athletic scholarships.

DEVRY UNIVERSITY (LONG BEACH, CA)

3880 Kilroy Airport Way, Long Beach, CA 90806-2449
Phone: 562-427-4162
E-mail: cblas@socal.devry.edu
Fax: 562-997-5371 • **Website:** www.devry.edu

This proprietary school was founded in 1931. It has a 25-acre campus.

RATINGS

Admissions Selectivity Rating: 60*   **Fire Safety Rating:** 60*

STUDENTS AND FACULTY

Enrollment: 1,928. **Student Body:** 26% female, 74% male, 2% international (11 countries represented). Asian 27%, African American 13%, Caucasian 19%, Hispanic 33%, Native American 1%
Retention and Graduation: 51% freshmen return for sophomore year. 25% freshmen graduate within 6 years. **Faculty:** 40 full-time faculty.

ACADEMICS

Degrees: associate, bachelor's, master's, post-bachelor's certificate, terminal associate. **Majors with Highest Enrollment:** Business Administration, Management and Operations. **Special Study Options:** Accelerated program, cooperative education program, distance learning, double major, weekend college. **Disability Services:** Special programs offered to physically disabled students include note-taking services, reader services, tape recorders, tutors. **Career services:** alumni services, career/job search classes.

FACILITIES

Housing: men's dorms, women's dorms. 90% of campus accessible to physically disabled. **Computers:** Students can register for classes online. Administrative functions (other than registration) can be performed online.

CAMPUS LIFE

Environment: Metropolis. **Activities:** Choral groups, concert band, music ensembles, student government, student newspaper, symphony orchestra, yearbook. 13 registered organizations, 5 honor societies.

ADMISSIONS

Freshman Academic Profile: Minimum paper TOEFL 500. **Basis for Candidate Selection:** *Important factors considered include:* interview. *Other factors considered include:* standardized test scores. **Freshman Admission Requirements:** High school diploma is required and GED is accepted. *Academic units required:* 1 mathematics. **Transfer Admission Requirements:** college

transcript(s), standardized test scores, Minimum college GPA of 2.0 required. Lowest grade transferable C. **General Admission Information:** Application Fee $50. Notification on a rolling basis, beginning on or about 11/2. Nonfall registration accepted. Admission may be deferred for a maximum of 12 months. Credit offered for CEEB Advanced Placement tests.

COSTS AND FINANCIAL AID

Annual tuition $11,870. Required fees $340. Average book expense $1,200. **Required Forms and Deadlines:** FAFSA. **Types of Aid:** *Need-based scholarships/grants:* Federal Pell, SEOG, state scholarships/grants, private scholarships, the school's own gift aid. *Loans:* Subsidized Stafford, Unsubsidized Stafford, PLUS, Federal Perkins, college/university loans from institutional funds. *Student Employment:* Federal Work-Study Program available. Institutional employment available. Highest amount earned per year from on-campus jobs $6,500. Off-campus job opportunities are good. **Financial Aid Statistics:** 72% freshmen, 69% undergrads receive need-based scholarship or grant aid. 0% freshmen, 0% undergrads receive non-need-based scholarship or grant aid. 98% freshmen, 98% undergrads receive need-based self-help aid. 0% freshmen, 0% undergrads receive athletic scholarships.

DEVRY UNIVERSITY (NORTH BRUNSWICK, NJ)

630 US Highway One, N. Brunswick, NJ 08902-3362
Phone: 732-435-4850
E-mail: admissions@devry.edu
Fax: 732-435-4850 • **Website:** www.devry.edu

This proprietary school was founded in 1931. It has a 15-acre campus.

RATINGS

Admissions Selectivity Rating: 60*   **Fire Safety Rating:** 60*

STUDENTS AND FACULTY

Enrollment: 2,517. **Student Body:** 21% female, 79% male, 1% international (23 countries represented). Asian 8%, African American 13%, Caucasian 43%, Hispanic 19%, Native American <1%
Retention and Graduation: 45% freshmen return for sophomore year. **Faculty:** 78 full-time faculty.

ACADEMICS

Degrees: associate, bachelor's, diploma, terminal associate. **Special Study Options:** Accelerated program, cooperative education program, distance learning, double major, weekend college. **Disability Services:** Special programs offered to physically disabled students include note-taking services, reader services, tape recorders, tutors. **Career services:** alumni services, career/job search classes.

FACILITIES

Housing: 90% of campus accessible to physically disabled. **Computers:** Students can register for classes online. Administrative functions (other than registration) can be performed online.

CAMPUS LIFE

Environment: Town. **Activities:** 13 registered organizations, 2 honor societies.

ADMISSIONS

Freshman Academic Profile: Minimum paper TOEFL 500. **Basis for Candidate Selection:** *Important factors considered include:* interview. *Other factors considered include:* standardized test scores. **Freshman Admission Requirements:** High school diploma is required and GED is accepted. *Academic units required:* 1 mathematics. **Transfer Admission Requirements:** college transcript(s), standardized test scores, Minimum college GPA of 2.0 required. Lowest grade transferable C. **General Admission Information:** Application Fee $50. Notification on a rolling basis, beginning on or about 11/2. Nonfall registration accepted. Admission may be deferred for a maximum of 12. Credit offered for CEEB Advanced Placement tests.

COSTS AND FINANCIAL AID

Annual tuition $11,330. Required fees $340. Average book expense $1,200. **Required Forms and Deadlines:** FAFSA. **Types of Aid:** *Need-based scholarships/grants:* Federal Pell, SEOG, private scholarships, the school's own gift aid. *Loans:* Subsidized Stafford, Unsubsidized Stafford, PLUS, Federal Perkins, college/university loans from institutional funds. *Student Employment:* Federal Work-Study Program available. Institutional employment available. Off-campus job opportunities are good. **Financial Aid Statistics:** 66% freshmen, 62% undergrads receive need-based scholarship or grant aid. 0% freshmen, 1% undergrads receive non-need-based scholarship or grant aid. 97% freshmen, 98% undergrads receive need-based self-help aid. 0% freshmen, 0% undergrads receive athletic scholarships.

DEVRY UNIVERSITY (ORLANDO,FL)

4000 Millenia Blvd., Orlando, FL 32839
Phone: 407-370-3131
E-mail: krochford@orl.devry.edu
Fax: 407-370-3198 • **Website:** www.devry.edu

This proprietary school was founded in 1931. It has a 11-acre campus.

RATINGS

Admissions Selectivity Rating: 60*   Fire Safety Rating: 60*

STUDENTS AND FACULTY

Enrollment: 1,346. **Student Body:** 29% female, 71% male, 3% international (13 countries represented). Asian 2%, African American 26%, Caucasian 30%, Hispanic 16%, Native American <1%
Retention and Graduation: 46% freshmen return for sophomore year. **Faculty:** 43 full-time faculty.

ACADEMICS

Degrees: associate, bachelor's, master's, post-bachelor's certificate, terminal associate. **Majors with Highest Enrollment:** Communication, Journalism, and Related Programs; Computer and Information Sciences and Support Services; Business, Management, Marketing, and Related Support Services. **Special Study Options:** Accelerated program, cooperative education program, distance learning, double major, weekend college. **Disability Services:** Special programs offered to physically disabled students include note-taking services, reader services, tape recorders, tutors. **Career services:** alumni services, career/job search classes.

FACILITIES

Housing: men's dorms, women's dorms, apartments for married students. 95% of campus accessible to physically disabled. **Computers:** Students can register for classes online. Administrative functions (other than registration) can be performed online.

CAMPUS LIFE

Environment: Metropolis. **Activities:** Choral groups, music ensembles, student government, yearbook. 6 registered organizations, 2 honor societies.

ADMISSIONS

Freshman Academic Profile: Minimum paper TOEFL 500. **Basis for Candidate Selection:** *Important factors considered include:* interview. *Other factors considered include:* standardized test scores. **Freshman Admission Requirements:** High school diploma is required and GED is accepted. *Academic units required:* 1 mathematics. **Transfer Admission Requirements:** college transcript(s), standardized test scores, Minimum college GPA of 2.0 required. Lowest grade transferable C. **General Admission Information:** Application Fee $50. Notification on a rolling basis, beginning on or about 11/2. Nonfall registration accepted. Admission may be deferred for a maximum of 12 months. Credit offered for CEEB Advanced Placement tests.

COSTS AND FINANCIAL AID

Annual tuition $11,870. Required fees $340. Average book expense $1,200. **Required Forms and Deadlines:** FAFSA. **Types of Aid:** *Need-based scholarships/grants:* Federal Pell, SEOG, private scholarships, the school's own gift aid. *Loans:* Subsidized Stafford, Unsubsidized Stafford, PLUS, Federal Perkins, college/university loans from institutional funds. *Student Employment:* Federal Work-Study Program available. Institutional employment available. Highest amount earned per year from on-campus jobs $6,916. Off-campus job opportunities are fair. **Financial Aid Statistics:** 71% freshmen, 66% undergrads receive need-based scholarship or grant aid. 0% freshmen, 0% undergrads receive non-need-based scholarship or grant aid. 98% freshmen, 98% undergrads receive need-based self-help aid. 0% freshmen, 0% undergrads receive athletic scholarships.

DEVRY UNIVERSITY (PHOENIX, AZ)

2149 West Dunlap, Phoenix, AZ 85021
Phone: 602-870-9222
E-mail: admissions@phx.devry.edu
Fax: 602-331-1494 • **Website:** www.devry.edu

This proprietary school was founded in 1931. It has a 12-acre campus.

RATINGS

Admissions Selectivity Rating: 60*   Fire Safety Rating: 60*

STUDENTS AND FACULTY

Enrollment: 1,496. **Student Body:** 24% female, 76% male, 0% international (4 countries represented). Asian 7%, African American 7%, Caucasian 58%, Hispanic 18%, Native American 6%
Faculty: 73 full-time faculty.

ACADEMICS

Degrees: associate, bachelor's, master's, post-bachelor's certificate, terminal associate. **Majors with Highest Enrollment:** Electrical, Electronic and Communications Engineering Technology/Technician. **Special Study Options:** Accelerated program, cooperative education program, distance learning, double major, weekend college. **Disability Services:** Special programs offered to physically disabled students include note-taking services, reader services, tape recorders, tutors. **Career services:** alumni services, career/job search classes.

FACILITIES

Housing: 100% of campus accessible to physically disabled. **Computers:** Students can register for classes online. Administrative functions (other than registration) can be performed online.

CAMPUS LIFE

Environment: Metropolis. **Activities:** student government. 19 registered organizations, 2 honor societies.

ADMISSIONS

Freshman Academic Profile: Minimum paper TOEFL 500. **Basis for Candidate Selection:** *Important factors considered include:* interview. *Other factors considered include:* standardized test scores. **Freshman Admission Requirements:** High school diploma is required and GED is accepted. **Transfer Admission Requirements:** college transcript(s), standardized test scores, Minimum college GPA of 2.0 required. Lowest grade transferable C. **General Admission Information:** Application Fee $50. Nonfall registration accepted. Admission may be deferred for a maximum of 12 months. Credit offered for CEEB Advanced Placement tests.

COSTS AND FINANCIAL AID

Annual tuition $11,240. Required fees $340. Average book expense $1,200. **Required Forms and Deadlines:** FAFSA. **Types of Aid:** *Need-based scholarships/grants:* Federal Pell, SEOG, private scholarships, the school's own gift aid. *Loans:* Subsidized Stafford, Unsubsidized Stafford, PLUS, Federal Perkins, college/university loans from institutional funds. *Student Employment:* Federal Work-Study Program available. Institutional employment available. Highest amount earned per year from on-campus jobs $6,500. Off-campus job opportunities are excellent. **Financial Aid Statistics:** 75% freshmen, 69% undergrads receive need-based scholarship or grant aid. 1% freshmen, 1% undergrads receive non-need-based scholarship or grant aid. 94% freshmen, 95% undergrads receive need-based self-help aid. 0% freshmen, 0% undergrads receive athletic scholarships. 94% undergrads borrow to pay for school. **Criteria for awarding institutional aid:** *Non-need-based:* academics.

DEVRY UNIVERSITY (POMONA, CA)

901 Corporate Center Drive, Pomona, CA 91768
Phone: 909-622-9800
E-mail: bchung@admin.pom.devry.edu
Fax: 909-868-4165 • **Website:** www.pom.devry.edu

This proprietary school was founded in 1931. It has a 13-acre campus.

RATINGS

Admissions Selectivity Rating: 60*   Fire Safety Rating: 60*

STUDENTS AND FACULTY

Enrollment: 1,491. **Student Body:** 23% female, 77% male, 4% international (19 countries represented). Asian 41%, African American 12%, Caucasian 33%, Hispanic 64%, Native American 1%
Retention and Graduation: 49% freshmen return for sophomore year. **Faculty:** 49 full-time faculty.

ACADEMICS

Degrees: associate, bachelor's, master's, post-bachelor's certificate, terminal associate. **Majors with Highest Enrollment:** Electrical, Electronic and Communications Engineering Technology/Technician. **Special Study Options:** Accelerated program, cooperative education program, distance learning, double major, weekend college. **Disability Services:** Special programs offered to physically disabled students include note-taking services, reader services, tape recorders, tutors. **Career services:** alumni services, career/job search classes.

FACILITIES

Housing: Private apartments, student plan housing, private rooms. 100% of campus accessible to physically disabled. **Computers:** Students can register for classes online. Administrative functions (other than registration) can be performed online.

CAMPUS LIFE

Environment: City. **Activities:** 15 registered organizations, 4 honor societies.

ADMISSIONS

Freshman Academic Profile: Minimum paper TOEFL 500. **Basis for Candidate Selection:** *Important factors considered include:* interview. *Other factors considered include:* standardized test scores. **Freshman Admission Requirements:** High school diploma is required and GED is accepted. *Academic units required:* 1 mathematics. 1 mathematics, **Transfer Admission Requirements:** High school transcript, standardized test scores, Minimum college GPA of 2.0 required. Lowest grade transferable C. **General Admission Information:** Application Fee $50. Notification on a rolling basis, beginning on or about 11/2. Nonfall registration accepted. Admission may be deferred for a maximum of 12 months. Credit offered for CEEB Advanced Placement tests.

COSTS AND FINANCIAL AID

Annual tuition $11,870. Required fees $340. Average book expense $1,200. **Types of Aid:** *Need-based scholarships/grants:* Federal Pell, SEOG, state scholarships/grants, private scholarships. *Loans:* Subsidized Stafford, Unsubsidized Stafford, PLUS, Federal Perkins. *Student Employment:* Federal Work-Study Program available. Institutional employment available. Highest amount earned per year from on-campus jobs $6,500. Off-campus job opportunities are good. **Financial Aid Statistics:** 70% freshmen, 66% undergrads receive need-based scholarship or grant aid. 0% freshmen, 0% undergrads receive non-need-based scholarship or grant aid. 98% freshmen, 98% undergrads receive need-based self-help aid. 0% freshmen, 0% undergrads receive athletic scholarships.

DEVRY UNIVERSITY (WEST HILLS, CA)

22801 Roscoe Boulevard, West Hills, CA 91304
Phone: 818-932-3001
E-mail: admissions@devry.com
Fax: 909-868-4165 • **Website:** www.devry.edu

This proprietary school was founded in 1931. It has a 20-acre campus.

RATINGS

Admissions Selectivity Rating: 60*   **Fire Safety Rating:** 60*

STUDENTS AND FACULTY

Enrollment: 1,161. **Student Body:** 26% female, 74% male, 3% international (13 countries represented). Asian 26%, African American 7%, Caucasian 32%, Hispanic 26%, Native American 1%
Retention and Graduation: 46% freshmen return for sophomore year. **Faculty:** 19 full-time faculty.

ACADEMICS

Degrees: associate, bachelor's, master's, post-bachelor's certificate, terminal associate. **Majors with Highest Enrollment:** General Studies; Youth Ministry; Psychology. **Special Study Options:** Accelerated program, cooperative education program, distance learning, double major, weekend college. **Disability Services:** Special programs offered to physically disabled students include note-taking services, reader services, tape recorders, tutors. **Career services:** alumni services, career/job search classes.

FACILITIES

Housing: special housing for disabled students, men's dorms, women's dorms. 100% of campus accessible to physically disabled. **Computers:** Students can register for classes online. Administrative functions (other than registration) can be performed online.

CAMPUS LIFE

Environment: Metropolis. **Activities:** dance, drama/theater, student government, student newspaper, yearbook. 14 registered organizations, 3 honor societies.

ADMISSIONS

Freshman Academic Profile: Minimum paper TOEFL 500. **Basis for Candidate Selection:** *Important factors considered include:* interview. *Other factors considered include:* standardized test scores. **Freshman Admission Requirements:** High school diploma is required and GED is accepted. *Academic units required:* 1 mathematics. 1 mathematics, **Transfer Admission Requirements:** college transcript(s), standardized test scores, Minimum college GPA of

4.0 required. Lowest grade transferable C. **General Admission Information:** Application Fee $50. Notification on a rolling basis, beginning on or about 11/2. Nonfall registration accepted. Admission may be deferred for a maximum of 12. Credit offered for CEEB Advanced Placement tests.

COSTS AND FINANCIAL AID

Annual tuition $11,870. Required fees $340. Average book expense $1,200. **Required Forms and Deadlines:** FAFSA. **Types of Aid:** *Need-based scholarships/grants:* Federal Pell, SEOG, private scholarships, the school's own gift aid. *Loans:* Subsidized Stafford, Unsubsidized Stafford, PLUS, Federal Perkins, college/university loans from institutional funds. *Student Employment:* Federal Work-Study Program available. Institutional employment available. Highest amount earned per year from on-campus jobs $6,075. Off-campus job opportunities are good. **Financial Aid Statistics:** 64% freshmen, 60% undergrads receive need-based scholarship or grant aid. 0% freshmen, 0% undergrads receive non-need-based scholarship or grant aid. 97% freshmen, 98% undergrads receive need-based self-help aid. 0% freshmen, 0% undergrads receive athletic scholarships.

DICKINSON COLLEGE

P.O. Box 1773, Carlisle, PA 17013-2896
Phone: 717-245-1231 • **Financial Aid Phone:** 717-245-1308
E-mail: admissions@dickinson.edu • **CEEB Code:** 2186
Fax: 717-245-1442 • **Website:** www.dickinson.edu/ • **ACT Code:** 3550

This private school was founded in 1783. It has a 308-acre campus.

RATINGS

Admissions Selectivity Rating: 91   **Fire Safety Rating:** 84

STUDENTS AND FACULTY

Enrollment: 2,315. **Student Body:** 58% female, 42% male, 77% out-of-state, 8% international (41 countries represented), Asian 2%, African American 4%, Caucasian 74%, Hispanic 6%, Native American <1%
Retention and Graduation: 90% freshmen return for sophomore year. 81% freshmen graduate within 4 years. 84% freshmen graduate within 6 years. 39% grads go on to further study within 1 year. 13% grads pursue arts and sciences degrees. 5% grads pursue law degrees. 2% grads pursue business degrees. 5% grads pursue medical degrees. **Faculty:** 224 full-time faculty, 92% hold PhDs, 47% are members of minority groups, 14% are women. 0% of classes are taught by teaching assistants.

ACADEMICS

Degrees: bachelor's. **Classes:** Most classes have 10–19 students. **Majors with Highest Enrollment:** International Business/Trade/Commerce; Political Science and Government; Biology/Biological Sciences. **Special Study Options:** Accelerated program, cross-registration, double major, English as a Second Language (ESL), exchange student program (domestic), independent study, internships, liberal arts/career combination, student-designed major, study abroad, teacher certification program. Combined degree programs: BA/JD, BA/MEng, 3-3 Dickinson School of Law (Penn State). **Disability Services:** Special programs offered to physically disabled students include note-taking services, reader services, tape recorders, tutors. **Career services:** Alumni network, alumni services, career/job search classes, career assessment, internships, regional alumni. Dickinson College believes in the power of experiential education. We maintain a database of over 1,200 business, government and social service internships for students to apply their education in a work setting. Internships can be done for credit. Over half of Dickinson College students do at least one internship during their four years. Over one quarter of our students who go overseas perform internships while in other countries. We have a rotational program set-up with local healthcare facilities for students to explore the medical fields. For those interested in law and government, we have many opportunities available in the county court, with local law firms and in the Pennsylvania state legislature.

FACILITIES

Housing: Coed dorms, special housing for disabled students, fraternity/sorority housing, apartments for single students, Theme HousingForeign languages, arts, environmental, multicultural, etc. 67% of campus accessible to physically disabled. **Special Academic Facilities/Equipment:** Art gallery, center for the arts, planetarium, observatory, scanning electron microscope, archeology.

Computers: 10% of classrooms, 100% of dorms, 100% of libraries, 100% of dining areas, 100% of student union, 5% of common outdoor areas have wireless network access. Students can register for classes online. Administrative functions (other than registration) can be performed online.

CAMPUS LIFE

Environment: City. **Activities:** Choral groups, concert band, dance, drama/theater, jazz band, literary magazine, music ensembles, musical theater, radio station, student government, student newspaper, student-run film society, symphony orchestra, yearbook, International Student Organization, Model UN. 112 registered organizations, 15 honor societies, 11 religious organization. 6 fraternities, 6 sororities. **Athletics (Intercollegiate):** *Men:* baseball, basketball, cross-country, football, golf, lacrosse, soccer, swimming, tennis, track/field (outdoor), track/field (indoor). *Women:* basketball, cross-country, field hockey, golf, lacrosse, soccer, softball, swimming, tennis, track/field (outdoor), track/field (indoor), volleyball. **On-Campus Highlights:** Old West, designed by Benjamin Latrobe, Rector Science Complex, Waidner Spahr Library, Stern Center for Global Education, Kline Athletic Center, The Quarry (coffee shop and late night party/gathering space),Weiss Center for the Arts, and the Trout Gallery. **Environmental Initiatives:** Integrating sustainability throughout the curriculum, supported by the Center for Sustainability Education. All new buildings and major renovations constructed to a LEED Silver certification standard or higher; all projects completed since this policy was adopted in 2007 have been certified LEED Gold Signed the American College and University Presidents Climate Commitment in 2007 and adopted a climate action plan in 2009 to become climate neutral by 2020.

ADMISSIONS

Freshman Academic Profile: 46% in top 10% of high school class, 80% in top 25% of high school class, 97% in top 50% of high school class. 59% from public high schools. SAT Math middle 50% range 600-690. SAT Critical Reading middle 50% range 590-680. SAT Writing middle 50% range 600-683. ACT middle 50% range 28-31. Minimum internet-based TOEFL 89. **Basis for Candidate Selection:** *Very important factors considered include:* academic GPA, rigor of secondary school record, extracurricular activities, talent/ability, volunteer work. *Important factors considered include:* Class rank, recommendation(s), standardized test scores, alumni/ae relation, work experience. *Other factors considered include:* application essay, character/personal qualities, first generation, geographical residence, interview, level of applicant's interest, racial/ethnic status, state residency. **Freshman Admission Requirements:** High school diploma is required and GED is accepted. *Academic units required:* 4 English, 3 mathematics, 3 science, (2 science labs), 2 foreign language, 2 social studies, 2 academic electives. **Freshman Admission Statistics:** 5,700 applied, 48% admitted, 23% enrolled. **Transfer Admission Requirements:** High school transcript, college transcript(s), essay or personal statement, statement of good standing from prior institution(s). Minimum college GPA of 2 required. Lowest grade transferable C. **General Admission Information:** Application Fee $65. Early decision application deadline 11/15. Regular application deadline 2/1. Regular notification 3/31. Nonfall registration not accepted. Admission may be deferred for a maximum of 2 years. Credit and/or placement offered for CEEB Advanced Placement tests.

COSTS AND FINANCIAL AID

Annual tuition $47,242. Room and board $11,972. Required fees $475. Average book expense $1,090. **Required Forms and Deadlines:** FAFSA, CSS/Financial Aid PROFILE, State aid form, Noncustodial PROFILE. **Notification of Awards:** Applicants will be notified of awards on or about 3/20. **Types of Aid:** *Need-based scholarships/grants:* Federal Pell, SEOG, state scholarships/grants, private scholarships, the school's own gift aid. *Loans:* Subsidized Stafford, Unsubsidized Stafford, PLUS, Federal Perkins, college/university loans from institutional funds. *Student Employment:* Federal Work-Study Program available. Institutional employment available. Off-campus job opportunities are good. **Financial Aid Statistics:** 96% freshmen, 96% undergrads receive need-based scholarship or grant aid. 10% freshmen, 8% undergrads receive non-need-based scholarship or grant aid. 86% freshmen, 88% undergrads receive need-based self-help aid. 0% freshmen, 0% undergrads receive athletic scholarships. 78% freshmen, 74% undergrads receive any aid. 57% undergrads borrow to pay for school. Average cumulative indebtedness $21,101. **Criteria for awarding institutional aid:** *Non-need-based:* academics, leadership.

DICKINSON STATE UNIVERSITY

Office of Enrollment Services, Dickinson, ND 58601-4896
Phone: 701-483-2175 · **Financial Aid Phone:** 701-483-2371
E-mail: dsu.hawks@dsu.nodak.edu
Fax: 701-483-2409 · **Website:** www.dickinsonstate.com · **ACT Code:** 3210

This public school was founded in 1918. It has a 137-acre campus.

RATINGS

Admissions Selectivity Rating: 73   **Fire Safety Rating:** 60*

STUDENTS AND FACULTY

Enrollment: 2,669. **Student Body:** 59% female, 41% male, 34% out-of-state, 12% international (30 countries represented). Asian 0%, African American 1%, Caucasian 71%, Hispanic 1%, Native American 2%
Retention and Graduation: 60% freshmen return for sophomore year. 9% freshmen graduate within 4 years. 31% freshmen graduate within 6 years. **Faculty:** 86 full-time faculty, 52% hold PhDs, 43% are members of minority groups, 6% are women.

ACADEMICS

Degrees: associate, bachelor's, certificate, terminal associate, transfer associate. **Classes:** Most classes have 10-19 students. **Majors with Highest Enrollment:** Teacher Education, Multiple Levels; Registered Nursing/Registered Nurse; Business/Commerce. **Special Study Options:** Accelerated program, distance learning, double major, dual enrollment, honors program, independent study, internships, liberal arts/career combination, student-designed major, study abroad, teacher certification program. **Career services:** Alumni network, alumni services, career/job search classes, career assessment, internships.

FACILITIES

Housing: Coed dorms, special housing for disabled students, men's dorms, women's dorms, apartments for married students, apartments for single students, Apartments for upperclassmen; apartments for scholars. **Special Academic Facilities/Equipment:** Art gallery, smart classrooms **Computers:** Students can register for classes online.

CAMPUS LIFE

Environment: Rural. **Activities:** Choral groups, concert band, dance, drama/theater, jazz band, literary magazine, marching band, music ensembles, musical theater, pep band, student government, student newspaper, student-run film society, yearbook, International Student Organization 51 registered organizations, 7 honor societies, 6 religious organizations. **Athletics (Intercollegiate):** *Men:* baseball, basketball, cheerleading, cross-country, football, golf, rodeo, track/field (outdoor), track/field (indoor), wrestling. *Women:* basketball, cheerleading, cross-country, golf, rodeo, softball, track/field (outdoor), track/field (indoor), volleyball. **On-Campus Highlights:** Murphy Hall, Student Center, Common Grounds Coffee Shop, Whitney Stadium.

ADMISSIONS

Freshman Academic Profile: Average high school GPA 3.24. 6% in top 10% of high school class, 19% in top 25% of high school class, 53% in top 50% of high school class. 98% from public high schools. SAT Math middle 50% range 470-590. SAT Critical Reading middle 50% range 430-530. ACT middle 50% range 18-23. Minimum paper TOEFL 525. **Freshman Admission Requirements:** High school diploma is required and GED is accepted. *Academic units required:* 4 English, 3 mathematics, 3 science, 3 History and/or Social Studies. **Freshman Admission Statistics:** 627 applied, 80% admitted, 75% enrolled. **Transfer Admission Requirements:** college transcript(s), Minimum college GPA of 2.0 required. Lowest grade transferable D. **General Admission Information:** Application Fee $35. Nonfall registration accepted. Admission may be deferred for a maximum of none. Neither credit nor placement offered for CEEB Advanced Placement tests.

COSTS AND FINANCIAL AID

Average book expense $900. **Required Forms and Deadlines:** FAFSA. **Notification of Awards:** Applicants will be notified of awards on a rolling basis beginning 4/30. **Types of Aid:** *Need-based scholarships/grants:* Federal Pell, SEOG, state scholarships/grants, private scholarships, the school's own gift aid. *Loans:* Subsidized Stafford, Unsubsidized Stafford, PLUS, Federal Perkins, Federal Nursing. *Student Employment:* Federal Work-Study Program available. Institutional employment available. Highest amount earned per year from on-campus jobs $1,304. Off-campus job opportunities are excellent. **Criteria for awarding institutional aid:** *Non-need-based:* academics, alumni affiliation, art, athletics, job skills, leadership, minority status, music/drama, state/district residency.

DIGIPEN INSTITUTE OF TECHNOLOGY

9931 Willows Road NE, Redmond, WA 98052
Phone: 425-629-5001 · **Financial Aid Phone:** 425-629-5002
E-mail: admissions@digipen.edu · **CEEB Code:** 37243
Fax: 425-558-0378 · **Website:** www.digipen.edu · **ACT Code:** 6659

This is a proprietary school.

RATINGS
Admissions Selectivity Rating: 81   **Fire Safety Rating:** 78

STUDENTS AND FACULTY
Enrollment: 0. **Student Body:** (31 countries represented).
Retention and Graduation: 66% freshmen return for sophomore year.
Faculty: 47 full-time faculty, 43% hold PhDs, 23% are members of minority groups. 0% of classes are taught by teaching assistants.

ACADEMICS
Degrees: Majors with Highest Enrollment: Animation, Interactive Technology, Video Graphics and Special Effects; Modeling, Virtual Environments and Simulation; Game and Interactive Media Design.

ADMISSIONS
Freshman Academic Profile: SAT Math middle 50% range 560-680. SAT Critical Reading middle 50% range 540-640. SAT Writing middle 50% range 490-600. ACT middle 50% range 25.5-31. Minimum internet-based TOEFL 80. Minimum paper TOEFL 550. **Freshman Admission Statistics:** 468 applied, 44% admitted, 73% enrolled.

COSTS AND FINANCIAL AID
Annual tuition $26,400. Room and board $10,441. Required fees $160. Average book expense $1,026. **Required Forms and Deadlines:** FAFSA, Institution's own financial aid form. **Financial Aid Statistics:** 100% freshmen, 100% undergrads receive need-based scholarship or grant aid. 100% freshmen, 100% undergrads receive non-need-based scholarship or grant aid. 100% freshmen, 100% undergrads receive need-based self-help aid. 0% freshmen, 0% undergrads receive athletic scholarships. 17% undergrads borrow to pay for school. Average cumulative indebtedness $21,500.

DILLARD UNIVERSITY

2601 Gentilly Boulevard, New Orleans, LA 70122
Phone: 504-816-4670 · **Financial Aid Phone:** 504-816-4677
E-mail: admissions@dillard.edu · **CEEB Code:** 6164
Fax: 504-816-4895 · **Website:** www.dillard.edu · **ACT Code:** 1578

This private school, affiliated with the United Church of Christ Church, was founded in 1869. It has a 55-acre campus.

RATINGS
Admissions Selectivity Rating: 83   **Fire Safety Rating:** 64

STUDENTS AND FACULTY
Enrollment: 2,155. **Student Body:** 78% female, 22% male, 54% out-of-state, 0% international (12 countries represented). Asian 0%, African American 99%, Caucasian 0%, Hispanic 0%, Native American <1%.
Retention and Graduation: 78% freshmen return for sophomore year. 36% freshmen graduate within 4 years. 47% freshmen graduate within 6 years. 39% grads go on to further study within 1 year. 34% grads pursue arts and sciences degrees. 1% grads pursue law degrees. 1% grads pursue business degrees. 3% grads pursue medical degrees. **Faculty:** 145 full-time faculty, 68% hold PhDs, 57% are members of minority groups, 91% are women. 0% of classes are taught by teaching assistants.

ACADEMICS
Degrees: bachelor's, terminal associate. **Classes:** Most classes have 10–19 students. Most lab/discussion sessions have 20–29 students. **Special Study Options:** double major, dual enrollment, honors program, independent study, internships, liberal arts/career combination, study abroad, teacher certification program. **Career services:** Alumni network, internships.

FACILITIES
Housing: Coed dorms, men's dorms, women's dorms, apartments for single students. 60% of campus accessible to physically disabled. **Special Academic Facilities/Equipment:** Art gallery, language lab, communication studies facilities, electron microscope, observatory, outdoor challenge course. **Computers:** Administrative functions (other than registration) can be performed online.

CAMPUS LIFE
Environment: Metropolis. **Activities:** Choral groups, dance, drama/theater, music ensembles, radio station, student government, student newspaper, yearbook. 67 registered organizations, 6 honor societies, 3 religious organizations. 4 fraternities, 4 sororities. **Athletics (Intercollegiate): Men:** basketball, cross-country, tennis. *Women:* basketball, cross-country, tennis, volleyball. **On-Campus Highlights:** Avenue of the Oaks, Lawless Memorial Chapel, Samuel DuBois Cook, Dent Hall.

ADMISSIONS
Freshman Academic Profile: Average high school GPA 3.2. 2% in top 10% of high school class, 44% in top 25% of high school class, 74% in top 50% of high school class. SAT Math middle 50% range 440-520. SAT Critical Reading middle 50% range 450-530. ACT middle 50% range 19-22. Minimum paper TOEFL 550. **Basis for Candidate Selection:** *Very important factors considered include:* application essay, recommendation(s), rigor of secondary school record, standardized test scores. *Other factors considered include:* Class rank, alumni/ae relation, extracurricular activities, interview. **Freshman Admission Requirements:** High school diploma is required and GED is accepted. *Academic units required:* 4 English, 3 mathematics, 3 science, 3 social studies, 6 academic electives. **Freshman Admission Statistics:** 3,106 applied, 47% admitted, 35% enrolled. **Transfer Admission Requirements:** college transcript(s), statement of good standing from prior institution(s). Minimum college GPA of 2.0 required. Lowest grade transferable C. **General Admission Information:** Application Fee $20. Regular application deadline 7/1. Nonfall registration accepted. Credit and/or placement offered for CEEB Advanced Placement tests.

COSTS AND FINANCIAL AID
Average book expense $1,000. **Required Forms and Deadlines:** FAFSA, Institution's own financial aid form. **Notification of Awards:** Applicants will be notified of awards on a rolling basis beginning 3/1. **Types of Aid:** *Need-based scholarships/grants:* Federal Pell, SEOG, state scholarships/grants, private scholarships, the school's own gift aid, United Negro College Fund, Federal Nursing Scholarships. *Loans:* Direct Subsidized Stafford, Direct Unsubsidized Stafford, Direct PLUS, Subsidized Stafford, Unsubsidized Stafford, PLUS, Federal Perkins, Federal Nursing. *Student Employment:* Federal Work-Study Program available. Highest amount earned per year from on-campus jobs $2,000. Off-campus job opportunities are good. **Financial Aid Statistics:** 83% freshmen, 66% undergrads receive need-based scholarship or grant aid. 0% freshmen, 0% undergrads receive non-need-based scholarship or grant aid. 110% freshmen, 112% undergrads receive need-based self-help aid. 3% freshmen, 2% undergrads receive athletic scholarships. 98% freshmen, 98% undergrads receive any aid. 90% undergrads borrow to pay for school. **Criteria for awarding institutional aid:** *Non-need-based:* academics, alumni affiliation, art, athletics, music/drama, religious affiliation.

DIVINE WORD COLLEGE

Office of Admissions, Epworth, IA 52045
Phone: 563-876-3332
E-mail: svdvocations@dwci.edu · **CEEB Code:** 6174
Fax: 563-876-5515

This private school, affiliated with the Roman Catholic Church, was founded in 1964. It has a 30-acre campus.

RATINGS
Admissions Selectivity Rating: 64   **Fire Safety Rating:** 60*

STUDENTS AND FACULTY
Enrollment: 65. **Student Body:** 100% out-of-state, (12 countries represented).
Faculty: 16 full-time faculty, 56% hold PhDs, 56% are members of minority groups, 25% are women. 0% of classes are taught by teaching assistants.

ACADEMICS
Degrees: associate, bachelor's. **Special Study Options:** double major, English as a Second Language (ESL), independent study, liberal arts/career combination.

FACILITIES
Housing: men's dorms.

CAMPUS LIFE
Environment: Rural. **Activities:** Choral groups, student government, yearbook, Campus Ministries, International Student Organization. **Athletics (Intercollegiate):** *Men:* soccer.

ADMISSIONS

Freshman Academic Profile: 0% in top 25% of high school class, Minimum paper TOEFL 550. **Basis for Candidate Selection:** *Very important factors considered include:* character/personal qualities, interview, level of applicant's interest, religious affiliation/commitment. *Important factors considered include:* application essay, academic GPA, recommendation(s). *Other factors considered include:* Class rank, rigor of secondary school record, standardized test scores, extracurricular activities, geographical residence, talent/ability, volunteer work, work experience. **Freshman Admission Requirements:** High school diploma is required and GED is accepted. **Freshman Admission Statistics:** 3 applied, 67% admitted, 0% enrolled. **Transfer Admission Requirements:** High school transcript, college transcript(s), essay or personal statement, interview, statement of good standing from prior institution(s). **General Admission Information:** Application Fee $25. Nonfall registration accepted. Admission may be deferred for a maximum of one semester. Credit and/or placement offered for CEEB Advanced Placement tests.

COSTS AND FINANCIAL AID

Annual tuition $10,400. Room and board $2,700. Required fees $120. Average book expense $500. **Types of Aid:** *Need-based scholarships/grants:* Federal Pell, SEOG, state scholarships/grants, private scholarships, the school's own gift aid. *Loans:* Direct Subsidized Stafford, Direct Unsubsidized Stafford, Subsidized Stafford, PLUS, Federal Perkins, state loans. *Student Employment:* Federal Work-Study Program available.

DOANE COLLEGE

1014 Boswell Avenue, Crete, NE 68333
Phone: 402-826-8222 · **Financial Aid Phone:** 402-826-8260
E-mail: admissions@doane.edu · **CEEB Code:** 6165
Fax: 402-826-8600 · **Website:** www.doane.edu · **ACT Code:** 2448

This private school, affiliated with the United Church of Christ Church, was founded in 1872. It has a 300-acre campus.

RATINGS

Admissions Selectivity Rating: 79   **Fire Safety Rating:** 85

STUDENTS AND FACULTY

Enrollment: 1,719. **Student Body:** 55% female, 45% male, 20% out-of-state, 1% international (16 countries represented). Asian 2%, African American 5%, Caucasian 83%, Hispanic 5%, Native American 1%
Retention and Graduation: 72% freshmen return for sophomore year. 54% freshmen graduate within 4 years. 59% freshmen graduate within 6 years. 32% grads go on to further study within 1 year. 15% grads pursue arts and sciences degrees. 1% grads pursue law degrees. 1% grads pursue business degrees. 5% grads pursue medical degrees. **Faculty:** 83 full-time faculty, 82% hold PhDs, 52% are members of minority groups, 1% are women. 0% of classes are taught by teaching assistants.

ACADEMICS

Degrees: bachelor's, master's. **Classes:** Most classes have fewer than 10 students. Most lab/discussion sessions have fewer than 10 students. **Majors with Highest Enrollment:** Biological and Physical Sciences; Elementary Education and Teaching; Business Administration and Management. **Special Study Options:** double major, English as a Second Language (ESL), honors program, independent study, internships, student-designed major, study abroad, teacher certification program. **Honors programs:** The Honors Program is designed to enrich, in a variety of ways, the educational experience of selected Doane students. Specialized, interdisciplinary, one-credit honors seminars form the intellectual core of the program. Another component is the study abroad experience undertaken during the junior or senior year. The culminating experience is a collaborative research project. Combined degree programs: BA/MEng. **Disability Services:** Special programs offered to physically disabled students include tutors. **Career services:** Alumni network, career assessment, internships. Career services highlights include the intenship program at Doane, which offers students quality internship that build upon their academic coursework. Up to 12 credit hours can apply toward graduation, giving students an edge in the job market and on graduate school acceptance.

FACILITIES

Housing: Coed dorms, men's dorms, women's dorms, Theme Housing. 60% of campus accessible to physically disabled. **Special Academic Facilities/Equipment:** Art gallery, language lab, communication studies facilities, electron microscope, observatory, outdoor challenge course. **Computers:** 90% of classrooms, 100% of dorms, 100% of libraries, 100% of dining areas, 100% of student union, 10% of common outdoor areas have wireless network access.

Students can register for classes online. Administrative functions (other than registration) can be performed online.

CAMPUS LIFE

Environment: Rural. **Activities:** Choral groups, concert band, dance, drama/theater, jazz band, literary magazine, marching band, music ensembles, musical theater, pep band, radio station, student government, student newspaper, television station, yearbook, Campus Ministries. 50 registered organizations, 8 honor societies, 2 religious organizations. 5 fraternities, 4 sororities. **Athletics (Intercollegiate):** *Men:* baseball, basketball, cross-country, football, golf, soccer, tennis, track/field (outdoor), track/field (indoor). *Women:* basketball, cheerleading, cross-country, golf, soccer, softball, tennis, track/field (outdoor), track/field (indoor), volleyball. **On-Campus Highlights:** Tiger Inn, Perkins Library, The Quads, Fuhrer Field House, Heckman Auditorium. **Environmental Initiatives:** Recycling

ADMISSIONS

Freshman Academic Profile: Average high school GPA 3.52. 17% in top 10% of high school class, 42% in top 25% of high school class, 76% in top 50% of high school class. 90% from public high schools. ACT middle 50% range 21-25. Minimum paper TOEFL 525. **Basis for Candidate Selection:** *Very important factors considered include:* academic GPA, standardized test scores. *Important factors considered include:* rigor of secondary school record, alumni/ae relation, character/personal qualities, level of applicant's interest. *Other factors considered include:* Class rank, recommendation(s), extracurricular activities, interview, racial/ethnic status, talent/ability, volunteer work, work experience. **Freshman Admission Requirements:** High school diploma is required and GED is accepted. **Freshman Admission Statistics:** 1,627 applied, 79% admitted, 21% enrolled. **Transfer Admission Requirements:** High school transcript, college transcript(s), statement of good standing from prior institution(s). Minimum college GPA of 2.0 required. Lowest grade transferable C-. **General Admission Information:** Notification on a rolling basis, beginning on or about 10/1. Nonfall registration accepted. Admission may be deferred for a maximum of one year. Credit offered for CEEB Advanced Placement tests.

COSTS AND FINANCIAL AID

Annual tuition $26,580. Room and board $8,030. Required fees $620. Average book expense $900. **Required Forms and Deadlines:** FAFSA. **Notification of Awards:** Applicants will be notified of awards on a rolling basis beginning 3/1. **Types of Aid:** *Need-based scholarships/grants:* Federal Pell, SEOG, state scholarships/grants, private scholarships, the school's own gift aid. *Loans:* Subsidized Stafford, Unsubsidized Stafford, PLUS, Federal Perkins. *Student Employment:* Federal Work-Study Program available. Institutional employment available. Highest amount earned per year from on-campus jobs $1,100. Off-campus job opportunities are fair. **Financial Aid Statistics:** 100% freshmen, 100% undergrads receive need-based scholarship or grant aid. 56% freshmen, 49% undergrads receive non-need-based scholarship or grant aid. 80% freshmen, 81% undergrads receive need-based self-help aid. 29% freshmen, 20% undergrads receive athletic scholarships. 100% freshmen, 98% undergrads receive any aid. 76% undergrads borrow to pay for school. Average cumulative indebtedness $27,136. **Criteria for awarding institutional aid:** *Non-need-based:* academics, art, athletics, leadership, music/drama.

DOMINICAN COLLEGE

470 Western Highway, Orangeburg, NY 10962-1210
Phone: 845-848-7901 · **Financial Aid Phone:** 845-848-7818
E-mail: admissions@dc.edu · **CEEB Code:** 2190
Fax: 845-365-3150 · **Website:** http://www.dc.edu · **ACT Code:** 2730

This private school was founded in 1952. It has a 70-acre campus.

RATINGS

Admissions Selectivity Rating: 71   **Fire Safety Rating:** 87

STUDENTS AND FACULTY

Enrollment: 1,559. **Student Body:** 67% female, 33% male, 25% out-of-state, 1% international (15 countries represented). Asian 8%, African American 16%, Caucasian 35%, Hispanic 24%, Native American <1%
Retention and Graduation: 64% freshmen return for sophomore year. 24% freshmen graduate within 4 years. 35% freshmen graduate within 6 years. **Faculty:** 75 full-time faculty, 56% hold PhDs, 72% are members of minority groups, 12% are women. 0% of classes are taught by teaching assistants.

ACADEMICS

Degrees: associate, bachelor's, doctoral, master's. **Classes:** Most classes have 20–29 students. **Majors with Highest Enrollment:** Social Sciences; Business/Commerce. **Special Study Options:** Accelerated program, cooperative education program, distance learning, dual enrollment, honors program, independent study, internships, liberal arts/career combination, teacher certification program, weekend college, Independent study. Combined degree programs: BS/MS Occupational Therapy. **Disability Services:** Special programs offered to physically disabled students include note-taking services, reader services, tutors. **Career services:** career/job search classes, career assessment, internships, regional alumni.

FACILITIES
Housing: Coed dorms. 100% of campus accessible to physically disabled. **Special Academic Facilities/Equipment:** New State of the Art Prusmack Center for Health Care Programs and Science Education **Computers:** 100% of classrooms, 100% of dorms, 100% of libraries, 100% of dining areas, have wireless network access.

CAMPUS LIFE
Environment: Metropolis. **Activities:** Choral groups, dance, drama/theater, literary magazine, musical theater, student government, student newspaper, yearbook, Campus Ministries, Model UN. 26 registered organizations, 8 honor societies, 1 religious organization. **Athletics (Intercollegiate):** *Men:* baseball, basketball, golf, lacrosse, soccer. *Women:* basketball, cross-country, lacrosse, soccer, softball, track/field (outdoor), volleyball. **On-Campus Highlights:** Prusmack Center for Health and Science Education, Granito Center: Book Store, Health Services, Hennessy Athletic Center, Sullivan Library, Rosary Hall Lounge, Wild Onion Lounge/Cafeteria in Casey Hall. **Environmental Initiatives:** Geothermal HVAC system installed in most recently constructed academic building; Campus-wide recycling program; Use of environmentally safe cleaning products throughout the Campus; All new construction projects incorporate as many green elements as possible.

ADMISSIONS
Freshman Academic Profile: Average high school GPA 2.67. 69% from public high schools. SAT Math middle 50% range 390-490. SAT Critical Reading middle 50% range 400-480. SAT Writing middle 50% range 400-490. ACT middle 50% range 17-20. Minimum paper TOEFL 550. **Basis for Candidate Selection:** *Important factors considered include:* academic GPA, recommendation(s), standardized test scores. *Other factors considered include:* application essay, rigor of secondary school record, character/personal qualities, extracurricular activities, interview, level of applicant's interest, talent/ability, volunteer work, work experience. **Freshman Admission Requirements:** High school diploma is required and GED is accepted. *Academic units required:* 4 English, 3 mathematics, 3 science, (1 science labs), 1 foreign language, 3 social studies, 3 history, 2 academic electives. **Freshman Admission Statistics:** 1,850 applied, 69% admitted, 23% enrolled. **Transfer Admission Requirements:** college transcript(s), Minimum college GPA of 2.0 required. Lowest grade transferable C. **General Admission Information:** Application Fee $35. Nonfall registration accepted. Admission may be deferred for a maximum of 1 year. Credit offered for CEEB Advanced Placement tests.

COSTS AND FINANCIAL AID
Average book expense $1,800. **Required Forms and Deadlines:** FAFSA, State aid form. **Notification of Awards:** Applicants will be notified of awards on a rolling basis beginning 2/1. **Types of Aid:** *Need-based scholarships/grants:* Federal Pell, SEOG, state scholarships/grants, private scholarships, the school's own gift aid. *Loans:* Subsidized Stafford, Unsubsidized Stafford, PLUS, Federal Perkins, Federal Nursing. *Student Employment:* Federal Work-Study Program available. Institutional employment available. Highest amount earned per year from on-campus jobs $2,000. Off-campus job opportunities are fair. **Financial Aid Statistics:** 100% freshmen, 93% undergrads receive need-based scholarship or grant aid. 8% freshmen, 7% undergrads receive non-need-based scholarship or grant aid. 83% freshmen, 84% undergrads receive need-based self-help aid. 6% freshmen, 5% undergrads receive athletic scholarships. 98% freshmen, 97% undergrads receive any aid. 95% undergrads borrow to pay for school. Average cumulative indebtedness $13,430. **Criteria for awarding institutional aid:** *Non-need-based:* academics, athletics.

DOMINICAN SCHOOL OF PHILOSOPHY AND THEOLOGY

2301 Vine Street, Berkeley, CA 94708
Phone: 510-883-2073
E-mail: admissions@dspt.edu
Fax: 510-849-1372 · **Website:** www.dspt.edu

This private school, affiliated with the Roman Catholic Church, was founded in 1932. It has a -1-acre campus.

RATINGS
Admissions Selectivity Rating: 60*   **Fire Safety Rating:** 60*

STUDENTS AND FACULTY
Enrollment: 5. **Student Body:** 40% female, 60% male, 0% international (6 countries represented). Asian 40%, African American 0%, Caucasian 20%, Hispanic 40%, Native American <1%
Retention and Graduation: 100% freshmen return for sophomore year. 50% grads go on to further study within 1 year. 60% grads pursue arts and sciences degrees. 10% grads pursue law degrees. 50% grads pursue medical degrees. **Faculty:** 12 full-time faculty, 100% hold PhDs, 17% are members of minority groups, 0% are women. 10% of classes are taught by teaching assistants.

ACADEMICS
Degrees: bachelor's, certificate, first professional, master's. **Classes:** Most classes have 10–19 students. **Special Study Options:** cross-registration, independent study, study abroad, Select graduate level courses available to undergradute students.

FACILITIES
Housing: men's dorms, women's dorms, apartments for married students, apartments for single students. 50% of campus accessible to physically disabled. **Computers:** Administrative functions (other than registration) can be performed online.

CAMPUS LIFE
Environment: City. **Activities:** Choral groups, concert band, music ensembles, student government, yearbook.

ADMISSIONS
Freshman Academic Profile: Minimum paper TOEFL 550. **Freshman Admission Requirements:** High school diploma is required and GED is accepted. **Transfer Admission Requirements:** college transcript(s), essay or personal statement, Minimum college GPA of 2.3 required. Lowest grade transferable C. **General Admission Information:** Application Fee $40. Nonfall registration not accepted. Admission may be deferred for a maximum of 1 year.

COSTS AND FINANCIAL AID
Average book expense $1,113. *Student Employment:* Highest amount earned per year from on-campus jobs $3,500.

DOMINICAN UNIVERSITY

7900 West Division, River Forest, IL 60305
Phone: 708-524-6800 · **Financial Aid Phone:** 708-524-6950
E-mail: domadmis@dom.edu · **CEEB Code:** 1667
Fax: 708-524-6864 · **Website:** www.dom.edu · **ACT Code:** 1126

This private school, affiliated with the Roman Catholic Church, was founded in 1901. It has a 37-acre campus.

RATINGS
Admissions Selectivity Rating: 83   **Fire Safety Rating:** 94

STUDENTS AND FACULTY
Enrollment: 2,149. **Student Body:** 66% female, 34% male, 7% out-of-state, 3% international (18 countries represented). Asian 3%, African American 6%, Caucasian 41%, Hispanic 44%, Native American <1%
Retention and Graduation: 48% freshmen graduate within 4 years. 63% freshmen graduate within 6 years. 34% grads go on to further study within 1 year. **Faculty:** 161 full-time faculty, 88% hold PhDs, 57% are members of minority groups, 18% are women. 0% of classes are taught by teaching assistants.

ACADEMICS
Degrees: bachelor's, certificate, master's, post-bachelor's certificate, post-master's certificate. **Classes:** Most classes have 10–19 students. Most lab/discussion

sessions have 10–19 students. **Majors with Highest Enrollment:** Business/Commerce; Psychology; Sociology. **Special Study Options:** Accelerated program, cross-registration, distance learning, double major, dual enrollment, English as a Second Language (ESL), honors program, independent study, internships, liberal arts/career combination, student-designed major, study abroad, teacher certification program. **Honors programs:** Honors seminars for high ability students Combined degree programs: BA/MA, BA/MBA; BA/MSLIS; BA/MSSPED; 5 yr. pr. w/ Rush U. **Disability Services:** Special programs offered to physically disabled students include note-taking services, reader services, tape recorders, tutors. **Career services:** career/job search classes, career assessment, internships. Career services highlights include our excellent Chicago internship program.

FACILITIES

Housing: Coed dorms, special housing for disabled students, co-ed by floor. 100% of campus accessible to physically disabled. **Special Academic Facilities/Equipment:** Art gallery, Technology Center, language lab, Recital Hall **Computers:** 70% of classrooms, 100% of libraries, 75% of dining areas, 100% of student union, have wireless network access. Students can register for classes online. Administrative functions (other than registration) can be performed online.

CAMPUS LIFE

Environment: Metropolis. **Activities:** Choral groups, dance, drama/theater, literary magazine, musical theater, student government, student newspaper, Campus Ministries, International Student Organization. 76 registered organizations, 14 honor societies, 2 religious organizations. **Athletics (Intercollegiate):** *Men:* baseball, basketball, cross-country, soccer, tennis. *Women:* basketball, cross-country, soccer, softball, tennis, volleyball. **On-Campus Highlights:** Cybercafe, New science building (Parmer Hall), Reading Room, Centennial Hall (residence hall), New parking pavillion. **Environmental Initiatives:** Over half the surface parking lots have permeable pavers Newest building built to Silver Leed standards Have replaced most lighting with flourescent bulbs, have retrofitted most original windows with energy saving windows

ADMISSIONS

Freshman Academic Profile: Average high school GPA 3.59. 22% in top 10% of high school class, 48% in top 25% of high school class, 85% in top 50% of high school class. 80% from public high schools. SAT Math middle 50% range 480-530. SAT Critical Reading middle 50% range 410-470. SAT Writing middle 50% range 470-530. ACT middle 50% range 20-24. Minimum internet-based TOEFL 79. Minimum paper TOEFL 550. **Basis for Candidate Selection:** *Very important factors considered include:* academic GPA. *Important factors considered include:* Class rank, rigor of secondary school record, standardized test scores. *Other factors considered include:* application essay, recommendation(s), alumni/ae relation, character/personal qualities, extracurricular activities, first generation, interview, talent/ability, volunteer work. **Freshman Admission Requirements:** High school diploma is required and GED is accepted. *Academic units required:* 4 English, 2 academic electives. **Freshman Admission Statistics:** 3,692 applied, 61% admitted, 21% enrolled. **Transfer Admission Requirements:** college transcript(s), essay or personal statement, Minimum college GPA of 2.5 required. Lowest grade transferable C-. **General Admission Information:** Application Fee $25. Notification on a rolling basis, beginning on or about 10/15. Nonfall registration accepted. Admission may be deferred for a maximum of 1 semester. Credit offered for CEEB Advanced Placement tests.

COSTS AND FINANCIAL AID

Annual tuition $30,300. Room and board $9,380. Required fees $370. Average book expense $1,200. **Required Forms and Deadlines:** FAFSA. **Notification of Awards:** Applicants will be notified of awards on a rolling basis beginning 3/15. **Types of Aid:** *Need-based scholarships/grants:* Federal Pell, SEOG, state scholarships/grants, private scholarships, the school's own gift aid. *Loans:* Subsidized Stafford, Unsubsidized Stafford, PLUS, Federal Perkins, state loans. *Student Employment:* Federal Work-Study Program available. Institutional employment available. Highest amount earned per year from on-campus jobs $7,730. Off-campus job opportunities are good. **Financial Aid Statistics:** 100% freshmen, 97% undergrads receive need-based scholarship or grant aid. 8% freshmen, 8% undergrads receive non-need-based scholarship or grant aid. 89% freshmen, 87% undergrads receive need-based self-help aid. 0% freshmen, 0% undergrads receive athletic scholarships. 100% freshmen, 91% undergrads receive any aid. 85% undergrads borrow to pay for school. Average cumulative indebtedness $25,541. **Criteria for awarding institutional aid:** *Non-need-based:* academics, alumni affiliation, leadership, music/drama, religious affiliation.

DOMINICAN UNIVERSITY OF CALIFORNIA

Admissions, San Rafael, CA 94901-2298
Phone: 415-485-3204 • **Financial Aid Phone:** 415-257-1302
E-mail: enroll@dominican.edu • **CEEB Code:** 4284
Fax: 415-485-3204 • **Website:** www.dominican.edu

This private school was founded in 1890. It has a 80-acre campus.

RATINGS

Admissions Selectivity Rating: 85   **Fire Safety Rating:** 99

STUDENTS AND FACULTY

Enrollment: 1,426. **Student Body:** 75% female, 25% male, 6% out-of-state, 2% international (20 countries represented). Asian 23%, African American 6%, Caucasian 38%, Hispanic 16%, Native American 1%
Retention and Graduation: 69% freshmen return for sophomore year. 31% freshmen graduate within 4 years. **Faculty:** 76 full-time faculty, 80% hold PhDs, 64% are members of minority groups, 14% are women. 0% of classes are taught by teaching assistants.

ACADEMICS

Degrees: bachelor's, master's, post-bachelor's certificate. **Classes:** Most classes have 10–19 students. Most lab/discussion sessions have fewer than 10 students. **Majors with Highest Enrollment:** Registered Nursing/Registered Nurse; Business Administration and Management; Psychology. **Special Study Options:** Accelerated program, cross-registration, distance learning, double major, dual enrollment, English as a Second Language (ESL), exchange student program (domestic), honors program, independent study, internships, study abroad, teacher certification program, weekend college. **Honors programs:** Honors Program Scholar in the World. **Disability Services:** Special programs offered to physically disabled students include note-taking services, reader services, tape recorders, tutors. **Career services:** Alumni network, alumni services, career/job search classes, career assessment, internships, regional alumni. Career services highlights include our Internship Program: Most programs at Dominican University of California require an internship of 45-135 hours, undertaken after completing some coursework in the major. The internship helps students clarify and test their career goals, obtain hands-on work experience related to their major, gain professional contacts, and develop self-confidence. In addition to the completion of the internship hours, students must maintain a journal, submit a paper or give an oral presentation, and evaluate the internship at midterm and upon completion.

FACILITIES

Housing: Coed dorms, Wellness Housing. 65% of campus accessible to physically disabled. **Special Academic Facilities/Equipment:** Art Gallery, Science Lab, Computer Labs, Nursing Skills Lab **Computers:** 10% of classrooms, 5% of dorms, 100% of libraries, 100% of dining areas, 100% of student union, have wireless network access. Administrative functions (other than registration) can be performed online.

CAMPUS LIFE

Environment: Town. **Activities:** Choral groups, dance, drama/theater, jazz band, literary magazine, music ensembles, musical theater, radio station, student government, student newspaper, yearbook, Campus Ministries. 19 registered organizations, 7 honor societies, 4 religious organizations. **Athletics (Intercollegiate):** *Men:* basketball, golf, lacrosse, soccer. *Women:* basketball, golf, soccer, softball, tennis, volleyball. **On-Campus Highlights:** Conlan Recreation Center, Caleruega Dining Hall, Guzman Lecture Hall, Alemany Library, Science Center. **Environmental Initiatives:** We established the Dominican Center for Sustainability. The Center serves as ground central for Dominican University's numerous green activities, including educational programs, scholarships, community outreach, and national and international partnerships. We created the Center to tap the wealth of intellectual capital in place at Dominican in order to support existing and emerging green programs. The Center identifies and promotes economically viable green business practices and serves as a think-tank for ongoing green projects on a community, regional, and global level. Dominican greatly expanded its academic programs focused on sustainability. We introduced a certificate program that enables nonprofit and corporate executives, as well as others who already hold an MBA, the Sustainable Enterprise Certificate provides individuals with the knowledge and tools to green their current workplaces while also advancing their careers. We also introduced a certificate program, offered through Dominicans Department of Professional and Continuing Education (PACE), designed for non-degree-seeking adults wanting to take positive steps to enhance their communities. The program offers three areas of concentration: Sustainable Careers and Advocacy, Sustainable Education, and Sustainable Lifestyles. Students will gain a high level of knowledge about sustainability issues as well as specific and practical skills to apply this knowledge to a particular area of specialization. The

Institution formally adopted a Green Statement to signal its ongoing commitment to sustainability: Dominican University of California will model and instill the values, theories and practices of reverence, interdependence, sustainability, social justice and stewardship into the entirety of its learning environment. The Dominican learning environment encompasses the education programs as well as maintaining green working and living spaces, and adopting policies and business practices that minimize our environmental footprint. Dominican University strives to increase the awareness, knowledge, skills and sense of purpose within our students, faculty, staff and community to best meet the needs of the present, while creating a future that is just and sustainable for all.

ADMISSIONS

Freshman Academic Profile: Average high school GPA 3.35. 19% in top 10% of high school class, 50% in top 25% of high school class, 80% in top 50% of high school class. SAT Math middle 50% range 470-560. SAT Critical Reading middle 50% range 460-560. SAT Writing middle 50% range 460-560. ACT middle 50% range 20-25. Minimum paper TOEFL 550. **Basis for Candidate Selection:** *Very important factors considered include:* application essay, academic GPA, recommendation(s), rigor of secondary school record, standardized test scores, character/personal qualities, first generation. *Important factors considered include:* Class rank, extracurricular activities, interview, talent/ability, volunteer work, work experience. *Other factors considered include:* alumni/ae relation. **Freshman Admission Requirements:** High school diploma is required and GED is accepted. *Academic units required:* 4 English, 2 mathematics, 2 foreign language, 1 history. **Freshman Admission Statistics:** 2,819 applied, 53% admitted, 18% enrolled. **Transfer Admission Requirements:** college transcript(s), essay or personal statement, Minimum college GPA of 2.0 required. Lowest grade transferable C. **General Admission Information:** Application Fee $40. Notification on a rolling basis, beginning on or about 10/15. Nonfall registration accepted. Admission may be deferred for a maximum of one term. Credit and/or placement offered for CEEB Advanced Placement tests.

COSTS AND FINANCIAL AID

Annual tuition $32,090. Room and board $12,560. Required fees $300. Average book expense $1,566. **Required Forms and Deadlines:** FAFSA, Institution's own financial aid form. **Notification of Awards:** Applicants will be notified of awards on a rolling basis beginning 3/15. **Types of Aid:** *Need-based scholarships/grants:* Federal Pell, SEOG, state scholarships/grants, private scholarships, the school's own gift aid. *Loans:* Subsidized Stafford, Unsubsidized Stafford, PLUS, Federal Perkins, Private Loans. *Student Employment:* Federal Work-Study Program available. Institutional employment available. Highest amount earned per year from on-campus jobs $3,834. Off-campus job opportunities are good. **Financial Aid Statistics:** 100% freshmen, 99% undergrads receive need-based scholarship or grant aid. 7% freshmen, 7% undergrads receive non-need-based scholarship or grant aid. 74% freshmen, 82% undergrads receive need-based self-help aid. 3% freshmen, 2% undergrads receive athletic scholarships. 98% freshmen, 84% undergrads receive any aid. 93% undergrads borrow to pay for school. Average cumulative indebtedness $13,903. **Criteria for awarding institutional aid:** *Non-need-based:* academics, alumni affiliation, athletics, leadership, minority status, music/drama.

DORDT COLLEGE

498 4th Avenue Northeast, Sioux Center, IA 51250
Phone: 712-722-6080 · **Financial Aid Phone:** 712-722-6087
E-mail: admissions@dordt.edu · **CEEB Code:** 6171
Fax: 712-722-6035 · **Website:** www.dordt.edu · **ACT Code:** 1301

This private school was founded in 1955. It has a 150-acre campus.

RATINGS

Admissions Selectivity Rating: 84   **Fire Safety Rating:** 81

STUDENTS AND FACULTY

Enrollment: 1,331. **Student Body:** 45% female, 55% male, 57% out-of-state, 7% international (21 countries represented). Asian 1%, African American 1%, Caucasian 76%, Hispanic 1%, Native American <1%
Retention and Graduation: 54% freshmen graduate within 4 years. 62% freshmen graduate within 6 years. 15% grads go on to further study within 1 year. 9% grads pursue arts and sciences degrees. 1% grads pursue law degrees. 3% grads pursue business degrees. 2% grads pursue medical degrees. **Faculty:** 81 full-time faculty, 68% hold PhDs, 15% are members of minority groups, 1% are women. 0% of classes are taught by teaching assistants.

ACADEMICS

Degrees: associate, bachelor's, master's, terminal associate. **Classes:** Most classes have 10–19 students. Most lab/discussion sessions have 10–19 students.

Majors with Highest Enrollment: Engineering; Education; Business/Commerce. **Special Study Options:** cooperative education program, double major, English as a Second Language (ESL), honors program, independent study, internships, liberal arts/career combination, student-designed major, study abroad, teacher certification program. **Disability Services:** Special programs offered to physically disabled students include note-taking services, reader services, tape recorders, tutors. **Career services:** Alumni network, alumni services, career/job search classes, career assessment, internships, regional alumni.

FACILITIES

Housing: special housing for disabled students, men's dorms, women's dorms, apartments for married students, apartments for single students. 100% of campus accessible to physically disabled. **Special Academic Facilities/Equipment:** observatories 160 acre research farm for Ag program, modern recreation facilities which include indoor track, swimming and ice arena. **Computers:** 100% of classrooms, 100% of dorms, 100% of libraries, 100% of dining areas, 100% of student union, 100% of common outdoor areas have wireless network access. Students can register for classes online. Administrative functions (other than registration) can be performed online.

CAMPUS LIFE

Environment: Village. **Activities:** Choral groups, concert band, dance, drama/theater, jazz band, literary magazine, music ensembles, musical theater, opera, pep band, radio station, student government, student newspaper, student-run film society, symphony orchestra, yearbook, Campus Ministries, International Student Organization. 40 registered organizations, 4 honor societies, 6 religious organizations. **Athletics (Intercollegiate):** *Men:* baseball, basketball, cross-country, football, golf, ice hockey, soccer, tennis, track/field (outdoor), track/field (indoor). *Women:* basketball, cross-country, soccer, softball, tennis, track/field (outdoor), track/field (indoor), volleyball. **On-Campus Highlights:** Campus Center, Recreation Center and De Wit Gymnasium, B J Haan Auditorium, Southview apartments, Covenant Hall.

ADMISSIONS

Freshman Academic Profile: Average high school GPA 3.54. 21.36% in top 10% of high school class, 44.01% in top 25% of high school class, 72.82% in top 50% of high school class. 30% from public high schools. SAT Math middle 50% range 500-630. SAT Critical Reading middle 50% range 450-610. SAT Writing middle 50% range 470-590. ACT middle 50% range 21-28. Minimum internet-based TOEFL 80. Minimum paper TOEFL 550. **Basis for Candidate Selection:** *Very important factors considered include:* rigor of secondary school record, standardized test scores, religious affiliation/commitment. *Other factors considered include:* Class rank, character/personal qualities, extracurricular activities, talent/ability. **Freshman Admission Requirements:** High school diploma is required and GED is accepted. *Academic units required:* 3 English, 2 mathematics, 2 science, 2 foreign language, 2 history, 6 academic electives. **Freshman Admission Statistics:** 1,356 applied, 75% admitted, 37% enrolled. **Transfer Admission Requirements:** High school transcript, college transcript(s), standardized test scores, Minimum college GPA of 2.0 required. Lowest grade transferable C. **General Admission Information:** Application Fee $25. Regular application deadline 8/1. Notification on a rolling basis, beginning on or about 10/1. Nonfall registration accepted. Credit offered for CEEB Advanced Placement tests.

COSTS AND FINANCIAL AID

Annual tuition $26,100. Room and board $7,620. Required fees $440. Average book expense $910. **Required Forms and Deadlines:** FAFSA, Institution's own financial aid form. **Notification of Awards:** Applicants will be notified of awards on a rolling basis beginning 3/15. **Types of Aid:** *Need-based scholarships/grants:* Federal Pell, SEOG, state scholarships/grants, private scholarships, the school's own gift aid. *Loans:* Direct Subsidized Stafford, Direct Unsubsidized Stafford, Direct PLUS, Subsidized Stafford, Unsubsidized Stafford, PLUS, Federal Perkins, college/university loans from institutional funds Alternate Loans. *Student Employment:* Highest amount earned per year from on-campus jobs $1,500. Off-campus job opportunities are good. **Financial Aid Statistics:** 100% freshmen, 100% undergrads receive need-based scholarship or grant aid. 14% freshmen, 14% undergrads receive non-need-based scholarship or grant aid. 99% freshmen, 100% undergrads receive need-based self-help aid. 8% freshmen, 7% undergrads receive athletic scholarships. 98% freshmen, 98% undergrads receive any aid. 85% undergrads borrow to pay for school. Average cumulative indebtedness $24,299. **Criteria for awarding institutional aid:** *Non-need-based:* academics, alumni affiliation, athletics, job skills, leadership, minority status, music/drama, religious affiliation, state/district residency.

DOWLING COLLEGE

Idle Hour Boulevard, Oakdale, NY 11769-1999
Phone: 800-369-5464 · **Financial Aid Phone:** 631-244-3303
E-mail: admissions@dowling.edu · **CEEB Code:** 2011
Fax: 631-563-3827 · **Website:** www.dowling.edu · **ACT Code:** 2665

This private school was founded in 1959. It has a 157-acre campus.

RATINGS

Admissions Selectivity Rating: 71   **Fire Safety Rating:** 73

STUDENTS AND FACULTY

Enrollment: 3,627. **Student Body:** 61% female, 39% male, 10% out-of-state, 4% international (53 countries represented). Asian 2%, African American 9%, Caucasian 59%, Hispanic 9%, Native American <1%
Retention and Graduation: 66% freshmen return for sophomore year. 17% freshmen graduate within 4 years. 34% freshmen graduate within 6 years. **Faculty:** 124 full-time faculty, 90% hold PhDs, 34% are members of minority groups, 9% are women. 0% of classes are taught by teaching assistants.

ACADEMICS

Degrees: bachelor's, master's, post-bachelor's certificate, post-master's certificate. **Classes:** Most classes have 10–19 students. **Majors with Highest Enrollment:** Special Education and Teaching; Elementary Education and Teaching; Business/Commerce. **Special Study Options:** Accelerated program, double major, English as a Second Language (ESL), honors program, independent study, internships, liberal arts/career combination, student-designed major, study abroad, teacher certification program, weekend college. **Honors programs:** The honor programs are for highly motivated, academically superior, and creative students. **Disability Services:** Special programs offered to physically disabled students include note-taking services, reader services, tape recorders, tutors.

FACILITIES

Housing: Coed dorms. 100% of campus accessible to physically disabled. **Special Academic Facilities/Equipment:** Art gallery, cultural study center, media center, human factors lab, meteorology lab. **Computers:** Students can register for classes online. Administrative functions (other than registration) can be performed online.

CAMPUS LIFE

Environment: Town. **Activities:** Choral groups, drama/theater, jazz band, literary magazine, music ensembles, musical theater, student government, student newspaper, symphony orchestra, yearbook. 29 registered organizations, 10 honor societies, 1 religious organization. **Athletics (Intercollegiate):** *Men:* baseball, basketball, crew/rowing, golf, lacrosse, soccer, tennis. *Women:* basketball, crew/rowing, cross-country, equestrian sports, soccer, softball, tennis, volleyball. **On-Campus Highlights:** Riverside Café, Giordano Gallery, Loft Theatre, Connetuot River, Henry Building Atrium.

ADMISSIONS

Freshman Academic Profile: Average high school GPA 2.8. 6% in top 10% of high school class, 19% in top 25% of high school class, 50% in top 50% of high school class. 89% from public high schools. SAT Math middle 50% range 410-520. SAT Critical Reading middle 50% range 410-520. **Basis for Candidate Selection:** *Very important factors considered include:* rigor of secondary school record. *Other factors considered include:* Class rank, application essay, academic GPA, recommendation(s), standardized test scores, alumni/ae relation, character/personal qualities, extracurricular activities, talent/ability. **Freshman Admission Requirements:** High school diploma is required and GED is accepted. **Freshman Admission Statistics:** 2,399 applied, 87% admitted, 22% enrolled. **Transfer Admission Requirements:** college transcript(s), Minimum college GPA of 2.0 required. Lowest grade transferable C. **General Admission Information:** Application Fee $25. Nonfall registration accepted. Admission may be deferred for a maximum of 1 year. Credit and/or placement offered for CEEB Advanced Placement tests.

COSTS AND FINANCIAL AID

Average book expense $1,000. **Required Forms and Deadlines:** FAFSA, State aid form. **Notification of Awards:** Applicants will be notified of awards on a rolling basis beginning 2/1. **Types of Aid:** *Need-based scholarships/grants:* Federal Pell, SEOG, state scholarships/grants, private scholarships, the school's own gift aid. *Loans:* Direct Subsidized Stafford, Direct Unsubsidized Stafford, Direct PLUS, Federal Perkins, Alternative Loans. *Student Employment:* Federal Work-Study Program available. Off-campus job opportunities are good. **Financial Aid Statistics:** 99% freshmen, 98% undergrads receive need-based scholarship or grant aid. 0% freshmen, 0% undergrads receive non-need-based scholarship or grant aid. 91% freshmen, 86% undergrads receive need-based self-help aid. 2% freshmen, 3% undergrads receive athletic scholarships. 87%

freshmen, 87% undergrads receive any aid. 81% undergrads borrow to pay for school. **Criteria for awarding institutional aid:** *Non-need-based:* academics, alumni affiliation, athletics.

DRAKE UNIVERSITY

2507 University Avenue, Des Moines, IA 50311-4505
Phone: 515-271-3181 · **Financial Aid Phone:** 515-271-2905
E-mail: admission@drake.edu · **CEEB Code:** 6168
Fax: 515-271-2831 · **Website:** www.drake.edu · **ACT Code:** 1302

This private school was founded in 1881. It has a 150-acre campus.

RATINGS

Admissions Selectivity Rating: 89   **Fire Safety Rating:** 97

STUDENTS AND FACULTY

Enrollment: 3,290. **Student Body:** 57% female, 43% male, 68% out-of-state, 7% international (34 countries represented). Asian 4%, African American 3%, Caucasian 79%, Hispanic 4%, Native American <1%
Retention and Graduation: 89% freshmen return for sophomore year. 70% freshmen graduate within 4 years. 78% freshmen graduate within 6 years. 22% grads go on to further study within 1 year. 9% grads pursue arts and sciences degrees. 4% grads pursue law degrees. 3% grads pursue business degrees. 4% grads pursue medical degrees. **Faculty:** 279 full-time faculty, 91% hold PhDs, 44% are members of minority groups, 17% are women. 0% of classes are taught by teaching assistants.

ACADEMICS

Degrees: bachelor's, certificate, first professional, first professional certificate, master's, post-bachelor's certificate. **Classes:** Most classes have 10–19 students. Most lab/discussion sessions have 10–19 students. **Majors with Highest Enrollment:** Marketing/Marketing Management; Actuarial Science; Psychology. **Special Study Options:** Accelerated program, cooperative education program, distance learning, double major, dual enrollment, English as a Second Language (ESL), honors program, independent study, internships, liberal arts/career combination, student-designed major, study abroad, teacher certification program. **Honors programs:** The Honors Program is designed for motivated students who want to participate in challenging, discussion-based courses on interdisciplinary and topical issues. The program provides a unique opportunity for intellectual enrichment both in and out of the classroom. Combined degree programs: BA/JD, PharmD/MBA, PharmD/MPA, PharmD/J.D.; AandS/J.D. **Disability Services:** Special programs offered to physically disabled students include note-taking services, reader services, tape recorders, tutors. **Career services:** Alumni network, alumni services, career/job search classes, career assessment, internships, regional alumni. Career services highlights include our Professional and Career Development Services, which provides exemplary programming that empowers students to pursue their professional objectives.

FACILITIES

Housing: Coed dorms, special housing for disabled students, fraternity/sorority housing, apartments for single students, Theme HousingThere are a total of 261 undergrad students and 58 Grad students residing in DWV Drake Realty houses 152 undergraduates and 46 graduate students Greek Life 324 undergraduate students Residence Life 831 EFR and 1795 undergraduate students. 93% of campus accessible to physically disabled. **Special Academic Facilities/Equipment:** Language lab, observatory, media service center, Anderson art gallery, Oreon E. Scott Chapel. **Computers:** 100% of classrooms, 100% of dorms, 100% of libraries, 100% of dining areas, 100% of student union, have wireless network access. Students can register for classes online. Administrative functions (other than registration) can be performed online.

CAMPUS LIFE

Environment: Metropolis. **Activities:** Choral groups, concert band, drama/theater, jazz band, literary magazine, marching band, music ensembles, musical theater, pep band, radio station, student government, student newspaper, symphony orchestra, Campus Ministries, International Student Organization, Model UN. 160 registered organizations, 24 honor societies, 10 religious organizations. 7 fraternities, 6 sororities. **Athletics (Intercollegiate):** *Men:* basketball, cheerleading, cross-country, football, golf, soccer, tennis, track/field (outdoor), track/field (indoor). *Women:* basketball, cheerleading, crew/rowing, cross-country, golf, soccer, softball, tennis, track/field (outdoor), track/field (indoor), volleyball. **On-Campus Highlights:** Athletic Facilities, Olmsted Center, Anderson Gallery, Helmick Commons, Residence Halls / Residence Life. **Environmental Initiatives:** Sustainable building practices. Employees and students receive unlimited, free bus transportation on Des Moines public transportation (DART) buses. Several academic programs include strong emphasis on environmental issues and long-term sustainability.

ADMISSIONS

Freshman Academic Profile: Average high school GPA 3.7. 41% in top 10% of high school class, 71% in top 25% of high school class, 94% in top 50% of high school class. SAT Math middle 50% range 530-670. SAT Critical Reading middle 50% range 530-640. ACT middle 50% range 25-30. Minimum internet-based TOEFL 71. Minimum paper TOEFL 530. **Basis for Candidate Selection:** *Very important factors considered include:* application essay, academic GPA, standardized test scores. *Important factors considered include:* recommendation(s), rigor of secondary school record, interview. *Other factors considered include:* Class rank, character/personal qualities, extracurricular activities, level of applicant's interest, talent/ability, volunteer work, work experience. **Freshman Admission Requirements:** High school diploma is required and GED is accepted. **Freshman Admission Statistics:** 6,476 applied, 69% admitted, 19% enrolled. **Transfer Admission Requirements:** college transcript(s), Minimum college GPA of 2.0 required. Lowest grade transferable C. **General Admission Information:** Application Fee $25. Notification on a rolling basis, beginning on or about 10/1. Nonfall registration accepted. Admission may be deferred for a maximum of 12 months. Credit and/or placement offered for CEEB Advanced Placement tests.

COSTS AND FINANCIAL AID

Annual tuition $30,734. Room and board $9,000. Required fees $146. Average book expense $1,100. **Required Forms and Deadlines:** FAFSA. **Notification of Awards:** Applicants will be notified of awards on a rolling basis beginning 3/1. **Types of Aid:** *Need-based scholarships/grants:* Federal Pell, SEOG, state scholarships/grants, private scholarships, the school's own gift aid. *Loans:* Subsidized Stafford, Unsubsidized Stafford, PLUS, Federal Perkins, college/university loans from institutional funds, Federal Health Professional Loans. *Student Employment:* Federal Work-Study Program available. Institutional employment available. Off-campus job opportunities are good. **Financial Aid Statistics:** 98% freshmen, 98% undergrads receive need-based scholarship or grant aid. 21% freshmen, 17% undergrads receive non-need-based scholarship or grant aid. 81% freshmen, 86% undergrads receive need-based self-help aid. 3% freshmen, 3% undergrads receive athletic scholarships. 63% undergrads borrow to pay for school. Average cumulative indebtedness $25,220. **Criteria for awarding institutional aid:** *Non-need-based:* academics, alumni affiliation, art, athletics, music/drama, state/district residency.

See page 1046.

DREW UNIVERSITY

Best 380

Office of College Admissions, Madison, NJ 07940-1493
Phone: 973-408-3739 · **Financial Aid Phone:** 973-408-3112
E-mail: cadm@drew.edu · **CEEB Code:** 2193
Fax: 973-408-3068 · **Website:** www.drew.edu · **ACT Code:** 2550

This private school, affiliated with the Methodist Church, was founded in 1868. It has a 186-acre campus.

RATINGS

Admissions Selectivity Rating: 85   **Fire Safety Rating:** 96

STUDENTS AND FACULTY

Enrollment: 1,453. **Student Body:** 62% female, 38% male, 31% out-of-state, 3% international (24 countries represented). Asian 5%, African American 11%, Caucasian 56%, Hispanic 14%, Native American <1%
Retention and Graduation: 76% freshmen return for sophomore year. 65% freshmen graduate within 4 years. 69% freshmen graduate within 6 years. 25% grads go on to further study within 1 year. 20% grads pursue arts and sciences degrees. 2% grads pursue law degrees. 2% grads pursue medical degrees. **Faculty:** 149 full-time faculty, 97% hold PhDs, 52% are members of minority groups, 19% are women. 0% of classes are taught by teaching assistants.

ACADEMICS

Degrees: bachelor's, first professional, master's, post-bachelor's certificate, post-master's certificate. **Classes:** Most classes have 10–19 students. Most lab/discussion sessions have 10–19 students. **Majors with Highest Enrollment:** Political Science and Government; English Language and Literature; Psychology. **Special Study Options:** Accelerated program, cross-registration, double major, exchange student program (domestic), independent study, internships, student-designed major, study abroad, teacher certification program,

Seven-year dual degree BA/MD program with UMDNJ-New Jersey Medical school. Five-year dual degree (B.A./B.S. or B.Eng.) programs in engineering and technologies with Columbia University, Stevens Institute of Technology, and Washington University. Five-year dual degree (B.A./Master of Forestry or Master of Environmental Management)program with Duke University. **Honors programs:** Phi Beta Kappa; Beta Beta Beta (biology), Delta Phi Alpha (German), Omicron Delta Epsilon (economics), Phi Alpha Theta (history), Pi Sigma Alpha (political science), Psi Chi (psychology), Dobro Slovo (Russian), Sigma Delta Pi (Spanish), Sigma Pi Sigma (physics), Pi Mu Epsilon (mathematics), Pi Delta Phi (French), Alpha Kappa Delta (sociology), Pinnacle (nontraditional continuing education students), and Epsilon Omega Psi (Educational Opportunity Scholars). Specialized Honors. Combined degree programs: BA/MD, Dual Degree Program with Columbia and Stevens Institute of Technology. **Disability Services:** Special programs offered to physically disabled students include note-taking services, tape recorders, tutors. **Career services:** Alumni network, alumni services, career/job search classes, internships.

FACILITIES

Housing: Coed dorms, special housing for disabled students, Wellness Housing, Theme Housing. **Special Academic Facilities/Equipment:** Art gallery, photography gallery, multimedia language lab, child development center, research greenhouse, arboretum, observatory, laser holography lab, nuclear magnetic resonator, electron microscope, optical and radio telescopes, computer graphics laboratory, New Jersey Shakespeare Festival (professional acting company). **Computers:** 90% of classrooms, 20% of dorms, 100% of libraries, 100% of dining areas, 100% of student union, 25% of common outdoor areas have wireless network access. Students can register for classes online. Administrative functions (other than registration) can be performed online. Undergraduates are required to own a computer.

CAMPUS LIFE

Environment: Village. **Activities:** Choral groups, dance, drama/theater, literary magazine, music ensembles, radio station, student government, student newspaper, student-run film society, symphony orchestra, television station, yearbook, Campus Ministries. 80 registered organizations, 17 honor societies, 9 religious organizations. **Athletics (Intercollegiate):** *Men:* baseball, basketball, cross-country, fencing, lacrosse, soccer, swimming, tennis. *Women:* basketball, cross-country, fencing, field hockey, lacrosse, soccer, softball, swimming, tennis. **On-Campus Highlights:** Dorothy Young Center for the Arts, Simon Forum, Rose Memorial Library, University Center, Commons. **Environmental Initiatives:** New residence hall, McLendon Hall, meets USGBC Leadership in Energy and Environmental Design; (LEED) Silver certification; Commitment to planting only native tree and plant species on campus grounds; Restoration of forest floor through annual fern planting (Fern Fest) in sections of campus and removal of turf to create "no-mow zones"; 100% composting/recycling of landscape waste.

ADMISSIONS

Freshman Academic Profile: Average high school GPA 3.4. 31% in top 10% of high school class, 62% in top 25% of high school class, 89% in top 50% of high school class. 66% from public high schools. SAT Math middle 50% range 500-610. SAT Critical Reading middle 50% range 490-610. SAT Writing middle 50% range 500-610. ACT middle 50% range 21.5-27. Minimum paper TOEFL 550. **Basis for Candidate Selection:** *Very important factors considered include:* academic GPA, rigor of secondary school record, talent/ability. *Important factors considered include:* application essay, recommendation(s), extracurricular activities, interview, level of applicant's interest. *Other factors considered include:* Class rank, standardized test scores, alumni/ae relation, character/personal qualities, first generation, geographical residence, racial/ethnic status, volunteer work, work experience. **Freshman Admission Requirements:** High school diploma or equivalent is not required. **Freshman Admission Statistics:** 3,430 applied, 77% admitted, 15% enrolled. **Transfer Admission Requirements:** High school transcript, college transcript(s), essay or personal statement, statement of good standing from prior institution(s). Lowest grade transferable C. **General Admission Information:** Application Fee $50. Early decision application deadline 12/1. Regular application deadline 2/15. Regular notification 3/21. Nonfall registration accepted. Admission may be deferred for a maximum of 1 year. Credit and/or placement offered for CEEB Advanced Placement tests.

COSTS AND FINANCIAL AID

Annual tuition $44,232. Room and board $12,302. Required fees $1,132. Average book expense $1,128. **Required Forms and Deadlines:** FAFSA. **Notification of Awards:** Applicants will be notified of awards on or about 4/1. **Types of Aid:** *Need-based scholarships/grants:* Federal Pell, SEOG, state scholarships/grants, private scholarships, the school's own gift aid. *Loans:* Subsidized Stafford, Unsubsidized Stafford, PLUS, Federal Perkins, state loans. *Student Employment:* Federal Work-Study Program available. Institutional employment available. Highest amount earned per year from on-campus jobs $5,800. Off-campus job opportunities are fair. **Financial Aid Statistics:** 100% freshmen, 100% undergrads receive need-based scholarship or grant aid. 9% freshmen,

8% undergrads receive non-need-based scholarship or grant aid. 78% freshmen, 83% undergrads receive need-based self-help aid. 0% freshmen, 0% undergrads receive athletic scholarships. 98% freshmen, 95% undergrads receive any aid. 70% undergrads borrow to pay for school. Average cumulative indebtedness $25,526. **Criteria for awarding institutional aid:** *Non-need-based:* academics, art, minority status, music/drama, state/district residency.

DREXEL UNIVERSITY

3141 Chestnut Street, Philadelphia, PA 19104
Phone: 215-895-2400 • **Financial Aid Phone:** 215-895-2537
E-mail: enroll@drexel.edu • **CEEB Code:** 2194
Fax: 215-895-1285 • **Website:** www.drexel.edu • **ACT Code:** 3556

This private school was founded in 1891. It has a 40-acre campus.

RATINGS

Admissions Selectivity Rating: 87   Fire Safety Rating: 86

STUDENTS AND FACULTY

Enrollment: 16,681. **Student Body:** 47% female, 53% male, 53% out-of-state, 13% international (104 countries represented). Asian 13%, African American 7%, Caucasian 56%, Hispanic 6%, Native American <1% **Retention and Graduation:** 84% freshmen return for sophomore year. 67% freshmen graduate within 6 years. **Faculty:** 1,174 full-time faculty, 46% are members of minority groups, 16% are women.

ACADEMICS

Degrees: associate, bachelor's, certificate, doctoral, master's, post-bachelor's certificate, post-master's certificate. **Classes:** Most classes have 10–19 students. **Majors with Highest Enrollment:** Registered Nursing/Registered Nurse; Mechanical Engineering; Business/Commerce. **Special Study Options:** Accelerated program, cooperative education program, distance learning, double major, dual enrollment, English as a Second Language (ESL), honors program, independent study, internships, study abroad, teacher certification program, weekend college, 3-3 programs in engineering with Lincoln University, Indiana Univ. of Penn. **Honors programs:** The Pennoni Honors College enriches the University experience for students from all majors with demonstrated academic achievement and broad intellectual interests. Consider the benefits: Individual attention paid to your academic progress; A variety of small group courses with Drexel's best faculty; The experience of being in a small college while enjoying the diverse academic opportunities offered by a major medical and technological research University; Opportunities to meet students from a variety of fields who share many of your interests; Preparation assistance for admission to graduate or professional school, and for fellowships to further your education at home or abroad; Social and cultural events; The option of taking part in a true living-learning community in the residence halls, which have locations set aside specifically for Honors students. Combined degree programs: BA/MD, BA/MA, Engineering BS/PhD, BS/DPT, BSN/MSN, BS/MBA, BS/MS. **Disability Services:** Special programs offered to physically disabled students include note-taking services, reader services, tape recorders, tutors. **Career services:** alumni services, career/job search classes, career assessment, internships. A pioneer in co-operative education since 1919, Drexel operates one of the largest co-operative education programs in the nation (in students placed annually). Over 1,500 business, industrial, governmental, and other institutions located in 27 states and 12 foreign countries "cooperate" with Drexel in offering students the opportunity to acquire practical experience in employment related to college studies.

FACILITIES

Housing: Coed dorms, special housing for disabled students, special housing for international students, fraternity/sorority housing, apartments for single students, Freshmen required to live on campus unless living with parents. 80% of campus accessible to physically disabled. **Special Academic Facilities/ Equipment:** Art museum, theatre, audiovisual center, TV studio, recreational center, center for automation technology, engineering center. **Computers:** 100% of classrooms, 100% of dorms, 100% of libraries, 100% of dining areas, 100% of student union, 100% of common outdoor areas have wireless network access. Students can register for classes online. Administrative functions (other than registration) can be performed online. Undergraduates are required to own a computer.

CAMPUS LIFE

Environment: Metropolis. **Activities:** Choral groups, concert band, dance, drama/theater, jazz band, literary magazine, music ensembles, musical theater, pep band, radio station, student government, student newspaper, student-run film society, television station, yearbook, Campus Ministries. 136 registered organizations, 8 honor societies, 8 religious organizations. 12 fraternities, 11 sorority. **Athletics (Intercollegiate):** *Men:* basketball, cheerleading, crew/rowing, diving, golf, lacrosse, soccer, swimming, tennis, wrestling. *Women:* basketball, cheerleading, crew/rowing, diving, field hockey, lacrosse, soccer, softball, swimming, tennis, volleyball. **On-Campus Highlights:** Ross Commons, University Bookstore, Creese Caf, Crossroads at the Handschumacher Dining Hall, The Quad. **Environmental Initiatives:** Green Power: In 2010, Drexel entered into a new agreement to purchase Renewable Energy Certificates equal to 100% of the Universitys total energy use (84,268 MWH) starting in January 2011. Around the same time, President John Fry signed the American College and University Presidents Climate Commitment (ACUPCC). Drexels purchase of 100% wind energy has reduced the Universitys operations carbon footprint by 81%, exceeding the ACUPCC goal 39 years early. In 2012, Drexel was awarded membership to the EPAs Green Power Leadership Club, which means its green power purchase requirements are 10 times those of the EPAs Green Power Partners. Recycling: With more than 600 tons of waste diverted from landfills, Drexels recycling diversion rate for 2011 was 35%, up from 28% in 2010. This total does not include the more than 12,000 tons of concrete and masonry diverted from two major projects in 2011: the demolition of Matheson Hall for the new LeBow College of Business building, and the renovation of the URBN Center for the new home of the Westphal College of Media Arts and Design. A total of 11,921.12 tons of materials were diverted from the Matheson demolition, compared to just 29.5 tons disposed as waste (99.75% diversion rate). A total of 342.26 tons were diverted from the URBN Center project, compared to 183.25 disposed as waste (65.13% diversion rate). The Papadakis Integrated Sciences Building, opened in September 2011, has been awarded 3 Green Globes from the Green Building Initiative and is registered for LEED Certification (anticipating LEED Gold). The building houses North Americas largest living biofilter wall and the only such structure installed at a U.S. university. The 75-foot high wall of living plants serves as a biological air filter, purifying, cooling, and humidifying the indoor air of the building. At Drexel, professors and students use the wall to examine its effect on the interior atmosphere and its potential health benefits for commercial and academic applications.

ADMISSIONS

Freshman Academic Profile: Average high school GPA 3.47. 29% in top 10% of high school class, 61% in top 25% of high school class, 90% in top 50% of high school class. SAT Math middle 50% range 560-670. SAT Critical Reading middle 50% range 530-630. SAT Writing middle 50% range 520-630. ACT middle 50% range 24-29. Minimum paper TOEFL 550. **Basis for Candidate Selection:** *Very important factors considered include:* Class rank, academic GPA, rigor of secondary school record, standardized test scores. *Important factors considered include:* application essay, recommendation(s), character/personal qualities. *Other factors considered include:* alumni/ae relation, extracurricular activities, first generation, interview, level of applicant's interest, talent/ability, volunteer work, work experience. **Freshman Admission Requirements:** High school diploma is required and GED is accepted. *Academic units required:* 3 mathematics, 1 science, (1 science labs). **Freshman Admission Statistics:** 47,477 applied, 76% admitted, 8% enrolled. **Transfer Admission Requirements:** college transcript(s), Minimum college GPA of 2.5 required. Lowest grade transferable C. **General Admission Information:** Application Fee $75. Regular application deadline 3/1. Nonfall registration accepted. Admission may be deferred for a maximum of 12 months. Credit and/or placement offered for CEEB Advanced Placement tests.

COSTS AND FINANCIAL AID

Annual tuition $44,646. Room and board $14,367. Required fees $2,405. Average book expense $2,053. **Required Forms and Deadlines:** FAFSA, CSS/ Financial Aid PROFILE. **Notification of Awards:** Applicants will be notified of awards on a rolling basis beginning 3/15. **Types of Aid:** *Need-based scholarships/grants:* Federal Pell, SEOG, state scholarships/grants, private scholarships, the school's own gift aid, United Negro College Fund. *Loans:* Subsidized Stafford, Unsubsidized Stafford, PLUS, Federal Perkins, Federal Nursing, college/university loans from institutional funds. *Student Employment:* Federal Work-Study Program available. **Financial Aid Statistics:** 100% freshmen, 94% undergrads receive need-based scholarship or grant aid. 11% freshmen, 3% undergrads receive non-need-based scholarship or grant aid. 78% freshmen, 86% undergrads receive need-based self-help aid. 0% freshmen, 0% undergrads receive athletic scholarships. Criteriafor awarding institutional aid: *Non-needbased:* academics, alumni affiliation, art, athletics, leadership, music/drama.

DRURY UNIVERSITY

900 North Benton Avenue, Springfield, MO 65802-3712
Phone: 417-873-7205 · **Financial Aid Phone:** 417-873-7312
E-mail: druryad@drury.edu · **CEEB Code:** 6169
Fax: 417-866-3873 · **Website:** www.drury.edu · **ACT Code:** 2292

This private school was founded in 1873. It has a 84-acre campus.

RATINGS

Admissions Selectivity Rating: 85   **Fire Safety Rating:** 73

STUDENTS AND FACULTY

Enrollment: 1,446. **Student Body:** 52% female, 48% male, 15% out-of-state, 11% international (41 countries represented). Asian 2%, African American 3%, Caucasian 78%, Hispanic 4%, Native American <1%
Retention and Graduation: 46% freshmen graduate within 4 years. 71% freshmen graduate within 6 years. 35% grads go on to further study within 1 year. 5% grads pursue arts and sciences degrees. 5% grads pursue law degrees. 9% grads pursue business degrees. 15% grads pursue medical degrees. **Faculty:** 140 full-time faculty, 90% hold PhDs, 43% are members of minority groups, 9% are women. 0% of classes are taught by teaching assistants.

ACADEMICS

Degrees: associate, bachelor's, master's. **Classes:** Most classes have 10–19 students. Most lab/discussion sessions have 20–29 students. **Majors with Highest Enrollment:** Psychology; Business Administration and Management; Biology/Biological Sciences. **Special Study Options:** Accelerated program, cooperative education program, distance learning, double major, dual enrollment, English as a Second Language (ESL), honors program, independent study, internships, liberal arts/career combination, student-designed major, study abroad, teacher certification program, Drury Center in Volos, Greece; Living-Learning Communities; Washington Semester. **Honors programs:** Drury Honors Program Combined degree programs: BA/MEng, 3+2 Occupational therapy with Washington Univ. **Disability Services:** Special programs offered to physically disabled students include note-taking services, reader services, tape recorders, tutors. **Career services:** Alumni network, alumni services, career/job search classes, career assessment, internships, regional alumni. Career services highlights include 75% of students complete at least one internship. Recent locations include National Public Radio in Washington, D.C.; state and federal legislators' offices, McSweeney's magazine, San Francisco; Fleishman-Hillard public relations, numerous not-for-profit organizations. Myriad opportunities are available thanks to Drury's widespread alumni base.

FACILITIES

Housing: Coed dorms, special housing for disabled students, fraternity/sorority housing, apartments for married students, apartments for single students, Living-learning communities; Leadership/community service. 97% of campus accessible to physically disabled. **Special Academic Facilities/Equipment:** Science center with greenhouse and astronomical observaton station, new visual art center with two galleries, TV studio, radio station, teleconference facility, language lab, electronic music lab, laser lab. **Computers:** 100% of classrooms, 30% of dorms, 100% of libraries, 100% of dining areas, 75% of student union, 20% of common outdoor areas have wireless network access. Students can register for classes online. Administrative functions (other than registration) can be performed online.

CAMPUS LIFE

Environment: City. **Activities:** Choral groups, concert band, dance, drama/theater, jazz band, literary magazine, music ensembles, musical theater, opera, pep band, radio station, student government, student newspaper, student-run film society, symphony orchestra, television station, Campus Ministries, International Student Organization. 90 registered organizations, 11 honor society, 7 religious organizations. 4 fraternities, 4 sororities. **Athletics (Intercollegiate):** *Men:* baseball, basketball, cheerleading, cross-country, diving, golf, soccer, softball, swimming, tennis. *Women:* basketball, cheerleading, cross-country, diving, golf, soccer, softball, swimming, tennis, volleyball. **On-Campus Highlights:** Trustee Science Center, Sunderland Hall (new student housing), Olin Library, Pool Art Center, College Park student housing, The Drury campus is impeccably maintained and is a registered tree farm; its overall appearance is the greatest highlight of a tour. **Environmental Initiatives:** Energy Management strategies on buildings upgrading lighting, HVAC systems). Bicycle rentals for students to use for the semester for $25. Expanded recycling program, launching a zero waste campaign and partnership with neighbor institutions. Sustainability across the curriculum developments and strengthening of academic majors in the Environmental Programs.

ADMISSIONS

Freshman Academic Profile: Average high school GPA 3.76. 31% in top 10% of high school class, 62% in top 25% of high school class, 89% in top 50%

of high school class. 85% from public high schools. ACT middle 50% range 23-29. Minimum internet-based TOEFL 72. **Basis for Candidate Selection:** *Very important factors considered include:* academic GPA. *Important factors considered include:* Class rank, application essay, recommendation(s), standardized test scores, character/personal qualities, interview. *Other factors considered include:* rigor of secondary school record, alumni/ae relation, extracurricular activities, geographical residence, level of applicant's interest, racial/ethnic status, talent/ability, volunteer work, work experience. **Freshman Admission Requirements:** High school diploma is required and GED is accepted. *Academic units required:* 4 English, 3 mathematics, 3 science, 2 foreign language, 3 social studies. **Freshman Admission Statistics:** 1,016 applied, 81% admitted, 33% enrolled. **Transfer Admission Requirements:** High school transcript, college transcript(s), essay or personal statement, Minimum college GPA of 2.0 required. Lowest grade transferable C. **General Admission Information:** Application Fee $25. Regular application deadline 8/1. Notification on a rolling basis, beginning on or about 10/1. Nonfall registration accepted. Admission may be deferred for a maximum of 1 semester. Credit and/or placement offered for CEEB Advanced Placement tests.

COSTS AND FINANCIAL AID

Annual tuition $22,750. Room and board $8,024. Required fees $1,135. Average book expense $1,200. **Required Forms and Deadlines:** FAFSA, Institution's own financial aid form. **Notification of Awards:** Applicants will be notified of awards on a rolling basis beginning 3/15. **Types of Aid:** *Need-based scholarships/grants:* Federal Pell, SEOG, state scholarships/grants, private scholarships, the school's own gift aid. *Loans:* Subsidized Stafford, Unsubsidized Stafford, PLUS, Federal Perkins. *Student Employment:* Federal Work-Study Program available. Institutional employment available. Highest amount earned per year from on-campus jobs $5,993. Off-campus job opportunities are good. **Financial Aid Statistics:** 100% freshmen, 99% undergrads receive need-based scholarship or grant aid. 20% freshmen, 13% undergrads receive non-need-based scholarship or grant aid. 77% freshmen, 82% undergrads receive need-based self-help aid. 11% freshmen, 10% undergrads receive athletic scholarships. 81% freshmen, 94% undergrads receive any aid. 59% undergrads borrow to pay for school. Average cumulative indebtedness $22,558. **Criteria for awarding institutional aid:** *Non-need-based:* academics, alumni affiliation, art, athletics, job skills, leadership, minority status, music/drama, religious affiliation.

DUKE UNIVERSITY

Best 380

2138 Campus Drive, Durham, NC 27708-0586
Phone: 919-684-3214
E-mail: undergrad-admissions@duke.edu · **CEEB Code:** 5156
Fax: 9196681661 · **Website:** www.duke.edu · **ACT Code:** 3088

This private school, affiliated with the Methodist Church, was founded in 1838. It has a 8500-acre campus.

RATINGS

Admissions Selectivity Rating: 98   **Fire Safety Rating:** 60*

STUDENTS AND FACULTY

Enrollment: 6,493. **Student Body:** 50% female, 50% male, 87% out-of-state, 8% international (89 countries represented). Asian 21%, African American 10%, Caucasian 46%, Hispanic 6%, Native American 1%
Retention and Graduation: 97% freshmen return for sophomore year. 87% freshmen graduate within 4 years. 94% freshmen graduate within 6 years. 38% grads go on to further study within 1 year. 14% grads pursue arts and sciences degrees. 11% grads pursue law degrees. 1% grads pursue business degrees. 12% grads pursue medical degrees. **Faculty:** 1,190 full-time faculty, 96% hold PhDs, 34% are members of minority groups, 19% are women. 4% of classes are taught by teaching assistants.

ACADEMICS

Degrees: associate, bachelor's. **Classes:** Most classes have 10–19 students. Most lab/discussion sessions have 10–19 students. **Majors with Highest Enrollment:** Psychology; Public Policy Analysis; Economics. **Special Study Options:** Accelerated program, cross-registration, distance learning, double major, exchange student program (domestic), honors program, independent study, internships, student-designed major, study abroad, teacher certification program, Undergrads may take grad level classes. **Off-Campus Study:** New

York Arts Program. Other Special Programs: Semester and summer programs in ecology, geology, oceanography, physiology, and zoology at marine laboratory in Beaufort. Combined degree programs: BA/MA, BA/MEng, 3-2 and 4-1 med-tech programs. **Disability Services:** Special programs offered to physically disabled students include note-taking services, reader services, tape recorders, tutors. **Career services:** alumni services, career/job search classes, career assessment, internships.

FACILITIES

Housing: Coed dorms, men's dorms, women's dorms, fraternity/sorority housing, apartments for single students, Theme houses. **Special Academic Facilities/Equipment:** Art museum, language lab, university forest, primate center, phytotron, electron laser, nuclear magnetic resonance machine, nuclear lab. **Computers:** Students can register for classes online.

CAMPUS LIFE

Environment: City. **Activities:** Choral groups, concert band, dance, drama/theater, jazz band, literary magazine, marching band, music ensembles, musical theater, opera, pep band, radio station, student government, student newspaper, student-run film society, symphony orchestra, television station, yearbook. 200 registered organizations, 10 honor societies, 25 religious organizations. 21 fraternity, 14 sororities. **Athletics (Intercollegiate):** *Men:* baseball, basketball, cross-country, diving, fencing, football, golf, lacrosse, soccer, swimming, tennis, track/field (outdoor), track/field (indoor), volleyball, wrestling. *Women:* basketball, crew/rowing, cross-country, diving, fencing, field hockey, golf, lacrosse, soccer, swimming, tennis, track/field (outdoor), track/field (indoor), volleyball. **On-Campus Highlights:** Duke Chapel, Primate Center, Sarah P. Duke Gardens, Duke Forest, Levine Science Research Center. **Environmental Initiatives:** Duke has signed the ACUPCC and made a commitment to make Duke a climate neutral institution. Duke signed a LEED building policy in 2003. The university now has 19 buildings that are certified or in the process of being certified. Sustainability has been a part of Dukes mission long before the word became fashionable. The Campus Master Plan, which guides all campus development, defines eight key principles including several that are related to the tenets of sustainability. Two of the most important of these principles are the commitment for Duke to be a university in the forest and a citizen of Durham and the region. Campus development is shaped by these goals of preserving our community within the forest while being a leader in environmental stewardship for our region. The current Strategic Plan highlights the universitys efforts to employ knowledge in service to society and to make Duke a leader in addressing pressing, global issues. The sustainability principles of environment, economy and society are embedded in these guiding documents of the university.

ADMISSIONS

Freshman Academic Profile: 90% in top 10% of high school class, 98% in top 25% of high school class, 100% in top 50% of high school class. 65% from public high schools. SAT Math middle 50% range 690-790. SAT Critical Reading middle 50% range 670-760. SAT Writing middle 50% range 680-780. ACT middle 50% range 30-34. **Basis for Candidate Selection:** *Very important factors considered include:* application essay, recommendation(s), rigor of secondary school record, standardized test scores, extracurricular activities, talent/ability. *Important factors considered include:* character/personal qualities. *Other factors considered include:* Class rank, academic GPA, alumni/ae relation, geographical residence, interview, racial/ethnic status, state residency, volunteer work, work experience. **Freshman Admission Requirements:** High school diploma is required and GED is not accepted. **Freshman Admission Statistics:** 30,374 applied, 13% admitted, 42% enrolled. **Transfer Admission Requirements:** High school transcript, college transcript(s), essay or personal statement, standardized test scores, Lowest grade transferable C. **General Admission Information:** Application Fee $65. Early decision application deadline 11/1. Regular application deadline 1/2. Regular notification 4/1. Nonfall registration not accepted. Admission may be deferred for a maximum of 1. Credit and/or placement offered for CEEB Advanced Placement tests.

COSTS AND FINANCIAL AID

Annual tuition $44,020. Room and board $12,902. Required fees $1,356. Average book expense $1,300. **Required Forms and Deadlines:** FAFSA, CSS/Financial Aid PROFILE, Noncustodial PROFILE, Business/Farm Supplement. **Notification of Awards:** Applicants will be notified of awards on or about 4/1. **Types of Aid:** *Need-based scholarships/grants:* Federal Pell, SEOG, state scholarships/grants, private scholarships, the school's own gift aid, ROTC. *Loans:* Subsidized Stafford, Unsubsidized Stafford, PLUS, Federal Perkins, college/university loans from institutional funds, Private loans. *Student Employment:* Federal Work-Study Program available. Institutional employment available. Highest amount earned per year from on-campus jobs $1,400. Off-campus job opportunities are good. **Financial Aid Statistics:** 95% freshmen, 95% undergrads receive need-based scholarship or grant aid. 10% freshmen, 7% undergrads receive non-need-based scholarship or grant aid. 83% freshmen, 89% undergrads receive need-based self-help aid. 0% freshmen, 0% undergrads receive athletic scholarships. 39% undergrads borrow to pay for school. Average

cumulative indebtedness $13,865. **Criteria for awarding institutional aid:** *Non-need-based:* academics, alumni affiliation, art, athletics, leadership, minority status, religious affiliation, state/district residency.

DUQUESNE UNIVERSITY

Best 380

600 Forbes Avenue, Pittsburgh, PA 15282
Phone: 412-396-6222 • **Financial Aid Phone:** 412-396-6607
E-mail: admissions@duq.edu
Fax: 412-396-6223 • **Website:** www.duq.edu

This private school, affiliated with the Roman Catholic Church, was founded in 1878. It has a 49-acre campus.

RATINGS

Admissions Selectivity Rating: 86   **Fire Safety Rating:** 99

STUDENTS AND FACULTY

Enrollment: 5,969. **Student Body:** 61% female, 39% male, 26% out-of-state, 4% international (50 countries represented). Asian 2%, African American 4%, Caucasian 83%, Hispanic 3%, Native American <1%
Retention and Graduation: 90% freshmen return for sophomore year. 65% freshmen graduate within 4 years. 76% freshmen graduate within 6 years. 45% grads go on to further study within 1 year. 29% grads pursue arts and sciences degrees. 1% grads pursue law degrees. 11% grads pursue business degrees. 2% grads pursue medical degrees. **Faculty:** 481 full-time faculty, 94% hold PhDs, 45% are members of minority groups, 7% are women.

ACADEMICS

Degrees: bachelor's, master's, post-bachelor's certificate, post-master's certificate. **Classes:** Most classes have 10–19 students. Most lab/discussion sessions have fewer than 10 students. **Majors with Highest Enrollment:** Pharmacy; Accounting; Registered Nursing/Registered Nurse. **Special Study Options:** Accelerated program, cross-registration, distance learning, double major, dual enrollment, English as a Second Language (ESL), exchange student program (domestic), external degree program, honors program, independent study, internships, liberal arts/career combination, student-designed major, study abroad, teacher certification program, weekend college. Students have the opportunity to study abroad on our Italian campus in Rome, Italy. **Honors programs:** Duquesne University offers it's most qualified and outstanding freshmen the opportunity to participate in the Honors College. This selective and intellectually challenging program is available by invitation only after review of the applicant's academic record. The Honors College combines liberal arts, with opportunities for professional studies while providing the thinking, writing, and speaking skill necessary for continuing success. The foundation of Duquesne's Honors College is the Integrated Honors Program, an enhanced track of the University Core Curriculum. Special honors sections of the core courses feature some of the University's most distinguished faculty. Integrated Honors Program courses focus on our essential human heritage and on the major ideas and issues forming the background and direction of modern life. They are taught in small class sections allowing for close interaction between students and teachers and encouraging individual initiative as well as collaborative learning. Combined degree programs: BA/JD, BA/MA, BS/MSEd, BSBA/JD, BSN/MSN, BS/MS, BSBA/MBA, BA/MBA, BS/MBA, BA/BS, BS/MA. **Disability Services:** Special programs offered to physically disabled students include note-taking services, reader services, tape recorders, tutors. **Career services:** Alumni network, alumni services, career/job search classes, career assessment, internships, regional alumni. Career services highlights include Duquesne University's Internship Program, which is designed to provide students with a professional, entry-level work experience as a valuable element of their academic curriculum. The Internship Program is open to all current students. Available internship positions are posted through the DuqConnection website on an on-going basis. In addition, companies seeking interns may participate in the On-Campus Recruiting Program. It is the responsibility of the student to apply for these positions according to the posted deadline dates. Students may also seek internship opportunities through other means, such as networking and application process.

FACILITIES

Housing: Coed dorms, special housing for disabled students, fraternity/sorority housing, apartments for married students, apartments for single students, Wellness HousingSorority and fraternity wings; club wings; international wings. 95% of campus accessible to physically disabled. **Special Academic Facilities/**

Equipment: Student Art Gallery. **Computers:** 10% of classrooms, 100% of libraries, 85% of dining areas, 100% of student union, 100% of common outdoor areas have wireless network access. Students can register for classes online. Administrative functions (other than registration) can be performed online.

CAMPUS LIFE

Environment: Metropolis. **Activities:** Choral groups, concert band, dance, drama/theater, jazz band, literary magazine, marching band, music ensembles, musical theater, opera, pep band, radio station, student government, student newspaper, student-run film society, symphony orchestra, television station, yearbook, Campus Ministries, International Student Organization, Model UN. 160 registered organizations, 34 honor societies, 7 religious organizations. 10 fraternities, 7 sororities. **Athletics (Intercollegiate):** *Men:* basketball, cross-country, football, soccer, tennis, track/field (outdoor). *Women:* basketball, crew/rowing, cross-country, lacrosse, soccer, swimming, tennis, track/field (outdoor), track/field (indoor), volleyball. **On-Campus Highlights:** Power Recreation Center, Starbucks, The Red Ring, Academic Walk, The Night Spot. The Power Recreation Center is a newly opened recreation and fitness center. Starbucks is a popular coffeehouse located in the Duquesne Union. The Red Ring is a new, full service restaurant/bar with nightly musical entertainment. Academic Walk is the main walkway through campus where many activities are held. There is also a new quiet Study Lounge located on the second floor of the Union.

ADMISSIONS

Freshman Academic Profile: Average high school GPA 3.73. 30% in top 10% of high school class, 58% in top 25% of high school class, 89% in top 50% of high school class. SAT Math middle 50% range 520-610. SAT Critical Reading middle 50% range 520-620. SAT Writing middle 50% range 510-610. ACT middle 50% range 23-28. Minimum internet-based TOEFL 90. Minimum paper TOEFL 575. **Basis for Candidate Selection:** *Very important factors considered include:* application essay, academic GPA, recommendation(s), rigor of secondary school record, standardized test scores. *Important factors considered include:* Class rank, character/personal qualities, extracurricular activities, interview, talent/ability, volunteer work. *Other factors considered include:* alumni/ae relation, first generation, level of applicant's interest, racial/ethnic status, work experience. **Freshman Admission Requirements:** High school diploma is required and GED is accepted. **Freshman Admission Statistics:** 6,534 applied, 73% admitted, 28% enrolled. **Transfer Admission Requirements:** High school transcript, college transcript(s), essay or personal statement, statement of good standing from prior institution(s). Minimum college GPA of 2.5 required. Lowest grade transferable C. **General Admission Information:** Application Fee $50. Early decision application deadline 11/1. Regular application deadline 7/1. Notification on a rolling basis, beginning on or about 9/15. Nonfall registration accepted. Admission may be deferred for a maximum of One academic year. Credit and/or placement offered for CEEB Advanced Placement tests.

COSTS AND FINANCIAL AID

Average book expense $1,000. **Required Forms and Deadlines:** FAFSA. **Notification of Awards:** Applicants will be notified of awards on a rolling basis beginning 3/1. **Types of Aid:** *Need-based scholarships/grants:* Federal Pell, SEOG, state scholarships/grants, private scholarships, the school's own gift aid, United Negro College Fund. *Loans:* Subsidized Stafford, Unsubsidized Stafford, PLUS, Federal Perkins, Federal Nursing, Private Alternative Loans. *Student Employment:* Federal Work-Study Program available. Institutional employment available. Off-campus job opportunities are good. **Financial Aid Statistics:** 100% freshmen, 99% undergrads receive need-based scholarship or grant aid. 100% freshmen, 94% undergrads receive non-need-based scholarship or grant aid. 88% freshmen, 87% undergrads receive need-based self-help aid. 5% freshmen, 5% undergrads receive athletic scholarships. 99% freshmen, 96% undergrads receive any aid. 75% undergrads borrow to pay for school. Average cumulative indebtedness $24,641. **Criteria for awarding institutional aid:** *Non-need-based:* academics, athletics, music/drama.

D'YOUVILLE COLLEGE

320 Porter Avenue, Buffalo, NY 14201
Phone: 716-829-7600 • **Financial Aid Phone:** 716-829-7500
E-mail: admissions@dyc.edu • **CEEB Code:** 2197
Fax: 716-829-7790 • **Website:** www.dyc.edu • **ACT Code:** 2732

This private school was founded in 1908. It has a 7-acre campus.

RATINGS

Admissions Selectivity Rating: 78   **Fire Safety Rating:** 74

STUDENTS AND FACULTY

Enrollment: 1,982. **Student Body:** 73% female, 27% male, 4% out-of-state, 7% international (55 countries represented). Asian 3%, African American 10%, Caucasian 70%, Hispanic 4%, Native American 1%
Retention and Graduation: 72% freshmen return for sophomore year. 32% freshmen graduate within 4 years. 52% freshmen graduate within 6 years. **Faculty:** 180 full-time faculty, 76% hold PhDs, 61% are members of minority groups, 8% are women. 0% of classes are taught by teaching assistants.

ACADEMICS

Degrees: bachelor's, first professional, master's, post-bachelor's certificate, post-master's certificate. **Classes:** Most classes have 10–19 students. Most lab/discussion sessions have 10–19 students. **Majors with Highest Enrollment:** Education; Registered Nursing/Registered Nurse; Business/Commerce. **Special Study Options:** Accelerated program, cooperative education program, cross-registration, distance learning, double major, dual enrollment, exchange student program (domestic), independent study, internships, liberal arts/career combination, study abroad, teacher certification program, weekend college. Combined degree programs: BS/MS. **Disability Services:** Special programs offered to physically disabled students include note-taking services, reader services, tape recorders, tutors.

FACILITIES

Housing: Coed dorms, special housing for disabled students, apartments for married students, apartments for single studentsQuiet floors for 3rd-5th year students. Separate male and female floors available. New apartment style housing opened 1/05. 100% of campus accessible to physically disabled. **Special Academic Facilities/Equipment:** Kavinoky Theatre (professional theatre). **Computers:** Students can register for classes online. Administrative functions (other than registration) can be performed online.

CAMPUS LIFE

Environment: City. **Activities:** Choral groups, drama/theater, literary magazine, student government, student newspaper, yearbook. 25 registered organizations, 3 honor societies, 1 religious organization. **Athletics (Intercollegiate):** *Men:* baseball, basketball, golf, soccer, volleyball. *Women:* basketball, crew/rowing, golf, soccer, softball, volleyball. **On-Campus Highlights:** New Academic Center, New Gym, Spot Spartian Café, Weight Room, Gross anatomy lab, New apartment style housing for junior level and up opening 1/05.

ADMISSIONS

Freshman Academic Profile: 18% in top 10% of high school class, 52% in top 25% of high school class, 87% in top 50% of high school class. 75% from public high schools. SAT Math middle 50% range 490-580. SAT Critical Reading middle 50% range 470-550. SAT Writing middle 50% range 450-540. ACT middle 50% range 21-25. Minimum paper TOEFL 500. **Basis for Candidate Selection:** *Very important factors considered include:* rigor of secondary school record, standardized test scores. *Important factors considered include:* Class rank. *Other factors considered include:* recommendation(s), alumni/ae relation, character/personal qualities, extracurricular activities, interview, talent/ability, volunteer work, work experience. **Freshman Admission Requirements:** High school diploma is required and GED is accepted. **Freshman Admission Statistics:** 1,023 applied, 80% admitted, 29% enrolled. **Transfer Admission Requirements:** High school transcript, college transcript(s), Minimum college GPA of 2.0 required. Lowest grade transferable C. **General Admission Information:** Application Fee $25. Nonfall registration accepted. Admission may be deferred for a maximum of 12 months. Credit offered for CEEB Advanced Placement tests.

COSTS AND FINANCIAL AID

Annual tuition $21,930. Room and board $10,250. Required fees $310. Average book expense $1,200. **Required Forms and Deadlines:** FAFSA, State aid form. **Notification of Awards:** Applicants will be notified of awards on a rolling basis beginning 4/15. **Types of Aid:** *Need-based scholarships/grants:* Federal Pell, SEOG, state scholarships/grants, private scholarships, the school's own gift aid, Federal Nursing Scholarships. *Loans:* Subsidized Stafford, Unsubsidized Stafford, PLUS, Federal Perkins, Federal Nursing, college/university loans from institutional funds. *Student Employment:* Federal Work-Study Program available. Institutional employment available. Highest amount earned per year from on-campus jobs $2,000. Off-campus job opportunities are excellent. **Financial Aid Statistics:** 100% freshmen, 115% undergrads receive need-based scholarship or grant aid. 10% freshmen, 5% undergrads receive non-need-based scholarship or grant aid. 88% freshmen, 92% undergrads receive need-based self-help aid. 0% freshmen, 0% undergrads receive athletic scholarships. 94% undergrads borrow to pay for school. Average cumulative indebtedness $34,899. **Criteria for awarding institutional aid:** *Non-need-based:* academics, alumni affiliation.

EARLHAM COLLEGE

Best 380

801 National Road West, Richmond, IN 47374-4095
Phone: 765-983-1600 · **Financial Aid Phone:** 765-983-1217
E-mail: admissions@earlham.edu · **CEEB Code:** 1195
Fax: 765-983-1560 · **Website:** www.earlham.edu · **ACT Code:** 1186

This private school, affiliated with the Quaker Church, was founded in 1847. It has a 800-acre campus.

RATINGS
Admissions Selectivity Rating: 88   **Fire Safety Rating:** 89

STUDENTS AND FACULTY
Enrollment: 942. **Student Body:** 55% female, 45% male, 77% out-of-state, 18% international (76 countries represented). Asian 6%, African American 13%, Caucasian 53%, Hispanic 6%, Native American 1%
Retention and Graduation: 65% freshmen graduate within 4 years. 72% freshmen graduate within 6 years. 20% grads go on to further study within 1 year. **Faculty:** 106 full-time faculty, 94% hold PhDs, 54% are members of minority groups, 20% are women. 0% of classes are taught by teaching assistants.

ACADEMICS
Degrees: bachelor's, first professional, master's. **Classes:** Most classes have 10–19 students. Most lab/discussion sessions have 20–29 students. **Majors with Highest Enrollment:** Biology/Biological Sciences; Psychology; Multi-/Interdisciplinary Studies. **Special Study Options:** Accelerated program, cross-registration, double major, dual enrollment, English as a Second Language (ESL), independent study, internships, student-designed major, study abroad, teacher certification program, Teacher certification at Master's Degree level only. Combined degree programs: 3-2 in Architecture. **Disability Services:** Special programs offered to physically disabled students include note-taking services, reader services, tape recorders, tutors.

FACILITIES
Housing: Coed dorms, special housing for disabled students, men's dorms, special housing for international students, women's dorms, Wellness Housing, Theme Housing, Friendship houses. 80% of campus accessible to physically disabled. **Special Academic Facilities/Equipment:** Major academic building Landrum Bolling Center for Interdisciplinary and Social Studies opened in 2002, natural history museum, cultural centers, language labs, greenhouse, observatory, planetarium. **Computers:** 95% of classrooms, have wireless network access. Administrative functions (other than registration) can be performed online.

CAMPUS LIFE
Environment: Town. **Activities:** Choral groups, concert band, dance, drama/theater, jazz band, literary magazine, music ensembles, radio station, student government, student newspaper, student-run film society, symphony orchestra, yearbook, Campus Ministries, International Student Organization, Model UN. 70 registered organizations, 1 honor society, 15 religious organizations. **Athletics (Intercollegiate):** *Men:* baseball, basketball, cross-country, football, soccer, tennis, track/field (outdoor), track/field (indoor). *Women:* basketball, cross-country, field hockey, soccer, tennis, track/field (outdoor), track/field (indoor), volleyball. **On-Campus Highlights:** Landrum Bolling Center - Interdisciplinary Studies, Athletics and Wellness Center, Runyan Center, Natural History Museum, Coffee Shop. **Environmental Initiatives:** Earlham recently spent the 2011-12 year in a planning process leading to the Earlham Sustainability Plan, a comprehensive public document. In 2012, Earlham hired its first full-time sustainability coordinator. In 2013 we launched a unique work-study program called student sustainability corps to employ students across the campus to work on sustainability projects.

ADMISSIONS
Freshman Academic Profile: Average high school GPA 3.5. 29% in top 10% of high school class, 60% in top 25% of high school class, 92% in top 50% of high school class. 73% from public high schools. SAT Math middle 50% range 580-680. SAT Critical Reading middle 50% range 570-690. SAT Writing middle 50% range 560-660. ACT middle 50% range 25-31. Minimum internet-based TOEFL 80. Minimum paper TOEFL 550. **Basis for Candidate Selection:** *Very important factors considered include:* Class rank, academic GPA, rigor of secondary school record, character/personal qualities. *Important factors considered include:* application essay, recommendation(s), standardized test scores, extracurricular activities, talent/ability, volunteer work. *Other factors considered*

include: interview, work experience. **Freshman Admission Requirements:** High school diploma is required and GED is accepted. *Academic units required:* 4 English, 3 mathematics, 3 science, (2 science labs), 2 foreign language, 4 social studies, 2 history, 1 visual/performing arts. **Freshman Admission Statistics:** 2,001 applied, 65% admitted, 21% enrolled. **Transfer Admission Requirements:** High school transcript, college transcript(s), essay or personal statement, standardized test scores, statement of good standing from prior institution(s). Minimum college GPA of 2.7 required. Lowest grade transferable C. **General Admission Information:** Early decision application deadline 12/1. Regular application deadline 2/15. Regular notification 3/15. Nonfall registration accepted. Admission may be deferred for a maximum of 1 year. Credit offered for CEEB Advanced Placement tests.

COSTS AND FINANCIAL AID
Annual tuition $42,000. Room and board $8,600. Required fees $870. Average book expense $1,200. **Required Forms and Deadlines:** FAFSA. **Notification of Awards:** Applicants will be notified of awards on a rolling basis beginning 2/15. **Types of Aid:** *Need-based scholarships/grants:* Federal Pell, SEOG, state scholarships/grants, private scholarships, the school's own gift aid. *Loans:* Direct Subsidized Stafford, Direct Unsubsidized Stafford, Direct PLUS, Federal Perkins, college/university loans from institutional funds. *Student Employment:* Highest amount earned per year from on-campus jobs $2,259. **Financial Aid Statistics:** 96% freshmen, 95% undergrads receive need-based scholarship or grant aid. 30% freshmen, 40% undergrads receive non-need-based scholarship or grant aid. 89% freshmen, 90% undergrads receive need-based self-help aid. 0% freshmen, 0% undergrads receive athletic scholarships. 97% freshmen, 94% undergrads receive any aid. 57% undergrads borrow to pay for school. Average cumulative indebtedness $27,107. **Criteria for awarding institutional aid:** *Non-need-based:* academics, minority status, religious affiliation.

EAST CAROLINA UNIVERSITY

Office of Undergraduate Admissions, Greenville, NC 27858-4353
Phone: 252-328-6640 · **Financial Aid Phone:** 252-328-4347
E-mail: admis@ecu.edu · **CEEB Code:** 5180
Fax: 252-328-6945 · **Website:** www.ecu.edu · **ACT Code:** 3094

This public school was founded in 1907. It has a 1379-acre campus.

RATINGS
Admissions Selectivity Rating: 79   **Fire Safety Rating:** 61

STUDENTS AND FACULTY
Enrollment: 21,207. **Student Body:** 58% female, 42% male, 12% out-of-state, 0% international (33 countries represented). Asian 3%, African American 16%, Caucasian 69%, Hispanic 6%, Native American 1%
Retention and Graduation: 33% freshmen graduate within 4 years. **Faculty:** 1,205 full-time faculty, 80% hold PhDs, 49% are members of minority groups, 14% are women.

ACADEMICS
Degrees: bachelor's, first professional, master's, post-bachelor's certificate, post-master's certificate. **Classes:** Most classes have fewer than 10 students. Most lab/discussion sessions have fewer than 10 students. **Majors with Highest Enrollment:** Speech Communication and Rhetoric; Elementary Education and Teaching; Registered Nursing/Registered Nurse. **Special Study Options:** Accelerated program, cooperative education program, distance learning, double major, dual enrollment, exchange student program (domestic), honors program, independent study, internships, student-designed major, study abroad, teacher certification program. Combined degree programs: BSA/MSA Accounting; MA/CAS in School Psychology. **Disability Services:** Special programs offered to physically disabled students include note-taking services, reader services, tape recorders, tutors. **Career services:** alumni services, career/job search classes, career assessment, internships.

FACILITIES
Housing: Coed dorms, men's dorms, women's dorms, fraternity/sorority housing, First-year students floor, leadership hall, extended quiet study hours floor, upper division, academic year residence halls, music student communities, service community, engineering. 94% of campus accessible to physically disabled. **Special Academic Facilities/Equipment:** Wellington B. Gray Gallery, Museum Without Walls, Ledonia Wright Cultural Center, A.J. Fletcher Recital Hall, Hendrix Theatre, Jenkins Fine Arts Center, McGinnis Theatre, and Mendenhall Student Center. **Computers:** 68% of classrooms, 20% of dorms, 100% of libraries, 100% of dining areas, 100% of student union, 25% of common outdoor areas have wireless network access. Students can register for classes online. Administrative functions (other than registration) can be performed online.

CAMPUS LIFE

Environment: Town. **Activities:** Choral groups, concert band, dance, drama/theater, jazz band, literary magazine, marching band, music ensembles, musical theater, radio station, student government, student newspaper, student-run film society, symphony orchestra, television station, yearbook, Campus Ministries, International Student Organization, Model UN. 297 registered organizations, 11 honor society, 27 religious organizations. 20 fraternities, 13 sororities. **Athletics (Intercollegiate):** *Men:* baseball, basketball, cheerleading, cross-country, diving, football, golf, swimming, tennis, track/field (outdoor). *Women:* basketball, cheerleading, cross-country, diving, golf, soccer, softball, swimming, tennis, track/field (outdoor), volleyball. **On-Campus Highlights:** Student Recreation Center, Wright Plaza, Mendenhall Student Center, Blounts Sports Complex, Science and Technology Building, Athletic facilities include: Dowdy-Ficklen Stadium, Williams Arena in Minges Coliseum and Harrington Field. **Environmental Initiatives:** Water conservation; Student life recycling; Construction guidelines for sustainable buildings.

ADMISSIONS

Freshman Academic Profile: Average high school GPA 3.67. 13% in top 10% of high school class, 40% in top 25% of high school class, 78% in top 50% of high school class. SAT Math middle 50% range 480-560. SAT Critical Reading middle 50% range 470-550. SAT Writing middle 50% range 440-530. ACT middle 50% range 19-23. Minimum internet-based TOEFL 80. Minimum paper TOEFL 500. **Basis for Candidate Selection:** *Very important factors considered include:* Class rank, rigor of secondary school record, standardized test scores. *Other factors considered include:* recommendation(s), alumni/ae relation, character/personal qualities, extracurricular activities, geographical residence, interview, state residency, talent/ability. **Freshman Admission Requirements:** High school diploma is required and GED is accepted. *Academic units required:* 4 English, 4 mathematics, 3 science, (1 science labs), 2 foreign language, 2 social studies. **Freshman Admission Statistics:** 14,223 applied, 77% admitted, 38% enrolled. **Transfer Admission Requirements:** High school transcript, college transcript(s), Minimum college GPA of 2.0 required. Lowest grade transferable C. **General Admission Information:** Application Fee $60. Regular application deadline 3/15. Notification on a rolling basis, beginning on or about 10/1. Nonfall registration accepted. Admission may be deferred for a maximum of 1 semester. Credit and/or placement offered for CEEB Advanced Placement tests.

COSTS AND FINANCIAL AID

Annual. Annual out-of-state tuition $19,156. Room and board $8,833. Required fees $2,184. Average book expense $1,234. **Required Forms and Deadlines:** FAFSA. **Notification of Awards:** Applicants will be notified of awards on a rolling basis beginning 3/15. **Types of Aid:** *Need-based scholarships/grants:* Federal Pell, SEOG, state scholarships/grants, private scholarships, the school's own gift aid. *Loans:* Subsidized Stafford, Unsubsidized Stafford, PLUS, Federal Perkins, Federal Nursing. *Student Employment:* Federal Work-Study Program available. Institutional employment available. **Financial Aid Statistics:** 71% freshmen, 74% undergrads receive need-based scholarship or grant aid. 23% freshmen, 15% undergrads receive non-need-based scholarship or grant aid. 85% freshmen, 84% undergrads receive need-based self-help aid. 2% freshmen, 2% undergrads receive athletic scholarships. 61% freshmen, 61% undergrads receive any aid. 67% undergrads borrow to pay for school. Average cumulative indebtedness $29,898. **Criteria for awarding institutional aid:** *Non-need-based:* academics, alumni affiliation, art, athletics.

EAST STROUDSBURG UNIVERSITY
OF PENNSYLVANIA

East Stroudsburg University, East Stroudsburg, PA 18301-2999
Phone: 570-422-3542 · **Financial Aid Phone:** 570-422-2800
E-mail: undergrads@po-box.esu.edu · **CEEB Code:** 2650
Fax: 570-422-3933 · **Website:** www4.esu.edu · **ACT Code:** 3700

This public school was founded in 1893. It has a 213-acre campus.

RATINGS

Admissions Selectivity Rating: 77   **Fire Safety Rating:** 98

STUDENTS AND FACULTY

Enrollment: 6,274. **Student Body:** 55% female, 45% male, 25% out-of-state, 1% international (24 countries represented). Asian 1%, African American 7%, Caucasian 76%, Hispanic 7%, Native American <1%

Retention and Graduation: 34% freshmen graduate within 4 years. **Faculty:** 330 full-time faculty, 74% hold PhDs, 51% are members of minority groups, 16% are women. 0% of classes are taught by teaching assistants.

ACADEMICS

Degrees: associate, bachelor's, master's. **Classes:** Most classes have 20–29 students. Most lab/discussion sessions have 10–19 students. **Majors with Highest Enrollment:** Elementary Education and Teaching; Physical Education Teaching and Coaching; Business Administration and Management. **Special Study Options:** Accelerated program, cross-registration, distance learning, double major, dual enrollment, exchange student program (domestic), honors program, independent study, internships, student-designed major, study abroad, teacher certification program. **Honors programs:** The Honors Program at ESU offers academically superior students an opportunity to challenge themselves intellectually both within and beyond the classroom setting. The focus of the Program was, and is, located in the area of the liberal arts general education curriculum. The goal of the program is to foster in the students an appreciation of the liberal arts perspective and a commitment to lifelong learning. **Disability Services:** Special programs offered to physically disabled students include note-taking services, reader services, tape recorders, tutors. **Career services:** career assessment. Career services highlights include several interns placed at Sanofi Pasteur, a major Parmaceutical company. Our individual career counseling services are rated very highly.

FACILITIES

Housing: Coed dorms. 95% of campus accessible to physically disabled. **Special Academic Facilities/Equipment:** Natural history museum, human performance lab, TV production studios, 119-acre student-owned/operated recreation area and wildlife sanctuary, observatory, electron microscopes. **Computers:** 50% of classrooms, 100% of dorms, 100% of libraries, 100% of student union, 10% of common outdoor areas have wireless network access. Students can register for classes online. Administrative functions (other than registration) can be performed online.

CAMPUS LIFE

Environment: Village. **Activities:** Choral groups, concert band, dance, drama/theater, jazz band, literary magazine, marching band, music ensembles, musical theater, pep band, radio station, student government, student newspaper, symphony orchestra, Campus Ministries, International Student Organization. 110 registered organizations, 28 honor societies, 3 religious organizations. 5 fraternities, 5 sororities. **Athletics (Intercollegiate):** *Men:* baseball, basketball, cross-country, football, soccer, tennis, track/field (outdoor), track/field (indoor), wrestling. *Women:* basketball, cross-country, field hockey, golf, lacrosse, soccer, softball, swimming, tennis, track/field (outdoor), track/field (indoor), volleyball. **On-Campus Highlights:** Recreation Center, Java CIty, University Center, Stoney Acres, The Quad.

ADMISSIONS

Freshman Academic Profile: 7.21% in top 10% of high school class, 30.14% in top 25% of high school class, 72.12% in top 50% of high school class. 90% from public high schools. SAT Math middle 50% range 460-550. SAT Critical Reading middle 50% range 440-530. SAT Writing middle 50% range 440-530. Minimum internet-based TOEFL 83. Minimum paper TOEFL 560. **Basis for Candidate Selection:** *Very important factors considered include:* Class rank, academic GPA, rigor of secondary school record, standardized test scores. **Freshman Admission Requirements:** High school diploma is required and GED is accepted. **Freshman Admission Statistics:** 7,258 applied, 63% admitted, 26% enrolled. **Transfer Admission Requirements:** college transcript(s), Minimum college GPA of 2.0 required. Lowest grade transferable C. **General Admission Information:** Application Fee $35. Regular application deadline 4/1. Notification on a rolling basis, beginning on or about 12/1. Nonfall registration accepted. Credit and/or placement offered for CEEB Advanced Placement tests.

COSTS AND FINANCIAL AID

Annual in-state tuition $5,804. Annual out-of-state tuition $14,510. Room and board $6,658. Required fees $1,974. Average book expense $1,200. **Required Forms and Deadlines:** FAFSA. **Notification of Awards:** Applicants will be notified of awards on or about 4/1. **Types of Aid:** *Need-based scholarships/grants:* Federal Pell, SEOG, state scholarships/grants, private scholarships, the school's own gift aid. *Loans:* Subsidized Stafford, Unsubsidized Stafford, PLUS, Federal Perkins. *Student Employment:* Federal Work-Study Program available. Institutional employment available. Highest amount earned per year from on-campus jobs $2,145. Off-campus job opportunities are fair. **Financial Aid Statistics:** 55% freshmen, 56% undergrads receive need-based scholarship or grant aid. 5% freshmen, 4% undergrads receive non-need-based scholarship or grant aid. 76% freshmen, 73% undergrads receive need-based self-help aid. 6% freshmen, 4% undergrads receive athletic scholarships. 75% freshmen, 84% undergrads receive any aid. 72% undergrads borrow to pay for school. Average cumulative indebtedness $19,477. **Criteria for awarding institutional aid:** *Non-need-based:* academics, alumni affiliation, art, athletics, leadership, minority status, music/drama, religious affiliation, state/district residency.

EAST TENNESSEE STATE UNIVERSITY

ETSU Box 70731, Johnson City, TN 37614
Phone: 423-439-4213 · **Financial Aid Phone:** 423-439-4300
E-mail: go2etsu@etsu.edu · **CEEB Code:** 1198
Fax: 423-439-4630 · **Website:** www.etsu.edu · **ACT Code:** 3958

This public school was founded in 1911. It has a 366-acre campus.

RATINGS

Admissions Selectivity Rating: 76   **Fire Safety Rating:** 60*

STUDENTS AND FACULTY

Enrollment: 11,162. **Student Body:** 57% female, 43% male, 13% out-of-state, 3% international (63 countries represented). Asian 1%, African American 6%, Caucasian 84%, Hispanic 2%, Native American <1%
Retention and Graduation: 20% freshmen graduate within 4 years. 43% freshmen graduate within 6 years. **Faculty:** 588 full-time faculty, 47% are members of minority groups, 18% are women.

ACADEMICS

Degrees: bachelor's, first professional, master's, post-bachelor's certificate, post-master's certificate. **Classes:** Most classes have 20–29 students. Most lab/discussion sessions have 20–29 students. **Majors with Highest Enrollment:** Business Administration and Management. **Special Study Options:** cooperative education program, distance learning, double major, dual enrollment, exchange student program (domestic), external degree program, honors program, independent study, internships, student-designed major, study abroad, teacher certification program. **Honors programs:** University Honors Program Honors-in-Discipline Programs. **Disability Services:** Special programs offered to physically disabled students include note-taking services, reader services, tape recorders, tutors. **Career services:** Alumni network, alumni services, career/job search classes, career assessment, internships, regional alumni.

FACILITIES

Housing: Coed dorms, special housing for disabled students, men's dorms, women's dorms, fraternity/sorority housing, apartments for married students, apartments for single students. 75% of campus accessible to physically disabled. **Special Academic Facilities/Equipment:** Regional history museum, art gallery, archives of Appalachia, planetarium. **Computers:** Students can register for classes online. Administrative functions (other than registration) can be performed online.

CAMPUS LIFE

Environment: Town. **Activities:** Choral groups, concert band, drama/theater, jazz band, literary magazine, music ensembles, pep band, radio station, student government, student newspaper, television station, Campus Ministries, International Student Organization. 200 registered organizations, 19 honor societies, 13 religious organizations. 9 fraternities, 7 sororities. **Athletics (Intercollegiate):** *Men:* baseball, basketball, cheerleading, cross-country, golf, soccer, tennis, track/field (outdoor), track/field (indoor). *Women:* basketball, cheerleading, cross-country, golf, soccer, softball, tennis, track/field (outdoor), track/field (indoor), volleyball. **On-Campus Highlights:** Memorial Center, New Sherrod Library, New Physical Activities Center, The Cave- a unique pizza pub located in the DP Culp Center. Built around a huge rock formation, indoors, Amphitheater—Natural stone + earth outdoor theater.

ADMISSIONS

Freshman Academic Profile: Average high school GPA 3.36. 18.93% in top 10% of high school class, 43.64% in top 25% of high school class, 75.79% in top 50% of high school class. 90% from public high schools. SAT Math middle 50% range 440-620. SAT Critical Reading middle 50% range 410-600. ACT middle 50% range 19-25. Minimum paper TOEFL 500. **Basis for Candidate Selection:** *Very important factors considered include:* academic GPA, standardized test scores. *Important factors considered include:* rigor of secondary school record. *Other factors considered include:* Class rank, geographical residence, state residency. **Freshman Admission Requirements:** High school diploma is required and GED is accepted. *Academic units required:* 4 English, 3 mathematics, 2 science, (1 science labs), 2 foreign language, 1 social studies, 1 history, 1 visual/performing arts. **Freshman Admission Statistics:** 5,252 applied, 92% admitted, 43% enrolled. **Transfer Admission Requirements:** High school transcript, college transcript(s), Minimum college GPA of 2.0 required. Lowest grade transferable D. **General Admission Information:** Application Fee $15. Nonfall registration accepted. Credit and/or placement offered for CEEB Advanced Placement tests.

COSTS AND FINANCIAL AID

Required Forms and Deadlines: FAFSA. **Notification of Awards:** Applicants will be notified of awards on a rolling basis beginning 4/15. **Types of Aid:** *Need-based scholarships/grants:* Federal Pell, SEOG, state scholarships/

grants, private scholarships, the school's own gift aid, Federal Nursing Scholarships. *Loans:* Direct Subsidized Stafford, Direct Unsubsidized Stafford, Direct PLUS, Federal Perkins, Federal Nursing, state loans, college/university loans from institutional funds. *Student Employment:* Federal Work-Study Program available. Institutional employment available. Off-campus job opportunities are excellent. **Financial Aid Statistics:** 0% freshmen, 0% undergrads receive athletic scholarships. *Criteria for awarding institutional aid: Non-need-based:* academics, alumni affiliation, art, athletics, leadership, minority status, music/drama, religious affiliation, state/district residency.

EAST TEXAS BAPTIST UNIVERSITY

One Tiger Drive, Marshall, TX 75670-1498
Phone: 903-923-2000 · **Financial Aid Phone:** 903-923-2137
E-mail: admissions@etbu.edu · **CEEB Code:** 6187
Fax: 903-923-2001 · **Website:** http://www.etbu.edu · **ACT Code:** 4086

This private school, affiliated with the Baptist Church, was founded in 1912. It has a 200-acre campus.

RATINGS

Admissions Selectivity Rating: 81   **Fire Safety Rating:** 73

STUDENTS AND FACULTY

Enrollment: 1,146. **Student Body:** 52% female, 48% male, 7% out-of-state, 2% international (13 countries represented). Asian 0%, African American 19%, Caucasian 64%, Hispanic 10%, Native American 1%
Retention and Graduation: 61% freshmen return for sophomore year. 29% freshmen graduate within 4 years. 38% freshmen graduate within 6 years. **Faculty:** 71 full-time faculty, 86% hold PhDs, 38% are members of minority groups, 4% are women. 0% of classes are taught by teaching assistants.

ACADEMICS

Degrees: bachelor's, certificate. **Classes:** Most classes have 10–19 students. Most lab/discussion sessions have 10–19 students. **Majors with Highest Enrollment:** Registered Nursing/Registered Nurse; Business/Commerce; Elementary Education and Teaching. **Special Study Options:** Accelerated program, cross-registration, distance learning, double major, dual enrollment, exchange student program (domestic), honors program, independent study, internships, liberal arts/career combination, student-designed major, study abroad, teacher certification program. **Disability Services:** Special programs offered to physically disabled students include reader services, tutors. **Career services:** alumni services, career assessment, internships. Career services highlights include internships.

FACILITIES

Housing: men's dorms, women's dorms, apartments for married students, Campus houses for married students. 95% of campus accessible to physically disabled. **Computers:** 100% of classrooms, 100% of dorms, 100% of libraries, 100% of dining areas, 100% of student union, 100% of common outdoor areas have wireless network access. Students can register for classes online. Administrative functions (other than registration) can be performed online.

CAMPUS LIFE

Environment: Village. **Activities:** Choral groups, concert band, drama/theater, jazz band, literary magazine, marching band, music ensembles, musical theater, pep band, radio station, student government, student newspaper, symphony orchestra, yearbook, Campus Ministries, International Student Organization, Model UN. 38 registered organizations, 7 honor societies, 3 religious organizations. 2 fraternities, 2 sororities. **Athletics (Intercollegiate):** *Men:* baseball, basketball, cross-country, football, soccer. *Women:* basketball, cross-country, soccer, softball, volleyball. **On-Campus Highlights:** Scarborough Hall, The Quad, Bennett Student Center, Dean Healthplex, Tiger Grrill.

ADMISSIONS

Freshman Academic Profile: Average high school GPA 3.36. 9% in top 10% of high school class, 39% in top 25% of high school class, 75% in top 50% of high school class. 80% from public high schools. SAT Math middle 50% range 450-530. SAT Critical Reading middle 50% range 420-510. ACT middle 50% range 18-22. Minimum internet-based TOEFL 61. Minimum paper TOEFL 500. **Basis for Candidate Selection:** *Very important factors considered include:* Class rank, standardized test scores. *Important factors considered include:* academic GPA. *Other factors considered include:* character/personal qualities. **Freshman Admission Requirements:** High school diploma is required and GED is accepted. **Freshman Admission Statistics:** 941 applied, 58% admitted, 67% enrolled. **Transfer Admission Requirements:** college transcript(s), statement of good standing from prior institution(s). Minimum college GPA of 2.00 required. Lowest grade transferable D. **General Admis-**

sion Information: Application Fee $25. Notification on a rolling basis, beginning on or about 9/1. Nonfall registration accepted. Admission may be deferred for a maximum of 1 year. Credit and/or placement offered for CEEB Advanced Placement tests.

COSTS AND FINANCIAL AID
Annual tuition $23,250. Room and board $8,629. Required fees $968. Average book expense $956. **Required Forms and Deadlines:** FAFSA, Institution's own financial aid form. **Notification of Awards:** Applicants will be notified of awards on a rolling basis beginning 1/1. **Types of Aid:** *Need-based scholarships/grants:* Federal Pell, SEOG, state scholarships/grants, private scholarships, the school's own gift aid, Federal Nursing Scholarships. *Loans:* Subsidized Stafford, Unsubsidized Stafford, PLUS, Federal Perkins, state loans. *Student Employment:* Federal Work-Study Program available. Institutional employment available. Highest amount earned per year from on-campus jobs $2,096. Off-campus job opportunities are fair. **Financial Aid Statistics:** 78% freshmen, 77% undergrads receive need-based scholarship or grant aid. 99% freshmen, 97% undergrads receive non-need-based scholarship or grant aid. 76% freshmen, 81% undergrads receive need-based self-help aid. 0% freshmen, 0% undergrads receive athletic scholarships. 99% freshmen, 99% undergrads receive any aid. 88% undergrads borrow to pay for school. Average cumulative indebtedness $25,926. **Criteria for awarding institutional aid:** *Non-need-based:* academics, alumni affiliation, leadership, music/drama, religious affiliation.

EASTERN CONNECTICUT STATE UNIVERSITY

83 Windham Street, Willimantic, CT 6226
Phone: 860-465-5286 • **Financial Aid Phone:** 860-365-5205
E-mail: admissions@easternct.edu • **CEEB Code:** 3966
Fax: 860-465-5286 • **Website:** www.easternct.edu

This public school was founded in 1889. It has a 182-acre campus.

RATINGS
Admissions Selectivity Rating: 77   **Fire Safety Rating:** 93

STUDENTS AND FACULTY
Enrollment: 5,035. **Student Body:** 53% female, 47% male, 7% out-of-state, 1% international (44 countries represented). Asian 2%, African American 7%, Caucasian 79%, Hispanic 7%, Native American <1%
Retention and Graduation: 77% freshmen return for sophomore year. 32% freshmen graduate within 4 years. 52% freshmen graduate within 6 years. 30% grads go on to further study within 1 year. **Faculty:** 198 full-time faculty, 96% hold PhDs, 44% are members of minority groups, 22% are women. 0% of classes are taught by teaching assistants.

ACADEMICS
Degrees: associate, bachelor's, master's. **Classes:** Most classes have 20–29 students. Most lab/discussion sessions have 10–19 students. **Majors with Highest Enrollment:** Business/Commerce; Psychology; Communication and Media Studies. **Special Study Options:** Accelerated program, cooperative education program, cross-registration, distance learning, double major, dual enrollment, exchange student program (domestic), honors program, independent study, internships, student-designed major, study abroad, teacher certification program, weekend college. **Honors programs:** University Honor Scholars Program offers interdisciplinary and independent study opportunities. **Disability Services:** Special programs offered to physically disabled students include note-taking services, reader services, tape recorders, tutors. **Career services:** Alumni network, alumni services, career/job search classes, career assessment, internships, regional alumni. Career services highlights include internships that lead to permanent employment.

FACILITIES
Housing: Coed dorms, apartments for single students. 95% of campus accessible to physically disabled. Art Gallery, Arboretum, Church Farm, Family/Child Development Center(2007), Green science bldg/labs(2008), electron microscope, planetarium,Media center with TV and radio station, Sports/Fitness Center and Studios,Center for Connecticut studies. **Computers:** 100% of libraries, 100% of dining areas, 100% of student union, 100% of common outdoor areas have wireless network access. Students can register for classes online. Administrative functions (other than registration) can be performed online.

CAMPUS LIFE
Environment: Village. **Activities:** Choral groups, concert band, dance, drama/theater, jazz band, literary magazine, music ensembles, musical theater, radio station, student government, student newspaper, television station, yearbook, International Student Organization. 68 registered organizations, 17 honor societies, 3 religious organizations. **Athletics (Intercollegiate):** *Men:* baseball,

basketball, cross-country, golf, lacrosse, soccer, track/field (outdoor), track/field (indoor). *Women:* basketball, cross-country, diving, field hockey, lacrosse, soccer, softball, swimming, track/field (outdoor), track/field (indoor), volleyball. **On-Campus Highlights:** Library, Student Center, Sports Center, Church Farm, Planetarium. **Environmental Initiatives:** Education Project http://www.ctenergyeducation.com/ Energy Solutions http://www.easternct.edu/depts/sustainenergy/energy_solutions/benchmarking.html Green Campus Initiative http://www.easternct.edu/depts/sustainenergy/colleges_n_uni/home_colleges_n_uni.html

ADMISSIONS
Freshman Academic Profile: Average high school GPA 3. 7% in top 10% of high school class, 25% in top 25% of high school class, 70% in top 50% of high school class. SAT Math middle 50% range 480-580. SAT Critical Reading middle 50% range 470-570. Minimum paper TOEFL 550. **Basis for Candidate Selection:** *Very important factors considered include:* Class rank, standardized test scores, talent/ability. *Important factors considered include:* academic GPA, recommendation(s), rigor of secondary school record, level of applicant's interest. *Other factors considered include:* application essay, character/personal qualities, extracurricular activities, interview, volunteer work, work experience. **Freshman Admission Requirements:** High school diploma is required and GED is accepted. *Academic units required:* 4 English, 3 mathematics, 2 science, (1 science labs), 2 foreign language, 2 social studies, 3 history. **Freshman Admission Statistics:** 3,493 applied, 65% admitted, 41% enrolled. **Transfer Admission Requirements:** High school transcript, college transcript(s), Minimum college GPA of 2.0 required. Lowest grade transferable C-. **General Admission Information:** Application Fee $50. Notification on a rolling basis, beginning on or about 12/1. Nonfall registration accepted. Credit offered for CEEB Advanced Placement tests.

COSTS AND FINANCIAL AID
Average book expense $1,554. **Required Forms and Deadlines:** FAFSA. **Types of Aid:** *Need-based scholarships/grants:* Federal Pell, SEOG, state scholarships/grants, private scholarships, the school's own gift aid. *Loans:* Subsidized Stafford, Unsubsidized Stafford, PLUS, Federal Perkins. *Student Employment:* Federal Work-Study Program available. Institutional employment available. Highest amount earned per year from on-campus jobs $5,500. Off-campus job opportunities are excellent. **Financial Aid Statistics:** 68% freshmen, 66% undergrads receive need-based scholarship or grant aid. 4% freshmen, 1% undergrads receive non-need-based scholarship or grant aid. 90% freshmen, 90% undergrads receive need-based self-help aid. 0% freshmen, 0% undergrads receive athletic scholarships. 69% freshmen, 75% undergrads receive any aid. 74% undergrads borrow to pay for school. Average cumulative indebtedness $17,448. **Criteria for awarding institutional aid:** *Non-need-based:* academics.

EASTERN ILLINOIS UNIVERSITY

600 Lincoln Avenue, Charleston, IL 61920
Phone: 217-581-2223 • **Financial Aid Phone:** 217-581-3713
E-mail: admissions@eiu.edu • **CEEB Code:** 1199
Fax: 217-581-7060 • **Website:** http://www.eiu.edu/ • **ACT Code:** 1016

This public school was founded in 1895. It has a 320-acre campus.

RATINGS
Admissions Selectivity Rating: 81   **Fire Safety Rating:** 93

STUDENTS AND FACULTY
Enrollment: 7,525. **Student Body:** 60% female, 40% male, 4% out-of-state, 1% international (31 countries represented). Asian 1%, African American 19%, Caucasian 70%, Hispanic 5%, Native American <1%
Retention and Graduation: 76% freshmen return for sophomore year. 33% freshmen graduate within 4 years. **Faculty:** 526 full-time faculty, 74% hold PhDs, 46% are members of minority groups, 13% are women. 3% of classes are taught by teaching assistants.

ACADEMICS
Degrees: bachelor's, master's, post-bachelor's certificate, post-master's certificate. **Classes:** Most classes have 20–29 students. **Majors with Highest Enrollment:** Kinesiology and Exercise Science; Communication; Liberal Arts and Sciences/Liberal Studies. **Special Study Options:** distance learning, double major, dual enrollment, exchange student program (domestic), external degree program, honors program, independent study, internships, study abroad, teacher certification program. **Honors programs:** Honors College. **Disability Services:** Special programs offered to physically disabled students include note-taking services, reader services, tape recorders, tutors. **Career services:** Alumni network, alumni services, career/job search classes, career assessment,

internships, regional alumni. Career services highlights include the externship program, which provides early professional direction and networking to students who are narrowing their major and career choices for further development, academically and experientially.

FACILITIES

Housing: Coed dorms, special housing for disabled students, men's dorms, women's dorms, fraternity/sorority housing, apartments for married students, apartments for single students. 80% of campus accessible to physically disabled. **Special Academic Facilities/Equipment:** Arts center, electron microscope. **Computers:** 100% of classrooms, 50% of dorms, 100% of libraries, 100% of dining areas, 100% of student union, have wireless network access. Students can register for classes online. Administrative functions (other than registration) can be performed online.

CAMPUS LIFE

Environment: Village. **Activities:** Choral groups, concert band, dance, drama/theater, jazz band, literary magazine, marching band, music ensembles, musical theater, opera, pep band, radio station, student government, student newspaper, symphony orchestra, television station, yearbook, Campus Ministries, International Student Organization. 232 registered organizations, 19 honor societies, 16 religious organizations. 15 fraternities, 11 sorority. **Athletics (Intercollegiate):** *Men:* baseball, basketball, cross-country, football, golf, soccer, swimming, tennis, track/field (outdoor), track/field (indoor). *Women:* basketball, cross-country, golf, rugby, soccer, softball, swimming, tennis, track/field (outdoor), track/field (indoor), volleyball. **On-Campus Highlights:** Doudna Fine Arts Building, Old Main, Martin Luther King Jr. University Union, Pemberton Hall, Student Recreation Center. **Environmental Initiatives:** Reduced campus water consumption by over 50%. Reduced campus energy consumption by over 30%. Opened the Renewable Energy Center replacing coal with renewable biomass.

ADMISSIONS

Freshman Academic Profile: Average high school GPA 3.05. 12% in top 10% of high school class, 33% in top 25% of high school class, 68% in top 50% of high school class. ACT middle 50% range 19-24. Minimum internet-based TOEFL 61. Minimum paper TOEFL 500. **Basis for Candidate Selection:** *Very important factors considered include:* academic GPA, rigor of secondary school record, standardized test scores, character/personal qualities. *Important factors considered include:* Class rank, extracurricular activities. *Other factors considered include:* application essay, recommendation(s). **Freshman Admission Requirements:** High school diploma is required and GED is accepted. *Academic units required:* 4 English, 3 mathematics, 3 science, (3 science labs), 3 social studies, 2 academic electives. **Freshman Admission Statistics:** 8,918 applied, 50% admitted, 25% enrolled. **Transfer Admission Requirements:** High school transcript, college transcript(s), standardized test scores, Minimum college GPA of 2.0 required. **General Admission Information:** Application Fee $30. Nonfall registration accepted. Admission may be deferred for a maximum of 1 year. Credit offered for CEEB Advanced Placement tests.

COSTS AND FINANCIAL AID

Annual in-state tuition $8,490. Annual out-of-state tuition $25,470. Room and board $9,358. Required fees $2,618. Average book expense $300. **Required Forms and Deadlines:** FAFSA. **Notification of Awards:** Applicants will be notified of awards on a rolling basis beginning 3/1. **Types of Aid:** *Need-based scholarships/grants:* Federal Pell, SEOG, state scholarships/grants, private scholarships, the school's own gift aid. *Loans:* Direct Subsidized Stafford, Direct Unsubsidized Stafford, Direct PLUS, Federal Perkins, college/university loans from institutional funds. *Student Employment:* Federal Work-Study Program available. Institutional employment available. Off-campus job opportunities are fair. **Financial Aid Statistics:** 78% freshmen, 74% undergrads receive need-based scholarship or grant aid. 58% freshmen, 43% undergrads receive non-need-based scholarship or grant aid. 84% freshmen, 85% undergrads receive need-based self-help aid. 2% freshmen, 2% undergrads receive athletic scholarships. 76% freshmen, 69% undergrads receive any aid. 82% undergrads borrow to pay for school. Average cumulative indebtedness $27,095. **Criteria for awarding institutional aid:** *Non-need-based:* academics, art, athletics, leadership, music/drama.

EASTERN KENTUCKY UNIVERSITY

SSB CPO 54, Richmond, KY 40475
Phone: 859-622-2106 · **Financial Aid Phone:** 859-622-2361
E-mail: admissions@eku.edu · **CEEB Code:** 1200
Fax: 859-622-8024 · **Website:** www.eku.edu · **ACT Code:** 1512

This public school was founded in 1906. It has a 675-acre campus.

STUDENTS AND FACULTY

Enrollment: 12,710. **Student Body:** 58% female, 42% male, 13% out-of-state, 1% international (36 countries represented). Asian 1%, African American 5%, Caucasian 99%, Hispanic 1%, Native American <1% **Faculty:** 599 full-time faculty, 69% hold PhDs, 48% are members of minority groups, 11% are women. 0% of classes are taught by teaching assistants.

ACADEMICS

Degrees: associate, bachelor's, certificate, master's, post-bachelor's certificate. **Classes:** Most classes have 10–19 students. **Majors with Highest Enrollment:** Elementary Education and Teaching; Criminal Justice/Law Enforcement Administration; Registered Nursing/Registered Nurse. **Special Study Options:** cooperative education program, distance learning, double major, English as a Second Language (ESL), honors program, independent study, internships, study abroad, teacher certification program. **Honors programs:** Honors Program: www.honors.eku.edu. **Disability Services:** Special programs offered to physically disabled students include note-taking services, reader services, tape recorders, tutors. **Career services:** Alumni network, alumni services, career/job search classes, career assessment, internships, regional alumni.

FACILITIES

Housing: Coed dorms, men's dorms, special housing for international students, women's dorms, fraternity/sorority housing, apartments for married students. 90% of campus accessible to physically disabled. **Special Academic Facilities/Equipment:** Hummel Planetarium, Giles Gallery. **Computers:** Students can register for classes online. Administrative functions (other than registration) can be performed online.

CAMPUS LIFE

Environment: Town. **Activities:** Choral groups, concert band, dance, drama/theater, jazz band, literary magazine, marching band, music ensembles, musical theater, pep band, radio station, student government, student newspaper, symphony orchestra. 178 registered organizations, 30 honor societies, 11 religious organization. 16 fraternities, 13 sororities. **Athletics (Intercollegiate):** *Men:* baseball, basketball, cheerleading, cross-country, football, golf, tennis, track/field (outdoor), track/field (indoor). *Women:* basketball, cheerleading, cross-country, golf, soccer, softball, tennis, track/field (outdoor), track/field (indoor), volleyball. **On-Campus Highlights:** Student Wellness Center (New), Library Café (New), Student Services Building (New), First Weekend Events.

ADMISSIONS

Freshman Academic Profile: SAT Math middle 50% range 440-450. SAT Critical Reading middle 50% range 440-450. SAT Writing middle 50% range 420-430. ACT middle 50% range 18-24. Minimum paper TOEFL 500. **Basis for Candidate Selection:** *Very important factors considered include:* academic GPA, standardized test scores. *Other factors considered include:* talent/ability. **Freshman Admission Requirements:** High school diploma is required and GED is accepted. *Academic units required:* 4 English, 3 mathematics, 3 science, (1 science labs), 2 foreign language, 3 social studies, 7 academic electives, 3 Health, Physical ED. = 0.5 and Art = 1. **Freshman Admission Statistics:** 6,928 applied, 69% admitted, 52% enrolled. **Transfer Admission Requirements:** college transcript(s), Minimum college GPA of 2.0 required. Lowest grade transferable D. **General Admission Information:** Application Fee $30. Regular application deadline 8/1. Notification on a rolling basis, beginning on or about 9/1. Nonfall registration accepted. Admission may be deferred for a maximum of 1 semester. Credit offered for CEEB Advanced Placement tests.

COSTS AND FINANCIAL AID

Annual out-of-state tuition $16,612. Room and board $5,288. Required fees $460. Average book expense $800. **Required Forms and Deadlines:** FAFSA. **Notification of Awards:** Applicants will be notified of awards on a rolling basis beginning 4/1. **Types of Aid:** *Need-based scholarships/grants:* Federal Pell, SEOG, state scholarships/grants, private scholarships, the school's own gift aid. *Loans:* Subsidized Stafford, Unsubsidized Stafford, PLUS, Federal Perkins, college/university loans from institutional funds. *Student Employment:* Federal Work-Study Program available. Institutional employment available. Highest amount earned per year from on-campus jobs $1,800. Off-campus job opportunities are good. **Financial Aid Statistics:** 60% freshmen, 58% undergrads receive need-based scholarship or grant aid. 80% freshmen, 51% undergrads receive non-need-based scholarship or grant aid. 74% freshmen, 81% undergrads receive need-based self-help aid. 2% freshmen, 1% undergrads receive athletic scholarships. 94% freshmen, 86% undergrads receive any aid. 69% undergrads borrow to pay for school. Average cumulative indebtedness $14,516. **Criteria for awarding institutional aid:** *Non-need-based:* academics, alumni affiliation, art, athletics, job skills, leadership, minority status, music/drama.

RATINGS

Admissions Selectivity Rating: 71   **Fire Safety Rating:** 83

EASTERN MENNONITE UNIVERSITY

1200 Park Rd., Harrisonburg, VA 22802
Phone: 540-432-4118 · **Financial Aid Phone:** 540-432-4137 · **CEEB Code:** 5181
Fax: 540-432-4444 · **Website:** www.emu.edu · **ACT Code:** 3708

This school, affiliated with the Mennonite Church, was founded in 1917. It has a 93-acre campus.

RATINGS
Admissions Selectivity Rating: 60*   **Fire Safety Rating:** 65

STUDENTS AND FACULTY
Student Body: (20 countries represented).
Retention and Graduation: 5% grads go on to further study within 1 year. 1% grads pursue arts and sciences degrees. 2% grads pursue medical degrees. **Faculty:** 0% of classes are taught by teaching assistants.

ACADEMICS
Degrees: Majors with Highest Enrollment: Psychology; Registered Nursing/Registered Nurse; Business Administration and Management. **Honors programs:** EMU's Honors Program accepts 10-14 academically-gifted first-year students into the selective Honors Program. Participation is renewable for up to 3 years. Honors students must maintain a 3.5 GPA and complete 9 SH of Honors Program Courses. Honors students gain access to many special educational opportunities and meet monthly for fellowship and discussion. **Disability Services:** Special programs offered to physically disabled students include note-taking services, reader services, tape recorders, tutors. **Career services:** alumni services, career/job search classes, career assessment, internships, regional alumni.

FACILITIES
Housing: 75% of campus accessible to physically disabled. **Special Academic Facilities/Equipment:** D. Ralph Hostetter Museum of Natural History, M. T. Brackbill Planetarium, arboretum, Menno Simons Historical Library. **Computers:** Administrative functions (other than registration) can be performed online.

CAMPUS LIFE
Environment: Town. **Activities:** 37 registered organizations, 2 honor societies, 4 religious organizations. **Athletics (Intercollegiate):** *Men:* baseball, basketball, cross-country, soccer, tennis, track/field (outdoor), track/field (indoor), volleyball. *Women:* basketball, cross-country, field hockey, soccer, softball, tennis, track/field (outdoor), track/field (indoor), volleyball. **On-Campus Highlights:** University Commons, Royals Den snack shop, Common Grounds coffeehouse, Campus Center Greeting Hall, Wood's Residence Halls, Park Woods.

ADMISSIONS
Freshman Academic Profile: 64% from public high schools. Minimum paper TOEFL 550. **General Admission Information:** Credit and/or placement offered for CEEB Advanced Placement tests.

COSTS AND FINANCIAL AID
Student Employment: Federal Work-Study Program available. Institutional employment available. Highest amount earned per year from on-campus jobs $3,500. Off-campus job opportunities are good. **Financial Aid Statistics:** 91% freshmen, 93% undergrads receive any aid.

EASTERN MICHIGAN UNIVERSITY

Eastern Michigan University, Ypsilanti, MI 48197
Phone: 734-487-3060 · **Financial Aid Phone:** 734-487-0455
E-mail: admissions@emich.edu · **CEEB Code:** 1201
Fax: 734-487-1484 · **Website:** www.emich.edu · **ACT Code:** 1990

This public school was founded in 1849. It has a 460-acre campus.

RATINGS
Admissions Selectivity Rating: 79   **Fire Safety Rating:** 78

STUDENTS AND FACULTY
Enrollment: 17,714. **Student Body:** 59% female, 41% male, 9% out-of-state, 2% international (80 countries represented). Asian 2%, African American 20%, Caucasian 66%, Hispanic 4%, Native American <1%.
Retention and Graduation: 13% freshmen graduate within 4 years. **Faculty:** 750 full-time faculty, 79% hold PhDs, 51% are members of minority groups, 19% are women. 3% of classes are taught by teaching assistants.

ACADEMICS
Degrees: bachelor's, doctoral, master's, post-bachelor's certificate, post-master's certificate. **Classes:** Most classes have 20-29 students. Most lab/discussion sessions have 20-29 students. **Majors with Highest Enrollment:** Registered Nursing/Registered Nurse; Psychology; Social Work. **Special Study Options:** Accelerated program, cooperative education program, distance learning, double major, dual enrollment, English as a Second Language (ESL), external degree program, honors program, independent study, internships, student-designed major, study abroad, teacher certification program, weekend college, Dual enrollment note: high school students may enroll in college courses while still enrolled in high school, but are required to apply for admission to Eastern. Combined degree programs: BA/MA, BA/BBA, BA/MSA, BS/MA, BS/MOT. **Disability Services:** Special programs offered to physically disabled students include note-taking services, reader services, tape recorders, tutors. **Career services:** Alumni network, alumni services, career/job search classes, career assessment, internships. We connect with area businesses to provide hands-on learning opportunities for our students. All three of the programs above work hand-in-hand toward helping students gain experience in their field of study (number one attributes employers look for in job candidates).

FACILITIES
Housing: Coed dorms, special housing for disabled students, special housing for international students, fraternity/sorority housing, apartments for married students, cooperative housing, apartments for single students, Theme Housing, house rental to sorority house. 80% of campus accessible to physically disabled. **Special Academic Facilities/Equipment:** Intermedia art gallery, paint research center, Sherzer observatory, Bruce T. Halle Library, Terrestial and Aquatics Ecology Research Facility, Coatings Research Institute, the John W. Porter Building housing the College of Education and the Marshall Building housing the College of Health and Human Services. **Computers:** 100% of classrooms, 25% of dorms, 100% of libraries, 100% of dining areas, 100% of student union, 15% of common outdoor areas have wireless network access. Students can register for classes online. Administrative functions (other than registration) can be performed online.

CAMPUS LIFE
Environment: City. **Activities:** Choral groups, concert band, dance, literary magazine, marching band, music ensembles, musical theater, pep band, radio station, student government, student newspaper, student-run film society, symphony orchestra, television station, Campus Ministries, International Student Organization. 220 registered organizations, 14 honor societies, 24 religious organizations. 11 fraternity, 13 sororities. **Athletics (Intercollegiate):** *Men:* basketball, diving, football, golf, swimming, track/field (outdoor), track/field (indoor), wrestling. *Women:* basketball, crew/rowing, diving, golf, gymnastics, soccer, softball, swimming, tennis, track/field (outdoor), track/field (indoor), volleyball. **On-Campus Highlights:** New Student Center, Recreations and Intramurals Building, The Lakehouse, Halle Library, Athletic Campus. **Environmental Initiatives:** Energy performance contract; Hiring an Energy & Sustainability Manager in March, 2008, position currently vacant as of February 2014; Recycling initiative.

ADMISSIONS
Freshman Academic Profile: Average high school GPA 3.27. 13% in top 10% of high school class, 39% in top 25% of high school class, 76% in top 50% of high school class. 85% from public high schools. SAT Math middle 50% range 450-560. SAT Critical Reading middle 50% range 420-560. SAT Writing middle 50% range 420-540. ACT middle 50% range 19-25. Minimum paper TOEFL 500. **Basis for Candidate Selection:** *Very important factors considered include:* academic GPA, standardized test scores. *Important factors considered include:* rigor of secondary school record, character/personal qualities. *Other factors considered include:* application essay, recommendation(s), extracurricular activities, interview, talent/ability. **Freshman Admission Requirements:** High school diploma is required and GED is accepted. **Freshman Admission Statistics:** 12,353 applied, 69% admitted, 43% enrolled. **Transfer Admission Requirements:** college transcript(s), Minimum college GPA of 2.0 required. Lowest grade transferable C. **General Admission Information:** Application Fee $30. Notification on a rolling basis, beginning on or about 10/1. Nonfall registration accepted. Admission may be deferred for a maximum of 1 year. Credit and/or placement offered for CEEB Advanced Placement tests.

COSTS AND FINANCIAL AID
Annual in-state tuition $8,244. Annual out-of-state tuition $24,287. Room and board $8,941. Required fees $1,419. Average book expense $1,000. **Required Forms and Deadlines:** FAFSA. **Notification of Awards:** Applicants will be notified of awards on a rolling basis beginning 3/1. **Types of Aid:** *Need-based scholarships/grants:* Federal Pell, SEOG, state scholarships/grants, private scholarships, the school's own gift aid. *Loans:* Subsidized Stafford, Unsubsidized Stafford, PLUS, Federal Perkins, state loans, college/university loans from institutional funds, Alternative (Private) Loans. *Student Employment:* Federal Work-Study Program available. Institutional employment available. Highest amount earned per year from on-campus jobs $13,375. Off-campus

job opportunities are excellent. **Financial Aid Statistics:** 71% freshmen, 74% undergrads receive need-based scholarship or grant aid. 79% freshmen, 44% undergrads receive non-need-based scholarship or grant aid. 71% freshmen, 80% undergrads receive need-based self-help aid. 3% freshmen, 3% undergrads receive athletic scholarships. 98% freshmen receive any aid. 69% undergrads borrow to pay for school. Average cumulative indebtedness $24,402. **Criteria for awarding institutional aid:** *Non-need-based:* academics, alumni affiliation, art, athletics, leadership, minority status, music/drama, state/district residency.

EASTERN NAZARENE COLLEGE

23 East Elm Avenue, Quincy, MA 02170-2999
Phone: 617-745-3711
E-mail: admissions@enc.edu · **CEEB Code:** 3365
Fax: 617-745-3992 · **Website:** www.enc.edu

This private school, affiliated with the Nazarene Church, was founded in 1918. It has a 19-acre campus.

RATINGS
Admissions Selectivity Rating: 60*   **Fire Safety Rating:** 60*

STUDENTS AND FACULTY
Student Body: 58% out-of-state.
Retention and Graduation: 22% grads go on to further study within 1 year. 17% grads pursue arts and sciences degrees. 1% grads pursue law degrees. 2% grads pursue business degrees. 2% grads pursue medical degrees. **Faculty:**

ACADEMICS
Degrees: associate, bachelor's, diploma, first professional certificate, master's. **Majors with Highest Enrollment:** Speech Communication and Rhetoric; Biology; Business/Commerce. **Special Study Options:** Accelerated program, cooperative education program, double major, honors program, independent study, internships, study abroad, teacher certification program. **Disability Services:** Special programs offered to physically disabled students include note-taking services, reader services, tape recorders, tutors. **Career services:** career assessment, internships.

FACILITIES
Housing: special housing for disabled students, men's dorms, women's dorms, apartments for married students, suites-men's and women's.

CAMPUS LIFE
Environment: Village. **Activities:** Choral groups, drama/theater, music ensembles, musical theater, radio station, student government, student newspaper, yearbook 1 religious organization. **Athletics (Intercollegiate):** *Men:* baseball, basketball, cross-country, soccer, tennis. *Women:* basketball, cross-country, soccer, softball, tennis, volleyball.

ADMISSIONS
Freshman Academic Profile: Minimum paper TOEFL 600. **Basis for Candidate Selection:** *Very important factors considered include:* application essay, recommendation(s), rigor of secondary school record, standardized test scores, interview. *Other factors considered include:* Class rank, character/personal qualities, extracurricular activities, religious affiliation/commitment, talent/ability, volunteer work, work experience. **Freshman Admission Requirements:** High school diploma is required and GED is accepted. *Academic units required:* 4 English, 2 mathematics, 1 science, 2 foreign language, 1 social studies, 1 history. **Transfer Admission Requirements:** High school transcript, college transcript(s), essay or personal statement, interview, standardized test scores, Minimum college GPA of 2.0 required. Lowest grade transferable c. **General Admission Information:** Application Fee $25. Nonfall registration accepted.

COSTS AND FINANCIAL AID
Average book expense $500. **Required Forms and Deadlines:** FAFSA, Institution's own financial aid form. **Types of Aid:** *Need-based scholarships/grants:* Federal Pell, SEOG, state scholarships/grants, private scholarships, the school's own gift aid, Church Scholarships. *Loans:* Subsidized Stafford, Unsubsidized Stafford, PLUS, Federal Perkins, state loans. *Student Employment:* Federal Work-Study Program available. Highest amount earned per year from on-campus jobs $3,000. **Financial Aid Statistics:** 34% freshmen, 22% undergrads receive need-based scholarship or grant aid. 97% freshmen, 99% undergrads receive non-need-based scholarship or grant aid. 85% freshmen, 75% undergrads receive need-based self-help aid. 0% freshmen, 0% undergrads receive athletic scholarships. Criteriafor awarding institutional aid: *Non-need-based:* academics, alumni affiliation, leadership, minority status, music/drama, religious affiliation, state/district residency.

EASTERN NEW MEXICO UNIVERSITY

Station #7, Portales, NM 88130
Phone: 575-562-2178 · **Financial Aid Phone:** 575-562-2194
E-mail: admissions@enmu.edu · **CEEB Code:** 4299
Fax: 575-562-2118 · **ACT Code:** 2636

This public school was founded in 1934. It has a 400-acre campus.

RATINGS
Admissions Selectivity Rating: 80   **Fire Safety Rating:** 87

STUDENTS AND FACULTY
Enrollment: 3,618. **Student Body:** 57% female, 43% male, 23% out-of-state, 3% international (23 countries represented). Asian 1%, African American 5%, Caucasian 54%, Hispanic 33%, Native American 3%
Retention and Graduation: 62% freshmen return for sophomore year. 11% freshmen graduate within 4 years. **Faculty:** 146 full-time faculty, 76% hold PhDs, 47% are members of minority groups, 14% are women. 3.4% of classes are taught by teaching assistants.

ACADEMICS
Degrees: associate, bachelor's, master's, terminal associate, transfer associate. **Classes:** Most classes have 10–19 students. Most lab/discussion sessions have 10–19 students. **Majors with Highest Enrollment:** Business Administration and Management; Elementary Education and Teaching; General Studies. **Special Study Options:** Accelerated program, distance learning, double major, dual enrollment, English as a Second Language (ESL), exchange student program (domestic), independent study, internships, student-designed major, teacher certification program. **Disability Services:** Special programs offered to physically disabled students include note-taking services, reader services, tape recorders, tutors. **Career services:** career assessment, internships.

FACILITIES
Housing: Coed dorms, special housing for disabled students, women's dorms, fraternity/sorority housing, apartments for married students, apartments for single students. 100% of campus accessible to physically disabled. **Special Academic Facilities/Equipment:** Natural history and historical museums, theatre, child development center, audiovisual center, electron microscopes, laser, KNEW Broadcast Center. **Computers:** Students can register for classes online. Administrative functions (other than registration) can be performed online.

CAMPUS LIFE
Environment: Village. **Activities:** Choral groups, concert band, dance, drama/theater, jazz band, literary magazine, marching band, music ensembles, radio station, student government, student newspaper, student-run film society, symphony orchestra, television station, Campus Ministries, International Student Organization. 55 registered organizations, 2 honor societies, 4 religious organizations. 4 fraternities, 2 sororities. **Athletics (Intercollegiate):** *Men:* baseball, basketball, cross-country, football, rodeo, soccer, track/field (outdoor). *Women:* basketball, cross-country, rodeo, soccer, softball, track/field (outdoor), volleyball. **On-Campus Highlights:** New Science facilities/Natural History Museum, Campus Union Building, Communications-Broadcast Center, Library, University Theatre Center. **Environmental Initiatives:** Water savings project Energy management project Development of solar energy project.

ADMISSIONS
Freshman Academic Profile: Average high school GPA 3.21. 11% in top 10% of high school class, 34% in top 25% of high school class, 68% in top 50% of high school class. 98% from public high schools. SAT Math middle 50% range 430-530. SAT Critical Reading middle 50% range 420-525. ACT middle 50% range 17-23. Minimum paper TOEFL 500. **Basis for Candidate Selection:** *Very important factors considered include:* academic GPA, standardized test scores. **Freshman Admission Requirements:** High school diploma is required and GED is accepted. **Freshman Admission Statistics:** 2,164 applied, 60% admitted, 48% enrolled. **Transfer Admission Requirements:** college transcript(s), statement of good standing from prior institution(s). Minimum college GPA of 2.0 required. Lowest grade transferable D. **General Admission Information:** Nonfall registration accepted. Admission may be deferred for a maximum of 0. Credit and/or placement offered for CEEB Advanced Placement tests.

COSTS AND FINANCIAL AID
Annual in-state tuition $2,688. Annual out-of-state tuition $8,220. Room and board $5,612. Required fees $1,212. Average book expense $500. **Required Forms and Deadlines:** FAFSA. **Notification of Awards:** Applicants will be notified of awards on a rolling basis beginning 4/15. **Types of Aid:** *Need-based scholarships/grants:* Federal Pell, SEOG, state scholarships/grants, the school's own gift aid. *Loans:* Subsidized Stafford, Unsubsidized Stafford, PLUS, Federal Perkins. *Student Employment:* Federal Work-Study Program available.

Institutional employment available. **Financial Aid Statistics:** 97% freshmen, 97% undergrads receive need-based scholarship or grant aid. 88% freshmen, 56% undergrads receive non-need-based scholarship or grant aid. 25% freshmen, 27% undergrads receive need-based self-help aid. 10% freshmen, 8% undergrads receive athletic scholarships. 99% freshmen, 91% undergrads receive any aid. 1% undergrads borrow to pay for school. Average cumulative indebtedness $11,911. **Criteria for awarding institutional aid:** *Non-need-based:* academics, alumni affiliation, art, athletics, leadership, music/drama, state/district residency.

EASTERN OREGON UNIVERSITY

One University Blvd, La Grande, OR 97850
Phone: 1-541-962-3393 · **Financial Aid Phone:** 1-800-452-8639
E-mail: admissions@eou.edu · **CEEB Code:** 4300
Fax: 541-962-3418 · **Website:** www.eou.edu · **ACT Code:** 3460

This public school was founded in 1929. It has a 121-acre campus.

RATINGS

Admissions Selectivity Rating: 78   **Fire Safety Rating:** 83

STUDENTS AND FACULTY

Enrollment: 2,997. **Student Body:** 63% female, 37% male, 28% out-of-state, 2% international (20 countries represented). Asian 2%, African American 3%, Caucasian 76%, Hispanic 6%, Native American 3%
Faculty: 106 full-time faculty, 75% hold PhDs, 42% are members of minority groups, 8% are women.

ACADEMICS

Degrees: bachelor's, master's. **Classes:** Most classes have 10–19 students. Most lab/discussion sessions have 10–19 students. **Majors with Highest Enrollment:** Business Administration, Management and Operations; Liberal Arts and Sciences/Liberal Studies; Education. **Special Study Options:** cooperative education program, cross-registration, distance learning, double major, dual enrollment, exchange student program (domestic), external degree program, honors program, independent study, internships, liberal arts/career combination, student-designed major, study abroad, teacher certification program, weekend college. **Disability Services:** Special programs offered to physically disabled students include note-taking services, reader services, tape recorders, tutors. **Career services:** alumni services, career/job search classes, career assessment, internships.

FACILITIES

Housing: Coed dorms, apartments for married students. 95% of campus accessible to physically disabled. **Special Academic Facilities/Equipment:** Art gallery, archaeological museum **Computers:** 40% of classrooms, 80% of libraries, 90% of dining areas, 90% of student union, 50% of common outdoor areas have wireless network access. Students can register for classes online.

CAMPUS LIFE

Environment: Village. **Activities:** Choral groups, concert band, dance, drama/theater, jazz band, literary magazine, music ensembles, musical theater, radio station, student government, student newspaper, symphony orchestra. 57 registered organizations, 2 honor societies, 4 religious organizations. **Athletics (Intercollegiate):** *Men:* basketball, cross-country, football, track/field (outdoor), track/field (indoor). *Women:* basketball, cross-country, soccer, softball, track/field (outdoor), track/field (indoor), volleyball. **On-Campus Highlights:** Loso Hall, Hoke Union, Community Stadium, Quinn Coliseum, Sports Practice Fields.

ADMISSIONS

Freshman Academic Profile: Average high school GPA 3.17. 8.9% in top 10% of high school class, 36.2% in top 25% of high school class, 73.7% in top 50% of high school class. SAT Math middle 50% range 410-520. SAT Critical Reading middle 50% range 410-530. SAT Writing middle 50% range 390-510. ACT middle 50% range 18-24. Minimum paper TOEFL 520. **Basis for Candidate Selection:** *Very important factors considered include:* academic GPA, rigor of secondary school record. *Important factors considered include:* recommendation(s), talent/ability. *Other factors considered include:* Class rank, application essay, standardized test scores, extracurricular activities, first generation, geographical residence, level of applicant's interest, volunteer work, work experience. **Freshman Admission Requirements:** High school diploma is required and GED is accepted. *Academic units required:* 4 English, 3 mathematics, 2 science, 2 foreign language. **Freshman Admission Statistics:** 1,530 applied, 64% admitted, 32% enrolled. **Transfer Admission Requirements:** college transcript(s), Minimum college GPA of 2.2 required. Lowest grade transferable D-. **General Admission Information:** Application Fee $50.

Regular application deadline 9/1. Notification on a rolling basis, beginning on or about 10/1. Nonfall registration accepted. Admission may be deferred for a maximum of 1 year. Credit offered for CEEB Advanced Placement tests.

COSTS AND FINANCIAL AID

Annual in-state tuition $6,030. Annual out-of-state tuition $16,110. Room and board $9,642. Required fees $1,410. Average book expense $1,425. **Required Forms and Deadlines:** FAFSA. **Notification of Awards:** Applicants will be notified of awards on a rolling basis beginning 4/1. **Types of Aid:** *Need-based scholarships/grants:* Federal Pell, SEOG, state scholarships/grants, private scholarships, the school's own gift aid. *Loans:* Subsidized Stafford, Unsubsidized Stafford, PLUS, Federal Perkins. *Student Employment:* Federal Work-Study Program available. Institutional employment available. Off-campus job opportunities are good. **Financial Aid Statistics:** 69% freshmen, 75% undergrads receive need-based scholarship or grant aid. 10% freshmen, 7% undergrads receive non-need-based scholarship or grant aid. 86% freshmen, 90% undergrads receive need-based self-help aid. 13% freshmen, 9% undergrads receive athletic scholarships. 72% undergrads borrow to pay for school. Average cumulative indebtedness $26,930. **Criteria for awarding institutional aid:** *Non-need-based:* academics, art, leadership, minority status, music/drama, state/district residency.

EASTERN UNIVERSITY

1300 Eagle Road, St. Davids, PA 19087-3696
Phone: 610-341-5967 · **Financial Aid Phone:** 610-341-5842
E-mail: ugadm@eastern.edu · **CEEB Code:** 2220
Fax: 610-341-1723 · **Website:** www.eastern.edu · **ACT Code:** 3562

This private school, affiliated with the American Baptist Church, was founded in 1952. It has a 107-acre campus.

RATINGS

Admissions Selectivity Rating: 82   **Fire Safety Rating:** 60*

STUDENTS AND FACULTY

Enrollment: 2,054. **Student Body:** 65% female, 35% male, 52% out-of-state, 1% international. Asian 1%, African American 12%, Caucasian 77%, Hispanic 5%, Native American <1%
Retention and Graduation: 77% freshmen return for sophomore year. 56% freshmen graduate within 4 years. 63% freshmen graduate within 6 years. 19% grads go on to further study within 1 year. 24% grads pursue arts and sciences degrees. 4% grads pursue law degrees. 4% grads pursue business degrees. **Faculty:** 79 full-time faculty, 78% hold PhDs, 42% are members of minority groups, 16% are women. 0% of classes are taught by teaching assistants.

ACADEMICS

Degrees: associate, bachelor's, master's, post-bachelor's certificate, post-master's certificate, transfer associate. **Classes:** Most classes have fewer than 10 students. Most lab/discussion sessions have 10–19 students. **Majors with Highest Enrollment:** Elementary Education and Teaching; Social Work; Business, Management, Marketing, and Related Support Services. **Special Study Options:** Accelerated program, cross-registration, double major, honors program, independent study, internships, student-designed major, study abroad, teacher certification program. **Disability Services:** Special programs offered to physically disabled students include note-taking services, reader services, tape recorders, tutors.

FACILITIES

Housing: Coed dorms, apartments for single students. 75% of campus accessible to physically disabled. **Special Academic Facilities/Equipment:** Planetarium. **Computers:** Students can register for classes online. Administrative functions (other than registration) can be performed online.

CAMPUS LIFE

Environment: Town. **Activities:** Choral groups, concert band, dance, drama/theater, jazz band, literary magazine, music ensembles, musical theater, pep band, student government, student newspaper, yearbook. 94 registered organizations, 10 honor societies, 20 religious organizations. **Athletics (Intercollegiate):** *Men:* baseball, basketball, golf, soccer, tennis. *Women:* basketball, field hockey, lacrosse, soccer, softball, tennis, volleyball.

ADMISSIONS

Freshman Academic Profile: Average high school GPA 3.34. 19% in top 10% of high school class, 47% in top 25% of high school class, 79% in top 50% of high school class. 75% from public high schools. SAT Math middle 50% range 490-590. SAT Critical Reading middle 50% range 510-610. ACT middle 50% range 19-31. Minimum paper TOEFL 213. **Basis for Candidate Selection:**

Very important factors considered include: Class rank, rigor of secondary school record, standardized test scores. *Important factors considered include:* application essay, recommendation(s), character/personal qualities, extracurricular activities, volunteer work. *Other factors considered include:* alumni/ae relation, interview, religious affiliation/commitment, talent/ability, work experience. **Freshman Admission Requirements:** High school diploma is required and GED is accepted. **Freshman Admission Statistics:** 1,174 applied, 77% admitted, 43% enrolled. **Transfer Admission Requirements:** High school transcript, college transcript(s), essay or personal statement, Minimum college GPA of 2.0 required. Lowest grade transferable C. **General Admission Information:** Application Fee $25. Nonfall registration accepted. Admission may be deferred for a maximum of 12 months. Credit and/or placement offered for CEEB Advanced Placement tests.

COSTS AND FINANCIAL AID

Annual tuition $17,700. Room and board $7,600. Required fees $40. Average book expense $830. **Required Forms and Deadlines:** FAFSA. **Types of Aid:** *Need-based scholarships/grants:* Federal Pell, SEOG, state scholarships/grants, private scholarships, the school's own gift aid. *Loans:* Subsidized Stafford, Unsubsidized Stafford, PLUS, Federal Perkins, Alternative loans. *Student Employment:* Highest amount earned per year from on-campus jobs $1,200. **Financial Aid Statistics:** 100% freshmen receive need-based scholarship or grant aid. 34% freshmen receive non-need-based scholarship or grant aid. 88% freshmen receive need-based self-help aid. 0% freshmen receive athletic scholarships. **Criteria for awarding institutional aid:** *Non-need-based:* academics, leadership, music/drama, religious affiliation, state/district residency.

EASTERN WASHINGTON UNIVERSITY

304 Sutton Hall, Cheney, WA 99004
Phone: 509-359-6692 · **Financial Aid Phone:** 509-359-2314
E-mail: admissions@ewu.edu · **CEEB Code:** 4301
Fax: 509-359-6692 · **Website:** www.ewu.edu · **ACT Code:** 4454

This public school was founded in 1882. It has a 335-acre campus.

RATINGS

Admissions Selectivity Rating: 71   **Fire Safety Rating:** 75

STUDENTS AND FACULTY

Enrollment: 12,402. **Student Body:** 54% female, 46% male, 6% out-of-state, 3% international (70 countries represented). Asian 3%, African American 3%, Caucasian 64%, Hispanic 14%, Native American 1%
Retention and Graduation: 20% freshmen graduate within 4 years. **Faculty:** 462 full-time faculty, 99% hold PhDs, 44% are members of minority groups, 17% are women. 0% of classes are taught by teaching assistants.

ACADEMICS

Degrees: bachelor's, certificate, master's, post-master's certificate. **Classes:** Most classes have 20–29 students. Most lab/discussion sessions have 20–29 students. **Majors with Highest Enrollment:** Business Administration and Management; Biology/Biological Sciences; Accounting. **Special Study Options:** distance learning, double major, English as a Second Language (ESL), honors program, independent study, internships, student-designed major, study abroad, teacher certification program. **Honors programs:** EWU Honors Combined degree programs: BA/MA. **Disability Services:** Special programs offered to physically disabled students include note-taking services, reader services, tape recorders.

FACILITIES

Housing: Coed dorms, special housing for disabled students, fraternity/sorority housing, apartments for married students, Wellness Housing, Theme Housing. 77% of campus accessible to physically disabled. **Special Academic Facilities/Equipment:** Anthropology museum, on-campus elementary school, education lab, primate research center, marine biology lab, ecological studies lab, wildlife refuge, planetarium. **Computers:** Students can register for classes online. Administrative functions (other than registration) can be performed online.

CAMPUS LIFE

Environment: Town. **Activities:** Choral groups, concert band, dance, drama/theater, jazz band, literary magazine, marching band, music ensembles, musical theater, pep band, radio station, student government, student newspaper, student-run film society, symphony orchestra, Campus Ministries, International Student Organization, Model UN. 100 registered organizations, 14 honor societies, 10 religious organizations. 5 fraternities, 5 sororities. **Athletics (Intercollegiate):** *Men:* basketball, cross-country, football, golf, tennis, track/field (outdoor), track/field (indoor). *Women:* basketball, cross-country, golf, soccer, tennis, track/field (outdoor), track/field (indoor), volleyball. **On-Campus High-**

lights: Pence Union Building, CyberCafe, Phase Athletic Facilities, Woodward Stadium, Central campus mall, EWU Gallery of Art. **Environmental Initiatives:** Facilities Maintenance. Energy Management Program: Limiting the greenhouse gas emission. Student Events: 1. Recycle Mania Competition http://www.ewu.edu/About/EWU-News/RecycleMania.xml 2. Human Powered paper vehicle competition http://www.ewu.edu/HPPV.xml 3. Campus wide recycling & composting. Ride Share/alternative transportation program http://access.ewu.edu/Commute-Trip-Reduction/CTR-Options.xml

ADMISSIONS

Freshman Academic Profile: Average high school GPA 3.23. 95% from public high schools. SAT Math middle 50% range 430-540. SAT Critical Reading middle 50% range 420-530. SAT Writing middle 50% range 400-510. ACT middle 50% range 17-23. Minimum internet-based TOEFL 71. Minimum paper TOEFL 525. **Basis for Candidate Selection:** *Very important factors considered include:* academic GPA, standardized test scores. *Important factors considered include:* application essay, rigor of secondary school record. *Other factors considered include:* character/personal qualities, extracurricular activities, interview, talent/ability, volunteer work, work experience. **Freshman Admission Requirements:** High school diploma or equivalent is not required. *Academic units required:* 4 English, 3 mathematics, 2 science, (1 science labs), 2 foreign language, 3 social studies, 1 visual/performing arts. **Freshman Admission Statistics:** 4,987 applied, 74% admitted, 44% enrolled. **Transfer Admission Requirements:** college transcript(s), essay or personal statement, Minimum college GPA of 2.0 required. Lowest grade transferable D-. **General Admission Information:** Application Fee $50. Regular application deadline 8/15. Notification on a rolling basis, beginning on or about 11/1. Nonfall registration accepted. Admission may be deferred for a maximum of 1 year. Credit and/or placement offered for CEEB Advanced Placement tests.

COSTS AND FINANCIAL AID

Required Forms and Deadlines: FAFSA. **Notification of Awards:** Applicants will be notified of awards on a rolling basis beginning 4/1. **Types of Aid:** *Need-based scholarships/grants:* Federal Pell, SEOG, state scholarships/grants, private scholarships, the school's own gift aid. *Loans:* Subsidized Stafford, Unsubsidized Stafford, PLUS, Federal Perkins. *Student Employment:* Highest amount earned per year from on-campus jobs $2,457. **Financial Aid Statistics:** 77% freshmen, 74% undergrads receive need-based scholarship or grant aid. 53% freshmen, 27% undergrads receive non-need-based scholarship or grant aid. 68% freshmen, 78% undergrads receive need-based self-help aid. 2% freshmen, 2% undergrads receive athletic scholarships. 69% freshmen, 59% undergrads receive any aid. 58% undergrads borrow to pay for school. Average cumulative indebtedness $24,673. **Criteria for awarding institutional aid:** *Non-need-based:* academics, alumni affiliation, athletics, state/district residency.

ECKERD COLLEGE

Best 380

4200 54th Avenue South, St.Petersburg, FL 33711
Phone: 727-864-8331 · **Financial Aid Phone:** 727-864-8854
E-mail: admissions@eckerd.edu
Fax: 727-866-2304 · **Website:** www.eckerd.edu · **ACT Code:** 731

This private school, affiliated with the Presbyterian Church, was founded in 1958. It has a 188-acre campus.

RATINGS

Admissions Selectivity Rating: 75   **Fire Safety Rating:** 75

STUDENTS AND FACULTY

Enrollment: 1,802. **Student Body:** 61% female, 39% male, 83% out-of-state, 4% international (39 countries represented). Asian 2%, African American 2%, Caucasian 80%, Hispanic 8%, Native American <1%
Retention and Graduation: 59% freshmen graduate within 4 years. 65% freshmen graduate within 6 years. **Faculty:** 114 full-time faculty, 95% hold PhDs, 39% are members of minority groups, 11% are women. 0% of classes are taught by teaching assistants.

ACADEMICS

Degrees: bachelor's. **Classes:** Most classes have 20–29 students. Most lab/discussion sessions have 10–19 students. **Majors with Highest Enrollment:** Environmental Studies; Marine Biology and Biological Oceanography; Psychology. **Special Study Options:** Accelerated program, double major, honors program, independent study, internships, liberal arts/career combination, student-designed major, study abroad. **Honors programs:** Ford Apprentice Scholar Program The Honors Program at Eckerd College. Combined degree programs: BA/MEng. **Disability Services:** Special programs offered to physically disabled students include reader services, tape recorders, tutors. **Career services:** Alumni network, alumni services, career assessment, internships, regional alumni. Career services highlights include our 90% success rate placing students in internship experiences.

FACILITIES

Housing: Coed dorms, women's dorms, suite-style dorms, wellness housing, pet dorms, community service dorms. 95% of campus accessible to physically disabled. **Special Academic Facilities/Equipment:** Language lab, oral communications lab, marine science center. **Computers:** 100% of classrooms, 100% of dorms, 100% of libraries, 100% of dining areas, 100% of student union, 90% of common outdoor areas have wireless network access. Students can register for classes online. Administrative functions (other than registration) can be performed online.

CAMPUS LIFE

Environment: City. **Activities:** Choral groups, concert band, dance, drama/theater, literary magazine, music ensembles, radio station, student government, student newspaper, television station, Campus Ministries, International Student Organization, Model UN. 74 registered organizations, 8 honor societies, 3 religious organizations. **Athletics (Intercollegiate):** *Men:* baseball, basketball, golf, sailing, soccer, tennis. *Women:* basketball, golf, sailing, soccer, softball, tennis, volleyball. **On-Campus Highlights:** Peter Armacost Library, Turley Athletic Complex, Gailbraith Marine Science Lab, Hough Campus Center/Campus Pub, Eckerd Waterfront/Wallace Boathouse, Awarded Phi Beta Kappa Chapter in Summer 2003. **Environmental Initiatives:** The yellow bike has in recent years become a new symbol of Eckerd College. The Yellow Bike Program started in the spring of 2004, and since then it has gained national recognition. Students, faculty, staff, and even the College President can be spotted riding them. The goal of the program is to have less vehicle traffic which decreases greenhouse gas emissions and reduces our harm to the environment. The bikes on campus will help lead to a mostly walking campus, and an eco-friendly campus. The Yellow Bike Program was recognized in 2005 by the National Wildlife Federation, and it has gained local and national news attention. The campus vegetable garden; The UHaul Car Share program.

ADMISSIONS

Freshman Academic Profile: Average high school GPA 3.39. SAT Math middle 50% range 500-610. SAT Critical Reading middle 50% range 510-630. ACT middle 50% range 23-29. Minimum internet-based TOEFL 79. Minimum paper TOEFL 550. **Basis for Candidate Selection:** *Very important factors considered include:* academic GPA, rigor of secondary school record. *Important factors considered include:* application essay, recommendation(s), standardized test scores, character/personal qualities, extracurricular activities, interview, talent/ability. *Other factors considered include:* Class rank, alumni/ae relation, first generation, level of applicant's interest, volunteer work, work experience. **Freshman Admission Requirements:** High school diploma is required and GED is accepted. **Freshman Admission Statistics:** 2,498 applied, 84% admitted, 24% enrolled. **Transfer Admission Requirements:** college transcript(s), essay or personal statement, statement of good standing from prior institution(s). Minimum college GPA of 2.5 required. Lowest grade transferable C. **General Admission Information:** Application Fee $35. Notification on a rolling basis, beginning on or about 10/1. Nonfall registration accepted. Admission may be deferred for a maximum of 1 year. Credit and/or placement offered for CEEB Advanced Placement tests.

COSTS AND FINANCIAL AID

Annual tuition $38,342. Room and board $10,550. Required fees $326. Average book expense $1,200. **Required Forms and Deadlines:** FAFSA. **Notification of Awards:** Applicants will be notified of awards on a rolling basis beginning 2/15. **Types of Aid:** *Need-based scholarships/grants:* Federal Pell, SEOG, state scholarships/grants, private scholarships, the school's own gift aid. *Loans:* Direct Subsidized Stafford, Direct Unsubsidized Stafford, Direct PLUS, Federal Perkins, college/university loans from institutional funds. *Student Employment:* Federal Work-Study Program available. Institutional employment available. Highest amount earned per year from on-campus jobs $2,500. Off-campus job opportunities are excellent. **Financial Aid Statistics:** 100% freshmen, 100% undergrads receive need-based scholarship or grant aid. 0% freshmen, 0% undergrads receive non-need-based scholarship or grant aid. 100% freshmen, 100% undergrads receive need-based self-help aid. 1% freshmen, 2% undergrads receive athletic scholarships. 97% freshmen, 95% undergrads receive any aid. 59% undergrads borrow to pay for school. Average cumulative indebtedness $25,791. **Criteria for awarding institutional aid:** *Non-need-based:* academics, art, athletics, music/drama, religious affiliation, state/district residency.

EDGEWOOD COLLEGE

1000 Edgewood College Drive, Madison, WI 53711-1997
Phone: 608-663-2294 · **Financial Aid Phone:** 608-663-4300
E-mail: admissions@edgewood.edu · **CEEB Code:** 1202
Fax: 608-663-2214 · **Website:** www.edgewood.edu · **ACT Code:** 4582

This private school, affiliated with the Roman Catholic Church, was founded in 1927. It has a 55-acre campus.

RATINGS

Admissions Selectivity Rating: 79   **Fire Safety Rating:** 78

STUDENTS AND FACULTY

Enrollment: 1,863. **Student Body:** 71% female, 29% male, 7% out-of-state, 4% international (44 countries represented). Asian 3%, African American 2%, Caucasian 80%, Hispanic 6%, Native American <1%
Retention and Graduation: 36% freshmen graduate within 4 years. 62% freshmen graduate within 6 years. **Faculty:** 158 full-time faculty, 72% hold PhDs, 58% are members of minority groups, 9% are women. 0% of classes are taught by teaching assistants.

ACADEMICS

Degrees: associate, bachelor's, master's. **Classes:** Most classes have 10–19 students. **Majors with Highest Enrollment:** Registered Nursing/Registered Nurse; Business/Commerce; Psychology. **Special Study Options:** Accelerated program, double major, dual enrollment, honors program, independent study, internships, liberal arts/career combination, student-designed major, study abroad, teacher certification program. **Honors programs:** We have an Honors Program for undergraduates. Combined degree programs: Undergraduate degrees from Edgewood and UW/Madison or Marquette. **Disability Services:** Special programs offered to physically disabled students include note-taking services, reader services, tape recorders, tutors. **Career services:** Alumni network, alumni services, career/job search classes, career assessment, internships, regional alumni. Career services highlights include career assessment, which is provided to all incoming students. Career services are available at no charge to alumni, and we provide an alumni mentor program.

FACILITIES

Housing: Coed dorms, special housing for disabled students, women's dorms, Theme Housing. **Special Academic Facilities/Equipment:** DeRicci Art Gallery, and Science Exploration Center. **Computers:** 90% of classrooms, 100% of dorms, 100% of libraries, 100% of dining areas, 100% of student union, 80% of common outdoor areas have wireless network access. Students can register for classes online. Administrative functions (other than registration) can be performed online.

CAMPUS LIFE

Environment: City. **Activities:** Choral groups, concert band, dance, drama/theater, jazz band, literary magazine, marching band, music ensembles, musical theater, pep band, student government, student newspaper, symphony orchestra, Campus Ministries, International Student Organization. 45 registered organizations, 4 honor societies, 1 religious organization. **Athletics (Intercollegiate):** *Men:* baseball, basketball, cross-country, golf, soccer, tennis, track/field (outdoor), track/field (indoor). *Women:* basketball, cross-country, golf, soccer, softball, tennis, track/field (outdoor), track/field (indoor), volleyball. **On-Campus Highlights:** Dominican Hall, Mazzuchelli Hall, Lake Wingra Boardwalk, Predolin Humanities Center, SondeRegger Science Center. **Environmental Initiatives:** The Campus Sustainability Coordinating Team has completed a Campus Sustainability Plan, components of which will be incorporated into the College's Master Plan. The recently completed Visual and Theater Arts Center (The Stream) is a registered LEED NC project, and is expected to receive Gold certification. We are a Founding Circle member of the Billion Dollar Green Challenge, a revolving fund to provide financing for campus sustainability projects. http://greenbillion.org/about/

ADMISSIONS

Freshman Academic Profile: Average high school GPA 3.4. 16.5% in top 10% of high school class, 44.1% in top 25% of high school class, 83.5% in top 50% of high school class. 92% from public high schools. SAT Math middle 50% range 550-580. SAT Critical Reading middle 50% range 320-400. ACT middle 50% range 20-25. Minimum internet-based TOEFL 71. Minimum paper TOEFL 525. **Basis for Candidate Selection:** *Very important factors considered include:* Class rank, academic GPA, standardized test scores. *Other factors considered include:* application essay, recommendation(s). **Freshman Admission Requirements:** High school diploma is required and GED is accepted. *Academic units required:* 4 English, 2 mathematics, 2 science, (1 science labs), 2 foreign language, 2 social studies, 1 history, 0 visual/performing arts, 0 computer science, 0 academic electives. **Freshman Admission Statistics:**

1,253 applied, 76% admitted, 30% enrolled. **Transfer Admission Requirements:** High school transcript, college transcript(s), Minimum college GPA of 2.0 required. Lowest grade transferable C-. **General Admission Information:** Application Fee $25. Regular application deadline 8/14. Notification on a rolling basis, beginning on or about 9/15. Nonfall registration accepted. Admission may be deferred for a maximum of 12 months. Credit and/or placement offered for CEEB Advanced Placement tests.

COSTS AND FINANCIAL AID

Annual tuition $25,590. Room and board $8,973. Average book expense $800. **Required Forms and Deadlines:** FAFSA. **Notification of Awards:** Applicants will be notified of awards on a rolling basis beginning 3/15. **Types of Aid:** *Need-based scholarships/grants:* Federal Pell, SEOG, state scholarships/grants, private scholarships, the school's own gift aid. *Loans:* Subsidized Stafford, Unsubsidized Stafford, PLUS, Federal Perkins, state loans, college/university loans from institutional funds. *Student Employment:* Federal Work-Study Program available. Institutional employment available. Highest amount earned per year from on-campus jobs $2,000. Off-campus job opportunities are good. **Financial Aid Statistics:** 100% freshmen, 98% undergrads receive need-based scholarship or grant aid. 7% freshmen, 6% undergrads receive non-need-based scholarship or grant aid. 92% freshmen, 94% undergrads receive need-based self-help aid. 0% freshmen, 0% undergrads receive athletic scholarships. 100% freshmen, 93% undergrads receive any aid. 77% undergrads borrow to pay for school. Average cumulative indebtedness $27,278. **Criteria for awarding institutional aid:** *Non-need-based:* academics, alumni affiliation, art, leadership, music/drama, religious affiliation.

EDINBORO UNIVERSITY OF PENNSYLVANIA

200 East Normal Street, Edinboro, PA 16444
Phone: 814-732-2761 · **Financial Aid Phone:** 814-732-3500
E-mail: eup_admissions@edinboro.edu · **CEEB Code:** 2651
Fax: 814-732-2420 · **Website:** http://www.edinboro.edu/ · **ACT Code:** 3702

This public school was founded in 1857. It has a 585-acre campus.

RATINGS

Admissions Selectivity Rating: 73   **Fire Safety Rating:** 95

STUDENTS AND FACULTY

Enrollment: 6,301. **Student Body:** 56% female, 44% male, 11% out-of-state, 1% international (31 countries represented). Asian 1%, African American 9%, Caucasian 87%, Hispanic 2%, Native American <1%
Retention and Graduation: 75% freshmen return for sophomore year. 24% freshmen graduate within 4 years. 47% freshmen graduate within 6 years.
Faculty: 346 full-time faculty, 46% are members of minority groups, 7% are women. 0% of classes are taught by teaching assistants.

ACADEMICS

Degrees: associate, bachelor's, master's, post-bachelor's certificate, post-master's certificate. **Classes:** Most classes have 20–29 students. **Majors with Highest Enrollment:** Fine/Studio Arts; Business Administration and Management; Criminal Justice/Safety Studies. **Special Study Options:** cooperative education program, cross-registration, distance learning, double major, dual enrollment, honors program, independent study, internships, liberal arts/career combination, student-designed major, study abroad, teacher certification program. **Honors programs:** Admission to the Upper Division Honors Program, may be made by any full time EUP student who has completed 63 credit hours with an overall GPA of 3.4 or higher. They must also provide letters of support from two faculty members, secure approval of their academic advisor, and complete a proposal for the Senior Project in consultation with the Honors Director, Academic Advisor and and Faculty Member who will supervise the Senior Project. Combined degree programs: BA/MEng. **Disability Services:** Special programs offered to physically disabled students include note-taking services, reader services, tape recorders, tutors. **Career services:** Alumni network, alumni services, career/job search classes, career assessment, internships, regional alumni. Career services highlights include extensive internship opportunities.

FACILITIES

Housing: Coed dorms, special housing for disabled students, Living-Learning and Suite Style housing. Choosing to become part of a living-learning community is a unique opportunity for any student to live on the same floor with others who share the same major, filed of study, or interest area. Participants will interact with faculty and staff outside of the classroom through programs, activities, and events. Residents are able to gain assistance and ideas from peers who share their strong commitment to the living-learning experience. 98% of campus accessible to physically disabled. **Special Academic Facilities/Equip-**

ment: Planetarium, Solar Observatory, Governor George Leader Speech and Hearing Center, Bates Art Gallery, Bruce Gallery. **Computers:** 90% of classrooms, 30% of dorms, 100% of libraries, 100% of dining areas, 75% of student union, 40% of common outdoor areas have wireless network access. Students can register for classes online. Administrative functions (other than registration) can be performed online.

CAMPUS LIFE

Environment: Rural. **Activities:** Choral groups, dance, drama/theater, jazz band, literary magazine, marching band, music ensembles, opera, radio station, student government, student newspaper, student-run film society, television station, Campus Ministries, International Student Organization. 157 registered organizations, 13 honor societies, 4 religious organizations. 10 fraternities, 7 sororities. **Athletics (Intercollegiate):** *Men:* basketball, cross-country, football, swimming, track/field (outdoor), track/field (indoor), wheel-chair basketball, wrestling. *Women:* basketball, cross-country, lacrosse, soccer, softball, swimming, track/field (outdoor), track/field (indoor), volleyball. **On-Campus Highlights:** Frank G. Pogue Student Center, Baron-Forness Library, R. Benjamin Wiley Arts & Sciences Center, Louis J. Cole Memorial Auditorium, McComb Fieldhouse, Planetarium.

ADMISSIONS

Freshman Academic Profile: Average high school GPA 3.15. 5% in top 10% of high school class, 20% in top 25% of high school class, 51% in top 50% of high school class. N/A% from public high schools. SAT Math middle 50% range 410-520. SAT Critical Reading middle 50% range 415-520. ACT middle 50% range 17-23. Minimum internet-based TOEFL 61. Minimum paper TOEFL 500. **Basis for Candidate Selection:** *Very important factors considered include:* Class rank, academic GPA, rigor of secondary school record, standardized test scores. *Other factors considered include:* application essay, recommendation(s), character/personal qualities, extracurricular activities, interview, talent/ability, volunteer work, work experience. **Freshman Admission Requirements:** High school diploma is required and GED is accepted. **Freshman Admission Statistics:** 4,411 applied, 73% admitted, 44% enrolled. **Transfer Admission Requirements:** High school transcript, college transcript(s), statement of good standing from prior institution(s). Minimum college GPA of 2.0 required. Lowest grade transferable C-. **General Admission Information:** Application Fee $30. Notification on a rolling basis, beginning on or about 9/15. Nonfall registration accepted. Admission may be deferred for a maximum of 1 year. Credit and/or placement offered for CEEB Advanced Placement tests.

COSTS AND FINANCIAL AID

Annual in-state tuition $5,554. Annual out-of-state tuition $8,332. Room and board $7,130. Required fees $1,762. Average book expense $900. **Required Forms and Deadlines:** FAFSA. **Notification of Awards:** Applicants will be notified of awards on a rolling basis beginning 3/22. **Types of Aid:** *Need-based scholarships/grants:* Federal Pell, SEOG, state scholarships/grants, private scholarships, the school's own gift aid. *Loans:* Direct Subsidized Stafford, Direct Unsubsidized Stafford, Subsidized Stafford, Unsubsidized Stafford, PLUS, Federal Perkins, Federal Nursing. *Student Employment:* Federal Work-Study Program available. Institutional employment available. Highest amount earned per year from on-campus jobs $7,233. Off-campus job opportunities are good. **Financial Aid Statistics:** 90% freshmen, 92% undergrads receive need-based scholarship or grant aid. 94% freshmen, 94% undergrads receive non-need-based scholarship or grant aid. 82% freshmen, 86% undergrads receive need-based self-help aid. 3% freshmen, 2% undergrads receive athletic scholarships. 91% freshmen, 88% undergrads receive any aid. 46% undergrads borrow to pay for school. Average cumulative indebtedness $16,297. **Criteria for awarding institutional aid:** *Non-need-based:* academics, alumni affiliation, art, athletics, job skills, leadership, minority status, music/drama, religious affiliation, state/district residency.

ELIZABETH CITY STATE UNIVERSITY

1704 Weeksville Road, Elizabeth City, NC 27909
Phone: 252-335-3305
E-mail: admissions@mail.ecsu.edu · **CEEB Code:** 5629
Fax: 252-335-3537 · **Website:** www.ecsu.edu · **ACT Code:** 3095

This public school was founded in 1891. It has a 114-acre campus.

RATINGS

Admissions Selectivity Rating: 70   **Fire Safety Rating:** 60*

STUDENTS AND FACULTY

Enrollment: 2,015. **Student Body:** 62% female, 38% male, 12% out-of-state, 0% international. Asian 0%, African American 77%, Caucasian 22%, Hispanic 1%, Native American <1%

Retention and Graduation: 39% freshmen graduate within 4 years. 51% freshmen graduate within 6 years. 20% grads go on to further study within 1 year. 20% grads pursue arts and sciences degrees. **Faculty:** 114 full-time faculty, 70% hold PhDs, 27% are members of minority groups, 80% are women.

ACADEMICS

Degrees: bachelor's, master's. **Classes:** Most classes have fewer than 10 students. **Special Study Options:** cooperative education program, distance learning, double major, honors program, independent study, internships, liberal arts/career combination, teacher certification program, weekend college. **Career services:** alumni services, career/job search classes, career assessment, internships.

FACILITIES

Housing: Coed dorms, men's dorms, women's dorms, apartments for single students, College-leased housing available. **Special Academic Facilities/Equipment:** Lab school, planetarium, science complex, music engineering station. **Computers:** Students can register for classes online. Administrative functions (other than registration) can be performed online.

CAMPUS LIFE

Environment: Village. **Activities:** Choral groups, concert band, dance, drama/theater, jazz band, literary magazine, marching band, music ensembles, musical theater, pep band, radio station, student government, student newspaper, symphony orchestra, television station, yearbook. 46 registered organizations, 3 honor societies, 4 religious organizations. 4 fraternities, 4 sororities. **Athletics (Intercollegiate):** *Men:* baseball, basketball, cheerleading, cross-country, football, golf, softball, tennis, track/field (outdoor), volleyball. *Women:* baseball, basketball, cheerleading, cross-country, golf, softball, tennis, track/field (outdoor), volleyball.

ADMISSIONS

Freshman Academic Profile: 99% from public high schools. SAT Math middle 50% range 360-450. SAT Critical Reading middle 50% range 360-450. Minimum paper TOEFL 550. **Basis for Candidate Selection:** *Very important factors considered include:* rigor of secondary school record, standardized test scores, character/personal qualities, geographical residence, state residency. *Important factors considered include:* Class rank, racial/ethnic status, talent/ability. *Other factors considered include:* application essay, recommendation(s), alumni/ae relation, extracurricular activities, interview, religious affiliation/commitment, work experience. **Freshman Admission Requirements:** High school diploma is required and GED is accepted. *Academic units required:* 4 English, 3 mathematics, 3 science, 1 social studies, 1 history, 8 academic electives. **Freshman Admission Statistics:** 1,262 applied, 77% admitted, 48% enrolled. **Transfer Admission Requirements:** High school transcript, college transcript(s), statement of good standing from prior institution(s). Minimum college GPA of 2.0 required. Lowest grade transferable C. **General Admission Information:** Application Fee $30. Regular application deadline 8/1. Nonfall registration accepted. Admission may be deferred for a maximum of one year. Credit and/or placement offered for CEEB Advanced Placement tests.

COSTS AND FINANCIAL AID

Required Forms and Deadlines: FAFSA, Institution's own financial aid form. **Notification of Awards:** Applicants will be notified of awards on or about 4/1. **Types of Aid:** *Need-based scholarships/grants:* Federal Pell, SEOG, state scholarships/grants, private scholarships, the school's own gift aid. *Loans:* Subsidized Stafford, Unsubsidized Stafford, PLUS, Federal Perkins, college/university loans from institutional funds. *Student Employment:* Federal Work-Study Program available. Highest amount earned per year from on-campus jobs $643. Off-campus job opportunities are fair.

ELIZABETHTOWN COLLEGE

Leffler House, Elizabethtown, PA 17022
Phone: 717-361-1400 • **Financial Aid Phone:** 717-361-1404
E-mail: admissions@etown.edu • **CEEB Code:** 2225
Fax: 717-361-1365 • **Website:** www.etown.edu • **ACT Code:** 3568

This private school, affiliated with the Church of Brethren Church, was founded in 1899. It has a 193-acre campus.

RATINGS

Admissions Selectivity Rating: 85   **Fire Safety Rating:** 62

STUDENTS AND FACULTY

Enrollment: 1,754. **Student Body:** 63% female, 37% male, 33% out-of-state, 4% international (17 countries represented). Asian 2%, African American 3%, Caucasian 86%, Hispanic 4%, Native American <1%

Retention and Graduation: 65% freshmen graduate within 4 years. 20% grads go on to further study within 1 year. **Faculty:** 137 full-time faculty, 92% hold PhDs, 47% are members of minority groups, 12% are women. 0% of classes are taught by teaching assistants.

ACADEMICS

Degrees: associate, bachelor's, certificate, diploma, master's, post-bachelor's certificate. **Classes:** Most classes have 10–19 students. Most lab/discussion sessions have 10–19 students. **Majors with Highest Enrollment:** Communication, Journalism, and Related Programs; Biology; Business/Commerce. **Special Study Options:** Accelerated program, cooperative education program, distance learning, double major, dual enrollment, English as a Second Language (ESL), exchange student program (domestic), honors program, independent study, internships, liberal arts/career combination, study abroad, teacher certification program, 2+2, 3+3 and 4+2 (PT docotorate) programs with Thomas Jefferson University in nursing, physical therapy, labratory sceinces, diagnostic imaging, 3+2 in engineering with Penn State University, 3+2 with Duke University in Forestry, 3+3 in physical therapy with Widener University and University of Maryland, Baltimore County, 3+1 in Invasive Cardiovascular Technology with Lancaster Institute for Health Education,articulation agreements with Lehigh Unversity, Rutgers Univesity, Loyola College (MD) and Penn State University, Harrisburg to satisfy 150-hour requriment in Accounting. Combined degree programs: BA/MD, BA/MA, 3+3 physical therapy with Thomas Jefferson Univers. **Disability Services:** Special programs offered to physically disabled students include tape recorders, tutors.

FACILITIES

Housing: Coed dorms, special housing for disabled students, special housing for international students, women's dorms, apartments for single students, off-campus houses for student service-learning groups. 75% of campus accessible to physically disabled. **Special Academic Facilities/Equipment:** Art gallery, Meetinghouse/center for Anabaptist and Pietist studies, chapel/performance center, Fourier transform multinuclear NMR spectrometer, blood gas analyzer, scanning densitometer, PCR machine, radiometer/data logger, automated ion analyzer, computerized language lab. **Computers:** Students can register for classes online. Administrative functions (other than registration) can be performed online.

CAMPUS LIFE

Environment: Village. **Activities:** Choral groups, concert band, dance, drama/theater, jazz band, literary magazine, music ensembles, musical theater, pep band, radio station, student government, student newspaper, student-run film society, symphony orchestra, television station, yearbook. 80 registered organizations, 16 honor societies, 6 religious organizations. **Athletics (Intercollegiate):** *Men:* baseball, basketball, cross-country, diving, golf, lacrosse, soccer, swimming, tennis, track/field (outdoor), track/field (indoor), wrestling. *Women:* basketball, cross-country, diving, field hockey, lacrosse, soccer, softball, swimming, tennis, track/field (outdoor), track/field (indoor), volleyball. **On-Campus Highlights:** Brossman Commons Students Center, The Jay's Nest Snack Bar, The Dell, The Blue Bean Café, The Ira R Herr Soccer Complex, During the academic year it is great to hang out in The Dell, located in the middle of campus, on a hot day for frisbee or just soaking up the sun. The Ira R Herr Soccer Complex is the place to be to see the Blue Jays men's or women's soccer team in action—either day or night—the stadium is one of the finest soccer venues in the East.

ADMISSIONS

Freshman Academic Profile: 31% in top 10% of high school class, 64% in top 25% of high school class, 92% in top 50% of high school class. 80% from public high schools. SAT Math middle 50% range 510-620. SAT Critical Reading middle 50% range 510-620. SAT Writing middle 50% range 480-600. ACT middle 50% range 22-28. Minimum paper TOEFL 525. **Basis for Candidate Selection:** *Very important factors considered include:* rigor of secondary school record. *Important factors considered include:* Class rank, recommendation(s), standardized test scores, interview, racial/ethnic status, volunteer work. *Other factors considered include:* application essay, alumni/ae relation, character/personal qualities, extracurricular activities, geographical residence, religious affiliation/commitment, state residency, talent/ability, work experience. **Freshman Admission Requirements:** High school diploma is required and GED is accepted. *Academic units required:* 4 English, 3 mathematics, 2 science, (2 science labs), 2 foreign language, 2 social studies, 2 history, 0 academic electives. **Freshman Admission Statistics:** 3,468 applied, 71% admitted, 18% enrolled. **Transfer Admission Requirements:** High school transcript, college transcript(s), essay or personal statement, standardized test scores, statement of good standing from prior institution(s). Minimum college GPA of 2.5 required. Lowest grade transferable C. **General Admission Information:** Application Fee $30. Notification on a rolling basis, beginning on or about 11/15. Nonfall registration accepted. Admission may be deferred for a maximum of 1 year. Credit and/or placement offered for CEEB Advanced Placement tests.

COSTS AND FINANCIAL AID

Annual tuition $39,920. Room and board $9,820. Required fees $0. Average book expense $1,100. **Required Forms and Deadlines:** FAFSA. **Notification of Awards:** Applicants will be notified of awards on a rolling basis beginning 3/1. **Types of Aid:** *Need-based scholarships/grants:* Federal Pell, SEOG, state scholarships/grants, private scholarships, the school's own gift aid. *Loans:* Subsidized Stafford, Unsubsidized Stafford, PLUS, Federal Perkins, state loans. **Financial Aid Statistics:** 100% freshmen, 100% undergrads receive need-based scholarship or grant aid. 23% freshmen, 15% undergrads receive non-need-based scholarship or grant aid. 76% freshmen, 82% undergrads receive need-based self-help aid. 0% freshmen, 0% undergrads receive athletic scholarships. 96% freshmen, 94% undergrads receive any aid. 75% undergrads borrow to pay for school. Average cumulative indebtedness $26,906. **Criteria for awarding institutional aid:** *Non-need-based:* academics, art, music/drama, religious affiliation.

ELMHURST COLLEGE

190 S Prospect Avenue, Elmhurst, IL 60126
Phone: 630-617-3400 • **Financial Aid Phone:** 630-617-3075
E-mail: admit@elmhurst.edu • **CEEB Code:** 1204
Fax: 630-617-5501 • **Website:** public.elmhurst.edu • **ACT Code:** 1020

This private school, affiliated with the United Church of Christ Church, was founded in 1871. It has a 38-acre campus.

RATINGS

Admissions Selectivity Rating: 76   **Fire Safety Rating:** 82

STUDENTS AND FACULTY

Enrollment: 2,773. **Student Body:** 60% female, 40% male, 10% out-of-state, 0% international (34 countries represented). Asian 5%, African American 4%, Caucasian 70%, Hispanic 16%, Native American <1%
Retention and Graduation: 61% freshmen graduate within 4 years. 74% freshmen graduate within 6 years. 17% grads go on to further study within 1 year. 1% grads pursue law degrees. 8% grads pursue business degrees. 2% grads pursue medical degrees. **Faculty:** 159 full-time faculty, 81% hold PhDs, 60% are members of minority groups, 13% are women. 0% of classes are taught by teaching assistants.

ACADEMICS

Degrees: bachelor's, master's. **Classes:** Most classes have 20–29 students. **Majors with Highest Enrollment:** Elementary Education and Teaching; Business Administration and Management. **Special Study Options:** Accelerated program, double major, dual enrollment, honors program, independent study, internships, liberal arts/career combination, student-designed major, study abroad, teacher certification program. **Honors programs:** The Elmhurst College Honors program provides a challenging set of educational experiences for the most academically students featuring small, stimulating seminar courses where class discussions are lively and engaging; opportunities to conduct and present professional-level research; private receptions with distinguished guest speakers; trips to theatre and dance performances, social events, and more. Combined degree programs: BA/MEng. **Disability Services:** Special programs offered to physically disabled students include note-taking services, reader services, tape recorders, tutors. **Career services:** Alumni network, career/job search classes, career assessment, internships. Career services highlights include Elmhurst College's Center for Professional Excellence, which provides a comprehensive suite of services to link students' academic experiences with opportunities to explore career options and to prepare for future careers.

FACILITIES

Housing: Coed dorms, apartments for single students. 95% of campus accessible to physically disabled. **Special Academic Facilities/Equipment:** Accelerator/art space, language lab, recording studio, computer science/technology center, four electron microscopes. **Computers:** Students can register for classes online. Administrative functions (other than registration) can be performed online.

CAMPUS LIFE

Environment: Town. **Activities:** Choral groups, concert band, dance, drama/theater, jazz band, literary magazine, music ensembles, musical theater, radio station, student government, student newspaper, symphony orchestra, yearbook, Campus Ministries, International Student Organization, Model UN. 106 registered organizations, 15 honor societies, 6 religious organizations. 3 fraternities, 6 sororities. **Athletics (Intercollegiate):** *Men:* baseball, basketball, cross-country, football, golf, soccer, tennis, track/field (outdoor), wrestling. *Women:* basketball, bowling, cross-country, golf, soccer, softball, tennis, track/field (outdoor), volleyball. **On-Campus Highlights:** Alumni Circle, Frick

Center, Library, Tyrrell Fitness Center, Circle Hall. **Environmental Initiatives:** Development and execution of our Sustainability Plan. It is a living document that continues to expand as goals are achieved. The construction of our LEED certified Residence Hall in 2008 with its surrounding native prairie garden and permeable paver parking lot. College/Community recycling events which include student leadership and have operated for the past two years. Within this framework we are expanding areas of cooperation to establishing a College/Community compostable material collection route and expanding initial electronic equipment recycling programs to include collection of bicycles, eye glasses, and other household products.

ADMISSIONS

Freshman Academic Profile: 92% from public high schools. SAT Math middle 50% range 450-630. SAT Critical Reading middle 50% range 460-600. SAT Writing middle 50% range 450-590. ACT middle 50% range 21-26. Minimum paper TOEFL 550. **Basis for Candidate Selection:** *Very important factors considered include:* Class rank, academic GPA, rigor of secondary school record, standardized test scores. *Important factors considered include:* application essay, recommendation(s), interview. *Other factors considered include:* alumni/ae relation, character/personal qualities, extracurricular activities, talent/ability. **Freshman Admission Requirements:** High school diploma is required and GED is accepted. *Academic units required:* 4 English, 2 mathematics, 2 science, (2 science labs), 0 foreign language, 2 social studies, 1 history, 4 academic electives. **Freshman Admission Statistics:** 3,193 applied, 68% admitted, 24% enrolled. **Transfer Admission Requirements:** High school transcript, college transcript(s), statement of good standing from prior institution(s). Minimum college GPA of 2.6 required. Lowest grade transferable C. **General Admission Information:** Regular application deadline 7/15. Notification on a rolling basis, beginning on or about 11/1. Nonfall registration accepted. Admission may be deferred for a maximum of 2 years. Credit offered for CEEB Advanced Placement tests.

COSTS AND FINANCIAL AID

Annual tuition $33,700. Room and board $9,386. Required fees $400. Average book expense $1,500. **Required Forms and Deadlines:** FAFSA. **Notification of Awards:** Applicants will be notified of awards on a rolling basis beginning 2/21. **Types of Aid:** *Need-based scholarships/grants:* Federal Pell, SEOG, state scholarships/grants, private scholarships, the school's own gift aid. *Loans:* Direct Subsidized Stafford, Direct Unsubsidized Stafford, Direct PLUS, Federal Perkins, Private alternative student loans. *Student Employment:* Federal Work-Study Program available. Institutional employment available. Highest amount earned per year from on-campus jobs $3,000. Off-campus job opportunities are excellent. **Financial Aid Statistics:** 100% freshmen, 100% undergrads receive need-based scholarship or grant aid. 38% freshmen, 36% undergrads receive non-need-based scholarship or grant aid. 85% freshmen, 85% undergrads receive need-based self-help aid. 0% freshmen, 0% undergrads receive athletic scholarships. 95% freshmen, 87% undergrads receive any aid. 74% undergrads borrow to pay for school. Average cumulative indebtedness $27,046. **Criteria for awarding institutional aid:** *Non-need-based:* academics, alumni affiliation, art, minority status, music/drama, religious affiliation, state/district residency.

See page 1048.

ELMIRA COLLEGE

One Park Place, Elmira, NY 14901
Phone: 607-735-1724 • **Financial Aid Phone:** 607-735-1728
E-mail: admissions@elmira.edu • **CEEB Code:** 2226
Fax: 607-735-1718 • **Website:** www.elmira.edu • **ACT Code:** 2736

This private school was founded in 1855. It has a 50-acre campus.

RATINGS

Admissions Selectivity Rating: 83   **Fire Safety Rating:** 81

STUDENTS AND FACULTY

Enrollment: 1,315. **Student Body:** 71% female, 29% male, 53% out-of-state, 3% international (22 countries represented). Asian 1%, African American 3%, Caucasian 70%, Hispanic 3%, Native American 1%
Retention and Graduation: 75% freshmen return for sophomore year. 60% freshmen graduate within 4 years. 63% freshmen graduate within 6 years. 39% grads go on to further study within 1 year. 4% grads pursue law degrees. 3% grads pursue business degrees. 3% grads pursue medical degrees. **Faculty:** 100 full-time faculty, 0% hold PhDs, 51% are members of minority groups, 7% are women. 0% of classes are taught by teaching assistants.

ACADEMICS

Degrees: bachelor's, master's. **Classes:** Most classes have 10–19 students. Most lab/discussion sessions have 10–19 students. **Majors with Highest Enroll-**

ment: Psychology; Education; Business Administration and Management. **Special Study Options:** Accelerated program, double major, English as a Second Language (ESL), exchange student program (domestic), independent study, internships, liberal arts/career combination, student-designed major, study abroad, teacher certification program. Combined degree programs: 3-2 Chemical Engineering with Clarkson University.

FACILITIES

Housing: Coed dorms, special housing for disabled students, women's dorms, apartments for single students. 25% of campus accessible to physically disabled. **Special Academic Facilities/Equipment:** Center for Mark Twain studies, American studies center.

CAMPUS LIFE

Environment: Town. **Activities:** Choral groups, concert band, dance, drama/theater, literary magazine, music ensembles, musical theater, pep band, radio station, student government, student newspaper, yearbook. 85 registered organizations, 13 honor societies, 3 religious organizations. **Athletics (Intercollegiate):** *Men:* basketball, cheerleading, golf, ice hockey, lacrosse, soccer, tennis. *Women:* basketball, cheerleading, field hockey, golf, ice hockey, lacrosse, soccer, softball, tennis, volleyball. **On-Campus Highlights:** Emerson Hall, Mark Twain Study, Towers, Campus Center, The Puddle.

ADMISSIONS

Freshman Academic Profile: Average high school GPA 3.24. 28% in top 10% of high school class, 58% in top 25% of high school class, 84% in top 50% of high school class. 65% from public high schools. SAT Math middle 50% range 470-580. SAT Critical Reading middle 50% range 470-580. ACT middle 50% range 20-27. Minimum internet-based TOEFL 64. Minimum paper TOEFL 500. **Basis for Candidate Selection:** *Very important factors considered include:* Class rank, academic GPA, rigor of secondary school record, character/personal qualities. *Important factors considered include:* application essay, recommendation(s), standardized test scores, extracurricular activities. *Other factors considered include:* alumni/ae relation, first generation, geographical residence, interview, level of applicant's interest, racial/ethnic status, talent/ability, volunteer work, work experience. **Freshman Admission Requirements:** High school diploma is required and GED is accepted. *Academic units required:* 4 English, 3 mathematics, 3 science, (2 science labs), 3 social studies, 1 history, 2 academic electives. **Freshman Admission Statistics:** 2,302 applied, 80% admitted, 17% enrolled. **Transfer Admission Requirements:** college transcript(s), essay or personal statement, statement of good standing from prior institution(s). Minimum college GPA of 2.0 required. Lowest grade transferable C-. **General Admission Information:** Application Fee $50. Early decision application deadline 11/15. Regular application deadline 3/1. Notification on a rolling basis, beginning on or about 10/15. Nonfall registration accepted. Admission may be deferred for a maximum of 1 year. Credit and/or placement offered for CEEB Advanced Placement tests.

COSTS AND FINANCIAL AID

Annual tuition $36,600. Room and board $11,800. Required fees $1,550. Average book expense $600. **Required Forms and Deadlines:** FAFSA, State aid form. **Notification of Awards:** Applicants will be notified of awards on a rolling basis beginning 2/1. **Types of Aid:** *Need-based scholarships/grants:* Federal Pell, SEOG, state scholarships/grants, private scholarships, the school's own gift aid. *Loans:* Subsidized Stafford, Unsubsidized Stafford, PLUS, Federal Perkins, college/university loans from institutional funds, GATE Student Loan; Private Alternative Loans. *Student Employment:* Federal Work-Study Program available. Institutional employment available. Highest amount earned per year from on-campus jobs $1,000. Off-campus job opportunities are good. **Financial Aid Statistics:** 100% freshmen, 100% undergrads receive need-based scholarship or grant aid. 17% freshmen, 15% undergrads receive non-need-based scholarship or grant aid. 79% freshmen, 81% undergrads receive need-based self-help aid. 0% freshmen, 0% undergrads receive athletic scholarships. 98% freshmen, 98% undergrads receive any aid. 79% undergrads borrow to pay for school. Average cumulative indebtedness $27,426. **Criteria for awarding institutional aid:** *Non-need-based:* academics, leadership.

See page 1050.

ELON UNIVERSITY

100 Campus Drive, Elon, NC 27244-2010
Phone: 336-278-3566 · **Financial Aid Phone:** 336-278-7640
E-mail: admissions@elon.edu · **CEEB Code:** 5183
Fax: 336-278-7699 · **Website:** www.elon.edu · **ACT Code:** 3096

This private school, affiliated with the United Church of Christ Church, was founded in 1889. It has a 575-acre campus.

RATINGS

Admissions Selectivity Rating: 89   **Fire Safety Rating:** 92

STUDENTS AND FACULTY

Enrollment: 5,782. **Student Body:** 59% female, 41% male, 79% out-of-state, 2% international (47 countries represented). Asian 2%, African American 6%, Caucasian 82%, Hispanic 5%, Native American <1% **Retention and Graduation:** 76% freshmen graduate within 4 years. 81% freshmen graduate within 6 years. 27% grads go on to further study within 1 year. 15% grads pursue arts and sciences degrees. 6% grads pursue law degrees. 3% grads pursue business degrees. 2% grads pursue medical degrees. **Faculty:** 402 full-time faculty, 89% hold PhDs, 47% are members of minority groups, 17% are women. 0% of classes are taught by teaching assistants.

ACADEMICS

Degrees: bachelor's, master's. **Classes:** Most classes have 10–19 students. Most lab/discussion sessions have 10–19 students. **Majors with Highest Enrollment:** Communication. **Special Study Options:** Accelerated program, cross-registration, distance learning, double major, dual enrollment, English as a Second Language (ESL), exchange student program (domestic), honors program, independent study, internships, liberal arts/career combination, student-designed major, study abroad, teacher certification program. **Honors programs:** Forty freshmen are selected for the Honors Fellows program, which has benefits of specialized courses, $2,500-$10,000 scholarship renewable annually based on academic performance and participation in the program, $1,000 study abroad grant, development and presentation of their honors thesis, and housing options such as a living-learning community for Fellows. Combined degree programs: BS/BS (3-2) Engineering. **Disability Services:** Special programs offered to physically disabled students include note-taking services, reader services, tape recorders, tutors. **Career services:** Alumni network, alumni services, career/job search classes, career assessment, internships, regional alumni. All students are required to particpate in an experiential learning experience and most Elon students particpate in internship/coop.

FACILITIES

Housing: Coed dorms, men's dorms, special housing for international students, women's dorms, fraternity/sorority housing, apartments for single students, Wellness Housing, Theme Housing. 80% of campus accessible to physically disabled. **Special Academic Facilities/Equipment:** Resource center, fine arts center with recital hall, theatre, television studios, music rooms, campus center, athletic center, art gallery. **Computers:** 100% of classrooms, 100% of dorms, 100% of libraries, 100% of dining areas, 100% of student union, 25% of common outdoor areas have wireless network access. Students can register for classes online. Administrative functions (other than registration) can be performed online.

CAMPUS LIFE

Environment: Town. **Activities:** Choral groups, concert band, dance, drama/theater, jazz band, literary magazine, marching band, music ensembles, musical theater, pep band, radio station, student government, student newspaper, student-run film society, symphony orchestra, television station, yearbook, Campus Ministries, International Student Organization, Model UN. 150 registered organizations, 27 honor societies, 10 religious organizations. 11 fraternity, 12 sororities. **Athletics (Intercollegiate):** *Men:* baseball, basketball, cheerleading, cross-country, football, golf, soccer, tennis. *Women:* basketball, cheerleading, cross-country, golf, soccer, softball, tennis, track/field (outdoor), track/field (indoor), volleyball. **On-Campus Highlights:** Belk Library, Rhodes Football Stadium, Koury Business Center, Moseley Student Center, Koury Athletic Center, Lindner Hall, Academic Village. **Environmental Initiatives:** Reducing greenhouse gas emissions; Conserving resources; Educating the community.

ADMISSIONS

Freshman Academic Profile: Average high school GPA 3.98. 25% in top 10% of high school class, 62% in top 25% of high school class, 91% in top 50% of

high school class. 60% from public high schools. SAT Math middle 50% range 570-660. SAT Critical Reading middle 50% range 560-660. SAT Writing middle 50% range 560-660. ACT middle 50% range 25-29. Minimum internet-based TOEFL 79. Minimum paper TOEFL 550. **Basis for Candidate Selection:** *Very important factors considered include:* academic GPA, rigor of secondary school record, standardized test scores. *Important factors considered include:* application essay, recommendation(s), alumni/ae relation, extracurricular activities, talent/ability, volunteer work, work experience. *Other factors considered include:* Class rank, character/personal qualities, first generation, geographical residence, level of applicant's interest, racial/ethnic status, state residency. **Freshman Admission Requirements:** High school diploma is required and GED is accepted. *Academic units required:* 4 English, 3 mathematics, 3 science, (1 science labs), 2 foreign language, 1 social studies, 2 history. **Freshman Admission Statistics:** 10,443 applied, 54% admitted, 27% enrolled. **Transfer Admission Requirements:** High school transcript, college transcript(s), standardized test scores, statement of good standing from prior institution(s). Minimum college GPA of 2.7 required. Lowest grade transferable C-. **General Admission Information:** Application Fee $50. Early decision application deadline 11/1. Regular application deadline 1/10. Regular notification 3/15. Nonfall registration not accepted. Admission may be deferred for a maximum of 1 year. Credit and/or placement offered for CEEB Advanced Placement tests.

COSTS AND FINANCIAL AID

Annual tuition $30,848. Room and board $10,667. Required fees $399. Average book expense $900. **Required Forms and Deadlines:** FAFSA, Institution's own financial aid form, CSS/Financial Aid PROFILE. **Notification of Awards:** Applicants will be notified of awards on a rolling basis beginning 3/30. **Types of Aid:** *Need-based scholarships/grants:* Federal Pell, SEOG, state scholarships/grants, private scholarships, the school's own gift aid. *Loans:* Subsidized Stafford, Unsubsidized Stafford, PLUS, Federal Perkins, state loans, Privately funded alternative loans. *Student Employment:* Federal Work-Study Program available. Institutional employment available. Highest amount earned per year from on-campus jobs $2,500. Off-campus job opportunities are good. **Financial Aid Statistics:** 87% freshmen, 90% undergrads receive need-based scholarship or grant aid. 43% freshmen, 43% undergrads receive non-need-based scholarship or grant aid. 79% freshmen, 81% undergrads receive need-based self-help aid. 4% freshmen, 5% undergrads receive athletic scholarships. 69% freshmen, 62% undergrads receive any aid. 43% undergrads borrow to pay for school. Average cumulative indebtedness $22,259. **Criteria for awarding institutional aid:** *Non-need-based:* academics, art, athletics, leadership, music/drama, state/district residency.

EMBRY RIDDLE AERONAUTICAL UNIVERSITY (FL)

600 South Clyde Morris Boulevard, Daytona Beach, FL 32114-3900
Phone: 386-226-6100 · **Financial Aid Phone:** 800-226-6307
E-mail: dbadmit@erau.edu · **CEEB Code:** 5190
Fax: 386-226-7070 · **Website:** www.embryriddle.edu · **ACT Code:** 725

This private school was founded in 1926. It has a 185-acre campus.

RATINGS

Admissions Selectivity Rating: 66   Fire Safety Rating: 77

STUDENTS AND FACULTY

Enrollment: 4,954. **Student Body:** 18% female, 82% male, 64% out-of-state, 15% international (98 countries represented). Asian 4%, African American 6%, Caucasian 53%, Hispanic 6%, Native American <1% **Retention and Graduation:** 79% freshmen return for sophomore year. 31% freshmen graduate within 4 years. 52% freshmen graduate within 6 years. **Faculty:** 0% of classes are taught by teaching assistants.

ACADEMICS

Degrees: associate, bachelor's, master's. **Classes:** Most classes have 20-29 students. Most lab/discussion sessions have 10-19 students. **Majors with Highest Enrollment:** Aerospace, Aeronautical and Astronautical/Space Engineering; Aeronautics/Aviation/Aerospace Science and Technology; Aircraft Powerplant Technology/Technician. **Special Study Options:** Accelerated program, cooperative education program, distance learning, double major, dual enrollment, English as a Second Language (ESL), honors program, independent study, internships, student-designed major, study abroad. **Honors programs:** The Embry-Riddle Honors Program is highly selective, offering its student members enriched educational experiences. Emphasizing Honors course work in General Education and in the majors, the Program involves selected faculty who develop innovative courses and establish mentoring relationships with students. The Program is designed to attract and retain top students and to develop their communicative, analytical, critical, and research skills, nurturing a love of life-

long learning, leadership, and service. **Disability Services:** Special programs offered to physically disabled students include reader services, tape recorders, tutors. **Career services:** Alumni network, alumni services, career/job search classes, career assessment, internships, regional alumni. Career services highlights include The Co-op/Internship program, which provides students with practical experience that reinforces the theoretical concepts learned in the classroom. The Co-op/Internship program aids in bridging the gap between student life and the world of work. This program combines students' academic and career interests with work experience in business, industry, government, or service organizations. Key elements of the Co-op/Internship program experience are: Professional level work assignments in areas related to the student's academic major. Supervision and evaluation of performance by professionals in a chosen career field. Completion of learning objectives designed to relate academic studies to the work world.

FACILITIES

Housing: Coed dorms, apartments for married students, apartments for single students. 80% of campus accessible to physically disabled. **Special Academic Facilities/Equipment:** Fully equipped aircraft, training simulators, airway science simulation lab, wind tunnel. **Computers:** 100% of classrooms, 100% of dorms, 100% of libraries, 100% of dining areas, 100% of student union, 15% of common outdoor areas have wireless network access. Students can register for classes online. Administrative functions (other than registration) can be performed online.

CAMPUS LIFE

Environment: Town. **Activities:** Choral groups, dance, drama/theater, music ensembles, pep band, radio station, student government, student newspaper, yearbook, Campus Ministries, International Student Organization, Model UN. 140 registered organizations, 12 honor societies, 5 religious organizations. 12 fraternities, 4 sororities. **Athletics (Intercollegiate):** *Men:* baseball, basketball, cheerleading, cross-country, golf, soccer, softball, tennis, track/field (outdoor), volleyball. *Women:* basketball, cheerleading, cross-country, golf, soccer, softball, tennis, track/field (outdoor), volleyball. **On-Campus Highlights:** Lehman Engineering and Technology Center, College of Aviation, Simulator Building, ICI Center (fieldhouse), The Green Garage - EcoCAR Challenge, The College of Aviation tour is a brief look at the Air Traffic Management Laboratory and its Pseudo-Pilots' Lab, the Aircraft Performance Lab, the Computer Flight Simulation Lab, the College of Aviation Student Success Center (Tutor Lab), and the Flight Tutor Lab. The COA building also contains a Weather Center and two Meteorology Labs, Basic and Advanced. **Environmental Initiatives:** Embry-Riddle Opens Green Garage Doors: EcoCAR Project Advances Universitys Environmental Commitment Daytona Beach, Fla., Dec. 10, 2009. Embry-Riddle Aeronautical University has opened the doors of a new green garage, where engineering students are using aerospace techniques to develop the car of tomorrow. The garage includes a rotary vehicle lift, dedicated high-voltage room, and integrated hardware-in-the-loop laboratory donated by National Instruments. It also showcases an environmental focus at Embry-Riddles College of Engineering. Every component in the lab was chosen to reduce environmental impact, including the floor covering, which is made from recycled tires. Interior design students from Daytona State College assisted in designing the new facility. http://givingto.erau.edu/givingnews/09releases/ecocar.html. The Green Flight Challenge is a competition that is sponsored by NASA and run by the CAFE Foundation, and involves helping General Aviation move toward a "greener" way of travel. The main requirements state that a new or modified aircraft must travel 200 miles while averaging 100 mph and obtaining at least 200 passenger-mpg. Embry Riddle was accepted into the competition several weeks ago as one of the 18 teams which will compete for the $1.5 million prize in July of 2011.

ADMISSIONS

Freshman Academic Profile: Minimum internet-based TOEFL 79. Minimum paper TOEFL 550. **Basis for Candidate Selection:** *Very important factors considered include:* Class rank, academic GPA, recommendation(s), standardized test scores. *Other factors considered include:* application essay, rigor of secondary school record, alumni/ae relation, character/personal qualities, extracurricular activities, interview, level of applicant's interest, volunteer work, work experience. **Freshman Admission Requirements:** High school diploma is required and GED is accepted. *Academic units required:* 4 English, 3 mathematics, 2 science, (2 science labs), 0 foreign language, 2 social studies, 1 history, 3 academic electives. **Freshman Admission Statistics:** 4,087 applied, 73% admitted, 73% enrolled. **Transfer Admission Requirements:** college transcript(s), Minimum college GPA of 2.0 required. Lowest grade transferable C. **General Admission Information:** Application Fee $50. Notification on a rolling basis, beginning on or about 11/1. Nonfall registration accepted. Admission may be deferred for a maximum of 1 year. Credit and/or placement offered for CEEB Advanced Placement tests.

COSTS AND FINANCIAL AID

Annual tuition $31,944. Room and board $10,382. Required fees $1,274. Average book expense $1,400. **Required Forms and Deadlines:** FAFSA. **Types of Aid:** *Need-based scholarships/grants:* Federal Pell, SEOG, state scholarships/

grants, private scholarships, the school's own gift aid. *Loans:* Direct Subsidized Stafford, Direct Unsubsidized Stafford, Direct PLUS, Subsidized Stafford. *Student Employment:* Federal Work-Study Program available. Institutional employment available. Off-campus job opportunities are good. **Financial Aid Statistics:** 99% freshmen, 95% undergrads receive need-based scholarship or grant aid. 0% freshmen, 0% undergrads receive non-need-based scholarship or grant aid. 60% freshmen, 67% undergrads receive need-based self-help aid. 5% freshmen, 5% undergrads receive athletic scholarships. Criteria for awarding institutional aid: *Non-need-based:* academics, alumni affiliation, athletics, leadership.

EMBRY RIDDLE AERONAUTICAL UNIVERSITY— PRESCOTT

3700 Willow Creek, Prescott, AZ 86301
Phone: 928-777-6600 · **Financial Aid Phone:** 800-888-3728
E-mail: pradmit@erau.edu · **CEEB Code:** 4305
Fax: 928-777-6606 · **Website:** www.embryriddle.edu · **ACT Code:** 725

This private school was founded in 1926. It has a 539-acre campus.

RATINGS
Admissions Selectivity Rating: 68   **Fire Safety Rating:** 62

STUDENTS AND FACULTY
Enrollment: 1,971. **Student Body:** 22% female, 78% male, 78% out-of-state, 10% international (31 countries represented). Asian 6%, African American 2%, Caucasian 58%, Hispanic 6%, Native American <1%
Retention and Graduation: 82% freshmen return for sophomore year. 35% freshmen graduate within 4 years. 58% freshmen graduate within 6 years. **Faculty:** 0% of classes are taught by teaching assistants.

ACADEMICS
Degrees: bachelor's, master's. **Classes:** Most classes have 10–19 students. Most lab/discussion sessions have 10–19 students. **Majors with Highest Enrollment:** Aerospace, Aeronautical and Astronautical/Space Engineering; Aeronautics/Aviation/Aerospace Science and Technology; International Relations and Affairs. **Special Study Options:** Accelerated program, cooperative education program, distance learning, double major, dual enrollment, English as a Second Language (ESL), exchange student program (domestic), honors program, independent study, internships, Flight Training. **Disability Services:** Special programs offered to physically disabled students include note-taking services, reader services, tape recorders, tutors. **Career services:** Alumni network, alumni services, career/job search classes, career assessment, internships, regional alumni.

FACILITIES
Housing: Coed dorms, apartments for single students. 50% of campus accessible to physically disabled. **Computers:** 100% of classrooms, 100% of dorms, 100% of libraries, 100% of dining areas, 100% of student union, 80% of common outdoor areas have wireless network access. Administrative functions (other than registration) can be performed online.

CAMPUS LIFE
Environment: Town. **Activities:** dance, literary magazine, music ensembles, radio station, student government, student newspaper. 85 registered organizations, 5 honor societies, 2 religious organizations. 5 fraternities, 3 sororities. **Athletics (Intercollegiate):** *Men:* wrestling. **On-Campus Highlights:** Flight Line Facilities, Wind Tunnel Labs, Outdoor Pool and Racquetball, Tennis Area, The Hangar - Cafeteria, Two athletic facilities and weight room, Embry-Riddle Prescott is culturally diverse with students representing 49 states and 24 countries for a combined total of approximately 1700 students. Embry-Riddle Prescott is home to the Golden Eagles Flight Team, a nationally ranked flight team. In the last 22 years, the Golden Eagles are undefeated at the regional level, and the National Championship has been secured six times.

ADMISSIONS
Freshman Academic Profile: Minimum internet-based TOEFL 79. Minimum paper TOEFL 550. **Basis for Candidate Selection:** *Very important factors considered include:* academic GPA, rigor of secondary school record, standardized test scores. *Other factors considered include:* Class rank, recommendation(s), extracurricular activities, first generation, talent/ability, volunteer work. **Freshman Admission Statistics:** 1,779 applied, 80% admitted, 35% enrolled. **Transfer Admission Requirements:** college transcript(s). **General Admission Information:** Application Fee $120. Regular application deadline 6/1. Notification on a rolling basis, beginning on or about 2/1. Nonfall registration not accepted. Admission may be deferred for a maximum of 1 year. Credit offered for CEEB Advanced Placement tests.

COSTS AND FINANCIAL AID
Annual tuition $31,944. Room and board $9,990. Required fees $1,200. Average book expense $1,400. **Required Forms and Deadlines:** FAFSA. **Types of Aid:** *Need-based scholarships/grants:* state scholarships/grants, private scholarships, the school's own gift aid, Federal Bursaries and Grants. *Loans:* Federal and provincial loan programs administered by governments. *Student Employment:* Off-campus job opportunities are good. **Criteria for awarding institutional aid:** *Non-need-based:* academics, alumni affiliation, art, athletics, leadership, minority status, music/drama, state/district residency.

EMERSON COLLEGE

120 Boylston Street, Boston, MA 02116-4624
Phone: 617-824-8600 · **Financial Aid Phone:** 617-824-8655
E-mail: admission@emerson.edu · **CEEB Code:** 3367
Fax: 617-824-8609 · **Website:** www.emerson.edu · **ACT Code:** 1820

This private school was founded in 1880. It has a 10-acre campus.

RATINGS
Admissions Selectivity Rating: 92   **Fire Safety Rating:** 76

STUDENTS AND FACULTY
Enrollment: 3,454. **Student Body:** 59% female, 41% male, 75% out-of-state, 3% international (45 countries represented). Asian 5%, African American 3%, Caucasian 62%, Hispanic 8%, Native American <1%
Retention and Graduation: 88% freshmen return for sophomore year. 74% freshmen graduate within 4 years. 78% freshmen graduate within 6 years. 10% grads go on to further study within 1 year. **Faculty:** 177 full-time faculty, 71% hold PhDs, 44% are members of minority groups, 18% are women. 3% of classes are taught by teaching assistants.

ACADEMICS
Degrees: bachelor's, certificate, master's. **Classes:** Most classes have 10–19 students. Most lab/discussion sessions have 10–19 students. **Majors with Highest Enrollment:** Cinematography and Film/Video Production Theatre/Theater. **Special Study Options:** cross-registration, double major, honors program, independent study, internships, liberal arts/career combination, student-designed major, study abroad, teacher certification program. Combined degree programs: BS/MSSp in Communication Disorders. **Disability Services:** Special programs offered to physically disabled students include note-taking services, reader services, tape recorders, tutors. **Career services:** Alumni network, alumni services, career/job search classes, career assessment, internships, regional alumni.

FACILITIES
Housing: Coed dorms, Optional Learning Communities, such as the Writers' Block, Film Immersion Community, and Digital Culture Floor. 80% of campus accessible to physically disabled. **Special Academic Facilities/Equipment:** Emerson is home to the historic 1,200-seat Cutler Majestic Theatre and WERS-FM, Boston's oldest noncommercial broadcaster. The College has an 11-story performance and production center, housing rehearsal space, a costume shop, makeup lab, theatre design/tech center, and sound-treated TV studios. There are also digital and audio post-production labs, recording studios, a film equipment distribution center, seven clinics/programs to observe speech and hearing therapy, an integrated digital newsroom, and marketing research suite. A new 14-story campus center and residence hall houses a gymnasium and space for student organizations. Current campus construction projects include new student residences in the renovated Colonial Building and a sound stage, scene shop, black box, and cinema in the refurbished Paramount Theatre complex. **Computers:** 100% of classrooms, 100% of dorms, 100% of libraries, 100% of dining areas, 100% of student union, 100% of common outdoor areas have wireless network access. Students can register for classes online. Administrative functions (other than registration) can be performed online.

CAMPUS LIFE
Environment: Metropolis. **Activities:** Choral groups, dance, drama/theater, literary magazine, music ensembles, musical theater, radio station, student government, student newspaper, student-run film society, television station, yearbook, Campus Ministries, International Student Organization. 60 registered organizations, 4 honor societies, 4 religious organizations. 4 fraternities, 3 sororities. **Athletics (Intercollegiate):** *Men:* baseball, basketball, cross-country, golf, lacrosse, soccer, tennis, track/field (indoor), volleyball. *Women:* basketball,

cross-country, golf, lacrosse, soccer, softball, tennis, track/field (indoor), volleyball. **On-Campus Highlights:** WERS-FM (Boston's oldest public radio), Historic Cutler Majestic Theatre, Tufte Performance and Production Center, Journalism's Integrated Digital Newsroom, Piano Row Residence Hall/College Center. Emerson is currently remodeling the Colonial Building into student residences and renovating the Paramount Theater complex to house a sound stage, scene shop, rehearsal space, and a student residence. **Environmental Initiatives:** LEED Certified residence hall (one of only two in the city of Boston), campus center, and gymnasium; Alternative energy sources; Major recycling programs.

ADMISSIONS

Freshman Academic Profile: Average high school GPA 3.59. 42.4% in top 10% of high school class, 76.6% in top 25% of high school class, 98% in top 50% of high school class. 70% from public high schools. SAT Math middle 50% range 540-640. SAT Critical Reading middle 50% range 570-670. SAT Writing middle 50% range 580-670. ACT middle 50% range 24-29. Minimum internet-based TOEFL 80. Minimum paper TOEFL 550. **Basis for Candidate Selection:** *Very important factors considered include:* academic GPA, standardized test scores. *Important factors considered include:* Class rank, application essay, recommendation(s), rigor of secondary school record, character/personal qualities, extracurricular activities, talent/ability. *Other factors considered include:* alumni/ae relation, first generation, geographical residence, racial/ethnic status, volunteer work, work experience. **Freshman Admission Requirements:** High school diploma is required and GED is accepted. *Academic units required:* 4 English, 3 mathematics, 3 science, 3 foreign language, 3 social studies. **Freshman Admission Statistics:** 6,943 applied, 42% admitted, 26% enrolled. **Transfer Admission Requirements:** High school transcript, college transcript(s), essay or personal statement, statement of good standing from prior institution(s). Minimum college GPA of 3.0 required. Lowest grade transferable C. **General Admission Information:** Application Fee $65. Regular application deadline 1/5. Regular notification 4/1. Nonfall registration accepted. Admission may be deferred for a maximum of 1 Year. Credit and/or placement offered for CEEB Advanced Placement tests.

COSTS AND FINANCIAL AID

Annual tuition $29,408. Room and board $12,280. Required fees $672. Average book expense $800. **Required Forms and Deadlines:** FAFSA, CSS/Financial Aid PROFILE, Noncustodial PROFILE, Business/Farm Supplement. **Notification of Awards:** Applicants will be notified of awards on or about 4/1. **Types of Aid:** *Need-based scholarships/grants:* Federal Pell, SEOG, state scholarships/grants, private scholarships, the school's own gift aid. *Loans:* Subsidized Stafford, Unsubsidized Stafford, PLUS, Federal Perkins, state loans. *Student Employment:* Federal Work-Study Program available. Institutional employment available. Highest amount earned per year from on-campus jobs $2,400. Off-campus job opportunities are excellent. **Financial Aid Statistics:** 84% freshmen, 79% undergrads receive need-based scholarship or grant aid. 4% freshmen, 3% undergrads receive non-need-based scholarship or grant aid. 84% freshmen, 94% undergrads receive need-based self-help aid. 0% freshmen, 0% undergrads receive athletic scholarships. 63% freshmen, 61% undergrads receive any aid. 59% undergrads borrow to pay for school. Average cumulative indebtedness $15,262. **Criteria for awarding institutional aid:** *Non-need-based:* academics, leadership, music/drama, state/district residency.

See page 1052.

EMILY CARR UNIVERSITY OF ART + DESIGN

1399 Johnston Street, Vancouver, BC V6H 3R9
Phone: 604-844-3897 · **Financial Aid Phone:** 1-604-844-3844
E-mail: admissions@ecuad.ca
Fax: 604-844-3089 · **Website:** www.ecuad.ca

This public school was founded in 1925. It has a 80-acre campus.

RATINGS

Admissions Selectivity Rating: 60*   **Fire Safety Rating:** 60*

STUDENTS AND FACULTY

Enrollment: 1,858. **Student Body:** 32% out-of-state, (53 countries represented).
Retention and Graduation: 85% freshmen return for sophomore year. **Faculty:** 0% of classes are taught by teaching assistants.

ACADEMICS

Degrees: bachelor's, master's. **Majors with Highest Enrollment:** Design and Visual Communications; Industrial and Product Design; Fine and Studio Arts. **Special Study Options:** cooperative education program, cross-registration,

distance learning, exchange student program (domestic), external degree program, independent study, internships, liberal arts/career combination, student-designed major, study abroad. **Disability Services:** Special programs offered to physically disabled students include note-taking services, reader services, tape recorders, tutors. **Career services:** Alumni network, alumni services, career/job search classes, career assessment, internships, regional alumni.

FACILITIES

Housing: Off campus housing assistance. 85% of campus accessible to physically disabled. **Special Academic Facilities/Equipment:** Two Galleries A Centre for Art and Technology.

CAMPUS LIFE

Activities: student government, student newspaper, yearbook. 12 registered organizations.

ADMISSIONS

Freshman Academic Profile: 85% from public high schools. Minimum internet-based TOEFL 84. Minimum paper TOEFL 570. **Basis for Candidate Selection:** *Very important factors considered include:* character/personal qualities, level of applicant's interest, talent/ability. *Important factors considered include:* academic GPA, rigor of secondary school record. *Other factors considered include:* extracurricular activities, volunteer work, work experience. **Freshman Admission Requirements:** High school diploma is required and GED is not accepted. *Academic units required:* 3 English, 6 visual/performing arts, 6 academic electives. **Transfer Admission Requirements:** college transcript(s), essay or personal statement, statement of good standing from prior institution(s). Minimum college GPA of 2.0 required. Lowest grade transferable C. **General Admission Information:** Application Fee $40. Early decision application deadline 1/30. Regular application deadline 2/1. Regular notification 4/1. Nonfall registration accepted. Admission may be deferred for a maximum of one year. Credit and/or placement offered for CEEB Advanced Placement tests.

COSTS AND FINANCIAL AID

Average book expense $3,000. *Student Employment:* Institutional employment available. Highest amount earned per year from on-campus jobs $1,200. Off-campus job opportunities are good.

EMMANUEL COLLEGE

400 The Fenway, Boston, MA 2115
Phone: 617-735-9715 · **Financial Aid Phone:** 617-735-9938
E-mail: enroll@emmanuel.edu · **CEEB Code:** 3368
Fax: 617-735-9801 · **Website:** www.emmanuel.edu · **ACT Code:** 1822

This private school, affiliated with the Roman Catholic Church, was founded in 1919. It has a 17-acre campus.

RATINGS

Admissions Selectivity Rating: 77   **Fire Safety Rating:** 91

STUDENTS AND FACULTY

Enrollment: 1,967. **Student Body:** 73% female, 27% male, 44% out-of-state, 1% international (48 countries represented). Asian 3%, African American 5%, Caucasian 72%, Hispanic 7%, Native American <1%
Retention and Graduation: 79% freshmen return for sophomore year. 56% freshmen graduate within 4 years. **Faculty:** 93 full-time faculty, 83% hold PhDs, 58% are members of minority groups, 17% are women. 0% of classes are taught by teaching assistants.

ACADEMICS

Degrees: bachelor's, master's, post-bachelor's certificate, post-master's certificate. **Classes:** Most classes have 10–19 students. Most lab/discussion sessions have 10–19 students. **Majors with Highest Enrollment:** Psychology; Business Administration and Management; Biology/Biological Sciences. **Special Study Options:** Accelerated program, cross-registration, distance learning, double major, exchange student program (domestic), honors program, independent study, internships, liberal arts/career combination, student-designed major, study abroad, teacher certification program. **Honors programs:** Emmanuel College's Honors Program is a four-year academic and co-curricular program that combines rigorous, discussion-based course work with special complementary opportunities such as cultural activities, faculty-directed research projects, and service in the community. The program begins with the yearlong Honors Colloquium, a forum for students to engage in an active and open dialogue with their peers and members of the College's faculty from across the disciplines. Students also participate in four interdisciplinary writing-intensive seminars over the course of their studies, as well as a research and presentation skills seminar in preparation for independent study as an upperclassman, and ultimately the opportunity to achieve Distinction in the Field. **Disability Services:** Special programs offered to physically disabled students include note-taking services, reader services, tape recorders, tutors. **Career services:** Alumni network, alumni services, career/job search classes, career assessment, internships, regional alumni. Career services highlights include a Part-time Job Fair the first week of school in September.

FACILITIES

Housing: Coed dorms, special housing for disabled students, Theme Housing. 90% of campus accessible to physically disabled. **Special Academic Facilities/Equipment:** Academic Science Center, Lillian Immig Gallery, Academic Resource Center, Jean Yawkey Center. **Computers:** Students can register for classes online. Administrative functions (other than registration) can be performed online.

CAMPUS LIFE

Environment: Metropolis. **Activities:** Choral groups, dance, drama/theater, jazz band, literary magazine, music ensembles, musical theater, pep band, radio station, student government, student newspaper, student-run film society, symphony orchestra, yearbook, Campus Ministries, International Student Organization, Model UN. 48 registered organizations, 11 honor society. **Athletics (Intercollegiate):** *Men:* basketball, cross-country, golf, soccer, track/field (outdoor), track/field (indoor), volleyball. *Women:* basketball, cross-country, lacrosse, soccer, softball, tennis, track/field (outdoor), track/field (indoor), volleyball. **On-Campus Highlights:** Jean Yawkey Center, Residence Halls, Academic Science Center, Chapel **Environmental Initiatives:** Signing onto the ACUPCC in September 2010 Making recycling units readily available across campus Pursuing sustainable practices that may result in benefits such as a healthier learning and work environment and financial savings.

ADMISSIONS

Freshman Academic Profile: Average high school GPA 3.62. 74% from public high schools. SAT Math middle 50% range 490-590. SAT Critical Reading middle 50% range 500-600. SAT Writing middle 50% range 500-600. ACT middle 50% range 22-26. Minimum internet-based TOEFL 79. Minimum paper TOEFL 550. **Basis for Candidate Selection:** *Very important factors considered include:* application essay, academic GPA, recommendation(s), rigor of secondary school record. *Important factors considered include:* standardized test scores, character/personal qualities, extracurricular activities, level of applicant's interest, volunteer work. *Other factors considered include:* Class rank, alumni/ae relation, first generation, geographical residence, interview, religious affiliation/commitment, talent/ability, work experience. **Freshman Admission Requirements:** High school diploma is required and GED is accepted. *Academic units required:* 4 English, 3 mathematics, 2 science, (2 science labs), 2 foreign language, 2 social studies. **Freshman Admission Statistics:** 5,899 applied, 69% admitted, 13% enrolled. **Transfer Admission Requirements:** High school transcript, college transcript(s), essay or personal statement, standardized test scores, statement of good standing from prior institution(s). Minimum college GPA of n/a required. Lowest grade transferable C. **General Admission Information:** Application Fee $40. Early decision application deadline 11/1. Regular application deadline 3/1. Notification on a rolling basis, beginning on or about 12/1. Nonfall registration accepted. Admission may be deferred for a maximum of 1 year. Credit and/or placement offered for CEEB Advanced Placement tests.

COSTS AND FINANCIAL AID

Annual tuition $35,312. Room and board $13,580. Required fees $500. Average book expense $880. **Required Forms and Deadlines:** FAFSA. **Notification of Awards:** Applicants will be notified of awards on a rolling basis beginning 3/15. **Types of Aid:** *Need-based scholarships/grants:* Federal Pell, SEOG, state scholarships/grants, private scholarships, the school's own gift aid. *Loans:* Direct Subsidized Stafford, Direct Unsubsidized Stafford, Direct PLUS, Federal Perkins, state loans. *Student Employment:* Federal Work-Study Program available. Institutional employment available. Highest amount earned per year from on-campus jobs $7,581. Off-campus job opportunities are excellent. **Financial Aid Statistics:** 100% freshmen, 100% undergrads receive need-based scholarship or grant aid. 100% freshmen, 98% undergrads receive non-need-based scholarship or grant aid. 85% freshmen, 84% undergrads receive need-based self-help aid. 0% freshmen, 0% undergrads receive athletic scholarships. 98 78% undergrads borrow to pay for school. **Criteria for awarding institutional aid:** *Non-need-based:* academics, alumni affiliation, leadership.

EMMANUEL COLLEGE (GA)

P.O. Box 129, Franklin Springs, GA 30639-0129
Phone: 706-245-7226 • **Financial Aid Phone:** 706-245-2844
E-mail: admissions@emmanuelcollege.edu • **CEEB Code:** 5184
Fax: 706-245-2876 • **Website:** http://www.ec.edu/

This private school, affiliated with the Pentecostal Church, was founded in 1919. It has a 150-acre campus.

RATINGS

Admissions Selectivity Rating: 85   **Fire Safety Rating:** 62

STUDENTS AND FACULTY

Enrollment: 613. **Student Body:** 54% female, 46% male, 22% out-of-state, 1% international (4 countries represented). Asian 1%, African American 16%, Caucasian 80%, Hispanic 2%, Native American <1%
Retention and Graduation: 61% freshmen return for sophomore year. 18% freshmen graduate within 4 years. 34% freshmen graduate within 6 years.
Faculty: 40 full-time faculty, 65% hold PhDs, 40% are members of minority groups, 3% are women. 0% of classes are taught by teaching assistants.

ACADEMICS

Degrees: associate, bachelor's, terminal associate, transfer associate. **Classes:** Most classes have fewer than 10 students. **Special Study Options:** dual enrollment, honors program, independent study, internships, teacher certification program. **Disability Services:** Special programs offered to physically disabled students include note-taking services, tutors.

FACILITIES

Housing: men's dorms, women's dorms, apartments for married students. 75% of campus accessible to physically disabled. **Computers:** Students can register for classes online.

CAMPUS LIFE

Environment: Rural. **Activities:** Choral groups, drama/theater, jazz band, literary magazine, music ensembles, musical theater, student government, student newspaper, yearbook. 25 registered organizations, 3 honor societies, 15 religious organizations. **Athletics (Intercollegiate):** *Men:* baseball, basketball, soccer, tennis. *Women:* basketball, soccer, softball, tennis. **On-Campus Highlights:** EC Café, Student Activities Center.

ADMISSIONS

Freshman Academic Profile: 10% in top 10% of high school class, 50% in top 25% of high school class, 60% in top 50% of high school class. 85% from public high schools. SAT Math middle 50% range 400-550. SAT Critical Reading middle 50% range 430-570. Minimum paper TOEFL 550. **Basis for Candidate Selection:** *Very important factors considered include:* academic GPA, standardized test scores. *Important factors considered include:* level of applicant's interest. *Other factors considered include:* recommendation(s). **Freshman Admission Requirements:** High school diploma is required and GED is accepted. **Freshman Admission Statistics:** 1,661 applied, 35% admitted, 45% enrolled. **Transfer Admission Requirements:** college transcript(s), standardized test scores, Lowest grade transferable D. **General Admission Information:** Application Fee $25. Regular application deadline 8/1. Notification on a rolling basis, beginning on or about 9/1. Nonfall registration accepted. Admission may be deferred for a maximum of 1 year. Credit offered for CEEB Advanced Placement tests.

COSTS AND FINANCIAL AID

Average book expense $600. **Required Forms and Deadlines:** FAFSA, Institution's own financial aid form, State aid form. **Notification of Awards:** Applicants will be notified of awards on a rolling basis beginning 3/1. **Types of Aid:** *Need-based scholarships/grants:* Federal Pell, SEOG, state scholarships/grants. *Loans:* Subsidized Stafford, Unsubsidized Stafford, PLUS. *Student Employment:* Federal Work-Study Program available. Institutional employment available. Off-campus job opportunities are good. **Financial Aid Statistics:** 84% freshmen, 92% undergrads receive need-based scholarship or grant aid. 51% freshmen, 50% undergrads receive non-need-based scholarship or grant aid. 74% freshmen, 56% undergrads receive need-based self-help aid. **Criteria for awarding institutional aid:** *Non-need-based:* academics, alumni affiliation, athletics, leadership, music/drama, religious affiliation.

EMORY AND HENRY COLLEGE

PO Box 10, Emory, VA 24327
Phone: 276-944-6133 · **Financial Aid Phone:** 866-794-0010
E-mail: ehadmiss@ehc.edu · **CEEB Code:** 5185
Fax: 276-944-6935 · **Website:** http://www.ehc.edu · **ACT Code:** 4350

This private school, affiliated with the Methodist Church, was founded in 1836. It has a 331-acre campus.

RATINGS
Admissions Selectivity Rating: 82   **Fire Safety Rating:** 60*

STUDENTS AND FACULTY
Enrollment: 900. **Student Body:** 47% female, 53% male, 36% out-of-state, 1% international (5 countries represented). Asian 0%, African American 10%, Caucasian 80%, Hispanic 2%, Native American <1%
Retention and Graduation: 74% freshmen return for sophomore year. 35% freshmen graduate within 4 years. 48% freshmen graduate within 6 years. 37% grads go on to further study within 1 year. 24% grads pursue arts and sciences degrees. 31% grads pursue law degrees. 23% grads pursue business degrees. 12% grads pursue medical degrees. **Faculty:** 72 full-time faculty, 82% hold PhDs, 49% are members of minority groups, 10% are women. 0% of classes are taught by teaching assistants.

ACADEMICS
Degrees: bachelor's, diploma, master's. **Classes:** Most classes have 10–19 students. **Majors with Highest Enrollment:** Education; Business Administration and Management; Pre-Medicine/Pre-Medical Studies. **Special Study Options:** cooperative education program, distance learning, double major, dual enrollment, honors program, independent study, internships, liberal arts/career combination, student-designed major, study abroad, teacher certification program. Combined degree programs: BA/MA. **Disability Services:** Special programs offered to physically disabled students include reader services, tape recorders, tutors. **Career services:** career/job search classes, career assessment, internships.

FACILITIES
Housing: Coed dorms, special housing for disabled students, men's dorms, women's dorms, Theme Housing. **Special Academic Facilities/Equipment:** Language lab, capillary gas chromatograph, DNA vertical slab gel electrophoretic equipment, infrared spectrophotometer. Theatre Studio, Art gallery. **Computers:** 100% of classrooms, 100% of dorms, 100% of libraries, 100% of dining areas, 100% of student union, 100% of common outdoor areas have wireless network access.

CAMPUS LIFE
Environment: Rural. **Activities:** Choral groups, drama/theater, literary magazine, music ensembles, musical theater, opera, pep band, radio station, student government, student newspaper, television station, yearbook, Campus Ministries, International Student Organization. 53 registered organizations, 7 honor societies, 4 religious organizations. 7 fraternities, 6 sororities. **Athletics (Intercollegiate):** *Men:* baseball, basketball, cross-country, football, golf, soccer, tennis. *Women:* basketball, cross-country, soccer, softball, swimming, tennis, volleyball. **On-Campus Highlights:** McGlothlin-Street Hall (new science buil, Memorial Chapel, Byars Hall (Arts, Music, and Theatre), King Athletic Center, Emory Mercantile (campus bookstore). **Environmental Initiatives:** Recycling is now in full swing, with a widespread distribution of recycling bins for paper, cardboard, aluminum, plastics and steel. There are thirty bins specially made for the college from sustainably-harvested local poplar. We have already reduced our trash volume significantly. We are a participant in the national Recyclemania competition, in the waste minimization category. All new campus construction will be LEED silver certified, including the use of local, sustainably harvested wood. The college food service has committed to buying a significant amount of local organic produce, eggs and meat from Appalachian Harvest, a cooperative of farmers in our region. This is for the fall semester of 2008. This is one of our most effective ways of reducing our college's environmental footprint.

ADMISSIONS
Freshman Academic Profile: Average high school GPA 3.5. 20% in top 10% of high school class, 45% in top 25% of high school class, 80% in top 50% of high school class. 92% from public high schools. SAT Math middle 50% range 445-560. SAT Critical Reading middle 50% range 430-555. SAT Writing middle 50% range 425-540. ACT middle 50% range 19-26. Minimum paper TOEFL 550. **Basis for Candidate Selection:** *Very important factors considered include:* academic GPA, recommendation(s), rigor of secondary school record, character/personal qualities, level of applicant's interest. *Important factors considered include:* application essay, standardized test scores, extracurricular activities, geographical residence, interview, state residency, talent/ability, volun-

teer work. *Other factors considered include:* Class rank, alumni/ae relation, first generation, racial/ethnic status, religious affiliation/commitment, work experience. **Freshman Admission Requirements:** High school diploma is required and GED is accepted. *Academic units required:* 4 English, 3 mathematics, 2 science, (2 science labs), 2 foreign language, 2 social studies, 0 history, 0 visual/performing arts, 0 computer science, 0 academic electives. **Freshman Admission Statistics:** 1,217 applied, 72% admitted, 28% enrolled. **Transfer Admission Requirements:** High school transcript, college transcript(s), statement of good standing from prior institution(s). Minimum college GPA of 2.5 required. Lowest grade transferable C. **General Admission Information:** Application Fee $30. Notification on a rolling basis, beginning on or about 8/1. Nonfall registration accepted. Admission may be deferred for a maximum of 1 year. Credit and/or placement offered for CEEB Advanced Placement tests.

COSTS AND FINANCIAL AID
Average book expense $800. **Required Forms and Deadlines:** FAFSA, State aid form. **Notification of Awards:** Applicants will be notified of awards on a rolling basis beginning 3/1. **Types of Aid:** *Need-based scholarships/grants:* Federal Pell, SEOG, state scholarships/grants, private scholarships, the school's own gift aid. *Loans:* Subsidized Stafford, Unsubsidized Stafford, PLUS, Federal Perkins. **Financial Aid Statistics:** 80% freshmen, 87% undergrads receive need-based scholarship or grant aid. 20% freshmen, 13% undergrads receive non-need-based scholarship or grant aid. 70% freshmen, 0% undergrads receive need-based self-help aid. 0% freshmen, 0% undergrads receive athletic scholarships. 79% undergrads borrow to pay for school. Average cumulative indebtedness $27,012. **Criteria for awarding institutional aid:** *Non-need-based:* academics, art, music/drama, religious affiliation, state/district residency.

EMORY UNIVERSITY

Best 380

Emory University, Boiseuillet Jones Ctr, Atlanta, GA 30322
Phone: 404-727-6036 · **Financial Aid Phone:** 404-727-6039
E-mail: admiss@emory.edu · **CEEB Code:** 5186
Fax: 404-727-4303 · **Website:** www.emory.edu · **ACT Code:** 851

This private school, affiliated with the Methodist Church, was founded in 1836. It has a 56-acre campus.

RATINGS
Admissions Selectivity Rating: 97   **Fire Safety Rating:** 74

STUDENTS AND FACULTY
Enrollment: 7,705. **Student Body:** 57% female, 43% male, 73% out-of-state, 15% international (106 countries represented). Asian 22%, African American 9%, Caucasian 40%, Hispanic 6%, Native American <1%
Retention and Graduation: 94% freshmen return for sophomore year. 84% freshmen graduate within 4 years. 91% freshmen graduate within 6 years. 43% grads go on to further study within 1 year. 22% grads pursue arts and sciences degrees. 16% grads pursue law degrees. 49% grads pursue medical degrees. **Faculty:** 1,004 full-time faculty, 94% hold PhDs, 40% are members of minority groups, 18% are women. 10% of classes are taught by teaching assistants.

ACADEMICS
Degrees: associate, bachelor's, first professional, master's. **Classes:** Most classes have 10–19 students. Most lab/discussion sessions have 10–19 students. **Majors with Highest Enrollment:** Economics; Business/Commerce; Biology/Biological Sciences. **Special Study Options:** cooperative education program, cross-registration, double major, dual enrollment, English as a Second Language (ESL), honors program, independent study, internships, liberal arts/career combination, study abroad, teacher certification program, Qualified undergraduates may take a semester of off-campus study in Washington D.C. Combined degree programs: BA/MA, 4 year BA/MA or BS/MS program. **Disability Services:** Special programs offered to physically disabled students include note-taking services, reader services, tape recorders, tutors. **Career services:** Alumni network, alumni services, career/job search classes, career assessment, internships, regional alumni.

FACILITIES
Housing: Coed dorms, special housing for disabled students, special housing for international students, women's dorms, fraternity/sorority housing, apartments for married students, apartments for single students, Theme Housing. **Computers:** Students can register for classes online. Administrative functions (other than registration) can be performed online.

CAMPUS LIFE

Environment: Town. **Activities:** Choral groups, concert band, dance, drama/theater, jazz band, literary magazine, marching band, music ensembles, musical theater, opera, pep band, radio station, student government, student newspaper, student-run film society, symphony orchestra, television station, Campus Ministries, International Student Organization 51 registered organizations, 30 honor societies, 27 religious organizations. 14 fraternities, 12 sororities. **Athletics (Intercollegiate):** *Men:* baseball, basketball, cross-country, diving, golf, soccer, swimming, tennis, track/field (outdoor). *Women:* basketball, cross-country, diving, soccer, softball, swimming, tennis, track/field (outdoor), volleyball. **On-Campus Highlights:** Michael C. Carlos Museum, Lullwater Park, Clifton Health Sciences Corridor, Top of Woodruff Library, Dooley's Den at the Depot, 6) Candler Library Reading Room. **Environmental Initiatives:** Emory has among the highest number of square feet of LEED-certified space of any campus in America. Emory constructed the first LEED-certified building in the Southeast in the 1990s, the first Good LEED-EB in the U.S., and since 2001 all new and future construction must be LEED (with Silver currently the minimum). We also are auditing and retrofitting exisiting buildings - roughly 1 million square feet are currently underway with additional 1 million in planning phase. Emory has set the goal of serving 75% local or sustainable ingredients in our campus and hospital cafeterias by 2015. To reach this ambitious target, we have hired a local farmer as Emorys Farm Liaison who is building a network of other local farmers to expand production and a Sustainable Food Educator to expand awareness of sustainable food. We are also working closely with the non-profit Georgia Organics and our vendor, Sodexho, to overcome barriers to distribution from farm to plate. Finally, weve started an on-campus Farmers Market and 8 educational food gardens on campus to allow students and staff the experience of growing their own local food. Emory has a robust alternative transportation program with one of the largest private bus fleets in metro Atlanta which is 100% alternatively fueled, running on a biodiesel blend made from the used cooking oil from our campus cafeterias and hospitals. Emory has also been named by global bike manufacturer, Fuji, as its first Fuji University and has a bike share program with free fleets of bikes at check-out locations around campus, discounted bikes for students and staff, and other incentives for biking (see www.bike.emory.edu). We give staff free public transit passes, and incentives for carpooling, walking, and vanpooling. We also have three park-n-ride facilities at shopping centers around Atlantas perimeter highway so that staff can take our free shuttle into work instead of driving into the heart of the city.

ADMISSIONS

Freshman Academic Profile: Average high school GPA 3.75. 75.8% in top 10% of high school class, 95.1% in top 25% of high school class, 99.2% in top 50% of high school class. 60% from public high schools. SAT Math middle 50% range 650-760. SAT Critical Reading middle 50% range 610-710. SAT Writing middle 50% range 630-730. ACT middle 50% range 29-32. Minimum paper TOEFL 600. **Basis for Candidate Selection:** *Very important factors considered include:* application essay, academic GPA, recommendation(s), rigor of secondary school record, standardized test scores, character/personal qualities, extracurricular activities, first generation, talent/ability. *Important factors considered include:* alumni/ae relation, geographical residence, level of applicant's interest, racial/ethnic status, volunteer work, work experience. *Other factors considered include:* Class rank, interview. **Freshman Admission Requirements:** High school diploma is required and GED is not accepted. *Academic units required:* 4 English, 3 mathematics, 2 science, (2 science labs), 2 foreign language, 2 social studies, 2 history, 1 visual/performing arts, 0 computer science, 2 academic electives. **Freshman Admission Statistics:** 17,681 applied, 26% admitted, 29% enrolled. **Transfer Admission Requirements:** High school transcript, college transcript(s), essay or personal statement, standardized test scores, statement of good standing from prior institution(s). Minimum college GPA of 3.00 required. Lowest grade transferable C. **General Admission Information:** Application Fee $50. Early decision application deadline 11/1. Regular application deadline 1/15. Regular notification 4/1. Nonfall registration not accepted. Admission may be deferred for a maximum of 1 year. Credit and/or placement offered for CEEB Advanced Placement tests.

COSTS AND FINANCIAL AID

Annual tuition $44,400. Room and board $12,760. Required fees $608. Average book expense $1,212. **Required Forms and Deadlines:** FAFSA, CSS/Financial Aid PROFILE, Noncustodial PROFILE. **Notification of Awards:** Applicants will be notified of awards on or about 4/1. **Types of Aid:** *Need-based scholarships/grants:* Federal Pell, SEOG, state scholarships/grants, private scholarships, the school's own gift aid. *Loans:* Subsidized Stafford, Unsubsidized Stafford, PLUS, Federal Perkins, Federal Nursing, state loans, college/university loans from institutional funds. **Financial Aid Statistics:** 90% freshmen, 92% undergrads receive need-based scholarship or grant aid. 37% freshmen, 30% undergrads receive non-need-based scholarship or grant aid. 95% freshmen, 93% undergrads receive need-based self-help aid. 0% freshmen, 0% undergrads receive athletic scholarships. 55% freshmen, 54% undergrads receive any aid. 49% undergrads borrow to pay for school. Average cumulative indebtedness $19,397. **Criteria for awarding institutional aid:** *Non-need-based:* academics, art, leadership, music/drama, religious affiliation, state/district residency.

EMPORIA STATE UNIVERSITY

1200 Commercial, Emporia, KS 66801-5087
Phone: 620-341-5465 • **Financial Aid Phone:** 620-341-5457
E-mail: go2esu@emporia.edu • **CEEB Code:** 6335
Fax: 620-341-5599 • **Website:** www.emporia.edu • **ACT Code:** 1430

This public school was founded in 1863. It has a 212-acre campus.

RATINGS

Admissions Selectivity Rating: 72   **Fire Safety Rating:** 71

STUDENTS AND FACULTY

Enrollment: 4,148. **Student Body:** 59% female, 41% male, 10% out-of-state, 6% international (40 countries represented). Asian 1%, African American 5%, Caucasian 79%, Hispanic 5%, Native American 1% **Retention and Graduation:** 22% freshmen graduate within 4 years. 47% freshmen graduate within 6 years. 20% grads go on to further study within 1 year. **Faculty:** 260 full-time faculty, 81% hold PhDs, 46% are members of minority groups, 9% are women. 9% of classes are taught by teaching assistants.

ACADEMICS

Degrees: bachelor's, master's, post-bachelor's certificate, post-master's certificate. **Classes:** Most classes have 20–29 students. Most lab/discussion sessions have 20–29 students. **Majors with Highest Enrollment:** Elementary Education and Teaching; Business/Commerce; Registered Nursing/Registered Nurse. **Special Study Options:** distance learning, double major, dual enrollment, honors program, independent study, internships, student-designed major, study abroad, teacher certification program, Continuing education courses, Evening courses, Interdisciplinary or interdepartmental course of study, Learning assistance program, Pass-Fail grading option, Student Exchange program, Summer sessions, Tutorial programs, Trio programs, Service members Opportunity College, Undergrads may take grad level classes, except 800 level. **Honors programs:** Honors Programs Combined degree programs: MLS Legal studies with KU. **Disability Services:** Special programs offered to physically disabled students include note-taking services, reader services, tape recorders, tutors. **Career services:** Alumni network, alumni services, career assessment, internships. Career services highlights include a formal, for-credit internship program available to any student, any major.

FACILITIES

Housing: Coed dorms, special housing for disabled students, special housing for international students, fraternity/sorority housing, apartments for married students, apartments for single students, Wellness Housing, Theme Housing. 100% of campus accessible to physically disabled. **Special Academic Facilities/Equipment:** Art gallery, geology and natural history museums, Great Plains study center, planetarium. **Computers:** 25% of classrooms, 100% of libraries, 50% of student union, have wireless network access. Students can register for classes online. Administrative functions (other than registration) can be performed online.

CAMPUS LIFE

Environment: Town. **Activities:** Choral groups, concert band, dance, drama/theater, jazz band, literary magazine, marching band, music ensembles, musical theater, opera, pep band, student government, student newspaper, student-run film society, symphony orchestra, yearbook, Campus Ministries, International Student Organization. 141 registered organizations, 15 honor societies, 11 religious organization. 6 fraternities, 4 sororities. **Athletics (Intercollegiate):** *Men:* baseball, basketball, cheerleading, cross-country, football, tennis, track/field (outdoor), track/field (indoor). *Women:* basketball, cheerleading, cross-country, soccer, softball, tennis, track/field (outdoor), track/field (indoor), volleyball. **On-Campus Highlights:** Student Recreation Center, The Memorial Student Union, Beach Music Hall, Wooster Lake, William Allen White Library.

ADMISSIONS

Freshman Academic Profile: Average high school GPA 3.28. 10% in top 10% of high school class, 34% in top 25% of high school class, 67% in top 50% of high school class. 96% from public high schools. ACT middle 50% range 19-25. Minimum paper TOEFL 450. **Basis for Candidate Selection:** *Very important factors considered include:* Class rank, academic GPA, standardized test scores. *Important factors considered include:* talent/ability. *Other factors considered include:* application essay, extracurricular activities. **Freshman Admission Requirements:** High school diploma is required and GED is accepted. *Academic units required:* 4 English, 3 mathematics, 3 science, 3 social studies, 1 computer science. **Freshman Admission Statistics:** 1,229 applied, 92% admitted, 61% enrolled. **Transfer Admission Requirements:** college transcript(s), Minimum college GPA of 2.0 required. Lowest grade transferable D. **General Admission Information:** Application Fee $30. Nonfall registration accepted. Admission may be deferred for a maximum of 1 year. Credit and/or placement offered for CEEB Advanced Placement tests.

COSTS AND FINANCIAL AID

Required Forms and Deadlines: FAFSA, State aid form. **Notification of Awards:** Applicants will be notified of awards on a rolling basis beginning 2/2. **Types of Aid:** *Need-based scholarships/grants:* Federal Pell, SEOG, state scholarships/grants, private scholarships, the school's own gift aid, Jones Foundation Grants. *Loans:* Subsidized Stafford, Unsubsidized Stafford, PLUS, Federal Perkins, Alaska Loans, alternative loans. *Student Employment:* Federal Work-Study Program available. Institutional employment available. Highest amount earned per year from on-campus jobs $3,500. Off-campus job opportunities are good. **Financial Aid Statistics:** 59% freshmen, 43% undergrads receive need-based scholarship or grant aid. 40% freshmen, 27% undergrads receive non-need-based scholarship or grant aid. 7% freshmen, 9% undergrads receive need-based self-help aid. 7% freshmen, 4% undergrads receive athletic scholarships. 61% freshmen, 57% undergrads receive any aid. 70% undergrads borrow to pay for school. Average cumulative indebtedness $16,725. **Criteria for awarding institutional aid:** *Non-need-based:* academics, alumni affiliation, art, athletics, job skills, leadership, minority status, music/drama, religious affiliation, state/district residency.

ENDICOTT COLLEGE

376 Hale Street, Beverly, MA 1915
Phone: 978-921-1000 · **Financial Aid Phone:** 978-232-2060
E-mail: admissio@endicott.edu · **CEEB Code:** 3369
Fax: 978-232-2520 · **Website:** www.endicott.edu · **ACT Code:** 1824

This private school was founded in 1939. It has a 231-acre campus.

RATINGS

Admissions Selectivity Rating: 82   Fire Safety Rating: 94

STUDENTS AND FACULTY

Enrollment: 2,795. **Student Body:** 62% female, 38% male, 52% out-of-state, 1% international (26 countries represented). Asian 1%, African American 3%, Caucasian 82%, Hispanic 4%, Native American <1%
Retention and Graduation: 83% freshmen return for sophomore year. 71% freshmen graduate within 4 years. 73% freshmen graduate within 6 years. 21% grads go on to further study within 1 year. **Faculty:** 91 full-time faculty, 70% hold PhDs, 56% are members of minority groups, 9% are women. 0% of classes are taught by teaching assistants.

ACADEMICS

Degrees: associate, bachelor's, master's, post-bachelor's certificate, terminal associate. **Classes:** Most classes have 10–19 students. Most lab/discussion sessions have 10–19 students. **Majors with Highest Enrollment:** Business Administration and Management; Sport and Fitness Administration/Management; Mass Communication/Media Studies. **Special Study Options:** Accelerated program, cross-registration, distance learning, dual enrollment, honors program, independent study, internships, liberal arts/career combination, student-designed major, study abroad, teacher certification program. **Honors programs:** Alpha Phi Sigma, Eta Sigma Delta, Kappa Delta Pi, Lambda Pi Eta, Communications Mortar Board, Psi Chi, Sigma Beta Delta, National Honor Society for Criminal Justice Students, Endicott College Honors Program, International Hospitality Management Society, National Honor Society for students in Senior Year. **Disability Services:** Special programs offered to physically disabled students include note-taking services, reader services, tape recorders, tutors. **Career services:** Alumni network, alumni services, career/job search classes, career assessment, internships, regional alumni. Career services highlights include internships that are required for all traditional undergraduate students.

FACILITIES

Housing: Coed dorms, special housing for disabled students, special housing for international students, women's dorms, apartments for single students, Theme Housing, Single parent housing, suites, healthy living, academic. 80% of campus accessible to physically disabled. **Special Academic Facilities/Equipment:** Center for the Arts (galleries, theaters) http://www.endicott.edu/centerforthearts, Endicott Archives Museum http://www.endicott.edu/archives, La Chanterelle, a student-run restaraunt http://www.endicott.edu/lachanterelle **Computers:** 100% of classrooms, 96% of dorms, 100% of libraries, 100% of dining areas, 100% of student union, have wireless network access. Students can register for classes online. Administrative functions (other than registration) can be performed online.

CAMPUS LIFE

Environment: Town. **Activities:** Choral groups, concert band, dance, drama/theater, jazz band, literary magazine, music ensembles, musical theater, student government, student newspaper, student-run film society, television station,

yearbook, Campus Ministries, International Student Organization, Model UN. 47 registered organizations, 7 honor societies, 1 religious organization. **Athletics (Intercollegiate):** *Men:* baseball, basketball, cross-country, equestrian sports, football, golf, lacrosse, soccer, tennis, volleyball. *Women:* basketball, cross-country, equestrian sports, field hockey, lacrosse, soccer, softball, tennis, volleyball. **On-Campus Highlights:** Center for the Arts, The Lodge, Post Center - Sports Complex, Callahan Center, Endicott Beaches.

ADMISSIONS

Freshman Academic Profile: Average high school GPA 3.22. 13% in top 10% of high school class, 40% in top 25% of high school class, 78% in top 50% of high school class. 79% from public high schools. SAT Math middle 50% range 490-590. SAT Critical Reading middle 50% range 490-580. SAT Writing middle 50% range 480-580. ACT middle 50% range 21-25. Minimum internet-based TOEFL 79. Minimum paper TOEFL 550. **Basis for Candidate Selection:** *Very important factors considered include:* academic GPA, rigor of secondary school record, character/personal qualities. *Important factors considered include:* Class rank, application essay, standardized test scores, alumni/ae relation, extracurricular activities, geographical residence, talent/ability, volunteer work, work experience. *Other factors considered include:* recommendation(s), first generation, interview, level of applicant's interest, racial/ethnic status, state residency. **Freshman Admission Requirements:** High school diploma is required and GED is accepted. **Freshman Admission Statistics:** 3,848 applied, 73% admitted, 27% enrolled. **Transfer Admission Requirements:** High school transcript, college transcript(s), essay or personal statement, standardized test scores, statement of good standing from prior institution(s). Minimum college GPA of 2.5 required. Lowest grade transferable C. **General Admission Information:** Application Fee $40. Regular application deadline 2/15. Notification on a rolling basis, beginning on or about 11/1. Nonfall registration accepted. Credit offered for CEEB Advanced Placement tests.

COSTS AND FINANCIAL AID

Annual tuition $28,994. Room and board $13,734. Required fees $500. Average book expense $1,170. **Required Forms and Deadlines:** FAFSA, Institution's own financial aid form. **Notification of Awards:** Applicants will be notified of awards on a rolling basis beginning 3/15. **Types of Aid:** *Loans:* Subsidized Stafford, Unsubsidized Stafford, PLUS, Federal Perkins, college/university loans from institutional funds. *Student Employment:* Federal Work-Study Program available. Institutional employment available. Highest amount earned per year from on-campus jobs $1,500. Off-campus job opportunities are good. **Financial Aid Statistics:** 84% freshmen, 83% undergrads receive need-based scholarship or grant aid. 73% freshmen, 64% undergrads receive non-need-based scholarship or grant aid. 94% freshmen, 94% undergrads receive need-based self-help aid. 0% freshmen, 0% undergrads receive athletic scholarships. 90% freshmen, 88% undergrads receive any aid. 74% undergrads borrow to pay for school. Average cumulative indebtedness $25,190. **Criteria for awarding institutional aid:** *Non-need-based:* academics, alumni affiliation, art, job skills, leadership, music/drama, religious affiliation, state/district residency.

ERSKINE COLLEGE

Erskine College, Due West, SC 29639
Phone: 864-379-8838 · **Financial Aid Phone:** 864-379-8832
E-mail: admissions@erskine.edu
Fax: 864-379-2172 · **Website:** www.erskine.edu

This private school, affiliated with the Presbyterian Church, was founded in 1839. It has a 85-acre campus.

RATINGS

Admissions Selectivity Rating: 84   Fire Safety Rating: 64

STUDENTS AND FACULTY

Enrollment: 548. **Student Body:** 53% female, 47% male, 24% out-of-state, 4% international (10 countries represented). Asian 1%, African American 8%, Caucasian 70%, Hispanic 1%, Native American <1%
Retention and Graduation: 77% freshmen return for sophomore year. 55% freshmen graduate within 4 years. 63% freshmen graduate within 6 years. **Faculty:** 41 full-time faculty, 85% hold PhDs, 39% are members of minority groups, 7% are women. 0% of classes are taught by teaching assistants.

ACADEMICS

Degrees: bachelor's, certificate, master's. **Classes:** Most classes have 10–19 students. Most lab/discussion sessions have 20–29 students. **Majors with Highest Enrollment:** Business/Commerce; Biology/Biological Sciences; Elementary Education and Teaching. **Special Study Options:** double major, independent study, internships, study abroad, teacher certification program. Combined degree programs: Medical Technology w/Medical Univ. of S. Carolina. **Disability Services:** Special programs offered to physically disabled students include tutors. **Career services:** career/job search classes.

FACILITIES

Housing: men's dorms, women's dorms. 75% of campus accessible to physically disabled. **Special Academic Facilities/Equipment:** Bowie Arts Center **Computers:**

CAMPUS LIFE

Environment: Rural. **Activities:** Choral groups, concert band, dance, drama/theater, jazz band, literary magazine, music ensembles, musical theater, radio station, student government, student newspaper, yearbook, Campus Ministries 51 registered organizations, 6 honor societies. **Athletics (Intercollegiate):** *Men:* baseball, basketball, cross-country, golf, soccer, tennis. *Women:* basketball, cross-country, golf, lacrosse, soccer, softball, tennis, volleyball. **On-Campus Highlights:** Java City, The Phoenix, Watkins Student Center, Bowie Arts Center.

ADMISSIONS

Freshman Academic Profile: 39% in top 10% of high school class, 65% in top 25% of high school class, 87% in top 50% of high school class. 85% from public high schools. SAT Math middle 50% range 480-605. SAT Critical Reading middle 50% range 460-590. ACT middle 50% range 21-26. Minimum paper TOEFL 550. **Basis for Candidate Selection:** *Very important factors considered include:* application essay, academic GPA, recommendation(s), rigor of secondary school record, standardized test scores, alumni/ae relation. *Important factors considered include:* character/personal qualities, extracurricular activities, talent/ability. *Other factors considered include:* Class rank, first generation, geographical residence, interview, level of applicant's interest, racial/ethnic status, religious affiliation/commitment, state residency, volunteer work, work experience. **Freshman Admission Requirements:** High school diploma is required and GED is accepted. *Academic units required:* 4 English, 2 mathematics, 2 science, (2 science labs). **Freshman Admission Statistics:** 500 applied, 75% admitted, 39% enrolled. **Transfer Admission Requirements:** college transcript(s), essay or personal statement, statement of good standing from prior institution(s). Minimum college GPA of 2.0 required. Lowest grade transferable C. **General Admission Information:** Application Fee $25. Notification on a rolling basis, beginning on or about 11/15. Nonfall registration accepted. Credit and/or placement offered for CEEB Advanced Placement tests.

COSTS AND FINANCIAL AID

Required Forms and Deadlines: FAFSA, Institution's own financial aid form, State aid form. **Notification of Awards:** Applicants will be notified of awards on a rolling basis beginning 12/15. **Types of Aid:** *Need-based scholarships/grants:* Federal Pell, SEOG, state scholarships/grants, private scholarships, the school's own gift aid Federal ACG, Smart & Teach Grants. *Loans:* Subsidized Stafford, Unsubsidized Stafford, PLUS, Federal Perkins, college/university loans from institutional funds, Alternative Loans. *Student Employment:* Federal Work-Study Program available. Institutional employment available. **Financial Aid Statistics:** 100% freshmen, 100% undergrads receive need-based scholarship or grant aid. 100% freshmen, 100% undergrads receive non-need-based scholarship or grant aid. 95% freshmen, 99% undergrads receive need-based self-help aid. 49% freshmen, 42% undergrads receive athletic scholarships. 72% undergrads borrow to pay for school. Average cumulative indebtedness $21,250. **Criteria for awarding institutional aid:** *Non-need-based:* academics, alumni affiliation, athletics, leadership, minority status, music/drama, religious affiliation, state/district residency.

EUGENE BIBLE COLLEGE

2155 Bailey Hill Road, Eugene, OR 97405-1194
Phone: 800-322-2638 · **Financial Aid Phone:** 800-322-2638
E-mail: admissions@ebc.edu · **CEEB Code:** 4274
Fax: 541-343-5801 · **Website:** http://www.ebc.edu/ · **ACT Code:** 3468

This private school was founded in 1925. It has a 33-acre campus.

RATINGS

Admissions Selectivity Rating: 84   Fire Safety Rating: 75

STUDENTS AND FACULTY

Enrollment: 180. **Student Body:** 44% female, 56% male, 54% out-of-state, (5 countries represented).
Retention and Graduation: 68% freshmen return for sophomore year. 31% freshmen graduate within 4 years. 41% freshmen graduate within 6 years. 35% grads go on to further study within 1 year. **Faculty:** 10 full-time faculty, 30% hold PhDs, 40% are members of minority groups, 20% are women. 0% of classes are taught by teaching assistants.

ACADEMICS

Degrees: bachelor's, certificate. **Classes:** Most classes have 10–19 students. Most lab/discussion sessions have 10–19 students. **Majors with Highest Enrollment:** Bible/Biblical Studies; Pastoral Studies/Counseling; Youth Ministry. **Special Study Options:** cooperative education program, distance learning, double major, dual enrollment, independent study, internships, liberal arts/career combination, One year Bible Certificate obtainable by external studies program. **Career services:**

FACILITIES

Housing: men's dorms, women's dorms, apartments for married students, apartments for single students. 75% of campus accessible to physically disabled. **Special Academic Facilities/Equipment:** Music lab, computer lab.

CAMPUS LIFE

Environment: City. **Activities:** Choral groups, drama/theater, music ensembles, student government, yearbook. **Athletics (Intercollegiate):** *Men:* basketball, soccer. *Women:* soccer, volleyball. **On-Campus Highlights:** Student Center, Cafeteria, Dorm Lounges, Computer Lab, Workout Room.

ADMISSIONS

Freshman Academic Profile: Average high school GPA 3.1. 8% in top 10% of high school class, 29% in top 25% of high school class, 67% in top 50% of high school class. 90% from public high schools. SAT Math middle 50% range 430-610. SAT Critical Reading middle 50% range 450-580. ACT middle 50% range 19-24. Minimum paper TOEFL 500. **Basis for Candidate Selection:** *Very important factors considered include:* application essay, recommendation(s), character/personal qualities, religious affiliation/commitment. *Important factors considered include:* rigor of secondary school record. *Other factors considered include:* Class rank, standardized test scores, extracurricular activities, talent/ability, volunteer work, work experience. **Freshman Admission Requirements:** High school diploma is required and GED is accepted. **Freshman Admission Statistics:** 217 applied, 47% admitted, 63% enrolled. **Transfer Admission Requirements:** college transcript(s), essay or personal statement, Minimum college GPA of 2.0 required. Lowest grade transferable C. **General Admission Information:** Application Fee $30. Regular application deadline 9/1. Notification on a rolling basis, beginning on or about 10/1. Nonfall registration accepted. Admission may be deferred for a maximum of 24 months. Credit offered for CEEB Advanced Placement tests.

COSTS AND FINANCIAL AID

Annual tuition $7,500. Room and board $4,575. Required fees $801. Average book expense $800. **Required Forms and Deadlines:** FAFSA. **Notification of Awards:** Applicants will be notified of awards on a rolling basis beginning 7/15. **Types of Aid:** *Need-based scholarships/grants:* Federal Pell, SEOG, the school's own gift aid. *Loans:* Direct Subsidized Stafford, Direct Unsubsidized Stafford, Direct PLUS, PLUS. **Financial Aid Statistics:** 100% freshmen, 100% undergrads receive need-based scholarship or grant aid. 16% freshmen, 13% undergrads receive non-need-based scholarship or grant aid. 100% freshmen, 100% undergrads receive need-based self-help aid. 1% freshmen, 0% undergrads receive athletic scholarships. 90% undergrads borrow to pay for school. **Criteria for awarding institutional aid:** *Non-need-based:* academics, alumni affiliation, athletics, leadership, music/drama.

EUGENE LANG COLLEGE THE NEW SCHOOL FOR LIBERAL ARTS

72 5th Avenue, 2nd Floor, New York, NY 10011
Phone: 212-229-5150 · **Financial Aid Phone:** 212 229 8930
E-mail: lang@newschool.edu · **CEEB Code:** 2521
Fax: 212-229-5355 · **Website:** www.newschool.edu/lang/ · **ACT Code:** 2828

This private school was founded in 1978.

RATINGS

Admissions Selectivity Rating: 84   Fire Safety Rating: 79

STUDENTS AND FACULTY

Enrollment: 1,441. **Student Body:** 70% female, 30% male, 72% out-of-state, 6% international (40 countries represented). Asian 5%, African American 7%, Caucasian 54%, Hispanic 13%, Native American <1%
Retention and Graduation: 76% freshmen return for sophomore year. 42% freshmen graduate within 4 years. 7% grads go on to further study within 1 year. **Faculty:** 64 full-time faculty, 88% hold PhDs, 58% are members of minority groups, 23% are women.

ACADEMICS

Degrees: bachelor's. **Classes:** Most classes have 10–19 students. Most lab/discussion sessions have 10–19 students. **Special Study Options:** Accelerated program, cross-registration, distance learning, double major, dual enrollment, English as a Second Language (ESL), exchange student program (domestic), independent study, internships, liberal arts/career combination, student-designed major, study abroad, Five year combined BA/BFA program. Combined degree programs: BA/BFA. **Disability Services:** Special programs offered to physically disabled students include note-taking services, reader services, tape recorders. **Career services:** Alumni network, alumni services, career/job search classes, career assessment, internships, regional alumni.

FACILITIES

Housing: Coed dorms, special housing for disabled students, apartments for single students. 99% of campus accessible to physically disabled. **Special Academic Facilities/Equipment:** Art gallery, photography gallery, extensive collections of contemporary art, concert hall, public lectures, conferences, cultural and intellectual events. **Computers:** 95% of classrooms, 100% of libraries, 100% of dining areas, na% of student union, 100% of common outdoor areas have wireless network access. Students can register for classes online. Administrative functions (other than registration) can be performed online.

CAMPUS LIFE

Environment: Metropolis. **Activities:** Choral groups, dance, drama/theater, jazz band, literary magazine, music ensembles, opera, radio station, student government, student newspaper, symphony orchestra, International Student Organization. 34 registered organizations. **On-Campus Highlights:** Harry Scherman Library, Raymond Fogelman Library, Lang Courtyard, University Welcome Center, Sheila C. Johnson Design Center. **Environmental Initiatives:** 1. In Fall 2010, The New School Facilities Management hired an engineering firm to conduct energy audits and to retro-commission five of the most energy-intensive owned buildings on campus. The result will be a phased capital plan to address needed upgrades in these buildings, equating to 500,000gsf, that will reduce carbon emissions. 2. The New School Office for Sustainability hired a consultant to conduct a waste audit of the entire campus in Fall 2009. A waste reduction strategy is currently being finalized. The immediate outcomes are new recycling signs and an enhanced post-consumer composting program in four buildings. Food scraps, napkins/paper towels and compostable cups and utensils will be collected in all food service locations plus a pilot location in a building with architecture and fine arts studios. The New School replaced two steam boilers, which were approximately 50 years old. Located in Johnson/Kaplan Hall, the universitys founding building, constructed in 1930, this boiler plant burned #6 heating oil, the dirtiest and most carbon-intensive heating oil. In the summer of 2010, Design, Construction, and Facilities Management upgraded the plant to house two new steam dual-fuel boilers with a thermal efficiency of 86 percent and the option to burn #2 heating oil or, eventually, natural gas, the least carbon intensive fossil fuel. This retrofit project also marks the phasing out of #6 heating oil on campus. In the summer of 2010, Design, Construction, and Facilities Management also replaced the roof at Johnson/Kaplan Hall with a white Thermoplastic Polyolefin (TPO) thermally bonded membrane with superior durability and an ENERGY STAR rating for its high reflectance. Insulation was also added to the roof. The new roof drastically reduces heat absorption in the summer months and also better insulates the building in the winter, resulting in lower cooling and heating loads and costs. Phasing out the use of T12 and incandescent lighting has been an ongoing initiative over the past two years and focused on 45 percent of the entire building portfolio (equivalent to 563,503 gross square feet, which represents nearly 72 percent of The New Schools owned buildings). In FY10, the Office for Sustainability began to install campus-wide (in all spaces where The New School has operational control) occupancy sensors in bathrooms, office kitchenettes, and conference rooms. By the end of FY12, the university will phase out T12s and incandescent lighting in all university-owned buildings and launch a LED lighting demonstration project.

ADMISSIONS

Freshman Academic Profile: Average high school GPA 3.29. 16% in top 10% of high school class, 51% in top 25% of high school class, 85% in top 50% of high school class. SAT Math middle 50% range 510-600. SAT Critical Reading middle 50% range 550-660. SAT Writing middle 50% range 550-650. ACT middle 50% range 25-29. Minimum internet-based TOEFL 92. **Basis for Candidate Selection:** *Very important factors considered include:* application essay, academic GPA, recommendation(s), rigor of secondary school record. *Important factors considered include:* standardized test scores, character/personal qualities, interview, level of applicant's interest, volunteer work. *Other factors considered include:* Class rank, alumni/ae relation, extracurricular activities, first generation, geographical residence, talent/ability, work experience. **Freshman Admission Requirements:** High school diploma is required and GED is accepted. *Academic units required:* 4 English. **Freshman Admission Statistics:** 1,642 applied, 81% admitted, 22% enrolled. **Transfer Admission Requirements:** High school transcript, college transcript(s), essay or personal statement, standardized test scores, Minimum college GPA of 3.0 required. Lowest grade transferable C. **General Admission Information:** Application Fee $50. Early decision application deadline 11/15. Regular application deadline 2/1.

Notification on a rolling basis, beginning on or about 3/25. Nonfall registration accepted. Admission may be deferred for a maximum of 1 year. Neither credit nor placement offered for CEEB Advanced Placement tests.

COSTS AND FINANCIAL AID

Annual tuition $39,030. Room and board $18,490. Required fees $886. Average book expense $920. **Required Forms and Deadlines:** FAFSA, State aid form. **Notification of Awards:** Applicants will be notified of awards on a rolling basis beginning 3/1. **Types of Aid:** *Need-based scholarships/grants:* Federal Pell, SEOG, state scholarships/grants, private scholarships, the school's own gift aid. *Loans:* Subsidized Stafford, Unsubsidized Stafford, PLUS, Federal Perkins. *Student Employment:* Federal Work-Study Program available. Institutional employment available. Off-campus job opportunities are excellent. **Financial Aid Statistics:** 97% freshmen, 93% undergrads receive need-based scholarship or grant aid. 14% freshmen, 17% undergrads receive non-need-based scholarship or grant aid. 96% freshmen, 94% undergrads receive need-based self-help aid. 0% freshmen, 0% undergrads receive athletic scholarships. 76% undergrads borrow to pay for school. Average cumulative indebtedness $19,264. **Criteria for awarding institutional aid:** *Non-need-based:* academics, leadership.

EUREKA COLLEGE

300 East College Avenue, Eureka, IL 61530-1500
Phone: 309-467-6350 • **Financial Aid Phone:** 309-467-6311
E-mail: admissions@eureka.edu • **CEEB Code:** 1206
Fax: 309-467-6576 • **Website:** http://www.eureka.edu/index.html • **ACT Code:** 1022

This private school, affiliated with the Disciples of Christ Church, was founded in 1855. It has a 112-acre campus.

RATINGS

Admissions Selectivity Rating: 78   **Fire Safety Rating:** 76

STUDENTS AND FACULTY

Enrollment: 654. **Student Body:** 56% female, 44% male, 10% out-of-state, 0% international (5 countries represented). Asian 1%, African American 3%, Caucasian 73%, Hispanic 2%, Native American <1%
Retention and Graduation: 74% freshmen return for sophomore year. 41% freshmen graduate within 4 years. 51% freshmen graduate within 6 years. 24% grads go on to further study within 1 year. 8% grads pursue arts and sciences degrees. 6% grads pursue law degrees. 2% grads pursue business degrees. 3% grads pursue medical degrees. **Faculty:** 35 full-time faculty, 80% hold PhDs, 34% are members of minority groups, 3% are women. 0% of classes are taught by teaching assistants.

ACADEMICS

Degrees: bachelor's, certificate. **Classes:** Most classes have 10–19 students. Most lab/discussion sessions have fewer than 10 students. **Majors with Highest Enrollment:** Elementary Education and Teaching; Psychology; Business/Commerce. **Special Study Options:** double major, dual enrollment, honors program, independent study, internships, liberal arts/career combination, student-designed major, study abroad, teacher certification program, weekend college, Weekend Degree Completion Cohort Program in Organizational Leadership Weekend Degree Certification in Special Education. **Honors programs:** Academic Honors Program, Reagan Leadership Program, Sandifer Mentorship Program Combined degree programs: BA/MEng, 2-2 nursing prog with Mennonite Coll of Nursing. **Disability Services:** Special programs offered to physically disabled students include tutors.

FACILITIES

Housing: Coed dorms, special housing for disabled students, men's dorms, women's dorms, fraternity/sorority housing. 60% of campus accessible to physically disabled. **Special Academic Facilities/Equipment:** Ronald Reagan Museum, Electron Microscope, Peace Garden. **Computers:** Administrative functions (other than registration) can be performed online.

CAMPUS LIFE

Environment: Village. **Activities:** Choral groups, concert band, dance, drama/theater, jazz band, literary magazine, musical theater, pep band, student government, student newspaper, student-run film society, yearbook. 41 registered organizations, 15 honor societies, 4 religious organizations. 3 fraternities, 3 sororities. **Athletics (Intercollegiate):** *Men:* baseball, basketball, cross-country, football, golf, soccer, swimming, tennis, track/field (outdoor). *Women:* basketball, cross-country, golf, soccer, softball, swimming, tennis, track/field (outdoor), volleyball. **On-Campus Highlights:** Ronald Reagan Museum and Peace Garden, Cerf College Center, National Historic Site: Administration Building, National Historic Site: The Chapel, Lilac Arboretum, Founded in 1855 by abolitionists, Eureka College is located on 130 acres of trees and gardens.

First college in Illinois to accept men and women on an equal basis. Small town setting located between two midsize cities—the best of both worlds! Personal. Faith-based. Liberal Arts. Pillow to Port internet access for all!

ADMISSIONS

Freshman Academic Profile: Average high school GPA 3.2. 17% in top 10% of high school class, 44% in top 25% of high school class, 96% in top 50% of high school class. 87% from public high schools. ACT middle 50% range 18-24. Minimum paper TOEFL 500. **Basis for Candidate Selection:** *Very important factors considered include:* Class rank, recommendation(s), rigor of secondary school record, standardized test scores, character/personal qualities, extracurricular activities, volunteer work. *Important factors considered include:* talent/ability. *Other factors considered include:* application essay, alumni/ae relation, interview, work experience. **Freshman Admission Requirements:** High school diploma is required and GED is accepted.High school diploma is required and GED is not accepted. **Freshman Admission Statistics:** 635 applied, 75% admitted, 31% enrolled. **Transfer Admission Requirements:** college transcript(s), statement of good standing from prior institution(s). Minimum college GPA of 2.0 required. Lowest grade transferable C. **General Admission Information:** Regular application deadline 8/1. Nonfall registration accepted. Admission may be deferred for a maximum of 1 year. Credit offered for CEEB Advanced Placement tests.

COSTS AND FINANCIAL AID

Annual tuition $15,673. Room and board $7,130. Required fees $580. Average book expense $1,000. **Required Forms and Deadlines:** FAFSA. **Notification of Awards:** Applicants will be notified of awards on or about 5/1. **Types of Aid:** *Need-based scholarships/grants:* Federal Pell, SEOG, state scholarships/grants, private scholarships, the school's own gift aid. *Loans:* Direct Subsidized Stafford, Direct Unsubsidized Stafford, Direct PLUS, Subsidized Stafford, Unsubsidized Stafford, PLUS, Federal Perkins, college/university loans from institutional funds, alternative loans. *Student Employment:* Federal Work-Study Program available. Institutional employment available. Highest amount earned per year from on-campus jobs $1,000. Off-campus job opportunities are excellent. **Financial Aid Statistics:** 100% freshmen, 100% undergrads receive need-based scholarship or grant aid. 0% freshmen, 0% undergrads receive non-need-based scholarship or grant aid. 91% freshmen, 89% undergrads receive need-based self-help aid. 0% freshmen, 0% undergrads receive athletic scholarships. 100% freshmen, 94% undergrads receive any aid. 86% undergrads borrow to pay for school. Average cumulative indebtedness $13,871. **Criteria for awarding institutional aid:** *Non-need-based:* academics, alumni affiliation, art, leadership, music/drama, religious affiliation.

EVANGEL UNIVERSITY

111 North Glenstone, Springfield, MO 65802
Phone: 417-865-2811
E-mail: admissions@evangel.edu · **CEEB Code:** 6198
Fax: 417-520-0545 · **Website:** www.evangel.edu · **ACT Code:** 2296

This private school was founded in 1955. It has a 80-acre campus.

RATINGS

Admissions Selectivity Rating: 61   **Fire Safety Rating:** 60*

STUDENTS AND FACULTY

Enrollment: 1,616. **Student Body:** 56% female, 44% male, 60% out-of-state, 1% international (13 countries represented). Asian 0%, African American 2%, Caucasian 64%, Hispanic 0%, Native American <1%
Retention and Graduation: 77% freshmen return for sophomore year. **Faculty:** 0% of classes are taught by teaching assistants.

ACADEMICS

Degrees: associate, bachelor's, master's. **Special Study Options:** cooperative education program, double major, dual enrollment, independent study, internships, teacher certification program. **Career services:** career/job search classes, career assessment, internships

FACILITIES

Housing: men's dorms, women's dorms, apartments for married students, Co-occupancy dorm with men and women in separate wings.

CAMPUS LIFE

Activities: Choral groups, concert band, drama/theater, jazz band, music ensembles, pep band, radio station, student government, student newspaper, television station, yearbook. 14 registered organizations, 10 honor societies, 3 religious organizations. **Athletics (Intercollegiate):** *Men:* baseball, basketball, cheerleading, cross-country, football, golf, track/field (outdoor), track/field

(indoor). *Women:* basketball, cheerleading, cross-country, golf, softball, track/field (outdoor), track/field (indoor), volleyball.

ADMISSIONS

Freshman Academic Profile: 76% from public high schools. Minimum paper TOEFL 490. **Basis for Candidate Selection:** *Very important factors considered include:* Class rank, recommendation(s), rigor of secondary school record, standardized test scores, religious affiliation/commitment. *Important factors considered include:* character/personal qualities. **Freshman Admission Requirements:** High school diploma is required and GED is accepted. **Freshman Admission Statistics:** 1,254 applied, 78% admitted, 0% enrolled. **Transfer Admission Requirements:** college transcript(s), statement of good standing from prior institution(s). Minimum college GPA of 2.0 required. Lowest grade transferable C. **General Admission Information:** Application Fee $35. Regular application deadline 8/15. Notification on a rolling basis, beginning on or about 9/1. Nonfall registration accepted. Admission may be deferred for a maximum of 1. Credit offered for CEEB Advanced Placement tests.

COSTS AND FINANCIAL AID

Annual tuition $13,530. Room and board $5,120. Required fees $660. Average book expense $800. **Required Forms and Deadlines:** FAFSA. **Notification of Awards:** Applicants will be notified of awards on a rolling basis beginning 4/1. **Types of Aid:** *Need-based scholarships/grants:* Federal Pell, SEOG, private scholarships. *Loans:* Direct Subsidized Stafford, Direct Unsubsidized Stafford, Direct PLUS, Subsidized Stafford, Unsubsidized Stafford, PLUS, Federal Perkins, college/university loans from institutional funds. *Student Employment:* Federal Work-Study Program available. Institutional employment available. Off-campus job opportunities are excellent. **Financial Aid Statistics:** 85% undergrads receive need-based scholarship or grant aid. 18% undergrads receive non-need-based scholarship or grant aid. 0% undergrads receive need-based self-help aid. 0% freshmen, 0% undergrads receive athletic scholarships.

THE EVERGREEN STATE COLLEGE

Best 380

2700 Evergreen Pkwy NW, Olympia, WA 98505
Phone: 360-867-6170 · **Financial Aid Phone:** 360-867-6205
E-mail: admissions@evergreen.edu · **CEEB Code:** 4292
Fax: 360-867-5114 · **Website:** www.evergreen.edu · **ACT Code:** 4457

This public school was founded in 1967. It has a 1000-acre campus.

RATINGS

Admissions Selectivity Rating: 71   **Fire Safety Rating:** 84

STUDENTS AND FACULTY

Enrollment: 3,802. **Student Body:** 54% female, 46% male, 25% out-of-state, 0% international (22 countries represented). Asian 2%, African American 6%, Caucasian 65%, Hispanic 8%, Native American 2%
Retention and Graduation: 69% freshmen return for sophomore year. 46% freshmen graduate within 4 years. 18% grads go on to further study within 1 year. 12% grads pursue arts and sciences degrees. 2% grads pursue business degrees. **Faculty:** 160 full-time faculty, 91% hold PhDs, 54% are members of minority groups, 25% are women. 0% of classes are taught by teaching assistants.

ACADEMICS

Degrees: bachelor's, certificate, master's. **Classes:** Most classes have 20–29 students. **Majors with Highest Enrollment:** Social Sciences; Liberal Arts and Sciences/Liberal Studies; Natural Sciences. **Special Study Options:** Accelerated program, double major, exchange student program (domestic), independent study, internships, student-designed major, study abroad, teacher certification program, weekend college, Learning disabilities services, summer session for credit, off-campus study. Combined degree programs: BA/BS Lib Arts/ Master Environ Stud/Pub Admin. **Disability Services:** Special programs offered to physically disabled students include note-taking services, tape recorders, tutors. **Career services:** Alumni network, alumni services, career/job search classes, career assessment, internships. Career services highlights include Community Opportunities & Internship Fair (COIF) http://www.evergreen.edu/advising/coif.

FACILITIES

Housing: Coed dorms, special housing for disabled students, special housing for international students, apartments for married students, apartments for single students, Wellness Housing, Theme **Housing:** First-Year/Freshman residence halls, Quiet housing, Substance-free housing, Gender Neutral Housing, Community Action House, Sustainability House. 85% of campus accessible to physically disabled. **Special Academic Facilities/Equipment:** Longhouse Cultural Center, 4 computer music labs, 3 digital studio production studios, 4 analog audio recording studio/control room clusters, digital still imaging lab, multimedia lab, 3 nonlinear video editing suites, 4 linear analog video editing suites, color and BandW photography labs, animation stand, 2 digital animation suites, film mixing studio with 5 editing suites, 2 flatbed film edit rooms, 3 A/V classrooms, 5 A/V lecture halls, Media Loan equipment checkout facility, academic sailing fleet (two 40' wooden sailboats), organic farm, scanning electron microscope, gas chromatography mass spectrometer, FTNMR, FTIR, scientific computing laboratory, printmaking studio, ceramics studio, academic wood and metal shops, weaving studio, fine metal studio, two art galleries. **Computers:** 100% of classrooms, 95% of dorms, 100% of libraries, 100% of dining areas, 100% of student union, 80% of common outdoor areas have wireless network access. Students can register for classes online. Administrative functions (other than registration) can be performed online.

CAMPUS LIFE
Environment: City. **Activities:** Choral groups, dance, drama/theater, literary magazine, music ensembles, pep band, radio station, student government, student newspaper, student-run film society, television station, Campus Ministries, Model UN. 61 registered organizations, 3 religious organizations. **Athletics (Intercollegiate):** *Men:* basketball, cross-country, soccer, track/field (outdoor), track/field (indoor). *Women:* basketball, cross-country, soccer, track/field (outdoor), track/field (indoor), volleyball. **On-Campus Highlights:** Longhouse Cultural and Education Center, Organic Farm, College Library, College Activities Building, New Seminar II Building, The Flaming Eggplant, a student-run café featuring organic, local, and vegan food. **Environmental Initiatives:** We have completed the planning and begun implementation of our Climate Action Plan—Carbon Neutrality by 2020. Integrating sustainability across the curriculum initiative. Free bus passes for all faculty/staff/students; first publicly funded LEED gold building in the state of Washington; 32% of food purchases from local/organic sources; campus waste diversion and composting programs; annual carbon inventory.

ADMISSIONS
Freshman Academic Profile: Average high school GPA 2.95. 9% in top 10% of high school class, 18% in top 25% of high school class, 55% in top 50% of high school class. SAT Math middle 50% range 420-570. SAT Critical Reading middle 50% range 460-630. SAT Writing middle 50% range 440-580. ACT middle 50% range 19-26. Minimum internet-based TOEFL 79. Minimum paper TOEFL 550. **Basis for Candidate Selection:** *Very important factors considered include:* application essay, academic GPA, rigor of secondary school record. *Important factors considered include:* standardized test scores, first generation, level of applicant's interest. *Other factors considered include:* recommendation(s), extracurricular activities, interview, volunteer work, work experience. **Freshman Admission Requirements:** High school diploma is required and GED is accepted. *Academic units required:* 4 English, 3 mathematics, 2 science, (1 science labs), 2 foreign language, 3 social studies, 1 academic electives, 1 Fine, visual or performing arts elective or other college prep elective from the areas above. **Freshman Admission Statistics:** 1,544 applied, 99% admitted, 35% enrolled. **Transfer Admission Requirements:** college transcript(s), Minimum college GPA of 2 required. Lowest grade transferable 2. **General Admission Information:** Application Fee $50. Notification on a rolling basis, beginning on or about 11/1. Nonfall registration accepted. Admission may be deferred for a maximum of One quarter. Credit offered for CEEB Advanced Placement tests.

COSTS AND FINANCIAL AID
Annual in-state tuition $7,845. Annual out-of-state tuition $20,901. Room and board $9,492. Required fees $853. Average book expense $1,032. **Required Forms and Deadlines:** FAFSA. **Notification of Awards:** Applicants will be notified of awards on a rolling basis beginning 4/1. **Types of Aid:** *Need-based scholarships/grants:* Federal Pell, SEOG, state scholarships/grants, private scholarships, the school's own gift aid, Federal Academic Competitiveness Grant (ACG); National Science and Mathematics Access to Retain Talent Grant(SMART Grant). *Loans:* Subsidized Stafford, Unsubsidized Stafford, PLUS, Federal Perkins, Private Alternative Loans. *Student Employment:* Federal Work-Study Program available. Institutional employment available. Highest amount earned per year from on-campus jobs $9,975. Off-campus job opportunities are good. **Financial Aid Statistics:** 65% freshmen, 77% undergrads receive need-based scholarship or grant aid. 1% undergrads receive non-need-based scholarship or grant aid. 68% freshmen, 77% undergrads receive need-based self-help aid. 0% freshmen, 0% undergrads receive athletic scholarships. 59% freshmen, 63% undergrads receive any aid. 51% undergrads borrow to pay for school. Average cumulative indebtedness $18,637. **Criteria for awarding institutional aid:** *Non-need-based:* academics, art, athletics, state/district residency.

EXCELSIOR COLLEGE

7 Columbia Circle, Albany, NY 12203-5159
Phone: 518-464-8500 · **Financial Aid Phone:** 518-464-8500
E-mail: admissions@excelsior.edu · **CEEB Code:** 759
Fax: 518-464-8777 · **Website:** https://www.excelsior.edu/ · **ACT Code:** 20214

This private school was founded in 1970.

RATINGS
Admissions Selectivity Rating: 60*   **Fire Safety Rating:** 60*

STUDENTS AND FACULTY
Enrollment: 32,133. **Student Body:** 58% female, 42% male, 90% out-of-state, 0% international (56 countries represented). Asian 4%, African American 17%, Caucasian 58%, Hispanic 5%, Native American 1%
Faculty:

ACADEMICS
Degrees: associate, bachelor's, master's, post-bachelor's certificate, post-master's certificate. **Classes:** Most classes have 10–19 students. **Majors with Highest Enrollment:** Liberal Arts and Sciences/Liberal Studies; Registered Nursing/Registered Nurse; Business Administration and Management. **Special Study Options:** Accelerated program, distance learning, external degree program, honors program, independent study. Combined degree programs: RN/MSN. **Career services:** Alumni network, alumni services, career assessment,

FACILITIES
Housing: No housing available on campus. **Computers:** Students can register for classes online. Administrative functions (other than registration) can be performed online.

CAMPUS LIFE
Environment: City. **Activities:** 1 honor society. **Environmental Initiatives:** EC has a staff created and led committee that looks for opportunites to create a more "green" environment.

ADMISSIONS
Freshman Admission Requirements: High school diploma is required and GED is accepted. Lowest grade transferable C. **General Admission Information:** Application Fee $75. Nonfall registration accepted.

COSTS AND FINANCIAL AID
Average book expense $0. **Required Forms and Deadlines:** FAFSA, Institution's own financial aid form, **Notification of Awards:** Applicants will be notified of awards on a rolling basis beginning 8/1. **Types of Aid:** *Need-based scholarships/grants:* Federal Pell, state scholarships/grants, private scholarships, the school's own gift aid. *Loans:* Direct Subsidized Stafford, Direct Unsubsidized Stafford, Direct PLUS. **Financial Aid Statistics:** 3% undergrads receive any aid.

FAIRFIELD UNIVERSITY

1073 North Benson Road, Fairfield, CT 6824
Phone: 203-254-4100 · **Financial Aid Phone:** 203-254-4125
E-mail: admis@fairfield.edu · **CEEB Code:** 3390
Fax: 203-254-4199 · **Website:** www.fairfield.edu · **ACT Code:** 560

This private school, affiliated with the Roman Catholic-Jesuit Church, was founded in 1942. It has a 200-acre campus.

RATINGS
Admissions Selectivity Rating: 79   **Fire Safety Rating:** 89

STUDENTS AND FACULTY
Enrollment: 3,841. **Student Body:** 59% female, 41% male, 71% out-of-state, 2% international (34 countries represented). Asian 2%, African American 2%, Caucasian 75%, Hispanic 7%, Native American <1%
Retention and Graduation: 89% freshmen return for sophomore year. 77% freshmen graduate within 4 years. 80% freshmen graduate within 6 years. 23% grads go on to further study within 1 year. 20% grads pursue arts and sciences

degrees. 12% grads pursue law degrees. 33% grads pursue business degrees. 7% grads pursue medical degrees. **Faculty:** 256 full-time faculty, 93% hold PhDs, 56% are members of minority groups, 9% are women. 0% of classes are taught by teaching assistants.

ACADEMICS

Degrees: associate, bachelor's, master's, post-master's certificate. **Classes:** Most classes have 20–29 students. **Majors with Highest Enrollment:** Registered Nursing/Registered Nurse; Speech Communication and Rhetoric; Marketing/Marketing Management. **Special Study Options:** cross-registration, double major, exchange student program (domestic), honors program, independent study, internships, liberal arts/career combination, student-designed major, study abroad, teacher certification program, 3/2 Program with UCONN, Rensselaer Polytechnic Institute of Technology, Columbia and Stevens Institute of Technology. **Honors programs:** Magis Scholars Four year Honors Program Corrigan Research Scholars Combined degree programs: BA/MEng, BS/MS Software Engineering. **Disability Services:** Special programs offered to physically disabled students include note-taking services, reader services, tape recorders, tutors. **Career services:** Alumni network, alumni services, career/job search classes, career assessment, internships. Career services highlights include Fairfield's proximity to NYC, Stamford, and Bridgeport, which maximizes student opportunities for internships in all majors from Finance to Psychology.

FACILITIES

Housing: Coed dorms, special housing for disabled students, apartments for single students, Wellness Floor; Sophomore College; Women in Math & Science; Freshmen Residence Halls; Diversity & Social Justice Floor (for Sophomores); Leadership House; Community Service House; The Green House; Empowering Women House; Extensive theme based living-learning options for sophomores. 70% of campus accessible to physically disabled. **Special Academic Facilities/Equipment:** Quick Center for the arts, 2 art galleries, media center, TV studio, language labs, computer center for teacher education, Business Experiential, Simulation & Trading Floor (BEST) at the School of Business. School of Nursing Learning Resouce center is a simulated hospital environment with a Human Patient Simulator (SimMan) for simulation based learning. **Computers:** 50% of classrooms, 100% of dorms, 100% of libraries, 100% of dining areas, 100% of student union, 5% of common outdoor areas have wireless network access. Students can register for classes online. Administrative functions (other than registration) can be performed online.

CAMPUS LIFE

Environment: Town. **Activities:** Choral groups, concert band, dance, drama/theater, jazz band, literary magazine, music ensembles, pep band, radio station, student government, student newspaper, student-run film society, television station, yearbook, Campus Ministries, International Student Organization, Model UN. 110 registered organizations, 21 honor society, 3 religious organizations. **Athletics (Intercollegiate):** Men: baseball, basketball, crew/rowing, cross-country, diving, golf, lacrosse, soccer, swimming, tennis. Women: basketball, crew/rowing, cross-country, diving, field hockey, golf, lacrosse, soccer, softball, swimming, tennis, volleyball. **On-Campus Highlights:** Quick Center for the Arts(includes Walsh Art Gallery, Kelley Theatre and Wien Theatre, Egan/Loyola Chapel, DiMenna-Nyselius Library, Leslie C. Quick, Jr. Recreation Complex, Barone Campus Center (Student Center), Jazzman's Coffee Bar. **Environmental Initiatives:** Built a Co-generation facility providing 90% of campus electricity; 60% campus heating. Large scale recycling and composting/biofuels initiative. While there is no Full-time dedicated staff person, sustainability efforts are performed by several people and overseen by the Environmental Steering Committees that was convened in 2006-07 and meets quarterly.

ADMISSIONS

Freshman Academic Profile: Average high school GPA 3.45. 57% from public high schools. SAT Math middle 50% range 550-640. SAT Critical Reading middle 50% range 540-620. SAT Writing middle 50% range 560-640. ACT middle 50% range 24-28. Minimum internet-based TOEFL 80. Minimum paper TOEFL 550. **Basis for Candidate Selection:** Very important factors considered include: application essay, academic GPA, recommendation(s), rigor of secondary school record. Important factors considered include: character/personal qualities, extracurricular activities, first generation, interview, talent/ability, volunteer work, work experience. Other factors considered include: Class rank, standardized test scores, alumni/ae relation, geographical residence, racial/ethnic status. **Freshman Admission Requirements:** High school diploma is required and GED is not accepted. Academic units required: 4 English, 3 mathematics, 2 science, (2 science labs), 2 foreign language, 2 social studies, 2 history, 1 academic electives. **Freshman Admission Statistics:** 9,978 applied, 72% admitted, 15% enrolled. **Transfer Admission Requirements:** High school transcript, college transcript(s), essay or personal statement, statement of good standing from prior institution(s). Minimum college GPA of .03 required. Lowest grade transferable C. **General Admission Information:** Application Fee $60. Regular application deadline 1/15. Regular notification 4/1. Nonfall registration not accepted. Admission may be deferred for a maximum of 1 Year. Credit and/or placement offered for CEEB Advanced Placement tests.

COSTS AND FINANCIAL AID

Annual tuition $43,170. Room and board $13,190. Required fees $600. Average book expense $1,150. **Required Forms and Deadlines:** FAFSA, CSS/Financial Aid PROFILE, Noncustodial PROFILE, Business/Farm Supplement. **Notification of Awards:** Applicants will be notified of awards on or about 4/1. *Types of Aid: Need-based scholarships/grants:* Federal Pell, SEOG, state scholarships/grants, private scholarships, the school's own gift aid, Federal Nursing Scholarships. *Loans:* Subsidized Stafford, Unsubsidized Stafford, PLUS, Federal Perkins, Federal Nursing, Alternative Loans. *Student Employment:* Federal Work-Study Program available. Institutional employment available. Highest amount earned per year from on-campus jobs $1,500. Off-campus job opportunities are good. **Financial Aid Statistics:** 86% freshmen, 88% undergrads receive need-based scholarship or grant aid. 89% freshmen, 80% undergrads receive non-need-based scholarship or grant aid. 78% freshmen, 82% undergrads receive need-based self-help aid. 7% freshmen, 7% undergrads receive athletic scholarships. 92% freshmen, 80% undergrads receive any aid. 65% undergrads borrow to pay for school. Average cumulative indebtedness $24,524. **Criteria for awarding institutional aid:** *Non-need-based:* academics, alumni affiliation, art, athletics, leadership, music/drama.

FAIRLEIGH DICKINSON UNIVERSITY, COLLEGE AT FLORHAM

285 Madison Ave, Madison, NJ 7940
Phone: 800-338-8803
E-mail: globaleducation@fdu.edu • **CEEB Code:** 226241
Fax: 973-443-8088 • **Website:** www.fdu.edu • **ACT Code:** 2554

This private school was founded in 1942. It has a 178-acre campus.

RATINGS

Admissions Selectivity Rating: 77   **Fire Safety Rating:** 85

STUDENTS AND FACULTY

Enrollment: 2,356. **Student Body:** 55% female, 45% male, 16% out-of-state, 1% international (25 countries represented). Asian 4%, African American 11%, Caucasian 62%, Hispanic 13%, Native American 1%
Retention and Graduation: 43% freshmen graduate within 4 years. 58% freshmen graduate within 6 years. **Faculty:** 141 full-time faculty, 45% are members of minority groups.

ACADEMICS

Degrees: bachelor's, master's, post-bachelor's certificate, post-master's certificate. **Majors with Highest Enrollment:** Business Administration and Management; Psychology; Speech Communication and Rhetoric. **Special Study Options:** Accelerated program, cooperative education program, cross-registration, distance learning, double major, external degree program, honors program, independent study, internships, liberal arts/career combination, student-designed major, teacher certification program, weekend college. Combined degree programs: BA/MD, BA/MA, BA/DDS, BA or BS/MAT, BA or BS/MBA, BA/MPA. **Disability Services:** Special programs offered to physically disabled students include note-taking services, reader services, tape recorders, tutors. **Career services:** Alumni network, alumni services, career/job search classes, career assessment, internships. Career services highlights include experiential learning.

FACILITIES

Housing: Coed dorms, special housing for disabled students. 34% of campus accessible to physically disabled. **Computers:** 100% of classrooms, 100% of libraries, 100% of dining areas, 100% of student union, have wireless network access. Students can register for classes online. Administrative functions (other than registration) can be performed online.

CAMPUS LIFE

Environment: Village. **Activities:** Choral groups, dance, drama/theater, literary magazine, musical theater, radio station, student government, student newspaper, student-run film society, yearbook, Campus Ministries, International Student Organization. 44 registered organizations, 9 honor societies, 3 religious organizations. 6 fraternities, 4 sororities. **Athletics (Intercollegiate):** Men: baseball, basketball, cross-country, football, golf, lacrosse, soccer, swimming, tennis. Women: basketball, cross-country, field hockey, lacrosse, soccer, softball, swimming, tennis, volleyball. **On-Campus Highlights:** Recreation Center, Bottle Hill Pub, Florham Perks, L'Orangerie of Library, Mansion gardens. **Environmental Initiatives:** Recyclemania, Recycling Bins, New contruction, LEED certification, HVAC upgrades will be energy efficient.

ADMISSIONS

Freshman Academic Profile: Average high school GPA 3.1. 14.3% in top 10% of high school class, 35.9% in top 25% of high school class, 74.6% in top 50% of high school class. SAT Math middle 50% range 460-570. SAT Critical Reading middle 50% range 450-560. SAT Writing middle 50% range 460-560. Minimum internet-based TOEFL 79. Minimum paper TOEFL 550. **Basis for Candidate Selection:** *Very important factors considered include:* academic GPA, rigor of secondary school record. *Important factors considered include:* standardized test scores. *Other factors considered include:* Class rank, recommendation(s), extracurricular activities, interview, volunteer work, work experience. **Freshman Admission Requirements:** High school diploma is required and GED is accepted. *Academic units required:* 4 English, 3 mathematics, 2 science, (2 science labs), 2 foreign language, 2 social studies, 2 history, 3 academic electives. **Freshman Admission Statistics:** 3,647 applied, 78% admitted, 21% enrolled. **Transfer Admission Requirements:** college transcript(s), Minimum college GPA of 2.0 required. Lowest grade transferable C. **General Admission Information:** Application Fee $40. Notification on a rolling basis, beginning on or about 11/15. Nonfall registration accepted. Admission may be deferred for a maximum of 1 year. Credit offered for CEEB Advanced Placement tests.

COSTS AND FINANCIAL AID

Annual tuition $36,386. Room and board $12,294. Required fees $958. *Student Employment:* Federal Work-Study Program available. Institutional employment available. Off-campus job opportunities are good. **Financial Aid Statistics:**

FAIRLEIGH DICKINSON UNIVERSITY, METROPOLITAN CAMPUS

1000 River Road, Teaneck, NJ 07666-1966
Phone: 201-692-2553
E-mail: globaleducation@fdu.edu • **CEEB Code:** 226341
Fax: 201-692-7319 • **Website:** www.fdu.edu • **ACT Code:** 2552

This private school was founded in 1942. It has a 68-acre campus.

RATINGS

Admissions Selectivity Rating: 78   **Fire Safety Rating:** 85

STUDENTS AND FACULTY

Enrollment: 4,101. **Student Body:** 57% female, 43% male, 14% out-of-state, 7% international (83 countries represented). Asian 5%, African American 14%, Caucasian 29%, Hispanic 34%, Native American <1%
Retention and Graduation: 28% freshmen graduate within 4 years. 47% freshmen graduate within 6 years. **Faculty:** 190 full-time faculty, 46% are members of minority groups.

ACADEMICS

Degrees: associate, bachelor's, certificate, master's, post-bachelor's certificate, post-master's certificate, terminal associate. **Majors with Highest Enrollment:** Psychology; Registered Nursing/Registered Nurse; Criminal Justice/Law Enforcement Administration. **Special Study Options:** Accelerated program, cooperative education program, cross-registration, distance learning, English as a Second Language (ESL), external degree program, honors program, independent study, internships, liberal arts/career combination, student-designed major, study abroad, teacher certification program, weekend college. Combined degree programs: BA/MD, BA/MA, BA/DDS, BA/MPA, BA/BS-MAT,BA/MBA,BS/DMD,BS/DC,BSEE/MSEE,BSEE/MSCE. **Disability Services:** Special programs offered to physically disabled students include note-taking services, reader services, tape recorders, tutors. **Career services:** Alumni network, alumni services, career/job search classes, career assessment, internships. Career services highlights include experiential learning.

FACILITIES

Housing: Coed dorms, special housing for disabled students, LIFE House - Substance Free Living, Global Scholars Hall, Honor's House, Academic Year Round Housing. 41% of campus accessible to physically disabled. **Computers:** 90% of classrooms, 100% of libraries, 100% of dining areas, 100% of student union, have wireless network access. Students can register for classes online. Administrative functions (other than registration) can be performed online.

CAMPUS LIFE

Environment: Town. **Activities:** Choral groups, dance, drama/theater, literary magazine, pep band, radio station, student government, student newspaper, student-run film society, yearbook, Campus Ministries, International Student Organization, Model UN. 72 registered organizations, 10 honor societies, 4 religious organizations. 5 fraternities, 7 sororities. **Athletics (Intercollegiate):**

Men: baseball, basketball, cross-country, golf, soccer, tennis, track/field (indoor). *Women:* basketball, bowling, cross-country, fencing, golf, soccer, softball, tennis, track/field (indoor), volleyball. **On-Campus Highlights:** Weiner Library, Fitness Center, Jeepers (Wireless Café), Knight Club, Hackensack River. **Environmental Initiatives:** Recyclemania, Recycling Bins, New construction, LEED certification, HVAC upgrades will be energy efficient.

ADMISSIONS

Freshman Academic Profile: Average high school GPA 3.2. 18.3% in top 10% of high school class, 44.6% in top 25% of high school class, 82.5% in top 50% of high school class. SAT Math middle 50% range 450-550. SAT Critical Reading middle 50% range 440-530. SAT Writing middle 50% range 430-540. Minimum internet-based TOEFL 79. Minimum paper TOEFL 550. **Basis for Candidate Selection:** *Very important factors considered include:* academic GPA, rigor of secondary school record. *Important factors considered include:* standardized test scores. *Other factors considered include:* Class rank, recommendation(s), extracurricular activities, interview, volunteer work, work experience. **Freshman Admission Requirements:** High school diploma is required and GED is accepted. *Academic units required:* 4 English, 3 mathematics, 2 science, (2 science labs), 2 foreign language, 2 social studies, 2 history, 3 academic electives. **Freshman Admission Statistics:** 5,193 applied, 73% admitted, 20% enrolled. **Transfer Admission Requirements:** college transcript(s), Minimum college GPA of 2.0 required. Lowest grade transferable C. **General Admission Information:** Application Fee $40. Notification on a rolling basis, beginning on or about 11/15. Nonfall registration accepted. Admission may be deferred for a maximum of 1 year. Credit offered for CEEB Advanced Placement tests.

COSTS AND FINANCIAL AID

Annual tuition $33,920. Room and board $12,742. Required fees $958. *Student Employment:* Federal Work-Study Program available. Off-campus job opportunities are good.

FAIRMONT STATE UNIVERSITY, INCLUDING PIERPONT COMMUNITY & TECHNICAL COLLEGE

Office of Admissions, Fairmont State, Fairmont, WV 26554
Phone: 304-367-4892 • **Financial Aid Phone:** 304-367-4813
E-mail: admit@fairmontstate.edu • **CEEB Code:** 4520
Website: http://www.fairmontstate.edu • **ACT Code:** 4520

This public school was founded in 1865.

RATINGS

Admissions Selectivity Rating: 72   **Fire Safety Rating:** 60*

STUDENTS AND FACULTY

Enrollment: 6,227. **Student Body:** 57% female, 43% male, 4% out-of-state, 1% international. Asian 0%, African American 4%, Caucasian 91%, Hispanic 1%, Native American <1%
Retention and Graduation: 70% freshmen return for sophomore year. 11% freshmen graduate within 4 years. 35% freshmen graduate within 6 years. **Faculty:** 232 full-time faculty, 48% hold PhDs, 45% are members of minority groups, 6% are women. 0% of classes are taught by teaching assistants.

ACADEMICS

Degrees: associate, bachelor's, certificate, master's, terminal associate, transfer associate. **Classes:** Most classes have 10–19 students. Most lab/discussion sessions have fewer than 10 students. **Majors with Highest Enrollment:** Business Administration and Management; Teacher Education and Professional Development, Specific Levels and Methods; Criminal Justice/Safety Studies. **Special Study Options:** Accelerated program, cooperative education program, cross-registration, distance learning, double major, dual enrollment, English as a Second Language (ESL), honors program, independent study, internships, liberal arts/career combination, study abroad, teacher certification program, weekend college. **Disability Services:** Special programs offered to physically disabled students include note-taking services, reader services, tutors. **Career services:** career/job search classes, career assessment.

FACILITIES

Housing: Coed dorms, men's dorms, women's dorms, apartments for married students, apartments for single students. 100% of campus accessible to physically disabled. **Special Academic Facilities/Equipment:** Folk Life Center. **Computers:** Students can register for classes online. Administrative functions (other than registration) can be performed online.

CAMPUS LIFE

Environment: Town. **Activities:** Choral groups, concert band, dance, drama/theater, jazz band, literary magazine, marching band, music ensembles, musical theater, student government, student newspaper, symphony orchestra, yearbook, Campus Ministries, International Student Organization, 90 registered organizations, 4 religious organizations, 4 fraternities, 3 sororities. **Athletics (Intercollegiate):** *Men:* baseball, basketball, cross-country, football, golf, swimming, tennis. *Women:* basketball, cheerleading, cross-country, golf, softball, tennis, volleyball.

ADMISSIONS

Freshman Academic Profile: Average high school GPA 3. 7% in top 10% of high school class, 24% in top 25% of high school class, 57% in top 50% of high school class. SAT Math middle 50% range 390-500. SAT Critical Reading middle 50% range 400-507.5. ACT middle 50% range 17-22. Minimum paper TOEFL 500. **Basis for Candidate Selection:** *Very important factors considered include:* academic GPA, standardized test scores. **Freshman Admission Requirements:** High school diploma is required and GED is accepted. *Academic units required:* 4 English, 3 mathematics, 3 science, (2 science labs), 3 social studies, 1 history. **Freshman Admission Statistics:** 3,400 applied, 79% admitted, 45% enrolled. **Transfer Admission Requirements:** college transcript(s), Minimum college GPA of 2.00 required. Lowest grade transferable D. **General Admission Information:** Notification on a rolling basis, beginning on or about 10/1. Nonfall registration accepted. Credit and/or placement offered for CEEB Advanced Placement tests.

COSTS AND FINANCIAL AID

Annual in-state tuition $4,656. Annual out-of-state tuition $9,956. Room and board $5,990. Average book expense $900. *Student Employment:* Federal Work-Study Program available. Institutional employment available. Off-campus job opportunities are good. **Financial Aid Statistics:** 85% freshmen, 80% undergrads receive any aid.

FAITH BAPTIST BIBLE COLLEGE AND THEOLOGICAL SEMINARY

1900 NW 4th Street, Ankeny, IA 50023
Phone: 1.888.faith.4.u · **Financial Aid Phone:** 515-964-0601
E-mail: admissions@faith.edu · **CEEB Code:** 6214
Fax: 515-964-1638 · **Website:** http://www.faith.edu/ · **ACT Code:** 1315

This private school, affiliated with the Baptist Church, was founded in 1921. It has a 52-acre campus.

RATINGS

Admissions Selectivity Rating: 82   **Fire Safety Rating:** 96

STUDENTS AND FACULTY

Enrollment: 232. **Student Body:** 55% female, 45% male, 56% out-of-state, 0% international. Asian 0%, African American 2%, Caucasian 92%, Hispanic 1%, Native American 1%
Retention and Graduation: 65% freshmen return for sophomore year. 39% freshmen graduate within 4 years. 23% grads go on to further study within 1 year. **Faculty:** 17 full-time faculty, 65% hold PhDs, 12% are members of minority groups, 0% are women. 0% of classes are taught by teaching assistants.

ACADEMICS

Degrees: associate, bachelor's, certificate, master's. **Classes:** Most classes have fewer than 10 students. **Majors with Highest Enrollment:** Elementary Education and Teaching; Bible/Biblical Studies; Religious Education. **Special Study Options:** independent study, internships, teacher certification program.

FACILITIES

Housing: special housing for disabled students, men's dorms, women's dorms, apartments for married students, apartments for single students. **Computers:** 75% of classrooms, 100% of dorms, 100% of libraries, 100% of dining areas, 100% of student union, 60% of common outdoor areas have wireless network access.

CAMPUS LIFE

Environment: Town. **Activities:** Choral groups, concert band, dance, drama/theater, music ensembles, student government, symphony orchestra, yearbook, Campus Ministries, International Student Organization 1 registered organization, 1 religious organization. **Athletics (Intercollegiate):** *Men:* basketball, soccer. *Women:* basketball, soccer, volleyball. **On-Campus Highlights:** Convocation Building, Benson Hall, Library, Gray Hall, Residence Halls.

ADMISSIONS

Freshman Academic Profile: Average high school GPA 3.46. 9% in top 10% of high school class, 40% in top 25% of high school class, 60% in top 50% of

high school class. 33% from public high schools. SAT Math middle 50% range 390-560. SAT Critical Reading middle 50% range 410-550. SAT Writing middle 50% range 400-470. ACT middle 50% range 19-24. Minimum internet-based TOEFL 173. Minimum paper TOEFL 500. **Basis for Candidate Selection:** *Very important factors considered include:* religious affiliation/commitment. *Important factors considered include:* application essay. *Other factors considered include:* Class rank, academic GPA, recommendation(s), standardized test scores, character/personal qualities, extracurricular activities, interview, level of applicant's interest, talent/ability, volunteer work. **Freshman Admission Requirements:** High school diploma is required and GED is accepted. **Freshman Admission Statistics:** 150 applied, 67% admitted, 87% enrolled. **Transfer Admission Requirements:** college transcript(s), essay or personal statement, statement of good standing from prior institution(s). Minimum college GPA of 2.0 required. Lowest grade transferable C. **General Admission Information:** Application Fee $25. Regular application deadline 8/1. Notification on a rolling basis, beginning on or about 9/1. Nonfall registration accepted. Admission may be deferred for a maximum of 1 year. Credit offered for CEEB Advanced Placement tests.

COSTS AND FINANCIAL AID

Required Forms and Deadlines: FAFSA. **Types of Aid:** *Need-based scholarships/grants:* Federal Pell, state scholarships/grants, private scholarships, the school's own gift aid. **Loans:** Subsidized Stafford, Unsubsidized Stafford, PLUS. *Student Employment:* Institutional employment available. Off-campus job opportunities are excellent. **Financial Aid Statistics:** 70% freshmen, 95% undergrads receive any aid. **Criteria for awarding institutional aid:** *Non-need-based:* academics, leadership, music/drama, state/district residency.

FARMINGDALE STATE COLLEGE

Admissions Office, Farmingdale, NY 11735
Phone: 631-420-2200 · **Financial Aid Phone:** 631-420-2578
E-mail: admissions@farmingdale.edu · **CEEB Code:** 2526
Fax: 631-420-2633 · **Website:** www.farmingdale.edu · **ACT Code:** 2918

This public school was founded in 1912. It has a 380-acre campus.

RATINGS

Admissions Selectivity Rating: 79   **Fire Safety Rating:** 60*

STUDENTS AND FACULTY

Enrollment: 7,768. **Student Body:** 42% female, 58% male, 0% out-of-state, 3% international. Asian 7%, African American 10%, Caucasian 60%, Hispanic 16%, Native American <1%
Retention and Graduation: 80% freshmen return for sophomore year. 26% freshmen graduate within 4 years. 43% freshmen graduate within 6 years. **Faculty:** 209 full-time faculty, 75% hold PhDs, 46% are members of minority groups. 0% of classes are taught by teaching assistants.

ACADEMICS

Degrees: associate, bachelor's, certificate, terminal associate, transfer associate. **Classes:** Most classes have 20–29 students. **Majors with Highest Enrollment:** Computer and Information Sciences and Support Services; Registered Nursing/Registered Nurse; Business, Management, Marketing, and Related Support Services. **Special Study Options:** distance learning, double major, dual enrollment, internships, study abroad. **Disability Services:** Special programs offered to physically disabled students include reader services, tutors. **Career services:** alumni services, career/job search classes, career assessment, internships,

FACILITIES

Housing: 90% of campus accessible to physically disabled. **Computers:** Students can register for classes online. Administrative functions (other than registration) can be performed online.

CAMPUS LIFE

Environment: Village. **Activities:** literary magazine. **Athletics (Intercollegiate):** *Men:* baseball, basketball, cross-country, golf, lacrosse, soccer, track/field (outdoor), track/field (indoor). *Women:* basketball, cross-country, soccer, softball, track/field (outdoor), track/field (indoor), volleyball.

ADMISSIONS

Freshman Academic Profile: Average high school GPA 3.2. 4% in top 10% of high school class, 24% in top 25% of high school class, 65% in top 50% of high school class. 92% from public high schools. SAT Math middle 50% range 460-540. SAT Critical Reading middle 50% range 440-520. ACT middle 50% range 19-23. **Basis for Candidate Selection:** *Very important factors considered include:* Class rank, rigor of secondary school record. *Important factors consid-*

ered include: talent/ability. *Other factors considered include:* application essay, recommendation(s), standardized test scores, alumni/ae relation, character/personal qualities, extracurricular activities, interview, volunteer work, work experience. **Freshman Admission Requirements:** High school diploma is required and GED is accepted. *Academic units required:* 4 English, 2 mathematics, 1 science, (1 science labs), 4 social studies. **Freshman Admission Statistics:** 5,183 applied, 47% admitted, 44% enrolled. **Transfer Admission Requirements:** High school transcript, college transcript(s), statement of good standing from prior institution(s). Minimum college GPA of 2.0 required. Lowest grade transferable C. **General Admission Information:** Application Fee $30. Notification on a rolling basis, beginning on or about 11/1. Nonfall registration accepted. Admission may be deferred for a maximum of 1 year. Credit and/or placement offered for CEEB Advanced Placement tests.

COSTS AND FINANCIAL AID
Annual in-state tuition $6,170. Annual out-of-state tuition $15,820. Room and board $12,190. Required fees $1,313. Average book expense $1,200. **Required Forms and Deadlines:** FAFSA. **Types of Aid:** *Need-based scholarships/grants:* Federal Pell, SEOG, state scholarships/grants. *Loans:* Direct Subsidized Stafford, Direct Unsubsidized Stafford, Direct PLUS, Subsidized Stafford, Unsubsidized Stafford, PLUS, Federal Perkins, Federal Nursing, state loans. *Student Employment:* Federal Work-Study Program available. Institutional employment available. Off-campus job opportunities are good. **Financial Aid Statistics:** 90% freshmen, 87% undergrads receive need-based scholarship or grant aid. 6% freshmen, 5% undergrads receive non-need-based scholarship or grant aid. 89% freshmen, 89% undergrads receive need-based self-help aid. 0% freshmen, 0% undergrads receive athletic scholarships.

FAULKNER UNIVERSITY

5345 Atlanta Highway, Montgomery, AL 36109-3398
Phone: 334-386-7200 · **Financial Aid Phone:** 334-386-7195
E-mail: admissions@faulkner.edu · **CEEB Code:** 1034
Fax: 334-386-7137 · **Website:** www.faulkner.edu · **ACT Code:** 3

This private school, affiliated with the Church of Christ Church, was founded in 1942. It has a 78-acre campus.

RATINGS
Admissions Selectivity Rating: 76   **Fire Safety Rating:** 72

STUDENTS AND FACULTY
Enrollment: 2,032. **Student Body:** 63% female, 37% male, 12% out-of-state, 1% international (15 countries represented). Asian 1%, African American 57%, Caucasian 63%, Hispanic 1%, Native American 1%
Retention and Graduation: 59% freshmen return for sophomore year. 8% freshmen graduate within 4 years. 22% freshmen graduate within 6 years. 80% grads go on to further study within 1 year. 35% grads pursue arts and sciences degrees. 12% grads pursue law degrees. 32% grads pursue business degrees. 19% grads pursue medical degrees. **Faculty:** 105 full-time faculty, 67% hold PhDs, 32% are members of minority groups, 10% are women. 0% of classes are taught by teaching assistants.

ACADEMICS
Degrees: associate, bachelor's, first professional, master's. **Classes:** Most classes have fewer than 10 students. Most lab/discussion sessions have fewer than 10 students. **Majors with Highest Enrollment:** Business/Commerce; Management Information Systems. **Special Study Options:** Accelerated program, cooperative education program, cross-registration, distance learning, double major, dual enrollment, honors program, independent study, internships, liberal arts/career combination, study abroad, teacher certification program, weekend college. **Honors programs:** Great Books Honors College. **Disability Services:** Special programs offered to physically disabled students include note-taking services, reader services, tape recorders, tutors. **Career services:** alumni services, career/job search classes, career assessment, internships. Career services highlights include internships for all undergraduate programs. In Fall 2009 the University is starting a Spiritual Formation Program with a service-learning component.

FACILITIES
Housing: special housing for disabled students, men's dorms, women's dorms, apartments for single students. 75% of campus accessible to physically disabled. **Computers:** 100% of classrooms, 100% of dorms, 100% of libraries, 100% of dining areas, 100% of student union, 100% of common outdoor areas have wireless network access. Administrative functions (other than registration) can be performed online.

CAMPUS LIFE
Environment: City. **Activities:** Choral groups, drama/theater, music ensembles, musical theater, pep band, student government, student newspaper, yearbook, Campus Ministries. 12 registered organizations, 5 honor societies, 3 religious organizations. 5 fraternities, 5 sororities. **Athletics (Intercollegiate):** *Men:* baseball, basketball, cheerleading, fishing, football, golf, soccer. *Women:* cheerleading, fishing, soccer, softball, volleyball. **On-Campus Highlights:** Café Sienna, Student Multiplex, Dorm Lobbies, Perry Cafeteria, Dinner Theatre.

ADMISSIONS
Freshman Academic Profile: Average high school GPA 3.08. 8% in top 10% of high school class, 10% in top 25% of high school class, 40% in top 50% of high school class. 75% from public high schools. SAT Math middle 50% range 430-550. SAT Critical Reading middle 50% range 440-560. ACT middle 50% range 18-22. Minimum paper TOEFL 450. **Basis for Candidate Selection:** *Very important factors considered include:* Class rank, recommendation(s), rigor of secondary school record, standardized test scores, character/personal qualities, extracurricular activities, interview. *Important factors considered include:* application essay, alumni/ae relation, religious affiliation/commitment, talent/ability. *Other factors considered include:* volunteer work, work experience. **Freshman Admission Requirements:** High school diploma is required and GED is accepted. **Freshman Admission Statistics:** 982 applied, 59% admitted, 48% enrolled. **Transfer Admission Requirements:** High school transcript, college transcript(s), standardized test scores, statement of good standing from prior institution(s). Minimum college GPA of 2.0 required. Lowest grade transferable C. **General Admission Information:** Application Fee $10. Notification on a rolling basis, beginning on or about 8/1. Nonfall registration accepted. Admission may be deferred for a maximum of 12. Credit and/or placement offered for CEEB Advanced Placement tests.

COSTS AND FINANCIAL AID
Annual tuition $12,720. Room and board $6,320. Required fees $1,170. Average book expense $1,200. **Required Forms and Deadlines:** FAFSA, Institution's own financial aid form, State aid form. **Notification of Awards:** Applicants will be notified of awards on a rolling basis beginning 6/1. **Types of Aid:** *Need-based scholarships/grants:* Federal Pell, SEOG, state scholarships/grants, private scholarships, the school's own gift aid. *Loans:* Subsidized Stafford, Unsubsidized Stafford, PLUS, Federal Perkins. *Student Employment:* Federal Work-Study Program available. Institutional employment available. Highest amount earned per year from on-campus jobs $1,250. **Financial Aid Statistics:** 74% freshmen, 74% undergrads receive need-based scholarship or grant aid. 59% freshmen, 59% undergrads receive non-need-based scholarship or grant aid. 87% freshmen, 87% undergrads receive need-based self-help aid. 12% freshmen, 11% undergrads receive athletic scholarships. 95% freshmen, 93% undergrads receive any aid. 87% undergrads borrow to pay for school. **Criteria for awarding institutional aid:** *Non-need-based:* academics, alumni affiliation, art, athletics, job skills, leadership, minority status, music/drama, religious affiliation, state/district residency.

FAYETTEVILLE STATE UNIVERSITY

Newbold Station, Fayetteville, NC 28301
Phone: 910-672-1371
E-mail: admissions@.uncfsu.edu · **CEEB Code:** 5212
Fax: 910-672-1414 · **Website:** www.uncfsu.edu · **ACT Code:** 3098

This public school was founded in 1867. It has a 136-acre campus.

RATINGS
Admissions Selectivity Rating: 69   **Fire Safety Rating:** 60*

STUDENTS AND FACULTY
Enrollment: 3,660. **Student Body:** 64% female, 36% male, 11% out-of-state, 0% international. Asian 1%, African American 80%, Caucasian 14%, Hispanic 4%, Native American 1%
Retention and Graduation: 74% freshmen return for sophomore year. 14% freshmen graduate within 4 years. 39% freshmen graduate within 6 years. 11% grads go on to further study within 1 year. 10% grads pursue arts and sciences degrees. 1% grads pursue business degrees. **Faculty:** 202 full-time faculty, 70% hold PhDs, 41% are members of minority groups, 77% are women. 0% of classes are taught by teaching assistants.

ACADEMICS
Degrees: bachelor's, master's. **Classes:** Most classes have 20-29 students. Most lab/discussion sessions have 20-29 students. **Majors with Highest Enrollment:** Elementary Education and Teaching; Criminal Justice/Police Science; Business/Commerce. **Special Study Options:** cooperative education

program, distance learning, double major, honors program, independent study, internships, liberal arts/career combination, study abroad, teacher certification program, weekend college. **Career services:** alumni services, career/job search classes, career assessment, internships.

FACILITIES

Housing: special housing for disabled students, men's dorms, women's dorms, apartments for married students, apartments for single students. 100% of campus accessible to physically disabled. **Special Academic Facilities/Equipment:** Planetarium; Observatory; Distance Learning Center; Science Labs; Health, Physical Education, and Recreation Complex; Art Gallery.

CAMPUS LIFE

Activities: Choral groups, concert band, dance, drama/theater, jazz band, marching band, music ensembles, musical theater, opera, pep band, radio station, student government, student newspaper, student-run film society, television station, yearbook. 56 registered organizations, 7 honor societies, 3 religious organizations. 4 fraternities, 4 sororities. **Athletics (Intercollegiate):** *Men:* basketball, cheerleading, cross-country, football, golf. *Women:* basketball, cheerleading, cross-country, softball, tennis, volleyball.

ADMISSIONS

Freshman Academic Profile: SAT Math middle 50% range 360-470. SAT Critical Reading middle 50% range 380-470. **Basis for Candidate Selection:** *Important factors considered include:* Class rank, rigor of secondary school record, standardized test scores, character/personal qualities, extracurricular activities, talent/ability. **Freshman Admission Requirements:** High school diploma is required and GED is accepted.High school diploma is required and GED is not accepted. *Academic units required:* 4 English, 3 mathematics, 3 science, 1 social studies, 1 history, 6 academic electives. **Freshman Admission Statistics:** 1,570 applied, 85% admitted, 58% enrolled. **Transfer Admission Requirements:** college transcript(s), statement of good standing from prior institution(s). Lowest grade transferable C. **General Admission Information:** Application Fee $25. Regular application deadline 8/15. Notification on a rolling basis, beginning on or about 11/1. Nonfall registration accepted. Credit and/or placement offered for CEEB Advanced Placement tests.

COSTS AND FINANCIAL AID

Annual in-state tuition $1,258. Annual out-of-state tuition $10,173. Room and board $3,820. Required fees $437. Average book expense $160. **Required Forms and Deadlines:** FAFSA, Institution's own financial aid form. **Notification of Awards:** Applicants will be notified of awards on or about 7/15. **Types of Aid:** *Need-based scholarships/grants:* Federal Pell, SEOG, state scholarships/grants, private scholarships, the school's own gift aid. *Loans:* Direct Subsidized Stafford, Direct Unsubsidized Stafford, Direct PLUS, Subsidized Stafford, Unsubsidized Stafford, PLUS, Federal Perkins, Federal Nursing, state loans. *Student Employment:* Federal Work-Study Program available. Off-campus job opportunities are excellent.

FELICIAN COLLEGE

262 South Main Street, Lodi, NJ 7644
Phone: 201-559-6131
E-mail: admissions@felician.edu • **CEEB Code:** 2321
Fax: 201-559-6138 • **Website:** www.felician.edu • **ACT Code:** 2559

This private school, affiliated with the Roman Catholic Church, was founded in 1942. It has a 27-acre campus.

RATINGS

Admissions Selectivity Rating: 62   **Fire Safety Rating:** 60*

STUDENTS AND FACULTY

Enrollment: 1,761. **Student Body:** 78% female, 22% male, 5% out-of-state. Asian 8%, African American 13%, Caucasian 43%, Hispanic 14%, Native American <1%
Retention and Graduation: 60% freshmen return for sophomore year. 17% freshmen graduate within 4 years. 33% freshmen graduate within 6 years. 20% grads go on to further study within 1 year. 40% grads pursue arts and sciences degrees. 10% grads pursue law degrees. 12% grads pursue business degrees. 5% grads pursue medical degrees. **Faculty:** 81 full-time faculty, 57% are members of minority groups. 0% of classes are taught by teaching assistants.

ACADEMICS

Degrees: associate, bachelor's, certificate, master's, post-bachelor's certificate. **Classes:** Most classes have greater than 100 students. **Majors with Highest Enrollment:** Psychology; Registered Nursing/Registered Nurse; Business/Commerce. **Special Study Options:** Accelerated program, cooperative

education program, cross-registration, distance learning, double major, dual enrollment, English as a Second Language (ESL), honors program, independent study, internships, liberal arts/career combination, student-designed major, study abroad, teacher certification program, weekend college. Combined degree programs: 3-2 Clinical lab science prog w/ U of Medicine NJ. **Disability Services:** Special programs offered to physically disabled students include note-taking services, reader services, tape recorders, tutors. **Career services:** alumni services, career/job search classes, internships.

FACILITIES

Housing: Coed dorms, special housing for disabled students, men's dorms, women's dorms. 90% of campus accessible to physically disabled. **Special Academic Facilities/Equipment:** On-campus elementary school for exceptional children.

CAMPUS LIFE

Activities: Choral groups, drama/theater, literary magazine, student government. 25 registered organizations, 2 honor societies, 3 religious organizations. 1 fraternity, 2 sororities. **Athletics (Intercollegiate):** *Men:* baseball, basketball, cheerleading, cross-country, soccer, track/field (outdoor). *Women:* basketball, cheerleading, cross-country, soccer, softball, track/field (outdoor).

ADMISSIONS

Freshman Academic Profile: 70% from public high schools. SAT Math middle 50% range 400-500. SAT Writing middle 50% range 390-490. **Basis for Candidate Selection:** *Very important factors considered include:* academic GPA, standardized test scores. *Important factors considered include:* application essay, rigor of secondary school record. *Other factors considered include:* Class rank, recommendation(s), character/personal qualities, extracurricular activities, interview, volunteer work, work experience. **Freshman Admission Requirements:** High school diploma is required and GED is accepted. **Freshman Admission Statistics:** 1,479 applied, 64% admitted, 28% enrolled. **Transfer Admission Requirements:** college transcript(s), essay or personal statement, Lowest grade transferable C. **General Admission Information:** Application Fee $30. Notification on a rolling basis, beginning on or about 3/15. Nonfall registration accepted. Admission may be deferred for a maximum of 1 year. Credit and/or placement offered for CEEB Advanced Placement tests.

COSTS AND FINANCIAL AID

Annual tuition $18,900. Room and board $7,432. Required fees $1,050. Average book expense $2,163. **Required Forms and Deadlines:** FAFSA. **Notification of Awards:** Applicants will be notified of awards on a rolling basis beginning 4/1. **Types of Aid:** *Need-based scholarships/grants:* Federal Pell, SEOG, state scholarships/grants, private scholarships, the school's own gift aid. *Loans:* Subsidized Stafford, Unsubsidized Stafford, PLUS, state loans. *Student Employment:* Federal Work-Study Program available. Off-campus job opportunities are good. **Financial Aid Statistics:** 65% freshmen, 65% undergrads receive need-based scholarship or grant aid. 20% freshmen, 20% undergrads receive non-need-based scholarship or grant aid. 66% freshmen, 66% undergrads receive need-based self-help aid. 13% freshmen, 7% undergrads receive athletic scholarships. 57% undergrads borrow to pay for school. **Criteria for awarding institutional aid:** *Non-need-based:* academics, alumni affiliation, athletics.

FERRIS STATE UNIVERSITY

1201 South State Street, Big Rapids, MI 49307
Phone: 231-591-2100 • **Financial Aid Phone:** 231-591-22115
E-mail: admissions@ferris.edu • **CEEB Code:** 1222
Fax: 231-591-3944 • **Website:** www.ferris.edu • **ACT Code:** 1994

This public school was founded in 1884. It has a 880-acre campus.

RATINGS

Admissions Selectivity Rating: 72   **Fire Safety Rating:** 78

STUDENTS AND FACULTY

Enrollment: 13,261. **Student Body:** 51% female, 49% male, 5% out-of-state, 1% international. Asian 1%, African American 7%, Caucasian 76%, Hispanic 3%, Native American 1%
Retention and Graduation: 70% freshmen return for sophomore year. 30% freshmen graduate within 4 years. 56% freshmen graduate within 6 years. **Faculty:** 567 full-time faculty, 42% hold PhDs, 42% are members of minority groups, 11% are women. 0% of classes are taught by teaching assistants.

ACADEMICS

Degrees: associate, bachelor's, certificate, first professional, master's, terminal associate, transfer associate. **Classes:** Most classes have 20–29 students. Most lab/discussion sessions have 10–19 students. **Majors with Highest**

Enrollment: Criminal Justice/Law Enforcement Administration; Pharmacy; Registered Nursing/Registered Nurse. **Special Study Options:** Accelerated program, cooperative education program, cross-registration, distance learning, double major, dual enrollment, exchange student program (domestic), external degree program, honors program, independent study, internships, liberal arts/career combination, study abroad, teacher certification program, weekend college. **Disability Services:** Special programs offered to physically disabled students include note-taking services, reader services, tape recorders, tutors.

FACILITIES

Housing: Coed dorms, special housing for disabled students, special housing for international students, apartments for married students, apartments for single students, Honors, smoke-free, alcohol-free, quiet residence halls, living/earning communities. 98% of campus accessible to physically disabled. **Special Academic Facilities/Equipment:** Rankin Art Gallery, Student Recreation Center, Card Wildlife Museum, Jim Crowe Museum, Elastomer Center, FLITE **Computers:** Students can register for classes online. Administrative functions (other than registration) can be performed online.

CAMPUS LIFE

Environment: Village. **Activities:** Choral groups, concert band, dance, drama/theater, jazz band, literary magazine, music ensembles, pep band, radio station, student government, student newspaper, symphony orchestra, television station. 180 registered organizations, 11 honor society, 14 religious organizations. 8 fraternities, 6 sororities. **Athletics (Intercollegiate):** *Men:* basketball, cheerleading, cross-country, football, golf, ice hockey, tennis, track/field (outdoor). *Women:* basketball, cheerleading, cross-country, golf, soccer, softball, tennis, track/field (outdoor), volleyball. **On-Campus Highlights:** FLITE Library, Student Recreation Center, Card Wildlife Center, Center for Student Services, Ewigleben Ice Arena.

ADMISSIONS

Freshman Academic Profile: Average high school GPA 3.22. 90% from public high schools. ACT middle 50% range 19-24. Minimum internet-based TOEFL 61. Minimum paper TOEFL 500. **Basis for Candidate Selection:** *Very important factors considered include:* academic GPA, standardized test scores. *Important factors considered include:* character/personal qualities. *Other factors considered include:* recommendation(s), rigor of secondary school record, alumni/ae relation, extracurricular activities, volunteer work. **Freshman Admission Requirements:** High school diploma is required and GED is accepted. **Freshman Admission Statistics:** 9,457 applied, 71% admitted, 38% enrolled. **Transfer Admission Requirements:** college transcript(s), statement of good standing from prior institution(s). Minimum college GPA of 2.0 required. Lowest grade transferable C. **General Admission Information:** Application Fee $30. Regular application deadline 8/4. Notification on a rolling basis, beginning on or about 7/1. Nonfall registration accepted. Credit and/or placement offered for CEEB Advanced Placement tests.

COSTS AND FINANCIAL AID

Annual in-state tuition $10,710. Annual out-of-state tuition $16,080. Room and board $8,744. Average book expense $1,050. **Required Forms and Deadlines:** FAFSA. **Notification of Awards:** Applicants will be notified of awards on a rolling basis beginning 4/1. **Types of Aid:** *Need-based scholarships/grants:* Federal Pell, SEOG, state scholarships/grants, private scholarships, the school's own gift aid. *Loans:* Direct Subsidized Stafford, Direct Unsubsidized Stafford, Direct PLUS, Federal Perkins, Federal Nursing, college/university loans from institutional funds, Key Loan, MI-Loan, Citi Assist. *Student Employment:* Highest amount earned per year from on-campus jobs $4,992. **Financial Aid Statistics:** 70% freshmen, 69% undergrads receive need-based scholarship or grant aid. 77% freshmen, 53% undergrads receive non-need-based scholarship or grant aid. 82% freshmen, 86% undergrads receive need-based self-help aid. 1% freshmen, 1% undergrads receive athletic scholarships. 86% freshmen, 81% undergrads receive any aid. 81% undergrads borrow to pay for school. Average cumulative indebtedness $27,466. **Criteria for awarding institutional aid:** *Non-need-based:* academics, alumni affiliation, art, athletics, leadership, minority status, music/drama, religious affiliation.

FISK UNIVERSITY

1000 17th Ave N, Nashville, TN 37208
Phone: 1-800-443-3475
Website: www.fisk.edu

RATINGS

Admissions Selectivity Rating: 83   **Fire Safety Rating:** 60*

ACADEMICS

Special Study Options: cross-registration, double major, exchange student program (domestic), honors program, independent study, internships, student-designed major, study abroad, teacher certification program.

ADMISSIONS

Freshman Academic Profile: Average high school GPA 3.33. 10% in top 10% of high school class, 30% in top 25% of high school class, 75% in top 50% of high school class. 92% from public high schools. SAT Math middle 50% range 455-540. SAT Critical Reading middle 50% range 467-546. SAT Writing middle 50% range 447-547. ACT middle 50% range 18-23. Minimum paper TOEFL 550. **Basis for Candidate Selection:** *Very important factors considered include:* rigor of secondary school record. *Important factors considered include:* Class rank, application essay, academic GPA, standardized test scores, character/personal qualities, extracurricular activities, interview. *Other factors considered include:* recommendation(s), alumni/ae relation, geographical residence, level of applicant's interest, talent/ability, volunteer work. **Freshman Admission Requirements:** High school diploma is required and GED is accepted. *Academic units required:* 4 English, 3 mathematics, 3 science, (2 science labs), 1 foreign language, 0 social studies, 1 history, 0 visual/performing arts, 0 computer science, 0 academic electives. **Freshman Admission Statistics:** 2,700 applied, 45% admitted, 51% enrolled. **Transfer Admission Requirements:** college transcript(s), essay or personal statement, statement of good standing from prior institution(s). Minimum college GPA of 2.5 required. Lowest grade transferable C, **General Admission Information:** Application Fee $50. Regular application deadline 3/1. Notification on a rolling basis, beginning on or about 9/1. Admission may be deferred for a maximum of 1 year. Credit and/or placement offered for CEEB Advanced Placement tests.

COSTS AND FINANCIAL AID

Annual tuition $15,140. Room and board $7,730. Required fees $1,100. Average book expense $1,500.

FITCHBURG STATE COLLEGE

160 Pearl Street, Fitchburg, MA 01420-2697
Phone: 978-665-3144 · **Financial Aid Phone:** 978-665-3156
E-mail: admissions@fitchburgstate.edu · **CEEB Code:** 3518
Fax: 978-665-4540 · **Website:** www.fitchburgstate.edu · **ACT Code:** 1902

This public school was founded in 1894. It has a 78-acre campus.

RATINGS

Admissions Selectivity Rating: 72   **Fire Safety Rating:** 91

STUDENTS AND FACULTY

Enrollment: 3,958. **Student Body:** 54% female, 46% male, 8% out-of-state, 0% international (6 countries represented). Asian 2%, African American 4%, Caucasian 81%, Hispanic 6%, Native American <1%
Retention and Graduation: 73% freshmen return for sophomore year. 21% freshmen graduate within 4 years. 47% freshmen graduate within 6 years. 10% grads go on to further study within 1 year. **Faculty:** 184 full-time faculty, 91% hold PhDs, 46% are members of minority groups, 11% are women. 0% of classes are taught by teaching assistants.

ACADEMICS

Degrees: bachelor's, certificate, master's, post-bachelor's certificate, post-master's certificate. **Classes:** Most classes have 20–29 students. **Majors with Highest Enrollment:** Business Administration and Management; Speech Communication and Rhetoric; Education. **Special Study Options:** cross-registration, distance learning, double major, dual enrollment, honors program, independent study, internships, liberal arts/career combination, student-designed major, study abroad, teacher certification program. **Honors programs:** Leadership Academy Honors Program. **Disability Services:** Special programs offered to physically disabled students include note-taking services, reader services, tape recorders, tutors. **Career services:** Alumni network, alumni services, career/job search classes, career assessment, internships

FACILITIES

Housing: Coed dorms, special housing for disabled students, apartments for single studentsAlcohol and Tobacco free housing. 80% of campus accessible to physically disabled. **Special Academic Facilities/Equipment:** Art gallery, on-campus teacher education school, 120-acre conservation area. **Computers:** 100% of classrooms, 10% of dorms, 100% of libraries, 40% of dining areas, 100% of student union, 90% of common outdoor areas have wireless network access. Students can register for classes online. Administrative functions (other than registration) can be performed online. Undergraduates are required to own a computer.

The Princeton Review's Complete Book of Colleges

CAMPUS LIFE

Environment: Town. **Activities:** Choral groups, concert band, dance, drama/theater, jazz band, radio station, student government, student newspaper, student-run film society, Campus Ministries, International Student Organization, Model UN. 60 registered organizations, 8 honor societies, 1 religious organization. 2 fraternities, 3 sororities. **Athletics (Intercollegiate):** *Men:* baseball, basketball, cross-country, football, ice hockey, soccer, track/field (outdoor), track/field (indoor). *Women:* basketball, cross-country, field hockey, lacrosse, soccer, softball, track/field (outdoor), track/field (indoor). **On-Campus Highlights:** Campus Recreation Center, Student Center Lounge, Campus Dining Hall, Commuter Café, Computer Labs. **Environmental Initiatives:** Single stream recycling program; Awarded LEED certification of newest residence hall; Campus-wide building level utility metering.

ADMISSIONS

Freshman Academic Profile: Average high school GPA 3.1. 90% from public high schools. SAT Math middle 50% range 460-560. SAT Critical Reading middle 50% range 450-560. SAT Writing middle 50% range 450-540. ACT middle 50% range 19-23. Minimum paper TOEFL 550. **Basis for Candidate Selection:** *Very important factors considered include:* rigor of secondary school record. *Important factors considered include:* application essay, academic GPA, standardized test scores. *Other factors considered include:* recommendation(s), alumni/ae relation, character/personal qualities, extracurricular activities, level of applicant's interest, talent/ability, volunteer work, work experience. **Freshman Admission Requirements:** High school diploma is required and GED is accepted. *Academic units required:* 4 English, 3 mathematics, 3 science, (2 science labs), 2 foreign language, 1 social studies, 1 history, 2 academic electives. **Freshman Admission Statistics:** 3,104 applied, 70% admitted, 32% enrolled. **Transfer Admission Requirements:** college transcript(s), essay or personal statement, Minimum college GPA of 2.0 required. Lowest grade transferable C. **General Admission Information:** Application Fee $25. Notification on a rolling basis, beginning on or about 12/1. Nonfall registration accepted. Admission may be deferred for a maximum of 1 year. Credit and/or placement offered for CEEB Advanced Placement tests.

COSTS AND FINANCIAL AID

Annual in-state tuition $970. Annual out-of-state tuition $7,050. Room and board $8,256. Required fees $7,330. Average book expense $800. **Required Forms and Deadlines:** FAFSA. **Notification of Awards:** Applicants will be notified of awards on a rolling basis beginning 3/15. **Types of Aid:** *Need-based scholarships/grants:* Federal Pell, SEOG, state scholarships/grants, private scholarships, the school's own gift aid. *Loans:* Direct Subsidized Stafford, Direct Unsubsidized Stafford, Direct PLUS, Federal Perkins, Federal Nursing, state loans. *Student Employment:* Federal Work-Study Program available. Institutional employment available. Off-campus job opportunities are good. **Criteria for awarding institutional aid:** *Non-need-based:* academics, alumni affiliation, job skills, leadership.

FIVE TOWNS COLLEGE

Five Towns College, Dix Hills, NY 11746
Phone: 631-656-2110 · **Financial Aid Phone:** 631-656-2164
E-mail: admissions@ftc.edu · **CEEB Code:** 3142
Fax: 631-656-2172 · **Website:** http://www.ftc.edu/

This proprietary school was founded in 1972. It has a 35-acre campus.

RATINGS

Admissions Selectivity Rating: 81   **Fire Safety Rating:** 99

STUDENTS AND FACULTY

Enrollment: 638. **Student Body:** 33% female, 67% male, 7% out-of-state, 0% international (4 countries represented). Asian 4%, African American 21%, Caucasian 50%, Hispanic 15%, Native American <1%.
Retention and Graduation: 60% freshmen return for sophomore year. 27% freshmen graduate within 4 years. 34% freshmen graduate within 6 years.
Faculty: 25 full-time faculty, 32% hold PhDs, 32% are members of minority groups, 16% are women. 0% of classes are taught by teaching assistants.

ACADEMICS

Degrees: associate, bachelor's, doctoral, master's. **Classes:** Most classes have 20-29 students. **Majors with Highest Enrollment:** Recording Arts Technology/Technician; Music; Film/Cinema/Video Studies. **Special Study Options:** distance learning, dual enrollment, internships, liberal arts/career combination, teacher certification program. **Disability Services:** Special programs offered to physically disabled students include note-taking services, reader services, tape recorders, tutors. **Career services:** career/job search classes, career assessment, internships.

FACILITIES

Housing: Coed dorms, Wellness Housing. **Computers:** 100% of classrooms, 100% of dorms, 100% of libraries, 100% of dining areas, 100% of common outdoor areas have wireless network access. Administrative functions (other than registration) can be performed online.

CAMPUS LIFE

Environment: Village. **Activities:** Choral groups, concert band, dance, drama/theater, jazz band, music ensembles, musical theater, radio station, student government, student newspaper, student-run film society, symphony orchestra, television station, yearbook. **On-Campus Highlights:** Student Center, Audio Studios, Film Video Studios, Radio Station, Court Yard.

ADMISSIONS

Freshman Academic Profile: Average high school GPA 83. 24% in top 10% of high school class, 39% in top 25% of high school class, 71% in top 50% of high school class. 91% from public high schools. SAT Math middle 50% range 360-500. SAT Critical Reading middle 50% range 400-500. SAT Writing middle 50% range 390-480. ACT middle 50% range 15-20. Minimum internet-based TOEFL 80. Minimum paper TOEFL 520. **Basis for Candidate Selection:** *Very important factors considered include:* application essay, academic GPA, recommendation(s), rigor of secondary school record, standardized test scores, character/personal qualities, talent/ability. *Important factors considered include:* Class rank, interview, level of applicant's interest. *Other factors considered include:* extracurricular activities, volunteer work, work experience. **Freshman Admission Requirements:** High school diploma is required and GED is accepted. **Freshman Admission Statistics:** 335 applied, 56% admitted, 63% enrolled. **Transfer Admission Requirements:** High school transcript, college transcript(s), essay or personal statement, statement of good standing from prior institution(s). Minimum college GPA of 2.5 required. Lowest grade transferable C. **General Admission Information:** Application Fee $35. Early decision application deadline 12/1. Notification on a rolling basis, beginning on or about 11/1. Nonfall registration accepted. Admission may be deferred for a maximum of 1 year. Placement offered for CEEB Advanced Placement tests.

COSTS AND FINANCIAL AID

Annual tuition $21,000. Room and board $13,200. Required fees $1,500. Average book expense $1,250. **Required Forms and Deadlines:** FAFSA, Institution's own financial aid form, State aid form. **Notification of Awards:** Applicants will be notified of awards on a rolling basis beginning 3/31. **Types of Aid:** *Need-based scholarships/grants:* Federal Pell, SEOG, state scholarships/grants, private scholarships, the school's own gift aid. *Loans:* Direct Subsidized Stafford, Direct Unsubsidized Stafford, Direct PLUS. *Student Employment:* Federal Work-Study Program available. Institutional employment available. **Financial Aid Statistics:** 53% freshmen, 58% undergrads receive need-based scholarship or grant aid. 97% freshmen, 92% undergrads receive non-need-based scholarship or grant aid. 72% freshmen, 76% undergrads receive need-based self-help aid. 0% freshmen, 0% undergrads receive athletic scholarships. 78% freshmen, 75% undergrads receive any aid. 96% undergrads borrow to pay for school. Average cumulative indebtedness $25,658. **Criteria for awarding institutional aid:** *Non-need-based:* academics, music/drama.

FLAGLER COLLEGE

74 King Street, St. Augustine, FL 32085-1027
Phone: 904-819-6220 · **Financial Aid Phone:** 904-819-6225
E-mail: admissions@flagler.edu · **CEEB Code:** 5235
Fax: 904-819-6466 · **Website:** www.flagler.edu · **ACT Code:** 772

This private school was founded in 1968. It has a 42-acre campus.

RATINGS

Admissions Selectivity Rating: 85   **Fire Safety Rating:** 76

STUDENTS AND FACULTY

Enrollment: 2,772. **Student Body:** 60% female, 40% male, 39% out-of-state, 4% international (43 countries represented). Asian 1%, African American 3%, Caucasian 74%, Hispanic 10%, Native American <1%.
Retention and Graduation: 47% freshmen graduate within 4 years. 58% freshmen graduate within 6 years. **Faculty:** 109 full-time faculty, 73% hold PhDs, 51% are members of minority groups, 11% are women. 0% of classes are taught by teaching assistants.

ACADEMICS

Degrees: bachelor's. **Classes:** Most classes have 20–29 students. **Majors with Highest Enrollment:** Psychology; Business Administration and Management; Communication, Journalism, and Related Programs. **Special Study Options:** double major, external degree program, independent study, internships, liberal arts/career combination, study abroad, teacher certification program. Combined degree programs: none. **Disability Services:** Special programs offered to physically disabled students include note-taking services, reader services, tape recorders, tutors. **Career services:** Alumni network, alumni services, career/job search classes, career assessment. Most majors require students to gain internship experience.

FACILITIES

Housing: men's dorms, women's dorms. 95% of campus accessible to physically disabled. **Special Academic Facilities/Equipment:** Museum/theatre; learning disabilities clinic for student teachers; NorthEast Florida Archeological Association; Crisp-Ellert Art Gallery. **Computers:** 30% of classrooms, 100% of dorms, 100% of libraries, 100% of dining areas, 100% of student union, 80% of common outdoor areas have wireless network access. Students can register for classes online. Administrative functions (other than registration) can be performed online.

CAMPUS LIFE

Environment: Town. **Activities:** Choral groups, drama/theater, literary magazine, radio station, student government, student newspaper, Campus Ministries 7 honor societies, 3 religious organizations. **Athletics (Intercollegiate):** *Men:* baseball, basketball, cross-country, golf, soccer, tennis. *Women:* basketball, cross-country, golf, soccer, softball, tennis, volleyball. **On-Campus Highlights:** The Student Center, Proctor Library, Campus Courtyard, Flagler College Tennis Complex, Flagler College Sports Complex. **Environmental Initiatives:** Chiller upgrades; Compact flourescents; and LED Green cleaning supplies.

ADMISSIONS

Freshman Academic Profile: Average high school GPA 3.39. 10.31% in top 10% of high school class, 38.16% in top 25% of high school class, 71.31% in top 50% of high school class. 78% from public high schools. SAT Math middle 50% range 470-560. SAT Critical Reading middle 50% range 490-580. SAT Writing middle 50% range 460-560. ACT middle 50% range 21-25. Minimum internet-based TOEFL 75. Minimum paper TOEFL 550. **Basis for Candidate Selection:** *Very important factors considered include:* rigor of secondary school record. *Important factors considered include:* application essay, academic GPA, standardized test scores, alumni/ae relation, extracurricular activities. *Other factors considered include:* Class rank, recommendation(s), character/personal qualities, first generation, interview, level of applicant's interest, talent/ability, volunteer work. **Freshman Admission Requirements:** High school diploma is required and GED is accepted. *Academic units required:* 4 English, 3 mathematics, 2 science, (1 science labs), 0 foreign language, 3 social studies, 1 history, 0 visual/performing arts, 0 computer science, 2 academic electives. **Freshman Admission Statistics:** 6,585 applied, 48% admitted, 21% enrolled. **Transfer Admission Requirements:** college transcript(s), essay or personal statement, Minimum college GPA of 2.0 required. Lowest grade transferable C. **General Admission Information:** Application Fee $40. Early decision application deadline 12/1. Regular application deadline 3/1. Regular notification 3/30. Nonfall registration accepted. Admission may be deferred for a maximum of 1 year. Credit and/or placement offered for CEEB Advanced Placement tests.

COSTS AND FINANCIAL AID

Annual tuition $16,800. Room and board $9,350. Required fees $100. Average book expense $1,000. **Required Forms and Deadlines:** FAFSA, State aid form. **Notification of Awards:** Applicants will be notified of awards on a rolling basis beginning 4/1. **Types of Aid:** *Need-based scholarships/grants:* Federal Pell, SEOG, state scholarships/grants, private scholarships, the school's own gift aid. *Loans:* Direct Subsidized Stafford, Direct Unsubsidized Stafford, Direct PLUS, Federal Perkins, Private Alternative Loans. *Student Employment:* Federal Work-Study Program available. Institutional employment available. Highest amount earned per year from on-campus jobs $1,400. Off-campus job opportunities are excellent. **Financial Aid Statistics:** 99% freshmen, 96% undergrads receive need-based scholarship or grant aid. 7% freshmen, 6% undergrads receive non-need-based scholarship or grant aid. 91% freshmen, 91% undergrads receive need-based self-help aid. 3% freshmen, 3% undergrads receive athletic scholarships. 91% freshmen, 88% undergrads receive any aid. 51% undergrads borrow to pay for school. Average cumulative indebtedness $25,968. **Criteria for awarding institutional aid:** *Non-need-based:* academics, art, athletics, job skills, leadership, minority status, music/drama, state/district residency.

FLORIDA A&M UNIVERSITY

Room 204, Tallahassee, FL 32307-3200
Phone: 850-599-3796 • **Financial Aid Phone:** 850-599-3730
E-mail: ugrdadmissions@famu.edu • **CEEB Code:** 5215
Fax: 850-599-3069 • **Website:** www.famu.edu • **ACT Code:** 726

This public school was founded in 1887. It has a 419-acre campus.

RATINGS

Admissions Selectivity Rating: 82   **Fire Safety Rating:** 92

STUDENTS AND FACULTY

Enrollment: 7,995. **Student Body:** 62% female, 38% male, 13% out-of-state, 1% international (46 countries represented). Asian 1%, African American 94%, Caucasian 3%, Hispanic 1%, Native American <1%
Retention and Graduation: 81% freshmen return for sophomore year. 38% grads go on to further study within 1 year. 8% grads pursue arts and sciences degrees. 3% grads pursue law degrees. 5% grads pursue business degrees. 4% grads pursue medical degrees. **Faculty:** 548 full-time faculty, 75% hold PhDs, 46% are members of minority groups, 82% are women. 0% of classes are taught by teaching assistants.

ACADEMICS

Degrees: associate, bachelor's, first professional, master's. **Classes:** Most classes have fewer than 10 students. **Majors with Highest Enrollment:** Criminal Justice/Safety Studies; Business Administration and Management; Biology/Biological Sciences. **Special Study Options:** Accelerated program, cooperative education program, distance learning, double major, dual enrollment, honors program, independent study, internships, study abroad, teacher certification program, weekend college. **Honors programs:** Florida Agricultural and Mechanical University Honors Program provides a series of challenging courses and academic enhancement experiences for undergraduate students who excel. Enhancement of academic performance in critical thinking skills, in essence, will lead to consummate intellectual engagement and strong research orientation as a launch to both graduate and professional schools, as well as career paths. The program stresses four major areas of concentration: academic achievement, development of leadership potential, community service and cultural enrichment. Combined degree programs: BA/JD, BA/MA, Pharmacy, Architecture, Occupational Therapy. **Disability Services:** Special programs offered to physically disabled students include note-taking services, reader services, tape recorders, tutors. **Career services:** Alumni network, alumni services, career/job search classes, career assessment, internships. Career services highlights include wonderful and successful interns.

FACILITIES

Housing: Coed dorms, men's dorms, women's dorms, apartments for married students, Outside housing (Apartment Complexes) agreement through the University. 100% of campus accessible to physically disabled. **Special Academic Facilities/Equipment:** Black Archives and Resource Ctr. Coleman Memorial Library Foster Tanner Music/Art Bldg. **Computers:** 90% of classrooms, 100% of dorms, 100% of libraries, 100% of dining areas, 100% of student union, 60% of common outdoor areas have wireless network access. Students can register for classes online. Administrative functions (other than registration) can be performed online.

CAMPUS LIFE

Environment: City. **Activities:** Choral groups, concert band, dance, drama/theater, jazz band, marching band, music ensembles, pep band, radio station, student government, student newspaper, symphony orchestra, television station, yearbook. 145 registered organizations, 16 honor societies, 11 religious organization. 4 fraternities, 4 sororities. **Athletics (Intercollegiate):** *Men:* baseball, basketball, cheerleading, cross-country, football, golf, swimming, tennis, track/field (outdoor), track/field (indoor). *Women:* basketball, bowling, cheerleading, cross-country, golf, softball, swimming, tennis, track/field (outdoor), track/field (indoor), volleyball. **On-Campus Highlights:** The Black Archives, FAMU/FSU College of Engineering, Athletic Department, Army/Navy ROTC, Alfred Lawson Jr. Multipurpose Center and Teaching Gymnasium. **Environmental Initiatives:** Establishment of an advisory body - the Environment & Sustainability Council to design and oversee the implementation of a sustainability strategic plan which informs and guides the various operatives on campus of the principles of sustainability as they apply specifically to the respective facets of the University - Administrative, Academic, Operations and Community Development of a comprehensive Recycling Program to facilitate the recycling needs of the faculty, staff, and students on campus. The recycling program engages collaborations with various external groups in the community including City and County Divisions with "green" student groups on campus. FAMU co-hosts the local staging of the annual National Conference of Mayors/Keep America Beautiful Cash for Cans Recycling Day. This is a major recycling event in Tallahassee, also co-hosted by both the City and County Recycling Divisions. FAMU's facilities planning and construction team has made the commitment to design and build all new renovation and construction projects to LEED standards.

ADMISSIONS

Freshman Academic Profile: Average high school GPA 3.29. 12.5% in top 10% of high school class, 36.1% in top 25% of high school class, 78% in top 50% of high school class. 87% from public high schools. SAT Math middle 50% range 420-510. SAT Critical Reading middle 50% range 430-523. SAT Writing middle 50% range 418-510. ACT middle 50% range 18-22. Minimum internet-based TOEFL 61. Minimum paper TOEFL 500. **Basis for Candidate Selection:** *Very important factors considered include:* application essay, academic GPA, rigor of secondary school record, standardized test scores. *Other factors considered include:* Class rank, alumni/ae relation, character/personal qualities, extracurricular activities, racial/ethnic status, state residency, talent/ability, volunteer work, work experience. **Freshman Admission Requirements:** High school diploma is required and GED is accepted. *Academic units required:* 4 English, 3 mathematics, 3 science, (1 science labs), 2 foreign language, 3 social studies, 3 academic electives. **Freshman Admission Statistics:** 5,017 applied, 49% admitted, 50% enrolled. **Transfer Admission Requirements:** college transcript(s), Minimum college GPA of 2.0 required. Lowest grade transferable C. **General Admission Information:** Application Fee $20. Regular application deadline 5/9. Nonfall registration accepted. Credit offered for CEEB Advanced Placement tests.

COSTS AND FINANCIAL AID

Annual in-state tuition $5,644. Annual out-of-state tuition $17,586. Room and board $9,576. Required fees $140. Average book expense $1,138. **Required Forms and Deadlines:** FAFSA. **Notification of Awards:** Applicants will be notified of awards on a rolling basis beginning 3/1. **Types of Aid:** *Need-based scholarships/grants:* Federal Pell, SEOG, state scholarships/grants, private scholarships, the school's own gift aid, United Negro College Fund, Federal Nursing Scholarships. *Loans:* Direct Subsidized Stafford, Direct Unsubsidized Stafford, Direct PLUS, Federal Perkins. *Student Employment:* Federal Work-Study Program available. Institutional employment available. Highest amount earned per year from on-campus jobs $9,800. Off-campus job opportunities are good. **Financial Aid Statistics:** 99% freshmen, 84% undergrads receive need-based scholarship or grant aid. 53% freshmen, 37% undergrads receive non-need-based scholarship or grant aid. 81% freshmen, 78% undergrads receive need-based self-help aid. 4% freshmen, 3% undergrads receive athletic scholarships. 95% freshmen, 86% undergrads receive any aid. 87% undergrads borrow to pay for school. Average cumulative indebtedness $30,427. **Criteria for awarding institutional aid:** *Non-need-based:* academics, art, leadership.

FLORIDA ATLANTIC UNIVERSITY

777 Glades Road, Boca Raton, FL 33431-0991
Phone: 561-297-3040 · **Financial Aid Phone:** 561-297-3530
E-mail: admissions@fau.edu · **CEEB Code:** 5229
Fax: 561-297-2758 · **Website:** www.fau.edu · **ACT Code:** 729

This public school was founded in 1961. It has a 860-acre campus.

RATINGS

Admissions Selectivity Rating: 86   **Fire Safety Rating:** 98

STUDENTS AND FACULTY

Enrollment: 24,228. **Student Body:** 57% female, 43% male, 5% out-of-state, 2% international. Asian 4%, African American 20%, Caucasian 45%, Hispanic 25%, Native American <1%
Retention and Graduation: 16% freshmen graduate within 4 years. **Faculty:** 730 full-time faculty, 87% hold PhDs, 42% are members of minority groups, 26% are women. 15% of classes are taught by teaching assistants.

ACADEMICS

Degrees: associate, bachelor's, certificate, master's, post-master's certificate. **Classes:** Most classes have 20–29 students. Most lab/discussion sessions have 20–29 students. **Majors with Highest Enrollment:** Education; Biology/Biological Sciences; Psychology. **Special Study Options:** Accelerated program, cooperative education program, cross-registration, distance learning, double major, dual enrollment, English as a Second Language (ESL), honors program, independent study, internships, liberal arts/career combination, study abroad, teacher certification program, weekend college. **Honors programs:** The Harriet L. Wilkes Honors College of Florida Atlantic University, which opened in the Fall of 1999, is the first public honors institution to be built from the ground up in the United States. Its intellectual foundation is a belief in liberal arts education as the best preparation for a full and productive life. The University

Scholars Program is the honors program located on the Boca Raton campus. It is for freshman and sophomore students. The historical mission of a liberal arts education has been to develop the qualities of a free and responsible citizen, one who can reason clearly, read analytically, argue persuasively in speech and in writing, and contribute in fundamental and innovative ways to a chosen field of study or work. Combined degree programs: BA/MEng. **Disability Services:** Special programs offered to physically disabled students include note-taking services, reader services, tape recorders, tutors. **Career services:** Alumni network, alumni services, career/job search classes, career assessment, internships, regional alumni.

FACILITIES

Housing: Coed dorms, apartments for married students, apartments for single students. 100% of campus accessible to physically disabled. **Special Academic Facilities/Equipment:** Art gallery, on-campus elementary school, robotics lab, marine research facilities. **Computers:** Students can register for classes online. Administrative functions (other than registration) can be performed online.

CAMPUS LIFE

Environment: City. **Activities:** Choral groups, dance, drama/theater, jazz band, literary magazine, marching band, music ensembles, musical theater, opera, radio station, student government, student newspaper, television station. 150 registered organizations, 11 honor society, 6 religious organizations. 9 fraternities, 4 sororities. **Athletics (Intercollegiate):** *Men:* baseball, basketball, cheerleading, cross-country, diving, football, golf, soccer, swimming, tennis. *Women:* basketball, cheerleading, cross-country, diving, golf, soccer, softball, swimming, tennis, track/field (outdoor), volleyball. **On-Campus Highlights:** Student Services Building, Student Union, Dining Hall, Breezeway, Residence Halls. **Environmental Initiatives:** All new construction is designed and built to a minimum LEED silver certification level. This has been surpassed on every project to date, FAU currently has 1 platinum, 5 gold, and 2 pending gold certified buildings. Replacement of the 2 main chillers that provide the majority of the HVAC to our main campus. This is a 1.9 million project that will reduce more than 632 metric tons of carbon and over 2500 MWH saved. Climate change has been recognized as one of the three main areas of research which FAU has committed to pursuing, and currently has more that 30 grant funded research projects dedicated to climate change in the Florida Region.

ADMISSIONS

Freshman Academic Profile: Average high school GPA 3.5. 11% in top 10% of high school class, 35% in top 25% of high school class, 78% in top 50% of high school class. SAT Math middle 50% range 490-580. SAT Critical Reading middle 50% range 480-570. SAT Writing middle 50% range 480-560. ACT middle 50% range 21-25. Minimum internet-based TOEFL 80. Minimum paper TOEFL 550. **Basis for Candidate Selection:** *Very important factors considered include:* academic GPA, standardized test scores. *Important factors considered include:* Class rank, rigor of secondary school record. *Other factors considered include:* application essay, recommendation(s), alumni/ae relation, character/personal qualities, extracurricular activities, first generation, level of applicant's interest, talent/ability, volunteer work. **Freshman Admission Requirements:** High school diploma is required and GED is accepted. *Academic units required:* 4 English, 3 mathematics, 3 science, (2 science labs), 2 foreign language, 3 social studies, 0 history, 0 visual/performing arts, 0 computer science, 3 academic electives. **Freshman Admission Statistics:** 27,888 applied, 39% admitted, 30% enrolled. **Transfer Admission Requirements:** college transcript(s), Minimum college GPA of 3.0 required. Lowest grade transferable D-. **General Admission Information:** Application Fee $30. Regular application deadline 6/1. Notification on a rolling basis, beginning on or about 9/1. Nonfall registration accepted. Admission may be deferred for a maximum of 2 semesters. Credit offered for CEEB Advanced Placement tests.

COSTS AND FINANCIAL AID

Annual in-state tuition $5,986. Annual out-of-state tuition $21,543. Room and board $11,353. Average book expense $1,203. **Required Forms and Deadlines:** FAFSA. **Notification of Awards:** Applicants will be notified of awards on a rolling basis beginning 4/1. **Types of Aid:** *Need-based scholarships/grants:* Federal Pell, SEOG, state scholarships/grants, private scholarships, the school's own gift aid, Federal Nursing Scholarships. *Loans:* Subsidized Stafford, Unsubsidized Stafford, PLUS, Federal Perkins, college/university loans from institutional funds. *Student Employment:* Federal Work-Study Program available. Institutional employment available. Highest amount earned per year from on-campus jobs $1,500. Off-campus job opportunities are excellent. **Financial Aid Statistics:** 91% freshmen, 86% undergrads receive need-based scholarship or grant aid. 7% freshmen, 4% undergrads receive non-need-based scholarship or grant aid. 71% freshmen, 73% undergrads receive need-based self-help aid. 1% freshmen, 1% undergrads receive athletic scholarships. 46% undergrads borrow to pay for school. Average cumulative indebtedness $17,666. **Criteria for awarding institutional aid:** *Non-need-based:* academics, athletics, music/drama, state/district residency.

See page 1056.

FLORIDA COLLEGE

Admissions Office, Temple Terrace, FL 33617-5578
Phone: 813-988-5131 · **Financial Aid Phone:** 813-988-5131
E-mail: Admissions@FloridaCollege.edu · **CEEB Code:** 1562
Fax: 813-899-6722 · **Website:** www.floridacollege.edu · **ACT Code:** 1482

This private school was founded in 1946.

RATINGS

Admissions Selectivity Rating: 76   **Fire Safety Rating:** 96

STUDENTS AND FACULTY

Enrollment: 558. **Student Body:** 50% female, 50% male, 67% out-of-state, 1% international (6 countries represented). Asian 1%, African American 5%, Caucasian 79%, Hispanic 5%, Native American 1%
Faculty: 39 full-time faculty, 36% hold PhDs, 26% are members of minority groups, 5% are women. 0% of classes are taught by teaching assistants.

ACADEMICS

Degrees: associate, bachelor's, transfer associate. **Classes:** Most classes have fewer than 10 students. Most lab/discussion sessions have 10–19 students. **Majors with Highest Enrollment:** Elementary Education and Teaching; Liberal Arts and Sciences/Liberal Studies; Business Administration and Management. **Special Study Options:** cross-registration, double major, independent study, teacher certification program. **Disability Services:** Special programs offered to physically disabled students include tape recorders, tutors. **Career services:**

FACILITIES

Housing: special housing for disabled students, men's dorms, women's dorms.

CAMPUS LIFE

Environment: Town. **Activities:** Choral groups, concert band, drama/theater, jazz band, literary magazine, music ensembles, musical theater, pep band, student government, yearbook. **Athletics (Intercollegiate):** *Men:* basketball, cross-country, soccer. *Women:* cheerleading, cross-country, soccer, volleyball. **On-Campus Highlights:** Riverwalk, Student Center.

ADMISSIONS

Freshman Academic Profile: SAT Math middle 50% range 460-570. SAT Critical Reading middle 50% range 470-590. SAT Writing middle 50% range 435-575. ACT middle 50% range 20-26. Minimum paper TOEFL 550. **Basis for Candidate Selection:** *Very important factors considered include:* academic GPA, recommendation(s), rigor of secondary school record, standardized test scores, character/personal qualities, religious affiliation/commitment. *Important factors considered include:* Class rank, level of applicant's interest. *Other factors considered include:* alumni/ae relation, talent/ability. **Freshman Admission Requirements:** High school diploma is required and GED is accepted. *Academic units required:* 4 English, 3 mathematics, 2 science, (2 science labs), 2 social studies. **Freshman Admission Statistics:** 344 applied, 74% admitted, 69% enrolled. **Transfer Admission Requirements:** High school transcript, college transcript(s), standardized test scores, statement of good standing from prior institution(s). Minimum college GPA of 2.0 required. Lowest grade transferable C. **General Admission Information:** Application Fee $30. Regular application deadline 8/1. Nonfall registration accepted. Placement offered for CEEB Advanced Placement tests.

COSTS AND FINANCIAL AID

Annual tuition $13,670. Room and board $7,760. Required fees $820. Average book expense $1,300. **Required Forms and Deadlines:** FAFSA, State aid form. **Notification of Awards:** Applicants will be notified of awards on a rolling basis beginning 3/1. **Types of Aid:** *Need-based scholarships/grants:* Federal Pell, SEOG, state scholarships/grants, private scholarships, the school's own gift aid. *Loans:* Subsidized Stafford, Unsubsidized Stafford, PLUS, Federal Perkins Alternative Loans. **Financial Aid Statistics:** 89% freshmen, 68% undergrads receive need-based scholarship or grant aid. 85% freshmen, 87% undergrads receive non-need-based scholarship or grant aid. 77% freshmen, 78% undergrads receive need-based self-help aid. 9% freshmen, 11% undergrads receive athletic scholarships. Criteria for awarding institutional aid: *Non-need-based:* academics, athletics, music/drama, state/district residency.

FLORIDA GULF COAST UNIVERSITY

10501 FGCU Blvd. South, Fort Myers, FL 33965-6565
Phone: 239-590-7878 · **Financial Aid Phone:** 239-590-7920
E-mail: admissions@fgcu.edu · **CEEB Code:** 5221
Fax: 239-590-7894 · **ACT Code:** 733

This public school was founded in 1991. It has a 760-acre campus.

RATINGS

Admissions Selectivity Rating: 79   **Fire Safety Rating:** 92

STUDENTS AND FACULTY

Enrollment: 12,773. **Student Body:** 55% female, 45% male, 7% out-of-state, 2% international (89 countries represented). Asian 2%, African American 7%, Caucasian 67%, Hispanic 19%, Native American <1%
Retention and Graduation: 76% freshmen return for sophomore year.
Faculty: 429 full-time faculty, 72% hold PhDs, 45% are members of minority groups, 17% are women. 0% of classes are taught by teaching assistants.

ACADEMICS

Degrees: associate, bachelor's, certificate, master's, transfer associate. **Classes:** Most classes have 20–29 students. **Majors with Highest Enrollment:** Elementary Education and Teaching; Liberal Arts and Sciences/Liberal Studies; Business/Commerce. **Special Study Options:** Accelerated program, cross-registration, distance learning, double major, dual enrollment, honors program, independent study, internships, student-designed major, study abroad, teacher certification program. **Honors programs:** The University Honors Program at Florida Gulf Coast University offers special opportunities for superior students to pursue academic work that challenges their interests and abilities. The program is university-wide, which gives students full access to the faculty and the entire range of programs at FGCU. Since the honors program at Florida Gulf Coast University is exclusive, we have the ability to design a unique program for each individual student. Scholarship opportunities and special programs that support the honors student's educational, intellectual, and personal goals will be designed individually with the student and his or her faculty mentor. Combined degree programs: Nursing, BS/MS. **Disability Services:** Special programs offered to physically disabled students include note-taking services, reader services, tape recorders, tutors. **Career services:** Alumni network, alumni services, career/job search classes, career assessment, internships.

FACILITIES

Housing: Coed dorms, special housing for disabled students, apartments for single students. 100% of campus accessible to physically disabled. **Special Academic Facilities/Equipment:** Art Gallery, Observatory. **Computers:** Students can register for classes online. Administrative functions (other than registration) can be performed online.

CAMPUS LIFE

Environment: City. **Activities:** Choral groups, dance, drama/theater, literary magazine, radio station, student government, student newspaper. 105 registered organizations, 7 honor societies, 8 religious organizations. 4 fraternities, 4 sororities. **Athletics (Intercollegiate):** *Men:* baseball, basketball, cross-country, golf, soccer, tennis. *Women:* basketball, cross-country, diving, golf, soccer, softball, swimming, tennis, volleyball. **On-Campus Highlights:** Alico Arena, Student Union, The Quad, The Library, Baseball/Softball fields.

ADMISSIONS

Freshman Academic Profile: Average high school GPA 3.34. 11% in top 10% of high school class, 36% in top 25% of high school class, 77% in top 50% of high school class. SAT Math middle 50% range 470-550. SAT Critical Reading middle 50% range 470-550. SAT Writing middle 50% range 450-540. ACT middle 50% range 20-24. Minimum internet-based TOEFL 79. Minimum paper TOEFL 550. **Basis for Candidate Selection:** *Very important factors considered include:* academic GPA, standardized test scores. *Important factors considered include:* rigor of secondary school record. *Other factors considered include:* Class rank, recommendation(s). **Freshman Admission Requirements:** High school diploma is required and GED is accepted. *Academic units required:* 4 English, 3 mathematics, 3 science, (2 science labs), 2 foreign language, 3 social studies, 3 academic electives. **Freshman Admission Statistics:** 10,804 applied, 66% admitted, 39% enrolled. **Transfer Admission Requirements:** college transcript(s), Minimum college GPA of 2.0 required. Lowest grade transferable D. **General Admission Information:** Application Fee $30. Regular application deadline 5/1. Nonfall registration accepted. Admission may be deferred for a maximum of 2 Semesters. Credit and/or placement offered for CEEB Advanced Placement tests.

COSTS AND FINANCIAL AID

Average book expense $1,200. **Required Forms and Deadlines:** FAFSA. **Types of Aid:** *Need-based scholarships/grants:* Federal Pell, SEOG, state scholarships/grants, private scholarships, the school's own gift aid. *Loans:* Subsidized Stafford, Unsubsidized Stafford, PLUS. **Financial Aid Statistics:** 62% freshmen, 64% undergrads receive need-based scholarship or grant aid. 67% freshmen, 31% undergrads receive non-need-based scholarship or grant aid. 61% freshmen, 66% undergrads receive need-based self-help aid. 1% freshmen, 1% undergrads receive athletic scholarships. 88% freshmen, 35% undergrads receive any aid. 47% undergrads borrow to pay for school. Average cumulative indebtedness $17,947. **Criteria for awarding institutional aid:** *Non-need-based:* academics, alumni affiliation, athletics, leadership, minority status, music/drama, religious affiliation, state/district residency.

FLORIDA INSTITUTE OF TECHNOLOGY

150 West University Boulevard, Melbourne, FL 32901-6975
Phone: 321-674-8030 • **Financial Aid Phone:** 800-666-4348
E-mail: admission@fit.edu • **CEEB Code:** 5080
Fax: 321-674-8004 • **Website:** http://www.fit.edu • **ACT Code:** 716

This private school was founded in 1958. It has a 130-acre campus.

RATINGS

Admissions Selectivity Rating: 87   **Fire Safety Rating:** 82

STUDENTS AND FACULTY

Enrollment: 3,348. **Student Body:** 28% female, 72% male, 45% out-of-state, 33% international (110 countries represented). Asian 3%, African American 6%, Caucasian 40%, Hispanic 7%, Native American <1%.
Retention and Graduation: 76% freshmen return for sophomore year. 39% freshmen graduate within 4 years. 55% freshmen graduate within 6 years. 47% grads go on to further study within 1 year. 13% grads pursue arts and sciences degrees. 1% grads pursue law degrees. 3% grads pursue business degrees. 2% grads pursue medical degrees. **Faculty:** 290 full-time faculty, 88% hold PhDs, 23% are members of minority groups, 18% are women. 0% of classes are taught by teaching assistants.

ACADEMICS

Degrees: associate, bachelor's, master's, post-master's certificate. **Classes:** Most classes have 10–19 students. Most lab/discussion sessions have 10–19 students. **Majors with Highest Enrollment:** Aerospace, Aeronautical and Astronautical/Space Engineering; Mechanical Engineering; Aviation/Airway Management and Operations. **Special Study Options:** Accelerated program, cooperative education program, cross-registration, distance learning, double major, dual enrollment, English as a Second Language (ESL), independent study, internships, study abroad, teacher certification program, Dual degrees in computer engineering/electrical engineering, chemical engineering/chemistry, molecular/marine biology. **Disability Services:** Special programs offered to physically disabled students include note-taking services, reader services, tutors. **Career services:** alumni services, career/job search classes, internships. Career services highlights include internships.

FACILITIES

Housing: Coed dorms, apartments for single students, Wellness Housing. 90% of campus accessible to physically disabled. **Special Academic Facilities/Equipment:** New facility openings have been the highlight of 2009, beginning in February with the dedication of the Emil Buehler Center for Aviation Training and Research at Melbourne International Airport. The center, valued at $5.1 million, consists of a main building and 17,600-square-foot hanger, located on eight acres at the airport. The new building houses the operations of F.I.T. Aviation. In August, the university's Department of Humanities got a boost with the opening of the 3,000-square-foot Ruth Funk Center for Textile Arts. The only textiles center in the state of Florida, the facility is dedicated to furthering the understanding of cultural and creative achievements in the textile and fine arts. October gave another boost to the College of Psychology and Liberal Arts with the opening of the Scott Center for Autism Treatment. The 18,000-square-foot center provides services for individuals with autism spectrum disorder, training for parents, teachers and other professionals and research on effective treatments for autism. The College of Engineering and College of Science also gained a new building in October with the opening of the Harris Center for Science and Engineering. While computer science and marine biology laboratories fill two-thirds of the building, the rest is dedicated to the Harris Institute for Assured Information. The institute is already recognized for its work and numerous government and national foundation contracts. The College of Business received a tremendous boost in 2009 with a $5 million gift from Nathan M. Bisk, a leader in continuing education and online learning. The gift enhances business programs offerings and strengthens online education and marks the start of fund-raising for a new building, to be named the Nathan M. Bisk College of Business. **Computers:** 100% of classrooms, 30% of dorms, 100% of

libraries, 100% of dining areas, 100% of student union, 5% of common outdoor areas have wireless network access. Students can register for classes online. Administrative functions (other than registration) can be performed online.

CAMPUS LIFE

Environment: Town. **Activities:** Choral groups, dance, drama/theater, literary magazine, pep band, radio station, student government, student newspaper, television station, Campus Ministries, International Student Organization. 106 registered organizations, 8 honor societies, 3 religious organizations. 7 fraternities, 3 sororities. **Athletics (Intercollegiate):** *Men:* baseball, basketball, cross-country, golf, soccer, tennis. *Women:* basketball, crew/rowing, cross-country, golf, soccer, softball, tennis, volleyball. **On-Campus Highlights:** Student Union Building, Clemente Center for Sports & Recreation, Olin Engineering Complex, Harris Village, Botanical Gardens. **Environmental Initiatives:** After a successful three year start with the minor program, a Bachelors of Science program in Sustainability Studies was launched in Fall 2013 with solid early enrollment from the beginning. An excellent curriculum and student capstone project program has already been field tested with the campus-wide sustainability minor program which has trained and graduated over 40 students from all five colleges and 15 different major tracks. All new construction to be LEED or near-LEED equivalent. Several buildings on campus undergoing LEED EBOM certification. One of the larger undertakings is the Siemens Campus-Wide Energy Savings Program. As part of this project, several major energy saving improvements were undertaken (reducing annual energy expenditures for these areas by approx. 25%). including installation of a localized chilled water plant to serve many of our new and aged heating and air-conditioning systems in some of the larger campus buildings (Crawford, Skurla Hall, the Gleason Center, the Link Building, Evans Library, Funk Center for Textile Arts, and the Student Union Building). Powered by two new-tech, high efficiency turbo-core chillers, the system has already been expanded to service the Clemente Athletics Center and the Panther Dining Hall.

ADMISSIONS

Freshman Academic Profile: Average high school GPA 3.62. 31% in top 10% of high school class, 32% in top 25% of high school class, 24% in top 50% of high school class. 41% from public high schools. SAT Math middle 50% range 530-660. SAT Critical Reading middle 50% range 510-610. ACT middle 50% range 23-30. Minimum internet-based TOEFL 80. Minimum paper TOEFL 550. **Basis for Candidate Selection:** *Very important factors considered include:* rigor of secondary school record. *Important factors considered include:* academic GPA, standardized test scores, level of applicant's interest. *Other factors considered include:* Class rank, application essay, recommendation(s), alumni/ae relation, character/personal qualities, extracurricular activities, interview, work experience. **Freshman Admission Requirements:** High school diploma is required and GED is accepted. *Academic units required:* 4 English, 3 mathematics, 3 science, (3 science labs), 1 social studies, 2 history, 7 academic electives. **Freshman Admission Statistics:** 8,573 applied, 62% admitted, 15% enrolled. **Transfer Admission Requirements:** college transcript(s), Minimum college GPA of 2.5 required. Lowest grade transferable C. **General Admission Information:** Application Fee $50. Notification on a rolling basis, beginning on or about 7/1. Nonfall registration accepted. Admission may be deferred for a maximum of 12 month. Credit and/or placement offered for CEEB Advanced Placement tests.

COSTS AND FINANCIAL AID

Required Forms and Deadlines: FAFSA, State aid form. **Notification of Awards:** Applicants will be notified of awards on a rolling basis beginning 2/15. **Types of Aid:** *Need-based scholarships/grants:* Federal Pell, SEOG, state scholarships/grants, private scholarships, the school's own gift aid. *Loans:* Subsidized Stafford, Unsubsidized Stafford, PLUS, Federal Perkins, state loans, college/university loans from institutional funds. *Student Employment:* Federal Work-Study Program available. Institutional employment available. Highest amount earned per year from on-campus jobs $15,715. Off-campus job opportunities are fair. **Financial Aid Statistics:** 100% freshmen, 100% undergrads receive need-based scholarship or grant aid. 99% freshmen, 97% undergrads receive non-need-based scholarship or grant aid. 67% freshmen, 72% undergrads receive need-based self-help aid. 4% freshmen, 5% undergrads receive athletic scholarships. 96% freshmen, 83% undergrads receive any aid. 60% undergrads borrow to pay for school. Average cumulative indebtedness $26,017. **Criteria for awarding institutional aid:** *Non-need-based:* academics, alumni affiliation, athletics, state/district residency.

FLORIDA INTERNATIONAL UNIVERSITY

Modesto Maidique Campus, Miami, FL 33199
Phone: 305-348-2363 · **Financial Aid Phone:** 305-348-7272
E-mail: admiss@fiu.edu · **CEEB Code:** 5206
Fax: 305-348-3648 · **Website:** www.fiu.edu · **ACT Code:** 776

This public school was founded in 1965. It has a 573-acre campus.

RATINGS

Admissions Selectivity Rating: 88   **Fire Safety Rating:** 83

STUDENTS AND FACULTY

Enrollment: 39,106. **Student Body:** 56% female, 44% male, 3% out-of-state, 5% international (151 countries represented). Asian 3%, African American 12%, Caucasian 10%, Hispanic 67%, Native American <1%
Faculty: 1,217 full-time faculty, 88% hold PhDs, 43% are members of minority groups, 37% are women.

ACADEMICS

Degrees: associate, bachelor's, certificate, master's, post-master's certificate.
Classes: Most classes have 20–29 students. Most lab/discussion sessions have 20–29 students. **Majors with Highest Enrollment:** Business Administration and Management; Biology/Biological Sciences; Psychology. **Special Study Options:** Accelerated program, cooperative education program, distance learning, double major, dual enrollment, exchange student program (domestic), honors program, independent study, internships, study abroad, teacher certification program, weekend college. Combined degree programs: BA/MA, BA/MEng, Economics, Asian Studies, International Relations, Liberal Studies. **Disability Services:** Special programs offered to physically disabled students include note-taking services, reader services, tape recorders, tutors. **Career services:** alumni services, career/job search classes, career assessment, internships, regional alumni. We are particularly proud of our Executive Protege Initiative that is designed for students who commit quality time to attend career readiness presentations and professional development actitivies. We are also proud of our yearly Federal Government Statewide Conference that brings together FIU students and federal agencies to help students freshman-graduate learn about internship and full-time opportunities in the federal government.

FACILITIES

Housing: Coed dorms, fraternity/sorority housing, apartments for married students, apartments for single students. 100% of campus accessible to physically disabled. **Special Academic Facilities/Equipment:** The Frost Art Museum, The Wolfsonian Art Museum, Natural Preserve, Biscayne Bay Preserve **Computers:** 100% of classrooms, 100% of dorms, 1000% of libraries, 100% of dining areas, 100% of student union, 100% of common outdoor areas have wireless network access. Students can register for classes online. Administrative functions (other than registration) can be performed online.

CAMPUS LIFE

Environment: Metropolis. **Activities:** Choral groups, drama/theater, jazz band, music ensembles, opera, radio station, student government, student newspaper, symphony orchestra, yearbook, Campus Ministries, International Student Organization, Model UN. 250 registered organizations, 40 honor societies, 5 religious organizations. 21 fraternity, 17 sororities. **Athletics (Intercollegiate):** *Men:* baseball, basketball, cross-country, football, soccer, track/field (outdoor), track/field (indoor). *Women:* basketball, cross-country, diving, golf, soccer, softball, swimming, tennis, track/field (outdoor), track/field (indoor), volleyball. **On-Campus Highlights:** The Frost Museum, The Wolfsonian Museum, Steven and Dorothea Green Library, Graham University Center, Biscayne Bay Campus Library, The Recreational Center. **Environmental Initiatives:** Spring 2011, FIU has officially become a smoking-free campus. Providing clean and smoke-free air to it's community. The latest initiative in FIUs commitment to going green, the web-based carpool program features award-winning software that makes signing up hassle-free and completely safe. Open to all FIU students, faculty and staff, university leaders are hoping the program will save money for participants, reduce traffic and relieve parking congestion, and help improve air quality and conserve energy. Installed sensor monitor for office light and installed new xerox machines which are energy efficient and are set for double-sided copying.

ADMISSIONS

Freshman Academic Profile: 21% in top 10% of high school class, 49% in top 25% of high school class, 86% in top 50% of high school class. SAT Math middle 50% range 510-600. SAT Critical Reading middle 50% range 510-600. SAT Writing middle 50% range 500-590. ACT middle 50% range 21-26. Minimum paper TOEFL 500. **Basis for Candidate Selection:** *Very important factors considered include:* Class rank, academic GPA, rigor of secondary school record, standardized test scores, first generation. *Other factors considered include:*

application essay, recommendation(s), alumni/ae relation, character/personal qualities, extracurricular activities, geographical residence, interview, level of applicant's interest, state residency, talent/ability, volunteer work, work experience. **Freshman Admission Requirements:** High school diploma is required and GED is accepted. *Academic units required:* 4 English, 3 mathematics, 3 science, (2 science labs), 2 foreign language, 3 social studies, 3 academic electives. **Freshman Admission Statistics:** 17,617 applied, 48% admitted, 36% enrolled. **Transfer Admission Requirements:** college transcript(s), statement of good standing from prior institution(s). Minimum college GPA of 2.0 required. Lowest grade transferable D. **General Admission Information:** Application Fee $30. Regular application deadline 5/1. Notification on a rolling basis, beginning on or about 12/1. Nonfall registration accepted. Credit offered for CEEB Advanced Placement tests.

COSTS AND FINANCIAL AID

Required Forms and Deadlines: FAFSA. *Student Employment:* Federal Work-Study Program available. Institutional employment available. Off-campus job opportunities are good. **Financial Aid Statistics:** 65% freshmen, 75% undergrads receive need-based scholarship or grant aid. 73% freshmen, 44% undergrads receive non-need-based scholarship or grant aid. 33% freshmen, 51% undergrads receive need-based self-help aid. 2% freshmen, 1% undergrads receive athletic scholarships. 49% undergrads borrow to pay for school. Average cumulative indebtedness $17,234.

FLORIDA SOUTHERN COLLEGE

111 Lake Hollingworth Drive, Lakeland, FL 33801
Phone: 863-680-4131 · **Financial Aid Phone:** 863-680-4140
E-mail: fscadm@flsouthern.edu · **CEEB Code:** 5218
Fax: 863-680-4120 · **Website:** www.flsouthern.edu · **ACT Code:** 732

This private school, affiliated with the Methodist Church, was founded in 1883. It has a 100-acre campus.

RATINGS

Admissions Selectivity Rating: 89   **Fire Safety Rating:** 88

STUDENTS AND FACULTY

Enrollment: 2,146. **Student Body:** 61% female, 39% male, 36% out-of-state, 5% international (38 countries represented). Asian 1%, African American 6%, Caucasian 73%, Hispanic 10%, Native American 1%
Retention and Graduation: 81% freshmen return for sophomore year. 56% freshmen graduate within 4 years. 65% freshmen graduate within 6 years. 18% grads go on to further study within 1 year. 9% grads pursue arts and sciences degrees. 1% grads pursue law degrees. 3% grads pursue business degrees. 1% grads pursue medical degrees. **Faculty:** 130 full-time faculty, 77% hold PhDs, 48% are members of minority groups, 16% are women. 0% of classes are taught by teaching assistants.

ACADEMICS

Degrees: bachelor's, master's. **Classes:** Most classes have 20–29 students. Most lab/discussion sessions have 10–19 students. **Majors with Highest Enrollment:** Business Administration and Management; Biology/Biological Sciences; Psychology. **Special Study Options:** double major, dual enrollment, honors program, independent study, internships, liberal arts/career combination, student-designed major, study abroad, teacher certification program, FSC Honors Program -- USF College of Medicine Medical Education Program. **Honors programs:** The mission of the Florida Southern College Honors Program is to offer academically talented and highly motivated students opportunities to explore special topics through carefully constructed courses. Professors employ innovative teaching techniques that challenge students to explore subjects through multiple perspectives. The Honors Program fosters an interactive learning environment within a community of scholars. Combined degree programs: BA/MD, Priority admittance to USF School of Medicine. **Career services:** Alumni network, alumni services, career/job search classes, career assessment, internships, regional alumni. Florida Southern College guarantees meaningful, real-world engaged learning experiences, including internships, to every student.

FACILITIES

Housing: Coed dorms, special housing for disabled students, men's dorms, women's dorms, fraternity/sorority housing, apartments for married students, apartments for single students, Theme Housing. 70% of campus accessible to physically disabled. **Special Academic Facilities/Equipment:** Campus designed by Frank Lloyd Wright; contains world's largest collection of Wright-designed structures at a single site. Also home to three buildings designed by world renowned architect Robert A.M. Stern: 2 residence halls and 1 classroom building, which includes an art gallery and film studies center. The science building features a planetarium; the communication building features a television studio. The latest two building additions are 1) a 24-hour, state-of-the-art Technology and Learning Center; and 2) a high-tech nursing building featuring virtual patient simulators. The college houses two newly renovated art galleries—the Melvin and Burke Galleries. Also of note, FSC has a world-class performing arts venue seating 2200. Students enjoy a Wellness Center accompanied by an outdoor pool and a boathouse for water-skiing, sailing, and kayaking. At the center of campus is a spectacular, 50-foot high Water Dome, which is next to the library's Cyber Café, which serves Starbuck's products. A spectacular Archives Center, also adjacent to the library, was completed within the past year. **Computers:** 20% of classrooms, 20% of dorms, 100% of libraries, 100% of dining areas, 50% of student union, 50% of common outdoor areas have wireless network access. Students can register for classes online. Administrative functions (other than registration) can be performed online.

CAMPUS LIFE

Environment: City. **Activities:** Choral groups, concert band, dance, drama/theater, jazz band, literary magazine, music ensembles, musical theater, opera, pep band, student government, student newspaper, symphony orchestra, television station, yearbook, Campus Ministries, International Student Organization. 70 registered organizations, 22 honor societies, 9 religious organizations. 7 fraternities, 7 sororities. **Athletics (Intercollegiate):** *Men:* baseball, basketball, cross-country, golf, lacrosse, soccer, swimming, tennis, track/field (outdoor). *Women:* basketball, cross-country, golf, soccer, softball, swimming, tennis, track/field (outdoor), volleyball. **On-Campus Highlights:** Tutu's Cyber Café, Wellness Center and Pool, Badcock Garden's "outdoor living room," The Terrace Café, Field House, Our sunny campus offers something for everyone, including more than 70 clubs and organizations that cater to every interest. On beautiful Lake Hollingsworth, students enjoy free kayaking, sailing, and canoeing. Our state-of-the-art Wellness Center offers classes in everything from yoga to Pilates to water aerobics in our Olympic-sized pool. If the arts are more your speed, visit the Melvin Art Gallery, which exhibits the works of students and internationally recognized artists. Take in an opera, play, or concert through the renowned Festival of Fine Arts series, or catch a movie on the Badcock Garden lawn. Our championship Division II NCAA sports programs mean there's always something to cheer about, and intramural sports such as flag football, tennis, and soccer give you a chance to get in the game. And if you've worked up an appetite, grab lunch from the Grillmaster in the Badcock Garden or enjoy a cup of Starbuck's coffee and a bagel on the patio overlooking the Water Dome at TuTu's Cyber Café. **Environmental Initiatives:** Florida Southern College has installed filtered water bottle stations throughout campus. These stations provide users with an opportunity to fill their individual bottle without purchasing filtered water bottles. Additionally, FSCs Student Government Association is in the process of distributing refillable water bottles, therefore, continuing to reduce FSCs carbon footprint. The new Sharp Family Tourism and Education Center uses ground-based, geothermal water heating to help maintain building temperatures. This year, the College installed a building-specific energy monitoring system with real-time displays available for student viewing.

ADMISSIONS

Freshman Academic Profile: Average high school GPA 3.69. 29% in top 10% of high school class, 58% in top 25% of high school class, 85% in top 50% of high school class. 79% from public high schools. SAT Math middle 50% range 520-600. SAT Critical Reading middle 50% range 520-620. SAT Writing middle 50% range 500-580. ACT middle 50% range 23-28. Minimum paper TOEFL 550. **Basis for Candidate Selection:** *Very important factors considered include:* academic GPA, rigor of secondary school record. *Important factors considered include:* application essay, recommendation(s), standardized test scores, character/personal qualities, extracurricular activities, level of applicant's interest, talent/ability. *Other factors considered include:* Class rank, alumni/ae relation, first generation, interview, racial/ethnic status, religious affiliation/commitment, volunteer work, work experience. **Freshman Admission Requirements:** High school diploma is required and GED is accepted. *Academic units required:* 4 English, 3 mathematics, 2 science, (2 science labs), 3 social studies, 3 history, 2 academic electives. **Freshman Admission Statistics:** 5,590 applied, 45% admitted, 50% enrolled. **Transfer Admission Requirements:** college transcript(s), essay or personal statement, statement of good standing from prior institution(s). Minimum college GPA of 2.0 required. Lowest grade transferable C. **General Admission Information:** Application Fee $30. Early decision application deadline 12/1. Regular application deadline 3/1. Notification on a rolling basis, beginning on or about 1/15. Nonfall registration accepted. Admission may be deferred for a maximum of 1 Year. Credit offered for CEEB Advanced Placement tests.

COSTS AND FINANCIAL AID

Required Forms and Deadlines: FAFSA, Institution's own financial aid form. **Notification of Awards:** Applicants will be notified of awards on a rolling basis beginning 3/1. **Types of Aid:** *Need-based scholarships/grants:* Federal Pell, SEOG, state scholarships/grants, private scholarships, the school's own gift aid, Federal Nursing Scholarships. *Loans:* Subsidized Stafford, Unsubsidized Stafford, PLUS, Federal Perkins. *Student Employment:* Federal Work-Study Program available. Institutional employment available. Highest amount earned per year from on-campus jobs $1,500. Off-campus job opportunities are good. **Financial Aid Statistics:** 100% freshmen, 99% undergrads receive need-based scholarship or grant aid. 60% freshmen, 68% undergrads receive non-need-based scholarship or grant aid. 7% freshmen, 23% undergrads receive need-based self-help aid. 4% freshmen, 5% undergrads receive athletic scholarships. 100% freshmen, 99% undergrads receive any aid. 71% undergrads borrow to pay for school. Average cumulative indebtedness $20,403. **Criteria for awarding institutional aid:** *Non-need-based:* academics, alumni affiliation, art, athletics, job skills, leadership, minority status, music/drama, religious affiliation, state/district residency.

FLORIDA STATE UNIVERSITY

PO Box 3062400, Tallahassee, FL 32306-2400
Phone: 850-644-6200 · **Financial Aid Phone:** 850-644-5716
E-mail: admissions@admin.fsu.edu · **CEEB Code:** 5219
Fax: 850-644-0197 · **Website:** www.fsu.edu · **ACT Code:** 734

This public school was founded in 1851. It has a 452-acre campus.

RATINGS

Admissions Selectivity Rating: 89   **Fire Safety Rating:** 78

STUDENTS AND FACULTY

Enrollment: 32,086. **Student Body:** 55% female, 45% male, 10% out-of-state, 1% international (142 countries represented). Asian 3%, African American 8%, Caucasian 67%, Hispanic 17%, Native American <1%
Retention and Graduation: 92% freshmen return for sophomore year. 57% freshmen graduate within 4 years. 77% freshmen graduate within 6 years. 42% grads go on to further study within 1 year. **Faculty:** 1,272 full-time faculty, 92% hold PhDs, 38% are members of minority groups, 19% are women. 28% of classes are taught by teaching assistants.

ACADEMICS

Degrees: associate, bachelor's, certificate, master's, post-bachelor's certificate, post-master's certificate, transfer associate. **Classes:** Most classes have 20–29 students. **Majors with Highest Enrollment:** Psychology; Criminal Justice/Safety Studies; English Language and Literature. **Special Study Options:** Accelerated program, cooperative education program, cross-registration, distance learning, double major, dual enrollment, English as a Second Language (ESL), honors program, independent study, internships, study abroad, teacher certification program. **Honors programs:** The Florida State University Honors Program provides an enriched curriculum and special opportunities for exceptional, high-achieving students who are entering college for the first time. Each fall, freshmen who are admitted into this program attend the University Honors Colloquium, a weekly forum that features stimulating lectures by distinguished faculty as well as informative presentations from directors of academic programs. As they work to meet their liberal study requirements, University Honors students then have the chance to take small, honors-only courses and special topic seminars with some of the university's best researchers and teachers. With its emphasis on small classes taught by top faculty, this program provides the atmosphere of a small liberal arts college within a large research university. Combined degree programs: BA/MA. **Disability Services:** Special programs offered to physically disabled students include note-taking services, reader services, tape recorders, tutors. **Career services:** Alumni network, alumni services, career/job search classes, career assessment, internships, regional alumni.

FACILITIES

Housing: Coed dorms, special housing for disabled students, women's dorms, fraternity/sorority housing, apartments for married students, apartments for single students, On-campus: Honors Residences; Living Learning Communities. Off-campus: Cooperative housing through Southern Scholarship Foundation; off-campus private residence halls. 99% of campus accessible to physically disabled. **Special Academic Facilities/Equipment:** Art gallery, museum, developmental research school, marine lab, oceanographic institute, tandem Van de Graaff accelerator, national high magnetic field lab. **Computers:** 50% of classrooms, 25% of dorms, 90% of libraries, 100% of dining areas, 90% of student union, 70% of common outdoor areas have wireless network access. Students can register for classes online. Administrative functions (other than registration) can be performed online. Undergraduates are required to own a computer.

CAMPUS LIFE

Environment: City. **Activities:** Choral groups, concert band, dance, drama/theater, jazz band, literary magazine, marching band, music ensembles, musical theater, opera, pep band, radio station, student government, student newspaper, student-run film society, symphony orchestra, television station, yearbook, Campus Ministries, International Student Organization, Model UN. 520 registered organizations, 23 honor societies, 30 religious organizations. 32 fraternities, 28 sororities. **Athletics (Intercollegiate):** *Men:* baseball, basketball, cheerleading, cross-country, diving, football, golf, swimming, tennis, track/field (outdoor), track/field (indoor). *Women:* basketball, cheerleading, cross-country, diving, golf, soccer, softball, swimming, tennis, track/field (outdoor), track/field (indoor), volleyball. **On-Campus Highlights:** Suwannee Dining Hall, Bobby E. Leach Student Recreation Center, Bobby Bowden Field at Doak Campbell Stadium, National High Magnetic Field Laboratory, FSU Reservation. **Environmental Initiatives:** Creation of the FSU Office of Sustainability and the hiring of a full-time Director of Campus Sustainability to help build a comprehensive sustainable campus program. Dedicated energy conservation fund ?û FSU has set aside some capital to be used exclusively for projects that have relatively short pay backs (less than 7 years on average). Our intention is to strive for a 10% energy reduction on campus over the next several years. Concentrated growth and expansion of sustainability-related outreach and engagement programs, including the creation of an Eco-Reps program and an increase in the number of volunteers and amount of recyclable material collected at our football game recycling program. Student-initiated projects are receiving more support from staff and administrators.

ADMISSIONS

Freshman Academic Profile: Average high school GPA 3.88. 41.8% in top 10% of high school class, 77% in top 25% of high school class, 97.2% in top 50% of high school class. SAT Math middle 50% range 550-640. SAT Critical Reading middle 50% range 560-640. SAT Writing middle 50% range 560-640. ACT middle 50% range 25-29. Minimum internet-based TOEFL 80. Minimum paper TOEFL 550. **Basis for Candidate Selection:** *Very important factors considered include:* academic GPA, rigor of secondary school record. *Important factors considered include:* standardized test scores, state residency, talent/ability. *Other factors considered include:* Class rank, application essay, recommendation(s), alumni/ae relation, character/personal qualities, extracurricular activities, first generation, geographical residence, volunteer work, work experience. **Freshman Admission Requirements:** High school diploma is required and GED is accepted. *Academic units required:* 4 English, 4 mathematics, 3 science, (2 science labs), 2 foreign language, 1 social studies, 2 history, 3 academic electives. **Freshman Admission Statistics:** 29,579 applied, 57% admitted, 36% enrolled. **Transfer Admission Requirements:** college transcript(s), Minimum college GPA of 3.0 required. Lowest grade transferable D-. **General Admission Information:** Application Fee $30. Regular application deadline 1/21. Nonfall registration accepted. Credit and/or placement offered for CEEB Advanced Placement tests.

COSTS AND FINANCIAL AID

Annual in-state tuition $4,640. Annual out-of-state tuition $19,806. Room and board $9,912. Required fees $1,867. Average book expense $1,000. **Required Forms and Deadlines:** FAFSA. **Notification of Awards:** Applicants will be notified of awards on a rolling basis beginning 3/15. **Types of Aid:** *Need-based scholarships/grants:* Federal Pell, SEOG, state scholarships/grants, private scholarships, the school's own gift aid. *Loans:* Subsidized Stafford, Unsubsidized Stafford, PLUS, Federal Perkins. *Student Employment:* Federal Work-Study Program available. Institutional employment available. Highest amount earned per year from on-campus jobs $10,000. Off-campus job opportunities are good. **Financial Aid Statistics:** 98% freshmen, 92% undergrads receive need-based scholarship or grant aid. 85% freshmen, 65% undergrads receive non-need-based scholarship or grant aid. 65% freshmen, 72% undergrads receive need-based self-help aid. 1% freshmen, 1% undergrads receive athletic scholarships. 96% freshmen, 87% undergrads receive any aid. 44% undergrads borrow to pay for school. Average cumulative indebtedness $22,086. **Criteria for awarding institutional aid:** *Non-need-based:* academics, athletics, state/district residency.

FONTBONNE UNIVERSITY

6800 Wydown Boulevard, St. Louis, MO 63105
Phone: 314-889-1400 • **Financial Aid Phone:** 314-889-1414
E-mail: fcadmis@fontbonne.edu • **CEEB Code:** 6216
Fax: 314-889-1451 • **Website:** www.fontbonne.edu • **ACT Code:** 2298

This private school, affiliated with the Roman Catholic Church, was founded in 1917. It has a 13-acre campus.

RATINGS

Admissions Selectivity Rating: 77   **Fire Safety Rating:** 84

STUDENTS AND FACULTY

Enrollment: 1,993. **Student Body:** 72% female, 28% male, 12% out-of-state, 1% international (23 countries represented). Asian 1%, African American 34%, Caucasian 62%, Hispanic 1%, Native American <1%
Retention and Graduation: 58% freshmen return for sophomore year. 33% freshmen graduate within 4 years. 49% freshmen graduate within 6 years. 25% grads go on to further study within 1 year. **Faculty:** 73 full-time faculty, 71% hold PhDs, 68% are members of minority groups, 10% are women. 0% of classes are taught by teaching assistants.

ACADEMICS

Degrees: bachelor's, certificate, master's, post-bachelor's certificate. **Classes:** Most classes have 10-19 students. Most lab/discussion sessions have 10-19 students. **Majors with Highest Enrollment:** Special Education and Teaching; Elementary Education and Teaching; Business Administration and Management. **Special Study Options:** Accelerated program, cooperative education program, cross-registration, distance learning, double major, English as a Second Language (ESL), exchange student program (domestic), honors program, independent study, internships, liberal arts/career combination, student-designed major, study abroad, teacher certification program, weekend college. Combined degree programs: BA/MEng, BS/MS with Washington University. **Disability Services:** Special programs offered to physically disabled students include note-taking services, reader services, tape recorders, tutors. **Career services:** alumni services, career/job search classes, career assessment, internships.

FACILITIES

Housing: Coed dorms, special housing for international students, apartments for single students, Off campus house which holds 13 females. 85% of campus accessible to physically disabled. **Special Academic Facilities/Equipment:** Art gallery. **Computers:** 75% of classrooms, 100% of dorms, 100% of libraries, 100% of dining areas, 100% of student union, 100% of common outdoor areas have wireless network access. Students can register for classes online. Administrative functions (other than registration) can be performed online.

CAMPUS LIFE

Environment: Metropolis. **Activities:** Choral groups, dance, drama/theater, literary magazine, music ensembles, radio station, student government, student newspaper, Campus Ministries. 34 registered organizations, 7 honor societies, 4 religious organizations. **Athletics (Intercollegiate):** *Men:* baseball, basketball, cross-country, field hockey, golf, lacrosse, soccer, tennis. *Women:* basketball, bowling, cross-country, field hockey, golf, lacrosse, soccer, softball, tennis, volleyball. **On-Campus Highlights:** Ryan Hall, Dunham Student Activity Center, Library, Medaille Hall, Fine Arts Center, Message from the President. On behalf of the entire Fontbonne University family, I am pleased to welcome you to our web site. As you navigate these electronic pages, I trust that you will find whatever information you seek about our University. When you explore the Fontbonne University campus, either in person or on a virtual visit like this, you will learn that Fontbonne has certain advantages that are evidenced in the following ways: Location Our campus is located in the heart of Clayton, Missouri, which is one of the most beautiful suburbs in the United States. There is easy access from our campus to Forest Park, the St. Louis Zoo, the Art Museum and the History Museum. In addition, you are approximately fifteen minutes from downtown St. Louis, home of the St. Louis Cardinals, NFL Rams and NHL Blues. Academics The academic programs are excellent, and they are taught in a values-based, student-centered context. Because of our student-faculty ratio, the faculty know you as an individual and will help you incorporate experiential learning in your academic program. Focus The individual student is the primary focus at Fontbonne University. You are the central focus of the administration, faculty and staff. We are dedicated to your academic, moral, emotional, spiritual, social, cultural, career and co-curricular development. Ultimate Goal At Fontbonne, we strive to achieve strength of curriculum and strength of character. Therefore, we will teach you not only how to make a living but also how to live a life so that you are prepared to face the challenges of the 21st century and to prevail. Fontbonne is a Catholic University sponsored by the Sisters of St. Joseph of Carondelet. We are co-educational with 2,800 students, and a student body comprised of both traditional-aged undergraduate students as well as adult learners. All of our students are taught to think critically, to act ethically and to assume responsibility as citizens and leaders for a world in need. If you are seeking a university education where the individual student is at the epicenter of all activity, then Fontbonne is for you. I invite you to visit our campus in person and come to know and value, as we do, the advantage that is a Fontbonne University education. Dennis C. Golden President.

ADMISSIONS

Freshman Academic Profile: Average high school GPA 3.05. 7% in top 10% of high school class, 28% in top 25% of high school class, 61% in top 50% of high school class. 56% from public high schools. SAT Math middle 50% range 470-625. SAT Critical Reading middle 50% range 500-625. ACT middle 50% range 18-24. Minimum paper TOEFL 525. **Basis for Candidate Selection:** *Very important factors considered include:* Class rank, academic GPA, rigor of secondary school record, standardized test scores, character/personal qualities. *Other factors considered include:* application essay, recommendation(s), alumni/ae relation, extracurricular activities, first generation, interview, level of applicant's interest, talent/ability, volunteer work, work experience. **Freshman Admission Requirements:** High school diploma is required and GED is accepted. *Academic units required:* 4 English, 3 mathematics, 3 science, (1 science labs), 3 social studies, 3 academic electives. **Freshman Admission Statistics:** 600 applied, 75% admitted, 42% enrolled. **Transfer Admission Requirements:** college transcript(s), essay or personal statement, Minimum college GPA of 2.0 required. Lowest grade transferable D. **General Admission Information:** Application Fee $25. Regular application deadline 8/1. Notification on a rolling basis, beginning on or about 8/15. Nonfall registration accepted. Admission may be deferred for a maximum of 1 year. Credit and/or placement offered for CEEB Advanced Placement tests.

COSTS AND FINANCIAL AID

Annual tuition $20,860. Room and board $8,319. Required fees $440. Average book expense $650. **Required Forms and Deadlines:** FAFSA, Institution's own financial aid form. **Types of Aid:** *Need-based scholarships/grants:* Federal Pell, SEOG, state scholarships/grants, private scholarships, the school's own gift aid. *Loans:* Subsidized Stafford, Unsubsidized Stafford, PLUS, Federal Perkins, state loans, college/university loans from institutional funds. *Student Employment:* Federal Work-Study Program available. **Financial Aid Statistics:** 96% freshmen, 98% undergrads receive need-based scholarship or grant aid. 99% freshmen, 67% undergrads receive non-need-based scholarship or grant aid. 93% freshmen, 90% undergrads receive need-based self-help aid. 0% freshmen, 0% undergrads receive athletic scholarships. 81% undergrads borrow to pay for school. Average cumulative indebtedness $19,377. **Criteria for awarding institutional aid:** *Non-need-based:* academics, alumni affiliation, art, job skills, leadership, minority status, religious affiliation.

FORDHAM UNIVERSITY

441 East Fordham Road, Bronx, NY 10458
Phone: 718-817-4000 · **Financial Aid Phone:** 718-817-3800
E-mail: enroll@fordham.edu · **CEEB Code:** 2259
Fax: 718-367-9404 · **Website:** www.fordham.edu · **ACT Code:** 2748

This private school, affiliated with the Roman Catholic Church, was founded in 1841. It has a 93-acre campus.

RATINGS

Admissions Selectivity Rating: 92   **Fire Safety Rating:** 91

STUDENTS AND FACULTY

Enrollment: 8,485. **Student Body:** 55% female, 45% male, 53% out-of-state, 6% international (66 countries represented). Asian 9%, African American 5%, Caucasian 60%, Hispanic 14%, Native American <1%
Retention and Graduation: 75% freshmen graduate within 4 years. 80% freshmen graduate within 6 years. 32% grads go on to further study within 1 year. 5% grads pursue arts and sciences degrees. 3% grads pursue law degrees. 3% grads pursue business degrees. 1% grads pursue medical degrees. **Faculty:** 747 full-time faculty, 93% hold PhDs, 42% are members of minority groups, 19% are women.

ACADEMICS

Degrees: bachelor's, first professional, master's, post-master's certificate.
Classes: Most classes have 10–19 students. Most lab/discussion sessions have 10–19 students. **Majors with Highest Enrollment:** Communication and Media Studies; Business Administration and Management; Social Sciences. **Special Study Options:** double major, English as a Second Language (ESL), exchange student program (domestic), honors program, independent study, internships, student-designed major, study abroad, teacher certification program, Globe Program in International Business. 3:2 Engineering Cooperative with Columbia University or Case Western Reserve University. **Honors programs:** Each undergraduate college has its own Honors Program. All four programs offer enriched academic opportunity for qualified and interested students. Additionally, there are major programs of study designated as selective. Students must be invited into those programs and meet minimum GPA requirements for consideration. Many more majors offer Honors designation at graduation usually based upon completion of a thesis or senior project. Combined degree programs: BA/JD, BA/MA, BS/MSW, BS/MBA, 3:2 Engineering. **Disability Services:** Special programs offered to physically disabled students include note-taking services, reader services, tape recorders, tutors.

FACILITIES

Housing: Coed dorms, special housing for disabled students, apartments for single students, Residential Colleges. 80% of campus accessible to physically disabled. **Special Academic Facilities/Equipment:** television station, radio station, theaters, white and black box studio spaces, media and visual arts labs and design space, art gallery, University Church, seismic station, 113 biological field station The Louis Calder Center, in Armonk, NY **Computers:** 90% of classrooms, 98% of dorms, 95% of libraries, 100% of dining areas, 80% of common outdoor areas have wireless network access. Students can register for classes online. Administrative functions (other than registration) can be performed online.

CAMPUS LIFE

Environment: Metropolis. **Activities:** Choral groups, concert band, dance, drama/theater, jazz band, literary magazine, music ensembles, musical theater, pep band, radio station, student government, student newspaper, student-run film society, symphony orchestra, television station, yearbook. 133 registered organizations, 12 honor societies, 3 religious organizations. **Athletics (Intercollegiate):** *Men:* baseball, basketball, cross-country, diving, football, golf, soccer, squash, swimming, tennis, track/field (outdoor), track/field (indoor), water polo. *Women:* basketball, cheerleading, crew/rowing, cross-country, diving, soccer, softball, swimming, tennis, track/field (outdoor), track/field (indoor), volleyball. **On-Campus Highlights:** William D. Walsh Family Library (Rose Hill), O'Hare Hall (Residential College at Rose Hill), Edwards Parade/Keating Hall (Rose Hill), McMahon Hall (Lincoln Center), Pope Auditorium (Lincoln Center), With three distinct campuses, there are numerous noteworthy buildings including new and recently renovated academic and extracurricular space, residence halls and athletic centers/fields. Additional space to note includes student-run coffee houses, white and black box studio spaces and historic buildings designated as NYC landmarks.

ADMISSIONS

Freshman Academic Profile: Average high school GPA 3.6. 47% in top 10% of high school class, 80% in top 25% of high school class, 97% in top 50% of high school class. SAT Math middle 50% range 580-680. SAT Critical Reading middle 50% range 570-670. SAT Writing middle 50% range 580-680. ACT middle 50% range 26-30. Minimum internet-based TOEFL 90. Minimum paper TOEFL 575. **Basis for Candidate Selection:** *Very important factors considered include:* Class rank, rigor of secondary school record, standardized test scores. *Important factors considered include:* application essay, recommendation(s), character/personal qualities, extracurricular activities, talent/ability. *Other factors considered include:* alumni/ae relation, first generation, geographical residence, racial/ethnic status, volunteer work, work experience. **Freshman Admission Requirements:** High school diploma is required and GED is accepted. *Academic units required:* 4 English, 3 mathematics, 3 science, 2 foreign language, 2 social studies, 2 history, 6 academic electives. **Freshman Admission Statistics:** 40,912 applied, 48% admitted, 12% enrolled. **Transfer Admission Requirements:** High school transcript, college transcript(s), essay or personal statement, statement of good standing from prior institution(s). Minimum college GPA of 3.0 required. Lowest grade transferable C. **General Admission Information:** Application Fee $50. Regular application deadline 1/15. Regular notification 4/1. Nonfall registration accepted. Admission may be deferred for a maximum of 1 year. Credit and/or placement offered for CEEB Advanced Placement tests.

COSTS AND FINANCIAL AID

Annual tuition $44,450. Room and board $15,965. Required fees $1,173. Average book expense $999. **Required Forms and Deadlines:** FAFSA, CSS/Financial Aid PROFILE, State aid form, Noncustodial PROFILE, Business/Farm Supplement. **Notification of Awards:** Applicants will be notified of awards on or about 4/1. **Types of Aid:** *Need-based scholarships/grants:* Federal Pell, SEOG, state scholarships/grants, private scholarships, the school's own gift aid. *Loans:* Subsidized Stafford, Unsubsidized Stafford, PLUS, Federal Perkins. **Financial Aid Statistics:** 98% freshmen, 96% undergrads receive need-based scholarship or grant aid. 20% freshmen, 17% undergrads receive non-need-based scholarship or grant aid. 70% freshmen, 71% undergrads receive need-based self-help aid. 2% freshmen, 2% undergrads receive athletic scholarships. 89% freshmen, 79% undergrads receive any aid. 62% undergrads borrow to pay for school. Average cumulative indebtedness $26,762. **Criteria for awarding institutional aid:** *Non-need-based:* academics, athletics.

FORT HAYS STATE UNIVERSITY

600 Park Street, Hays, KS 67601-4099
Phone: 785.628.3478 • **Financial Aid Phone:** 785-628-4408
E-mail: tigers@fhsu.edu • **CEEB Code:** 6218
Fax: 800.432.0248 • **Website:** www.fhsu.edu • **ACT Code:** 1408

This public school was founded in 1902. It has a 4160-acre campus.

RATINGS
Admissions Selectivity Rating: 73   Fire Safety Rating: 70

STUDENTS AND FACULTY
Enrollment: 11,298. **Student Body:** 60% female, 40% male, 29% out-of-state, 29% international. Asian 1%, African American 4%, Caucasian 56%, Hispanic 7%, Native American <1%
Retention and Graduation: 18% freshmen graduate within 4 years. 42% freshmen graduate within 6 years. 20% grads go on to further study within 1 year. **Faculty:** 304 full-time faculty, 69% hold PhDs, 47% are members of minority groups, 9% are women. 1% of classes are taught by teaching assistants.

ACADEMICS
Degrees: associate, bachelor's, certificate, master's, post-master's certificate. **Classes:** Most classes have 10–19 students. Most lab/discussion sessions have fewer than 10 students. **Majors with Highest Enrollment:** Elementary Education and Teaching; Health and Physical Education/Fitness; Business/Commerce. **Special Study Options:** distance learning, double major, dual enrollment, English as a Second Language (ESL), exchange student program (domestic), external degree program, independent study, internships, liberal arts/career combination, student-designed major, study abroad, teacher certification program. Combined degree programs: BA/MEng, 3-1 progs in allied health, dentistry, and eng. **Disability Services:** Special programs offered to physically disabled students include note-taking services, reader services, tutors. **Career services:** Alumni network, alumni services, career/job search classes, career assessment, internships.

FACILITIES
Housing: Coed dorms, men's dorms, women's dorms, fraternity/sorority housing, apartments for married students, apartments for single students. 100% of campus accessible to physically disabled. **Special Academic Facilities/Equipment:** Paleontology, natural history, visual arts and media center, farm, NMR gas analyzer, telescope (HG). **Computers:** 100% of classrooms, 100% of dorms, 100% of libraries, 100% of dining areas, 100% of student union, 100% of common outdoor areas have wireless network access.

CAMPUS LIFE
Environment: Village. **Activities:** Choral groups, concert band, dance, drama/theater, jazz band, marching band, music ensembles, musical theater, pep band, radio station, student government, student newspaper, symphony orchestra, television station, yearbook. 103 registered organizations, 20 honor societies, 2 religious organizations. 3 fraternities, 3 sororities. **Athletics (Intercollegiate):** *Men:* baseball, basketball, cheerleading, cross-country, football, golf, track/field (outdoor), track/field (indoor), wrestling. *Women:* basketball, cheerleading, cross-country, golf, softball, tennis, track/field (outdoor), track/field (indoor), volleyball. **On-Campus Highlights:** www.tigersportszone.com, www.fhsu.edu/sternberg/, www.fhsu.edu/int/kfhsradio/, www.fhsu.edu/int/kfhstv/, www.fhsu.edu/leader. **Environmental Initiatives:** Clean up of Big Creek; Clean up of area neighborhoods; Recycling of paper, newspapers and aluminum all over campus.

ADMISSIONS
Freshman Academic Profile: Average high school GPA 3.3. 11% in top 10% of high school class, 30% in top 25% of high school class, 62% in top 50% of high school class. 95% from public high schools. ACT middle 50% range 18-24. Minimum internet-based TOEFL 61. Minimum paper TOEFL 500. **Basis for Candidate Selection:** *Other factors considered include:* Class rank, academic GPA, rigor of secondary school record, standardized test scores. **Freshman Admission Requirements:** High school diploma is required and GED is accepted. **Freshman Admission Statistics:** 2,427 applied, 88% admitted, 48% enrolled. **Transfer Admission Requirements:** college transcript(s), Minimum college GPA of 2.0 required. Lowest grade transferable D. **General Admission Information:** Application Fee $30. Nonfall registration accepted. Admission may be deferred for a maximum of 1 year. Credit offered for CEEB Advanced Placement tests.

COSTS AND FINANCIAL AID
Annual in-state tuition $3,314. Annual out-of-state tuition $12,003. Room and board $7,003. Required fees $926. Average book expense $920. **Required Forms and Deadlines:** FAFSA, Institution's own financial aid form. **Types of Aid:** *Need-based scholarships/grants:* Federal Pell, SEOG, state scholarships/grants, private scholarships, the school's own gift aid. *Loans:* Subsidized Stafford, Unsubsidized Stafford, PLUS, Federal Perkins, college/university loans from institutional funds. *Student Employment:* Federal Work-Study Program available. Highest amount earned per year from on-campus jobs $2,000. Off-campus job opportunities are fair. **Financial Aid Statistics:** 94% freshmen, 79% undergrads receive need-based scholarship or grant aid. 10% freshmen, 3% undergrads receive non-need-based scholarship or grant aid. 73% freshmen, 80% undergrads receive need-based self-help aid. 5% freshmen, 4% undergrads receive athletic scholarships. 71% undergrads borrow to pay for school. Average cumulative indebtedness $24,453. **Criteria for awarding institutional aid:** *Non-need-based:* academics, alumni affiliation, art, athletics, job skills, leadership, minority status, music/drama, religious affiliation, state/district residency.

FORT LEWIS COLLEGE

1000 Rim Drive, Durango, CO 81301
Phone: 970-247-7184 • **Financial Aid Phone:** 970-247-7142
E-mail: admisson@fortlewis.edu • **CEEB Code:** 4310
Fax: 970-247-7179 • **Website:** www.fortlewis.edu • **ACT Code:** 510

This public school was founded in 1911. It has a 362-acre campus.

RATINGS
Admissions Selectivity Rating: 75   Fire Safety Rating: 84

STUDENTS AND FACULTY
Enrollment: 3,615. **Student Body:** 48% female, 52% male, 47% out-of-state, 1% international (17 countries represented). Asian 1%, African American 1%, Caucasian 55%, Hispanic 10%, Native American 24%
Retention and Graduation: 18% freshmen graduate within 4 years. 15% grads go on to further study within 1 year. **Faculty:** 167 full-time faculty, 82% hold PhDs, 52% are members of minority groups, 8% are women. 0% of classes are taught by teaching assistants.

ACADEMICS
Degrees: bachelor's. **Classes:** Most classes have 10–19 students. Most lab/discussion sessions have 10–19 students. **Majors with Highest Enrollment:** Biology/Biological Sciences; Business Administration and Management; Psychology. **Special Study Options:** Accelerated program, cooperative education program, distance learning, double major, dual enrollment, English as a Second Language (ESL), exchange student program (domestic), honors program, independent study, internships, liberal arts/career combination, student-designed major, study abroad, teacher certification program. **Honors programs:** The John F. Reed honors program selects outstanding first and second-year students who demonstrate ability and interest in pursuing additional academic achievements and challenges. The program requires honors courses called forums which ask students to study innovative thinkers, intellectual foundations, and multidisciplinary perspectives. All of the student"s work culminates in an honors thesis presented in a public forum. Students in the honors program also benefit from the honors lounge (computers, tv, fridge, reference materials, etc.), free tickets to events and mentoring by professional associates. Upon graduation, the students receive a minor in Honors called "Rhetoric of Inquiry." **Disability Services:** Special programs offered to physically disabled students include note-taking services, reader services, tape recorders, tutors. **Career services:** Alumni network, alumni services, career/job search classes, career assessment, internships, regional alumni. Career services highlights include The Skyhawks Job Source: Our new on-line, web-based system allows students to search for positions, post resumes and cover letters for employers to view. The system also allows students to apply for positions on-line. Students who up-load a resume to the site will be included in candidate searches by employers and by the Career Services Office. Students can keep track of and manage their job search activities as well.

FACILITIES
Housing: Coed dorms, special housing for disabled students, apartments for married students, apartments for single students, Wellness Housing, Theme Housing. 100% of campus accessible to physically disabled. **Special Academic Facilities/Equipment:** Center of Southwest Studies, Community Concert Hall **Computers:** 100% of classrooms, 100% of dorms, 100% of libraries, 100% of dining areas, 100% of student union, 10% of common outdoor areas have wireless network access. Students can register for classes online. Administrative functions (other than registration) can be performed online.

CAMPUS LIFE

Environment: Town. **Activities:** Choral groups, concert band, drama/theater, jazz band, literary magazine, musical theater, pep band, radio station, student government, student newspaper, Campus Ministries. 65 registered organizations, 5 honor societies, 3 religious organizations. **Athletics (Intercollegiate):** *Men:* basketball, cross-country, football, golf, soccer. *Women:* basketball, cross-country, lacrosse, soccer, softball, volleyball. **On-Campus Highlights:** Center of Southwest Studies, Student Life Center, College Union Building, Residence Halls, Academic buildings, Highly qualified, committed faculty who are available, helpful, and engaged. Emphasis on active, experiential learning through community service, undergraduate research, study abroad, and internships. Student-faculty ratio of 17:1. Collaborative campus culture where student voices are heard and respected. Graduates who are twice as likely as those other schools to say their education was "excellent." Cultural diversity is a core value and key feature of Fort Lewis College. Approximately 28% of our students are from ethnic minority backgrounds. **Environmental Initiatives:** All new construction or renovation follow at minimum LEED Silver standards Waste minimization including a full-scale recycling program, event recycling, and composting within campus dining Promotion of alternative transportation options. All students and faculty receive a free bus pass, green cars receive a parking permit discount, and there is an extensive trail system for biking and walking to campus.

ADMISSIONS

Freshman Academic Profile: Average high school GPA 3.21. 11% in top 10% of high school class, 31% in top 25% of high school class, 69% in top 50% of high school class. 99% from public high schools. SAT Math middle 50% range 465-565. SAT Critical Reading middle 50% range 460-632. SAT Writing middle 50% range 423-520. ACT middle 50% range 19-24. Minimum internet-based TOEFL 61. Minimum paper TOEFL 500. **Basis for Candidate Selection:** *Very important factors considered include:* Class rank, academic GPA, rigor of secondary school record, standardized test scores. *Other factors considered include:* application essay, recommendation(s), alumni/ae relation, character/personal qualities, extracurricular activities, first generation, interview, level of applicant's interest, talent/ability, volunteer work, work experience. **Freshman Admission Requirements:** High school diploma is required and GED is accepted. *Academic units required:* 4 English, 4 mathematics, 3 science, (2 science labs), 1 foreign language, 2 social studies, 1 history, 2 academic electives. **Freshman Admission Statistics:** 2,439 applied, 91% admitted, 35% enrolled. **Transfer Admission Requirements:** college transcript(s), Minimum college GPA of 2.40 required. Lowest grade transferable C-. **General Admission Information:** Application Fee $40. Regular application deadline 8/10. Notification on a rolling basis, beginning on or about 10/10. Nonfall registration accepted. Admission may be deferred for a maximum of 1 semester. Credit and/or placement offered for CEEB Advanced Placement tests.

COSTS AND FINANCIAL AID

Annual in-state tuition $5,544. Annual out-of-state tuition $16,072. Room and board $8,850. Required fees $1,708. Average book expense $1,208. **Required Forms and Deadlines:** FAFSA. **Notification of Awards:** Applicants will be notified of awards on a rolling basis beginning 3/15. **Types of Aid:** *Need-based scholarships/grants:* Federal Pell, SEOG, state scholarships/grants, private scholarships, the school's own gift aid. *Loans:* Subsidized Stafford, Unsubsidized Stafford, PLUS, Federal Perkins, college/university loans from institutional funds. *Student Employment:* Federal Work-Study Program available. Institutional employment available. Highest amount earned per year from on-campus jobs $6,905. Off-campus job opportunities are good. **Financial Aid Statistics:** 89% freshmen, 86% undergrads receive need-based scholarship or grant aid. 7% freshmen, 4% undergrads receive non-need-based scholarship or grant aid. 72% freshmen, 73% undergrads receive need-based self-help aid. 6% freshmen, 8% undergrads receive athletic scholarships. 91% freshmen, 83% undergrads receive any aid. 62% undergrads borrow to pay for school. Average cumulative indebtedness $18,944. **Criteria for awarding institutional aid:** *Non-need-based:* academics, alumni affiliation, art, athletics, leadership, minority status, music/drama, state/district residency.

FRAMINGHAM STATE UNIVERSITY

100 State Street, Framingham, MA 01701-9101
Phone: 508-626-4500 · **Financial Aid Phone:** 508-626-4534
E-mail: admissions@framingham.edu · **CEEB Code:** 3519
Fax: 508-626-4017 · **Website:** www.framingham.edu · **ACT Code:** 1904

This public school was founded in 1839. It has a 73-acre campus.

RATINGS

Admissions Selectivity Rating: 77   **Fire Safety Rating:** 99

STUDENTS AND FACULTY

Enrollment: 4,329. **Student Body:** 64% female, 36% male, 4% out-of-state, 0% international (21 countries represented). Asian 3%, African American 8%, Caucasian 74%, Hispanic 9%, Native American <1%
Retention and Graduation: 33% freshmen graduate within 4 years. 51% freshmen graduate within 6 years. **Faculty:** 186 full-time faculty, 90% hold PhDs, 59% are members of minority groups, 18% are women. 0% of classes are taught by teaching assistants.

ACADEMICS

Degrees: bachelor's, master's, post-bachelor's certificate. **Classes:** Most classes have 20–29 students. **Majors with Highest Enrollment:** Business/Commerce; Family and Consumer Sciences/Human Sciences; Sociology. **Special Study Options:** cross-registration, distance learning, double major, honors program, independent study, internships, liberal arts/career combination, study abroad, teacher certification program, Pre-engineering program in conjunction with University of Massachusetts Amherst, University of Massachusetts Dartmouth, and University of Massachusetts Lowell. **Honors programs:** The Honors Program offers challenging courses and projects for qualified students,and sponsors events which contribute to the intellectual life of the College community. **Disability Services:** Special programs offered to physically disabled students include note-taking services, reader services, tape recorders, tutors. **Career services:** Alumni network, alumni services, career/job search classes, career assessment, internships. Career services highlights include our current working relationships with key employers in the MetroWest area with plans to expand in MetroWest, Boston, and Worcester.

FACILITIES

Housing: Coed dorms, women's dorms, Wellness Housing, Theme Housing. 95% of campus accessible to physically disabled. **Special Academic Facilities/Equipment:** Mazmanian Art Gallery, McAuliffe Challenger Learning Center, Greenhouse, Early Childhood Development Lab, Education Curriculum Library,Planetarium **Computers:** 100% of classrooms, 100% of dorms, 100% of libraries, 100% of dining areas, 100% of student union, have wireless network access. Students can register for classes online. Administrative functions (other than registration) can be performed online. Undergraduates are required to own a computer.

CAMPUS LIFE

Environment: City. **Activities:** Choral groups, dance, drama/theater, literary magazine, musical theater, radio station, student government, student newspaper, Campus Ministries, International Student Organization. 55 registered organizations, 11 honor society, 4 religious organizations. **Athletics (Intercollegiate):** *Men:* baseball, basketball, cross-country, football, ice hockey, soccer. *Women:* basketball, cross-country, field hockey, lacrosse, soccer, softball, volleyball. **On-Campus Highlights:** Residence Halls, Athletic Facility, College Center, Academic Buildings, Library. **Environmental Initiatives:** Conversion of our power plant from #6 oil to natural gas, decreasing our carbon footprint from the plant by 30%. Increase of renewable power from less than 1% to 17.82%. Added new course time blocks allowing for commuters, students and faculty, to deduce the number of commuting days.

ADMISSIONS

Freshman Academic Profile: Average high school GPA 3.21. 7% in top 10% of high school class, 25% in top 25% of high school class, 67% in top 50% of high school class. SAT Math middle 50% range 460-550. SAT Critical Reading middle 50% range 460-550. SAT Writing middle 50% range 440-540. ACT middle 50% range 20-24. Minimum internet-based TOEFL 79. Minimum paper TOEFL 550. **Basis for Candidate Selection:** *Very important factors considered include:* academic GPA, rigor of secondary school record, standardized test scores. *Important factors considered include:* Class rank, application essay, recommendation(s). *Other factors considered include:* alumni/ae relation, character/personal qualities, extracurricular activities, first generation, level of applicant's interest, state residency, talent/ability, volunteer work, work experience. **Freshman Admission Requirements:** High school diploma is required and GED is accepted. *Academic units required:* 4 English, 3 mathematics, 3 science, (2 science labs), 2 foreign language, 1 social studies, 1 history, 2 academic electives. **Freshman Admission Statistics:** 5,207 applied, 62% admitted, 25% enrolled. **Transfer Admission Requirements:** High school transcript, college transcript(s), essay or personal statement, Minimum college GPA of 2.5 required. Lowest grade transferable C-. **General Admission Information:** Application Fee $50. Notification on a rolling basis, beginning on or about 1/15. Nonfall registration accepted. Admission may be deferred for a maximum of 12 months. Credit and/or placement offered for CEEB Advanced Placement tests.

COSTS AND FINANCIAL AID

Annual out-of-state tuition $7,050. Room and board $10,534. Required fees $7,530. Average book expense $1,000. **Required Forms and Deadlines:** FAFSA. **Notification of Awards:** Applicants will be notified of awards on a rolling basis beginning 3/15. **Types of Aid:** *Need-based scholarships/grants:* Federal Pell, SEOG, state scholarships/grants, private scholarships, the school's own gift aid. *Loans:* Subsidized Stafford, Unsubsidized Stafford, PLUS, Federal Perkins, state loans. *Student Employment:* Federal Work-Study Program available. Institutional employment available. Highest amount earned per year from on-campus jobs $1,000. Off-campus job opportunities are excellent. **Financial Aid Statistics:** 82% freshmen, 78% undergrads receive need-based scholarship or grant aid. 1% freshmen, 1% undergrads receive non-need-based scholarship or grant aid. 81% freshmen, 77% undergrads receive need-based self-help aid. 0% freshmen, 0% undergrads receive athletic scholarships. 88% freshmen, 80% undergrads receive any aid. 81% undergrads borrow to pay for school. Average cumulative indebtedness $17,230. **Criteria for awarding institutional aid:** *Non-need-based:* academics.

THE FRANCISCAN UNIVERSITY

400 North Bluff Blvd, Clinton, IA 52733-2967
Phone: 563-242-4153
E-mail: admissns@tfu.edu • **CEEB Code:** 6418
Fax: 563-243-6102 • **Website:** www.tfu.edu • **ACT Code:** 1342

This private school was founded in 1918. It has a 25-acre campus.

RATINGS

Admissions Selectivity Rating: 72   **Fire Safety Rating:** 60*

STUDENTS AND FACULTY

Enrollment: 416. **Student Body:** 56% female, 44% male, 46% out-of-state, 3% international (10 countries represented). Asian 1%, African American 6%, Caucasian 87%, Hispanic 3%, Native American <1%
Retention and Graduation: 69% freshmen return for sophomore year. 25% freshmen graduate within 4 years. 34% freshmen graduate within 6 years. 25% grads go on to further study within 1 year. **Faculty:** 27 full-time faculty, 48% hold PhDs, 44% are members of minority groups, 4% are women. 0% of classes are taught by teaching assistants.

ACADEMICS

Degrees: associate, bachelor's, master's, transfer associate. **Classes:** Most classes have 10–19 students. Most lab/discussion sessions have fewer than 10 students. **Majors with Highest Enrollment:** Education; Liberal Arts and Sciences Studies and Humanities; Social Sciences. **Special Study Options:** distance learning, double major, dual enrollment, honors program, independent study, internships, student-designed major, study abroad, teacher certification program, Advanced Placement Program Summer School off-campus study senior capstone or culminating academic experiences undergraduate research/ creative projects writing in the disciplines. **Disability Services:** Special programs offered to physically disabled students include tutors.

FACILITIES

Housing: Coed dorms, Durham Hall = 2 bedroom suites (one side floors are designated for men and one side designated for women. Sides of building joined by common lounge area), Regis Hall = single bedrooms (1 floor for women and 1 floor for men). 95% of campus accessible to physically disabled. **Special Academic Facilities/Equipment:** On-campus preschool. Indoor swimming pool, multipurpose educ. center, resident halls, 1 bedroom suites or 2 single rooms **Computers:** Administrative functions (other than registration) can be performed online.

CAMPUS LIFE

Environment: Town. **Activities:** Choral groups, music ensembles, student government, student newspaper. 20 registered organizations, 2 honor societies. **Athletics (Intercollegiate):** *Men:* baseball, basketball, cross-country, golf, soccer, track/field (outdoor). *Women:* basketball, cross-country, soccer, softball, track/field (outdoor), volleyball.

ADMISSIONS

Freshman Academic Profile: Average high school GPA 2.84. 8% in top 10% of high school class, 16% in top 25% of high school class, 50% in top 50% of high school class. ACT middle 50% range 16-22. Minimum paper TOEFL 430. **Basis for Candidate Selection:** *Very important factors considered include:* Class rank, rigor of secondary school record, standardized test scores. *Other factors considered include:* recommendation(s). **Freshman Admission Requirements:** High school diploma is required and GED is accepted. **Freshman Admission Statistics:** 246 applied, 77% admitted, 28% enrolled. **Transfer Admission Requirements:** college transcript(s), statement of good standing from prior institution(s). Minimum college GPA of 2.0 required. Lowest grade transferable c. **General Admission Information:** Application Fee $20. Regular application deadline 8/15. Nonfall registration accepted. Admission may be deferred for a maximum of 1academic year. Credit and/or placement offered for CEEB Advanced Placement tests.

COSTS AND FINANCIAL AID

Annual tuition $13,920. Room and board $5,250. Required fees $130. Average book expense $600. **Required Forms and Deadlines:** FAFSA. **Notification of Awards:** Applicants will be notified of awards on a rolling basis beginning 3/15. **Types of Aid:** *Need-based scholarships/grants:* Federal Pell, SEOG, state scholarships/grants, private scholarships, the school's own gift aid. *Loans:* Subsidized Stafford, Unsubsidized Stafford, PLUS, Federal Perkins, Private Loan Company. **Financial Aid Statistics:** 100% freshmen, 100% undergrads receive need-based scholarship or grant aid. 13% freshmen, 13% undergrads receive non-need-based scholarship or grant aid. 78% freshmen, 80% undergrads receive need-based self-help aid. 23% freshmen, 12% undergrads receive athletic scholarships. 88% undergrads borrow to pay for school. **Criteria for awarding institutional aid:** *Non-need-based:* academics, alumni affiliation, art, athletics, job skills, leadership, minority status, music/drama, religious affiliation.

FRANCISCAN UNIVERSITY OF STEUBENVILLE

1235 University Boulevard, Steubenville, OH 43952-1763
Phone: 740-283-6226 • **Financial Aid Phone:** 740-283-6226
E-mail: admissions@franciscan.edu • **CEEB Code:** 1133
Fax: 740-284-5456 • **Website:** www.franciscan.edu • **ACT Code:** 3258

This private school, affiliated with the Roman Catholic Church, was founded in 1946. It has a 124-acre campus.

RATINGS

Admissions Selectivity Rating: 86   **Fire Safety Rating:** 68

STUDENTS AND FACULTY

Enrollment: 2,038. **Student Body:** 61% female, 39% male, 79% out-of-state, 1% international (20 countries represented). Asian 1%, African American 1%, Caucasian 80%, Hispanic 9%, Native American <1%
Retention and Graduation: 87% freshmen return for sophomore year. 70% freshmen graduate within 4 years. 73% freshmen graduate within 6 years. 13% grads go on to further study within 1 year. 9% grads pursue arts and sciences degrees. 1% grads pursue business degrees. 1% grads pursue medical degrees. **Faculty:** 108 full-time faculty, 81% hold PhDs, 26% are members of minority groups, 1% are women. 0% of classes are taught by teaching assistants.

ACADEMICS

Degrees: associate, bachelor's, master's. **Classes:** Most classes have 10–19 students. Most lab/discussion sessions have 10–19 students. **Majors with Highest Enrollment:** Elementary Education and Teaching; Theology/Theological Studies; Business/Commerce. **Special Study Options:** Accelerated program, distance learning, double major, dual enrollment, honors program, independent study, internships, liberal arts/career combination, study abroad, teacher certification program. **Honors programs:** We have a Great Books program. Combined degree programs: BA/MA, 4+1 in Business and Philosophy. **Disability Services:** Special programs offered to physically disabled students include note-taking services, reader services, tape recorders, tutors. **Career services:** career/job search classes, career assessment, internships.

FACILITIES

Housing: men's dorms, women's dorms, apartments for single students. 75% of campus accessible to physically disabled. **Special Academic Facilities/ Equipment:** Art Gallery. **Computers:** Students can register for classes online. Administrative functions (other than registration) can be performed online.

CAMPUS LIFE

Environment: Village. **Activities:** Choral groups, drama/theater, literary magazine, music ensembles, radio station, student government, student newspaper, yearbook, Campus Ministries, International Student Organization. 31 registered organizations, 3 honor societies, 6 religious organizations. 1 fraternity, 1 sorority. **On-Campus Highlights:** Heavenly Grounds Coffee Shop, Sts. Cosmas and Damian Hall-Science Building, Finnegan Fieldhouse, Christ The King Chapel, Portiuncula Chapel.

ADMISSIONS

Freshman Academic Profile: Average high school GPA 3.69. 22% in top 10% of high school class, 53% in top 25% of high school class, 81% in top 50% of high school class. 42% from public high schools. SAT Math middle 50% range 520-620. SAT Critical Reading middle 50% range 540-650. SAT Writing middle 50% range 520-630. ACT middle 50% range 22-29. Minimum paper TOEFL 550. **Basis for Candidate Selection:** *Very important factors considered include:* application essay, academic GPA, rigor of secondary school record, standardized test scores, character/personal qualities, interview. *Important factors considered include:* extracurricular activities, level of applicant's interest, talent/ability. *Other factors considered include:* recommendation(s). **Freshman Admission Requirements:** High school diploma is required and GED is accepted. **Freshman Admission Statistics:** 1,787 applied, 76% admitted, 32% enrolled. **Transfer Admission Requirements:** High school transcript, college transcript(s), essay or personal statement, Minimum college GPA of 2.2 required. Lowest grade transferable C. **General Admission Information:** Application Fee $20. Regular application deadline 5/1. Notification on a rolling basis, beginning on or about 9/1. Nonfall registration accepted. Admission may be deferred for a maximum of one year. Credit and/or placement offered for CEEB Advanced Placement tests.

COSTS AND FINANCIAL AID

Required Forms and Deadlines: FAFSA. **Notification of Awards:** Applicants will be notified of awards on a rolling basis beginning 3/15. **Types of Aid:** *Need-based scholarships/grants:* Federal Pell, SEOG, state scholarships/grants, private scholarships, the school's own gift aid. *Loans:* Subsidized Stafford, Unsubsidized Stafford, PLUS, Federal Perkins, Alternative Loans. *Student Employment:* Federal Work-Study Program available. Institutional employment available. Highest amount earned per year from on-campus jobs $3,090. Off-campus job opportunities are good. **Financial Aid Statistics:** 98% freshmen, 96% undergrads receive need-based scholarship or grant aid. 11% freshmen, 7% undergrads receive non-need-based scholarship or grant aid. 89% freshmen, 92% undergrads receive need-based self-help aid. 0% freshmen, 0% undergrads receive athletic scholarships. 63% freshmen, 62% undergrads receive any aid. 76% undergrads borrow to pay for school. Average cumulative indebtedness $22,257. **Criteria for awarding institutional aid:** *Non-need-based:* academics, leadership, religious affiliation.

FRANCIS MARION UNIVERSITY

Office of Admissions, Florence, SC 29502-0547
Phone: 843-661-1231 · **Financial Aid Phone:** 843-661-1190
E-mail: admissions@fmarion.edu · **CEEB Code:** 5442
Fax: 843-661-4635 · **Website:** www.fmarion.edu · **ACT Code:** 3856

This public school was founded in 1970. It has a 300-acre campus.

RATINGS

Admissions Selectivity Rating: 78 **Fire Safety Rating:** 76

STUDENTS AND FACULTY

Enrollment: 3,380. **Student Body:** 68% female, 32% male, 3% out-of-state, 1% international (19 countries represented). Asian 1%, African American 50%, Caucasian 45%, Hispanic 1%, Native American <1%
Retention and Graduation: 67% freshmen return for sophomore year. 16% freshmen graduate within 4 years. 41% freshmen graduate within 6 years. **Faculty:** 204 full-time faculty, 79% hold PhDs, 49% are members of minority groups, 11% are women. 0% of classes are taught by teaching assistants.

ACADEMICS

Degrees: bachelor's, master's. **Classes:** Most classes have 20–29 students. **Majors with Highest Enrollment:** Registered Nursing/Registered Nurse; Biology/Biological Sciences; Psychology. **Special Study Options:** Accelerated program, cross-registration, distance learning, double major, dual enrollment, honors program, independent study, internships, study abroad, teacher certification program. Combined degree programs: 2-2 Forestry prog with Clemson U.; engineering, BSN. **Disability Services:** Special programs offered to physically disabled students include note-taking services, reader services, tape recorders, tutors.

FACILITIES

Housing: special housing for disabled students, men's dorms, women's dorms, apartments for single students. 100% of campus accessible to physically disabled. **Special Academic Facilities/Equipment:** Media center, planetarium, observatory. **Computers:** Students can register for classes online.

CAMPUS LIFE

Environment: Rural. **Activities:** Choral groups, drama/theater, jazz band, literary magazine, music ensembles, student government, student newspaper, television station. 56 registered organizations, 13 honor societies, 5 religious organizations. 7 fraternities, 7 sororities. **Athletics (Intercollegiate):** *Men:* baseball, basketball, cross-country, golf, soccer, tennis, track/field (outdoor). *Women:* basketball, cross-country, soccer, softball, tennis, track/field (outdoor), volleyball. **On-Campus Highlights:** The Cottage, The Smith University Center, The Dooley Planetarium, The Hyman Fine Arts Center, The Hewn Timber Cabins.

ADMISSIONS

Freshman Academic Profile: Average high school GPA 3.611. 15.1% in top 10% of high school class, 14.8% in top 25% of high school class, 80.8% in top 50% of high school class. 91% from public high schools. SAT Math middle 50% range 420-530. SAT Critical Reading middle 50% range 410-530. SAT Writing middle 50% range 390-500. ACT middle 50% range 17-22. Minimum internet-based TOEFL 61. Minimum paper TOEFL 500. **Basis for Candidate Selection:** *Very important factors considered include:* rigor of secondary school record, standardized test scores. *Important factors considered include:* Class rank. *Other factors considered include:* recommendation(s). **Freshman Admission Requirements:** High school diploma is required and GED is accepted. *Academic units required:* 4 English, 3 mathematics, 3 science, (3 science labs), 2 foreign language, 2 social studies, 1 history, 4 academic electives, 1 PE or ROTC. **Freshman Admission Statistics:** 3,952 applied, 57% admitted, 33% enrolled. **Transfer Admission Requirements:** High school transcript, college transcript(s), statement of good standing from prior institution(s). Minimum college GPA of 2.0 required. Lowest grade transferable C. **General Admission Information:** Application Fee $30. Notification on a rolling basis, beginning on or about 9/1. Nonfall registration accepted. Admission may be deferred for a maximum of 1 semester. Credit offered for CEEB Advanced Placement tests.

COSTS AND FINANCIAL AID

Annual in-state tuition $9,266. Annual out-of-state tuition $18,532. Room and board $7,256. Required fees $472. Average book expense $999. **Required Forms and Deadlines:** FAFSA. **Notification of Awards:** Applicants will be notified of awards on a rolling basis beginning 4/15. **Types of Aid:** *Need-based scholarships/grants:* Federal Pell, SEOG, state scholarships/grants, private scholarships, the school's own gift aid. *Loans:* Subsidized Stafford, Unsubsidized Stafford, PLUS, Federal Perkins, state loans, college/university loans from institutional funds. **Financial Aid Statistics:** 99% freshmen, 76% undergrads receive need-based scholarship or grant aid. 7% freshmen, 4% undergrads receive non-need-based scholarship or grant aid. 75% freshmen, 88% undergrads receive need-based self-help aid. 0% freshmen, 0% undergrads receive athletic scholarships. 88% freshmen, 82% undergrads receive any aid. 94% undergrads borrow to pay for school. Average cumulative indebtedness $32,118. **Criteria for awarding institutional aid:** *Non-need-based:* academics.

FRANKLIN AND MARSHALL COLLEGE

P.O. Box 3003, Lancaster, PA 17604-3003
Phone: 717-291-3953 · **Financial Aid Phone:** 717-291-3991
E-mail: admission@fandm.edu · **CEEB Code:** 2261
Fax: 717-291-4389 · **Website:** www.fandm.edu · **ACT Code:** 3574

This private school was founded in 1787. It has a 180-acre campus.

RATINGS

Admissions Selectivity Rating: 92 **Fire Safety Rating:** 95

STUDENTS AND FACULTY

Enrollment: 2,182. **Student Body:** 50% female, 50% male, 76% out-of-state, 14% international (49 countries represented). Asian 5%, African American 6%, Caucasian 59%, Hispanic 8%, Native American <1%
Retention and Graduation: 91% freshmen return for sophomore year. 82% freshmen graduate within 4 years. 87% freshmen graduate within 6 years. 31% grads go on to further study within 1 year. **Faculty:** 226 full-time faculty, 92% hold PhDs, 46% are members of minority groups, 12% are women. 0% of classes are taught by teaching assistants.

ACADEMICS

Degrees: bachelor's. **Classes:** Most classes have 10–19 students. Most lab/discussion sessions have 10–19 students. **Majors with Highest Enrollment:** Political Science and Government; Business/Commerce; Psychology. **Special Study Options:** Accelerated program, cross-registration, double major, dual enrollment, exchange student program (domestic), honors program, independent study, internships, student-designed major, study abroad, teacher certification program. **Disability Services:** Special programs offered to physically disabled students include note-taking services, tutors. **Career services:** Alumni network, alumni services, career/job search classes, career assessment, internships, regional alumni.

FACILITIES

Housing: Coed dorms, special housing for disabled students, men's dorms, special housing for international students, women's dorms, fraternity/sorority housing, apartments for single students, Arts House, French House, Community Outreach House, Sustainability House. 80% of campus accessible to physically disabled. **Special Academic Facilities/Equipment:** Art gallery, associated with natural history museums, bronze casting foundry, retail sales complex, psychology and language labs, TV and radio station, observatory/planetarium, Writers House **Computers:** 100% of classrooms, 100% of dorms, 100% of libraries, 100% of dining areas, 100% of student union, 100% of common outdoor areas have wireless network access. Students can register for classes online. Administrative functions (other than registration) can be performed online.

CAMPUS LIFE

Environment: Town. **Activities:** Choral groups, concert band, dance, drama/theater, jazz band, literary magazine, music ensembles, musical theater, radio station, student government, student newspaper, symphony orchestra, yearbook, Campus Ministries, International Student Organization, Model UN. 90 registered organizations, 13 honor societies, 8 religious organizations. 7 fraternities, 3 sororities. **Athletics (Intercollegiate):** *Men:* baseball, basketball, crew/rowing, cross-country, football, golf, lacrosse, soccer, squash, swimming, tennis, track/field (outdoor), track/field (indoor), wrestling. *Women:* basketball, crew/rowing, cross-country, field hockey, golf, lacrosse, soccer, softball, squash, swimming, tennis, track/field (outdoor), track/field (indoor), volleyball. **On-Campus Highlights:** Alumni Sport and Fitness Center, Barshinger Center in Hensel Hall, Barnes and Noble Bookstore and Jazzman's Café, Roschel Performing Arts Center, Writers House. **Environmental Initiatives:** We have established the Wohlsen Center for the Sustainable Environment, including a Director, student staff member, and Artist-in-Residence, and partnership with the Millport Conservancy. We have a Student Sustainability House, are incorporating sustainability into 1st year orientation and support very active clubs: The Environmental Action Alliance, Fair Trade Café, and Dirt Army (organic garden). We have majors in Environmental Studies and Environmental Science and integrate interdisciplinary collaboration in sustainability across the curriculum.

ADMISSIONS

Freshman Academic Profile: Average high school GPA 3.8. 62% from public high schools. SAT Math middle 50% range 630-710. SAT Critical Reading middle 50% range 590-680. ACT middle 50% range 27-30. Minimum paper TOEFL 600. **Basis for Candidate Selection:** *Very important factors considered include:* Class rank, academic GPA, rigor of secondary school record, character/personal qualities. *Important factors considered include:* application essay, recommendation(s), standardized test scores, extracurricular activities, interview, talent/ability, volunteer work. *Other factors considered include:* alumni/ae relation, geographical residence, level of applicant's interest, racial/ethnic status, work experience. **Freshman Admission Requirements:** High school diploma is required and GED is accepted. *Academic units required:* 4 English, 3 mathematics, 2 science, (2 science labs), 2 foreign language, 1 social studies, 2 history, 1 visual/performing arts. **Freshman Admission Statistics:** 5,472 applied, 39% admitted, 28% enrolled. **Transfer Admission Requirements:** High school transcript, college transcript(s), essay or personal statement, interview, standardized test scores, statement of good standing from prior institution(s). Lowest grade transferable C-. **General Admission Information:** Application Fee $60. Early decision application deadline 11/15. Regular application deadline 2/1. Regular notification 4/1. Nonfall registration accepted. Admission may be deferred for a maximum of one year. Credit and/or placement offered for CEEB Advanced Placement tests.

COSTS AND FINANCIAL AID

Annual tuition $48,414. Room and board $12,285. Required fees $100. Average book expense $1,200. **Required Forms and Deadlines:** FAFSA, CSS/Financial Aid PROFILE, Noncustodial PROFILE. **Notification of Awards:** Applicants will be notified of awards on or about 4/1. **Types of Aid:** *Need-based scholarships/grants:* Federal Pell, SEOG, state scholarships/grants, private scholarships, the school's own gift aid. *Loans:* Subsidized Stafford, Unsubsidized Stafford, PLUS, Federal Perkins, college/university loans from institutional funds. *Student Employment:* Federal Work-Study Program available. Highest amount earned per year from on-campus jobs $2,175. **Financial Aid Statistics:** 98% freshmen, 96% undergrads receive need-based scholarship or grant aid. 24% freshmen, 27% undergrads receive non-need-based scholarship or grant aid. 96% freshmen, 96% undergrads receive need-based self-help aid. 0% freshmen, 0% undergrads receive athletic scholarships. 58% freshmen, 53% undergrads receive any aid. 50% undergrads borrow to pay for school. Average cumulative indebtedness $21,705. **Criteria for awarding institutional aid:** *Non-need-based:* academics, art, leadership, minority status.

FRANKLIN COLLEGE

101 Branigin Blvd, Franklin, IN 46131-2623
Phone: 317-738-8062 · **Financial Aid Phone:** 317-738-8075
E-mail: admissions@franklincollege.edu · **CEEB Code:** 1228
Fax: 317-738-8274 · **Website:** www.franklincollege.edu · **ACT Code:** 1194

This private school, affiliated with the American Baptist Church, was founded in 1834. It has a 156-acre campus.

RATINGS

Admissions Selectivity Rating: 81   **Fire Safety Rating:** 76

STUDENTS AND FACULTY

Enrollment: 1,022. **Student Body:** 53% female, 47% male, 9% out-of-state, 2% international (15 countries represented). Asian 1%, African American 4%, Caucasian 84%, Hispanic 2%, Native American <1%. **Retention and Graduation:** 79% freshmen return for sophomore year. 54% freshmen graduate within 4 years. 61% freshmen graduate within 6 years. 18% grads go on to further study within 1 year. 13% grads pursue arts and sciences degrees. 3% grads pursue law degrees. 2% grads pursue medical degrees. **Faculty:** 74 full-time faculty, 82% hold PhDs, 47% are members of minority groups, 9% are women. 0% of classes are taught by teaching assistants.

ACADEMICS

Degrees: bachelor's. **Classes:** Most classes have 10–19 students. **Majors with Highest Enrollment:** Elementary Education and Teaching; Biology/Biological Sciences; Journalism. **Special Study Options:** double major, dual enrollment, exchange student program (domestic), independent study, internships, study abroad, teacher certification program. **Honors programs:** The intercultural Honors Experience is a freshman-year program designed to attract and retain superior students and faculty to FC while internationalizing the FC community. The program is designed to help FC students build a solid intercultural foundation, introduce them to interdisciplinary learning, and provide them with opportunities and incentives to study abroad. Faculty development is an integral part of the project. **Disability Services:** Special programs offered to physically disabled students include note-taking services, reader services, tape recorders, tutors. **Career services:** alumni services, career/job search classes, career assessment.

FACILITIES

Housing: Coed dorms, special housing for disabled students, men's dorms, women's dorms, fraternity/sorority housing. 100% of campus accessible to physically disabled. **Special Academic Facilities/Equipment:** Pulliam School of Journalism, Dietz Center for Professional Development, Leadership Center. **Computers:** 100% of classrooms, 100% of libraries, 100% of dining areas, 100% of student union, have wireless network access. Students can register for classes online. Administrative functions (other than registration) can be performed online.

CAMPUS LIFE

Environment: Village. **Activities:** Choral groups, dance, drama/theater, literary magazine, musical theater, pep band, radio station, student government, student newspaper, yearbook. 66 registered organizations, 13 honor societies, 3 religious organizations. 5 fraternities, 4 sororities. **Athletics (Intercollegiate):** *Men:* baseball, basketball, cross-country, diving, football, golf, soccer, swimming, tennis, track/field (outdoor). *Women:* basketball, cheerleading, cross-country, diving, golf, soccer, softball, swimming, tennis, track/field (outdoor), volleyball. **On-Campus Highlights:** Student Center, Spurlock Center (athletic facility), library, residence hall, fraternity houses. **Environmental Initiatives:** Completing green house car emissions inventory; Star purchase policy; Recycling, composting program.

ADMISSIONS

Freshman Academic Profile: Average high school GPA 3.4. 18% in top 10% of high school class, 47% in top 25% of high school class, 86% in top 50% of high school class. 93% from public high schools. SAT Math middle 50% range 470-560. SAT Critical Reading middle 50% range 450-560. SAT Writing middle 50% range 440-540. ACT middle 50% range 20-25. Minimum paper TOEFL 550. **Basis for Candidate Selection:** *Very important factors considered include:* Class rank, academic GPA, rigor of secondary school record, standardized test scores. *Important factors considered include:* application essay, alumni/ae relation, character/personal qualities, extracurricular activities. *Other factors considered include:* recommendation(s), first generation, geographical residence, interview, level of applicant's interest, racial/ethnic status, religious affiliation/commitment, state residency, talent/ability, volunteer work, work experience. **Freshman Admission Requirements:** High school diploma is required and GED is accepted. *Academic units required:* 4 English, 4 mathematics, 2 science, 3 social studies. **Freshman Admission Statistics:** 2,050 applied,

69% admitted, 23% enrolled. **Transfer Admission Requirements:** High school transcript, college transcript(s), essay or personal statement, statement of good standing from prior institution(s). Minimum college GPA of 2.0 required. Lowest grade transferable C-. **General Admission Information:** Application Fee $30. Regular notification 9/1. Nonfall registration accepted. Admission may be deferred for a maximum of 1 year. Credit and/or placement offered for CEEB Advanced Placement tests.

COSTS AND FINANCIAL AID

Annual tuition $28,000. Room and board $8,775. Required fees $185. Average book expense $1,200. **Required Forms and Deadlines:** FAFSA, Institution's own financial aid form. **Notification of Awards:** Applicants will be notified of awards on or about 4/1. **Types of Aid:** *Need-based scholarships/grants:* Federal Pell, SEOG, state scholarships/grants, private scholarships, the school's own gift aid. *Loans:* Subsidized Stafford, Unsubsidized Stafford, PLUS, Federal Perkins, college/university loans from institutional funds. *Student Employment:* Federal Work-Study Program available. Institutional employment available. Highest amount earned per year from on-campus jobs $2,000. Off-campus job opportunities are good. **Financial Aid Statistics:** 100% freshmen, 100% undergrads receive need-based scholarship or grant aid. 90% freshmen, 89% undergrads receive non-need-based scholarship or grant aid. 100% freshmen, 100% undergrads receive need-based self-help aid. 0% freshmen, 0% undergrads receive athletic scholarships. 100% freshmen, 96% undergrads receive any aid. 80% undergrads borrow to pay for school. Average cumulative indebtedness $27,524. **Criteria for awarding institutional aid:** *Non-need-based:* academics, alumni affiliation, leadership, minority status, religious affiliation, state/district residency.

FRANKLIN PIERCE UNIVERSITY

Admissions Office, Rindge, NH 3461
Phone: 603-899-4050 • **Financial Aid Phone:** 603-899-4180
E-mail: admissions@franklinpierce.edu • **CEEB Code:** 3395
Fax: 603-889-4394 • **Website:** www.franklinpierce.edu • **ACT Code:** 2509

This private school was founded in 1962. It has a 1200-acre campus.

RATINGS

Admissions Selectivity Rating: 71   Fire Safety Rating: 89

STUDENTS AND FACULTY

Enrollment: 2,061. **Student Body:** 49% female, 51% male, 78% out-of-state. **Retention and Graduation:** 26% grads go on to further study within 1 year. 5% grads pursue arts and sciences degrees. 3% grads pursue law degrees. 7% grads pursue business degrees. 1% grads pursue medical degrees. **Faculty:** 100 full-time faculty, 68% hold PhDs, 45% are members of minority groups, 1% are women. 0% of classes are taught by teaching assistants.

ACADEMICS

Degrees: associate, bachelor's, certificate, first professional, master's, post-master's certificate. **Classes:** Most classes have 10–19 students. Most lab/discussion sessions have fewer than 10 students. **Majors with Highest Enrollment:** Education; Criminal Justice/Safety Studies; Mass Communication/Media Studies. **Special Study Options:** distance learning, double major, dual enrollment, English as a Second Language (ESL), exchange student program (domestic), honors program, independent study, internships, liberal arts/career combination, student-designed major, study abroad, teacher certification program, Walk Across Europe Program, Washington Semester, Arcadia Study Abroad. **Honors programs:** Honors Program. **Disability Services:** Special programs offered to physically disabled students include note-taking services, reader services, tape recorders, tutors. **Career services:** Alumni network, alumni services, career/job search classes, career assessment, internships, regional alumni. For career services highlights see http://franklinpierce.edu/academics/career/ugrad_rindge_cpp.htm.

FACILITIES

Housing: Coed dorms, special housing for disabled students, apartments for single students, Wellness Housing, Condominiums (townhouses). 67% of campus accessible to physically disabled. **Special Academic Facilities/Equipment:** Thoreau Art Gallery; Flynt Center; Fitzwater Communications Center; Dance Studio; Pottery Kiln; Glass Blowing Studio; TV Station; Radio Station; Grimshaw-Gudewicz Activities Center: Lakeside Activity Center **Computers:** 20% of classrooms, 20% of dorms, 100% of libraries, 80% of dining areas, 100% of student union, 50% of common outdoor areas have wireless network access. Administrative functions (other than registration) can be performed online.

CAMPUS LIFE

Environment: Rural. **Activities:** Choral groups, dance, drama/theater, literary magazine, music ensembles, musical theater, radio station, student government,

student newspaper, television station, yearbook, Campus Ministries. 35 registered organizations, 8 honor societies, 3 religious organizations. **Athletics (Intercollegiate):** *Men:* baseball, basketball, crew/rowing, golf, ice hockey, rugby, soccer, tennis. *Women:* basketball, crew/rowing, cross-country, field hockey, lacrosse, soccer, softball, volleyball. **On-Campus Highlights:** Peterson Hall, The Campus Center, The Northfields Activity Center, The Fitzwater Center for Communications, The Pub. **Environmental Initiatives:** Development of on enhanced on-campus recycling program; Conversion to online format materials; reducing paper waste (online catalogue, billing, forms, etc); Conversion of incandescent lighting to compact flourescent throughout campus.

ADMISSIONS

Freshman Academic Profile: Average high school GPA 2.78. 7% in top 10% of high school class, 20% in top 25% of high school class, 54% in top 50% of high school class. 89% from public high schools. SAT Math middle 50% range 430-540. SAT Critical Reading middle 50% range 440-550. SAT Writing middle 50% range 420-520. Minimum internet-based TOEFL 61. Minimum paper TOEFL 500. **Basis for Candidate Selection:** *Very important factors considered include:* academic GPA, recommendation(s), character/personal qualities. *Important factors considered include:* application essay, rigor of secondary school record, standardized test scores. *Other factors considered include:* Class rank, extracurricular activities, interview, talent/ability, volunteer work, work experience. **Freshman Admission Requirements:** High school diploma is required and GED is accepted. *Academic units required:* 4 English, 3 mathematics, 2 science, (2 science labs), 0 foreign language, 3 social studies, 0 history, 4 academic electives. **Transfer Admission Requirements:** college transcript(s), essay or personal statement, Minimum college GPA of 2.0 required. Lowest grade transferable C-. **General Admission Information:** Application Fee $40. Notification on a rolling basis, beginning on or about 10/15. Nonfall registration accepted. Admission may be deferred for a maximum of 1 year. Credit and/or placement offered for CEEB Advanced Placement tests.

COSTS AND FINANCIAL AID

Annual tuition $27,700. Room and board $9,800. Required fees $1,300. Average book expense $1,000. **Required Forms and Deadlines:** FAFSA. **Notification of Awards:** Applicants will be notified of awards on a rolling basis beginning 2/1. **Types of Aid:** *Need-based scholarships/grants:* Federal Pell, SEOG, state scholarships/grants, private scholarships, the school's own gift aid. *Loans:* Subsidized Stafford, Unsubsidized Stafford, PLUS, Federal Perkins. *Student Employment:* Federal Work-Study Program available. Institutional employment available. Highest amount earned per year from on-campus jobs $2,200. Off-campus job opportunities are fair. **Financial Aid Statistics:** 99% freshmen, 99% undergrads receive need-based scholarship or grant aid. 9% freshmen, 9% undergrads receive non-need-based scholarship or grant aid. 90% freshmen, 90% undergrads receive need-based self-help aid. 4% freshmen, 5% undergrads receive athletic scholarships. 99% freshmen, 87% undergrads receive any aid. 67% undergrads borrow to pay for school. Average cumulative indebtedness $3,500. **Criteria for awarding institutional aid:** *Non-need-based:* academics, alumni affiliation, athletics, leadership, minority status, music/drama.

FRANKLIN UNIVERSITY

201 S Grant Ave, Columbus, OH 43215
Phone: 614-797-4700
E-mail: info@franklin.edu • **CEEB Code:** 1229
Fax: 614-224-8027 • **Website:** 201 S Grant Ave • **ACT Code:** 3275

This private school was founded in 1902. It has a 14-acre campus.

RATINGS

Admissions Selectivity Rating: 60*   Fire Safety Rating: 60*

STUDENTS AND FACULTY

Enrollment: 5,682. **Student Body:** 55% female, 45% male, 26% out-of-state, 5% international. Asian 3%, African American 19%, Caucasian 66%, Hispanic 2%, Native American <1%
Retention and Graduation: 72% freshmen return for sophomore year. **Faculty:** 36 full-time faculty, 64% hold PhDs, 44% are members of minority groups, 6% are women.

ACADEMICS

Degrees: associate, bachelor's, master's. **Classes:** Most classes have 10–19 students. **Majors with Highest Enrollment:** Computer and Information Sciences; Business/Commerce; Accounting. **Special Study Options:** Accelerated program, cooperative education program, cross-registration, distance learning, double major, dual enrollment, English as a Second Language (ESL), independent study, internships, study abroad, weekend college. Combined degree programs: BS/MBA. **Disability Services:** Special programs offered to physically disabled students include note-taking services, reader services, tape recorders, tutors. **Career services:** Alumni network, alumni services, internships.

FACILITIES

Housing: 100% of campus accessible to physically disabled. **Computers:** Students can register for classes online.

CAMPUS LIFE

Activities: 6 registered organizations.

ADMISSIONS

Freshman Academic Profile: Minimum paper TOEFL 430. **Freshman Admission Requirements:** High school diploma is required and GED is accepted. **Freshman Admission Statistics:** 262 applied, 100% admitted, 47% enrolled. **Transfer Admission Requirements:** college transcript(s), Lowest grade transferable C-. **General Admission Information:** Nonfall registration accepted. Admission may be deferred for a maximum of indefinite. Credit and/or placement offered for CEEB Advanced Placement tests.

COSTS AND FINANCIAL AID

Annual tuition $6,990. Required fees $0. Average book expense $0. **Required Forms and Deadlines:** FAFSA. **Types of Aid:** *Need-based scholarships/ grants:* Federal Pell, SEOG, state scholarships/grants, private scholarships, the school's own gift aid. *Loans:* Subsidized Stafford, Unsubsidized Stafford, PLUS, college/university loans from institutional funds. *Student Employment:* Federal Work-Study Program available. Institutional employment available. Off-campus job opportunities are good. **Financial Aid Statistics:** 72% freshmen, 64% undergrads receive need-based scholarship or grant aid. 85% freshmen, 82% undergrads receive non-need-based scholarship or grant aid. 92% freshmen, 94% undergrads receive need-based self-help aid. 0% freshmen, 0% undergrads receive athletic scholarships. Criteria for awarding institutional aid: *Non-need-based:* academics, leadership, minority status.

FRANKLIN W. OLIN COLLEGE OF ENGINEERING

Olin Way, Needham, MA 02492
Phone: 781-292-2222 · **Financial Aid Phone:** 781-292-2343
E-mail: info@olin.edu · **CEEB Code:** 2824
Fax: 781-292-2210 · **Website:** www.olin.edu · **ACT Code:** 1883

This private school was founded in 1997.

RATINGS

Admissions Selectivity Rating: 96   **Fire Safety Rating:** 85

STUDENTS AND FACULTY

Enrollment: 334. **Student Body:** 50% female, 50% male, 85% out-of-state, 7% international (18 countries represented). Asian 15%, African American 1%, Caucasian 56%, Hispanic 4%, Native American <1%
Retention and Graduation: 96% freshmen return for sophomore year. 83% freshmen graduate within 4 years. 95% freshmen graduate within 6 years. 18% grads go on to further study within 1 year. 14% grads pursue arts and sciences degrees. 1% grads pursue law degrees. 1% grads pursue business degrees. 1% grads pursue medical degrees. **Faculty:** 35 full-time faculty, 100% hold PhDs, 46% are members of minority groups, 23% are women. 0% of classes are taught by teaching assistants.

ACADEMICS

Degrees: bachelor's. **Classes:** Most classes have 20–29 students. **Majors with Highest Enrollment:** Engineering; Electrical and Electronics Engineering; Mechanical Engineering. **Special Study Options:** cross-registration, exchange student program (domestic), independent study, internships, liberal arts/career combination, student-designed major, study abroad, Passionate Pursuits program. **Career services:** Alumni network, alumni services, career/job search classes, internships, regional alumni. Because we are a fairly new school, our network of alumni remains small but powerful. Many are now at prestigious companies or graduate school programs, and they often return to campus to talk about their company, career, grad school experience, or they perform mock interviews and/or provide advice to our current students. Due to our young age, our students are especially interested in hearing of our alumni's tales of continued development and success.

FACILITIES

Housing: Coed dorms, special housing for disabled students. **Computers:** 100% of classrooms, 100% of dorms, 100% of libraries, 100% of dining areas,

100% of student union, 100% of common outdoor areas have wireless network access. Students can register for classes online. Administrative functions (other than registration) can be performed online. Undergraduates are required to own a computer.

CAMPUS LIFE

Environment: Town. **Activities:** Choral groups, dance, drama/theater, jazz band, music ensembles, musical theater, student government, student-run film society, symphony orchestra, yearbook. 55 registered organizations. **Environmental Initiatives:** Replacing site-wide external lighting with LED's; Installing site-wide lighting and heating sensors (60% of interior).

ADMISSIONS

Freshman Academic Profile: Average high school GPA 4. SAT Math middle 50% range 720-790. SAT Critical Reading middle 50% range 690-760. SAT Writing middle 50% range 685-760. ACT middle 50% range 32-34. **Basis for Candidate Selection:** *Very important factors considered include:* academic GPA, rigor of secondary school record, interview, talent/ability. *Important factors considered include:* standardized test scores, character/personal qualities, extracurricular activities. *Other factors considered include:* Class rank, application essay, recommendation(s), alumni/ae relation, level of applicant's interest, volunteer work, work experience. **Freshman Admission Requirements:** High school diploma is required and GED is accepted. *Academic units required:* 4 English, 3 mathematics, 2 science, (1 science labs), 0 foreign language, 2 social studies, 1 history, 0 visual/performing arts, 0 computer science, 4 academic electives, 0 two years of algebra recommended. **Freshman Admission Statistics:** 983 applied, 12% admitted, 67% enrolled. **Transfer Admission Requirements:** college transcript(s), Minimum college GPA of 2.0 required. Lowest grade transferable C. **General Admission Information:** Application Fee $30. Regular application deadline 7/15. Notification on a rolling basis, beginning on or about 10/1. Nonfall registration accepted. Admission may be deferred for a maximum of 1 year. Credit and/or placement offered for CEEB Advanced Placement tests.

COSTS AND FINANCIAL AID

Annual tuition $45,000. Room and board $15,600. Required fees $3,181. Average book expense $300. **Required Forms and Deadlines:** FAFSA. **Notification of Awards:** Applicants will be notified of awards on a rolling basis beginning 2/1. **Types of Aid:** *Need-based scholarships/grants:* Federal Pell, SEOG, state scholarships/grants, private scholarships, the school's own gift aid. *Loans:* Subsidized Stafford, Unsubsidized Stafford, PLUS, Federal Perkins. *Student Employment:* Federal Work-Study Program available. Institutional employment available. Highest amount earned per year from on-campus jobs $1,450. Off-campus job opportunities are good. **Financial Aid Statistics:** 100% freshmen, 100% undergrads receive need-based scholarship or grant aid. 100% freshmen, 100% undergrads receive non-need-based scholarship or grant aid. 83% freshmen, 85% undergrads receive need-based self-help aid. 0% freshmen, 0% undergrads receive athletic scholarships. 100% freshmen, 100% undergrads receive any aid. 44% undergrads borrow to pay for school. Average cumulative indebtedness $18,566. **Criteria for awarding institutional aid:** *Non-need-based:* academics, alumni affiliation, leadership.

FREED-HARDEMAN UNIVERSITY

158 East Main Street, Henderson, TN 38340
Phone: 731-989-6651 · **Financial Aid Phone:** 731-989-6662
E-mail: jathoms1@yahoo.com · **CEEB Code:** 1230
Fax: 731-989-6047 · **Website:** web.fhu.edu · **ACT Code:** 3962

This private school, affiliated with the Church of Christ Church, was founded in 1869. It has a 122-acre campus.

RATINGS

Admissions Selectivity Rating: 87   **Fire Safety Rating:** 63

STUDENTS AND FACULTY

Enrollment: 1,428. **Student Body:** 55% female, 45% male, 50% out-of-state, 3% international (26 countries represented). Asian 0%, African American 4%, Caucasian 91%, Hispanic 1%, Native American <1%
Retention and Graduation: 74% freshmen return for sophomore year. 41% freshmen graduate within 4 years. 58% freshmen graduate within 6 years. 40% grads go on to further study within 1 year. **Faculty:** 108 full-time faculty, 69% hold PhDs, 31% are members of minority groups, 5% are women. 0% of classes are taught by teaching assistants.

ACADEMICS

Degrees: bachelor's, first professional, master's, post-bachelor's certificate, post-master's certificate, terminal associate. **Classes:** Most classes have 10–19

students. Most lab/discussion sessions have 10–19 students. **Majors with Highest Enrollment:** Liberal Arts and Sciences Studies and Humanities; Biology/Biological Sciences; Bible/Biblical Studies. **Special Study Options:** Accelerated program, cooperative education program, cross-registration, distance learning, double major, dual enrollment, honors program, independent study, internships, liberal arts/career combination, student-designed major, study abroad, teacher certification program, 3-2 engineering, Honors College, study abroad in Belgium and Italy. **Honors programs:** Exceptional students may be admitted to the Honors College, where he or she may graduate as an Honors College Scholar, or as an Honors College Scholar with University Honors. Combined degree programs: BBA/MBA. **Disability Services:** Special programs offered to physically disabled students include note-taking services, reader services, tutors. **Career services:** Alumni network, career assessment, internships.

FACILITIES

Housing: men's dorms, women's dorms, apartments for single students. Some student teacher housing is available. 70% of campus accessible to physically disabled. **Special Academic Facilities/Equipment:** Child development lab, nursery school. **Computers:** Students can register for classes online. Administrative functions (other than registration) can be performed online.

CAMPUS LIFE

Environment: Rural. **Activities:** Choral groups, concert band, drama/theater, jazz band, music ensembles, musical theater, pep band, radio station, student government, student newspaper, television station, yearbook. 52 registered organizations, 4 honor societies, 5 religious organizations. 6 fraternities, 6 sororities. **Athletics (Intercollegiate):** *Men:* baseball, basketball, cheerleading, soccer. *Women:* basketball, cheerleading, soccer, softball, volleyball. **On-Campus Highlights:** The Commons, The Student Center, The Sports Center, Brown-Kopel Business Center, The Library.

ADMISSIONS

Freshman Academic Profile: Average high school GPA 3.37. 25% in top 10% of high school class, 51% in top 25% of high school class, 79% in top 50% of high school class. SAT Math middle 50% range 480-600. SAT Critical Reading middle 50% range 480-640. ACT middle 50% range 20-26. **Basis for Candidate Selection:** *Very important factors considered include:* academic GPA, rigor of secondary school record, standardized test scores. *Other factors considered include:* recommendation(s), alumni/ae relation, character/personal qualities, extracurricular activities, racial/ethnic status, religious affiliation/commitment, volunteer work, work experience. **Freshman Admission Requirements:** High school diploma is required and GED is accepted. **Freshman Admission Statistics:** 1,326 applied, 55% admitted, 53% enrolled. **Transfer Admission Requirements:** college transcript(s), statement of good standing from prior institution(s). Lowest grade transferable D. **General Admission Information:** Notification on a rolling basis, beginning on or about 5/2. Nonfall registration accepted. Admission may be deferred for a maximum of 2 years. Credit and/or placement offered for CEEB Advanced Placement tests.

COSTS AND FINANCIAL AID

Annual tuition $13,192. Room and board $6,560. Average book expense $1,710. **Required Forms and Deadlines:** FAFSA. **Notification of Awards:** Applicants will be notified of awards on a rolling basis beginning 3/1. **Types of Aid:** *Need-based scholarships/grants:* Federal Pell, SEOG, state scholarships/grants, private scholarships, the school's own gift aid. *Loans:* Subsidized Stafford, Unsubsidized Stafford, PLUS, Federal Perkins, Alternative loan programs. *Student Employment:* Federal Work-Study Program available. Institutional employment available. Off-campus job opportunities are fair. **Financial Aid Statistics:** 97% freshmen, 91% undergrads receive need-based scholarship or grant aid. 19% freshmen, 17% undergrads receive non-need-based scholarship or grant aid. 73% freshmen, 78% undergrads receive need-based self-help aid. 4% freshmen, 4% undergrads receive athletic scholarships. 86 76% undergrads borrow to pay for school. Average cumulative indebtedness $25,687. **Criteria for awarding institutional aid:** *Non-need-based:* academics, art, athletics, leadership, minority status, music/drama, state/district residency.

FRESNO PACIFIC UNIVERSITY

1717 S. Chestnut Ave, Fresno, CA 93702
Phone: 559-453-2039 · **Financial Aid Phone:** 559-453-2041
E-mail: ugadmis@fresno.edu · **CEEB Code:**
Fax: 559-453-2007 · **Website:** http://www.fresno.edu/

This private school, affiliated with the Mennonite Church, was founded in 1944. It has a 42-acre campus.

RATINGS

Admissions Selectivity Rating: 60*   Fire Safety Rating: 60*

STUDENTS AND FACULTY

Enrollment: 1,459. **Student Body:** 68% female, 32% male, 2% international. Asian 4%, African American 4%, Caucasian 53%, Hispanic 26%, Native American 1%
Retention and Graduation: 70% freshmen return for sophomore year. 48% freshmen graduate within 4 years. 62% freshmen graduate within 6 years.

ACADEMICS

Degrees: associate, bachelor's, certificate, master's, post-bachelor's certificate. **Classes:** Most classes have fewer than 10 students. Most lab/discussion sessions have fewer than 10 students. **Majors with Highest Enrollment:** Education; Bible/Biblical Studies; Business/Commerce. **Special Study Options:** Accelerated program, cooperative education program, cross-registration, distance learning, double major, English as a Second Language (ESL), independent study, internships, liberal arts/career combination, student-designed major, study abroad, teacher certification program. **Disability Services:** Special programs offered to physically disabled students include note-taking services, reader services, tutors. **Career services:** alumni services, career/job search classes, career assessment, internships.

FACILITIES

Housing: special housing for disabled students, men's dorms, women's dorms, apartments for single students, Houses. 100% of campus accessible to physically disabled. **Special Academic Facilities/Equipment:** English Language Training Institute.

CAMPUS LIFE

Environment: Metropolis. **Activities:** Choral groups, concert band, dance, drama/theater, jazz band, music ensembles, pep band, student government, student newspaper, yearbook. 36 registered organizations, 1 honor society, 11 religious organization. **Athletics (Intercollegiate):** *Men:* baseball, basketball, cross-country, soccer, tennis, track/field (outdoor). *Women:* basketball, cross-country, soccer, tennis, track/field (outdoor), volleyball. **On-Campus Highlights:** Special Events Center (Gym), Steinert Campus Center, The Green (students hang out there), Bookshop, New AIMS Building.

ADMISSIONS

Basis for Candidate Selection: *Very important factors considered include:* rigor of secondary school record, standardized test scores. *Important factors considered include:* Class rank, application essay, academic GPA, recommendation(s), religious affiliation/commitment. *Other factors considered include:* character/personal qualities. **Freshman Admission Requirements:** High school diploma is required and GED is accepted. *Academic units required:* 4 English, 3 mathematics, 1 science, (1 science labs), 2 foreign language, 2 social studies. **Transfer Admission Requirements:** High school transcript, college transcript(s), essay or personal statement, Minimum college GPA of 2.4 required. Lowest grade transferable C. **General Admission Information:** Application Fee $40. Regular application deadline 7/31. Notification on a rolling basis, beginning on or about 12/1. Nonfall registration accepted. Admission may be deferred for a maximum of NA. Credit offered for CEEB Advanced Placement tests.

COSTS AND FINANCIAL AID

Annual tuition $24,960. Room and board $11,230. Required fees $276. Average book expense $1,665. **Required Forms and Deadlines:** FAFSA. **Notification of Awards:** Applicants will be notified of awards on a rolling basis beginning 3/2. **Types of Aid:** *Need-based scholarships/grants:* Federal Pell, SEOG, state scholarships/grants, private scholarships, the school's own gift aid. *Loans:* Subsidized Stafford, Unsubsidized Stafford, PLUS, Federal Perkins. *Student Employment:* Federal Work-Study Program available. Institutional employment available. Off-campus job opportunities are good. **Financial Aid Statistics:** 81% freshmen, 81% undergrads receive need-based scholarship or grant aid. 98% freshmen, 51% undergrads receive non-need-based scholarship or grant aid. 74% freshmen, 79% undergrads receive need-based self-help aid. 14% freshmen, 9% undergrads receive athletic scholarships. 75% undergrads borrow to pay for school. Average cumulative indebtedness $19,176. **Criteria for awarding institutional aid:** *Non-need-based:* academics, alumni affiliation, art, athletics, leadership, minority status, music/drama, religious affiliation, state/district residency.

FRIENDS UNIVERSITY

2100 University Avenue, Wichita, KS 67213
Phone: 316-295-5100 · **Financial Aid Phone:** 316-295-5200
E-mail: learn@friends.edu · **CEEB Code:** 6224
Fax: 316-295-5101 · **Website:** www.friends.edu · **ACT Code:** 1918

This private school, affiliated with the Quaker Church, was founded in 1898. It has a 45-acre campus.

RATINGS
Admissions Selectivity Rating: 83   **Fire Safety Rating:** 81

STUDENTS AND FACULTY
Enrollment: 1,737. **Student Body:** 56% female, 44% male, 19% out-of-state, 0% international (13 countries represented). Asian 3%, African American 11%, Caucasian 71%, Hispanic 4%, Native American 2%
Retention and Graduation: 60% freshmen return for sophomore year. 10% freshmen graduate within 4 years. 33% freshmen graduate within 6 years. **Faculty:** 75 full-time faculty, 71% hold PhDs, 41% are members of minority groups, 5% are women. 0% of classes are taught by teaching assistants.

ACADEMICS
Degrees: bachelor's, master's, terminal associate, transfer associate. **Majors with Highest Enrollment:** Business Administration and Management; Wildlife Biology; Psychology. **Special Study Options:** cooperative education program, cross-registration, double major, dual enrollment, external degree program, honors program, independent study, internships, student-designed major, study abroad, teacher certification program, Degree completion program for working adults. **Career services:** career/job search classes, internships.

FACILITIES
Housing: men's dorms, women's dorms, apartments for married students, apartments for single students, University-owned houses.

CAMPUS LIFE
Activities: Choral groups, concert band, dance, drama/theater, jazz band, literary magazine, music ensembles, musical theater, pep band, student government, symphony orchestra, yearbook. 32 registered organizations, 4 honor societies, 3 religious organizations. 2 fraternities, 1 sorority. **Athletics (Intercollegiate):** *Men:* baseball, basketball, cheerleading, cross-country, football, golf, soccer, tennis, track/field (outdoor). *Women:* basketball, cheerleading, cross-country, soccer, softball, tennis, track/field (outdoor), volleyball.

ADMISSIONS
Freshman Academic Profile: Average high school GPA 3.38. 20% in top 10% of high school class, 36% in top 25% of high school class, 68% in top 50% of high school class. 84% from public high schools. SAT Math middle 50% range 400-510. SAT Critical Reading middle 50% range 390-515. ACT middle 50% range 18-26. Minimum internet-based TOEFL 63. Minimum paper TOEFL 500. **Basis for Candidate Selection:** *Very important factors considered include:* rigor of secondary school record, standardized test scores. *Important factors considered include:* recommendation(s), interview. *Other factors considered include:* alumni/ae relation, extracurricular activities, racial/ethnic status, religious affiliation/commitment, talent/ability. **Freshman Admission Requirements:** High school diploma is required and GED is accepted. **Freshman Admission Statistics:** 786 applied, 58% admitted, 43% enrolled. **Transfer Admission Requirements:** college transcript(s), statement of good standing from prior institution(s). Minimum college GPA of 2.0 required. Lowest grade transferable C. **General Admission Information:** Application Fee $15. Nonfall registration accepted. Credit and/or placement offered for CEEB Advanced Placement tests.

COSTS AND FINANCIAL AID
Annual tuition $23,250. Room and board $6,800. Required fees $180. Average book expense $1,500. **Required Forms and Deadlines:** FAFSA. **Types of Aid:** *Need-based scholarships/grants:* Federal Pell, SEOG, private scholarships. *Loans:* Direct Subsidized Stafford, Direct Unsubsidized Stafford, Direct PLUS, Federal Perkins. *Student Employment:* Federal Work-Study Program available. Institutional employment available. Off-campus job opportunities are excellent. **Financial Aid Statistics:** 100% freshmen, 84% undergrads receive need-based scholarship or grant aid. 24% freshmen, 13% undergrads receive non-need-based scholarship or grant aid. 78% freshmen, 89% undergrads receive need-based self-help aid. 21% freshmen, 3% undergrads receive athletic scholarships. 87% freshmen, 77% undergrads receive any aid. 86% undergrads borrow to pay for school. Average cumulative indebtedness $18,000. **Criteria for awarding institutional aid:** *Non-need-based:* academics, alumni affiliation, athletics, leadership, minority status, music/drama, religious affiliation.

FROSTBURG STATE UNIVERSITY

FSU, 101 Braddock Road, Frostburg, MD 21532
Phone: 301-687-4201 · **Financial Aid Phone:** 301-687-4301
E-mail: fsuadmissions@frostburg.edu · **CEEB Code:** 5402
Fax: 301-687-7074 · **Website:** www.frostburg.edu · **ACT Code:** 1714

This public school was founded in 1898. It has a 260-acre campus.

RATINGS
Admissions Selectivity Rating: 79   **Fire Safety Rating:** 79

STUDENTS AND FACULTY
Enrollment: 4,522. **Student Body:** 49% female, 51% male, 8% out-of-state, 1% international (25 countries represented). Asian 1%, African American 26%, Caucasian 64%, Hispanic 3%, Native American <1%
Retention and Graduation: 72% freshmen return for sophomore year. 20% freshmen graduate within 4 years. 45% freshmen graduate within 6 years. **Faculty:** 245 full-time faculty, 41% are members of minority groups, 13% are women.

ACADEMICS
Degrees: bachelor's, certificate, master's, post-bachelor's certificate, post-master's certificate. **Classes:** Most classes have 20–29 students. Most lab/discussion sessions have 10–19 students. **Majors with Highest Enrollment:** Elementary Education and Teaching; Psychology; Business/Commerce. **Special Study Options:** Accelerated program, distance learning, double major, dual enrollment, honors program, independent study, internships, liberal arts/career combination, study abroad, teacher certification program, Learning Communities, Dual Degree Program. Combined degree programs: MBA/BS in Accounting. **Disability Services:** Special programs offered to physically disabled students include note-taking services, reader services, tape recorders, tutors.

FACILITIES
Housing: Coed dorms, women's dorms, Special interest **Housing:** Leadership Hall, Honors Housing, Community Service. 100% of campus accessible to physically disabled. **Special Academic Facilities/Equipment:** Art gallery, planetarium, electron microscope. **Computers:** Students can register for classes online. Administrative functions (other than registration) can be performed online.

CAMPUS LIFE
Environment: Rural. **Activities:** Choral groups, concert band, dance, drama/theater, jazz band, literary magazine, marching band, music ensembles, musical theater, pep band, radio station, student government, student newspaper, symphony orchestra, television station. 95 registered organizations, 18 honor societies, 6 religious organizations. 9 fraternities, 6 sororities. **Athletics (Intercollegiate):** *Men:* baseball, basketball, cross-country, diving, football, golf, soccer, swimming, tennis, track/field (outdoor), track/field (indoor). *Women:* basketball, cross-country, diving, field hockey, lacrosse, soccer, softball, swimming, tennis, track/field (outdoor), track/field (indoor), volleyball. **On-Campus Highlights:** Lane University Center, Cordts PE Center, Performing Arts Center, Stephanie Roper Art Gallery, Compton Science Center. **Environmental Initiatives:** Adopted an energy-efficient appliance purchasing policy requiring purchase of ENERGY STAR-certified products in all areas for which such ratings exist. Purchasing or producing at least 15 percent of our institutions electricity consumption from renewable resources. Participating in the Waste Minimization component of the national Recyclemania competition, and adopt three or more associated measures to reduce waste.

ADMISSIONS
Freshman Academic Profile: Average high school GPA 3.2. 11% in top 10% of high school class, 31% in top 25% of high school class, 66% in top 50% of high school class. SAT Math middle 50% range 440-540. SAT Critical Reading middle 50% range 440-530. SAT Writing middle 50% range 420-520. ACT middle 50% range 18-22. Minimum paper TOEFL 550. **Basis for Candidate Selection:** *Very important factors considered include:* academic GPA, rigor of secondary school record, standardized test scores. *Important factors considered include:* recommendation(s), interview. *Other factors considered include:* alumni/ae relation, character/personal qualities, extracurricular activities, talent/ability. **Freshman Admission Requirements:** High school diploma is required and GED is accepted. *Academic units required:* 4 English, 3 mathematics, 3 science, (2 science labs), 2 foreign language, 3 social studies. **Freshman Admission Statistics:** 3,951 applied, 59% admitted, 35% enrolled. **Transfer Admission Requirements:** college transcript(s), Minimum college GPA of 2.0 required. Lowest grade transferable C. **General Admission Information:** Application Fee $30. Early decision application deadline 12/15. Notification on a rolling basis, beginning on or about 11/1. Nonfall registration accepted. Credit and/or placement offered for CEEB Advanced Placement tests.

COSTS AND FINANCIAL AID

Annual in-state tuition $5,464. Annual out-of-state tuition $15,652. Room and board $7,796. Required fees $1,972. Average book expense $1,200. **Required Forms and Deadlines:** FAFSA. **Notification of Awards:** Applicants will be notified of awards on a rolling basis beginning 3/15. **Types of Aid:** *Need-based scholarships/grants:* Federal Pell, SEOG, state scholarships/grants, private scholarships, the school's own gift aid. *Loans:* Direct Subsidized Stafford, Direct Unsubsidized Stafford, Direct PLUS, PLUS, Federal Perkins, college/university loans from institutional funds. *Student Employment:* Highest amount earned per year from on-campus jobs $1,000. **Financial Aid Statistics:** 75% freshmen, 73% undergrads receive need-based scholarship or grant aid. 30% freshmen, 28% undergrads receive non-need-based scholarship or grant aid. 78% freshmen, 80% undergrads receive need-based self-help aid. 0% freshmen, 0% undergrads receive athletic scholarships. 72% freshmen, 65% undergrads receive any aid. 64% undergrads borrow to pay for school. Average cumulative indebtedness $15,724. **Criteria for awarding institutional aid:** *Non-need-based:* academics, alumni affiliation, art, leadership, music/drama, state/district residency.

FULL SAIL UNIVERSITY

3300 University Blvd, Winter Park, FL 32792
Phone: 800-226-7625
E-mail: admissions@fullsail.com
Website: http://www.fullsail.edu/

This proprietary school was founded in 1979. It has a 91-acre campus.

RATINGS

Admissions Selectivity Rating: 60*   Fire Safety Rating: 60*

STUDENTS AND FACULTY

Enrollment: 4,628.

ACADEMICS

Degrees: associate, bachelor's, master's, terminal associate. **Majors with Highest Enrollment:** Recording Arts Technology/Technician; Animation, Interactive Technology, Video Graphics and Special Effects; Cinematography and Film/Video Production. **Special Study Options:** Accelerated program.

FACILITIES

Housing: Full Sail does not feature on-campus living arrangements, but does employ a Housing Manager who is dedicated to providing information about affordable accommodations in one of the many apartment complexes near the school. The Housing Manager can also help with information regarding roommates (other incoming Full Sail students), power, phones, furniture, and helpful community programs in the Central Florida area.

CAMPUS LIFE

Environment: Metropolis.

ADMISSIONS

Basis for Candidate Selection: *Very important factors considered include:* application essay, level of applicant's interest, talent/ability. *Important factors considered include:* academic GPA, recommendation(s), standardized test scores, character/personal qualities. *Other factors considered include:* Class rank, rigor of secondary school record, extracurricular activities, interview, volunteer work. **Freshman Admission Requirements:** High school diploma is required and GED is accepted. **Transfer Admission Requirements:** college transcript(s), essay or personal statement, statement of good standing from prior institution(s). Minimum college GPA of 2.6 required. Lowest grade transferable c. **General Admission Information:** Application Fee $50. Regular application deadline 7/15. Notification on a rolling basis, beginning on or about 1/1. Nonfall registration accepted. Admission may be deferred for a maximum of 1 semester. Credit offered for CEEB Advanced Placement tests.

COSTS AND FINANCIAL AID

Notification of Awards: Applicants will be notified of awards on a rolling basis beginning 5/1. **Types of Aid:** *Need-based scholarships/grants:* Federal Pell, SEOG, state scholarships/grants, private scholarships, the school's own gift aid. *Loans:* Subsidized Stafford, Unsubsidized Stafford, PLUS. *Student Employment:* Federal Work-Study Program available. Institutional employment available. Off-campus job opportunities are good. **Criteria for awarding institutional aid:** *Non-need-based:* academics, art.

FURMAN UNIVERSITY

3300 Poinsett Highway, Greenville, SC 29613
Phone: 864-294-2034 · **Financial Aid Phone:** 864-294-2204
E-mail: admissions@furman.edu · **CEEB Code:** 5222
Fax: 864-294-2018 · **Website:** www.furman.edu · **ACT Code:** 3858

This private school was founded in 1826. It has a 800-acre campus.

RATINGS

Admissions Selectivity Rating: 88   Fire Safety Rating: 84

STUDENTS AND FACULTY

Enrollment: 2,796. **Student Body:** 57% female, 43% male, 72% out-of-state, 5% international (55 countries represented). Asian 2%, African American 5%, Caucasian 80%, Hispanic 4%, Native American <1%
Retention and Graduation: 80% freshmen graduate within 4 years. 42% grads go on to further study within 1 year. 32% grads pursue arts and sciences degrees. 4% grads pursue law degrees. 2% grads pursue business degrees. 4% grads pursue medical degrees. **Faculty:** 234 full-time faculty, 96% hold PhDs, 35% are members of minority groups, 6% are women. 0% of classes are taught by teaching assistants.

ACADEMICS

Degrees: bachelor's, master's, post-bachelor's certificate. **Classes:** Most classes have 10–19 students. **Majors with Highest Enrollment:** Political Science and Government; Business/Commerce; Health Professions and Related Clinical Sciences. **Special Study Options:** double major, independent study, internships, student-designed major, study abroad, teacher certification program. Combined degree programs: BA/MD, BA/MA, BA/DDS, Environmental Studies, Pharmacy, Nursing. **Disability Services:** Special programs offered to physically disabled students include note-taking services, reader services, tape recorders, tutors. **Career services:** Alumni network, career/job search classes, career assessment, internships. Career services highlights include Furman's internships, which are both paid and unpaid, and available to virtually every student. They run the gamut from medical research to international business opportunities.

FACILITIES

Housing: Coed dorms, men's dorms, special housing for international students, women's dorms, apartments for single students, Wellness Housing, Theme Housing, lakeside cottages, language houses, eco-cottage. 98% of campus accessible to physically disabled. **Special Academic Facilities/Equipment:** Visual arts gallery and teaching facility, language lab. Astronomical lab; Center for Engaged Learning; and Center for Collaborative Learning and Communication. **Computers:** 100% of classrooms, 100% of libraries, 100% of dining areas, 100% of student union, have wireless network access. Students can register for classes online. Administrative functions (other than registration) can be performed online.

CAMPUS LIFE

Environment: City. **Activities:** Choral groups, concert band, dance, drama/theater, jazz band, literary magazine, marching band, music ensembles, musical theater, opera, pep band, radio station, student government, student newspaper, student-run film society, symphony orchestra, television station, yearbook, Campus Ministries, International Student Organization. 143 registered organizations, 29 honor societies, 17 religious organizations. 7 fraternities, 7 sororities. **Athletics (Intercollegiate):** *Men:* baseball, basketball, cheerleading, cross-country, football, golf, soccer, tennis, track/field (outdoor), track/field (indoor). *Women:* basketball, cheerleading, cross-country, golf, soccer, softball, tennis, track/field (outdoor), track/field (indoor), volleyball. **On-Campus Highlights:** Charles Townes Science Center, Timmons Arena, Library, 18-hole Golf Course, Physical Activities Center, Place of Peace, David Shi Center for Sustainability. **Environmental Initiatives:** Sustainable Furman: The approval of Sustainable Furman, the universitys comprehensive sustainability master plan. The plan covers all aspects of the university; the 8 goals of Sustainable Furman address sustainability in the curriculum, co-curricular activities, campus culture, renewable energy, efficiency in operations and maintenance, transportation, sustainability service, and continuing national leadership in the sustainability arena. In addition, the plan sets out a path for the university to reach carbon neutrality by 2026. Sustainability curriculum development: In recent years Furman has sought to infuse sustainability and environmental issues across the curriculum. The university offers a wide range of sustainability-related courses at all levels. The new university-wide curriculum, inaugurated in the fall of 2008, requires all students to take at least one course that focuses on the relationship between "Humans and the Natural Environment." In 2009-2010, 31 courses in 11 departments were offered to fulfill the Humans and the Natural Environment credit. Nine departments in the natural sciences, social sciences, and humanities contribute faculty members to a multi-disciplinary Concentration in Environmental Studies. Students in the capstone course for the concentration are also involved in service learning projects in the community. The most recent new courses in sustainability have included several first-year seminars and an environmental policy course that focuses on campus/community connections. Finally, the faculty approved a new major in Sustainability Science in November 2010. Creation of the David E. Shi Center for Sustainability

ADMISSIONS

Freshman Academic Profile: 38% in top 10% of high school class, 72% in top 25% of high school class, 92% in top 50% of high school class. 59% from public high schools. SAT Math middle 50% range 570-670. SAT Critical Reading middle 50% range 560-670. SAT Writing middle 50% range 560-660. ACT middle 50% range 25-30. Minimum paper TOEFL 570. **Basis for Candidate Selection:** *Very important factors considered include:* rigor of secondary school record. *Important factors considered include:* Class rank, application essay, academic GPA, standardized test scores, character/personal qualities, extracurricular activities. *Other factors considered include:* recommendation(s), alumni/ae relation, first generation, level of applicant's interest, racial/ethnic status, talent/ability, volunteer work, work experience. **Freshman Admission Requirements:** High school diploma is required and GED is accepted. *Academic units required:* 4 English, 3 mathematics, 2 science, (2 science labs), 2 foreign language, 3 social studies. **Freshman Admission Statistics:** 4,583 applied, 69% admitted, 23% enrolled. **Transfer Admission Requirements:** High school transcript, college transcript(s), essay or personal statement, standardized test scores, statement of good standing from prior institution(s). Minimum college GPA of 3.0 required. Lowest grade transferable C. **General Admission Information:** Application Fee $50. Early decision application deadline 11/15. Regular application deadline 1/15. Regular notification 3/15. Nonfall registration not accepted. Credit and/or placement offered for CEEB Advanced Placement tests.

COSTS AND FINANCIAL AID

Average book expense $1,200. **Required Forms and Deadlines:** FAFSA, Institution's own financial aid form, CSS/Financial Aid PROFILE, State aid form. **Notification of Awards:** Applicants will be notified of awards on or about 3/15. **Types of Aid:** *Need-based scholarships/grants:* Federal Pell, SEOG, state scholarships/grants, private scholarships, the school's own gift aid, Donor sponsored loans for study abroad. *Loans:* Subsidized Stafford, Unsubsidized Stafford, PLUS, Federal Perkins, state loans, Federal SMART and ACG grants. *Student Employment:* Federal Work-Study Program available. Institutional employment available. Highest amount earned per year from on-campus jobs $1,500. Off-campus job opportunities are excellent. **Financial Aid Statistics:** 100% freshmen, 99% undergrads receive need-based scholarship or grant aid. 100% freshmen, 99% undergrads receive non-need-based scholarship or grant aid. 54% freshmen, 58% undergrads receive need-based self-help aid. 11% freshmen, 11% undergrads receive athletic scholarships. 93% freshmen, 88% undergrads receive any aid. 42% undergrads borrow to pay for school. Average cumulative indebtedness $22,546. **Criteria for awarding institutional aid:** *Non-need-based:* academics, alumni affiliation, art, athletics, leadership, music/drama, religious affiliation, state/district residency.

GALLAUDET UNIVERSITY

800 Florida Avenue, NE, Washington DC, DC 20002
Phone: 202-651-5750 · **Financial Aid Phone:** 202-651-5290
E-mail: admissions.office@gallaudet.edu · **CEEB Code:** 5240
Fax: 202-651-5744 · **Website:** http://www.gallaudet.edu/ · **ACT Code:** 662

This private school was founded in 1864. It has a 99-acre campus.

RATINGS

Admissions Selectivity Rating: 75   **Fire Safety Rating:** 86

STUDENTS AND FACULTY

Enrollment: 1,001. **Student Body:** 54% female, 46% male, 97% out-of-state, 8% international (31 countries represented). Asian 4%, African American 12%, Caucasian 56%, Hispanic 15%, Native American <1%.
Retention and Graduation: 67% freshmen return for sophomore year. 16% freshmen graduate within 4 years. 46% freshmen graduate within 6 years.
Faculty: 181 full-time faculty, 88% hold PhDs, 62% are members of minority groups, 24% are women.

ACADEMICS

Degrees: bachelor's, master's, post-bachelor's certificate. **Classes:** Most classes have 10–19 students. Most lab/discussion sessions have fewer than 10 students.

Majors with Highest Enrollment: Psychology; Business Administration and Management; Ethnic, Cultural Minority, Gender, and Group Studies. **Special Study Options:** Accelerated program, cross-registration, distance learning, double major, English as a Second Language (ESL), exchange student program (domestic), honors program, independent study, internships, student-designed major, study abroad, teacher certification program, Experiential programs off-campus including orientation program for employers of deaf students and para-professional jobs on campus, programs for interpreter-assisted mainstreaming of students into area colleges such as Georgetown University, George Mason University, Catholic University, and Howard University. **Honors programs:** The Gallaudet Honors Program is a Learning Community for the most academically capable and motivated students. The overall goal is to foster skills, work habits, and attitudes conducive to future achievement and lifelong learning. To this end, the Program focuses on linking rigorous, challenging, and innovative curricular offerings with co-curricular activities. It also serves as a leader in and test laboratory of curricular, co-curricular, and extracurricular innovations; successes may then be replicated for all students. Combined degree programs: BA/MA, BA or BS (Education) with MA in Teaching. **Disability Services:** Special programs offered to physically disabled students include tutors. **Career services:** Alumni network, alumni services, career/job search classes, career assessment, internships. Career services highlights include our internship program.

FACILITIES

Housing: Coed dorms, special housing for disabled students, apartments for married students, Theme Housing. 100% of campus accessible to physically disabled. **Special Academic Facilities/Equipment:** Kendall Demonstration Elementary School and Model Secondary School for the Deaf **Computers:** 100% of classrooms, 100% of dorms, 100% of libraries, 100% of dining areas, 100% of student union, 20% of common outdoor areas have wireless network access. Students can register for classes online. Administrative functions (other than registration) can be performed online.

CAMPUS LIFE

Environment: Metropolis. **Activities:** dance, drama/theater, literary magazine, student government, student newspaper, student-run film society, yearbook, Campus Ministries, International Student Organization. 25 registered organizations, 1 honor society, 1 religious organization. 5 fraternities, 4 sororities. **Athletics (Intercollegiate):** *Men:* baseball, basketball, cross-country, diving, football, soccer, swimming, tennis, track/field (outdoor), wrestling. *Women:* basketball, cross-country, diving, soccer, softball, swimming, tennis, track/field (outdoor), volleyball. **On-Campus Highlights:** Rathskellar, Cafeteria, Bison Shop, Starbucks, Student Academic Center.

ADMISSIONS

Freshman Academic Profile: Average high school GPA 3.19. SAT Math middle 50% range 405-485. SAT Critical Reading middle 50% range 385-475. ACT middle 50% range 15-20. **Basis for Candidate Selection:** *Very important factors considered include:* application essay, academic GPA, recommendation(s), rigor of secondary school record, standardized test scores. *Important factors considered include:* Class rank, first generation. *Other factors considered include:* alumni/ae relation, extracurricular activities, talent/ability. **Freshman Admission Requirements:** High school diploma is required and GED is accepted. **Freshman Admission Statistics:** 496 applied, 65% admitted, 56% enrolled. **Transfer Admission Requirements:** college transcript(s), essay or personal statement, Lowest grade transferable C-. **General Admission Information:** Application Fee $50. Nonfall registration accepted. Credit and/or placement offered for CEEB Advanced Placement tests.

COSTS AND FINANCIAL AID

Annual tuition $15,078. Room and board $12,630. Required fees $526. Average book expense $1,800. **Required Forms and Deadlines:** FAFSA. **Notification of Awards:** Applicants will be notified of awards on a rolling basis beginning 3/1. **Types of Aid:** *Need-based scholarships/grants:* Federal Pell, SEOG, state scholarships/grants, private scholarships, the school's own gift aid. *Loans:* Subsidized Stafford, Unsubsidized Stafford, PLUS, Federal Perkins. *Student Employment:* Federal Work-Study Program available. Institutional employment available. **Financial Aid Statistics:** 99% freshmen, 91% undergrads receive need-based scholarship or grant aid. 18% freshmen, 16% undergrads receive non-need-based scholarship or grant aid. 45% freshmen, 43% undergrads receive need-based self-help aid. 0% freshmen, 0% undergrads receive athletic scholarships. 94% freshmen, 85% undergrads receive any aid. 62% undergrads borrow to pay for school. Average cumulative indebtedness $15,157. **Criteria for awarding institutional aid:** *Non-need-based:* academics, leadership, minority status.

GANNON UNIVERSITY

109 University Square, Erie, PA 16541
Phone: 814-871-7240 · **Financial Aid Phone:** 814-871-7337
E-mail: admissions@gannon.edu · **CEEB Code:** 2270
Fax: 814-871-5803 · **Website:** www.gannon.edu · **ACT Code:** 3576

This private school, affiliated with the Roman Catholic Church, was founded in 1925. It has a 13-acre campus.

RATINGS

Admissions Selectivity Rating: 81   **Fire Safety Rating:** 95

STUDENTS AND FACULTY

Enrollment: 2,763. **Student Body:** 57% female, 43% male, 27% out-of-state, 8% international (34 countries represented). Asian 2%, African American 5%, Caucasian 79%, Hispanic 3%, Native American <1%
Retention and Graduation: 50% freshmen graduate within 4 years. 65% freshmen graduate within 6 years. 44% grads go on to further study within 1 year. 36% grads pursue arts and sciences degrees. 2% grads pursue law degrees. 3% grads pursue business degrees. 2% grads pursue medical degrees. **Faculty:** 207 full-time faculty, 74% hold PhDs, 45% are members of minority groups, 12% are women. 0.76% of classes are taught by teaching assistants.

ACADEMICS

Degrees: associate, bachelor's, certificate, master's, post-bachelor's certificate, post-master's certificate. **Classes:** Most classes have 10–19 students. Most lab/discussion sessions have 10–19 students. **Majors with Highest Enrollment:** Health Professions and Related Clinical Sciences; Registered Nursing/Registered Nurse; Biology/Biological Sciences. **Special Study Options:** Accelerated program, distance learning, double major, dual enrollment, honors program, independent study, internships, liberal arts/career combination, study abroad, teacher certification program. **Honors programs:** Gannon offers an honors program for the academically talented and highly motivated students. Last year, 246 students participated in honors classes that were small in size and staffed by Gannon's best teachers. Combined degree programs: BA/MD, BA/JD, BA/MA, BS/MBA. **Disability Services:** Special programs offered to physically disabled students include note-taking services, reader services, tape recorders, tutors. **Career services:** Alumni network, alumni services, career/job search classes, career assessment, internships, regional alumni. Career services highlights include The Career Road Show program we offer, which has the Career Development staff making over 55 in-class career and job search presentations each year. The program continues to grow and students benefit from learning valuable career information taught in classes within their major.

FACILITIES

Housing: Coed dorms, special housing for disabled students, apartments for single students. 85% of campus accessible to physically disabled. **Special Academic Facilities/Equipment:** Laser and spectrographic labs, Patient Simulation Center, metallurgy institute, computer-integrated manufacturing facilities, Schuster Art Gallery, Schuster Theatres, Erie Technology Incubator. **Computers:** 100% of classrooms, 100% of dorms, 100% of libraries, 100% of dining areas, 100% of student union, 100% of common outdoor areas have wireless network access. Students can register for classes online. Administrative functions (other than registration) can be performed online.

CAMPUS LIFE

Environment: City. **Activities:** Choral groups, concert band, dance, drama/theater, literary magazine, music ensembles, musical theater, pep band, radio station, student government, student newspaper, yearbook, Campus Ministries, International Student Organization, Model UN. 71 registered organizations, 11 honor society, 6 religious organizations. 5 fraternities, 5 sororities. **Athletics (Intercollegiate):** *Men:* baseball, basketball, cheerleading, cross-country, football, golf, soccer, swimming, water polo, wrestling. *Women:* basketball, cheerleading, cross-country, golf, lacrosse, soccer, softball, swimming, volleyball, water polo. **On-Campus Highlights:** Multi-purpose Athletic Field, Waldron Campus Center, A.J. Palumbo Academic Center, Carnaval Athletic Pavilion, Zurn Science Center, Schuster Art Gallery, Morosky College of Health Professions and Science. **Environmental Initiatives:** Switching out all campus light bulbs to compact flourescent; Experimenting with and have switched to green cleaning products.

ADMISSIONS

Freshman Academic Profile: Average high school GPA 3.52. 17% in top 10% of high school class, 45.21% in top 25% of high school class, 78.36% in top 50% of high school class. 77% from public high schools. SAT Math middle 50% range 470-570. SAT Critical Reading middle 50% range 460-560. SAT Writing middle 50% range 440-540. ACT middle 50% range 20-25. Minimum internet-based TOEFL 79. Minimum paper TOEFL 550. **Basis for Candidate Selec-**

tion: *Very important factors considered include:* Class rank, academic GPA, rigor of secondary school record, standardized test scores. *Important factors considered include:* recommendation(s), level of applicant's interest. *Other factors considered include:* application essay, extracurricular activities, interview, talent/ability, volunteer work. **Freshman Admission Requirements:** High school diploma is required and GED is accepted. *Academic units required:* 4 English, 0 foreign language, 2 social studies, 1 history, 3 academic electives. **Freshman Admission Statistics:** 4,097 applied, 78% admitted, 19% enrolled. **Transfer Admission Requirements:** college transcript(s), statement of good standing from prior institution(s). Minimum college GPA of 2.0 required. Lowest grade transferable C. **General Admission Information:** Application Fee $25. Notification on a rolling basis, beginning on or about 9/15. Nonfall registration accepted. Admission may be deferred for a maximum of 1 year. Credit and/or placement offered for CEEB Advanced Placement tests.

COSTS AND FINANCIAL AID

Required Forms and Deadlines: FAFSA. **Notification of Awards:** Applicants will be notified of awards on a rolling basis beginning 11/1. **Types of Aid:** *Need-based scholarships/grants:* Federal Pell, SEOG, state scholarships/grants, private scholarships, the school's own gift aid. *Loans:* Direct Subsidized Stafford, Direct Unsubsidized Stafford, Direct PLUS, Subsidized Stafford, Unsubsidized Stafford, PLUS, Federal Perkins. *Student Employment:* Federal Work-Study Program available. Institutional employment available. Highest amount earned per year from on-campus jobs $2,300. Off-campus job opportunities are good. **Financial Aid Statistics:** 98% freshmen, 100% undergrads receive need-based scholarship or grant aid. 16% freshmen, 14% undergrads receive non-need-based scholarship or grant aid. 83% freshmen, 80% undergrads receive need-based self-help aid. 4% freshmen, 4% undergrads receive athletic scholarships. 97% freshmen, 95% undergrads receive any aid. 76% undergrads borrow to pay for school. Average cumulative indebtedness $27,560. **Criteria for awarding institutional aid:** *Non-need-based:* academics, athletics, leadership, music/drama, religious affiliation.

GARDNER-WEBB UNIVERSITY

PO Box 817, Boiling Springs, NC 28017
Phone: 704-406-4498 · **Financial Aid Phone:** 704-406-4243
E-mail: admissions@gardner-webb.edu · **CEEB Code:** 5242
Fax: 704-406-4488 · **Website:** www.gardner-webb.edu · **ACT Code:** 3102

This private school, affiliated with the Baptist Church, was founded in 1905. It has a 250-acre campus.

RATINGS

Admissions Selectivity Rating: 85   **Fire Safety Rating:** 85

STUDENTS AND FACULTY

Enrollment: 2,640. **Student Body:** 65% female, 35% male, 21% out-of-state, 0% international (22 countries represented). Asian 0%, African American 19%, Caucasian 73%, Hispanic 2%, Native American 1%
Retention and Graduation: 36% freshmen graduate within 4 years. 49% freshmen graduate within 6 years. **Faculty:** 140 full-time faculty, 80% hold PhDs, 46% are members of minority groups, 4% are women. 0% of classes are taught by teaching assistants.

ACADEMICS

Degrees: associate, bachelor's, doctoral, master's. **Classes:** Most classes have fewer than 10 students. **Majors with Highest Enrollment:** Social Sciences; Business/Commerce; Religion/Religious Studies. **Special Study Options:** Accelerated program, distance learning, double major, dual enrollment, English as a Second Language (ESL), honors program, independent study, internships, liberal arts/career combination, study abroad, teacher certification program. **Honors programs:** Alpha Chi Honors Program Beta Beta Beta Delta Mu Delta Sigma Delta Pi Sigma Tau Delta Theta Alpha Kappa Pi Delta Phi Psi Chi Sigma Zeta Sigma Theta Tau Who's Who Combined degree programs: Music-Business - BM/MBA. **Disability Services:** Special programs offered to physically disabled students include note-taking services, reader services, tape recorders, tutors. **Career services:** Alumni network, career/job search classes, career assessment, internships. Career services highlights include a mock formal dinner interview and the Metrolina Career Fair and a Nursing Career Fair, both organized by our Career Services office.

FACILITIES

Housing: special housing for disabled students, men's dorms, women's dorms, apartments for single students, Wellness HousingHousing for Honor Students. 100% of campus accessible to physically disabled. **Special Academic Facilities/Equipment:** Williams Observatory, Millennium Playhouse, Broyhill

Adventure Course, Lake Hollifield Complex and Carillon **Computers:** 100% of classrooms, 100% of dorms, 100% of libraries, 100% of dining areas, 100% of student union, 100% of common outdoor areas have wireless network access. Students can register for classes online. Administrative functions (other than registration) can be performed online.

CAMPUS LIFE

Environment: Rural. **Activities:** Choral groups, concert band, dance, drama/theater, jazz band, literary magazine, marching band, music ensembles, musical theater, opera, pep band, radio station, student government, student newspaper, symphony orchestra, yearbook, Campus Ministries, International Student Organization. 65 registered organizations, 12 honor societies, 11 religious organization. **Athletics (Intercollegiate):** *Men:* baseball, basketball, cheerleading, cross-country, football, golf, soccer, swimming, tennis, track/field (outdoor), track/field (indoor), wrestling. *Women:* basketball, cheerleading, cross-country, golf, soccer, softball, swimming, tennis, track/field (outdoor), track/field (indoor), volleyball. **On-Campus Highlights:** Dover Campus Center, Suttle Wellness Center, Cafeteria, Lutz-Yelton Convocation Center, Kennel Snack Bar. **Environmental Initiatives:** recycling programs; environmental science major with student projects.

ADMISSIONS

Freshman Academic Profile: Average high school GPA 3.47. 32% in top 10% of high school class, 49% in top 25% of high school class, 72% in top 50% of high school class. 84% from public high schools. SAT Math middle 50% range 420-550. SAT Critical Reading middle 50% range 440-560. ACT middle 50% range 18-23. Minimum internet-based TOEFL 61. Minimum paper TOEFL 500. **Basis for Candidate Selection:** *Very important factors considered include:* academic GPA, rigor of secondary school record, standardized test scores, level of applicant's interest. *Important factors considered include:* Class rank, recommendation(s), character/personal qualities, extracurricular activities. *Other factors considered include:* application essay, interview, talent/ability, volunteer work. **Freshman Admission Requirements:** High school diploma is required and GED is accepted. **Freshman Admission Statistics:** 3,277 applied, 62% admitted, 22% enrolled. **Transfer Admission Requirements:** college transcript(s), statement of good standing from prior institution(s). Minimum college GPA of 2.25 required. Lowest grade transferable C. **General Admission Information:** Application Fee $40. Notification on a rolling basis, beginning on or about 9/1. Nonfall registration accepted. Admission may be deferred for a maximum of 2 Semesters. Credit and/or placement offered for CEEB Advanced Placement tests.

COSTS AND FINANCIAL AID

Annual tuition $22,050. Room and board $7,195. Required fees $465. Average book expense $1,000. **Required Forms and Deadlines:** FAFSA, State aid form. **Notification of Awards:** Applicants will be notified of awards on a rolling basis beginning 3/1. **Types of Aid:** *Need-based scholarships/grants:* Federal Pell, SEOG, state scholarships/grants, private scholarships, the school's own gift aid. *Loans:* Subsidized Stafford, Unsubsidized Stafford, PLUS, Federal Perkins, Federal Nursing, state loans. *Student Employment:* Federal Work-Study Program available. Institutional employment available. Off-campus job opportunities are good. **Financial Aid Statistics:** 96% freshmen, 34% undergrads receive need-based scholarship or grant aid. 77% freshmen, 70% undergrads receive non-need-based scholarship or grant aid. 66% freshmen, 75% undergrads receive need-based self-help aid. 100% freshmen receive any aid. **Criteria for awarding institutional aid:** *Non-need-based:* academics, athletics, leadership, music/drama, state/district residency.

GENEVA COLLEGE

3200 College Avenue, Beaver Falls, PA 15010
Phone: 724-847-6500 · **Financial Aid Phone:** 724-847-6530
E-mail: admissions@geneva.edu · **CEEB Code:** 2273
Fax: 724-847-6776 · **Website:** http://www.geneva.edu/ · **ACT Code:** 33578

This private school was founded in 1848. It has a 55-acre campus.

RATINGS

Admissions Selectivity Rating: 81   **Fire Safety Rating:** 70

STUDENTS AND FACULTY

Enrollment: 1,340. **Student Body:** 54% female, 46% male, 26% out-of-state, 1% international (7 countries represented). Asian 1%, African American 15%, Caucasian 105%, Hispanic 1%, Native American <1%.
Retention and Graduation: 78% freshmen return for sophomore year. 45% freshmen graduate within 4 years. 58% freshmen graduate within 6 years. 32% grads go on to further study within 1 year. **Faculty:** 84 full-time faculty, 76% hold PhDs, 35% are members of minority groups, 8% are women. 0% of classes are taught by teaching assistants.

ACADEMICS

Degrees: associate, bachelor's, master's. **Classes:** Most classes have 10–19 students. **Majors with Highest Enrollment:** Elementary Education and Teaching; Bible/Biblical Studies; Business/Commerce. **Special Study Options:** Accelerated program, cooperative education program, cross-registration, double major, dual enrollment, honors program, independent study, internships, student-designed major, study abroad, teacher certification program. **Honors programs:** Freshmen Honors Program Combined degree programs: BA/MA, Psychology and Business. **Disability Services:** Special programs offered to physically disabled students include note-taking services, reader services, tape recorders, tutors. **Career services:** Alumni network, alumni services, career/job search classes, career assessment, internships.

FACILITIES

Housing: men's dorms, women's dorms, apartments for single students. 85% of campus accessible to physically disabled. **Special Academic Facilities/Equipment:** Center for Technology Development. **Computers:** Students can register for classes online. Administrative functions (other than registration) can be performed online.

CAMPUS LIFE

Environment: Village. **Activities:** Choral groups, concert band, dance, drama/theater, jazz band, literary magazine, marching band, music ensembles, pep band, radio station, student government, student newspaper, yearbook. 56 registered organizations, 5 honor societies, 11 religious organization. **Athletics (Intercollegiate):** *Men:* baseball, basketball, cross-country, football, soccer, track/field (outdoor), track/field (indoor). *Women:* basketball, cheerleading, cross-country, soccer, softball, tennis, track/field (outdoor), track/field (indoor), volleyball. **On-Campus Highlights:** The Riverview Café (Coffee Shop), The Briagadoon (Café-Casual Dining), The Fitness Center, Track/Soccer Field, Skye Lounge (Student Center).

ADMISSIONS

Freshman Academic Profile: Average high school GPA 3.4. 16% in top 10% of high school class, 37% in top 25% of high school class, 71% in top 50% of high school class. 72% from public high schools. SAT Math middle 50% range 480-590. SAT Critical Reading middle 50% range 490-610. ACT middle 50% range 20-25. Minimum paper TOEFL 480. **Basis for Candidate Selection:** *Very important factors considered include:* application essay, academic GPA, rigor of secondary school record, standardized test scores. *Other factors considered include:* Class rank, recommendation(s), alumni/ae relation, character/personal qualities, extracurricular activities, interview. **Freshman Admission Requirements:** High school diploma is required and GED is accepted. *Academic units required:* 4 English, 2 mathematics, 1 science, 2 foreign language, 3 social studies, 4 academic electives. **Freshman Admission Statistics:** 1,329 applied, 64% admitted, 35% enrolled. **Transfer Admission Requirements:** High school transcript, college transcript(s), essay or personal statement, Minimum college GPA of 2.0 required. Lowest grade transferable C-. **General Admission Information:** Application Fee $40. Notification on a rolling basis, beginning on or about 9/1. Nonfall registration accepted. Admission may be deferred for a maximum of 3 years. Credit and/or placement offered for CEEB Advanced Placement tests.

COSTS AND FINANCIAL AID

Annual tuition $19,430. Room and board $7,200. Average book expense $800. **Required Forms and Deadlines:** FAFSA. **Notification of Awards:** Applicants will be notified of awards on a rolling basis beginning 3/15. **Types of Aid:** *Need-based scholarships/grants:* Federal Pell, SEOG, state scholarships/grants, private scholarships, the school's own gift aid, FSEOG. *Loans:* Subsidized Stafford, Unsubsidized Stafford, PLUS, Federal Perkins. *Student Employment:* Federal Work-Study Program available. Institutional employment available. Highest amount earned per year from on-campus jobs $2,000. Off-campus job opportunities are fair. **Financial Aid Statistics:** 100% freshmen, 99% undergrads receive need-based scholarship or grant aid. 12% freshmen, 11% undergrads receive non-need-based scholarship or grant aid. 84% freshmen, 85% undergrads receive need-based self-help aid. 0% freshmen, 3% undergrads receive athletic scholarships. 95% freshmen, 92% undergrads receive any aid. 96% undergrads borrow to pay for school. Average cumulative indebtedness $22,000. **Criteria for awarding institutional aid:** *Non-need-based:* academics, athletics, music/drama, religious affiliation.

GEORGE FOX UNIVERSITY

414 N. Meridian St., Newberg, OR 97132
Phone: 503-554-2240 · **Financial Aid Phone:** 503-554-2300
E-mail: admissions@georgefox.edu · **CEEB Code:** 4325
Fax: 503-554-3110 · **Website:** www.georgefox.edu · **ACT Code:** 3462

This private school was founded in 1891. It has a 85-acre campus.

RATINGS

Admissions Selectivity Rating: 85   **Fire Safety Rating:** 81

STUDENTS AND FACULTY

Enrollment: 2,358. **Student Body:** 57% female, 43% male, 35% out-of-state, 6% international (43 countries represented). Asian 4%, African American 2%, Caucasian 70%, Hispanic 7%, Native American <1%
Retention and Graduation: 82% freshmen return for sophomore year. 52% freshmen graduate within 4 years. 62% freshmen graduate within 6 years. 11% grads go on to further study within 1 year. 6% grads pursue arts and sciences degrees. 2% grads pursue business degrees. 2% grads pursue medical degrees. **Faculty:** 168 full-time faculty, 76% hold PhDs, 40% are members of minority groups, 14% are women. 0% of classes are taught by teaching assistants.

ACADEMICS

Degrees: bachelor's, master's, post-bachelor's certificate, post-master's certificate. **Classes:** Most classes have 10–19 students. Most lab/discussion sessions have 10–19 students. **Majors with Highest Enrollment:** Business Administration and Management; Registered Nursing/Registered Nurse; Elementary Education and Teaching. **Special Study Options:** Accelerated program, cross-registration, double major, dual enrollment, English as a Second Language (ESL), exchange student program (domestic), honors program, independent study, internships, student-designed major, study abroad, teacher certification program. **Honors programs:** University Scholars, Richter Scholars, Honors Scholarships, Advance Leadership Development Program Combined degree programs: 3-1 coop. program in design and merchandising. **Disability Services:** Special programs offered to physically disabled students include note-taking services, reader services, tape recorders, tutors. **Career services:** Alumni network, alumni services, career/job search classes, career assessment, internships, regional alumni.

FACILITIES

Housing: special housing for disabled students, men's dorms, women's dorms, apartments for single students, Wellness Housing, Theme HousingHouses. 98% of campus accessible to physically disabled. **Special Academic Facilities/Equipment:** nuclear magnetic resonance spectrometer, Providence Nursing Learning Lab, language lab, electron microscope. **Computers:** 100% of classrooms, 90% of dorms, 100% of libraries, 100% of dining areas, 100% of student union, 50% of common outdoor areas have wireless network access. Students can register for classes online. Administrative functions (other than registration) can be performed online.

CAMPUS LIFE

Environment: Village. **Activities:** Choral groups, concert band, drama/theater, jazz band, literary magazine, music ensembles, musical theater, pep band, radio station, student government, student newspaper, symphony orchestra, yearbook, Campus Ministries, International Student Organization. 20 registered organizations, 3 honor societies, 3 religious organizations. **Athletics (Intercollegiate):** *Men:* baseball, basketball, cross-country, golf, soccer, tennis, track/field (outdoor). *Women:* basketball, cross-country, golf, soccer, softball, tennis, track/field (outdoor), volleyball. **On-Campus Highlights:** Bruin Den-Café in the Student Union Bldg, The Foxhole-Student-run coffee house, Dorm Movie Rooms—most have movie areas, Wheeler Sports Center. **Environmental Initiatives:** LEED-certified residence hall; Fleet vehicle hybrid purchases; Progressive recycling program.

ADMISSIONS

Freshman Academic Profile: Average high school GPA 3.56. 27.27% in top 10% of high school class, 57.22% in top 25% of high school class, 84.76% in top 50% of high school class. 73% from public high schools. SAT Math middle 50% range 470-600. SAT Critical Reading middle 50% range 470-600. SAT Writing middle 50% range 460-590. ACT middle 50% range 20-26. Minimum internet-based TOEFL 80. Minimum paper TOEFL 550. **Basis for Candidate Selection:** *Very important factors considered include:* rigor of secondary school record. *Important factors considered include:* application essay, academic GPA, recommendation(s), standardized test scores. *Other factors considered include:* character/personal qualities, extracurricular activities, interview, religious affiliation/commitment, talent/ability, volunteer work, work experience. **Freshman Admission Requirements:** High school diploma is required and GED is accepted. **Freshman Admission Statistics:** 2,431 applied, 75% admitted, 34%

enrolled. **Transfer Admission Requirements:** college transcript(s), essay or personal statement, statement of good standing from prior institution(s). Minimum college GPA of 2.6 required. Lowest grade transferable C-. **General Admission Information:** Application Fee $40. Notification on a rolling basis, beginning on or about 10/1. Nonfall registration accepted. Admission may be deferred for a maximum of 1 yr. Credit and/or placement offered for CEEB Advanced Placement tests.

COSTS AND FINANCIAL AID

Annual tuition $30,770. Room and board $9,630. Required fees $350. Average book expense $950. **Required Forms and Deadlines:** FAFSA, State aid form. **Notification of Awards:** Applicants will be notified of awards on a rolling basis beginning 3/1. **Types of Aid:** *Need-based scholarships/grants:* Federal Pell, SEOG, state scholarships/grants, private scholarships, the school's own gift aid, ACG & SMART, TEACH Grants. *Loans:* Direct Subsidized Stafford, Direct Unsubsidized Stafford, Direct PLUS, Federal Perkins, Alternative loans. *Student Employment:* Federal Work-Study Program available. Institutional employment available. Highest amount earned per year from on-campus jobs $3,715. Off-campus job opportunities are good. **Financial Aid Statistics:** 84% freshmen, 89% undergrads receive need-based scholarship or grant aid. 98% freshmen, 86% undergrads receive non-need-based scholarship or grant aid. 100% freshmen, 99% undergrads receive need-based self-help aid. 0% freshmen, 0% undergrads receive athletic scholarships. 100% freshmen, 96% undergrads receive any aid. 86% undergrads borrow to pay for school. Average cumulative indebtedness $22,170. **Criteria for awarding institutional aid:** *Non-need-based:* academics, alumni affiliation, art, job skills, leadership, minority status, music/drama, religious affiliation.

GEORGE MASON UNIVERSITY

Best 380

4400 University Drive, Fairfax, VA 22030-4444
Phone: 703-993-2400 · **Financial Aid Phone:** 703-993-2349
E-mail: admissions@gmu.edu · **CEEB Code:** 5827
Fax: 703-993-4622 · **Website:** http://www.gmu.edu · **ACT Code:** 4357

This public school was founded in 1972. It has a 806-acre campus.

RATINGS

Admissions Selectivity Rating: 87   **Fire Safety Rating:** 90

STUDENTS AND FACULTY

Enrollment: 21,672. **Student Body:** 51% female, 49% male, 11% out-of-state, 4% international (122 countries represented). Asian 18%, African American 10%, Caucasian 45%, Hispanic 12%, Native American <1%
Retention and Graduation: 43% freshmen graduate within 4 years. 67% freshmen graduate within 6 years. 8% grads go on to further study within 1 year. 34% grads pursue arts and sciences degrees. 13% grads pursue law degrees. 8% grads pursue business degrees. 8% grads pursue medical degrees. **Faculty:** 1,236 full-time faculty, 91% hold PhDs, 43% are members of minority groups, 15% are women. 5.1% of classes are taught by teaching assistants.

ACADEMICS

Degrees: bachelor's, first professional, master's, post-bachelor's certificate, post-master's certificate. **Classes:** Most classes have 20–29 students. Most lab/discussion sessions have 20–29 students. **Majors with Highest Enrollment:** Biology/Biological Sciences; Psychology; Accounting. **Special Study Options:** Accelerated program, cooperative education program, cross-registration, distance learning, double major, dual enrollment, English as a Second Language (ESL), exchange student program (domestic), external degree program, honors program, independent study, internships, liberal arts/career combination, student-designed major, study abroad, teacher certification program. **Honors programs:** Honors Program in General Education provides small courses with outstanding faculty. The University Scholars program provides an elite group of students with exceptional academic and research oppotunities in a dynamic community of learners. Combined degree programs: BS/MS. **Disability Services:** Special programs offered to physically disabled students include note-taking services, reader services, tape recorders. **Career services:** Alumni network, alumni services, career/job search classes, career assessment, internships, regional alumni. Career services highlights include a current initiative to increase student uptake of federal government internship opportunities (Federal Student Career Experience Program-SCEP). Students enroll for SCEP positions through Mason's Cooperative Education program. Cooperative

Education employs students in the DC metro area and adds value to student degree. Internships can be taken in concert with Co-op or stand alone.

FACILITIES

Housing: Coed dorms, special housing for disabled students, men's dorms, women's dorms, apartments for single students. 95% of campus accessible to physically disabled. **Special Academic Facilities/Equipment:** Center for the Arts, science/technology building, television studio, art galleries in Mason Hall and Johnson Center, astronomy observatory, Smithsonian Conservation and Research Center. **Computers:** 30% of classrooms, 100% of dorms, 100% of libraries, 100% of dining areas, 100% of student union, 5% of common outdoor areas have wireless network access. Students can register for classes online. Administrative functions (other than registration) can be performed online.

CAMPUS LIFE

Environment: City. **Activities:** Choral groups, concert band, dance, drama/theater, jazz band, literary magazine, music ensembles, musical theater, opera, pep band, radio station, student government, student newspaper, student-run film society, symphony orchestra, television station, yearbook, Campus Ministries, International Student Organization. 250 registered organizations, 7 honor societies, 29 religious organizations. 22 fraternities, 13 sororities. **Athletics (Intercollegiate):** *Men:* baseball, basketball, cheerleading, cross-country, diving, golf, soccer, swimming, tennis, track/field (outdoor), track/field (indoor), volleyball, wrestling. *Women:* basketball, cheerleading, crew/rowing, cross-country, diving, lacrosse, soccer, softball, swimming, tennis, track/field (outdoor), track/field (indoor), volleyball. **On-Campus Highlights:** Johnson Center, Aquatic and Fitness Center, Center for the Arts, Patriot Center, Freedom Aquatic Center at Prince William. **Environmental Initiatives:** Climate neutrality: Have signed on to the American College and University Presidents Climate Committment. Our inaugural Climate Action Plan was published (last year) on the ACUPCC website (http://acupcc.aashe.org/cap/84/.) Work toward executing this plan began in January 2010. Built **Environment:** Have committed all new buildings to be built to the USGBC LEED Silver standard, and have 6 registered projects in the queue for certification at this time. LEED standards are being worked into our Design Manual guidelines for all contractors. Transportation: Have put in place multiple shuttles to the metro and to off-campus lots; provide transportation credits to employees; free local bus rides to all Mason ID holders; bike committee examining ways to increase cycling accessibility on campus; Bike to Mason day on Earth Day being planned; van pool is offered to employees coming in from far away at a reduced monthly cost versus driving and parking; rideshare and carpooling is being promoted. Mason also offers Gunstons Go-Bus, a social shuttle service provided free to all Mason community members who travel to local establishments.

ADMISSIONS

Freshman Academic Profile: Average high school GPA 3.65. 26% in top 10% of high school class, 65% in top 25% of high school class, 95% in top 50% of high school class. 90% from public high schools. SAT Math middle 50% range 530-630. SAT Critical Reading middle 50% range 520-620. ACT middle 50% range 23-28. Minimum internet-based TOEFL 88. Minimum paper TOEFL 570. **Basis for Candidate Selection:** *Very important factors considered include:* academic GPA, rigor of secondary school record. *Important factors considered include:* Class rank, application essay, recommendation(s), alumni/ae relation, character/personal qualities, talent/ability. *Other factors considered include:* standardized test scores, extracurricular activities, first generation, level of applicant's interest, volunteer work, work experience. **Freshman Admission Requirements:** High school diploma is required and GED is accepted. *Academic units required:* 4 English, 3 mathematics, 3 science, (3 science labs), 2 foreign language, 3 social studies, 3 academic electives. **Freshman Admission Statistics:** 22,532 applied, 67% admitted, 20% enrolled. **Transfer Admission Requirements:** college transcript(s), Minimum college GPA of 2.0 required. Lowest grade transferable C. **General Admission Information:** Application Fee $70. Regular application deadline 1/15. Regular notification 4/1. Nonfall registration accepted. Admission may be deferred for a maximum of one semester. Credit and/or placement offered for CEEB Advanced Placement tests.

COSTS AND FINANCIAL AID

Annual in-state tuition $7,562. Annual out-of-state tuition $27,140. Room and board $10,100. Required fees $2,820. Average book expense $1,136. **Required Forms and Deadlines:** FAFSA. **Notification of Awards:** Applicants will be notified of awards on a rolling basis beginning 4/1. **Types of Aid:** *Need-based scholarships/grants:* Federal Pell, SEOG, state scholarships/grants, private scholarships, the school's own gift aid, Federal ACG and SMART Grants. *Loans:* Subsidized Stafford, Unsubsidized Stafford, PLUS, Federal Perkins, Federal Nursing. *Student Employment:* Federal Work-Study Program available. Institutional employment available. Highest amount earned per year from on-campus jobs $7,200. Off-campus job opportunities are excellent. **Financial Aid Statistics:** 81% freshmen, 78% undergrads receive need-based scholarship or grant aid. 31% freshmen, 15% undergrads receive non-need-based scholarship or grant aid. 76% freshmen, 76% undergrads receive need-based self-help aid. 2% freshmen, 2% undergrads receive athletic scholarships. 68% freshmen, 58%

undergrads receive any aid. 60% undergrads borrow to pay for school. Average cumulative indebtedness $22,178. **Criteria for awarding institutional aid:** *Non-need-based:* academics, athletics, minority status, music/drama, state/district residency.

THE GEORGE WASHINGTON UNIVERSITY

2121 Eye Street NW, Suite 201, Washington, DC 20052
Phone: 202-994-6040
E-mail: gwadm@gwu.edu • **CEEB Code:** 5246
Fax: 202-994-0325 • **Website:** www.gwu.edu • **ACT Code:** 664

This private school was founded in 1821. It has a 45-acre campus.

RATINGS

Admissions Selectivity Rating: 94   Fire Safety Rating: 60*

STUDENTS AND FACULTY

Enrollment: 10,184. **Student Body:** 56% female, 44% male, 98% out-of-state, 7% international (122 countries represented). Asian 10%, African American 7%, Caucasian 57%, Hispanic 7%, Native American <1%
Retention and Graduation: 94% freshmen return for sophomore year. 76% freshmen graduate within 4 years. 22% grads go on to further study within 1 year. 48% grads pursue arts and sciences degrees. 31% grads pursue law degrees. 2% grads pursue business degrees. 18% grads pursue medical degrees. **Faculty:** 942 full-time faculty, 92% hold PhDs, 40% are members of minority groups, 21% are women. 3% of classes are taught by teaching assistants.

ACADEMICS

Degrees: associate, bachelor's, certificate, master's, post-bachelor's certificate, post-master's certificate. **Classes:** Most classes have 10–19 students. Most lab/discussion sessions have 20–29 students. **Majors with Highest Enrollment:** International Relations and Affairs; Business Administration and Management; Psychology. **Special Study Options:** Accelerated program, cooperative education program, cross-registration, distance learning, double major, dual enrollment, honors program, independent study, internships, liberal arts/career combination, student-designed major, study abroad. Combined degree programs: BA/MD, BA/JD, BA/MA. **Disability Services:** Special programs offered to physically disabled students include note-taking services, reader services, tape recorders, tutors.

FACILITIES

Housing: Coed dorms, fraternity/sorority housing, apartments for single students, Theme Housing. **Special Academic Facilities/Equipment:** Art gallery, language lab, word processing center. **Computers:** Students can register for classes online. Administrative functions (other than registration) can be performed online.

CAMPUS LIFE

Environment: Metropolis. **Activities:** Choral groups, concert band, dance, drama/theater, jazz band, literary magazine, marching band, music ensembles, musical theater, pep band, radio station, student government, student newspaper, student-run film society, television station, yearbook, International Student Organization, Model UN. 220 registered organizations, 3 honor societies, 5 religious organizations. 12 fraternities, 9 sororities. **Athletics (Intercollegiate):** *Men:* baseball, basketball, crew/rowing, cross-country, diving, fencing, golf, rugby, soccer, squash, swimming, tennis, water polo. *Women:* basketball, crew/rowing, cross-country, fencing, gymnastics, soccer, swimming, tennis, volleyball. **On-Campus Highlights:** The Smith Center, The Hippo, Media and Public Affairs Building, Kogan Plaza, Gelman Library. **Environmental Initiatives:** 1. GWs mission is to be the premier university on policy and governance for sustainable systems through practice, teaching, research, and outreach. The University is deploying a pan-university approach that bridges traditional disciplines. In Fall 2012 GW will offer an interdisciplinary Minor in Sustainability to all undergraduate students. The minor is a pan-university offering that provides students with inter-disciplinary teaching (with a team-taught course taught by faculty representing several schools) and experiential learning (which challenges students to apply knowledge, theory and methods learned in the classroom to analyze a real-world sustainability issue and/or practice). 2. Strategic Plan and Targets including GWater Plan Commitment and ACUPCC/Climate Action Plan Commitment. In Spring 2011 GW released a comprehensive plan for water sustainability. The GWater Plan takes a holistic look at GWs water footprint.

GW was one of the first universities to disclose its full water footprint and has set goals and targets to address its water sustainability across its potable water, rainfall capture, water quality and bottled water footprints. The full plan can be found here: http://www.gwu.edu/staticfile/GW/News%20and%20Events/6.%20 Initiatives/1.%20Sustainability/Resources/GWater%20Plan.pdf The University's commitment to developing a plan towards carbon neutrality represents GWs environmental commitment. As an urban school with many older buildings, becoming carbon neutral will require a significant investment in order to develop the appropriate infrastructure. 3. Commitment to LEED. GW is committed to achieving a minimum of LEED Silver certification on all new construction and GWs two newest buildings—both residence halls—are LEED Gold certified. GWs commitment to designing buildings that are both comfortable for GWs students as well as environmentally friendly is part of GWs commitment to becoming a leader in urban sustainability.

ADMISSIONS

Freshman Academic Profile: 58% in top 10% of high school class, 86% in top 25% of high school class, 99% in top 50% of high school class. 70% from public high schools. SAT Math middle 50% range 610-700. SAT Critical Reading middle 50% range 600-700. SAT Writing middle 50% range 620-710. ACT middle 50% range 27-31. Minimum paper TOEFL 550. **Basis for Candidate Selection:** *Very important factors considered include:* academic GPA, rigor of secondary school record. *Important factors considered include:* Class rank, application essay, recommendation(s), standardized test scores, extracurricular activities, interview, talent/ability, volunteer work. *Other factors considered include:* alumni/ae relation, character/personal qualities, first generation, geographical residence, level of applicant's interest, racial/ethnic status, work experience. **Freshman Admission Requirements:** High school diploma is required and GED is not accepted. *Academic units required:* 4 English, 2 mathematics, 2 science, (1 science labs), 2 foreign language, 2 social studies. **Freshman Admission Statistics:** 21,591 applied, 33% admitted, 31% enrolled. **Transfer Admission Requirements:** High school transcript, college transcript(s), essay or personal statement, standardized test scores, Lowest grade transferable C. **General Admission Information:** Application Fee $65. Early decision application deadline 11/10. Regular application deadline 1/10. Regular notification 4/1. Nonfall registration accepted. Credit and/or placement offered for CEEB Advanced Placement tests.

COSTS AND FINANCIAL AID

Annual tuition $48,700. Room and board $11,700. Required fees $60. Average book expense $1,275. **Required Forms and Deadlines:** FAFSA, CSS/Financial Aid PROFILE. **Notification of Awards:** Applicants will be notified of awards on a rolling basis beginning 3/24. **Types of Aid:** *Need-based scholarships/grants:* Federal Pell, SEOG, state scholarships/grants, the school's own gift aid. *Loans:* Subsidized Stafford, Unsubsidized Stafford, PLUS, Federal Perkins. *Student Employment:* Federal Work-Study Program available. Institutional employment available. Highest amount earned per year from on-campus jobs $3,160. Off-campus job opportunities are excellent. **Financial Aid Statistics:** 93% freshmen, 92% undergrads receive need-based scholarship or grant aid. 47% freshmen, 27% undergrads receive non-need-based scholarship or grant aid. 75% freshmen, 78% undergrads receive need-based self-help aid. 2% freshmen, 2% undergrads receive athletic scholarships. Average cumulative indebtedness $23,390. **Criteria for awarding institutional aid:** *Non-need-based:* academics, art, athletics, music/drama.

GEORGETOWN COLLEGE

400 East College Street, Georgetown, KY 40324
Phone: 502-863-8009 · **Financial Aid Phone:** 502-863-8027
E-mail: admissions@georgetowncollege.edu · **CEEB Code:** 1249
Fax: 502-868-7733 · **Website:** www.georgetowncollege.edu · **ACT Code:** 1514

This private school was founded in 1787. It has a 104-acre campus.

RATINGS

Admissions Selectivity Rating: 79   Fire Safety Rating: 63

STUDENTS AND FACULTY

Enrollment: 965. **Student Body:** 53% female, 47% male, 26% out-of-state, 2% international (12 countries represented). Asian 1%, African American 6%, Caucasian 58%, Hispanic 3%, Native American <1%
Retention and Graduation: 70% freshmen return for sophomore year. 46% freshmen graduate within 4 years. **Faculty:** 98 full-time faculty, 96% hold PhDs, 50% are members of minority groups, 7% are women. 0% of classes are taught by teaching assistants.

ACADEMICS

Degrees: bachelor's, master's. **Classes:** Most classes have 20–29 students. Most lab/discussion sessions have 10–19 students. **Majors with Highest Enrollment:** Psychology; Biology/Biological Sciences; Athletic Training/Trainer. **Special Study Options:** Accelerated program, cooperative education program, double major, dual enrollment, honors program, independent study, internships, liberal arts/career combination, student-designed major, study abroad, teacher certification program. **Honors programs:** Georgetown College Academic Honors Program. **Disability Services:** Special programs offered to physically disabled students include note-taking services, reader services, tape recorders, tutors. **Career services:** Alumni network, alumni services, career/job search classes, career assessment, internships, regional alumni.

FACILITIES

Housing: men's dorms, women's dorms, fraternity/sorority housing, Apartments for upper classmen. **Special Academic Facilities/Equipment:** To name only some: the Anna Ashcraft Ensor Learning Resource Center, an aboretum, three antebellum buildings, the Asher Science Center, the Anne Wright Wilson Fine Arts Building, and the Wilson Laboratory Theatre. **Computers:** 10% of classrooms, 60% of dorms, 90% of libraries, 100% of dining areas, 100% of student union, have wireless network access. Students can register for classes online. Administrative functions (other than registration) can be performed online.

CAMPUS LIFE

Environment: Town. **Activities:** Choral groups, concert band, dance, drama/theater, literary magazine, music ensembles, musical theater, pep band, radio station, student government, student newspaper, yearbook, Campus Ministries. 110 registered organizations, 20 honor societies, 8 religious organizations. 5 fraternities, 4 sororities. **Athletics (Intercollegiate):** *Men:* baseball, basketball, cross-country, football, golf, soccer, tennis, track/field (outdoor), track/field (indoor). *Women:* basketball, cheerleading, cross-country, golf, soccer, softball, tennis, track/field (outdoor), track/field (indoor), volleyball. **On-Campus Highlights:** The Ensor Learning Resource Center, Starbucks—in the Learning Resource Center, The Grille **Environmental Initiatives:** Student led "Green Team" Sustainability themed student activities Community garden

ADMISSIONS

Freshman Academic Profile: Average high school GPA 3.37. 26% in top 10% of high school class, 49% in top 25% of high school class, 82% in top 50% of high school class. 84% from public high schools. SAT Math middle 50% range 490-570. SAT Critical Reading middle 50% range 435-580. ACT middle 50% range 21-27. Minimum internet-based TOEFL 68. Minimum paper TOEFL 520. **Basis for Candidate Selection:** *Very important factors considered include:* academic GPA, rigor of secondary school record. *Important factors considered include:* Class rank, recommendation(s), standardized test scores, character/personal qualities, extracurricular activities, talent/ability. *Other factors considered include:* application essay, alumni/ae relation, geographical residence, interview, level of applicant's interest, religious affiliation/commitment, state residency, volunteer work. **Freshman Admission Requirements:** High school diploma is required and GED is accepted. **Freshman Admission Statistics:** 2,089 applied, 89% admitted, 15% enrolled. **Transfer Admission Requirements:** High school transcript, college transcript(s), statement of good standing from prior institution(s). Minimum college GPA of 2.5 required. Lowest grade transferable C. **General Admission Information:** Application Fee $30. Regular application deadline 8/1. Notification on a rolling basis, beginning on or about 10/1. Nonfall registration accepted. Admission may be deferred for a maximum of 1 year. Credit and/or placement offered for CEEB Advanced Placement tests.

COSTS AND FINANCIAL AID

Annual tuition $32,960. Room and board $8,480. Required fees $0. Average book expense $1,250. **Required Forms and Deadlines:** FAFSA. **Notification of Awards:** Applicants will be notified of awards on a rolling basis beginning 3/15. **Types of Aid:** *Need-based scholarships/grants:* Federal Pell, SEOG, state scholarships/grants, private scholarships, the school's own gift aid. *Loans:* Subsidized Stafford, Unsubsidized Stafford, PLUS, Federal Perkins, college/university loans from institutional funds. *Student Employment:* Federal Work-Study Program available. Institutional employment available. Highest amount earned per year from on-campus jobs $2,500. Off-campus job opportunities are good. **Financial Aid Statistics:** 100% freshmen, 100% undergrads receive need-based scholarship or grant aid. 15% freshmen, 18% undergrads receive non-need-based scholarship or grant aid. 75% freshmen, 77% undergrads receive need-based self-help aid. 5% freshmen, 4% undergrads receive athletic scholarships. 95% freshmen, 96% undergrads receive any aid. 68% undergrads borrow to pay for school. Average cumulative indebtedness $15,171. **Criteria for awarding institutional aid:** *Non-need-based:* academics, alumni affiliation, art, athletics, leadership, minority status, music/drama, religious affiliation, state/district residency.

GEORGETOWN UNIVERSITY

Best 380

103 White Gravenor Hall, 37th and O, Washington, DC 20057
Phone: 202-687-3600 · **Financial Aid Phone:** 202-687-4547
E-mail: guadmiss@georgetown.edu · **CEEB Code:** 5244
Fax: 202-687-5084 · **Website:** www.georgetown.edu · **ACT Code:** 668

This private school, affiliated with the Roman Catholic Church, was founded in 1789. It has a 104-acre campus.

RATINGS
Admissions Selectivity Rating: 98   **Fire Safety Rating:** 80

STUDENTS AND FACULTY
Enrollment: 7,211. **Student Body:** 55% female, 45% male, 98% out-of-state, 12% international (138 countries represented). Asian 10%, African American 6%, Caucasian 58%, Hispanic 8%, Native American <1%
Retention and Graduation: 96% freshmen return for sophomore year. 91% freshmen graduate within 4 years. **Faculty:** 1,001 full-time faculty, 87% hold PhDs, 45% are members of minority groups, 13% are women. 8% of classes are taught by teaching assistants.

ACADEMICS
Degrees: bachelor's, certificate, first professional, master's. **Majors with Highest Enrollment:** Political Science and Government; International Relations and Affairs; English Language and Literature. **Special Study Options:** cross-registration, double major, English as a Second Language (ESL), honors program, independent study, internships, student-designed major, study abroad. **Honors programs:** The John Carroll Programs guide and support a highly selective group of academically talented and ambitious students from around the world. The Programs seek individuals who desire to make a lasting difference in the fields and communities they touch. For these young men and women, the Programs provide models and skills to help them make the most effective use of their undergraduate years, and to assists them in moving from the undergraduate experience to their post-graduate academic and professional lives. The Programs invite students to take as their own the Carroll motto, mentis vita pro vita mundi: the life of the mind for the life of the world. Combined degree programs: BA/MA. **Disability Services:** Special programs offered to physically disabled students include note-taking services, reader services, tape recorders, tutors. **Career services:** Alumni network, alumni services, career/job search classes, career assessment, internships, regional alumni.

FACILITIES
Housing: Coed dorms, special housing for disabled students, apartments for single students, Freshmen and sophomores are required to live on campus. 92% of campus accessible to physically disabled. **Special Academic Facilities/Equipment:** Language lab, seismological observatory. **Computers:** Students can register for classes online. Administrative functions (other than registration) can be performed online.

CAMPUS LIFE
Environment: Metropolis. **Activities:** Choral groups, concert band, dance, drama/theater, jazz band, literary magazine, music ensembles, musical theater, pep band, radio station, student government, student newspaper, student-run film society, symphony orchestra, television station, yearbook. 139 registered organizations, 14 honor societies, 20 religious organizations. **Athletics (Intercollegiate):** *Men:* baseball, basketball, crew/rowing, cross-country, diving, football, golf, lacrosse, sailing, soccer, swimming, tennis, track/field (outdoor), track/field (indoor). *Women:* basketball, crew/rowing, cross-country, diving, field hockey, golf, lacrosse, sailing, soccer, softball, swimming, tennis, track/field (outdoor), track/field (indoor), volleyball. **On-Campus Highlights:** Yates Field House, Uncommon Grounds, The Observatory, The Quadrangle, Healy Hall. **Environmental Initiatives:** Set LEED certification as the standard for new constructions & major renovations Implemented energy construction programs in utility operations Expanded recycling program to include construction waste

ADMISSIONS
Freshman Academic Profile: 92% in top 10% of high school class, 99% in top 25% of high school class, 100% in top 50% of high school class. 49% from public high schools. SAT Math middle 50% range 660-760. SAT Critical Reading middle 50% range 660-760. ACT middle 50% range 30-33. **Basis for Candidate Selection:** *Very important factors considered include:* Class rank, application essay, academic GPA, recommendation(s), rigor of secondary school record, standardized test scores, character/personal qualities, talent/ability.

Important factors considered include: extracurricular activities, interview, volunteer work. *Other factors considered include:* alumni/ae relation, geographical residence, racial/ethnic status, state residency, work experience. **Freshman Admission Requirements:** High school diploma is required and GED is accepted. **Freshman Admission Statistics:** 19,505 applied, 17% admitted, 47% enrolled. **Transfer Admission Requirements:** High school transcript, college transcript(s), essay or personal statement, standardized test scores, statement of good standing from prior institution(s). Minimum college GPA of 3.0 required. Lowest grade transferable C. **General Admission Information:** Application Fee $65. Regular application deadline 1/10. Regular notification 4/1. Nonfall registration not accepted. Admission may be deferred for a maximum of 1 year. Credit and/or placement offered for CEEB Advanced Placement tests. COSTS AND FINANCIAL AID **Required Forms and Deadlines:** FAFSA, CSS/Financial Aid PROFILE, Business/Farm Supplement. **Notification of Awards:** Applicants will be notified of awards on or about 4/1. **Types of Aid:** *Need-based scholarships/grants:* Federal Pell, SEOG, state scholarships/grants, private scholarships, the school's own gift aid. *Loans:* Subsidized Stafford, Unsubsidized Stafford, PLUS, Federal Perkins, Federal Nursing, Alternative loans. *Student Employment:* Federal Work-Study Program available. Institutional employment available. Off-campus job opportunities are excellent. **Financial Aid Statistics:** 93% freshmen, 92% undergrads receive need-based scholarship or grant aid. 40% freshmen, 30% undergrads receive non-need-based scholarship or grant aid. 99% freshmen, 85% undergrads receive need-based self-help aid. 4% freshmen, 4% undergrads receive athletic scholarships. 39% undergrads borrow to pay for school. Average cumulative indebtedness $16,711. **Criteria for awarding institutional aid:** *Non-need-based:* athletics.

GEORGIA COLLEGE & STATE UNIVERSITY

Campus Box 23, Milledgeville, GA 31061
Phone: 478-445-1283 · **Financial Aid Phone:** 478-445-5149
E-mail: admissions@gcsu.edu · **CEEB Code:** 5252
Fax: 478-445-1914 · **Website:** www.gcsu.edu · **ACT Code:** 828

This public school was founded in 1889. It has a 590-acre campus.

RATINGS
Admissions Selectivity Rating: 75   **Fire Safety Rating:** 98

STUDENTS AND FACULTY
Enrollment: 5,916. **Student Body:** 61% female, 39% male, 1% out-of-state, 1% international (36 countries represented). Asian 1%, African American 5%, Caucasian 84%, Hispanic 5%, Native American <1%
Retention and Graduation: 40% freshmen graduate within 4 years. 61% freshmen graduate within 6 years. **Faculty:** 323 full-time faculty, 73% hold PhDs, 55% are members of minority groups, 15% are women.

ACADEMICS
Degrees: bachelor's, master's, post-master's certificate. **Classes:** Most classes have 20–29 students. Most lab/discussion sessions have 20–29 students. **Majors with Highest Enrollment:** Registered Nursing/Registered Nurse; Business Administration and Management; Biology/Biological Sciences. **Special Study Options:** Accelerated program, distance learning, double major, English as a Second Language (ESL), honors program, independent study, internships, study abroad, teacher certification program. **Honors programs:** Honors and/or Scholars Program. **Disability Services:** Special programs offered to physically disabled students include note-taking services, reader services, tape recorders, tutors. **Career services:** Alumni network, career/job search classes, career assessment, internships.

FACILITIES
Housing: Coed dorms, special housing for international students, apartments for single students, Theme Housing. 90% of campus accessible to physically disabled. **Special Academic Facilities/Equipment:** Education archives museum, old governor's mansion, Museum of Fine Arts, Natural History Museum and Planetarium **Computers:** 98% of classrooms, 98% of dorms, 100% of libraries, 98% of dining areas, 100% of student union, 100% of common outdoor areas have wireless network access. Students can register for classes online. Administrative functions (other than registration) can be performed online.

CAMPUS LIFE
Environment: Town. **Activities:** Choral groups, concert band, dance, drama/theater, jazz band, literary magazine, music ensembles, musical theater, radio station, student government, student newspaper, television station, Campus Ministries, International Student Organization. 238 registered organizations, 8 religious organizations. 8 fraternities, 6 sororities. **Athletics (Intercollegiate):** *Men:* baseball, basketball, cross-country, golf, tennis. *Women:* basketball, cross-

country, softball, speed skating, tennis. **On-Campus Highlights:** The Depot (Wellness Center), The Centennial Center (Gymnasium), Cafeteria, Libary and Information Technology Center. **Environmental Initiatives:** recycling program; efficient HVAC; landscaping.

ADMISSIONS

Freshman Academic Profile: Average high school GPA 3.45. SAT Math middle 50% range 520-610. SAT Critical Reading middle 50% range 530-610. SAT Writing middle 50% range 510-600. ACT middle 50% range 23-26. Minimum internet-based TOEFL 61. Minimum paper TOEFL 500. **Basis for Candidate Selection:** *Very important factors considered include:* academic GPA, rigor of secondary school record, standardized test scores. *Important factors considered include:* Class rank, application essay, recommendation(s), extracurricular activities, talent/ability. *Other factors considered include:* alumni/ae relation, character/personal qualities, first generation, geographical residence, level of applicant's interest, racial/ethnic status, state residency, volunteer work, work experience. **Freshman Admission Requirements:** High school diploma is required and GED is accepted. *Academic units required:* 4 English, 4 mathematics, 3 science, (2 science labs), 2 foreign language, 3 social studies. **Freshman Admission Statistics:** 3,978 applied, 76% admitted, 48% enrolled. **Transfer Admission Requirements:** college transcript(s), statement of good standing from prior institution(s). Minimum college GPA of 2.0 required. **General Admission Information:** Application Fee $40. Regular application deadline 4/1. Nonfall registration accepted. Admission may be deferred for a maximum of 1 year. Credit offered for CEEB Advanced Placement tests.

COSTS AND FINANCIAL AID

Annual in-state tuition $6,634. Annual out-of-state tuition $24,098. Room and board $9,268. Required fees $1,984. Average book expense $1,350. **Required Forms and Deadlines:** FAFSA. **Notification of Awards:** Applicants will be notified of awards on a rolling basis beginning 3/1. **Types of Aid:** *Need-based scholarships/grants:* Federal Pell, SEOG, state scholarships/grants, private scholarships, the school's own gift aid. *Loans:* Direct PLUS, Subsidized Stafford, Unsubsidized Stafford, PLUS, Federal Perkins, state loans. *Student Employment:* Federal Work-Study Program available. Institutional employment available. Highest amount earned per year from on-campus jobs $6,812. Off-campus job opportunities are good. **Financial Aid Statistics:** 34% freshmen, 40% undergrads receive need-based scholarship or grant aid. 94% freshmen, 76% undergrads receive non-need-based scholarship or grant aid. 52% freshmen, 61% undergrads receive need-based self-help aid. 2% freshmen, 2% undergrads receive athletic scholarships. 96% freshmen, 86% undergrads receive any aid. **Criteria for awarding institutional aid:** *Non-need-based:* academics, alumni affiliation, art, athletics, leadership, music/drama, state/district residency.

GEORGIA INSTITUTE OF TECHNOLOGY

Office of Undergraduate Admissions, Atlanta, GA 30332-0320
Phone: 404-894-4154 · **Financial Aid Phone:** 404-894-4160
E-mail: admission@gatech.edu · **CEEB Code:** 5248
Fax: 404-894-9511 · **Website:** www.gatech.edu · **ACT Code:** 818

This public school was founded in 1885. It has a 450-acre campus.

RATINGS

Admissions Selectivity Rating: 96   **Fire Safety Rating:** 93

STUDENTS AND FACULTY

Enrollment: 13,996. **Student Body:** 34% female, 66% male, 31% out-of-state, 11% international (95 countries represented). Asian 18%, African American 6%, Caucasian 53%, Hispanic 7%, Native American <1%
Retention and Graduation: 96% freshmen return for sophomore year. 37% freshmen graduate within 4 years. 22% grads go on to further study within 1 year. 2% grads pursue arts and sciences degrees. 1% grads pursue business degrees. 2% grads pursue medical degrees. **Faculty:** 1,054 full-time faculty, 88% hold PhDs, 25% are members of minority groups, 28% are women. 2.95% of classes are taught by teaching assistants.

ACADEMICS

Degrees: bachelor's, master's. **Classes:** Most classes have 20–29 students. Most lab/discussion sessions have 20–29 students. **Majors with Highest Enrollment:** Mechanical Engineering; Industrial Engineering; Computer and Information Sciences. **Special Study Options:** Accelerated program, cooperative education program, cross-registration, distance learning, double major, dual enrollment, English as a Second Language (ESL), honors program, independent study, internships, student-designed major, study abroad, Dual degree program (3-2); Regent's Engineering Transfer Program with 14 colleges in the University System of Georgia; Georgia Tech Regional Engineering Program (GTREP) offers undergraduate and graduate Engineering degrees in collaboration with Armstrong Atlantic state University, Georgia Southern University, and Savannah State University. **Honors programs:** The Georgia Tech Honors Program combines the challenging academic standards of one of the finest technological universities in the world with the closer connections between students and faculty that one might expect to find in a smaller college. Our mission is to create a lively environment in which students and faculty members learn from each other through a common commitment to intellectual inquiry, careful analysis, and energetic exchange of ideas. To promote and sustain this close engagement between students and faculty, the Honors Program will offer unique opportunities to students in the first two years of their studies at Georgia Tech: 1) An Honors Program Residence where first-year students can find a supportive community of interesting people, continue their conversations beyond the classroom, and develop connections to Georgia Tech and the surrounding community; 2) Small sections of introductory core courses designed to emphasize not just mastery of the material, but innovative inquiry and exploration within the discipline and often beyond; 3) A selection of small special topics courses, each with an enrollment limit of twenty HP students, that encourage critical thinking and an interdisciplinary approach to some of the most significant issues facing the world today; 4) A program of well-coordinated advising that will help students build upon their first two years in the Honors Program as they move into their chosen undergraduate majors in the third and fourth years. Combined degree programs: BS/MS, BS/MCRP. **Disability Services:** Special programs offered to physically disabled students include note-taking services, reader services, tape recorders, tutors. **Career services:** Alumni network, alumni services, career/job search classes, career assessment, internships, regional alumni. Career services highlights include Georgia Tech's co-op program, which has more than 2,700 students participating, is currently the largest optional co-op program in the United States, and has perennially been listed in U.S. News & World Report as one of the "Top Ten" co-op programs in America.

FACILITIES

Housing: Coed dorms, special housing for disabled students, men's dorms, special housing for international students, women's dorms, fraternity/sorority housing, apartments for married students, apartments for single students, Theme Housing. First Year housing is guaranteed to all new freshman and transfer students who submit an application by May 1. 75% of campus accessible to physically disabled. **Special Academic Facilities/Equipment:** Nuclear Magnetic Resonance Spectroscopy Center, Georgia Tech Research Institute, Ovarian Cancer Institute, Paper Museum, Mechanical Properties Research Laboratory with scanning electron microscope, Virtual Factory Laboratory, Ferris-Goldsmith Trading Floor, Advanced Technology Development Center, Klaus Advanced Computing Building, Electron Microscope, Marcus Nanotechnology Research Center, Solar Decathlon House at College of Architecture, Wind Tunnel, GT Smart House, Clough Undergraduates Learning Commons (under construction). **Computers:** 100% of classrooms, 100% of dorms, 100% of libraries, 100% of dining areas, 100% of student union, 65% of common outdoor areas have wireless network access. Students can register for classes online. Administrative functions (other than registration) can be performed online. Undergraduates are required to own a computer.

CAMPUS LIFE

Environment: Metropolis. **Activities:** Choral groups, concert band, dance, drama/theater, jazz band, literary magazine, marching band, music ensembles, musical theater, pep band, radio station, student government, student newspaper, student-run film society, symphony orchestra, television station, yearbook, Campus Ministries, International Student Organization, Model UN. 429 registered organizations, 24 honor societies, 39 religious organizations. 38 fraternities, 14 sororities. **Athletics (Intercollegiate):** *Men:* baseball, basketball, cheerleading, cross-country, diving, football, golf, swimming, tennis, track/field (outdoor), track/field (indoor). *Women:* basketball, cheerleading, cross-country, diving, softball, swimming, tennis, track/field (outdoor), track/field (indoor), volleyball. **On-Campus Highlights:** Tech Square—Bookstore/Hotel, Olympic Aquatic Center/Campus Recreation, The Hill/Tech Tower, Student Center Commons and the Library W, Ferst Center for the Arts. **Environmental Initiatives:** Education: Over 350 courses across all colleges with a goal of having every student who graduates have at least one sustainability course. 23 degree programs at the undergraduate level, even more at the graduate level, many continuing education and certificate programs also focus on sustainability and major areas of sustainability. In the process of adding additional minors related to sustainability. Energy minor already implemented. Sustainability included in Mission Statement and Strategic Plan since 1994. Updated Strategic Plan in 2010. Have included addressing the Grand Challenges in the Strategic Plan to go along with Improving the Human Condition and a Sustainable Global Economy. Are implementing an option for a flexible cross disciplinary degree offering to address Grand Challenge. Research: 21 endowed chairs and 30 research centers focusing on sustainability, Georgia Tech is home to the Strategic Energy Institute, which focuses on alternative energy and energy efficiency, the Institute of Sustainable Systems, the Sustainable Design and Manufacturing Center, and much more. Georgia Tech works at the intersection of technology, business, policy, and sustainability. The Institute has over 20 student sustainability groups on campus plus over 20 student professional organizations related to sustainability. Campus as a Living Laboratory and immersive green role model: 1. Water Leadership (100% low flow fixtures, 2,225,000+gallons of cistern capacity, stormwater runoff management (including 80+ acre Eco-Commons in process)Largest campus cistern in US, at 1.4 million gallons, collects building condensate and Stormwater runoff for flushing toilets and use in our smart irrigation systems. 2. Energy efficiency (over 7,300,000 sf of energy efficient building space (via energy retrofit, and retro commissioned and new construction) resulting in an energy efficiency). We use less energy per sf than the average of our peer very high research universities. Green building with LEED Gold as a minimum is a subset of our building and construction design standard. 17 LEED certified buildings with many more in process. Most are LEED Gold certified. Two are LEED Platinum certified buildings: Carbon Neutral Energy Solutions Laboratory Building and the G Wayne Clough Undergraduate Learning Commons. Largest campus residence hall in the world to be LEED Existing Building: Operations and Maintenance certified including being certified at the LEED Gold level. LEED Gold dining hall. All dining halls compost food and are 98% waste neutral. Thirteen LEED certified building in the US. First historical building in the U niversity System of Georgia (public higher education campuses) to be LEED certified. LEED Gold certified renovation of the first research building on Georgia Techs campus. LEED certified buildings in all types of buildings on campus: athletics, academic, research, housing, administration, recreation and auxiliary services o Recognized leaders in recycling, green cleaning, green dorms, green computing, green building, alternative transportation offerings, etc. Early adapter of alternative fuel vehicles and integrating with city mass transit systems to demonstrate and facilities clean and efficient transportation options for our students and city. Students are engaged in activities such as the EcoCar Challenge (design and build the next generation environmentally friendly car) and Solar Jackets (solar race car building and competition). Georgia Techs ATDC has been named in the Top 12 Technology Incubators Changing the world by the WSJ. A graduate of our clean tech incubator, Suniva, has been No.2 on WSJ's clean tech list for 2 years.

ADMISSIONS

Freshman Academic Profile: Average high school GPA 3.95. 79.21% in top 10% of high school class, 96.75% in top 25% of high school class, 99.37% in top 50% of high school class. SAT Math middle 50% range 680-770. SAT Critical Reading middle 50% range 630-720. SAT Writing middle 50% range 630-730. ACT middle 50% range 30-33. **Basis for Candidate Selection:** *Very important factors considered include:* academic GPA, rigor of secondary school record, extracurricular activities. *Important factors considered include:* application essay, standardized test scores, character/personal qualities, geographical residence, state residency, talent/ability, volunteer work, work experience. *Other factors considered include:* alumni/ae relation, racial/ethnic status. **Freshman Admission Requirements:** High school diploma is required and GED is accepted. *Academic units required:* 4 English, 4 mathematics, 3 science, (3 science labs), 2 foreign language, 3 social studies. **Freshman Admission Statistics:** 25,884 applied, 33% admitted, 33% enrolled. **Transfer Admission Requirements:** college transcript(s), statement of good standing from prior institution(s). Minimum college GPA of 2.7 required. Lowest grade transferable C. **General Admission Information:** Application Fee $65. Regular application deadline 1/15. Regular notification 3/15. Nonfall registration accepted. Credit and/or placement offered for CEEB Advanced Placement tests.

COSTS AND FINANCIAL AID

Annual in-state tuition $9,002. Annual out-of-state tuition $28,306. Room and board $10,434. Required fees $2,392. Average book expense $1,200. **Required Forms and Deadlines:** FAFSA, Institution's own financial aid form, CSS/Financial Aid PROFILE. **Notification of Awards:** Applicants will be notified of awards on or about 4/1. **Types of Aid:** *Need-based scholarships/grants:* Federal Pell, SEOG, state scholarships/grants, private scholarships, the school's own gift aid. *Loans:* Direct Subsidized Stafford, Direct Unsubsidized Stafford, Direct PLUS, Federal Perkins, college/university loans from institutional funds. *Student Employment:* Federal Work-Study Program available. Institutional employment available. Off-campus job opportunities are excellent. **Financial Aid Statistics:** 93% freshmen, 86% undergrads receive need-based scholarship or grant aid. 74% freshmen, 58% undergrads receive non-need-based scholarship or grant aid. 49% freshmen, 61% undergrads receive need-based self-help aid. 3% freshmen, 2% undergrads receive athletic scholarships. 72% freshmen, 74% undergrads receive any aid. 43% undergrads borrow to pay for school. Average cumulative indebtedness $20,972. **Criteria for awarding institutional aid:** *Non-need-based:* academics, athletics, leadership, music/drama, state/district residency.

P.O. Box 8024, Statesboro, GA 30460
Phone: 912-478-5391 · **Financial Aid Phone:** 912-478-5413
E-mail: admissions@georgiasouthern.edu · **CEEB Code:** 5253
Fax: 912-478-7240 · **Website:** http://www.georgiasouthern.edu/ · **ACT Code:** 830

This public school was founded in 1906. It has a 700-acre campus.

RATINGS

Admissions Selectivity Rating: 83   **Fire Safety Rating:** 94

STUDENTS AND FACULTY

Enrollment: 17,232. **Student Body:** 50% female, 50% male, 3% out-of-state, 1% international (65 countries represented). Asian 1%, African American 26%, Caucasian 63%, Hispanic 5%, Native American <1%
Retention and Graduation: 81% freshmen return for sophomore year. 27% freshmen graduate within 4 years. 51% freshmen graduate within 6 years. 13% grads go on to further study within 1 year. **Faculty:** 775 full-time faculty, 82% hold PhDs, 47% are members of minority groups, 21% are women. 3% of classes are taught by teaching assistants.

ACADEMICS

Degrees: bachelor's, master's, post-master's certificate. **Classes:** Most classes have 20–29 students. Most lab/discussion sessions have 20–29 students. **Majors with Highest Enrollment:** General Studies; Biology/Biological Sciences; Registered Nursing/Registered Nurse. **Special Study Options:** Accelerated program, cooperative education program, distance learning, double major, English as a Second Language (ESL), honors program, independent study, internships, student-designed major, study abroad, teacher certification program. **Honors programs:** Georgia Southern offers University Honors Program (UHP) and 1906 Scholars. The UHP is designed to offer exceptionally able and diligent students the opportunity to enroll in particularly stimulating classes and to integrate their classroom learning with the needs of the community in which they live. The 1906 Scholars, a selective group within the UHP, accepts 15-18 freshmen from the pool of approximately 400 UHP applicants. The program offers interdisciplinary course options. Weekly seminars and colloquia emphasize discussion and independent endeavor, and nurture curiosity and the sharing of ideas among students and faculty. Selected students receive a full tuition scholarship, including out-of-state fees. Combined degree programs: Bachelor's/Graduate in Accounting and Nursing. **Disability Services:** Special programs offered to physically disabled students include note-taking services, reader services, tape recorders, tutors. **Career services:** Alumni network, alumni services, career/job search classes, career assessment, internships, regional alumni. Career services highlights include our Cooperative Education Program.

FACILITIES

Housing: Coed dorms, special housing for disabled students, special housing for international students, apartments for single students, Theme Housing. 97% of campus accessible to physically disabled. **Special Academic Facilities/Equipment:** Art galleries, teaching museum, performing arts center, wildlife education center, eagle cinema, broadcasting studios, planetarium, botanical garden, radio station, black box theatre, and Recreation Activity Center. **Computers:** 80% of classrooms, 45% of dorms, 100% of libraries, 100% of dining areas, 100% of student union, 20% of common outdoor areas have wireless network access. Students can register for classes online. Administrative functions (other than registration) can be performed online.

CAMPUS LIFE

Environment: Village. **Activities:** Choral groups, concert band, dance, drama/theater, jazz band, literary magazine, marching band, music ensembles, musical theater, pep band, radio station, student government, student newspaper, student-run film society, symphony orchestra, television station, Campus Ministries, International Student Organization. 235 registered organizations, 17 honor societies, 20 religious organizations. 20 fraternities, 9 sororities. **Athletics (Intercollegiate):** *Men:* baseball, basketball, cheerleading, football, golf, soccer, tennis. *Women:* basketball, cheerleading, cross-country, diving, soccer, softball, swimming, tennis, track/field (outdoor), volleyball. **On-Campus Highlights:** Russell Union, Recreation Activity Center, Center for Wildlife Education, Georgia Southern Museum, Paulson Stadium, Performing Arts Center, Lamar Q. Ball Raptor Center, Georgia Southern Planetarium, Gallery 303, the Georgia Southern Botanical Gardens, Eagle Cinema, College of Information Technology and Eagle Village. **Environmental Initiatives:** $10 sustainability fee per semester passed by student body to support sustainability efforts at Georgia Southern (75% majority); Three new green buildings completed in 2013 and two repurposed buildings brought up to high efficiency standards; Signed an MOU with Region 4 Environmental Protection Agency to strengthen partnerships between Georgia Southern and the EPA regarding research, education and outreach on the environment.

ADMISSIONS

Freshman Academic Profile: Average high school GPA 3.27. 19% in top 10% of high school class, 47% in top 25% of high school class, 77% in top 50% of high school class. SAT Math middle 50% range 510-590. SAT Critical Reading middle 50% range 520-590. SAT Writing middle 50% range 480-570. ACT middle 50% range 22-25. Minimum internet-based TOEFL 69. Minimum paper TOEFL 523. **Basis for Candidate Selection:** *Very important factors considered include:* academic GPA, rigor of secondary school record, standardized test scores. *Other factors considered include:* Class rank. **Freshman Admission Requirements:** High school diploma is required and GED is not accepted. *Academic units required:* 4 English, 4 mathematics, 3 science, (2 science labs), 2 foreign language, 3 social studies. **Freshman Admission Statistics:** 9,679 applied, 63% admitted, 57% enrolled. **Transfer Admission Requirements:** college transcript(s), statement of good standing from prior institution(s). Minimum college GPA of 2.0 required. Lowest grade transferable D. **General Admission Information:** Application Fee $30. Regular application deadline 5/1. Nonfall registration accepted. Admission may be deferred for a maximum of circumstantial. Placement offered for CEEB Advanced Placement tests.

COSTS AND FINANCIAL AID

Annual in-state tuition $5,098. Annual out-of-state tuition $17,994. Room and board $9,752. Required fees $2,092. Average book expense $1,200. **Required Forms and Deadlines:** FAFSA. **Notification of Awards:** Applicants will be notified of awards on a rolling basis beginning 4/20. **Types of Aid:** *Need-based scholarships/grants:* Federal Pell, SEOG, state scholarships/grants, private scholarships, the school's own gift aid, Hope Scholarships°, Federal Work Study, TEACH Grant°, ACG, SMART Grant. *Loans:* Direct Subsidized Stafford, Direct Unsubsidized Stafford, Direct PLUS, Federal Perkins, state loans, Service-Cancelable State Direct Student Loans, External Alternative Loans. *Student Employment:* Federal Work-Study Program available. Institutional employment available. Highest amount earned per year from on-campus jobs $2,142. Off-campus job opportunities are excellent. **Financial Aid Statistics:** 87% freshmen, 81% undergrads receive need-based scholarship or grant aid. 2% freshmen, 1% undergrads receive non-need-based scholarship or grant aid. 74% freshmen, 82% undergrads receive need-based self-help aid. 1% freshmen, 1% undergrads receive athletic scholarships. 92% freshmen, 89% undergrads receive any aid. 72% undergrads borrow to pay for school. Average cumulative indebtedness $23,367. **Criteria for awarding institutional aid:** *Non-need-based:* academics, alumni affiliation, art, athletics, leadership, minority status, music/drama, state/district residency.

GEORGIA SOUTHWESTERN STATE UNIVERSITY

800 Georgia Southwestern State University Dr., Americus, GA 31709-4693
Phone: 229-928-1273 · **Financial Aid Phone:** 229-928-1378
E-mail: admissions@gsw.edu · **CEEB Code:** 5250
Fax: 229-931-2983 · **Website:** www.gsw.edu · **ACT Code:** 824

This public school was founded in 1906. It has a 325-acre campus.

RATINGS

Admissions Selectivity Rating: 78 **Fire Safety Rating:** 80

STUDENTS AND FACULTY

Enrollment: 2,419. **Student Body:** 63% female, 37% male, 3% out-of-state, 2% international (34 countries represented). Asian 1%, African American 28%, Caucasian 63%, Hispanic 4%, Native American <1%
Retention and Graduation: 10% freshmen graduate within 4 years. 32% freshmen graduate within 6 years. **Faculty:** 109 full-time faculty, 74% hold PhDs, 50% are members of minority groups, 14% are women. 0% of classes are taught by teaching assistants.

ACADEMICS

Degrees: bachelor's, master's, post-bachelor's certificate, post-master's certificate. **Classes:** Most classes have 20–29 students. **Majors with Highest Enrollment:** Registered Nursing/Registered Nurse; Business Administration and Management; Accounting. **Special Study Options:** Accelerated program, cooperative education program, distance learning, double major, dual enrollment, English as a Second Language (ESL), honors program, internships, study abroad, teacher certification program. **Disability Services:** Special programs offered to physically disabled students include note-taking services, reader services, tape recorders, tutors.

FACILITIES

Housing: Coed dorms, Apartment housing for upperclassmen. 100% of campus accessible to physically disabled. **Special Academic Facilities/Equipment:** Observatory, Glass-blowing studio. **Computers:** Students can register for classes online. Administrative functions (other than registration) can be performed online.

CAMPUS LIFE

Environment: Village. **Activities:** Choral groups, concert band, drama/theater, jazz band, literary magazine, music ensembles, musical theater, student government, student newspaper, television station, International Student Organization. 12 honor societies, 7 fraternities, 6 sororities. **Athletics (Intercollegiate):** *Men:* baseball, basketball, golf, soccer, tennis. *Women:* basketball, cross-country, soccer, softball, tennis.

ADMISSIONS

Freshman Academic Profile: Average high school GPA 3.24. 15% in top 10% of high school class, 42% in top 25% of high school class, 74% in top 50% of high school class. 82% from public high schools. SAT Math middle 50% range 440-520. SAT Critical Reading middle 50% range 440-540. SAT Writing middle 50% range 430-520. ACT middle 50% range 18-23. Minimum internet-based TOEFL 70. Minimum paper TOEFL 523. **Basis for Candidate Selection:** *Very important factors considered include:* academic GPA, rigor of secondary school record, standardized test scores. *Important factors considered include:* Class rank. *Other factors considered include:* application essay, recommendation(s), extracurricular activities, interview, talent/ability. **Freshman Admission Requirements:** High school diploma is required and GED is accepted. *Academic units required:* 4 English, 4 mathematics, 3 science, (2 science labs), 2 foreign language, 1 social studies, 2 history, 2 academic electives. **Freshman Admission Statistics:** 1,179 applied, 70% admitted, 48% enrolled. **Transfer Admission Requirements:** college transcript(s), Minimum college GPA of 2.0 required. Lowest grade transferable D. **General Admission Information:** Application Fee $25. Early decision application deadline 12/15. Notification on a rolling basis, beginning on or about 8/1. Nonfall registration accepted. Admission may be deferred for a maximum of 12 months. Credit and/or placement offered for CEEB Advanced Placement tests.

COSTS AND FINANCIAL AID

Annual out-of-state tuition $17,246. Room and board $7,140. Required fees $1,366. Average book expense $1,400. **Required Forms and Deadlines:** FAFSA, Institution's own financial aid form, State aid form. **Notification of Awards:** Applicants will be notified of awards on a rolling basis beginning 3/1. **Types of Aid:** *Need-based scholarships/grants:* Federal Pell, SEOG, state scholarships/grants, the school's own gift aid. *Loans:* Subsidized Stafford, Unsubsidized Stafford, PLUS, Federal Perkins. *Student Employment:* Federal Work-Study Program available. Institutional employment available. Off-campus job opportunities are fair. **Criteria for awarding institutional aid:** *Non-need-based:* academics, athletics, leadership.

GEORGIA STATE UNIVERSITY

PO Box 4009, Atlanta, GA 30302-4009
Phone: 404-413-2500 · **Financial Aid Phone:** 404-413-2600
E-mail: admissions@gsu.edu · **CEEB Code:** 5251
Fax: 404-413-2002 · **Website:** www.gsu.edu · **ACT Code:** 826

This public school was founded in 1913. It has a 33-acre campus.

RATINGS

Admissions Selectivity Rating: 82 **Fire Safety Rating:** 80

STUDENTS AND FACULTY

Enrollment: 24,638. **Student Body:** 59% female, 41% male, 4% out-of-state, 2% international (159 countries represented). Asian 12%, African American 41%, Caucasian 29%, Hispanic 5%, Native American <1%
Retention and Graduation: 22% freshmen graduate within 4 years. **Faculty:** 1,206 full-time faculty, 91% hold PhDs, 47% are members of minority groups, 12% are women.

ACADEMICS

Degrees: bachelor's, certificate, first professional, master's, post-bachelor's certificate, post-master's certificate. **Classes:** Most classes have 20–29 students. **Majors with Highest Enrollment:** Biology/Biological Sciences; Registered Nursing/Registered Nurse; Computer Science. **Special Study Options:** Accelerated program, cooperative education program, cross-registration, distance learning, double major, dual enrollment, English as a Second Language (ESL), honors program, independent study, internships, student-designed major, study abroad, teacher certification program, Freshman Learning Communities. **Honors programs:** Students have the advantage of small classes and close contact with faculty members. Combined degree programs: BA/MA, BA/MIB in French, German or Spanish. **Disability Services:** Special programs offered to physically disabled students include note-taking services, reader services, tape recorders, tutors.

FACILITIES

Housing: Coed dorms, special housing for disabled students, special housing for international students, apartments for married students, apartments for single students, Some arrangments for visiting faculty/scholars. 100% of campus accessible to physically disabled. **Special Academic Facilities/Equipment:** Cartography Production Laboratory, Commuter Student Services, Cooperative Learning Laboratory, Economic Forecasting Center, Ernest G. Welch School of Art and Design Gallery, Instructional Technology Center, James M. Cox, Jr. Multi-Media Instructional Lab and Satellite Downlink Facility, Kopleff Recital Hall, Lanette L. Suttles Child Development Center, Language Acquisition and Resource Center, Mathematics Assistance Complex, Mathematics Interactive Learning Environment, Music Media Center, Rialto Center for the Performing Arts, Small Business Development Center, Visual Resource Center, Writing Studio. **Computers:** Students can register for classes online. Administrative functions (other than registration) can be performed online.

CAMPUS LIFE

Environment: Metropolis. **Activities:** Choral groups, concert band, dance, drama/theater, jazz band, literary magazine, music ensembles, pep band, radio station, student government, student newspaper, student-run film society, television station. 201 registered organizations, 19 honor societies, 21 religious organization. 9 fraternities, 15 sororities. **Athletics (Intercollegiate):** *Men:* baseball, basketball, cross-country, golf, soccer, tennis, track/field (outdoor), volleyball. *Women:* basketball, cross-country, golf, soccer, softball, tennis, track/field (outdoor), volleyball. **On-Campus Highlights:** Recreatoin Center, Student Housing, Aderhold Learning Center, The Rialto Center for the Performing Arts, The Student Center.

ADMISSIONS

Freshman Academic Profile: Average high school GPA 3.36. SAT Math middle 50% range 470-580. SAT Critical Reading middle 50% range 480-600. ACT middle 50% range 20-24. Minimum internet-based TOEFL 79. Minimum paper TOEFL 550. **Basis for Candidate Selection:** *Very important factors considered include:* academic GPA, rigor of secondary school record, standardized test scores. *Other factors considered include:* application essay, recommendation(s), alumni/ae relation, character/personal qualities, extracurricular activities, first generation, geographical residence, interview, level of applicant's interest, state residency, talent/ability, volunteer work, work experience. **Freshman Admission Requirements:** High school diploma is required and GED is not accepted. *Academic units required:* 4 English, 4 mathematics, 3 science, (2 science labs), 2 foreign language, 2 social studies, 1 history, 0 academic electives. **Freshman Admission Statistics:** 12,518 applied, 57% admitted, 52% enrolled. **Transfer Admission Requirements:** college transcript(s), Minimum college GPA of 2.5 required. Lowest grade transferable D. **General Admission Information:** Application Fee $50. Regular application deadline 3/1. Notification on a rolling basis, beginning on or about 10/1. Nonfall registration accepted. Admission may be deferred for a maximum of 2 terms. Credit offered for CEEB Advanced Placement tests.

COSTS AND FINANCIAL AID

Annual in-state tuition $8,112. Annual out-of-state tuition $26,322. Room and board $13,342. Required fees $2,128. Average book expense $1,200. **Required Forms and Deadlines:** FAFSA. **Notification of Awards:** Applicants will be notified of awards on a rolling basis beginning 3/30. **Types of Aid:** *Need-based scholarships/grants:* Federal Pell, SEOG, state scholarships/grants, private scholarships, the school's own gift aid. *Loans:* Direct Subsidized Stafford, Direct Unsubsidized Stafford, Direct PLUS, PLUS, Federal Perkins, state loans. *Student Employment:* Federal Work-Study Program available. Institutional employment available. Off-campus job opportunities are good. **Financial Aid Statistics:** 87% freshmen, 89% undergrads receive need-based scholarship or grant aid. 93% freshmen, 86% undergrads receive non-need-based scholarship or grant aid. 59% freshmen, 67% undergrads receive need-based self-help aid. 0% freshmen, 0% undergrads receive athletic scholarships. Criteriafor awarding institutional aid: *Non-need-based:* academics, alumni affiliation, art, athletics, minority status, music/drama, state/district residency.

GEORGIAN COURT UNIVERSITY

900 Lakewood Avenue, Lakewood, NJ 08701-2697
Phone: 732-987-2700 · **Financial Aid Phone:** 732-987-2258
E-mail: admissions@georgian.edu · **CEEB Code:** 2274
Fax: 732-987-2000 · **Website:** www.georgian.edu · **ACT Code:** 2562

This private school, affiliated with the Roman Catholic Church, was founded in 1908. It has a 156-acre campus.

RATINGS

Admissions Selectivity Rating: 60*   Fire Safety Rating: 60*

STUDENTS AND FACULTY

Enrollment: 1,422. **Student Body:** 81% female, 19% male, 5% out-of-state, 1% international (13 countries represented). Asian 2%, African American 14%, Caucasian 56%, Hispanic 11%, Native American <1%
Retention and Graduation: 70% freshmen return for sophomore year. 25% freshmen graduate within 4 years. **Faculty:** 96 full-time faculty, 90% hold PhDs, 65% are members of minority groups, 18% are women. 0% of classes are taught by teaching assistants.

ACADEMICS

Degrees: bachelor's, certificate, master's, post-bachelor's certificate, post-master's certificate. **Classes:** Most classes have 10–19 students. **Majors with Highest Enrollment:** Registered Nursing/Registered Nurse; English Language and Literature. **Special Study Options:** Accelerated program, distance learning, double major, dual enrollment, English as a Second Language (ESL), honors program, independent study, internships, liberal arts/career combination, study abroad, teacher certification program, Undergrads may take grad level classes. Co-Op Programs: Arts, Business, Health Professions, Natural Science, Social/Behavioral Science. **Honors programs:** Members of the University Honors Program receive an enriched academic curriculum featuring: Faculty chosen for their excellence as teaching-scholars; Challenging interactive classroom format; Emphasis on primary texts and sources; Rigorous scholarly writing assignments and oral presentations; Close faculty mentoring; Preference in academic advisement and course registration; A strong sense of belonging to a community of scholars; Sponsorship in funding presentations at regional and national conferences; Special advisement by faculty regarding graduate and professional school applications and prestigious fellowship opportunities; Special recognition at commencement ceremonies Combined degree programs: BS/MBA. **Disability Services:** Special programs offered to physically disabled students include note-taking services, reader services, tape recorders, tutors. **Career services:** Alumni network, alumni services, career/job search classes, career assessment, internships. Career services highlights include Career Connections, GCU's new online job board with research tools for students and alumni. Members can search for jobs, view the calendar of events and register for them, network with alumni, and upload their resumes. Employers can post jobs and internships directly online and search through resumes.

FACILITIES

Housing: women's dorms, Wellness Housing. 77% of campus accessible to physically disabled. **Special Academic Facilities/Equipment:** Art gallery, arboretum, Wellness Center, NASA ERC. **Computers:** 98% of classrooms, 77% of dorms, 100% of libraries, 50% of dining areas, 100% of student union, have wireless network access. Students can register for classes online. Administrative functions (other than registration) can be performed online.

CAMPUS LIFE

Environment: Town. **Activities:** Choral groups, concert band, dance, jazz band, literary magazine, music ensembles, student government, student newspaper, yearbook, Campus Ministries, International Student Organization, Model UN. 48 registered organizations, 18 honor societies, 1 religious organization. **Athletics (Intercollegiate):** *Women:* basketball, cross-country, lacrosse, soccer, softball, tennis, track/field (outdoor), volleyball. **On-Campus Highlights:** Arboretum, NASA Educational Resource Center, Art Gallery, Library, Wellness Center. **Environmental Initiatives:** We have included a sustainability commitment in our strategic plan. Our president was the 8th signatory of ACUPCC in New Jersey. GCU purchased Green-E certified renewable energy certificates equivalent to 100% of our projected campus electrical usage for 2009-10.

ADMISSIONS

Freshman Academic Profile: Average high school GPA 3.21. 6% in top 10% of high school class, 29% in top 25% of high school class, 66% in top 50% of high school class. 84% from public high schools. SAT Math middle 50% range 430-540. SAT Critical Reading middle 50% range 410-510. SAT Writing middle 50% range 410-500. Minimum internet-based TOEFL 79. Minimum paper TOEFL 550. **Basis for Candidate Selection:** *Very important factors considered include:* academic GPA, rigor of secondary school record. *Important factors considered include:* standardized test scores. *Other factors considered include:* Class rank, application essay, recommendation(s), alumni/ae relation, character/personal qualities, extracurricular activities, first generation, interview, level of applicant's interest, talent/ability, volunteer work, work experience. **Freshman Admission Requirements:** High school diploma is required and GED is accepted. *Academic units required:* 4 English, 2 mathematics, (1 science labs), 2 foreign language, 1 history, 6 academic electives. **Freshman Admission Statistics:** 1,290 applied, 68% admitted, 26% enrolled. **Transfer Admission Requirements:** college transcript(s), Minimum college GPA of 2.0 required. Lowest grade transferable c. **General Admission Information:** Application Fee $40. Regular application deadline 8/1. Notification on a rolling basis, beginning on or about 10/1. Nonfall registration accepted. Credit and/or placement offered for CEEB Advanced Placement tests.

COSTS AND FINANCIAL AID

Annual tuition $29,566. Room and board $10,596. Required fees $1,432. Average book expense $1,350. **Required Forms and Deadlines:** FAFSA. **Notification of Awards:** Applicants will be notified of awards on a rolling basis beginning 2/1. **Types of Aid:** *Need-based scholarships/grants:* Federal Pell, SEOG, state scholarships/grants, private scholarships, the school's own gift aid. *Loans:* Subsidized Stafford, Unsubsidized Stafford, PLUS, Federal Perkins, state loans. *Student Employment:* Federal Work-Study Program available. Institutional employment available. Highest amount earned per year from on-campus jobs $2,000. Off-campus job opportunities are good. **Financial Aid Statistics:** 98% freshmen, 95% undergrads receive need-based scholarship or grant aid. 10% freshmen, 7% undergrads receive non-need-based scholarship or grant aid. 77% freshmen, 81% undergrads receive need-based self-help aid. 3% freshmen, 2% undergrads receive athletic scholarships. 90% undergrads borrow to pay for school. Average cumulative indebtedness $28,904. **Criteria for awarding institutional aid:** *Non-need-based:* academics, alumni affiliation, art, athletics, leadership, minority status, music/drama, religious affiliation.

GETTYSBURG COLLEGE

Admissions Office, Gettysburg, PA 17325-1484
Phone: 717-337-6100 · **Financial Aid Phone:** 717-337-6611
E-mail: admiss@gettysburg.edu · **CEEB Code:** 2275
Fax: 717-337-6145 · **Website:** www.gettysburg.edu · **ACT Code:** 3580

This private school, affiliated with the Lutheran Church, was founded in 1832. It has a 200-acre campus.

RATINGS

Admissions Selectivity Rating: 93   **Fire Safety Rating:** 85

STUDENTS AND FACULTY

Enrollment: 2,435. **Student Body:** 52% female, 48% male, 73% out-of-state, 4% international (28 countries represented). Asian 2%, African American 4%, Caucasian 80%, Hispanic 5%, Native American <1% **Retention and Graduation:** 89% freshmen return for sophomore year. 80% freshmen graduate within 4 years. 30% grads go on to further study within 1 year. **Faculty:** 225 full-time faculty, 96% hold PhDs, 42% are members of minority groups, 16% are women. 0% of classes are taught by teaching assistants.

ACADEMICS

Degrees: bachelor's. **Classes:** Most classes have 10–19 students. **Majors with Highest Enrollment:** Psychology; Political Science and Government; Business/Commerce. **Special Study Options:** double major, independent study, internships, student-designed major, study abroad, teacher certification program. Combined degree programs: Optometry, Physical Therapy, Nursing. **Disability Services:** Special programs offered to physically disabled students include tape recorders. **Career services:** Alumni network, alumni services, career/job search classes, career assessment, internships, regional alumni.

FACILITIES

Housing: Coed dorms, women's dorms, fraternity/sorority housing, apartments for single students, Theme HousingSpecial interest and theme housing. **Special Academic Facilities/Equipment:** Art gallery, language lab, Child Study lab, Majestic Theatre, Sunderman Conservatory, planetarium, observatory, electron microscopes, NMR spectrometer, greenhouse,digital classrooms, wireless network, Plasma Physics labs, Science Center. **Computers:** 100% of classrooms, 100% of dorms, 100% of libraries, 100% of dining areas, 100% of student union, 90% of common outdoor areas have wireless network access. Students can register for classes online. Administrative functions (other than registration) can be performed online.

CAMPUS LIFE

Environment: Village. **Activities:** Choral groups, concert band, dance, drama/theater, jazz band, literary magazine, marching band, music ensembles, radio station, student government, student newspaper, student-run film society, symphony orchestra, television station, yearbook, Campus Ministries, International Student Organization, Model UN. 120 registered organizations, 16 honor societies, 7 religious organizations. 10 fraternities, 6 sororities. **Athletics (Intercollegiate):** *Men:* baseball, basketball, cheerleading, cross-country, football, golf, lacrosse, soccer, swimming, tennis, track/field (outdoor), track/field (indoor), wrestling. *Women:* basketball, cheerleading, cross-country, field hockey, golf,

lacrosse, soccer, softball, swimming, tennis, track/field (outdoor), track/field (indoor), volleyball. **On-Campus Highlights:** Beautiful 200-acre campus, Musselman Library, Science Center, Center for Athletics, Recreation, and Fitness, College Union Building. **Environmental Initiatives:** The Center for Athletics, Recreation, and Fitness has received LEED Gold certification; Buying 50% of electric from renewable resources; Installed water retention system under new parking lot for campus irrigation.

ADMISSIONS

Freshman Academic Profile: 70% in top 10% of high school class, 88% in top 25% of high school class, 99% in top 50% of high school class. 70% from public high schools. SAT Math middle 50% range 610-680. SAT Critical Reading middle 50% range 600-680. **Basis for Candidate Selection:** *Very important factors considered include:* Class rank, academic GPA, recommendation(s), rigor of secondary school record. *Important factors considered include:* application essay, standardized test scores, character/personal qualities, extracurricular activities, interview, talent/ability, volunteer work. *Other factors considered include:* alumni/ae relation, first generation, geographical residence, level of applicant's interest, racial/ethnic status, work experience. **Freshman Admission Requirements:** High school diploma is required and GED is accepted. *Academic units required:* 4 English, 3 mathematics, 3 science, (3 science labs), 3 foreign language, 3 social studies, 3 history. **Transfer Admission Requirements:** High school transcript, college transcript(s), essay or personal statement, standardized test scores, statement of good standing from prior institution(s). Minimum college GPA of 2.5 required. Lowest grade transferable C. **General Admission Information:** Application Fee $55. Early decision application deadline 11/15. Regular application deadline 2/1. Regular notification 4/1. Nonfall registration accepted. Admission may be deferred for a maximum of 1 year. Credit and/or placement offered for CEEB Advanced Placement tests.

COSTS AND FINANCIAL AID

Annual tuition $47,480. Room and board $11,340. Average book expense $500. **Required Forms and Deadlines:** FAFSA, CSS/Financial Aid PROFILE. **Notification of Awards:** Applicants will be notified of awards on or about 3/26. **Types of Aid:** *Need-based scholarships/grants:* Federal Pell, SEOG, state scholarships/grants, private scholarships, the school's own gift aid. *Loans:* Subsidized Stafford, Unsubsidized Stafford, PLUS, Federal Perkins, college/university loans from institutional funds. *Student Employment:* Federal Work-Study Program available. Institutional employment available. Highest amount earned per year from on-campus jobs $1,500. Off-campus job opportunities are excellent. **Financial Aid Statistics:** 96% freshmen, 96% undergrads receive need-based scholarship or grant aid. 49% freshmen, 50% undergrads receive non-need-based scholarship or grant aid. 89% freshmen, 87% undergrads receive need-based self-help aid. 0% freshmen, 0% undergrads receive athletic scholarships. 60% freshmen, 60% undergrads receive any aid. 57% undergrads borrow to pay for school. Average cumulative indebtedness $20,787. **Criteria for awarding institutional aid:** *Non-need-based:* academics, music/drama.

GIBBS COLLEGE

85 Garfield Ave., Cranston, RI 2920
Phone: 401-824-5300 · **Financial Aid Phone:** 401-824-5327
E-mail: psimonin@gbbsRI.edu
Fax: 401-824-5376 · **Website:** http://www.gibbsri.edu/

This proprietary school was founded in 1911. It has a 30-acre campus.

RATINGS

Admissions Selectivity Rating: 60*   **Fire Safety Rating:** 60*

STUDENTS AND FACULTY

Enrollment: 613. **Student Body:** 72% female, 28% male, 0% international (0 countries represented). Asian 5%, African American 6%, Caucasian 57%, Hispanic 22%, Native American <1% **Faculty:** 17 full-time faculty, 47% hold PhDs, 41% are members of minority groups, 12% are women. 0% of classes are taught by teaching assistants.

ACADEMICS

Degrees: associate, certificate, terminal associate, transfer associate. **Majors with Highest Enrollment:** Computer and Information Systems Security/Information Assurance; Criminal Justice/Law Enforcement Administration; Medical/Clinical Assistant. **Special Study Options:** internships, liberal arts/career combination. **Disability Services:** Special programs offered to physically disabled students include tape recorders, tutors. **Career services:** Alumni network, alumni services, career/job search classes, career assessment.

FACILITIES

Housing: None. 100% of campus accessible to physically disabled.

CAMPUS LIFE

Environment: City. **Activities:** student government.

ADMISSIONS

Basis for Candidate Selection: *Very important factors considered include:* interview, level of applicant's interest. *Important factors considered include:* character/personal qualities. *Other factors considered include:* recommendation(s), talent/ability. **Freshman Admission Requirements:** High school diploma is required and GED is accepted. **Transfer Admission Requirements:** High school transcript, college transcript(s), interview, Lowest grade transferable C. **General Admission Information:** Application Fee $50. Nonfall registration accepted. Admission may be deferred for a maximum of 1 year. Credit and/or placement offered for CEEB Advanced Placement tests.

COSTS AND FINANCIAL AID

Annual tuition $11,250. Required fees $450.

GLENVILLE STATE COLLEGE

200 High Street, Glenville, WV 26351
Phone: 304-462-4128
E-mail: admissions@glenville.edu · **CEEB Code:**
Fax: 304-462-8619 · **Website:** www.glenville.edu · **ACT Code:** 4522

This public school was founded in 1872.

RATINGS

Admissions Selectivity Rating: 60*   **Fire Safety Rating:** 64

STUDENTS AND FACULTY

Enrollment: 1,374. **Student Body:** 54% female, 46% male,
Retention and Graduation: 49% freshmen return for sophomore year.
Faculty: 53 full-time faculty, 30% hold PhDs, 36% are members of minority groups, 6% are women. 0% of classes are taught by teaching assistants.

ACADEMICS

Degrees: associate, bachelor's, certificate. **Special Study Options:** cooperative education program, double major, honors program, internships, student-designed major, teacher certification program. **Disability Services:** Special programs offered to physically disabled students include reader services, tape recorders, tutors.

FACILITIES

Housing: Coed dorms, special housing for disabled students, men's dorms, women's dorms, apartments for married students, apartments for single students.

CAMPUS LIFE

Environment: Rural. **Activities:** Choral groups, concert band, drama/theater, jazz band, marching band, music ensembles, student government, student newspaper, yearbook. 30 registered organizations, 2 religious organizations. 2 fraternities, 2 sororities. **Athletics (Intercollegiate):** *Men:* basketball, cross-country, football, golf, track/field (outdoor). *Women:* basketball, cross-country, golf, softball, track/field (outdoor), volleyball. **On-Campus Highlights:** High Adventure, GSC Fitness Center, Fine Arts Building, PG's Snack Bar, Pioneer Village.

ADMISSIONS

Freshman Academic Profile: Minimum paper TOEFL 550. **Basis for Candidate Selection:** *Very important factors considered include:* rigor of secondary school record, standardized test scores. *Other factors considered include:* Class rank, academic GPA, recommendation(s), talent/ability. **Freshman Admission Requirements:** High school diploma is required and GED is accepted. *Academic units required:* 4 English, 3 mathematics, 3 science, (2 science labs), 3 social studies. **Freshman Admission Statistics:** 1,132 applied, 100% admitted, 41% enrolled. **Transfer Admission Requirements:** college transcript(s), Minimum college GPA of 2.0 required. Lowest grade transferable C. **General Admission Information:** Nonfall registration accepted. Admission may be deferred for a maximum of 1 year. Credit offered for CEEB Advanced Placement tests.

COSTS AND FINANCIAL AID

Average book expense $350. **Required Forms and Deadlines:** FAFSA. **Types of Aid:** *Need-based scholarships/grants:* Federal Pell, SEOG, state scholarships/grants, private scholarships, the school's own gift aid. *Loans:* Direct Subsidized Stafford, Direct Unsubsidized Stafford, Direct PLUS, Federal Perkins. *Student Employment:* Federal Work-Study Program available. Highest amount earned per year from on-campus jobs $900. Off-campus job opportunities are fair. **Financial Aid Statistics:** 81% freshmen, 82% undergrads receive

---

need-based scholarship or grant aid. 21% freshmen, 19% undergrads receive non-need-based scholarship or grant aid. 61% freshmen, 70% undergrads receive need-based self-help aid. 1% freshmen, 3% undergrads receive athletic scholarships. 71% undergrads borrow to pay for school. **Criteria for awarding institutional aid:** *Non-need-based:* academics, art, athletics, music/drama.

GOLDEN GATE UNIVERSITY

536 Mission Street, San Francisco, CA 94105
Phone: 415-442-7800
E-mail: info@ggu.edu · **CEEB Code:** 4329
Fax: 415-442-7807 · **Website:** www.ggu.edu · **ACT Code:** 278

This private school was founded in 1901.

RATINGS

Admissions Selectivity Rating: 60*   **Fire Safety Rating:** 60*

STUDENTS AND FACULTY

Enrollment: 421. **Student Body:** 5% out-of-state, (61 countries represented). **Retention and Graduation:** 15% grads go on to further study within 1 year. 30% grads pursue business degrees. **Faculty:** 81 full-time faculty. 0% of classes are taught by teaching assistants.

ACADEMICS

Degrees: bachelor's, certificate, first professional, master's, post-bachelor's certificate, post-master's certificate. **Classes:** Most classes have 10–19 students. **Special Study Options:** Accelerated program, cooperative education program, distance learning, dual enrollment, English as a Second Language (ESL), independent study, internships, weekend college. **Disability Services:** Special programs offered to physically disabled students include tape recorders. **Career services:** Alumni network, alumni services, career/job search classes, career assessment, internships. Career services highlights include Virtual career center at www.ggucareer.com. 27/7 access to career maanagement tools and resources including self assessment, company contact databases, industry reports and job board.

FACILITIES

Housing: 100% of campus accessible to physically disabled. **Computers:** Students can register for classes online. Administrative functions (other than registration) can be performed online.

CAMPUS LIFE

Activities: student government, student newspaper. 16 registered organizations, 5 honor societies.

ADMISSIONS

Freshman Academic Profile: Average high school GPA 2.7. Minimum paper TOEFL 525. **Basis for Candidate Selection:** *Very important factors considered include:* rigor of secondary school record. *Other factors considered include:* Class rank, application essay, recommendation(s), standardized test scores. **Freshman Admission Requirements:** High school diploma is required and GED is accepted. **Transfer Admission Requirements:** college transcript(s), Minimum college GPA of 2.0 required. Lowest grade transferable C-. **General Admission Information:** Application Fee $55. Notification on a rolling basis, beginning on or about 1/15. Nonfall registration accepted. Admission may be deferred for a maximum of 12 months. Credit offered for CEEB Advanced Placement tests.

COSTS AND FINANCIAL AID

Average book expense $1,920. **Required Forms and Deadlines:** FAFSA, Institution's own financial aid form. **Types of Aid:** *Need-based scholarships/grants:* Federal Pell, SEOG, the school's own gift aid. *Loans:* Direct Subsidized Stafford, Direct Unsubsidized Stafford, Federal Perkins, state loans. *Student Employment:* Federal Work-Study Program available. Institutional employment available. Highest amount earned per year from on-campus jobs $2,480. Off-campus job opportunities are good. **Financial Aid Statistics:** 20% undergrads receive need-based scholarship or grant aid. 24% undergrads receive non-need-based scholarship or grant aid. 100% undergrads receive need-based self-help aid. 0% undergrads receive athletic scholarships. 73% undergrads borrow to pay for school. Average cumulative indebtedness $37,500. **Criteria for awarding institutional aid:** *Non-need-based:* academics, alumni affiliation, leadership.

GOLDEY-BEACOM COLLEGE

4701 Limestone Road, Wilmington, DE 19808
Phone: 302-998-8814
E-mail: admissions@gbc.edu · **CEEB Code:** 5255
Fax: 302-996-5408 · **Website:** www.goldey.gbc.edu

This private school was founded in 1886. It has a 27-acre campus.

RATINGS

Admissions Selectivity Rating: 71   Fire Safety Rating: 60*

STUDENTS AND FACULTY

Enrollment: 385. **Student Body:** 100% female, 0% male, 50% out-of-state, 8% international (60 countries represented). Asian 2%, African American 6%, Caucasian 64%, Hispanic 2%, Native American <1%.
Retention and Graduation: 5% grads go on to further study within 1 year. 1% grads pursue law degrees. 4% grads pursue business degrees. **Faculty:** 0% of classes are taught by teaching assistants.

ACADEMICS

Degrees: associate, bachelor's, master's. **Special Study Options:** Accelerated program, cooperative education program, distance learning, independent study, internships.

FACILITIES

Housing: Coed dorms, fraternity/sorority housing, apartments for single students.

CAMPUS LIFE

Environment: Village **Activities:** drama/theater, student government, student newspaper 4 religious organizations. **Athletics (Intercollegiate):** *Men:* soccer, softball. *Women:* softball.

ADMISSIONS

Freshman Academic Profile: 90% from public high schools. SAT Math middle 50% range 440-593. SAT Critical Reading middle 50% range 400-512. Minimum paper TOEFL 500. **Basis for Candidate Selection:** *Very important factors considered include:* rigor of secondary school record, standardized test scores. *Important factors considered include:* Class rank, recommendation(s). *Other factors considered include:* character/personal qualities, interview. **Freshman Admission Requirements:** High school diploma is required and GED is accepted. *Academic units required:* 4 English, 3 mathematics, 3 science. **Freshman Admission Statistics:** 689 applied, 77% admitted, 56% enrolled. **Transfer Admission Requirements:** High school transcript, college transcript(s), Minimum college GPA of 2.0 required. Lowest grade transferable 2. **General Admission Information:** Application Fee $30. Regular application deadline 8/15. Notification on a rolling basis, beginning on or about 10/1. Nonfall registration accepted. Admission may be deferred for a maximum of 12. Credit and/or placement offered for CEEB Advanced Placement tests.

COSTS AND FINANCIAL AID

Room and board $3,422. Average book expense $700. **Types of Aid:** *Need-based scholarships/grants:* Federal Pell, SEOG, state scholarships/grants, private scholarships, the school's own gift aid. *Loans:* Subsidized Stafford, Unsubsidized Stafford, PLUS, Federal Perkins, state loans, college/university loans from institutional funds. *Student Employment:* Federal Work-Study Program available. Off-campus job opportunities are excellent. **Financial Aid Statistics:**

GONZAGA UNIVERSITY

502 E. Boone Avenue, Spokane, WA 99258
Phone: 509-313-6572 · **Financial Aid Phone:** 509-313-6582
E-mail: admissions@gonzaga.edu · **CEEB Code:** 4330
Fax: 509-313-5780 · **Website:** www.gonzaga.edu · **ACT Code:** 4458

This private school, affiliated with the Roman Catholic Church and the Catholic-Jesuit Church, was founded in 1887. It has a 108-acre campus.

RATINGS

Admissions Selectivity Rating: 89   Fire Safety Rating: 93

STUDENTS AND FACULTY

Enrollment: 4,754. **Student Body:** 54% female, 46% male, 50% out-of-state, 2% international (34 countries represented). Asian 5%, African American 1%, Caucasian 73%, Hispanic 9%, Native American 1%
Retention and Graduation: 73% freshmen graduate within 4 years. 83% freshmen graduate within 6 years. **Faculty:** 427 full-time faculty, 83% hold PhDs, 44% are members of minority groups, 12% are women. 0% of classes are taught by teaching assistants.

ACADEMICS

Degrees: bachelor's, master's. **Classes:** Most classes have 20-29 students. Most lab/discussion sessions have 10-19 students. **Majors with Highest Enrollment:** Business/Commerce; Psychology; Biology/Biological Sciences. **Special Study Options:** Accelerated program, double major, dual enrollment, English as a Second Language (ESL), exchange student program (domestic), honors program, independent study, internships, study abroad, teacher certification program. **Honors programs:** Hogan Entrepreneurial Leadership Program—Immerses students in the fundamentals of creating and managing new ventures in the public and private sectors Combined degree programs: MAcc/JD, MBA/JD, BSN/MSN. **Disability Services:** Special programs offered to physically disabled students include note-taking services, reader services, tape recorders. **Career services:** Alumni network, alumni services, career/job search classes, career assessment, internships, regional alumni.

FACILITIES

Housing: Coed dorms, special housing for disabled students, men's dorms, special housing for international students, women's dorms, apartments for married students, apartments for single students, Theme Housing. 90% of campus accessible to physically disabled. **Special Academic Facilities/Equipment:** Art center, museum, language lab, TV production center, educational center, two electron microscopes. **Computers:** 75% of classrooms, 90% of dorms, 100% of libraries, 100% of student union, 75% of common outdoor areas have wireless network access. Students can register for classes online. Administrative functions (other than registration) can be performed online.

CAMPUS LIFE

Environment: City. **Activities:** Choral groups, concert band, dance, drama/theater, jazz band, literary magazine, music ensembles, pep band, radio station, student government, student newspaper, symphony orchestra, television station, yearbook, Campus Ministries. 86 registered organizations, 10 honor societies, 4 religious organizations. **Athletics (Intercollegiate):** *Men:* baseball, basketball, crew/rowing, cross-country, golf, soccer, tennis, track/field (outdoor). *Women:* basketball, crew/rowing, cross-country, golf, soccer, tennis, track/field (outdoor), volleyball. **On-Campus Highlights:** St Aloysius Cathedral, McCarthy Athletic Center, Jundt Art Museum, Bing Crosby Museum in the Crosby Student Center, The Gonzaga University Bookstore. **Environmental Initiatives:** Developing an emission inventory and a comprehensive Climate Action Plan. Formation of the Advisory Council on Stewardship and Sustainability, which reports directly to the President and has a dedicated budget. Participation in the Curriculum for the Bioregion initiative, which will expand the incorporation of sustainability across the curriculum.

ADMISSIONS

Freshman Academic Profile: Average high school GPA 3.7. 38% in top 10% of high school class, 71% in top 25% of high school class, 95% in top 50% of high school class. 68% from public high schools. SAT Math middle 50% range 560-650. SAT Critical Reading middle 50% range 540-640. ACT middle 50% range 25-29. Minimum paper TOEFL 550. **Basis for Candidate Selection:** *Very important factors considered include:* academic GPA, rigor of secondary school record, character/personal qualities, first generation. *Important factors considered include:* application essay, recommendation(s), standardized test scores, extracurricular activities, talent/ability. *Other factors considered include:* Class rank, alumni/ae relation, interview, level of applicant's interest, racial/ethnic status, volunteer work, work experience. **Freshman Admission Requirements:** High school diploma is required and GED is not accepted. *Academic units required:* 4 English, 3 mathematics, 3 science, (3 science labs), 3 foreign language, 2 social studies, 2 history, 2 academic electives. **Freshman Admission Statistics:** 7,162 applied, 68% admitted, 22% enrolled. **Transfer Admission Requirements:** college transcript(s), essay or personal statement, statement of good standing from prior institution(s). Minimum college GPA of 2.7 required. Lowest grade transferable C. **General Admission Information:** Application Fee $50. Regular application deadline 2/1. Regular notification 3/15. Nonfall registration accepted. Admission may be deferred for a maximum of 1 year. Credit and/or placement offered for CEEB Advanced Placement tests.

COSTS AND FINANCIAL AID

Annual tuition $37,480. Room and board $10,835. Required fees $510. Average book expense $1,092. **Required Forms and Deadlines:** FAFSA. **Notification of Awards:** Applicants will be notified of awards on a rolling basis beginning 3/1. **Types of Aid:** *Need-based scholarships/grants:* Federal Pell, SEOG, state scholarships/grants, private scholarships, the school's own gift aid, United Negro College Fund, Federal Nursing Scholarships. *Loans:* Subsidized Stafford, Unsubsidized Stafford, PLUS, Federal Perkins, Federal Nursing, state loans, college/university loans from institutional funds. *Student Employment:* Federal Work-Study Program available. Institutional employment available. Off-campus job opportunities are excellent. **Financial Aid Statistics:** 100% freshmen, 100% undergrads receive need-based scholarship or grant aid. 22% freshmen, 19% undergrads receive non-need-based scholarship or grant aid. 65% freshmen, 69% undergrads receive need-based self-help aid. 2% freshmen, 4% undergrads receive athletic scholarships. 99% freshmen, 98% undergrads receive any aid. 60% undergrads borrow to pay for school. Average cumulative indebtedness $25,753. **Criteria for awarding institutional aid:** *Non-need-based:* academics, alumni affiliation, athletics, leadership, minority status, music/drama.

See page 1058.

GORDON COLLEGE

255 Grapevine Road, Wenham, MA 01984-1899
Phone: 978-867-4218 · **Financial Aid Phone:** 978-867-4246
E-mail: admissions@gordon.edu · **CEEB Code:** 3417
Fax: 978-867-4682 · **Website:** www.gordon.edu · **ACT Code:** 1838

This private school, affiliated with the Protestant Church, was founded in 1889. It has a 500-acre campus.

RATINGS

Admissions Selectivity Rating: 87   **Fire Safety Rating:** 89

STUDENTS AND FACULTY

Enrollment: 1,704. **Student Body:** 61% female, 39% male, 66% out-of-state, 7% international (39 countries represented). Asian 4%, African American 4%, Caucasian 75%, Hispanic 7%, Native American <1%
Retention and Graduation: 81% freshmen return for sophomore year. 61% freshmen graduate within 4 years. 71% freshmen graduate within 6 years. 37% grads go on to further study within 1 year. 7% grads pursue arts and sciences degrees. 4% grads pursue law degrees. 4% grads pursue business degrees. 5% grads pursue medical degrees. **Faculty:** 97 full-time faculty, 88% hold PhDs, 36% are members of minority groups, 15% are women. 0% of classes are taught by teaching assistants.

ACADEMICS

Degrees: bachelor's, master's. **Classes:** Most classes have 10–19 students. Most lab/discussion sessions have 10–19 students. **Majors with Highest Enrollment:** English Language and Literature; Psychology; Business/Commerce. **Special Study Options:** cooperative education program, cross-registration, double major, honors program, independent study, internships, liberal arts/career combination, student-designed major, study abroad, teacher certification program, Gordon-in-Boston Urban Semester; Gordon-in-France; Italian Semester in Orvieto, Italy; Oregon Extension; Outdoor Education Immersion Semester; LaVida Wilderness Expedition; Co-Op Programs: Arts, Business, Computer Science, Education, Engineering, Health Professions, Humanities, Natural Science, Social/Behavioral Science. **Honors programs:** The Jerusalem and Athens Forum is a new interdisciplinary honors program at Gordon College, beginning in the academic year 2004-05. Through a variety of program components, but principally a great books course in the history of Christian thought and literature, the program strives to help students reflect on the relationship between faith and intellect, deepen their own sense of vocation, and awaken their capacities for intellectual and moral leadership. (Description taken from www.gordon.edu/jaf) The Kenneth L. Pike Honors Program provides exceptional students with an opportunity to meet unique academic goals not possible under existing Gordon programs by designing individualized, disciplined and chalenging interdisciplinary academic experiences. (Description taken from the Gordon College Academic Catalog) Combined degree programs: BA/MA, 2-2 allied health sciences prog with Thomas Jeffer. **Disability Services:** Special programs offered to physically disabled students include tape recorders, tutors. **Career services:** Alumni network, career/job search classes, career assessment, internships. Career services highlights include the Harmeling Physical Therapy Clinic located on campus, which provides Movement Science students hands-on experience.

FACILITIES

Housing: Coed dorms, special housing for disabled students, men's dorms, apartments for married students, apartments for single students, Theme Housing, International hall, mentoring hall. Also Gordon's dorms are coed by floors and/or wings. Men and women do not live together or share facilities. 99% of campus accessible to physically disabled. **Special Academic Facilities/Equipment:** Barrington Center for the Arts; Phillips Music Center; Center for Balance and Mobility; an electron microscope; a gene sequencer; papers of British Statesman/Reformer, William Wilberforce; East-West Institute; Center for Student Leadership; Center for Christian Studies; international office for Christians in the Visual Arts (CIVA). **Computers:** Administrative functions (other than registration) can be performed online.

CAMPUS LIFE

Environment: Village. **Activities:** Choral groups, concert band, drama/theater, jazz band, literary magazine, music ensembles, musical theater, student government, student newspaper, student-run film society, symphony orchestra, yearbook, Campus Ministries, International Student Organization, Model UN. 35 registered organizations, 17 honor societies, 15 religious organizations. **Athletics (Intercollegiate):** *Men:* baseball, basketball, cross-country, lacrosse, soccer, swimming, tennis, track/field (outdoor), track/field (indoor). *Women:* basketball, cross-country, field hockey, lacrosse, soccer, softball, swimming, tennis, track/field (outdoor), track/field (indoor), volleyball. **On-Campus Highlights:** Gillies Lounge/Claymore Café, Hiking/biking/cross country ski trails, Bennett Athletic and Recreation Center, Barrington Center for the Arts, Canoeing/swimming ponds, Gordon's campus had many lakes and trails for use by the student body. On campus recreational activities are regularly planned and/or available. **Environmental Initiatives:** Winner of MA College/University Recycling Award 2008; Green Chemistry practice and teaching; Frost Hall Wetland Restoration Project, Conservation—native plant garden, wetland restoration, 400 acres of conservation land with trails.

ADMISSIONS

Freshman Academic Profile: Average high school GPA 3.6. 36% in top 10% of high school class, 67% in top 25% of high school class, 91% in top 50% of high school class. 61% from public high schools. SAT Math middle 50% range 510-640. SAT Critical Reading middle 50% range 520-640. SAT Writing middle 50% range 520-630. ACT middle 50% range 23-29. Minimum internet-based TOEFL 85. **Basis for Candidate Selection:** *Very important factors considered include:* application essay, academic GPA, recommendation(s), rigor of secondary school record, standardized test scores, character/personal qualities, extracurricular activities, interview, religious affiliation/commitment. *Important factors considered include:* Class rank, talent/ability. *Other factors considered include:* alumni/ae relation, racial/ethnic status, volunteer work, work experience. **Freshman Admission Requirements:** High school diploma is required and GED is accepted. *Academic units required:* 4 English, 2 mathematics, 2 science, (1 science labs), 2 foreign language, 2 social studies, 5 academic electives. **Freshman Admission Statistics:** 1,892 applied, 88% admitted, 24% enrolled. **Transfer Admission Requirements:** college transcript(s), essay or personal statement, interview, statement of good standing from prior institution(s). Minimum college GPA of 2.0 required. Lowest grade transferable C. **General Admission Information:** Application Fee $50. Early decision application deadline 11/15. Notification on a rolling basis, beginning on or about 12/15. Nonfall registration accepted. Admission may be deferred for a maximum of 12 months. Credit offered for CEEB Advanced Placement tests.

COSTS AND FINANCIAL AID

Average book expense $800. **Required Forms and Deadlines:** FAFSA. **Notification of Awards:** Applicants will be notified of awards on a rolling basis beginning 4/15. **Types of Aid:** *Need-based scholarships/grants:* Federal Pell, SEOG, state scholarships/grants, private scholarships, the school's own gift aid. *Loans:* Subsidized Stafford, Unsubsidized Stafford, PLUS, Federal Perkins, state loans, college/university loans from institutional funds. *Student Employment:* Federal Work-Study Program available. Highest amount earned per year from on-campus jobs $1,500. Off-campus job opportunities are good. **Financial Aid Statistics:** 100% freshmen, 100% undergrads receive need-based scholarship or grant aid. 13% freshmen, 11% undergrads receive non-need-based scholarship or grant aid. 80% freshmen, 86% undergrads receive need-based self-help aid. 0% freshmen, 0% undergrads receive athletic scholarships. 100% freshmen, 97% undergrads receive any aid. 80% undergrads borrow to pay for school. Average cumulative indebtedness $25,130. **Criteria for awarding institutional aid:** *Non-need-based:* academics, alumni affiliation, art, leadership, minority status, music/drama, religious affiliation.

GOSHEN COLLEGE

1700 South Main Street, Goshen, IN 46526-4794
Phone: 574-535-7535 · **Financial Aid Phone:** 574-535-7525
E-mail: admission@goshen.edu · **CEEB Code:** 1251
Fax: 574-535-7609 · **Website:** www.goshen.edu · **ACT Code:** 1196

This private school, affiliated with the Mennonite Church, was founded in 1894. It has a 135-acre campus.

RATINGS

Admissions Selectivity Rating: 89   **Fire Safety Rating:** 96

STUDENTS AND FACULTY

Enrollment: 750. **Student Body:** 58% female, 42% male, 48% out-of-state, 9% international (25 countries represented). Asian 2%, African American 4%, Caucasian 68%, Hispanic 13%, Native American <1%
Retention and Graduation: 56% freshman graduate within 4 years. 72% freshmen graduate within 6 years. 15% grads go on to further study within 1 year. 13% grads pursue arts and sciences degrees. 3% grads pursue law degrees. 1% grads pursue business degrees. 3% grads pursue medical degrees. **Faculty:** 65 full-time faculty, 66% hold PhDs, 49% are members of minority groups, 9% are women. 0% of classes are taught by teaching assistants.

ACADEMICS

Degrees: bachelor's, certificate, master's. **Classes:** Most classes have 10–19 students. Most lab/discussion sessions have 10–19 students. **Majors with Highest Enrollment:** Biology/Biological Sciences; Registered Nursing/Registered Nurse; Music. **Special Study Options:** cross-registration, double major, dual enrollment, independent study, internships, liberal arts/career combination, student-designed major, study abroad, teacher certification program, Adult degree completion program (one evening per week, concentrated study). Combined degree programs: BA/BS Eng. **Disability Services:** Special programs offered to physically disabled students include note-taking services, reader services, tape recorders, tutors. **Career services:** Alumni network, career/job search classes, internships, regional alumni.

FACILITIES

Housing: Coed dorms, special housing for disabled students, men's dorms, women's dorms, apartments for married students, apartments for single students, Wellness Housing. 88% of campus accessible to physically disabled. **Special Academic Facilities/Equipment:** X-ray precision lab, lab kindergarten, Mennonite Historical Library. **Computers:** 100% of classrooms, 25% of dorms, 80% of libraries, 75% of dining areas, 100% of student union, have wireless network access. Students can register for classes online. Administrative functions (other than registration) can be performed online.

CAMPUS LIFE

Environment: Town. **Activities:** Choral groups, concert band, drama/theater, jazz band, music ensembles, musical theater, opera, radio station, student government, student newspaper, student-run film society, symphony orchestra, yearbook, Campus Ministries, International Student Organization. 21 registered organizations, 4 religious organizations. **Athletics (Intercollegiate):** *Men:* baseball, basketball, cross-country, golf, soccer, tennis, track/field (outdoor), track/field (indoor). *Women:* basketball, cross-country, soccer, softball, tennis, track/field (outdoor), track/field (indoor), volleyball. **On-Campus Highlights:** Music Center, Gingerich Rec-Fitness Center, Science Building, Residential Halls Connector, Good Library. **Environmental Initiatives:** Built the first Platinum LEED Certified facility in Indiana at our Merry Lea Environmental Center. www.goshen.edu/merrylea Signing the President's Climate Commitment and the formation of the Ecological Stewardship Committee Have reduced campus wide gas use by 31% and electric use by 17% over the last six years during a time when actual square footage of buildings increased by 20%.

ADMISSIONS

Freshman Academic Profile: Average high school GPA 3.5. 38% in top 10% of high school class, 63% in top 25% of high school class, 85% in top 50% of high school class. 90% from public high schools. SAT Math middle 50% range 500-635. SAT Critical Reading middle 50% range 475-620. SAT Writing middle 50% range 450-610. ACT middle 50% range 21-28. Minimum internet-based TOEFL 79. Minimum paper TOEFL 550. **Basis for Candidate Selection:** *Very important factors considered include:* academic GPA, rigor of secondary school record, standardized test scores. *Important factors considered include:* Class rank, recommendation(s), character/personal qualities, interview. *Other factors considered include:* application essay, alumni/ae relation, extracurricular activities, level of applicant's interest, religious affiliation/commitment, talent/ability, volunteer work, work experience. **Freshman Admission Requirements:** High school diploma is required and GED is accepted. *Academic units required:* 4 English, 2 mathematics, 2 science, 2 foreign language, 2 social stud-

ies, 2 history. **Freshman Admission Statistics:** 900 applied, 54% admitted, 33% enrolled. **Transfer Admission Requirements:** college transcript(s), essay or personal statement, statement of good standing from prior institution(s). Lowest grade transferable C. **General Admission Information:** Application Fee $25. Regular application deadline 8/1. Notification on a rolling basis, beginning on or about 9/15. Nonfall registration accepted. Admission may be deferred for a maximum of 1 year. Credit and/or placement offered for CEEB Advanced Placement tests.

COSTS AND FINANCIAL AID

Annual tuition $29,700. Room and board $9,700. Required fees $0. Average book expense $900. **Required Forms and Deadlines:** FAFSA. **Notification of Awards:** Applicants will be notified of awards on a rolling basis beginning 3/1. **Types of Aid:** *Need-based scholarships/grants:* Federal Pell, SEOG, state scholarships/grants, private scholarships, the school's own gift aid. *Loans:* Direct Subsidized Stafford, Direct Unsubsidized Stafford, Direct PLUS, Federal Perkins, Federal Nursing, college/university loans from institutional funds. *Student Employment:* Federal Work-Study Program available. Institutional employment available. Highest amount earned per year from on-campus jobs $1,001. Off-campus job opportunities are poor. **Financial Aid Statistics:** 100% freshmen, 98% undergrads receive need-based scholarship or grant aid. 20% freshmen, 16% undergrads receive non-need-based scholarship or grant aid. 77% freshmen, 81% undergrads receive need-based self-help aid. 5% freshmen, 9% undergrads receive athletic scholarships. 100% freshmen, 99% undergrads receive any aid. 73% undergrads borrow to pay for school. Average cumulative indebtedness $23,270. **Criteria for awarding institutional aid:** *Non-need-based:* academics, art, athletics, leadership, music/drama.

GOUCHER COLLEGE

1021 Dulaney Valley Road, Baltimore, MD 21204-2794
Phone: 410-337-6100 · **Financial Aid Phone:** 410-337-6141
E-mail: admissions@goucher.edu · **CEEB Code:** 5257
Fax: 410-337-6354 · **Website:** www.goucher.edu · **ACT Code:** 1696

This private school was founded in 1885. It has a 287-acre campus.

RATINGS

Admissions Selectivity Rating: 85   **Fire Safety Rating:** 90

STUDENTS AND FACULTY

Enrollment: 1,463. **Student Body:** 67% female, 33% male, 73% out-of-state, 2% international (16 countries represented). Asian 3%, African American 10%, Caucasian 67%, Hispanic 8%, Native American <1%
Retention and Graduation: 77% freshmen return for sophomore year. 51% freshmen graduate within 4 years. 63% freshmen graduate within 6 years. 25% grads go on to further study within 1 year. **Faculty:** 136 full-time faculty, 93% hold PhDs, 58% are members of minority groups, 17% are women. 0% of classes are taught by teaching assistants.

ACADEMICS

Degrees: bachelor's, master's, post-bachelor's certificate. **Classes:** Most classes have 10–19 students. **Majors with Highest Enrollment:** Psychology; English Language and Literature; Business Administration and Management. **Special Study Options:** cross-registration, distance learning, double major, dual enrollment, independent study, internships, student-designed major, study abroad, teacher certification program. Combined degree programs: BA/MEng. **Career services:** Alumni network, alumni services, career assessment, internships. Goucher has been linking liberal arts education with internships for more than 75 years. Through our internship program, we help students explore career paths, enhance skills, and experience the world of work.

FACILITIES

Housing: Coed dorms, special housing for disabled students, women's dorms, apartments for single students, Wellness Housing, Theme Housing. **Special Academic Facilities/Equipment:** The Athenaeum is a 103,000-square-foot building which is open 24 hours a day and features a new, technologically superior library; a spacious open forum for performances, public discussions, and other events; a café; art gallery; a center for community service and multicultural affairs programming; and spaces for exercise, conversation, and quiet reflection and relaxation. Goucher, in collaboration with the architecture firm RMJM, approached every aspect of the Athenaeum project with an eye toward sustainable design strategies, and the project is in the process of applying for Silver certification from the Leadership in Energy and Environmental Design (LEED) Green-Building Rating System. The Silber Art Gallery in the Athenaeum provides a suitably secure gallery dedicated solely to the exhibition of art, both from the Goucher collection and from contemporary artists and collectors outside the campus. The 1,000-square-foot gallery is the new home to Goucher's permanent collection and its critically acclaimed program of contemporary art exhibitions. In addition to enabling us to display selections from the college's permanent collection, the gallery hosts a range of programming, from the traditional to the experimental, featuring the work of students, emerging artists, and established names alike. Additionally, Goucher has the Rosenberg Art Gallery and the Scientific Visualization Lab. **Computers:** 95% of classrooms, 40% of dorms, 100% of libraries, 100% of dining areas, 100% of student union, 80% of common outdoor areas have wireless network access. Students can register for classes online. Administrative functions (other than registration) can be performed online.

CAMPUS LIFE

Environment: City. **Activities:** Choral groups, dance, drama/theater, jazz band, literary magazine, music ensembles, musical theater, opera, radio station, student government, student newspaper, student-run film society, symphony orchestra, television station, yearbook, Campus Ministries, International Student Organization, Model UN. 60 registered organizations, 1 honor society, 8 religious organizations. **Athletics (Intercollegiate):** *Men:* basketball, cross-country, lacrosse, soccer, swimming, tennis, track/field (outdoor), track/field (indoor). *Women:* basketball, cross-country, equestrian sports, field hockey, lacrosse, soccer, swimming, tennis, track/field (outdoor), track/field (indoor), volleyball. **On-Campus Highlights:** The Library at the Athenaeum, Alice's Café, Sports and Recreation Center, Pearlstone Café, Gopher Hole. **Environmental Initiatives:** Our newest building, the Athenaeum, was awarded Gold certification from the Leadership in Energy and Environmental Design (LEED) rating system, the national recognized standard for measuring a building's environmental sustainability, and committing that future buildings and renovations will also be LEED certified. Goucher, in collaboration with the architecture firm RMJM, approached every aspect of the Athenaeum project with an eye toward sustainable design strategies. Goucher has completed its Greenhouse Gas Emissions Inventory (and subsequent progress reports) and Climate Action Plan, as required by the American College and University Presidents Climate Commitment. In the fall 2010 semester, Goucher College launched an interdisciplinary environmental studies major. The program includes two concentrations-environmental science or environment and society-to give students a firm background in all facets of environmental studies. The major is designed so that all the students will be able to apply principles from the social sciences and the natural sciences to address complex environmental problems," said German Mora, the Robert and Jane Meyerhoff Associate Professor of Environmental Science and the chair of the environmental studies program.

ADMISSIONS

Freshman Academic Profile: Average high school GPA 3.17. 27.39% in top 10% of high school class, 52.87% in top 25% of high school class, 80.89% in top 50% of high school class. 90% from public high schools. SAT Math middle 50% range 500-635. SAT Critical Reading middle 50% range 475-620. SAT Writing middle 50% range 450-610. ACT middle 50% range 21-28. Minimum internet-based TOEFL 79. Minimum paper TOEFL 550. **Basis for Candidate Selection:** *Very important factors considered include:* academic GPA, rigor of secondary school record, standardized test scores. *Important factors considered include:* Class rank, recommendation(s), character/personal qualities, interview. *Other factors considered include:* application essay, alumni/ae relation, extracurricular activities, level of applicant's interest, religious affiliation/commitment, talent/ability, volunteer work, work experience. **Freshman Admission Requirements:** High school diploma is required and GED is accepted. *Academic units required:* 4 English, 2 mathematics, 2 science, 2 foreign language, 2 social studies, 2 history. **Freshman Admission Statistics:** 900 applied, 54% admitted, 33% enrolled. **Transfer Admission Requirements:** college transcript(s), essay or personal statement, statement of good standing from prior institution(s). Lowest grade transferable C. **General Admission Information:** Application Fee $25. Regular application deadline 8/1. Notification on a rolling basis, beginning on or about 9/15. Nonfall registration accepted. Admission may be deferred for a maximum of 1 year. Credit and/or placement offered for CEEB Advanced Placement tests.

COSTS AND FINANCIAL AID

Annual tuition $29,700. Room and board $9,700. Required fees $0. Average book expense $900. **Required Forms and Deadlines:** FAFSA. **Notification of Awards:** Applicants will be notified of awards on a rolling basis beginning 3/1. **Types of Aid:** *Need-based scholarships/grants:* Federal Pell, SEOG, state scholarships/grants, private scholarships, the school's own gift aid. *Loans:* Direct Subsidized Stafford, Direct Unsubsidized Stafford, Direct PLUS, Federal Perkins, Federal Nursing, college/university loans from institutional funds. *Student Employment:* Federal Work-Study Program available. Institutional

employment available. Highest amount earned per year from on-campus jobs $1,001. Off-campus job opportunities are poor. **Financial Aid Statistics:** 100% freshmen, 98% undergrads receive need-based scholarship or grant aid. 20% freshmen, 16% undergrads receive non-need-based scholarship or grant aid. 77% freshmen, 81% undergrads receive need-based self-help aid. 5% freshmen, 9% undergrads receive athletic scholarships. 100% freshmen, 99% undergrads receive any aid. 73% undergrads borrow to pay for school. Average cumulative indebtedness $23,270. **Criteria for awarding institutional aid:** *Non-need-based:* academics, art, athletics, leadership, music/drama.

GOVERNORS STATE UNIVERSITY

1 University Parkway, University Park, IL 60484
Phone: 708-534-4490 · **Financial Aid Phone:** 708-534-4480
E-mail: gsunow@govst.edu
Fax: 708-534-1640 · **Website:** www.govst.edu

This public school was founded in 1969. It has a 720-acre campus.

RATINGS

Admissions Selectivity Rating: 60*   **Fire Safety Rating:** 60*

STUDENTS AND FACULTY

Enrollment: 3,103. **Student Body:** 68% female, 32% male, 3% out-of-state, 0% international (17 countries represented). Asian 2%, African American 37%, Caucasian 44%, Hispanic 10%, Native American <1%
Retention and Graduation: 34% grads go on to further study within 1 year. 17% grads pursue arts and sciences degrees. 1% grads pursue law degrees. 16% grads pursue business degrees. **Faculty:** 211 full-time faculty, 59% hold PhDs, 59% are members of minority groups, 37% are women. 0% of classes are taught by teaching assistants.

ACADEMICS

Degrees: bachelor's, master's, post-master's certificate. **Majors with Highest Enrollment:** Communication and Media Studies; Elementary Education and Teaching; Business/Commerce. **Special Study Options:** cross-registration, distance learning, dual enrollment, external degree program, honors program, independent study, internships, student-designed major, study abroad, teacher certification program. **Disability Services:** Special programs offered to physically disabled students include note-taking services, reader services, tape recorders, tutors. **Career services:** Alumni network, alumni services, career/job search classes, career assessment, internships.

FACILITIES

Housing: 99% of campus accessible to physically disabled. **Special Academic Facilities/Equipment:** Manilow Sculpture Park. **Computers:** Students can register for classes online. Administrative functions (other than registration) can be performed online.

CAMPUS LIFE

Environment: Village. **Activities:** drama/theater, literary magazine, student government, student newspaper, student-run film society 7 honor societies.

ADMISSIONS

Freshman Academic Profile: 0% from public high schools. **Transfer Admission Requirements:** college transcript(s), statement of good standing from prior institution(s). Minimum college GPA of 2.0 required. Lowest grade transferable C. **General Admission Information:** Nonfall registration not accepted.

COSTS AND FINANCIAL AID

Types of Aid: *Need-based scholarships/grants:* Federal Pell, SEOG, state scholarships/grants, private scholarships, the school's own gift aid, Federal Nursing Scholarships. *Loans:* Direct Subsidized Stafford, Federal Perkins, Federal Nursing, state loans, college/university loans from institutional funds. *Student Employment:* Federal Work-Study Program available. Institutional employment available. **Criteria for awarding institutional aid:** *Non-need-based:* academics.

GRACE BIBLE COLLEGE

1011 Aldon Street SW, Grand Rapids, MI 49509-1921
Phone: 616-538-2330
E-mail: enrollment@gbcol.edu
Fax: 616-538-0599 • **Website:** www.gbcol.edu

This is a private school.

RATINGS

Admissions Selectivity Rating: 65   **Fire Safety Rating:** 60*

STUDENTS AND FACULTY

Enrollment: 153. **Student Body:** 52% female, 48% male,
Retention and Graduation: 45% freshmen return for sophomore year. 13% freshmen graduate within 4 years. 31% freshmen graduate within 6 years.
Faculty:

ACADEMICS

Degrees: associate, bachelor's.

CAMPUS LIFE

Environment: Village.

ADMISSIONS

Basis for Candidate Selection: *Very important factors considered include:* application essay, rigor of secondary school record, standardized test scores. *Important factors considered include:* Class rank, recommendation(s), character/personal qualities, religious affiliation/commitment. *Other factors considered include:* extracurricular activities, talent/ability, volunteer work, work experience. **Freshman Admission Requirements:** High school diploma is required and GED is accepted. **Freshman Admission Statistics:** 166 applied, 43% admitted, 56% enrolled. **General Admission Information:**

COSTS AND FINANCIAL AID

Types of Aid: *Need-based scholarships/grants:* Federal Pell, SEOG, state scholarships/grants, private scholarships, the school's own gift aid. *Loans:* Subsidized Stafford, Unsubsidized Stafford, PLUS, state loans. **Criteria for awarding institutional aid:** *Non-need-based:* academics.

GRACE COLLEGE AND SEMINARY

200 Seminary Drive, Winona Lake, IN 46590
Phone: 800-544-7223 • **Financial Aid Phone:** 574-372-5100
E-mail: enroll@grace.edu • **CEEB Code:** 1252
Fax: 574-372-5120 • **Website:** www.grace.edu • **ACT Code:** 1198

This private school was founded in 1948. It has a 150-acre campus.

RATINGS

Admissions Selectivity Rating: 82   **Fire Safety Rating:** 74

STUDENTS AND FACULTY

Enrollment: 1,507. **Student Body:** 55% female, 45% male, 28% out-of-state, 1% international (9 countries represented). Asian 1%, African American 5%, Caucasian 76%, Hispanic 4%, Native American <1%
Retention and Graduation: 81% freshmen return for sophomore year. 62% freshmen graduate within 4 years. 65% freshmen graduate within 6 years.
Faculty: 44 full-time faculty, 55% hold PhDs, 32% are members of minority groups, 2% are women. 0% of classes are taught by teaching assistants.

ACADEMICS

Degrees: associate, bachelor's, certificate, diploma, master's. **Classes:** Most classes have 10–19 students. Most lab/discussion sessions have 10–19 students. **Majors with Highest Enrollment:** Elementary Education and Teaching; Business/Commerce; Psychology. **Special Study Options:** cooperative education program, cross-registration, distance learning, double major, dual enrollment, exchange student program (domestic), honors program, independent study, internships, liberal arts/career combination, study abroad, teacher certification program, Degree completion. **Disability Services:** Special programs offered to physically disabled students include note-taking services, reader services, tape recorders, tutors. **Career services:** career assessment.

FACILITIES

Housing: men's dorms, women's dorms, apartments for single students. 85% of campus accessible to physically disabled. **Special Academic Facilities/Equipment:** Reneker Museum of Winona History. **Computers:** 100% of classrooms,

100% of dorms, 100% of libraries, 100% of dining areas, 100% of student union, 33% of common outdoor areas have wireless network access. Students can register for classes online. Administrative functions (other than registration) can be performed online.

CAMPUS LIFE

Environment: Village. **Activities:** Choral groups, concert band, drama/theater, music ensembles, musical theater, opera, pep band, student government, student newspaper, symphony orchestra, yearbook, Campus Ministries. 9 registered organizations, 1 honor society, 8 religious organizations. **Athletics (Intercollegiate):** *Men:* baseball, basketball, cheerleading, cross-country, golf, soccer, tennis, track/field (outdoor). *Women:* basketball, cheerleading, cross-country, soccer, softball, tennis, track/field (outdoor), volleyball. **On-Campus Highlights:** Gordon Recreation Center, Tree of Life Coffee shop, Westminster Grille, Orthopedic Capital Center.

ADMISSIONS

Freshman Academic Profile: Average high school GPA 3.5. 21% in top 10% of high school class, 48% in top 25% of high school class, 81% in top 50% of high school class. 71% from public high schools. SAT Math middle 50% range 470-590. SAT Critical Reading middle 50% range 460-580. ACT middle 50% range 21-27. **Basis for Candidate Selection:** *Very important factors considered include:* application essay, recommendation(s), rigor of secondary school record, standardized test scores, religious affiliation/commitment. *Important factors considered include:* academic GPA, character/personal qualities. *Other factors considered include:* Class rank, alumni/ae relation, extracurricular activities, interview, talent/ability. **Freshman Admission Requirements:** High school diploma is required and GED is accepted. **Freshman Admission Statistics:** 3,517 applied, 80% admitted, 26% enrolled. **Transfer Admission Requirements:** college transcript(s), essay or personal statement, standardized test scores, Minimum college GPA of 2.0 required. Lowest grade transferable C-. **General Admission Information:** Application Fee $20. Regular application deadline 8/15. Notification on a rolling basis, beginning on or about 9/1. Nonfall registration accepted. Admission may be deferred for a maximum of 1 semester. Credit offered for CEEB Advanced Placement tests.

COSTS AND FINANCIAL AID

Annual tuition $24,670. Room and board $6,030. Average book expense $1,000. **Required Forms and Deadlines:** FAFSA. **Notification of Awards:** Applicants will be notified of awards on a rolling basis beginning 3/1. **Types of Aid:** *Need-based scholarships/grants:* Federal Pell, SEOG, state scholarships/grants, private scholarships, the school's own gift aid. *Loans:* Subsidized Stafford, Unsubsidized Stafford, PLUS, Federal Perkins, Alternative Educational Loan Program. *Student Employment:* Federal Work-Study Program available. Institutional employment available. Off-campus job opportunities are good. **Financial Aid Statistics:** 89% freshmen, 89% undergrads receive need-based scholarship or grant aid. 99% freshmen, 84% undergrads receive non-need-based scholarship or grant aid. 77% freshmen, 75% undergrads receive need-based self-help aid. 0% freshmen, 0% undergrads receive athletic scholarships. Criteria for awarding institutional aid: *Non-need-based:* academics, art, athletics, leadership, music/drama.

GRACE UNIVERSITY

1311 S 9th St, Omaha, NE 68108
Phone: 402-449-2831
E-mail: admissions@graceu.com • **CEEB Code:**
Fax: 402-341-9587 • **Website:** www.graceuniversity.com • **ACT Code:** 2454

This private school, affiliated with the Christian (Nondenominational) Church, was founded in 1943. It has a 20-acre campus.

RATINGS

Admissions Selectivity Rating: 60*   **Fire Safety Rating:** 69

STUDENTS AND FACULTY

Enrollment: 427. **Student Body:** 57% female, 43% male, 60% out-of-state, 1% international (7 countries represented). Asian 0%, African American 5%, Caucasian 99%, Hispanic 2%, Native American <1%
Faculty: 25 full-time faculty, 100% hold PhDs, 28% are members of minority groups, 8% are women. 0% of classes are taught by teaching assistants.

ACADEMICS

Degrees: associate, bachelor's, certificate, master's, terminal associate, transfer associate. **Majors with Highest Enrollment:** Education; Bible/Biblical Studies; Youth Ministry. **Special Study Options:** Accelerated program, cooperative education program, distance learning, double major, dual enrollment, independent study, student-designed major, study abroad, teacher certification program. **Disability Services:** Special programs offered to physically disabled students include note-taking services, tape recorders. **Career services:** career assessment, internships

FACILITIES

Housing: men's dorms, women's dorms, apartments for married students. 100% of campus accessible to physically disabled. **Computers:** Administrative functions (other than registration) can be performed online.

CAMPUS LIFE

Environment: Metropolis. **Activities:** Choral groups, concert band, drama/theater, music ensembles, musical theater, pep band, radio station, student government, student newspaper, yearbook. 6 registered organizations, 1 religious organization. **Athletics (Intercollegiate):** *Men:* basketball, soccer. *Women:* basketball, volleyball. **On-Campus Highlights:** Dirk Lounge, Health and Fitness Center, Dorms, Dining Commons, Royal's Court.

ADMISSIONS

Freshman Academic Profile: Minimum paper TOEFL 550. **Basis for Candidate Selection:** *Very important factors considered include:* application essay, recommendation(s), rigor of secondary school record, religious affiliation/commitment. *Important factors considered include:* Class rank, standardized test scores, character/personal qualities. *Other factors considered include:* alumni/ae relation, extracurricular activities, interview, talent/ability, volunteer work, work experience. **Freshman Admission Requirements:** High school diploma is required and GED is accepted. **Transfer Admission Requirements:** High school transcript, college transcript(s), essay or personal statement, Minimum college GPA of 2.0 required. Lowest grade transferable C. **General Admission Information:** Application Fee $35. Nonfall registration accepted. Admission may be deferred for a maximum of 1 year. Credit offered for CEEB Advanced Placement tests.

COSTS AND FINANCIAL AID

Required Forms and Deadlines: FAFSA, Institution's own financial aid form. **Notification of Awards:** Applicants will be notified of awards on or about 4/1. **Types of Aid:** *Need-based scholarships/grants:* Federal Pell, SEOG, state scholarships/grants, private scholarships, the school's own gift aid, United Negro College Fund. *Loans:* Subsidized Stafford, Unsubsidized Stafford, PLUS, Alternative Loans. *Student Employment:* Federal Work-Study Program available. Institutional employment available. Highest amount earned per year from on-campus jobs $3,750. Off-campus job opportunities are excellent. **Financial Aid Statistics:** 94% freshmen, 89% undergrads receive need-based scholarship or grant aid. 9% freshmen, 9% undergrads receive non-need-based scholarship or grant aid. 82% freshmen, 80% undergrads receive need-based self-help aid. 0% freshmen, 0% undergrads receive athletic scholarships. 77% freshmen, 78% undergrads receive any aid. 72% undergrads borrow to pay for school. **Criteria for awarding institutional aid:** *Non-need-based:* academics, alumni affiliation, leadership, music/drama, religious affiliation.

GRACELAND UNIVERSITY

1 University Place, Lamoni, IA 50140
Phone: 641-784-5196 · **Financial Aid Phone:** 641-784-5140
E-mail: admissions@graceland.edu · **CEEB Code:** 6249
Fax: 641-784-5480 · **Website:** www.graceland.edu · **ACT Code:** 1314

This private school was founded in 1895. It has a 170-acre campus.

RATINGS

Admissions Selectivity Rating: 82   **Fire Safety Rating:** 82

STUDENTS AND FACULTY

Enrollment: 1,415. **Student Body:** 54% female, 46% male, 75% out-of-state, 6% international (32 countries represented). Asian 1%, African American 10%, Caucasian 64%, Hispanic 9%, Native American <1%

Retention and Graduation: 36% freshmen graduate within 4 years. 54% freshmen graduate within 6 years. 27% grads go on to further study within 1 year. 3% grads pursue arts and sciences degrees. 3% grads pursue law degrees. 5% grads pursue business degrees. 5% grads pursue medical degrees. **Faculty:** 90 full-time faculty, 76% hold PhDs, 57% are members of minority groups, 10% are women. 0% of classes are taught by teaching assistants.

ACADEMICS

Degrees: bachelor's, master's, post-bachelor's certificate, post-master's certificate. **Classes:** Most classes have 10–19 students. Most lab/discussion sessions have 20–29 students. **Majors with Highest Enrollment:** Elementary Education and Teaching; Business Administration and Management; Registered Nursing/Registered Nurse. **Special Study Options:** Accelerated program,

distance learning, double major, dual enrollment, English as a Second Language (ESL), honors program, independent study, internships, liberal arts/career combination, student-designed major, study abroad, teacher certification program. **Honors programs:** The Graceland University Honors Program includes courses in Honors English, Honors Humanities, Honors Advanced Composition, the combined Jr. and Sr. Honors Seminar, a Sr. Honors Thesis, and Honors Contracts to be created with instructors in any academic course the students choose. Completion of the Honors Program requires 21 hours of honors credit, completion of the Jr. and Sr. Honors Seminars, a Sr. Honors Thesis, and a minimum 3.5 gpa overall and in their honors work. Honors Students with a 3.75 gpa or higher are eligible for an Honors Scholarship. Incoming students with a 3.75 gap and an ACT of 27 or higher may apply for full tuition Prestigious Honors Scholarship, which are available on a competitive basis, and require an interview. Graceland University offers an Excellent Education in a caring community. So we believe the best reason to participate in the Honors Program is the people in it, and to participate in the Honors community. Combined degree programs: BSN/MSN. **Disability Services:** Special programs offered to physically disabled students include note-taking services, reader services, tape recorders, tutors. **Career services:** Alumni network, alumni services, career/job search classes, career assessment, internships. Career services highlights include our own job posting site for students and alumni. We offer our career exploration and job search classes online each semester.

FACILITIES

Housing: men's dorms, women's dorms, apartments for married students. 95% of campus accessible to physically disabled. **Computers:** 100% of classrooms, 91% of dorms, 100% of libraries, 100% of dining areas, 100% of student union, 30% of common outdoor areas have wireless network access. Students can register for classes online. Administrative functions (other than registration) can be performed online.

CAMPUS LIFE

Environment: Rural. **Activities:** Choral groups, concert band, dance, drama/theater, jazz band, music ensembles, musical theater, pep band, radio station, student government, student newspaper, symphony orchestra, yearbook, Campus Ministries, International Student Organization. 54 registered organizations, 1 religious organization. **Athletics (Intercollegiate):** *Men:* baseball, basketball, cross-country, football, golf, soccer, tennis, track/field (outdoor), track/field (indoor), volleyball. *Women:* basketball, cross-country, golf, soccer, softball, tennis, track/field (outdoor), track/field (indoor), volleyball. **On-Campus Highlights:** Resch Science & Technology Hall, The Helene Center for Visual Arts, The Closson Center, The Shaw Center for Performing Arts, The Higdon Administration Building. **Environmental Initiatives:** Installation of Hoop House garden to produce vegetables for campus dining services. Shared bike program Car Share Program

ADMISSIONS

Freshman Academic Profile: Average high school GPA 3.08. 9.4% in top 10% of high school class, 25% in top 25% of high school class, 55% in top 50% of high school class. 99% from public high schools. SAT Math middle 50% range 380-490. SAT Critical Reading middle 50% range 380-470. ACT middle 50% range 18-23. Minimum internet-based TOEFL 79. Minimum paper TOEFL 550. **Basis for Candidate Selection:** *Very important factors considered include:* Class rank, academic GPA, rigor of secondary school record, standardized test scores, character/personal qualities, talent/ability. *Important factors considered include:* extracurricular activities, interview. *Other factors considered include:* application essay, recommendation(s), alumni/ae relation, religious affiliation/commitment. **Freshman Admission Requirements:** High school diploma is required and GED is accepted. **Freshman Admission Statistics:** 2,169 applied, 50% admitted, 26% enrolled. **Transfer Admission Requirements:** college transcript(s), Minimum college GPA of 2.0 required. Lowest grade transferable D. **General Admission Information:** Application Fee $50. Nonfall registration accepted. Credit and/or placement offered for CEEB Advanced Placement tests.

COSTS AND FINANCIAL AID

Annual tuition $25,420. Room and board $8,100. Required fees $470. Average book expense $1,040. **Required Forms and Deadlines:** FAFSA. **Notification of Awards:** Applicants will be notified of awards on a rolling basis beginning 3/1. **Types of Aid:** *Need-based scholarships/grants:* Federal Pell, SEOG, state scholarships/grants, private scholarships, the school's own gift aid. *Loans:* Direct Subsidized Stafford, Direct Unsubsidized Stafford, Direct PLUS, Federal Perkins, state loans, college/university loans from institutional funds, Alternative loans. *Student Employment:* Federal Work-Study Program available. Institutional employment available. Highest amount earned per year from on-campus jobs $6,062. Off-campus job opportunities are poor. **Financial Aid Statistics:** 99% freshmen, 94% undergrads receive need-based scholarship or grant aid. 25% freshmen, 28% undergrads receive non-need-based scholarship or grant aid. 87% freshmen, 84% undergrads receive need-based self-help aid. 9% freshmen, 12% undergrads receive athletic scholarships. 99% freshmen, 93% undergrads receive any aid. 78% undergrads borrow to pay for school. Average cumulative indebtedness $33,050. **Criteria for awarding institutional aid:** *Non-need-based:* academics, alumni affiliation, art, athletics, job skills, leadership, music/drama, religious affiliation.

See page 1060.

GRAMBLING STATE UNIVERSITY

P. O. Box 864, Grambling, LA 71245
Phone: (318) 274-6423
E-mail: taylorn@gram.edu · **CEEB Code:** 6250
Fax: 318-274-3292 · **Website:** www.gram.edu · **ACT Code:** 1582

This public school was founded in 1901. It has a 340-acre campus.

RATINGS

Admissions Selectivity Rating: 63   **Fire Safety Rating:** 69

STUDENTS AND FACULTY

Enrollment: 4,171. **Student Body:** 57% female, 43% male, 34% out-of-state, 2% international (21 countries represented). Asian 0%, African American 105%, Caucasian 4%, Hispanic 0%, Native American <1%
Retention and Graduation: 68% freshmen return for sophomore year. 20% freshmen graduate within 4 years. 39% freshmen graduate within 6 years. 33% grads go on to further study within 1 year. 33% grads pursue arts and sciences degrees. **Faculty:** 243 full-time faculty, 57% hold PhDs, 42% are members of minority groups, 78% are women.

ACADEMICS

Degrees: associate, bachelor's, master's. **Special Study Options:** Accelerated program, cooperative education program, distance learning, double major, exchange student program (domestic), honors program, independent study, internships, study abroad, teacher certification program. **Career services:** career assessment.

FACILITIES

Housing: men's dorms, women's dorms, fraternity/sorority housing, Graduate Dorm. **Special Academic Facilities/Equipment:** Audiovisual and TV center, lab schools. **Computers:**

CAMPUS LIFE

Environment: Village. **Activities:** Choral groups, dance, drama/theater, jazz band, marching band, music ensembles, radio station, student government, student newspaper, television station, yearbook. 50 registered organizations, 11 honor society, 3 religious organizations. 4 fraternities, 5 sororities. **Athletics (Intercollegiate):** *Men:* baseball, basketball, cross-country, football, golf, tennis, track/field (outdoor), track/field (indoor). *Women:* basketball, cross-country, golf, soccer, softball, tennis, track/field (outdoor), track/field (indoor).

ADMISSIONS

Freshman Academic Profile: Average high school GPA 2.65. **Basis for Candidate Selection:** *Very important factors considered include:* standardized test scores. *Other factors considered include:* recommendation(s), alumni/ae relation, extracurricular activities, talent/ability. **Freshman Admission Requirements:** High school diploma is required and GED is accepted. *Academic units required:* 4 English, 3 mathematics, 3 science, 3 social studies, 8 academic electives, 2 Health and Physical Education. **Freshman Admission Statistics:** 2,923 applied, 62% admitted, 57% enrolled. **Transfer Admission Requirements:** college transcript(s), statement of good standing from prior institution(s). Minimum college GPA of 2.0 required. Lowest grade transferable C. **General Admission Information:** Application Fee $20. Early decision application deadline 4/15. Regular application deadline 8/1. Nonfall registration accepted. Admission may be deferred for a maximum of 6mos.

COSTS AND FINANCIAL AID

Average book expense $600. **Required Forms and Deadlines:** FAFSA. **Notification of Awards:** Applicants will be notified of awards on a rolling basis beginning 3/1. **Types of Aid:** *Need-based scholarships/grants:* Federal Pell, SEOG, state scholarships/grants. *Loans:* Direct Subsidized Stafford, Direct Unsubsidized Stafford, Direct PLUS, Subsidized Stafford, Unsubsidized Stafford, PLUS, Federal Perkins, college/university loans from institutional funds, Non-Federal Alternative/Private Loans. *Student Employment:* Federal Work-Study Program available. Institutional employment available. Highest amount earned per year from on-campus jobs $4,648. Off-campus job opportunities are good. **Financial Aid Statistics:** 84% freshmen, 87% undergrads receive need-based scholarship or grant aid. 28% freshmen, 25% undergrads receive non-need-based scholarship or grant aid. 90% freshmen, 89% undergrads receive need-based self-help aid. 4% freshmen, 5% undergrads receive athletic scholarships. 90% freshmen, 92% undergrads receive any aid. 90% undergrads borrow to pay

for school. **Criteria for awarding institutional aid:** *Non-need-based:* academics, alumni affiliation, athletics, leadership, minority status, music/drama, state/district residency.

GRAND CANYON UNIVERSITY

3300 W Camelback Rd, Phoenix, AZ 85017
Phone: 602-589-2855
E-mail: admissions@grand-canyon.edu · **CEEB Code:** 4331
Fax: 602-589-2580 · **Website:** www.grand-canyon.edu · **ACT Code:** 92

This private school was founded in 1949. It has a 90-acre campus.

RATINGS

Admissions Selectivity Rating: 61   **Fire Safety Rating:** 60*

STUDENTS AND FACULTY

Enrollment: 1,609. **Student Body:** 64% female, 36% male, 19% out-of-state, 3% international. Asian 2%, African American 3%, Caucasian 56%, Hispanic 7%, Native American 1%
Retention and Graduation: 76% freshmen return for sophomore year. 32% freshmen graduate within 4 years. 50% freshmen graduate within 6 years. **Faculty:** 97 full-time faculty, 58% hold PhDs, 52% are members of minority groups, 3% are women.

ACADEMICS

Degrees: bachelor's, diploma, master's. **Classes:** Most classes have fewer than 10 students. Most lab/discussion sessions have 10–19 students. **Special Study Options:** Accelerated program, cooperative education program, distance learning, double major, dual enrollment, English as a Second Language (ESL), exchange student program (domestic), honors program, independent study, internships, study abroad, teacher certification program. **Disability Services:** Special programs offered to physically disabled students include note-taking services, reader services, tape recorders, tutors. **Career services:** alumni services, career assessment, internships.

FACILITIES

Housing: men's dorms, women's dorms, apartments for married students, apartments for single students. 99% of campus accessible to physically disabled. **Special Academic Facilities/Equipment:** Art gallery, dynamical systems laboratory.

CAMPUS LIFE

Activities: Choral groups, concert band, drama/theater, jazz band, literary magazine, music ensembles, musical theater, opera, student government, student newspaper. 20 registered organizations, 3 honor societies, 4 religious organizations. **Athletics (Intercollegiate):** *Men:* baseball, basketball, golf, soccer. *Women:* basketball, soccer, tennis, volleyball. **On-Campus Highlights:** New Student Union, New Student Suites, Athletic Facilities, Ethington Theatre, Medical Cadaver Lab.

ADMISSIONS

Freshman Academic Profile: Minimum paper TOEFL 500. **Basis for Candidate Selection:** *Very important factors considered include:* rigor of secondary school record, standardized test scores. *Important factors considered include:* Class rank. *Other factors considered include:* application essay, recommendation(s), character/personal qualities, extracurricular activities, interview, talent/ability. **Freshman Admission Requirements:** High school diploma is required and GED is accepted. *Academic units required:* 4 English, 3 mathematics, 2 science, (2 science labs), 2 social studies. **Freshman Admission Statistics:** 823 applied, 69% admitted, 44% enrolled. **Transfer Admission Requirements:** college transcript(s), Minimum college GPA of 2.0 required. Lowest grade transferable C. **General Admission Information:** Application Fee $50. Nonfall registration accepted. Credit offered for CEEB Advanced Placement tests.

COSTS AND FINANCIAL AID

Room and board $7,130. Required fees $100. Average book expense $780. **Required Forms and Deadlines:** FAFSA. **Notification of Awards:** Applicants will be notified of awards on a rolling basis beginning 3/15. **Types of Aid:** *Need-based scholarships/grants:* Federal Pell, SEOG, state scholarships/grants, private scholarships, the school's own gift aid, Bureau of Indian Affairs Grant. *Loans:* Subsidized Stafford, Unsubsidized Stafford, PLUS, Federal Perkins, state loans, Alternative loans. *Student Employment:* Federal Work-Study Program available. Institutional employment available. Highest amount earned per year from on-campus jobs $1,500. Off-campus job opportunities are excellent. **Financial Aid Statistics:** 35% freshmen, 46% undergrads receive need-based scholarship or grant aid. 87% freshmen, 72% undergrads receive non-need-based scholarship or grant aid. 58% freshmen, 76% undergrads receive need-based self-help aid. 4% freshmen, 5% undergrads receive athletic scholarships. 61% undergrads borrow to pay for school. **Criteria for awarding institutional aid:** *Non-need-based:* academics, alumni affiliation, art, athletics, job skills, leadership, minority status, music/drama, religious affiliation, state/district residency.

GRAND RAPIDS THEOLOGICAL SEMINARY

1001 E Beltline Ave. NE, Grand Rapids, MI 49525
Phone: 1-800-697-1133 · **Financial Aid Phone:** 616-949-5300
E-mail: grts@cornerstone.edu
Fax: 616-254-1623 · **Website:** http://grts.cornerstone.edu

This is a private school.

RATINGS
Admissions Selectivity Rating: 60*   Fire Safety Rating: 94

STUDENTS AND FACULTY
Enrollment: 0. **Student Body:**
Retention and Graduation: 15% grads go on to further study within 1 year. 10% grads pursue arts and sciences degrees. 1% grads pursue law degrees. 3% grads pursue business degrees. 1% grads pursue medical degrees. **Faculty:** 9 full-time faculty, 56% are members of minority groups. 0% of classes are taught by teaching assistants.

ACADEMICS
Degrees: certificate, master's. **Majors with Highest Enrollment:** Education; Psychology; Business/Commerce. **Special Study Options:** distance learning, double major, dual enrollment, honors program, independent study, internships, study abroad. **Honors programs:** Honors Program based on a "great books" curriculum. **Disability Services:** Special programs offered to physically disabled students include note-taking services, reader services, tape recorders, tutors. **Career services:** career/job search classes, career assessment, internships. Career services highlights include the required internship of all students as part of the graduation requirements.

FACILITIES
Housing: special housing for disabled students, men's dorms, women's dorms, apartments for married students, apartments for single students. 100% of campus accessible to physically disabled. **Computers:** Students can register for classes online. Administrative functions (other than registration) can be performed online. Undergraduates are required to own a computer.

CAMPUS LIFE
Activities: student government, Campus Ministries, International Student Organization. 11 registered organizations, 2 honor societies, 1 religious organization. **Athletics (Intercollegiate):** *Men:* basketball, cross-country, golf, soccer, track/field (outdoor), track/field (indoor). *Women:* basketball, cross-country, golf, soccer, softball, track/field (outdoor), track/field (indoor), volleyball. **On-Campus Highlights:** Corum Student Union, Bernice Hansen Athletic Center, Campus Bookstore Atrium, Faber Hall Seating Area, Gordon Music Hall. **Environmental Initiatives:** On campus dialogue and focus on sustainability issues. Joining a community organization.

ADMISSIONS
Freshman Academic Profile: 60% from public high schools. Minimum paper TOEFL 500. **Basis for Candidate Selection:** *Very important factors considered include:* application essay, academic GPA, recommendation(s), religious affiliation/commitment. *Important factors considered include:* standardized test scores, character/personal qualities, extracurricular activities, level of applicant's interest, volunteer work. *Other factors considered include:* rigor of secondary school record, talent/ability, work experience. **Freshman Admission Requirements:** High school diploma is required and GED is accepted. **Transfer Admission Requirements:** college transcript(s), essay or personal statement, Minimum college GPA of 2.5 required. Lowest grade transferable C. **General Admission Information:** Credit and/or placement offered for CEEB Advanced Placement tests.

COSTS AND FINANCIAL AID
Types of Aid: *Need-based scholarships/grants:* state scholarships/grants, private scholarships, the school's own gift aid. *Loans:* Direct Subsidized Stafford, Direct Unsubsidized Stafford. *Student Employment:* Federal Work-Study Program available. Highest amount earned per year from on-campus jobs $5,500. Off-campus job opportunities are good. **Financial Aid Statistics:** 100% freshmen, 98% undergrads receive any aid. **Criteria for awarding institutional aid:** *Non-need-based:* academics, job skills, leadership, minority status, religious affiliation.

GRAND VALLEY STATE UNIVERSITY

1 Campus Drive, Allendale, MI 49401
Phone: 616-331-2025 · **Financial Aid Phone:** 616-331-3234
E-mail: admissions@gvsu.edu · **CEEB Code:** 1258
Fax: 616-331-2000 · **Website:** www.gvsu.edu · **ACT Code:** 2005

This public school was founded in 1960. It has a 1275-acre campus.

RATINGS
Admissions Selectivity Rating: 80   Fire Safety Rating: 83

STUDENTS AND FACULTY
Enrollment: 21,561. **Student Body:** 58% female, 42% male, 6% out-of-state, 1% international (82 countries represented). Asian 2%, African American 5%, Caucasian 83%, Hispanic 5%, Native American <1%
Retention and Graduation: 83% freshmen return for sophomore year. **Faculty:** 1,113 full-time faculty, 78% hold PhDs, 50% are members of minority groups, 16% are women. 0% of classes are taught by teaching assistants.

ACADEMICS
Degrees: bachelor's, certificate, master's, post-bachelor's certificate, post-master's certificate. **Classes:** Most classes have 20–29 students. Most lab/discussion sessions have 20–29 students. **Majors with Highest Enrollment:** Health Services/Allied Health/Health Sciences; Business/Commerce. **Special Study Options:** distance learning, double major, dual enrollment, English as a Second Language (ESL), honors program, independent study, internships, student-designed major, study abroad, teacher certification program. **Honors programs:** Honor's College Combined degree programs: BA/JD, BA/MEng, Physical therapy program; Occupational Therapy; Ph. **Disability Services:** Special programs offered to physically disabled students include reader services, tape recorders, tutors. **Career services:** Alumni network, alumni services, career/job search classes, career assessment, internships, regional alumni. Career services highlights include a very strong cooperative education program in engineering that is mature and provides one year of full-time work for students. We also have very strong internship programs in the following departments: computer science, hospitality, communications, education, health majors, and social work.

FACILITIES
Housing: Coed dorms, fraternity/sorority housing, apartments for married students, apartments for single students, Theme Housing. 99% of campus accessible to physically disabled. **Special Academic Facilities/Equipment:** two Great Lakes research vessels, audio-visual center, performance/recital hall, pipe organ, physical therapy/human performance lab. **Computers:** 100% of classrooms, 63% of dorms, 100% of libraries, 100% of dining areas, 100% of student union, have wireless network access. Students can register for classes online. Administrative functions (other than registration) can be performed online.

CAMPUS LIFE
Environment: City. **Activities:** Choral groups, concert band, dance, drama/theater, jazz band, literary magazine, marching band, music ensembles, musical theater, pep band, radio station, student government, student newspaper, symphony orchestra, television station, Campus Ministries, International Student Organization. 301 registered organizations, 20 honor societies, 20 religious organizations. 11 fraternity, 11 sorority. **Athletics (Intercollegiate):** *Men:* baseball, basketball, cross-country, diving, football, golf, swimming, tennis, track/field (outdoor), track/field (indoor). *Women:* basketball, cross-country, diving, golf, soccer, softball, swimming, tennis, track/field (outdoor), track/field (indoor), volleyball. **On-Campus Highlights:** Living Centers, Cook DeVos Center for Health Sciences, Recreation Center and Fieldhouse, Laker Turf Building, Kirkhof Center. **Environmental Initiatives:** Climate Mitigation: GVSU is a signatory to American College and University Presidents Climate Commitment and has recently completed its Climate Action Plan and set a goal of climate neutrality by 2037. The climate action plan is available online. Currently there are over 650 colleges and universities that have signed on to this agreement. LEED construction projects and bus transportation are both important climate mitigation strategies. GVSU has completed and certified 10 LEED projects with 2 more LEED projects under construction. These 12 LEED projects represent over 925,000 square feet and ~19% of total square footage. Annual bus ridership is over ~ 2MM bus rides per year for faculty and students and saves millions of dollars in annual fuel purchases and vehicle maintenance costs while reducing our carbon footprint. Waste Minimization: GVSU's currently diverts over 600 TPY of waste on our main campus from the landfill. Our recycling rate is over 30% and we have entered the national Recylemania competition again this year in a number of waste categories. We have also begun to divert waste from the landfill by composting our campus food waste. In a pilot project at a few locations, we have been able to compost ~50 tons of food waste per month. Local, fair trade, organic food purchases continue to track at a 25% +

annualized rate with additional healthy, nutritional and local food options being offered. A Farmers Market is available on campus during the growing season as well as the development of a campus community garden.

ADMISSIONS
Freshman Academic Profile: Average high school GPA 3.34. 18% in top 10% of high school class, 48% in top 25% of high school class, 86% in top 50% of high school class. ACT middle 50% range 21-26. Minimum paper TOEFL 550. **Basis for Candidate Selection:** *Very important factors considered include:* academic GPA, rigor of secondary school record. *Important factors considered include:* standardized test scores. *Other factors considered include:* Class rank, application essay, recommendation(s), alumni/ae relation, extracurricular activities, first generation, talent/ability, volunteer work, work experience. **Freshman Admission Requirements:** High school diploma is required and GED is accepted. *Academic units required:* 4 English, 3 mathematics, 3 science, (1 science labs), 2 foreign language, 3 social studies. **Freshman Admission Statistics:** 16,884 applied, 80% admitted, 31% enrolled. **Transfer Admission Requirements:** college transcript(s), statement of good standing from prior institution(s). Minimum college GPA of 2.5 required. Lowest grade transferable D. **General Admission Information:** Application Fee $30. Nonfall registration accepted. Credit and/or placement offered for CEEB Advanced Placement tests.

COSTS AND FINANCIAL AID
Required Forms and Deadlines: FAFSA. **Notification of Awards:** Applicants will be notified of awards on a rolling basis beginning 3/10. **Types of Aid:** *Need-based scholarships/grants:* Federal Pell, SEOG, state scholarships/grants, private scholarships, the school's own gift aid. *Loans:* Direct Subsidized Stafford, Direct Unsubsidized Stafford, Direct PLUS, Federal Perkins, Federal Nursing. *Student Employment:* Federal Work-Study Program available. Institutional employment available. Highest amount earned per year from on-campus jobs $5,200. Off-campus job opportunities are good. **Financial Aid Statistics:** 87% freshmen, 82% undergrads receive need-based scholarship or grant aid. 4% freshmen, 3% undergrads receive non-need-based scholarship or grant aid. 87% freshmen, 88% undergrads receive need-based self-help aid. 1% freshmen, 1% undergrads receive athletic scholarships. 86% freshmen, 83% undergrads receive any aid. 73% undergrads borrow to pay for school. Average cumulative indebtedness $26,698. **Criteria for awarding institutional aid:** *Non-need-based:* academics, alumni affiliation, art, athletics, music/drama, state/district residency.

GRAND VIEW UNIVERSITY

1200 Grandview Avenue, Des Moines, IA 50316-1599
Phone: 515-263-2810 · **Financial Aid Phone:** 515-263-2963
E-mail: admissions@GrandView.edu · **CEEB Code:** 6251
Fax: 515-263-2974 · **Website:** www.admissions.grandview.edu · **ACT Code:** 1316

This private school, affiliated with the Lutheran Church, was founded in 1896. It has a 35-acre campus.

RATINGS
Admissions Selectivity Rating: 71   Fire Safety Rating: 60*

STUDENTS AND FACULTY
Enrollment: 2,079. **Student Body:** 58% female, 42% male, 13% out-of-state, 2% international (16 countries represented). Asian 3%, African American 8%, Caucasian 74%, Hispanic 3%, Native American <1%
Retention and Graduation: 69% freshmen return for sophomore year. 28% freshmen graduate within 4 years. 48% freshmen graduate within 6 years. **Faculty:** 95 full-time faculty, 68% hold PhDs, 56% are members of minority groups, 7% are women. 0% of classes are taught by teaching assistants.

ACADEMICS
Degrees: associate, bachelor's, certificate, master's, post-bachelor's certificate, terminal associate, transfer associate. **Classes:** Most classes have 10–19 students. Most lab/discussion sessions have 10–19 students. **Majors with Highest Enrollment:** Education; Registered Nursing/Registered Nurse; Business/Commerce. **Special Study Options:** Accelerated program, cooperative education program, cross-registration, distance learning, double major, dual enrollment, honors program, independent study, internships, liberal arts/career combination, student-designed major, study abroad, teacher certification program, weekend college. **Honors programs:** Logos Honors Program. Combined degree programs: Dual Degrees.

FACILITIES
Housing: Coed dorms, apartments for single students. **Special Academic Facilities/Equipment:** Danish American Archives. **Computers:** Administrative functions (other than registration) can be performed online.

CAMPUS LIFE
Activities: Choral groups, concert band, dance, drama/theater, literary magazine, music ensembles, radio station, student government, student newspaper, television station, Campus Ministries, International Student Organization. 28 registered organizations, 1 religious organization. **Athletics (Intercollegiate):** *Men:* baseball, basketball, cross-country, golf, soccer. *Women:* basketball, cross-country, golf, soccer, softball, volleyball.

ADMISSIONS
Freshman Academic Profile: Average high school GPA 3.2. 15% in top 10% of high school class, 33% in top 25% of high school class, 64% in top 50% of high school class. SAT Math middle 50% range 400-480. SAT Critical Reading middle 50% range 380-450. SAT Writing middle 50% range 360-440. ACT middle 50% range 19-23. Minimum paper TOEFL 550. **Basis for Candidate Selection:** *Very important factors considered include:* Class rank, academic GPA, rigor of secondary school record, character/personal qualities. *Important factors considered include:* standardized test scores. *Other factors considered include:* alumni/ae relation, extracurricular activities, talent/ability, volunteer work, work experience. **Freshman Admission Requirements:** High school diploma is required and GED is accepted. **Freshman Admission Statistics:** 805 applied, 96% admitted, 39% enrolled. **Transfer Admission Requirements:** college transcript(s), Minimum college GPA of 2.0 required. Lowest grade transferable D. **General Admission Information:** Application Fee $35. Regular application deadline 8/15. Notification on a rolling basis, beginning on or about 9/15. Nonfall registration accepted. Admission may be deferred for a maximum of 1 SEMESTER. Credit and/or placement offered for CEEB Advanced Placement tests.

COSTS AND FINANCIAL AID
Annual tuition $22,986. Room and board $7,554. Required fees $530. Average book expense $880. **Required Forms and Deadlines:** FAFSA. **Notification of Awards:** Applicants will be notified of awards on a rolling basis beginning 3/1. **Types of Aid:** *Need-based scholarships/grants:* Federal Pell, SEOG, state scholarships/grants, private scholarships, the school's own gift aid. *Loans:* Subsidized Stafford, Unsubsidized Stafford, PLUS, Federal Perkins, Federal Nursing. *Student Employment:* Federal Work-Study Program available. Institutional employment available. Highest amount earned per year from on-campus jobs $1,500. Off-campus job opportunities are excellent. **Financial Aid Statistics:** 88% freshmen, 92% undergrads receive need-based scholarship or grant aid. 20% freshmen, 11% undergrads receive non-need-based scholarship or grant aid. 80% freshmen, 88% undergrads receive need-based self-help aid. 63% freshmen, 10% undergrads receive athletic scholarships. 97% freshmen, 99% undergrads receive any aid. 85% undergrads borrow to pay for school. Average cumulative indebtedness $28,639. **Criteria for awarding institutional aid:** *Non-need-based:* academics, alumni affiliation, art, athletics, leadership, music/drama.

GRANTHAM UNIVERSITY

7200 NW 86th Street, Kansas City, MO 64153
E-mail: admissions@grantham.edu
Fax: 816-595-5757 · **Website:** http://www.grantham.edu/

This is a proprietary school.

RATINGS
Admissions Selectivity Rating: 60*   Fire Safety Rating: 60*

ACADEMICS
Degrees: associate, bachelor's, master's. **Special Study Options:** Accelerated program, distance learning, external degree program, independent study.

ADMISSIONS
Basis for Candidate Selection: *Very important factors considered include:* Class rank, rigor of secondary school record, interview. *Other factors considered include:* application essay, recommendation(s), standardized test scores, character/personal qualities, extracurricular activities, talent/ability, volunteer work, work experience. **Freshman Admission Requirements:** High school diploma is required and GED is accepted. **Transfer Admission Requirements:** High school transcript, college transcript(s), Minimum college GPA of 2.0 required. Lowest grade transferable C. **General Admission Information:** Application Fee $30. Nonfall registration accepted. Admission may be deferred for a maximum of Unlimited.

COSTS AND FINANCIAL AID
Types of Aid: *Need-based scholarships/grants:* Federal Pell, SEOG, state scholarships/grants, private scholarships, the school's own gift aid. *Loans:* Subsidized Stafford, Unsubsidized Stafford, PLUS, Federal Perkins. **Criteria for awarding institutional aid:** *Non-need-based:* academics, art, athletics, state/district residency.

GRATZ COLLEGE

7605 Old York Road, Melrose Park, PA 19027
Phone: 215-635-7300, x140
E-mail: admissions@gratz.edu
Fax: 215-635-7399 · **Website:** www.gratz.edu

This is a private school.

RATINGS

Admissions Selectivity Rating: 61   **Fire Safety Rating:** 60*

STUDENTS AND FACULTY

Enrollment: 12. **Student Body:** 92% female, 8% male, 25% out-of-state, 0% international. Asian 8%, African American 0%, Caucasian 100%, Hispanic 0%, Native American <1%
Retention and Graduation: 88% freshmen return for sophomore year. **Faculty:** 8 full-time faculty, 100% hold PhDs, 50% are members of minority groups, 0% are women. 0% of classes are taught by teaching assistants.

ACADEMICS

Degrees: bachelor's, master's, post-bachelor's certificate. **Classes:** Most classes have fewer than 10 students. Most lab/discussion sessions have fewer than 10 students. **Special Study Options:** cross-registration, double major, dual enrollment, independent study, internships, liberal arts/career combination, study abroad, teacher certification program, Joint programs with area colleges and universities are offered only at the Master's level. **Career services:** alumni services, career/job search classes, internships,

FACILITIES

Housing: The College does not offer housing. All students live off campus. 100% of campus accessible to physically disabled. **Computers:**

CAMPUS LIFE

Activities: Choral groups, music ensembles.

ADMISSIONS

Freshman Academic Profile: Minimum paper TOEFL 450. **Basis for Candidate Selection:** *Very important factors considered include:* application essay, recommendation(s), character/personal qualities, religious affiliation/commitment, talent/ability. *Important factors considered include:* rigor of secondary school record, interview, volunteer work. *Other factors considered include:* Class rank, standardized test scores, alumni/ae relation, extracurricular activities, racial/ethnic status, work experience. **Freshman Admission Requirements:** High school diploma is required and GED is accepted. *Academic units required:* 3 English, 2 mathematics, 2 science, (1 science labs), 2 foreign language, 3 social studies, 3 history, 2 academic electives. **Freshman Admission Statistics:** 7 applied, 71% admitted, 100% enrolled. **Transfer Admission Requirements:** High school transcript, college transcript(s), essay or personal statement, Minimum college GPA of 0 required. Lowest grade transferable C. **General Admission Information:** Application Fee $50. Nonfall registration accepted. Admission may be deferred for a maximum of 2 years. Neither credit nor placement offered for CEEB Advanced Placement tests.

COSTS AND FINANCIAL AID

Average book expense $550. **Required Forms and Deadlines:** FAFSA, Institution's own financial aid form. **Types of Aid:** *Need-based scholarships/grants:* Federal Pell, private scholarships. *Loans:* Subsidized Stafford, Unsubsidized Stafford, PLUS. *Student Employment:* Institutional employment available. Off-campus job opportunities are good. **Financial Aid Statistics:** 100% undergrads receive need-based scholarship or grant aid. 0% undergrads receive non-need-based scholarship or grant aid. 100% undergrads receive need-based self-help aid.

GREEN MOUNTAIN COLLEGE

One Brennan Circle, Poultney, VT 05764-1199
Phone: 802-287-8000 · **Financial Aid Phone:** 802-287-8209
E-mail: admiss@greenmtn.edu · **CEEB Code:** 3418
Fax: 802-287-8099 · **Website:** www.greenmtn.edu · **ACT Code:** 4302

This private school, affiliated with the Methodist Church, was founded in 1834. It has a 155-acre campus.

RATINGS

Admissions Selectivity Rating: 76   **Fire Safety Rating:** 83

STUDENTS AND FACULTY

Enrollment: 557. **Student Body:** 51% female, 49% male, 86% out-of-state, 3% international (14 countries represented). Asian 1%, African American 5%, Caucasian 60%, Hispanic 60%, Native American 1%
Retention and Graduation: 69% freshmen return for sophomore year. 41% freshmen graduate within 4 years. 48% freshmen graduate within 6 years. 18% grads go on to further study within 1 year. **Faculty:** 41 full-time faculty, 90% hold PhDs, 37% are members of minority groups, 5% are women. 0% of classes are taught by teaching assistants.

ACADEMICS

Degrees: bachelor's, certificate, master's. **Classes:** Most classes have 10–19 students. Most lab/discussion sessions have 10–19 students. **Majors with Highest Enrollment:** Environmental Studies; Parks, Recreation and Leisure Studies; Agroecology and Sustainable Agriculture. **Special Study Options:** cooperative education program, distance learning, double major, exchange student program (domestic), honors program, independent study, internships, liberal arts/career combination, student-designed major, study abroad, teacher certification program. **Honors programs:** College Honors Program. **Disability Services:** Special programs offered to physically disabled students include note-taking services, tape recorders, tutors. Career services highlights include two Co-Ops that all Resort Management students participate in. Last year, 384 students completed 5,829 hours of service with 54 community partners. GMC has an active internship program and requires many students to complete an internship within their chosen field.

FACILITIES

Housing: Coed dorms, special housing for disabled students, substance free theme floors—recreation, education, community, Honors. **Special Academic Facilities/Equipment:** Welsh Heritage Collection, Rare Books Room, Feick Arts Center. **Computers:** Students can register for classes online. Administrative functions (other than registration) can be performed online.

CAMPUS LIFE

Environment: Rural. **Activities:** Choral groups, concert band, drama/theater, jazz band, literary magazine, music ensembles, radio station, student government, student newspaper, student-run film society, yearbook. 25 registered organizations, 2 honor societies, 2 religious organizations. **Athletics (Intercollegiate):** *Men:* basketball, cross-country, golf, lacrosse, skiing (downhill/alpine), soccer, tennis. *Women:* basketball, cross-country, lacrosse, skiing (downhill/alpine), soccer, softball, tennis, volleyball. **On-Campus Highlights:** Withey Student Center, Moses Coffeehouse, Surdam Art Building, Griswold Library, The Farm. **Environmental Initiatives:** 1. In 2011, Green Mountain College became the second college in the country to achieve climate neutrality under the ACUPCC agreement and the first to do it by reducing emissions by 50%. The reductions came from an integrated approach of replacing windows, upgrading to more efficient lights and appliances, and building a $5.8 million combined heat and power plant to shift the primary heat source from number six fuel oil to locally sourced woodchips, while also producing electricity with high pressure steam. 2. The College is now planning to move beyond climate neutrality and is striving to achieve authentic sustainability by the year 2020. The goal requires the College to give back more than it takes across the three capital stocks of environmental, social, and economic capital. The goal, developed by a campus-wide strategic planning process, recognizes that true sustainability requires resilient social and economic systems to support environmental efforts. In the environmental domain, the college aims to produce all of its required energy on campus with alternative energy technologies or locally sourced sustainable fuel, to help re-build the natural capital of the region, and to produce highly skilled students with hands-on experience that can be leaders in the field. To measure progress toward authentic sustainability a task force comprised of the Provost, professors, staff members, and students has been working to develop a comprehensive set of metrics that will measure the Colleges impact on stocks. A thirty-page white paper has been written by the group explaining their first draft of metrics, and community wide consultation will help refine the list. 3. Green Mountain College integrates sustainability thoroughly across curriculum. In addition to the comprehensive Environmental Liberal Arts core curriculum, other interdisciplinary academic degree offerings include a new Sustainable Agriculture and Food Production degree and a new Renewable Energy and Ecological Design Degree Program. A REED block course last fall designed and built a solar garage from the ground up that now stands on the south end of campus, boasting a 3.8 kW, grid-tied array and a passive heat system comprised of a heat slab and a south-facing wall of e-glazed windows. Other successful environmental degree programs include Adventure Education, Environmental Studies, Natural Resources Management, Environmental Management, and Biology. The relatively new graduate programs also include a Master of Science in Environmental Studies, a Sustainable MBA, and a Master of Science in Sustainable Food Systems.

ADMISSIONS

Freshman Academic Profile: SAT Math middle 50% range 450-560. SAT Critical Reading middle 50% range 470-600. SAT Writing middle 50% range 450-580. ACT middle 50% range 19-27. Minimum internet-based TOEFL 61. Minimum paper TOEFL 500. **Basis for Candidate Selection:** *Very important factors considered include:* application essay, academic GPA, rigor of secondary school record, character/personal qualities. *Important factors considered include:* Class rank, recommendation(s), extracurricular activities, interview, volunteer work. *Other factors considered include:* standardized test scores, level of applicant's interest, talent/ability, work experience. **Freshman Admission Requirements:** High school diploma is required and GED is accepted. *Academic units required:* 4 English, 3 mathematics, 3 science, (2 science labs), 2 foreign language, 3 social studies, 1 history, 5 academic electives. **Freshman Admission Statistics:** 973 applied, 68% admitted, 20% enrolled. **Transfer Admission Requirements:** High school transcript, college transcript(s), essay or personal statement, statement of good standing from prior institution(s). Minimum college GPA of 2.0 required. Lowest grade transferable C-. **General Admission Information:** Application Fee $30. Notification on a rolling basis, beginning on or about 9/1. Nonfall registration accepted. Admission may be deferred for a maximum of 1 year. Credit and/or placement offered for CEEB Advanced Placement tests.

COSTS AND FINANCIAL AID

Annual tuition $32,594. Room and board $11,492. Required fees $1,142. Average book expense $980. **Required Forms and Deadlines:** FAFSA. **Notification of Awards:** Applicants will be notified of awards on a rolling basis beginning 1/1. **Types of Aid:** *Need-based scholarships/grants:* Federal Pell, SEOG, state scholarships/grants, private scholarships, the school's own gift aid. *Loans:* Subsidized Stafford, Unsubsidized Stafford, PLUS, state loans, Alternative Loans. **Financial Aid Statistics:** 100% freshmen, 97% undergrads receive need-based scholarship or grant aid. 2% freshmen, 6% undergrads receive non-need-based scholarship or grant aid. 93% freshmen, 85% undergrads receive need-based self-help aid. 0% freshmen, 0% undergrads receive athletic scholarships. 98% freshmen, 94% undergrads receive any aid. 75% undergrads borrow to pay for school. Average cumulative indebtedness $25,346. **Criteria for awarding institutional aid:** *Non-need-based:* academics, alumni affiliation, art, leadership, music/drama, religious affiliation.

GREENVILLE COLLEGE

315 East College Avenue, Greenville, IL 62246
Phone: 618-664-7100 · **Financial Aid Phone:** 618-664-7110
E-mail: admissions@greenville.edu · **CEEB Code:** 1256
Fax: 618-664-9841 · **Website:** www.greenville.edu · **ACT Code:** 1032

This private school, affiliated with the Free Methodist Church, was founded in 1892. It has a 40-acre campus.

RATINGS

Admissions Selectivity Rating: 84   **Fire Safety Rating:** 94

STUDENTS AND FACULTY

Enrollment: 1,055. **Student Body:** 49% female, 51% male, 35% out-of-state, 2% international (14 countries represented). Asian 1%, African American 9%, Caucasian 76%, Hispanic 5%, Native American <1%
Retention and Graduation: 40% freshmen graduate within 4 years. 48% freshmen graduate within 6 years. **Faculty:** 62 full-time faculty, 79% hold PhDs, 35% are members of minority groups, 11% are women. 0% of classes are taught by teaching assistants.

ACADEMICS

Degrees: bachelor's, master's. **Classes:** Most classes have 10–19 students. **Majors with Highest Enrollment:** Elementary Education and Teaching; Visual and Performing Arts; Organizational Behavior Studies. **Special Study Options:** Accelerated program, cooperative education program, cross-registration, double major, external degree program, honors program, independent study, internships, liberal arts/career combination, student-designed major, study abroad, teacher certification program. **Honors programs:** Greenville College's Honors Program is an academic program that was established in 1995 to provide a "value-added" dimension to the excellent, Christ-centered education students regularly receive at Greenville College. The Honors Program consists of a blend of enriched sections of several general education classes, special honors seminars, and experiential learning opportunities offered in an enhanced educational environment that strives for small class sizes to encourage total student participation, facilitate spirited discussions and promote greater student-faculty interaction. Outside the classroom, the Honors Programs offers a co-curricular program consisting of diversified cultural, social and educationally-oriented activities and events developed especially for program members. The Honors Program encourages its members to be persons with multi-dimensional interests who participate in a wide range of College sponsored events, activities, and organizations. Students admitted to The Honors Program automatically become members of The Honors Society, the student organization within the program which elects officers who assist with the planning and implementation of the aforementioned activities and other community building opportunities. The Greenville College Honors Program strives to emulate the guidelines, "Basic Characteristics of a Fully-Developed Honors Program," developed by the National Collegiate Honors Council. It, also, cooperates with member institutions of the Council of Christian Colleges and Universities by encouraging GC students to participate in one of the nearly twenty semester-long academic programs coordinated and promoted by CCCU that are offered at off-campus sites, both domestic and abroad. Locally, The Honors Program is administered by a director who is assisted by an Honors Council composed of faculty and students. To graduate with Honors Program recognition, students must fulfill the requirements of their academic major, earn a minimum of 25 credit hours of honors work, maintain a cumulative grade point average of 3.50 and complete a Departmental Honors Thesis under the supervision of a three-person faculty thesis committee. Graduates of the Honors Program are awarded a special medallion and receive special recognition at commencement. For additional information about The Honors Program, contact the director at 618-664-6610. **Disability Services:** Special programs offered to physically disabled students include note-taking services, reader services, tutors.

FACILITIES

Housing: men's dorms, women's dorms, apartments for single students, All single students not living at home must live in college approved housing. 40% of campus accessible to physically disabled. **Special Academic Facilities/Equipment:** Sculpture museum, sports training annex. **Computers:** Administrative functions (other than registration) can be performed online.

CAMPUS LIFE

Environment: Village. **Activities:** Choral groups, concert band, drama/theater, jazz band, music ensembles, musical theater, pep band, radio station, student government, student newspaper, yearbook. 25 registered organizations, 6 honor societies, 2 religious organizations. **Athletics (Intercollegiate):** *Men:* baseball, basketball, cross-country, football, soccer, tennis, track/field (outdoor), track/field (indoor). *Women:* basketball, cross-country, soccer, softball, tennis, track/field (outdoor), track/field (indoor), volleyball. **On-Campus Highlights:** Hogue Hall, Family Christian Bookstore, Jo's Java, Maves Art Center, Fitness Center.

ADMISSIONS

Freshman Academic Profile: Average high school GPA 3.38. 16% in top 10% of high school class, 39% in top 25% of high school class, 75% in top 50% of high school class. SAT Math middle 50% range 440-550. SAT Critical Reading middle 50% range 425-550. SAT Writing middle 50% range 400-530. ACT middle 50% range 20-26. Minimum paper TOEFL 500. **Basis for Candidate Selection:** *Very important factors considered include:* Class rank, application essay, academic GPA, rigor of secondary school record, character/personal qualities, religious affiliation/commitment, talent/ability. *Important factors considered include:* recommendation(s), standardized test scores. *Other factors considered include:* alumni/ae relation, extracurricular activities, first generation, geographical residence, interview, level of applicant's interest, racial/ethnic status, volunteer work, work experience. **Freshman Admission Requirements:** High school diploma is required and GED is accepted. *Academic units required:* 0 English, 0 mathematics, 0 science, (0 science labs), 0 foreign language, 0 social studies, 0 history, 0 academic electives. **Freshman Admission Statistics:** 2,321 applied, 56% admitted, 21% enrolled. **Transfer Admission Requirements:** High school transcript, college transcript(s), essay or personal statement, Minimum college GPA of 2.0 required. Lowest grade transferable C. **General Admission Information:** Application Fee $25. Regular application deadline 8/1. Notification on a rolling basis, beginning on or about 10/15. Nonfall registration accepted. Admission may be deferred for a maximum of One year. Credit and/or placement offered for CEEB Advanced Placement tests.

COSTS AND FINANCIAL AID

Average book expense $150. **Required Forms and Deadlines:** FAFSA. **Notification of Awards:** Applicants will be notified of awards on a rolling basis beginning 3/15. **Types of Aid:** *Need-based scholarships/grants:* Federal Pell, SEOG, state scholarships/grants, private scholarships, the school's own gift aid. *Loans:* Direct Subsidized Stafford, Direct Unsubsidized Stafford, Direct PLUS, Subsidized Stafford, Unsubsidized Stafford, PLUS, Federal Perkins, college/university loans from institutional funds. *Student Employment:* Federal Work-Study Program available. Institutional employment available. Highest amount earned per year from on-campus jobs $2,407. Off-campus job opportunities are fair. **Financial Aid Statistics:** 100% freshmen, 97% undergrads receive need-based scholarship or grant aid. 10% freshmen, 9% undergrads receive non-need-based scholarship or grant aid. 85% freshmen, 84% undergrads receive need-based self-help aid. 0% freshmen, 0% undergrads receive athletic scholarships. 94% freshmen, 92% undergrads receive any aid. 78% undergrads borrow to pay for school. Average cumulative indebtedness $28,562. **Criteria for awarding institutional aid:** *Non-need-based:* academics, alumni affiliation, art, leadership, minority status, music/drama, religious affiliation, state/district residency.

GRIGGS UNIVERSITY

PO Box 4437, Silver Spring, MD 20914-4437
Phone: 301-680-6579
E-mail: enrollmentservices@griggs.edu
Fax: 301-680-6526 • **Website:** www.griggs.edu

This private school, affiliated with the Seventh Day Adventist Church, was founded in 1909.

RATINGS
Admissions Selectivity Rating: 60*   **Fire Safety Rating:** 60*

STUDENTS AND FACULTY
Enrollment: 1,076. **Student Body:** 50% female, 50% male, 0% international. Asian 0%, African American 0%, Caucasian 0%, Hispanic 0%, Native American <1%

ACADEMICS
Degrees: associate, bachelor's. **Majors with Highest Enrollment:** Computer and Information Sciences; Business/Commerce; Accounting and Business/Management. **Special Study Options:** Accelerated program, distance learning, independent study.

CAMPUS LIFE
Environment: City.

ADMISSIONS
Basis for Candidate Selection: *Very important factors considered include:* rigor of secondary school record. *Important factors considered include:* application essay, religious affiliation/commitment, work experience. *Other factors considered include:* recommendation(s), standardized test scores, alumni/ae relation, character/personal qualities, extracurricular activities, interview, talent/ability, volunteer work. **Freshman Admission Requirements:** *Academic units required:* 4 English, 3 mathematics, 2 science, 3 social studies, 3 academic electives, 7 Bible, Health, Word Processing. **Transfer Admission Requirements:** college transcript(s), essay or personal statement, Minimum college GPA of 2.0 required. Lowest grade transferable C. **General Admission Information:** Application Fee $60. Nonfall registration accepted.

COSTS AND FINANCIAL AID
Average book expense $1,000. **Types of Aid:** *Need-based scholarships/grants:* the school's own gift aid.

GRINNELL COLLEGE

1103 Park Street, Grinnell, IA 50112-1690
Phone: 641-269-3600 • **Financial Aid Phone:** 641-269-3250
E-mail: askgrin@grinnell.edu • **CEEB Code:** 6252
Fax: 641-269-4800 • **Website:** www.grinnell.edu • **ACT Code:** 1318

This private school was founded in 1846. It has a 120-acre campus.

RATINGS
Admissions Selectivity Rating: 95   **Fire Safety Rating:** 86

STUDENTS AND FACULTY
Enrollment: 1,670. **Student Body:** 55% female, 45% male, 92% out-of-state, 14% international (47 countries represented). Asian 7%, African American 6%, Caucasian 58%, Hispanic 8%, Native American <1%
Retention and Graduation: 94% freshmen return for sophomore year. 85% freshmen graduate within 4 years. 31% grads go on to further study within 1 year. 29% grads pursue arts and sciences degrees. 3% grads pursue law degrees. 1% grads pursue business degrees. 3% grads pursue medical degrees. **Faculty:** 168 full-time faculty, 98% hold PhDs, 47% are members of minority groups, 18% are women. 0% of classes are taught by teaching assistants.

ACADEMICS
Degrees: bachelor's. **Classes:** Most classes have 10–19 students. Most lab/discussion sessions have 10–19 students. **Majors with Highest Enrollment:** Political Science and Government; Economics; Biology/Biological Sciences. **Special Study Options:** Accelerated program, double major, independent study, internships, liberal arts/career combination, student-designed major, study abroad, teacher certification program, Study abroad available in 32 countries, including Grinnell-in-London, Grinnell-in-Washington program, 3-2 programs available in engineering, architecture, and law. Combined degree programs: Architecture With Washington Univ,St.Louis Law Col. **Disability Services:** Special programs offered to physically disabled students include note-taking services, reader services, tape recorders, tutors. **Career services:** Alumni network, alumni services, career assessment, internships, regional alumni. Career services highlights include support for 12+ funded internships each summer.

FACILITIES
Housing: Coed dorms, special housing for disabled students, cooperative housing, Wellness Housing, Theme Housing. 67% of campus accessible to physically disabled. **Special Academic Facilities/Equipment:** Art galleries, language lab, nuclear magnetic resonance spectrometer, electron microscope, 24-inch reflecting telescope, 365-acre environmental research area. **Computers:** 100% of classrooms, 100% of dorms, 100% of libraries, 100% of dining areas, 100% of student union, 100% of common outdoor areas have wireless network access. Administrative functions (other than registration) can be performed online.

CAMPUS LIFE
Environment: Village. **Activities:** Choral groups, concert band, dance, drama/theater, jazz band, literary magazine, music ensembles, musical theater, pep band, radio station, student government, student newspaper, student-run film society, symphony orchestra, yearbook, Campus Ministries, International Student Organization, Model UN. 240 registered organizations, 2 honor societies, 12 religious organizations. **Athletics (Intercollegiate):** *Men:* baseball, basketball, cross-country, diving, football, golf, soccer, swimming, tennis, track/field (outdoor), track/field (indoor). *Women:* basketball, cross-country, diving, golf, soccer, softball, swimming, tennis, track/field (outdoor), track/field (indoor), volleyball. **On-Campus Highlights:** Two building on campus are listed on the National Register of Historic Places: Mears Cottage and Goodnow Hall, Faulconer Gallery, Burling Library, Joe Rosenfield '25 Center, Bucksbaum Center for the Arts, Robert N. Noyce '49 Science Center; Athletic Center. **Environmental Initiatives:** All new buildings are LEED certified. The college has committed to building a wind farm near campus which will provide 50% of the campus' electricity. The college has dedicated one of its student houses as an Ecohouse and will use that house to demonstrate green technologies, energy conservation, water conservation, and local foods to the Grinnell community.

ADMISSIONS
Freshman Academic Profile: 69% in top 10% of high school class, 89% in top 25% of high school class, 99% in top 50% of high school class. 67% from public high schools. SAT Math middle 50% range 660-760. SAT Critical Reading middle 50% range 630-740. ACT middle 50% range 30-33. **Basis

for Candidate Selection: *Very important factors considered include:* Class rank, academic GPA, recommendation(s), rigor of secondary school record, standardized test scores, extracurricular activities, talent/ability. *Important factors considered include:* application essay, interview, racial/ethnic status. *Other factors considered include:* alumni/ae relation, character/personal qualities, first generation, geographical residence, level of applicant's interest, state residency, volunteer work, work experience. **Freshman Admission Requirements:** High school diploma is required and GED is accepted. **Freshman Admission Statistics:** 6,058 applied, 28% admitted, 26% enrolled. **Transfer Admission Requirements:** High school transcript, college transcript(s), essay or personal statement, standardized test scores, statement of good standing from prior institution(s). Lowest grade transferable C. **General Admission Information:** Application Fee $30. Early decision application deadline 11/15. Regular application deadline 1/2. Regular notification 4/1. Nonfall registration not accepted. Admission may be deferred for a maximum of 1 year. Credit offered for CEEB Advanced Placement tests.

COSTS AND FINANCIAL AID
Average book expense $900. **Required Forms and Deadlines:** FAFSA, CSS/Financial Aid PROFILE, Noncustodial PROFILE. **Notification of Awards:** Applicants will be notified of awards on or about 4/1. **Types of Aid:** *Need-based scholarships/grants:* Federal Pell, SEOG, state scholarships/grants, private scholarships, the school's own gift aid. *Loans:* Subsidized Stafford, Unsubsidized Stafford, PLUS, Federal Perkins, college/university loans from institutional funds. *Student Employment:* Federal Work-Study Program available. Institutional employment available. Highest amount earned per year from on-campus jobs $2,500. Off-campus job opportunities are excellent. **Financial Aid Statistics:** 98% freshmen, 99% undergrads receive need-based scholarship or grant aid. 14% freshmen, 10% undergrads receive non-need-based scholarship or grant aid. 84% freshmen, 86% undergrads receive need-based self-help aid. 0% freshmen, 0% undergrads receive athletic scholarships. 86% freshmen, 86% undergrads receive any aid. 56% undergrads borrow to pay for school. Average cumulative indebtedness $12,834. **Criteria for awarding institutional aid:** *Non-need-based:* academics.

GROVE CITY COLLEGE

Best 380

100 Campus Drive, Grove City, PA 16127-2104
Phone: 724-458-2100 · **Financial Aid Phone:** 724-458-3300
E-mail: admissions@gcc.edu · **CEEB Code:** 2277
Fax: 724-458-3395 · **Website:** www.gcc.edu · **ACT Code:** 3582

This private school, affiliated with the Presbyterian Church, was founded in 1876. It has a 150-acre campus.

RATINGS
Admissions Selectivity Rating: 88   **Fire Safety Rating:** 87

STUDENTS AND FACULTY
Enrollment: 2,472. **Student Body:** 50% female, 50% male, 49% out-of-state, 1% international (11 countries represented). Asian 2%, African American 1%, Caucasian 93%, Hispanic 1%, Native American <1%.
Retention and Graduation: 91% freshmen return for sophomore year. 77% freshmen graduate within 4 years. 83% freshmen graduate within 6 years. 11% grads go on to further study within 1 year. 8% grads pursue arts and sciences degrees. 1% grads pursue law degrees. 1% grads pursue business degrees. 1% grads pursue medical degrees. **Faculty:** 150 full-time faculty, 80% hold PhDs, 32% are members of minority groups, 5% are women. 0% of classes are taught by teaching assistants.

ACADEMICS
Degrees: bachelor's. **Classes:** Most classes have 20–29 students. Most lab/discussion sessions have 20–29 students. **Majors with Highest Enrollment:** Mechanical Engineering; Biology/Biological Sciences; Speech Communication and Rhetoric. **Special Study Options:** Accelerated program, double major, independent study, internships, study abroad, teacher certification program. **Disability Services:** Special programs offered to physically disabled students include tutors. **Career services:** Alumni network, alumni services, career/job search classes, career assessment, internships, regional alumni. Career services highlights include Entrepreneurship Internships required of most majors.

FACILITIES
Housing: men's dorms, women's dorms, fraternity/sorority housing, apartments for single students, Theme Housing. 100% of campus accessible to physically disabled. **Special Academic Facilities/Equipment:** Fine arts center, language lab, on-campus preschool, technological learning center. **Computers:** 100% of classrooms, 15% of dorms, 100% of libraries, 33% of dining areas, 100% of student union, 10% of common outdoor areas have wireless network access. Students can register for classes online. Administrative functions (other than registration) can be performed online. Undergraduates are required to own a computer.

CAMPUS LIFE
Environment: Rural. **Activities:** Choral groups, concert band, dance, drama/theater, jazz band, literary magazine, marching band, music ensembles, musical theater, opera, pep band, radio station, student government, student newspaper, symphony orchestra, television station, yearbook, Campus Ministries, International Student Organization. 130 registered organizations, 19 honor societies, 22 religious organizations. 8 fraternities, 8 sororities. **Athletics (Intercollegiate):** *Men:* baseball, basketball, cross-country, diving, football, golf, soccer, swimming, tennis, track/field (outdoor). *Women:* basketball, cheerleading, cross-country, diving, golf, soccer, softball, swimming, tennis, track/field (outdoor), volleyball, water polo. **On-Campus Highlights:** Student Union, Chapel, Hall of Arts and Letters, Fitness Center, Ketler Recreation Room. **Environmental Initiatives:** Use of high-efficiency condensing boilers in new construction or existing retrofits. Use of chilled beams and heat recovery in new construction. Allowing students and employees to participate in annual e-waste recycling collection.

ADMISSIONS
Freshman Academic Profile: Average high school GPA 3.73. 45% in top 10% of high school class, 79% in top 25% of high school class, 93% in top 50% of high school class. 60% from public high schools. SAT Math middle 50% range 632-661. SAT Critical Reading middle 50% range 538-673. ACT middle 50% range 24-29. Minimum internet-based TOEFL 79. Minimum paper TOEFL 550. **Basis for Candidate Selection:** *Very important factors considered include:* application essay, academic GPA, rigor of secondary school record, standardized test scores, character/personal qualities, interview, level of applicant's interest, religious affiliation/commitment. *Important factors considered include:* recommendation(s), extracurricular activities, geographical residence. *Other factors considered include:* Class rank, alumni/ae relation, first generation, racial/ethnic status, state residency, talent/ability, volunteer work, work experience. **Freshman Admission Requirements:** High school diploma is required and GED is accepted. **Freshman Admission Statistics:** 1,492 applied, 88% admitted, 49% enrolled. **Transfer Admission Requirements:** High school transcript, college transcript(s), essay or personal statement, standardized test scores, statement of good standing from prior institution(s). Minimum college GPA of 2.0 required. Lowest grade transferable C. **General Admission Information:** Application Fee $50. Early decision application deadline 11/15. Regular application deadline 2/1. Regular notification 3/15. Nonfall registration accepted. Admission may be deferred for a maximum of 1 year. Credit offered for CEEB Advanced Placement tests.

COSTS AND FINANCIAL AID
Average book expense $1,000. **Required Forms and Deadlines:** Institution's own financial aid form. **Notification of Awards:** Applicants will be notified of awards on or about 3/26. **Types of Aid:** *Need-based scholarships/grants:* state scholarships/grants, private scholarships, the school's own gift aid. *Loans:* state loans, Private loans. *Student Employment:* Institutional employment available. Highest amount earned per year from on-campus jobs $1,500. Off-campus job opportunities are good. **Financial Aid Statistics:** 98% freshmen, 98% undergrads receive need-based scholarship or grant aid. 9% freshmen, 8% undergrads receive non-need-based scholarship or grant aid. 62% freshmen, 65% undergrads receive need-based self-help aid. 0% freshmen, 0% undergrads receive athletic scholarships. 70% freshmen, 71% undergrads receive any aid. 56% undergrads borrow to pay for school. Average cumulative indebtedness $0. **Criteria for awarding institutional aid:** *Non-need-based:* academics, leadership, minority status.

GUILFORD COLLEGE

5800 West Friendly Avenue, Greensboro, NC 27410
Phone: 336-316-2100 • **Financial Aid Phone:** 336-316-2410
E-mail: admission@guilford.edu • **CEEB Code:** 5261
Fax: 336-316-2954 • **Website:** http://www.guilford.edu/ • **ACT Code:** 3106

This private school, affiliated with the Quaker Church, was founded in 1837. It has a 340-acre campus.

RATINGS
Admissions Selectivity Rating: 82   **Fire Safety Rating:** 81

STUDENTS AND FACULTY
Enrollment: 1,999. **Student Body:** 53% female, 47% male, 45% out-of-state, 2% international (23 countries represented). Asian 2%, African American 23%, Caucasian 63%, Hispanic 6%, Native American <1%
Retention and Graduation: 50% freshmen graduate within 4 years. 20% grads go on to further study within 1 year. 55% grads pursue arts and sciences degrees. 1% grads pursue law degrees. 18% grads pursue business degrees. 1% grads pursue medical degrees. **Faculty:** 116 full-time faculty, 91% hold PhDs, 48% are members of minority groups, 8% are women. 0% of classes are taught by teaching assistants.

ACADEMICS
Degrees: bachelor's, certificate. **Classes:** Most classes have 10–19 students. Most lab/discussion sessions have 10–19 students. **Majors with Highest Enrollment:** Psychology; Criminal Justice/Safety Studies; Business Administration and Management. **Special Study Options:** Accelerated program, cooperative education program, cross-registration, double major, honors program, independent study, internships, liberal arts/career combination, student-designed major, study abroad, teacher certification program, weekend college, There are 3-2 degree programs available in forestry and environmental studies with Duke University, and in physician assistant training with Bowman Gray School of Medicine at Wake Forest University. Guilford also offers many internships, a Washington semester, work-study programs, accelerated degree programs in business management, computer information systems, psychology, and biology, dual majors, student-designed majors, study abroad in 9 countries, and cross-registration with members of the Greater Greensboro Consortium (8 colleges/universities). **Honors programs:** Guilford College is a participating member of the National Collegiate Honors Council. Membership in the NCHC means that students in the Guilford College Honors Program can participate in the NCHC Honors Semesters. These semester programs are regularly offered in different sites around the world and enable Honors students from across the country to meet and learn in unique settings. In recent years, Guilford College students have participated in the Study Abroad programs sponsored by Honors Programs at other colleges and universities. The University of North Carolina at Wilmington offers an Honors Semester Program at the University of Wales Swansea. For more information visit the following site: www.swan.ac.uk. Eastern Illinois University offers a n Honors Summer Program at the Universite Catholique de Louvain in Belgium that features archaeological study of historic sites. For more information, one can visit: www.eiu.edu/~honprog/abroad.htm. Both these programs offer college credit courses that are transferable. Combined degree programs: 3-1 Physician's asst program, 3-2 Forestry/environ. **Disability Services:** Special programs offered to physically disabled students include note-taking services, reader services, tape recorders, tutors. **Career services:** Alumni network, alumni services, career/job search classes, career assessment, internships. Career services highlights include internships that offer students up to 12 credit hours. Local, national, and international opportunities are available. Program is centralized and provides a coordinator to assist students with the process and reflection.

FACILITIES
Housing: Coed dorms, special housing for disabled students, men's dorms, special housing for international students, women's dorms, cooperative housing, apartments for single students, Theme HousingSpecial interest housing available. Alternative houses with themes and community service project requirements. 97% of campus accessible to physically disabled. Friends Historical Collection, Frank Family Science Center, art gallery, language lab, research-grade observatory + planetarium, **Computers:** 15% of classrooms, 10% of dorms, 100% of libraries, 100% of dining areas, 50% of student union, 10% of common outdoor areas have wireless network access. Students can register for classes online. Administrative functions (other than registration) can be performed online.

CAMPUS LIFE
Environment: City. **Activities:** Choral groups, concert band, dance, drama/theater, jazz band, literary magazine, music ensembles, musical theater, pep band, radio station, student government, student newspaper, student-run film society, yearbook, Campus Ministries. 47 registered organizations, 1 honor society, 8 religious organizations. **Athletics (Intercollegiate):** *Men:* baseball, basketball, cross-country, football, golf, lacrosse, rugby, soccer, tennis. *Women:* basketball, cross-country, lacrosse, rugby, soccer, softball, swimming, tennis, volleyball. **On-Campus Highlights:** Hege Library and Art Gallery, Community Center, Frank Family Science Center, Founders Student Center and the new Grill 155, The Greenleaf Café—coffee co-op. The Guilford College campus is a beautiful 340 acre campus situated in the western residential area of Greensboro, North Carolina. The college is bordered by woods on one end and easy access to stores on the other. **Environmental Initiatives:** Purchasing policy that only allows Energy Star rated appliances. Renovations and new building required to be built to LEED silver standards. Zero food waste due to composting and a food waste digester.

ADMISSIONS
Freshman Academic Profile: Average high school GPA 3.13. 12% in top 10% of high school class, 34% in top 25% of high school class, 71% in top 50% of high school class. 75% from public high schools. SAT Math middle 50% range 460-580. SAT Critical Reading middle 50% range 450-590. SAT Writing middle 50% range 430-560. ACT middle 50% range 19-26. Minimum paper TOEFL 550. **Basis for Candidate Selection:** *Very important factors considered include:* application essay, academic GPA, rigor of secondary school record, character/personal qualities. *Important factors considered include:* Class rank, recommendation(s), standardized test scores, extracurricular activities, interview, level of applicant's interest, talent/ability, volunteer work, work experience. *Other factors considered include:* alumni/ae relation, first generation, geographical residence, racial/ethnic status, state residency. **Freshman Admission Requirements:** High school diploma is required and GED is accepted. **Freshman Admission Statistics:** 3,001 applied, 62% admitted, 19% enrolled. **Transfer Admission Requirements:** High school transcript, college transcript(s), essay or personal statement, standardized test scores, statement of good standing from prior institution(s). Minimum college GPA of 2.5 required. Lowest grade transferable C. **General Admission Information:** Application Fee $25. Regular application deadline 8/10. Notification on a rolling basis, beginning on or about 10/1. Nonfall registration accepted. Admission may be deferred for a maximum of 12 months. Credit and/or placement offered for CEEB Advanced Placement tests.

COSTS AND FINANCIAL AID
Required Forms and Deadlines: FAFSA. **Notification of Awards:** Applicants will be notified of awards on a rolling basis beginning 2/15. **Types of Aid:** *Need-based scholarships/grants:* Federal Pell, SEOG, state scholarships/grants, private scholarships, the school's own gift aid. *Loans:* Subsidized Stafford, Unsubsidized Stafford, PLUS, Federal Perkins, college/university loans from institutional funds. *Student Employment:* Federal Work-Study Program available. Institutional employment available. Highest amount earned per year from on-campus jobs $6,911. Off-campus job opportunities are fair. **Financial Aid Statistics:** 91% freshmen, 92% undergrads receive need-based scholarship or grant aid. 96% freshmen, 56% undergrads receive non-need-based scholarship or grant aid. 76% freshmen, 72% undergrads receive need-based self-help aid. 0% freshmen, 0% undergrads receive athletic scholarships. 98% freshmen, 86% undergrads receive any aid. 79% undergrads borrow to pay for school. Average cumulative indebtedness $13,253. **Criteria for awarding institutional aid:** *Non-need-based:* academics.

GUSTAVUS ADOLPHUS COLLEGE

800 College Avenue, Saint Peter, MN 56082
Phone: 507-933-7676 • **Financial Aid Phone:** 507-933-7527
E-mail: admission@gustavus.edu • **CEEB Code:** 6253
Fax: 507-933-7474 • **Website:** www.gustavus.edu • **ACT Code:** 2112

This private school, affiliated with the Lutheran Church, was founded in 1862. It has a 340-acre campus.

RATINGS
Admissions Selectivity Rating: 89   **Fire Safety Rating:** 82

STUDENTS AND FACULTY
Enrollment: 2,454. **Student Body:** 54% female, 46% male, 19% out-of-state, 3% international (19 countries represented). Asian 4%, African American 2%, Caucasian 83%, Hispanic 3%, Native American <1%
Retention and Graduation: 90% freshmen return for sophomore year. 81% freshmen graduate within 4 years. 82% freshmen graduate within 6 years. 26%

grads go on to further study within 1 year. 9% grads pursue arts and sciences degrees. 2% grads pursue law degrees. 2% grads pursue business degrees. 3% grads pursue medical degrees. **Faculty:** 193 full-time faculty, 98% hold PhDs, 53% are members of minority groups, 16% are women. 0% of classes are taught by teaching assistants.

ACADEMICS

Degrees: bachelor's. **Classes:** Most classes have 10–19 students. Most lab/discussion sessions have 10–19 students. **Majors with Highest Enrollment:** Psychology; Business/Commerce; Biology/Biological Sciences. **Special Study Options:** cooperative education program, cross-registration, double major, dual enrollment, exchange student program (domestic), honors program, independent study, internships, liberal arts/career combination, student-designed major, study abroad, teacher certification program. **Honors programs:** Curriculum II. **Disability Services:** Special programs offered to physically disabled students include note-taking services, reader services, tape recorders, tutors. **Career services:** Alumni network, alumni services, career assessment, internships. Career services highlights include a well developed internship program offering month-long career explorations as well as full-semester and summer full-time and part-time internships for academic credit. Forty-eight percent of our graduates participate in an internship for academic credit and 93.4% participated in some type of experiential learning during their college experience.

FACILITIES

Housing: Coed dorms, special housing for disabled students, special housing for international students, apartments for single students, Wellness Housing, Theme Housing. 95% of campus accessible to physically disabled. **Special Academic Facilities/Equipment:** Art gallery, mineral museum, electron microscopes, arboretum, 14-inch computer-guided Celestron telescope, artificial intelligence laboratory, materials science laboratory, 300-MHz NMR spectrometer, five-section greenhouse. **Computers:** 100% of dorms, 100% of libraries, 100% of dining areas, 100% of student union, 50% of common outdoor areas have wireless network access. Students can register for classes online. Administrative functions (other than registration) can be performed online.

CAMPUS LIFE

Environment: Village. **Activities:** Choral groups, concert band, dance, drama/theater, jazz band, literary magazine, music ensembles, musical theater, pep band, radio station, student government, student newspaper, symphony orchestra, television station, yearbook. 120 registered organizations, 11 honor society, 8 religious organizations. 5 fraternities, 5 sororities. **Athletics (Intercollegiate):** *Men:* baseball, basketball, cross-country, diving, football, golf, ice hockey, skiing (nordic/cross-country), soccer, swimming, tennis, track/field (outdoor), track/field (indoor). *Women:* basketball, cross-country, diving, golf, gymnastics, ice hockey, skiing (nordic/cross-country), soccer, softball, swimming, tennis, track/field (outdoor), track/field (indoor), volleyball. **On-Campus Highlights:** Campus Center, Courtyard Café, Lund Athletic Center, Christ Chapel, Linnaeus Arboretum, With over 75% of students remaining on campus during a typical weekend (according to our Dining Service), our students actively use the entire campus. As there are no city streets intersecting our campus, Gusties enjoy their home on the hill. **Environmental Initiatives:** Seeking to acquire 5 MW of wind generator capacity Established the Johnson Center for Environmental Innovation Strong institutional commitment to recycling & energy conservation

ADMISSIONS

Freshman Academic Profile: Average high school GPA 3.63. 31% in top 10% of high school class, 64% in top 25% of high school class, 94% in top 50% of high school class. 93% from public high schools. SAT Math middle 50% range 550-680. SAT Critical Reading middle 50% range 550-680. ACT middle 50% range 24-30. Minimum internet-based TOEFL 80. Minimum paper TOEFL 550. **Basis for Candidate Selection:** *Very important factors considered include:* rigor of secondary school record. *Important factors considered include:* application essay, academic GPA, recommendation(s), standardized test scores. *Other factors considered include:* alumni/ae relation, extracurricular activities, first generation, geographical residence, interview, level of applicant's interest, racial/ethnic status, religious affiliation/commitment, state residency, talent/ability, volunteer work, work experience. **Freshman Admission Requirements:** High school diploma is required and GED is accepted. *Academic units required:* 4 English, 3 mathematics, 2 science, (2 science labs), 2 foreign language, 2 social studies, 2 history. **Freshman Admission Statistics:** 5,199 applied, 61% admitted, 19% enrolled. **Transfer Admission Requirements:** High school transcript, college transcript(s), essay or personal statement, standardized test scores, statement of good standing from prior institution(s). Minimum college GPA of 2.4 required. Lowest grade transferable 2. **General Admission Information:** Notification on a rolling basis, beginning on or about 11/20. Nonfall registration accepted. Admission may be deferred for a maximum of 1 year. Credit and/or placement offered for CEEB Advanced Placement tests.

COSTS AND FINANCIAL AID

Annual tuition $39,550. Room and board $9,250. Required fees $460. Average book expense $900. **Required Forms and Deadlines:** FAFSA. **Notification**

of Awards: Applicants will be notified of awards on a rolling basis beginning 1/20. **Types of Aid:** *Need-based scholarships/grants:* Federal Pell, SEOG, state scholarships/grants, private scholarships, the school's own gift aid. *Loans:* Direct Subsidized Stafford, Direct Unsubsidized Stafford, Direct PLUS, Federal Perkins, state loans, Alternative loans from private lenders. *Student Employment:* Federal Work-Study Program available. Institutional employment available. Highest amount earned per year from on-campus jobs $1,800. Off-campus job opportunities are good. **Financial Aid Statistics:** 98% freshmen, 98% undergrads receive need-based scholarship or grant aid. 10% freshmen, 9% undergrads receive non-need-based scholarship or grant aid. 98% freshmen, 99% undergrads receive need-based self-help aid. 0% freshmen, 0% undergrads receive athletic scholarships. 96% freshmen, 95% undergrads receive any aid. 76% undergrads borrow to pay for school. Average cumulative indebtedness $26,274. **Criteria for awarding institutional aid:** *Non-need-based:* academics, alumni affiliation, art, music/drama, religious affiliation.

GWYNEDD-MERCY COLLEGE

1325 Sumneytown Pike, Gwynedd Valley, PA 19437-0901
Phone: 215-641-5510 • **Financial Aid Phone:** 215-646-7300
E-mail: admissions@gmc.edu • **CEEB Code:** 2278
Fax: 215-641-5556 • **Website:** www.gmc.edu

This private school, affiliated with the Roman Catholic Church, was founded in 1948. It has a 160-acre campus.

RATINGS

Admissions Selectivity Rating: 73   **Fire Safety Rating:** 74

STUDENTS AND FACULTY

Enrollment: 2,130. **Student Body:** 74% female, 26% male, 8% out-of-state, 0% international (28 countries represented). Asian 2%, African American 21%, Caucasian 69%, Hispanic 1%, Native American <1%
Retention and Graduation: 76% freshmen return for sophomore year. 50% freshmen graduate within 4 years. 69% freshmen graduate within 6 years. 60% grads go on to further study within 1 year. **Faculty:** 75 full-time faculty, 63% hold PhDs, 71% are members of minority groups, 0% are women. 0% of classes are taught by teaching assistants.

ACADEMICS

Degrees: associate, bachelor's, certificate, master's, post-bachelor's certificate, post-master's certificate. **Classes:** Most classes have 10–19 students. Most lab/discussion sessions have 10–19 students. **Majors with Highest Enrollment:** Education; Business Administration and Management; Registered Nursing, Nursing Administration, Nursing Research and Clinical Nursing. **Special Study Options:** Accelerated program, cross-registration, double major, English as a Second Language (ESL), honors program, independent study, internships, liberal arts/career combination, study abroad, teacher certification program, weekend college. **Honors programs:** The Honors Program in Liberal Studies consists of six interdisciplinary, team-taught courses developing the theme of "The Quest for Community and Freedom: The Individual and Society." Combined degree programs: BSN/MSN. **Disability Services:** Special programs offered to physically disabled students include reader services, tutors. **Career services:** alumni services, career assessment, internships.

FACILITIES

Housing: Coed dorms, special housing for international students. 95% of campus accessible to physically disabled. **Special Academic Facilities/Equipment:** Keiss Hall (Health and Science Center), television production room and small theater, computer labs. **Computers:** Students can register for classes online.

CAMPUS LIFE

Environment: City. **Activities:** Choral groups, literary magazine, student government, student newspaper, yearbook, Campus Ministries. 22 registered organizations, 10 honor societies, 1 religious organization. **Athletics (Intercollegiate):** *Men:* baseball, basketball, cross-country, golf, soccer, tennis, track/field (outdoor), track/field (indoor). *Women:* basketball, cross-country, field hockey, lacrosse, soccer, softball, tennis, track/field (outdoor), track/field (indoor), volleyball. **On-Campus Highlights:** Assumption Hall, The Sister Isabelle Keiss Center for Health and Sciences, The Griffin Complex Student Union and Athletic Facility, Saint Bernard Lobby and Snack Bar, Loyola Hall and Saint Brigid's Hall—Residence Halls.

ADMISSIONS

Freshman Academic Profile: 4% in top 10% of high school class, 14% in top 25% of high school class, 40% in top 50% of high school class. 57% from public high schools. SAT Math middle 50% range 430-530. SAT Critical Reading middle 50% range 440-530. Minimum paper TOEFL 525. **Basis for Candidate Selection:** *Very important factors considered include:* rigor of secondary school record. *Important factors considered include:* Class rank, academic GPA, recommendation(s), standardized test scores, extracurricular activities. *Other factors considered include:* application essay, alumni/ae relation, character/ personal qualities, interview, volunteer work, work experience. **Freshman Admission Requirements:** High school diploma is required and GED is accepted. *Academic units required:* 4 English, 3 mathematics, 3 science, 0 foreign language, 1 history, 3 academic electives. 4 English, 3 mathematics, 3 science, 0 foreign language, 1 history, 3 academic electives. **Freshman Admission Statistics:** 1,844 applied, 67% admitted, 25% enrolled. **Transfer Admission Requirements:** High school transcript, college transcript(s), Minimum college GPA of 2.0 required. Lowest grade transferable c. **General Admission Information:** Application Fee $25. Regular application deadline 8/20. Notification on a rolling basis, beginning on or about 9/20. Nonfall registration accepted. Admission may be deferred for a maximum of 12 months. Credit and/or placement offered for CEEB Advanced Placement tests.

COSTS AND FINANCIAL AID
Annual tuition $25,160. Room and board $9,760. Required fees $450. Average book expense $600. **Required Forms and Deadlines:** FAFSA, Institution's own financial aid form. **Notification of Awards:** Applicants will be notified of awards on a rolling basis beginning 3/1. **Types of Aid:** *Need-based scholarships/ grants:* Federal Pell, SEOG, state scholarships/grants, private scholarships, the school's own gift aid. *Loans:* Direct Subsidized Stafford, Direct Unsubsidized Stafford, Direct PLUS, Subsidized Stafford, Unsubsidized Stafford, PLUS, Federal Perkins, Federal Nursing, Alternative loan through banks. *Student Employment:* Federal Work-Study Program available. Off-campus job opportunities are fair. **Financial Aid Statistics:** 97% freshmen, 98% undergrads receive need-based scholarship or grant aid. 77% freshmen, 77% undergrads receive non-need-based scholarship or grant aid. 91% freshmen, 83% undergrads receive need-based self-help aid. 0% freshmen, 0% undergrads receive athletic scholarships. 97% freshmen, 92% undergrads receive any aid. 90% undergrads borrow to pay for school. Average cumulative indebtedness $26,160. **Criteria for awarding institutional aid:** *Non-need-based:* academics, leadership.

HAMILTON COLLEGE

Office of Admission, Clinton, NY 13323
Phone: 315-859-4421 · **Financial Aid Phone:** 800-859-4413
E-mail: admission@hamilton.edu · **CEEB Code:** 2286
Fax: 315-859-4457 · **Website:** www.hamilton.edu · **ACT Code:** 2754

This private school was founded in 1812. It has a 1300-acre campus.

RATINGS
Admissions Selectivity Rating: 96   **Fire Safety Rating:** 87

STUDENTS AND FACULTY
Enrollment: 1,890. **Student Body:** 51% female, 49% male, 70% out-of-state, 5% international (45 countries represented). Asian 7%, African American 4%, Caucasian 64%, Hispanic 8%, Native American <1%
Retention and Graduation: 96% freshmen return for sophomore year. 86% freshmen graduate within 4 years. 91% freshmen graduate within 6 years. 14% grads go on to further study within 1 year. 8% grads pursue arts and sciences degrees. 1% grads pursue law degrees. 1% grads pursue business degrees. 2% grads pursue medical degrees. **Faculty:** 191 full-time faculty, 95% hold PhDs, 43% are members of minority groups, 18% are women. 0% of classes are taught by teaching assistants.

ACADEMICS
Degrees: bachelor's. **Classes:** Most classes have 10–19 students. Most lab/ discussion sessions have 10–19 students. **Majors with Highest Enrollment:** Economics; Biology/Biological Sciences; International Relations and Affairs. **Special Study Options:** Accelerated program, cross-registration, double major, English as a Second Language (ESL), independent study, internships, student-designed major, study abroad, 3-2 program in Engineering with Columbia University, Rensselaer Polytechnic Institute, and Washington University(St. Louis); 3-3 program in Law with Columbia University. Combined degree programs: BA/JD, BA/MEng, Cooperative Program with Columbia University. **Disability Services:** Special programs offered to physically disabled students include note-taking services, reader services, tape recorders, tutors. **Career services:**

Alumni network, alumni services, career/job search classes, career assessment, internships, regional alumni. Career services highlights include the Summer Internship Fund, launched with a $1.6 million endowment in 2006, which provides cost-of-living stipends each summer to a number of undergraduates who accept unpaid internships in any career field.

FACILITIES
Housing: Coed dorms, special housing for disabled students, apartments for married students, cooperative housing, apartments for single students, Wellness Housing. **Special Academic Facilities/Equipment:** Art gallery, language lab, fitness center, observatory, two electron microscopes. Arthur Levitt Public Affairs Center. **Computers:** 100% of classrooms, 100% of dorms, 100% of libraries, 100% of dining areas, 100% of student union, 100% of common outdoor areas have wireless network access. Students can register for classes online. Administrative functions (other than registration) can be performed online.

CAMPUS LIFE
Environment: Rural. **Activities:** Choral groups, concert band, dance, drama/ theater, jazz band, literary magazine, music ensembles, musical theater, radio station, student government, student newspaper, student-run film society, symphony orchestra, yearbook, Campus Ministries, International Student Organization, Model UN. 117 registered organizations, 8 honor societies, 4 religious organizations. 11 fraternity, 7 sororities. **Athletics (Intercollegiate):** *Men:* baseball, basketball, crew/rowing, cross-country, diving, football, golf, ice hockey, lacrosse, soccer, squash, swimming, tennis, track/field (outdoor), track/ field (indoor). *Women:* basketball, crew/rowing, cross-country, diving, field hockey, ice hockey, lacrosse, soccer, softball, squash, swimming, tennis, track/ field (outdoor), track/field (indoor), volleyball. **On-Campus Highlights:** Blood Fitness and Dance Center, Kirner-Johnson Commons, Outdoor Leadership Center/Root Glen, Science Center, Café Opus.

ADMISSIONS
Freshman Academic Profile: 75% in top 10% of high school class, 94% in top 25% of high school class, 99% in top 50% of high school class. 61% from public high schools. SAT Math middle 50% range 660-740. SAT Critical Reading middle 50% range 650-730. SAT Writing middle 50% range 650-740. ACT middle 50% range 30-33. **Basis for Candidate Selection:** *Very important factors considered include:* Class rank, academic GPA, rigor of secondary school record. *Important factors considered include:* application essay, recommendation(s), standardized test scores, character/personal qualities, extracurricular activities, interview. *Other factors considered include:* alumni/ae relation, first generation, geographical residence, level of applicant's interest, racial/ethnic status, talent/ ability, volunteer work, work experience. **Freshman Admission Requirements:** High school diploma is required and GED is accepted. **Freshman Admission Statistics:** 5,071 applied, 26% admitted, 35% enrolled. **Transfer Admission Requirements:** High school transcript, college transcript(s), essay or personal statement, standardized test scores, statement of good standing from prior institution(s). Lowest grade transferable C. **General Admission Information:** Application Fee $75. Early decision application deadline 11/15. Regular application deadline 1/1. Regular notification 4/1. Nonfall registration accepted. Admission may be deferred for a maximum of 2 years. Credit and/or placement offered for CEEB Advanced Placement tests.

COSTS AND FINANCIAL AID
Average book expense $1,300. **Required Forms and Deadlines:** FAFSA, Institution's own financial aid form, CSS/Financial Aid PROFILE, State aid form, Noncustodial PROFILE, Business/Farm Supplement. **Notification of Awards:** Applicants will be notified of awards on or about 4/1. **Types of Aid:** *Need-based scholarships/grants:* Federal Pell, SEOG, state scholarships/ grants, private scholarships, the school's own gift aid. *Loans:* Subsidized Stafford, Unsubsidized Stafford, PLUS, Federal Perkins, college/university loans from institutional funds. *Student Employment:* Federal Work-Study Program available. Institutional employment available. Highest amount earned per year from on-campus jobs $1,800. **Financial Aid Statistics:** 100% freshmen, 100% undergrads receive need-based scholarship or grant aid. 0% freshmen, 0% undergrads receive non-need-based scholarship or grant aid. 84% freshmen, 83% undergrads receive need-based self-help aid. 0% freshmen, 0% undergrads receive athletic scholarships. 52% freshmen, 47% undergrads receive any aid. 44% undergrads borrow to pay for school. Average cumulative indebtedness $15,441. **Criteria for awarding institutional aid:** *Non-need-based:* state/ district residency.

HAMLINE UNIVERSITY

1536 Hewitt Ave, St Paul, MN 55104
Phone: 651-523-2207 · **Financial Aid Phone:** 651-523-3000
E-mail: CLA-admis@hamline.edu · **CEEB Code:** 6265
Fax: 651-523-2458 · **Website:** www.hamline.edu · **ACT Code:** 2114

This private school, affiliated with the Methodist Church, was founded in 1854. It has a 77-acre campus.

RATINGS

Admissions Selectivity Rating: 83   **Fire Safety Rating:** 82

STUDENTS AND FACULTY

Enrollment: 1,986. **Student Body:** 58% female, 42% male, 15% out-of-state, 3% international (53 countries represented). Asian 6%, African American 5%, Caucasian 75%, Hispanic 2%, Native American 1%
Retention and Graduation: 82% freshmen return for sophomore year. 61% freshmen graduate within 4 years. 68% freshmen graduate within 6 years. 27% grads go on to further study within 1 year. 17% grads pursue arts and sciences degrees. 4% grads pursue law degrees. 2% grads pursue business degrees. 1% grads pursue medical degrees. **Faculty:** 173 full-time faculty, 87% hold PhDs, 49% are members of minority groups, 11% are women. 0% of classes are taught by teaching assistants.

ACADEMICS

Degrees: bachelor's, first professional, master's, post-bachelor's certificate. **Classes:** Most classes have 10–19 students. Most lab/discussion sessions have 10–19 students. **Majors with Highest Enrollment:** Psychology; Criminal Justice/Police Science; Business/Commerce. **Special Study Options:** cross-registration, double major, dual enrollment, English as a Second Language (ESL), exchange student program (domestic), honors program, independent study, internships, student-designed major, study abroad, teacher certification program. Combined degree programs: BA/JD, BA/MEng, 3-3 prog with Hamline School of Law. **Disability Services:** Special programs offered to physically disabled students include note-taking services, reader services, tape recorders, tutors. **Career services:** Alumni network, alumni services, career/job search classes, career assessment, internships, regional alumni. Career services highlights include the Leadership, Education, and Development (LEAD) requirement that all students must fulfill, which integrates the liberal arts with the world of work. Most students choose an internship to fulfill this requirement.

FACILITIES

Housing: Coed dorms, fraternity/sorority housing, apartments for married students, cooperative housing, apartments for single students, PRIDE (African-American), Spectrum (GLBT), Hmong, foreign language interest, theme housing (floors organized around areas like Arts, Weekends on Campus, GLBT, and Social Justice). 80% of campus accessible to physically disabled. **Special Academic Facilities/Equipment:** theatre, music hall, art gallery, science center. **Computers:** 100% of classrooms, 100% of dorms, 100% of libraries, 100% of dining areas, 100% of student union, 100% of common outdoor areas have wireless network access. Students can register for classes online. Administrative functions (other than registration) can be performed online.

CAMPUS LIFE

Environment: Metropolis. **Activities:** Choral groups, concert band, dance, drama/theater, jazz band, literary magazine, music ensembles, musical theater, pep band, radio station, student government, student newspaper, symphony orchestra, television station, yearbook, Campus Ministries, International Student Organization, Model UN. 77 registered organizations, 11 honor society, 9 religious organizations. 1 fraternity, 2 sororities. **Athletics (Intercollegiate):** *Men:* baseball, basketball, cross-country, diving, football, ice hockey, soccer, swimming, tennis, track/field (outdoor), track/field (indoor). *Women:* basketball, cross-country, diving, gymnastics, ice hockey, soccer, softball, swimming, tennis, track/field (outdoor), track/field (indoor), volleyball. **On-Campus Highlights:** Klas Center (stadium and food service), Walker Field House, Sorin Dining Hall, Sundin Music Hall, Bush Student Center. **Environmental Initiatives:** Recycling program Energy saving projects such as chiller replacement, boiler burner replacement and lighting retrofits. Transportation initiatives (increases in bike parking and the use of electric vehicles in mail services and safety and security services, discounted transit pass).

ADMISSIONS

Freshman Academic Profile: Average high school GPA 3.4. 20% in top 10% of high school class, 49% in top 25% of high school class, 79% in top 50% of high school class. 90% from public high schools. SAT Math middle 50% range 540-640. SAT Critical Reading middle 50% range 512.5-645. SAT Writing middle 50% range 510-615. ACT middle 50% range 21-27. Minimum paper TOEFL 550. **Basis for Candidate Selection:** *Very important factors considered include:* Class rank, rigor of secondary school record. *Important factors considered include:* application essay, academic GPA, recommendation(s), standardized test scores, extracurricular activities, interview, talent/ability. *Other factors considered include:* alumni/ae relation, character/personal qualities, first generation, racial/ethnic status, volunteer work, work experience. **Freshman Admission Requirements:** High school diploma is required and GED is accepted. **Freshman Admission Statistics:** 2,018 applied, 78% admitted, 29% enrolled. **Transfer Admission Requirements:** college transcript(s), essay or personal statement, Minimum college GPA of 2.0 required. Lowest grade transferable C-. **General Admission Information:** Notification on a rolling basis, beginning on or about 12/20. Nonfall registration accepted. Admission may be deferred for a maximum of 2 years. Credit and/or placement offered for CEEB Advanced Placement tests.

COSTS AND FINANCIAL AID

Required Forms and Deadlines: FAFSA. **Notification of Awards:** Applicants will be notified of awards on a rolling basis beginning 3/15. **Types of Aid:** *Need-based scholarships/grants:* Federal Pell, SEOG, state scholarships/grants, private scholarships, the school's own gift aid, Federal ACG and SMART grants. *Loans:* Subsidized Stafford, Unsubsidized Stafford, PLUS, Federal Perkins, state loans, Non-federal alternative loans. *Student Employment:* Federal Work-Study Program available. Institutional employment available. Highest amount earned per year from on-campus jobs $3,250. Off-campus job opportunities are excellent. **Financial Aid Statistics:** 100% freshmen, 99% undergrads receive need-based scholarship or grant aid. 15% freshmen, 10% undergrads receive non-need-based scholarship or grant aid. 87% freshmen, 91% undergrads receive need-based self-help aid. 0% freshmen, 0% undergrads receive athletic scholarships. 98% freshmen, 95% undergrads receive any aid. 79% undergrads borrow to pay for school. Average cumulative indebtedness $18,888. **Criteria for awarding institutional aid:** *Non-need-based:* academics, alumni affiliation, art, job skills, leadership, minority status, music/drama, religious affiliation, state/district residency.

HAMPDEN-SYDNEY COLLEGE

PO Box 667, Hampden-Sydney, VA 23943-0667
Phone: 434-223-6120 · **Financial Aid Phone:** 434-223-6119
E-mail: hsapp@hsc.edu · **CEEB Code:** 5291
Fax: 434-223-6346 · **Website:** www.hsc.edu · **ACT Code:** 4356

This private school, affiliated with the Presbyterian Church, was founded in 1775. It has a 1200-acre campus.

RATINGS

Admissions Selectivity Rating: 84   **Fire Safety Rating:** 80

STUDENTS AND FACULTY

Enrollment: 1,105. **Student Body:** 0% female, 100% male, 30% out-of-state, 0% international (14 countries represented). Asian 2%, African American 8%, Caucasian 82%, Hispanic 2%, Native American <1%
Retention and Graduation: 63% freshmen graduate within 4 years. 67% freshmen graduate within 6 years. 20% grads go on to further study within 1 year. 7% grads pursue arts and sciences degrees. 7% grads pursue law degrees. 5% grads pursue business degrees. 4% grads pursue medical degrees. **Faculty:** 85 full-time faculty, 88% hold PhDs, 29% are members of minority groups, 7% are women. 0% of classes are taught by teaching assistants.

ACADEMICS

Degrees: bachelor's. **Classes:** Most classes have 10–19 students. **Majors with Highest Enrollment:** Economics; History; Psychology. **Special Study Options:** cooperative education program, cross-registration, double major, dual enrollment, exchange student program (domestic), honors program, independent study, internships, study abroad, Appalachian semester, junior year exchange with members of Virginia consortium. Semester at sea and Washington semester also available. **Honors programs:** Student Summer Research programs, Departmental Honors. **Disability Services:** Special programs offered to physically disabled students include note-taking services, reader services, tape recorders, tutors. **Career services:** Alumni network, alumni services, career/job search classes, career assessment, internships, regional alumni. Career services highlights include Internships; our goal is to assist all of our students who want internships with finding them.

FACILITIES

Housing: men's dorms, special housing for international students, fraternity/sorority housing, apartments for married students, apartments for single students, Theme Housing, Language Houses. 90% of campus accessible to physically disabled. **Special Academic Facilities/Equipment:** History museum, language lab, international communications center, observatory. **Computers:** 15% of classrooms, 100% of libraries, 100% of dining areas, 100% of student union, 20% of common outdoor areas have wireless network access. Students can register for classes online. Administrative functions (other than registration) can be performed online.

CAMPUS LIFE

Environment: Rural. **Activities:** Choral groups, drama/theater, literary magazine, music ensembles, pep band, radio station, student government, student newspaper, yearbook, Campus Ministries, International Student Organization. 45 registered organizations, 14 honor societies, 6 religious organizations. 11 fraternity. **Athletics (Intercollegiate):** *Men:* baseball, basketball, cross-country, football, golf, lacrosse, soccer, tennis. **On-Campus Highlights:** Bortz Library, Kirby Fieldhouse (athletic facility), Gammon gym/Hall of Fame, Tiger Inn, Campus Museum. **Environmental Initiatives:** Electrical energy conservation; Removal of all underground fossil fuel tanks; Conversion from heating oil to propane for improved air quality.

ADMISSIONS

Freshman Academic Profile: Average high school GPA 3.38. 8% in top 10% of high school class, 30% in top 25% of high school class, 70% in top 50% of high school class. 64% from public high schools. SAT Math middle 50% range 500-610. SAT Critical Reading middle 50% range 495-600. SAT Writing middle 50% range 460-570. ACT middle 50% range 21-26. Minimum internet-based TOEFL 100. Minimum paper TOEFL 600. **Basis for Candidate Selection:** *Very important factors considered include:* application essay, academic GPA, recommendation(s), rigor of secondary school record, standardized test scores, character/personal qualities. *Important factors considered include:* Class rank, extracurricular activities. *Other factors considered include:* first generation, interview, level of applicant's interest, talent/ability, volunteer work, work experience. **Freshman Admission Requirements:** High school diploma is required and GED is accepted. *Academic units required:* 4 English, 3 mathematics, 2 science, (1 science labs), 2 foreign language, 1 social studies, 1 history, 3 academic electives. **Freshman Admission Statistics:** 3,639 applied, 47% admitted, 19% enrolled. **Transfer Admission Requirements:** High school transcript, college transcript(s), essay or personal statement, standardized test scores, statement of good standing from prior institution(s). Minimum college GPA of 2.5 required. Lowest grade transferable C. **General Admission Information:** Application Fee $30. Early decision application deadline 11/15. Regular application deadline 3/1. Regular notification 4/15. Nonfall registration accepted. Credit and/or placement offered for CEEB Advanced Placement tests.

COSTS AND FINANCIAL AID

Annual tuition $38,018. Room and board $12,312. Required fees $1,586. Average book expense $1,298. **Required Forms and Deadlines:** FAFSA, State aid form. **Notification of Awards:** Applicants will be notified of awards on or about 3/15. **Types of Aid:** *Need-based scholarships/grants:* Federal Pell, SEOG, state scholarships/grants, private scholarships, the school's own gift aid. *Loans:* Subsidized Stafford, Unsubsidized Stafford, PLUS, Federal Perkins, college/university loans from institutional funds. *Student Employment:* Federal Work-Study Program available. Institutional employment available. Highest amount earned per year from on-campus jobs $2,884. Off-campus job opportunities are fair. **Financial Aid Statistics:** 103% freshmen, 100% undergrads receive need-based scholarship or grant aid. 17% freshmen, 14% undergrads receive non-need-based scholarship or grant aid. 83% freshmen, 82% undergrads receive need-based self-help aid. 0% freshmen, 0% undergrads receive athletic scholarships. 100% freshmen, 99% undergrads receive any aid. 59% undergrads borrow to pay for school. Average cumulative indebtedness $26,811. **Criteria for awarding institutional aid:** *Non-need-based:* academics, leadership, minority status, religious affiliation, state/district residency.

HAMPSHIRE COLLEGE

Admissions Office, Amherst, MA 1002
Phone: 413-559-5471 • **Financial Aid Phone:** 413-559-5484
E-mail: admissions@hampshire.edu • **CEEB Code:** 3447
Fax: 413-559-5631 • **Website:** https://www.hampshire.edu/ • **ACT Code:** 1842

This private school was founded in 1965. It has a 850-acre campus.

RATINGS

Admissions Selectivity Rating: 82   **Fire Safety Rating:** 72

STUDENTS AND FACULTY

Enrollment: 1,358. **Student Body:** 59% female, 41% male, 5% international (31 countries represented). Asian 2%, African American 4%, Caucasian 68%, Hispanic 9%, Native American <1%
Retention and Graduation: 78% freshmen return for sophomore year. 63% freshmen graduate within 4 years. 74% freshmen graduate within 6 years. 10% grads go on to further study within 1 year. 8% grads pursue arts and sciences degrees. 1% grads pursue law degrees. 1% grads pursue medical degrees. **Faculty:** 112 full-time faculty. 0% of classes are taught by teaching assistants.

ACADEMICS

Degrees: bachelor's. **Classes:** Most classes have 10–19 students. Most lab/discussion sessions have 10–19 students. **Majors with Highest Enrollment:** Film/Video and Photographic Arts; Creative Writing; Cultural Studies/Critical Theory and Analysis. **Special Study Options:** exchange student program (domestic), independent study, internships, student-designed major, study abroad, teacher certification program. **Disability Services:** Special programs offered to physically disabled students include note-taking services, reader services, tape recorders. **Career services:** Alumni network, alumni services, career/job search classes, career assessment, internships.

FACILITIES

Housing: Coed dorms, special housing for disabled students, special housing for international students, women's dorms, apartments for single students, Theme Housing. 50% of campus accessible to physically disabled. **Special Academic Facilities/Equipment:** Performing and visual arts center, bioshelter (integrated greenhouse/aquaculture facility), farm center, electronic music and TV production studios, extensive film and photography facilities, multimedia center. **Computers:** 100% of classrooms, 10% of dorms, 100% of libraries, 100% of dining areas, n/a% of student union, 50% of common outdoor areas have wireless network access. Students can register for classes online. Administrative functions (other than registration) can be performed online.

CAMPUS LIFE

Environment: Town. **Activities:** Choral groups, dance, drama/theater, jazz band, student newspaper, student-run film society, International Student Organization. 94 registered organizations, 3 religious organizations. **On-Campus Highlights:** Bridge Café, Bookstore, Library, Eric Carle Museum of Picture Book Art, Liebling Center—Film/Photo. **Environmental Initiatives:** Constructing a new facility addition to LEED standards (minimum silver; hopefully gold); constructing a condominium community to be LEED certified. ACUPCC signatory, establishing an environmental committee and mandating emissions inventory. Formed a committee on sustainability that will engage all administrative areas, including Facilities and Grounds, Purchasing, Environmental Health and Safety, Dining Services, Campus Planning, and Information Technology. The campus sustainability committment has also been re-emphasized at the trustee committee level.

ADMISSIONS

Freshman Academic Profile: Average high school GPA 3.47. 74% from public high schools. SAT Math middle 50% range 530-660. SAT Critical Reading middle 50% range 580-700. SAT Writing middle 50% range 560-670. ACT middle 50% range 25-30. Minimum internet-based TOEFL 91. Minimum paper TOEFL 577. **Basis for Candidate Selection:** *Very important factors considered include:* application essay, character/personal qualities. *Important factors considered include:* recommendation(s), rigor of secondary school record, extracurricular activities, level of applicant's interest, talent/ability. *Other factors considered include:* Class rank, academic GPA, standardized test scores, alumni/ae relation, interview, racial/ethnic status, volunteer work, work experience. **Freshman Admission Requirements:** High school diploma is required and GED is accepted. *Academic units required:* 4 English, 3 mathematics, 3 science, (2 science labs), 3 foreign language, 3 history. **Freshman Admission Statistics:** 2,671 applied, 67% admitted, 19% enrolled. **Transfer Admission Requirements:** High school transcript, college transcript(s), essay or personal statement, Lowest grade transferable C. **General Admission Information:** Application Fee $60. Early decision application deadline 11/15. Regular application deadline 1/1. Regular notification 4/1. Nonfall registration accepted. Admission may be deferred for a maximum of 1 year. Placement offered for CEEB Advanced Placement tests.

COSTS AND FINANCIAL AID

Annual tuition $47,620. Room and board $12,950. Required fees $1,740. Average book expense $850. **Required Forms and Deadlines:** FAFSA, CSS/Financial Aid PROFILE, Noncustodial PROFILE. **Notification of Awards:** Applicants will be notified of awards on or about 4/1. **Types of Aid:** *Need-based scholarships/grants:* Federal Pell, SEOG, state scholarships/grants, private scholarships, the school's own gift aid. *Loans:* Direct Subsidized Stafford, Direct Unsubsidized Stafford, Direct PLUS, PLUS, Federal Perkins. *Student Employment:* Federal Work-Study Program available. Highest amount earned per year from on-campus jobs $2,600. **Financial Aid Statistics:** 97% freshmen, 98% undergrads receive need-based scholarship or grant aid. 14% freshmen, 14%

undergrads receive non-need-based scholarship or grant aid. 96% freshmen, 96% undergrads receive need-based self-help aid. 0% freshmen, 0% undergrads receive athletic scholarships. 70% freshmen, 76% undergrads receive any aid. 65% undergrads borrow to pay for school. Average cumulative indebtedness $19,706. **Criteria for awarding institutional aid:** *Non-need-based:* academics, leadership, minority status.

HAMPTON UNIVERSITY

Office of Admissions, Hampton, VA 23668
Phone: 757-727-5328 · **Financial Aid Phone:** 757-727-5332
E-mail: admit@hamptonu.edu · **CEEB Code:** 5292
Fax: 757-727-5095 · **Website:** www.hamptonu.edu · **ACT Code:** 4358

This private school was founded in 1868. It has a 255-acre campus.

RATINGS

Admissions Selectivity Rating: 88   **Fire Safety Rating:** 67

STUDENTS AND FACULTY

Enrollment: 3,851. **Student Body:** 64% female, 36% male, 51% out-of-state, 1% international (33 countries represented). Asian 1%, African American 89%, Caucasian 2%, Hispanic 1%, Native American <1%
Retention and Graduation: 76% freshmen return for sophomore year. **Faculty:** 363 full-time faculty, 75% hold PhDs, 58% are members of minority groups, 79% are women. 0% of classes are taught by teaching assistants.

ACADEMICS

Degrees: associate, bachelor's, certificate, first professional, master's, post-master's certificate. **Classes:** Most classes have 20–29 students. Most lab/discussion sessions have 10–19 students. **Majors with Highest Enrollment:** Psychology; Business Administration, Management and Operations; Biology. **Special Study Options:** Accelerated program, cooperative education program, cross-registration, distance learning, double major, dual enrollment, honors program, independent study, internships, study abroad, teacher certification program, Undergrads may take grad level programs. Co-Op Programs: Arts, Business, Education, Engineering,Social/Behavioral Science, Pre-college, Army ROTC, Navy ROTC. Member Tidewater Consortium. **Honors programs:** Honors College-Designed to augment, enhance and extend the undergraduate academic experience through community, exposure and expectations. Leadership Institute offers the undergraduate student a curricular option that enhances the university experience. Combined degree programs: Bachelor of Arts/Master in Teaching. **Disability Services:** Special programs offered to physically disabled students include note-taking services, reader services, tape recorders, tutors. **Career services:** Alumni network, alumni services, career/job search classes, career assessment, internships. Students who experience jobs through Cooperative Education have a chance to determine their life's work while earning academic credit.

FACILITIES

Housing: Coed dorms, men's dorms, special housing for international students, women's dorms. 90% of campus accessible to physically disabled. **Special Academic Facilities/Equipment:** African, Native American, and Oceanic museums, and gallery. New Student Center **Computers:** 100% of classrooms, 100% of dorms, 100% of libraries, 100% of dining areas, 100% of student union, 100% of common outdoor areas have wireless network access. Students can register for classes online. Administrative functions (other than registration) can be performed online.

CAMPUS LIFE

Environment: City. **Activities:** Choral groups, concert band, dance, drama/theater, jazz band, marching band, music ensembles, musical theater, opera, pep band, radio station, student government, student newspaper, symphony orchestra, television station, yearbook. 85 registered organizations, 16 honor societies, 3 religious organizations. 6 fraternities, 3 sororities. **Athletics (Intercollegiate):** *Men:* basketball, cross-country, football, golf, sailing, tennis, track/field (outdoor), track/field (indoor). *Women:* basketball, bowling, cross-country, golf, sailing, softball, tennis, track/field (outdoor), track/field (indoor), volleyball. **On-Campus Highlights:** Emancipation Oak, Memorial Chapel, Huntington Memorial Museum, Booker T. Washington Monument, Student Center: bowling, fitness and movie.

ADMISSIONS

Freshman Academic Profile: Average high school GPA 3.3. 20% in top 10% of high school class, 45% in top 25% of high school class, 90% in top 50% of high school class. 90% from public high schools. SAT Math middle 50% range 510-530. SAT Critical Reading middle 50% range 525-540. ACT middle 50% range 18-23. Minimum paper TOEFL 525. **Basis for Candidate Selection:** *Very important factors considered include:* application essay, rigor of secondary school record, standardized test scores, character/personal qualities. *Important factors considered include:* Class rank, recommendation(s). *Other factors considered include:* alumni/ae relation, extracurricular activities, talent/ability, volunteer work. **Freshman Admission Requirements:** High school diploma is required and GED is accepted. *Academic units required:* 4 English, 3 mathematics, 2 science, (2 science labs), 2 social studies, 6 academic electives. **Freshman Admission Statistics:** 14,503 applied, 36% admitted, 16% enrolled. **Transfer Admission Requirements:** college transcript(s), essay or personal statement, statement of good standing from prior institution(s). Minimum college GPA of 2.3 required. Lowest grade transferable C. **General Admission Information:** Application Fee $35. Nonfall registration accepted. Admission may be deferred for a maximum of one year. Credit and/or placement offered for CEEB Advanced Placement tests.

COSTS AND FINANCIAL AID

Annual tuition $17,732. Room and board $8,790. Required fees $2,006. Average book expense $1,100. **Required Forms and Deadlines:** FAFSA. **Notification of Awards:** Applicants will be notified of awards on a rolling basis beginning 4/15. **Types of Aid:** *Need-based scholarships/grants:* Federal Pell, SEOG, state scholarships/grants, private scholarships, the school's own gift aid, Federal Nursing Scholarships. *Loans:* Direct Subsidized Stafford, Direct Unsubsidized Stafford, Direct PLUS, Subsidized Stafford, Unsubsidized Stafford, PLUS, Federal Perkins, Alternative Loans. *Student Employment:* Federal Work-Study Program available. Off-campus job opportunities are excellent. **Financial Aid Statistics:** 94% freshmen, 95% undergrads receive need-based scholarship or grant aid. 37% freshmen, 26% undergrads receive non-need-based scholarship or grant aid. 81% freshmen, 83% undergrads receive need-based self-help aid. 5% freshmen, 5% undergrads receive athletic scholarships. 44% freshmen, 100% undergrads receive any aid. 93% undergrads borrow to pay for school. Average cumulative indebtedness $1,853. **Criteria for awarding institutional aid:** *Non-need-based:* academics, athletics, leadership, music/drama.

HANNIBAL-LAGRANGE UNIVERSITY

2800 Palmyra Road, Hannibal, MO 63401
Phone: 573-221-3113 · **Financial Aid Phone:** 573-629-3280
E-mail: admissio@hlg.edu
Fax: 573-221-6594 · **Website:** http://www.hlg.edu/ · **ACT Code:** 2320

This private school, affiliated with the Southern Baptist Church, was founded in 1858. It has a 110-acre campus.

RATINGS

Admissions Selectivity Rating: 72   **Fire Safety Rating:** 71

STUDENTS AND FACULTY

Enrollment: 1,246. **Student Body:** 26% out-of-state, (11 countries represented).
Retention and Graduation: 58% freshmen return for sophomore year. **Faculty:** 60 full-time faculty, 28% hold PhDs, 52% are members of minority groups, 2% are women. 0% of classes are taught by teaching assistants.

ACADEMICS

Degrees: associate, bachelor's, master's. **Majors with Highest Enrollment:** Secondary Education and Teaching; Elementary Education and Teaching; Non-Profit/Public/Organizational Management. **Special Study Options:** Accelerated program, distance learning, dual enrollment, English as a Second Language (ESL), honors program, independent study, internships, liberal arts/career combination, student-designed major, study abroad, teacher certification program, weekend college, Adult Program. **Honors programs:** Honors Program qualifies a student for a semester of study at Harlaxton College, Grantham, England. **Disability Services:** Special programs offered to physically disabled students include tape recorders, tutors. **Career services:** career assessment, internships. Career services highlights include the FOCUS online career exploration program.

FACILITIES

Housing: special housing for disabled students, men's dorms, women's dorms, apartments for single students. 98% of campus accessible to physically disabled. **Special Academic Facilities/Equipment:** L.A. Foster Library, T.M. Matthews Science Building, Mary Wiehe Science Building, Partee Tech. Center, Roland Fine Arts Center. **Computers:** Students can register for classes online.

CAMPUS LIFE

Environment: Village. **Activities:** Choral groups, concert band, drama/theater, jazz band, music ensembles, musical theater, student government, student newspaper, yearbook, Campus Ministries, International Student Organization. 22 registered organizations, 1 honor society, 3 religious organizations. **Athletics (Intercollegiate):** *Men:* baseball, basketball, cross-country, golf, soccer, swimming, track/field (outdoor), volleyball, wrestling. *Women:* basketball, cheerleading, cross-country, golf, soccer, softball, swimming, track/field (outdoor), volleyball. **On-Campus Highlights:** Roland Fine Arts Center, Mabee Sports Complex, Common Grounds, Snack Shack, Carroll Mission Center.

ADMISSIONS

Freshman Academic Profile: 21% in top 10% of high school class, 37% in top 25% of high school class, 52% in top 50% of high school class. SAT Math middle 50% range 440-480. SAT Critical Reading middle 50% range 260-490. SAT Writing middle 50% range 420-480. ACT middle 50% range 19-24. Minimum paper TOEFL 520. **Basis for Candidate Selection:** *Very important factors considered include:* academic GPA, standardized test scores. *Important factors considered include:* rigor of secondary school record. *Other factors considered include:* Class rank, recommendation(s), character/personal qualities, level of applicant's interest, religious affiliation/commitment, talent/ability. **Freshman Admission Requirements:** High school diploma is required and GED is accepted. **Transfer Admission Requirements:** college transcript(s), Minimum college GPA of 2.0 required. Lowest grade transferable 1. **General Admission Information:** Application Fee $25. Nonfall registration accepted. Admission may be deferred for a maximum of 1 semester. Neither credit nor placement offered for CEEB Advanced Placement tests.

COSTS AND FINANCIAL AID

Average book expense $800. **Required Forms and Deadlines:** FAFSA, Institution's own financial aid form. **Types of Aid:** *Need-based scholarships/grants:* Federal Pell, SEOG, state scholarships/grants, private scholarships, the school's own gift aid. *Loans:* Subsidized Stafford, Unsubsidized Stafford, PLUS, Federal Perkins. *Student Employment:* Federal Work-Study Program available. Institutional employment available. Off-campus job opportunities are fair. **Criteria for awarding institutional aid:** *Non-need-based:* academics, art, athletics, music/drama, religious affiliation.

HANOVER COLLEGE

Best 380

P.O. Box 108, Hanover, IN 47243-0108
Phone: 800-213-2178 · **Financial Aid Phone:** 812-866-7029
E-mail: admission@hanover.edu · **CEEB Code:** 1290
Fax: 812-866-7098 · **Website:** www.hanover.edu · **ACT Code:** 1200

This private school, affiliated with the Presbyterian Church, was founded in 1827. It has a 650-acre campus.

RATINGS

Admissions Selectivity Rating: 87   **Fire Safety Rating:** 90

STUDENTS AND FACULTY

Enrollment: 1,136. **Student Body:** 58% female, 42% male, 29% out-of-state, 5% international (56 countries represented). Asian 1%, African American 5%, Caucasian 82%, Hispanic 2%, Native American 1%
Retention and Graduation: 82% freshmen return for sophomore year. 66% freshmen graduate within 4 years. 69% freshmen graduate within 6 years. 24% grads go on to further study within 1 year. 16% grads pursue arts and sciences degrees. 3% grads pursue law degrees. 2% grads pursue business degrees. 2% grads pursue medical degrees. **Faculty:** 98 full-time faculty, 99% hold PhDs, 44% are members of minority groups, 8% are women. 0% of classes are taught by teaching assistants.

ACADEMICS

Degrees: bachelor's. **Classes:** Most classes have 10–19 students. **Majors with Highest Enrollment:** Psychology; Biology/Biological Sciences; Speech Communication and Rhetoric. **Special Study Options:** double major, dual enrollment, independent study, internships, student-designed major, study abroad, teacher certification program, CBP (Center for Business Preparation) Business Scholar Program, Philadelphia Center and Washington Center Internship

Programs. **Disability Services:** Special programs offered to physically disabled students include note-taking services, tutors. **Career services:** Alumni network, alumni services, career/job search classes, career assessment, internships, regional alumni. Hanover College curriculum teaches students to communicate effectively, think critically, and solve problems creatively. Through a variety of experiential learning opportunities and networking events, the CBP builds upon the liberal arts foundation by emphasizing personal leadership development and team working skills.

FACILITIES

Housing: Coed dorms, men's dorms, women's dorms, fraternity/sorority housing, apartments for single students, Wellness Housing, Theme Housing. 50% of campus accessible to physically disabled. **Special Academic Facilities/Equipment:** cadaver lab, geological museum, electronic language lab, observatory. **Computers:** 80% of classrooms, 100% of dorms, 50% of libraries, 100% of dining areas, 100% of student union, 20% of common outdoor areas have wireless network access. Students can register for classes online. Administrative functions (other than registration) can be performed online.

CAMPUS LIFE

Environment: Rural. **Activities:** Choral groups, concert band, dance, drama/theater, jazz band, literary magazine, music ensembles, musical theater, pep band, radio station, student government, student newspaper, student-run film society, symphony orchestra, television station, yearbook, Campus Ministries, International Student Organization. 60 registered organizations, 8 honor societies, 4 religious organizations. 4 fraternities, 4 sororities. **Athletics (Intercollegiate):** *Men:* baseball, basketball, cross-country, football, golf, lacrosse, soccer, tennis, track/field (outdoor). *Women:* basketball, cross-country, golf, soccer, softball, tennis, track/field (outdoor), volleyball. **On-Campus Highlights:** Science Center, Horner Health and Recreation Center (Collier Arena), Campus Center, The Shoebox, The Point-River View, The Shoebox serves food and drinks, as does the new coffee house in Crowe Hall. **Environmental Initiatives:** As part of the long range Strategic Plan the College has identified Environmental Sustainability as a core value; Developed a Board of Trustees approved Environmental Policy for the campus and are continuing to work on implementing an Environmental Management System across campus; Conducted an analysis and complete overhaul of our solid waste management system to improve our recycling rate as well as our waste diversion rate.

ADMISSIONS

Freshman Academic Profile: Average high school GPA 3.62. 29% in top 10% of high school class, 62% in top 25% of high school class, 93% in top 50% of high school class. 80% from public high schools. SAT Math middle 50% range 470-580. SAT Critical Reading middle 50% range 470-590. SAT Writing middle 50% range 450-550. ACT middle 50% range 23-28. Minimum internet-based TOEFL 80. Minimum paper TOEFL 550. **Basis for Candidate Selection:** *Very important factors considered include:* Class rank, academic GPA, rigor of secondary school record. *Important factors considered include:* recommendation(s), standardized test scores, talent/ability. *Other factors considered include:* application essay, alumni/ae relation, character/personal qualities, extracurricular activities, first generation, geographical residence, interview, level of applicant's interest, racial/ethnic status, state residency, volunteer work, work experience. **Freshman Admission Requirements:** High school diploma is required and GED is not accepted. *Academic units required:* 4 English, 3 mathematics, 3 science, (2 science labs), 2 foreign language, 2 social studies, 2 history, 2 academic electives. **Freshman Admission Statistics:** 2,888 applied, 64% admitted, 16% enrolled. **Transfer Admission Requirements:** High school transcript, college transcript(s), essay or personal statement, standardized test scores, statement of good standing from prior institution(s). Minimum college GPA of 2.0 required. Lowest grade transferable C-. **General Admission Information:** Application Fee $40. Regular application deadline 3/1. Notification on a rolling basis, beginning on or about 9/1. Nonfall registration accepted. Admission may be deferred for a maximum of 1 year. Credit and/or placement offered for CEEB Advanced Placement tests.

COSTS AND FINANCIAL AID

Annual tuition $32,423. Room and board $10,050. Required fees $600. Average book expense $1,200. **Required Forms and Deadlines:** FAFSA. **Notification of Awards:** Applicants will be notified of awards on a rolling basis beginning 3/1. **Types of Aid:** *Need-based scholarships/grants:* Federal Pell, SEOG, state scholarships/grants, private scholarships, the school's own gift aid. *Loans:* Subsidized Stafford, Unsubsidized Stafford, PLUS, college/university loans from institutional funds. *Student Employment:* Institutional employment available. Highest amount earned per year from on-campus jobs $3,000. Off-campus job opportunities are fair. **Financial Aid Statistics:** 100% freshmen, 100% undergrads receive need-based scholarship or grant aid. 17% freshmen, 14% undergrads receive non-need-based scholarship or grant aid. 82% freshmen, 85% undergrads receive need-based self-help aid. 0% freshmen, 0% undergrads receive athletic scholarships. 100% freshmen, 100% undergrads receive any aid. 79% undergrads borrow to pay for school. Average cumulative indebtedness $25,839. **Criteria for awarding institutional aid:** *Non-need-based:* academics, alumni affiliation, art, leadership, minority status, music/drama, religious affiliation, state/district residency.

HARDING UNIVERSITY

Box 12255, Searcy, AR 72149
Phone: 501-279-4407 • **Financial Aid Phone:** 501-279-4257
E-mail: admissions@harding.edu • **CEEB Code:** 10311
Fax: 501-279-4129 • **Website:** www.harding.edu • **ACT Code:** 124

This private school, affiliated with the Church of Christ Church, was founded in 1924. It has a 275-acre campus.

RATINGS

Admissions Selectivity Rating: 82   **Fire Safety Rating:** 86

STUDENTS AND FACULTY

Enrollment: 4,469. **Student Body:** 55% female, 45% male, 69% out-of-state, 6% international (44 countries represented). Asian 1%, African American 4%, Caucasian 84%, Hispanic 3%, Native American 1%
Retention and Graduation: 43% freshmen graduate within 4 years. 63% freshmen graduate within 6 years. **Faculty:** 289 full-time faculty, 67% hold PhDs, 35% are members of minority groups, 5% are women. 0% of classes are taught by teaching assistants.

ACADEMICS

Degrees: bachelor's, master's, post-master's certificate. **Classes:** Most classes have 10–19 students. Most lab/discussion sessions have 10–19 students. **Majors with Highest Enrollment:** Early Childhood Education and Teaching; Business Administration and Management; Accounting. **Special Study Options:** Accelerated program, cooperative education program, distance learning, double major, dual enrollment, English as a Second Language (ESL), honors program, independent study, internships, liberal arts/career combination, study abroad, teacher certification program. Combined degree programs: BA/PharmD. **Disability Services:** Special programs offered to physically disabled students include note-taking services, reader services, tape recorders, tutors. **Career services:** alumni services, career/job search classes, career assessment, internships.

FACILITIES

Housing: special housing for disabled students, men's dorms, women's dorms, apartments for married students, apartments for single students, Approved Off-Campus Housing. 95% of campus accessible to physically disabled. **Special Academic Facilities/Equipment:** On-campus academy (prep school grades K-12). **Computers:** 95% of classrooms, 100% of libraries, 100% of dining areas, 100% of student union, 80% of common outdoor areas have wireless network access. Students can register for classes online. Administrative functions (other than registration) can be performed online.

CAMPUS LIFE

Environment: Village. **Activities:** Choral groups, concert band, drama/theater, jazz band, marching band, music ensembles, pep band, radio station, student government, student newspaper, symphony orchestra, television station, yearbook, Campus Ministries, International Student Organization. 100 registered organizations, 12 honor societies, 10 religious organizations. 14 fraternities, 15 sororities. **Athletics (Intercollegiate):** *Men:* baseball, basketball, cross-country, football, golf, soccer, tennis, track/field (outdoor). *Women:* basketball, cheerleading, cross-country, golf, soccer, tennis, track/field (outdoor), volleyball. **On-Campus Highlights:** Cyber Café in Student Center, Front Lawn with Swings, Campus Dining until 9:00pm, Rhodes Memorial Field House, First Security Stadium. **Environmental Initiatives:** Recycling, Composting, Trayless Dining.

ADMISSIONS

Freshman Academic Profile: Average high school GPA 3.63. 27% in top 10% of high school class, 55% in top 25% of high school class, 82% in top 50% of high school class. 65% from public high schools. SAT Math middle 50% range 470-610. SAT Critical Reading middle 50% range 480-610. ACT middle 50% range 22-28. Minimum internet-based TOEFL 79. Minimum paper TOEFL 550. **Basis for Candidate Selection:** *Very important factors considered include:* recommendation(s), rigor of secondary school record, standardized test scores, character/personal qualities, interview. *Important factors considered include:* Class rank, academic GPA, talent/ability. *Other factors considered include:* application essay, alumni/ae relation, extracurricular activities, first generation, geographical residence, level of applicant's interest, state residency, volunteer work, work experience. **Freshman Admission Requirements:** High school diploma is required and GED is accepted. *Academic units required:* 4 English, 3 mathematics, 2 science, 3 social studies, 3 academic electives.

Freshman Admission Statistics: 2,269 applied, 99% admitted, 47% enrolled. **Transfer Admission Requirements:** college transcript(s), essay or personal statement, statement of good standing from prior institution(s). Minimum college GPA of 2 required. Lowest grade transferable C. **General Admission Information:** Application Fee $40. Notification on a rolling basis, beginning on or about 5/1. Nonfall registration accepted. Admission may be deferred for a maximum of One Year. Credit and/or placement offered for CEEB Advanced Placement tests.

COSTS AND FINANCIAL AID

Annual tuition $17,190. Room and board $6,700. Required fees $480. Average book expense $900. **Required Forms and Deadlines:** FAFSA. **Notification of Awards:** Applicants will be notified of awards on a rolling basis beginning 2/15. **Types of Aid:** *Need-based scholarships/grants:* Federal Pell, SEOG, state scholarships/grants, private scholarships, the school's own gift aid, Stephens Scholars Program for African-American students. *Loans:* Subsidized Stafford, Unsubsidized Stafford, PLUS, Federal Perkins, Federal Nursing, college/university loans from institutional funds. *Student Employment:* Federal Work-Study Program available. Institutional employment available. **Financial Aid Statistics:** 98% freshmen, 92% undergrads receive need-based scholarship or grant aid. 20% freshmen, 17% undergrads receive non-need-based scholarship or grant aid. 69% freshmen, 76% undergrads receive need-based self-help aid. 5% freshmen, 4% undergrads receive athletic scholarships. 99% freshmen, 94% undergrads receive any aid. 63% undergrads borrow to pay for school. Average cumulative indebtedness $20,597. **Criteria for awarding institutional aid:** *Non-need-based:* academics, alumni affiliation, art, athletics, leadership, music/drama, religious affiliation, state/district residency.

HARDIN-SIMMONS UNIVERSITY

Box 16050, Abilene, TX 79698
Phone: 325-670-1206 • **Financial Aid Phone:** 325-670-1206
E-mail: enroll@hsutx.edu • **CEEB Code:** 6268
Fax: 325-671-2115 • **Website:** www.hsutx.edu • **ACT Code:** 4096

This private school was founded in 1891. It has a 209-acre campus.

RATINGS

Admissions Selectivity Rating: 84   **Fire Safety Rating:** 67

STUDENTS AND FACULTY

Enrollment: 1,591. **Student Body:** 52% female, 48% male, 4% out-of-state, 2% international (20 countries represented). Asian 1%, African American 7%, Caucasian 71%, Hispanic 15%, Native American <1%
Retention and Graduation: 64% freshmen return for sophomore year. 36% freshmen graduate within 4 years. 53% freshmen graduate within 6 years. 45% grads go on to further study within 1 year. 17% grads pursue arts and sciences degrees. 3% grads pursue law degrees. 2% grads pursue business degrees. 7% grads pursue medical degrees. **Faculty:** 141 full-time faculty, 92% hold PhDs, 37% are members of minority groups, 5% are women. 0% of classes are taught by teaching assistants.

ACADEMICS

Degrees: bachelor's, doctoral, master's, post-bachelor's certificate. **Classes:** Most classes have 10–19 students. Most lab/discussion sessions have 20–29 students. **Majors with Highest Enrollment:** Registered Nursing/Registered Nurse; Business, Management, Marketing, and Related Support Services; Education. **Special Study Options:** Accelerated program, cross-registration, distance learning, double major, dual enrollment, honors program, independent study, internships, study abroad, teacher certification program. **Honors programs:** The Hardin-Simmons University Honors Program provides an enriched educational environment for undergraduate students of exceptional promise who have a wide variety of interests and seek an enhanced learning opportunity. The Honors Program promotes creative and critical thinking skills to equip individuals for success in today's world. The Program, which serves as an integral part of the academic community, includes courses taught by selected faculty members interested in working with highly motivated students. The Honors Program expects participants to strive for excellence and assume personal accountability for their intellectual growth. **Disability Services:** Special programs offered to physically disabled students include note-taking services, reader services, tape recorders, tutors. **Career services:** Alumni network, alumni services, career/job search classes, career assessment, internships, regional alumni. Career services highlights include the Internship program—the Office of Career Services at HSU hosts internship listings through our online service, Career Connection. In addition, many academic departments have a specific faculty person designated to help students find internship opportunities within their field of study.

FACILITIES

Housing: special housing for disabled students, men's dorms, women's dorms, apartments for married students, apartments for single students, Single and Duplex housing with priority given to families. 100% of campus accessible to physically disabled. **Special Academic Facilities/Equipment:** Art center, observatory with 14-inch telescope, rare and fine book room, SIX WHITE HORSE facility, Holland Health Science Medical High School. **Computers:** 90% of classrooms, 100% of dorms, 80% of libraries, 100% of dining areas, 100% of student union, 50% of common outdoor areas have wireless network access.

CAMPUS LIFE

Environment: City. **Activities:** Choral groups, concert band, drama/theater, jazz band, literary magazine, marching band, music ensembles, musical theater, opera, student government, student newspaper, symphony orchestra, yearbook, Campus Ministries, International Student Organization, Model UN. 15 honor societies, 1 religious organization. 4 fraternities, 4 sororities. **Athletics (Intercollegiate):** *Men:* baseball, basketball, cheerleading, cross-country, football, golf, soccer, tennis, track/field (outdoor). *Women:* basketball, cheerleading, cross-country, golf, soccer, softball, tennis, track/field (outdoor), volleyball. **On-Campus Highlights:** Moody Center (Student Center), Java City Coffee House, The Pond/Gazebo, Dorm Lobbies, The Pool, Gym/Fitness Center; Connally Mission Center; Skiles Social Science Building. **Environmental Initiatives:** Establishing a recycling program; Educating the student body, faculty, staff and alumni on sustainability; Installing Hydration Station in multiple locations on campus to encourage students, faculty, and staff to refill their reusable water bottles.

ADMISSIONS

Freshman Academic Profile: Average high school GPA 3.59. 17% in top 10% of high school class, 46% in top 25% of high school class, 83% in top 50% of high school class. 87% from public high schools. SAT Math middle 50% range 460-570. SAT Critical Reading middle 50% range 450-565. SAT Writing middle 50% range 430-550. ACT middle 50% range 20-25. Minimum internet-based TOEFL 75. Minimum paper TOEFL 550. **Basis for Candidate Selection:** *Very important factors considered include:* Class rank, academic GPA, standardized test scores. *Important factors considered include:* recommendation(s), rigor of secondary school record, character/personal qualities, talent/ability. *Other factors considered include:* alumni/ae relation, extracurricular activities, level of applicant's interest, religious affiliation/commitment. **Freshman Admission Requirements:** High school diploma is required and GED is accepted. *Academic units required:* 3 English, 2 mathematics, 2 science, 2 social studies, 7 academic electives. **Freshman Admission Statistics:** 1,456 applied, 57% admitted, 41% enrolled. **Transfer Admission Requirements:** college transcript(s), Minimum college GPA of 2.0 required. Lowest grade transferable C. **General Admission Information:** Application Fee $50. Notification on a rolling basis, beginning on or about 9/1. Nonfall registration accepted. Admission may be deferred for a maximum of 1 Year. Credit offered for CEEB Advanced Placement tests.

COSTS AND FINANCIAL AID

Annual tuition $24,500. Room and board $7,740. Average book expense $800. **Required Forms and Deadlines:** FAFSA. **Notification of Awards:** Applicants will be notified of awards on a rolling basis beginning 2/1. **Types of Aid:** *Need-based scholarships/grants:* Federal Pell, SEOG, state scholarships/grants, private scholarships, the school's own gift aid, ACG/SMART (federal grants). *Loans:* Subsidized Stafford, Unsubsidized Stafford, PLUS, Federal Perkins, state loans, college/university loans from institutional funds. *Student Employment:* Federal Work-Study Program available. Institutional employment available. Highest amount earned per year from on-campus jobs $2,400. Off-campus job opportunities are excellent. **Financial Aid Statistics:** 71% freshmen, 72% undergrads receive need-based scholarship or grant aid. 97% freshmen, 91% undergrads receive non-need-based scholarship or grant aid. 86% freshmen, 89% undergrads receive need-based self-help aid. 0% freshmen, 0% undergrads receive athletic scholarships. 97% freshmen, 91% undergrads receive any aid. 75% undergrads borrow to pay for school. Average cumulative indebtedness $29,303. **Criteria for awarding institutional aid:** *Non-need-based:* academics, art, job skills, music/drama, religious affiliation.

HARRINGTON COLLEGE OF DESIGN

200 West Madison, Chicago, IL 60606-3433
Phone: 877-939-4975
E-mail: hiid@interiordesign.edu · **CEEB Code:**
Fax: 312-697-8032 · **Website:** www.harringtoncollege.com · **ACT Code:** 6641

This proprietary school was founded in 1931.

RATINGS

Admissions Selectivity Rating: 60*   Fire Safety Rating: 60*

STUDENTS AND FACULTY

Enrollment: 512. **Student Body:** 9% out-of-state.

ACADEMICS

Degrees: associate, bachelor's, certificate, diploma. **Special Study Options:** Accelerated program, internships, study abroad.

FACILITIES

Housing: apartments for single students, Independent referral housing Shared Apartment housing.

CAMPUS LIFE

Activities: student government.

ADMISSIONS

Freshman Academic Profile: Minimum paper TOEFL 500. **Basis for Candidate Selection:** *Very important factors considered include:* interview. *Important factors considered include:* character/personal qualities, talent/ability. *Other factors considered include:* Class rank, application essay, recommendation(s), rigor of secondary school record, standardized test scores, extracurricular activities, geographical residence, volunteer work, work experience. **Freshman Admission Requirements:** High school diploma is required and GED is accepted. **Freshman Admission Statistics:** 568 applied, 90% admitted, 7% enrolled. **Transfer Admission Requirements:** college transcript(s), interview, Lowest grade transferable C. **General Admission Information:** Application Fee $60. Nonfall registration accepted.

COSTS AND FINANCIAL AID

Average book expense $900. **Required Forms and Deadlines:** FAFSA. **Types of Aid:** *Need-based scholarships/grants:* Federal Pell, SEOG. *Loans:* Subsidized Stafford, Unsubsidized Stafford, PLUS. *Student Employment:* Off-campus job opportunities are excellent.

HARRISBURG UNIVERSITY OF SCIENCE AND TECHNOLOGY

326 Market Street, Harrisburg, PA 17101
Phone: 717-901-5101 · **Financial Aid Phone:** 717-901-5115
E-mail: admissions@HarrisburgU.edu · **CEEB Code:** 4511
Fax: 717-901-3101 · **Website:** www.HarrisburgU.edu · **ACT Code:** 3637

This private school was founded in 2001. It has a 2-acre campus.

RATINGS

Admissions Selectivity Rating: 80   Fire Safety Rating: 60*

STUDENTS AND FACULTY

Enrollment: 272. **Student Body:** 46% female, 54% male, 17% out-of-state, 1% international (3 countries represented). Asian 4%, African American 32%, Caucasian 49%, Hispanic 8%, Native American <1%. **Retention and Graduation:** 54% freshmen return for sophomore year. 12% freshmen graduate within 4 years. 20% freshmen graduate within 6 years. 10% grads go on to further study within 1 year. 10% grads pursue arts and sciences degrees. **Faculty:** 10 full-time faculty, 100% hold PhDs, 50% are members of minority groups, 40% are women. 0% of classes are taught by teaching assistants.

ACADEMICS

Degrees: bachelor's, master's. **Majors with Highest Enrollment:** Computer and Information Sciences; Biotechnology; Physical Sciences. **Special Study Options:** dual enrollment, internships, student-designed major. **Career services:** internships.

FACILITIES

Housing: 100% of campus accessible to physically disabled. **Computers:** 100% of classrooms, 100% of libraries, 100% of dining areas, 100% of student union, 100% of common outdoor areas have wireless network access. Students can register for classes online. Administrative functions (other than registration) can be performed online. Undergraduates are required to own a computer.

CAMPUS LIFE

Environment: City. **On-Campus Highlights:** Conference Center.

ADMISSIONS

Freshman Academic Profile: 90% from public high schools. SAT Math middle 50% range 420-550. SAT Critical Reading middle 50% range 440-530. SAT Writing middle 50% range 390-510. ACT middle 50% range 20-24. Minimum paper TOEFL 80. **Freshman Admission Statistics:** 1,827 applied, 47% admitted, 15% enrolled. **General Admission Information:**

COSTS AND FINANCIAL AID

Annual tuition $23,800. Room and board $6,340. Required fees $0. Average book expense $1,500. **Required Forms and Deadlines:** FAFSA. **Financial Aid Statistics:** 99% freshmen, 100% undergrads receive need-based scholarship or grant aid. 9% freshmen, 6% undergrads receive non-need-based scholarship or grant aid. 87% freshmen, 82% undergrads receive need-based self-help aid. 0% freshmen, 0% undergrads receive athletic scholarships. 98% freshmen, 94% undergrads receive any aid. 80% undergrads borrow to pay for school. Average cumulative indebtedness $36,164.

HARTWICK COLLEGE

PO Box 4022, Oneonta, NY 13820-4020
Phone: 607-431-4154 · **Financial Aid Phone:** 607-431-4130
E-mail: admissions@hartwick.edu · **CEEB Code:** 2288
Fax: 607-431-4102 · **Website:** www.hartwick.edu/ · **ACT Code:** 2756

This private school was founded in 1797. It has a 425-acre campus.

RATINGS

Admissions Selectivity Rating: 77   **Fire Safety Rating:** 88

STUDENTS AND FACULTY

Enrollment: 1,529. **Student Body:** 61% female, 39% male, 22% out-of-state, 3% international (35 countries represented). Asian 2%, African American 8%, Caucasian 68%, Hispanic 7%, Native American <1%
Retention and Graduation: 53% freshmen graduate within 4 years. 61% freshmen graduate within 6 years. 22% grads go on to further study within 1 year. **Faculty:** 0% of classes are taught by teaching assistants.

ACADEMICS

Degrees: bachelor's. **Classes:** Most classes have 10–19 students. Most lab/discussion sessions have 30-39 students. **Majors with Highest Enrollment:** Psychology; Business Administration and Management; Registered Nursing, Nursing Administration, Nursing Research and Clinical Nursing. **Special Study Options:** Accelerated program, cross-registration, double major, exchange student program (domestic), honors program, independent study, internships, student-designed major, study abroad, teacher certification program, January thematic term, study abroad/international internships. **Honors programs:** Requirements for the Honors Program are: Challenges—4 must be completed by graduation Divisions, 3 must be represented in Challenges Honors Forum; a presentation of a project Academic Excellence; a 3.50 Grade Point Average. Also, students in the Honors program can choose to live on the Honors floor in a campus residence hall. Combined degree programs: BA/JD, BA/MEng, JD with Albany Law School. **Disability Services:** Special programs offered to physically disabled students include reader services, tape recorders, tutors. **Career services:** career/job search classes, internships. Career services highlights include learning outside the classroom, an integral part of preparing our students for careers after graduation and why we've designed our curriculum and teaching approaches to break down the barriers that separate the classroom from the world. As a Hartwick student, you'll get to learn "out there" and bring that experience back, making your time in the classroom more engaging and effective.

FACILITIES

Housing: Coed dorms, women's dorms, fraternity/sorority housing, apartments for single students, Housing at Pine Lake environmental campus (lodge and cabins) also available. 50% of campus accessible to physically disabled. **Special Academic Facilities/Equipment:** Art and history museums, Indian artifact collection, environmental center, observatory, electron microscope, tissue culture lab, spectrophotometers. **Computers:** 100% of classrooms, 100%

of dorms, 100% of libraries, 50% of dining areas, 50% of student union, have wireless network access. Students can register for classes online. Administrative functions (other than registration) can be performed online.

CAMPUS LIFE

Environment: Village. **Activities:** Choral groups, dance, drama/theater, literary magazine, music ensembles, pep band, radio station, student government, student newspaper, yearbook, Campus Ministries. 70 registered organizations, 30 honor societies, 3 religious organizations. 3 fraternities, 3 sororities. **Athletics (Intercollegiate):** *Men:* basketball, cross-country, diving, football, lacrosse, soccer, swimming, tennis. *Women:* basketball, cheerleading, cross-country, diving, equestrian sports, field hockey, lacrosse, soccer, swimming, tennis, volleyball, water polo. **On-Campus Highlights:** Yager Museum, Stevens-German Library, Johnstone Science Center, Binder Athletic Facility, Dewar Student Union. **Environmental Initiatives:** Hartwick is a signatory of the Talloires Declaration and is a member of the Association for the Advancement of Sustainability in Higher Education. In 2005, the College received a Kresge Green Building Iniative planning grant to partially fund green design of its first LEED-certified building, Golisano Hall. In keeping with Hartwick's emphasis on hands-on learning, the project provided the basis for a course entitled "Sustainable Design", taught by Richard Rittelman, FAIA principal architect and Karl Seeley, PhD. of Hartwick's economics department. The LEED-certification process for Golisano Hall is currently underway. The process involves commissioning the building's systems, which are estimated to use 75% less energy than the average building on Hartwick's campus. As an institution, Hartwick has a long history of environmental awareness and action. The 125 acre Pine Lake Environmental Campus (which borders 3,000 acres of state park) was created in 1971, offering students a unique living laboratory for sustainability where ecological principles such as energy conservation, organic gardening, composting, waste reduction, and recycling are practiced every day. The lake, forests, trails, and mud bog have been the sites of more than 40 courses and 30 ongoing student/faculty research projects. Pine Lake is also a residence for 30-35 students. In 2002, students in the class "Architecture of the Sacred," finished construction on a 900-square foot strawbale house at the Lake. Built of compressed strawbale and finished with natural plaster, the house is economical and environmentally friendly and was the first "green" building constructed by Hartwick. Subsequently, students constructed a cob house, also at Pine Lake. Since 2002-03 Hartwick's academic year theme fas focused on sustainablilty, including annual themes on sustainable living, food in our lives, health and the human experience, globalization, water works, climate change and balance. Several leaders in the sustainability movement, including Vandura Shiva, Bill McKibben, Peter Finn, David Orr, Winona LaDuke, and Oren Lyons have spent time on campus, led college activities, and made public presentations. The Pine Lake Institute (PLI) for Environmental and Sustainability Studies sets an example for the College and community as to how to live sustainably.

ADMISSIONS

Freshman Academic Profile: Average high school GPA 3.13. 15% in top 10% of high school class, 45% in top 25% of high school class, 79% in top 50% of high school class. 86% from public high schools. SAT Math middle 50% range 510-590. SAT Critical Reading middle 50% range 500-610. SAT Writing middle 50% range 480-610. ACT middle 50% range 21-26. Minimum internet-based TOEFL 79. Minimum paper TOEFL 550. **Basis for Candidate Selection:** *Very important factors considered include:* rigor of secondary school record. *Important factors considered include:* Class rank, academic GPA, recommendation(s). *Other factors considered include:* application essay, standardized test scores, alumni/ae relation, character/personal qualities, extracurricular activities, first generation, geographical residence, interview, level of applicant's interest, racial/ethnic status, state residency, talent/ability, volunteer work, work experience. **Freshman Admission Requirements:** High school diploma is required and GED is accepted. **Freshman Admission Statistics:** 5,036 applied, 90% admitted, 9% enrolled. **Transfer Admission Requirements:** college transcript(s), essay or personal statement, statement of good standing from prior institution(s). Minimum college GPA of 2.0 required. Lowest grade transferable C-. **General Admission Information:** Application Fee $35. Early decision application deadline 11/15. Regular application deadline 2/15. Nonfall registration accepted. Admission may be deferred for a maximum of 12 months. Credit offered for CEEB Advanced Placement tests.

COSTS AND FINANCIAL AID

Average book expense $700. **Required Forms and Deadlines:** FAFSA. **Notification of Awards:** Applicants will be notified of awards on or about 3/15. **Types of Aid:** *Need-based scholarships/grants:* Federal Pell, SEOG, state scholarships/grants, private scholarships, the school's own gift aid. *Loans:* Subsidized Stafford, Unsubsidized Stafford, PLUS, Federal Perkins, Federal Nursing. *Student Employment:* Federal Work-Study Program available. Institutional employment available. Highest amount earned per year from on-campus jobs $2,000. Off-campus job opportunities are good. **Financial Aid Statistics:** 98% freshmen, 96% undergrads receive need-based scholarship or grant aid. 2% freshmen, 4% undergrads receive non-need-based scholarship or grant aid.

87% freshmen, 86% undergrads receive need-based self-help aid. 1% freshmen, 2% undergrads receive athletic scholarships. 100% freshmen, 95% undergrads receive any aid. 72% undergrads borrow to pay for school. Average cumulative indebtedness $26,153. **Criteria for awarding institutional aid:** *Non-need-based:* academics, alumni affiliation, art, athletics, leadership, music/drama, state/district residency.

HARVARD COLLEGE

86 Brattle Street, Cambridge, MA 2138
Phone: 617-495-1551 · **Financial Aid Phone:** 617-495-1581
E-mail: college@fas.harvard.edu · **CEEB Code:** 3434
Fax: 617-495-8821 · **Website:** www.college.harvard.edu · **ACT Code:** 1840

This private school was founded in 1636. It has a 380-acre campus.

RATINGS

Admissions Selectivity Rating: 99   **Fire Safety Rating:** 60*

STUDENTS AND FACULTY

Enrollment: 6,636. **Student Body:** 47% female, 53% male, 84% out-of-state, 11% international (100 countries represented). Asian 19%, African American 7%, Caucasian 44%, Hispanic 10%, Native American <1%
Retention and Graduation: 97% freshmen return for sophomore year. 86% freshmen graduate within 4 years. 98% freshmen graduate within 6 years. **Faculty:** 971 full-time faculty, 83% hold PhDs, 34% are members of minority groups, 20% are women. 0% of classes are taught by teaching assistants.

ACADEMICS

Degrees: bachelor's, master's, post-master's certificate. **Classes:** Most classes have fewer than 10 students. **Majors with Highest Enrollment:** Political Science and Government; Economics; Social Sciences. **Special Study Options:** Accelerated program, cross-registration, double major, exchange student program (domestic), honors program, independent study, internships, student-designed major, study abroad, teacher certification program. Combined degree programs: BA/MA, BA/MEng. **Disability Services:** Special programs offered to physically disabled students include note-taking services, reader services, tape recorders, tutors. **Career services:** Alumni network, alumni services.

FACILITIES

Housing: Coed dorms, special housing for disabled students, apartments for married students, cooperative housing. **Special Academic Facilities/Equipment:** Museums (University Arts Museums, Museums of Cultural History, many others), language labs, observatory, many science and research laboratories and facilities, new state-of-the-art computer science facility. **Computers:** 98% of classrooms, 100% of dorms, 100% of libraries, have wireless network access. Students can register for classes online. Administrative functions (other than registration) can be performed online.

CAMPUS LIFE

Environment: City. **Activities:** Choral groups, concert band, dance, drama/theater, jazz band, literary magazine, marching band, music ensembles, musical theater, opera, pep band, radio station, student government, student newspaper, student-run film society, symphony orchestra, television station, yearbook, Campus Ministries, International Student Organization, Model UN. 393 registered organizations, 1 honor society, 28 religious organizations. **Athletics (Intercollegiate):** *Men:* baseball, basketball, crew/rowing, cross-country, diving, fencing, football, golf, ice hockey, lacrosse, sailing, skiing (downhill/alpine), skiing (nordic/cross-country), soccer, squash, swimming, tennis, track/field (outdoor), track/field (indoor), volleyball, water polo, wrestling. *Women:* basketball, crew/rowing, cross-country, diving, fencing, field hockey, golf, ice hockey, lacrosse, sailing (downhill/alpine), skiing (nordic/cross-country), soccer, softball, squash, swimming, tennis, track/field (outdoor), track/field (indoor), volleyball, water polo. **On-Campus Highlights:** Widener Library, Harvard Yard, Fogg Museum, Annenburg/Memorial Hall, Science Center. **Environmental Initiatives:** Campus-wide Sustainability Principles that provide a broad vision to guide University operations and planning (adopted in 2004) and an established University-wide Office for Sustainability (green.harvard.edu) that oversees implementation of Harvards GHG reduction goal and sustainability commitments. The University has had a formal sustainability office for a decade initially created by a faculty and staff initiative with strong student involvement. Greenhouse Gas (GHG) Reduction Goal to reduce GHG emissions 30% below

a 2006 baseline by 2016, including growth (adopted in 2008). University-wide GHG emissions have declined by 7% from FY06-FY09, including growth. When growth is excluded, emissions declined by 14% in the same time period. Comprehensive Green Building Standards for capital projects, renovations and building system upgrades that require a smart design process incorporating life cycle costing, integrated design, energy modeling when applicable and other elements that ensure all sustainable design and operations opportunities are vetted and that performance requirements are achieved in a cost-effective manner (Adopted 2009, building on the 2007 Green Building Guidelines).

ADMISSIONS

Freshman Academic Profile: Average high school GPA 4.03. 95% in top 10% of high school class, 100% in top 25% of high school class, 100% in top 50% of high school class. 64% from public high schools. SAT Math middle 50% range 710-800. SAT Critical Reading middle 50% range 700-800. SAT Writing middle 50% range 710-800. ACT middle 50% range 32-35. **Basis for Candidate Selection:** *Other factors considered include:* application essay, academic GPA, recommendation(s), rigor of secondary school record, standardized test scores, alumni/ae relation, character/personal qualities, extracurricular activities, first generation, geographical residence, interview, racial/ethnic status, talent/ability, volunteer work, work experience. **Freshman Admission Requirements:** High school diploma or equivalent is not required. **Freshman Admission Statistics:** 34,919 applied, 6% admitted, 85% enrolled. **General Admission Information:** Application Fee $75. Regular application deadline 1/1. Regular notification 4/1. Nonfall registration not accepted. Admission may be deferred for a maximum of 12 months. Credit and/or placement offered for CEEB Advanced Placement tests.

COSTS AND FINANCIAL AID

Average book expense $1,000. **Required Forms and Deadlines:** FAFSA, CSS/Financial Aid PROFILE. **Notification of Awards:** Applicants will be notified of awards on or about 4/1. **Types of Aid:** *Need-based scholarships/grants:* Federal Pell, SEOG, state scholarships/grants, private scholarships, the school's own gift aid. *Loans:* Direct Subsidized Stafford, Direct Unsubsidized Stafford, Direct PLUS, Federal Perkins, college/university loans from institutional funds. *Student Employment:* Federal Work-Study Program available. Institutional employment available. Highest amount earned per year from on-campus jobs $19,967. Off-campus job opportunities are excellent. **Financial Aid Statistics:** 99% freshmen, 99% undergrads receive need-based scholarship or grant aid. 0% freshmen, 0% undergrads receive non-need-based scholarship or grant aid. 65% freshmen, 84% undergrads receive need-based self-help aid. 0% freshmen, 0% undergrads receive athletic scholarships. 73% freshmen, 66% undergrads receive any aid. 26% undergrads borrow to pay for school. Average cumulative indebtedness $9,818.

HARVEY MUDD COLLEGE

301 Platt Boulevard, Claremont, CA 91711-5990
Phone: 909-621-8011 · **Financial Aid Phone:** 909-621-8055
E-mail: admission@hmc.edu · **CEEB Code:** 4341
Fax: 909-621-8360 · **Website:** www.hmc.edu

This private school was founded in 1955. It has a 33-acre campus.

RATINGS

Admissions Selectivity Rating: 98   **Fire Safety Rating:** 75

STUDENTS AND FACULTY

Enrollment: 779. **Student Body:** 44% female, 56% male, 63% out-of-state, 6% international (18 countries represented). Asian 16%, African American 1%, Caucasian 43%, Hispanic 5%, Native American <1%
Retention and Graduation: 98% freshmen return for sophomore year. 84% freshmen graduate within 4 years. 88% freshmen graduate within 6 years. **Faculty:** 86 full-time faculty, 100% hold PhDs, 40% are members of minority groups, 22% are women. 0% of classes are taught by teaching assistants.

ACADEMICS

Degrees: bachelor's. **Classes:** Most classes have 10–19 students. Most lab/discussion sessions have 10–19 students. **Majors with Highest Enrollment:** Engineering; Computer and Information Sciences; Mathematics. **Special Study Options:** cross-registration, double major, dual enrollment, exchange student program (domestic), independent study, internships, liberal arts/career combination, student-designed major, study abroad, Innovative client-sponsored design projects. Combined degree programs: BS/MS math, BS/MBA, BS/MIS, BA/BS. **Career services:** Alumni network, alumni services, career assessment, internships. For career services highlights see http://www.hmc.edu/academic-sclinicresearch/clinicprogram1/history.html.

FACILITIES

Housing: Coed dorms, apartments for married students, apartments for single students, Housing exchange program w/ Pomona College, Pitzer College, Scripps College, and Claremont McKenna College. 80% of campus accessible to physically disabled. **Computers:** 100% of classrooms, 100% of dorms, 100% of libraries, 100% of dining areas, 100% of student union, 75% of common outdoor areas have wireless network access. Students can register for classes online. Administrative functions (other than registration) can be performed online.

CAMPUS LIFE

Environment: Town. **Activities:** Choral groups, concert band, dance, drama/ theater, jazz band, literary magazine, music ensembles, musical theater, pep band, radio station, student government, student newspaper, student-run film society, symphony orchestra, yearbook, Campus Ministries, International Student Organization, Model UN. 109 registered organizations, 4 honor societies, 6 religious organizations. **Athletics (Intercollegiate):** *Men:* baseball, basketball, cross-country, diving, football, golf, soccer, swimming, tennis, track/field (outdoor), water polo. *Women:* basketball, cross-country, diving, golf, lacrosse, soccer, softball, swimming, tennis, track/field (outdoor), volleyball, water polo. **On-Campus Highlights:** Dorm Lounges, Platt Campus Center Living Room, Liquidamber mall, Jay's Pizza Place, Linde Student Activities Center. **Environmental Initiatives:** In February 2008 Harvey Mudd College President Maria Klawe signed the American College & University Presidents Climate Commitment and Harvey Mudd College Board of Trustees adopted HMC Sustainability Policy Statement. Additionally, the Board of Trustees passed a resolution where the standard for new buildings will be at least U.S. Green Building Council LEED Silver standard or equivalent and premium rated or ENERGY STAR certified products are purchased for use on campus where possible. In 2007 a team of students lead by faculty advisers documented the historical usage of key resources and utilities ?ù electricity, natural gas, and water for Harvey Mudd College and the other Claremont Colleges ?ù in order to establish baselines against which to compare future usage, and to identify targets for conservation programs. The team also studied emissions, waste disposal, and recycling programs with the ultimate goal of assessing the feasibility of achieving carbon neutrality within the next decade or two. Finally the team developed recommendations for creating a more sustainable Claremont Colleges Community. The Center for Environmental Studies at Harvey Mudd College was created in May 1999 to create and coordinate interdepartmental programs related to environmental studies. The Center provides a framework through which students, faculty, and alumni can come together to identify critical issues in the relationship between human life and both natural and human-built environments, to investigate those issues, and to help articulate the important roles that science, mathematics, and engineering will take in addressing those issues. Through this framework, the Center seeks to perpetuate creative and responsible professional practices in an increasingly fragile world.

ADMISSIONS

Freshman Academic Profile: 96% in top 10% of high school class, 100% in top 25% of high school class, 100% in top 50% of high school class. 67% from public high schools. SAT Math middle 50% range 740-800. SAT Critical Reading middle 50% range 680-770. SAT Writing middle 50% range 680-760. ACT middle 50% range 33-35. Minimum internet-based TOEFL 100. Minimum paper TOEFL 600. **Basis for Candidate Selection:** *Very important factors considered include:* application essay, academic GPA, recommendation(s), rigor of secondary school record, character/personal qualities, talent/ability. *Important factors considered include:* Class rank, standardized test scores, extracurricular activities. *Other factors considered include:* alumni/ae relation, first generation, geographical residence, interview, level of applicant's interest, racial/ethnic status, state residency, volunteer work, work experience. **Freshman Admission Requirements:** High school diploma is required and GED is accepted. High school diploma or equivalent is not required. *Academic units required:* 4 English, 3 mathematics, 3 science, 1 history. **Freshman Admission Statistics:** 3,336 applied, 19% admitted, 31% enrolled. **Transfer Admission Requirements:** High school transcript, college transcript(s), essay or personal statement, statement of good standing from prior institution(s). Minimum college GPA of 3.0 required. Lowest grade transferable C. **General Admission Information:** Application Fee $60. Early decision application deadline 11/15. Regular application deadline 1/2. Regular notification 4/1. Nonfall registration not accepted. Admission may be deferred for a maximum of 12 months. Placement offered for CEEB Advanced Placement tests.

COSTS AND FINANCIAL AID

Annual tuition $48,315. Room and board $15,833. Required fees $379. Average book expense $800. **Required Forms and Deadlines:** FAFSA, CSS/Financial Aid PROFILE, State aid form, Noncustodial PROFILE, Business/Farm Sup-

plement. **Notification of Awards:** Applicants will be notified of awards on or about 4/1. **Types of Aid:** *Need-based scholarships/grants:* Federal Pell, SEOG, state scholarships/grants, private scholarships, the school's own gift aid Federal ACG and SMART Grants. *Loans:* Subsidized Stafford, Unsubsidized Stafford, PLUS, Federal Perkins, college/university loans from institutional funds, Alternative Loans. *Student Employment:* Federal Work-Study Program available. Institutional employment available. Highest amount earned per year from on-campus jobs $11,776. Off-campus job opportunities are excellent. **Financial Aid Statistics:** 96% freshmen, 97% undergrads receive need-based scholarship or grant aid. 40% freshmen, 44% undergrads receive non-need-based scholarship or grant aid. 61% freshmen, 74% undergrads receive need-based self-help aid. 0% freshmen, 0% undergrads receive athletic scholarships. 58% undergrads borrow to pay for school. Average cumulative indebtedness $23,139. **Criteria for awarding institutional aid:** *Non-need-based:* academics.

HASTINGS COLLEGE

Hastings College, Hastings, NE 68901
Phone: 402-461-7403 • **Financial Aid Phone:** 402-461-7431
E-mail: mmolliconi@hastings.edu • **CEEB Code:** 6270
Fax: 402-461-7490 • **Website:** www.hastings.edu • **ACT Code:** 2456

This private school, affiliated with the Presbyterian Church, was founded in 1882. It has a 109-acre campus.

RATINGS

Admissions Selectivity Rating: 79   **Fire Safety Rating:** 72

STUDENTS AND FACULTY

Enrollment: 1,067. **Student Body:** 46% female, 54% male, 28% out-of-state, 1% international (7 countries represented). Asian 1%, African American 2%, Caucasian 91%, Hispanic 3%, Native American <1%
Retention and Graduation: 76% freshmen return for sophomore year. 52% freshmen graduate within 4 years. 61% freshmen graduate within 6 years. 24% grads go on to further study within 1 year. 16% grads pursue arts and sciences degrees. 2% grads pursue law degrees. 1% grads pursue business degrees. 1% grads pursue medical degrees. **Faculty:** 87 full-time faculty, 71% hold PhDs, 34% are members of minority groups, 1% are women. 0% of classes are taught by teaching assistants.

ACADEMICS

Degrees: bachelor's, master's. **Classes:** Most classes have 10–19 students. Most lab/discussion sessions have fewer than 10 students. **Majors with Highest Enrollment:** Education; Psychology; Business/Commerce. **Special Study Options:** double major, exchange student program (domestic), independent study, internships, student-designed major, study abroad, teacher certification program. Combined degree programs: BA/BM. **Disability Services:** Special programs offered to physically disabled students include note-taking services, reader services, tape recorders, tutors. **Career services:** Alumni network, alumni services, career/job search classes, career assessment, internships, regional alumni. Career services highlights include the Service Learning program.

FACILITIES

Housing: Coed dorms, men's dorms, women's dorms, apartments for single students, Honors housing, one apartment complex is for quiet and alcohol-free living. 90% of campus accessible to physically disabled. **Special Academic Facilities/Equipment:** center for communication arts, glass-blowing studio, observatory, art gallery. **Computers:** 95% of classrooms, 100% of libraries, 100% of dining areas, 100% of student union, have wireless network access. Administrative functions (other than registration) can be performed online.

CAMPUS LIFE

Environment: Village. **Activities:** Choral groups, concert band, dance, drama/ theater, jazz band, literary magazine, marching band, music ensembles, musical theater, pep band, radio station, student government, student newspaper, symphony orchestra, television station, yearbook, Campus Ministries. 85 registered organizations, 13 honor societies, 10 religious organizations. 4 fraternities, 4 sororities. **Athletics (Intercollegiate):** *Men:* baseball, basketball, cross-country, football, golf, soccer, tennis, track/field (outdoor), track/field (indoor), wrestling. *Women:* basketball, cheerleading, cross-country, golf, soccer, softball, tennis, track/field (outdoor), track/field (indoor), volleyball. **On-Campus Highlights:** Fleharty Educational Center and weight room, Hazelrigg Student Union, Perkins Library, Gray Center of Communication Arts, Dorm lounges.

ADMISSIONS

Freshman Academic Profile: Average high school GPA 3.2. 16% in top 10% of high school class, 40% in top 25% of high school class, 65% in top 50% of high school class. 88% from public high schools. SAT Math middle 50% range

490-605. SAT Critical Reading middle 50% range 500-600. ACT middle 50% range 20-26. Minimum paper TOEFL 600. **Basis for Candidate Selection:** *Very important factors considered include:* Class rank, academic GPA, recommendation(s), rigor of secondary school record, standardized test scores. *Important factors considered include:* character/personal qualities, extracurricular activities, talent/ability. *Other factors considered include:* application essay, alumni/ae relation, interview, level of applicant's interest, racial/ethnic status. **Freshman Admission Requirements:** High school diploma is required and GED is accepted. *Academic units required:* 3 English, 3 mathematics, 3 science, (3 science labs), 0 foreign language, 4 social studies, 3 history. **Freshman Admission Statistics:** 1,564 applied, 78% admitted, 25% enrolled. **Transfer Admission Requirements:** High school transcript, college transcript(s), statement of good standing from prior institution(s). Minimum college GPA of 2.0 required. Lowest grade transferable C. **General Admission Information:** Application Fee $20. Notification on a rolling basis, beginning on or about 10/15. Nonfall registration accepted. Credit and/or placement offered for CEEB Advanced Placement tests.

COSTS AND FINANCIAL AID

Average book expense $730. **Required Forms and Deadlines:** FAFSA, Institution's own financial aid form. **Notification of Awards:** Applicants will be notified of awards on a rolling basis beginning 3/1. **Types of Aid:** *Need-based scholarships/grants:* Federal Pell, SEOG, state scholarships/grants, private scholarships, the school's own gift aid. *Loans:* Subsidized Stafford, Unsubsidized Stafford, PLUS, Federal Perkins. *Student Employment:* Federal Work-Study Program available. Institutional employment available. Highest amount earned per year from on-campus jobs $1,000. Off-campus job opportunities are good. **Financial Aid Statistics:** 100% freshmen, 98% undergrads receive need-based scholarship or grant aid. 20% freshmen, 16% undergrads receive non-need-based scholarship or grant aid. 73% freshmen, 79% undergrads receive need-based self-help aid. 23% freshmen, 16% undergrads receive athletic scholarships. 97% freshmen, 98% undergrads receive any aid. Average cumulative indebtedness $18,939. **Criteria for awarding institutional aid:** *Non-need-based:* academics, art, athletics, leadership, music/drama.

HAVERFORD COLLEGE

370 Lancaster Avenue, Haverford, PA 19041
Phone: 610-896-1350 • **Financial Aid Phone:** 610-896-1350
E-mail: http://www.haverford.edu/admission/ • **CEEB Code:** 2289
Fax: 610-896-1338 • **Website:** www.haverford.edu • **ACT Code:** 3409

This private school was founded in 1833. It has a 200-acre campus.

RATINGS

Admissions Selectivity Rating: 99   **Fire Safety Rating:** 81

STUDENTS AND FACULTY

Enrollment: 1,187. **Student Body:** 53% female, 47% male, 88% out-of-state, 6% international (39 countries represented). Asian 9%, African American 6%, Caucasian 64%, Hispanic 9%, Native American <1%
Retention and Graduation: 97% freshmen return for sophomore year. 88% freshmen graduate within 4 years. 94% freshmen graduate within 6 years. 20% grads go on to further study within 1 year. 14% grads pursue arts and sciences degrees. 3% grads pursue law degrees. 2% grads pursue medical degrees. **Faculty:** 129 full-time faculty, 98% hold PhDs, 48% are members of minority groups, 24% are women. 0% of classes are taught by teaching assistants.

ACADEMICS

Degrees: bachelor's. **Classes:** Most classes have fewer than 10 students. Most lab/discussion sessions have fewer than 10 students. **Majors with Highest Enrollment:** Biology/Biological Sciences; English Language and Literature; Psychology. **Special Study Options:** cross-registration, double major, exchange student program (domestic), independent study, internships, liberal arts/career combination, student-designed major, study abroad, teacher certification program. Combined degree programs: BA/MEng. **Disability Services:** Special programs offered to physically disabled students include note-taking services, tape recorders. **Career services:** Alumni network, alumni services, career assessment, internships, regional alumni.

FACILITIES

Housing: Coed dorms, men's dorms, women's dorms, apartments for single students, Theme HousingTheme houses. 60% of campus accessible to physi-

cally disabled. **Special Academic Facilities/Equipment:** Art gallery, center for cross-cultural study of religion, arboretum, observatory, foundry. **Computers:** 75% of classrooms, 75% of libraries, 100% of dining areas, 100% of student union, 80% of common outdoor areas have wireless network access. Students can register for classes online. Administrative functions (other than registration) can be performed online.

CAMPUS LIFE

Environment: Town. **Activities:** Choral groups, dance, drama/theater, literary magazine, music ensembles, musical theater, student government, student newspaper, yearbook, Campus Ministries, International Student Organization. 144 registered organizations, 1 honor society, 6 religious organizations. **Athletics (Intercollegiate):** *Men:* baseball, basketball, cross-country, fencing, lacrosse, soccer, squash, tennis, track/field (outdoor), track/field (indoor). *Women:* basketball, cross-country, fencing, field hockey, lacrosse, soccer, softball, squash, tennis, track/field (outdoor), track/field (indoor), volleyball. **On-Campus Highlights:** Integrated Natural Sciences Center, John Whitehead Campus Center, Cantor Fitzgerald Gallery, Arboretum, Douglas B. Gardner Athletic Center. **Environmental Initiatives:** The athletic center is the 1st gold LEED certified recreation center in the US (opened in 2005). We have reached 98% for grounds recycling. We have completed a master plan to identify utility and powerhouse improvements, and will commence work on these improvements immediately.

ADMISSIONS

Freshman Academic Profile: 94% in top 10% of high school class, 98% in top 25% of high school class, 100% in top 50% of high school class. SAT Math middle 50% range 660-740. SAT Critical Reading middle 50% range 670-750. SAT Writing middle 50% range 660-750. ACT middle 50% range 31-34. Minimum internet-based TOEFL 250. Minimum paper TOEFL 600. **Basis for Candidate Selection:** *Very important factors considered include:* application essay, academic GPA, recommendation(s), rigor of secondary school record, character/personal qualities, extracurricular activities. *Important factors considered include:* Class rank, standardized test scores, talent/ability, volunteer work, work experience. *Other factors considered include:* alumni/ae relation, first generation, geographical residence, interview, level of applicant's interest, racial/ethnic status. **Freshman Admission Requirements:** High school diploma or equivalent is not required. **Freshman Admission Statistics:** 3,496 applied, 13% admitted, 73% enrolled. **Transfer Admission Requirements:** college transcript(s), essay or personal statement, standardized test scores, statement of good standing from prior institution(s). Minimum college GPA of 3.0 required. Lowest grade transferable C. **General Admission Information:** Application Fee $60. Early decision application deadline 11/15. Regular application deadline 1/15. Regular notification 4/15. Nonfall registration not accepted. Admission may be deferred for a maximum of 12 months.

COSTS AND FINANCIAL AID

Annual tuition $48,656. Room and board $14,888. Required fees $672. Average book expense $1,194. **Required Forms and Deadlines:** FAFSA, CSS/Financial Aid PROFILE, Noncustodial PROFILE, Business/Farm Supplement. **Notification of Awards:** Applicants will be notified of awards on or about 4/1. **Types of Aid:** *Need-based scholarships/grants:* Federal Pell, SEOG, state scholarships/grants, the school's own gift aid. *Loans:* Subsidized Stafford, Unsubsidized Stafford, PLUS, Federal Perkins. *Student Employment:* Federal Work-Study Program available. Institutional employment available. Highest amount earned per year from on-campus jobs $2,300. Off-campus job opportunities are good. **Financial Aid Statistics:** 95% freshmen, 96% undergrads receive need-based scholarship or grant aid. 0% freshmen, 0% undergrads receive non-need-based scholarship or grant aid. 90% freshmen, 90% undergrads receive need-based self-help aid. 0% freshmen, 0% undergrads receive athletic scholarships. 53% freshmen, 51% undergrads receive any aid. 26% undergrads borrow to pay for school. Average cumulative indebtedness $14,720.

See page 1062.

HAWAI'I PACIFIC UNIVERSITY

1164 Bishop Street, Honolulu, HI 96813
Phone: 808-544-0238 • **Financial Aid Phone:** 808-544-0253
E-mail: admissions@hpu.edu • **CEEB Code:** 4352
Fax: 808-544-1136 • **Website:** www.hpu.edu • **ACT Code:** 4352

This private school was founded in 1965. It has a 135-acre campus.

RATINGS

Admissions Selectivity Rating: 78   **Fire Safety Rating:** 77

STUDENTS AND FACULTY

Enrollment: 6,262. **Student Body:** 61% female, 39% male, 40% out-of-state, 10% international (102 countries represented). Asian 31%, African American 7%, Caucasian 34%, Hispanic 7%, Native American 1%

Retention and Graduation: 66% freshmen return for sophomore year. 68% grads go on to further study within 1 year. 20% grads pursue arts and sciences degrees. 5% grads pursue law degrees. 45% grads pursue business degrees. 3% grads pursue medical degrees. **Faculty:** 264 full-time faculty, 66% hold PhDs, 46% are members of minority groups, 25% are women. 0% of classes are taught by teaching assistants.

ACADEMICS

Degrees: associate, bachelor's, certificate, master's, post-bachelor's certificate, post-master's certificate. **Classes:** Most classes have 10–19 students. Most lab/discussion sessions have fewer than 10 students. **Majors with Highest Enrollment:** Registered Nursing/Registered Nurse; Management Information Systems; Business, Management, Marketing, and Related Support Services. **Special Study Options:** Accelerated program, cooperative education program, distance learning, double major, dual enrollment, English as a Second Language (ESL), honors program, independent study, internships, liberal arts/career combination, student-designed major, study abroad, weekend college. **Honors programs:** University Scholars Honors Program: During the freshman and sophomore years University Scholars enroll in honors sections of many courses required in the general education curriculum. Normally, University Scholars are required to complete at least six of these courses, but exceptions can be made for students who have completed certain requirements through AP courses in high school or for majors with different general education requirements. At the upper-division level, University Scholars enroll in three honors seminars. The Certificate of Merit is awarded at the time of graduation to students who fulfill the University Scholars requirements. Combined degree programs: BA/MA.

FACILITIES

Housing: Coed dorms, women's dorms, apartments for married students, apartments for single students, Apartment search and referral service. 90% of campus accessible to physically disabled. **Special Academic Facilities/Equipment:** Hawaii Pacific University Art Gallery, Hawaii Pacific University Theatre. **Computers:** Students can register for classes online. Administrative functions (other than registration) can be performed online.

CAMPUS LIFE

Environment: Metropolis. **Activities:** Choral groups, dance, drama/theater, literary magazine, music ensembles, musical theater, pep band, student government, student newspaper, student-run film society. 80 registered organizations, 18 honor societies, 3 religious organizations. **Athletics (Intercollegiate):** *Men:* baseball, basketball, cheerleading, cross-country, golf, tennis. *Women:* cheerleading, cross-country, golf, softball, tennis, volleyball. **On-Campus Highlights:** Frear Center, Sea Warrior Center, Windward Campus, Art Gallery, Fort Street Mall.

ADMISSIONS

Freshman Academic Profile: Average high school GPA 3.26. 20% in top 10% of high school class, 45% in top 25% of high school class, 80% in top 50% of high school class. 60% from public high schools. SAT Math middle 50% range 430-560. SAT Critical Reading middle 50% range 420-550. SAT Writing middle 50% range 350-540. ACT middle 50% range 17-24. Minimum paper TOEFL 550. **Basis for Candidate Selection:** *Very important factors considered include:* academic GPA, rigor of secondary school record. *Important factors considered include:* standardized test scores, extracurricular activities, interview. *Other factors considered include:* Class rank, application essay, recommendation(s), character/personal qualities, first generation, talent/ability, volunteer work, work experience. **Freshman Admission Requirements:** High school diploma is required and GED is accepted. **Freshman Admission Statistics:** 2,991 applied, 80% admitted, 29% enrolled. **Transfer Admission Requirements:** college transcript(s), Minimum college GPA of 2.0 required. Lowest grade transferable C. **General Admission Information:** Application Fee $50. Notification on a rolling basis, beginning on or about 1/1. Nonfall registration accepted. Admission may be deferred for a maximum of 24 months. Credit and/or placement offered for CEEB Advanced Placement tests.

COSTS AND FINANCIAL AID

Annual tuition $20,930. Room and board $12,550. Required fees $80. Average book expense $2,096. **Required Forms and Deadlines:** FAFSA. **Notification of Awards:** Applicants will be notified of awards on a rolling basis beginning 4/1. **Types of Aid:** *Need-based scholarships/grants:* Federal Pell, SEOG, state scholarships/grants, the school's own gift aid, Federal Nursing Scholarships. *Loans:* Subsidized Stafford, Unsubsidized Stafford, PLUS, Federal Perkins, Federal Nursing, Alternative loans. *Student Employment:* Highest amount earned per year from on-campus jobs $3,800. **Financial Aid Statistics:** 41% freshmen, 45% undergrads receive need-based scholarship or grant aid. 38% freshmen, 28% undergrads receive non-need-based scholarship or grant aid. 87% freshmen, 93% undergrads receive need-based self-help aid. 0% freshmen,

0% undergrads receive athletic scholarships. 75% freshmen, 67% undergrads receive any aid. 36% undergrads borrow to pay for school. **Criteria for awarding institutional aid:** *Non-need-based:* academics, alumni affiliation, athletics, job skills, leadership, music/drama, religious affiliation.

HEBREW COLLEGE

160 Herrick Road, Newton Centre, MA 2459
Phone: 617-559-8610 • **Financial Aid Phone:** 617-559-8642
E-mail: admissions@hebrewcollege.edu • **CEEB Code:**
Fax: 617-559-8601 • **Website:** www.hebrewcollege.edu

This private school, affiliated with the Jewish Church, was founded in 1921.

RATINGS

Admissions Selectivity Rating: 60* **Fire Safety Rating:** 60*

STUDENTS AND FACULTY

Enrollment: 4. **Student Body:** 50% female, 50% male, 1% out-of-state, 25% international.

Retention and Graduation: 40% grads go on to further study within 1 year.

ACADEMICS

Degrees: bachelor's, certificate, master's. **Majors with Highest Enrollment:** Education; Psychology; Business Administration and Management. **Special Study Options:** cross-registration, distance learning, independent study, internships, student-designed major, Semester in Israel is encouraged.

CAMPUS LIFE

Environment: City. **Activities:** Choral groups. **On-Campus Highlights:** Library.

ADMISSIONS

Freshman Academic Profile: Minimum paper TOEFL 400. **Basis for Candidate Selection:** *Very important factors considered include:* application essay, religious affiliation/commitment, talent/ability. *Important factors considered include:* Class rank, recommendation(s), rigor of secondary school record, standardized test scores, character/personal qualities, extracurricular activities, interview, volunteer work, work experience. *Other factors considered include:* alumni/ae relation, geographical residence, state residency. **Transfer Admission Requirements:** college transcript(s), essay or personal statement, interview, Lowest grade transferable C. **General Admission Information:** Regular application deadline 4/15. Nonfall registration accepted.

COSTS AND FINANCIAL AID

Annual tuition $7,920. Required fees $75. *Student Employment:* Off-campus job opportunities are good.

HEBREW UNION COLLEGE— JEWISH INSTITUTE OF RELIGION

One W. 4th Street, New York, NY 10012
Phone: 212-824-2207
E-mail: fdantowitz@huc.edu
Fax: 212-388-1720 • **Website:** www.huc.edu

This private school, affiliated with the Jewish Church, was founded in 1875.

RATINGS

Admissions Selectivity Rating: 60* **Fire Safety Rating:** 60*

STUDENTS AND FACULTY

Student Body: 1 country represented.

ACADEMICS

Degrees: certificate, first professional, master's, post-bachelor's certificate. **Special Study Options:** cooperative education program, double major, independent study, internships. **Career services:** alumni services, internships.

CAMPUS LIFE

Activities: 1 religious organization.

ADMISSIONS

General Admission Information: Application Fee $55. Regular application deadline 3/1. Notification on a rolling basis, beginning on or about 1/1.

COSTS AND FINANCIAL AID

Average book expense $0. **Types of Aid:** *Need-based scholarships/grants:* private scholarships. *Loans:* Subsidized Stafford, Unsubsidized Stafford, college/university loans from institutional funds. **Criteria for awarding institutional aid:** *Non-need-based:* academics, music/drama, religious affiliation.

HEIDELBERG UNIVERSITY

310 East Market Street, Tiffin, OH 44883
Phone: 419-448-2330 · **Financial Aid Phone:** 419-448-2293
E-mail: adminfo@heidelberg.edu · **CEEB Code:** 1292
Fax: 419-448-2334 · **Website:** www.heidelberg.edu · **ACT Code:** 3278

This private school, affiliated with the United Church of Christ Church, was founded in 1850. It has a 120-acre campus.

RATINGS

Admissions Selectivity Rating: 78   **Fire Safety Rating:** 62

STUDENTS AND FACULTY

Enrollment: 1,089. **Student Body:** 48% female, 52% male, 15% out-of-state, 1% international. Asian 1%, African American 7%, Caucasian 78%, Hispanic 2%, Native American <1%
Retention and Graduation: 61% freshmen return for sophomore year. 39% freshmen graduate within 4 years. 51% freshmen graduate within 6 years. 25% grads go on to further study within 1 year. 15% grads pursue arts and sciences degrees. 2% grads pursue law degrees. 5% grads pursue business degrees. 3% grads pursue medical degrees. **Faculty:** 50 full-time faculty, 86% hold PhDs, 46% are members of minority groups, 6% are women. 0% of classes are taught by teaching assistants.

ACADEMICS

Degrees: bachelor's, master's. **Classes:** Most classes have fewer than 10 students. Most lab/discussion sessions have 10–19 students. **Majors with Highest Enrollment:** Education; Biological and Physical Sciences; Business/Commerce. **Special Study Options:** cross-registration, double major, dual enrollment, English as a Second Language (ESL), exchange student program (domestic), honors program, independent study, internships, liberal arts/career combination, study abroad, teacher certification program. **Honors programs:** The Honors Program, entitled "The Life of the Mind," integrates learning and life experiences, stems from the mission of the University. It features extensive contact with the fundamental values that underpin self-worth and integrity, free inquiry, and intellectual rigor, an understanding of other cultures and traditions, and a lifelong habit of commitment to the community and concern for social responsibility. **Disability Services:** Special programs offered to physically disabled students include tutors. **Career services:** Alumni network, career assessment, internships.

FACILITIES

Housing: Coed dorms, special housing for disabled students, women's dorms, cooperative housing, apartments for single students, Theme Housing. 65% of campus accessible to physically disabled. **Special Academic Facilities/Equipment:** Forest research lots, water quality lab, Center for Historic and Military Archaeology. **Computers:** 80% of classrooms, 70% of dorms, 100% of libraries, 100% of dining areas, 100% of student union, have wireless network access. Students can register for classes online. Administrative functions (other than registration) can be performed online.

CAMPUS LIFE

Environment: Village. **Activities:** Choral groups, concert band, dance, drama/theater, jazz band, literary magazine, music ensembles, musical theater, opera, pep band, radio station, student government, student newspaper, student-run film society, symphony orchestra, television station, yearbook, Campus Ministries, International Student Organization, Model UN. 75 registered organizations, 6 honor societies, 3 religious organizations. 5 fraternities, 4 sororities. **Athletics (Intercollegiate):** *Men:* baseball, basketball, cheerleading, cross-country, football, golf, soccer, tennis, track/field (outdoor), track/field (indoor), wrestling. *Women:* basketball, cheerleading, cross-country, golf, soccer, softball, tennis, track/field (outdoor), track/field (indoor), volleyball. **On-Campus Highlights:** Gillmor Science Center, Campus Center, Seiberling Gymnasium, Education Center

ADMISSIONS

Freshman Academic Profile: Average high school GPA 3.22. 14% in top 10% of high school class, 33% in top 25% of high school class, 62% in top 50% of

high school class. 61% from public high schools. SAT Math middle 50% range 420-570. SAT Critical Reading middle 50% range 420-590. SAT Writing middle 50% range 400-550. ACT middle 50% range 19-25. Minimum paper TOEFL 550. **Basis for Candidate Selection:** *Very important factors considered include:* academic GPA, rigor of secondary school record, standardized test scores, character/personal qualities, talent/ability. *Important factors considered include:* Class rank, extracurricular activities, interview, level of applicant's interest. *Other factors considered include:* application essay, recommendation(s), alumni/ae relation, first generation, geographical residence, religious affiliation/commitment, state residency, volunteer work, work experience. **Freshman Admission Requirements:** High school diploma is required and GED is accepted. **Freshman Admission Statistics:** 1,726 applied, 71% admitted, 29% enrolled. **Transfer Admission Requirements:** High school transcript, college transcript(s), standardized test scores, statement of good standing from prior institution(s). Minimum college GPA of 2.0 required. Lowest grade transferable C-. **General Admission Information:** Application Fee $25. Regular application deadline 8/1. Notification on a rolling basis, beginning on or about 8/1. Nonfall registration accepted. Admission may be deferred for a maximum of 1 year. Credit and/or placement offered for CEEB Advanced Placement tests.

COSTS AND FINANCIAL AID

Average book expense $1,500. **Required Forms and Deadlines:** FAFSA. **Notification of Awards:** Applicants will be notified of awards on a rolling basis beginning 3/1. **Types of Aid:** *Need-based scholarships/grants:* Federal Pell, SEOG, state scholarships/grants, private scholarships, the school's own gift aid. *Loans:* Subsidized Stafford, Unsubsidized Stafford, PLUS, Federal Perkins. *Student Employment:* Federal Work-Study Program available. Institutional employment available. Highest amount earned per year from on-campus jobs $1,500. Off-campus job opportunities are good. **Financial Aid Statistics:** 100% freshmen, 100% undergrads receive need-based scholarship or grant aid. 89% freshmen, 70% undergrads receive non-need-based scholarship or grant aid. 89% freshmen, 89% undergrads receive need-based self-help aid. 0% freshmen, 0% undergrads receive athletic scholarships. 99% freshmen, 97% undergrads receive any aid. 86% undergrads borrow to pay for school. Average cumulative indebtedness $26,884. **Criteria for awarding institutional aid:** *Non-need-based:* academics, music/drama, religious affiliation, state/district residency.

HELLENIC COLLEGE

50 Goddard Avenue, Brookline, MA 2445
Phone: 617-850-1260 · **Financial Aid Phone:** 617-850-1317
E-mail: admissions@hchc.edu · **CEEB Code:**
Fax: 617-850-1460 · **Website:** www.hchc.edu · **ACT Code:** 1843

This private school, affiliated with the Greek Orthodox Church, was founded in 1937. It has a 59-acre campus.

RATINGS

Admissions Selectivity Rating: 75   **Fire Safety Rating:** 82

STUDENTS AND FACULTY

Enrollment: 99. **Student Body:** 38% female, 62% male, 80% out-of-state, 8% international (9 countries represented). Caucasian 90%, Hispanic 2%
Retention and Graduation: 50% grads go on to further study within 1 year.
Faculty: 18 full-time faculty.

ACADEMICS

Degrees: bachelor's, master's. **Classes:** Most classes have 20–29 students. **Majors with Highest Enrollment:** Religion/Religious Studies. **Special Study Options:** honors program, liberal arts/career combination. Combined degree programs: BA/MA. **Disability Services:** Special programs offered to physically disabled students include tutors. **Career services:** alumni services, regional alumni.

FACILITIES

Housing: Coed dorms, apartments for married students. 20% of campus accessible to physically disabled. **Computers:** 100% of dorms, have wireless network access.

CAMPUS LIFE

Environment: Village. **Activities:** Choral groups, student government, yearbook, Campus Ministries. **Athletics (Intercollegiate):** *Men:* basketball. *Women:* tennis.

ADMISSIONS

Freshman Academic Profile: Average high school GPA 3.104. 100% from public high schools. SAT Math middle 50% range 390-750. SAT Critical Reading middle 50% range 400-700. SAT Writing middle 50% range 390-640. ACT middle 50% range 20-23. Minimum internet-based TOEFL 61. Minimum paper TOEFL 500. **Basis for Candidate Selection:** *Very important factors considered include:* application essay, academic GPA, recommendation(s), rigor of secondary school record, standardized test scores, interview. *Important factors considered include:* Class rank. *Other factors considered include:* alumni/ae relation, character/personal qualities, extracurricular activities. **Freshman Admission Requirements:** High school diploma is required and GED is accepted. *Academic units required:* 4 English, 2 mathematics, 2 science, 2 foreign language, 2 social studies, 2 history. **Freshman Admission Statistics:** 64 applied, 81% admitted, 73% enrolled. **Transfer Admission Requirements:** college transcript(s), essay or personal statement, interview, Minimum college GPA of 2.0 required. Lowest grade transferable C+. **General Admission Information:** Application Fee $50. Regular application deadline 8/15. Notification on a rolling basis, beginning on or about 9/1. Nonfall registration accepted. Admission may be deferred for a maximum of 2. Credit offered for CEEB Advanced Placement tests.

COSTS AND FINANCIAL AID

Average book expense $1,000. **Required Forms and Deadlines:** FAFSA, Institution's own financial aid form. **Notification of Awards:** Applicants will be notified of awards on a rolling basis beginning 4/1. **Types of Aid:** *Need-based scholarships/grants:* Federal Pell, SEOG, state scholarships/grants, private scholarships, the school's own gift aid. *Loans:* Subsidized Stafford, Unsubsidized Stafford, PLUS. *Student Employment:* Highest amount earned per year from on-campus jobs $1,600. **Financial Aid Statistics:** 100% freshmen, 100% undergrads receive need-based scholarship or grant aid. 0% freshmen, 0% undergrads receive non-need-based scholarship or grant aid. 0% freshmen, 0% undergrads receive need-based self-help aid. 0% freshmen, 0% undergrads receive athletic scholarships. 98% freshmen, 96% undergrads receive any aid. 68% undergrads borrow to pay for school. Average cumulative indebtedness $23,000. **Criteria for awarding institutional aid:** *Non-need-based:* academics, alumni affiliation, religious affiliation.

HENDERSON STATE UNIVERSITY

1100 Henderson Street, Arkadelphia, AR 71999-0001
Phone: 870-230-5028 · **Financial Aid Phone:** 870-230-5148
E-mail: admissions@hsu.edu · **CEEB Code:** 6272
Fax: 870-230-5066 · **ACT Code:** 126

This public school was founded in 1890. It has a 151-acre campus.

RATINGS

Admissions Selectivity Rating: 80   **Fire Safety Rating:** 81

STUDENTS AND FACULTY

Enrollment: 3,190. **Student Body:** 56% female, 44% male, 13% out-of-state, 1% international (35 countries represented). Asian 1%, African American 24%, Caucasian 66%, Hispanic 3%, Native American <1%
Retention and Graduation: 58% freshmen return for sophomore year. 15% freshmen graduate within 4 years. 29% freshmen graduate within 6 years.
Faculty: 164 full-time faculty, 69% hold PhDs, 44% are members of minority groups, 17% are women. 0% of classes are taught by teaching assistants.

ACADEMICS

Degrees: associate, bachelor's, master's. **Majors with Highest Enrollment:** Business/Commerce; Biology/Biological Sciences; General Studies. **Special Study Options:** cross-registration, distance learning, English as a Second Language (ESL), honors program, internships, liberal arts/career combination, teacher certification program. **Honors programs:** The overarching purpose of the Honors College is summed up in the single ancient Greek word, aretÃ© (highest excellence), which the students and faculty of the College have taken as their motto. In working to achieve this purpose, the Honors College shares the university's goal "to excel in undergraduate education, always striving to enrich the quality of learning and teaching." The program is directly involved in "actively recruiting, challenging, and supporting those students" who are among the most "highly motivated toward achieving academic success." **Disability Services:** Special programs offered to physically disabled students include note-taking services, tutors. **Career services:** alumni services, career assessment, internships.

FACILITIES

Housing: Coed dorms, men's dorms, special housing for international students, women's dorms, cooperative housing, honors dorm. 72% of campus accessible to physically disabled. **Special Academic Facilities/Equipment:** closed-circuit TV studio, Planetarium **Computers:** Students can register for classes online. Administrative functions (other than registration) can be performed online.

CAMPUS LIFE

Environment: Rural. **Activities:** Choral groups, concert band, dance, drama/theater, jazz band, literary magazine, marching band, music ensembles, radio station, student government, student newspaper, symphony orchestra, television station, yearbook, International Student Organization. 80 registered organizations, 11 honor society, 7 religious organizations. 9 fraternities, 6 sororities. **Athletics (Intercollegiate):** *Men:* baseball, basketball, cross-country, football, golf, swimming. *Women:* basketball, cross-country, golf, softball, swimming, tennis, volleyball. **On-Campus Highlights:** HSU Planetarium, New Reddie Athletic Center, Newly Renovated Arkansas Hall, Henderson House Bed and Breakfast, Java Spot Coffee House. **Environmental Initiatives:** Recycling paper, cans and bottles on campus. On-going "Green News" newsletter to faculty and staff that promotes living green and ways to do so.

ADMISSIONS

Freshman Academic Profile: Average high school GPA 3.19. 12% in top 10% of high school class, 26% in top 25% of high school class, 52% in top 50% of high school class. 92% from public high schools. SAT Math middle 50% range 485-573. SAT Critical Reading middle 50% range 465-538. ACT middle 50% range 19-24. Minimum internet-based TOEFL 61. Minimum paper TOEFL 500. **Basis for Candidate Selection:** *Very important factors considered include:* academic GPA, rigor of secondary school record, standardized test scores. *Other factors considered include:* Class rank, application essay, recommendation(s), character/personal qualities, interview. **Freshman Admission Requirements:** High school diploma is required and GED is accepted. *Academic units required:* 4 English, 2 mathematics, 2 science, 2 social studies, 1 history. **Freshman Admission Statistics:** 3,388 applied, 62% admitted, 33% enrolled. **Transfer Admission Requirements:** college transcript(s), Lowest grade transferable C. **General Admission Information:** Regular application deadline 7/15. Nonfall registration accepted. Admission may be deferred for a maximum of 1+. Neither credit nor placement offered for CEEB Advanced Placement tests.

COSTS AND FINANCIAL AID

Annual in-state tuition $5,730. Annual out-of-state tuition $11,850. Room and board $6,350. Required fees $1,554. Average book expense $1,200. **Required Forms and Deadlines:** FAFSA. **Notification of Awards:** Applicants will be notified of awards on a rolling basis beginning 3/1. **Types of Aid:** *Need-based scholarships/grants:* Federal Pell, SEOG, state scholarships/grants, private scholarships, the school's own gift aid. *Loans:* Direct Subsidized Stafford, Direct Unsubsidized Stafford, Direct PLUS, Subsidized Stafford, Unsubsidized Stafford, PLUS, Federal Perkins. *Student Employment:* Federal Work-Study Program available. Off-campus job opportunities are good. **Financial Aid Statistics:** 69% freshmen, 69% undergrads receive need-based scholarship or grant aid. 87% freshmen, 71% undergrads receive non-need-based scholarship or grant aid. 63% freshmen, 70% undergrads receive need-based self-help aid. 8% freshmen, 8% undergrads receive athletic scholarships. **Criteria for awarding institutional aid:** *Non-need-based:* academics, alumni affiliation, art, athletics, leadership, minority status, music/drama.

HENDRIX COLLEGE

1600 Washington Avenue, Conway, AR 72032
Phone: 501-450-1362 · **Financial Aid Phone:** 501-450-1368
E-mail: adm@hendrix.edu · **CEEB Code:** 6273
Fax: 501-450-3843 · **Website:** www.hendrix.edu · **ACT Code:** 128

This private school, affiliated with the Methodist Church, was founded in 1876. It has a 160-acre campus.

RATINGS

Admissions Selectivity Rating: 89   **Fire Safety Rating:** 73

STUDENTS AND FACULTY

Enrollment: 1,416. **Student Body:** 55% female, 45% male, 53% out-of-state, 4% international (13 countries represented). Asian 5%, African American 5%, Caucasian 71%, Hispanic 5%, Native American 2%
Retention and Graduation: 63% freshmen graduate within 4 years. 68% freshmen graduate within 6 years. 63% grads go on to further study within 1 year. 43% grads pursue arts and sciences degrees. 10% grads pursue law degrees. 3% grads pursue business degrees. 6% grads pursue medical degrees.
Faculty: 108 full-time faculty, 90% hold PhDs, 45% are members of minority groups, 11% are women. 0% of classes are taught by teaching assistants.

ACADEMICS

Degrees: bachelor's, master's. **Classes:** Most classes have 10–19 students. Most lab/discussion sessions have 20–29 students. **Majors with Highest Enrollment:** Psychology; Biology/Biological Sciences. **Special Study Options:**

cooperative education program, double major, English as a Second Language (ESL), independent study, internships, student-designed major, study abroad, teacher certification program, Hendrix-in-Brussels (Belgium), Hendrix-in-Costa Rica, Hendrix-in-Heilongjiang (China), Hendrix-in-Graz (Austria), Hendrix-in-London (UK), Hendrix-in-Madrid (Spain), Hendrix-in-Oxford (UK), Accademia dell'Arte, other programs with 140 colleges and universities on 6 continents including countries such as Australia, Finland, France, Ghana, Japan etc. Combined degree programs: BA/MEng, 4-1 BA/MPH Program in Public Health with UAMS. **Disability Services:** Special programs offered to physically disabled students include note-taking services, reader services, tape recorders, tutors. **Career services:** Alumni network, alumni services, career/job search classes, career assessment, internships, regional alumni. Career services highlights include ASK, The Alumni Sharing Knowledge Program, Internships, Grad Expo, Career Week/Fair.

FACILITIES

Housing: Coed dorms, special housing for disabled students, men's dorms, women's dorms, cooperative housing, apartments for single students, Wellness Housing, Theme Housing: co-educational foreign language house (Spanish, German, French alternating years) available; suite-style small houses; Ecology house; Christian House. 49% of campus accessible to physically disabled. **Special Academic Facilities/Equipment:** Herbarium, Wilbur A. Mills Library. **Computers:** 100% of classrooms, 100% of dorms, 100% of libraries, 100% of dining areas, 100% of student union, 100% of common outdoor areas have wireless network access. Students can register for classes online. Administrative functions (other than registration) can be performed online.

CAMPUS LIFE

Environment: Town. **Activities:** Choral groups, concert band, dance, drama/theater, jazz band, literary magazine, music ensembles, musical theater, pep band, radio station, student government, student newspaper, student-run film society, symphony orchestra, yearbook, Campus Ministries, International Student Organization, Model UN. 80 registered organizations, 6 honor societies, 5 religious organizations. **Athletics (Intercollegiate):** *Men:* baseball, basketball, cross-country, diving, golf, lacrosse, soccer, swimming, tennis, track/field (outdoor). *Women:* basketball, cross-country, diving, field hockey, golf, soccer, softball, swimming, tennis, track/field (outdoor), volleyball. **On-Campus Highlights:** Student Life & Technology Center, Village at Hendrix Apartments, Wellness & Athletic Center, Charles D. Morgan Center for Physical Sc, D.W. Reynolds building for the life scie, Art Complex, Butler Plaza Fountain, the Burrow (campus center). **Environmental Initiatives:** Reduction in paper utilization; Maintaining and building environmentally sound buildings; Recycling.

ADMISSIONS

Freshman Academic Profile: Average high school GPA 3.9. 51% in top 10% of high school class, 77% in top 25% of high school class, 96% in top 50% of high school class. 77% from public high schools. SAT Math middle 50% range 540-670. SAT Critical Reading middle 50% range 550-680. ACT middle 50% range 26-32. Minimum internet-based TOEFL 79. Minimum paper TOEFL 550. **Basis for Candidate Selection:** *Very important factors considered include:* application essay, academic GPA, rigor of secondary school record, standardized test scores. *Important factors considered include:* Class rank, recommendation(s), extracurricular activities, interview. *Other factors considered include:* racial/ethnic status, talent/ability, volunteer work. **Freshman Admission Requirements:** High school diploma is required and GED is accepted. **Freshman Admission Statistics:** 1,656 applied, 83% admitted, 27% enrolled. **Transfer Admission Requirements:** college transcript(s), essay or personal statement, statement of good standing from prior institution(s). Minimum college GPA of 2.5 required. Lowest grade transferable C. **General Admission Information:** Application Fee $40. Regular application deadline 8/1. Notification on a rolling basis, beginning on or about 11/1. Nonfall registration accepted. Admission may be deferred for a maximum of 1 year. Credit and/or placement offered for CEEB Advanced Placement tests.

COSTS AND FINANCIAL AID

Annual tuition $37,516. Room and board $10,620. Required fees $300. Average book expense $1,100. **Required Forms and Deadlines:** FAFSA. **Notification of Awards:** Applicants will be notified of awards on a rolling basis beginning 2/15. **Types of Aid:** *Need-based scholarships/grants:* Federal Pell, SEOG, state scholarships/grants, private scholarships, the school's own gift aid. *Loans:* Direct Subsidized Stafford, Direct Unsubsidized Stafford, Direct PLUS, Subsidized Stafford, Unsubsidized Stafford, PLUS, Federal Perkins, Private alternative loans as selected by the student. *Student Employment:* Federal Work-Study Program available. Institutional employment available. Highest amount earned per year from on-campus jobs $1,500. Off-campus job opportunities are good. **Financial Aid Statistics:** 100% freshmen, 100% undergrads receive need-based scholarship or grant aid. 38% freshmen, 34% undergrads receive non-need-based scholarship or grant aid. 62% freshmen, 65% undergrads receive need-based self-help aid. 0% freshmen, 0% undergrads receive athletic scholarships. 100% freshmen, 100% undergrads receive any aid. 52% undergrads borrow to pay for school. Average cumulative indebtedness $21,715. **Criteria for awarding institutional aid:** *Non-need-based:* academics, art, leadership, music/drama, state/district residency.

HERITAGE UNIVERSITY

3240 Fort Road, Toppenish, WA 98948
Phone: 509-865-8508 • **Financial Aid Phone:** 509-865-8502
E-mail: 3w_Admissions@heritage.edu • **CEEB Code:** 3777
Fax: 509-865-8659 • **Website:** http://www.heritage.edu/

This private school was founded in 1982. It has a 20-acre campus.

RATINGS

Admissions Selectivity Rating: 62   Fire Safety Rating: 60*

STUDENTS AND FACULTY

Enrollment: 756. **Student Body:** 73% female, 27% male, 0% out-of-state, 0% international. Asian 1%, African American 1%, Caucasian 35%, Hispanic 56%, Native American 11%
Retention and Graduation: 49% freshmen return for sophomore year. 30% freshmen graduate within 6 years. **Faculty:** 47 full-time faculty, 38% hold PhDs, 49% are members of minority groups, 23% are women. 0% of classes are taught by teaching assistants.

ACADEMICS

Degrees: associate, bachelor's, certificate, master's, post-bachelor's certificate, post-master's certificate, terminal associate, transfer associate. **Classes:** Most classes have fewer than 10 students. **Special Study Options:** cooperative education program, distance learning, double major, English as a Second Language (ESL), honors program, independent study, internships, liberal arts/career combination, teacher certification program. **Honors programs:** Students take Honors seminar, Honors sections of general education requirements, and have frequent interactions with faculty, other scholars, and community leaders; develop and implement strategies for community improvement and participate in cultural events. Combined degree programs: N/A. **Disability Services:** Special programs offered to physically disabled students include note-taking services, reader services, tape recorders, tutors.

FACILITIES

Housing: 90% of campus accessible to physically disabled.

CAMPUS LIFE

Environment: Rural. **Activities:** drama/theater, literary magazine, music ensembles, student government, student newspaper. **On-Campus Highlights:** Student Services Center, Jewett Center, Library, Academic Skills Center.

ADMISSIONS

Freshman Academic Profile: 95% from public high schools. Minimum paper TOEFL 500. **Freshman Admission Requirements:** High school diploma is required and GED is accepted. **Freshman Admission Statistics:** 475 applied, 60% admitted, 31% enrolled. **Transfer Admission Requirements:** college transcript(s), Lowest grade transferable C-. **General Admission Information:** Regular application deadline 9/1. Nonfall registration accepted. Admission may be deferred for a maximum of 3. Credit and/or placement offered for CEEB Advanced Placement tests.

COSTS AND FINANCIAL AID

Required Forms and Deadlines: FAFSA, Institution's own financial aid form. **Types of Aid:** *Need-based scholarships/grants:* Federal Pell, SEOG, state scholarships/grants, private scholarships, the school's own gift aid. *Loans:* Subsidized Stafford, Unsubsidized Stafford, PLUS, Federal Perkins. **Financial Aid Statistics:** 90% freshmen, 86% undergrads receive need-based scholarship or grant aid. 2% freshmen, 2% undergrads receive non-need-based scholarship or grant aid. 52% freshmen, 65% undergrads receive need-based self-help aid. 92% undergrads borrow to pay for school.

HIGH POINT UNIVERSITY

University Station 3598, High Point, NC 27262-3598
Phone: 336-841-9216 • **Financial Aid Phone:** 336-841-9128
E-mail: admiss@highpoint.edu • **CEEB Code:** 5293
Fax: 336-888-6382 • **Website:** www.highpoint.edu • **ACT Code:** 3108

This private school, affiliated with the Methodist Church, was founded in 1924. It has a 135-acre campus.

RATINGS

Admissions Selectivity Rating: 83   Fire Safety Rating: 78

STUDENTS AND FACULTY

Enrollment: 4,197. **Student Body:** 59% female, 41% male, 78% out-of-state, 2% international (30 countries represented). Asian 1%, African American 5%, Caucasian 81%, Hispanic 4%, Native American <1% **Retention and Graduation:** 59% freshmen graduate within 4 years. 63% freshmen graduate within 6 years. 28% grads go on to further study within 1 year. 19% grads pursue arts and sciences degrees. 3% grads pursue law degrees. 2% grads pursue business degrees. 1% grads pursue medical degrees. **Faculty:** 252 full-time faculty, 79% hold PhDs, 47% are members of minority groups, 10% are women. 0% of classes are taught by teaching assistants.

ACADEMICS

Degrees: bachelor's, master's, post-bachelor's certificate. **Classes:** Most classes have 10–19 students. **Majors with Highest Enrollment:** Business/Commerce; Speech Communication and Rhetoric; Biology/Biological Sciences. **Special Study Options:** Accelerated program, cooperative education program, cross-registration, double major, dual enrollment, English as a Second Language (ESL), honors program, independent study, internships, liberal arts/career combination, student-designed major, study abroad, teacher certification program, Joint degree programs in environmental science, forestry and medical technology. **Honors programs:** More than 200 students are enrolled in the university's Honors Program. In addition to enrollment in honors courses, members of the Honors Program often present the results of their research at the Honors Symposium sponsored annually by the university's Odyssey Club, an organization of students enrolled in the Honors Program. In addition to activities for members of the Honors Program, the Odyssey Club sponsors a number of activities annually for the campus at large, including academic bowls and visiting lecturers. Combined degree programs: 3-2 programs: med tech; environ sci; forestry. **Disability Services:** Special programs offered to physically disabled students include tape recorders, tutors. **Career services:** career/job search classes, career assessment, internships. Career services highlights include the civic engagement program, the mission of which is to increase students' understanding of their diverse responsibilities as stewards of their communities by: providing students with opportunities to participate in activities that contribute to the public good; encouraging students to reflect on their experiences as a means of making more permanent the practical lessons they learn in the field; instilling in students an awareness of the mutually beneficial relationship that exists between social institutions and centers of higher learning; teaching students to think critically, speak clearly, and write effectively as a means of becoming productive members of society.

FACILITIES

Housing: Coed dorms, special housing for disabled students, men's dorms, women's dorms, fraternity/sorority housing, apartments for married students, cooperative housing, apartments for single studentsThe number of apartments/houses are available for married students is limited. 98% of campus accessible to physically disabled. **Special Academic Facilities/Equipment:** Hayworth Chapel; Hayworth Fine Arts Center; Sechrest Gallery; Smith Library; Campus Television Studio; Radio Studio/Station (WHPU) Beginning a $100 million new-construction and renovation program, the campus of High Point University is currently experiencing the greatest period of growth in our 81-year history. Currently under construction are: Blessing Residence Hall is a $10-million facility which is made possible by the generous lead gift of one anonymous donor who requested we call it the "Blessing" residence hall. It will be loaded with amenities that make it a prototype for 21st Century college residence halls. It will offer 240 fully furnished, private bedrooms arranged in suites with living rooms,kitchens and dining areas. Residents will enjoy spacious common areas, computer lounges, conference areas, laundry rooms and elevators. Slane Student Life & Wellness Center will be a centerpiece of campus. This $6.5 million, 45,000-square-foot building will connect to the current Slane Student Center via a two-story atrium, and will feature a high-performance aerobics room, rock-climbing wall, indoor track, fully equipped weight room, food court, dramatic inside & outside basketball courts, outdoor swimming pool, sand volleyball courts, and a grand student atrium with billiard tables and sitting areas. The Earl N. Phillips School of Business will be a new 27,000-square-foot building which will become the home for the more than 1,000 undergraduate students pursuing a degree in one of High Point University's 12 undergraduate majors and Master of Business Administration graduate degree. The facility will feature a 200-seat, tiered lecture hall, four smaller lecture rooms, as well as traditional classrooms, a spacious auditorium, private study rooms, computer labs and faculty offices. The Jerry & Kitty Steele Sports Center will be a $5 million, 2-story, 27,000-square-foot facility featuring training & weight rooms, a hospitality/conference room, locker rooms, and an academic services room. In addition, another $5 million is being invested to build a new soccer stadium, baseball stadium, and eight-lane track. University Park will be an extraordinary outdoor experience. Featuring a network of trails and bridges, spectacular waterfalls, a 15-foot overhead trellis, multi-level reflecting pools, 65' covered walkway, and an amphitheatre, this will be the perfect place for an outdoor class, receptions, plays and programs. **Computers:** 100% of classrooms, 100% of dorms, 100% of libraries, 100% of dining areas, 100% of student union, 100% of common

outdoor areas have wireless network access. Students can register for classes on-line. Administrative functions (other than registration) can be performed online.

CAMPUS LIFE

Environment: City. **Activities:** Choral groups, concert band, dance, drama/theater, literary magazine, music ensembles, musical theater, pep band, radio station, student government, student newspaper, symphony orchestra, television station, yearbook, Campus Ministries, Model UN. 109 registered organizations, 14 honor societies, 8 religious organizations. 4 fraternities, 5 sororities. **Athletics (Intercollegiate):** *Men:* baseball, basketball, cheerleading, cross-country, golf, soccer, tennis, track/field (outdoor), track/field (indoor). *Women:* basketball, cheerleading, cross-country, golf, soccer, tennis, track/field (outdoor), track/field (indoor), volleyball. **On-Campus Highlights:** Slane University Center, Hayworth Fine Arts Center, Millis Athletic/Convocation Center, Hayworth Chapel, The International Promenade, High Point University is in the midst of a 5-year, $250 million campus development plan that will result in the construction of a new building for the School of Business, a new Student Activity Center, a new soccer stadium and track, a new residence hall, a new Sports Center, a new University Park, and dozens of renovations across campus. **Environmental Initiatives:** Arboreatum and Tree Campus; USA Recycling Program; Free Bike Rentals to students.

ADMISSIONS

Freshman Academic Profile: Average high school GPA 3.23. 21.5% in top 10% of high school class, 47.4% in top 25% of high school class, 79.2% in top 50% of high school class. 64% from public high schools. SAT Math middle 50% range 510-601. SAT Critical Reading middle 50% range 499-591. SAT Writing middle 50% range 489-591. ACT middle 50% range 21-26. Minimum internet-based TOEFL 79. Minimum paper TOEFL 500. **Basis for Candidate Selection:** *Very important factors considered include:* rigor of secondary school record, standardized test scores. *Important factors considered include:* Class rank, academic GPA. *Other factors considered include:* application essay, recommendation(s), extracurricular activities, interview, talent/ability, volunteer work, work experience. **Freshman Admission Requirements:** High school diploma is required and GED is accepted. *Academic units required:* 4 English, 3 mathematics, 2 science, (2 science labs), 2 social studies, 2 history, 1 academic electives. **Freshman Admission Statistics:** 7,410 applied, 80% admitted, 23% enrolled. **Transfer Admission Requirements:** High school transcript, college transcript(s), standardized test scores, statement of good standing from prior institution(s). Minimum college GPA of 2.0 required. Lowest grade transferable C. **General Admission Information:** Application Fee $40. Early decision application deadline 11/7. Regular application deadline 8/15. Notification on a rolling basis, beginning on or about 11/6. Nonfall registration accepted. Admission may be deferred for a maximum of 1 year. Credit and/or placement offered for CEEB Advanced Placement tests.

COSTS AND FINANCIAL AID

Annual tuition $27,775. Room and board $11,480. Required fees $3,705. Average book expense $1,500. **Required Forms and Deadlines:** FAFSA, State aid form. **Notification of Awards:** Applicants will be notified of awards on a rolling basis beginning 4/1. **Types of Aid:** *Need-based scholarships/grants:* Federal Pell, SEOG, state scholarships/grants, private scholarships, the school's own gift aid. *Loans:* Direct Subsidized Stafford, Direct Unsubsidized Stafford, Direct PLUS, Subsidized Stafford, Unsubsidized Stafford, PLUS, Federal Perkins. *Student Employment:* Federal Work-Study Program available. Institutional employment available. Off-campus job opportunities are good. **Financial Aid Statistics:** 96% freshmen, 71% undergrads receive need-based scholarship or grant aid. 70% freshmen, 61% undergrads receive non-need-based scholarship or grant aid. 100% freshmen, 100% undergrads receive need-based self-help aid. 5% freshmen, 5% undergrads receive athletic scholarships. 80% freshmen, 78% undergrads receive any aid. 70% undergrads borrow to pay for school. Average cumulative indebtedness $11,767. **Criteria for awarding institutional aid:** *Non-need-based:* academics, alumni affiliation, art, athletics, leadership, music/drama, religious affiliation, state/district residency.

HILBERT COLLEGE

5200 South Park Avenue, Hamburg, NY 14075-1597
Phone: 716-649-7900 • **Financial Aid Phone:** 716-649-7900
E-mail: admissions@hilbert.edu • **CEEB Code:** 2334
Fax: 716-649-0702 • **Website:** www.hilbert.edu • **ACT Code:** 2759

This private school, affiliated with the Roman Catholic Church, was founded in 1957. It has a 40-acre campus.

RATINGS

Admissions Selectivity Rating: 70 **Fire Safety Rating:** 86

STUDENTS AND FACULTY

Enrollment: 998. **Student Body:** 60% female, 40% male, 10% out-of-state, 0% international (4 countries represented). Asian 0%, African American 6%, Caucasian 82%, Hispanic 2%, Native American 2%.
Retention and Graduation: 70% freshmen return for sophomore year. 49% freshmen graduate within 4 years. 50% freshmen graduate within 6 years. 15% grads go on to further study within 1 year. 4% grads pursue arts and sciences degrees. 4% grads pursue law degrees. 4% grads pursue business degrees. **Faculty:** 48 full-time faculty, 50% hold PhDs, 48% are members of minority groups, 2% are women. 0% of classes are taught by teaching assistants.

ACADEMICS

Degrees: associate, bachelor's, certificate, terminal associate. **Classes:** Most classes have 10–19 students. Most lab/discussion sessions have fewer than 10 students. **Majors with Highest Enrollment:** Criminal Justice/Law Enforcement Administration; Forensic Science and Technology; Business/Commerce. **Special Study Options:** cross-registration, distance learning, dual enrollment, honors program, independent study, internships, study abroad, Member of Western New York consortium of colleges. **Honors programs:** About the Honors Program The Hilbert Honors Program will give you more from your college experience. You will enroll in regular classes and fulfill honors credit requirements by doing advanced work, or in lieu of projects. These special projects allow you to work one-on-one with Hilbert's outstanding honors faculty in your major and in other academic areas. As an honors student, you will also have a student mentor for your first semester and personal faculty advisement. **Disability Services:** Special programs offered to physically disabled students include note-taking services, reader services, tape recorders, tutors. **Career services:** Alumni network, alumni services, career assessment, internships. Career services highlights include internships available with agencies in most majors.

FACILITIES

Housing: Coed dorms, apartments for single studentsCampus Apartments. 95% of campus accessible to physically disabled. Honors Lounge, Institute for Law and Justice, Center for Creative Media, **Computers:** 100% of classrooms, 100% of dorms, 100% of libraries, 100% of dining areas, 100% of student union, 100% of common outdoor areas have wireless network access. Students can register for classes online. Administrative functions (other than registration) can be performed online.

CAMPUS LIFE

Environment: Village. **Activities:** Choral groups, drama/theater, literary magazine, student government, student newspaper, Campus Ministries. 20 registered organizations, 5 honor societies, 1 religious organization. **Athletics (Intercollegiate):** *Men:* baseball, basketball, cross-country, golf, soccer, volleyball. *Women:* basketball, cross-country, golf, soccer, softball, volleyball. **On-Campus Highlights:** Hafner Recreation Center, Franciscan Hall Atrium, Campus Apartments, Swan Auditorium, Paczesny Hall.

ADMISSIONS

Freshman Academic Profile: Average high school GPA 2.8. 2% in top 10% of high school class, 13% in top 25% of high school class, 40% in top 50% of high school class. 85% from public high schools. SAT Math middle 50% range 400-510. SAT Critical Reading middle 50% range 400-510. ACT middle 50% range 17-22. Minimum paper TOEFL 500. **Basis for Candidate Selection:** *Very important factors considered include:* academic GPA, rigor of secondary school record. *Important factors considered include:* recommendation(s). *Other factors considered include:* application essay, character/personal qualities, extracurricular activities, interview, talent/ability, volunteer work, work experience. **Freshman Admission Requirements:** High school diploma is required and GED is accepted. *Academic units required:* 4 English, 2 mathematics, 2 science, (1 science labs), 0 foreign language, 2 social studies, 2 history, 4 academic electives. **Freshman Admission Statistics:** 726 applied, 85% admitted, 35% enrolled. **Transfer Admission Requirements:** High school transcript, college transcript(s), Minimum college GPA of 2.0 required. Lowest grade transferable C. **General Admission Information:** Application Fee $20. Regular application deadline 9/1. Nonfall registration accepted. Admission may be deferred for a maximum of 1 year. Credit offered for CEEB Advanced Placement tests.

COSTS AND FINANCIAL AID

Annual tuition $16,000. Room and board $6,600. Required fees $600. Average book expense $700. **Required Forms and Deadlines:** FAFSA, State aid form. **Notification of Awards:** Applicants will be notified of awards on a rolling basis beginning 3/1. **Types of Aid:** *Need-based scholarships/grants:* Federal Pell, SEOG, state scholarships/grants, private scholarships, the school's own gift aid. *Loans:* Subsidized Stafford, Unsubsidized Stafford, PLUS, Federal Perkins. *Student Employment:* Federal Work-Study Program available. Institutional employment available. Highest amount earned per year from on-campus jobs $1,250. Off-campus job opportunities are excellent. **Financial Aid Statistics:** 99% freshmen, 98% undergrads receive need-based scholarship or grant aid. 4% freshmen, 5% undergrads receive non-need-based scholarship or grant aid.

90% freshmen, 88% undergrads receive need-based self-help aid. 0% freshmen, 0% undergrads receive athletic scholarships. 92% freshmen, 87% undergrads receive any aid. 93% undergrads borrow to pay for school. Average cumulative indebtedness $20,513. **Criteria for awarding institutional aid:** *Non-need-based:* academics, leadership, minority status.

HILLSDALE COLLEGE

33 East College Street, Hillsdale, MI 49242
Phone: 517-607-2327 • **Financial Aid Phone:** 517-607-2350
E-mail: admissions@hillsdale.edu • **CEEB Code:** 1295
Fax: 517-607-2223 • **Website:** www.hillsdale.edu • **ACT Code:** 2010

This private school was founded in 1844. It has a 200-acre campus.

RATINGS

Admissions Selectivity Rating: 93   **Fire Safety Rating:** 79

STUDENTS AND FACULTY

Enrollment: 1,469. **Student Body:** 52% female, 48% male, 66% out-of-state, (9 countries represented).
Retention and Graduation: 70% freshmen graduate within 4 years. 17% grads go on to further study within 1 year. 8% grads pursue arts and sciences degrees. 2% grads pursue law degrees. 2% grads pursue business degrees. 4% grads pursue medical degrees. **Faculty:** 133 full-time faculty, 87% hold PhDs, 26% are members of minority groups. 0% of classes are taught by teaching assistants.

ACADEMICS

Degrees: bachelor's. **Classes:** Most classes have fewer than 10 students. Most lab/discussion sessions have 20–29 students. **Majors with Highest Enrollment:** Biology/Biological Sciences; History; English Language and Literature. **Special Study Options:** double major, dual enrollment, honors program, independent study, internships, student-designed major, study abroad, teacher certification program. **Honors programs:** Honors Program available. **Career services:** Alumni network, alumni services, career assessment, internships. Career services highlights include a National Professional Sales Internship Program.

FACILITIES

Housing: men's dorms, women's dorms, fraternity/sorority housing, apartments for single students **Special Academic Facilities/Equipment:** Early childhood education lab, media center, K-8 private academy, Slayton Arboretum, rare books library. **Computers:** 100% of classrooms, 85% of dorms, 100% of libraries, 100% of dining areas, 100% of student union, 100% of common outdoor areas have wireless network access.

CAMPUS LIFE

Environment: Village. **Activities:** Choral groups, concert band, dance, drama/theater, jazz band, literary magazine, music ensembles, musical theater, pep band, student government, student newspaper, symphony orchestra, yearbook, Campus Ministries, International Student Organization. 50 registered organizations, 26 honor societies, 4 religious organizations. 3 fraternities, 3 sororities. **Athletics (Intercollegiate):** *Men:* baseball, basketball, cheerleading, cross-country, football, track/field (outdoor), track/field (indoor). *Women:* basketball, cheerleading, cross-country, diving, equestrian sports, softball, swimming, track/field (outdoor), track/field (indoor), volleyball. **On-Campus Highlights:** Student Union, Quad (outdoor quadrangle), Sage Center for the Arts, Howard Music Hall, Sports Complex. **Environmental Initiatives:** Central heating and cooling efficiency plan; High efficiency lighting in all new facilities; Environmental controls in all buildings for energy management.

ADMISSIONS

Freshman Academic Profile: Average high school GPA 3.81. 50% in top 10% of high school class, 82% in top 25% of high school class, 97% in top 50% of high school class. 51% from public high schools. SAT Math middle 50% range 590-690. SAT Critical Reading middle 50% range 617-730. SAT Writing middle 50% range 590-693. ACT middle 50% range 27-31. Minimum internet-based TOEFL 83. Minimum paper TOEFL 580. **Basis for Candidate Selection:** *Very important factors considered include:* academic GPA, rigor of secondary school record, standardized test scores, character/personal qualities, interview. *Important factors considered include:* Class rank, application essay, recommendation(s), extracurricular activities, level of applicant's interest, volunteer work, work experience. *Other factors considered include:* alumni/ae relation, talent/ability. **Freshman Admission Requirements:** High school diploma is required and GED is accepted. **Freshman Admission Statistics:** 1,833 applied, 53% admitted, 37% enrolled. **Transfer Admission Requirements:** High school transcript, college transcript(s), essay or personal statement, standardized test scores, statement of good standing from prior institution(s). Minimum college GPA of 3.25 required. Lowest grade transferable C. **General Admission Information:** Application Fee $35. Early decision application deadline 11/15. Regular application deadline 2/15. Nonfall registration accepted. Admission may be deferred for a maximum of one year. Credit and/or placement offered for CEEB Advanced Placement tests.

COSTS AND FINANCIAL AID
Required Forms and Deadlines: Institution's own financial aid form. **Notification of Awards:** Applicants will be notified of awards on a rolling basis beginning 2/15. **Types of Aid:** *Need-based scholarships/grants:* private scholarships, the school's own gift aid. *Loans:* college/university loans from institutional funds. *Student Employment:* Institutional employment available. Highest amount earned per year from on-campus jobs $1,300. Off-campus job opportunities are good. **Financial Aid Statistics:** 65% freshmen, 61% undergrads receive need-based scholarship or grant aid. 77% freshmen, 76% undergrads receive non-need-based scholarship or grant aid. 101% freshmen, 66% undergrads receive need-based self-help aid. 15% freshmen, 14% undergrads receive athletic scholarships. 91% freshmen, 95% undergrads receive any aid. 56% undergrads borrow to pay for school. Average cumulative indebtedness $0. **Criteria for awarding institutional aid:** *Non-need-based:* academics, alumni affiliation, art, athletics, leadership, music/drama.

See page 1064.

HIRAM COLLEGE

PO Box 96, Hiram, OH 44234
CEEB Code: 1297
Website: www.hiram.edu • **ACT Code:** 3280

This private school, affiliated with the Disciples of Christ Church, was founded in 1850. It has a 110-acre campus.

RATINGS
Admissions Selectivity Rating: 82   **Fire Safety Rating:** 61

STUDENTS AND FACULTY
Enrollment: 1,260. **Student Body:** 55% female, 45% male, 18% out-of-state, 4% international (17 countries represented). Asian 1%, African American 14%, Caucasian 71%, Hispanic 4%, Native American <1%
Retention and Graduation: 76% freshmen return for sophomore year. 60% freshmen graduate within 4 years. 36% grads go on to further study within 1 year. 30% grads pursue arts and sciences degrees. 3% grads pursue law degrees. 5% grads pursue business degrees. 3% grads pursue medical degrees. **Faculty:** 80 full-time faculty, 89% hold PhDs, 58% are members of minority groups, 11% are women. 0% of classes are taught by teaching assistants.

ACADEMICS
Degrees: bachelor's, master's. **Classes:** Most classes have 10–19 students. Most lab/discussion sessions have 10–19 students. **Majors with Highest Enrollment:** Education; Accounting and Business/Management; Registered Nursing/Registered Nurse. **Special Study Options:** Accelerated program, cross-registration, double major, English as a Second Language (ESL), exchange student program (domestic), independent study, internships, student-designed major, study abroad, teacher certification program, weekend college. Combined degree programs: BA(Hiram)/BS(Engineering) 5 years. **Disability Services:** Special programs offered to physically disabled students include note-taking services, reader services, tape recorders, tutors. **Career services:** Alumni network, alumni services, career/job search classes, career assessment, internships. Career services highlights include internships including participation in the regional ClevelandIntern.net, biomedical research, and virtual internships.

FACILITIES
Housing: Coed dorms, special housing for disabled students, women's dorms, Theme Housing, suite style housing. 55% of campus accessible to physically disabled. **Special Academic Facilities/Equipment:** Psychology lab, language lab, international center, center for literature and medicine, fitness center, health center, observatory, electron microscope, two field stations for study and research.

CAMPUS LIFE
Environment: Rural. **Activities:** Choral groups, concert band, dance, drama/theater, jazz band, literary magazine, marching band, music ensembles, opera,

pep band, radio station, student government, student newspaper, symphony orchestra, yearbook, Campus Ministries, International Student Organization, Model UN. 55 registered organizations, 7 honor societies, 6 religious organizations. 3 fraternities, 3 sororities. **Athletics (Intercollegiate):** *Men:* baseball, basketball, cheerleading, cross-country, diving, football, golf, soccer, swimming, tennis, track/field (outdoor), track/field (indoor). *Women:* basketball, cheerleading, cross-country, diving, golf, soccer, softball, swimming, tennis, track/field (outdoor), track/field (indoor), volleyball. **On-Campus Highlights:** James H. Barrow Field Station, The Hiram College Library, Kennedy Center (Food Court, Bookstore, ballroom,and other facilities), Hiram Church, Stevens Memorial Observatory.

ADMISSIONS
Freshman Academic Profile: Average high school GPA 3.21. 12% in top 10% of high school class, 37% in top 25% of high school class, 67% in top 50% of high school class. 86% from public high schools. SAT Math middle 50% range 450-580. SAT Critical Reading middle 50% range 430-600. SAT Writing middle 50% range 430-560. ACT middle 50% range 19-25. Minimum paper TOEFL 550. **Freshman Admission Statistics:** 2,530 applied, 57% admitted, 20% enrolled. **General Admission Information:** Credit and/or placement offered for CEEB Advanced Placement tests.

COSTS AND FINANCIAL AID
Annual tuition $29,065. Room and board $9,860. Required fees $975. Average book expense $700. **Required Forms and Deadlines:** FAFSA. **Notification of Awards:** Applicants will be notified of awards on a rolling basis beginning 3/1. **Types of Aid:** *Need-based scholarships/grants:* Federal Pell, SEOG, state scholarships/grants, private scholarships, the school's own gift aid, United Negro College Fund. *Loans:* Subsidized Stafford, Unsubsidized Stafford, PLUS, Federal Perkins, college/university loans from institutional funds. *Student Employment:* Highest amount earned per year from on-campus jobs $500. **Financial Aid Statistics:** 100% freshmen, 97% undergrads receive need-based scholarship or grant aid. 100% freshmen, 92% undergrads receive non-need-based scholarship or grant aid. 92% freshmen, 89% undergrads receive need-based self-help aid. 0% freshmen, 0% undergrads receive athletic scholarships.91% undergrads receive any aid. 42% undergrads borrow to pay for school. Average cumulative indebtedness $27,055. **Criteria for awarding institutional aid:** *Non-need-based:* academics, alumni affiliation, music/drama, religious affiliation, state/district residency.

HOBART AND WILLIAM SMITH COLLEGES

629 South Main Street, Geneva, NY 14456
Phone: 315-781-3622 • **Financial Aid Phone:** 315-781-3315
E-mail: admissions@hws.edu • **CEEB Code:** 2294
Fax: 315-781-3914 • **Website:** www.hws.edu • **ACT Code:** 2758

This private school was founded in 1822. It has a 170-acre campus.

RATINGS
Admissions Selectivity Rating: 89   **Fire Safety Rating:** 92

STUDENTS AND FACULTY
Enrollment: 2,344. **Student Body:** 53% female, 47% male, 59% out-of-state, 5% international (32 countries represented). Asian 3%, African American 5%, Caucasian 70%, Hispanic 6%, Native American 1%
Retention and Graduation: 88% freshmen return for sophomore year. 74% freshmen graduate within 4 years. 29% grads go on to further study within 1 year. 5% grads pursue law degrees. 2% grads pursue medical degrees. **Faculty:** 223 full-time faculty, 98% hold PhDs, 48% are members of minority groups, 17% are women. 0% of classes are taught by teaching assistants.

ACADEMICS
Degrees: bachelor's, master's. **Classes:** Most classes have 10–19 students. **Majors with Highest Enrollment:** Economics; Political Science and Government; Psychology. **Special Study Options:** cross-registration, double major, dual enrollment, English as a Second Language (ESL), exchange student program (domestic), honors program, independent study, internships, student-designed major, study abroad, teacher certification program. Combined degree programs: BA/MA, 3-2 Engineer; 3-4 Architect; 4-1 MBA; 4-1 MAT. **Disability Services:** Special programs offered to physically disabled students include note-taking services, reader services, tape recorders, tutors. **Career services:**

Alumni network, alumni services, career/job search classes, career assessment, internships.

FACILITIES

Housing: Coed dorms, men's dorms, special housing for international students, women's dorms, fraternity/sorority housing, cooperative housing, apartments for single students, Upperclass townhouses; Theme Houses; Honors Houses. **Special Academic Facilities/Equipment:** Houghton Gallery, HWS Explorer (resesarch vessel), 100 Acre Nature Preserve, Melly Academic Center, Rosenberg science center. **Computers:** Students can register for classes online. Administrative functions (other than registration) can be performed online.

CAMPUS LIFE

Environment: Village. **Activities:** Choral groups, dance, drama/theater, jazz band, literary magazine, music ensembles, radio station; student government, student newspaper, student-run film society, symphony orchestra, yearbook. 77 registered organizations, 12 honor societies, 4 religious organizations. 5 fraternities. **Athletics (Intercollegiate):** *Men:* basketball, crew/rowing, cross-country, football, golf, ice hockey, lacrosse, sailing, soccer, squash, tennis. *Women:* basketball, crew/rowing, cross-country, diving, field hockey, golf, lacrosse, sailing, soccer, squash, swimming, tennis. **On-Campus Highlights:** Scandling Center, South Hall, Stern Hall, North Hall, Bristol Field House, Trinity Hall, with the newly remodeled Salisbury Center, houses the Offices of Career Development, Public Service and Global Education. The building re-opened in January 2004. **Environmental Initiatives:** Integrating the Colleges Sustainability living laboratory approach in the Climate Action Plan. The living laboratory approach is exemplified through student projects—class, independent study or volunteer that directly effect the colleges impact on the environment and culture of environmental sustainability. For example, The Finger Lakes Institutes renovation was directed by a first year Energy class project that identified specific environmental parameters to be incorporated into the building. These students vision and project qualified the Finger Lakes Institute for the Energy Star Small Business Award. This living laboratory, student oriented learning approach is at the core of the Colleges Sustainability Program and enhanced by the Colleges Climate Action Plan. The Climate Task Force (Colleges Sustainability Executive Committee) created an Energy and Climate Committee, an outcome of the Climate Action Plan. The Energy and Climate Committee is charged to reduce HWS greenhouse gas emissions through electricity and heat conservation initiatives. The Committee decreased emissions resulting from energy consumption by 10%, saving over $300,000 through investment in energy efficiency technologies ?û including, but certainly not limited to L.E.D. lighting, high efficiency boilers, variable speed drives, and refined building scheduling through building automation systems. The student led overhaul of the Colleges waste management program led the Colleges to institutionalize composting, add over 1000 recycling bins and implement a year round E-Waste management program. The Colleges now compost nearly 100% of pre-consumer & post-consumer (must be a clean stream) food-waste from its dining facilities sending nearly 2 tons of foodwaste and compostable serviceware (used in our retail Café and Pub operations as well as at all catered events) to the compost facility weekly. In addition, the Colleges raised its recycling rate by 25% through front end awareness building and a transition to a single stream recycling program.

ADMISSIONS

Freshman Academic Profile: Average high school GPA 3.41. 30% in top 10% of high school class, 70% in top 25% of high school class, 90% in top 50% of high school class. 62% from public high schools. SAT Math middle 50% range 580-660. SAT Critical Reading middle 50% range 560-660. ACT middle 50% range 26-31. Minimum internet-based TOEFL 80. Minimum paper TOEFL 550. **Basis for Candidate Selection:** *Very important factors considered include:* rigor of secondary school record. *Important factors considered include:* Class rank, application essay, academic GPA, recommendation(s), standardized test scores, character/personal qualities, extracurricular activities, volunteer work, work experience. *Other factors considered include:* alumni/ae relation, first generation, geographical residence, interview, level of applicant's interest, racial/ethnic status, talent/ability. **Freshman Admission Requirements:** High school diploma is required and GED is accepted. *Academic units required:* 4 English, 3 mathematics, 3 science, (2 science labs), 2 foreign language, 2 social studies, 2 history, 2 academic electives. **Freshman Admission Statistics:** 5,093 applied, 50% admitted, 26% enrolled. **Transfer Admission Requirements:** High school transcript, college transcript(s), essay or personal statement, standardized test scores, Minimum college GPA of 2.5 required. Lowest grade transferable C. **General Admission Information:** Application Fee $45. Early decision application deadline 11/15. Regular application deadline 2/1. Regular notification 4/1. Nonfall registration not accepted. Admission may be deferred for a maximum of 2 Years. Credit offered for CEEB Advanced Placement tests.

COSTS AND FINANCIAL AID

Average book expense $1,300. **Required Forms and Deadlines:** FAFSA, CSS/Financial Aid PROFILE, State aid form, Noncustodial PROFILE. **Notification of Awards:** Applicants will be notified of awards on or about 4/1. **Types of Aid:** *Need-based scholarships/grants:* Federal Pell, SEOG, state scholar-

ships/grants, private scholarships, the school's own gift aid. *Loans:* Subsidized Stafford, Unsubsidized Stafford, PLUS, Federal Perkins. *Student Employment:* Federal Work-Study Program available. Institutional employment available. Highest amount earned per year from on-campus jobs $600. Off-campus job opportunities are good. **Financial Aid Statistics:** 99% freshmen, 98% undergrads receive need-based scholarship or grant aid. 19% freshmen, 14% undergrads receive non-need-based scholarship or grant aid. 80% freshmen, 84% undergrads receive need-based self-help aid. 0% freshmen, 0% undergrads receive athletic scholarships. 86% freshmen, 89% undergrads receive any aid. 57% undergrads borrow to pay for school. Average cumulative indebtedness $26,022. **Criteria for awarding institutional aid:** *Non-need-based:* academics, art, leadership, music/drama.

HODGES UNIVERSITY

2655 Northbrooke Drive, Naples, FL 34119
Phone: 239-513-1122 · **Financial Aid Phone:** 239-513-1122
E-mail: admit@internationalcollege.edu · **CEEB Code:** 7113
Fax: 239-598-6254 · **Website:** www.hodges.edu · **ACT Code:** 4775

This private school was founded in 1990.

RATINGS

Admissions Selectivity Rating: 61   **Fire Safety Rating:** 60*

STUDENTS AND FACULTY

Enrollment: 1,475. **Student Body:** 68% female, 32% male, 0% out-of-state, 0% international (40 countries represented). Asian 2%, African American 16%, Caucasian 55%, Hispanic 24%, Native American <1%
Faculty: 61 full-time faculty, 66% hold PhDs, 33% are members of minority groups, 8% are women. 0% of classes are taught by teaching assistants.

ACADEMICS

Degrees: associate, bachelor's, certificate, master's. **Classes:** Most classes have 10–19 students. **Majors with Highest Enrollment:** Business, Management, Marketing, and Related Support Services; Multi-/Interdisciplinary Studies; Health Professions and Related Clinical Sciences. **Special Study Options:** Accelerated program, cooperative education program, distance learning, double major, English as a Second Language (ESL), independent study, internships, weekend college. **Career services:** alumni services, career/job search classes, career assessment.

FACILITIES

Housing: 100% of campus accessible to physically disabled. **Computers:** 100% of classrooms, 100% of libraries, have wireless network access. Students can register for classes online. Administrative functions (other than registration) can be performed online.

CAMPUS LIFE

Environment: City. **Activities:** literary magazine 1 honor society. **Environmental Initiatives:** Reduction in energy usage; Recycling Programs.

ADMISSIONS

Freshman Academic Profile: Minimum paper TOEFL 500. **Basis for Candidate Selection:** *Important factors considered include:* interview, level of applicant's interest. **Freshman Admission Requirements:** High school diploma is required and GED is accepted. **Freshman Admission Statistics:** 210 applied, 79% admitted, 94% enrolled. **Transfer Admission Requirements:** High school transcript, essay or personal statement, Lowest grade transferable C. **General Admission Information:** Application Fee $20. Nonfall registration accepted. Admission may be deferred for a maximum of 1 year. Credit offered for CEEB Advanced Placement tests.

COSTS AND FINANCIAL AID

Required Forms and Deadlines: FAFSA. **Types of Aid:** *Need-based scholarships/grants:* Federal Pell, SEOG, state scholarships/grants, private scholarships, the school's own gift aid. *Loans:* Subsidized Stafford, Unsubsidized Stafford, PLUS. *Student Employment:* Federal Work-Study Program available. Institutional employment available. Off-campus job opportunities are good. **Financial Aid Statistics:** 90% freshmen, 94% undergrads receive need-based scholarship or grant aid. 41% freshmen, 66% undergrads receive non-need-based scholarship or grant aid. 87% freshmen, 91% undergrads receive need-based self-help aid. 0% freshmen, 0% undergrads receive athletic scholarships. 81% undergrads borrow to pay for school. Average cumulative indebtedness $18,025. **Criteria for awarding institutional aid:** *Non-need-based:* academics, leadership.

HOFSTRA UNIVERSITY

Best 380

100 Hofstra University, Hempstead, NY 11549
Phone: 516-463-6700 · **Financial Aid Phone:** 516-463-8000
E-mail: admission@hofstra.edu · **CEEB Code:** 2295
Fax: 516-463-5100 · **Website:** http://www.hofstra.edu · **ACT Code:** 2760

This private school was founded in 1935. It has a 240-acre campus.

RATINGS

Admissions Selectivity Rating: 87   **Fire Safety Rating:** 97

STUDENTS AND FACULTY

Enrollment: 6,803. **Student Body:** 54% female, 46% male, 35% out-of-state, 4% international (51 countries represented). Asian 9%, African American 9%, Caucasian 56%, Hispanic 14%, Native American <1% **Retention and Graduation:** 80% freshmen return for sophomore year. 50% freshmen graduate within 4 years. 60% freshmen graduate within 6 years. 29% grads go on to further study within 1 year. 3% grads pursue arts and sciences degrees. 3% grads pursue law degrees. 3% grads pursue business degrees. 2% grads pursue medical degrees. **Faculty:** 498 full-time faculty, 93% hold PhDs, 44% are members of minority groups, 20% are women. 0% of classes are taught by teaching assistants.

ACADEMICS

Degrees: bachelor's, certificate, doctoral, master's, post-bachelor's certificate, post-master's certificate. **Classes:** Most classes have 10–19 students. Most lab/discussion sessions have 10–19 students. **Majors with Highest Enrollment:** Biology/Biological Sciences; Psychology; Accounting. **Special Study Options:** Accelerated program, cross-registration, distance learning, double major, dual enrollment, English as a Second Language (ESL), external degree program, honors program, independent study, internships, liberal arts/career combination, student-designed major, study abroad, teacher certification program. **Honors programs:** Hofstra University's Honors College (HUHC) is the leading edge of Hofstra University's pursuit of academic excellence. Serving the highly motivated, high achieving student, every aspect of its curriculum is designed to provide them with the resources they need to meet their academic objectives. Combining the support of a strong community with the freedom to pursue individual goals HUHC emphasizes student ownership and direction of their own education. At the same time, HUHC recognizes its responsibility to support students so that they can explore, reflect upon and achieve their educational objectives. HUHC is an intimate community of students, faculty and administrators committed to challenging and supporting one another in the pursuit of excellence at all levels. Its students are connected to every college, department, major and program on campus and engaged in every aspect of campus life. All entering HUHC students begin their Hofstra careers with Culture and Expression (C&E) a four-course, year-long sequence designed specifically for the honors college community. C&E is our primary tool for establishing a community among the students of each entering class. Together, they follow a common reading list, attend common lectures and take ownership of the materials via small group discussions with some of Hofstra's best faculty. C&E addresses life's biggest questions with rigor. Most importantly, it provides a broad foundation for a lifetime of learning in college and beyond. After the first year, Honors College students pursue honors work in those Hofstra courses that they find most exciting. Each semester HUHC offers an array of small, discussion based seminars, taught by professors from around the university, who are invited to offer their dream course. In addition, HUHC's Honors Option program allows students to enrich regular courses that align with their personal and intellectual passions. These honors experiences are all recognized on the transcript and count toward completion of an HUHC designation which is applied to both the student's transcript and diploma. Thus, HUHC students may choose from among any of Hofstra's more than 145 undergraduate majors and upon graduation receive a bachelor's degree with a special designation marking it as having been achieved with an extraordinary level of distinction. HUHC sponsors a rich array of cultural and social experiences, including trips to New York City to visit museums, Broadway shows, concerts, and major league sporting events. Given our location, HUHC faculty mentors regularly organize outdoor adventures, such as sea kayaking, hiking and visits to ocean beaches. A significant percentage of HUHC students participate in a variety of HUHC-based social service programs, including those focused on serving the homeless, promoting early literacy and working toward environmental responsibility. HUHC students can be found in leadership roles in virtually every club and activity on the Hofstra campus. They are student government leaders, newspaper editors, and champi-

ons of social and political causes. They are committed to the arts and to sports (including Division I) and can be found in just about every form of meaningful activity imaginable. They come from across the United States, and increasingly from abroad. Most of all, they are curious about one another and the wider world. Many HUHC students opt to live in honors housing, where they enjoy an even greater sense of community and an exceptional level of support from a professional staff and specially selected student leaders. HUHC graduates have won prestigious grants and fellowships such as the Fulbright, the National Science Fellowship, and the Jack Kent Cooke fellowship. They've also been admitted to the most prestigious graduate and professional schools. Hofstra University also recognizes high-achieving students in many other ways, including Dean's List, Provost's Scholars, Phi Beta Kappa, Phi Eta Sigma, Golden Key, and the chance to earn baccalaureate degrees with distinction and departmental honors. Combined degree programs: BA/JD, BBA/MS, BBA/MBA. **Disability Services:** Special programs offered to physically disabled students include note-taking services, reader services, tape recorders, tutors. **Career services:** Alumni network, alumni services, career/job search classes, career assessment, internships. Career services highlights include Comprehensive on-campus job fairs and recruiting program including internship opportunities for all majors with Fortune 500, media outlets, government, law, not-for-profit, and education, many of which lead to job opportunities for graduates.

FACILITIES

Housing: Coed dorms, special housing for disabled students, apartments for single students, Theme **Housing:** Living-Learning Center, Honors Housing, Quiet Floors, and Women's Floors. 100% of campus accessible to physically disabled. **Special Academic Facilities/Equipment:** New state-of-the-art medical school, financial trading room, multi-media converged news room, comprehensive media production facility including a 24 hour radio station, linux beowolf cluster, digital language lab, technology, science and engineering labs, a rooftop observatory, 6 theaters including a black box teaching theater, assessment centers for client observation and counseling, child care institute, cultural center, museum, arboretum, and bird sanctuary. **Computers:** 57% of classrooms, 100% of dorms, 100% of libraries, 100% of dining areas, 100% of student union, 60% of common outdoor areas have wireless network access. Students can register for classes online. Administrative functions (other than registration) can be performed online.

CAMPUS LIFE

Environment: City. **Activities:** Choral groups, concert band, dance, drama/theater, jazz band, literary magazine, music ensembles, musical theater, opera, pep band, radio station, student government, student newspaper, student-run film society, symphony orchestra, television station, yearbook, Campus Ministries, International Student Organization. 135 registered organizations, 32 honor societies, 9 religious organizations. 13 fraternities, 12 sororities. **Athletics (Intercollegiate):** *Men:* baseball, basketball, cross-country, golf, lacrosse, soccer, tennis, wrestling. *Women:* basketball, cross-country, field hockey, golf, lacrosse, soccer, softball, tennis, volleyball. **Environmental Initiatives:** New construction complies with LEED standards where feasible. The new School of Medicine Building has been committed to be LEED Silver Certified. In August 2011, Hofstra University installed a 9 KW solar array on the Living Green Learning Living Community residence house. The University is looking into expanding solar technology to more buildings on campus. Hofstra is offering a Bachelor of Arts, a Bachelor of Science and a minor in Sustainability Studies. A cornerstone of the curriculum is a strong applied focus such that students will be involved with sustainability projects on campus and in the surrounding area.

ADMISSIONS

Freshman Academic Profile: Average high school GPA 3.55. 28% in top 10% of high school class, 57% in top 25% of high school class, 86% in top 50% of high school class. SAT Math middle 50% range 530-620. SAT Critical Reading middle 50% range 520-610. ACT middle 50% range 23-28. Minimum internet-based TOEFL 80. Minimum paper TOEFL 550. **Basis for Candidate Selection:** *Very important factors considered include:* Class rank, application essay, academic GPA, recommendation(s), rigor of secondary school record, standardized test scores. *Important factors considered include:* character/personal qualities, extracurricular activities, interview, talent/ability. *Other factors considered include:* alumni/ae relation, geographical residence, level of applicant's interest, racial/ethnic status, volunteer work, work experience. **Freshman Admission Requirements:** High school diploma is required and GED is accepted. *Academic units required:* 4 English, 3 mathematics, 3 science, (1 science labs), 2 foreign language, 3 social studies. **Freshman Admission Statistics:** 26,388 applied, 62% admitted, 11% enrolled. **Transfer Admission Requirements:** college transcript(s), statement of good standing from prior institution(s). Lowest grade transferable C-. **General Admission Information:** Application Fee $70. Notification on a rolling basis, beginning on or about 2/1. Nonfall registration accepted. Admission may be deferred for a maximum of 1 year. Credit and/or placement offered for CEEB Advanced Placement tests.

COSTS AND FINANCIAL AID

Annual tuition $37,850. Room and board $13,510. Required fees $1,050. Average book expense $1,000. **Required Forms and Deadlines:** FAFSA, State aid form. **Notification of Awards:** Applicants will be notified of awards on a rolling basis beginning 3/1. **Types of Aid:** *Need-based scholarships/grants:* Federal Pell, SEOG, state scholarships/grants, private scholarships, the school's own gift aid, ACG & SMART. *Loans:* Subsidized Stafford, Unsubsidized Stafford, PLUS, Federal Perkins, college/university loans from institutional funds. *Student Employment:* Federal Work-Study Program available. Institutional employment available. Highest amount earned per year from on-campus jobs $22,795. Off-campus job opportunities are excellent. **Financial Aid Statistics:** 96% freshmen, 93% undergrads receive need-based scholarship or grant aid. 17% freshmen, 13% undergrads receive non-need-based scholarship or grant aid. 83% freshmen, 78% undergrads receive need-based self-help aid. 1% freshmen, 1% undergrads receive athletic scholarships. 97% freshmen, 91% undergrads receive any aid. 67% undergrads borrow to pay for school. **Criteria for awarding institutional aid:** *Non-need-based:* academics, alumni affiliation, art, athletics, leadership, music/drama, state/district residency.

See page 1066.

HOLLINS UNIVERSITY

PO Box 9707, Roanoke, VA 24020-1707
Phone: 540-362-6401 · **Financial Aid Phone:** 540-362-6332
E-mail: huadm@hollins.edu · **CEEB Code:** 5294
Fax: 540-362-6218 · **Website:** www.hollins.edu · **ACT Code:** 4360

This private school was founded in 1842. It has a 475-acre campus.

RATINGS

Admissions Selectivity Rating: 85   **Fire Safety Rating:** 77

STUDENTS AND FACULTY

Enrollment: 588. **Student Body:** 100% female, 0% male, 44% out-of-state, 6% international (17 countries represented). Asian 3%, African American 11%, Caucasian 71%, Hispanic 5%, Native American 1%
Retention and Graduation: 80% freshmen return for sophomore year. 60% freshmen graduate within 4 years. 24% grads go on to further study within 1 year. 16% grads pursue arts and sciences degrees. 1% grads pursue law degrees. 1% grads pursue business degrees. 3% grads pursue medical degrees. **Faculty:** 71 full-time faculty, 97% hold PhDs, 58% are members of minority groups, 15% are women. 1.4% of classes are taught by teaching assistants.

ACADEMICS

Degrees: bachelor's, master's, post-bachelor's certificate, post-master's certificate. **Classes:** Most classes have 10–19 students. Most lab/discussion sessions have 10–19 students. **Majors with Highest Enrollment:** English Language and Literature; Psychology; Business/Commerce. **Special Study Options:** Accelerated program, cross-registration, double major, dual enrollment, exchange student program (domestic), independent study, internships, student-designed major, study abroad, teacher certification program. **Honors programs:** A number of university departments offer honors programs. The specific nature of departmental honors varies from department to department. The programs, which are undertaken for at least the full senior year, may involve research, theses, oral or written examinations, seminars, reading programs, or any combination thereof. **Disability Services:** Special programs offered to physically disabled students include tape recorders. **Career services:** Alumni network, alumni services, career/job search classes, career assessment, internships, regional alumni.

FACILITIES

Housing: special housing for disabled students, women's dorms, apartments for single students, Wellness Housing, Theme Housing. 38% of campus accessible to physically disabled. **Special Academic Facilities/Equipment:** Athletic complex, a writing center, language labs, campus-wide computer network, scientific equipment and instrumentation, art museum, and a state-of-the-art library. **Computers:** 90% of classrooms, 100% of dorms, 100% of libraries, 100% of dining areas, 100% of student union, 100% of common outdoor areas have wireless network access. Students can register for classes online. Administrative functions (other than registration) can be performed online.

CAMPUS LIFE

Environment: City. **Activities:** Choral groups, dance, drama/theater, literary magazine, music ensembles, musical theater, student government, student newspaper, student-run film society, television station, yearbook, Campus Ministries, International Student Organization, Model UN. 28 registered organiza-

tions, 15 honor societies, 5 religious organizations. **Athletics (Intercollegiate):** *Women:* basketball, equestrian sports, golf, lacrosse, soccer, swimming, tennis. **On-Campus Highlights:** Front Quadrangle, Wetherill Visual Arts Center and Wilson Museum, Wyndham Robertson Library, Moody Center, Gymnasium, Northen Swim Cntrr, Taylee Fitness Cntr. **Environmental Initiatives:** Signing the President's Climate Agreement Completed a strategic plan (April 2009) with target of 3% annual reduction of green gasses for five years. Hollins University and Emory & Henry College have hired an energy manager for both institutions; a key component of a joint, three-year energy conservation project, supported by a grant from the Jesse Ball duPont Fund and intended to foster a culture of sustainability. The energy manager is conducting a comprehensive assessment of energy consumption on each campus; identifying strategies to further decrease energy use; developing and implementing energy policies for each institution; and enhancing educational activities to promote energy conservation by members of each campus community.

ADMISSIONS

Freshman Academic Profile: Average high school GPA 3.6. 15% in top 10% of high school class, 38% in top 25% of high school class, 30% in top 50% of high school class. 85% from public high schools. SAT Math middle 50% range 460-570. SAT Critical Reading middle 50% range 500-630. SAT Writing middle 50% range 490-590. ACT middle 50% range 20-27. Minimum internet-based TOEFL 80. Minimum paper TOEFL 550. **Basis for Candidate Selection:** *Very important factors considered include:* academic GPA, standardized test scores. *Important factors considered include:* application essay, recommendation(s), talent/ability. *Other factors considered include:* Class rank, rigor of secondary school record, alumni/ae relation, character/personal qualities, extracurricular activities, first generation, interview, level of applicant's interest, volunteer work, work experience. **Freshman Admission Requirements:** High school diploma is required and GED is accepted. *Academic units required:* 4 English, 3 mathematics, 3 science, 3 foreign language, 3 social studies. **Freshman Admission Statistics:** 1,782 applied, 57% admitted, 16% enrolled. **Transfer Admission Requirements:** High school transcript, college transcript(s), essay or personal statement, Minimum college GPA of 2.5 required. Lowest grade transferable C. **General Admission Information:** Application Fee $40. Early decision application deadline 12/1. Notification on a rolling basis, beginning on or about 12/15. Nonfall registration accepted. Admission may be deferred for a maximum of usually one year. Credit and/or placement offered for CEEB Advanced Placement tests.

COSTS AND FINANCIAL AID

Annual tuition $33,660. Room and board $11,940. Required fees $860. Average book expense $1,000. **Required Forms and Deadlines:** FAFSA, State aid form. **Notification of Awards:** Applicants will be notified of awards on a rolling basis beginning 3/1. **Types of Aid:** *Need-based scholarships/grants:* Federal Pell, SEOG, state scholarships/grants, private scholarships, the school's own gift aid. *Loans:* Direct Subsidized Stafford, Direct Unsubsidized Stafford, Direct PLUS, Federal Perkins, college/university loans from institutional funds, PLATO, CitiAssist, SallieMae, Nelnet, Campus Door. *Student Employment:* Federal Work-Study Program available. Institutional employment available. Highest amount earned per year from on-campus jobs $3,067. Off-campus job opportunities are good. **Financial Aid Statistics:** 100% freshmen, 100% undergrads receive need-based scholarship or grant aid. 100% freshmen, 100% undergrads receive non-need-based scholarship or grant aid. 78% freshmen, 82% undergrads receive need-based self-help aid. 0% freshmen, 0% undergrads receive athletic scholarships. 99% freshmen, 96% undergrads receive any aid. 77% undergrads borrow to pay for school. Average cumulative indebtedness $29,471. **Criteria for awarding institutional aid:** *Non-need-based:* academics, alumni affiliation, art, leadership, music/drama, state/district residency.

HOLY FAMILY UNIVERSITY

9801 Frankford Avenue, Philadephia, PA 19114-2009
Phone: 215-637-7700 · **Financial Aid Phone:** 267-341-3234
E-mail: admissions@holyfamily.edu gradstudy@holyfamily.edu · **CEEB Code:** 2297
Fax: 215-281-1022 · **Website:** www.holyfamily.edu · **ACT Code:** 3592

This private school, affiliated with the Roman Catholic Church, was founded in 1954. It has a 46-acre campus.

RATINGS

Admissions Selectivity Rating: 75   **Fire Safety Rating:** 86

STUDENTS AND FACULTY

Enrollment: 2,018. **Student Body:** 74% female, 26% male, 16% out-of-state, 0% international (12 countries represented). Asian 4%, African American 7%, Caucasian 56%, Hispanic 6%, Native American <1%

Retention and Graduation: 78% freshmen return for sophomore year. 39% freshmen graduate within 4 years. 24% grads go on to further study within 1 year. **Faculty:** 84 full-time faculty, 83% hold PhDs, 68% are members of minority groups, 14% are women. 0% of classes are taught by teaching assistants.

ACADEMICS

Degrees: associate, bachelor's, certificate, master's, post-bachelor's certificate. **Classes:** Most classes have 10–19 students. **Majors with Highest Enrollment:** Business Administration and Management; Psychology; Registered Nursing/Registered Nurse. **Special Study Options:** Accelerated program, cooperative education program, double major, dual enrollment, English as a Second Language (ESL), independent study, internships, study abroad, teacher certification program. **Disability Services:** Special programs offered to physically disabled students include note-taking services, reader services, tape recorders, tutors. **Career services:** alumni services, career/job search classes, career assessment, internships. Career services highlights include our Co-op Program. Refer to website for more details.

FACILITIES

Housing: Coed dorms. 100% of campus accessible to physically disabled. **Special Academic Facilities/Equipment:** On-campus nursery school, art gallery. **Computers:** 100% of classrooms, 100% of dorms, 100% of libraries, 100% of dining areas, 100% of student union, 100% of common outdoor areas have wireless network access. Students can register for classes online. Administrative functions (other than registration) can be performed online.

CAMPUS LIFE

Environment: Metropolis. **Activities:** Choral groups, drama/theater, literary magazine, radio station, student government, student newspaper, television station, yearbook, Campus Ministries, International Student Organization. 15 registered organizations, 14 honor societies, 1 religious organization. **Athletics (Intercollegiate):** *Men:* basketball, cross-country, golf, soccer, track/field (outdoor), track/field (indoor). *Women:* basketball, cross-country, lacrosse, soccer, softball, tennis, track/field (outdoor), track/field (indoor), volleyball. **On-Campus Highlights:** Campus Center, Education / Technology Center, Library, Student Residence Halls, Nurse Education Building.

ADMISSIONS

Freshman Academic Profile: Average high school GPA 3.12. 11% in top 10% of high school class, 35% in top 25% of high school class, 70% in top 50% of high school class. 60% from public high schools. SAT Math middle 50% range 430-520. SAT Critical Reading middle 50% range 420-510. SAT Writing middle 50% range 410-510. ACT middle 50% range 16-22. Minimum paper TOEFL 550. **Basis for Candidate Selection:** *Very important factors considered include:* Class rank, rigor of secondary school record, interview. *Important factors considered include:* academic GPA, standardized test scores, alumni/ae relation, character/personal qualities, level of applicant's interest. *Other factors considered include:* application essay, recommendation(s), extracurricular activities, talent/ability, volunteer work, work experience. **Freshman Admission Requirements:** High school diploma is required and GED is accepted. *Academic units required:* 4 English, 3 mathematics, 2 science, 2 history, 3 academic electives. **Freshman Admission Statistics:** 1,287 applied, 78% admitted, 29% enrolled. **Transfer Admission Requirements:** High school transcript, college transcript(s), essay or personal statement, statement of good standing from prior institution(s). Minimum college GPA of 2.5 required. Lowest grade transferable C. **General Admission Information:** Application Fee $25. Nonfall registration not accepted. Admission may be deferred for a maximum of 1 year. Neither credit nor placement offered for CEEB Advanced Placement tests.

COSTS AND FINANCIAL AID

Annual tuition $26,200. Room and board $12,930. Required fees $900. Average book expense $1,050. **Required Forms and Deadlines:** FAFSA. **Notification of Awards:** Applicants will be notified of awards on a rolling basis beginning 4/1. **Types of Aid:** *Need-based scholarships/grants:* Federal Pell, SEOG, state scholarships/grants, private scholarships, the school's own gift aid. *Loans:* Subsidized Stafford, Unsubsidized Stafford, PLUS, Federal Perkins, Federal Nursing, college/university loans from institutional funds. *Student Employment:* Federal Work-Study Program available. Off-campus job opportunities are excellent. **Financial Aid Statistics:** 99% freshmen, 97% undergrads receive need-based scholarship or grant aid. 92% freshmen, 85% undergrads receive non-need-based scholarship or grant aid. 85% freshmen, 83% undergrads receive need-based self-help aid. 12% freshmen, 9% undergrads receive athletic scholarships. 90% freshmen, 86% undergrads receive any aid. 85% undergrads borrow to pay for school. Average cumulative indebtedness $28,044. **Criteria for awarding institutional aid:** *Non-need-based:* academics, alumni affiliation, athletics.

HOLY NAMES UNIVERSITY

3500 Mountain Boulevard, Oakland, CA 94619-1699
Phone: 510-436-1351
E-mail: admissions@hnu.edu • **CEEB Code:** 4059
Fax: 510-436-1325 • **Website:** www.hnu.edu • **ACT Code:** 230

This private school, affiliated with the Roman Catholic Church, was founded in 1868. It has a 60-acre campus.

RATINGS

Admissions Selectivity Rating: 78   **Fire Safety Rating:** 63

STUDENTS AND FACULTY

Enrollment: 592. **Student Body:** 78% female, 22% male, 4% out-of-state, 3% international (25 countries represented). Asian 6%, African American 32%, Caucasian 28%, Hispanic 16%, Native American 1% **Retention and Graduation:** 62% freshmen return for sophomore year. 30% freshmen graduate within 4 years. 46% freshmen graduate within 6 years. **Faculty:** 31 full-time faculty, 90% hold PhDs, 68% are members of minority groups, 23% are women. 0% of classes are taught by teaching assistants.

ACADEMICS

Degrees: bachelor's, master's, post-bachelor's certificate. **Classes:** Most classes have 10–19 students. Most lab/discussion sessions have 10–19 students. **Majors with Highest Enrollment:** Psychology; Registered Nursing/Registered Nurse; Business/Commerce. **Special Study Options:** Accelerated program, cross-registration, distance learning, double major, English as a Second Language (ESL), exchange student program (domestic), independent study, internships, liberal arts/career combination, student-designed major, study abroad, teacher certification program, weekend college, academic remediating, independent study, learning disabled services, off campus study. Combined degree programs: BA/MA. **Disability Services:** Special programs offered to physically disabled students include note-taking services, tape recorders, tutors. **Career services:** Alumni network, alumni services, career/job search classes, career assessment, internships, regional alumni. Assistance is available for researching and obtaining positions in business, government, education and non-profits. All students are encouraged to enhance their professional development. They can earn a maximum of 6 units for internship credit.

FACILITIES

Housing: Coed dorms, Single sex floor and wings. 30% of campus accessible to physically disabled. **Special Academic Facilities/Equipment:** Valley Center for the Performing Arts and The J.D. Kennedy Arts Center Gallery.

CAMPUS LIFE

Environment: Metropolis. **Activities:** Choral groups, drama/theater, music ensembles, student government, symphony orchestra. 16 registered organizations, 11 honor society, 1 religious organization. **Athletics (Intercollegiate):** *Men:* basketball, cross-country, golf, soccer. *Women:* basketball, cross-country, soccer, volleyball. **On-Campus Highlights:** Green Banana Café, Gym, Soda Commons, Cafeteria, Valley Center for Performing Arts.

ADMISSIONS

Freshman Academic Profile: Average high school GPA 3.22. 12% in top 10% of high school class, 40% in top 25% of high school class, 79% in top 50% of high school class. 62% from public high schools. SAT Math middle 50% range 440-540. SAT Critical Reading middle 50% range 450-510. ACT middle 50% range 16-23. Minimum paper TOEFL 490. **Basis for Candidate Selection:** *Very important factors considered include:* rigor of secondary school record. *Important factors considered include:* application essay, recommendation(s), standardized test scores. *Other factors considered include:* Class rank, alumni/ae relation, character/personal qualities, extracurricular activities, interview, talent/ability, volunteer work, work experience. **Freshman Admission Requirements:** High school diploma is required and GED is accepted. *Academic units required:* 4 English, 3 mathematics, 1 science, (1 science labs), 2 foreign language, 1 history, 4 academic electives. **Freshman Admission Statistics:** 211 applied, 62% admitted, 44% enrolled. **Transfer Admission Requirements:** college transcript(s), essay or personal statement, statement of good standing from prior institution(s). Minimum college GPA of 2.2 required. Lowest grade transferable C-. **General Admission Information:** Application Fee $35. Regular application deadline 8/1. Notification on a rolling basis, beginning on or about 10/1. Nonfall registration accepted. Admission may be deferred for a maximum of 1 year. Credit offered for CEEB Advanced Placement tests.

COSTS AND FINANCIAL AID

Average book expense $946. **Required Forms and Deadlines:** FAFSA, Institution's own financial aid form, State aid form. **Notification of Awards:** Applicants will be notified of awards on a rolling basis beginning 4/1. **Types of Aid:** *Need-based scholarships/grants:* Federal Pell, SEOG, state scholarships/

grants, private scholarships, the school's own gift aid. *Loans:* Subsidized Stafford, Unsubsidized Stafford, PLUS, Federal Perkins, Alternative loans. *Student Employment:* Federal Work-Study Program available. Institutional employment available. Off-campus job opportunities are good. **Financial Aid Statistics:** 93% freshmen, 92% undergrads receive need-based scholarship or grant aid. 100% freshmen, 75% undergrads receive non-need-based scholarship or grant aid. 100% freshmen, 92% undergrads receive need-based self-help aid. 42% freshmen, 20% undergrads receive athletic scholarships. 79% freshmen, 57% undergrads receive any aid. 95% undergrads borrow to pay for school. **Criteria for awarding institutional aid:** *Non-need-based:* academics, alumni affiliation, athletics, leadership, music/drama, religious affiliation.

HOOD COLLEGE

401 Rosemont Avenue, Frederick, MD 21701
Phone: 301-696-3400 • **Financial Aid Phone:** 301-696-3411
E-mail: admission@hood.edu • **CEEB Code:** 5296
Fax: 301-696-3819 • **Website:** www.hood.edu • **ACT Code:** 1702

This private school, affiliated with the United Church of Christ Church, was founded in 1893. It has a 50-acre campus.

RATINGS

Admissions Selectivity Rating: 77   **Fire Safety Rating:** 93

STUDENTS AND FACULTY

Enrollment: 1,330. **Student Body:** 63% female, 37% male, 24% out-of-state, 2% international (36 countries represented). Asian 4%, African American 13%, Caucasian 65%, Hispanic 8%, Native American <1%
Retention and Graduation: 58% freshmen graduate within 4 years. 71% freshmen graduate within 6 years. 35% grads go on to further study within 1 year. 35% grads pursue arts and sciences degrees. 4% grads pursue law degrees. 15% grads pursue business degrees. **Faculty:** 97 full-time faculty, 95% hold PhDs, 59% are members of minority groups, 18% are women. 0% of classes are taught by teaching assistants.

ACADEMICS

Degrees: bachelor's, master's, post-bachelor's certificate. **Classes:** Most classes have 10–19 students. Most lab/discussion sessions have 10–19 students. **Majors with Highest Enrollment:** Business Administration and Management; Psychology; Biology/Biological Sciences. **Special Study Options:** double major, dual enrollment, honors program, independent study, internships, liberal arts/career combination, student-designed major, study abroad, teacher certification program. **Honors programs:** Our award-winning program offers exceptional undergraduate students four years of exciting coursework and co-curriuclar activities. Classes are small, discussion oriented, and enhanced by guest speakers and field trips. Interdisciplinary in approach, students are encouraged to engage in personal and intellectual development in the context of community memebership and service. Combined degree programs: BA Biology/MS Biomed Sci with Montgomery CC. **Disability Services:** Special programs offered to physically disabled students include note-taking services, reader services, tape recorders, tutors. **Career services:** Alumni network, alumni services, career assessment, internships, regional alumni. Career services highlights include a very active internship program. In 2008–09, more than 100 students completed internships at a variety of sites throughout the Baltimore/Washington/Frederick area.

FACILITIES

Housing: Coed dorms, women's dorms, Theme Housing. 30% of campus accessible to physically disabled. **Special Academic Facilities/Equipment:** Art gallery, child development lab, language lab, observatory, science labs. **Computers:** 100% of classrooms, 100% of dorms, 100% of libraries, 100% of dining areas, 100% of student union, 100% of common outdoor areas have wireless network access. Students can register for classes online. Administrative functions (other than registration) can be performed online.

CAMPUS LIFE

Environment: Town. **Activities:** Choral groups, dance, drama/theater, jazz band, literary magazine, music ensembles, musical theater, radio station, student government, student newspaper, student-run film society, Campus Ministries, International Student Organization, Model UN. 92 registered organizations, 14 honor societies, 6 religious organizations. **Athletics (Intercollegiate):** *Men:* basketball, cross-country, golf, lacrosse, soccer, swimming, tennis, track/field (outdoor). *Women:* basketball, cross-country, field hockey, golf, lacrosse, soccer, softball, swimming, tennis, track/field (outdoor), volleyball. **On-Campus Highlights:** Whitaker Campus Center, Hodson Science and Technology Building, Coblentz Dining Hall, Beneficial-Hodson Library, The Residence Halls.

Environmental Initiatives: Reduction of natural gas consumption through the use of new decentralized building heating boilers and software controls programming. Reduction of solid waste steam through campus recycling efforts for single stream recycling for applicable recyclables. Reduction in electric energy usage through lighting technologies of CFL's and LED lighting replacements.

ADMISSIONS

Freshman Academic Profile: Average high school GPA 3.44. 14% in top 10% of high school class, 32% in top 25% of high school class, 70% in top 50% of high school class. 82% from public high schools. SAT Math middle 50% range 460-570. SAT Critical Reading middle 50% range 460-570. SAT Writing middle 50% range 450-560. ACT middle 50% range 19-25. Minimum internet-based TOEFL 79. Minimum paper TOEFL 550. **Basis for Candidate Selection:** *Very important factors considered include:* academic GPA, rigor of secondary school record. *Important factors considered include:* standardized test scores. *Other factors considered include:* Class rank, application essay, recommendation(s), alumni/ae relation, extracurricular activities, first generation, interview, level of applicant's interest. **Freshman Admission Requirements:** High school diploma is required and GED is accepted. *Academic units required:* 4 English, 3 mathematics, 3 science, (2 science labs), 2 foreign language, 2 social studies, 1 history, 0 visual/performing arts, 0 computer science, 1 academic electives. **Freshman Admission Statistics:** 1,590 applied, 81% admitted, 23% enrolled. **Transfer Admission Requirements:** college transcript(s), Minimum college GPA of 2.5 required. Lowest grade transferable C-. **General Admission Information:** Application Fee $35. Notification on a rolling basis, beginning on or about 12/1. Nonfall registration accepted. Admission may be deferred for a maximum of 1 yr. Credit and/or placement offered for CEEB Advanced Placement tests.

COSTS AND FINANCIAL AID

Required Forms and Deadlines: FAFSA. **Notification of Awards:** Applicants will be notified of awards on a rolling basis beginning 2/15. **Types of Aid:** *Need-based scholarships/grants:* Federal Pell, SEOG, state scholarships/grants, private scholarships, the school's own gift aid. *Loans:* Direct Subsidized Stafford, Direct Unsubsidized Stafford, Direct PLUS, Subsidized Stafford, Unsubsidized Stafford, PLUS, Federal Perkins. *Student Employment:* Federal Work-Study Program available. Institutional employment available. Highest amount earned per year from on-campus jobs $1,800. Off-campus job opportunities are good. **Financial Aid Statistics:** 100% freshmen, 100% undergrads receive need-based scholarship or grant aid. 11% freshmen, 12% undergrads receive non-need-based scholarship or grant aid. 82% freshmen, 82% undergrads receive need-based self-help aid. 0% freshmen, 0% undergrads receive athletic scholarships. 99% freshmen, 98% undergrads receive any aid. 66% undergrads borrow to pay for school. Average cumulative indebtedness $28,190. **Criteria for awarding institutional aid:** *Non-need-based:* academics, alumni affiliation, music/drama.

HOPE COLLEGE

69 East 10th, Holland, MI 49422-9000
Phone: 616-395-7850 • **Financial Aid Phone:** 616-395-7765
E-mail: admissions@hope.edu • **CEEB Code:** 1301
Fax: 616-395-7130 • **Website:** www.hope.edu • **ACT Code:** 2012

This private school, affiliated with the Reformed Church Church, was founded in 1862. It has a 120-acre campus.

RATINGS

Admissions Selectivity Rating: 86   **Fire Safety Rating:** 82

STUDENTS AND FACULTY

Enrollment: 3,251. **Student Body:** 60% female, 40% male, 32% out-of-state, 2% international (35 countries represented). Asian 2%, African American 2%, Caucasian 85%, Hispanic 6%, Native American <1%
Retention and Graduation: 90% freshmen return for sophomore year. 67% freshmen graduate within 4 years. 77% freshmen graduate within 6 years. 25% grads go on to further study within 1 year. 8% grads pursue arts and sciences degrees. 1% grads pursue law degrees. 1% grads pursue business degrees. 10% grads pursue medical degrees. **Faculty:** 226 full-time faculty, 78% hold PhDs, 47% are members of minority groups, 13% are women. 0% of classes are taught by teaching assistants.

ACADEMICS

Degrees: bachelor's. **Classes:** Most classes have 10–19 students. Most lab/discussion sessions have 20–29 students. **Majors with Highest Enrollment:** Business/Commerce; Speech Communication and Rhetoric; Psychology. **Special Study Options:** distance learning, double major, English as a Second

Language (ESL), independent study, internships, student-designed major, study abroad, teacher certification program. **Disability Services:** Special programs offered to physically disabled students include note-taking services, reader services, tape recorders, tutors. **Career services:** Alumni network, alumni services, career/job search classes, career assessment, internships, regional alumni. Career services highlights include an extensive undergraduate research program engaging more than 200 students each summer.

FACILITIES

Housing: Coed dorms, special housing for disabled students, men's dorms, special housing for international students, women's dorms, fraternity/sorority housing, apartments for single students, Wellness Housing, Theme Housing. 95% of campus accessible to physically disabled. **Special Academic Facilities/Equipment:** Art gallery, particle accelerator, computational chemistry lab, electron microscopes, spectrometers, ultracentrifuge, observatory, new $38M science building. **Computers:** 70% of classrooms, 100% of libraries, 34% of dining areas, 100% of student union, 40% of common outdoor areas have wireless network access. Students can register for classes online. Administrative functions (other than registration) can be performed online.

CAMPUS LIFE

Environment: Town. **Activities:** Choral groups, concert band, dance, drama/theater, jazz band, literary magazine, music ensembles, radio station, student government, student newspaper, symphony orchestra, television station, yearbook, Campus Ministries, International Student Organization, Model UN. 67 registered organizations, 22 honor societies, 6 religious organizations. 6 fraternities, 7 sororities. **Athletics (Intercollegiate):** *Men:* baseball, basketball, cheerleading, cross-country, diving, football, golf, soccer, swimming, tennis, track/field (outdoor), track/field (indoor). *Women:* basketball, cheerleading, cross-country, diving, golf, soccer, softball, swimming, tennis, track/field (outdoor), track/field (indoor), volleyball. **On-Campus Highlights:** DeWitt Student Center, Martha Miller Center for Global Communic, Library, Paul A Schaap Science Center, DeVos Fieldhouse, Kletz—student grill. **Environmental Initiatives:** electrical use reduction; water use reduction; expanded recycling.

ADMISSIONS

Freshman Academic Profile: Average high school GPA 3.77. 37% in top 10% of high school class, 64% in top 25% of high school class, 92% in top 50% of high school class. 88% from public high schools. SAT Math middle 50% range 520-670. SAT Critical Reading middle 50% range 510-660. ACT middle 50% range 23-29. Minimum internet-based TOEFL 80. **Basis for Candidate Selection:** *Very important factors considered include:* academic GPA, rigor of secondary school record, standardized test scores. *Important factors considered include:* Class rank, application essay. *Other factors considered include:* recommendation(s), alumni/ae relation, character/personal qualities, extracurricular activities, first generation, geographical residence, interview, racial/ethnic status, religious affiliation/commitment, state residency, talent/ability, volunteer work, work experience. **Freshman Admission Requirements:** High school diploma is required and GED is accepted. **Freshman Admission Statistics:** 3,491 applied, 85% admitted, 30% enrolled. **Transfer Admission Requirements:** High school transcript, college transcript(s), essay or personal statement, standardized test scores, statement of good standing from prior institution(s). Minimum college GPA of 2.5 required. Lowest grade transferable C. **General Admission Information:** Application Fee $35. Notification on a rolling basis, beginning on or about 12/15. Nonfall registration accepted. Admission may be deferred for a maximum of 1 year. Credit offered for CEEB Advanced Placement tests.

COSTS AND FINANCIAL AID

Annual tuition $28,550. Room and board $8,810. Required fees $170. Average book expense $820. **Required Forms and Deadlines:** FAFSA, Institution's own financial aid form. **Notification of Awards:** Applicants will be notified of awards on a rolling basis beginning 3/15. **Types of Aid:** *Need-based scholarships/grants:* Federal Pell, SEOG, state scholarships/grants, private scholarships, the school's own gift aid. *Loans:* Direct Subsidized Stafford, Direct Unsubsidized Stafford, Direct PLUS, Federal Perkins, college/university loans from institutional funds. *Student Employment:* Federal Work-Study Program available. Institutional employment available. Highest amount earned per year from on-campus jobs $7,455. Off-campus job opportunities are good. **Financial Aid Statistics:** 86% freshmen, 84% undergrads receive need-based scholarship or grant aid. 74% freshmen, 68% undergrads receive non-need-based scholarship or grant aid. 83% freshmen, 82% undergrads receive need-based self-help aid. 0% freshmen, 0% undergrads receive athletic scholarships. 96% freshmen, 92% undergrads receive any aid. 65% undergrads borrow to pay for school. Average cumulative indebtedness $23,717. **Criteria for awarding institutional aid:** *Non-need-based:* academics, art, minority status, music/drama, religious affiliation.

HOPE INTERNATIONAL UNIVERSITY

Undergraduate Admissions, Fullerton, CA 92831
Phone: 866-722-4673 • **Financial Aid Phone:** 714-879-3901
E-mail: pccadmissions@hiu.edu • **CEEB Code:**
Fax: 714-681-7423 • **Website:** www.hiu.edu • **ACT Code:** 356

This private school, affiliated with the Church of Christ Church, was founded in 1928. It has a 18-acre campus.

RATINGS

Admissions Selectivity Rating: 80   **Fire Safety Rating:** 65

STUDENTS AND FACULTY

Enrollment: 521. **Student Body:** 60% female, 40% male, 24% out-of-state, 2% international. Asian 5%, African American 5%, Caucasian 61%, Hispanic 16%, Native American 1%
Retention and Graduation: 71% freshmen return for sophomore year. 1% freshmen graduate within 4 years. 50% freshmen graduate within 6 years. **Faculty:** 32 full-time faculty, 59% hold PhDs, 25% are members of minority groups, 6% are women. 0% of classes are taught by teaching assistants.

ACADEMICS

Degrees: associate, bachelor's, certificate, master's, post-bachelor's certificate. **Classes:** Most classes have fewer than 10 students. Most lab/discussion sessions have fewer than 10 students. **Majors with Highest Enrollment:** Teacher Education, Multiple Levels; Youth Ministry; Psychology. **Special Study Options:** Accelerated program, cross-registration, distance learning, double major, dual enrollment, English as a Second Language (ESL), independent study, internships, liberal arts/career combination, student-designed major, study abroad, teacher certification program. **Disability Services:** Special programs offered to physically disabled students include note-taking services, tape recorders, tutors.

FACILITIES

Housing: men's dorms, women's dorms. 95% of campus accessible to physically disabled.

CAMPUS LIFE

Environment: City. **Activities:** Choral groups, drama/theater, jazz band, music ensembles, musical theater, student government, student newspaper, yearbook. **Athletics (Intercollegiate):** *Men:* basketball, soccer, tennis, volleyball. *Women:* basketball, soccer, softball, tennis, volleyball. **On-Campus Highlights:** Lawson-Fulton Student Center, Darling Library, Lambda Lounge, Auditorium, The Commons.

ADMISSIONS

Freshman Academic Profile: Average high school GPA 3.3. 20% in top 10% of high school class, 37% in top 25% of high school class, 77% in top 50% of high school class. 95% from public high schools. SAT Math middle 50% range 420-530. SAT Critical Reading middle 50% range 440-540. SAT Writing middle 50% range 420-520. ACT middle 50% range 18-21. Minimum paper TOEFL 500. **Basis for Candidate Selection:** *Very important factors considered include:* Class rank, application essay, academic GPA, recommendation(s), rigor of secondary school record, standardized test scores. *Important factors considered include:* level of applicant's interest. *Other factors considered include:* character/personal qualities, extracurricular activities, interview, religious affiliation/commitment, talent/ability, volunteer work. **Freshman Admission Requirements:** High school diploma is required and GED is accepted. **Freshman Admission Statistics:** 413 applied, 71% admitted, 59% enrolled. **Transfer Admission Requirements:** college transcript(s), essay or personal statement, statement of good standing from prior institution(s). Minimum college GPA of 2.5 required. Lowest grade transferable C. **General Admission Information:** Application Fee $40. Notification on a rolling basis, beginning on or about 8/1. Nonfall registration accepted. Credit and/or placement offered for CEEB Advanced Placement tests.

COSTS AND FINANCIAL AID

Annual tuition $21,560. Average book expense $1,386. **Required Forms and Deadlines:** FAFSA, Institution's own financial aid form. **Notification of Awards:** Applicants will be notified of awards on a rolling basis beginning 3/15. **Types of Aid:** *Need-based scholarships/grants:* Federal Pell, SEOG, state scholarships/grants, private scholarships, the school's own gift aid. *Loans:* Direct Subsidized Stafford, Direct Unsubsidized Stafford, Direct PLUS, Subsidized Stafford, Unsubsidized Stafford, PLUS, Federal Perkins, state loans, college/university loans from institutional funds. *Student Employment:* Federal Work-Study Program available. Institutional employment available. Off-campus job opportunities are good. **Financial Aid Statistics:** 98% freshmen, 96% undergrads receive need-based scholarship or grant aid. 19% freshmen, 14% undergrads receive non-need-based scholarship or grant aid. 74% freshmen, 77% undergrads receive need-based self-help aid. 0% freshmen, 0% undergrads receive athletic scholarships. 67% freshmen, 73% undergrads receive any aid. 92% undergrads borrow to pay for school. **Criteria for awarding institutional aid:** *Non-need-based:* academics, alumni affiliation, athletics, leadership, music/drama, religious affiliation.

HOUGHTON COLLEGE

PO Box 128, Houghton, NY 14744
Phone: 585-567-9353 • **Financial Aid Phone:** 585-567-9328
E-mail: admission@houghton.edu • **CEEB Code:** 2299
Fax: 716-567-9522 • **Website:** www.houghton.edu • **ACT Code:** 2766

This private school, affiliated with the Wesleyan Church, was founded in 1883. It has a 1300-acre campus.

RATINGS

Admissions Selectivity Rating: 83   **Fire Safety Rating:** 74

STUDENTS AND FACULTY

Enrollment: 1,047. **Student Body:** 65% female, 35% male, 38% out-of-state, 6% international (31 countries represented). Asian 1%, African American 3%, Caucasian 85%, Hispanic 2%, Native American <1%.
Retention and Graduation: 65% freshmen graduate within 4 years. 73% freshmen graduate within 6 years. 18% grads go on to further study within 1 year. 11% grads pursue arts and sciences degrees. 1% grads pursue business degrees. 1% grads pursue medical degrees. **Faculty:** 73 full-time faculty, 88% hold PhDs, 36% are members of minority groups, 4% are women. 0% of classes are taught by teaching assistants.

ACADEMICS

Degrees: associate, bachelor's, master's. **Classes:** Most classes have 10–19 students. Most lab/discussion sessions have 10–19 students. **Majors with Highest Enrollment:** Business Administration and Management; Biology/Biological Sciences; Digital Communication and Media/Multimedia. **Special Study Options:** cross-registration, double major, exchange student program (domestic), honors program, independent study, internships, liberal arts/career combination, study abroad, teacher certification program. **Honors programs:** First-year honors program in London, England; first-year honors program in Eastern Europe; first-year honors program in math and science. **Disability Services:** Special programs offered to physically disabled students include note-taking services, tape recorders, tutors. **Career services:** Alumni network, alumni services, career/job search classes, career assessment, internships.

FACILITIES

Housing: men's dorms, special housing for international students, women's dorms, apartments for married students, apartments for single students. 80% of campus accessible to physically disabled. **Special Academic Facilities/Equipment:** Electron microscope, Art Gallery, Greenhouse. **Computers:** 100% of classrooms, 100% of dorms, 100% of libraries, 100% of dining areas, 100% of student union, 50% of common outdoor areas have wireless network access. Students can register for classes online. Administrative functions (other than registration) can be performed online.

CAMPUS LIFE

Environment: Rural. **Activities:** Choral groups, concert band, dance, drama/theater, jazz band, literary magazine, music ensembles, musical theater, opera, student government, student newspaper, symphony orchestra, yearbook, Campus Ministries, International Student Organization. 34 registered organizations, 2 honor societies, 9 religious organizations. **Athletics (Intercollegiate):** *Men:* basketball, cross-country, soccer, track/field (outdoor), track/field (indoor). *Women:* basketball, cross-country, field hockey, soccer, track/field (outdoor), track/field (indoor), volleyball. **On-Campus Highlights:** Center for the Arts, Nielsen Physical Education Center, Wesley Chapel, Campus Center, Library. **Environmental Initiatives:** Achieving carbon neutrality by 2050. We are in process of constructing a LEED silver specification (not certified) field house this spring. Educating students about sustainability.

ADMISSIONS

Freshman Academic Profile: Average high school GPA 3.53. 35.2% in top 10% of high school class, 61.4% in top 25% of high school class, 87.6% in top 50% of high school class. 66% from public high schools. SAT Math middle 50% range 490-605. SAT Critical Reading middle 50% range 490-630. SAT Writing middle 50% range 470-600. ACT middle 50% range 21-28. Minimum internet-based TOEFL 80. Minimum paper TOEFL 550. **Basis for Candidate Selection:** *Very important factors considered include:* academic GPA, religious affiliation/commitment. *Important factors considered include:* Class rank, application essay, recommendation(s), rigor of secondary school record, standardized test scores, character/personal qualities. *Other factors considered include:* alumni/

ae relation, extracurricular activities, interview, level of applicant's interest, racial/ethnic status, talent/ability, volunteer work, work experience. **Freshman Admission Requirements:** High school diploma is required and GED is accepted. **Freshman Admission Statistics:** 807 applied, 91% admitted, 30% enrolled. **Transfer Admission Requirements:** college transcript(s), essay or personal statement, Lowest grade transferable C-. **General Admission Information:** Application Fee $40. Notification on a rolling basis, beginning on or about 1/1. Nonfall registration accepted. Admission may be deferred for a maximum of 2 years. Credit and/or placement offered for CEEB Advanced Placement tests.

COSTS AND FINANCIAL AID

Annual tuition $27,578. Room and board $8,012. Required fees $150. Average book expense $1,000. **Required Forms and Deadlines:** FAFSA, State aid form. **Notification of Awards:** Applicants will be notified of awards on a rolling basis beginning 3/15. **Types of Aid:** *Need-based scholarships/grants:* Federal Pell, SEOG, state scholarships/grants, private scholarships, the school's own gift aid. *Loans:* Subsidized Stafford, Unsubsidized Stafford, PLUS, Federal Perkins. *Student Employment:* Federal Work-Study Program available. Institutional employment available. Highest amount earned per year from on-campus jobs $4,283. Off-campus job opportunities are poor. **Financial Aid Statistics:** 90% freshmen, 88% undergrads receive need-based scholarship or grant aid. 76% freshmen, 76% undergrads receive non-need-based scholarship or grant aid. 90% freshmen, 89% undergrads receive need-based self-help aid. 0% freshmen, 5% undergrads receive athletic scholarships. 100% freshmen, 98% undergrads receive any aid. 72% undergrads borrow to pay for school. Average cumulative indebtedness $22,081. **Criteria for awarding institutional aid:** *Non-need-based:* academics, alumni affiliation, art, athletics, music/drama, religious affiliation.

HOUSTON BAPTIST UNIVERSITY

7502 Fondren Road, Houston, TX 77074
Phone: 281-649-3211 • **Financial Aid Phone:** 281-649-3471
E-mail: unadm@hbu.edu • **CEEB Code:** 6282
Fax: 281-649-3217 • **Website:** www.hbu.edu • **ACT Code:** 4101

This private school, affiliated with the Southern Baptist Church, was founded in 1960. It has a 100-acre campus.

RATINGS

Admissions Selectivity Rating: 83   **Fire Safety Rating:** 78

STUDENTS AND FACULTY

Enrollment: 1,916. **Student Body:** 67% female, 33% male, 3% out-of-state, 6% international (36 countries represented). Asian 13%, African American 20%, Caucasian 46%, Hispanic 14%, Native American <1%.
Retention and Graduation: 74% freshmen return for sophomore year. 32% freshmen graduate within 4 years. 59% freshmen graduate within 6 years. **Faculty:** 103 full-time faculty, 81% hold PhDs, 48% are members of minority groups, 10% are women. 0% of classes are taught by teaching assistants.

ACADEMICS

Degrees: associate, bachelor's, master's. **Classes:** Most classes have 10–19 students. Most lab/discussion sessions have fewer than 10 students. **Majors with Highest Enrollment:** Biology/Biological Sciences; Psychology; Business/Commerce. **Special Study Options:** Accelerated program, double major, dual enrollment, English as a Second Language (ESL), independent study, internships, liberal arts/career combination, teacher certification program. Combined degree programs: Accelerated MATS degree Program (with BA or BS). **Career services:** Alumni network, alumni services, career/job search classes, career assessment, internships, regional alumni. Career services highlights include our internship program , which provides opportunities for student to work with early stage companies at the BU incubators, as well as in the community. One particularly unusual aspect of the program is that we provide opportunities for non-business students to "intern" with startups our business students are creating. One such program this year had Graphic Design students working with MBA student entrepreneurs to develop corporate identity programs for them.

FACILITIES

Housing: men's dorms, women's dorms, apartments for single students. 90% of campus accessible to physically disabled. **Special Academic Facilities/Equipment:** Museum of architecture/decorative arts, language lab, research center. **Computers:** Students can register for classes online.

CAMPUS LIFE

Environment: Metropolis. **Activities:** Choral groups, concert band, drama/theater, music ensembles, pep band, student government, student newspaper, yearbook. 36 registered organizations, 9 honor societies, 3 religious organizations. 2 fraternities, 2 sororities. **Athletics (Intercollegiate):** *Men:* baseball, basketball, cheerleading. *Women:* basketball, cheerleading, softball, volleyball. **On-Campus Highlights:** Hinton Center, Baugh Center and the Bone Appetit Café, Bible Museum, Wellness Center, Admissions Office.

ADMISSIONS

Freshman Academic Profile: 24% in top 10% of high school class, 44% in top 25% of high school class, 79% in top 50% of high school class. 79% from public high schools. SAT Math middle 50% range 500-620. SAT Critical Reading middle 50% range 500-610. ACT middle 50% range 19-25. Minimum paper TOEFL 550. **Basis for Candidate Selection:** *Very important factors considered include:* application essay, recommendation(s), rigor of secondary school record, standardized test scores. *Important factors considered include:* Class rank, extracurricular activities, geographical residence, religious affiliation/commitment, talent/ability, volunteer work. *Other factors considered include:* alumni/ae relation, character/personal qualities, interview. **Freshman Admission Requirements:** High school diploma is required and GED is accepted. **Freshman Admission Statistics:** 867 applied, 65% admitted, 55% enrolled. **Transfer Admission Requirements:** college transcript(s), essay or personal statement, statement of good standing from prior institution(s). Minimum college GPA of 2.0 required. Lowest grade transferable C. **General Admission Information:** Application Fee $25. Nonfall registration accepted. Admission may be deferred for a maximum of None. Credit offered for CEEB Advanced Placement tests.

COSTS AND FINANCIAL AID

Required Forms and Deadlines: FAFSA. **Notification of Awards:** Applicants will be notified of awards on a rolling basis beginning 3/10. **Types of Aid:** *Need-based scholarships/grants:* Federal Pell, SEOG, state scholarships/grants, private scholarships, the school's own gift aid. *Loans:* Subsidized Stafford, Unsubsidized Stafford, PLUS, state loans, Private, non federal. *Student Employment:* Federal Work-Study Program available. Highest amount earned per year from on-campus jobs $1,800. **Financial Aid Statistics:** 99% freshmen, 97% undergrads receive need-based scholarship or grant aid. 14% freshmen, 7% undergrads receive non-need-based scholarship or grant aid. 73% freshmen, 82% undergrads receive need-based self-help aid. 3% freshmen, 1% undergrads receive athletic scholarships. 64% freshmen, 85% undergrads receive any aid. **Criteria for awarding institutional aid:** *Non-need-based:* academics, alumni affiliation, art, athletics, leadership, music/drama, religious affiliation.

HOWARD PAYNE UNIVERSITY

Howard Payne Station, Brownwood, TX 76801
Phone: 325-649-8027 · **Financial Aid Phone:** 325-649-8015
E-mail: enroll@hputx.edu
Fax: 325-649-8901 · **Website:** www.hputx.edu · **ACT Code:** 4102

This private school, affiliated with the Baptist Church, was founded in 1889. It has a 30-acre campus.

RATINGS

Admissions Selectivity Rating: 75 · **Fire Safety Rating:** 72

STUDENTS AND FACULTY

Enrollment: 1,303. **Student Body:** 50% female, 50% male, 3% out-of-state, 1% international (6 countries represented). Asian 1%, African American 8%, Caucasian 75%, Hispanic 12%, Native American 1%
Retention and Graduation: 61% freshmen return for sophomore year. 21% freshmen graduate within 4 years. 35% freshmen graduate within 6 years. 15% grads go on to further study within 1 year. 2% grads pursue law degrees. 2% grads pursue business degrees. 2% grads pursue medical degrees. **Faculty:** 75 full-time faculty, 59% hold PhDs, 36% are members of minority groups, 5% are women. 0% of classes are taught by teaching assistants.

ACADEMICS

Degrees: associate, bachelor's, certificate. **Classes:** Most classes have fewer than 10 students. **Majors with Highest Enrollment:** Education; Bible/Biblical Studies; Business/Commerce. **Special Study Options:** Accelerated program, cooperative education program, distance learning, double major, dual enrollment, English as a Second Language (ESL), honors program, independent study, internships, liberal arts/career combination, study abroad, teacher certification program, Extension campuses are located in El Paso, Corpus Christi, Weatherford,and Harlingen,Texas. **Honors programs:** The Douglas MacArthur Academy of Freedom is designed for academically gifted students who aspire to leadership roles in a variety of careers. The Academy program prepares students to read critically, think analytically, and communicate ideas

effectively. Through a broad-based liberal arts education that emphasizes Judeo-Christian values, western civilization, free enterprise principles, and political awareness, the Academy explores the meaning and significance of traditional American values and seeks to understand the problems of contemporary society. Students develop critical thinking skills by analyzing current issues through the multidisciplinary Academy major, which includes courses from the School of Humanities, the School of Christian Studies, and the School of Business. **Disability Services:** Special programs offered to physically disabled students include tutors. **Career services:** Alumni network, career assessment.

FACILITIES

Housing: men's dorms, women's dorms, apartments for single students. 95% of campus accessible to physically disabled. **Special Academic Facilities/Equipment:** Douglas MacArthur Academy of Freedom and Museum. **Computers:** Administrative functions (other than registration) can be performed online.

CAMPUS LIFE

Environment: Rural. **Activities:** Choral groups, concert band, drama/theater, jazz band, literary magazine, marching band, music ensembles, musical theater, opera, radio station, student government, student newspaper, yearbook. 32 registered organizations, 3 honor societies, 4 religious organizations. 5 fraternities, 5 sororities. **Athletics (Intercollegiate):** *Men:* baseball, basketball, cheerleading, cross-country, football, tennis, track/field (outdoor). *Women:* basketball, cheerleading, cross-country, softball, tennis, track/field (outdoor), volleyball. **On-Campus Highlights:** Elliston-Castle Wellness Center, Mabee University Center, Douglas macArthur Academy of Freedom, Muse Mall and Plaza, Old Main Park.

ADMISSIONS

Freshman Academic Profile: Average high school GPA 3.3. 15% in top 10% of high school class, 39% in top 25% of high school class, 71% in top 50% of high school class. 94% from public high schools. SAT Math middle 50% range 440-550. SAT Critical Reading middle 50% range 440-570. ACT middle 50% range 17-23. Minimum paper TOEFL 550. **Basis for Candidate Selection:** *Very important factors considered include:* rigor of secondary school record, standardized test scores. *Important factors considered include:* recommendation(s), interview. *Other factors considered include:* Class rank, character/personal qualities, work experience. **Freshman Admission Requirements:** High school diploma is required and GED is accepted. **Freshman Admission Statistics:** 640 applied, 78% admitted, 62% enrolled. **Transfer Admission Requirements:** college transcript(s), Minimum college GPA of 2.0 required. Lowest grade transferable D. **General Admission Information:** Application Fee $25. Regular application deadline 8/31. Nonfall registration accepted. Admission may be deferred for a maximum of 1 year. Credit and/or placement offered for CEEB Advanced Placement tests.

COSTS AND FINANCIAL AID

Annual tuition $12,000. Room and board $4,615. Required fees $1,000. Average book expense $1,000. **Required Forms and Deadlines:** FAFSA, Institution's own financial aid form. **Notification of Awards:** Applicants will be notified of awards on a rolling basis beginning 3/1. **Types of Aid:** *Need-based scholarships/grants:* Federal Pell, SEOG, state scholarships/grants, private scholarships, the school's own gift aid. *Loans:* Subsidized Stafford, Unsubsidized Stafford, PLUS, Federal Perkins, state loans. *Student Employment:* Federal Work-Study Program available. Institutional employment available. Off-campus job opportunities are good. **Financial Aid Statistics:** 98% freshmen, 98% undergrads receive need-based scholarship or grant aid. 10% freshmen, 10% undergrads receive non-need-based scholarship or grant aid. 72% freshmen, 76% undergrads receive need-based self-help aid. 0% freshmen, 0% undergrads receive athletic scholarships. 69% undergrads borrow to pay for school. **Criteria for awarding institutional aid:** *Non-need-based:* academics, alumni affiliation, art, leadership, music/drama, religious affiliation.

HOWARD UNIVERSITY

Best 380

2400 Sixth Street, NW, Suite 111, Washington, DC 20059
Phone: 202-806-2755 · **Financial Aid Phone:** 202-806-2840
E-mail: admission@howard.edu · **CEEB Code:** 5297
Fax: 202-806-4465 · **Website:** www.howard.edu · **ACT Code:** 674

This private school was founded in 1867. It has a 258-acre campus.

RATINGS

Admissions Selectivity Rating: 88 · **Fire Safety Rating:** 97

STUDENTS AND FACULTY

Enrollment: 6,921. **Student Body:** 67% female, 33% male, 95% out-of-state, 3% international (86 countries represented). Asian 1%, African American 91%, Caucasian 1%, Hispanic 0%, Native American 2%

Retention and Graduation: 83% freshmen return for sophomore year. 40% freshmen graduate within 4 years. 60% grads go on to further study within 1 year. 42% grads pursue arts and sciences degrees. 12% grads pursue law degrees. 15% grads pursue business degrees. 11% grads pursue medical degrees. **Faculty:** 1,149 full-time faculty, 81% hold PhDs, 45% are members of minority groups, 78% are women.

ACADEMICS

Degrees: bachelor's, certificate, first professional, first professional certificate, master's, post-master's certificate. **Classes:** Most classes have fewer than 10 students. Most lab/discussion sessions have 10–19 students. **Majors with Highest Enrollment:** Journalism; Radio and Television; Biology/Biological Sciences. **Special Study Options:** Accelerated program, cooperative education program, distance learning, double major, English as a Second Language (ESL), exchange student program (domestic), honors program, independent study, internships, study abroad, teacher certification program, Tutorial program, advanced placement, continuing education. Combined degree programs: BA/MD, BA/DDS, MBA / JD, MD / PHD. **Disability Services:** Special programs offered to physically disabled students include note-taking services, reader services. **Career services:** career/job search classes, career assessment, internships. Career services highlights include Rangel Scholars Program Internships, which offer exposure to Capital Hii and countries abroad. Students get personal experiences regarding the working of our political system and those of other countries from experienced state department professionals and elected government officials.

FACILITIES

Housing: Coed dorms, men's dorms, women's dorms, apartments for married students, apartments for single students. 100% of campus accessible to physically disabled. **Special Academic Facilities/Equipment:** Three art galleries, language labs, hospital. Research center with comprehensive collection on Africa and persons of African descent. **Computers:** 10% of classrooms, 100% of dorms, 100% of libraries, 10% of dining areas, 50% of student union, 10% of common outdoor areas have wireless network access. Students can register for classes online. Administrative functions (other than registration) can be performed online.

CAMPUS LIFE

Environment: Metropolis. **Activities:** Choral groups, concert band, dance, drama/theater, jazz band, literary magazine, marching band, music ensembles, musical theater, opera, pep band, radio station, student government, student newspaper, student-run film society, symphony orchestra, television station, yearbook, Campus Ministries, International Student Organization. 150 registered organizations, 15 honor societies, 3 religious organizations. 10 fraternities, 8 sororities. **Athletics (Intercollegiate):** *Men:* basketball, cheerleading, cross-country, diving, football, soccer, swimming, tennis, track/field (outdoor). *Women:* basketball, bowling, boxing, cheerleading, cross-country, diving, lacrosse, soccer, softball, swimming, tennis, track/field (outdoor), volleyball. **On-Campus Highlights:** Founders Library, Rankin Chapel, Punchout, Ira Aldridge Theatre, Burr Gymnasium.

ADMISSIONS

Freshman Academic Profile: Average high school GPA 3.3. 23% in top 10% of high school class, 54% in top 25% of high school class, 85% in top 50% of high school class. 80% from public high schools. SAT Math middle 50% range 490-590. SAT Critical Reading middle 50% range 490-600. SAT Writing middle 50% range 490-600. ACT middle 50% range 21-26. Minimum paper TOEFL 550. **Basis for Candidate Selection:** *Very important factors considered include:* Class rank, rigor of secondary school record, standardized test scores. *Important factors considered include:* recommendation(s), character/personal qualities. *Other factors considered include:* application essay, alumni/ae relation, extracurricular activities, talent/ability, volunteer work, work experience. **Freshman Admission Requirements:** High school diploma is required and GED is accepted. *Academic units required:* 4 English, 2 mathematics, 2 science, (0 science labs), 2 foreign language, 2 social studies, 2 history, 0 any other academic courses counted towards graduation. **Freshman Admission Statistics:** 11,599 applied, 57% admitted, 24% enrolled. **Transfer Admission Requirements:** college transcript(s), statement of good standing from prior institution(s). Minimum college GPA of 2.5 required. Lowest grade transferable C. **General Admission Information:** Application Fee $45. Early decision application deadline 11/1. Regular application deadline 2/15. Nonfall registration accepted. Admission may be deferred for a maximum of 1. Credit and/or placement offered for CEEB Advanced Placement tests.

COSTS AND FINANCIAL AID

Annual tuition $22,737. Room and board $13,646. Required fees $1,233. Average book expense $3,000. **Required Forms and Deadlines:** FAFSA. **Notification of Awards:** Applicants will be notified of awards on a rolling basis

beginning 4/1. **Types of Aid:** *Need-based scholarships/grants:* Federal Pell, SEOG, state scholarships/grants, private scholarships, the school's own gift aid, Federal Nursing Scholarships. *Loans:* Direct Subsidized Stafford, Direct Unsubsidized Stafford, Direct PLUS, Federal Perkins, Federal Nursing. *Student Employment:* Federal Work-Study Program available. Institutional employment available. Highest amount earned per year from on-campus jobs $3,500. Off-campus job opportunities are excellent. **Financial Aid Statistics:** 61% freshmen, 63% undergrads receive need-based scholarship or grant aid. 50% freshmen, 45% undergrads receive non-need-based scholarship or grant aid. 67% freshmen, 76% undergrads receive need-based self-help aid. 5% freshmen, 4% undergrads receive athletic scholarships. 96% freshmen, 96% undergrads receive any aid. 83% undergrads borrow to pay for school. Average cumulative indebtedness $23,749. **Criteria for awarding institutional aid:** *Non-need-based:* academics, art, athletics, job skills, music/drama, state/district residency.

HUMBOLDT STATE UNIVERSITY

1 Harpst Street, Arcata, CA 95521-8299
Phone: 707-826-4402 · **Financial Aid Phone:** 707-826-4321
E-mail: hsuinfo@humboldt.edu · **CEEB Code:** 4345
Fax: 707-826-6190 · **Website:** www.humboldt.edu · **ACT Code:** 286

This public school was founded in 1913. It has a 161-acre campus.

RATINGS

Admissions Selectivity Rating: 76   **Fire Safety Rating:** 86

STUDENTS AND FACULTY

Enrollment: 7,942. **Student Body:** 54% female, 46% male, 6% out-of-state, 1% international (40 countries represented). Asian 3%, African American 4%, Caucasian 47%, Hispanic 30%, Native American 1%

Retention and Graduation: 13% freshmen graduate within 4 years. 44% freshmen graduate within 6 years. **Faculty:** 219 full-time faculty, 99% hold PhDs, 42% are members of minority groups, 14% are women.

ACADEMICS

Degrees: bachelor's, master's, post-bachelor's certificate. **Classes:** Most classes have 20–29 students. Most lab/discussion sessions have 20–29 students. **Majors with Highest Enrollment:** Biology/Biological Sciences; Business Administration and Management; Psychology. **Special Study Options:** double major, English as a Second Language (ESL), exchange student program (domestic), student-designed major, study abroad, teacher certification program. **Disability Services:** Special programs offered to physically disabled students include note-taking services, reader services, tape recorders, tutors. **Career services:** alumni services, career/job search classes, career assessment, internships, regional alumni. Career services highlights include internships that allow students to get jobs in their fields after they graduate. The Career Center connects students with the internships that work best for them.

FACILITIES

Housing: Coed dorms. 75% of campus accessible to physically disabled. **Special Academic Facilities/Equipment:** Art and geology museums, marine research lab, fish hatchery, wildlife game pen, observatory, First Street Gallery **Computers:** 55% of classrooms, 100% of dorms, 100% of libraries, 100% of dining areas, 100% of student union, 80% of common outdoor areas have wireless network access. Students can register for classes online. Administrative functions (other than registration) can be performed online.

CAMPUS LIFE

Environment: Village. **Activities:** Choral groups, concert band, dance, drama/theater, jazz band, literary magazine, music ensembles, pep band, radio station, student government, student newspaper, symphony orchestra, International Student Organization, Model UN. 160 registered organizations, 6 honor societies, 8 religious organizations. 2 fraternities, 4 sororities. **Athletics (Intercollegiate):** *Men:* basketball, cross-country, football, soccer, track/field (outdoor). *Women:* basketball, crew/rowing, cross-country, soccer, softball, track/field (outdoor), volleyball. **On-Campus Highlights:** Founders Hall, Campus Center for Appropriate Technology, University Center, Redwood Bowl, University Library. **Environmental Initiatives:** Campus Center for Appropriate Technology (CCAT): For 35 years, the Campus Center for Appropriate Technologys live-in demonstration home for sustainability annually exposes over 2,000 students, faculty, staff, and visitors through tours, student-taught courses, workshops, presentations and hands-on projects. The first of its kind, CCAT has been the inspiration for similar projects on college campuses across the nation. http://www.humboldt.edu/~ccat/ Established in 1989, Humboldt States Schatz Energy Research Center has been an international leader in the development of clean and renewable energy. Most recently, the Center unveiled a hydrogen fueling station upgrade that powers two hydrogen fueled Toyota Highlanders. http://www.schatzlab.org/ Humbodlt Energy Independent Fund (HEIF): HEIF seeks to reduce the environmental impacts of energy use at HSU through student created, designed, and implemented projects. The funds for these projects come from a $10 per semester student fee (students approved the fee via a university-wide vote). Projects educate about energy, save energy or generate energy. So far, seventeen projects been commissioned, with two notable ones being: a 10.5 kW solar installation along with a student-designed interpretive sign; a re-lamp of the sports stadium reducing electrical use and associated light pollution, in addition to saving $9,000/yr in energy costs. http://www.humboldt.edu/~heif/

ADMISSIONS

Freshman Academic Profile: Average high school GPA 3.21. 13% in top 10% of high school class, 46% in top 25% of high school class, 80% in top 50% of high school class. 90% from public high schools. SAT Math middle 50% range 440-560. SAT Critical Reading middle 50% range 430-540. SAT Writing middle 50% range 430-540. ACT middle 50% range 18-24. Minimum internet-based TOEFL 71. Minimum paper TOEFL 525. **Basis for Candidate Selection:** *Very important factors considered include:* academic GPA, standardized test scores. *Important factors considered include:* rigor of secondary school record. *Other factors considered include:* state residency. **Freshman Admission Requirements:** High school diploma is required and GED is accepted. *Academic units required:* 4 English, 3 mathematics, 2 science, (1 science labs), 2 foreign language, 1 social studies, 1 history, 1 visual/performing arts, 1 academic electives. **Freshman Admission Statistics:** 11,912 applied, 77% admitted, 15% enrolled. **Transfer Admission Requirements:** college transcript(s), statement of good standing from prior institution(s). Minimum college GPA of 2.00 required. Lowest grade transferable D-. **General Admission Information:** Application Fee $55. Regular application deadline 11/30. Notification on a rolling basis, beginning on or about 12/1. Nonfall registration not accepted. Credit and/or placement offered for CEEB Advanced Placement tests.

COSTS AND FINANCIAL AID

Annual in-state tuition $7,190. Annual out-of-state tuition $16,118. Room and board $12,380. Average book expense $1,628. **Required Forms and Deadlines:** FAFSA. **Notification of Awards:** Applicants will be notified of awards on a rolling basis beginning 4/1. **Types of Aid:** *Need-based scholarships/grants:* Federal Pell, SEOG, state scholarships/grants, private scholarships, the school's own gift aid. *Loans:* Direct Subsidized Stafford, Direct Unsubsidized Stafford, Direct PLUS, Federal Perkins. *Student Employment:* Federal Work-Study Program available. Institutional employment available. Off-campus job opportunities are good. **Financial Aid Statistics:** 83% freshmen, 84% undergrads receive need-based scholarship or grant aid. 1% freshmen, 1% undergrads receive non-need-based scholarship or grant aid. 77% freshmen, 75% undergrads receive need-based self-help aid. 1% freshmen, 1% undergrads receive athletic scholarships. 72% freshmen, 74% undergrads receive any aid. 74% undergrads borrow to pay for school. Average cumulative indebtedness $18,407. **Criteria for awarding institutional aid:** *Non-need-based:* academics, alumni affiliation, athletics, leadership, minority status, music/drama, religious affiliation.

HUMPHREYS COLLEGE

6650 Inglewood Avenue, Stockton, CA 95207
Phone: 209-478-0800 · **Financial Aid Phone:** 209-478-0800
E-mail: slopez@humphreys.edu
Fax: 209-478-0800 · **Website:** http://www.humphreys.edu/

This private school was founded in 1896. It has a 10-acre campus.

RATINGS

Admissions Selectivity Rating: 60*   **Fire Safety Rating:** 60*

STUDENTS AND FACULTY

Enrollment: 692. **Student Body:** 85% female, 15% male, 0% out-of-state, 0% international. Asian 12%, African American 15%, Caucasian 25%, Hispanic 33%, Native American 1%
Retention and Graduation: 64% freshmen return for sophomore year. 100% freshmen graduate within 4 years. 100% freshmen graduate within 6 years. 54% grads go on to further study within 1 year. 20% grads pursue arts and sciences degrees. 30% grads pursue law degrees. 40% grads pursue business degrees. 1% grads pursue medical degrees. **Faculty:** 18 full-time faculty, 17% hold PhDs, 67% are members of minority groups, 6% are women. 0% of classes are taught by teaching assistants.

ACADEMICS

Degrees: associate, bachelor's, certificate, first professional. **Classes:** Most classes have greater than 100 students. **Special Study Options:** distance learn-

ing, double major, dual enrollment, independent study, internships. **Career services:** alumni services, internships. Career services highlights include internships.

FACILITIES

Housing: apartments for single students. 100% of campus accessible to physically disabled.

CAMPUS LIFE

Environment: Village. **Activities:** literary magazine, student newspaper. 3 registered organizations.

ADMISSIONS

Freshman Academic Profile: Average high school GPA 3. 0% in top 10% of high school class, 0% in top 25% of high school class, 15% in top 50% of high school class. 95% from public high schools. Minimum paper TOEFL 450. **Basis for Candidate Selection:** *Very important factors considered include:* interview. *Important factors considered include:* character/personal qualities. *Other factors considered include:* level of applicant's interest. **Freshman Admission Requirements:** High school diploma is required and GED is accepted. **Freshman Admission Statistics:** 143 applied, 81% admitted, 100% enrolled. **Transfer Admission Requirements:** High school transcript, college transcript(s), interview, Minimum college GPA of 2.0 required. Lowest grade transferable C-. **General Admission Information:** Application Fee $35. Nonfall registration accepted. Admission may be deferred for a maximum of 5. Placement offered for CEEB Advanced Placement tests.

COSTS AND FINANCIAL AID

Required Forms and Deadlines: FAFSA. **Types of Aid:** *Need-based scholarships/grants:* Federal Pell, SEOG, state scholarships/grants, private scholarships. *Loans:* Subsidized Stafford, Unsubsidized Stafford, PLUS. *Student Employment:* Highest amount earned per year from on-campus jobs $1,603. Off-campus job opportunities are fair. **Financial Aid Statistics:** 100% freshmen, 100% undergrads receive need-based scholarship or grant aid. 0% freshmen, 0% undergrads receive non-need-based scholarship or grant aid. 23% freshmen, 7% undergrads receive need-based self-help aid. 0% freshmen, 0% undergrads receive athletic scholarships. 98% freshmen, 98% undergrads receive any aid. 8% undergrads borrow to pay for school.

HUNTINGDON COLLEGE

1500 East Fairview Avenue, Montgomery, AL 36106-2148
Phone: 334-833-4497 · **Financial Aid Phone:** 334-833-4428
E-mail: admiss@huntingdon.edu · **CEEB Code:** 1303
Fax: 334-833-4347 · **Website:** www.huntingdon.edu · **ACT Code:** 18

This private school, affiliated with the Methodist Church, was founded in 1854. It has a 71-acre campus.

RATINGS

Admissions Selectivity Rating: 82   **Fire Safety Rating:** 92

STUDENTS AND FACULTY

Enrollment: 1,149. **Student Body:** 49% female, 51% male, 18% out-of-state, 1% international (8 countries represented). Asian 1%, African American 20%, Caucasian 64%, Hispanic 2%, Native American 1%
Retention and Graduation: 30% freshmen graduate within 4 years. 45% freshmen graduate within 6 years. **Faculty:** 41 full-time faculty, 85% hold PhDs, 46% are members of minority groups, 5% are women. 0% of classes are taught by teaching assistants.

ACADEMICS

Degrees: bachelor's. **Classes:** Most classes have fewer than 10 students. Most lab/discussion sessions have 10–19 students. **Majors with Highest Enrollment:** Kinesiology and Exercise Science; Biology/Biological Sciences; Business/Commerce. **Special Study Options:** cross-registration, double major, honors program, independent study, internships, liberal arts/career combination, student-designed major, study abroad, teacher certification program, Adult Degree Completion Program in which students take classes only in the evening, all year long, dual engineering degree with Auburn University and exchange student program with universities Ireland; travel opportunities to all full-time junior and seniors within regular educational costs or for nominal additional fees. **Honors programs:** Program Honors—An outstanding student in a particular major has the opportunity to create an individualized honors project within the major to meet a particular need and interest. **Disability Services:** Special programs offered to physically disabled students include note-taking services, reader services, tape recorders, tutors. **Career services:** Alumni network, alumni services, career/job search classes, career assessment, internships. Career services highlights include an exceptional internship program. The Center for Career and Vocation currently has more internships and jobs than there are students and alumni needing such opportunities. Huntingdon College's partnership with the community and local business and industry is paying huge dividends for Huntingdon students, alumni and the College.

FACILITIES

Housing: Coed dorms, men's dorms, women's dorms. 85% of campus accessible to physically disabled. **Special Academic Facilities/Equipment:** 1. The Bowman Ecological Center is a protected area in Prattville, AL that provides space for students to collect and study samples of plants, trees, and aquatic life. 2. Sybil Smith Hall is a fully equipped music facility housing the Lucile Crowell Delchamps Recital Hall, the Julia Lightfoot Sellers Reception Hall, faculty offices and studios, rehersal rooms, classrooms, a modern electronic music laboratory, and one of the most extensive music collections in the South, with more than 10,000 records, CDs and tapes. 3. The Staton Center for Learning Enrichment Center oversees the Academic Success Centers, advises students who have not declared majors, provides academic counseling for students with provisional enrollment, serves as a resource for study halls as related to study skills and time management skills, and advises staff and faculty serving the First Year Experience (FYEx) program. 4. Leon and Myra Allman Ligon Chapel contains the newly expanded and installed Bellingrath Memorial Organ, which Dr. Harold Rohlig, professor of music, designed. The Bellingrath Memorial Organ is one of the largest of its kind among private colleges in the Southeast, with 141 ranks and a four-manual keyboard. The Chapel's Green Window, revered by alumni as a symbol of the Huntingdon experience, is framed by the new organ pipes, some of which are 32 feet in length. Ligon Chapel is the site of pageants, performances, lectures, convocations, concerts, and countless traditions at Huntingdon College. **Computers:** 40% of classrooms, 33% of dorms, 100% of libraries, 100% of dining areas, 100% of student union, have wireless network access. Administrative functions (other than registration) can be performed online. Undergraduates are required to own a computer.

CAMPUS LIFE

Environment: City. **Activities:** Choral groups, concert band, dance, drama/theater, literary magazine, marching band, music ensembles, pep band, student government, student newspaper, yearbook, Campus Ministries, International Student Organization, Model UN. 50 registered organizations, 15 honor societies, 3 religious organizations. 4 fraternities, 4 sororities. **Athletics (Intercollegiate):** *Men:* baseball, basketball, cross-country, football, golf, soccer, tennis. *Women:* basketball, cross-country, golf, soccer, softball, tennis, volleyball. **On-Campus Highlights:** Flowers Hall, Houghton Memorial Library, Wilson Center, Carolyn & Wynton Blount (Residence) Hall, Julia Walker Russell Dining Hall.

ADMISSIONS

Freshman Academic Profile: Average high school GPA 3.44. 14% in top 10% of high school class, 32% in top 25% of high school class, 78% in top 50% of high school class. 78% from public high schools. SAT Math middle 50% range 450-530. SAT Critical Reading middle 50% range 460-560. ACT middle 50% range 20-24. Minimum internet-based TOEFL 45. Minimum paper TOEFL 500. **Basis for Candidate Selection:** *Very important factors considered include:* academic GPA, standardized test scores. *Important factors considered include:* rigor of secondary school record. *Other factors considered include:* Class rank, application essay, recommendation(s), interview. **Freshman Admission Requirements:** High school diploma is required and GED is accepted. **Freshman Admission Statistics:** 1,437 applied, 58% admitted, 27% enrolled. **Transfer Admission Requirements:** High school transcript, college transcript(s), statement of good standing from prior institution(s). Minimum college GPA of 2.25 required. Lowest grade transferable C. **General Admission Information:** Regular application deadline 8/15. Notification on a rolling basis, beginning on or about 9/7. Nonfall registration accepted. Admission may be deferred for a maximum of 2 semesters. Credit and/or placement offered for CEEB Advanced Placement tests.

COSTS AND FINANCIAL AID

Required Forms and Deadlines: FAFSA. **Notification of Awards:** Applicants will be notified of awards on a rolling basis beginning 3/1. **Types of Aid:** *Need-based scholarships/grants:* Federal Pell, SEOG, state scholarships/grants, private scholarships, the school's own gift aid. *Loans:* Subsidized Stafford, Unsubsidized Stafford, PLUS, Federal Perkins. *Student Employment:* Federal Work-Study Program available. Institutional employment available. Off-campus job opportunities are excellent. **Financial Aid Statistics:** 100% freshmen, 99% undergrads receive need-based scholarship or grant aid. 11% freshmen, 10% undergrads receive non-need-based scholarship or grant aid. 81% freshmen, 79% undergrads receive need-based self-help aid. 0% freshmen, 0% undergrads receive athletic scholarships. 100% freshmen, 100% undergrads receive any aid. 77% undergrads borrow to pay for school. Average cumulative indebtedness $25,714. **Criteria for awarding institutional aid:** *Non-need-based:* academics, alumni affiliation, leadership, music/drama, religious affiliation, state/district residency.

HUNTINGTON UNIVERSITY

2303 College Avenue, Huntington, IN 46750
Phone: (260) 359-4000 • **Financial Aid Phone:** 800-642-6493
E-mail: admissions@huntington.edu • **CEEB Code:** 1304
Fax: (260) 358-3699 • **Website:** www.huntington.edu • **ACT Code:** 1202

This private school, affiliated with the Protestant Church, was founded in 1897. It has a 170-acre campus.

RATINGS

Admissions Selectivity Rating: 79   **Fire Safety Rating:** 93

STUDENTS AND FACULTY

Enrollment: 968. **Student Body:** 57% female, 43% male, 35% out-of-state, 4% international (20 countries represented). Asian 1%, African American 2%, Caucasian 94%, Hispanic 4%, Native American <1%.
Retention and Graduation: 79% freshmen return for sophomore year. 57% freshmen graduate within 4 years. 62% freshmen graduate within 6 years. 14% grads go on to further study within 1 year. 13% grads pursue arts and sciences degrees. 1% grads pursue medical degrees. **Faculty:** 55 full-time faculty, 87% hold PhDs, 38% are members of minority groups, 2% are women. 0% of classes are taught by teaching assistants.

ACADEMICS

Degrees: associate, bachelor's, diploma, master's, terminal associate, transfer associate. **Classes:** Most classes have 10–19 students. Most lab/discussion sessions have 10–19 students. **Majors with Highest Enrollment:** Animation, Interactive Technology, Video Graphics and Special Effects; Practical Nursing, Vocational Nursing and Nursing Assistants; Cinematography and Film/Video Production. **Special Study Options:** Accelerated program, double major, independent study, internships, study abroad, teacher certification program, Bible and religion. **Disability Services:** Special programs offered to physically disabled students include note-taking services, reader services, tutors. **Career services:** Alumni network, alumni services, career/job search classes, career assessment, internships, regional alumni. Career services highlights include www.huntington.edu/erc/.

FACILITIES

Housing: special housing for disabled students, men's dorms, women's dorms, apartments for single students, college-owned houses. 62% of campus accessible to physically disabled. **Special Academic Facilities/Equipment:** Thornhill Nature Preserve **Computers:** 100% of classrooms, 100% of dorms, 100% of libraries, 100% of dining areas, 100% of student union, have wireless network access. Students can register for classes online. Administrative functions (other than registration) can be performed online.

CAMPUS LIFE

Environment: Town. **Activities:** Choral groups, concert band, dance, drama/theater, jazz band, literary magazine, music ensembles, musical theater, pep band, radio station, student government, student newspaper, student-run film society, television station, yearbook, Campus Ministries, International Student Organization 6 honor societies, 4 religious organizations. **Athletics (Intercollegiate):** *Men:* baseball, basketball, cheerleading, cross-country, golf, soccer, tennis, track/field (outdoor), track/field (indoor). *Women:* basketball, cheerleading, cross-country, golf, soccer, softball, tennis, track/field (outdoor), track/field (indoor), volleyball. **On-Campus Highlights:** Residence Halls-lounges, Habecker Dining Commons, Norm's Place-snack lounge, Merillat Complex for Physical Education and Recreation, Merillat Centre for the Arts. **Environmental Initiatives:** Campus recycling program.

ADMISSIONS

Freshman Academic Profile: Average high school GPA 3.46. 26% in top 10% of high school class, 53% in top 25% of high school class, 80% in top 50% of high school class. 81% from public high schools. SAT Math middle 50% range 440-560. SAT Critical Reading middle 50% range 440-570. SAT Writing middle 50% range 423-550. ACT middle 50% range 21-27. Minimum internet-based TOEFL 65. Minimum paper TOEFL 525. **Basis for Candidate Selection:** *Very important factors considered include:* academic GPA, rigor of secondary school record, standardized test scores, religious affiliation/commitment. *Important factors considered include:* Class rank, application essay, character/personal qualities, extracurricular activities. *Other factors considered include:* recommendation(s), alumni/ae relation, first generation, interview, level of applicant's interest, racial/ethnic status, talent/ability, volunteer work, work experience. **Freshman Admission Requirements:** High school diploma is required and GED is accepted. *Academic units required:* 4 English, 3 mathematics, 2 science, (1 science labs), 0 foreign language, 2 social studies, 2 history, 0 academic electives. **Freshman Admission Statistics:** 780 applied, 97% admitted, 30% enrolled. **Transfer Admission Requirements:** college transcript(s), essay or personal statement, Minimum college GPA of 2.0 required. Lowest grade transferable C. **General Admission Information:** Application Fee $20. Regular application deadline 8/1. Notification on a rolling basis, beginning on or about 10/1. Nonfall registration accepted. Admission may be deferred for a maximum of 1 year. Credit and/or placement offered for CEEB Advanced Placement tests.

COSTS AND FINANCIAL AID

Annual tuition $23,976. Room and board $8,306. Required fees $795. Average book expense $1,000. **Required Forms and Deadlines:** FAFSA. **Notification of Awards:** Applicants will be notified of awards on a rolling basis beginning 3/1. **Types of Aid:** *Need-based scholarships/grants:* Federal Pell, SEOG, state scholarships/grants, private scholarships, the school's own gift aid. *Loans:* Subsidized Stafford, Unsubsidized Stafford, PLUS, Federal Perkins. *Student Employment:* Federal Work-Study Program available. Institutional employment available. Highest amount earned per year from on-campus jobs $3,500. Off-campus job opportunities are good. **Financial Aid Statistics:** 94% freshmen, 94% undergrads receive need-based scholarship or grant aid. 22% freshmen, 17% undergrads receive non-need-based scholarship or grant aid. 88% freshmen, 90% undergrads receive need-based self-help aid. 6% freshmen, 5% undergrads receive athletic scholarships. 98% freshmen, 94% undergrads receive any aid. 66% undergrads borrow to pay for school. Average cumulative indebtedness $25,806. **Criteria for awarding institutional aid:** *Non-need-based:* academics, alumni affiliation, art, athletics, leadership, music/drama, religious affiliation.

HUSSON UNIVERSITY

1 College Circle, Bangor, ME 4401
Phone: 207-941-7100 • **Financial Aid Phone:** 207-941-7156
E-mail: admit@husson.edu • **CEEB Code:** 3440
Fax: 207-941-7935 • **Website:** www.husson.edu • **ACT Code:** 1646

This private school was founded in 1898. It has a 170-acre campus.

RATINGS

Admissions Selectivity Rating: 79   **Fire Safety Rating:** 98

STUDENTS AND FACULTY

Enrollment: 2,291. **Student Body:** 59% female, 41% male, 16% out-of-state, 3% international (19 countries represented). Asian 1%, African American 4%, Caucasian 88%, Hispanic 1%, Native American 1%
Retention and Graduation: 71% freshmen return for sophomore year. 25% freshmen graduate within 4 years. 20% grads go on to further study within 1 year. 1% grads pursue arts and sciences degrees. 2% grads pursue law degrees. 10% grads pursue business degrees. 1% grads pursue medical degrees. **Faculty:** 121 full-time faculty, 66% hold PhDs, 50% are members of minority groups, 3% are women. 0% of classes are taught by teaching assistants.

ACADEMICS

Degrees: associate, bachelor's, certificate, diploma, master's, post-master's certificate, terminal associate. **Classes:** Most classes have 20–29 students. Most lab/discussion sessions have fewer than 10 students. **Majors with Highest Enrollment:** Business/Commerce; Registered Nursing/Registered Nurse; Criminal Justice/Law Enforcement Administration. **Special Study Options:** Accelerated program, cooperative education program, distance learning, double major, dual enrollment, independent study, internships, liberal arts/career combination, student-designed major, teacher certification program, weekend college. Combined degree programs: BS/BS, BS/MS, DPT/BS. **Disability Services:** Special programs offered to physically disabled students include note-taking services, tape recorders, tutors. **Career services:** Alumni network, career/job search classes, internships.

FACILITIES

Housing: Coed dorms, special housing for disabled students. 85% of campus accessible to physically disabled. **Special Academic Facilities/Equipment:** White Art Gallery, Dahl Anatomy Lab, Kenduskeag Research Institute, Gracie Theater. **Computers:** 100% of classrooms, 100% of dorms, 100% of libraries, 100% of student union, have wireless network access. Students can register for classes online. Administrative functions (other than registration) can be performed online.

CAMPUS LIFE

Environment: City. **Activities:** drama/theater, literary magazine, pep band, radio station, student government, student newspaper, television station, yearbook, Campus Ministries, International Student Organization. 30 registered organizations, 1 honor society, 2 religious organizations. 2 fraternities, 3 sororities. **Athletics (Intercollegiate):** *Men:* baseball, basketball, football, golf, lacrosse,

soccer. *Women:* basketball, field hockey, lacrosse, soccer, softball, swimming, tennis, volleyball. **On-Campus Highlights:** Swan Fitness Center, Campus Center, Student Lounge, Newman Gym, Library, The Meeting House, a new academic building, opened in the fall of 2008. The attached 500-seat balconied, performing arts center opened in the fall of 2009. **Environmental Initiatives:** Green Cleaning Supplies; Recycle paper and plastic and glass; Reduce printing by setting a maximum limit.

ADMISSIONS

Freshman Academic Profile: Average high school GPA 3.22. 18% in top 10% of high school class, 59% in top 25% of high school class, 84% in top 50% of high school class. 87% from public high schools. SAT Math middle 50% range 430-550. SAT Critical Reading middle 50% range 420-530. SAT Writing middle 50% range 420-530. ACT middle 50% range 17-21. Minimum paper TOEFL 500. **Basis for Candidate Selection:** *Very important factors considered include:* recommendation(s), rigor of secondary school record, interview. *Important factors considered include:* Class rank, application essay, academic GPA, standardized test scores, character/personal qualities, extracurricular activities. *Other factors considered include:* alumni/ae relation, first generation, level of applicant's interest, volunteer work, work experience. **Freshman Admission Requirements:** High school diploma is required and GED is accepted. **Freshman Admission Statistics:** 1,581 applied, 80% admitted, 35% enrolled. **Transfer Admission Requirements:** High school transcript, college transcript(s), essay or personal statement, Minimum college GPA of 2.0 required. Lowest grade transferable C. **General Admission Information:** Application Fee $25. Notification on a rolling basis, beginning on or about 12/1. Nonfall registration accepted. Admission may be deferred for a maximum of 1 year. Credit and/or placement offered for CEEB Advanced Placement tests.

COSTS AND FINANCIAL AID

Annual tuition $15,210. Room and board $8,604. Required fees $380. Average book expense $1,150. **Required Forms and Deadlines:** FAFSA. **Notification of Awards:** Applicants will be notified of awards on a rolling basis beginning 3/1. **Types of Aid:** *Need-based scholarships/grants:* Federal Pell, SEOG, state scholarships/grants, private scholarships, the school's own gift aid. *Loans:* Subsidized Stafford, Unsubsidized Stafford, PLUS, Federal Perkins, state loans. *Student Employment:* Federal Work-Study Program available. Institutional employment available. Highest amount earned per year from on-campus jobs $1,600. Off-campus job opportunities are good. **Financial Aid Statistics:** 96% freshmen, 83% undergrads receive need-based scholarship or grant aid. 3% freshmen, 2% undergrads receive non-need-based scholarship or grant aid. 93% freshmen, 84% undergrads receive need-based self-help aid. 0% freshmen, 0% undergrads receive athletic scholarships. 79% freshmen, 59% undergrads receive any aid. 88% undergrads borrow to pay for school. Average cumulative indebtedness $31,327. **Criteria for awarding institutional aid:** *Non-need-based:* academics, leadership.

HUSTON-TILLOTSON UNIVERSITY

900 Chicon Street, Austin, TX 78702
Phone: 512-505-3028 • **Financial Aid Phone:** 512-505-3028
E-mail: admission@htu.edu • **CEEB Code:** 6280
Fax: 512-505-3192 • **Website:** www.htu.edu./ • **ACT Code:** 4104

This private school was founded in 1875. It has a 35-acre campus.

RATINGS

Admissions Selectivity Rating: 67   **Fire Safety Rating:** 60*

STUDENTS AND FACULTY

Enrollment: 889. **Student Body:** 51% female, 49% male, 3% out-of-state, 3% international (11 countries represented). African American 72%, Caucasian 5%, Hispanic 19%
Retention and Graduation: 50% freshmen return for sophomore year. 12% freshmen graduate within 4 years. 24% freshmen graduate within 6 years. **Faculty:** 47 full-time faculty, 70% hold PhDs, 53% are members of minority groups, 57% are women. 0% of classes are taught by teaching assistants.

ACADEMICS

Degrees: bachelor's, post-bachelor's certificate. **Classes:** Most classes have fewer than 10 students. Most lab/discussion sessions have fewer than 10 students. **Majors with Highest Enrollment:** Computer and Information Sciences; Education; Business/Commerce. **Special Study Options:** cross-registration, distance learning, double major, dual enrollment, external degree program, honors program, independent study, internships, liberal arts/career combination, study abroad, teacher certification program, 3-2 Engineering Program with Prairie View A&M University.

FACILITIES

Housing: men's dorms, women's dorms.

CAMPUS LIFE

Activities: Choral groups, dance, jazz band, literary magazine, music ensembles, student government, student-run film society, Campus Ministries, International Student Organization. 17 registered organizations, 5 honor societies, 5 religious organizations. **Athletics (Intercollegiate):** *Men:* baseball, basketball, soccer, track/field (outdoor). *Women:* basketball, track/field (outdoor), volleyball.

ADMISSIONS

Freshman Academic Profile: Average high school GPA 2.79. 6% in top 10% of high school class, 12% in top 25% of high school class, 53% in top 50% of high school class. SAT Math middle 50% range 360-460. SAT Critical Reading middle 50% range 350-460. ACT middle 50% range 14-19. Minimum internet-based TOEFL 61. Minimum paper TOEFL 500. **Basis for Candidate Selection:** *Very important factors considered include:* rigor of secondary school record, standardized test scores. *Important factors considered include:* application essay, academic GPA, interview, religious affiliation/commitment. *Other factors considered include:* recommendation(s), alumni/ae relation, extracurricular activities, talent/ability. **Freshman Admission Requirements:** High school diploma is required and GED is accepted. *Academic units required:* 4 English, 3 mathematics, 2 science, 3 social studies, 1 computer science, 2 Health,P.E. **Freshman Admission Statistics:** 652 applied, 96% admitted, 43% enrolled. **Transfer Admission Requirements:** college transcript(s), essay or personal statement, Minimum college GPA of 2.0 required. Lowest grade transferable C. **General Admission Information:** Application Fee $25. Regular application deadline 7/1. Notification on a rolling basis, beginning on or about 1/1. Nonfall registration accepted. Admission may be deferred for a maximum of 1 Year. Credit and/or placement offered for CEEB Advanced Placement tests.

COSTS AND FINANCIAL AID

Annual tuition $10,396. Room and board $6,946. Required fees $2,034. Average book expense $600. **Required Forms and Deadlines:** FAFSA. **Notification of Awards:** Applicants will be notified of awards on a rolling basis beginning 4/1. **Types of Aid:** *Need-based scholarships/grants:* Federal Pell, SEOG, state scholarships/grants, private scholarships, the school's own gift aid, United Negro College Fund. *Loans:* Direct Subsidized Stafford, Direct Unsubsidized Stafford, Direct PLUS, Subsidized Stafford, Unsubsidized Stafford, PLUS, state loans, Private Loans. *Student Employment:* Federal Work-Study Program available. Off-campus job opportunities are good. **Financial Aid Statistics:** 25% freshmen, 33% undergrads receive need-based scholarship or grant aid. 33% freshmen, 35% undergrads receive non-need-based scholarship or grant aid. 100% freshmen, 100% undergrads receive need-based self-help aid. 15% freshmen, 14% undergrads receive athletic scholarships.97% undergrads receive any aid. 89% undergrads borrow to pay for school. Average cumulative indebtedness $10,750. **Criteria for awarding institutional aid:** *Non-need-based:* academics, alumni affiliation, art, athletics, job skills, leadership, minority status, music/drama, religious affiliation, state/district residency.

IDAHO STATE UNIVERSITY

Museum of National History 319, Pocatello, ID 83209-8270
Phone: 208-282-2475 · **Financial Aid Phone:** 208-282-2981
E-mail: info@isu.edu · **CEEB Code:** 4355
Fax: 208-282-4231 · **Website:** www.isu.edu · **ACT Code:** 918

This public school was founded in 1901. It has a 1100-acre campus.

RATINGS

Admissions Selectivity Rating: 75   **Fire Safety Rating:** 68

STUDENTS AND FACULTY

Enrollment: 10,034. **Student Body:** 54% female, 46% male, 6% out-of-state, 1% international (63 countries represented). Asian 2%, African American 1%, Caucasian 82%, Hispanic 6%, Native American 2%
Retention and Graduation: 60% freshmen return for sophomore year. 4% freshmen graduate within 4 years. 18% freshmen graduate within 6 years.
Faculty: 602 full-time faculty, 76% hold PhDs, 43% are members of minority groups, 7% are women.

ACADEMICS

Degrees: associate, bachelor's, certificate, doctoral, master's, post-bachelor's certificate, post-master's certificate. **Classes:** Most classes have 10–19 students. Most lab/discussion sessions have 20–29 students. **Majors with Highest Enrollment:** Secondary Education and Teaching; Elementary Education and

---

Teaching; Biology/Biological Sciences. **Special Study Options:** Accelerated program, cooperative education program, cross-registration, distance learning, double major, dual enrollment, English as a Second Language (ESL), exchange student program (domestic), honors program, independent study, internships, liberal arts/career combination, student-designed major, study abroad, teacher certification program, weekend college. **Honors programs:** Honors courses are offered in small classes and deal with interdisciplinary issues and confront some aspect of the human condition. Innovative teaching and assignments are encourages and interaction with faculty and class members is lively. Combined degree programs: BA/MA, BS/MS in chemistry. **Disability Services:** Special programs offered to physically disabled students include note-taking services, reader services, tape recorders, tutors.

FACILITIES

Housing: Coed dorms, special housing for disabled students, men's dorms, women's dorms, fraternity/sorority housing, apartments for married students, apartments for single students, Graduate Student Housing. 100% of campus accessible to physically disabled. **Special Academic Facilities/Equipment:** Museum of Natural History, Idaho Accelerator Center, Rendezvous Center. **Computers:** Students can register for classes online. Administrative functions (other than registration) can be performed online.

CAMPUS LIFE

Environment: Town. **Activities:** Choral groups, concert band, dance, drama/theater, jazz band, marching band, music ensembles, musical theater, opera, pep band, radio station, student government, student newspaper, symphony orchestra, television station, yearbook, Campus Ministries, International Student Organization. 134 registered organizations, 8 honor societies, 7 religious organizations. 2 fraternities, 3 sororities. **Athletics (Intercollegiate):** *Men:* basketball, cheerleading, cross-country, football, golf, tennis, track/field (outdoor). *Women:* basketball, cheerleading, cross-country, golf, soccer, softball, tennis, track/field (outdoor), volleyball. **On-Campus Highlights:** Idaho Museum of Natural History, Rock Climbing Wall at Reed Gym, L.E. and Thelma E Stephens performing Ar, Rendezvous Center, Particle Accelerator.

ADMISSIONS

Freshman Academic Profile: Average high school GPA 3.21. 13% in top 10% of high school class, 31% in top 25% of high school class, 61% in top 50% of high school class. SAT Math middle 50% range 470-570. SAT Writing middle 50% range 460-600. ACT middle 50% range 18-24. Minimum internet-based TOEFL 61. Minimum paper TOEFL 500. **Basis for Candidate Selection:** *Other factors considered include:* academic GPA, standardized test scores. **Freshman Admission Requirements:** High school diploma is required and GED is accepted. *Academic units required:* 4 English, 3 mathematics, 3 science, (1 science labs), 1 foreign language, 0 history, 0 computer science, 0 academic electives. **Freshman Admission Statistics:** 3,889 applied, 73% admitted, 67% enrolled. **Transfer Admission Requirements:** High school transcript, college transcript(s), standardized test scores, Minimum college GPA of 2.0 required. Lowest grade transferable D. **General Admission Information:** Application Fee $40. Notification on a rolling basis, beginning on or about 3/1. Nonfall registration accepted. Admission may be deferred for a maximum of 3 years. Credit and/or placement offered for CEEB Advanced Placement tests.

COSTS AND FINANCIAL AID

Annual in-state tuition $3,318. Annual out-of-state tuition $13,120. Room and board $5,050. Required fees $1,650. Average book expense $900. **Required Forms and Deadlines:** FAFSA. **Notification of Awards:** Applicants will be notified of awards on a rolling basis beginning 4/1. **Types of Aid:** *Need-based scholarships/grants:* Federal Pell, SEOG, state scholarships/grants, private scholarships, the school's own gift aid, Federal Nursing Scholarships. *Loans:* Direct Subsidized Stafford, Direct Unsubsidized Stafford, Direct PLUS, Federal Perkins. *Student Employment:* Off-campus job opportunities are good. **Criteria for awarding institutional aid:** *Non-need-based:* academics, alumni affiliation, art, athletics, leadership, minority status, music/drama, state/district residency.

ILLINOIS COLLEGE

1101 West College, Jacksonville, IL 62650
Phone: 217-245-3030
E-mail: admissions@ic.edu · **CEEB Code:** 1315
Fax: 217-245-3034 · **Website:** www.ic.edu · **ACT Code:** 1034

This private school, affiliated with the Presbyterian Church, was founded in 1829. It has a 62-acre campus.

RATINGS

Admissions Selectivity Rating: 86   **Fire Safety Rating:** 60*

STUDENTS AND FACULTY

Enrollment: 854. **Student Body:** 50% female, 50% male, 10% out-of-state, 3% international. Asian 1%, African American 5%, Caucasian 82%, Hispanic 2%, Native American 1%

Retention and Graduation: 83% freshmen return for sophomore year. 50% freshmen graduate within 4 years. 60% freshmen graduate within 6 years. 22% grads go on to further study within 1 year. 13% grads pursue arts and sciences degrees. 5% grads pursue law degrees. 2% grads pursue business degrees. 4% grads pursue medical degrees. **Faculty:** 74 full-time faculty, 84% hold PhDs, 50% are members of minority groups, 9% are women.

ACADEMICS

Degrees: bachelor's. **Classes:** Most classes have 10–19 students. Most lab/discussion sessions have 10–19 students. **Special Study Options:** cross-registration, double major, dual enrollment, independent study, internships, liberal arts/career combination, student-designed major, study abroad, teacher certification program. Combined degree programs: 3-2 nursing, 3-2 occupational ther and 3-1 med-tech. **Career services:** career/job search classes, career assessment, internships.

FACILITIES

Housing: Coed dorms, men's dorms, women's dorms, apartments for single students **Special Academic Facilities/Equipment:** Art gallery, language lab.

CAMPUS LIFE

Environment: Rural. **Activities:** Choral groups, concert band, drama/theater, literary magazine, music ensembles, student government, student newspaper, yearbook, Campus Ministries, International Student Organization, Model UN. 72 registered organizations, 12 honor societies, 3 religious organizations. 4 fraternities, 3 sororities. **Athletics (Intercollegiate):** *Men:* baseball, basketball, cross-country, football, golf, soccer, tennis, track/field (outdoor), track/field (indoor), wrestling. *Women:* basketball, cheerleading, cross-country, golf, soccer, softball, tennis, track/field (outdoor), track/field (indoor), volleyball.

ADMISSIONS

Freshman Academic Profile: Average high school GPA 3.39. 26% in top 10% of high school class, 56% in top 25% of high school class, 85% in top 50% of high school class. 80% from public high schools. ACT middle 50% range 21-27. Minimum paper TOEFL 550. **Basis for Candidate Selection:** *Very important factors considered include:* academic GPA, rigor of secondary school record, character/personal qualities. *Important factors considered include:* Class rank, application essay, recommendation(s), extracurricular activities, interview, state residency, talent/ability. *Other factors considered include:* standardized test scores, alumni/ae relation, first generation, geographical residence, level of applicant's interest, racial/ethnic status, volunteer work, work experience. **Freshman Admission Requirements:** High school diploma is required and GED is accepted. *Academic units required:* 4 English, 3 mathematics, 2 science, (2 science labs), 0 foreign language, 1 social studies, 1 history, 3 academic electives. **Freshman Admission Statistics:** 1,313 applied, 55% admitted, 31% enrolled. **Transfer Admission Requirements:** High school transcript, college transcript(s), Minimum college GPA of 2.50 required. Lowest grade transferable C. **General Admission Information:** Notification on a rolling basis, beginning on or about 11/15. Nonfall registration accepted. Admission may be deferred for a maximum of 1 year. Credit and/or placement offered for CEEB Advanced Placement tests.

COSTS AND FINANCIAL AID

Annual tuition $26,000. Room and board $8,500. Required fees $500. Average book expense $900. **Required Forms and Deadlines:** FAFSA. **Notification of Awards:** Applicants will be notified of awards on a rolling basis beginning 3/1. **Types of Aid:** *Need-based scholarships/grants:* Federal Pell, SEOG, state scholarships/grants, private scholarships, the school's own gift aid. *Loans:* Direct Subsidized Stafford, Direct Unsubsidized Stafford, Direct PLUS, Federal Perkins. *Student Employment:* Federal Work-Study Program available. Institutional employment available. Highest amount earned per year from on-campus jobs $800. Off-campus job opportunities are good. **Financial Aid Statistics:** 100% freshmen, 100% undergrads receive need-based scholarship or grant aid. 15% freshmen, 13% undergrads receive non-need-based scholarship or grant aid. 84% freshmen, 86% undergrads receive need-based self-help aid. 0% freshmen, 0% undergrads receive athletic scholarships. 79% undergrads borrow to pay for school. Average cumulative indebtedness $25,758. **Criteria for awarding institutional aid:** *Non-need-based:* academics, art, minority status, music/drama.

ILLINOIS INSTITUTE OF TECHNOLOGY

10 West 33rd Street, Chicago, IL 60616
Phone: 312-567-3025 • **Financial Aid Phone:** 312-567-7219
E-mail: admission@iit.edu • **CEEB Code:** 1318
Fax: 312-567-6939 • **Website:** http://www.iit.edu/ • **ACT Code:** 1040

This private school was founded in 1892. It has a 120-acre campus.

RATINGS

Admissions Selectivity Rating: 91   **Fire Safety Rating:** 74

STUDENTS AND FACULTY

Enrollment: 3,046. **Student Body:** 31% female, 69% male, 20% out-of-state, 30% international (74 countries represented). Asian 11%, African American 6%, Caucasian 33%, Hispanic 14%, Native American <1%

Retention and Graduation: 91% freshmen return for sophomore year. 28% freshmen graduate within 4 years. 65% freshmen graduate within 6 years. 12% grads go on to further study within 1 year. 2% grads pursue arts and sciences degrees. 1% grads pursue business degrees. **Faculty:** 424 full-time faculty, 87% hold PhDs, 27% are members of minority groups, 20% are women. 0% of classes are taught by teaching assistants.

ACADEMICS

Degrees: bachelor's, master's. **Classes:** Most classes have 10–19 students. Most lab/discussion sessions have 20–29 students. **Majors with Highest Enrollment:** Architecture; Mechanical Engineering; Electrical and Electronics Engineering. **Special Study Options:** cooperative education program, cross-registration, distance learning, double major, English as a Second Language (ESL), independent study, liberal arts/career combination, study abroad, teacher certification program, Joint **Enrollment:** Enrollment at 2 institutions for 2 degrees. **Honors programs:** Honors Pharmacy Program, and Honors Medical Program, Honors Law Program, Business Honors Law Program Combined degree programs: BS/MBA; BS/JD; BArch/MS; BArch/MBA; BS/MS; BS/MPA. **Disability Services:** Special programs offered to physically disabled students include note-taking services, reader services, tape recorders, tutors. **Career services:** Alumni network, alumni services, career/job search classes, career assessment, internships, regional alumni. Career services highlights include Co-operative Education.

FACILITIES

Housing: Coed dorms, fraternity/sorority housing, Men's/women's floors in residence halls, university apartments, arrangements for disabled students. 90% of campus accessible to physically disabled. **Special Academic Facilities/Equipment:** The Center for Accelerator and Particle Physics (CAPP), The Center for Complex Systems and Dynamics (CCSD), The Center for Digital Design and Manufacturing (CDDM), The Center for Electrochemical Science and Engineering, The Center for Excellence in Polymer Science and Engineering, The Center for Integrative Neuroscience and Neuroengineering Research, The Center for the Management of Medical Technology (CMMT), The Center for Molecular Study of Soft Condensed Matter (CMS2), The Center for Strategic Competitiveness (CSC), The Center for the Study of Ethics in the Professions (CSEP), The Center for Synchrotron Radiation Research and Instrumentation, The Center for Work Zone Safety and Mobility (CWZSM), Electric Power and Power Electronics Center (EPPEC), Energy + Power Center, Energy and Sustainability Institute, The Engineering Center For Diabetes Research and Education (ECDRE), The Fluid Dynamics Research Center, The High Performance Computing Center (HPCC), IIT Research Institute (IITRI), The International Center for Sensor Science and Engineering (ICSSE), The International Center for Sustainable New Cities (ICSNC), The Medical Imaging Research Center (MIRC), The National Center for Food Safety and Technology (NCFST), The Particle Technology and Crystallization Center (PTCC), The Pritzker Institute of Biomedical Science and Engineering, The Thermal Processing Technology Center (TPTC), The Wireless Network and Communications Research Center (WiNCom), Main Campus design by Ludwig Mies van der Rohe, McCormick Tribune Campus Center (MTCC) design by Rem Koolhaas, residence hall designed by Helmut Jahn, IIT Research Institute (IITRI), University Technology Park At IIT (UTP), Kemper Room Art Gallery, Illinois Tech Model Railroad (ITMR) **Computers:** 100% of classrooms, 100% of dorms, 100% of libraries, 100% of dining areas, 100% of student union, have wireless network access. Students can register for classes online. Administrative functions (other than registration) can be performed online.

CAMPUS LIFE

Environment: Metropolis. **Activities:** Choral groups, concert band, dance, drama/theater, literary magazine, music ensembles, musical theater, radio station, student government, student newspaper, student-run film society, television station, yearbook, Campus Ministries, International Student Organization. 100 registered organizations, 4 honor societies, 10 religious organizations. 7 fraternities, 3 sororities. **Athletics (Intercollegiate):** *Men:* baseball, cross-country, diving, soccer, swimming. *Women:* cross-country, diving, soccer, swimming, volleyball. **On-Campus Highlights:** S.R. Crown Hall (Architecture Building), McCormick Tribune Center, Keating Athletic Center, Hermann Hall, State Street Village. **Environmental Initiatives:** Creation of an Office of Campus Energy and Sustainability and the Wanger Institute of Sustainable Energy Research bringing students, faculty, staff, and alumni together to address complex sustainability issues. Implementation of a smart-micro grid on campus encompassing smart metering, energy efficiency, wind power, solar and on-site storage. Recycling Expansion: In 2008, IIT re-invigorated its recycling program under the banner of IIT Hawk Recycling and expanded into other areas to include other recyclables such as glass, cans, and batteries in addition to the paper and e-waste programs already in existence. In 2009, the program was expanded to include all campus academic, support and residence buildings and is anticipated to include all research buildings by May 2010. IIT projects an annual improvement between 5-10% in recycling rates due to the expanded program. The recycling effort will avoid approximately 750 cubic yards of land-fill waste per year. Recycling reports are available to the campus community, as well as details on where recycled material ends up, at www.iit.edu/recycling. In addition, IIT has implemented commercial composting and on-site composting to eliminate landfilling of recyclable food waste.

ADMISSIONS

Freshman Academic Profile: Average high school GPA 3.62. 45% in top 10% of high school class, 74% in top 25% of high school class, 96% in top 50% of high school class. 90% from public high schools. SAT Math middle 50% range 640-740. SAT Critical Reading middle 50% range 520-640. SAT Writing middle 50% range 520-640. ACT middle 50% range 25-31. Minimum internet-based TOEFL 80. Minimum paper TOEFL 550. **Basis for Candidate Selection:** *Very important factors considered include:* academic GPA, rigor of secondary school record. *Important factors considered include:* Class rank, application essay, recommendation(s), standardized test scores. *Other factors considered include:* alumni/ae relation, character/personal qualities, extracurricular activities, first generation, interview, level of applicant's interest, talent/ability, volunteer work, work experience. **Freshman Admission Requirements:** High school diploma is required and GED is accepted. *Academic units required:* 4 English, 4 mathematics, 3 science, (2 science labs), 2 foreign language, 2 social studies. **Freshman Admission Statistics:** 3,559 applied, 51% admitted, 24% enrolled. **Transfer Admission Requirements:** college transcript(s), essay or personal statement, statement of good standing from prior institution(s). Minimum college GPA of 3.0 required. Lowest grade transferable C. **General Admission Information:** Early decision application deadline 11/9. Notification on a rolling basis, beginning on or about 10/10. Nonfall registration accepted. Admission may be deferred for a maximum of 1 Year. Credit and/or placement offered for CEEB Advanced Placement tests.

COSTS AND FINANCIAL AID

Annual tuition $39,975. Room and board $10,900. Required fees $1,670. Average book expense $1,200. **Required Forms and Deadlines:** FAFSA. **Notification of Awards:** Applicants will be notified of awards on a rolling basis beginning 3/1. **Types of Aid:** *Need-based scholarships/grants:* Federal Pell, SEOG, state scholarships/grants, private scholarships, the school's own gift aid. *Loans:* Subsidized Stafford, Unsubsidized Stafford, PLUS, Federal Perkins, college/university loans from institutional funds. *Student Employment:* Federal Work-Study Program available. Institutional employment available. Off-campus job opportunities are good. **Financial Aid Statistics:** 99% freshmen, 99% undergrads receive need-based scholarship or grant aid. 19% freshmen, 11% undergrads receive non-need-based scholarship or grant aid. 66% freshmen, 73% undergrads receive need-based self-help aid. 0% freshmen, 1% undergrads receive athletic scholarships. 100% freshmen, 100% undergrads receive any aid. 58% undergrads borrow to pay for school. Average cumulative indebtedness $26,378. **Criteria for awarding institutional aid:** *Non-need-based:* academics, alumni affiliation, athletics, leadership, minority status.

ILLINOIS STATE UNIVERSITY

Office of Admissions, Normal, IL 61790-2200
Phone: 309-438-2181 · **Financial Aid Phone:** 309-438-2231
E-mail: admissions@illinoisstate.edu · **CEEB Code:** 1319
Fax: 309-438-3932 · **Website:** www.ilstu.edu · **ACT Code:** 1042

This public school was founded in 1857. It has a 850-acre campus.

RATINGS

Admissions Selectivity Rating: 78   **Fire Safety Rating:** 76

STUDENTS AND FACULTY

Enrollment: 18,526. **Student Body:** 55% female, 45% male, 2% out-of-state, 1% international (59 countries represented). Asian 2%, African American 6%, Caucasian 82%, Hispanic 6%, Native American <1% **Retention and Graduation:** 85% freshmen return for sophomore year. 44% freshmen graduate within 4 years. **Faculty:** 882 full-time faculty, 84% hold PhDs, 48% are members of minority groups, 15% are women. 7% of classes are taught by teaching assistants.

ACADEMICS

Degrees: bachelor's, master's, post-bachelor's certificate, post-master's certificate. **Classes:** Most classes have 20–29 students. Most lab/discussion sessions have 20–29 students. **Majors with Highest Enrollment:** Special Education and Teaching; Elementary Education and Teaching; Business Administration and Management. **Special Study Options:** Accelerated program, cooperative education program, distance learning, double major, dual enrollment, English as a Second Language (ESL), exchange student program (domestic), honors program, independent study, internships, student-designed major, study abroad, teacher certification program. Combined degree programs: BS/MPA. **Disability Services:** Special programs offered to physically disabled students include note-taking services, reader services, tape recorders, tutors. **Career services:** alumni services, internships.

FACILITIES

Housing: Coed dorms, special housing for disabled students, special housing for international students, women's dorms, fraternity/sorority housing, apartments for married students, apartments for single students. 100% of campus accessible to physically disabled. **Special Academic Facilities/Equipment:** Art gallery, cultural museums, on-campus elementary and secondary schools, greenhouse, farm, planetarium. **Computers:** 100% of classrooms, 100% of dorms, 100% of libraries, 100% of dining areas, 100% of student union, have wireless network access. Students can register for classes online. Administrative functions (other than registration) can be performed online. Undergraduates are required to own a computer.

CAMPUS LIFE

Environment: City. **Activities:** Choral groups, concert band, dance, drama/theater, jazz band, literary magazine, marching band, music ensembles, musical theater, pep band, radio station, student government, student newspaper, student-run film society, symphony orchestra, television station. 270 registered organizations, 23 honor societies, 22 religious organizations. 21 fraternity, 17 sororities. **Athletics (Intercollegiate):** *Men:* baseball, basketball, cheerleading, cross-country, football, golf, tennis, track/field (outdoor), track/field (indoor). *Women:* basketball, cheerleading, cross-country, diving, golf, gymnastics, soccer, softball, swimming, tennis, track/field (outdoor), track/field (indoor), volleyball. **On-Campus Highlights:** College of Business Building, Science Laboratory Building, Redbird Arena. **Environmental Initiatives:** Establishing a formal Office of Sustainability with 2 full time staff, 1 graduate assistant and multiple interns. The development of a sustainability across the curriculum summer workshop for faculty Launch of a community wide food waste composting operation at the University Farm.

ADMISSIONS

Freshman Academic Profile: Average high school GPA 3.33. 87% from public high schools. ACT middle 50% range 22-26. Minimum paper TOEFL 550. **Basis for Candidate Selection:** *Very important factors considered include:* academic GPA, rigor of secondary school record, standardized test scores. *Important factors considered include:* application essay. *Other factors considered include:* Class rank, character/personal qualities, first generation, talent/ability. **Freshman Admission Requirements:** High school diploma is required and GED is accepted. *Academic units required:* 4 English, 3 mathematics, 2 science, (2 science labs), 2 foreign language, 2 social studies, 2 academic electives. **Freshman Admission Statistics:** 13,156 applied, 63% admitted, 40% enrolled. **Transfer Admission Requirements:** college transcript(s), essay or personal statement, Minimum college GPA of 3.0 required. Lowest grade transferable D. **General Admission Information:** Application Fee $40. Regular application deadline 3/1. Notification on a rolling basis, beginning on or about 9/1. Nonfall registration accepted. Credit and/or placement offered for CEEB Advanced Placement tests.

The Princeton Review's Complete Book of Colleges

COSTS AND FINANCIAL AID

Annual in-state tuition $9,630. Annual out-of-state tuition $16,590. Room and board $9,090. Required fees $2,600. Average book expense $1,074. **Required Forms and Deadlines:** FAFSA. **Notification of Awards:** Applicants will be notified of awards on a rolling basis beginning 4/1. **Types of Aid:** *Need-based scholarships/grants:* Federal Pell, SEOG, state scholarships/grants, private scholarships, the school's own gift aid, Federal Nursing Scholarships. *Loans:* Direct Subsidized Stafford, Direct Unsubsidized Stafford, Direct PLUS, Federal Perkins, Federal Nursing, college/university loans from institutional funds. *Student Employment:* Off-campus job opportunities are excellent. **Financial Aid Statistics:** 58% freshmen, 55% undergrads receive need-based scholarship or grant aid. 32% freshmen, 22% undergrads receive non-need-based scholarship or grant aid. 88% freshmen, 83% undergrads receive need-based self-help aid. 1% freshmen, 1% undergrads receive athletic scholarships. 74% freshmen, 75% undergrads receive any aid. 65% undergrads borrow to pay for school. Average cumulative indebtedness $20,862. **Criteria for awarding institutional aid:** *Non-need-based:* academics, art, athletics, music/drama.

ILLINOIS WESLEYAN UNIVERSITY

P.O. Box 2900, Bloomington, IL 61702-2900
Phone: 309-556-3031 · **Financial Aid Phone:** 309-556-3096
E-mail: iwuadmit@iwu.edu · **CEEB Code:** 1320
Fax: 309-556-3820 · **Website:** www.iwu.edu · **ACT Code:** 1044

This private school was founded in 1850. It has a 80-acre campus.

RATINGS

Admissions Selectivity Rating: 88   **Fire Safety Rating:** 89

STUDENTS AND FACULTY

Enrollment: 1,883. **Student Body:** 56% female, 44% male, 11% out-of-state, 8% international (24 countries represented). Asian 4%; African American 5%; Caucasian 71%, Hispanic 7%, Native American <1%
Retention and Graduation: 92% freshmen return for sophomore year. 75% freshmen graduate within 4 years. 30% grads go on to further study within 1 year. **Faculty:** 155 full-time faculty, 90% hold PhDs, 45% are members of minority groups, 10% are women. 0% of classes are taught by teaching assistants.

ACADEMICS

Degrees: bachelor's. **Classes:** Most classes have 10–19 students. Most lab/discussion sessions have 10–19 students. **Majors with Highest Enrollment:** Business/Commerce; Psychology; Biology/Biological Sciences. **Special Study Options:** double major, exchange student program (domestic), honors program, independent study, internships, student-designed major, study abroad, teacher certification program. **Honors programs:** IWU offers a research honors designation to eligible senior students who successfully complete and defend an intensive, advanced research or creative project under the direction of an interdisciplinary faculty committee. Performance Honors designations are also available in the Art, Music, and Theatre Arts. Combined degree programs: 3-2 prgrms--Engrng, Forestry, or Environ. **Disability Services:** Special programs offered to physically disabled students include note-taking services, reader services, tape recorders, tutors. **Career services:** Alumni network, alumni services, career/job search classes, career assessment, internships, regional alumni. Career services highlights include The Action Research Center, which links students in seminar and internships classes with community partners, such as social service and non-profit agencies. Students in these classes work with the partners on major projects intended to have a lasting, positive impact on the community. Projects have been as varied as those on environmental issues, historic preservation, pre-school education, crisis intervention, mentoring troubled youth, drug courts, living wage legislation, and ESL tutoring. See http://www2.iwu.edu/action/ for more details.

FACILITIES

Housing: Coed dorms, special housing for disabled students, special housing for international students, fraternity/sorority housing, apartments for single students, Groups of students with common curricular or cocurricular interests can propose and implement theme housing consistent with their educational goals in a limited number of residential buildings. Examples of past and current interest areas include the arts, languages, environmentalism, multi-faith issues, wellness, culinary arts, and internationalism. 80% of campus accessible to physically disabled. **Special Academic Facilities/Equipment:** observa-

tory, computerized music lab, graphic design studio, Ames Library archives and special collections, visual anthropology lab, social science lab. **Computers:** 60% of classrooms, 100% of libraries, 100% of dining areas, 100% of student union, have wireless network access. Students can register for classes online. Administrative functions (other than registration) can be performed online.

CAMPUS LIFE

Environment: City. **Activities:** Choral groups, concert band, dance, drama/theater, jazz band, literary magazine, music ensembles, musical theater, opera, pep band, radio station, student government, student newspaper, student-run film society, symphony orchestra, television station, yearbook, Campus Ministries, International Student Organization, Model UN. 165 registered organizations, 29 honor societies, 15 religious organizations. 6 fraternities, 5 sororities. **Athletics (Intercollegiate):** *Men:* baseball, basketball, cross-country, diving, football, golf, soccer, swimming, tennis, track/field (outdoor), track/field (indoor). *Women:* basketball, cross-country, diving, golf, soccer, softball, swimming, tennis, track/field (outdoor), track/field (indoor), volleyball. **On-Campus Highlights:** Ames Library, Hansen Student Center, Shirk Center for Athletics and Wellness, Center for Natural Science, The Dugout (snack bar and coffee shop). **Environmental Initiatives:** IWU has a commitment to environmental sustainability in its mission statement. IWU signed the Talloires Declaration. IWU signed the Illinois Sustainability Compact on July 22, 2009. Our Welcome Center (admissions office) is LEED certified.

ADMISSIONS

Freshman Academic Profile: Average high school GPA 3.77. 38% in top 10% of high school class, 76% in top 25% of high school class, 99% in top 50% of high school class. 73% from public high schools. SAT Math middle 50% range 660-760. SAT Critical Reading middle 50% range 490-620. ACT middle 50% range 25-30. Minimum internet-based TOEFL 80. Minimum paper TOEFL 550. **Basis for Candidate Selection:** *Very important factors considered include:* academic GPA, rigor of secondary school record, interview. *Important factors considered include:* Class rank, application essay, standardized test scores, character/personal qualities, extracurricular activities, talent/ability. *Other factors considered include:* recommendation(s), alumni/ae relation, first generation, geographical residence, level of applicant's interest, racial/ethnic status, state residency, volunteer work, work experience. **Freshman Admission Requirements:** High school diploma is required and GED is accepted. **Freshman Admission Statistics:** 3,427 applied, 60% admitted, 22% enrolled. **Transfer Admission Requirements:** High school transcript, college transcript(s), essay or personal statement, standardized test scores, Minimum college GPA of 2.0 required. Lowest grade transferable C-. **General Admission Information:** Notification on a rolling basis, beginning on or about 12/15. Nonfall registration accepted. Admission may be deferred for a maximum of 1 year. Credit and/or placement offered for CEEB Advanced Placement tests.

COSTS AND FINANCIAL AID

Annual tuition $37,774. Room and board $8,838. Required fees $180. Average book expense $800. **Required Forms and Deadlines:** FAFSA, Institution's own financial aid form. **Notification of Awards:** Applicants will be notified of awards on a rolling basis beginning 2/15. **Types of Aid:** *Need-based scholarships/grants:* Federal Pell, SEOG, state scholarships/grants, private scholarships, the school's own gift aid. *Loans:* Subsidized Stafford, Unsubsidized Stafford, PLUS, Federal Perkins, Federal Nursing, college/university loans from institutional funds. *Student Employment:* Federal Work-Study Program available. Institutional employment available. Off-campus job opportunities are good. **Financial Aid Statistics:** 100% freshmen, 100% undergrads receive need-based scholarship or grant aid. 14% freshmen, 9% undergrads receive non-need-based scholarship or grant aid. 79% freshmen, 86% undergrads receive need-based self-help aid. 0% freshmen, 0% undergrads receive athletic scholarships. 100% freshmen, 98% undergrads receive any aid. 69% undergrads borrow to pay for school. Average cumulative indebtedness $25,085. **Criteria for awarding institutional aid:** *Non-need-based:* academics, art, music/drama.

IMMACULATA UNIVERSITY

1145 King Road, Immaculata, PA 19345-0642
Phone: 610-647-4400 x3060 · **Financial Aid Phone:** 877-428-6329
E-mail: admiss@immaculata.edu · **CEEB Code:** 2320
Fax: 610-640-0836 · **Website:** www.immaculata.edu · **ACT Code:** 3596

This private school, affiliated with the Roman Catholic Church, was founded in 2000. It has a 400-acre campus.

RATINGS

Admissions Selectivity Rating: 72   **Fire Safety Rating:** 78

STUDENTS AND FACULTY

Enrollment: 2,012. **Student Body:** 75% female, 25% male, 26% out-of-state, 1% international. Asian 2%, African American 15%, Caucasian 73%, Hispanic 5%, Native American <1%
Retention and Graduation: 80% freshmen return for sophomore year. 51% freshmen graduate within 4 years. **Faculty:** 98 full-time faculty, 82% hold PhDs, 74% are members of minority groups, 5% are women. 0% of classes are taught by teaching assistants.

ACADEMICS

Degrees: associate, bachelor's, certificate, post-bachelor's certificate. **Majors with Highest Enrollment:** Registered Nursing/Registered Nurse; Business Administration and Management; Human Resources Management and Services. **Special Study Options:** Accelerated program, cooperative education program, cross-registration, distance learning, double major, dual enrollment, external degree program, honors program, independent study, internships, liberal arts/career combination, study abroad, teacher certification program. **Disability Services:** Special programs offered to physically disabled students include note-taking services, reader services, tape recorders, tutors. **Career services:** career assessment, internships.

FACILITIES

Housing: No housing is available for CLL students. 100% of campus accessible to physically disabled. **Special Academic Facilities/Equipment:** Annual art show on-campus. **Computers:** Administrative functions (other than registration) can be performed online.

CAMPUS LIFE

Environment: Town. **Activities:** Choral groups, dance, drama/theater, literary magazine, music ensembles, musical theater, student government, student newspaper, symphony orchestra, yearbook. 28 registered organizations, 14 honor societies, 1 religious organization. **Athletics (Intercollegiate):** *Men:* basketball, golf, soccer, tennis. *Women:* basketball, cross-country, field hockey, golf, lacrosse, soccer, softball, tennis, volleyball. **On-Campus Highlights:** Java Hut, Pool, Weight Room.

ADMISSIONS

Freshman Academic Profile: Average high school GPA 3.21. SAT Math middle 50% range 430-530. SAT Critical Reading middle 50% range 440-530. SAT Writing middle 50% range 430-540. ACT middle 50% range 17-23. Minimum paper TOEFL 500. **Basis for Candidate Selection:** *Important factors considered include:* level of applicant's interest. *Other factors considered include:* character/personal qualities, interview, work experience. **Freshman Admission Requirements:** High school diploma is required and GED is accepted. **Freshman Admission Statistics:** 1,729 applied, 76% admitted, 17% enrolled. **Transfer Admission Requirements:** High school transcript, college transcript(s), Minimum college GPA of 2.0 required. Lowest grade transferable C. **General Admission Information:** Application Fee $50. Nonfall registration accepted. Admission may be deferred for a maximum of 1 Year. Credit and/or placement offered for CEEB Advanced Placement tests.

COSTS AND FINANCIAL AID

Annual tuition $29,000. Room and board $11,740. Required fees $0. Average book expense $1,790. **Required Forms and Deadlines:** FAFSA. **Notification of Awards:** Applicants will be notified of awards on a rolling basis beginning 2/1. **Types of Aid:** *Need-based scholarships/grants:* Federal Pell, state scholarships/grants, private scholarships, United Negro College Fund. *Loans:* Subsidized Stafford, Unsubsidized Stafford, PLUS, Federal Perkins. *Student Employment:* Federal Work-Study Program available. Institutional employment available. Highest amount earned per year from on-campus jobs $1,053. Off-campus job opportunities are good. **Financial Aid Statistics:** 35% undergrads receive need-based scholarship or grant aid. 5% undergrads receive non-need-based scholarship or grant aid. 73% undergrads receive need-based self-help aid. 0% undergrads receive athletic scholarships. 34% undergrads receive any aid. 80% undergrads borrow to pay for school.

INDIANA INSTITUTE OF TECHNOLOGY

1600 East Washington Blvd, Fort Wayne, IN 46803
Phone: 260-422-5561
E-mail: admissions@indtech.edu · **CEEB Code:** 1805
Fax: 260-422-7696 · **Website:** www.indianatech.edu · **ACT Code:** 1208

This private school was founded in 1930. It has a 57-acre campus.

RATINGS

Admissions Selectivity Rating: 61   Fire Safety Rating: 60*

STUDENTS AND FACULTY

Enrollment: 2,985. **Student Body:** 56% female, 44% male, 13% out-of-state, 1% international (14 countries represented). Asian 1%, African American 17%, Caucasian 63%, Hispanic 2%, Native American 1%
Retention and Graduation: 56% freshmen return for sophomore year. 11% freshmen graduate within 4 years. 16% freshmen graduate within 6 years. **Faculty:** 40 full-time faculty, 38% hold PhDs, 30% are members of minority groups, 15% are women. 0% of classes are taught by teaching assistants.

ACADEMICS

Degrees: associate, bachelor's, master's. **Classes:** Most classes have 10–19 students. **Majors with Highest Enrollment:** Electrical and Electronics Engineering; Engineering; Business/Commerce. **Special Study Options:** Accelerated program, cooperative education program, distance learning, double major, external degree program, independent study, internships. **Career services:** alumni services, career assessment, internships.

FACILITIES

Housing: Coed dorms, fraternity/sorority housing, apartments for single students. **Computers:** Students can register for classes online. Undergraduates are required to own a computer.

CAMPUS LIFE

Activities: Choral groups, dance, pep band, student government, student newspaper. 14 registered organizations, 1 honor society, 3 fraternities, 1 sorority. **Athletics (Intercollegiate):** *Men:* baseball, basketball, soccer. *Women:* basketball, soccer, softball.

ADMISSIONS

Freshman Academic Profile: Average high school GPA 2.93. 8% in top 10% of high school class, 27% in top 25% of high school class, 57% in top 50% of high school class. 80% from public high schools. Minimum paper TOEFL 500. **Basis for Candidate Selection:** *Very important factors considered include:* rigor of secondary school record, alumni/ae relation. *Important factors considered include:* Class rank, standardized test scores, interview, racial/ethnic status. *Other factors considered include:* application essay, recommendation(s), character/personal qualities, extracurricular activities, talent/ability, volunteer work, work experience. **Freshman Admission Requirements:** High school diploma is required and GED is accepted. *Academic units required:* 4 English, 3 mathematics, 2 science. **Freshman Admission Statistics:** 1,989 applied, 92% admitted, 13% enrolled. **Transfer Admission Requirements:** college transcript(s), Minimum college GPA of 2.0 required. Lowest grade transferable C. **General Admission Information:** Application Fee $50. Regular application deadline 9/1. Notification on a rolling basis, beginning on or about 10/15. Nonfall registration accepted. Admission may be deferred for a maximum of 2 years. Credit and/or placement offered for CEEB Advanced Placement tests.

COSTS AND FINANCIAL AID

Average book expense $0. **Required Forms and Deadlines:** FAFSA, Institution's own financial aid form. **Notification of Awards:** Applicants will be notified of awards on a rolling basis beginning 2/2. **Types of Aid:** *Need-based scholarships/grants:* Federal Pell, SEOG, state scholarships/grants, private scholarships, the school's own gift aid, United Negro College Fund. *Loans:* Subsidized Stafford, Unsubsidized Stafford, PLUS, Federal Perkins. *Student Employment:* Federal Work-Study Program available. Institutional employment available. Off-campus job opportunities are good. **Financial Aid Statistics:** 92% freshmen, 82% undergrads receive need-based scholarship or grant aid. 8% freshmen, 5% undergrads receive non-need-based scholarship or grant aid. 89% freshmen, 87% undergrads receive need-based self-help aid. 6% freshmen, 4% undergrads receive athletic scholarships. 73% undergrads borrow to pay for school. **Criteria for awarding institutional aid:** *Non-need-based:* academics, alumni affiliation, athletics, leadership, minority status, music/drama, state/district residency.

INDIANA STATE UNIVERSITY

Office of Admissions, 318 N 6th Street, Terre Haute, IN 47809
Phone: 812-237-2121 · **Financial Aid Phone:** 812-237-2215
E-mail: http://cms.indstate.edu/admissions · **CEEB Code:** 1322
Fax: 812-237-8023 · **Website:** www.indstate.edu · **ACT Code:** 1206

This public school was founded in 1865. It has a 92-acre campus.

RATINGS

Admissions Selectivity Rating: 72   Fire Safety Rating: 86

STUDENTS AND FACULTY

Enrollment: 10,497. **Student Body:** 54% female, 46% male, 15% out-of-state, 6% international (73 countries represented). Asian 1%, African American 19%,

Caucasian 66%, Hispanic 3%, Native American <1%
Retention and Graduation: 20% freshmen graduate within 4 years. 40% freshmen graduate within 6 years. **Faculty:** 477 full-time faculty, 73% hold PhDs, 46% are members of minority groups, 17% are women. 4% of classes are taught by teaching assistants.

ACADEMICS

Degrees: associate, bachelor's, certificate, master's, post-bachelor's certificate, post-master's certificate, terminal associate, transfer associate. **Classes:** Most classes have 20–29 students. **Majors with Highest Enrollment:** Business Administration and Management; Criminology; Registered Nursing/Registered Nurse. **Special Study Options:** Accelerated program, cooperative education program, distance learning, double major, dual enrollment, English as a Second Language (ESL), honors program, independent study, internships, study abroad, teacher certification program. **Honors programs:** University Honors Program. **Disability Services:** Special programs offered to physically disabled students include note-taking services, tape recorders, tutors. **Career services:** alumni services, career assessment, internships. At Indiana State, students from every discipline are able to apply what they are learning through hands-on inquiry and research, and life-changing field experiences. Our students program robots, conduct research alongside expert faculty, assist K-12 teachers in the classroom, analyze artifacts from a major archaeological dig, compose, dance, write and perform. They assist non-profit organizations, sample deep-ocean sediments off the California coast, and care for patients at our community health education center. Experiential learning brings knowledge to life and gives student the kind of real-world understanding that sets you apart from students at other institutions.

FACILITIES

Housing: Coed dorms, special housing for disabled students, men's dorms, women's dorms, fraternity/sorority housing, apartments for married students, apartments for single students, Theme Housing, Special housing for freshmen, and apartments for students with dependent children. 98% of campus accessible to physically disabled. **Special Academic Facilities/Equipment:** Music hall, art gallery, civic center, museum, flight simulator, audio-visual center, observatory, theaters. **Computers:** 100% of classrooms, 100% of dorms, 100% of libraries, 100% of dining areas, 100% of student union, have wireless network access. Students can register for classes online. Administrative functions (other than registration) can be performed online. Undergraduates are required to own a computer.

CAMPUS LIFE

Environment: Town. **Activities:** Choral groups, concert band, dance, drama/theater, jazz band, literary magazine, marching band, music ensembles, musical theater, pep band, radio station, student government, student newspaper, student-run film society, symphony orchestra, yearbook, Campus Ministries, International Student Organization. 130 registered organizations, 19 honor societies, 13 religious organizations. 11 fraternity, 10 sororities. **Athletics (Intercollegiate):** *Men:* baseball, basketball, cross-country, football, track/field (outdoor), track/field (indoor). *Women:* basketball, cross-country, golf, soccer, softball, track/field (outdoor), track/field (indoor), volleyball. **On-Campus Highlights:** Hulman Memorial Student Union, Student Recreation Center, John C. Hook's Memorial Observatory, Cunningham Memorial Library, Three Art Galleries, The Hulman Memorial Student Union Building contains the University Bookstore, The Commons(food court), Le Club(exercise club),etc. Various Libraries—Cunningham Memorial (main), Women Study, Arts and Science, etc. **Environmental Initiatives:** The signing of the American Colleges & Universities President's Climate Commitment that resulted in the development of a Climate Action Plan and three rounds of carbon footprint analyses. ISU's commitment to sustainability through a $1 million internal grant over the next five years for the Institute for Community Sustainability (http://unboundedpossibilities.com/ICS); Public and Campus Recycling efforts since 1989.

ADMISSIONS

Freshman Academic Profile: Average high school GPA 3.07. 9% in top 10% of high school class, 27% in top 25% of high school class, 64% in top 50% of high school class. SAT Math middle 50% range 400-510. SAT Critical Reading middle 50% range 410-510. SAT Writing middle 50% range 390-480. ACT middle 50% range 16-22. Minimum internet-based TOEFL 61. Minimum paper TOEFL 500. **Basis for Candidate Selection:** *Very important factors considered include:* Class rank, academic GPA, rigor of secondary school record. *Important factors considered include:* application essay, recommendation(s), standardized test scores. *Other factors considered include:* character/personal qualities, extracurricular activities, interview, talent/ability. **Freshman Admission Requirements:** High school diploma is required and GED is accepted. **Freshman Admission Statistics:** 11,258 applied, 83% admitted, 29% enrolled. **Transfer Admission Requirements:** college transcript(s), Minimum college GPA of 2.0 required. Lowest grade transferable C. **General Admission Information:** Application Fee $25. Regular application deadline 8/15. Nonfall registration accepted. Admission may be deferred for a maximum of 12 months. Credit offered for CEEB Advanced Placement tests.

COSTS AND FINANCIAL AID

Annual in-state tuition $8,216. Annual out-of-state tuition $18,146. Room and board $9,182. Required fees $200. Average book expense $1,110. **Required Forms and Deadlines:** FAFSA. **Notification of Awards:** Applicants will be notified of awards on a rolling basis beginning 4/15. **Types of Aid:** *Need-based scholarships/grants:* Federal Pell, SEOG, state scholarships/grants, private scholarships, the school's own gift aid. *Loans:* Subsidized Stafford, Unsubsidized Stafford, PLUS, Federal Perkins, Alternative Loans. *Student Employment:* Federal Work-Study Program available. Institutional employment available. Highest amount earned per year from on-campus jobs $13,370. Off-campus job opportunities are good. **Financial Aid Statistics:** 70% freshmen, 65% undergrads receive need-based scholarship or grant aid. 78% freshmen, 59% undergrads receive non-need-based scholarship or grant aid. 73% freshmen, 75% undergrads receive need-based self-help aid. 2% freshmen, 3% undergrads receive athletic scholarships. 80% freshmen, 72% undergrads receive any aid. 72% undergrads borrow to pay for school. Average cumulative indebtedness $23,847. **Criteria for awarding institutional aid:** *Non-need-based:* academics, alumni affiliation, art, athletics, minority status, music/drama, state/district residency.

INDIANA UNIVERSITY—BLOOMINGTON

300 North Jordan Avenue, Bloomington, IN 47405-1106
Phone: 812-855-0661 · **Financial Aid Phone:** 812-855-6500
E-mail: iuadmit@indiana.edu · **CEEB Code:** 1324
Fax: 812-855-5102 · **Website:** www.iub.edu · **ACT Code:** 1210

This public school was founded in 1820. It has a 1937-acre campus.

RATINGS

Admissions Selectivity Rating: 87   **Fire Safety Rating:** 81

STUDENTS AND FACULTY

Enrollment: 32,252. **Student Body:** 50% female, 50% male, 27% out-of-state, 11% international (148 countries represented). Asian 4%, African American 4%, Caucasian 72%, Hispanic 5%, Native American <1%
Retention and Graduation: 59% freshmen graduate within 4 years. 78% freshmen graduate within 6 years. **Faculty:** 2,047 full-time faculty, 78% hold PhDs, 39% are members of minority groups, 19% are women.

ACADEMICS

Degrees: bachelor's, certificate, diploma, doctoral, master's, post-bachelor's certificate, post-master's certificate. **Classes:** Most classes have 20–29 students. Most lab/discussion sessions have 20–29 students. **Majors with Highest Enrollment:** Business/Commerce; Kinesiology and Exercise Science; Public Administration. **Special Study Options:** Accelerated program, cooperative education program, distance learning, double major, dual enrollment, English as a Second Language (ESL), external degree program, honors program, independent study, internships, liberal arts/career combination, student-designed major, study abroad, teacher certification program. **Honors programs:** Hutton Honors College and the Hudson/Holland Scholar Programs. **Disability Services:** Special programs offered to physically disabled students include note-taking services, reader services, tape recorders, tutors. **Career services:** Alumni network, career/job search classes, career assessment, internships. Career services highlights include the New IU Alumni Connections Program that we initated this year, which brings back successful alumni to work with current students.

FACILITIES

Housing: Coed dorms, special housing for disabled students, men's dorms, special housing for international students, women's dorms, fraternity/sorority housing, apartments for married students, cooperative housing, apartments for single students, Apartments for students with dependent children. Residential language houses, and living/learning centers available, wellness center, African-American living/learning. Honor College floors, First-Year Academic Interest Group Housing; Suites for 2, 3 students. 95% of campus accessible to physically disabled. **Special Academic Facilities/Equipment:** Art Gallery, folklore, radio station, natural history museum, TV station, art museum, Mathers Museum of World Cultures, Kirkwood Observatory, Hilltop Garden and Nature Center, Arboretum, Student Recreational Sports and Aquatic Center, Auditorium, Beck Chapel, Golf Driving Range, Musical Arts Center, Health Physical Education and Recreation facilities (HPER), indoor swimming, outdoor swimming, Wildermuth Intramural Center (in HPER complex), cyclotron, Lilly Library, and more than 70 research centers. **Computers:** Students can register for classes online. Administrative functions (other than registration) can be performed online.

CAMPUS LIFE

Environment: City. **Activities:** Choral groups, concert band, dance, drama/theater, jazz band, literary magazine, marching band, music ensembles, musical theater, opera, radio station, student government, student newspaper, symphony orchestra, television station, yearbook, Campus Ministries, International Student Organization 9 religious organizations. **Athletics (Intercollegiate):** *Men:* baseball, basketball, cheerleading, cross-country, diving, football, golf, soccer, swimming, tennis, track/field (outdoor), wrestling. *Women:* basketball, cheerleading, cross-country, diving, field hockey, golf, soccer, softball, swimming, tennis, track/field (outdoor), volleyball, water polo. **On-Campus Highlights:** Indiana Memorial Union, Art Museum, Lilly Library, Assembly Hall, Student Recreational Sports Center. **Environmental Initiatives:** Established an office of sustainability in 2009 with two full time staff and 18 interns. Director of Sustainability reports to the Provost and the Vice President for Capital Projects and Facilities. A Campus Sustainability Advisory Board composed of 40 representatives of faculty, staff and students includes seven working groups staffed by nearly 200 volunteers. A Student Sustainability Council, with 22 member student organizations, advises the Office of Sustainability and also administers its own initiatives. Energy Challenge is an annual competition, conceived of and ran by student sustainability interns, to see which campus unit can most reduce its energy and water consumption based on a 3-year baseline for their own buildings. The 2010 competition included all 11 residence halls on the Bloomington campus, 26 Greek houses and 8 academic buildings competing in three separate divisions. Community based social marketing techniques are used to improve peer-to-peer learning. The Residence Hall Association is the student group most active in the residence hall competition, Greeks Go Green assist with influencing normative behavior in the Greek houses and Green Teams trade best practices in the academic buildings. In four weeks, these 14,000 participants saved over 2.5 million gallons of water and over 1 million kilowatt hours of electricity, or the equivalent of over 1000 households. The high profile of this competition, which has become a campus tradition leading up to Earth Day, has led to accelerated implementation of metering on campus and drawn attention to the need for and the paths to energy and water conservation. The Fall Energy challenge involved 11 residence halls, 27 Greek houses and 19 academic buildings encompassing over 6 million square feet and 18,000 occupants. In total, the four Energy Challenge competitions since 2008 have conserved 2,753,850 kWh of electricity and 6,061,365 gallons of water. This is enough electricity to power 2,753 average American homes for 12 weeks and enough water to fill more than 10 Olympic sized swimming pools! Approximately 4,392,252 pounds of CO_2 emissions have been avoided and $199,469 in utility savings have been achieved because of the Energy Challenge. E-Waste Days Sustainability Interns Kristin Hanks and Laura Knudsen wanted to create an electronic waste recycling program in a manner that would allow certification that the waste did not get shipped overseas to sweat shops or wind up in landfills. Another Sustainability Intern, Susan Coleman Morse, worked with various campus departments to strengthen campus e-waste recycling efforts. In collaboration with various IU departments, campuses and communities, Apple Inc and Sims Recycling, these dedicated students organized an effort that in two years has diverted more than a million pounds of electronic waste from the landfill at locations on this campus and other IU regional campuses. E-Waste Days were three-day events that invited corporations, institutions and the general public to participate. Apple Inc officials called this one of the best organized e-waste recycling efforts in the United States.

ADMISSIONS

Freshman Academic Profile: Average high school GPA 3.63. 33.1% in top 10% of high school class, 68.8% in top 25% of high school class, 95.3% in top 50% of high school class. SAT Math middle 50% range 540-660. SAT Critical Reading middle 50% range 520-630. SAT Writing middle 50% range 510-620. ACT middle 50% range 24-30. Minimum internet-based TOEFL 79. Minimum paper TOEFL 550. **Basis for Candidate Selection:** *Very important factors considered include:* Class rank, academic GPA, rigor of secondary school record. *Important factors considered include:* standardized test scores. *Other factors considered include:* application essay, recommendation(s), alumni/ae relation, character/personal qualities, extracurricular activities, first generation, geographical residence, interview, level of applicant's interest, racial/ethnic status, state residency, talent/ability, volunteer work, work experience. **Freshman Admission Requirements:** High school diploma is required and GED is accepted. *Academic units required:* 4 English, 3 mathematics, 1 science, (1 science labs), 2 social studies, 4 academic electives. **Freshman Admission Statistics:** 36,362 applied, 76% admitted, 28% enrolled. **Transfer Admission Requirements:** college transcript(s), Minimum college GPA of 2.0 required. Lowest grade transferable C. **General Admission Information:** Application Fee $55. Nonfall registration accepted. Admission may be deferred for a maximum of 1 year. Credit and/or placement offered for CEEB Advanced Placement tests.

COSTS AND FINANCIAL AID

Annual in-state tuition $9,087. Annual out-of-state tuition $31,940. Room and board $9,493. Required fees $1,301. Average book expense $1,500. **Required**

Forms and Deadlines: FAFSA. **Notification of Awards:** Applicants will be notified of awards on a rolling basis beginning 4/1. **Types of Aid:** *Need-based scholarships/grants:* Federal Pell, SEOG, state scholarships/grants, private scholarships, the school's own gift aid. *Loans:* Direct Subsidized Stafford, Direct Unsubsidized Stafford, Direct PLUS, Federal Perkins, college/university loans from institutional funds. *Student Employment:* Federal Work-Study Program available. Institutional employment available. Off-campus job opportunities are good. **Financial Aid Statistics:** 77% freshmen, 80% undergrads receive need-based scholarship or grant aid. 17% freshmen, 12% undergrads receive non-need-based scholarship or grant aid. 51% freshmen, 61% undergrads receive need-based self-help aid. 1% freshmen, 1% undergrads receive athletic scholarships. 71% freshmen receive any aid. 51% undergrads borrow to pay for school. Average cumulative indebtedness $22,462. **Criteria for awarding institutional aid:** *Non-need-based:* academics, art, athletics, leadership, minority status, music/drama, religious affiliation.

INDIANA UNIVERSITY EAST

2325 Chester Boulevard, Richmond, IN 47374-1289
Phone: 765-973-8208 · **Financial Aid Phone:** 765-973-8206
E-mail: applynow@iue.edu · **CEEB Code:** 1194
Fax: 765-973-8209 · **Website:** www.iue.edu · **ACT Code:** 1216

This public school was founded in 1971. It has a 182-acre campus.

RATINGS

Admissions Selectivity Rating: 78   **Fire Safety Rating:** 60*

STUDENTS AND FACULTY

Enrollment: 3,200. **Student Body:** 65% female, 35% male, 25% out-of-state, 1% international (37 countries represented). Asian 1%, African American 4%, Caucasian 88%, Hispanic 3%, Native American <1%
Retention and Graduation: 9% freshmen graduate within 4 years. 27% freshmen graduate within 6 years. **Faculty:** 105 full-time faculty, 63% hold PhDs, 65% are members of minority groups, 18% are women.

ACADEMICS

Degrees: associate, bachelor's, master's, post-bachelor's certificate. **Classes:** Most classes have 10-19 students. **Majors with Highest Enrollment:** Psychology; Registered Nursing/Registered Nurse; Business/Commerce. **Special Study Options:** cooperative education program, cross-registration, distance learning, double major, dual enrollment, external degree program, honors program, independent study, internships, teacher certification program, weekend college, State-wide technology program with Purdue University. **Disability Services:** Special programs offered to physically disabled students include note-taking services, reader services, tape recorders, tutors.

FACILITIES

Computers: Students can register for classes online. Administrative functions (other than registration) can be performed online.

CAMPUS LIFE

Environment: Town. **Activities:** drama/theater, literary magazine, student government, student newspaper, television station. **Athletics (Intercollegiate):** *Men:* basketball, golf. *Women:* volleyball.

ADMISSIONS

Freshman Academic Profile: Average high school GPA 3.2. 10.9% in top 10% of high school class, 36.9% in top 25% of high school class, 72.9% in top 50% of high school class. SAT Math middle 50% range 420-520. SAT Critical Reading middle 50% range 410-510. SAT Writing middle 50% range 390-490. ACT middle 50% range 18-23. Minimum internet-based TOEFL 79. Minimum paper TOEFL 550. **Basis for Candidate Selection:** *Very important factors considered include:* rigor of secondary school record, standardized test scores. *Important factors considered include:* Class rank, academic GPA. *Other factors considered include:* geographical residence, state residency. **Freshman Admission Requirements:** High school diploma is required and GED is accepted. *Academic units required:* 4 English, 3 mathematics, 1 science, (1 science labs), 2 social studies. **Freshman Admission Statistics:** 1,388 applied, 64% admitted, 47% enrolled. **Transfer Admission Requirements:** college transcript(s), Minimum college GPA of 2.0 required. Lowest grade transferable C. **General Admission Information:** Application Fee $35. Notification on a rolling basis, beginning on or about 9/1. Nonfall registration accepted. Admission may be deferred for a maximum of Contact campus.

COSTS AND FINANCIAL AID

Annual in-state tuition $6,196. Annual out-of-state tuition $17,490. Required fees $591. **Required Forms and Deadlines:** FAFSA, Institution's own financial aid form. **Notification of Awards:** Applicants will be notified of awards on a rolling basis beginning 5/1. **Types of Aid:** *Need-based scholarships/grants:* Federal Pell, SEOG, state scholarships/grants, private scholarships, the school's own gift aid. *Loans:* Direct Subsidized Stafford, Direct Unsubsidized Stafford, Direct PLUS, Federal Perkins, college/university loans from institutional funds. **Financial Aid Statistics:** 87% freshmen, 83% undergrads receive need-based scholarship or grant aid. 5% freshmen, 3% undergrads receive non-need-based scholarship or grant aid. 51% freshmen, 68% undergrads receive need-based self-help aid. 4% freshmen, 2% undergrads receive athletic scholarships. 95% freshmen receive any aid. 78% undergrads borrow to pay for school. Average cumulative indebtedness $29,179. **Criteria for awarding institutional aid:** *Non-need-based:* academics, alumni affiliation, leadership.

Types of Aid: *Need-based scholarships/grants:* Federal Pell, SEOG, state scholarships/grants, private scholarships, the school's own gift aid. *Loans:* Direct Subsidized Stafford, Direct Unsubsidized Stafford, Direct PLUS, Federal Perkins, Federal Nursing, college/university loans from institutional funds. *Student Employment:* Federal Work-Study Program available. Institutional employment available. **Financial Aid Statistics:** 83% freshmen, 81% undergrads receive need-based scholarship or grant aid. 3% freshmen, 2% undergrads receive non-need-based scholarship or grant aid. 48% freshmen, 66% undergrads receive need-based self-help aid. 0% freshmen, 0% undergrads receive athletic scholarships. 86% freshmen receive any aid. 74% undergrads borrow to pay for school. Average cumulative indebtedness $25,394. **Criteria for awarding institutional aid:** *Non-need-based:* academics.

INDIANA UNIVERSITY—KOKOMO

2300 South Washington Street, Kokomo, IN 46904-9003
Phone: 765-455-9217 · **Financial Aid Phone:** 765-455-9216
E-mail: iuadmis@iuk.edu · **CEEB Code:** 1337
Fax: 765-455-9537 · **Website:** www.iuk.edu · **ACT Code:** 1219

This public school was founded in 1945. It has a 51-acre campus.

RATINGS

Admissions Selectivity Rating: 75   **Fire Safety Rating:** 60*

STUDENTS AND FACULTY

Enrollment: 2,724. **Student Body:** 68% female, 32% male, 0% out-of-state, 0% international (25 countries represented). Asian 1%, African American 4%, Caucasian 84%, Hispanic 5%, Native American <1%
Retention and Graduation: 64% freshmen return for sophomore year. 9% freshmen graduate within 4 years. 27% freshmen graduate within 6 years. **Faculty:** 114 full-time faculty, 60% hold PhDs, 61% are members of minority groups, 14% are women.

ACADEMICS

Degrees: associate, bachelor's, certificate, master's, post-bachelor's certificate. **Classes:** Most classes have 20–29 students. Most lab/discussion sessions have 20–29 students. **Majors with Highest Enrollment:** Business/Commerce; Registered Nursing/Registered Nurse; Psychology. **Special Study Options:** Accelerated program, cross-registration, distance learning, double major, dual enrollment, external degree program, honors program, independent study, internships, liberal arts/career combination, study abroad, teacher certification program. **Disability Services:** Special programs offered to physically disabled students include note-taking services, reader services, tutors. **Career services:** alumni services, career/job search classes, career assessment, internships.

FACILITIES

Housing: Special Academic Facilities/Equipment: Observatory, Art Gallery. **Computers:** Students can register for classes online. Administrative functions (other than registration) can be performed online.

CAMPUS LIFE

Environment: Village. **Activities:** Choral groups, drama/theater, music ensembles, student government, student newspaper.

ADMISSIONS

Freshman Academic Profile: Average high school GPA 3.08. 8.16% in top 10% of high school class, 30.54% in top 25% of high school class, 70.29% in top 50% of high school class. SAT Math middle 50% range 420-520. SAT Critical Reading middle 50% range 410-520. SAT Writing middle 50% range 400-490. ACT middle 50% range 17-22. Minimum internet-based TOEFL 61. Minimum paper TOEFL 530. **Basis for Candidate Selection:** *Very important factors considered include:* Class rank, rigor of secondary school record. *Important factors considered include:* standardized test scores. *Other factors considered include:* recommendation(s). **Freshman Admission Requirements:** High school diploma is required and GED is accepted. *Academic units required:* 4 English, 3 mathematics, 1 science, 2 social studies. **Freshman Admission Statistics:** 1,408 applied, 67% admitted, 56% enrolled. **Transfer Admission Requirements:** college transcript(s), Minimum college GPA of 2.0 required. Lowest grade transferable C. **General Admission Information:** Application Fee $45. Nonfall registration accepted. Admission may be deferred for a maximum of Contact admissions. Credit and/or placement offered for CEEB Advanced Placement tests.

COSTS AND FINANCIAL AID

Annual in-state tuition $6,220. Annual out-of-state tuition $17,490. Required fees $591. **Required Forms and Deadlines:** FAFSA. **Notification of Awards:** Applicants will be notified of awards on a rolling basis beginning 5/1.

INDIANA UNIVERSITY NORTHWEST

3400 Broadway, Gary, IN 46408-1197
Phone: 219-980-6991 · **Financial Aid Phone:** 209-980-6778
E-mail: admit@iun.edu · **CEEB Code:** 1338
Fax: 219-981-4219 · **Website:** www.iun.edu · **ACT Code:** 1218

This public school was founded in 1948. It has a 38-acre campus.

RATINGS

Admissions Selectivity Rating: 72   **Fire Safety Rating:** 60*

STUDENTS AND FACULTY

Enrollment: 4,370. **Student Body:** 69% female, 31% male, 2% out-of-state, 0% international (34 countries represented). Asian 2%, African American 18%, Caucasian 56%, Hispanic 19%, Native American <1%
Retention and Graduation: 9% freshmen graduate within 4 years. 29% freshmen graduate within 6 years. **Faculty:** 176 full-time faculty, 71% hold PhDs, 53% are members of minority groups, 27% are women.

ACADEMICS

Degrees: associate, bachelor's, certificate, master's, post-bachelor's certificate. **Classes:** Most classes have 20–29 students. Most lab/discussion sessions have 20–29 students. **Majors with Highest Enrollment:** Business/Commerce; Registered Nursing/Registered Nurse; General Studies. **Special Study Options:** Accelerated program, cooperative education program, distance learning, double major, dual enrollment, external degree program, independent study, internships, liberal arts/career combination, student-designed major, study abroad, teacher certification program, weekend college. **Disability Services:** Special programs offered to physically disabled students include reader services, tape recorders, tutors. **Career services:** alumni services, career/job search classes, career assessment, internships.

FACILITIES

Computers: Students can register for classes online. Administrative functions (other than registration) can be performed online.

CAMPUS LIFE

Activities: Choral groups, dance, drama/theater, literary magazine, musical theater, radio station, student government, student newspaper, International Student Organization. 60 registered organizations, 4 honor societies, 2 religious organizations. 2 fraternities, 3 sororities. **Athletics (Intercollegiate):** *Men:* baseball, basketball, cheerleading, golf. *Women:* basketball, cheerleading, volleyball.

ADMISSIONS

Freshman Academic Profile: Average high school GPA 2.88. 7.89% in top 10% of high school class, 27.51% in top 25% of high school class, 62.92% in top 50% of high school class. SAT Math middle 50% range 400-510. SAT Critical Reading middle 50% range 390-510. SAT Writing middle 50% range 390-490. ACT middle 50% range 17-22. Minimum internet-based TOEFL 71. Minimum paper TOEFL 530. **Basis for Candidate Selection:** *Very important factors considered include:* Class rank, academic GPA, rigor of secondary school record, standardized test scores. *Other factors considered include:* recommendation(s). **Freshman Admission Requirements:** High school diploma is required and GED is accepted. *Academic units required:* 4 English, 3 mathematics, 2 science, 2 social studies, 4 academic electives. **Freshman Admission Statistics:** 1,658 applied, 77% admitted, 56% enrolled. **Transfer Admission Requirements:** High school transcript, college transcript(s), Minimum college GPA of 2.0 required. Lowest grade transferable C. **General Admission Information:** Application Fee $25. Nonfall registration accepted. Admission may be deferred for a maximum of 2 years. Credit offered for CEEB Advanced Placement tests.

COSTS AND FINANCIAL AID

Annual in-state tuition $6,263. Annual out-of-state tuition $17,490. Required fees $591. **Required Forms and Deadlines:** FAFSA. **Notification of**

Awards: Applicants will be notified of awards on a rolling basis beginning 5/1. **Types of Aid:** *Need-based scholarships/grants:* Federal Pell, SEOG, state scholarships/grants, private scholarships, the school's own gift aid, Federal Nursing Scholarships. *Loans:* Direct Subsidized Stafford, Direct Unsubsidized Stafford, Direct PLUS, Federal Perkins, college/university loans from institutional funds. *Student Employment:* Federal Work-Study Program available. Off-campus job opportunities are good. **Financial Aid Statistics:** 77% freshmen, 79% undergrads receive need-based scholarship or grant aid. 2% freshmen, 1% undergrads receive non-need-based scholarship or grant aid. 46% freshmen, 66% undergrads receive need-based self-help aid. 1% freshmen, 0% undergrads receive athletic scholarships. 81% freshmen receive any aid. 78% undergrads borrow to pay for school. Average cumulative indebtedness $32,094. **Criteria for awarding institutional aid:** *Non-need-based:* academics, athletics.

INDIANA UNIVERSITY OF PENNSYLVANIA

1011 South Drive, Indiana, PA 15705
Phone: 724-357-2230 · **Financial Aid Phone:** 724-357-2218
E-mail: admissions-inquiry@iup.edu · **CEEB Code:** 2652
Fax: 724-357-6281 · **Website:** www.iup.edu · **ACT Code:** 3704

This public school was founded in 1875. It has a 342-acre campus.

RATINGS

Admissions Selectivity Rating: 70   **Fire Safety Rating:** 94

STUDENTS AND FACULTY

Enrollment: 11,774. **Student Body:** 55% female, 45% male, 6% out-of-state, 3% international (62 countries represented). Asian 1%, African American 11%, Caucasian 77%, Hispanic 4%, Native American <1%
Faculty: 616 full-time faculty, 48% are members of minority groups, 17% are women. 0% of classes are taught by teaching assistants.

ACADEMICS

Degrees: associate, bachelor's, certificate, master's, post-bachelor's certificate, post-master's certificate. **Classes:** Most classes have 20–29 students. Most lab/discussion sessions have 10–19 students. **Majors with Highest Enrollment:** Health and Physical Education/Fitness; Criminology; Speech Communication and Rhetoric. **Special Study Options:** Accelerated program, cooperative education program, cross-registration, distance learning, double major, dual enrollment, English as a Second Language (ESL), exchange student program (domestic), external degree program, honors program, independent study, internships, liberal arts/career combination, student-designed major, study abroad, teacher certification program, weekend college. **Honors programs:** Robert E. Cook Honors College. **Disability Services:** Special programs offered to physically disabled students include note-taking services, reader services, tape recorders. **Career services:** Alumni network, alumni services, internships. Career services highlights include a Mock Interview Simulation Program that has 800 participants each year.

FACILITIES

Housing: Coed dorms, special housing for disabled students, special housing for international students, apartments for married students, apartments for single students, Wellness Housing, Theme Housing, Living Learning Communities. 98% of campus accessible to physically disabled. **Special Academic Facilities/Equipment:** Art museum, natural history museum, on-campus elementary school, lodge, farm, co-generation plant, ski slope, sailing base. **Computers:** 90% of classrooms, 60% of dorms, 100% of libraries, 100% of dining areas, 80% of student union, 100% of common outdoor areas have wireless network access. Students can register for classes online. Administrative functions (other than registration) can be performed online.

CAMPUS LIFE

Environment: Village. **Activities:** Choral groups, concert band, dance, drama/theater, jazz band, marching band, music ensembles, musical theater, radio station, student government, student newspaper, symphony orchestra, television station, Campus Ministries, International Student Organization. 210 registered organizations, 23 honor societies, 18 religious organizations. 18 fraternities, 14 sororities. **Athletics (Intercollegiate):** *Men:* baseball, basketball, cross-country, diving, football, golf, swimming, track/field (outdoor), track/field (indoor). *Women:* basketball, cross-country, diving, field hockey, lacrosse, soccer, softball, swimming, tennis, track/field (outdoor), track/field (indoor), volleyball.

On-Campus Highlights: Suites on Grant, Oak Grove, Hadley Union Building Fitness Center/Foo, Stapleton Library, Miller Stadium.

ADMISSIONS

Freshman Academic Profile: 8% in top 10% of high school class, 26% in top 25% of high school class, 60% in top 50% of high school class. SAT Math middle 50% range 430-530. SAT Critical Reading middle 50% range 430-530. SAT Writing middle 50% range 403-510. Minimum internet-based TOEFL 61. Minimum paper TOEFL 500. **Basis for Candidate Selection:** *Very important factors considered include:* academic GPA, standardized test scores. *Important factors considered include:* rigor of secondary school record. *Other factors considered include:* Class rank, application essay, recommendation(s), extracurricular activities. **Freshman Admission Requirements:** High school diploma is required and GED is accepted. **Freshman Admission Statistics:** 8,754 applied, 95% admitted, 33% enrolled. **Transfer Admission Requirements:** High school transcript, college transcript(s), statement of good standing from prior institution(s). Minimum college GPA of 2.0 required. Lowest grade transferable C-. **General Admission Information:** Application Fee $35. Notification on a rolling basis, beginning on or about 9/15. Nonfall registration accepted. Admission may be deferred for a maximum of 1 year. Credit offered for CEEB Advanced Placement tests.

COSTS AND FINANCIAL AID

Annual in-state tuition $6,820. Annual out-of-state tuition $17,050. Room and board $11,490. Required fees $2,650. Average book expense $1,100. **Required Forms and Deadlines:** FAFSA. **Notification of Awards:** Applicants will be notified of awards on a rolling basis beginning 3/15. **Types of Aid:** *Need-based scholarships/grants:* Federal Pell, SEOG, state scholarships/grants, private scholarships, the school's own gift aid, United Negro College Fund. *Loans:* Subsidized Stafford, Unsubsidized Stafford, PLUS, Federal Perkins, Private Alternative Loans. *Student Employment:* Federal Work-Study Program available. Institutional employment available. Highest amount earned per year from on-campus jobs $8,043. Off-campus job opportunities are good. **Financial Aid Statistics:** 65% freshmen, 64% undergrads receive need-based scholarship or grant aid. 32% freshmen, 20% undergrads receive non-need-based scholarship or grant aid. 91% freshmen, 90% undergrads receive need-based self-help aid. 2% freshmen, 2% undergrads receive athletic scholarships. 79% freshmen, 82% undergrads receive any aid. 82% undergrads borrow to pay for school. Average cumulative indebtedness $33,476. **Criteria for awarding institutional aid:** *Non-need-based:* academics, alumni affiliation, art, athletics, job skills, leadership, music/drama, state/district residency.

INDIANA UNIVERSITY—PURDUE UNIVERSITY FORT WAYNE

2101 East Coliseum Boulevard, Fort Wayne, IN 46805-1499
Phone: 260-481-6812
E-mail: ipfwadms@ipfw.edu · **CEEB Code:** 1336
Fax: 260-481-6880 · **Website:** www.ipfw.edu · **ACT Code:** 1217

This public school was founded in 1917. It has a 565-acre campus.

RATINGS

Admissions Selectivity Rating: 70   **Fire Safety Rating:** 60*

STUDENTS AND FACULTY

Enrollment: 10,587. **Student Body:** 58% female, 42% male, 5% out-of-state, 2% international (71 countries represented). Asian 2%, African American 5%, Caucasian 87%, Hispanic 2%, Native American <1%
Retention and Graduation: 60% freshmen return for sophomore year.
Faculty: 329 full-time faculty, 83% hold PhDs, 37% are members of minority groups, 13% are women. 1% of classes are taught by teaching assistants.

ACADEMICS

Degrees: associate, bachelor's, certificate, master's, post-bachelor's certificate, post-master's certificate, terminal associate, transfer associate. **Classes:** Most classes have 20–29 students. Most lab/discussion sessions have 20–29 students. **Majors with Highest Enrollment:** Elementary Education and Teaching; Registered Nursing/Registered Nurse; Business/Commerce. **Special Study Options:** cooperative education program, distance learning, double major, English as a Second Language (ESL), exchange student program (domestic), honors program, independent study, internships, liberal arts/career combination, student-designed major, study abroad, teacher certification program, weekend college. **Disability Services:** Special programs offered to physically disabled students include note-taking services, reader services, tape recorders, tutors. **Career services:** Alumni network, alumni services, career/job search classes, career assessment, internships, regional alumni.

The Princeton Review's Complete Book of Colleges

FACILITIES

Housing: Coed dorms. 100% of campus accessible to physically disabled. **Special Academic Facilities/Equipment:** Williams theatre. recital hall anthropology and geology exhibits art gallery **Computers:** Students can register for classes online. Administrative functions (other than registration) can be performed online.

CAMPUS LIFE

Environment: Village. **Activities:** Choral groups, concert band, dance, drama/theater, jazz band, literary magazine, music ensembles, musical theater, opera, pep band, student government, student newspaper, symphony orchestra, television station. 65 registered organizations, 7 honor societies, 3 religious organizations. 2 fraternities, 3 sororities. **Athletics (Intercollegiate):** *Men:* baseball, basketball, cross-country, soccer, tennis, track/field (outdoor), volleyball. *Women:* basketball, cross-country, soccer, softball, tennis, track/field (outdoor), volleyball.

ADMISSIONS

Freshman Academic Profile: Average high school GPA 2.59. 7% in top 10% of high school class, 24% in top 25% of high school class, 57% in top 50% of high school class. SAT Math middle 50% range 430-550. SAT Critical Reading middle 50% range 420-540. ACT middle 50% range 17-23. Minimum paper TOEFL 550. **Basis for Candidate Selection:** *Very important factors considered include:* Class rank, rigor of secondary school record, standardized test scores. *Other factors considered include:* recommendation(s), state residency. **Freshman Admission Requirements:** High school diploma is required and GED is accepted. *Academic units required:* 4 English, 3 mathematics, 1 science, 1 foreign language, 1 social studies. **Freshman Admission Statistics:** 2,471 applied, 97% admitted, 71% enrolled. **Transfer Admission Requirements:** High school transcript, college transcript(s), Minimum college GPA of 2.0 required. Lowest grade transferable C-. **General Admission Information:** Application Fee $30. Regular application deadline 8/1. Notification on a rolling basis, beginning on or about 12/1. Nonfall registration accepted. Credit and/or placement offered for CEEB Advanced Placement tests.

COSTS AND FINANCIAL AID

Annual in-state tuition $3,508. Annual out-of-state tuition $8,136. Required fees $384. Average book expense $800. **Required Forms and Deadlines:** FAFSA. **Notification of Awards:** Applicants will be notified of awards on or about 4/30. **Types of Aid:** *Need-based scholarships/grants:* Federal Pell, SEOG, state scholarships/grants, private scholarships, Federal Nursing Scholarships. *Loans:* Subsidized Stafford, Unsubsidized Stafford, PLUS, Federal Perkins, Federal Nursing. *Student Employment:* Federal Work-Study Program available. Institutional employment available. Highest amount earned per year from on-campus jobs $1,200. Off-campus job opportunities are excellent. **Financial Aid Statistics:** 56% freshmen, 69% undergrads receive need-based scholarship or grant aid. 22% freshmen, 19% undergrads receive non-need-based scholarship or grant aid. 37% freshmen, 40% undergrads receive need-based self-help aid. 3% freshmen, 3% undergrads receive athletic scholarships. 59% undergrads borrow to pay for school. **Criteria for awarding institutional aid:** *Non-need-based:* academics, alumni affiliation, art, athletics.

INDIANA UNIVERSITY—PURDUE UNIVERSITY INDIANAPOLIS

420 N University Boulevard, Indianapolis, IN 46202
Phone: 317-274-4591 · **Financial Aid Phone:** 317-274-4162
E-mail: apply@iupui.edu · **CEEB Code:** 1325
Fax: 317-278-1862 · **Website:** www.iupui.edu · **ACT Code:** 1214

This public school was founded in 1969. It has a 509-acre campus.

RATINGS

Admissions Selectivity Rating: 79   **Fire Safety Rating:** 89

STUDENTS AND FACULTY

Enrollment: 21,777. **Student Body:** 56% female, 44% male, 2% out-of-state, 4% international (149 countries represented). Asian 4%, African American 10%, Caucasian 72%, Hispanic 6%, Native American <1%
Retention and Graduation: 71% freshmen return for sophomore year. 18% freshmen graduate within 4 years. 44% freshmen graduate within 6 years.
Faculty: 2,220 full-time faculty, 84% hold PhDs, 41% are members of minority groups, 24% are women.

ACADEMICS

Degrees: associate, bachelor's, certificate, doctoral, master's, post-bachelor's certificate. **Classes:** Most classes have 20–29 students. Most lab/discussion sessions have 10–19 students. **Majors with Highest Enrollment:** Registered Nursing/Registered Nurse; Business/Commerce; Psychology. **Special Study Options:** Accelerated program, cooperative education program, cross-registration, distance learning, double major, dual enrollment, English as a Second Language (ESL), exchange student program (domestic), external degree program, honors program, independent study, internships, student-designed major, study abroad, teacher certification program, weekend college. **Honors programs:** The Honors Program provides a challenging campus-wide program for high achieving students from all academic disciplines. Honors Program students have the opportunity to enroll in smaller dynamic classes and to collaborate with faculty in independent study and research projects. Participants in the IUPUI Honors Program will be required to complete at least three credit hours of honors course work each semester. Combined degree programs: BA/MEng, BS /MS;MD/PhD; MA/MPA; MBA/JD. **Disability Services:** Special programs offered to physically disabled students include note-taking services, reader services, tape recorders, tutors.

FACILITIES

Housing: Coed dorms, special housing for international students, apartments for married students, apartments for single students. 90% of campus accessible to physically disabled. **Special Academic Facilities/Equipment:** Inlow Hall-Law School Eskenazi Hall-Herron School of Art and Design Cavanaugh Hall-School of Liberal Arts and IUPUI Enrollment Center University Library-Most high tech library in North America IUPUI Sport Complex-host of 11 Olympic Team Trails White River State Park-Indianapolis' version of the mall in Washington, D.C. **Computers:** 100% of classrooms, 100% of dorms, 100% of libraries, 100% of dining areas, 100% of student union, 100% of common outdoor areas have wireless network access. Students can register for classes online. Administrative functions (other than registration) can be performed online.

CAMPUS LIFE

Environment: Metropolis. **Activities:** Choral groups, concert band, dance, drama/theater, jazz band, literary magazine, music ensembles, pep band, student government, student newspaper, Campus Ministries, International Student Organization. 154 registered organizations, 9 honor societies, 10 religious organizations. 2 fraternities, 1 sorority. **Athletics (Intercollegiate):** *Men:* basketball, cross-country, diving, golf, soccer, swimming, tennis. *Women:* basketball, cross-country, diving, golf, soccer, softball, swimming, tennis, volleyball. **On-Campus Highlights:** IUPUI Sport Complex, University College, Cavanaugh Hall, University Library, Eskenazi Hall, IU Medical Center.

ADMISSIONS

Freshman Academic Profile: Average high school GPA 3.34. 14.89% in top 10% of high school class, 41.96% in top 25% of high school class, 85.54% in top 50% of high school class. SAT Math middle 50% range 440-570. SAT Critical Reading middle 50% range 440-550. SAT Writing middle 50% range 430-530. ACT middle 50% range 19-25. Minimum internet-based TOEFL 79. Minimum paper TOEFL 550. **Basis for Candidate Selection:** *Very important factors considered include:* rigor of secondary school record. *Important factors considered include:* academic GPA. *Other factors considered include:* Class rank, application essay, recommendation(s), standardized test scores, character/personal qualities, first generation, volunteer work, work experience. **Freshman Admission Requirements:** High school diploma is required and GED is accepted. *Academic units required:* 4 English, 3 mathematics, 3 science, (3 science labs), 2 social studies, 2 history, 4 academic electives. **Freshman Admission Statistics:** 12,920 applied, 70% admitted, 43% enrolled. **Transfer Admission Requirements:** college transcript(s), Minimum college GPA of 2.0 required. Lowest grade transferable C. **General Admission Information:** Application Fee $50. Nonfall registration accepted. Admission may be deferred for a maximum of 1 year. Credit and/or placement offered for CEEB Advanced Placement tests.

COSTS AND FINANCIAL AID

Annual in-state tuition $7,878. Annual out-of-state tuition $29,058. Room and board $7,981. Required fees $1,031. Average book expense $1,400. **Required Forms and Deadlines:** FAFSA. **Notification of Awards:** Applicants will be notified of awards on a rolling basis beginning 4/1. **Types of Aid:** *Need-based scholarships/grants:* Federal Pell, SEOG, state scholarships/grants, private scholarships, the school's own gift aid. *Loans:* Direct Subsidized Stafford, Direct Unsubsidized Stafford, Direct PLUS, Federal Perkins, Federal Nursing, college/university loans from institutional funds. *Student Employment:* Federal Work-Study Program available. Institutional employment available. **Financial Aid Statistics:** 83% freshmen, 79% undergrads receive need-based scholarship or grant aid. 7% freshmen, 4% undergrads receive non-need-based scholarship or grant aid. 63% freshmen, 72% undergrads receive need-based self-help aid. 1% freshmen, 1% undergrads receive athletic scholarships. 89% freshmen receive any aid. 73% undergrads borrow to pay for school. Average cumulative indebtedness $28,485. **Criteria for awarding institutional aid:** *Non-need-based:* academics.

INDIANA UNIVERSITY SOUTH BEND

1700 Mishawaka Avenue, South Bend, IN 46634-7111
Phone: 574-520-4834 • **Financial Aid Phone:** 574-520-4357
E-mail: admissions@iusb.edu • **CEEB Code:** 1339
Fax: 574-520-4834 • **Website:** www.iusb.edu • **ACT Code:** 1225

This public school was founded in 1922. It has a 80-acre campus.

RATINGS

Admissions Selectivity Rating: 73   **Fire Safety Rating:** 85

STUDENTS AND FACULTY

Enrollment: 5,398. **Student Body:** 61% female, 39% male, 3% out-of-state, 3% international (76 countries represented). Asian 1%, African American 8%, Caucasian 75%, Hispanic 8%, Native American <1%
Retention and Graduation: 6% freshmen graduate within 4 years. 26% freshmen graduate within 6 years. **Faculty:** 283 full-time faculty, 67% hold PhDs, 48% are members of minority groups, 22% are women.

ACADEMICS

Degrees: associate, bachelor's, certificate, diploma, master's, post-bachelor's certificate. **Classes:** Most classes have 20–29 students. Most lab/discussion sessions have 20–29 students. **Majors with Highest Enrollment:** Registered Nursing/Registered Nurse; Business/Commerce; Elementary Education and Teaching. **Special Study Options:** Accelerated program, cross-registration, distance learning, double major, English as a Second Language (ESL), external degree program, honors program, internships, liberal arts/career combination, study abroad, teacher certification program, weekend college, Electrical, Mechanical Engineering, Computer Technology with Purdue University on Indiana University South Bend Campus. Northern Indiana Consortium for Education (NICE); IUSB is one of six member institutions sharing library resources, faculty expertise, and academic strengths resulting in broadened course opportunities to students. **Disability Services:** Special programs offered to physically disabled students include note-taking services, reader services, tape recorders, tutors. **Career services:** alumni services, career/job search classes, career assessment, internships.

FACILITIES

Housing: Coed dorms, special housing for international students, apartments for single students. **Computers:** Students can register for classes online. Administrative functions (other than registration) can be performed online.

CAMPUS LIFE

Activities: Choral groups, drama/theater, jazz band, literary magazine, music ensembles, musical theater, opera, student government, student newspaper, student-run film society, symphony orchestra. 30 registered organizations, 1 religious organization. 2 fraternities, 1 sorority. **Athletics (Intercollegiate):** *Men:* basketball. *Women:* basketball.

ADMISSIONS

Freshman Academic Profile: Average high school GPA 3.07. 7.07% in top 10% of high school class, 28.44% in top 25% of high school class, 67.76% in top 50% of high school class. SAT Math middle 50% range 420-520. SAT Critical Reading middle 50% range 420-520. SAT Writing middle 50% range 400-500. ACT middle 50% range 17-23. Minimum internet-based TOEFL 71. Minimum paper TOEFL 530. **Basis for Candidate Selection:** *Very important factors considered include:* rigor of secondary school record. *Important factors considered include:* Class rank, academic GPA. *Other factors considered include:* recommendation(s), standardized test scores, extracurricular activities, interview, state residency. **Freshman Admission Requirements:** High school diploma is required and GED is accepted. *Academic units required:* 4 English, 3 mathematics, 1 science, (1 science labs), 2 social studies. **Freshman Admission Statistics:** 2,430 applied, 73% admitted, 53% enrolled. **Transfer Admission Requirements:** college transcript(s), Minimum college GPA of 2.0 required. Lowest grade transferable C. **General Admission Information:** Application Fee $45. Nonfall registration accepted. Admission may be deferred for a maximum of Contact admissions. Neither credit nor placement offered for CEEB Advanced Placement tests.

COSTS AND FINANCIAL AID

Annual in-state tuition $6,314. Annual out-of-state tuition $17,490. Room and board $7,150. Required fees $591. Average book expense $1,300. **Required Forms and Deadlines:** FAFSA, Institution's own financial aid form. **Notification of Awards:** Applicants will be notified of awards on a rolling basis beginning 5/1. **Types of Aid:** *Need-based scholarships/grants:* Federal Pell, SEOG, state scholarships/grants, private scholarships, the school's own gift aid. *Loans:* Direct Subsidized Stafford, Direct Unsubsidized Stafford, Direct PLUS, Federal Perkins, college/university loans from institutional funds. *Student Employment:* Federal Work-Study Program available. Off-campus job opportunities

are good. **Financial Aid Statistics:** 88% freshmen, 83% undergrads receive need-based scholarship or grant aid. 4% freshmen, 2% undergrads receive non-need-based scholarship or grant aid. 55% freshmen, 66% undergrads receive need-based self-help aid. 6% freshmen, 1% undergrads receive athletic scholarships. 89% freshmen receive any aid. 75% undergrads borrow to pay for school. Average cumulative indebtedness $29,529. **Criteria for awarding institutional aid:** *Non-need-based:* academics, athletics.

INDIANA UNIVERSITY SOUTHEAST

4201 Grant Line Road, New Albany, IN 47150
Phone: 812-941-2212 • **Financial Aid Phone:** 812-941-2246
E-mail: admissions@ius.edu • **CEEB Code:** 1314
Fax: 812-941-2595 • **Website:** www.ius.edu • **ACT Code:** 1229

This public school was founded in 1941. It has a 177-acre campus.

RATINGS

Admissions Selectivity Rating: 74   **Fire Safety Rating:** 85

STUDENTS AND FACULTY

Enrollment: 5,476. **Student Body:** 59% female, 41% male, 28% out-of-state, 0% international (43 countries represented). Asian 1%, African American 6%, Caucasian 86%, Hispanic 3%, Native American <1%
Retention and Graduation: 62% freshmen return for sophomore year. 9% freshmen graduate within 4 years. 32% freshmen graduate within 6 years. **Faculty:** 213 full-time faculty, 69% hold PhDs, 52% are members of minority groups, 16% are women.

ACADEMICS

Degrees: associate, bachelor's, certificate, master's, post-bachelor's certificate. **Classes:** Most classes have 20–29 students. Most lab/discussion sessions have 10–19 students. **Majors with Highest Enrollment:** Registered Nursing/Registered Nurse; Business/Commerce; Psychology. **Special Study Options:** Accelerated program, cross-registration, distance learning, double major, dual enrollment, external degree program, honors program, independent study, internships, student-designed major, study abroad, teacher certification program, weekend college. **Disability Services:** Special programs offered to physically disabled students include note-taking services, reader services, tutors. **Career services:** alumni services, career/job search classes, career assessment, internships.

FACILITIES

Housing: Coed dorms. 95% of campus accessible to physically disabled. **Special Academic Facilities/Equipment:** Paul W. Ogle Center, Concert Hall, Theatre, Recital Hall, Japanese Cultural Center, Ronald L. Barr Art Gallery. **Computers:** Students can register for classes online. Administrative functions (other than registration) can be performed online.

CAMPUS LIFE

Environment: Village. **Activities:** Choral groups, concert band, drama/theater, literary magazine, music ensembles, student government, student newspaper, symphony orchestra. 76 registered organizations, 1 religious organization. 2 fraternities, 4 sororities. **Athletics (Intercollegiate):** *Men:* baseball, basketball, cross-country, tennis. *Women:* basketball, cross-country, softball, tennis, volleyball. **Environmental Initiatives:** Single stream waste recycling Campus Beautification Day. Volunteers assist grounds personnel in planting flowers and other plant life. Energy reduction capital project (completed in 2006).

ADMISSIONS

Freshman Academic Profile: Average high school GPA 3.04. 9.93% in top 10% of high school class, 31.02% in top 25% of high school class, 69.25% in top 50% of high school class. SAT Math middle 50% range 420-520. SAT Critical Reading middle 50% range 430-530. SAT Writing middle 50% range 410-510. ACT middle 50% range 18-23. Minimum internet-based TOEFL 75. Minimum paper TOEFL 530. **Basis for Candidate Selection:** *Very important factors considered include:* Class rank, rigor of secondary school record. *Important factors considered include:* academic GPA, standardized test scores. *Other factors considered include:* recommendation(s), interview. **Freshman Admission Requirements:** High school diploma is required and GED is accepted. *Academic units required:* 4 English, 3 mathematics, 1 science, (1 science labs), 2 social studies, 4 academic electives. **Freshman Admission Statistics:** 2,038 applied, 80% admitted, 60% enrolled. **Transfer Admission Requirements:** college transcript(s), Lowest grade transferable C. **General Admission Information:** Application Fee $30. Nonfall registration accepted. Admission may be deferred for a maximum of Contact admissions. Credit offered for CEEB Advanced Placement tests.

COSTS AND FINANCIAL AID

Annual in-state tuition $6,236. Annual out-of-state tuition $17,490. Room and board $6,280. Required fees $591. Average book expense $1,300. **Required Forms and Deadlines:** FAFSA. **Notification of Awards:** Applicants will be notified of awards on a rolling basis beginning 5/1. **Types of Aid:** *Need-based scholarships/grants:* Federal Pell, SEOG, state scholarships/grants, private scholarships, the school's own gift aid. *Loans:* Direct Subsidized Stafford, Direct Unsubsidized Stafford, Direct PLUS, Federal Perkins, Federal Nursing, college/university loans from institutional funds. *Student Employment:* Federal Work-Study Program available. Institutional employment available. Off-campus job opportunities are excellent. **Financial Aid Statistics:** 93% freshmen, 82% undergrads receive need-based scholarship or grant aid. 5% freshmen, 3% undergrads receive non-need-based scholarship or grant aid. 53% freshmen, 64% undergrads receive need-based self-help aid. 1% freshmen, 1% undergrads receive athletic scholarships. 91% freshmen receive any aid. 67% undergrads borrow to pay for school. Average cumulative indebtedness $25,294. **Criteria for awarding institutional aid:** *Non-need-based:* academics, art, athletics, leadership, minority status, music/drama.

INDIANA WESLEYAN UNIVERSITY

4201 South Washington Street, Marion, IN 46953
Phone: 765-677-2138 · **Financial Aid Phone:** 765-677-2137
E-mail: admissions@indwes.edu · **CEEB Code:** 1446
Fax: 765-677-2333 · **Website:** www.indwes.edu · **ACT Code:** 1226

This private school, affiliated with the Wesleyan Church, was founded in 1920. It has a 220-acre campus.

RATINGS

Admissions Selectivity Rating: 81   **Fire Safety Rating:** 94

STUDENTS AND FACULTY

Enrollment: 2,815. **Student Body:** 65% female, 35% male, 54% out-of-state, 0% international (21 countries represented). Asian 1%, African American 2%, Caucasian 90%, Hispanic 3%, Native American <1%
Retention and Graduation: 79% freshmen return for sophomore year. 55% freshmen graduate within 4 years. **Faculty:** 167 full-time faculty, 65% hold PhDs, 39% are members of minority groups, 12% are women. 0% of classes are taught by teaching assistants.

ACADEMICS

Degrees: associate, bachelor's. **Classes:** Most classes have 10–19 students. Most lab/discussion sessions have 10–19 students. **Majors with Highest Enrollment:** Registered Nursing/Registered Nurse; Business Administration and Management; Psychology. **Special Study Options:** double major, dual enrollment, honors program, independent study, internships, study abroad, teacher certification program. **Honors programs:** John Wesley Honors College Combined degree programs: BA/MA, MA/Ed.D. in Leadership. **Disability Services:** Special programs offered to physically disabled students include note-taking services, reader services, tape recorders, tutors. **Career services:** Alumni network, alumni services, career/job search classes, career assessment, internships, regional alumni. Career services highlights include The Center for Life Calling and Leadership, which enables individuals to find an overriding purpose for their lives, equips them to make life decisions based on this purpose, and empowers them to develop this purpose into world changing leadership.

FACILITIES

Housing: men's dorms, women's dorms, apartments for married students, apartments for single students. 99% of campus accessible to physically disabled. **Special Academic Facilities/Equipment:** Lee Howard art collection (European artists), Lewis Jackson Library (2003), Tom and Joanne Phillippe Performing Arts Center (1998), Bronze statues from Israel (1998-2002), Williams chapel—medieval replica (2001), Burns Hall of Science and Nursing (2000), Luckey Recreation and Wellness Center (2001), John Maxwell Business Center (1999). **Computers:** 100% of classrooms, 100% of dorms, 100% of libraries, 100% of dining areas, 100% of student union, 100% of common outdoor areas have wireless network access. Students can register for classes online. Administrative functions (other than registration) can be performed online.

CAMPUS LIFE

Environment: Town. **Activities:** Choral groups, concert band, drama/theater, jazz band, literary magazine, music ensembles, musical theater, pep band, radio station, student government, student newspaper, symphony orchestra, television station, yearbook, Campus Ministries, International Student Organization. 35 registered organizations, 1 honor society, 5 religious organizations. **Athletics**

(Intercollegiate): *Men:* baseball, basketball, cheerleading, cross-country, golf, soccer, tennis, track/field (outdoor), track/field (indoor). *Women:* basketball, cheerleading, cross-country, soccer, softball, tennis, track/field (outdoor), track/field (indoor), volleyball. **On-Campus Highlights:** McConn Coffee Shop, Recreation and Wellness Center, Globe Theater, The 1920 Art Gallery, Williams Chapel, The McCoon Coffee Shop is one of the more striking facilities on any college campus—situated in a long indoor mall area of the student center—and includes a fireplace and numerous seating configurations. **Environmental Initiatives:** Creation of a multi-disciplinary Task Force for Campus Sustainabilty; Researching grant opportunities for alternative energy projects; Currently developing an RFP to calculate our carbon footprint.

ADMISSIONS

Freshman Academic Profile: Average high school GPA 3.59. 28% in top 10% of high school class, 57% in top 25% of high school class, 85% in top 50% of high school class. SAT Math middle 50% range 480-590. SAT Critical Reading middle 50% range 470-580. SAT Writing middle 50% range 460-570. ACT middle 50% range 21-27. Minimum internet-based TOEFL 79. Minimum paper TOEFL 550. **Basis for Candidate Selection:** *Very important factors considered include:* academic GPA, recommendation(s), standardized test scores, character/personal qualities. *Important factors considered include:* Class rank, rigor of secondary school record. *Other factors considered include:* application essay, alumni/ae relation, extracurricular activities, first generation, interview, level of applicant's interest, religious affiliation/commitment, talent/ability, volunteer work, work experience. **Freshman Admission Requirements:** High school diploma is required and GED is accepted. **Freshman Admission Statistics:** 2,606 applied, 97% admitted, 28% enrolled. **Transfer Admission Requirements:** college transcript(s), statement of good standing from prior institution(s). Minimum college GPA of 2.0 required. Lowest grade transferable C. **General Admission Information:** Application Fee $25. Regular application deadline 8/1. Notification on a rolling basis, beginning on or about 10/1. Nonfall registration accepted. Admission may be deferred for a maximum of 1 year. Credit offered for CEEB Advanced Placement tests.

COSTS AND FINANCIAL AID

Annual tuition $24,102. Room and board $7,713. Average book expense $1,392. **Required Forms and Deadlines:** FAFSA, Institution's own financial aid form. **Notification of Awards:** Applicants will be notified of awards on or about 4/1. **Types of Aid:** *Need-based scholarships/grants:* Federal Pell, SEOG, state scholarships/grants, private scholarships, the school's own gift aid, *Loans:* Subsidized Stafford, Unsubsidized Stafford, PLUS, Federal Perkins, Federal Nursing, college/university loans from institutional funds. *Student Employment:* Federal Work-Study Program available. Institutional employment available. Off-campus job opportunities are good. **Financial Aid Statistics:** 10% freshmen, 99% undergrads receive need-based scholarship or grant aid. 14% freshmen, 11% undergrads receive non-need-based scholarship or grant aid. 71% freshmen, 78% undergrads receive need-based self-help aid. 4% freshmen, 4% undergrads receive athletic scholarships. 99% freshmen, 93% undergrads receive any aid. 77% undergrads borrow to pay for school. Average cumulative indebtedness $22,778. **Criteria for awarding institutional aid:** *Non-need-based:* academics, alumni affiliation, art, athletics, leadership, music/drama.

IONA COLLEGE

715 North Avenue, New Rochelle, NY 10801
Phone: 914-633-2502 · **Financial Aid Phone:** 914-633-2497
E-mail: admissions@iona.edu · **CEEB Code:** 2324
Fax: 914-633-2182 · **Website:** www.iona.edu · **ACT Code:** 2770

This private school, affiliated with the Roman Catholic Church, was founded in 1940. It has a 35-acre campus.

RATINGS

Admissions Selectivity Rating: 76   **Fire Safety Rating:** 93

STUDENTS AND FACULTY

Enrollment: 2,988. **Student Body:** 57% female, 43% male, 24% out-of-state, 2% international (25 countries represented). Asian 2%, African American 6%, Caucasian 63%, Hispanic 18%, Native American <1%
Retention and Graduation: 81% freshmen return for sophomore year. 56% freshmen graduate within 4 years. 65% freshmen graduate within 6 years. **Faculty:** 176 full-time faculty, 90% hold PhDs, 38% are members of minority groups, 16% are women. 0% of classes are taught by teaching assistants.

ACADEMICS

Degrees: bachelor's, master's, post-bachelor's certificate, post-master's certificate. **Classes:** Most classes have 20–29 students. Most lab/discussion sessions have 10–19 students. **Majors with Highest Enrollment:** Psychology; Mass Communication/Media Studies; Marketing/Marketing Management. **Special Study Options:** Accelerated program, distance learning, double major, honors program, independent study, internships, liberal arts/career combination, study abroad, teacher certification program, weekend college. **Honors programs:** The Iona College Honors Degree Program is designed to meet the educational needs of the ablest and most highly motivated students at Iona. Grounded in a challenging curriculum, the program offers gifted students the resources and opportunities to develop their talents and to perform at the peak of their capabilities. The course of study is designed to develop intellectual curiosity, analytic abilities, and awareness of ethical and civic responsibilities. The program encourages the development of a nucleus of independent learners able to inspire each other academically and fosters a sense of self-respect in students, encouraging them to stretch their abilities in pursuit of lifelong learning, independent thinking, and personal fulfillment. The Honors Degree Program seeks to establish a core academic community that enriches and serves the wider college community. The program endeavors to create an intellectual atmosphere to attract and challenge superior students and faculty and to enhance the public image of the College by promoting the concept of excellence in education. The curriculum promotes an appreciation and understanding of the interrelatedness of knowledge and culture by providing a wide range of interdisciplinary courses and opportunities to study abroad. Students in the program take specially designed honors courses and advanced courses in other areas, and engage in independent research under the guidance of faculty mentors. Small class sizes encourage student participation and promote a close student-faculty relationship. Students are offered close individual guidance, both academically and in terms of career preparation. There is a faculty committee that works with students interested in applying for competitive grants and fellowships and advises them regarding graduate and professional studies. A career mentoring program affords students a unique chance to explore career opportunities by matching them with an appropriate alumnus/alumna or corporate liaison. Combined degree programs: BA/MA. **Disability Services:** Special programs offered to physically disabled students include note-taking services, reader services, tape recorders, tutors. **Career services:** Alumni network, alumni services, career/job search classes, career assessment, internships, regional alumni.

FACILITIES

Housing: Coed dorms, special housing for disabled students, apartments for single students, Living learning communities in Science, Education, wellness housing to Honors Program Students. 100% of campus accessible to physically disabled. **Special Academic Facilities/Equipment:** Iona College Art Center, Br. Kenneth Chapman Public Art Gallary, Murphy Science Technology Center, Hynes Natural Science Center, Advanced Computer Laboratory, TV Production Studio, LaPenta Student Union, Hynes Athletic Center, Rowing tank, Arrigoni center. **Computers:** 100% of classrooms, 100% of dorms, 100% of libraries, 100% of dining areas, 100% of student union, 100% of common outdoor areas have wireless network access. Students can register for classes online. Administrative functions (other than registration) can be performed online.

CAMPUS LIFE

Environment: City. **Activities:** Choral groups, dance, drama/theater, literary magazine, musical theater, pep band, radio station, student government, student newspaper, student-run film society, television station, yearbook, Campus Ministries, International Student Organization, Model UN. 65 registered organizations, 9 honor societies, 4 religious organizations. 4 fraternities, 6 sororities. **Athletics (Intercollegiate):** *Men:* baseball, basketball, crew/rowing, cross-country, diving, golf, soccer, swimming, track/field (outdoor), track/field (indoor), water polo. *Women:* basketball, crew/rowing, cross-country, diving, lacrosse, soccer, softball, swimming, track/field (outdoor), track/field (indoor), volleyball, water polo. **On-Campus Highlights:** Lapenta Student Union, Hynes Athletics Center, Ryan Library, North Residence Hall, Loftus Courtyard.

ADMISSIONS

Freshman Academic Profile: Average high school GPA 3.1. 17% in top 10% of high school class, 44% in top 25% of high school class, 76% in top 50% of high school class. 58% from public high schools. SAT Math middle 50% range 460-560. SAT Critical Reading middle 50% range 450-550. ACT middle 50% range 20-25. Minimum internet-based TOEFL 80. Minimum paper TOEFL 550. **Basis for Candidate Selection:** *Very important factors considered include:* academic GPA, rigor of secondary school record. *Important factors considered include:* Class rank, application essay, standardized test scores, character/personal qualities, interview. *Other factors considered include:* recommendation(s), alumni/ae relation, extracurricular activities, first generation, geographical residence, level of applicant's interest, talent/ability, volunteer work, work experience. **Freshman Admission Requirements:** High school diploma is required and GED is accepted. *Academic units required:* 4 English, 3 mathematics, 2 science, (2 science labs), 2 foreign language, 1 social studies, 1 history, 1 academic electives. **Freshman Admission Statistics:** 8,741 applied, 86% admitted, 10% enrolled. **Transfer Admission Requirements:** High school transcript, college transcript(s), essay or personal statement, Minimum

college GPA of 2.5 required. Lowest grade transferable C. **General Admission Information:** Application Fee $50. Regular application deadline 2/15. Regular notification 3/20. Nonfall registration accepted. Admission may be deferred for a maximum of 12 months. Credit and/or placement offered for CEEB Advanced Placement tests.

COSTS AND FINANCIAL AID

Annual tuition $30,670. Room and board $13,175. Required fees $2,100. Average book expense $1,500. **Required Forms and Deadlines:** FAFSA, State aid form. **Notification of Awards:** Applicants will be notified of awards on a rolling basis beginning 12/20. **Types of Aid:** *Need-based scholarships/grants:* Federal Pell, SEOG, state scholarships/grants, private scholarships, the school's own gift aid. *Loans:* Subsidized Stafford, Unsubsidized Stafford, PLUS, Federal Perkins, Alternative Loans. *Student Employment:* Federal Work-Study Program available. Institutional employment available. Highest amount earned per year from on-campus jobs $9,729. Off-campus job opportunities are good. **Financial Aid Statistics:** 77% freshmen, 70% undergrads receive need-based scholarship or grant aid. 97% freshmen, 97% undergrads receive non-need-based scholarship or grant aid. 82% freshmen, 83% undergrads receive need-based self-help aid. 7% freshmen, 7% undergrads receive athletic scholarships. 98% freshmen, 96% undergrads receive any aid. 71% undergrads borrow to pay for school. Average cumulative indebtedness $22,877. **Criteria for awarding institutional aid:** *Non-need-based:* academics, alumni affiliation, athletics.

IOWA STATE UNIVERSITY

100 Enrollment Services Center, Ames, IA 50011-2011
Phone: 515-294-5836 · **Financial Aid Phone:** 515-294-2223
E-mail: admissions@iastate.edu · **CEEB Code:** 6306
Fax: 515-294-2592 · **Website:** www.iastate.edu · **ACT Code:** 1320

This public school was founded in 1858. It has a 1794-acre campus.

RATINGS

Admissions Selectivity Rating: 84   **Fire Safety Rating:** 86

STUDENTS AND FACULTY

Enrollment: 28,336. **Student Body:** 43% female, 57% male, 31% out-of-state, 7% international (106 countries represented). Asian 3%, African American 3%, Caucasian 77%, Hispanic 4%, Native American <1%
Retention and Graduation: 39% freshmen graduate within 4 years. 20% grads go on to further study within 1 year. 7% grads pursue arts and sciences degrees. 1% grads pursue law degrees. 3% grads pursue business degrees. 2% grads pursue medical degrees. **Faculty:** 1,516 full-time faculty, 92% hold PhDs, 36% are members of minority groups, 21% are women. 11% of classes are taught by teaching assistants.

ACADEMICS

Degrees: bachelor's, master's. **Classes:** Most classes have 20–29 students. Most lab/discussion sessions have 20–29 students. **Majors with Highest Enrollment:** Mechanical Engineering; Kinesiology and Exercise Science; Finance. **Special Study Options:** Accelerated program, cooperative education program, cross-registration, distance learning, double major, dual enrollment, English as a Second Language (ESL), exchange student program (domestic), external degree program, honors program, independent study, internships, liberal arts/career combination, student-designed major, study abroad, teacher certification program, weekend college. **Honors programs:** ISU offers both a University Honors Program and a Freshman Honors Program. Each program promotes an enhanced academic environment for students of high ability and emphasizes the development of an enriched, individualized program study that meets each student's particular needs, interests and abilities. Honors gives students a supportive community in which to pursue their goals and stretch their horizons. Benefits include uniques courses, small class sizes, research opportunities and funding, access to graduate-level courses, and priority registration. Combined degree programs: BA/MEng, BS/MS. **Disability Services:** Special programs offered to physically disabled students include note-taking services, reader services, tape recorders, tutors. **Career services:** Alumni network, alumni services, career/job search classes, career assessment, internships. Career services highlights include our Learning Communities, in which students who have similar career goals live together and share academic courses, are ranked high nationally.

FACILITIES

Housing: Coed dorms, special housing for disabled students, men's dorms, special housing for international students, women's dorms, fraternity/sorority housing, apartments for married students, apartments for single students, Theme HousingLearning Communities; family housing; quiet, non-smoking, or alcohol-free floors; graduate/adult undergraduate housing. 95% of campus accessible to physically disabled. **Special Academic Facilities/Equipment:** Brunnier art museum, Farm House museum, observatory, numerous institutes, research centers, College of Design Gallery, Virtual Reality Application Center, Pappajohn Center for Entrepreneurship. **Computers:** 100% of classrooms, 75% of dorms, 100% of libraries, 100% of dining areas, 100% of student union, 40% of common outdoor areas have wireless network access. Students can register for classes online. Administrative functions (other than registration) can be performed online.

CAMPUS LIFE

Environment: Town. **Activities:** Choral groups, concert band, dance, drama/theater, jazz band, literary magazine, marching band, music ensembles, musical theater, opera, pep band, radio station, student government, student newspaper, student-run film society, symphony orchestra, television station. 799 registered organizations, 43 honor societies, 34 religious organizations. 34 fraternities, 19 sororities. **Athletics (Intercollegiate):** *Men:* basketball, cross-country, football, golf, track/field (outdoor), track/field (indoor), wrestling. *Women:* basketball, cross-country, diving, golf, gymnastics, soccer, softball, swimming, tennis, track/field (outdoor), track/field (indoor), volleyball. **On-Campus Highlights:** Union Drive Community Center (dining center), Reiman Gardens, Lied Recreation Center, Memorial Union, Virtual Reality Lab (available to visitors also), Campanile. **Environmental Initiatives:** Establishment of the Live Green Initiative (http://www.livegreen.iastate.edu/about/) that has included: 1. Hiring of a Director of Sustainability (http://www.iastate.edu/Inside/2008/1212/rankin.shtml) 2. Creation of a 13 member (students, staff, and faculty) President's Advisory Committee on Energy Conservation and Global Climate Change (http://www.committees.iastate.edu/comm-info.php?id=136) 3. Creation of a Live Green Loan Fund for energy conservation and sustainability projects (http://www.livegreen.iastate.edu/loan/) 4. Completion of an annual Symposium on Sustainability (http://www.livegreen.iastate.edu/symposium/archive/). Commitment to Sustainable Operations highlighted by: 1. Energy—through a joint contract with the City of Ames, allowing up to 10% of Iowa State University's energy to be derived from wind. In addition, there is ongoing evaluation and testing of renewable fuel sources. 2. Building and Construction—LEED Gold Certification Requirement for all new construction and major renovation projects. Specific Iowa State University required LEED credits have also been designated. In addition, for all other campus projects the incorporation of sustainable design standards is required. Currently ISU has one platinum, two gold, and one silver LEED buildings. 3. Dining Services—12% of purchases are local, organic, or environmentally-preferable. Trayless dining in three dining centers has reduced food waste by 50%. Food waste is composted at the university's compost facility and utilized for on-campus projects. Prepared leftover food is donated to a free meal program in the Ames community. Waste in packaging is reduced through a reusable mug program, keeping 42,796 disposable coffee cups out of the landfill in 2011, and a "green" to go reusable takeway container program, currently serving 3,312 customers. 4. Campus Green Teams—Development of campus green teams dedicated to increasing sustainability efforts as related to a specific campus building, college, department, or operation. To date, there are 33 Iowa State University Green Teams. 5. Community partnership to bring 12 hybrid buses, Cybrids (17% of the total fleet), to the University and Ames community bus system; CyRide. Government of the Student Body is very active in supporting and expanding sustainability efforts including: the creation a cabinet postion of Director of Sustainability, formation of a Sustainability Committee, addition of a sustainability section to their website (http://www.gsb.iastate.edu/en/projects_and_issues/sustainability_efforts/), and the development and launching of an online Ride Share database to increase sustainability in travel and commuting for students, faculty, and staff.

ADMISSIONS

Freshman Academic Profile: Average high school GPA 3.55. 26% in top 10% of high school class, 58% in top 25% of high school class, 91% in top 50% of high school class. 93% from public high schools. SAT Math middle 50% range 530-680. SAT Critical Reading middle 50% range 460-630. ACT middle 50% range 21-29. Minimum internet-based TOEFL 71. Minimum paper TOEFL 530. **Basis for Candidate Selection:** *Very important factors considered include:* Class rank, academic GPA, rigor of secondary school record, standardized test scores. *Other factors considered include:* application essay, recommendation(s), character/personal qualities, extracurricular activities, geographical residence, interview, state residency, talent/ability, volunteer work, work experience. **Freshman Admission Requirements:** High school diploma is required and GED is accepted. *Academic units required:* 4 English, 3 mathematics, 3 science, (2 science labs), 2 foreign language, 2 social studies. **Freshman Admission Statistics:** 18,399 applied, 87% admitted, 38% enrolled. **Transfer Admission Requirements:** college transcript(s), statement of good

standing from prior institution(s). Minimum college GPA of 2.0 required. Lowest grade transferable D. **General Admission Information:** Application Fee $30. Regular application deadline 7/1. Notification on a rolling basis, beginning on or about 7/1. Nonfall registration accepted. Admission may be deferred for a maximum of 1 year. Credit and/or placement offered for CEEB Advanced Placement tests.

COSTS AND FINANCIAL AID

Annual in-state tuition $6,648. Annual out-of-state tuition $19,768. Room and board $8,070. Required fees $1,088. **Required Forms and Deadlines:** FAFSA. **Notification of Awards:** Applicants will be notified of awards on a rolling basis beginning 4/1. **Types of Aid:** *Need-based scholarships/grants:* Federal Pell, SEOG, state scholarships/grants, the school's own gift aid. *Loans:* Direct Subsidized Stafford, Direct Unsubsidized Stafford, Direct PLUS, Federal Perkins, state loans, college/university loans from institutional funds, Private alternative loans. *Student Employment:* Federal Work-Study Program available. Institutional employment available. Highest amount earned per year from on-campus jobs $1,877. Off-campus job opportunities are excellent. **Financial Aid Statistics:** 98% freshmen, 98% undergrads receive need-based scholarship or grant aid. 47% freshmen, 45% undergrads receive non-need-based scholarship or grant aid. 66% freshmen, 75% undergrads receive need-based self-help aid. 1% freshmen, 2% undergrads receive athletic scholarships. 86% freshmen, 79% undergrads receive any aid. 62% undergrads borrow to pay for school. Average cumulative indebtedness $24,787. **Criteria for awarding institutional aid:** *Non-need-based:* academics, art, athletics, leadership, minority status, music/drama, state/district residency.

ITHACA COLLEGE

Ithaca College, Office of Admission, Ithaca, NY 14850-7002
Phone: (607) 274-3124 · **Financial Aid Phone:** 607-274-3131
E-mail: admission@ithaca.edu · **CEEB Code:** 2325
Fax: (607) 274-1900 · **Website:** www.ithaca.edu · **ACT Code:** 2772

This private school was founded in 1892. It has a 650-acre campus.

RATINGS

Admissions Selectivity Rating: 88   **Fire Safety Rating:** 89

STUDENTS AND FACULTY

Enrollment: 6,085. **Student Body:** 57% female, 43% male, 55% out-of-state, 2% international (51 countries represented). Asian 4%, African American 5%, Caucasian 71%, Hispanic 8%, Native American <1%
Retention and Graduation: 71% freshmen graduate within 4 years. 78% freshmen graduate within 6 years. 29% grads go on to further study within 1 year. **Faculty:** 501 full-time faculty, 86% hold PhDs, 46% are members of minority groups, 12% are women. 2% of classes are taught by teaching assistants.

ACADEMICS

Degrees: bachelor's, certificate, master's. **Classes:** Most classes have fewer than 10 students. Most lab/discussion sessions have 10-19 students. **Majors with Highest Enrollment:** Radio and Television; Music; Business Administration, Management and Operations. **Special Study Options:** Accelerated program, cross-registration, distance learning, double major, dual enrollment, honors program, independent study, internships, liberal arts/career combination, student-designed major, study abroad, teacher certification program, London Center (London, England), Los Angeles Program, Washington D.C. semester program, Walkabout Down Under Program(Australia),opportunities to study in over 50 countries around the world. **Honors programs:** Students in the Humanities and Sciences Honors Program participate in a series of special intensive seminars complemented by an array of out-of-class activities. Starting in the fall of the first year, honors students begin a sequence of eight honors seminar courses that help them meet general requirements of the school. The sequence includes: a first-year seminar taken in the first semester, four intermediate seminars normally taken in the second, third and fourth semesters, a seminar on cultural themes taken in the junior year, and a capstone seminar on contemporary issues, taken in the senior year. Combined degree programs: BS/MS-Occup. Therapy and BS/DPT in Physical Therapy. **Disability Services:** Special programs offered to physically disabled students include note-taking services, reader services, tape recorders. **Career services:** Alumni network, alumni services, career/job search classes, career assessment, internships, regional alumni. Career services highlights include Park School of Communication Internships, normally taken during a students senior year. Sponsors include local, regional, national, and international TV, radio, advertising, public relations, motion picture, education and corporate media organizations and many corporations and non-profit organizations.

FACILITIES

Housing: Coed dorms, special housing for disabled students, women's dorms, fraternity/sorority housing, apartments for single students, Theme Housing. **Special Academic Facilities/Equipment:** Two newly-constructed Platinum LEED certified buildings (the Business School and the Peggy Williams Center), Art Gallery, Radio and TV stations, digital technology throughout Communications building, Observatory, Wellness Clinic, Fitness Center, Trading Room, Speech and Hearing Handicapped Clinic, Physical Therapy Clinic, Performing Arts Centers (Music And Theater), Music Recording Facility. **Computers:** 50% of classrooms, 100% of dorms, 100% of libraries, 100% of dining areas, 100% of student union, have wireless network access. Students can register for classes online. Administrative functions (other than registration) can be performed online.

CAMPUS LIFE

Environment: Town. **Activities:** Choral groups, concert band, dance, drama/theater, jazz band, literary magazine, music ensembles, musical theater, opera, pep band, radio station, student government, student newspaper, student-run film society, symphony orchestra, television station, yearbook, Campus Ministries, International Student Organization. 180 registered organizations, 28 honor societies, 8 religious organizations. 3 fraternities, 1 sorority. **Athletics (Intercollegiate):** *Men:* baseball, basketball, crew/rowing, cross-country, diving, football, lacrosse, soccer, swimming, tennis, track/field (outdoor), wrestling. *Women:* basketball, crew/rowing, cross-country, diving, field hockey, golf, gymnastics, lacrosse, soccer, softball, swimming, tennis, track/field (outdoor), volleyball. **On-Campus Highlights:** IC Square and Food Court, Handwerker Gallery, Fitness Center, Business School Atrium, Library. **Environmental Initiatives:** Sustainability Initiative that spurs and chronicles progress in three separate but highly inter-related areas: development of curriculum to infuse considerations of sustainability and applied research opportunities to study and solve sustainability challenges; modification of campus operations to incorporate more sustainable decision-making; and campus in-reach and community outreach to share our experiences as a learning organization seeking to become more sustainable. Ithaca College participated as a charter member in the Sustainability Tracking, Assessment and Rating System (STARS) developed by the Association for the Advancement of Sustainability in Higher Education (AASHE). Using the STARS campus sustainability evaluation system, Ithaca College achieved a GOLD rating. We have collaborated with our regional Sodexo Facilities Management group to implement the recommendations of a comprehensive energy and resource audit and sustainability assessment of all of our dining services-related facilities including board dining halls and retail operations.

ADMISSIONS

Freshman Academic Profile: 29.4% in top 10% of high school class, 67.5% in top 25% of high school class, 91.8% in top 50% of high school class. 83% from public high schools. SAT Math middle 50% range 550-650. SAT Critical Reading middle 50% range 550-650. SAT Writing middle 50% range 540-640. Minimum internet-based TOEFL 80. Minimum paper TOEFL 550. **Basis for Candidate Selection:** *Very important factors considered include:* academic GPA, rigor of secondary school record, standardized test scores. *Important factors considered include:* Class rank, application essay, recommendation(s), character/personal qualities, extracurricular activities, talent/ability. *Other factors considered include:* alumni/ae relation, first generation, level of applicant's interest, volunteer work, work experience. **Freshman Admission Requirements:** High school diploma is required and GED is accepted. *Academic units required:* 4 English, 3 mathematics, 3 science, 2 foreign language, 4 social studies, 1 academic electives. **Freshman Admission Statistics:** 18,207 applied, 59% admitted, 14% enrolled. **Transfer Admission Requirements:** High school transcript, college transcript(s), essay or personal statement, statement of good standing from prior institution(s). Minimum college GPA of 2.75 required. Lowest grade transferable C-. **General Admission Information:** Application Fee $60. Early decision application deadline 11/1. Regular application deadline 2/1. Regular notification 4/15. Notification on a rolling basis, beginning on or about 11/15. Nonfall registration accepted. Admission may be deferred for a maximum of 1 year. Credit and/or placement offered for CEEB Advanced Placement tests.

COSTS AND FINANCIAL AID

Annual tuition $39,532. Room and board $14,332. Required fees $0. Average book expense $1,502. **Required Forms and Deadlines:** FAFSA, CSS/Financial Aid PROFILE. **Notification of Awards:** Applicants will be notified of awards on a rolling basis beginning 2/15. **Types of Aid:** *Need-based scholarships/grants:* Federal Pell, SEOG, state scholarships/grants, private scholarships, the school's own gift aid. *Loans:* Subsidized Stafford, Unsubsidized Stafford, PLUS, Federal Perkins, Alternative Loans. *Student Employment:*

Federal Work-Study Program available. Institutional employment available. Highest amount earned per year from on-campus jobs $2,400. Off-campus job opportunities are good. **Financial Aid Statistics:** 96% freshmen, 97% undergrads receive need-based scholarship or grant aid. 34% freshmen, 23% undergrads receive non-need-based scholarship or grant aid. 91% freshmen, 93% undergrads receive need-based self-help aid. 0% freshmen, 0% undergrads receive athletic scholarships. 95% freshmen, 92% undergrads receive any aid. **Criteria for awarding institutional aid:** *Non-need-based:* academics, alumni affiliation, leadership, minority status, music/drama.

JACKSON STATE UNIVERSITY

1400 J. R. Lynch Street, Jackson, MS 39217
Phone: (601) 979-2100 · **Financial Aid Phone:** 601-979-2227
E-mail: admappl@jsums.edu · **CEEB Code:** 1341
Fax: 601-979-3445 · **Website:** www.jsums.edu · **ACT Code:** 2204

This public school was founded in 1877. It has a 150-acre campus.

RATINGS

Admissions Selectivity Rating: 70   **Fire Safety Rating:** 82

STUDENTS AND FACULTY

Enrollment: 6,844. **Student Body:** 62% female, 38% male, 17% out-of-state, 2% international (35 countries represented). Asian 0%, African American 93%, Caucasian 3%, Hispanic 0%, Native American <1%
Retention and Graduation: 78% freshmen return for sophomore year. 22% freshmen graduate within 4 years. 42% freshmen graduate within 6 years.
Faculty: 378 full-time faculty, 81% hold PhDs, 46% are members of minority groups, 81% are women.

ACADEMICS

Degrees: bachelor's, master's, post-master's certificate. **Majors with Highest Enrollment:** Elementary Education and Teaching; Biology/Biological Sciences; Criminal Justice/Safety Studies. **Special Study Options:** cooperative education program, distance learning, double major, dual enrollment, English as a Second Language (ESL), honors program, independent study, internships, study abroad, teacher certification program, weekend college, Undergrads may take grad level classes. Off-Campus Programs: Research semester at Lawrence Berkeley Lab. Co-Op Programs: Business, Computer Science, Natural Science. **Honors programs:** Honors College. **Disability Services:** Special programs offered to physically disabled students include note-taking services, tape recorders, tutors. **Career services:** career/job search classes, career assessment. These are both important in assisting students for job placement after graduation.

FACILITIES

Housing: men's dorms, women's dorms. 100% of campus accessible to physically disabled. **Special Academic Facilities/Equipment:** Research center. **Computers:** Students can register for classes online. Administrative functions (other than registration) can be performed online.

CAMPUS LIFE

Environment: Metropolis. **Activities:** Choral groups, concert band, dance, drama/theater, jazz band, literary magazine, marching band, music ensembles, opera, pep band, radio station, student government, student newspaper, student-run film society, symphony orchestra, television station, yearbook. 150 registered organizations, 20 honor societies, 11 religious organization. 4 fraternities, 4 sororities. **Athletics (Intercollegiate):** *Men:* baseball, basketball, cross-country, football, golf, soccer, tennis, track/field (outdoor), track/field (indoor), volleyball. *Women:* basketball, cross-country, golf, soccer, softball, tennis, track/field (outdoor), track/field (indoor), volleyball.

ADMISSIONS

Freshman Academic Profile: Average high school GPA 2.9. 85% from public high schools. ACT middle 50% range 17-20. Minimum paper TOEFL 525. **Basis for Candidate Selection:** *Very important factors considered include:* academic GPA, rigor of secondary school record, standardized test scores. *Important factors considered include:* level of applicant's interest. **Freshman Admission Requirements:** High school diploma is required and GED is accepted. *Academic units required:* 4 English, 3 mathematics, 3 science, 3 social studies, 2 academic electives. **Freshman Admission Statistics:** 7,265 applied, 74% admitted, 19% enrolled. **Transfer Admission Requirements:** High school transcript, college transcript(s), Minimum college GPA of 2.0 required. Lowest grade transferable C. **General Admission Information:** Nonfall registration accepted.

COSTS AND FINANCIAL AID

Average book expense $800. **Required Forms and Deadlines:** FAFSA, Institution's own financial aid form, State aid form. **Notification of Awards:** Applicants will be notified of awards on a rolling basis beginning 2/15. **Types of Aid:** *Need-based scholarships/grants:* Federal Pell, SEOG, state scholarships/grants, private scholarships, the school's own gift aid. *Loans:* Subsidized Stafford, Unsubsidized Stafford, PLUS, Federal Perkins, college/university loans from institutional funds. *Student Employment:* Federal Work-Study Program available. Institutional employment available. Highest amount earned per year from on-campus jobs $2,200. Off-campus job opportunities are good.

JACKSONVILLE STATE UNIVERSITY

700 Pelham Road North, Jacksonville, AL 36265
Phone: 256-782-5268 · **Financial Aid Phone:** 256-782-5006
E-mail: info@jsu.edu
Fax: 256-782-5953 · **Website:** www.jsu.edu · **ACT Code:** 20

This public school was founded in 1883. It has a 459-acre campus.

RATINGS

Admissions Selectivity Rating: 70   **Fire Safety Rating:** 65

STUDENTS AND FACULTY

Enrollment: 7,096. **Student Body:** 58% female, 42% male, 12% out-of-state, 1% international (73 countries represented). Asian 1%, African American 22%, Caucasian 71%, Hispanic 1%, Native American 1%
Retention and Graduation: 63% freshmen return for sophomore year. 15% freshmen graduate within 4 years. 35% freshmen graduate within 6 years. **Faculty:** 300 full-time faculty, 66% hold PhDs, 44% are members of minority groups, 11% are women. 0% of classes are taught by teaching assistants.

ACADEMICS

Degrees: bachelor's, master's, post-master's certificate. **Classes:** Most classes have 20–29 students. **Majors with Highest Enrollment:** Elementary Education and Teaching; Criminal Justice/Safety Studies; Registered Nursing/Registered Nurse. **Special Study Options:** Accelerated program, cooperative education program, distance learning, double major, dual enrollment, honors program, independent study, internships, teacher certification program. **Disability Services:** Special programs offered to physically disabled students include note-taking services, reader services, tape recorders, tutors.

FACILITIES

Housing: Coed dorms, men's dorms, special housing for international students, women's dorms, fraternity/sorority housing, apartments for married students, apartments for single students, apartments for students with dependent children. 90% of campus accessible to physically disabled. **Computers:** Students can register for classes online.

CAMPUS LIFE

Environment: Village. **Activities:** Choral groups, concert band, dance, drama/theater, jazz band, marching band, music ensembles, musical theater, pep band, radio station, student government, student newspaper, symphony orchestra, yearbook. 100 registered organizations, 13 honor societies, 8 religious organizations. 11 fraternity, 9 sororities. **Athletics (Intercollegiate): Men:** baseball, basketball, cheerleading, football, golf, riflery, tennis. **Women:** basketball, cheerleading, cross-country, golf, riflery, soccer, softball, tennis, track/field (outdoor), volleyball. **On-Campus Highlights:** Houston Cole Library, Theron Montgomery Bldg—Student Life, Stephenson Gym, Bibb Graves—Adm Bldg, Paul Snow Stadium.

ADMISSIONS

Freshman Academic Profile: Average high school GPA 2.99. 3% in top 10% of high school class, 13% in top 25% of high school class, 34% in top 50% of high school class. 99% from public high schools. SAT Math middle 50% range 400-530. SAT Critical Reading middle 50% range 420-530. ACT middle 50% range 17-23. Minimum paper TOEFL 500. **Basis for Candidate Selection:** *Very important factors considered include:* rigor of secondary school record, standardized test scores. **Freshman Admission Requirements:** High school diploma is required and GED is accepted. *Academic units required:* 3 English, 4 academic electives. **Freshman Admission Statistics:** 2,419 applied, 88% admitted, 50% enrolled. **Transfer Admission Requirements:** college transcript(s), Lowest grade transferable D. **General Admission Information:** Application Fee $20. Nonfall registration accepted. Admission may be deferred for a maximum of 4. Credit and/or placement offered for CEEB Advanced Placement tests.

COSTS AND FINANCIAL AID

Annual in-state tuition $4,040. Annual out-of-state tuition $8,080. Room and board $3,312. Required fees $20. Average book expense $1,008. **Required Forms and Deadlines:** FAFSA, Institution's own financial aid form. **Notification of Awards:** Applicants will be notified of awards on a rolling basis beginning 5/15. **Types of Aid:** *Need-based scholarships/grants:* Federal Pell, SEOG, state scholarships/grants, private scholarships, Federal Nursing Scholarships. *Loans:* Direct Subsidized Stafford, Direct Unsubsidized Stafford, Direct PLUS, college/university loans from institutional funds.

JACKSONVILLE UNIVERSITY

Office of Admissions, Jacksonville, FL 32211
Phone: 904-256-7000 · **Financial Aid Phone:** 800-558-3467
E-mail: admissions@ju.edu · **CEEB Code:** 5331
Website: http://www.ju.edu/ · **ACT Code:** 740

This private school was founded in 1934. It has a 198-acre campus.

RATINGS

Admissions Selectivity Rating: 87   **Fire Safety Rating:** 74

STUDENTS AND FACULTY

Enrollment: 3,122. **Student Body:** 59% female, 41% male, 29% out-of-state, 1% international (50 countries represented). Asian 4%, African American 19%, Caucasian 60%, Hispanic 7%, Native American 1%
Retention and Graduation: 60% freshmen return for sophomore year. 23% freshmen graduate within 4 years. 40% freshmen graduate within 6 years. 22% grads go on to further study within 1 year. **Faculty:** 180 full-time faculty, 79% hold PhDs, 43% are members of minority groups, 9% are women. 0% of classes are taught by teaching assistants.

ACADEMICS

Degrees: bachelor's, master's. **Classes:** Most classes have 10–19 students. **Majors with Highest Enrollment:** Aviation/Airway Management and Operations; Registered Nursing/Registered Nurse; Business/Commerce. **Special Study Options:** Accelerated program, cooperative education program, distance learning, double major, dual enrollment, honors program, independent study, internships, liberal arts/career combination, student-designed major, study abroad, teacher certification program. **Honors programs:** University Honors Program. **Disability Services:** Special programs offered to physically disabled students include note-taking services, reader services, tutors.

FACILITIES

Housing: Coed dorms, special housing for disabled students, men's dorms, women's dorms, fraternity/sorority housing, apartments for single students **Special Academic Facilities/Equipment:** Art museum, dance pavilion, concert hall, on-campus pre-school. **Computers:** Students can register for classes online. Administrative functions (other than registration) can be performed online.

CAMPUS LIFE

Environment: Metropolis. **Activities:** Choral groups, concert band, dance, drama/theater, jazz band, literary magazine, music ensembles, musical theater, pep band, radio station, student government, student newspaper, symphony orchestra, television station, yearbook, Campus Ministries, International Student Organization. 60 registered organizations, 16 honor societies, 9 fraternities, 6 sororities. **Athletics (Intercollegiate): Men:** baseball, basketball, crew/rowing, cross-country, football, golf, soccer, tennis. **Women:** basketball, crew/rowing, cross-country, golf, soccer, softball, tennis, track/field (outdoor), track/field (indoor), volleyball. **On-Campus Highlights:** Alexander Brest Fine Arts Museum, Davis College of Business/ Jazzman's Café (New), JU Baseball Complex, Lazzara Health Sciences Center (New), Residential Apartment Village (New).

ADMISSIONS

Freshman Academic Profile: Average high school GPA 3.47. SAT Math middle 50% range 480-570. SAT Critical Reading middle 50% range 470-560. ACT middle 50% range 20-26. Minimum paper TOEFL 540. **Basis for Candidate Selection:** *Very important factors considered include:* academic GPA, standardized test scores. *Important factors considered include:* rigor of secondary school record, talent/ability. *Other factors considered include:* application essay, recommendation(s), character/personal qualities, extracurricular activities, interview, volunteer work, work experience. **Freshman Admission Requirements:** High school diploma is required and GED is accepted. *Academic units required:* 4 English, 3 mathematics, 3 science, (2 science labs), 3 social studies. **Freshman Admission Statistics:** 8,096 applied, 42% admitted, 16% enrolled. **Transfer Admission Requirements:** college transcript(s), essay or personal statement, statement of good standing from prior institution(s). Minimum college GPA of 2.0 required. Lowest grade transferable C. **General**

Admission Information: Notification on a rolling basis, beginning on or about 10/1. Nonfall registration accepted. Admission may be deferred for a maximum of NA. Credit and/or placement offered for CEEB Advanced Placement tests.

COSTS AND FINANCIAL AID
Required Forms and Deadlines: FAFSA, Institution's own financial aid form, State aid form. **Notification of Awards:** Applicants will be notified of awards on a rolling basis beginning 2/15. **Types of Aid:** *Need-based scholarships/grants:* Federal Pell, SEOG, state scholarships/grants, private scholarships, the school's own gift aid, ACG/SMART. *Loans:* Subsidized Stafford, Unsubsidized Stafford, PLUS, Federal Perkins, state loans, college/university loans from institutional funds. *Student Employment:* Highest amount earned per year from on-campus jobs $4,677. **Financial Aid Statistics:** 98% freshmen, 99% undergrads receive need-based scholarship or grant aid. 1% freshmen, 1% undergrads receive non-need-based scholarship or grant aid. 62% freshmen, 69% undergrads receive need-based self-help aid. 2% freshmen, 4% undergrads receive athletic scholarships. 97% freshmen, 87% undergrads receive any aid. Average cumulative indebtedness $20,937. **Criteria for awarding institutional aid:** *Non-need-based:* academics, art, athletics, job skills, leadership, music/drama, state/district residency.

JAMES MADISON UNIVERSITY

Sonner Hall, MSC 0101, Harrisonburg, VA 22807
Phone: 540-568-5681 · **Financial Aid Phone:** 540-568-7820
E-mail: admissions@jmu.edu · **CEEB Code:** 5392
Fax: 540-568-3332 · **Website:** www.jmu.edu · **ACT Code:** 4370

This public school was founded in 1908. It has a 712-acre campus.

RATINGS

Admissions Selectivity Rating: 83   **Fire Safety Rating:** 76

STUDENTS AND FACULTY
Enrollment: 18,695. **Student Body:** 59% female, 41% male, 25% out-of-state, 2% international (70 countries represented). Asian 4%, African American 4%, Caucasian 78%, Hispanic 5%, Native American <1%
Retention and Graduation: 29% grads go on to further study within 1 year. 14% grads pursue arts and sciences degrees. 1% grads pursue law degrees. 2% grads pursue business degrees. 1% grads pursue medical degrees. **Faculty:** 960 full-time faculty, 74% hold PhDs, 48% are members of minority groups, 10% are women. 1% of classes are taught by teaching assistants.

ACADEMICS
Degrees: bachelor's, master's, post-master's certificate. **Classes:** Most classes have 20–29 students. Most lab/discussion sessions have 20–29 students. **Majors with Highest Enrollment:** Community Health Services/Liaison/Counseling; Speech Communication and Rhetoric; Psychology. **Special Study Options:** Accelerated program, distance learning, double major, English as a Second Language (ESL), honors program, independent study, internships, study abroad, teacher certification program, Continuing education programs offered on campus. **Honors programs:** Academic honors program, honors scholars (3.25 or above),honors courses, and senior honors project (3.25) Combined degree programs: BS in Bio. JMU/Master of Forestry VA Tech 3-2. **Disability Services:** Special programs offered to physically disabled students include note-taking services, reader services, tape recorders. **Career services:** Alumni network, alumni services, career/job search classes, career assessment, internships. Career services highlights include a course designed for first and second year students who have not selected a major called Life and Career Planning. It is offered for academic credit and serves over 10% of the freshman class. Our assessment data has demonstrated the effectiveness of this course in enhancing students' understanding of career decision-making processes, career decisiveness and career decision-making self-efficacy.

FACILITIES
Housing: Coed dorms, special housing for disabled students, fraternity/sorority housing, apartments for single students, Wellness Housing, Theme Housing. 90% of campus accessible to physically disabled. **Special Academic Facilities/Equipment:** language lab, music and fine arts buildings, herbarium, university farm, planetarium, arboretum,mineral museum,Science on a Sphere. **Computers:** 25% of classrooms, 100% of dorms, 100% of libraries, 50% of dining areas, 100% of student union, 25% of common outdoor areas have wireless network

access. Students can register for classes online. Administrative functions (other than registration) can be performed online.

CAMPUS LIFE
Environment: Town. **Activities:** Choral groups, concert band, dance, drama/theater, jazz band, literary magazine, marching band, music ensembles, musical theater, opera, pep band, radio station, student government, student newspaper, student-run film society, symphony orchestra, yearbook, Campus Ministries, International Student Organization. 298 registered organizations, 28 honor societies, 28 religious organizations. 15 fraternities, 9 sororities **Athletics (Intercollegiate):** *Men:* baseball, basketball, cheerleading, football, golf, soccer, tennis. *Women:* basketball, cheerleading, cross-country, diving, field hockey, golf, lacrosse, soccer, softball, swimming, tennis, track/field (outdoor), volleyball. **On-Campus Highlights:** Quad, Taylor Down Under, UREC, East Campus Library, Festival Student Center. **Environmental Initiatives:** Development of student learning outcomes for environmental literacy and an assessment. Transformation of the campus transportation system and integration with the community transportation system to facilitate use of alternatives to driving single-occupancy vehicles. Greening of buildings, grounds, and operations, including an emphasis on energy management, stormwater best practices, and waste reduction.

ADMISSIONS
Freshman Academic Profile: 26% in top 10% of high school class, 43% in top 25% of high school class, 97% in top 50% of high school class. 60% from public high schools. SAT Math middle 50% range 530-620. SAT Critical Reading middle 50% range 520-610. ACT middle 50% range 25-27. Minimum paper TOEFL 550. **Basis for Candidate Selection:** *Very important factors considered include:* academic GPA, rigor of secondary school record. *Important factors considered include:* standardized test scores. *Other factors considered include:* Class rank, application essay, recommendation(s), alumni/ae relation, character/personal qualities, extracurricular activities, geographical residence, state residency, talent/ability, volunteer work, work experience. **Freshman Admission Requirements:** High school diploma is required and GED is accepted. *Academic units required:* 4 English, 4 mathematics, 3 science, (3 science labs), 2 foreign language, 3 social studies. **Transfer Admission Requirements:** High school transcript, college transcript(s), Minimum college GPA of 2.0 required. Lowest grade transferable C. **General Admission Information:** Application Fee $50. Regular application deadline 1/15. Regular notification 4/1. Nonfall registration not accepted. Admission may be deferred for a maximum of 1 year with. Credit offered for CEEB Advanced Placement tests.

COSTS AND FINANCIAL AID
Annual out-of-state tuition $20,266. Room and board $8,828. Required fees $4,256. Average book expense $876. **Required Forms and Deadlines:** FAFSA. **Notification of Awards:** Applicants will be notified of awards on a rolling basis beginning 4/1. **Types of Aid:** *Need-based scholarships/grants:* Federal Pell, SEOG, state scholarships/grants, private scholarships, the school's own gift aid. *Loans:* Direct Subsidized Stafford, Direct Unsubsidized Stafford, Direct PLUS, Federal Perkins, Federal Nursing. *Student Employment:* Federal Work-Study Program available. Institutional employment available. Highest amount earned per year from on-campus jobs $3,640. Off-campus job opportunities are good. **Financial Aid Statistics:** 50% freshmen, 44% undergrads receive need-based scholarship or grant aid. 13% freshmen, 19% undergrads receive non-need-based scholarship or grant aid. 74% freshmen, 68% undergrads receive need-based self-help aid. 2% freshmen, 2% undergrads receive athletic scholarships. 61% freshmen, 49% undergrads receive any aid. 52% undergrads borrow to pay for school. Average cumulative indebtedness $20,054. **Criteria for awarding institutional aid:** *Non-need-based:* academics, alumni affiliation, art, athletics, leadership, minority status, music/drama, state/district residency.

JARVIS CHRISTIAN COLLEGE

P.O.BOX 1470, Hawkins, TX 75765-1470
Phone: 903-769-5730 · **Financial Aid Phone:** 903-769-5740
E-mail: felecia_tyiska@jarvis.edu
Fax: 903-769-1282 · **Website:** http://www.jarvis.edu/ · **ACT Code:** 4110

This private school, affiliated with the Disciples of Christ Church, was founded in 1912. It has a 243-acre campus.

RATINGS

Admissions Selectivity Rating: 60*   **Fire Safety Rating:** 86

STUDENTS AND FACULTY
Enrollment: 547. **Student Body:** 60% female, 40% male, 15% out-of-state, 0% international (2 countries represented). Asian 0%, African American 107%,

Caucasian 2%, Hispanic 4%, Native American <1%.
Retention and Graduation: 41% freshmen return for sophomore year. 17% freshmen graduate within 4 years. 19% freshmen graduate within 6 years. 2% grads go on to further study within 1 year. 1% grads pursue business degrees. **Faculty:** 35 full-time faculty, 46% hold PhDs, 49% are members of minority groups, 63% are women. 0% of classes are taught by teaching assistants.

ACADEMICS

Degrees: bachelor's. **Classes:** Most classes have fewer than 10 students. Most lab/discussion sessions have 10–19 students. **Majors with Highest Enrollment:** Biology/Biological Sciences; Criminal Justice/Law Enforcement Administration; Health and Physical Education/Fitness. **Special Study Options:** cross-registration, distance learning, double major, dual enrollment, English as a Second Language (ESL), honors program, independent study, internships, liberal arts/career combination, student-designed major, teacher certification program. **Honors programs:** JETS Honors Program. **Disability Services:** Special programs offered to physically disabled students include reader services, tutors. **Career services:** Alumni network, alumni services.

FACILITIES

Housing: special housing for disabled students, men's dorms, women's dorms, apartments for married students, apartments for single students. 95% of campus accessible to physically disabled. **Special Academic Facilities/Equipment:** ARCHIVES **Computers:** 100% of classrooms, 100% of dorms, 100% of libraries, 100% of dining areas, 100% of student union, 20% of common outdoor areas have wireless network access. Students can register for classes online.

CAMPUS LIFE

Environment: Rural. **Activities:** Choral groups, drama/theater, music ensembles, pep band, student government, International Student Organization. 33 registered organizations, 6 honor societies, 5 religious organizations. 4 fraternities, 4 sororities. **Athletics (Intercollegiate):** *Men:* baseball, basketball. *Women:* basketball, volleyball. **On-Campus Highlights:** E. W. Rand Health, Physical Education, and Recreat, J. N. Ervin Religion Center, Walk of Fame, Community and Technology Center, Meyer Science and Mathematics Center, Archives of the Texas Christian Missionary Fellowship of the Christian Church (Disciples of Christ).

ADMISSIONS

Freshman Academic Profile: Average high school GPA 2.63. 0% in top 10% of high school class, 6% in top 25% of high school class, 23% in top 50% of high school class. 99% from public high schools. ACT middle 50% range 100-. Minimum paper TOEFL 500. **Basis for Candidate Selection:** *Other factors considered include:* Class rank, academic GPA, rigor of secondary school record, standardized test scores, character/personal qualities, extracurricular activities, talent/ability. **Freshman Admission Requirements:** High school diploma is required and GED is accepted. *Academic units required:* 3 English, 2 mathematics, 1 science, (0 science labs), 0 foreign language, 3 social studies, 0 history, 7 academic electives. **Freshman Admission Statistics:** 525 applied, 92% admitted, 25% enrolled. **Transfer Admission Requirements:** High school transcript, college transcript(s), standardized test scores, Lowest grade transferable F. **General Admission Information:** Application Fee $50. Notification on a rolling basis, beginning on or about 8/1. Nonfall registration accepted. Admission may be deferred for a maximum of one year. Neither credit nor placement offered for CEEB Advanced Placement tests.

COSTS AND FINANCIAL AID

Annual tuition $8,528. Room and board $6,715. Required fees $1,080. Average book expense $1,000. **Required Forms and Deadlines:** FAFSA, Institution's own financial aid form, State aid form. **Notification of Awards:** Applicants will be notified of awards on a rolling basis beginning 5/1. **Types of Aid:** *Need-based scholarships/grants:* Federal Pell, SEOG, state scholarships/grants, private scholarships, the school's own gift aid, United Negro College Fund. *Loans:* Direct Subsidized Stafford, Direct Unsubsidized Stafford, Direct PLUS, Subsidized Stafford, Unsubsidized Stafford, PLUS, Federal Perkins, UNCF INSTITUTIONAL. *Student Employment:* Federal Work-Study Program available. Highest amount earned per year from on-campus jobs $1,729. Off-campus job opportunities are fair. **Financial Aid Statistics:** 94% freshmen, 100% undergrads receive need-based scholarship or grant aid. 41% freshmen, 23% undergrads receive non-need-based scholarship or grant aid. 79% freshmen, 89% undergrads receive need-based self-help aid. 3% freshmen, 6% undergrads receive athletic scholarships. 98% freshmen, 98% undergrads receive any aid. 93% undergrads borrow to pay for school. Average cumulative indebtedness $15,000. **Criteria for awarding institutional aid:** *Non-need-based:* academics, athletics, religious affiliation, state/district residency.

JEWISH THEOLOGICAL SEMINARY, ALBERT A. LIST COLLEGE

3080 Broadway, New York, NY 10027
Phone: 212-678-8832 • **Financial Aid Phone:** 212-678-8007
E-mail: lcadmissions@jtsa.edu • **CEEB Code:** 2339
Fax: 212-280-6022 • **Website:** www.jtsa.edu • **ACT Code:** 2776

This private school, affiliated with the Jewish Church, was founded in 1886. It has a 1-acre campus.

RATINGS

Admissions Selectivity Rating: 89   **Fire Safety Rating:** 61

STUDENTS AND FACULTY

Enrollment: 177. **Student Body:** 54% female, 46% male, 84% out-of-state, 3% international (10 countries represented). Asian 0%, African American 0%, Caucasian 94%, Hispanic 1%, Native American <1%.
Retention and Graduation: 89% freshmen return for sophomore year. 15% grads go on to further study within 1 year. 6% grads pursue arts and sciences degrees. 6% grads pursue law degrees. 3% grads pursue medical degrees. **Faculty:** 52 full-time faculty, 29% are members of minority groups, 0% are women. 0% of classes are taught by teaching assistants.

ACADEMICS

Degrees: bachelor's, master's. **Classes:** Most classes have fewer than 10 students. **Majors with Highest Enrollment:** Jewish/Judaic Studies; Bible/Biblical Studies; Talmudic Studies. **Special Study Options:** cross-registration, distance learning, double major, exchange student program (domestic), honors program, independent study, internships, liberal arts/career combination, student-designed major, study abroad, BA/MA program with JTS Graduate School or William Davidson School of Jewish Education. Combined degree programs: BA/MA, BA/BA and BA/BS programs with Columbia University and Barnard College. **Disability Services:** Special programs offered to physically disabled students include tape recorders, tutors. **Career services:** Alumni network, alumni services, career/job search classes, internships. Career services highlights include Career/Job search classes and alumni network.

FACILITIES

Housing: Coed dorms, apartments for married students, apartments for single students **Special Academic Facilities/Equipment:** The Jewish Museum and the Rare Book Room of the Library. **Computers:** 100% of classrooms, 100% of dorms, 80% of libraries, 100% of dining areas, 50% of common outdoor areas have wireless network access. Students can register for classes online. Administrative functions (other than registration) can be performed online.

CAMPUS LIFE

Environment: Metropolis. **Activities:** Choral groups, concert band, dance, drama/theater, jazz band, literary magazine, music ensembles, musical theater, radio station, student government, student newspaper, yearbook 1 religious organization. **Athletics (Intercollegiate):** *Men:* baseball, basketball, crew/rowing, soccer, tennis, track/field (outdoor), volleyball. *Women:* baseball, basketball, crew/rowing, soccer, tennis, track/field (outdoor), volleyball. **On-Campus Highlights:** The Library of the Jewish Theological Seminary. **Environmental Initiatives:** 4-Day work week to save on electricity; The cafeteria has replaced styrofoam products with paper products and promotes the use of reusable plates, bowls and utensils; Energy saving film applied to all windows.

ADMISSIONS

Freshman Academic Profile: Average high school GPA 3.7. SAT Math middle 50% range 620-660. SAT Critical Reading middle 50% range 640-700. SAT Writing middle 50% range 620-720. ACT middle 50% range 30-32. Minimum paper TOEFL 600. **Basis for Candidate Selection:** *Very important factors considered include:* academic GPA, rigor of secondary school record, standardized test scores. *Important factors considered include:* Class rank, application essay, recommendation(s), interview. *Other factors considered include:* alumni/ae relation, character/personal qualities, extracurricular activities, first generation, level of applicant's interest, religious affiliation/commitment, talent/ability, volunteer work. **Freshman Admission Requirements:** High school diploma is required and GED is not accepted. **Freshman Admission Statistics:** 102 applied, 62% admitted, 65% enrolled. **Transfer Admission Requirements:** High school transcript, college transcript(s), essay or personal statement, standardized test scores, statement of good standing from prior institution(s). **General Admission Information:** Application Fee $65. Early decision application deadline 11/15. Regular application deadline 2/15. Regular notification 4/1. Nonfall registration accepted. Admission may be deferred for a maximum of 1. Credit and/or placement offered for CEEB Advanced Placement tests.

COSTS AND FINANCIAL AID

Annual tuition $14,200. Room and board $9,200. Required fees $800. Average book expense $500. **Required Forms and Deadlines:** FAFSA, Institution's own financial aid form, CSS/Financial Aid PROFILE, State aid form, Non-custodial PROFILE, Business/Farm Supplement. **Notification of Awards:** Applicants will be notified of awards on a rolling basis beginning 4/1. **Types of Aid:** *Need-based scholarships/grants:* private scholarships, the school's own gift aid. *Loans:* Direct Subsidized Stafford, Direct Unsubsidized Stafford, college/university loans from institutional funds. *Student Employment:* Federal Work-Study Program available. Institutional employment available. Off-campus job opportunities are excellent. **Financial Aid Statistics:** 100% freshmen, 100% undergrads receive need-based scholarship or grant aid. 50% freshmen, 41% undergrads receive non-need-based scholarship or grant aid. 86% freshmen, 97% undergrads receive need-based self-help aid. 0% freshmen, 0% undergrads receive athletic scholarships. 42% undergrads borrow to pay for school. Average cumulative indebtedness $16,892. **Criteria for awarding institutional aid:** *Non-need-based:* academics, alumni affiliation, leadership.

JOHN BROWN UNIVERSITY

2000 West University Street, Siloam Springs, AR 72761
Phone: 479-524-7157 · **Financial Aid Phone:** 479-524-7424
E-mail: jbuinfo@jbu.edu · **CEEB Code:** 6321
Fax: 479-524-4196 · **Website:** www.jbu.edu · **ACT Code:** 130

This private school was founded in 1919. It has a 200-acre campus.

RATINGS

Admissions Selectivity Rating: 88   **Fire Safety Rating:** 60*

STUDENTS AND FACULTY

Enrollment: 1,742. **Student Body:** 57% female, 43% male, 57% out-of-state, 6% international (40 countries represented). Asian 1%, African American 3%, Caucasian 76%, Hispanic 6%, Native American 2%
Retention and Graduation: 84% freshmen return for sophomore year. 50% freshmen graduate within 4 years. 61% freshmen graduate within 6 years. 18% grads go on to further study within 1 year. **Faculty:** 80 full-time faculty, 74% hold PhDs, 25% are members of minority groups, 4% are women. 0% of classes are taught by teaching assistants.

ACADEMICS

Degrees: bachelor's, master's. **Classes:** Most classes have 10–19 students. Most lab/discussion sessions have 10–19 students. **Majors with Highest Enrollment:** Graphic Design; Business Administration and Management; Digital Communication and Media/Multimedia. **Special Study Options:** Accelerated program, distance learning, double major, dual enrollment, English as a Second Language (ESL), honors program, independent study, internships, liberal arts/career combination, student-designed major, study abroad, teacher certification program. **Honors programs:** The Honors Scholars Program consists of enriched Core Curriculum courses developed especially for gifted and highly motivated students. Emphasizing the use of primary texts, instructors challenge students through individual research, critical reflection, incisive discussion, interactive projects, and professional presentations. **Disability Services:** Special programs offered to physically disabled students include note-taking services, reader services, tutors. **Career services:** Alumni network, career/job search classes, career assessment.

FACILITIES

Housing: Coed dorms, men's dorms, women's dorms, apartments for married students, apartments for single students. 80% of campus accessible to physically disabled. **Special Academic Facilities/Equipment:** Art Gallery, Human Anatomy Lab, TV Studio, Radio Station, Outdoor Learning Center, Center for Relationship Enrichment, Soderquist Center for Business and Ethics **Computers:** 100% of classrooms, 100% of dorms, 100% of libraries, 100% of dining areas, 100% of student union, 30% of common outdoor areas have wireless network access. Students can register for classes online. Administrative functions (other than registration) can be performed online.

CAMPUS LIFE

Environment: Village. **Activities:** Choral groups, dance, drama/theater, jazz band, literary magazine, music ensembles, musical theater, pep band, radio station, student government, student newspaper, student-run film society, yearbook, Campus Ministries, International Student Organization. 20 registered organizations, 3 honor societies. **Athletics (Intercollegiate):** *Men:* basketball, golf, soccer, tennis. *Women:* basketball, soccer, swimming, tennis, volleyball. **On-Campus Highlights:** Walker Student Center, California Café, Chapel, Walton Lifetime Health Complex, Intramural Sports.

ADMISSIONS

Freshman Academic Profile: Average high school GPA 3.7. 30% in top 10% of high school class, 59% in top 25% of high school class, 85% in top 50% of high school class. SAT Math middle 50% range 510-620. SAT Critical Reading middle 50% range 515-640. SAT Writing middle 50% range 490-600. ACT middle 50% range 23-29. Minimum internet-based TOEFL 85. Minimum paper TOEFL 560. **Basis for Candidate Selection:** *Very important factors considered include:* academic GPA, recommendation(s), standardized test scores. *Important factors considered include:* Class rank, application essay, character/personal qualities, interview, religious affiliation/commitment. *Other factors considered include:* rigor of secondary school record, alumni/ae relation, extracurricular activities, first generation, level of applicant's interest, talent/ability. **Freshman Admission Requirements:** High school diploma is required and GED is accepted. **Freshman Admission Statistics:** 1,201 applied, 69% admitted, 38% enrolled. **Transfer Admission Requirements:** High school transcript, college transcript(s), essay or personal statement, Minimum college GPA of 2.5 required. Lowest grade transferable C. **General Admission Information:** Application Fee $25. Notification on a rolling basis, beginning on or about 11/1. Nonfall registration accepted. Admission may be deferred for a maximum of 1 year. Neither credit nor placement offered for CEEB Advanced Placement tests.

COSTS AND FINANCIAL AID

Annual tuition $22,552. Room and board $8,468. Required fees $1,036. Average book expense $800. **Required Forms and Deadlines:** FAFSA, State aid form. **Notification of Awards:** Applicants will be notified of awards on or about 3/1. **Types of Aid:** *Need-based scholarships/grants:* Federal Pell, SEOG, state scholarships/grants, private scholarships, the school's own gift aid. *Loans:* Direct Subsidized Stafford, Direct Unsubsidized Stafford, Direct PLUS, Subsidized Stafford, Unsubsidized Stafford, PLUS, Federal Perkins, college/university loans from institutional funds. *Student Employment:* Federal Work-Study Program available. Institutional employment available. Highest amount earned per year from on-campus jobs $1,415. Off-campus job opportunities are fair. **Financial Aid Statistics:** 93% freshmen, 93% undergrads receive need-based scholarship or grant aid. 93% freshmen, 80% undergrads receive non-need-based scholarship or grant aid. 61% freshmen, 43% undergrads receive need-based self-help aid. 5% freshmen, 5% undergrads receive athletic scholarships. 90% freshmen, 91% undergrads receive any aid. 61% undergrads borrow to pay for school. Average cumulative indebtedness $23,487. **Criteria for awarding institutional aid:** *Non-need-based:* academics, alumni affiliation, art, athletics, leadership, music/drama.

JOHN CARROLL UNIVERSITY

1 John Carroll Boulevard, University Heights, OH 44118-4581
Phone: 216-397-4294 · **Financial Aid Phone:** 216-397-4270 · **CEEB Code:** 1342
Fax: 216-397-4981 · **Website:** http://sites.jcu.edu/ · **ACT Code:** 3282

This private school, affiliated with the Roman Catholic Church, was founded in 1886. It has a 60-acre campus.

RATINGS

Admissions Selectivity Rating: 81   **Fire Safety Rating:** 77

STUDENTS AND FACULTY

Enrollment: 3,081. **Student Body:** 47% female, 53% male, 31% out-of-state, 2% international (23 countries represented). Asian 2%, African American 4%, Caucasian 85%, Hispanic 3%, Native American <1%
Retention and Graduation: 60% freshmen graduate within 4 years. 28% grads go on to further study within 1 year. 48% grads pursue arts and sciences degrees. 7% grads pursue law degrees. 28% grads pursue business degrees. 9% grads pursue medical degrees. **Faculty:** 190 full-time faculty, 98% hold PhDs, 43% are members of minority groups, 17% are women. 1% of classes are taught by teaching assistants.

ACADEMICS

Degrees: bachelor's, master's, post-bachelor's certificate. **Classes:** Most classes have 20–29 students. Most lab/discussion sessions have 10–19 students. **Majors with Highest Enrollment:** Speech Communication and Rhetoric; Psychology; Marketing/Marketing Management. **Special Study Options:** Accelerated program, cooperative education program, cross-registration, double major, dual enrollment, exchange student program (domestic), honors program, independent study, internships, liberal arts/career combination, student-designed major, study abroad, teacher certification program, Undergrads may take grad level classes. Co-Op Programs: All majors. Combined degree programs: 3-4 Doctor of Nursing prog with Case Western Reserve U. **Disability Services:** Special programs offered to physically disabled students include note-taking services, reader services, tape recorders. **Career services:** Alumni network, alumni services, career/job search classes, career assessment, internships, regional alumni. Career services highlights include internships that are available to our students for 0-3 credits and they can be paid or unpaid. We have a large number of students working at non-profits who are eligible for scholarships.

FACILITIES
Housing: Coed dorms, special housing for disabled students, women's dorms, fraternity/sorority housing, apartments for single students, Theme Housing. 94% of campus accessible to physically disabled. **Computers:** 100% of classrooms, 100% of dorms, 100% of libraries, 100% of dining areas, 100% of student union, 100% of common outdoor areas have wireless network access. Students can register for classes online. Administrative functions (other than registration) can be performed online.

CAMPUS LIFE
Environment: Metropolis. **Activities:** Choral groups, dance, drama/theater, literary magazine, music ensembles, pep band, radio station, student government, student newspaper, television station, yearbook, Campus Ministries. 95 registered organizations, 12 honor societies, 2 religious organizations. 4 fraternities, 5 sororities. **Athletics (Intercollegiate):** *Men:* baseball, basketball, cross-country, diving, football, golf, soccer, swimming, tennis, track/field (outdoor), track/field (indoor), wrestling. *Women:* basketball, cheerleading, cross-country, diving, golf, soccer, softball, swimming, tennis, track/field (outdoor), track/field (indoor), volleyball. **On-Campus Highlights:** Einstein Bagel Bros, Dolan Center for Science and Technology, Inn-Between Café, Grasselli Library, Student Center Atrium. **Environmental Initiatives:** Reuse building materials on campus or divert from landfills; Reduce energy and water consumption; LEED design principles used in all renovations or new buildings.

ADMISSIONS
Freshman Academic Profile: Average high school GPA 3.51. 20% in top 10% of high school class, 44% in top 25% of high school class, 79% in top 50% of high school class. 57% from public high schools. SAT Math middle 50% range 500-610. SAT Critical Reading middle 50% range 500-590. SAT Writing middle 50% range 480-590. ACT middle 50% range 22-27. Minimum internet-based TOEFL 79. Minimum paper TOEFL 550. **Basis for Candidate Selection:** *Very important factors considered include:* academic GPA, rigor of secondary school record. *Important factors considered include:* application essay, standardized test scores, character/personal qualities, extracurricular activities, talent/ability, volunteer work, work experience. *Other factors considered include:* Class rank, recommendation(s), alumni/ae relation, first generation, geographical residence, interview. **Freshman Admission Requirements:** High school diploma is required and GED is accepted. *Academic units required:* 4 English, 3 mathematics, 2 science, (2 science labs), 2 foreign language, 2 social studies, 0 history, 3 academic electives, 2 units must be distributed between social studies and/or history; 4 recommended. **Freshman Admission Statistics:** 3,873 applied, 83% admitted, 25% enrolled. **Transfer Admission Requirements:** High school transcript, college transcript(s), essay or personal statement, standardized test scores, statement of good standing from prior institution(s). Lowest grade transferable 2. **General Admission Information:** Regular application deadline 2/1. Notification on a rolling basis, beginning on or about 12/15. Nonfall registration accepted. Admission may be deferred for a maximum of 1-2 terms. Credit and/or placement offered for CEEB Advanced Placement tests.

COSTS AND FINANCIAL AID
Annual tuition $35,930. Room and board $10,920. Required fees $1,250. Average book expense $1,000. **Required Forms and Deadlines:** FAFSA. **Notification of Awards:** Applicants will be notified of awards on a rolling basis beginning 2/15. **Types of Aid:** *Need-based scholarships/grants:* Federal Pell, SEOG, state scholarships/grants, private scholarships, the school's own gift aid. *Loans:* Subsidized Stafford, Unsubsidized Stafford, PLUS, Federal Perkins. *Student Employment:* Federal Work-Study Program available. Institutional employment available. Highest amount earned per year from on-campus jobs $2,747. Off-campus job opportunities are good. **Financial Aid Statistics:** 92% freshmen, 98% undergrads receive need-based scholarship or grant aid. 93% freshmen, 99% undergrads receive non-need-based scholarship or grant aid. 78% freshmen, 85% undergrads receive need-based self-help aid. 0% freshmen, 0% undergrads receive athletic scholarships. 100% freshmen, 95% undergrads receive any aid. 82% undergrads borrow to pay for school. Average cumulative indebtedness $25,818. **Criteria for awarding institutional aid:** *Non-need-based:* academics, alumni affiliation, leadership, minority status, state/district residency.

JOHNS HOPKINS UNIVERSITY

3400 North Charles Street, Baltimore, MD 21218
Phone: 410-516-8171 · **Financial Aid Phone:** 410-516-8028
E-mail: gotojhu@jhu.edu · **CEEB Code:** 5332
Fax: 410-516-6025 · **Website:** www.jhu.edu

This private school was founded in 1876. It has a 140-acre campus.

RATINGS
Admissions Selectivity Rating: 99   **Fire Safety Rating:** 95

STUDENTS AND FACULTY
Enrollment: 5,312. **Student Body:** 49% female, 51% male, 88% out-of-state, 9% international (65 countries represented). Asian 21%, African American 5%, Caucasian 44%, Hispanic 13%, Native American <1%
Retention and Graduation: 88% freshmen graduate within 4 years. 94% freshmen graduate within 6 years. 36% grads go on to further study within 1 year. 8% grads pursue arts and sciences degrees. 1% grads pursue law degrees. 1% grads pursue business degrees. 6% grads pursue medical degrees. **Faculty:** 576 full-time faculty, 93% hold PhDs, 31% are members of minority groups, 14% are women.

ACADEMICS
Degrees: bachelor's, certificate, diploma, master's, post-bachelor's certificate, post-master's certificate. **Classes:** Most classes have 10–19 students. Most lab/discussion sessions have 20–29 students. **Majors with Highest Enrollment:** Bioengineering and Biomedical Engineering; Neuroscience; International Relations and Affairs. **Special Study Options:** cross-registration, double major, dual enrollment, independent study, internships, student-designed major, study abroad, Combined Bachelor's/Master's programs. Combined degree programs: BA/MA, BA/MEng, Accelerated Bachelor's/Masters Programs. **Disability Services:** Special programs offered to physically disabled students include note-taking services, reader services, tape recorders, tutors. **Career services:** Alumni network, alumni services, career/job search classes, career assessment, internships, regional alumni. Career services highlights include Second Decade Society summer internship grants; Medical tutorial program, wherein students shadow physicians.

FACILITIES
Housing: Coed dorms, men's dorms, women's dorms, fraternity/sorority housing, apartments for single students **Special Academic Facilities/Equipment:** Baltimore Museum of Art, on-campus Digital Media Center, art gallery, electron microscope, Space Telescope Science Institute, four major research centers. **Computers:** 95% of classrooms, 100% of dorms, 100% of libraries, 90% of dining areas, 100% of student union, 50% of common outdoor areas have wireless network access. Students can register for classes online. Administrative functions (other than registration) can be performed online.

CAMPUS LIFE
Environment: Metropolis. **Activities:** Choral groups, concert band, dance, drama/theater, jazz band, literary magazine, music ensembles, musical theater, pep band, radio station, student government, student newspaper, student-run film society, symphony orchestra, yearbook, Campus Ministries, Model UN. 250 registered organizations, 17 honor societies, 20 religious organizations. 12 fraternities, 7 sororities. **Athletics (Intercollegiate):** *Men:* baseball, basketball, cross-country, diving, fencing, football, lacrosse, soccer, swimming, tennis, track/field (outdoor), track/field (indoor), water polo, wrestling. *Women:* basketball, cross-country, diving, fencing, field hockey, lacrosse, soccer, swimming, tennis, track/field (outdoor), track/field (indoor), volleyball. **On-Campus Highlights:** Mason Hall—new Visitor's Center, Mattin Student Arts Center, Homewood House Museum, Lacrosse Hall of Fame and Museum, Ralph S. O'Connor Recreation Center, Also, Charles Commons, a new building that houses 618 upperclassmen, as well as a new dining facility and retail spaces, opened in the Fall of 2007. **Environmental Initiatives:** Comprehensive climate commitment includes reaching a 51% reduction in GHG by 2025, investing over $73 million in GHG reduction projects, and seed grants for climate researchers. Created the Energy, Environment, Health, and Sustainability Institute (EESHI) to advance greater collaboration among researchers on areas of opportunity. Strong commitment to the surrounding community through conducting sustainability assessments, facilitating collegetown sustainability networks, and providing workshops and training for community members.

ADMISSIONS

Freshman Academic Profile: Average high school GPA 3.88. 88% in top 10% of high school class, 98% in top 25% of high school class, 100% in top 50% of high school class. 59% from public high schools. SAT Math middle 50% range 690-780. SAT Critical Reading middle 50% range 670-750. SAT Writing middle 50% range 680-770. ACT middle 50% range 32-34. Minimum paper TOEFL 600. **Basis for Candidate Selection:** *Very important factors considered include:* academic GPA, recommendation(s), rigor of secondary school record, character/personal qualities. *Important factors considered include:* Class rank, application essay, standardized test scores, extracurricular activities, talent/ability, volunteer work, work experience. *Other factors considered include:* alumni/ae relation, first generation, geographical residence, interview, racial/ethnic status, state residency. **Freshman Admission Requirements:** High school diploma or equivalent is not required. **Freshman Admission Statistics:** 23,877 applied, 15% admitted, 39% enrolled. **Transfer Admission Requirements:** High school transcript, college transcript(s), essay or personal statement, statement of good standing from prior institution(s). Minimum college GPA of 3.0 required. Lowest grade transferable C. **General Admission Information:** Application Fee $70. Early decision application deadline 11/1. Regular application deadline 1/1. Regular notification 4/1. Nonfall registration not accepted. Admission may be deferred for a maximum of 2 Years. Credit offered for CEEB Advanced Placement tests.

COSTS AND FINANCIAL AID

Annual tuition $47,060. Room and board $14,246. Required fees $500. Average book expense $1,223. **Required Forms and Deadlines:** FAFSA, CSS/Financial Aid PROFILE, Noncustodial PROFILE, Business/Farm Supplement. **Notification of Awards:** Applicants will be notified of awards on or about 4/1. **Types of Aid:** *Need-based scholarships/grants:* Federal Pell, SEOG, state scholarships/grants, private scholarships, the school's own gift aid. *Loans:* Direct Subsidized Stafford, Direct Unsubsidized Stafford, Direct PLUS, Federal Perkins, college/university loans from institutional funds. *Student Employment:* Federal Work-Study Program available. Institutional employment available. Off-campus job opportunities are good. **Financial Aid Statistics:** 92% freshmen, 92% undergrads receive need-based scholarship or grant aid. 11% freshmen, 8% undergrads receive non-need-based scholarship or grant aid. 82% freshmen, 88% undergrads receive need-based self-help aid. 1% freshmen, 1% undergrads receive athletic scholarships. 58% freshmen, 55% undergrads receive any aid. 45% undergrads borrow to pay for school. Average cumulative indebtedness $17,438. **Criteria for awarding institutional aid:** *Non-need-based:* academics, athletics, leadership, state/district residency.

See page 1068.

JOHNSON AND WALES UNIVERSITY AT NORTH MIAMI

1701 NE 127th Street, North Miami, FL 33181
Phone: 1-866-598-3567
E-mail: admissions.mia@jwu.edu
Fax: 305-892-7020 • **Website:** www.jwu.edu

This is a private school.

RATINGS

Admissions Selectivity Rating: 65   **Fire Safety Rating:** 60*

STUDENTS AND FACULTY

Enrollment: 2,152. **Student Body:** 57% female, 43% male, 56% out-of-state, 9% international. Asian 1%, African American 24%, Caucasian 23%, Hispanic 21%, Native American 1%
Retention and Graduation: 67% freshmen return for sophomore year. 34% freshmen graduate within 4 years. **Faculty:** 64 full-time faculty, 34% are members of minority groups.

ACADEMICS

Degrees: associate, bachelor's. **Classes:** Most classes have 10–19 students. Most lab/discussion sessions have 20–29 students. **Special Study Options:** Accelerated program, cooperative education program, honors program, independent study, internships, study abroad, weekend college.

FACILITIES

Housing: Coed dorms, special housing for disabled students.

CAMPUS LIFE

Activities: dance, drama/theater, student government, student newspaper, yearbook.

ADMISSIONS

Freshman Academic Profile: Average high school GPA 3.11. **Basis for Candidate Selection:** *Very important factors considered include:* Class rank, rigor of secondary school record, interview. *Important factors considered include:* extracurricular activities, work experience. *Other factors considered include:* academic GPA, recommendation(s), standardized test scores, alumni/ae relation, volunteer work. **Freshman Admission Requirements:** High school diploma is required and GED is accepted. **Freshman Admission Statistics:** 5,414 applied, 63% admitted, 19% enrolled. **Transfer Admission Requirements:** High school transcript, college transcript(s), Minimum college GPA of 2.0 required. Lowest grade transferable C. **General Admission Information:** Notification on a rolling basis, beginning on or about 11/1. Nonfall registration accepted. Admission may be deferred for a maximum of 1 year.

COSTS AND FINANCIAL AID

Annual tuition $26,112. Room and board $10,728. Required fees $300. Average book expense $1,800. **Required Forms and Deadlines:** FAFSA. **Notification of Awards:** Applicants will be notified of awards on a rolling basis beginning 3/1. **Types of Aid:** *Need-based scholarships/grants:* Federal Pell, SEOG, state scholarships/grants, private scholarships, the school's own gift aid. *Loans:* Subsidized Stafford, Unsubsidized Stafford, PLUS, Federal Perkins, state loans, college/university loans from institutional funds. **Financial Aid Statistics:** 94% undergrads receive need-based scholarship or grant aid. 71% freshmen, 63% undergrads receive non-need-based scholarship or grant aid. 98% freshmen, 97% undergrads receive need-based self-help aid. 0% freshmen, 0% undergrads receive athletic scholarships. 82% undergrads borrow to pay for school. Average cumulative indebtedness $26,588. **Criteria for awarding institutional aid:** *Non-need-based:* academics, alumni affiliation, job skills, leadership, state/district residency.

JOHNSON AND WALES UNIVERSITY—DENVER

7150 Montview Boulevard, Denver, CO 80220
Phone: 303-256-9300
Fax: 303-256-9333 • **Website:** http://www.jwu.edu/denver

This private school was founded in 1914.

RATINGS

Admissions Selectivity Rating: 63   **Fire Safety Rating:** 60*

STUDENTS AND FACULTY

Enrollment: 1,672. **Student Body:** 59% female, 41% male, 56% out-of-state, 1% international. Asian 3%, African American 5%, Caucasian 49%, Hispanic 11%, Native American 1%
Retention and Graduation: 39% freshmen graduate within 4 years. **Faculty:** 54 full-time faculty, 37% are members of minority groups.

ACADEMICS

Degrees: associate, bachelor's. **Classes:** Most classes have 10–19 students. Most lab/discussion sessions have 20–29 students. **Majors with Highest Enrollment:** Business/Commerce; Hotel/Motel Administration/Management; Restaurant/Food Services Management. **Special Study Options:** cooperative education program, double major, honors program, independent study, internships, study abroad.

FACILITIES

Housing: Coed dorms, Living-Learning Communities (LLCs) and Theme Floors, are an exciting approach to combining residential and academic life at Johnson & Wales University, Denver. LLCs and theme floors provide students with an opportunity to interact with faculty, staff, and other students around a theme or academic discipline in an active and collaborative program that enhances the teaching and learning process by incorporating all aspects of a Student's collegiate experience.

CAMPUS LIFE

Activities: Choral groups, dance, literary magazine, student government, yearbook.

ADMISSIONS

Freshman Academic Profile: Average high school GPA 3.16. **Basis for Candidate Selection:** *Very important factors considered include:* Class rank, rigor of secondary school record, interview. *Important factors considered include:* extracurricular activities, work experience. *Other factors considered include:* academic GPA, recommendation(s), standardized test scores, alumni/ae relation, level of applicant's interest, volunteer work. **Freshman Admission Requirements:** High school diploma is required and GED is accepted. **Freshman Admission Statistics:** 2,520 applied, 70% admitted, 24% enrolled. **Trans-**

fer Admission Requirements: High school transcript, college transcript(s), Minimum college GPA of 2.0 required. Lowest grade transferable C. **General Admission Information:** Notification on a rolling basis, beginning on or about 11/1. Nonfall registration accepted. Admission may be deferred for a maximum of 1 year.

COSTS AND FINANCIAL AID

Annual tuition $26,112. Room and board $9,750. Required fees $300. **Required Forms and Deadlines:** FAFSA. **Notification of Awards:** Applicants will be notified of awards on a rolling basis beginning 3/1. **Types of Aid:** *Need-based scholarships/grants:* Federal Pell, SEOG, state scholarships/grants, private scholarships, the school's own gift aid. *Loans:* Subsidized Stafford, Unsubsidized Stafford, PLUS, Federal Perkins, state loans, college/university loans from institutional funds. **Financial Aid Statistics:** 91% freshmen, 84% undergrads receive need-based scholarship or grant aid. 85% freshmen, 74% undergrads receive non-need-based scholarship or grant aid. 90% freshmen, 94% undergrads receive need-based self-help aid. 0% freshmen, 0% undergrads receive athletic scholarships. 74% undergrads borrow to pay for school. Average cumulative indebtedness $19,547. **Criteria for awarding institutional aid:** *Non-need-based:* academics, alumni affiliation, job skills, leadership, state/district residency.

JOHNSON AND WALES UNIVERSITY— PROVIDENCE CAMPUS

8 Abbott Park Place, Providence, RI 02903-3703
Phone: 401-598-2310
E-mail: admissions.pvd@jwu.edu
Fax: 401-598-2948 • **Website:** www.jwu.edu • **ACT Code:** 3804

This private school was founded in 1914. It has a 50-acre campus.

RATINGS

Admissions Selectivity Rating: 63   Fire Safety Rating: 60*

STUDENTS AND FACULTY

Enrollment: 9,756. **Student Body:** 56% female, 44% male, 81% out-of-state, 10% international. Asian 2%, African American 8%, Caucasian 48%, Hispanic 8%, Native American <1%
Retention and Graduation: 74% freshmen return for sophomore year. 41% freshmen graduate within 4 years. **Faculty:** 308 full-time faculty, 42% are members of minority groups.

ACADEMICS

Degrees: associate, bachelor's, certificate, master's, post-master's certificate. **Classes:** Most classes have 10–19 students. Most lab/discussion sessions have 10–19 students. **Special Study Options:** Accelerated program, cooperative education program, English as a Second Language (ESL), exchange student program (domestic), external degree program, honors program, independent study, study abroad, weekend college.

FACILITIES

Housing: Coed dorms, special housing for disabled students, special housing for international students, Technology Living/Learning Community at Snowden Hall—a wing for first-year technology majors (among other upperclassman technology majors) interested in living with other students in the same academic program. The floor Resident Assistant is an upperclassman Technology Major. Faculty from the School of Technology will be involved in programming and mentorship in this community, providing out of classroom contact with instructors and academic program content. **Special Academic Facilities/ Equipment:** Culinary Archives and Museum. **Computers:** Students can register for classes online. Administrative functions (other than registration) can be performed online.

CAMPUS LIFE

Environment: City. **Activities:** Choral groups, dance, drama/theater, pep band, student government, student newspaper, yearbook. **Athletics (Intercollegiate):** *Men:* baseball, basketball, cheerleading, cross-country, equestrian sports, golf, ice hockey, soccer, tennis, volleyball, wrestling. *Women:* basketball, cheerleading, cross-country, equestrian sports, golf, ice hockey, soccer, softball, tennis, volleyball.

ADMISSIONS

Freshman Academic Profile: Average high school GPA 3.12. **Basis for Candidate Selection:** *Very important factors considered include:* Class rank, rigor of secondary school record, interview. *Important factors considered include:* extracurricular activities, work experience. *Other factors considered include:*

academic GPA, recommendation(s), standardized test scores, level of applicant's interest, volunteer work. **Freshman Admission Requirements:** High school diploma is required and GED is accepted. **Freshman Admission Statistics:** 11,830 applied, 76% admitted, 26% enrolled. **Transfer Admission Requirements:** High school transcript, college transcript(s), Minimum college GPA of 2.0 required. Lowest grade transferable C. **General Admission Information:** Notification on a rolling basis, beginning on or about 11/1. Nonfall registration accepted. Admission may be deferred for a maximum of 1 year.

COSTS AND FINANCIAL AID

Annual tuition $27,156. Room and board $10,728. Required fees $300. Average book expense $1,800. **Required Forms and Deadlines:** FAFSA. **Notification of Awards:** Applicants will be notified of awards on a rolling basis beginning 3/1. **Types of Aid:** *Need-based scholarships/grants:* Federal Pell, SEOG, state scholarships/grants, private scholarships, the school's own gift aid. *Loans:* Subsidized Stafford, Unsubsidized Stafford, PLUS, Federal Perkins, state loans, college/university loans from institutional funds. **Financial Aid Statistics:** 90% freshmen, 84% undergrads receive need-based scholarship or grant aid. 71% freshmen, 59% undergrads receive non-need-based scholarship or grant aid. 93% freshmen, 95% undergrads receive need-based self-help aid. 0% freshmen, 0% undergrads receive athletic scholarships. 77% undergrads borrow to pay for school. Average cumulative indebtedness $20,148. **Criteria for awarding institutional aid:** *Non-need-based:* academics, alumni affiliation, job skills, leadership, state/district residency.

JOHNSON STATE COLLEGE

337 College Hill, Johnson, VT 05656-9408
Phone: 802-635-1219 • **Financial Aid Phone:** 802-635-1380
E-mail: jscadmissions@jsc.edu • **CEEB Code:** 3766
Fax: 802-635-1230 • **Website:** www.jsc.edu • **ACT Code:** 4316

This public school was founded in 1828. It has a 350-acre campus.

RATINGS

Admissions Selectivity Rating: 78   Fire Safety Rating: 72

STUDENTS AND FACULTY

Enrollment: 1,640. **Student Body:** 62% female, 38% male, 28% out-of-state, 0% international (2 countries represented). Asian 1%, African American 3%, Caucasian 85%, Hispanic 1%, Native American 1%
Retention and Graduation: 64% freshmen return for sophomore year. 15% freshmen graduate within 4 years. 35% freshmen graduate within 6 years. **Faculty:** 50 full-time faculty, 98% hold PhDs, 36% are members of minority groups, 4% are women. 0% of classes are taught by teaching assistants.

ACADEMICS

Degrees: associate, bachelor's, master's, post-bachelor's certificate, terminal associate. **Classes:** Most classes have 10–19 students. **Majors with Highest Enrollment:** Elementary Education and Teaching; Visual and Performing Arts; Tourism and Travel Services Management. **Special Study Options:** cross-registration, double major, dual enrollment, English as a Second Language (ESL), exchange student program (domestic), external degree program, honors program, independent study, internships, study abroad, teacher certification program. **Disability Services:** Special programs offered to physically disabled students include note-taking services, reader services, tape recorders, tutors. **Career services:** Alumni network, alumni services, career/job search classes, career assessment, internships, regional alumni. Career services highlights include internships.

FACILITIES

Housing: Coed dorms, apartments for married students, apartments for single students, Apartments for students who have 60 credits and a 3.0 average GPA. 65% of campus accessible to physically disabled. **Special Academic Facilities/ Equipment:** Art gallery, visual arts center, child development center, human performance lab, 1,000-acre nature preserve, snowboard terrain park, dance studio. **Computers:** Students can register for classes online. Administrative functions (other than registration) can be performed online.

CAMPUS LIFE

Environment: Rural. **Activities:** Choral groups, concert band, dance, drama/theater, jazz band, literary magazine, music ensembles, musical theater, pep band, radio station, student government, student newspaper, yearbook, International Student Organization. 30 registered organizations, 1 honor society, 4 religious organizations. **Athletics (Intercollegiate):** *Men:* basketball, cross-country, golf, lacrosse, soccer, tennis. *Women:* basketball, cross-country, soccer, softball, tennis, volleyball. **On-Campus Highlights:** Dibden Center For the Arts, Snowboarding Hill, Baselodge, Disc Golf Course, SHAPE Athletic Facility, Located in the heart of the Green Mountains, 1 hour from Vermont largest city, Burlington. JSC has 14 buildings on 1,350 acres (including our nature preserve). **Environmental Initiatives:** We compost. We owned a 1000 acres preserved land. Bio-Diesel school bus for students' transportation.

ADMISSIONS

Freshman Academic Profile: 34% in top 10% of high school class, 66% in top 25% of high school class, 68% in top 50% of high school class. SAT Math middle 50% range 430-550. SAT Critical Reading middle 50% range 430-550. ACT middle 50% range 20-28. Minimum internet-based TOEFL 61. Minimum paper TOEFL 500. **Basis for Candidate Selection:** *Very important factors considered include:* rigor of secondary school record, standardized test scores. *Important factors considered include:* Class rank, application essay, academic GPA, recommendation(s), character/personal qualities, talent/ability. *Other factors considered include:* extracurricular activities, interview, volunteer work, work experience. **Freshman Admission Requirements:** High school diploma is required and GED is accepted. *Academic units required:* 4 English, 2 mathematics, 2 science, (1 science labs), 0 foreign language, 3 social studies, 2 history. **Transfer Admission Requirements:** High school transcript, college transcript(s), essay or personal statement, statement of good standing from prior institution(s). Minimum college GPA of 2.0 required. Lowest grade transferable C-. **General Admission Information:** Application Fee $39. Notification on a rolling basis, beginning on or about 12/1. Nonfall registration accepted. Admission may be deferred for a maximum of 1 year. Credit and/or placement offered for CEEB Advanced Placement tests.

COSTS AND FINANCIAL AID

Average book expense $1,000. **Required Forms and Deadlines:** FAFSA, State aid form. **Notification of Awards:** Applicants will be notified of awards on a rolling basis beginning 4/1. **Types of Aid:** *Need-based scholarships/grants:* Federal Pell, SEOG, state scholarships/grants, private scholarships, the school's own gift aid. *Loans:* Subsidized Stafford, Unsubsidized Stafford, PLUS, Federal Perkins. *Student Employment:* Federal Work-Study Program available. Institutional employment available. Off-campus job opportunities are good. **Financial Aid Statistics:** 93% freshmen, 89% undergrads receive need-based scholarship or grant aid. 4% freshmen, 3% undergrads receive non-need-based scholarship or grant aid. 95% freshmen, 95% undergrads receive need-based self-help aid. 0% freshmen, 0% undergrads receive athletic scholarships. 87% freshmen, 82% undergrads receive any aid. **Criteria for awarding institutional aid:** *Non-need-based:* academics, art, leadership, music/drama, state/district residency.

JOHNSON UNIVERSITY

7900 Johnson Drive, Knoxville, TN 37998
Phone: 800-827-2122 · **Financial Aid Phone:** 865-251-2303
E-mail: http://www.johnsonu.edu/ · **CEEB Code:** 1345
Fax: 865-251-2336 · **Website:** http://www.johnsonu.edu/ · **ACT Code:** 3968

This private school, affiliated with the Christian (Nondenominational) Church, was founded in 1893. It has a 350-acre campus.

RATINGS

Admissions Selectivity Rating: 80   **Fire Safety Rating:** 73

STUDENTS AND FACULTY

Student Body: 78% out-of-state, (12 countries represented).
Retention and Graduation: 73% freshmen return for sophomore year. 57% freshmen graduate within 6 years. **Faculty:** 30 full-time faculty, 63% hold PhDs, 17% are members of minority groups, 0% are women. 0% of classes are taught by teaching assistants.

ACADEMICS

Degrees: associate, bachelor's, certificate, master's. **Special Study Options:** Accelerated program, cooperative education program, distance learning, double major, English as a Second Language (ESL), honors program, independent study, internships, teacher certification program. **Disability Services:** Special programs offered to physically disabled students include reader services, tape recorders.

FACILITIES

Housing: men's dorms, women's dorms, apartments for married students.
Computers: Students can register for classes online. Administrative functions (other than registration) can be performed online.

CAMPUS LIFE

Environment: Rural. **Activities:** Choral groups, music ensembles, musical theater, radio station, student government, yearbook 3 honor societies, 3 religious organizations. **Athletics (Intercollegiate):** *Men:* baseball, basketball,

cheerleading, soccer. *Women:* basketball, cheerleading, volleyball. **On-Campus Highlights:** women's residence hall, men's residence hall, global-education-tech building.

ADMISSIONS

Freshman Academic Profile: Average high school GPA 3. 21% in top 10% of high school class, 48% in top 25% of high school class, 78% in top 50% of high school class. SAT Math middle 50% range 470-560. SAT Critical Reading middle 50% range 480-612. SAT Writing middle 50% range 487-562. ACT middle 50% range 20-26. Minimum paper TOEFL 500. **Basis for Candidate Selection:** *Very important factors considered include:* Class rank, recommendation(s), rigor of secondary school record, standardized test scores, character/personal qualities, religious affiliation/commitment. *Important factors considered include:* application essay, interview. *Other factors considered include:* alumni/ae relation, extracurricular activities, talent/ability, volunteer work. **Freshman Admission Requirements:** High school diploma is required and GED is accepted. **Freshman Admission Statistics:** 213 applied, 95% admitted, 58% enrolled. **Transfer Admission Requirements:** High school transcript, college transcript(s), essay or personal statement, statement of good standing from prior institution(s). Lowest grade transferable C. **General Admission Information:** Application Fee $35. Regular application deadline 7/1. Regular notification 9/1. Nonfall registration accepted. Admission may be deferred for a maximum of one year.

COSTS AND FINANCIAL AID

Average book expense $1,300. **Required Forms and Deadlines:** FAFSA, Institution's own financial aid form. **Notification of Awards:** Applicants will be notified of awards on or about 3/30. **Types of Aid:** *Need-based scholarships/grants:* Federal Pell, SEOG, state scholarships/grants, private scholarships, the school's own gift aid. *Loans:* Subsidized Stafford, Unsubsidized Stafford, PLUS. *Student Employment:* Federal Work-Study Program available. Institutional employment available. Highest amount earned per year from on-campus jobs $1,240. **Financial Aid Statistics:** 97% freshmen, 98% undergrads receive need-based scholarship or grant aid. 24% freshmen, 26% undergrads receive non-need-based scholarship or grant aid. 59% freshmen, 58% undergrads receive need-based self-help aid. 0% freshmen, 0% undergrads receive athletic scholarships. 97% undergrads receive any aid. 63% undergrads borrow to pay for school. **Criteria for awarding institutional aid:** *Non-need-based:* academics, minority status, music/drama, religious affiliation, state/district residency.

JONES INTERNATIONAL UNIVERSITY

9697 E. Mineral Avenue, Centennial, CO 80112
Phone: 800-811-5663
E-mail: admissions@international.edu
Fax: 303-799-0966 · **Website:** www.jonesinternational.edu

This is a private school.

RATINGS

Admissions Selectivity Rating: 60*   **Fire Safety Rating:** 60*

STUDENTS AND FACULTY

Enrollment: 22. **Student Body:** 50% female, 50% male,
Retention and Graduation: 97% freshmen return for sophomore year.
Faculty:

ACADEMICS

Degrees: bachelor's, certificate, master's. **Special Study Options:** Accelerated program, distance learning, external degree program.

ADMISSIONS

Basis for Candidate Selection: *Very important factors considered include:* rigor of secondary school record, interview. *Important factors considered include:* standardized test scores. *Other factors considered include:* Class rank, academic GPA, recommendation(s), character/personal qualities, extracurricular activities, talent/ability, volunteer work, work experience. **Freshman Admission Requirements:** High school diploma is required and GED is accepted. **Freshman Admission Statistics:** 22 applied, 100% admitted, 86% enrolled. **Transfer Admission Requirements:** High school transcript, college transcript(s), Lowest grade transferable C. **General Admission Information:** Application Fee $50. Nonfall registration accepted. Credit and/or placement offered for CEEB Advanced Placement tests.

COSTS AND FINANCIAL AID

Average book expense $100. **Notification of Awards:** Applicants will be notified of awards on a rolling basis beginning 3/1. **Types of Aid:** *Need-based scholarships/grants:* Federal Pell, SEOG, state scholarships/grants, private scholarships, the school's own gift aid. *Loans:* Subsidized Stafford, Unsubsidized Stafford, PLUS, state loans. **Criteria for awarding institutional aid:** *Non-need-based:* academics, alumni affiliation.

JUDSON COLLEGE (AL)

302 Bibb Street, Marion, AL 36756
Phone: 334-683-5110 · **Financial Aid Phone:** 334-683-5157
E-mail: admissions@judson.edu · **CEEB Code:** 1349
Fax: 334-683-5282 · **Website:** www.judson.edu · **ACT Code:** 22

This private school, affiliated with the Baptist Church, was founded in 1838. It has a 80-acre campus.

RATINGS

Admissions Selectivity Rating: 80   **Fire Safety Rating:** 70

STUDENTS AND FACULTY

Enrollment: 315. **Student Body:** 97% female, 3% male, 29% out-of-state, 1% international (3 countries represented). Asian 0%, African American 12%, Caucasian 83%, Hispanic 1%, Native American 1%
Retention and Graduation: 61% freshmen return for sophomore year. 49% freshmen graduate within 4 years. 49% freshmen graduate within 6 years. 15% grads go on to further study within 1 year. 83% grads pursue arts and sciences degrees. 17% grads pursue medical degrees. **Faculty:** 18 full-time faculty, 83% hold PhDs, 39% are members of minority groups, 0% are women. 0% of classes are taught by teaching assistants.

ACADEMICS

Degrees: bachelor's. **Classes:** Most classes have fewer than 10 students. Most lab/discussion sessions have fewer than 10 students. **Majors with Highest Enrollment:** Elementary Education and Teaching; Biology/Biological Sciences; Psychology. **Special Study Options:** Accelerated program, cross-registration, distance learning, double major, dual enrollment, independent study, internships, student-designed major, study abroad, teacher certification program. **Disability Services:** Special programs offered to physically disabled students include tutors. **Career services:** alumni services, career assessment, internships,

FACILITIES

Housing: women's dorms. 50% of campus accessible to physically disabled. **Special Academic Facilities/Equipment:** Alabama Women's Hall of Fame. **Computers:** 50% of classrooms, 100% of dorms, 100% of libraries, 100% of student union, have wireless network access.

CAMPUS LIFE

Environment: Rural. **Activities:** Choral groups, drama/theater, literary magazine, marching band, music ensembles, student government, student newspaper, yearbook, Campus Ministries. 23 registered organizations, 8 honor societies, 1 religious organization. **Athletics (Intercollegiate):** *Women:* basketball, equestrian sports, soccer, softball, volleyball. **On-Campus Highlights:** Residence Hall Lobbies, Gym, Computer Labs, Club House, Student Center.

ADMISSIONS

Freshman Academic Profile: Average high school GPA 3.41. 32% in top 10% of high school class, 22% in top 25% of high school class, 84% in top 50% of high school class. 78% from public high schools. SAT Math middle 50% range 470-590. SAT Critical Reading middle 50% range 540-590. SAT Writing middle 50% range 520-630. ACT middle 50% range 19-26. Minimum paper TOEFL 500. **Basis for Candidate Selection:** *Very important factors considered include:* Class rank, academic GPA, standardized test scores. *Other factors considered include:* recommendation(s), rigor of secondary school record, alumni/ae relation, character/personal qualities, extracurricular activities, level of applicant's interest, talent/ability. **Freshman Admission Requirements:** High school diploma is required and GED is accepted. *Academic units required:* 4 English, 2 mathematics, 2 science, 3 social studies, 5 academic electives. **Freshman Admission Statistics:** 306 applied, 84% admitted, 38% enrolled. **Transfer Admission Requirements:** college transcript(s), Minimum college GPA of 2.0 required. Lowest grade transferable C-. **General Admission Information:** Application Fee $35. Notification on a rolling basis, beginning on or about 8/1. Nonfall registration accepted. Admission may be deferred for a maximum of 1 Year. Credit and/or placement offered for CEEB Advanced Placement tests.

COSTS AND FINANCIAL AID

Annual tuition $12,327. Room and board $7,969. Required fees $330. Average book expense $1,200. **Required Forms and Deadlines:** FAFSA, Institution's own financial aid form, State aid form. **Notification of Awards:** Applicants will be notified of awards on a rolling basis beginning 11/15. **Types of Aid:**

Need-based scholarships/grants: Federal Pell, SEOG, state scholarships/grants, private scholarships, the school's own gift aid. *Loans:* Subsidized Stafford, Unsubsidized Stafford, PLUS, Federal Perkins, college/university loans from institutional funds. *Student Employment:* Federal Work-Study Program available. Institutional employment available. Highest amount earned per year from on-campus jobs $1,750. Off-campus job opportunities are poor. **Financial Aid Statistics:** 97% freshmen, 97% undergrads receive need-based scholarship or grant aid. 11% freshmen, 12% undergrads receive non-need-based scholarship or grant aid. 75% freshmen, 86% undergrads receive need-based self-help aid. 12% freshmen, 12% undergrads receive athletic scholarships. 99% freshmen, 96% undergrads receive any aid. 74% undergrads borrow to pay for school. Average cumulative indebtedness $16,920. **Criteria for awarding institutional aid:** *Non-need-based:* academics, alumni affiliation, art, athletics, music/drama, religious affiliation, state/district residency.

JUDSON UNIVERSITY (IL)

1151 North State Street, Elgin, IL 60123
Phone: 847-628-2510 · **Financial Aid Phone:** 847-628-2530
E-mail: admission@JudsonU.edu · **CEEB Code:** 1700
Fax: 847-628-2526 · **Website:** www.JudsonU.edu · **ACT Code:** 1101

This private school, affiliated with the Baptist Church, was founded in 1963. It has a 84-acre campus.

RATINGS

Admissions Selectivity Rating: 77   **Fire Safety Rating:** 77

STUDENTS AND FACULTY

Enrollment: 1,132. **Student Body:** 58% female, 42% male, 35% out-of-state, 3% international (25 countries represented). Asian 1%, African American 4%, Caucasian 69%, Hispanic 5%, Native American <1%
Retention and Graduation: 72% freshmen return for sophomore year. **Faculty:** 54 full-time faculty, 74% hold PhDs, 30% are members of minority groups, 13% are women. 0% of classes are taught by teaching assistants.

ACADEMICS

Degrees: bachelor's, certificate, master's. **Classes:** Most classes have 10–19 students. Most lab/discussion sessions have fewer than 10 students. **Majors with Highest Enrollment:** Elementary Education and Teaching; Business/Commerce. **Special Study Options:** Accelerated program, distance learning, double major, English as a Second Language (ESL), honors program, independent study, internships, study abroad, teacher certification program. **Honors programs:** GEN101H Faith and Learning: The Consecrated Genius MAT 211H Functions and Calculus Combined degree programs: BA/MA, Architecture. **Disability Services:** Special programs offered to physically disabled students include tutors. **Career services:** Alumni network, alumni services, career/job search classes, career assessment, internships. Career services highlights include internships in the following areas: Architecture, Business, Education, Worship Arts, Youth Ministry.

FACILITIES

Housing: Coed dorms, special housing for disabled students, men's dorms, women's dorms, apartments for married students. **Computers:** Students can register for classes online. Administrative functions (other than registration) can be performed online.

CAMPUS LIFE

Environment: City. **Activities:** Choral groups, drama/theater, music ensembles, student government. 23 registered organizations, 1 honor society. **Athletics (Intercollegiate):** *Men:* baseball, basketball, cheerleading, soccer. *Women:* basketball, cheerleading, soccer, softball, volleyball. **On-Campus Highlights:** Harm A. Weber Academic Center, Lindner Fitness Center, Lindner Commons, Eyrie Coffee House.

ADMISSIONS

Freshman Academic Profile: Average high school GPA 3.27. 7% in top 10% of high school class, 35% in top 25% of high school class, 59% in top 50% of high school class. SAT Math middle 50% range 440-660. SAT Critical Reading middle 50% range 430-600. ACT middle 50% range 20-26. Minimum paper TOEFL 550. **Basis for Candidate Selection:** *Very important factors considered include:* rigor of secondary school record, standardized test scores. *Important factors considered include:* character/personal qualities. *Other factors considered include:* Class rank, recommendation(s), talent/ability. **Freshman Admission Requirements:** High school diploma is required and GED is accepted. **Freshman Admission Statistics:** 520 applied, 73% admitted, 44% enrolled. **Transfer Admission Requirements:** college transcript(s), Minimum college GPA of 2.0 required. Lowest grade transferable C-. **General**

Admission Information: Application Fee $30. Notification on a rolling basis, beginning on or about 7/1. Nonfall registration accepted. Admission may be deferred for a maximum of 1 semester. Credit and/or placement offered for CEEB Advanced Placement tests.

COSTS AND FINANCIAL AID

Annual tuition $13,872. Room and board $5,570. Required fees $550. Average book expense $680. **Required Forms and Deadlines:** FAFSA. **Types of Aid:** *Need-based scholarships/grants:* Federal Pell, SEOG, state scholarships/grants, private scholarships, the school's own gift aid. *Loans:* Direct Subsidized Stafford, Direct Unsubsidized Stafford, Direct PLUS, Federal Perkins. *Student Employment:* Federal Work-Study Program available. Institutional employment available. Highest amount earned per year from on-campus jobs $1,200. Off-campus job opportunities are excellent. **Financial Aid Statistics:** 0% freshmen, 0% undergrads receive athletic scholarships. 90% freshmen, 90% undergrads receive any aid. **Criteria for awarding institutional aid:** *Non-need-based:* academics, art, athletics, music/drama.

THE JUILLIARD SCHOOL

60 Lincoln Center Plaza, New York, NY 10023-6588
Phone: 212-799-2000 ext.223 · **Financial Aid Phone:** 212-799-5000
E-mail: admissions@juilliard.edu · **CEEB Code:** 2340
Fax: 212-769-6420 · **Website:** www.juilliard.edu

This private school was founded in 1905.

RATINGS
Admissions Selectivity Rating: 71   **Fire Safety Rating:** 65

STUDENTS AND FACULTY

Enrollment: 510. **Student Body:** 45% female, 55% male, 32% out-of-state, 26% international (40 countries represented). Asian 13%, African American 5%, Caucasian 43%, Hispanic 6%, Native American <1%
Faculty: 130 full-time faculty, 33% are members of minority groups, 17% are women.

ACADEMICS

Degrees: bachelor's, diploma, master's, post-master's certificate. **Classes:** Most classes have fewer than 10 students. **Majors with Highest Enrollment:** Keyboard Instruments; Voice and Opera; Stringed Instruments.

FACILITIES

Housing: Coed dorms. **Special Academic Facilities/Equipment:** 2 recital halls, 1 theater (1000 ppl), 1 drama theater (200 ppl), 15 two-story studios, 35 private teaching studios, 106 practice rooms, organ studios, 200+ pianos, recording studio, The Peter Jay Sharp Special Collections Room. **Computers:** Students can register for classes online. Administrative functions (other than registration) can be performed online.

CAMPUS LIFE

Environment: Metropolis. **Activities:** student government. 5 registered organizations, 2 religious organizations. **On-Campus Highlights:** Lila Acheson Wallace Library, Lincoln Center, Rose Building—cafeteria, Juilliard Bookstore.

ADMISSIONS

Freshman Academic Profile: Minimum paper TOEFL 533. **Basis for Candidate Selection:** *Very important factors considered include:* interview, talent/ability. *Other factors considered include:* application essay, academic GPA, recommendation(s). **Freshman Admission Requirements:** High school diploma is required and GED is accepted. **Freshman Admission Statistics:** 2,385 applied, 8% admitted, 67% enrolled. **Transfer Admission Requirements:** college transcript(s), essay or personal statement, interview, Lowest grade transferable C. **General Admission Information:** Application Fee $100. Regular application deadline 12/1. Regular notification 4/1. Nonfall registration not accepted. Neither credit nor placement offered for CEEB Advanced Placement tests.

COSTS AND FINANCIAL AID

Annual tuition $38,190. Room and board $14,290. Required fees $450. Average book expense $560. **Required Forms and Deadlines:** FAFSA, Institution's own financial aid form. **Notification of Awards:** Applicants will be notified of awards on or about 4/1. **Types of Aid:** *Need-based scholarships/grants:* Federal Pell, SEOG, state scholarships/grants, private scholarships, the school's own gift aid. *Loans:* Direct Subsidized Stafford, Direct Unsubsidized Stafford, Direct PLUS, PLUS, Federal Perkins. *Student Employment:* Highest amount earned per year from on-campus jobs $4,500. **Financial Aid Statistics:** 95% freshmen, 97% undergrads receive need-based scholarship or grant aid. 0% freshmen, 0%

undergrads receive non-need-based scholarship or grant aid. 95% freshmen, 97% undergrads receive need-based self-help aid. 0% freshmen, 0% undergrads receive athletic scholarships. 53% undergrads borrow to pay for school. Average cumulative indebtedness $22,605. **Criteria for awarding institutional aid:** *Non-need-based:* music/drama.

JUNIATA COLLEGE

1700 Moore Street, Huntingdon, PA 16652
Phone: 814-641-3420 · **Financial Aid Phone:** 814-641-3142
E-mail: admissions@juniata.edu · **CEEB Code:** 2341
Fax: 814-641-3100 · **Website:** www.juniata.edu · **ACT Code:** 3600

This private school was founded in 1876. It has a 800-acre campus.

RATINGS
Admissions Selectivity Rating: 88   **Fire Safety Rating:** 81

STUDENTS AND FACULTY

Enrollment: 1,503. **Student Body:** 55% female, 45% male, 36% out-of-state, 8% international (44 countries represented). Asian 3%, African American 3%, Caucasian 74%, Hispanic 4%, Native American <1%
Retention and Graduation: 88% freshmen return for sophomore year. 72% freshmen graduate within 4 years. 75% freshmen graduate within 6 years. 34% grads go on to further study within 1 year. 62% grads pursue arts and sciences degrees. 3% grads pursue law degrees. 5% grads pursue business degrees. 20% grads pursue medical degrees. **Faculty:** 106 full-time faculty, 93% hold PhDs, 42% are members of minority groups, 7% are women. 0% of classes are taught by teaching assistants.

ACADEMICS

Degrees: bachelor's. **Classes:** Most classes have 10–19 students. Most lab/discussion sessions have 10–19 students. **Majors with Highest Enrollment:** Biology/Biological Sciences; Business/Commerce; Psychology. **Special Study Options:** double major, dual enrollment, English as a Second Language (ESL), exchange student program (domestic), honors program, independent study, internships, student-designed major, study abroad, teacher certification program, Philadelphia Urban Semester, Marine Science Semester, Washington Semester, Cooperative Degree Programs (3-1, 3-2, etc.). **Honors programs:** Entire college is considered to be an honors program. Combined degree programs: BA/MD, BA/JD, BA/MA, BA/DDS, BA/MEng, Dentistry,Optometry,Podiatry,Allied Health,Nursing. **Disability Services:** Special programs offered to physically disabled students include reader services, tape recorders, tutors. **Career services:** Alumni network, alumni services, career/job search classes, career assessment, internships. Career services highlights include countless opportunities to learn by doing. Whether students are participating in internships, studying abroad, volunteering for local charities, leading student organizations, starting their own business, designing a play, or working on individual research, Juniata students learn early in their education how to make things happen.

FACILITIES

Housing: Coed dorms, special housing for international students, women's dorms, apartments for single students, Substance-Free Housing. 75% of campus accessible to physically disabled. **Special Academic Facilities/Equipment:** Environmental Studies Field Station, Juniata Museum of Art, Early Childhood Education Center, Ceramics studio and Anagama Kiln, Nature preserve and Peace Chapel, Observatory, Electron microscopes, Nuclear magnetic resonance spectrometers, Human Interaction Lab. three story, free form theater. **Computers:** 100% of classrooms, 100% of dorms, 100% of libraries, 100% of dining areas, 100% of student union, 100% of common outdoor areas have wireless network access. Students can register for classes online. Administrative functions (other than registration) can be performed online. Undergraduates are required to own a computer.

CAMPUS LIFE

Environment: Village. **Activities:** Choral groups, concert band, dance, drama/theater, jazz band, literary magazine, music ensembles, musical theater, radio station, student government, student newspaper, symphony orchestra, television station, Campus Ministries, International Student Organization, Model UN. 94 registered organizations, 12 honor societies, 7 religious organizations. **Athletics (Intercollegiate):** *Men:* baseball, basketball, cross-country, football, soccer, tennis, track/field (outdoor), track/field (indoor), volleyball. *Women:* basketball, cross-country, field hockey, soccer, softball, swimming, tennis, track/field (outdoor), track/field (indoor), volleyball. **On-Campus Highlights:** von Liebig Science Center, Juniata College Museum of Art, Ceramics Studio w/Anagama Kiln, Sill Business Incubator and Juniata College Center, Suzanne von Liebig Theatre. **Environmental Initiatives:** 60% today and 75% by 2012 Electric in Wind RECS 2 LEED Certified Buildings, one Gold with Geothermal Goals part of campus strategic plan.

ADMISSIONS

Freshman Academic Profile: Average high school GPA 3.75. 34% in top 10% of high school class, 73% in top 25% of high school class, 98% in top 50% of high school class. 78% from public high schools. SAT Math middle 50% range 520-630. SAT Critical Reading middle 50% range 520-630. Minimum internet-based TOEFL 79. Minimum paper TOEFL 550. **Basis for Candidate Selection:** *Very important factors considered include:* application essay, academic GPA, recommendation(s), rigor of secondary school record, standardized test scores, character/personal qualities. *Important factors considered include:* extracurricular activities, first generation, interview, talent/ability, volunteer work. *Other factors considered include:* alumni/ae relation, geographical residence, level of applicant's interest, racial/ethnic status, state residency. **Freshman Admission Requirements:** High school diploma is required and GED is accepted. *Academic units required:* 4 English, 3 mathematics, 3 science, (2 science labs), 2 foreign language, 1 social studies, 3 history. **Freshman Admission Statistics:** 2,227 applied, 74% admitted, 24% enrolled. **Transfer Admission Requirements:** High school transcript, college transcript(s), essay or personal statement, Minimum college GPA of 2.5 required. Lowest grade transferable C-. **General Admission Information:** Application Fee $30. Early decision application deadline 12/1. Regular application deadline 3/15. Notification on a rolling basis, beginning on or about 2/28. Nonfall registration accepted. Admission may be deferred for a maximum of 12 months. Credit and/or placement offered for CEEB Advanced Placement tests.

COSTS AND FINANCIAL AID

Annual tuition $37,870. Room and board $10,710. Required fees $760. Average book expense $1,000. **Required Forms and Deadlines:** FAFSA. **Notification of Awards:** Applicants will be notified of awards on a rolling basis beginning 2/28. **Types of Aid:** *Need-based scholarships/grants:* Federal Pell, SEOG, state scholarships/grants, private scholarships, the school's own gift aid. *Loans:* Subsidized Stafford, Unsubsidized Stafford, PLUS, Federal Perkins, college/university loans from institutional funds. *Student Employment:* Federal Work-Study Program available. Institutional employment available. Highest amount earned per year from on-campus jobs $4,596. Off-campus job opportunities are good. **Financial Aid Statistics:** 100% freshmen, 99% undergrads receive need-based scholarship or grant aid. 14% freshmen, 13% undergrads receive non-need-based scholarship or grant aid. 86% freshmen, 86% undergrads receive need-based self-help aid. 0% freshmen, 0% undergrads receive athletic scholarships. 100% freshmen, 100% undergrads receive any aid. 81% undergrads borrow to pay for school. Average cumulative indebtedness $26,573. **Criteria for awarding institutional aid:** *Non-need-based:* academics, art, leadership.

KALAMAZOO COLLEGE

Best 380

1200 Academy Street, Kalamazoo, MI 49006
Phone: 269-337-7166 · **Financial Aid Phone:** 269-337-7192
E-mail: admission@kzoo.edu · **CEEB Code:** 1365
Fax: 269-337-7390 · **Website:** www.kzoo.edu · **ACT Code:** 2018

This private school was founded in 1833. It has a 60-acre campus.

RATINGS

Admissions Selectivity Rating: 89 **Fire Safety Rating:** 72

STUDENTS AND FACULTY

Enrollment: 1,431. **Student Body:** 56% female, 44% male, 31% out-of-state, 6% international (32 countries represented). Asian 6%, African American 5%, Caucasian 62%, Hispanic 9%, Native American <1%
Retention and Graduation: 92% freshmen return for sophomore year. 76% freshmen graduate within 4 years. 18% grads go on to further study within 1 year. **Faculty:** 102 full-time faculty, 92% hold PhDs, 52% are members of minority groups, 23% are women. 0% of classes are taught by teaching assistants.

ACADEMICS

Degrees: bachelor's. **Classes:** Most classes have 10–19 students. Most lab/discussion sessions have fewer than 10 students. **Majors with Highest Enroll-**

ment: English Language and Literature; Psychology; Economics. **Special Study Options:** cross-registration, double major, dual enrollment, English as a Second Language (ESL), exchange student program (domestic), independent study, internships, student-designed major, study abroad. **Disability Services:** Special programs offered to physically disabled students include note-taking services, tape recorders, tutors. **Career services:** Alumni network, alumni services, career/job search classes, career assessment, internships, regional alumni. For career services highlights see www.kzoo.edu/careerdevelopment/.

FACILITIES

Housing: Coed dorms, Wellness Housing, Theme Housing. 25% of campus accessible to physically disabled. **Special Academic Facilities/Equipment:** Science center, Rare book room. **Computers:** 100% of classrooms, 70% of dorms, 100% of libraries, 100% of dining areas, 100% of student union, have wireless network access. Students can register for classes online. Administrative functions (other than registration) can be performed online.

CAMPUS LIFE

Environment: City. **Activities:** Choral groups, concert band, dance, drama/theater, jazz band, literary magazine, music ensembles, musical theater, pep band, radio station, student government, student newspaper, symphony orchestra, yearbook, Campus Ministries, International Student Organization, Model UN. 50 registered organizations, 3 honor societies, 5 religious organizations. **Athletics (Intercollegiate):** *Men:* baseball, basketball, cross-country, diving, football, golf, soccer, swimming, tennis. *Women:* basketball, cross-country, diving, golf, soccer, softball, swimming, tennis, volleyball. **On-Campus Highlights:** Upjohn Library Commons, The Quad, Biggby Coffee Shop, Hicks Student Center, Anderson Athletic Center. **Environmental Initiatives:** The College is currently involved in a LEED registered expansion and renovation of Hicks Student Center. The project is expected to receive Silver certification when completed in summer 2008. The College has had an active recycling operation since 1988 and is participating in Recyclemania 2012 for the eighth consecutive year. The College has consistently garnered top 5 finishes in multiple categories each year it has participated. A student initiative in early 2010 intituted a food waste composting program in campus dining services. The program is in its second full yeear of operation and diverts 1,500 punds of food waste every week.

ADMISSIONS

Freshman Academic Profile: Average high school GPA 3.78. 35% in top 10% of high school class, 75% in top 25% of high school class, 96% in top 50% of high school class. 80% from public high schools. SAT Math middle 50% range 550-700. SAT Critical Reading middle 50% range 527.5-680. SAT Writing middle 50% range 540-670. ACT middle 50% range 25-30. Minimum internet-based TOEFL 84. Minimum paper TOEFL 550. **Basis for Candidate Selection:** *Very important factors considered include:* academic GPA, rigor of secondary school record, extracurricular activities, volunteer work, work experience. *Important factors considered include:* application essay, recommendation(s), standardized test scores. *Other factors considered include:* alumni/ae relation, character/personal qualities, first generation, geographical residence, interview, level of applicant's interest, racial/ethnic status, talent/ability. **Freshman Admission Requirements:** High school diploma is required and GED is accepted. *Academic units required:* 4 English, 3 mathematics, 3 science, 3 foreign language, 2 social studies, 2 history. **Freshman Admission Statistics:** 2,366 applied, 70% admitted, 22% enrolled. **Transfer Admission Requirements:** High school transcript, college transcript(s), essay or personal statement, standardized test scores, statement of good standing from prior institution(s). Lowest grade transferable C. **General Admission Information:** Application Fee $40. Early decision application deadline 11/10. Regular application deadline 2/1. Regular notification 4/1. Nonfall registration not accepted. Admission may be deferred for a maximum of 1 year. Credit and/or placement offered for CEEB Advanced Placement tests.

COSTS AND FINANCIAL AID

Annual tuition $40,728. Room and board $8,679. Required fees $433. Average book expense $705. **Required Forms and Deadlines:** FAFSA, Institution's own financial aid form. **Notification of Awards:** Applicants will be notified of awards on a rolling basis beginning 3/21. **Types of Aid:** *Need-based scholarships/grants:* Federal Pell, SEOG, state scholarships/grants, private scholarships, the school's own gift aid. *Loans:* Direct Subsidized Stafford, Direct Unsubsidized Stafford, Direct PLUS, Federal Perkins. *Student Employment:* Federal Work-Study Program available. Institutional employment available. Off-campus job opportunities are good. **Financial Aid Statistics:** 98% freshmen, 98% undergrads receive need-based scholarship or grant aid. 23% freshmen, 19% undergrads receive non-need-based scholarship or grant aid. 81% freshmen, 82% undergrads receive need-based self-help aid. 0% freshmen, 0% undergrads receive athletic scholarships. 98% freshmen, 97% undergrads receive any aid. 58% undergrads borrow to pay for school. Average cumulative indebtedness $25,020.

KANSAS CITY ART INSTITUTE

4415 Warwick Boulevard, Kansas City, MO 64111
Phone: 800-522-5224 · **Financial Aid Phone:** 816-802-3337
E-mail: admiss@kcai.edu · **CEEB Code:** 6330
Fax: 816-802-3309 · **Website:** www.kcai.edu · **ACT Code:** 2277

This private school was founded in 1885. It has a 15-acre campus.

RATINGS

Admissions Selectivity Rating: 83   **Fire Safety Rating:** 66

STUDENTS AND FACULTY

Enrollment: 671. **Student Body:** 55% female, 45% male, 62% out-of-state, 1% international (6 countries represented). Asian 4%, African American 3%, Caucasian 80%, Hispanic 6%, Native American 1%
Retention and Graduation: 78% freshmen return for sophomore year. 43% freshmen graduate within 4 years. 53% freshmen graduate within 6 years. 40% grads go on to further study within 1 year. **Faculty:** 51 full-time faculty, 84% hold PhDs, 37% are members of minority groups, 2% are women. 0% of classes are taught by teaching assistants.

ACADEMICS

Degrees: bachelor's. **Classes:** Most classes have 20–29 students. **Majors with Highest Enrollment:** Design and Visual Communications; Film/Video and Photographic Arts; Painting. **Special Study Options:** cross-registration, double major, exchange student program (domestic), independent study, internships, student-designed major, study abroad. **Disability Services:** Special programs offered to physically disabled students include tape recorders, tutors. **Career services:** Alumni network, alumni services, career/job search classes, career assessment, internships, regional alumni. Career services highlights include Community Arts and Service Learning program (CASL).

FACILITIES

Housing: Coed dorms, apartments for single students **Special Academic Facilities/Equipment:** H and R Block Art Space **Computers:** Students can register for classes online. Administrative functions (other than registration) can be performed online.

CAMPUS LIFE

Environment: Metropolis. **Activities:** student government. **On-Campus Highlights:** Dodge Painting Building, Café Nerman, Jannes Library-Learning Center, H&R Block Artspace, Green space in center of campus.

ADMISSIONS

Freshman Academic Profile: Average high school GPA 3.2. 11% in top 10% of high school class, 39% in top 25% of high school class, 73% in top 50% of high school class. 80% from public high schools. SAT Math middle 50% range 430-590. SAT Critical Reading middle 50% range 430-580. SAT Writing middle 50% range 420-570. ACT middle 50% range 20-25. Minimum internet-based TOEFL 79. Minimum paper TOEFL 550. **Basis for Candidate Selection:** *Very important factors considered include:* recommendation(s). *Important factors considered include:* application essay, academic GPA, rigor of secondary school record, standardized test scores. *Other factors considered include:* character/personal qualities, extracurricular activities, first generation, interview, level of applicant's interest, talent/ability, volunteer work, work experience. **Freshman Admission Requirements:** High school diploma is required and GED is accepted. **Freshman Admission Statistics:** 537 applied, 63% admitted, 41% enrolled. **Transfer Admission Requirements:** High school transcript, college transcript(s), essay or personal statement, statement of good standing from prior institution(s). Minimum college GPA of 2.5 required. Lowest grade transferable C. **General Admission Information:** Application Fee $35. Notification on a rolling basis, beginning on or about 9/1. Nonfall registration accepted. Admission may be deferred for a maximum of 12. Credit offered for CEEB Advanced Placement tests.

COSTS AND FINANCIAL AID

Annual tuition $27,220. Room and board $8,294. Average book expense $1,500. **Required Forms and Deadlines:** FAFSA. **Notification of Awards:** Applicants will be notified of awards on a rolling basis beginning 4/1. **Types of Aid:** *Need-based scholarships/grants:* Federal Pell, SEOG, state scholarships/grants, the school's own gift aid. *Loans:* Subsidized Stafford, Unsubsidized Stafford, PLUS, Federal Perkins, Alternative Loans. *Student Employment:* Federal Work-Study Program available. Institutional employment available. Highest amount earned per year from on-campus jobs $1,000. Off-campus job opportunities are good. **Financial Aid Statistics:** 100% freshmen, 100% undergrads receive need-based scholarship or grant aid. 15% freshmen, 9% undergrads receive non-need-based scholarship or grant aid. 78% freshmen, 87% undergrads receive need-based self-help aid. 0% freshmen, 0% undergrads receive athletic scholarships. 99% freshmen, 95% undergrads receive any aid. 84% undergrads

borrow to pay for school. Average cumulative indebtedness $21,607. **Criteria for awarding institutional aid:** *Non-need-based:* academics, art.

KANSAS STATE UNIVERSITY

Best 380

119 Anderson Hall, Manhattan, KS 66506
Phone: 785-532-6250 · **Financial Aid Phone:** 785-532-6420
E-mail: k-state@k-state.edu · **CEEB Code:** 6334
Fax: 785-532-6393 · **Website:** www.k-state.edu · **ACT Code:** 1428

This public school was founded in 1863. It has a 668-acre campus.

RATINGS

Admissions Selectivity Rating: 78   **Fire Safety Rating:** 70

STUDENTS AND FACULTY

Enrollment: 19,727. **Student Body:** 48% female, 52% male, 17% out-of-state, 6% international (107 countries represented). Asian 1%, African American 4%, Caucasian 78%, Hispanic 6%, Native American <1%
Retention and Graduation: 28% freshmen graduate within 4 years. 59% freshmen graduate within 6 years. 22% grads go on to further study within 1 year. **Faculty:** 1,081 full-time faculty, 83% hold PhDs, 41% are members of minority groups, 15% are women. 17% of classes are taught by teaching assistants.

ACADEMICS

Degrees: associate, bachelor's, master's, post-bachelor's certificate. **Classes:** Most classes have fewer than 10 students. **Majors with Highest Enrollment:** Business Administration and Management; Animal Sciences; Mechanical Engineering. **Special Study Options:** Accelerated program, cooperative education program, distance learning, double major, English as a Second Language (ESL), exchange student program (domestic), honors program, independent study, internships, study abroad, teacher certification program, Minors. **Honors programs:** The University Honors Program is an opportunity for undergraduate students from all colleges to enhance their education with special classes and opportunities for personal growth. Combined degree programs: BS/MS Architectural Engineering, BS/MS Industrial Engineering. **Disability Services:** Special programs offered to physically disabled students include note-taking services, reader services, tape recorders, tutors. **Career services:** career/job search classes, career assessment. Career services highlights include an alumni career services partnership with the k-state alumni association that provides lifelong career services.

FACILITIES

Housing: Coed dorms, men's dorms, women's dorms, fraternity/sorority housing, apartments for married students, cooperative housing, apartments for single students. 100% of campus accessible to physically disabled. **Special Academic Facilities/Equipment:** South Asian area study center, education communications center, center for cancer research, planetarium, nuclear reactor/accelerator, Beach Art museum. **Computers:** 85% of classrooms, 100% of dorms, 100% of libraries, 100% of dining areas, 100% of student union, 10% of common outdoor areas have wireless network access. Students can register for classes online. Administrative functions (other than registration) can be performed online.

CAMPUS LIFE

Environment: Town. **Activities:** Choral groups, concert band, dance, drama/theater, jazz band, marching band, music ensembles, musical theater, pep band, radio station, student government, student newspaper, symphony orchestra, television station, yearbook, Campus Ministries, International Student Organization, Model UN. 594 registered organizations, 36 honor societies, 37 religious organizations. 28 fraternities, 16 sororities. **Athletics (Intercollegiate):** *Men:* baseball, basketball, cheerleading, cross-country, football, golf, track/field (outdoor), track/field (indoor). *Women:* basketball, cheerleading, crew/rowing, cross-country, equestrian sports, golf, tennis, track/field (outdoor), track/field (indoor), volleyball. **On-Campus Highlights:** Peters Recreation Complex, Sports Complexes: Wagner Field, Bramlage Coliseum, K-State Student Union, Ahearn Fieldhouse, Beach Museum of Art. **Environmental Initiatives:** A university-wide task force for long-term visioning and planning in all areas of the university, including campus operations, curriculum, research, and external relations/outreach. Development of a new 10,000 square foot recycling facility on campus. Planning to install a used functional 750kW wind turbine donated by our local utility for research and education as well as feeding renewable energy into our campus grid.

ADMISSIONS

Freshman Academic Profile: Average high school GPA 3.49. 22% in top 10% of high school class, 47% in top 25% of high school class, 75% in top 50% of high school class. 81% from public high schools. ACT middle 50% range 22-28. **Basis for Candidate Selection:** *Very important factors considered include:* Class rank, academic GPA, rigor of secondary school record, standardized test scores. *Other factors considered include:* recommendation(s). **Freshman Admission Requirements:** High school diploma is required and GED is accepted. **Freshman Admission Statistics:** 9,614 applied, 95% admitted, 41% enrolled. **Transfer Admission Requirements:** college transcript(s), Minimum college GPA of 2.0 required. Lowest grade transferable C. **General Admission Information:** Application Fee $30. Nonfall registration accepted. Credit and/or placement offered for CEEB Advanced Placement tests.

COSTS AND FINANCIAL AID

Annual in-state tuition $8,223. Annual out-of-state tuition $21,813. Room and board $8,060. Required fees $811. Average book expense $1,100. **Required Forms and Deadlines:** FAFSA. **Notification of Awards:** Applicants will be notified of awards on a rolling basis beginning 4/1. **Types of Aid:** *Need-based scholarships/grants:* Federal Pell, SEOG, state scholarships/grants, private scholarships, the school's own gift aid. *Loans:* Direct Subsidized Stafford, Direct Unsubsidized Stafford, Direct PLUS, Subsidized Stafford, Unsubsidized Stafford, PLUS, Federal Perkins, college/university loans from institutional funds, Alternative Student Loans. *Student Employment:* Federal Work-Study Program available. Institutional employment available. Off-campus job opportunities are good. **Financial Aid Statistics:** 54% freshmen, 56% undergrads receive need-based scholarship or grant aid. 71% freshmen, 47% undergrads receive non-need-based scholarship or grant aid. 69% freshmen, 77% undergrads receive need-based self-help aid. 3% freshmen, 2% undergrads receive athletic scholarships. 63% undergrads borrow to pay for school. Average cumulative indebtedness $24,879. **Criteria for awarding institutional aid:** *Non-need-based:* academics, alumni affiliation, art, athletics, leadership, music/drama, state/district residency.

KANSAS WESLEYAN UNIVERSITY

100 E. Claflin, Salina, KS 67401
Phone: ext 1285 · **Financial Aid Phone:** 785-827-5541 · **CEEB Code:**
Fax: 785-827-0927 · **Website:** www.kwu.edu · **ACT Code:** 1434

This private school, affiliated with the Methodist Church, was founded in 1886. It has a 28-acre campus.

RATINGS

Admissions Selectivity Rating: 79   Fire Safety Rating: 72

STUDENTS AND FACULTY

Enrollment: 742. **Student Body:** 57% female, 43% male, 29% out-of-state, 2% international (8 countries represented). Asian 1%, African American 7%, Caucasian 58%, Hispanic 7%, Native American 1%
Retention and Graduation: 30% grads go on to further study within 1 year. 24% grads pursue arts and sciences degrees. **Faculty:** 42 full-time faculty, 67% hold PhDs, 38% are members of minority groups. 0% of classes are taught by teaching assistants.

ACADEMICS

Degrees: associate, bachelor's, master's. **Classes:** Most classes have 10–19 students. **Special Study Options:** cross-registration, double major, honors program, independent study, internships, student-designed major, study abroad, teacher certification program. **Honors programs:** Alpha Chi Beta Beta Beta Sigma Pi Sigma Alpha Psi Omega Phi Alpha Theta. **Career services:** alumni services, career assessment, internships, regional alumni.

FACILITIES

Housing: Coed dorms, special housing for disabled students, men's dorms, women's dorms, apartments for married students, apartments for single students. 95% of campus accessible to physically disabled.

CAMPUS LIFE

Environment: Town. **Activities:** Choral groups, concert band, dance, drama/theater, jazz band, literary magazine, music ensembles, musical theater, pep band, student government, student newspaper, symphony orchestra, yearbook, Campus Ministries, International Student Organization, Model UN. 20 registered organizations, 5 honor societies, 3 religious organizations. **Athletics (Intercollegiate):** *Men:* baseball, basketball, cheerleading, cross-country, football, golf, racquetball, soccer, tennis, track/field (outdoor). *Women:* basketball, cheerleading, cross-country, golf, racquetball, soccer, softball, tennis, track/field (outdoor), volleyball. **On-Campus Highlights:** NEW Student Center & Gym, Sam's Chapel, dorms, library, Science Hall.

ADMISSIONS

Freshman Academic Profile: Average high school GPA 3.207. 9.3% in top 10% of high school class, 32% in top 25% of high school class, 62% in top 50% of high school class. SAT Math middle 50% range 500-590. SAT Critical Reading middle 50% range 420-520. ACT middle 50% range 22-. **Basis for Candidate Selection:** *Very important factors considered include:* academic GPA, standardized test scores. **Freshman Admission Requirements:** High school diploma is required and GED is accepted. **Freshman Admission Statistics:** 442 applied, 61% admitted, 43% enrolled. **Transfer Admission Requirements:** college transcript(s), Minimum college GPA of 2.0 required. Lowest grade transferable D. **General Admission Information:** Application Fee $20. Nonfall registration accepted.

COSTS AND FINANCIAL AID

Average book expense $800. **Required Forms and Deadlines:** FAFSA. **Types of Aid:** *Need-based scholarships/grants:* Federal Pell, SEOG, state scholarships/grants, private scholarships, the school's own gift aid. *Loans:* Direct Subsidized Stafford, Direct Unsubsidized Stafford, Direct PLUS, Federal Perkins. *Student Employment:* Federal Work-Study Program available. Off-campus job opportunities are excellent. **Financial Aid Statistics:** 0% freshmen, 0% undergrads receive athletic scholarships.75% undergrads receive any aid. 75% undergrads borrow to pay for school. **Criteria for awarding institutional aid:** *Non-need-based:* academics, alumni affiliation, art, athletics, music/drama.

KEAN UNIVERSITY

Undergraduate Admissions, PO Box 411, Union, NJ 07083-0411
Phone: 908-737-7100 · **Financial Aid Phone:** 908-737-3220
E-mail: admitme@kean.edu · **CEEB Code:** 2517
Fax: 908-737-7105 · **Website:** www.kean.edu · **ACT Code:** 2582

This public school was founded in 1855. It has a 186-acre campus.

RATINGS

Admissions Selectivity Rating: 74   Fire Safety Rating: 98

STUDENTS AND FACULTY

Enrollment: 11,938. **Student Body:** 60% female, 40% male, 2% out-of-state, 1% international (59 countries represented). Asian 6%, African American 20%, Caucasian 38%, Hispanic 25%, Native American <1%
Retention and Graduation: 75% freshmen return for sophomore year. 18% freshmen graduate within 4 years. 48% freshmen graduate within 6 years. **Faculty:** 351 full-time faculty, 85% hold PhDs, 52% are members of minority groups, 27% are women. 0% of classes are taught by teaching assistants.

ACADEMICS

Degrees: bachelor's, master's, post-master's certificate. **Classes:** Most classes have 20–29 students. **Majors with Highest Enrollment:** Business Administration and Management; Psychology; Speech Communication and Rhetoric. **Special Study Options:** Accelerated program, cooperative education program, distance learning, double major, dual enrollment, English as a Second Language (ESL), honors program, independent study, internships, liberal arts/career combination, study abroad, teacher certification program, weekend college, 2-year bachelor's degree program for RNs, Foreign Transfer Programs, Travelearn. **Honors programs:** NJCSTME—The New Jersey Center for Science, Technology and Mathematics Education: 5 year B.S./M.S.; B.S./M.A. Scholars programs—There is a critical and immediate need for highly qualified Science and Mathematics teachers in New Jersey, especially in urban school districts. There is also a need for highly trained research technicians to work in the pharmaceutical and biotechnology industries in New Jersey. Kean University created The New Jersey Center for Science, Technology and Mathematics Education (NJCSTME) to respond to both these needs. Through NJCSTME, Kean University offers an innovative and rigorous five year combined bachelor/master degree program to qualified students who are interested either in teaching science or mathematics (teacher track) or in a career in biotechnology or computational mathematics (research track). This program prepares graduates for immediate, well paid employment, and helps future generations of New Jersey students by putting highly qualified science and math teachers in the classroom and researchers in industry laboratories. These are some of the programs important features: It is the only program in New Jersey that offers a core curriculum that links science and math laboratory courses with a team teaching approach. This program is a great opportunity for any student interested in both mathematics and science. Each student has both an academic advisor and a career mentor. The progress of every student in the program is closely tracked by dedicated faculty who offer personal attention and support. It is a rigorous but highly structured and very supportive program that is designed for ensuring student success. Students participate in research seminars and presentations, team research projects under faculty leadership, and educational outreach enrichment programs at area schools to help them appreciate the career choice between teaching and research. 4 + 4 B.S. / M.D. Scholars Program-Kean University's NJ Center for Science, Technology and Mathematics Education (NJCSTME), Drexel University College of Medicine and St. Peter's University Hospital have partnered to offer a four-plus-four Bachelor of Science/Medical Degree (4 + 4 B.S./M.D.) Scholars Program to highly qualified incoming freshmen. Students who meet all the requirements of this joint program while in college are awarded the B.S. in science and technology degree from NJCSTME at the end of their fourth year, then proceed to enter the first year medical school class at DCOM. Combined degree programs: BA/MA, BA/MPA,BA/MS,BS/ MS,BS/MA, BS/DPT,BS/MD, BA/DPM,MSN/MPA. **Disability Services:** Special programs offered to physically disabled students include note-taking services, reader services, tape recorders, tutors. **Career services:** alumni services, career/job search classes, career assessment, internships. Career services highlights include an interviewing workshop.

FACILITIES

Housing: Coed dorms, special housing for disabled students, apartments for single students, Freshmen Housing, Floor for women-only housing. 100% of campus accessible to physically disabled. **Special Academic Facilities/Equipment:** Liberty Hall Museum, Holocaust Resource Center, Center for Academic Success, Harwood Arena,Human Rights Institute Wynona Moore Lipman Ethnic Studies Center **Computers:** 100% of classrooms, 100% of dorms, 100% of libraries, 100% of dining areas, 100% of student union, 100% of common outdoor areas have wireless network access. Students can register for classes online. Administrative functions (other than registration) can be performed online.

CAMPUS LIFE

Environment: City. **Activities:** Choral groups, concert band, dance, drama/ theater, jazz band, literary magazine, music ensembles, musical theater, pep band, radio station, student government, student newspaper, student-run film society, symphony orchestra, television station, yearbook, Campus Ministries, International Student Organization. 143 registered organizations, 23 honor societies, 6 religious organizations. 16 fraternities, 17 sororities. **Athletics (Intercollegiate):** *Men:* baseball, basketball, football, lacrosse, soccer, track/field (outdoor). *Women:* basketball, field hockey, lacrosse, soccer, softball, tennis, track/field (outdoor), volleyball. **On-Campus Highlights:** University Center, Harwood Arena and Football Field, Center for Academic Success (CAS), Kean Hall, One Stop Service Center, Liberty Hall Museum Weather Station Holocaust Resource Center Wynona Moore Lipman Ethnic Studies Center Planetarium CAS and Vaughn Eames - Art Gallaries. **Environmental Initiatives:** Creation of a bachelor of science degree in sustainability. Composting all of our food waste, plates, and compostable utensils on campus. LEED Certified renovation of our Center for Academic Success building.

ADMISSIONS

Freshman Academic Profile: Average high school GPA 3.0 8% in top 10% of high school class, 26% in top 25% of high school class, 64% in top 50% of high school class. SAT Math middle 50% range 420-510. SAT Critical Reading middle 50% range 400-490. ACT middle 50% range 15-22. Minimum internet-based TOEFL 80. Minimum paper TOEFL 550. **Basis for Candidate Selection:** *Very important factors considered include:* academic GPA, rigor of secondary school record. *Important factors considered include:* standardized test scores. *Other factors considered include:* Class rank, application essay, recommendation(s), alumni/ae relation, character/personal qualities, extracurricular activities, interview, talent/ability, volunteer work, work experience. **Freshman Admission Requirements:** High school diploma is required and GED is accepted. *Academic units required:* 4 English, 3 mathematics, 2 science, (2 science labs), 2 history, 5 academic electives. **Freshman Admission Statistics:** 5,718 applied, 70% admitted, 37% enrolled. **Transfer Admission Requirements:** college transcript(s), statement of good standing from prior institution(s). Minimum college GPA of 2.0 required. Lowest grade transferable C. **General Admission Information:** Application Fee $50. Regular application deadline 5/31. Notification on a rolling basis, beginning on or about 11/1. Nonfall registration accepted. Credit and/or placement offered for CEEB Advanced Placement tests.

COSTS AND FINANCIAL AID

Required Forms and Deadlines: FAFSA. **Notification of Awards:** Applicants will be notified of awards on a rolling basis beginning 3/15. **Types of Aid:** *Need-based scholarships/grants:* Federal Pell, SEOG, state scholarships/ grants, private scholarships, the school's own gift aid. *Loans:* Direct Subsidized Stafford, Direct Unsubsidized Stafford, Direct PLUS, Federal Perkins. *Student Employment:* Federal Work-Study Program available. Institutional employment available. Highest amount earned per year from on-campus jobs $6,290. Off-campus job opportunities are excellent. **Financial Aid Statistics:** 68% freshmen, 70% undergrads receive need-based scholarship or grant aid. 13% freshmen, 10% undergrads receive non-need-based scholarship or grant aid. 88% freshmen, 93% undergrads receive need-based self-help aid. 0% freshmen, 0% undergrads receive athletic scholarships. 80% freshmen, 74% undergrads receive any aid. 73% undergrads borrow to pay for school. Average cumulative indebtedness $27,355. **Criteria for awarding institutional aid:** *Non-need-based:* academics, alumni affiliation, art, leadership, music/drama.

KEENE STATE COLLEGE

229 Main Street, Keene, NH 03435-2604
Phone: 603-358-2276 · **Financial Aid Phone:** 603-358-2280
E-mail: admissions@keene.edu · **CEEB Code:** 3472
Fax: 603-358-2767 · **Website:** www.keene.edu · **ACT Code:** 2510

This public school was founded in 1909. It has a 150-acre campus.

RATINGS

Admissions Selectivity Rating: 73   **Fire Safety Rating:** 98

STUDENTS AND FACULTY

Enrollment: 4,648. **Student Body:** 58% female, 42% male, 51% out-of-state, 0% international (10 countries represented). Asian 1%, African American 1%, Caucasian 82%, Hispanic 3%, Native American <1%
Retention and Graduation: 76% freshmen return for sophomore year. 52% freshmen graduate within 4 years. 63% freshmen graduate within 6 years.
Faculty: 217 full-time faculty, 90% hold PhDs, 48% are members of minority groups, 9% are women. 0% of classes are taught by teaching assistants.

ACADEMICS

Degrees: associate, bachelor's, certificate, master's, post-bachelor's certificate, post-master's certificate. **Classes:** Most classes have 10–19 students. **Majors with Highest Enrollment:** Elementary Education and Teaching; Occupational Safety and Health Technology/Technician; Business Administration and Management. **Special Study Options:** cooperative education program, double major, English as a Second Language (ESL), exchange student program (domestic), honors program, independent study, internships, liberal arts/career combination, student-designed major, study abroad, teacher certification program. **Honors programs:** The Keene State College Honors Program; National Society of Collegiate Scholars in addition to Honors Programs in: Psychology, Safety Studies. **Disability Services:** Special programs offered to physically disabled students include note-taking services, reader services, tape recorders, tutors. **Career services:** alumni services, career/job search classes, career assessment, internships. Career services highlights include experiential learning/ service learning and commitment to the community. Students apply what they learn from their course work by working in the local community. These real-life working situations enhance student learning and help students meet their course goals.

FACILITIES

Housing: Coed dorms, women's dorms, fraternity/sorority housing, apartments for married students, apartments for single students, Wellness Housing, Theme Housing: Honors, Language/Culture, Leadership, Quiet Study, Substance Free. 98% of campus accessible to physically disabled. **Special Academic Facilities/Equipment:** Thorne-Sagendorph Art gallery, Redfern Arts Center, Recreational Center, Science Center, Mason Library, Media Arts Center, Cohen Center for Holocaust Studies, Center for Writing, Child Development Center. **Computers:** 10% of classrooms, 100% of libraries, 50% of dining areas, 80% of student union, have wireless network access. Students can register for classes online. Administrative functions (other than registration) can be performed online.

CAMPUS LIFE

Environment: Village. **Activities:** Choral groups, concert band, dance, drama/ theater, jazz band, literary magazine, music ensembles, musical theater, radio station, student government, student newspaper, student-run film society, television station, yearbook, Campus Ministries, International Student Organization. 100 registered organizations, 21 honor society, 4 religious organizations. 4 fraternities, 5 sororities. **Athletics (Intercollegiate):** *Men:* baseball, basketball, cheerleading, cross-country, diving, lacrosse, soccer, swimming, track/field (outdoor), track/field (indoor). *Women:* basketball, cheerleading, cross-country, diving, field hockey, lacrosse, soccer, softball, swimming, track/field (outdoor), track/field (indoor), volleyball. **On-Campus Highlights:** Science Building, Mason Library, Young Student Center, Night Owl Café, Arts Center on Brickyard Pond, Spaulding Gymnasium, Zorn Dining Commons new facility, New Pondside residence hall,Bodyworks Fitness Center, New Alumni Center in progress. **Environmental Initiatives:** LEED Silver residence hall (awarded 2008); Development of cogeneration capability in steam heat plant (combined heat and power); President's Council for a Sustainable Future.

ADMISSIONS

Freshman Academic Profile: Average high school GPA 2.92. 4% in top 10% of high school class, 19% in top 25% of high school class, 56% in top 50% of high school class. SAT Math middle 50% range 440-540. SAT Critical Reading middle 50% range 430-540. SAT Writing middle 50% range 440-530. Minimum internet-based TOEFL 61. Minimum paper TOEFL 550. **Basis for Candidate Selection:** *Very important factors considered include:* rigor of secondary school record. *Important factors considered include:* application essay, academic GPA, recommendation(s), standardized test scores. *Other factors considered include:* Class rank, alumni/ae relation, character/personal qualities, extracurricular activities, first generation, level of applicant's interest, racial/ethnic status, talent/ability, volunteer work, work experience. **Freshman Admission Requirements:** High school diploma is required and GED is accepted. *Academic units required:* 4 English, 3 mathematics, 3 science, 2 social studies, 2 academic electives. **Freshman Admission Statistics:** 6,144 applied, 82% admitted, 25% enrolled. **Transfer Admission Requirements:** High school transcript, college transcript(s), essay or personal statement, statement of good standing from prior institution(s). Minimum college GPA of 2.0 required. Lowest grade transferable C. **General Admission Information:** Application Fee $40. Regular application deadline 4/1. Nonfall registration accepted. Admission may be deferred for a maximum of 1 year. Credit and/or placement offered for CEEB Advanced Placement tests.

COSTS AND FINANCIAL AID

Annual. Annual out-of-state tuition $18,330. Room and board $9,368. Required fees $2,454. Average book expense $900. **Required Forms and Deadlines:** FAFSA. **Types of Aid:** *Need-based scholarships/grants:* Federal Pell, SEOG, state scholarships/grants, private scholarships, the school's own gift aid. *Loans:* Subsidized Stafford, Unsubsidized Stafford, PLUS, Federal Perkins, college/university loans from institutional funds. *Student Employment:* Federal Work-Study Program available. Institutional employment available. Off-campus job opportunities are excellent. **Financial Aid Statistics:** 71% freshmen, 68% undergrads receive need-based scholarship or grant aid. 45% freshmen, 30% undergrads receive non-need-based scholarship or grant aid. 92% freshmen, 93% undergrads receive need-based self-help aid. 0% freshmen, 0% undergrads receive athletic scholarships. 92% freshmen, 88% undergrads receive any aid. 83% undergrads borrow to pay for school. Average cumulative indebtedness $23,844. **Criteria for awarding institutional aid:** *Non-need-based:* academics, alumni affiliation, art, music/drama.

KENDALL COLLEGE

900 N. North Branch Street, Chicago, IL 60622
Phone: 877-588-8860 · **Financial Aid Phone:** 866-803-9988
E-mail: admissions@kendall.edu
Fax: 312-752-2021 · **Website:** www.kendall.edu · **ACT Code:** 1703

This private school, affiliated with the Methodist Church, was founded in 1934.

RATINGS

Admissions Selectivity Rating: 60*   Fire Safety Rating: 71

STUDENTS AND FACULTY

Enrollment: 950. **Student Body:** 12% out-of-state, (19 countries represented).
Faculty: 37 full-time faculty, 38% are members of minority groups, 14% are women. 0% of classes are taught by teaching assistants.

ACADEMICS

Degrees: associate, bachelor's, certificate. **Majors with Highest Enrollment:** Culinary Arts and Related Services; Hospitality Administration/Management; Hospitality Administration/Management. **Special Study Options:** Accelerated program, cooperative education program, distance learning, double major, internships, student-designed major, study abroad, teacher certification program. **Disability Services:** Special programs offered to physically disabled students include tutors. **Career services:** Alumni network, alumni services, career/job search classes, career assessment, internships, regional alumni.

FACILITIES

Housing: Coed dorms, special housing for disabled students.

CAMPUS LIFE

Environment: Metropolis. **Activities:** student government, student newspaper. **On-Campus Highlights:** Kitchens, Hyatt Suite, Formal Dining Room, Student-Run Cafeteria.

ADMISSIONS

Freshman Academic Profile: Average high school GPA 3.2. Minimum paper TOEFL 525. **Basis for Candidate Selection:** *Very important factors considered include:* Class rank, academic GPA, recommendation(s), rigor of secondary school record, standardized test scores. *Important factors considered include:* character/personal qualities. *Other factors considered include:* application essay, extracurricular activities, geographical residence, interview, talent/ability, work experience. **Freshman Admission Requirements:** High school diploma is required and GED is accepted. *Academic units required:* 4 English, 2 math-

ematics, 2 science, 2 foreign language, 2 social studies. **Transfer Admission Requirements:** college transcript(s), statement of good standing from prior institution(s). Minimum college GPA of 2.0 required. Lowest grade transferable C. **General Admission Information:** Application Fee $50. Nonfall registration accepted. Admission may be deferred for a maximum of 2 years. Credit and/or placement offered for CEEB Advanced Placement tests.

COSTS AND FINANCIAL AID

Annual tuition $21,510. Room and board $10,200. Required fees $440. **Required Forms and Deadlines:** FAFSA, Institution's own financial aid form. **Notification of Awards:** Applicants will be notified of awards on or about 4/1. **Types of Aid:** *Need-based scholarships/grants:* Federal Pell, SEOG, state scholarships/grants, private scholarships, the school's own gift aid. *Loans:* Direct Subsidized Stafford, Direct Unsubsidized Stafford, Direct PLUS, Subsidized Stafford, Unsubsidized Stafford, PLUS, Federal Perkins, college/university loans from institutional funds. *Student Employment:* Federal Work-Study Program available. Institutional employment available. Off-campus job opportunities are excellent. **Financial Aid Statistics:** 87% undergrads receive any aid. **Criteria for awarding institutional aid:** *Non-need-based:* academics, athletics, leadership, religious affiliation.

KENDALL COLLEGE OF ART AND DESIGN OF FERRIS STATE UNIVERSITY

17 Fountain Street NW, Grand Rapids, MI 49503-3002
Phone: 616-451-2787 · **Financial Aid Phone:** 616-451-2787
E-mail: brittons@ferris.edu · **CEEB Code:** 1983
Fax: 616-831-9689 · **Website:** www.kcad.edu · **ACT Code:** 1983

This public school was founded in 1928. It has a 2-acre campus.

RATINGS

Admissions Selectivity Rating: 60*   Fire Safety Rating: 60*

STUDENTS AND FACULTY

Enrollment: 1,141. **Student Body:** 13% out-of-state, (15 countries represented).
Retention and Graduation: 12% grads go on to further study within 1 year. 12% grads pursue arts and sciences degrees. **Faculty:** 50 full-time faculty, 6% hold PhDs, 4% are women. 0% of classes are taught by teaching assistants.

ACADEMICS

Degrees: bachelor's, master's. **Majors with Highest Enrollment:** Interior Design; Graphic Design; Illustration. **Special Study Options:** cooperative education program, double major, dual enrollment, independent study, internships, liberal arts/career combination, study abroad, teacher certification program. **Disability Services:** Special programs offered to physically disabled students include note-taking services, reader services, tape recorders, tutors. **Career services:** Alumni network, alumni services, career/job search classes, internships, regional alumni.

FACILITIES

Housing: apartments for married students, apartments for single students, Fabulous historic district with rental apartments nearby. 100% of campus accessible to physically disabled. **Computers:** 100% of classrooms, 100% of libraries, 100% of student union, have wireless network access. Students can register for classes online. Administrative functions (other than registration) can be performed online. Undergraduates are required to own a computer.

CAMPUS LIFE

Environment: Metropolis. **Activities:** 12 registered organizations, 1 religious organization. **On-Campus Highlights:** Studio Spaces, Studio Class Rooms, Library, Student Commons, Labs.

ADMISSIONS

Freshman Academic Profile: Average high school GPA 3.1. 10% in top 10% of high school class, 20% in top 25% of high school class, 75% in top 50% of high school class. Minimum internet-based TOEFL 61. Minimum paper TOEFL 500. **Basis for Candidate Selection:** *Very important factors considered include:* application essay, academic GPA, rigor of secondary school record, standardized test scores, talent/ability. *Important factors considered include:* character/personal qualities, interview. *Other factors considered include:* Class rank, recommendation(s), extracurricular activities. **Freshman Admission Requirements:** High school diploma is required and GED is accepted. **Transfer Admission Requirements:** High school transcript, college transcript(s), essay or personal statement, Lowest grade transferable C. **General Admission Information:** Application Fee $30. Nonfall registration accepted. Admission may be deferred for a maximum of one semester. Credit offered for CEEB Advanced Placement tests.

COSTS AND FINANCIAL AID

Annual in-state tuition $12,674. Annual out-of-state tuition $19,220. Required fees $420. Average book expense $3,604. **Required Forms and Deadlines:** FAFSA. **Notification of Awards:** Applicants will be notified of awards on a rolling basis beginning 4/1. **Types of Aid:** *Need-based scholarships/grants:* Federal Pell, SEOG, state scholarships/grants, private scholarships, the school's own gift aid. *Loans:* Direct Subsidized Stafford, Direct Unsubsidized Stafford, Direct PLUS, Federal PerkinsKey Alternative Loan CitiAssist Student Loan Michigan Alternative Loan. *Student Employment:* Federal Work-Study Program available. Institutional employment available. Highest amount earned per year from on-campus jobs $2,000. **Criteria for awarding institutional aid:** *Non-need-based:* academics, alumni affiliation, art.

KENNESAW STATE UNIVERSITY

3391 Town Point Drive, Suite 1000, Kennesaw, GA 30144-5591
Phone: 770-423-6300 · **Financial Aid Phone:** 770-423-6074
E-mail: ksuadmit@kennesaw.edu · **CEEB Code:** 5359
Fax: 470-578-9169 · **Website:** www.kennesaw.edu · **ACT Code:** 833

This public school was founded in 1963. It has a 384-acre campus.

RATINGS

Admissions Selectivity Rating: 85   **Fire Safety Rating:** 99

STUDENTS AND FACULTY

Enrollment: 23,435. **Student Body:** 57% female, 43% male, 6% out-of-state, 2% international (131 countries represented). Asian 3%, African American 19%, Caucasian 61%, Hispanic 8%, Native American <1%
Retention and Graduation: 79% freshmen return for sophomore year. 16% freshmen graduate within 4 years. 43% freshmen graduate within 6 years.
Faculty: 755 full-time faculty, 78% hold PhDs, 56% are members of minority groups, 21% are women. 0% of classes are taught by teaching assistants.

ACADEMICS

Degrees: bachelor's, doctoral, master's. **Classes:** Most classes have 20–29 students. Most lab/discussion sessions have 20–29 students. **Majors with Highest Enrollment:** Registered Nursing/Registered Nurse; Psychology; Speech Communication and Rhetoric. **Special Study Options:** cooperative education program, cross-registration, distance learning, double major, English as a Second Language (ESL), honors program, internships, study abroad, teacher certification program, weekend college. **Honors programs:** The Honors Program at KSU provides a unique opportunity for exceptional students to customize their college experience. Through colloquia, seminars and directed studies, honor students can tailor their experience to meet their needs and interest. Instead of being restricted to the guidelines of a course catalog, students are encouraged to think outside the box and stretch themselves in academic directions that appeal to them. To guide them in their journey, a faculty mentor is assigned to each student. Most students only know faculty in a classroom setting, but honor students develop a one-on-one relationship designed to enhance their collegiate experience. **Disability Services:** Special programs offered to physically disabled students include note-taking services, reader services, tape recorders, tutors. **Career services:** Alumni network, alumni services, internships. Career services highlights include internships that are on the rise and fully supported by campus administration. The president of KSU has expressed he wants to see a 10% annual increase in the number of students participating in this program from now on.

FACILITIES

Housing: apartments for single students. 100% of campus accessible to physically disabled. **Computers:** 100% of classrooms, 100% of libraries, 100% of dining areas, 100% of student union, 5% of common outdoor areas have wireless network access. Students can register for classes online. Administrative functions (other than registration) can be performed online.

CAMPUS LIFE

Environment: Town. **Activities:** Choral groups, concert band, dance, drama/theater, jazz band, music ensembles, musical theater, radio station, student government, student newspaper, symphony orchestra, Campus Ministries, International Student Organization, Model UN. 151 registered organizations, 20 honor societies, 18 religious organizations. 10 fraternities, 8 sororities. **Athletics (Intercollegiate):** *Men:* baseball, basketball, cross-country, golf, tennis, track/field (outdoor), track/field (indoor). *Women:* basketball, cheerleading, cross-country, golf, soccer, softball, tennis, track/field (outdoor), track/field (indoor), volleyball. **On-Campus Highlights:** Student Dining Hall, Lounge in Student Center, Game Room in Student Center, Student Recreation Center, Campus Green. **Environmental Initiatives:** Commitment by KSU President Daniel S. Papp to reduce the university's carbon footprint, in line with a national coalition of college and university presidents. Naming of a campus Director of Sustain-

ability who will oversee the university's "green" initiatives and teach students as a member of the faculty. Launching an undergraduate degree program with emphases in environmental science or environmental polity within KSU's existing Interdisciplinary Studies program.

ADMISSIONS

Freshman Academic Profile: Average high school GPA 3.23. 27% in top 10% of high school class, 35% in top 25% of high school class, 98% in top 50% of high school class. 90% from public high schools. SAT Math middle 50% range 490-580. SAT Critical Reading middle 50% range 500-590. SAT Writing middle 50% range 460-560. ACT middle 50% range 21-24. Minimum internet-based TOEFL 75. Minimum paper TOEFL 527. **Basis for Candidate Selection:** *Very important factors considered include:* academic GPA, standardized test scores. **Freshman Admission Requirements:** High school diploma is required and GED is not accepted. *Academic units required:* 4 English, 4 mathematics, 3 science, (3 science labs), 2 foreign language, 3 social studies. **Freshman Admission Statistics:** 11,309 applied, 54% admitted, 62% enrolled. **Transfer Admission Requirements:** college transcript(s), Minimum college GPA of 2.0 required. Lowest grade transferable D. **General Admission Information:** Application Fee $40. Regular application deadline 5/14. Notification on a rolling basis, beginning on or about 1/1. Nonfall registration accepted. Admission may be deferred for a maximum of 12 months. Credit offered for CEEB Advanced Placement tests.

COSTS AND FINANCIAL AID

Required Forms and Deadlines: FAFSA. **Notification of Awards:** Applicants will be notified of awards on a rolling basis beginning 4/1. **Types of Aid:** *Need-based scholarships/grants:* Federal Pell, SEOG, state scholarships/grants, private scholarships. *Loans:* Subsidized Stafford, Unsubsidized Stafford, PLUS, Federal Perkins, Federal Nursing, state loans. *Student Employment:* Federal Work-Study Program available. Institutional employment available. Highest amount earned per year from on-campus jobs $15,732. Off-campus job opportunities are good. **Financial Aid Statistics:** 78% freshmen, 86% undergrads receive need-based scholarship or grant aid. 70% freshmen, 43% undergrads receive non-need-based scholarship or grant aid. 1% freshmen, 1% undergrads receive need-based self-help aid. 2% freshmen, 2% undergrads receive athletic scholarships. 65% freshmen, 64% undergrads receive any aid. 63% undergrads borrow to pay for school. Average cumulative indebtedness $9,679. **Criteria for awarding institutional aid:** *Non-need-based:* academics, alumni affiliation, art, athletics, job skills, leadership, minority status, music/drama, state/district residency.

KENT STATE UNIVERSITY—KENT CAMPUS

161 Michael Schwartz Center, Kent, OH 44242-0001
Phone: 330-672-2444 · **Financial Aid Phone:** 330-672-2972
E-mail: kentadm@kent.edu · **CEEB Code:** 1367
Fax: 330-672-2499 · **Website:** www.kent.edu · **ACT Code:** 3284

This public school was founded in 1910. It has a 1200-acre campus.

RATINGS

Admissions Selectivity Rating: 76   **Fire Safety Rating:** 87

STUDENTS AND FACULTY

Enrollment: 22,530. **Student Body:** 59% female, 41% male, 13% out-of-state, 6% international (96 countries represented). Asian 1%, African American 9%, Caucasian 75%, Hispanic 3%, Native American <1%
Retention and Graduation: 31% freshmen graduate within 4 years. **Faculty:** 958 full-time faculty, 52% are members of minority groups, 12% are women. 10% of classes are taught by teaching assistants.

ACADEMICS

Degrees: associate, bachelor's, certificate, doctoral, master's, post-bachelor's certificate, post-master's certificate, terminal associate, transfer associate. **Classes:** Most classes have 20–29 students. **Majors with Highest Enrollment:** Business Administration and Management; Psychology; Registered Nursing/Registered Nurse. **Special Study Options:** Accelerated program, cooperative education program, cross-registration, distance learning, double major, dual enrollment, English as a Second Language (ESL), exchange student program (domestic), external degree program, honors program, independent study, internships, liberal arts/career combination, student-designed major, study abroad, teacher certification program, weekend college. **Honors programs:** Honors College membership at Kent State University is open to all majors and hosts approximately 1,350 students at the Kent Campus and five Regional Campuses. Honors College classes emphasize the intellectual value in the pursuit of knowledge. Every effort is made to show students the connections between disciplines. Honors College classes are small, taught by carefully chosen faculty, and emphasize students' active involvement in their learning. Plentiful opportunities for individual study, including the Senior Honors Thesis/ Project give students exciting experiences in following their intellectual curiosity. An Honors College residence complex, state-of-the-art facilities, experiences including study abroad/away opportunities and cultural programming all support bright and motivated students seeking an intellectual home within the larger university. Combined degree programs: BA/MD, BA/MA. **Disability Services:** Special programs offered to physically disabled students include note-taking services, reader services, tape recorders, tutors. **Career services:** Alumni network, alumni services, career/job search classes, career assessment, internships, regional alumni. Career services highlights include the first academic trading floor with live derivatives exchange data. The Olga A. Mural Financial Engineering Trading Floor cost $2.2M to build and has an annual operating budget of $450,000. The Kent State Financial Engineering students are provided experience through Industry-based Projects (Internships). Internships are ten weeks in length and begin in May.

FACILITIES

Housing: Coed dorms, special housing for disabled students, men's dorms, special housing for international students, women's dorms, fraternity/sorority housing, apartments for married students, apartments for single students. 95% of campus accessible to physically disabled. **Special Academic Facilities/ Equipment:** Fashion museum, herbarium, liquid crystal institute, planetarium, airport. **Computers:** 90% of classrooms, 20% of dorms, 40% of libraries, 70% of dining areas, 100% of student union, 10% of common outdoor areas have wireless network access. Students can register for classes online. Administrative functions (other than registration) can be performed online.

CAMPUS LIFE

Environment: Town. **Activities:** Choral groups, concert band, dance, drama/ theater, jazz band, literary magazine, marching band, music ensembles, pep band, radio station, student government, student newspaper, television station, Campus Ministries, International Student Organization. 214 registered organizations, 10 honor societies, 15 religious organizations. 17 fraternities, 6 sororities. **Athletics (Intercollegiate):** *Men:* baseball, basketball, cheerleading, cross-country, football, golf, track/field (outdoor), track/field (indoor), wrestling. *Women:* basketball, cheerleading, cross-country, field hockey, football, golf, gymnastics, soccer, softball, track/field (outdoor), track/field (indoor), volleyball. **On-Campus Highlights:** Student Recreation and Wellness Center, Kent State University Museum, Kent Student Center Plaza, Pan African Center Gallery, May 4 Memorial. **Environmental Initiatives:** Energy production on campus including a combined heat and power plant and a solar array installed in spring 2012 as part of our renewable energy master plan. Ongoing energy efficiency improvement at all campuses, including performance contracting. Supporting alternative transportation by providing a free bike sharing program, supporting walk-ability on campus, and providing free public transit for students.

ADMISSIONS

Freshman Academic Profile: Average high school GPA 3.34. 15% in top 10% of high school class, 40% in top 25% of high school class, 77% in top 50% of high school class. SAT Math middle 50% range 470-580. SAT Critical Reading middle 50% range 470-580. SAT Writing middle 50% range 460-560. ACT middle 50% range 20-25. Minimum internet-based TOEFL 71. Minimum paper TOEFL 525. **Basis for Candidate Selection:** *Very important factors considered include:* academic GPA, rigor of secondary school record, standardized test scores. *Other factors considered include:* Class rank, recommendation(s). **Freshman Admission Requirements:** High school diploma is required and GED is accepted. **Freshman Admission Statistics:** 16,125 applied, 84% admitted, 32% enrolled. **Transfer Admission Requirements:** college transcript(s), Minimum college GPA of 2.0 required. Lowest grade transferable C. **General Admission Information:** Application Fee $40. Regular application deadline 8/1. Notification on a rolling basis, beginning on or about 10/1. Nonfall registration accepted. Admission may be deferred for a maximum of 1 year. Credit and/or placement offered for CEEB Advanced Placement tests.

COSTS AND FINANCIAL AID

Required Forms and Deadlines: FAFSA. **Notification of Awards:** Applicants will be notified of awards on or about 3/15. **Types of Aid:** *Need-based scholarships/grants:* Federal Pell, SEOG, state scholarships/grants, private scholarships, the school's own gift aid. *Loans:* Direct Subsidized Stafford, Direct Unsubsidized Stafford, Direct PLUS, Federal Perkins, Federal Nursing, state loans, college/university loans from institutional funds, Alternative Loans. *Student Employment:* Federal Work-Study Program available. Institutional employment available. Highest amount earned per year from on-campus jobs $14,000. Off-campus job opportunities are excellent. **Financial Aid Statistics:** 52% freshmen, 55% undergrads receive need-based scholarship or grant aid. 76% freshmen, 50% undergrads receive non-need-based scholarship or grant aid. 80% freshmen, 82% undergrads receive need-based self-help aid. 1% freshmen, 1% undergrads receive athletic scholarships. 93% freshmen, 85% undergrads receive any aid. 75% undergrads borrow to pay for school. Average cumulative indebtedness $28,613. **Criteria for awarding institutional aid:**

Non-need-based: academics, alumni affiliation, art, athletics, leadership, minority status, music/drama, state/district residency.

KENTUCKY STATE UNIVERSITY

400 East Main Street, Frankfort, KY 40601
Phone: 502-597-6813 • **Financial Aid Phone:** 502-597-5960
E-mail: admissions@kysu.edu • **CEEB Code:** 1368
Fax: 502-597-5814 • **Website:** www.kysu.edu • **ACT Code:** 1516

This public school was founded in 1886. It has a 915-acre campus.

RATINGS

Admissions Selectivity Rating: 78   **Fire Safety Rating:** 77

STUDENTS AND FACULTY

Enrollment: 1,627. **Student Body:** 62% female, 38% male, 42% out-of-state, 0% international (4 countries represented). Asian 0%, African American 58%, Caucasian 25%, Hispanic 2%, Native American <1%
Retention and Graduation: 7% freshmen graduate within 4 years. 20% freshmen graduate within 6 years. **Faculty:** 124 full-time faculty, 75% hold PhDs, 38% are members of minority groups, 31% are women. 0% of classes are taught by teaching assistants.

ACADEMICS

Degrees: associate, bachelor's, master's. **Classes:** Most classes have 20–29 students. Most lab/discussion sessions have fewer than 10 students. **Majors with Highest Enrollment:** Registered Nursing/Registered Nurse; Business/Commerce; Criminal Justice/Safety Studies. **Special Study Options:** cooperative education program, distance learning, double major, dual enrollment, English as a Second Language (ESL), honors program, independent study, internships, liberal arts/career combination, student-designed major, study abroad, teacher certification program. **Honors programs:** The Whitney Young School of Honors and Liberal Studies. The Honors Program is an integrated liberal arts program that emphasizes student discussion of excellent books. **Disability Services:** Special programs offered to physically disabled students include note-taking services, reader services, tape recorders, tutors. **Career services:** Alumni network, alumni services, career assessment, internships, regional alumni. Career services highlights include the KSU Intern and Cooperative Education program. The students gain hands on experience and 85% are offered positions after graduation.

FACILITIES

Housing: Coed dorms, men's dorms, women's dorms. 100% of campus accessible to physically disabled. **Special Academic Facilities/Equipment:** Art gallery, nutrition lab, agriculture research building, research farm, fish hatchery, electron microscope. **Computers:** 100% of classrooms, 100% of dorms, 100% of libraries, 100% of dining areas, 100% of student union, 60% of common outdoor areas have wireless network access. Students can register for classes online. Administrative functions (other than registration) can be performed online.

CAMPUS LIFE

Environment: Town. **Activities:** Choral groups, concert band, dance, drama/ theater, jazz band, marching band, music ensembles, musical theater, opera, pep band, student government, student newspaper, Campus Ministries, International Student Organization. 30 registered organizations, 5 honor societies, 4 religious organizations. 6 fraternities, 5 sororities. **Athletics (Intercollegiate):** *Men:* baseball, basketball, cross-country, football, golf, track/field (outdoor), track/field (indoor). *Women:* basketball, cross-country, softball, track/field (outdoor), track/field (indoor), volleyball. **On-Campus Highlights:** Jackson Hall, Carl Hill Student Center, William Exum Building, Whitney Young Residence Hall, Hume Hall. **Environmental Initiatives:** Energy efficient fixtures for power & water; Recycling Program for trash and cardboard.

ADMISSIONS

Freshman Academic Profile: Average high school GPA 2.8. 9% in top 10% of high school class, 24% in top 25% of high school class, 55% in top 50% of high school class. SAT Math middle 50% range 323-478. SAT Critical Reading middle 50% range 360-480. SAT Writing middle 50% range 350-440. ACT middle 50% range 16-21. Minimum internet-based TOEFL 70. Minimum paper TOEFL 525. **Basis for Candidate Selection:** *Very important factors considered include:* academic GPA, standardized test scores. *Important factors considered include:* rigor of secondary school record, first generation, level of applicant's interest, state residency. *Other factors considered include:* application essay, recommendation(s), alumni/ae relation, character/personal qualities, extracurricular activities, geographical residence, interview. **Freshman Admission Requirements:** High school diploma is required and GED is accepted. *Academic units required:* 4 English, 3 mathematics, 3 science, 2 foreign language, 3 social studies, 1 visual/performing arts, 1 Physical Education and 0.5 Health Education. **Freshman Admission Statistics:** 6,415 applied, 48% admitted, 9% enrolled. **Transfer Admission Requirements:** college transcript(s), Minimum college GPA of 2.0 required. Lowest grade transferable C. **General Admission Information:** Application Fee $30. Nonfall registration accepted. Credit and/or placement offered for CEEB Advanced Placement tests.

COSTS AND FINANCIAL AID
Annual out-of-state tuition $16,824. Room and board $6,690. Required fees $390. Average book expense $1,300. **Required Forms and Deadlines:** FAFSA. **Notification of Awards:** Applicants will be notified of awards on or about 4/1. **Types of Aid:** *Need-based scholarships/grants:* Federal Pell, SEOG, state scholarships/grants, private scholarships, the school's own gift aid, United Negro College Fund, Federal Nursing Scholarships. *Loans:* Direct Subsidized Stafford, Direct Unsubsidized Stafford, Direct PLUS. *Student Employment:* Federal Work-Study Program available. Institutional employment available. Highest amount earned per year from on-campus jobs $2,500. Off-campus job opportunities are good. **Financial Aid Statistics:** 95% freshmen, 93% undergrads receive need-based scholarship or grant aid. 6% freshmen, 4% undergrads receive non-need-based scholarship or grant aid. 75% freshmen, 80% undergrads receive need-based self-help aid. 2% freshmen, 2% undergrads receive athletic scholarships. 95% freshmen, 94% undergrads receive any aid. 54% undergrads borrow to pay for school. Average cumulative indebtedness $34,110. **Criteria for awarding institutional aid:** *Non-need-based:* academics, alumni affiliation, art, athletics, minority status, music/drama.

KENTUCKY WESLEYAN COLLEGE

3000 Frederica Street, Owensboro, KY 42301
Phone: 270-852-3120 • **Financial Aid Phone:** 270-852-3130
E-mail: http://www.kwc.edu/page.php?page=353 • **CEEB Code:** 1369
Fax: 270-852-3133 • **Website:** www.kwc.edu • **ACT Code:** 1518

This private school, affiliated with the Methodist Church, was founded in 1858. It has a 52-acre campus.

RATINGS
Admissions Selectivity Rating: 82   **Fire Safety Rating:** 77

STUDENTS AND FACULTY
Enrollment: 657. **Student Body:** 48% female, 52% male, 28% out-of-state, 2% international (8 countries represented). Asian 0%, African American 12%, Caucasian 73%, Hispanic 2%, Native American <1%
Retention and Graduation: 54% freshmen return for sophomore year. 29% freshmen graduate within 4 years. 25% grads go on to further study within 1 year. **Faculty:** 48 full-time faculty, 71% hold PhDs, 48% are members of minority groups, 6% are women. 0% of classes are taught by teaching assistants.

ACADEMICS
Degrees: bachelor's. **Classes:** Most classes have 10–19 students. Most lab/discussion sessions have 10–19 students. **Majors with Highest Enrollment:** Business/Commerce; Biology/Biological Sciences; Criminal Justice/Safety Studies. **Special Study Options:** double major, independent study, internships, liberal arts/career combination, student-designed major, study abroad, teacher certification program, Online Program. **Combined degree programs:** University of Louisville and Auburn University. **Disability Services:** Special programs offered to physically disabled students include note-taking services, tutors. **Career services:** Alumni network, career/job search classes, career assessment, internships.

FACILITIES
Housing: Coed dorms, special housing for disabled students, men's dorms, women's dorms, fraternity/sorority housing, apartments for married students, apartments for single students. 100% of campus accessible to physically disabled. **Special Academic Facilities/Equipment:** President's Hall/Library Learning Center Ralph Center for Fine Arts. Woodward Health and Recreation Center. Yu Hak Hahn Center for the Sciences. **Computers:** 100% of classrooms, 100% of dorms, 100% of libraries, 100% of dining areas, 100% of student union, have wireless network access. Students can register for classes online. Administrative functions (other than registration) can be performed online.

CAMPUS LIFE
Environment: Town. **Activities:** Choral groups, dance, drama/theater, literary magazine, music ensembles, pep band, radio station, student government, student newspaper, yearbook, Campus Ministries. 42 registered organizations, 6 honor societies, 6 religious organizations. 3 fraternities, 2 sororities. **Athletics**

(Intercollegiate): *Men:* baseball, basketball, cheerleading, cross-country, football, golf, soccer. *Women:* basketball, cheerleading, cross-country, golf, soccer, softball, tennis, volleyball. **On-Campus Highlights:** Winchester Center-New Campus Center, Ralph Fine Arts Center, Yu Hak Hahn Center for the Sciences, Woodward Health and Recreation Center, The Quad. For virtual tours, visit www.kwc.edu.

ADMISSIONS
Freshman Academic Profile: Average high school GPA 3.24. 20% in top 10% of high school class, 44% in top 25% of high school class, 68% in top 50% of high school class. 90% from public high schools. SAT Math middle 50% range 410-555. SAT Critical Reading middle 50% range 410-540. SAT Writing middle 50% range 450-660. ACT middle 50% range 19-25. Minimum paper TOEFL 500. **Basis for Candidate Selection:** *Very important factors considered include:* academic GPA, standardized test scores. *Important factors considered include:* rigor of secondary school record, extracurricular activities, interview. *Other factors considered include:* Class rank, recommendation(s), alumni/ae relation, character/personal qualities, level of applicant's interest, talent/ability, volunteer work, work experience. **Freshman Admission Requirements:** High school diploma is required and GED is accepted. *Academic units required:* 4 English, 3 mathematics, 3 science, 3 social studies. **Freshman Admission Statistics:** 1,006 applied, 67% admitted, 24% enrolled. **Transfer Admission Requirements:** college transcript(s), Minimum college GPA of 2.0 required. Lowest grade transferable C. **General Admission Information:** Notification on a rolling basis, beginning on or about 9/1. Nonfall registration accepted. Admission may be deferred for a maximum of 12 mo. Credit and/or placement offered for CEEB Advanced Placement tests.

COSTS AND FINANCIAL AID
Annual tuition $21,400. Room and board $7,800. Required fees $800. Average book expense $1,400. **Required Forms and Deadlines:** FAFSA. **Notification of Awards:** Applicants will be notified of awards on a rolling basis beginning 2/15. **Types of Aid:** *Need-based scholarships/grants:* Federal Pell, SEOG, state scholarships/grants, private scholarships, the school's own gift aid. *Loans:* Subsidized Stafford, Unsubsidized Stafford, PLUS, Federal Perkins, college/university loans from institutional funds, Alternative Education Loans. *Student Employment:* Federal Work-Study Program available. Institutional employment available. Off-campus job opportunities are good. **Financial Aid Statistics:** 99% freshmen, 98% undergrads receive need-based scholarship or grant aid. 7% freshmen, 11% undergrads receive non-need-based scholarship or grant aid. 80% freshmen, 76% undergrads receive need-based self-help aid. 0% freshmen, 0% undergrads receive athletic scholarships. 99% freshmen, 85% undergrads receive any aid. 0% undergrads borrow to pay for school. Average cumulative indebtedness $0. **Criteria for awarding institutional aid:** *Non-need-based:* academics, alumni affiliation, art, athletics, leadership, music/drama, religious affiliation, state/district residency.

KENYON COLLEGE

Kenyon College Admissions Office, Gambier, OH 43022-9623
Phone: 740-427-5776 • **Financial Aid Phone:** 740-427-5240
E-mail: admissions@kenyon.edu • **CEEB Code:** 1370
Fax: 740-427-5770 • **Website:** www.kenyon.edu • **ACT Code:** 3286

This private school was founded in 1824. It has a 1200-acre campus.

RATINGS
Admissions Selectivity Rating: 96   **Fire Safety Rating:** 82

STUDENTS AND FACULTY
Enrollment: 1,651. **Student Body:** 55% female, 45% male, 78% out-of-state, 4% international (41 countries represented). Asian 5%, African American 4%, Caucasian 74%, Hispanic 6%, Native American 1%
Retention and Graduation: 86% freshmen graduate within 4 years. 25% grads go on to further study within 1 year. **Faculty:** 159 full-time faculty, 99% hold PhDs, 43% are members of minority groups, 21% are women. 0% of classes are taught by teaching assistants.

ACADEMICS
Degrees: bachelor's. **Classes:** Most classes have 10–19 students. **Majors with Highest Enrollment:** Economics; Psychology; English Language and Literature. **Special Study Options:** Accelerated program, double major, exchange

student program (domestic), honors program, independent study, internships, liberal arts/career combination, student-designed major, study abroad. **Honors programs:** Honors programs are offered by all departmental and interdepartmental majors. **Combined degree programs:** Education, Environmental Studies. **Disability Services:** Special programs offered to physically disabled students include note-taking services, reader services, tape recorders, tutors. **Career services:** Alumni network, alumni services, career/job search classes, career assessment, internships, regional alumni. Career services highlights include our Extern program, which enables students to explore career options through an experiential week of job-showing during winter or spring breaks. This often helps students decide what internships and/or career paths they'd like to pursue while building a network of contacts.

FACILITIES

Housing: Coed dorms, special housing for disabled students, women's dorms, fraternity/sorority housing, apartments for single students, Wellness Housing. Theme **Housing:** housing options for community service, substance-free, wellness, international wing, Kosher. 41% of campus accessible to physically disabled. **Special Academic Facilities/Equipment:** Horn and Olin art galleries; Bolton and Hill theaters; Black Box Theater; Rosse and Storer halls for music; new sciences quadrangle; greenhouse and observatory; environmental center; $70-million fitness, recreation, and athletics facility. new art history building under construction **Computers:** 100% of classrooms, 100% of dorms, 100% of libraries, 100% of dining areas, NA% of student union, 33% of common outdoor areas have wireless network access. Administrative functions (other than registration) can be performed online.

CAMPUS LIFE

Environment: Rural. **Activities:** Choral groups, concert band, dance, drama/theater, jazz band, literary magazine, music ensembles, musical theater, opera, pep band, radio station, student government, student newspaper, student-run film society, symphony orchestra, yearbook, Campus Ministries, International Student Organization, Model UN. 140 registered organizations, 5 honor societies, 6 religious organizations. 8 fraternities, 4 sororities. **Athletics (Intercollegiate):** *Men:* baseball, basketball, cross-country, diving, football, golf, lacrosse, soccer, swimming, tennis, track/field (outdoor), track/field (indoor). *Women:* basketball, cross-country, diving, field hockey, lacrosse, soccer, softball, swimming, tennis, track/field (outdoor), track/field (indoor), volleyball. **On-Campus Highlights:** Kenyon College Bookstore, Fitness,/Recreation, Athletic Facility, Middle Ground Coffee Shop, Brown Family Environmental Center, Horn Gallery. **Environmental Initiatives:** 1 Food for Thought (purchase of local foods for dining hall and building a county-wide sustainable food system) http://rurallife.kenyon.edu 2 Brown Family Environmental Center (academic and public sustainability programs) http://bfec.kenyon.edu 3 Kenyon Environmental Sustainability Council http://www.kenyon.edu/about-kenyon/sustainability/contact/sustainability-council/ 4 Paper/can/bottle recycling program campus wide

ADMISSIONS

Freshman Academic Profile: Average high school GPA 3.94. 65% in top 10% of high school class, 86% in top 25% of high school class, 99% in top 50% of high school class. 55% from public high schools. SAT Math middle 50% range 610-690. SAT Critical Reading middle 50% range 620-730. SAT Writing middle 50% range 620-720. ACT middle 50% range 28-32. Minimum internet-based TOEFL 100. **Basis for Candidate Selection:** *Very important factors considered include:* application essay, academic GPA, recommendation(s), rigor of secondary school record, character/personal qualities. *Important factors considered include:* Class rank, standardized test scores, extracurricular activities, interview, level of applicant's interest, talent/ability. *Other factors considered include:* alumni/ae relation, first generation, geographical residence, racial/ethnic status, state residency, volunteer work, work experience. **Freshman Admission Requirements:** High school diploma is required and GED is accepted. *Academic units required:* 4 English, 3 mathematics, 3 science, (3 science labs), 3 foreign language, 1 social studies, 2 history, 3 academic electives. **Freshman Admission Statistics:** 6,635 applied, 25% admitted, 27% enrolled. **Transfer Admission Requirements:** High school transcript, college transcript(s), essay or personal statement, standardized test scores, statement of good standing from prior institution(s). Minimum college GPA of 3.0 required. Lowest grade transferable C. **General Admission Information:** Application Fee $45. Early decision application deadline 11/15. Regular application deadline 1/15. Regular notification 4/1. Nonfall registration not accepted. Admission may be deferred for a maximum of 1 year. Credit and/or placement offered for CEEB Advanced Placement tests.

COSTS AND FINANCIAL AID

Annual tuition $47,220. Room and board $11,890. Required fees $1,920. Average book expense $1,900. **Required Forms and Deadlines:** FAFSA, CSS/Financial Aid PROFILE, Noncustodial PROFILE. **Notification of Awards:** Applicants will be notified of awards on or about 4/1. **Types of Aid:** *Need-based scholarships/grants:* Federal Pell, SEOG, state scholarships/grants, private scholarships, the school's own gift aid. *Loans:* Subsidized Stafford, Unsubsidized Stafford, PLUS, Federal Perkins, college/university loans from institutional funds. *Student Employment:* Federal Work-Study Program available. Institutional employment available. Highest amount earned per year from on-campus jobs $1,255. Off-campus job opportunities are poor. **Financial Aid Statistics:** 96% freshmen, 96% undergrads receive need-based scholarship or grant aid. 19% freshmen, 15% undergrads receive non-need-based scholarship or grant aid. 87% freshmen, 80% undergrads receive need-based self-help aid. 0% freshmen, 0% undergrads receive athletic scholarships. 49% freshmen, 42% undergrads receive any aid. 46% undergrads borrow to pay for school. Average cumulative indebtedness $15,705. **Criteria for awarding institutional aid:** *Non-need-based:* academics, minority status.

KETTERING UNIVERSITY

1700 University Ave., Flint, MI 48504-6214
Phone: 810-762-9865 · **Financial Aid Phone:** 810-762-7859
E-mail: admissions@kettering.edu · **CEEB Code:** 1246
Fax: 810-762-9837 · **Website:** www.kettering.edu · **ACT Code:** 1998

This private school was founded in 1919. It has a 85-acre campus.

RATINGS

Admissions Selectivity Rating: 88   **Fire Safety Rating:** 71

STUDENTS AND FACULTY

Enrollment: 1,698. **Student Body:** 18% female, 82% male, 18% out-of-state, 5% international (29 countries represented). Asian 3%, African American 4%, Caucasian 76%, Hispanic 3%, Native American <1%
Retention and Graduation: 12% freshmen graduate within 4 years. **Faculty:** 119 full-time faculty, 84% hold PhDs, 27% are members of minority groups, 15% are women. 0% of classes are taught by teaching assistants.

ACADEMICS

Degrees: bachelor's, master's. **Classes:** Most classes have 20–29 students. Most lab/discussion sessions have 10–19 students. **Majors with Highest Enrollment:** Mechanical Engineering; Electrical and Electronics Engineering; Chemical Engineering. **Special Study Options:** Accelerated program, cooperative education program, distance learning, double major, dual enrollment, independent study, study abroad, Co-op is required of all undergraduate students and typically begins in the first year. Each 24 week semester is divided into 11-weeks of classes and 12-13 weeks of paid professional co-op experience in industry. Students co-op with employers in 43 states and several countries. Income from co-op is a major resource for Kettering students whose total co-op income over their 4 and 1/2-year program typically ranges between $40,000 and $65,000. In addition to study abroad some Kettering students also gain experience in foreign locations for their co-op employer. Accelerated Program, Cooperative (work-study)program, distance learning, double major, independent study. Distance learing is for graduate students only. **Combined degree programs:** BS/MS Engineering. **Disability Services:** Special programs offered to physically disabled students include note-taking services, reader services, tape recorders, tutors. Kettering University is a preimere cooperative education program. All students are required to complete a specified number of co-op terms to graduate. Students may start their co-op experience as early as their freshmen year.

FACILITIES

Housing: Coed dorms, fraternity/sorority housing, apartments for single students. 100% of campus accessible to physically disabled. **Special Academic Facilities/Equipment:** Art museum, Scharschburg Archieves and Industrial History Museum (principal repository for SAE Patents and Technical Papers). Kettering is renown for the variety and quality of its laboratories for student use and teaching. Labs are required in nearly all science and engineering courses. Of special note are the Bosch Automotive Electronics Systems Lab, Ford Design Simulation Studio, the GM/PACE e-Design and e-Manufacturing Studio, Center for Fuel Cell Systems and Powertrain Integration, the Crash Test Safety, Computer Intergrated Manufacturing (CIM), Polymer Processing, and Mechatronics Labs, the Lubrizol Engine Test Center, SAE Project Vehicle facilities, Biomedical, and the Environmental Scanning Electron Microscopy Lab. The Connie and Jim John Recreation Center and Kettering Park (outdoor recreation). **Computers:** 100% of classrooms, 100% of libraries, 100% of dining areas, have wireless network access. Students can register for classes online. Administrative functions (other than registration) can be performed online.

CAMPUS LIFE

Environment: City. **Activities:** drama/theater, music ensembles, radio station, student government, student newspaper, yearbook. 43 registered organizations, 13 honor societies, 1 religious organization. 13 fraternities, 6 sororities. **On-Campus Highlights:** CS Mott Engineering and Science Center, Connie and Jim John Recreation Center, Frances Willson Thompson Residence Hall,

Cemistry and Physics Laboratories, Engineering Laboratories, Kettering University takes great pride in our TOP ranked programs and one-of-a kind co-op program. Kettering students earn on average $40,000-$65,000 and up to 2 1/2 years of relevant work experience while working for one of our 600+ co-op employers. Prospective students are encouraged to visit campus to learn more about our academic programs, one-of-a-kind co-op program and to meet our faculty, students and staff.

ADMISSIONS

Freshman Academic Profile: Average high school GPA 3.65. 34% in top 10% of high school class, 71% in top 25% of high school class, 93.5% in top 50% of high school class. 68% from public high schools. SAT Math middle 50% range 590-660. SAT Critical Reading middle 50% range 520-650. ACT middle 50% range 25-29. Minimum internet-based TOEFL 79. Minimum paper TOEFL 550. **Basis for Candidate Selection:** *Very important factors considered include:* academic GPA, rigor of secondary school record, standardized test scores. *Important factors considered include:* Class rank, extracurricular activities. *Other factors considered include:* application essay, recommendation(s), interview, racial/ethnic status, volunteer work, work experience. **Freshman Admission Requirements:** High school diploma is required and GED is not accepted. *Academic units required:* 3 English, 4 mathematics, 2 science, (2 science labs), 0 foreign language, 0 social studies, 0 history, 0 visual/performing arts, 0 computer science, 0 academic electives. **Freshman Admission Statistics:** 1,587 applied, 72% admitted, 32% enrolled. **Transfer Admission Requirements:** college transcript(s), Minimum college GPA of 3.0 required. Lowest grade transferable C. **General Admission Information:** Application Fee $35. Notification on a rolling basis, beginning on or about 10/15. Nonfall registration accepted. Admission may be deferred for a maximum of 1 year. Credit offered for CEEB Advanced Placement tests.

COSTS AND FINANCIAL AID

Required Forms and Deadlines: FAFSA. **Notification of Awards:** Applicants will be notified of awards on a rolling basis beginning 1/15. **Types of Aid:** *Need-based scholarships/grants:* Federal Pell, SEOG, state scholarships/grants, private scholarships, the school's own gift aid. *Loans:* Direct Subsidized Stafford, Direct Unsubsidized Stafford, Direct PLUS, Subsidized Stafford, Unsubsidized Stafford, PLUS. *Student Employment:* Federal Work-Study Program available. Institutional employment available. Highest amount earned per year from on-campus jobs $1,200. Off-campus job opportunities are fair. **Financial Aid Statistics:** 100% freshmen, 99% undergrads receive need-based scholarship or grant aid. 7% freshmen, 8% undergrads receive non-need-based scholarship or grant aid. 93% freshmen, 91% undergrads receive need-based self-help aid. 0% freshmen, 98% freshmen, 88% undergrads receive any aid. **Criteria for awarding institutional aid:** *Non-need-based:* academics, alumni affiliation, leadership, state/district residency.

See page 1070.

KEUKA COLLEGE

Office of Admissions, Keuka Park, NY 14478-0098
Phone: 315-279-5254 · **Financial Aid Phone:** 315-279-5646
E-mail: admissions@mail.keuka.edu · **CEEB Code:** 2744
Fax: 315-536-5386 · **Website:** www.keuka.edu · **ACT Code:** 2782

This private school, affiliated with the American Baptist Church, was founded in 1890. It has a 203-acre campus.

RATINGS

Admissions Selectivity Rating: 72   Fire Safety Rating: 79

STUDENTS AND FACULTY

Enrollment: 1,738. **Student Body:** 76% female, 24% male, 6% out-of-state, 0% international (3 countries represented). Asian 0%, African American 3%, Caucasian 35%, Hispanic 0%, Native American <1%
Retention and Graduation: 36% freshmen graduate within 4 years. 48% freshmen graduate within 6 years. 28% grads go on to further study within 1 year. **Faculty:** 90 full-time faculty, 70% hold PhDs, 61% are members of minority groups, 18% are women. 0% of classes are taught by teaching assistants.

ACADEMICS

Degrees: bachelor's, master's. **Classes:** Most classes have 20–29 students. Most lab/discussion sessions have 10–19 students. **Majors with Highest Enrollment:** Special Education and Teaching; Occupational Therapy/Therapist; Business Administration and Management. **Special Study Options:** Accelerated program, cooperative education program, cross-registration, double major, dual enrollment, independent study, internships, student-designed major, study abroad, teacher certification program. **Combined degree programs:** Clinical Science to Chiropractic with NY Chiroprac. **Disability Services:** Special

programs offered to physically disabled students include note-taking services, reader services, tape recorders, tutors. **Career services:** Alumni network, alumni services, career/job search classes, career assessment, internships, regional alumni. Career services highlights include Experiential learning. We are a national leader in Experiential, Hands-on Learning.

FACILITIES

Housing: Coed dorms, special housing for disabled students, men's dorms, women's dorms, cooperative housing, Theme housing. 61% of campus accessible to physically disabled. **Special Academic Facilities/Equipment:** Bird Museum, Lightner Gallery.

CAMPUS LIFE

Environment: Rural. **Activities:** Choral groups, concert band, dance, drama/theater, literary magazine, musical theater, radio station, student government, student newspaper, student-run film society, yearbook. 32 registered organizations, 7 honor societies, 2 religious organizations. **Athletics (Intercollegiate):** *Men:* baseball, basketball, cross-country, golf, lacrosse, soccer, tennis. *Women:* basketball, cross-country, golf, lacrosse, soccer, softball, synchronized swimming, tennis, volleyball. **On-Campus Highlights:** The Weed Physical Arts Center (Gym, pool, fitness rooms, coaches offices), Dahstrom Student Center (bookstore, club offices, student affairs), Ostrander Field (soccer, lacrosse games), Hegeman Hall (classes, faculty offices), Jephson Hall (sciences, greenhouse, labs, electronic classroom).

ADMISSIONS

Freshman Academic Profile: Average high school GPA 3.14. 7% in top 10% of high school class, 27% in top 25% of high school class, 74.9% in top 50% of high school class. 96% from public high schools. SAT Math middle 50% range 430-530. SAT Critical Reading middle 50% range 430-520. SAT Writing middle 50% range 400-500. ACT middle 50% range 18-23. Minimum paper TOEFL 500. **Basis for Candidate Selection:** *Very important factors considered include:* rigor of secondary school record. *Important factors considered include:* Class rank, application essay, academic GPA, recommendation(s), character/personal qualities, extracurricular activities, interview. *Other factors considered include:* standardized test scores, alumni/ae relation, level of applicant's interest, talent/ability, volunteer work, work experience. **Freshman Admission Requirements:** High school diploma is required and GED is accepted. **Freshman Admission Statistics:** 1,371 applied, 83% admitted, 19% enrolled. **Transfer Admission Requirements:** college transcript(s), essay or personal statement, Minimum college GPA of 2.0 required. Lowest grade transferable C. **General Admission Information:** Application Fee $30. Notification on a rolling basis, beginning on or about 9/1. Nonfall registration accepted. Admission may be deferred for a maximum of 12. Credit and/or placement offered for CEEB Advanced Placement tests.

COSTS AND FINANCIAL AID

Annual tuition $26,490. Room and board $10,590. Required fees $790. Average book expense $1,500. **Required Forms and Deadlines:** FAFSA. **Notification of Awards:** Applicants will be notified of awards on a rolling basis beginning 3/1. **Types of Aid:** *Need-based scholarships/grants:* Federal Pell, SEOG, state scholarships/grants, the school's own gift aid. *Loans:* Subsidized Stafford, Unsubsidized Stafford, PLUS, Federal Perkins. *Student Employment:* Highest amount earned per year from on-campus jobs $1,800. Off-campus job opportunities are good. **Financial Aid Statistics:** 91% freshmen, 80% undergrads receive need-based scholarship or grant aid. 83% freshmen, 57% undergrads receive non-need-based scholarship or grant aid. 97% freshmen, 91% undergrads receive need-based self-help aid. 0% freshmen, 0% undergrads receive athletic scholarships. 92% freshmen, 93% undergrads receive any aid. 95% undergrads borrow to pay for school. Average cumulative indebtedness $17,852. **Criteria for awarding institutional aid:** *Non-need-based:* academics, alumni affiliation, leadership, minority status, religious affiliation.

KEYSTONE COLLEGE

One College Green, La Plume, PA 18440
Phone: 570-945-8111 · **Financial Aid Phone:** 570-945-8132
E-mail: admissions@keystone.edu · **CEEB Code:** 2351
Fax: 570-945-7916 · **Website:** www.keystone.edu · **ACT Code:** 2602

This private school was founded in 1868. It has a 270-acre campus.

RATINGS

Admissions Selectivity Rating: 71   Fire Safety Rating: 95

STUDENTS AND FACULTY

Enrollment: 1,647. **Student Body:** 60% female, 40% male, 13% out-of-state, 1% international (9 countries represented). Asian 1%, African American 5%, Caucasian 72%, Hispanic 3%, Native American <1%

Retention and Graduation: 29% freshmen graduate within 4 years. 42% freshmen graduate within 6 years. 25% grads go on to further study within 1 year. 1% grads pursue arts and sciences degrees. 1% grads pursue law degrees. 1% grads pursue business degrees. 1% grads pursue medical degrees. **Faculty:** 68 full-time faculty, 49% hold PhDs, 63% are members of minority groups, 1% are women. 0% of classes are taught by teaching assistants.

ACADEMICS

Degrees: associate, bachelor's, certificate, post-bachelor's certificate, terminal associate, transfer associate. **Classes:** Most classes have 10–19 students. Most lab/discussion sessions have fewer than 10 students. **Majors with Highest Enrollment:** Business Administration and Management; Homeland Security, Law Enforcement, Firefighting and Related Protective Services; Education. **Special Study Options:** cooperative education program, cross-registration, distance learning, double major, dual enrollment, English as a Second Language (ESL), honors program, independent study, internships, study abroad, teacher certification program, weekend college. **Honors programs:** Freshmen Honor's Program. **Disability Services:** Special programs offered to physically disabled students include note-taking services, reader services, tutors. **Career services:** Alumni network, alumni services, career/job search classes, career assessment, internships, regional alumni. Career services highlights include student internship placements that have included NBC Dateline, Late Night with Conan O'Brien, US Olympic Training Committee, US Secret Service, ESPN Radio, Atlantic Records, and placements abroad in several countries.

FACILITIES

Housing: Coed dorms, special housing for disabled students, women's dorms. 80% of campus accessible to physically disabled. **Special Academic Facilities/ Equipment:** Linder Art Gallery; Cupillari Astronomical Observatory; Willary Water Resource Center **Computers:** 100% of classrooms, 50% of dorms, 100% of libraries, 100% of dining areas, 100% of student union, 50% of common outdoor areas have wireless network access. Students can register for classes online. Administrative functions (other than registration) can be performed online.

CAMPUS LIFE

Environment: Rural. **Activities:** Choral groups, drama/theater, literary magazine, musical theater, radio station, student government, student newspaper, yearbook, Campus Ministries, International Student Organization. 22 registered organizations, 1 religious organization. **Athletics (Intercollegiate):** *Men:* baseball, basketball, cross-country, golf, soccer, tennis, track/field (outdoor), track/field (indoor). *Women:* basketball, cross-country, field hockey, soccer, softball, tennis, track/field (outdoor), track/field (indoor), volleyball. **On-Campus Highlights:** Linder Art Gallery, 270 acre woodlands campus (trail system), Astronomical Observatory, Giants' Den, Keystone Commons. **Environmental Initiatives:** A recycling program Water reduction Energy Star Appliance policy

ADMISSIONS

Freshman Academic Profile: SAT Math middle 50% range 400-500. SAT Critical Reading middle 50% range 400-500. SAT Writing middle 50% range 380-480. ACT middle 50% range 17-22. Minimum internet-based TOEFL 80. Minimum paper TOEFL 550. **Basis for Candidate Selection:** *Very important factors considered include:* academic GPA, standardized test scores. *Important factors considered include:* recommendation(s), extracurricular activities, state residency, talent/ability. *Other factors considered include:* application essay, alumni/ae relation, character/personal qualities, geographical residence, interview, work experience. **Freshman Admission Requirements:** High school diploma is required and GED is accepted. **Freshman Admission Statistics:** 1,192 applied, 70% admitted, 43% enrolled. **Transfer Admission Requirements:** college transcript(s), essay or personal statement, standardized test scores, statement of good standing from prior institution(s). Minimum college GPA of 2 required. Lowest grade transferable 2. **General Admission Information:** Application Fee $45. Regular application deadline 5/15. Notification on a rolling basis, beginning on or about 7/20. Nonfall registration accepted.

COSTS AND FINANCIAL AID

Annual tuition $20,300. Room and board $9,800. Required fees $1,400. Average book expense $1,900. **Required Forms and Deadlines:** FAFSA, State aid form. **Notification of Awards:** Applicants will be notified of awards on or about 8/15. **Types of Aid:** *Need-based scholarships/grants:* private scholarships, the school's own gift aid. *Loans:* **Financial Aid Statistics:** 100% freshmen, 99% undergrads receive need-based scholarship or grant aid. 76% freshmen, 72% undergrads receive non-need-based scholarship or grant aid. 90% freshmen, 91% undergrads receive need-based self-help aid. 0% freshmen, 0% undergrads receive athletic scholarships. 88% freshmen, 91% undergrads receive any aid. 92% undergrads borrow to pay for school. Average cumulative indebtedness $7,754. **Criteria for awarding institutional aid:** *Non-need-based:* academics, art, athletics, leadership, music/drama, state/district residency.

KING'S COLLEGE (PA)

133 North River Street, Wilkes-Barre, PA 18711
Phone: 570-208-5858 · **Financial Aid Phone:** 570-208-5868
E-mail: admissions@kings.edu · **CEEB Code:** 2353
Fax: 570-208-5971 · **Website:** www.kings.edu · **ACT Code:** 3604

This private school, affiliated with the Roman Catholic Church, was founded in 1946. It has a 48-acre campus.

RATINGS

Admissions Selectivity Rating: 82   **Fire Safety Rating:** 94

STUDENTS AND FACULTY

Enrollment: 1,865. **Student Body:** 47% female, 53% male, 29% out-of-state, 1% international (2 countries represented). Asian 2%, African American 3%, Caucasian 76%, Hispanic 6%, Native American <1%
Retention and Graduation: 56% freshmen graduate within 4 years. 62% freshmen graduate within 6 years. 25% grads go on to further study within 1 year. 17% grads pursue arts and sciences degrees. 1% grads pursue law degrees. 1% grads pursue business degrees. **Faculty:** 141 full-time faculty, 86% hold PhDs, 45% are members of minority groups, 4% are women. 0% of classes are taught by teaching assistants.

ACADEMICS

Degrees: associate, bachelor's, certificate, master's, post-bachelor's certificate. **Classes:** Most classes have 10–19 students. Most lab/discussion sessions have 10–19 students. **Majors with Highest Enrollment:** Physician Assistant; Criminal Justice/Safety Studies; Accounting. **Special Study Options:** Accelerated program, cross-registration, distance learning, double major, dual enrollment, English as a Second Language (ESL), honors program, independent study, internships, student-designed major, study abroad, teacher certification program, weekend college. **Combined degree programs:** BS Med Studies/ MS Phys Asst. **Disability Services:** Special programs offered to physically disabled students include note-taking services, reader services, tape recorders, tutors. **Career services:** Alumni network, alumni services, career/job search classes, career assessment, internships, regional alumni.

FACILITIES

Housing: Coed dorms, special housing for disabled students, men's dorms, women's dorms, apartments for single students, Wellness Housing, Theme Housing. 99% of campus accessible to physically disabled. **Special Academic Facilities/Equipment:** Electron microscope, rooftop greenhouse, molecular biology lab, computer graphics lab. **Computers:** 50% of classrooms, 25% of dorms, 100% of libraries, 100% of dining areas, 100% of student union, 100% of common outdoor areas have wireless network access. Students can register for classes online. Administrative functions (other than registration) can be performed online.

CAMPUS LIFE

Environment: City. **Activities:** Choral groups, dance, drama/theater, literary magazine, music ensembles, pep band, radio station, student government, student newspaper, yearbook, Campus Ministries. 50 registered organizations, 15 honor societies, 2 religious organizations. **Athletics (Intercollegiate):** *Men:* baseball, basketball, cheerleading, cross-country, football, golf, lacrosse, soccer, swimming, tennis, wrestling. *Women:* basketball, cheerleading, cross-country, field hockey, lacrosse, soccer, softball, swimming, tennis, volleyball. **On-Campus Highlights:** Sheehy-Farmer Campus Center, McGowan School of Business, Scandlon Physical Education Center, Betzler Fields (Athletic Complex), Gateway Corners.

ADMISSIONS

Freshman Academic Profile: Average high school GPA 3.3. 14% in top 10% of high school class, 39% in top 25% of high school class, 67% in top 50% of high school class. 74% from public high schools. SAT Math middle 50% range 470-590. SAT Critical Reading middle 50% range 450-550. SAT Writing middle 50% range 440-550. Minimum internet-based TOEFL 71. Minimum paper TOEFL 530. **Basis for Candidate Selection:** *Very important factors considered include:* Class rank, academic GPA, rigor of secondary school record. *Important factors considered include:* application essay, standardized test scores, character/personal qualities. *Other factors considered include:* recommendation(s), alumni/ae relation, extracurricular activities, interview, volunteer work, work experience. **Freshman Admission Requirements:** High school diploma is required and GED is accepted. *Academic units required:* 4 English, 3 mathematics, 3 science, (2 science labs), 2 foreign language, 3 social studies, 1 history, 0 computer science, 0 academic electives. **Freshman Admission Statistics:** 3,150 applied, 67% admitted, 23% enrolled. **Transfer Admission Requirements:** High school transcript, college transcript(s), essay or personal statement, Minimum college GPA of 2.0 required. Lowest grade transferable C. **General Admission Information:** Application Fee $30.

Notification on a rolling basis, beginning on or about 10/1. Nonfall registration accepted. Admission may be deferred for a maximum of 1 year. Neither credit nor placement offered for CEEB Advanced Placement tests.

COSTS AND FINANCIAL AID

Required Forms and Deadlines: FAFSA. **Notification of Awards:** Applicants will be notified of awards on a rolling basis beginning 3/1. **Types of Aid:** *Need-based scholarships/grants:* Federal Pell, SEOG, state scholarships/grants, private scholarships, the school's own gift aid. *Loans:* Subsidized Stafford, Unsubsidized Stafford, PLUS, Federal Perkins, Private Loans. *Student Employment:* Federal Work-Study Program available. Institutional employment available. Highest amount earned per year from on-campus jobs $2,000. Off-campus job opportunities are fair. **Financial Aid Statistics:** 98% freshmen, 98% undergrads receive need-based scholarship or grant aid. 11% freshmen, 9% undergrads receive non-need-based scholarship or grant aid. 86% freshmen, 88% undergrads receive need-based self-help aid. 0% freshmen, 0% undergrads receive athletic scholarships. 99% freshmen, 96% undergrads receive any aid. 86% undergrads borrow to pay for school. Average cumulative indebtedness $19,450. **Criteria for awarding institutional aid:** *Non-need-based:* academics, leadership.

KING UNIVERSITY

1350 King College Road, Bristol, TN 37620-2699
Phone: 423-652-4861 · **Financial Aid Phone:** 423-652-4728
E-mail: admissions@king.edu · **CEEB Code:** 1371
Fax: 423-652-4727 · **Website:** www.king.edu · **ACT Code:** 3970

This private school, affiliated with the Presbyterian Church, was founded in 1867. It has a 135-acre campus.

RATINGS

Admissions Selectivity Rating: 81   **Fire Safety Rating:** 65

STUDENTS AND FACULTY

Enrollment: 1,866. **Student Body:** 64% female, 36% male, 37% out-of-state, 3% international (29 countries represented). Asian 0%, African American 5%, Caucasian 80%, Hispanic 2%, Native American <1%
Retention and Graduation: 36% freshmen graduate within 4 years. 50% freshmen graduate within 6 years. 32% grads go on to further study within 1 year. 39% grads pursue arts and sciences degrees. 3% grads pursue law degrees. 42% grads pursue business degrees. 5% grads pursue medical degrees. **Faculty:** 86 full-time faculty, 60% hold PhDs, 53% are members of minority groups, 6% are women. 0% of classes are taught by teaching assistants.

ACADEMICS

Degrees: bachelor's, master's. **Classes:** Most classes have 10–19 students. Most lab/discussion sessions have fewer than 10 students. **Special Study Options:** Accelerated program, cross-registration, double major, dual enrollment, exchange student program (domestic), honors program, independent study, internships, student-designed major, study abroad, teacher certification program. **Honors programs:** The Jack E. Snider Honors Center allows students to interact with other students and faculty of diverse interests. Participants take selected courses that stimulate thinking and allow for creative response while engaging in special opportunities such as meeting with faculty members and outside guests. Other courses may allow honors students, for extra credit, to develop more extensive research projects. The honors seminars also examine ideas from a variety of academic disciplines. Participants serve both the campus and the larger community by tutoring and mentoring and are encouraged to explore other perspectives through study abroad experiences. **Combined degree programs:** BA/MEng, 3-1 Pharmacyprogram 3-1 Medical Technology program. **Disability Services:** Special programs offered to physically disabled students include tutors. **Career services:** Alumni network, alumni services, career assessment, internships.

FACILITIES

Housing: special housing for disabled students, men's dorms, women's dorms. 80% of campus accessible to physically disabled. **Special Academic Facilities/Equipment:** Electron microscope, observatory with two reflecting telescopes, solar telescope.

CAMPUS LIFE

Environment: Town. **Activities:** Choral groups, concert band, dance, drama/theater, literary magazine, music ensembles, musical theater, pep band, student government, student newspaper, yearbook, Campus Ministries, International Student Organization. 35 registered organizations, 5 honor societies, 9 religious organizations. **Athletics (Intercollegiate):** *Men:* baseball, basketball, bowling, cheerleading, cross-country, cycling, diving, golf, soccer, swimming, tennis, track/field (outdoor), track/field (indoor), wrestling. *Women:* basketball, bowling, cheerleading, cross-country, cycling, diving, golf, soccer, softball, swimming,

tennis, track/field (outdoor), track/field (indoor), volleyball, wrestling. **On-Campus Highlights:** New Student Center/Athletic Complex, Campus oval, Library, Residence hall lobbies, Entrance way and sporting fields.

ADMISSIONS

Freshman Academic Profile: Average high school GPA 3.37. 17% in top 10% of high school class, 42% in top 25% of high school class, 74% in top 50% of high school class. 89% from public high schools. SAT Math middle 50% range 450-560. SAT Critical Reading middle 50% range 440-540. SAT Writing middle 50% range 415-520. ACT middle 50% range 19-24. Minimum internet-based TOEFL 84. Minimum paper TOEFL 563. **Basis for Candidate Selection:** *Very important factors considered include:* academic GPA, standardized test scores. *Other factors considered include:* Class rank, application essay, recommendation(s), rigor of secondary school record, character/personal qualities, extracurricular activities, interview, level of applicant's interest. **Freshman Admission Requirements:** High school diploma is required and GED is accepted. *Academic units required:* 4 English, 3 mathematics, 1 science, (1 science labs), 2 foreign language, 0 social studies, 2 history, 0 visual/performing arts, 0 computer science, 4 academic electives. **Freshman Admission Statistics:** 1,090 applied, 72% admitted, 27% enrolled. **Transfer Admission Requirements:** college transcript(s), Minimum college GPA of 2.0 required. Lowest grade transferable C-. **General Admission Information:** Application Fee $20. Nonfall registration accepted. Admission may be deferred for a maximum of 1 semester. Credit and/or placement offered for CEEB Advanced Placement tests.

COSTS AND FINANCIAL AID

Annual tuition $23,608. Room and board $8,180. Required fees $1,352. Average book expense $600. **Required Forms and Deadlines:** FAFSA. **Notification of Awards:** Applicants will be notified of awards on a rolling basis beginning 3/1. **Types of Aid:** *Need-based scholarships/grants:* Federal Pell, SEOG, state scholarships/grants, the school's own gift aid. *Loans:* Subsidized Stafford, Unsubsidized Stafford, PLUS, Federal Perkins, state loans, college/university loans from institutional funds. *Student Employment:* Federal Work-Study Program available. Institutional employment available. Highest amount earned per year from on-campus jobs $1,236. Off-campus job opportunities are good. **Financial Aid Statistics:** 95% freshmen, 85% undergrads receive need-based scholarship or grant aid. 12% freshmen, 8% undergrads receive non-need-based scholarship or grant aid. 87% freshmen, 92% undergrads receive need-based self-help aid. 12% freshmen, 6% undergrads receive athletic scholarships. 98% freshmen, 94% undergrads receive any aid. 95% undergrads borrow to pay for school. Average cumulative indebtedness $27,578. **Criteria for awarding institutional aid:** *Non-need-based:* academics, athletics, music/drama.

KNOX COLLEGE

2 East South Street, Campus Box 148, Galesburg, IL 61401
Phone: 309-341-7100 · **Financial Aid Phone:** 309-341-7149
E-mail: admission@knox.edu · **CEEB Code:** 1372
Fax: 309-341-7070 · **Website:** www.knox.edu · **ACT Code:** 1052

This private school was founded in 1837. It has a 82-acre campus.

RATINGS

Admissions Selectivity Rating: 87   **Fire Safety Rating:** 89

STUDENTS AND FACULTY

Enrollment: 1,376. **Student Body:** 58% female, 42% male, 43% out-of-state, 13% international (46 countries represented). Asian 6%, African American 8%, Caucasian 53%, Hispanic 13%, Native American <1%
Retention and Graduation: 88% freshmen return for sophomore year. 73% freshmen graduate within 4 years. 80% freshmen graduate within 6 years. 24% grads go on to further study within 1 year. 13% grads pursue arts and sciences degrees. 1% grads pursue law degrees. 2% grads pursue business degrees. 3% grads pursue medical degrees. **Faculty:** 116 full-time faculty, 96% hold PhDs, 42% are members of minority groups, 15% are women. 0% of classes are taught by teaching assistants.

ACADEMICS

Degrees: bachelor's. **Classes:** Most classes have 10–19 students. Most lab/discussion sessions have 10–19 students. **Majors with Highest Enrollment:** Creative Writing; Economics; Psychology. **Special Study Options:** double major, dual enrollment, honors program, independent study, internships, student-designed major, study abroad, teacher certification program. **Honors**

programs: Knox College is an "honors college". If you compare Knox's academic requirements, student profile, educational opportunities, and student experiences with those of an honors program at a university, Knox provides comparable and often much richer opportunities for its students. **Combined degree programs:** BA/JD, BA/MEng, Architecture, Environment Management, Medical Tec. **Disability Services:** Special programs offered to physically disabled students include note-taking services, tape recorders, tutors. **Career services:** career assessment, internships. Career services highlights include Kemper Scholars Program.

FACILITIES

Housing: Coed dorms, special housing for disabled students, men's dorms, special housing for international students, women's dorms, fraternity/sorority housing, apartments for single students, Wellness Housing, Theme Housing. 60% of campus accessible to physically disabled. **Special Academic Facilities/ Equipment:** Anthropology, art, and field museums, theatre with revolving stage and computerized lighting, ceramics, sculpture, painting, and printmaking studios, 760-acre biological field station, environmental climate chambers, electron microscope. **Computers:** 100% of classrooms, 100% of dorms, 100% of libraries, 100% of dining areas, 100% of student union, 90% of common outdoor areas have wireless network access. Students can register for classes online. Administrative functions (other than registration) can be performed online.

CAMPUS LIFE

Environment: Town. **Activities:** Choral groups, dance, drama/theater, jazz band, literary magazine, music ensembles, radio station, student government, student newspaper, symphony orchestra, Campus Ministries, International Student Organization, Model UN. 102 registered organizations, 8 honor societies, 6 religious organizations. 5 fraternities, 3 sororities. **Athletics (Intercollegiate):** *Men:* baseball, basketball, cross-country, football, golf, soccer, swimming, tennis, track/field (outdoor), track/field (indoor), wrestling. *Women:* basketball, cross-country, golf, soccer, softball, swimming, tennis, track/field (outdoor), track/field (indoor), volleyball. **On-Campus Highlights:** Gizmo Snack Bar, Andrew Fitness Center, Hard Knox Café, Gizmo Patio, Seymour Library. **Environmental Initiatives:** In 2008, Knox College created the President's Sustainability Task Force and students approved a fee to be added to their bills to support sustainability projects on campus. This Student Sustainability Fund, administered by the Student Senate Sustainability Committee, has been used to subsidize purchase of bicycles and equipment for the on-campus bike share program, Energy Star washers and dryers, low-flow shower heads for residences, a vermicomposting system for the dining center, and compostable serving ware for the campus café (in Fall 2012 all styrofoam and plasticware was removed from campus and replaced with compostable products). This Fund allows students to have a direct impact on campus sustainability and in 2012 they used it to hire a Sustainability Coordinator and create an Office of Sustainability - centrally located in the student union. Knox College has been reducing its energy usage continuously through lighting upgrades and sensors, utility refurbishments, etc. The first LEED-certified building on campus is expected to be finished within two years. Knox College is working on a Bike/Pedestrian Plan, a Sustainability Plan, and is currently investigating additional investment in its sustainability profile, including a wind turbine on campus, car sharing program, green roof, and other projects. Student have championed various projects on campus including the Eco House (theme house for 8 students interested in sustainable living), Knox Community Garden (space for students to grow produce and learn about farming and composting), a Bike Share, a vermicomposting system at the cafeteria, trayless dining, local produce and meat, organic, vegetarian, and vegan meals, and many more. A new on-campus Bike Shop is a space where student mechanics repair the Bike Share fleet as well as teach workshops and provide repair and safety guidance to those who have their own bikes. An expanded Bike Share now offers both long-term bicycles (up to a student's entire time at Knox) or per day check outs (both programs are free). In 2012, Knox launched the Knox-Corps program which sends over a dozen students and recent graduates into the Galesburg community for a year of in-depth engagement with local non-profits and social service agencies. This real world experience not only complements the students education, but helps build partnerships and strengthens the local community. During New Student Orientation, a full day of local tours (themes include historical landmarks, arts & culture, local food, are offered so that new students can learn more about their new home and get more involved in the city. Once per term a Day of Service sends hundreds of students off campus to volunteer in the community. In fact, over half the student body volunteers regularly. The Knox community is very active with the Galesburg Farmers Market and other local food producers. Galesburg recently went to 100% renewable electric power for all residences. A Free Store on campus provides a year-round repository for items no longer wanted by students, faculty, and staff. Anyone can visit the FreeStore to take these items and those left for more than a year go to local charities. Items include clothing, furniture, appliances, electronics, books, household items, decor, shoes, office supplies, etc. Recycling on campus has increased as more containers have been placed throughout all buildings and residence hall rooms. New programs to collect cardboard during move-in and items during special events will continue this progress. Student workers collect the recycling and transport it to dumpsters using a bike-drawn trailer.

Knox College Dining Services won the Illinois Stewardship Alliance's Golden Beet Award in 2011 for incorporating local food into the menu on campus. The Cafeteria offers many local, vegetarian, vegan, gluten-free, and other more sustainable dishes. One night a week is Local Burger Night, featuring beef and vegetables from local farms. Dining Services used "eco clamshells" which are reusable, washable take-out containers rather than the disposable type. They also went trayless in 2010 to save on water, detergent, and reduce food waste. A vermicomposting bin and dehydrator compost 100% of the food waste (about 60,000 lbs. per year) at the on-campus cafeteria. Two gardens on campus provide hands-on urban agriculture and gardening experience for students and also provides produce for use in the dining hall.

ADMISSIONS

Freshman Academic Profile: 31% in top 10% of high school class, 58% in top 25% of high school class, 89% in top 50% of high school class. 75% from public high schools. SAT Math middle 50% range 540-670. SAT Critical Reading middle 50% range 580-690. SAT Writing middle 50% range 560-670. ACT middle 50% range 23-30. Minimum internet-based TOEFL 80. Minimum paper TOEFL 550. **Basis for Candidate Selection:** *Very important factors considered include:* academic GPA, rigor of secondary school record. *Important factors considered include:* Class rank, application essay, recommendation(s), character/personal qualities. *Other factors considered include:* standardized test scores, alumni/ae relation, extracurricular activities, first generation, geographical residence, interview, level of applicant's interest, racial/ethnic status, state residency, talent/ability, volunteer work. **Freshman Admission Requirements:** High school diploma is required and GED is accepted. **Freshman Admission Statistics:** 3,221 applied, 68% admitted, 17% enrolled. **Transfer Admission Requirements:** High school transcript, college transcript(s), essay or personal statement, statement of good standing from prior institution(s). Minimum college GPA of 3.0 required. Lowest grade transferable C. **General Admission Information:** Application Fee $40. Regular application deadline 2/1. Regular notification 3/31. Admission may be deferred for a maximum of 1 year. Credit and/or placement offered for CEEB Advanced Placement tests.

COSTS AND FINANCIAL AID

Required Forms and Deadlines: FAFSA, Institution's own financial aid form. **Notification of Awards:** Applicants will be notified of awards on a rolling basis beginning 3/15. **Types of Aid:** *Need-based scholarships/grants:* Federal Pell, SEOG, state scholarships/grants, private scholarships, the school's own gift aid. *Loans:* Direct Subsidized Stafford, Direct Unsubsidized Stafford, Direct PLUS, Federal Perkins, college/university loans from institutional funds. *Student Employment:* Federal Work-Study Program available. Institutional employment available. Highest amount earned per year from on-campus jobs $5,479. Off-campus job opportunities are fair. **Financial Aid Statistics:** 98% freshmen, 98% undergrads receive need-based scholarship or grant aid. 20% freshmen, 14% undergrads receive non-need-based scholarship or grant aid. 88% freshmen, 89% undergrads receive need-based self-help aid. 0% freshmen, 0% undergrads receive athletic scholarships. 99% freshmen, 98% undergrads receive any aid. 68% undergrads borrow to pay for school. Average cumulative indebtedness $26,151. **Criteria for awarding institutional aid:** *Non-need-based:* academics, art, music/drama.

See page 1072.

KUTZTOWN UNIVERSITY OF PENNSYLVANIA

Admissions Office, Kutztown, PA 19530-0730
Phone: 610-683-4060 • **Financial Aid Phone:** 610-683-4032
E-mail: admissions@kutztown.edu • **CEEB Code:** 2653
Fax: 610-683-1375 • **Website:** www.kutztown.edu • **ACT Code:** 3706

This public school was founded in 1866. It has a 325-acre campus.

RATINGS

Admissions Selectivity Rating: 82   Fire Safety Rating: 85

STUDENTS AND FACULTY

Enrollment: 8,516. **Student Body:** 56% female, 44% male, 11% out-of-state, 1% international (30 countries represented). Asian 1%, African American 8%, Caucasian 79%, Hispanic 7%, Native American <1%

Retention and Graduation: 73% freshmen return for sophomore year. 38% freshmen graduate within 4 years. 56% freshmen graduate within 6 years. 29% grads go on to further study within 1 year. 26% grads pursue arts and sciences degrees. 4% grads pursue law degrees. 4% grads pursue business degrees. 16% grads pursue medical degrees. **Faculty:** 413 full-time faculty, 81% hold PhDs, 48% are members of minority groups, 18% are women. 0% of classes are taught by teaching assistants.

ACADEMICS

Degrees: bachelor's, master's, post-bachelor's certificate. **Classes:** Most classes have 20–29 students. Most lab/discussion sessions have 20–29 students. **Majors with Highest Enrollment:** Psychology; Business Administration and Management; Criminal Justice/Safety Studies. **Special Study Options:** cross-registration, distance learning, double major, dual enrollment, honors program, independent study, internships, liberal arts/career combination, student-designed major, study abroad, teacher certification program. **Honors programs:** 1)University Honors Program 2)Various Honor Societies **Combined degree programs:** BS/MS Computer Information Science. **Disability Services:** Special programs offered to physically disabled students include note-taking services, reader services, tape recorders, tutors. **Career services:** Alumni network, alumni services, career/job search classes, career assessment, internships, regional alumni. Career services highlights include the wide array of services and events for Kutztown University students.

FACILITIES

Housing: Coed dorms, women's dorms, cooperative housing, apartments for single students, apartment units. 90% of campus accessible to physically disabled. **Special Academic Facilities/Equipment:** Art Gallery, German Cultural Heritage Center, Early Childhood Learning Center, Cartography Lab, Observatory, Planetarium, Daycare Center **Computers:** 25% of classrooms, 95% of dorms, 100% of libraries, 75% of dining areas, 100% of student union, 65% of common outdoor areas have wireless network access. Students can register for classes online. Administrative functions (other than registration) can be performed online.

CAMPUS LIFE

Environment: Rural. **Activities:** Choral groups, concert band, dance, drama/theater, jazz band, literary magazine, marching band, music ensembles, musical theater, radio station, student government, student newspaper, student-run film society, symphony orchestra, television station, yearbook, Campus Ministries, International Student Organization, Model UN. 218 registered organizations, 15 honor societies, 11 religious organization. 9 fraternities, 8 sororities. **Athletics (Intercollegiate):** *Men:* baseball, basketball, cross-country, football, tennis, track/field (outdoor), track/field (indoor), wrestling. *Women:* basketball, bowling, cross-country, field hockey, golf, lacrosse, soccer, softball, swimming, tennis, track/field (outdoor), track/field (indoor), volleyball. **On-Campus Highlights:** Taylor and Burnes Gourmet Coffee, Student Rec Center, Alumni Plaza-new walkway with outdoor amphitheater, Pennsylvania German Cultural Heritage Center, Academic Forum. **Environmental Initiatives:** Recycling program; Guaranteed energy savings agreement.

ADMISSIONS

Freshman Academic Profile: Average high school GPA 3.13. 4.8% in top 10% of high school class, 17.3% in top 25% of high school class, 51.6% in top 50% of high school class. 99% from public high schools. SAT Math middle 50% range 430-530. SAT Critical Reading middle 50% range 440-530. SAT Writing middle 50% range 420-510. ACT middle 50% range 17-22. Minimum internet-based TOEFL 79. Minimum paper TOEFL 550. **Basis for Candidate Selection:** *Very important factors considered include:* Class rank, rigor of secondary school record, standardized test scores. *Other factors considered include:* academic GPA, recommendation(s), character/personal qualities, extracurricular activities, geographical residence, interview, racial/ethnic status, state residency, talent/ability, volunteer work, work experience. **Freshman Admission Requirements:** High school diploma is required and GED is accepted. **Freshman Admission Statistics:** 8,061 applied, 39% admitted, 57% enrolled. **Transfer Admission Requirements:** college transcript(s), statement of good standing from prior institution(s). Minimum college GPA of 2.0 required. Lowest grade transferable C-. **General Admission Information:** Application Fee $35. Notification on a rolling basis, beginning on or about 10/1. Nonfall registration accepted. Admission may be deferred for a maximum of 1 year. Credit and/or placement offered for CEEB Advanced Placement tests.

COSTS AND FINANCIAL AID

Annual in-state tuition $6,820. Annual out-of-state tuition $17,050. Room and board $8,430. Required fees $2,251. Average book expense $1,107. **Required Forms and Deadlines:** FAFSA. **Notification of Awards:** Applicants will be notified of awards on a rolling basis beginning 3/30. **Types of Aid:** *Need-based scholarships/grants:* Federal Pell, SEOG, state scholarships/grants, private scholarships, the school's own gift aid. *Loans:* Subsidized Stafford, Unsubsidized Stafford, PLUS, Federal Perkins. *Student Employment:* Federal Work-Study Program available. Institutional employment available. Highest amount earned per year from on-campus jobs $9,999. Off-campus job opportunities are fair. **Financial Aid Statistics:** 59% freshmen, 60% undergrads receive need-based scholarship or grant aid. 7% freshmen, 8% undergrads receive non-need-based scholarship or grant aid. 88% freshmen, 88% undergrads receive need-based self-help aid. 5% freshmen, 3% undergrads receive athletic scholarships. 88% freshmen, 82% undergrads receive any aid. 81% undergrads borrow to pay for school. Average cumulative indebtedness $26,324. **Criteria for awarding institutional aid:** *Non-need-based:* academics, art, athletics, leadership, minority status, music/drama.

LA ROCHE COLLEGE

9000 Babcock Boulevard, Pittsburgh, PA 15237
Phone: 412-536-1271 · **Financial Aid Phone:** 412-536-1120
E-mail: admissions@laroche.edu · **CEEB Code:** 2379
Fax: 412-847-1820 · **Website:** www.laroche.edu · **ACT Code:** 3607

This private school, affiliated with the Roman Catholic Church, was founded in 1963. It has a 43-acre campus.

RATINGS

Admissions Selectivity Rating: 72   **Fire Safety Rating:** 88

STUDENTS AND FACULTY

Enrollment: 1,269. **Student Body:** 55% female, 45% male, 6% out-of-state, 14% international (35 countries represented). Asian 1%, African American 7%, Caucasian 63%, Hispanic 2%, Native American <1%
Retention and Graduation: 72% freshmen return for sophomore year. 29% freshmen graduate within 4 years. 45% freshmen graduate within 6 years.
Faculty: 61 full-time faculty, 82% hold PhDs, 57% are members of minority groups, 10% are women. 0% of classes are taught by teaching assistants.

ACADEMICS

Degrees: associate, bachelor's, certificate, master's, post-bachelor's certificate, terminal associate. **Classes:** Most classes have 10–19 students. Most lab/discussion sessions have 10–19 students. **Majors with Highest Enrollment:** Psychology; Criminal Justice/Safety Studies; Accounting. **Special Study Options:** Accelerated program, cross-registration, distance learning, double major, English as a Second Language (ESL), honors program, independent study, internships, student-designed major, study abroad, teacher certification program. **Combined degree programs:** BA/MA. **Disability Services:** Special programs offered to physically disabled students include note-taking services, reader services, tutors. **Career services:** career/job search classes, career assessment, internships, regional alumni.

FACILITIES

Housing: Coed dorms. 100% of campus accessible to physically disabled. **Special Academic Facilities/Equipment:** Cantellopes Art Gallery; College Center extension has state of the art smart classrooms **Computers:** 100% of classrooms, 10% of dorms, 100% of libraries, 100% of dining areas, 100% of student union, 25% of common outdoor areas have wireless network access. Students can register for classes online. Administrative functions (other than registration) can be performed online.

CAMPUS LIFE

Environment: City. **Activities:** Choral groups, dance, drama/theater, literary magazine, musical theater, radio station, student government, student newspaper, Campus Ministries, International Student Organization. 40 registered organizations, 4 honor societies, 2 religious organizations. **Athletics (Intercollegiate):** *Men:* baseball, basketball, cross-country, golf, lacrosse, soccer. *Women:* basketball, cheerleading, cross-country, soccer, softball, tennis, volleyball. **On-Campus Highlights:** Sports and Fitness Center, College bookstore, Magdalen Chapel, College Center Annex.

ADMISSIONS

Freshman Academic Profile: Average high school GPA 3.3. 14% in top 10% of high school class, 37% in top 25% of high school class, 74% in top 50% of high school class. 72% from public high schools. SAT Math middle 50% range 420-530. SAT Critical Reading middle 50% range 420-480. SAT Writing middle 50% range 410-530. ACT middle 50% range 16-23. **Basis for Candidate Selection:** *Very important factors considered include:* academic GPA, standardized test scores. *Important factors considered include:* level of applicant's interest. *Other factors considered include:* application essay, recommendation(s), rigor of secondary school record, character/personal qualities, interview, talent/ability, volunteer work. **Freshman Admission Requirements:** High school diploma is required and GED is accepted. *Academic units required:* 4 English, 3 mathematics, 3 science, (2 science labs), 0 foreign language, 3 social studies, 3 history. **Freshman Admission Statistics:** 990 applied, 94% admitted, 24% enrolled. **Transfer Admission Requirements:** college transcript(s), essay or personal statement, Minimum college GPA of 2.0 required. Lowest grade transferable C. **General Admission Information:** Application Fee $50. Notification on a rolling basis, beginning on or about 9/15. Nonfall registration accepted. Admission may be deferred for a maximum of 1 year. Credit offered for CEEB Advanced Placement tests.

COSTS AND FINANCIAL AID

Annual tuition $23,328. Room and board $9,732. Required fees $730. Average book expense $1,200. **Required Forms and Deadlines:** FAFSA. **Notification of Awards:** Applicants will be notified of awards on a rolling basis beginning 3/1. **Types of Aid:** *Need-based scholarships/grants:* Federal Pell, SEOG, state scholarships/grants, private scholarships, the school's own gift aid. *Loans:* Subsidized Stafford, Unsubsidized Stafford, PLUS, Federal Perkins, Private loans. *Student Employment:* Federal Work-Study Program available. Institutional employment available. Off-campus job opportunities are excellent. **Financial Aid Statistics:** 95% freshmen, 77% undergrads receive need-based scholarship or grant aid. 97% freshmen, 100% undergrads receive non-need-based scholarship or grant aid. 85% freshmen, 92% undergrads receive need-based self-help aid. 0% freshmen, 0% undergrads receive athletic scholarships. 91% freshmen, 91% undergrads receive any aid. 75% undergrads borrow to pay for school. Average cumulative indebtedness $23,102. **Criteria for awarding institutional aid:** *Non-need-based:* academics.

See page 1074.

LA SALLE UNIVERSITY

1900 West Olney Avenue, Philadelphia, PA 19141-1199
Phone: 215-951-1500 • **Financial Aid Phone:** 215-951-1070
E-mail: admiss@lasalle.edu • **CEEB Code:** 2363
Fax: 215-951-1656 • **Website:** http://www.lasalle.edu • **ACT Code:** 3608

This private school, affiliated with the Roman Catholic Church, was founded in 1863. It has a 120-acre campus.

RATINGS

Admissions Selectivity Rating: 77   **Fire Safety Rating:** 77

STUDENTS AND FACULTY

Enrollment: 4,122. **Student Body:** 63% female, 37% male, 33% out-of-state, 2% international (13 countries represented). Asian 5%, African American 19%, Caucasian 55%, Hispanic 10%, Native American <1%
Retention and Graduation: 81% freshmen return for sophomore year. 56% freshmen graduate within 4 years. 67% freshmen graduate within 6 years.
Faculty: 247 full-time faculty, 83% hold PhDs, 53% are members of minority groups, 10% are women. 0% of classes are taught by teaching assistants.

ACADEMICS

Degrees: associate, bachelor's, certificate, master's, post-bachelor's certificate, post-master's certificate. **Classes:** Most classes have 20–29 students. Most lab/discussion sessions have fewer than 10 students. **Majors with Highest Enrollment:** Health Services/Allied Health/Health Sciences; Accounting; Biological and Physical Sciences. **Special Study Options:** Accelerated program, cooperative education program, cross-registration, double major, dual enrollment, English as a Second Language (ESL), exchange student program (domestic), honors program, independent study, internships, student-designed major, study abroad, teacher certification program, 2+2 with Thomas Jefferson University. **Combined degree programs:** BS/MS (5 year)Speech/Language Path. and Audiology. **Disability Services:** Special programs offered to physically disabled students include note-taking services, reader services, tape recorders, tutors.

FACILITIES

Housing: Coed dorms, special housing for disabled students, fraternity/sorority housing, apartments for single students. 95% of campus accessible to physically disabled. **Special Academic Facilities/Equipment:** Art museum, Japanese tea house, language lab, child development center. **Computers:** Students can register for classes online. Administrative functions (other than registration) can be performed online.

CAMPUS LIFE

Environment: Metropolis. **Activities:** Choral groups, concert band, drama/theater, jazz band, literary magazine, music ensembles, musical theater, pep band, radio station, student government, student newspaper, student-run film society, television station, yearbook. 100 registered organizations, 10 honor societies, 4 religious organizations. 7 fraternities, 5 sororities. **Athletics (Intercollegiate):** *Men:* baseball, basketball, cheerleading, crew/rowing, cross-country, diving, football, golf, soccer, swimming, tennis, track/field (outdoor), wrestling. *Women:* basketball, cheerleading, crew/rowing, cross-country, diving, field hockey, golf, lacrosse, soccer, softball, swimming, tennis, track/field (outdoor), volleyball. **On-Campus Highlights:** Hayman Center (sports facility), Connelly Library, Student Union Building-food court, coffee house, restaurant, La Salle University Art Museum, Japanese Tea Ceremony House.

ADMISSIONS

Freshman Academic Profile: Average high school GPA 3.33. 15% in top 10% of high school class, 35% in top 25% of high school class, 68% in top 50% of high school class. 35% from public high schools. SAT Math middle 50% range 450-550. SAT Critical Reading middle 50% range 450-550. ACT middle 50% range 18-24. Minimum internet-based TOEFL 76. Minimum paper TOEFL 540. *Basis for Candidate Selection: Very important factors considered*

include: rigor of secondary school record. *Important factors considered include:* Class rank, application essay, standardized test scores. *Other factors considered include:* recommendation(s), alumni/ae relation, character/personal qualities, extracurricular activities, interview, talent/ability, volunteer work, work experience. **Freshman Admission Requirements:** High school diploma is required and GED is accepted. *Academic units required:* 4 English, 3 mathematics, 1 science, (1 science labs), 2 foreign language, 0 social studies, 1 history, 5 academic electives. **Freshman Admission Statistics:** 5,778 applied, 78% admitted, 20% enrolled. **Transfer Admission Requirements:** High school transcript, college transcript(s), essay or personal statement, standardized test scores, statement of good standing from prior institution(s). Minimum college GPA of 2.5 required. Lowest grade transferable C. **General Admission Information:** Application Fee $35. Notification on a rolling basis, beginning on or about 11/15. Nonfall registration accepted. Admission may be deferred for a maximum of info. not available.

COSTS AND FINANCIAL AID

Average book expense $500. **Required Forms and Deadlines:** FAFSA. **Notification of Awards:** Applicants will be notified of awards on a rolling basis beginning 3/15. **Types of Aid:** *Need-based scholarships/grants:* Federal Pell, SEOG, state scholarships/grants, private scholarships, the school's own gift aid. *Loans:* Subsidized Stafford, Unsubsidized Stafford, PLUS, Federal Perkins. **Financial Aid Statistics:** 99% freshmen, 98% undergrads receive need-based scholarship or grant aid. 9% freshmen, 8% undergrads receive non-need-based scholarship or grant aid. 79% freshmen, 81% undergrads receive need-based self-help aid. 5% freshmen, 5% undergrads receive athletic scholarships. 97% freshmen, 93% undergrads receive any aid. 79% undergrads borrow to pay for school. Average cumulative indebtedness $20,176. **Criteria for awarding institutional aid:** *Non-need-based:* academics, athletics.

LAFAYETTE COLLEGE

118 Markle Hall, Easton, PA 18042
Phone: 610-330-5100 • **Financial Aid Phone:** 610-330-5055
E-mail: admissions@lafayette.edu • **CEEB Code:** 2361
Fax: 610-330-5355 • **Website:** http://www.lafayette.edu/

This private school, affiliated with the Presbyterian Church, was founded in 1826. It has a 340-acre campus.

RATINGS

Admissions Selectivity Rating: 95   **Fire Safety Rating:** 95

STUDENTS AND FACULTY

Enrollment: 2,471. **Student Body:** 47% female, 53% male, 79% out-of-state, 8% international (42 countries represented). Asian 3%, African American 5%, Caucasian 68%, Hispanic 7%, Native American <1%
Retention and Graduation: 93% freshmen return for sophomore year. 88% freshmen graduate within 4 years. 26% grads go on to further study within 1 year. 3% grads pursue law degrees. 4% grads pursue medical degrees. **Faculty:** 221 full-time faculty, 97% hold PhDs, 35% are members of minority groups, 14% are women. 0% of classes are taught by teaching assistants.

ACADEMICS

Degrees: bachelor's. **Classes:** Most classes have 10–19 students. Most lab/discussion sessions have 10–19 students. **Majors with Highest Enrollment:** Economics; Political Science and Government; Mechanical Engineering. **Special Study Options:** cross-registration, double major, dual enrollment, exchange student program (domestic), honors program, independent study, internships, student-designed major, study abroad, interim sessions here and abroad. **Disability Services:** Special programs offered to physically disabled students include tutors. **Career services:** alumni services, career/job search classes, career assessment, internships.

FACILITIES

Housing: Coed dorms, special housing for disabled students, men's dorms, women's dorms, fraternity/sorority housing, apartments for single students, Wellness Housing, Theme Housingscholars houses, Hillel House, arts houses. 100% of campus accessible to physically disabled. **Special Academic Facilities/Equipment:** Art and geological museums, center for the arts, engineering labs, INSTRON materials testing machine, electron microscopes, transform nuclear magnetic resonance spectrometer, computerized gas chromatograph/mass spectrometer. **Computers:** Students can register for classes online. Administrative functions (other than registration) can be performed online.

CAMPUS LIFE

Environment: Village. **Activities:** Choral groups, concert band, dance, drama/theater, jazz band, literary magazine, music ensembles, musical theater, pep band, radio station, student government, student newspaper, student-run film society, symphony orchestra, yearbook, Campus Ministries, International Student Organization. 250 registered organizations, 14 honor societies, 7 religious organizations. 7 fraternities, 6 sororities. **Athletics (Intercollegiate):** *Men:* baseball, basketball, cheerleading, crew/rowing, cross-country, diving, equestrian sports, fencing, football, golf, gymnastics, ice hockey, lacrosse, soccer, softball, swimming, tennis, track/field (outdoor), track/field (indoor), volleyball, wrestling. *Women:* basketball, cheerleading, crew/rowing, cross-country, diving, equestrian sports, fencing, field hockey, golf, gymnastics, softball, swimming, tennis, track/field (outdoor), track/field (indoor), volleyball. **On-Campus Highlights:** Skillman and Kirby Libraries, Farinon College Center, Williams Center for the Arts. **Environmental Initiatives:** In addition to signing American College and University Presidents Climate Commitment, three undertakings summarize the Colleges efforts towards responsible stewardship of the environment: Waste Reduction—Recycling, including composting; Purchases of materials/goods made from recycled materials and/or virgin material that is recyclable and produced from renewable sources. Resource Conservation—Seeking to enhance our energy use portfolios renewable energy sources (i.e. electric power suppliers with more sustainable product offerings); Installation of conservation/efficiency technology to reduce consumption of water, electric power, and natural gas; Purchases of materials/goods made from recycled materials and/or virgin material that is recyclable and produced from renewable sources. Commitment to education and information dissemination of sustainable practices: Information dissemination through College website, public discussions, and campus publications; Inclusion of sustainability in our curriculum offerings (i.e. Environmental Engineerings composting initiative) and as a cornerstone of orientation week for new students (beginning in the Fall of 2008); New curriculum initiative at Metzgar property involving the growing of vegetables through sustainable and organic methods.

ADMISSIONS

Freshman Academic Profile: Average high school GPA 3.46. 62% in top 10% of high school class, 89% in top 25% of high school class, 97% in top 50% of high school class. 65% from public high schools. SAT Math middle 50% range 610-700. SAT Critical Reading middle 50% range 570-670. SAT Writing middle 50% range 580-690. ACT middle 50% range 27-31. Minimum internet-based TOEFL 80. Minimum paper TOEFL 550. **Basis for Candidate Selection:** *Very important factors considered include:* academic GPA, rigor of secondary school record. *Important factors considered include:* Class rank, application essay, recommendation(s), standardized test scores, character/personal qualities, extracurricular activities, talent/ability. *Other factors considered include:* alumni/ae relation, first generation, geographical residence, interview, level of applicant's interest, racial/ethnic status, volunteer work, work experience. **Freshman Admission Requirements:** High school diploma or equivalent is not required. **Freshman Admission Statistics:** 6,766 applied, 34% admitted, 27% enrolled. **Transfer Admission Requirements:** High school transcript, college transcript(s), essay or personal statement, statement of good standing from prior institution(s). Lowest grade transferable C. **General Admission Information:** Application Fee $60. Early decision application deadline 2/15. Regular application deadline 1/1. Regular notification 4/1. Nonfall registration accepted. Admission may be deferred for a maximum of 1 year. Credit and/or placement offered for CEEB Advanced Placement tests.

COSTS AND FINANCIAL AID

Annual tuition $45,230. Room and board $13,520. Required fees $405. Average book expense $1,000. **Required Forms and Deadlines:** FAFSA, CSS/Financial Aid PROFILE, Noncustodial PROFILE. **Notification of Awards:** Applicants will be notified of awards on or about 4/1. **Types of Aid:** *Need-based scholarships/grants:* Federal Pell, SEOG, state scholarships/grants, private scholarships, the school's own gift aid. *Loans:* Subsidized Stafford, Unsubsidized Stafford, PLUS, Federal Perkins, college/university loans from institutional funds, HELP loan to parents (Lafayette Loan Program). *Student Employment:* Federal Work-Study Program available. Institutional employment available. Highest amount earned per year from on-campus jobs $1,000. Off-campus job opportunities are good. **Financial Aid Statistics:** 97% freshmen, 97% undergrads receive need-based scholarship or grant aid. 29% freshmen, 22% undergrads receive non-need-based scholarship or grant aid. 92% freshmen, 93% undergrads receive need-based self-help aid. 9% freshmen, 4% undergrads receive athletic scholarships. 62% freshmen, 61% undergrads receive any aid. 54% undergrads borrow to pay for school. Average cumulative indebtedness $21,264. **Criteria for awarding institutional aid:** *Non-need-based:* academics, athletics, leadership.

LAGRANGE COLLEGE

Office of Admission, LaGrange, GA 30240
Phone: 706-880-8005 • **Financial Aid Phone:** 888-253-9918
E-mail: lgcadmis@lagrange.edu • **CEEB Code:** 5362
Fax: 706-880-8010 • **Website:** www.lagrange.edu • **ACT Code:** 834

This private school, affiliated with the Methodist Church, was founded in 1831. It has a 120-acre campus.

RATINGS

Admissions Selectivity Rating: 85   **Fire Safety Rating:** 60*

STUDENTS AND FACULTY

Enrollment: 860. **Student Body:** 55% female, 45% male, 11% out-of-state, 2% international (10 countries represented). Asian 1%, African American 22%, Caucasian 72%, Hispanic 2%, Native American <1%
Retention and Graduation: 71% freshmen return for sophomore year. 39% freshmen graduate within 4 years. 55% freshmen graduate within 6 years. **Faculty:** 65 full-time faculty, 83% hold PhDs, 48% are members of minority groups. 0% of classes are taught by teaching assistants.

ACADEMICS

Degrees: associate, bachelor's, master's. **Classes:** Most classes have 10–19 students. Most lab/discussion sessions have 10–19 students. **Majors with Highest Enrollment:** Organizational Behavior Studies; Business Administration and Management; Teacher Education, Multiple Levels. **Special Study Options:** double major, dual enrollment, independent study, internships, liberal arts/career combination, study abroad, teacher certification program. **Career services:** Alumni network, alumni services, career/job search classes, career assessment, internships.

FACILITIES

Housing: Coed dorms, men's dorms, women's dorms, fraternity/sorority housing, apartments for single students, Theme Housing. 75% of campus accessible to physically disabled. **Special Academic Facilities/Equipment:** Lamar Dodd Art Center, Price Theater, Callaway Auditorium. **Computers:** Students can register for classes online. Administrative functions (other than registration) can be performed online.

CAMPUS LIFE

Environment: Village. **Activities:** Choral groups, drama/theater, literary magazine, music ensembles, musical theater, pep band, student government, student newspaper, symphony orchestra, yearbook, Campus Ministries, International Student Organization. 49 registered organizations, 11 honor society, 8 religious organizations. 3 fraternities, 6 sororities. **Athletics (Intercollegiate):** *Men:* baseball, basketball, cross-country, football, golf, soccer, swimming, tennis. *Women:* basketball, cheerleading, cross-country, soccer, softball, swimming, tennis, volleyball. **On-Campus Highlights:** Turner Student Center, Smith Hall, Academic Quadrangle, Smith Patio, Callaway Sports Facilities. **Environmental Initiatives:** Building a LEED library; Conserving water; Relamped buildings along with HVAC retrofitting.

ADMISSIONS

Freshman Academic Profile: Average high school GPA 3.47. 25% in top 10% of high school class, 54% in top 25% of high school class, 92% in top 50% of high school class. SAT Math middle 50% range 460-570. SAT Critical Reading middle 50% range 460-570. ACT middle 50% range 20-25. Minimum paper TOEFL 500. **Basis for Candidate Selection:** *Very important factors considered include:* academic GPA, standardized test scores, character/personal qualities. *Important factors considered include:* Class rank, recommendation(s), extracurricular activities, level of applicant's interest. *Other factors considered include:* application essay, rigor of secondary school record, alumni/ae relation, geographical residence, interview, talent/ability, volunteer work. **Freshman Admission Requirements:** High school diploma is required and GED is accepted. *Academic units required:* 4 English, 4 mathematics, 3 science, 3 social studies. **Freshman Admission Statistics:** 1,342 applied, 65% admitted, 27% enrolled. **Transfer Admission Requirements:** college transcript(s), statement of good standing from prior institution(s). Minimum college GPA of 2.0 required. Lowest grade transferable 1. **General Admission Information:** Application Fee $30. Notification on a rolling basis, beginning on or about 9/15. Nonfall registration accepted. Admission may be deferred for a maximum of one term. Credit and/or placement offered for CEEB Advanced Placement tests.

COSTS AND FINANCIAL AID

Annual tuition $19,900. Room and board $8,168. **Required Forms and Deadlines:** FAFSA, State aid form. **Notification of Awards:** Applicants will be notified of awards on a rolling basis beginning 3/15. **Types of Aid:** *Need-based scholarships/grants:* Federal Pell, SEOG, state scholarships/grants, private scholarships, the school's own gift aid. *Loans:* Subsidized Stafford, Unsubsidized Stafford, PLUS, Federal Perkins, state loans. *Student Employment:* Federal Work-Study Program available. Institutional employment available. Off-campus job opportunities are excellent. **Financial Aid Statistics:** 100% freshmen, 100% undergrads receive need-based scholarship or grant aid. 24% freshmen, 17% undergrads receive non-need-based scholarship or grant aid. 69% freshmen, 77% undergrads receive need-based self-help aid. 0% freshmen, 0% undergrads receive athletic scholarships. 75% undergrads borrow to pay for school. Average cumulative indebtedness $21,000. **Criteria for awarding institutional aid:** *Non-need-based:* academics, art, leadership, music/drama, religious affiliation, state/district residency.

LAKE ERIE COLLEGE

391 West Washington Street, Painesville, OH 44077-3389
Phone: 440-375-7050 · **Financial Aid Phone:** 440-375-7100
E-mail: admissions@lec.edu · **CEEB Code:** 1391
Fax: 440-375-7005 · **Website:** www.lec.edu

This is a private school.

RATINGS

Admissions Selectivity Rating: 72   **Fire Safety Rating:** 89

STUDENTS AND FACULTY

Enrollment: 762. **Student Body:** 45% female, 55% male, 28% out-of-state, 3% international. Asian 0%, African American 12%, Caucasian 77%, Hispanic 2%, Native American <1%
Retention and Graduation: 35% freshmen graduate within 4 years. 47% freshmen graduate within 6 years. 23% grads go on to further study within 1 year. **Faculty:** 44 full-time faculty, 77% hold PhDs, 59% are members of minority groups. 0% of classes are taught by teaching assistants.

ACADEMICS

Degrees: bachelor's, certificate, master's, post-bachelor's certificate. **Classes:** Most classes have fewer than 10 students. **Majors with Highest Enrollment:** Biology; Business Administration and Management; Criminal Justice/Law Enforcement Administration. **Special Study Options:** Accelerated program, cross-registration, double major, dual enrollment, honors program, independent study, internships, liberal arts/career combination, student-designed major, study abroad, teacher certification program, weekend college. **Honors programs:** LEC Scholars Program. **Disability Services:** Special programs offered to physically disabled students include note-taking services, reader services, tape recorders, tutors. **Career services:** Alumni network, alumni services, career/job search classes, career assessment, internships.

FACILITIES

Housing: Coed dorms, women's dorms, apartments for single students, Theme Housing. 90% of campus accessible to physically disabled. **Computers:** Students can register for classes online. Administrative functions (other than registration) can be performed online.

CAMPUS LIFE

Activities: Choral groups, dance, drama/theater, pep band, student government, student newspaper, yearbook, International Student Organization. 15 registered organizations, 3 honor societies, 1 sorority. **Athletics (Intercollegiate):** *Men:* baseball, basketball, cross-country, equestrian sports, football, golf, soccer. *Women:* basketball, cross-country, equestrian sports, soccer, softball, volleyball.

ADMISSIONS

Freshman Academic Profile: Average high school GPA 3.02. 89% from public high schools. SAT Math middle 50% range 435-540. SAT Critical Reading middle 50% range 395-535. SAT Writing middle 50% range 390-515. ACT middle 50% range 18-23. Minimum internet-based TOEFL 79. Minimum paper TOEFL 550. **Basis for Candidate Selection:** *Very important factors considered include:* application essay, academic GPA, recommendation(s), rigor of secondary school record, standardized test scores, character/personal qualities, level of applicant's interest. *Important factors considered include:* Class rank, interview, talent/ability. *Other factors considered include:* alumni/ae relation, extracurricular activities, first generation, geographical residence, religious affiliation/commitment, state residency, volunteer work, work experience. **Freshman Admission Requirements:** High school diploma is required and GED is accepted. *Academic units required:* 4 English, 3 mathematics, 3 science, (2 science labs), 2 foreign language, 3 social studies, 0 history. **Freshman Admission Statistics:** 891 applied, 69% admitted, 30% enrolled. **Transfer Admission Requirements:** High school transcript, college transcript(s), statement of good standing from prior institution(s). Minimum college GPA of 2.0 required. Lowest grade transferable C. **General Admission Information:**

Application Fee $30. Notification on a rolling basis, beginning on or about 7/1. Nonfall registration accepted. Admission may be deferred for a maximum of 12 months. Credit and/or placement offered for CEEB Advanced Placement tests.

COSTS AND FINANCIAL AID

Annual tuition $27,770. Room and board $9,178. Required fees $1,392. Average book expense $1,100. **Required Forms and Deadlines:** FAFSA. **Notification of Awards:** Applicants will be notified of awards on a rolling basis beginning 1/20. **Types of Aid:** *Need-based scholarships/grants:* Federal Pell, SEOG, state scholarships/grants, private scholarships, the school's own gift aid. *Loans:* Subsidized Stafford, Unsubsidized Stafford, PLUS, Federal Perkins, Payment plans. *Student Employment:* Federal Work-Study Program available. Institutional employment available. Highest amount earned per year from on-campus jobs $1,200. Off-campus job opportunities are good. **Financial Aid Statistics:** 99% freshmen, 100% undergrads receive need-based scholarship or grant aid. 9% freshmen, 13% undergrads receive non-need-based scholarship or grant aid. 90% freshmen, 86% undergrads receive need-based self-help aid. 8% freshmen, 12% undergrads receive athletic scholarships. 100% freshmen, 91% undergrads receive any aid. 83% undergrads borrow to pay for school. Average cumulative indebtedness $28,134. **Criteria for awarding institutional aid:** *Non-need-based:* academics, art, leadership, music/drama, state/district residency.

LAKE FOREST COLLEGE

Best 380

555 North Sheridan Road, Lake Forest, IL 60045
Phone: 847-735-5000 · **Financial Aid Phone:** 847-725-5103
E-mail: admissions@lakeforest.edu · **CEEB Code:** 1392
Fax: 847-735-6291 · **Website:** www.lakeforest.edu   •   **ACT Code:** 1054

This private school was founded in 1857. It has a 107-acre campus.

RATINGS

Admissions Selectivity Rating: 88   **Fire Safety Rating:** 74

STUDENTS AND FACULTY

Enrollment: 1,600. **Student Body:** 57% female, 43% male, 36% out-of-state, 9% international (73 countries represented). Asian 5%, African American 7%, Caucasian 58%, Hispanic 15%, Native American <1%
Retention and Graduation: 85% freshmen return for sophomore year. 64% freshmen graduate within 4 years. 73% freshmen graduate within 6 years. 25% grads go on to further study within 1 year. 53% grads pursue arts and sciences degrees. 9% grads pursue law degrees. 6% grads pursue business degrees. 13% grads pursue medical degrees. **Faculty:** 101 full-time faculty, 99% hold PhDs, 44% are members of minority groups, 13% are women. 0% of classes are taught by teaching assistants.

ACADEMICS

Degrees: bachelor's, master's. **Classes:** Most classes have 10–19 students. Most lab/discussion sessions have 10–19 students. **Majors with Highest Enrollment:** Business/Commerce; Speech Communication and Rhetoric; Biology/Biological Sciences. **Special Study Options:** Accelerated program, double major, honors program, independent study, internships, liberal arts/career combination, student-designed major, study abroad, teacher certification program. **Honors programs:** The Honors Fellows program recognizes those students admitted to Lake Forest College with exemplary high school careers and high promise for independent study and research at the College. Fellows are expected to think deeply and broadly, and to join their teachers and fellow students in serious intellectual inquiry and debate. They will produce independent work, research, Student Symposium presentations, Independent Scholar majors, distinguished senior theses, and provide intellectual leadership. The Richter Apprentice Scholars Program provides students, early in their academic careers, with the opportunity to conduct independent, individual research with Lake Forest College faculty. In the summer between their first and second year, each student in the Richter Program is employed for a ten week period and works one-on-one with a faculty member, doing independent research in a particular field. As the Richter Apprentice Scholars live and work together and participate in a weekly colloquium, they become a community of peers providing encouragement and support for each other's present and future intellectual and research endeavors. **Combined degree programs:** BA/JD, BA/MA, Accelerated BA/JD with select law schools - Acc. BA/MA with Monterey Inst. **Disability Services:** Special programs offered to physically disabled students include note-taking services, reader services, tape recorders, tutors. **Career**

services: Alumni network, alumni services, career/job search classes, career assessment, internships, regional alumni. Career services highlights include: 1) Internships—due to our location near Chicago and the many partnerships Lake Forest College has developed with Chicago institutions over the years, there are a myriad of internship opportunities available to our students. 2) Experiential learning—again, due to our location near Chicago and the relationships with area insitutions we offer dozens of courses that have been developed to utilize the rich resources of Chicago to enhance the curriculum. Beginning with our innovative First-Year Studies program students travel downtown to Chicago with professors and take advantage of the many resources.

FACILITIES

Housing: Coed dorms, special housing for disabled students, women's dorms, apartments for single students, Wellness Housing. 80% of campus accessible to physically disabled. **Special Academic Facilities/Equipment:** Center for Chicago Programs, art galleries, language labs, technology resource center, speech and video production room, "smart" classrooms, music/recording studio with synthesizers, public access computer labs, electron microscope, computer molecular modeling equipment, high-resolution FT-IR, NMR spectrometer, neutron howitzer, digital storage oscilloscopes, flourescence microscope **Computers:** 90% of classrooms, 100% of dorms, 100% of libraries, 75% of dining areas, 100% of student union, 10% of common outdoor areas have wireless network access. Administrative functions (other than registration) can be performed online.

CAMPUS LIFE

Environment: Village. **Activities:** Choral groups, concert band, dance, drama/theater, jazz band, literary magazine, music ensembles, musical theater, radio station, student government, student newspaper, symphony orchestra, Campus Ministries, International Student Organization, Model UN. 80 registered organizations, 12 honor societies, 6 religious organizations. 2 fraternities, 4 sororities. **Athletics (Intercollegiate):** *Men:* basketball, cross-country, diving, football, handball, ice hockey, soccer, swimming, tennis. *Women:* basketball, cross-country, diving, handball, ice hockey, soccer, softball, swimming, tennis, volleyball. **On-Campus Highlights:** Donnelley and Lee Library, Mohr Student Center, Sports Center, Center for Chicago Programs, Career Advancement Center. **Environmental Initiatives:** The organic campus garden provides internship opportunities for students and it supplies the campus cafeteria with food during the summer and fall; Restoration initiatives for ravine and savannah ecosystems; The expansion of offerings of environmental studies courses.

ADMISSIONS

Freshman Academic Profile: Average high school GPA 3.67. 27% in top 10% of high school class, 56% in top 25% of high school class, 86% in top 50% of high school class. 70% from public high schools. SAT Math middle 50% range 500-630. SAT Critical Reading middle 50% range 500-620. SAT Writing middle 50% range 490-620. ACT middle 50% range 23-28. Minimum paper TOEFL 550. **Basis for Candidate Selection:** *Very important factors considered include:* academic GPA, recommendation(s), rigor of secondary school record, interview. *Important factors considered include:* application essay, character/personal qualities, extracurricular activities, level of applicant's interest, talent/ability. *Other factors considered include:* Class rank, standardized test scores, alumni/ae relation, first generation, geographical residence, volunteer work, work experience. **Freshman Admission Requirements:** High school diploma is required and GED is accepted. *Academic units required:* 4 English, 3 mathematics, 3 science, (3 science labs), 2 foreign language, 2 social studies, 2 history, 0 visual/performing arts, 0 computer science, 3 academic electives, 0 Honors or AP courses. **Freshman Admission Statistics:** 3,451 applied, 55% admitted, 22% enrolled. **Transfer Admission Requirements:** High school transcript, college transcript(s), essay or personal statement, Minimum college GPA of 2.5 required. Lowest grade transferable C-. **General Admission Information:** Application Fee $40. Early decision application deadline 12/1. Regular notification 3/20. Nonfall registration accepted. Admission may be deferred for a maximum of 12 months. Credit and/or placement offered for CEEB Advanced Placement tests.

COSTS AND FINANCIAL AID

Annual tuition $41,920. Room and board $9,570. Required fees $724. Average book expense $1,000. **Required Forms and Deadlines:** FAFSA. **Notification of Awards:** Applicants will be notified of awards on a rolling basis beginning 2/1. **Types of Aid:** *Need-based scholarships/grants:* Federal Pell, SEOG, state scholarships/grants, private scholarships, the school's own gift aid. *Loans:* Subsidized Stafford, Unsubsidized Stafford, PLUS, Federal Perkins, Private loans. *Student Employment:* Federal Work-Study Program available. Institutional employment available. Off-campus job opportunities are good. **Financial Aid Statistics:** 100% freshmen, 99% undergrads receive need-based scholarship or grant aid. 0% freshmen, 0% undergrads receive non-need-based scholarship or grant aid. 82% freshmen, 83% undergrads receive need-based self-help aid. 0% freshmen, 0% undergrads receive athletic scholarships. 94% freshmen, 95% undergrads receive any aid. 71% undergrads borrow to pay for school. Average cumulative indebtedness $28,509. **Criteria for awarding institutional aid:**

Non-need-based: academics, alumni affiliation, art, leadership, music/drama, state/district residency.

See page 1076.

LAKE REGION STATE COLLEGE

1801 College Drive N, Devils Lake, ND 58301-1598
Phone: 701-662-1514 • **Financial Aid Phone:** 701-662-1516
E-mail: lrsc.admissions@lrsc.edu
Fax: 701-662-1581 • **Website:** www.lrsc.edu • **ACT Code:** 3198

This public school was founded in 1941. It has a 120-acre campus.

RATINGS

Admissions Selectivity Rating: 67   **Fire Safety Rating:** 94

STUDENTS AND FACULTY

Enrollment: 696. **Student Body:** 53% female, 47% male, 12% out-of-state, 3% international (14 countries represented). Asian 2%, African American 4%, Caucasian 82%, Hispanic 2%, Native American 5%
Faculty: 35 full-time faculty, 14% hold PhDs, 51% are members of minority groups, 3% are women. 0% of classes are taught by teaching assistants.

ACADEMICS

Degrees: associate, certificate, diploma, terminal associate, transfer associate. **Classes:** Most classes have fewer than 10 students. **Majors with Highest Enrollment:** Liberal Arts and Sciences/Liberal Studies; Criminal Justice/Police Science; Business Administration and Management. **Special Study Options:** cooperative education program, cross-registration, distance learning, dual enrollment, English as a Second Language (ESL), internships, liberal arts/career combination. **Disability Services:** Special programs offered to physically disabled students include note-taking services, reader services, tape recorders, tutors. **Career services:** career/job search classes, internships.

FACILITIES

Housing: special housing for disabled students, men's dorms, women's dorms, apartments for married students, apartments for single students, Coed dorms for adult students. 100% of campus accessible to physically disabled. **Special Academic Facilities/Equipment:** Paul Hoghaug Library and Law Library **Computers:** 100% of classrooms, 100% of dorms, 100% of libraries, 100% of dining areas, 100% of student union, have wireless network access. Students can register for classes online. Administrative functions (other than registration) can be performed online.

CAMPUS LIFE

Environment: Village. **Activities:** drama/theater, literary magazine, musical theater, student government, symphony orchestra. 12 registered organizations, 1 religious organization. **Athletics (Intercollegiate):** *Men:* basketball. *Women:* basketball. **On-Campus Highlights:** Student Union, Computer Lab, Recreational Area, Library, Gymnasium.

ADMISSIONS

Freshman Academic Profile: 98% from public high schools. ACT middle 50% range 18-25. Minimum internet-based TOEFL 65. Minimum paper TOEFL 510. **Freshman Admission Requirements:** High school diploma is required and GED is accepted. **Freshman Admission Statistics:** 233 applied, 99% admitted, 95% enrolled. **Transfer Admission Requirements:** High school transcript, college transcript(s), statement of good standing from prior institution(s). Minimum college GPA of 2.0 required. Lowest grade transferable D. **General Admission Information:** Application Fee $35. Nonfall registration accepted. Admission may be deferred for a maximum of one semester. Credit offered for CEEB Advanced Placement tests.

COSTS AND FINANCIAL AID

Annual in-state tuition $3,065. Annual out-of-state tuition $3,065. Room and board $5,230. Required fees $843. Average book expense $900. **Required Forms and Deadlines:** FAFSA. **Notification of Awards:** Applicants will be notified of awards on a rolling basis beginning 5/15. **Types of Aid:** *Need-based scholarships/grants:* Federal Pell, SEOG, state scholarships/grants, private scholarships, the school's own gift aid, Academic Competitiveness Grant. *Loans:* Subsidized Stafford, Unsubsidized Stafford, PLUS, Federal Perkins, state loans. *Student Employment:* Federal Work-Study Program available. Institutional employment available. Off-campus job opportunities are good. **Financial Aid Statistics:** 93% freshmen, 87% undergrads receive need-based scholarship or grant aid. 1% freshmen, 0% undergrads receive non-need-based scholarship or grant aid. 85% freshmen, 89% undergrads receive need-based self-help aid. 6% freshmen, 6% undergrads receive athletic scholarships. 80% undergrads receive any aid. 71% undergrads borrow to pay for school. Average cumulative indebtedness $8,521. **Criteria for awarding institutional aid:** *Non-need-based:* academics, athletics, leadership, minority status, music/drama.

LAKE SUPERIOR STATE UNIVERSITY

650 W. Easterday Avenue, Sault Ste. Marie, MI 49783-1699
Phone: 906-635-2231 · **Financial Aid Phone:** 906-635-2678
E-mail: admissions@lssu.edu · **CEEB Code:** 1421
Fax: 906-635-6669 • **ACT Code:** 2031

This public school was founded in 1946. It has a 115-acre campus.

RATINGS

Admissions Selectivity Rating: 73   **Fire Safety Rating:** 60*

STUDENTS AND FACULTY

Enrollment: 2,440. **Student Body:** 50% female, 50% male, 5% out-of-state, 7% international. Asian 1%, African American 1%, Caucasian 79%, Hispanic 2%, Native American 8%
Retention and Graduation: 70% freshmen return for sophomore year. 13% freshmen graduate within 4 years. 33% freshmen graduate within 6 years. **Faculty:** 114 full-time faculty, 53% hold PhDs, 46% are members of minority groups, 5% are women. 0% of classes are taught by teaching assistants.

ACADEMICS

Degrees: associate, bachelor's, certificate, master's. **Classes:** Most classes have 20–29 students. Most lab/discussion sessions have 10–19 students. **Special Study Options:** cooperative education program, cross-registration, distance learning, double major, dual enrollment, honors program, independent study, internships, student-designed major, teacher certification program, weekend college. **Disability Services:** Special programs offered to physically disabled students include note-taking services, reader services, tape recorders, tutors.

FACILITIES

Housing: Coed dorms, men's dorms, women's dorms, fraternity/sorority housing, apartments for married students, apartments for single students. 90% of campus accessible to physically disabled. **Special Academic Facilities/Equipment:** Natural science, Michigan history, and Great Lakes shipping museums, planetarium, industrial robots, atomic absorption/flame emission spectrophotometer. **Computers:** Students can register for classes online.

CAMPUS LIFE

Environment: City. **Activities:** Choral groups, concert band, dance, drama/theater, jazz band, literary magazine, music ensembles, pep band, radio station, student government, student newspaper, symphony orchestra. 60 registered organizations, 4 fraternities, 4 sororities. **Athletics (Intercollegiate):** *Men:* basketball, cross-country, ice hockey, tennis, track/field (outdoor), track/field (indoor). *Women:* basketball, cross-country, softball, tennis, track/field (outdoor), track/field (indoor), volleyball.

ADMISSIONS

Freshman Academic Profile: Average high school GPA 3.29. 14% in top 10% of high school class, 40% in top 25% of high school class, 75% in top 50% of high school class. ACT middle 50% range 20-25. Minimum paper TOEFL 550. **Basis for Candidate Selection:** *Very important factors considered include:* academic GPA, rigor of secondary school record, standardized test scores. *Other factors considered include:* Class rank, recommendation(s), geographical residence, interview. **Freshman Admission Requirements:** High school diploma is required and GED is accepted. **Freshman Admission Statistics:** 1,425 applied, 90% admitted, 34% enrolled. **Transfer Admission Requirements:** college transcript(s), Minimum college GPA of 2.0 required. Lowest grade transferable C-. **General Admission Information:** Application Fee $20. Regular application deadline 8/15. Notification on a rolling basis, beginning on or about 9/15. Nonfall registration accepted. Admission may be deferred for a maximum of 1 Year. Credit offered for CEEB Advanced Placement tests.

COSTS AND FINANCIAL AID

Annual. Annual out-of-state tuition $14,410. Room and board $8,481. Required fees $350. Average book expense $1,200. **Required Forms and Deadlines:** FAFSA. **Notification of Awards:** Applicants will be notified of awards on a rolling basis beginning 11/1. **Types of Aid:** *Need-based scholarships/grants:* Federal Pell, SEOG, state scholarships/grants, private scholarships, the school's own gift aid, Federal Nursing Scholarships., third party payments. *Loans:* Direct Subsidized Stafford, Direct Unsubsidized Stafford, Direct PLUS, Federal Perkins, Federal Nursing, state loans. *Student Employment:* Highest amount earned per year from on-campus jobs $2,400. Off-campus job opportunities are good. **Financial Aid Statistics:** 75% freshmen, 75% undergrads receive need-based scholarship or grant aid. 61% freshmen, 40% undergrads receive non-need-based scholarship or grant aid. 82% freshmen, 90% undergrads

receive need-based self-help aid. 10% freshmen, 9% undergrads receive athletic scholarships.83% undergrads receive any aid. 71% undergrads borrow to pay for school. Average cumulative indebtedness $22,896.

LAKEHEAD UNIVERSITY

955 Oliver Road, Thunder Bay, ON P7B 5E1
Phone: 807-343-8500 · **Financial Aid Phone:** 807-343-8206
E-mail: admissions@lakeheadu.ca
Fax: 807-766-7209 · **Website:** www.lakeheadu.ca

This public school was founded in 1965. It has a 288-acre campus.

RATINGS

Admissions Selectivity Rating: 60*   **Fire Safety Rating:** 60*

STUDENTS AND FACULTY

Enrollment: 7,139.
Retention and Graduation: 85% freshmen return for sophomore year.

ACADEMICS

Degrees: bachelor's, certificate, diploma, first professional, master's. **Classes:** Most classes have 30-39 students. **Majors with Highest Enrollment:** Engineering; Forestry; Business Administration and Management.

FACILITIES

Housing: Coed dorms, special housing for disabled students, apartments for single students, Wellness Housing. **Computers:** Students can register for classes online.

CAMPUS LIFE

Environment: City. **Activities:** Choral groups, concert band, dance, drama/theater, jazz band, literary magazine, music ensembles, musical theater, radio station, student government, student newspaper, Campus Ministries, International Student Organization, Model UN. **Athletics (Intercollegiate):** *Men:* basketball, cross-country, ice hockey, skiing (nordic/cross-country), track/field (outdoor), track/field (indoor), wrestling. *Women:* basketball, cross-country, skiing (nordic/cross-country), track/field (outdoor), track/field (indoor), volleyball, wrestling.

ADMISSIONS

Freshman Admission Requirements: High school diploma is required and GED is accepted. **General Admission Information:** Application Fee $105. Regular application deadline 9/24. Nonfall registration accepted. Admission may be deferred for a maximum of one year.

LAMAR UNIVERSITY

P.O. Box 10009, Beaumont, TX 77710
Phone: 409-880-8888
E-mail: admissions@hal.lamar.edu · **CEEB Code:** 6360
Fax: 409-880-8463 · **Website:** www.lamar.edu • **ACT Code:** 4114

This public school was founded in 1923. It has a 200-acre campus.

RATINGS

Admissions Selectivity Rating: 60*   **Fire Safety Rating:** 60*

STUDENTS AND FACULTY

Enrollment: 9,057. **Student Body:** 55% female, 45% male, 1% out-of-state, 1% international. Asian 3%, African American 22%, Caucasian 74%, Hispanic 5%, Native American 1%
Faculty:

ACADEMICS

Degrees: bachelor's, master's. **Special Study Options:** cooperative education program, distance learning, double major, dual enrollment, English as a Second Language (ESL), honors program, internships, study abroad, teacher certification program, Texas Academy for Leadership in the Humanities, a two-year residential, early admission program for gifted high school students. Students are selected during the sophomore year of high school and enter the University at the end of their junior year. **Combined degree programs:** 3-1 program Medicine/Dentistry 3-2 Pharmacy prog. **Disability Services:** Special programs offered to physically disabled students include note-taking services, reader services, tape recorders, tutors. **Career services:** alumni services, career/job search classes, career assessment.

FACILITIES

Housing: Coed dorms, men's dorms, women's dorms, fraternity/sorority housing, apartments for single students. **Special Academic Facilities/Equipment:** Museum.

CAMPUS LIFE

Environment: Village. **Activities:** student government, student newspaper. 145 registered organizations, 11 fraternity, 8 sororities. **Athletics (Intercollegiate):** *Men:* baseball, basketball, cross-country, golf, tennis, track/field (outdoor). *Women:* basketball, cross-country, golf, tennis, track/field (outdoor), volleyball.

ADMISSIONS

Freshman Academic Profile: 10% in top 10% of high school class, 27% in top 25% of high school class, 90% in top 50% of high school class. 96% from public high schools. Minimum paper TOEFL 500. **Freshman Admission Requirements:** High school diploma is required and GED is accepted.High school diploma is required and GED is not accepted. Minimum college GPA of 2.0 required. Lowest grade transferable D. **General Admission Information:** Regular application deadline 8/1. Nonfall registration accepted. Credit and/or placement offered for CEEB Advanced Placement tests.

COSTS AND FINANCIAL AID

Required fees $840. **Required Forms and Deadlines:** FAFSA, Institution's own financial aid form, State aid form. **Types of Aid:** *Loans:* Subsidized Stafford, PLUS. *Student Employment:* Federal Work-Study Program available. Institutional employment available. Highest amount earned per year from on-campus jobs $1,200. Off-campus job opportunities are good.

LAMBUTH UNIVERSITY

705 Lambuth Boulevard, Jackson, TN 38301-5296
Phone: 731-425-3223 · **Financial Aid Phone:** 731-425-3332
E-mail: admit@lambuth.edu · **CEEB Code:** 1394
Fax: 731-425-3496 · **Website:** www.lambuth.edu · **ACT Code:** 3974

This private school, affiliated with the Methodist Church, was founded in 1843. It has a 50-acre campus.

RATINGS

Admissions Selectivity Rating: 83   Fire Safety Rating: 78

STUDENTS AND FACULTY

Enrollment: 765. **Student Body:** 47% female, 53% male, 21% out-of-state, (9 countries represented).
Retention and Graduation: 60% freshmen return for sophomore year. 29% freshmen graduate within 4 years. 39% freshmen graduate within 6 years. 20% grads go on to further study within 1 year. 5% grads pursue arts and sciences degrees. 5% grads pursue law degrees. 5% grads pursue business degrees. 5% grads pursue medical degrees. **Faculty:** 51 full-time faculty, 78% hold PhDs, 41% are members of minority groups, 2% are women. 0% of classes are taught by teaching assistants.

ACADEMICS

Degrees: bachelor's. **Classes:** Most classes have fewer than 10 students. Most lab/discussion sessions have 20–29 students. **Majors with Highest Enrollment:** Business/Commerce; Psychology; Health and Physical Education/Fitness. **Special Study Options:** cross-registration, double major, honors program, independent study, internships, student-designed major, study abroad, teacher certification program, Washington Semester. Tennessee Legislative Internship. Interdisciplinary courses. Lambuth in London. **Honors programs:** University Honors is a 3 semester sequence of courses designed to offer more in-depth study of classic literature and themes. Various topics are considered including art, psychology, ecology, history, ethics, politics, science, sociology, business, religion, and literature. Honors study is available in most disciplines and consists of an 8 hour sequence of research over the last 3 semesters of study in a particular discipline. **Disability Services:** Special programs offered to physically disabled students include tape recorders, tutors. **Career services:** Alumni network, alumni services, career/job search classes, career assessment, internships, regional alumni. Career services highlights include excellent internships for business, communications, psychology, education and social science majors.

FACILITIES

Housing: Coed dorms, special housing for disabled students, men's dorms, women's dorms, fraternity/sorority housing, apartments for single students. 80% of campus accessible to physically disabled. **Special Academic Facilities/Equipment:** Academic Support Center, Interior Design lab, M.D. Anderson Planetarium, Oxley Biological Field Station. **Computers:** 40% of classrooms,

10% of dorms, 100% of libraries, 100% of dining areas, 100% of student union, 50% of common outdoor areas have wireless network access.

CAMPUS LIFE

Environment: City. **Activities:** Choral groups, concert band, dance, drama/theater, jazz band, literary magazine, music ensembles, musical theater, student government, student newspaper, yearbook, Campus Ministries, International Student Organization, Model UN. 41 registered organizations, 6 honor societies, 3 religious organizations. 3 fraternities, 3 sororities. **Athletics (Intercollegiate):** *Men:* baseball, basketball, football, golf, soccer, tennis. *Women:* basketball, golf, soccer, softball, tennis. **On-Campus Highlights:** Eagle's Nest Bistro, E/MI Studio, The Quadrangle, Eickoff Plaza, M.D. Anderson Planetarium, Oxley Square (apartment-style dorms), Computer Center, Hamilton Performing Arts Center, R. E. Womack Memorial Chapel, Greek houses, Wellness Center, Athletic Center/Olympic Pool.

ADMISSIONS

Freshman Academic Profile: Average high school GPA 3.3, 21% in top 10% of high school class, 42% in top 25% of high school class, 71% in top 50% of high school class. 85% from public high schools. SAT Math middle 50% range 460-570. SAT Critical Reading middle 50% range 440-570. ACT middle 50% range 20-25. Minimum paper TOEFL 425. **Basis for Candidate Selection:** *Very important factors considered include:* academic GPA, rigor of secondary school record, standardized test scores. *Important factors considered include:* application essay, recommendation(s), extracurricular activities, interview, level of applicant's interest. *Other factors considered include:* Class rank, alumni/ae relation, first generation, geographical residence, religious affiliation/commitment, state residency, talent/ability, volunteer work, work experience. **Freshman Admission Requirements:** High school diploma is required and GED is accepted. **Freshman Admission Statistics:** 679 applied, 62% admitted, 49% enrolled. **Transfer Admission Requirements:** college transcript(s), essay or personal statement, statement of good standing from prior institution(s). Minimum college GPA of 2.0 required. Lowest grade transferable D. **General Admission Information:** Application Fee $25. Notification on a rolling basis, beginning on or about 10/1. Nonfall registration accepted. Admission may be deferred for a maximum of one year. Credit and/or placement offered for CEEB Advanced Placement tests.

COSTS AND FINANCIAL AID

Annual tuition $17,000. Room and board $7,160. Required fees $400. Average book expense $1,200. **Required Forms and Deadlines:** FAFSA, Institution's own financial aid form. **Notification of Awards:** Applicants will be notified of awards on a rolling basis beginning 2/15. **Types of Aid:** *Need-based scholarships/grants:* Federal Pell, SEOG, state scholarships/grants, private scholarships, the school's own gift aid, Tennessee Hope Lottery Programs. *Loans:* Subsidized Stafford, Unsubsidized Stafford, PLUS, Federal Perkins. *Student Employment:* Federal Work-Study Program available. Institutional employment available. Highest amount earned per year from on-campus jobs $1,404. Off-campus job opportunities are excellent. **Financial Aid Statistics:** 98% freshmen, 97% undergrads receive need-based scholarship or grant aid. 23% freshmen, 22% undergrads receive non-need-based scholarship or grant aid. 66% freshmen, 68% undergrads receive need-based self-help aid. 9% freshmen, 9% undergrads receive athletic scholarships. 99% freshmen, 99% undergrads receive any aid. 64% undergrads borrow to pay for school. Average cumulative indebtedness $18,000. **Criteria for awarding institutional aid:** *Non-need-based:* academics, alumni affiliation, art, athletics, job skills, leadership, music/drama, religious affiliation.

LANCASTER BIBLE COLLEGE

901 Eden Rd, Lancaster, PA 17601-5036
Phone: 717-560-8271 · **Financial Aid Phone:** 717-560-8254
E-mail: admissions@lbc.edu · **CEEB Code:** 2388
Fax: 717-560-8213 · **Website:** www.lbc.edu · **ACT Code:** 3707

This private school was founded in 1933. It has a 100-acre campus.

RATINGS

Admissions Selectivity Rating: 60*   Fire Safety Rating: 70

STUDENTS AND FACULTY

Enrollment: 702. **Student Body:** 47% female, 53% male, 26% out-of-state, 1% international. Asian 1%, African American 3%, Caucasian 71%, Hispanic 1%, Native American <1%
Faculty: 48 full-time faculty, 52% hold PhDs, 25% are members of minority groups, 2% are women. 0% of classes are taught by teaching assistants.

ACADEMICS

Degrees: associate, bachelor's, certificate, master's, post-bachelor's certificate. **Classes:** Most classes have fewer than 10 students. Most lab/discussion sessions have 10–19 students. **Majors with Highest Enrollment:** Elementary Education and Teaching; Bible/Biblical Studies; Theology and Religious Vocations. **Special Study Options:** Accelerated program, double major, independent study, internships, study abroad, teacher certification program. **Disability Services:** Special programs offered to physically disabled students include note-taking services, reader services, tape recorders, tutors. **Career services:** Alumni network, internships.

FACILITIES

Housing: men's dorms, women's dorms. 80% of campus accessible to physically disabled.

CAMPUS LIFE

Environment: Village. **Activities:** Choral groups, concert band, drama/theater, music ensembles, musical theater, student government, student newspaper, yearbook. 20 registered organizations. **Athletics (Intercollegiate):** *Men:* baseball, basketball, cheerleading, soccer, volleyball. *Women:* basketball, cheerleading, lacrosse, soccer, volleyball.

ADMISSIONS

Freshman Academic Profile: 60% from public high schools. Minimum paper TOEFL 550. **Basis for Candidate Selection:** *Very important factors considered include:* application essay, recommendation(s), rigor of secondary school record, standardized test scores, character/personal qualities, religious affiliation/commitment. *Important factors considered include:* extracurricular activities. *Other factors considered include:* interview, talent/ability, volunteer work. **Freshman Admission Requirements:** High school diploma is required and GED is accepted. **Freshman Admission Statistics:** 314 applied, 97% admitted, 44% enrolled. **Transfer Admission Requirements:** High school transcript, college transcript(s), essay or personal statement, standardized test scores, statement of good standing from prior institution(s). Minimum college GPA of 2.0 required. Lowest grade transferable C. **General Admission Information:** Application Fee $25. Notification on a rolling basis, beginning on or about 9/1. Nonfall registration accepted. Admission may be deferred for a maximum of 1 year.

COSTS AND FINANCIAL AID

Annual tuition $15,930. Room and board $7,110. Required fees $630. Average book expense $1,000. **Required Forms and Deadlines:** FAFSA, State aid form. **Notification of Awards:** Applicants will be notified of awards on a rolling basis beginning 3/1. **Types of Aid:** *Need-based scholarships/grants:* Federal Pell, SEOG, state scholarships/grants, private scholarships, the school's own gift aid, Office of Vocational Rehabilitation Blindness and Visual Services Awards. *Loans:* Subsidized Stafford, Unsubsidized Stafford, PLUS, Federal Perkins, Alternative Loans. *Student Employment:* Federal Work-Study Program available. Institutional employment available. Highest amount earned per year from on-campus jobs $1,400. Off-campus job opportunities are good. **Financial Aid Statistics:** 98% freshmen, 94% undergrads receive need-based scholarship or grant aid. 96% freshmen, 79% undergrads receive non-need-based scholarship or grant aid. 82% freshmen, 88% undergrads receive need-based self-help aid. 0% freshmen, 0% undergrads receive athletic scholarships. 27% undergrads borrow to pay for school. Average cumulative indebtedness $17,329. **Criteria for awarding institutional aid:** *Non-need-based:* academics, alumni affiliation, leadership, music/drama.

LANDER UNIVERSITY

320 Stanley Avenue, Greenwood, SC 29649
Phone: 864-388-8307 · **Financial Aid Phone:** 864-388-8340
E-mail: admissions@lander.edu · **CEEB Code:** 5363
Fax: 864-388-8125 · **Website:** www.lander.edu · **ACT Code:** 3860

This public school was founded in 1872. It has a 100-acre campus.

RATINGS

Admissions Selectivity Rating: 72   **Fire Safety Rating:** 62

STUDENTS AND FACULTY

Enrollment: 2,655. **Student Body:** 67% female, 33% male, 3% out-of-state, 2% international (21 countries represented). Asian 1%, African American 22%, Caucasian 74%, Hispanic 1%, Native American <1%
Retention and Graduation: 65% freshmen return for sophomore year. 28% freshmen graduate within 4 years. 43% freshmen graduate within 6 years.
Faculty: 117 full-time faculty, 72% hold PhDs, 44% are members of minority groups, 8% are women. 0% of classes are taught by teaching assistants.

ACADEMICS

Degrees: bachelor's, certificate, master's. **Classes:** Most classes have 20–29 students. **Majors with Highest Enrollment:** Elementary Education and Teaching; Registered Nursing/Registered Nurse; Business/Commerce. **Special Study Options:** cooperative education program, distance learning, double major, dual enrollment, honors program, independent study, internships, liberal arts/career combination, student-designed major, study abroad, teacher certification program, Nursing (R.N. to B.S.N. completion) program courses now offered on the web. M.B.A. from Clemson U. offered on campus. M.Ed. Counseling/School Administration from Clemson U. offered on campus. M.Ed. Elementary Education. M.A.T. Master of Art in Teaching. Dual degree in Engineering offered in conjunction with Clemson University. **Combined degree programs:** BA/MEng. **Disability Services:** Special programs offered to physically disabled students include note-taking services, reader services, tape recorders, tutors. **Career services:** internships.

FACILITIES

Housing: Coed dorms, women's dorms, apartments for single students. 100% of campus accessible to physically disabled. **Special Academic Facilities/Equipment:** Art gallery, continuing education center, media center, electronic piano instruction facility, amphitheatre. **Computers:** Students can register for classes online. Administrative functions (other than registration) can be performed online.

CAMPUS LIFE

Environment: Village. **Activities:** Choral groups, concert band, dance, drama/theater, jazz band, literary magazine, music ensembles, student government, student newspaper. 65 registered organizations, 6 honor societies, 7 religious organizations. 6 fraternities, 6 sororities. **Athletics (Intercollegiate):** *Men:* baseball, basketball, golf, soccer, tennis. *Women:* basketball, cross-country, soccer, softball, tennis, volleyball. **On-Campus Highlights:** Student Center, Grill Works, Cafeteria, Student Atrium, Library.

ADMISSIONS

Freshman Academic Profile: Average high school GPA 3.4. 8% in top 10% of high school class, 30% in top 25% of high school class, 68% in top 50% of high school class. SAT Math middle 50% range 440-540. SAT Critical Reading middle 50% range 430-530. ACT middle 50% range 17-22. Minimum paper TOEFL 550. **Basis for Candidate Selection:** *Very important factors considered include:* Class rank, rigor of secondary school record, standardized test scores. *Other factors considered include:* application essay, recommendation(s), alumni/ae relation, character/personal qualities, extracurricular activities, interview, talent/ability, volunteer work, work experience. **Freshman Admission Requirements:** High school diploma is required and GED is accepted. *Academic units required:* 4 English, 3 mathematics, 3 science, (3 science labs), 2 foreign language, 2 social studies, 1 history, 4 academic electives, 1 Phys. Educ./Rotc. **Freshman Admission Statistics:** 1,750 applied, 85% admitted, 45% enrolled. **Transfer Admission Requirements:** college transcript(s), statement of good standing from prior institution(s). Minimum college GPA of 2.0 required. Lowest grade transferable C. **General Admission Information:** Application Fee $35. Regular application deadline 8/5. Nonfall registration accepted. Admission may be deferred as decided on a case-by-case basis. Credit and/or placement offered for CEEB Advanced Placement tests.

COSTS AND FINANCIAL AID

Average book expense $840. **Required Forms and Deadlines:** FAFSA. **Notification of Awards:** Applicants will be notified of awards on or about 6/1. **Types of Aid:** *Need-based scholarships/grants:* Federal Pell, SEOG, state scholarships/grants, private scholarships, the school's own gift aid, Federal Nursing Scholarships. *Loans:* Subsidized Stafford, Unsubsidized Stafford, PLUS, Federal Perkins, state loans. *Student Employment:* Federal Work-Study Program available. Highest amount earned per year from on-campus jobs $4,500. Off-campus job opportunities are good. **Financial Aid Statistics:** 57% freshmen, 58% undergrads receive need-based scholarship or grant aid. 48% freshmen, 48% undergrads receive non-need-based scholarship or grant aid. 73% freshmen, 72% undergrads receive need-based self-help aid. 0% freshmen, 0% undergrads receive athletic scholarships. 80% freshmen, 80% undergrads receive any aid. 49% undergrads borrow to pay for school. **Criteria for awarding institutional aid:** *Non-need-based:* academics, art, athletics, leadership, music/drama, state/district residency.

LANDMARK COLLEGE

P.O. Box 820, Putney, VT 05346-0820
Phone: 802-387-6718 · **Financial Aid Phone:** 802-387-6736
E-mail: admissions@landmark.edu
Fax: 802-387-6868 · **Website:** http://www.landmark.edu/ · **ACT Code:** 4317

This private school was founded in 1984. It has a 128-acre campus.

RATINGS

Admissions Selectivity Rating: 66   **Fire Safety Rating:** 75

STUDENTS AND FACULTY

Enrollment: 487. **Student Body:** 32% female, 68% male, 95% out-of-state, 3% international (14 countries represented). Asian 1%, African American 5%, Caucasian 70%, Hispanic 3%, Native American <1%
Retention and Graduation: 95% grads go on to further study within 1 year. **Faculty:** 86 full-time faculty, 64% are members of minority groups, 1% are women. 0% of classes are taught by teaching assistants.

ACADEMICS

Degrees: associate, terminal associate, transfer associate. **Classes:** Most classes have 10–19 students. **Special Study Options:** internships, study abroad.

FACILITIES

Housing: Coed dorms, special housing for disabled students, Wellness Housing. 65% of campus accessible to physically disabled.

CAMPUS LIFE

Environment: Rural. **Activities:** Choral groups, dance, drama/theater, jazz band, literary magazine, music ensembles, radio station, student government.

ADMISSIONS

Freshman Academic Profile: 70% from public high schools. Minimum paper TOEFL 200. **Basis for Candidate Selection:** *Very important factors considered include:* recommendation(s), interview. *Important factors considered include:* character/personal qualities, level of applicant's interest. *Other factors considered include:* Class rank, application essay, academic GPA, rigor of secondary school record, standardized test scores, extracurricular activities, talent/ability. **Freshman Admission Requirements:** High school diploma is required and GED is accepted. **Freshman Admission Statistics:** 395 applied, 54% admitted, 54% enrolled. **Transfer Admission Requirements:** High school transcript, college transcript(s), essay or personal statement, interview, Lowest grade transferable C-. **General Admission Information:** Application Fee $75. Notification on a rolling basis, beginning on or about 12/1. Nonfall registration accepted. Admission may be deferred for a maximum of 1 calendar year.

COSTS AND FINANCIAL AID

Annual tuition $48,210. Room and board $8,620. Required fees $500. Average book expense $1,200. **Required Forms and Deadlines:** FAFSA. **Notification of Awards:** Applicants will be notified of awards on a rolling basis beginning 4/15. **Types of Aid:** *Need-based scholarships/grants:* Federal Pell, SEOG, state scholarships/grants, private scholarships, the school's own gift aid, Vocational Rehabilitation Grants. *Loans:* Subsidized Stafford, Unsubsidized Stafford, PLUS. *Student Employment:* Federal Work-Study Program available. Institutional employment available. Highest amount earned per year from on-campus jobs $1,500. Off-campus job opportunities are good. **Financial Aid Statistics:**100% undergrads receive need-based scholarship or grant aid.4% undergrads receive non-need-based scholarship or grant aid.100% undergrads receive need-based self-help aid.0% undergrads receive athletic scholarships. 35% freshmen, 42% undergrads receive any aid. 51% undergrads borrow to pay for school. Average cumulative indebtedness $6,308. **Criteria for awarding institutional aid:** *Non-need-based:* academics, art, athletics, leadership, minority status, music/drama.

LANE COLLEGE

545 Lane Avenue, Jackson, TN 38301
Phone: 731-426-7532 · **Financial Aid Phone:** 731-426-7536
E-mail: admissions@lanecollege.edu
Fax: 731-426-7559 · **Website:** www.lanecollege.edu · **ACT Code:** 3976

This private school, affiliated with the Methodist Church, was founded in 1882. It has a 25-acre campus.

RATINGS

Admissions Selectivity Rating: 77   **Fire Safety Rating:** 92

STUDENTS AND FACULTY

Enrollment: 1,512. **Student Body:** 51% female, 49% male, 37% out-of-state, 0% international (1 countries represented). Asian %, African American 100%, Caucasian 0%, Hispanic 0%, Native American <1%
Retention and Graduation: 50% freshmen return for sophomore year. 22% freshmen graduate within 4 years. 38% freshmen graduate within 6 years. 35% grads go on to further study within 1 year. 37% grads pursue arts and sciences degrees. 6% grads pursue law degrees. 10% grads pursue business degrees. 7% grads pursue medical degrees. **Faculty:** 90 full-time faculty. 0% of classes are taught by teaching assistants.

ACADEMICS

Degrees: bachelor's. **Classes:** Most classes have 20–29 students. **Majors with Highest Enrollment:** Criminal Justice/Law Enforcement Administration; Business/Commerce; Biology/Biological Sciences. **Special Study Options:** Accelerated program, independent study, internships, study abroad, teacher certification program. **Disability Services:** Special programs offered to physically disabled students include tutors. **Career services:** alumni services, career/job search classes, career assessment, internships.

FACILITIES

Housing: men's dorms, women's dorms. 98% of campus accessible to physically disabled. **Special Academic Facilities/Equipment:** The Grand Student Center; The Cyber Café. **Computers:** 50% of classrooms, 100% of libraries, 100% of student union, 25% of common outdoor areas have wireless network access.

CAMPUS LIFE

Environment: Town. **Activities:** Choral groups, concert band, dance, drama/theater, marching band, music ensembles, student government, student newspaper, yearbook, Campus Ministries. 21 registered organizations, 6 honor societies, 4 religious organizations. 4 fraternities, 4 sororities. **Athletics (Intercollegiate):** *Men:* baseball, basketball, cross-country, football, tennis, track/field (outdoor). *Women:* basketball, cheerleading, cross-country, softball, tennis, track/field (outdoor), volleyball. **On-Campus Highlights:** Pond at the Plain, Williams/Boyd Campus Center, The Cyber Café, Phillips Dining Hall, The Grand. **Environmental Initiatives:** LEEDS TP3-Pollution; Tennessee Pollution Prevention Partnership; EPA Environmental Self-audit Program.

ADMISSIONS

Freshman Academic Profile: Average high school GPA 2.8. 3% in top 10% of high school class, 12% in top 25% of high school class, 39% in top 50% of high school class. 96% from public high schools. ACT middle 50% range 14-17. Minimum paper TOEFL 339. **Basis for Candidate Selection:** *Very important factors considered include:* recommendation(s), rigor of secondary school record, character/personal qualities. *Important factors considered include:* standardized test scores. *Other factors considered include:* academic GPA, interview, level of applicant's interest, talent/ability. **Freshman Admission Requirements:** High school diploma is required and GED is accepted. **Freshman Admission Statistics:** 5,324 applied, 33% admitted, 18% enrolled. **Transfer Admission Requirements:** college transcript(s), standardized test scores, statement of good standing from prior institution(s). Lowest grade transferable C. **General Admission Information:** Regular application deadline 8/1. Notification on a rolling basis, beginning on or about 2/1. Nonfall registration accepted. Admission may be deferred for a maximum of one semester. Credit offered for CEEB Advanced Placement tests.

COSTS AND FINANCIAL AID

Annual tuition $8,380. Room and board $6,520. Required fees $800. Average book expense $1,100. **Required Forms and Deadlines:** FAFSA. **Notification of Awards:** Applicants will be notified of awards on a rolling basis beginning 3/31. **Types of Aid:** *Need-based scholarships/grants:* Federal Pell, SEOG, state scholarships/grants, private scholarships, the school's own gift aid, United Negro College Fund. *Loans:* Direct Subsidized Stafford, Direct Unsubsidized Stafford, Direct PLUS. *Student Employment:* Federal Work-Study Program available. Institutional employment available. Off-campus job opportunities are excellent. **Financial Aid Statistics:** 94% freshmen, 98% undergrads receive need-based scholarship or grant aid. 0% freshmen, 0% undergrads receive non-need-based scholarship or grant aid. 94% freshmen, 97% undergrads receive need-based self-help aid. 348% freshmen, 0% undergrads receive athletic scholarships. 96% freshmen, 98% undergrads receive any aid. 82% undergrads borrow to pay for school. Average cumulative indebtedness $13,248. **Criteria for awarding institutional aid:** *Non-need-based:* academics, athletics, religious affiliation.

LASELL COLLEGE

Office of Undergraduate Admissions, Newton, MA 2466
Phone: 617-243-2225 · **Financial Aid Phone:** 617-243-2227
E-mail: info@lasell.edu · **CEEB Code:** 3481
Fax: 617-243-2380 · **Website:** www.lasell.edu · **ACT Code:** 1848

This private school was founded in 1851. It has a 55-acre campus.

RATINGS

Admissions Selectivity Rating: 72   **Fire Safety Rating:** 71

STUDENTS AND FACULTY

Enrollment: 1,667. **Student Body:** 64% female, 36% male, 44% out-of-state, 3% international (15 countries represented). Asian 2%, African American 7%, Caucasian 71%, Hispanic 9%, Native American <1%
Retention and Graduation: 47% freshmen graduate within 4 years. 53% freshmen graduate within 6 years. 18% grads go on to further study within 1 year. 13% grads pursue arts and sciences degrees. 5% grads pursue business degrees. **Faculty:** 79 full-time faculty, 68% hold PhDs, 65% are members of minority groups, 19% are women. 0% of classes are taught by teaching assistants.

ACADEMICS

Degrees: bachelor's, master's, post-bachelor's certificate. **Classes:** Most classes have 10–19 students. Most lab/discussion sessions have 10–19 students. **Majors with Highest Enrollment:** Psychology; Criminology; Fashion/Apparel Design. **Special Study Options:** double major, honors program, internships, liberal arts/career combination, study abroad. **Honors programs:** Lasell College Honor's Program. **Career services:** alumni services, career/job search classes, career assessment, internships.

FACILITIES

Housing: Coed dorms, women's dorms, Special interst (human services). Some houses Alcohol free. All houses Smoke free. 30% of campus accessible to physically disabled. **Special Academic Facilities/Equipment:** Center for Public Service, Yamawaki Art/Cultural Center.

CAMPUS LIFE

Environment: City. **Activities:** Choral groups, dance, drama/theater, literary magazine, music ensembles, musical theater, radio station, student government, student newspaper, television station, yearbook. 30 registered organizations, 1 honor society. **Athletics (Intercollegiate):** *Men:* basketball, cross-country, lacrosse, soccer, volleyball. *Women:* basketball, cross-country, field hockey, lacrosse, soccer, softball, volleyball. **On-Campus Highlights:** Yamawaki Art and Cultural Center, Campus Center, Athletic Center, Winslow Academic Center, Edwards Student Center.

ADMISSIONS

Freshman Academic Profile: Average high school GPA 2.83. 85% from public high schools. SAT Math middle 50% range 440-530. SAT Critical Reading middle 50% range 440-540. SAT Writing middle 50% range 440-520. ACT middle 50% range 18-23. Minimum paper TOEFL 500. **Basis for Candidate Selection:** *Very important factors considered include:* recommendation(s), rigor of secondary school record. *Important factors considered include:* standardized test scores, extracurricular activities, interview. *Other factors considered include:* Class rank, application essay, alumni/ae relation, character/personal qualities, talent/ability, volunteer work, work experience. **Freshman Admission Requirements:** High school diploma is required and GED is accepted. *Academic units required:* 4 English, 3 mathematics, 2 science, (2 science labs), 0 foreign language, 2 social studies, 2 history. **Freshman Admission Statistics:** 3,584 applied, 76% admitted, 18% enrolled. **Transfer Admission Requirements:** college transcript(s), standardized test scores, statement of good standing from prior institution(s). Minimum college GPA of 2.3 required. Lowest grade transferable C. **General Admission Information:** Application Fee $40. Notification on a rolling basis, beginning on or about 12/15. Nonfall registration accepted. Admission may be deferred for a maximum of 1 year. Credit offered for CEEB Advanced Placement tests.

COSTS AND FINANCIAL AID

Annual tuition $29,800. Room and board $12,750. Required fees $1,200. Average book expense $1,000. **Required Forms and Deadlines:** FAFSA. **Notification of Awards:** Applicants will be notified of awards on a rolling basis beginning 2/15. **Types of Aid:** *Need-based scholarships/grants:* Federal Pell, SEOG, state scholarships/grants, private scholarships, the school's own gift aid. *Loans:* Subsidized Stafford, Unsubsidized Stafford, PLUS, Federal Perkins, state loans. *Student Employment:* Federal Work-Study Program available. Institutional employment available. Off-campus job opportunities are excellent. **Financial Aid Statistics:** 99% freshmen, 100% undergrads receive need-based scholarship or grant aid. 11% freshmen, 9% undergrads receive non-need-based scholarship or grant aid. 99% freshmen, 92% undergrads receive need-based

self-help aid. 0% freshmen, 0% undergrads receive athletic scholarships. 87% freshmen, 85% undergrads receive any aid. 86% undergrads borrow to pay for school. Average cumulative indebtedness $26,888. **Criteria for awarding institutional aid:** *Non-need-based:* academics, alumni affiliation.

LAURA AND ALVIN SIEGAL COLLEGE OF JUDAIC STUDIES

26500 Shaker Boulevard, Beachwood, OH 44122-7116
Phone: 216-464-4050 · **Financial Aid Phone:** 216-464-4050
E-mail: admissions@siegalcollege.edu
Fax: 216-464-5827

This private school, affiliated with the Jewish Church, was founded in 1963.

RATINGS

Admissions Selectivity Rating: 60*   **Fire Safety Rating:** 60*

STUDENTS AND FACULTY

Enrollment: 12. **Student Body:** 67% female, 33% male, 90% out-of-state, 0% international (1 countries represented). Asian 0%, African American 0%, Caucasian 100%, Hispanic 0%, Native American <1%
Retention and Graduation: 100% freshmen return for sophomore year. **Faculty:** 11 full-time faculty, 82% hold PhDs, 36% are members of minority groups, 0% are women. 0% of classes are taught by teaching assistants.

ACADEMICS

Degrees: bachelor's, certificate, master's. **Majors with Highest Enrollment:** Bible/Biblical Studies. **Special Study Options:** distance learning, double major, independent study, internships.

FACILITIES

Housing: no housing available on campus. 100% of campus accessible to physically disabled. **Computers:** Students can register for classes online.

CAMPUS LIFE

Environment: Village. **Activities:** 1 registered organization. **On-Campus Highlights:** library, video conferencing rooms, student lounge, language media center, professors offices.

ADMISSIONS

Basis for Candidate Selection: *Very important factors considered include:* application essay, recommendation(s), interview, level of applicant's interest. *Important factors considered include:* academic GPA, rigor of secondary school record. *Other factors considered include:* Class rank, standardized test scores, character/personal qualities, extracurricular activities, talent/ability, work experience. **Freshman Admission Requirements:** High school diploma is required and GED is accepted. **Freshman Admission Statistics:** 3 applied, 100% admitted, 100% enrolled. **Transfer Admission Requirements:** college transcript(s), essay or personal statement, interview, Minimum college GPA of 2.7 required. Lowest grade transferable c. **General Admission Information:** Application Fee $50. Nonfall registration accepted. Admission may be deferred for a maximum of 1 year.

COSTS AND FINANCIAL AID

Annual tuition $12,600. Required fees $25. **Required Forms and Deadlines:** Institution's own financial aid form. **Notification of Awards:** Applicants will be notified of awards on a rolling basis beginning 9/5. **Types of Aid:** *Need-based scholarships/grants:* Federal Pell, the school's own gift aid. *Loans:* Subsidized Stafford, Unsubsidized Stafford, PLUS. *Student Employment:* Off-campus job opportunities are good. **Financial Aid Statistics:** 100% freshmen receive need-based scholarship or grant aid. 0% freshmen receive non-need-based scholarship or grant aid. 0% freshmen receive need-based self-help aid. 0% freshmen receive athletic scholarships. 0% undergrads borrow to pay for school.

LAWRENCE TECHNOLOGICAL UNIVERSITY

21000 West Ten Mile Rd., Southfield, MI 48075-1058
Phone: 248-204-3160 · **Financial Aid Phone:** 248-204-2280
E-mail: admissions@ltu.edu · **CEEB Code:** 1399
Fax: 248-204-3188 · **Website:** www.ltu.edu · **ACT Code:** 2020

This private school was founded in 1932. It has a 102-acre campus.

RATINGS

Admissions Selectivity Rating: 86   **Fire Safety Rating:** 88

STUDENTS AND FACULTY

Enrollment: 1,978. **Student Body:** 27% female, 73% male, 4% out-of-state, 8% international (60 countries represented). Asian 7%, African American 8%, Caucasian 67%, Hispanic 3%, Native American <1%
Retention and Graduation: 82% freshmen return for sophomore year. 27% grads go on to further study within 1 year. **Faculty:** 122 full-time faculty, 66% hold PhDs, 26% are members of minority groups, 24% are women. 0% of classes are taught by teaching assistants.

ACADEMICS

Degrees: associate, bachelor's, certificate, doctoral, master's, post-bachelor's certificate. **Classes:** Most classes have 10–19 students. Most lab/discussion sessions have fewer than 10 students. **Majors with Highest Enrollment:** Mechanical Engineering; Computer Science; Architecture. **Special Study Options:** cooperative education program, cross-registration, distance learning, double major, dual enrollment, English as a Second Language (ESL), honors program, independent study, internships, liberal arts/career combination, study abroad, weekend college. **Honors programs:** The LTU Honors Program is designed for highly qualified students who want an educational experience that will take full advantage of the challenging curricula offered at Lawrence Tech. **Combined degree programs:** Many dual degree combinations. **Disability Services:** Special programs offered to physically disabled students include note-taking services, reader services, tape recorders, tutors. **Career services:** Alumni network, alumni services, career/job search classes, career assessment, internships, regional alumni. Career services highlights include "Find Your First Professional Job." A 10 week program to develop student skills to locate and secure their career goals. Classes are taught by leading employers, and each student is assigned a career counselor to help develop an individualized approach to their quest.

FACILITIES

Housing: special housing for disabled students, fraternity/sorority housing, apartments for married students, apartments for single students. 97% of campus accessible to physically disabled. **Special Academic Facilities/Equipment:** Albert Kahn Library, Center for Innovative Materials Research. **Computers:** 100% of classrooms, 100% of dorms, 100% of libraries, 100% of dining areas, 100% of student union, 75% of common outdoor areas have wireless network access. Students can register for classes online. Administrative functions (other than registration) can be performed online. Undergraduates are required to own a computer.

CAMPUS LIFE

Environment: City. **Activities:** drama/theater, literary magazine, music ensembles, student government, student newspaper. 54 registered organizations, 7 honor societies, 1 religious organization. 6 fraternities, 3 sororities. **On-Campus Highlights:** Atrium, Field House, Engineering Lounge, Larry Joe Coffee Bar, Housing. **Environmental Initiatives:** A. Alfred Taubman Student Services Center is a green building including geothermal wells and a vegetated roof. It serves as a living laboratory for sustainability education of architects and engineers. Establishment of the Center for Sustainability including campus standards for sustainability, a speaker series, and recycling. Academic programming including Formula Zero international competitions.

ADMISSIONS

Freshman Academic Profile: Average high school GPA 3.43. 24% in top 10% of high school class, 50% in top 25% of high school class, 81% in top 50% of high school class. SAT Math middle 50% range 540-650. SAT Critical Reading middle 50% range 500-580. SAT Writing middle 50% range 450-580. ACT middle 50% range 21-28. Minimum internet-based TOEFL 79. Minimum paper TOEFL 550. **Basis for Candidate Selection:** *Very important factors considered include:* academic GPA, rigor of secondary school record, standardized test scores. *Other factors considered include:* application essay, recommendation(s), interview. **Freshman Admission Requirements:** High school diploma is required and GED is accepted. *Academic units required:* 4 English, 3 mathematics, 2 science, 3 social studies. **Freshman Admission Statistics:** 2,285 applied, 57% admitted, 26% enrolled. **Transfer Admission Requirements:** High school transcript, college transcript(s), Minimum college GPA of 2.2 required. Lowest grade transferable C. **General Admission Information:** Application

Fee $30. Nonfall registration accepted. Credit and/or placement offered for CEEB Advanced Placement tests.

COSTS AND FINANCIAL AID

Annual tuition $29,580. Room and board $8,986. Required fees $620. Average book expense $1,405. **Required Forms and Deadlines:** FAFSA. **Notification of Awards:** Applicants will be notified of awards on a rolling basis beginning 3/1. **Types of Aid:** *Need-based scholarships/grants:* Federal Pell, SEOG, state scholarships/grants, private scholarships, the school's own gift aid. *Loans:* Direct Subsidized Stafford, Direct Unsubsidized Stafford, Direct PLUS, Federal Perkins, state loans, college/university loans from institutional funds, Private Alternative Loans. *Student Employment:* Federal Work-Study Program available. Institutional employment available. Highest amount earned per year from on-campus jobs $13,110. Off-campus job opportunities are excellent. **Financial Aid Statistics:** 98% freshmen, 97% undergrads receive need-based scholarship or grant aid. 90% freshmen, 78% undergrads receive non-need-based scholarship or grant aid. 80% freshmen, 84% undergrads receive need-based self-help aid. 19% freshmen, 12% undergrads receive athletic scholarships. 95% freshmen, 53% undergrads receive any aid. 69% undergrads borrow to pay for school. Average cumulative indebtedness $27,768. **Criteria for awarding institutional aid:** *Non-need-based:* academics, alumni affiliation, art, job skills, leadership, minority status, state/district residency.

See page 1078.

LAWRENCE UNIVERSITY

Best 380

711 East Boldt Way, Appleton, WI 54911-5699
Phone: 920-832-6500 · **Financial Aid Phone:** 920-832-6583
E-mail: admissions@lawrence.edu · **CEEB Code:** 1398
Fax: 920-832-6782 · **Website:** www.lawrence.edu · **ACT Code:** 4596

This private school was founded in 1847. It has a 84-acre campus.

RATINGS

Admissions Selectivity Rating: 89   **Fire Safety Rating:** 77

STUDENTS AND FACULTY

Enrollment: 1,483. **Student Body:** 54% female, 46% male, 65% out-of-state, 9% international (31 countries represented). Asian 4%, African American 3%, Caucasian 71%, Hispanic 7%, Native American 1%
Retention and Graduation: 90% freshmen return for sophomore year. 66% freshmen graduate within 4 years. 22% grads go on to further study within 1 year. 11% grads pursue arts and sciences degrees. 3% grads pursue law degrees. 2% grads pursue medical degrees. **Faculty:** 159 full-time faculty, 92% hold PhDs, 40% are members of minority groups, 11% are women. 0% of classes are taught by teaching assistants.

ACADEMICS

Degrees: bachelor's. **Classes:** Most classes have 10–19 students. **Majors with Highest Enrollment:** Music Performance; Biology/Biological Sciences; Psychology. **Special Study Options:** double major, independent study, internships, student-designed major, study abroad, teacher certification program. **Combined degree programs:** BA/B-MUS. **Disability Services:** Special programs offered to physically disabled students include note-taking services, reader services, tape recorders, tutors. **Career services:** Alumni network, alumni services, career assessment, internships, regional alumni.

FACILITIES

Housing: Coed dorms, special housing for disabled students, men's dorms, women's dorms, apartments for married students, Theme Housingtheme/group houses available. 70% of campus accessible to physically disabled. **Special Academic Facilities/Equipment:** Art galleries, anthropology collection, 425-acre estate on Lake Michigan hosting retreats and seminars for students, new student center (Warch Center), electron microscope, laser physics lab, physics/computational graphics lab, nuclear magnetic resonance spectrometer. **Computers:** 100% of classrooms, 20% of dorms, 100% of libraries, 100% of dining areas, 100% of student union, have wireless network access. Students can register for classes online. Administrative functions (other than registration) can be performed online.

CAMPUS LIFE

Environment: City. **Activities:** Choral groups, concert band, dance, drama/theater, jazz band, literary magazine, music ensembles, musical theater, opera, pep band, radio station, student government, student newspaper, student-run film society, symphony orchestra, yearbook, Campus Ministries, International Student Organization, Model UN. 90 registered organizations, 5 honor societies, 3 religious organizations. 5 fraternities, 3 sororities. **Athletics (Intercollegiate):** *Men:* baseball, basketball, cross-country, diving, fencing, football, golf, ice hockey, soccer, swimming, tennis, track/field (outdoor), track/field (indoor), wrestling. *Women:* basketball, cross-country, diving, fencing, soccer, softball, swimming, tennis, track/field (outdoor), track/field (indoor), volleyball. **On-Campus Highlights:** Wriston Art Gallery, Music Conservatory, New Warch Campus Center -opening '09, New $18 million Science Building, Hiett Hall (new $8 million residence hall). **Environmental Initiatives:** Construction of LEED certified Student Center—Gold!; Campus Garden (SLUG) (http://blogs.lawrence.edu/SLUG/) which provides produce to the dining hall and composts all food prep waste. Also serves an educational garden for the Community Garden Partnership of the Fox Cities. Lawrence has a long standing Environmental Studies Program and offers Majors and Minors. http:www.lawrence.edu/academics/enst/

ADMISSIONS

Freshman Academic Profile: Average high school GPA 3.51. 42% in top 10% of high school class, 70% in top 25% of high school class, 94% in top 50% of high school class. 70% from public high schools. SAT Math middle 50% range 560-720. SAT Critical Reading middle 50% range 580-690. SAT Writing middle 50% range 570-680. ACT middle 50% range 25-31. Minimum internet-based TOEFL 90. Minimum paper TOEFL 577. **Basis for Candidate Selection:** *Very important factors considered include:* Class rank, academic GPA, rigor of secondary school record. *Important factors considered include:* application essay, recommendation(s), character/personal qualities, extracurricular activities, talent/ability. *Other factors considered include:* standardized test scores, alumni/ae relation, first generation, interview, racial/ethnic status, volunteer work, work experience. **Freshman Admission Requirements:** High school diploma is required and GED is not accepted. *Academic units required:* 4 English. **Freshman Admission Statistics:** 2,747 applied, 73% admitted, 19% enrolled. **Transfer Admission Requirements:** High school transcript, college transcript(s), essay or personal statement, Minimum college GPA of 2.75 required. Lowest grade transferable C-. **General Admission Information:** Application Fee $40. Early decision application deadline 11/15. Regular application deadline 1/15. Regular notification 4/1. Nonfall registration not accepted. Admission may be deferred for a maximum of 12 mo. Credit and/or placement offered for CEEB Advanced Placement tests.

COSTS AND FINANCIAL AID

Annual tuition $43,440. Room and board $9,210. Required fees $100. **Required Forms and Deadlines:** FAFSA, CSS/Financial Aid PROFILE, Noncustodial PROFILE. **Notification of Awards:** Applicants will be notified of awards on a rolling basis beginning 3/1. **Types of Aid:** *Need-based scholarships/grants:* Federal Pell, SEOG, state scholarships/grants, private scholarships, the school's own gift aid. *Loans:* Direct Subsidized Stafford, Direct Unsubsidized Stafford, Direct PLUS, Federal Perkins. *Student Employment:* Federal Work-Study Program available. Institutional employment available. Highest amount earned per year from on-campus jobs $4,189. Off-campus job opportunities are good. **Financial Aid Statistics:** 100% freshmen, 100% undergrads receive need-based scholarship or grant aid. 2% freshmen, 4% undergrads receive non-need-based scholarship or grant aid. 83% freshmen, 82% undergrads receive need-based self-help aid. 0% freshmen, 0% undergrads receive athletic scholarships. 97% freshmen, 97% undergrads receive any aid. 62% undergrads borrow to pay for school. Average cumulative indebtedness $28,280. **Criteria for awarding institutional aid:** *Non-need-based:* academics, alumni affiliation, leadership, minority status, music/drama.

LE MOYNE COLLEGE

Best 380

1419 Salt Springs Rd., Syracuse, NY 13214-1301
Phone: 315-445-4300 · **Financial Aid Phone:** 315-445-4400
E-mail: admission@lemoyne.edu · **CEEB Code:** 2366
Fax: 315-445-4711 · **Website:** www.lemoyne.edu · **ACT Code:** 2790

This private school, affiliated with the Roman Catholic Church, was founded in 1946. It has a 161-acre campus.

RATINGS

Admissions Selectivity Rating: 83   Fire Safety Rating: 84

STUDENTS AND FACULTY

Enrollment: 2,728. **Student Body:** 58% female, 42% male, 6% out-of-state, 1% international (39 countries represented). Asian 3%, African American 6%, Caucasian 79%, Hispanic 5%, Native American <1%
Retention and Graduation: 86% freshmen return for sophomore year. 61% freshmen graduate within 4 years. 72% freshmen graduate within 6 years. 36% grads go on to further study within 1 year. 13% grads pursue arts and sciences degrees. 2% grads pursue law degrees. 2% grads pursue business degrees. 7% grads pursue medical degrees. **Faculty:** 149 full-time faculty, 93% hold PhDs, 41% are members of minority groups, 16% are women. 0% of classes are taught by teaching assistants.

ACADEMICS

Degrees: bachelor's, master's, post-master's certificate. **Classes:** Most classes have 20–29 students. Most lab/discussion sessions have 10–19 students. **Majors with Highest Enrollment:** Biology/Biological Sciences; Psychology; Accounting. **Special Study Options:** Accelerated program, double major, dual enrollment, honors program, independent study, internships, study abroad, teacher certification program, Certificate of Advanced Studies in Educational Leadership and Certificate of Advanced Studies in Nursing. **Honors programs:** Students in the program complete a 21-hour sequence of interdisciplinary humanities courses that replaces the standard core requirements in English, history, philosophy, and religious studies. Seniors complete an honors project working in close collaboration with a faculty advisor. **Combined degree programs:** BA/MA, BA/DDS, BA/MEng, 3-4:Pre-Optmtry (PA Coll) Pre-Podiatry (NY Coll);3-3:Dr of Physcl Thrpy. **Disability Services:** Special programs offered to physically disabled students include note-taking services, reader services, tape recorders, tutors. **Career services:** Alumni network, alumni services, career/job search classes, career assessment, internships, regional alumni. Career services highlights include Business and Science Internship Programs and Mock Interview week.

FACILITIES

Housing: Coed dorms, special housing for disabled students, men's dorms, women's dorms, apartments for single students, Living/Learning Communities. 96% of campus accessible to physically disabled. **Special Academic Facilities/Equipment:** Art gallery, audiovisual center, electron microscopes and Academic Support Center. **Computers:** 100% of classrooms, 75% of dorms, 100% of libraries, 100% of dining areas, 100% of student union, 100% of common outdoor areas have wireless network access. Students can register for classes online. Administrative functions (other than registration) can be performed online.

CAMPUS LIFE

Environment: City. **Activities:** Choral groups, concert band, dance, drama/theater, jazz band, literary magazine, music ensembles, musical theater, pep band, radio station, student government, student newspaper, student-run film society, television station, yearbook, Campus Ministries, International Student Organization, Model UN. 70 registered organizations, 14 honor societies, 11 religious organization. **Athletics (Intercollegiate):** *Men:* baseball, basketball, cross-country, diving, golf, lacrosse, soccer, swimming, tennis. *Women:* basketball, cross-country, diving, golf, lacrosse, soccer, softball, swimming, tennis, volleyball. **On-Campus Highlights:** The Thomas J. Niland Athletic Complex, Campus Center, The W.Carroll Coyne Center for the Performing Arts, Panasci Family Chapel, Noreen Reale Falcone Library. **Environmental Initiatives:** LEED GOLD certification on new science building. Project for LED lighting. Dining Services Food Composting.

ADMISSIONS

Freshman Academic Profile: Average high school GPA 3.43. 21% in top 10% of high school class, 50% in top 25% of high school class, 85% in top 50% of high school class. 83% from public high schools. SAT Math middle 50% range 480-590. SAT Critical Reading middle 50% range 470-570. ACT middle 50% range 21-27. Minimum internet-based TOEFL 79. Minimum paper TOEFL 550. **Basis for Candidate Selection:** *Very important factors considered include:* academic GPA, rigor of secondary school record. *Important factors considered include:* Class rank, application essay, recommendation(s), standardized test scores, extracurricular activities, interview, talent/ability, work experience. *Other factors considered include:* alumni/ae relation, character/personal qualities, geographical residence, level of applicant's interest, state residency, volunteer work. **Freshman Admission Requirements:** High school diploma is required and GED is accepted. *Academic units required:* 4 English, 3 mathematics, 3 science, 3 foreign language, 4 social studies. **Freshman Admission Statistics:** 6,253 applied, 66% admitted, 16% enrolled. **Transfer Admission Requirements:** college transcript(s), essay or personal statement, Minimum college GPA of 2.6 required. Lowest grade transferable C-. **General Admission Information:** Application Fee $35. Early decision application deadline 12/1. Notification on a rolling basis, beginning on or about 1/1. Nonfall registration accepted. Admission may be deferred for a maximum of 12 months. Credit and/or placement offered for CEEB Advanced Placement tests.

COSTS AND FINANCIAL AID

Annual tuition $30,350. Room and board $12,130. Required fees $990. Average book expense $1,300. **Required Forms and Deadlines:** FAFSA, State aid form. **Notification of Awards:** Applicants will be notified of awards on or about 3/15. **Types of Aid:** *Need-based scholarships/grants:* Federal Pell, SEOG, state scholarships/grants, private scholarships, the school's own gift aid. *Loans:* Subsidized Stafford, Unsubsidized Stafford, PLUS, Federal Perkins. *Student Employment:* Federal Work-Study Program available. Institutional employment available. Highest amount earned per year from on-campus jobs $2,000. Off-campus job opportunities are excellent. **Financial Aid Statistics:** 100% freshmen, 100% undergrads receive need-based scholarship or grant aid. 18% freshmen, 13% undergrads receive non-need-based scholarship or grant aid. 78% freshmen, 82% undergrads receive need-based self-help aid. 7% freshmen, 8% undergrads receive athletic scholarships. 90% freshmen, 92% undergrads receive any aid. 88% undergrads borrow to pay for school. Average cumulative indebtedness $24,739. **Criteria for awarding institutional aid:** *Non-need-based:* academics, alumni affiliation, athletics, leadership, minority status.

See page 1080.

LEBANON VALLEY COLLEGE

101 North College Avenue, Annville, PA 17003-1400
Phone: 717-867-6181 · **Financial Aid Phone:** 717-867-6126
E-mail: admission@lvc.edu · **CEEB Code:** 2364
Fax: 717-867-6026 · **Website:** www.lvc.edu · **ACT Code:** 3610

This private school, affiliated with the Methodist Church, was founded in 1866. It has a 340-acre campus.

RATINGS
Admissions Selectivity Rating: 85   **Fire Safety Rating:** 88

STUDENTS AND FACULTY
Enrollment: 1,627. **Student Body:** 54% female, 46% male, 20% out-of-state, 0% international (4 countries represented). Asian 2%, African American 3%, Caucasian 83%, Hispanic 5%, Native American <1%
Retention and Graduation: 85% freshmen return for sophomore year. 70% freshmen graduate within 4 years. 75% freshmen graduate within 6 years. 42% grads go on to further study within 1 year. 35% grads pursue arts and sciences degrees. 1% grads pursue law degrees. 2% grads pursue medical degrees. **Faculty:** 106 full-time faculty, 90% hold PhDs, 39% are members of minority groups, 9% are women. 0% of classes are taught by teaching assistants.

ACADEMICS
Degrees: associate, bachelor's, certificate, master's, post-bachelor's certificate, terminal associate. **Classes:** Most classes have 10–19 students. Most lab/discussion sessions have 10–19 students. **Majors with Highest Enrollment:** Health Services/Allied Health/Health Sciences; Early Childhood Education and Teaching; Business/Commerce. **Special Study Options:** double major, dual enrollment, independent study, internships, liberal arts/career combination, student-designed major, study abroad, teacher certification program. **Combined degree programs:** Forestry/Environmental Studies - 3+2 w/ Duke. **Disability Services:** Special programs offered to physically disabled students include note-taking services, reader services, tape recorders, tutors. **Career services:** Alumni network, alumni services, career assessment, internships. Career services highlights include Career Connections, our on-line mentoring/networking system for connecting students with almuni who can assist in career planning and the job search.

FACILITIES
Housing: Coed dorms, special housing for disabled students, women's dorms, apartments for single students, Theme Housing, suites. 80% of campus accessible to physically disabled. **Special Academic Facilities/Equipment:** Electric pianos, sound recording studio, transmission electron microscope, scanning electron microscope, Fourier transform infrared spectrometer, atomic absorption spectrometer, nuclear magnetic resonance spectrometer, molecular modeling lab, campus Arboretum, art gallery, therapy pool. **Computers:** 100% of classrooms, 100% of dorms, 100% of libraries, 100% of dining areas, 100% of student union, 90% of common outdoor areas have wireless network access. Students can register for classes online. Administrative functions (other than registration) can be performed online.

CAMPUS LIFE
Environment: Rural. **Activities:** Choral groups, drama/theater, jazz band, literary magazine, marching band, music ensembles, musical theater, radio station, student government, student newspaper, symphony orchestra, yearbook, Campus Ministries. 79 registered organizations, 6 honor societies, 14 religious organizations. 4 fraternities, 4 sororities. **Athletics (Intercollegiate):** *Men:* baseball, basketball, cross-country, football, golf, ice hockey, lacrosse, soccer,

swimming, tennis, track/field (outdoor), track/field (indoor). *Women:* basketball, cross-country, field hockey, lacrosse, soccer, softball, swimming, tennis, track/field (outdoor), track/field (indoor), volleyball. **On-Campus Highlights:** Neidig Garber Science Center, Lynch Memorial - Synodinos Commons, The Peace Garden, Bishop Library, Suzanne Arnold Art Gallery and Zimmerman Recital Hall, Athletic fields are outstanding. Stanson Residence Hall, with 148 beds, was opened in Fall 2009. **Environmental Initiatives:** energy conservation recycling green products used in cleaning and grounds care

ADMISSIONS
Freshman Academic Profile: 32% in top 10% of high school class, 66% in top 25% of high school class, 91% in top 50% of high school class. SAT Math middle 50% range 500-620. SAT Critical Reading middle 50% range 470-590. SAT Writing middle 50% range 470-580. ACT middle 50% range 21-26. Minimum internet-based TOEFL 80. Minimum paper TOEFL 550. **Basis for Candidate Selection:** *Very important factors considered include:* Class rank, rigor of secondary school record. *Important factors considered include:* academic GPA, character/personal qualities, extracurricular activities, interview, level of applicant's interest, talent/ability. *Other factors considered include:* application essay, recommendation(s), standardized test scores, alumni/ae relation, first generation, geographical residence, racial/ethnic status, state residency, volunteer work, work experience. **Freshman Admission Requirements:** High school diploma is required and GED is accepted. *Academic units required:* 4 English, 3 mathematics, 2 science, 2 foreign language, 1 social studies. **Freshman Admission Statistics:** 3,643 applied, 71% admitted, 16% enrolled. **Transfer Admission Requirements:** High school transcript, college transcript(s), essay or personal statement, statement of good standing from prior institution(s). Minimum college GPA of 2.0 required. Lowest grade transferable C-. **General Admission Information:** Application Fee $30. Notification on a rolling basis, beginning on or about 10/15. Nonfall registration accepted. Credit offered for CEEB Advanced Placement tests.

COSTS AND FINANCIAL AID
Annual tuition $36,470. Room and board $10,100. Required fees $1,000. Average book expense $1,100. **Required Forms and Deadlines:** FAFSA. **Notification of Awards:** Applicants will be notified of awards on a rolling basis beginning 3/1. **Types of Aid:** *Need-based scholarships/grants:* Federal Pell, SEOG, state scholarships/grants, private scholarships, the school's own gift aid. *Loans:* Subsidized Stafford, Unsubsidized Stafford, PLUS, Federal Perkins. *Student Employment:* Federal Work-Study Program available. Institutional employment available. Highest amount earned per year from on-campus jobs $901. Off-campus job opportunities are good. **Financial Aid Statistics:** 99% freshmen, 99% undergrads receive need-based scholarship or grant aid. 8% freshmen, 9% undergrads receive non-need-based scholarship or grant aid. 91% freshmen, 87% undergrads receive need-based self-help aid. 0% freshmen, 0% undergrads receive athletic scholarships. 99% freshmen, 99% undergrads receive any aid. 80% undergrads borrow to pay for school. Average cumulative indebtedness $26,069. **Criteria for awarding institutional aid:** *Non-need-based:* academics, alumni affiliation, music/drama.

LEE UNIVERSITY

P.O. Box 3450, Cleveland, TN 37320-3450
Phone: 423-614-8500 · **Financial Aid Phone:** 423-614-8300
E-mail: admissions@leeuniversity.edu · **CEEB Code:** 1401
Fax: 423-614-8533 · **Website:** www.leeuniversity.edu · **ACT Code:** 3978

This private school, affiliated with the Church of God Church, was founded in 1918. It has a 115-acre campus.

RATINGS
Admissions Selectivity Rating: 81   **Fire Safety Rating:** 72

STUDENTS AND FACULTY
Enrollment: 4,117. **Student Body:** 58% female, 42% male, 57% out-of-state, 5% international (50 countries represented). Asian 1%, African American 6%, Caucasian 79%, Hispanic 4%, Native American <1%
Retention and Graduation: 39% freshmen graduate within 4 years. 54% freshmen graduate within 6 years. 20% grads go on to further study within 1 year. **Faculty:** 168 full-time faculty, 77% hold PhDs, 33% are members of minority groups, 11% are women. 0% of classes are taught by teaching assistants.

ACADEMICS
Degrees: bachelor's, master's, post-master's certificate. **Classes:** Most classes have 20–29 students. Most lab/discussion sessions have fewer than 10 students. **Majors with Highest Enrollment:** Curriculum and Instruction; Psychology; Elementary Education and Teaching. **Special Study Options:** distance learn-

ing, double major, dual enrollment, English as a Second Language (ESL), exchange student program (domestic), external degree program, honors program, independent study, internships, liberal arts/career combination, study abroad, teacher certification program. **Honors programs:** The Kairos Scholars Honors Program. Also, several academic subject honors societies like Psychology, Business, Music and Pre-Med. **Disability Services:** Special programs offered to physically disabled students include reader services, tape recorders, tutors. **Career services:** alumni services, career assessment, internships.

FACILITIES

Housing: men's dorms, women's dorms, apartments for married students, apartments for single students, Wellness Housing. Lee University leases apartments and houses for students. 71% of campus accessible to physically disabled. **Special Academic Facilities/Equipment:** Curriculum Library in the College of Education. **Computers:** 80% of classrooms, 50% of dorms, 100% of libraries, 100% of dining areas, 100% of student union, 50% of common outdoor areas have wireless network access. Students can register for classes online. Administrative functions (other than registration) can be performed online.

CAMPUS LIFE

Environment: Town. **Activities:** Choral groups, concert band, drama/theater, jazz band, literary magazine, music ensembles, musical theater, opera, pep band, student government, student newspaper, symphony orchestra, yearbook, Campus Ministries, International Student Organization, Model UN. 72 registered organizations, 16 honor societies, 10 religious organizations. 5 fraternities, 4 sororities. **Athletics (Intercollegiate):** *Men:* baseball, basketball, cheerleading, cross-country, golf, soccer, tennis. *Women:* basketball, cheerleading, cross-country, soccer, softball, tennis, volleyball. **On-Campus Highlights:** Paul Conn Student Union-Bookstore, Pizza Hut, Chickfil, Conn Center-Home of Chapels, Concerts, etc., Dixon Center plays, recitals, community events, De Vos Recreaction Center, The House—Coffee House, and Jazzman's Café.

ADMISSIONS

Freshman Academic Profile: Average high school GPA 3.56. 19.91% in top 10% of high school class, 48.74% in top 25% of high school class, 75.29% in top 50% of high school class. 75% from public high schools. SAT Math middle 50% range 420-540. SAT Critical Reading middle 50% range 450-590. ACT middle 50% range 21-27. Minimum paper TOEFL 450. **Basis for Candidate Selection:** *Very important factors considered include:* academic GPA, rigor of secondary school record, standardized test scores. *Important factors considered include:* Class rank, character/personal qualities, level of applicant's interest. *Other factors considered include:* recommendation(s), alumni/ae relation, extracurricular activities, first generation, interview, talent/ability. **Freshman Admission Requirements:** High school diploma is required and GED is accepted. *Academic units required:* 4 English, 3 mathematics, 2 science, (0 science labs), 1 foreign language, 2 social studies, 1 history, 0 academic electives. **Freshman Admission Statistics:** 1,745 applied, 89% admitted, 49% enrolled. **Transfer Admission Requirements:** college transcript(s), Minimum college GPA of 2.0 required. Lowest grade transferable D. **General Admission Information:** Application Fee $25. Regular application deadline 9/1. Notification on a rolling basis, beginning on or about 9/1. Nonfall registration accepted. Admission may be deferred for a maximum of 1 semester. Credit and/or placement offered for CEEB Advanced Placement tests.

COSTS AND FINANCIAL AID

Annual tuition $14,400. Room and board $7,045. Required fees $600. Average book expense $1,200. **Required Forms and Deadlines:** FAFSA. **Notification of Awards:** Applicants will be notified of awards on a rolling basis beginning 2/1. **Types of Aid:** *Need-based scholarships/grants:* Federal Pell, SEOG, state scholarships/grants, private scholarships, the school's own gift aid. *Loans:* Subsidized Stafford, Unsubsidized Stafford, PLUS, Federal Perkins, college/university loans from institutional funds. *Student Employment:* Federal Work-Study Program available. Institutional employment available. Off-campus job opportunities are good. **Financial Aid Statistics:** 93% freshmen, 88% undergrads receive need-based scholarship or grant aid. 15% freshmen, 8% undergrads receive non-need-based scholarship or grant aid. 80% freshmen, 82% undergrads receive need-based self-help aid. 5% freshmen, 3% undergrads receive athletic scholarships. 94% freshmen, 89% undergrads receive any aid. 62% undergrads borrow to pay for school. Average cumulative indebtedness $28,930. **Criteria for awarding institutional aid:** *Non-need-based:* academics, alumni affiliation, athletics, leadership, minority status, music/drama, religious affiliation, state/district residency.

LEHIGH UNIVERSITY

27 Memorial Drive West, Bethlehem, PA 18015
Phone: 610-758-3100 · **Financial Aid Phone:** 610-758-3181
E-mail: admissions@lehigh.edu · **CEEB Code:** 2365
Fax: 610-758-4361 · **Website:** www.lehigh.edu · **ACT Code:** 3612

This private school was founded in 1865. It has a 1600-acre campus.

RATINGS

Admissions Selectivity Rating: 94   Fire Safety Rating: 83

STUDENTS AND FACULTY

Enrollment: 5,034. **Student Body:** 45% female, 55% male, 73% out-of-state, 7% international (63 countries represented). Asian 8%, African American 4%, Caucasian 67%, Hispanic 8%, Native American <1%. **Retention and Graduation:** 96% freshmen return for sophomore year. 76% freshmen graduate within 4 years. 87% freshmen graduate within 6 years. 29% grads go on to further study within 1 year. 27% grads pursue arts and sciences degrees. 7% grads pursue law degrees. 11% grads pursue business degrees. 8% grads pursue medical degrees. **Faculty:** 506 full-time faculty, 96% hold PhDs, 31% are members of minority groups, 20% are women.

ACADEMICS

Degrees: bachelor's, doctoral, master's, post-bachelor's certificate, post-master's certificate. **Classes:** Most classes have 10–19 students. Most lab/discussion sessions have 10–19 students. **Majors with Highest Enrollment:** Mechanical Engineering; Finance; Chemical Engineering. **Special Study Options:** Accelerated program, cooperative education program, cross-registration, distance learning, double major, English as a Second Language (ESL), exchange student program (domestic), external degree program, honors program, independent study, internships, liberal arts/career combination, study abroad. **Honors programs:** Integrated Business and Engineering (IBE) Honors Program, program description available http://www.lehigh.edu/~inibep/ **Combined degree programs:** BA/MD, BA/DDS, 7-year BA/OD Program with SUNY Optometry. **Disability Services:** Special programs offered to physically disabled students include note-taking services, reader services, tape recorders, tutors. **Career services:** Alumni network, alumni services, career/job search classes, career assessment, internships, regional alumni. Career services highlights include Lehigh University's Integrated Business and Engineering Honors Program, which infuses engineering thinking into the world of entrepreneurship and business. The interdisciplinary four-year program ends with a year-long experiential capstone project usually involving a high-tech startup. This senior project incorporates marketing, strategic planning and competitive analysis, along with product, process and system design issues.

FACILITIES

Housing: Coed dorms, special housing for disabled students, special housing for international students, fraternity/sorority housing, apartments for married students, apartments for single students, Wellness Housing, Theme Housing. **Special Academic Facilities/Equipment:** Art Museum, Zoellner Arts Center, Electron optical labs, civil engineering lab, particle accelerator, electron optical labs. **Computers:** 70% of classrooms, 100% of dorms, 100% of libraries, 100% of dining areas, 75% of student union, 80% of common outdoor areas have wireless network access. Students can register for classes online. Administrative functions (other than registration) can be performed online.

CAMPUS LIFE

Environment: City. **Activities:** Choral groups, concert band, dance, drama/theater, jazz band, literary magazine, marching band, music ensembles, musical theater, pep band, radio station, student government, student newspaper, student-run film society, symphony orchestra, yearbook, Campus Ministries, International Student Organization, Model UN. 18 honor societies, 10 religious organizations. 21 fraternity, 9 sororities. **Athletics (Intercollegiate):** *Men:* baseball, basketball, cross-country, diving, football, golf, lacrosse, soccer, swimming, tennis, track/field (outdoor), track/field (indoor), wrestling. *Women:* basketball, crew/rowing, cross-country, diving, field hockey, golf, lacrosse, soccer, softball, swimming, tennis, track/field (outdoor), track/field (indoor), volleyball. **On-Campus Highlights:** Zoellner Arts Center LU Art Galleries, Campus Square, Taylor Gymnasium, Ulrich Student Center, Goodman Campus. **Environmental Initiatives:** Lehigh's Eco-Rep program, a peer-to-peer education program focused on educating students in residential halls about sustainable lifestyles, has grown from 12 students and 2 residential halls in 2010 to 27 Eco-Reps in 14 Residential Halls and 11 Greek Houses in the 2011-2012 academic year. Sustainability Plan finalized in Spring 2012. A new sustainability-focused excursion, SustainabLEHIGH, was added to Lehigh's pre-orientation program. http://www.lehigh.edu/sustainability/sustainablehigh.html

ADMISSIONS

Freshman Academic Profile: 62.1% in top 10% of high school class, 88.9% in top 25% of high school class, 99.1% in top 50% of high school class. SAT Math middle 50% range 640–740. SAT Critical Reading middle 50% range 590–670. ACT middle 50% range 28–32. Minimum internet-based TOEFL 90. Minimum paper TOEFL 570. **Basis for Candidate Selection:** *Very important factors considered include:* recommendation(s), rigor of secondary school record. *Important factors considered include:* application essay, standardized test scores, character/personal qualities, extracurricular activities, level of applicant's interest, talent/ability, volunteer work. *Other factors considered include:* Class rank, academic GPA, alumni/ae relation, first generation, geographical residence, racial/ethnic status, work experience. **Freshman Admission Requirements:** High school diploma or equivalent is not required. *Academic units required:* 4 English, 3 mathematics, 2 science, (2 science labs), 2 foreign language, 2 social studies, 3 academic electives. **Freshman Admission Statistics:** 11,512 applied, 34% admitted, 33% enrolled. **Transfer Admission Requirements:** High school transcript, college transcript(s), essay or personal statement, statement of good standing from prior institution(s). Minimum college GPA of 3.25 required. **General Admission Information:** Application Fee $70. Early decision application deadline 11/15. Regular application deadline 1/1. Regular notification 4/1. Nonfall registration accepted. Admission may be deferred for a maximum of 1 year. Credit and/or placement offered for CEEB Advanced Placement tests.

COSTS AND FINANCIAL AID

Annual tuition $44,520. Room and board $11,880. Required fees $370. Average book expense $1,000. **Required Forms and Deadlines:** FAFSA, CSS/Financial Aid PROFILE, Noncustodial PROFILE, Business/Farm Supplement. **Notification of Awards:** Applicants will be notified of awards on or about 3/30. **Types of Aid:** *Need-based scholarships/grants:* Federal Pell, SEOG, state scholarships/grants, private scholarships, the school's own gift aid, United Negro College Fund. *Loans:* Subsidized Stafford, Unsubsidized Stafford, PLUS, Federal Perkins, college/university loans from institutional funds. *Student Employment:* Federal Work-Study Program available. Institutional employment available. Off-campus job opportunities are good. **Financial Aid Statistics:** 97% freshmen, 98% undergrads receive need-based scholarship or grant aid. 12% freshmen, 14% undergrads receive non-need-based scholarship or grant aid. 95% freshmen, 95% undergrads receive need-based self-help aid. 5% freshmen, 4% undergrads receive athletic scholarships. 57% freshmen, 59% undergrads receive any aid. 52% undergrads borrow to pay for school. Average cumulative indebtedness $22,025. **Criteria for awarding institutional aid:** *Non-need-based:* academics, art, athletics, leadership, music/drama.

LEMOYNE-OWEN COLLEGE

807 Walker Avenue, Memphis, TN 38126
Phone: 901-942-7302 · **Financial Aid Phone:** 901-942-7313
E-mail: admission@loc.edu · **CEEB Code:** 1403
Fax: 901-942-6233 · **Website:** www.loc.edu · **ACT Code:** 3980

This private school was founded in 1862. It has a 15-acre campus.

RATINGS

Admissions Selectivity Rating: 70   Fire Safety Rating: 71

STUDENTS AND FACULTY

Enrollment: 720. **Student Body:** 0% female, 100% male, 3% out-of-state, 2% international. Asian 0%, African American 98%, Caucasian 0%, Hispanic 0%, Native American <1%
Retention and Graduation: 38% freshmen graduate within 4 years. 49% freshmen graduate within 6 years. **Faculty:** 54 full-time faculty, 80% hold PhDs, 50% are members of minority groups, 89% are women. 85% of classes are taught by teaching assistants.

ACADEMICS

Degrees: bachelor's, post-bachelor's certificate. **Classes:** Most classes have 20–29 students. **Majors with Highest Enrollment:** Education; Business/Commerce. **Special Study Options:** cross-registration, double major, honors program, independent study, internships, student-designed major, study abroad, teacher certification program, Undergrads may take Grad level courses. **Combined degree programs:** BA/MEng, Dual Degree Program in English. **Career services:** Alumni network, alumni services, career/job search classes, career assessment, internships, regional alumni.

FACILITIES

Housing: Coed dorms, men's dorms, women's dorms. 85% of campus accessible to physically disabled. **Special Academic Facilities/Equipment:** Museum/gallery, language lab.

CAMPUS LIFE

Environment: Metropolis. **Activities:** Choral groups, drama/theater, jazz band, music ensembles, student government, student newspaper, yearbook 5 honor societies, 6 religious organizations. 4 fraternities, 3 sororities. **Athletics (Intercollegiate):** *Men:* baseball, basketball, cross-country, tennis. *Women:* basketball, cross-country, softball, tennis, volleyball.

ADMISSIONS

Freshman Academic Profile: 95% from public high schools. Minimum paper TOEFL 475. **Basis for Candidate Selection:** *Very important factors considered include:* standardized test scores. **Freshman Admission Requirements:** High school diploma is required and GED is accepted. **Freshman Admission Statistics:** 1,118 applied, 17% admitted, 63% enrolled. **Transfer Admission Requirements:** college transcript(s), standardized test scores, Minimum college GPA of 2.0 required. Lowest grade transferable C. **General Admission Information:** Application Fee $25. Regular application deadline 6/15. Nonfall registration accepted. Credit and/or placement offered for CEEB Advanced Placement tests.

COSTS AND FINANCIAL AID

Annual tuition $8,250. Required fees $200. Average book expense $700. **Required Forms and Deadlines:** FAFSA. **Types of Aid:** *Need-based scholarships/grants:* United Negro College Fund. *Loans:* Subsidized Stafford, PLUS. *Student Employment:* Federal Work-Study Program available. Institutional employment available. **Financial Aid Statistics:** 0% freshmen, 0% undergrads receive athletic scholarships.

LENOIR-RHYNE COLLEGE

Admissions Office, Hickory, NC 28603
Phone: 828-328-7300
E-mail: admission@lrc.edu · **CEEB Code:** 5365
Fax: 828-328-7378 · **Website:** www.lrc.edu · **ACT Code:** 2941

This private school, affiliated with the Lutheran Church, was founded in 1891. It has a 100-acre campus.

RATINGS

Admissions Selectivity Rating: 71   Fire Safety Rating: 60*

STUDENTS AND FACULTY

Enrollment: 1,358. **Student Body:** 64% female, 36% male, 29% out-of-state, 0% international. Asian 1%, African American 7%, Caucasian 91%, Hispanic 1%, Native American <1%
Retention and Graduation: 80% freshmen return for sophomore year. 40% grads go on to further study within 1 year. 1% grads pursue arts and sciences degrees. 4% grads pursue law degrees. 5% grads pursue business degrees. 4% grads pursue medical degrees. **Faculty:** 107 full-time faculty, 45% are members of minority groups. 0% of classes are taught by teaching assistants.

ACADEMICS

Degrees: bachelor's, certificate, master's. **Special Study Options:** Accelerated program, double major, dual enrollment, English as a Second Language (ESL), honors program, independent study, internships, student-designed major, study abroad, teacher certification program. **Combined degree programs:** BA/MEng. **Disability Services:** Special programs offered to physically disabled students include note-taking services, tutors. **Career services:** alumni services, career/job search classes, career assessment, internships.

FACILITIES

Housing: Coed dorms, special housing for disabled students, men's dorms, women's dorms, fraternity/sorority housing, Honors, Hearing Impaired. 90% of campus accessible to physically disabled. **Special Academic Facilities/Equipment:** Language lab.

CAMPUS LIFE

Environment: Village. **Activities:** Choral groups, concert band, dance, drama/theater, jazz band, music ensembles, musical theater, pep band, radio station, student government, student newspaper, television station, yearbook. 54 registered organizations, 10 honor societies, 6 religious organizations. 4 fraternities, 4 sororities. **Athletics (Intercollegiate):** *Men:* baseball, basketball, cheerleading, cross-country, football, golf, soccer. *Women:* basketball, cheerleading, cross-country, golf, soccer, softball, volleyball. **On-Campus Highlights:** McCrorie Center, Cromer College Center, Shuford Fitness Center, Living and Learning Center, Quad.

ADMISSIONS

Freshman Academic Profile: 90% from public high schools. SAT Math middle 50% range 470-580. SAT Critical Reading middle 50% range 460-570. ACT middle 50% range 17-24. Minimum paper TOEFL 500. **Basis for Candidate Selection:** *Very important factors considered include:* rigor of secondary school record, standardized test scores. *Important factors considered include:* Class rank, interview. *Other factors considered include:* application essay, recommendation(s), character/personal qualities, extracurricular activities, volunteer work, work experience. **Freshman Admission Requirements:** High school diploma is required and GED is accepted. *Academic units required:* 4 English, 3 mathematics, 1 science, (1 science labs), 2 foreign language, 1 social studies, 1 history. **Freshman Admission Statistics:** 915 applied, 85% admitted, 35% enrolled. **Transfer Admission Requirements:** college transcript(s), statement of good standing from prior institution(s). Minimum college GPA of 2.5 required. Lowest grade transferable C. **General Admission Information:** Application Fee $25. Notification on a rolling basis, beginning on or about 9/1. Nonfall registration accepted. Admission may be deferred for a maximum of 1 year. Credit offered for CEEB Advanced Placement tests.

COSTS AND FINANCIAL AID

Annual tuition $12,870. Room and board $4,920. Required fees $486. Average book expense $700. **Required Forms and Deadlines:** FAFSA, Institution's own financial aid form, State aid form. **Types of Aid:** *Need-based scholarships/grants:* Federal Pell, SEOG, state scholarships/grants, the school's own gift aid. *Loans:* Direct Subsidized Stafford, Direct Unsubsidized Stafford, Direct PLUS, Federal Perkins. *Student Employment:* Federal Work-Study Program available. Institutional employment available. Highest amount earned per year from on-campus jobs $1,000. Off-campus job opportunities are excellent. **Financial Aid Statistics:** 0% freshmen receive athletic scholarships. **Criteria for awarding institutional aid:** *Non-need-based:* academics, alumni affiliation, athletics, leadership, minority status, music/drama, religious affiliation, state/district residency.

LESLEY UNIVERSITY

Office of Admissions, Cambridge, MA 2138
Phone: 617-349-8800 · **Financial Aid Phone:** 617-349-8710
E-mail: lcadmissions@lesley.edu · **CEEB Code:** 3483
Fax: 617-349-8810 · **Website:** www.lesley.edu · **ACT Code:** 1850

This private school was founded in 1909. It has a 1-acre campus.

RATINGS

Admissions Selectivity Rating: 81   **Fire Safety Rating:** 85

STUDENTS AND FACULTY

Enrollment: 1,450. **Student Body:** 76% female, 24% male, 56% out-of-state, 2% international (30 countries represented). Asian 4%, African American 3%, Caucasian 72%, Hispanic 8%, Native American <1%
Retention and Graduation: 79% freshmen return for sophomore year. 35% freshmen graduate within 4 years. **Faculty:** 74 full-time faculty, 88% hold PhDs, 57% are members of minority groups, 9% are women. 0% of classes are taught by teaching assistants.

ACADEMICS

Degrees: associate, bachelor's, certificate, diploma, master's, post-bachelor's certificate, post-master's certificate. **Classes:** Most classes have 10–19 students. **Majors with Highest Enrollment:** Elementary Education and Teaching Marketing/Marketing Management. **Special Study Options:** Accelerated program, cross-registration, distance learning, double major, dual enrollment, exchange student program (domestic), honors program, independent study, internships, liberal arts/career combination, student-designed major, study abroad, teacher certification program, Studio courses. **Combined degree programs:** BA/MA, BS/M.Ed. **Disability Services:** Special programs offered to physically disabled students include note-taking services, reader services, tape recorders, tutors. **Career services:** Alumni network, alumni services, career/job search classes, career assessment, internships, regional alumni. Wellesley College funded at least one internship for more than half the class of 2009. This included grants of up $3,500 for what otherwise would have been unpaid internships over the summer.

FACILITIES

Housing: Coed dorms, women's dorms, Special Interest and themed housing. 85% of campus accessible to physically disabled. **Special Academic Facilities/Equipment:** Kresge Center for Teaching Resources and Educational Software Collection, Marran Art Gallery, Porter Exchange Gallery, AIB Main Gallery **Computers:** 100% of classrooms, 100% of libraries, 100% of dining areas,

100% of student union, 20% of common outdoor areas have wireless network access. Students can register for classes online. Administrative functions (other than registration) can be performed online.

CAMPUS LIFE

Environment: Metropolis. **Activities:** Choral groups, dance, drama/theater, literary magazine, musical theater, student government, student newspaper, Campus Ministries, International Student Organization. 25 registered organizations, 2 honor societies, 2 religious organizations. **Athletics (Intercollegiate):** *Men:* basketball, cross-country, soccer, tennis, volleyball. *Women:* basketball, crew/rowing, cross-country, soccer, softball, tennis, volleyball. **On-Campus Highlights:** Student Center, Ludke Library, Porter Exchange Building, Stebbins Fitness Room, Kresge Center for Teaching Resources. **Environmental Initiatives:** The continual enhancement of recycling, waste management and composting programs on campus. The formation of sustainability recommendations for faculty, staff and students. Student groups on campus are involved with and sponsor sustainability events.

ADMISSIONS

Freshman Academic Profile: Average high school GPA 3.02. 10% in top 10% of high school class, 36% in top 25% of high school class, 80% in top 50% of high school class. 83% from public high schools. SAT Math middle 50% range 460-570. SAT Critical Reading middle 50% range 490-600. SAT Writing middle 50% range 490-590. ACT middle 50% range 21-26. Minimum internet-based TOEFL 61. Minimum paper TOEFL 500. **Basis for Candidate Selection:** *Very important factors considered include:* academic GPA, rigor of secondary school record. *Important factors considered include:* Class rank, application essay, recommendation(s), standardized test scores, character/personal qualities, extracurricular activities, interview, talent/ability, volunteer work. *Other factors considered include:* alumni/ae relation, first generation, geographical residence, level of applicant's interest, racial/ethnic status, work experience. **Freshman Admission Requirements:** High school diploma is required and GED is accepted. *Academic units required:* 4 English, 3 mathematics, 3 science, (2 science labs), 0 foreign language, 1 social studies, 1 history, 0 visual/performing arts, 0 computer science, 4 academic electives. **Freshman Admission Statistics:** 2,605 applied, 67% admitted, 18% enrolled. **Transfer Admission Requirements:** High school transcript, college transcript(s), essay or personal statement, statement of good standing from prior institution(s). Minimum college GPA of 2.5 required. Lowest grade transferable C. **General Admission Information:** Application Fee $50. Notification on a rolling basis, beginning on or about 1/15. Nonfall registration accepted. Admission may be deferred for a maximum of 1 year. Credit and/or placement offered for CEEB Advanced Placement tests.

COSTS AND FINANCIAL AID

Annual tuition $24,000. Room and board $14,000. **Required Forms and Deadlines:** FAFSA. **Notification of Awards:** Applicants will be notified of awards on a rolling basis beginning 2/15. **Types of Aid:** *Need-based scholarships/grants:* Federal Pell, SEOG, state scholarships/grants, private scholarships, the school's own gift aid. *Loans:* Direct Subsidized Stafford, Direct Unsubsidized Stafford, Direct PLUS, Federal Perkins, state loans. *Student Employment:* Federal Work-Study Program available. Institutional employment available. Highest amount earned per year from on-campus jobs $1,200. Off-campus job opportunities are excellent. **Financial Aid Statistics:** 99% freshmen, 98% undergrads receive need-based scholarship or grant aid. 8% freshmen, 7% undergrads receive non-need-based scholarship or grant aid. 99% freshmen, 88% undergrads receive need-based self-help aid. 0% freshmen, 0% undergrads receive athletic scholarships. 70% freshmen, 70% undergrads receive any aid. 75% undergrads borrow to pay for school. Average cumulative indebtedness $23,000. **Criteria for awarding institutional aid:** *Non-need-based:* academics, art, leadership, minority status, state/district residency.

LETOURNEAU UNIVERSITY

PO Box 7001, Longview, TX 75607-7001
Phone: 903-233-4300
E-mail: admissions@letu.edu · **CEEB Code:** 6365
Fax: 903-233-4301 · **Website:** www.letu.edu · **ACT Code:** 4120

This private school was founded in 1946. It has a 162-acre campus.

RATINGS

Admissions Selectivity Rating: 89   **Fire Safety Rating:** 60*

STUDENTS AND FACULTY

Enrollment: 2,015. **Student Body:** 46% female, 54% male, 43% out-of-state, 4% international (37 countries represented). Asian 1%, African American 10%, Caucasian 66%, Hispanic 9%, Native American <1%

Retention and Graduation: 83% freshmen return for sophomore year.
Faculty: 90 full-time faculty, 78% hold PhDs, 23% are members of minority groups, 16% are women.

ACADEMICS

Degrees: associate, bachelor's, master's. **Classes:** Most classes have fewer than 10 students. Most lab/discussion sessions have 10–19 students. **Special Study Options:** Accelerated program, cooperative education program, distance learning, double major, dual enrollment, honors program, independent study, internships, study abroad, teacher certification program, weekend college. **Career services:** alumni services, career/job search classes, career assessment, internships.

FACILITIES

Housing: special housing for disabled students, men's dorms, special housing for international students, women's dorms, apartments for married students, apartments for single students, Theme Housing, Residential societies available. **Special Academic Facilities/Equipment:** Longview Citizens Resource Center; R.G. LeTourneau Memorial Museum. **Computers:** Students can register for classes online. Administrative functions (other than registration) can be performed online.

CAMPUS LIFE

Environment: Town. **Activities:** Choral groups, drama/theater, jazz band, literary magazine, music ensembles, musical theater, student government, student newspaper, student-run film society, yearbook, Campus Ministries, International Student Organization. 44 registered organizations, 4 honor societies, 10 religious organizations. **Athletics (Intercollegiate):** *Men:* baseball, basketball, cross-country, golf, soccer, tennis. *Women:* basketball, cross-country, golf, soccer, softball, tennis, volleyball.

ADMISSIONS

Freshman Academic Profile: Average high school GPA 3.59. 32% in top 10% of high school class, 56% in top 25% of high school class, 87% in top 50% of high school class. SAT Math middle 50% range 530-650. SAT Critical Reading middle 50% range 500-660. SAT Writing middle 50% range 470-610. ACT middle 50% range 22-30. **Basis for Candidate Selection:** *Very important factors considered include:* academic GPA, rigor of secondary school record, standardized test scores. *Important factors considered include:* Class rank, application essay, character/personal qualities, religious affiliation/commitment. *Other factors considered include:* recommendation(s), alumni/ae relation, extracurricular activities, first generation, interview, racial/ethnic status, talent/ability, volunteer work. **Freshman Admission Requirements:** High school diploma is required and GED is accepted. *Academic units required:* 4 English, 3 mathematics, 3 science, (3 science labs), 2 social studies, 1 history. **Freshman Admission Statistics:** 1,761 applied, 49% admitted, 42% enrolled. **Transfer Admission Requirements:** college transcript(s), essay or personal statement, Minimum college GPA of 2.0 required. Lowest grade transferable C. **General Admission Information:** Application Fee $25. Regular notification 8/26. Notification on a rolling basis, beginning on or about 9/15. Nonfall registration accepted. Credit and/or placement offered for CEEB Advanced Placement tests.

COSTS AND FINANCIAL AID

Annual tuition $26,390. Room and board $9,300. Required fees $520. Average book expense $1,520. **Required Forms and Deadlines:** FAFSA. **Notification of Awards:** Applicants will be notified of awards on a rolling basis beginning 3/1. **Types of Aid:** *Need-based scholarships/grants:* Federal Pell, SEOG, state scholarships/grants, private scholarships, the school's own gift aid. *Loans:* Subsidized Stafford, Unsubsidized Stafford, PLUS, Federal Perkins, state loans. *Student Employment:* Federal Work-Study Program available. Institutional employment available. Off-campus job opportunities are excellent. **Financial Aid Statistics:** 100% freshmen, 98% undergrads receive need-based scholarship or grant aid. 16% freshmen, 7% undergrads receive non-need-based scholarship or grant aid. 56% freshmen, 52% undergrads receive need-based self-help aid. 0% freshmen, 0% undergrads receive athletic scholarships. 77% undergrads borrow to pay for school. Average cumulative indebtedness $27,446. **Criteria for awarding institutional aid:** *Non-need-based:* academics, leadership.

LEWIS & CLARK COLLEGE

Best 380

0615 SW Palatine Hill Road, Portland, OR 97219-7899
Phone: 503-768-7040 • **Financial Aid Phone:** 503-768-7090
E-mail: admissions@lclark.edu • **CEEB Code:** 4384
Fax: 503-768-7055 • **Website:** www.lclark.edu • **ACT Code:** 3464

This private school was founded in 1867. It has a 137-acre campus.

RATINGS

Admissions Selectivity Rating: 90   **Fire Safety Rating:** 76

STUDENTS AND FACULTY

Enrollment: 2,039. **Student Body:** 61% female, 39% male, 80% out-of-state, 5% international (80 countries represented). Asian 7%, African American 2%, Caucasian 68%, Hispanic 9%, Native American 1%
Retention and Graduation: 85% freshmen return for sophomore year. 71% freshmen graduate within 4 years. 79% freshmen graduate within 6 years. **Faculty:** 239 full-time faculty, 90% hold PhDs, 49% are members of minority groups, 15% are women. 0% of classes are taught by teaching assistants.

ACADEMICS

Degrees: bachelor's, first professional, master's, post-master's certificate. **Classes:** Most classes have 20–29 students. Most lab/discussion sessions have 20–29 students. **Majors with Highest Enrollment:** Psychology; International Relations and Affairs; Biology/Biological Sciences. **Special Study Options:** Accelerated program, cross-registration, double major, dual enrollment, English as a Second Language (ESL), honors program, independent study, internships, student-designed major, study abroad, teacher certification program, Teacher certification is graduate level only. **Honors programs:** Honors are designated by each department **Combined degree programs:** BA/MA, BA/MAT, 4+1 yr Masters Degree and credential. **Disability Services:** Special programs offered to physically disabled students include note-taking services, reader services, tape recorders, tutors. **Career services:** Alumni network, alumni services, career assessment, internships, regional alumni.

FACILITIES

Housing: Coed dorms, women's dorms, Theme Floors, Apartment-style residence halls for upper-class students. 85% of campus accessible to physically disabled. **Special Academic Facilities/Equipment:** Art gallery, observatory, world music room, 85 Rank Casavant organ, renovated greenhouse. **Computers:** 50% of classrooms, 20% of dorms, 100% of libraries, 25% of common outdoor areas have wireless network access. Students can register for classes online. Administrative functions (other than registration) can be performed online.

CAMPUS LIFE

Environment: City. **Activities:** Choral groups, concert band, dance, drama/theater, jazz band, literary magazine, music ensembles, musical theater, radio station, student government, student newspaper, symphony orchestra, television station, yearbook, Campus Ministries, International Student Organization, Model UN. 70 registered organizations, 5 honor societies, 9 religious organizations. **Athletics (Intercollegiate):** *Men:* baseball, basketball, crew/rowing, cross-country, football, golf, swimming, tennis, track/field (outdoor). *Women:* basketball, crew/rowing, cross-country, golf, soccer, softball, swimming, tennis, track/field (outdoor), volleyball. **On-Campus Highlights:** Gallery of Contemporary Art, New residence halls/Maggie's Café, Library, Templeton Student Center, Pamplin Sports Center, Howard Hall, newest academic building. **Environmental Initiatives:** Lewis & Clark provides students, faculty, and staff with a fare-free shuttle bus system that allows access to downtown Portland, local neighborhoods, and retail stores. We installed a 100KW photovoltaic system. Students funds are used to purchase green power. Lewis & Clark established an Environmental Council in the late 1990's that has since been renamed as the Sustainability Council. The trustee investment committee has made a $3 million committment to fund sustainable energy development. Since 1991 Lewis & Clark has invested in energy conservation projects that have resulted in a current annual reduction in use of 4,000,000 kWh of electricity and 230,000 Therms of natural gas with a corresponding decrease in carbon footprint.

ADMISSIONS

Freshman Academic Profile: Average high school GPA 3.91. 38% in top 10% of high school class, 79% in top 25% of high school class, 96% in top 50% of high school class. 76% from public high schools. SAT Math middle 50% range 580-670. SAT Critical Reading middle 50% range 610-710. SAT Writing middle 50% range 590-680. ACT middle 50% range 27-31. Minimum internet-based TOEFL 91. Minimum paper TOEFL 575. **Basis for Candidate Selection:**

Very important factors considered include: academic GPA, rigor of secondary school record, racial/ethnic status. *Important factors considered include:* Class rank, application essay, recommendation(s), standardized test scores, alumni/ae relation, character/personal qualities, extracurricular activities, first generation, talent/ability, volunteer work. *Other factors considered include:* geographical residence, interview, level of applicant's interest, state residency, work experience. **Freshman Admission Requirements:** High school diploma is required and GED is accepted. **Freshman Admission Statistics:** 6,243 applied, 67% admitted, 14% enrolled. **Transfer Admission Requirements:** High school transcript, college transcript(s), essay or personal statement, statement of good standing from prior institution(s). Minimum college GPA of 2.0 required. Lowest grade transferable C. **General Admission Information:** Application Fee $50. Regular application deadline 2/1. Regular notification 4/1. Nonfall registration accepted. Admission may be deferred for a maximum of One year. Credit and/or placement offered for CEEB Advanced Placement tests.

COSTS AND FINANCIAL AID

Annual tuition $43,022. Room and board $11,000. Required fees $360. Average book expense $1,050. **Required Forms and Deadlines:** FAFSA, CSS/Financial Aid PROFILE. **Notification of Awards:** Applicants will be notified of awards on a rolling basis beginning 3/1. **Types of Aid:** *Need-based scholarships/grants:* Federal Pell, SEOG, state scholarships/grants, private scholarships, the school's own gift aid. *Loans:* Direct Subsidized Stafford, Direct Unsubsidized Stafford, Direct PLUS, Subsidized Stafford, Unsubsidized Stafford, PLUS, Federal Perkins. *Student Employment:* Federal Work-Study Program available. Institutional employment available. Highest amount earned per year from on-campus jobs $1,800. Off-campus job opportunities are fair. **Financial Aid Statistics:** 99% freshmen, 99% undergrads receive need-based scholarship or grant aid. 11% freshmen, 9% undergrads receive non-need-based scholarship or grant aid. 91% freshmen, 94% undergrads receive need-based self-help aid. 0% freshmen, 0% undergrads receive athletic scholarships. 92% freshmen, 87% undergrads receive any aid. 56% undergrads borrow to pay for school. Average cumulative indebtedness $23,619. **Criteria for awarding institutional aid:** *Non-need-based:* academics, leadership, music/drama.

See page 1082.

LEWIS-CLARK STATE COLLEGE

500 Eighth Avenue, Lewiston, ID 83501
Phone: 208-792-2210 · **Financial Aid Phone:** 208-792-2224
E-mail: admissions@lcsc.edu · **CEEB Code:** 4385
Fax: 208-792-2876 · **Website:** www.lcsc.edu · **ACT Code:** 920

This public school was founded in 1893. It has a 44-acre campus.

RATINGS

Admissions Selectivity Rating: 70   **Fire Safety Rating:** 71

STUDENTS AND FACULTY

Enrollment: 3,172. **Student Body:** 61% female, 39% male, 20% out-of-state, 3% international (32 countries represented). Asian 1%, African American 1%, Caucasian 80%, Hispanic 5%, Native American 2%
Retention and Graduation: 61% freshmen return for sophomore year. 18% freshmen graduate within 4 years. 31% freshmen graduate within 6 years. 7% grads go on to further study within 1 year. **Faculty:** 159 full-time faculty, 47% hold PhDs, 53% are members of minority groups, 4% are women. 0% of classes are taught by teaching assistants.

ACADEMICS

Degrees: associate, bachelor's, certificate, diploma, terminal associate, transfer associate. **Classes:** Most classes have fewer than 10 students. **Majors with Highest Enrollment:** Elementary Education and Teaching; Registered Nursing/Registered Nurse; Business/Commerce. **Special Study Options:** Accelerated program, cooperative education program, distance learning, double major, dual enrollment, English as a Second Language (ESL), independent study, internships, study abroad, teacher certification program. **Disability Services:** Special programs offered to physically disabled students include note-taking services, reader services, tape recorders, tutors.

FACILITIES

Housing: Coed dorms, apartments for married students, apartments for single students. 95% of campus accessible to physically disabled. **Special Academic Facilities/Equipment:** Museum/art gallery, Media Services. **Computers:** Students can register for classes online. Administrative functions (other than registration) can be performed online.

CAMPUS LIFE

Environment: Town. **Activities:** drama/theater, jazz band, literary magazine, radio station, student government, student newspaper, Campus Ministries, In-

ternational Student Organization. 52 registered organizations, 1 honor society, 3 religious organizations. **Athletics (Intercollegiate):** *Men:* baseball, basketball, cross-country, golf, tennis. *Women:* basketball, cross-country, golf, tennis, volleyball. **On-Campus Highlights:** Information Commons in the Library, Student Union Building, Athletic Center which is under construction, Centennial Mall, Yo Espresso or Jitterz.

ADMISSIONS

Freshman Academic Profile: Average high school GPA 3.13. 5% in top 10% of high school class, 18% in top 25% of high school class, 46% in top 50% of high school class. 99% from public high schools. SAT Math middle 50% range 400-520. SAT Critical Reading middle 50% range 410-510. ACT middle 50% range 17-22. Minimum paper TOEFL 500. **Basis for Candidate Selection:** *Very important factors considered include:* academic GPA, rigor of secondary school record, standardized test scores. **Freshman Admission Requirements:** High school diploma is required and GED is accepted. *Academic units required:* 4 English, 3 mathematics, 3 science, (2 science labs). **Freshman Admission Statistics:** 852 applied, 99% admitted, 61% enrolled. **Transfer Admission Requirements:** college transcript(s), Minimum college GPA of 2.0 required. Lowest grade transferable D. **General Admission Information:** Application Fee $35. Nonfall registration accepted. Admission may be deferred for a maximum of 1 year. Credit and/or placement offered for CEEB Advanced Placement tests.

COSTS AND FINANCIAL AID

Annual in-state tuition $9,132. Room and board $6,194. Required fees $2,724. **Required Forms and Deadlines:** FAFSA. **Notification of Awards:** Applicants will be notified of awards on a rolling basis beginning 4/15. **Types of Aid:** *Need-based scholarships/grants:* Federal Pell, SEOG, state scholarships/grants, private scholarships, the school's own gift aid. *Loans:* Subsidized Stafford, Unsubsidized Stafford, PLUS, Federal Perkins, Federal Nursing. *Student Employment:* Federal Work-Study Program available. Institutional employment available. **Financial Aid Statistics:** 58% freshmen, 66% undergrads receive need-based scholarship or grant aid. 52% freshmen, 24% undergrads receive non-need-based scholarship or grant aid. 73% freshmen, 81% undergrads receive need-based self-help aid. 5% freshmen, 8% undergrads receive athletic scholarships. 85% freshmen, 76% undergrads receive any aid. 61% undergrads borrow to pay for school. **Criteria for awarding institutional aid:** *Non-need-based:* academics, alumni affiliation, art, athletics, leadership, minority status, music/drama.

LEWIS UNIVERSITY

One University Parkway, Romeoville, IL 60446
Phone: 815-836-5250 · **Financial Aid Phone:** 815-836-5263
E-mail: admissions@lewisu.edu · **CEEB Code:** 1404
Fax: 815-836-5002 · **Website:** www.lewisu.edu · **ACT Code:** 1058

This private school, affiliated with the Roman Catholic Church, was founded in 1932. It has a 375-acre campus.

RATINGS

Admissions Selectivity Rating: 83   **Fire Safety Rating:** 96

STUDENTS AND FACULTY

Enrollment: 4,605. **Student Body:** 57% female, 43% male, 6% out-of-state, 1% international (20 countries represented). Asian 3%, African American 7%, Caucasian 66%, Hispanic 18%, Native American <1%
Retention and Graduation: 82% freshmen return for sophomore year. 42% freshmen graduate within 4 years. 62% freshmen graduate within 6 years. **Faculty:** 221 full-time faculty, 74% hold PhDs, 52% are members of minority groups, 13% are women. 0% of classes are taught by teaching assistants.

ACADEMICS

Degrees: associate, bachelor's, certificate, master's, post-master's certificate. **Classes:** Most classes have 10–19 students. Most lab/discussion sessions have 10–19 students. **Majors with Highest Enrollment:** Criminal Justice/Safety Studies; Registered Nursing/Registered Nurse; Biology/Biological Sciences. **Special Study Options:** Accelerated program, distance learning, double major, dual enrollment, English as a Second Language (ESL), exchange student program (domestic), honors program, independent study, internships, liberal arts/career combination, student-designed major, study abroad, teacher certification program. **Honors programs:** Honors Program offers academically motivated students opportunities for active and collaborative learning. Students have the opporuntiy to fulfill many of their general education requirements in a "paired course" arrangement that allows for greater integration of material and content. **Combined degree programs:** BA/MA, MSN-MBA / BS - MBA. **Disability Services:** Special programs offered to physically disabled students include note-taking services, tape recorders, tutors. **Career services:** Alumni network, alumni services, career/job search classes, career assessment, internships, regional alumni. Career services highlights include our Alumni Volunteer Network, which pairs current stduents with professionals active in their field of interest for mentoring and career search guidance.

FACILITIES

Housing: Coed dorms, special housing for disabled students, Theme Housing. 95% of campus accessible to physically disabled. **Special Academic Facilities/Equipment:** Lewis University is located immediately adjacent to the Lewis University airport, and contains an aviation complex, which includes a Boeing 737 located on campus for use by students studying aviation maintenance. Special collections on campus include: Curriculum Collection, Eva White Memorial Aviation Collection, Library of American Civilization (ultrafiche), Library of English Literature (ultrafiche), ERIC fiche, Government Documents (Lewis University has housed a selective Federal Depository since 1952, and possesses a strong collection of the public documents generated during each decennial census), and Canal and Regional History Collection/I and M Canal Archives (one of the largest collections of documents, photographs, and artifacts pertaining to the canal era in the U.S.). **Computers:** 100% of classrooms, 100% of dorms, 100% of libraries, 100% of dining areas, 100% of student union, 100% of common outdoor areas have wireless network access. Students can register for classes online. Administrative functions (other than registration) can be performed online.

CAMPUS LIFE

Environment: Metropolis. **Activities:** Choral groups, dance, drama/theater, jazz band, literary magazine, music ensembles, musical theater, radio station, student government, student newspaper, television station, Campus Ministries, International Student Organization. 45 registered organizations, 10 honor societies, 7 religious organizations. 7 fraternities, 6 sororities. **Athletics (Intercollegiate):** *Men:* baseball, basketball, cheerleading, cross-country, golf, soccer, swimming, tennis, track/field (outdoor), track/field (indoor), volleyball. *Women:* basketball, cheerleading, cross-country, golf, soccer, softball, swimming, tennis, track/field (outdoor), track/field (indoor), volleyball. **On-Campus Highlights:** Harold E. White Aviation Center, Student Recreation and Fitness Center, Philip Lynch Theatre, Student Union/Bookstore, Flyer's Den. **Environmental Initiatives:** The Lewis University Environment and Energy Conservation Council sponsors annual events such as an Earth Day event in spring where we clear out Buckthorn (an invasive plant species) from the nature trail here on campus and the Arbor Day Initiative in which we plant an assortment of native trees back into the University nature trail. Lewis sponsors an annual Come Clean, Go Green Sustainability Contest. One-half of the prize money goes toward the creation and implementation of the winning projects, which are then publicized. The other half of the prize money goes directly to the winner(s). There is an awards ceremony to honor the winning proposals and to distribute prizes. The Illinois Green Governments Coordinating Council has recognized Lewis University for achieving the bronze standard recognition level of sustainability goals in higher education as established by the Illinois Campus Sustainability Compact. The goal of the Illinois Campus Sustainability Compact is to encourage universities and colleges within the state to incorporate sustainability into their campus operations, academic and research programs, student activities and community outreach. Lewis has pledged a commitment to achieve Silver Level.

ADMISSIONS

Freshman Academic Profile: Average high school GPA 3.38. 18% in top 10% of high school class, 44% in top 25% of high school class, 83% in top 50% of high school class. 86% from public high schools. SAT Math middle 50% range 490-570. SAT Critical Reading middle 50% range 500-570. SAT Writing middle 50% range 480-570. ACT middle 50% range 21-25. Minimum internet-based TOEFL 79. Minimum paper TOEFL 550. **Basis for Candidate Selection:** *Very important factors considered include:* academic GPA, rigor of secondary school record, standardized test scores. *Important factors considered include:* application essay. *Other factors considered include:* Class rank, recommendation(s), alumni/ae relation, character/personal qualities, extracurricular activities, first generation, geographical residence, interview, level of applicant's interest, racial/ethnic status, talent/ability, volunteer work, work experience. **Freshman Admission Requirements:** High school diploma is required and GED is accepted. *Academic units required:* 3 English. **Freshman Admission Statistics:** 5,786 applied, 62% admitted, 21% enrolled. **Transfer Admission Requirements:** college transcript(s), Minimum college GPA of 2.0 required. Lowest grade transferable D. **General Admission Information:** Application Fee $40. Notification on a rolling basis, beginning on or about 10/1. Nonfall registration accepted. Admission may be deferred for a maximum of 12 months. Credit and/or placement offered for CEEB Advanced Placement tests.

COSTS AND FINANCIAL AID

Annual tuition $28,940. Room and board $9,930. Required fees $100. Average book expense $1,000. **Required Forms and Deadlines:** FAFSA. **Notification of Awards:** Applicants will be notified of awards on a rolling basis beginning 2/1. **Types of Aid:** *Need-based scholarships/grants:* Federal Pell, SEOG, state

scholarships/grants, private scholarships, the school's own gift aid, Federal Nursing Scholarships. *Loans:* Subsidized Stafford, Unsubsidized Stafford, PLUS, Federal Perkins. *Student Employment:* Federal Work-Study Program available. Institutional employment available. Highest amount earned per year from on-campus jobs $3,000. Off-campus job opportunities are good. **Financial Aid Statistics:** 100% freshmen, 95% undergrads receive need-based scholarship or grant aid. 13% freshmen, 12% undergrads receive non-need-based scholarship or grant aid. 87% freshmen, 89% undergrads receive need-based self-help aid. 3% freshmen, 3% undergrads receive athletic scholarships. 98% freshmen, 80% undergrads receive any aid. 81% undergrads borrow to pay for school. Average cumulative indebtedness $26,833. **Criteria for awarding institutional aid:** *Non-need-based:* academics, alumni affiliation, art, athletics, leadership, music/drama, religious affiliation.

LIBERTY UNIVERSITY

1971 University Blvd, Lynchburg, VA 24515
Phone: 434-582-2000 • **Financial Aid Phone:** 434-582-2270
E-mail: admissions@liberty.edu • **CEEB Code:** 5385
Fax: 800-628-7977 • **Website:** https://www.liberty.edu/ • **ACT Code:** 4364

This private school, affiliated with the Baptist Church, was founded in 1971. It has a 4400-acre campus.

RATINGS

Admissions Selectivity Rating: 89   **Fire Safety Rating:** 76

STUDENTS AND FACULTY

Enrollment: 12,577. **Student Body:** 52% female, 48% male, 60% out-of-state, 6% international (125 countries represented). Asian 1%, African American 6%, Caucasian 67%, Hispanic 2%, Native American <1%
Retention and Graduation: 78% freshmen return for sophomore year. 29% freshmen graduate within 4 years. 53% freshmen graduate within 6 years. **Faculty:** 0% of classes are taught by teaching assistants.

ACADEMICS

Degrees: associate, bachelor's, certificate, doctoral, master's, post-master's certificate, terminal associate. **Classes:** Most classes have 20–29 students. **Majors with Highest Enrollment:** Religion/Religious Studies; Psychology; Business/Commerce. **Special Study Options:** Accelerated program, cooperative education program, distance learning, double major, dual enrollment, English as a Second Language (ESL), external degree program, honors program, independent study, internships, student-designed major, teacher certification program, weekend college. **Honors programs:** An early class registration period, smaller class size (15:1) for general education Honors seminars, and a generous scholarship based on grade point average are just a few of the benefits enjoyed by our Honors students. Once Honors students reach junior status, they petition one Honors course per semester in their desired major field of study. **Disability Services:** Special programs offered to physically disabled students include tutors. **Career services:** career assessment, internships. Career services highlights include https://www.liberty.edu/academics/general/career/index.cfm?PID=6149.

FACILITIES

Housing: special housing for disabled students, men's dorms, women's dorms, apartments for single students. 94% of campus accessible to physically disabled. **Special Academic Facilities/Equipment:** Displays from the Museum of Life and Earth History are located in the Library. The Jerry Falwell Museum located in the main lobby of DeMoss Hall. **Computers:** 90% of classrooms, have wireless network access. Students can register for classes online. Administrative functions (other than registration) can be performed online.

CAMPUS LIFE

Environment: Town. **Activities:** Choral groups, concert band, drama/theater, literary magazine, marching band, music ensembles, musical theater, pep band, radio station, student government, student newspaper, symphony orchestra, television station, yearbook, Campus Ministries. 25 registered organizations, 8 honor societies, 10 religious organizations. **Athletics (Intercollegiate):** *Men:* baseball, basketball, cheerleading, cross-country, football, golf, soccer, tennis, track/field (outdoor), track/field (indoor), wrestling. *Women:* basketball, cheerleading, cross-country, soccer, softball, tennis, track/field (outdoor), track/field (indoor), volleyball. **On-Campus Highlights:** LaHaye Student Center, Bookstore, Hangar (Food Court), ILRC Computer Lab, LaHaye Ice Center (Ice Arena).

ADMISSIONS

Freshman Academic Profile: Average high school GPA 3.39. 18.28% in top 10% of high school class, 42.03% in top 25% of high school class, 72.29% in top

50% of high school class. SAT Math middle 50% range 450-570. SAT Critical Reading middle 50% range 460-590. SAT Writing middle 50% range 450-570. ACT middle 50% range 20-26. Minimum internet-based TOEFL 60. Minimum paper TOEFL 500. **Basis for Candidate Selection:** *Very important factors considered include:* rigor of secondary school record, standardized test scores. *Important factors considered include:* application essay, academic GPA. *Other factors considered include:* Class rank, recommendation(s), character/personal qualities, extracurricular activities, level of applicant's interest, talent/ability. **Freshman Admission Requirements:** High school diploma is required and GED is accepted. **Freshman Admission Statistics:** 29,490 applied, 20% admitted, 46% enrolled. **Transfer Admission Requirements:** High school transcript, college transcript(s), essay or personal statement, statement of good standing from prior institution(s). Minimum college GPA of 2.0 required. Lowest grade transferable C. **General Admission Information:** Application Fee $40. Nonfall registration accepted. Admission may be deferred for a maximum of 12 months. Credit and/or placement offered for CEEB Advanced Placement tests.

COSTS AND FINANCIAL AID

Required Forms and Deadlines: FAFSA, State aid form. **Notification of Awards:** Applicants will be notified of awards on a rolling basis beginning 3/15. **Types of Aid:** *Need-based scholarships/grants:* Federal Pell, SEOG, state scholarships/grants, private scholarships, the school's own gift aid. *Loans:* Subsidized Stafford, Unsubsidized Stafford, PLUS. *Student Employment:* Off-campus job opportunities are good. **Financial Aid Statistics:** 100% freshmen, 98% undergrads receive need-based scholarship or grant aid. 18% freshmen, 17% undergrads receive non-need-based scholarship or grant aid. 71% freshmen, 74% undergrads receive need-based self-help aid. 0% freshmen, 1% undergrads receive athletic scholarships. 95% freshmen, 87% undergrads receive any aid. 66% undergrads borrow to pay for school. Average cumulative indebtedness $17,028. **Criteria for awarding institutional aid:** *Non-need-based:* academics, alumni affiliation, athletics, leadership, music/drama, religious affiliation, state/district residency.

LIFE PACIFIC COLLEGE

1100 Covina Blvd., San Dimas, CA 91773
Phone: 909-599-5433 · **Financial Aid Phone:** 909-599-5433
E-mail: adm@lifepacific.edu
Fax: 909-599-6690 · **Website:** http://www.lifepacific.edu/ • **ACT Code:** 489

This private school, affiliated with the Protestant Church, was founded in 1923. It has a 9-acre campus.

RATINGS

Admissions Selectivity Rating: 72   **Fire Safety Rating:** 71

STUDENTS AND FACULTY

Enrollment: 528. **Student Body:** 46% female, 54% male, 48% out-of-state, 0% international (2 countries represented). Asian 0%, African American 0%, Caucasian 0%, Hispanic 0%, Native American <1% **Retention and Graduation:** 69% freshmen return for sophomore year. 18% freshmen graduate within 4 years. 32% freshmen graduate within 6 years. 48% grads go on to further study within 1 year. **Faculty:** 12 full-time faculty, 17% hold PhDs, 17% are members of minority groups, 8% are women. 0% of classes are taught by teaching assistants.

ACADEMICS

Degrees: associate, bachelor's. **Classes:** Most classes have 10–19 students. Most lab/discussion sessions have 20–29 students. **Special Study Options:** Accelerated program, distance learning, dual enrollment, external degree program, independent study, internships. **Disability Services:** Special programs offered to physically disabled students include note-taking services, tape recorders, tutors. **Career services:** alumni services, career/job search classes, internships. Career services highlights include our service learning program, which is required for all students.

FACILITIES

Housing: men's dorms, women's dorms. 100% of campus accessible to physically disabled. **Special Academic Facilities/Equipment:** New gymnasium and work out facilities; New computer lab; New Student Center; New Music Facilities. **Computers:** Students can register for classes online.

CAMPUS LIFE

Environment: Town. **Activities:** Choral groups, dance, drama/theater, music ensembles, student government, yearbook. **Athletics (Intercollegiate):** *Men:* basketball. *Women:* volleyball. **On-Campus Highlights:** The Cove Student Center, New Gymnasium, New Work-out room, Music Wing (new).

ADMISSIONS

Freshman Academic Profile: Average high school GPA 2.87. 5% in top 10% of high school class, 21% in top 25% of high school class, 38% in top 50% of high school class. SAT Math middle 50% range 410-510. SAT Critical Reading middle 50% range 430-540. ACT middle 50% range 14-23. Minimum paper TOEFL 550. **Basis for Candidate Selection:** *Very important factors considered include:* application essay, academic GPA, recommendation(s), standardized test scores, character/personal qualities, level of applicant's interest, religious affiliation/commitment. *Other factors considered include:* alumni/ae relation, extracurricular activities, talent/ability. **Freshman Admission Requirements:** High school diploma is required and GED is accepted. **Freshman Admission Statistics:** 102 applied, 87% admitted, 70% enrolled. **Transfer Admission Requirements:** college transcript(s), essay or personal statement, statement of good standing from prior institution(s). Minimum college GPA of 2.0 required. Lowest grade transferable C. **General Admission Information:** Application Fee $35. Regular application deadline 6/1. Nonfall registration accepted. Admission may be deferred for a maximum of 1 yr. Credit and/or placement offered for CEEB Advanced Placement tests.

COSTS AND FINANCIAL AID

Annual tuition $9,750. Room and board $5,000. Required fees $350. Average book expense $1,242. **Required Forms and Deadlines:** FAFSA. **Notification of Awards:** Applicants will be notified of awards on a rolling basis beginning 6/1. **Types of Aid:** *Need-based scholarships/grants:* Federal Pell, SEOG, state scholarships/grants, private scholarships, the school's own gift aid. *Loans:* Subsidized Stafford, Unsubsidized Stafford, PLUS. *Student Employment:* Federal Work-Study Program available. Institutional employment available. Off-campus job opportunities are excellent. **Financial Aid Statistics:** 68% freshmen, 78% undergrads receive need-based scholarship or grant aid. 16% freshmen, 4% undergrads receive non-need-based scholarship or grant aid. 70% freshmen, 76% undergrads receive need-based self-help aid. 0% freshmen, 0% undergrads receive athletic scholarships. 70% undergrads borrow to pay for school. **Criteria for awarding institutional aid:** *Non-need-based:* academics, alumni affiliation, leadership, religious affiliation.

LIM COLLEGE

12 East 53rd Street, New York, NY 10022
Phone: 212-752-1530 · **Financial Aid Phone:** 212-752-1530
E-mail: admissions@limcollege.edu · **CEEB Code:** 2380
Fax: 212-750-3432 · **Website:** www.limcollege.edu • **ACT Code:** 4807

This proprietary school was founded in 1939.

RATINGS

Admissions Selectivity Rating: 79   **Fire Safety Rating:** 73

STUDENTS AND FACULTY

Enrollment: 1,308. **Student Body:** 94% female, 6% male, 57% out-of-state, 1% international (13 countries represented). Asian 6%, African American 11%, Caucasian 68%, Hispanic 14%, Native American <1% **Retention and Graduation:** 64% freshmen return for sophomore year. 53% freshmen graduate within 4 years. **Faculty:** 26 full-time faculty, 38% hold PhDs, 46% are members of minority groups, 31% are women. 0% of classes are taught by teaching assistants.

ACADEMICS

Degrees: associate, bachelor's, master's. **Classes:** Most classes have 10–19 students. **Majors with Highest Enrollment:** Marketing/Marketing Management; Fashion Merchandising. **Special Study Options:** cooperative education program, internships, study abroad, 3 credit trip in winter/summer to Europe. **Disability Services:** Special programs offered to physically disabled students include tape recorders, tutors. **Career services:** Alumni network, alumni services, career/job search classes, career assessment, internships. Career services highlights include a 5 week internship between Thanksgiving and Christmas that all first and second year students must participate in. All seniors must participate in a full-semester co-op.

FACILITIES

Housing: Coed dorms. 100% of campus accessible to physically disabled. **Computers:** 100% of classrooms, 100% of dorms, 100% of libraries, 100% of dining areas, 100% of student union, have wireless network access. Students can register for classes online. Administrative functions (other than registration) can be performed online.

CAMPUS LIFE

Environment: Metropolis. **Activities:** student government, yearbook. 12 registered organizations, 1 honor society. **On-Campus Highlights:** Library, Café 45, Cyber Lounge, 1760 Third Ave.

ADMISSIONS

Freshman Academic Profile: Average high school GPA 84.5. 3% in top 10% of high school class, 17% in top 25% of high school class, 55% in top 50% of high school class. 73% from public high schools. SAT Math middle 50% range 420-510. SAT Critical Reading middle 50% range 440-520. SAT Writing middle 50% range 500-520. ACT middle 50% range 19-23. Minimum paper TOEFL 550. **Basis for Candidate Selection:** *Very important factors considered include:* academic GPA, interview, level of applicant's interest. *Important factors considered include:* Class rank, application essay, recommendation(s), rigor of secondary school record, standardized test scores, alumni/ae relation, character/personal qualities, extracurricular activities, talent/ability, volunteer work, work experience. *Other factors considered include:* geographical residence, racial/ethnic status, state residency. **Freshman Admission Requirements:** High school diploma is required and GED is accepted. **Freshman Admission Statistics:** 1,069 applied, 56% admitted, 51% enrolled. **Transfer Admission Requirements:** High school transcript, college transcript(s), essay or personal statement, Minimum college GPA of 2.0 required. Lowest grade transferable D-. **General Admission Information:** Application Fee $40. Notification on a rolling basis, beginning on or about 12/15. Nonfall registration accepted. Admission may be deferred for a maximum of 1 Semester. Credit offered for CEEB Advanced Placement tests.

COSTS AND FINANCIAL AID

Annual tuition $23,070. Room and board $19,850. Required fees $575. Average book expense $900. **Required Forms and Deadlines:** FAFSA, State aid form. **Notification of Awards:** Applicants will be notified of awards on a rolling basis beginning 2/15. **Types of Aid:** *Need-based scholarships/grants:* Federal Pell, SEOG, state scholarships/grants, private scholarships, the school's own gift aid. *Loans:* Direct Subsidized Stafford, Direct Unsubsidized Stafford, Direct PLUS. *Student Employment:* Federal Work-Study Program available. Institutional employment available. Off-campus job opportunities are excellent. **Financial Aid Statistics:** 77% freshmen, 79% undergrads receive need-based scholarship or grant aid. 18% freshmen, 27% undergrads receive non-need-based scholarship or grant aid. 97% freshmen, 95% undergrads receive need-based self-help aid. 0% freshmen, 0% undergrads receive athletic scholarships. 85% freshmen, 85% undergrads receive any aid. 73% undergrads borrow to pay for school. Average cumulative indebtedness $23,618. **Criteria for awarding institutional aid:** *Non-need-based:* academics.

See page 1084.

LIMESTONE COLLEGE

1115 College Drive, Gaffney, SC 29340-3799
Phone: 864-488-4549 · **Financial Aid Phone:** 864-488-8800
E-mail: admiss@limestone.edu · **CEEB Code:** 5366
Fax: 864-487-8706 · **Website:** www.limestone.edu · **ACT Code:** 3862

This private school was founded in 1845. It has a 115-acre campus.

RATINGS

Admissions Selectivity Rating: 80   **Fire Safety Rating:** 73

STUDENTS AND FACULTY

Enrollment: 1,052. **Student Body:** 38% female, 62% male, 42% out-of-state, 9% international. Asian 0%, African American 29%, Caucasian 54%, Hispanic 4%, Native American <1%
Retention and Graduation: 21% freshmen graduate within 4 years. 37% freshmen graduate within 6 years. **Faculty:** 75 full-time faculty, 80% hold PhDs, 51% are members of minority groups, 5% are women. 0% of classes are taught by teaching assistants.

ACADEMICS

Degrees: bachelor's, transfer associate. **Classes:** Most classes have 20–29 students. Most lab/discussion sessions have fewer than 10 students. **Majors with Highest Enrollment:** Business/Managerial Economics; Elementary Education and Teaching; Health and Physical Education/Fitness. **Special Study Options:** Accelerated program, distance learning, double major, honors program, independent study, internships, liberal arts/career combination, student-designed major, teacher certification program. **Honors programs:** The Honors Program was established at Limestone College in 1983 to create a challenging academic environment for gifted and special ability students. **Disability Services:** Special programs offered to physically disabled students include tape recorders, tutors. **Career services:** alumni services, career assessment, Career services highlights include student placement in a local private or public enterprise to gain work-related experience consistent with their field of study.

FACILITIES

Housing: men's dorms, women's dorms, apartments for single students. 90% of campus accessible to physically disabled. **Special Academic Facilities/Equipment:** Computer graphic arts lab; museum of Southern history in Winnie Davis Hall. **Computers:** 20% of classrooms, 20% of dorms, 100% of libraries, 100% of student union, 5% of common outdoor areas have wireless network access. Students can register for classes online. Administrative functions (other than registration) can be performed online.

CAMPUS LIFE

Environment: Town. **Activities:** Choral groups, concert band, drama/theater, jazz band, literary magazine, music ensembles, musical theater, pep band, student government, yearbook, Campus Ministries. 2 religious organizations. **Athletics (Intercollegiate):** *Men:* baseball, basketball, cross-country, golf, lacrosse, soccer, swimming, tennis, track/field (outdoor), volleyball, wrestling. *Women:* basketball, cross-country, field hockey, golf, lacrosse, soccer, softball, swimming, tennis, track/field (outdoor), volleyball. **On-Campus Highlights:** Dixie Lodge, Stephenson Dining Hall, Timken Gym and Pool, Eastwood Library, Curtis Administration Building, The Walt Griffin Physical Education Center, Limestone Learning Center, Winnie Davis Hall of History. **Environmental Initiatives:** Community Garden.

ADMISSIONS

Freshman Academic Profile: Average high school GPA 3.18. 2.75% in top 10% of high school class, 18.68% in top 25% of high school class, 51.37% in top 50% of high school class. 90% from public high schools. SAT Math middle 50% range 480-560. SAT Critical Reading middle 50% range 450-530. Minimum internet-based TOEFL 75. Minimum paper TOEFL 500. **Basis for Candidate Selection:** *Very important factors considered include:* academic GPA, rigor of secondary school record, standardized test scores. *Important factors considered include:* Class rank. *Other factors considered include:* recommendation(s), interview. **Freshman Admission Requirements:** High school diploma is required and GED is accepted. *Academic units required:* 4 English, 3 mathematics, 2 science, (2 science labs), 3 social studies. **Freshman Admission Statistics:** 2,318 applied, 54% admitted, 33% enrolled. **Transfer Admission Requirements:** college transcript(s), statement of good standing from prior institution(s). Minimum college GPA of 2.0 required. Lowest grade transferable C. **General Admission Information:** Application Fee $25. Regular application deadline 8/26. Notification on a rolling basis, beginning on or about 6/1. Nonfall registration accepted. Admission may be deferred for a maximum of 18 months. Credit offered for CEEB Advanced Placement tests.

COSTS AND FINANCIAL AID

Annual tuition $23,000. Room and board $7,800. Average book expense $2,304. **Required Forms and Deadlines:** FAFSA. **Notification of Awards:** Applicants will be notified of awards on a rolling basis beginning 1/15. **Types of Aid:** *Need-based scholarships/grants:* Federal Pell, SEOG, state scholarships/grants, private scholarships, the school's own gift aid. *Loans:* Subsidized Stafford, Unsubsidized Stafford, PLUS, Federal Perkins. *Student Employment:* Federal Work-Study Program available. Institutional employment available. Highest amount earned per year from on-campus jobs $8,300. Off-campus job opportunities are good. **Financial Aid Statistics:** 100% freshmen, 100% undergrads receive need-based scholarship or grant aid. 8% freshmen, 10% undergrads receive non-need-based scholarship or grant aid. 86% freshmen, 85% undergrads receive need-based self-help aid. 12% freshmen, 16% undergrads receive athletic scholarships. 98% freshmen, 98% undergrads receive any aid. 90% undergrads borrow to pay for school. Average cumulative indebtedness $27,173. **Criteria for awarding institutional aid:** *Non-need-based:* academics, art, athletics, job skills, leadership, music/drama, state/district residency.

LINCOLN CHRISTIAN COLLEGE AND SEMINARY

100 Campus View Dr, Lincoln, IL 62656-2167
Phone: 217-732-3168 x:2251 · **Financial Aid Phone:** 217-732-3168
E-mail: coladmis@lccs.edu · **CEEB Code:**
Fax: 217-732-4199 · **Website:** www.lccs.edu · **ACT Code:** 1060

This private school, affiliated with the Church of Christ Church, was founded in 1944. It has a 100-acre campus.

RATINGS

Admissions Selectivity Rating: 78   **Fire Safety Rating:** 76

STUDENTS AND FACULTY

Enrollment: 601. **Student Body:** 51% female, 49% male, 40% out-of-state, 0% international (19 countries represented). Asian 0%, African American 5%, Caucasian 91%, Hispanic 2%, Native American <1%
Retention and Graduation: 17% grads go on to further study within 1 year.

The Princeton Review's Complete Book of Colleges

Faculty: 44 full-time faculty, 45% hold PhDs, 18% are members of minority groups, 5% are women. 0% of classes are taught by teaching assistants.

ACADEMICS

Degrees: associate, bachelor's, certificate, first professional, master's. **Special Study Options:** distance learning, double major, honors program, independent study, internships, study abroad, teacher certification program, weekend college, Teacher preparatory program through University of Illinois at Springfield, Illinois State University, and Greenville College. **Honors programs:** Students with at least sophomore standing and a cumulative grade average of 3.5 or higher may apply for acceptance into an honors degree program. The honors degree requires 5 additional semester hours of study under a mentoring professor and the completion of a capstone project. The additional work may be completed in the area of the student's ministry specialization or in an area of interest outside the specialization. Since the program is funded by memorial gifts, honors degree students do not pay tuition for the additional 5 hours. For students who complet the honors degree requirements, special recognition will be given at the Commencement service, and an honors designation will be included on the academic transcript. **Disability Services:** Special programs offered to physically disabled students include reader services, tape recorders, tutors. Career services highlights include https://secure.lccs.edu/internship/.

FACILITIES

Housing: men's dorms, women's dorms, apartments for married students. 80% of campus accessible to physically disabled. **Computers:** 90% of classrooms, 100% of dorms, 80% of libraries, have wireless network access. Students can register for classes online. Administrative functions (other than registration) can be performed online.

CAMPUS LIFE

Environment: Village. **Activities:** Choral groups, drama/theater, music ensembles, musical theater, student government, student newspaper, Campus Ministries, International Student Organization. 7 registered organizations. **Athletics (Intercollegiate):** *Men:* baseball, basketball, soccer. *Women:* basketball, softball, volleyball. **On-Campus Highlights:** The Warehouse, The Coffee Shop.

ADMISSIONS

Freshman Academic Profile: 19% in top 10% of high school class, 45% in top 25% of high school class, 76% in top 50% of high school class. ACT middle 50% range 19-25. Minimum internet-based TOEFL 75. Minimum paper TOEFL 550. **Basis for Candidate Selection:** *Very important factors considered include:* application essay, rigor of secondary school record, standardized test scores, level of applicant's interest, religious affiliation/commitment, state residency. *Important factors considered include:* Class rank, academic GPA, alumni/ae relation, character/personal qualities, extracurricular activities, geographical residence, racial/ethnic status, volunteer work. *Other factors considered include:* recommendation(s), interview, talent/ability, work experience. **Freshman Admission Requirements:** High school diploma is required and GED is accepted. **Freshman Admission Statistics:** 195 applied, 84% admitted, 65% enrolled. **Transfer Admission Requirements:** High school transcript, college transcript(s), essay or personal statement, Minimum college GPA of 2.0 required. Lowest grade transferable 2. **General Admission Information:** Application Fee $25. Nonfall registration accepted. Admission may be deferred for a maximum of 1 semester. Credit offered for CEEB Advanced Placement tests.

COSTS AND FINANCIAL AID

Annual tuition $11,790. Room and board $5,355. **Required Forms and Deadlines:** FAFSA. **Notification of Awards:** Applicants will be notified of awards on a rolling basis beginning 3/1. **Types of Aid:** *Need-based scholarships/grants:* Federal Pell, SEOG, state scholarships/grants. *Loans:* Subsidized Stafford, Unsubsidized Stafford, PLUS, Federal Perkins, college/university loans from institutional funds. *Student Employment:* Federal Work-Study Program available. Institutional employment available. Off-campus job opportunities are good. **Financial Aid Statistics:** 55% freshmen, 64% undergrads receive need-based scholarship or grant aid. 84% freshmen, 78% undergrads receive non-need-based scholarship or grant aid. 66% freshmen, 71% undergrads receive need-based self-help aid. 0% freshmen, 0% undergrads receive athletic scholarships. 80% freshmen, 80% undergrads receive any aid. 71% undergrads borrow to pay for school. Average cumulative indebtedness $17,625. **Criteria for awarding institutional aid:** *Non-need-based:* academics.

LINCOLN COLLEGE

300 Keokuk St, Lincoln, IL 62656
Phone: 800-569-0556
E-mail: admission@lincolncollege.com
Fax: 217-732-7715 • **Website:** www.lincolncollege.edu • **ACT Code:** 1062

This private school was founded in 1865. It has a 60-acre campus.

RATINGS

Admissions Selectivity Rating: 60* **Fire Safety Rating:** 67

STUDENTS AND FACULTY

Faculty: 0% of classes are taught by teaching assistants.

ACADEMICS

Degrees: associate, transfer associate. **Disability Services:** Special programs offered to physically disabled students include tape recorders, tutors.

FACILITIES

Housing: 90% of campus accessible to physically disabled. **Computers:** Students can register for classes online. Administrative functions (other than registration) can be performed online.

CAMPUS LIFE

Environment: Village. **Activities:** 10 registered organizations, 1 honor society. **Athletics (Intercollegiate):** *Men:* baseball, basketball, cheerleading, cross-country, diving, golf, soccer, swimming, wrestling. *Women:* basketball, cheerleading, cross-country, diving, golf, soccer, softball, swimming, volleyball. **On-Campus Highlights:** Meyer-Evans Student Center, Library-Museum, Heritage Resident Halls, Dooley Hall, University Hall, Johnston Center for Performing Arts.

ADMISSIONS

Freshman Academic Profile: 80% from public high schools. Minimum paper TOEFL 480. **General Admission Information:** Placement offered for CEEB Advanced Placement tests.

COSTS AND FINANCIAL AID

Student Employment: Federal Work-Study Program available. Institutional employment available. Highest amount earned per year from on-campus jobs $1,500. Off-campus job opportunities are fair. **Financial Aid Statistics:** 92% freshmen, 92% undergrads receive any aid.

LINCOLN MEMORIAL UNIVERSITY

6965 Cumberland Gap Parkway, Harrogate, TN 37752
Phone: 423-869-6280 • **Financial Aid Phone:** 423-869-6465
E-mail: admissions@lmunet.edu • **CEEB Code:** 1408
Fax: 423-869-6250 • **Website:** www.lmunet.edu • **ACT Code:** 3982

This private school was founded in 1897. It has a 1000-acre campus.

RATINGS

Admissions Selectivity Rating: 76 **Fire Safety Rating:** 60*

STUDENTS AND FACULTY

Enrollment: 1,749. **Student Body:** 73% female, 27% male, 36% out-of-state, 2% international (27 countries represented). Asian 1%, African American 4%, Caucasian 80%, Hispanic 2%, Native American <1%
Retention and Graduation: 66% freshmen return for sophomore year.
Faculty: 191 full-time faculty, 65% hold PhDs, 50% are members of minority groups, 5% are women. 0% of classes are taught by teaching assistants.

ACADEMICS

Degrees: associate, bachelor's, master's, post-bachelor's certificate, post-master's certificate. **Classes:** Most classes have fewer than 10 students. Most lab/discussion sessions have 10–19 students. **Majors with Highest Enrollment:** Athletic Training/Trainer; Biology/Biological Sciences. **Special Study Options:** Accelerated program, distance learning, double major, dual enrollment, English as a Second Language (ESL), internships, teacher certification program. **Career services:** alumni services.

FACILITIES

Housing: Coed dorms, special housing for disabled students, men's dorms, women's dorms, apartments for married students, apartments for single students. 60% of campus accessible to physically disabled. **Special Academic Facilities/Equipment:** Civil War museum, including Abraham Lincoln memorabilia collection of over 6,000 books, paintings, and manuscripts.

CAMPUS LIFE

Environment: Rural. **Activities:** Choral groups, dance, drama/theater, literary magazine, music ensembles, pep band, radio station, student government, television station, yearbook, Campus Ministries, International Student Organization. 26 registered organizations, 5 honor societies, 3 religious organizations. 3 fraternities, 3 sororities. **Athletics (Intercollegiate):** *Men:* baseball, basketball, cross-country, golf, soccer, tennis. *Women:* basketball, cross-country, golf, soccer, softball, tennis, volleyball.

ADMISSIONS

Freshman Academic Profile: Average high school GPA 3.44. 90% from public high schools. SAT Math middle 50% range 430-560. SAT Critical Reading middle 50% range 420-550. ACT middle 50% range 20-25. Minimum paper TOEFL 500. **Basis for Candidate Selection:** *Very important factors considered include:* academic GPA, rigor of secondary school record, standardized test scores. *Important factors considered include:* Class rank, alumni/ae relation, character/personal qualities. *Other factors considered include:* extracurricular activities, first generation, racial/ethnic status, religious affiliation/commitment, volunteer work. **Freshman Admission Requirements:** High school diploma is required and GED is accepted. *Academic units required:* 4 English, 3 mathematics, 2 science, 2 foreign language, 1 social studies, 1 history, 1 visual/performing arts. **Freshman Admission Statistics:** 984 applied, 65% admitted, 39% enrolled. **Transfer Admission Requirements:** High school transcript, college transcript(s), standardized test scores, Minimum college GPA of 2.0 required. Lowest grade transferable C. **General Admission Information:** Application Fee $25. Notification on a rolling basis, beginning on or about 9/1. Nonfall registration accepted. Credit offered for CEEB Advanced Placement tests.

COSTS AND FINANCIAL AID

Annual tuition $18,240. Room and board $6,480. Required fees $500. Average book expense $1,250. **Required Forms and Deadlines:** FAFSA. **Notification of Awards:** Applicants will be notified of awards on a rolling basis beginning 4/15. **Types of Aid:** *Need-based scholarships/grants:* Federal Pell, SEOG, state scholarships/grants, private scholarships, the school's own gift aid. *Loans:* Subsidized Stafford, Unsubsidized Stafford, PLUS, Federal Perkins. *Student Employment:* Federal Work-Study Program available. Highest amount earned per year from on-campus jobs $1,500. Off-campus job opportunities are fair. **Financial Aid Statistics:** 100% freshmen, 97% undergrads receive need-based scholarship or grant aid. 17% freshmen, 9% undergrads receive non-need-based scholarship or grant aid. 42% freshmen, 59% undergrads receive need-based self-help aid. 2% freshmen, 1% undergrads receive athletic scholarships. 60% undergrads borrow to pay for school. Average cumulative indebtedness $22,439. **Criteria for awarding institutional aid:** *Non-need-based:* academics, alumni affiliation, art, athletics, leadership, music/drama.

LINCOLN UNIVERSITY (CA)

401 15th Street, Oakland, CA 94612
Phone: 510-628-8010 · **Financial Aid Phone:** 510-628-8023
E-mail: admissions@lincolnuca.edu
Fax: 510-628-8012 · **Website:** www.lincolnuca.edu

This private school was founded in 1919.

RATINGS

Admissions Selectivity Rating: 60*   **Fire Safety Rating:** 60*

STUDENTS AND FACULTY

Enrollment: 91. **Student Body:** 57% female, 43% male,
Faculty: 11 full-time faculty, 82% hold PhDs, 9% are members of minority groups.

ACADEMICS

Degrees: associate, bachelor's, certificate, master's. **Majors with Highest Enrollment:** Education; Bible/Biblical Studies; Youth Ministry. **Special Study Options:** cross-registration, double major, English as a Second Language (ESL), internships, student-designed major. **Career services:** Alumni network, internships.

FACILITIES

Housing: Universal Student Housing Placement.

CAMPUS LIFE

Environment: Metropolis. **Activities:** student government.

ADMISSIONS

Freshman Academic Profile: Minimum paper TOEFL 500. **Basis for Candidate Selection:** *Very important factors considered include:* rigor of

secondary school record. *Important factors considered include:* academic GPA. *Other factors considered include:* Class rank, standardized test scores. **Freshman Admission Requirements:** High school diploma is required and GED is accepted. **Freshman Admission Statistics:** 130 applied, 82% admitted, 40% enrolled. **Transfer Admission Requirements:** college transcript(s), Minimum college GPA of 2.0 required. Lowest grade transferable C. **General Admission Information:** Application Fee $75. Regular application deadline 8/15. Nonfall registration accepted. Admission may be deferred for a maximum of 3 semester.

COSTS AND FINANCIAL AID

Average book expense $400. **Types of Aid:** *Need-based scholarships/grants:* Federal Pell.

LINCOLN UNIVERSITY (MO)

820 Chestnut Street, Jefferson City, MO 65101
Phone: 573-681-5599 · **Financial Aid Phone:** 573-681-6156
E-mail: enroll@lincolnu.edu
Fax: 573-681-5889 · **Website:** www.lincolnu.edu • **ACT Code:** 2322

This public school was founded in 1866. It has a 165-acre campus.

RATINGS

Admissions Selectivity Rating: 74   **Fire Safety Rating:** 99

STUDENTS AND FACULTY

Enrollment: 2,377. **Student Body:** 56% female, 44% male, 15% out-of-state, 2% international (16 countries represented). Asian 0%, African American 49%, Caucasian 38%, Hispanic 2%, Native American <1%
Retention and Graduation: 64% freshmen return for sophomore year. 9% freshmen graduate within 4 years. 25% freshmen graduate within 6 years.
Faculty: 115 full-time faculty, 48% are members of minority groups, 20% are women.

ACADEMICS

Degrees: associate, bachelor's, master's, post-master's certificate, terminal associate, transfer associate. **Classes:** Most classes have 20–29 students. **Majors with Highest Enrollment:** Business Administration and Management; Criminal Justice/Law Enforcement Administration; Registered Nursing/Registered Nurse. **Special Study Options:** Accelerated program, distance learning, double major, dual enrollment, exchange student program (domestic), honors program, independent study, internships, study abroad, teacher certification program, Senior Citizen Program; Learning in Retirement, Inc.; Intersession courses. **Honors programs:** Lincoln University offers a 24-credit-hour Honors Program which features small classes, unique academic challenges, individual attention from Honors faculty, and association with other like-minded students. An Honors student has opportunities to compete for summer mentorships, work closely with a faculty member on a research or creative project; to do sustained research or creative work leading to a thesis in the student's major; and to present his/her work at regional, national, and international conferences. These students also qualify for Honors housing, certain restricted courses, and other activities. **Disability Services:** Special programs offered to physically disabled students include note-taking services, reader services, tape recorders, tutors. **Career services:** alumni services, career assessment, internships.

FACILITIES

Housing: Coed dorms, men's dorms, women's dorms, Wellness Housing, Honors Student Housing. 100% of campus accessible to physically disabled. **Special Academic Facilities/Equipment:** University Archives/Ethnic Studies Center, Media Center, Student Support Services, Center for Academic Enrichment, Agriculture and Extension Information, Center Education Curriculum Library. **Computers:** 100% of classrooms, 100% of dorms, 100% of libraries, 100% of dining areas, 100% of student union, have wireless network access. Students can register for classes online. Administrative functions (other than registration) can be performed online.

CAMPUS LIFE

Environment: Town. **Activities:** Choral groups, concert band, dance, drama/theater, jazz band, literary magazine, marching band, music ensembles, pep band, radio station, student newspaper, television station, yearbook, Campus Ministries, International Student Organization. 24 registered organizations, 6 honor societies, 2 religious organizations. 4 fraternities, 2 sororities. **Athletics (Intercollegiate):** *Men:* baseball, basketball, football, golf, track/field (outdoor). *Women:* basketball, cheerleading, cross-country, golf, softball, tennis, track/field (outdoor). **On-Campus Highlights:** Clifford G. Scruggs University Center (SUC), Inman E. Page Library, Stamper Hall (Business and Economics), Richardson Fine Arts Center, Dwight T. Reed Stadium, University Farms used for agricultural research include: Busby Research Farm (273 acres);

Carver Research Farm (173 acres); and Freeman Research Farm (199 acres). **Environmental Initiatives:** Lincoln University Composting Facility built to divert cafeteria food waste from landfills and convert it to soil amendment. Campus-wide recycling program. Environmental Health & Safety Management provides resources and services to ensure the proper management and disposal of hazardous materials around campus.

ADMISSIONS

Freshman Academic Profile: Average high school GPA 2.65. 5% in top 10% of high school class, 17% in top 25% of high school class, 48% in top 50% of high school class. SAT Math middle 50% range 335–460. SAT Critical Reading middle 50% range 345–430. ACT middle 50% range 15–21. Minimum internet-based TOEFL 61. Minimum paper TOEFL 500. **Basis for Candidate Selection:** *Other factors considered include:* academic GPA, state residency. **Freshman Admission Requirements:** High school diploma is required and GED is accepted. **Freshman Admission Statistics:** 3,940 applied, 54% admitted, 25% enrolled. **Transfer Admission Requirements:** college transcript(s), Minimum college GPA of 2.0 required. Lowest grade transferable C. **General Admission Information:** Application Fee $20. Regular application deadline 7/15. Nonfall registration accepted. Credit and/or placement offered for CEEB Advanced Placement tests.

COSTS AND FINANCIAL AID

Required Forms and Deadlines: FAFSA, Institution's own financial aid form. **Notification of Awards:** Applicants will be notified of awards on a rolling basis beginning 3/15. **Types of Aid:** *Need-based scholarships/grants:* Federal Pell, SEOG, state scholarships/grants, private scholarships, the school's own gift aid. *Loans:* Subsidized Stafford, Unsubsidized Stafford, PLUS. *Student Employment:* Federal Work-Study Program available. Institutional employment available. Off-campus job opportunities are fair. **Financial Aid Statistics:** 94% freshmen, 90% undergrads receive need-based scholarship or grant aid. 1% freshmen, 2% undergrads receive non-need-based scholarship or grant aid. 91% freshmen, 90% undergrads receive need-based self-help aid. 9% freshmen, 10% undergrads receive athletic scholarships. 93% freshmen, 88% undergrads receive any aid. 73% undergrads borrow to pay for school. Average cumulative indebtedness $30,541. **Criteria for awarding institutional aid:** *Non-need-based:* academics, art, athletics, job skills, leadership, minority status, music/drama, state/district residency.

THE LINCOLN UNIVERSITY (PA)

1570 Balitmore Pike, Lincoln University, PA 19352
Phone: 484-365-7206 · **Financial Aid Phone:** 800-561-2606
E-mail: admiss@lincoln.edu · **CEEB Code:** 2367
Fax: 484-365-8109 · **Website:** www.lincoln.edu · **ACT Code:** 3614

This public school was founded in 1854. It has a 422-acre campus.

RATINGS

Admissions Selectivity Rating: 75   **Fire Safety Rating:** 70

STUDENTS AND FACULTY

Enrollment: 1,583. **Student Body:** 61% female, 39% male, 57% out-of-state, 4% international (28 countries represented). Asian 0%, African American 81%, Caucasian 2%, Hispanic 2%, Native American <1%
Retention and Graduation: 23% freshmen graduate within 4 years. 20% grads go on to further study within 1 year. **Faculty:** 91 full-time faculty, 86% hold PhDs, 38% are members of minority groups, 59% are women. 0% of classes are taught by teaching assistants.

ACADEMICS

Degrees: bachelor's, master's. **Classes:** Most classes have 20–29 students. Most lab/discussion sessions have 10–19 students. **Majors with Highest Enrollment:** Criminal Justice/Safety Studies; Human Services; Biology/Biological Sciences. **Special Study Options:** double major, exchange student program (domestic), honors program, independent study, internships, study abroad, teacher certification program, 3-2 in advanced science/engineering with Drexel University, Pennsylvania State University, Howard University, University of Delaware, Temple University, Widener University, and New Jersey Institute of Technology. **Combined degree programs:** 2-2 nursing prog with West Chester U. **Disability Services:** Special programs offered to physically disabled students include reader services, tutors. **Career services:** alumni services, internships.

FACILITIES

Housing: Coed dorms, men's dorms, women's dorms, apartments for single students. 90% of campus accessible to physically disabled. **Special Academic Facilities/Equipment:** African museum, fine arts center, hall for life sciences, learning resource center. **Computers:**

CAMPUS LIFE

Environment: Rural. **Activities:** Choral groups, dance, drama/theater, jazz band, music ensembles, radio station, student government, student newspaper, television station, yearbook. 30 registered organizations, 9 honor societies, 4 fraternities, 3 sororities. **Athletics (Intercollegiate):** *Men:* baseball, basketball, cross-country, soccer, tennis, track/field (outdoor), track/field (indoor). *Women:* basketball, cross-country, soccer, tennis, track/field (outdoor), track/field (indoor), volleyball. **On-Campus Highlights:** Langston Hughes Memorial Library, Thurgood Marshall Living and Learning Center, John Miller Dickey Hall, Student Union Building, Fredrick Douglass Memorial statue area.

ADMISSIONS

Freshman Academic Profile: Average high school GPA 2.86. SAT Math middle 50% range 390–470. SAT Critical Reading middle 50% range 382–470. SAT Writing middle 50% range 360–450. ACT middle 50% range 16–21. Minimum paper TOEFL 500. **Basis for Candidate Selection:** *Very important factors considered include:* Class rank, rigor of secondary school record. *Important factors considered include:* academic GPA, recommendation(s), standardized test scores, talent/ability. *Other factors considered include:* application essay, alumni/ae relation, character/personal qualities, extracurricular activities, first generation, geographical residence, interview, level of applicant's interest, religious affiliation/commitment, state residency, volunteer work, work experience. **Freshman Admission Requirements:** High school diploma is required and GED is accepted. *Academic units required:* 4 English, 3 mathematics, 3 science, 3 social studies, 5 academic electives, 3 arts or humanities, and 1 health and physical education is required. **Freshman Admission Statistics:** 2,793 applied, 50% admitted, 23% enrolled. **Transfer Admission Requirements:** college transcript(s), essay or personal statement, statement of good standing from prior institution(s). Minimum college GPA of 2.0 required. Lowest grade transferable C. **General Admission Information:** Application Fee $20. Notification on a rolling basis, beginning on or about 2/15. Nonfall registration accepted. Admission may be deferred for a maximum of 1 year. Credit offered for CEEB Advanced Placement tests.

COSTS AND FINANCIAL AID

Annual in-state tuition $7,160. Annual out-of-state tuition $11,836. Room and board $8,686. Required fees $3,782. Average book expense $1,520. **Required Forms and Deadlines:** FAFSA. **Notification of Awards:** Applicants will be notified of awards on a rolling basis beginning 4/1. **Types of Aid:** *Need-based scholarships/grants:* Federal Pell, SEOG, state scholarships/grants, private scholarships, the school's own gift aid, United Negro College Fund. *Loans:* Subsidized Stafford, Unsubsidized Stafford, PLUS, Federal Perkins. *Student Employment:* Federal Work-Study Program available. Institutional employment available. Highest amount earned per year from on-campus jobs $3,500. Off-campus job opportunities are fair. **Financial Aid Statistics:** 0% freshmen, 0% undergrads receive athletic scholarships. 99% freshmen, 93% undergrads receive any aid. 91% undergrads borrow to pay for school. Average cumulative indebtedness $11,445. **Criteria for awarding institutional aid:** *Non-need-based:* academics, alumni affiliation, leadership, music/drama.

LINDENWOOD UNIVERSITY

209 South Kingshighway, Saint Charles, MO 63301-1695
Phone: 314-949-4949
E-mail: admissions@lindenwood.edu · **CEEB Code:** 6367
Fax: 314-949-4989 · **Website:** www.lindenwood.edu · **ACT Code:** 2324

This private school, affiliated with the Presbyterian Church, was founded in 1827. It has a 172-acre campus.

RATINGS

Admissions Selectivity Rating: 83   **Fire Safety Rating:** 60*

STUDENTS AND FACULTY

Enrollment: 6,330. **Student Body:** 56% female, 44% male, 20% out-of-state, 10% international. Asian 1%, African American 11%, Caucasian 62%, Hispanic 2%, Native American <1%
Retention and Graduation: 66% freshmen return for sophomore year. 26% freshmen graduate within 4 years. 43% freshmen graduate within 6 years. 20% grads go on to further study within 1 year. 8% grads pursue arts and sciences degrees. 1% grads pursue law degrees. 10% grads pursue business degrees. 1% grads pursue medical degrees. **Faculty:** 190 full-time faculty, 65% hold PhDs, 40% are members of minority groups, 8% are women. 0% of classes are taught by teaching assistants.

ACADEMICS

Degrees: bachelor's, certificate, master's, post-bachelor's certificate, post-master's certificate. **Classes:** Most classes have 10–19 students. Most lab/discussion sessions have 20–29 students. **Special Study Options:** Accelerated program, cross-registration, double major, dual enrollment, English as a Second Language (ESL), honors program, independent study, internships, student-designed major, study abroad, teacher certification program. **Disability Services:** Special programs offered to physically disabled students include reader services, tutors. **Career services:** alumni services, career assessment, internships.

FACILITIES

Housing: men's dorms, women's dorms, apartments for married students, apartments for single students. **Special Academic Facilities/Equipment:** University archives. Daniel Boone Campus

CAMPUS LIFE

Activities: Choral groups, concert band, dance, drama/theater, jazz band, literary magazine, marching band, music ensembles, musical theater, pep band, radio station, student government, student newspaper, symphony orchestra, television station, Campus Ministries, International Student Organization. 72 registered organizations, 8 honor societies, 13 religious organizations. 1 fraternity, 1 sorority. **Athletics (Intercollegiate):** *Men:* baseball, basketball, cheerleading, cross-country, diving, football, golf, ice hockey, lacrosse, riflery, soccer, swimming, tennis, track/field (outdoor), track/field (indoor), volleyball, water polo, wrestling. *Women:* basketball, cheerleading, cross-country, diving, field hockey, golf, ice hockey, lacrosse, riflery, soccer, softball, swimming, tennis, track/field (outdoor), track/field (indoor), volleyball, water polo. **Environmental Initiatives:** Paper recycling; Lighting.

ADMISSIONS

Freshman Academic Profile: Average high school GPA 3.12. 10% in top 10% of high school class, 30% in top 25% of high school class, 62% in top 50% of high school class. 75% from public high schools. SAT Math middle 50% range 480-560. SAT Critical Reading middle 50% range 410-490. ACT middle 50% range 20-24. Minimum paper TOEFL 500. **Basis for Candidate Selection:** *Very important factors considered include:* academic GPA, standardized test scores. *Important factors considered include:* Class rank, rigor of secondary school record, character/personal qualities, extracurricular activities, interview, talent/ability. *Other factors considered include:* application essay, recommendation(s), alumni/ae relation, first generation, level of applicant's interest, volunteer work. **Freshman Admission Requirements:** High school diploma is required and GED is accepted. **Freshman Admission Statistics:** 4,020 applied, 40% admitted, 69% enrolled. **Transfer Admission Requirements:** college transcript(s), Minimum college GPA of 2.0 required. Lowest grade transferable D. **General Admission Information:** Application Fee $30. Nonfall registration accepted. Admission may be deferred for a maximum of Eval Indiviudally. Credit and/or placement offered for CEEB Advanced Placement tests.

COSTS AND FINANCIAL AID

Annual tuition $12,960. Room and board $6,700. Required fees $300. **Required Forms and Deadlines:** FAFSA. *Types of Aid: Need-based scholarships/grants:* Federal Pell, SEOG, state scholarships/grants, private scholarships, the school's own gift aid. *Loans:* Subsidized Stafford, Unsubsidized Stafford, PLUS, Federal Perkins. *Student Employment:* Federal Work-Study Program available. Institutional employment available. Off-campus job opportunities are good. **Financial Aid Statistics:** 67% freshmen, 67% undergrads receive need-based scholarship or grant aid. 26% freshmen, 30% undergrads receive non-need-based scholarship or grant aid. 91% freshmen, 93% undergrads receive need-based self-help aid. 0% freshmen, 0% undergrads receive athletic scholarships. **Criteria for awarding institutional aid:** *Non-need-based:* academics, alumni affiliation, art, job skills, leadership, music/drama.

LINDSEY WILSON COLLEGE

210 Lindsey Wilson Street, Columbia, KY 42728
Phone: 800-264-0138
E-mail: admissions@lindsey.edu • **CEEB Code:** 1409
Fax: 270-384-8591 • **Website:** www.lindsey.edu • **ACT Code:** 1522

This private school, affiliated with the Methodist Church, was founded in 1903. It has a 43-acre campus.

RATINGS

Admissions Selectivity Rating: 63   **Fire Safety Rating:** 60*

STUDENTS AND FACULTY

Enrollment: 1,335. **Student Body:** 6% out-of-state.
Retention and Graduation: 49% freshmen return for sophomore year.

ACADEMICS

Degrees: associate, bachelor's, master's. **Majors with Highest Enrollment:** Elementary Education and Teaching; Biology; Social Sciences. **Special Study**

Options: cooperative education program, English as a Second Language (ESL), internships, study abroad. **Disability Services:** Special programs offered to physically disabled students include reader services, tutors. **Career services:** alumni services, career assessment, internships.

FACILITIES

Housing: men's dorms, women's dorms, apartments for single students. **Computers:** Students can register for classes online. Administrative functions (other than registration) can be performed online.

CAMPUS LIFE

Environment: Rural. **Activities:** Choral groups, literary magazine, student government, student newspaper, yearbook. 28 registered organizations. **Athletics (Intercollegiate):** *Men:* baseball, basketball, cross-country, golf, soccer, tennis, track/field (outdoor). *Women:* basketball, cross-country, golf, soccer, softball, tennis, track/field (outdoor), volleyball.

ADMISSIONS

Freshman Academic Profile: Minimum paper TOEFL 490. **Freshman Admission Requirements:** High school diploma is required and GED is accepted. **Freshman Admission Statistics:** 1,335 applied, 57% admitted, 55% enrolled. **Transfer Admission Requirements:** college transcript(s), standardized test scores, statement of good standing from prior institution(s). Lowest grade transferable D. **General Admission Information:** Nonfall registration accepted. Placement offered for CEEB Advanced Placement tests.

COSTS AND FINANCIAL AID

Annual tuition $12,456. Average book expense $350. **Required Forms and Deadlines:** FAFSA, Institution's own financial aid form, State aid form. **Types of Aid:** *Need-based scholarships/grants:* Federal Pell, SEOG, state scholarships/grants, private scholarships, the school's own gift aid. *Loans:* Subsidized Stafford, PLUS, Federal Perkins, college/university loans from institutional funds. *Student Employment:* Federal Work-Study Program available. Institutional employment available. Off-campus job opportunities are good.

LINFIELD COLLEGE

900 South East Baker Street, McMinnville, OR 97128-6894
Phone: 503-883-2213 • **Financial Aid Phone:** 503-883-2269
E-mail: admission@linfield.edu • **CEEB Code:** 4387
Fax: 503-883-2472 • **Website:** www.linfield.edu • **ACT Code:** 3466

This private school, affiliated with the American Baptist Church, was founded in 1858. It has a 193-acre campus.

RATINGS

Admissions Selectivity Rating: 82   **Fire Safety Rating:** 97

STUDENTS AND FACULTY

Enrollment: 1,643. **Student Body:** 61% female, 39% male, 52% out-of-state, 4% international (25 countries represented). Asian 6%, African American 2%, Caucasian 64%, Hispanic 10%, Native American 1%
Retention and Graduation: 88% freshmen return for sophomore year. 61% freshmen graduate within 4 years. 69% freshmen graduate within 6 years. 22% grads go on to further study within 1 year. 5% grads pursue arts and sciences degrees. 2% grads pursue law degrees. 10% grads pursue business degrees. 1% grads pursue medical degrees. **Faculty:** 116 full-time faculty, 95% hold PhDs, 51% are members of minority groups, 10% are women. 0% of classes are taught by teaching assistants.

ACADEMICS

Degrees: bachelor's. **Classes:** Most classes have 10–19 students. **Majors with Highest Enrollment:** Elementary Education and Teaching; Kinesiology and Exercise Science; Psychology. **Special Study Options:** cross-registration, distance learning, double major, English as a Second Language (ESL), external degree program, independent study, internships, liberal arts/career combination, student-designed major, study abroad, teacher certification program, Unique January Term courses, widespread participation in off-campus international study. **Disability Services:** Special programs offered to physically disabled students include note-taking services, reader services, tape recorders, tutors. **Career services:** Alumni network, alumni services, career/job search classes, internships, regional alumni.

FACILITIES

Housing: Coed dorms, special housing for disabled students, men's dorms, women's dorms, fraternity/sorority housing, apartments for single students, Wellness Housing. 80% of campus accessible to physically disabled. **Special Academic Facilities/Equipment:** New library, art gallery, anthropology museum, language classroom with murals, environmental field station, undergraduate research institute, electron microscope. **Computers:** 90% of classrooms,

90% of dorms, 100% of libraries, have wireless network access. Students can register for classes online. Administrative functions (other than registration) can be performed online.

CAMPUS LIFE

Environment: Town. **Activities:** Choral groups, concert band, dance, drama/theater, jazz band, literary magazine, music ensembles, musical theater, opera, pep band, radio station, student government, student newspaper, symphony orchestra, Campus Ministries, International Student Organization, Model UN. 41 registered organizations, 18 honor societies, 5 religious organizations. 4 fraternities, 4 sororities. **Athletics (Intercollegiate):** *Men:* baseball, basketball, cross-country, football, golf, soccer, swimming, tennis, track/field (outdoor). *Women:* basketball, cross-country, golf, lacrosse, soccer, softball, swimming, tennis, track/field (outdoor), volleyball. **On-Campus Highlights:** Nicholson Library, Modern language rooms (Walker Hall, 3rd floor), Elkington and Terrell Halls, Food services and coffee shop, Athletic complex. **Environmental Initiatives:** Signatory on ACUPCC; Established sustainability office; Completed part I of carbon footprint survey, Climate Action Plan 2010 & GHG Reports 2007 & 2010.

ADMISSIONS

Freshman Academic Profile: Average high school GPA 3.65. 27% in top 10% of high school class, 56% in top 25% of high school class, 94% in top 50% of high school class. 90% from public high schools. SAT Math middle 50% range 480-600. SAT Critical Reading middle 50% range 480-600. SAT Writing middle 50% range 460-580. ACT middle 50% range 21-26. Minimum internet-based TOEFL 80. Minimum paper TOEFL 550. **Basis for Candidate Selection:** *Very important factors considered include:* academic GPA, rigor of secondary school record, standardized test scores. *Important factors considered include:* Class rank, application essay, recommendation(s). *Other factors considered include:* alumni/ae relation, character/personal qualities, extracurricular activities, first generation, geographical residence, level of applicant's interest, racial/ethnic status, talent/ability, volunteer work, work experience. **Freshman Admission Requirements:** High school diploma is required and GED is accepted. **Freshman Admission Statistics:** 2,054 applied, 94% admitted, 24% enrolled. **Transfer Admission Requirements:** college transcript(s), essay or personal statement, Lowest grade transferable C. **General Admission Information:** Application Fee $40. Regular notification 4/1. Nonfall registration accepted. Admission may be deferred for a maximum of 1 YEAR. Credit offered for CEEB Advanced Placement tests.

COSTS AND FINANCIAL AID

Annual tuition $37,000. Room and board $10,330. Required fees $346. Average book expense $750. **Required Forms and Deadlines:** FAFSA. **Notification of Awards:** Applicants will be notified of awards on or about 4/1. **Types of Aid:** *Need-based scholarships/grants:* Federal Pell, SEOG, state scholarships/grants, private scholarships, the school's own gift aid. *Loans:* Direct Subsidized Stafford, Direct Unsubsidized Stafford, Direct PLUS, Federal Perkins, private loans from multiple lenders. *Student Employment:* Federal Work-Study Program available. Institutional employment available. Highest amount earned per year from on-campus jobs $2,250. Off-campus job opportunities are fair. **Financial Aid Statistics:** 84% freshmen, 82% undergrads receive need-based scholarship or grant aid. 85% freshmen, 87% undergrads receive non-need-based scholarship or grant aid. 80% freshmen, 84% undergrads receive need-based self-help aid. 0% freshmen, 0% undergrads receive athletic scholarships. 92% freshmen, 97% undergrads receive any aid. 70% undergrads borrow to pay for school. Average cumulative indebtedness $25,384. **Criteria for awarding institutional aid:** *Non-need-based:* academics, minority status, music/drama.

LIPSCOMB UNIVERSITY

One University Park Dr., Nashville, TN 37204-3951
Phone: 615-966-1776 · **Financial Aid Phone:** 615-966-1791
E-mail: admissions@lipscomb.edu · **CEEB Code:** 1161
Fax: 615-966-1804 · **Website:** http://www.lipscomb.edu · **ACT Code:** 3956

This private school, affiliated with the Church of Christ Church, was founded in 1891. It has a 65-acre campus.

RATINGS

Admissions Selectivity Rating: 88   **Fire Safety Rating:** 96

STUDENTS AND FACULTY

Enrollment: 2,875. **Student Body:** 61% female, 39% male, 34% out-of-state, 2% international (39 countries represented). Asian 3%, African American 7%, Caucasian 77%, Hispanic 6%, Native American <1%
Retention and Graduation: 45% freshmen graduate within 4 years. 30% grads go on to further study within 1 year. **Faculty:** 196 full-time faculty, 84%

hold PhDs, 40% are members of minority groups, 5% are women. 0% of classes are taught by teaching assistants.

ACADEMICS

Degrees: bachelor's, first professional, master's, post-bachelor's certificate. **Classes:** Most classes have 10–19 students. Most lab/discussion sessions have 20–29 students. **Majors with Highest Enrollment:** Biology/Biological Sciences; Business Administration and Management; Registered Nursing/Registered Nurse. **Special Study Options:** cross-registration, distance learning, double major, dual enrollment, honors program, independent study, internships, study abroad, teacher certification program, weekend college. **Disability Services:** Special programs offered to physically disabled students include note-taking services, reader services, tape recorders, tutors. **Career services:** Alumni network, alumni services, career/job search classes, career assessment, internships.

FACILITIES

Housing: men's dorms, women's dormsOut-of-town undergraduates required to live on campus except for seniors, students over 21, and married students. 100% of campus accessible to physically disabled. **Special Academic Facilities/Equipment:** On-campus elementary, middle, and secondary schools. **Computers:** 100% of classrooms, 100% of dorms, 100% of libraries, 100% of dining areas, 100% of student union, 100% of common outdoor areas have wireless network access. Students can register for classes online. Administrative functions (other than registration) can be performed online.

CAMPUS LIFE

Environment: Metropolis. **Activities:** Choral groups, concert band, drama/theater, jazz band, literary magazine, marching band, music ensembles, musical theater, pep band, radio station, student government, student newspaper, yearbook, Campus Ministries, International Student Organization. 65 registered organizations. **Athletics (Intercollegiate):** *Men:* baseball, basketball, cross-country, golf, soccer, tennis, track/field (outdoor). *Women:* basketball, cheerleading, cross-country, soccer, softball, tennis, track/field (outdoor), track/field (indoor), volleyball. **On-Campus Highlights:** Student Center, SAC —Student Activity Center, Allen Arena, Willard Collins Alumni Auditorium, Bison Square. **Environmental Initiatives:** Internal Sustainability Practices: Geothermal heating and cooling in all new building and rennovation since 2005 (currently three buildings); hybrid cars for VP's; a green housekeeping program. Established SE region's first SE Sustainability Academic Program: New Institute for Sustainable Practice, TN's first green MBA, TN's first sustainability undergrad degree and TN's first sustainability minor. Since 2007, Leader in State and Local Dialogue and Awareness on Sustainabilty: Hosted Tennessee's first two state wide conferences on sustainability policy and sponsored TN's first five green business summits and expos with international sustainability speakers (Dr. Brian Nattrass of Natural Step; Gary Hirshberg, CEO Stonyfield Farms; Joel Makower of Greenbiz.com; L. Hunter Lovins formerly of Rocky Mtn Institute; Don Mosely, Walmart Sustainable Facilities; Tom Szaky of Terracyle and the Biomimicry Institute's Janine Benyus.

ADMISSIONS

Freshman Academic Profile: Average high school GPA 3.55. 25% in top 10% of high school class, 51% in top 25% of high school class, 78% in top 50% of high school class. 70% from public high schools. SAT Math middle 50% range 518-620. SAT Critical Reading middle 50% range 510-640. ACT middle 50% range 23-29. Minimum internet-based TOEFL 80. Minimum paper TOEFL 550. **Basis for Candidate Selection:** *Very important factors considered include:* Class rank, standardized test scores, interview. *Important factors considered include:* academic GPA, recommendation(s), rigor of secondary school record, character/personal qualities. *Other factors considered include:* extracurricular activities, first generation, talent/ability, volunteer work, work experience. **Freshman Admission Requirements:** High school diploma is required and GED is accepted. *Academic units required:* 4 English, 2 mathematics, 2 science, 2 foreign language, 2 social studies, 2 academic electives. **Freshman Admission Statistics:** 3,699 applied, 56% admitted, 31% enrolled. **Transfer Admission Requirements:** college transcript(s), interview, statement of good standing from prior institution(s). Minimum college GPA of 2.0 required. Lowest grade transferable C. **General Admission Information:** Application Fee $25. Nonfall registration accepted. Credit and/or placement offered for CEEB Advanced Placement tests.

COSTS AND FINANCIAL AID

Annual tuition $22,978. Room and board $9,224. Required fees $1,676. Average book expense $1,500. **Required Forms and Deadlines:** FAFSA. **Notification of Awards:** Applicants will be notified of awards on a rolling basis beginning 2/15. **Types of Aid:** *Need-based scholarships/grants:* Federal Pell, SEOG, state scholarships/grants, private scholarships, the school's own gift aid. *Loans:* Subsidized Stafford, Unsubsidized Stafford, PLUS, Federal Perkins, Federal Nursing, alternative. **Financial Aid Statistics:** 36% freshmen, 33% undergrads receive need-based scholarship or grant aid. 99% freshmen, 87% undergrads receive non-need-based scholarship or grant aid. 62% freshmen, 61% undergrads receive need-based self-help aid. 3% freshmen, 3% undergrads receive athletic scholarships. 100% freshmen, 75% undergrads receive any aid. 61% undergrads borrow to pay for school. Average cumulative indebtedness $25,805. **Criteria** for awarding institutional aid: *Non-need-based:* academics, alumni affiliation, art, athletics, leadership, minority status, music/drama, religious affiliation, state/district residency.

LIVINGSTONE COLLEGE

701 West Monroe Street, Salisbury, NC 28144-5213
Phone: 704-216-6001 · **Financial Aid Phone:** 707-216-6273
E-mail: admissions@livingstone.edu
Fax: 704-216-6215 · **Website:** www.livingstone.edu

This private school, affiliated with the African Methodist Episcopal Church, was founded in 1879. It has a 272-acre campus.

RATINGS
Admissions Selectivity Rating: 70   **Fire Safety Rating:** 65

STUDENTS AND FACULTY
Enrollment: 907. **Student Body:** 43% female, 57% male, 1% international (5 countries represented). Asian 0%, African American 67%, Caucasian 1%, Hispanic 0%, Native American <1%
Retention and Graduation: 61% freshmen return for sophomore year. 50% grads go on to further study within 1 year. 25% grads pursue arts and sciences degrees. 5% grads pursue law degrees. 15% grads pursue business degrees. 5% grads pursue medical degrees. **Faculty:** 54 full-time faculty, 50% hold PhDs, 44% are members of minority groups, 33% are women. 0% of classes are taught by teaching assistants.

ACADEMICS
Degrees: bachelor's. **Classes:** Most classes have fewer than 10 students. Most lab/discussion sessions have 10–19 students. **Majors with Highest Enrollment:** Computer and Information Sciences; Criminal Justice/Safety Studies; Business Administration and Management. **Special Study Options:** Accelerated program, cross-registration, double major, independent study, internships, teacher certification program, Community Service.

FACILITIES
Housing: special housing for disabled students, men's dorms, special housing for international students, women's dorms, apartments for married students, apartments for single students. 90% of campus accessible to physically disabled. **Special Academic Facilities/Equipment:** Heritage Hall; Poets and Dreamers Garden; NASA SEMAA Lab; and the Elizabeth Koontz Center. **Computers:** Students can register for classes online. Administrative functions (other than registration) can be performed online.

CAMPUS LIFE
Environment: Town. **Activities:** Choral groups, concert band, dance, drama/theater, jazz band, marching band, music ensembles, musical theater, pep band, radio station, student government, student-run film society, yearbook. 16 registered organizations, 4 honor societies, 2 religious organizations. 4 fraternities, 4 sororities. **Athletics (Intercollegiate):** *Men:* basketball, cross-country, football, track/field (outdoor). *Women:* basketball, bowling, cheerleading, cross-country, softball, tennis, track/field (outdoor), volleyball.

ADMISSIONS
Freshman Academic Profile: SAT Math middle 50% range 320-430. SAT Critical Reading middle 50% range 323-420. SAT Writing middle 50% range 320-400. ACT middle 50% range 12-16. Minimum paper TOEFL 500. **Basis for Candidate Selection:** *Important factors considered include:* academic GPA, recommendation(s). *Other factors considered include:* Class rank, application essay, rigor of secondary school record, alumni/ae relation, character/personal qualities, extracurricular activities, first generation, geographical residence, interview, level of applicant's interest, state residency, talent/ability, volunteer work, work experience. **Freshman Admission Requirements:** High school diploma is required and GED is accepted. *Academic units required:* 4 English, 3 mathematics, 2 science, 2 foreign language, 2 social studies, 1 history. **Freshman Admission Statistics:** 1,587 applied, 58% admitted, 28% enrolled. **Transfer Admission Requirements:** college transcript(s), statement of good standing from prior institution(s). Minimum college GPA of 2.0 required. Lowest grade transferable C. **General Admission Information:** Application Fee $25. Nonfall registration accepted. Credit and/or placement offered for CEEB Advanced Placement tests.

COSTS AND FINANCIAL AID
Required Forms and Deadlines: FAFSA, Institution's own financial aid form, State aid form. **Types of Aid:** *Loans:* Subsidized Stafford, PLUS. *Student Employment:* Highest amount earned per year from on-campus jobs $1,200. **Financial Aid Statistics:** 94% freshmen, 96% undergrads receive need-based scholarship or grant aid. 8% freshmen, 6% undergrads receive non-need-based

scholarship or grant aid. 74% freshmen, 85% undergrads receive need-based self-help aid. 0% freshmen, 0% undergrads receive athletic scholarships. 97% undergrads borrow to pay for school.

LOCK HAVEN UNIVERSITY OF PENNSYLVANIA

LHU Office of Admissions, Lock Haven, PA 17745
Phone: 570-484-2027
E-mail: admissions@lhup.edu · **CEEB Code:** 2654
Fax: 570-484-2201 · **Website:** www.lhup.edu · **ACT Code:** 3708

This public school was founded in 1870. It has a 175-acre campus.

RATINGS
Admissions Selectivity Rating: 71   **Fire Safety Rating:** 62

STUDENTS AND FACULTY
Enrollment: 4,448. **Student Body:** 56% female, 44% male, 6% out-of-state, 0% international (39 countries represented). Asian 1%, African American 9%, Caucasian 85%, Hispanic 2%, Native American <1%
Retention and Graduation: 28% freshmen graduate within 4 years. **Faculty:** 210 full-time faculty, 81% hold PhDs, 50% are members of minority groups, 15% are women. 0% of classes are taught by teaching assistants.

ACADEMICS
Degrees: associate, bachelor's, master's. **Classes:** Most classes have 20–29 students. Most lab/discussion sessions have 20–29 students. **Majors with Highest Enrollment:** Elementary Education and Teaching; Health and Physical Education/Fitness; Health Professions and Related Clinical Sciences. **Special Study Options:** cross-registration, distance learning, double major, dual enrollment, honors program, independent study, internships, student-designed major, study abroad, teacher certification program. **Honors programs:** The University Honors Program provides students and faculty opportunities for creative intellectual engagement through a mix of special curricular and co-curricular opportunities. Students may apply for entry as a first-year freshman or after completing 1–4 semesters of college-level work. Entry as a first-year freshman may be either directly into the University Honors or through the First Year Excellence Program. Students successfully completing the First Year Excellence Program receive certificate recognition. Students completing the University Honors Program receive recognition on their transcript, on their diploma and at commencement. Students in both the First Year Excellence and University Honors programs must participate in co-curricular activities and community service in addition to their curriculum. Engaging activity groups and Speaker Series allow students in the Honors Program to bond together and learn from each other, creating a community of both friends and scholars. **Disability Services:** Special programs offered to physically disabled students include note-taking services, reader services, tape recorders, tutors. **Career services:** Alumni network, alumni services, career/job search classes, career assessment, internships, regional alumni.

FACILITIES
Housing: Coed dorms, apartments for single students. 98% of campus accessible to physically disabled. **Special Academic Facilities/Equipment:** Planetarium, Sloan Art Gallery, Library Archives. **Computers:** Students can register for classes online. Administrative functions (other than registration) can be performed online. Undergraduates are required to own a computer.

CAMPUS LIFE
Environment: Village. **Activities:** Choral groups, concert band, dance, drama/theater, jazz band, literary magazine, marching band, music ensembles, musical theater, pep band, radio station, student government, student newspaper, symphony orchestra, television station, yearbook, Campus Ministries, International Student Organization. 96 registered organizations, 10 honor societies, 7 religious organizations. 6 fraternities, 4 sororities. **Athletics (Intercollegiate):** *Men:* baseball, basketball, football, soccer, track/field (outdoor), track/field (indoor), wrestling. *Women:* basketball, field hockey, lacrosse, soccer, softball, swimming, track/field (outdoor), track/field (indoor), volleyball. **On-Campus Highlights:** Student Recreation Center, Parsons Union Building, Library, Residence Halls, Bentley Dining Hall.

ADMISSIONS
Freshman Academic Profile: Average high school GPA 3.26. 9% in top 10% of high school class, 30% in top 25% of high school class, 61% in top 50% of high school class. SAT Math middle 50% range 430-530. SAT Critical Reading middle 50% range 420-520. SAT Writing middle 50% range 390-490. ACT middle 50% range 16-22. Minimum paper TOEFL 550. **Basis for Candidate Selection:** *Very important factors considered include:* Class rank, academic GPA, rigor of secondary school record, character/personal qualities, talent/ability. *Important factors considered include:* standardized test scores, racial/ethnic

status. *Other factors considered include:* application essay, recommendation(s), extracurricular activities, first generation, interview, level of applicant's interest, volunteer work, work experience. **Freshman Admission Requirements:** High school diploma is required and GED is accepted. *Academic units required:* 4 English, 3 mathematics, 3 science, (2 science labs), 0 foreign language, 2 social studies, 2 history. **Freshman Admission Statistics:** 3,436 applied, 93% admitted, 29% enrolled. **Transfer Admission Requirements:** college transcript(s), statement of good standing from prior institution(s). Minimum college GPA of 2.0 required. Lowest grade transferable C. **General Admission Information:** Application Fee $25. Notification on a rolling basis, beginning on or about 10/1. Nonfall registration accepted. Admission may be deferred for a maximum of 1 year. Credit and/or placement offered for CEEB Advanced Placement tests.

COSTS AND FINANCIAL AID

Annual out-of-state tuition $15,050. Room and board $8,752. Required fees $2,456. Average book expense $1,313. **Required Forms and Deadlines:** FAFSA, State aid form. **Notification of Awards:** Applicants will be notified of awards on a rolling basis beginning 4/1. **Types of Aid:** *Need-based scholarships/ grants:* Federal Pell, SEOG, state scholarships/grants, private scholarships, United Negro College Fund. *Loans:* Subsidized Stafford, Unsubsidized Stafford, PLUS, Federal Perkins, college/university loans from institutional funds. *Student Employment:* Federal Work-Study Program available. Institutional employment available. Off-campus job opportunities are good. **Financial Aid Statistics:** 78% freshmen, 87% undergrads receive need-based scholarship or grant aid. 21% freshmen, 12% undergrads receive non-need-based scholarship or grant aid. 87% freshmen, 90% undergrads receive need-based self-help aid. 6% freshmen, 4% undergrads receive athletic scholarships. 82% undergrads borrow to pay for school. Average cumulative indebtedness $25,879. **Criteria for awarding institutional aid:** *Non-need-based:* academics, art, athletics, leadership, minority status, music/drama, state/district residency.

LOMA LINDA UNIVERSITY

Office of Admissions, Loma Linda, CA 92350
Phone: 909-824-4599
Fax: 909-824-4291 • **Website:** http://www.llu.edu/

This private school, affiliated with the Seventh Day Adventist Church, was founded in 1905.

RATINGS

Admissions Selectivity Rating: 60*   **Fire Safety Rating:** 60*

STUDENTS AND FACULTY

Enrollment: 1,129. **Student Body:** (80 countries represented).

ACADEMICS

Degrees: associate, bachelor's, certificate, master's, post-bachelor's certificate. **Special Study Options:** distance learning, double major.

FACILITIES

Housing: Coed dorms, men's dorms, women's dorms, apartments for single students.

CAMPUS LIFE

Environment: Village. **Activities:** student government, student newspaper, yearbook. 1 honor society, 1 religious organization.

ADMISSIONS

Basis for Candidate Selection: *Very important factors considered include:* application essay, recommendation(s), character/personal qualities, interview, religious affiliation/commitment. *Important factors considered include:* talent/ ability, volunteer work, work experience. *Other factors considered include:* alumni/ae relation, extracurricular activities. **Freshman Admission Requirements:** High school diploma is required and GED is accepted. **Transfer Admission Requirements:** High school transcript, college transcript(s), essay or personal statement, interview, Minimum college GPA of 2.0 required. Lowest grade transferable c. **General Admission Information:** Application Fee $50. Nonfall registration not accepted. Admission may be deferred for a maximum of 1.

COSTS AND FINANCIAL AID

Types of Aid: *Loans:* Subsidized Stafford, PLUS.

LONGWOOD UNIVERSITY

Admissions Office, Farmville, VA 23909
Phone: 434-395-2060 • **Financial Aid Phone:** 800-281-4677
E-mail: admissions@longwood.edu • **CEEB Code:** 5368
Fax: 434-395-2332 • **Website:** www.whylongwood.com • **ACT Code:** 4366

This public school was founded in 1839. It has a 160-acre campus.

RATINGS

Admissions Selectivity Rating: 77   **Fire Safety Rating:** 82

STUDENTS AND FACULTY

Enrollment: 4,185. **Student Body:** 66% female, 34% male, 3% out-of-state, 1% international (46 countries represented). Asian 1%, African American 7%, Caucasian 81%, Hispanic 4%, Native American <1%
Retention and Graduation: 79% freshmen return for sophomore year. 40% freshmen graduate within 4 years. **Faculty:** 222 full-time faculty, 85% hold PhDs, 48% are members of minority groups, 8% are women. 0% of classes are taught by teaching assistants.

ACADEMICS

Degrees: bachelor's, master's. **Classes:** Most classes have 20–29 students. Most lab/discussion sessions have 20–29 students. **Majors with Highest Enrollment:** Elementary Education and Teaching; Psychology; Business/Commerce. **Special Study Options:** Accelerated program, cross-registration, distance learning, double major, dual enrollment, English as a Second Language (ESL), honors program, independent study, internships, study abroad, teacher certification program. **Honors programs:** The Longwood University Honors Program is designed to meet the needs of academically gifted and talented undergraduate students. Challenging courses with high academic standards enable students to expand their intellectual and creative horizons. The Honors Program focuses on the exchange of ideas and the enrichment of students' educational and cultural experiences. Learning takes place not only in the classroom, but also through cultural events, conferences, field trips, and study abroad. In keeping with the University's mission, the Longwood Honors Program strives to develop citizens who are committed to using their learning to provide service to their local communities as well as to the larger national and global communities. The concept of linking learning with the practice of citizenship is the distinctive feature of our Program. **Combined degree programs:** BA/MA, Special Education BA/MS and BS/MS. **Disability Services:** Special programs offered to physically disabled students include note-taking services, reader services, tape recorders, tutors. **Career services:** career/job search classes, career assessment, internships. Career services highlights include a requirement that students must complete either an internship, study abroad program, or work on a research project to graduate.

FACILITIES

Housing: Coed dorms, special housing for disabled students, women's dorms, fraternity/sorority housing, apartments for single students, Honor Student Housing. 100% of campus accessible to physically disabled. **Special Academic Facilities/Equipment:** Longwood Center for the Visual Arts. **Computers:** 100% of classrooms, 100% of libraries, 100% of dining areas, 100% of student union, have wireless network access. Students can register for classes online. Administrative functions (other than registration) can be performed online. Undergraduates are required to own a computer.

CAMPUS LIFE

Environment: Village. **Activities:** Choral groups, concert band, dance, drama/ theater, jazz band, literary magazine, music ensembles, pep band, radio station, student government, student newspaper, yearbook, Campus Ministries, International Student Organization. 129 registered organizations, 17 honor societies, 11 religious organization. 9 fraternities, 12 sororities. **Athletics (Intercollegiate):** *Men:* baseball, basketball, cheerleading, cross-country, golf, soccer, tennis. *Women:* basketball, cheerleading, cross-country, field hockey, golf, lacrosse, soccer, softball, tennis. **On-Campus Highlights:** Brock Commons, Lankford Student Union, Health and Fitness Center, Greenwood Library, Dorrill Dining Hall, Science Building.

ADMISSIONS

Freshman Academic Profile: Average high school GPA 3.39. 12% in top 10% of high school class, 39% in top 25% of high school class, 79% in top 50% of high school class. 92% from public high schools. SAT Math middle 50% range 470-560. SAT Critical Reading middle 50% range 480-570. ACT middle 50% range 20-24. Minimum internet-based TOEFL 79. Minimum paper TOEFL 550. **Basis for Candidate Selection:** *Very important factors considered include:* application essay, academic GPA, rigor of secondary school record, standardized test scores. *Important factors considered include:* Class rank, alumni/ae relation, character/personal qualities, extracurricular activities, first generation, geographical residence, racial/ethnic status, talent/ability, volunteer work. *Other factors considered include:* recommendation(s), state residency. **Freshman Admission Requirements:** High school diploma is required and GED is accepted. *Academic units required:* 4 English, 3 mathematics, 3 science, (2 science labs), 2 foreign language, 2 social studies, 2 history, 1 visual/performing arts. **Freshman Admission Statistics:** 4,166 applied, 78% admitted, 32% enrolled. **Transfer Admission Requirements:** High school transcript, college transcript(s), essay or personal statement, Minimum college GPA of 2.50 required. Lowest grade transferable C-. **General Admission Information:** Application Fee $40. Notification on a rolling basis, beginning on or about 1/15. Nonfall registration accepted. Admission may be deferred for a maximum of 1 year. Credit offered for CEEB Advanced Placement tests.

COSTS AND FINANCIAL AID
Annual in-state tuition $7,800. Annual out-of-state tuition $24,210. Room and board $9,584. Required fees $4,890. Average book expense $1,000. **Required Forms and Deadlines:** FAFSA. **Notification of Awards:** Applicants will be notified of awards on or about 4/1. **Types of Aid:** *Need-based scholarships/grants:* Federal Pell, SEOG, state scholarships/grants, private scholarships, the school's own gift aid. *Loans:* Direct Subsidized Stafford, Direct Unsubsidized Stafford, Direct PLUS, Federal Perkins. *Student Employment:* Federal Work-Study Program available. Institutional employment available. Off-campus job opportunities are good. **Financial Aid Statistics:** 85% freshmen, 79% undergrads receive need-based scholarship or grant aid. 2% freshmen, 2% undergrads receive non-need-based scholarship or grant aid. 85% freshmen, 84% undergrads receive need-based self-help aid. 3% freshmen, 3% undergrads receive athletic scholarships. 60% freshmen receive any aid. 64% undergrads borrow to pay for school. Average cumulative indebtedness $23,218. **Criteria for awarding institutional aid:** *Non-need-based:* academics, alumni affiliation, art, athletics, leadership, music/drama, state/district residency.

LORAS COLLEGE

1450 Alta Vista, Dubuque, IA 52001
Phone: 563-588-7236 · **Financial Aid Phone:** 563-588-7136
E-mail: admissions@loras.edu · **CEEB Code:** 6370
Fax: 563-588-7119 · **Website:** www.loras.edu · **ACT Code:** 1328

This private school, affiliated with the Roman Catholic Church, was founded in 1839. It has a 60-acre campus.

RATINGS
Admissions Selectivity Rating: 77   **Fire Safety Rating:** 94

STUDENTS AND FACULTY
Enrollment: 1,468. **Student Body:** 48% female, 52% male, 63% out-of-state, 2% international (10 countries represented). Asian 1%, African American 3%, Caucasian 84%, Hispanic 6%, Native American <1%
Retention and Graduation: 51% freshmen graduate within 4 years. 64% freshmen graduate within 6 years. 16% grads go on to further study within 1 year. 2% grads pursue arts and sciences degrees. **Faculty:** 110 full-time faculty, 94% hold PhDs, 42% are members of minority groups, 5% are women. 0% of classes are taught by teaching assistants.

ACADEMICS
Degrees: associate, bachelor's, master's. **Classes:** Most classes have 20–29 students. Most lab/discussion sessions have fewer than 10 students. **Majors with Highest Enrollment:** Psychology; Biology/Biological Sciences; Sport and Fitness Administration/Management. **Special Study Options:** cooperative education program, cross-registration, double major, dual enrollment, English as a Second Language (ESL), honors program, independent study, internships, liberal arts/career combination, student-designed major, study abroad, teacher certification program, Undergrads may take graduate level classes if certain qualifications are met. **Combined degree programs:** BA/MA, 2-2 nursing prog with U of Iowa. **Disability Services:** Special programs offered to physically disabled students include note-taking services, reader services, tape recorders. **Career services:** internships.

FACILITIES
Housing: Coed dorms, men's dorms, women's dorms, apartments for single students. 95% of campus accessible to physically disabled. **Special Academic Facilities/Equipment:** Language lab, television studio, observatory and planetarium. **Computers:** Students can register for classes online. Administrative functions (other than registration) can be performed online. Undergraduates are required to own a computer.

CAMPUS LIFE
Environment: Town. **Activities:** Choral groups, concert band, dance, drama/theater, jazz band, music ensembles, musical theater, radio station, student government, student newspaper, television station, yearbook. 71 registered organizations, 710 honor societies, 5 religious organizations. 2 fraternities, 2 sororities. **Athletics (Intercollegiate):** *Men:* baseball, basketball, cross-country, diving, football, golf, soccer, swimming, tennis, track/field (outdoor), track/field (indoor), wrestling. *Women:* basketball, cross-country, diving, golf, soccer, softball, swimming, tennis, track/field (outdoor), track/field (indoor), volleyball. **On-Campus Highlights:** Academic Resource Center, Alumni Campus Center, The Pub and Cafeteria, The Grotto.

ADMISSIONS
Freshman Academic Profile: Average high school GPA 3.37. 16% in top 10% of high school class, 40% in top 25% of high school class, 73% in top 50% of high school class. 64% from public high schools. SAT Math middle 50% range 417.5-615. SAT Critical Reading middle 50% range 395-567.5. ACT middle 50% range 21-26. Minimum internet-based TOEFL 79. Minimum paper TOEFL 550. **Basis for Candidate Selection:** *Very important factors considered include:* academic GPA, rigor of secondary school record, standardized test scores. *Important factors considered include:* Class rank. *Other factors considered include:* application essay, recommendation(s), character/personal qualities, extracurricular activities, racial/ethnic status, volunteer work. **Freshman Admission Requirements:** High school diploma is required and GED is accepted. **Freshman Admission Statistics:** 1,293 applied, 95% admitted, 30% enrolled. **Transfer Admission Requirements:** High school transcript, college transcript(s), standardized test scores, Minimum college GPA of 2.0 required. Lowest grade transferable C. **General Admission Information:** Application Fee $25. Nonfall registration accepted. Admission may be deferred for a maximum of Two Terms. Credit offered for CEEB Advanced Placement tests.

COSTS AND FINANCIAL AID
Annual tuition $28,340. Room and board $8,353. Required fees $1,389. Average book expense $1,100. **Required Forms and Deadlines:** FAFSA. **Notification of Awards:** Applicants will be notified of awards on a rolling basis beginning 3/1. **Types of Aid:** *Need-based scholarships/grants:* Federal Pell, SEOG, state scholarships/grants, private scholarships, the school's own gift aid. *Loans:* Subsidized Stafford, Unsubsidized Stafford, PLUS, Federal Perkins, college/university loans from institutional funds. *Student Employment:* Highest amount earned per year from on-campus jobs $1,500. **Financial Aid Statistics:** 100% freshmen, 96% undergrads receive need-based scholarship or grant aid. 100% freshmen, 100% undergrads receive non-need-based scholarship or grant aid. 79% freshmen, 79% undergrads receive need-based self-help aid. 0% freshmen, 0% undergrads receive athletic scholarships. 100% freshmen, 98% undergrads receive any aid. 73% undergrads borrow to pay for school. Average cumulative indebtedness $27,263. **Criteria for awarding institutional aid:** *Non-need-based:* academics, alumni affiliation, music/drama.

LOUISIANA COLLEGE

1140 College Drive, Pineville, LA 71359-0560
Phone: 318-487-7259
E-mail: admissions@lacollege.edu · **CEEB Code:** 6371
Fax: 318-487-7550 · **Website:** www.lacollege.edu · **ACT Code:** 1586

This private school, affiliated with the Baptist Church, was founded in 1906. It has a 81-acre campus.

RATINGS
Admissions Selectivity Rating: 79   **Fire Safety Rating:** 67

STUDENTS AND FACULTY
Enrollment: 1,014. **Student Body:** 56% female, 44% male, 9% out-of-state, 1% international. Asian 1%, African American 7%, Caucasian 89%, Hispanic 2%, Native American <1%
Retention and Graduation: 59% freshmen return for sophomore year. 25% freshmen graduate within 4 years. 46% freshmen graduate within 6 years. **Faculty:** 68 full-time faculty, 60% hold PhDs, 46% are members of minority groups, 0% are women. 0% of classes are taught by teaching assistants.

ACADEMICS
Degrees: bachelor's. **Classes:** Most classes have fewer than 10 students. Most lab/discussion sessions have 10–19 students. **Majors with Highest Enrollment:** Elementary Education and Teaching; Biology; Psychology. **Special Study Options:** double major, honors program, independent study, internships, liberal arts/career combination, student-designed major, study abroad, teacher certification program. **Honors programs:** London Semester. **Disability Services:** Special programs offered to physically disabled students include note-taking services, reader services, tutors. **Career services:** career/job search classes, career assessment, internships. Career services highlights include Several majors require internships to fulfill graduation requirements. Academic

credit may be available to students who wish to pursue internship opportunities outside major requirements.

FACILITIES

Housing: men's dorms, women's dorms, apartments for married students, apartments for single students. 95% of campus accessible to physically disabled. **Special Academic Facilities/Equipment:** Art gallery, radio station, performing arts center, theater.

CAMPUS LIFE

Environment: Village. **Activities:** Choral groups, concert band, drama/theater, jazz band, literary magazine, music ensembles, musical theater, opera, pep band, radio station, student government, student newspaper, symphony orchestra, yearbook. 60 registered organizations, 13 honor societies, 8 religious organizations. 4 fraternities, 3 sororities. **Athletics (Intercollegiate):** *Men:* baseball, basketball, cheerleading, football, golf, soccer. *Women:* basketball, cheerleading, cross-country, soccer, softball, tennis. **On-Campus Highlights:** Healthplex/Wellness Center, Student Center, Martin Performing Arts Center, Weathersby Fine Arts Building, Alexandria Hall.

ADMISSIONS

Freshman Academic Profile: Average high school GPA 3.48. 29% in top 10% of high school class, 54% in top 25% of high school class, 87% in top 50% of high school class. SAT Math middle 50% range 440-600. SAT Critical Reading middle 50% range 440-570. ACT middle 50% range 21-26. Minimum internet-based TOEFL 61. Minimum paper TOEFL 500. **Basis for Candidate Selection:** *Very important factors considered include:* Class rank, rigor of secondary school record, standardized test scores. *Other factors considered include:* recommendation(s), alumni/ae relation, character/personal qualities, extracurricular activities, geographical residence, interview, racial/ethnic status, religious affiliation/commitment, state residency, talent/ability, volunteer work, work experience. **Freshman Admission Requirements:** High school diploma is required and GED is accepted. *Academic units required:* 4 English, 3 mathematics, 3 science, (2 science labs), 2 social studies, 1 history, 4 academic electives. **Freshman Admission Statistics:** 727 applied, 85% admitted, 43% enrolled. **Transfer Admission Requirements:** college transcript(s), Minimum college GPA of 2.0 required. Lowest grade transferable D. **General Admission Information:** Application Fee $25. Regular application deadline 8/15. Notification on a rolling basis, beginning on or about 1/1. Nonfall registration accepted. Admission may be deferred for a maximum of 1 year. Credit and/or placement offered for CEEB Advanced Placement tests.

COSTS AND FINANCIAL AID

Average book expense $750. **Required Forms and Deadlines:** FAFSA, Institution's own financial aid form. **Notification of Awards:** Applicants will be notified of awards on a rolling basis beginning 3/1. **Types of Aid:** *Need-based scholarships/grants:* Federal Pell, SEOG, state scholarships/grants, private scholarships, the school's own gift aid, LEAP. *Loans:* Direct Subsidized Stafford, Direct Unsubsidized Stafford, Direct PLUS, Subsidized Stafford, Unsubsidized Stafford, PLUS, college/university loans from institutional funds. *Student Employment:* Federal Work-Study Program available. Institutional employment available. Highest amount earned per year from on-campus jobs $400. Off-campus job opportunities are excellent. **Financial Aid Statistics:** 44% freshmen, 45% undergrads receive need-based scholarship or grant aid. 100% freshmen, 97% undergrads receive non-need-based scholarship or grant aid. 57% freshmen, 57% undergrads receive need-based self-help aid. 0% freshmen, 0% undergrads receive athletic scholarships. 98% freshmen, 82% undergrads receive any aid. 54% undergrads borrow to pay for school. **Criteria for awarding institutional aid:** *Non-need-based:* academics, art, leadership, music/drama.

LOUISIANA STATE UNIVERSITY

Best 380

1146 Pleasant Hall, Baton Rouge, LA 70803
Phone: 225-578-1175 · **Financial Aid Phone:** 225-578-3103
E-mail: admissions@lsu.edu · **CEEB Code:** 6373
Fax: 225-578-4433 · **Website:** www.lsu.edu · **ACT Code:** 1590

This public school was founded in 1860. It has a 2000-acre campus.

RATINGS

Admissions Selectivity Rating: 84   Fire Safety Rating: 96

STUDENTS AND FACULTY

Enrollment: 23,990. **Student Body:** 52% female, 48% male, 19% out-of-state, 2% international (76 countries represented). Asian 3%, African American 11%, Caucasian 76%, Hispanic 5%, Native American <1%
Retention and Graduation: 40% freshmen graduate within 4 years. **Faculty:** 1,232 full-time faculty, 88% hold PhDs, 36% are members of minority groups, 18% are women. 7% of classes are taught by teaching assistants.

ACADEMICS

Degrees: bachelor's, doctoral, master's, post-master's certificate. **Classes:** Most classes have 20–29 students. Most lab/discussion sessions have 20–29 students. **Majors with Highest Enrollment:** Biology/Biological Sciences; Mass Communication/Media Studies; Physical Education Teaching and Coaching. **Special Study Options:** Accelerated program, cooperative education program, cross-registration, distance learning, double major, dual enrollment, English as a Second Language (ESL), exchange student program (domestic), honors program, independent study, internships, liberal arts/career combination, student-designed major, study abroad, teacher certification program. **Honors programs:** Admissions to the Honors College **Combined degree programs:** BS/MED Elementary Education/Holmes. **Disability Services:** Special programs offered to physically disabled students include note-taking services, reader services, tape recorders. **Career services:** Alumni network, alumni services, career/job search classes, career assessment, internships. Career services highlights include a newly initiated Fellows Program, which will bring our Institute the creme of the crop in both students from around campus and in internships for those students. We are committed to teaching entrepreneurship to students in order that they are prepared to start new, innovative ventures sometime in their lives.

FACILITIES

Housing: Coed dorms, special housing for disabled students, men's dorms, women's dorms, fraternity/sorority housing, apartments for married students, apartments for single students, Theme Housing. 75% of campus accessible to physically disabled. **Special Academic Facilities/Equipment:** Art Museum, NAtural Science Museum, Rural Life Museum, Lichen/Bryophyte Mycological and Vascular Plant herbariums, on campus K-12 schools, geoscience and mycological museums, electron microscope, nuclear science center and civil war center. **Computers:** 100% of classrooms, 100% of dorms, 100% of libraries, 90% of dining areas, 100% of student union, 90% of common outdoor areas have wireless network access. Students can register for classes online. Administrative functions (other than registration) can be performed online.

CAMPUS LIFE

Environment: Metropolis. **Activities:** Choral groups, concert band, dance, drama/theater, jazz band, literary magazine, marching band, music ensembles, musical theater, opera, pep band, radio station, student government, student newspaper, student-run film society, symphony orchestra, television station, yearbook, Campus Ministries, International Student Organization. 300 registered organizations, 32 honor societies, 25 religious organizations. 23 fraternities, 15 sororities. **Athletics (Intercollegiate):** *Men:* baseball, basketball, cheerleading, cross-country, diving, football, golf, swimming, tennis, track/field (outdoor), track/field (indoor). *Women:* basketball, cheerleading, cross-country, diving, golf, gymnastics, soccer, softball, swimming, tennis, track/field (outdoor), track/field (indoor), volleyball. **On-Campus Highlights:** LSU Student Union, Mike VI Tiger Habitat, Indian Mounds, Tiger Stadium, Alex Box Stadium, FACES Laboratory. **Environmental Initiatives:** Energy efficiency programs including Recommissioning, Utility insulation, LED lighting, Class Utilization Study and IT power management enforcement; Programs reducing vehicles on campus by 60%, new bus service using low-sulphur diesel and increasing ridership, new bike facility master plan; Advanced Recycling Program, athletics in-stadium recycling increased by 77%, composting during fall festival events, sustainable Christmas tree.

ADMISSIONS

Freshman Academic Profile: Average high school GPA 3.45. 25% in top 10% of high school class, 53% in top 25% of high school class, 82% in top 50% of high school class. 60% from public high schools. SAT Math middle 50% range 510-625. SAT Critical Reading middle 50% range 500-600. ACT middle 50% range 23-28. Minimum internet-based TOEFL 79. Minimum paper TOEFL 550. **Basis for Candidate Selection:** *Very important factors considered include:* academic GPA, rigor of secondary school record, standardized test scores. *Important factors considered include:* Class rank, talent/ability. *Other factors considered include:* application essay, recommendation(s), extracurricular activities, first generation. **Freshman Admission Requirements:** High school diploma is required and GED is accepted. *Academic units required:* 4 English, 3 mathematics, 3 science, 2 foreign language, 1 social studies, 2 history. **Freshman Admission Statistics:** 16,005 applied, 75% admitted, 46% enrolled. **Transfer Admission Requirements:** college transcript(s), Minimum college GPA of 2.5 required. Lowest grade transferable D. **General Admission Information:** Application Fee $40. Regular application deadline 4/15. Nonfall registration accepted. Admission may be deferred for a maximum of 1 year. Credit offered for CEEB Advanced Placement tests.

COSTS AND FINANCIAL AID

Annual in-state tuition $6,678. Annual out-of-state tuition $24,395. Room and board $10,804. Required fees $2,072. Average book expense $1,500. **Required Forms and Deadlines:** FAFSA, Institution's own financial aid form. **Notification of Awards:** Applicants will be notified of awards on a rolling basis beginning 3/1. **Types of Aid:** *Need-based scholarships/grants:* Federal Pell, SEOG, state scholarships/grants, private scholarships, the school's own gift aid, ACG/SMART. *Loans:* Subsidized Stafford, Unsubsidized Stafford, PLUS, Federal Perkins, Alternative/Grad Plus. *Student Employment:* Federal Work-Study Program available. Institutional employment available. Off-campus job opportunities are excellent. **Financial Aid Statistics:** 95% freshmen, 87% undergrads receive need-based scholarship or grant aid. 4% freshmen, 2% undergrads receive non-need-based scholarship or grant aid. 68% freshmen, 74% undergrads receive need-based self-help aid. 2% freshmen, 2% undergrads receive athletic scholarships. 94% freshmen, 81% undergrads receive any aid. 39% undergrads borrow to pay for school. Average cumulative indebtedness $19,704. **Criteria for awarding institutional aid:** *Non-need-based:* academics, alumni affiliation, art, athletics, leadership, music/drama, state/district residency.

LOUISIANA STATE UNIVERSITY IN SHREVEPORT

One University Place, Shreveport, LA 71115-2399
Phone: 318-797-5061
E-mail: admissions@pilot.lsus.edu · **CEEB Code:** 6355
Fax: 318-797-5204 · **Website:** www.lsus.edu · **ACT Code:** 1593

This public school was founded in 1965. It has a 200-acre campus.

RATINGS

Admissions Selectivity Rating: 71   Fire Safety Rating: 60*

STUDENTS AND FACULTY

Enrollment: 3,594. **Student Body:** 62% female, 38% male, 2% out-of-state, 1% international. Asian 2%, African American 22%, Caucasian 65%, Hispanic 2%, Native American 1%
Retention and Graduation: 53% freshmen return for sophomore year. **Faculty:** 155 full-time faculty, 72% hold PhDs, 39% are members of minority groups, 12% are women.

ACADEMICS

Degrees: bachelor's, master's, post-master's certificate. **Classes:** Most classes have 20–29 students. **Majors with Highest Enrollment:** Elementary Education and Teaching; General Studies; Business/Commerce. **Special Study Options:** cooperative education program, study abroad, teacher certification program, Undergrads may take grad level courses and evening Courses. **Combined degree programs:** Combined social work program w/ Grambling State U. **Disability Services:** Special programs offered to physically disabled students include note-taking services, reader services, tape recorders, tutors. **Career services:** alumni services, career/job search classes, career assessment, internships.

FACILITIES

Housing: apartments for married students, apartments for single students. 100% of campus accessible to physically disabled. **Special Academic Facilities/Equipment:** Art center, life science museum, pioneer heritage center. **Computers:** Students can register for classes online. Administrative functions (other than registration) can be performed online.

CAMPUS LIFE

Activities: student government, student newspaper. 52 registered organizations, 4 honor societies, 3 religious organizations. 5 fraternities, 3 sororities. **Athletics (Intercollegiate):** *Men:* baseball.

ADMISSIONS

Freshman Academic Profile: Average high school GPA 3.06. 90% from public high schools. ACT middle 50% range 18-23. Minimum paper TOEFL 500. **Basis for Candidate Selection:** *Other factors considered include:* rigor of secondary school record, standardized test scores. **Freshman Admission Requirements:** High school diploma is required and GED is accepted. **Freshman Admission Statistics:** 848 applied, 65% admitted, 106% enrolled. **Transfer Admission Requirements:** college transcript(s), Minimum college GPA of 2.0 required. Lowest grade transferable D. **General Admission Information:** Application Fee $10. Regular application deadline 8/1. Nonfall registration accepted. Credit offered for CEEB Advanced Placement tests.

COSTS AND FINANCIAL AID

Required Forms and Deadlines: FAFSA, Institution's own financial aid form. **Types of Aid:** *Need-based scholarships/grants:* state scholarships/grants.

Loans: Subsidized Stafford, PLUS. *Student Employment:* Federal Work-Study Program available. Institutional employment available. Highest amount earned per year from on-campus jobs $2,000. Off-campus job opportunities are good.

LOUISIANA TECH UNIVERSITY

P. O. Box 3178, Ruston, LA 71272
Phone: 318-257-3036
E-mail: bulldog@latech.edu
Fax: 318-257-2499 · **Website:** www.latech.edu

This is a public school.

RATINGS

Admissions Selectivity Rating: 83   Fire Safety Rating: 60*

STUDENTS AND FACULTY

Enrollment: 7,047. **Student Body:** 43% female, 57% male, 10% out-of-state, 4% international. Asian 1%, African American 15%, Caucasian 68%, Hispanic 1%, Native American <1%
Retention and Graduation: 29% freshmen graduate within 4 years. **Faculty:** 352 full-time faculty, 79% hold PhDs, 39% are members of minority groups.

ACADEMICS

Degrees: associate, bachelor's, master's, post-bachelor's certificate. **Career services:** Alumni network, alumni services, career/job search classes, career assessment, internships, regional alumni. The mission of the Career Center is to educate and to serve the students and graduates of Louisiana Tech University in the career education, planning, and development processes. In support of the mission of the University, the Career Center functions as a vital component in the total educational experience of students, primarily in the development, evaluation, initiation, and implementation of career plans and opportunities. Career Center services and resources provide assistance to students in the cultivation and enhancement of skills to explore career options, master job search techniques and strategies, and research employment opportunities. The Career Center provides effective and efficient service to employers in recruitment programs and activities.

ADMISSIONS

Freshman Academic Profile: Average high school GPA 3.43. 24% in top 10% of high school class, 51% in top 25% of high school class, 80% in top 50% of high school class. 82% from public high schools. SAT Math middle 50% range 490-600. SAT Critical Reading middle 50% range 450-590. ACT middle 50% range 21-26. Minimum internet-based TOEFL 88. Minimum paper TOEFL 570. **Freshman Admission Statistics:** 5,077 applied, 67% admitted, 45% enrolled. **General Admission Information:** Credit offered for CEEB Advanced Placement tests.

COSTS AND FINANCIAL AID

Required Forms and Deadlines: FAFSA, Institution's own financial aid form. **Financial Aid Statistics:** 94% freshmen, 89% undergrads receive need-based scholarship or grant aid. 17% freshmen, 15% undergrads receive non-need-based scholarship or grant aid. 49% freshmen, 60% undergrads receive need-based self-help aid. 1% freshmen, 2% undergrads receive athletic scholarships. 58% undergrads borrow to pay for school. Average cumulative indebtedness $19,696.

LOURDES UNIVERSITY

6832 Convent Road, Sylvania, OH 43560-2898
Phone: 419-885-5291 · **Financial Aid Phone:** 419-824-3732
E-mail: AdmissionsLCAdmits@lourdes.edu · **CEEB Code:** 1427
Fax: 419-824-3916 · **Website:** www.lourdes.edu · **ACT Code:** 3598

This private school, affiliated with the Roman Catholic Church, was founded in 1958. It has a 94-acre campus.

RATINGS

Admissions Selectivity Rating: 75   Fire Safety Rating: 76

STUDENTS AND FACULTY

Enrollment: 1,666. **Student Body:** 71% female, 29% male, 14% out-of-state, 0% international. Asian 1%, African American 21%, Caucasian 84%, Hispanic 7%, Native American <1%

Retention and Graduation: 63% freshmen return for sophomore year. **Faculty:** 100 full-time faculty, 59% hold PhDs, 67% are members of minority groups, 10% are women. 2% of classes are taught by teaching assistants.

ACADEMICS

Degrees: associate, bachelor's, certificate, master's, post-bachelor's certificate. **Classes:** Most classes have 10–19 students. Most lab/discussion sessions have fewer than 10 students. **Majors with Highest Enrollment:** Registered Nursing/Registered Nurse; Social Work; Business Administration and Management. **Special Study Options:** distance learning, double major, dual enrollment, independent study, internships, liberal arts/career combination, student-designed major, study abroad, teacher certification program. **Disability Services:** Special programs offered to physically disabled students include note-taking services, reader services, tape recorders, tutors. **Career services:** career/job search classes, career assessment.

FACILITIES

Housing: Special Academic Facilities/Equipment: Planetarium, Life Lab. **Computers:** 100% of classrooms, 100% of libraries, 100% of dining areas, 100% of student union, have wireless network access. Students can register for classes online. Administrative functions (other than registration) can be performed online.

CAMPUS LIFE

Environment: Village. **Activities:** Choral groups, drama/theater, literary magazine, student government, Campus Ministries. 25 registered organizations, 2 honor societies. **Athletics (Intercollegiate):** *Men:* basketball, golf. *Women:* golf, volleyball. **On-Campus Highlights:** McAlear Hall, Ebied Center.

ADMISSIONS

Freshman Academic Profile: Average high school GPA 3. 8% in top 10% of high school class, 27% in top 25% of high school class, 59% in top 50% of high school class. SAT Math middle 50% range 350-500. SAT Critical Reading middle 50% range 410-540. ACT middle 50% range 17-22. Minimum internet-based TOEFL 173. Minimum paper TOEFL 500. **Basis for Candidate Selection:** *Very important factors considered include:* academic GPA. *Other factors considered include:* interview. **Freshman Admission Requirements:** High school diploma is required and GED is accepted. **Freshman Admission Statistics:** 1,296 applied, 68% admitted, 29% enrolled. **Transfer Admission Requirements:** college transcript(s), Minimum college GPA of 2.0 required. Lowest grade transferable C. **General Admission Information:** Application Fee $25. Nonfall registration accepted. Admission may be deferred for a maximum of 4 years. Credit and/or placement offered for CEEB Advanced Placement tests.

COSTS AND FINANCIAL AID

Annual tuition $17,455. Room and board $8,400. Required fees $200. Average book expense $1,275. **Required Forms and Deadlines:** FAFSA. **Notification of Awards:** Applicants will be notified of awards on a rolling basis beginning 3/1. *Types of Aid: Need-based scholarships/grants:* Federal Pell, SEOG, state scholarships/grants, private scholarships, the school's own gift aid. *Loans:* Direct Subsidized Stafford, Direct Unsubsidized Stafford, Direct PLUS, Federal Perkins, state loans, college/university loans from institutional funds. *Student Employment:* Federal Work-Study Program available. Institutional employment available. Off-campus job opportunities are excellent. **Financial Aid Statistics:** 88% freshmen, 82% undergrads receive need-based scholarship or grant aid. 89% freshmen, 63% undergrads receive non-need-based scholarship or grant aid. 92% freshmen, 91% undergrads receive need-based self-help aid. 28% freshmen, 18% undergrads receive athletic scholarships. 96% freshmen, 84% undergrads receive any aid. 87% undergrads borrow to pay for school. Average cumulative indebtedness $40,574. **Criteria for awarding institutional aid:** *Non-need-based:* academics, art, minority status, state/district residency.

LOYOLA MARYMOUNT UNIVERSITY

1 LMU Drive, Los Angeles, CA 90045-8350
Phone: 310-338-2750 · **Financial Aid Phone:** 310-338-2753
E-mail: admissions@lmu.edu · **CEEB Code:** 4403
Fax: 310-338-2797 · **Website:** www.lmu.edu · **ACT Code:** 326

This private school, affiliated with the Roman Catholic Church, was founded in 1911. It has a 128-acre campus.

RATINGS

Admissions Selectivity Rating: 89   **Fire Safety Rating:** 82

STUDENTS AND FACULTY

Enrollment: 6,064. **Student Body:** 57% female, 43% male, 22% out-of-state, 7% international (83 countries represented). Asian 11%, African American 6%, Caucasian 47%, Hispanic 22%, Native American <1%
Retention and Graduation: 69% freshmen graduate within 4 years. 78% freshmen graduate within 6 years. 27% grads go on to further study within 1 year. 10% grads pursue arts and sciences degrees. 3% grads pursue law degrees. 1% grads pursue business degrees. 1% grads pursue medical degrees. **Faculty:** 522 full-time faculty, 102% hold PhDs, 47% are members of minority groups, 29% are women. 1% of classes are taught by teaching assistants.

ACADEMICS

Degrees: bachelor's, first professional, first professional certificate, master's, post-bachelor's certificate, post-master's certificate. **Classes:** Most classes have 20–29 students. Most lab/discussion sessions have 10–19 students. **Majors with Highest Enrollment:** Speech Communication and Rhetoric; Finance; Psychology. **Special Study Options:** cross-registration, double major, dual enrollment, honors program, independent study, internships, liberal arts/career combination, student-designed major, study abroad, teacher certification program, Encore program for adult students. **Disability Services:** Special programs offered to physically disabled students include note-taking services, reader services, tape recorders, tutors. **Career services:** alumni services, career assessment, internships.

FACILITIES

Housing: Coed dorms, special housing for disabled students, men's dorms, women's dorms, apartments for single students. 99% of campus accessible to physically disabled. **Special Academic Facilities/Equipment:** Art gallery, theater, TV production labs, computer graphics lab. **Computers:** Students can register for classes online. Administrative functions (other than registration) can be performed online.

CAMPUS LIFE

Environment: Metropolis. **Activities:** Choral groups, dance, drama/theater, literary magazine, music ensembles, musical theater, pep band, radio station, student government, student newspaper, student-run film society, television station, yearbook. 120 registered organizations, 12 honor societies, 2 religious organizations. 6 fraternities, 8 sororities. **Athletics (Intercollegiate):** *Men:* baseball, basketball, crew/rowing, cross-country, golf, soccer, tennis, water polo. *Women:* basketball, crew/rowing, cross-country, soccer, softball, swimming, tennis, volleyball, water polo. **Environmental Initiatives:** LEED Building Program: LMU's new $64 million library incorporates state-of-the-art technologies and energy efficiency features, complementing other LEED-certified campus buildings and signifying LMU's commitment to continued leadership in environmental stewardship. The library will also act as a 'living lab' for students studying Information Systems and IT in the context of building automation systems applications. LMU's solar energy program was the first, and is still one of the largest of its kind in the entire City of Los Angeles. Integrating on-site renewable energy generation together with extensive retro-fitting and efficiency features is a natural extension of our commitment to reducing our carbon footprint. The creation of the Environmental Stewardship and Sustainability Committee represents a tremendous step in establishing comprehensive, campus-wide policies and governance over every aspect of campus operations by instituting sustainability considerations and decision variables to be used across the university, from purchasing and procurement to academics and student life. The committee seeks to emphasize the inextricable link between ecological justice and social justice within our mission as a Jesuit university.

ADMISSIONS

Freshman Academic Profile: Average high school GPA 3.75. 36% in top 10% of high school class, 74% in top 25% of high school class, 96% in top 50% of high school class. 51% from public high schools. SAT Math middle 50% range 560-660. SAT Critical Reading middle 50% range 540-640. SAT Writing middle 50% range 545-650. ACT middle 50% range 25-30. Minimum internet-based TOEFL 80. Minimum paper TOEFL 550. **Basis for Candidate Selection:** *Very important factors considered include:* academic GPA, rigor of secondary school record. *Important factors considered include:* Class rank, application essay, standardized test scores, character/personal qualities, talent/ability. *Other factors considered include:* recommendation(s), alumni/ae relation, extracurricular activities, first generation, geographical residence, interview, volunteer work, work experience. **Freshman Admission Requirements:** High school diploma is required and GED is accepted. **Freshman Admission Statistics:** 12,117 applied, 53% admitted, 21% enrolled. **Transfer Admission Requirements:** college transcript(s), essay or personal statement, statement of good standing from prior institution(s). Minimum college GPA of 2.8 required. Lowest grade transferable C. **General Admission Information:** Application Fee $50. Notification on a rolling basis, beginning on or about 1/1. Nonfall registration accepted. Admission may be deferred for a maximum of 12. Credit and/or placement offered for CEEB Advanced Placement tests.

COSTS AND FINANCIAL AID

Annual tuition $40,680. Room and board $13,690. Required fees $917. Average book expense $1,710. **Required Forms and Deadlines:** FAFSA. **Notification of Awards:** Applicants will be notified of awards on a rolling basis beginning

3/15. **Types of Aid:** *Need-based scholarships/grants:* Federal Pell, SEOG, state scholarships/grants, private scholarships, the school's own gift aid. *Loans:* Subsidized Stafford, Unsubsidized Stafford, PLUS, Federal Perkins, college/university loans from institutional funds. *Student Employment:* Federal Work-Study Program available. Institutional employment available. Off-campus job opportunities are excellent. **Financial Aid Statistics:** 98% freshmen, 93% undergrads receive need-based scholarship or grant aid. 12% freshmen, 12% undergrads receive non-need-based scholarship or grant aid. 77% freshmen, 79% undergrads receive need-based self-help aid. 3% freshmen, 3% undergrads receive athletic scholarships. 95% freshmen, 86% undergrads receive any aid. 59% undergrads borrow to pay for school. Average cumulative indebtedness $22,802.

LOYOLA UNIVERSITY CHICAGO

820 North Michigan Avenue, Chicago, IL 60611
Phone: 312-915-6500 · **Financial Aid Phone:** 773-508-7704
E-mail: admission@luc.edu · **CEEB Code:** 1412
Fax: 312-915-7216 · **Website:** www.luc.edu/

This private school, affiliated with the Roman Catholic-Jesuit Church, was founded in 1870. It has a 105-acre campus.

RATINGS

Admissions Selectivity Rating: 89   **Fire Safety Rating:** 83

STUDENTS AND FACULTY

Enrollment: 10,042. **Student Body:** 65% female, 35% male, 35% out-of-state, 4% international (87 countries represented). Asian 11%, African American 4%, Caucasian 60%, Hispanic 13%, Native American <1%
Retention and Graduation: 65% freshmen graduate within 4 years. 73% freshmen graduate within 6 years. **Faculty:** 749 full-time faculty, 93% hold PhDs, 49% are members of minority groups, 13% are women. 0% of classes are taught by teaching assistants.

ACADEMICS

Degrees: bachelor's, certificate, master's, post-bachelor's certificate, post-master's certificate. **Classes:** Most classes have 10–19 students. Most lab/discussion sessions have 10–19 students. **Majors with Highest Enrollment:** Registered Nursing/Registered Nurse; Biology/Biological Sciences; Psychology. **Special Study Options:** Accelerated program, distance learning, double major, dual enrollment, English as a Second Language (ESL), exchange student program (domestic), honors program, independent study, internships, study abroad, teacher certification program. **Honors programs:** Loyola University Chicago offers an Interdisciplinary Honors Program that integrates a challenging academic program with service-learning opportunities. Taking a series of team-taught, interdisciplinary courses, students learn to perceive unexpected convergences among discrete facts, to synthesize information from many sources, and to use their knowledge to benefit society. **Combined degree programs:** BA/JD, BA/MA, BA/MEng, B.B.A/M.B.A. Business Administration; B.S. Biology/M.B.A.; B.B.A./M.S.A. Ac. **Disability Services:** Special programs offered to physically disabled students include note-taking services, reader services, tape recorders, tutors. **Career services:** Alumni network, alumni services, career/job search classes, career assessment, internships, regional alumni. Career services highlights include the Career Development Center counselors, who teach 4 sections each semester of the "Career and Life Planning" course. This unique course takes students through a thorough self assessment, exploration of their passions and calling, and provides detailed information on job search skills. This self-reflective course encourages students to research and explore a variety of industries and employment options so they are more focused and confident in their internship choices and their future career goals.

FACILITIES

Housing: Coed dorms, special housing for disabled students, apartments for single students, Honors floors, Living Learning Community floors. 90% of campus accessible to physically disabled. **Special Academic Facilities/Equipment:** Renaissance art gallery, Loyola University Museum of Art (LUMA), Madonna Della Strada Chapel, The Quinlin Life Sciences Building's Bio Deisel Labs, Mock Trial Room, Mundelein Auditorium. **Computers:** 75% of classrooms, 60% of dorms, 95% of libraries, 50% of dining areas, 100% of student union, 40% of common outdoor areas have wireless network access. Students can register for classes online. Administrative functions (other than registration) can be performed online.

CAMPUS LIFE

Environment: Metropolis. **Activities:** concert band, dance, drama/theater, jazz band, literary magazine, music ensembles, musical theater, pep band, radio station, student government, student newspaper, student-run film society, television station, Campus Ministries, International Student Organization, Model UN. 185 registered organizations, 11 honor society, 9 religious organizations. 6 fraternities, 9 sororities. **Athletics (Intercollegiate):** *Men:* basketball, cheerleading, cross-country, golf, soccer, track/field (outdoor), track/field (indoor), volleyball. *Women:* basketball, cheerleading, cross-country, golf, soccer, softball, track/field (outdoor), track/field (indoor), volleyball. **On-Campus Highlights:** Information Commons, Lake front Residence Halls, Joseph J. Gentile Center, Halas Athletic Center/Alumni Gym, Quinlan Life Sciences Center. LAKE SHORE CAMPUS Loyola's main residential campus is located on Chicago's North Side, minutes from downtown Chicago and the Water Tower Campus, and is set along the shore of Lake Michigan. It's home to the College of Arts and Sciences, Graduate School and Marcella Niehoff School of Nursing. The School of Education offers academic courses, programs and student advising. More than 3,000 students live in residence halls. The Lake Shore Campus includes Cudahy Library, Madonna della Strada Chapel, Joseph J. Gentile Center and the Halas Sports Center. WATER TOWER CAMPUS Loyola's downtown campus is located along Pearson Street, just off North Michigan Avenue, Chicago's "Magnificent Mile." Here, both residential and commuter students can complete one of many undergraduate degree programs, as well as take advantage of internships at many of Chicago's business and cultural institutions. The Water Tower Campus is home to the Schools of Business Administration, Education, Law and Social Work, and to selected programs in the College of Arts and Sciences. **Environmental Initiatives:** Energy reduction and conservation, transportation: Adopt green building design standards for all new construction. Lighting, heating/cooling retrofits. Biodiesel production from dining hall's waste vegetable oil used in campus shuttles. (www.luc.edu/biodiesel) Transportation: walk-to-work program, bicycle program, electric vehicles, public transit passes for students, car sharing program. Education and Research: Launching an Institute for Environmental Sustainability and a new center, Center for Urban Sustainable Living in 2013; Courses and programs with multidisciplinary, problem solving,research-based, and experiential focus to include co-curricular activities; Undergraduate interdisciplinary environmental research fellowships -Urban food demonstration program -Sustainable agriculture courses; Green Living Learning Community; Environmental Science Department; Biodiesel production courses; Professional non-credit sustainability education courses/workshops; Environmental topics and themes across the disciplines; Design projects that directly involve students with community organizations on environmental sustainable projects and outreach. Waste Reduction, Reuse and Recycle programs: BioSoap production made from the glycerin, a by-product of biodiesel production (http://www.luc.edu/biodiesel/BioSoap.shtml); small farm to supply food in dining hall at the Retreat and Ecology Campus; Rainwater cistern, permeable walkways, semi-permeable artificial turf and track walkway, expanded recycling to include batteries, inkjet/printer cartridges, and small personal electronics; Trayfree dining halls, nondisposable water bottle campaign and water bottle refill stations, recyclable collection during fall move-in and a spring move-out collection for students to donate reusable items (clothing, toiletries, nonperishable foods) to charities which divert items from landfills. 2011 began investigating off-site composting of dining hall plate waste.

ADMISSIONS

Freshman Academic Profile: Average high school GPA 3.8. 34.2% in top 10% of high school class, 72.2% in top 25% of high school class, 95.8% in top 50% of high school class. 68% from public high schools. SAT Math middle 50% range 530-630. SAT Critical Reading middle 50% range 520-630. SAT Writing middle 50% range 520-620. ACT middle 50% range 25-29. Minimum internet-based TOEFL 79. Minimum paper TOEFL 550. **Basis for Candidate Selection:** *Very important factors considered include:* academic GPA, rigor of secondary school record, standardized test scores. *Important factors considered include:* application essay, recommendation(s), character/personal qualities, extracurricular activities, level of applicant's interest, volunteer work. *Other factors considered include:* Class rank, alumni/ae relation, first generation, geographical residence, interview, state residency, talent/ability, work experience. **Freshman Admission Requirements:** High school diploma is required and GED is accepted. *Academic units required:* 4 English, 3 mathematics, 3 science, (0 science labs), 2 foreign language, 2 social studies, 1 history, 0 visual/performing arts, 0 computer science, 0 academic electives. **Freshman Admission Statistics:** 20,414 applied, 63% admitted, 18% enrolled. **Transfer Admission Requirements:** college transcript(s), Minimum college GPA of 2.0 required. Lowest grade transferable C. **General Admission Information:** Application Fee $25. Notification on a rolling basis, beginning on or about 10/1. Nonfall registration accepted. Credit and/or placement offered for CEEB Advanced Placement tests.

COSTS AND FINANCIAL AID

Annual tuition $39,130. Room and board $13,310. Required fees $1,296. Average book expense $1,200. **Required Forms and Deadlines:** FAFSA. **Notification of Awards:** Applicants will be notified of awards on a rolling basis beginning 2/15. **Types of Aid:** *Need-based scholarships/grants:* Federal Pell, SEOG, state scholarships/grants, private scholarships, the school's own gift aid. *Loans:* Subsidized Stafford, Unsubsidized Stafford, PLUS, Federal Perkins, Federal Nursing. *Student Employment:* Federal Work-Study Program available. Institutional employment available. Highest amount earned per year from on-campus jobs $9,803. Off-campus job opportunities are good. **Financial Aid Statistics:** 99% freshmen, 95% undergrads receive need-based scholarship or grant aid. 12% freshmen, 9% undergrads receive non-need-based scholarship or grant aid. 83% freshmen, 83% undergrads receive need-based self-help aid. 1% freshmen, 1% undergrads receive athletic scholarships. 96% freshmen, 86% undergrads receive any aid. 72% undergrads borrow to pay for school. **Criteria for awarding institutional aid:** *Non-need-based:* academics, athletics, leadership, music/drama, religious affiliation.

See page 1086.

LOYOLA UNIVERSITY IN MARYLAND

4501 North Charles Street, Baltimore, MD 21210
Phone: 410-617-5012 · **Financial Aid Phone:** 410-617-2576
E-mail: admissions@loyola.edu · **CEEB Code:** 5370
Fax: 410-617-2176 · **Website:** www.loyola.edu

This private school, affiliated with the Roman Catholic Church, was founded in 1852. It has a 89-acre campus.

RATINGS

Admissions Selectivity Rating: 89   **Fire Safety Rating:** 89

STUDENTS AND FACULTY
Enrollment: 4,062. **Student Body:** 58% female, 42% male, 83% out-of-state, 0% international (37 countries represented). Asian 3%, African American 5%, Caucasian 79%, Hispanic 9%, Native American <1%
Retention and Graduation: 88% freshmen return for sophomore year. 77% freshmen graduate within 4 years. 83% freshmen graduate within 6 years. 25% grads go on to further study within 1 year. 35% grads pursue arts and sciences degrees. 13% grads pursue law degrees. 11% grads pursue business degrees. 2% grads pursue medical degrees. **Faculty:** 364 full-time faculty, 85% hold PhDs, 48% are members of minority groups, 17% are women. 0% of classes are taught by teaching assistants.

ACADEMICS
Degrees: bachelor's, master's, post-master's certificate. **Classes:** Most classes have 20–29 students. Most lab/discussion sessions have 10–19 students. **Majors with Highest Enrollment:** Business Administration and Management; Psychology; Communication. **Special Study Options:** cross-registration, double major, dual enrollment, exchange student program (domestic), honors program, independent study, internships, liberal arts/career combination, study abroad, teacher certification program. **Honors programs:** http://www.loyola.edu/undergraduate/academics/honors.aspx. **Disability Services:** Special programs offered to physically disabled students include note-taking services, reader services, tape recorders, tutors. **Career services:** Alumni network, alumni services, career/job search classes, career assessment, internships.

FACILITIES
Housing: Coed dorms, cooperative housing, apartments for single students, Wellness Housing, Theme Housing. 100% of campus accessible to physically disabled. **Special Academic Facilities/Equipment:** Art gallery, advanced biology lab, humanities building, speech pathology lab and audiology center, black box theater. **Computers:** 75% of classrooms, 80% of dorms, 100% of libraries, 100% of dining areas, 50% of student union, 50% of common outdoor areas have wireless network access. Students can register for classes online. Administrative functions (other than registration) can be performed online.

CAMPUS LIFE
Environment: Village. **Activities:** Choral groups, dance, drama/theater, literary magazine, music ensembles, musical theater, radio station, student government, student newspaper, television station, yearbook, Campus Ministries, International Student Organization. 185 registered organizations, 25 honor societies, 4 religious organizations. **Athletics (Intercollegiate):** *Men:* basketball, crew/rowing, cross-country, diving, golf, lacrosse, soccer, swimming, tennis. *Women:* basketball, crew/rowing, cross-country, diving, lacrosse, soccer, swimming, tennis, track/field (outdoor), track/field (indoor), volleyball.

On-Campus Highlights: Loyola/Notre Dame Library, The Loyola University Art Gallery, Fitness and Aquatic Center, Boulder Garden Café, Primo's: The New Marketplace. **Environmental Initiatives:** Our commitment responsible building can be seen in our 100,000 sq. ft. green residential hall that was built in 2007. In 2010 we completed construction of an athletic facility that was built on a landfill and is considered an example of smart growth. Our waste management & diversion program currently diverts about 65% of our waste from a landfill. 55% of that is recycling and the other 10% is compost. We passed an energy management plan that has successfully reduced energy by 12% in the last 4 years. We are currently looking at making the plan more robust to include retrofits and possibly a greater commitment to renewable energy.

ADMISSIONS
Freshman Academic Profile: Average high school GPA 3.4. 27% in top 10% of high school class, 65% in top 25% of high school class, 87% in top 50% of high school class. 51% from public high schools. SAT Math middle 50% range 560-640. SAT Critical Reading middle 50% range 540-630. ACT middle 50% range 25-29. Minimum internet-based TOEFL 79. Minimum paper TOEFL 550. **Basis for Candidate Selection:** *Very important factors considered include:* application essay, recommendation(s), rigor of secondary school record, character/personal qualities. *Important factors considered include:* Class rank, alumni/ae relation, extracurricular activities, first generation, talent/ability, volunteer work. *Other factors considered include:* academic GPA, standardized test scores, geographical residence, interview, level of applicant's interest, racial/ethnic status, work experience. **Freshman Admission Requirements:** High school diploma is required and GED is accepted. *Academic units required:* 4 English, 3 mathematics, 3 science, 3 foreign language, 2 social studies, 2 history, 0 visual/performing arts, 0 computer science. **Freshman Admission Statistics:** 13,863 applied, 60% admitted, 14% enrolled. **Transfer Admission Requirements:** High school transcript, college transcript(s), essay or personal statement, statement of good standing from prior institution(s). Minimum college GPA of 2.7 required. Lowest grade transferable C. **General Admission Information:** Application Fee $50. Regular application deadline 6/1. Nonfall registration accepted. Admission may be deferred for a maximum of 1. Credit and/or placement offered for CEEB Advanced Placement tests.

COSTS AND FINANCIAL AID
Required Forms and Deadlines: FAFSA, CSS/Financial Aid PROFILE, Noncustodial PROFILE. **Notification of Awards:** Applicants will be notified of awards on or about 4/1. **Types of Aid:** *Need-based scholarships/grants:* Federal Pell, SEOG, state scholarships/grants, private scholarships, the school's own gift aid. *Loans:* Direct Subsidized Stafford, Direct Unsubsidized Stafford, Direct PLUS, Federal Perkins, college/university loans from institutional funds. *Student Employment:* Federal Work-Study Program available. Institutional employment available. Highest amount earned per year from on-campus jobs $2,420. Off-campus job opportunities are good. **Financial Aid Statistics:** 92% freshmen, 88% undergrads receive need-based scholarship or grant aid. 47% freshmen, 33% undergrads receive non-need-based scholarship or grant aid. 89% freshmen, 90% undergrads receive need-based self-help aid. 3% freshmen, 3% undergrads receive athletic scholarships. 75% freshmen, 70% undergrads receive any aid. 63% undergrads borrow to pay for school. Average cumulative indebtedness $25,505. **Criteria for awarding institutional aid:** *Non-need-based:* academics, athletics, minority status.

LOYOLA UNIVERSITY NEW ORLEANS

6363 St. Charles Avenue, New Orleans, LA 70118-6195
Phone: 504-865-3240 · **Financial Aid Phone:** 504-865-3231
E-mail: admit@loyno.edu · **CEEB Code:** 6374
Fax: 504-865-3383 · **Website:** www.loyno.edu · **ACT Code:** 1592

This private school, affiliated with the Roman Catholic Church,, affiliated with the Jesuit Church, was founded in 1912. It has a 26-acre campus.

RATINGS

Admissions Selectivity Rating: 80   **Fire Safety Rating:** 98

STUDENTS AND FACULTY
Enrollment: 2,734. **Student Body:** 59% female, 41% male, 57% out-of-state, 3% international (44 countries represented). Asian 4%, African American 16%, Caucasian 51%, Hispanic 16%, Native American 1%
Retention and Graduation: 51% freshmen graduate within 4 years. 64% grads go on to further study within 1 year. **Faculty:** 272 full-time faculty, 89%

hold PhDs, 44% are members of minority groups, 15% are women. 0% of classes are taught by teaching assistants.

ACADEMICS

Degrees: bachelor's, master's, post-bachelor's certificate, post-master's certificate. **Classes:** Most classes have 10–19 students. Most lab/discussion sessions have fewer than 10 students. **Majors with Highest Enrollment:** Psychology; Mass Communication/Media Studies; Music Management. **Special Study Options:** Accelerated program, cross-registration, distance learning, double major, dual enrollment, English as a Second Language (ESL), exchange student program (domestic), honors program, independent study, internships, liberal arts/career combination, student-designed major, study abroad, teacher certification program, Advance placement credit. Limited weekend courses available. Evening Courses available. Also teacher certification program is available in music only. **Honors programs:** The Loyola University Honors Program offers the opportunity for academically superior, highly motivated students to take challenging Honors courses and to participate in special cultural and intellectual enrichment activities. The University Honors Program is open to qualified students of all undergraduate colleges and majors. The Honors courses replace other required courses, and therefore do not add to the number of requirements for graduation. **Combined degree programs:** RN/MSN/DNP, JD/MBA, MPS/MS, Early Law Admission. **Disability Services:** Special programs offered to physically disabled students include note-taking services, reader services, tape recorders, tutors. **Career services:** Alumni network, alumni services, career/job search classes, career assessment, internships, regional alumni.

FACILITIES

Housing: Coed dorms, special housing for disabled students, apartments for single students, Wellness Housing, Theme Housing, Honors floor available. 95% of campus accessible to physically disabled. **Special Academic Facilities/Equipment:** Collins C. Diboll Art Gallery, Humanities Lab with Perseus Project and TLG TV, Multimedia Classrooms, 24-hour Microcomputer Labs, Computer Science Lab, Graphics Lab, Visual Arts Lab, Ad Club/Communications Lab, RATHE Business Computer Lab, Multi-Media Training Center, Donnelley Center for Non-Profit Communications, Chemistry Wing, Television Broadcast Studio, Multimedia Studio, Audio Recording Studio, Editing Studio, Library Learning Commons, Multimedia Exhibit Room, Satchmo's Deli and Performance Area, Center for International Education, University Sports Complex with Suspended Pool, Career Development Center, Jesuit Social Research Institute, Learning Communities. **Computers:** 50% of classrooms, 100% of dorms, 100% of libraries, 100% of dining areas, 100% of student union, 100% of common outdoor areas have wireless network access. Students can register for classes online. Administrative functions (other than registration) can be performed online.

CAMPUS LIFE

Environment: City. **Activities:** Choral groups, concert band, dance, drama/theater, jazz band, literary magazine, music ensembles, musical theater, opera, pep band, radio station, student government, student newspaper, student-run film society, symphony orchestra, yearbook, Campus Ministries, International Student Organization 90 registered organizations, 13 honor societies, 4 religious organizations. 7 fraternities, 7 sororities. **Athletics (Intercollegiate):** *Men:* baseball, basketball, cross-country, track/field (outdoor), track/field (indoor). *Women:* basketball, cross-country, track/field (outdoor), track/field (indoor), volleyball. **On-Campus Highlights:** J. Edgar and Louise S. Monroe Library, Danna Student Center, Recreational Sports Complex, Peace Quad, Residential Quad, Collins C. Diboll Art Gallery, Humanities Lab with Perseus Project and TLG TV, Multimedia Classrooms, 24-hour Microcomputer Labs, Computer Science Lab, Graphics Lab, Visual Arts Lab, Ad Club/Communications Lab, RATHE Business Computer Lab, Multi-Media Training Center, Donnelley Center for Non-Profit Communications, Chemistry Wing, Television Broadcast Studio, Multimedia Studio, Audio Recording Studio, Editing Studio, Library Learning Commons, Multimedia Exhibit Room, Satchmo''s Deli and Performance Area, Center for International Education, University Sports Complex with Suspended Pool, Career Development Center, Jesuit Social Research Institute, Learning Communities. **Environmental Initiatives:** Formation of a committee that has representatives from important units on campus, including SGA and other student organizations. Full support of the Administration, starting with the President and Provost. Have signed on to the leading sustainable action groups (Talloires Sustainability Declaration, EPA WasteWise Team, President's Climate Change,NWF Campus Ecology Program, etc.) Implemented major inventories of sustainable operations across campus.

ADMISSIONS

Freshman Academic Profile: Average high school GPA 3.51. 19% in top 10% of high school class, 39% in top 25% of high school class, 74% in top 50% of high school class. 48% from public high schools. SAT Math middle 50% range 490-600. SAT Critical Reading middle 50% range 520-630. ACT middle 50% range 22-28. Minimum internet-based TOEFL 79. Minimum paper TOEFL 550. **Basis for Candidate Selection:** *Very important factors considered include:* academic GPA, rigor of secondary school record, standardized test scores. *Important factors considered include:* application essay, recommendation(s),

extracurricular activities, talent/ability. *Other factors considered include:* Class rank, alumni/ae relation, character/personal qualities, geographical residence, interview, level of applicant's interest, state residency, volunteer work, work experience. **Freshman Admission Requirements:** High school diploma is required and GED is accepted. *Academic units required:* 4 English, 2 mathematics, 2 science, 2 social studies. **Freshman Admission Statistics:** 4,491 applied, 90% admitted, 15% enrolled. **Transfer Admission Requirements:** college transcript(s), essay or personal statement, statement of good standing from prior institution(s). Minimum college GPA of 2.25 required. Lowest grade transferable C. **General Admission Information:** Application Fee $20. Notification on a rolling basis, beginning on or about 10/20. Nonfall registration accepted. Credit and/or placement offered for CEEB Advanced Placement tests.

COSTS AND FINANCIAL AID

Annual tuition $36,214. Room and board $12,808. Required fees $1,366. Average book expense $1,220. **Required Forms and Deadlines:** FAFSA. **Notification of Awards:** Applicants will be notified of awards on a rolling basis beginning 3/1. **Types of Aid:** *Need-based scholarships/grants:* Federal Pell, SEOG, private scholarships, the school's own gift aid. *Loans:* Subsidized Stafford, Unsubsidized Stafford, PLUS, Federal Perkins. *Student Employment:* Federal Work-Study Program available. Institutional employment available. Highest amount earned per year from on-campus jobs $1,920. Off-campus job opportunities are excellent. **Financial Aid Statistics:** 100% freshmen, 99% undergrads receive need-based scholarship or grant aid. 7% freshmen, 10% undergrads receive non-need-based scholarship or grant aid. 90% freshmen, 85% undergrads receive need-based self-help aid. 1% freshmen, 2% undergrads receive athletic scholarships. 92% freshmen, 92% undergrads receive any aid. 64% undergrads borrow to pay for school. Average cumulative indebtedness $25,404. **Criteria for awarding institutional aid:** *Non-need-based:* academics, alumni affiliation, art, leadership.

LUBBOCK CHRISTIAN UNIVERSITY

5601 19th Street, Lubbock, TX 79407
Phone: 800-720-7151 · **Financial Aid Phone:** 806-720-7176
E-mail: admissions@lcu.edu · **CEEB Code:** 6378
Fax: 806-720-7162 · **Website:** www.lcu.edu • **ACT Code:** 4123

This private school, affiliated with the Church of Christ Church, was founded in 1957. It has a 120-acre campus.

RATINGS

| Admissions Selectivity Rating: 77 | Fire Safety Rating: 66 |

STUDENTS AND FACULTY

Enrollment: 1,728. **Student Body:** 56% female, 44% male, 9% out-of-state, 0% international. Asian 1%, African American 6%, Caucasian 79%, Hispanic 14%, Native American 1%

Retention and Graduation: 67% freshmen return for sophomore year. 27% freshmen graduate within 4 years. 43% freshmen graduate within 6 years.
Faculty: 79 full-time faculty, 59% hold PhDs, 39% are members of minority groups, 0% are women. 0% of classes are taught by teaching assistants.

ACADEMICS

Degrees: bachelor's, master's. **Classes:** Most classes have 10–19 students. Most lab/discussion sessions have fewer than 10 students. **Majors with Highest Enrollment:** Elementary Education and Teaching; Humanities/Humanistic Studies; Small Business Administration/Management. **Special Study Options:** distance learning, double major, dual enrollment, honors program, internships, liberal arts/career combination, student-designed major, study abroad, teacher certification program, weekend college. **Honors programs:** Honors program available to all majors. **Disability Services:** Special programs offered to physically disabled students include tape recorders, tutors. **Career services:** alumni services, career/job search classes, career assessment, internships. Career services highlights include experiential learning opportunities in local schools that are required with each education course.

FACILITIES

Housing: special housing for disabled students, men's dorms, women's dorms, apartments for married students, apartments for single students. 78% of campus accessible to physically disabled. **Computers:** Students can register for classes online.

CAMPUS LIFE

Environment: City. **Activities:** Choral groups, drama/theater, music ensembles, student government, student newspaper, yearbook. 24 registered organizations, 3 honor societies, 4 fraternities, 4 sororities. **Athletics (Intercollegiate):** *Men:* baseball, basketball, cheerleading, golf. *Women:* basketball, cheerleading, golf, volleyball. **On-Campus Highlights:** Student Union Building, Ramona Perrin Fitness Center, Rip Griffin Athletic Center, Library, Snackbar.

ADMISSIONS

Freshman Academic Profile: Average high school GPA 3.48. 18% in top 10% of high school class, 44% in top 25% of high school class, 76% in top 50% of high school class. 76% from public high schools. SAT Math middle 50% range 440-572. SAT Critical Reading middle 50% range 450-582. ACT middle 50% range 18-24. Minimum paper TOEFL 500. **Basis for Candidate Selection:** *Very important factors considered include:* standardized test scores. *Important factors considered include:* rigor of secondary school record, character/personal qualities. *Other factors considered include:* Class rank, recommendation(s), alumni/ae relation, racial/ethnic status, religious affiliation/commitment, talent/ability, volunteer work. **Freshman Admission Requirements:** High school diploma is required and GED is accepted. **Freshman Admission Statistics:** 771 applied, 77% admitted, 45% enrolled. **Transfer Admission Requirements:** college transcript(s), statement of good standing from prior institution(s). Lowest grade transferable C. **General Admission Information:** Application Fee $20. Regular application deadline 8/15. Notification on a rolling basis, beginning on or about 9/1. Nonfall registration accepted. Credit and/or placement offered for CEEB Advanced Placement tests.

COSTS AND FINANCIAL AID

Annual tuition $11,644. Room and board $2,125. Required fees $916. Average book expense $832. **Required Forms and Deadlines:** FAFSA, Institution's own financial aid form. **Notification of Awards:** Applicants will be notified of awards on a rolling basis beginning 3/1. **Types of Aid:** *Need-based scholarships/grants:* Federal Pell, SEOG, state scholarships/grants. *Loans:* Subsidized Stafford, Unsubsidized Stafford, PLUS, Federal Perkins. *Student Employment:* Federal Work-Study Program available. Off-campus job opportunities are excellent. **Financial Aid Statistics:** 100% freshmen, 97% undergrads receive need-based scholarship or grant aid. 13% freshmen, 6% undergrads receive non-need-based scholarship or grant aid. 85% freshmen, 91% undergrads receive need-based self-help aid. 5% freshmen, 36% undergrads receive athletic scholarships. 78% freshmen, 72% undergrads receive any aid. 76% undergrads borrow to pay for school. **Criteria for awarding institutional aid:** *Non-need-based:* academics, athletics, leadership, music/drama.

LUTHER COLLEGE

700 College Drive, Decorah, IA 52101-1042
Phone: 563-387-1287 · **Financial Aid Phone:** 563-387-1018
E-mail: admissions@luther.edu · **CEEB Code:** 6375
Fax: 563-387-2159 · **Website:** www.luther.edu · **ACT Code:** 1330

This private school, affiliated with the Lutheran Church, was founded in 1861. It has a 175-acre campus.

RATINGS

Admissions Selectivity Rating: 88   **Fire Safety Rating:** 80

STUDENTS AND FACULTY

Enrollment: 2,402. **Student Body:** 56% female, 44% male, 68% out-of-state, 5% international (46 countries represented). Asian 2%, African American 1%, Caucasian 86%, Hispanic 3%, Native American <1%
Retention and Graduation: 68% freshmen graduate within 4 years. 77% freshmen graduate within 6 years. 18% grads go on to further study within 1 year. 6% grads pursue arts and sciences degrees. 1% grads pursue law degrees. 3% grads pursue medical degrees. **Faculty:** 178 full-time faculty, 93% hold PhDs, 45% are members of minority groups, 6% are women. 0% of classes are taught by teaching assistants.

ACADEMICS

Degrees: bachelor's. **Classes:** Most classes have 10–19 students. Most lab/discussion sessions have 10–19 students. **Majors with Highest Enrollment:** Biology/Biological Sciences; Music; Psychology. **Special Study Options:** double major, dual enrollment, honors program, independent study, internships, student-designed major, study abroad, teacher certification program. **Disability Services:** Special programs offered to physically disabled students include note-taking services, reader services, tutors. **Career services:** Alumni network, career/job search classes, internships.

FACILITIES

Housing: Coed dorms, special housing for disabled students, apartments for married students, apartments for single students, Wellness Housing. 95% of campus accessible to physically disabled. **Special Academic Facilities/Equipment:** Natural history museum, Norwegian-American museum, five art galleries, planetarium, live animal center, archaeological research center, computer music lab, two electron microscopes. **Computers:** 90% of classrooms, 75%

of dorms, 90% of libraries, 90% of dining areas, 90% of student union, 25% of common outdoor areas have wireless network access. Students can register for classes online. Administrative functions (other than registration) can be performed online.

CAMPUS LIFE

Environment: Village. **Activities:** Choral groups, concert band, dance, drama/theater, jazz band, literary magazine, music ensembles, musical theater, pep band, radio station, student government, student newspaper, symphony orchestra, yearbook, Campus Ministries, International Student Organization, Model UN. 83 registered organizations, 13 honor societies, 8 religious organizations. 1 fraternity, 3 sororities. **Athletics (Intercollegiate):** *Men:* baseball, basketball, cross-country, diving, football, golf, soccer, swimming, tennis, track/field (outdoor), track/field (indoor), wrestling. *Women:* basketball, cross-country, diving, golf, soccer, softball, swimming, tennis, track/field (outdoor), track/field (indoor), volleyball. **On-Campus Highlights:** Marty's Cyber Café, Legends Fitness Center, The Cafeteria, Residence Hall Lounges, Sunnyside Café in the Center for the Arts. **Environmental Initiatives:** Energy audit and efficiency upgrades totaling $1.5 million and has reduced campus carbon footprint by 15%; Built new science facility to LEED gold certification; Wind turbine is expected to generate 1/3 of our electricity consumption; Geothermal energy heats and cools two of the facilities on campus reducing our need for fossil fuel heating and cooling.

ADMISSIONS

Freshman Academic Profile: Average high school GPA 3.63. 31.8% in top 10% of high school class, 59.3% in top 25% of high school class, 89.7% in top 50% of high school class. 91% from public high schools. SAT Math middle 50% range 500-620. SAT Critical Reading middle 50% range 450-605. SAT Writing middle 50% range 450-595. ACT middle 50% range 23-28. Minimum internet-based TOEFL 80. Minimum paper TOEFL 550. **Basis for Candidate Selection:** *Very important factors considered include:* Class rank, academic GPA, recommendation(s), rigor of secondary school record, standardized test scores. *Important factors considered include:* character/personal qualities, extracurricular activities, talent/ability. *Other factors considered include:* application essay, alumni/ae relation, first generation, interview, level of applicant's interest, racial/ethnic status, volunteer work. **Freshman Admission Requirements:** High school diploma is required and GED is accepted. **Freshman Admission Statistics:** 3,556 applied, 70% admitted, 26% enrolled. **Transfer Admission Requirements:** High school transcript, college transcript(s), essay or personal statement, standardized test scores, Minimum college GPA of 2.50 required. Lowest grade transferable C. **General Admission Information:** Application Fee $25. Nonfall registration accepted. Admission may be deferred for a maximum of 1 year. Credit and/or placement offered for CEEB Advanced Placement tests.

COSTS AND FINANCIAL AID

Annual tuition $37,330. Room and board $6,850. Required fees $150. Average book expense $1,040. **Required Forms and Deadlines:** FAFSA, Institution's own financial aid form. **Notification of Awards:** Applicants will be notified of awards on a rolling basis beginning 3/15. **Types of Aid:** *Need-based scholarships/grants:* Federal Pell, SEOG, state scholarships/grants, private scholarships, the school's own gift aid. *Loans:* Direct Subsidized Stafford, Direct Unsubsidized Stafford, Direct PLUS, Federal Perkins, college/university loans from institutional funds. *Student Employment:* Federal Work-Study Program available. Institutional employment available. Highest amount earned per year from on-campus jobs $3,190. Off-campus job opportunities are good. **Financial Aid Statistics:** 100% freshmen, 100% undergrads receive need-based scholarship or grant aid. 21% freshmen, 17% undergrads receive non-need-based scholarship or grant aid. 77% freshmen, 82% undergrads receive need-based self-help aid. 0% freshmen, 0% undergrads receive athletic scholarships. 98% freshmen, 97% undergrads receive any aid. 78% undergrads borrow to pay for school. Average cumulative indebtedness $25,573. **Criteria for awarding institutional aid:** *Non-need-based:* academics, alumni affiliation, art, minority status, music/drama.

LYCOMING COLLEGE

700 College Place, Williamsport, PA 17701
Phone: 570-321-4026 · **Financial Aid Phone:** 570-321-4040
E-mail: admissions@lycoming.edu · **CEEB Code:** 2372
Fax: 570-321-4317 · **Website:** www.lycoming.edu · **ACT Code:** 3622

This private school, affiliated with the Methodist Church, was founded in 1812. It has a 39-acre campus.

RATINGS

Admissions Selectivity Rating: 82   **Fire Safety Rating:** 81

STUDENTS AND FACULTY

Enrollment: 1,338. **Student Body:** 53% female, 47% male, 34% out-of-state, 4% international (16 countries represented). Asian 1%, African American 7%, Caucasian 76%, Hispanic 4%, Native American <1%
Retention and Graduation: 52% freshmen graduate within 4 years. 62% freshmen graduate within 6 years. 20% grads go on to further study within 1 year. 10% grads pursue arts and sciences degrees. 1% grads pursue law degrees. 1% grads pursue business degrees. 6% grads pursue medical degrees. **Faculty:** 82 full-time faculty, 95% hold PhDs, 44% are members of minority groups, 5% are women. 0% of classes are taught by teaching assistants.

ACADEMICS

Degrees: bachelor's. **Classes:** Most classes have 10–19 students. Most lab/discussion sessions have 10–19 students. **Majors with Highest Enrollment:** Biology/Biological Sciences; Business Administration and Management; Psychology. **Special Study Options:** Accelerated program, cross-registration, double major, honors program, independent study, internships, student-designed major, study abroad, teacher certification program. **Honors programs:** Scholars Program offered to students through admissions process; each major also provides an Honors major option for students who wish to graduate with honors within their field of study. **Disability Services:** Special programs offered to physically disabled students include note-taking services, reader services, tape recorders, tutors. **Career services:** Alumni network, career/job search classes, career assessment, internships. Career services highlights include a successful internship program with local businesses. Williamsport, PA serves as the County Seat and offers a rich array of business and government opportunities for students. In addition, Lycoming has successfully placed students in nationally competitive internship programs with the FBI, top 5 accounting firms, Datatel, and the National Science Foundation.

FACILITIES

Housing: Coed dorms, special housing for disabled students, women's dorms, fraternity/sorority housing, apartments for single students, Theme **Housing:** Substance-free housing, Study-intensive housing, Creative Arts Society housing. 85% of campus accessible to physically disabled. **Special Academic Facilities/Equipment:** Language lab, tissue culture lab, TV studio, planetarium, video conferencing. **Computers:** 100% of classrooms, 100% of dorms, 100% of libraries, 100% of dining areas, 100% of student union, 100% of common outdoor areas have wireless network access. Students can register for classes online. Administrative functions (other than registration) can be performed online.

CAMPUS LIFE

Environment: Town. **Activities:** Choral groups, concert band, dance, drama/theater, jazz band, literary magazine, music ensembles, musical theater, pep band, radio station, student government, student newspaper, student-run film society, symphony orchestra, television station, yearbook, Campus Ministries, International Student Organization. 78 registered organizations, 20 honor societies, 3 religious organizations. 5 fraternities, 5 sororities. **Athletics (Intercollegiate):** *Men:* basketball, cross-country, football, golf, lacrosse, soccer, swimming, tennis, wrestling. *Women:* basketball, cross-country, golf, lacrosse, soccer, softball, swimming, tennis, volleyball. **On-Campus Highlights:** Quad, Dining Hall, Jack's Place, Lamade Gymnasium, Recreation Center. **Environmental Initiatives:** The College has a Sustainability Committee that is comprised of faculty, administrators and students. Several initiatives have emerged from this group including using the grease waste from campus dining and converting it into biodiesel. The College has replaced older less efficient lighting systems on campus to more energy efficient systems. All residence halls and many of the other campus buildings have been retrofitted to include high EER rated lighting equipment. This has cut our energy costs in half for many buildings. New and renovated buildings are updated to include the latest technology in energy efficiency.

ADMISSIONS

Freshman Academic Profile: Average high school GPA 3.43. 20.4% in top 10% of high school class, 45.5% in top 25% of high school class, 82.8% in top 50% of high school class. 90% from public high schools. SAT Math middle 50% range 470-590. SAT Critical Reading middle 50% range 460-563. SAT Writing middle 50% range 440-530. ACT middle 50% range 19-26. Minimum internet-based TOEFL 70. Minimum paper TOEFL 525. **Basis for Candidate Selection:** *Very important factors considered include:* rigor of secondary school record. *Important factors considered include:* Class rank, application essay, academic GPA, recommendation(s), standardized test scores, interview, racial/ethnic status. *Other factors considered include:* alumni/ae relation, character/personal qualities, extracurricular activities, first generation, geographical residence, level of applicant's interest, talent/ability, volunteer work, work experience. **Freshman Admission Requirements:** High school diploma is required and GED is accepted. *Academic units required:* 4 English, 3 mathematics, 3 science, (2 science labs), 2 foreign language, 4 social studies, 3 history, 2 academic electives. **Freshman Admission Statistics:** 1,782 applied, 72% admitted, 31% enrolled. **Transfer Admission Requirements:** college transcript(s), statement of good standing from prior institution(s). Minimum college GPA of 2.0 required. Lowest grade transferable C-. **General Admission Information:**

Application Fee $35. Regular application deadline 7/1. Notification on a rolling basis, beginning on or about 12/15. Nonfall registration accepted. Admission may be deferred for a maximum of 1 year. Credit offered for CEEB Advanced Placement tests.

COSTS AND FINANCIAL AID

Average book expense $1,000. **Required Forms and Deadlines:** FAFSA. **Notification of Awards:** Applicants will be notified of awards on a rolling basis beginning 3/1. **Types of Aid:** *Need-based scholarships/grants:* Federal Pell, SEOG, state scholarships/grants, private scholarships, the school's own gift aid. *Loans:* Subsidized Stafford, Unsubsidized Stafford, PLUS, Federal Perkins, college/university loans from institutional funds. *Student Employment:* Federal Work-Study Program available. Institutional employment available. Highest amount earned per year from on-campus jobs $4,004. Off-campus job opportunities are good. **Financial Aid Statistics:** 100% freshmen, 100% undergrads receive need-based scholarship or grant aid. 18% freshmen, 15% undergrads receive non-need-based scholarship or grant aid. 76% freshmen, 82% undergrads receive need-based self-help aid. 0% freshmen, 0% undergrads receive athletic scholarships. 100% freshmen, 100% undergrads receive any aid. **Criteria for awarding institutional aid:** *Non-need-based:* academics, art, leadership, minority status, music/drama.

LYME ACADEMY COLLEGE OF FINE ARTS

84 Lyme St, Old Lyme, CT 6371
Phone: 860-434-3571 x118 • **Financial Aid Phone:** 860-434-5232
E-mail: admissions@lymeacademy.edu • **CEEB Code:** 1971
Fax: 860-434-8725 • **Website:** http://www.lymeacademy.edu/

This private school was founded in 1976. It has a 47-acre campus.

RATINGS

Admissions Selectivity Rating: 75   **Fire Safety Rating:** 60*

STUDENTS AND FACULTY

Enrollment: 92. **Student Body:** 63% female, 37% male, 47% out-of-state, 0% international (0 countries represented). Asian 1%, African American 3%, Caucasian 74%, Hispanic 1%, Native American 2%
Retention and Graduation: 89% freshmen return for sophomore year. 53% freshmen graduate within 4 years. 10% grads go on to further study within 1 year. **Faculty:** 8 full-time faculty, 75% hold PhDs, 38% are members of minority groups, 0% are women. 0% of classes are taught by teaching assistants.

ACADEMICS

Degrees: bachelor's, certificate, post-bachelor's certificate. **Classes:** Most classes have 10–19 students. **Majors with Highest Enrollment:** Sculpture; Painting; Illustration. **Special Study Options:** independent study.

FACILITIES

Housing: Currently, all housing is Off-campus. Students live in local homes as well as apartments. Contact Patti Broedlin in Student Services for assistance, lists and referrals. 95% of campus accessible to physically disabled. **Special Academic Facilities/Equipment:** Sill House Gallery, Chauncey Stillman Gallery, Academy Wood Shop, Sculpture Casting rooms. **Computers:** 20% of classrooms, 100% of libraries, 100% of dining areas, 100% of student union, 40% of common outdoor areas have wireless network access.

CAMPUS LIFE

Environment: Village. **Activities:** literary magazine, student government, student-run film society. **On-Campus Highlights:** Chauncey Stillman Art Gallery, Café, Student Commons, Library, Sill House Art Gallery.

ADMISSIONS

Freshman Academic Profile: Average high school GPA 3.22. 85% from public high schools. SAT Math middle 50% range 395-555. SAT Critical Reading middle 50% range 440-650. SAT Writing middle 50% range 450-595. Minimum paper TOEFL 550. **Basis for Candidate Selection:** *Very important factors considered include:* academic GPA, character/personal qualities, interview, level of applicant's interest, talent/ability. *Important factors considered include:* application essay, recommendation(s), rigor of secondary school record. *Other factors considered include:* standardized test scores, racial/ethnic status. **Freshman Admission Requirements:** High school diploma is required and GED is accepted. **Freshman Admission Statistics:** 82 applied, 68% admitted, 41% enrolled. **Transfer Admission Requirements:** college transcript(s), essay or personal statement, interview, Minimum college GPA of 2.0 required. Lowest grade transferable C. **General Admission Information:** Application Fee $55. Notification on a rolling basis, beginning on or about 12/1. Nonfall registration accepted. Admission may be deferred for a maximum of 1 year. Credit and/or placement offered for CEEB Advanced Placement tests.

COSTS AND FINANCIAL AID

Annual tuition $25,248. Required fees $1,536. Average book expense $1,500. **Required Forms and Deadlines:** FAFSA. **Notification of Awards:** Applicants will be notified of awards on a rolling basis beginning 3/1. **Types of Aid:** *Need-based scholarships/grants:* Federal Pell, SEOG, state scholarships/grants, private scholarships, the school's own gift aid. *Loans:* Subsidized Stafford, Unsubsidized Stafford, PLUS. *Student Employment:* Federal Work-Study Program available. Institutional employment available. Off-campus job opportunities are good. **Financial Aid Statistics:** 0% freshmen, 0% undergrads receive athletic scholarships. 88% freshmen, 84% undergrads receive any aid. **Criteria for awarding institutional aid:** *Non-need-based:* academics, art, leadership.

LYNCHBURG COLLEGE

Best 380

1501 Lakeside Drive, Lynchburg, VA 24501
Phone: 434-544-8300 · **Financial Aid Phone:** 434-544-8229
E-mail: admissions@lynchburg.edu · **CEEB Code:** 5372
Fax: 434-544-8653 · **Website:** www.lynchburg.edu · **ACT Code:** 4368

This private school, affiliated with the Disciples of Christ Church, was founded in 1903. It has a 214-acre campus.

RATINGS

Admissions Selectivity Rating: 74   Fire Safety Rating: 80

STUDENTS AND FACULTY

Enrollment: 2,079. **Student Body:** 59% female, 41% male, 31% out-of-state, 3% international (13 countries represented). Asian 1%, African American 11%, Caucasian 73%, Hispanic 5%, Native American 1%
Retention and Graduation: 70% freshmen return for sophomore year. 42% freshmen graduate within 4 years. **Faculty:** 172 full-time faculty, 81% hold PhDs, 51% are members of minority groups, 8% are women. 0% of classes are taught by teaching assistants.

ACADEMICS

Degrees: bachelor's, master's, post-bachelor's certificate. **Classes:** Most classes have 10–19 students. Most lab/discussion sessions have 10–19 students. **Majors with Highest Enrollment:** Teacher Education and Professional Development, Specific Levels and Methods; Speech Communication and Rhetoric; Registered Nursing, Nursing Administration, Nursing Research and Clinical Nursing. **Special Study Options:** Accelerated program, cross-registration, double major, dual enrollment, honors program, independent study, internships, study abroad, teacher certification program. **Honors programs:** Westover Honors Program. **Disability Services:** Special programs offered to physically disabled students include note-taking services, reader services, tape recorders, tutors. **Career services:** Alumni network, alumni services, career/job search classes, career assessment, internships, regional alumni. Career services highlights include experiential learning and internship programs that are so numerous and diverse that it is impossible to select one that is most outstanding.

FACILITIES

Housing: Coed dorms, special housing for disabled students, men's dorms, special housing for international students, women's dorms, fraternity/sorority housing, apartments for single students, Wellness Housing, Theme Housing. 83% of campus accessible to physically disabled. **Special Academic Facilities/Equipment:** Daura Art Gallery, Claytor Nature Study Center, Ramsey-Freer Herbarium, Forensics cadaver lab; Centennial Hall audio-visual and television studios, Dillard Fine Arts Center. **Computers:** 20% of dorms, 100% of libraries, 100% of dining areas, 100% of student union, have wireless network access. Students can register for classes online. Administrative functions (other than registration) can be performed online.

CAMPUS LIFE

Environment: City. **Activities:** Choral groups, concert band, dance, drama/theater, jazz band, literary magazine, music ensembles, musical theater, pep band, student government, student newspaper, student-run film society, symphony orchestra, yearbook, Campus Ministries, International Student Organization, Model UN. 90 registered organizations, 14 honor societies, 10 religious organizations. 4 fraternities, 6 sororities. **Athletics (Intercollegiate):** *Men:* baseball, basketball, cheerleading, cross-country, golf, lacrosse, soccer, tennis, track/field (outdoor), track/field (indoor). *Women:* basketball, cheerleading, cross-country, equestrian sports, field hockey, lacrosse, soccer, softball, tennis, track/field (outdoor), track/field (indoor), volleyball. **On-Campus Highlights:**

Shellenberger Field, Burton Student Center, Claytor Nature Study Center, Stingers Coffee House, Schewel Hall. **Environmental Initiatives:** Recovery of College Lake. Working with the Army Corp of Engineers, and the state of Virginia, Lynchburg College is attempting to restore College Lake. During January 2014, LC joined four other state schools to begin using methane gas from landfills for electricity needs. The College is scheduled to receive 100% of its electricity from landfill gas by the end of 2014. Lynchburg College has saved 3.6 million kWH in electricity and 13.3 million gallons of water in 2010 and 2011, for a 2-year savings of about $454,000, thanks primarily to continuing campus-wide retrofits completed as part of LC's commitment to reducing energy use.

ADMISSIONS

Freshman Academic Profile: Average high school GPA 3.27. 85% from public high schools. SAT Math middle 50% range 440-540. SAT Critical Reading middle 50% range 460-550. SAT Writing middle 50% range 430-530. ACT middle 50% range 19-24. Minimum internet-based TOEFL 78. Minimum paper TOEFL 550. **Basis for Candidate Selection:** *Very important factors considered include:* academic GPA, rigor of secondary school record, standardized test scores. *Important factors considered include:* Class rank, interview. *Other factors considered include:* application essay, recommendation(s), extracurricular activities, level of applicant's interest, talent/ability, volunteer work. **Freshman Admission Requirements:** High school diploma is required and GED is accepted. *Academic units required:* 4 English, 3 mathematics, 3 science, (2 science labs), 2 foreign language, 2 social studies, 2 history. **Freshman Admission Statistics:** 5,515 applied, 67% admitted, 14% enrolled. **Transfer Admission Requirements:** college transcript(s), Minimum college GPA of 2.0 required. Lowest grade transferable C. **General Admission Information:** Application Fee $30. Early decision application deadline 11/15. Notification on a rolling basis, beginning on or about 9/1. Nonfall registration accepted. Admission may be deferred for a maximum of 1 year. Credit offered for CEEB Advanced Placement tests.

COSTS AND FINANCIAL AID

Annual tuition $33,600. Room and board $9,330. Required fees $945. Average book expense $1,000. **Required Forms and Deadlines:** FAFSA. **Notification of Awards:** Applicants will be notified of awards on a rolling basis beginning 3/5. **Types of Aid:** *Need-based scholarships/grants:* Federal Pell, SEOG, state scholarships/grants, private scholarships, the school's own gift aid. *Loans:* Subsidized Stafford, Unsubsidized Stafford, PLUS, Federal Perkins. *Student Employment:* Federal Work-Study Program available. Institutional employment available. Off-campus job opportunities are good. **Financial Aid Statistics:** 100% freshmen, 99% undergrads receive need-based scholarship or grant aid. 13% freshmen, 11% undergrads receive non-need-based scholarship or grant aid. 84% freshmen, 75% undergrads receive need-based self-help aid. 0% freshmen, 0% undergrads receive athletic scholarships. 85% freshmen, 75% undergrads receive any aid. 83% undergrads borrow to pay for school. Average cumulative indebtedness $28,819. **Criteria for awarding institutional aid:** *Non-need-based:* academics, leadership, music/drama, religious affiliation.

LYNDON STATE COLLEGE

P O Box 919, Lyndonville, VT 5851
Phone: 802-626-6413
E-mail: admissions@lyndonstate.edu · **CEEB Code:** 3767
Fax: 802-626-6335 · **Website:** www.lyndonstate.edu · **ACT Code:** 4318

This public school was founded in 1911. It has a 175-acre campus.

RATINGS

Admissions Selectivity Rating: 71   Fire Safety Rating: 60*

STUDENTS AND FACULTY

Enrollment: 1,273. **Student Body:** 49% female, 51% male, 40% out-of-state, 0% international. Asian 0%, African American 1%, Caucasian 52%, Hispanic 1%, Native American <1%
Retention and Graduation: 67% freshmen return for sophomore year. 24% freshmen graduate within 4 years. 43% freshmen graduate within 6 years. 10% grads go on to further study within 1 year. **Faculty:** 59 full-time faculty, 90% hold PhDs, 34% are members of minority groups, 0% are women. 0% of classes are taught by teaching assistants.

ACADEMICS

Degrees: associate, bachelor's, certificate, master's. **Classes:** Most classes have 10–19 students. Most lab/discussion sessions have 10–19 students. **Special Study Options:** Accelerated program, cooperative education program, double major, dual enrollment, exchange student program (domestic), independent study, internships, liberal arts/career combination, student-designed major, study abroad, teacher certification program. **Disability Services:** Special programs offered to physically disabled students include note-taking services, tape recorders, tutors. **Career services:** Alumni network, alumni services, career/job search classes, career assessment, internships, regional alumni.

FACILITIES
Housing: Coed dorms, special housing for disabled students, women's dorms, Substance free dorms. 100% of campus accessible to physically disabled. **Special Academic Facilities/Equipment:** Museum of college history, weather satellite lab, television studio, radio station, science labs: geology, chemistry, physics; GIS/GPS lab.

CAMPUS LIFE
Environment: Rural. **Activities:** Choral groups, dance, drama/theater, literary magazine, musical theater, radio station, student government, student newspaper, television station. 26 registered organizations, 1 honor society, 1 religious organization. **Athletics (Intercollegiate):** *Men:* baseball, basketball, cross-country, soccer, tennis. *Women:* basketball, cross-country, soccer, softball, tennis.

ADMISSIONS
Freshman Academic Profile: Average high school GPA 2.5. 12% in top 10% of high school class, 22% in top 25% of high school class, 69% in top 50% of high school class. SAT Math middle 50% range 410-530. SAT Critical Reading middle 50% range 418-520. Minimum paper TOEFL 500. **Basis for Candidate Selection:** *Very important factors considered include:* rigor of secondary school record. *Important factors considered include:* Class rank, recommendation(s), character/personal qualities, interview, talent/ability. *Other factors considered include:* application essay, standardized test scores, alumni/ae relation, extracurricular activities, volunteer work, work experience. **Freshman Admission Requirements:** High school diploma is required and GED is accepted. *Academic units required:* 4 English, 3 mathematics, 2 science, (2 science labs), 2 social studies, 2 history. **Freshman Admission Statistics:** 994 applied, 94% admitted, 36% enrolled. **Transfer Admission Requirements:** college transcript(s), essay or personal statement, statement of good standing from prior institution(s). Minimum college GPA of 2.2 required. Lowest grade transferable C-. **General Admission Information:** Application Fee $35. Notification on a rolling basis, beginning on or about 12/1. Nonfall registration accepted. Admission may be deferred for a maximum of 1 year. Credit and/or placement offered for CEEB Advanced Placement tests.

COSTS AND FINANCIAL AID
Average book expense $600. **Required Forms and Deadlines:** FAFSA. **Notification of Awards:** Applicants will be notified of awards on a rolling basis beginning 4/1. **Types of Aid:** *Need-based scholarships/grants:* Federal Pell, SEOG, state scholarships/grants, private scholarships, the school's own gift aid. *Loans:* Direct Subsidized Stafford, Direct Unsubsidized Stafford, Direct PLUS, Federal Perkins, state loans. *Student Employment:* Federal Work-Study Program available. Institutional employment available. Highest amount earned per year from on-campus jobs $700. Off-campus job opportunities are good. **Financial Aid Statistics:** 53% freshmen, 53% undergrads receive need-based scholarship or grant aid. 21% freshmen, 8% undergrads receive non-need-based scholarship or grant aid. 99% freshmen, 100% undergrads receive need-based self-help aid. 0% freshmen, 0% undergrads receive athletic scholarships. Criteria for awarding institutional aid: *Non-need-based:* academics, leadership.

LYNN UNIVERSITY

3601 North Military Trail, Boca Raton, FL 33431-5598
Phone: 561-237-7900 · **Financial Aid Phone:** 561-237-7973
E-mail: admission@lynn.edu · **CEEB Code:** 5437
Fax: 561-237-7100 · **Website:** www.lynn.edu · **ACT Code:** 706

This private school was founded in 1962. It has a 123-acre campus.

RATINGS
Admissions Selectivity Rating: 75   **Fire Safety Rating:** 98

STUDENTS AND FACULTY
Enrollment: 1,911. **Student Body:** 47% female, 53% male, 53% out-of-state, 23% international (89 countries represented). Asian 1%, African American 9%, Caucasian 43%, Hispanic 14%, Native American 1% **Retention and Graduation:** 35% freshmen graduate within 4 years. 40% freshmen graduate within 6 years. **Faculty:** 101 full-time faculty, 59% hold PhDs, 38% are members of minority groups, 5% are women. 0% of classes are taught by teaching assistants.

ACADEMICS
Degrees: bachelor's, certificate, master's, post-bachelor's certificate, post-master's certificate. **Classes:** Most classes have 10–19 students. **Majors with**

Highest Enrollment: Business Administration and Management. **Special Study Options:** Accelerated program, cooperative education program, distance learning, double major, dual enrollment, English as a Second Language (ESL), honors program, independent study, internships, liberal arts/career combination, study abroad, teacher certification program. **Honors programs:** Honors Program. **Disability Services:** Special programs offered to physically disabled students include note-taking services, reader services, tape recorders. **Career services:** alumni services, career/job search classes, career assessment, internships, regional alumni. Career services highlights include a well developed internship program, with approximately 300 internship students for whom we provide services in all program areas, excluding Education and Aviation.

FACILITIES
Housing: Coed dorms, special housing for disabled students, special housing for international students, women's dorms. 100% of campus accessible to physically disabled. **Computers:** Students can register for classes online. Administrative functions (other than registration) can be performed online.

CAMPUS LIFE
Environment: City. **Activities:** Choral groups, dance, drama/theater, literary magazine, music ensembles, radio station, student government, student newspaper, student-run film society, symphony orchestra, television station, yearbook, Campus Ministries, International Student Organization. 25 registered organizations, 4 honor societies, 4 religious organizations. 2 fraternities, 1 sorority. **Athletics (Intercollegiate):** *Men:* baseball, basketball, golf, soccer, tennis. *Women:* basketball, golf, soccer, softball, tennis, volleyball. **On-Campus Highlights:** The de Hoernle Sports Complex, The de Hoernle Sports and Cultural Center, The Coleman Electronic Lab, The Lynn Student Center, The Eugene M. and Christine E. Lynn Library. **Environmental Initiatives:** Lynns Going Green initiatives includes a complete campus retrofit of water fixtures and lighting equipment (over 7,500 light bulbs changed out in 2012). These projects also include: building a new Central Energy Plant, complete retrofit of campus A/C equipment, boilers and hot water heaters, as well as other measures to save energy. Lynn has 123 acres of campus; recently we switched to using reclaimed water for irrigation as opposed to water from the aquifer. This prevents a significant amount of water from being drawn out of the aquifer. During the January term of 2013 the University engaged more than 300 students in our Citizenship Project to help do trash clean-ups of campus, the nearby roadways, the campus nature preserve and the adjacent canals. Through this project the University also re-planted the landscaping to the west of the Schmidt College Center to more native, drought tolerant plants. Also, a herb garden was planted for the use of students, staff, and faculty. Lastly, the Universitys certified butterfly garden was revitalized.

ADMISSIONS
Freshman Academic Profile: Average high school GPA 2.92. 10% in top 10% of high school class, 19% in top 25% of high school class, 45% in top 50% of high school class. SAT Math middle 50% range 430-535. SAT Critical Reading middle 50% range 440-540. SAT Writing middle 50% range 430-530. ACT middle 50% range 19-23. Minimum paper TOEFL 525. **Basis for Candidate Selection:** *Very important factors considered include:* academic GPA, rigor of secondary school record, standardized test scores. *Important factors considered include:* Class rank, application essay, recommendation(s), character/personal qualities, work experience. *Other factors considered include:* alumni/ae relation, extracurricular activities, first generation, interview, state residency, talent/ability, volunteer work. **Freshman Admission Requirements:** High school diploma is required and GED is accepted. *Academic units required:* 4 English, 4 mathematics, 4 science, 2 social studies, 2 history. **Freshman Admission Statistics:** 3,557 applied, 75% admitted, 20% enrolled. **Transfer Admission Requirements:** college transcript(s), essay or personal statement, statement of good standing from prior institution(s). Minimum college GPA of 2.0 required. Lowest grade transferable C. **General Admission Information:** Application Fee $35. Nonfall registration accepted. Credit offered for CEEB Advanced Placement tests.

COSTS AND FINANCIAL AID
Annual tuition $33,450. Room and board $11,300. Required fees $1,750. Average book expense $800. **Required Forms and Deadlines:** FAFSA. **Notification of Awards:** Applicants will be notified of awards on a rolling basis beginning 2/1. **Types of Aid:** *Need-based scholarships/grants:* Federal Pell, SEOG, state scholarships/grants, private scholarships, the school's own gift aid. *Loans:* Direct Subsidized Stafford, Direct Unsubsidized Stafford, Direct PLUS, Subsidized Stafford, Unsubsidized Stafford, PLUS, Federal Perkins, state loans, college/university loans from institutional funds. *Student Employment:* Federal Work-Study Program available. Institutional employment available. Highest amount earned per year from on-campus jobs $16,420. Off-campus job opportunities are excellent. **Financial Aid Statistics:** 79% freshmen, 79% undergrads receive need-based scholarship or grant aid. 92% freshmen, 87% undergrads receive non-need-based scholarship or grant aid. 69% freshmen, 68% undergrads receive need-based self-help aid. 24% freshmen, 13% undergrads receive athletic scholarships. 84% freshmen, 79% undergrads receive any aid. 38% undergrads borrow to pay for school. Average cumulative indebted-

ness $22,839. **Criteria for awarding institutional aid:** *Non-need-based:* academics, athletics, leadership, music/drama, religious affiliation, state/district residency.

LYON COLLEGE

P.O. Box 2317, Batesville, AR 72503-2317
Phone: 870-307-7250 • **Financial Aid Phone:** 870-307-7257
E-mail: admissions@lyon.edu • **CEEB Code:** 1088
Fax: 870-307-7542 • **Website:** www.lyon.edu • **ACT Code:** 112

This private school, affiliated with the Presbyterian Church, was founded in 1872. It has a 136-acre campus.

RATINGS

Admissions Selectivity Rating: 86   **Fire Safety Rating:** 75

STUDENTS AND FACULTY

Enrollment: 706. **Student Body:** 47% female, 53% male, 29% out-of-state, 3% international (8 countries represented). Asian 2%, African American 7%, Caucasian 73%, Hispanic 6%, Native American 1%
Retention and Graduation: 43% freshmen graduate within 4 years. 48% freshmen graduate within 6 years. **Faculty:** 42 full-time faculty, 95% hold PhDs, 26% are members of minority groups, 10% are women. 0% of classes are taught by teaching assistants.

ACADEMICS

Degrees: bachelor's. **Classes:** Most classes have 10–19 students. Most lab/discussion sessions have fewer than 10 students. **Majors with Highest Enrollment:** Biology/Biological Sciences; Psychology; English Language and Literature. **Special Study Options:** Accelerated program, cross-registration, double major, dual enrollment, independent study, internships, liberal arts/career combination, student-designed major, study abroad, teacher certification program. **Combined degree programs:** BA/MEng, BS/BEng (with U. MO. Rolla). **Disability Services:** Special programs offered to physically disabled students include tape recorders. **Career services:** Alumni network, alumni services, career/job search classes, career assessment, internships, regional alumni.

FACILITIES

Housing: Coed dorms, special housing for disabled students, men's dorms, women's dorms, apartments for single students, Limited College-owned off-campus housing. 80% of campus accessible to physically disabled. **Special Academic Facilities/Equipment:** Ozark Regional Studies Center **Computers:** 100% of classrooms, 100% of dorms, 100% of libraries, 100% of dining areas, 100% of student union, 100% of common outdoor areas have wireless network access. Students can register for classes online. Administrative functions (other than registration) can be performed online.

CAMPUS LIFE

Environment: Village. **Activities:** Choral groups, concert band, drama/theater, literary magazine, music ensembles, student government, student newspaper, yearbook, Campus Ministries, Model UN. 44 registered organizations, 9 honor societies, 7 religious organizations. 3 fraternities, 2 sororities. **Athletics (Intercollegiate):** *Men:* baseball, basketball, cheerleading, cross-country, golf, soccer. *Women:* basketball, cheerleading, cross-country, golf, soccer, softball, volleyball. **On-Campus Highlights:** Derby Center for Science and Mathematics, Becknell Gymnasium, Holloway Theater, Edwards Commons/Bookstore, Mabee Simpson Library.

ADMISSIONS

Freshman Academic Profile: Average high school GPA 3.57. 23.38% in top 10% of high school class, 55.19% in top 25% of high school class, 85.71% in top 50% of high school class. SAT Math middle 50% range 480-560. SAT Critical Reading middle 50% range 440-550. SAT Writing middle 50% range 430-510. ACT middle 50% range 22-27. Minimum internet-based TOEFL 79. Minimum paper TOEFL 550. **Basis for Candidate Selection:** *Very important factors considered include:* academic GPA, standardized test scores. *Important factors considered include:* rigor of secondary school record. *Other factors considered include:* Class rank, application essay, recommendation(s), character/personal qualities, extracurricular activities, interview, level of applicant's interest, talent/ability, volunteer work, work experience. **Freshman Admission Requirements:** High school diploma is required and GED is accepted. *Academic units required:* 4 English, 3 mathematics, 3 science, (2 science labs), 2 foreign language, 1 social studies, 2 history, 1 academic electives. **Freshman Admission Statistics:** 1,952 applied, 61% admitted, 22% enrolled. **Transfer Admission Requirements:** college transcript(s), statement of good standing from prior institution(s). Minimum college GPA of 2.75 required. Lowest grade transferable C. **General Admission Information:** Application Fee $25. Nonfall registration accepted. Admission may be deferred for a maximum of 1 year. Credit and/or placement offered for CEEB Advanced Placement tests.

COSTS AND FINANCIAL AID

Annual tuition $24,070. Room and board $7,790. Required fees $230. Average book expense $1,000. **Required Forms and Deadlines:** FAFSA. **Notification of Awards:** Applicants will be notified of awards on a rolling basis beginning 3/1. **Types of Aid:** *Need-based scholarships/grants:* Federal Pell, SEOG, state scholarships/grants, private scholarships, the school's own gift aid. *Loans:* Subsidized Stafford, Unsubsidized Stafford, PLUS, Federal Perkins. *Student Employment:* Highest amount earned per year from on-campus jobs $5,600. Off-campus job opportunities are good. **Financial Aid Statistics:** 100% freshmen, 100% undergrads receive need-based scholarship or grant aid. 24% freshmen, 22% undergrads receive non-need-based scholarship or grant aid. 72% freshmen, 71% undergrads receive need-based self-help aid. 15% freshmen, 15% undergrads receive athletic scholarships. 100% freshmen, 99% undergrads receive any aid. 78% undergrads borrow to pay for school. Average cumulative indebtedness $21,617. **Criteria for awarding institutional aid:** *Non-need-based:* academics, art, athletics, job skills, leadership, music/drama, religious affiliation.

MACALESTER COLLEGE

1600 Grand Avenue, St. Paul, MN 55105
Phone: 651-696-6357 • **Financial Aid Phone:** 651-696-6214
E-mail: admissions@macalester.edu • **CEEB Code:** 6390
Fax: 651-696-6724 • **Website:** www.macalester.edu • **ACT Code:** 2122

This private school, affiliated with the Presbyterian Church, was founded in 1874. It has a 53-acre campus.

RATINGS

Admissions Selectivity Rating: 94   **Fire Safety Rating:** 97

STUDENTS AND FACULTY

Enrollment: 2,053. **Student Body:** 60% female, 40% male, 82% out-of-state, 13% international (91 countries represented). Asian 7%, African American 2%, Caucasian 66%, Hispanic 6%, Native American <1%
Retention and Graduation: 94% freshmen return for sophomore year. 85% freshmen graduate within 4 years. 90% freshmen graduate within 6 years. 22% grads go on to further study within 1 year. 17% grads pursue arts and sciences degrees. 2% grads pursue law degrees. 1% grads pursue business degrees. 1% grads pursue medical degrees. **Faculty:** 180 full-time faculty, 94% hold PhDs, 51% are members of minority groups, 20% are women. 0% of classes are taught by teaching assistants.

ACADEMICS

Degrees: bachelor's. **Classes:** Most classes have 10–19 students. Most lab/discussion sessions have 10–19 students. **Majors with Highest Enrollment:** Biology/Biological Sciences; Economics; International/Global Studies. **Special Study Options:** cross-registration, double major, honors program, independent study, internships, student-designed major, study abroad, Combined bachelors/graduate programs: -BA/Master's in Architecture with Washington University, St. Louis, Missouri -BA/BS in Engineering with Washington University, St. Louis or the University of Minnesota. **Combined degree programs:** 3/3 Architecture Washington U. **Disability Services:** Special programs offered to physically disabled students include note-taking services, reader services, tape recorders, tutors. **Career services:** Alumni network, alumni services, career assessment, internships, regional alumni. Students at Macalester are civically engaged through a broad range of experientially focused programs. Last year, 302 students did internships for academic credit, 22 classes were offered that included a significant civic engagement component, 42 students worked in non-profit settings through an off-campus student employment program, and students contributed almost 50,000 hours of volunteer service to the community. This is possible due to the college's vibrant urban location and the strongly held belief of faculty, staff, and administration that experiential education and civic engagement are vital elements in a quality liberal arts education.

FACILITIES

Housing: Coed dorms, cooperative housing, apartments for single students, Theme HousingLanguage Houses, Kosher Residence, EcoHouse. 75% of campus accessible to physically disabled. **Special Academic Facilities/Equipment:** Humanities learning center, econometrics lab, cartography lab, 250-acre nature preserve, observatory and planetarium, two electron microscopes, nuclear magnetic resonance spectrometer, laser spectroscopy lab, X-ray diffractometer, International Center, Center for Scholarship and Teaching, Ethnographic lab, GIS lab, State-of-the-Art science labs. **Computers:** 100% of classrooms, 98% of dorms, 100% of libraries, 100% of dining areas, 100% of student union, 90% of common outdoor areas have wireless network access. Students can register for classes online. Administrative functions (other than registration) can be performed online.

CAMPUS LIFE

Environment: Metropolis. **Activities:** Choral groups, concert band, dance, drama/theater, jazz band, literary magazine, music ensembles, radio station, student government, student newspaper, symphony orchestra, Campus Ministries, International Student Organization, Model UN. 80 registered organizations, 15 honor societies, 10 religious organizations. **Athletics (Intercollegiate):** *Men:* baseball, basketball, cross-country, diving, football, golf, soccer, swimming, tennis, track/field (outdoor), track/field (indoor). *Women:* basketball, cross-country, diving, golf, soccer, softball, swimming, tennis, track/field (outdoor), track/field (indoor), volleyball, water polo. **On-Campus Highlights:** Second Floor Campus Center, Bateman Plaza (our front patio), The Quad (our front yard), Shaw Field, Smail Gallery in the Science Center. **Environmental Initiatives:** Developed a comprehensive sustainability plan; Hired a sustainability Manager; Built a LEED Platinum Building.

ADMISSIONS

Freshman Academic Profile: 65% in top 10% of high school class, 93% in top 25% of high school class, 100% in top 50% of high school class. 63% from public high schools. SAT Math middle 50% range 630-735. SAT Critical Reading middle 50% range 640-730. SAT Writing middle 50% range 640-720. ACT middle 50% range 28-32. Minimum internet-based TOEFL 100. Minimum paper TOEFL 600. **Basis for Candidate Selection:** *Very important factors considered include:* academic GPA, rigor of secondary school record. *Important factors considered include:* application essay, recommendation(s), standardized test scores, character/personal qualities, extracurricular activities. *Other factors considered include:* Class rank, alumni/ae relation, first generation, interview, racial/ethnic status, talent/ability, volunteer work, work experience. **Freshman Admission Requirements:** High school diploma or equivalent is not required. **Freshman Admission Statistics:** 6,463 applied, 36% admitted, 23% enrolled. **Transfer Admission Requirements:** High school transcript, college transcript(s), essay or personal statement, standardized test scores, statement of good standing from prior institution(s). Lowest grade transferable C-. **General Admission Information:** Application Fee $40. Early decision application deadline 11/15. Regular application deadline 1/15. Regular notification 3/30. Nonfall registration not accepted. Admission may be deferred for a maximum of 1 year. Credit and/or placement offered for CEEB Advanced Placement tests.

COSTS AND FINANCIAL AID

Average book expense $1,096. **Required Forms and Deadlines:** FAFSA, CSS/Financial Aid PROFILE, Noncustodial PROFILE. **Notification of Awards:** Applicants will be notified of awards on or about 4/1. **Types of Aid:** *Need-based scholarships/grants:* Federal Pell, SEOG, state scholarships/grants, private scholarships, the school's own gift aid. *Loans:* Direct Subsidized Stafford, Direct Unsubsidized Stafford, Direct PLUS, Federal Perkins, state loans. *Student Employment:* Federal Work-Study Program available. Institutional employment available. Highest amount earned per year from on-campus jobs $2,800. Off-campus job opportunities are excellent. **Financial Aid Statistics:** 100% freshmen, 99% undergrads receive need-based scholarship or grant aid. 6% freshmen, 5% undergrads receive non-need-based scholarship or grant aid. 91% freshmen, 92% undergrads receive need-based self-help aid. 0% freshmen, 0% undergrads receive athletic scholarships. 84% freshmen, 78% undergrads receive any aid. 68% undergrads borrow to pay for school. Average cumulative indebtedness $21,902. **Criteria for awarding institutional aid:** *Non-need-based:* academics, minority status.

MACMURRAY COLLEGE

447 East College, Jacksonville, IL 62650
Phone: 217-479-7056 · **Financial Aid Phone:** 217-479-7041
E-mail: admissions@mac.edu · **CEEB Code:** 1435
Fax: 217-291-0702 · **Website:** www.mac.edu · **ACT Code:** 1068

This private school, affiliated with the Methodist Church, was founded in 1846. It has a 60-acre campus.

RATINGS

Admissions Selectivity Rating: 76   Fire Safety Rating: 67

STUDENTS AND FACULTY

Enrollment: 581. **Student Body:** 66% female, 34% male, 11% out-of-state, 0% international (2 countries represented). Asian 1%, African American 13%, Caucasian 73%, Hispanic 3%, Native American <1%.

Retention and Graduation: 72% freshmen return for sophomore year. 26% freshmen graduate within 4 years. 37% freshmen graduate within 6 years. 25% grads go on to further study within 1 year. 9% grads pursue arts and sciences degrees. 1% grads pursue law degrees. 12% grads pursue business degrees. 1% grads pursue medical degrees. **Faculty:** 35 full-time faculty, 63% hold PhDs, 74% are members of minority groups, 3% are women. 0% of classes are taught by teaching assistants.

ACADEMICS

Degrees: associate, bachelor's. **Classes:** Most classes have 10–19 students. Most lab/discussion sessions have 10–19 students. **Majors with Highest Enrollment:** Special Education and Teaching; Registered Nursing/Registered Nurse; Business/Commerce. **Special Study Options:** cooperative education program, double major, dual enrollment, independent study, internships, liberal arts/career combination, student-designed major, study abroad, teacher certification program. **Combined degree programs:** BA/MEng, 3-2 Occupational Therapy prog. w/Washington U. **Disability Services:** Special programs offered to physically disabled students include note-taking services, reader services, tape recorders, tutors. **Career services:** Alumni network, alumni services, career/job search classes, career assessment, internships, regional alumni.

FACILITIES

Housing: Coed dorms, special housing for disabled students, women's dorms. 50% of campus accessible to physically disabled. Art gallery, language lab., music hall, nursing labs.

CAMPUS LIFE

Environment: Village. **Activities:** Choral groups, dance, drama/theater, literary magazine, student government, yearbook, Campus Ministries. 37 registered organizations, 2 honor societies, 2 religious organizations. 2 fraternities, 1 sorority. **Athletics (Intercollegiate):** *Men:* baseball, basketball, football, golf, soccer, wrestling. *Women:* basketball, golf, soccer, softball, volleyball. **On-Campus Highlights:** Gamble Campus, Education Complex, Jane Hall, Putnam Center for the Arts, McClelland Dining Hall.

ADMISSIONS

Freshman Academic Profile: Average high school GPA 2.84. 4% in top 10% of high school class, 28% in top 25% of high school class, 55% in top 50% of high school class. 75% from public high schools. SAT Math middle 50% range 430-500. SAT Critical Reading middle 50% range 370-470. SAT Writing middle 50% range 340-430. ACT middle 50% range 17-23. Minimum paper TOEFL 550. **Basis for Candidate Selection:** *Very important factors considered include:* academic GPA, rigor of secondary school record, standardized test scores. *Important factors considered include:* Class rank, character/personal qualities, extracurricular activities. *Other factors considered include:* application essay, recommendation(s), interview, volunteer work, work experience. **Freshman Admission Requirements:** High school diploma is required and GED is accepted. **Freshman Admission Statistics:** 800 applied, 61% admitted, 19% enrolled. **Transfer Admission Requirements:** college transcript(s), Minimum college GPA of 2.0 required. Lowest grade transferable C. **General Admission Information:** Application Fee $25. Notification on a rolling basis, beginning on or about 9/1. Nonfall registration accepted. Admission may be deferred for a maximum of 12. Credit and/or placement offered for CEEB Advanced Placement tests.

COSTS AND FINANCIAL AID

Annual tuition $15,500. Room and board $5,998. Required fees $250. Average book expense $775. **Required Forms and Deadlines:** FAFSA. **Notification of Awards:** Applicants will be notified of awards on a rolling basis beginning 2/1. **Types of Aid:** *Need-based scholarships/grants:* Federal Pell, SEOG, state scholarships/grants, private scholarships, the school's own gift aid, Federal Nursing Scholarships. *Loans:* Subsidized Stafford, Unsubsidized Stafford, PLUS, Federal Perkins. *Student Employment:* Federal Work-Study Program available. Institutional employment available. Highest amount earned per year from on-campus jobs $945. **Financial Aid Statistics:** 100% freshmen, 100% undergrads receive need-based scholarship or grant aid. 9% freshmen, 7% undergrads receive non-need-based scholarship or grant aid. 79% freshmen, 86% undergrads receive need-based self-help aid. 0% freshmen, 0% undergrads receive athletic scholarships. 95% freshmen, 97% undergrads receive any aid. 95% undergrads borrow to pay for school. Average cumulative indebtedness $18,543. **Criteria for awarding institutional aid:** *Non-need-based:* academics, alumni affiliation, art, leadership, music/drama, religious affiliation.

MAHARISHI UNIVERSITY OF MANAGEMENT

1000 North Fourth Street, Fairfield, IA 52557
Phone: 641-472-1110 · **Financial Aid Phone:** 641-472-1156
E-mail: admissions@mum.edu
Fax: 641-472-1179 · **Website:** www.mum.edu · **ACT Code:** 1317

This private school was founded in 1971. It has a 242-acre campus.

RATINGS

Admissions Selectivity Rating: 68   **Fire Safety Rating:** 60*

STUDENTS AND FACULTY

Enrollment: 199. **Student Body:** 43% female, 57% male, 65% out-of-state, 17% international. Asian 4%, African American 2%, Caucasian 71%, Hispanic 7%, Native American <1%. **Retention and Graduation:** 84% grads go on to further study within 1 year. **Faculty:** 52 full-time faculty, 98% hold PhDs, 21% are members of minority groups, 13% are women. 0% of classes are taught by teaching assistants.

ACADEMICS

Degrees: associate, bachelor's, certificate, doctoral, master's. **Majors with Highest Enrollment:** Fine/Studio Arts; Business/Commerce; Environmental Studies. **Special Study Options:** double major, independent study, internships, study abroad, teacher certification program, Rotating University: several one-month blocks out of each academic year, a course is offered abroad-e.g. students spend a month with professor studying Art in Italy, Literature in Switzerland, or Business in Japan.

FACILITIES

Housing: special housing for disabled students, men's dorms, women's dorms, apartments for married students, apartments for single students, Apartments for students with dependent children; "quiet" dorms. 80% of campus accessible to physically disabled. **Special Academic Facilities/Equipment:** art gallery; scanning electron microscope; real-time cell-imaging computer system; DNA synthesizer; rock-climbing wall.

CAMPUS LIFE

Environment: Village. **Activities:** Choral groups, dance, drama/theater, music ensembles, musical theater, radio station, student government, student newspaper, yearbook. 25 registered organizations, 3 honor societies, 1 religious organization. **Athletics (Intercollegiate):** *Men:* golf. *Women:* golf. **On-Campus Highlights:** Golden Domes, Vedic Architecture, 60,000 sq. ft. Recreation Center, Student Café, Vedic Organic Greenhouses. **Environmental Initiatives:** Four-year bachelors of Science degree offered in Sustainable Living; Construction of new Sustainable Living Center; Implementation of Climate Action Plan.

ADMISSIONS

Freshman Academic Profile: Average high school GPA 3.61. 0% in top 10% of high school class, 0% in top 25% of high school class, 80% in top 50% of high school class. Minimum paper TOEFL 550. **Basis for Candidate Selection:** *Very important factors considered include:* character/personal qualities, interview. *Important factors considered include:* application essay, academic GPA, recommendation(s), rigor of secondary school record, extracurricular activities, level of applicant's interest, talent/ability. *Other factors considered include:* standardized test scores, alumni/ae relation, volunteer work, work experience. **Freshman Admission Requirements:** High school diploma is required and GED is accepted. **Freshman Admission Statistics:** 126 applied, 41% admitted, 87% enrolled. **Transfer Admission Requirements:** High school transcript, college transcript(s), essay or personal statement, interview, Minimum college GPA of 2.5 required. Lowest grade transferable 2. **General Admission Information:** Application Fee $30. Notification on a rolling basis, beginning on or about 12/1. Nonfall registration accepted. Admission may be deferred for a maximum of one semester. Credit offered for CEEB Advanced Placement tests.

COSTS AND FINANCIAL AID

Annual tuition $24,000. Room and board $6,000. Required fees $430. Average book expense $800. **Required Forms and Deadlines:** FAFSA. **Notification of Awards:** Applicants will be notified of awards on a rolling basis beginning 3/1. **Types of Aid:** *Need-based scholarships/grants:* Federal Pell, SEOG, state scholarships/grants, private scholarships, the school's own gift aid, Federal Work Study, Veterans, Benefits. *Loans:* Subsidized Stafford, Unsubsidized Stafford, PLUS, Federal Perkins, college/university loans from institutional funds. *Student Employment:* Federal Work-Study Program available. Off-campus job opportunities are fair. **Financial Aid Statistics:** 100% freshmen, 100% undergrads receive need-based scholarship or grant aid. 0% freshmen, 7% undergrads receive non-need-based scholarship or grant aid. 100% freshmen, 100% undergrads receive need-based self-help aid. 0% freshmen, 0% undergrads receive athletic scholarships. 93% freshmen, 98% undergrads receive any aid. 83% undergrads borrow to pay for school. Average cumulative indebtedness $16,814.

Criteria for awarding institutional aid: *Non-need-based:* academics, alumni affiliation, music/drama, state/district residency.

MAINE COLLEGE OF ART

97 Spring Street, Portland, ME 4101
Phone: 207-775-3052 · **Financial Aid Phone:** 207-775-5157
E-mail: admissions@meca.edu · **CEEB Code:** 3701
Fax: 207-772-5069 · **Website:** www.meca.edu · **ACT Code:** 6908

This private school was founded in 1882.

RATINGS

Admissions Selectivity Rating: 76   **Fire Safety Rating:** 68

STUDENTS AND FACULTY

Enrollment: 425. **Student Body:** 62% female, 38% male, 2% international (7 countries represented). Asian 0%, African American 0%, Caucasian 49%, Hispanic 2%, Native American <1%. **Retention and Graduation:** 73% freshmen return for sophomore year. 32% freshmen graduate within 4 years. 34% freshmen graduate within 6 years. **Faculty:** 30 full-time faculty, 93% hold PhDs, 63% are members of minority groups, 3% are women.

ACADEMICS

Degrees: bachelor's, master's. **Classes:** Most classes have 10–19 students. **Special Study Options:** cross-registration, double major, exchange student program (domestic), independent study, internships, student-designed major, study abroad, teacher certification program, Mobility program with 36 AICAD (Associated Independent Colleges of Art and Design) institutions in USA and Canada; cross-registration program with 4 other colleges and universites in the greater Portland area; BFA credit available through Provincetown, MA Fine Arts Work Center. **Disability Services:** Special programs offered to physically disabled students include note-taking services, reader services, tape recorders, tutors. **Career services:** Alumni network, alumni services, career/job search classes, career assessment, internships, regional alumni.

FACILITIES

Housing: Coed dorms, cooperative housing. 80% of campus accessible to physically disabled. **Special Academic Facilities/Equipment:** Institute of Contemporary Art at Maine College of Art; June Fitzpatrick Gallery; ArtMart (art supply store).

CAMPUS LIFE

Environment: City. **Activities:** student government, student-run film society. **On-Campus Highlights:** The Gorman Student Center ("Living Room"), The Student Gallery, Individual Major Spaces, Institute of Contemporary Art at MECA, Computer Labs.

ADMISSIONS

Freshman Academic Profile: Average high school GPA 3.18. 8% in top 10% of high school class, 19% in top 25% of high school class, 48% in top 50% of high school class. SAT Math middle 50% range 440-560. SAT Critical Reading middle 50% range 480-610. ACT middle 50% range 17-23. Minimum paper TOEFL 500. **Basis for Candidate Selection:** *Very important factors considered include:* rigor of secondary school record, talent/ability. *Important factors considered include:* application essay, recommendation(s), character/personal qualities. *Other factors considered include:* Class rank, standardized test scores, alumni/ae relation, extracurricular activities, geographical residence, interview, racial/ethnic status, state residency, volunteer work, work experience. **Freshman Admission Requirements:** High school diploma is required and GED is accepted. **Freshman Admission Statistics:** 440 applied, 64% admitted, 35% enrolled. **Transfer Admission Requirements:** college transcript(s), essay or personal statement, statement of good standing from prior institution(s). Lowest grade transferable C. **General Admission Information:** Application Fee $40. Nonfall registration accepted. Admission may be deferred for a maximum of 12 months. Credit and/or placement offered for CEEB Advanced Placement tests.

COSTS AND FINANCIAL AID

Required Forms and Deadlines: FAFSA. **Notification of Awards:** Applicants will be notified of awards on a rolling basis beginning 2/15. **Types of Aid:** *Need-based scholarships/grants:* Federal Pell, SEOG, state scholarships/grants, the school's own gift aid. *Loans:* Subsidized Stafford, Unsubsidized Stafford, PLUS, Federal Perkins. **Financial Aid Statistics:** 100% freshmen, 99% undergrads receive need-based scholarship or grant aid. 5% freshmen, 4% undergrads receive non-need-based scholarship or grant aid. 93% freshmen, 91% undergrads receive need-based self-help aid. 0% freshmen, 0% undergrads receive athletic scholarships. 79% undergrads borrow to pay for school. **Criteria for awarding institutional aid:** *Non-need-based:* academics, art.

MAINE MARITIME ACADEMY

Pleasant Street, Castine, ME 4420
Phone: 207-326-2206
E-mail: admissions@mma.edu • **CEEB Code:** 3505
Fax: 207-326-2515 • **Website:** www.mainemaritime.edu • **ACT Code:** 1648

This public school was founded in 1941. It has a 35-acre campus.

RATINGS

Admissions Selectivity Rating: 66   Fire Safety Rating: 60*

STUDENTS AND FACULTY

Enrollment: 814. **Student Body:** 15% female, 85% male, 39% out-of-state, 0% international (10 countries represented). Asian 1%, African American 0%, Caucasian 95%, Hispanic 1%, Native American 1%
Retention and Graduation: 75% freshmen return for sophomore year. 2% grads go on to further study within 1 year. 1% grads pursue arts and sciences degrees. 1% grads pursue law degrees. **Faculty:** 55 full-time faculty. 0% of classes are taught by teaching assistants.

ACADEMICS

Degrees: associate, bachelor's, master's. **Classes:** Most classes have 10–19 students. Most lab/discussion sessions have 10–19 students. **Special Study Options:** cooperative education program, internships, Annual Training Cruises. **Career services:** alumni services, career/job search classes, internships.

FACILITIES

Housing: Coed dorms, apartments for single students. 90% of campus accessible to physically disabled. **Computers:** Administrative functions (other than registration) can be performed online. Undergraduates are required to own a computer.

CAMPUS LIFE

Environment: Rural. **Activities:** concert band, drama/theater, jazz band, marching band, student government, yearbook. 28 registered organizations. **Athletics (Intercollegiate):** *Men:* basketball, cross-country, football, golf, lacrosse, sailing, soccer. *Women:* basketball, cross-country, golf, sailing, soccer, softball.

ADMISSIONS

Freshman Academic Profile: 28% in top 10% of high school class, 48% in top 25% of high school class, 74% in top 50% of high school class. Minimum paper TOEFL 550. **Basis for Candidate Selection:** *Very important factors considered include:* rigor of secondary school record, character/personal qualities. *Important factors considered include:* interview. *Other factors considered include:* Class rank, recommendation(s), alumni/ae relation, extracurricular activities, talent/ability, volunteer work, work experience. **Freshman Admission Requirements:** High school diploma is required and GED is accepted. *Academic units required:* 4 English, 3 mathematics, 2 science, (2 science labs), 0 foreign language, 0 Computer Literacy. **Freshman Admission Statistics:** 613 applied, 76% admitted, 49% enrolled. **Transfer Admission Requirements:** High school transcript, college transcript(s), standardized test scores, statement of good standing from prior institution(s). Minimum college GPA of 2.0 required. Lowest grade transferable C. **General Admission Information:** Application Fee $15. Early decision application deadline 12/20. Regular application deadline 7/1. Notification on a rolling basis, beginning on or about 10/1. Nonfall registration accepted. Admission may be deferred for a maximum of 1 year. Credit offered for CEEB Advanced Placement tests.

COSTS AND FINANCIAL AID

Average book expense $700. **Types of Aid:** *Loans:* Subsidized Stafford, PLUS. *Student Employment:* Federal Work-Study Program available. Institutional employment available. Highest amount earned per year from on-campus jobs $1,200. Off-campus job opportunities are fair.

MALONE UNIVERSITY

2600 Cleveland Avenue NW, Canton, OH 44709
Phone: 330-471-8145 • **Financial Aid Phone:** 330-471-8161
E-mail: admissions@malone.edu • **CEEB Code:** 1439
Fax: 330-471-8149 • **Website:** www.malone.edu • **ACT Code:** 3289

This private school was founded in 1892. It has a 87-acre campus.

RATINGS

Admissions Selectivity Rating: 80   Fire Safety Rating: 78

STUDENTS AND FACULTY

Enrollment: 1,496. **Student Body:** 58% female, 42% male, 14% out-of-state, 1% international (17 countries represented). Asian 1%, African American 8%, Caucasian 84%, Hispanic 2%, Native American <1%
Retention and Graduation: 38% freshmen graduate within 4 years. 51% freshmen graduate within 6 years. **Faculty:** 95 full-time faculty, 78% hold PhDs, 52% are members of minority groups, 4% are women. 0% of classes are taught by teaching assistants.

ACADEMICS

Degrees: bachelor's, master's, post-bachelor's certificate. **Classes:** Most classes have 10–19 students. Most lab/discussion sessions have 10–19 students. **Majors with Highest Enrollment:** Early Childhood Education and Teaching; Business/Commerce; Registered Nursing, Nursing Administration, Nursing Research and Clinical Nursing. **Special Study Options:** Accelerated program, cross-registration, distance learning, double major, dual enrollment, exchange student program (domestic), honors program, independent study, internships, student-designed major, study abroad, teacher certification program, weekend college, 2 degree-completion programs for adults; management, nursing. NOTE: Weekend college is only for degree-completion programs and graduate programs. NOTE: Cooperative education credits are available; but, not entire program. **Honors programs:** The purpose of the Malone University Honors Program is to support the university's intellectually gifted and highly motivated students, to create a community of students and faculty engaged in serious, substantive, and sustained critical inquiry, and to underscore the university's commitment to academic excellence. The Honors Program fulfills this purpose through pursuit of the following goals: 1. Challenging students to fulfill their intellectual and personal potential through enriching and stimulating experiences in and out of the classroom. 2. Cultivating an esprit de corps, committed to an earnest, cooperative, free, and open pursuit of truth. 3. Developing students' understanding of the unity of knowledge and the interrelationship of the academic disciplines. 4. Providing students the occasion for mentoring relationships with faculty. 5. Preparing students for the pursuit of original and advanced research, scholarship, and performance. 6. Equipping students for outstanding leadership in service to God, their communities, and the world. **Combined degree programs:** 3-1 Medical Technology program. **Disability Services:** Special programs offered to physically disabled students include note-taking services, reader services, tape recorders, tutors. **Career services:** alumni services, career/job search classes, career assessment, internships. The highest number of graduates who are hired by the employer providing experiential learning is in Nursing.

FACILITIES

Housing: special housing for disabled students, men's dorms, women's dorms, Theme Housing. **Special Academic Facilities/Equipment:** Child development center. **Computers:** 100% of classrooms, 85% of dorms, 100% of libraries, 100% of dining areas, 100% of student union, 40% of common outdoor areas have wireless network access. Students can register for classes online. Administrative functions (other than registration) can be performed online.

CAMPUS LIFE

Environment: City. **Activities:** Choral groups, concert band, dance, drama/theater, jazz band, literary magazine, marching band, music ensembles, musical theater, radio station, student government, student newspaper, student-run film society, television station, yearbook, Campus Ministries, International Student Organization. 53 registered organizations, 11 honor society, 9 religious organizations. **Athletics (Intercollegiate):** *Men:* baseball, basketball, cheerleading, cross-country, diving, football, golf, soccer, swimming, tennis, track/field (outdoor), track/field (indoor). *Women:* basketball, cheerleading, cross-country, diving, golf, soccer, softball, swimming, tennis, track/field (outdoor), track/field (indoor), volleyball. **On-Campus Highlights:** Hoover Dining Commons, Brehme Centennial Center, Randall Campus Center, Wellness Center, Froggy's & Regula Café, Classsrooms, Randall Campus Center houses the Office of Student Development; a game room, among other features. The Wellness Center houses equipment and laboratories to support the programs of the majors in the Health and Human Performance Department. Also, its aerobic exercise and weight room are available for all Malone University, students, faculty, and staff. It was opened in Fall 2004. **Environmental Initiatives:** Recycling, Reducing, Conservation.

ADMISSIONS

Freshman Academic Profile: Average high school GPA 3.31. 18% in top 10% of high school class, 44% in top 25% of high school class, 76% in top 50% of high school class. 80% from public high schools. SAT Math middle 50% range 472.5-570. SAT Critical Reading middle 50% range 430-570. ACT middle 50% range 20-25. Minimum internet-based TOEFL 79. Minimum paper TOEFL 550. **Basis for Candidate Selection:** *Very important factors considered include:* academic GPA, rigor of secondary school record, standardized test scores, character/personal qualities. *Important factors considered include:* Class rank, level of applicant's interest, religious affiliation/commitment, talent/ability. *Other factors considered include:* application essay, recommendation(s), alumni/ae relation, extracurricular activities, interview, racial/ethnic status, volunteer work. **Freshman Admission Requirements:** High school diploma is required and GED is accepted. *Academic units required:* 4 English, 3 mathematics, 3 science, (1 science labs), 2 foreign language, 2 social studies, 1 history, 1 visual/performing arts, 2 academic electives. **Freshman Admission Statistics:** 1,327 applied, 72% admitted, 33% enrolled. **Transfer Admission Requirements:** High school transcript, college transcript(s), statement of good standing from prior institution(s). Minimum college GPA of 2.0 required. **General Admission Information:** Application Fee $20. Regular application deadline 7/1. Notification on a rolling basis, beginning on or about 9/1. Nonfall registration accepted. Admission may be deferred for a maximum of 2 years. Credit and/or placement offered for CEEB Advanced Placement tests.

COSTS AND FINANCIAL AID

Annual tuition $26,456. Room and board $9,266. Required fees $984. Average book expense $1,200. **Required Forms and Deadlines:** FAFSA. **Notification of Awards:** Applicants will be notified of awards on a rolling basis beginning 3/1. **Types of Aid:** *Need-based scholarships/grants:* Federal Pell, SEOG, state scholarships/grants, private scholarships, the school's own gift aid, Academic Competetiveness and Smart Grant. *Loans:* Subsidized Stafford, Unsubsidized Stafford, PLUS, Federal Perkins, state loans, college/university loans from institutional funds, Private Loans. *Student Employment:* Federal Work-Study Program available. Institutional employment available. Highest amount earned per year from on-campus jobs $2,500. Off-campus job opportunities are good. **Financial Aid Statistics:** 100% freshmen, 98% undergrads receive need-based scholarship or grant aid. 13% freshmen, 13% undergrads receive non-need-based scholarship or grant aid. 82% freshmen, 81% undergrads receive need-based self-help aid. 12% freshmen, 10% undergrads receive athletic scholarships. 100% freshmen, 95% undergrads receive any aid. 83% undergrads borrow to pay for school. Average cumulative indebtedness $25,910. **Criteria for awarding institutional aid:** *Non-need-based:* academics, alumni affiliation, athletics, leadership, music/drama, religious affiliation.

MANCHESTER UNIVERSITY

604 E. College Avenue, N. Manchester, IN 46962
Phone: 260-982-5055 • **Financial Aid Phone:** 260-982-5066
E-mail: admitinfo@manchester.edu • **CEEB Code:** 1440
Fax: 260-982-5239 • **Website:** www.manchester.edu • **ACT Code:** 1222

This private school was founded in 1889. It has a 124-acre campus.

RATINGS

Admissions Selectivity Rating: 79   Fire Safety Rating: 75

STUDENTS AND FACULTY

Enrollment: 1,240. **Student Body:** 52% female, 48% male, 12% out-of-state, 2% international (15 countries represented). Asian 1%, African American 4%, Caucasian 84%, Hispanic 5%, Native American <1%
Retention and Graduation: 48% freshmen graduate within 4 years. 19% grads go on to further study within 1 year. 15% grads pursue arts and sciences degrees. 1% grads pursue law degrees. 3% grads pursue business degrees. 4% grads pursue medical degrees. **Faculty:** 74 full-time faculty, 86% hold PhDs, 7% are women. 0% of classes are taught by teaching assistants.

ACADEMICS

Degrees: associate, bachelor's, master's. **Classes:** Most classes have 20–29 students. **Majors with Highest Enrollment:** Accounting and Business/Management; Education; Health Services/Allied Health/Health Sciences. **Special Study Options:** Accelerated program, cross-registration, double major, dual enrollment, exchange student program (domestic), honors program, independent study, internships, liberal arts/career combination, student-designed major, study abroad, teacher certification program. **Honors programs:** An Honors Program for top students. **Disability Services:** Special programs offered to physically disabled students include reader services, tape recorders, tutors. **Career services:** Alumni network, alumni services, career/job search classes, career assessment, internships, regional alumni. Career services highlights include college-paid internships in regional businesses.

FACILITIES

Housing: Coed dorms, special housing for disabled students, apartments for married students, apartments for single students. **Special Academic Facilities/Equipment:** Language lab, observatory, environmental center and labs. **Computers:** 50% of classrooms, 100% of libraries, 100% of dining areas, 100% of student union, 5% of common outdoor areas have wireless network access. Students can register for classes online. Administrative functions (other than registration) can be performed online.

CAMPUS LIFE

Environment: Rural. **Activities:** Choral groups, concert band, dance, drama/theater, jazz band, literary magazine, music ensembles, musical theater, opera, pep band, radio station, student government, student newspaper, symphony orchestra, yearbook, Campus Ministries, International Student Organization, Model UN. 47 registered organizations, 3 honor societies, 5 religious organizations. **Athletics (Intercollegiate):** *Men:* baseball, basketball, cheerleading, cross-country, football, golf, soccer, tennis, track/field (outdoor), wrestling. *Women:* basketball, cheerleading, cross-country, golf, soccer, softball, tennis, track/field (outdoor), volleyball. **On-Campus Highlights:** Athletic Facilities, Residence Halls, College Union, Petersime Chapel, Science Center, The campus is located on a well maintained wooded 125 acres. **Environmental Initiatives:** Over 25 years of active recyling on campus; One of the oldest envirnmental studies majors in the country. Manchester University environmental studies program director Jerry Sweeten is 2009 Indiana Professor of the Year; see http://www.manchester.edu/OCA/PR/Files/News/SweetenPoY.htm over 25 years of dedication to reduction in energy consumption

ADMISSIONS

Freshman Academic Profile: Average high school GPA 3.36. 16% in top 10% of high school class, 45% in top 25% of high school class, 84% in top 50% of high school class. SAT Math middle 50% range 450-560. SAT Critical Reading middle 50% range 440-540. SAT Writing middle 50% range 420-515. ACT middle 50% range 19-24. Minimum internet-based TOEFL 79. Minimum paper TOEFL 550. **Basis for Candidate Selection:** *Very important factors considered include:* rigor of secondary school record. *Important factors considered include:* academic GPA, recommendation(s), standardized test scores. *Other factors considered include:* Class rank, alumni/ae relation, character/personal qualities, interview, religious affiliation/commitment, talent/ability. **Freshman Admission Requirements:** High school diploma is required and GED is accepted. *Academic units required:* 4 English, 2 mathematics, 2 science, (2 science labs), 2 foreign language, 2 social studies, 1 history, 0 visual/performing arts, 0 computer science, 1 academic electives. **Freshman Admission Statistics:** 2,551 applied, 74% admitted, 23% enrolled. **Transfer Admission Requirements:** High school transcript, college transcript(s), statement of good standing from prior institution(s). Minimum college GPA of 2.0 required. **General Admission Information:** Application Fee $25. Notification on a rolling basis, beginning on or about 9/1. Nonfall registration accepted. Admission may be deferred for a maximum of 1 year. Credit and/or placement offered for CEEB Advanced Placement tests.

COSTS AND FINANCIAL AID

Annual tuition $27,000. Room and board $9,250. Required fees $920. Average book expense $1,000. **Required Forms and Deadlines:** FAFSA. **Notification of Awards:** Applicants will be notified of awards on a rolling basis beginning 3/30. **Types of Aid:** *Need-based scholarships/grants:* Federal Pell, SEOG, state scholarships/grants, private scholarships, the school's own gift aid. *Loans:* Subsidized Stafford, Unsubsidized Stafford, PLUS, Federal Perkins. *Student Employment:* Highest amount earned per year from on-campus jobs $2,000. Off-campus job opportunities are fair. **Financial Aid Statistics:** 100% freshmen, 100% undergrads receive need-based scholarship or grant aid. 11% freshmen, 11% undergrads receive non-need-based scholarship or grant aid. 89% freshmen, 89% undergrads receive need-based self-help aid. 0% freshmen, 0% undergrads receive athletic scholarships. 100% freshmen, 99% undergrads receive any aid. 82% undergrads borrow to pay for school. Average cumulative indebtedness $24,826. **Criteria for awarding institutional aid:** *Non-need-based:* academics, alumni affiliation, minority status, religious affiliation.

MANHATTAN CHRISTIAN COLLEGE

1415 Anderson, Manhattan, KS 66502-4081
Phone: 877-246-4622 • **Financial Aid Phone:** 785-539-3571
E-mail: admit@mccks.edu
Fax: 785-776-9251 • **Website:** www.mccks.edu • **ACT Code:** 1436

This private school, affiliated with the Christian (Nondenominational) Church, was founded in 1927. It has a 1-acre campus.

RATINGS

Admissions Selectivity Rating: 78   Fire Safety Rating: 70

STUDENTS AND FACULTY

Enrollment: 310. **Student Body:** 51% female, 49% male, 35% out-of-state, 0% international. Asian 0%, African American 4%, Caucasian 99%, Hispanic 2%, Native American <1%
Retention and Graduation: 51% freshmen return for sophomore year. 36% freshmen graduate within 6 years. 3% grads go on to further study within 1 year.

Faculty: 10 full-time faculty, 40% hold PhDs, 20% are members of minority groups, 10% are women. 0% of classes are taught by teaching assistants.

ACADEMICS
Degrees: associate, bachelor's, certificate, post-bachelor's certificate, transfer associate. **Classes:** Most classes have 10–19 students. **Majors with Highest Enrollment:** Bible/Biblical Studies; Pastoral Counseling and Specialized Ministries; Management Science. **Special Study Options:** double major, dual enrollment, internships. **Combined degree programs:** Dual-degree program with Kansas State University. **Disability Services:** Special programs offered to physically disabled students include tutors. **Career services:** career assessment, internships. Career services highlights include internships that are required as a Directed Field Experience and that must be at least 10-weeks long.

FACILITIES
Housing: men's dorms, women's dorms, apartments for married students, apartments for single students. 100% of campus accessible to physically disabled.

CAMPUS LIFE
Environment: Town. **Activities:** dance, music ensembles, student government, yearbook 2 honor societies, 10 religious organizations. **Athletics (Intercollegiate):** *Men:* baseball, basketball, soccer. *Women:* basketball, soccer, volleyball. **On-Campus Highlights:** Coffin Memorial Hall, Campus Center, Residence Halls.

ADMISSIONS
Freshman Academic Profile: Average high school GPA 3.38. 30% in top 10% of high school class, 40% in top 25% of high school class, 70% in top 50% of high school class. 95% from public high schools. ACT middle 50% range 19-25. Minimum paper TOEFL 550. **Basis for Candidate Selection:** *Very important factors considered include:* recommendation(s), character/personal qualities, religious affiliation/commitment. *Important factors considered include:* application essay, rigor of secondary school record, standardized test scores, talent/ability. *Other factors considered include:* extracurricular activities, interview, volunteer work. **Freshman Admission Requirements:** High school diploma is required and GED is accepted. **Freshman Admission Statistics:** 155 applied, 79% admitted, 66% enrolled. **Transfer Admission Requirements:** college transcript(s), essay or personal statement, Minimum college GPA of 2.0 required. Lowest grade transferable C. **General Admission Information:** Application Fee $25. Regular application deadline 8/1. Notification on a rolling basis, beginning on or about 10/1. Nonfall registration accepted. Admission may be deferred for a maximum of 1 year. Credit and/or placement offered for CEEB Advanced Placement tests.

COSTS AND FINANCIAL AID
Average book expense $1,150. **Required Forms and Deadlines:** FAFSA. **Notification of Awards:** Applicants will be notified of awards on a rolling basis beginning 5/1. **Types of Aid:** *Need-based scholarships/grants:* Federal Pell, SEOG, state scholarships/grants, private scholarships, the school's own gift aid. *Loans:* Direct Subsidized Stafford, Direct Unsubsidized Stafford, Direct PLUS, Federal Perkins. *Student Employment:* Federal Work-Study Program available. Off-campus job opportunities are good. **Financial Aid Statistics:** 53% freshmen, 89% undergrads receive need-based scholarship or grant aid. 96% freshmen, 84% undergrads receive non-need-based scholarship or grant aid. 78% freshmen, 97% undergrads receive need-based self-help aid. 0% freshmen, 0% undergrads receive athletic scholarships. 55% undergrads borrow to pay for school. **Criteria for awarding institutional aid:** *Non-need-based:* academics, alumni affiliation, leadership, music/drama, religious affiliation.

MANHATTAN COLLEGE

Manhattan College Parkway, Riverdale, NY 10471
Phone: 718-862-7200 · **Financial Aid Phone:** 718-862-7100
E-mail: admit@manhattan.edu · **CEEB Code:** 2395
Fax: 718-862-8019 · **Website:** www.manhattan.edu

This private school, affiliated with the Roman Catholic Church, was founded in 1853. It has a 22-acre campus.

RATINGS
Admissions Selectivity Rating: 84   **Fire Safety Rating:** 75

STUDENTS AND FACULTY
Enrollment: 3,471. **Student Body:** 44% female, 56% male, 28% out-of-state, 3% international (46 countries represented). Asian 4%, African American 4%, Caucasian 56%, Hispanic 19%, Native American <1%
Retention and Graduation: 64% freshmen graduate within 4 years. 74% freshmen graduate within 6 years. 28% grads go on to further study within 1

year. 1% grads pursue law degrees. 2% grads pursue business degrees. 1% grads pursue medical degrees. **Faculty:** 225 full-time faculty, 98% hold PhDs, 43% are members of minority groups, 13% are women. 0% of classes are taught by teaching assistants.

ACADEMICS
Degrees: bachelor's, master's. **Classes:** Most classes have 20–29 students. Most lab/discussion sessions have 10–19 students. **Majors with Highest Enrollment:** Special Education and Teaching; Civil Engineering; Marketing/Marketing Management. **Special Study Options:** Accelerated program, cooperative education program, cross-registration, distance learning, double major, English as a Second Language (ESL), exchange student program (domestic), honors program, independent study, internships, liberal arts/career combination, student-designed major, study abroad, teacher certification program. **Honors programs:** Honors Enrichment Program **Combined degree programs:** BA/MA, BA/MEng, Education. **Disability Services:** Special programs offered to physically disabled students include note-taking services, reader services, tape recorders, tutors. **Career services:** alumni services, career/job search classes, career assessment, internships.

FACILITIES
Housing: Coed dorms. 100% of campus accessible to physically disabled. **Special Academic Facilities/Equipment:** Research and learning center, 24-hour Internet café. **Computers:** 100% of classrooms, 50% of dorms, 100% of libraries, 100% of dining areas, 100% of student union, 100% of common outdoor areas have wireless network access. Students can register for classes online. Administrative functions (other than registration) can be performed online.

CAMPUS LIFE
Environment: Metropolis. **Activities:** Choral groups, concert band, dance, drama/theater, jazz band, literary magazine, music ensembles, musical theater, radio station, student government, student newspaper, symphony orchestra, television station, yearbook, Campus Ministries, International Student Organization, Model UN. 64 registered organizations, 30 honor societies, 2 religious organizations. 2 fraternities, 2 sororities. **Athletics (Intercollegiate):** *Men:* baseball, basketball, cross-country, golf, lacrosse, soccer, tennis, track/field (outdoor), track/field (indoor). *Women:* basketball, cross-country, lacrosse, soccer, softball, swimming, tennis, track/field (outdoor), track/field (indoor), volleyball. **On-Campus Highlights:** Quadrangle, O'Malley Library, Internet Café, Galligan Exercise Center, Thomas Hall.

ADMISSIONS
Freshman Academic Profile: Average high school GPA 88.96. 23% in top 10% of high school class, 52% in top 25% of high school class, 85% in top 50% of high school class. 57% from public high schools. SAT Math middle 50% range 500-610. SAT Critical Reading middle 50% range 490-580. SAT Writing middle 50% range 480-590. ACT middle 50% range 22-27. Minimum internet-based TOEFL 80. Minimum paper TOEFL 550. **Basis for Candidate Selection:** *Very important factors considered include:* academic GPA, rigor of secondary school record, standardized test scores. *Important factors considered include:* Class rank, application essay, recommendation(s), extracurricular activities, interview. *Other factors considered include:* alumni/ae relation, character/personal qualities, talent/ability, volunteer work, work experience. **Freshman Admission Requirements:** High school diploma is required and GED is accepted. *Academic units required:* 4 English, 3 mathematics, 2 science, 2 foreign language, 3 social studies, 2 academic electives. **Freshman Admission Statistics:** 8,199 applied, 67% admitted, 14% enrolled. **Transfer Admission Requirements:** High school transcript, college transcript(s), standardized test scores, statement of good standing from prior institution(s). Minimum college GPA of 2.5 required. Lowest grade transferable C. **General Admission Information:** Application Fee $60. Early decision application deadline 11/15. Notification on a rolling basis, beginning on or about 12/15. Nonfall registration accepted. Admission may be deferred for a maximum of 1 year. Credit and/or placement offered for CEEB Advanced Placement tests.

COSTS AND FINANCIAL AID
Annual tuition $33,000. Room and board $13,080. Required fees $3,250. Average book expense $1,200. **Required Forms and Deadlines:** FAFSA. **Notification of Awards:** Applicants will be notified of awards on a rolling basis beginning 2/15. **Types of Aid:** *Need-based scholarships/grants:* Federal Pell, SEOG, state scholarships/grants, private scholarships, the school's own gift aid. *Loans:* Direct Subsidized Stafford, Direct Unsubsidized Stafford, Direct PLUS, Subsidized Stafford, Unsubsidized Stafford, PLUS, Federal Perkins. *Student Employment:* Highest amount earned per year from on-campus jobs $1,500. **Financial Aid Statistics:** 14% freshmen, 13% undergrads receive non-need-based scholarship or grant aid. 70% freshmen, 71% undergrads receive need-based self-help aid. 3% freshmen, 3% undergrads receive athletic scholarships. 88% freshmen, 86% undergrads receive any aid. 75% undergrads borrow to pay for school. Average cumulative indebtedness $25,762. **Criteria for awarding institutional aid:** *Non-need-based:* academics, athletics.

See page 1088.

MANHATTAN SCHOOL OF MUSIC

120 Claremont Ave, New York, NY 10027
Phone: 212-749-2802 • **Financial Aid Phone:** 917-493-4463
E-mail: admission@msmnyc.edu • **CEEB Code:** 2396
Fax: 212-749-3025 • **Website:** www.msmnyc.edu • **ACT Code:** 2809

This private school was founded in 1917. It has a 1-acre campus.

RATINGS

Admissions Selectivity Rating: 67   **Fire Safety Rating:** 74

STUDENTS AND FACULTY

Enrollment: 408. **Student Body:** 48% female, 52% male, 69% out-of-state, 20% international (27 countries represented). Asian 9%, African American 3%, Caucasian 44%, Hispanic 4%, Native American <1% **Retention and Graduation:** 82% freshmen return for sophomore year. 90% grads go on to further study within 1 year. 75% grads pursue arts and sciences degrees. 1% grads pursue law degrees. 1% grads pursue business degrees. 1% grads pursue medical degrees. **Faculty:** 1% of classes are taught by teaching assistants.

ACADEMICS

Degrees: bachelor's, diploma, master's, post-master's certificate. **Special Study Options:** cross-registration, English as a Second Language (ESL), study abroad. **Disability Services:** Special programs offered to physically disabled students include note-taking services, reader services, tape recorders, tutors. **Career services:** Alumni network, alumni services, career/job search classes. Career services highlights include training in educational and community outreach.

FACILITIES

Housing: apartments for married students, apartments for single students. 75% of campus accessible to physically disabled. **Special Academic Facilities/Equipment:** Electronic music studios, electronic piano lab, recording studio, practice rooms, 1,000-seat auditorium, 3 recital halls.

CAMPUS LIFE

Environment: Metropolis. **Activities:** Choral groups, dance, drama/theater, jazz band, literary magazine, music ensembles, student government, symphony orchestra. 8 registered organizations. **On-Campus Highlights:** Library, Residence Hall, Practice Rooms, Concert Halls, Cafeteria.

ADMISSIONS

Freshman Academic Profile: 75% from public high schools. Minimum paper TOEFL 550. **Basis for Candidate Selection:** *Very important factors considered include:* rigor of secondary school record, interview, talent/ability. *Important factors considered include:* application essay, recommendation(s), character/personal qualities, extracurricular activities, volunteer work. *Other factors considered include:* Class rank, standardized test scores, alumni/ae relation, racial/ethnic status, work experience. **Freshman Admission Requirements:** High school diploma is required and GED is accepted. *Academic units required:* 2 English, 2 mathematics, 2 science, (0 science labs), 0 foreign language, 3 social studies, 3 history. **Freshman Admission Statistics:** 794 applied, 40% admitted, 32% enrolled. **Transfer Admission Requirements:** college transcript(s), essay or personal statement, interview, Minimum college GPA of 3 required. Lowest grade transferable C. **General Admission Information:** Application Fee $100. Regular application deadline 12/1. Regular notification 4/1. Nonfall registration not accepted. Admission may be deferred for a maximum of 2 semesters. Credit offered for CEEB Advanced Placement tests.

COSTS AND FINANCIAL AID

Annual tuition $26,000. Room and board $14,250. Required fees $460. Average book expense $850. **Required Forms and Deadlines:** FAFSA, Institution's own financial aid form, CSS/Financial Aid PROFILE. **Notification of Awards:** Applicants will be notified of awards on or about 4/1. **Types of Aid:** *Need-based scholarships/grants:* Federal Pell, SEOG, state scholarships/grants, the school's own gift aid. *Loans:* Subsidized Stafford, Unsubsidized Stafford, PLUS, Federal Perkins. *Student Employment:* Federal Work-Study Program available. Institutional employment available. Highest amount earned per year from on-campus jobs $4,000. Off-campus job opportunities are excellent. **Financial Aid Statistics:** 89% freshmen, 75% undergrads receive need-based scholarship or grant aid. 6% freshmen, 10% undergrads receive non-need-based scholarship or grant aid. 77% freshmen, 84% undergrads receive need-based self-help aid. 0% freshmen, 0% undergrads receive athletic scholarships. 66% freshmen, 75% undergrads receive any aid. 58% undergrads borrow to pay for school. **Criteria for awarding institutional aid:** *Non-need-based:* academics, alumni affiliation, art, music/drama.

MANHATTANVILLE COLLEGE

2900 Purchase Street, Purchase, NY 10577
Phone: 914-323-5464 • **Financial Aid Phone:** 914-323-5357
E-mail: admissions@mville.edu • **CEEB Code:** 2397
Fax: 914-694-1732 • **Website:** www.mville.edu • **ACT Code:** 2800

This private school was founded in 1841. It has a 100-acre campus.

RATINGS

Admissions Selectivity Rating: 73   **Fire Safety Rating:** 98

STUDENTS AND FACULTY

Enrollment: 1,754. **Student Body:** 64% female, 36% male, 30% out-of-state, 9% international (47 countries represented). Asian 1%, African American 8%, Caucasian 29%, Hispanic 13%, Native American <1% **Retention and Graduation:** 79% freshmen return for sophomore year. 57% freshmen graduate within 4 years. 24% grads go on to further study within 1 year. 6% grads pursue arts and sciences degrees. 1% grads pursue law degrees. 1% grads pursue business degrees. 2% grads pursue medical degrees. **Faculty:** 105 full-time faculty, 82% hold PhDs, 51% are members of minority groups, 13% are women. 0% of classes are taught by teaching assistants.

ACADEMICS

Degrees: bachelor's, master's, post-bachelor's certificate, post-master's certificate. **Classes:** Most classes have 10–19 students. **Majors with Highest Enrollment:** Business/Commerce; Psychology; Communication. **Special Study Options:** Accelerated program, cross-registration, double major, dual enrollment, English as a Second Language (ESL), exchange student program (domestic), honors program, independent study, internships, student-designed major, study abroad, teacher certification program, weekend college. **Honors programs:** The Castle Scholars Program offers students of exceptional ability a broader and more intensive program of study than the usual college curriculum. It provides motivated students in any major field with challenging, cross-disciplinary courses that encourage their academic and personal growth. Participation in the Castle Scholars Program encourages intellectual exchange among students and faculty and fosters independent initiative in academic and creative realms. Advised and mentored by the Program Director, Castle Scholars are well prepared for success in graduate and professional schools, as well as in the professional world. Castle Scholars build relationships with each other and with the college's faculty in specially-designed Honors Seminars and other unique academic opportunities, as well as in a host of social events throughout the year. Through their studies, research, and service, the Scholars contribute to the intellectual and social life of the college. Studies are augmented by participation in the wider New York City community. The Castle Scholars Program complements a student's chosen major and minor and is distinct from honors options within the major. Castle Scholars are recognized annually at college-wide awards receptions, and honors courses are noted on student academic transcripts. Successful completion of the program will be noted on the final transcript as well as on printed graduation materials. **Combined degree programs:** BA/MA, Dual BS programs. **Disability Services:** Special programs offered to physically disabled students include note-taking services, reader services, tape recorders, tutors. **Career services:** Alumni network, career/job search classes, career assessment, internships, regional alumni. Career services highlights include internships involving career-related work that enhances a student's academic program.

FACILITIES

Housing: Coed dorms. 95% of campus accessible to physically disabled. **Special Academic Facilities/Equipment:** Art gallery, art and music studios, Environmental Park, English language institute, two electron microscopes, library. **Computers:** Students can register for classes online. Administrative functions (other than registration) can be performed online.

CAMPUS LIFE

Environment: Town. **Activities:** Choral groups, concert band, dance, drama/theater, jazz band, literary magazine, music ensembles, musical theater, opera, radio station, student government, student newspaper, student-run film society, symphony orchestra, television station, yearbook, Campus Ministries, International Student Organization. 46 registered organizations, 2 honor societies, 5 religious organizations. **Athletics (Intercollegiate):** *Men:* baseball, basketball, golf, ice hockey, lacrosse, soccer, tennis. *Women:* basketball, cheerleading, field hockey, ice hockey, lacrosse, soccer, softball, tennis, volleyball. **On-Campus Highlights:** The Castle, Library Café, Richard Berman Student Center, Kennedy Gymnasium, Quad, New Student Center. **Environmental Initiatives:**

Environmental Classroom Building's Platinum Rating (LEED); New Student Center's Gold Rating (LEED); Green Cleaning.

ADMISSIONS

Freshman Academic Profile: SAT Math middle 50% range 480-580. SAT Critical Reading middle 50% range 490-580. SAT Writing middle 50% range 480-590. ACT middle 50% range 21-26. Minimum internet-based TOEFL 80. Minimum paper TOEFL 550. **Basis for Candidate Selection:** *Very important factors considered include:* rigor of secondary school record. *Important factors considered include:* application essay, recommendation(s), extracurricular activities, interview. *Other factors considered include:* alumni/ae relation, character/personal qualities, geographical residence, talent/ability, volunteer work, work experience. **Freshman Admission Requirements:** High school diploma is required and GED is accepted. *Academic units required:* 4 English, 3 mathematics, 2 science, 2 social studies, 5 academic electives. **Freshman Admission Statistics:** 3,929 applied, 74% admitted, 16% enrolled. **Transfer Admission Requirements:** college transcript(s), statement of good standing from prior institution(s). Minimum college GPA of 2.5 required. Lowest grade transferable C. **General Admission Information:** Application Fee $70. Early decision application deadline 12/1. Regular application deadline 3/1. Notification on a rolling basis, beginning on or about 1/5. Nonfall registration accepted. Admission may be deferred for a maximum of 1 year. Credit and/or placement offered for CEEB Advanced Placement tests.

COSTS AND FINANCIAL AID

Annual tuition $34,870. Room and board $14,520. Required fees $1,350. Average book expense $800. **Required Forms and Deadlines:** FAFSA, State aid form. **Notification of Awards:** Applicants will be notified of awards on a rolling basis beginning 3/1. **Types of Aid:** *Need-based scholarships/grants:* Federal Pell, SEOG, state scholarships/grants, private scholarships, the school's own gift aid. *Loans:* Direct Subsidized Stafford, Direct Unsubsidized Stafford, Direct PLUS. *Student Employment:* Federal Work-Study Program available. Institutional employment available. Off-campus job opportunities are excellent. **Financial Aid Statistics:** 69% freshmen, 77% undergrads receive need-based scholarship or grant aid. 95% freshmen, 99% undergrads receive non-need-based scholarship or grant aid. 71% freshmen, 73% undergrads receive need-based self-help aid. 0% freshmen, 0% undergrads receive athletic scholarships. 97% freshmen, 94% undergrads receive any aid. 72% undergrads borrow to pay for school. Average cumulative indebtedness $26,299. **Criteria for awarding institutional aid:** *Non-need-based:* academics, alumni affiliation, art, leadership, music/drama.

MANNES COLLEGE—
THE NEW SCHOOL FOR MUSIC

72 Fifth Avenue, New York, NY 10011
Phone: 212-580-5150 • **Financial Aid Phone:** 212-229-8930
E-mail: mannesadmission@newschool.edu • **CEEB Code:** 2521
Website: www.mannes.edu • **ACT Code:** 2828

This private school was founded in 1916.

RATINGS

Admissions Selectivity Rating: 70   **Fire Safety Rating:** 79

STUDENTS AND FACULTY

Enrollment: 150. **Student Body:** 53% female, 47% male, 61% out-of-state, 39% international (31 countries represented). Asian 8%, African American 1%, Caucasian 38%, Hispanic 5%, Native American %
Retention and Graduation: 73% freshmen return for sophomore year. 60% freshmen graduate within 4 years. 5% grads go on to further study within 1 year. **Faculty:** 17 full-time faculty, 18% hold PhDs, 47% are members of minority groups, 12% are women. 0% of classes are taught by teaching assistants.

ACADEMICS

Degrees: bachelor's, diploma, master's, post-bachelor's certificate, post-master's certificate. **Classes:** Most classes have fewer than 10 students. **Special Study Options:** Accelerated program, double major, English as a Second Language (ESL), independent study, internships. **Disability Services:** Special programs offered to physically disabled students include note-taking services, reader services, tape recorders. **Career services:** Alumni network, alumni services, career/job search classes, career assessment, internships, regional alumni.

FACILITIES

Housing: Coed dorms, special housing for disabled students, apartments for single students. 99% of campus accessible to physically disabled. **Special

Academic Facilities/Equipment: Art gallery, photography gallery, extensive collections of contemporary art, concert hall, public lectures, conferences, cultural and intellectual events. **Computers:** 95% of classrooms, 100% of libraries, 100% of dining areas, na% of student union, 100% of common outdoor areas have wireless network access. Students can register for classes online. Administrative functions (other than registration) can be performed online.

CAMPUS LIFE

Environment: Metropolis. **Activities:** Choral groups, dance, drama/theater, jazz band, literary magazine, music ensembles, opera, radio station, student government, student newspaper, symphony orchestra, International Student Organization. 39 registered organizations. **On-Campus Highlights:** Mannes Concert Hall **Environmental Initiatives:** 1. In Fall 2010, The New School Facilities Management hired an engineering firm to conduct energy audits and to retro-commission five of the most energy-intensive owned buildings on campus. The result will be a phased capital plan to address needed upgrades in these buildings, equating to 500,000gsf, that will reduce carbon emissions. 2. The New School Office for Sustainability hired a consultant to conduct a waste audit of the entire campus in Fall 2009. A waste reduction strategy is currently being finalized. The immediate outcomes are new recycling signs and an enhanced post-consumer composting program in four buildings. Food scraps, napkins/paper towels and compostable cups and utensils will be collected in all food service locations plus a pilot location in a building with architecture and fine arts studios. The New School replaced two steam boilers, which were approximately 50 years old. Located in Johnson/Kaplan Hall, the universitys founding building, constructed in 1930, this boiler plant burned #6 heating oil, the dirtiest and most carbon-intensive heating oil. In the summer of 2010, Design, Construction, and Facilities Management upgraded the plant to house two new steam dual-fuel boilers with a thermal efficiency of 86 percent and the option to burn #2 heating oil or, eventually, natural gas, the least carbon intensive fossil fuel. This retrofit project also marks the phasing out of #6 heating oil on campus. In the summer of 2010, Design, Construction, and Facilities Management also replaced the roof at Johnson/Kaplan Hall with a white Thermoplastic Polyolefin (TPO) thermally bonded membrane with superior durability and an ENERGY STAR rating for its high reflectance. Insulation was also added to the roof. The new roof drastically reduces heat absorption in the summer months and also better insulates the building in the winter, resulting in lower cooling and heating loads and costs. Phasing out the use of T12 and incandescent lighting has been an ongoing initiative over the past two years and focused on 45 percent of the entire building portfolio (equivalent to 563,503 gross square feet, which represents nearly 72 percent of The New Schools owned buildings). In FY10, the Office for Sustainability began to install campus-wide (in all spaces where The New School has operational control) occupancy sensors in bathrooms, office kitchenettes, and conference rooms. By the end of FY12, the university will phase out T12s and incandescent lighting in all university-owned buildings and launch a LED lighting demonstration project.

ADMISSIONS

Freshman Academic Profile: Average high school GPA 3.37. **Basis for Candidate Selection:** *Very important factors considered include:* level of applicant's interest, talent/ability. *Important factors considered include:* academic GPA, recommendation(s), rigor of secondary school record. *Other factors considered include:* Class rank, application essay, character/personal qualities, extracurricular activities, interview. **Freshman Admission Requirements:** High school diploma is required and GED is accepted. *Academic units required:* 4 English, 4 mathematics, 4 science, (2 science labs), 2 social studies. **Freshman Admission Statistics:** 410 applied, 36% admitted, 23% enrolled. **Transfer Admission Requirements:** college transcript(s), essay or personal statement, Minimum college GPA of 2.0 required. Lowest grade transferable C. **General Admission Information:** Application Fee $100. Regular application deadline 12/1. Notification on a rolling basis, beginning on or about 4/1. Nonfall registration not accepted. Credit and/or placement offered for CEEB Advanced Placement tests.

COSTS AND FINANCIAL AID

Annual tuition $37,950. Room and board $18,490. Required fees $886. Average book expense $920. **Required Forms and Deadlines:** FAFSA, State aid form. **Notification of Awards:** Applicants will be notified of awards on a rolling basis beginning 3/1. **Types of Aid:** *Need-based scholarships/grants:* Federal Pell, SEOG, state scholarships/grants, private scholarships, the school's own gift aid. *Loans:* Subsidized Stafford, Unsubsidized Stafford, PLUS, Federal Perkins. *Student Employment:* Federal Work-Study Program available. Institutional employment available. Off-campus job opportunities are good. **Financial Aid Statistics:** 93% freshmen, 77% undergrads receive need-based scholarship or grant aid. 20% freshmen, 11% undergrads receive non-need-based scholarship or grant aid. 93% freshmen, 93% undergrads receive need-based self-help aid. 0% freshmen, 0% undergrads receive athletic scholarships. 36% undergrads borrow to pay for school. Average cumulative indebtedness $17,860. **Criteria for awarding institutional aid:** *Non-need-based:* music/drama.

MANSFIELD UNIVERSITY

71 Academy Street, Mansfield, PA 16933
Phone: 570-662-4243 • **Financial Aid Phone:** 570-664-4129
E-mail: admissions@mansfield.edu • **CEEB Code:** 2655
Fax: 570-662-4121 • **Website:** mansfield.edu • **ACT Code:** 3710

This public school was founded in 1857. It has a 174-acre campus.

RATINGS

Admissions Selectivity Rating: 72   Fire Safety Rating: 71

STUDENTS AND FACULTY

Enrollment: 2,640. **Student Body:** 59% female, 41% male, 20% out-of-state, 1% international (15 countries represented). Asian 1%, African American 9%, Caucasian 81%, Hispanic 3%, Native American <1%
Retention and Graduation: 72% freshmen return for sophomore year. 35% freshmen graduate within 4 years. 50% freshmen graduate within 6 years. 23% grads go on to further study within 1 year. **Faculty:** 140 full-time faculty, 84% hold PhDs, 46% are members of minority groups, 10% are women. 0% of classes are taught by teaching assistants.

ACADEMICS

Degrees: associate, bachelor's, certificate, diploma, master's. **Classes:** Most classes have 20–29 students. Most lab/discussion sessions have 20–29 students. **Majors with Highest Enrollment:** Education; Music Teacher Education; Criminal Justice/Law Enforcement Administration. **Special Study Options:** cross-registration, distance learning, double major, dual enrollment, exchange student program (domestic), honors program, independent study, internships, liberal arts/career combination, student-designed major, study abroad, teacher certification program. **Disability Services:** Special programs offered to physically disabled students include note-taking services, reader services, tape recorders, tutors. **Career services:** career/job search classes, career assessment, internships.

FACILITIES

Housing: Coed dorms, fraternity/sorority housing. 90% of campus accessible to physically disabled. **Special Academic Facilities/Equipment:** Science museum, two art galleries, animal collection, planetarium, solar collector. **Computers:** Students can register for classes online.

CAMPUS LIFE

Environment: Rural. **Activities:** Choral groups, concert band, dance, drama/theater, jazz band, literary magazine, marching band, music ensembles, musical theater, pep band, radio station, student government, student newspaper, symphony orchestra, television station. 108 registered organizations, 10 honor societies, 4 religious organizations. 6 fraternities, 4 sororities. **Athletics (Intercollegiate):** *Men:* baseball, basketball, cross-country, football, track/field (outdoor), track/field (indoor). *Women:* basketball, cheerleading, cross-country, diving, field hockey, soccer, softball, swimming, track/field (outdoor), track/field (indoor). **On-Campus Highlights:** North Hall Library, Fitness Center, Student Union.

ADMISSIONS

Freshman Academic Profile: Average high school GPA 3.31. 8% in top 10% of high school class, 29% in top 25% of high school class, 63% in top 50% of high school class. SAT Math middle 50% range 430-540. SAT Critical Reading middle 50% range 420-530. SAT Writing middle 50% range 390-470. Minimum internet-based TOEFL 61. Minimum paper TOEFL 500. **Basis for Candidate Selection:** *Very important factors considered include:* Class rank, academic GPA, rigor of secondary school record, standardized test scores. *Other factors considered include:* application essay, recommendation(s), alumni/ae relation, character/personal qualities, extracurricular activities, first generation, geographical residence, interview, talent/ability, volunteer work, work experience. **Freshman Admission Requirements:** High school diploma is required and GED is accepted. *Academic units required:* 4 English, 3 mathematics, 2 science, (2 science labs), 2 foreign language, 4 history, 6 academic electives. **Freshman Admission Statistics:** 2,023 applied, 92% admitted, 34% enrolled. **Transfer Admission Requirements:** college transcript(s), Minimum college GPA of 2.0 required. Lowest grade transferable D. **General Admission Information:** Application Fee $25. Notification on a rolling basis, beginning on or about 7/1. Nonfall registration accepted. Admission may be deferred for a maximum of 12. Credit offered for CEEB Advanced Placement tests.

COSTS AND FINANCIAL AID

Annual in-state tuition $6,622. Annual out-of-state tuition $16,556. Room and board $10,276. Required fees $2,570. Average book expense $1,200. **Required Forms and Deadlines:** FAFSA, State aid form. **Notification of Awards:** Applicants will be notified of awards on a rolling basis beginning 3/15. **Types of Aid:** *Need-based scholarships/grants:* Federal Pell, SEOG, state scholarships/grants, private scholarships, the school's own gift aid, United Negro College Fund, Federal Nursing Scholarships. *Loans:* Subsidized Stafford, Unsubsidized Stafford, PLUS, Federal Perkins, Federal Nursing, state loans. *Student Employment:* Federal Work-Study Program available. Institutional employment available. Highest amount earned per year from on-campus jobs $1,236. Off-campus job opportunities are fair. **Financial Aid Statistics:** 71% freshmen, 73% undergrads receive need-based scholarship or grant aid. 80% freshmen, 82% undergrads receive non-need-based scholarship or grant aid. 98% freshmen, 97% undergrads receive need-based self-help aid. 2% freshmen, 1% undergrads receive athletic scholarships. 90% freshmen, 90% undergrads receive any aid. 89% undergrads borrow to pay for school. Average cumulative indebtedness $28,485. **Criteria for awarding institutional aid:** *Non-need-based:* academics, art, athletics, leadership, music/drama, state/district residency.

MARIAN UNIVERSITY

3200 Cold Spring Rd., Indianapolis, IN 46222-1997
Phone: 317-955-6300 • **Financial Aid Phone:** 317-955-6040
E-mail: admissions@marian.edu • **CEEB Code:** 1442
Fax: 317-955-6401 • **Website:** www.marian.edu • **ACT Code:** 1224

This private school is, affiliated with the Roman Catholic Church.

RATINGS

Admissions Selectivity Rating: 79   Fire Safety Rating: 60*

STUDENTS AND FACULTY

Enrollment: 1,999. **Student Body:** 64% female, 36% male, 14% out-of-state, 1% international (10 countries represented). Asian 1%, African American 13%, Caucasian 73%, Hispanic 5%, Native American <1%
Retention and Graduation: 74% freshmen return for sophomore year. 34% freshmen graduate within 4 years. 13% grads go on to further study within 1 year. 33% grads pursue arts and sciences degrees. 3% grads pursue law degrees. 8% grads pursue business degrees. 18% grads pursue medical degrees. **Faculty:** 137 full-time faculty, 64% hold PhDs, 50% are members of minority groups, 11% are women. 0% of classes are taught by teaching assistants.

ACADEMICS

Degrees: associate, bachelor's, certificate, master's, terminal associate, transfer associate. **Classes:** Most classes have fewer than 10 students. Most lab/discussion sessions have 10–19 students. **Majors with Highest Enrollment:** Registered Nursing/Registered Nurse; Business Administration and Management; Elementary Education and Teaching. **Special Study Options:** Accelerated program, cooperative education program, cross-registration, double major, dual enrollment, honors program, independent study, internships, liberal arts/career combination, study abroad, teacher certification program. **Disability Services:** Special programs offered to physically disabled students include note-taking services, reader services, tape recorders, tutors. **Career services:** Alumni network, alumni services, career/job search classes, career assessment, internships.

FACILITIES

Housing: Coed dorms, cooperative housing, On-campus seminary, housing for Peace and Justice. **Computers:** 15% of classrooms, 100% of dorms, 100% of libraries, 100% of dining areas, 100% of student union, 50% of common outdoor areas have wireless network access. Administrative functions (other than registration) can be performed online.

CAMPUS LIFE

Environment: Metropolis. **Activities:** Choral groups, concert band, dance, drama/theater, marching band, music ensembles, musical theater, pep band, student government, student newspaper, yearbook, Campus Ministries, International Student Organization. **Athletics (Intercollegiate):** *Men:* baseball, basketball, cheerleading, cross-country, cycling, football, golf, tennis, track/field (outdoor), track/field (indoor). *Women:* basketball, cheerleading, cross-country, cycling, golf, softball, tennis, track/field (outdoor), track/field (indoor), volleyball.

ADMISSIONS

Freshman Academic Profile: Average high school GPA 3.8. 17% in top 10% of high school class, 39% in top 25% of high school class, 75% in top 50% of high school class. 80% from public high schools. SAT Math middle 50% range 460-560. SAT Critical Reading middle 50% range 460-560. SAT Writing middle 50% range 430-530. ACT middle 50% range 20-26. Minimum internet-based TOEFL 80. Minimum paper TOEFL 550. **Basis for Candidate Selection:** *Very important factors considered include:* academic GPA, rigor of secondary school record, standardized test scores. *Important factors considered include:* Class rank, recommendation(s). *Other factors considered include:* application essay, alumni/ae relation, extracurricular activities, interview, level of applicant's interest, talent/ability. **Freshman Admission Requirements:** High school diploma is required and GED is accepted. *Academic units required:* 4 English, 2 mathematics, 2 science, (2 science labs), 1 foreign language, 2 social studies, 9 academic electives. **Freshman Admission Statistics:** 1,825 applied, 75% admitted, 23% enrolled. **Transfer Admission Requirements:** college transcript(s), Minimum college GPA of 2 required. Lowest grade transferable C-. **General Admission Information:** Application Fee $20. Regular application deadline 8/1. Notification on a rolling basis, beginning on or about 9/15. Nonfall registration accepted. Admission may be deferred for a maximum of 1 yr. Credit and/or placement offered for CEEB Advanced Placement tests.

COSTS AND FINANCIAL AID

Annual tuition $29,400. Room and board $9,140. Average book expense $1,200. **Required Forms and Deadlines:** FAFSA. **Types of Aid:** *Need-based scholarships/grants:* Federal Pell, SEOG, state scholarships/grants, private scholarships, the school's own gift aid. *Loans:* Direct Subsidized Stafford, Direct Unsubsidized Stafford, Direct PLUS, Subsidized Stafford, Unsubsidized Stafford, PLUS, Federal Perkins, state loans. *Student Employment:* Federal Work-Study Program available. **Criteria for awarding institutional aid:** *Non-need-based:* academics, alumni affiliation, art, athletics, leadership, music/drama, religious affiliation.

MARIAN UNIVERSITY

45 South National Avenue, Fond du Lac, WI 54935
Phone: 920-923-7650 · **Financial Aid Phone:** 920-923-7614
E-mail: admissions@marianuniversity.edu · **CEEB Code:** 1443
Fax: 920-923-8755 · **Website:** www.marianuniversity.edu · **ACT Code:** 4606

This private school, affiliated with the Roman Catholic Church, was founded in 1936. It has a 100-acre campus.

RATINGS

Admissions Selectivity Rating: 71   **Fire Safety Rating:** 64

STUDENTS AND FACULTY

Enrollment: 1,903. **Student Body:** 75% female, 25% male, 7% out-of-state, 1% international (13 countries represented). Asian 1%, African American 5%, Caucasian 88%, Hispanic 2%, Native American 1%
Retention and Graduation: 21% freshmen graduate within 4 years. 41% freshmen graduate within 6 years. 16% grads go on to further study within 1 year. **Faculty:** 83 full-time faculty, 60% hold PhDs, 55% are members of minority groups, 6% are women. 0% of classes are taught by teaching assistants.

ACADEMICS

Degrees: bachelor's, master's. **Classes:** Most classes have 10–19 students. Most lab/discussion sessions have 10–19 students. **Majors with Highest Enrollment:** Teacher Education and Professional Development, Specific Levels and Methods; Registered Nursing/Registered Nurse; Business/Commerce. **Special Study Options:** Accelerated program, cooperative education program, distance learning, double major, dual enrollment, honors program, independent study, internships, liberal arts/career combination, student-designed major, study abroad, teacher certification program, Accelerated programs for adults in business, criminal justice, nursing, operations management, and radiologic technology. **Honors programs:** Honors. **Disability Services:** Special programs offered to physically disabled students include note-taking services, reader services, tape recorders, tutors. **Career services:** career/job search classes, career assessment, internships. Career services highlights include 97% of students receive field experience.

FACILITIES

Housing: Coed dorms, special housing for disabled students, fraternity/sorority housing, apartments for single students, Townhouses, Penthouses and Suites. 95% of campus accessible to physically disabled. **Special Academic Facilities/Equipment:** On-campus child-care center, electron microscope. **Computers:** Students can register for classes online. Administrative functions (other than registration) can be performed online.

CAMPUS LIFE

Environment: Town. **Activities:** Choral groups, concert band, dance, drama/theater, jazz band, literary magazine, music ensembles, pep band, student government, student newspaper, symphony orchestra, Campus Ministries, Model UN. 40 registered organizations, 6 honor societies, 1 religious organization. 1 fraternity, 2 sororities. **Athletics (Intercollegiate):** *Men:* baseball, basketball, cross-country, golf, ice hockey, soccer, tennis. *Women:* basketball, cross-country, golf, ice hockey, soccer, softball, tennis, volleyball. **On-Campus Highlights:** Housing, Coffee House, Student Center, Stayer Center, Library and Academic buildings.

ADMISSIONS

Freshman Academic Profile: Average high school GPA 3.02. 9% in top 10% of high school class, 30% in top 25% of high school class, 66% in top 50% of high school class. 87% from public high schools. ACT middle 50% range 18-22. Minimum paper TOEFL 525. **Basis for Candidate Selection:** *Very important factors considered include:* Class rank, academic GPA, rigor of secondary school record, standardized test scores. *Important factors considered include:* character/personal qualities, interview, level of applicant's interest. *Other factors considered include:* application essay, recommendation(s), alumni/ae relation, extracurricular activities, talent/ability, volunteer work, work experience. **Freshman Admission Requirements:** High school diploma is required and GED is accepted. *Academic units required:* 4 English, 2 mathematics, 1 science, (1 science labs), 1 history. **Freshman Admission Statistics:** 843 applied, 86% admitted, 40% enrolled. **Transfer Admission Requirements:** High school transcript, college transcript(s), Minimum college GPA of 2.0 required. Lowest grade transferable C. **General Admission Information:** Application Fee $20. Notification on a rolling basis, beginning on or about 9/15. Nonfall registration accepted. Admission may be deferred for a maximum of case by case. Credit and/or placement offered for CEEB Advanced Placement tests.

COSTS AND FINANCIAL AID

Annual tuition $19,590. Room and board $5,380. Required fees $350. Average book expense $700. **Required Forms and Deadlines:** FAFSA, Institution's own financial aid form. **Notification of Awards:** Applicants will be notified of awards on a rolling basis beginning 3/1. **Types of Aid:** *Need-based scholarships/grants:* Federal Pell, SEOG, state scholarships/grants, private scholarships, the school's own gift aid. *Loans:* Subsidized Stafford, Unsubsidized Stafford, PLUS, Federal Perkins, Federal Nursing. *Student Employment:* Federal Work-Study Program available. Institutional employment available. Highest amount earned per year from on-campus jobs $2,000. Off-campus job opportunities are fair. **Financial Aid Statistics:** 100% freshmen, 97% undergrads receive need-based scholarship or grant aid. 91% freshmen, 85% undergrads receive non-need-based scholarship or grant aid. 89% freshmen, 91% undergrads receive need-based self-help aid. 0% freshmen, 0% undergrads receive athletic scholarships. 99% freshmen, 94% undergrads receive any aid. 90% undergrads borrow to pay for school. **Criteria for awarding institutional aid:** *Non-need-based:* academics, state/district residency.

MARIETTA COLLEGE

215 Fifth Street, Marietta, OH 45750
Phone: 740-376-4600 · **Financial Aid Phone:** 740-376-4712
E-mail: admit@marietta.edu · **CEEB Code:** 1444
Fax: 740-376-8888 · **Website:** www.marietta.edu · **ACT Code:** 3290

This private school was founded in 1835. It has a 90-acre campus.

RATINGS

Admissions Selectivity Rating: 86   **Fire Safety Rating:** 80

STUDENTS AND FACULTY

Enrollment: 1,470. **Student Body:** 43% female, 57% male, 36% out-of-state, 12% international (15 countries represented). Asian 1%, African American 6%, Caucasian 71%, Hispanic 2%, Native American <1%
Retention and Graduation: 75% freshmen return for sophomore year. 54% freshmen graduate within 4 years. 63% freshmen graduate within 6 years. 20% grads go on to further study within 1 year. 9% grads pursue arts and sciences degrees. 3% grads pursue law degrees. 2% grads pursue business degrees. 2% grads pursue medical degrees. **Faculty:** 110 full-time faculty, 89% hold PhDs, 45% are members of minority groups, 7% are women. 0% of classes are taught by teaching assistants.

ACADEMICS

Degrees: associate, bachelor's, certificate, master's. **Classes:** Most classes have 10–19 students. **Majors with Highest Enrollment:** Education; Petroleum Engineering; Athletic Training/Trainer. **Special Study Options:** double major, dual enrollment, English as a Second Language (ESL), exchange student program (domestic), honors program, independent study, internships, liberal arts/career combination, student-designed major, study abroad, teacher certification program. **Honors programs:** Four Year Program for Top Scholarship Winners. **Combined degree programs:** BA/MA. **Disability Services:** Special programs offered to physically disabled students include note-taking services, reader services, tape recorders, tutors. **Career services:** Alumni network, alumni services, career/job search classes, career assessment, internships, regional alumni.

FACILITIES

Housing: Coed dorms, special housing for disabled students, men's dorms, women's dorms, fraternity/sorority housing, apartments for single students, Wellness Housing, Theme Housing. 90% of campus accessible to physically disabled. **Special Academic Facilities/Equipment:** Mass media building, fine arts center, natural science field camp, observatory, special collections in library **Computers:** 100% of classrooms, 100% of dorms, 100% of libraries, 100% of dining areas, 100% of student union, have wireless network access. Students can register for classes online. Administrative functions (other than registration) can be performed online.

CAMPUS LIFE

Environment: Town. **Activities:** Choral groups, concert band, dance, drama/ theater, jazz band, literary magazine, music ensembles, musical theater, radio station, student government, student newspaper, television station, yearbook, Campus Ministries, International Student Organization, Model UN. 80 registered organizations, 23 honor societies, 2 religious organizations. 3 fraternities, 3 sororities. **Athletics (Intercollegiate):** *Men:* baseball, basketball, crew/ rowing, cross-country, football, soccer, tennis, track/field (outdoor), track/field (indoor). *Women:* basketball, crew/rowing, cross-country, soccer, softball, tennis, track/field (outdoor), track/field (indoor), volleyball. **On-Campus Highlights:** Gathering Place, new Upper Class Residence Hall, Legacy Library, Hermann Fine Arts Center, Dyson Baudo Recreation Center, New Rickey Science Center, New Soccer and Softball Fields, Andrews Hall, Izzy's Snack Place. **Environmental Initiatives:** Added Sustainable Energy Minor under the Petroleum Engineering Program. Energy and the Environment selected as this year's theme for campus and community awareness events. Offer a sustainable living life style theme house.

ADMISSIONS

Freshman Academic Profile: Average high school GPA 3.45. 30% in top 10% of high school class, 56% in top 25% of high school class, 84% in top 50% of high school class. 89% from public high schools. SAT Math middle 50% range 490-610. SAT Critical Reading middle 50% range 480-610. SAT Writing middle 50% range 450-580. ACT middle 50% range 21-26. Minimum internet-based TOEFL 79. Minimum paper TOEFL 550. **Basis for Candidate Selection:** *Very important factors considered include:* Class rank, academic GPA, rigor of secondary school record, standardized test scores. *Important factors considered include:* application essay, recommendation(s), character/personal qualities, interview. *Other factors considered include:* alumni/ae relation, extracurricular activities, first generation, geographical residence, level of applicant's interest, racial/ethnic status, state residency, talent/ability, volunteer work, work experience. **Freshman Admission Requirements:** High school diploma is required and GED is accepted. *Academic units required:* 4 English, 3 mathematics, 3 science, (2 science labs), 2 foreign language, 2 social studies, 2 history. **Freshman Admission Statistics:** 4,157 applied, 68% admitted, 14% enrolled. **Transfer Admission Requirements:** college transcript(s), essay or personal statement, statement of good standing from prior institution(s). Minimum college GPA of 2.3 required. Lowest grade transferable C. **General Admission Information:** Application Fee $25. Notification on a rolling basis, beginning on or about 9/1. Nonfall registration accepted. Admission may be deferred for a maximum of 12 months. Credit and/or placement offered for CEEB Advanced Placement tests.

COSTS AND FINANCIAL AID

Annual tuition $30,090. Room and board $9,560. Required fees $850. Average book expense $1,136. **Required Forms and Deadlines:** FAFSA. **Notification of Awards:** Applicants will be notified of awards on a rolling basis beginning 3/15. **Types of Aid:** *Need-based scholarships/grants:* Federal Pell, SEOG, state scholarships/grants, private scholarships, the school's own gift aid. *Loans:* Direct Subsidized Stafford, Direct Unsubsidized Stafford, Direct PLUS, Subsidized Stafford, Unsubsidized Stafford, PLUS, Federal Perkins, college/university loans from institutional funds. *Student Employment:* Federal Work-Study Program available. Institutional employment available. Highest amount earned per year from on-campus jobs $2,000. Off-campus job opportunities are good. **Financial Aid Statistics:** 98% freshmen, 97% undergrads receive need-based scholarship or grant aid. 71% freshmen, 85% undergrads receive non-need-based scholarship or grant aid. 86% freshmen, 86% undergrads receive need-based self-help aid. 0% freshmen, 0% undergrads receive athletic scholarships. 98% freshmen, 94% undergrads receive any aid. 82% undergrads borrow to pay for school. Average cumulative indebtedness $22,130. **Criteria for awarding institutional aid:** *Non-need-based:* academics, alumni affiliation, art, leadership, minority status, music/drama, state/district residency.

MARIST COLLEGE

3399 North Road, Poughkeepsie, NY 12601-1387
Phone: 845-575-3226 · **Financial Aid Phone:** 845-575-3230
E-mail: admission@marist.edu · **CEEB Code:** 2400
Fax: 845-575-3215 · **Website:** http://www.marist.edu/ · **ACT Code:** 2804

This private school was founded in 1929. It has a 180-acre campus.

RATINGS

Admissions Selectivity Rating: 89   **Fire Safety Rating:** 92

STUDENTS AND FACULTY

Enrollment: 5,240. **Student Body:** 59% female, 41% male, 43% out-of-state, 2% international (44 countries represented). Asian 3%, African American 4%, Caucasian 78%, Hispanic 9%, Native American <1% **Retention and Graduation:** 68% freshmen graduate within 4 years. 24% grads go on to further study within 1 year. 6% grads pursue law degrees. 4% grads pursue business degrees. 2% grads pursue medical degrees. **Faculty:** 233 full-time faculty, 76% hold PhDs, 52% are members of minority groups, 15% are women. 0% of classes are taught by teaching assistants.

ACADEMICS

Degrees: bachelor's, certificate, master's, post-bachelor's certificate. **Classes:** Most classes have 20–29 students. Most lab/discussion sessions have 20–29 students. **Majors with Highest Enrollment:** Business Administration and Management; Communication; Psychology. **Special Study Options:** Accelerated program, cooperative education program, cross-registration, distance learning, double major, dual enrollment, English as a Second Language (ESL), honors program, independent study, internships, liberal arts/career combination, study abroad, teacher certification program, weekend college, Undergrads may take grad level classes. Cooperative ed- Arts, Business, Computer Science, Education, Humanities, Natural Science, Social/Behavioral Science, Technologies. **Honors programs:** The Marist College Honors Program brings together talented students in honors-enriched classes that often coordinate with co-curricular activities such as field trips and lectures. The cultural enrichment exchange is a highlight of the Program. It encourages students to move beyond standard curricula and engage in a broader range of experience consonant with their interests. **Combined degree programs:** BA/MA, BS/MS. **Disability Services:** Special programs offered to physically disabled students include note-taking services, reader services, tape recorders, tutors. **Career services:** Alumni network, alumni services, career/job search classes, career assessment, internships, regional alumni. Career services highlights include an extensive internship program that provides students with practical work experience and reinforces the lessons from the classroom.

FACILITIES

Housing: Coed dorms, special housing for disabled students, apartments for single students, Wellness Housing, garden apartments, townhouses, suites. 88% of campus accessible to physically disabled. **Special Academic Facilities/ Equipment:** Art gallery, language lab, estuarine and environmental studies lab, public opinion institute, audiovisual/TV center, communications center, high tech classroom, digital state of the art library. **Computers:** 100% of classrooms, 100% of dorms, 100% of libraries, 100% of dining areas, 100% of student union, 57% of common outdoor areas have wireless network access. Students can register for classes online. Administrative functions (other than registration) can be performed online.

CAMPUS LIFE

Environment: Town. **Activities:** Choral groups, concert band, dance, drama/ theater, jazz band, literary magazine, marching band, music ensembles, musical theater, pep band, radio station, student government, student newspaper, student-run film society, television station, yearbook, Campus Ministries. 86 registered organizations, 16 honor societies, 6 religious organizations. 3 fraternities, 4 sororities. **Athletics (Intercollegiate):** *Men:* baseball, basketball, crew/ rowing, cross-country, diving, football, lacrosse, soccer, swimming, tennis, track/ field (outdoor). *Women:* basketball, crew/rowing, cross-country, diving, lacrosse, soccer, softball, swimming, tennis, track/field (outdoor), volleyball, water polo. **On-Campus Highlights:** James A Cannavino Library, James J McCann Recreation Center, Student Center, Newly Renovated Freshman Residence Halls, Tenney Stadium at Leonidoff Field. **Environmental Initiatives:** Sustainable food purchases; Energy efficiency/reduction (electricity and heat); Composting; Recycling; Green information technology initiatives.

ADMISSIONS

Freshman Academic Profile: Average high school GPA 3.3. 30% in top 10% of high school class, 58% in top 25% of high school class, 87% in top 50% of high school class. 70% from public high schools. SAT Math middle 50% range 550-640. SAT Critical Reading middle 50% range 540-630. SAT Writing middle 50% range 540-640. ACT middle 50% range 25-29. Minimum internet-based TOEFL 80. Minimum paper TOEFL 550. **Basis for Candidate Selection:** *Very important factors considered include:* academic GPA, rigor of secondary school record, standardized test scores. *Important factors considered include:* Class rank, application essay, recommendation(s), character/personal qualities, extracurricular activities, geographical residence, state residency, talent/ability, volunteer work, work experience. *Other factors considered include:* alumni/ae relation, level of applicant's interest, racial/ethnic status. **Freshman Admission Requirements:** High school diploma is required and GED is accepted. *Academic units required:* 4 English, 3 mathematics, 3 science, (2 science labs), 2 foreign language, 2 social studies, 1 history, 2 academic electives. **Freshman Admission Statistics:** 9,751 applied, 39% admitted, 30% enrolled. **Transfer Admission Requirements:** High school transcript, college transcript(s), essay or personal statement, Minimum college GPA of 2.8 required. Lowest grade transferable 2. **General Admission Information:** Application Fee $50. Early decision application deadline 11/15. Regular application deadline 2/15. Regular notification 3/30. Nonfall registration accepted. Admission may be deferred for a maximum of 12 months. Credit and/or placement offered for CEEB Advanced Placement tests.

COSTS AND FINANCIAL AID

Annual tuition $32,000. Room and board $13,600. Required fees $590. Average book expense $1,500. **Required Forms and Deadlines:** FAFSA, Institution's own financial aid form. **Notification of Awards:** Applicants will be notified of awards on a rolling basis beginning 3/15. **Types of Aid:** *Need-based scholarships/grants:* Federal Pell, SEOG, state scholarships/grants, private scholarships, the school's own gift aid. *Loans:* Subsidized Stafford, Unsubsidized Stafford, PLUS, Federal Perkins, Alternative Loans. *Student Employment:* Federal Work-Study Program available. Institutional employment available. Highest amount earned per year from on-campus jobs $7,920. Off-campus job opportunities are excellent. **Financial Aid Statistics:** 74% freshmen, 72% undergrads receive need-based scholarship or grant aid. 97% freshmen, 83% undergrads receive non-need-based scholarship or grant aid. 82% freshmen, 85% undergrads receive need-based self-help aid. 7% freshmen, 6% undergrads receive athletic scholarships. 86% freshmen, 84% undergrads receive any aid. 68% undergrads borrow to pay for school. Average cumulative indebtedness $24,197. **Criteria for awarding institutional aid:** *Non-need-based:* academics, athletics, music/drama, state/district residency.

MARLBORO COLLEGE

Best 380

PO Box A, Marlboro, VT 05344-0300
Phone: 802-258-9236 · **Financial Aid Phone:** 802-258-9312
E-mail: admissions@marlboro.edu · **CEEB Code:** 3509
Fax: 802-451-7555 · **Website:** www.marlboro.edu · **ACT Code:** 4304

This private school was founded in 1946. It has a 350-acre campus.

RATINGS

Admissions Selectivity Rating: 77   **Fire Safety Rating:** 74

STUDENTS AND FACULTY

Enrollment: 238. **Student Body:** 48% female, 52% male, 92% out-of-state, 1% international (8 countries represented). Asian 3%, African American 1%, Caucasian 63%, Hispanic 0%, Native American 1%
Retention and Graduation: 68% freshmen return for sophomore year. 59% freshmen graduate within 4 years. 69% grads go on to further study within 1 year. **Faculty:** 39 full-time faculty, 90% hold PhDs, 44% are members of minority groups, 10% are women. 0% of classes are taught by teaching assistants.

ACADEMICS

Degrees: bachelor's, master's. **Classes:** Most classes have fewer than 10 students. Most lab/discussion sessions have fewer than 10 students. **Majors with Highest Enrollment:** English Language and Literature; Social Sciences; Visual and Performing Arts. **Special Study Options:** double major, dual enrollment, independent study, internships, student-designed major, study abroad, World Studies Program for students interested in international relations while also integrating an internship with study abroad opportunities. **Disability**

Services: Special programs offered to physically disabled students include note-taking services, reader services, tape recorders, tutors. **Career services:** alumni services, career/job search classes, career assessment,

FACILITIES

Housing: Coed dorms, special housing for disabled students, women's dorms, apartments for married students, cooperative housing, apartments for single students, Housing is to a human scale; the largest residence hall accommodates about 30 students. 80% of campus accessible to physically disabled. **Special Academic Facilities/Equipment:** Serkin Center for the Performing Arts, Drury art gallery, theater, dance studio, observatory, darkroom, art studios, music practice and performance spaces. **Computers:** 80% of classrooms, 85% of dorms, 100% of libraries, 100% of dining areas, 100% of student union, 80% of common outdoor areas have wireless network access. Students can register for classes online. Administrative functions (other than registration) can be performed online.

CAMPUS LIFE

Environment: Rural. **Activities:** Choral groups, dance, drama/theater, literary magazine, music ensembles, musical theater, radio station, student government, student newspaper, student-run film society. 22 registered organizations. **On-Campus Highlights:** The Rice-Aron Library, Whittemore Theatre, Rod Gander World Studies Center, Serkin Center for the Performing Arts, Persons Auditorium. **Environmental Initiatives:** Energy audits of all campus buildings in preparation for efficiency upgrades. Solar-powered water heater in new Total Health Center facility. Recycling.

ADMISSIONS

Freshman Academic Profile: Average high school GPA 3.11. 70% from public high schools. SAT Math middle 50% range 520-650. SAT Critical Reading middle 50% range 560-730. SAT Writing middle 50% range 530-680. Minimum internet-based TOEFL 90. Minimum paper TOEFL 577. **Basis for Candidate Selection:** *Very important factors considered include:* application essay, academic GPA, rigor of secondary school record, character/personal qualities. *Important factors considered include:* extracurricular activities, interview. *Other factors considered include:* Class rank, recommendation(s), standardized test scores, alumni/ae relation, first generation, geographical residence, level of applicant's interest, state residency, talent/ability, volunteer work, work experience. **Freshman Admission Requirements:** High school diploma is required and GED is accepted. **Freshman Admission Statistics:** 256 applied, 79% admitted, 24% enrolled. **Transfer Admission Requirements:** High school transcript, college transcript(s), essay or personal statement, Minimum college GPA of 2.0 required. Lowest grade transferable C-. **General Admission Information:** Application Fee $50. Early decision application deadline 12/1. Regular application deadline 3/1. Notification on a rolling basis, beginning on or about 12/1. Nonfall registration accepted. Admission may be deferred for a maximum of 1 year. Credit offered for CEEB Advanced Placement tests.

COSTS AND FINANCIAL AID

Annual tuition $36,300. Room and board $9,930. Required fees $1,340. Average book expense $1,200. **Required Forms and Deadlines:** FAFSA. **Notification of Awards:** Applicants will be notified of awards on a rolling basis beginning 3/15. **Types of Aid:** *Need-based scholarships/grants:* Federal Pell, SEOG, state scholarships/grants, private scholarships, the school's own gift aid. *Loans:* Subsidized Stafford, Unsubsidized Stafford, PLUS. *Student Employment:* Federal Work-Study Program available. Institutional employment available. Highest amount earned per year from on-campus jobs $2,050. Off-campus job opportunities are fair. **Financial Aid Statistics:** 100% freshmen, 99% undergrads receive need-based scholarship or grant aid. 85% freshmen, 90% undergrads receive non-need-based scholarship or grant aid. 100% freshmen, 97% undergrads receive need-based self-help aid. 0% freshmen, 0% undergrads receive athletic scholarships. 98% freshmen, 94% undergrads receive any aid. 71% undergrads borrow to pay for school. Average cumulative indebtedness $7,212. **Criteria for awarding institutional aid:** *Non-need-based:* academics, leadership.

See page 1090.

MARQUETTE UNIVERSITY

Best 380

PO Box 1881, Milwaukee, WI 53201-1881
Phone: 414-288-7302 · **Financial Aid Phone:** 414-288-7390
E-mail: admissions@Marquette.edu · **CEEB Code:** 1448
Fax: 414-288-3764 · **Website:** www.marquette.edu · **ACT Code:** 4610

This private school, affiliated with the Roman Catholic-Jesuit Church,, affiliated with the Jesuit Church, was founded in 1881. It has a 93-acre campus.

RATINGS

Admissions Selectivity Rating: 88   **Fire Safety Rating:** 90

STUDENTS AND FACULTY

Enrollment: 8,212. **Student Body:** 52% female, 48% male, 66% out-of-state, 4% international (44 countries represented). Asian 5%, African American 4%, Caucasian 74%, Hispanic 10%, Native American <1%
Retention and Graduation: 89% freshmen return for sophomore year. 59% freshmen graduate within 4 years. 79% freshmen graduate within 6 years. **Faculty:** 634 full-time faculty, 90% hold PhDs, 42% are members of minority groups, 15% are women.

ACADEMICS

Degrees: bachelor's, doctoral, master's, post-master's certificate. **Classes:** Most classes have 10–19 students. Most lab/discussion sessions have 20–29 students. **Majors with Highest Enrollment:** Biomedical Sciences; Registered Nursing/Registered Nurse; Accounting. **Special Study Options:** Accelerated program, cooperative education program, cross-registration, double major, dual enrollment, honors program, independent study, internships, student-designed major, study abroad, teacher certification program, weekend college. **Honors programs:** Pre-Law Scholars Program Pre-Dental Scholars Program **Combined degree programs:** BA/JD, BA/MA, BA/DDS, Physical Therapy, Physician Assistant Studies. **Disability Services:** Special programs offered to physically disabled students include note-taking services, reader services, tape recorders, tutors.

FACILITIES

Housing: Coed dorms, special housing for disabled students, men's dorms, special housing for international students, women's dorms, fraternity/sorority housing, apartments for married students, apartments for single students, Specialty housing for honor students, engineering students, nursing students. 90% of campus accessible to physically disabled. **Special Academic Facilities/Equipment:** Haggerty Museum of Art, Helfaer Theatre, Al McGuire Center Broadcast Facilities, Dental School/Clinic. **Computers:** 30% of classrooms, 100% of dorms, 100% of libraries, 100% of dining areas, 100% of student union, 10% of common outdoor areas have wireless network access. Students can register for classes online. Administrative functions (other than registration) can be performed online.

CAMPUS LIFE

Environment: Metropolis. **Activities:** Choral groups, concert band, dance, drama/theater, jazz band, literary magazine, music ensembles, musical theater, pep band, radio station, student government, student newspaper, symphony orchestra, television station, yearbook, Campus Ministries, International Student Organization, Model UN. 230 registered organizations, 21 honor society, 11 religious organization. 11 fraternity, 11 sorority. **Athletics (Intercollegiate):** *Men:* basketball, cheerleading, cross-country, golf, soccer, tennis, track/field (outdoor), track/field (indoor). *Women:* basketball, cheerleading, cross-country, soccer, tennis, track/field (outdoor), track/field (indoor), volleyball. **On-Campus Highlights:** The Raynor Memorial Library and the Law, Gesu Church, Haggerty Museum of Art, Al McGuire Center, Helfaer Recreation Center, Other places of interest Alumni Memorial Union and the Golden Eagle giftshop. (Located in the AMU). **Environmental Initiatives:** All Full-Time undergraduate Students receive a UPASS (Allows unlimited use of Milwaukee County Transit System Buses); Recycling garbage and electronic equipment; Marquette uses steam from the power company (waste heat) for 90% of campus heating; Marquette participates in the State of Wisconsin's Focus on Energy Program; In collaboration with Johnson Controls, Marquette was able to reduce energy use by 1,547,000 kWh (2,320,500 lbs of CO2) and annual water consumption by 13,400,000 gallons.

ADMISSIONS

Freshman Academic Profile: 32% in top 10% of high school class, 67% in top 25% of high school class, 94% in top 50% of high school class. 59% from public high schools. SAT Math middle 50% range 560-650. SAT Critical Reading middle 50% range 540-640. SAT Writing middle 50% range 520-620. ACT middle 50% range 25-29. Minimum internet-based TOEFL 78. Minimum paper TOEFL 530. **Basis for Candidate Selection:** *Very important factors considered include:* academic GPA, rigor of secondary school record. *Important factors considered include:* Class rank, application essay, recommendation(s), standardized test scores. *Other factors considered include:* alumni/ae relation, character/personal qualities, extracurricular activities, first generation, geographical residence, racial/ethnic status, state residency, talent/ability, volunteer work. **Freshman Admission Requirements:** High school diploma is required and GED is accepted. *Academic units required:* 4 English, 2 mathematics, 2 science, (2 science labs), 2 social studies, 0 history, 2 academic electives. **Freshman Admission Statistics:** 21,755 applied, 67% admitted, 14% enrolled. **Transfer Admission Requirements:** High school transcript, college transcript(s), essay or personal statement, Lowest grade transferable C. **General Admission Information:** Application Fee $30. Regular application deadline 12/1. Regular notification 1/31. Nonfall registration accepted. Admission may be deferred for a maximum of 1 year. Credit and/or placement offered for CEEB Advanced Placement tests.
COSTS AND FINANCIAL AID Required Forms and Deadlines: FAFSA. **Notification of Awards:** Applicants will be notified of awards on a rolling basis beginning 3/20. **Types of Aid:** *Need-based scholarships/grants:* Federal Pell, SEOG, state scholarships/grants, private scholarships, the school's own gift aid, Marquette Merit Based aid is not based on need, but is used to cover need. *Loans:* Direct Subsidized Stafford, Direct Unsubsidized Stafford, Direct PLUS, Federal Perkins, Federal Nursing, state loans, college/university loans from institutional funds, Private educational/alternative loans. *Student Employment:* Highest amount earned per year from on-campus jobs $2,500. Off-campus job opportunities are excellent. **Financial Aid Statistics:** 98% freshmen, 98% undergrads receive need-based scholarship or grant aid. 12% freshmen, 11% undergrads receive non-need-based scholarship or grant aid. 81% freshmen, 82% undergrads receive need-based self-help aid. 2% freshmen, 2% undergrads receive athletic scholarships. 99% freshmen, 99% undergrads receive any aid. 63% undergrads borrow to pay for school. Average cumulative indebtedness $26,708. **Criteria for awarding institutional aid:** *Non-need-based:* academics, athletics, leadership, music/drama.

MARS HILL COLLEGE

PO Box 370, Mars Hill, NC 28754
Phone: 828-689-1201 · **Financial Aid Phone:** 828-689-1123
E-mail: admissions@mhc.edu · **CEEB Code:** 5395
Fax: 828-689-1473 · **ACT Code:** 3124

This private school, affiliated with the Baptist Church, was founded in 1856. It has a 180-acre campus.

RATINGS

Admissions Selectivity Rating: 60*   **Fire Safety Rating:** 60*

STUDENTS AND FACULTY

Enrollment: 1,177. **Student Body:** 56% female, 44% male, 35% out-of-state, 3% international (20 countries represented). Asian 0%, African American 8%, Caucasian 99%, Hispanic 1%, Native American 1%
Retention and Graduation: 71% freshmen return for sophomore year. **Faculty:** 78 full-time faculty, 63% hold PhDs, 36% are members of minority groups, 1% are women. 0% of classes are taught by teaching assistants.

ACADEMICS

Degrees: bachelor's, diploma. **Majors with Highest Enrollment:** Elementary Education and Teaching; Biology/Biological Sciences; Business/Commerce. **Special Study Options:** Accelerated program, cooperative education program, distance learning, double major, dual enrollment, English as a Second Language (ESL), honors program, independent study, internships, liberal arts/career combination, study abroad, teacher certification program. **Honors programs:** http://www.mhc.edu/honors.asp. **Disability Services:** Special programs offered to physically disabled students include note-taking services, reader services, tape recorders, tutors.

FACILITIES

Housing: special housing for disabled students, men's dorms, women's dorms, apartments for married students, apartments for single students **Special Academic Facilities/Equipment:** Language lab, Appalachian artifacts museum, rural life museum. **Computers:** Students can register for classes online. Administrative functions (other than registration) can be performed online.

CAMPUS LIFE

Environment: Rural. **Activities:** Choral groups, concert band, dance, drama/theater, jazz band, literary magazine, marching band, music ensembles, musical theater, radio station, student government, student newspaper, symphony orchestra, yearbook. 45 registered organizations, 9 honor societies, 5 religious organizations. 6 fraternities, 5 sororities. **Athletics (Intercollegiate):** *Men:* baseball, basketball, cheerleading, cross-country, football, golf, lacrosse, soccer, tennis, track/field (outdoor). *Women:* basketball, cheerleading, cross-country, golf, soccer, softball, swimming, tennis, track/field (outdoor), volleyball. **On-Campus Highlights:** Wren Student Union, The Loft, The Ice Cream Shoppe, Cafeteria, Gym.

ADMISSIONS

Freshman Academic Profile: Average high school GPA 3.38. **Basis for Candidate Selection:** *Very important factors considered include:* rigor of secondary school record, standardized test scores. *Important factors considered include:* Class rank, recommendation(s), character/personal qualities, extracurricular activities, interview, talent/ability. *Other factors considered include:* alumni/ae relation, religious affiliation/commitment, volunteer work, work experience. **Freshman Admission Requirements:** High school diploma is required and GED is accepted. *Academic units required:* 4 English, 3 mathematics, 2 science, (1 science labs), 2 social studies, 2 history. **Transfer Admission Requirements:** college transcript(s), statement of good standing from prior institution(s). Minimum college GPA of 2.0 required. Lowest grade transferable C. **General Admission Information:** Application Fee $25. Nonfall registration accepted.

COSTS AND FINANCIAL AID

Average book expense $600. **Required Forms and Deadlines:** FAFSA, State aid form. **Types of Aid:** *Need-based scholarships/grants:* state scholarships/grants. *Loans:* Subsidized Stafford, PLUS. **Financial Aid Statistics:** 99% freshmen, 90% undergrads receive any aid.

MARSHALL UNIVERSITY

One John Marshall Drive, Huntington, WV 25755
Phone: 304-696-3160 · **Financial Aid Phone:** 304-696-3162
E-mail: admissions@marshall.edu · **CEEB Code:** 5396
Fax: 304-696-3135 · **Website:** www.marshall.edu · **ACT Code:** 4526

This public school was founded in 1837. It has a 70-acre campus.

RATINGS

Admissions Selectivity Rating: 72   Fire Safety Rating: 64

STUDENTS AND FACULTY

Enrollment: 8,871. **Student Body:** 56% female, 44% male, 23% out-of-state, 1% international. Asian 1%, African American 7%, Caucasian 85%, Hispanic 2%, Native American <1%
Retention and Graduation: 69% freshmen return for sophomore year. 25% freshmen graduate within 4 years. 45% freshmen graduate within 6 years. 27% grads go on to further study within 1 year. **Faculty:** 494 full-time faculty, 75% hold PhDs, 46% are members of minority groups, 18% are women.

ACADEMICS

Degrees: associate, bachelor's, master's, post-bachelor's certificate, post-master's certificate. **Classes:** Most classes have 20–29 students. **Majors with Highest Enrollment:** Elementary Education and Teaching; Psychology; Business/Commerce. **Special Study Options:** Accelerated program, cooperative education program, cross-registration, distance learning, double major, dual enrollment, English as a Second Language (ESL), exchange student program (domestic), honors program, independent study, internships, study abroad, teacher certification program. **Honors programs:** John Marshall Scholars, Society of Yeager Scholars **Combined degree programs:** BS/MF Forestry (w/ Duke), BS/MEM Env Mgmt (w/ Duke). **Disability Services:** Special programs offered to physically disabled students include note-taking services, reader services, tutors. **Career services:** Alumni network, alumni services, career/job search classes, career assessment, internships, regional alumni.

FACILITIES

Housing: Coed dorms, special housing for disabled students, women's dorms. 100% of campus accessible to physically disabled. **Special Academic Facilities/Equipment:** Art gallery, audiovisual center, language lab, superconducting nuclear magnetic resonance spectrometer. **Computers:** Students can register for classes online. Administrative functions (other than registration) can be performed online.

CAMPUS LIFE

Environment: Town. **Activities:** Choral groups, concert band, dance, drama/theater, jazz band, literary magazine, marching band, music ensembles, musical theater, opera, pep band, radio station, student government, student newspaper, symphony orchestra, television station, Campus Ministries, International Stu-

dent Organization, Model UN. 100 registered organizations, 11 honor society, 10 religious organizations. 12 fraternities, 7 sororities. **Athletics (Intercollegiate):** *Men:* baseball, basketball, cross-country, football, golf, soccer, track/field (outdoor). *Women:* basketball, cross-country, golf, soccer, softball, swimming, tennis, track/field (outdoor), volleyball. **On-Campus Highlights:** Memorial Student Center Plaza, Drinko Library, Marshall Stadium, Henderson Center, Buskirk Field.

ADMISSIONS

Freshman Academic Profile: Average high school GPA 3.4. SAT Math middle 50% range 440-550. SAT Critical Reading middle 50% range 430-550. ACT middle 50% range 19-24.5. Minimum paper TOEFL 500. **Basis for Candidate Selection:** *Very important factors considered include:* academic GPA, standardized test scores. *Other factors considered include:* rigor of secondary school record. **Freshman Admission Requirements:** High school diploma is required and GED is accepted. *Academic units required:* 4 English, 4 mathematics, 3 science, (3 science labs), 2 foreign language, 3 social studies, 1 visual/performing arts. **Freshman Admission Statistics:** 2,863 applied, 77% admitted, 84% enrolled. **Transfer Admission Requirements:** college transcript(s). **General Admission Information:** Application Fee $30. Notification on a rolling basis, beginning on or about 9/1. Nonfall registration accepted. Admission may be deferred for a maximum of 1 year. Credit offered for CEEB Advanced Placement tests.

COSTS AND FINANCIAL AID

Annual in-state tuition $5,450. Annual out-of-state tuition $13,950. Room and board $9,546. Required fees $1,076. Average book expense $1,100. **Required Forms and Deadlines:** FAFSA, State aid form. **Notification of Awards:** Applicants will be notified of awards on a rolling basis beginning 5/1. **Types of Aid:** *Need-based scholarships/grants:* Federal Pell, SEOG, state scholarships/grants, private scholarships, the school's own gift aid. *Loans:* Direct Subsidized Stafford, Direct Unsubsidized Stafford, Direct PLUS, Federal Perkins. *Student Employment:* Off-campus job opportunities are good. **Financial Aid Statistics:** 79% freshmen, 77% undergrads receive need-based scholarship or grant aid. 58% freshmen, 40% undergrads receive non-need-based scholarship or grant aid. 70% freshmen, 75% undergrads receive need-based self-help aid. 4% freshmen, 4% undergrads receive athletic scholarships. 67% undergrads borrow to pay for school. Average cumulative indebtedness $25,401. **Criteria for awarding institutional aid:** *Non-need-based:* academics, art, athletics, minority status, music/drama, state/district residency.

MARY BALDWIN COLLEGE

PO Box 1500, Staunton, VA 24402
Phone: 540-887-7019 · **Financial Aid Phone:** 540-887-7022
E-mail: admit@mbc.edu · **CEEB Code:** 5397
Fax: 540-887-7292 · **Website:** www.mbc.edu · **ACT Code:** 4374

This private school, affiliated with the Presbyterian Church, was founded in 1842. It has a 54-acre campus.

RATINGS

Admissions Selectivity Rating: 84   Fire Safety Rating: 79

STUDENTS AND FACULTY

Enrollment: 1,298. **Student Body:** 94% female, 6% male, 31% out-of-state, 0% international (4 countries represented). Asian 3%, African American 25%, Caucasian 57%, Hispanic 7%, Native American <1%
Retention and Graduation: 68% freshmen return for sophomore year. 43% freshmen graduate within 4 years. 20% grads go on to further study within 1 year. 5% grads pursue law degrees. 5% grads pursue business degrees. 2% grads pursue medical degrees. **Faculty:** 86 full-time faculty, 84% hold PhDs, 63% are members of minority groups, 19% are women. 0% of classes are taught by teaching assistants.

ACADEMICS

Degrees: bachelor's, certificate, master's. **Classes:** Most classes have 10–19 students. Most lab/discussion sessions have 10–19 students. **Majors with Highest Enrollment:** Social Sciences; Psychology; Multi-/Interdisciplinary Studies. **Special Study Options:** Accelerated program, cooperative education program, cross-registration, distance learning, double major, dual enrollment, English as a Second Language (ESL), exchange student program (domestic), external degree program, honors program, independent study, internships, liberal arts/career combination, student-designed major, study abroad, teacher certification program, Summer exchange program with Doshisha Women's College in Kyoto, Japan. **Disability Services:** Special programs offered to physically disabled students include tape recorders, tutors. **Career services:** alumni services, career/job search classes, career assessment, internships.

FACILITIES

Housing: special housing for international students, women's dorms, apartments for single students, Special interest (club) housing focuses on students,honors,leadership and community services available. 75% of campus accessible to physically disabled. **Special Academic Facilities/Equipment:** Audiovisual center, TV studio, communications lab, electron microscope, gas chromatoscope, greenhouse. **Computers:** 100% of classrooms, 100% of dorms, 100% of libraries, 100% of common outdoor areas have wireless network access. Students can register for classes online. Administrative functions (other than registration) can be performed online.

CAMPUS LIFE

Environment: Village. **Activities:** Choral groups, dance, drama/theater, literary magazine, marching band, music ensembles, musical theater, radio station, student government, student newspaper, student-run film society, television station, yearbook. 34 registered organizations, 9 honor societies, 4 religious organizations. **Athletics (Intercollegiate):** *Women:* basketball, field hockey, soccer, softball, swimming, tennis, volleyball. **On-Campus Highlights:** Coffee House (The Nut House), SMA (VWIL) Museum, The Library, Spencer Center for Civic & Global Engage, Computer Center Labs. **Environmental Initiatives:** Trayless dining hall; enhancing native landscaping.

ADMISSIONS

Freshman Academic Profile: Average high school GPA 3.39. 14% in top 10% of high school class, 42% in top 25% of high school class, 82% in top 50% of high school class. 75% from public high schools. SAT Math middle 50% range 410-530. SAT Critical Reading middle 50% range 440-560. SAT Writing middle 50% range 420-540. ACT middle 50% range 19-24. Minimum paper TOEFL 500. **Basis for Candidate Selection:** *Very important factors considered include:* rigor of secondary school record, standardized test scores. *Important factors considered include:* character/personal qualities, extracurricular activities, interview. *Other factors considered include:* Class rank, application essay, recommendation(s), alumni/ae relation, talent/ability, volunteer work, work experience. **Freshman Admission Requirements:** High school diploma is required and GED is accepted. *Academic units required:* 4 English, 3 mathematics, 2 science, (1 science labs), 2 foreign language, 3 social studies. **Freshman Admission Statistics:** 5,860 applied, 51% admitted, 9% enrolled. **Transfer Admission Requirements:** High school transcript, college transcript(s), statement of good standing from prior institution(s). Minimum college GPA of 2.0 required. Lowest grade transferable C-. **General Admission Information:** Application Fee $35. Early decision application deadline 11/8. Notification on a rolling basis, beginning on or about 9/8. Nonfall registration accepted. Admission may be deferred for a maximum of 1 semester. Credit offered for CEEB Advanced Placement tests.

COSTS AND FINANCIAL AID

Annual tuition $29,210. Room and board $8,650. Required fees $385. Average book expense $1,000. **Required Forms and Deadlines:** FAFSA, State aid form. **Notification of Awards:** Applicants will be notified of awards on a rolling basis beginning 1/1. **Types of Aid:** *Need-based scholarships/grants:* Federal Pell, SEOG, state scholarships/grants, private scholarships, the school's own gift aid. *Loans:* Subsidized Stafford, Unsubsidized Stafford, PLUS, Federal Perkins, Private alternative loans. *Student Employment:* Federal Work-Study Program available. Institutional employment available. Highest amount earned per year from on-campus jobs $1,356. Off-campus job opportunities are excellent. **Financial Aid Statistics:** 98% freshmen, 99% undergrads receive need-based scholarship or grant aid. 7% freshmen, 7% undergrads receive non-need-based scholarship or grant aid. 87% freshmen, 88% undergrads receive need-based self-help aid. 0% freshmen, 0% undergrads receive athletic scholarships. 90% freshmen, 95% undergrads receive any aid. 89% undergrads borrow to pay for school. Average cumulative indebtedness $34,938. **Criteria for awarding institutional aid:** *Non-need-based:* academics, leadership, state/district residency.

STUDENTS AND FACULTY

Enrollment: 662. **Student Body:** 79% female, 21% male, 2% out-of-state, 1% international. Asian 0%, African American 70%, Caucasian 5%, Hispanic 2%, Native American <1%
Retention and Graduation: 61% freshmen return for sophomore year. 30% grads go on to further study within 1 year. 30% grads pursue arts and sciences degrees. **Faculty:** 65 full-time faculty, 66% hold PhDs, 65% are members of minority groups, 25% are women. 0% of classes are taught by teaching assistants.

ACADEMICS

Degrees: associate, bachelor's, certificate, master's, post-bachelor's certificate. **Classes:** Most classes have fewer than 10 students. **Majors with Highest Enrollment:** Computer and Information Sciences; Social Work; Business/Commerce. **Special Study Options:** cooperative education program, distance learning, double major, honors program, independent study, student-designed major, study abroad, teacher certification program. **Honors programs:** Honors program. **Disability Services:** Special programs offered to physically disabled students include tutors. **Career services:** Alumni network, alumni services, career/job search classes, career assessment, internships, regional alumni.

FACILITIES

Housing: Coed dorms. 95% of campus accessible to physically disabled. **Special Academic Facilities/Equipment:** conference center, chapel, theatre, art gallery. **Computers:** Students can register for classes online. Administrative functions (other than registration) can be performed online.

CAMPUS LIFE

Environment: Metropolis. **Activities:** Choral groups, dance, music ensembles, student government. 17 registered organizations, 6 honor societies. **On-Campus Highlights:** Theater, Chapel, Conference Center, Art Gallery.

ADMISSIONS

Freshman Academic Profile: Average high school GPA 2.87. 10% in top 10% of high school class, 75% in top 25% of high school class, 100% in top 50% of high school class. 80% from public high schools. ACT middle 50% range 16-21. Minimum paper TOEFL 520. **Basis for Candidate Selection:** *Important factors considered include:* rigor of secondary school record, standardized test scores, character/personal qualities, interview, talent/ability. *Other factors considered include:* recommendation(s), extracurricular activities, volunteer work, work experience. **Freshman Admission Requirements:** High school diploma is required and GED is accepted. **Freshman Admission Statistics:** 290 applied, 40% admitted, 36% enrolled. **Transfer Admission Requirements:** college transcript(s), statement of good standing from prior institution(s). Minimum college GPA of 2.7 required. Lowest grade transferable C. **General Admission Information:** Application Fee $25. Regular application deadline 8/15. Regular notification 8/15. Nonfall registration accepted. Admission may be deferred for a maximum of 12 Months. Credit and/or placement offered for CEEB Advanced Placement tests.

COSTS AND FINANCIAL AID

Annual tuition $12,190. Room and board $6,000. Required fees $250. Average book expense $1,180. **Required Forms and Deadlines:** FAFSA, Institution's own financial aid form. **Notification of Awards:** Applicants will be notified of awards on a rolling basis beginning 5/1. **Types of Aid:** *Need-based scholarships/grants:* Federal Pell, SEOG, state scholarships/grants, private scholarships, the school's own gift aid. *Loans:* Direct Subsidized Stafford, Direct Unsubsidized Stafford, Direct PLUS, Subsidized Stafford, Unsubsidized Stafford, PLUS, Federal Perkins, state loans. *Student Employment:* Federal Work-Study Program available. Highest amount earned per year from on-campus jobs $2,700. Off-campus job opportunities are good. **Financial Aid Statistics:** 0% freshmen, 0% undergrads receive athletic scholarships. Criteriafor awarding institutional aid: *Non-need-based:* academics, art, leadership, music/drama.

MARYGROVE COLLEGE

8425 West McNichols R, Detroit, MI 48221-2599
Phone: 313-927-1240
E-mail: info@marygrove.edu · **CEEB Code:** 1452
Fax: 313-927-1345 · **Website:** www.marygrove.edu · **ACT Code:** 2024

This private school, affiliated with the Roman Catholic Church, was founded in 1927. It has a 50-acre campus.

RATINGS

Admissions Selectivity Rating: 84   **Fire Safety Rating:** 60*

MARYLAND INSTITUTE COLLEGE OF ART

1300 West Mount Royal Avenue, Baltimore, MD 21217
Phone: 410-225-2222 · **Financial Aid Phone:** 410-225-2285
E-mail: admissions@mica.edu · **CEEB Code:** 5399
Fax: 410-225-2337 · **Website:** www.mica.edu · **ACT Code:** 1710

This private school was founded in 1826. It has a 12-acre campus.

RATINGS

Admissions Selectivity Rating: 84   **Fire Safety Rating:** 87

STUDENTS AND FACULTY

Enrollment: 1,842. **Student Body:** 72% female, 28% male, 80% out-of-state, 12% international (62 countries represented). Asian 13%, African American 6%, Caucasian 52%, Hispanic 4%, Native American <1%

Retention and Graduation: 87% freshmen return for sophomore year. 64% freshmen graduate within 4 years. 72% freshmen graduate within 6 years. **Faculty:** 150 full-time faculty, 77% hold PhDs, 51% are members of minority groups, 15% are women. 0% of classes are taught by teaching assistants.

ACADEMICS

Degrees: bachelor's, master's, post-bachelor's certificate. **Classes:** Most classes have 10–19 students. **Majors with Highest Enrollment:** Illustration; Graphic Design; Painting. **Special Study Options:** Accelerated program, cross-registration, distance learning, double major, dual enrollment, exchange student program (domestic), independent study, internships, student-designed major, study abroad, teacher certification program, Cooperative exchange programs with Johns Hopkins University, Goucher College, The Peabody Conservatory of Music, University of Baltimore, Loyola College, Notre Dame College, University of Maryland Baltimore County, Morgan State University, and Towson University; 5-year BFA/MAT program is available. **Combined degree programs:** BA/MA, BFA/MAT. **Disability Services:** Special programs offered to physically disabled students include note-taking services, tape recorders, tutors. **Career services:** Alumni network, alumni services, career/job search classes, career assessment, internships, regional alumni.

FACILITIES

Housing: Coed dorms, special housing for disabled students, special housing for international students, apartments for single students. 85% of campus accessible to physically disabled. **Special Academic Facilities/Equipment:** There are seven art galleries open to the public year-round featuring work by MICA faculty, students, and nationally/internationally known artists; a nature library; and an extensive slide library containing over 220,000 slides. **Computers:** 100% of libraries, 100% of dining areas, 80% of common outdoor areas have wireless network access. Students can register for classes online. Administrative functions (other than registration) can be performed online.

CAMPUS LIFE

Environment: Metropolis. **Activities:** Choral groups, dance, drama/theater, literary magazine, radio station, student government, student-run film society, International Student Organization. 50 registered organizations, 3 religious organizations. **On-Campus Highlights:** The Gateway, our new dormitory, The Brown Center, our Digital Arts cente, The Meyerhoff House dormitory & dining, Various on-campus galleries/exhibitiions, Café Doris and Java Corner, two eateries. **Environmental Initiatives:** Single-Stream recycling of recyclable waste. Using an independent auditor to track the Colleges energy for an energy-use audit. MICA does not use chemical drain cleaners and openers to unclog plumbing because these products are highly acidic and detrimental to the environment, persons handling the products, as well as the plumbing.

ADMISSIONS

Freshman Academic Profile: 70% from public high schools. SAT Math middle 50% range 510-630. SAT Critical Reading middle 50% range 520-670. SAT Writing middle 50% range 520-650. Minimum internet-based TOEFL 80. Minimum paper TOEFL 550. **Basis for Candidate Selection:** *Very important factors considered include:* academic GPA, rigor of secondary school record, level of applicant's interest, talent/ability. *Important factors considered include:* Class rank, application essay, standardized test scores, extracurricular activities, interview. *Other factors considered include:* recommendation(s), alumni/ae relation, character/personal qualities, racial/ethnic status, volunteer work. **Freshman Admission Requirements:** High school diploma is required and GED is accepted. *Academic units required:* 4 English, 2 mathematics, 2 science, (1 science labs), 4 social studies, 3 history, 6 academic electives, 2 Studio Art 2, 4 studio art recommended, 1 Art History recommended. **Freshman Admission Statistics:** 3,067 applied, 54% admitted, 27% enrolled. **Transfer Admission Requirements:** High school transcript, college transcript(s), essay or personal statement, Minimum college GPA of 2.8 required. Lowest grade transferable C. **General Admission Information:** Application Fee $60. Early decision application deadline 11/14. Regular application deadline 2/13. Regular notification 3/13. Nonfall registration accepted. Admission may be deferred for a maximum of 1 year. Credit and/or placement offered for CEEB Advanced Placement tests.

COSTS AND FINANCIAL AID

Annual tuition $40,850. Room and board $11,710. Required fees $1,540. Average book expense $1,450. **Required Forms and Deadlines:** FAFSA, Institution's own financial aid form. **Notification of Awards:** Applicants will be notified of awards on or about 4/10. *Types of Aid: Need-based scholarships/grants:* Federal Pell, SEOG, state scholarships/grants, private scholarships, school's own gift aid. *Loans:* Subsidized Stafford, Unsubsidized Stafford, PLUS, Federal Perkins. *Student Employment:* Federal Work-Study Program available. Institutional employment available. Off-campus job opportunities are excellent. **Criteria for awarding institutional aid:** *Non-need-based:* academics, art.

MARYLHURST UNIVERSITY

PO Box 261, Marylhurst, OR 97036
Phone: 503-699-6268 • **Financial Aid Phone:** 503-699-6253
E-mail: admissions@marylhurst.edu • **CEEB Code:** 440
Fax: 503-636-9526 • **Website:** www.marylhurst.edu • **ACT Code:** 3470

This private school, affiliated with the Roman Catholic Church, was founded in 1893. It has a 68-acre campus.

RATINGS

Admissions Selectivity Rating: 60*	**Fire Safety Rating:** 60*

STUDENTS AND FACULTY

Enrollment: 597. **Student Body:** 72% female, 28% male, 27% out-of-state. **Faculty:** 0% of classes are taught by teaching assistants.

ACADEMICS

Degrees: bachelor's, certificate, first professional, master's, post-bachelor's certificate, post-master's certificate. **Classes:** Most classes have fewer than 10 students. **Majors with Highest Enrollment:** Multi-/Interdisciplinary Studies; Business Administration and Management; Interior Design. **Special Study Options:** Accelerated program, cooperative education program, cross-registration, distance learning, double major, English as a Second Language (ESL), independent study, internships, student-designed major, study abroad, teacher certification program, weekend college. **Disability Services:** Special programs offered to physically disabled students include note-taking services, reader services, tape recorders, tutors.

FACILITIES

Housing: 90% of campus accessible to physically disabled. **Special Academic Facilities/Equipment:** Art Gym Art Gallery Streff Gallery **Computers:** Students can register for classes online. Administrative functions (other than registration) can be performed online.

CAMPUS LIFE

Environment: City. **Activities:** Choral groups, jazz band, literary magazine, music ensembles, symphony orchestra. 6 registered organizations, 1 honor society.

ADMISSIONS

Basis for Candidate Selection: *Other factors considered include:* academic GPA, recommendation(s), interview. **Freshman Admission Requirements:** High school diploma is required and GED is accepted. **Transfer Admission Requirements:** High school transcript, college transcript(s), Minimum college GPA of 2.0 required. Lowest grade transferable C-. **General Admission Information:** Application Fee $20. Nonfall registration accepted. Admission may be deferred for a maximum of 1 yr. Credit and/or placement offered for CEEB Advanced Placement tests.

COSTS AND FINANCIAL AID

Annual tuition $20,295. **Required Forms and Deadlines:** FAFSA, Institution's own financial aid form. **Notification of Awards:** Applicants will be notified of awards on a rolling basis beginning 4/15. *Types of Aid: Need-based scholarships/grants:* Federal Pell, SEOG, state scholarships/grants, private scholarships, the school's own gift aid. *Loans:* Subsidized Stafford, Unsubsidized Stafford, PLUS, Federal Perkins. **Financial Aid Statistics:** 97% undergrads receive need-based scholarship or grant aid.2% undergrads receive non-need-based scholarship or grant aid.89% undergrads receive need-based self-help aid.0% undergrads receive athletic scholarships. 100% undergrads borrow to pay for school. Average cumulative indebtedness $34,399. **Criteria for awarding institutional aid:** *Non-need-based:* academics.

MARYMOUNT CALIFORNIA UNIVERSITY

Marymount California University, 30800 Palos Verdes Drive East, CA 90275
Phone: 310-377-5501 • **Financial Aid Phone:** 310-303-7311
E-mail: admissions@marymountcalifornia.edu • **CEEB Code:** 4515
Fax: 310-265-0962 • **Website:** http://www.marymountcalifornia.edu/
ACT Code: 316

This private school, affiliated with the Roman Catholic Church, was founded in 1932. It has a 22-acre campus.

RATINGS

Admissions Selectivity Rating: 73	**Fire Safety Rating:** 86

STUDENTS AND FACULTY

Enrollment: 1,034. **Student Body:** 55% female, 45% male, 5% out-of-state, 14% international (42 countries represented). Asian 5%, African American 8%, Caucasian 25%, Hispanic 36%, Native American <1%
Retention and Graduation: 68% freshmen return for sophomore year.
Faculty: 28 full-time faculty, 68% hold PhDs, 43% are members of minority groups, 18% are women. 0% of classes are taught by teaching assistants.

ACADEMICS

Degrees: associate, bachelor's. **Classes:** Most classes have 10–19 students.
Majors with Highest Enrollment: Business, Management, Marketing, and Related Support Services; Liberal Arts and Sciences Studies and Humanities; Psychology. **Special Study Options:** dual enrollment, English as a Second Language (ESL), honors program, internships, study abroad, weekend college. **Honors programs:** Marymount Honors Program, Phi Theta Kappa. **Disability Services:** Special programs offered to physically disabled students include note-taking services, reader services, tape recorders, tutors.

FACILITIES

Housing: Coed dorms, special housing for disabled students. 100% of campus accessible to physically disabled. **Computers:** 100% of classrooms, 100% of dorms, 100% of libraries, 100% of dining areas, 100% of student union, 75% of common outdoor areas have wireless network access. Administrative functions (other than registration) can be performed online.

CAMPUS LIFE

Environment: Town. **Activities:** Choral groups, dance, drama/theater, jazz band, literary magazine, musical theater, radio station, student government, student newspaper, student-run film society, Campus Ministries, International Student Organization 2 honor societies, 2 religious organizations. **Athletics (Intercollegiate):** *Men:* soccer. *Women:* soccer.

ADMISSIONS

Freshman Academic Profile: Average high school GPA 2.95. 30% from public high schools. SAT Math middle 50% range 390-520. SAT Critical Reading middle 50% range 410-520. SAT Writing middle 50% range 400-520. ACT middle 50% range 16-22. Minimum internet-based TOEFL 61. **Basis for Candidate Selection:** *Very important factors considered include:* academic GPA, rigor of secondary school record. *Other factors considered include:* Class rank, application essay, recommendation(s), standardized test scores, alumni/ae relation, character/personal qualities, extracurricular activities, interview, level of applicant's interest, talent/ability, volunteer work. **Freshman Admission Requirements:** High school diploma is required and GED is accepted. **Freshman Admission Statistics:** 1,612 applied, 59% admitted, 30% enrolled. **Transfer Admission Requirements:** High school transcript, college transcript(s), Lowest grade transferable C-. **General Admission Information:** Application Fee $40. Notification on a rolling basis, beginning on or about 12/1. Nonfall registration accepted. Admission may be deferred for a maximum of 1 year. Credit and/or placement offered for CEEB Advanced Placement tests.

COSTS AND FINANCIAL AID

Required Forms and Deadlines: FAFSA. **Notification of Awards:** Applicants will be notified of awards on or about 3/1. **Types of Aid:** *Need-based scholarships/grants:* Federal Pell, SEOG, state scholarships/grants, private scholarships, the school's own gift aid. *Loans:* Subsidized Stafford, Unsubsidized Stafford, PLUS. *Student Employment:* Federal Work-Study Program available. Institutional employment available. Highest amount earned per year from on-campus jobs $3,840. Off-campus job opportunities are good. **Financial Aid Statistics:** 100% freshmen, 100% undergrads receive need-based scholarship or grant aid. 86% freshmen, 88% undergrads receive non-need-based scholarship or grant aid. 1% freshmen, 6% undergrads receive need-based self-help aid. 5% freshmen, 5% undergrads receive athletic scholarships. 84% freshmen, 74% undergrads receive any aid. 57% undergrads borrow to pay for school. Average cumulative indebtedness $7,473. **Criteria for awarding institutional aid:** *Non-need-based:* academics, art, athletics, leadership.

MARYMOUNT MANHATTAN COLLEGE

221 East 71 Street, New York, NY 10021
Phone: 212-517-0430 · **Financial Aid Phone:** 212-517-0500
E-mail: admissions@mmm.edu · **CEEB Code:** 2405
Fax: 212-517-0448 · **Website:** www.mmm.edu · **ACT Code:** 2810

This private school was founded in 1936. It has a 1-acre campus.

RATINGS

Admissions Selectivity Rating: 78   **Fire Safety Rating:** 88

STUDENTS AND FACULTY

Enrollment: 1,727. **Student Body:** 84% female, 16% male, 57% out-of-state, 3% international (36 countries represented). Asian 8%, African American 13%, Caucasian 71%, Hispanic 13%, Native American <1%
Retention and Graduation: 34% freshmen graduate within 4 years. 33% grads go on to further study within 1 year. 9% grads pursue arts and sciences degrees. 7% grads pursue law degrees. 12% grads pursue business degrees. 5% grads pursue medical degrees. **Faculty:** 103 full-time faculty, 90% hold PhDs, 63% are members of minority groups.

ACADEMICS

Degrees: associate, bachelor's, certificate. **Classes:** Most classes have 10–19 students. **Majors with Highest Enrollment:** Dance; Drama and Dramatics/Theatre Arts; Communication and Media Studies. **Special Study Options:** Accelerated program, distance learning, double major, dual enrollment, exchange student program (domestic), independent study, internships, liberal arts/career combination, study abroad, teacher certification program. **Disability Services:** Special programs offered to physically disabled students include note-taking services, reader services, tape recorders, tutors. **Career services:** Alumni network, alumni services, career assessment, internships.

FACILITIES

Housing: Coed dorms. 100% of campus accessible to physically disabled. **Special Academic Facilities/Equipment:** Gallery, communications and learning center, theatre, media center, college skills center, mathematics lab, Samuel Freeman science center,Comm Arts multimedia suite. **Computers:** 40% of classrooms, 100% of libraries, have wireless network access. Students can register for classes online. Administrative functions (other than registration) can be performed online.

CAMPUS LIFE

Environment: Metropolis. **Activities:** Choral groups, dance, drama/theater, literary magazine, musical theater, radio station, student government, student newspaper, yearbook, International Student Organization. 30 registered organizations, 7 honor societies, 2 religious organizations. **On-Campus Highlights:** Theresa Lang Theatre, Hewitt Gallery of Art, Science Laboratories, 55th Street Residence Hall, Shanahan Library, Student cafeterias. **Environmental Initiatives:** purchase of renewable energy recycling of paper and bottles awareness campaigns to get students and faculty and staff moving in a green direction

ADMISSIONS

Freshman Academic Profile: Average high school GPA 3.36. 70% from public high schools. SAT Math middle 50% range 510-620. SAT Critical Reading middle 50% range 540-650. SAT Writing middle 50% range 510-630. ACT middle 50% range 21-26. Minimum internet-based TOEFL 80. Minimum paper TOEFL 550. **Basis for Candidate Selection:** *Very important factors considered include:* academic GPA, rigor of secondary school record, standardized test scores. *Important factors considered include:* application essay, recommendation(s), character/personal qualities, extracurricular activities, talent/ability. *Other factors considered include:* Class rank, interview, volunteer work, work experience. **Freshman Admission Requirements:** High school diploma is required and GED is accepted. *Academic units required:* 4 English, 3 mathematics, 3 science, 3 social studies, 4 academic electives. **Freshman Admission Statistics:** 4,174 applied, 72% admitted, 17% enrolled. **Transfer Admission Requirements:** High school transcript, college transcript(s), essay or personal statement, statement of good standing from prior institution(s). Minimum college GPA of 2.5 required. Lowest grade transferable C-. **General Admission Information:** Application Fee $60. Notification on a rolling basis, beginning on or about 9/1. Nonfall registration accepted. Admission may be deferred for a maximum of 1 Semester. Credit and/or placement offered for CEEB Advanced Placement tests.

COSTS AND FINANCIAL AID

Annual tuition $24,482. Room and board $14,430. Required fees $1,206. Average book expense $1,000. **Required Forms and Deadlines:** FAFSA. **Notification of Awards:** Applicants will be notified of awards on a rolling basis beginning 3/15. **Types of Aid:** *Need-based scholarships/grants:* Federal Pell, SEOG, state scholarships/grants, private scholarships, the school's own gift aid. *Loans:* Subsidized Stafford, Unsubsidized Stafford, PLUS. *Student Employment:* Federal Work-Study Program available. Institutional employment available. Highest amount earned per year from on-campus jobs $2,000. Off-campus job opportunities are excellent. **Financial Aid Statistics:** 100% freshmen, 100% undergrads receive need-based scholarship or grant aid. 26% freshmen, 26% undergrads receive non-need-based scholarship or grant aid. 68% freshmen, 75% undergrads receive need-based self-help aid. 0% freshmen, 0% undergrads receive athletic scholarships. 79% freshmen, 65% undergrads receive any aid. 77% undergrads borrow to pay for school. Average cumulative indebtedness $9,673.

MARYMOUNT UNIVERSITY

2807 North Glebe Road, Arlington, VA 22207
Phone: 703-284-1500 · **Financial Aid Phone:** 703-284-1530
E-mail: admissions@marymount.edu · **CEEB Code:** 5405
Fax: 703-522-0349 · **Website:** http://www.marymount.edu · **ACT Code:** 4378

This private school, affiliated with the Roman Catholic Church, was founded in 1950. It has a 21-acre campus.

RATINGS

Admissions Selectivity Rating: 77   **Fire Safety Rating:** 77

STUDENTS AND FACULTY

Enrollment: 2,199. **Student Body:** 75% female, 25% male, 42% out-of-state, 6% international (70 countries represented). Asian 8%, African American 15%, Caucasian 46%, Hispanic 12%, Native American 1%
Retention and Graduation: 71% freshmen return for sophomore year. **Faculty:** 138 full-time faculty, 89% hold PhDs, 74% are members of minority groups, 5% are women. 0% of classes are taught by teaching assistants.

ACADEMICS

Degrees: bachelor's, certificate, master's, post-bachelor's certificate, post-master's certificate. **Classes:** Most classes have 10–19 students. **Majors with Highest Enrollment:** Business Administration and Management; Fashion/Apparel Design; Biology/Biological Sciences. **Special Study Options:** Accelerated program, cross-registration, distance learning, double major, English as a Second Language (ESL), honors program, independent study, internships, student-designed major, study abroad, teacher certification program. **Honors programs:** The Honors Program at Marymount University **Combined degree programs:** BBA/MBA, Health Promotion Mgt. BS/MS. **Disability Services:** Special programs offered to physically disabled students include note-taking services, reader services, tape recorders, tutors. **Career services:** Alumni network, career/job search classes, internships.

FACILITIES

Housing: Coed dorms, men's dorms, women's dorms. 75% of campus accessible to physically disabled. **Special Academic Facilities/Equipment:** Art gallery, learning resource center, audiovisual center, studio, and computer labs. **Computers:** Students can register for classes online. Administrative functions (other than registration) can be performed online.

CAMPUS LIFE

Environment: City. **Activities:** Choral groups, dance, drama/theater, literary magazine, student government, student newspaper, yearbook, Campus Ministries, International Student Organization. 33 registered organizations, 11 honor society, 2 religious organizations. **Athletics (Intercollegiate):** *Men:* basketball, cross-country, golf, lacrosse, soccer, swimming. *Women:* basketball, cross-country, lacrosse, soccer, swimming, volleyball. **On-Campus Highlights:** Student Center, Gym, Bernie's Café, Turf field, Ballston campus. **Environmental Initiatives:** Recycling program; Public transportation available; Car pool incentives.

ADMISSIONS

Freshman Academic Profile: Average high school GPA 3.1. 15% in top 10% of high school class, 41% in top 25% of high school class, 81% in top 50% of high school class. 68% from public high schools. SAT Math middle 50% range 450-550. SAT Critical Reading middle 50% range 450-560. SAT Writing middle 50% range 450-550. ACT middle 50% range 18-24. Minimum internet-based TOEFL 79. Minimum paper TOEFL 550. **Basis for Candidate Selection:** *Very important factors considered include:* academic GPA, rigor of secondary school record, standardized test scores. *Important factors considered include:* Class rank, recommendation(s), interview, talent/ability. *Other factors considered include:* application essay, alumni/ae relation, character/personal qualities, extracurricular activities, first generation, level of applicant's interest, volunteer work, work experience. **Freshman Admission Requirements:** High school diploma is required and GED is accepted. **Freshman Admission Statistics:** 1,904 applied, 81% admitted, 26% enrolled. **Transfer Admission Requirements:** college transcript(s), statement of good standing from prior institution(s). Minimum college GPA of 2.0 required. Lowest grade transferable C. **General Admission Information:** Application Fee $40. Nonfall registration accepted. Admission may be deferred for a maximum of 1 year. Credit offered for CEEB Advanced Placement tests.

COSTS AND FINANCIAL AID

Annual tuition $23,700. Room and board $8,705. Required fees $220. Average book expense $800. **Required Forms and Deadlines:** FAFSA. **Notification of Awards:** Applicants will be notified of awards on a rolling basis beginning 3/15. **Types of Aid:** *Need-based scholarships/grants:* Federal Pell, SEOG, state scholarships/grants, private scholarships, the school's own gift aid. *Loans:*

Direct Subsidized Stafford, Direct Unsubsidized Stafford, Subsidized Stafford, Unsubsidized Stafford, PLUS, Federal Perkins. *Student Employment:* Federal Work-Study Program available. Institutional employment available. Off-campus job opportunities are good. **Financial Aid Statistics:** 83% freshmen, 74% undergrads receive need-based scholarship or grant aid. 79% freshmen, 73% undergrads receive non-need-based scholarship or grant aid. 77% freshmen, 82% undergrads receive need-based self-help aid. 0% freshmen, 0% undergrads receive athletic scholarships. 92% freshmen, 84% undergrads receive any aid. 70% undergrads borrow to pay for school. Average cumulative indebtedness $16,940. **Criteria for awarding institutional aid:** *Non-need-based:* academics, alumni affiliation, leadership, state/district residency.

MARYVILLE COLLEGE

502 East Lamar Alexander Parkway, Maryville, TN 37804-5907
Phone: 865-981-8092 · **Financial Aid Phone:** 865-981-8100
E-mail: admissions@maryvillecollege.edu · **CEEB Code:** 1454
Fax: 865-981-8005 · **Website:** www.maryvillecollege.edu · **ACT Code:** 3988

This private school, affiliated with the Presbyterian Church, was founded in 1819. It has a 370-acre campus.

RATINGS

Admissions Selectivity Rating: 86   **Fire Safety Rating:** 87

STUDENTS AND FACULTY

Enrollment: 1,114. **Student Body:** 55% female, 45% male, 24% out-of-state, 4% international (20 countries represented). Asian 1%, African American 5%, Caucasian 86%, Hispanic 2%, Native American <1%
Retention and Graduation: 67% freshmen return for sophomore year. 43% freshmen graduate within 4 years. 51% freshmen graduate within 6 years. 28% grads go on to further study within 1 year. **Faculty:** 79 full-time faculty, 76% hold PhDs, 54% are members of minority groups, 4% are women. 0% of classes are taught by teaching assistants.

ACADEMICS

Degrees: bachelor's. **Classes:** Most classes have 10–19 students. Most lab/discussion sessions have 10–19 students. **Majors with Highest Enrollment:** Education; Biology/Biological Sciences; Business/Commerce. **Special Study Options:** double major, English as a Second Language (ESL), honors program, independent study, internships, liberal arts/career combination, student-designed major, study abroad, teacher certification program. **Honors programs:** Presidential and Deans scholars participate in honors courses and honors tutorial practicum. Most courses may be taken with "honors" status. **Combined degree programs:** BA/MSN. **Disability Services:** Special programs offered to physically disabled students include note-taking services, reader services, tape recorders, tutors. **Career services:** Alumni network, alumni services, career/job search classes, career assessment, internships, regional alumni. Career services highlights include internships and practica available in almost all major fields.

FACILITIES

Housing: Coed dorms, special housing for disabled students, men's dorms, women's dorms, apartments for single students, Special Interest groups. 90% of campus accessible to physically disabled. **Special Academic Facilities/Equipment:** Art gallery, theatre, greenhouse, College Woods. **Computers:** 100% of classrooms, 100% of dorms, 100% of libraries, 100% of dining areas, 100% of student union, 50% of common outdoor areas have wireless network access. Students can register for classes online. Administrative functions (other than registration) can be performed online.

CAMPUS LIFE

Environment: Town. **Activities:** Choral groups, concert band, dance, drama/theater, jazz band, literary magazine, music ensembles, musical theater, student government, student newspaper, symphony orchestra, yearbook, Campus Ministries. 63 registered organizations, 15 honor societies, 5 religious organizations. **Athletics (Intercollegiate):** *Men:* baseball, basketball, cross-country, equestrian sports, football, soccer, tennis. *Women:* basketball, cross-country, equestrian sports, soccer, softball, tennis, volleyball. **On-Campus Highlights:** Isaacs Student Center, Mountain Challenge, Lloyd Beach, New Lloyd Residence Hall, Center for Calling and Career, Mountain Challenge includes a 60' Alpine Tower, rock climbing wall, ropes course, and kayak roll sessions on campus. In addition there are trips offered every Saturday to nearby attractions, i.e. rock climbing, white water rafting, camping, and caving. **Environmental Initiatives:** Steam plant boiler is fueled by recycled wood products; Campus-wide recycling program; Purchase of green power for selected campus buildings.

ADMISSIONS

Freshman Academic Profile: Average high school GPA 3.59. 34% in top 10% of high school class, 65% in top 25% of high school class, 89% in top 50% of high school class. 91% from public high schools. SAT Math middle 50% range 480-610. SAT Critical Reading middle 50% range 470-630. SAT Writing middle 50% range 450-610. ACT middle 50% range 21-28. Minimum paper TOEFL 525. **Basis for Candidate Selection:** *Very important factors considered include:* Class rank, rigor of secondary school record, standardized test scores. *Important factors considered include:* academic GPA, recommendation(s), extracurricular activities, interview. *Other factors considered include:* application essay, alumni/ae relation, character/personal qualities, first generation, level of applicant's interest, talent/ability, volunteer work. **Freshman Admission Requirements:** High school diploma is required and GED is accepted. *Academic units required:* 4 English, 3 mathematics, 2 science, (1 science labs), 2 foreign language, 2 social studies, 1 academic electives. **Freshman Admission Statistics:** 1,621 applied, 75% admitted, 24% enrolled. **Transfer Admission Requirements:** college transcript(s), statement of good standing from prior institution(s). Minimum college GPA of 2.0 required. Lowest grade transferable C. **General Admission Information:** Early decision application deadline 11/15. Notification on a rolling basis, beginning on or about 12/1. Nonfall registration accepted. Admission may be deferred for a maximum of 1 year. Credit and/or placement offered for CEEB Advanced Placement tests.

COSTS AND FINANCIAL AID

Annual tuition $26,272. Room and board $8,240. Required fees $675. Average book expense $880. **Required Forms and Deadlines:** FAFSA. **Types of Aid:** *Need-based scholarships/grants:* Federal Pell, SEOG, state scholarships/grants, private scholarships, the school's own gift aid. *Loans:* Direct Subsidized Stafford, Direct Unsubsidized Stafford, Direct PLUS, Subsidized Stafford, Unsubsidized Stafford, PLUS, Federal Perkins, state loans, college/university loans from institutional funds. *Student Employment:* Federal Work-Study Program available. Highest amount earned per year from on-campus jobs $2,617. Off-campus job opportunities are good. **Financial Aid Statistics:** 75% freshmen, 98% undergrads receive need-based scholarship or grant aid. 31% freshmen, 25% undergrads receive non-need-based scholarship or grant aid. 78% freshmen, 61% undergrads receive need-based self-help aid. 0% freshmen, 0% undergrads receive athletic scholarships. 100% freshmen, 98% undergrads receive any aid. 92% undergrads borrow to pay for school. Average cumulative indebtedness $13,023. **Criteria for awarding institutional aid:** *Non-need-based:* academics, art, leadership, minority status, music/drama, religious affiliation, state/district residency.

MARYVILLE UNIVERSITY OF SAINT LOUIS

650 Maryville University Drive, St. Louis, MO 63141-7299
Phone: 314-529-9350 · **Financial Aid Phone:** 314-529-9360
E-mail: admissions@maryville.edu · **CEEB Code:** 6399
Fax: 314-529-9927 • **ACT Code:** 2326

This private school was founded in 1872. It has a 130-acre campus.

RATINGS

Admissions Selectivity Rating: 86   Fire Safety Rating: 88

STUDENTS AND FACULTY

Enrollment: 2,736. **Student Body:** 71% female, 29% male, 21% out-of-state, 3% international (14 countries represented). Asian 2%, African American 8%, Caucasian 76%, Hispanic 3%, Native American <1%
Retention and Graduation: 87% freshmen return for sophomore year. 49% freshmen graduate within 4 years. **Faculty:** 121 full-time faculty, 80% hold PhDs, 64% are members of minority groups, 14% are women. 0% of classes are taught by teaching assistants.

ACADEMICS

Degrees: bachelor's, certificate, master's. **Classes:** Most classes have 10–19 students. Most lab/discussion sessions have fewer than 10 students. **Majors with Highest Enrollment:** Registered Nursing/Registered Nurse; Physical Therapy/Therapist; Business/Commerce. **Special Study Options:** Accelerated program, cooperative education program, cross-registration, distance learning, double major, dual enrollment, honors program, independent study, internships, liberal arts/career combination, student-designed major, study abroad, teacher certification program, weekend college, Washington Center, Semester at Sea. **Honors programs:** Bascom Honors Program **Combined degree programs:** MU-St. Louis Univ. M.S.W. Joint Degree Program. **Disability Services:** Special programs offered to physically disabled students include note-taking services, reader services, tape recorders, tutors. **Career services:** career/job search classes, career assessment, internships. Career services highlights include Cooperative Education—over 80 students per year participate in a co-op experience.

College Directory

FACILITIES

Housing: Coed dorms, apartments for single students, Wellness Housing, Theme Housing. 90% of campus accessible to physically disabled. **Special Academic Facilities/Equipment:** University Center, art galleries, auditorium, chapel, observatory, teaching lab, clinical labs, art and design labs, videoconferencing facility with downlinking and electronic multi-media capability for presentations. **Computers:** 100% of classrooms, 100% of dorms, 100% of libraries, 100% of dining areas, 100% of student union, 100% of common outdoor areas have wireless network access. Students can register for classes online. Administrative functions (other than registration) can be performed online.

CAMPUS LIFE

Environment: Metropolis. **Activities:** Choral groups, dance, drama/theater, jazz band, literary magazine, music ensembles, pep band, student government, student newspaper, symphony orchestra, Campus Ministries. 40 registered organizations, 3 honor societies, 4 religious organizations. **Athletics (Intercollegiate):** *Men:* baseball, basketball, cheerleading, cross-country, golf, soccer, tennis. *Women:* basketball, cheerleading, cross-country, golf, soccer, softball, tennis, volleyball.

ADMISSIONS

Freshman Academic Profile: Average high school GPA 3.7. 28% in top 10% of high school class, 61% in top 25% of high school class, 89% in top 50% of high school class. 77% from public high schools. SAT Math middle 50% range 480-590. SAT Critical Reading middle 50% range 460-560. ACT middle 50% range 23-27. Minimum paper TOEFL 500. **Basis for Candidate Selection:** *Very important factors considered include:* academic GPA, standardized test scores. *Important factors considered include:* rigor of secondary school record, extracurricular activities. *Other factors considered include:* Class rank, application essay, recommendation(s), character/personal qualities, interview, talent/ability. **Freshman Admission Requirements:** High school diploma is required and GED is accepted. *Academic units required:* 4 English, 3 mathematics, 2 science, 2 social studies, 8 academic electives. **Freshman Admission Statistics:** 1,576 applied, 72% admitted, 36% enrolled. **Transfer Admission Requirements:** college transcript(s), Minimum college GPA of 2.0 required. Lowest grade transferable C-. **General Admission Information:** Application Fee $30. Regular application deadline 8/15. Nonfall registration accepted. Admission may be deferred for a maximum of 1 year. Credit offered for CEEB Advanced Placement tests.

COSTS AND FINANCIAL AID

Annual tuition $24,694. Room and board $9,972. Required fees $1,190. Average book expense $1,800. **Required Forms and Deadlines:** FAFSA. **Notification of Awards:** Applicants will be notified of awards on a rolling basis beginning 3/1. **Types of Aid:** *Need-based scholarships/grants:* Federal Pell, SEOG, state scholarships/grants, private scholarships, the school's own gift aid, TEACH Grant, Academic Competitiveness Grant, Smart Grant. *Loans:* Direct Subsidized Stafford, Direct Unsubsidized Stafford, Direct PLUS, Federal Perkins, Five Month Installment Deferred Payment Program. *Student Employment:* Federal Work-Study Program available. **Financial Aid Statistics:** 99% freshmen, 96% undergrads receive need-based scholarship or grant aid. 25% freshmen, 19% undergrads receive non-need-based scholarship or grant aid. 76% freshmen, 80% undergrads receive need-based self-help aid. 7% freshmen, 5% undergrads receive athletic scholarships. 72% freshmen, 65% undergrads receive any aid. 69% undergrads borrow to pay for school. Average cumulative indebtedness $26,464. **Criteria for awarding institutional aid:** *Non-need-based:* academics, alumni affiliation, art, athletics, leadership, minority status.

MARYWOOD UNIVERSITY

Office of University Admissions, Scranton, PA 18509
Phone: 570-348-6234 · **Financial Aid Phone:** 866-279-9663
E-mail: yourfuture@marywood.edu · **CEEB Code:** 2407
Fax: 570-961-4763 · **Website:** www.marywood.edu • **ACT Code:** 3626

This private school, affiliated with the Roman Catholic Church, was founded in 1915. It has a 115-acre campus.

RATINGS

Admissions Selectivity Rating: 81   Fire Safety Rating: 92

STUDENTS AND FACULTY

Enrollment: 1,878. **Student Body:** 67% female, 33% male, 30% out-of-state, 1% international (8 countries represented). Asian 2%, African American 2%, Caucasian 79%, Hispanic 6%, Native American <1%
Retention and Graduation: 80% freshmen return for sophomore year. 56% freshmen graduate within 4 years. 27% grads go on to further study within 1 year. 22% grads pursue arts and sciences degrees. 1% grads pursue medical de-

grees. **Faculty:** 163 full-time faculty, 91% hold PhDs, 55% are members of minority groups, 10% are women. 0% of classes are taught by teaching assistants.

ACADEMICS

Degrees: bachelor's, master's, post-bachelor's certificate, post-master's certificate. **Classes:** Most classes have 10–19 students. **Majors with Highest Enrollment:** Psychology; Architecture; Dietetics/Dietitian. **Special Study Options:** cross-registration, double major, dual enrollment, English as a Second Language (ESL), honors program, independent study, internships, student-designed major, study abroad, teacher certification program. **Honors programs:** Open Door Honors program. **Disability Services:** Special programs offered to physically disabled students include note-taking services, reader services, tape recorders, tutors. **Career services:** alumni services, career/job search classes, career assessment, internships, regional alumni.

FACILITIES

Housing: Coed dorms, special housing for disabled students, men's dorms, women's dorms, apartments for single students. 100% of campus accessible to physically disabled. **Special Academic Facilities/Equipment:** Mellow Athletic and Fitness Center, Mahady Gallery, Suraci Gallery, The Maslow Study Gallery for Contemporary Art, Performing Arts Center, O'Neill Center for Healthy Families, Insalaco Studio Arts Center, Center for Architectural Studies, Marywood University Arboretum, Curriculum Lab, electronic learning labs, Broadcast Studios, instructional media lab, interactive video lab, computerized editing facility, center for natural and health sciences, psycho-physiology experimental lab, psychology/education research lab, science multi-media lab, language lab, center for justice and peace, on-campus preschool and day care, video tele-conferencing lab. **Computers:** 75% of classrooms, 75% of dorms, 100% of libraries, 100% of dining areas, 100% of student union, 75% of common outdoor areas have wireless network access. Students can register for classes online. Administrative functions (other than registration) can be performed online.

CAMPUS LIFE

Environment: City. **Activities:** Choral groups, concert band, dance, drama/theater, jazz band, literary magazine, music ensembles, musical theater, radio station, student government, student newspaper, television station, Campus Ministries, International Student Organization. 43 registered organizations, 31 honor society, 1 religious organization. 1 sorority. **Athletics (Intercollegiate):** *Men:* baseball, basketball, cross-country, diving, lacrosse, soccer, swimming, tennis. *Women:* basketball, cross-country, diving, field hockey, lacrosse, soccer, softball, swimming, tennis, volleyball. **On-Campus Highlights:** Mellow Center for Athletics and Wellness, Insalaco Center for Studio Arts, Liberal Arts Center Rotunda, Café Ritazza/Main Dining Room, Nazareth Student Center. **Environmental Initiatives:** Use of geothermal technology using "mine Water"; geothermal harvesting for chilled Beam cooling; Purchase of wind energy and installation of a windmill on campus; Construction of our LEED Gold certified Center for Architectural Studies and commitment to pursue LEED certification for all future new construction projects.

ADMISSIONS

Freshman Academic Profile: Average high school GPA 3.5. 17.7% in top 10% of high school class, 44.7% in top 25% of high school class, 84.4% in top 50% of high school class. 89% from public high schools. SAT Math middle 50% range 470-570. SAT Critical Reading middle 50% range 460-560. SAT Writing middle 50% range 450-560. Minimum internet-based TOEFL 71. Minimum paper TOEFL 530. **Basis for Candidate Selection:** *Very important factors considered include:* Class rank, academic GPA, rigor of secondary school record, standardized test scores, character/personal qualities. *Important factors considered include:* application essay, recommendation(s), interview, talent/ability. *Other factors considered include:* extracurricular activities, level of applicant's interest, volunteer work. **Freshman Admission Requirements:** High school diploma is required and GED is accepted. *Academic units required:* 4 English, 2 mathematics, 1 science, (1 science labs), 3 social studies, 6 academic electives. **Freshman Admission Statistics:** 2,111 applied, 74% admitted, 24% enrolled. **Transfer Admission Requirements:** High school transcript, college transcript(s), Minimum college GPA of 2.25 required. Lowest grade transferable C. **General Admission Information:** Application Fee $35. Notification on a rolling basis, beginning on or about 10/1. Nonfall registration accepted. Credit and/or placement offered for CEEB Advanced Placement tests.

COSTS AND FINANCIAL AID

Annual tuition $30,942. Room and board $13,900. Required fees $1,750. Average book expense $1,000. **Required Forms and Deadlines:** FAFSA, State aid form. **Notification of Awards:** Applicants will be notified of awards on a rolling basis beginning 2/15. **Types of Aid:** *Need-based scholarships/grants:* Federal Pell, SEOG, state scholarships/grants, private scholarships, the school's own gift aid, Federal Nursing Scholarships. *Loans:* Subsidized Stafford, Unsubsidized Stafford, PLUS, Federal Perkins, state loans, Private Alternative Loans. *Student Employment:* Federal Work-Study Program available. **Financial Aid Statistics:** 84% freshmen, 83% undergrads receive need-based scholarship or grant aid.

100% freshmen, 100% undergrads receive non-need-based scholarship or grant aid. 82% freshmen, 83% undergrads receive need-based self-help aid. 0% freshmen, 0% undergrads receive athletic scholarships. 99% freshmen, 99% undergrads receive any aid. 86% undergrads borrow to pay for school. Average cumulative indebtedness $27,290. **Criteria for awarding institutional aid:** *Non-need-based:* academics, art, leadership, music/drama, state/district residency.

MASSACHUSETTS COLLEGE OF ART AND DESIGN

621 Huntington Avenue, Boston, MA 2115
Phone: 617-879-7222 • **Financial Aid Phone:** 617-879-7850
E-mail: admissions@massart.edu • **CEEB Code:** 3516
Fax: 617-879-7250 • **ACT Code:** 1846

This public school was founded in 1873. It has a 5-acre campus.

RATINGS

Admissions Selectivity Rating: 75   **Fire Safety Rating:** 74

STUDENTS AND FACULTY

Enrollment: 1,788. **Student Body:** 70% female, 30% male, 31% out-of-state, 3% international. Asian 7%, African American 3%, Caucasian 64%, Hispanic 8%, Native American <1%
Retention and Graduation: 89% freshmen return for sophomore year. 52% freshmen graduate within 4 years. **Faculty:** 103 full-time faculty. 0% of classes are taught by teaching assistants.

ACADEMICS

Degrees: bachelor's, certificate, master's, post-bachelor's certificate. **Classes:** Most classes have 10–19 students. **Majors with Highest Enrollment:** Illustration; Graphic Design; Painting. **Special Study Options:** cross-registration, double major, exchange student program (domestic), independent study, internships, liberal arts/career combination, student-designed major, study abroad, teacher certification program. **Disability Services:** Special programs offered to physically disabled students include note-taking services, reader services, tutors. **Career services:** Alumni network, alumni services, career/job search classes, career assessment, internships.

FACILITIES

Housing: Coed dorms, apartments for single students, Off campus housing assistance from school. Additional housing available in Simmons College dorms. 95% of campus accessible to physically disabled. **Special Academic Facilities/Equipment:** Ten art galleries, foundry, glass furnaces, ceramic kilns, video and film studios, performance spaces, Polaroid 20x24 camera, individual studio spaces, design research unit, printmaking facilities, video and photography equipment and facilities, specialized computer labs, specialized equipment and facilities for all art and design programs and levels. **Computers:** 100% of classrooms, 100% of dorms, 100% of libraries, 100% of dining areas, 100% of student union, 100% of common outdoor areas have wireless network access. Students can register for classes online. Administrative functions (other than registration) can be performed online.

CAMPUS LIFE

Environment: Metropolis. **Activities:** dance, drama/theater, music ensembles, radio station, student government, student newspaper, student-run film society, television station, yearbook. 30 registered organizations, 1 honor society, 3 religious organizations. **Athletics (Intercollegiate):** *Men:* baseball, basketball, cross-country, golf, lacrosse, soccer, softball, tennis, volleyball. *Women:* basketball, cross-country, golf, lacrosse, soccer, softball, tennis, volleyball. **On-Campus Highlights:** 10 art galleries, student studios, courtyard, cafes, student center, see http://inside.massart.edu/x942.xml for a description of student activities. **Environmental Initiatives:** See http://inside.massart.edu/Administration/Administration_and_Finance/Facilities/Sustainability.html.

ADMISSIONS

Freshman Academic Profile: Average high school GPA 3.42. SAT Math middle 50% range 460-580. SAT Critical Reading middle 50% range 490-610. SAT Writing middle 50% range 470-590. ACT middle 50% range 22-27. Minimum internet-based TOEFL 85. Minimum paper TOEFL 530. **Basis for Candidate Selection:** *Very important factors considered include:* application essay, academic GPA, rigor of secondary school record, talent/ability. *Important factors considered include:* standardized test scores, state residency. *Other factors considered include:* Class rank, recommendation(s), character/personal qualities, extracurricular activities, geographical residence, volunteer work, work experience. **Freshman Admission Requirements:** High school diploma is required and GED is accepted. *Academic units required:* 4 English,

2 mathematics, 2 science, (2 science labs), 2 foreign language, 2 social studies, 0 history, 2 academic electives, 2 Art electives. **Freshman Admission Statistics:** 1,345 applied, 73% admitted, 33% enrolled. **Transfer Admission Requirements:** college transcript(s), essay or personal statement, statement of good standing from prior institution(s). Minimum college GPA of 2.5 required. Lowest grade transferable C. **General Admission Information:** Application Fee $65. Regular application deadline 2/1. Notification on a rolling basis, beginning on or about 2/1. Nonfall registration not accepted. Admission may be deferred for a maximum of 12 months. Credit and/or placement offered for CEEB Advanced Placement tests.

COSTS AND FINANCIAL AID

Annual out-of-state tuition $29,925. Room and board $13,000. Required fees $0. Average book expense $2,100. **Required Forms and Deadlines:** FAFSA. **Notification of Awards:** Applicants will be notified of awards on or about 2/1. **Types of Aid:** *Need-based scholarships/grants:* Federal Pell, SEOG, state scholarships/grants, private scholarships, the school's own gift aid. *Loans:* Direct Subsidized Stafford, Direct Unsubsidized Stafford, Direct PLUS, Subsidized Stafford, Unsubsidized Stafford, PLUS, Federal Perkins, state loans, college/university loans from institutional funds, Alternative loans (credit Based). *Student Employment:* Federal Work-Study Program available. Institutional employment available. Highest amount earned per year from on-campus jobs $800. Off-campus job opportunities are good. **Financial Aid Statistics:** 79% freshmen, 70% undergrads receive need-based scholarship or grant aid. 16% freshmen, 8% undergrads receive non-need-based scholarship or grant aid. 95% freshmen, 93% undergrads receive need-based self-help aid. 0% freshmen, 0% undergrads receive athletic scholarships. 73% undergrads borrow to pay for school. **Criteria for awarding institutional aid:** *Non-need-based:* academics, art, leadership.

MASSACHUSETTS INSTITUTE OF TECHNOLOGY

77 Massachusetts Avenue, Cambridge, MA 2139
Phone: 617-253-3400 · **Financial Aid Phone:** 617-258-8600
E-mail: admissions@mit.edu · **CEEB Code:** 3514
Fax: 617-258-8304 · **Website:** web.mit.edu · **ACT Code:** 1858

This private school was founded in 1861. It has a 168-acre campus.

RATINGS

Admissions Selectivity Rating: 99   **Fire Safety Rating: 74**

STUDENTS AND FACULTY

Enrollment: 4,476. **Student Body:** 46% female, 54% male, 91% out-of-state, 10% international (91 countries represented). Asian 25%, African American 6%, Caucasian 37%, Hispanic 16%, Native American <1%
Retention and Graduation: 99% freshmen return for sophomore year. 81% freshmen graduate within 4 years. 91% freshmen graduate within 6 years. 35% grads go on to further study within 1 year. 29% grads pursue arts and sciences degrees. 1% grads pursue law degrees. 1% grads pursue business degrees. 12% grads pursue medical degrees. **Faculty:** 1,228 full-time faculty, 91% hold PhDs, 24% are members of minority groups, 17% are women.

ACADEMICS

Degrees: bachelor's, master's. **Classes:** Most classes have fewer than 10 students. Most lab/discussion sessions have 10–19 students. **Majors with Highest Enrollment:** Computer Science; Mechanical Engineering; Mathematics. **Special Study Options:** cooperative education program, cross-registration, double major, internships, study abroad, teacher certification program, Undergraduate Research Opportunities Program (UROP); Independent Activities Period (IAP); freshman learning communities. **Combined degree programs:** Two Bachelor's, SB/SM, SB/MEng, SB/MCP. **Disability Services:** Special programs offered to physically disabled students include note-taking services, reader services, tape recorders. **Career services:** Alumni network, alumni services, career/job search classes, career assessment, internships, regional alumni. Career services highlights include a very strong on-campus recruiting system, with over 397 employers who came to our Careers Office to interview students.

FACILITIES

Housing: Coed dorms, special housing for disabled students, women's dorms, fraternity/sorority housing, apartments for married students, cooperative housing, apartments for single students, Theme Housing independent living group housing, apartments for students with dependent children, and living learning communities available. **Special Academic Facilities/Equipment:** List

Visual Arts Center; MIT Museum; Ray and Maria Stata Center for Computer, Information and Intelligence Sciences; numerous labs and centers. **Computers:** 100% of classrooms, 100% of dorms, 100% of libraries, 100% of dining areas, 100% of student union, 80-98% of common outdoor areas have wireless network access. Administrative functions (other than registration) can be performed online.

CAMPUS LIFE

Environment: City. **Activities:** Choral groups, concert band, dance, drama/theater, jazz band, literary magazine, marching band, music ensembles, musical theater, radio station, student government, student newspaper, student-run film society, symphony orchestra, television station, yearbook, Campus Ministries, International Student Organization, Model UN. 400 registered organizations, 10 honor societies, 29 religious organizations. 27 fraternities, 6 sororities. **Athletics (Intercollegiate):** *Men:* baseball, basketball, crew/rowing, cross-country, diving, fencing, football, golf, gymnastics, lacrosse, pistol, riflery, sailing, skiing (downhill/alpine), skiing (nordic/cross-country), soccer, squash, swimming, tennis, track/field (outdoor), track/field (indoor), volleyball, water polo, wrestling. *Women:* basketball, crew/rowing, cross-country, diving, fencing, field hockey, gymnastics, ice hockey, lacrosse, pistol, riflery, sailing, skiing (downhill/alpine), skiing (nordic/cross-country), soccer, softball, swimming, tennis, track/field (outdoor), track/field (indoor), volleyball. **On-Campus Highlights:** Ray and Maria Stata Center, Zesiger Sports and Fitness Center, Killian Court, The Infinite Corridor, The Student Center (W20), Stata Center is a 720,000 square foot building designed by Frank Gehry. Zesiger Sports and Fitness Center is our state-of-the-art athletics facility. At 778.8 feet, the Infinite Corridor is reputed to be the longest straight hallway in the world—it connects many of the buildings on central campus and runs though two popular gathering spots: Lobbies 7 and 10. **Environmental Initiatives:** In 2010, MIT established MIT Efficiency Forward, a ground-breaking, multi-million dollar collaborative energy conservation and efficiency program with their electric and gas utility company NSTAR. The program is a first-ever-of-its-kind with a utility company and is the single largest energy efficiency program NSTAR has developed with a customer. The program is investing nearly $14 million over the next three years, with an innovative funding strategy that leverages funds from MIT, NSTAR incentive payments, and reinvestment of energy savings. MIT has committed to a goal of reducing annual electrical use on campus by 34 million kilowatt hours within three years, equivalent to 15% of MITs current electrical use. The total estimated savings over the lifetime of the efficiency measures is estimated in excess of $50 million. In 2011, MIT surpassed its two year goal by saving over 23 million kWh; Addition of cogeneration for central power supply reduced greenhouse gas emissions by over 30%; 60kw installed capacity of solar power. Recycling (47% recycling rate with new composting services offered for post-consumer food waste. Over 10% increase in recycling rate; trash reductions achieved also Green building (LEED) for new and existing buildings. In 2011, MIT certified two LEED Gold buildings (an admistrative building and a laboratory), that use 45% and 35% less energy, respectively, than a typical building of the same size.

ADMISSIONS

Freshman Academic Profile: 97% in top 10% of high school class, 100% in top 25% of high school class, 100% in top 50% of high school class. 67% from public high schools. SAT Math middle 50% range 740-800. SAT Critical Reading middle 50% range 680-770. SAT Writing middle 50% range 690-780. ACT middle 50% range 33-35. Minimum internet-based TOEFL 90. **Basis for Candidate Selection:** *Very important factors considered include:* character/personal qualities. *Important factors considered include:* Class rank, academic GPA, recommendation(s), rigor of secondary school record, standardized test scores, extracurricular activities, interview, talent/ability. *Other factors considered include:* application essay, alumni/ae relation, first generation, geographical residence, racial/ethnic status, volunteer work, work experience. **Freshman Admission Requirements:** High school diploma or equivalent is not required. **Freshman Admission Statistics:** 18,356 applied, 8% admitted, 72% enrolled. **Transfer Admission Requirements:** High school transcript, college transcript(s), essay or personal statement, standardized test scores, statement of good standing from prior institution(s). Lowest grade transferable B. **General Admission Information:** Application Fee $75. Regular application deadline 1/1. Regular notification 3/20. Nonfall registration not accepted. Admission may be deferred for a maximum of 2 years. Credit and/or placement offered for CEEB Advanced Placement tests.

COSTS AND FINANCIAL AID

Annual tuition $44,720. Room and board $13,224. Required fees $296. Average book expense $1,000. **Required Forms and Deadlines:** FAFSA, CSS/Financial Aid PROFILE, Noncustodial PROFILE, Business/Farm Supplement. **Notification of Awards:** Applicants will be notified of awards on or about 4/1. **Types of Aid:** *Need-based scholarships/grants:* Federal Pell, SEOG, state scholarships/grants, private scholarships, the school's own gift aid. *Loans:* Direct Subsidized Stafford, Direct Unsubsidized Stafford, Direct PLUS, Federal Perkins, college/university loans from institutional funds. *Student Employment:* Federal Work-Study Program available. Institutional employment available.

Highest amount earned per year from on-campus jobs $25,990. Off-campus job opportunities are excellent. **Financial Aid Statistics:** 96% freshmen, 96% undergrads receive need-based scholarship or grant aid. 4% freshmen, 2% undergrads receive non-need-based scholarship or grant aid. 84% freshmen, 87% undergrads receive need-based self-help aid. 0% freshmen, 0% undergrads receive athletic scholarships. 87% freshmen, 75% undergrads receive any aid. 41% undergrads borrow to pay for school. Average cumulative indebtedness $13,883.

MASSACHUSETTS MARITIME ACADEMY

101 Academy Drive, Buzzards Bay, MA 2532
Phone: 800-544-3411
E-mail: admissions@maritime.edu
Fax: 508-830-5077 • **Website:** www.maritime.edu

This public school was founded in 1891. It has a 55-acre campus.

RATINGS

Admissions Selectivity Rating: 63   Fire Safety Rating: 60*

STUDENTS AND FACULTY

Enrollment: 923. **Student Body:** 12% female, 88% male, 28% out-of-state, 0% international (6 countries represented). Asian 0%, African American 0%, Caucasian 0%, Hispanic 0%, Native American <1%
Retention and Graduation: 30% grads go on to further study within 1 year. 10% grads pursue arts and sciences degrees. 4% grads pursue law degrees. 15% grads pursue business degrees. 1% grads pursue medical degrees. **Faculty:** 0% of classes are taught by teaching assistants.

ACADEMICS

Degrees: bachelor's, first professional certificate, master's. **Majors with Highest Enrollment:** Environmental Science; Environmental/Environmental Health Engineering; Ocean Engineering. **Special Study Options:** cooperative education program, double major, internships, Semester-at-Sea. **Career services:** Alumni network, alumni services, career/job search classes, internships

FACILITIES

Housing: Coed dorms. 80% of campus accessible to physically disabled. **Special Academic Facilities/Equipment:** Maritime Ship Model Museum; Training Ship Enterprise. **Computers:** Undergraduates are required to own a computer.

CAMPUS LIFE

Environment: Village. **Activities:** drama/theater, jazz band, marching band, music ensembles, student government, student newspaper, yearbook. 12 registered organizations, 1 honor society, 1 religious organization. **Athletics (Intercollegiate):** *Men:* baseball, crew/rowing, cross-country, football, lacrosse, riflery, rugby, sailing, soccer. *Women:* crew/rowing, cross-country, riflery, rugby, sailing, softball, volleyball.

ADMISSIONS

Freshman Academic Profile: Average high school GPA 2.8. 0% in top 10% of high school class, 0% in top 25% of high school class, 0% in top 50% of high school class. 65% from public high schools. Minimum paper TOEFL 500. **Basis for Candidate Selection:** *Very important factors considered include:* rigor of secondary school record, standardized test scores. *Important factors considered include:* application essay, character/personal qualities. *Other factors considered include:* recommendation(s), alumni/ae relation, extracurricular activities, interview, talent/ability, volunteer work, work experience. **Freshman Admission Requirements:** High school diploma is required and GED is accepted. *Academic units required:* 4 English, 3 mathematics, 3 science, (2 science labs), 2 foreign language, 2 history, 2 academic electives. **Freshman Admission Statistics:** 808 applied, 60% admitted, 56% enrolled. **Transfer Admission Requirements:** High school transcript, college transcript(s), essay or personal statement, Minimum college GPA of 2.0 required. Lowest grade transferable c. **General Admission Information:** Application Fee $50. Notification on a rolling basis, beginning on or about 12/15. Nonfall registration not accepted. Admission may be deferred for a maximum of 1. Credit and/or placement offered for CEEB Advanced Placement tests.

COSTS AND FINANCIAL AID

Annual in-state tuition $11,500. Annual out-of-state tuition $22,000. Average book expense $700. **Required Forms and Deadlines:** FAFSA, Institution's own financial aid form. **Notification of Awards:** Applicants will be notified of awards on a rolling basis beginning 3/1. **Types of Aid:** *Need-based scholarships/grants:* Federal Pell, SEOG, state scholarships/grants, private scholarships, the school's own gift aid. *Loans:* Direct Subsidized Stafford, Direct Unsubsidized Stafford, Direct PLUS. *Student Employment:* Federal Work-Study Program

available. Highest amount earned per year from on-campus jobs $650. Off-campus job opportunities are good. **Financial Aid Statistics:** 12% freshmen, 18% undergrads receive need-based scholarship or grant aid. 8% freshmen, 37% undergrads receive non-need-based scholarship or grant aid. 53% freshmen, 60% undergrads receive need-based self-help aid. 0% freshmen, 0% undergrads receive athletic scholarships. 82% undergrads borrow to pay for school. **Criteria for awarding institutional aid:** *Non-need-based:* academics, leadership.

THE MASTER'S COLLEGE AND SEMINARY

21726 Placerita Canyon Road, Santa Clarita, CA 91321
Phone: 661-259-3540 • **Financial Aid Phone:** 661-259-3540
E-mail: admissions@masters.edu • **CEEB Code:** 4411
Fax: 661-288-1037 • **Website:** www.masters.edu • **ACT Code:** 303

This private school was founded in 1927. It has a 95-acre campus.

RATINGS

Admissions Selectivity Rating: 84   Fire Safety Rating: 88

STUDENTS AND FACULTY

Enrollment: 1,098. **Student Body:** 48% female, 52% male, 27% out-of-state, 4% international (19 countries represented). Asian 6%, African American 2%, Caucasian 57%, Hispanic 8%, Native American <1%
Retention and Graduation: 81% freshmen return for sophomore year. 48% freshmen graduate within 4 years. 54% freshmen graduate within 6 years. **Faculty:** 58 full-time faculty, 74% hold PhDs, 14% are members of minority groups, 10% are women. 0% of classes are taught by teaching assistants.

ACADEMICS

Degrees: bachelor's, certificate, first professional, first professional certificate, master's. **Classes:** Most classes have fewer than 10 students. **Majors with Highest Enrollment:** Bible/Biblical Studies; Business/Commerce; Communication. **Special Study Options:** Accelerated program, cooperative education program, distance learning, double major, independent study, internships, liberal arts/career combination, study abroad, teacher certification program, Israel semester. **Disability Services:** Special programs offered to physically disabled students include note-taking services, reader services, tape recorders, tutors. **Career services:** Alumni network, alumni services, career/job search classes, career assessment, internships.

FACILITIES

Housing: men's dorms, special housing for international students, women's dorms, Wellness Housing. 95% of campus accessible to physically disabled. **Computers:** 100% of classrooms, 100% of dorms, 100% of libraries, 100% of dining areas, 100% of student union, 95% of common outdoor areas have wireless network access. Students can register for classes online. Administrative functions (other than registration) can be performed online. Undergraduates are required to own a computer.

CAMPUS LIFE

Environment: City. **Activities:** Choral groups, concert band, drama/theater, jazz band, music ensembles, opera, pep band, student government, symphony orchestra. 15 registered organizations, 1 honor society, 11 religious organization. **Athletics (Intercollegiate):** *Men:* baseball, basketball, cross-country, golf, soccer, track/field (outdoor). *Women:* basketball, cross-country, soccer, tennis, track/field (outdoor), volleyball. **On-Campus Highlights:** New All-Weather Field (2005), Dining Center Remodeled (2005), Music Center, Smith Hall Dormitory, Canyon Café.

ADMISSIONS

Freshman Academic Profile: Average high school GPA 3.7. 28% in top 10% of high school class, 55% in top 25% of high school class, 82% in top 50% of high school class. 52% from public high schools. SAT Math middle 50% range 450-610. SAT Critical Reading middle 50% range 490-590. SAT Writing middle 50% range 480-600. ACT middle 50% range 21-26. Minimum internet-based TOEFL 80. **Basis for Candidate Selection:** *Very important factors considered include:* application essay, academic GPA, recommendation(s), rigor of secondary school record, standardized test scores, character/personal qualities, interview, religious affiliation/commitment. *Other factors considered include:* alumni/ae relation, extracurricular activities, level of applicant's interest, talent/ability. **Freshman Admission Requirements:** High school diploma is required and GED is accepted. *Academic units required:* 4 English, 3 mathematics, 2 science, 2 history. **Freshman Admission Statistics:** 556 applied, 78% admitted, 43% enrolled. **Transfer Admission Requirements:** High school transcript, college transcript(s), essay or personal statement, interview, statement of good standing from prior institution(s). Minimum college GPA of 2.5 required. Lowest grade transferable C. **General Admission Information:** Application Fee $40. Notification on a rolling basis, beginning on or about 3/15.

Nonfall registration accepted. Admission may be deferred for a maximum of 2 semesters. Credit and/or placement offered for CEEB Advanced Placement tests.

COSTS AND FINANCIAL AID
Annual tuition $28,380. Room and board $9,360. Required fees $550. Average book expense $1,710. **Required Forms and Deadlines:** FAFSA, Institution's own financial aid form, State aid form. **Notification of Awards:** Applicants will be notified of awards on a rolling basis beginning 2/18. **Types of Aid:** *Need-based scholarships/grants:* Federal Pell, SEOG, state scholarships/grants, private scholarships, the school's own gift aid. *Loans:* Subsidized Stafford, Unsubsidized Stafford, PLUS, Federal Perkins, Alternative private loans. *Student Employment:* Federal Work-Study Program available. Institutional employment available. Highest amount earned per year from on-campus jobs $5,000. Off-campus job opportunities are excellent. **Financial Aid Statistics:** 99% freshmen, 97% undergrads receive need-based scholarship or grant aid. 11% freshmen, 8% undergrads receive non-need-based scholarship or grant aid. 87% freshmen, 81% undergrads receive need-based self-help aid. 3% freshmen, 5% undergrads receive athletic scholarships. 68% freshmen, 64% undergrads receive any aid. 40% undergrads borrow to pay for school. Average cumulative indebtedness $16,453. **Criteria for awarding institutional aid:** *Non-need-based:* academics, alumni affiliation, art, athletics, leadership, music/drama.

MAYNOOTH UNIVERSITY

International Office, Maynooth, Co Kildare, Ireland
Phone: 35317083868 international.office@nuim.ie
Fax: 35317086113 • **Website:** www.nuim.ie/international • **ACT Code:** 5483

This is a public school.

RATINGS

STUDENTS AND FACULTY
Student Body: 90 countries represented.
Retention and Graduation: 95% freshmen return for sophomore year.

ACADEMICS
<BODY **Majors with Highest Enrollment:** Liberal Arts and Sciences Studies and Humanities; Business/Commerce; Multi-/Interdisciplinary Studies.

CAMPUS LIFE
Environmental Initiatives: To provide and co-ordinate the travel strategy at NUIM to enable a lasting and maintained shift to sustainable travel in line with the University's vision of becoming a sustainable campus by providing the best range of travel options to staff, students and visitors. Implementation and promotion of a Cycle to Work scheme for staff. Launching and promotion of the Car Share database. Implementation of recycling policy and provision of waste receptacles for general, recyclable paper and plastics, and food waste.

ADMISSIONS
Freshman Academic Profile: Average high school GPA 3.4. Minimum web-based TOEFL 80. Minimum paper TOEFL 550.

MAYVILLE STATE UNIVERSITY

330 Third Street Northeast, Mayville, ND 58257-1299
Phone: 701-788-4842 • **Financial Aid Phone:** 701-788-4767
E-mail: MaSU.admissions@mayvillestate.edu • **CEEB Code:** 6478
Fax: 701-788-4656 • **Website:** www.mayvillestate.edu • **ACT Code:** 3212

This public school was founded in 1889. It has a 55-acre campus.

RATINGS

STUDENTS AND FACULTY
Enrollment: 784. **Student Body:** 53% female, 47% male, 41% out-of-state, 4% international (7 countries represented). Asian 0%, African American 9%, Caucasian 107%, Hispanic 7%, Native American 2%

Retention and Graduation: 54% freshmen return for sophomore year. 19% freshmen graduate within 4 years. 42% freshmen graduate within 6 years. 15% grads go on to further study within 1 year. 2% grads pursue arts and sciences degrees. 5% grads pursue business degrees. **Faculty:** 46 full-time faculty, 37% hold PhDs, 43% are members of minority groups, 2% are women. 0% of classes are taught by teaching assistants.

ACADEMICS
Degrees: bachelor's, transfer associate. **Classes:** Most classes have 10–19 students. **Majors with Highest Enrollment:** Elementary Education and Teaching; Physical Education Teaching and Coaching; Business/Commerce. **Special Study Options:** Accelerated program, cooperative education program, distance learning, double major, dual enrollment, independent study, internships, student-designed major, teacher certification program. **Disability Services:** Special programs offered to physically disabled students include note-taking services, tape recorders, tutors. **Career services:** Alumni network, alumni services, career/job search classes, career assessment, internships, regional alumni. Career services highlights include the internship program, which provides opportunities for students to have related work experience with a variety of local, regional and national employers.

FACILITIES
Housing: men's dorms, women's dorms, apartments for married students, apartments for single students. 80% of campus accessible to physically disabled. **Special Academic Facilities/Equipment:** Art gallery available in the Campus Center. **Computers:** 100% of classrooms, 25% of dorms, 100% of libraries, 100% of dining areas, 100% of student union, 25% of common outdoor areas have wireless network access. Students can register for classes online. Administrative functions (other than registration) can be performed online. Undergraduates are required to own a computer.

CAMPUS LIFE
Environment: Rural. **Activities:** Choral groups, concert band, drama/theater, jazz band, music ensembles, musical theater, radio station, student government, student newspaper. 118 registered organizations, 1 honor society, 2 religious organizations. **Athletics (Intercollegiate):** *Men:* baseball, basketball, football. *Women:* basketball, softball, volleyball. **On-Campus Highlights:** Lewy Lee Fieldhouse, Campus Center, Residence Halls, Library, West Hall.

ADMISSIONS
Freshman Academic Profile: Average high school GPA 2.99. 95% from public high schools. ACT middle 50% range 17-22. Minimum internet-based TOEFL 68. Minimum paper TOEFL 520. **Basis for Candidate Selection:** *Very important factors considered include:* academic GPA. *Important factors considered include:* rigor of secondary school record, standardized test scores. *Other factors considered include:* character/personal qualities, interview. **Freshman Admission Requirements:** High school diploma is required and GED is accepted. *Academic units required:* 4 English, 3 mathematics, 3 science, (3 science labs), 3 social studies. **Freshman Admission Statistics:** 413 applied, 57% admitted, 74% enrolled. **Transfer Admission Requirements:** college transcript(s), statement of good standing from prior institution(s). Minimum college GPA of 2.0 required. Lowest grade transferable d. **General Admission Information:** Application Fee $35. Notification on a rolling basis, beginning on or about 1/1. Nonfall registration accepted. Admission may be deferred for a maximum of NA. Credit and/or placement offered for CEEB Advanced Placement tests.

COSTS AND FINANCIAL AID
Annual in-state tuition $4,810. Annual out-of-state tuition $7,215. Room and board $5,430. Required fees $1,679. Average book expense $1,000. **Required Forms and Deadlines:** FAFSA. **Notification of Awards:** Applicants will be notified of awards on a rolling basis beginning 5/1. **Types of Aid:** *Need-based scholarships/grants:* Federal Pell, SEOG, state scholarships/grants, private scholarships, the school's own gift aid. *Loans:* Subsidized Stafford, Unsubsidized Stafford, PLUS, Federal Perkins. *Student Employment:* Federal Work-Study Program available. Institutional employment available. Highest amount earned per year from on-campus jobs $1,500. Off-campus job opportunities are fair. **Financial Aid Statistics:** 88% freshmen, 84% undergrads receive need-based scholarship or grant aid. 28% freshmen, 20% undergrads receive non-need-based scholarship or grant aid. 87% freshmen, 85% undergrads receive need-based self-help aid. 24% freshmen, 20% undergrads receive athletic scholarships. 67% freshmen, 60% undergrads receive any aid. 75% undergrads borrow to pay for school. Average cumulative indebtedness $29,820. **Criteria for awarding institutional aid:** *Non-need-based:* academics, athletics, leadership, minority status, music/drama, state/district residency.

MCDANIEL COLLEGE

2 College Hill, Westminster, MD 21157
Financial Aid **Phone:** 410-857-2233
E-mail: admissions@mcdaniel.edu • **CEEB Code:** 5898
• **Website:** www.mcdaniel.edu • **ACT Code:** 1756

This is a private school.

RATINGS

Admissions Selectivity Rating: 84   **Fire Safety Rating:** 78

STUDENTS AND FACULTY

Enrollment: 1,667. **Student Body:** 53% female, 47% male, 64% out-of-state, 1% international (11 countries represented). Asian 3%, African American 12%, Caucasian 73%, Hispanic 6%, Native American <1%
Retention and Graduation: 60% freshmen graduate within 4 years. 68% freshmen graduate within 6 years. **Faculty:** 110 full-time faculty, 97% hold PhDs, 54% are members of minority groups, 12% are women. 0% of classes are taught by teaching assistants.

ACADEMICS

Degrees: Majors with Highest Enrollment: Health and Physical Education/Fitness; Psychology; Biology/Biological Sciences. **Disability Services:** Special programs offered to physically disabled students include note-taking services, reader services, tape recorders, tutors. **Career services:** Alumni network, career/job search classes, career assessment, internships.

FACILITIES

Housing: Coed dorms, special housing for disabled students, men's dorms, women's dorms, fraternity/sorority housing, apartments for married students, apartments for single studentsSingle family homes shared by 3-10 students. 80% of campus accessible to physically disabled. **Special Academic Facilities/Equipment:** Art gallery, computer graphics and physiology labs, electron microscope, math spectrometer. **Computers:** Students can register for classes online. Administrative functions (other than registration) can be performed online.

CAMPUS LIFE

Activities: Choral groups, concert band, dance, drama/theater, jazz band, literary magazine, music ensembles, musical theater, pep band, radio station, student government, student newspaper, symphony orchestra, television station, yearbook. 136 registered organizations, 22 honor societies, 5 religious organizations. 6 fraternities, 4 sororities. **Athletics (Intercollegiate):** *Men:* baseball, basketball, cross-country, football, golf, lacrosse, soccer, swimming, tennis, track/field (outdoor), track/field (indoor), volleyball, wrestling. *Women:* basketball, cross-country, field hockey, golf, lacrosse, soccer, softball, swimming, tennis, track/field (outdoor), track/field (indoor), volleyball. **On-Campus Highlights:** The Hoover Library, Peterson Hall, Golf course, Bair stadium, Academic Hall. **Environmental Initiatives:** Our strategy aims to implement low-cost actions first, which will jumpstart carbon reductions and save the College significant operating costs. Aspects of the College that warrant immediate investment include: (1) Information Technology; (2) recycling programs; (3) dining services; and (4) individual behaviors of community members. Once the aforementioned conservation measures are in place, McDaniel College should pursue generating electricity from renewable sources. Future emissions reductions should focus on the contributions from oil and natural gas purchases (primarily used for heating) and from transportation.

ADMISSIONS

Freshman Academic Profile: Average high school GPA 3.46. 26% in top 10% of high school class, 50% in top 25% of high school class, 85% in top 50% of high school class. 72% from public high schools. SAT Math middle 50% range 490-600. SAT Critical Reading middle 50% range 490-600. ACT middle 50% range 21-27. Minimum internet-based TOEFL 80. Minimum paper TOEFL 550. **Freshman Admission Statistics:** 2,966 applied, 76% admitted, 18% enrolled. **General Admission Information:** Credit and/or placement offered for CEEB Advanced Placement tests.

COSTS AND FINANCIAL AID

Average book expense $1,200. **Required Forms and Deadlines:** FAFSA. **Financial Aid Statistics:** 100% freshmen, 100% undergrads receive need-based scholarship or grant aid. 18% freshmen, 15% undergrads receive non-need-based scholarship or grant aid. 77% freshmen, 80% undergrads receive need-based self-help aid. 0% freshmen, 0% undergrads receive athletic scholarships. 100% freshmen, 98% undergrads receive any aid. 68% undergrads borrow to pay for school. Average cumulative indebtedness $31,568.

MCGILL UNIVERSITY

Best 380

3415 McTavish St., Montreal, QC H3A 0C8
Phone: 514-398-7878 • **Financial Aid Phone:** 514-398-6013
E-mail: admissions@mcgill.ca • **CEEB Code:** 935
Fax: 514-398-5544 • **Website:** http://www.mcgill.ca/admissions/ • **ACT Code:** 5231

This public school was founded in 1821. It has a 80-acre campus.

RATINGS

Admissions Selectivity Rating: 91   **Fire Safety Rating:** 72

STUDENTS AND FACULTY

Enrollment: 20,831. **Student Body:** 59% female, 41% male, 37% out-of-state, 17% international (136 countries represented). Asian 0%, African American 0%, Caucasian 0%, Hispanic 0%, Native American <1%
Retention and Graduation: 93% freshmen return for sophomore year. 67% freshmen graduate within 4 years. 85% freshmen graduate within 6 years. **Faculty:** 1,689 full-time faculty, 95% hold PhDs, 29% are members of minority groups.

ACADEMICS

Degrees: bachelor's, certificate, diploma, first professional, master's, post-bachelor's certificate. **Classes:** Most classes have 10–19 students. Most lab/discussion sessions have 20–29 students. **Majors with Highest Enrollment:** Political Science and Government; Psychology; Business/Commerce. **Special Study Options:** Accelerated program, cooperative education program, cross-registration, distance learning, double major, English as a Second Language (ESL), exchange student program (domestic), honors program, independent study, internships, study abroad, teacher certification program. **Honors programs:** McGill's Faculties of Arts, Science, and Engineering, the Desautels Faculty of Management, and the McGill School of Environment offer many outstanding honours and joint honours programs. Honours programs offer specialization and research in one academic discipline while joint honours programs offer specialization and research in a combination of disciplines. **Combined degree programs:** BSc/BEd;BMus/BEd;BCL/LLB;MSW/Law;MDCM;MBA;MDCM/PhD. **Disability Services:** Special programs offered to physically disabled students include note-taking services, reader services, tape recorders, tutors. **Career services:** career/job search classes, career assessment. Career services highlights include a Bilingual Mining and Materials Co-op Program.

FACILITIES

Housing: Coed dorms, special housing for disabled students, women's dorms, apartments for single students, Shared Facilities **Housing:** Similar to Cooperative Housing but chores and costs are not shared amongst the students. 90% of campus accessible to physically disabled. **Special Academic Facilities/Equipment:** McCord Museum of Canadian History, Redpath Museum of Natural History, Lyman Entomological Museum and Research Laboratory, Ecomuseum, Rutherford Museum, Lawrence Lande Collection of Canadiana, Canadian Architecture Collection, Morgan Arboretum, Gault Nature Reserve, Herbarium, McGill Archives (Canadian History), Islamic Studies Library, Bellairs Research Institute, McConnell Brain Imaging Centre, McConnell Winter Arena, McGill Sports Centre Gymnasiums, Percival Molson Stadium, Memorial Pool, Richard Tomlinson Fieldhouse, Outdoor Tennis Courts, McGill Arctic Research Station, McGill Subarctic Research Station, Phytotron, Schulich School of Music (world-class sound stage, recording studio), McGill Centre for Interdisciplinary Research in Music, Media and Technology, Research Greenhouse, J. S. Marshall Weather Radar Observatory, Mountain and Glen Campuses (McGill University Health Centre Teaching Hospitals), McGill Medical Simulation Centre, McGill Reproductive Centre, McGill University and Genome Quebec Innovation Centre. **Computers:** 100% of classrooms, 100% of dorms, 100% of libraries, 100% of dining areas, 100% of student union, 100% of common outdoor areas have wireless network access. Students can register for classes online. Administrative functions (other than registration) can be performed online.

CAMPUS LIFE

Environment: Metropolis. **Activities:** Choral groups, concert band, dance, drama/theater, jazz band, literary magazine, marching band, music ensembles, musical theater, opera, pep band, radio station, student government, student newspaper, student-run film society, symphony orchestra, television station, yearbook, International Student Organization. 250 registered organizations, 2 honor societies, 10 religious organizations. 8 fraternities, 4 sororities. **Athletics (Intercollegiate):** *Men:* badminton, baseball, basketball, cheerleading, crew/rowing, cross-country, curling, cycling, fencing, football, golf, ice hockey, lacrosse, rugby, sailing, skiing (downhill/alpine), skiing (nordic/cross-country), soccer, squash, swimming, tennis, track/field (indoor), ultimate frisbee, volleyball, wrestling. *Women:* badminton, basketball, cheerleading, crew/rowing, cross-country, curling, cycling, fencing, field hockey, golf, ice hockey, lacrosse, rugby, sailing, skiing (downhill/alpine), skiing (nordic/cross-country), soccer, squash, swimming, synchronized swimming, tennis, track/field (indoor), ultimate frisbee, volleyball, wrestling. **On-Campus Highlights:** Arts Building, Schulich School of Music, McGill Bookstore, MacDonald Campus, Redpath Museum, To get a big-picture view of the entire campus, take a walk up Mont-Royal. From the Chateau look-out it is possible to see the entire downtown campus. **Environmental Initiatives:** Excellence in environmental research and teaching (e.g. School of Environment, GEC3, Brace, VERT, etc.); Continual investment in energy infrastructure improvements to efficiency and reduce resource consumption; Conservation efforts (including Gault Reserve, Morgan Arboretum, EcoMuseum, etc.).

ADMISSIONS

Freshman Academic Profile: Average high school GPA 3.52. SAT Math middle 50% range 650-720. SAT Critical Reading middle 50% range 640-740. SAT Writing middle 50% range 650-730. ACT middle 50% range 29-32. Minimum internet-based TOEFL 90. Minimum paper TOEFL 577. **Basis for Candidate Selection:** *Very important factors considered include:* academic GPA, rigor of secondary school record, standardized test scores. *Important factors considered include:* Class rank. *Other factors considered include:* recommendation(s). **Freshman Admission Requirements:** High school diploma is required and GED is not accepted. **Freshman Admission Statistics:** 21,242 applied, 54% admitted, 44% enrolled. **Transfer Admission Requirements:** High school transcript, college transcript(s), Minimum college GPA of 3.00 required. Lowest grade transferable C. **General Admission Information:** Application Fee $85. Regular application deadline 1/15. Notification on a rolling basis, beginning on or about 1/30. Nonfall registration accepted. Admission may be deferred for a maximum of 1 year. Credit and/or placement offered for CEEB Advanced Placement tests.

COSTS AND FINANCIAL AID

Annual. Annual out-of-state tuition $5,500. Room and board $11,000. Required fees $1,500. Average book expense $1,000. **Required Forms and Deadlines:** Institution's own financial aid form. **Notification of Awards:** Applicants will be notified of awards on a rolling basis beginning 3/1. **Types of Aid:** *Need-based scholarships/grants:* private scholarships, the school's own gift aid, Canadian (Federal & Provincial) Student Assistance. *Loans:* Subsidized Stafford, Unsubsidized Stafford, PLUS, college/university loans from institutional funds. *Student Employment:* Institutional employment available. Off-campus job opportunities are fair. **Financial Aid Statistics:** 63% undergrads receive need-based scholarship or grant aid. 31% undergrads receive non-need-based scholarship or grant aid. 89% undergrads receive need-based self-help aid. 0% undergrads receive athletic scholarships. 28% undergrads receive any aid. 24% undergrads borrow to pay for school. **Criteria for awarding institutional aid:** *Non-need-based:* academics, art, athletics, leadership, music/drama, state/district residency.

MCKENDREE COLLEGE

701 College Road, Lebanon, IL 62254
Phone: 618-537-6831 · **Financial Aid Phone:** 618-537-6828
E-mail: inquiry@mckendree.edu · **CEEB Code:** 1456
Fax: 618-537-6496 · **Website:** www.mckendree.edu · **ACT Code:** 1076

This private school, affiliated with the Methodist Church, was founded in 1828. It has a 100-acre campus.

RATINGS

Admissions Selectivity Rating: 82   Fire Safety Rating: 66

STUDENTS AND FACULTY

Enrollment: 2,118. **Student Body:** 57% female, 43% male, 13% out-of-state, 2% international (24 countries represented). Asian 1%, African American 12%, Caucasian 81%, Hispanic 2%, Native American <1%
Retention and Graduation: 73% freshmen return for sophomore year. 37% freshmen graduate within 4 years. 58% freshmen graduate within 6 years. 14% grads go on to further study within 1 year. 5% grads pursue arts and sciences degrees. 3% grads pursue law degrees. 6% grads pursue business degrees. 1% grads pursue medical degrees. **Faculty:** 70 full-time faculty, 81% hold PhDs, 51% are members of minority groups, 4% are women. 0% of classes are taught by teaching assistants.

ACADEMICS

Degrees: associate, bachelor's, master's. **Classes:** Most classes have 10–19 students. Most lab/discussion sessions have 10–19 students. **Special Study Options:** Accelerated program, cooperative education program, double major,

external degree program, honors program, independent study, internships, liberal arts/career combination, student-designed major, study abroad, teacher certification program, evening programs in accounting, business administration, organizational communication, 3-2 occupational therapy program with Washington University. **Disability Services:** Special programs offered to physically disabled students include note-taking services, reader services, tutors. **Career services:** alumni services, career/job search classes, career assessment, internships. Career services highlights include internships.

FACILITIES

Housing: Coed dorms, special housing for disabled students, women's dorms, apartments for single students Suite-style apartments are available for both men and women. 80% of campus accessible to physically disabled. **Computers:** Students can register for classes online. Administrative functions (other than registration) can be performed online.

CAMPUS LIFE

Environment: Rural. **Activities:** Choral groups, concert band, dance, drama/theater, jazz band, literary magazine, marching band, music ensembles, musical theater, pep band, student government, student newspaper, student-run film society, yearbook. 59 registered organizations, 9 honor societies, 3 religious organizations. 4 fraternities, 3 sororities. **Athletics (Intercollegiate):** *Men:* baseball, basketball, bowling, cheerleading, cross-country, football, golf, ice hockey, soccer, tennis, track/field (outdoor), track/field (indoor), wrestling. *Women:* basketball, bowling, cheerleading, cross-country, golf, ice hockey, soccer, softball, tennis, track/field (outdoor), track/field (indoor), volleyball. **On-Campus Highlights:** Marion K. Piper Academic Center, Bothwell Chapel, Melvin Price Convocation Center, The Lair-student lounge and snack bar, McKendree West Clubhouse.

ADMISSIONS

Freshman Academic Profile: Average high school GPA 3.6. 25% in top 10% of high school class, 54% in top 25% of high school class, 91% in top 50% of high school class. SAT Math middle 50% range 430-630. SAT Critical Reading middle 50% range 420-530. ACT middle 50% range 20-27. Minimum paper TOEFL 500. **Basis for Candidate Selection:** *Very important factors considered include:* rigor of secondary school record. *Important factors considered include:* Class rank, recommendation(s), standardized test scores, character/personal qualities. *Other factors considered include:* application essay, alumni/ae relation, extracurricular activities, interview, talent/ability, volunteer work, work experience. **Freshman Admission Requirements:** High school diploma is required and GED is accepted. **Freshman Admission Statistics:** 1,150 applied, 69% admitted, 43% enrolled. **Transfer Admission Requirements:** High school transcript, college transcript(s), statement of good standing from prior institution(s). Minimum college GPA of 2.2 required. Lowest grade transferable C. **General Admission Information:** Application Fee $40. Nonfall registration accepted. Admission may be deferred for a maximum of 6. Credit and/or placement offered for CEEB Advanced Placement tests.

COSTS AND FINANCIAL AID

Annual tuition $16,400. Room and board $6,480. Required fees $200. Average book expense $1,000. **Required Forms and Deadlines:** FAFSA, Institution's own financial aid form. **Notification of Awards:** Applicants will be notified of awards on a rolling basis beginning 3/1. **Types of Aid:** *Need-based scholarships/grants:* Federal Pell, SEOG, state scholarships/grants. *Loans:* Subsidized Stafford, Unsubsidized Stafford, PLUS, Federal Perkins, college/university loans from institutional funds. *Student Employment:* Federal Work-Study Program available. Institutional employment available. Highest amount earned per year from on-campus jobs $2,326. Off-campus job opportunities are good. **Financial Aid Statistics:** 100% freshmen, 99% undergrads receive need-based scholarship or grant aid. 19% freshmen, 18% undergrads receive non-need-based scholarship or grant aid. 75% freshmen, 75% undergrads receive need-based self-help aid. 12% freshmen, 12% undergrads receive athletic scholarships. 99% freshmen, 97% undergrads receive any aid. 58% undergrads borrow to pay for school. **Criteria for awarding institutional aid:** *Non-need-based:* academics, art, athletics, leadership, minority status, music/drama, religious affiliation.

MCNEESE STATE UNIVERSITY

Box 91740, Lake Charles, LA 70609
Phone: 337-475-5504 · **Financial Aid Phone:** 337 475-5065
E-mail: admissions@mcneese.edu
Fax: 337-475-5151 · **Website:** www.mcneese.edu · **ACT Code:** 1594

This is a public school.

RATINGS

Admissions Selectivity Rating: 80   Fire Safety Rating: 60*

STUDENTS AND FACULTY

Enrollment: 6,735. **Student Body:** 62% female, 38% male, 7% out-of-state, 4% international (53 countries represented). Asian 1%, African American 19%, Caucasian 71%, Hispanic 2%, Native American 1%
Retention and Graduation: 69% freshmen return for sophomore year.
Faculty: 272 full-time faculty, 62% hold PhDs, 46% are members of minority groups, 9% are women.

ACADEMICS

Degrees: associate, bachelor's, master's, post-master's certificate. **Classes:** Most classes have 20–29 students. Most lab/discussion sessions have 10–19 students. **Special Study Options:** Accelerated program, cooperative education program, distance learning, double major, dual enrollment, English as a Second Language (ESL), honors program, independent study, internships, study abroad, teacher certification program.

FACILITIES

Housing: Coed dorms, apartments for married students, apartments for single students.

CAMPUS LIFE

Activities: drama/theater, marching band, student government, student newspaper, yearbook.

ADMISSIONS

Freshman Academic Profile: 18% in top 10% of high school class, 41% in top 25% of high school class, 72% in top 50% of high school class. SAT Math middle 50% range 460-610. ACT middle 50% range 20-24. Minimum internet-based TOEFL 61. Minimum paper TOEFL 500. **Basis for Candidate Selection:** *Very important factors considered include:* rigor of secondary school record, standardized test scores. *Important factors considered include:* Class rank, academic GPA. *Other factors considered include:* character/personal qualities, extracurricular activities, talent/ability, volunteer work, work experience. **Freshman Admission Requirements:** High school diploma is required and GED is accepted. **Freshman Admission Statistics:** 3,638 applied, 60% admitted, 61% enrolled. **Transfer Admission Requirements:** college transcript(s), statement of good standing from prior institution(s). Minimum college GPA of 2.00 required. Lowest grade transferable C. **General Admission Information:** Application Fee $20. Nonfall registration accepted. Credit and/or placement offered for CEEB Advanced Placement tests.

COSTS AND FINANCIAL AID

Notification of Awards: Applicants will be notified of awards on a rolling basis beginning 4/15. **Criteria for awarding institutional aid:** *Non-need-based:* academics, alumni affiliation, art, athletics, leadership, minority status, music/drama, state/district residency.

MCPHERSON COLLEGE

P.O. Box 1402, McPherson, KS 67460
Phone: 620-241-0731 · **Financial Aid Phone:** 800-365-7402
E-mail: admiss@mcpherson.edu · **CEEB Code:** 6404
Fax: 620-241-8443 · **ACT Code:** 1440

This private school, affiliated with the Church of Brethren Church, was founded in 1887. It has a 23-acre campus.

RATINGS

Admissions Selectivity Rating: 72   **Fire Safety Rating:** 60*

STUDENTS AND FACULTY

Enrollment: 573. **Student Body:** 43% female, 57% male, 5% out-of-state, 1% international. Asian 2%, African American 9%, Caucasian 76%, Hispanic 7%, Native American 3%
Retention and Graduation: 67% freshmen return for sophomore year. 36% freshmen graduate within 4 years. 48% freshmen graduate within 6 years. 9% grads go on to further study within 1 year. 9% grads pursue medical degrees.
Faculty: 34 full-time faculty, 82% hold PhDs, 32% are members of minority groups, 12% are women. 0% of classes are taught by teaching assistants.

ACADEMICS

Degrees: bachelor's. **Classes:** Most classes have 10–19 students. Most lab/discussion sessions have 10–19 students. **Special Study Options:** cross-registration, double major, dual enrollment, English as a Second Language (ESL), independent study, internships, student-designed major, study abroad, teacher certification program. **Combined degree programs:** 2-2 program with Hutchinson Com Col.

FACILITIES

Housing: Coed dorms, special housing for disabled students, men's dorms, women's dorms. **Special Academic Facilities/Equipment:** Natural history museum.

CAMPUS LIFE

Environment: Village. **Activities:** Choral groups, concert band, dance, drama/theater, jazz band, music ensembles, musical theater, pep band, student government, student newspaper, yearbook, Campus Ministries. **Athletics (Intercollegiate):** *Women:* basketball, cross-country, golf, tennis, track/field (outdoor), volleyball.

ADMISSIONS

Freshman Academic Profile: Average high school GPA 3.16. 9% in top 10% of high school class, 25% in top 25% of high school class, 60% in top 50% of high school class. 99% from public high schools. SAT Math middle 50% range 450-563. SAT Critical Reading middle 50% range 448-560. ACT middle 50% range 19-24. Minimum paper TOEFL 550. **Basis for Candidate Selection:** *Very important factors considered include:* academic GPA, rigor of secondary school record, standardized test scores. *Other factors considered include:* Class rank, recommendation(s), character/personal qualities, extracurricular activities, first generation, interview, level of applicant's interest, talent/ability, volunteer work, work experience. **Freshman Admission Requirements:** High school diploma is required and GED is accepted. **Freshman Admission Statistics:** 474 applied, 87% admitted, 54% enrolled. **Transfer Admission Requirements:** High school transcript, college transcript(s), statement of good standing from prior institution(s). Minimum college GPA of 2.0 required. Lowest grade transferable C. **General Admission Information:** Application Fee $25. Nonfall registration accepted. Admission may be deferred for a maximum of i year. Credit offered for CEEB Advanced Placement tests.

COSTS AND FINANCIAL AID

Annual tuition $17,900. Room and board $6,910. Required fees $500. Average book expense $1,170. **Required Forms and Deadlines:** FAFSA, State aid form. **Notification of Awards:** Applicants will be notified of awards on a rolling basis beginning 3/1. **Types of Aid:** *Need-based scholarships/grants:* Federal Pell, SEOG, state scholarships/grants, private scholarships, the school's own gift aid, United Negro College Fund. *Loans:* Subsidized Stafford, Unsubsidized Stafford, PLUS, Federal Perkins. *Student Employment:* Federal Work-Study Program available. Institutional employment available. Highest amount earned per year from on-campus jobs $400. Off-campus job opportunities are good. **Financial Aid Statistics:** 85% freshmen, 85% undergrads receive need-based scholarship or grant aid. 95% freshmen, 98% undergrads receive non-need-based scholarship or grant aid. 86% freshmen, 88% undergrads receive need-based self-help aid. 66% freshmen, 38% undergrads receive athletic scholarships. 91% undergrads borrow to pay for school. Average cumulative indebtedness $24,690. **Criteria for awarding institutional aid:** *Non-need-based:* academics, alumni affiliation, art, athletics, music/drama, religious affiliation, state/district residency.

MCPHS UNIVERSITY

Office of Admissions, Boston, MA 2115
Phone: 617-732-2850 · **Financial Aid Phone:** 617-732-2864
E-mail: admissions@mcphs.edu · **CEEB Code:** 3512
Fax: 617-732-2118 · **Website:** www.mcphs.edu · **ACT Code:** 1860

This private school was founded in 1823. It has a 3-acre campus.

RATINGS

Admissions Selectivity Rating: 83   **Fire Safety Rating:** 96

STUDENTS AND FACULTY

Enrollment: 3,850. **Student Body:** 67% female, 33% male, 62% out-of-state, 11% international (32 countries represented). Asian 26%, African American 5%, Caucasian 38%, Hispanic 2%, Native American <1%
Retention and Graduation: 89% freshmen return for sophomore year. 61% freshmen graduate within 4 years. 71% freshmen graduate within 6 years. **Faculty:** 0% of classes are taught by teaching assistants.

ACADEMICS

Degrees: bachelor's, certificate, master's, post-bachelor's certificate. **Classes:** Most classes have 20–29 students. Most lab/discussion sessions have 10–19 students. **Majors with Highest Enrollment:** Registered Nursing/Registered Nurse; Pharmacy; Pre-Medicine/Pre-Medical Studies. **Special Study Options:** Accelerated program, cross-registration, distance learning, double major, independent study, internships, study abroad. **Combined degree programs:** BS/MS Pharmaceutical Chemistry. **Disability Services:** Special programs offered to physically disabled students include note-taking services, reader services, tape recorders, tutors. **Career services:** Alumni network, alumni services, regional alumni. Career services highlights include Students in most majors have "rotations" in hospitals, pharmacies, clinics.

FACILITIES

Housing: Coed dorms, Wellness Housing, Separate all-women floors. 100% of campus accessible to physically disabled. **Special Academic Facilities/Equipment:** Museum of Fine Arts and Isabella Stewart Gardner museum next door. **Computers:** 100% of classrooms, 100% of dorms, 100% of libraries, 100% of dining areas, 100% of student union, 100% of common outdoor areas have wireless network access. Students can register for classes online. Administrative functions (other than registration) can be performed online.

CAMPUS LIFE

Environment: Metropolis. **Activities:** Choral groups, concert band, dance, drama/theater, literary magazine, music ensembles, musical theater, student government, student newspaper, yearbook, International Student Organization. 66 registered organizations, 5 honor societies, 2 religious organizations. **On-Campus Highlights:** New Building, residence hall, labs, Pharmacy Laboratory, Dental Hygiene Clinic, Cafeteria (located in Mass. College of Art), Student Lounge, In addition to the Boston campus, there are campuses in Worcester and Manchester NH with expanding program offerings.

ADMISSIONS

Freshman Academic Profile: Average high school GPA 3.52. SAT Math middle 50% range 510-630. SAT Critical Reading middle 50% range 480-570. SAT Writing middle 50% range 480-590. ACT middle 50% range 21-26. Minimum internet-based TOEFL 79. Minimum paper TOEFL 550. **Basis for Candidate Selection:** *Very important factors considered include:* academic GPA, rigor of secondary school record, standardized test scores. *Other factors considered include:* Class rank, application essay, recommendation(s), alumni/ae relation, character/personal qualities, extracurricular activities, first generation, level of applicant's interest, talent/ability, volunteer work, work experience. **Freshman Admission Requirements:** High school diploma is required and GED is accepted. *Academic units required:* 4 English, 3 mathematics, 2 science, (2 science labs), 1 social studies, 1 history, 5 academic electives. **Freshman Admission Statistics:** 5,265 applied, 89% admitted, 19% enrolled. **Transfer Admission Requirements:** college transcript(s), essay or personal statement, Minimum college GPA of 2.5 required. Lowest grade transferable C. **General Admission Information:** Application Fee $70. Regular notification 2/15. Nonfall registration not accepted. Admission may be deferred for a maximum of one year. Credit and/or placement offered for CEEB Advanced Placement tests.

COSTS AND FINANCIAL AID

Annual tuition $28,470. Room and board $13,950. Required fees $938. Average book expense $922. **Required Forms and Deadlines:** FAFSA. **Notification of Awards:** Applicants will be notified of awards on a rolling basis beginning 2/1. **Types of Aid:** *Need-based scholarships/grants:* Federal Pell, SEOG, state scholarships/grants, private scholarships, the school's own gift aid. *Loans:* Direct Subsidized Stafford, Direct Unsubsidized Stafford, Direct PLUS, Subsidized Stafford, Unsubsidized Stafford, PLUS, Federal Perkins, Health Professions Loans. *Student Employment:* Federal Work-Study Program available. Off-campus job opportunities are excellent. **Financial Aid Statistics:** 91% freshmen, 81% undergrads receive need-based scholarship or grant aid. 0% freshmen, 0% undergrads receive non-need-based scholarship or grant aid. 88% freshmen, 91% undergrads receive need-based self-help aid. 0% freshmen, 0% undergrads receive athletic scholarships. 90% freshmen, 90% undergrads receive any aid. 78% undergrads borrow to pay for school. Average cumulative indebtedness $5,112. **Criteria for awarding institutional aid:** *Non-need-based:* academics.

MEDAILLE COLLEGE

18 Agassiz Circle, Buffalo, NY 14214
Phone: 716-884-3281
E-mail: jmatheny@medaille.edu • **CEEB Code:** 2422
Fax: 716-884-0291 • **Website:** www.medaille.edu • **ACT Code:** 2822

This private school was founded in 1937. It has a 13-acre campus.

RATINGS

Admissions Selectivity Rating: 77   **Fire Safety Rating:** 69

STUDENTS AND FACULTY

Enrollment: 1,650. **Student Body:** 67% female, 33% male, 1% out-of-state, 3% international (2 countries represented). Asian 1%, African American 16%, Caucasian 65%, Hispanic 3%, Native American 1%. **Retention and Graduation:** 70% freshmen return for sophomore year. 15%

freshmen graduate within 4 years. 24% freshmen graduate within 6 years. 24% grads go on to further study within 1 year. 4% grads pursue arts and sciences degrees. 1% grads pursue law degrees. 5% grads pursue business degrees. 1% grads pursue medical degrees. **Faculty:** 70 full-time faculty, 56% hold PhDs, 43% are members of minority groups, 7% are women. 0% of classes are taught by teaching assistants.

ACADEMICS

Degrees: associate, bachelor's, certificate, master's. **Classes:** Most classes have 10–19 students. Most lab/discussion sessions have 10–19 students. **Special Study Options:** Accelerated program, cross-registration, double major, honors program, independent study, internships, liberal arts/career combination, student-designed major, teacher certification program, weekend college, Module system for full-time evening studies. **Honors programs:** Theodore Roosevelt Scholars PRogram **Combined degree programs:** B.S. / M.B.A. **Disability Services:** Special programs offered to physically disabled students include note-taking services, reader services, tape recorders, tutors. **Career services:** alumni services, career/job search classes, career assessment, internships. Career services highlights include internships that are available in each academic program and required for most academic programs.

FACILITIES

Housing: Coed dorms, men's dorms, women's dorms, apartments for married students, apartments for single students. 100% of campus accessible to physically disabled. **Special Academic Facilities/Equipment:** Veterinary technology labs, New Media Institute, Childrens Literature Collection.

CAMPUS LIFE

Environment: City. **Activities:** drama/theater, literary magazine, musical theater, radio station, student government, student newspaper, student-run film society, television station, yearbook. 18 registered organizations, 2 honor societies. **Athletics (Intercollegiate):** *Men:* baseball, basketball, cheerleading, lacrosse, soccer, volleyball. *Women:* basketball, cheerleading, cross-country, lacrosse, soccer, softball, volleyball. **On-Campus Highlights:** Kevin I. Sullivan Campus Center, Cafeteria, New Media Laboratory, Computer Lab, Radio Station.

ADMISSIONS

Freshman Academic Profile: Average high school GPA 2.8. 14% in top 10% of high school class, 45% in top 25% of high school class, 75% in top 50% of high school class. 85% from public high schools. SAT Math middle 50% range 410-500. SAT Critical Reading middle 50% range 420-520. ACT middle 50% range 17-21. Minimum paper TOEFL 550. **Basis for Candidate Selection:** *Very important factors considered include:* rigor of secondary school record, standardized test scores, interview. *Important factors considered include:* application essay, recommendation(s), extracurricular activities. *Other factors considered include:* Class rank, alumni/ae relation, character/personal qualities, talent/ability, volunteer work, work experience. **Freshman Admission Requirements:** High school diploma is required and GED is accepted. *Academic units required:* 4 English, 2 mathematics, 2 science, 4 social studies. **Freshman Admission Statistics:** 763 applied, 68% admitted, 55% enrolled. **Transfer Admission Requirements:** High school transcript, college transcript(s), essay or personal statement, Minimum college GPA of 2.0 required. Lowest grade transferable C. **General Admission Information:** Application Fee $25. Notification on a rolling basis, beginning on or about 10/1. Nonfall registration accepted. Admission may be deferred for a maximum of 1year. Credit and/or placement offered for CEEB Advanced Placement tests.

COSTS AND FINANCIAL AID

Annual tuition $13,350. Room and board $6,400. Required fees $310. Average book expense $930. **Required Forms and Deadlines:** FAFSA, Institution's own financial aid form, State aid form. **Notification of Awards:** Applicants will be notified of awards on a rolling basis beginning 5/1. **Types of Aid:** *Need-based scholarships/grants:* Federal Pell, SEOG, state scholarships/grants, private scholarships, the school's own gift aid. *Loans:* Subsidized Stafford, Unsubsidized Stafford, PLUS. *Student Employment:* Federal Work-Study Program available. Institutional employment available. Highest amount earned per year from on-campus jobs $1,500. Off-campus job opportunities are good. **Financial Aid Statistics:** 96% freshmen, 82% undergrads receive need-based scholarship or grant aid. 37% freshmen, 13% undergrads receive non-need-based scholarship or grant aid. 100% freshmen, 90% undergrads receive need-based self-help aid. 0% freshmen, 0% undergrads receive athletic scholarships. 85% freshmen, 85% undergrads receive any aid. 75% undergrads borrow to pay for school. **Criteria for awarding institutional aid:** *Non-need-based:* academics.

MEDCENTER ONE COLLEGE OF NURSING

512 North 7th Street, Bismarck, ND 58501
Phone: 701-323-6271 · **Financial Aid Phone:** 701-323-6270
E-mail: msmith@mohs.org
Fax: 701-323-6289 · **Website:** www.medcenterone.com/collegeofnursing
ACT Code: 3197

This private school was founded in 1988.

RATINGS

Admissions Selectivity Rating: 60*   **Fire Safety Rating:** 60*

STUDENTS AND FACULTY

Enrollment: 91. **Student Body:** 91% female, 9% male, 6% out-of-state, 0% international (0 countries represented). Asian 1%, African American 4%, Caucasian 90%, Hispanic 1%, Native American <1%
Faculty: 10 full-time faculty, 10% hold PhDs, 100% are members of minority groups. 0% of classes are taught by teaching assistants.

ACADEMICS

Degrees: bachelor's. **Classes:** Most classes have 40-49 students. Most lab/discussion sessions have fewer than 10 students. **Majors with Highest Enrollment:** Registered Nursing/Registered Nurse. **Special Study Options:** independent study, internships.

FACILITIES

Special Academic Facilities/Equipment: Alumni Corner. **Computers:** 100% of classrooms, 100% of libraries, 100% of common outdoor areas have wireless network access.

CAMPUS LIFE

Environment: Rural. **Activities:** student government. 2 registered organizations, 1 honor society. **On-Campus Highlights:** Simulation Lab

ADMISSIONS

Freshman Admission Requirements: High school diploma is required and GED is accepted. **Transfer Admission Requirements:** High school transcript, college transcript(s), essay or personal statement, interview, Minimum college GPA of 2.5 required. Lowest grade transferable C. **General Admission Information:** Application Fee $40. Notification on a rolling basis, beginning on or about 11/4. Nonfall registration not accepted.

COSTS AND FINANCIAL AID

Average book expense $1,169. **Notification of Awards:** Applicants will be notified of awards on a rolling basis beginning 6/1. **Types of Aid:** *Need-based scholarships/grants:* Federal Pell, SEOG, state scholarships/grants, private scholarships, the school's own gift aid. *Loans:* Subsidized Stafford, Unsubsidized Stafford, PLUS, Federal Perkins, Federal Nursing, college/university loans from institutional funds. *Student Employment:* Federal Work-Study Program available. Off-campus job opportunities are good. **Financial Aid Statistics:** 78% undergrads receive need-based scholarship or grant aid. 29% undergrads receive non-need-based scholarship or grant aid. 77% undergrads receive need-based self-help aid. 0% undergrads receive athletic scholarships. 0% freshmen receive any aid. 0% undergrads borrow to pay for school. **Criteria for awarding institutional aid:** *Non-need-based:* academics, alumni affiliation, leadership.

MEDICAL UNIVERSITY OF SOUTH CAROLINA

41 Bee Street, Charleston, SC 29425-0203
Phone: 843-792-3281 · **Financial Aid Phone:** 843-792-2536
E-mail: oesadmis@musc.edu
Fax: 843-792-6615 · **Website:** www.musc.edu · **ACT Code:** 6440

This public school was founded in 1824. It has a 80-acre campus.

RATINGS

Admissions Selectivity Rating: 60*   **Fire Safety Rating:** 60*

STUDENTS AND FACULTY

Enrollment: 198. **Student Body:** 79% female, 21% male, 12% out-of-state, 0% international (26 countries represented). Asian 3%, African American 11%, Caucasian 73%, Hispanic 6%, Native American 1%
Faculty: 153 full-time faculty, 92% hold PhDs, 56% are members of minority groups, 10% are women. 0% of classes are taught by teaching assistants.

ACADEMICS

Degrees: bachelor's, doctoral, master's, post-bachelor's certificate, post-master's certificate. **Classes:** Most classes have 50-59 students. **Majors with Highest Enrollment:** Registered Nursing/Registered Nurse. **Special Study Options:** Accelerated program, distance learning, Varies with the academic program selected. **Disability Services:** Special programs offered to physically disabled students include note-taking services, reader services, tape recorders, tutors. **Career services:** internships. We are an academic health science center and each specialty has various programs for placement of these highly specialized graduates. Internship refers to post-graduate programs and are not part of the degree curriculum.

FACILITIES

Housing: No on-campus housing available. Housing available in community and promoted to students via the Off-Campus Housing Service's website. 97% of campus accessible to physically disabled. **Special Academic Facilities/Equipment:** Dental Museum, and Medical Museum, and Pharmacy Museum. **Computers:** 100% of classrooms, n/a% of dorms, 100% of libraries, 100% of dining areas, n/a% of student union, 100% of common outdoor areas have wireless network access. Students can register for classes online. Administrative functions (other than registration) can be performed online.

CAMPUS LIFE

Environment: City. **Activities:** Choral groups, dance, literary magazine, music ensembles, student government, Campus Ministries, International Student Organization. 77 registered organizations, 4 honor societies. **On-Campus Highlights:** Student Activity and Fitness Center, Library, Various Student Lounges, Classroom and Laboratories **Environmental Initiatives:** Installed ground source heat pump as first renewable energy project Recycling program since 1992 with four clealy stated recycling goals that are a part of the campus wide sustainability plan: reduce, re-use, recycle, and green packaging. Green Building Projects include: energy performance contract (in progress from January 09); Constructing first LEED building (opened in 2011)

ADMISSIONS

Freshman Academic Profile: Minimum internet-based TOEFL 80. Minimum paper TOEFL 550.

COSTS AND FINANCIAL AID

Required Forms and Deadlines: FAFSA, Institution's own financial aid form. **Notification of Awards:** Applicants will be notified of awards on a rolling basis beginning 4/21. **Types of Aid:** *Need-based scholarships/grants:* Federal Pell, SEOG, state scholarships/grants, private scholarships, the school's own gift aid, Federal Nursing Scholarships. *Loans:* Subsidized Stafford, Unsubsidized Stafford, PLUS, Federal Perkins, Federal Nursing, college/university loans from institutional funds. *Student Employment:* Federal Work-Study Program available. Off-campus job opportunities are good. **Financial Aid Statistics:** 49% undergrads receive need-based scholarship or grant aid. 23% undergrads receive non-need-based scholarship or grant aid. 98% undergrads receive need-based self-help aid.0% undergrads receive athletic scholarships. 0% freshmen, 75% undergrads receive any aid. **Criteria for awarding institutional aid:** *Non-need-based:* academics, alumni affiliation, minority status, state/district residency.

MEMORIAL UNIVERSITY OF NEWFOUNDLAND

Memorial University of Newfoundland, St. Johns, NF A1B 3V6
Phone: 709-777-6615
E-mail: munmed@mun.ca
Fax: 709-777-6615 · **Website:** www.med.mun.ca/admissions

This public school was founded in 1925. It has a 220-acre campus.

RATINGS

Admissions Selectivity Rating: 61   **Fire Safety Rating:** 60*

STUDENTS AND FACULTY

Student Body: 40% out-of-state.
Faculty: 1,012 full-time faculty, 26% are members of minority groups. 3% of classes are taught by teaching assistants.

ACADEMICS

Degrees: Special Study Options: Accelerated program, cooperative education program, distance learning, double major, English as a Second Language (ESL), exchange student program (domestic), honors program, internships, liberal arts/career combination, study abroad, teacher certification program. **Combined degree programs:** BA/BBA, BM/BEd. **Disability Services:** Special programs offered to physically disabled students include note-taking services, reader services, tape recorders, tutors. **Career services:** alumni services, career/job search classes, career assessment, internships.

FACILITIES

Housing: Special Academic Facilities/Equipment: Olympic sized swimming pool, complete fitness centre, student eating area, indoor aerobics, track and field, soccer field, basketball courts. **Computers:** Students can register for classes online. Administrative functions (other than registration) can be performed online.

CAMPUS LIFE

Activities: student government 81 registered organizations. **Athletics (Intercollegiate)** *Men:* basketball, fencing, ice hockey, riflery, rugby, skiing (downhill/alpine), soccer, softball, squash, swimming, track/field (outdoor), volleyball, wrestling. *Women:* basketball, fencing, ice hockey, riflery, rugby, skiing (downhill/alpine), soccer, softball, squash, swimming, track/field (outdoor), volleyball, wrestling.

ADMISSIONS

Freshman Academic Profile: Minimum paper TOEFL 550. **Freshman Admission Requirements:** High school diploma is required and GED is accepted. *Academic units required:* 3 English, 4 mathematics, 4 science, (4 science labs), 2 social studies, 2 academic electives. **Freshman Admission Statistics:** 3,900 applied, 86% admitted, 116% enrolled. **Transfer Admission Requirements:** High school transcript, college transcript(s), standardized test scores. **General Admission Information:** Application Fee $80. Regular application deadline 3/1. Notification on a rolling basis, beginning on or about 6/21. Nonfall registration accepted.

COSTS AND FINANCIAL AID

Types of Aid: *Need-based scholarships/grants:* Universities Scholarships awarded for academic excellence. *Loans:* Canada/Newfoundland Government Student Loans. *Student Employment:* Institutional employment available. Off-campus job opportunities are good. **Financial Aid Statistics:** 63% undergrads borrow to pay for school. **Criteria for awarding institutional aid:** *Non-need-based:* academics, athletics, leadership, minority status, music/drama, state/district residency.

MEMPHIS COLLEGE OF ART

Overton Park, 1930 Poplar Avenue, Memphis, TN 38104-2764
Phone: 901-272-5151 · **Financial Aid Phone:** 901-272-5136
E-mail: info@mca.edu · **CEEB Code:** 1511
Fax: 901-272-5158 · **Website:** www.mca.edu · **ACT Code:** 3991

This private school was founded in 1936. It has a 340-acre campus.

RATINGS

Admissions Selectivity Rating: 80   **Fire Safety Rating:** 74

STUDENTS AND FACULTY

Enrollment: 367. **Student Body:** 66% female, 34% male, 55% out-of-state, 1% international (13 countries represented). Asian 2%, African American 25%, Caucasian 60%, Hispanic 7%, Native American <1%
Retention and Graduation: 69% freshmen return for sophomore year. 29% freshmen graduate within 4 years. 47% freshmen graduate within 6 years. 10% grads go on to further study within 1 year. **Faculty:** 21 full-time faculty, 90% hold PhDs, 62% are members of minority groups, 14% are women. 0% of classes are taught by teaching assistants.

ACADEMICS

Degrees: bachelor's, master's. **Classes:** Most classes have 10–19 students. **Special Study Options:** cross-registration, double major, exchange student program (domestic), independent study, internships, study abroad, teacher certification program, New York Studies Program. Arts Exchange possible with othe AICAD schools. **Disability Services:** Special programs offered to physically disabled students include note-taking services, reader services, tape recorders, tutors. **Career services:** Alumni network, alumni services, career/job search classes, internships, regional alumni.

FACILITIES

Housing: Coed dorms, apartments for single students. 100% of campus accessible to physically disabled. **Special Academic Facilities/Equipment:** Art museum, numerous galleries for student exhibition, Computer writing lab. **Computers:** 100% of classrooms, 100% of dorms, 100% of libraries, 100% of dining areas, have wireless network access.

CAMPUS LIFE

Environment: Metropolis. **Activities:** student government, student newspaper.

ADMISSIONS

Freshman Academic Profile: Average high school GPA 3.29. 80% from public high schools. Minimum paper TOEFL 500. **Basis for Candidate Selection:** *Very important factors considered include:* academic GPA, talent/ability. *Important factors considered include:* rigor of secondary school record, standardized test scores, interview. *Other factors considered include:* Class rank, application essay, recommendation(s), character/personal qualities, extracurricular activities, level of applicant's interest, volunteer work, work experience. **Freshman Admission Requirements:** High school diploma is required and GED is accepted. **Freshman Admission Statistics:** 847 applied, 40% admitted, 34% enrolled. **Transfer Admission Requirements:** college transcript(s), Minimum college GPA of 2.0 required. Lowest grade transferable C. **General Admission Information:** Application Fee $25. Notification on a rolling basis, beginning on or about 12/1. Nonfall registration accepted. Admission may be deferred for a maximum of 1 year. Credit and/or placement offered for CEEB Advanced Placement tests.

COSTS AND FINANCIAL AID

Annual tuition $28,170. Room and board $8,500. Required fees $650. Average book expense $1,650. **Required Forms and Deadlines:** FAFSA. **Notification of Awards:** Applicants will be notified of awards on a rolling basis beginning 1/15. **Types of Aid:** *Need-based scholarships/grants:* Federal Pell, SEOG, state scholarships/grants, private scholarships, the school's own gift aid. *Loans:* Direct Subsidized Stafford, Direct Unsubsidized Stafford, Direct PLUS, Subsidized Stafford, Unsubsidized Stafford, PLUS, Federal Perkins, college/university loans from institutional funds. *Student Employment:* Federal Work-Study Program available. Highest amount earned per year from on-campus jobs $1,000. Off-campus job opportunities are good. **Financial Aid Statistics:** 58% freshmen, 64% undergrads receive need-based scholarship or grant aid. 97% freshmen, 97% undergrads receive non-need-based scholarship or grant aid. 71% freshmen, 71% undergrads receive need-based self-help aid. 0% freshmen, 0% undergrads receive athletic scholarships. 95% freshmen, 95% undergrads receive any aid. 100% undergrads borrow to pay for school. **Criteria for awarding institutional aid:** *Non-need-based:* academics, art.

MENLO COLLEGE

1000 El Camino Real, Atherton, CA 94027
Phone: 650-543-3753 · **Financial Aid Phone:** 650-543-3880
E-mail: admissions@menlo.edu · **CEEB Code:** 1236
Fax: 650-543-4103 · **Website:** www.menlo.edu · **ACT Code:** 330

This private school was founded in 1927. It has a 45-acre campus.

RATINGS

Admissions Selectivity Rating: 78   **Fire Safety Rating:** 69

STUDENTS AND FACULTY

Enrollment: 771. **Student Body:** 40% female, 60% male, 17% out-of-state, 13% international (33 countries represented). Asian 7%, African American 7%, Caucasian 34%, Hispanic 21%, Native American 1%
Retention and Graduation: 80% freshmen return for sophomore year. 48% freshmen graduate within 4 years. 59% freshmen graduate within 6 years. **Faculty:** 28 full-time faculty, 86% hold PhDs, 43% are members of minority groups, 29% are women. 0% of classes are taught by teaching assistants.

ACADEMICS

Degrees: bachelor's. **Classes:** Most classes have 20–29 students. Most lab/discussion sessions have 10–19 students. **Majors with Highest Enrollment:** Sport and Fitness Administration/Management; Accounting; Marketing/Marketing Management. **Special Study Options:** Accelerated program, double major, independent study, internships, student-designed major, study abroad, Advanced Placement credit Learning disability services. **Disability Services:** Special programs offered to physically disabled students include note-taking services, reader services, tape recorders, tutors. **Career services:** Alumni network, alumni services, career/job search classes, career assessment, internships, regional alumni.

FACILITIES

Housing: Coed dorms, special housing for disabled students, men's dorms, women's dorms. 95% of campus accessible to physically disabled. **Computers:** 33% of classrooms, 100% of libraries, 100% of dining areas, 100% of student union, have wireless network access. Students can register for classes online. Administrative functions (other than registration) can be performed online.

CAMPUS LIFE

Environment: Town. **Activities:** radio station, student government, student newspaper, student-run film society, television station, yearbook, International Student Organization. 30 registered organizations, 2 honor societies. **Athletics (Intercollegiate)** *Men:* baseball, basketball, cross-country, football, golf, soccer, wrestling. *Women:* basketball, cross-country, soccer, softball, volleyball, wrestling. **On-Campus Highlights:** Library, Student Union, Dining commons. **Environmental Initiatives:** Plastic bottle free campus.

ADMISSIONS

Freshman Academic Profile: Average high school GPA 3.2. 74% from public high schools. SAT Math middle 50% range 458-560. SAT Critical Reading middle 50% range 440-535. SAT Writing middle 50% range 448-528. ACT middle 50% range 19-23. Minimum internet-based TOEFL 61. Minimum paper TOEFL 500. **Basis for Candidate Selection:** *Very important factors considered include:* rigor of secondary school record, character/personal qualities. *Important factors considered include:* Class rank, application essay, academic GPA, recommendation(s), standardized test scores, alumni/ae relation, extracurricular activities, level of applicant's interest, volunteer work. *Other factors considered include:* interview, talent/ability, work experience. **Freshman Admission Requirements:** High school diploma is required and GED is accepted. **Freshman Admission Statistics:** 3,935 applied, 45% admitted, 11% enrolled. **Transfer Admission Requirements:** college transcript(s), essay or personal statement, statement of good standing from prior institution(s). Minimum college GPA of 2.0 required. Lowest grade transferable C-. **General Admission Information:** Application Fee $40. Notification on a rolling basis, beginning on or about 12/1. Nonfall registration accepted. Admission may be deferred for a maximum of 2 semesters. Credit and/or placement offered for CEEB Advanced Placement tests.

COSTS AND FINANCIAL AID

Annual tuition $38,100. Room and board $12,630. Required fees $650. Average book expense $1,764. **Required Forms and Deadlines:** FAFSA, State aid form. **Notification of Awards:** Applicants will be notified of awards on a rolling basis beginning 12/15. **Types of Aid:** *Need-based scholarships/grants:* Federal Pell, SEOG, state scholarships/grants, the school's own gift aid, Federal ACG Grant. *Loans:* Direct Subsidized Stafford, Direct Unsubsidized Stafford, Direct PLUS, Subsidized Stafford, Unsubsidized Stafford, PLUS. *Student Employment:* Federal Work-Study Program available. Institutional employment available. Highest amount earned per year from on-campus jobs $2,000. Off-campus job opportunities are excellent. **Financial Aid Statistics:** 100% freshmen, 100% undergrads receive need-based scholarship or grant aid. 9% freshmen, 10% undergrads receive non-need-based scholarship or grant aid. 90% freshmen, 87% undergrads receive need-based self-help aid. 13% freshmen, 16% undergrads receive athletic scholarships. 97% freshmen, 96% undergrads receive any aid. 77% undergrads borrow to pay for school. Average cumulative indebtedness $24,926. **Criteria for awarding institutional aid:** *Non-need-based:* academics.

MERCER UNIVERSITY—MACON

Admissions Office, Macon, GA 31207-0001
Phone: 478-301-2650 • **Financial Aid Phone:** 478-301-2670
E-mail: admissions@mercer.edu • **CEEB Code:** 5409
Fax: 478-301-2828 • **Website:** www.mercer.edu • **ACT Code:** 838

This private school, affiliated with the Baptist Church, was founded in 1833. It has a 150-acre campus.

RATINGS

Admissions Selectivity Rating: 88   **Fire Safety Rating:** 82

STUDENTS AND FACULTY

Enrollment: 2,663. **Student Body:** 49% female, 51% male, 19% out-of-state, 4% international (38 countries represented). Asian 7%, African American 19%, Caucasian 58%, Hispanic 5%, Native American <1%
Retention and Graduation: 80% freshmen return for sophomore year. 50% freshmen graduate within 4 years. 64% freshmen graduate within 6 years. 37% grads go on to further study within 1 year. **Faculty:** 401 full-time faculty, 92% hold PhDs, 46% are members of minority groups, 21% are women. 0% of classes are taught by teaching assistants.

ACADEMICS

Degrees: bachelor's, master's, post-master's certificate. **Classes:** Most classes have 10–19 students. Most lab/discussion sessions have 20–29 students. **Majors with Highest Enrollment:** Engineering; Business/Commerce; Biology/Biological Sciences. **Special Study Options:** Accelerated program, cooperative education program, cross-registration, double major, dual enrollment, honors

program, independent study, internships, liberal arts/career combination, student-designed major, study abroad, teacher certification program, Great Books program. **Honors programs:** Qualified students may be admitted to the Honors Program in the College of Liberal Arts, the Stetson School of Business and Economics, the School of Engineering, and the Tift College of Education. The Honors Program includes honors courses, out of classroom activities, independent study, and other opportunities. **Combined degree programs:** BA/MEng, Pharmacy (D. Pharm), Medicine (MD), Law (JD). **Disability Services:** Special programs offered to physically disabled students include note-taking services, reader services, tape recorders, tutors. **Career services:** Alumni network, alumni services, career/job search classes, career assessment, internships. Aproximately 65% of undergraduate students participate in some form of structured experiential education prior to graduation. These experiences serve to enhance the students' academic and leadership skills and also prepares them well for their chosen career paths.

FACILITIES

Housing: Coed dorms, special housing for disabled students, men's dorms, special housing for international students, women's dorms, fraternity/sorority housing, apartments for married students, apartments for single students. 85% of campus accessible to physically disabled. **Special Academic Facilities/Equipment:** McCorkle Music Building **Computers:** 100% of classrooms, 100% of dorms, 100% of libraries, 100% of dining areas, 100% of student union, 100% of common outdoor areas have wireless network access. Students can register for classes online. Administrative functions (other than registration) can be performed online.

CAMPUS LIFE

Environment: City. **Activities:** Choral groups, concert band, dance, drama/theater, jazz band, literary magazine, music ensembles, musical theater, opera, pep band, student government, student newspaper, television station, Campus Ministries, International Student Organization. 115 registered organizations, 18 honor societies, 7 religious organizations. 9 fraternities, 7 sororities. **Athletics (Intercollegiate):** *Men:* baseball, basketball, cross-country, golf, riflery, soccer, tennis. *Women:* basketball, cross-country, golf, soccer, softball, tennis, volleyball. **On-Campus Highlights:** University Center, Connell Student Center, Greek Village, Porter Patch, Jesse Mercer Plaza. **Environmental Initiatives:** We have long-standing community partnerships to improve and rehabilitate housing and commerical stock in Macon proper, which has significant positive impact on the sustability of the community. We have an active mixed paper, aluminum can, and plastic recycling program. We provide subsidies for faculty and staff to purchase homes that are within walking distance of the university. We provide free tolley service from the Macon Campus to downtown Macon.

ADMISSIONS

Freshman Academic Profile: Average high school GPA 3.75. 38% in top 10% of high school class, 70% in top 25% of high school class, 93% in top 50% of high school class. SAT Math middle 50% range 550-650. SAT Critical Reading middle 50% range 540-640. SAT Writing middle 50% range 510-610. ACT middle 50% range 25-29. Minimum internet-based TOEFL 80. Minimum paper TOEFL 550. **Basis for Candidate Selection:** *Very important factors considered include:* academic GPA, rigor of secondary school record, standardized test scores, level of applicant's interest. *Important factors considered include:* character/personal qualities, extracurricular activities, talent/ability, volunteer work. *Other factors considered include:* Class rank, recommendation(s), alumni/ae relation, interview, work experience. **Freshman Admission Requirements:** High school diploma is required and GED is accepted. *Academic units required:* 4 English, 4 mathematics, 3 science, (2 science labs), 2 foreign language, 1 social studies, 2 history. **Freshman Admission Statistics:** 4,375 applied, 67% admitted, 28% enrolled. **Transfer Admission Requirements:** college transcript(s), statement of good standing from prior institution(s). Minimum college GPA of 2.5 required. Lowest grade transferable C. **General Admission Information:** Application Fee $50. Regular application deadline 7/1. Notification on a rolling basis, beginning on or about 11/1. Nonfall registration not accepted. Admission may be deferred for a maximum of 1 year. Credit and/or placement offered for CEEB Advanced Placement tests.

COSTS AND FINANCIAL AID

Annual tuition $33,480. Room and board $10,678. Required fees $300. Average book expense $1,200. **Required Forms and Deadlines:** FAFSA, Institution's own financial aid form, State aid form. **Notification of Awards:** Applicants will be notified of awards on a rolling basis beginning 3/15. **Types of Aid:** *Need-based scholarships/grants:* Federal Pell, SEOG, state scholarships/grants, the school's own gift aid, Federal Nursing Scholarships. *Loans:* Direct Subsidized Stafford, Direct Unsubsidized Stafford, Direct PLUS, Federal Perkins, Federal Nursing, college/university loans from institutional funds. *Student Employment:* Federal Work-Study Program available. Institutional employment available. Off-campus job opportunities are good. **Financial Aid Statistics:** 100% freshmen, 99% undergrads receive need-based scholarship or grant aid. 42% freshmen, 34% undergrads receive non-need-based scholarship or grant aid. 55% freshmen, 54% undergrads receive need-based self-help aid. 5% freshmen, 5% undergrads receive athletic scholarships. 99% freshmen, 97% undergrads receive any aid. 64% undergrads borrow to pay for school. Average cumulative indebtedness $26,164. **Criteria for awarding institutional aid:** *Non-need-based:* academics, art, athletics, job skills, leadership, music/drama, state/district residency.

See page 1092.

MERCY COLLEGE

555 Broadway, Dobbs Ferry, NY 10522
Phone: (877) 637-2946 · **Financial Aid Phone:** 1-888-464-6737
E-mail: admissions@mercy.edu · **CEEB Code:** 2409
Fax: 914-674-7382 · **Website:** www.mercy.edu · **ACT Code:** 2814

This private school was founded in 1950. It has a 90-acre campus.

RATINGS

Admissions Selectivity Rating: 61   **Fire Safety Rating:** 96

STUDENTS AND FACULTY

Enrollment: 6,402. **Student Body:** 69% female, 31% male, 7% out-of-state, 1% international (37 countries represented). Asian 3%, African American 27%, Caucasian 27%, Hispanic 36%, Native American <1%
Retention and Graduation: 66% freshmen return for sophomore year. 15% freshmen graduate within 4 years. **Faculty:** Student/faculty ratio :1. 196 full-time faculty, 84% hold PhDs, 62% are are members of minority groups, 23% are women. 0% of classes are taught by teaching assistants.

ACADEMICS

Degrees: associate, bachelor's, certificate, master's, post-bachelor's certificate, post-master's certificate, terminal associate, transfer associate. **Classes:** Most classes have 10-19 students. **Majors with Highest Enrollment:** Psychology; Social Sciences; Business Administration and Management. **Special Study Options:** Accelerated program, cooperative education program, distance learning, double major, dual enrollment, honors program, internships, teacher certification program, weekend college, Program for college students with learning disabilities. **Honors programs:** Admission criteria to the Honors Program is a 87 or above high school average. One hundred and thirty new and transfer students were admitted in 2009-10. Students in the Honors Program take Honors versions of General Education courses (e.g., English, speech, and math) at the lower level and complete individualized Honors project in connection with their major for a total of 24 Honors credits. **Combined degree programs:** BA/MA, Accounting, Education, Nursing. **Disability Services:** Special programs offered to physically disabled students include note-taking services, reader services, tape recorders, tutors. **Career services:** Alumni network, alumni services, career/job search classes, career assessment, internships. Career services highlights include Cooperative Learning.

FACILITIES

Housing: Coed dorms 100% of campus accessible to physically diasbled. **Special Academic Facilities/Equipment:** Childcare center located at the Bronx campus. **Computers:** 40% of classrooms, 100% of dorms, 60% of libraries, 60% of dining areas, 60% of student union, have wireless network access. Students can register for classes online. Administrative functions (other than registration) can be performed online.

CAMPUS LIFE

Environment: Village. **Activities:** dance, student government, student newspaper, Campus Ministries, Model UN. 20 registered organizations, 1 religious organizations. **Athletics (Intercollegiate):** *Men:* baseball, basketball, cross-country, lacrosse, soccer, tennis, track/field (outdoor). *Women:* basketball, cross-country, lacrosse, soccer, softball, track/field (outdoor), volleyball. **On-Campus Highlights:** Waterfront campus on the Hudson River, New State-of-the-Art Library, Student Cafe, Music and Recording Studio, Roy Disney Center for Computer Animation.

ADMISSIONS

Freshman Academic Profile: Average high school GPA 2.99. Minimum internet-based TOEFL 79. Minimum paper TOEFL 550. **Basis for Candidate Selection:** *Very important factors considered include:* academic GPA, character/personal qualities, extracurricular activities, talent/ability. *Important factors considered include:* Class rank, application essay, recommendation(s), rigor of secondary school record, standardized test scores, interview, level of applicant's interest. *Other factors considered include:* alumni/ae relation, volunteer work, work experience. **Freshman Admission Requirements:** High school diploma is required and GED is accepted. *Academic units required:* 4 English, 4 mathematics, 3 science, (1 science labs), 3 foreign language, 2 social studies, 2 history, 3 academic electives. **Freshman Admission Statistics:** 5,728 applied, 72% admitted, 18% enrolled. **Transfer Admission Requirements:** college

transcript(s), Minimum college GPA of 2.0 required. Lowest grade transferable C. **General Admission Information:** Application Fee $40. Notification on a rolling basis, beginning on or about 12/1. Nonfall registration accepted. Credit offered for CEEB Advanced Placement tests.

COSTS AND FINANCIAL AID

Annual tuition $17,166. Room and board $12,690. Required fees $600. Average book expense $1,742. **Required Forms and Deadlines:** FAFSA, State aid form. **Notification of Awards:** Applicants will be notified of awards on a rolling basis beginning 4/1. **Types of Aid:** *Need-based scholarships/grants:* Federal Pell, SEOG, state scholarships/grants, private scholarships, the school's own gift aid, Federal Nursing Scholarships. *Loans:* Subsidized Stafford, Unsubsidized Stafford, PLUS, Federal Nursing, Private Educational Loans. *Student Employment:* Federal Work-Study Program available. Institutional employment available. Highest amount earned per year from on-campus jobs $5,342. Off-campus job opportunities are good. **Financial Aid Statistics:** 90% freshmen, 89% undergrads receive need-based scholarship or grant aid. 46% freshmen, 25% undergrads receive non-need-based scholarship or grant aid. 76% freshmen, 80% undergrads receive need-based self-help aid. 7% freshmen, 4% undergrads receive athletic scholarships. 82% freshmen, 82% undergrads receive any aid. 82% undergrads borrow to pay for school. Average cumulative indebtedness $15,278. **Criteria for awarding institutional aid:** *Non-need-based:* academics, athletics.

MERCYHURST UNIVERSITY

Admissions, Erie, PA 16546
Phone: 814-824-2202 · **Financial Aid Phone:** 814-824-2288
E-mail: admissions@mercyhurst.edu · **CEEB Code:** 2410
Fax: 814-824-2071 · **Website:** www.mercyhurst.edu · **ACT Code:** 3629

This private school, affiliated with the Roman Catholic Church, was founded in 1926. It has a 88-acre campus.

RATINGS

Admissions Selectivity Rating: 81   **Fire Safety Rating:** 84

STUDENTS AND FACULTY

Enrollment: 2,680. **Student Body:** 56% female, 44% male, 48% out-of-state, 8% international. Asian 1%, African American 4%, Caucasian 77%, Hispanic 2%, Native American <1%
Retention and Graduation: 79% freshmen return for sophomore year. 55% freshmen graduate within 4 years. 61% freshmen graduate within 6 years. **Faculty:** 164 full-time faculty, 68% hold PhDs, 44% are members of minority groups, 9% are women. 0% of classes are taught by teaching assistants.

ACADEMICS

Degrees: associate, bachelor's, certificate, master's, post-bachelor's certificate, terminal associate, transfer associate. **Classes:** Most classes have fewer than 10 students. Most lab/discussion sessions have 10–19 students. **Majors with Highest Enrollment:** Elementary Education and Teaching; International/Global Studies; Business Administration and Management. **Special Study Options:** Accelerated program, cooperative education program, cross-registration, double major, exchange student program (domestic), honors program, independent study, internships, liberal arts/career combination, student-designed major, study abroad, teacher certification program, weekend college, Arts, Business, Computer Science, Education, Health Professions, History, English Home Economics, Humanities, Natural Science, Social/Behavioral Science. Off Campus Study: Washington D.C. Undergrads may take grad level classes. **Combined degree programs:** 3+4 Medical school program. **Disability Services:** Special programs offered to physically disabled students include note-taking services, reader services, tape recorders, tutors. **Career services:** Alumni network, alumni services, career/job search classes, career assessment, internships.

FACILITIES

Housing: special housing for disabled students, men's dorms, women's dorms, apartments for single students. **Special Academic Facilities/Equipment:** Art gallery, college-owned restaurant for hotel/restaurant management department, observatory, archaeology lab. **Computers:** Students can register for classes online. Administrative functions (other than registration) can be performed online.

CAMPUS LIFE

Environment: Village. **Activities:** Choral groups, concert band, dance, drama/theater, literary magazine, music ensembles, musical theater, pep band, radio station, student government, student newspaper, television station, yearbook 9 honor societies, 2 religious organizations. **Athletics (Intercollegiate):** *Men:* baseball, basketball, cheerleading, crew/rowing, cross-country, football, golf, ice hockey, lacrosse, soccer, tennis, volleyball, water polo, wrestling. *Women:* basketball, cheerleading, crew/rowing, cross-country, field hockey, golf, ice hockey, lacrosse, soccer, softball, tennis, volleyball, water polo. **On-Campus Highlights:** Performing Arts Center, Mercyhurst Athletic Center, Library, Student Union, Ice Rink.

ADMISSIONS
Freshman Academic Profile: Average high school GPA 3.37. 21% in top 10% of high school class, 29% in top 25% of high school class, 87% in top 50% of high school class. 55% from public high schools. SAT Math middle 50% range 470-570. SAT Critical Reading middle 50% range 470-580. SAT Writing middle 50% range 460-560. ACT middle 50% range 21-26. Minimum internet-based TOEFL 79. Minimum paper TOEFL 550. **Basis for Candidate Selection:** *Very important factors considered include:* rigor of secondary school record. *Important factors considered include:* Class rank, standardized test scores, character/personal qualities, interview, talent/ability. *Other factors considered include:* application essay, recommendation(s), alumni/ae relation, extracurricular activities, geographical residence, racial/ethnic status, religious affiliation/commitment, state residency, volunteer work, work experience. **Freshman Admission Requirements:** High school diploma is required and GED is accepted. **Freshman Admission Statistics:** 2,938 applied, 75% admitted, 27% enrolled. **Transfer Admission Requirements:** High school transcript, college transcript(s), standardized test scores, Minimum college GPA of 2.0 required. Lowest grade transferable C. **General Admission Information:** Application Fee $30. Notification on a rolling basis, beginning on or about 11/15. Nonfall registration accepted. Admission may be deferred for a maximum of 1 year. Credit and/or placement offered for CEEB Advanced Placement tests.

COSTS AND FINANCIAL AID
Annual tuition $29,600. Room and board $10,800. Required fees $1,885. Average book expense $1,000. **Notification of Awards:** Applicants will be notified of awards on a rolling basis beginning 2/15. **Types of Aid:** *Need-based scholarships/grants:* Federal Pell, SEOG, state scholarships/grants, private scholarships, the school's own gift aid. *Loans:* Subsidized Stafford, Unsubsidized Stafford, PLUS, Federal Perkins. *Student Employment:* Federal Work-Study Program available. Institutional employment available. Highest amount earned per year from on-campus jobs $1,200. **Financial Aid Statistics:** 95% freshmen, 94% undergrads receive need-based scholarship or grant aid. 75% freshmen, 66% undergrads receive non-need-based scholarship or grant aid. 82% freshmen, 87% undergrads receive need-based self-help aid. 5% freshmen, 5% undergrads receive athletic scholarships. 93% freshemn receive any aid. 73% undergrads borrow to pay for school. Average cumulative indebtedness $20,114. **Criteria for awarding institutional aid:** *Non-need-based:* academics, alumni affiliation, art, athletics, leadership, minority status, music/drama, religious affiliation.

MEREDITH COLLEGE

3800 Hillsborough Street, Raleigh, NC 27607
Phone: 919-760-8581 · **Financial Aid Phone:** 919-760-8565
E-mail: admissions@meredith.edu · **CEEB Code:** 5410
Fax: 919-760-2348 · **Website:** www.meredith.edu · **ACT Code:** 3126

This private school was founded in 1891. It has a 225-acre campus.

RATINGS
Admissions Selectivity Rating: 82   **Fire Safety Rating:** 81

STUDENTS AND FACULTY
Enrollment: 1,618. **Student Body:** 100% female, 0% male, 12% out-of-state, 4% international (24 countries represented). Asian 3%, African American 11%, Caucasian 72%, Hispanic 4%, Native American 1%
Retention and Graduation: 79% freshmen return for sophomore year. 49% freshmen graduate within 4 years. 62% freshmen graduate within 6 years.
Faculty: 120 full-time faculty, 89% hold PhDs, 70% are members of minority groups, 12% are women. 0% of classes are taught by teaching assistants.

ACADEMICS
Degrees: bachelor's, master's, post-bachelor's certificate. **Classes:** Most classes have 10–19 students. Most lab/discussion sessions have fewer than 10 students. **Majors with Highest Enrollment:** Psychology; Biology/Biological Sciences; Interior Design. **Special Study Options:** Accelerated program, cooperative education program, cross-registration, double major, dual enrollment, honors program, independent study, internships, liberal arts/career combination, student-designed major, study abroad, teacher certification program, Semester Programs at American U., Drew U., Marymount Manhattan. **Honors programs:** Meredith offers an enriched academic and co-curricular Honors Program that spans the four years and involves honors courses in general education, in the major field, and a thesis or equivalent project. Interdisciplinary honors courses and weekend trips/programs enrich the experience, and a Focus

on Excellence series offers a variety of outings to cultural/intellectual/entertainment venues. Scholarships are provided for Honors Program participants. **Combined degree programs:** BA/MEng, BS/MBA in accounting. **Disability Services:** Special programs offered to physically disabled students include note-taking services, reader services, tape recorders, tutors. **Career services:** Alumni network, alumni services, career/job search classes, career assessment, internships.

FACILITIES
Housing: women's dorms, apartments for married students, apartments for single students. 80% of campus accessible to physically disabled. **Special Academic Facilities/Equipment:** Art gallery, amphitheatre, child-care lab, learning center and fitness center. Experimental and clinical psychology labs including an autism lab. A new Science and Mathematics Building provides a roof top telescope platform for astronomy observations, an electron microscope suite, greenhouse, and 15 student/faculty research labs. **Computers:** Students can register for classes online. Administrative functions (other than registration) can be performed online.

CAMPUS LIFE
Environment: Metropolis. **Activities:** Choral groups, concert band, dance, drama/theater, literary magazine, music ensembles, musical theater, student government, student newspaper, symphony orchestra, yearbook, Model UN 91 registered organizations, 22 honor societies, 7 religious organizations. **Athletics (Intercollegiate):** *Women:* basketball, cross-country, soccer, softball, tennis, volleyball. **On-Campus Highlights:** Science and Math Building, McIver Ampitheatre and Meredith Lake, Weatherspoon Physical Education -Dance Building, Belk Dining Hall, Cate Student Center/Bee Hive (snack bar).

ADMISSIONS
Freshman Academic Profile: Average high school GPA 3.28. 18% in top 10% of high school class, 46% in top 25% of high school class, 83% in top 50% of high school class. SAT Math middle 50% range 450-560. SAT Critical Reading middle 50% range 470-570. ACT middle 50% range 20-25. Minimum paper TOEFL 500. **Basis for Candidate Selection:** *Very important factors considered include:* Class rank, academic GPA, rigor of secondary school record. *Important factors considered include:* recommendation(s), standardized test scores, character/personal qualities. *Other factors considered include:* application essay, alumni/ae relation, extracurricular activities, interview, talent/ability, volunteer work, work experience. **Freshman Admission Requirements:** High school diploma is required and GED is not accepted. *Academic units required:* 4 English, 3 mathematics, 3 science, 2 foreign language. **Freshman Admission Statistics:** 1,797 applied, 61% admitted, 43% enrolled. **Transfer Admission Requirements:** High school transcript, college transcript(s), statement of good standing from prior institution(s). Minimum college GPA of 2.0 required. Lowest grade transferable C. **General Admission Information:** Application Fee $40. Early decision application deadline 10/15. Notification on a rolling basis, beginning on or about 11/1. Nonfall registration accepted. Admission may be deferred for a maximum of One year. Credit offered for CEEB Advanced Placement tests.

COSTS AND FINANCIAL AID
Annual tuition $32,140. Room and board $9,516. Average book expense $850. **Required Forms and Deadlines:** FAFSA. **Notification of Awards:** Applicants will be notified of awards on a rolling basis beginning 3/15. **Types of Aid:** *Need-based scholarships/grants:* Federal Pell, SEOG, state scholarships/grants, private scholarships, the school's own gift aid. *Loans:* Subsidized Stafford, Unsubsidized Stafford, PLUS, Federal Perkins, college/university loans from institutional funds. **Financial Aid Statistics:** 100% freshmen, 100% undergrads receive need-based scholarship or grant aid. 0% freshmen, 0% undergrads receive non-need-based scholarship or grant aid. 78% freshmen, 81% undergrads receive need-based self-help aid. 0% freshmen, 0% undergrads receive athletic scholarships. 72% undergrads borrow to pay for school. Average cumulative indebtedness $26,734. **Criteria for awarding institutional aid:** *Non-need-based:* academics, art, leadership, minority status, music/drama, religious affiliation, state/district residency.

MERRIMACK COLLEGE

315 Turnpike St, Office of Admission, North Andover, MA 1845
Phone: 978-837-5100 · **Financial Aid Phone:** 978-837-5186
E-mail: admission@merrimack.edu · **CEEB Code:** 3525
Fax: 978-837-5133 · **Website:** www.merrimack.edu

This private school, affiliated with the Roman Catholic Church, was founded in 1947. It has a 220-acre campus.

RATINGS
Admissions Selectivity Rating: 64   **Fire Safety Rating:** 98

STUDENTS AND FACULTY

Enrollment: 2,722. **Student Body:** 50% female, 50% male, 27% out-of-state, 6% international (22 countries represented). Asian 2%, African American 3%, Caucasian 67%, Hispanic 6%, Native American <1%

Retention and Graduation: 81% freshmen return for sophomore year. 53% freshmen graduate within 4 years. 59% freshmen graduate within 6 years. 24% grads go on to further study within 1 year. **Faculty:** 142 full-time faculty, 85% hold PhDs, 44% are members of minority groups, 9% are women. 0% of classes are taught by teaching assistants.

ACADEMICS

Degrees: associate, bachelor's, master's. **Classes:** Most classes have 10–19 students. **Majors with Highest Enrollment:** Business Administration and Management; Criminal Justice/Law Enforcement Administration; Communication. **Special Study Options:** Accelerated program, cooperative education program, cross-registration, double major, dual enrollment, English as a Second Language (ESL), independent study, internships, liberal arts/career combination, student-designed major, study abroad, teacher certification program, Five-year combined BA/BS program, continuing education program, center for corporate education. ESL available through Kaplan with offices on the college campus. Cross-registration available through college's membership in 10-college consortium. **Honors programs:** The Honors Program offers students with strong academic credentials, class standing, and leadership qualities the opportunity to study with other exceptional students in smaller classes. It is an innovative and exciting approach to fulfilling the college"s general education requirements and includes a variety of social and co-curricular activities. **Disability Services:** Special programs offered to physically disabled students include note-taking services, reader services, tape recorders, tutors. **Career services:** Alumni network, alumni services, career/job search classes, career assessment, internships, regional alumni. Career services highlights include experiential opportunities for students in each major: Traditional 5 year cooperative education program; Full-time paid summer internships; Part-time paid internship opportunities during the academic year; In conjunction with academic departments, unpaid but for-academic credit internships; Service learning volunteer opportunities with local non-profit agencies.

FACILITIES

Housing: Coed dorms, special housing for disabled students, apartments for single students, Wellness Housing, Theme Housing 90% of campus accessible to physically disabled. **Special Academic Facilities/Equipment:** Observatory, Rogers Center for the Arts. **Computers:** 100% of classrooms, 100% of libraries, 100% of dining areas, 100% of student union, have wireless network access. Students can register for classes online. Administrative functions (other than registration) can be performed online.

CAMPUS LIFE

Environment: Town. **Activities:** Choral groups, dance, drama/theater, jazz band, music ensembles, musical theater, pep band, student government, student newspaper, student-run film society, television station, yearbook, Campus Ministries, International Student Organization, Model UN. 47 registered organizations, 3 honor societies, 5 religious organizations. 2 fraternities, 3 sororities. **Athletics (Intercollegiate):** *Men:* baseball, basketball, cross-country, football, ice hockey, lacrosse, soccer, tennis. *Women:* basketball, cross-country, field hockey, lacrosse, soccer, softball, tennis, volleyball. **On-Campus Highlights:** Sakowich Student Center, Rogers Center for the Arts, Santagati Hall, McQuade Library, Volpe Athletic Complex, Campus observatory open one night a week to the public. Rogers Center and the McQuade Library have art gallerys. McQuade Gallery frequently displays student art. **Environmental Initiatives:** Roll-out of the new interdisciplinary Environmental Studies and Sustainability Major in fall 2011. The new major has an integrated curriculum across the Colleges four Schools, Science and Engineering, Liberal Arts, Business, and Education. Adoption of a new College Strategic Plan (2011-2022) that includes a new commitment to sustainability and sustainable campus operations (see question (1) 3. Development of a Campus Energy Plan that includes energy efficiency improvements, increased commitment to renewable energy and cataloging our greenhouse gas emissions.

ADMISSIONS

Freshman Academic Profile: Average high school GPA 2.91. 11% in top 10% of high school class, 34% in top 25% of high school class, 69% in top 50% of high school class. 73% from public high schools. Minimum internet-based TOEFL 80. Minimum paper TOEFL 550. **Basis for Candidate Selection:** *Very important factors considered include:* application essay, academic GPA, rigor of secondary school record. *Important factors considered include:* Class rank, recommendation(s), character/personal qualities, talent/ability. *Other factors considered include:* alumni/ae relation, extracurricular activities, interview, level of applicant's interest, volunteer work, work experience. **Freshman Admission Requirements:** High school diploma is required and GED is accepted. *Academic units required:* 4 English, 3 mathematics, 3 science, (3 science labs), 2 foreign language, 1 social studies, 1 history, 3 academic electives. **Freshman Admission Statistics:** 6,314 applied, 79% admitted, 16% enrolled.

Transfer Admission Requirements: college transcript(s), essay or personal statement, Minimum college GPA of 2.5 required. Lowest grade transferable C. **General Admission Information:** Application Fee $60. Regular application deadline 2/1. Regular notification 4/1. Nonfall registration accepted. Admission may be deferred for a maximum of 12 months. Credit and/or placement offered for CEEB Advanced Placement tests.

COSTS AND FINANCIAL AID

Required Forms and Deadlines: FAFSA, Noncustodial PROFILE, Business/Farm Supplement. **Notification of Awards:** Applicants will be notified of awards on or about 3/15. **Types of Aid:** *Need-based scholarships/grants:* Federal Pell, SEOG, state scholarships/grants, private scholarships, the school's own gift aid. *Loans:* Subsidized Stafford, Unsubsidized Stafford, PLUS, Federal Perkins, state loans, college/university loans from institutional funds, Alternative Loans. *Student Employment:* Federal Work-Study Program available. Highest amount earned per year from on-campus jobs $1,500. Off-campus job opportunities are good. **Financial Aid Statistics:** 100% freshmen, 98% undergrads receive need-based scholarship or grant aid. 7% freshmen, 9% undergrads receive non-need-based scholarship or grant aid. 88% freshmen, 86% undergrads receive need-based self-help aid. 6% freshmen, 6% undergrads receive athletic scholarships. Criteriafor awarding institutional aid: *Non-need-based:* academics, athletics, leadership, minority status, religious affiliation.

MESSIAH COLLEGE

One College Avenue, Mechanicsburg, PA 17055
Phone: (717) 691-6000 · **Financial Aid Phone:** 717-691-6007
E-mail: admiss@messiah.edu · **CEEB Code:** 2411
Fax: 717-691-2307 · **Website:** www.messiah.edu · **ACT Code:** 3630

This private school was founded in 1909. It has a 471-acre campus.

RATINGS

Admissions Selectivity Rating: 86   **Fire Safety Rating:** 77

STUDENTS AND FACULTY

Enrollment: 2,713. **Student Body:** 60% female, 40% male, 37% out-of-state, 3% international (23 countries represented). Asian 2%, African American 2%, Caucasian 85%, Hispanic 4%, Native American <1%

Retention and Graduation: 74% freshmen graduate within 4 years. 80% freshmen graduate within 6 years. 16% grads go on to further study within 1 year. 51% grads pursue arts and sciences degrees. 3% grads pursue law degrees. 2% grads pursue business degrees. 35% grads pursue medical degrees. **Faculty:** 179 full-time faculty, 85% hold PhDs, 41% are members of minority groups, 7% are women. 0% of classes are taught by teaching assistants.

ACADEMICS

Degrees: bachelor's. **Classes:** Most classes have 20–29 students. Most lab/discussion sessions have 10–19 students. **Majors with Highest Enrollment:** Engineering; Registered Nursing/Registered Nurse; Business Administration and Management. **Special Study Options:** Accelerated program, double major, dual enrollment, English as a Second Language (ESL), exchange student program (domestic), honors program, independent study, internships, student-designed major, study abroad, teacher certification program, Pass/Fail option. **Honors programs:** The College Honors Program is designed for students who demonstrate high scholarly ability early in their academic career. The program provides a series of interdisciplinary honors courses which satisfy selected general education requirements. In addition, various campus activities are designed each semester for participants in the College Honors Program. Participation in the program culminates in an honors research project, typically during the senior year. Admission to the program is highly competitive and students selected for the College Honors Program receive either full tuition or partial tuition scholarships. **Disability Services:** Special programs offered to physically disabled students include note-taking services, reader services, tape recorders, tutors. **Career services:** Alumni network, alumni services, career assessment, internships. Career services highlights include an internship program that supports roughly 150 students each year.

FACILITIES

Housing: Coed dorms, special housing for disabled students, men's dorms, special housing for international students, women's dorms, apartments for single students. 80% of campus accessible to physically disabled. **Special Academic Facilities/Equipment:** Boyer Center for Advanced Studies; Brethren in Christ Historical Society and Archives; Oakes Museum of Natural History. **Computers:** 100% of classrooms, 100% of dorms, 100% of libraries, 100% of dining areas, 100% of student union, have wireless network access. Students can register for classes online. Administrative functions (other than registration) can be performed online.

CAMPUS LIFE

Environment: Village. **Activities:** Choral groups, concert band, dance, drama/theater, jazz band, literary magazine, music ensembles, musical theater, pep band, radio station, student government, student newspaper, student-run film society, symphony orchestra, yearbook, Campus Ministries, International Student Organization 71 registered organizations, 7 honor societies, 10 religious organizations. **Athletics (Intercollegiate):** *Men:* baseball, basketball, cross-country, golf, lacrosse, soccer, swimming, tennis, track/field (outdoor), track/field (indoor), ultimate frisbee, wrestling. *Women:* basketball, cross-country, field hockey, lacrosse, soccer, softball, swimming, tennis, track/field (outdoor), track/field (indoor), volleyball. **On-Campus Highlights:** Boyer Hall (Schools of Humanities, Ed. and Soc. Sci., Eisenhower Campus Center/Sollenberger Sports Cent, Oakes Museum of Natural History, Stone Covered Bridge, Starry Athletic Complex, The scenic Yellow Breeches Creek runs through the 471 acre campus. It is a nationally recognized trout fishing stream, complete with covered bridge and swinging foot bridge. **Environmental Initiatives:** Sunflower Power Project—A full cycle of process of growing sunflowers on campus, pressing and processing cooking oil on campus for dining hall, and recycling used oil on campus into biodiesel fuel for on campus use (http://www.sunflowernsa.com/magazine/details.asp?ID=771 http://www.youtube.com/watch?v=w5_4LvNZu9M&feature=player_embedded); Creation Care Community Garden—Community Supported Agriculture that is student run by the EarthKeepers Delivery of educational mock energy bills to students (http://www.messiah.edu/sustainability/turn_it_off/index.html); Recycling and composting of wastes by Facilities Management and Conference Services & Digital energy management system across campus buildings which is yielding solid energy savings.

ADMISSIONS

Freshman Academic Profile: Average high school GPA 3.74. 29% in top 10% of high school class, 63% in top 25% of high school class, 89% in top 50% of high school class. 75% from public high schools. SAT Math middle 50% range 518-620. SAT Critical Reading middle 50% range 500-620. SAT Writing middle 50% range 490-600. ACT middle 50% range 22-27. Minimum internet-based TOEFL 80. Minimum paper TOEFL 550. **Basis for Candidate Selection:** *Very important factors considered include:* Class rank, academic GPA, recommendation(s), rigor of secondary school record, standardized test scores, character/personal qualities, extracurricular activities, religious affiliation/commitment, talent/ability. *Important factors considered include:* application essay, volunteer work. *Other factors considered include:* alumni/ae relation, interview, level of applicant's interest, racial/ethnic status, work experience. **Freshman Admission Requirements:** High school diploma is required and GED is accepted. *Academic units required:* 4 English, 2 mathematics, 2 science, (2 science labs), 2 foreign language, 2 social studies, 0 history, 4 academic electives. **Freshman Admission Statistics:** 2,472 applied, 80% admitted, 35% enrolled. **Transfer Admission Requirements:** college transcript(s), essay or personal statement, statement of good standing from prior institution(s). Minimum college GPA of 2.5 required. Lowest grade transferable C. **General Admission Information:** Application Fee $30. Notification on a rolling basis, beginning on or about 7/1. Nonfall registration accepted. Admission may be deferred for a maximum of 2 years. Credit and/or placement offered for CEEB Advanced Placement tests.

COSTS AND FINANCIAL AID

Required Forms and Deadlines: FAFSA. **Notification of Awards:** Applicants will be notified of awards on a rolling basis beginning 3/15. **Types of Aid:** *Need-based scholarships/grants:* Federal Pell, SEOG, state scholarships/grants, private scholarships, the school's own gift aid. *Loans:* Direct Subsidized Stafford, Direct Unsubsidized Stafford, Direct PLUS, Subsidized Stafford, Unsubsidized Stafford, PLUS, Federal Perkins, Federal Nursing. *Student Employment:* Federal Work-Study Program available. Institutional employment available. Highest amount earned per year from on-campus jobs $5,730. Off-campus job opportunities are good. **Financial Aid Statistics:** 99% freshmen, 99% undergrads receive need-based scholarship or grant aid. 14% freshmen, 11% undergrads receive non-need-based scholarship or grant aid. 79% freshmen, 80% undergrads receive need-based self-help aid. 0% freshmen, 0% undergrads receive athletic scholarships. 100% freshmen, 98% undergrads receive any aid. 71% undergrads borrow to pay for school. Average cumulative indebtedness $24,391. **Criteria for awarding institutional aid:** *Non-need-based:* academics, art, leadership, music/drama, religious affiliation.

METHODIST UNIVERSITY

5400 Ramsey Street, Fayetteville, NC 28311
Phone: 910-630-7027 • **Financial Aid Phone:** 910-630-7192
E-mail: admissions@methodist.edu • **CEEB Code:** 5426
Fax: 910-630-7285 • **Website:** www.methodist.edu • **ACT Code:** 3127

This private school, affiliated with the Methodist Church, was founded in 1956. It has a 600-acre campus.

RATINGS

Admissions Selectivity Rating: 81   **Fire Safety Rating:** 71

STUDENTS AND FACULTY

Enrollment: 2,226. **Student Body:** 48% female, 52% male, 30% out-of-state, 5% international (53 countries represented). Asian 1%, African American 24%, Caucasian 48%, Hispanic 6%, Native American 1%

Retention and Graduation: 62% freshmen return for sophomore year. 16% freshmen graduate within 4 years. 44% freshmen graduate within 6 years. 38% grads go on to further study within 1 year. 8% grads pursue arts and sciences degrees. 1% grads pursue law degrees. 12% grads pursue business degrees. 7% grads pursue medical degrees. **Faculty:** 142 full-time faculty, 69% hold PhDs, 49% are members of minority groups, 13% are women. 0% of classes are taught by teaching assistants.

ACADEMICS

Degrees: associate, bachelor's, master's, terminal associate. **Classes:** Most classes have fewer than 10 students. Most lab/discussion sessions have 20–29 students. **Majors with Highest Enrollment:** Secondary Education and Teaching; Cell/Cellular and Molecular Biology; Business/Commerce. **Special Study Options:** cooperative education program, distance learning, double major, dual enrollment, English as a Second Language (ESL), honors program, independent study, internships, liberal arts/career combination, student-designed major, study abroad, teacher certification program, weekend college, distance learning is on-line coursework available. **Honors programs:** The Methodist College Honors Program is based on the "Great Books" and is an outstanding opportunity for high acheiving students. **Disability Services:** Special programs offered to physically disabled students include note-taking services, reader services, tape recorders, tutors. **Career services:** career/job search classes, career assessment, internships.

FACILITIES

Housing: Coed dorms, men's dorms, women's dorms, apartments for single students, first year experience hall. 80% of campus accessible to physically disabled. **Special Academic Facilities/Equipment:** Art gallery, Nature Trail, 18 hole golf course with practice facilities for PGM students, Academic Developement Center **Computers:** Administrative functions (other than registration) can be performed online.

CAMPUS LIFE

Environment: City. **Activities:** Choral groups, concert band, dance, drama/theater, jazz band, literary magazine, marching band, music ensembles, musical theater, opera, pep band, radio station, student government, student newspaper, symphony orchestra, yearbook, Campus Ministries, Model UN. 72 registered organizations, 15 honor societies, 8 religious organizations. 3 fraternities, 2 sororities. **Athletics (Intercollegiate):** *Men:* baseball, basketball, cheerleading, cross-country, football, golf, soccer, tennis, track/field (outdoor). *Women:* basketball, cheerleading, cross-country, golf, lacrosse, soccer, softball, tennis, track/field (outdoor), volleyball.

ADMISSIONS

Freshman Academic Profile: Average high school GPA 3.28. 9% in top 10% of high school class, 34% in top 25% of high school class, 73% in top 50% of high school class. 86% from public high schools. SAT Math middle 50% range 450-550. SAT Critical Reading middle 50% range 430-520. SAT Writing middle 50% range 400-490. ACT middle 50% range 17-23. Minimum paper TOEFL 500. **Basis for Candidate Selection:** *Very important factors considered include:* academic GPA, rigor of secondary school record. *Important factors considered include:* Class rank, standardized test scores, interview. *Other factors considered include:* application essay, recommendation(s), alumni/ae relation, character/personal qualities, extracurricular activities, first generation, talent/ability. **Freshman Admission Requirements:** High school diploma is required and GED is accepted. *Academic units required:* 4 English, 3 mathematics, 3 science, (1 science labs), 0 foreign language, 1 social studies, 2 history, 4 academic electives. **Freshman Admission Statistics:** 3,823 applied, 61% admitted, 21% enrolled. **Transfer Admission Requirements:** High school transcript, college transcript(s), statement of good standing from prior institution(s). Minimum college GPA of 2.0 required. Lowest grade transferable C. **General Admission Information:** Application Fee $25. Notification on a rolling basis, beginning on or about 9/1. Nonfall registration accepted. Admission may be deferred for a maximum of 1 academic year. Credit and/or placement offered for CEEB Advanced Placement tests.

COSTS AND FINANCIAL AID

Annual tuition $25,160. Room and board $9,521. Required fees $465. Average book expense $1,200. **Required Forms and Deadlines:** FAFSA. **Notification of Awards:** Applicants will be notified of awards on a rolling basis beginning 3/1. **Types of Aid:** *Need-based scholarships/grants:* Federal Pell, SEOG, state scholarships/grants, private scholarships, the school's own gift aid. *Loans:* Subsidized Stafford, Unsubsidized Stafford, PLUS, Federal Perkins. *Student Employment:* Federal Work-Study Program available. Highest amount earned per year from on-campus jobs $1,600. Off-campus job opportunities are good. **Financial Aid Statistics:** 96% freshmen, 90% undergrads receive need-based scholarship or grant aid. 71% freshmen, 79% undergrads receive non-need-based scholarship or grant aid. 92% freshmen, 87% undergrads receive need-based self-help aid. 0% freshmen, 0% undergrads receive athletic scholarships. 90% freshmen, 86% undergrads receive any aid. 81% undergrads borrow to pay for school. Average cumulative indebtedness $20,026. **Criteria for awarding institutional aid:** *Non-need-based:* academics, alumni affiliation, leadership, music/drama, religious affiliation, state/district residency.

METROPOLITAN COLLEGE OF NEW YORK

75 Varick Street, New York, NY 10013
Phone: 212-343-1234
E-mail: admissions@metropolitan.edu · **CEEB Code:** 4802
Fax: 212-343-8470 · **Website:** www.metropolitan.edu

This private school was founded in 1964.

RATINGS

Admissions Selectivity Rating: 61   **Fire Safety Rating:** 60*

STUDENTS AND FACULTY

Enrollment: 1,093. **Student Body:** 80% female, 20% male, 10% out-of-state, 0% international (12 countries represented). Asian 1%, African American %, Caucasian 5%, Hispanic 18%, Native American 1%
Retention and Graduation: 72% freshmen return for sophomore year. 60% grads go on to further study within 1 year. 15% grads pursue law degrees. 24% grads pursue business degrees. **Faculty:** 26 full-time faculty. 0% of classes are taught by teaching assistants.

ACADEMICS

Degrees: associate, bachelor's, certificate, master's, transfer associate. **Classes:** Most classes have 10–19 students. **Special Study Options:** Accelerated program, cooperative education program, distance learning, honors program, internships, weekend college. **Combined degree programs:** MS/MBA. **Disability Services:** Special programs offered to physically disabled students include tutors. **Career services:** alumni services, internships.

FACILITIES

Housing: 4% of campus accessible to physically disabled. **Computers:** Administrative functions (other than registration) can be performed online.

CAMPUS LIFE

Activities: student government, student newspaper. 10 registered organizations.

ADMISSIONS

Freshman Academic Profile: 70% from public high schools. Minimum paper TOEFL 550. **Basis for Candidate Selection:** *Very important factors considered include:* interview. *Important factors considered include:* extracurricular activities, talent/ability, volunteer work, work experience. *Other factors considered include:* recommendation(s), character/personal qualities. **Freshman Admission Requirements:** High school diploma is required and GED is accepted. **Freshman Admission Statistics:** 399 applied, 78% admitted, 62% enrolled. **Transfer Admission Requirements:** High school transcript, essay or personal statement, interview, Lowest grade transferable C. **General Admission Information:** Application Fee $30. Early decision application deadline 5/2. Nonfall registration accepted. Admission may be deferred for a maximum of 12. Neither credit nor placement offered for CEEB Advanced Placement tests.

COSTS AND FINANCIAL AID

Average book expense $1,500. **Required Forms and Deadlines:** FAFSA, State aid form, Noncustodial PROFILE. **Types of Aid:** *Need-based scholarships/grants:* Federal Pell, SEOG, state scholarships/grants, private scholarships, the school's own gift aid. *Loans:* Subsidized Stafford, Unsubsidized

Stafford, PLUS, signature loan. *Student Employment:* Federal Work-Study Program available. Off-campus job opportunities are good. **Financial Aid Statistics:** 70% freshmen, 75% undergrads receive need-based scholarship or grant aid. 14% freshmen, 13% undergrads receive non-need-based scholarship or grant aid. 70% freshmen, 71% undergrads receive need-based self-help aid. 0% freshmen, 0% undergrads receive athletic scholarships. 80% undergrads borrow to pay for school. **Criteria for awarding institutional aid:** *Non-need-based:* academics, leadership.

METROPOLITAN STATE UNIVERSITY

700 Seventh St E, St Paul, MN 55106
Phone: 651-793-1300
Website: http://www.metrostate.edu

This public school was founded in 1971.

RATINGS

Admissions Selectivity Rating: 60*   **Fire Safety Rating:** 60*

STUDENTS AND FACULTY

Enrollment: 7,787.

ACADEMICS

Degrees: bachelor's, certificate, master's.

CAMPUS LIFE

Environment: City. **Activities:** student government, student newspaper.

ADMISSIONS

Basis for Candidate Selection: *Very important factors considered include:* application essay, academic GPA, recommendation(s), rigor of secondary school record, standardized test scores, character/personal qualities, first generation, interview, level of applicant's interest, talent/ability, work experience. *Important factors considered include:* Class rank, extracurricular activities, racial/ethnic status. *Other factors considered include:* alumni/ae relation, geographical residence, state residency, volunteer work. **Freshman Admission Requirements:** High school diploma is required and GED is accepted. **Transfer Admission Requirements:** High school transcript, college transcript(s), essay or personal statement, standardized test scores, Lowest grade transferable C. **General Admission Information:** Application Fee $65. Regular application deadline 6/1. Notification on a rolling basis, beginning on or about 2/1. Nonfall registration accepted. Admission may be deferred for a maximum of 2 semesters. Credit and/or placement offered for CEEB Advanced Placement tests.

COSTS AND FINANCIAL AID

Types of Aid: *Need-based scholarships/grants:* Federal Pell, SEOG, state scholarships/grants, private scholarships, the school's own gift aid. *Loans:* Subsidized Stafford, Unsubsidized Stafford, Federal Perkins, college/university loans from institutional funds. *Student Employment:* Federal Work-Study Program available. Institutional employment available. Off-campus job opportunities are excellent. **Criteria for awarding institutional aid:** *Non-need-based:* academics.

MIAMI UNIVERSITY (OH)

301 S. Campus Ave., Oxford, OH 45056
Phone: 513-529-2531 · **Financial Aid Phone:** 513-529-8734
E-mail: admission@miamioh.edu · **CEEB Code:** 1463
Fax: 513-529-1550 · **Website:** http://www.miamioh.edu/ · **ACT Code:** 3294

This public school was founded in 1809. It has a 2000-acre campus.

RATINGS

Admissions Selectivity Rating: 89   **Fire Safety Rating:** 85

STUDENTS AND FACULTY

Enrollment: 15,378. **Student Body:** 52% female, 48% male, 32% out-of-state, 6% international (73 countries represented). Asian 2%, African American 4%, Caucasian 81%, Hispanic 3%, Native American <1%

Retention and Graduation: 90% freshmen return for sophomore year. 68% freshmen graduate within 4 years. 81% freshmen graduate within 6 years. **Faculty:** 843 full-time faculty, 86% hold PhDs, 43% are members of minority groups, 18% are women. 5% of classes are taught by teaching assistants.

ACADEMICS

Degrees: associate, bachelor's, certificate, doctoral, master's, post-master's certificate, terminal associate, transfer associate. **Classes:** Most classes have 20–29 students. Most lab/discussion sessions have 20–29 students. **Majors with Highest Enrollment:** Accounting; Marketing/Marketing Management; Psychology. **Special Study Options:** cooperative education program, cross-registration, distance learning, double major, exchange student program (domestic), honors program, independent study, internships, liberal arts/career combination, student-designed major, study abroad, teacher certification program. **Honors programs:** Miami has a University Honors Program. Students selected to participate receive a renewable scholarship, priority registration, and other special opportunities. **Combined degree programs:** 3-2 forestry/env. studies with Duke; 3-1 Arts/Prof. Degree, 3-2 engineering. **Disability Services:** Special programs offered to physically disabled students include note-taking services, reader services, tape recorders, tutors. **Career services:** Alumni network, alumni services, career/job search classes, career assessment, internships, regional alumni.

FACILITIES

Housing: Coed dorms, special housing for disabled students, men's dorms, special housing for international students, women's dorms, fraternity/sorority housing, apartments for married students, cooperative housing, apartments for single students, Wellness Housing, Theme Housing. 100% of campus accessible to physically disabled. **Special Academic Facilities/Equipment:** Geology, art, anthropology, and zoology museums, performing arts center, herbarium, ecology research center, 400-acre nature preserve, electron microscope center. **Computers:** 100% of classrooms, 100% of dorms, 100% of libraries, 100% of dining areas, 100% of student union, 65% of common outdoor areas have wireless network access. Students can register for classes online. Administrative functions (other than registration) can be performed online.

CAMPUS LIFE

Environment: Village. **Activities:** Choral groups, concert band, dance, drama/theater, jazz band, literary magazine, marching band, music ensembles, musical theater, opera, pep band, radio station, student government, student newspaper, student-run film society, symphony orchestra, television station, yearbook, Campus Ministries, International Student Organization, Model UN. 304 registered organizations, 38 honor societies, 22 religious organizations. 32 fraternities, 23 sororities. **Athletics (Intercollegiate):** *Men:* baseball, basketball, cross-country, diving, football, golf, ice hockey, swimming, track/field (outdoor). *Women:* basketball, cross-country, diving, field hockey, soccer, softball, swimming, tennis, track/field (outdoor), volleyball. **On-Campus Highlights:** Farmer School of Business, McGuffey Museum, Center for the Performing Arts, Recreational Sports Center, Peabody Hall (National Historical Landmark), Formal Gardens. **Environmental Initiatives:** We are currently itemizing and scheduling implementation of our Sustainability Goals and Commitments announced in 2011. Among the major goals is 20% reduction in GHG emissions by 2020 and a phase-out of coal burning for steam heat by 2025. To achieve these and related goals, Miami is developing an energy/utility master plan that will provide a basis for a climate action plan. As part of this process, Miami has begun a major shift to geothermal heating/cooling to reduce loadings on our steam plant, beginning with energy efficient retrofits of our two oldest campus buildings (1825 and 1836). Much new construction and renovation as part of our Long Range Housing Master Plan will be heated/cooled by geothermal. A number of related planning processes will make the Miami campus more sustainable. Miami has set a minimum standard of Leadership in Energy and Environmental Design (LEED) certification for all new projects and major renovations. In support of this effort, we have recently completed Miami's first comprehensive Storm Water Master Plan to reduce runoff and introduce best management practices (including cisterns, green roofing technology, permeable paving, etc.). Also in support has been a new Campus Circulation Master Plan, which identifies ways to make walking, biking, and transit safer and more convenient on campus. Phased implementation of crosswalk improvements, bicycle routes and parking, and efficiency improvements in our transit service has begun. A set of energy efficiency and waste reduction strategies are underway. Miami continues to compete in Recyclemania, which now covers all campus buildings. Housing Dining and Guest Services continues to participate in the Campus Conservation Nationals competition. Building energy consumption is now metered and available publicly on-line, and will soon be communicated to building users by updated bulletin boards. An "eco-reps" program has been instituted in residence halls by Residence Life, recruiting students to provide leadership in communicating and modeling sustainable practices. We have launched a parallel program "Sustainability Champions" so that faculty and staff in diverse units can provide points of contact and leadership in creating a workplace culture of sustainability.

ADMISSIONS

Freshman Academic Profile: Average high school GPA 3.72. 39.2% in top 10% of high school class, 71.4% in top 25% of high school class, 95.5% in top 50% of high school class. 73% from public high schools. SAT Math middle 50% range 580-680. SAT Critical Reading middle 50% range 540-650. ACT middle 50% range 25-30. Minimum internet-based TOEFL 80. Minimum paper TOEFL 550. **Basis for Candidate Selection:** *Very important factors considered include:* Class rank, application essay, academic GPA, recommendation(s), rigor of secondary school record, standardized test scores, character/personal qualities, talent/ability. *Other factors considered include:* alumni/ae relation, extracurricular activities, first generation, geographical residence, state residency, volunteer work, work experience. **Freshman Admission Requirements:** High school diploma is required and GED is accepted. **Freshman Admission Statistics:** 22,520 applied, 67% admitted, 24% enrolled. **Transfer Admission Requirements:** High school transcript, college transcript(s), essay or personal statement, statement of good standing from prior institution(s). Minimum college GPA of 2.0 required. Lowest grade transferable C. **General Admission Information:** Application Fee $50. Early decision application deadline 11/1. Regular application deadline 2/1. Regular notification 3/15. Nonfall registration accepted. Admission may be deferred for a maximum of 1 year. Credit offered for CEEB Advanced Placement tests.

COSTS AND FINANCIAL AID

Annual in-state tuition $13,533. Annual out-of-state tuition $29,640. Room and board $11,109. Required fees $754. Average book expense $1,250. **Required Forms and Deadlines:** FAFSA. **Notification of Awards:** Applicants will be notified of awards on a rolling basis beginning 3/20. **Types of Aid:** *Need-based scholarships/grants:* Federal Pell, SEOG, state scholarships/grants, private scholarships, the school's own gift aid. *Loans:* Direct Subsidized Stafford, Direct Unsubsidized Stafford, Direct PLUS, Federal Perkins, Federal Nursing, college/university loans from institutional funds, Bank Education Loans. *Student Employment:* Federal Work-Study Program available. Institutional employment available. Off-campus job opportunities are good. **Financial Aid Statistics:** 63% freshmen, 66% undergrads receive need-based scholarship or grant aid. 19% freshmen, 10% undergrads receive non-need-based scholarship or grant aid. 62% freshmen, 75% undergrads receive need-based self-help aid. 3% freshmen, 3% undergrads receive athletic scholarships. 54% undergrads borrow to pay for school. Average cumulative indebtedness $23,487. **Criteria for awarding institutional aid:** *Non-need-based:* academics, art, athletics, leadership, minority status, music/drama, state/district residency.

MICHIGAN STATE UNIVERSITY

250 Administration Building, East Lansing, MI 48824-1046
Phone: 517-355-8332 • **Financial Aid Phone:** 517-353-5940
E-mail: admis@msu.edu • **CEEB Code:** 1465
Fax: 517-353-1647 • **Website:** www.msu.edu • **ACT Code:** 2032

This public school was founded in 1855. It has a 5200-acre campus.

RATINGS

Admissions Selectivity Rating: 87	**Fire Safety Rating:** 60*

STUDENTS AND FACULTY

Enrollment: 38,395. **Student Body:** 50% female, 50% male, 11% out-of-state, 13% international (105 countries represented). Asian 4%, African American 7%, Caucasian 68%, Hispanic 4%, Native American <1%
Retention and Graduation: 92% freshmen return for sophomore year. 29% grads go on to further study within 1 year. 6% grads pursue law degrees. 33% grads pursue business degrees. 5% grads pursue medical degrees. **Faculty:** 2,413 full-time faculty, 90% hold PhDs, 39% are members of minority groups, 22% are women.

ACADEMICS

Degrees: bachelor's, certificate, master's, post-master's certificate. **Classes:** Most classes have 20–29 students. Most lab/discussion sessions have 20–29 students. **Special Study Options:** Accelerated program, cooperative education program, distance learning, double major, dual enrollment, English as a Second Language (ESL), exchange student program (domestic), honors program, independent study, internships, liberal arts/career combination, student-designed major, study abroad, teacher certification program, weekend college. **Honors programs:** MSU's Honors College embodies MSU's long-standing commitment to provide programs of study that attract and challenge unusually talented undergraduates utilizing carefully planned, highly individualized programs of study that will meet the needs of academically talented students. **Combined degree programs:** BA/MA, Computer Science. **Disability Services:** Special programs offered to physically disabled students include note-taking services, reader services, tape recorders, tutors. **Career services:** Alumni network, alumni services, career/job search classes, career assessment, internships, regional alumni.

FACILITIES

Housing: Coed dorms, special housing for disabled students, special housing for international students, women's dorms, fraternity/sorority housing, apartments for married students, cooperative housing, apartments for single students, Theme Housing **Special Academic Facilities/Equipment:** Art, natural history, Michigan history and anthropology museums, art center, on-campus preschool and elementary school, biological station, experimental farms, botanical garden, planetarium, two superconducting cyclotrons, observatory. **Computers:** Students can register for classes online. Administrative functions (other than registration) can be performed online. Undergraduates are required to own a computer.

CAMPUS LIFE

Environment: Town. **Activities:** Choral groups, concert band, dance, drama/theater, jazz band, literary magazine, marching band, music ensembles, musical theater, opera, pep band, radio station, student government, student newspaper, student-run film society, symphony orchestra, television station, yearbook, Campus Ministries, International Student Organization, Model UN. 500 registered organizations, 47 honor societies, 50 religious organizations. 31 fraternity, 19 sororities. **Athletics (Intercollegiate):** *Men:* baseball, basketball, cheerleading, cross-country, diving, football, golf, ice hockey, soccer, swimming, tennis, track/field (outdoor), track/field (indoor), wrestling. *Women:* basketball, cheerleading, crew/rowing, cross-country, diving, field hockey, golf, gymnastics, soccer, softball, swimming, tennis, track/field (outdoor), track/field (indoor), volleyball. **On-Campus Highlights:** MSU Student Union, Jack Breslin Student Events Center, MSU Main Library and Cyber Caf, The International Center, Wharton Center for the Performing Arts. **Environmental Initiatives:** Chicago Climate Exchange; Implementing an Office of Campus Sustainability; Fair Trade Products Preference.

ADMISSIONS

Freshman Academic Profile: Average high school GPA 3.66. 31% in top 10% of high school class, 68% in top 25% of high school class, 95% in top 50% of high school class. SAT Math middle 50% range 540-690. SAT Critical Reading middle 50% range 430-580. SAT Writing middle 50% range 460-570. ACT middle 50% range 23-28. Minimum internet-based TOEFL 79. Minimum paper TOEFL 550. **Basis for Candidate Selection:** *Very important factors considered include:* academic GPA, rigor of secondary school record, standardized test scores. *Important factors considered include:* application essay, extracurricular activities, first generation, geographical residence. *Other factors considered include:* Class rank, recommendation(s), alumni/ae relation, character/personal qualities, level of applicant's interest, state residency, talent/ability, volunteer work, work experience. **Freshman Admission Requirements:** High school diploma is required and GED is accepted. *Academic units required:* 4 English, 3 mathematics, 2 science, 2 foreign language, 2 social studies, 1 history. **Freshman Admission Statistics:** 33,211 applied, 66% admitted, 37% enrolled. **Transfer Admission Requirements:** college transcript(s), essay or personal statement, statement of good standing from prior institution(s). Minimum college GPA of 2.0 required. Lowest grade transferable C. **General Admission Information:** Application Fee $35. Nonfall registration accepted. Credit and/or placement offered for CEEB Advanced Placement tests.

COSTS AND FINANCIAL AID

Annual out-of-state tuition $34,965. Room and board $9,154. Average book expense $1,060. **Required Forms and Deadlines:** FAFSA. **Notification of Awards:** Applicants will be notified of awards on a rolling basis beginning 3/15. **Types of Aid:** *Need-based scholarships/grants:* Federal Pell, SEOG, state scholarships/grants, private scholarships, the school's own gift aid, United Negro College Fund. *Loans:* Direct Subsidized Stafford, Direct Unsubsidized Stafford, Direct PLUS, Federal Perkins, college/university loans from institutional funds. *Student Employment:* Federal Work-Study Program available. Institutional employment available. Off-campus job opportunities are excellent. **Financial Aid Statistics:** 68% freshmen, 71% undergrads receive need-based scholarship or grant aid. 44% freshmen, 28% undergrads receive non-need-based scholarship or grant aid. 75% freshmen, 82% undergrads receive need-based self-help aid. 1% freshmen, 1% undergrads receive athletic scholarships. 45% freshmen, 46% undergrads receive any aid. 45% undergrads borrow to pay for school. **Criteria for awarding institutional aid:** *Non-need-based:* academics, alumni affiliation, art, athletics, leadership, music/drama, state/district residency.

MICHIGAN TECHNOLOGICAL UNIVERSITY

1400 Townsend Drive, Houghton, MI 49931
Phone: 906-487-2335 • **Financial Aid Phone:** 906-487-2622
E-mail: mtu4u@mtu.edu • **CEEB Code:** 1464
Fax: 906-487-2125 • **Website:** www.mtu.edu • **ACT Code:** 2030

This public school was founded in 1885. It has a 925-acre campus.

RATINGS

Admissions Selectivity Rating: 87   **Fire Safety Rating:** 86

STUDENTS AND FACULTY

Enrollment: 5,576. **Student Body:** 25% female, 75% male, 23% out-of-state, 5% international (33 countries represented). Asian 1%, African American 1%, Caucasian 85%, Hispanic 2%, Native American 1%
Retention and Graduation: 85% freshmen return for sophomore year. 25% freshmen graduate within 4 years. 64% freshmen graduate within 6 years. 11% grads go on to further study within 1 year. 2% grads pursue arts and sciences degrees. 1% grads pursue business degrees. 1% grads pursue medical degrees. **Faculty:** 410 full-time faculty, 87% hold PhDs, 30% are members of minority groups, 19% are women. 5% of classes are taught by teaching assistants.

ACADEMICS

Degrees: associate, bachelor's, certificate, master's, post-bachelor's certificate, terminal associate. **Classes:** Most classes have 10–19 students. Most lab/discussion sessions have 10–19 students. **Majors with Highest Enrollment:** Mechanical Engineering; Civil Engineering; Electrical and Electronics Engineering. **Special Study Options:** cooperative education program, distance learning, double major, dual enrollment, English as a Second Language (ESL), exchange student program (domestic), honors program, independent study, internships, study abroad, teacher certification program, Dual degrees with Northwestern MI College, Adrian College, Albion College, Augsburg College (MN), College of St. Scholastica (MN), Mount Senario College, Olivet College, Northland College, University of Wisconsin-Superior, St. Norbert College (WI), Northcentral Technical College (WI), College of Lake County (IL), and Macomb Community College (MI). **Honors programs:** Qualifying students are invited to apply to Michigan Tech's Honors Institute. Membership focuses on activities and enrichment for top scholars, rather than separate honors courses. More details are at http://honors.mtu.edu/. **Disability Services:** Special programs offered to physically disabled students include note-taking services, reader services, tape recorders, tutors. **Career services:** alumni services, career/job search classes, career assessment, internships. Career services highlights include the MTU Career Center, which is proud to be able to provide career advising. We want to have students focus on a career verses a job. Advising includes graduate school, military, and professional employment. 96% of the 2007-08 graduates were placed either in a job relevant to their degree, graduate school, or military education.

FACILITIES

Housing: Coed dorms, special housing for disabled students, special housing for international students, fraternity/sorority housing, apartments for married students, apartments for single students, Wellness Housing, Theme Housing: Alcohol Free, Research, Scholar, Honors Housing, ROTC. Learning Communities: Computer Science; First-year Experience; Health Summit; Forest Resources & Environmental Science; International House; Visual & Performing Arts; Leadership. 90% of campus accessible to physically disabled. **Special Academic Facilities/Equipment:** Mineralogical Museum, 4,700 Acre Research Forest, Scanning Electron Microscope, PUMA Robots, X-ray Fluorescence Spectrometer, Process Simulation and Control Center, Rozsa Center for the Performing Arts, Cleanrooms, MEMS Fabrication Facility, Environmental Scanning Electron Microscope, Transmission Electron Microscope, Radiofrequency Plasma-Assisted Deposition Chamber, Electron Lithography Equipment. **Computers:** 93% of classrooms, 10% of dorms, 100% of libraries, 100% of dining areas, 100% of student union, 10% of common outdoor areas have wireless network access. Students can register for classes online. Administrative functions (other than registration) can be performed online.

CAMPUS LIFE

Environment: Village. **Activities:** Choral groups, concert band, dance, drama/theater, jazz band, literary magazine, music ensembles, musical theater, opera, pep band, radio station, student government, student newspaper, student-run film society, symphony orchestra, Campus Ministries, International Student Organization. 210 registered organizations, 16 honor societies, 16 religious organizations. 13 fraternities, 8 sororities. **Athletics (Intercollegiate):** *Men:*

basketball, cross-country, football, ice hockey, skiing (nordic/cross-country), tennis, track/field (outdoor). *Women:* basketball, cross-country, skiing (nordic/cross-country), tennis, track/field (outdoor), volleyball. **On-Campus Highlights:** Student Development Complex, Rozsa Center for the Performing Arts, Mont Ripley Ski Hill, Portage Lake Golf Course, Memorial Union Building. **Environmental Initiatives:** Emphasis on multidisciplinary sustainability research (http://www.sfi.mtu.edu/research.php/), education (http://www.sfi.mtu.edu/education.php), and outreach, such as Sustainable Futures Institute, Center for Water and Society, Environmentally Responsible Design and Manufacturing Research Group, National Institute for Climatic Change Research (Midwestern Region), Advanced Power Systems Research Center, Materials in Sustainable Transportation Infrastructure, Power and Energy Research Center, International Sustainable Engineering Initiative, IGERT for Sustainable Futures, Graduate Certificate in Sustainability, D80 Center, Peace Corps Masters International Program, International Sustainable Development Engineering Certificate, International Senior Design Programs, Sustainability Research Experience for Undergraduates, Wood-to-Wheels Graduate Enterprise, sustainability-based undergraduate Enterprise Programs (Challenge X, Clean Snowmobile, Alternative Fuels Group, Aqua Terra Tech, Efficiency Through Engineering and Construction), Undergraduate and Graduate Colloquium in Sustainability, Sustainable Futures 1 and 2 courses Commitment of Administration to sustainability in strategic plan and NCA AQIP accreditation project to move toward a carbon-neutral campus (as referenced above). Sustainability Strategic Faculty Hiring Initiative (www.mtu.edu/sfhi/) and other development efforts that are focused on strengthening Michigan Techs sustainability infrastructure.

ADMISSIONS

Freshman Academic Profile: Average high school GPA 3.69. 30.87% in top 10% of high school class, 64.93% in top 25% of high school class, 90.92% in top 50% of high school class. 90% from public high schools. SAT Math middle 50% range 570-680. SAT Critical Reading middle 50% range 530-673. SAT Writing middle 50% range 498-633. ACT middle 50% range 25-30. Minimum internet-based TOEFL 79. Minimum paper TOEFL 550. **Basis for Candidate Selection:** *Very important factors considered include:* academic GPA, rigor of secondary school record, standardized test scores. *Important factors considered include:* Class rank. *Other factors considered include:* application essay, recommendation(s), alumni/ae relation, character/personal qualities, extracurricular activities, interview, talent/ability, volunteer work, work experience. **Freshman Admission Requirements:** High school diploma is required and GED is accepted. *Academic units required:* 3 English, 3 mathematics, 2 science. **Freshman Admission Statistics:** 5,111 applied, 76% admitted, 31% enrolled. **Transfer Admission Requirements:** college transcript(s), statement of good standing from prior institution(s). Minimum college GPA of 2.75 required. Lowest grade transferable C. **General Admission Information:** Notification on a rolling basis, beginning on or about 9/15. Nonfall registration accepted. Admission may be deferred for a maximum of 1 year. Credit and/or placement offered for CEEB Advanced Placement tests.

COSTS AND FINANCIAL AID

Annual in-state tuition $13,740. Annual out-of-state tuition $29,220. Room and board $9,516. Required fees $300. Average book expense $1,200. **Required Forms and Deadlines:** FAFSA. **Types of Aid:** *Need-based scholarships/grants:* Federal Pell, SEOG, state scholarships/grants, private scholarships, the school's own gift aid. *Loans:* Direct Subsidized Stafford, Direct Unsubsidized Stafford, Direct PLUS, Federal Perkins, college/university loans from institutional funds, External Private Loans. *Student Employment:* Federal Work-Study Program available. Institutional employment available. Highest amount earned per year from on-campus jobs $4,500. Off-campus job opportunities are excellent. **Financial Aid Statistics:** 82% freshmen, 77% undergrads receive need-based scholarship or grant aid. 84% freshmen, 73% undergrads receive non-need-based scholarship or grant aid. 80% freshmen, 85% undergrads receive need-based self-help aid. 5% freshmen, 5% undergrads receive athletic scholarships. 93% freshmen, 92% undergrads receive any aid. 73% undergrads borrow to pay for school. Average cumulative indebtedness $26,371. **Criteria for awarding institutional aid:** *Non-need-based:* academics, alumni affiliation, art, athletics, job skills, leadership, music/drama, state/district residency.

See page 1094.

MID-AMERICA CHRISTIAN UNIVERSITY

3500 SW 119th Street, Oklahoma City, OK 73170
Phone: 405-691-3188
E-mail: info@macu.edu · **CEEB Code:** 6942
Fax: 405-692-3165 · **Website:** www.macu.edu · **ACT Code:** 4097

This private school, affiliated with the Church of God Church, was founded in 1953.

RATINGS

Admissions Selectivity Rating: 60*   **Fire Safety Rating:** 63

STUDENTS AND FACULTY

Enrollment: 512. **Student Body:** (3 countries represented).
Faculty: 0% of classes are taught by teaching assistants.

ACADEMICS

Degrees: associate, bachelor's. **Majors with Highest Enrollment:** Pastoral Studies/Counseling; Theology and Religious Vocations; Business/Commerce. **Special Study Options:** Accelerated program, distance learning, double major, external degree program, internships, liberal arts/career combination, student-designed major, teacher certification program. **Combined degree programs:** Multidisciplinary. **Career services:** internships.

FACILITIES

Housing: special housing for disabled students, men's dorms, women's dorms. 100% of campus accessible to physically disabled.

CAMPUS LIFE

Environment: Metropolis. **Activities:** Choral groups, student government, student newspaper, yearbook 1 honor society, 5 religious organizations. **Athletics (Intercollegiate):** *Men:* baseball, basketball, soccer. *Women:* basketball, softball, volleyball. **On-Campus Highlights:** Gaulke Activity Center, President's Chapel, Fowler Student Center, Charles Ewing Brown Library.

ADMISSIONS

Freshman Academic Profile: Minimum paper TOEFL 500. **Transfer Admission Requirements:** college transcript(s), Lowest grade transferable D. **General Admission Information:** Credit and/or placement offered for CEEB Advanced Placement tests.

COSTS AND FINANCIAL AID

Average book expense $500. **Types of Aid:** *Loans:* Subsidized Stafford, PLUS. *Student Employment:* Federal Work-Study Program available. Off-campus job opportunities are excellent.

MIDAMERICA NAZARENE UNIVERSITY

2030 College Way, Olathe, KS 66062
Phone: 913-791-3380 · **Financial Aid Phone:** 913-971-3298
E-mail: admissions@mnu.edu · **CEEB Code:** 6437
Fax: 913-791-3481 · **Website:** www.mnu.edu · **ACT Code:** 1445

This private school, affiliated with the Nazarene Church, was founded in 1966. It has a 105-acre campus.

RATINGS

Admissions Selectivity Rating: 76   **Fire Safety Rating:** 73

STUDENTS AND FACULTY

Enrollment: 1,347. **Student Body:** 57% female, 43% male, 31% out-of-state, 2% international (12 countries represented). Asian 1%, African American 11%, Caucasian 76%, Hispanic 4%, Native American 1%
Retention and Graduation: 76% freshmen return for sophomore year. 33% freshmen graduate within 4 years. **Faculty:** 86 full-time faculty, 50% hold PhDs, 41% are members of minority groups, 5% are women. 0% of classes are taught by teaching assistants.

ACADEMICS

Degrees: associate, bachelor's, master's, post-master's certificate. **Classes:** Most classes have 10–19 students. Most lab/discussion sessions have 10–19 students. **Majors with Highest Enrollment:** Elementary Education and Teaching; Registered Nursing/Registered Nurse; Business/Commerce. **Special Study Options:** Accelerated program, cross-registration, distance learning, double major, dual enrollment, independent study, internships, student-designed major, study abroad, teacher certification program, weekend college.

Disability Services: Special programs offered to physically disabled students include note-taking services, reader services, tape recorders, tutors. **Career services:** career assessment.

FACILITIES

Housing: special housing for disabled students, men's dorms, women's dorms, apartments for single students. 90% of campus accessible to physically disabled. **Computers:** Students can register for classes online. Administrative functions (other than registration) can be performed online.

CAMPUS LIFE

Environment: City. **Activities:** Choral groups, concert band, drama/theater, jazz band, literary magazine, music ensembles, musical theater, pep band, radio station, student government, student newspaper, television station, yearbook, Campus Ministries, International Student Organization. 43 registered organizations, 6 honor societies, 4 religious organizations. **Athletics (Intercollegiate):** *Men:* baseball, basketball, cheerleading, cross-country, football, soccer, track/field (outdoor), track/field (indoor). *Women:* basketball, cheerleading, cross-country, soccer, softball, track/field (outdoor), track/field (indoor), volleyball. **On-Campus Highlights:** Cook Center, Land Memorial Gym, Fitness Center, Campus Center, Bell Cultural Events Center.

ADMISSIONS

Freshman Academic Profile: Average high school GPA 3.37. 2% in top 10% of high school class, 5% in top 25% of high school class, 27% in top 50% of high school class. 88% from public high schools. SAT Math middle 50% range 440-550. SAT Critical Reading middle 50% range 410-540. ACT middle 50% range 20-25. Minimum paper TOEFL 550. **Basis for Candidate Selection:** *Very important factors considered include:* Class rank, rigor of secondary school record, standardized test scores, character/personal qualities. *Important factors considered include:* academic GPA, recommendation(s), level of applicant's interest. *Other factors considered include:* application essay, extracurricular activities, interview, talent/ability. **Freshman Admission Requirements:** High school diploma is required and GED is accepted. **Freshman Admission Statistics:** 617 applied, 65% admitted, 58% enrolled. **Transfer Admission Requirements:** college transcript(s), Minimum college GPA of 2.0 required. Lowest grade transferable D. **General Admission Information:** Application Fee $25. Regular application deadline 8/1. Nonfall registration not accepted. Admission may be deferred for a maximum of 2 years. Credit offered for CEEB Advanced Placement tests.

COSTS AND FINANCIAL AID

Annual tuition $20,500. Room and board $7,000. Required fees $1,000. Average book expense $1,180. **Required Forms and Deadlines:** FAFSA. **Notification of Awards:** Applicants will be notified of awards on a rolling basis beginning 2/1. **Types of Aid:** *Need-based scholarships/grants:* Federal Pell, SEOG, state scholarships/grants, private scholarships, the school's own gift aid. *Loans:* Subsidized Stafford, Unsubsidized Stafford, PLUS, Federal Perkins. *Student Employment:* Off-campus job opportunities are good. **Financial Aid Statistics:** 77% freshmen, 94% undergrads receive need-based scholarship or grant aid. 53% freshmen, 41% undergrads receive non-need-based scholarship or grant aid. 75% freshmen, 79% undergrads receive need-based self-help aid. 46% freshmen, 36% undergrads receive athletic scholarships. 92% freshmen, 86% undergrads receive any aid. 77% undergrads borrow to pay for school. Average cumulative indebtedness $22,195. **Criteria for awarding institutional aid:** *Non-need-based:* academics, athletics, leadership, minority status, music/drama, religious affiliation, state/district residency.

MIDDLE TENNESSEE STATE UNIVERSITY

Cope Administration Building 208, Murfreesboro, TN 37132
Phone: 615-898-2111
E-mail: admissions@mtsu.edu
Fax: 615-898-5478 · **Website:** www.mtsu.edu

This is a public school.

RATINGS

Admissions Selectivity Rating: 81   Fire Safety Rating: 60*

STUDENTS AND FACULTY

Enrollment: 22,121. **Student Body:** 53% female, 47% male, 4% out-of-state. Asian 3%, African American 19%, Caucasian 69%, Hispanic 4%, Native American <1%
Faculty: 938 full-time faculty, 46% are members of minority groups, 16% are women.

ACADEMICS

Degrees: bachelor's, master's, post-bachelor's certificate, post-master's certificate. **Classes:** Most classes have 20–29 students. Most lab/discussion sessions have fewer than 10 students. **Special Study Options:** distance learning, double major, dual enrollment, honors program, independent study, internships, study abroad, teacher certification program.

FACILITIES

Housing: Coed dorms, special housing for disabled students, men's dorms, special housing for international students, women's dorms, fraternity/sorority housing, apartments for married students, cooperative housing, apartments for single students, Wellness Housing, Theme HousingWellness housing.

CAMPUS LIFE

Activities: Choral groups, concert band, dance, drama/theater, jazz band, literary magazine, marching band, music ensembles, musical theater, opera, pep band, radio station, student government, student newspaper, symphony orchestra, television station, Campus Ministries, International Student Organization, Model UN.

ADMISSIONS

Freshman Academic Profile: Average high school GPA 3.31. 17% in top 10% of high school class, 42% in top 25% of high school class, 78% in top 50% of high school class. SAT Math middle 50% range 460-580. SAT Critical Reading middle 50% range 460-590. ACT middle 50% range 19-24. Minimum paper TOEFL 500. **Basis for Candidate Selection:** *Very important factors considered include:* academic GPA, rigor of secondary school record, standardized test scores. *Important factors considered include:* racial/ethnic status, talent/ability. *Other factors considered include:* Class rank, recommendation(s), character/personal qualities, extracurricular activities, first generation, level of applicant's interest, volunteer work, work experience. **Freshman Admission Requirements:** High school diploma is required and GED is accepted. *Academic units required:* 4 English, 3 mathematics, 2 science, 2 foreign language, 1 social studies, 1 history, 1 visual/performing arts. **Freshman Admission Statistics:** 9,405 applied, 67% admitted, 50% enrolled. **Transfer Admission Requirements:** college transcript(s), Minimum college GPA of 2.0 required. Lowest grade transferable D. **General Admission Information:** Application Fee $25. Nonfall registration accepted. Credit offered for CEEB Advanced Placement tests.

COSTS AND FINANCIAL AID

Required Forms and Deadlines: FAFSA. **Financial Aid Statistics:** 65% freshmen, 66% undergrads receive need-based scholarship or grant aid. 88% freshmen, 59% undergrads receive non-need-based scholarship or grant aid. 55% freshmen, 67% undergrads receive need-based self-help aid. 1% freshmen, 1% undergrads receive athletic scholarships. 59% undergrads borrow to pay for school. Average cumulative indebtedness $21,224.

MIDDLEBURY COLLEGE

The Emma Willard House, Middlebury, VT 05753-6002
Phone: 802-443-3000 · **Financial Aid Phone:** 802-443-5158
E-mail: admissions@middlebury.edu · **CEEB Code:** 3526
Fax: 802-443-2056 · **Website:** www.middlebury.edu · **ACT Code:** 4306

This private school was founded in 1800. It has a 350-acre campus.

RATINGS

Admissions Selectivity Rating: 95   Fire Safety Rating: 93

STUDENTS AND FACULTY

Enrollment: 2,498. **Student Body:** 51% female, 49% male, 94% out-of-state, 10% international (74 countries represented). Asian 7%, African American 3%, Caucasian 65%, Hispanic 9%, Native American <1%
Retention and Graduation: 96% freshmen return for sophomore year. 89% freshmen graduate within 4 years. 94% freshmen graduate within 6 years. 12% grads go on to further study within 1 year. **Faculty:** 270 full-time faculty, 94% hold PhDs, 44% are members of minority groups, 18% are women. 0% of classes are taught by teaching assistants.

ACADEMICS

Degrees: bachelor's, master's. **Classes:** Most classes have 10–19 students. **Majors with Highest Enrollment:** Economics; Environmental Studies; Political Science and Government. **Special Study Options:** Accelerated program, double major, exchange student program (domestic), honors program, independent study, internships, student-designed major, study abroad, teacher certification program, Williams College-Mystic Seaport Program in American Maritime Studies, Oxford University summer Program,independent scholar programs with Berea College and Swarthmore College, 3-year international major. **Disability Services:** Special programs offered to physically disabled students include note-taking services, reader services, tape recorders, tutors. **Career services:** Alumni network, alumni services, career/job search classes, career assessment, internships, regional alumni.

FACILITIES

Housing: Coed dorms, special housing for disabled students, apartments for single students, Multi-cultural house, environmental house, foreign language house, 5 co-ed social houses. Commons System organizes residence halls into 5 groups,each with its own budget, government, faculty, and staff associates. 60% of campus accessible to physically disabled. **Special Academic Facilities/ Equipment:** Art museum, theatres, language lab, observatory, electron microscope, mountain campus, downhill and cross-country ski areas, golf course, Franklin Environmental Center, organic garden. **Computers:** Students can register for classes online. Administrative functions (other than registration) can be performed online.

CAMPUS LIFE

Environment: Village. **Activities:** Choral groups, dance, drama/theater, jazz band, literary magazine, music ensembles, musical theater, radio station, student government, student newspaper, student-run film society, symphony orchestra, yearbook. 100 registered organizations. **Athletics (Intercollegiate):** *Men:* baseball, basketball, cross-country, diving, football, golf, ice hockey, lacrosse, skiing (downhill/alpine), skiing (nordic/cross-country), soccer, swimming, tennis, track/field (outdoor), track/field (indoor). *Women:* basketball, cross-country, diving, field hockey, golf, ice hockey, lacrosse, skiing (downhill/alpine), skiing (nordic/cross-country), soccer, softball, squash, swimming, tennis, track/field (outdoor), track/field (indoor), volleyball. **On-Campus Highlights:** Science - Bicentennial Hall, The Center for the Arts, Athletic Facilities, The Commons System, Middlebury College Snow Bowl (Ski Area). **Environmental Initiatives:** Student initiated effort that led to Trustees resolution in 2007 charging the entire college community to work together to achieve carbon neutrality by 2016. A similar effort modeled on this one is also in progress with regard to divesting the college endowment from fossil fuel related companies. Thus far, it has led to new proxy voting policies in support of open and transparent governance and environmental and social responsibility, a student member of the Advisory Committee on Socially Responsible Investing has been appointed to the Investment Committee of the Board, and the question of divesting from fossil fuels is currently being given full and open consideration by the Trustees with significant community involvement in the discussion. Completion of a $12 million biomass gasification system that burns renewable wood chips, reduces carbon emissions by 40% and fuel oil consumption by 1,000,000 gallons, has saved us over $1 million annually in fuel costs and has shifted nearly a million dollars of spending into the local economy through purchase of woodchips within 75 miles of the campus Our Franklin Environmental Center at Hillcrest which received LEED Platinum certification. The first in Vermont and only the seventh nationwide. Through this Center we have provided annual two day workshops for non-environmental faculty who want to integrate sustainability into their courses and have had 35 faculty do so—more than 10% of the entire faculty. This is in addition to 12 core environmental studies (ES) faculty and 50 others who are affiliated with the ES program.

ADMISSIONS

Freshman Academic Profile: SAT Math middle 50% range 630-740. SAT Critical Reading middle 50% range 630-730. SAT Writing middle 50% range 650-750. ACT middle 50% range 30-33. **Basis for Candidate Selection:** *Very important factors considered include:* Class rank, academic GPA, rigor of secondary school record, character/personal qualities, extracurricular activities, talent/ability. *Important factors considered include:* application essay, recommendation(s), standardized test scores, racial/ethnic status. *Other factors considered include:* alumni/ae relation, first generation, geographical residence, interview, level of applicant's interest, volunteer work, work experience. **Freshman Admission Requirements:** High school diploma or equivalent is not required. **Freshman Admission Statistics:** 8,195 applied, 17% admitted, 41% enrolled. **Transfer Admission Requirements:** High school transcript, college transcript(s), essay or personal statement, statement of good standing from prior institution(s). Minimum college GPA of 3.0 required. Lowest grade transferable C-. **General Admission Information:** Application Fee $65. Early decision application deadline 11/1. Regular application deadline 1/1. Regular notification 4/1. Nonfall registration accepted. Admission may be deferred for a maximum of 1 year. Credit and/or placement offered for CEEB Advanced Placement tests.

COSTS AND FINANCIAL AID

Annual tuition $45,637. Room and board $13,116. Required fees $407. **Required Forms and Deadlines:** FAFSA, CSS/Financial Aid PROFILE, Non-

custodial PROFILE. **Notification of Awards:** Applicants will be notified of awards on or about 4/1. **Types of Aid:** *Need-based scholarships/grants:* Federal Pell, SEOG, state scholarships/grants, private scholarships, the school's own gift aid. *Loans:* Subsidized Stafford, Unsubsidized Stafford, PLUS, Federal Perkins, college/university loans from institutional funds. **Financial Aid Statistics:** 98% freshmen, 97% undergrads receive need-based scholarship or grant aid. 0% freshmen, 0% undergrads receive non-need-based scholarship or grant aid. 89% freshmen, 90% undergrads receive need-based self-help aid. 0% freshmen, 0% undergrads receive athletic scholarships. 48% freshmen, 42% undergrads receive any aid. 44% undergrads borrow to pay for school. Average cumulative indebtedness $15,517.

MIDWAY COLLEGE

512 East Stephen Street., Midway, KY 40347-1120
Phone: 859-846-5347 · **Financial Aid Phone:** 859-846-5410
E-mail: admissions@midway.edu · **CEEB Code:** 1975
Fax: 859-846-5787 · **Website:** www.midway.edu · **ACT Code:** 1528

This private school, affiliated with the Disciples of Christ Church, was founded in 1847. It has a 105-acre campus.

RATINGS

Admissions Selectivity Rating: 76   **Fire Safety Rating:** 63

STUDENTS AND FACULTY

Enrollment: 1,395. **Student Body:** 91% female, 9% male, 9% out-of-state, 0% international (1 countries represented). Asian 0%, African American 7%, Caucasian 68%, Hispanic 1%, Native American 1%
Retention and Graduation: 76% freshmen return for sophomore year. 26% freshmen graduate within 4 years. 32% freshmen graduate within 6 years. **Faculty:** 41 full-time faculty, 46% hold PhDs, 39% are members of minority groups. 0% of classes are taught by teaching assistants.

ACADEMICS

Degrees: associate, bachelor's, master's. **Classes:** Most classes have 10–19 students. Most lab/discussion sessions have 10–19 students. **Majors with Highest Enrollment:** Elementary Education and Teaching; Registered Nursing/ Registered Nurse. **Special Study Options:** Accelerated program, distance learning, double major, dual enrollment, honors program, study abroad, teacher certification program, weekend college. **Honors programs:** Ruth Slack Roach Leadership, President's Ambassadors, Gamma Beta Phi, Tri Beta. **Disability Services:** Special programs offered to physically disabled students include note-taking services, reader services, tape recorders, tutors.

FACILITIES

Housing: women's dorms. 75% of campus accessible to physically disabled.

CAMPUS LIFE

Environment: Rural. **Activities:** Choral groups, music ensembles, student government, student newspaper, yearbook. **Athletics (Intercollegiate):** *Women:* basketball, cross-country, equestrian sports, soccer, softball, tennis, volleyball. **On-Campus Highlights:** Anne Hart Raymond Center, Little Memorial Library, Equestrian Center, McManus Student Center, Piper Dining Hall.

ADMISSIONS

Freshman Academic Profile: Average high school GPA 3.15. 12% in top 10% of high school class, 25% in top 25% of high school class, 64% in top 50% of high school class. SAT Math middle 50% range 400-560. SAT Critical Reading middle 50% range 420-560. ACT middle 50% range 18-22. Minimum paper TOEFL 500. **Basis for Candidate Selection:** *Very important factors considered include:* rigor of secondary school record, standardized test scores. *Important factors considered include:* alumni/ae relation. *Other factors considered include:* Class rank, application essay, recommendation(s), character/personal qualities, extracurricular activities, interview, talent/ability, volunteer work, work experience. **Freshman Admission Requirements:** High school diploma is required and GED is accepted. *Academic units required:* 4 English. **Freshman Admission Statistics:** 456 applied, 71% admitted, 63% enrolled. **Transfer Admission Requirements:** High school transcript, college transcript(s), Minimum college GPA of 2.0 required. Lowest grade transferable c. **General Admission Information:** Application Fee $25. Notification on a rolling basis, beginning on or about 9/5. Nonfall registration accepted. Admission may be deferred for a maximum of 0. Credit and/or placement offered for CEEB Advanced Placement tests.

COSTS AND FINANCIAL AID

Annual tuition $15,750. Room and board $6,000. Required fees $150. Average book expense $1,200. **Required Forms and Deadlines:** FAFSA, Institution's own financial aid form. **Types of Aid:** *Need-based scholarships/grants:* Federal Pell, SEOG, state scholarships/grants, private scholarships, the school's own gift aid. *Loans:* Subsidized Stafford, Unsubsidized Stafford, PLUS, Federal Perkins, college/university loans from institutional funds. *Student Employment:* Federal Work-Study Program available. Institutional employment available. Off-campus job opportunities are good. **Financial Aid Statistics:** 100% freshmen, 93% undergrads receive need-based scholarship or grant aid. 8% freshmen, 8% undergrads receive non-need-based scholarship or grant aid. 81% freshmen, 88% undergrads receive need-based self-help aid. 1% freshmen, 1% undergrads receive athletic scholarships. 85% freshmen, 81% undergrads receive any aid. 86% undergrads borrow to pay for school. Average cumulative indebtedness $18,182. **Criteria for awarding institutional aid:** *Non-need-based:* academics, alumni affiliation, athletics, leadership, religious affiliation.

MIDWESTERN STATE UNIVERSITY

3410 Taft Blvd., Wichita Falls, TX 76308-2099
Phone: 940-397-4334 · **Financial Aid Phone:** 940-397-4119
E-mail: admissions@mwsu.edu · **CEEB Code:** 6408
Fax: 940-397-4672 · **Website:** www.mwsu.edu · **ACT Code:** 4132

This public school was founded in 1922. It has a 255-acre campus.

RATINGS

Admissions Selectivity Rating: 78   **Fire Safety Rating:** 85

STUDENTS AND FACULTY

Enrollment: 5,358. **Student Body:** 58% female, 42% male, 5% out-of-state, 5% international (41 countries represented). Asian 4%, African American 13%, Caucasian 67%, Hispanic 9%, Native American 1%
Retention and Graduation: 66% freshmen return for sophomore year. 9% freshmen graduate within 4 years. 28% freshmen graduate within 6 years.
Faculty: 206 full-time faculty, 68% hold PhDs, 47% are members of minority groups, 11% are women. 2% of classes are taught by teaching assistants.

ACADEMICS

Degrees: associate, bachelor's, master's, post-bachelor's certificate. **Classes:** Most classes have 20–29 students. Most lab/discussion sessions have 10–19 students. **Majors with Highest Enrollment:** Marketing/Marketing Management; Social Sciences; Journalism. **Special Study Options:** distance learning, double major, dual enrollment, English as a Second Language (ESL), honors program, independent study, internships, liberal arts/career combination, study abroad, teacher certification program. **Honors programs:** First established in 1964 and developed upon Midwestern State University's Tradition of Excellence, the University Honors Program offers high achieving MSU students a challenging premier undergraduate learning experience. From the Honors Introductory Seminar at the beginning, through Honors designated classes taught by outstanding faculty, to the Honors Capstone Course and Graduation with Honors at the end, the MSU Honors Program serves as a powerful program from start to finish. **Combined degree programs:** Accounting/MBA. **Disability Services:** Special programs offered to physically disabled students include note-taking services, reader services, tape recorders, tutors. **Career services:** Alumni network, alumni services, career/job search classes, internships. Career services highlights include career and job search.

FACILITIES

Housing: Coed dorms, special housing for disabled students, men's dorms, women's dorms, apartments for married students, apartments for single students, Housing for Honor students Biology Cooperative Housing. 99% of campus accessible to physically disabled. **Special Academic Facilities/Equipment:** Language lab, technology lab, video lab, planetarium, art museum. **Computers:** Students can register for classes online. Administrative functions (other than registration) can be performed online.

CAMPUS LIFE

Environment: City. **Activities:** Choral groups, concert band, dance, drama/theater, jazz band, literary magazine, marching band, music ensembles, pep band, student government, student newspaper, student-run film society, television station, yearbook. 145 registered organizations, 23 honor societies, 15 religious organizations. 8 fraternities, 8 sororities. **Athletics (Intercollegiate):** *Men:* basketball, football, golf, soccer, tennis. *Women:* basketball, cross-country, soccer, softball, tennis, volleyball. **On-Campus Highlights:** Clark Student Center, D.L. Ligon Coliseum, Corner Perk Coffee Shop, Wellness Center, Library, Sikes Lake, an art meseuon.

ADMISSIONS

Freshman Academic Profile: Average high school GPA 3.41. 12% in top 10% of high school class, 37% in top 25% of high school class, 73% in top 50% of

high school class. 96% from public high schools. SAT Math middle 50% range 450-560. SAT Critical Reading middle 50% range 440-550. SAT Writing middle 50% range 440-540. ACT middle 50% range 18-23. Minimum paper TOEFL 550. **Basis for Candidate Selection:** *Very important factors considered include:* Class rank, academic GPA, rigor of secondary school record, standardized test scores. *Other factors considered include:* application essay, alumni/ae relation, character/personal qualities, extracurricular activities, first generation, geographical residence, interview, level of applicant's interest, racial/ethnic status, state residency, talent/ability, volunteer work, work experience. **Freshman Admission Requirements:** High school diploma is required and GED is accepted. *Academic units required:* 4 English, 3 mathematics, 2 science, 6 academic electives. **Freshman Admission Statistics:** 1,407 applied, 69% admitted, 70% enrolled. **Transfer Admission Requirements:** college transcript(s), statement of good standing from prior institution(s). Minimum college GPA of 2.0 required. Lowest grade transferable D. **General Admission Information:** Application Fee $25. Regular application deadline 8/7. Notification on a rolling basis, beginning on or about 9/1. Nonfall application accepted. Credit and/or placement offered for CEEB Advanced Placement tests.

COSTS AND FINANCIAL AID

Required Forms and Deadlines: FAFSA, Institution's own financial aid form. **Notification of Awards:** Applicants will be notified of awards on a rolling basis beginning 3/15. **Types of Aid:** *Need-based scholarships/grants:* Federal Pell, SEOG, state scholarships/grants, private scholarships, the school's own gift aid. *Loans:* Subsidized Stafford, Unsubsidized Stafford, PLUS, Federal Perkins, state loans, college/university loans from institutional funds, Alternative Private Loans. *Student Employment:* Federal Work-Study Program available. Institutional employment available. Highest amount earned per year from on-campus jobs $9,120. Off-campus job opportunities are good. **Financial Aid Statistics:** 84% freshmen, 83% undergrads receive need-based scholarship or grant aid. 2% freshmen, 2% undergrads receive non-need-based scholarship or grant aid. 77% freshmen, 81% undergrads receive need-based self-help aid. 5% freshmen, 3% undergrads receive athletic scholarships. 72% freshmen, 76% undergrads receive any aid. 54% undergrads borrow to pay for school. Average cumulative indebtedness $18,971. **Criteria for awarding institutional aid:** *Non-need-based:* academics, alumni affiliation, art, athletics, leadership, minority status, music/drama.

MILES COLLEGE

5500 Myron Massey Blvd., Fairfield, AL 35064
Phone: 205-929-1656
E-mail: admissions@mail.miles.edu
Fax: 205-929-1627 · **Website:** miles.edu

This private school, affiliated with the Episcopal Church, was founded in 1905. It has a 37-acre campus.

RATINGS

Admissions Selectivity Rating: 61   **Fire Safety Rating:** 60*

STUDENTS AND FACULTY

Enrollment: 1,660. **Student Body:** 57% female, 43% male, 33% out-of-state, 0% international. Asian 0%, African American 98%, Caucasian 1%, Hispanic 0%, Native American <1%
Retention and Graduation: 70% freshmen return for sophomore year. 26% freshmen graduate within 4 years. 71% freshmen graduate within 6 years.
Faculty: 94 full-time faculty, 35% hold PhDs, 51% are members of minority groups.

ACADEMICS

Degrees: bachelor's. **Special Study Options:** cooperative education program, double major, honors program, internships, study abroad, teacher certification program, weekend college.

FACILITIES

Housing: Coed dorms, men's dorms, women's dorms, apartments for single students.

CAMPUS LIFE

Activities: Choral groups, concert band, drama/theater, jazz band, marching band, music ensembles, pep band, student government, student newspaper, television station 8 honor societies, 1 religious organization. **Athletics (Intercollegiate):** *Men:* baseball, basketball, cheerleading, football, tennis, track/field (outdoor). *Women:* basketball, cheerleading, softball, tennis, track/field (outdoor), volleyball.

ADMISSIONS

Freshman Academic Profile: Average high school GPA 2.35. 15% in top 10% of high school class, 31% in top 25% of high school class, 48% in top

50% of high school class. Minimum paper TOEFL 450. **Basis for Candidate Selection:** *Other factors considered include:* standardized test scores, alumni/ae relation. **Freshman Admission Requirements:** High school diploma is required and GED is accepted. **Transfer Admission Requirements:** Lowest grade transferable C. **General Admission Information:** Application Fee $25. Regular application deadline 8/23. Nonfall registration accepted. Admission may be deferred for a maximum of 1 year.

COSTS AND FINANCIAL AID

Annual tuition $5,008. Room and board $2,950. Required fees $350. Average book expense $600. **Required Forms and Deadlines:** FAFSA, State aid form. **Types of Aid:** *Need-based scholarships/grants:* Federal Pell, SEOG, state scholarships/grants, private scholarships, the school's own gift aid, United Negro College Fund. *Loans:* Direct Subsidized Stafford, Direct Unsubsidized Stafford, Direct PLUS, Subsidized Stafford, Unsubsidized Stafford, PLUS, Federal Perkins, state loans, college/university loans from institutional funds. *Student Employment:* Federal Work-Study Program available. Highest amount earned per year from on-campus jobs $1,000. **Criteria for awarding institutional aid:** *Non-need-based:* academics, job skills, religious affiliation, state/district residency.

MILLERSVILLE UNIVERSITY OF PENNSYLVANIA

P.O. Box 1002, Millersville, PA 17551-0302
Phone: 717-871-4625 • **Financial Aid Phone:** 717-871-5100
E-mail: admissions@millersville.edu • **CEEB Code:** 2656
Fax: 717-871-2147 • **Website:** www.millersville.edu • **ACT Code:** 3712

This public school was founded in 1855. It has a 250-acre campus.

RATINGS

Admissions Selectivity Rating: 76   Fire Safety Rating: 99

STUDENTS AND FACULTY

Enrollment: 7,070. **Student Body:** 56% female, 44% male, 5% out-of-state, 0% international (54 countries represented). Asian 2%, African American 10%, Caucasian 77%, Hispanic 8%, Native American <1%
Retention and Graduation: 39% freshmen graduate within 4 years. 64% freshmen graduate within 6 years. **Faculty:** 287 full-time faculty, 98% hold PhDs, 46% are members of minority groups, 19% are women, 0% of classes are taught by teaching assistants.

ACADEMICS

Degrees: associate, bachelor's, master's, post-bachelor's certificate, post-master's certificate. **Classes:** Most classes have 30-39 students. Most lab/discussion sessions have 20–29 students. **Majors with Highest Enrollment:** Business Administration and Management; Biology/Biological Sciences; Psychology. **Special Study Options:** Accelerated program, cooperative education program, cross-registration, distance learning, double major, dual enrollment, honors program, independent study, internships, study abroad, teacher certification program, Academic Remediation; Advanced Placement Credit; Off-Campus Study; Learning Disabilities Services; Adult and Continuing Education (ACE) Program; Internet Courses; Summer Session for credit. **Honors programs:** Honors College **Combined degree programs:** AS/Pre-Pharmacy; BS/Pre-Optometry; BS/Pre-Podiatry; BS/Pre-Athl. Training. **Disability Services:** Special programs offered to physically disabled students include note-taking services, reader services, tape recorders, tutors. **Career services:** alumni services, career/job search classes, career assessment Career services highlights include internships and co-ops that are a winning strategy for students, employers and the university. Students develop their professional proficiency and self-confidence and get a chance to "test drive" their career choice. Employers get a highly motivated employee for a specific amount of time. The university gains valuable feedback regarding its instruction, curriculum, and programs.

FACILITIES

Housing: Coed dorms, Wellness Housing, Theme Housing, Academic Interest Housing for several subject areas. 85% of campus accessible to physically disabled. **Special Academic Facilities/Equipment:** Art galleries, foreign language lab, extensive inventory of scientific & technological instrumentation, weather station, T.V. studio, radio station, teleconferencing center, Distance Learning **Computers:** 100% of classrooms, 100% of dorms, 100% of libraries, 100% of dining areas, 100% of student union, 100% of common outdoor areas have wireless network access. Students can register for classes online. Administrative functions (other than registration) can be performed online.

CAMPUS LIFE

Environment: Village. **Activities:** Choral groups, concert band, dance, drama/theater, jazz band, literary magazine, marching band, music ensembles, musical theater, pep band, radio station, student government, student newspaper, sym-

phony orchestra, television station, yearbook, Campus Ministries. 120 registered organizations, 11 honor society, 12 religious organizations. 9 fraternities, 10 sororities. **Athletics (Intercollegiate):** *Men:* baseball, basketball, cross-country, football, golf, soccer, tennis, track/field (outdoor), track/field (indoor), wrestling. *Women:* basketball, cheerleading, cross-country, field hockey, lacrosse, soccer, softball, swimming, tennis, track/field (outdoor), track/field (indoor), volleyball. **On-Campus Highlights:** Student Memorial Center, Ganser Library, Science and Technology Building, Biemesderfer Executive Center, Gordinier Dining Hall. **Environmental Initiatives:** Constructed a LEEDS certifiable building; Campus recycling program; Energy Conservation Program.

ADMISSIONS

Freshman Academic Profile: 12.5% in top 10% of high school class, 36.6% in top 25% of high school class, 72.9% in top 50% of high school class. SAT Math middle 50% range 460-560. SAT Critical Reading middle 50% range 460-550. SAT Writing middle 50% range 440-530. ACT middle 50% range 19-23. Minimum internet-based TOEFL 79. Minimum paper TOEFL 550. **Basis for Candidate Selection:** *Very important factors considered include:* Class rank, rigor of secondary school record, standardized test scores. *Important factors considered include:* character/personal qualities, extracurricular activities, talent/ability, volunteer work, work experience. *Other factors considered include:* application essay, recommendation(s), alumni/ae relation, geographical residence, interview, racial/ethnic status, state residency. **Freshman Admission Requirements:** High school diploma is required and GED is accepted. *Academic units required:* 4 English, 3 mathematics, 3 science, (1 science labs), 0 foreign language, 3 social studies, 2 history, 0 visual/performing arts, 0 computer science, 0 academic electives. **Freshman Admission Statistics:** 6,184 applied, 69% admitted, 32% enrolled. **Transfer Admission Requirements:** High school transcript, college transcript(s), statement of good standing from prior institution(s). Minimum college GPA of 2.0 required. Lowest grade transferable C. **General Admission Information:** Application Fee $50. Notification on a rolling basis, beginning on or about 9/15. Nonfall registration accepted. Admission may be deferred for a maximum of 1 semester. Credit and/or placement offered for CEEB Advanced Placement tests.

COSTS AND FINANCIAL AID

Annual in-state tuition $7,920. Annual out-of-state tuition $21,300. Room and board $11,380. Required fees $2,348. Average book expense $1,000. **Required Forms and Deadlines:** FAFSA. **Notification of Awards:** Applicants will be notified of awards on a rolling basis beginning 3/19. **Types of Aid:** *Need-based scholarships/grants:* Federal Pell, SEOG, state scholarships/grants, private scholarships, the school's own gift aid, Schock Scholarship. *Loans:* Subsidized Stafford, Unsubsidized Stafford, PLUS, Federal Perkins, college/university loans from institutional funds. *Student Employment:* Federal Work-Study Program available. Institutional employment available. Highest amount earned per year from on-campus jobs $12,787. Off-campus job opportunities are excellent. **Financial Aid Statistics:** 73% freshmen, 70% undergrads receive need-based scholarship or grant aid. 15% freshmen, 10% undergrads receive non-need-based scholarship or grant aid. 83% freshmen, 86% undergrads receive need-based self-help aid. 1% freshmen, 1% undergrads receive athletic scholarships. 86% freshmen, 83% undergrads receive any aid. 70% undergrads borrow to pay for school. Average cumulative indebtedness $24,883. **Criteria for awarding institutional aid:** *Non-need-based:* academics, athletics, minority status.

MILLIGAN COLLEGE

P.O. Box 210, Milligan College, TN 37682
Phone: 423-461-8730 • **Financial Aid Phone:** 423-461-8968
E-mail: admissions@milligan.edu • **CEEB Code:** 1469
Fax: 423-461-8982 • **Website:** http://www.milligan.edu/ • **ACT Code:** 3996

This private school was founded in 1866. It has a 181-acre campus.

RATINGS

Admissions Selectivity Rating: 87   Fire Safety Rating: 96

STUDENTS AND FACULTY

Enrollment: 938. **Student Body:** 60% female, 40% male, 35% out-of-state, 3% international (15 countries represented). Asian 1%, African American 6%, Caucasian 84%, Hispanic 4%, Native American <1%
Retention and Graduation: 80% freshmen return for sophomore year. 65% freshmen graduate within 6 years. 9% grads pursue arts and sciences degrees. 2% grads pursue law degrees. 2% grads pursue business degrees. 6% grads pursue medical degrees. **Faculty:** 68 full-time faculty, 79% hold PhDs, 50% are members of minority groups, 3% are women. 0% of classes are taught by teaching assistants.

ACADEMICS

Degrees: bachelor's, master's. **Classes:** Most classes have fewer than 10 students. Most lab/discussion sessions have fewer than 10 students. **Majors with Highest Enrollment:** Bible/Biblical Studies; Registered Nursing/Registered Nurse; Business Administration and Management. **Special Study Options:** cross-registration, double major, independent study, internships, study abroad, teacher certification program. **Disability Services:** Special programs offered to physically disabled students include note-taking services, tape recorders, tutors. **Career services:** Alumni network, career/job search classes, career assessment, regional alumni.

FACILITIES

Housing: men's dorms, women's dorms, apartments for married students, apartments for single students. 80% of campus accessible to physically disabled. **Computers:** 95% of classrooms, 95% of dorms, 100% of libraries, 100% of dining areas, 100% of student union, 25% of common outdoor areas have wireless network access. Students can register for classes online. Administrative functions (other than registration) can be performed online.

CAMPUS LIFE

Environment: Town. **Activities:** Choral groups, concert band, drama/theater, jazz band, literary magazine, music ensembles, musical theater, pep band, radio station, student government, student newspaper, symphony orchestra, yearbook. 36 registered organizations, 5 honor societies, 5 religious organizations. **Athletics (Intercollegiate):** *Men:* baseball, basketball, cross-country, golf, mountain biking, soccer, swimming, tennis, track/field (outdoor), track/field (indoor). *Women:* basketball, cross-country, soccer, softball, swimming, tennis, track/field (outdoor), track/field (indoor), volleyball. **On-Campus Highlights:** The Gregory Center, Student Center, Residence Halls/ Dining Hall, Seeger Chapel, Athletic Facilities. **Environmental Initiatives:** Campuswide recycling; Construction of a new LEED certified Wellness Center opened in March; 2010 Campuswide energy audit.

ADMISSIONS

Freshman Academic Profile: Average high school GPA 3.7. 37% in top 10% of high school class, 65% in top 25% of high school class, 89% in top 50% of high school class. 80% from public high schools. SAT Math middle 50% range 490-610. SAT Critical Reading middle 50% range 490-600. SAT Writing middle 50% range 480-560. ACT middle 50% range 21-27. Minimum internet-based TOEFL 79. Minimum paper TOEFL 550. **Basis for Candidate Selection:** *Very important factors considered include:* application essay, academic GPA, rigor of secondary school record, standardized test scores, character/personal qualities, religious affiliation/commitment. *Important factors considered include:* recommendation(s), extracurricular activities. *Other factors considered include:* Class rank, alumni/ae relation, interview, racial/ethnic status, talent/ability, volunteer work, work experience. **Freshman Admission Requirements:** High school diploma is required and GED is accepted. **Freshman Admission Statistics:** 603 applied, 70% admitted, 48% enrolled. **Transfer Admission Requirements:** college transcript(s), essay or personal statement, Minimum college GPA of 2.0 required. Lowest grade transferable C-. **General Admission Information:** Application Fee $30. Regular application deadline 8/1. Notification on a rolling basis, beginning on or about 10/1. Nonfall registration accepted. Admission may be deferred for a maximum of 1 year. Credit and/or placement offered for CEEB Advanced Placement tests.

COSTS AND FINANCIAL AID

Annual tuition $24,360. Room and board $5,650. Required fees $900. Average book expense $900. **Required Forms and Deadlines:** FAFSA. **Notification of Awards:** Applicants will be notified of awards on a rolling basis beginning 3/15. **Types of Aid:** *Need-based scholarships/grants:* Federal Pell, SEOG, state scholarships/grants, private scholarships, the school's own gift aid. *Loans:* Subsidized Stafford, Unsubsidized Stafford, PLUS, Federal Perkins. *Student Employment:* Federal Work-Study Program available. Institutional employment available. Off-campus job opportunities are excellent. **Financial Aid Statistics:** 100% freshmen, 98% undergrads receive need-based scholarship or grant aid. 30% freshmen, 21% undergrads receive non-need-based scholarship or grant aid. 58% freshmen, 69% undergrads receive need-based self-help aid. 21% freshmen, 16% undergrads receive athletic scholarships. 97% freshmen, 92% undergrads receive any aid. 72% undergrads borrow to pay for school. Average cumulative indebtedness $15,296. **Criteria for awarding institutional aid:** *Non-need-based:* academics, alumni affiliation, art, athletics, job skills, minority status, music/drama, religious affiliation, state/district residency.

MILLIKIN UNIVERSITY

1184 West Main Street, Decatur, IL 62522-2084
Phone: 217-424-6210 · **Financial Aid Phone:** 217-424-6317
E-mail: admis@millikin.edu · **CEEB Code:** 1470
Fax: 217-425-4669 · **Website:** www.millikin.edu · **ACT Code:** 1080

This private school, affiliated with the Presbyterian Church, was founded in 1901. It has a 75-acre campus.

RATINGS

Admissions Selectivity Rating: 82   **Fire Safety Rating:** 98

STUDENTS AND FACULTY

Enrollment: 2,082. **Student Body:** 59% female, 41% male, 13% out-of-state, 1% international (19 countries represented). Asian 1%, African American 14%, Caucasian 74%, Hispanic 6%, Native American <1% **Retention and Graduation:** 51% freshmen graduate within 4 years. 61% freshmen graduate within 6 years. 19% grads go on to further study within 1 year. 13% grads pursue arts and sciences degrees. 1% grads pursue law degrees. 3% grads pursue business degrees. 1% grads pursue medical degrees. **Faculty:** 146 full-time faculty, 79% hold PhDs, 51% are members of minority groups, 7% are women. 0% of classes are taught by teaching assistants.

ACADEMICS

Degrees: bachelor's, master's. **Classes:** Most classes have 10–19 students. Most lab/discussion sessions have 10–19 students. **Majors with Highest Enrollment:** Registered Nursing/Registered Nurse; Drama and Dramatics/Theatre Arts; Music Performance. **Special Study Options:** Accelerated program, double major, exchange student program (domestic), honors program, independent study, internships, student-designed major, study abroad, teacher certification program. **Honors programs:** Presidential Scholars are Millikin's best and brightest students; selection is based upon outstanding academic performance and demonstrated leadership; they receive a full tuition scholarship, renewable for up to four years. Millikin's Honors Program introduces students to college-level scholarship, research, critical thinking, and writing during the freshman and sophomore years; classes are taught as seminars - sessions involving intense discussion and requiring active participation; Millikin's strongest juniors are invited to join the next phase of the Honors Program to become James Millikin Scholars.; James Millikin Scholars Program; Honors Program. **Disability Services:** Special programs offered to physically disabled students include note-taking services, reader services, tape recorders, tutors. **Career services:** Alumni network, alumni services, career/job search classes, career assessment, internships. Career services highlights include Millikin's Blue Connection, a retail art gallery, which serves as the practical laboratory for Millikin's innovative Art of Entrepreneurship curriculum. This gallery sells, original art, produced by Millikin alumni, faculty, staff and students. The Blue Connection retail art store is fully operated by Millikin students, a majority of which are from Art, Business and Music programs. The talents of the various majors are integrated with the concept of business ownership. The success of the venture is in the hands of the Millikin students.

FACILITIES

Housing: Coed dorms, special housing for disabled students, men's dorms, special housing for international students, women's dorms, fraternity/sorority housing, apartments for married students, apartments for single students, Wellness HousingLearning Communities. 66% of campus accessible to physically disabled. **Special Academic Facilities/Equipment:** Art galleries, art museum, fitness/wellness center, recording studio, indoor sports center, greenhouse, observatory, 2 indoor sports centers, 2000 seat performance center. **Computers:** 75% of classrooms, 75% of dorms, 100% of libraries, 100% of dining areas, 100% of student union, 5% of common outdoor areas have wireless network access. Students can register for classes online. Administrative functions (other than registration) can be performed online.

CAMPUS LIFE

Environment: City. **Activities:** Choral groups, concert band, dance, drama/theater, jazz band, literary magazine, music ensembles, musical theater, opera, pep band, radio station, student government, student newspaper, student-run film society, symphony orchestra, International Student Organization, Model UN. 96 registered organizations, 7 honor societies, 2 religious organizations. 5 fraternities, 4 sororities. **Athletics (Intercollegiate):** *Men:* baseball, basketball, cheerleading, cross-country, football, golf, soccer, swimming, track/field (outdoor), track/field (indoor). *Women:* basketball, cheerleading, cross-country, golf, soccer, softball, swimming, tennis, track/field (outdoor), track/field (indoor), volleyball. **On-Campus Highlights:** ADM-Scovill Hall, Perkinson Music Center, Albert Taylor Theatre, Decatur Indoor Sports Center, Kirkland Fine Arts Center.

ADMISSIONS

Freshman Academic Profile: Average high school GPA 3.299. 14% in top 10% of high school class, 40% in top 25% of high school class, 71% in top 50% of high school class. 91% from public high schools. SAT Math middle 50% range 380-620. SAT Critical Reading middle 50% range 430-570. SAT Writing middle 50% range 390-550. ACT middle 50% range 19-26. Minimum internet-based TOEFL 79. Minimum paper TOEFL 550. **Basis for Candidate Selection:** *Very important factors considered include:* rigor of secondary school record. *Important factors considered include:* Class rank, academic GPA, recommendation(s), standardized test scores, interview. *Other factors considered include:* alumni/ae relation, character/personal qualities, extracurricular activities, level of applicant's interest, talent/ability, volunteer work, work experience. **Freshman Admission Requirements:** High school diploma is required and GED is accepted. **Freshman Admission Statistics:** 3,255 applied, 63% admitted, 23% enrolled. **Transfer Admission Requirements:** High school transcript, college transcript(s), Minimum college GPA of 2.0 required. Lowest grade transferable C-. **General Admission Information:** Notification on a rolling basis, beginning on or about 9/15. Nonfall registration accepted. Admission may be deferred for a maximum of 1 year. Credit and/or placement offered for CEEB Advanced Placement tests.

COSTS AND FINANCIAL AID

Annual tuition $27,852. Room and board $8,950. Required fees $892. Average book expense $1,000. **Required Forms and Deadlines:** FAFSA. **Notification of Awards:** Applicants will be notified of awards on a rolling basis beginning 3/15. **Types of Aid:** *Need-based scholarships/grants:* Federal Pell, SEOG, state scholarships/grants, private scholarships, the school's own gift aid. *Loans:* Subsidized Stafford, Unsubsidized Stafford, PLUS, Federal Perkins, state loans. *Student Employment:* Federal Work-Study Program available. Institutional employment available. Highest amount earned per year from on-campus jobs $4,285. Off-campus job opportunities are good. **Financial Aid Statistics:** 90% freshmen, 90% undergrads receive need-based scholarship or grant aid. 99% freshmen, 92% undergrads receive non-need-based scholarship or grant aid. 80% freshmen, 83% undergrads receive need-based self-help aid. 0% freshmen, 0% undergrads receive athletic scholarships. 100% freshmen, 98% undergrads receive any aid. 81% undergrads borrow to pay for school. Average cumulative indebtedness $26,965. **Criteria for awarding institutional aid:** *Non-need-based:* academics, alumni affiliation, art, leadership, minority status, music/drama.

MILLS COLLEGE

5000 MacArthur Boulevard, Oakland, CA 94613
Phone: 510-430-2135 · **Financial Aid Phone:** 510-430-2000
E-mail: admission@mills.edu · **CEEB Code:** 4485
Fax: 510-430-3314 · **Website:** www.mills.edu · **ACT Code:** 4485

This private school was founded in 1852. It has a 135-acre campus.

RATINGS

Admissions Selectivity Rating: 86   Fire Safety Rating: 71

STUDENTS AND FACULTY

Enrollment: 909. **Student Body:** 100% female, 0% male, 24% out-of-state, 1% international (7 countries represented). Asian 11%, African American 7%, Caucasian 45%, Hispanic 23%, Native American 1%
Retention and Graduation: 71% freshmen return for sophomore year. 60% freshmen graduate within 4 years. 24% grads go on to further study within 1 year. 12% grads pursue arts and sciences degrees. 2% grads pursue law degrees. 1% grads pursue business degrees. 1% grads pursue medical degrees. **Faculty:** 107 full-time faculty, 93% hold PhDs, 68% are members of minority groups, 31% are women. 0% of classes are taught by teaching assistants.

ACADEMICS

Degrees: bachelor's, certificate, master's, post-bachelor's certificate. **Classes:** Most classes have 10–19 students. Most lab/discussion sessions have 10–19 students. **Majors with Highest Enrollment:** Psychology; English Language and Literature; Biology/Biological Sciences. **Special Study Options:** cooperative education program, cross-registration, double major, exchange student program (domestic), independent study, internships, liberal arts/career combination, student-designed major, study abroad, teacher certification program. **Combined degree programs:** BA/MA, BA/MEng, BA/MBA; BA/MPP; BA/MA/Teaching Credential. **Disability Services:** Special programs offered to physically

disabled students include note-taking services, reader services, tape recorders, tutors. **Career services:** Alumni network, alumni services, career/job search classes, career assessment, internships, regional alumni. Career services highlights include our expanding internship services program within career services. In 2006, we hired a dedicated internship coordinator for the campus and this position has focused on increasing access to local and national internships for our student population. We have also worked to track student success related to internship completion and to make the process more user friendly.

FACILITIES

Housing: Coed dorms, special housing for disabled students, women's dorms, apartments for married students, cooperative housing, apartments for single students, Wellness Housing, Theme Housing, Resumer Student Housing. 90% of campus accessible to physically disabled. **Special Academic Facilities/Equipment:** Art Museum, Center for contemporary Music, on-campus elementary school, botanical gardens. **Computers:** 100% of classrooms, 100% of dorms, 100% of libraries, 100% of dining areas, 100% of student union, 100% of common outdoor areas have wireless network access. Students can register for classes online. Administrative functions (other than registration) can be performed online.

CAMPUS LIFE

Environment: Metropolis. **Activities:** Choral groups, dance, drama/theater, literary magazine, music ensembles, musical theater, radio station, student government, student newspaper, student-run film society, yearbook, Campus Ministries, International Student Organization, Model UN. 47 registered organizations, 2 honor societies, 4 religious organizations. **Athletics (Intercollegiate):** *Women:* crew/rowing, cross-country, soccer, swimming, tennis, track/field (outdoor), volleyball. **On-Campus Highlights:** The Mills College Art Museum, Haas Pavilion & Trefethen Aquatic Center, Rothwell Student Center, Lorrie Lokey Graduate School of Business, Littlefield Concert Hall. **Environmental Initiatives:** Mills recycles, composts and reuses all consumer materials to the extent possible. www.mills.edu/green/recycling Mills students, staff and faculty participate in Recycle Mania. Mills builds to LEED standards of silver or higher. Mills has been awarded a LEED Platinum for new science building and has just broken ground on a business school designed to achieve LEED Gold. Mills encourages the use and provides access to public and shared transportation by offering a Mills Shuttle service, car share and web based carpool system. Public Transit passes available to all undergraduate students, funded through student fees.

ADMISSIONS

Freshman Academic Profile: Average high school GPA 3.66. 29% in top 10% of high school class, 64% in top 25% of high school class, 97% in top 50% of high school class. 85% from public high schools. SAT Math middle 50% range 490-610. SAT Critical Reading middle 50% range 530-640. SAT Writing middle 50% range 520-610. ACT middle 50% range 23-29. Minimum internet-based TOEFL 80. Minimum paper TOEFL 550. **Basis for Candidate Selection:** *Very important factors considered include:* rigor of secondary school record. *Important factors considered include:* Class rank, application essay, academic GPA, recommendation(s), standardized test scores, character/personal qualities, extracurricular activities. *Other factors considered include:* alumni/ae relation, first generation, interview, level of applicant's interest, talent/ability, volunteer work, work experience. **Freshman Admission Requirements:** High school diploma is required and GED is accepted. *Academic units required:* 4 English, 3 mathematics, 2 science, (2 science labs), 2 foreign language, 2 social studies, 2 history. **Freshman Admission Statistics:** 1,869 applied, 76% admitted, 13% enrolled. **Transfer Admission Requirements:** High school transcript, college transcript(s), essay or personal statement, Lowest grade transferable C-. **General Admission Information:** Application Fee $50. Regular application deadline 8/1. Notification on a rolling basis, beginning on or about 11/1. Nonfall registration accepted. Admission may be deferred for a maximum of 1 year. Credit and/or placement offered for CEEB Advanced Placement tests.

COSTS AND FINANCIAL AID

Annual tuition $41,618. Room and board $12,118. Required fees $1,300. Average book expense $1,490. **Required Forms and Deadlines:** FAFSA, Institution's own financial aid form, State aid form. **Notification of Awards:** Applicants will be notified of awards on a rolling basis beginning 3/1. **Types of Aid:** *Need-based scholarships/grants:* Federal Pell, SEOG, state scholarships/grants, private scholarships, the school's own gift aid. *Loans:* Subsidized Stafford, Unsubsidized Stafford, PLUS, Federal Perkins, college/university loans from institutional funds. *Student Employment:* Federal Work-Study Program available. Institutional employment available. Highest amount earned per year from on-campus jobs $2,700. Off-campus job opportunities are excellent. **Financial Aid Statistics:** 97% freshmen, 96% undergrads receive need-based scholarship or grant aid. 6% freshmen, 4% undergrads receive non-need-based scholarship or grant aid. 88% freshmen, 88% undergrads receive need-based self-help aid. 0% freshmen, 0% undergrads receive athletic scholarships. 88% freshmen, 86% undergrads receive any aid. 68% undergrads borrow to pay for school. Average cumulative indebtedness $24,861. **Criteria for awarding institutional aid:** *Non-need-based:* academics, leadership, minority status, music/drama.

MILLSAPS COLLEGE

Best 380

1701 North State Street, Jackson, MS 39210
Phone: 601-974-1050 • **Financial Aid Phone:** 800-352-1050
E-mail: admissions@millsaps.edu • **CEEB Code:** 1471
Fax: 601-974-1059 • **Website:** www.millsaps.edu • **ACT Code:** 2212

This private school, affiliated with the Methodist Church, was founded in 1890. It has a 100-acre campus.

RATINGS

Admissions Selectivity Rating: 84   **Fire Safety Rating:** 84

STUDENTS AND FACULTY

Enrollment: 760. **Student Body:** 49% female, 51% male, 55% out-of-state, 4% international (16 countries represented). Asian 4%, African American 11%, Caucasian 74%, Hispanic 2%, Native American 1%
Retention and Graduation: 80% freshmen return for sophomore year. 62% freshmen graduate within 4 years. 44% grads go on to further study within 1 year. 15% grads pursue arts and sciences degrees. 6% grads pursue law degrees. 9% grads pursue business degrees. 5% grads pursue medical degrees. **Faculty:** 82 full-time faculty, 95% hold PhDs, 49% are members of minority groups, 12% are women. 0% of classes are taught by teaching assistants.

ACADEMICS

Degrees: bachelor's, master's. **Classes:** Most classes have 10–19 students. Most lab/discussion sessions have 10–19 students. **Majors with Highest Enrollment:** Biology/Biological Sciences; Psychology; Business Administration, Management and Operations. **Special Study Options:** Accelerated program, double major, honors program, independent study, internships, liberal arts/career combination, student-designed major, study abroad, teacher certification program, The Millsaps Faith & Work Initiative offers an array of curricular and extracurricular programs to help students discern their vocation or call in life and to pursue that call with passion, integrity and an eye toward the needs of the world. Faith & Work options include service-learning courses and the Meaning of Work course, immersion and service experiences, discussion programs with faculty and professionals, leadership and service clubs, internships, and public lecture series. Other interdisciplinary programs or concentrations are available in American studies, Christian education, environmental studies, film studies, human services, international studies, women's and gender studies, and church music. Undergraduate research is available in most academic departments, including field research opportunities in the Pacific Northwest, Yellowstone, the Mexico, and Europe. Millsaps' nonprofit biocultural reserve on 4500 acres in the Yucatan Peninsula of Mexico offers multi-disciplinary options for study, including archaeology, business, ecology, education, geology, history, literature, math and socio-cultural anthropology. Students may also choose among other STUDY ABROAD programs developed by Millsaps faculty—in Albania, Belgium, China, Costa Rica, England, France, Germany, Ghana, Greece, Ireland, Israel, Italy, Japan, Mexico (Yucatan), and Tanzania. Pre-professional programs include dentistry, engineering, law, medicine, ministry, and social work. Millsaps students may work towards dual degrees in engineering, applied science or nursing through agreements with Auburn University, Columbia University, Vanderbilt University, Washington University, and the University of Mississippi Medical Health Center. Other distinctive programs include the Ford Teaching Fellows program (research and internships for students interested in college teaching), and the Weiner Pre-Medical Fellows program (summer research). **Honors programs:** The Honors Program, Ford Teaching Fellows program (research and internships for students interested in college teaching), Weiner Pre-Medical Fellows Program (summer research), Lilly Fellows Faith and Work Initiative (connecting individual passions with learning, meaning, service, and career) **Combined degree programs:** BA/MBA-Millsaps, 3-2 BSN nursing-Univ.of Miss., 4-2 MSN nursing-Vanderbilt.
Disability Services: Special programs offered to physically disabled students include note-taking services, reader services, tutors. **Career services:** Alumni network, alumni services, career assessment, internships, regional alumni. Career services highlights include The Millsaps Career Center which sponsors an internship-for-credit program designed to assist students with career choices and relate student work experiences to their education. Initially, the Career Center offers orientation and internship search assistance. During the internships, students maintain work logs, write monthly journals of their work experiences, and receive monthly feedback from the Career Center. Interns also obtain written evaluations from their supervisors and write final reports, evaluating their work sites and relating their work experiences to their education and career objectives.

FACILITIES

Housing: Coed dorms, special housing for disabled students, women's dorms, fraternity/sorority housing, Wellness Housing, Theme Housing. Our theme housing is community service housing. 90% of campus accessible to physically disabled. **Special Academic Facilities/Equipment:** Millsaps' W.M. Keck Center for Instrumental and Biochemical Comparative Archaeology is the only undergraduate facility of its kind in the world. The new multi-disciplinary research laboratory provides undergraduate students with the opportunity to explore complex archeological questions using advanced bioanalytical and biochemical techniques. 4-6 Keck Fellows assist each year in gathering the artifacts studied in the lab from the College's archaeological field programs in Yucatán, Mexico, and northern Albania. The lab houses an inductively-coupled plasma spectrometer with laser ablation, a gas-chromotography spectrometer, a liquid-chromatography spectrometer, and a portable x-ray fluorescence spectrometer. In addition, the college's other labs include a unique array of spectrometers for measuring atomic absorption, infrared transitional modes, nuclear magnetic resonance, and other forms of energy; high performance chromatographs for separation and identification of compounds; electrophoresis instruments for analyzing biomolecules and other biological materials; and an inert atmosphere reaction chamber. Other facilities include a state-of-the-art molecular biology/functional genomics research laboratory; a fluorescence microscopy suite and imaging facility; a GIS workstation with Rockware and Arcview 9.1 GIS Software; a specially-designed automated 24-hour food monitoring system for rats; a microsurgical lab for animal surgeries; an on-campus hydrogeologic monitoring station to measure the water table and water levels in four on-campus wells; and a computational modeling lab for math, chemistry and physics students which provides numerical and graphical solutions in three dimensions. The College Sorbent and Environmental Laboratory provides undergraduates with opportunities for oil spill and stormwater remediation research. Another unique facility is the college's 4,000-acre biocultural reserve and learning center in the state of Yucatan, Mexico. Here students excavate ancient Mayan archaeological sites, conduct environmental studies of the jungle, research the biology and geology of the area, and live in a sustainable solar-powered facility constructed of materials inspired by the native Mayan architecture. Millsaps' Yucatan program also includes a newly-renovated teaching and living facility for international business studies which is located in the large city of Merida. In addition, Millsaps' newly-renovated digital Language Resource Center has been equipped with 25 network computers and satellite connections for international programming.
Computers: 100% of classrooms, 100% of dorms, 100% of libraries, 100% of dining areas, 100% of student union, 100% of common outdoor areas have wireless network access. Students can register for classes online. Administrative functions (other than registration) can be performed online.

CAMPUS LIFE

Environment: Metropolis. **Activities:** Choral groups, dance, drama/theater, literary magazine, music ensembles, musical theater, student government, student newspaper, yearbook, Campus Ministries, International Student Organization, Model UN. 85 registered organizations, 28 honor societies, 12 religious organizations. 6 fraternities, 6 sororities. **Athletics (Intercollegiate):** *Men:* baseball, basketball, cross-country, football, golf, lacrosse, soccer, tennis, track/field (outdoor). *Women:* basketball, cross-country, golf, lacrosse, soccer, softball, tennis, track/field (outdoor), volleyball. **On-Campus Highlights:** Hall Activities Center (fitness/athletic facility), Campbell College Center (student activities), The Bowl (outdoor green space/campus center), Millsaps Wilson Library (study center), Fraternity Row, The Campbell College Center includes a cafeteria, a coffeehouse, live entertainment and game areas, and a bookstore. The Bowl is a natural, outdoor space in the heart of the campus where students congregate between classes to relax and to participate in outdoor activities. **Environmental Initiatives:** The College supports the Center for Research and Learning at the H. Moyers Biocultural Reserve operated by Kaxil Kiuic, Yucatan, Mexico. The Center is an off the grid facility built using sustainable design and technology. Applied Ecological Design, taught by Millsaps faculty at the Center, focuses on topics critical to planning, designing, and creating a sustainable home including sustainable construction, solar power, energy efficiency, water supply, waste and wastewater management, and agriculture/ permaculture; coursework includes on-site project experimentation, design, and construction.

ADMISSIONS

Freshman Academic Profile: Average high school GPA 3.68. 55% from public high schools. SAT Math middle 50% range 520-630. SAT Critical Reading middle 50% range 510-640. ACT middle 50% range 23-29. Minimum internet-based TOEFL 80. Minimum paper TOEFL 550. **Basis for Candidate Selection:** *Very important factors considered include:* academic GPA, rigor of secondary school record, standardized test scores, character/personal qualities. *Important factors considered include:* Class rank, application essay, recommendation(s), extracurricular activities, interview, talent/ability, volunteer work. *Other factors considered include:* work experience. **Freshman Admission Requirements:** High school diploma is required and GED is accepted. *Academic units required:* 4 English, 3 mathematics, 3 science, (1 science labs), 2 social studies, 2 history. **Freshman Admission Statistics:** 2,861 applied,

57% admitted, 14% enrolled. **Transfer Admission Requirements:** college transcript(s), essay or personal statement, standardized test scores, statement of good standing from prior institution(s). Minimum college GPA of 2.75 required. Lowest grade transferable C. **General Admission Information:** Notification on a rolling basis, beginning on or about 10/1. Nonfall registration accepted. Admission may be deferred for a maximum of 1 year. Credit and/or placement offered for CEEB Advanced Placement tests.

COSTS AND FINANCIAL AID
Annual tuition $31,872. Room and board $11,878. Required fees $2,110. Average book expense $1,100. **Required Forms and Deadlines:** FAFSA. **Notification of Awards:** Applicants will be notified of awards on a rolling basis beginning 3/15. **Types of Aid:** *Need-based scholarships/grants:* Federal Pell, SEOG, state scholarships/grants, private scholarships, the school's own gift aid. *Loans:* Subsidized Stafford, Unsubsidized Stafford, PLUS, Federal Perkins, college/university loans from institutional funds. *Student Employment:* Federal Work-Study Program available. Institutional employment available. Highest amount earned per year from on-campus jobs $8,429. Off-campus job opportunities are good. **Financial Aid Statistics:** 100% freshmen, 100% undergrads receive need-based scholarship or grant aid. 26% freshmen, 20% undergrads receive non-need-based scholarship or grant aid. 70% freshmen, 75% undergrads receive need-based self-help aid. 0% freshmen, 0% undergrads receive athletic scholarships. 100% freshmen, 98% undergrads receive any aid. 59% undergrads borrow to pay for school. Average cumulative indebtedness $25,538. **Criteria for awarding institutional aid:** *Non-need-based:* academics, art, leadership, music/drama, religious affiliation.

MILWAUKEE INSTITUTE OF ART AND DESIGN

273 East Erie Street, Milwaukee, WI 53202
Phone: 414-847-3200 · **Financial Aid Phone:** 414-291-8272
E-mail: admissions@miad.edu · **CEEB Code:** 1506
Fax: 414-291-8077 · **Website:** 273 E. Erie Street · **ACT Code:** 4701

This private school was founded in 1974. It has a 2-acre campus.

RATINGS
Admissions Selectivity Rating: 64   **Fire Safety Rating:** 69

STUDENTS AND FACULTY
Enrollment: 643. **Student Body:** 50% female, 50% male, 37% out-of-state, 4% international (3 countries represented). Asian 3%, African American 3%, Caucasian 80%, Hispanic 9%, Native American 1%
Retention and Graduation: 81% freshmen return for sophomore year. 38% freshmen graduate within 4 years. 46% freshmen graduate within 6 years. 6% grads go on to further study within 1 year. 4% grads pursue arts and sciences degrees. **Faculty:** 33 full-time faculty, 67% hold PhDs, 42% are members of minority groups, 6% are women. 0% of classes are taught by teaching assistants.

ACADEMICS
Degrees: bachelor's. **Classes:** Most classes have 10–19 students. Most lab/discussion sessions have fewer than 10 students. **Majors with Highest Enrollment:** Industrial and Product Design; Graphic Design; Illustration. **Special Study Options:** double major, exchange student program (domestic), independent study, internships, study abroad. **Disability Services:** Special programs offered to physically disabled students include note-taking services, reader services, tape recorders, tutors. **Career services:** Alumni network, alumni services, career assessment, internships.

FACILITIES
Housing: Coed dorms. 100% of campus accessible to physically disabled. **Special Academic Facilities/Equipment:** Eisner Museum of Advertising and Design, Brook Stevens Gallery of Industrial design, Frederick Layton Gallery.

CAMPUS LIFE
Environment: Metropolis. **Activities:** drama/theater, literary magazine, student government, student newspaper. 12 registered organizations, 2 honor societies, 1 religious organization.

ADMISSIONS
Freshman Academic Profile: Average high school GPA 3.04. 6% in top 10% of high school class, 25% in top 25% of high school class, 56% in top 50% of high school class. Minimum paper TOEFL 550. **Basis for Candidate Selection:** *Very important factors considered include:* application essay, academic GPA, character/personal qualities, interview, level of applicant's interest, talent/ability. *Other factors considered include:* Class rank, recommendation(s), rigor of secondary school record, standardized test scores, extracurricular activities, volunteer work, work experience. **Freshman Admission Requirements:** High school diploma is required and GED is accepted. **Freshman Admission Statistics:** 416 applied, 75% admitted, 62% enrolled. **Transfer Admission**

Requirements: essay or personal statement, interview, Minimum college GPA of 2.0 required. Lowest grade transferable C. **General Admission Information:** Application Fee $25. Notification on a rolling basis, beginning on or about 9/1. Nonfall registration accepted. Admission may be deferred for a maximum of 2 years. Neither credit nor placement offered for CEEB Advanced Placement tests.

COSTS AND FINANCIAL AID
Required Forms and Deadlines: FAFSA. **Notification of Awards:** Applicants will be notified of awards on a rolling basis beginning 4/1. **Types of Aid:** *Need-based scholarships/grants:* Federal Pell, SEOG, state scholarships/grants, private scholarships, the school's own gift aid. *Loans:* Direct Subsidized Stafford, Direct Unsubsidized Stafford, Direct PLUS. *Student Employment:* Federal Work-Study Program available. Institutional employment available. Highest amount earned per year from on-campus jobs $1,200. Off-campus job opportunities are good. **Financial Aid Statistics:** 99% freshmen, 98% undergrads receive need-based scholarship or grant aid. 9% freshmen, 6% undergrads receive non-need-based scholarship or grant aid. 91% freshmen, 94% undergrads receive need-based self-help aid. 0% freshmen, 0% undergrads receive athletic scholarships. 95% freshmen, 92% undergrads receive any aid. 100% undergrads borrow to pay for school. Average cumulative indebtedness $322,900. **Criteria for awarding institutional aid:** *Non-need-based:* academics, art.

MILWAUKEE SCHOOL OF ENGINEERING

1025 North Broadway, Milwaukee, WI 53202-3109
Phone: 414-277-6763 · **Financial Aid Phone:** 800-778-7223
E-mail: explore@msoe.edu · **CEEB Code:** 1476
Fax: 414-277-7475 · **Website:** www.msoe.edu · **ACT Code:** 4616

This private school was founded in 1903. It has a 15-acre campus.

RATINGS
Admissions Selectivity Rating: 82   **Fire Safety Rating:** 98

STUDENTS AND FACULTY
Enrollment: 2,596. **Student Body:** 24% female, 76% male, 33% out-of-state, 12% international (31 countries represented). Asian 3%, African American 2%, Caucasian 69%, Hispanic 4%, Native American <1%
Retention and Graduation: 82% freshmen return for sophomore year. 33% freshmen graduate within 4 years. 56% freshmen graduate within 6 years. 7% grads go on to further study within 1 year. 1% grads pursue law degrees. 3% grads pursue business degrees. **Faculty:** 134 full-time faculty, 77% hold PhDs, 30% are members of minority groups, 11% are women. 0% of classes are taught by teaching assistants.

ACADEMICS
Degrees: bachelor's, master's. **Classes:** Most classes have 20–29 students. Most lab/discussion sessions have 10–19 students. **Majors with Highest Enrollment:** Architectural Engineering; Electrical and Electronics Engineering; Mechanical Engineering. **Special Study Options:** Accelerated program, distance learning, double major, dual enrollment, English as a Second Language (ESL), independent study, internships, study abroad, BS in international business and in electrical and mechanical engineering with Fachhochschule Lubeck, Germany. All students may apply to study at Czech Technical University, Prague, Czech Republic. **Combined degree programs:** BA/MEng, Architectural Eng. and Construction Management. **Disability Services:** Special programs offered to physically disabled students include note-taking services, reader services, tape recorders, tutors. **Career services:** Alumni network, alumni services, career/job search classes, career assessment, internships, regional alumni. Career services highlights include internship experience for approximatly 85% of graduates.

FACILITIES
Housing: Coed dorms, special housing for disabled students. 85% of campus accessible to physically disabled. **Special Academic Facilities/Equipment:** Grohmann Museum, Kern Center Health, Wellness and Recreation Facility, Rader School of Business, Johnson Controls Software Engineering Lab, Fluid Power Institute, Rapid Prototyping Center, Applied Technology Center, Center for BioMolecular Modeling, Warren P. Knowles Nursing Lab, Harley Davidson Design Lab, Johnson Controls Environmental Systems Lab **Computers:** 100% of classrooms, 10% of dorms, 100% of libraries, 100% of dining areas, 100% of student union, 100% of common outdoor areas have wireless network access. Students can register for classes online. Administrative functions (other than registration) can be performed online. Undergraduates are required to own a computer. ·

CAMPUS LIFE
Environment: Metropolis. **Activities:** dance, drama/theater, jazz band, literary magazine, pep band, radio station, student government, symphony orchestra,

Campus Ministries, International Student Organization. 61 registered organizations, 6 honor societies, 4 religious organizations. 3 fraternities, 3 sororities. **Athletics (Intercollegiate):** *Men:* baseball, basketball, cheerleading, crew/rowing, cross-country, golf, ice hockey, lacrosse, soccer, tennis, track/field (outdoor), track/field (indoor), volleyball, wrestling. *Women:* basketball, cheerleading, cross-country, golf, soccer, softball, tennis, track/field (outdoor), track/field (indoor), volleyball. **On-Campus Highlights:** Kern Center—Health and Wellness Center, Student Life and Campus Center (dining and game room), The Grohmann Museum, Rapid Prototyping Center, School of Nursing Simulation Lab. **Environmental Initiatives:** In the Fall of 2010, MSOE initiated a compostable service ware program in the school's café. It included replacing hot and cold beverage cups, plates and soup bowls. At the time, there was also a dedicated collection stream setup to help divert an estimated 150 cubic yards of waste per year from going into local landfills. Efforts have been made to increase MSOE's recycling rate from 10% in 6/09 to over 60% in 1/11. In January of 2011, MSOE implemented a chemical inventory database for all chemicals on campus. The database enables the school to bar code and track chemical containers on campus. It also provides an opportunity for chemical surplus sharing across campus. The system is expected to reduce redundant purchasing and foster waste minimization on campus. Installed $320,000 of renewable energy generation capacity on campus 2008–2011.

ADMISSIONS

Freshman Academic Profile: Average high school GPA 3.62. 92% from public high schools. SAT Math middle 50% range 580-680. SAT Critical Reading middle 50% range 550-670. ACT middle 50% range 25-30. Minimum internet-based TOEFL 82. Minimum paper TOEFL 550. **Basis for Candidate Selection:** *Very important factors considered include:* academic GPA, rigor of secondary school record, standardized test scores. *Other factors considered include:* recommendation(s), character/personal qualities, extracurricular activities, level of applicant's interest, volunteer work, work experience. **Freshman Admission Requirements:** High school diploma is required and GED is accepted. *Academic units required:* 4 English, 4 mathematics, 2 science, (0 science labs), 0 foreign language, 0 social studies, 0 history, 0 academic electives. **Freshman Admission Statistics:** 2,574 applied, 69% admitted, 33% enrolled. **Transfer Admission Requirements:** college transcript(s), Minimum college GPA of 2.5 required. Lowest grade transferable C. **General Admission Information:** Application Fee $25. Notification on a rolling basis, beginning on or about 10/15. Nonfall registration accepted. Admission may be deferred for a maximum of 2 year. Placement offered for CEEB Advanced Placement tests.

COSTS AND FINANCIAL AID

Annual tuition $34,890. Room and board $8,613. Required fees $1,650. Average book expense $1,200. **Required Forms and Deadlines:** FAFSA. **Notification of Awards:** Applicants will be notified of awards on a rolling basis beginning 3/1. **Types of Aid:** *Need-based scholarships/grants:* Federal Pell, SEOG, state scholarships/grants, private scholarships, the school's own gift aid. *Loans:* Subsidized Stafford, Unsubsidized Stafford, PLUS, Federal Perkins, state loans. *Student Employment:* Federal Work-Study Program available. Institutional employment available. Highest amount earned per year from on-campus jobs $14,141. Off-campus job opportunities are excellent. **Financial Aid Statistics:** 100% freshmen, 100% undergrads receive need-based scholarship or grant aid. 20% freshmen, 14% undergrads receive non-need-based scholarship or grant aid. 77% freshmen, 83% undergrads receive need-based self-help aid. 0% freshmen, 0% undergrads receive athletic scholarships. 94% freshmen, 93% undergrads receive any aid. 85% undergrads borrow to pay for school. Average cumulative indebtedness $28,338. **Criteria for awarding institutional aid:** *Non-need-based:* academics.

MINNEAPOLIS COLLEGE OF ART AND DESIGN

2501 Stevens Avenue, Minneapolis, MN 55404
Phone: 612-874-3760 · **Financial Aid Phone:** 612-874-3782
E-mail: admissions@mcad.edu · **CEEB Code:** 6411
Fax: 612-874-3701 · **Website:** www.mcad.edu • **ACT Code:** 2130

This private school was founded in 1886. It has a 3-acre campus.

RATINGS

Admissions Selectivity Rating: 80   **Fire Safety Rating:** 60*

STUDENTS AND FACULTY

Enrollment: 594. **Student Body:** 61% female, 39% male, 36% out-of-state, 1% international (10 countries represented). Asian 6%, African American 2%, Caucasian 72%, Hispanic 6%, Native American 1%
Retention and Graduation: 70% freshmen return for sophomore year. 10% grads go on to further study within 1 year. 10% grads pursue arts and sciences degrees. **Faculty:** 42 full-time faculty, 100% hold PhDs, 31% are members of minority groups. 0% of classes are taught by teaching assistants.

ACADEMICS

Degrees: bachelor's, master's, post-bachelor's certificate. **Classes:** Most classes have 10–19 students. **Special Study Options:** cooperative education program, cross-registration, distance learning, independent study, internships, study abroad, **Off-Campus Study:** Arts Program in New York. Co-Op Programs: Arts. **Disability Services:** Special programs offered to physically disabled students include note-taking services, reader services, tape recorders, tutors. **Career services:** alumni services, career assessment, internships.

FACILITIES

Housing: Coed dorms, apartments for single students. 95% of campus accessible to physically disabled. **Special Academic Facilities/Equipment:** Art gallery.

CAMPUS LIFE

Environment: Metropolis. **Activities:** radio station, student government, student-run film society. **On-Campus Highlights:** Main gallery, Student Center.

ADMISSIONS

Freshman Academic Profile: Average high school GPA 3.25. 89% from public high schools. SAT Math middle 50% range 430-604. SAT Critical Reading middle 50% range 503-680. SAT Writing middle 50% range 467-644. ACT middle 50% range 21-27. Minimum paper TOEFL 550. **Basis for Candidate Selection:** *Very important factors considered include:* application essay, academic GPA, recommendation(s), standardized test scores, talent/ability. *Important factors considered include:* character/personal qualities, interview. **Freshman Admission Requirements:** High school diploma is required and GED is accepted. **Freshman Admission Statistics:** 406 applied, 64% admitted, 33% enrolled. **Transfer Admission Requirements:** High school transcript, college transcript(s), essay or personal statement, standardized test scores, Minimum college GPA of 2.5 required. Lowest grade transferable C-. **General Admission Information:** Application Fee $50. Regular application deadline 5/1. Nonfall registration accepted. Admission may be deferred for a maximum of 1 semester. Credit offered for CEEB Advanced Placement tests.

COSTS AND FINANCIAL AID

Annual tuition $31,450. Room and board $4,650. Required fees $200. Average book expense $2,724. **Required Forms and Deadlines:** FAFSA. **Notification of Awards:** Applicants will be notified of awards on a rolling basis beginning 4/1. **Types of Aid:** *Need-based scholarships/grants:* Federal Pell, SEOG, state scholarships/grants, private scholarships, the school's own gift aid. *Loans:* Subsidized Stafford, Unsubsidized Stafford, PLUS, Federal Perkins, state loans. *Student Employment:* Federal Work-Study Program available. Institutional employment available. Highest amount earned per year from on-campus jobs $1,656. Off-campus job opportunities are good. **Financial Aid Statistics:** 99% freshmen, 96% undergrads receive need-based scholarship or grant aid. 3% freshmen, 4% undergrads receive non-need-based scholarship or grant aid. 97% freshmen, 95% undergrads receive need-based self-help aid. 0% freshmen, 0% undergrads receive athletic scholarships. 85% undergrads borrow to pay for school. Average cumulative indebtedness $26,001. **Criteria for awarding institutional aid:** *Non-need-based:* academics, alumni affiliation, art, leadership.

MINNESOTA STATE UNIVERSITY, MANKATO

122 Taylor Center, Mankato, MN 56001
Phone: 507-389-1822 · **Financial Aid Phone:** 507-389-1866
E-mail: admissions@mnsu.edu · **CEEB Code:** 6677
Fax: 507-389-1511 · **Website:** www.mnsu.edu • **ACT Code:** 2126

This public school was founded in 1868. It has a 354-acre campus.

RATINGS

Admissions Selectivity Rating: 76   **Fire Safety Rating:** 68

STUDENTS AND FACULTY

Enrollment: 12,292. **Student Body:** 51% female, 49% male, 14% out-of-state, 5% international (94 countries represented). Asian 4%, African American 5%, Caucasian 78%, Hispanic 4%, Native American <1%
Retention and Graduation: 19% freshmen graduate within 4 years. 21% grads go on to further study within 1 year. 21% grads pursue arts and sciences degrees. 8% grads pursue business degrees. **Faculty:** 479 full-time faculty, 88% hold PhDs, 47% are members of minority groups, 18% are women. 4% of classes are taught by teaching assistants.

ACADEMICS

Degrees: associate, bachelor's, certificate, master's, post-master's certificate. **Classes:** most classes have 20–29 students. Most lab/discussion sessions have 20–29 students. **Majors with highest enrollment:** business administration and management; biology/biological sciences; elementary education and teaching. **Special Study Options:** cross-registration, distance learning, double major, dual enrollment, English as a second language (ESL), exchange student program (domestic), external degree program, honors program, independent study, internships, student-designed major, study abroad, teacher certification program. **Disability Services:** special programs offered to physically disabled students include note-taking services, reader services, tape recorders. **Career services:** alumni network, alumni services, career/job search classes, career assessment, internships. Career services highlights include walk-in hours for student résumé review and other services.

FACILITIES

Housing: Coed dorms, special housing for disabled students. 90% of campus accessible to physically disabled. **Special Academic Facilities/Equipment:** Two art galleries, day care facility, two astronomy observ- atories, main stage and studio theatres **Computers:** 100% of classrooms, 10% of dorms, 100% of libraries, 100% of dining areas, 100% of student union, 80% of common outdoor areas have wireless network access. Students can register for classes online. Administrative functions (other than registration) can be performed online.

CAMPUS LIFE

Environment: Town. **Activities:** Choral groups, concert band, dance, drama/ theater, jazz band, literary magazine, music ensembles, musical theater, pep band, radio station, student government, student newspaper, symphony orchestra, Campus Ministries, International Student Organization. 178 registered organizations, 18 honor societies, 15 religious organizations. 7 fraternities, 4 sororities. **Athletics (Intercollegiate):** *Men:* baseball, basketball, cross-country, diving, football, golf, ice hockey, swimming, tennis, track/field (outdoor), track/ field (indoor), wrestling. *Women:* basketball, bowling, cross-country, diving, golf, ice hockey, soccer, softball, swimming, tennis, track/field (outdoor), track/ field (indoor), volleyball. **On-Campus Highlights:** Student Union, Myers Field House, Campus Recreation Center, Julia Sears Residence Hall, Memorial Library. **Environmental Initiatives:** Energy retrofit of building for lighting and motors; All new buildings exceed LEED compliance; Purchase of three electric cars for University Security and Environmental Health and Safety Offices.

ADMISSIONS

Freshman Academic Profile: Average high school GPA 3.21. 7% in top 10% of high school class, 24% in top 25% of high school class, 67% in top 50% of high school class. 95% from public high schools. ACT middle 50% range 19-24. Minimum internet-based TOEFL 61. Minimum paper TOEFL 500. **Basis for Candidate Selection:** *Very important factors considered include:* Class rank, standardized test scores. *Other factors considered include:* academic GPA, recommendation(s). **Freshman Admission Requirements:** High school diploma is required and GED is accepted. *Academic units required:* 4 English, 3 mathematics, 3 science, (3 science labs), 2 foreign language, 2 social studies, 1 history, 1 visual/performing arts. **Freshman Admission Statistics:** 9,984 applied, 67% admitted, 34% enrolled. **Transfer Admission Requirements:** college transcript(s), statement of good standing from prior institution(s). Minimum college GPA of 2.0 required. Lowest grade transferable D. **General Admission Information:** Application Fee $20. Nonfall registration accepted. Admission may be deferred for a maximum of No set time frame. Credit offered for CEEB Advanced Placement tests.

COSTS AND FINANCIAL AID

Annual in-state tuition $6,668. Annual out-of-state tuition $15,052. Room and board $8,042. Required fees $906. Average book expense $910. **Required Forms and Deadlines:** FAFSA. **Notification of Awards:** Applicants will be notified of awards on a rolling basis beginning 3/30. **Types of Aid:** *Need-based scholarships/grants:* Federal Pell, SEOG, state scholarships/grants, private scholarships, the school's own gift aid, Federal ACG/SMART. *Loans:* Subsidized Stafford, Unsubsidized Stafford, PLUS, Federal Perkins, state loans, Alternative Loans. *Student Employment:* Federal Work-Study Program available. Institutional employment available. Off-campus job opportunities are fair. **Financial Aid Statistics:** 78% freshmen, 73% undergrads receive need-based scholarship or grant aid. 11% freshmen, 2% undergrads receive non-need-based scholarship or grant aid. 97% freshmen, 98% undergrads receive need-based self-help aid. 2% freshmen, 2% undergrads receive athletic scholarships. 67% freshmen, 72% undergrads receive any aid. **Criteria for awarding institutional aid:** *Non-need-based:* academics, art, athletics, leadership, minority status, music/drama.

MINNESOTA STATE UNIVERSITY MOORHEAD

Owens Hall, Moorhead, MN 56563
Phone: 218-477-2161 · **Financial Aid Phone:** 218-477-2251
E-mail: dragon@mnstate.edu · **CEEB Code:** 6678
Fax: 218-477-4374 · **Website:** www.mnstate.edu · **ACT Code:** 2134

This public school was founded in 1887. It has a 140-acre campus.

RATINGS

Admissions Selectivity Rating: 74   Fire Safety Rating: 60*

STUDENTS AND FACULTY

Enrollment: 6,582. **Student Body:** 57% female, 43% male, 5% international (56 countries represented). Asian 1%, African American 3%, Caucasian 84%, Hispanic 1%, Native American 1%
Faculty: 286 full-time faculty, 45% are members of minority groups.

ACADEMICS

Degrees: associate, bachelor's, certificate, master's, post-bachelor's certificate, post-master's certificate, transfer associate. **Classes:** Most classes have 20–29 students. Most lab/discussion sessions have 20–29 students. **Majors with Highest Enrollment:** Elementary Education and Teaching; Mass Communication/ Media Studies; Business Administration and Management. **Special Study Options:** cross-registration, distance learning, double major, dual enrollment, exchange student program (domestic), external degree program, honors program, independent study, internships, student-designed major, study abroad, teacher certification program. **Honors programs:** Honors Program to reward and encourage superior academic achievement. **Combined degree programs:** Dual degree programs w/University of MN in depts of chemistry & physics. **Disability Services:** Special programs offered to physically disabled students include note-taking services, reader services, tape recorders, tutors. **Career services:** career/job search classes, career assessment, internships.

FACILITIES

Housing: Coed dorms, special housing for disabled students, men's dorms, women's dorms, apartments for single students, Theme Housing, Sorority housing. 95% of campus accessible to physically disabled. **Special Academic Facilities/Equipment:** Art and biology museums on-campus, planetarium, regional science center, Center for Business, new Science Building, Center for Business, Wellness Center. **Computers:** Students can register for classes online. Administrative functions (other than registration) can be performed online.

CAMPUS LIFE

Environment: City. **Activities:** Choral groups, concert band, dance, drama/ theater, jazz band, literary magazine, music ensembles, musical theater, radio station, student government, student newspaper, student-run film society, symphony orchestra, television station, Campus Ministries, International Student Organization, Model UN. 109 registered organizations, 6 honor societies, 11 religious organization. 2 sororities. **Athletics (Intercollegiate):** *Men:* basketball, cross-country, football, track/field (outdoor), track/field (indoor), wrestling. *Women:* basketball, cross-country, golf, soccer, softball, swimming, tennis, track/ field (outdoor), track/field (indoor), volleyball. **On-Campus Highlights:** Underground Night Club, Comstock Memorial Student Union, Regional Science Center, Nemzek Athletic Complex, Planetarium, New Science Lab Building, New Wellness Center.

ADMISSIONS

Freshman Academic Profile: 7% in top 10% of high school class, 24% in top 25% of high school class, 57% in top 50% of high school class. SAT Math middle 50% range 500-610. SAT Critical Reading middle 50% range 440-570. ACT middle 50% range 20-24. Minimum paper TOEFL 500. **Basis for Candidate Selection:** *Very important factors considered include:* Class rank, rigor of secondary school record, standardized test scores. **Freshman Admission Requirements:** High school diploma is required and GED is accepted. *Academic units required:* 4 English, 3 mathematics, 3 science, (1 science labs), 2 foreign language, 3 social studies, 1 World culture or the arts. **Freshman Admission Statistics:** 3,393 applied, 73% admitted, 50% enrolled. **Transfer Admission Requirements:** college transcript(s), statement of good standing from prior institution(s). Minimum college GPA of 2.0 required. Lowest grade transferable D. **General Admission Information:** Application Fee $20. Regular application deadline 8/1. Notification on a rolling basis, beginning on or about 10/1. Nonfall registration accepted. Admission may be deferred for a maximum of case by case. Credit and/or placement offered for CEEB Advanced Placement tests.

COSTS AND FINANCIAL AID

Annual in-state tuition $6,140. Annual out-of-state tuition $6,140. Room and board $6,468. Required fees $587. Average book expense $800. **Notification of Awards:** Applicants will be notified of awards on a rolling basis beginning 6/1. **Types of Aid:** *Need-based scholarships/grants:* Federal Pell, SEOG, state scholarships/grants, private scholarships, the school's own gift aid. *Loans:* Direct Subsidized Stafford, Direct Unsubsidized Stafford, Direct PLUS, Federal Perkins, state loans. *Student Employment:* Federal Work-Study Program available. Institutional employment available. Highest amount earned per year from on-campus jobs $2,200. Off-campus job opportunities are excellent. **Financial Aid Statistics:** 75% freshmen, 58% undergrads receive any aid. **Criteria for awarding institutional aid:** *Non-need-based:* academics, art, athletics, leadership, minority status, music/drama, state/district residency.

MISERICORDIA UNIVERSITY

301 Lake Street, Dallas, PA 18612
Phone: 570-674-6264 • **Financial Aid Phone:** 570-674-6222
E-mail: admiss@misericordia.edu • **CEEB Code:** 2087
Fax: 570-675-2441 • **Website:** www.misericordia.edu • **ACT Code:** 3539

This private school, affiliated with the Roman Catholic Church, was founded in 1924. It has a 120-acre campus.

RATINGS
Admissions Selectivity Rating: 85   **Fire Safety Rating:** 93

STUDENTS AND FACULTY
Enrollment: 2,350. **Student Body:** 68% female, 32% male, 24% out-of-state, 0% international (4 countries represented). Asian 1%, African American 2%, Caucasian 93%, Hispanic 3%, Native American <1%
Retention and Graduation: 80% freshmen return for sophomore year. 63% freshmen graduate within 4 years. 71% freshmen graduate within 6 years. 33% grads go on to further study within 1 year. 25% grads pursue arts and sciences degrees. 8% grads pursue business degrees. **Faculty:** 123 full-time faculty, 78% hold PhDs, 59% are members of minority groups, 8% are women. 0% of classes are taught by teaching assistants.

ACADEMICS
Degrees: bachelor's, certificate, master's, post-bachelor's certificate, post-master's certificate. **Classes:** Most classes have 10–19 students. Most lab/discussion sessions have 10–19 students. **Majors with Highest Enrollment:** Registered Nursing/Registered Nurse; Business Administration and Management; Health/Health Care Administration/Management. **Special Study Options:** Accelerated program, cross-registration, distance learning, double major, dual enrollment, honors program, independent study, internships, student-designed major, study abroad, teacher certification program, weekend college. **Honors programs:** The Honors Program is an interdisciplinary community of undergraduate students and faculty working together to create an intellectually stimulating and challenging environment for learning. Honors students take a common sequence of core curriculum courses in place of regular core offerings, participate each semester in our Honors Explorations Seminar, and procuce a professional quality paper or project as part of the Honors Capstone. **Combined degree programs:** BS/MSPT and BS/MSOT and BS/MSSLP. **Disability Services:** Special programs offered to physically disabled students include tape recorders, tutors. **Career services:** Alumni network, alumni services, career/job search classes, career assessment, internships.

FACILITIES
Housing: Coed dorms, Leadership House, Women with Children House. 100% of campus accessible to physically disabled. **Computers:** 5% of classrooms, 100% of libraries, 100% of dining areas, 100% of student union, 10% of common outdoor areas have wireless network access. Students can register for classes online. Administrative functions (other than registration) can be performed online.

CAMPUS LIFE
Environment: Town. **Activities:** Choral groups, dance, drama/theater, jazz band, literary magazine, music ensembles, radio station, student government, student newspaper, television station, yearbook, Campus Ministries. 27 registered organizations, 1 honor society, 1 religious organization. **Athletics (Intercollegiate):** *Men:* baseball, basketball, cross-country, golf, lacrosse, soccer, swimming, tennis, track/field (outdoor). *Women:* basketball, cheerleading, cross-country, field hockey, lacrosse, soccer, softball, swimming, tennis, track/field (outdoor), volleyball. **On-Campus Highlights:** Anderson Sports and Health Center, Banks Student Life Center, Mangelsdorf Field, Bevevino Library.

ADMISSIONS
Freshman Academic Profile: Average high school GPA 3.34. 30% in top 10% of high school class, 60% in top 25% of high school class, 84% in top 50% of high school class. 82% from public high schools. SAT Math middle 50% range 490-590. SAT Critical Reading middle 50% range 480-580. ACT middle 50% range 21-26. Minimum paper TOEFL 500. **Basis for Candidate Selection:** *Very important factors considered include:* academic GPA, rigor

of secondary school record. *Important factors considered include:* Class rank, standardized test scores. *Other factors considered include:* application essay, recommendation(s), character/personal qualities, extracurricular activities, interview, racial/ethnic status, volunteer work, work experience. **Freshman Admission Requirements:** High school diploma is required and GED is accepted. *Academic units required:* 4 English, 4 mathematics, 4 science, 4 social studies. **Freshman Admission Statistics:** 2,050 applied, 71% admitted, 30% enrolled. **Transfer Admission Requirements:** college transcript(s), Minimum college GPA of 2.0 required. Lowest grade transferable C. **General Admission Information:** Application Fee $25. Notification on a rolling basis, beginning on or about 10/1. Nonfall registration accepted. Admission may be deferred for a maximum of 12 months. Credit and/or placement offered for CEEB Advanced Placement tests.

COSTS AND FINANCIAL AID
Annual tuition $27,470. Room and board $12,050. Required fees $1,540. Average book expense $1,150. **Required Forms and Deadlines:** FAFSA, Institution's own financial aid form. **Notification of Awards:** Applicants will be notified of awards on a rolling basis beginning 3/15. **Types of Aid:** *Need-based scholarships/grants:* Federal Pell, SEOG, state scholarships/grants, private scholarships, the school's own gift aid, Federal Nursing Scholarships. *Loans:* Subsidized Stafford, Unsubsidized Stafford, PLUS, Federal Perkins, Federal Nursing, state loans. *Student Employment:* Federal Work-Study Program available. Institutional employment available. Highest amount earned per year from on-campus jobs $1,600. Off-campus job opportunities are good. **Financial Aid Statistics:** 99% freshmen, 100% undergrads receive need-based scholarship or grant aid. 21% freshmen, 16% undergrads receive non-need-based scholarship or grant aid. 82% freshmen, 82% undergrads receive need-based self-help aid. 0% freshmen, 0% undergrads receive athletic scholarships. 99% freshmen, 99% undergrads receive any aid. 88% undergrads borrow to pay for school. Average cumulative indebtedness $24,008. **Criteria for awarding institutional aid:** *Non-need-based:* academics, alumni affiliation, leadership, minority status, state/district residency.

MISSISSIPPI COLLEGE

Box 4026, Clinton, MS 39058-0001
Phone: 601-925-3800 • **Financial Aid Phone:** 601-925-3212
E-mail: enrollment-services@mc.edu • **CEEB Code:** 1477
Fax: 601-925-3950 • **Website:** http://www.mc.edu • **ACT Code:** 2214

This private school, affiliated with the Southern Baptist Church, was founded in 1826. It has a 320-acre campus.

RATINGS
Admissions Selectivity Rating: 87   **Fire Safety Rating:** 93

STUDENTS AND FACULTY
Enrollment: 3,030. **Student Body:** 61% female, 39% male, 24% out-of-state, 3% international (21 countries represented). Asian 1%, African American 24%, Caucasian 67%, Hispanic 2%, Native American 1%
Retention and Graduation: 73% freshmen return for sophomore year. 40% freshmen graduate within 4 years. 62% freshmen graduate within 6 years. **Faculty:** 205 full-time faculty, 78% hold PhDs, 48% are members of minority groups, 9% are women. 0% of classes are taught by teaching assistants.

ACADEMICS
Degrees: bachelor's, doctoral, master's, post-bachelor's certificate, post-master's certificate. **Classes:** Most classes have 10–19 students. Most lab/discussion sessions have fewer than 10 students. **Majors with Highest Enrollment:** Business Administration and Management; Biomedical Sciences; Elementary Education and Teaching. **Special Study Options:** Accelerated program, distance learning, double major, dual enrollment, English as a Second Language (ESL), honors program, independent study, internships, study abroad, teacher certification program, Academic remediation, Advance Placement credit, Work-Study program, Learning disabilities services. **Honors programs:** Honors programs open to freshmen, sophomores, juniors, and seniors and administered by the Honors Council. Freshmen who have a high ACT score (established each year) are invited to participate in a program of study called Freshman Honors Seminar (IDS161), it is an interdisciplinary study dealing with contemporary issues and interests. Upperclassmen who maintain a high GPA may also participate in Sophomore and Senior Honors Seminars (IDS 261, 461). Successful completion of the Junior-Senior Honors Program leads to a degree "With Honors" or "With High Honors." **Combined degree programs:** BA/JD. **Disability Services:** Special programs offered to physically disabled students include note-taking services, reader services, tape recorders, tutors. **Career services:** alumni services, career/job search classes, career assessment, internships.

FACILITIES

Housing: special housing for disabled students, men's dorms, women's dorms, apartments for single students. 90% of campus accessible to physically disabled. **Computers:** 60% of classrooms, 100% of dorms, 100% of libraries, 100% of dining areas, 60% of common outdoor areas have wireless network access. Students can register for classes online. Administrative functions (other than registration) can be performed online.

CAMPUS LIFE

Environment: Metropolis. **Activities:** Choral groups, concert band, dance, drama/theater, jazz band, literary magazine, marching band, music ensembles, musical theater, opera, radio station, student government, student newspaper, yearbook, Campus Ministries, International Student Organization. 66 registered organizations, 22 honor societies, 6 religious organizations. 5 fraternities, 4 sororities. **Athletics (Intercollegiate):** *Men:* baseball, basketball, cross-country, football, golf, soccer, tennis, track/field (outdoor). *Women:* basketball, cheerleading, cross-country, equestrian sports, soccer, softball, tennis, track/field (outdoor), volleyball. **On-Campus Highlights:** Gore Gallery, Healthplex, Men's Rotunda and New Women's Residence Hall, Provine Chapel, Anderson Hall in BCR Student Center, Nelson Hall-Administration Building Robinson-Wright Field House.

ADMISSIONS

Freshman Academic Profile: Average high school GPA 3.43. 33% in top 10% of high school class, 57% in top 25% of high school class, 74% in top 50% of high school class. SAT Math middle 50% range 470-580. SAT Critical Reading middle 50% range 470-613. ACT middle 50% range 20-27. Minimum internet-based TOEFL 69. **Basis for Candidate Selection:** *Very important factors considered include:* standardized test scores. *Important factors considered include:* rigor of secondary school record, character/personal qualities, extracurricular activities, level of applicant's interest. *Other factors considered include:* Class rank, academic GPA, recommendation(s), alumni/ae relation, interview, talent/ability, volunteer work, work experience. **Freshman Admission Requirements:** High school diploma is required and GED is accepted. **Freshman Admission Statistics:** 2,178 applied, 58% admitted, 38% enrolled. **Transfer Admission Requirements:** college transcript(s), essay or personal statement, statement of good standing from prior institution(s). Minimum college GPA of 2.0 required. Lowest grade transferable C. **General Admission Information:** Early decision application deadline 12/1. Nonfall registration accepted. Admission may be deferred for a maximum of 1 year. Credit offered for CEEB Advanced Placement tests.

COSTS AND FINANCIAL AID

Annual tuition $14,120. Room and board $7,150. Required fees $748. Average book expense $1,100. **Required Forms and Deadlines:** FAFSA, State aid form. **Notification of Awards:** Applicants will be notified of awards on a rolling basis beginning 3/1. **Types of Aid:** *Need-based scholarships/grants:* Federal Pell, SEOG, state scholarships/grants, private scholarships, the school's own gift aid, Federal Nursing Scholarships. *Loans:* Subsidized Stafford, Unsubsidized Stafford, PLUS, Federal Perkins, Federal Nursing, college/university loans from institutional funds. *Student Employment:* Federal Work-Study Program available. Highest amount earned per year from on-campus jobs $3,000. Off-campus job opportunities are good. **Financial Aid Statistics:** 89% freshmen, 86% undergrads receive need-based scholarship or grant aid. 96% freshmen, 86% undergrads receive non-need-based scholarship or grant aid. 81% freshmen, 84% undergrads receive need-based self-help aid. 0% freshmen, 0% undergrads receive athletic scholarships. 98% freshmen, 94% undergrads receive any aid. 53% undergrads borrow to pay for school. Average cumulative indebtedness $23,888. **Criteria for awarding institutional aid:** *Non-need-based:* academics, alumni affiliation, art, leadership, music/drama, religious affiliation.

MISSISSIPPI STATE UNIVERSITY

P. O. Box 6334, Mississippi State, MS 39762
Phone: 662-325-2224 · **Financial Aid Phone:** 662-325-2450
E-mail: admit@msstate.edu · **CEEB Code:** 1480
Fax: 662-325-1MSU · **Website:** www.msstate.edu · **ACT Code:** 2220

This public school was founded in 1878. It has a 4200-acre campus.

RATINGS

Admissions Selectivity Rating: 87   Fire Safety Rating: 85

STUDENTS AND FACULTY

Enrollment: 15,786. **Student Body:** 49% female, 51% male, 98% out-of-state, 2% international (84 countries represented). Asian 1%, African American 20%, Caucasian 72%, Hispanic 2%, Native American 1%
Faculty: 861 full-time faculty, 81% hold PhDs, 39% are members of minority groups, 17% are women.

ACADEMICS

Degrees: bachelor's, doctoral, master's. **Classes:** Most classes have 20–29 students. Most lab/discussion sessions have fewer than 10 students. **Majors with Highest Enrollment:** Physical Education Teaching and Coaching; Business Administration and Management; Geology/Earth Science. **Special Study Options:** cooperative education program, distance learning, double major, dual enrollment, English as a Second Language (ESL), exchange student program (domestic), external degree program, honors program, independent study, internships, liberal arts/career combination, student-designed major, study abroad, teacher certification program, weekend college. **Honors programs:** University Honors Program. **Disability Services:** Special programs offered to physically disabled students include note-taking services, reader services, tape recorders, tutors. **Career services:** Alumni network, alumni services, career/job search classes, career assessment, internships, regional alumni. Career services highlights include a diversified Co-op program. Students are participating from several colleges and schools at the university.

FACILITIES

Housing: special housing for disabled students, men's dorms, women's dorms, fraternity/sorority housing, apartments for married students, apartments for single students, Theme Housing, co-residential. 95% of campus accessible to physically disabled. **Special Academic Facilities/Equipment:** Geology, archeology, music, entomological museums; art gallery; flight research lab. **Computers:** 100% of classrooms, 100% of dorms, 100% of libraries, 100% of dining areas, 100% of student union, 100% of common outdoor areas have wireless network access. Students can register for classes online. Administrative functions (other than registration) can be performed online.

CAMPUS LIFE

Environment: Town. **Activities:** Choral groups, concert band, dance, drama/theater, jazz band, literary magazine, marching band, music ensembles, musical theater, pep band, radio station, student government, student newspaper, television station, yearbook, Campus Ministries, International Student Organization, Model UN. 326 registered organizations, 42 honor societies, 30 religious organizations. 17 fraternities, 11 sorority. **Athletics (Intercollegiate):** *Men:* baseball, basketball, cheerleading, cross-country, football, golf, tennis, track/field (outdoor). *Women:* basketball, cheerleading, cross-country, golf, soccer, softball, tennis, track/field (outdoor), volleyball. **On-Campus Highlights:** Scott Field Stadium, Dudy Noble Field, Humphrey Coliseum, Barnes and Noble Campus Bookstore, Sanderson Student Recreation Center. **Environmental Initiatives:** Recycling; Bicycle Program; Environmental Sustainability; Research Center.

ADMISSIONS

Freshman Academic Profile: Average high school GPA 3.35. 28% in top 10% of high school class, 54% in top 25% of high school class, 81% in top 50% of high school class. SAT Math middle 50% range 500-640. SAT Critical Reading middle 50% range 490-630. ACT middle 50% range 21-28. Minimum internet-based TOEFL 71. Minimum paper TOEFL 525. **Basis for Candidate Selection:** *Very important factors considered include:* academic GPA, standardized test scores. *Important factors considered include:* Class rank. *Other factors considered include:* rigor of secondary school record, talent/ability. **Freshman Admission Requirements:** High school diploma is required and GED is accepted. *Academic units required:* 4 English, 3 mathematics, 3 science, (2 science labs), 1 social studies, 2 history, 2 academic electives. **Freshman Admission Statistics:** 10,766 applied, 71% admitted, 39% enrolled. **Transfer Admission Requirements:** college transcript(s), statement of good standing from prior institution(s). Minimum college GPA of 2.0 required. Lowest grade transferable D. **General Admission Information:** Application Fee $35. Notification on a rolling basis, beginning on or about 9/1. Nonfall registration accepted. Credit offered for CEEB Advanced Placement tests.

COSTS AND FINANCIAL AID

Annual. Annual out-of-state tuition $18,478. Room and board $8,954. Average book expense $1,200. **Required Forms and Deadlines:** FAFSA, State aid form. **Notification of Awards:** Applicants will be notified of awards on a rolling basis beginning 12/1. **Types of Aid:** *Need-based scholarships/grants:* Federal Pell, SEOG, state scholarships/grants, private scholarships, the school's own gift aid, United Negro College Fund. *Loans:* Subsidized Stafford, Unsubsidized Stafford, PLUS, Federal Perkins, college/university loans from institutional funds. *Student Employment:* Federal Work-Study Program available. Institutional employment available. Off-campus job opportunities are good. **Financial Aid Statistics:** 91% freshmen, 87% undergrads receive need-based scholarship or grant aid. 15% freshmen, 7% undergrads receive non-need-based scholarship or grant aid. 68% freshmen, 76% undergrads receive need-based self-help aid. 3% freshmen, 3% undergrads receive athletic scholarships. 53% undergrads borrow to pay for school. Average cumulative indebtedness $29,355. **Criteria for awarding institutional aid:** *Non-need-based:* academics, alumni affiliation, art, athletics, job skills, leadership, minority status, music/drama, state/district residency.

MISSISSIPPI VALLEY STATE UNIVERSITY

14000 Highway 82 West, Itta Bena, MS 38941-1400
Phone: 662-254-3344 · **Financial Aid Phone:** 662-254-3338
E-mail: nbtaylor@mvsu.edu · **CEEB Code:** 1482
Fax: 662-254-3759 · **Website:** www.mvsu.edu · **ACT Code:** 2224

This public school was founded in 1950. It has a 250-acre campus.

RATINGS
Admissions Selectivity Rating: 80   **Fire Safety Rating:** 75

STUDENTS AND FACULTY
Enrollment: 2,357. **Student Body:** 62% female, 38% male, 11% out-of-state, 0% international (2 countries represented). Asian 0%, African American 93%, Caucasian 4%, Hispanic 1%, Native American <1%
Retention and Graduation: 55% freshmen return for sophomore year. 18% freshmen graduate within 4 years. 35% freshmen graduate within 6 years.
Faculty: 133 full-time faculty, 58% hold PhDs, 46% are members of minority groups, 30% are women. 0% of classes are taught by teaching assistants.

ACADEMICS
Degrees: bachelor's, master's. **Classes:** Most classes have fewer than 10 students. Most lab/discussion sessions have 20–29 students. **Majors with Highest Enrollment:** Kindergarten/Preschool Education and Teaching; Business, Management, Marketing, and Related Support Services; Social Work. **Special Study Options:** cooperative education program, distance learning, double major, honors program, internships, teacher certification program, weekend college, Co-Op Programs: Business, Computer Science, Natural Science, Social/Behavioral Science. **Disability Services:** Special programs offered to physically disabled students include tape recorders, tutors. **Career services:** alumni services. Many of our students have received internships with the Environmental Protection Agency in Washington, DC.

FACILITIES
Housing: men's dorms, women's dorms, apartments for married students, apartments for single students. **Computers:** Students can register for classes online.

CAMPUS LIFE
Environment: Rural. **Activities:** Choral groups, concert band, drama/theater, marching band, radio station, student government, student newspaper, yearbook. 35 registered organizations, 19 honor societies, 4 religious organizations. 4 fraternities, 2 sororities. **Athletics (Intercollegiate):** *Men:* baseball, basketball, cross-country, football, golf, tennis, track/field (outdoor). *Women:* basketball, cross-country, golf, soccer, softball, tennis, track/field (outdoor), volleyball. **On-Campus Highlights:** Student Union, Student Pavillion, Administration Building, Library.

ADMISSIONS
Freshman Academic Profile: Average high school GPA 2.58. 0% in top 10% of high school class,% in top 50% of high school class. 96% from public high schools. ACT middle 50% range 15-19. Minimum paper TOEFL 525. **Basis for Candidate Selection:** *Very important factors considered include:* Class rank, rigor of secondary school record, standardized test scores, state residency. *Other factors considered include:* recommendation(s), extracurricular activities, interview, talent/ability. **Freshman Admission Requirements:** High school diploma is required and GED is accepted. *Academic units required:* 4 English, 3 mathematics, 3 science, (2 science labs), 1 foreign language, 3 social studies, 2 academic electives, 1 Computer Applications. **Freshman Admission Statistics:** 6,086 applied, 30% admitted, 23% enrolled. **Transfer Admission Requirements:** college transcript(s), Minimum college GPA of 2.0 required. Lowest grade transferable C. **General Admission Information:** Nonfall registration accepted.

COSTS AND FINANCIAL AID
Average book expense $1,400. **Required Forms and Deadlines:** FAFSA, Institution's own financial aid form. **Notification of Awards:** Applicants will be notified of awards on or about 7/15. **Types of Aid:** *Need-based scholarships/grants:* Federal Pell, SEOG, state scholarships/grants, private scholarships, the school's own gift aid. *Loans:* Direct Unsubsidized Stafford, Direct PLUS. *Student Employment:* Federal Work-Study Program available. **Financial Aid Statistics:** 95% freshmen, 95% undergrads receive any aid.

MISSOURI SOUTHERN STATE UNIVERSITY—JOPLIN

3950 E. Newman Road, Joplin, MO 64801-1595
Phone: 417-625-9378 · **Financial Aid Phone:** 417-625-9325
E-mail: admissions@mssu.edu · **CEEB Code:** 6322
Fax: 417-659-4429 · **ACT Code:** 2304

This public school was founded in 1937. It has a 365-acre campus.

RATINGS
Admissions Selectivity Rating: 70   **Fire Safety Rating:** 65

STUDENTS AND FACULTY
Enrollment: 5,135. **Student Body:** 59% female, 41% male, 15% out-of-state, 1% international (31 countries represented). Asian 1%, African American 3%, Caucasian 89%, Hispanic 2%, Native American 3%
Retention and Graduation: 63% freshmen return for sophomore year. 18% freshmen graduate within 4 years. 36% freshmen graduate within 6 years.
Faculty: 208 full-time faculty, 64% hold PhDs, 37% are members of minority groups, 9% are women. 0% of classes are taught by teaching assistants.

ACADEMICS
Degrees: associate, bachelor's, certificate, master's. **Classes:** Most classes have 20–29 students. Most lab/discussion sessions have fewer than 10 students. **Majors with Highest Enrollment:** Education; Criminal Justice/Law Enforcement Administration; Business/Commerce. **Special Study Options:** Accelerated program, cooperative education program, distance learning, double major, dual enrollment, English as a Second Language (ESL), exchange student program (domestic), honors program, independent study, internships, liberal arts/career combination, study abroad, teacher certification program, weekend college. **Honors programs:** MSSU Honors Program. **Disability Services:** Special programs offered to physically disabled students include note-taking services, reader services, tape recorders, tutors.

FACILITIES
Housing: Coed dorms, special housing for disabled students, men's dorms, women's dorms, apartments for single students. 100% of campus accessible to physically disabled. **Special Academic Facilities/Equipment:** spiva art gallery, biology pond, forensics laboratory, child development center, indoor "livefire" firearms range, green house, law library, cyber coffee shop, international trade and quality center, graduate center, tv station, radio station, small business development center, Thomas E. Taylor Performing Arts Center, health center. **Computers:** Administrative functions (other than registration) can be performed online.

CAMPUS LIFE
Environment: Town. **Activities:** Choral groups, concert band, dance, drama/theater, jazz band, literary magazine, marching band, music ensembles, musical theater, pep band, radio station, student government, student newspaper, student-run film society, symphony orchestra, television station. 82 registered organizations, 12 honor societies, 9 religious organizations. 2 fraternities, 2 sororities. **Athletics (Intercollegiate):** *Men:* baseball, basketball, cheerleading, cross-country, football, golf, soccer, track/field (outdoor). *Women:* basketball, cheerleading, cross-country, soccer, softball, tennis, track/field (outdoor), volleyball. **On-Campus Highlights:** Cyber Coffee Shop, Lion's Den, Student Life Activity Center, Leggett and Platt Athletic Center, Spiva Art Gallery, In addition to MSSU's campus facilities, Missouri Southern's low crime rate, well lit campus, 24 hour security and emergency phones located in key spots help to ensure the safety of students as they enjoy Missouri Southern's campus.

ADMISSIONS
Freshman Academic Profile: 17% in top 10% of high school class, 40% in top 25% of high school class, 72% in top 50% of high school class. 98% from public high schools. ACT middle 50% range 17-19. Minimum paper TOEFL 535. **Basis for Candidate Selection:** *Very important factors considered include:* Class rank, academic GPA, rigor of secondary school record, standardized test scores. *Other factors considered include:* recommendation(s). **Freshman Admission Requirements:** High school diploma is required and GED is accepted. **Freshman Admission Statistics:** 2,669 applied, 98% admitted, 36% enrolled. **Transfer Admission Requirements:** college transcript(s), Minimum college GPA of 2.0 required. Lowest grade transferable D. **General Admission Information:** Application Fee $15. Notification on a rolling basis, beginning on or about 9/1. Nonfall registration accepted. Admission may be deferred for a maximum of 1 year. Credit and/or placement offered for CEEB Advanced Placement tests.

COSTS AND FINANCIAL AID
Average book expense $600. **Required Forms and Deadlines:** FAFSA. **Notification of Awards:** Applicants will be notified of awards on a rolling basis beginning 2/15. **Types of Aid:** *Need-based scholarships/grants:* Federal Pell,

SEOG, state scholarships/grants, private scholarships. *Loans:* Direct Subsidized Stafford, Direct Unsubsidized Stafford, Direct PLUS, Federal Perkins, state loans. **Criteria for awarding institutional aid:** *Non-need-based:* academics, alumni affiliation, art, athletics, job skills, leadership, minority status, music/drama, state/district residency.

MISSOURI STATE UNIVERSITY

901 S. National, Springfield, MO 65897
Phone: 417-836-5517 · **Financial Aid Phone:** 417-835-5262
E-mail: info@missouristate.edu · **CEEB Code:** 6665
Fax: 417-836-6334 · **Website:** www.missouristate.edu · **ACT Code:** 2370

This public school was founded in 1905. It has a 450-acre campus.

RATINGS

Admissions Selectivity Rating: 78   Fire Safety Rating: 83

STUDENTS AND FACULTY

Enrollment: 14,463. **Student Body:** 56% female, 44% male, 7% out-of-state, 2% international. Asian 1%, African American 2%, Caucasian 77%, Hispanic 1%, Native American 1%
Retention and Graduation: 73% freshmen return for sophomore year. 20% grads go on to further study within 1 year. 2% grads pursue arts and sciences degrees. 2% grads pursue law degrees. 10% grads pursue business degrees. 2% grads pursue medical degrees. **Faculty:** 728 full-time faculty, 78% hold PhDs, 40% are members of minority groups, 7% are women. 8% of classes are taught by teaching assistants.

ACADEMICS

Degrees: bachelor's, master's, post-bachelor's certificate, post-master's certificate. **Classes:** Most classes have 20–29 students. Most lab/discussion sessions have 20–29 students. **Majors with Highest Enrollment:** Elementary Education and Teaching; Management Information Systems; Marketing/Marketing Management. **Special Study Options:** Accelerated program, cooperative education program, distance learning, double major, dual enrollment, English as a Second Language (ESL), exchange student program (domestic), honors program, independent study, internships, student-designed major, study abroad, teacher certification program. **Honors programs:** The Honors College is to provide a program of enhanced, advanced study and recognition for students of unusually strong academic achievement and motivation. The Honors College is to provide these students with intellectual opportunities beyond those generally found in the more traditional programs: smaller and enriched classes, direct contact with outstanding faculty members, and the option to pursue their own intellectual, research, and creative interests. The Honors College is to provide the means whereby individual departments may develop departmental honors opportunities. These opportunities will allow students with higher academic achievement and motivation to develop their individual interests more fully through contact with faculty and students of similar interests and abilities while maintaining involvement in the University community as a whole. **Disability Services:** Special programs offered to physically disabled students include note-taking services, reader services, tape recorders, tutors.

FACILITIES

Housing: Coed dorms, special housing for disabled students, special housing for international students, fraternity/sorority housing, apartments for married students, apartments for single students, graduate student housing, non-traditional student housing, upper-class student housing, honor student housing, transfer student housing and family housing. 95% of campus accessible to physically disabled. **Special Academic Facilities/Equipment:** On-campus laboratory school (K-12), 125-acre Darr Agricultrual Center, Baker Observatory, Bull Shoals Field Station, electron microscope, molecular beam epitaxy laboratory, Ion implantation laboratory, Art and Design Gallery, Student Exhibition Center, Coger Theatre, Ellis Recital Hall, Instructional TV Studio, Computer Animation Studio, Foundry, Wehr Band Hall, Multimedia Lab, Language Lab, Juanita K. Hammons Hall for the Performing Arts. **Computers:** Students can register for classes online. Administrative functions (other than registration) can be performed online.

CAMPUS LIFE

Environment: City. **Activities:** Choral groups, concert band, dance, drama/theater, jazz band, literary magazine, marching band, music ensembles, musical theater, pep band, radio station, student government, student newspaper, student-run film society, symphony orchestra, television station. 270 registered organizations, 26 honor societies, 28 religious organizations. 15 fraternities, 9 sororities. **Athletics (Intercollegiate):** *Men:* baseball, basketball, cross-country, diving, football, golf, soccer, swimming, tennis, track/field (outdoor), track/field (indoor), volleyball. *Women:* basketball, cross-country, diving, field hockey, golf, soccer, softball, swimming, tennis, track/field (outdoor), track/field (indoor), vol-

leyball. **On-Campus Highlights:** Plaster Student Union, Meyer Library, Baker Bookstore, Hammons Fountains, Plaster Sports Complex.

ADMISSIONS

Freshman Academic Profile: Average high school GPA 3.57. 22% in top 10% of high school class, 49% in top 25% of high school class, 81% in top 50% of high school class. ACT middle 50% range 21-26. Minimum paper TOEFL 500. **Basis for Candidate Selection:** *Very important factors considered include:* Class rank, rigor of secondary school record, standardized test scores. *Other factors considered include:* application essay, recommendation(s), alumni/ae relation, character/personal qualities, extracurricular activities, interview, racial/ethnic status, talent/ability, volunteer work, work experience. **Freshman Admission Requirements:** High school diploma is required and GED is accepted. *Academic units required:* 4 English, 3 mathematics, 2 science, (1 science labs), 3 social studies, 3 academic electives. **Freshman Admission Statistics:** 6,866 applied, 77% admitted, 50% enrolled. **Transfer Admission Requirements:** college transcript(s), Minimum college GPA of 2.0 required. Lowest grade transferable D. **General Admission Information:** Application Fee $30. Regular application deadline 7/20. Nonfall registration accepted. Credit and/or placement offered for CEEB Advanced Placement tests.

COSTS AND FINANCIAL AID

Annual in-state tuition $4,920. Annual out-of-state tuition $9,840. Room and board $5,294. Required fees $534. Average book expense $800. **Required Forms and Deadlines:** FAFSA. **Notification of Awards:** Applicants will be notified of awards on a rolling basis beginning 4/1. **Types of Aid:** *Need-based scholarships/grants:* Federal Pell, SEOG, state scholarships/grants, private scholarships, the school's own gift aid. *Loans:* Subsidized Stafford, Unsubsidized Stafford, PLUS, Federal Perkins, college/university loans from institutional funds. **Financial Aid Statistics:** 78% freshmen, 67% undergrads receive need-based scholarship or grant aid. 14% freshmen, 7% undergrads receive non-need-based scholarship or grant aid. 73% freshmen, 78% undergrads receive need-based self-help aid. 3% freshmen, 3% undergrads receive athletic scholarships. 66% undergrads borrow to pay for school. **Criteria for awarding institutional aid:** *Non-need-based:* academics, alumni affiliation, art, athletics, job skills, leadership, minority status, music/drama, state/district residency.

MISSOURI UNIVERSITY OF SCIENCE AND TECHNOLOGY

300 W. 13th Street; 106 Parker Hall, Rolla, MO 65409-1060
Phone: 573-341-4165 · **Financial Aid Phone:** 573-341-4282
E-mail: admissions@mst.edu · **CEEB Code:** 6876
Fax: 573-341-4082 · **Website:** www.mst.edu · **ACT Code:** 2398

This public school was founded in 1870. It has a 284-acre campus.

RATINGS

Admissions Selectivity Rating: 87   Fire Safety Rating: 80

STUDENTS AND FACULTY

Enrollment: 6,415. **Student Body:** 23% female, 77% male, 19% out-of-state, 7% international (60 countries represented). Asian 3%, African American 4%, Caucasian 81%, Hispanic 2%, Native American <1%
Retention and Graduation: 23% freshmen graduate within 4 years. 63% freshmen graduate within 6 years. **Faculty:** 379 full-time faculty, 90% hold PhDs, 26% are members of minority groups, 32% are women. 12% of classes are taught by teaching assistants.

ACADEMICS

Degrees: bachelor's, certificate, master's, post-bachelor's certificate. **Classes:** Most classes have 20–29 students. Most lab/discussion sessions have 20–29 students. **Majors with Highest Enrollment:** Civil Engineering; Electrical and Electronics Engineering; Mechanical Engineering. **Special Study Options:** distance learning, double major, dual enrollment, English as a Second Language (ESL), honors program, independent study, internships, liberal arts/career combination, study abroad, teacher certification program. **Honors programs:** Honors Academy and Master Student Fellowship Programs; for more information see: http://ugs.mst.edu/honors.html. **Combined degree programs:** BA/MEng. **Disability Services:** Special programs offered to physically disabled students include note-taking services, reader services, tape recorders, tutors.

Career services: Alumni network, alumni services, career/job search classes, career assessment, internships, regional alumni.

FACILITIES

Housing: Coed dorms, special housing for disabled students, fraternity/sorority housing, apartments for married students, cooperative housing, apartments for single students, Wellness Housing, Theme Housing. 95% of campus accessible to physically disabled. **Special Academic Facilities/Equipment:** Writing Center, Student Design Center, Nuclear Reactor, Observatory, Explosives Testing Lab, Underground Mine, Museum of Rocks, Minerals, and Gemstones, Centers for Environmental Research, Water Resources, Industrial Research, and Rock Mechanics Research, Geophysical Observatory, Computerized Manufacturing System, Millenium Arch, and Stonehenge. **Computers:** 100% of classrooms, 100% of dorms, 100% of libraries, 66% of dining areas, 100% of student union, 80% of common outdoor areas have wireless network access. Students can register for classes online. Administrative functions (other than registration) can be performed online.

CAMPUS LIFE

Environment: Village. **Activities:** Choral groups, concert band, dance, drama/theater, jazz band, literary magazine, marching band, music ensembles, musical theater, pep band, radio station, student government, student newspaper, symphony orchestra, yearbook, Campus Ministries, International Student Organization. 202 registered organizations, 29 honor societies, 13 religious organizations. 21 fraternity, 4 sororities. **Athletics (Intercollegiate):** *Men:* baseball, basketball, cross-country, football, soccer, swimming, track/field (outdoor), track/field (indoor). *Women:* basketball, cross-country, soccer, softball, track/field (outdoor), track/field (indoor), volleyball. **On-Campus Highlights:** Havener Student Center, Residential College, Student Design Team Center, Castleman Performing Arts Center, Student Recreation Center. **Environmental Initiatives:** Reducing amount of paper being consumed. Reducing amount of energy being consumed. Reducing solid waste.

ADMISSIONS

Freshman Academic Profile: Average high school GPA 3.5. 40% in top 10% of high school class, 72% in top 25% of high school class, 95% in top 50% of high school class. 85% from public high schools. SAT Math middle 50% range 600-700. SAT Critical Reading middle 50% range 535-670. ACT middle 50% range 26-31. Minimum internet-based TOEFL 79. Minimum paper TOEFL 550. **Basis for Candidate Selection:** *Very important factors considered include:* Class rank, academic GPA, rigor of secondary school record, standardized test scores. *Important factors considered include:* recommendation(s). *Other factors considered include:* application essay, character/personal qualities, extracurricular activities, interview, talent/ability, volunteer work, work experience. **Freshman Admission Requirements:** High school diploma is required and GED is accepted. *Academic units required:* 4 English, 4 mathematics, 3 science, (1 science labs), 2 foreign language, 3 social studies, 1 visual/performing arts. **Freshman Admission Statistics:** 3,577 applied, 86% admitted, 42% enrolled. **Transfer Admission Requirements:** college transcript(s), Minimum college GPA of 2.5 required. **General Admission Information:** Application Fee $45. Regular application deadline 7/1. Notification on a rolling basis, beginning on or about 10/1. Nonfall registration accepted. Admission may be deferred for a maximum of 2 year. Credit and/or placement offered for CEEB Advanced Placement tests.

COSTS AND FINANCIAL AID

Annual. Annual out-of-state tuition $22,482. Room and board $9,396. Required fees $774. Average book expense $896. **Required Forms and Deadlines:** FAFSA. **Types of Aid:** *Need-based scholarships/grants:* Federal Pell, state scholarships/grants, private scholarships, the school's own gift aid. *Loans:* Subsidized Stafford, Unsubsidized Stafford, PLUS, Federal Perkins. *Student Employment:* Federal Work-Study Program available. Institutional employment available. Off-campus job opportunities are good. **Financial Aid Statistics:** 95% freshmen, 91% undergrads receive need-based scholarship or grant aid. 28% freshmen, 33% undergrads receive non-need-based scholarship or grant aid. 17% freshmen, 29% undergrads receive need-based self-help aid. 5% freshmen, 5% undergrads receive athletic scholarships. 91% freshmen, 85% undergrads receive any aid. 47% undergrads borrow to pay for school. Average cumulative indebtedness $23,416. **Criteria for awarding institutional aid:** *Non-need-based:* academics, alumni affiliation, athletics, job skills, leadership, minority status, music/drama, religious affiliation, state/district residency.

MISSOURI VALLEY COLLEGE

500 East College Street, Marshall, MO 65340
Phone: 660-831-4114
E-mail: admissions@moval.edu
Fax: 660-831-4233 • **Website:** www.moval.edu • **ACT Code:** 2330

This private school, affiliated with the Presbyterian Church, was founded in 1889. It has a 150-acre campus.

RATINGS

Admissions Selectivity Rating: 77   **Fire Safety Rating:** 60*

STUDENTS AND FACULTY

Enrollment: 1,425. **Student Body:** 43% female, 57% male, 34% out-of-state, 8% international (29 countries represented). Asian 4%, African American 13%, Caucasian 70%, Hispanic 4%, Native American 1%
Retention and Graduation: 45% freshmen return for sophomore year. 11% freshmen graduate within 4 years. 21% freshmen graduate within 6 years. 20% grads go on to further study within 1 year. **Faculty:** 66 full-time faculty, 53% hold PhDs, 35% are members of minority groups, 3% are women. 0% of classes are taught by teaching assistants.

ACADEMICS

Degrees: associate, bachelor's. **Classes:** Most classes have 20–29 students. Most lab/discussion sessions have 20–29 students. **Majors with Highest Enrollment:** Elementary Education and Teaching; Criminal Justice/Law Enforcement Administration; Business/Commerce. **Special Study Options:** double major, dual enrollment, internships, teacher certification program. **Disability Services:** Special programs offered to physically disabled students include reader services, tutors. **Career services:** internships. Career services highlights include required internships for many of our majors.

FACILITIES

Housing: men's dorms, women's dorms, fraternity/sorority housing, apartments for married students, apartments for single students.

CAMPUS LIFE

Environment: Rural. **Activities:** Choral groups, dance, drama/theater, literary magazine, music ensembles, musical theater, pep band, radio station, student government, student newspaper, television station, yearbook. 28 registered organizations, 8 honor societies, 7 religious organizations. 4 fraternities, 2 sororities. **Athletics (Intercollegiate):** *Men:* baseball, basketball, cheerleading, cross-country, football, golf, rodeo, soccer, tennis, track/field (outdoor), track/field (indoor), volleyball, wrestling. *Women:* basketball, cheerleading, cross-country, golf, rodeo, soccer, softball, tennis, track/field (outdoor), track/field (indoor), volleyball, wrestling. **On-Campus Highlights:** Burns Gym, Eckilson-Mabee Theater, Black Box Theater, Student Lounge (basement of MacDonald Hall), Tech Center Computer Lab.

ADMISSIONS

Freshman Academic Profile: Average high school GPA 2.9. 4% in top 10% of high school class, 38% in top 25% of high school class, 54% in top 50% of high school class. SAT Math middle 50% range 412-597. SAT Critical Reading middle 50% range 372-537. ACT middle 50% range 19-27. Minimum paper TOEFL 450. **Basis for Candidate Selection:** *Very important factors considered include:* character/personal qualities, interview. *Important factors considered include:* extracurricular activities, talent/ability, volunteer work. *Other factors considered include:* Class rank, recommendation(s), rigor of secondary school record, standardized test scores, alumni/ae relation, work experience. **Freshman Admission Requirements:** High school diploma is required and GED is accepted. **Freshman Admission Statistics:** 1,345 applied, 67% admitted, 45% enrolled. **Transfer Admission Requirements:** High school transcript, college transcript(s), standardized test scores, Minimum college GPA of 2.0 required. Lowest grade transferable C. **General Admission Information:** Application Fee $15. Regular application deadline 9/1. Nonfall registration accepted.

COSTS AND FINANCIAL AID

Annual tuition $13,000. Room and board $5,200. Required fees $500. Average book expense $1,300. **Required Forms and Deadlines:** FAFSA, State aid form. **Types of Aid:** *Need-based scholarships/grants:* Federal Pell, SEOG, state scholarships/grants, private scholarships, the school's own gift aid. *Loans:* Subsidized Stafford, Unsubsidized Stafford, PLUS, Federal Perkins. *Student Employment:* Federal Work-Study Program available. Institutional employment available. Off-campus job opportunities are excellent. **Financial Aid Statistics:** 100% freshmen, 100% undergrads receive need-based scholarship or grant aid. 100% freshmen, 100% undergrads receive non-need-based scholarship or grant aid. 87% freshmen, 87% undergrads receive need-based self-help aid. 0% freshmen, 0% undergrads receive athletic scholarships. 98% freshmen, 92% undergrads receive any aid. 86% undergrads borrow to pay for school.

MISSOURI WESTERN STATE COLLEGE

4525 Downs Drive, Saint Joseph, MO 64507
Phone: 816-271-4266
E-mail: admissn@mwsc.edu
Fax: 816-271-5833 · **Website:** www.mwsc.edu · **ACT Code:** 2344

This public school was founded in 1969. It has a 740-acre campus.

RATINGS

Admissions Selectivity Rating: 69   **Fire Safety Rating:** 60*

STUDENTS AND FACULTY

Enrollment: 4,652. **Student Body:** 61% female, 39% male, 9% out-of-state, 0% international (5 countries represented). Asian 1%, African American 11%, Caucasian 85%, Hispanic 2%, Native American 1%
Retention and Graduation: 55% freshmen return for sophomore year. 16% freshmen graduate within 4 years. 35% freshmen graduate within 6 years. 20% grads go on to further study within 1 year. 11% grads pursue arts and sciences degrees. 1% grads pursue law degrees. 6% grads pursue business degrees. 2% grads pursue medical degrees. **Faculty:** 180 full-time faculty, 75% hold PhDs, 41% are members of minority groups, 6% are women. 0% of classes are taught by teaching assistants.

ACADEMICS

Degrees: associate, bachelor's, certificate, terminal associate, transfer associate. **Classes:** Most classes have 20–29 students. Most lab/discussion sessions have 20–29 students. **Majors with Highest Enrollment:** Criminal Justice/Law Enforcement Administration; Registered Nursing/Registered Nurse; Business/Commerce. **Special Study Options:** distance learning, double major, dual enrollment, honors program, internships, liberal arts/career combination, teacher certification program, weekend college. **Disability Services:** Special programs offered to physically disabled students include note-taking services, reader services, tutors. **Career services:** career/job search classes, career assessment.

FACILITIES

Housing: Coed dorms, fraternity/sorority housing, apartments for single students. 99% of campus accessible to physically disabled. **Special Academic Facilities/Equipment:** Multi-media classroom building, Planetarium.

CAMPUS LIFE

Environment: Village. **Activities:** Choral groups, concert band, dance, drama/theater, jazz band, marching band, music ensembles, pep band, student government, student newspaper, yearbook. 64 registered organizations, 5 honor societies, 7 religious organizations. 5 fraternities, 6 sororities. **Athletics (Intercollegiate):** *Men:* baseball, basketball, football, golf. *Women:* basketball, golf, softball, tennis, volleyball.

ADMISSIONS

Freshman Academic Profile: 8% in top 10% of high school class, 25% in top 25% of high school class, 55% in top 50% of high school class. 95% from public high schools. ACT middle 50% range 16–22. Minimum paper TOEFL 500. **Freshman Admission Requirements:** High school diploma is required and GED is accepted. *Academic units required:* 4 English, 3 mathematics, 2 science, (1 science labs), 3 social studies, 3 academic electives, 1 Visual/Perf Arts. **Freshman Admission Statistics:** 2,421 applied, 100% admitted, 43% enrolled. **Transfer Admission Requirements:** college transcript(s), Lowest grade transferable D. **General Admission Information:** Application Fee $15. Regular application deadline 8/15. Notification on a rolling basis, beginning on or about 10/1. Nonfall registration accepted. Credit offered for CEEB Advanced Placement tests.

COSTS AND FINANCIAL AID

Annual in-state tuition $4,098. Annual out-of-state tuition $7,674. Room and board $4,058. Required fees $366. Average book expense $700. **Required Forms and Deadlines:** FAFSA, Institution's own financial aid form. **Notification of Awards:** Applicants will be notified of awards on a rolling basis beginning 3/2. **Types of Aid:** *Need-based scholarships/grants:* Federal Pell, SEOG, state scholarships/grants, private scholarships, the school's own gift aid. *Loans:* Subsidized Stafford, Unsubsidized Stafford, PLUS, Federal Perkins. *Student Employment:* Federal Work-Study Program available. Institutional employment available. Highest amount earned per year from on-campus jobs $1,400. Off-campus job opportunities are good. **Financial Aid Statistics:** 66% freshmen, 67% undergrads receive need-based scholarship or grant aid. 48% freshmen, 37% undergrads receive non-need-based scholarship or grant aid. 66% freshmen, 79% undergrads receive need-based self-help aid. 3% freshmen, 5% undergrads receive athletic scholarships. 68% undergrads borrow to pay for school. **Criteria for awarding institutional aid:** *Non-need-based:* academics, alumni affiliation, art, athletics, job skills, leadership, minority status, music/drama, state/district residency.

MITCHELL COLLEGE

437 Pequot Avenue, New London, CT 6320
Phone: 860-701-5011 · **Financial Aid Phone:** 800-443-2811
E-mail: admissions@mitchell.edu · **CEEB Code:** 3528
Fax: 860-444-1209 · **Website:** http://www.mitchell.edu/ · **ACT Code:** 572

This private school was founded in 1938. It has a 68-acre campus.

RATINGS

Admissions Selectivity Rating: 64   **Fire Safety Rating:** 67

STUDENTS AND FACULTY

Enrollment: 785. **Student Body:** 47% female, 53% male, 42% out-of-state, 0% international. Asian 2%, African American 11%, Caucasian 68%, Hispanic 13%, Native American 1%
Retention and Graduation: 57% freshmen return for sophomore year. **Faculty:** 35 full-time faculty, 74% hold PhDs, 51% are members of minority groups. 0% of classes are taught by teaching assistants.

ACADEMICS

Degrees: associate, bachelor's, certificate. **Special Study Options:** dual enrollment, English as a Second Language (ESL), internships, teacher certification program. **Disability Services:** Special programs offered to physically disabled students include note-taking services, reader services, tape recorders, tutors.

FACILITIES

Housing: Coed dorms, special housing for disabled students, Four residence halls are Victorian and Colonial houses located on the waterfront. Three other residence halls are of traditional design. 50% of campus accessible to physically disabled. **Special Academic Facilities/Equipment:** Private dock w/fleet of sailboats, 2 private beaches, 26 acres of woods.

CAMPUS LIFE

Environment: Town. **Activities:** Choral groups, dance, drama/theater, literary magazine, student government, student newspaper, yearbook. 30 registered organizations, 2 honor societies, 2 religious organizations. **Athletics (Intercollegiate):** *Men:* baseball, basketball, cross-country, golf, lacrosse, soccer, tennis. *Women:* basketball, cross-country, golf, soccer, softball, tennis, volleyball.

ADMISSIONS

Freshman Academic Profile: Average high school GPA 2.68. Minimum paper TOEFL 500. **Basis for Candidate Selection:** *Very important factors considered include:* recommendation(s), rigor of secondary school record, interview. *Important factors considered include:* application essay, standardized test scores, character/personal qualities, extracurricular activities, talent/ability. *Other factors considered include:* Class rank, alumni/ae relation, volunteer work, work experience. **Freshman Admission Requirements:** High school diploma is required and GED is accepted. **Freshman Admission Statistics:** 1,041 applied, 60% admitted, 24% enrolled. **Transfer Admission Requirements:** High school transcript, college transcript(s), essay or personal statement, standardized test scores, Minimum college GPA of 2.0 required. Lowest grade transferable C-. **General Admission Information:** Application Fee $30. Early decision application deadline 11/15. Notification on a rolling basis, beginning on or about 12/15. Nonfall registration accepted. Admission may be deferred for a maximum of 1 year. Credit and/or placement offered for CEEB Advanced Placement tests.

COSTS AND FINANCIAL AID

Annual tuition $26,774. Room and board $12,492. Required fees $1,720. Average book expense $1,500. **Required Forms and Deadlines:** FAFSA. **Notification of Awards:** Applicants will be notified of awards on a rolling basis beginning 3/1. **Types of Aid:** *Need-based scholarships/grants:* Federal Pell, SEOG, state scholarships/grants, private scholarships, the school's own gift aid. *Loans:* Subsidized Stafford, Unsubsidized Stafford, PLUS, Federal Perkins, Plato. **Financial Aid Statistics:** 100% freshmen, 99% undergrads receive need-based scholarship or grant aid. 93% freshmen, 87% undergrads receive non-need-based scholarship or grant aid. 93% freshmen, 95% undergrads receive need-based self-help aid. 0% freshmen, 0% undergrads receive athletic scholarships. 73% undergrads borrow to pay for school. Average cumulative indebtedness $28,416. **Criteria for awarding institutional aid:** *Non-need-based:* academics, alumni affiliation, art, leadership, state/district residency.

MOLLOY COLLEGE

1000 Hempstead Avenue, Rockville Centre, NY 11570
Phone: 516-323-4000 · **Financial Aid Phone:** 516-323-4209
E-mail: admissions@molloy.edu · **CEEB Code:** 2415
Website: http://www.molloy.edu/ · **ACT Code:** 2820

This private school, affiliated with the Roman Catholic Church, was founded in 1955. It has a 35-acre campus.

RATINGS

Admissions Selectivity Rating: 82   **Fire Safety Rating:** 66

STUDENTS AND FACULTY

Enrollment: 3,293. **Student Body:** 75% female, 25% male, 2% out-of-state, 0% international (5 countries represented). Asian 7%, African American 12%, Caucasian 63%, Hispanic 14%, Native American <1% **Retention and Graduation:** 90% freshmen return for sophomore year. 40% freshmen graduate within 4 years. 70% freshmen graduate within 6 years. **Faculty:** 187 full-time faculty, 75% hold PhDs, 73% are members of minority groups, 18% are women. 0% of classes are taught by teaching assistants.

ACADEMICS

Degrees: associate, bachelor's, master's, post-master's certificate. **Classes:** Most classes have 10–19 students. Most lab/discussion sessions have 10–19 students. **Majors with Highest Enrollment:** Registered Nursing/Registered Nurse; Criminal Justice/Safety Studies; Registered Nursing, Nursing Administration, Nursing Research and Clinical Nursing. **Special Study Options:** double major, English as a Second Language (ESL), honors program, independent study, internships, liberal arts/career combination, student-designed major, study abroad, teacher certification program. **Combined degree programs:** BSW/MSW, BS/MS, BS/MBA. **Disability Services:** Special programs offered to physically disabled students include note-taking services, reader services, tape recorders, tutors. **Career services:** Alumni network, alumni services, internships, regional alumni.

FACILITIES

Housing: 100% of campus accessible to physically disabled. **Special Academic Facilities/Equipment:** Professional Repertory Theatre Company in residence, dance studio, institute of cross-cultural and cross-ethnic studies, institute of gerontology, cablevision studio. **Computers:** 100% of classrooms, 100% of libraries, 100% of dining areas, 100% of student union, 100% of common outdoor areas have wireless network access. Students can register for classes online. Administrative functions (other than registration) can be performed online.

CAMPUS LIFE

Environment: Village. **Activities:** Choral groups, dance, drama/theater, jazz band, literary magazine, music ensembles, student government, student newspaper, yearbook, Campus Ministries 21 registered organizations, 18 honor societies, 1 religious organization. **Athletics (Intercollegiate):** *Men:* baseball, basketball, cross-country, lacrosse, soccer, track/field (outdoor), track/field (indoor). *Women:* basketball, cross-country, lacrosse, soccer, softball, tennis, track/field (outdoor), track/field (indoor), volleyball. **On-Campus Highlights:** The Anselma Room, The Fitness Center, Center for Social and Ethical Concerns, Media Center. **Environmental Initiatives:** The Sustainability Institute at Molloy College. http://www.molloy.edu/si/index.asp

ADMISSIONS

Freshman Academic Profile: Average high school GPA 3. 34% in top 10% of high school class, 54% in top 25% of high school class, 93% in top 50% of high school class. 60% from public high schools. SAT Math middle 50% range 490-580. SAT Critical Reading middle 50% range 490-560. SAT Writing middle 50% range 470-570. ACT middle 50% range 22-26. Minimum paper TOEFL 500. **Basis for Candidate Selection:** *Very important factors considered include:* academic GPA, rigor of secondary school record, standardized test scores. *Other factors considered include:* Class rank, application essay, recommendation(s), extracurricular activities, interview, talent/ability, volunteer work, work experience. **Freshman Admission Requirements:** High school diploma is required and GED is accepted. *Academic units required:* 4 English, 3 mathematics, 3 science, 3 foreign language, 4 social studies. **Freshman Admission Statistics:** 3,277 applied, 75% admitted, 20% enrolled. **Transfer Admission Requirements:** college transcript(s), Minimum college GPA of 2.0 required. Lowest grade transferable c. **General Admission Information:** Application Fee $30. Notification on a rolling basis, beginning on or about 10/15. Nonfall registration accepted. Admission may be deferred for a maximum of One Year. Credit offered for CEEB Advanced Placement tests.

COSTS AND FINANCIAL AID

Annual tuition $25,800. Room and board $13,590. Required fees $1,050. Average book expense $1,444. **Required Forms and Deadlines:** FAFSA, State aid

form. **Notification of Awards:** Applicants will be notified of awards on a rolling basis beginning 2/1. **Types of Aid:** *Need-based scholarships/grants:* Federal Pell, SEOG, state scholarships/grants, private scholarships, the school's own gift aid, Federal Nursing Scholarships. *Loans:* Subsidized Stafford, Unsubsidized Stafford, PLUS, Federal Perkins, Federal Nursing. *Student Employment:* Federal Work-Study Program available. Off-campus job opportunities are good. **Financial Aid Statistics:** 97% freshmen, 93% undergrads receive need-based scholarship or grant aid. 7% freshmen, 6% undergrads receive non-need-based scholarship or grant aid. 79% freshmen, 82% undergrads receive need-based self-help aid. 3% freshmen, 2% undergrads receive athletic scholarships. 97% freshmen, 82% undergrads receive any aid. 73% undergrads borrow to pay for school. **Criteria for awarding institutional aid:** *Non-need-based:* academics, alumni affiliation, art, athletics, leadership, music/drama, religious affiliation.

See page 1096.

MONMOUTH COLLEGE

700 East Broadway, Monmouth, IL 61462
Phone: 309-457-2131 · **Financial Aid Phone:** 309-457-2129
E-mail: admissions@monmouthcollege.edu · **CEEB Code:** 1484
Fax: 309-457-2141 · **Website:** www.monmouthcollege.edu · **ACT Code:** 1084

This private school, affiliated with the Presbyterian Church, was founded in 1853. It has a 80-acre campus.

RATINGS

Admissions Selectivity Rating: 80   **Fire Safety Rating:** 84

STUDENTS AND FACULTY

Enrollment: 1,280. **Student Body:** 55% female, 45% male, 8% out-of-state, 3% international (24 countries represented). Asian 1%, African American 11%, Caucasian 64%, Hispanic 13%, Native American 1% **Retention and Graduation:** 78% freshmen return for sophomore year. 48% freshmen graduate within 4 years. 15% grads go on to further study within 1 year. 10% grads pursue arts and sciences degrees. 1% grads pursue law degrees. 1% grads pursue medical degrees. **Faculty:** 92 full-time faculty, 85% hold PhDs, 43% are members of minority groups, 7% are women. 0% of classes are taught by teaching assistants.

ACADEMICS

Degrees: bachelor's. **Classes:** Most classes have 20–29 students. Most lab/discussion sessions have 10–19 students. **Majors with Highest Enrollment:** Speech Communication and Rhetoric; Business Administration and Management; Psychology. **Special Study Options:** double major, English as a Second Language (ESL), exchange student program (domestic), honors program, independent study, internships, student-designed major, study abroad, teacher certification program. **Honors programs:** The Monmouth Coillege Honors Program is intended for a select group of academically well-prepared and intellectually ambitious students. Acceptance into the program is determined competitively,normally occurring at the end of the first semester of the freshman year. The program consists of three levels: exploration of the history of the liberal arts as a field of inquiry, in-depth seminars upon historically significant persons, events, movements and ideas, and a senior capstone course. **Combined degree programs:** 3/3 and 3/4 agreements in architecture, nursing, phys. therapy, med. tech. **Disability Services:** Special programs offered to physically disabled students include note-taking services, reader services, tape recorders, tutors. **Career services:** Alumni network, alumni services, career/job search classes, career assessment, internships, regional alumni. All Monmouth students are encouraged to seek out rigorous, academically-grounded internship opportunities. The Career Center provides pre-internship orientation to professional office conduct, placement advising, maintenance of contacts with internship sponsors, and quality-control oversight of internship experiences. The Career Center coordinates closely with academic departments in selecting internship opportunities and in assisting students with placements.

FACILITIES

Housing: Coed dorms, special housing for disabled students, men's dorms, special housing for international students, women's dorms, fraternity/sorority housing, apartments for single students, Wellness Housing, Theme Housing. 70% of campus accessible to physically disabled. **Special Academic Facilities/Equipment:** Shields Art & Antiquities Collection, Wackerle Career & Leadership Center, Mellinger Teaching & Learning Center, MC-TV (student-run television station), WMCR (student-run radio station). **Computers:** 100% of classrooms, 100% of dorms, 100% of libraries, 100% of dining areas, 100% of student union, 80% of common outdoor areas have wireless network access. Students can register for classes online. Administrative functions (other than registration) can be performed online.

CAMPUS LIFE

Environment: Village. **Activities:** Choral groups, concert band, dance, drama/theater, jazz band, literary magazine, marching band, music ensembles, musical theater, radio station, student government, student newspaper, symphony orchestra, television station, Campus Ministries, International Student Organization. 67 registered organizations, 16 honor societies, 6 religious organizations. 4 fraternities, 3 sororities. **Athletics (Intercollegiate):** *Men:* baseball, basketball, cross-country, diving, football, golf, soccer, swimming, tennis, track/field (outdoor), track/field (indoor). *Women:* basketball, cross-country, diving, golf, soccer, softball, swimming, tennis, track/field (outdoor), track/field (indoor), volleyball. **On-Campus Highlights:** Stockdale Student Center, Hewes Library (including coffee shop!), Huff Athletic Center, Mellinger Teaching and Learning Center, Wallace Hall—main floor coffee/study, The nature trail at LeSuer Nature Preserve offers many opportunities for recreation and scientific study. The new Monmouth College athletic fields are available for team practice, of course, but also open to ad hoc student groups and individuals. **Environmental Initiatives:** The College has a comprehensive recycling and waste diversion program. We provide recycling receptacles for paper, glass, plastic and aluminum in every office and every bedroom in all academic buildings and residence halls, with a recycling center for electronics, flourescent lights and cell phones in the Stockdale Center (the student center). We recycle all cardboard generated at the dining service. We have a fleet of 5 hybrid cars for use by Monmouth faculty and staff for college purposes. In 2007 we retrofitted light fixtures in all of our academic buildings, and, in 2008, placed energy-efficient boilers in five buildings. Our new academic building will meet LEEDS Silver certification standards. We offer a popular organic-foods meal plan. We provide 'trayless' dining in the main cafeteria.

ADMISSIONS

Freshman Academic Profile: Average high school GPA 3.3. 13% in top 10% of high school class, 35% in top 25% of high school class, 75% in top 50% of high school class. 80% from public high schools. SAT Math middle 50% range 500-580. SAT Critical Reading middle 50% range 480-600. SAT Writing middle 50% range 410-510. ACT middle 50% range 19-25. Minimum internet-based TOEFL 79. Minimum paper TOEFL 550. **Basis for Candidate Selection:** *Very important factors considered include:* rigor of secondary school record. *Important factors considered include:* Class rank, academic GPA, standardized test scores, character/personal qualities, extracurricular activities, interview, talent/ability. *Other factors considered include:* application essay, recommendation(s), alumni/ae relation, first generation, geographical residence, state residency, volunteer work, work experience. **Freshman Admission Requirements:** High school diploma is required and GED is accepted. *Academic units required:* 4 English, 3 mathematics, 2 science, (1 science labs), 2 foreign language, 2 social studies, 1 history. **Freshman Admission Statistics:** 2,849 applied, 69% admitted, 20% enrolled. **Transfer Admission Requirements:** college transcript(s), Minimum college GPA of 2.5 required. Lowest grade transferable C-. **General Admission Information:** Notification on a rolling basis, beginning on or about 9/15. Nonfall registration accepted. Admission may be deferred for a maximum of 1 year. Placement offered for CEEB Advanced Placement tests.

COSTS AND FINANCIAL AID

Annual tuition $34,200. Room and board $8,060. Required fees $190. Average book expense $1,200. **Required Forms and Deadlines:** FAFSA. **Notification of Awards:** Applicants will be notified of awards on a rolling basis beginning 3/1. **Types of Aid:** *Need-based scholarships/grants:* Federal Pell, SEOG, state scholarships/grants, private scholarships, the school's own gift aid. *Loans:* Direct Subsidized Stafford, Direct Unsubsidized Stafford, Direct PLUS, Subsidized Stafford, Unsubsidized Stafford, PLUS, Federal Perkins, college/university loans from institutional funds. *Student Employment:* Federal Work-Study Program available. Institutional employment available. Highest amount earned per year from on-campus jobs $2,325. Off-campus job opportunities are fair. **Financial Aid Statistics:** 100% freshmen, 100% undergrads receive need-based scholarship or grant aid. 10% freshmen, 12% undergrads receive non-need-based scholarship or grant aid. 85% freshmen, 82% undergrads receive need-based self-help aid. 0% freshmen, 0% undergrads receive athletic scholarships. 100% freshmen, 100% undergrads receive any aid. 89% undergrads borrow to pay for school. Average cumulative indebtedness $28,036. **Criteria for awarding institutional aid:** *Non-need-based:* academics, art, leadership, music/drama.

MONMOUTH UNIVERSITY (NJ)

Admission, Monmouth University, West Long Branch, NJ 07764-1898
Phone: 732-571-3456 · **Financial Aid Phone:** 732-571-3463
E-mail: admission@monmouth.edu · **CEEB Code:** 2416
Fax: 732-263-5166 · **Website:** www.monmouth.edu · **ACT Code:** 2571

This private school was founded in 1933. It has a 156-acre campus.

RATINGS

Admissions Selectivity Rating: 81   **Fire Safety Rating:** 97

STUDENTS AND FACULTY

Enrollment: 4,584. **Student Body:** 59% female, 41% male, 12% out-of-state, 1% international (24 countries represented). Asian 3%, African American 5%, Caucasian 76%, Hispanic 10%, Native American <1%
Retention and Graduation: 49% freshmen graduate within 4 years. 67% freshmen graduate within 6 years. **Faculty:** 278 full-time faculty, 83% hold PhDs, 55% are members of minority groups, 17% are women. 0% of classes are taught by teaching assistants.

ACADEMICS

Degrees: associate, bachelor's, certificate, master's, post-bachelor's certificate, post-master's certificate. **Classes:** Most classes have 10–19 students. **Majors with Highest Enrollment:** Business Administration and Management; Computer and Information Sciences; Education. **Special Study Options:** Accelerated program, cooperative education program, cross-registration, distance learning, double major, dual enrollment, honors program, independent study, internships, liberal arts/career combination, student-designed major, study abroad, teacher certification program, Clinical Lab Science Program in collaboration with UMDNJ. Air Force ROTC at Rutgers University. Affiliated with Washington Center providing semester and summer internships and shorter symposia. Monmouth Medical Scholars Program allows five incoming freshmen to complete undergraduate degree at Monmouth, including nine credit clinical requirement at Monmouth Medical Center, and commence medical studies at Drexel University School of Medicine. Study Abroad in London at Regent's College and Sydney, Australia at Macquarie University. **Honors programs:** The Honors School is committed to providing motivated students with a unique learning environment in a community of scholars. By supporting both disciplinary and interdisciplinary approaches to education, the Honors School seeks to help students develop not only depth within their intended field of study, but also an appreciation for how that knowledge is embedded within a broader context of intellectual inquiry. The Honors School also is dedicated to raising students' level of cultural, ethical, and societal awareness as its participants develop into well-rounded scholars and citizens within a global community. **Combined degree programs:** BA/MD, BA/MA, 5 yr programs BS/MBA, BS//MS, BA/MA, BSW/MSW, BA/MEd, BA/MSEd. **Disability Services:** Special programs offered to physically disabled students include note-taking services, reader services, tape recorders, tutors. **Career services:** Alumni network, alumni services, career/job search classes, career assessment, internships, regional alumni. Career services highlights include an Experiential Education graduation requirement.

FACILITIES

Housing: Coed dorms, apartments for single students, Wellness Housing, Theme Housing, Honor Program Housing, Health & Wellness housing, Community Service housing. 95% of campus accessible to physically disabled. **Special Academic Facilities/Equipment:** Art gallery, instructional media center with TV and Radio stations, theatre. **Computers:** 100% of classrooms, 100% of dorms, 100% of libraries, 100% of dining areas, 100% of student union, 90% of common outdoor areas have wireless network access. Students can register for classes online. Administrative functions (other than registration) can be performed online.

CAMPUS LIFE

Environment: Village. **Activities:** Choral groups, concert band, dance, drama/theater, jazz band, literary magazine, music ensembles, musical theater, pep band, radio station, student government, student newspaper, television station, yearbook, Campus Ministries, International Student Organization, Model UN. 67 registered organizations, 19 honor societies, 3 religious organizations. 7 fraternities, 6 sororities. **Athletics (Intercollegiate):** *Men:* baseball, basketball, cross-country, football, golf, soccer, tennis, track/field (outdoor), track/field (indoor). *Women:* basketball, cross-country, field hockey, golf, lacrosse, soccer, softball, tennis, track/field (outdoor), track/field (indoor). **On-Campus Highlights:** Woodrow Wilson Hall, Plangere Center for Communication, Rebecca

Stafford Student Center, Multipurpose Activity Center **Environmental Initiatives:** EPA MOU discussed above Solar power 454.5 KW solar installation on four university buildings, additional 700 KW installation on 7 buildings in 2012 Establishment of the Sustainability Advisory Council. The Monmouth University Sustainability Advisory Council (SAC) is an interdisciplinary work group comprised of students, faculty, staff & administrators that promotes environmental awareness & encourages the development of an environmentally responsible & sustainable campus community in its operations, education, research, outreach & services.

ADMISSIONS

Freshman Academic Profile: Average high school GPA 3.37. 18.6% in top 10% of high school class, 49% in top 25% of high school class, 81.4% in top 50% of high school class. 85% from public high schools. SAT Math middle 50% range 490-580. SAT Critical Reading middle 50% range 470-560. SAT Writing middle 50% range 480-580. ACT middle 50% range 22-25. Minimum internet-based TOEFL 79. Minimum paper TOEFL 550. **Basis for Candidate Selection:** *Very important factors considered include:* academic GPA, rigor of secondary school record, standardized test scores. *Important factors considered include:* extracurricular activities, volunteer work, work experience. *Other factors considered include:* application essay, recommendation(s), alumni/ae relation, character/personal qualities. **Freshman Admission Requirements:** High school diploma is required and GED is accepted. *Academic units required:* 4 English, 3 mathematics, 2 science, (1 science labs), 2 history, 5 academic electives. **Freshman Admission Statistics:** 7,691 applied, 74% admitted, 19% enrolled. **Transfer Admission Requirements:** college transcript(s), statement of good standing from prior institution(s). Minimum college GPA of 2.25 required. Lowest grade transferable C. **General Admission Information:** Application Fee $50. Regular application deadline 3/1. Nonfall registration accepted. Admission may be deferred for a maximum of 2 semesters. Credit and/or placement offered for CEEB Advanced Placement tests.

COSTS AND FINANCIAL AID

Annual tuition $31,682. Room and board $11,798. Required fees $628. Average book expense $1,100. **Required Forms and Deadlines:** FAFSA. **Notification of Awards:** Applicants will be notified of awards on a rolling basis beginning 2/15. **Types of Aid:** *Need-based scholarships/grants:* Federal Pell, SEOG, state scholarships/grants, private scholarships, the school's own gift aid, Federal Nursing Scholarships. *Loans:* Direct Subsidized Stafford, Direct Unsubsidized Stafford, Direct PLUS, PLUS, Federal Perkins, state loans, college/university loans from institutional funds, Alternative Loans. *Student Employment:* Federal Work-Study Program available. Institutional employment available. Highest amount earned per year from on-campus jobs $5,000. Off-campus job opportunities are good. **Financial Aid Statistics:** 60% freshmen, 52% undergrads receive need-based scholarship or grant aid. 98% freshmen, 94% undergrads receive non-need-based scholarship or grant aid. 84% freshmen, 84% undergrads receive need-based self-help aid. 7% freshmen, 9% undergrads receive athletic scholarships. 99% freshmen, 97% undergrads receive any aid. 77% undergrads borrow to pay for school. Average cumulative indebtedness $30,385. **Criteria for awarding institutional aid:** *Non-need-based:* academics, alumni affiliation, art, athletics, leadership, religious affiliation, state/district residency.

MONROE COLLEGE

2501 Jerome Ave, Bronx, NY 10468
Phone: 718-933-6700
E-mail: cpatrick@monroecollege.edu
Fax: 718-364-3552 · **Website:** http://www.monroecollege.edu/

This is a proprietary school.

RATINGS

Admissions Selectivity Rating: 61   Fire Safety Rating: 60*

STUDENTS AND FACULTY

Enrollment: 6,713. **Student Body:** 64% female, 36% male, 2% out-of-state, 4% international. Asian 1%, African American 46%, Caucasian 2%, Hispanic 42%, Native American <1%
Retention and Graduation: 75% freshmen return for sophomore year. **Faculty:** 70 full-time faculty, 40% hold PhDs, 44% are members of minority groups, 57% are women.

ACADEMICS

Degrees: associate, bachelor's, master's. **Classes:** Most classes have 20–29 students. **Special Study Options:** distance learning, honors program, independent study, internships, weekend college.

FACILITIES
Housing: Coed dorms.
CAMPUS LIFE
Activities: literary magazine.
ADMISSIONS
Basis for Candidate Selection: *Very important factors considered include:* application essay, academic GPA, recommendation(s), rigor of secondary school record, character/personal qualities, extracurricular activities, level of applicant's interest, talent/ability. *Important factors considered include:* Class rank, standardized test scores, racial/ethnic status, volunteer work. *Other factors considered include:* first generation, geographical residence, interview, state residency, work experience. **Freshman Admission Requirements:** High school diploma or equivalent is not required. **Freshman Admission Statistics:** 2,108 applied, 67% admitted, 95% enrolled. **General Admission Information:** Application Fee $80. Regular application deadline 1/1. Regular notification 3/22. Nonfall registration not accepted. Admission may be deferred for a maximum of 1 year.

COSTS AND FINANCIAL AID
Average book expense $900. **Required Forms and Deadlines:** FAFSA. **Notification of Awards:** Applicants will be notified of awards on a rolling basis beginning 4/1. **Types of Aid:** *Need-based scholarships/grants:* Federal Pell, SEOG, private scholarships, the school's own gift aid. *Loans:* Subsidized Stafford, Unsubsidized Stafford, PLUS. *Student Employment:* Institutional employment available. **Financial Aid Statistics:** 97% freshmen, 100% undergrads receive need-based scholarship or grant aid. 1% freshmen, 1% undergrads receive non-need-based scholarship or grant aid. 41% freshmen, 43% undergrads receive need-based self-help aid. 1% freshmen, 0% undergrads receive athletic scholarships. 27% undergrads borrow to pay for school. **Criteria for awarding institutional aid:** *Non-need-based:* academics, leadership.

MONTANA STATE UNIVERSITY

PO Box 172190, Bozeman, MT 59717-2190
Phone: 406-994-2452 · **Financial Aid Phone:** 406-994-2845
E-mail: admissions@montana.edu · **CEEB Code:** 4488
Fax: 406-994-1923 · **Website:** http://www.montana.edu · **ACT Code:** 2420

This public school was founded in 1893. It has a 1780-acre campus.

RATINGS

Admissions Selectivity Rating: 81   Fire Safety Rating: 88

STUDENTS AND FACULTY
Enrollment: 13,132. **Student Body:** 45% female, 55% male, 39% out-of-state, 3% international (55 countries represented). Asian 0%, African American 1%, Caucasian 1%, Hispanic 3%, Native American 1%
Retention and Graduation: 76% freshmen return for sophomore year. 20% freshmen graduate within 4 years. 31% grads go on to further study within 1 year. **Faculty:** 549 full-time faculty, 78% hold PhDs, 41% are members of minority groups, 6% are women. 6% of classes are taught by teaching assistants.

ACADEMICS
Degrees: bachelor's, certificate, doctoral, master's, post-master's certificate. **Classes:** Most classes have 10–19 students. Most lab/discussion sessions have 10–19 students. **Majors with Highest Enrollment:** Liberal Arts and Sciences/Liberal Studies; Marketing/Marketing Management; Registered Nursing/Registered Nurse. **Special Study Options:** cooperative education program, cross-registration, distance learning, double major, English as a Second Language (ESL), exchange student program (domestic), honors program, independent study, internships, student-designed major, study abroad, teacher certification program. **Honors programs:** http://www.montana.edu/wwwuhp/. **Combined degree programs:** BA/MEng, BA in Environmental Design/Master of Architecture. **Disability Services:** Special programs offered to physically disabled students include note-taking services, reader services, tape recorders, tutors. **Career services:** Alumni network, career/job search classes, career assessment, internships.

FACILITIES
Housing: Coed dorms, men's dorms, women's dorms, fraternity/sorority housing, apartments for married students, apartments for single students, Wellness Housing, Theme Housing, Wellness floors, non-smoking, older student floors. 90% of campus accessible to physically disabled. **Special Academic Facilities/Equipment:** Museum of the Rockies (History & Paleontology Museum); Planetarium; Studio 1080 (multi-media, interactive learning center); Subzero Lab; Wind Tunnel; Clean Laboratory; Nano Laboratory; Ion Beam Laboratory; Electron Microscopes; Center for Biofilm Engineering; Plant Growth Center

(29 green houses); Fitness Center ($11.7 million student funded renovation completed in 2008); Chemistry & Biochemistry Research Facility; Copeland Art Gallery (Art Gallery); Exit Art Gallery (Student Art Gallery); Wild Trout Research Laboratory; Burns Telecommunications Center; Plant and Animal Bioscience Research Facilities. **Computers:** Students can register for classes online. Administrative functions (other than registration) can be performed online.

CAMPUS LIFE

Environment: Town. **Activities:** Choral groups, concert band, dance, drama/theater, jazz band, literary magazine, marching band, music ensembles, musical theater, pep band, radio station, student newspaper, student-run film society, television station, Campus Ministries, International Student Organization. 140 registered organizations, 18 honor societies, 12 religious organizations. 9 fraternities, 4 sororities. **Athletics (Intercollegiate):** *Men:* basketball, cheerleading, cross-country, football, rodeo, skiing (downhill/alpine), skiing (nordic/cross-country), tennis, track/field (outdoor), track/field (indoor). *Women:* basketball, cheerleading, cross-country, golf, rodeo, skiing (downhill/alpine), skiing (nordic/cross-country), tennis, track/field (outdoor), track/field (indoor), volleyball. **On-Campus Highlights:** Museum of the Rockies, Planetarium, Fitness Center ($11.7 million student funded renovation completed in 2008, Burns Telecommunications Center, Chemistry & Biochemistry Research Facility, Blackbox Theatre, Student Union Building, Exit Art Gallery (Student Art Gallery), Copeland Art Gallery (Art Gallery). **Environmental Initiatives:** Building Lighting Retrofit projects; Recycling to reduce waste stream—we have increased diversion 3% by weight in each of the last three years; Reduce the building's energy consumption by nearly 50% and save over 4,000,000 gallons of municipal water annually.

ADMISSIONS

Freshman Academic Profile: Average high school GPA 3.3. 19% in top 10% of high school class, 44% in top 25% of high school class, 72% in top 50% of high school class. SAT Math middle 50% range 510-630. SAT Critical Reading middle 50% range 500-630. SAT Writing middle 50% range 490-600. ACT middle 50% range 21-27. Minimum internet-based TOEFL 71. Minimum paper TOEFL 525. **Basis for Candidate Selection:** *Very important factors considered include:* Class rank, rigor of secondary school record, standardized test scores. **Freshman Admission Requirements:** High school diploma is required and GED is accepted. *Academic units required:* 4 English, 3 mathematics, 2 science, (2 science labs), 3 social studies, 2 years chosen from the following: foreign language, computer science, visual/performing arts. **Freshman Admission Statistics:** 12,578 applied, 85% admitted, 27% enrolled. **Transfer Admission Requirements:** college transcript(s), standardized test scores, statement of good standing from prior institution(s). Minimum college GPA of 2.0 required. Lowest grade transferable D-. **General Admission Information:** Application Fee $30. Nonfall registration accepted. Admission may be deferred for a maximum of one year. Credit and/or placement offered for CEEB Advanced Placement tests.

COSTS AND FINANCIAL AID

Annual out-of-state tuition $19,157. Room and board $8,220. Required fees $1,491. Average book expense $1,200. **Required Forms and Deadlines:** FAFSA. **Notification of Awards:** Applicants will be notified of awards on a rolling basis beginning 4/1. **Types of Aid:** *Need-based scholarships/grants:* Federal Pell, SEOG, state scholarships/grants, private scholarships, the school's own gift aid, Federal Nursing Scholarships. *Loans:* Subsidized Stafford, Unsubsidized Stafford, PLUS, Federal Perkins, Federal Nursing, college/university loans from institutional funds. *Student Employment:* Institutional employment available. Highest amount earned per year from on-campus jobs $11,700. Off-campus job opportunities are good. **Financial Aid Statistics:** 77% freshmen, 73% undergrads receive need-based scholarship or grant aid. 5% freshmen, 3% undergrads receive non-need-based scholarship or grant aid. 69% freshmen, 79% undergrads receive need-based self-help aid. 1% freshmen, 1% undergrads receive athletic scholarships. 55% freshmen, 52% undergrads receive any aid. 65% undergrads borrow to pay for school. Average cumulative indebtedness $25,253. **Criteria for awarding institutional aid:** *Non-need-based:* academics, alumni affiliation, art, athletics, job skills, leadership, minority status, music/drama, state/district residency.

MONTANA STATE UNIVERSITY BILLINGS

1500 University Drive, Billings, MT 59101
Phone: 406-657-2158 • **Financial Aid Phone:** 406-657-1617 • **CEEB Code:** 4298
Fax: 406-657-2302 • **Website:** www.msubillings.edu • **ACT Code:** 2416

This public school was founded in 1927. It has a 92-acre campus.

RATINGS

Admissions Selectivity Rating: 70   Fire Safety Rating: 74

STUDENTS AND FACULTY

Enrollment: 4,091. **Student Body:** 62% female, 38% male, 11% out-of-state, 3% international (21 countries represented). Asian 1%, African American 1%, Caucasian 81%, Hispanic 5%, Native American 4%
Retention and Graduation: 10% grads go on to further study within 1 year. 70% grads pursue arts and sciences degrees. 14% grads pursue business degrees. 1% grads pursue medical degrees. **Faculty:** 165 full-time faculty, 0% hold PhDs, 41% are members of minority groups, 5% are women. 0% of classes are taught by teaching assistants.

ACADEMICS

Degrees: associate, bachelor's, certificate, master's, post-bachelor's certificate, terminal associate, transfer associate. **Classes:** Most classes have 20–29 students. Most lab/discussion sessions have 10–19 students. **Majors with Highest Enrollment:** Elementary Education and Teaching; Liberal Arts and Sciences/Liberal Studies; Business/Commerce. **Special Study Options:** Accelerated program, cooperative education program, cross-registration, distance learning, double major, dual enrollment, English as a Second Language (ESL), external degree program, honors program, independent study, internships, student-designed major, study abroad, teacher certification program, weekend college, On-line degrees and extensive on-line course offerings. Evening College. **Honors programs:** The MSU-Billings University Honors Program is designed for curious students who are eager to participate actively in their education. Classes in the University Honors Program tend to be smaller than other classes and emphasize class discussion. Often these classes are interdisciplinary in nature; this helps students study issues from several perspectives. Some classes are team-taught, which also enriches the discussion. **Disability Services:** Special programs offered to physically disabled students include note-taking services, reader services, tape recorders, tutors. **Career services:** career/job search classes, career assessment, internships.

FACILITIES

Housing: Coed dorms, special housing for disabled students, men's dorms, women's dorms, apartments for married students, apartments for students with dependent children. 99% of campus accessible to physically disabled. **Special Academic Facilities/Equipment:** Montana Center for Disabilities, Business Enterprise, Small Business Institute, Urban Institute, Public Radio, Applied Economic Research, Biological Station, Northern Plains Studies Center, Montana Business Connections, Information Commons, Academic Support Center, Advising Center, TRIO Programs, SOS Programs, Northcutt Steele Gallery, Cisel Recital Hall, Petro Theatre, MSU-Billings Downtown. **Computers:** 30% of classrooms, 100% of dorms, 100% of libraries, 100% of dining areas, 100% of student union, have wireless network access. Students can register for classes online. Administrative functions (other than registration) can be performed online.

CAMPUS LIFE

Environment: City. **Activities:** Choral groups, concert band, drama/theater, jazz band, literary magazine, music ensembles, musical theater, pep band, radio station, student government, student newspaper, symphony orchestra, Campus Ministries, International Student Organization. 53 registered organizations, 10 honor societies, 8 religious organizations. **Athletics (Intercollegiate):** *Men:* baseball, basketball, cross-country, golf, soccer, tennis, track/field (outdoor), track/field (indoor). *Women:* basketball, cross-country, golf, soccer, softball, tennis, track/field (outdoor), track/field (indoor), volleyball. **On-Campus Highlights:** Alterowitz Gym, MSU Billings Downtown, SUB Coffee Shop, Liberal Arts Coffee Shop, Library.

ADMISSIONS

Freshman Academic Profile: 9% in top 10% of high school class, 27% in top 25% of high school class, 63% in top 50% of high school class. 96% from public high schools. SAT Math middle 50% range 430-540. SAT Critical Reading middle 50% range 430-550. ACT middle 50% range 18-23. Minimum internet-based TOEFL 68. Minimum paper TOEFL 515. **Basis for Candidate Selection:** *Very important factors considered include:* Class rank, academic GPA, rigor of secondary school record, standardized test scores, level of applicant's interest. *Other factors considered include:* character/personal qualities. **Freshman Admission Requirements:** High school diploma is required and GED is accepted. *Academic units required:* 4 English, 3 mathematics, 2 science, (2 science labs), 3 social studies, 2 For Lang, Vis Arts, Comp Sci. **Freshman Admission Statistics:** 1,602 applied, 100% admitted, 49% enrolled. **Transfer Admission Requirements:** college transcript(s), statement of good standing from prior institution(s). Minimum college GPA of 2.0 required. Lowest grade transferable C-. **General Admission Information:** Application Fee $30. Regular application deadline 7/1. Notification on a rolling basis, beginning on or about 7/1. Nonfall registration accepted. Credit and/or placement offered for CEEB Advanced Placement tests.

COSTS AND FINANCIAL AID

Annual in-state tuition $4,397. Annual out-of-state tuition $15,959. Room and board $6,980. Required fees $1,383. Average book expense $1,460. **Required Forms and Deadlines:** FAFSA, Institution's own financial aid form. **Notification of Awards:** Applicants will be notified of awards on or about 5/1. **Types of**

Aid: *Need-based scholarships/grants:* Federal Pell, SEOG, state scholarships/ grants, private scholarships, the school's own gift aid, Montana State University-Billings Foundation. *Loans:* Subsidized Stafford, Unsubsidized Stafford, PLUS, Federal Perkins, college/university loans from institutional funds. *Student Employment:* Federal Work-Study Program available. Institutional employment available. Highest amount earned per year from on-campus jobs $2,000. Off-campus job opportunities are excellent. **Financial Aid Statistics:** 87% freshmen, 81% undergrads receive need-based scholarship or grant aid. 4% freshmen, 3% undergrads receive non-need-based scholarship or grant aid. 73% freshmen, 79% undergrads receive need-based self-help aid. 2% freshmen, 4% undergrads receive athletic scholarships. 78% undergrads borrow to pay for school. Average cumulative indebtedness $26,638. **Criteria for awarding institutional aid:** *Non-need-based:* academics, alumni affiliation, art, athletics, job skills, leadership, minority status, music/drama, state/district residency.

MONTANA TECH OF THE UNIVERSITY OF MONTANA

Best 380

1300 West Park Street, Butte, MT 59701
Phone: 406-496-4256 · **Financial Aid Phone:** 406-496-4213
E-mail: enrollment@mtech.edu · **CEEB Code:** 4487
Fax: 406-496-4710 · **Website:** www.mtech.edu · **ACT Code:** 24180

This public school was founded in 1893. It has a 113-acre campus.

RATINGS

Admissions Selectivity Rating: 81   **Fire Safety Rating:** 97

STUDENTS AND FACULTY

Enrollment: 2,437. **Student Body:** 37% female, 63% male, 15% out-of-state, 9% international (14 countries represented). Asian 1%, African American 1%, Caucasian 81%, Hispanic 2%, Native American 2%
Retention and Graduation: 71% freshmen return for sophomore year. 17% freshmen graduate within 4 years. 42% freshmen graduate within 6 years. 13% grads go on to further study within 1 year. 11% grads pursue arts and sciences degrees. 1% grads pursue business degrees. 2% grads pursue medical degrees. **Faculty:** 148 full-time faculty, 59% hold PhDs, 34% are members of minority groups, 8% are women.

ACADEMICS

Degrees: associate, bachelor's, certificate, master's, post-bachelor's certificate. **Classes:** Most classes have fewer than 10 students. Most lab/discussion sessions have 10–19 students. **Majors with Highest Enrollment:** Petroleum Engineering; Engineering; Management Information Systems and Services. **Special Study Options:** cooperative education program, distance learning, double major, dual enrollment, honors program, independent study, internships, teacher certification program. **Honors programs:** Honors program provided for all programs. Consists of honors seminar and a few extra courses. **Combined degree programs:** BA/MA. **Disability Services:** Special programs offered to physically disabled students include note-taking services, reader services, tape recorders, tutors. **Career services:** alumni services, career/job search classes, career assessment, internships, regional alumni. Career services highlights include internships.

FACILITIES

Housing: Coed dorms, special housing for disabled students, special housing for international students, apartments for married students, apartments for single students, apartments for families (don't have to be married if have children). 75% of campus accessible to physically disabled. **Special Academic Facilities/Equipment:** Mineral Museum; World Museum of Mining. **Computers:** 30% of classrooms, 100% of libraries, 100% of dining areas, 100% of student union, have wireless network access. Students can register for classes online. Administrative functions (other than registration) can be performed online.

CAMPUS LIFE

Environment: Town. **Activities:** concert band, pep band, radio station, student government, student newspaper, yearbook, Campus Ministries. 58 registered organizations, 2 honor societies, 3 religious organizations. **Athletics (Intercollegiate):** *Men:* basketball, football, golf. *Women:* basketball, golf, volleyball. **On-Campus Highlights:** Mineral Museum, Mil Building (which houses Starbucks and, HPER, an athletic facility), Student Union, Mall area (outdoor located in the center).

ADMISSIONS

Freshman Academic Profile: Average high school GPA 3.48. 24% in top 10% of high school class, 57% in top 25% of high school class, 85% in top 50% of high school class. SAT Math middle 50% range 540-630. SAT Critical Reading middle 50% range 490-590. SAT Writing middle 50% range 450-560. ACT middle 50% range 22-27. Minimum internet-based TOEFL 71. Minimum paper TOEFL 525. **Basis for Candidate Selection:** *Other factors considered include:* Class rank, academic GPA, standardized test scores. **Freshman Admission Requirements:** High school diploma is required and GED is accepted. *Academic units required:* 4 English, 3 mathematics, 2 science, (2 science labs), 3 social studies, 2 Combined 2 years of foreign language, visual and performing arts, computer science, or vocational ed. **Freshman Admission Statistics:** 952 applied, 90% admitted, 52% enrolled. **Transfer Admission Requirements:** college transcript(s), Minimum college GPA of 2.0 required. Lowest grade transferable C. **General Admission Information:** Application Fee $30. Notification on a rolling basis, beginning on or about 8/30. Nonfall registration accepted. Admission may be deferred for a maximum of 1 year. Credit and/or placement offered for CEEB Advanced Placement tests.

COSTS AND FINANCIAL AID

Annual out-of-state tuition $19,147. Room and board $8,238. Average book expense $1,050. **Required Forms and Deadlines:** FAFSA. **Notification of Awards:** Applicants will be notified of awards on a rolling basis beginning 3/15. **Types of Aid:** *Need-based scholarships/grants:* Federal Pell, SEOG, state scholarships/grants, private scholarships, the school's own gift aid. *Loans:* Subsidized Stafford, Unsubsidized Stafford, PLUS, Federal Perkins, college/university loans from institutional funds. *Student Employment:* Federal Work-Study Program available. Institutional employment available. Highest amount earned per year from on-campus jobs $4,200. Off-campus job opportunities are good. **Financial Aid Statistics:** 90% freshmen, 89% undergrads receive need-based scholarship or grant aid. 10% freshmen, 5% undergrads receive non-need-based scholarship or grant aid. 73% freshmen, 80% undergrads receive need-based self-help aid. 4% freshmen, 3% undergrads receive athletic scholarships. 72% freshmen, 67% undergrads receive any aid. 85% undergrads borrow to pay for school. Average cumulative indebtedness $23,315. **Criteria for awarding institutional aid:** *Non-need-based:* academics, alumni affiliation, athletics, job skills, minority status, state/district residency.

MONTCLAIR STATE UNIVERSITY

One Normal Avenue, Montclair, NJ 07043-1624
Phone: 973-655-4444 · **Financial Aid Phone:** 973-655-4461
E-mail: undergraduate.admissions@montclair.edu · **CEEB Code:** 2520
Fax: 973-655-7700 · **Website:** www.montclair.edu/ · **ACT Code:** 2572

This public school was founded in 1908. It has a 275-acre campus.

RATINGS

Admissions Selectivity Rating: 77   **Fire Safety Rating:** 98

STUDENTS AND FACULTY

Enrollment: 15,676. **Student Body:** 61% female, 39% male, 3% out-of-state, 2% international (85 countries represented). Asian 5%, African American 10%, Caucasian 46%, Hispanic 24%, Native American <1%
Retention and Graduation: 36% freshmen graduate within 4 years. 17% grads go on to further study within 1 year. **Faculty:** 612 full-time faculty, 92% hold PhDs, 48% are members of minority groups, 28% are women.

ACADEMICS

Degrees: bachelor's, certificate, master's, post-bachelor's certificate. **Majors with Highest Enrollment:** Business Administration and Management; Psychology; Family and Consumer Sciences/Human Sciences. **Special Study Options:** cooperative education program, double major, English as a Second Language (ESL), honors program, independent study, internships, study abroad, teacher certification program. **Combined degree programs:** BA/MA, 5yr BA/MA, 5yr BA/M practical anthropolo. **Disability Services:** Special programs offered to physically disabled students include note-taking services, reader services, tape recorders, tutors. **Career services:** Alumni network, alumni services, career/job search classes, career assessment, internships, regional alumni. All of our career services programs are exceptional.

FACILITIES

Housing: Coed dorms, special housing for disabled students, special housing for international students, women's dorms, apartments for single students, Theme Housing. 90% of campus accessible to physically disabled. **Special Academic Facilities/Equipment:** The Dumont Television Center, Yogi Berra Museum and Stadium, Floyd Hall Arena **Computers:** 70% of classrooms, 20% of dorms, 100% of libraries, 75% of dining areas, 50% of student union, 10%

of common outdoor areas have wireless network access. Students can register for classes online. Administrative functions (other than registration) can be performed online.

CAMPUS LIFE

Environment: Town. **Activities:** Choral groups, concert band, dance, drama/theater, jazz band, literary magazine, marching band, music ensembles, musical theater, opera, pep band, radio station, student government, student newspaper, symphony orchestra, television station, yearbook, Campus Ministries, International Student Organization 121 registered organizations, 28 honor societies, 8 religious organizations. 13 fraternities, 16 sororities. **Athletics (Intercollegiate):** *Men:* baseball, basketball, diving, football, lacrosse, soccer, swimming, track/field (outdoor). *Women:* basketball, diving, field hockey, lacrosse, soccer, softball, swimming, track/field (outdoor), volleyball. **On-Campus Highlights:** Café Diem, University Hall, Student Center, Recreation Center, Kasser Theater. **Environmental Initiatives:** Recycling Program—campus-wide; New Cogen Plant to begin operation for April 2013; Green products used in housekeeping (this was built into the recent contract that was awarded); Solar farm installation in 2012; Food waste composter (Transitions Dining Services food waste into compost that is used by Grounds Services in plantings around campus); Three more new buildings for prospective LEED certification.

ADMISSIONS

Freshman Academic Profile: Average high school GPA 3.2. 12% in top 10% of high school class, 37% in top 25% of high school class, 78% in top 50% of high school class. SAT Math middle 50% range 450-540. SAT Critical Reading middle 50% range 430-530. SAT Writing middle 50% range 440-540. Minimum internet-based TOEFL 80. Minimum paper TOEFL 550. **Basis for Candidate Selection:** *Very important factors considered include:* academic GPA, rigor of secondary school record. *Important factors considered include:* Class rank, standardized test scores. *Other factors considered include:* recommendation(s), extracurricular activities, first generation, talent/ability, volunteer work, work experience. **Freshman Admission Requirements:** High school diploma is required and GED is accepted. *Academic units required:* 4 English, 3 mathematics, 2 science, (2 science labs), 2 foreign language, 2 social studies, 3 academic electives. **Freshman Admission Statistics:** 12,462 applied, 67% admitted, 48% enrolled. **Transfer Admission Requirements:** college transcript(s), statement of good standing from prior institution(s). Minimum college GPA of 2.0 required. Lowest grade transferable C-. **General Admission Information:** Application Fee $60. Regular application deadline 3/1. Notification on a rolling basis, beginning on or about 10/1. Nonfall registration accepted. Admission may be deferred for a maximum of 1 semester. Credit offered for CEEB Advanced Placement tests.

COSTS AND FINANCIAL AID

Annual in-state tuition $8,346. Annual out-of-state tuition $17,060. Room and board $14,010. Required fees $3,194. Average book expense $1,334. **Required Forms and Deadlines:** FAFSA. **Notification of Awards:** Applicants will be notified of awards on a rolling basis beginning 4/1. **Types of Aid:** *Need-based scholarships/grants:* Federal Pell, SEOG, state scholarships/grants, private scholarships, the school's own gift aid. *Loans:* Subsidized Stafford, Unsubsidized Stafford, PLUS, Federal Perkins, state loans. *Student Employment:* Federal Work-Study Program available. Institutional employment available. Highest amount earned per year from on-campus jobs $2,297. Off-campus job opportunities are good. **Financial Aid Statistics:** 58% freshmen, 60% undergrads receive need-based scholarship or grant aid. 6% freshmen, 6% undergrads receive non-need-based scholarship or grant aid. 72% freshmen, 79% undergrads receive need-based self-help aid. 0% freshmen, 0% undergrads receive athletic scholarships. 66% freshmen, 55% undergrads receive any aid. 71% undergrads borrow to pay for school. Average cumulative indebtedness $21,241. **Criteria for awarding institutional aid:** *Non-need-based:* academics, alumni affiliation, art, leadership, minority status, music/drama, religious affiliation, state/district residency.

MONTREAT COLLEGE

310 Gaither Circle, Montreat, NC 28757-1267
Phone: 828-669-8011 · **Financial Aid Phone:** 800-545-4656
E-mail: admissions@montreat.edu · **CEEB Code:** 5423
Fax: 828-669-0120 · **Website:** www.montreat.edu · **ACT Code:** 3130

This private school, affiliated with the Christian (Nondenominational) Church, was founded in 1916. It has a 162-acre campus.

RATINGS

Admissions Selectivity Rating: 70   **Fire Safety Rating:** 60*

STUDENTS AND FACULTY

Enrollment: 937. **Student Body:** 60% female, 40% male, 20% out-of-state, (12 countries represented).
Faculty: 46 full-time faculty, 67% hold PhDs, 35% are members of minority groups, 13% are women. 0% of classes are taught by teaching assistants.

ACADEMICS

Degrees: associate, bachelor's, master's. **Classes:** Most classes have 10–19 students. Most lab/discussion sessions have 10–19 students. **Majors with Highest Enrollment:** Environmental Studies; Bible/Biblical Studies; Business Administration and Management. **Special Study Options:** Accelerated program, double major, dual enrollment, independent study, internships, student-designed major, study abroad, teacher certification program, American Studies Program (Washington, D.C.). L.A. Film Studies Center (Los Angeles, CA). Martha's Vineyard Semester. **Disability Services:** Special programs offered to physically disabled students include reader services, tutors.

FACILITIES

Housing: men's dorms, women's dorms. 100% of campus accessible to physically disabled. **Special Academic Facilities/Equipment:** Hamilton Art Gallery, Chapel of the Prodigal. **Computers:** Administrative functions (other than registration) can be performed online.

CAMPUS LIFE

Environment: Village. **Activities:** Choral groups, dance, drama/theater, music ensembles, musical theater, student government, student newspaper 11 registered organizations. **Athletics (Intercollegiate):** *Men:* baseball, basketball, cross-country, golf, soccer. *Women:* basketball, cross-country, golf, soccer, softball, volleyball. **On-Campus Highlights:** Gaither Chapel, Chapel of the Prodigal (contains original Fresco), Student Game Area with LCD Flat Panel TV, Student Lounge Area with 24 Hr. Computer Access, Cavalier Grill—relaxing café-style eatery.

ADMISSIONS

Freshman Academic Profile: Average high school GPA 3.01. 7% in top 10% of high school class, 20% in top 25% of high school class, 59% in top 50% of high school class. SAT Math middle 50% range 430-540. SAT Critical Reading middle 50% range 410-560. ACT middle 50% range 18-22. Minimum paper TOEFL 500. **Basis for Candidate Selection:** *Very important factors considered include:* application essay, academic GPA, rigor of secondary school record, standardized test scores. *Important factors considered include:* recommendation(s), character/personal qualities, interview. *Other factors considered include:* Class rank, alumni/ae relation, extracurricular activities, first generation, level of applicant's interest, talent/ability, volunteer work, work experience. **Freshman Admission Requirements:** High school diploma is required and GED is accepted. *Academic units required:* 4 English, 3 mathematics, 3 science, 1 foreign language, 3 history. **Transfer Admission Requirements:** college transcript(s), essay or personal statement, statement of good standing from prior institution(s). Minimum college GPA of 2.5 required. Lowest grade transferable C. **General Admission Information:** Application Fee $30. Regular application deadline 8/1. Notification on a rolling basis, beginning on or about 9/1. Nonfall registration accepted. Admission may be deferred for a maximum of 1 semester. Credit and/or placement offered for CEEB Advanced Placement tests.

COSTS AND FINANCIAL AID

Annual tuition $20,196. Room and board $6,540. Average book expense $1,000. **Required Forms and Deadlines:** FAFSA. **Notification of Awards:** Applicants will be notified of awards on a rolling basis beginning 2/1. **Types of Aid:** *Need-based scholarships/grants:* Federal Pell, SEOG, state scholarships/grants, private scholarships, the school's own gift aid. *Loans:* Subsidized Stafford, Unsubsidized Stafford, PLUS, Federal Perkins. *Student Employment:* Highest amount earned per year from on-campus jobs $2,212. **Financial Aid Statistics:** 95% freshmen, 98% undergrads receive need-based scholarship or grant aid. 81% freshmen, 94% undergrads receive non-need-based scholarship or grant aid. 72% freshmen, 88% undergrads receive need-based self-help aid. 68% freshmen, 62% undergrads receive athletic scholarships. 98% freshmen, 98% undergrads receive any aid. 89% undergrads borrow to pay for school. **Criteria for awarding institutional aid:** *Non-need-based:* academics, alumni affiliation, athletics, leadership, music/drama, state/district residency.

MONTSERRAT COLLEGE OF ART

23 Essex Street, Beverly, MA 1915
Phone: 978-921-4242
E-mail: admiss@montserrat.edu · **CEEB Code:** 9101
Fax: 978-921-4241 · **Website:** www.montserrat.edu · **ACT Code:** 1847

This private school was founded in 1970. It has a 12-acre campus.

RATINGS

Admissions Selectivity Rating: 71   **Fire Safety Rating:** 69

STUDENTS AND FACULTY

Enrollment: 298. **Student Body:** 62% female, 38% male, 50% out-of-state, 0% international. Asian 2%, African American 1%, Caucasian 76%, Hispanic 2%, Native American <1%
Retention and Graduation: 51% freshmen return for sophomore year. 45% freshmen graduate within 4 years. 55% freshmen graduate within 6 years.
Faculty: 26 full-time faculty, 62% hold PhDs, 58% are members of minority groups, 4% are women.

ACADEMICS

Degrees: bachelor's, certificate, diploma. **Classes:** Most classes have 10–19 students. **Majors with Highest Enrollment:** Graphic Design; Illustration; Painting. **Special Study Options:** cross-registration, dual enrollment, exchange student program (domestic), independent study, internships, student-designed major, study abroad, teacher certification program. **Disability Services:** Special programs offered to physically disabled students include reader services, tape recorders. **Career services:** career/job search classes, internships.

FACILITIES

Housing: special housing for disabled students, apartment style: coed buildings with single sex apartments. **Special Academic Facilities/Equipment:** Montserrat Gallery, 301 Gallery, Carol Schlosberg Alumni Gallery, 292 Gallery.

CAMPUS LIFE

Environment: Town. **Activities:** literary magazine, student government. 5 registered organizations. **On-Campus Highlights:** Student Lounge, Hardie Building, 292 Cabot, Montserrat Gallery, 301 Gallery.

ADMISSIONS

Freshman Academic Profile: Average high school GPA 2.8. SAT Math middle 50% range 372-589. SAT Critical Reading middle 50% range 416-642. ACT middle 50% range 18-22. Minimum paper TOEFL 550. **Basis for Candidate Selection:** *Very important factors considered include:* application essay, recommendation(s), rigor of secondary school record, character/personal qualities, interview, talent/ability. *Important factors considered include:* standardized test scores. *Other factors considered include:* Class rank, extracurricular activities, volunteer work, work experience. **Freshman Admission Requirements:** High school diploma is required and GED is accepted. **Freshman Admission Statistics:** 326 applied, 85% admitted, 27% enrolled. **Transfer Admission Requirements:** college transcript(s), essay or personal statement, Minimum college GPA of 2.2 required. Lowest grade transferable C. **General Admission Information:** Application Fee $40. Notification on a rolling basis, beginning on or about 12/20. Nonfall registration accepted. Admission may be deferred for a maximum of one year. Credit offered for CEEB Advanced Placement tests.

COSTS AND FINANCIAL AID

Required Forms and Deadlines: FAFSA, Institution's own financial aid form, Noncustodial PROFILE. **Notification of Awards:** Applicants will be notified of awards on a rolling basis beginning 3/1. **Types of Aid:** *Need-based scholarships/grants:* Federal Pell, SEOG, state scholarships/grants, private scholarships, the school's own gift aid. *Loans:* Subsidized Stafford, Unsubsidized Stafford, PLUS, state loans. *Student Employment:* Federal Work-Study Program available. Institutional employment available. Highest amount earned per year from on-campus jobs $1,500. Off-campus job opportunities are good. **Financial Aid Statistics:** 96% freshmen, 91% undergrads receive need-based scholarship or grant aid. 93% freshmen, 78% undergrads receive non-need-based scholarship or grant aid. 100% freshmen, 100% undergrads receive need-based self-help aid. 0% freshmen, 0% undergrads receive athletic scholarships. 96% freshmen, 79% undergrads receive any aid. 84% undergrads borrow to pay for school. **Criteria for awarding institutional aid:** *Non-need-based:* academics, art.

MOORE COLLEGE OF ART AND DESIGN

20th Street and The Parkway, Philadelphia, PA 19103-1179
Phone: 215-965-4017 · **Financial Aid Phone:** 215-965-4042
E-mail: enroll@moore.edu · **CEEB Code:** 2417
Fax: 215-568-3547 · **Website:** www.moore.edu · **ACT Code:** 2417

This private school was founded in 1848.

RATINGS

Admissions Selectivity Rating: 78   **Fire Safety Rating:** 94

STUDENTS AND FACULTY

Enrollment: 482. **Student Body:** 100% female, 0% male, 42% out-of-state, 3% international (15 countries represented). Asian 4%, African American 16%, Caucasian 65%, Hispanic 5%, Native American 1%
Retention and Graduation: 73% freshmen return for sophomore year. 48% freshmen graduate within 4 years. 56% freshmen graduate within 6 years.
Faculty: 24 full-time faculty, 50% hold PhDs, 67% are members of minority groups, 8% are women. 0% of classes are taught by teaching assistants.

ACADEMICS

Degrees: bachelor's, post-bachelor's certificate. **Classes:** Most classes have 10–19 students. **Majors with Highest Enrollment:** Fashion/Apparel Design; Fine/Studio Arts; Illustration. **Special Study Options:** double major, independent study, internships, study abroad, teacher certification program, arts, education student travel courses. **Disability Services:** Special programs offered to physically disabled students include tape recorders, tutors. **Career services:** alumni services, internships, regional alumni. Career services highlights include a required internship before senior year for all majors.

FACILITIES

Housing: women's dorms. **Special Academic Facilities/Equipment:** Paley, Graham and Levy Galleries. **Computers:** 100% of classrooms, 100% of dorms, 100% of libraries, 100% of dining areas, have wireless network access. Students can register for classes online. Administrative functions (other than registration) can be performed online. Undergraduates are required to own a computer.

CAMPUS LIFE

Environment: Metropolis. **Activities:** student government, yearbook. 8 registered organizations. **On-Campus Highlights:** Three art galleries, Outdoor coffee shop, Internships, Leadership Fellowships, Locks Career Center for Women.

ADMISSIONS

Freshman Academic Profile: Average high school GPA 3.2. SAT Math middle 50% range 420-520. SAT Critical Reading middle 50% range 450-560. ACT middle 50% range 17-22. Minimum paper TOEFL 527. **Basis for Candidate Selection:** *Very important factors considered include:* academic GPA, rigor of secondary school record, standardized test scores, character/personal qualities, interview, level of applicant's interest, talent/ability. *Important factors considered include:* application essay, recommendation(s), extracurricular activities. *Other factors considered include:* Class rank, volunteer work, work experience. **Freshman Admission Requirements:** High school diploma is required and GED is accepted. **Freshman Admission Statistics:** 607 applied, 54% admitted, 33% enrolled. **Transfer Admission Requirements:** High school transcript, college transcript(s), essay or personal statement, statement of good standing from prior institution(s). Minimum college GPA of 2.5 required. Lowest grade transferable C. **General Admission Information:** Application Fee $40. Early decision application deadline 11/15. Regular application deadline 8/15. Notification on a rolling basis, beginning on or about 11/15. Nonfall registration accepted. Admission may be deferred for a maximum of 1 year. Credit offered for CEEB Advanced Placement tests.

COSTS AND FINANCIAL AID

Annual tuition $31,654. Room and board $12,298. Required fees $1,084. Average book expense $2,000. **Required Forms and Deadlines:** FAFSA. **Notification of Awards:** Applicants will be notified of awards on a rolling basis beginning 2/15. **Types of Aid:** *Need-based scholarships/grants:* Federal Pell, SEOG, state scholarships/grants, private scholarships, the school's own gift aid. *Loans:* Subsidized Stafford, Unsubsidized Stafford, PLUS, Federal Perkins, Alternative loans. *Student Employment:* Federal Work-Study Program available. Off-campus job opportunities are good. **Financial Aid Statistics:** 97% undergrads receive any aid. **Criteria for awarding institutional aid:** *Non-need-based:* academics, art, leadership.

MORAVIAN COLLEGE

1200 Main Street, Bethlehem, PA 18018
Phone: 610-861-1320 · **Financial Aid Phone:** 610-861-1330
E-mail: admissions@moravian.edu · **CEEB Code:** 3301
Fax: 610-625-7930 · **Website:** www.moravian.edu · **ACT Code:** 3634

This private school, affiliated with the Moravian Church, was founded in 1742. It has a 60-acre campus.

RATINGS

Admissions Selectivity Rating: 78   **Fire Safety Rating:** 94

STUDENTS AND FACULTY

Enrollment: 1,570. **Student Body:** 58% female, 42% male, 33% out-of-state, 3% international (11 countries represented). Asian 2%, African American 4%, Caucasian 75%, Hispanic 9%, Native American <1% **Retention and Graduation:** 79% freshmen return for sophomore year. 66% freshmen graduate within 4 years. 26% grads go on to further study within 1 year. 54% grads pursue arts and sciences degrees. 6% grads pursue law degrees. 4% grads pursue business degrees. 9% grads pursue medical degrees. **Faculty:** 97 full-time faculty, 90% hold PhDs, 57% are members of minority groups, 8% are women. 0% of classes are taught by teaching assistants.

ACADEMICS

Degrees: bachelor's, first professional, master's, post-bachelor's certificate. **Classes:** Most classes have 20–29 students. Most lab/discussion sessions have 10–19 students. **Majors with Highest Enrollment:** Psychology; Registered Nursing, Nursing Administration, Nursing Research and Clinical Nursing; Business Administration and Management. **Special Study Options:** cross-registration, double major, honors program, independent study, internships, student-designed major, study abroad, teacher certification program. **Honors programs:** Students can do honors projects within their selected major **Combined degree programs:** BA/MEng, Occ. Therapy (TJU); MBA (Moravian College). **Disability Services:** Special programs offered to physically disabled students include note-taking services, reader services, tape recorders, tutors. **Career services:** Alumni network, alumni services, career/job search classes, career assessment, internships, regional alumni.

FACILITIES

Housing: Coed dorms, men's dorms, women's dorms, fraternity/sorority housing, apartments for single students, Wellness Housing, Theme Housing. **Special Academic Facilities/Equipment:** Payne [art] Gallery, Foy [concert] Hall, greenhouse, student art studios, observation room for psychology classes, Leadership Center **Computers:** 80% of classrooms, 100% of libraries, 100% of dining areas, 100% of student union, 25% of common outdoor areas have wireless network access. Administrative functions (other than registration) can be performed online.

CAMPUS LIFE

Environment: City. **Activities:** Choral groups, concert band, dance, drama/theater, jazz band, literary magazine, marching band, music ensembles, musical theater, radio station, student government, student newspaper, symphony orchestra, yearbook, Campus Ministries, International Student Organization. 80 registered organizations, 16 honor societies, 4 religious organizations. 3 fraternities, 4 sororities. **Athletics (Intercollegiate):** *Men:* baseball, basketball, cross-country, football, golf, lacrosse, soccer, tennis, track/field (outdoor), track/field (indoor). *Women:* basketball, cross-country, field hockey, lacrosse, soccer, softball, tennis, track/field (outdoor), track/field (indoor), volleyball. **On-Campus Highlights:** Alternative (on campus club/hang out), Afterwords Café (Library Coffe Shop), Priscilla Payne Hurd Academic Complex, Fitness Center, The Quad. **Environmental Initiatives:** The Sustainability Committee initiated a strategic planning process during 2012 that will culminate in the first Campus Sustainability Plan. The committe hosted three workshops and invited participants from across the campus community including students, staff and faculty to share current practices, envision a sustainable campus, and create ambitious and measurable goals. Moravian College was selected to serve as a "civil society observer" at the annual United Nations Framework Climate Change Conference (UNFCCC) meetings. The College is one of just six private liberal arts or predominantly undergraduate institutions in the U.S to serve in that capacity. Over the past three years, faculty and students have attended the UN Climate Change Conferences in Copehhagen, Cancun, South Africa. The Moravian delegations blogs about their experiences while attending the meetings to keep the campus informed. The goal of the meetings is to find a binding agreement to replace or modify the KYOTO protocol, which ended in 2012. In partnership with dining services the College has reduced waste in the following areas: paper napkin use (by using new dispensers), plastic bags (by replacing with reusable bags), and food (by instituting a no tray day). In addition pre-consumer food waste is now being diverted for composting at the Rodale Institute Experimental Farm. Another outcome of collaborating with dining servces are expanded vegan meal options.

ADMISSIONS

Freshman Academic Profile: Average high school GPA 3.39. 17% in top 10% of high school class, 45% in top 25% of high school class, 77% in top 50% of high school class. 85% from public high schools. SAT Math middle 50% range 460-570. SAT Critical Reading middle 50% range 450-560. SAT Writing middle 50% range 450-560. ACT middle 50% range 18-26. Minimum internet-based TOEFL 80. Minimum paper TOEFL 550. **Basis for Candidate Selection:** *Very important factors considered include:* Class rank, academic GPA, rigor of secondary school record, alumni/ae relation, character/personal qualities. *Important factors considered include:* application essay, recommendation(s), standardized test scores, extracurricular activities, first generation, level of applicant's interest, racial/ethnic status, talent/ability, volunteer work. *Other factors considered include:* geographical residence, interview, work experience. **Freshman Admission Requirements:** High school diploma is required and GED is accepted. *Academic units required:* 4 English, 3 mathematics, 3 science, (2 science labs), 2 foreign language, 4 social studies. **Freshman Admission Statistics:** 1,536 applied, 86% admitted, 29% enrolled. **Transfer Admission Requirements:** High school transcript, college transcript(s), essay or personal statement, statement of good standing from prior institution(s). Minimum college GPA of 3.0 required. Lowest grade transferable C. **General Admission Information:** Application Fee $40. Early decision application deadline 2/1. Regular application deadline 3/1. Regular notification 3/15. Nonfall registration accepted. Admission may be deferred for a maximum of 1 year. Placement offered for CEEB Advanced Placement tests.

COSTS AND FINANCIAL AID

Required Forms and Deadlines: FAFSA, Institution's own financial aid form. **Notification of Awards:** Applicants will be notified of awards on or about 4/1. **Types of Aid:** *Need-based scholarships/grants:* Federal Pell, SEOG, state scholarships/grants, the school's own gift aid. *Loans:* Subsidized Stafford, Unsubsidized Stafford, PLUS, Federal Perkins. *Student Employment:* Highest amount earned per year from on-campus jobs $3,000. **Financial Aid Statistics:** 100% freshmen, 100% undergrads receive need-based scholarship or grant aid. 10% freshmen, 9% undergrads receive non-need-based scholarship or grant aid. 90% freshmen, 91% undergrads receive need-based self-help aid. 0% freshmen, 0% undergrads receive athletic scholarships. 96% freshmen, 95% undergrads receive any aid. 82% undergrads borrow to pay for school. Average cumulative indebtedness $28,368. **Criteria for awarding institutional aid:** *Non-need-based:* academics, alumni affiliation, leadership, minority status, music/drama, religious affiliation.

MOREHEAD STATE UNIVERSITY

Admissions Center, Morehead, KY 40351
Phone: 606-783-2000 · **Financial Aid Phone:** 606-783-2011
E-mail: admissions@moreheadstate.edu
Fax: 606-783-5038 · **Website:** http://www.moreheadstate.edu/ · **ACT Code:** 1530

This public school was founded in 1922. It has a 1016-acre campus.

RATINGS

Admissions Selectivity Rating: 77   **Fire Safety Rating:** 81

STUDENTS AND FACULTY

Enrollment: 7,212. **Student Body:** 60% female, 40% male, 14% out-of-state, 1% international (35 countries represented). Asian 0%, African American 4%, Caucasian 90%, Hispanic 1%, Native American <1% **Faculty:** 359 full-time faculty, 48% are members of minority groups, 7% are women.

ACADEMICS

Degrees: associate, bachelor's, master's, post-bachelor's certificate, post-master's certificate. **Classes:** Most classes have 20–29 students. Most lab/discussion sessions have 10–19 students. **Majors with Highest Enrollment:** Elementary Education and Teaching; General Studies; Registered Nursing/Registered Nurse. **Special Study Options:** Accelerated program, cooperative education program, cross-registration, distance learning, double major, dual enrollment, exchange student program (domestic), honors program, independent study, internships, student-designed major, study abroad, teacher certification program, weekend college. **Disability Services:** Special programs offered to physically disabled students include note-taking services, reader services, tutors. **Career services:** Alumni network, alumni services, career/job search classes, career assessment, internships.

FACILITIES

Housing: Coed dorms, special housing for disabled students, special housing for international students, fraternity/sorority housing, apartments for married students, apartments for single students, Limited housing available at agriculture complex for agriculture science students. Housing for handicapped students and private rooms available. 90% of campus accessible to physically disabled. **Special Academic Facilities/Equipment:** KY Folk Art Center, 320-acre agricultural complex, Space Science Center, KY Center for Traditional Music. **Computers:** 100% of classrooms, 20% of dorms, 100% of libraries, 100% of dining areas, 100% of student union, 100% of common outdoor areas have wireless network access. Students can register for classes online. Administrative functions (other than registration) can be performed online.

CAMPUS LIFE

Environment: Village. **Activities:** Choral groups, concert band, dance, drama/theater, jazz band, literary magazine, marching band, music ensembles, musical theater, opera, pep band, radio station, student government, student newspaper, symphony orchestra, television station, yearbook 101 registered organizations, 11 honor society, 7 religious organizations. 10 fraternities, 9 sororities. **Athletics (Intercollegiate):** *Men:* baseball, basketball, cheerleading, cross-country, football, golf, riflery, tennis, track/field (outdoor). *Women:* basketball, cheerleading, cross-country, golf, riflery, soccer, softball, tennis, track/field (outdoor), track/field (indoor), volleyball. **On-Campus Highlights:** Adron Doran University Center, Eagle Lake, MSU Wellness Center, Laughlin Health Building. **Environmental Initiatives:** Environmental Education Center—Organizes educational workshops, Earth Day Activities, and community outreach.

ADMISSIONS

Freshman Academic Profile: Average high school GPA 3.321. 17% in top 10% of high school class, 42% in top 25% of high school class, 76% in top 50% of high school class. SAT Math middle 50% range 450-560. SAT Critical Reading middle 50% range 450-535. SAT Writing middle 50% range 410-530. ACT middle 50% range 19-25. Minimum paper TOEFL 500. **Basis for Candidate Selection:** *Very important factors considered include:* academic GPA, rigor of secondary school record, standardized test scores. *Other factors considered include:* recommendation(s). **Freshman Admission Requirements:** High school diploma is required and GED is accepted. *Academic units required:* 4 English, 3 mathematics, 3 science, (1 science labs), 2 foreign language, 3 social studies, 1 history, 1 visual/performing arts, 7 academic electives, 1 1 unit history & appreciation of fine arts required. **Freshman Admission Statistics:** 5,236 applied, 84% admitted, 34% enrolled. **Transfer Admission Requirements:** college transcript(s), statement of good standing from prior institution(s). Minimum college GPA of 2.0 required. Lowest grade transferable C. **General Admission Information:** Application Fee $30. Nonfall registration accepted. Admission may be deferred for a maximum of one semester. Credit offered for CEEB Advanced Placement tests.

COSTS AND FINANCIAL AID

Average book expense $1,200. **Required Forms and Deadlines:** FAFSA, Institution's own financial aid form. **Types of Aid:** *Need-based scholarships/grants:* Federal Pell, SEOG, state scholarships/grants, private scholarships, the school's own gift aid. *Loans:* Direct Subsidized Stafford, Direct Unsubsidized Stafford, Direct PLUS, Subsidized Stafford, Unsubsidized Stafford, PLUS, Federal Perkins, college/university loans from institutional funds. *Student Employment:* Federal Work-Study Program available. Institutional employment available. **Financial Aid Statistics:** 67% freshmen, 69% undergrads receive need-based scholarship or grant aid. 45% freshmen, 62% undergrads receive non-need-based scholarship or grant aid. 65% freshmen, 73% undergrads receive need-based self-help aid. 6% freshmen, 5% undergrads receive athletic scholarships. 69% undergrads borrow to pay for school. Average cumulative indebtedness $28,238. **Criteria for awarding institutional aid:** *Non-need-based:* academics, alumni affiliation, art, athletics, leadership, minority status, music/drama, state/district residency.

MOREHOUSE COLLEGE

830 Westview Drive, SW, Atlanta, GA 30314
Phone: 404-215-2632
E-mail: janderso@morehouse.edu · **CEEB Code:** 5415
Fax: 404-524-5635 · **Website:** www.morehouse.edu · **ACT Code:** 792

This private school was founded in 1867. It has a 61-acre campus.

RATINGS

Admissions Selectivity Rating: 83   **Fire Safety Rating:** 60*

STUDENTS AND FACULTY

Enrollment: 2,891. **Student Body:** 0% female, 100% male, 70% out-of-state, 3% international. Asian 0%, African American 94%, Caucasian 0%, Hispanic 0%, Native American <1%
Retention and Graduation: 84% freshmen return for sophomore year. 32% freshmen graduate within 4 years. 50% freshmen graduate within 6 years. 25% grads go on to further study within 1 year. 22% grads pursue arts and sciences degrees. 5% grads pursue law degrees. 10% grads pursue business degrees. 14% grads pursue medical degrees. **Faculty:** 159 full-time faculty, 81% hold PhDs, 31% are members of minority groups, 77% are women.

ACADEMICS

Degrees: bachelor's. **Classes:** Most classes have fewer than 10 students. **Majors with Highest Enrollment:** Computer and Information Sciences; Biology; Business/Commerce. **Special Study Options:** cooperative education program, cross-registration, double major, dual enrollment, exchange student program (domestic), honors program, internships, study abroad, dual degree program in engineering and architecture with other institutions. **Combined degree programs:** BA/MEng, degree architecture w/ michigan u. **Disability Services:** Special programs offered to physically disabled students include reader services, tape recorders, tutors. **Career services:** career/job search classes, career assessment, internships.

FACILITIES

Housing: men's dorms, apartments for single students. 100% of campus accessible to physically disabled. **Special Academic Facilities/Equipment:** Three chapels, a meditation room, and an arena that was built by and used for the Oplympic games in 1996. **Computers:** Students can register for classes online. Administrative functions (other than registration) can be performed online.

CAMPUS LIFE

Activities: Choral groups, concert band, drama/theater, jazz band, literary magazine, marching band, music ensembles, pep band, student government, student newspaper, yearbook. 34 registered organizations, 7 honor societies, 4 religious organizations. 6 fraternities. **Athletics (Intercollegiate):** *Men:* basketball, cross-country, football, track/field (outdoor). **On-Campus Highlights:** Forbes Arena, Graves Hall, Martin Luther King International Chapel, Century Yard, Technology Tower.

ADMISSIONS

Freshman Academic Profile: Average high school GPA 3.24. 20% in top 10% of high school class, 47% in top 25% of high school class, 77% in top 50% of high school class. 80% from public high schools. SAT Math middle 50% range 470-590. SAT Critical Reading middle 50% range 470-580. ACT middle 50% range 19-24. Minimum paper TOEFL 500. **Basis for Candidate Selection:** *Very important factors considered include:* standardized test scores. *Important factors considered include:* Class rank, application essay, recommendation(s), rigor of secondary school record. *Other factors considered include:* alumni/ae relation, character/personal qualities, extracurricular activities, geographical residence, interview, racial/ethnic status, talent/ability, volunteer work. **Freshman Admission Requirements:** High school diploma is required and GED is accepted. *Academic units required:* 4 English, 3 mathematics, 2 science, 2 foreign language, 2 social studies. **Freshman Admission Statistics:** 2,277 applied, 67% admitted, 46% enrolled. **Transfer Admission Requirements:** college transcript(s), essay or personal statement, standardized test scores, statement of good standing from prior institution(s). Minimum college GPA of 2.5 required. Lowest grade transferable c. **General Admission Information:** Application Fee $45. Early decision application deadline 10/15. Regular application deadline 2/15. Regular notification 4/1. Nonfall registration not accepted. Admission may be deferred for a maximum of 2.

COSTS AND FINANCIAL AID

Annual tuition $14,318. Room and board $8,748. Required fees $1,422. Average book expense $850. **Required Forms and Deadlines:** FAFSA, Institution's own financial aid form, CSS/Financial Aid PROFILE. **Notification of Awards:** Applicants will be notified of awards on or about 5/1. **Types of Aid:** *Need-based scholarships/grants:* Federal Pell, SEOG, state scholarships/grants, private scholarships, the school's own gift aid, United Negro College Fund. *Loans:* Direct Subsidized Stafford, Direct Unsubsidized Stafford, Direct PLUS, Subsidized Stafford, Unsubsidized Stafford, PLUS, Federal Perkins, state loans, college/university loans from institutional funds. *Student Employment:* Federal Work-Study Program available. Institutional employment available. Highest amount earned per year from on-campus jobs $1,500. Off-campus job opportunities are good. **Financial Aid Statistics:** 41% freshmen, 41% undergrads receive need-based scholarship or grant aid. 78% freshmen, 79% undergrads receive non-need-based scholarship or grant aid. 56% freshmen, 61% undergrads receive need-based self-help aid. 3% freshmen, 4% undergrads receive athletic scholarships. 53% undergrads borrow to pay for school. **Criteria for awarding institutional aid:** *Non-need-based:* academics, alumni affiliation, art, athletics, leadership, music/drama, state/district residency.

MORGAN STATE UNIVERSITY

1700 East Cold Spring Lane,
Phone: 800-332-6674
E-mail: tjenness@moac.morgan.edu • **CEEB Code:** 5416
Fax: 410-319-3684 • **Website:** www.morgan.edu • **ACT Code:** 1722

This public school was founded in 1867. It has a 122-acre campus.

RATINGS

Admissions Selectivity Rating: 65   **Fire Safety Rating:** 60*

STUDENTS AND FACULTY

Enrollment: 7,546. **Student Body:** 40% out-of-state.
Retention and Graduation: 76% freshmen return for sophomore year.
Faculty:

ACADEMICS

Degrees: bachelor's, master's. **Special Study Options:** cooperative education program, business, education, engineering, social/behavioral science. **Combined degree programs:** 3-3 pharmacy, 3-4 predental/premed. **Disability Services:** Special programs offered to physically disabled students include tutors. **Career services:** career/job search classes, career assessment, internships.

FACILITIES

Housing: Coed dorms, men's dorms, women's dorms, apartments for single students. **Special Academic Facilities/Equipment:** African-American collection, new science complex and school of engineering.

CAMPUS LIFE

Activities: radio station, student government, student newspaper, television station, yearbook. 250 registered organizations, 1 religious organization. 4 fraternities, 4 sororities. **Athletics (Intercollegiate):** *Men:* basketball, cross-country, football, tennis, track/field (outdoor), volleyball. *Women:* basketball, cross-country, tennis, track/field (outdoor), volleyball. **On-Campus Highlights:** Fine Arts Center, Hughes Stadium, Mitchell Building, Research Facility, University Museum.

ADMISSIONS

Freshman Academic Profile: 10% in top 10% of high school class, 80% in top 25% of high school class, 96% in top 50% of high school class. 82% from public high schools. Minimum internet-based TOEFL 88. Minimum paper TOEFL 570. **Freshman Admission Requirements:** High school diploma is required and GED is accepted. High school diploma is required and GED is not accepted. Lowest grade transferable C. **General Admission Information:** Early decision application deadline 4/15. Regular application deadline 4/15. Nonfall registration accepted. Credit offered for CEEB Advanced Placement tests.

COSTS AND FINANCIAL AID

Required fees $762. Average book expense $1,500. **Required Forms and Deadlines:** FAFSA, Institution's own financial aid form, State aid form. **Types of Aid:** *Need-based scholarships/grants:* state scholarships/grants, United Negro College Fund. *Loans:* Subsidized Stafford, PLUS. *Student Employment:* Federal Work-Study Program available. Institutional employment available. Off-campus job opportunities are good.

MORNINGSIDE COLLEGE

1501 Morningside Avenue, Sioux City, IA 51106-1751
Phone: 712-274-5511 • **Financial Aid Phone:** 712-274-5159
E-mail: mscadm@morningside.edu • **CEEB Code:** 6415
Fax: 712-274-5101 • **Website:** www.morningside.edu • **ACT Code:** 1338

This private school, affiliated with the Methodist Church, was founded in 1894. It has a 68-acre campus.

RATINGS

Admissions Selectivity Rating: 79   **Fire Safety Rating:** 65

STUDENTS AND FACULTY

Enrollment: 1,180. **Student Body:** 54% female, 46% male, 32% out-of-state, 1% international (4 countries represented). Asian 2%, African American 1%, Caucasian 84%, Hispanic 3%, Native American 1%.
Retention and Graduation: 70% freshmen return for sophomore year. 31% freshmen graduate within 4 years. 44% freshmen graduate within 6 years. 11% grads go on to further study within 1 year. 48% grads pursue arts and sciences degrees. 10% grads pursue law degrees. **Faculty:** 69 full-time faculty, 77% hold

PhDs, 45% are members of minority groups, 3% are women. 0% of classes are taught by teaching assistants.

ACADEMICS

Degrees: bachelor's, master's. **Classes:** Most classes have 10–19 students. Most lab/discussion sessions have 10–19 students. **Majors with Highest Enrollment:** Biology/Biological Sciences; Elementary Education and Teaching; Business Administration and Management. **Special Study Options:** distance learning, double major, dual enrollment, English as a Second Language (ESL), honors program, independent study, internships, liberal arts/career combination, student-designed major, study abroad, teacher certification program, health professions. **Combined degree programs:** BA/MA. **Disability Services:** Special programs offered to physically disabled students include note-taking services, reader services, tape recorders, tutors. **Career services:** Alumni network, alumni services, career/job search classes, career assessment, internships, regional alumni.

FACILITIES

Housing: Coed dorms, fraternity/sorority housing, apartments for married students, apartments for single students. 50% of campus accessible to physically disabled. **Special Academic Facilities/Equipment:** media-enhanced "smart classroom", high-speed campus internet connection, art gallery, theatre, totally renovated science facility **Computers:** 100% of classrooms, 100% of dorms, 100% of libraries, 100% of dining areas, 100% of student union, 100% of common outdoor areas have wireless network access. Students can register for classes online. Administrative functions (other than registration) can be performed online. Undergraduates are required to own a computer.

CAMPUS LIFE

Environment: City. **Activities:** Choral groups, concert band, dance, drama/theater, jazz band, literary magazine, marching band, music ensembles, musical theater, pep band, radio station, student government, student newspaper, television station, yearbook, Campus Ministries, International Student Organization. 40 registered organizations, 15 honor societies, 10 religious organizations. 2 fraternities, 1 sorority. **Athletics (Intercollegiate):** *Men:* baseball, basketball, cheerleading, cross-country, football, golf, soccer, swimming, tennis, track/field (outdoor), track/field (indoor), wrestling. *Women:* basketball, cheerleading, cross-country, golf, soccer, softball, swimming, tennis, track/field (outdoor), track/field (indoor), volleyball. **On-Campus Highlights:** New Student Apartments, Health-Fitness Center, Eppley Auditorium, Olsen Student Center, Walker Science Center.

ADMISSIONS

Freshman Academic Profile: Average high school GPA 3.37. 15% in top 10% of high school class, 42% in top 25% of high school class, 78% in top 50% of high school class. 94% from public high schools. ACT middle 50% range 20-25. Minimum paper TOEFL 450. **Basis for Candidate Selection:** *Very important factors considered include:* Class rank, academic GPA, recommendation(s), rigor of secondary school record, standardized test scores. *Important factors considered include:* extracurricular activities, interview, talent/ability. *Other factors considered include:* application essay. **Freshman Admission Requirements:** High school diploma and GED is accepted. **Freshman Admission Statistics:** 1,349 applied, 74% admitted, 30% enrolled. **Transfer Admission Requirements:** High school transcript, college transcript(s), statement of good standing from prior institution(s). Minimum college GPA of 2.25 required. Lowest grade transferable C-. **General Admission Information:** Application Fee $25. Nonfall registration accepted. Admission may be deferred for a maximum of no limit. Credit and/or placement offered for CEEB Advanced Placement tests.

COSTS AND FINANCIAL AID

Annual tuition $21,116. Room and board $6,729. Required fees $1,130. Average book expense $800. **Required Forms and Deadlines:** FAFSA. **Notification of Awards:** Applicants will be notified of awards on a rolling basis beginning 3/31. **Types of Aid:** *Need-based scholarships/grants:* Federal Pell, SEOG, state scholarships/grants, private scholarships, the school's own gift aid. *Loans:* Subsidized Stafford, Unsubsidized Stafford, PLUS, Federal Perkins, state loans, college/university loans from institutional funds. *Student Employment:* Federal Work-Study Program available. Institutional employment available. Highest amount earned per year from on-campus jobs $9,536. Off-campus job opportunities are excellent. **Financial Aid Statistics:** 73% freshmen, 76% undergrads receive need-based scholarship or grant aid. 83% freshmen, 86% undergrads receive need-based self-help aid. 56% freshmen, 45% undergrads receive athletic scholarships. 100% freshmen, 100% undergrads receive any aid. 88% undergrads borrow to pay for school. Average cumulative indebtedness $21,466. **Criteria for awarding institutional aid:** *Non-need-based:* academics, alumni affiliation, art, athletics, job skills, leadership, music/drama, religious affiliation, state/district residency.

MORRIS COLLEGE

100 West College Street, Sumter, SC 29150
Phone: 803-934-3225 • **Financial Aid Phone:** 803-934-3238
E-mail: gscriven@morris.edu • **CEEB Code:** 5418
Fax: 803-773-8241 • **Website:** http://www.morris.edu/ • **ACT Code:** 3868

This private school, affiliated with the Baptist Church, was founded in 1908. It has a 34-acre campus.

RATINGS

Admissions Selectivity Rating: 63   **Fire Safety Rating:** 72

STUDENTS AND FACULTY

Enrollment: 774. **Student Body:** 57% female, 43% male, 20% out-of-state, 0% international (0 countries represented). Asian 0%, African American 98%, Caucasian 0%, Hispanic 1%, Native American <1%
Retention and Graduation: 52% freshmen return for sophomore year. 13% freshmen graduate within 4 years. 31% freshmen graduate within 6 years. 12% grads go on to further study within 1 year. 1% grads pursue arts and sciences degrees. 1% grads pursue law degrees. 2% grads pursue business degrees. 2% grads pursue medical degrees. **Faculty:** 47 full-time faculty, 70% hold PhDs, 47% are members of minority groups, 62% are women.

ACADEMICS

Degrees: bachelor's. **Classes:** Most classes have 10–19 students. Most lab/discussion sessions have fewer than 10 students. **Majors with Highest Enrollment:** Business Administration and Management; Criminal Justice/Law Enforcement Administration; Biology/Biological Sciences. **Special Study Options:** Accelerated program, cooperative education program, double major, honors program, internships, liberal arts/career combination, study abroad, teacher certification program, Advanced degree program available for adults aged 25 and older with 60 earned credit hours. **Combined degree programs:** Dual degree, math/engineering with NC A&T State U. **Career services:** Alumni network, alumni services, career/job search classes, career assessment, internships. Career services highlights include the cooperative education internship program, which allows students to gain invaluable paid work experience closely related to their chosen field of study while earning their undergraduate degrees. The majority of these students are hired full-time by their co-op employers upon graduation from the college.

FACILITIES

Housing: men's dorms, women's dorms. 73% of campus accessible to physically disabled. **Special Academic Facilities/Equipment:** WMMC-640AM Student Radio Station **Computers:** 100% of classrooms, 100% of dorms, 100% of libraries, 100% of dining areas, 100% of student union, 95% of common outdoor areas have wireless network access. Administrative functions (other than registration) can be performed online.

CAMPUS LIFE

Environment: Town. **Activities:** Choral groups, dance, drama/theater, literary magazine, pep band, radio station, student government, student newspaper, yearbook. 55 registered organizations, 7 honor societies, 2 religious organizations. 4 fraternities, 4 sororities. **Athletics (Intercollegiate):** *Men:* baseball, basketball, cheerleading, cross-country, golf, tennis, track/field (outdoor). *Women:* basketball, cheerleading, cross-country, softball, tennis, track/field (outdoor), volleyball. **On-Campus Highlights:** Student Center, Library, Human Development Center, Outdoor Basketball Court, Auditorium, Computer Labs.

ADMISSIONS

Freshman Academic Profile: Average high school GPA 2.68. 2% in top 10% of high school class, 9% in top 25% of high school class, 34% in top 50% of high school class. 98% from public high schools. Minimum paper TOEFL 500. **Basis for Candidate Selection:** *Very important factors considered include:* academic GPA. *Important factors considered include:* Class rank, rigor of secondary school record, standardized test scores. **Freshman Admission Requirements:** High school diploma is required and GED is accepted. *Academic units required:* 4 English, 4 mathematics, 3 science, 1 foreign language, 2 social studies, 1 history, 7 academic electives, 1 Government-1/2, Economics-1/2. **Freshman Admission Statistics:** 2,031 applied, 62% admitted, 18% enrolled. **Transfer Admission Requirements:** High school transcript, college transcript(s), standardized test scores, statement of good standing from prior institution(s). Minimum college GPA of 2.0 required. Lowest grade transferable C. **General Admission Information:** Application Fee $20. Notification on a rolling basis, beginning on or about 11/1. Nonfall registration accepted. Admission may be deferred for a maximum of 1 semester. Credit offered for CEEB Advanced Placement tests.

COSTS AND FINANCIAL AID

Required Forms and Deadlines: FAFSA, Institution's own financial aid form. **Notification of Awards:** Applicants will be notified of awards on a rolling basis beginning 6/1. **Types of Aid:** *Need-based scholarships/grants:* Federal Pell, SEOG, state scholarships/grants, private scholarships, the school's own gift aid, United Negro College Fund. *Loans:* Direct Subsidized Stafford, Direct Unsubsidized Stafford, Direct PLUS, Federal Perkins. *Student Employment:* Federal Work-Study Program available. Off-campus job opportunities are good. **Financial Aid Statistics:** 98% freshmen, 97% undergrads receive need-based scholarship or grant aid. 20% freshmen, 20% undergrads receive non-need-based scholarship or grant aid. 94% freshmen, 97% undergrads receive need-based self-help aid. 6% freshmen, 10% undergrads receive athletic scholarships. 98% freshmen, 98% undergrads receive any aid. 98% undergrads borrow to pay for school. Average cumulative indebtedness $23,000. **Criteria for awarding institutional aid:** *Non-need-based:* academics, athletics, state/district residency.

MOUNT ALLISON UNIVERSITY

65 York Street, Sackville, NB E4L1E4
Phone: 506-364-2269 • **Financial Aid Phone:** 506-364-2258
E-mail: admissions@mta.ca • **CEEB Code:**
Fax: 506-364-2272 • **Website:** www.mta.ca

This public school was founded in 1839. It has a 25-acre campus.

RATINGS

Admissions Selectivity Rating: 66   **Fire Safety Rating:** 86

STUDENTS AND FACULTY

Enrollment: 2,396. **Student Body:** 60% female, 40% male, 45% out-of-state, 0% international (40 countries represented). Asian 0%, African American 0%, Caucasian 0%, Hispanic 0%, Native American <1%
Retention and Graduation: 45% freshmen graduate within 4 years. 58% freshmen graduate within 6 years. 30% grads go on to further study within 1 year. 10% grads pursue arts and sciences degrees. 3% grads pursue law degrees. 5% grads pursue business degrees. 12% grads pursue medical degrees. **Faculty:** 124 full-time faculty, 100% hold PhDs, 31% are members of minority groups. 0% of classes are taught by teaching assistants.

ACADEMICS

Degrees: bachelor's, master's. **Classes:** Most classes have fewer than 10 students. **Majors with Highest Enrollment:** Sociology; Business/Commerce. **Special Study Options:** distance learning, double major, English as a Second Language (ESL), exchange student program (domestic), honors program, independent study, internships, student-designed major, study abroad. **Disability Services:** Special programs offered to physically disabled students include reader services, tutors. **Career services:** career/job search classes,

FACILITIES

Housing: Coed dorms, special housing for disabled students, special housing for international students, women's dorms, cooperative housing, Zero environment Footprint Housing, Pet Friendly Housing. (one residence fosters pets for humane society). 80% of campus accessible to physically disabled. **Special Academic Facilities/Equipment:** Art gallery **Computers:** 100% of classrooms, 100% of dorms, 100% of libraries, 100% of dining areas, 100% of student union, 85% of common outdoor areas have wireless network access. Students can register for classes online. Administrative functions (other than registration) can be performed online.

CAMPUS LIFE

Environment: Rural. **Activities:** Choral groups, concert band, dance, drama/theater, jazz band, music ensembles, musical theater, radio station, student government, student newspaper, student-run film society, symphony orchestra, yearbook, International Student Organization. 106 registered organizations. **Athletics (Intercollegiate):** *Men:* badminton, basketball, football, rugby, soccer, swimming. *Women:* badminton, basketball, rugby, soccer, swimming, volleyball. **On-Campus Highlights:** Ownes Art Gallery, Jenings Dinning Hall, Library, Student Center **Environmental Initiatives:** Residence Climate Change Challenge expanded this year to include academic and administrative buildings—buildings reduced their consumption of utilities during the month of February from 10 to 25%; New campus Green Plan which studied the waste generated on campus and identified waste reduction and waste diversion programs to increase our waste diversion from 45% to 70%; Introduced a clean plate program in the dining hall—students scrape their plates just like at home, and a 44% reduction in food waste is the result of this "waste in your face" project.

ADMISSIONS

Freshman Academic Profile: 99% from public high schools. Minimum paper TOEFL 550. **Basis for Candidate Selection:** *Very important factors considered include:* academic GPA, rigor of secondary school record, extracurricular activities, interview, talent/ability. *Important factors considered include:* recommendation(s), character/personal qualities, volunteer work. *Other factors* considered include: Class rank, application essay, standardized test scores, work experience. **Freshman Admission Requirements:** High school diploma is required and GED is accepted. **Freshman Admission Statistics:** 1,997 applied, 46% admitted, 83% enrolled. **Transfer Admission Requirements:** High school transcript, college transcript(s), essay or personal statement, statement of good standing from prior institution(s). Lowest grade transferable c-. **General Admission Information:** Application Fee $50. Regular application deadline 5/1. Nonfall registration accepted.

COSTS AND FINANCIAL AID

Average book expense $1,200. **Required Forms and Deadlines:** FAFSA, Institution's own financial aid form. **Types of Aid:** *Need-based scholarships/grants:* private scholarships, the school's own gift aid. *Loans:* Subsidized Stafford, Unsubsidized Stafford, PLUS, Canada/Provincial Loan Program. *Student Employment:* Off-campus job opportunities are good. **Financial Aid Statistics:** 100% freshmen, 100% undergrads receive need-based scholarship or grant aid. 0% freshmen, 0% undergrads receive non-need-based scholarship or grant aid. 0% freshmen, 0% undergrads receive need-based self-help aid. 0% freshmen, 0% undergrads receive athletic scholarships. Criteriafor awarding institutional aid: *Non-need-based:* academics, alumni affiliation, art, athletics, job skills, leadership, minority status, music/drama, state/district residency.

MOUNT ALOYSIUS COLLEGE

7373 Admiral Peary Highway, Cresson, PA 16630
Phone: 814-886-6383 • **Financial Aid Phone:** 814-886-6463
E-mail: admissions@mtaloy.edu • **CEEB Code:** 2420
Fax: 814-886-6441 • **ACT Code:** 3635

This private school, affiliated with the Roman Catholic Church, was founded in 1939. It has a 125-acre campus.

RATINGS

Admissions Selectivity Rating: 71   Fire Safety Rating: 60*

STUDENTS AND FACULTY

Enrollment: 1,565. **Student Body:** 74% female, 26% male, 5% out-of-state, 1% international. Asian 0%, African American 3%, Caucasian 78%, Hispanic 1%, Native American <1%
Faculty: 75 full-time faculty, 47% hold PhDs, 75% are members of minority groups, 4% are women. 0% of classes are taught by teaching assistants.

ACADEMICS

Degrees: associate, bachelor's, certificate, master's, terminal associate. **Classes:** Most classes have 10–19 students. Most lab/discussion sessions have fewer than 10 students. **Majors with Highest Enrollment:** Medical Radiologic Technology/Science; Registered Nursing/Registered Nurse; Business Administration and Management. **Special Study Options:** Accelerated program, distance learning, honors program, independent study, internships, student-designed major, teacher certification program. **Career services:** alumni services, career/job search classes, career assessment, internships.

FACILITIES

Housing: Coed dorms. 90% of campus accessible to physically disabled. **Computers:** 100% of classrooms, 100% of dorms, 100% of libraries, 100% of dining areas, 100% of student union, 100% of common outdoor areas have wireless network access.

CAMPUS LIFE

Environment: Rural. **Activities:** Choral groups, drama/theater, student government, student newspaper. 16 registered organizations, 2 honor societies, 1 religious organization. **Athletics (Intercollegiate):** *Men:* basketball, golf, soccer. *Women:* basketball, soccer, volleyball.

ADMISSIONS

Freshman Academic Profile: Average high school GPA 3.2. SAT Math middle 50% range 430-500. SAT Critical Reading middle 50% range 410-510. SAT Writing middle 50% range 383-480. ACT middle 50% range 16-20. **Basis for Candidate Selection:** *Very important factors considered include:* academic GPA, rigor of secondary school record, character/personal qualities, extracurricular activities, first generation, interview, talent/ability, volunteer work. *Important factors considered include:* Class rank, recommendation(s), standardized test scores, level of applicant's interest. *Other factors considered include:* application essay. **Freshman Admission Requirements:** High school diploma is required and GED is accepted. *Academic units required:* 4 English, 3 mathematics, 3 science, 3 social studies, 3 computer science. **Freshman Admission Statistics:** 1,572 applied, 74% admitted, 33% enrolled. **Transfer Admission Requirements:** High school transcript, college transcript(s), Minimum college GPA of 2.0 required. Lowest grade transferable C. **General Admission Information:** Application Fee $30. Notification on a rolling basis, beginning

on or about 8/1. Nonfall registration accepted. Admission may be deferred for a maximum of 1 semester. Credit and/or placement offered for CEEB Advanced Placement tests.

COSTS AND FINANCIAL AID

Average book expense $2,500. **Required Forms and Deadlines:** FAFSA. **Notification of Awards:** Applicants will be notified of awards on a rolling basis beginning 3/15. **Types of Aid:** *Need-based scholarships/grants:* Federal Pell, SEOG, state scholarships/grants, private scholarships, the school's own gift aid. *Loans:* Subsidized Stafford, Unsubsidized Stafford, PLUS, Federal Perkins, Federal Nursing, Alternative loans. *Student Employment:* Federal Work-Study Program available. Institutional employment available. Off-campus job opportunities are poor. **Financial Aid Statistics:** 100% freshmen, 100% undergrads receive need-based scholarship or grant aid. 10% freshmen, 8% undergrads receive non-need-based scholarship or grant aid. 100% freshmen, 100% undergrads receive need-based self-help aid. 0% freshmen, 0% undergrads receive athletic scholarships. 90% undergrads borrow to pay for school. **Criteria for awarding institutional aid:** *Non-need-based:* academics, art, leadership, music/drama, religious affiliation.

See page 1098.

MOUNT HOLYOKE COLLEGE

Best 380

Newhall Center, South Hadley, MA 1075
Phone: 413-538-2023 • **Financial Aid Phone:** 413-538-2291
E-mail: admission@mtholyoke.edu • **CEEB Code:** 3529
Fax: 413-538-2409 • **Website:** www.mtholyoke.edu • **ACT Code:** 1866

This private school was founded in 1837. It has a 800-acre campus.

RATINGS

Admissions Selectivity Rating: 93   Fire Safety Rating: 77

STUDENTS AND FACULTY

Enrollment: 2,161. **Student Body:** 100% female, 0% male, 77% out-of-state, 25% international (72 countries represented). Asian 10%, African American 6%, Caucasian 47%, Hispanic 8%, Native American <1%
Retention and Graduation: 76% freshmen graduate within 4 years. 80% freshmen graduate within 6 years. 19% grads go on to further study within 1 year. 14% grads pursue arts and sciences degrees. 1% grads pursue law degrees. 2% grads pursue medical degrees. **Faculty:** 208 full-time faculty, 94% hold PhDs, 56% are members of minority groups, 23% are women. 0% of classes are taught by teaching assistants.

ACADEMICS

Degrees: bachelor's, certificate, master's, post-bachelor's certificate. **Classes:** Most classes have 10–19 students. Most lab/discussion sessions have 10–19 students. **Majors with Highest Enrollment:** English Language and Literature; Economics; International Relations and Affairs. **Special Study Options:** cooperative education program, cross-registration, double major, exchange student program (domestic), independent study, internships, liberal arts/career combination, student-designed major, study abroad, teacher certification program, Community-based learning courses and First-Year seminars. **Disability Services:** Special programs offered to physically disabled students include note-taking services, reader services, tape recorders, tutors. **Career services:** Alumni network, alumni services, career/job search classes, career assessment, internships, regional alumni. For career services highlights see http://www.mtholyoke.edu/cdc/internships.html.

FACILITIES

Housing: special housing for disabled students, women's dorms, apartments for single students, Special housing arrangements are available upon request. 95% of campus accessible to physically disabled. **Special Academic Facilities/Equipment:** Art and historical museums, bronze-casting foundry, child study center, audio-visual center, language learning center, greenhouse, Japanese meditation garden, equestrian center, observatory, linear accelerator, electron microscope, refracting telescope, nuclear magnetic resonance equipment, MCulloch Center for Global Initiatives, Weissman Center for Leadership and the Liberal Arts, Center for the Environment. **Computers:** 20% of classrooms, 100% of dorms, 100% of libraries, 100% of dining areas, 100% of student union, 4% of common outdoor areas have wireless network access. Students can register for classes online. Administrative functions (other than registration) can be performed online.

CAMPUS LIFE

Environment: Town. **Activities:** Choral groups, dance, drama/theater, jazz band, literary magazine, music ensembles, musical theater, radio station, student government, student newspaper, student-run film society, symphony orchestra, yearbook, Campus Ministries, International Student Organization, Model UN. 150 registered organizations, 4 honor societies, 12 religious organizations. **Athletics (Intercollegiate):** *Women:* basketball, crew/rowing, cross-country, diving, equestrian sports, field hockey, golf, horseback riding, lacrosse, soccer, squash, swimming, tennis, track/field (outdoor), track/field (indoor), volleyball. **On-Campus Highlights:** Unified Science Center, Kendall Sports and Dance Complex, The Equestrian Center, Blanchard Campus Center, Williston Memorial Library, The entire campus is an exquisitely maintained botanic garden which includes an arboretum, numerous gardens, and the Talcott Greenhouse. **Environmental Initiatives:** Bottled water free commencement—Funded by the Campus Sustainability Fund the students of Think Outside the Bottle organized a bottle water free commencement. All attendees were provided with a reusable bottle filled with local water. War-of-the-Watts—Funded by the Campus Sustainability Fund, the Eco-reps and sustainability office organized a one month energy competition among the 21 residence hall culminating in an event called Nutella with Pasquerella with President Lynn Pasquerella attending a nutella party for the winning hall. (http://www.youtube.com/watch?v=S4RhqG502Z0). Sustainable Food for the Five—Mount Holyoke has joined the other 4 colleges in the consortium to work collectively with local farmers and businesses to source more local and sustainable food.

ADMISSIONS

Freshman Academic Profile: Average high school GPA 3.75. 56% in top 10% of high school class, 82% in top 25% of high school class, 95% in top 50% of high school class. 60% from public high schools. SAT Math middle 50% range 610-730. SAT Critical Reading middle 50% range 610-720. SAT Writing middle 50% range 620-710. ACT middle 50% range 28-31. Minimum internet-based TOEFL 100. **Basis for Candidate Selection:** *Very important factors considered include:* Class rank, application essay, academic GPA, recommendation(s), rigor of secondary school record. *Important factors considered include:* character/personal qualities, extracurricular activities, first generation, interview, talent/ability, volunteer work, work experience. *Other factors considered include:* standardized test scores, alumni/ae relation, geographical residence, level of applicant's interest, racial/ethnic status. **Freshman Admission Requirements:** High school diploma is required and GED is accepted. **Freshman Admission Statistics:** 3,201 applied, 55% admitted, 31% enrolled. **Transfer Admission Requirements:** High school transcript, college transcript(s), essay or personal statement, statement of good standing from prior institution(s). Minimum college GPA of 3.0 required. Lowest grade transferable C-. **General Admission Information:** Application Fee $60. Early decision application deadline 11/15. Regular application deadline 1/15. Regular notification 4/1. Nonfall registration accepted. Credit and/or placement offered for CEEB Advanced Placement tests.

COSTS AND FINANCIAL AID

Annual tuition $42,470. Room and board $12,490. Required fees $186. Average book expense $950. **Required Forms and Deadlines:** FAFSA, CSS/Financial Aid PROFILE, Noncustodial PROFILE. **Notification of Awards:** Applicants will be notified of awards on or about 4/1. **Types of Aid:** *Need-based scholarships/grants:* Federal Pell, SEOG, state scholarships/grants, private scholarships, the school's own gift aid. *Loans:* Direct Subsidized Stafford, Direct Unsubsidized Stafford, Direct PLUS, Federal Perkins, state loans, college/university loans from institutional funds. *Student Employment:* Federal Work-Study Program available. Institutional employment available. Highest amount earned per year from on-campus jobs $2,100. Off-campus job opportunities are fair. **Financial Aid Statistics:** 100% freshmen, 99% undergrads receive need-based scholarship or grant aid. 23% freshmen, 18% undergrads receive non-need-based scholarship or grant aid. 85% freshmen, 88% undergrads receive need-based self-help aid. 0% freshmen, 0% undergrads receive athletic scholarships. 80% freshmen, 80% undergrads receive any aid. 73% undergrads borrow to pay for school. Average cumulative indebtedness $22,399. **Criteria for awarding institutional aid:** *Non-need-based:* academics, leadership.

MOUNT IDA COLLEGE

777 Dedham Street, Newton, MA 2459
Phone: 617-928-4553 • **Financial Aid Phone:** 617-928-4785
E-mail: admissions@mountida.edu • **CEEB Code:** 3530
Fax: 617-928-4507 • **Website:** www.mountida.edu • **ACT Code:** 1868

This private school was founded in 1899. It has a 72-acre campus.

RATINGS

Admissions Selectivity Rating: 71   Fire Safety Rating: 60*

STUDENTS AND FACULTY

Enrollment: 1,445. **Student Body:** 67% female, 33% male, 40% out-of-state, 5% international (32 countries represented). Asian 2%, African American 10%, Caucasian 56%, Hispanic 6%, Native American <1%
Retention and Graduation: 57% freshmen return for sophomore year. **Faculty:** 63 full-time faculty, 57% hold PhDs, 60% are members of minority groups, 8% are women. 0% of classes are taught by teaching assistants.

ACADEMICS

Degrees: associate, bachelor's, certificate, terminal associate, transfer associate. **Classes:** Most classes have 10–19 students. **Special Study Options:** Accelerated program, distance learning, English as a Second Language (ESL), honors program, independent study, internships, student-designed major, study abroad, teacher certification program. **Disability Services:** Special programs offered to physically disabled students include tape recorders, tutors. **Career services:** Alumni network, alumni services, career assessment, internships.

FACILITIES

Housing: Coed dorms, special housing for disabled students, men's dorms, women's dorms. **Special Academic Facilities/Equipment:** Mount Ida College Art Gallery.

CAMPUS LIFE

Environment: Village. **Activities:** Choral groups, dance, drama/theater, literary magazine, radio station, student government, student newspaper, yearbook, International Student Organization. 22 registered organizations, 6 honor societies. **Athletics (Intercollegiate):** *Men:* basketball, football, lacrosse, soccer, volleyball. *Women:* basketball, cheerleading, cross-country, equestrian sports, soccer, softball, volleyball.

ADMISSIONS

Freshman Academic Profile: SAT Math middle 50% range 380-490. SAT Critical Reading middle 50% range 390-490. SAT Writing middle 50% range 400-500. ACT middle 50% range 15-20. Minimum internet-based TOEFL 70. Minimum paper TOEFL 525. **Basis for Candidate Selection:** *Very important factors considered include:* academic GPA. *Important factors considered include:* recommendation(s), rigor of secondary school record. *Other factors considered include:* application essay, standardized test scores, character/personal qualities, extracurricular activities, interview, talent/ability, volunteer work, work experience. **Freshman Admission Requirements:** High school diploma is required and GED is accepted. **Freshman Admission Statistics:** 2,222 applied, 74% admitted, 25% enrolled. **Transfer Admission Requirements:** High school transcript, college transcript(s), essay or personal statement, statement of good standing from prior institution(s). Minimum college GPA of 2.0 required. Lowest grade transferable C. **General Admission Information:** Application Fee $45. Nonfall registration accepted. Admission may be deferred for a maximum of 1 year. Credit offered for CEEB Advanced Placement tests.

COSTS AND FINANCIAL AID

Average book expense $1,000. **Required Forms and Deadlines:** FAFSA. **Notification of Awards:** Applicants will be notified of awards on a rolling basis beginning 3/1. **Types of Aid:** *Need-based scholarships/grants:* Federal Pell, SEOG, state scholarships/grants, private scholarships, the school's own gift aid. *Loans:* Subsidized Stafford, Unsubsidized Stafford, PLUS, state loans. *Student Employment:* Federal Work-Study Program available. Institutional employment available. Highest amount earned per year from on-campus jobs $1,500. **Financial Aid Statistics:** 99% freshmen, 97% undergrads receive need-based scholarship or grant aid. 6% freshmen, 6% undergrads receive non-need-based scholarship or grant aid. 96% freshmen, 95% undergrads receive need-based self-help aid. 0% freshmen, 0% undergrads receive athletic scholarships. **Criteria for awarding institutional aid:** *Non-need-based:* academics, art, leadership.

MOUNT MARY UNIVERSITY

2900 North Menomonee River Parkway, Milwaukee, WI 53222-4597
Phone: 414-256-1219 • **Financial Aid Phone:** 414-256-1258
E-mail: mmu-admiss@mtmary.edu • **CEEB Code:** 1490
Fax: 414-256-0180 • **Website:** http://www.mtmary.edu/ • **ACT Code:** 4620

This private school, affiliated with the Roman Catholic Church, was founded in 1913. It has a 80-acre campus.

RATINGS

Admissions Selectivity Rating: 85   Fire Safety Rating: 71

STUDENTS AND FACULTY

Enrollment: 774. **Student Body:** 100% female, 0% male, 6% out-of-state, 0% international (16 countries represented). Asian 7%, African American 23%, Caucasian 52%, Hispanic 14%, Native American 1%

Retention and Graduation: 78% freshmen return for sophomore year. 26% freshmen graduate within 4 years. **Faculty:** Student/faculty ratio :1. 65 full-time faculty, 75% hold PhDs, 91% are are members of minority groups. 0% of classes are taught by teaching assistants.

ACADEMICS
Degrees: bachelor's, master's, post-bachelor's certificate, post-master's certificate. **Classes:** Most classes have 10-19 students. Most lab/discussion sessions have 10-19 students. **Majors with Highest Enrollment:** Occupational Therapy/Therapist; Fashion/Apparel Design; Fashion Merchandising. **Special Study Options:** Accelerated program, double major, honors program, independent study, internships, liberal arts/career combination, student-designed major, study abroad, teacher certification program. **Honors programs:** The purpose of the Mount Mary College Honors Program is to reward superior scholarly achievement and to provide special challenges to serious students who wish to achieve maximum benefit from their college education. **Disability Services:** Special programs offered to physically disabled students include note-taking services, reader services, tape recorders, tutors. **Career services:** career/job search classes, career assessment, internships.

FACILITIES
Housing: women's dorms 90% of campus accessible to physically diasbled. **Special Academic Facilities/Equipment:** Hagerty Library, Marian Art Gallery, Walter and Olive Stiemke Memorial Hall and Conference Center. **Computers:** 100% of dorms, have wireless network access. Students can register for classes online. Administrative functions (other than registration) can be performed online.

CAMPUS LIFE
Environment: Metropolis. **Activities:** Choral groups, dance, literary magazine, music ensembles, student government, student newspaper, Campus Ministries, International Student Organization, Model UN. 42 registered organizations, 14 honor societies, 1 religious organizations. **Athletics (Intercollegiate):** *Women:* basketball, cross-country, soccer, softball, tennis, volleyball. **On-Campus Highlights:** Cyber Cafe, Gerhardinger Science and Technology Center, Haggerty Library, Notre Dame Hall, Bloechl Recreation Center.

ADMISSIONS
Freshman Academic Profile: Average high school GPA 3.08. 20% in top 10% of high school class, 45% in top 25% of high school class, 78% in top 50% of high school class. ACT middle 50% range 17-22. Minimum internet-based TOEFL 61. **Basis for Candidate Selection:** *Very important factors considered include:* academic GPA, rigor of secondary school record. *Important factors considered include:* Class rank, standardized test scores, character/personal qualities, talent/ability. *Other factors considered include:* application essay, recommendation(s), extracurricular activities, interview, volunteer work, work experience. **Freshman Admission Requirements:** High school diploma is required and GED is accepted. *Academic units required:* 4 English, 2 mathematics, 2 science, (2 science labs), 0 foreign language, 2 social studies, 2 history, 2 academic electives. **Freshman Admission Statistics:** 638 applied, 35% admitted, 69% enrolled. **Transfer Admission Requirements:** High school transcript, college transcript(s), Minimum college GPA of 2.0 required. Lowest grade transferable C. **General Admission Information:** Application Fee $25. Notification on a rolling basis, beginning on or about 9/15. Nonfall registration accepted. Admission may be deferred for a maximum of 1 year. Credit and/or placement offered for CEEB Advanced Placement tests.

COSTS AND FINANCIAL AID
Required Forms and Deadlines: FAFSA. **Notification of Awards:** Applicants will be notified of awards on a rolling basis beginning 3/1. **Types of Aid:** *Need-based scholarships/grants:* Federal Pell, SEOG, state scholarships/grants, private scholarships, the school's own gift aid. *Loans:* Subsidized Stafford, Unsubsidized Stafford, PLUS, Federal Perkins, state loans. *Student Employment:* Federal Work-Study Program available. Institutional employment available. Highest amount earned per year from on-campus jobs $1,152. **Financial Aid Statistics:** 100% freshmen, 100% undergrads receive need-based scholarship or grant aid. 6% freshmen, 5% undergrads receive non-need-based scholarship or grant aid. 87% freshmen, 94% undergrads receive need-based self-help aid. 0% freshmen, 0% undergrads receive athletic scholarships. 100% freshmen, 95% undergrads receive any aid. 89% undergrads borrow to pay for school. Average cumulative indebtedness $29,759. **Criteria for awarding institutional aid:** *Non-need-based:* academics, alumni affiliation, art, leadership; music/drama.

MOUNT MERCY COLLEGE

1330 Elmhurst Drive Northeast, Cedar Rapids, IA 52402-4797
Phone: 319-368-6460
E-mail: admission@mtmercy.edu
Fax: 319-363-5270 • **Website:** www.mtmercy.edu

This is a private school.

RATINGS
Admissions Selectivity Rating: 75   **Fire Safety Rating:** 60*

STUDENTS AND FACULTY
Enrollment: 1,434. **Student Body:** 70% female, 30% male, 6% out-of-state, 0% international. Asian 1%, African American 2%, Caucasian 87%, Hispanic 1%, Native American <1%
Retention and Graduation: 77% freshmen return for sophomore year. 49% freshmen graduate within 4 years. 61% freshmen graduate within 6 years. 9% grads go on to further study within 1 year. 6% grads pursue arts and sciences degrees. 1% grads pursue law degrees. 2% grads pursue business degrees. **Faculty:** 72 full-time faculty, 61% hold PhDs, 57% are members of minority groups, 6% are women. 0% of classes are taught by teaching assistants.

ACADEMICS
Degrees: bachelor's. **Classes:** Most classes have 10–19 students. **Majors with Highest Enrollment:** Education; Registered Nursing/Registered Nurse; Business/Commerce. **Special Study Options:** Accelerated program, cooperative education program, cross-registration, double major, dual enrollment, honors program, independent study, internships, liberal arts/career combination, student-designed major, study abroad, teacher certification program, weekend college. **Combined degree programs:** 2-2 programs with Kirkwood Community College. **Disability Services:** Special programs offered to physically disabled students include note-taking services, reader services, tape recorders, tutors. **Career services:** Alumni network, alumni services, career/job search classes, career assessment, internships, regional alumni.

FACILITIES
Housing: Coed dorms, apartments for single students. 95% of campus accessible to physically disabled.

CAMPUS LIFE
Activities: Choral groups, drama/theater, literary magazine, pep band, student government, student newspaper. 35 registered organizations, 16 honor societies, 7 religious organizations. **Athletics (Intercollegiate):** *Men:* baseball, basketball, cross-country, golf, soccer, track/field (outdoor). *Women:* basketball, cross-country, golf, soccer, softball, track/field (outdoor), volleyball. **On-Campus Highlights:** Lundy Commons: Game Room, TV Room, Convenience Store, Bookstore, Lounges, Hilltop Grill and Dining Hall, Busse Library, Andrea's House—144 bed, suite style campus residence, Entire campus is connected by underground tunnels.

ADMISSIONS
Freshman Academic Profile: Average high school GPA 3.43. 18% in top 10% of high school class, 44% in top 25% of high school class, 82% in top 50% of high school class. 83% from public high schools. ACT middle 50% range 20-25. Minimum paper TOEFL 550. **Basis for Candidate Selection:** *Very important factors considered include:* Class rank, rigor of secondary school record, standardized test scores. *Important factors considered include:* application essay, recommendation(s), extracurricular activities. *Other factors considered include:* character/personal qualities, interview, talent/ability, volunteer work. **Freshman Admission Requirements:** High school diploma is required and GED is accepted. **Freshman Admission Statistics:** 488 applied, 84% admitted, 48% enrolled. **Transfer Admission Requirements:** college transcript(s), statement of good standing from prior institution(s). Minimum college GPA of 2.5 required. Lowest grade transferable D. **General Admission Information:** Application Fee $20. Regular application deadline 8/30. Nonfall registration accepted. Admission may be deferred for a maximum of 1 year. Credit and/or placement offered for CEEB Advanced Placement tests.

COSTS AND FINANCIAL AID
Required Forms and Deadlines: FAFSA. **Notification of Awards:** Applicants will be notified of awards on a rolling basis beginning 3/15. **Types of Aid:** *Need-based scholarships/grants:* Federal Pell, SEOG, state scholarships/grants, the school's own gift aid. *Loans:* Direct Subsidized Stafford, Direct Unsubsidized Stafford, Direct PLUS, Federal Perkins, state loans, college/university loans from institutional funds. *Student Employment:* Federal Work-Study Program available. Institutional employment available. Off-campus job opportunities are excellent. **Financial Aid Statistics:** 100% freshmen, 99% undergrads receive need-based scholarship or grant aid. 14% freshmen, 8% undergrads receive non-need-based scholarship or grant aid. 84% freshmen, 89% undergrads

receive need-based self-help aid. 0% freshmen, 0% undergrads receive athletic scholarships. 71% undergrads borrow to pay for school. **Criteria for awarding institutional aid:** *Non-need-based:* academics, art, leadership, music/drama.

MOUNT OLIVE COLLEGE

634 Henderson Street, Mount Olive, NC 28365
Phone: 919-658-2502
E-mail: admissions@moc.edu • **CEEB Code:** 5435
Fax: 919-658-9816 • **Website:** www.moc.edu • **ACT Code:** 3131

This private school, affiliated with the Baptist Church, was founded in 1951. It has a 138-acre campus.

RATINGS
Admissions Selectivity Rating: 79 **Fire Safety Rating:** 60*

STUDENTS AND FACULTY
Enrollment: 3,305. **Student Body:** 68% female, 32% male, 4% out-of-state. Asian 1%, African American 35%, Caucasian 51%, Hispanic 3%, Native American <1%
Retention and Graduation: 68% freshmen return for sophomore year. 20% grads go on to further study within 1 year. **Faculty:** 80 full-time faculty, 96% hold PhDs, 35% are members of minority groups, 15% are women.

ACADEMICS
Degrees: associate, bachelor's, terminal associate, transfer associate. **Special Study Options:** Accelerated program, cooperative education program, distance learning, double major, dual enrollment, external degree program, honors program, independent study, internships, liberal arts/career combination, teacher certification program. **Disability Services:** Special programs offered to physically disabled students include tutors. **Career services:** alumni services, career/job search classes, career assessment, internships,

FACILITIES
Housing: men's dorms, women's dorms, apartments for single students. 95% of campus accessible to physically disabled.

CAMPUS LIFE
Environment: Rural. **Activities:** Choral groups, concert band, music ensembles, musical theater, student government, Campus Ministries, International Student Organization. 33 registered organizations, 4 honor societies, 6 religious organizations. **Athletics (Intercollegiate):** *Men:* baseball, basketball, cross-country, golf, soccer, tennis. *Women:* basketball, cross-country, soccer, softball, tennis, volleyball.

ADMISSIONS
Freshman Academic Profile: Average high school GPA 3.05. 9% in top 10% of high school class, 26% in top 25% of high school class, 59% in top 50% of high school class. SAT Math middle 50% range 420-520. SAT Critical Reading middle 50% range 410-490. ACT middle 50% range 15-20. Minimum paper TOEFL 500. **Basis for Candidate Selection:** *Very important factors considered include:* academic GPA, rigor of secondary school record, character/personal qualities. *Important factors considered include:* Class rank, standardized test scores, extracurricular activities, interview, level of applicant's interest, talent/ability. *Other factors considered include:* recommendation(s), alumni/ae relation, geographical residence. **Freshman Admission Requirements:** High school diploma is required and GED is accepted. *Academic units required:* 4 English, 3 mathematics, 3 science, (1 science labs), 0 foreign language, 3 social studies, 0 visual/performing arts, 0 computer science, 3 academic electives. **Freshman Admission Statistics:** 1,838 applied, 50% admitted, 37% enrolled. **Transfer Admission Requirements:** High school transcript, college transcript(s), Minimum college GPA of 2.0 required. **General Admission Information:** Nonfall registration accepted.

COSTS AND FINANCIAL AID
Annual tuition $7,223. Room and board $2,775. Required fees $0. Average book expense $656. **Required Forms and Deadlines:** FAFSA, State aid form. **Notification of Awards:** Applicants will be notified of awards on a rolling basis beginning 2/14. **Types of Aid:** *Need-based scholarships/grants:* Federal Pell, SEOG, state scholarships/grants, private scholarships, the school's own gift aid. *Loans:* Subsidized Stafford, Unsubsidized Stafford, PLUS, Federal Perkins, Federal Nursing, state loans. *Student Employment:* Federal Work-Study Program available. Off-campus job opportunities are excellent. **Financial Aid Statistics:** 97% freshmen, 93% undergrads receive need-based scholarship or grant aid. 5% freshmen, 4% undergrads receive non-need-based scholarship or grant aid. 82% freshmen, 84% undergrads receive need-based self-help aid. 7% freshmen, 2% undergrads receive athletic scholarships. 93% undergrads borrow to pay for school. Average cumulative indebtedness $15,343. **Criteria**

for awarding institutional aid: *Non-need-based:* academics, art, athletics, leadership, music/drama, religious affiliation.

MOUNT SAINT MARY COLLEGE

330 Powell Avenue, Newburgh, NY 12550
Phone: 845-569-3488 • **Financial Aid Phone:** 845-569-3298
E-mail: admissions@msmc.edu • **CEEB Code:** 2423
Fax: 845-569-3520 • **Website:** www.msmc.edu • **ACT Code:** 2819

This private school was founded in 1959. It has a 70-acre campus.

RATINGS
Admissions Selectivity Rating: 74 **Fire Safety Rating:** 96

STUDENTS AND FACULTY
Enrollment: 2,096. **Student Body:** 71% female, 29% male, 11% out-of-state, 0% international (14 countries represented). Asian 2%, African American 8%, Caucasian 63%, Hispanic 13%, Native American 1%
Retention and Graduation: 74% freshmen return for sophomore year. 44% freshmen graduate within 4 years. 35% grads go on to further study within 1 year. 9% grads pursue arts and sciences degrees. 1% grads pursue law degrees. 8% grads pursue business degrees. **Faculty:** 83 full-time faculty, 93% hold PhDs, 58% are members of minority groups, 6% are women. 0% of classes are taught by teaching assistants.

ACADEMICS
Degrees: bachelor's, certificate, master's, post-master's certificate. **Classes:** Most classes have 20–29 students. Most lab/discussion sessions have fewer than 10 students. **Majors with Highest Enrollment:** Registered Nursing/Registered Nurse; Business Administration and Management; Teacher Education and Professional Development, Specific Levels and Methods. **Special Study Options:** Accelerated program, cooperative education program, cross-registration, distance learning, double major, dual enrollment, exchange student program (domestic), honors program, independent study, internships, liberal arts/career combination, student-designed major, study abroad, teacher certification program. **Honors programs:** The Honors Program comprises academic, cultural, and social activities, each of which complements and reinforces the others. **Combined degree programs:** BA/MA. **Disability Services:** Special programs offered to physically disabled students include tape recorders, tutors. **Career services:** alumni services, career/job search classes, career assessment. Career services highlights include the Co-op program, which helps many students get a jump start on their career choice as well as help clarify their goals.

FACILITIES
Housing: Coed dorms, special housing for disabled students, men's dorms, women's dorms. 95% of campus accessible to physically disabled. **Special Academic Facilities/Equipment:** On-campus elementary school, television studio, and radio station. Multi-media lab. **Computers:** 100% of classrooms, 100% of dorms, 100% of libraries, 100% of dining areas, 100% of student union, 40% of common outdoor areas have wireless network access. Students can register for classes online. Administrative functions (other than registration) can be performed online.

CAMPUS LIFE
Environment: Town. **Activities:** Choral groups, concert band, dance, drama/theater, literary magazine, music ensembles, musical theater, radio station, student government, student newspaper, student-run film society, yearbook, Campus Ministries. 30 registered organizations, 12 honor societies, 1 religious organization. **Athletics (Intercollegiate):** *Men:* baseball, basketball, cross-country, lacrosse, soccer, swimming, tennis. *Women:* basketball, cross-country, lacrosse, soccer, softball, swimming, tennis, volleyball. **On-Campus Highlights:** Athletic Center with indoor pool, cardio/weight rm, Knight Court Cyber Café', Library with wireless internet access, Multi-media production laboratory, Theater with student productions/music events. **Environmental Initiatives:** Use of high efficiency boilers; Purchase and use of water conserving plumbing fixtures, faucets, and appliances; Natural products for flooring such as cork or marmoleum.

ADMISSIONS
Freshman Academic Profile: Average high school GPA 3.2. 10% in top 10% of high school class, 37% in top 25% of high school class, 75% in top 50% of high school class. 71% from public high schools. SAT Math middle 50% range 460-560. SAT Critical Reading middle 50% range 450-540. SAT Writing middle 50% range 440-540. ACT middle 50% range 20-24. TOEFL Minimum internet-based TOEFL 79. Minimum paper TOEFL 550. **Basis for Candidate Selection:** *Very important factors considered include:* academic GPA, rigor of secondary school record. *Important factors considered include:* Class rank, application

essay, recommendation(s), standardized test scores, character/personal qualities, interview, talent/ability. *Other factors considered include:* alumni/ae relation, extracurricular activities, first generation, level of applicant's interest, volunteer work, work experience. **Freshman Admission Requirements:** High school diploma is required and GED is accepted. **Freshman Admission Statistics:** 3,742 applied, 89% admitted, 12% enrolled. **Transfer Admission Requirements:** High school transcript, college transcript(s), standardized test scores, statement of good standing from prior institution(s). Minimum college GPA of 2.0 required. Lowest grade transferable C. **General Admission Information:** Application Fee $45. Regular application deadline 8/15. Notification on a rolling basis, beginning on or about 9/15. Nonfall registration accepted. Admission may be deferred for a maximum of 1 year. Credit and/or placement offered for CEEB Advanced Placement tests.

COSTS AND FINANCIAL AID

Required Forms and Deadlines: FAFSA. **Notification of Awards:** Applicants will be notified of awards on a rolling basis beginning 3/15. **Types of Aid:** *Need-based scholarships/grants:* Federal Pell, SEOG, state scholarships/grants, private scholarships, the school's own gift aid, Federal Nursing Scholarships., Academic Competitiveness Grant (ACG) and National Science and Mathematics Access to Retain Talent Grant (National SMART or NSG). *Loans:* Subsidized Stafford, Unsubsidized Stafford, PLUS, Federal Perkins, Federal Nursing. *Student Employment:* Federal Work-Study Program available. Institutional employment available. Highest amount earned per year from on-campus jobs $4,204. Off-campus job opportunities are good. **Financial Aid Statistics:** 100% freshmen, 98% undergrads receive need-based scholarship or grant aid. 14% freshmen, 12% undergrads receive non-need-based scholarship or grant aid. 87% freshmen, 87% undergrads receive need-based self-help aid. 0% freshmen, 0% undergrads receive athletic scholarships. 99% freshmen, 93% undergrads receive any aid. 84% undergrads borrow to pay for school. Average cumulative indebtedness $25,852. **Criteria for awarding institutional aid:** *Non-need-based:* academics.

MOUNT SAINT MARY'S UNIVERSITY (CA)

12001 Chalon Road, Los Angeles, CA 90049-1597
Financial Aid Phone: 310-954-4190
E-mail: admissions@msmu.edu · **CEEB Code:** 4493
Fax: 310-954-4259 · **Website:** www.msmu.edu · **ACT Code:** 338

This private school, affiliated with the Roman Catholic Church, was founded in 1925. It has a 53-acre campus.

RATINGS

Admissions Selectivity Rating: 75 **Fire Safety Rating:** 85

STUDENTS AND FACULTY

Enrollment: 2,659. **Student Body:** 93% female, 7% male, 1% out-of-state, 0% international (9 countries represented). Asian 17%, African American 7%, Caucasian 10%, Hispanic 60%, Native American <1%
Retention and Graduation: 77% freshmen return for sophomore year. 30% grads go on to further study within 1 year. **Faculty:** 118 full-time faculty, 59% hold PhDs, 76% are members of minority groups, 22% are women. 0% of classes are taught by teaching assistants.

ACADEMICS

Degrees: associate, bachelor's, certificate, master's, post-bachelor's certificate, post-master's certificate, terminal associate, transfer associate. **Classes:** Most classes have 10–19 students. Most lab/discussion sessions have 10–19 students. **Majors with Highest Enrollment:** Registered Nursing/Registered Nurse; Psychology; Biology/Biological Sciences. **Special Study Options:** Accelerated program, cross-registration, double major, exchange student program (domestic), honors program, independent study, internships, student-designed major, study abroad, teacher certification program, weekend college. **Honors programs:** Honors program is available to qualifying incoming freshmen and college students meeting eligibility requirements. **Combined degree programs:** BA/MA, ADN to MSN. **Disability Services:** Special programs offered to physically disabled students include note-taking services, reader services, tape recorders, tutors. **Career services:** alumni services, career/job search classes, career assessment, internships.

FACILITIES

Housing: men's dorms, women's dorms, limited men's housing. 100% of campus accessible to physically disabled. **Special Academic Facilities/Equipment:** Drudis-Biada Art Gallery **Computers:** 100% of classrooms, 100% of dorms, 100% of libraries, 100% of dining areas, have wireless network access. Students can register for classes online. Administrative functions (other than registration) can be performed online.

CAMPUS LIFE

Environment: Metropolis. **Activities:** Choral groups, dance, drama/theater, literary magazine, music ensembles, student government, student newspaper, yearbook, Campus Ministries. 29 registered organizations, 3 honor societies, 1 religious organization. 3 sororities. **On-Campus Highlights:** Humanities Building, Chapel, Fitness Center **Environmental Initiatives:** Water Conservation: Bottled water deliveries virtually canceled on both campuses; Activated Carbon Water filters added to bottle-free water dispensers on both campuses. Carbon Footprint: Gas-powered golf carts replaced with electric vehicles on both campuses; Facilities Management offices using only "Green-Certified" vendors; Full deployment of recycling containers in offices, classrooms and throughout both campuses; Reusable containers offered for take away food from the café, paper take away products are no longer offered.

ADMISSIONS

Freshman Academic Profile: Average high school GPA 3.4. 14% in top 10% of high school class, 42% in top 25% of high school class, 83% in top 50% of high school class. 53% from public high schools. SAT Math middle 50% range 400-510. SAT Critical Reading middle 50% range 410-510. SAT Writing middle 50% range 420-520. ACT middle 50% range 15-21. Minimum paper TOEFL 550. **Basis for Candidate Selection:** *Very important factors considered include:* application essay, academic GPA, standardized test scores. *Important factors considered include:* recommendation(s), rigor of secondary school record. *Other factors considered include:* alumni/ae relation, character/personal qualities, extracurricular activities, first generation, geographical residence, racial/ethnic status, religious affiliation/commitment, state residency, talent/ability, volunteer work, work experience. **Freshman Admission Requirements:** High school diploma is required and GED is accepted. *Academic units required:* 4 English, 3 mathematics, 2 science, (2 science labs), 2 foreign language, 2 social studies, 2 history. **Freshman Admission Statistics:** 2,161 applied, 78% admitted, 27% enrolled. **Transfer Admission Requirements:** college transcript(s), essay or personal statement, statement of good standing from prior institution(s). Minimum college GPA of 2.4 required. Lowest grade transferable D. **General Admission Information:** Application Fee $40. Notification on a rolling basis, beginning on or about 11/15. Nonfall registration accepted. Admission may be deferred for a maximum of 1 year. Credit and/or placement offered for CEEB Advanced Placement tests.

COSTS AND FINANCIAL AID

Annual tuition $32,882. Room and board $10,530. Required fees $990. Average book expense $1,774. **Required Forms and Deadlines:** FAFSA, Institution's own financial aid form. **Notification of Awards:** Applicants will be notified of awards on a rolling basis beginning 3/15. **Types of Aid:** *Need-based scholarships/grants:* Federal Pell, SEOG, state scholarships/grants, private scholarships, the school's own gift aid. *Loans:* Subsidized Stafford, Unsubsidized Stafford, PLUS, Federal Nursing, college/university loans from institutional funds. *Student Employment:* Federal Work-Study Program available. Institutional employment available. Off-campus job opportunities are good. **Financial Aid Statistics:** 100% freshmen, 95% undergrads receive need-based scholarship or grant aid. 100% freshmen, 43% undergrads receive non-need-based scholarship or grant aid. 97% freshmen, 96% undergrads receive need-based self-help aid. 0% freshmen, 0% undergrads receive athletic scholarships. 85% undergrads borrow to pay for school. Average cumulative indebtedness $27,053. **Criteria for awarding institutional aid:** *Non-need-based:* academics, alumni affiliation, minority status, religious affiliation, state/district residency.

MOUNT ST. JOSEPH UNIVERSITY

5701 Delhi Road, Cincinnati, OH 45233
Phone: 513-244-4531 · **Financial Aid Phone:** 513-244-4418
E-mail: admissions@msj.edu · **CEEB Code:** 1129
Fax: 513-244-4629 · **Website:** www.msj.edu · **ACT Code:** 3254

This private school, affiliated with the Roman Catholic Church, was founded in 1920. It has a 92-acre campus.

RATINGS

Admissions Selectivity Rating: 74 **Fire Safety Rating:** 99

STUDENTS AND FACULTY

Enrollment: 1,463. **Student Body:** 59% female, 41% male, 16% out-of-state, 0% international (3 countries represented). Asian 1%, African American 11%, Caucasian 80%, Hispanic 2%, Native American <1%
Retention and Graduation: 67% freshmen return for sophomore year. 39% freshmen graduate within 4 years. 57% freshmen graduate within 6 years. 17% grads go on to further study within 1 year. 12% grads pursue arts and sciences degrees. 4% grads pursue business degrees. **Faculty:** 109 full-time faculty, 66%

hold PhDs, 61% are members of minority groups, 4% are women. 0% of classes are taught by teaching assistants.

ACADEMICS

Degrees: associate, bachelor's, certificate, master's, post-bachelor's certificate. **Classes:** Most classes have 10–19 students. Most lab/discussion sessions have 10–19 students. **Majors with Highest Enrollment:** Business Administration and Management; Sport and Fitness Administration/Management; Registered Nursing, Nursing Administration, Nursing Research and Clinical Nursing. **Special Study Options:** Accelerated program, cooperative education program, cross-registration, distance learning, double major, dual enrollment, honors program, independent study, internships, liberal arts/career combination, study abroad, teacher certification program. **Honors programs:** Designed to meet the interests of highly motivated students who are able to take responsibility for their own learning under the guidance of experienced faculty members. **Disability Services:** Special programs offered to physically disabled students include note-taking services, reader services, tape recorders, tutors. **Career services:** alumni services, career/job search classes, career assessment, internships. Career services highlights include the opportunity for qualified students to gain career related, paid work experience. Co-ops earn academic credit that will complement classroom training by integrating theory and practice.

FACILITIES

Housing: Coed dorms, special housing for disabled students. 95% of campus accessible to physically disabled. **Special Academic Facilities/Equipment:** Art studio/gallery, Student Scholar Center, Computer Labs, Theatre. **Computers:** 100% of classrooms, 100% of dorms, 100% of libraries, 100% of dining areas, 100% of common outdoor areas have wireless network access. Students can register for classes online. Administrative functions (other than registration) can be performed online.

CAMPUS LIFE

Environment: Metropolis. **Activities:** Choral groups, concert band, dance, drama/theater, jazz band, literary magazine, music ensembles, musical theater, pep band, student government, student newspaper, Campus Ministries, International Student Organization. 35 registered organizations, 10 honor societies, 1 religious organization. **Athletics (Intercollegiate): Men:** baseball, basketball, cross-country, football, golf, lacrosse, soccer, tennis, track/field (outdoor), track/field (indoor), volleyball, wrestling. **Women:** basketball, cheerleading, cross-country, golf, lacrosse, soccer, softball, tennis, track/field (outdoor), track/field (indoor), volleyball. **On-Campus Highlights:** Harrington Student Center/Sports Complex, Starbucks Gallery, Residential Suites, Computer Learning Center, Project EXCEL. **Environmental Initiatives:** New green roof installed on Library (2008); Switch to trayless dining in cafeteria (2008); less food waste (450 lbs/day); water conservation (250 gallons/day); Recycling across campus and increased amounts/types of materials.

ADMISSIONS

Freshman Academic Profile: Average high school GPA 3.31. 9% in top 10% of high school class, 34% in top 25% of high school class, 59% in top 50% of high school class. 73% from public high schools. SAT Math middle 50% range 420-550. SAT Critical Reading middle 50% range 440-560. ACT middle 50% range 19-24. Minimum internet-based TOEFL 64. Minimum paper TOEFL 510. **Basis for Candidate Selection:** *Very important factors considered include:* academic GPA, rigor of secondary school record, standardized test scores. *Other factors considered include:* application essay, recommendation(s), alumni/ae relation, character/personal qualities, extracurricular activities, first generation, geographical residence, interview, level of applicant's interest, racial/ethnic status, religious affiliation/commitment, state residency, talent/ability, volunteer work, work experience. **Freshman Admission Requirements:** High school diploma is required and GED is accepted. *Academic units required:* 4 English, 3 mathematics, 3 science, (1 science labs), 2 foreign language, 1 social studies, 1 history, 1 visual/performing arts, 1 academic electives, 1 Academic Elective. **Freshman Admission Statistics:** 1,010 applied, 88% admitted, 34% enrolled. **Transfer Admission Requirements:** college transcript(s), Minimum college GPA of 2.0 required. Lowest grade transferable C. **General Admission Information:** Application Fee $25. Regular application deadline 8/15. Notification on a rolling basis, beginning on or about 10/1. Nonfall registration accepted. Admission may be deferred for a maximum of 12 months. Credit and/or placement offered for CEEB Advanced Placement tests.

COSTS AND FINANCIAL AID

Annual tuition $25,850. Room and board $8,710. Required fees $1,000. Average book expense $1,000. **Required Forms and Deadlines:** FAFSA. **Notification of Awards:** Applicants will be notified of awards on a rolling basis beginning 1/31. **Types of Aid:** *Need-based scholarships/grants:* Federal Pell, SEOG, state scholarships/grants, private scholarships, the school's own gift aid. *Loans:* Subsidized Stafford, Unsubsidized Stafford, PLUS, Federal Perkins, Federal Nursing, state loans. *Student Employment:* Federal Work-Study Program available. Institutional employment available. Highest amount earned per year from on-campus jobs $1,500. Off-campus job opportunities are good. **Financial Aid Statistics:** 100% freshmen, 98% undergrads receive need-based scholarship or grant aid. 14% freshmen, 13% undergrads receive non-need-based scholarship or grant aid. 89% freshmen, 90% undergrads receive need-based self-help aid. 0% freshmen, 0% undergrads receive athletic scholarships. 99% freshmen, 80% undergrads receive any aid. **Criteria for awarding institutional aid:** *Non-need-based:* academics, alumni affiliation, art, leadership, music/drama, state/district residency.

MOUNT ST. MARY'S UNIVERSITY

16300 Old Emmitsburg Road, Emmitsburg, MD 21727
Phone: 301-447-5214 · **Financial Aid Phone:** 301-447-5207
E-mail: admissions@msmary.edu · **CEEB Code:** 5421
Fax: 301-447-5860 · **Website:** www.msmary.edu · **ACT Code:** 1726

This private school, affiliated with the Roman Catholic Church, was founded in 1808. It has a 1400-acre campus.

RATINGS

Admissions Selectivity Rating: 83   **Fire Safety Rating:** 84

STUDENTS AND FACULTY

Enrollment: 1,806. **Student Body:** 56% female, 44% male, 49% out-of-state, 1% international (13 countries represented). Asian 2%, African American 11%, Caucasian 71%, Hispanic 9%, Native American <1%
Retention and Graduation: 79% freshmen return for sophomore year. 58% freshmen graduate within 4 years. 33% grads go on to further study within 1 year. 16% grads pursue arts and sciences degrees. 2% grads pursue law degrees. 11% grads pursue business degrees. 2% grads pursue medical degrees. **Faculty:** 118 full-time faculty, 92% hold PhDs, 40% are members of minority groups, 6% are women. 0% of classes are taught by teaching assistants.

ACADEMICS

Degrees: bachelor's, master's, post-bachelor's certificate, post-master's certificate. **Classes:** Most classes have 20–29 students. Most lab/discussion sessions have 10–19 students. **Majors with Highest Enrollment:** Business/Commerce; Elementary Education and Teaching; Accounting. **Special Study Options:** Accelerated program, cross-registration, double major, dual enrollment, honors program, independent study, internships, liberal arts/career combination, student-designed major, study abroad, teacher certification program, weekend college, 3-2 with Johns Hopkins Univ. (BS in Biology; BS in Nursing) 3-3 with Sacred Heart Univ. (BS in Biology; Ph.D in PT) 4-2 with Sacred Heart Univ. (BS in Biology; MS in OT). **Honors programs:** The Honors Program offers talented and motivated students an educational experience that integrates curricular, co-curricular, and extra-curricular learning in both interdisciplinary and major areas of study. **Combined degree programs:** BS Bio, BS Nursing; BS Bio, Ph.D PT; BS Bio, MS OT. **Disability Services:** Special programs offered to physically disabled students include note-taking services, reader services, tape recorders, tutors. **Career services:** Alumni network, alumni services, career/job search classes, career assessment, internships. Career services highlights include The Mount's Internship Program, which provides excellent learning and networking experiences for either credit or non-credit. Internships are tailored to students' majors. "Mount in Washington" offers full time internships in Washington D.C. The Career Center has also introduced International Internships to London, Dublin and Florence.

FACILITIES

Housing: Coed dorms, special housing for disabled students, apartments for single students, Wellness Housing, Theme Housing. 85% of campus accessible to physically disabled. **Special Academic Facilities/Equipment:** Historical art collection reflecting Catholic history in America and Marylandia. **Computers:** 100% of classrooms, 100% of dorms, 100% of libraries, 100% of dining areas, 100% of student union, 50% of common outdoor areas have wireless network access. Students can register for classes online. Administrative functions (other than registration) can be performed online.

CAMPUS LIFE

Environment: Rural. **Activities:** Choral groups, concert band, dance, drama/theater, jazz band, literary magazine, music ensembles, musical theater, pep band, radio station, student government, student newspaper, television station, yearbook, Campus Ministries, International Student Organization. 68 registered organizations, 19 honor societies, 8 religious organizations. **Athletics (Intercollegiate): Men:** baseball, basketball, cross-country, golf, lacrosse, soccer, tennis, track/field (outdoor), track/field (indoor). **Women:** basketball, cross-country, golf, lacrosse, soccer, softball, swimming, tennis, track/field (outdoor), track/field (indoor). **On-Campus Highlights:** McGowan Student Center - Patriot Hall, Knott Athletic Recreation Convocation Complex, Knott Academic Center, Phillips Library, National Shrine Grotto of Lourdes. **Environmental Initiatives:** We have 1.1 MW photovoltaic panels being installed that will be online in summer 2012 and provide a substantial fraction of our electricity needs. Our newest dorm is a green building that uses groundwater-source geothermal heating and cooling. We have eliminated the coal-burning furnace and replaced it with a high-efficiency gas furnace. We are also decentralizing our heating/steam systems to prevent leaks and reduce transmission losses.

ADMISSIONS

Freshman Academic Profile: Average high school GPA 3.39. 12.93% in top 10% of high school class, 39.12% in top 25% of high school class, 71.43% in top 50% of high school class. 64% from public high schools. SAT Math middle 50% range 470-570. SAT Critical Reading middle 50% range 480-580. SAT Writing middle 50% range 460-570. ACT middle 50% range 20-24. Minimum internet-based TOEFL 83. Minimum paper TOEFL 550. **Basis for Candidate Selection:** *Important factors considered include:* academic GPA, rigor of secondary school record, standardized test scores, extracurricular activities, talent/ability, volunteer work. *Other factors considered include:* application essay, recommendation(s), character/personal qualities, interview, level of applicant's interest, racial/ethnic status, work experience. **Freshman Admission Requirements:** High school diploma is required and GED is accepted. *Academic units required:* 4 English, 3 mathematics, 3 science, (2 science labs), 2 foreign language, 3 social studies, 1 academic electives. **Freshman Admission Statistics:** 6,142 applied, 67% admitted, 12% enrolled. **Transfer Admission Requirements:** college transcript(s), statement of good standing from prior institution(s). Minimum college GPA of 2.0 required. Lowest grade transferable C. **General Admission Information:** Application Fee $35. Notification on a rolling basis, beginning on or about 12/1. Nonfall registration accepted. Admission may be deferred for a maximum of 1 yr. Credit and/or placement offered for CEEB Advanced Placement tests.

COSTS AND FINANCIAL AID

Annual tuition $36,250. Room and board $12,400. Required fees $1,250. Average book expense $1,300. **Required Forms and Deadlines:** FAFSA. **Notification of Awards:** Applicants will be notified of awards on a rolling basis beginning 2/15. **Types of Aid:** *Need-based scholarships/grants:* Federal Pell, SEOG, state scholarships/grants, private scholarships, the school's own gift aid. *Loans:* Subsidized Stafford, Unsubsidized Stafford, PLUS, Federal Perkins. *Student Employment:* Federal Work-Study Program available. Institutional employment available. Off-campus job opportunities are fair. **Financial Aid Statistics:** 100% freshmen, 99% undergrads receive need-based scholarship or grant aid. 23% freshmen, 19% undergrads receive non-need-based scholarship or grant aid. 73% freshmen, 78% undergrads receive need-based self-help aid. 5% freshmen, 7% undergrads receive athletic scholarships. 98% freshmen, 99% undergrads receive any aid. 72% undergrads borrow to pay for school. Average cumulative indebtedness $24,988. **Criteria for awarding institutional aid:** *Non-need-based:* academics, art, athletics, leadership, minority status, music/drama.

MOUNT VERNON NAZARENE UNIVERSITY

800 Martinsburg Road, Mount Vernon, OH 43050
Phone: 740-392-6868 · **Financial Aid Phone:** 866-686-8243
E-mail: admissions@mvnu.edu · **CEEB Code:** 1531
Fax: 740-393-0511 · **Website:** www.mvnu.edu · **ACT Code:** 3372

This private school, affiliated with the Nazarene Church, was founded in 1964. It has a 401-acre campus.

RATINGS

Admissions Selectivity Rating: 80   **Fire Safety Rating:** 70

STUDENTS AND FACULTY

Enrollment: 1,705. **Student Body:** 64% female, 36% male, 13% out-of-state, 1% international (17 countries represented). Asian 0%, African American 4%, Caucasian 83%, Hispanic 2%, Native American <1%
Retention and Graduation: 82% freshmen return for sophomore year. 50% freshmen graduate within 4 years. 59% freshmen graduate within 6 years. 11% grads go on to further study within 1 year. 8% grads pursue arts and sciences degrees. 11% grads pursue business degrees. 3% grads pursue medical degrees. **Faculty:** 72 full-time faculty, 74% hold PhDs, 36% are members of minority groups, 4% are women. 0% of classes are taught by teaching assistants.

ACADEMICS

Degrees: associate, bachelor's, master's. **Classes:** Most classes have 10–19 students. **Majors with Highest Enrollment:** Registered Nursing/Registered Nurse; Biology/Biological Sciences; Business Administration and Management. **Special Study Options:** cooperative education program, cross-registration, distance learning, double major, dual enrollment, honors program, independent study, internships, liberal arts/career combination, study abroad, teacher certi-

fication program, Cooperative pre-engineering program with Olivet Nazarene University, cooperative pre-occupational therapy/physical therapy/physician's assistant programs with Chatham University, and articulation agreements with Columbus State Community College, Marion Technical College, Zane State College, Central Ohio Technical College, and North Central State College. Several opportunities for students to participate in service learning or mission trips. During the academic year, students may participate in one of the following trips: Germany, Hungary, Venezuela, Costa Rica, Nicaragua, Belize, Benin, Romania, or several out-of-state USA trips. **Honors programs:** Honors Program for outstandning students is designed to provide rewarding challenges for the academically gifted. Specific courses, seminars, and other out-of-the ordinary experiences, both on and off campus, are offered by the Honors Program. A $250 scholarship the first year, increases to $400 in the fourth year. The Honors Program adds depth to your academic development and allows you to have input in designing your own curiculum by proposing study topics for Honors courses and by developing independent projects. You will work closely with a faculty mentor to complete an Honors Project in your major. There are also opportunities for off-campus culural enrichment and entertainment, including travel to musuems, ballet and music performances, or dinner theater. **Disability Services:** Special programs offered to physically disabled students include note-taking services, reader services, tape recorders, tutors. **Career services:** alumni services, career/job search classes, career assessment Career services highlights include missions and ministry opportunities, and study aboard.

FACILITIES

Housing: special housing for disabled students, men's dorms, women's dorms, apartments for single students, Wellness Housing. 95% of campus accessible to physically disabled. **Special Academic Facilities/Equipment:** Art gallery, nature reserve. **Computers:** 95% of classrooms, 5% of dorms, 100% of libraries, 100% of dining areas, 100% of student union, 10% of common outdoor areas have wireless network access. Administrative functions (other than registration) can be performed online.

CAMPUS LIFE

Environment: Rural. **Activities:** Choral groups, concert band, drama/theater, jazz band, literary magazine, music ensembles, musical theater, opera, pep band, radio station, student government, student newspaper, yearbook, Campus Ministries, International Student Organization. 26 registered organizations, 4 honor societies, 16 religious organizations. **Athletics (Intercollegiate):** *Men:* baseball, basketball, cross-country, golf, soccer. *Women:* basketball, cross-country, soccer, softball, volleyball. **On-Campus Highlights:** The Prince Student Union, The Chapel, The Cafeteria, The Quad, The Grove. **Environmental Initiatives:** The President has made a public commitment for the University to minimize its "mark" on the environment. Dialogue on how to best develop a University-wide environmental stewardship plan has begun. The University is in the process of finalizing a comprehensive environmental stewardship plan and has recent efforts to increase campus-wide recycling, and conversion of used vegetable oil into biodisel fuel.

ADMISSIONS

Freshman Academic Profile: Average high school GPA 3.38. 22% in top 10% of high school class, 44% in top 25% of high school class, 71% in top 50% of high school class. 80% from public high schools. SAT Math middle 50% range 450-530. SAT Critical Reading middle 50% range 450-540. ACT middle 50% range 20-25. Minimum internet-based TOEFL 80. **Basis for Candidate Selection:** *Very important factors considered include:* academic GPA, standardized test scores. *Important factors considered include:* recommendation(s), rigor of secondary school record. *Other factors considered include:* application essay. **Freshman Admission Requirements:** High school diploma is required and GED is accepted. *Academic units required:* 2 foreign language. **Freshman Admission Statistics:** 1,020 applied, 76% admitted, 40% enrolled. **Transfer Admission Requirements:** High school transcript, college transcript(s), essay or personal statement, statement of good standing from prior institution(s). Minimum college GPA of 2.0 required. Lowest grade transferable C-. **General Admission Information:** Application Fee $25. Regular application deadline 7/15. Notification on a rolling basis, beginning on or about 9/1. Nonfall registration accepted. Admission may be deferred for a maximum of 1 year. Credit offered for CEEB Advanced Placement tests.

COSTS AND FINANCIAL AID

Annual tuition $24,400. Room and board $7,260. Required fees $250. Average book expense $1,400. **Required Forms and Deadlines:** FAFSA. **Notification of Awards:** Applicants will be notified of awards on a rolling basis beginning 3/15. **Types of Aid:** *Need-based scholarships/grants:* Federal Pell, SEOG, state scholarships/grants, private scholarships, the school's own gift aid. *Loans:* Direct Subsidized Stafford, Direct Unsubsidized Stafford, Direct PLUS. *Student Employment:* Federal Work-Study Program available. Institutional employment available. Highest amount earned per year from on-campus jobs $5,866. Off-campus job opportunities are good. **Financial Aid Statistics:** 88% undergrads borrow to pay for school. Average cumulative indebtedness $27,742. **Criteria for awarding institutional aid:** *Non-need-based:* academics, athletics, minority status, music/drama, religious affiliation, state/district residency.

MUHLENBERG COLLEGE

Best 380

2400 West Chew Street, Allentown, PA 18104-5596
Phone: 484-664-3200 · **Financial Aid Phone:** 484-664-3175
E-mail: admission@muhlenberg.edu · **CEEB Code:** 2424
Fax: 484-664-3234 · **Website:** www.muhlenberg.edu · **ACT Code:** 3640

This private school, affiliated with the Lutheran Church, was founded in 1848. It has a 81-acre campus.

RATINGS

Admissions Selectivity Rating: 92   **Fire Safety Rating:** 94

STUDENTS AND FACULTY

Enrollment: 2,357. **Student Body:** 59% female, 41% male, 78% out-of-state, 1% international (14 countries represented). Asian 3%, African American 3%, Caucasian 77%, Hispanic 5%, Native American <1% **Retention and Graduation:** 81% freshmen graduate within 4 years. 86% freshmen graduate within 6 years. 29% grads go on to further study within 1 year. 20% grads pursue arts and sciences degrees. 4% grads pursue law degrees. 1% grads pursue business degrees. 5% grads pursue medical degrees. **Faculty:** 173 full-time faculty, 88% hold PhDs, 50% are members of minority groups, 8% are women. 0% of classes are taught by teaching assistants.

ACADEMICS

Degrees: associate, bachelor's, certificate, transfer associate. **Classes:** Most classes have 10–19 students. Most lab/discussion sessions have 10–19 students. **Majors with Highest Enrollment:** Business/Commerce; Psychology; Drama and Dramatics/Theatre Arts. **Special Study Options:** Accelerated program, cross-registration, double major, exchange student program (domestic), honors program, independent study, internships, student-designed major, study abroad, teacher certification program. **Honors programs:** Muhlenberg Scholar, Dana Associate, R.J. Fellow (each provides a $4,000 annual stipend, dedicated freshman seminar, and mentored research) **Combined degree programs:** BA/MD, BA/DDS, BA/DDS University of Pennsylvania, BS/MD Drexel Un. **Disability Services:** Special programs offered to physically disabled students include note-taking services, tutors. **Career services:** Alumni network, alumni services, career/job search classes, career assessment, internships, regional alumni. Career services highlights include The Muhlenberg Shadow Program, which matches students with alumni in their field of interest to spend a day on the job over winter break. Students are able to learn first-hand about career options of interest to them, and alumni enjoy the feeling of helping a student and remembering why they enjoy their jobs.

FACILITIES

Housing: Coed dorms, special housing for disabled students, special housing for international students, women's dorms, fraternity/sorority housing, apartments for single students, College-owned houses in the neighborhood surrounding the campus. 95% of campus accessible to physically disabled. **Special Academic Facilities/Equipment:** Martin art gallery, biology museum, Graver arboretum, greenhouse, mainstage theatre, recital hall, 20-foot boat for marine studies, 40-acre Raker environmental field station, two electron microscopes, dance studios, experimental theatres, proscenium theatres. **Computers:** 10% of classrooms, 20% of dorms, 100% of libraries, 100% of dining areas, 100% of student union, 10% of common outdoor areas have wireless network access. Students can register for classes online. Administrative functions (other than registration) can be performed online.

CAMPUS LIFE

Environment: City. **Activities:** concert band, dance, drama/theater, jazz band, literary magazine, music ensembles, musical theater, pep band, radio station, student government, student newspaper, student-run film society, symphony orchestra, yearbook. 100 registered organizations, 12 honor societies, 7 religious organizations. 4 fraternities, 4 sororities. **Athletics (Intercollegiate):** *Men:* baseball, basketball, cheerleading, cross-country, football, golf, lacrosse, soccer, tennis, track/field (outdoor), track/field (indoor), wrestling. *Women:* basketball, cheerleading, cross-country, field hockey, golf, lacrosse, soccer, softball, tennis, track/field (outdoor), track/field (indoor), volleyball. **On-Campus Highlights:** Seegers Union by fireplace & Java Joe's, The Life Sports Center-Athletic Facility, Parents Plaza-Outdoor Courtyard, GQ, Seegers Union, Trexler Pavilion for Threatre & Dance. **Environmental Initiatives:** Muhlenberg College supports the initiatives of the Office of Campus Sustainability, which executes the vision of the Greening Committee and Muhlenberg College Strategic Plan to further the College's sustainability stewardship. The Office of Campus Sustainability brings together students, faculty and staff with a diversity of perspectives and areas of expertise to seek creative solutions for campus sustainability. Staffed by

the Director of Sustainability Studies and The Campus Sustainability Coordinator, its mission is to facilitate the linkage between academic and facilities-based sustainability efforts, to create student internship opportunities in the area of campus sustainability, to support the Campus Greening Committee and student environmental groups, and to seek out external funding and maintain resources to further the integration of sustainability into the curriculum and across campus. The College also supports the efforts of the Sustainability Studies program. Sustainability is most commonly defined as meeting the needs of the present generation without compromising the ability of future generations to meet their own needs. The field of Sustainability Studies explores and critiques ways to do this in the context of maintaining ecological and environmental health while generating economic welfare and ensuring social justice. The minor in Sustainability Studies integrates across disciplines with its goal of instilling understanding, appreciation, and thoughtful problem solving skills in students regarding the relationships and interactions of human society and the environment. The Sustainability Studies Minor highlights issues related to sustainability and explore how those issues impact and are addressed at local, national, and global levels. This minor will provide the interdisciplinary background that is needed to understand many of the complex challenges facing our world, and will equip students with the skills needed to develop solutions to these problems. An additional goal is to build a community of faculty and students with a diversity of perspectives and areas of expertise committed to seeking creative solutions for sustainability. Sustainability is a major component of the Muhlenberg College Strategic Plan and one of the major strategic goals is to improve sustainability on campus. The College is in the process of replacing desktop hardware with at least 85% EPeat Gold-rated hardware, is evaluating and proposing applications to insure responsible use of consumables campus-wide, undergoing wide-ranging reductions in energy including replacing existing steam to water converters with a gas fired heating system, conducting detailed energy audits for all major buildings on campus in accordance with the detailed American Society of Heating Refrigerating and AIr-Conditioning Engineers (ASHRAE) Level II Audit program, installing occupancy sensors, and installing steam meters.

ADMISSIONS

Freshman Academic Profile: Average high school GPA 3.33. 45% in top 10% of high school class, 73% in top 25% of high school class, 92% in top 50% of high school class. 78% from public high schools. SAT Math middle 50% range 570-670. SAT Critical Reading middle 50% range 570-670. SAT Writing middle 50% range 570-670. ACT middle 50% range 25-30. Minimum internet-based TOEFL 79. Minimum paper TOEFL 550. **Basis for Candidate Selection:** *Very important factors considered include:* academic GPA, rigor of secondary school record. *Important factors considered include:* application essay, recommendation(s), standardized test scores, character/personal qualities, extracurricular activities, interview, talent/ability. *Other factors considered include:* Class rank, alumni/ae relation, first generation, level of applicant's interest, racial/ethnic status, volunteer work, work experience. **Freshman Admission Requirements:** High school diploma is required and GED is accepted. *Academic units required:* 4 English, 3 mathematics, 2 science, 2 foreign language, 2 history. **Freshman Admission Statistics:** 5,170 applied, 46% admitted, 24% enrolled. **Transfer Admission Requirements:** High school transcript, college transcript(s), essay or personal statement, interview, standardized test scores, statement of good standing from prior institution(s). Minimum college GPA of 2.5 required. Lowest grade transferable C. **General Admission Information:** Application Fee $50. Early decision application deadline 2/1. Regular application deadline 2/15. Regular notification 4/1. Nonfall registration accepted. Admission may be deferred for a maximum of 1 year. Credit and/or placement offered for CEEB Advanced Placement tests.

COSTS AND FINANCIAL AID

Average book expense $1,300. **Required Forms and Deadlines:** FAFSA, Institution's own financial aid form, CSS/Financial Aid PROFILE, Noncustodial PROFILE, Business/Farm Supplement. **Notification of Awards:** Applicants will be notified of awards on or about 4/1. **Types of Aid:** *Need-based scholarships/grants:* Federal Pell, SEOG, state scholarships/grants, private scholarships, the school's own gift aid. *Loans:* Subsidized Stafford, Unsubsidized Stafford, PLUS, Federal Perkins, Private. *Student Employment:* Federal Work-Study Program available. Institutional employment available. Highest amount earned per year from on-campus jobs $1,800. Off-campus job opportunities are excellent. **Financial Aid Statistics:** 97% freshmen, 94% undergrads receive need-based scholarship or grant aid. 23% freshmen, 17% undergrads receive non-need-based scholarship or grant aid. 68% freshmen, 72% undergrads receive need-based self-help aid. 0% freshmen, 0% undergrads receive athletic scholarships. 88% freshmen, 85% undergrads receive any aid. 55% undergrads borrow to pay for school. Average cumulative indebtedness $23,041. **Criteria for awarding institutional aid:** *Non-need-based:* academics, art, leadership, music/drama.

MULTNOMAH UNIVERSITY

8435 NE Glisan Street, Portland, OR 97220-5898
Phone: 503-251-6485 · **Financial Aid Phone:** 503-251-5335
E-mail: admiss@multnomah.edu
Fax: 503-254-1268 · **Website:** http://www.multnomah.edu/

This private school, affiliated with the Christian (Nondenominational) Church, was founded in 1936. It has a 25-acre campus.

RATINGS

Admissions Selectivity Rating: 86   **Fire Safety Rating:** 63

STUDENTS AND FACULTY

Enrollment: 418. **Student Body:** 46% female, 54% male, 50% out-of-state, 0% international (13 countries represented). Asian 1%, African American 3%, Caucasian 69%, Hispanic 6%, Native American 1%
Retention and Graduation: 35% freshmen graduate within 4 years. 54% freshmen graduate within 6 years. **Faculty:** 26 full-time faculty, 81% hold PhDs, 19% are members of minority groups, 12% are women. 0% of classes are taught by teaching assistants.

ACADEMICS

Degrees: bachelor's, master's, post-bachelor's certificate. **Classes:** Most classes have fewer than 10 students. Most lab/discussion sessions have 10–19 students. **Special Study Options:** cooperative education program, distance learning, double major, internships, liberal arts/career combination, teacher certification program. **Career services:** career/job search classes, career assessment.

FACILITIES

Housing: special housing for disabled students, men's dorms, women's dorms, apartments for married students, apartments for single students, Houses for students with spouses or dependents. **Computers:** 100% of classrooms, 100% of dorms, 100% of libraries, 100% of dining areas, 30% of common outdoor areas have wireless network access. Students can register for classes online. Administrative functions (other than registration) can be performed online.

CAMPUS LIFE

Environment: Metropolis. **Activities:** Choral groups, drama/theater, music ensembles, student government, student newspaper. **Athletics (Intercollegiate):** *Men:* basketball. *Women:* volleyball. **On-Campus Highlights:** Solid Rock Café, A-Frame Community Lounge, STUGO Game Room, Cafeteria, Commuter Lounge, The Solid Rock Café, STUGO Game Room and cafeteria are all centrally located in our JCA Student Center along with a computer lab, post-office, and health center.

ADMISSIONS

Freshman Academic Profile: Average high school GPA 3.43. 10.5% in top 10% of high school class, 36.8% in top 25% of high school class, 79% in top 50% of high school class. SAT Math middle 50% range 490-580. SAT Critical Reading middle 50% range 500-650. SAT Writing middle 50% range 490-590. ACT middle 50% range 22-27. Minimum paper TOEFL 550. **Basis for Candidate Selection:** *Very important factors considered include:* academic GPA, recommendation(s), rigor of secondary school record, standardized test scores, religious affiliation/commitment. *Important factors considered include:* application essay, character/personal qualities. *Other factors considered include:* Class rank, alumni/ae relation, extracurricular activities, talent/ability, volunteer work, work experience. **Freshman Admission Requirements:** High school diploma is required and GED is accepted. **Freshman Admission Statistics:** 176 applied, 54% admitted, 58% enrolled. **Transfer Admission Requirements:** college transcript(s), essay or personal statement, statement of good standing from prior institution(s). Minimum college GPA of 2.0 required. Lowest grade transferable C-. **General Admission Information:** Application Fee $40. Regular application deadline 7/15. Notification on a rolling basis, beginning on or about 9/1. Nonfall registration accepted. Admission may be deferred for a maximum of one semester. Credit offered for CEEB Advanced Placement tests.

COSTS AND FINANCIAL AID

Annual tuition $21,600. Room and board $7,600. Required fees $125. Average book expense $1,000. **Required Forms and Deadlines:** FAFSA. **Notification of Awards:** Applicants will be notified of awards on a rolling basis beginning 4/1. **Types of Aid:** *Need-based scholarships/grants:* Federal Pell, SEOG, private scholarships, the school's own gift aid. *Loans:* Direct Subsidized Stafford, Subsidized Stafford, Unsubsidized Stafford, PLUS. *Student Employment:* Federal Work-Study Program available. Institutional employment available. Off-campus job opportunities are good. **Financial Aid Statistics:** 100% freshmen, 93% undergrads receive need-based scholarship or grant aid. 6% freshmen, 4% undergrads receive non-need-based scholarship or grant aid. 97% freshmen, 95% undergrads receive need-based self-help aid. 0% freshmen, 0% undergrads receive athletic scholarships. 48% freshmen, 89% undergrads receive any aid.

Criteria for awarding institutional aid: *Non-need-based:* academics, alumni affiliation, leadership, music/drama.

MURRAY STATE UNIVERSITY

102 Curris Center, Murray, KY 42071-0009
Phone: 270-809-3741 · **Financial Aid Phone:** 270-809-2546
E-mail: msu.admissions@murraystate.edu · **CEEB Code:** 1494
Fax: 270-809-3780 · **Website:** www.murraystate.edu · **ACT Code:** 1532

This public school was founded in 1922. It has a 350-acre campus.

RATINGS

Admissions Selectivity Rating: 79   **Fire Safety Rating:** 87

STUDENTS AND FACULTY

Enrollment: 8,126. **Student Body:** 58% female, 42% male, 31% out-of-state, 4% international (50 countries represented). Asian 1%, African American 8%, Caucasian 82%, Hispanic 2%, Native American <1%
Retention and Graduation: 72% freshmen return for sophomore year. 29% freshmen graduate within 4 years. 41% grads go on to further study within 1 year. **Faculty:** 445 full-time faculty, 77% hold PhDs, 41% are members of minority groups, 16% are women. 0.3% of classes are taught by teaching assistants.

ACADEMICS

Degrees: associate, bachelor's, master's, post-master's certificate. **Classes:** Most classes have fewer than 10 students. Most lab/discussion sessions have 10–19 students. **Majors with Highest Enrollment:** Registered Nursing/Registered Nurse; Veterinary/Animal Health Technology/Technician and Veterinary Assistant; Business/Commerce. **Special Study Options:** Accelerated program, cooperative education program, cross-registration, distance learning, double major, dual enrollment, English as a Second Language (ESL), exchange student program (domestic), external degree program, honors program, independent study, internships, study abroad, teacher certification program, weekend college, agriculture, arts, business/marketing, biological sciences, communications/communication technologies, computer and information sciences, education, engineering/engineering technologies, English, foreign languages, health professions and related sciences, history, home economics, humanities and liberal arts, library sciences, mathematics, natural resources and environmental sciences, natural sciences, parks and recreation, philosophy, physical sciences, protective sciences/public administration, psychology, social/behavioral sciences, technologies, trade and industry, visual and performing arts. **Honors programs:** The Honors Program offers a unique educational experience designed to teach able students how to learn, how to think critically and creatively, and how to communicate effectively. **Combined degree programs:** engineering program w/ U of L. and U. of KY. **Disability Services:** Special programs offered to physically disabled students include note-taking services, tape recorders, tutors. **Career services:** Alumni network, alumni services, career/job search classes, career assessment, internships, regional alumni.

FACILITIES

Housing: Coed dorms, special housing for disabled students, men's dorms, women's dorms, fraternity/sorority housing, apartments for married students, apartments for single students. All housing is operated under a Residential College system. 96% of campus accessible to physically disabled. **Special Academic Facilities/Equipment:** State-of-the-art 73000 square-foot Student Recreation and Wellness Center nestled in the Residential College housing complex, West Kentucky Museum, 8,500 seat Regional Special Events Center. **Computers:** 95% of classrooms, 90% of dorms, 100% of libraries, 100% of dining areas, 100% of student union, have wireless network access. Students can register for classes online. Administrative functions (other than registration) can be performed online.

CAMPUS LIFE

Environment: Village. **Activities:** Choral groups, concert band, dance, drama/theater, jazz band, literary magazine, marching band, music ensembles, musical theater, pep band, radio station, student government, student newspaper, student-run film society, symphony orchestra, television station, yearbook, Campus Ministries, International Student Organization. 175 registered organizations, 30 honor societies, 15 religious organizations. 15 fraternities, 7 sororities. **Athletics (Intercollegiate):** *Men:* baseball, basketball, bowling, cheerleading, cross-country, equestrian sports, football, golf, horseback riding, riflery, rodeo, tennis. *Women:* basketball, cheerleading, cross-country, equestrian sports, golf, horseback riding, riflery, rodeo, soccer, softball, tennis, track/field (outdoor), volleyball. **On-Campus Highlights:** New Student Fitness Center, Curris Student Center, Regional Special Events Center, Equine Center, Residential Colleges. Environmental Initiatives: Renewable Fuels, BioDiesel, g-35, e-10 Recycling Program Diverting 30% of waste stream from landfill.

ADMISSIONS

Freshman Academic Profile: Average high school GPA 3.4. 18% in top 10% of high school class, 43% in top 25% of high school class, 77% in top 50% of high school class. SAT Math middle 50% range 460-560. SAT Critical Reading middle 50% range 430-550. ACT middle 50% range 20-26. Minimum internet-based TOEFL 71. Minimum paper TOEFL 527. **Basis for Candidate Selection:** *Very important factors considered include:* Class rank, academic GPA, rigor of secondary school record, standardized test scores. *Important factors considered include:* alumni/ae relation, talent/ability. *Other factors considered include:* character/personal qualities, extracurricular activities, geographical residence, interview, racial/ethnic status, state residency, volunteer work, work experience. **Freshman Admission Requirements:** High school diploma is required and GED is accepted. *Academic units required:* 4 English, 3 mathematics, 3 science, (1 science labs), 2 foreign language, 3 social studies, 5 academic electives, 2 Art Appreciation, 1/2 PE, 1/2 Health. **Freshman Admission Statistics:** 4,760 applied, 80% admitted, 40% enrolled. **Transfer Admission Requirements:** college transcript(s), statement of good standing from prior institution(s). Minimum college GPA of 2.0 required. Lowest grade transferable d. **General Admission Information:** Application Fee $30. Regular application deadline 8/3. Nonfall registration accepted. Admission may be deferred for a maximum of 1 year. Credit offered for CEEB Advanced Placement tests.

COSTS AND FINANCIAL AID

Annual in-state tuition $6,360. Annual out-of-state tuition $10,073. Room and board $7,912. Required fees $1,032. Average book expense $1,314. **Required Forms and Deadlines:** FAFSA, Institution's own financial aid form. **Notification of Awards:** Applicants will be notified of awards on a rolling basis beginning 4/15. **Types of Aid:** *Need-based scholarships/grants:* Federal Pell, SEOG, state scholarships/grants, private scholarships, the school's own gift aid, Federal Nursing Scholarships. A wide variety of private and Foundation scholarships available. Check out the website www.murraystate.edu. *Loans:* Direct Subsidized Stafford, Direct Unsubsidized Stafford, Direct PLUS, Subsidized Stafford, Unsubsidized Stafford, PLUS, Federal Perkins, Federal Nursing, state loans, college/university loans from institutional funds. *Student Employment:* Federal Work-Study Program available. Institutional employment available. Highest amount earned per year from on-campus jobs $3,500. Off-campus job opportunities are good. **Financial Aid Statistics:** 91% freshmen, 84% undergrads receive need-based scholarship or grant aid. 12% freshmen, 7% undergrads receive non-need-based scholarship or grant aid. 69% freshmen, 77% undergrads receive need-based self-help aid. 3% freshmen, 3% undergrads receive athletic scholarships. 94% freshmen, 76% undergrads receive any aid. 47% undergrads borrow to pay for school. Average cumulative indebtedness $24,108. **Criteria for awarding institutional aid:** *Non-need-based:* academics, alumni affiliation, art, athletics, job skills, leadership, minority status, music/drama, state/district residency.

MUSICIANS INSTITUTE

1655 McCadden Place, Hollywood, CA 90028
Phone: 800-255-7529 • **Financial Aid Phone:** 323-462-1121
E-mail: admissions@mi.edu
Fax: 323-462-6978

This private school was founded in 1977.

RATINGS

Admissions Selectivity Rating: 60*   **Fire Safety Rating:** 60*

STUDENTS AND FACULTY

Enrollment: 489. **Student Body:** 14% female, 86% male, 26% out-of-state. Asian 11%, African American 7%, Caucasian 56%, Hispanic 12%, Native American <1%
Faculty: 69 full-time faculty, 0% hold PhDs, 16% are members of minority groups, 14% are women.

ACADEMICS

Degrees: associate, bachelor's, certificate. **Majors with Highest Enrollment:** General Studies; Multi-/Interdisciplinary Studies. **Career services:** Alumni network, internships.

FACILITIES

Housing: Musicians Institute's Housing Services department assists students and their parents in locating safe, comfortable, affordable, and accessible off-campus housing. MI does not own or operate student housing, but Housing Services manages a vacancy listing service for housing in a variety of locations ad difference price levels.

CAMPUS LIFE

Environment: Metropolis.

ADMISSIONS

Basis for Candidate Selection: *Very important factors considered include:* level of applicant's interest, talent/ability. *Important factors considered include:* recommendation(s), character/personal qualities, extracurricular activities, interview, work experience. *Other factors considered include:* Class rank, application essay, academic GPA, rigor of secondary school record, standardized test scores, alumni/ae relation, first generation, volunteer work. **Freshman Admission Requirements:** High school diploma is required and GED is accepted. **Freshman Admission Statistics:** 1,057 applied, 98% admitted, 64% enrolled. **Transfer Admission Requirements:** college transcript(s), essay or personal statement, Minimum college GPA of 2.0 required. Lowest grade transferable C. **General Admission Information:** Application Fee $100. Notification on a rolling basis, beginning on or about 10/1. Nonfall registration accepted. Admission may be deferred for a maximum of 1 year.

COSTS AND FINANCIAL AID

Required Forms and Deadlines: FAFSA. **Types of Aid:** *Need-based scholarships/grants:* Federal Pell, SEOG, state scholarships/grants, private scholarships. *Loans:* Subsidized Stafford, Unsubsidized Stafford, PLUS, Alternative loans. **Financial Aid Statistics:** 44% freshmen, 66% undergrads receive need-based scholarship or grant aid. 0% freshmen, 0% undergrads receive non-need-based scholarship or grant aid. 28% freshmen, 53% undergrads receive need-based self-help aid. 0% freshmen, 0% undergrads receive athletic scholarships. 25% undergrads borrow to pay for school.

MUSKINGUM UNIVERSITY

163 Stormont Street, New Concord, OH 43762
Phone: 740-826-8137 • **Financial Aid Phone:** 740-826-8137
E-mail: jzellers@muskingum.edu • **CEEB Code:** 1496
Fax: 614-826-8100 • **ACT Code:** 3305

This private school, affiliated with the Presbyterian Church, was founded in 1837. It has a 245-acre campus.

RATINGS

Admissions Selectivity Rating: 78   **Fire Safety Rating:** 60*

STUDENTS AND FACULTY

Enrollment: 1,641. **Student Body:** 55% female, 45% male, 8% out-of-state, 4% international (10 countries represented). Asian 0%, African American 6%, Caucasian 82%, Hispanic 2%, Native American <1%
Retention and Graduation: 69% freshmen return for sophomore year. 29% freshmen graduate within 4 years. 48% freshmen graduate within 6 years. 25% grads go on to further study within 1 year. 5% grads pursue arts and sciences degrees. 3% grads pursue law degrees. 4% grads pursue business degrees. 2% grads pursue medical degrees. **Faculty:** 96 full-time faculty, 96% hold PhDs, 45% are members of minority groups, 11% are women. 0% of classes are taught by teaching assistants.

ACADEMICS

Degrees: bachelor's, master's. **Classes:** Most classes have fewer than 10 students. Most lab/discussion sessions have 20–29 students. **Majors with Highest Enrollment:** Early Childhood Education and Teaching; Registered Nursing/Registered Nurse; Business Administration and Management. **Special Study Options:** Accelerated program, distance learning, double major, dual enrollment, English as a Second Language (ESL), exchange student program (domestic), independent study, internships, liberal arts/career combination, student-designed major, study abroad, teacher certification program, weekend college. **Combined degree programs:** BA/MEng, BA, BS, MAE. **Disability Services:** Special programs offered to physically disabled students include note-taking services, reader services, tape recorders, tutors. **Career services:** Alumni network, alumni services, career assessment, internships, regional alumni. Career services highlights include the Muskingum Leadership Initiative, through which alumni identify relevant national and regional internships and communicate those opportunities to Muskingum students and faculty.

FACILITIES

Housing: Coed dorms, men's dorms, women's dorms, fraternity/sorority housing, cooperative housing, apartments for single students, Theme Housing. 50% of campus accessible to physically disabled. **Special Academic Facilities/Equipment:** Art gallery, on-campus nursery school, electron microscope, 57-acre biology field station and mobile biology lab. **Computers:** 15% of classrooms, 100% of libraries, 33% of dining areas, 100% of student union, 10% of common outdoor areas have wireless network access. Students can register for classes online. Administrative functions (other than registration) can be performed online.

CAMPUS LIFE
Environment: Rural. **Activities:** Choral groups, concert band, dance, drama/theater, jazz band, literary magazine, marching band, music ensembles, musical theater, pep band, radio station, student government, student newspaper, symphony orchestra, television station, yearbook, Campus Ministries, International Student Organization, Model UN. 95 registered organizations, 16 honor societies, 4 religious organizations. 5 fraternities, 5 sororities. **Athletics (Intercollegiate):** *Men:* baseball, basketball, cheerleading, cross-country, football, golf, soccer, tennis, track/field (outdoor), track/field (indoor), wrestling. *Women:* basketball, cheerleading, cross-country, golf, soccer, softball, tennis, track/field (outdoor), track/field (indoor), volleyball. **On-Campus Highlights:** Philip and Betsey Caldwell Hall, Boyd Science Center, Rec Center, Patton Dining Center/Kelly Coffee House, Walter K. Chess Student Center, New music classroom building opening Fall 2010.

ADMISSIONS
Freshman Academic Profile: Average high school GPA 3.1. 28% in top 10% of high school class, 43% in top 25% of high school class, 70% in top 50% of high school class. 92% from public high schools. SAT Math middle 50% range 420-540. SAT Critical Reading middle 50% range 400-520. SAT Writing middle 50% range 380-500. ACT middle 50% range 18-24. Minimum internet-based TOEFL 79. Minimum paper TOEFL 550. **Basis for Candidate Selection:** *Very important factors considered include:* academic GPA, rigor of secondary school record. *Important factors considered include:* Class rank, recommendation(s), standardized test scores. *Other factors considered include:* application essay, alumni/ae relation, character/personal qualities, extracurricular activities, geographical residence, interview, racial/ethnic status, talent/ability, work experience. **Freshman Admission Requirements:** High school diploma is required and GED is accepted. *Academic units required:* 4 English, 2 mathematics, 2 science, (1 science labs), 2 foreign language, 1 social studies, 2 history. **Freshman Admission Statistics:** 2,001 applied, 76% admitted, 27% enrolled. **Transfer Admission Requirements:** High school transcript, college transcript(s), Minimum college GPA of 2.0 required. Lowest grade transferable C. **General Admission Information:** Regular application deadline 8/1. Notification on a rolling basis, beginning on or about 10/1. Nonfall registration accepted. Admission may be deferred for a maximum of 1 year. Credit and/or placement offered for CEEB Advanced Placement tests.

COSTS AND FINANCIAL AID
Annual tuition $24,000. Room and board $9,760. Required fees $1,066. Average book expense $1,100. **Required Forms and Deadlines:** FAFSA. **Notification of Awards:** Applicants will be notified of awards on a rolling basis beginning 3/1. **Types of Aid:** *Need-based scholarships/grants:* Federal Pell, SEOG, state scholarships/grants, private scholarships, the school's own gift aid. *Loans:* Subsidized Stafford, Unsubsidized Stafford, PLUS, Federal Perkins, college/university loans from institutional funds. *Student Employment:* Federal Work-Study Program available. Institutional employment available. Highest amount earned per year from on-campus jobs $1,500. Off-campus job opportunities are fair. **Financial Aid Statistics:** 100% freshmen, 100% undergrads receive need-based scholarship or grant aid. 99% freshmen, 92% undergrads receive non-need-based scholarship or grant aid. 90% freshmen, 87% undergrads receive need-based self-help aid. 0% freshmen, 0% undergrads receive athletic scholarships. 98% freshmen, 98% undergrads receive any aid. 80% undergrads borrow to pay for school. Average cumulative indebtedness $25,685. **Criteria for awarding institutional aid:** *Non-need-based:* academics, alumni affiliation, art, leadership, minority status, music/drama, religious affiliation, state/district residency.

NAROPA UNIVERSITY

2130 Araphahoe Avenue, Boulder, CO 80302
Phone: 303-546-3572 • **Financial Aid Phone:** 303-546-3534
E-mail: admissions@naropa.edu • **CEEB Code:** 908
Fax: 303-546-3583 • **Website:** www.naropa.edu/ • **ACT Code:** 4853

This private school was founded in 1974. It has a 12-acre campus.

RATINGS
Admissions Selectivity Rating: 61   Fire Safety Rating: 61

STUDENTS AND FACULTY
Enrollment: 464. **Student Body:** 61% female, 39% male, 74% out-of-state, 3% international (24 countries represented). Asian 3%, African American 2%, Caucasian 75%, Hispanic 4%, Native American 3%

Retention and Graduation: 64% freshmen return for sophomore year. 19% freshmen graduate within 4 years. 42% freshmen graduate within 6 years. **Faculty:** 51 full-time faculty, 51% hold PhDs, 57% are members of minority groups, 12% are women. 0% of classes are taught by teaching assistants.

ACADEMICS
Degrees: bachelor's, certificate, first professional, master's. **Classes:** Most classes have 10–19 students. **Majors with Highest Enrollment:** Psychology; Visual and Performing Arts; English Language and Literature. **Special Study Options:** double major, independent study, internships, student-designed major, study abroad, Some courses available on-line. **Disability Services:** Special programs offered to physically disabled students include note-taking services, reader services, tape recorders, tutors.

FACILITIES
Housing: apartments for married students, apartments for single students, Themed housing (living and learning concept). 85% of campus accessible to physically disabled. **Special Academic Facilities/Equipment:** Maitri Rooms, meditation halls, Allen Ginsberg library and a preschool **Computers:** 100% of classrooms, 100% of dorms, 100% of libraries, 100% of dining areas, 100% of student union, 100% of common outdoor areas have wireless network access. Students can register for classes online. Administrative functions (other than registration) can be performed online.

CAMPUS LIFE
Environment: City. **Activities:** Choral groups, dance, drama/theater, jazz band, literary magazine, music ensembles, student government. 20 registered organizations, 2 religious organizations. **On-Campus Highlights:** Lincoln Building, Nalanda Event Center, Meditation Hall, Naropa Café, Visual Arts Studio. **Environmental Initiatives:** We compost all of our paper towels in public restrooms diverting 25% of our landfill waste into compost. The caf?? composts which will divert 20-25% of organics into compost from the landfill. CFL installed in the residential halls, and are converting burned out bulbs to green bulbs throughout the campuses.

ADMISSIONS
Freshman Academic Profile: Average high school GPA 3.026. Minimum paper TOEFL 550. **Basis for Candidate Selection:** *Very important factors considered include:* application essay, academic GPA, recommendation(s), rigor of secondary school record, interview. *Important factors considered include:* character/personal qualities, extracurricular activities, talent/ability, volunteer work. *Other factors considered include:* alumni/ae relation, first generation, racial/ethnic status, work experience. **Freshman Admission Requirements:** High school diploma is required and GED is accepted. **Freshman Admission Statistics:** 139 applied, 93% admitted, 53% enrolled. **Transfer Admission Requirements:** college transcript(s), essay or personal statement, interview, Lowest grade transferable C. **General Admission Information:** Application Fee $50. Nonfall registration accepted. Admission may be deferred for a maximum of 1 year. Credit and/or placement offered for CEEB Advanced Placement tests.

COSTS AND FINANCIAL AID
Annual tuition $23,420. Room and board $8,478. Required fees $100. Average book expense $1,200. **Required Forms and Deadlines:** FAFSA. **Notification of Awards:** Applicants will be notified of awards on a rolling basis beginning 3/1. **Types of Aid:** *Need-based scholarships/grants:* Federal Pell, SEOG, private scholarships, the school's own gift aid. *Loans:* Subsidized Stafford, Unsubsidized Stafford, PLUS, Federal Perkins. *Student Employment:* Federal Work-Study Program available. Off-campus job opportunities are good. **Financial Aid Statistics:** 87% freshmen, 88% undergrads receive need-based scholarship or grant aid. 0% freshmen, 0% undergrads receive non-need-based scholarship or grant aid. 94% freshmen, 91% undergrads receive need-based self-help aid. 0% freshmen, 0% undergrads receive athletic scholarships. 71% freshmen, 71% undergrads receive any aid. 7% undergrads borrow to pay for school. Average cumulative indebtedness $17,825.

NATIONAL AMERICAN UNVERSITY (NM)

4775 Indian School Rd NE, Albuquerque, NM 87110
Phone: 505-348-3700
E-mail: NPointer@national.edu
Fax: 505-348-3705

This proprietary school was founded in 1941. It has a 15-acre campus.

RATINGS
Admissions Selectivity Rating: 60*   Fire Safety Rating: 60*

STUDENTS AND FACULTY

Enrollment: 611. **Student Body:** 42% female, 58% male, 0% out-of-state, 1% international (2 countries represented). Asian 2%, African American 5%, Caucasian 42%, Hispanic 38%, Native American 6%
Retention and Graduation: 5% grads go on to further study within 1 year. 1% grads pursue law degrees. 5% grads pursue business degrees. **Faculty:** 6 full-time faculty, 33% hold PhDs, 50% are members of minority groups, 0% are women. 0% of classes are taught by teaching assistants.

ACADEMICS

Degrees: associate, bachelor's, master's. **Classes:** Most classes have fewer than 10 students. **Majors with Highest Enrollment:** Information Technology; Business/Commerce; Accounting. **Special Study Options:** Accelerated program, cooperative education program, distance learning, double major, dual enrollment, independent study, weekend college. **Career services:** Alumni network, career/job search classes, internships.

FACILITIES

Housing: 100% of campus accessible to physically disabled. **Computers:** Students can register for classes online. Administrative functions (other than registration) can be performed online.

CAMPUS LIFE

Environment: Metropolis. **Activities:** student government 1 registered organization, 1 honor society.

ADMISSIONS

Freshman Academic Profile: 99% from public high schools. Minimum paper TOEFL 500. **Freshman Admission Requirements:** High school diploma is required and GED is accepted. **Transfer Admission Requirements:** High school transcript, college transcript(s), Lowest grade transferable C. **General Admission Information:** Application Fee $25. Regular application deadline 9/13. Nonfall registration accepted. Admission may be deferred for a maximum of 12 months.

COSTS AND FINANCIAL AID

Annual tuition $8,100. Required fees $390. **Types of Aid:** *Need-based scholarships/grants:* Federal Pell, SEOG, state scholarships/grants, private scholarships, the school's own gift aid. *Loans:* Direct Subsidized Stafford, Direct Unsubsidized Stafford, Direct PLUS, Subsidized Stafford, Unsubsidized Stafford, PLUS, Federal Perkins, state loans, college/university loans from institutional funds. *Student Employment:* Federal Work-Study Program available. Institutional employment available. Off-campus job opportunities are good.

NATIONAL UNIVERSITY

11255 North Torrey Pinos Road, La Jolla, CA 92037
Phone: 858-642-8180
E-mail: advisor@nu.edu • **CEEB Code:** 4557
Fax: 858-642-8710 • **Website:** www.nu.edu • **ACT Code:** 20015

This private school was founded in 1971.

RATINGS

Admissions Selectivity Rating: 60*   Fire Safety Rating: 60*

STUDENTS AND FACULTY

Enrollment: 4,776. **Student Body:** 57% female, 43% male, 0% out-of-state, 1% international. Asian 9%, African American 13%, Caucasian 52%, Hispanic 18%, Native American 1%
Retention and Graduation: 40% freshmen return for sophomore year. 70% freshmen graduate within 6 years. **Faculty:** 151 full-time faculty, 87% hold PhDs, 42% are members of minority groups, 19% are women. 0% of classes are taught by teaching assistants.

ACADEMICS

Degrees: associate, bachelor's, certificate, diploma, master's, post-bachelor's certificate, terminal associate, transfer associate. **Classes:** Most classes have 10–19 students. **Majors with Highest Enrollment:** Multi-/Interdisciplinary Studies; Criminal Justice/Law Enforcement Administration; Business/Commerce. **Special Study Options:** Accelerated program, distance learning, double major, dual enrollment, English as a Second Language (ESL), teacher certification program, extensive online offerings are available. **Disability Services:** Special programs offered to physically disabled students include note-taking services, reader services, tutors. **Career services:** career assessment, regional alumni.

FACILITIES

Housing: 100% of campus accessible to physically disabled. **Computers:** Students can register for classes online. Administrative functions (other than registration) can be performed online.

CAMPUS LIFE

Activities: literary magazine.

ADMISSIONS

Freshman Academic Profile: Minimum paper TOEFL 525. **Basis for Candidate Selection:** *Important factors considered include:* interview, work experience. *Other factors considered include:* application essay, extracurricular activities. **Freshman Admission Requirements:** High school diploma is required and GED is accepted. **Freshman Admission Statistics:** 156 applied, 100% admitted, 36% enrolled. **General Admission Information:** Application Fee $60. Nonfall registration accepted. Admission may be deferred for a maximum of 12 months. Neither credit nor placement offered for CEEB Advanced Placement tests.

COSTS AND FINANCIAL AID

Annual tuition $7,965. Required fees $60. **Required Forms and Deadlines:** FAFSA, Institution's own financial aid form, State aid form. **Types of Aid:** *Need-based scholarships/grants:* Federal Pell, SEOG, state scholarships/grants, private scholarships, the school's own gift aid. *Loans:* Direct Subsidized Stafford, Direct Unsubsidized Stafford, Subsidized Stafford, Unsubsidized Stafford, PLUS, Federal Perkins. *Student Employment:* Institutional employment available. Off-campus job opportunities are good. **Financial Aid Statistics:** 65% undergrads borrow to pay for school.

NATIONAL UNIVERSITY OF HEALTH SCIENCES

200 E. Roosevelt Road, Lombard, IL 60148
Phone: 630-889-6566 • **Financial Aid Phone:** 630-889-6700
E-mail: admissions@nuhs.edu
Fax: 630-889-6554 • **Website:** www.nuhs.edu

This private school was founded in 1906. It has a 32-acre campus.

RATINGS

Admissions Selectivity Rating: 60*   Fire Safety Rating: 60*

STUDENTS AND FACULTY

Enrollment: 74. **Student Body:** 16% female, 84% male, 70% out-of-state, 9% international (9 countries represented). Asian 11%, African American 35%, Caucasian 141%, Hispanic 11%, Native American <1%
Retention and Graduation: 90% freshmen return for sophomore year. **Faculty:** 46 full-time faculty, 93% hold PhDs, 17% are members of minority groups.

ACADEMICS

Degrees: bachelor's, certificate, master's. **Classes:** Most classes have 40-49 students. Most lab/discussion sessions have 20–29 students. **Majors with Highest Enrollment:** Biomedical Sciences; Massage Therapy/Therapeutic Massage. **Special Study Options:** internships, Accelerated science prerequisite program. **Combined degree programs:** BS/DC.

FACILITIES

Housing: Coed dorms, men's dorms, women's dorms, apartments for married students, apartments for single students, Studio apartments. **Special Academic Facilities/Equipment:** Museum, Fitness Center, Learning Resource Center, Health Care Clinic. **Computers:** 88% of classrooms, 100% of libraries, 100% of common outdoor areas have wireless network access. Students can register for classes online.

CAMPUS LIFE

Environment: Town. **Activities:** student government, student newspaper, yearbook. 24 registered organizations, 1 religious organization. 2 fraternities, 1 sorority. **On-Campus Highlights:** Janse Hall, Student Center, Clinic, Learning Resource Center, Dormitories.

ADMISSIONS

Freshman Academic Profile: Minimum internet-based TOEFL 79. Minimum paper TOEFL 550. **Freshman Admission Requirements:** High school diploma is required and GED is accepted. **Transfer Admission Requirements:** college transcript(s), statement of good standing from prior institution(s). Minimum college GPA of 2.5 required. Lowest grade transferable C. **General Admission Information:** Application Fee $55. Nonfall registration accepted. Credit offered for CEEB Advanced Placement tests.

COSTS AND FINANCIAL AID

Types of Aid: *Need-based scholarships/grants:* Federal Pell, SEOG, state scholarships/grants, private scholarships, the school's own gift aid. *Loans:* Subsidized Stafford, Unsubsidized Stafford, PLUS, Federal Perkins. *Student Employment:* Federal Work-Study Program available. Institutional employment available. Off-campus job opportunities are excellent. **Financial Aid**

Statistics: 62% undergrads receive need-based scholarship or grant aid. 10% undergrads receive non-need-based scholarship or grant aid. 62% undergrads receive need-based self-help aid.

NAZARETH COLLEGE

4245 East Avenue, Rochester, NY 14618-3790
Phone: 585-389-2860 · **Financial Aid Phone:** 585-389-2310
E-mail: admissions@naz.edu · **CEEB Code:** 2511
Fax: 585-389-2826 · **Website:** www.naz.edu · **ACT Code:** 2826

This private school was founded in 1924. It has a 150-acre campus.

RATINGS

Admissions Selectivity Rating: 84   Fire Safety Rating: 88

STUDENTS AND FACULTY

Enrollment: 2,017. **Student Body:** 72% female, 28% male, 8% out-of-state, 2% international (34 countries represented). Asian 3%, African American 7%, Caucasian 74%, Hispanic 4%, Native American <1%
Retention and Graduation: 65% freshmen graduate within 4 years. **Faculty:** 180 full-time faculty, 82% hold PhDs, 62% are members of minority groups, 13% are women. 0% of classes are taught by teaching assistants.

ACADEMICS

Degrees: bachelor's, master's, post-master's certificate. **Classes:** Most classes have 10–19 students. Most lab/discussion sessions have 10–19 students. **Majors with Highest Enrollment:** Education; Physical Therapy/Therapist; Business Administration, Management and Operations. **Special Study Options:** cross-registration, distance learning, double major, exchange student program (domestic), honors program, independent study, internships, study abroad, teacher certification program. **Combined degree programs:** BS/DPT Physical Therapy. **Disability Services:** Special programs offered to physically disabled students include note-taking services, reader services, tape recorders, tutors. **Career services:** Alumni network, alumni services, career/job search classes, career assessment, internships, regional alumni.

FACILITIES

Housing: Coed dorms, special housing for disabled students, apartments for single students, Substance Free, Quiet Floors, Language House, Honors, First-year Experience. 80% of campus accessible to physically disabled. **Special Academic Facilities/Equipment:** Arts center, speech/hearing/language clinic, reading clinic, psychology center, center for service learning, Center for Teaching Excellence, and Center for International Education. **Computers:** Students can register for classes online.

CAMPUS LIFE

Environment: Village. **Activities:** Choral groups, concert band, dance, drama/theater, jazz band, literary magazine, music ensembles, musical theater, opera, radio station, student government, student newspaper, symphony orchestra, yearbook, Campus Ministries, International Student Organization, 50 registered organizations, 19 honor societies, 5 religious organizations. **Athletics (Intercollegiate):** *Men:* basketball, cross-country, diving, equestrian sports, golf, lacrosse, soccer, swimming, tennis, track/field (outdoor), track/field (indoor), volleyball. *Women:* basketball, cross-country, diving, equestrian sports, field hockey, golf, lacrosse, soccer, softball, swimming, tennis, track/field (outdoor), track/field (indoor), volleyball. **On-Campus Highlights:** Cabaret- informal dining/coffee house, Athletic Facilities, Shults Community Center, Colie's Café, Library.

ADMISSIONS

Freshman Academic Profile: Average high school GPA 3.4. 23% in top 10% of high school class, 56% in top 25% of high school class, 86% in top 50% of high school class. 90% from public high schools. SAT Math middle 50% range 490-600. SAT Critical Reading middle 50% range 490-590. SAT Writing middle 50% range 470-580. ACT middle 50% range 22-27. Minimum internet-based TOEFL 79. Minimum paper TOEFL 550. **Basis for Candidate Selection:** *Very important factors considered include:* Class rank, application essay, academic GPA, recommendation(s), rigor of secondary school record. *Important factors considered include:* character/personal qualities, extracurricular activities, geographical residence, interview, level of applicant's interest, racial/ethnic status, state residency, talent/ability, volunteer work, work experience. *Other factors considered include:* standardized test scores, alumni/ae relation, first generation. **Freshman Admission Requirements:** High school diploma is re-

quired and GED is accepted. *Academic units required:* 4 English, 3 mathematics, 3 science, (2 science labs), 3 foreign language, 3 social studies. **Freshman Admission Statistics:** 4,185 applied, 70% admitted, 16% enrolled. **Transfer Admission Requirements:** college transcript(s), essay or personal statement, Minimum college GPA of 2.5 required. Lowest grade transferable C. **General Admission Information:** Application Fee $40. Early decision application deadline 11/15. Regular application deadline 2/15. Regular notification 3/1. Nonfall registration accepted. Admission may be deferred for a maximum of 1 year. Credit and/or placement offered for CEEB Advanced Placement tests.

COSTS AND FINANCIAL AID

Required Forms and Deadlines: FAFSA, State aid form. **Notification of Awards:** Applicants will be notified of awards on a rolling basis beginning 2/20. **Types of Aid:** *Need-based scholarships/grants:* Federal Pell, SEOG, state scholarships/grants, private scholarships, the school's own gift aid. *Loans:* Subsidized Stafford, Unsubsidized Stafford, PLUS, Federal Perkins. *Student Employment:* Federal Work-Study Program available. Institutional employment available. Off-campus job opportunities are excellent. **Financial Aid Statistics:** 100% freshmen, 100% undergrads receive need-based scholarship or grant aid. 39% freshmen, 32% undergrads receive non-need-based scholarship or grant aid. 97% freshmen, 94% undergrads receive need-based self-help aid. 0% freshmen, 0% undergrads receive athletic scholarships. 85% undergrads borrow to pay for school. Average cumulative indebtedness $25,546. **Criteria for awarding institutional aid:** *Non-need-based:* academics, alumni affiliation, art, minority status, music/drama, state/district residency.

See page 1100.

NEBRASKA CHRISTIAN COLLEGE

1800 Syracuse Avenue, Norfolk, NE 68701
Phone: 402-379-5000
E-mail: admissions@nechristian.edu · **CEEB Code:**
Fax: 402-379-5100 · **ACT Code:** 2473

This private school was founded in 1945. It has a 40-acre campus.

RATINGS

Admissions Selectivity Rating: 62   Fire Safety Rating: 60*

STUDENTS AND FACULTY

Enrollment: 146. **Student Body:** 45% female, 55% male, 10% out-of-state. **Faculty:** 0% of classes are taught by teaching assistants.

ACADEMICS

Degrees: associate, bachelor's. **Special Study Options:** distance learning, internships, study abroad.

FACILITIES

Housing: Private apartments, student plan housing, private rooms.

CAMPUS LIFE

Environment: Rural. **Activities:** student newspaper. **Athletics (Intercollegiate):** *Men:* basketball, soccer. *Women:* basketball, volleyball.

ADMISSIONS

Basis for Candidate Selection: *Very important factors considered include:* recommendation(s), standardized test scores, character/personal qualities. *Important factors considered include:* Class rank, rigor of secondary school record, extracurricular activities, interview, talent/ability, volunteer work. *Other factors considered include:* alumni/ae relation, work experience. **Freshman Admission Requirements:** High school diploma is required and GED is accepted. **Freshman Admission Statistics:** 148 applied, 60% admitted, 67% enrolled. **Transfer Admission Requirements:** High school transcript, college transcript(s). **General Admission Information:** Application Fee $25. Nonfall registration accepted. Admission may be deferred for a maximum of 1 year.

COSTS AND FINANCIAL AID

Annual tuition $4,500. Room and board $2,960. Required fees $450. Average book expense $400. **Required Forms and Deadlines:** FAFSA, Institution's own financial aid form. **Types of Aid:** *Need-based scholarships/grants:* Federal Pell, SEOG, state scholarships/grants, private scholarships, the school's own gift aid. *Loans:* Subsidized Stafford, Unsubsidized Stafford, PLUS. *Student Employment:* Federal Work-Study Program available. Institutional employment available. Highest amount earned per year from on-campus jobs $1,625. Off-campus job opportunities are excellent. **Financial Aid Statistics:** 93% freshmen, 93% undergrads receive need-based scholarship or grant aid. 0% freshmen, 0% undergrads receive non-need-based scholarship or grant aid. 59% freshmen, 53% undergrads receive need-based self-help aid. 0% freshmen, 0%

undergrads receive athletic scholarships. 90% undergrads borrow to pay for school. **Criteria for awarding institutional aid:** *Non-need-based:* academics, leadership, music/drama.

NEBRASKA METHODIST COLLEGE

720 North 87th Street, Omaha, NE 68114
Phone: 402-354-7200 • **Financial Aid Phone:** 402-354-7225
E-mail: admissions@methodistcollege.edu • **CEEB Code:** 6510
Fax: 402-354-7020 • **ACT Code:** 2465

This private school, affiliated with the Methodist Church, was founded in 1891. It has a 6-acre campus.

RATINGS

Admissions Selectivity Rating: 74   **Fire Safety Rating:** 64

STUDENTS AND FACULTY

Enrollment: 504. **Student Body:** 92% female, 8% male, 35% out-of-state, 0% international (3 countries represented). Asian 3%, African American 3%, Caucasian 87%, Hispanic 1%, Native American 1%
Retention and Graduation: 81% freshmen return for sophomore year. 10% grads go on to further study within 1 year. 10% grads pursue arts and sciences degrees. **Faculty:** 43 full-time faculty, 28% hold PhDs, 91% are members of minority groups, 7% are women. 0% of classes are taught by teaching assistants.

ACADEMICS

Degrees: associate, bachelor's, certificate, master's, post-master's certificate. **Classes:** Most classes have 10–19 students. Most lab/discussion sessions have 10–19 students. **Majors with Highest Enrollment:** Diagnostic Medical Sonography/Sonographer and Ultrasound Technician; Radiologic Technology/Science; Registered Nursing/Registered Nurse. **Special Study Options:** Accelerated program, distance learning, independent study. **Disability Services:** Special programs offered to physically disabled students include note-taking services, reader services, tape recorders, tutors. **Career services:** Alumni network, alumni services, career/job search classes,

FACILITIES

Housing: apartments for single students. 90% of campus accessible to physically disabled. **Computers:** 100% of classrooms, 100% of libraries, 100% of dining areas, 100% of student union, have wireless network access. Students can register for classes online. Administrative functions (other than registration) can be performed online.

CAMPUS LIFE

Environment: City. **Activities:** student government 11 registered organizations, 2 honor societies. **On-Campus Highlights:** Student Center, Library, Human Cadaver Lab, Chapel.

ADMISSIONS

Freshman Academic Profile: Average high school GPA 3.31. 11% in top 10% of high school class, 11% in top 25% of high school class, 50% in top 50% of high school class. 90% from public high schools. ACT middle 50% range 19-23. Minimum internet-based TOEFL 80. Minimum paper TOEFL 550. **Basis for Candidate Selection:** *Very important factors considered include:* academic GPA, rigor of secondary school record, standardized test scores. *Important factors considered include:* Class rank, application essay, recommendation(s), character/personal qualities, interview. *Other factors considered include:* alumni/ae relation, first generation, geographical residence, level of applicant's interest, racial/ethnic status, state residency, volunteer work, work experience. **Freshman Admission Requirements:** High school diploma is required and GED is accepted. *Academic units required:* 4 English, 3 mathematics, 2 science, (2 science labs), 2 social studies. **Freshman Admission Statistics:** 96 applied, 76% admitted, 70% enrolled. **Transfer Admission Requirements:** High school transcript, college transcript(s), essay or personal statement, interview, statement of good standing from prior institution(s). Minimum college GPA of 2.5 required. Lowest grade transferable C. **General Admission Information:** Application Fee $25. Regular application deadline 3/1. Notification on a rolling basis, beginning on or about 1/15. Nonfall registration accepted. Admission may be deferred for a maximum of 12 months. Neither credit nor placement offered for CEEB Advanced Placement tests.

COSTS AND FINANCIAL AID

Annual tuition $12,840. Room and board $2,625. Required fees $600. Average book expense $1,300. **Required Forms and Deadlines:** FAFSA, Institution's own financial aid form. **Notification of Awards:** Applicants will be notified of awards on a rolling basis beginning 3/1. **Types of Aid:** *Need-based scholarships/grants:* Federal Pell, SEOG, state scholarships/grants, private scholarships, the

school's own gift aid. *Loans:* Subsidized Stafford, Unsubsidized Stafford, PLUS, Federal Perkins, Federal Nursing, state loans, college/university loans from institutional funds, Alternative loans. *Student Employment:* Federal Work-Study Program available. Institutional employment available. Off-campus job opportunities are good. **Financial Aid Statistics:** 38% freshmen, 51% undergrads receive need-based scholarship or grant aid. 3% freshmen, 4% undergrads receive non-need-based scholarship or grant aid. 34% freshmen, 56% undergrads receive need-based self-help aid. 0% freshmen, 0% undergrads receive athletic scholarships. 85% freshmen, 69% undergrads receive any aid. 86% undergrads borrow to pay for school. Average cumulative indebtedness $24,383. **Criteria for awarding institutional aid:** *Non-need-based:* academics, minority status, religious affiliation.

NEBRASKA WESLEYAN UNIVERSITY

5000 Saint Paul Ave., Lincoln, NE 68504
Phone: 402-465-2218 • **Financial Aid Phone:** 402-465-2212
E-mail: admissions@nebrwesleyan.edu • **CEEB Code:** 6470
Fax: 402-465-2177 • **Website:** http://www.nebrwesleyan.edu • **ACT Code:** 2474

This private school, affiliated with the Methodist Church, was founded in 1887. It has a 50-acre campus.

RATINGS

Admissions Selectivity Rating: 83   **Fire Safety Rating:** 81

STUDENTS AND FACULTY

Enrollment: 1,803. **Student Body:** 62% female, 38% male, 14% out-of-state, 1% international (20 countries represented). Asian 2%, African American 3%, Caucasian 84%, Hispanic 5%, Native American <1%
Retention and Graduation: 81% freshmen return for sophomore year. 55% freshmen graduate within 4 years. **Faculty:** 106 full-time faculty, 92% hold PhDs, 54% are members of minority groups, 2% are women. 0% of classes are taught by teaching assistants.

ACADEMICS

Degrees: bachelor's, certificate, master's, post-bachelor's certificate, post-master's certificate. **Classes:** Most classes have 20–29 students. Most lab/discussion sessions have 10–19 students. **Majors with Highest Enrollment:** Business Administration and Management; Biology/Biological Sciences; Psychology. **Special Study Options:** double major, dual enrollment, independent study, internships, liberal arts/career combination, study abroad, teacher certification program, weekend college, 3-2 Engineering Program with Washington Univ., Columbia Univ., or Univ. of Nebraska-Lincoln; Capitol Hill Internship Program; Chicago Center for Urban Life & Culture. **Disability Services:** Special programs offered to physically disabled students include note-taking services, reader services, tape recorders, tutors. **Career services:** Alumni network, alumni services, career/job search classes, career assessment, internships, regional alumni. Career services highlights include national and international service learning trips; service learning as part of coursework.

FACILITIES

Housing: Coed dorms, women's dorms, fraternity/sorority housing, apartments for single students, Townhouses; residence hall suites. 92% of campus accessible to physically disabled. **Special Academic Facilities/Equipment:** Art galleries, psychology/sleep lab, observatory and planetarium, green house, laboratory theatre, herbarium, nuclear magnetic resonance laboratory. **Computers:** Students can register for classes online. Administrative functions (other than registration) can be performed online.

CAMPUS LIFE

Environment: City. **Activities:** Choral groups, concert band, drama/theater, jazz band, literary magazine, marching band, music ensembles, musical theater, opera, pep band, radio station, student government, student newspaper, symphony orchestra, Campus Ministries, International Student Organization. 80 registered organizations, 18 honor societies, 5 religious organizations. 3 fraternities, 4 sororities. **Athletics (Intercollegiate):** *Men:* baseball, basketball, cross-country, football, golf, soccer, tennis, track/field (outdoor), track/field (indoor). *Women:* basketball, cross-country, golf, soccer, softball, tennis, track/field (outdoor), track/field (indoor), volleyball. **On-Campus Highlights:** Weary Center for Health and Fitness, Wesleyan Coffee House, Old Main, Roy G Story Student Center, Great Hall, Smith-Curtis. **Environmental Initiatives:** Completed light inventory; retrofitted 80% of all lights. Recycling including cans, plastic bottles, paper Updated central heating plant.

ADMISSIONS

Freshman Academic Profile: Average high school GPA 3.65. 21% in top 10% of high school class, 54% in top 25% of high school class, 81% in top 50% of high school class. SAT Math middle 50% range 460-650. SAT Critical

Reading middle 50% range 480-600. ACT middle 50% range 22-27. Minimum paper TOEFL 525. **Basis for Candidate Selection:** *Very important factors considered include:* Class rank, standardized test scores. *Important factors considered include:* academic GPA, character/personal qualities, extracurricular activities, talent/ability. *Other factors considered include:* application essay, recommendation(s), rigor of secondary school record, alumni/ae relation, first generation, geographical residence, interview, racial/ethnic status, volunteer work. **Freshman Admission Requirements:** High school diploma is required and GED is accepted. **Freshman Admission Statistics:** 1,775 applied, 78% admitted, 27% enrolled. **Transfer Admission Requirements:** college transcript(s), statement of good standing from prior institution(s). Minimum college GPA of 2.0 required. Lowest grade transferable C-. **General Admission Information:** Application Fee $20. Regular application deadline 8/15. Regular notification 1/15. Nonfall registration accepted. Admission may be deferred for a maximum of 1 year. Credit offered for CEEB Advanced Placement tests.

COSTS AND FINANCIAL AID

Average book expense $1,000. **Required Forms and Deadlines:** FAFSA. **Types of Aid:** *Need-based scholarships/grants:* Federal Pell, SEOG, state scholarships/grants, private scholarships, the school's own gift aid. *Loans:* Subsidized Stafford, Unsubsidized Stafford, PLUS, Federal Perkins. *Student Employment:* Federal Work-Study Program available. Institutional employment available. Highest amount earned per year from on-campus jobs $7,664. Off-campus job opportunities are good. **Financial Aid Statistics:** 98% freshmen, 98% undergrads receive need-based scholarship or grant aid. 14% freshmen, 10% undergrads receive non-need-based scholarship or grant aid. 79% freshmen, 84% undergrads receive need-based self-help aid. 0% freshmen, 0% undergrads receive athletic scholarships. 99% freshmen, 96% undergrads receive any aid. 73% undergrads borrow to pay for school. Average cumulative indebtedness $26,063. **Criteria for awarding institutional aid:** *Non-need-based:* academics, art, minority status, music/drama.

NEUMANN UNIVERSITY

One Neumann Drive, Aston, PA 19014
Phone: 610-558-5616 • **Financial Aid Phone:** 610-558-5521
E-mail: neumann@neumann.edu • **CEEB Code:** 2628
Fax: 610-558-5652 • **Website:** www.neumann.edu • **ACT Code:** 3649

This private school, affiliated with the Roman Catholic Church, was founded in 1965. It has a 55-acre campus.

RATINGS

Admissions Selectivity Rating: 68   Fire Safety Rating: 89

STUDENTS AND FACULTY

Enrollment: 2,462. **Student Body:** 64% female, 36% male, 34% out-of-state, 2% international (16 countries represented). Asian 0%, African-American 18%, Caucasian 52%, Hispanic 3%, Native American 1%
Retention and Graduation: 66% freshmen return for sophomore year. 29% freshmen graduate within 4 years. 50% freshmen graduate within 6 years. 20% grads go on to further study within 1 year. 7% grads pursue arts and sciences degrees. 1% grads pursue law degrees. 6% grads pursue business degrees. 1% grads pursue medical degrees. **Faculty:** 104 full-time faculty, 79% hold PhDs, 63% are members of minority groups. 0% of classes are taught by teaching assistants.

ACADEMICS

Degrees: associate, bachelor's, certificate, master's, post-bachelor's certificate, post-master's certificate, terminal associate. **Classes:** Most classes have 20–29 students. Most lab/discussion sessions have 10–19 students. **Majors with Highest Enrollment:** Elementary Education and Teaching; Registered Nursing, Nursing Administration, Nursing Research and Clinical Nursing; Psychology. **Special Study Options:** Accelerated program, cooperative education program, distance learning, double major, exchange student program (domestic), honors program, independent study, internships, liberal arts/career combination, student-designed major, study abroad, teacher certification program, weekend college. **Disability Services:** Special programs offered to physically disabled students include note-taking services, reader services, tape recorders, tutors. **Career services:** Alumni network, alumni services, career/job search classes, career assessment, internships.

FACILITIES

Housing: Coed dorms, special housing for disabled students, Off campus housing. 100% of campus accessible to physically disabled. **Special Academic Facilities/Equipment:** Child development center. **Computers:** 100% of classrooms, 100% of libraries, have wireless network access. Administrative functions (other than registration) can be performed online.

CAMPUS LIFE

Environment: Town. **Activities:** Choral groups, dance, drama/theater, jazz band, literary magazine, music ensembles, musical theater, radio station, student government, student newspaper, yearbook, Campus Ministries, Model UN. 14 registered organizations, 4 honor societies, 2 religious organizations. **Athletics (Intercollegiate):** *Men:* baseball, basketball, cross-country, golf, ice hockey, lacrosse, soccer, tennis. *Women:* basketball, cross-country, field hockey, ice hockey, lacrosse, soccer, softball, tennis, volleyball. **On-Campus Highlights:** Life Center, Training room, On campus Chapel, Library, Computer Labs.

ADMISSIONS

Freshman Academic Profile: Average high school GPA 2.91. 68% from public high schools. SAT Math middle 50% range 380-480. SAT Critical Reading middle 50% range 390-470. SAT Writing middle 50% range 380-470. ACT middle 50% range 16-20. Minimum internet-based TOEFL 84. **Basis for Candidate Selection:** *Very important factors considered include:* recommendation(s), rigor of secondary school record, extracurricular activities, talent/ability. *Important factors considered include:* Class rank, standardized test scores, alumni/ae relation, character/personal qualities, interview, level of applicant's interest. *Other factors considered include:* application essay, racial/ethnic status, religious affiliation/commitment, volunteer work. **Freshman Admission Requirements:** High school diploma is required and GED is accepted. *Academic units required:* 4 English, 2 mathematics, 2 science, 2 foreign language, 2 social studies, 4 academic electives. **Freshman Admission Statistics:** 2,637 applied, 94% admitted, 20% enrolled. **Transfer Admission Requirements:** college transcript(s), Minimum college GPA of 2.0 required. Lowest grade transferable C. **General Admission Information:** Application Fee $35. Nonfall registration accepted. Admission may be deferred for a maximum of one year. Credit offered for CEEB Advanced Placement tests.

COSTS AND FINANCIAL AID

Notification of Awards: Applicants will be notified of awards on a rolling basis beginning 3/1. **Types of Aid:** *Need-based scholarships/grants:* Federal Pell, SEOG, state scholarships/grants, private scholarships, the school's own gift aid, Federal Nursing Scholarships. *Loans:* Direct Subsidized Stafford, Direct Unsubsidized Stafford, Direct PLUS, Subsidized Stafford, Unsubsidized Stafford, PLUS, Federal Nursing. *Student Employment:* Federal Work-Study Program available. Highest amount earned per year from on-campus jobs $5,000. Off-campus job opportunities are excellent. **Financial Aid Statistics:** 100% freshmen, 95% undergrads receive need-based scholarship or grant aid. 119% freshmen, 131% undergrads receive non-need-based scholarship or grant aid. 94% freshmen, 90% undergrads receive need-based self-help aid. 0% freshmen, 0% undergrads receive athletic scholarships. 97% freshmen, 95% undergrads receive any aid. 95% undergrads borrow to pay for school. Average cumulative indebtedness $27,000. **Criteria for awarding institutional aid:** *Non-need-based:* academics.

NEUMONT UNIVERSITY

10701 S. River Front Parkway, South Jordan, UT 84095
Phone: 888-638-6668 • **Financial Aid Phone:** 801-302-2870
E-mail: admissions@neumont.edu
Fax: 801-302-2880 • **Website:** www.neumont.edu

This proprietary school was founded in 2003.

RATINGS

Admissions Selectivity Rating: 61   Fire Safety Rating: 60*

STUDENTS AND FACULTY

Enrollment: 366. **Student Body:** 10% female, 90% male, (40 countries represented).
Retention and Graduation: 69% freshmen return for sophomore year. **Faculty:** 13 full-time faculty, 15% are members of minority groups.

ACADEMICS

Degrees: bachelor's, master's. **Special Study Options:** Accelerated program, internships. **Disability Services:** Special programs offered to physically disabled students include note-taking services, reader services, tape recorders, tutors. **Career services:** career/job search classes, career assessment, internships.

FACILITIES

Housing: apartments for married students, apartments for single students **Computers:** 100% of classrooms, 100% of libraries, 100% of dining areas, 100% of student union, have wireless network access. Students can register for classes online. Undergraduates are required to own a computer.

CAMPUS LIFE

Environment: Metropolis. **Activities:** student government. 8 registered organizations.

ADMISSIONS

Freshman Admission Statistics: 596 applied, 81% admitted, 35% enrolled.

COSTS AND FINANCIAL AID

Annual tuition $21,600. Room and board $4,230. Required fees $1,500. Average book expense $1,080. **Required Forms and Deadlines:** FAFSA, Institution's own financial aid form.

NEW COLLEGE OF FLORIDA

Best 380

5800 Bay Shore Rd, Sarasota, FL 34243-2109
Phone: 941-487-5000 · **Financial Aid Phone:** 941-487-5000
E-mail: admissions@ncf.edu · **CEEB Code:** 39574
Fax: 941-487-5001 · **Website:** www.ncf.edu · **ACT Code:** 750

This public school was founded in 1960. It has a 118.6-acre campus.

RATINGS

Admissions Selectivity Rating: 91   **Fire Safety Rating:** 84

STUDENTS AND FACULTY

Enrollment: 834. **Student Body:** 59% female, 41% male, 19% out-of-state, 2% international (23 countries represented). Asian 2%, African American 3%, Caucasian 71%, Hispanic 15%, Native American <1%
Retention and Graduation: 80% freshmen return for sophomore year. 57% freshmen graduate within 4 years. 69% freshmen graduate within 6 years. 13% grads go on to further study within 1 year. **Faculty:** 73 full-time faculty, 97% hold PhDs, 52% are members of minority groups, 12% are women. 0% of classes are taught by teaching assistants.

ACADEMICS

Degrees: bachelor's. **Classes:** Most classes have 10–19 students. Most lab/discussion sessions have 10–19 students. **Majors with Highest Enrollment:** Biology/Biological Sciences; Psychology; Political Science and Government. **Special Study Options:** cross-registration, double major, exchange student program (domestic), honors program, independent study, internships, student-designed major, study abroad, Academic contract, January interterm (independent study), Narrative evaluation/pass-fail, Senior thesis, Tutorials, Undergraduate research. Special or unique academic programs: (1) The New College academic contract whereby each student develops her/his individual academic program of coursework, tutorials, field and lab research, study abroad, and so on, in close consultation with a faculty member. See the General Catalog on the web. http://www.ncf.edu/resources-for-students. (2) Non-graded, narrative evaluation which encourages exploration and mastery. (3) Intensive "Independent Study Projects" during January which can be highly individual but can also involve group activities, such as an acting workshop or an ecological tour of Florida. (4) Competitive grants programs to support student research. **Honors programs:** New College of Florida is the state's officially-designated "honors college for the liberal arts." **Disability Services:** Special programs offered to physically disabled students include note-taking services, reader services, tape recorders. **Career services:** Alumni network, alumni services, career/job search classes, career assessment, internships, regional alumni. Career services highlights include The National Student Exchange program.

FACILITIES

Housing: Coed dorms, special housing for disabled students, apartments for single students, specialized housing options may be arranged in response to student interest. 60% of campus accessible to physically disabled. **Special Academic Facilities/Equipment:** Anthropology and psychology labs. Electronic music lab. Individual studio space for senior art students. Marine biology research center with Living Ecosystem Teaching and Research Aquarium, wet lab, and seawater on tap. NMR, scanning electron microscope, inert atmosphere glovebox, transparent fume hoods, greenhouse. **Computers:** 95% of classrooms, 100% of dorms, 100% of libraries, 100% of dining areas, 100% of student union, 20% of common outdoor areas have wireless network access. Students can register for classes online. Administrative functions (other than registration) can be performed online.

CAMPUS LIFE

Environment: Town. **Activities:** Choral groups, dance, drama/theater, literary magazine, music ensembles, musical theater, radio station, student government,

student newspaper, student-run film society, Campus Ministries. 90 registered organizations, 5 religious organizations. **Athletics (Intercollegiate):** *Men:* sailing. *Women:* sailing. **On-Campus Highlights:** The R.V. Heiser Natural Sciences Complex, Pritzker Marine Biology Research Center, The Caples Fine Arts Complex, Four Winds Café (Student owned and operated), Jane Bancroft Cook Library, Historic bayfront mansions. **Environmental Initiatives:** We've had an environmental studies program since 1972. Students have voted for a green fee and have paid a lump sum to make County buses service free. We use no nitrogen fertilizer and have just replaced about 1/50 of the campus area with native grasses and wildflowers.

ADMISSIONS

Freshman Academic Profile: Average high school GPA 4. 45% in top 10% of high school class, 78% in top 25% of high school class, 99% in top 50% of high school class. 79% from public high schools. SAT Math middle 50% range 560-670. SAT Critical Reading middle 50% range 620-710. SAT Writing middle 50% range 590-680. ACT middle 50% range 26-30. Minimum internet-based TOEFL 83. Minimum paper TOEFL 560. **Basis for Candidate Selection:** *Very important factors considered include:* application essay, academic GPA, rigor of secondary school record. *Important factors considered include:* recommendation(s), standardized test scores, character/personal qualities. *Other factors considered include:* Class rank, alumni/ae relation, extracurricular activities, first generation, geographical residence, interview, level of applicant's interest, state residency, talent/ability, volunteer work, work experience. **Freshman Admission Requirements:** High school diploma is required and GED is accepted. *Academic units required:* 4 English, 4 mathematics, 3 science, (2 science labs), 2 foreign language, 3 social studies, 2 academic electives. **Freshman Admission Statistics:** 1,570 applied, 60% admitted, 25% enrolled. **Transfer Admission Requirements:** college transcript(s), essay or personal statement, Minimum college GPA of 2.0 required. Lowest grade transferable C. **General Admission Information:** Application Fee $30. Regular application deadline 4/15. Nonfall registration accepted. Admission may be deferred for a maximum of 1 year. Neither credit nor placement offered for CEEB Advanced Placement tests.

COSTS AND FINANCIAL AID

Annual in-state tuition $5,227. Annual out-of-state tuition $28,255. Room and board $8,856. Required fees $1,645. Average book expense $1,200. **Required Forms and Deadlines:** FAFSA. **Notification of Awards:** Applicants will be notified of awards on a rolling basis beginning 10/1. **Types of Aid:** *Need-based scholarships/grants:* Federal Pell, SEOG, state scholarships/grants, private scholarships, the school's own gift aid, Federal Academic Competitiveness Grant. *Loans:* Subsidized Stafford, Unsubsidized Stafford, PLUS, Alternative Loans. *Student Employment:* Federal Work-Study Program available. Institutional employment available. Highest amount earned per year from on-campus jobs $5,358. Off-campus job opportunities are good. **Financial Aid Statistics:** 100% freshmen, 98% undergrads receive need-based scholarship or grant aid. 23% freshmen, 17% undergrads receive non-need-based scholarship or grant aid. 77% freshmen, 78% undergrads receive need-based self-help aid. 0% freshmen, 0% undergrads receive athletic scholarships. 100% freshmen, 97% undergrads receive any aid. 39% undergrads borrow to pay for school. Average cumulative indebtedness $16,559. **Criteria for awarding institutional aid:** *Non-need-based:* academics, state/district residency.

NEW ENGLAND COLLEGE

102 Bridge Street, Henniker, NH 3242
Phone: 603-428-2223 · **Financial Aid Phone:** 603-428-2226
E-mail: admission@nec.edu · **CEEB Code:** 3657
Fax: 603-428-3155 · **Website:** www.nec.edu · **ACT Code:** 2513

This private school was founded in 1946. It has a 225-acre campus.

RATINGS

Admissions Selectivity Rating: 71   **Fire Safety Rating:** 98

STUDENTS AND FACULTY

Enrollment: 1,599. **Student Body:** 56% female, 44% male, 76% out-of-state, 4% international. Asian 1%, African American 19%, Caucasian 59%, Hispanic 3%, Native American 1%
Retention and Graduation: 60% freshmen return for sophomore year. 34% freshmen graduate within 4 years. 40% freshmen graduate within 6 years. 19% grads go on to further study within 1 year. 12% grads pursue arts and sciences degrees. 1% grads pursue law degrees. 3% grads pursue business degrees. **Faculty:** 63 full-time faculty, 71% hold PhDs, 41% are members of minority groups, 3% are women. 0% of classes are taught by teaching assistants.

ACADEMICS

Degrees: associate, bachelor's, master's. **Classes:** Most classes have 10–19 students. Most lab/discussion sessions have 10–19 students. **Majors with Highest Enrollment:** Elementary Education and Teaching; Sport and Fitness Administration/Management; Business/Commerce. **Special Study Options:** Accelerated program, cross-registration, distance learning, double major, dual enrollment, English as a Second Language (ESL), exchange student program (domestic), external degree program, honors program, independent study, internships, liberal arts/career combination, student-designed major, study abroad, teacher certification program. **Honors programs:** Honors Program for community college honors transfers **Combined degree programs:** BA/JD, NEC and New York Law 3 + 3 Program. **Disability Services:** Special programs offered to physically disabled students include note-taking services, tape recorders, tutors. **Career services:** Alumni network, career/job search classes, career assessment, internships, regional alumni. Career services highlights include internships and practical experience throughout the curriculum.

FACILITIES

Housing: Coed dorms, fraternity/sorority housing, Theme Housing, Resident freshmen and sophomores are required to live in College housing. Quiet study options, special interest housing is available. 75% of campus accessible to physically disabled. **Special Academic Facilities/Equipment:** New England Art Gallery, Graphic Design and Imaging Lab, Center for Educational Innovation (High Tech Building). **Computers:** 100% of classrooms, 100% of dorms, 100% of libraries, 100% of dining areas, 100% of student union, 75% of common outdoor areas have wireless network access. Students can register for classes online. Administrative functions (other than registration) can be performed online.

CAMPUS LIFE

Environment: Rural. **Activities:** Choral groups, dance, drama/theater, literary magazine, radio station, student government, student newspaper, yearbook, International Student Organization. 26 registered organizations, 2 honor societies, 1 religious organization. 2 fraternities, 2 sororities. **Athletics (Intercollegiate):** *Men:* baseball, basketball, cross-country, ice hockey, lacrosse, soccer. *Women:* basketball, cheerleading, cross-country, field hockey, ice hockey, lacrosse, soccer, softball. **On-Campus Highlights:** Simon Center (Student Center), Center of Education Innovation, Fitness Center, Gilmore Dining Hall, Coffee House. **Environmental Initiatives:** Addition of sustainability to the mission statement. A complete overhaul of lighting at the College for energy efficiency. Completion of a campus wide facilities plan. Environmental Action Committee Capital budgeting to include green projects

ADMISSIONS

Freshman Academic Profile: Average high school GPA 2.63. 2% in top 10% of high school class, 12% in top 25% of high school class, 36% in top 50% of high school class. 90% from public high schools. SAT Math middle 50% range 410-520. SAT Critical Reading middle 50% range 400-500. SAT Writing middle 50% range 390-490. ACT middle 50% range 19-23. Minimum internet-based TOEFL 13. Minimum paper TOEFL 550. **Basis for Candidate Selection:** *Very important factors considered include:* application essay, recommendation(s), rigor of secondary school record, extracurricular activities, interview, level of applicant's interest, talent/ability. *Important factors considered include:* character/personal qualities, volunteer work. *Other factors considered include:* Class rank, academic GPA, standardized test scores, alumni/ae relation, work experience. **Freshman Admission Requirements:** High school diploma is required and GED is accepted. *Academic units required:* 4 English, 2 mathematics, 2 science, (1 science labs), 0 foreign language, 2 social studies, 0 history, 0 visual/performing arts, 0 computer science, 0 academic electives. **Freshman Admission Statistics:** 5,843 applied, 90% admitted, 8% enrolled. **Transfer Admission Requirements:** High school transcript, college transcript(s), essay or personal statement, statement of good standing from prior institution(s). Lowest grade transferable C-. **General Admission Information:** Application Fee $30. Regular application deadline 9/1. Notification on a rolling basis, beginning on or about 11/1. Nonfall registration accepted. Admission may be deferred for a maximum of 1 year. Credit and/or placement offered for CEEB Advanced Placement tests.

COSTS AND FINANCIAL AID

Annual tuition $32,650. Room and board $12,930. Required fees $350. Average book expense $1,000. **Required Forms and Deadlines:** FAFSA. **Notification of Awards:** Applicants will be notified of awards on a rolling basis beginning 1/12. **Types of Aid:** *Need-based scholarships/grants:* Federal Pell, SEOG, state scholarships/grants, private scholarships, the school's own gift aid. *Loans:* Direct Subsidized Stafford, Direct Unsubsidized Stafford, Direct PLUS, Subsidized Stafford, Unsubsidized Stafford, PLUS, Federal Perkins, state loans. *Student Employment:* Federal Work-Study Program available. Institutional employment available. Highest amount earned per year from on-campus jobs $2,500. Off-campus job opportunities are good. **Financial Aid Statistics:** 97% freshmen, 91% undergrads receive need-based scholarship or grant aid. 3% freshmen, 2% undergrads receive non-need-based scholarship or grant aid. 100% freshmen, 99% undergrads receive need-based self-help aid. 0% freshmen, 0% undergrads

receive athletic scholarships. 93% freshmen, 88% undergrads receive any aid. 76% undergrads borrow to pay for school. Average cumulative indebtedness $9,849. **Criteria for awarding institutional aid:** *Non-need-based:* academics, alumni affiliation, art, job skills, leadership, music/drama.

NEW ENGLAND CONSERVATORY OF MUSIC

290 Huntington Avenue, Boston, MA 2115
Phone: 617-585-1101
E-mail: admissions@newenglandconservatory.edu • **CEEB Code:** 3659
Fax: 617-585-1115 • **Website:** www.newenglandconservatory.edu • **ACT Code:** 1872

This private school was founded in 1867.

RATINGS

Admissions Selectivity Rating: 70   **Fire Safety Rating:** 60*

STUDENTS AND FACULTY

Enrollment: 378. **Student Body:** 45% female, 55% male, 85% out-of-state, 6% international. Asian 3%, African American 1%, Caucasian 13%, Hispanic 1%, Native American <1%
Retention and Graduation: 98% freshmen return for sophomore year. 56% freshmen graduate within 4 years. 69% freshmen graduate within 6 years.
Faculty: 88 full-time faculty, 26% hold PhDs, 33% are members of minority groups, 6% are women.

ACADEMICS

Degrees: bachelor's, diploma, master's. **Classes:** Most classes have 10–19 students. Most lab/discussion sessions have fewer than 10 students. **Majors with Highest Enrollment:** Voice and Opera; Jazz/Jazz Studies; Stringed Instruments. **Special Study Options:** cross-registration, dual enrollment, English as a Second Language (ESL), independent study, internships, study abroad. **Disability Services:** Special programs offered to physically disabled students include note-taking services, tutors. **Career services:** Alumni network, alumni services, career/job search classes, career assessment, internships.

FACILITIES

Housing: Coed dorms. 100% of campus accessible to physically disabled. **Special Academic Facilities/Equipment:** Rare instrument collection of over 200 pieces, recording and electronic music studios. over 200 pieces, recording and electronic music studios. Jordan Hall, the Main Concert Hall, is a national Historic Landmark.

CAMPUS LIFE

Activities: Choral groups, concert band, jazz band, music ensembles, musical theater, opera, student government, symphony orchestra. 7 registered organizations, 1 honor society, 1 religious organization. 1 fraternity.

ADMISSIONS

Freshman Academic Profile: Minimum paper TOEFL 500. **Basis for Candidate Selection:** *Very important factors considered include:* talent/ability. *Important factors considered include:* rigor of secondary school record, standardized test scores. *Other factors considered include:* application essay, academic GPA, recommendation(s), character/personal qualities. **Freshman Admission Requirements:** High school diploma is required and GED is accepted. **Freshman Admission Statistics:** 1,022 applied, 28% admitted, 28% enrolled. **Transfer Admission Requirements:** college transcript(s), essay or personal statement, interview, Minimum college GPA of 2.7 required. Lowest grade transferable B. **General Admission Information:** Application Fee $100. Notification on a rolling basis, beginning on or about 4/1. Nonfall registration accepted. Admission may be deferred for a maximum of 1 year. Credit offered for CEEB Advanced Placement tests.

COSTS AND FINANCIAL AID

Annual tuition $30,650. Room and board $11,300. Required fees $325. Average book expense $700. **Required Forms and Deadlines:** FAFSA, Institution's own financial aid form. **Notification of Awards:** Applicants will be notified of awards on a rolling basis beginning 4/1. **Types of Aid:** *Need-based scholarships/grants:* Federal Pell, SEOG, state scholarships/grants, private scholarships, the school's own gift aid. *Loans:* Subsidized Stafford, Unsubsidized Stafford, PLUS, Federal Perkins, state loans. *Student Employment:* Federal Work-Study Program available. Institutional employment available. Off-campus job opportunities are good. **Financial Aid Statistics:** 86% freshmen, 88% undergrads receive need-based scholarship or grant aid. 39% freshmen, 50% undergrads receive non-need-based scholarship or grant aid. 64% freshmen, 70% undergrads receive need-based self-help aid. 0% freshmen, 0% undergrads receive athletic scholarships. 61% undergrads borrow to pay for school. Average cumulative indebtedness $19,545. **Criteria for awarding institutional aid:** *Non-need-based:* academics, music/drama.

NEW JERSEY CITY UNIVERSITY

2039 Kennedy Boulevard, Jersey City, NJ 7305
Phone: 888-441-6528 · **Financial Aid Phone:** 201-200-3378
E-mail: admissions@njcu.edu · **CEEB Code:** 2316
Fax: 201-200-2044 · **Website:** www.njcu.edu

This public school was founded in 1927. It has a 17-acre campus.

RATINGS

Admissions Selectivity Rating: 73   **Fire Safety Rating:** 77

STUDENTS AND FACULTY

Enrollment: 6,163. **Student Body:** 60% female, 40% male, 1% out-of-state, 1% international (17 countries represented). Asian 9%, African American 21%, Caucasian 25%, Hispanic 35%, Native American <1%
Retention and Graduation: 74% freshmen return for sophomore year. 7% freshmen graduate within 4 years. 32% freshmen graduate within 6 years.
Faculty: 258 full-time faculty, 50% are members of minority groups, 32% are women. 0% of classes are taught by teaching assistants.

ACADEMICS

Degrees: bachelor's, certificate, master's, post-bachelor's certificate, post-master's certificate. **Classes:** Most classes have 20–29 students. **Majors with Highest Enrollment:** Psychology; Corrections and Criminal Justice; Registered Nursing/Registered Nurse. **Special Study Options:** Accelerated program, cooperative education program, cross-registration, distance learning, double major, dual enrollment, English as a Second Language (ESL), honors program, independent study, internships, study abroad, teacher certification program, weekend college. **Honors programs:** Honors program in the William Maxwell College of Arts and Sciences. **Combined degree programs:** BA/MA. **Disability Services:** Special programs offered to physically disabled students include reader services, tape recorders, tutors. **Career services:** career assessment, internships. Career services highlights include Cooperative education.

FACILITIES

Housing: Coed dorms. 100% of campus accessible to physically disabled.
Special Academic Facilities/Equipment: Art galleries, lab school for special education, criminal justice institute, electron microscope, Raimondo Center for Urban Research and Public Policy. **Computers:** Students can register for classes online. Administrative functions (other than registration) can be performed online.

CAMPUS LIFE

Environment: City. **Activities:** Choral groups, concert band, dance, drama/theater, jazz band, literary magazine, music ensembles, musical theater, opera, radio station, student government, student newspaper, symphony orchestra, yearbook, Campus Ministries, International Student Organization. 50 registered organizations, 2 religious organizations. 7 fraternities, 5 sororities. **Athletics (Intercollegiate):** *Men:* baseball, basketball, cross-country, soccer, track/field (outdoor), track/field (indoor), volleyball. *Women:* basketball, bowling, cross-country, soccer, softball, track/field (outdoor), track/field (indoor), volleyball.
On-Campus Highlights: Student Union, Physical fitness center, Library, Cafeteria.

ADMISSIONS

Freshman Academic Profile: Average high school GPA 2.95. 13% in top 10% of high school class, 33% in top 25% of high school class, 61% in top 50% of high school class. SAT Math middle 50% range 410-500. SAT Critical Reading middle 50% range 390-480. Minimum internet-based TOEFL 79. **Basis for Candidate Selection:** *Very important factors considered include:* rigor of secondary school record, standardized test scores, level of applicant's interest, volunteer work. *Important factors considered include:* application essay, academic GPA, recommendation(s), extracurricular activities. *Other factors considered include:* character/personal qualities, interview, talent/ability. **Freshman Admission Requirements:** High school diploma is required and GED is accepted. *Academic units required:* 4 English, 4 mathematics, 4 science, (2 science labs), 0 foreign language, 4 social studies. **Freshman Admission Statistics:** 2,618 applied, 77% admitted, 34% enrolled. **Transfer Admission Requirements:** college transcript(s), Minimum college GPA of 2.0 required. Lowest grade transferable C. **General Admission Information:** Application Fee $35. Nonfall registration accepted. Credit and/or placement offered for CEEB Advanced Placement tests.

COSTS AND FINANCIAL AID

Average book expense $1,000. **Required Forms and Deadlines:** FAFSA. **Notification of Awards:** Applicants will be notified of awards on or about 5/15. **Types of Aid:** *Need-based scholarships/grants:* Federal Pell, SEOG, state scholarships/grants, private scholarships, the school's own gift aid, United Negro College Fund. *Loans:* Subsidized Stafford, Unsubsidized Stafford, PLUS, Federal Perkins, state loans. *Student Employment:* Federal Work-Study Program

available. Institutional employment available. Off-campus job opportunities are good. **Financial Aid Statistics:** 83% freshmen, 78% undergrads receive need-based scholarship or grant aid. 19% freshmen, 9% undergrads receive non-need-based scholarship or grant aid. 40% freshmen, 61% undergrads receive need-based self-help aid. 0% freshmen, 0% undergrads receive athletic scholarships. 71% undergrads borrow to pay for school. Average cumulative indebtedness $20,701.

NEW JERSEY INSTITUTE OF TECHNOLOGY

Best 380

Office of University Admissions, Newark, NJ 7102
Phone: 973-596-3300 · **Financial Aid Phone:** 973-596-3479
E-mail: admissions@njit.edu · **CEEB Code:** 2580
Fax: 973-596-3461 · **Website:** www.njit.edu · **ACT Code:** 2513

This public school was founded in 1881. It has a 48-acre campus.

RATINGS

Admissions Selectivity Rating: 83   **Fire Safety Rating:** 99

STUDENTS AND FACULTY

Enrollment: 6,154. **Student Body:** 21% female, 79% male, 9% out-of-state, 5% international (83 countries represented). Asian 21%, African American 9%, Caucasian 37%, Hispanic 15%, Native American <1%
Retention and Graduation: 82% freshmen return for sophomore year. 19% freshmen graduate within 4 years. 55% freshmen graduate within 6 years. 17% grads go on to further study within 1 year. 1% grads pursue arts and sciences degrees. 1% grads pursue business degrees. **Faculty:** 398 full-time faculty, 100% hold PhDs, 19% are members of minority groups, 26% are women. 0% of classes are taught by teaching assistants.

ACADEMICS

Degrees: bachelor's, doctoral, master's, post-bachelor's certificate. **Classes:** Most classes have 20–29 students. **Majors with Highest Enrollment:** Mechanical Engineering; Civil Engineering; Architecture. **Special Study Options:** Accelerated program, cooperative education program, cross-registration, distance learning, double major, English as a Second Language (ESL), honors program, independent study, internships, study abroad. **Honors programs:** The Albert Dorman Honors College at the New Jersey Institute of Technology (NJIT) enrolls over 500 exceptional students who excel in the fields of engineering, architecture, computing sciences, management, and the sciences. **Combined degree programs:** BA/MD, BA/MA, BS/MD,BS/DMD,BS/OD,BArch/MS Mang. **Disability Services:** Special programs offered to physically disabled students include note-taking services, reader services, tape recorders, tutors. **Career services:** Alumni network, alumni services, career/job search classes, career assessment, internships, regional alumni. Career services highlights include Cooperative Education at NJIT, an academically integrated program that gives students the opportunity to gain paid professional work experience before graduation. Although not mandatory, over 400 students choose to participate each year. Most co-op students work fulltime for one or two semesters. The average wage for co-op students exceeds $15.00 per hour Nearly 2600 different companies have hired NJIT students over the past decade. Employers range from large multinationals to small start-up companies. Students have completed their co-op assignments in New Jersey, ten other states, and four foreign countries.

FACILITIES

Housing: Coed dorms. 100% of campus accessible to physically disabled. **Special Academic Facilities/Equipment:** New Jersey Literary Hall of Fame and more than 50 research centers and sponsored research laboratories, including computer chip manufacturing center, manufacturing systems center, and many others. **Computers:** 100% of classrooms, 100% of dorms, 100% of libraries, 100% of dining areas, 100% of student union, 100% of common outdoor areas have wireless network access. Students can register for classes online. Administrative functions (other than registration) can be performed online. Undergraduates are required to own a computer.

CAMPUS LIFE

Environment: Metropolis. **Activities:** concert band, dance, drama/theater, literary magazine, marching band, musical theater, radio station, student government, student newspaper, yearbook, International Student Organization. 70 registered organizations, 10 honor societies, 5 religious organizations. 15 fraternities, 7 sororities. **Athletics (Intercollegiate):** *Men:* baseball, basketball, cheerleading, cross-country, fencing, soccer, swimming, tennis, track/field (outdoor), track/field (indoor), volleyball. *Women:* basketball, cheerleading, cross-country, fencing, soccer, swimming, tennis, track/field (outdoor), track/field (indoor), volleyball. **On-Campus Highlights:** Campus Center, Van Houten Library, Zoom Fleisher Athletic Center, East Building—Admissions, Student Mall. **Environmental Initiatives:** Recycling; Energy efficiencies on equipment; Water conservation devices.

ADMISSIONS

Freshman Academic Profile: 20% in top 10% of high school class, 52% in top 25% of high school class, 85% in top 50% of high school class. 85% from public high schools. SAT Math middle 50% range 550-660. SAT Critical Reading middle 50% range 470-600. SAT Writing middle 50% range 470-590. Minimum internet-based TOEFL 79. Minimum paper TOEFL 550. **Basis for Candidate Selection:** *Very important factors considered include:* Class rank, rigor of secondary school record, standardized test scores. *Important factors considered include:* academic GPA. *Other factors considered include:* application essay, recommendation(s), alumni/ae relation, character/personal qualities, extracurricular activities, geographical residence, interview, level of applicant's interest, racial/ethnic status, religious affiliation/commitment, state residency, talent/ability, volunteer work, work experience. **Freshman Admission Requirements:** High school diploma is required and GED is accepted. *Academic units required:* 4 English, 4 mathematics, 2 science, (2 science labs), 0 foreign language, 0 social studies, 0 history, 0 academic electives. **Freshman Admission Statistics:** 4,216 applied, 64% admitted, 38% enrolled. **Transfer Admission Requirements:** college transcript(s), Minimum college GPA of 2.0 required. Lowest grade transferable C. **General Admission Information:** Application Fee $50. Regular application deadline 4/1. Notification on a rolling basis, beginning on or about 11/15. Nonfall registration accepted. Admission may be deferred for a maximum of 1 semester. Credit offered for CEEB Advanced Placement tests.

COSTS AND FINANCIAL AID

Annual in-state tuition $11,756. Annual out-of-state tuition $23,116. Room and board $11,000. Required fees $2,218. Average book expense $1,900. **Required Forms and Deadlines:** FAFSA. **Notification of Awards:** Applicants will be notified of awards on a rolling basis beginning 12/20. **Types of Aid:** *Need-based scholarships/grants:* Federal Pell, SEOG, state scholarships/grants, private scholarships, the school's own gift aid. *Loans:* Direct Subsidized Stafford, Direct Unsubsidized Stafford, Direct PLUS, Federal Perkins, state loans, college/university loans from institutional funds. *Student Employment:* Federal Work-Study Program available. Institutional employment available. Highest amount earned per year from on-campus jobs $5,500. Off-campus job opportunities are good. **Financial Aid Statistics:** 63% freshmen, 70% undergrads receive need-based scholarship or grant aid. 15% freshmen, 7% undergrads receive non-need-based scholarship or grant aid. 59% freshmen, 67% undergrads receive need-based self-help aid. 3% freshmen, 2% undergrads receive athletic scholarships. 87% freshmen, 72% undergrads receive any aid. 61% undergrads borrow to pay for school. Average cumulative indebtedness $20,246. **Criteria for awarding institutional aid:** *Non-need-based:* academics, athletics, job skills, leadership, state/district residency.

NEW MEXICO INSTITUTE OF MINING AND TECHNOLOGY

Campus Station, Socorro, NM 87801
Phone: 575-835-5424 · **Financial Aid Phone:** 575-835-5333
E-mail: admission@admin.nmt.edu · **CEEB Code:** 4533
Fax: 575-835-5989 · **Website:** www.nmt.edu · **ACT Code:** 2642

This public school was founded in 1889. It has a 320-acre campus.

RATINGS

Admissions Selectivity Rating: 91   **Fire Safety Rating:** 60*

STUDENTS AND FACULTY

Enrollment: 1,525. **Student Body:** 27% female, 73% male, 16% out-of-state, 4% international. Asian 3%, African American 2%, Caucasian 56%, Hispanic 28%, Native American 3%
Retention and Graduation: 22% freshmen graduate within 4 years. 45% freshmen graduate within 6 years. **Faculty:** 121 full-time faculty.

ACADEMICS

Degrees: bachelor's, master's, terminal associate. **Classes:** Most classes have fewer than 10 students. Most lab/discussion sessions have 10–19 students. **Majors with Highest Enrollment:** Computer and Information Sciences; Electrical and Electronics Engineering; Mechanical Engineering. **Special Study Options:** Accelerated program, cooperative education program, distance learning, double major, dual enrollment, exchange student program (domestic),

independent study, internships, student-designed major, teacher certification program. **Combined degree programs:** BS/MS Geology, Hydrology. **Disability Services:** Special programs offered to physically disabled students include note-taking services, reader services, tape recorders, tutors. **Career services:** career/job search classes, career assessment, internships.

FACILITIES

Housing: Coed dorms, men's dorms, women's dorms, apartments for married students, apartments for single students. **Special Academic Facilities/Equipment:** Mineral museum, observatory, radio telescope, seismic observatory and library, explosives labs. **Computers:** Students can register for classes online. Administrative functions (other than registration) can be performed online.

CAMPUS LIFE

Environment: Village. **Activities:** Choral groups, concert band, dance, drama/theater, jazz band, music ensembles, musical theater, radio station, student government, student newspaper. 60 registered organizations, 7 honor societies, 3 religious organizations. **On-Campus Highlights:** Fidel Student Center, Skeen Library, Workman Center.

ADMISSIONS

Freshman Academic Profile: Average high school GPA 3.64. 35.9% in top 10% of high school class, 63.6% in top 25% of high school class, 85.6% in top 50% of high school class. 80% from public high schools. SAT Math middle 50% range 570-670. SAT Critical Reading middle 50% range 550-640. ACT middle 50% range 23-29. Minimum paper TOEFL 540. **Basis for Candidate Selection:** *Very important factors considered include:* academic GPA, rigor of secondary school record, standardized test scores. *Other factors considered include:* Class rank, extracurricular activities, talent/ability. **Freshman Admission Requirements:** High school diploma is required and GED is accepted. *Academic units required:* 4 English, 3 mathematics, 2 science, (2 science labs), 0 foreign language, 2 social studies, 1 history, 3 academic electives. **Freshman Admission Statistics:** 1,003 applied, 36% admitted, 79% enrolled. **Transfer Admission Requirements:** High school transcript, college transcript(s), statement of good standing from prior institution(s). Minimum college GPA of 2.0 required. Lowest grade transferable D. **General Admission Information:** Application Fee $15. Regular application deadline 8/1. Notification on a rolling basis, beginning on or about 3/1. Nonfall registration accepted. Admission may be deferred for a maximum of 1 year. Credit and/or placement offered for CEEB Advanced Placement tests.

COSTS AND FINANCIAL AID

Annual out-of-state tuition $17,226. Room and board $7,336. Required fees $958. Average book expense $1,066. **Required Forms and Deadlines:** FAFSA. **Notification of Awards:** Applicants will be notified of awards on a rolling basis beginning 4/1. **Types of Aid:** *Need-based scholarships/grants:* Federal Pell, SEOG, state scholarships/grants, private scholarships, the school's own gift aid. *Loans:* Subsidized Stafford, Unsubsidized Stafford, PLUS, Federal Perkins, state loans. *Student Employment:* Federal Work-Study Program available. Institutional employment available. Highest amount earned per year from on-campus jobs $3,500. Off-campus job opportunities are fair. **Financial Aid Statistics:** 61% freshmen, 63% undergrads receive need-based scholarship or grant aid. 83% freshmen, 71% undergrads receive non-need-based scholarship or grant aid. 50% freshmen, 62% undergrads receive need-based self-help aid. 0% freshmen, 0% undergrads receive athletic scholarships. 43% undergrads borrow to pay for school. Average cumulative indebtedness $19,367. **Criteria for awarding institutional aid:** *Non-need-based:* academics, alumni affiliation, minority status, state/district residency.

NEW MEXICO STATE UNIVERSITY

Box 30001, Las Cruces, NM 88003-8001
Phone: 575-646-3121
E-mail: admissions@nmsu.edu · **CEEB Code:** 4531
Fax: 575-646-6330 · **Website:** www.nmsu.edu · **ACT Code:** 2638

This public school was founded in 1888. It has a 900-acre campus.

RATINGS

Admissions Selectivity Rating: 78   **Fire Safety Rating:** 60*

STUDENTS AND FACULTY

Enrollment: 12,886. **Student Body:** 53% female, 47% male, 25% out-of-state, 4% international (72 countries represented). Asian 1%, African American 3%, Caucasian 32%, Hispanic 52%, Native American 2%
Retention and Graduation: 74% freshmen return for sophomore year. 16% freshmen graduate within 4 years. 46% freshmen graduate within 6 years.
Faculty: 699 full-time faculty, 89% hold PhDs, 44% are members of minority groups, 28% are women.

ACADEMICS

Degrees: associate, bachelor's, doctoral, master's, post-bachelor's certificate, post-master's certificate. **Classes:** Most classes have 20–29 students. Most lab/discussion sessions have 20–29 students. **Majors with Highest Enrollment:** Curriculum and Instruction; Electrical and Electronics Engineering; Business/Commerce. **Special Study Options:** Accelerated program, cooperative education program, cross-registration, distance learning, double major, dual enrollment, English as a Second Language (ESL), exchange student program (domestic), external degree program, honors program, independent study, internships, student-designed major, study abroad, teacher certification program, weekend college. **Disability Services:** Special programs offered to physically disabled students include note-taking services, reader services, tape recorders, tutors. **Career services:** alumni services, career/job search classes, career assessment, internships.

FACILITIES

Housing: Coed dorms, special housing for disabled students, men's dorms, women's dorms, fraternity/sorority housing, apartments for married students, apartments for single students. 95% of campus accessible to physically disabled. **Special Academic Facilities/Equipment:** University and art department museums, theatre, horse farm, sports medicine training clinic, observatory, electron microscope, CRAY supercomputer. **Computers:** Students can register for classes online. Administrative functions (other than registration) can be performed online.

CAMPUS LIFE

Environment: City. **Activities:** Choral groups, concert band, dance, drama/theater, jazz band, literary magazine, marching band, music ensembles, musical theater, opera, pep band, radio station, student government, student newspaper, symphony orchestra, television station, Campus Ministries. 263 registered organizations, 24 honor societies, 23 religious organizations. 14 fraternities, 5 sororities. **Athletics (Intercollegiate):** *Men:* baseball, basketball, cross-country, football, golf, tennis. *Women:* basketball, cross-country, golf, softball, swimming, tennis, track/field (outdoor), volleyball.

ADMISSIONS

Freshman Academic Profile: Average high school GPA 3.39. 21% in top 10% of high school class, 47% in top 25% of high school class, 80% in top 50% of high school class. SAT Math middle 50% range 430-530. SAT Critical Reading middle 50% range 410-540. SAT Writing middle 50% range 400-520. ACT middle 50% range 18-24. Minimum paper TOEFL 500. **Basis for Candidate Selection:** *Very important factors considered include:* rigor of secondary school record, standardized test scores. *Other factors considered include:* academic GPA. **Freshman Admission Requirements:** High school diploma is required and GED is accepted. *Academic units required:* 4 English, 3 mathematics, 2 science, (2 science labs), 1 foreign language. **Freshman Admission Statistics:** 5,362 applied, 85% admitted, 42% enrolled. **Transfer Admission Requirements:** college transcript(s), Minimum college GPA of 2.0 required. Lowest grade transferable C. **General Admission Information:** Application Fee $20. Nonfall registration accepted. Admission may be deferred for a maximum of 1 year. Credit offered for CEEB Advanced Placement tests.

COSTS AND FINANCIAL AID

Average book expense $1,084. **Required Forms and Deadlines:** FAFSA. **Notification of Awards:** Applicants will be notified of awards on or about 3/1. **Types of Aid:** *Need-based scholarships/grants:* the school's own gift aid. *Loans:* Subsidized Stafford, Unsubsidized Stafford, PLUS, Federal Perkins, college/university loans from institutional funds. *Student Employment:* Federal Work-Study Program available. Institutional employment available. Off-campus job opportunities are good. **Financial Aid Statistics:** 98% freshmen, 94% undergrads receive need-based scholarship or grant aid. 10% freshmen, 7% undergrads receive non-need-based scholarship or grant aid. 52% freshmen, 68% undergrads receive need-based self-help aid. 2% freshmen, 2% undergrads receive athletic scholarships. 55% undergrads borrow to pay for school. Average cumulative indebtedness $19,366. **Criteria for awarding institutional aid:** *Non-need-based:* academics, alumni affiliation, athletics, leadership, minority status, state/district residency.

THE NEW SCHOOL FOR JAZZ AND CONTEMPORARY MUSIC

55 W 13th St, New York, NY 10011
Phone: 212-229-5896 x4589 • **Financial Aid Phone:** 212-229-8930
E-mail: jazzadm@newschool.edu • **CEEB Code:** 2521
Fax: 212-229-8936 • **Website:** jazz.newschool.edu • **ACT Code:** 2828

This private school was founded in 1986.

RATINGS

Admissions Selectivity Rating: 84   Fire Safety Rating: 79

STUDENTS AND FACULTY

Enrollment: 269. **Student Body:** 19% female, 81% male, 74% out-of-state, 33% international (29 countries represented). Asian 3%, African American 9%, Caucasian 40%, Hispanic 7%, Native American %
Retention and Graduation: 58% freshmen graduate within 4 years. 3% grads go on to further study within 1 year. **Faculty:** 3 full-time faculty, 0% hold PhDs, 33% are members of minority groups, 33% are women. 0% of classes are taught by teaching assistants.

ACADEMICS

Degrees: bachelor's. **Classes:** Most classes have fewer than 10 students. **Majors with Highest Enrollment:** Jazz/Jazz Studies. **Special Study Options:** Accelerated program, cross-registration, dual enrollment, English as a Second Language (ESL), exchange student program (domestic), independent study, internships, study abroad, five year combined BA/BFA. **Combined degree programs:** BA/BFA. **Disability Services:** Special programs offered to physically disabled students include note-taking services, reader services, tape recorders. **Career services:** Alumni network, alumni services, career/job search classes, career assessment, internships, regional alumni.

FACILITIES

Housing: Coed dorms, special housing for disabled students, apartments for single students. 99% of campus accessible to physically disabled. **Computers:** 95% of classrooms, 100% of libraries, 100% of dining areas, na% of student union, 100% of common outdoor areas have wireless network access. Students can register for classes online. Administrative functions (other than registration) can be performed online.

CAMPUS LIFE

Environment: Metropolis. **Activities:** Choral groups, dance, drama/theater, jazz band, literary magazine, music ensembles, opera, radio station, student government, student newspaper, symphony orchestra, International Student Organization. 34 registered organizations. **On-Campus Highlights:** Jazz Center, University Welcome Center **Environmental Initiatives:** 1. In Fall 2010, The New School Facilities Management hired an engineering firm to conduct energy audits and to retro-commission five of the most energy-intensive owned buildings on campus. The result will be a phased capital plan to address needed upgrades in these buildings, equating to 500,000gsf, that will reduce carbon emissions. 2. The New School Office for Sustainability hired a consultant to conduct a waste audit of the entire campus in Fall 2009. A waste reduction strategy is currently being finalized. The immediate outcomes are new recycling signs and an enhanced post-consumer composting program in four buildings. Food scraps, napkins/paper towels and compostable cups and utensils will be collected in all food service locations plus a pilot location in a building with architecture and fine arts studios. The New School replaced two steam boilers, which were approximately 50 years old. Located in Johnson/Kaplan Hall, the universitys founding building, constructed in 1930, this boiler plant burned #6 heating oil, the dirtiest and most carbon-intensive heating oil. In the summer of 2010, Design, Construction, and Facilities Management upgraded the plant to house two new steam dual-fuel boilers with a thermal efficiency of 86 percent and the option to burn #2 heating oil or, eventually, natural gas, the least carbon intensive fossil fuel. This retrofit project also marks the phasing out of #6 heating oil on campus. In the summer of 2010, Design, Construction, and Facilities Management also replaced the roof at Johnson/Kaplan Hall with a white Thermoplastic Polyolefin (TPO) thermally bonded membrane with superior durability and an ENERGY STAR rating for its high reflectance. Insulation was also added to the roof. The new roof drastically reduces heat absorption in the summer months and also better insulates the building in the winter, resulting in lower cooling and heating loads and costs. Phasing out the use of T12 and incandescent lighting has been an ongoing initiative over the past two years and focused on 45 percent of the entire building portfolio (equivalent to 563,503 gross square feet, which represents nearly 72 percent of The New Schools owned buildings). In FY10, the Office for Sustainability began to install campus-wide (in all spaces where The New School has operational control) occupancy sensors in bathrooms, office kitchenettes, and conference rooms. By the end of FY12, the university will phase out T12s and incandescent lighting in all university-owned buildings and launch a LED lighting demonstration project.

ADMISSIONS

Freshman Academic Profile: Average high school GPA 3.23. 11.8% in top 10% of high school class, 41.18% in top 25% of high school class, 64.71% in top 50% of high school class. N/a% from public high schools. SAT Math middle 50% range 553-608. SAT Critical Reading middle 50% range 563-635. SAT Writing middle 50% range 528-588. Minimum internet-based TOEFL 79. **Basis for Candidate Selection:** *Very important factors considered include:* level of applicant's interest, talent/ability. *Important factors considered include:* rigor of secondary school record. *Other factors considered include:* application essay, academic GPA, recommendation(s), extracurricular activities. **Freshman Admission Requirements:** High school diploma is required and GED is accepted. **Freshman Admission Statistics:** 285 applied, 69% admitted, 25% enrolled. **Transfer Admission Requirements:** college transcript(s), essay or personal statement, Lowest grade transferable C. **General Admission Information:** Application Fee $100. Notification on a rolling basis, beginning on or about 4/1. Nonfall registration accepted.

COSTS AND FINANCIAL AID

Notification of Awards: Applicants will be notified of awards on a rolling basis beginning 3/1. **Types of Aid:** *Need-based scholarships/grants:* Federal Pell, SEOG, state scholarships/grants, private scholarships, the school's own gift aid. *Loans:* Subsidized Stafford, Unsubsidized Stafford, PLUS, Federal Perkins. *Student Employment:* Federal Work-Study Program available. Institutional employment available. Off-campus job opportunities are excellent. **Financial Aid Statistics:** 91% freshmen, 81% undergrads receive need-based scholarship or grant aid. 4% freshmen, 5% undergrads receive non-need-based scholarship or grant aid. 91% freshmen, 84% undergrads receive need-based self-help aid. 0% freshmen, 0% undergrads receive athletic scholarships. 69% undergrads borrow to pay for school. Average cumulative indebtedness $14,475. **Criteria for awarding institutional aid:** *Non-need-based:* academics, music/drama.

NEW WORLD SCHOOL OF THE ARTS

300 NE 2nd Avenue, Miami, FL 33132
Phone: 305-237-7007
E-mail: nwsaadm@mdc.edu
Fax: 305-237-3794 • **Website:** www.mdc.edu/nwsa

This public school was founded in 1984. It has a 2-acre campus.

RATINGS

Admissions Selectivity Rating: 60*   **Fire Safety Rating:** 60*

STUDENTS AND FACULTY

Enrollment: 359. **Student Body:** 52% female, 48% male, 17% out-of-state, 0% international (17 countries represented). Asian 4%, African American 11%, Caucasian 31%, Hispanic 51%, Native American <1%
Retention and Graduation: 50% grads pursue arts and sciences degrees. **Faculty:** 20 full-time faculty, 100% hold PhDs, 35% are members of minority groups, 20% are women. 0% of classes are taught by teaching assistants.

ACADEMICS

Degrees: associate, bachelor's. **Majors with Highest Enrollment:** Dance; Graphic Design. **Special Study Options:** cooperative education program, distance learning, English as a Second Language (ESL), independent study, liberal arts/career combination.

FACILITIES

Housing: 100% of campus accessible to physically disabled. **Special Academic Facilities/Equipment:** black box theater art gallery dance recital hall **Computers:** Students can register for classes online. Administrative functions (other than registration) can be performed online.

CAMPUS LIFE

Environment: Metropolis. **Activities:** dance, drama/theater, music ensembles, musical theater, opera, student government, symphony orchestra.

ADMISSIONS

Freshman Academic Profile: 99% from public high schools. Minimum paper TOEFL 550. **Basis for Candidate Selection:** *Very important factors considered include:* talent/ability. *Other factors considered include:* application essay, recommendation(s), rigor of secondary school record, character/personal qualities, interview. **Freshman Admission Requirements:** High school diploma is required and GED is accepted. **Transfer Admission Requirements:** High school transcript, college transcript(s), essay or personal statement, interview, Lowest grade transferable C. **General Admission Information:** Nonfall

registration not accepted. Credit and/or placement offered for CEEB Advanced Placement tests.

COSTS AND FINANCIAL AID

Average book expense $600. **Required Forms and Deadlines:** FAFSA. **Types of Aid:** *Need-based scholarships/grants:* Federal Pell, SEOG, state scholarships/grants, private scholarships, the school's own gift aid. *Loans:* Direct Subsidized Stafford, Direct Unsubsidized Stafford, Direct PLUS, PLUS, Federal Perkins, state loans, college/university loans from institutional funds. *Student Employment:* Federal Work-Study Program available. Off-campus job opportunities are excellent. **Criteria for awarding institutional aid:** *Non-need-based:* art, music/drama.

NEW YORK INSTITUTE OF TECHNOLOGY

PO Box 8000, Old Westbury, NY 11568
Phone: 516-686-7520
E-mail: admissions@nyit.edu • **CEEB Code:** 2561
Fax: 516-686-7613 • **Website:** www.nyit.edu • **ACT Code:** 2832

This private school was founded in 1955. It has a 525-acre campus.

RATINGS

Admissions Selectivity Rating: 72   **Fire Safety Rating:** 69

STUDENTS AND FACULTY

Enrollment: 5,141. **Student Body:** 38% female, 62% male, 10% out-of-state, 7% international. Asian 10%, African American 11%, Caucasian 33%, Hispanic 10%, Native American <1%
Retention and Graduation: 71% freshmen return for sophomore year. 14% freshmen graduate within 4 years. 32% freshmen graduate within 6 years. 29% grads go on to further study within 1 year. 21% grads pursue arts and sciences degrees. 1% grads pursue law degrees. 33% grads pursue business degrees. 2% grads pursue medical degrees. **Faculty:** 218 full-time faculty, 89% hold PhDs, 23% are members of minority groups, 22% are women. 0% of classes are taught by teaching assistants.

ACADEMICS

Degrees: associate, bachelor's, certificate, first professional, master's, post-bachelor's certificate, post-master's certificate, terminal associate, transfer associate. **Classes:** Most classes have 10–19 students. Most lab/discussion sessions have 10–19 students. **Majors with Highest Enrollment:** Speech Communication and Rhetoric; Business, Management, Marketing, and Related Support Services. **Special Study Options:** Accelerated program, cooperative education program, cross-registration, distance learning, double major, dual enrollment, English as a Second Language (ESL), honors program, independent study, internships, liberal arts/career combination, study abroad, teacher certification program, weekend college, Combined bachelor's/professional degree program in Life Sciences (BS)/Osteopathic Medicine (DO); Architectural Technology (BS)/ Energy Managment (MS); Architectural Technology (BS)/MBA; Mechanical Engineering (BS)/Energy Managment (MS); Life Sciences (BS)/Physical Therapy (MS) Life Sciences (BS)/Occupational Therapy (MS); Behavioral Sciences (BS)/Law at Touro Law Center (JD). **Combined degree programs:** BA/JD, BA/MA, BS/MS, BS/MBA. **Disability Services:** Special programs offered to physically disabled students include tutors. **Career services:** Alumni network, alumni services, career/job search classes, career assessment, internships, regional alumni.

FACILITIES

Housing: Coed dorms, special housing for international students, fraternity/sorority housing, apartments for single students, Housing for graduate, life sciences, first-year experience, student leaders, student government, international, Greek Life organizations and architecture students provided. For the Manhattan Campus, housing is available off-campus. 100% of campus accessible to physically disabled. **Special Academic Facilities/Equipment:** Center for Urban/Suburban Studies; Center for Neighborhood Revitalization; Parkinson's Disease Treatment Center; Center for Energy Policy and Research; Academic Computing Labs; Center for Labor and Industrial Relations; Carleton Group (Advertising) LI News Tonight; Education Enterprise Zone; Center for Teaching and Learning with Technology, Production House, Motion Graphics Laboratory; Academic Health Care Center; Center for Business Information Technologies; de Seversky Culinary Arts Center. **Computers:** Students can register for classes online. Administrative functions (other than registration) can be performed online. Undergraduates are required to own a computer.

CAMPUS LIFE

Environment: Village. **Activities:** Choral groups, dance, drama/theater, literary magazine, musical theater, radio station, student government, student newspaper, student-run film society, television station, yearbook. 100 registered organizations, 14 honor societies, 4 religious organizations. 5 fraternities, 3 sororities. **Athletics (Intercollegiate):** *Men:* baseball, basketball, cross-country, lacrosse, soccer, track/field (outdoor). *Women:* basketball, cross-country, soccer, softball, track/field (outdoor), volleyball. **On-Campus Highlights:** Libraries, Computer clusters, Radio/Television studios, CAD rooms, Motion Graphics Laboratory, Enginnering labs, Allied Health facilities, de Seversky Culinary Arts Center.

ADMISSIONS

Freshman Academic Profile: Average high school GPA 3.1. 0% in top 10% of high school class, 0% in top 25% of high school class, 0% in top 50% of high school class. 60% from public high schools. SAT Math middle 50% range 510-630. SAT Critical Reading middle 50% range 470-580. ACT middle 50% range 20-27. Minimum paper TOEFL 550. **Basis for Candidate Selection:** *Very important factors considered include:* rigor of secondary school record. *Important factors considered include:* application essay, standardized test scores, interview. *Other factors considered include:* Class rank, recommendation(s), character/personal qualities, extracurricular activities, talent/ability, volunteer work, work experience. **Freshman Admission Requirements:** High school diploma is required and GED is accepted. *Academic units required:* 4 English, 2 mathematics, 1 science, (1 science labs), 2 social studies, 7 academic electives. **Freshman Admission Statistics:** 3,511 applied, 76% admitted, 33% enrolled. **Transfer Admission Requirements:** college transcript(s), essay or personal statement, Minimum college GPA of 2.0 required. Lowest grade transferable C-. **General Admission Information:** Application Fee $50. Notification on a rolling basis, beginning on or about 1/1. Nonfall registration accepted. Admission may be deferred for a maximum of 1 year. Credit and/or placement offered for CEEB Advanced Placement tests.

COSTS AND FINANCIAL AID

Annual tuition $16,926. Room and board $7,780. Required fees $300. Average book expense $1,200. **Required Forms and Deadlines:** FAFSA. **Notification of Awards:** Applicants will be notified of awards on a rolling basis beginning 3/15. **Types of Aid:** *Need-based scholarships/grants:* Federal Pell, SEOG, state scholarships/grants, private scholarships, the school's own gift aid. *Loans:* Subsidized Stafford, Unsubsidized Stafford, PLUS, Federal Perkins, Federal Nursing, Alternative loans. *Student Employment:* Federal Work-Study Program available. Institutional employment available. Highest amount earned per year from on-campus jobs $2,200. Off-campus job opportunities are good. **Financial Aid Statistics:** 66% freshmen, 85% undergrads receive need-based scholarship or grant aid. 73% freshmen, 68% undergrads receive non-need-based scholarship or grant aid. 88% freshmen, 89% undergrads receive need-based self-help aid. 5% freshmen, 5% undergrads receive athletic scholarships. 75% undergrads borrow to pay for school. **Criteria for awarding institutional aid:** *Non-need-based:* academics, alumni affiliation, athletics.

NEW YORK SCHOOL OF INTERIOR DESIGN

170 East 70th Street, New York, NY 10021
Phone: 212-472-1500 · **Financial Aid Phone:** 212-472-1500 x212
E-mail: admissions@nysid.edu · **CEEB Code:** 333
Fax: 212-472-1867 · **ACT Code:** 2829

This private school was founded in 1916.

RATINGS

Admissions Selectivity Rating: 83   Fire Safety Rating: 60*

STUDENTS AND FACULTY

Enrollment: 429. **Student Body:** 88% female, 12% male, 33% out-of-state, 16% international. Asian 7%, African American 3%, Caucasian 49%, Hispanic 8%, Native American <1%
Faculty: 8 full-time faculty, 88% hold PhDs, 50% are members of minority groups. 0% of classes are taught by teaching assistants.

ACADEMICS

Degrees: associate, bachelor's, certificate, first professional, master's, transfer associate. **Classes:** Most classes have 10–19 students. **Majors with Highest Enrollment:** Interior Design. **Special Study Options:** independent study, internships, study abroad. **Disability Services:** Special programs offered to physically disabled students include tutors. **Career services:** Alumni network, alumni services, internships,

FACILITIES

Housing: 100% of campus accessible to physically disabled. **Special Academic Facilities/Equipment:** Three galleries, lighting laboratory, student atelier.

CAMPUS LIFE

Environment: Metropolis. **Activities:** 1 registered organization.

ADMISSIONS

Freshman Academic Profile: Average high school GPA 3. 0% in top 10% of high school class, 9% in top 25% of high school class, 55% in top 50% of high school class. SAT Math middle 50% range 450-600. SAT Critical Reading middle 50% range 440-570. SAT Writing middle 50% range 430-540. ACT middle 50% range 20-24. Minimum internet-based TOEFL 79. Minimum paper TOEFL 550. **Basis for Candidate Selection:** *Very important factors considered include:* application essay, rigor of secondary school record. *Important factors considered include:* academic GPA, recommendation(s), level of applicant's interest. *Other factors considered include:* Class rank, standardized test scores, alumni/ae relation, character/personal qualities, extracurricular activities, interview, work experience. **Freshman Admission Requirements:** High school diploma is required and GED is accepted. **Freshman Admission Statistics:** 156 applied, 38% admitted, 59% enrolled. **Transfer Admission Requirements:** High school transcript, college transcript(s), essay or personal statement, Minimum college GPA of 3.0 required. Lowest grade transferable C. **General Admission Information:** Application Fee $50. Regular notification 4/1. Nonfall registration accepted. Admission may be deferred for a maximum of 1 year. Credit offered for CEEB Advanced Placement tests.

COSTS AND FINANCIAL AID

Annual tuition $28,413. Required fees $570. Average book expense $1,000. **Required Forms and Deadlines:** FAFSA, Institution's own financial aid form, State aid form. **Notification of Awards:** Applicants will be notified of awards on a rolling basis beginning 2/1. **Types of Aid:** *Need-based scholarships/grants:* Federal Pell, SEOG, state scholarships/grants, the school's own gift aid. *Loans:* Subsidized Stafford, Unsubsidized Stafford, PLUS. *Student Employment:* Federal Work-Study Program available. Off-campus job opportunities are excellent. **Financial Aid Statistics:** 100% freshmen, 79% undergrads receive need-based scholarship or grant aid. 0% freshmen, 1% undergrads receive non-need-based scholarship or grant aid. 92% freshmen, 91% undergrads receive need-based self-help aid. 0% freshmen, 0% undergrads receive athletic scholarships. 67% undergrads borrow to pay for school. Average cumulative indebtedness $35,502.

NEW YORK UNIVERSITY

665 Broadway, New York, NY 10012
Phone: 212-998-4500 · **Financial Aid Phone:** 212-998-4444
E-mail: admissions@nyu.edu · **CEEB Code:** 2562
Fax: 212-995-4902 · **Website:** www.nyu.edu · **ACT Code:** 2838

This private school was founded in 1831.

RATINGS

Admissions Selectivity Rating: 93   Fire Safety Rating: 97

STUDENTS AND FACULTY

Enrollment: 24,539. **Student Body:** 57% female, 43% male, 64% out-of-state, 15% international (139 countries represented). Asian 20%, African American 5%, Caucasian 36%, Hispanic 12%, Native American <1%
Retention and Graduation: 92% freshmen return for sophomore year. 72% freshmen graduate within 4 years. 83% freshmen graduate within 6 years. 15% grads go on to further study within 1 year. 1% grads pursue arts and sciences degrees. 2% grads pursue law degrees. 1% grads pursue business degrees. 3% grads pursue medical degrees. **Faculty:** 2,843 full-time faculty, 72% hold PhDs, 41% are members of minority groups, 24% are women.

ACADEMICS

Degrees: associate, bachelor's, certificate, diploma, doctoral, master's, post-bachelor's certificate, post-master's certificate, terminal associate, transfer associate. **Classes:** Most classes have 10–19 students. Most lab/discussion sessions have 10–19 students. **Majors with Highest Enrollment:** Liberal Arts and Sciences/Liberal Studies; Drama and Dramatics/Theatre Arts; Business/Commerce. **Special Study Options:** cross-registration, distance learning, double major, English as a Second Language (ESL), exchange student program (domestic), honors program, independent study, internships, liberal arts/career combination, student-designed major, study abroad, teacher certification program, Exchange program with several historically black colleges. **Combined degree programs:** BA/DDS. **Disability Services:** Special programs offered to physically disabled students include note-taking services, reader services, tape recorders. **Career services:** Alumni network, alumni services, career/

job search classes, career assessment, internships, regional alumni. Career services highlights include multiple opportunites for students to advance their entrepreneurial learning through course work, business planning competitions, workshops, mentoring and coaching.

FACILITIES

Housing: Coed dorms, special housing for disabled students, fraternity/sorority housing, apartments for single students, Wellness Housing, Theme Housing Choices: Substance Free Communities; FYRE: First Year Residential Experience; Sophomore Year Residential Experience; Explorations Learning Communities; Mixed Sex Housing. 95% of campus accessible to physically disabled. **Special Academic Facilities/Equipment:** Bobst Library and study center; Grey Art Gallery and study center; Special academic facilities for arts, business, culture, education, international relations, language, law, media, music, public service, research, and social policy, and Skirball Center for Performing Arts. **Computers:** 70% of classrooms, 100% of libraries, 100% of dining areas, 100% of student union, 50% of common outdoor areas have wireless network access. Students can register for classes online. Administrative functions (other than registration) can be performed online.

CAMPUS LIFE

Environment: Metropolis. **Activities:** Choral groups, concert band, dance, drama/theater, jazz band, literary magazine, music ensembles, musical theater, opera, pep band, radio station, student government, student newspaper, student-run film society, symphony orchestra, television station, yearbook, Campus Ministries, International Student Organization, Model UN. 407 registered organizations, 3 honor societies, 31 religious organization. 14 fraternities, 10 sororities. **Athletics (Intercollegiate):** *Men:* basketball, cross-country, diving, fencing, golf, soccer, swimming, tennis, track/field (outdoor), track/field (indoor), volleyball, wrestling. *Women:* basketball, cross-country, diving, fencing, golf, soccer, swimming, tennis, track/field (outdoor), track/field (indoor), volleyball. **On-Campus Highlights:** Kimmel Center for Student Life, Silver Center for Arts and Science, Coles Athletic Center, Palladium Athletic Facility, Skirball Center for the Performing Arts. **Environmental Initiatives:** Reduce Energy Intensity: NYU will reduce the amount of energy used in buildings through conservation, "green" construction and renovation, retrofits and upgrades, and operational innovations to run buildings more effectively. Initial efforts have already resulted in 20% emissions cuts. Generate and Use Cleaner Energy: NYU will generate cleaner energy on-site with a new cogeneration power plant, which will mitigate 23 percent of NYU's baseline FY 2006 emissions. NYU will also minimize the use of fuel oil to heat buildings, replacing it with cleaner, more efficient energy sources. Generate Renewable Energy & Reduce/Offset Remaining Emissions: NYU is exploring options to develop on-site distributed renewable energy generation projects on its buildings, including wind and solar technologies. Given the constraints of a dense urban environment, it is likely that NYU will purchase high-quality, credible offsets to accomplish long-term climate goals.

ADMISSIONS

Freshman Academic Profile: Average high school GPA 3.7. 59% from public high schools. SAT Math middle 50% range 630-740. SAT Critical Reading middle 50% range 610-710. SAT Writing middle 50% range 620-720. ACT middle 50% range 28-32. Minimum internet-based TOEFL 100. **Basis for Candidate Selection:** *Very important factors considered include:* application essay, academic GPA, recommendation(s), rigor of secondary school record, standardized test scores, extracurricular activities, talent/ability. *Important factors considered include:* Class rank, alumni/ae relation, character/personal qualities, first generation, geographical residence. *Other factors considered include:* racial/ethnic status, volunteer work, work experience. **Freshman Admission Requirements:** High school diploma is required and GED is accepted. *Academic units required:* 4 English, 3 mathematics, 3 science, 2 foreign language, 4 history. **Freshman Admission Statistics:** 50,804 applied, 35% admitted, 33% enrolled. **Transfer Admission Requirements:** High school transcript, college transcript(s), essay or personal statement, statement of good standing from prior institution(s). Lowest grade transferable C. **General Admission Information:** Application Fee $65. Early decision application deadline 11/1. Regular application deadline 1/1. Regular notification 4/1. Nonfall registration not accepted. Admission may be deferred for a maximum of 12 months. Credit offered for CEEB Advanced Placement tests.

COSTS AND FINANCIAL AID

Average book expense $1,070. **Required Forms and Deadlines:** FAFSA, CSS/Financial Aid PROFILE, Noncustodial PROFILE. **Notification of Awards:** Applicants will be notified of awards on a rolling basis beginning 4/1. **Types of Aid:** *Need-based scholarships/grants:* Federal Pell, SEOG, state scholarships/grants, private scholarships, the school's own gift aid. *Loans:* Subsidized Stafford, Unsubsidized Stafford, PLUS, Federal Perkins, Federal Nursing. *Student Employment:* Federal Work-Study Program available. Institutional employment available. Highest amount earned per year from on-campus jobs $24,026. Off-campus job opportunities are excellent. **Criteria for awarding institutional aid:** *Non-need-based:* academics.

See page 1102.

NEWBERRY COLLEGE

2100 College Street, Newberry, SC 29108
Phone: 803-321-5127
E-mail: admissions@newberry.edu • **CEEB Code:** 5493
Fax: 803-321-5138 • **Website:** www.newberry.edu • **ACT Code:** 3870

This private school, affiliated with the Lutheran Church, was founded in 1856. It has a 60-acre campus.

RATINGS

Admissions Selectivity Rating: 70   **Fire Safety Rating:** 63

STUDENTS AND FACULTY

Enrollment: 764. **Student Body:** 43% female, 57% male, 25% out-of-state, 2% international (8 countries represented). Asian 0%, African American 27%, Caucasian 71%, Hispanic 1%, Native American 1% **Retention and Graduation:** 58% freshmen return for sophomore year. 36% freshmen graduate within 4 years. 49% freshmen graduate within 6 years. 15% grads go on to further study within 1 year. **Faculty:** 46 full-time faculty, 61% hold PhDs, 37% are members of minority groups, 9% are women. 0% of classes are taught by teaching assistants.

ACADEMICS

Degrees: bachelor's. **Classes:** Most classes have fewer than 10 students. Most lab/discussion sessions have 20–29 students. **Majors with Highest Enrollment:** Speech Communication and Rhetoric; Elementary Education and Teaching; Business/Commerce. **Special Study Options:** cooperative education program, double major, dual enrollment, honors program, independent study, internships, liberal arts/career combination, student-designed major, study abroad, teacher certification program. **Honors programs:** Summerland Honors Program- Focus is on human identity-honors credit may substitute for cored curriculum. **Disability Services:** Special programs offered to physically disabled students include tutors. **Career services:** alumni services, career/job search classes, internships.

FACILITIES

Housing: Coed dorms, men's dorms, women's dorms. 90% of campus accessible to physically disabled. **Special Academic Facilities/Equipment:** TV Studio.

CAMPUS LIFE

Environment: Rural. **Activities:** Choral groups, concert band, drama/theater, jazz band, literary magazine, marching band, music ensembles, radio station, student government, student newspaper, television station, yearbook. 50 registered organizations, 11 honor society, 4 religious organizations. 5 fraternities, 4 sororities. **Athletics (Intercollegiate):** *Men:* baseball, basketball, cross-country, football, golf, soccer, tennis. *Women:* basketball, cheerleading, cross-country, golf, soccer, softball, tennis, volleyball. **On-Campus Highlights:** The Quad-grassy lawln area, Steele Student Center-snack bar, game room, Fitness Center in Physical Education Complex, John F. Clarkson Swimming Pool, Weber Ministries House.

ADMISSIONS

Freshman Academic Profile: Average high school GPA 3.2. 7% in top 10% of high school class, 22% in top 25% of high school class, 61% in top 50% of high school class. 88% from public high schools. SAT Math middle 50% range 460-600. SAT Critical Reading middle 50% range 490-570. ACT middle 50% range 17-22. Minimum paper TOEFL 525. **Basis for Candidate Selection:** *Very important factors considered include:* rigor of secondary school record, standardized test scores. *Important factors considered include:* Class rank. *Other factors considered include:* application essay, recommendation(s), alumni/ae relation, character/personal qualities, extracurricular activities, geographical residence, interview, racial/ethnic status, religious affiliation/commitment, state residency, talent/ability, volunteer work, work experience. **Freshman Admission Requirements:** High school diploma is required and GED is accepted. *Academic units required:* 4 English, 3 mathematics, 2 science, (2 science labs), 2 foreign language, 2 social studies, 1 history, 1 academic electives. **Freshman Admission Statistics:** applied, % admitted, 41% enrolled. **Transfer Admission Requirements:** college transcript(s), Minimum college GPA of 2.0 required. Lowest grade transferable C. **General Admission Information:** Application Fee $30. Notification on a rolling basis, beginning on or about 9/30. Nonfall registration accepted. Admission may be deferred for a maximum of 2 years. Credit and/or placement offered for CEEB Advanced Placement tests.

COSTS AND FINANCIAL AID

Annual tuition $17,470. Room and board $5,890. Required fees $631. Average book expense $1,195. **Required Forms and Deadlines:** FAFSA, Institution's own financial aid form. **Types of Aid:** *Need-based scholarships/grants:* Federal Pell, SEOG, state scholarships/grants, private scholarships, the school's own gift aid. *Loans:* Subsidized Stafford, Unsubsidized Stafford, PLUS, Federal Perkins, state loans. *Student Employment:* Federal Work-Study Program available. Institutional employment available. Off-campus job opportunities are poor. **Financial Aid Statistics:** 100% freshmen, 99% undergrads receive need-based scholarship or grant aid. 24% freshmen, 22% undergrads receive non-need-based scholarship or grant aid. 68% freshmen, 69% undergrads receive need-based self-help aid. 16% freshmen, 11% undergrads receive athletic scholarships. 98% undergrads borrow to pay for school. **Criteria for awarding institutional aid:** *Non-need-based:* academics, alumni affiliation, athletics, music/drama, religious affiliation, state/district residency.

NEWMAN UNIVERSITY

3100 McCormick Avenue, Wichita, KS 67213-2097
Phone: 316-942-4291
E-mail: admissions@newmanu.edu · **CEEB Code:** 6615
Fax: 316-942-4483 · **Website:** www.newmanu.edu • **ACT Code:** 1452

This private school, affiliated with the Roman Catholic Church, was founded in 1933. It has a 53-acre campus.

RATINGS
Admissions Selectivity Rating: 61   **Fire Safety Rating:** 60*

STUDENTS AND FACULTY
Enrollment: 1,843. **Student Body:** 62% female, 38% male, 11% out-of-state, 6% international (26 countries represented). Asian 3%, African American 5%, Caucasian 77%, Hispanic 7%, Native American 2%
Faculty: 66 full-time faculty. 0% of classes are taught by teaching assistants.

ACADEMICS
Degrees: associate, bachelor's, master's, terminal associate, transfer associate. **Classes:** Most classes have 10–19 students. Most lab/discussion sessions have 10–19 students. **Special Study Options:** cooperative education program, cross-registration, distance learning, double major, dual enrollment, independent study, internships, liberal arts/career combination, student-designed major, study abroad, teacher certification program, weekend college. **Disability Services:** Special programs offered to physically disabled students include note-taking services, reader services, tape recorders, tutors.

FACILITIES
Housing: Coed dorms, special housing for disabled students, apartments for married students, apartments for single students, Freshmen required to live in college housng first 2 years if not living with parents. 95% of campus accessible to physically disabled. **Special Academic Facilities/Equipment:** Cadaver lab; art gallery.

CAMPUS LIFE
Activities: Choral groups, drama/theater, literary magazine, radio station, student government, student newspaper. 25 registered organizations, 3 honor societies, 2 religious organizations. **Athletics (Intercollegiate):** *Men:* baseball, basketball, golf, soccer. *Women:* basketball, golf, soccer, softball, volleyball.

ADMISSIONS
Freshman Academic Profile: Average high school GPA 3.35. 12% in top 10% of high school class, 26% in top 25% of high school class, 52% in top 50% of high school class. 78% from public high schools. Minimum paper TOEFL 530. **Basis for Candidate Selection:** *Very important factors considered include:* rigor of secondary school record, standardized test scores. *Other factors considered include:* recommendation(s). **Freshman Admission Requirements:** High school diploma is required and GED is accepted. **Transfer Admission Requirements:** college transcript(s), Minimum college GPA of 2.0 required. Lowest grade transferable D. **General Admission Information:** Application Fee $20. Notification on a rolling basis, beginning on or about 6/1. Nonfall registration accepted. Admission may be deferred for a maximum of 2 years. Credit offered for CEEB Advanced Placement tests.

COSTS AND FINANCIAL AID
Average book expense $800. **Required Forms and Deadlines:** FAFSA, Institution's own financial aid form. **Notification of Awards:** Applicants will be notified of awards on a rolling basis beginning 1/2. **Types of Aid:** *Need-based scholarships/grants:* Federal Pell, SEOG, state scholarships/grants, private scholarships, the school's own gift aid. *Loans:* Subsidized Stafford, Unsubsidized Stafford, PLUS, Federal Perkins. *Student Employment:* Highest amount earned per year from on-campus jobs $1,200. **Financial Aid Statistics:** 79% freshmen, 79% undergrads receive need-based scholarship or grant aid. 82% freshmen, 47% undergrads receive non-need-based scholarship or grant aid. 73% freshmen, 80% undergrads receive need-based self-help aid. 36% freshmen, 29% undergrads receive athletic scholarships. 69% undergrads borrow to pay for

school. **Criteria for awarding institutional aid:** *Non-need-based:* academics, alumni affiliation, athletics, leadership, minority status, music/drama, religious affiliation.

NIAGARA UNIVERSITY

Gacioch Family Center, Niagara University, NY 14109
Phone: 716-286-8700 · **Financial Aid Phone:** 716-286-8669
E-mail: admissions@niagara.edu · **CEEB Code:** 2558
Fax: 716-286-8710 · **Website:** www.niagara.edu • **ACT Code:** 2842

This private school, affiliated with the Roman Catholic Church, was founded in 1856. It has a 160-acre campus.

RATINGS
Admissions Selectivity Rating: 83   **Fire Safety Rating:** 76

STUDENTS AND FACULTY
Enrollment: 3,130. **Student Body:** 61% female, 39% male, 9% out-of-state, 9% international (24 countries represented). Asian 2%, African American 6%, Caucasian 71%, Hispanic 4%, Native American 1%
Retention and Graduation: 84% freshmen return for sophomore year. 59% freshmen graduate within 4 years. 32% grads go on to further study within 1 year. 9% grads pursue arts and sciences degrees. 1% grads pursue law degrees. 10% grads pursue business degrees. 1% grads pursue medical degrees. **Faculty:** Student/faculty ratio :1. 157 full-time faculty, 91% hold PhDs, 40% are are members of minority groups, 17% are women. 0% of classes are taught by teaching assistants.

ACADEMICS
Degrees: associate, bachelor's, certificate, master's, post-bachelor's certificate, post-master's certificate. **Classes:** Most classes have 10-19 students. Most lab/discussion sessions have 10-19 students. **Majors with Highest Enrollment:** Teacher Education, Multiple Levels; Criminal Justice/Law Enforcement Administration; Business/Commerce. **Special Study Options:** Accelerated program, cooperative education program, cross-registration, double major, dual enrollment, English as a Second Language (ESL), exchange student program (domestic), honors program, independent study, internships, liberal arts/career combination, study abroad, teacher certification program. **Combined degree programs:** BA/MA, BBA/MBA. **Disability Services:** Special programs offered to physically disabled students include note-taking services, reader services, tape recorders, tutors. **Career services:** Alumni network, career/job search classes, career assessment, internships, regional alumni. Career services highlights include a cooperative educaton experience that enables students to explore the world of work firsthand by providing a unique oportunity for them to earn while they learn. Students majoring in liberal arts, business or hospitality are eligible to particiapte in the co-op program in their junior or senior year, enabling them to gain academic credit as well as paid work experiences in their majors.

FACILITIES
Housing: Coed dorms, apartments for single students. **Special Academic Facilities/Equipment:** Castellani Art Museum. **Computers:** Students can register for classes online.

CAMPUS LIFE
Environment: Town. **Activities:** Choral groups, dance, drama/theater, musical theater, radio station, student government, student newspaper, yearbook, Campus Ministries, International Student Organization. 70 registered organizations, 14 honor societies, 2 religious organizations. 3 fraternities, 2 sororities. **Athletics (Intercollegiate):** *Men:* baseball, basketball, cross-country, diving, golf, ice hockey, soccer, swimming, tennis. *Women:* basketball, cross-country, diving, golf, ice hockey, lacrosse, soccer, softball, swimming, tennis, volleyball. **On-Campus Highlights:** Gallagher Center, St.Vincent's Hall, Castellani Art Museum, Clet Hall, Dwyer Arena, Student Apartments. **Environmental Initiatives:** 60000 sq. ft. academic complex opened in Fall 2007 is LEED certifiable. 98% of the university's electricity is hydro-non carbon based. 50000 sq. ft. science complex opened in Fall 2013 is LEED certifiable.

ADMISSIONS
Freshman Academic Profile: 19% in top 10% of high school class, 44% in top 25% of high school class, 76% in top 50% of high school class. 95% from public high schools. SAT Math middle 50% range 480-570. SAT Critical Reading middle 50% range 460-560. SAT Writing middle 50% range -. ACT middle 50% range 20-25. Minimum internet-based TOEFL 79. Minimum paper TOEFL 500. **Basis for Candidate Selection:** *Very important factors considered include:* rigor of secondary school record. *Important factors considered include:* recommendation(s), standardized test scores, interview. *Other factors considered include:* Class rank, application essay, alumni/ae relation,

character/personal qualities, extracurricular activities, talent/ability, volunteer work. **Freshman Admission Requirements:** High school diploma is required and GED is accepted. *Academic units required:* 4 English, 2 mathematics, 2 science, 2 foreign language, 2 social studies, 4 academic electives. **Freshman Admission Statistics:** 3,565 applied, 66% admitted, 26% enrolled. **Transfer Admission Requirements:** High school transcript, college transcript(s), Minimum college GPA of 2.0 required. Lowest grade transferable C. **General Admission Information:** Application Fee $30. Regular application deadline 8/1. Nonfall registration accepted. Admission may be deferred for a maximum of 12. Credit offered for CEEB Advanced Placement tests.

COSTS AND FINANCIAL AID

Annual tuition $27,700. Room and board $11,950. Required fees $1,560. Average book expense $1,050. **Required Forms and Deadlines:** FAFSA, State aid form. **Notification of Awards:** Applicants will be notified of awards on a rolling basis beginning 3/1. **Types of Aid:** *Need-based scholarships/grants:* Federal Pell, SEOG, state scholarships/grants, private scholarships, the school's own gift aid. *Loans:* Direct Subsidized Stafford, Direct Unsubsidized Stafford, Direct PLUS, Federal Perkins, Federal Nursing, state loans, college/university loans from institutional funds. *Student Employment:* Federal Work-Study Program available. Highest amount earned per year from on-campus jobs $1,800. Off-campus job opportunities are excellent. **Financial Aid Statistics:** 99% freshmen, 98% undergrads receive need-based scholarship or grant aid. 82% freshmen, 77% undergrads receive non-need-based scholarship or grant aid. 81% freshmen, 80% undergrads receive need-based self-help aid. 0% freshmen, 4% undergrads receive athletic scholarships. 98% freshmen, 94% undergrads receive any aid. 72% undergrads borrow to pay for school. Average cumulative indebtedness $25,976. **Criteria for awarding institutional aid:** *Non-need-based:* academics, athletics.

See page 1104.

NICHOLLS STATE UNIVERSITY

P.O. Box 2004, Thibodaux, LA 70310
Phone: 985-448-4507 · **Financial Aid Phone:** 985-448-4048
E-mail: nicholls@nicholls.edu · **CEEB Code:** 6221
Fax: 985-448-4929 · **Website:** www.nicholls.edu · **ACT Code:** 1580

This public school was founded in 1948. It has a 210-acre campus.

RATINGS

Admissions Selectivity Rating: 76   **Fire Safety Rating:** 77

STUDENTS AND FACULTY

Enrollment: 6,246. **Student Body:** 61% female, 39% male, 4% out-of-state, 2% international (40 countries represented). Asian 1%, African American 18%, Caucasian 73%, Hispanic 1%, Native American 2%
Faculty: 295 full-time faculty, 54% hold PhDs, 51% are members of minority groups, 11% are women. 1% of classes are taught by teaching assistants.

ACADEMICS

Degrees: associate, bachelor's, certificate, master's, post-master's certificate. **Classes:** Most classes have 20–29 students. **Majors with Highest Enrollment:** General Studies; Registered Nursing/Registered Nurse; Business Administration and Management. **Special Study Options:** cooperative education program, cross-registration, distance learning, dual enrollment, honors program, independent study, internships, study abroad, teacher certification program. **Honors programs:** You can learn advanced material in small classes taught by outstanding professors. You can enrich your college experience through intellectually stimulating courses that allow you to reach your potential. The Honors Program invites all academically talented and intellectually curious students to participate. By joining the program you can become a select member of the campus community and associate with students who share similar goals and interests. The Program is designed to meet students' needs and interests. Therefore, students in the program determine their degree of involvement. You may take as many honors courses as you choose or simply successfully complete one-three hour honors course each year. And because honors classes fit degree requirements for all majors, participants graduate on time. **Combined degree programs:** BA/MA. **Disability Services:** Special programs offered to physically disabled students include note-taking services, reader services, tape recorders, tutors. **Career services:** Alumni network, alumni services, career/job search classes, career assessment, internships.

FACILITIES

Housing: special housing for disabled students, men's dorms, special housing for international students, women's dorms, apartments for married students, apartments for single students, Wellness Housing. **Special Academic Facilities/Equipment:** Ameen Art Gallery. **Computers:** 100% of classrooms, 100%

of dorms, 100% of libraries, 100% of dining areas, 100% of student union, 100% of common outdoor areas have wireless network access. Students can register for classes online. Administrative functions (other than registration) can be performed online.

CAMPUS LIFE

Environment: Village. **Activities:** Choral groups, concert band, dance, drama/theater, jazz band, literary magazine, marching band, music ensembles, musical theater, radio station, student government, student newspaper, student-run film society, television station, yearbook. 121 registered organizations, 24 honor societies, 6 religious organizations. 10 fraternities, 5 sororities. **Athletics (Intercollegiate):** *Men:* baseball, basketball, cross-country, football, golf, tennis. *Women:* basketball, cross-country, golf, soccer, softball, tennis, track/field (outdoor), track/field (indoor), volleyball. **On-Campus Highlights:** Admissions Office, Student Union, Ellender Memorial Library, Guidry Stadium.

ADMISSIONS

Freshman Academic Profile: Average high school GPA 3.17. 18% in top 10% of high school class, 43% in top 25% of high school class, 73% in top 50% of high school class. 68% from public high schools. ACT middle 50% range 24-20. Minimum internet-based TOEFL 61. Minimum paper TOEFL 500. **Basis for Candidate Selection:** *Very important factors considered include:* rigor of secondary school record. *Important factors considered include:* standardized test scores. *Other factors considered include:* Class rank, academic GPA, talent/ability. **Freshman Admission Requirements:** High school diploma is required and GED is accepted. *Academic units required:* 4 English, 3 mathematics, 3 science, 2 foreign language, 1 social studies, 2 history, 2 academic electives. **Freshman Admission Statistics:** 2,420 applied, 82% admitted, 63% enrolled. **Transfer Admission Requirements:** college transcript(s), Minimum college GPA of 2.0 required. Lowest grade transferable D. **General Admission Information:** Application Fee $20. Notification on a rolling basis, beginning on or about 9/1. Nonfall registration accepted. Admission may be deferred for a maximum of 1 semester. Credit and/or placement offered for CEEB Advanced Placement tests.

COSTS AND FINANCIAL AID

Annual in-state tuition $2,231. Annual out-of-state tuition $7,679. Room and board $4,556. Required fees $1,364. Average book expense $1,200. **Required Forms and Deadlines:** FAFSA, Institution's own financial aid form, State aid form, Noncustodial PROFILE. **Types of Aid:** *Need-based scholarships/grants:* Federal Pell, SEOG, state scholarships/grants, private scholarships, the school's own gift aid. *Loans:* Subsidized Stafford, Unsubsidized Stafford, PLUS, Federal Perkins. *Student Employment:* Federal Work-Study Program available. Institutional employment available. Highest amount earned per year from on-campus jobs $8,112. Off-campus job opportunities are fair. **Financial Aid Statistics:** 93% freshmen, 86% undergrads receive need-based scholarship or grant aid. 68% freshmen, 32% undergrads receive non-need-based scholarship or grant aid. 50% freshmen, 69% undergrads receive need-based self-help aid. 3% freshmen, 3% undergrads receive athletic scholarships. 77% freshmen, 74% undergrads receive any aid. **Criteria for awarding institutional aid:** *Non-need-based:* academics, athletics, state/district residency.

NICHOLS COLLEGE

PO Box 5000, Dudley, MA 01571-5000
Phone: 508-213-2203 · **Financial Aid Phone:** 508-213-2276
E-mail: admissions@nichols.edu · **CEEB Code:** 3666
Fax: 508-943-9885 · **Website:** www.nichols.edu · **ACT Code:** 1878

This private school was founded in 1815. It has a 200-acre campus.

RATINGS

Admissions Selectivity Rating: 71   **Fire Safety Rating:** 75

STUDENTS AND FACULTY

Enrollment: 1,214. **Student Body:** 40% female, 60% male, 35% out-of-state, 0% international (4 countries represented). Asian 1%, African American 4%, Caucasian 78%, Hispanic 3%, Native American <1%
Retention and Graduation: 43% freshmen graduate within 4 years. 46% freshmen graduate within 6 years. 7% grads go on to further study within 1 year. 2% grads pursue business degrees. **Faculty:** 34 full-time faculty, 56% hold PhDs, 29% are members of minority groups, 3% are women. 0% of classes are taught by teaching assistants.

ACADEMICS

Degrees: associate, bachelor's, master's. **Classes:** Most classes have 20–29 students. Most lab/discussion sessions have 10–19 students. **Majors with Highest Enrollment:** Sport and Fitness Administration/Management; Criminal Justice/

Law Enforcement Administration; Business/Commerce. **Special Study Options:** cooperative education program, distance learning, double major, honors program, independent study, internships, liberal arts/career combination, study abroad, teacher certification program. **Combined degree programs:** Five year BSBA/MBA Program. **Disability Services:** Special programs offered to physically disabled students include tutors. **Career services:** Alumni network, alumni services, career/job search classes, career assessment, internships, regional alumni.

FACILITIES

Housing: Coed dorms, men's dorms, women's dorms, apartments for single students. 80% of campus accessible to physically disabled. **Computers:** 10% of classrooms, 100% of libraries, 100% of dining areas, have wireless network access. Students can register for classes online. Administrative functions (other than registration) can be performed online.

CAMPUS LIFE

Environment: Village. **Activities:** drama/theater, literary magazine, musical theater, radio station, student government, student newspaper, yearbook. 25 registered organizations, 5 honor societies, 1 religious organization. **Athletics (Intercollegiate):** *Men:* baseball, basketball, football, golf, ice hockey, lacrosse, soccer, tennis. *Women:* basketball, field hockey, golf, ice hockey, lacrosse, soccer, softball, tennis. **On-Campus Highlights:** Athletic and Recreation Complex, The Currier Center, Snack Bar in Alumni Hall, Davis Café, WNRC Radio Station.

ADMISSIONS

Freshman Academic Profile: Average high school GPA 2.61. 0% in top 10% of high school class, 0% in top 25% of high school class, 0% in top 50% of high school class. 82% from public high schools. SAT Math middle 50% range 420-520. SAT Critical Reading middle 50% range 400-490. SAT Writing middle 50% range 418-473. Minimum paper TOEFL 550. **Basis for Candidate Selection:** *Very important factors considered include:* application essay, recommendation(s), rigor of secondary school record. *Important factors considered include:* academic GPA, standardized test scores, interview. *Other factors considered include:* Class rank, character/personal qualities, extracurricular activities, level of applicant's interest, talent/ability, volunteer work, work experience. **Freshman Admission Requirements:** High school diploma is required and GED is accepted. *Academic units required:* 4 English, 3 mathematics, 2 science, (2 science labs), 2 social studies, 5 academic electives. **Freshman Admission Statistics:** 1,894 applied, 77% admitted, 30% enrolled. **Transfer Admission Requirements:** High school transcript, college transcript(s), essay or personal statement, Minimum college GPA of 2.0 required. Lowest grade transferable C. **General Admission Information:** Application Fee $25. Notification on a rolling basis, beginning on or about 10/1. Nonfall registration accepted. Admission may be deferred for a maximum of 1 year. Neither credit nor placement offered for CEEB Advanced Placement tests.

COSTS AND FINANCIAL AID

Annual tuition $25,400. Room and board $8,960. Required fees $300. Average book expense $1,050. **Required Forms and Deadlines:** FAFSA. **Notification of Awards:** Applicants will be notified of awards on a rolling basis beginning 3/15. **Types of Aid:** *Need-based scholarships/grants:* Federal Pell, SEOG, state scholarships/grants, private scholarships. *Loans:* Subsidized Stafford, Unsubsidized Stafford, PLUS, state loans. *Student Employment:* Federal Work-Study Program available. Institutional employment available. Highest amount earned per year from on-campus jobs $3,000. Off-campus job opportunities are fair. **Financial Aid Statistics:** 100% freshmen, 100% undergrads receive need-based scholarship or grant aid. 6% freshmen, 6% undergrads receive non-need-based scholarship or grant aid. 91% freshmen, 93% undergrads receive need-based self-help aid. 0% freshmen, 0% undergrads receive athletic scholarships. 70% freshmen, 73% undergrads receive any aid. 84% undergrads borrow to pay for school. **Criteria for awarding institutional aid:** *Non-need-based:* academics.

NORTH CAROLINA A&T STATE UNIVERSITY

1601 East Market Street, Greensboro, NC 27411
Phone: 336-334-7946
E-mail: uadmit@ncat.edu
Fax: 336-334-7478 • **Website:** www.ncat.edu

This is a public school.

RATINGS

Admissions Selectivity Rating: 72 **Fire Safety Rating:** 60*

STUDENTS AND FACULTY

Enrollment: 8,921. **Student Body:** 54% female, 46% male, 16% out-of-state, 1% international. Asian 1%, African American 89%, Caucasian 4%, Hispanic 2%, Native American <1%

Retention and Graduation: 17% freshmen graduate within 4 years. **Faculty:** 532 full-time faculty, 77% hold PhDs, 44% are members of minority groups, 73% are women.

ACADEMICS

Degrees: bachelor's, master's. **Classes:** Most classes have 20–29 students. **Special Study Options:** cooperative education program, cross-registration, distance learning, double major, external degree program, honors program, independent study, internships, study abroad, teacher certification program.

FACILITIES

Housing: Coed dorms, men's dorms, women's dorms, Theme Housing, Graduate housing.

CAMPUS LIFE

Activities: Choral groups, concert band, dance, drama/theater, jazz band, literary magazine, marching band, music ensembles, musical theater, opera, pep band, radio station, student government, student newspaper, student-run film society, symphony orchestra, television station, yearbook, International Student Organization, Model UN.

ADMISSIONS

Freshman Academic Profile: Average high school GPA 3.13. 0% in top 10% of high school class, 6% in top 25% of high school class, 34% in top 50% of high school class. 82% from public high schools. SAT Math middle 50% range 410-500. SAT Critical Reading middle 50% range 390-480. SAT Writing middle 50% range 370-460. ACT middle 50% range 17-21. Minimum internet-based TOEFL 88. Minimum paper TOEFL 570. **Basis for Candidate Selection:** *Very important factors considered include:* rigor of secondary school record, state residency. *Important factors considered include:* standardized test scores. *Other factors considered include:* Class rank, recommendation(s), alumni/ae relation, character/personal qualities, extracurricular activities, geographical residence, talent/ability, volunteer work, work experience. **Freshman Admission Requirements:** High school diploma is required and GED is accepted. *Academic units required:* 4 English, 3 mathematics, 3 science, 2 social studies, 4 academic electives. **Freshman Admission Statistics:** 6,692 applied, 66% admitted, 42% enrolled. **Transfer Admission Requirements:** High school transcript, Minimum college GPA of 2.0 required. Lowest grade transferable C. **General Admission Information:** Application Fee $35. Notification on a rolling basis, beginning on or about 9/15. Nonfall registration accepted. Admission may be deferred for a maximum of 1 semester. Credit offered for CEEB Advanced Placement tests.

COSTS AND FINANCIAL AID

Annual in-state tuition $2,791. Annual out-of-state tuition $12,425. Room and board $7,225. Required fees $1,877. Average book expense $1,400. **Required Forms and Deadlines:** FAFSA. **Notification of Awards:** Applicants will be notified of awards on a rolling basis beginning 4/15. **Types of Aid:** *Need-based scholarships/grants:* Federal Pell, SEOG, state scholarships/grants, private scholarships, the school's own gift aid, United Negro College Fund, Federal Nursing Scholarships. *Loans:* Direct Subsidized Stafford, Direct Unsubsidized Stafford, Direct PLUS, Federal Perkins, alternative loans. **Financial Aid Statistics:** 78% freshmen, 75% undergrads receive need-based scholarship or grant aid. 92% freshmen, 84% undergrads receive non-need-based scholarship or grant aid. 84% freshmen, 84% undergrads receive need-based self-help aid. 3% freshmen, 2% undergrads receive athletic scholarships. 74% undergrads borrow to pay for school. **Criteria for awarding institutional aid:** *Non-need-based:* academics, alumni affiliation, athletics, minority status, music/drama, state/district residency.

NORTH CAROLINA CENTRAL UNIVERSITY

Fayetteville Street, Durham, NC 27707
Phone: 919-560-6298
E-mail: ebridges@wpo.nccu.edu • **CEEB Code:** 5495
Fax: 919-530-7625 • **Website:** www.nccu.edu • **ACT Code:** 3132

This public school was founded in 1910. It has a 130-acre campus.

RATINGS

Admissions Selectivity Rating: 70 **Fire Safety Rating:** 60*

STUDENTS AND FACULTY

Enrollment: 5,439. **Student Body:** 66% female, 34% male, 10% out-of-state, 0% international (17 countries represented). Asian 0%, African American 79%, Caucasian 3%, Hispanic 1%, Native American <1%
Retention and Graduation: 78% freshmen return for sophomore year.
Faculty: 231 full-time faculty, 67% hold PhDs, 47% are members of minority groups, 77% are women.

ACADEMICS

Degrees: bachelor's, first professional, master's. **Classes:** Most classes have fewer than 10 students. Most lab/discussion sessions have fewer than 10 students. **Special Study Options:** cooperative education program, double major, honors program, independent study, internships, study abroad, teacher certification program, weekend college. **Disability Services:** Special programs offered to physically disabled students include note-taking services, reader services, tape recorders, tutors. **Career services:** alumni services, career/job search classes, internships.

FACILITIES

Housing: Coed dorms, men's dorms, women's dorms, Coed houses dormitory available. **Special Academic Facilities/Equipment:** Treasury Room collection of primary resources on black life and culture, art museum with works of Afro-American culture. **Computers:** Administrative functions (other than registration) can be performed online.

CAMPUS LIFE

Activities: Choral groups, concert band, dance, drama/theater, jazz band, literary magazine, marching band, radio station, student government, student newspaper, yearbook 4 fraternities, 4 sororities. **Athletics (Intercollegiate):** *Men:* basketball, cross-country, football, golf, tennis, track/field (outdoor). *Women:* basketball, cross-country, golf, softball, tennis, track/field (outdoor), volleyball.

ADMISSIONS

Freshman Academic Profile: Average high school GPA 2.6. 4% in top 10% of high school class, 19% in top 25% of high school class, 53% in top 50% of high school class. SAT Math middle 50% range 380-470. SAT Critical Reading middle 50% range 380-470. ACT middle 50% range 14-18. Minimum paper TOEFL 500. **Basis for Candidate Selection:** *Very important factors considered include:* rigor of secondary school record. *Important factors considered include:* Class rank, standardized test scores. *Other factors considered include:* application essay, recommendation(s), alumni/ae relation, extracurricular activities, interview, racial/ethnic status, state residency, talent/ability. **Freshman Admission Requirements:** High school diploma is required and GED is accepted. *Academic units required:* 4 English, 3 mathematics, 3 science, (1 science labs), 2 social studies, 2 history. **Freshman Admission Statistics:** 2,801 applied, 83% admitted, 50% enrolled. **Transfer Admission Requirements:** High school transcript, college transcript(s), statement of good standing from prior institution(s). Minimum college GPA of 2.0 required. Lowest grade transferable C. **General Admission Information:** Application Fee $30. Regular application deadline 7/1. Nonfall registration accepted. Admission may be deferred for a maximum of 4. Credit offered for CEEB Advanced Placement tests.

COSTS AND FINANCIAL AID

Required Forms and Deadlines: FAFSA. **Types of Aid:** *Need-based scholarships/grants:* Federal Pell, SEOG, state scholarships/grants, private scholarships, the school's own gift aid, United Negro College Fund, Federal Nursing Scholarships. *Loans:* Direct Subsidized Stafford, Direct Unsubsidized Stafford, Direct PLUS, Federal Perkins. *Student Employment:* Federal Work-Study Program available. Off-campus job opportunities are fair. **Financial Aid Statistics:** 73% freshmen, 72% undergrads receive need-based scholarship or grant aid. 87% freshmen, 47% undergrads receive non-need-based scholarship or grant aid. 83% freshmen, 87% undergrads receive need-based self-help aid. 4% freshmen, 2% undergrads receive athletic scholarships. Criteria for awarding institutional aid: *Non-need-based:* academics, alumni affiliation, athletics.

NORTH CAROLINA STATE UNIVERSITY

Box 7103, Raleigh, NC 27695
Phone: 919-515-2434 • **Financial Aid Phone:** 919-515-2421
E-mail: undergrad_admissions@ncsu.edu • **CEEB Code:** 5496
Fax: 919-515-5039 • **Website:** http://www.ncsu.edu/ • **ACT Code:** 3164

This public school was founded in 1887. It has a 2110-acre campus.

RATINGS

Admissions Selectivity Rating: 91   **Fire Safety Rating:** 97

STUDENTS AND FACULTY

Enrollment: 22,925. **Student Body:** 44% female, 56% male, 10% out-of-state, 3% international (117 countries represented). Asian 5%, African American 7%, Caucasian 75%, Hispanic 4%, Native American <1%

Retention and Graduation: 31% grads go on to further study within 1 year. 46% grads pursue arts and sciences degrees. 6% grads pursue law degrees. 16% grads pursue business degrees. 1% grads pursue medical degrees. **Faculty:** 1,484 full-time faculty, 88% hold PhDs, 37% are members of minority groups, 17% are women. 17% of classes are taught by teaching assistants.

ACADEMICS

Degrees: associate, bachelor's, certificate, master's, post-bachelor's certificate. **Classes:** Most classes have 20–29 students. Most lab/discussion sessions have 20–29 students. **Majors with Highest Enrollment:** Mechanical Engineering; Biology/Biological Sciences; Business Administration and Management. **Special Study Options:** Accelerated program, cooperative education program, cross-registration, distance learning, double major, dual enrollment, exchange student program (domestic), honors program, independent study, internships, liberal arts/career combination, student-designed major, study abroad. **Honors programs:** The University Honors Program recruits and provides programmatic support for a diverse group of nationally outstanding students, ensuring that they benefit fully from the resources of a major land-grant, research university and the Research Triangle by emphasizing inquiry-, creativity-, and discovery-based learning. The program offers interdisciplinary seminars and a variety of credit-earning opportunites for out-of-classroom experiences. The program emphasizes participation in research by students from all disciplines. Entering students may instead choose to participate in the University Scholars program, which emphasizes enrichment activities and leadership development. There are over 30 honors programs located in the colleges or departments that invite students in their sophomore or junior years. These programs include honors sections of courses, honors seminars, and honors research. Some programs require a senior honor thesis. **Combined degree programs:** BA/BS Humanities/Engineering Humanities/Design. **Disability Services:** Special programs offered to physically disabled students include note-taking services, reader services, tape recorders. **Career services:** career/job search classes, career assessment, internships, regional alumni.

FACILITIES

Housing: Coed dorms, special housing for disabled students, men's dorms, special housing for international students, women's dorms, fraternity/sorority housing, apartments for married students, apartments for single students, Theme Housing, Living/Learning Dormitories. 87% of campus accessible to physically disabled. **Special Academic Facilities/Equipment:** Art and arts/crafts galleries, research farms and forest, phytotronon with controlled atmosphere growth chambers. pulp/paper and wood products labs, processing equipment for fiber, fabric, and garment manufacture, electron microscopes, nuclear reactor, stable isotope lab. **Computers:** 94% of classrooms, 100% of libraries, 92% of dining areas, 100% of student union, 52% of common outdoor areas have wireless network access. Students can register for classes online. Administrative functions (other than registration) can be performed online.

CAMPUS LIFE

Environment: Metropolis. **Activities:** Choral groups, concert band, dance, drama/theater, jazz band, literary magazine, marching band, music ensembles, musical theater, pep band, radio station, student government, student newspaper, symphony orchestra, yearbook, Campus Ministries, International Student Organization. 560 registered organizations, 26 honor societies, 25 religious organizations. 33 fraternities, 17 sororities. **Athletics (Intercollegiate):** *Men:* baseball, basketball, cheerleading, cross-country, diving, football, golf, riflery, soccer, swimming, tennis, track/field (outdoor), track/field (indoor), wrestling. *Women:* basketball, cheerleading, cross-country, diving, golf, gymnastics, riflery, soccer, softball, swimming, tennis, track/field (outdoor), track/field (indoor), volleyball. **On-Campus Highlights:** RBC Center—Sports Arena, Gallery of Art and Design, Carter Finley Stadium, Talley Student Center, University Theatre. **Environmental Initiatives:** Completion and acceptance by the Chancellor of a Sustainability Strategic Plan that will help guide sustainability policies and procedures on campus. This plan is supported by a Climate Action Plan and an Energy Management Plan. Committment to a minimum of LEED Silver for all new buildings and major renovations. Currently underway is a $61 million performance contract, part of which will install an 11 Megawatt (MW) Combined Heat and Power (CHP) system on the campus.

ADMISSIONS

Freshman Academic Profile: Average high school GPA 3.63. 52% in top 10% of high school class, 86% in top 25% of high school class, 99% in top 50% of high school class. 80% from public high schools. SAT Math middle 50% range 600-680. SAT Critical Reading middle 50% range 560-650. SAT Writing middle 50% range 540-630. ACT middle 50% range 26-31. Minimum internet-based TOEFL 85. Minimum paper TOEFL 563. **Basis for Candidate Selection:** *Very important factors considered include:* Class rank, academic GPA, rigor of secondary school record, standardized test scores. *Other factors considered include:* application essay, recommendation(s), alumni/ae relation, character/personal qualities, extracurricular activities, first generation, geographical residence, racial/ethnic status, state residency, talent/ability, volunteer work, work experience. **Freshman Admission Requirements:** High school diploma is required and GED is not accepted. *Academic units required:* 4 English, 4 mathematics, 3 science, (1 science labs), 2 foreign language, 1 social studies, 1 history, 1 academic electives. **Freshman Admission Statistics:** 20,208 applied, 51% admitted, 42% enrolled. **Transfer Admission Requirements:** college transcript(s), Minimum college GPA of 2.0 required. Lowest grade transferable C-. **General Admission Information:** Application Fee $70. Regular application deadline 2/1. Notification on a rolling basis, beginning on or about 10/15. Nonfall registration accepted. Admission may be deferred for a maximum of 1 year. Credit and/or placement offered for CEEB Advanced Placement tests.

COSTS AND FINANCIAL AID

Annual in-state tuition $6,038. Annual out-of-state tuition $21,293. Room and board $10,030. Required fees $2,258. Average book expense $1,076. **Required Forms and Deadlines:** FAFSA. **Notification of Awards:** Applicants will be notified of awards on a rolling basis beginning 4/1. **Types of Aid:** *Need-based scholarships/grants:* Federal Pell, SEOG, state scholarships/grants, private scholarships, the school's own gift aid, United Negro College Fund. *Loans:* Subsidized Stafford, Unsubsidized Stafford, PLUS, Federal Perkins, state loans, college/university loans from institutional funds. *Student Employment:* Federal Work-Study Program available. Institutional employment available. Highest amount earned per year from on-campus jobs $7,300. Off-campus job opportunities are excellent. **Financial Aid Statistics:** 94% freshmen, 91% undergrads receive need-based scholarship or grant aid. 19% freshmen, 11% undergrads receive non-need-based scholarship or grant aid. 70% freshmen, 73% undergrads receive need-based self-help aid. 2% freshmen, 2% undergrads receive athletic scholarships. 75% freshmen, 69% undergrads receive any aid. 57% undergrads borrow to pay for school. Average cumulative indebtedness $20,839. **Criteria for awarding institutional aid:** *Non-need-based:* academics, alumni affiliation, athletics, leadership, state/district residency.

NORTH CAROLINA WESLEYAN COLLEGE

3400 North Wesleyan Boulevard, Rocky Mount, NC 27804
Phone: 252-985-5200
E-mail: adm@ncwc.edu
Fax: 252-985-5309 • **Website:** www.ncwc.edu

This private school, affiliated with the Methodist Church, was founded in 1956.

RATINGS

Admissions Selectivity Rating: 61   Fire Safety Rating: 63

STUDENTS AND FACULTY

Enrollment: 1,695. **Student Body:** 59% female, 41% male, 12% out-of-state, 0% international (1 countries represented). Asian 1%, African American 40%, Caucasian 48%, Hispanic 1%, Native American 1%
Retention and Graduation: 57% freshmen return for sophomore year. 26% freshmen graduate within 4 years. 38% freshmen graduate within 6 years.
Faculty: 45 full-time faculty, 62% hold PhDs, 51% are members of minority groups, 0% are women. 0% of classes are taught by teaching assistants.

ACADEMICS

Degrees: bachelor's, certificate. **Classes:** Most classes have 10–19 students.
Majors with Highest Enrollment: Computer and Information Sciences; Psychology; Business/Commerce. **Special Study Options:** Accelerated program, cooperative education program, cross-registration, distance learning, double major, dual enrollment, honors program, independent study, internships, liberal arts/career combination, teacher certification program, weekend college.
Disability Services: Special programs offered to physically disabled students include note-taking services, reader services, tape recorders, tutors. **Career services:** career/job search classes, career assessment, internships. Career services highlights include North Carolina Wesleyan College's Internship and Career Services Center (ICSC), which complements the academic program of the College. The ICSC at Wesleyan assists our students' professional development and serves as a resource to students, faculty, and the business community. By emphasizing hands-on learning as an important tool for both full time employment and in developing a career path, the ICSC helps students realize their career goals. The ICSC offers a variety of services that allows students to assess their skills and abilities, make the major declaration, and explore the world of work. Through our resource library and employer files students are able to research possible majors, minors, and careers. To prepare our students for the world of work, the ICSC offers the Career Development Workshop as a required component of the internship for traditional day students. The workshop includes resume and cover letter writing, the value of networking, interviewing skills, appropriate business attire, how to deal with racial discrimination and sexual harassment, and social etiquette. The relevance of practical experience will become evident as students begin to explore their career goals through the Extended Internship (EI) program.

FACILITIES

Housing: Coed dorms, special housing for disabled students, men's dorms, women's dorms. 70% of campus accessible to physically disabled. **Special Academic Facilities/Equipment:** Mims Gallery, Dunn Center for the Performaing Arts. **Computers:** Administrative functions (other than registration) can be performed online.

CAMPUS LIFE

Environment: Village. **Activities:** Choral groups, drama/theater, literary magazine, music ensembles, student government, student newspaper, yearbook. 30 registered organizations, 2 honor societies, 2 religious organizations. 3 fraternities, 3 sororities. **Athletics (Intercollegiate):** *Men:* baseball, basketball, football, golf, soccer, tennis. *Women:* basketball, soccer, softball, tennis, volleyball. **On-Campus Highlights:** Dunn Center for the Performing Arts, Mims Gallery, Serpentine Wall, College Fountain, Bellmonte House.

ADMISSIONS

Freshman Academic Profile: Average high school GPA 2.79. 8% in top 10% of high school class, 18% in top 25% of high school class, 59% in top 50% of high school class. 85% from public high schools. Minimum paper TOEFL 500.
Basis for Candidate Selection: *Very important factors considered include:* recommendation(s), rigor of secondary school record, standardized test scores, talent/ability. *Important factors considered include:* application essay, alumni/ae relation, character/personal qualities, extracurricular activities, interview, volunteer work, work experience. *Other factors considered include:* Class rank.
Freshman Admission Requirements: High school diploma is required and GED is accepted. **Freshman Admission Statistics:** 651 applied, 83% admitted, 37% enrolled. **Transfer Admission Requirements:** High school transcript, college transcript(s), standardized test scores, Minimum college GPA of 2.0 required. Lowest grade transferable C. **General Admission Information:** Application Fee $25. Nonfall registration accepted. Credit and/or placement offered for CEEB Advanced Placement tests.

COSTS AND FINANCIAL AID

Annual tuition $11,225. Room and board $5,555. Required fees $1,218. Average book expense $800. **Required Forms and Deadlines:** FAFSA, State aid form. **Notification of Awards:** Applicants will be notified of awards on a rolling basis beginning 2/1. **Types of Aid:** *Need-based scholarships/grants:* Federal Pell, SEOG, state scholarships/grants, private scholarships, the school's own gift aid. *Loans:* Subsidized Stafford, Unsubsidized Stafford, PLUS, Federal Perkins, Alternative Loans. *Student Employment:* Federal Work-Study Program available. Highest amount earned per year from on-campus jobs $800. **Financial Aid Statistics:** 0% freshmen, 0% undergrads receive athletic scholarships. 100% undergrads borrow to pay for school. **Criteria for awarding institutional aid:** *Non-need-based:* academics, religious affiliation, state/district residency.

NORTH CENTRAL COLLEGE

Office of Admissions, Naperville, IL 60566-7063
Phone: 630-637-5800 • **Financial Aid Phone:** 630-637-5600
E-mail: admissions@noctrl.edu • **CEEB Code:** 1555
Fax: 630-637-5819 • **Website:** www.northcentralcollege.edu • **ACT Code:** 1096

This private school, affiliated with the Methodist Church, was founded in 1861. It has a 59-acre campus.

RATINGS

Admissions Selectivity Rating: 86   Fire Safety Rating: 88

STUDENTS AND FACULTY

Enrollment: 2,686. **Student Body:** 56% female, 44% male, 7% out-of-state, 2% international (32 countries represented). Asian 2%, African American 4%, Caucasian 73%, Hispanic 10%, Native American <1%
Retention and Graduation: 78% freshmen return for sophomore year. 50% freshmen graduate within 4 years. **Faculty:** 138 full-time faculty, 91% hold PhDs, 54% are members of minority groups, 12% are women. 0% of classes are taught by teaching assistants.

ACADEMICS

Degrees: bachelor's, master's, post-bachelor's certificate. **Classes:** Most classes have 20–29 students. Most lab/discussion sessions have 20–29 students.
Majors with Highest Enrollment: Business Administration, Management and Operations; Psychology; Sociology. **Special Study Options:** Accelerated program, cross-registration, double major, dual enrollment, English as a Second Language (ESL), exchange student program (domestic), honors program, independent study, internships, student-designed major, study abroad, teacher certification program, 3-2 Engineering program with University of Illinois, University of Minnesota; Integrated 5 year Bachelor's/Master's degree programs.
Honors programs: The College Scholars is a comprehensive four year integra-

tive program culminating in a senior honors thesis. The program is open to students from all academic disciplines. **Combined degree programs:** BA/MA, BA in Acc/MBA; Bachelor's Degree/Masters in Web and Internet Applications. **Disability Services:** Special programs offered to physically disabled students include note-taking services, reader services, tape recorders, tutors. **Career services:** Alumni network, alumni services, career/job search classes, career assessment, internships, regional alumni. Because career-related experiences support the mission of the college, the CDC actively assists students in developing Internship opportunities. We have found that real hands on experience within the workforce increases graduates marketability following graduation, be it for seeking employment or pursuing graduate school. Today's job market is competitive and we offer a strong resource in helping students get involved in these types of opportunities which ultimately helps them reach their goals.

FACILITIES

Housing: Coed dorms, special housing for disabled students, women's dorms, Substance-free housing. 85% of campus accessible to physically disabled. **Special Academic Facilities/Equipment:** None **Computers:** 50% of classrooms, 30% of dorms, 100% of libraries, 100% of dining areas, 100% of student union, 100% of common outdoor areas have wireless network access. Students can register for classes online. Administrative functions (other than registration) can be performed online.

CAMPUS LIFE

Environment: City. **Activities:** Choral groups, concert band, dance, drama/theater, jazz band, literary magazine, music ensembles, musical theater, opera, pep band, radio station, student government, student newspaper, Campus Ministries, International Student Organization, Model UN. 54 registered organizations, 14 honor societies, 6 religious organizations. **Athletics (Intercollegiate):** *Men:* baseball, basketball, cross-country, football, golf, soccer, swimming, tennis, track/field (outdoor), track/field (indoor), wrestling. *Women:* basketball, cheerleading, cross-country, golf, lacrosse, soccer, softball, swimming, tennis, track/field (outdoor), track/field (indoor), volleyball. **On-Campus Highlights:** Old Main—historic home of North Central College, Benedtti-Wehrli Stadium, Res/Rec Center, Fine Arts Center & Wentz Concert Hall, Oesterle Library, Rolland Boilerhouse Café is also a popular on-campus hangout. **Environmental Initiatives:** The College committed to building a one of a kind building with a residence hall wrapped-around a rec center and NCAA regulation sized indoor track. The building was built to LEED silver certification standards with heating and cooling from a geothermal field, occupancy sensors, precast walls made of recycled material, water efficient fixtures, bike storage, and more. The College committed to hiring a full-time sustainbility coordinator to increase program development and campus-wide involvement with sustainability issues. The College hired a sustainability consulting group in Fall 2010 to further investigate quick-win projects, benchmarking, student involvement, and the College's sustainability mission.

ADMISSIONS

Freshman Academic Profile: Average high school GPA 3.59. 22% in top 10% of high school class, 52% in top 25% of high school class, 81% in top 50% of high school class. 88% from public high schools. ACT middle 50% range 22-27. Minimum internet-based TOEFL 68. Minimum paper TOEFL 520. **Basis for Candidate Selection:** *Very important factors considered include:* academic GPA, rigor of secondary school record, standardized test scores, character/personal qualities. *Important factors considered include:* extracurricular activities, talent/ability, volunteer work. *Other factors considered include:* application essay, recommendation(s), alumni/ae relation, first generation, interview, level of applicant's interest, work experience. **Freshman Admission Requirements:** High school diploma is required and GED is accepted. *Academic units required:* 4 English, 3 mathematics, 3 science, (1 science labs), 0 foreign language, 2 social studies, 1 history, 3 academic electives. **Freshman Admission Statistics:** 5,807 applied, 60% admitted, 17% enrolled. **Transfer Admission Requirements:** college transcript(s), Minimum college GPA of 2.25 required. Lowest grade transferable D. **General Admission Information:** Application Fee $25. Notification on a rolling basis, beginning on or about 10/1. Nonfall registration accepted. Admission may be deferred for a maximum of 1 year. Credit and/or placement offered for CEEB Advanced Placement tests.

COSTS AND FINANCIAL AID

Annual tuition $34,050. Room and board $9,795. Required fees $180. Average book expense $1,200. **Required Forms and Deadlines:** FAFSA, Institution's own financial aid form. **Notification of Awards:** Applicants will be notified of awards on a rolling basis beginning 3/1. **Types of Aid:** *Need-based scholarships/grants:* Federal Pell, SEOG, state scholarships/grants, private scholarships, the school's own gift aid. *Loans:* Subsidized Stafford, Unsubsidized Stafford, PLUS, Federal Perkins, state loans, college/university loans from institutional funds. *Student Employment:* Federal Work-Study Program available. Institutional employment available. Off-campus job opportunities are excellent. **Financial Aid Statistics:** 100% freshmen, 99% undergrads receive need-based scholarship or grant aid. 16% freshmen, 11% undergrads receive non-need-based scholarship or grant aid. 79% freshmen, 84% undergrads receive need-based self-help aid.

0% freshmen, 0% undergrads receive athletic scholarships. 99% freshmen, 97% undergrads receive any aid. 80% undergrads borrow to pay for school. Average cumulative indebtedness $23,768. **Criteria for awarding institutional aid:** *Non-need-based:* academics, art, leadership, minority status, music/drama, religious affiliation, state/district residency.

NORTH CENTRAL UNIVERSITY

Admissions Office, Minneapolis, MN 55404
Phone: 612-343-4460
E-mail: admissions@northcentral.edu
Fax: 612-343-4146 · **Website:** www.northcentral.edu

This private school, affiliated with the Pentecostal Church, was founded in 1930. It has a 9-acre campus.

RATINGS

Admissions Selectivity Rating: 70   **Fire Safety Rating:** 69

STUDENTS AND FACULTY

Enrollment: 1,217. **Student Body:** 57% female, 43% male, 60% out-of-state, (11 countries represented).
Retention and Graduation: 75% freshmen return for sophomore year. 45% freshmen graduate within 6 years. **Faculty:** 40 full-time faculty, 43% hold PhDs, 38% are members of minority groups, 13% are women. 0% of classes are taught by teaching assistants.

ACADEMICS

Degrees: associate, bachelor's, certificate, diploma. **Classes:** Most classes have 10–19 students. **Majors with Highest Enrollment:** Education; Youth Ministry; Digital Arts. **Special Study Options:** distance learning, double major, exchange student program (domestic), independent study, internships. **Disability Services:** Special programs offered to physically disabled students include note-taking services, reader services, tape recorders, tutors.

FACILITIES

Housing: men's dorms, women's dorms, apartments for married students, apartments for single students.

CAMPUS LIFE

Environment: Metropolis. **Activities:** Choral groups, concert band, drama/theater, jazz band, music ensembles, radio station, student government, student newspaper, television station. 30 registered organizations, 15 religious organizations. **Athletics (Intercollegiate):** *Men:* basketball, cross-country, soccer, track/field (outdoor). *Women:* basketball, cross-country, soccer, track/field (outdoor), volleyball. **On-Campus Highlights:** Chapel, Library, Cafetria, Philipps Hall, Clay Commons.

ADMISSIONS

Freshman Academic Profile: Average high school GPA 3.1. 2% in top 10% of high school class, 11% in top 25% of high school class, 32% in top 50% of high school class. SAT Math middle 50% range 440-300. SAT Critical Reading middle 50% range 480-630. ACT middle 50% range 18-24. Minimum paper TOEFL 500. **Basis for Candidate Selection:** *Very important factors considered include:* application essay, academic GPA, recommendation(s), rigor of secondary school record, standardized test scores, character/personal qualities, religious affiliation/commitment. *Important factors considered include:* extracurricular activities, talent/ability, volunteer work. *Other factors considered include:* Class rank, interview. **Freshman Admission Requirements:** High school diploma is required and GED is accepted. **Freshman Admission Statistics:** 422 applied, 98% admitted, 58% enrolled. **Transfer Admission Requirements:** High school transcript, college transcript(s), essay or personal statement, Minimum college GPA of 2.0 required. Lowest grade transferable C. **General Admission Information:** Application Fee $25. Regular application deadline 6/1. Notification on a rolling basis, beginning on or about 1/1. Nonfall registration accepted. Admission may be deferred for a maximum of 1 year.

COSTS AND FINANCIAL AID

Annual tuition $12,060. Room and board $4,612. Required fees $1,001. Average book expense $600. **Required Forms and Deadlines:** FAFSA, State aid form. **Notification of Awards:** Applicants will be notified of awards on a rolling basis beginning 3/1. **Types of Aid:** *Need-based scholarships/grants:* Federal Pell, SEOG, state scholarships/grants, private scholarships, the school's own gift aid. *Loans:* Subsidized Stafford, Unsubsidized Stafford, PLUS, Federal Perkins, state loans.

NORTH DAKOTA STATE UNIVERSITY

PO Box 6050 Dept 5230, Fargo, ND 58108
Phone: 701-231-8643 • **Financial Aid Phone:** 800-726-3188
E-mail: ndsu.admission@ndsu.edu • **CEEB Code:** 6474
Fax: 701-231-8802 • **Website:** www.ndsu.edu • **ACT Code:** 3202

This public school was founded in 1890. It has a 258-acre campus.

RATINGS

Admissions Selectivity Rating: 80   **Fire Safety Rating:** 72

STUDENTS AND FACULTY

Enrollment: 12,028. **Student Body:** 45% female, 55% male, 55% out-of-state, 4% international (79 countries represented). Asian 1%, African American 2%, Caucasian 88%, Hispanic 1%, Native American 1%
Retention and Graduation: 24% freshmen graduate within 4 years. 52% freshmen graduate within 6 years. **Faculty:** 643 full-time faculty, 84% hold PhDs, 37% are members of minority groups, 16% are women.

ACADEMICS

Degrees: bachelor's, certificate, first professional, master's, post-master's certificate. **Classes:** Most classes have 20–29 students. Most lab/discussion sessions have 20–29 students. **Majors with Highest Enrollment:** Civil Engineering; Mechanical Engineering; Business, Management, Marketing, and Related Support Services. **Special Study Options:** cooperative education program, cross-registration, distance learning, double major, dual enrollment, English as a Second Language (ESL), honors program, independent study, internships, student-designed major, study abroad, teacher certification program, Tri-College Collaboration and Registration with Minnesota State University and Concordia College. Collaboration with North Dakota University System institutions. **Honors programs:** Scholars Program. **Disability Services:** Special programs offered to physically disabled students include note-taking services, reader services, tape recorders, tutors. **Career services:** career/job search classes, internships. Career services highlights include Cooperative Education opportunities available for most majors. Students are paid for their work experience and earn credit.

FACILITIES

Housing: Coed dorms, men's dorms, women's dorms, apartments for married students, apartments for single students, Designated floors for engineering and architecture students. Learning communities. Wellness community. Freshmen under 19 years of age not living with a parent or guardian must live on campus. Housing is guaranteed for freshmen required to live on campus. Handicapped accessible. 100% of campus accessible to physically disabled. **Special Academic Facilities/Equipment:** Art gallery, language lab, genetics institute, regional studies institute. **Computers:** Students can register for classes online. Administrative functions (other than registration) can be performed online.

CAMPUS LIFE

Environment: City. **Activities:** Choral groups, concert band, drama/theater, jazz band, marching band, music ensembles, musical theater, pep band, radio station, student government, student newspaper. 218 registered organizations, 22 honor societies, 18 religious organizations. 10 fraternities, 5 sororities. **Athletics (Intercollegiate):** *Men:* baseball, basketball, cross-country, football, golf, track/field (outdoor), track/field (indoor), wrestling. *Women:* basketball, cross-country, golf, soccer, softball, track/field (outdoor), track/field (indoor), volleyball. **On-Campus Highlights:** Wellness Center, Memorial Union, FargoDome, Alumni Center, Industrial Agricultural Communications Center, Residence Halls/Living Learning Center, Newman Outdoor Field, Technology Park.

ADMISSIONS

Freshman Academic Profile: Average high school GPA 3.39. 16.21% in top 10% of high school class, 40.12% in top 25% of high school class, 73.69% in top 50% of high school class. SAT Math middle 50% range 490-620. SAT Critical Reading middle 50% range 480-610. ACT middle 50% range 20-26. Minimum paper TOEFL 525. **Basis for Candidate Selection:** *Very important factors considered include:* academic GPA, rigor of secondary school record, standardized test scores. *Other factors considered include:* Class rank, recommendation(s). **Freshman Admission Requirements:** High school diploma is required and GED is accepted. *Academic units required:* 4 English, 3 mathematics, 3 science, (3 science labs), 3 social studies. **Freshman Admission Statistics:** 5,562 applied, 84% admitted, 53% enrolled. **Transfer Admission Requirements:** college transcript(s), Minimum college GPA of 2.0 required. Lowest grade transferable D. **General Admission Information:** Application Fee $35. Regular application deadline 8/15. Notification on a rolling basis, beginning on or about 9/1. Nonfall registration accepted. Admission may be deferred for a maximum of 3 years. Credit and/or placement offered for CEEB Advanced Placement tests.

COSTS AND FINANCIAL AID

Annual out-of-state tuition $16,381. Room and board $6,910. Required fees $1,218. Average book expense $1,100. **Required Forms and Deadlines:** FAFSA. **Notification of Awards:** Applicants will be notified of awards on a rolling basis beginning 3/15. **Types of Aid:** *Need-based scholarships/grants:* Federal Pell, SEOG, state scholarships/grants, private scholarships, the school's own gift aid, Diversity Waivers. *Loans:* Subsidized Stafford, Unsubsidized Stafford, PLUS, Federal Perkins, Federal Nursing, Private loans from various lending institutions. *Student Employment:* Federal Work-Study Program available. Institutional employment available. Off-campus job opportunities are good. **Financial Aid Statistics:** 77% freshmen, 69% undergrads receive need-based scholarship or grant aid. 3% freshmen, 1% undergrads receive non-need-based scholarship or grant aid. 86% freshmen, 87% undergrads receive need-based self-help aid. 3% freshmen, 3% undergrads receive athletic scholarships. 85% undergrads borrow to pay for school. Average cumulative indebtedness $22,571. **Criteria for awarding institutional aid:** *Non-need-based:* academics, alumni affiliation, art, athletics, leadership, minority status, music/drama, state/district residency.

NORTH GREENVILLE COLLEGE

PO Box 1892, Tigerville, SC 29688-1892
Phone: 864-977-7001
E-mail: admissions@ngc.edu
Fax: 864-977-7177 • **Website:** www.ngc.edu

This private school, affiliated with the Southern Baptist Church, was founded in 1892.

RATINGS

Admissions Selectivity Rating: 74   **Fire Safety Rating:** 60*

STUDENTS AND FACULTY

Enrollment: 1,570. **Student Body:** 49% female, 51% male, 19% out-of-state, 2% international (19 countries represented). Asian 0%, African American 10%, Caucasian 90%, Hispanic 0%, Native American <1%
Faculty: 70 full-time faculty, 37% are members of minority groups.

ACADEMICS

Degrees: associate, bachelor's, transfer associate. **Classes:** Most classes have 10–19 students. Most lab/discussion sessions have 10–19 students. **Special Study Options:** Accelerated program, cooperative education program, cross-registration, double major, English as a Second Language (ESL), external degree program, honors program, independent study, internships, student-designed major, study abroad, teacher certification program. **Disability Services:** Special programs offered to physically disabled students include tutors.

FACILITIES

Housing: men's dorms, women's dorms.

CAMPUS LIFE

Environment: Rural. **Activities:** Choral groups, concert band, drama/theater, jazz band, literary magazine, marching band, music ensembles, radio station, student government, student newspaper, television station, yearbook. **Athletics (Intercollegiate):** *Men:* baseball, basketball, cross-country, football, golf, soccer, softball, tennis. *Women:* basketball, cross-country, soccer, softball, tennis, volleyball.

ADMISSIONS

Freshman Academic Profile: Average high school GPA 3.8. 16% in top 10% of high school class, 43% in top 25% of high school class, 70% in top 50% of high school class. SAT Math middle 50% range 460-570. SAT Critical Reading middle 50% range 470-580. ACT middle 50% range 20-24. Minimum paper TOEFL 500. **Basis for Candidate Selection:** *Very important factors considered include:* Class rank, rigor of secondary school record, standardized test scores. *Other factors considered include:* application essay, recommendation(s). **Freshman Admission Requirements:** High school diploma is required and GED is accepted. **Freshman Admission Statistics:** 769 applied, 95% admitted, 56% enrolled. **Transfer Admission Requirements:** college transcript(s), Minimum college GPA of 2.0 required. Lowest grade transferable C. **General Admission Information:** Application Fee $25. Regular application deadline 8/25. Nonfall registration accepted. Admission may be deferred for a maximum of 1 year.

COSTS AND FINANCIAL AID

Required Forms and Deadlines: FAFSA. **Notification of Awards:** Applicants will be notified of awards on a rolling basis beginning 2/1. **Types of Aid:** *Need-based scholarships/grants:* Federal Pell, SEOG, state scholarships/grants, private scholarships, the school's own gift aid. *Loans:* Subsidized Stafford,

Unsubsidized Stafford, PLUS, Federal Perkins, state loans, college/university loans from institutional funds. **Financial Aid Statistics:** 97% freshmen, 95% undergrads receive need-based scholarship or grant aid. 0% freshmen, 0% undergrads receive non-need-based scholarship or grant aid. 25% freshmen, 23% undergrads receive need-based self-help aid. 20% freshmen, 30% undergrads receive athletic scholarships. 50% undergrads borrow to pay for school. **Criteria for awarding institutional aid:** *Non-need-based:* academics, art, athletics, music/drama, religious affiliation.

NORTH PARK UNIVERSITY

3225 West Foster Avenue, Chicago, IL 60625-4895
Phone: 773-244-5500 · **Financial Aid Phone:** 773-244-5506
E-mail: admission@northpark.edu · **CEEB Code:** 1556
Fax: 773-244-5243 · **Website:** www.northpark.edu · **ACT Code:** 1098

This private school was founded in 1891. It has a 30-acre campus.

RATINGS

Admissions Selectivity Rating: 79   **Fire Safety Rating:** 70

STUDENTS AND FACULTY

Enrollment: 2,188. **Student Body:** 63% female, 37% male, 31% out-of-state, 4% international (31 countries represented). Asian 7%, African American 9%, Caucasian 60%, Hispanic 10%, Native American <1%
Retention and Graduation: 71% freshmen return for sophomore year. 45% freshmen graduate within 4 years. 55% freshmen graduate within 6 years. 15% grads go on to further study within 1 year. 15% grads pursue arts and sciences degrees. 2% grads pursue law degrees. 10% grads pursue business degrees. 3% grads pursue medical degrees. **Faculty:** 125 full-time faculty, 88% hold PhDs, 50% are members of minority groups, 17% are women. 0% of classes are taught by teaching assistants.

ACADEMICS

Degrees: bachelor's, first professional, master's, post-bachelor's certificate. **Classes:** Most classes have 10–19 students. Most lab/discussion sessions have 20–29 students. **Majors with Highest Enrollment:** Business Administration and Management; Education; Biology/Biological Sciences. **Special Study Options:** Accelerated program, distance learning, double major, English as a Second Language (ESL), honors program, independent study, internships, liberal arts/career combination, student-designed major, study abroad, teacher certification program. **Honors programs:** The North Park University Honors Congress brings together students of high academic ability with faculty in a learning community designed to promote academic excellence, rigorous intellectual development, community involvement, service to others, and vocational direction. As Honors Congress Scholars, students of promise are provided opportunities to excel during their first two years of undergraduate study. Honors courses during the second two years are offered in individual departments. We strive to take the words of Jesus, "To whom much is given, much is required," and give them special consideration in the Honors Congress. Our philosophy is simply this: The Honors Congress gives students of high intellectual ability an array of learning experiences from which to choose, places them side-by-side with faculty mentors who care, and offers them guidance and encouragement along the way. **Combined degree programs:** MDiv/MBA dual degree. **Disability Services:** Special programs offered to physically disabled students include note-taking services, reader services, tape recorders, tutors. **Career services:** Alumni network, career/job search classes, career assessment, internships. Career services highlights include hundreds of internship opportunities available throughout the Chicago area. Students can decide between public and private, nonprofit and for profit organizations.

FACILITIES

Housing: special housing for disabled students, men's dorms, women's dorms, apartments for single students. **Special Academic Facilities/Equipment:** Art gallery, language lab, Swedish Historical Society Archives. **Computers:** 100% of libraries, 25% of dining areas, have wireless network access. Students can register for classes online. Administrative functions (other than registration) can be performed online.

CAMPUS LIFE

Environment: Metropolis. **Activities:** Choral groups, concert band, drama/theater, jazz band, literary magazine, music ensembles, musical theater, opera, pep band, student government, student newspaper, symphony orchestra, yearbook, Campus Ministries, International Student Organization 4 honor societies, 1 religious organization. **Athletics (Intercollegiate):** *Men:* baseball, basketball, cross-country, football, golf, soccer, track/field (outdoor), track/field (indoor). *Women:* basketball, crew/rowing, cross-country, golf, soccer, softball, track/field (outdoor), track/field (indoor), volleyball. **On-Campus Highlights:** New Stu-

dent Recreation Center, Brandel Library, New state of the art outdoor athletic facilities, Beautiful New Campus Quadrangle, Diverse neighborhood.

ADMISSIONS

Freshman Academic Profile: Average high school GPA 3.1. 11% in top 10% of high school class, 35% in top 25% of high school class, 66% in top 50% of high school class. 80% from public high schools. SAT Math middle 50% range 460-590. SAT Critical Reading middle 50% range 470-580. ACT middle 50% range 19-24. Minimum paper TOEFL 550. **Basis for Candidate Selection:** *Very important factors considered include:* Class rank, application essay, academic GPA, recommendation(s), rigor of secondary school record, standardized test scores, character/personal qualities, talent/ability. *Important factors considered include:* extracurricular activities, first generation, interview, racial/ethnic status, volunteer work. *Other factors considered include:* alumni/ae relation, geographical residence, level of applicant's interest, work experience. **Freshman Admission Requirements:** High school diploma is required and GED is accepted. **Freshman Admission Statistics:** 1,402 applied, 71% admitted, 42% enrolled. **Transfer Admission Requirements:** college transcript(s), essay or personal statement, statement of good standing from prior institution(s). Minimum college GPA of 2.0 required. Lowest grade transferable D. **General Admission Information:** Application Fee $40. Regular application deadline 7/1. Notification on a rolling basis, beginning on or about 9/15. Nonfall registration accepted. Admission may be deferred for a maximum of 1 year. Credit and/or placement offered for CEEB Advanced Placement tests.

COSTS AND FINANCIAL AID

Annual tuition $23,290. Room and board $8,600. Average book expense $1,000. **Required Forms and Deadlines:** FAFSA. **Notification of Awards:** Applicants will be notified of awards on a rolling basis beginning 3/15. **Types of Aid:** *Need-based scholarships/grants:* Federal Pell, SEOG, state scholarships/grants, private scholarships, the school's own gift aid, Federal Nursing Scholarships. *Loans:* Direct Subsidized Stafford, Direct Unsubsidized Stafford, Direct PLUS, Subsidized Stafford, Unsubsidized Stafford, PLUS, Federal Perkins, Federal Nursing. *Student Employment:* Federal Work-Study Program available. Institutional employment available. Highest amount earned per year from on-campus jobs $1,600. Off-campus job opportunities are excellent. **Financial Aid Statistics:** 70% freshmen, 42% freshmen, 64% freshmen, 0% freshmen, 0% undergrads receive athletic scholarships. 90% freshmen, 90% undergrads receive any aid. 79% undergrads borrow to pay for school. Average cumulative indebtedness $17,454. **Criteria for awarding institutional aid:** *Non-need-based:* academics, art, music/drama, religious affiliation, state/district residency.

NORTHEASTERN ILLINOIS UNIVERSITY

5500 North St. Louis Avenue, Chicago, IL 60625-4699
Phone: 773-442-4000 · **Financial Aid Phone:** 773-442-5000
E-mail: admrec@neiu.edu · **CEEB Code:** 1090
Fax: 773-442-4020 · **Website:** www.neiu.edu · **ACT Code:** 993

This public school was founded in 1961. It has a 63-acre campus.

RATINGS

Admissions Selectivity Rating: 74   **Fire Safety Rating:** 60*

STUDENTS AND FACULTY

Enrollment: 8,284. **Student Body:** 56% female, 44% male, 2% out-of-state, 4% international (91 countries represented). Asian 9%, African American 10%, Caucasian 36%, Hispanic 36%, Native American <1%
Retention and Graduation: 5% freshmen graduate within 4 years. **Faculty:** 374 full-time faculty, 82% hold PhDs, 53% are members of minority groups, 30% are women.

ACADEMICS

Degrees: bachelor's, master's. **Classes:** Most classes have 20–29 students. **Majors with Highest Enrollment:** Psychology; Biology/Biological Sciences; Social Work. **Special Study Options:** cooperative education program, distance learning, double major, dual enrollment, exchange student program (domestic), honors program, independent study, student-designed major, study abroad, teacher certification program. **Disability Services:** Special programs offered to physically disabled students include note-taking services, reader services, tape recorders, tutors. **Career services:** career assessment, internships.

FACILITIES

Housing: 98% of campus accessible to physically disabled. **Special Academic Facilities/Equipment:** Learning center with audiovisual, TV, multimedia, film, photography, graphic arts, and electronic instructional equipment, listening room. **Computers:** 50% of classrooms, n/a% of dorms, 100% of libraries, 80% of dining areas, 100% of student union, 50% of common outdoor areas have wireless network access. Students can register for classes online. Administrative functions (other than registration) can be performed online.

CAMPUS LIFE

Environment: Metropolis. **Activities:** Choral groups, concert band, dance, drama/theater, jazz band, literary magazine, music ensembles, musical theater, radio station, student government, student newspaper. 42 registered organizations, 12 honor societies, 6 religious organizations. 3 fraternities, 3 sororities. **On-Campus Highlights:** International Day, Fine Arst Building/ Art Gallery, Ensemble Dance Company, Health and Wellness Center, Library. **Environmental Initiatives:** Recycling; Environmentally Friendly Chemicals; Lighting upgrades.

ADMISSIONS

Freshman Academic Profile: Average high school GPA 2.8. 8% in top 10% of high school class, 23% in top 25% of high school class, 55% in top 50% of high school class. 90% from public high schools. ACT middle 50% range 16–21. Minimum paper TOEFL 500. **Basis for Candidate Selection:** *Very important factors considered include:* Class rank, standardized test scores. **Freshman Admission Requirements:** High school diploma is required and GED is accepted. *Academic units required:* 4 English, 3 mathematics, 3 science, 3 social studies, 2 Fine Arts, Foreign Lang. or Voc. Ed (only 1 yr voc. ed. allowed). **Freshman Admission Statistics:** 4,986 applied, 57% admitted, 27% enrolled. **Transfer Admission Requirements:** college transcript(s), statement of good standing from prior institution(s). Minimum college GPA of 2.0 required. Lowest grade transferable D. **General Admission Information:** Application Fee $25. Regular application deadline 7/1. Regular notification 9/1. Nonfall registration accepted. Admission may be deferred for a maximum of 1 semester. Credit offered for CEEB Advanced Placement tests.

COSTS AND FINANCIAL AID

Annual out-of-state tuition $19,320. Required fees $1,644. **Required Forms and Deadlines:** FAFSA. **Notification of Awards:** Applicants will be notified of awards on a rolling basis beginning 4/1. **Types of Aid:** *Need-based scholarships/grants:* Federal Pell, SEOG, state scholarships/grants, private scholarships, the school's own gift aid, Federal ACG, SMART. *Loans:* Subsidized Stafford, Unsubsidized Stafford, PLUS, Federal Perkins. *Student Employment:* Federal Work-Study Program available. Institutional employment available. Off-campus job opportunities are good. **Financial Aid Statistics:** 89% freshmen, 78% undergrads receive need-based scholarship or grant aid. 8% freshmen, 15% undergrads receive non-need-based scholarship or grant aid. 15% freshmen, 36% undergrads receive need-based self-help aid. 0% freshmen, 0% undergrads receive athletic scholarships. 72% freshmen, 64% undergrads receive any aid. 18% undergrads borrow to pay for school. Average cumulative indebtedness $12,800. **Criteria for awarding institutional aid:** *Non-need-based:* academics, art, leadership, music/drama.

NORTHEASTERN STATE UNIVERSITY

Office of Admissions and Records, Tahlequah, OK 74464-2399
Phone: 918-444-2200 • **Financial Aid Phone:** 918-444-6402
E-mail: nsuinfo@nsuok.edu • **CEEB Code:** 6485
Fax: 918-458-2342 • **ACT Code:** 3408

This public school was founded in 1846. It has a 200-acre campus.

RATINGS

Admissions Selectivity Rating: 67   Fire Safety Rating: 60*

STUDENTS AND FACULTY

Enrollment: 8,485. **Student Body:** 61% female, 39% male, 3% out-of-state, 3% international (41 countries represented). Asian 1%, African American 6%, Caucasian 59%, Hispanic 2%, Native American 29%
Retention and Graduation: 64% freshmen return for sophomore year. 12% freshmen graduate within 4 years. 33% freshmen graduate within 6 years.
Faculty: 306 full-time faculty, 70% hold PhDs, 46% are members of minority groups, 13% are women. 2% of classes are taught by teaching assistants.

ACADEMICS

Degrees: bachelor's, first professional, master's, post-bachelor's certificate, post-master's certificate. **Classes:** Most classes have 20–29 students. Most lab/discussion sessions have 10–19 students. **Majors with Highest Enrollment:** Elementary Education and Teaching; Business Administration and Management; Accounting. **Special Study Options:** cooperative education program, distance learning, double major, dual enrollment, honors program, independent study, internships, student-designed major, weekend college.
Honors programs: NSU Honors Program: The Honors Program at NSU is a challenging educational option for academically talented students who enjoy learning. Honor students work with distinguished faculty members and peers in enhanced courses, pursue independent research, and participate in co-curricular cultural experiences. NSU President's Leadership Class: The President's Leadership Class is a unique scholarship/leadership program designed to

identify and cultivate outstanding potential in selected freshmen entering NSU. Membership in the PLC allows students to develop close associations with University administrators, meet scholars and dignitaries who frequently visit campus, take advantage of some of the most talented faculty members at NSU who teach special sections of selected required courses, and receive scholarship assistance which includes a tuition waiver and a stipend. The PLC Scholarship is renewable for four years if members maintain high academic standards while exercising practical leadership in University activities. **Disability Services:** Special programs offered to physically disabled students include note-taking services, reader services, tape recorders, tutors. **Career services:** alumni services, career/job search classes, career assessment.

FACILITIES

Housing: Coed dorms, special housing for disabled students, fraternity/sorority housing, apartments for married students, apartments for single students. **Computers:** Administrative functions (other than registration) can be performed online.

CAMPUS LIFE

Environment: Rural. **Activities:** Choral groups, concert band, dance, drama/theater, jazz band, literary magazine, marching band, music ensembles, musical theater, pep band, student government, student newspaper, symphony orchestra, television station. 77 registered organizations, 9 honor societies, 5 religious organizations. 7 fraternities, 6 sororities. **Athletics (Intercollegiate):** *Men:* baseball, basketball, football, golf, soccer. *Women:* basketball, golf, soccer, softball, tennis. **On-Campus Highlights:** Seminary Hall, University Center, New Science Lab Building, NET Building, Seminary Suites.

ADMISSIONS

Freshman Academic Profile: Average high school GPA 3.24. ACT middle 50% range 18–23. Minimum paper TOEFL 500. **Basis for Candidate Selection:** *Very important factors considered include:* Class rank, academic GPA, rigor of secondary school record, standardized test scores. *Other factors considered include:* first generation, geographical residence, state residency. **Freshman Admission Requirements:** High school diploma is required and GED is accepted. *Academic units required:* 4 English, 3 mathematics, 2 science, (2 science labs), 2 history, 4 academic electives. **Freshman Admission Statistics:** applied, % admitted, 69% enrolled. **Transfer Admission Requirements:** college transcript(s), Minimum college GPA of 2.0 required. Lowest grade transferable D. **General Admission Information:** Regular application deadline 8/1. Nonfall registration accepted. Admission may be deferred for a maximum of one semester. Credit offered for CEEB Advanced Placement tests.

COSTS AND FINANCIAL AID

Average book expense $950. **Required Forms and Deadlines:** FAFSA, Institution's own financial aid form. **Notification of Awards:** Applicants will be notified of awards on a rolling basis beginning 2/15. **Types of Aid:** *Need-based scholarships/grants:* Federal Pell, SEOG, state scholarships/grants, private scholarships, the school's own gift aid. *Loans:* Subsidized Stafford, Unsubsidized Stafford, PLUS, Federal Perkins. *Student Employment:* Federal Work-Study Program available. Institutional employment available. **Financial Aid Statistics:** 68% freshmen, 70% undergrads receive need-based scholarship or grant aid. 66% freshmen, 86% undergrads receive non-need-based scholarship or grant aid. 28% freshmen, 62% undergrads receive need-based self-help aid. 4% freshmen, 13% undergrads receive athletic scholarships. 75% freshmen, 75% undergrads receive any aid. 61% undergrads borrow to pay for school. Average cumulative indebtedness $18,992. **Criteria for awarding institutional aid:** *Non-need-based:* academics, alumni affiliation, art, athletics, job skills, leadership, minority status, music/drama, religious affiliation, state/district residency.

NORTHEASTERN UNIVERSITY

360 Huntington Avenue, Boston, MA 2115
Phone: 617-373-2200 • **Financial Aid Phone:** 617-373-3190
E-mail: admissions@neu.edu • **CEEB Code:** 3667
Fax: 617-373-8780 • **Website:** www.northeastern.edu • **ACT Code:** 1880

This private school was founded in 1898. It has a 73-acre campus.

RATINGS

Admissions Selectivity Rating: 95   Fire Safety Rating: 90

STUDENTS AND FACULTY

Enrollment: 17,382. **Student Body:** 50% female, 50% male, 68% out-of-state, 18% international (140 countries represented). Asian 11%, African American 3%, Caucasian 50%, Hispanic 7%, Native American <1%
Retention and Graduation: 96% freshmen return for sophomore year. 21% grads go on to further study within 1 year.

ACADEMICS

Degrees: bachelor's, master's, post-master's certificate. **Classes:** Most classes have 10–19 students. **Majors with Highest Enrollment:** Engineering; Health Services/Allied Health/Health Sciences. **Special Study Options:** Accelerated program, cooperative education program, cross-registration, distance learning, double major, English as a Second Language (ESL), exchange student program (domestic), honors program, independent study, internships, liberal arts/career combination, student-designed major, study abroad, teacher certification program, ROTC. **Honors programs:** The University Honors Program offers exceptionally motivated students an undergraduate experience charted by meeting academic challenge. The program includes demanding and challenging academic opportunities, connections to an active community of thinkers committed to making a difference, and Living and Learning in the Honors Program thematic communities. The University Honors Program frames opportunities that are intellectually rigorous; promotes global awareness and civic engagement; and empowers students. **Combined degree programs:** BA/MA, BA/MEng. **Disability Services:** Special programs offered to physically disabled students include note-taking services, reader services, tape recorders. **Career services:** Alumni network, alumni services, career/job search classes, career assessment, internships, regional alumni. Career services highlights include our inclusion in Princeton Review's Top 5 in Job Placement Career Services for 2 consecutive years; we host one of the largest Career Fairs in the region each semester—over 500 employers participated in Fall '08 & Spring '09 Career Fairs. We have an "Employer in Residence" program where IBM, Raytheon, and Shawmut Design & Construction make available a company rep one day a week to meet with students to assist in career related topics: résumés, interviews, job openings, and career paths. We also participate in "Call to Serve" (Partnership for Public Service) which educates a new generation about the importance of strong civil service, helps re-establish links between federal agencies and campus, and provides students with information about federal jobs.

FACILITIES

Housing: Coed dorms, special housing for disabled students, special housing for international students, apartments for single students, Wellness Housing, Theme Housing. 95% of campus accessible to physically disabled. **Special Academic Facilities/Equipment:** John D. O'Bryant African American Institute, Egan Science/Engineering Research Center, Behrakis Health Sciences Center, Marine Science Center at Nahant, Center for Subsurfacing Sensing and Imaging Systems (CenSSIS), Center for Complex Network Research, Center for Drug Discovery, Barnett Institute of Chemical and Biological Analysis, Behrakis Health Sciences Center, Center for High Rate Nanomanufacturing, Center for Subsurface Sensing and Imaging Systems (CenSSIS), Egan Science/Engineering Research Center, Institute for Information Assurance, Institute on Urban Health Research, Dukakis Center for Urban and Regional Policy, John D. O'Bryant African-American Institute, Institute on Race and Justice, Institute for Global Innovation Management, Marine Science Center, Marino Recreation Center. **Computers:** 100% of classrooms, 20% of dorms, 100% of libraries, 75% of dining areas, 100% of student union, 100% of common outdoor areas have wireless network access. Students can register for classes online. Administrative functions (other than registration) can be performed online.

CAMPUS LIFE

Environment: Metropolis. **Activities:** Choral groups, concert band, dance, drama/theater, jazz band, literary magazine, music ensembles, musical theater, pep band, radio station, student government, student newspaper, symphony orchestra, television station, yearbook, Campus Ministries, International Student Organization, Model UN. 225 registered organizations, 15 honor societies, 20 religious organizations. 9 fraternities, 8 sororities. **Athletics (Intercollegiate):** *Men:* baseball, basketball, crew/rowing, cross-country, ice hockey, soccer, track/field (outdoor), track/field (indoor). *Women:* basketball, crew/rowing, cross-country, diving, field hockey, ice hockey, soccer, swimming, track/field (outdoor), track/field (indoor), volleyball. **On-Campus Highlights:** International Village, Curry Student Center, Marino Health and Fitness Center, Levine Marketplace & Stetson West Dining, Cyber Café. **Environmental Initiatives:** ACUPCC Presidents Climate Committee LEED certification for new buildings and major renovations Aggressive energy efficiency, conservation, and use of energy management systems; recycling; composting; expanding procurement of dining services items including local produce and fair trade certified products, zero transfat, antibiotic-free poultry, pork, and locally raised beef burger, sustainable seafood, cage free eggs; corporate responsibility partnerships; active engagement with student groups, individual students, staff, and faculty; and expanding community partnerships that further demonstrate NU's sustainability commitment.

ADMISSIONS

Freshman Academic Profile: 65.8% in top 10% of high school class, 91.9% in top 25% of high school class, 98.7% in top 50% of high school class. SAT Math middle 50% range 680-760. SAT Critical Reading middle 50% range 660-740. SAT Writing middle 50% range 640-730. ACT middle 50% range 31-33. Minimum internet-based TOEFL 92. **Basis for Candidate Selection:** *Very important factors considered include:* academic GPA, rigor of secondary school record. *Important factors considered include:* application essay, recommendation(s), standardized test scores, character/personal qualities, extracurricular activities, first generation, talent/ability, volunteer work. *Other factors considered include:* Class rank, alumni/ae relation, geographical residence, interview, racial/ethnic status, state residency, work experience. **Freshman Admission Requirements:** High school diploma is required and GED is accepted. *Academic units required:* 4 English, 3 mathematics, 3 science, (2 science labs), 2 foreign language, 3 social studies, 2 history. **Freshman Admission Statistics:** 59,819 applied, 27% admitted, 18% enrolled. **Transfer Admission Requirements:** college transcript(s), essay or personal statement, statement of good standing from prior institution(s). Minimum college GPA of 2.0 required. Lowest grade transferable C. **General Admission Information:** Application Fee $70. Regular application deadline 1/15. Nonfall registration accepted. Admission may be deferred for a maximum of 1 year. Credit and/or placement offered for CEEB Advanced Placement tests.

COSTS AND FINANCIAL AID

Annual tuition $42,534. Room and board $14,570. Required fees $906. Average book expense $1,000. **Required Forms and Deadlines:** FAFSA, CSS/Financial Aid PROFILE, Noncustodial PROFILE. **Notification of Awards:** Applicants will be notified of awards on a rolling basis beginning 3/15. **Types of Aid:** *Need-based scholarships/grants:* Federal Pell, SEOG, state scholarships/grants, private scholarships, the school's own gift aid. *Loans:* Direct Subsidized Stafford, Direct Unsubsidized Stafford, Direct PLUS, Federal Perkins, Federal Nursing, state loans. *Student Employment:* Federal Work-Study Program available. Institutional employment available. Off-campus job opportunities are excellent. **Criteria for awarding institutional aid:** *Non-need-based:* academics, athletics, minority status.

See page 1106.

NORTHERN ARIZONA UNIVERSITY

PO Box 4084, Flagstaff, AZ 86011-4084
Phone: 928-523-5511 · **Financial Aid Phone:** 855-628-6333
E-mail: admissions@nau.edu · **CEEB Code:** 4006
Fax: 928-523-0226 · **Website:** www.nau.edu · **ACT Code:** 86

This public school was founded in 1899. It has a 740-acre campus.

RATINGS

Admissions Selectivity Rating: 78 **Fire Safety Rating:** 81

STUDENTS AND FACULTY

Enrollment: 23,705. **Student Body:** 58% female, 42% male, 28% out-of-state, 5% international (72 countries represented). Asian 2%, African American 3%, Caucasian 61%, Hispanic 20%, Native American 3%
Retention and Graduation: 74% freshmen return for sophomore year. 33% freshmen graduate within 4 years. 52% freshmen graduate within 6 years.
Faculty: 1,055 full-time faculty, 50% are members of minority groups, 15% are women.

ACADEMICS

Degrees: bachelor's, certificate, master's, post-bachelor's certificate. **Classes:** Most classes have 20–29 students. Most lab/discussion sessions have 20–29 students. **Majors with Highest Enrollment:** Registered Nursing/Registered Nurse; Psychology; Elementary Education and Teaching. **Special Study Options:** Accelerated program, cooperative education program, distance learning, double major, dual enrollment, English as a Second Language (ESL), exchange student program (domestic), honors program, independent study, internships, study abroad, teacher certification program. **Honors programs:** Honors Program. **Disability Services:** Special programs offered to physically disabled students include note-taking services, reader services, tape recorders, tutors. **Career services:** alumni services, career/job search classes, career assessment, internships.

FACILITIES

Housing: Coed dorms, men's dorms, special housing for international students, women's dorms, fraternity/sorority housing, apartments for married students, apartments for single students. 90% of campus accessible to physically disabled. **Special Academic Facilities/Equipment:** Art gallery, art and music studios, observatory, multidisciplinary research center, 4,000-acre experimental forest. **Computers:** 100% of classrooms, 100% of dorms, 100% of libraries, 100% of dining areas, 100% of student union, 25% of common outdoor areas have wireless network access. Students can register for classes online. Administrative functions (other than registration) can be performed online.

CAMPUS LIFE
Environment: Town. **Activities:** Choral groups, concert band, dance, drama/theater, jazz band, marching band, music ensembles, musical theater, opera, radio station, student government, student newspaper, symphony orchestra, television station, yearbook, Campus Ministries, International Student Organization. 193 registered organizations, 20 honor societies, 7 religious organizations. 14 fraternities, 9 sororities. **Athletics (Intercollegiate):** *Men:* basketball, cheerleading, cross-country, football, tennis, track/field (outdoor). *Women:* basketball, cheerleading, cross-country, diving, golf, soccer, swimming, tennis, track/field (outdoor), volleyball. **On-Campus Highlights:** University Union, NAU Dome, Wall Aquatic Center, Cline Library, Old Main. **Environmental Initiatives:** Green Building commitment; Fifty percent of campus landscaping served by reclaimed/non-potable water; ecoPass—Free city bus passes offered to all faculty and staff.

ADMISSIONS
Freshman Academic Profile: Average high school GPA 3.49. 21% in top 10% of high school class, 50% in top 25% of high school class, 83% in top 50% of high school class. SAT Math middle 50% range 460-570. SAT Critical Reading middle 50% range 470-580. SAT Writing middle 50% range 450-560. ACT middle 50% range 20-25. Minimum internet-based TOEFL 70. Minimum paper TOEFL 525. **Basis for Candidate Selection:** *Important factors considered include:* Class rank, academic GPA, rigor of secondary school record, standardized test scores. **Freshman Admission Requirements:** High school diploma is required and GED is accepted. *Academic units required:* 4 English, 4 mathematics, 3 science, (1 science labs), 2 foreign language, 1 social studies, 1 history, 1 Fine Arts. **Freshman Admission Statistics:** 27,780 applied, 91% admitted, 20% enrolled. Minimum college GPA of 2.0 required. Lowest grade transferable C. **General Admission Information:** Application Fee $25. Non-fall registration accepted. Admission may be deferred for a maximum of 2 years. Credit and/or placement offered for CEEB Advanced Placement tests.

COSTS AND FINANCIAL AID
Annual in-state tuition $9,120. Annual out-of-state tuition $21,640. Room and board $9,020. Required fees $870. Average book expense $1,000. **Required Forms and Deadlines:** FAFSA. **Notification of Awards:** Applicants will be notified of awards on a rolling basis beginning 3/15. **Types of Aid:** *Need-based scholarships/grants:* Federal Pell, SEOG, state scholarships/grants, private scholarships, the school's own gift aid, Federal Nursing Scholarships. *Loans:* Direct Subsidized Stafford, Direct Unsubsidized Stafford, Direct PLUS, Federal Perkins, Federal Nursing, state loans, college/university loans from institutional funds. *Student Employment:* Federal Work-Study Program available. Institutional employment available. Off-campus job opportunities are good. **Financial Aid Statistics:** 69% freshmen, 71% undergrads receive need-based scholarship or grant aid. 54% freshmen, 43% undergrads receive non-need-based scholarship or grant aid. 69% freshmen, 71% undergrads receive need-based self-help aid. 2% freshmen, 2% undergrads receive athletic scholarships. 62% freshmen, 65% undergrads receive any aid. 65% undergrads borrow to pay for school. Average cumulative indebtedness $22,422. **Criteria for awarding institutional aid:** *Non-need-based:* academics, alumni affiliation, art, athletics, leadership, minority status, music/drama, state/district residency.

NORTHERN ILLINOIS UNIVERSITY

Office of Admissions, DeKalb, IL 60115-2857
Phone: 815-753-0446 · **Financial Aid Phone:** 815-753-1395
E-mail: admissions-info@niu.edu · **CEEB Code:** 1559
Fax: 815-753-1783 · **Website:** www.reg.niu.edu · **ACT Code:** 1102

This public school was founded in 1895. It has a 546-acre campus.

RATINGS
Admissions Selectivity Rating: 80   **Fire Safety Rating:** 60*

STUDENTS AND FACULTY
Enrollment: 28,551. **Student Body:** 29% female, 71% male, 2% out-of-state, 1% international. Asian 3%, African American 9%, Caucasian 35%, Hispanic 7%, Native American <1%
Retention and Graduation: 28% freshmen graduate within 4 years. 54% freshmen graduate within 6 years. **Faculty:** 891 full-time faculty, 82% hold PhDs, 46% are members of minority groups, 13% are women.

ACADEMICS
Degrees: bachelor's, first professional, master's. **Classes:** Most classes have 20–29 students. Most lab/discussion sessions have 20–29 students. **Special Study Options:** cooperative education program, distance learning, double major, dual enrollment, external degree program, honors program, independent study, internships, liberal arts/career combination, student-designed major, study abroad, teacher certification program. **Combined degree programs:** BA/JD. **Disability Services:** Special programs offered to physically disabled students include note-taking services, tape recorders, tutors. **Career services:** Alumni network, alumni services, career/job search classes, internships, regional alumni. Career services highlights include Comprehensive internship and Cooperative ed. program.

FACILITIES
Housing: Coed dorms, special housing for disabled students, special housing for international students, fraternity/sorority housing, apartments for married studentsQuiet and alcohol-free lifestyle floors, 21 and over/graduates student floors, honors floors. Fllors with visitation policies, computer science residential program. 90% of campus accessible to physically disabled. **Special Academic Facilities/Equipment:** Art and anthropology museums, plant molecular biology center. **Computers:** Students can register for classes online.

CAMPUS LIFE
Environment: Rural. **Activities:** Choral groups, concert band, dance, drama/theater, jazz band, marching band, opera, radio station, student government, student newspaper, student-run film society, symphony orchestra, television station. 200 registered organizations, 13 religious organizations. 22 fraternities, 14 sororities. **Athletics (Intercollegiate):** *Men:* baseball, basketball, diving, football, golf, soccer, swimming, tennis, wrestling. *Women:* basketball, cross-country, golf, gymnastics, soccer, softball, swimming, tennis, volleyball. **On-Campus Highlights:** Barsema Hall, Convocation Center, Holmes Student Center, Campus Life Building, Recreation Center.

ADMISSIONS
Freshman Academic Profile: 11% in top 10% of high school class, 33% in top 25% of high school class, 70% in top 50% of high school class. ACT middle 50% range 19-25. Minimum paper TOEFL 525. **Basis for Candidate Selection:** *Very important factors considered include:* Class rank, rigor of secondary school record, standardized test scores. *Other factors considered include:* application essay, recommendation(s), extracurricular activities, racial/ethnic status, talent/ability. **Freshman Admission Requirements:** High school diploma is required and GED is accepted. *Academic units required:* 4 English, 2 mathematics, 2 science, (1 science labs), 1 foreign language, 2 social studies, 1 history. **Freshman Admission Statistics:** 17,842 applied, 52% admitted, 29% enrolled. **Transfer Admission Requirements:** college transcript(s), Minimum college GPA of 2.0 required. Lowest grade transferable c. **General Admission Information:** Regular application deadline 8/1. Nonfall registration accepted. Credit and/or placement offered for CEEB Advanced Placement tests.

COSTS AND FINANCIAL AID
Room and board $10,648. Average book expense $1,400. **Required Forms and Deadlines:** FAFSA, Institution's own financial aid form, Noncustodial PROFILE. **Notification of Awards:** Applicants will be notified of awards on a rolling basis beginning 4/15. **Types of Aid:** *Need-based scholarships/grants:* Federal Pell, SEOG, state scholarships/grants, private scholarships, the school's own gift aid, Federal Nursing Scholarships. *Loans:* Subsidized Stafford, Unsubsidized Stafford, PLUS, Federal Perkins. *Student Employment:* Off-campus job opportunities are good. **Financial Aid Statistics:** 96% freshmen, 74% undergrads receive need-based scholarship or grant aid. 1% freshmen, 2% undergrads receive non-need-based scholarship or grant aid. 87% freshmen, 88% undergrads receive need-based self-help aid. 3% freshmen, 2% undergrads receive athletic scholarships. 78% freshmen, 68% undergrads receive any aid. 72% undergrads borrow to pay for school. Average cumulative indebtedness $24,769. **Criteria for awarding institutional aid:** *Non-need-based:* academics, athletics.

NORTHERN KENTUCKY UNIVERSITY

Administrative Center 401, Highland Heights, KY 41099
Phone: 859-572-5220 · **Financial Aid Phone:** 859-572-6437
E-mail: admitnku@nku.edu · **CEEB Code:** 1574
Website: www.nku.edu · **ACT Code:** 1566

This public school was founded in 1968. It has a 397-acre campus.

RATINGS
Admissions Selectivity Rating: 78   **Fire Safety Rating:** 81

STUDENTS AND FACULTY

Enrollment: 12,658. **Student Body:** 56% female, 44% male, 31% out-of-state, 1% international (48 countries represented). Asian 1%, African American 7%, Caucasian 84%, Hispanic 2%, Native American <1%
Retention and Graduation: 68% freshmen return for sophomore year. 8% freshmen graduate within 4 years. **Faculty:** 530 full-time faculty, 68% hold PhDs, 51% are members of minority groups, 12% are women. 0% of classes are taught by teaching assistants.

ACADEMICS

Degrees: associate, bachelor's, certificate, first professional, master's, post-bachelor's certificate. **Classes:** Most classes have 20–29 students. Most lab/discussion sessions have 10–19 students. **Majors with Highest Enrollment:** Registered Nursing/Registered Nurse; Psychology; Biology/Biological Sciences. **Special Study Options:** cooperative education program, cross-registration, distance learning, double major, dual enrollment, exchange student program (domestic), honors program, independent study, internships, liberal arts/career combination, study abroad, teacher certification program, weekend college, Web-based Programs. **Honors programs:** The NKU Honors Program provides qualified students a 21-hour minor, which includes 15 semester hours of seminars, each having a maximum enrollment of 15 students, plus 6 semester hours for completing the Honors Thesis. At the core of the Honors experience, the seminars emphasize discussion and discovery of ideas. NKU's Honors Program is university-wide. The program showcases open-ended seminars not conforming to the boundaries traditionally dividing fields of experise. Honors learning affords the intellectual challenges of interdisciplinary education. **Combined degree programs:** MBA/JD. **Disability Services:** Special programs offered to physically disabled students include note-taking services, reader services, tape recorders, tutors. **Career services:** alumni services, career/job search classes, career assessment, internships. Career services highlights include Cooperative Education—a well organized co-op learning program out of the Career Development Center. This program has grown significantly (55%) in the last two years.

FACILITIES

Housing: Coed dorms, special housing for disabled students, men's dorms, women's dorms, cooperative housing, apartments for single students. One-Third of all college housing accessible to handicapped. 100% of campus accessible to physically disabled. **Special Academic Facilities/Equipment:** Art gallery, biology, geology, and anthropology museums, research/technical center, two electron microscopes. **Computers:** Students can register for classes online. Administrative functions (other than registration) can be performed online.

CAMPUS LIFE

Environment: Metropolis. **Activities:** Choral groups, concert band, dance, drama/theater, jazz band, literary magazine, music ensembles, musical theater, opera, pep band, radio station, student government, student newspaper, symphony orchestra, television station. 125 registered organizations, 14 honor societies, 9 religious organizations. 8 fraternities, 8 sororities. **Athletics (Intercollegiate):** *Men:* baseball, basketball, cheerleading, cross-country, golf, soccer, tennis. *Women:* basketball, cheerleading, cross-country, golf, soccer, softball, tennis, volleyball. **On-Campus Highlights:** Natural Science Center, University Suites (housing), Starbucks Café, Albright Health Center, a full service U.S. Bank Branch. **Environmental Initiatives:** NKU has a $4.5 million ESCO (energy savings performance contract to improve lighting, HVAC and water use). Originally expected to pay for itself within 11.7 years, it has been so successful that it will pay for itself in 10 years. NKU partnered with the Transit Authority of Northern Kentucky (TANK) to provide free, unlimited bus rides to students and faculty/staff with a valid university ID. August 2007 through March 2011, this program, called U-PASS, has provided over 900,000 free rides on TANK and NKU shuttle buses for an avoidance of 2,425 metric tons of CO2 equivalent in the Northern Kentucky atmosphere. Since 2007, the campus recycling program has expanded and now includes high-grade paper, cardboard, aluminum, steel cans, plastic/glass bottles, light bulbs, magazines, newspapers, books, and sorted office paper. Some of the more unusual things we recycle are tires and oil from the campus vehicles, plant materials for compost, wood pallets, telephone books, computer equipment, printer cartridges, plates from the print shop and carpet. As an ACUPCC signatory, NKU has participated in RecycleMania for the past four years. Each year, students, faculty/staff and visitors to campus are encouraged to limit their waste and increase their percentage of recyclables.

ADMISSIONS

Freshman Academic Profile: Average high school GPA 3.1. 9.2% in top 10% of high school class, 28.82% in top 25% of high school class, 63.32% in top 50% of high school class. SAT Math middle 50% range 435-555. SAT Critical Reading middle 50% range 430-550. ACT middle 50% range 19-24. Minimum internet-based TOEFL 61. Minimum paper TOEFL 500. **Basis for Candidate Selection:** *Very important factors considered include:* Class rank, academic GPA, standardized test scores. **Freshman Admission Requirements:** High school diploma is required and GED is accepted. *Academic units required:* 4 English, 3 mathematics, 3 science, (1 science labs), 2 foreign language, 3

social studies, 6 academic electives, 1 Health/Physical Education. **Freshman Admission Statistics:** 7,202 applied, 66% admitted, 49% enrolled. **Transfer Admission Requirements:** college transcript(s), Minimum college GPA of 2.0 required. Lowest grade transferable D. **General Admission Information:** Application Fee $30. Regular application deadline 8/1. Notification on a rolling basis, beginning on or about 10/1. Nonfall registration accepted. Credit offered for CEEB Advanced Placement tests.

COSTS AND FINANCIAL AID

Required Forms and Deadlines: FAFSA. **Notification of Awards:** Applicants will be notified of awards on a rolling basis beginning 4/1. **Types of Aid:** *Need-based scholarships/grants:* Federal Pell, SEOG, state scholarships/grants, private scholarships, the school's own gift aid. *Loans:* Subsidized Stafford, Unsubsidized Stafford, PLUS, Federal Perkins, Private Loans. *Student Employment:* Federal Work-Study Program available. Institutional employment available. Highest amount earned per year from on-campus jobs $5,625. Off-campus job opportunities are good. **Financial Aid Statistics:** 53% freshmen, 52% undergrads receive need-based scholarship or grant aid. 71% freshmen, 47% undergrads receive non-need-based scholarship or grant aid. 87% freshmen, 89% undergrads receive need-based self-help aid. 3% freshmen, 2% undergrads receive athletic scholarships. 66% freshmen, 57% undergrads receive any aid. 69% undergrads borrow to pay for school. Average cumulative indebtedness $19,412. **Criteria for awarding institutional aid:** *Non-need-based:* academics, alumni affiliation, art, athletics, job skills, leadership, minority status, music/drama, state/district residency.

NORTHERN MICHIGAN UNIVERSITY

1401 Presque Isle Avenue, Marquette, MI 49855
Phone: 906-227-2650 • **Financial Aid Phone:** 800-682-9797
E-mail: admiss@nmu.edu • **CEEB Code:** 1560
Fax: 906-227-1747 • **Website:** www.nmu.edu • **ACT Code:** 2038

This public school was founded in 1899. It has a 350-acre campus.

RATINGS

Admissions Selectivity Rating: 73   Fire Safety Rating: 70

STUDENTS AND FACULTY

Enrollment: 7,977. **Student Body:** 53% female, 47% male, 19% out-of-state, 1% international (30 countries represented). Asian 1%, African American 2%, Caucasian 81%, Hispanic 1%, Native American 2%
Retention and Graduation: 20% freshmen graduate within 4 years. 47% freshmen graduate within 6 years. **Faculty:**

ACADEMICS

Degrees: associate, bachelor's, certificate, diploma, master's, post-bachelor's certificate, post-master's certificate, terminal associate, transfer associate. **Classes:** Most classes have 20–29 students. **Majors with Highest Enrollment:** Art/Art Studies; Criminal Justice/Safety Studies; Nursing Science. **Special Study Options:** distance learning, double major, dual enrollment, English as a Second Language (ESL), honors program, independent study, internships, liberal arts/career combination, student-designed major, study abroad, teacher certification program, weekend college. **Honors programs:** Honors Program for eligible freshmen and transfer students. **Disability Services:** Special programs offered to physically disabled students include note-taking services, reader services, tape recorders, tutors. **Career services:** Alumni network, career/job search classes, internships. Career services highlights include internships specific to each academic department.

FACILITIES

Housing: Coed dorms, special housing for disabled students, apartments for married students, apartments for single students, Wellness Housing, Theme Housing. 100% of campus accessible to physically disabled. **Special Academic Facilities/Equipment:** Seaborg Science Center, New Science facility, new and remodeled Music and Art and Design instructional rooms, DeVos Art Gallery. **Computers:** 100% of classrooms, 100% of dorms, 100% of libraries, 100% of dining areas, 100% of student union, 100% of common outdoor areas have wireless network access. Students can register for classes online. Administrative functions (other than registration) can be performed online.

CAMPUS LIFE

Environment: Village. **Activities:** Choral groups, concert band, dance, drama/theater, jazz band, literary magazine, marching band, music ensembles, musical theater, opera, pep band, radio station, student government, student newspaper, student-run film society, symphony orchestra, television station, Campus Ministries, International Student Organization, Model UN. 308 registered organizations, 11 honor society, 19 religious organizations. 3 fraternities, 4 sororities. **Athletics (Intercollegiate):** *Men:* basketball, football, golf, ice hockey, skiing (nordic/cross-country). *Women:* basketball, cross-country, diving, skiing (nordic/cross-country), soccer, swimming, track/field (outdoor), track/field (indoor), volleyball. **On-Campus Highlights:** Hedgcock Student Service Center, Superior Dome, New Science Facility, Market Place Dining Facility, De Vos Art Galleries, The Starbucks coffee lounge located in the library is a very popular place and doubles as a study lounge. **Environmental Initiatives:** Northern is a member of the Association for the Advancement of Sustainability in Higher Education and USGBC. Reduced energy consumption by providing computer controlled heating and cooling, thermal efficient windows for the dormitories,individual heating controls in dorm rooms, new efficient lighting and controls technology, new energy efficient architectural design components, water efficient fixtures, wells for irrigation and waterless urinals In 2007 Meyland Hall's renovation received LEED certification, a first for any building in the Upper Peninsula and the first certified residence hall in the states of MI, WI, MN, OH & IN. A total of four residence halls are now certified by LEED.

ADMISSIONS
Freshman Academic Profile: Average high school GPA 3.13. ACT middle 50% range 19-24. Minimum internet-based TOEFL 61. Minimum paper TOEFL 500. **Basis for Candidate Selection:** *Very important factors considered include:* academic GPA, standardized test scores. **Freshman Admission Requirements:** High school diploma is required and GED is accepted. **Freshman Admission Statistics:** 6,841 applied, 68% admitted, 36% enrolled. **Transfer Admission Requirements:** college transcript(s), statement of good standing from prior institution(s). Minimum college GPA of 2.0 required. Lowest grade transferable C-. **General Admission Information:** Application Fee $30. Notification on a rolling basis, beginning on or about 9/15. Nonfall registration accepted. Admission may be deferred for a maximum of 1 year. Credit and/or placement offered for CEEB Advanced Placement tests.

COSTS AND FINANCIAL AID
Annual in-state tuition $8,646. Annual out-of-state tuition $13,542. Room and board $8,404. Average book expense $900. **Required Forms and Deadlines:** FAFSA. **Notification of Awards:** Applicants will be notified of awards on a rolling basis beginning 4/1. **Types of Aid:** *Need-based scholarships/grants:* Federal Pell, SEOG, state scholarships/grants, private scholarships, the school's own gift aid, Federal Nursing Scholarships. *Loans:* Direct Subsidized Stafford, Direct Unsubsidized Stafford, Direct PLUS, Federal Perkins, state loans, Private loans. *Student Employment:* Federal Work-Study Program available. Institutional employment available. Off-campus job opportunities are fair. **Financial Aid Statistics:** 60% freshmen, 61% undergrads receive need-based scholarship or grant aid. 45% freshmen, 36% undergrads receive non-need-based scholarship or grant aid. 77% freshmen, 84% undergrads receive need-based self-help aid. 1% freshmen, 0% undergrads receive athletic scholarships. 68% undergrads borrow to pay for school. Average cumulative indebtedness $23,950. **Criteria for awarding institutional aid:** *Non-need-based:* academics, art, athletics, leadership, minority status, music/drama, religious affiliation, state/district residency.

NORTHERN STATE UNIVERSITY

1200 South Jay Street, Aberdeen, SD 57401-7198
Phone: 605-626-2544 • **Financial Aid Phone:** 605-626-2640
E-mail: admission2@northern.edu • **CEEB Code:** 6487
Fax: 605-626-2531 • **Website:** www.northern.edu • **ACT Code:** 3916

This public school was founded in 1901. It has a 72-acre campus.

RATINGS
Admissions Selectivity Rating: 72   **Fire Safety Rating:** 71

STUDENTS AND FACULTY
Enrollment: 1,693. **Student Body:** 57% female, 43% male, 18% out-of-state, 4% international (35 countries represented). Asian 1%, African American 2%, Caucasian 84%, Hispanic 3%, Native American 2%
Retention and Graduation: 67% freshmen return for sophomore year. 20% freshmen graduate within 4 years. 33% grads go on to further study within 1 year. **Faculty:** 90 full-time faculty, 86% hold PhDs, 37% are members of minority groups, 8% are women. 0% of classes are taught by teaching assistants.

ACADEMICS
Degrees: associate, bachelor's, certificate, master's. **Classes:** Most classes have 10–19 students. **Majors with Highest Enrollment:** Elementary Education and Teaching; Sociology; Business/Commerce. **Special Study Options:** Accelerated program, cooperative education program, cross-registration, distance learning, double major, dual enrollment, English as a Second Language (ESL), exchange student program (domestic), external degree program, honors program, independent study, internships, liberal arts/career combination, student-designed major, study abroad, teacher certification program, weekend college, International Business E-Learning Certification. **Honors programs:** Honors Program **Combined degree programs:** Bachelor's/MBA w/ U of South Dakota. **Disability Services:** Special programs offered to physically disabled students include note-taking services, reader services, tape recorders, tutors. **Career services:** Alumni network, alumni services, career/job search classes, career assessment, internships, regional alumni. Career services highlights include School of Business Programs and School of Education Programs.

FACILITIES
Housing: Coed dorms, men's dorms, women's dorms, apartments for married students, apartments for single students. 90% of campus accessible to physically disabled. **Special Academic Facilities/Equipment:** State-Wide E-Learning Center; Art galleries. **Computers:** 100% of classrooms, 100% of dorms, 100% of libraries, 100% of dining areas, 100% of student union, have wireless network access. Students can register for classes online. Administrative functions (other than registration) can be performed online.

CAMPUS LIFE
Environment: Rural. **Activities:** Choral groups, concert band, dance, drama/theater, jazz band, marching band, music ensembles, musical theater, pep band, student government, student newspaper, symphony orchestra, television station, yearbook, Campus Ministries, International Student Organization. 100 registered organizations, 5 honor societies, 6 religious organizations. **Athletics (Intercollegiate):** *Men:* baseball, basketball, cheerleading, cross-country, football, golf, track/field (outdoor), track/field (indoor), wrestling. *Women:* basketball, cheerleading, cross-country, golf, soccer, softball, swimming, tennis, track/field (outdoor), track/field (indoor), volleyball. **On-Campus Highlights:** NSU Student Center, NSU State-Wide E-Learning Center, NSU Barnett Athletic Center, NSU Johnson Fine Arts Center, NSU International Center of Excellence.

ADMISSIONS
Freshman Academic Profile: Average high school GPA 3.25. 7% in top 10% of high school class, 20% in top 25% of high school class, 60% in top 50% of high school class. SAT Math middle 50% range 370-580. SAT Critical Reading middle 50% range 420-540. ACT middle 50% range 19-25. Minimum internet-based TOEFL 61. Minimum paper TOEFL 525. **Basis for Candidate Selection:** *Very important factors considered include:* Class rank, rigor of secondary school record, standardized test scores. *Other factors considered include:* interview, talent/ability. **Freshman Admission Requirements:** High school diploma is required and GED is accepted. *Academic units required:* 4 English, 3 mathematics, 3 science, (3 science labs), 3 social studies. **Freshman Admission Statistics:** 1,379 applied, 83% admitted, 32% enrolled. **Transfer Admission Requirements:** High school transcript, college transcript(s), statement of good standing from prior institution(s). Minimum college GPA of 2.0 required. Lowest grade transferable C. **General Admission Information:** Application Fee $20. Nonfall registration accepted. Credit and/or placement offered for CEEB Advanced Placement tests.

COSTS AND FINANCIAL AID
Annual in-state tuition $3,993. Annual out-of-state tuition $5,992. Room and board $6,942. Required fees $3,570. Average book expense $1,200. **Required Forms and Deadlines:** FAFSA. **Notification of Awards:** Applicants will be notified of awards on or about 4/15. **Types of Aid:** *Need-based scholarships/grants:* Federal Pell, SEOG, state scholarships/grants, private scholarships, the school's own gift aid. *Loans:* Subsidized Stafford, Unsubsidized Stafford, PLUS, Federal Perkins, college/university loans from institutional funds. *Student Employment:* Federal Work-Study Program available. Institutional employment available. Off-campus job opportunities are excellent. **Financial Aid Statistics:** 92% freshmen, 83% undergrads receive need-based scholarship or grant aid. 8% freshmen, 6% undergrads receive non-need-based scholarship or grant aid. 86% freshmen, 88% undergrads receive need-based self-help aid. 12% freshmen, 9% undergrads receive athletic scholarships. 74% undergrads borrow to pay for school. Average cumulative indebtedness $28,223. **Criteria for awarding institutional aid:** *Non-need-based:* academics, art, athletics, leadership, minority status, music/drama, state/district residency.

NORTHLAND COLLEGE

1411 Ellis Avenue, Ashland, WI 54806-3999
Phone: 715-682-1224 · **Financial Aid Phone:** 715-682-1254
E-mail: admit@northland.edu · **CEEB Code:** 1561
Fax: 715-682-1258 · **Website:** www.northland.edu · **ACT Code:** 4624

This private school, affiliated with the United Church of Christ Church, was founded in 1892. It has a 130-acre campus.

RATINGS

Admissions Selectivity Rating: 84   **Fire Safety Rating:** 73

STUDENTS AND FACULTY

Enrollment: 575. **Student Body:** 50% female, 50% male, 50% out-of-state, 1% international (4 countries represented). Asian 0%, African American 1%, Caucasian 59%, Hispanic 3%, Native American 2%
Retention and Graduation: 66% freshmen return for sophomore year. 41% freshmen graduate within 4 years. 46% freshmen graduate within 6 years. **Faculty:** 47 full-time faculty, 89% hold PhDs, 40% are members of minority groups, 6% are women. 0% of classes are taught by teaching assistants.

ACADEMICS

Degrees: bachelor's. **Classes:** Most classes have 10–19 students. Most lab/discussion sessions have 10–19 students. **Majors with Highest Enrollment:** Natural Resources and Conservation; Biology/Biological Sciences; Community Organization and Advocacy. **Special Study Options:** distance learning, double major, dual enrollment, exchange student program (domestic), honors program, independent study, internships, student-designed major, teacher certification program, 3-2 cooperative programs in Forestry and Engineering with Michigan Technological University and Washington University Eco League consortium with 6 environmental liberal arts colleges around the country (Prescott, Green Mountain, Alaska Pacific University, Antioch College, College of the Atlantic, Northland College) engaging in student semester exchanges. **Combined degree programs:** 3-2 engineering. **Disability Services:** Special programs offered to physically disabled students include note-taking services, reader services, tape recorders, tutors. **Career services:** internships.

FACILITIES

Housing: Coed dorms, women's dorms, cooperative housing, apartments for single students, Theme Housing. **Special Academic Facilities/Equipment:** Native American museum, language lab, field stations in nearby national forest, observatory. **Computers:** 20% of classrooms, 20% of dorms, 100% of libraries, 100% of dining areas, 100% of student union, 75% of common outdoor areas have wireless network access. Students can register for classes online. Administrative functions (other than registration) can be performed online.

CAMPUS LIFE

Environment: Village. **Activities:** Choral groups, concert band, drama/theater, jazz band, music ensembles, radio station, student government, student newspaper, symphony orchestra, yearbook, International Student Organization. 30 registered organizations, 1 honor society, 2 religious organizations. **Athletics (Intercollegiate):** *Men:* baseball, basketball, cross-country, ice hockey, skiing (nordic/cross-country), soccer. *Women:* basketball, cross-country, skiing (nordic/cross-country), soccer, softball, volleyball. **On-Campus Highlights:** Campus Center, Science Center, The Fire Ring, The Environmental Living and Learning Center, The Ravine. **Environmental Initiatives:** Founding member of the Billion Dollar Green Challenge Northland promotes outreach through the Regional Sustainability Coordinator and inreach through student involvement in every major sustainability effort on campus. Northland College has integrated liberal arts studies with an environmental emphasis since 1972.

ADMISSIONS

Freshman Academic Profile: Average high school GPA 3.4. 13% in top 10% of high school class, 43% in top 25% of high school class, 82% in top 50% of high school class. SAT Math middle 50% range 460-580. SAT Critical Reading middle 50% range 488-600. SAT Writing middle 50% range 430-570. ACT middle 50% range 21-26. Minimum paper TOEFL 525. **Basis for Candidate Selection:** *Very important factors considered include:* rigor of secondary school record. *Important factors considered include:* Class rank, application essay, academic GPA, recommendation(s), standardized test scores. *Other factors considered include:* alumni/ae relation, character/personal qualities, extracurricular activities, first generation, geographical residence, interview, level of applicant's interest, talent/ability, volunteer work, work experience. **Freshman Admission Requirements:** High school diploma is required and GED is accepted. *Academic units required:* 4 English, 3 mathematics, 3 science, (2 science labs), 0 foreign language, 3 social studies, 0 history, 0 visual/performing arts, 0 computer science, 3 academic electives. **Freshman Admission Statistics:** 1,020 applied, 63% admitted, 23% enrolled. **Transfer Admission Requirements:** High

school transcript, college transcript(s), essay or personal statement, statement of good standing from prior institution(s). Minimum college GPA of 2.0 required. Lowest grade transferable C-. **General Admission Information:** Application Fee $25. Notification on a rolling basis, beginning on or about 9/1. Nonfall registration accepted. Admission may be deferred for a maximum of 2 years. Credit and/or placement offered for CEEB Advanced Placement tests.

COSTS AND FINANCIAL AID

Annual tuition $30,450. Room and board $7,858. Required fees $1,030. Average book expense $800. **Required Forms and Deadlines:** FAFSA. **Notification of Awards:** Applicants will be notified of awards on a rolling basis beginning 3/1. **Types of Aid:** *Need-based scholarships/grants:* Federal Pell, SEOG, state scholarships/grants, private scholarships, the school's own gift aid, Bureau of Indian Affairs Grants. *Loans:* Direct Subsidized Stafford, Direct Unsubsidized Stafford, Direct PLUS, Subsidized Stafford, Unsubsidized Stafford, PLUS, Federal Perkins. *Student Employment:* Federal Work-Study Program available. Institutional employment available. Highest amount earned per year from on-campus jobs $1,600. Off-campus job opportunities are good. **Financial Aid Statistics:** 100% freshmen, 99% undergrads receive need-based scholarship or grant aid. 19% freshmen, 17% undergrads receive non-need-based scholarship or grant aid. 77% freshmen, 80% undergrads receive need-based self-help aid. 0% freshmen, 0% undergrads receive athletic scholarships. 99% freshmen, 99% undergrads receive any aid. 82% undergrads borrow to pay for school. Average cumulative indebtedness $26,938. **Criteria for awarding institutional aid:** *Non-need-based:* academics, alumni affiliation, art, job skills, leadership, minority status, music/drama, religious affiliation, state/district residency.

NORTHWEST CHRISTIAN COLLEGE

828 East 11th Avenue, Eugene, OR 97401
Phone: 541-684-7201 · **Financial Aid Phone:** 541-684-7203
E-mail: admissions@nwcc.edu · **CEEB Code:** 4543
Fax: 541-628-7317 · **ACT Code:** 10101

This private school was founded in 1895. It has a 8-acre campus.

RATINGS

Admissions Selectivity Rating: 81   **Fire Safety Rating:** 64

STUDENTS AND FACULTY

Enrollment: 380. **Student Body:** 61% female, 39% male, 10% out-of-state, 0% international (0 countries represented). Asian 2%, African American 1%, Caucasian 64%, Hispanic 4%, Native American 2%
Retention and Graduation: 66% freshmen return for sophomore year. 23% freshmen graduate within 4 years. 29% freshmen graduate within 6 years. **Faculty:** 21 full-time faculty, 43% hold PhDs, 52% are members of minority groups, 0% are women. 0% of classes are taught by teaching assistants.

ACADEMICS

Degrees: associate, bachelor's, certificate, master's, post-bachelor's certificate. **Classes:** Most classes have fewer than 10 students. Most lab/discussion sessions have 10–19 students. **Majors with Highest Enrollment:** Teacher Education, Multiple Levels; Business/Commerce. **Special Study Options:** Accelerated program, distance learning, double major, English as a Second Language (ESL), independent study, internships, liberal arts/career combination, student-designed major, study abroad, teacher certification program. **Disability Services:** Special programs offered to physically disabled students include note-taking services, tape recorders, tutors. **Career services:** career/job search classes, career assessment, internships. Career services highlights include internships that are required of all undergraduate students.

FACILITIES

Housing: Coed dorms, apartments for single students. 80% of campus accessible to physically disabled. **Special Academic Facilities/Equipment:** Morse Event Center with gym, athletic facilities, and weight training room plus Student Life and Athletic Offices. Library Museum and Rare Book Collections. **Computers:** Administrative functions (other than registration) can be performed online.

CAMPUS LIFE

Environment: City. **Activities:** Choral groups, concert band, drama/theater, literary magazine, music ensembles, student government, student newspaper, yearbook. 10 registered organizations, 1 honor society, 2 religious organizations. **Athletics (Intercollegiate):** *Men:* basketball, cross-country, soccer. *Women:* basketball, cross-country, soccer, softball, volleyball. **On-Campus Highlights:** Morse Event Center, Bookstore/Internet Café in Dormitory, Chapel, Library, Pomajevich Faculty Building.

ADMISSIONS

Freshman Academic Profile: Average high school GPA 3.34. 11% in top 10% of high school class, 42% in top 25% of high school class, 74% in top 50% of high school class. 89% from public high schools. SAT Math middle 50% range 470-560. SAT Critical Reading middle 50% range 440-540. SAT Writing middle 50% range 410-510. ACT middle 50% range 21-23. Minimum paper TOEFL 500. **Basis for Candidate Selection:** *Very important factors considered include:* academic GPA. *Important factors considered include:* Class rank, application essay, recommendation(s), standardized test scores. *Other factors considered include:* rigor of secondary school record, character/personal qualities, work experience. **Freshman Admission Requirements:** High school diploma is required and GED is accepted. *Academic units required:* 4 English, 3 mathematics, 2 science, (1 science labs), 2 foreign language, 2 social studies, 1 history. **Freshman Admission Statistics:** 232 applied, 61% admitted, 46% enrolled. **Transfer Admission Requirements:** college transcript(s), essay or personal statement, statement of good standing from prior institution(s). Minimum college GPA of 2.2 required. Lowest grade transferable C-. **General Admission Information:** Notification on a rolling basis, beginning on or about 10/15. Nonfall registration accepted. Admission may be deferred for a maximum of 2 years. Credit and/or placement offered for CEEB Advanced Placement tests.

COSTS AND FINANCIAL AID

Average book expense $525. **Required Forms and Deadlines:** FAFSA. **Notification of Awards:** Applicants will be notified of awards on a rolling basis beginning 4/1. **Types of Aid:** *Need-based scholarships/grants:* Federal Pell, SEOG, state scholarships/grants, private scholarships, the school's own gift aid. *Loans:* Subsidized Stafford, Unsubsidized Stafford, PLUS, Federal Perkins. *Student Employment:* Federal Work-Study Program available. Institutional employment available. Off-campus job opportunities are fair. **Financial Aid Statistics:** 100% freshmen, 100% undergrads receive need-based scholarship or grant aid. 13% freshmen, 6% undergrads receive non-need-based scholarship or grant aid. 75% freshmen, 85% undergrads receive need-based self-help aid. 14% freshmen, 5% undergrads receive athletic scholarships. 97% freshmen, 96% undergrads receive any aid. 79% undergrads borrow to pay for school. **Criteria for awarding institutional aid:** *Non-need-based:* academics, athletics, leadership, music/drama, religious affiliation.

NORTHWEST COLLEGE

PO Box 579, Kirkland, WA 98083-0579
Phone: 425-889-5231
E-mail: admissions@ncag.edu • **CEEB Code:** 4541
Fax: 425-889-5224 • **Website:** www.nwcollege.edu • **ACT Code:** 4466

This private school, affiliated with the Assemblies of God Church, was founded in 1934. It has a 56-acre campus.

RATINGS

Admissions Selectivity Rating: 60*   Fire Safety Rating: 60*

STUDENTS AND FACULTY

Enrollment: 1,054. **Student Body:** 62% female, 38% male, 18% out-of-state, 2% international (9 countries represented). Asian 4%, African American 3%, Caucasian 84%, Hispanic 3%, Native American 1%
Retention and Graduation: 66% freshmen return for sophomore year. 35% freshmen graduate within 4 years. 43% freshmen graduate within 6 years. **Faculty:** 50 full-time faculty, 48% hold PhDs, 42% are members of minority groups, 10% are women. 0% of classes are taught by teaching assistants.

ACADEMICS

Degrees: associate, bachelor's, certificate, diploma, master's, post-bachelor's certificate. **Classes:** Most classes have 20–29 students. Most lab/discussion sessions have 10–19 students. **Special Study Options:** Accelerated program, double major, English as a Second Language (ESL), independent study, internships, liberal arts/career combination, study abroad, teacher certification program. **Disability Services:** Special programs offered to physically disabled students include note-taking services, reader services, tape recorders, tutors. **Career services:** career/job search classes, career assessment, internships.

FACILITIES

Housing: men's dorms, women's dorms, apartments for married students, apartments for single students, Apartments for students with dependent children. 80% of campus accessible to physically disabled. **Computers:** Students can register for classes online.

CAMPUS LIFE

Environment: Village. **Activities:** Choral groups, concert band, drama/theater, jazz band, music ensembles, musical theater, radio station, student government,

---

student newspaper, symphony orchestra, yearbook. 15 registered organizations, 9 religious organizations. **Athletics (Intercollegiate):** *Men:* basketball, cross-country, soccer, track/field (outdoor). *Women:* basketball, cross-country, track/field (outdoor), volleyball.

ADMISSIONS

Freshman Academic Profile: Average high school GPA 3.33. 75% from public high schools. Minimum paper TOEFL 500. **Basis for Candidate Selection:** *Very important factors considered include:* application essay, recommendation(s), rigor of secondary school record, standardized test scores, character/personal qualities. *Important factors considered include:* Class rank, extracurricular activities, religious affiliation/commitment. *Other factors considered include:* alumni/ae relation, interview, talent/ability, volunteer work. **Freshman Admission Requirements:** High school diploma is required and GED is accepted. **Freshman Admission Statistics:** 308 applied, 90% admitted, 60% enrolled. **Transfer Admission Requirements:** High school transcript, college transcript(s), essay or personal statement, statement of good standing from prior institution(s). Minimum college GPA of 2.3 required. Lowest grade transferable C. **General Admission Information:** Application Fee $30. Regular application deadline 8/1. Notification on a rolling basis, beginning on or about 10/1. Nonfall registration accepted. Admission may be deferred for a maximum of 12 months. Credit offered for CEEB Advanced Placement tests.

COSTS AND FINANCIAL AID

Annual tuition $13,200. Room and board $6,142. Required fees $324. Average book expense $850. **Required Forms and Deadlines:** FAFSA, Institution's own financial aid form. **Notification of Awards:** Applicants will be notified of awards on a rolling basis beginning 4/15. **Types of Aid:** *Need-based scholarships/grants:* Federal Pell, SEOG, state scholarships/grants, private scholarships, the school's own gift aid. *Loans:* Subsidized Stafford, Unsubsidized Stafford, PLUS, Federal Perkins, state loans, alternative(private) loans. *Student Employment:* Federal Work-Study Program available. Institutional employment available. Highest amount earned per year from on-campus jobs $3,308. Off-campus job opportunities are excellent. **Financial Aid Statistics:** 99% freshmen, 94% undergrads receive need-based scholarship or grant aid. 13% freshmen, 10% undergrads receive non-need-based scholarship or grant aid. 86% freshmen, 87% undergrads receive need-based self-help aid. 4% freshmen, 4% undergrads receive athletic scholarships. 91% undergrads borrow to pay for school. **Criteria for awarding institutional aid:** *Non-need-based:* academics, art, athletics, leadership, music/drama, religious affiliation.

NORTHWEST MISSOURI STATE UNIVERSITY

800 University Drive, Maryville, MO 64468
Phone: 800-633-1175
E-mail: admissions@nwmissouri.edu • **CEEB Code:** 6488
Fax: 660-562-1121 • **ACT Code:** 2338

This public school was founded in 1905. It has a 240-acre campus.

RATINGS

Admissions Selectivity Rating: 80   Fire Safety Rating: 60*

STUDENTS AND FACULTY

Enrollment: 4,956. **Student Body:** 55% female, 45% male, 26% out-of-state, 2% international. Asian 1%, African American 4%, Caucasian 86%, Hispanic 2%, Native American <1%
Retention and Graduation: 74% freshmen return for sophomore year. **Faculty:** 249 full-time faculty, 64% hold PhDs, 45% are members of minority groups, 6% are women. 0% of classes are taught by teaching assistants.

ACADEMICS

Degrees: bachelor's, master's, post-master's certificate. **Classes:** Most classes have 20–29 students. Most lab/discussion sessions have 20–29 students. **Special Study Options:** Accelerated program, distance learning, double major, dual enrollment, English as a Second Language (ESL), honors program, independent study, internships, study abroad, teacher certification program. **Disability Services:** Special programs offered to physically disabled students include note-taking services, reader services, tape recorders, tutors. **Career services:** alumni services, career/job search classes, career assessment, internships.

FACILITIES

Housing: Coed dorms, special housing for disabled students, fraternity/sorority housing, apartments for single students. **Special Academic Facilities/Equipment:** State history and art collections, earth/science museum, broadcasting museum, on-campus elementary lab school, biomass energy plant. **Computers:** Students can register for classes online.

CAMPUS LIFE

Environment: Rural. **Activities:** Choral groups, concert band, dance, drama/theater, jazz band, literary magazine, marching band, music ensembles, musical theater, pep band, radio station, student government, student newspaper, student-run film society, symphony orchestra, television station, yearbook. 174 registered organizations, 13 honor societies, 9 religious organizations. 10 fraternities, 6 sororities. **Athletics (Intercollegiate):** *Men:* baseball, basketball, cheerleading, cross-country, football, rodeo, tennis, track/field (outdoor), track/field (indoor). *Women:* basketball, cheerleading, cross-country, rodeo, soccer, softball, tennis, track/field (outdoor), track/field (indoor), volleyball.

ADMISSIONS

Freshman Academic Profile: Average high school GPA 3.34. 13% in top 10% of high school class, 41% in top 25% of high school class, 80% in top 50% of high school class. 90% from public high schools. SAT Math middle 50% range 480-610. SAT Critical Reading middle 50% range 450-600. ACT middle 50% range 19-24. Minimum paper TOEFL 500. **Basis for Candidate Selection:** *Very important factors considered include:* Class rank, rigor of secondary school record, standardized test scores. *Important factors considered include:* academic GPA. *Other factors considered include:* application essay, recommendation(s), character/personal qualities, extracurricular activities, interview, level of applicant's interest, state residency. **Freshman Admission Requirements:** High school diploma is required and GED is accepted. *Academic units required:* 4 English, 3 mathematics, 2 science, (1 science labs), 3 social studies, 4 academic electives. **Freshman Admission Statistics:** 3,759 applied, 75% admitted, 45% enrolled. **Transfer Admission Requirements:** college transcript(s), statement of good standing from prior institution(s). Minimum college GPA of 2.0 required. Lowest grade transferable D. **General Admission Information:** Application Fee $25. Nonfall registration accepted.

COSTS AND FINANCIAL AID

Average book expense $500. **Required Forms and Deadlines:** FAFSA. **Notification of Awards:** Applicants will be notified of awards on or about 4/15. **Types of Aid:** *Need-based scholarships/grants:* Federal Pell, SEOG, state scholarships/grants, private scholarships, the school's own gift aid. *Loans:* Direct Subsidized Stafford, Direct Unsubsidized Stafford, Direct PLUS, Federal Perkins, college/university loans from institutional funds. *Student Employment:* Federal Work-Study Program available. Institutional employment available. Off-campus job opportunities are fair. **Financial Aid Statistics:** 53% freshmen, 51% undergrads receive need-based scholarship or grant aid. 74% freshmen, 50% undergrads receive non-need-based scholarship or grant aid. 88% freshmen, 87% undergrads receive need-based self-help aid. 0% freshmen, 0% undergrads receive athletic scholarships. 58% undergrads borrow to pay for school. **Criteria for awarding institutional aid:** *Non-need-based:* academics, alumni affiliation, art, athletics, leadership, music/drama, state/district residency.

NORTHWEST NAZARENE UNIVERSITY

623 S. University Blvd., Nampa, ID 83686
Phone: 208-467-8000 · **Financial Aid Phone:** 208-467-8641
E-mail: admissions@nnu.edu · **CEEB Code:** 4544
Fax: 208-467-8645 · **Website:** www.nnu.edu · **ACT Code:** 924

This private school, affiliated with the Nazarene Church, was founded in 1913. It has a 85-acre campus.

RATINGS

Admissions Selectivity Rating: 86   Fire Safety Rating: 65

STUDENTS AND FACULTY

Enrollment: 1,263. **Student Body:** 59% female, 41% male, 51% out-of-state, 2% international (20 countries represented). Asian 2%, African American 1%, Caucasian 68%, Hispanic 6%, Native American <1%
Faculty: 103 full-time faculty, 73% hold PhDs, 45% are members of minority groups, 6% are women. 0% of classes are taught by teaching assistants.

ACADEMICS

Degrees: bachelor's, master's. **Majors with Highest Enrollment:** Education; Registered Nursing/Registered Nurse; Business/Commerce. **Special Study Options:** cooperative education program, cross-registration, distance learning, double major, English as a Second Language (ESL), exchange student program (domestic), honors program, independent study, internships, liberal arts/career combination, student-designed major, study abroad, teacher certification program, Many service and ministry programs and opportunities. **Combined degree programs:** 3-2 engineering program with any co-op institution. **Disability Services:** Special programs offered to physically disabled students include reader services, tape recorders, tutors. **Career services:** Alumni network, career/job search classes, internships, regional alumni.

FACILITIES

Housing: Coed dorms, men's dorms, women's dorms, apartments for married students, apartments for single students, Off-campus housing owned the by University include rental homes and units. 70% of campus accessible to physically disabled. **Computers:** 100% of classrooms, have wireless network access. Administrative functions (other than registration) can be performed online.

CAMPUS LIFE

Environment: City. **Activities:** Choral groups, concert band, drama/theater, jazz band, literary magazine, music ensembles, musical theater, pep band, student government, student newspaper, symphony orchestra, yearbook, Campus Ministries, International Student Organization 21 registered organizations, 6 honor societies, 8 religious organizations. **Athletics (Intercollegiate):** *Men:* baseball, basketball, cross-country, golf, soccer, track/field (outdoor), track/field (indoor). *Women:* basketball, cross-country, soccer, softball, track/field (outdoor), track/field (indoor), volleyball. **On-Campus Highlights:** Helstrom Business Center, The Brandt Center, Ford Hall, Johnson Sports Center, Student Center.

ADMISSIONS

Freshman Academic Profile: Average high school GPA 3.54. 29% in top 10% of high school class, 52% in top 25% of high school class, 81% in top 50% of high school class. SAT Math middle 50% range 470-620. SAT Critical Reading middle 50% range 470-600. SAT Writing middle 50% range 470-570. ACT middle 50% range 21-27. Minimum paper TOEFL 500. **Basis for Candidate Selection:** *Very important factors considered include:* Class rank, academic GPA, standardized test scores, character/personal qualities. *Other factors considered include:* recommendation(s), rigor of secondary school record, alumni/ae relation, extracurricular activities, religious affiliation/commitment, talent/ability. **Freshman Admission Requirements:** High school diploma is required and GED is accepted. **Freshman Admission Statistics:** 984 applied, 69% admitted, 41% enrolled. **Transfer Admission Requirements:** college transcript(s), Minimum college GPA of 2.0 required. Lowest grade transferable C-. **General Admission Information:** Application Fee $25. Regular application deadline 8/15. Nonfall registration accepted. Credit and/or placement offered for CEEB Advanced Placement tests.

COSTS AND FINANCIAL AID

Annual tuition $26,150. Room and board $6,400. Required fees $400. Average book expense $1,160. **Required Forms and Deadlines:** FAFSA. **Notification of Awards:** Applicants will be notified of awards on a rolling basis beginning 4/1. **Types of Aid:** *Need-based scholarships/grants:* Federal Pell, SEOG, state scholarships/grants, private scholarships, the school's own gift aid. *Loans:* Subsidized Stafford, Unsubsidized Stafford, PLUS, Federal Perkins, college/university loans from institutional funds, Bank Loans. *Student Employment:* Federal Work-Study Program available. Institutional employment available. Highest amount earned per year from on-campus jobs $8,739. Off-campus job opportunities are good. **Financial Aid Statistics:** 100% freshmen, 95% undergrads receive need-based scholarship or grant aid. 14% freshmen, 8% undergrads receive non-need-based scholarship or grant aid. 72% freshmen, 79% undergrads receive need-based self-help aid. 9% freshmen, 9% undergrads receive athletic scholarships. 64% undergrads borrow to pay for school. Average cumulative indebtedness $24,799. **Criteria for awarding institutional aid:** *Non-need-based:* academics, alumni affiliation, art, athletics, leadership, minority status, music/drama, religious affiliation, state/district residency.

NORTHWESTERN COLLEGE (IA)

101 7th St SW, Orange City, IA 51041
Phone: 712-707-7130 · **Financial Aid Phone:** 712-707-7131
E-mail: admissions@nwciowa.edu · **CEEB Code:** 6490
Fax: 712-707-7164 · **Website:** www.nwciowa.edu · **ACT Code:** 1346

This private school, affiliated with the Reformed Church Church, was founded in 1882. It has a 100-acre campus.

RATINGS

Admissions Selectivity Rating: 84   Fire Safety Rating: 91

STUDENTS AND FACULTY

Enrollment: 1,113. **Student Body:** 57% female, 43% male, 47% out-of-state, 3% international (23 countries represented). Asian 1%, African American 1%, Caucasian 84%, Hispanic 5%, Native American <1%
Retention and Graduation: 77% freshmen return for sophomore year. 54% freshmen graduate within 4 years. 63% freshmen graduate within 6 years. 14% grads go on to further study within 1 year. **Faculty:** 83 full-time faculty, 83% hold PhDs, 39% are members of minority groups. 0% of classes are taught by teaching assistants.

ACADEMICS

Degrees: bachelor's, certificate. **Classes:** Most classes have 10–19 students. **Majors with Highest Enrollment:** Education; Registered Nursing/Registered Nurse; Business/Commerce. **Special Study Options:** double major, English as a Second Language (ESL), honors program, independent study, internships, liberal arts/career combination, student-designed major, study abroad, teacher certification program, Off Campus Study Programs: American Studies Program (Washington, D.C.), AuSable Inst of Environmental Studies Program (Michigan), Los Angeles Film Studies Semester, Chicago Metropolitan Studies Program (Chicago), China Studies Program (Xiaman, China), Middle East Studies Program (Cairo, Egypt), Oxford Summer Program (Oxford, England), Romanian Studies Program, Russian Studies Program, Contemporary Music Center (Martha's Vineyard, MA), Latin American Studies Program (Costa Rica), Oxford Honours Programme (England), Trinity Christian College: Semester in Spain, and Creation Care Study Program. **Honors programs:** Honors Program: Affords students an interdisciplinary approach to understanding perennial and contemporary issues, such as technology, war and peace, gender roles, work and calling, and humor. Affords students th eopportunity to delve more deeply into a topic of their choice, workinh with selected faculty members to complete a project that goes beyond the normal upper-division work at the college. Encourages graduate education by sponsoring trips to regional graduate schools and financially supporting graduate school applications. **Disability Services:** Special programs offered to physically disabled students include note-taking services, reader services, tape recorders, tutors. **Career services:** alumni services, career/job search classes, career assessment, internships. Career services highlights include internships.

FACILITIES

Housing: special housing for disabled students, men's dorms, women's dorms, apartments for single students, Theme housing (i.e., Spanish house, etc.). 90% of campus accessible to physically disabled. **Special Academic Facilities/Equipment:** Thea G Korver Visual Arts Center-Art Gallery; DeWitt Theatre Arts Center-Proscenium Theatre, Black Box Theatre, Costume Shop. **Computers:** 75% of classrooms, 30% of dorms, 100% of libraries, 100% of dining areas, 100% of student union, 30% of common outdoor areas have wireless network access. Students can register for classes online. Administrative functions (other than registration) can be performed online.

CAMPUS LIFE

Environment: Rural. **Activities:** Choral groups, concert band, dance, drama/theater, jazz band, literary magazine, music ensembles, musical theater, pep band, student government, student newspaper, symphony orchestra, television station, yearbook. 30 registered organizations, 2 honor societies, 5 religious organizations. **Athletics (Intercollegiate):** *Men:* baseball, basketball, cheerleading, cross-country, football, golf, soccer, track/field (outdoor), track/field (indoor), wrestling. *Women:* basketball, cheerleading, cross-country, golf, soccer, softball, track/field (outdoor), track/field (indoor), volleyball. **On-Campus Highlights:** Rowenhorst Student Center, Bultman Center Gym, DeWitt Theatre Arts Center, Korver Visual Arts Center

ADMISSIONS

Freshman Academic Profile: Average high school GPA 3.6. 23% in top 10% of high school class, 55% in top 25% of high school class, 87% in top 50% of high school class. 74% from public high schools. SAT Math middle 50% range 490-640. SAT Critical Reading middle 50% range 455-600. SAT Writing middle 50% range 420-590. ACT middle 50% range 21-27. Minimum paper TOEFL 475. **Basis for Candidate Selection:** *Very important factors considered include:* Class rank, rigor of secondary school record, standardized test scores. *Important factors considered include:* application essay, academic GPA, recommendation(s), character/personal qualities, first generation, interview, level of applicant's interest, talent/ability. *Other factors considered include:* extracurricular activities, religious affiliation/commitment. **Freshman Admission Requirements:** High school diploma is required and GED is accepted. **Freshman Admission Statistics:** 1,254 applied, 78% admitted, 32% enrolled. **Transfer Admission Requirements:** college transcript(s), Minimum college GPA of 2.2 required. Lowest grade transferable C. **General Admission Information:** Application Fee $25. Notification on a rolling basis, beginning on or about 10/1. Nonfall registration accepted. Admission may be deferred for a maximum of 4 years. Credit and/or placement offered for CEEB Advanced Placement tests.

COSTS AND FINANCIAL AID

Annual tuition $28,750. Room and board $8,750. Required fees $300. Average book expense $1,200. **Required Forms and Deadlines:** FAFSA. **Notification of Awards:** Applicants will be notified of awards on a rolling basis beginning 3/15. **Types of Aid:** *Need-based scholarships/grants:* Federal Pell, SEOG, state scholarships/grants, private scholarships, the school's own gift aid, United Negro College Fund. *Loans:* Subsidized Stafford, Unsubsidized Stafford, PLUS, Federal Perkins, college/university loans from institutional funds. *Student Employment:* Highest amount earned per year from on-campus jobs $2,100. Off-campus job opportunities are fair. **Financial Aid Statistics:** 97% freshmen, 95% undergrads receive need-based scholarship or grant aid. 95% freshmen, 97% undergrads receive non-need-based scholarship or grant aid. 79% fresh-men, 81% undergrads receive need-based self-help aid. 11% freshmen, 8% undergrads receive athletic scholarships. 100% freshmen, 99% undergrads receive any aid. 85% undergrads borrow to pay for school. Average cumulative indebtedness $24,128. **Criteria for awarding institutional aid:** *Non-need-based:* academics, art, athletics, music/drama, religious affiliation.

NORTHWESTERN STATE UNIVERSITY

South Hall, Natchitoches, LA 71497
Phone: 318-357-4078 · **Financial Aid Phone:** 800-823-3008
E-mail: applications@nsula.edu · **CEEB Code:** 6492
Fax: 318-357-4660 · **Website:** www.nsula.edu • **ACT Code:** 1600

This public school was founded in 1884. It has a 916-acre campus.

RATINGS

Admissions Selectivity Rating: 75   **Fire Safety Rating:** 81

STUDENTS AND FACULTY

Enrollment: 7,333. **Student Body:** 68% female, 32% male, 9% out-of-state, 1% international (34 countries represented). Asian 1%, African American 30%, Caucasian 57%, Hispanic 3%, Native American 1%
Retention and Graduation: 71% freshmen return for sophomore year. 17% freshmen graduate within 4 years. 36% freshmen graduate within 6 years. **Faculty:** 291 full-time faculty, 60% hold PhDs, 55% are members of minority groups, 8% are women. 1% of classes are taught by teaching assistants.

ACADEMICS

Degrees: associate, bachelor's, master's, post-master's certificate. **Classes:** Most classes have 10–19 students. Most lab/discussion sessions have fewer than 10 students. **Majors with Highest Enrollment:** General Studies; Registered Nursing/Registered Nurse; Business Administration and Management. **Special Study Options:** cooperative education program, distance learning, double major, dual enrollment, honors program, independent study, internships, study abroad, teacher certification program. **Honors programs:** The Louisiana Scholar's College is a special institution at Northwestern that enrolls students in a strong liberal arts program while simultaneously letting them take part in the other great areas of NSU. **Disability Services:** Special programs offered to physically disabled students include note-taking services, reader services, tape recorders, tutors. **Career services:** alumni services, career/job search classes, career assessment, internships.

FACILITIES

Housing: Coed dorms, special housing for disabled students, fraternity/sorority housing, apartments for married students, apartments for single students, Theme Housing. 96% of campus accessible to physically disabled. **Special Academic Facilities/Equipment:** Cammie G. Henry Research Center; Louisiana Creole Heritage Center; Louisiana Folklife Center; Louisiana Regional Folklife Center; The Space Science Group; Williamson Museum. **Computers:** 50% of classrooms, 100% of dorms, 100% of libraries, 50% of dining areas, 100% of student union, 75% of common outdoor areas have wireless network access. Students can register for classes online. Administrative functions (other than registration) can be performed online.

CAMPUS LIFE

Environment: Village. **Activities:** Choral groups, concert band, dance, drama/theater, jazz band, literary magazine, marching band, music ensembles, musical theater, opera, pep band, radio station, student government, student newspaper, symphony orchestra, television station, yearbook, Campus Ministries, International Student Organization. 109 registered organizations, 11 honor society, 6 religious organizations. 10 fraternities, 7 sororities. **Athletics (Intercollegiate):** *Men:* baseball, basketball, cheerleading, cross-country, football, soccer, track/field (outdoor), track/field (indoor). *Women:* basketball, cheerleading, cross-country, soccer, softball, tennis, track/field (outdoor), track/field (indoor), volleyball. **On-Campus Highlights:** Wellness, Recreation, and Activity Center, Student Union, University Place Apartments, University Columns Apartments, BCM/CSO/Wellesley Foundation. **Environmental Initiatives:** NSU student groups and organizations participate in recycling, liter-abatement, campus beautification, and related Green service (and service-learning) activities. Professors of courses in the Arts and the Sciences have adopted Green topics for class assignments and projects. All Freshman are invited to attend a seminar that addresses conservation, recycling, and other sustainable practices on campus.

ADMISSIONS

Freshman Academic Profile: Average high school GPA 3.16. 16% in top 10% of high school class, 39% in top 25% of high school class, 72% in top 50% of high school class. SAT Math middle 50% range 435-555. SAT Critical Reading middle 50% range 435-550. ACT middle 50% range 19-23. Minimum internet-based TOEFL 61. Minimum paper TOEFL 500. **Basis for Candi-**

date Selection: *Very important factors considered include:* rigor of secondary school record, standardized test scores. *Important factors considered include:* Class rank, academic GPA. *Other factors considered include:* alumni/ae relation, extracurricular activities, geographical residence, state residency, talent/ability. **Freshman Admission Requirements:** High school diploma is required and GED is accepted. *Academic units required:* 4 English, 3 mathematics, 3 science, (3 science labs), 2 foreign language, 1 social studies, 2 history, 1 visual/performing arts, 1 Other: One additional math or science. **Freshman Admission Statistics:** 2,633 applied, 83% admitted, 51% enrolled. **Transfer Admission Requirements:** college transcript(s), statement of good standing from prior institution(s). Minimum college GPA of 2.0 required. Lowest grade transferable D. **General Admission Information:** Application Fee $20. Regular application deadline 7/6. Notification on a rolling basis, beginning on or about 1/1. Nonfall registration accepted. Admission may be deferred for a maximum of 3 Semesters w/o Fee. Credit and/or placement offered for CEEB Advanced Placement tests.

COSTS AND FINANCIAL AID

Required Forms and Deadlines: FAFSA, Institution's own financial aid form. **Notification of Awards:** Applicants will be notified of awards on a rolling basis beginning 5/1. **Types of Aid:** *Need-based scholarships/grants:* Federal Pell, SEOG, state scholarships/grants, private scholarships, the school's own gift aid, United Negro College Fund, Federal Nursing Scholarships, Third Party Scholarships. *Loans:* Subsidized Stafford, Unsubsidized Stafford, PLUS, Federal Perkins, Alternative Loans. *Student Employment:* Federal Work-Study Program available. Institutional employment available. Highest amount earned per year from on-campus jobs $9,218. Off-campus job opportunities are fair. **Financial Aid Statistics:** 64% freshmen, 65% undergrads receive need-based scholarship or grant aid. 67% freshmen, 45% undergrads receive non-need-based scholarship or grant aid. 56% freshmen, 64% undergrads receive need-based self-help aid. 6% freshmen, 5% undergrads receive athletic scholarships. 91% freshmen, 82% undergrads receive any aid. 67% undergrads borrow to pay for school. Average cumulative indebtedness $22,453. **Criteria for awarding institutional aid:** *Non-need-based:* academics, alumni affiliation, art, athletics, job skills, leadership, minority status, music/drama, religious affiliation, state/district residency.

NORTHWESTERN UNIVERSITY

1801 Hinman Ave, Evanston, IL 60208
Phone: 847-491-7271 · **Financial Aid Phone:** 847-491-7400
E-mail: ug-admission@northwestern.edu · **CEEB Code:** 1565
Website: www.northwestern.edu · **ACT Code:** 1106

This private school was founded in 1851. It has a 240-acre campus.

RATINGS

Admissions Selectivity Rating: 98   Fire Safety Rating: 75

STUDENTS AND FACULTY

Enrollment: 8,936. **Student Body:** 50% female, 50% male, 67% out-of-state, 8% international (77 countries represented). Asian 17%, African American 6%, Caucasian 53%, Hispanic 11%, Native American <1%
Retention and Graduation: 97% freshmen return for sophomore year. 23% grads go on to further study within 1 year. 7% grads pursue arts and sciences degrees. 3% grads pursue law degrees. 1% grads pursue business degrees. 7% grads pursue medical degrees. **Faculty:** 1,422 full-time faculty, 100% hold PhDs, 37% are members of minority groups, 17% are women. 2% of classes are taught by teaching assistants.

ACADEMICS

Degrees: bachelor's, certificate, first professional, master's, post-master's certificate. **Classes:** Most classes have fewer than 10 students. Most lab/discussion sessions have 10–19 students. **Majors with Highest Enrollment:** Economics; Engineering; Journalism. **Special Study Options:** Accelerated program, cooperative education program, double major, honors program, independent study, internships, liberal arts/career combination, student-designed major, study abroad, teacher certification program. **Honors programs:** Honors Program in Medical Education, Integrated Science Program, MENU, MMSS **Combined degree programs:** BA/MD, BA/MA, BM/MS, BA/BS, BA/BM, BS/BM, BS/MS. **Disability Services:** Special programs offered to physically disabled students include note-taking services, reader services, tape recorders, tutors. **Career services:** Alumni network, alumni services, career/job search classes, career assessment, internships, regional alumni. Career services highlights

include the opportunity for all undergraduates to gain real-world experience through internships, field studies programs, and practicums. These programs place students in corporations, newsrooms, archaeological dig sites, and laboratories throughout Chicago, the United States, and the world.

FACILITIES

Housing: Coed dorms, men's dorms, women's dorms, fraternity/sorority housing, Wellness Housing, Theme Housing. 100% of campus accessible to physically disabled. **Special Academic Facilities/Equipment:** Art gallery, learning sciences institute, communicative disorders and materials and life sciences buildings, catalysis center, astronomical research center. Ford Motor Compay Engineering Design Center for engineering students. **Computers:** 100% of classrooms, 100% of dorms, 100% of libraries, 100% of dining areas, 100% of student union, 100% of common outdoor areas have wireless network access. Students can register for classes online.

CAMPUS LIFE

Environment: Town. **Activities:** Choral groups, concert band, dance, drama/theater, jazz band, literary magazine, marching band, music ensembles, musical theater, opera, pep band, radio station, student government, student newspaper, student-run film society, symphony orchestra, television station, yearbook, Campus Ministries, International Student Organization, Model UN. 415 registered organizations, 23 honor societies, 29 religious organizations. 17 fraternities, 19 sororities. **Athletics (Intercollegiate):** *Men:* baseball, basketball, cheerleading, diving, football, golf, soccer, swimming, tennis, wrestling. *Women:* basketball, cheerleading, cross-country, diving, fencing, field hockey, golf, lacrosse, soccer, softball, swimming, tennis, volleyball. **On-Campus Highlights:** Shakespeare Garden, Dearborn Observatory, Norris Student Center, Henry Crown Sports Pavilion and Acquatic Center, The lakefill on Lake Michigan. **Environmental Initiatives:** The development of a Strategic Plan for sustainability that will detail the long-term sustainability vision and goals for Northwestern University as well as putting in place the governance and accountability for the implementation of that plan and communicating our progress to stakeholders at all levels. A comprehensive approach to Energy Efficiency and Alternative Energy consisting of several phases of energy efficiency initiatives ranging from prescriptive programs to upgrade lighting and controls to a $15M–$22M fund set-aside for the completion of campus-wide energy conservation measures identified through 3rd party audits. In addition, the University has increased its commitment to purchase of renewable energy credits to 30% of the University's usage or almost 75,000 MWh placing NU 6th nationally in green power purchases (US EPA Green Power Partnership) as well as the installation of a 17kW solar PV array on the Ford Engineering Design Center (LEED certified) A commitment to LEED certification in all new construction and major renovations; of the last six major projects, five were awarded LEED Gold and one was awarded LEED silver. The next three major projects; the Bienen school of music, the new visitors center and the new Kellogg School of Business have all targeted LEED Gold or higher.

ADMISSIONS

Freshman Academic Profile: 90% in top 10% of high school class, 100% in top 25% of high school class, 65% from public high schools. SAT Math middle 50% range 700-790. SAT Critical Reading middle 50% range 690-770. ACT middle 50% range 31-34. **Basis for Candidate Selection:** *Very important factors considered include:* Class rank, application essay, academic GPA, rigor of secondary school record, standardized test scores. *Important factors considered include:* recommendation(s), character/personal qualities, extracurricular activities, talent/ability. *Other factors considered include:* alumni/ae relation, first generation, interview, level of applicant's interest, racial/ethnic status, volunteer work, work experience. **Freshman Admission Requirements:** High school diploma or equivalent is not required. **Freshman Admission Statistics:** 33,673 applied, 13% admitted, 46% enrolled. **Transfer Admission Requirements:** High school transcript, college transcript(s), essay or personal statement, standardized test scores, statement of good standing from prior institution(s). Minimum college GPA of 3.0 required. Lowest grade transferable C. **General Admission Information:** Application Fee $65. Early decision application deadline 11/1. Regular application deadline 1/1. Regular notification 4/15. Nonfall registration accepted. Admission may be deferred for a maximum of 1 year. Credit and/or placement offered for CEEB Advanced Placement tests.

COSTS AND FINANCIAL AID

Annual tuition $46,836. Room and board $14,389. Required fees $415. Average book expense $1,914. **Required Forms and Deadlines:** FAFSA, CSS/Financial Aid PROFILE, Noncustodial PROFILE. **Notification of Awards:** Applicants will be notified of awards on or about 4/15. **Types of Aid:** *Need-based scholarships/grants:* Federal Pell, SEOG, state scholarships/grants, private scholarships, the school's own gift aid, United Negro College Fund. *Loans:* Subsidized Stafford, Unsubsidized Stafford, PLUS, Federal Perkins, college/university loans from institutional funds. *Student Employment:* Federal Work-Study Program available. Institutional employment available. Off-campus job opportunities are excellent. **Financial Aid Statistics:** 98% freshmen, 97% undergrads receive need-based scholarship or grant aid. 0% freshmen, 0% undergrads receive non-need-based scholarship or grant aid. 75% freshmen,

78% undergrads receive need-based self-help aid. 5% freshmen, 5% undergrads receive athletic scholarships. 46% undergrads borrow to pay for school. Average cumulative indebtedness $17,197. **Criteria for awarding institutional aid:** *Non-need-based:* academics, athletics, music/drama.

NORTHWOOD UNIVERSITY

4000 Whiting Drive, Midland, MI 48640
Phone: 989-837-4273 · **Financial Aid Phone:** 989-837-4320
E-mail: miadmit@northwood.edu · **CEEB Code:** 1568
Fax: 989-837-4273 · **Website:** www.northwood.edu · **ACT Code:** 2041

This private school was founded in 1959. It has a 434-acre campus.

RATINGS

Admissions Selectivity Rating: 79   **Fire Safety Rating:** 76

STUDENTS AND FACULTY

Enrollment: 1,530. **Student Body:** 38% female, 62% male, 11% out-of-state, 9% international (26 countries represented). Asian 1%, African American 8%, Caucasian 71%, Hispanic 3%, Native American <1%
Retention and Graduation: 77% freshmen return for sophomore year. 33% freshmen graduate within 4 years. 54% freshmen graduate within 6 years.
Faculty: 53 full-time faculty, 38% hold PhDs, 32% are members of minority groups, 9% are women. 0% of classes are taught by teaching assistants.

ACADEMICS

Degrees: bachelor's, master's. **Classes:** Most classes have 10–19 students. **Majors with Highest Enrollment:** Sport and Fitness Administration/Management; Business Administration and Management. **Special Study Options:** Accelerated program, distance learning, double major, dual enrollment, external degree program, honors program, independent study, internships, study abroad, weekend college. **Honors programs:** An Honors Program began in Fall Term, 1991. In it, honors sections of six critically important courses are offered. The best instructors and the most demanding material and expectations are used. Additionally, special one credit hour seminars, which include outside speakers, are offered to sophomores and juniors. **Disability Services:** Special programs offered to physically disabled students include tutors. **Career services:** Alumni network, alumni services, career/job search classes, career assessment, internships.

FACILITIES

Housing: men's dorms, women's dorms, apartments for single students **Special Academic Facilities/Equipment:** Hach Student Life Center, Gerstacker Student Union **Computers:** 100% of classrooms, 100% of dorms, 100% of libraries, 100% of dining areas, 100% of student union, have wireless network access. Students can register for classes online. Administrative functions (other than registration) can be performed online.

CAMPUS LIFE

Environment: Town. **Activities:** Choral groups, dance, drama/theater, pep band, student government, student newspaper, yearbook, International Student Organization. 42 registered organizations, 2 honor societies, 2 religious organizations. 9 fraternities, 3 sororities. **Athletics (Intercollegiate):** *Men:* baseball, basketball, cheerleading, cross-country, football, golf, soccer, tennis, track/field (outdoor), track/field (indoor). *Women:* basketball, cheerleading, cross-country, golf, soccer, softball, tennis, track/field (outdoor), track/field (indoor), volleyball. **On-Campus Highlights:** Hach Student Life Center, Mid-Caf @ Northwood, Bennett Sports Center.

ADMISSIONS

Freshman Academic Profile: Average high school GPA 3.26. 12% in top 10% of high school class, 40% in top 25% of high school class, 71% in top 50% of high school class. 70% from public high schools. SAT Math middle 50% range 470-580. SAT Critical Reading middle 50% range 410-540. ACT middle 50% range 20-25. Minimum paper TOEFL 500. **Basis for Candidate Selection:** *Very important factors considered include:* level of applicant's interest. *Important factors considered include:* academic GPA, standardized test scores. *Other factors considered include:* Class rank, application essay, recommendation(s), rigor of secondary school record, alumni/ae relation, character/personal qualities, extracurricular activities, interview. **Freshman Admission Requirements:** High school diploma is required and GED is accepted. **Freshman Admission Statistics:** 1,258 applied, 68% admitted, 39% enrolled. **Transfer Admission Requirements:** college transcript(s), Minimum college GPA of 2.0 required. Lowest grade transferable C. **General Admission Information:** Application Fee $25. Notification on a rolling basis, beginning on or about 1/1. Nonfall registration accepted. Admission may be deferred for a maximum of 1 term. Credit and/or placement offered for CEEB Advanced Placement tests.

COSTS AND FINANCIAL AID

Required Forms and Deadlines: FAFSA, State aid form. **Notification of Awards:** Applicants will be notified of awards on a rolling basis beginning 3/1. **Types of Aid:** *Need-based scholarships/grants:* Federal Pell, SEOG, state scholarships/grants, private scholarships, the school's own gift aid. *Loans:* Subsidized Stafford, Unsubsidized Stafford, PLUS, state loans. *Student Employment:* Federal Work-Study Program available. Institutional employment available. Off-campus job opportunities are fair. **Financial Aid Statistics:** 91% freshmen, 88% undergrads receive need-based scholarship or grant aid. 41% freshmen, 38% undergrads receive non-need-based scholarship or grant aid. 84% freshmen, 87% undergrads receive need-based self-help aid. 9% freshmen, 7% undergrads receive athletic scholarships. 74% undergrads borrow to pay for school. Average cumulative indebtedness $25,588. **Criteria for awarding institutional aid:** *Non-need-based:* academics, athletics, leadership, minority status.

NORTHWOOD UNIVERSITY, FLORIDA CAMPUS

2600 North Military Trail, West Palm Beach, FL 33409-2911
Phone: (561) 478-5500 · **Financial Aid Phone:** 561-478-5590
E-mail: fladmit@northwood.edu · **CEEB Code:** 4072
Fax: 561-681-7901 · **Website:** northwood.edu · **ACT Code:** 6736

This private school was founded in 1982. It has a 90-acre campus.

RATINGS

Admissions Selectivity Rating: 82   **Fire Safety Rating:** 76

STUDENTS AND FACULTY

Enrollment: 490. **Student Body:** 36% female, 64% male, 37% out-of-state, 39% international (40 countries represented). Asian 1%, African American 10%, Caucasian 25%, Hispanic 11%, Native American 1%
Retention and Graduation: 60% freshmen return for sophomore year. 24% freshmen graduate within 4 years. **Faculty:** 16 full-time faculty, 38% hold PhDs, 38% are members of minority groups. 0% of classes are taught by teaching assistants.

ACADEMICS

Degrees: bachelor's. **Classes:** Most classes have 10–19 students. **Majors with Highest Enrollment:** Marketing/Marketing Management; Banking and Financial Support Services. **Special Study Options:** Accelerated program, distance learning, double major, dual enrollment, external degree program, honors program, independent study, internships, study abroad, weekend college. **Honors programs:** An Honors Program began in fall term 1991. In it, honors sections of a variety of critically important courses are offered. The best instructors and the most demanding material and expectations are used. Additionally, special one-credit-hour seminars, which include outside speakers, are offered to sophomores and juniors. Honor students having completed 17 credit hours in honors courses may apply for honors admission to Term in Europe, Term in Asia, or Term in Northern Europe and are eligible for a partial scholarship to support these travel abroad programs. This also provides a powerful incentive for students to successfully compete in the Honors Program. **Disability Services:** Special programs offered to physically disabled students include note-taking services. **Career services:** Alumni network, alumni services, career/job search classes, career assessment, internships.

FACILITIES

Housing: men's dorms, women's dorms. **Special Academic Facilities/Equipment:** Art Gallery. **Computers:** 100% of classrooms, 100% of dorms, 100% of libraries, 100% of dining areas, 100% of student union, have wireless network access. Students can register for classes online. Administrative functions (other than registration) can be performed online.

CAMPUS LIFE

Environment: City. **Activities:** dance, drama/theater, student government, student newspaper, International Student Organization. 23 registered organizations, 1 honor society. **Athletics (Intercollegiate):** *Men:* baseball, basketball, golf, soccer, tennis. *Women:* basketball, golf, soccer, softball, tennis, volleyball. **On-Campus Highlights:** Countess de Hoernle Student Life Center. **Environmental Initiatives:** We keep use of paper to a minimum (e-mail attachments/files, Blackboard portal); Advertising promotions in small numbers in key locations (as opposed to making up 50 flyers and posting them everywhere!); We are just starting a campus-wide paper recycling program with recycling boxes in key locations and a large bin on campus.

ADMISSIONS

Freshman Academic Profile: Average high school GPA 3.24. 13% in top 10% of high school class, 27% in top 25% of high school class, 57% in top 50% of high school class. 70% from public high schools. SAT Math middle 50% range

440-550. SAT Critical Reading middle 50% range 430-510. SAT Writing middle 50% range 390-480. ACT middle 50% range 18-21. Minimum paper TOEFL 500. **Basis for Candidate Selection:** *Very important factors considered include:* academic GPA, level of applicant's interest. *Important factors considered include:* Class rank, rigor of secondary school record, standardized test scores. *Other factors considered include:* application essay, recommendation(s), alumni/ae relation, character/personal qualities, extracurricular activities, geographical residence, interview, talent/ability, volunteer work, work experience. **Freshman Admission Requirements:** High school diploma is required and GED is accepted. **Freshman Admission Statistics:** 628 applied, 54% admitted, 31% enrolled. **Transfer Admission Requirements:** High school transcript, college transcript(s), Minimum college GPA of 2.0 required. Lowest grade transferable C. **General Admission Information:** Application Fee $25. Notification on a rolling basis, beginning on or about 10/1. Nonfall registration accepted. Admission may be deferred for a maximum of 1 year. Credit and/or placement offered for CEEB Advanced Placement tests.

COSTS AND FINANCIAL AID
Required Forms and Deadlines: FAFSA, State aid form. **Notification of Awards:** Applicants will be notified of awards on a rolling basis beginning 3/1. **Types of Aid:** *Need-based scholarships/grants:* Federal Pell, SEOG, state scholarships/grants, private scholarships, the school's own gift aid. *Loans:* Subsidized Stafford, Unsubsidized Stafford, PLUS. **Financial Aid Statistics:** 87% freshmen, 86% undergrads receive need-based scholarship or grant aid. 27% freshmen, 21% undergrads receive non-need-based scholarship or grant aid. 84% freshmen, 90% undergrads receive need-based self-help aid. 20% freshmen, 19% undergrads receive athletic scholarships. 61% undergrads borrow to pay for school. Average cumulative indebtedness $23,407. **Criteria for awarding institutional aid:** *Non-need-based:* academics, alumni affiliation, athletics, leadership, minority status, state/district residency.

NORTHWOOD UNIVERSITY, TEXAS CAMPUS

1114 West FM 1382, Cedar Hill, TX 75104-1204
Phone: 800-622-9000 · **Financial Aid Phone:** 972-293-5430 · **CEEB Code:** 6499
Website: northwood.edu · **ACT Code:** 4135

This private school was founded in 1966. It has a 360-acre campus.

RATINGS
Admissions Selectivity Rating: 77   **Fire Safety Rating:** 66

STUDENTS AND FACULTY
Enrollment: 531. **Student Body:** 42% female, 58% male, 27% international (18 countries represented). Asian 2%, African American 15%, Caucasian 20%, Hispanic 26%, Native American <1%
Retention and Graduation: 31% freshmen graduate within 4 years. **Faculty:** 20 full-time faculty, 25% hold PhDs, 45% are members of minority groups, 15% are women. 0% of classes are taught by teaching assistants.

ACADEMICS
Degrees: bachelor's. **Classes:** Most classes have 10–19 students. **Majors with Highest Enrollment:** Entrepreneurship/Entrepreneurial Studies; International Business/Trade/Commerce; Marketing/Marketing Management. **Special Study Options:** Accelerated program, distance learning, double major, dual enrollment, external degree program, honors program, independent study, internships, study abroad, weekend college. **Honors programs:** An Honors Program begain in Fall Term, 1991. In it, honors sections of six critically important courses are offered. The best instructors and the most demanding material and expectations are used. Additionally, special one credit hour seminars, which include outside speakers, are offered to sophomores and juniors. **Disability Services:** Special programs offered to physically disabled students include tutors. **Career services:** Alumni network, alumni services, career assessment, internships.

FACILITIES
Housing: men's dorms, women's dorms, apartments for single students **Special Academic Facilities/Equipment:** Butler Gallery, Hopkins Display Cases, Hach Library **Computers:** 100% of classrooms, 100% of dorms, 100% of libraries, 100% of dining areas, 100% of student union, have wireless network access. Students can register for classes online. Administrative functions (other than registration) can be performed online.

CAMPUS LIFE
Environment: Village. **Activities:** Choral groups, dance, drama/theater, student newspaper, Campus Ministries, International Student Organization. 17 registered organizations, 1 honor society, 2 religious organizations. 1 fraternity, 1 sorority. **Athletics (Intercollegiate):** *Men:* baseball, cross-country, golf, soccer, track/field (outdoor), track/field (indoor). *Women:* cross-country, golf, soccer,

softball, track/field (outdoor), track/field (indoor). **Environmental Initiatives:** Paper recycling. We have two large bins in one of the parking lots. The paper is collected twice a week from offices and common areas. During the month of April and for Earth Day, we plan other activities and provide educational flyers about what everyone can do on their own.

ADMISSIONS
Freshman Academic Profile: Average high school GPA 3.32. 8% in top 10% of high school class, 27% in top 25% of high school class, 65% in top 50% of high school class. 90% from public high schools. SAT Math middle 50% range 420-520. SAT Critical Reading middle 50% range 390-500. SAT Writing middle 50% range 390-460. ACT middle 50% range 17-22. Minimum paper TOEFL 500. **Basis for Candidate Selection:** *Very important factors considered include:* Class rank, application essay, academic GPA, recommendation(s), rigor of secondary school record, standardized test scores, character/personal qualities, extracurricular activities, interview, level of applicant's interest. *Important factors considered include:* talent/ability, volunteer work, work experience. *Other factors considered include:* alumni/ae relation, first generation. **Freshman Admission Requirements:** High school diploma is required and GED is accepted. **Freshman Admission Statistics:** 452 applied, 59% admitted, 65% enrolled. **Transfer Admission Requirements:** High school transcript, college transcript(s), essay or personal statement, Minimum college GPA of 2.0 required. Lowest grade transferable C. **General Admission Information:** Application Fee $25. Notification on a rolling basis, beginning on or about 1/1. Nonfall registration accepted. Admission may be deferred for a maximum of 1 year. Credit and/or placement offered for CEEB Advanced Placement tests.

COSTS AND FINANCIAL AID
Required Forms and Deadlines: FAFSA. **Notification of Awards:** Applicants will be notified of awards on a rolling basis beginning 3/1. **Types of Aid:** *Need-based scholarships/grants:* Federal Pell, SEOG, private scholarships, the school's own gift aid. *Loans:* Subsidized Stafford, Unsubsidized Stafford, PLUS. **Financial Aid Statistics:** 92% freshmen, 89% undergrads receive need-based scholarship or grant aid. 24% freshmen, 22% undergrads receive non-need-based scholarship or grant aid. 90% freshmen, 91% undergrads receive need-based self-help aid. 11% freshmen, 12% undergrads receive athletic scholarships. 81% undergrads borrow to pay for school. Average cumulative indebtedness $24,171. **Criteria for awarding institutional aid:** *Non-need-based:* academics, alumni affiliation, athletics, leadership, minority status, state/district residency.

NORWICH UNIVERSITY

Admissions Office, Northfield, VT 5663
Phone: 802-485-2001
E-mail: nuadm@norwich.edu
Fax: 802-485-2032 · **Website:** www.norwich.edu

This private school was founded in 1819. It has a 1125-acre campus.

RATINGS
Admissions Selectivity Rating: 77   **Fire Safety Rating:** 60*

STUDENTS AND FACULTY
Enrollment: 2,201. **Student Body:** 26% female, 74% male, 84% out-of-state, 2% international. Asian 2%, African American 3%, Caucasian 74%, Hispanic 4%, Native American 1%
Retention and Graduation: 85% freshmen return for sophomore year. 45% freshmen graduate within 4 years. 55% freshmen graduate within 6 years. 10% grads go on to further study within 1 year. 2% grads pursue arts and sciences degrees. 2% grads pursue law degrees. 2% grads pursue business degrees. 1% grads pursue medical degrees. **Faculty:** 140 full-time faculty, 36% are members of minority groups, 9% are women. 0% of classes are taught by teaching assistants.

ACADEMICS
Degrees: bachelor's, master's, post-bachelor's certificate. **Classes:** Most classes have 10–19 students. **Majors with Highest Enrollment:** Liberal Arts and Sciences/Liberal Studies; Criminal Justice/Law Enforcement Administration. **Special Study Options:** cooperative education program, distance learning, double major, English as a Second Language (ESL), honors program, independent study, internships, study abroad. **Disability Services:** Special programs offered to physically disabled students include tutors. **Career services:** career/job search classes,

FACILITIES
Housing: Coed dorms. 95% of campus accessible to physically disabled. **Special Academic Facilities/Equipment:** museum, architecture and art building w/galery, new library.

CAMPUS LIFE

Environment: Rural. **Activities:** Choral groups, concert band, drama/theater, jazz band, literary magazine, marching band, pep band, radio station, student government, student newspaper, yearbook. 40 registered organizations, 8 honor societies, 4 religious organizations. **Athletics (Intercollegiate):** *Men:* baseball, basketball, cross-country, diving, football, ice hockey, lacrosse, riflery, rugby, soccer, swimming, track/field (outdoor), volleyball, wrestling. *Women:* basketball, cross-country, diving, riflery, rugby, soccer, softball, swimming, track/field (outdoor), volleyball.

ADMISSIONS

Freshman Academic Profile: Average high school GPA 3.12. 11% in top 10% of high school class, 37% in top 25% of high school class, 74% in top 50% of high school class. 90% from public high schools. SAT Math middle 50% range 500-640. SAT Critical Reading middle 50% range 480-580. SAT Writing middle 50% range 460-620. ACT middle 50% range 21-26. Minimum paper TOEFL 500. **Basis for Candidate Selection:** *Very important factors considered include:* rigor of secondary school record. *Important factors considered include:* extracurricular activities, talent/ability. *Other factors considered include:* Class rank, application essay, recommendation(s), standardized test scores, alumni/ae relation, character/personal qualities, interview, volunteer work, work experience. **Freshman Admission Requirements:** High school diploma is required and GED is accepted. *Academic units required:* 4 English, 3 mathematics, 2 science, (2 science labs), 0 foreign language. **Freshman Admission Statistics:** 1,473 applied, 91% admitted, 37% enrolled. **Transfer Admission Requirements:** High school transcript, college transcript(s), Lowest grade transferable C-. **General Admission Information:** Application Fee $35. Early decision application deadline 11/15. Notification on a rolling basis, beginning on or about 10/1. Nonfall registration accepted. Admission may be deferred for a maximum of 1. Credit offered for CEEB Advanced Placement tests.

COSTS AND FINANCIAL AID

Annual tuition $30,048. Room and board $10,976. Required fees $1,734. Average book expense $1,000. **Required Forms and Deadlines:** FAFSA. **Types of Aid:** *Need-based scholarships/grants:* Federal Pell, SEOG. *Loans:* Direct Subsidized Stafford, Direct Unsubsidized Stafford, Subsidized Stafford, Unsubsidized Stafford, PLUS, Federal Perkins. *Student Employment:* Federal Work-Study Program available. Institutional employment available. Off-campus job opportunities are fair. **Financial Aid Statistics:** 100% freshmen, 100% undergrads receive need-based scholarship or grant aid. 18% freshmen, 17% undergrads receive non-need-based scholarship or grant aid. 79% freshmen, 79% undergrads receive need-based self-help aid. 0% freshmen, 0% undergrads receive athletic scholarships.

NOTRE DAME COLLEGE

4545 College Road, South Euclid, OH 44121
Phone: 216-381-1680 · **Financial Aid Phone:** 216-373-5213
E-mail: admissions@ndc.edu · **CEEB Code:** 3085
Fax: 216-373-5278 · **Website:** www.notredamecollege.edu · **ACT Code:** 3302

This private school, affiliated with the Roman Catholic Church, was founded in 1922. It has a 53-acre campus.

RATINGS

Admissions Selectivity Rating: 78   **Fire Safety Rating:** 67

STUDENTS AND FACULTY

Enrollment: 835. **Student Body:** 63% female, 37% male, 3% out-of-state, 4% international. Asian 0%, African American 24%, Caucasian 62%, Hispanic 3%, Native American <1%
Retention and Graduation: 65% freshmen return for sophomore year. 60% grads go on to further study within 1 year. 10% grads pursue arts and sciences degrees. 5% grads pursue law degrees. 10% grads pursue business degrees. 5% grads pursue medical degrees. **Faculty:** 36 full-time faculty, 53% hold PhDs, 58% are members of minority groups, 3% are women. 0% of classes are taught by teaching assistants.

ACADEMICS

Degrees: associate, bachelor's, certificate, master's, post-bachelor's certificate. **Classes:** Most classes have 10–19 students. Most lab/discussion sessions have 10–19 students. **Majors with Highest Enrollment:** Secondary Education and Teaching; Psychology; Business/Commerce. **Special Study Options:** cooperative education program, cross-registration, distance learning, double major, independent study, internships, student-designed major, study abroad, teacher certification program, weekend college. **Disability Services:** Special programs offered to physically disabled students include tutors. **Career services:** alumni services, career/job search classes, career assessment, internships.

FACILITIES

Housing: Coed dorms, men's dorms, women's dorms. 100% of campus accessible to physically disabled. **Special Academic Facilities/Equipment:** Tolerance Resource Center.

CAMPUS LIFE

Environment: Town. **Activities:** Choral groups, dance, drama/theater, literary magazine, pep band, student government, student newspaper, yearbook. 22 registered organizations, 6 honor societies, 1 religious organization. **Athletics (Intercollegiate):** *Men:* baseball, basketball, cross-country, golf, soccer, tennis, track/field (outdoor). *Women:* basketball, cross-country, golf, lacrosse, soccer, softball, track/field (outdoor), volleyball. **On-Campus Highlights:** Smart Classroom, Legacy Walkway, Joseph H. Keller Fitness Center, Tolerance Resource Center, Coffee Shop, Several new construction and renovations projects underway beginning in 2005. Check back for updates.

ADMISSIONS

Freshman Academic Profile: Average high school GPA 2.95. 4% in top 10% of high school class, 22% in top 25% of high school class, 62% in top 50% of high school class. 60% from public high schools. SAT Math middle 50% range 393-520. SAT Critical Reading middle 50% range 440-528. ACT middle 50% range 17-21. Minimum paper TOEFL 550. **Basis for Candidate Selection:** *Very important factors considered include:* academic GPA, rigor of secondary school record, standardized test scores. *Important factors considered include:* Class rank, interview, level of applicant's interest. *Other factors considered include:* application essay, recommendation(s), alumni/ae relation, character/personal qualities, extracurricular activities, talent/ability, volunteer work, work experience. **Freshman Admission Requirements:** High school diploma is required and GED is accepted. **Freshman Admission Statistics:** 1,004 applied, 51% admitted, 29% enrolled. **Transfer Admission Requirements:** High school transcript, college transcript(s), interview, Minimum college GPA of 2.5 required. Lowest grade transferable C. **General Admission Information:** Application Fee $30. Notification on a rolling basis, beginning on or about 9/1. Nonfall registration accepted. Admission may be deferred for a maximum of 1 year. Credit offered for CEEB Advanced Placement tests.

COSTS AND FINANCIAL AID

Annual tuition $18,670. Room and board $6,648. Required fees $550. Average book expense $1,270. **Required Forms and Deadlines:** FAFSA. **Notification of Awards:** Applicants will be notified of awards on a rolling basis beginning 1/1. **Types of Aid:** *Need-based scholarships/grants:* Federal Pell, SEOG, state scholarships/grants, private scholarships, the school's own gift aid. *Loans:* Subsidized Stafford, Unsubsidized Stafford, PLUS, Federal Perkins, state loans, college/university loans from institutional funds. *Student Employment:* Federal Work-Study Program available. Institutional employment available. Off-campus job opportunities are good. **Financial Aid Statistics:** 100% freshmen, 100% undergrads receive need-based scholarship or grant aid. 100% freshmen, 100% undergrads receive non-need-based scholarship or grant aid. 100% freshmen, 100% undergrads receive need-based self-help aid. 0% freshmen, 6% undergrads receive athletic scholarships. 93% freshmen, 63% undergrads receive any aid. 90% undergrads borrow to pay for school. **Criteria for awarding institutional aid:** *Non-need-based:* academics, art, leadership, state/district residency.

See page 1108.

NOTRE DAME DE NAMUR UNIVERSITY

1500 Ralston Avenue, Belmont, CA 94002-1908
Phone: 650-508-3600 · **Financial Aid Phone:** 650-508-3600
E-mail: admiss@ndnu.edu · **CEEB Code:** 4063
Fax: 650-508-3426 · **Website:** www.ndnu.edu · **ACT Code:** 236

This private school, affiliated with the Roman Catholic Church, was founded in 1851. It has a 80-acre campus.

RATINGS

Admissions Selectivity Rating: 75   **Fire Safety Rating:** 61

STUDENTS AND FACULTY

Enrollment: 1,177. **Student Body:** 67% female, 33% male, 6% out-of-state, 3% international. Asian 12%, African American 6%, Caucasian 25%, Hispanic 37%, Native American 1%
Retention and Graduation: 75% freshmen return for sophomore year. 43% freshmen graduate within 4 years. 53% freshmen graduate within 6 years. **Faculty:** 60 full-time faculty, 95% hold PhDs, 55% are members of minority groups, 22% are women. 0% of classes are taught by teaching assistants.

ACADEMICS

Degrees: bachelor's, master's, post-bachelor's certificate. **Classes:** Most classes have 10–19 students. **Majors with Highest Enrollment:** Psychology; Human

Services; Business Administration and Management. **Special Study Options:** Accelerated program, double major, English as a Second Language (ESL), exchange student program (domestic), independent study, internships, liberal arts/career combination, student-designed major, study abroad, teacher certification program. **Disability Services:** Special programs offered to physically disabled students include note-taking services, reader services. **Career services:** career/job search classes, internships.

FACILITIES

Housing: Coed dorms, 2 or 3 person apartments 4-person suites. **Special Academic Facilities/Equipment:** Student art museum, professional art gallery, archives of modern Christian art, theatre, early learning center for Montessori credential training, on-campus elementary school.

CAMPUS LIFE

Environment: Village. **Activities:** Choral groups, dance, literary magazine, music ensembles, musical theater, student government, student newspaper. 15 registered organizations, 3 honor societies, 1 religious organization. **Athletics (Intercollegiate):** *Men:* basketball, cheerleading, soccer, tennis, track/field (outdoor). *Women:* basketball, cheerleading, cross-country, soccer, softball, tennis, track/field (outdoor), volleyball.

ADMISSIONS

Freshman Academic Profile: Average high school GPA 3.18. 13% in top 10% of high school class, 35% in top 25% of high school class, 76% in top 50% of high school class. 62% from public high schools. SAT Math middle 50% range 420-520. SAT Critical Reading middle 50% range 430-520. SAT Writing middle 50% range 420-510. ACT middle 50% range 17-21. Minimum internet-based TOEFL 61. Minimum paper TOEFL 500. **Basis for Candidate Selection:** *Very important factors considered include:* academic GPA, rigor of secondary school record, character/personal qualities. *Important factors considered include:* Class rank, application essay, recommendation(s), standardized test scores, extracurricular activities, talent/ability, volunteer work. *Other factors considered include:* first generation, interview, work experience. **Freshman Admission Requirements:** High school diploma is required and GED is accepted. *Academic units required:* 4 English, 2 mathematics, 1 science, (1 science labs), 2 foreign language, 2 social studies, 1 history, 3 academic electives. **Freshman Admission Statistics:** 2,167 applied, 78% admitted, 11% enrolled. **Transfer Admission Requirements:** college transcript(s), essay or personal statement, statement of good standing from prior institution(s). Minimum college GPA of 2.0 required. Lowest grade transferable C. **General Admission Information:** Application Fee $40. Notification on a rolling basis, beginning on or about 12/1. Nonfall registration accepted. Admission may be deferred for a maximum of 12 months. Credit offered for CEEB Advanced Placement tests.

COSTS AND FINANCIAL AID

Annual tuition $32,208. Room and board $13,006. Required fees $400. Average book expense $1,790. **Required Forms and Deadlines:** FAFSA. **Types of Aid:** *Need-based scholarships/grants:* Federal Pell, SEOG, state scholarships/grants, private scholarships. *Loans:* Subsidized Stafford, Unsubsidized Stafford, PLUS, Federal Perkins. *Student Employment:* Federal Work-Study Program available. Institutional employment available. Highest amount earned per year from on-campus jobs $1,300. Off-campus job opportunities are excellent. **Financial Aid Statistics:** 100% freshmen, 100% undergrads receive need-based scholarship or grant aid. 5% freshmen, 3% undergrads receive non-need-based scholarship or grant aid. 87% freshmen, 80% undergrads receive need-based self-help aid. 3% freshmen, 1% undergrads receive athletic scholarships. 77% undergrads borrow to pay for school. Average cumulative indebtedness $28,632. **Criteria for awarding institutional aid:** *Non-need-based:* academics, alumni affiliation, art, athletics, leadership, music/drama.

NOVA SCOTIA COLLEGE OF ART AND DESIGN

5163 Duke Street, Halifax, NS B3J3J6
Phone: 902-494-8129 · **Financial Aid Phone:** 902-494-8130
E-mail: admissions@nscad.ca · **CEEB Code:**
Fax: 902-425-2987 · **Website:** www.nscad.ca

This public school was founded in 1887. It has a 1-acre campus.

RATINGS

Admissions Selectivity Rating: 65   Fire Safety Rating: 60*

STUDENTS AND FACULTY

Enrollment: 896. **Student Body:** 64% female, 36% male.
Faculty: 68 full-time faculty, 28% are members of minority groups. 19% of classes are taught by teaching assistants.

ACADEMICS

Degrees: bachelor's, master's. **Special Study Options:** cooperative education program, distance learning, double major, exchange student program (domestic), independent study, internships, study abroad. **Combined degree programs:** BFA/BD. **Disability Services:** Special programs offered to physically disabled students include note-taking services, tape recorders.

FACILITIES

Housing: men's dorms, women's dorms, apartments for married students. 25% of campus accessible to physically disabled.

CAMPUS LIFE

Environment: City. **Activities:** Choral groups, concert band, drama/theater, music ensembles, musical theater, student government, yearbook.

ADMISSIONS

Freshman Academic Profile: Minimum paper TOEFL 575. **Basis for Candidate Selection:** *Very important factors considered include:* application essay, rigor of secondary school record, talent/ability. *Other factors considered include:* recommendation(s), standardized test scores, character/personal qualities, interview, volunteer work, work experience. **Freshman Admission Statistics:** 247 applied, 43% admitted, 0% enrolled. **Transfer Admission Requirements:** college transcript(s), essay or personal statement, statement of good standing from prior institution(s). **General Admission Information:** Application Fee $50. Regular application deadline 5/15. Notification on a rolling basis, beginning on or about 3/15. Nonfall registration not accepted. Admission may be deferred for a maximum of 1 year. Placement offered for CEEB Advanced Placement tests.

NOVA SOUTHEASTERN UNIVERSITY

3301 College Avenue, Fort Lauderdale, FL 33314
Phone: 954-262-8000 · **Financial Aid Phone:** 954-262-7456
E-mail: admissions@nova.edu · **CEEB Code:** 5514
Fax: 954-262-3811 · **Website:** www.nova.edu • **ACT Code:** 6706

This private school was founded in 1964. It has a 300-acre campus.

RATINGS

Admissions Selectivity Rating: 80   Fire Safety Rating: 88

STUDENTS AND FACULTY

Enrollment: 6,246. **Student Body:** 71% female, 29% male, 16% out-of-state, 4% international. Asian 6%, African American 24%, Caucasian 28%, Hispanic 32%, Native American <1%
Retention and Graduation: 70% freshmen return for sophomore year.
Faculty: 814 full-time faculty, 88% hold PhDs, 49% are members of minority groups, 30% are women. 0% of classes are taught by teaching assistants.

ACADEMICS

Degrees: associate, bachelor's, master's, post-bachelor's certificate, post-master's certificate. **Classes:** Most classes have 10–19 students. **Majors with Highest Enrollment:** Biology/Biological Sciences; Business Administration and Management; Psychology. **Special Study Options:** distance learning, double major, honors program, independent study, internships, study abroad, teacher certification program, Dual admission programs with NSU graduate and professional schools. **Honors programs:** http://undergrad.nova.edu/honors/index.cfm For the academically motivated student, the NSU Honors program provides a value added experience. Students enjoy greater interaction with faculty through curricular and co-curricular activities, special invitations to events, and enhanced engagement in disciplinary inquiry. **Combined degree programs:** BA/MD, BA/JD, BA/MA, BA/DDS, See http://www.undergrad.nova.edu/majors.cfm for more information. **Disability Services:** Special programs offered to physically disabled students include note-taking services, reader services, tape recorders, tutors. **Career services:** alumni services, career assessment, internships, regional alumni. Career services highlights include Our comprehensive career development program encompassing career planning, advisement services, employment and career resources, campus relations, and employer recruitment program.

FACILITIES

Housing: Coed dorms, special housing for disabled students, special housing for international students, fraternity/sorority housing, apartments for married students, apartments for single students, Wellness Housing, Theme Housing. **Special Academic Facilities/Equipment:** Institute for Early Childhood Studies, University School for pre-kindergarten to grade 12, Oceanographic Center and Lab, Biofeedback and Learning Technology Labs, Audiology and Speech Language Pathology, and Psychology Clinics. **Computers:** 100% of classrooms, 100% of dorms, 100% of libraries, 80% of dining areas, 100% of student union, 70% of common outdoor areas have wireless network access. Students can register for classes online. Administrative functions (other than registration) can be performed online.

CAMPUS LIFE
Environment: City. **Activities:** Choral groups, dance, drama/theater, jazz band, literary magazine, music ensembles, musical theater, pep band, radio station, student government, student newspaper, International Student Organization. 292 registered organizations. **Athletics (Intercollegiate):** *Men:* baseball, basketball, cross-country, golf, soccer, track/field (outdoor). *Women:* basketball, cheerleading, crew/rowing, cross-country, golf, soccer, softball, tennis, track/field (outdoor), volleyball. **On-Campus Highlights:** University Center and Performing Arts Wi, Alvin Sherman Library, Research & Inform, Health Professions Division Museum, Miniaci Performing Arts Center, Law School, University Center includes the sports arena, fitness center, flight deck, shark mural, and mall-style food court. Performing Arts Wing includes multiple theaters, costume and scenery shops, performance practice rooms for music and dance, dressing rooms, and a gallery.

ADMISSIONS
Freshman Academic Profile: SAT Math middle 50% range 470-590. SAT Critical Reading middle 50% range 460-570. ACT middle 50% range 20-25. Minimum paper TOEFL 550. **Basis for Candidate Selection:** *Very important factors considered include:* academic GPA, standardized test scores. *Important factors considered include:* rigor of secondary school record. *Other factors considered include:* application essay, recommendation(s), character/personal qualities, extracurricular activities, interview, talent/ability, volunteer work. **Freshman Admission Requirements:** High school diploma is required and GED is accepted. **Freshman Admission Statistics:** 3,780 applied, 58% admitted, 31% enrolled. **Transfer Admission Requirements:** college transcript(s), statement of good standing from prior institution(s). Minimum college GPA of 2.50 required. Lowest grade transferable D. **General Admission Information:** Application Fee $50. Regular application deadline 8/1. Nonfall registration accepted. Admission may be deferred for a maximum of 1 year. Credit and/or placement offered for CEEB Advanced Placement tests.

COSTS AND FINANCIAL AID
Annual tuition $21,600. Room and board $9,086. Required fees $550. Average book expense $1,500. **Required Forms and Deadlines:** FAFSA, State aid form. **Notification of Awards:** Applicants will be notified of awards on a rolling basis beginning 3/15. **Types of Aid:** *Need-based scholarships/grants:* Federal Pell, SEOG, state scholarships/grants, private scholarships, the school's own gift aid. *Loans:* Subsidized Stafford, Unsubsidized Stafford, PLUS, Federal Perkins. *Student Employment:* Federal Work-Study Program available. Institutional employment available. Off-campus job opportunities are good. **Financial Aid Statistics:** 97% freshmen, 96% undergrads receive need-based scholarship or grant aid. 99% freshmen, 99% undergrads receive non-need-based scholarship or grant aid. 83% freshmen, 87% undergrads receive need-based self-help aid. 12% freshmen, 7% undergrads receive athletic scholarships. 92% freshmen, 83% undergrads receive any aid. 76% undergrads borrow to pay for school. Average cumulative indebtedness $34,113. **Criteria for awarding institutional aid:** *Non-need-based:* academics, athletics, leadership, music/drama.

OAK HILLS CHRISTIAN COLLEGE

1600 Oak Hills Rd SW, Bemidji, MN 56601
Phone: 218-751-8670 · **Financial Aid Phone:** 218-751-8670
E-mail: admissions@oakhills.edu
Fax: 218-751-8825 · **Website:** www.oakhills.edu · **ACT Code:** 2167

This private school was founded in 1946. It has a 180-acre campus.

RATINGS
Admissions Selectivity Rating: 74   **Fire Safety Rating:** 66

STUDENTS AND FACULTY
Enrollment: 131. **Student Body:** 53% female, 47% male, 33% out-of-state, 1% international (1 countries represented). Asian 2%, African American 1%, Caucasian 79%, Hispanic %, Native American 1%
Retention and Graduation: 55% freshmen return for sophomore year. 38% freshmen graduate within 6 years. **Faculty:** 6 full-time faculty, 67% hold PhDs, 33% are members of minority groups, 0% are women. 0% of classes are taught by teaching assistants.

ACADEMICS
Degrees: associate, bachelor's, certificate, diploma. **Classes:** Most classes have fewer than 10 students. **Majors with Highest Enrollment:** Bible/Biblical Studies; Pastoral Studies/Counseling; Youth Ministry. **Special Study Options:** cooperative education program, double major, independent study, internships. **Disability Services:** Special programs offered to physically disabled students include note-taking services, reader services, tape recorders, tutors. **Career**

services: Alumni network, career/job search classes, career assessment, internships.

FACILITIES
Housing: special housing for disabled students, men's dorms, women's dorms, apartments for married students, apartments for single students. 85% of campus accessible to physically disabled. **Special Academic Facilities/Equipment:** American Indian Resource Center **Computers:** 50% of classrooms, 100% of dorms, 100% of libraries, 100% of student union, 50% of common outdoor areas have wireless network access. Students can register for classes online. Administrative functions (other than registration) can be performed online.

CAMPUS LIFE
Environment: Village. **Activities:** Choral groups, music ensembles, student government, Campus Ministries. **Athletics (Intercollegiate):** *Men:* basketball. *Women:* basketball, volleyball. **On-Campus Highlights:** The Fellowship Center Lounge, Schreiber Activity Center (SAC) Gym, Library, Chapel, Lake Front.

ADMISSIONS
Freshman Academic Profile: 5% in top 10% of high school class, 5% in top 25% of high school class, 47% in top 50% of high school class. 79% from public high schools. ACT middle 50% range 16-21. Minimum paper TOEFL 500. **Basis for Candidate Selection:** *Very important factors considered include:* Class rank, application essay, academic GPA, recommendation(s). *Other factors considered include:* rigor of secondary school record, interview. **Freshman Admission Requirements:** High school diploma is required and GED is accepted. **Freshman Admission Statistics:** 70 applied, 56% admitted, 79% enrolled. **Transfer Admission Requirements:** High school transcript, college transcript(s), essay or personal statement, Minimum college GPA of 2.0 required. Lowest grade transferable C. **General Admission Information:** Application Fee $25. Notification on a rolling basis, beginning on or about 9/1. Nonfall registration accepted. Admission may be deferred for a maximum of 2 years. Credit and/or placement offered for CEEB Advanced Placement tests.

COSTS AND FINANCIAL AID
Annual tuition $14,420. Room and board $5,180. Average book expense $990. **Required Forms and Deadlines:** FAFSA, Institution's own financial aid form. **Notification of Awards:** Applicants will be notified of awards on a rolling basis beginning 3/1. **Types of Aid:** *Need-based scholarships/grants:* Federal Pell, SEOG, state scholarships/grants, private scholarships, the school's own gift aid. *Loans:* Subsidized Stafford, Unsubsidized Stafford, PLUS, state loans, Alternative Loan programs. *Student Employment:* Federal Work-Study Program available. Institutional employment available. Highest amount earned per year from on-campus jobs $9. Off-campus job opportunities are excellent. **Financial Aid Statistics:** 100% freshmen, 100% undergrads receive need-based scholarship or grant aid. 0% freshmen, 0% undergrads receive non-need-based scholarship or grant aid. 75% freshmen, 86% undergrads receive need-based self-help aid. 0% freshmen, 0% undergrads receive athletic scholarships. 100% freshmen, 100% undergrads receive any aid. 100% undergrads borrow to pay for school. Average cumulative indebtedness $24,876. **Criteria for awarding institutional aid:** *Non-need-based:* academics, alumni affiliation.

OAKLAND CITY UNIVERSITY

138 N. Lucretia Street, Oakland City, IN 47660
Phone: 812-749-1221
E-mail: ocuadmit@oak.edu
Fax: 812-749-1433 · **Website:** http://www.oak.edu

This is a private school.

RATINGS
Admissions Selectivity Rating: 77   **Fire Safety Rating:** 60*

STUDENTS AND FACULTY
Enrollment: 1,492. **Student Body:** 53% female, 47% male, 17% out-of-state, 1% international. Asian 1%, African American 13%, Caucasian 98%, Hispanic 0%, Native American 1%
Retention and Graduation: 66% freshmen return for sophomore year. 46% freshmen graduate within 4 years. 64% freshmen graduate within 6 years. **Faculty:** 58 full-time faculty, 47% are members of minority groups, 0% are women.

ACADEMICS
Degrees: associate, bachelor's, certificate, doctoral, master's. **Classes:** Most classes have 10–19 students. Most lab/discussion sessions have fewer than 10 students. **Special Study Options:** distance learning, double major, dual enrollment, independent study, internships, teacher certification program.

FACILITIES

Housing: men's dorms, women's dorms, apartments for married students, apartments for single students.

CAMPUS LIFE

Activities: Choral groups, drama/theater, pep band, student government, student newspaper, yearbook, Campus Ministries.

ADMISSIONS

Freshman Academic Profile: Average high school GPA 3.15. 9% in top 10% of high school class, 16% in top 25% of high school class, 41% in top 50% of high school class. SAT Math middle 50% range 420-530. SAT Critical Reading middle 50% range 400-510. SAT Writing middle 50% range 398-500. ACT middle 50% range 17-23. **Basis for Candidate Selection:** *Very important factors considered include:* academic GPA, rigor of secondary school record, standardized test scores. *Other factors considered include:* Class rank, alumni/ae relation, character/personal qualities, interview, level of applicant's interest. **Freshman Admission Requirements:** High school diploma is required and GED is accepted. **Freshman Admission Statistics:** 620 applied, 56% admitted, 100% enrolled. **Transfer Admission Requirements:** High school transcript, college transcript(s), standardized test scores, Minimum college GPA of 2.0 required. Lowest grade transferable C. **General Admission Information:** Application Fee $35. Regular application deadline 9/5. Nonfall registration accepted.

COSTS AND FINANCIAL AID

Annual tuition $15,200. Room and board $6,000. Required fees $360. Average book expense $1,500. **Required Forms and Deadlines:** FAFSA. **Notification of Awards:** Applicants will be notified of awards on a rolling basis beginning 5/1. **Types of Aid:** *Need-based scholarships/grants:* Federal Pell, SEOG, state scholarships/grants, private scholarships, the school's own gift aid. *Loans:* Subsidized Stafford, Unsubsidized Stafford, PLUS, Federal Perkins. **Financial Aid Statistics:** 0% freshmen, 0% undergrads receive athletic scholarships. Criteria for awarding institutional aid: *Non-need-based:* academics, alumni affiliation, art, athletics, minority status, music/drama, religious affiliation.

OAKLAND UNIVERSITY

Office of Admissions, Rochester, MI 48309-4401
Phone: 248-370-3360 · **Financial Aid Phone:** 248-370-2550
E-mail: visit@oakland.edu · **CEEB Code:** 1497
Fax: 248-370-4462 · **Website:** http://www.oakland.edu · **ACT Code:** 2033

This public school was founded in 1957. It has a 1444-acre campus.

RATINGS

Admissions Selectivity Rating: 81   **Fire Safety Rating:** 83

STUDENTS AND FACULTY

Enrollment: 16,528. **Student Body:** 58% female, 42% male, 1% out-of-state, 2% international (98 countries represented). Asian 4%, African American 8%, Caucasian 75%, Hispanic 3%, Native American <1%.
Retention and Graduation: 16% freshmen graduate within 4 years. **Faculty:** 565 full-time faculty, 89% hold PhDs, 45% are members of minority groups, 22% are women. 1% of classes are taught by teaching assistants.

ACADEMICS

Degrees: bachelor's, doctoral, master's, post-bachelor's certificate, post-master's certificate. **Classes:** Most classes have 20–29 students. Most lab/discussion sessions have 10–19 students. **Majors with Highest Enrollment:** Health Professions and Related Clinical Sciences; Business/Commerce; Registered Nursing/Registered Nurse. **Special Study Options:** Accelerated program, cooperative education program, cross-registration, distance learning, double major, English as a Second Language (ESL), honors program, independent study, internships, student-designed major, study abroad, teacher certification program. **Honors programs:** Honors College **Combined degree programs:** 5 year MBA program. **Disability Services:** Special programs offered to physically disabled students include note-taking services, reader services, tape recorders, tutors. **Career services:** Alumni network, alumni services, internships.

FACILITIES

Housing: Coed dorms, special housing for disabled students, special housing for international students, fraternity/sorority housing, apartments for married students, cooperative housing, apartments for single students, Wellness Housing, Theme Housing, Living/Learning Community. 90% of campus accessible to physically disabled. **Special Academic Facilities/Equipment:** Art gallery, robotics lab, Eye Research institute, Professional theater, Meadowbrook Hall, Meadowbrook Music Festival, two golf courses, Pawley Learning center, Lowry

Early Childhood Education Center, Jack's Place for Autism at OU. **Computers:** Students can register for classes online. Administrative functions (other than registration) can be performed online.

CAMPUS LIFE

Environment: Town. **Activities:** Choral groups, concert band, dance, drama/theater, jazz band, literary magazine, music ensembles, musical theater, pep band, radio station, student government, student newspaper, student-run film society, symphony orchestra, television station, Campus Ministries, International Student Organization. 170 registered organizations, 9 honor societies, 12 religious organizations. 6 fraternities, 6 sororities. **Athletics (Intercollegiate):** *Men:* baseball, basketball, cross-country, diving, golf, soccer, swimming, track/field (outdoor). *Women:* basketball, cross-country, diving, golf, soccer, softball, swimming, tennis, track/field (outdoor), volleyball. **On-Campus Highlights:** Recreation Center, Pawley Hall, Oakland Center, Library, Honors College. **Environmental Initiatives:** $8 million Facility upgrade from 1998 to save on energy costs; Solar electric power roof installed on the student apartment buildings; Investigating Biomass energy and/ or wind power for campus heating and cooling.

ADMISSIONS

Freshman Academic Profile: Average high school GPA 3.4. 16% in top 10% of high school class, 44% in top 25% of high school class, 81% in top 50% of high school class. 90% from public high schools. ACT middle 50% range 20-26. Minimum internet-based TOEFL 79. Minimum paper TOEFL 550. **Basis for Candidate Selection:** *Very important factors considered include:* Class rank, academic GPA, rigor of secondary school record. *Important factors considered include:* recommendation(s), character/personal qualities, extracurricular activities, talent/ability, volunteer work. *Other factors considered include:* application essay, standardized test scores, alumni/ae relation, first generation, interview, level of applicant's interest, work experience. **Freshman Admission Requirements:** High school diploma is required and GED is accepted. *Academic units required:* 4 English, 3 mathematics, 3 science, 3 social studies. **Freshman Admission Statistics:** 12,403 applied, 67% admitted, 31% enrolled. **Transfer Admission Requirements:** college transcript(s), statement of good standing from prior institution(s). Minimum college GPA of 2.50 required. Lowest grade transferable C. **General Admission Information:** Notification on a rolling basis, beginning on or about 9/15. Nonfall registration accepted. Admission may be deferred for a maximum of 1 year. Placement offered for CEEB Advanced Placement tests.

COSTS AND FINANCIAL AID

Annual in-state tuition $10,613. Annual out-of-state tuition $23,873. Room and board $8,895. Average book expense $1,054. **Required Forms and Deadlines:** FAFSA. **Notification of Awards:** Applicants will be notified of awards on a rolling basis beginning 3/15. **Types of Aid:** *Need-based scholarships/grants:* Federal Pell, SEOG, state scholarships/grants, private scholarships, the school's own gift aid. *Loans:* Direct Subsidized Stafford, Direct Unsubsidized Stafford, Direct PLUS, Federal Perkins, Private loans. *Student Employment:* Federal Work-Study Program available. Institutional employment available. Off-campus job opportunities are good. **Criteria for awarding institutional aid:** *Non-need-based:* academics, art, athletics, leadership, music/drama, state/district residency.

OBERLIN COLLEGE

Best 380

101 North Professor Street, Oberlin, OH 44074
Phone: 440-775-8411 · **Financial Aid Phone:** 440-775-8142
E-mail: college.admissions@oberlin.edu · **CEEB Code:** 1587
Fax: 440-775-6905 · **Website:** www.oberlin.edu · **ACT Code:** 3304

This private school was founded in 1833. It has a 450-acre campus.

RATINGS

Admissions Selectivity Rating: 96   **Fire Safety Rating:** 71

STUDENTS AND FACULTY

Enrollment: 2,894. **Student Body:** 54% female, 46% male, 92% out-of-state, 7% international. Asian 4%, African American 5%, Caucasian 70%, Hispanic 7%, Native American <1%.
Retention and Graduation: 93% freshmen return for sophomore year. 76% freshmen graduate within 4 years. 88% freshmen graduate within 6 years. 16%

grads go on to further study within 1 year. 8% grads pursue arts and sciences degrees. 3% grads pursue law degrees. 2% grads pursue business degrees. 3% grads pursue medical degrees. **Faculty:** 296 full-time faculty, 94% hold PhDs, 40% are members of minority groups, 16% are women. 0% of classes are taught by teaching assistants.

ACADEMICS

Degrees: bachelor's, diploma, master's, post-master's certificate. **Classes:** Most classes have 10–19 students. Most lab/discussion sessions have fewer than 10 students. **Majors with Highest Enrollment:** English Language and Literature; Biology; History. **Special Study Options:** cross-registration, double major, dual enrollment, English as a Second Language (ESL), exchange student program (domestic), honors program, independent study, internships, student-designed major, study abroad, teacher certification program, 5 year double degree program with Conservatory of Music and College of Arts and Sciences; 3-2 engineering. **Combined degree programs:** BA/B.Music. **Disability Services:** Special programs offered to physically disabled students include note-taking services, reader services, tape recorders, tutors.

FACILITIES

Housing: Coed dorms, men's dorms, women's dorms, cooperative housing, Theme Housing. 90% of campus accessible to physically disabled. **Special Academic Facilities/Equipment:** Allen Memorial Art museum, Theaters, music performance halls. **Computers:** Students can register for classes online. Administrative functions (other than registration) can be performed online.

CAMPUS LIFE

Environment: Rural. **Activities:** Choral groups, concert band, dance, drama/theater, jazz band, literary magazine, marching band, music ensembles, musical theater, opera, radio station, student government, student newspaper, student-run film society, symphony orchestra, yearbook, Campus Ministries, International Student Organization. 125 registered organizations, 3 honor societies, 10 religious organizations. **Athletics (Intercollegiate):** *Men:* baseball, basketball, cross-country, diving, football, golf, lacrosse, soccer, swimming, tennis, track/field (outdoor), track/field (indoor). *Women:* basketball, cross-country, diving, field hockey, golf, lacrosse, soccer, softball, swimming, tennis, track/field (outdoor), track/field (indoor), volleyball. **On-Campus Highlights:** Allen Art Museum, Oberlin College Science Center, Adam Joseph Lewis Center for Environmental Studies, Mudd Library, Jesse Philips Recreational Center. **Environmental Initiatives:** Development of Campus Resource Monitoring System, oberlin.edu/dormenergy; Building of social capital on campus and in the larger community, http://www.oberlin.edu/sustainability/portfolio/social_capital.html; Adam Joseph Lewis Center for Environmental Studies, oberlin.edu/ajlc.

ADMISSIONS

Freshman Academic Profile: Average high school GPA 3.59. 62% in top 10% of high school class, 87% in top 25% of high school class, 99% in top 50% of high school class. 60% from public high schools. SAT Math middle 50% range 620-715. SAT Critical Reading middle 50% range 650-740. SAT Writing middle 50% range 645-730. ACT middle 50% range 28-32. Minimum paper TOEFL 600. **Basis for Candidate Selection:** *Very important factors considered include:* Class rank, academic GPA, rigor of secondary school record, standardized test scores. *Important factors considered include:* application essay, recommendation(s), character/personal qualities, extracurricular activities, first generation, talent/ability. *Other factors considered include:* alumni/ae relation, interview, level of applicant's interest, racial/ethnic status, volunteer work, work experience. **Freshman Admission Requirements:** High school diploma is required and GED is accepted. *Academic units required:* 4 English, 4 mathematics, 3 science, 3 foreign language, 3 social studies. **Freshman Admission Statistics:** 7,438 applied, 30% admitted, 35% enrolled. **Transfer Admission Requirements:** High school transcript, college transcript(s), essay or personal statement, standardized test scores, statement of good standing from prior institution(s). Minimum college GPA of 3.0 required. Lowest grade transferable C-. **General Admission Information:** Application Fee $35. Early decision application deadline 11/15. Regular application deadline 1/15. Regular notification 4/1. Nonfall registration not accepted. Admission may be deferred for a maximum of 1 year. Credit and/or placement offered for CEEB Advanced Placement tests.

COSTS AND FINANCIAL AID

Annual tuition $48,054. Room and board $13,106. Required fees $628. Average book expense $930. **Required Forms and Deadlines:** FAFSA, Institution's own financial aid form, CSS/Financial Aid PROFILE, Noncustodial PROFILE. **Notification of Awards:** Applicants will be notified of awards on or about 4/1. **Types of Aid:** *Need-based scholarships/grants:* Federal Pell, SEOG, state scholarships/grants, private scholarships, the school's own gift aid. *Loans:* Subsidized Stafford, Unsubsidized Stafford, PLUS, Federal Perkins, college/university loans from institutional funds. *Student Employment:* Highest amount earned per year from on-campus jobs $1,750. **Financial Aid Statistics:** 96% freshmen, 99% undergrads receive need-based scholarship or grant aid. 81% freshmen, 73% undergrads receive non-need-based scholarship or grant aid. 79% freshmen, 89% undergrads receive need-based self-help aid. 0% freshmen, 0% undergrads receive athletic scholarships. 61% freshmen, 60% undergrads

receive any aid. **Criteria for awarding institutional aid:** *Non-need-based:* academics, music/drama.

OCCIDENTAL COLLEGE

1600 Campus Road, Los Angeles, CA 90041-3314
Phone: 323-259-2700 · **Financial Aid Phone:** 323-259-2548
E-mail: admission@oxy.edu · **CEEB Code:** 4581
Fax: 323-341-4875 · **Website:** www.oxy.edu · **ACT Code:** 350

This private school was founded in 1887. It has a 120-acre campus.

RATINGS

Admissions Selectivity Rating: 93   **Fire Safety Rating:** 73

STUDENTS AND FACULTY

Enrollment: 2,101. **Student Body:** 56% female, 44% male, 48% out-of-state, 5% international (33 countries represented). Asian 12%, African American 5%, Caucasian 51%, Hispanic 15%, Native American <1%
Retention and Graduation: 80% freshmen graduate within 4 years. 10% grads go on to further study within 1 year. **Faculty:** 169 full-time faculty, 95% hold PhDs, 50% are members of minority groups, 30% are women. 0% of classes are taught by teaching assistants.

ACADEMICS

Degrees: bachelor's, master's. **Classes:** Most classes have 10–19 students. Most lab/discussion sessions have 10–19 students. **Majors with Highest Enrollment:** Economics; International Relations and Affairs; Biology/Biological Sciences. **Special Study Options:** cross-registration, double major, exchange student program (domestic), honors program, independent study, internships, student-designed major, study abroad, Richter fellowships for international research; summer undergraduate research program; endowment investment management program (Blyth Fund). **Combined degree programs:** BA/JD, law, Columbia; biotech with Keck Grad Institute. **Disability Services:** Special programs offered to physically disabled students include note-taking services, tape recorders. **Career services:** Alumni network, alumni services, career/job search classes, internships, regional alumni.

FACILITIES

Housing: Coed dorms, women's dorms, fraternity/sorority housing, Theme Housing. 75% of campus accessible to physically disabled. **Special Academic Facilities/Equipment:** Keck Theater; Mullin Studio and Art Gallery; Moore Ornithology Collection; Smiley Geological Collection; Morse Collection of Astronomical Instruments; superconducting magnet; vivarium; greenhouses. **Computers:** 100% of classrooms, 100% of dorms, 90% of libraries, 100% of dining areas, 80% of student union, 50% of common outdoor areas have wireless network access. Students can register for classes online. Administrative functions (other than registration) can be performed online.

CAMPUS LIFE

Environment: Metropolis. **Activities:** Choral groups, concert band, dance, drama/theater, jazz band, literary magazine, music ensembles, musical theater, radio station, student government, student newspaper, student-run film society, symphony orchestra, yearbook, International Student Organization. 8 honor societies, 5 religious organizations. 4 fraternities, 4 sororities. **Athletics (Intercollegiate):** *Men:* baseball, basketball, cross-country, diving, football, golf, soccer, swimming, tennis, track/field (outdoor), water polo. *Women:* basketball, cross-country, diving, golf, lacrosse, soccer, softball, swimming, tennis, track/field (outdoor), volleyball, water polo. **On-Campus Highlights:** Johnson Student Center, Student Quad, Samuelson Pavilion, Clapp Library, Alumni Gymnasium. **Environmental Initiatives:** Sustainability coordinator; Solar array that provides 11% of campus power needs; LEED silver standard for new construction.

ADMISSIONS

Freshman Academic Profile: Average high school GPA 3.65. 55% in top 10% of high school class, 85% in top 25% of high school class, 99% in top 50% of high school class. 60% from public high schools. SAT Math middle 50% range 610-700. SAT Critical Reading middle 50% range 600-690. SAT Writing middle 50% range 610-700. ACT middle 50% range 27-31. Minimum paper TOEFL 600. **Basis for Candidate Selection:** *Very important factors considered include:* rigor of secondary school record, extracurricular activities, volunteer work, work experience. *Important factors considered include:* Class rank, application essay, recommendation(s), standardized test scores. *Other factors* *considered include:* academic GPA, alumni/ae relation, character/personal qualities, first generation, geographical residence, interview, level of applicant's interest, racial/ethnic status, talent/ability. **Freshman Admission Requirements:** High school diploma is required and GED is accepted. **Freshman Admission Statistics:** 6,071 applied, 42% admitted, 21% enrolled. **Transfer Admission Requirements:** High school transcript, college transcript(s), essay or personal statement, statement of good standing from prior institution(s). Minimum college GPA of 3.0 required. Lowest grade transferable D. **General Admission Information:** Application Fee $50. Early decision application deadline 11/15. Regular application deadline 1/10. Regular notification 4/1. Nonfall registration not accepted. Admission may be deferred for a maximum of 1 year. Credit and/or placement offered for CEEB Advanced Placement tests.

COSTS AND FINANCIAL AID
Annual tuition $46,952. Room and board $13,450. Required fees $570. Average book expense $1,252. **Required Forms and Deadlines:** FAFSA, CSS/Financial Aid PROFILE, State aid form, Noncustodial PROFILE. **Notification of Awards:** Applicants will be notified of awards on a rolling basis beginning 4/1. **Types of Aid:** *Need-based scholarships/grants:* Federal Pell, SEOG, state scholarships/grants, private scholarships, the school's own gift aid. *Loans:* Subsidized Stafford, Unsubsidized Stafford, PLUS, Federal Perkins, college/university loans from institutional funds. *Student Employment:* Federal Work-Study Program available. Institutional employment available. Off-campus job opportunities are good. **Financial Aid Statistics:** 92% freshmen, 87% undergrads receive need-based scholarship or grant aid. 14% freshmen, 14% undergrads receive non-need-based scholarship or grant aid. 85% freshmen, 92% undergrads receive need-based self-help aid. 0% freshmen, 0% undergrads receive athletic scholarships. 72% freshmen, 74% undergrads receive any aid. 64% undergrads borrow to pay for school. Average cumulative indebtedness $22,786. **Criteria for awarding institutional aid:** *Non-need-based:* academics, leadership, music/drama, state/district residency.

OGLETHORPE UNIVERSITY

4484 Peachtree Road N.E., Atlanta, GA 30319
Phone: 404-364-8307 · **Financial Aid Phone:** 404-364-8356
E-mail: admission@oglethorpe.edu · **CEEB Code:** 5521
Fax: 404-364-8491 · **Website:** www.oglethorpe.edu · **ACT Code:** 850

This private school was founded in 1835. It has a 102-acre campus.

RATINGS
Admissions Selectivity Rating: 87   **Fire Safety Rating:** 75

STUDENTS AND FACULTY
Enrollment: 1,021. **Student Body:** 57% female, 43% male, 27% out-of-state, 5% international (24 countries represented). Asian 4%, African American 18%, Caucasian 35%, Hispanic 10%, Native American <1%
Retention and Graduation: 55% freshmen graduate within 4 years. 62% freshmen graduate within 6 years. 40% grads go on to further study within 1 year. 19% grads pursue arts and sciences degrees. 9% grads pursue law degrees. 10% grads pursue business degrees. 2% grads pursue medical degrees. **Faculty:** 60 full-time faculty, 92% hold PhDs, 40% are members of minority groups, 13% are women. 0% of classes are taught by teaching assistants.

ACADEMICS
Degrees: bachelor's, master's. **Classes:** Most classes have 10–19 students. **Majors with Highest Enrollment:** English Language and Literature; Psychology; Business/Commerce. **Special Study Options:** Accelerated program, cooperative education program, cross-registration, double major, dual enrollment, exchange student program (domestic), honors program, independent study, internships, liberal arts/career combination, student-designed major, study abroad. **Disability Services:** Special programs offered to physically disabled students include note-taking services, tutors. **Career services:** alumni services, career/job search classes, career assessment, internships.

FACILITIES
Housing: Coed dorms, fraternity/sorority housing. 60% of campus accessible to physically disabled. **Special Academic Facilities/Equipment:** Art museum, scanning electron microscope. **Computers:** 100% of classrooms, 100% of dorms, 100% of libraries, 100% of student union, 25% of common outdoor areas have wireless network access. Administrative functions (other than registration) can be performed online.

CAMPUS LIFE
Environment: Metropolis. **Activities:** Choral groups, dance, drama/theater, jazz band, literary magazine, music ensembles, musical theater, pep band, radio station, student government, student newspaper, student-run film society, yearbook, Campus Ministries, International Student Organization. 57 registered

organizations, 10 honor societies, 5 religious organizations. 4 fraternities, 3 sororities. **Athletics (Intercollegiate):** *Men:* baseball, basketball, cross-country, golf, lacrosse, soccer, tennis, track/field (outdoor). *Women:* basketball, cheerleading, cross-country, golf, lacrosse, soccer, tennis, track/field (outdoor), volleyball. **On-Campus Highlights:** Oglethorpe University Museum, Phillip Weltner Library, Conant Performing Arts Center, Hermance Stadium, New Residence Halls. **Environmental Initiatives:** New buildings are built according to LEED requirements; use of green cleaning chemicals; recycling program on campus—student organized and student run.

ADMISSIONS
Freshman Academic Profile: Average high school GPA 3.49. 20% in top 10% of high school class, 55% in top 25% of high school class, 86% in top 50% of high school class. 79% from public high schools. SAT Math middle 50% range 510-610. SAT Critical Reading middle 50% range 520-630. SAT Writing middle 50% range 490-610. ACT middle 50% range 22-27. Minimum paper TOEFL 550. **Basis for Candidate Selection:** *Very important factors considered include:* academic GPA, rigor of secondary school record, standardized test scores. *Important factors considered include:* Class rank, application essay, recommendation(s), extracurricular activities, interview, level of applicant's interest, volunteer work. *Other factors considered include:* alumni/ae relation, character/personal qualities, first generation, talent/ability, work experience. **Freshman Admission Requirements:** High school diploma is required and GED is accepted. *Academic units required:* 4 English, 3 mathematics, 2 science, 3 social studies. **Freshman Admission Statistics:** 4,403 applied, 56% admitted, 11% enrolled. **Transfer Admission Requirements:** college transcript(s), statement of good standing from prior institution(s). Minimum college GPA of 2.8 required. Lowest grade transferable C. **General Admission Information:** Application Fee $40. Notification on a rolling basis, beginning on or about 12/1. Nonfall registration accepted, Admission may be deferred for a maximum of 1 year. Credit and/or placement offered for CEEB Advanced Placement tests.

COSTS AND FINANCIAL AID
Annual tuition $32,200. Room and board $11,700. Required fees $300. Average book expense $1,100. **Required Forms and Deadlines:** FAFSA. **Notification of Awards:** Applicants will be notified of awards on a rolling basis beginning 3/1. **Types of Aid:** *Need-based scholarships/grants:* Federal Pell, SEOG, state scholarships/grants, private scholarships, the school's own gift aid. *Loans:* Direct Subsidized Stafford, Direct Unsubsidized Stafford, Direct PLUS, Federal Perkins. *Student Employment:* Federal Work-Study Program available. Institutional employment available. Off-campus job opportunities are excellent. **Financial Aid Statistics:** 100% freshmen, 100% undergrads receive need-based scholarship or grant aid. 14% freshmen, 10% undergrads receive non-need-based scholarship or grant aid. 70% freshmen, 74% undergrads receive need-based self-help aid. 0% freshmen, 0% undergrads receive athletic scholarships. 95% freshmen, 95% undergrads receive any aid. 68% undergrads borrow to pay for school. Average cumulative indebtedness $24,162. **Criteria for awarding institutional aid:** *Non-need-based:* academics, music/drama.

OHIO DOMINICAN UNIVERSITY

1216 Sunbury Road, Coumbus, OH 42319-2099
Phone: 614-251-4500 · **Financial Aid Phone:** 614-251-4778
E-mail: admissions@ohiodominican.edu · **CEEB Code:** 1131
Fax: 614-251-0156 · **Website:** http://www.ohiodominican.edu · **ACT Code:** 3256

This private school, affiliated with the Roman Catholic Church, was founded in 1911. It has a 75-acre campus.

RATINGS
Admissions Selectivity Rating: 85   **Fire Safety Rating:** 84

STUDENTS AND FACULTY
Enrollment: 1,483. **Student Body:** 57% female, 43% male, 3% out-of-state, 1% international (9 countries represented). Asian 1%, African American 26%, Caucasian 63%, Hispanic 3%, Native American <1%
Retention and Graduation: 66% freshmen return for sophomore year. 29% freshmen graduate within 4 years. 42% freshmen graduate within 6 years. **Faculty:** 73 full-time faculty, 90% hold PhDs, 49% are members of minority groups, 10% are women. 0% of classes are taught by teaching assistants.

ACADEMICS
Degrees: associate, bachelor's, certificate, master's, transfer associate. **Classes:** Most classes have 10–19 students. **Majors with Highest Enrollment:** Psychology; Secondary Education and Teaching; Education/Teaching of Individuals with Multiple Disabilities. **Special Study Options:** Accelerated program, cross-registration, distance learning, double major, dual enrollment, exchange student program (domestic), honors program, independent study, internships,

study abroad, teacher certification program. **Honors programs:** The Honors Program is designed for high-ability, motivated students. Honors-designed courses will be offered to specifically challenge and engage students in the program. **Career services:** Alumni network, alumni services, career/job search classes, career assessment, internships. Career services highlights include vital practical experience for students who participate in internships.

FACILITIES

Housing: Coed dorms. 90% of campus accessible to physically disabled. **Special Academic Facilities/Equipment:** Wehrle Art Gallery. **Computers:** 90% of classrooms, 100% of libraries, 100% of dining areas, na% of student union, 5% of common outdoor areas have wireless network access. Students can register for classes online. Administrative functions (other than registration) can be performed online.

CAMPUS LIFE

Environment: Metropolis. **Activities:** Choral groups, concert band, dance, drama/theater, literary magazine, marching band, music ensembles, musical theater, pep band, radio station, student government, student newspaper, Campus Ministries, Model UN. 40 registered organizations, 2 honor societies, 1 religious organization. **Athletics (Intercollegiate):** *Men:* baseball, basketball, cross-country, football, golf, soccer, tennis. *Women:* basketball, cross-country, golf, soccer, softball, tennis, volleyball. **On-Campus Highlights:** Student Center opened Fall 2009, Panther Plaza, Alumni Hall, Wehrle Hall, The Underground in Fitzpatrick Hall. **Environmental Initiatives:** New buildings are to be LEED silver certified. Recycling program is now in place.

ADMISSIONS

Freshman Academic Profile: Average high school GPA 3.343. 22% in top 10% of high school class, 46% in top 25% of high school class, 80% in top 50% of high school class. 86% from public high schools. SAT Math middle 50% range 480-580. SAT Critical Reading middle 50% range 440-540. SAT Writing middle 50% range 430-520. ACT middle 50% range 20-24. Minimum internet-based TOEFL 78. Minimum paper TOEFL 550. **Basis for Candidate Selection:** *Very important factors considered include:* academic GPA, rigor of secondary school record. *Important factors considered include:* standardized test scores. *Other factors considered include:* Class rank, application essay, recommendation(s), character/personal qualities, extracurricular activities, interview, talent/ability, volunteer work, work experience. **Freshman Admission Requirements:** High school diploma is required and GED is accepted. **Freshman Admission Statistics:** 2,652 applied, 49% admitted, 18% enrolled. **Transfer Admission Requirements:** college transcript(s), Lowest grade transferable C. **General Admission Information:** Application Fee $25. Notification on a rolling basis, beginning on or about 9/4. Nonfall registration accepted. Admission may be deferred for a maximum of 1-year. Credit and/or placement offered for CEEB Advanced Placement tests.

COSTS AND FINANCIAL AID

Annual tuition $24,116. Room and board $7,900. Required fees $500. Average book expense $1,000. **Required Forms and Deadlines:** FAFSA. **Notification of Awards:** Applicants will be notified of awards on a rolling basis beginning 3/1. **Types of Aid:** *Need-based scholarships/grants:* Federal Pell, SEOG, state scholarships/grants, private scholarships, the school's own gift aid. *Loans:* Subsidized Stafford, Unsubsidized Stafford, PLUS, Federal Perkins. *Student Employment:* Federal Work-Study Program available. Off-campus job opportunities are good. **Financial Aid Statistics:** 100% freshmen, 72% undergrads receive any aid. 59% undergrads borrow to pay for school. **Criteria for awarding institutional aid:** *Non-need-based:* academics, athletics, music/drama.

OHIO NORTHERN UNIVERSITY

525 South Main Street, Ada, OH 45810
Phone: 419-772-2260 · **Financial Aid Phone:** 419-772-2272
E-mail: admissions-ug@onu.edu · **CEEB Code:** 1591
Fax: 419-772-2821 · **Website:** www.onu.edu · **ACT Code:** 3310

This private school, affiliated with the Methodist Church, was founded in 1871. It has a 300-acre campus.

RATINGS

Admissions Selectivity Rating: 87   Fire Safety Rating: 62

STUDENTS AND FACULTY

Enrollment: 2,232. **Student Body:** 47% female, 53% male, 13% out-of-state, 4% international (17 countries represented). Asian 1%, African American 4%, Caucasian 84%, Hispanic 1%, Native American <1%
Retention and Graduation: 88% freshmen return for sophomore year. 51% freshmen graduate within 4 years. 65% freshmen graduate within 6 years.
Faculty: 210 full-time faculty, 84% hold PhDs, 40% are members of minority groups, 12% are women. 0% of classes are taught by teaching assistants.

ACADEMICS

Degrees: bachelor's, post-bachelor's certificate. **Classes:** Most classes have 20-29 students. **Majors with Highest Enrollment:** Mechanical Engineering; Biology/Biological Sciences; Registered Nursing/Registered Nurse. **Special Study Options:** cooperative education program, distance learning, double major, dual enrollment, English as a Second Language (ESL), exchange student program (domestic), honors program, independent study, internships, liberal arts/career combination, study abroad, teacher certification program, Washington semester. **Honors programs:** Honors Program consists of a First-Year Honors Seminar and 3 additional Honors Seminars, 2 "contract" courses and a final Honors project. **Combined degree programs:** BA/JD, Pharm D. **Disability Services:** Special programs offered to physically disabled students include note-taking services, reader services, tape recorders, tutors. **Career services:** Alumni network, alumni services, career/job search classes, career assessment, internships.

FACILITIES

Housing: Coed dorms, special housing for disabled students, men's dorms, special housing for international students, women's dorms, fraternity/sorority housing, apartments for married students, cooperative housing, apartments for single students, Wellness Housing, Theme Housing, Honors Residence Halls. 95% of campus accessible to physically disabled. **Special Academic Facilities/Equipment:** Art gallery, performing arts center, language lab, sports center, pharmacy museum. **Computers:** 100% of classrooms, 100% of dorms, 100% of libraries, 100% of dining areas, 100% of student union, have wireless network access. Students can register for classes online. Administrative functions (other than registration) can be performed online.

CAMPUS LIFE

Environment: Village. **Activities:** Choral groups, concert band, dance, drama/theater, jazz band, literary magazine, marching band, music ensembles, musical theater, opera, pep band, radio station, student government, student newspaper, symphony orchestra, television station, yearbook, Campus Ministries, International Student Organization, Model UN. 200 registered organizations, 40 honor societies, 27 religious organizations. 6 fraternities, 4 sororities. **Athletics (Intercollegiate):** *Men:* baseball, basketball, cross-country, diving, football, golf, soccer, swimming, tennis, track/field (outdoor), track/field (indoor), wrestling. *Women:* basketball, cross-country, diving, golf, soccer, softball, swimming, tennis, track/field (outdoor), track/field (indoor), volleyball. **On-Campus Highlights:** ONU Sports Center, Northern on Main Coffee Café, Performing Arts Center, New Student Apartments, James F. Dicke Hall.

ADMISSIONS

Freshman Academic Profile: Average high school GPA 3.7. 35% in top 10% of high school class, 62% in top 25% of high school class, 90% in top 50% of high school class. SAT Math middle 50% range 530-650. SAT Critical Reading middle 50% range 520-620. SAT Writing middle 50% range 510-600. ACT middle 50% range 23-29. Minimum internet-based TOEFL 54. Minimum paper TOEFL 480. **Basis for Candidate Selection:** *Very important factors considered include:* academic GPA, rigor of secondary school record, standardized test scores. *Important factors considered include:* Class rank, extracurricular activities, interview. *Other factors considered include:* application essay, recommendation(s), alumni/ae relation, character/personal qualities, first generation, level of applicant's interest, talent/ability, volunteer work. **Freshman Admission Requirements:** High school diploma is required and GED is accepted. *Academic units required:* 4 English, 2 mathematics, 2 science, (2 science labs), 2 social studies, 2 history, 4 academic electives. **Freshman Admission Statistics:** 3,337 applied, 69% admitted, 27% enrolled. **Transfer Admission Requirements:** High school transcript, college transcript(s), statement of good standing from prior institution(s). Minimum college GPA of 2.0 required. Lowest grade transferable C. **General Admission Information:** Application Fee $30. Regular application deadline 8/15. Notification on a rolling basis, beginning on or about 7/15. Nonfall registration accepted. Admission may be deferred for a maximum of 1 year. Credit and/or placement offered for CEEB Advanced Placement tests.

COSTS AND FINANCIAL AID

Annual tuition $27,500. Room and board $10,910. Required fees $550. Average book expense $1,800. **Required Forms and Deadlines:** FAFSA. **Notification of Awards:** Applicants will be notified of awards on a rolling basis beginning 3/1. **Types of Aid:** *Need-based scholarships/grants:* Federal Pell, SEOG, state scholarships/grants, private scholarships, the school's own gift aid, External Scholarships. *Loans:* Subsidized Stafford, Unsubsidized Stafford, PLUS, Federal Perkins, college/university loans from institutional funds, Alternative Loans, Federal Health Professions Loan. *Student Employment:* Federal Work-Study Program available. Institutional employment available. Off-campus job opportunities are good. **Criteria for awarding institutional aid:** *Non-need-based:* academics, alumni affiliation, art, leadership, minority status, music/drama, state/district residency.

THE OHIO STATE UNIVERSITY AT MANSFIELD

1680 University Drive, Mansfield, OH 44906
Phone: 419-755-4011 • **Financial Aid Phone:** 614-292-0330
E-mail: askabuckeye@osu.edu • **CEEB Code:** 744
Website: www.mansfield.ohio.edu • **ACT Code:** 3312

This public school was founded in 1958. It has a 640-acre campus.

RATINGS

Admissions Selectivity Rating: 71   **Fire Safety Rating:** 75

STUDENTS AND FACULTY

Enrollment: 1,092. **Student Body:** 55% female, 45% male, (0 countries represented). Asian 2%, African American 9%, Caucasian 81%, Hispanic 3%, Native American <1%
Retention and Graduation: 23% freshmen graduate within 4 years. 42% freshmen graduate within 6 years. **Faculty:** 39 full-time faculty, 97% hold PhDs, 49% are members of minority groups, 10% are women.

ACADEMICS

Degrees: associate, bachelor's, master's. **Classes:** Most classes have 10–19 students. Most lab/discussion sessions have 40-49 students. **Special Study Options:** Accelerated program, cooperative education program, cross-registration, distance learning, double major, dual enrollment, English as a Second Language (ESL), exchange student program (domestic), honors program, independent study, internships, liberal arts/career combination, student-designed major, study abroad, teacher certification program, weekend college. **Honors programs:** The University Honors Program is dedicated to promoting the intellectual and personal development of high-performing students. It strives to promote a more active and enriching relationship between Honors students and the University by connecting them with resources and opportunities that will encourage them to maximize their potential. The University Scholars Program enables talented and motivated students to be part of smaller, selective communities within the larger university environment. Each of the fourteen programs focuses on a common theme or academic area of interest designed to foster learning and involvement. Scholars live together, attend classes together, and experience diverse opportunities outside the classroom. **Combined degree programs:** BA/MD, BA/DDS. **Disability Services:** Special programs offered to physically disabled students include note-taking services, reader services, tape recorders, tutors. **Career services:** Alumni network, alumni services.

FACILITIES

Housing: special housing for disabled students, apartments for single students, Wellness Housing. 90% of campus accessible to physically disabled. **Computers:** 100% of classrooms, 100% of dorms, 100% of libraries, 100% of dining areas, 100% of student union, 50% of common outdoor areas have wireless network access. Students can register for classes online. Administrative functions (other than registration) can be performed online.

CAMPUS LIFE

Environment: Town. **Activities:** Choral groups, dance, drama/theater, student newspaper, student-run film society. 16 registered organizations, 2 honor societies, 2 religious organizations. **Athletics (Intercollegiate):** *Men:* baseball, basketball, soccer. *Women:* basketball, cheerleading, volleyball.

ADMISSIONS

Freshman Academic Profile: 10% in top 10% of high school class, 33% in top 25% of high school class, 69% in top 50% of high school class. 92% from public high schools. SAT Math middle 50% range 470-600. SAT Critical Reading middle 50% range 440-570. SAT Writing middle 50% range 420-560. Minimum internet-based TOEFL 79. Minimum paper TOEFL 550. **Basis for Candidate Selection:** *Other factors considered include:* recommendation(s), rigor of secondary school record. **Freshman Admission Requirements:** *Academic units required:* 4 English, 3 mathematics, 2 science, (2 science labs), 2 foreign language, 2 social studies, 1 visual/performing arts, 1 academic electives. **Freshman Admission Statistics:** 1,626 applied, 99% admitted, 30% enrolled. **Transfer Admission Requirements:** college transcript(s), Minimum college GPA of 2.0 required. Lowest grade transferable C-. **General Admission Information:** Application Fee $40. Regular application deadline 7/1. Notification on a rolling basis, beginning on or about 12/1. Nonfall registration accepted. Credit and/or placement offered for CEEB Advanced Placement tests.

COSTS AND FINANCIAL AID

Average book expense $1,248. **Required Forms and Deadlines:** FAFSA. **Notification of Awards:** Applicants will be notified of awards on or about 4/5. **Types of Aid:** *Need-based scholarships/grants:* Federal Pell, SEOG, state scholarships/grants, private scholarships, the school's own gift aid. *Loans:* Direct Subsidized Stafford, Direct Unsubsidized Stafford, Direct PLUS, Federal Perkins, Federal Nursing, college/university loans from institutional funds. *Student Employment:* Federal Work-Study Program available. Institutional employment available. Off-campus job opportunities are good. **Financial Aid Statistics:** 83% freshmen, 79% undergrads receive need-based scholarship or grant aid. 1% freshmen, 1% undergrads receive non-need-based scholarship or grant aid. 93% freshmen, 91% undergrads receive need-based self-help aid. 0% freshmen, 0% undergrads receive athletic scholarships. 91% freshmen, 87% undergrads receive any aid. **Criteria for awarding institutional aid:** *Non-need-based:* academics, alumni affiliation, art, athletics, job skills, leadership, minority status, music/drama, state/district residency.

THE OHIO STATE UNIVERSITY AT MARION

1465 Mount Vernon Avenue, Marion, OH 43302
Phone: 740-725-6337 • **Financial Aid Phone:** 614-292-0300
E-mail: askabuckeye@osu.edu • **CEEB Code:** 752
Website: www.marion.ohio-state.edu • **ACT Code:** 3312

This public school was founded in 1957. It has a 188-acre campus.

RATINGS

Admissions Selectivity Rating: 71   **Fire Safety Rating:** 60*

STUDENTS AND FACULTY

Enrollment: 1,146. **Student Body:** 53% female, 47% male, 0% international (0 countries represented). Asian 4%, African American 5%, Caucasian 82%, Hispanic 4%, Native American <1%
Retention and Graduation: 21% freshmen graduate within 4 years. 43% freshmen graduate within 6 years. **Faculty:** 38 full-time faculty, 97% hold PhDs, 45% are members of minority groups, 11% are women.

ACADEMICS

Degrees: associate, bachelor's, master's. **Classes:** Most classes have 20–29 students. Most lab/discussion sessions have 20–29 students. **Special Study Options:** Accelerated program, cooperative education program, cross-registration, distance learning, double major, dual enrollment, English as a Second Language (ESL), exchange student program (domestic), honors program, independent study, internships, liberal arts/career combination, student-designed major, study abroad, teacher certification program, weekend college. **Honors programs:** The University Honors Program is dedicated to promoting the intellectual and personal development of high-performing students. It strives to promote a more active and enriching relationship between Honors students and the University by connecting them with resources and opportunities that will encourage them to maximize their potential. The University Scholars Program enables talented and motivated students to be part of smaller, selective communities within the larger university environment. Each of the fourteen programs focuses on a common theme or academic area of interest designed to foster learning and involvement. Scholars live together, attend classes together, and experience diverse opportunities outside the classroom. **Combined degree programs:** BA/MD, BA/DDS, BA/MEng. **Disability Services:** Special programs offered to physically disabled students include note-taking services, reader services, tape recorders, tutors. **Career services:** Alumni network, alumni services, career/job search classes, career assessment, internships, regional alumni.

FACILITIES

Housing: 100% of campus accessible to physically disabled. **Special Academic Facilities/Equipment:** Kuhn Art Gallery **Computers:** 100% of classrooms, 100% of libraries, have wireless network access. Students can register for classes online. Administrative functions (other than registration) can be performed online.

CAMPUS LIFE

Environment: Town. **Activities:** Choral groups, literary magazine, music ensembles, student government, Campus Ministries. 33 registered organizations, 1 honor society, 3 religious organizations. **Athletics (Intercollegiate):** *Men:* basketball, gymnastics, volleyball. *Women:* gymnastics.

ADMISSIONS

Freshman Academic Profile: 9% in top 10% of high school class, 34% in top 25% of high school class, 67% in top 50% of high school class. 95% from public high schools. SAT Math middle 50% range 490-590. SAT Critical Reading middle 50% range 470-550. SAT Writing middle 50% range 430-570. Minimum

The Princeton Review's Complete Book of Colleges

internet-based TOEFL 79. Minimum paper TOEFL 550. **Basis for Candidate Selection:** *Other factors considered include:* recommendation(s), rigor of secondary school record. **Freshman Admission Requirements:** *Academic units required:* 4 English, 3 mathematics, 2 science, (2 science labs), 2 foreign language, 2 social studies, 1 visual/performing arts, 1 academic electives. **Freshman Admission Statistics:** 960 applied, 99% admitted, 47% enrolled. **Transfer Admission Requirements:** college transcript(s), Minimum college GPA of 2.0 required. Lowest grade transferable C-. **General Admission Information:** Application Fee $40. Regular application deadline 7/1. Regular notification 12/1. Nonfall registration accepted. Credit and/or placement offered for CEEB Advanced Placement tests.

COSTS AND FINANCIAL AID

Average book expense $1,248. **Required Forms and Deadlines:** FAFSA. **Notification of Awards:** Applicants will be notified of awards on or about 4/5. **Types of Aid:** *Need-based scholarships/grants:* Federal Pell, SEOG, state scholarships/grants, private scholarships, the school's own gift aid. *Loans:* Direct Subsidized Stafford, Direct Unsubsidized Stafford, Direct PLUS, Federal Perkins, Federal Nursing, college/university loans from institutional funds. *Student Employment:* Federal Work-Study Program available. Institutional employment available. Off-campus job opportunities are good. **Financial Aid Statistics:** 84% freshmen, 80% undergrads receive need-based scholarship or grant aid. 2% freshmen, 1% undergrads receive non-need-based scholarship or grant aid. 85% freshmen, 88% undergrads receive need-based self-help aid. 0% freshmen, 0% undergrads receive athletic scholarships. 91% freshmen, 86% undergrads receive any aid. **Criteria for awarding institutional aid:** *Non-need-based:* academics, alumni affiliation, art, athletics, job skills, leadership, minority status, music/drama, state/district residency.

THE OHIO STATE UNIVERSITY—COLUMBUS

Student Academic Services Building, Columbus, OH 43210
Phone: 614-292-3980 • **Financial Aid Phone:** 614-292-0300
E-mail: askabuckeye@osu.edu • **CEEB Code:** 1592
Fax: 614-292-4818 • **Website:** www.osu.edu • **ACT Code:** 3312

This public school was founded in 1870. It has a 3469-acre campus.

RATINGS

Admissions Selectivity Rating: 91   **Fire Safety Rating:** 60*

STUDENTS AND FACULTY

Enrollment: 43,733. **Student Body:** 47% female, 53% male, 16% out-of-state, 8% international (109 countries represented). Asian 6%, African American 6%, Caucasian 72%, Hispanic 3%, Native American <1%
Retention and Graduation: 61% freshmen graduate within 4 years. 84% freshmen graduate within 6 years. **Faculty:** 3,710 full-time faculty, 99% hold PhDs, 37% are members of minority groups, 23% are women.

ACADEMICS

Degrees: associate, bachelor's, certificate, doctoral, master's, post-bachelor's certificate, post-master's certificate. **Classes:** Most classes have 20–29 students. Most lab/discussion sessions have 20–29 students. **Majors with Highest Enrollment:** Psychology; Finance; Communication. **Special Study Options:** Accelerated program, cooperative education program, cross-registration, distance learning, double major, dual enrollment, English as a Second Language (ESL), exchange student program (domestic), honors program, independent study, internships, liberal arts/career combination, student-designed major, study abroad, teacher certification program, weekend college. **Honors programs:** The University Honors Program is dedicated to promoting the intellectual and personal development of high-performing students. It strives to promote a more active and enriching relationship between Honors students and the University by connecting them with resources and opportunities that will encourage them to maximize their potential. The University Scholars Program enables talented and motivated students to be part of smaller, selective communnities within the larger university environment. Each of the fourteen programs focuses on a common theme or academic area of interest designed to foster learning and involvement. Scholars live together, attend classes together, and experience diverse opportunities outside the classroom. **Combined degree programs:** BA/MD, BA/DDS. **Disability Services:** Special programs offered to physically disabled students include note-taking services, reader services, tape recorders, tutors. **Career services:** Alumni network, alumni services, career/job search classes, career assessment, internships, regional alumni.

FACILITIES

Housing: Coed dorms, special housing for disabled students, special housing for international students, women's dorms, fraternity/sorority housing, apartments for married students, cooperative housing, apartments for single students, Wellness Housing, Theme Housing. 90% of campus accessible to physically disabled. **Special Academic Facilities/Equipment:** Wexner center for the Arts, zoology museum, geology museum, art and photography galleries, nuclear research reactor, electroscience lab, biomedical engineering center, cartoon art museum **Computers:** 100% of dorms, 90% of libraries, 100% of dining areas, 100% of student union, 4% of common outdoor areas have wireless network access. Students can register for classes online. Administrative functions (other than registration) can be performed online.

CAMPUS LIFE

Environment: Metropolis. **Activities:** Choral groups, dance, drama/theater, jazz band, literary magazine, marching band, music ensembles, musical theater, opera, pep band, radio station, student government, student newspaper, student-run film society, symphony orchestra, television station, yearbook, International Student Organization. 950 registered organizations, 39 honor societies, 93 religious organizations. 42 fraternities, 25 sororities. **Athletics (Intercollegiate):** *Men:* baseball, basketball, cheerleading, cross-country, diving, fencing, football, golf, gymnastics, ice hockey, lacrosse, pistol, riflery, soccer, swimming, tennis, track/field (outdoor), track/field (indoor), volleyball, wrestling. *Women:* baseball, basketball, cheerleading, cross-country, diving, fencing, field hockey, golf, gymnastics, ice hockey, lacrosse, pistol, riflery, soccer, softball, swimming, synchronized swimming, tennis, track/field (outdoor), track/field (indoor), volleyball. **On-Campus Highlights:** Hale Cultural Center, Chadwick Arboretum, Jack Nicklaus Golf Museum, Schottenstein Center and Value City Arena, Wexner Center for the Arts. **Environmental Initiatives:** Building Energy Auditing Program, http://president.osu.edu/sustainability, iee.osu.edu; http://fod.osu.edu/afp/; All-In-One Campus Recycling System, http://president. osu.edu/sustainability, iee.osu.edu, http://fod.osu.edu/afp/. Ohio State boasts a holistic approach to sustainability endeavors: in-depth planning, programs for the physical environment and programs for the community. The 'One Ohio State Framework Plan' is the structure for guiding the ever improving university, of which, sustainability plays a major role. The Sustainability Plan, the Climate Action Plan and the Energy and Infrastructure Plan, key elements of the Framework Plan, serve as references for the forthcoming Integrated Energy and Environment Implementation Strategy. This strategy will provide direction for all energy and environment initiatives from development of university level policies to support for individual projects and programs. Existing plans come into action on Ohio State's campus through the university's aggressive building energy auditing program and expansive "All-In-One" recycling program. The true reach of Ohio State's planning is seen through research, curriculum and engagement programs. Several research incubators, including the Institute for Energy and the Environment, champion sustainability innovation from professors and students alike. Ohio State also demonstrates a strong commitment to developing environmentally conscious students by offering sustainability focused degrees, concentrations and courses while providing strong support for its over two dozen sustainability oriented student groups.

ADMISSIONS

Freshman Academic Profile: 61% in top 10% of high school class, 94% in top 25% of high school class, 99% in top 50% of high school class. 85% from public high schools. SAT Math middle 50% range 620-730. SAT Critical Reading middle 50% range 540-660. SAT Writing middle 50% range 560-660. ACT middle 50% range 27-31. Minimum internet-based TOEFL 79. Minimum paper TOEFL 550. **Basis for Candidate Selection:** *Very important factors considered include:* Class rank, academic GPA, rigor of secondary school record, standardized test scores. *Important factors considered include:* application essay, extracurricular activities, first generation, talent/ability, volunteer work, work experience. *Other factors considered include:* recommendation(s), character/personal qualities, geographical residence, racial/ethnic status, state residency. **Freshman Admission Requirements:** High school diploma is required and GED is accepted. *Academic units required:* 4 English, 3 mathematics, 2 science, (2 science labs), 2 foreign language, 2 social studies, 1 visual/performing arts, 1 academic electives. **Freshman Admission Statistics:** 36,788 applied, 53% admitted, 36% enrolled. **Transfer Admission Requirements:** college transcript(s), Minimum college GPA of 2.0 required. Lowest grade transferable C-. **General Admission Information:** Application Fee $40. Regular application deadline 2/1. Notification on a rolling basis, beginning on or about 12/1. Nonfall registration accepted. Credit and/or placement offered for CEEB Advanced Placement tests.

COSTS AND FINANCIAL AID

Average book expense $1,248. **Required Forms and Deadlines:** FAFSA. **Notification of Awards:** Applicants will be notified of awards on or about 4/5. **Types of Aid:** *Need-based scholarships/grants:* Federal Pell, SEOG, state scholarships/grants, private scholarships, the school's own gift aid. *Loans:* Direct Subsidized Stafford, Direct Unsubsidized Stafford, Direct PLUS, Federal Perkins, Federal Nursing, college/university loans from institutional funds. *Student*

Employment: Federal Work-Study Program available. Institutional employment available. Off-campus job opportunities are good. **Financial Aid Statistics:** 90% freshmen, 78% undergrads receive need-based scholarship or grant aid. 10% freshmen, 4% undergrads receive non-need-based scholarship or grant aid. 79% freshmen, 88% undergrads receive need-based self-help aid. 1% freshmen, 1% undergrads receive athletic scholarships. 88% freshmen, 79% undergrads receive any aid. 56% undergrads borrow to pay for school. Average cumulative indebtedness $22,756. **Criteria for awarding institutional aid:** *Non-need-based:* academics, alumni affiliation, art, athletics, job skills, leadership, minority status, music/drama, state/district residency.

THE OHIO STATE UNIVERSITY—LIMA CAMPUS

4240 Campus Drive, Lima, OH 45804-3596
Phone: 419-995-8434 • **Financial Aid Phone:** 614-292-0300
E-mail: lima-askabuckeye@osu.edu • **CEEB Code:** 1541
Fax: 419-995-8483 • **Website:** www.lima.osu.edu • **ACT Code:** 3312

This public school was founded in 1960. It has a 565-acre campus.

RATINGS
Admissions Selectivity Rating: 71   Fire Safety Rating: 60*

STUDENTS AND FACULTY
Enrollment: 928. **Student Body:** 57% female, 43% male, 0% out-of-state, 0% international (2 countries represented). Asian 2%, African American 4%, Caucasian 91%, Hispanic 3%, Native American <1%
Retention and Graduation: 21% freshmen graduate within 4 years. 33% freshmen graduate within 6 years. **Faculty:** 35 full-time faculty, 97% hold PhDs, 37% are members of minority groups, 17% are women. 0% of classes are taught by teaching assistants.

ACADEMICS
Degrees: associate, bachelor's, master's. **Classes:** Most classes have 20–29 students. Most lab/discussion sessions have 20–29 students. **Majors with Highest Enrollment:** Elementary Education and Teaching; Psychology; Biology/Biological Sciences. **Special Study Options:** Accelerated program, cooperative education program, cross-registration, distance learning, double major, dual enrollment, English as a Second Language (ESL), exchange student program (domestic), honors program, independent study, internships, liberal arts/career combination, student-designed major, study abroad, teacher certification program, weekend college. **Honors programs:** The University Honors Program is dedicated to promoting the intellectual and personal development of high-performing students. It strives to promote a more active and enriching relationship between Honors students and the University by connecting them with resources and opportunities that will encourage them to maximize their potential. The University Scholars Program enables talented and motivated students to be part of smaller, selective communnities within the larger university environment. Each of the fourteen programs focuses on a common theme or academic area of interest designed to foster learning and involvement. Scholars live together, attend classes together, and experience diverse opportunities outside the classroom. **Disability Services:** Special programs offered to physically disabled students include note-taking services, reader services, tape recorders, tutors. **Career services:** Alumni network, alumni services, career/job search classes, career assessment, internships, regional alumni.

FACILITIES
Housing: 100% of campus accessible to physically disabled. **Special Academic Facilities/Equipment:** OhioSeis seismological network: http://seismic.lima.ohio-state.edu/ Geological Museum Observatory **Computers:** 75% of classrooms, 100% of libraries, 100% of dining areas, 100% of student union, 100% of common outdoor areas have wireless network access. Students can register for classes online. Administrative functions (other than registration) can be performed online.

CAMPUS LIFE
Environment: Rural. **Activities:** Choral groups, dance, drama/theater, musical theater, pep band, student government, student-run film society, Campus Ministries, International Student Organization. 32 registered organizations, 1 honor society, 2 religious organizations.

ADMISSIONS
Freshman Academic Profile: 7% in top 10% of high school class, 31% in top 25% of high school class, 65% in top 50% of high school class. 94% from public high schools. SAT Math middle 50% range 460-650. SAT Critical Reading middle 50% range 528-630. SAT Writing middle 50% range 498-563. ACT middle 50% range 19-25. Minimum internet-based TOEFL 79. Minimum paper TOEFL 550. **Basis for Candidate Selection:** *Other factors considered*

include: recommendation(s), rigor of secondary school record. **Freshman Admission Requirements:** *Academic units required:* 4 English, 3 mathematics, 2 science, (2 science labs), 2 foreign language, 2 social studies, 1 visual/performing arts, 1 academic electives. **Freshman Admission Statistics:** 1,257 applied, 99% admitted, 35% enrolled. **Transfer Admission Requirements:** college transcript(s), Minimum college GPA of 2.0 required. Lowest grade transferable C-. **General Admission Information:** Application Fee $40. Regular application deadline 7/1. Notification on a rolling basis, beginning on or about 12/1. Credit and/or placement offered for CEEB Advanced Placement tests.

COSTS AND FINANCIAL AID
Average book expense $1,248. **Required Forms and Deadlines:** FAFSA. **Notification of Awards:** Applicants will be notified of awards on or about 4/5. **Types of Aid:** *Need-based scholarships/grants:* Federal Pell, SEOG, state scholarships/grants, private scholarships, the school's own gift aid. *Loans:* Direct Subsidized Stafford, Direct Unsubsidized Stafford, Direct PLUS, Federal Perkins, Federal Nursing, college/university loans from institutional funds. *Student Employment:* Federal Work-Study Program available. Institutional employment available. Off-campus job opportunities are good. **Financial Aid Statistics:** 83% freshmen, 76% undergrads receive need-based scholarship or grant aid. 3% freshmen, 2% undergrads receive non-need-based scholarship or grant aid. 90% freshmen, 90% undergrads receive need-based self-help aid. 0% freshmen, 0% undergrads receive athletic scholarships. 94% freshmen, 91% undergrads receive any aid. **Criteria for awarding institutional aid:** *Non-need-based:* academics, alumni affiliation, art, athletics, job skills, leadership, minority status, music/drama, state/district residency.

THE OHIO STATE UNIVERSITY—NEWARK

1179 University Drive, Newark, OH 43055
Phone: 740-366-9333 • **Financial Aid Phone:** 614-292-0300
E-mail: askabuckeye@osu.edu • **CEEB Code:** 752
Fax: 740-364-9645 • **Website:** http://www.newark.osu.edu/Pages/Index/as
ACT Code: 3312

This public school was founded in 1957. It has a 106-acre campus.

RATINGS
Admissions Selectivity Rating: 70   Fire Safety Rating: 90

STUDENTS AND FACULTY
Enrollment: 2,311. **Student Body:** 50% female, 50% male, 1% out-of-state. Asian 4%, African American 13%, Caucasian 73%, Hispanic 3%, Native American <1%
Retention and Graduation: 20% freshmen graduate within 4 years. 39% freshmen graduate within 6 years. **Faculty:** 53 full-time faculty, 98% hold PhDs, 38% are members of minority groups, 17% are women.

ACADEMICS
Degrees: associate, bachelor's, master's. **Classes:** Most classes have 20–29 students. Most lab/discussion sessions have 20–29 students. **Majors with Highest Enrollment:** Psychology; Elementary Education and Teaching; Registered Nursing/Registered Nurse. **Special Study Options:** Accelerated program, cooperative education program, cross-registration, distance learning, double major, dual enrollment, English as a Second Language (ESL), exchange student program (domestic), honors program, independent study, internships, liberal arts/career combination, student-designed major, study abroad, teacher certification program, weekend college. **Honors programs:** The University Honors Program is dedicated to promoting the intellectual and personal development of high-performing students. It strives to promote a more active and enriching relationship between Honors students and the University by connecting them with resources and opportunities that will encourage them to maximize their potential. The University Scholars Program enables talented and motivated students to be part of smaller, selective communnities within the larger university environment. Each of the fourteen programs focuses on a common theme or academic area of interest designed to foster learning and involvement. Scholars live together, attend classes together, and experience diverse opportunities outside the classroom. **Combined degree programs:** BA/MD, BA/DDS, BA/MEng. **Disability Services:** Special programs offered to physically disabled students include note-taking services, reader services, tape recorders, tutors. **Career services:** career assessment, internships.

FACILITIES
Housing: Coed dorms, apartments for single students, Wellness Housing. 100% of campus accessible to physically disabled. **Computers:** 100% of classrooms, 100% of dorms, 100% of libraries, 100% of dining areas, 100% of student union, have wireless network access. Students can register for classes

online. Administrative functions (other than registration) can be performed online.

CAMPUS LIFE

Environment: Village. **Activities:** Choral groups, drama/theater, literary magazine, music ensembles, student government, Campus Ministries. 33 registered organizations, 2 honor societies, 2 religious organizations. **Athletics (Intercollegiate):** Men: basketball, golf, soccer. Women: basketball, soccer, softball, volleyball.

ADMISSIONS

Freshman Academic Profile: 4% in top 10% of high school class, 21% in top 25% of high school class, 59% in top 50% of high school class. 90% from public high schools. SAT Math middle 50% range 473-590. SAT Critical Reading middle 50% range 460-570. SAT Writing middle 50% range 440-550. ACT middle 50% range 20-25. **Basis for Candidate Selection:** *Other factors considered include:* recommendation(s), rigor of secondary school record. **Freshman Admission Requirements:** High school diploma is required and GED is accepted. *Academic units required:* 4 English, 3 mathematics, 2 science, (2 science labs), 2 foreign language, 2 social studies, 1 academic electives, 1 visual/performing arts. **Freshman Admission Statistics:** 3,105 applied, 99% admitted, 40% enrolled. **Transfer Admission Requirements:** college transcript(s), Minimum college GPA of 2.0 required. Lowest grade transferable C-. **General Admission Information:** Application Fee $40. Regular application deadline 7/1. Notification on a rolling basis, beginning on or about 12/1. Nonfall registration accepted. Credit and/or placement offered for CEEB Advanced Placement tests.

COSTS AND FINANCIAL AID

Average book expense $1,248. **Required Forms and Deadlines:** FAFSA. **Notification of Awards:** Applicants will be notified of awards on or about 4/5. **Types of Aid:** *Need-based scholarships/grants:* Federal Pell, SEOG, state scholarships/grants, private scholarships, the school's own gift aid. *Loans:* Direct Subsidized Stafford, Direct Unsubsidized Stafford, Direct PLUS, Federal Perkins, Federal Nursing, college/university loans from institutional funds. *Student Employment:* Federal Work-Study Program available. Institutional employment available. Off-campus job opportunities are good. **Financial Aid Statistics:** 69% freshmen, 68% undergrads receive need-based scholarship or grant aid. 43% freshmen, 0% undergrads receive non-need-based scholarship or grant aid. 93% freshmen, 92% undergrads receive need-based self-help aid. 0% freshmen, 0% undergrads receive athletic scholarships. 86% freshmen, 82% undergrads receive any aid. **Criteria for awarding institutional aid:** *Non-need-based:* academics, alumni affiliation, art, athletics, job skills, leadership, minority status, music/drama, state/district residency.

OHIO UNIVERSITY—ATHENS

Best 380

120 Chubb Hall, Athens, OH 45701
Phone: 740-593-4100 · **Financial Aid Phone:** 740-593-4141
E-mail: admissions@ohio.edu · **CEEB Code:** 1593
Fax: 740-593-0560 · **Website:** www.ohio.edu · **ACT Code:** 3314

This public school was founded in 1804. It has a 1762-acre campus.

RATINGS

Admissions Selectivity Rating: 80   **Fire Safety Rating:** 77

STUDENTS AND FACULTY

Enrollment: 23,390. **Student Body:** 60% female, 40% male, 15% out-of-state, 4% international (117 countries represented). Asian 1%, African American 5%, Caucasian 83%, Hispanic 3%, Native American <1%
Retention and Graduation: 80% freshmen return for sophomore year. 49% freshmen graduate within 4 years. 67% freshmen graduate within 6 years. 24% grads go on to further study within 1 year. 6% grads pursue arts and sciences degrees. 1% grads pursue law degrees. 1% grads pursue business degrees. 1% grads pursue medical degrees. **Faculty:** 933 full-time faculty, 78% hold PhDs, 40% are members of minority groups, 16% are women. 12% of classes are taught by teaching assistants.

ACADEMICS

Degrees: associate, bachelor's, master's. **Classes:** Most classes have 10–19 students. Most lab/discussion sessions have 10–19 students. **Majors with Highest Enrollment:** Biology/Biological Sciences; Journalism; Psychology.

Special Study Options: Accelerated program, cooperative education program, cross-registration, distance learning, double major, dual enrollment, English as a Second Language (ESL), external degree program, honors program, independent study, internships, liberal arts/career combination, student-designed major, study abroad, teacher certification program. **Honors programs:** Honors Tutorial College: The most selective of Ohio University's nine undergraduate colleges the Honor's Tutorial College is the oldest, largest, and most academically diverse degree-only degree-granting college in the country. Based on Oxbridge systems of tutorial education developed in England, it offers highly motivated, talented students the opportunity to receive a substantial part of their education through tutorials (one-on-one classes or small seminars). There are generally 220 students in the Honors Tutorial College spread over 26 programs of study. To preserve the tutorial experience, HTC enrolls about 60 new students each year, and admission is highly competitive. **Disability Services:** Special programs offered to physically disabled students include reader services, tape recorders, tutors. **Career services:** Alumni network, alumni services, career/job search classes, career assessment, regional alumni. Career services highlights include Most internships/co-ops coordinated through college departments as our office focuses on full-time positions.

FACILITIES

Housing: Coed dorms, special housing for disabled students, special housing for international students, women's dorms, apartments for married students. 89% of campus accessible to physically disabled. **Special Academic Facilities/Equipment:** Museum of American Art, Innovation Center, Nuclear Accelerator, Electron Microscope, Biotech Center, Kennedy Museum of Art, Trisolini Gallery, Art Gallery in Multicultural Programs, Voinovich Center, Academic Research Center. **Computers:** 100% of classrooms, 100% of dorms, 100% of libraries, 100% of dining areas, 100% of student union, 100% of common outdoor areas have wireless network access. Students can register for classes online. Administrative functions (other than registration) can be performed online.

CAMPUS LIFE

Environment: Village. **Activities:** Choral groups, concert band, dance, drama/theater, jazz band, literary magazine, marching band, music ensembles, musical theater, opera, pep band, radio station, student government, student newspaper, student-run film society, symphony orchestra, television station, yearbook, Campus Ministries, International Student Organization. 323 registered organizations, 16 honor societies, 27 religious organizations. 17 fraternities, 12 sororities. **Athletics (Intercollegiate):** Men: baseball, basketball, cheerleading, cross-country, football, golf, wrestling. Women: basketball, cheerleading, cross-country, diving, field hockey, golf, soccer, softball, swimming, track/field (outdoor), volleyball. **On-Campus Highlights:** Charles J. Ping Recreation Center, Kennedy Museum of Art, Templeton-Blackburn Memorial Auditorium, Convocation Center, Alden Library, Baker University Center. **Environmental Initiatives:** Ohio University is currently expanding its invessel composting system, already the largest at any college or university in the nation, to handle all organic waste at the university. The Presidential Advisory Council for Sustainability Planning prepared a Sustainability Plan that was approved by the university last summer, allowing the group to now develop a climate action plan aimed at providing guidance toward institutional climate neutrality. The OHIO Ecohouse demonstrates affordable green technology & sustainable living to inform, engage & inspire campus & community members.

ADMISSIONS

Freshman Academic Profile: Average high school GPA 3.43. 15% in top 10% of high school class, 43% in top 25% of high school class, 82% in top 50% of high school class. 82% from public high schools. SAT Math middle 50% range 490-600. SAT Critical Reading middle 50% range 490-600. SAT Writing middle 50% range 470-580. ACT middle 50% range 22-26. **Basis for Candidate Selection:** *Very important factors considered include:* academic GPA, rigor of secondary school record. *Important factors considered include:* Class rank, standardized test scores. *Other factors considered include:* application essay, recommendation(s), alumni/ae relation, character/personal qualities, extracurricular activities, talent/ability, volunteer work, work experience. **Freshman Admission Requirements:** High school diploma is required and GED is accepted. *Academic units required:* 4 English, 3 mathematics, 3 science, 2 foreign language, 3 social studies, 1 Visual or Performing Arts. **Freshman Admission Statistics:** 20,934 applied, 74% admitted, 28% enrolled. **Transfer Admission Requirements:** college transcript(s), Minimum college GPA of 2.0 required. Lowest grade transferable C-. **General Admission Information:** Application Fee $45. Regular application deadline 2/1. Notification on a rolling basis, beginning on or about 9/15. Nonfall registration accepted. Admission may be deferred for a maximum of 12 months. Credit and/or placement offered for CEEB Advanced Placement tests.

COSTS AND FINANCIAL AID

Annual in-state tuition $10,602. Annual out-of-state tuition $19,566. Room and board $10,478. Average book expense $916. **Required Forms and Deadlines:** FAFSA. **Notification of Awards:** Applicants will be notified of awards on or about 4/1. **Types of Aid:** *Need-based scholarships/grants:* Federal Pell,

SEOG, state scholarships/grants, private scholarships, the school's own gift aid. *Loans:* Direct Subsidized Stafford, Direct Unsubsidized Stafford, Direct PLUS, Federal Perkins, Institutional short term loans are repaid in 30-60 days. *Student Employment:* Federal Work-Study Program available. Institutional employment available. Highest amount earned per year from on-campus jobs $1,784. **Financial Aid Statistics:** 91% freshmen, 74% undergrads receive need-based scholarship or grant aid. 13% freshmen, 6% undergrads receive non-need-based scholarship or grant aid. 98% freshmen, 92% undergrads receive need-based self-help aid. 0% freshmen, 1% undergrads receive athletic scholarships. 92% freshmen, 73% undergrads receive any aid. 66% undergrads borrow to pay for school. Average cumulative indebtedness $23,425. **Criteria for awarding institutional aid:** *Non-need-based:* academics, art, athletics, minority status, music/drama, religious affiliation.

OHIO UNIVERSITY—SOUTHERN

Office of Enrollment Services, Ironton, OH 45638-2214
Phone: 740-533-4600
E-mail: askousc@mail.southern.ohiou.edu · **CEEB Code:**
Fax: 740-533-4632 · **Website:** www.southern.ohiou.edu

This public school was founded in 1956. It has a 9-acre campus.

RATINGS

Admissions Selectivity Rating: 60*   Fire Safety Rating: 60*

STUDENTS AND FACULTY

Enrollment: 1,963. **Student Body:** 11% out-of-state.
Faculty:

ACADEMICS

Degrees: associate, bachelor's, master's, terminal associate, transfer associate. **Special Study Options:** distance learning, double major, independent study, student-designed major, teacher certification program, weekend college.

FACILITIES

Computers: Students can register for classes online. Administrative functions (other than registration) can be performed online.

CAMPUS LIFE

Environment: Village. **Activities:** Choral groups, concert band, drama/theater, literary magazine, music ensembles, radio station, student government, television station.

ADMISSIONS

Transfer Admission Requirements: college transcript(s), Lowest grade transferable C. **General Admission Information:** Application Fee $20.

COSTS AND FINANCIAL AID

Average book expense $700. **Required Forms and Deadlines:** FAFSA. **Types of Aid:** *Need-based scholarships/grants:* Federal Pell, SEOG, state scholarships/grants, private scholarships, the school's own gift aid. *Loans:* Direct Subsidized Stafford, Direct Unsubsidized Stafford, Direct PLUS, Federal Perkins.

OHIO VALLEY UNIVERSITY

#1 Campus View Drive, Vienna, WV 26105
Phone: 304-865-6200
E-mail: admissions@ovu.edu
Fax: 304-865-6001 • **ACT Code:** 4548

This private school was founded in 1960. It has a 267-acre campus.

RATINGS

Admissions Selectivity Rating: 79   Fire Safety Rating: 69

STUDENTS AND FACULTY

Enrollment: 512. **Student Body:** 53% female, 47% male, 6% out-of-state, 7% international (12 countries represented). Asian 1%, African American 4%, Caucasian 86%, Hispanic 1%, Native American 1%
Retention and Graduation: 72% freshmen return for sophomore year.
Faculty: 26 full-time faculty, 38% hold PhDs, 38% are members of minority groups. 0% of classes are taught by teaching assistants.

ACADEMICS

Degrees: associate, bachelor's. **Classes:** Most classes have fewer than 10 students. Most lab/discussion sessions have fewer than 10 students. **Majors with Highest Enrollment:** Elementary Education and Teaching; Psychology; Business/Commerce. **Special Study Options:** double major, English as a Second Language (ESL), study abroad, teacher certification program, weekend college, Adult Education: Degree completion program in Business Administration and Saturday college available. **Disability Services:** Special programs offered to physically disabled students include tutors.

FACILITIES

Housing: men's dorms, women's dorms, apartments for married students, apartments for single students. 50% of campus accessible to physically disabled.

CAMPUS LIFE

Environment: Village. **Activities:** Choral groups, concert band, drama/theater, jazz band, literary magazine, music ensembles, musical theater, student government, student newspaper, symphony orchestra, yearbook. 10 registered organizations, 2 honor societies, 3 religious organizations. 4 fraternities, 4 sororities. **Athletics (Intercollegiate):** *Men:* baseball, basketball, cross-country, golf, soccer. *Women:* basketball, cheerleading, cross-country, soccer, softball, volleyball. **On-Campus Highlights:** New men and women's dorm, Memorial Fountain.

ADMISSIONS

Freshman Academic Profile: Average high school GPA 3. 10% in top 10% of high school class, 32% in top 25% of high school class, 57% in top 50% of high school class. 95% from public high schools. SAT Math middle 50% range 540-460. SAT Critical Reading middle 50% range 600-510. ACT middle 50% range 23-17. Minimum paper TOEFL 500. **Basis for Candidate Selection:** *Very important factors considered include:* rigor of secondary school record, standardized test scores, character/personal qualities. *Important factors considered include:* recommendation(s), alumni/ae relation, talent/ability. *Other factors considered include:* Class rank, application essay, extracurricular activities, interview, religious affiliation/commitment. **Freshman Admission Requirements:** High school diploma is required and GED is accepted. **Freshman Admission Statistics:** 326 applied, 59% admitted, 50% enrolled. **Transfer Admission Requirements:** High school transcript, college transcript(s), standardized test scores, Minimum college GPA of 2.0 required. Lowest grade transferable D. **General Admission Information:** Application Fee $20. Regular application deadline 8/20. Nonfall registration accepted. Admission may be deferred for a maximum of 1 year. Credit and/or placement offered for CEEB Advanced Placement tests.

COSTS AND FINANCIAL AID

Annual tuition $12,750. Room and board $5,850. Required fees $1,512. Average book expense $1,000. **Required Forms and Deadlines:** FAFSA. **Notification of Awards:** Applicants will be notified of awards on a rolling basis beginning 3/15. **Types of Aid:** *Need-based scholarships/grants:* Federal Pell, SEOG, state scholarships/grants, private scholarships, the school's own gift aid. *Loans:* Subsidized Stafford, Unsubsidized Stafford, PLUS, Federal Perkins, Signature student loans. *Student Employment:* Federal Work-Study Program available. Institutional employment available. Highest amount earned per year from on-campus jobs $800. Off-campus job opportunities are good. **Financial Aid Statistics:** 100% freshmen, 86% undergrads receive need-based scholarship or grant aid. 11% freshmen, 12% undergrads receive non-need-based scholarship or grant aid. 89% freshmen, 86% undergrads receive need-based self-help aid. 16% freshmen, 12% undergrads receive athletic scholarships. 81% freshmen, 89% undergrads receive any aid. 80% undergrads borrow to pay for school. Average cumulative indebtedness $12,154. **Criteria for awarding institutional aid:** *Non-need-based:* academics, athletics, job skills, leadership, music/drama, religious affiliation.

OHIO WESLEYAN UNIVERSITY

61 South Sandusky Street, Delaware, OH 43015
Phone: 740-368-3020 · **Financial Aid Phone:** 740-368-3050
E-mail: owuadmit@owu.edu · **CEEB Code:** 1594
Fax: 740-368-3314 · **Website:** www.owu.edu • **ACT Code:** 3316

This private school, affiliated with the Methodist Church, was founded in 1842. It has a 200-acre campus.

RATINGS

Admissions Selectivity Rating: 85   Fire Safety Rating: 78

STUDENTS AND FACULTY

Enrollment: 1,729. **Student Body:** 53% female, 47% male, 54% out-of-state, 7% international (41 countries represented). Asian 2%, African American 7%, Caucasian 72%, Hispanic 4%, Native American <1%
Retention and Graduation: 60% freshmen graduate within 4 years. 65% freshmen graduate within 6 years. 32% grads go on to further study within 1 year. 14% grads pursue arts and sciences degrees. 3% grads pursue law degrees. 2% grads pursue business degrees. 14% grads pursue medical degrees. **Faculty:** 143 full-time faculty, 99% hold PhDs, 40% are members of minority groups, 6% are women. 0% of classes are taught by teaching assistants.

ACADEMICS

Degrees: bachelor's. **Classes:** Most classes have 10–19 students. Most lab/discussion sessions have 10–19 students. **Majors with Highest Enrollment:** Psychology; Economics; Zoology/Animal Biology. **Special Study Options:** double major, dual enrollment, exchange student program (domestic), honors program, independent study, internships, student-designed major, study abroad, teacher certification program. **Honors programs:** The Leland F. and Helen Schubert Honors Program recognizes the most talented students among Ohio Wesleyan's community of scholars and challenges them through Honors Tutorials, Honors Seminars, and Honors Scholarships. **Combined degree programs:** Pre-Medical Tech,Pre-Optometry,Pre-Physical Therap. **Disability Services:** Special programs offered to physically disabled students include note-taking services, tape recorders, tutors. **Career services:** Alumni network, alumni services, career assessment. Career services highlights include our Alumni Networking System.

FACILITIES

Housing: Coed dorms, special housing for international students, women's dorms, fraternity/sorority housing, apartments for single students, Small Living Units (SLUs) offer unique living opportunities to groups of 10-15 OWU students. In these theme houses, students create a small community centered on promoting specific interests and concerns. 60% of campus accessible to physically disabled. **Special Academic Facilities/Equipment:** Perkins and Student Observatories Scanning electron microscope Woltemade Center for Economics, Business and Entrepreneurship Nine inch refractor telescope Ross Art Museum Newly renovated fine arts facilities Newly renovated 150,000 square foot science center with state-of-the art classrooms and equipment. Wireless Internet in some areas. Fiber optic network **Computers:** 10% of classrooms, 100% of libraries, 10% of dining areas, 10% of common outdoor areas have wireless network access. Administrative functions (other than registration) can be performed online.

CAMPUS LIFE

Environment: Town. **Activities:** Choral groups, dance, drama/theater, jazz band, literary magazine, music ensembles, musical theater, opera, pep band, radio station, student government, student newspaper, symphony orchestra, yearbook, Campus Ministries, International Student Organization, Model UN. 86 registered organizations, 26 honor societies, 10 religious organizations. 11 fraternity, 7 sororities. **Athletics (Intercollegiate):** *Men:* baseball, basketball, cross-country, diving, football, golf, lacrosse, sailing, soccer, swimming, tennis, track/field (outdoor), track/field (indoor). *Women:* basketball, cross-country, diving, field hockey, lacrosse, sailing, soccer, softball, swimming, tennis, track/field (outdoor), track/field (indoor), volleyball. **On-Campus Highlights:** Science Center, Hamilton Williams Campus Center, Selby Stadium, R.W. Corns Building, Sanborn Hall (music), Beeghly Library and Ross Museum are additional popular places on campus. **Environmental Initiatives:** Waste reduction; Energy efficiency and conservation; Water conservation.

ADMISSIONS

Freshman Academic Profile: Average high school GPA 3.46. 24% in top 10% of high school class, 56% in top 25% of high school class, 88% in top 50% of high school class. 77% from public high schools. SAT Math middle 50% range 500-610. SAT Critical Reading middle 50% range 500-610. SAT Writing middle 50% range 490-600. ACT middle 50% range 22-28. Minimum paper TOEFL 550. **Basis for Candidate Selection:** *Very important factors considered include:* application essay, academic GPA, recommendation(s), rigor of secondary school record, character/personal qualities, interview. *Important factors considered include:* Class rank, standardized test scores, extracurricular activities, talent/ability. *Other factors considered include:* alumni/ae relation, first generation, geographical residence, level of applicant's interest, racial/ethnic status, volunteer work, work experience. **Freshman Admission Requirements:** High school diploma is required and GED is accepted. *Academic units required:* 4 English, 3 mathematics, 3 science, 2 foreign language, 3 social studies. **Freshman Admission Statistics:** 3,981 applied, 74% admitted, 15% enrolled. **Transfer Admission Requirements:** High school transcript, college transcript(s), essay or personal statement, statement of good standing from prior institution(s). Minimum college GPA of 2.5 required. Lowest grade transferable C-. **General Admission Information:** Application Fee $35. Early decision application deadline 12/1. Notification on a rolling basis, beginning on or about 10/1. Nonfall registration accepted. Admission may be deferred for a maximum

of 2 years. Credit and/or placement offered for CEEB Advanced Placement tests.

COSTS AND FINANCIAL AID

Annual tuition $41,660. Room and board $11,210. Required fees $260. Average book expense $1,300. **Required Forms and Deadlines:** FAFSA. **Notification of Awards:** Applicants will be notified of awards on a rolling basis beginning 2/15. **Types of Aid:** *Need-based scholarships/grants:* Federal Pell, SEOG, state scholarships/grants, private scholarships, the school's own gift aid. *Loans:* Subsidized Stafford, Unsubsidized Stafford, PLUS, Federal Perkins, college/university loans from institutional funds. *Student Employment:* Federal Work-Study Program available. Institutional employment available. Highest amount earned per year from on-campus jobs $2,400. Off-campus job opportunities are excellent. **Financial Aid Statistics:** 100% freshmen, 100% undergrads receive need-based scholarship or grant aid. 24% freshmen, 22% undergrads receive non-need-based scholarship or grant aid. 84% freshmen, 82% undergrads receive need-based self-help aid. 0% freshmen, 0% undergrads receive athletic scholarships. 97% freshmen, 97% undergrads receive any aid. 68% undergrads borrow to pay for school. Average cumulative indebtedness $21,671. **Criteria for awarding institutional aid:** *Non-need-based:* academics, alumni affiliation, art, leadership, minority status, music/drama, religious affiliation, state/district residency.

OKLAHOMA BAPTIST UNIVERSITY

500 West University, Shawnee, OK 74804
Phone: 800-654-3285 · **Financial Aid Phone:** 405-878-2016
E-mail: admissions@okbu.edu · **CEEB Code:** 6541
Fax: 405-585-5017 · **Website:** www.okbu.edu · **ACT Code:** 3414

This private school, affiliated with the Southern Baptist Church, was founded in 1910. It has a 200-acre campus.

RATINGS

Admissions Selectivity Rating: 87   **Fire Safety Rating:** 74

STUDENTS AND FACULTY

Enrollment: 1,824. **Student Body:** 60% female, 40% male, 44% out-of-state, 3% international (25 countries represented). Asian 1%, African American 6%, Caucasian 71%, Hispanic 2%, Native American 5%
Retention and Graduation: 78% freshmen return for sophomore year. 41% freshmen graduate within 4 years. 51% freshmen graduate within 6 years. **Faculty:** 122 full-time faculty, 72% hold PhDs, 37% are members of minority groups, 11% are women. 0% of classes are taught by teaching assistants.

ACADEMICS

Degrees: associate, bachelor's, master's. **Classes:** Most classes have fewer than 10 students. Most lab/discussion sessions have fewer than 10 students. **Majors with Highest Enrollment:** Elementary Education and Teaching; Bible/Biblical Studies; Registered Nursing/Registered Nurse. **Special Study Options:** cooperative education program, double major, English as a Second Language (ESL), exchange student program (domestic), honors program, independent study, internships, student-designed major, study abroad, teacher certification program, Semester-away programs available. **Honors programs:** The OBU Honors Program is a curricular program designed to enhance the undergraduate study experience for certain exceptionally well-qualified students. Students completing all of the requirements for gradulation in the Honors Program earn the designation "with Honors" on their OBU diplomas. **Combined degree programs:** BA/MA. **Disability Services:** Special programs offered to physically disabled students include note-taking services, reader services, tape recorders, tutors. **Career services:** Alumni network, regional alumni.

FACILITIES

Housing: men's dorms, women's dorms, apartments for married students, apartments for single students. 95% of campus accessible to physically disabled. **Special Academic Facilities/Equipment:** planetarium, Baptist Historical Society Archives, Avery T. Willis Center for Global Outreach **Computers:** Students can register for classes online. Administrative functions (other than registration) can be performed online.

CAMPUS LIFE

Environment: Town. **Activities:** Choral groups, concert band, drama/theater, jazz band, literary magazine, music ensembles, musical theater, opera, pep band, student government, student newspaper, symphony orchestra, television station, yearbook, Campus Ministries. 80 registered organizations, 15 honor societies, 5 religious organizations. 5 fraternities, 5 sororities. **Athletics (Intercollegiate):** *Men:* baseball, basketball, cheerleading, cross-country, golf, soccer, tennis, track/field (outdoor), track/field (indoor). *Women:* basketball, cheerleading, cross-country, golf, soccer, softball, tennis, track/field (outdoor), track/field (indoor), volleyball. **On-Campus Highlights:** Geiger Center (Student Building), Recreation and Wellness Center, Noble Complex (athletics), Mabee Learning Center (Library), Intramural Field.

ADMISSIONS

Freshman Academic Profile: 23% in top 10% of high school class, 49.2% in top 25% of high school class, 89.5% in top 50% of high school class. 90% from public high schools. SAT Math middle 50% range 517-559. SAT Critical Reading middle 50% range 489-661. ACT middle 50% range 22.2-29.5. Minimum paper TOEFL 500. **Basis for Candidate Selection:** *Very important factors considered include:* academic GPA, rigor of secondary school record. *Important factors considered include:* Class rank, recommendation(s), standardized test scores, character/personal qualities, extracurricular activities. *Other factors considered include:* application essay, alumni/ae relation, geographical residence, interview, level of applicant's interest, religious affiliation/commitment, state residency, talent/ability, volunteer work, work experience. **Freshman Admission Requirements:** High school diploma is required and GED is accepted. **Freshman Admission Statistics:** 5,984 applied, 60% admitted, 13% enrolled. **Transfer Admission Requirements:** college transcript(s), Minimum college GPA of 2.5 required. Lowest grade transferable D. **General Admission Information:** Application Fee $25. Regular application deadline 8/1. Regular notification 9/1. Nonfall registration accepted. Admission may be deferred for a maximum of one year. Credit and/or placement offered for CEEB Advanced Placement tests.

COSTS AND FINANCIAL AID

Annual tuition $21,630. Room and board $6,780. Required fees $2,370. Average book expense $1,200. **Required Forms and Deadlines:** FAFSA. **Notification of Awards:** Applicants will be notified of awards on or about 3/1. **Types of Aid:** *Need-based scholarships/grants:* Federal Pell, SEOG, state scholarships/grants, private scholarships, the school's own gift aid, Federal Nursing Scholarships., ACG SMART. *Loans:* Subsidized Stafford, Unsubsidized Stafford, PLUS, Federal Perkins, college/university loans from institutional funds. *Student Employment:* Highest amount earned per year from on-campus jobs $3,200. **Financial Aid Statistics:** 82% freshmen, 85% undergrads receive need-based scholarship or grant aid. 97% freshmen, 96% undergrads receive non-need-based scholarship or grant aid. 79% freshmen, 78% undergrads receive need-based self-help aid. 26% freshmen, 33% undergrads receive athletic scholarships. 87% freshmen, 90% undergrads receive any aid. 62% undergrads borrow to pay for school. Average cumulative indebtedness $24,623. **Criteria for awarding institutional aid:** *Non-need-based:* academics, alumni affiliation, art, athletics, job skills, leadership, music/drama, religious affiliation.

OKLAHOMA CHRISTIAN UNIVERSITY

P.O. Box 11000, Oklahoma City, OK 73136-1100
Phone: 405-425-5050 · **Financial Aid Phone:** 405-425-5190
E-mail: info@oc.edu
Fax: 405-425-5069 · **Website:** www.oc.edu · **ACT Code:** 3415

This private school, affiliated with the Church of Christ Church, was founded in 1950. It has a 240-acre campus.

RATINGS

Admissions Selectivity Rating: 89   Fire Safety Rating: 73

STUDENTS AND FACULTY

Enrollment: 1,910. **Student Body:** 49% female, 51% male, 63% out-of-state, 11% international (38 countries represented). Asian 1%, African American 3%, Caucasian 63%, Hispanic 3%, Native American 4%
Retention and Graduation: 73% freshmen return for sophomore year. 31% freshmen graduate within 4 years. 48% freshmen graduate within 6 years.
Faculty: 116 full-time faculty, 73% hold PhDs, 30% are members of minority groups. 0% of classes are taught by teaching assistants.

ACADEMICS

Degrees: bachelor's, master's. **Classes:** Most classes have 10–19 students. **Majors with Highest Enrollment:** Registered Nursing/Registered Nurse; Elementary Education and Teaching; Liberal Arts and Sciences/Liberal Studies. **Special Study Options:** cross-registration, distance learning, double major, English as a Second Language (ESL), honors program, independent study, internships, student-designed major, study abroad, teacher certification program. **Career services:** Alumni network, alumni services, career/job search classes, career assessment, internships. Career services highlights include government sponsored internships with DISA, FBI, CIA, homeland security and more, along with more companies than we can list.

FACILITIES

Housing: special housing for disabled students, men's dorms, women's dorms, apartments for married students, apartments for single students. **Special Academic Facilities/Equipment:** Art Museum Art Gallery. **Computers:** 100% of classrooms, 100% of dorms, 100% of libraries, 100% of dining areas, 100% of student union, 95% of common outdoor areas have wireless network access. Students can register for classes online. Administrative functions (other than registration) can be performed online.

CAMPUS LIFE

Environment: Metropolis. **Activities:** Choral groups, concert band, drama/theater, jazz band, literary magazine, music ensembles, musical theater, opera, pep band, radio station, student government, student newspaper, symphony orchestra, television station, yearbook, Campus Ministries, International Student Organization. 20 registered organizations, 5 honor societies, 2 religious organizations. 6 fraternities, 6 sororities. **Athletics (Intercollegiate):** *Men:* baseball, basketball, cross-country, golf, soccer, tennis, track/field (outdoor). *Women:* basketball, cheerleading, cross-country, soccer, softball, tennis, track/field (outdoor). **On-Campus Highlights:** Gaylord University Center, University House Commons, Lawson Commons, Payne Athletic & Fitness Center, Mabee Learning Center. **Environmental Initiatives:** Trayless Cafeteria.

ADMISSIONS

Freshman Academic Profile: Average high school GPA 3.56. 30% in top 10% of high school class, 54% in top 25% of high school class, 80% in top 50% of high school class. SAT Math middle 50% range 470-640. SAT Critical Reading middle 50% range 440-620. SAT Writing middle 50% range 470-600. ACT middle 50% range 21-28. Minimum internet-based TOEFL 61. Minimum paper TOEFL 500. **Basis for Candidate Selection:** *Other factors considered include:* Class rank, academic GPA, recommendation(s), rigor of secondary school record, standardized test scores, character/personal qualities, extracurricular activities, interview, talent/ability, volunteer work. **Freshman Admission Requirements:** High school diploma is required and GED is accepted. **Freshman Admission Statistics:** 2,156 applied, 45% admitted, 47% enrolled. **Transfer Admission Requirements:** High school transcript, college transcript(s), standardized test scores, statement of good standing from prior institution(s). Lowest grade transferable D. **General Admission Information:** Application Fee $25. Notification on a rolling basis, beginning on or about 9/1. Nonfall registration accepted. Admission may be deferred for a maximum of 1 year. Credit offered for CEEB Advanced Placement tests.

COSTS AND FINANCIAL AID

Annual tuition $18,800. Room and board $6,775. Average book expense $1,000. **Required Forms and Deadlines:** FAFSA. **Notification of Awards:** Applicants will be notified of awards on a rolling basis beginning 2/2. **Types of Aid:** *Need-based scholarships/grants:* Federal Pell, SEOG, state scholarships/grants, private scholarships, the school's own gift aid. *Loans:* Subsidized Stafford, Unsubsidized Stafford, PLUS, Federal Perkins. *Student Employment:* Federal Work-Study Program available. Institutional employment available. Highest amount earned per year from on-campus jobs $9,905. Off-campus job opportunities are excellent. **Financial Aid Statistics:** 58% freshmen, 58% undergrads receive need-based scholarship or grant aid. 82% freshmen, 77% undergrads receive non-need-based scholarship or grant aid. 60% freshmen, 42% undergrads receive need-based self-help aid. 9% freshmen, 9% undergrads receive athletic scholarships. 100% freshmen, 98% undergrads receive any aid. 65% undergrads borrow to pay for school. Average cumulative indebtedness $24,797. **Criteria for awarding institutional aid:** *Non-need-based:* academics, alumni affiliation, art, athletics, leadership, music/drama.

OKLAHOMA CITY UNIVERSITY

2501 North Blackwelder, Oklahoma City, OK 73106
Phone: 405-208-5055 · **Financial Aid Phone:** 405-208-5848
E-mail: uadmissions@okcu.edu · **CEEB Code:** 6543
Fax: 405-208-5916 · **Website:** www.okcu.edu · **ACT Code:** 3416

This private school, affiliated with the Methodist Church, was founded in 1904. It has a 78-acre campus.

RATINGS

Admissions Selectivity Rating: 76   Fire Safety Rating: 87

STUDENTS AND FACULTY

Enrollment: 1,766. **Student Body:** 63% female, 37% male, 47% out-of-state, 13% international (57 countries represented). Asian 2%, African American 5%, Caucasian 61%, Hispanic 8%, Native American 2%
Retention and Graduation: 49% freshmen graduate within 4 years. 59% freshmen graduate within 6 years. **Faculty:** 205 full-time faculty, 62% hold

PhDs, 48% are members of minority groups, 16% are women. 0% of classes are taught by teaching assistants.

ACADEMICS

Degrees: bachelor's, master's. **Classes:** Most classes have 10–19 students. Most lab/discussion sessions have fewer than 10 students. **Majors with Highest Enrollment:** Business/Commerce; Dance; Nursing Practice. **Special Study Options:** Accelerated program, cooperative education program, distance learning, double major, dual enrollment, English as a Second Language (ESL), exchange student program (domestic), external degree program, honors program, independent study, internships, student-designed major, study abroad, teacher certification program. **Honors programs:** University Honors Program: The mission of the University Honors program is to provide an enhanced learning environment for academically gifted undergraduate students. Each new class of Honors students at OCU will be a spcial community of scholars. Students will have the opportunity to become acquainted with one another and the Honors program in the Honors Colloquium, a course required for all new honors students during their first semester in the program. Honors students will have the opportunities to meet with visiting scholars and participate in special events. As part of a network of honors programs through the National Collegiate Honors Council and the Great Plains Honors Council, students may present research at national and regional honors conferences and participate in exciting summer and semester programs. **Combined degree programs:** BA/JD, MBA/JD. **Disability Services:** Special programs offered to physically disabled students include reader services, tape recorders, tutors. **Career services:** Alumni network, alumni services, career/job search classes, career assessment, internships, regional alumni. Career services highlights include Career Fairs hosting over 200+ employers on campus.

FACILITIES

Housing: Coed dorms, special housing for disabled students, men's dorms, women's dorms, fraternity/sorority housing, apartments for married students, apartments for single students, Learning Communities. 96% of campus accessible to physically disabled. **Special Academic Facilities/Equipment:** Art museum, audiovisual center, language lab. **Computers:** 100% of classrooms, 100% of dorms, 100% of libraries, 100% of dining areas, 100% of student union, 90% of common outdoor areas have wireless network access. Students can register for classes online. Administrative functions (other than registration) can be performed online.

CAMPUS LIFE

Environment: Metropolis. **Activities:** Choral groups, concert band, dance, drama/theater, jazz band, literary magazine, music ensembles, musical theater, opera, pep band, student government, student newspaper, symphony orchestra, television station, yearbook, Campus Ministries, International Student Organization. 64 registered organizations, 14 honor societies, 6 religious organizations. 2 fraternities, 4 sororities. **Athletics (Intercollegiate):** *Men:* baseball, basketball, cheerleading, crew/rowing, golf, soccer, track/field (outdoor), wrestling. *Women:* basketball, cheerleading, crew/rowing, golf, soccer, softball, track/field (outdoor), volleyball, wrestling. **On-Campus Highlights:** Tom and Brenda McDaniel Univ Center, Henry J Freede Wellness and Activity Center, Meinders' School of Business, Walker Center for Arts and Sciences, Norick Art Center. **Environmental Initiatives:** Computer recycling program, community garden Purchasing maximum % of wind power allowable by energy supplying and trading company. Install sprinkler system on well system saving city water.

ADMISSIONS

Freshman Academic Profile: Average high school GPA 3.61. 40% in top 10% of high school class, 64% in top 25% of high school class, 90% in top 50% of high school class. 88% from public high schools. Minimum internet-based TOEFL 80. Minimum paper TOEFL 550. **Basis for Candidate Selection:** *Very important factors considered include:* Class rank, application essay, academic GPA, recommendation(s), standardized test scores. *Important factors considered include:* rigor of secondary school record, extracurricular activities. *Other factors considered include:* character/personal qualities, talent/ability, volunteer work, work experience. **Freshman Admission Requirements:** High school diploma is required and GED is accepted. *Academic units required:* 4 English, 3 mathematics, 3 science, (1 science labs), 2 foreign language, 3 social studies, 3 history. **Freshman Admission Statistics:** 1,505 applied, 68% admitted, 29% enrolled. **Transfer Admission Requirements:** college transcript(s), essay or personal statement, statement of good standing from prior institution(s). Minimum college GPA of 2.0 required. Lowest grade transferable C-. **General Admission Information:** Application Fee $40. Regular application deadline 8/21. Notification on a rolling basis, beginning on or about 10/15. Nonfall registration accepted. Admission may be deferred for a maximum of 1 year. Credit and/or placement offered for CEEB Advanced Placement tests.

COSTS AND FINANCIAL AID

Annual tuition $27,276. Room and board $9,750. Required fees $3,450. Average book expense $1,500. **Required Forms and Deadlines:** FAFSA. **Notification of Awards:** Applicants will be notified of awards on a rolling basis beginning

2/20. **Types of Aid:** *Need-based scholarships/grants:* Federal Pell, SEOG, state scholarships/grants, private scholarships, the school's own gift aid, United Negro College Fund, Native American Grants. *Loans:* Subsidized Stafford, Unsubsidized Stafford, PLUS, Federal Perkins. *Student Employment:* Federal Work-Study Program available. Institutional employment available. Highest amount earned per year from on-campus jobs $10,800. Off-campus job opportunities are good. **Financial Aid Statistics:** 100% freshmen, 95% undergrads receive need-based scholarship or grant aid. 56% freshmen, 63% undergrads receive non-need-based scholarship or grant aid. 68% freshmen, 70% undergrads receive need-based self-help aid. 8% freshmen, 9% undergrads receive athletic scholarships. 98% freshmen, 84% undergrads receive any aid. 62% undergrads borrow to pay for school. Average cumulative indebtedness $24,292. **Criteria for awarding institutional aid:** *Non-need-based:* academics, alumni affiliation, art, athletics, job skills, leadership, music/drama, religious affiliation, state/district residency.

OKLAHOMA STATE UNIVERSITY

219 Student Union, Stillwater, OK 74078
Phone: 405-744-5358 • **Financial Aid Phone:** 405-744-6604
E-mail: admissions@okstate.edu • **CEEB Code:** 6546
Fax: 405-744-7092 • **Website:** http://go.okstate.edu • **ACT Code:** 3424

This public school was founded in 1890. It has a 840-acre campus.

RATINGS

Admissions Selectivity Rating: 85   **Fire Safety Rating:** 93

STUDENTS AND FACULTY

Enrollment: 20,581. **Student Body:** 49% female, 51% male, 27% out-of-state, 3% international (92 countries represented). Asian 2%, African American 5%, Caucasian 71%, Hispanic 6%, Native American 5%
Retention and Graduation: 34% freshmen graduate within 4 years. 61% freshmen graduate within 6 years. **Faculty:** 1,037 full-time faculty, 89% hold PhDs, 34% are members of minority groups, 19% are women. 17% of classes are taught by teaching assistants.

ACADEMICS

Degrees: bachelor's, master's, post-bachelor's certificate, post-master's certificate. **Classes:** Most classes have 10–19 students. Most lab/discussion sessions have 10–19 students. **Majors with Highest Enrollment:** Marketing/Marketing Management; Accounting; Business Administration and Management. **Special Study Options:** Accelerated program, cross-registration, distance learning, double major, dual enrollment, English as a Second Language (ESL), exchange student program (domestic), honors program, independent study, internships, student-designed major, study abroad, teacher certification program. **Combined degree programs:** BS/MS Accounting. **Disability Services:** Special programs offered to physically disabled students include note-taking services, reader services, tape recorders, tutors. **Career services:** Alumni network, alumni services, career/job search classes, career assessment, internships, regional alumni. Career services highlights include our Entrepreneurship Empowerment in South Africa (EESA) Program, which involves taking 20 OSU students, pairing them with 20 South African students, and spending six weeks working with a group of historically disadvantaged, township-based entrepreneurs helping them growth their businesses. The students are taught and coached by three of our entrepreneurship faculty members. Over the years we have assisted over 120 entrepreneurs in meaningful ways.

FACILITIES

Housing: Coed dorms, special housing for disabled students, men's dorms, women's dorms, fraternity/sorority housing, apartments for married students, apartments for single students, Wellness Housing, Theme Housing. 97% of campus accessible to physically disabled. **Special Academic Facilities/Equipment:** Art, history, and natural science museums, wellness center, laser research center. **Computers:** 80% of classrooms, 80% of dorms, 100% of libraries, 80% of student union, have wireless network access. Students can register for classes online. Administrative functions (other than registration) can be performed online.

CAMPUS LIFE

Environment: Town. **Activities:** Choral groups, concert band, dance, drama/theater, jazz band, literary magazine, marching band, music ensembles, musical theater, opera, pep band, radio station, student government, student newspaper, symphony orchestra, television station, Campus Ministries, International Student Organization. 300 registered organizations. **Athletics (Intercollegiate):** *Men:* baseball, basketball, cross-country, football, golf, tennis, track/field (outdoor), wrestling. *Women:* basketball, cross-country, equestrian sports, golf, soccer, softball, tennis, track/field (outdoor). **On-Campus Highlights:** Colvin Recreational Center, Gallagher/Iba Arena and Museum, Student Union Building, Library, ConocoPhillips Alumni Center. **Environmental Initiatives:** Energy conservation—turning off lights, computers, monitors, speakers, printers, etc when not in use. Reducing thermostat settings during winter and turning it up during summer. This program has saved over $30 million since 2007. OSU now has a wind farm that provided 70% of electricity for the campus in 2013. Rolled out a new campus-wide recycling program called OSU Recycles.

ADMISSIONS

Freshman Academic Profile: Average high school GPA 3.54. 26% in top 10% of high school class, 54% in top 25% of high school class, 85% in top 50% of high school class. SAT Math middle 50% range 510-620. SAT Critical Reading middle 50% range 480-600. ACT middle 50% range 22-28. Minimum internet-based TOEFL 61. Minimum paper TOEFL 500. **Basis for Candidate Selection:** *Very important factors considered include:* Class rank, academic GPA, standardized test scores. *Other factors considered include:* application essay, recommendation(s), rigor of secondary school record, character/personal qualities, extracurricular activities, interview, talent/ability. **Freshman Admission Requirements:** High school diploma is required and GED is accepted. *Academic units required:* 4 English, 3 mathematics, 2 science, (2 science labs), 2 social studies, 1 history, 3 academic electives. **Freshman Admission Statistics:** 12,259 applied, 75% admitted, 44% enrolled. **Transfer Admission Requirements:** college transcript(s), Minimum college GPA of 2.25 required. Lowest grade transferable D. **General Admission Information:** Application Fee $40. Nonfall registration accepted. Admission may be deferred for a maximum of military. Credit offered for CEEB Advanced Placement tests.

COSTS AND FINANCIAL AID

Annual in-state tuition $4,425. Annual out-of-state tuition $17,010. Room and board $7,390. Required fees $3,017. Average book expense $1,030. **Required Forms and Deadlines:** FAFSA. **Notification of Awards:** Applicants will be notified of awards on a rolling basis beginning 10/1. **Types of Aid:** *Need-based scholarships/grants:* Federal Pell, SEOG, state scholarships/grants, private scholarships, the school's own gift aid, TEACH, ACG, SMART. *Loans:* Direct Subsidized Stafford, Direct Unsubsidized Stafford, Direct PLUS, Federal Perkins. *Student Employment:* Institutional employment available. Off-campus job opportunities are good. **Financial Aid Statistics:** 76% freshmen, 76% undergrads receive need-based scholarship or grant aid. 9% freshmen, 5% undergrads receive non-need-based scholarship or grant aid. 56% freshmen, 67% undergrads receive need-based self-help aid. 2% freshmen, 2% undergrads receive athletic scholarships. 89% freshmen, 83% undergrads receive any aid. 51% undergrads borrow to pay for school. Average cumulative indebtedness $21,901. **Criteria for awarding institutional aid:** *Non-need-based:* academics, alumni affiliation, art, athletics, leadership, minority status, music/drama, state/district residency.

OKLAHOMA WESLEYAN UNIVERSITY

2201 Silver Lake Road, Bartlesville, OK 74006
Phone: 918-335-6219
E-mail: admissions@okwu.edu · **CEEB Code:** 6135
Fax: 918-335-6229 · **Website:** www.okwu.edu · **ACT Code:** 3387

This private school was founded in 1972. It has a 127-acre campus.

RATINGS

Admissions Selectivity Rating: 75   Fire Safety Rating: 60*

STUDENTS AND FACULTY

Enrollment: 571. **Student Body:** 43% out-of-state, (12 countries represented).
Retention and Graduation: 10% grads go on to further study within 1 year. 2% grads pursue arts and sciences degrees. 2% grads pursue law degrees. 5% grads pursue business degrees. 2% grads pursue medical degrees. **Faculty:** 0% of classes are taught by teaching assistants.

ACADEMICS

Degrees: associate, bachelor's, certificate, master's. **Special Study Options:** double major, English as a Second Language (ESL), independent study, internships, student-designed major, study abroad. **Disability Services:** Special programs offered to physically disabled students include tutors. **Career services:**

FACILITIES

Housing: men's dorms, women's dorms. 70% of campus accessible to physically disabled. **Special Academic Facilities/Equipment:** LaQuinta Mansion. **Computers:** Undergraduates are required to own a computer.

CAMPUS LIFE

Environment: Village. **Activities:** Choral groups, music ensembles, pep band, student government, student newspaper, yearbook. 10 registered organizations, 2 honor societies, 3 religious organizations. **Athletics (Intercollegiate):** *Men:* baseball, basketball, cheerleading, golf, soccer. *Women:* basketball, cheerleading, soccer, softball, volleyball.

ADMISSIONS

Freshman Academic Profile: 90% from public high schools. ACT middle 50% range 19-25. Minimum paper TOEFL 500. **Basis for Candidate Selection:** *Very important factors considered include:* Class rank, recommendation(s), rigor of secondary school record, standardized test scores, character/personal qualities, religious affiliation/commitment, state residency. *Important factors considered include:* alumni/ae relation, geographical residence, interview, racial/ethnic status. *Other factors considered include:* extracurricular activities, talent/ability. **Freshman Admission Requirements:** High school diploma is required and GED is accepted. *Academic units required:* 4 English, 2 mathematics, 1 science, (1 science labs), 1 social studies, 1 history, 6 academic electives. **Freshman Admission Statistics:** 317 applied, 60% admitted, 62% enrolled. **Transfer Admission Requirements:** High school transcript, college transcript(s), essay or personal statement, statement of good standing from prior institution(s). Minimum college GPA of 2.0 required. Lowest grade transferable D. **General Admission Information:** Application Fee $25. Nonfall registration accepted. Admission may be deferred for a maximum of 12. Credit and/or placement offered for CEEB Advanced Placement tests.

COSTS AND FINANCIAL AID

Annual tuition $8,200. Room and board $3,800. Required fees $500. **Types of Aid:** *Need-based scholarships/grants:* Federal Pell, SEOG, state scholarships/grants, private scholarships, the school's own gift aid. *Loans:* Direct Subsidized Stafford, Direct Unsubsidized Stafford, Direct PLUS, Federal Perkins. *Student Employment:* Federal Work-Study Program available. Institutional employment available. Highest amount earned per year from on-campus jobs $1,913. Off-campus job opportunities are excellent.

OLD DOMINION UNIVERSITY

108 Rollins Hall, Norfolk, VA 23529-0050
Phone: 757-683-3685 · **Financial Aid Phone:** 757-683-3683
E-mail: admissions@odu.edu · **CEEB Code:** 5126
Fax: 757-683-3255 · **Website:** www.odu.edu

This public school was founded in 1930. It has a 188-acre campus.

RATINGS

Admissions Selectivity Rating: 74   Fire Safety Rating: 82

STUDENTS AND FACULTY

Enrollment: 19,842. **Student Body:** 54% female, 46% male, 8% out-of-state, 1% international (118 countries represented). Asian 4%, African American 27%, Caucasian 50%, Hispanic 7%, Native American <1%
Retention and Graduation: 81% freshmen return for sophomore year. 24% freshmen graduate within 4 years. 52% freshmen graduate within 6 years.
Faculty: 787 full-time faculty, 76% hold PhDs, 43% are members of minority groups, 20% are women.

ACADEMICS

Degrees: bachelor's, doctoral, master's, post-master's certificate. **Classes:** Most classes have 10–19 students. Most lab/discussion sessions have 20–29 students. **Majors with Highest Enrollment:** Multi-/Interdisciplinary Studies; Psychology; Criminology. **Special Study Options:** Accelerated program, cooperative education program, cross-registration, distance learning, double major, dual enrollment, English as a Second Language (ESL), exchange student program (domestic), honors program, independent study, internships, liberal arts/career combination, student-designed major, study abroad, teacher certification program, weekend college, Experiential Learning. **Honors programs:** Honors College. The Honors College was established to further the University's commitment to excellence in education. With an emphasis on teaching, innovation, and small classes, the college offers the experience of a small liberal arts college within the framework of the large university. The four-year experience offers specially designed, low-enrollment courses to honors students and selected juniors and seniors. Several out-of-class and off-campus experiences are often part of these courses '– at no extra cost to students. A one credit honors tutorial is required in the junior year, and a senior honors colloquium is taken in the final year of study. All Honors College students are awarded an annual honors stipend. **Combined degree programs:** BA/MD, BA/JD, BA/MA, BA/DDS, BA/MEng, 5-year Master's degree program in education. **Disability Services:** Special programs offered to physically disabled students include note-taking services, reader services, tutors. **Career services:** Alumni network, alumni services, career/job search classes, career assessment, internships, regional alumni. Career services highlights include The Career Advantage Program, a comprehensive series of programs, services, professional seminars, appointments, and work assignments geared toward helping you determine your future career. The cornerstone of the Career Advantage Program is the Guaranteed Practicum. All undergraduates are guaranteed a practical experience, or classroom experience working in a "real world" setting. More information is available at http://www.odu.edu/ao/cmc/cap.html.

FACILITIES

Housing: Coed dorms, special housing for disabled students, special housing for international students, apartments for single students. 95% of campus accessible to physically disabled. **Special Academic Facilities/Equipment:** Centers for urban research/service, economic education, and child study, planetarium, marine science research vessel, random wave pool. **Computers:** 100% of classrooms, 100% of dorms, 100% of libraries, 100% of dining areas, 100% of student union, 20% of common outdoor areas have wireless network access. Students can register for classes online. Administrative functions (other than registration) can be performed online.

CAMPUS LIFE

Environment: City. **Activities:** Choral groups, concert band, dance, drama/theater, jazz band, marching band, music ensembles, musical theater, pep band, radio station, student government, student newspaper, symphony orchestra, television station, Campus Ministries, International Student Organization, Model UN. 155 registered organizations, 16 honor societies, 25 religious organizations. 14 fraternities, 10 sororities. **Athletics (Intercollegiate): Men:** baseball, basketball, diving, football, golf, sailing, soccer, tennis, wrestling. **Women:** basketball, crew/rowing, diving, field hockey, golf, lacrosse, sailing, soccer, tennis. **On-Campus Highlights:** Webb Student Center, Engineering/Computational Bldg, University Village, Constant Convocation Center, Kaufman Mall. **Environmental Initiatives:** All new contruction and major renovations are designed to LEED Silver standards at a minimum. We completed two projects this year, one new construction and one renovation. We recycled over 1.7 million pounds of materials last year that would have otherwise gone to landfill. Established the ODU Climate Change and Sea Level Ride Initiative (CCSLRI) which is an effort by researcher and local policy makers to identify the multifaceted impact climate change and rising sea levels will have on our region.

ADMISSIONS

Freshman Academic Profile: Average high school GPA 3.29. 10% in top 10% of high school class, 33% in top 25% of high school class, 76% in top 50% of high school class. 93% from public high schools. SAT Math middle 50% range 460-560. SAT Critical Reading middle 50% range 460-560. ACT middle 50% range 18-23. Minimum internet-based TOEFL 79. Minimum paper TOEFL 550. **Basis for Candidate Selection:** *Very important factors considered include:* academic GPA, rigor of secondary school record, standardized test scores, extracurricular activities. *Important factors considered include:* Class rank, application essay, recommendation(s), volunteer work, work experience. *Other factors considered include:* alumni/ae relation, character/personal qualities, first generation, interview, level of applicant's interest, talent/ability. **Freshman Admission Requirements:** High school diploma is required and GED is accepted. *Academic units required:* 4 English, 3 mathematics, 3 science, 3 foreign language, 3 social studies. **Freshman Admission Statistics:** 9,161 applied, 82% admitted, 37% enrolled. **Transfer Admission Requirements:** college transcript(s), Minimum college GPA of 2.2 required. Lowest grade transferable c. **General Admission Information:** Application Fee $50. Regular application deadline 2/1. Notification on a rolling basis, beginning on or about 1/15. Nonfall registration accepted. Admission may be deferred for a maximum of 12 months. Credit and/or placement offered for CEEB Advanced Placement tests.

COSTS AND FINANCIAL AID

Annual in-state tuition $8,970. Annual out-of-state tuition $25,140. Room and board $10,233. Required fees $280. Average book expense $1,000. **Required Forms and Deadlines:** FAFSA. **Notification of Awards:** Applicants will be notified of awards on a rolling basis beginning 2/1. **Types of Aid:** *Need-based scholarships/grants:* Federal Pell, SEOG, state scholarships/grants, private scholarships, the school's own gift aid, United Negro College Fund, Federal Nursing Scholarships. *Loans:* Direct Subsidized Stafford, Direct Unsubsidized Stafford, Direct PLUS, Federal Perkins, Federal Nursing, college/university loans from institutional funds. *Student Employment:* Federal Work-Study Program available. Institutional employment available. Highest amount earned per year from on-campus jobs $5,382. Off-campus job opportunities are excellent. **Financial Aid Statistics:** 82% freshmen, 75% undergrads receive need-based scholarship or grant aid. 40% freshmen, 20% undergrads receive non-need-based scholarship or grant aid. 80% freshmen, 80% undergrads receive need-based self-help aid. 2% freshmen, 2% undergrads receive athletic scholarships. 85% freshmen, 73% undergrads receive any aid. 69% undergrads borrow to pay for school. Average cumulative indebtedness $26,404. **Criteria for awarding institutional aid:** *Non-need-based:* academics, alumni affiliation, art, athletics, leadership, music/drama, state/district residency.

OLIVET COLLEGE

320 S. Main St., Olivet, MI 49076
Phone: 269-749-7635
E-mail: admissions@olivetcollege.edu • **CEEB Code:** 1595
Fax: 269-749-6617 • **Website:** www.olivetcollege.edu • **ACT Code:** 2042

This private school, affiliated with the United Church of Christ Church, was founded in 1844. It has a 45-acre campus.

RATINGS

Admissions Selectivity Rating: 60*   **Fire Safety Rating:** 60*

STUDENTS AND FACULTY

Enrollment: 1,070. **Student Body:** 42% female, 58% male, 5% out-of-state, 3% international. Asian 1%, African American 16%, Caucasian 76%, Hispanic 2%, Native American 1%
Retention and Graduation: 65% grads go on to further study within 1 year. 72% grads pursue arts and sciences degrees. 20% grads pursue law degrees. 45% grads pursue business degrees. 10% grads pursue medical degrees. **Faculty:** 46 full-time faculty, 46% hold PhDs, 37% are members of minority groups, 26% are women. 1% of classes are taught by teaching assistants.

ACADEMICS

Degrees: bachelor's, master's. **Special Study Options:** cooperative education program, dual enrollment, honors program, independent study, internships, liberal arts/career combination, student-designed major, study abroad, teacher certification program, Freshman Year Experience, Portfolio Assessment, Senior Experience, and Service Learning programs. **Disability Services:** Special programs offered to physically disabled students include reader services, tape recorders, tutors. **Career services:** career/job search classes, career assessment, internships.

FACILITIES

Housing: Coed dorms, men's dorms, special housing for international students, women's dorms, fraternity/sorority housing, apartments for married students, apartments for single students. 30% of campus accessible to physically disabled. **Computers:** Students can register for classes online. Administrative functions (other than registration) can be performed online.

CAMPUS LIFE

Environment: Rural. **Activities:** Choral groups, concert band, drama/theater, jazz band, music ensembles, musical theater, pep band, radio station, student government, student newspaper, yearbook. 12 registered organizations, 1 honor society, 1 religious organization. 3 fraternities, 3 sororities. **Athletics (Intercollegiate): Men:** baseball, basketball, cross-country, diving, football, golf, soccer, swimming, track/field (outdoor), wrestling. **Women:** basketball, cheerleading, cross-country, diving, golf, soccer, softball, swimming, tennis, track/field (outdoor), volleyball.

ADMISSIONS

Freshman Academic Profile: Average high school GPA 2.92. Minimum internet-based TOEFL 79. Minimum paper TOEFL 550. **Basis for Candidate Selection:** *Very important factors considered include:* rigor of secondary school record, standardized test scores, alumni/ae relation, character/personal qualities, extracurricular activities, volunteer work, work experience. *Important factors considered include:* recommendation(s), racial/ethnic status. *Other factors considered include:* Class rank, application essay, geographical residence, interview, religious affiliation/commitment, state residency, talent/ability. **Freshman Admission Requirements:** High school diploma is required and GED is accepted. **Transfer Admission Requirements:** High school transcript, college transcript(s), Minimum college GPA of 2.0 required. Lowest grade transferable C-. **General Admission Information:** Application Fee $25. Notification on a rolling basis, beginning on or about 8/15. Nonfall registration accepted. Admission may be deferred for a maximum of 1 year. Credit and/or placement offered for CEEB Advanced Placement tests.

COSTS AND FINANCIAL AID

Annual tuition $17,994. Room and board $6,346. Required fees $664. Average book expense $800. **Required Forms and Deadlines:** FAFSA. **Notification of Awards:** Applicants will be notified of awards on a rolling basis beginning 2/1. **Types of Aid:** *Need-based scholarships/grants:* Federal Pell, SEOG, state scholarships/grants, private scholarships, the school's own gift aid. *Loans:* Subsidized Stafford, Unsubsidized Stafford, PLUS, Federal Perkins, state loans. *Student Employment:* Federal Work-Study Program available. Institutional employment available. Highest amount earned per year from on-campus jobs $850. Off-campus job opportunities are fair. **Financial Aid Statistics:** 100% freshmen, 100% undergrads receive need-based scholarship or grant aid. 6% freshmen, 4% undergrads receive non-need-based scholarship or grant aid. 93% freshmen, 93% undergrads receive need-based self-help aid. 0% freshmen, 0% undergrads receive athletic scholarships. 80% undergrads borrow to pay for school. **Criteria for awarding institutional aid:** *Non-need-based:* academics, art, leadership, music/drama, religious affiliation.

OLIVET NAZARENE UNIVERSITY

One University Avenue, Bourbonnais, IL 60914
Phone: 815-939-5603 · **Financial Aid Phone:** 815-939-5249
E-mail: admissions@olivet.edu · **CEEB Code:** 32
Fax: 815-935-4998 · **Website:** www.olivet.edu · **ACT Code:** 1112

This private school, affiliated with the Nazarene Church, was founded in 1907. It has a 225-acre campus.

RATINGS

Admissions Selectivity Rating: 85   **Fire Safety Rating:** 66

STUDENTS AND FACULTY

Enrollment: 2,633. **Student Body:** 60% female, 40% male, 55% out-of-state, 1% international (18 countries represented). Asian 1%, African American 9%, Caucasian 86%, Hispanic 3%, Native American <1%
Retention and Graduation: 79% freshmen return for sophomore year. 39% grads go on to further study within 1 year. 27% grads pursue arts and sciences degrees. 3% grads pursue law degrees. 13% grads pursue business degrees. 9% grads pursue medical degrees. **Faculty:** 94 full-time faculty, 68% hold PhDs, 34% are members of minority groups, 3% are women. 0% of classes are taught by teaching assistants.

ACADEMICS

Degrees: associate, bachelor's, master's. **Classes:** Most classes have 20–29 students. **Majors with Highest Enrollment:** Education; Health/Medical Preparatory Programs; Business/Commerce. **Special Study Options:** Accelerated program, distance learning, double major, honors program, independent study, internships, student-designed major, study abroad, teacher certification program. **Honors programs:** Phi Delta Lambda Psi Chi (Psychology); Dappa Delta Pi (Education); Kappa Omicron Nu (FACS); Sigma Tau Delta (English); Sigma Theta Tau (Nursing); Kappa Sigma Chapter (Nursing); Phi Alpha Theta (History); Departmental Honors. **Disability Services:** Special programs offered to physically disabled students include note-taking services, reader services, tape recorders, tutors.

FACILITIES

Housing: special housing for disabled students, men's dorms, women's dorms, apartments for married students, apartments for single students. 100% of campus accessible to physically disabled. **Special Academic Facilities/Equipment:** Planetarium, "Smart" Classrooms, Radio Station **Computers:** Students can register for classes online. Administrative functions (other than registration) can be performed online.

CAMPUS LIFE

Environment: Town. **Activities:** Choral groups, concert band, dance, drama/theater, jazz band, literary magazine, marching band, music ensembles, musical theater, opera, pep band, radio station, student government, student newspaper, student-run film society, symphony orchestra, television station, yearbook. 79 registered organizations, 8 honor societies, 23 religious organizations. **Athletics (Intercollegiate):** *Men:* baseball, basketball, cheerleading, cross-country, football, golf, soccer, tennis, track/field (outdoor), track/field (indoor). *Women:* basketball, cheerleading, cross-country, soccer, softball, tennis, track/field (outdoor), track/field (indoor), volleyball. **On-Campus Highlights:** Common Grounds (coffee shop), Ludwig Center (student center), McHie Arena, Fitness Center, Red Room (student lounge).

ADMISSIONS

Freshman Academic Profile: Average high school GPA 3.3. 22% in top 10% of high school class, 45% in top 25% of high school class, 75% in top 50% of high school class. 85% from public high schools. SAT Math middle 50% range 480-590. SAT Critical Reading middle 50% range 490-620. ACT middle 50% range 20-26. Minimum paper TOEFL 500. **Basis for Candidate Selection:** *Very important factors considered include:* Class rank, recommendation(s), rigor of secondary school record, standardized test scores, character/personal qualities. *Important factors considered include:* application essay, extracurricular activities, interview, talent/ability. *Other factors considered include:* religious affiliation/commitment, volunteer work, work experience. **Freshman Admission Requirements:** High school diploma is required and GED is accepted. *Academic units required:* 4 English, 3 mathematics, 3 science, 3 social studies, 2 history, 0 academic electives. **Freshman Admission Statistics:** 2,747 applied, 64% admitted, 40% enrolled. **Transfer Admission Requirements:** college transcript(s), essay or personal statement, statement of good standing from prior institution(s). Minimum college GPA of 2.0 required. Lowest grade transfer-

able D-. **General Admission Information:** Regular application deadline 5/15. Notification on a rolling basis, beginning on or about 6/1. Nonfall registration accepted. Credit and/or placement offered for CEEB Advanced Placement tests.

COSTS AND FINANCIAL AID

Annual tuition $16,750. Room and board $6,400. Required fees $840. Average book expense $800. **Required Forms and Deadlines:** FAFSA, Institution's own financial aid form. **Notification of Awards:** Applicants will be notified of awards on a rolling basis beginning 2/1. **Types of Aid:** *Need-based scholarships/grants:* Federal Pell, SEOG, state scholarships/grants, private scholarships, the school's own gift aid. *Loans:* Direct Subsidized Stafford, Direct Unsubsidized Stafford, Direct PLUS, Subsidized Stafford, Unsubsidized Stafford, PLUS, Federal Perkins. *Student Employment:* Federal Work-Study Program available. **Financial Aid Statistics:** 99% freshmen, 98% undergrads receive need-based scholarship or grant aid. 95% freshmen, 91% undergrads receive non-need-based scholarship or grant aid. 82% freshmen, 86% undergrads receive need-based self-help aid. 15% freshmen, 15% undergrads receive athletic scholarships.96% undergrads receive any aid. 68% undergrads borrow to pay for school. **Criteria for awarding institutional aid:** *Non-need-based:* academics, art, athletics, leadership, music/drama, religious affiliation.

ONONDAGA COMMUNITY COLLEGE

4941, Syracuse, NY 13215
Phone: 315-498-2201
E-mail: occinfo@sunyocc.edu
Fax: 315-469-2107 · **Website:** www.sunyocc.edu

This public school was founded in 1961. It has a 181-acre campus.

RATINGS

Admissions Selectivity Rating: 61   **Fire Safety Rating:** 60*

STUDENTS AND FACULTY

Enrollment: 5,097. **Student Body:** 54% female, 46% male, 0% out-of-state, 0% international. Asian 0%, African American 0%, Caucasian 0%, Hispanic 0%, Native American <1%
Faculty: 179 full-time faculty, 52% are members of minority groups, 9% are women.

ACADEMICS

Degrees: associate, certificate. **Classes:** Most classes have 10–19 students. **Special Study Options:** cooperative education program, double major, dual enrollment, English as a Second Language (ESL), honors program, independent study, internships, liberal arts/career combination, study abroad. **Disability Services:** Special programs offered to physically disabled students include note-taking services, reader services, tape recorders, tutors. **Career services:** alumni services, career/job search classes.

CAMPUS LIFE

Environment: Village. **Activities:** Choral groups, music ensembles, radio station, student government, student newspaper, television station 1 honor society. **Athletics (Intercollegiate):** *Men:* baseball, basketball, cross-country, lacrosse, tennis. *Women:* basketball, cross-country, softball, tennis, volleyball.

ADMISSIONS

Freshman Academic Profile: 95% from public high schools. Minimum paper TOEFL 500. **Basis for Candidate Selection:** *Very important factors considered include:* rigor of secondary school record. *Other factors considered include:* recommendation(s), character/personal qualities, interview. **Freshman Admission Requirements:** High school diploma is required and GED is accepted.High school diploma or equivalent is not required. **Freshman Admission Statistics:** 2,899 applied, 79% admitted, 217% enrolled. **Transfer Admission Requirements:** High school transcript, college transcript(s), Lowest grade transferable C. **General Admission Information:** Application Fee $30. Nonfall registration accepted. Admission may be deferred for a maximum of 2 semesters.

COSTS AND FINANCIAL AID

Required Forms and Deadlines: FAFSA, State aid form. **Notification of Awards:** Applicants will be notified of awards on or about 4/15. **Types of Aid:** *Need-based scholarships/grants:* Federal Pell, SEOG, state scholarships/grants, Federal work study. *Loans:* Subsidized Stafford, Unsubsidized Stafford, PLUS. *Student Employment:* Federal Work-Study Program available. Off-campus job opportunities are excellent. **Financial Aid Statistics:** 60% freshmen, 60% undergrads receive need-based scholarship or grant aid. 1% freshmen, 1% undergrads receive non-need-based scholarship or grant aid. 73% freshmen,

73% undergrads receive need-based self-help aid. 0% freshmen, 0% undergrads receive athletic scholarships. **Criteria for awarding institutional aid:** *Non-need-based:* academics, alumni affiliation.

ORAL ROBERTS UNIVERSITY

7777 S. Lewis Avenue, Tulsa, OK 74171
Phone: 918-495-6518
E-mail: admissions@oru.edu • **CEEB Code:** 6552
Fax: 918-495-6222 • **Website:** www.oru.edu • **ACT Code:** 3427

This is a private school. It has a 500-acre campus.

RATINGS

Admissions Selectivity Rating: 79   **Fire Safety Rating:** 60*

STUDENTS AND FACULTY

Enrollment: 2,944. **Student Body:** 57% female, 43% male, 58% out-of-state, 2% international. Asian 1%, African American 4%, Caucasian 16%, Hispanic 3%, Native American 1%
Retention and Graduation: 81% freshmen return for sophomore year. 50% grads go on to further study within 1 year. 25% grads pursue arts and sciences degrees. 1% grads pursue law degrees. 10% grads pursue business degrees. 5% grads pursue medical degrees. **Faculty:** 163 full-time faculty, 63% hold PhDs, 36% are members of minority groups, 20% are women. 0% of classes are taught by teaching assistants.

ACADEMICS

Degrees: bachelor's, first professional, master's. **Classes:** Most classes have 10–19 students. Most lab/discussion sessions have 20–29 students. **Majors with Highest Enrollment:** Mass Communication/Media Studies; Theology/Theological Studies; Marketing/Marketing Management. **Special Study Options:** Accelerated program, distance learning, double major, dual enrollment, English as a Second Language (ESL), external degree program, honors program, independent study, internships, liberal arts/career combination, student-designed major, study abroad, teacher certification program, weekend college. **Honors programs:** ORU HOnors Program includes "Scholars" and "Fellows" a Highly selective Includes Beta Gamma Phi and others **Combined degree programs:** 3-2 bachelor's/ MBA and bachelor's/MA.Ed. programs. **Disability Services:** Special programs offered to physically disabled students include note-taking services, reader services, tape recorders, tutors.

FACILITIES

Housing: men's dorms, women's dorms. 100% of campus accessible to physically disabled. **Special Academic Facilities/Equipment:** Dial Access Information Retrieval System, programmed learning facilities, early learning center, TV production studio.

CAMPUS LIFE

Activities: Choral groups, concert band, dance, drama/theater, jazz band, music ensembles, musical theater, pep band, radio station, student government, student newspaper, television station, yearbook, Campus Ministries, International Student Organization, Model UN. **Athletics (Intercollegiate):** *Men:* baseball, basketball, cheerleading, cross-country, soccer, swimming, tennis, track/field (outdoor). *Women:* basketball, cheerleading, cross-country, soccer, swimming, tennis, track/field (outdoor), volleyball. **On-Campus Highlights:** Eagle's Nest, Aerobics Center, Prayer Tower, Mabee Center (Multi-purpose Event Complex), Gabrielle Christian Salem Hall.

ADMISSIONS

Freshman Academic Profile: 75% from public high schools. SAT Math middle 50% range 450-560. SAT Critical Reading middle 50% range 460-570. ACT middle 50% range 20-25. Minimum paper TOEFL 500. **Basis for Candidate Selection:** *Very important factors considered include:* application essay, academic GPA, rigor of secondary school record, standardized test scores. *Important factors considered include:* Class rank, recommendation(s). *Other factors considered include:* alumni/ae relation, character/personal qualities, religious affiliation/commitment. **Freshman Admission Requirements:** High school diploma is required and GED is accepted. **Freshman Admission Statistics:** 1,417 applied, 44% admitted, 65% enrolled. **Transfer Admission Requirements:** High school transcript, college transcript(s), essay or personal statement, Minimum college GPA of 2.0 required. Lowest grade transferable 2. **General Admission Information:** Application Fee $35. Nonfall registration accepted. Credit and/or placement offered for CEEB Advanced Placement tests.

COSTS AND FINANCIAL AID

Required Forms and Deadlines: FAFSA. **Types of Aid:** *Need-based scholarships/grants:* Federal Pell, SEOG, state scholarships/grants, private scholarships, the school's own gift aid. *Loans:* Subsidized Stafford, Unsubsi-

dized Stafford, PLUS, Federal Perkins. *Student Employment:* Highest amount earned per year from on-campus jobs $1,800. **Financial Aid Statistics:** 100% freshmen, 99% undergrads receive need-based scholarship or grant aid. 32% freshmen, 36% undergrads receive non-need-based scholarship or grant aid. 93% freshmen, 92% undergrads receive need-based self-help aid. 3% freshmen, 4% undergrads receive athletic scholarships. 47% undergrads borrow to pay for school. Average cumulative indebtedness $31,588. **Criteria for awarding institutional aid:** *Non-need-based:* academics, alumni affiliation, art, athletics, job skills, leadership, music/drama.

OREGON COLLEGE OF ART AND CRAFT

8245 Southwest Barnes Road, Portland, OR 97225
Phone: 971-255-4192 • **Financial Aid Phone:** 971-255-4224
E-mail: admissions@ocac.edu • **CEEB Code:** 4236
Fax: 503-297-9651 • **Website:** www.ocac.edu • **ACT Code:** 3471

This private school was founded in 1907. It has a 9-acre campus.

RATINGS

Admissions Selectivity Rating: 62   **Fire Safety Rating:** 64

STUDENTS AND FACULTY

Enrollment: 151. **Student Body:** 73% female, 27% male, 18% out-of-state, 0% international (2 countries represented). Asian 2%, African American 0%, Caucasian 70%, Hispanic 5%, Native American 3%
Retention and Graduation: 65% freshmen return for sophomore year. 25% freshmen graduate within 4 years. 38% freshmen graduate within 6 years. 9% grads pursue arts and sciences degrees. **Faculty:** 10 full-time faculty, 90% hold PhDs, 50% are members of minority groups, 10% are women. 0% of classes are taught by teaching assistants.

ACADEMICS

Degrees: bachelor's, certificate, post-bachelor's certificate. **Classes:** Most classes have fewer than 10 students. **Majors with Highest Enrollment:** Fine Arts and Art Studies. **Special Study Options:** cross-registration, exchange student program (domestic), independent study, internships, study abroad.

FACILITIES

Housing: cooperative housing, The college offers a small number of on-campus housing for new students straight from high school. In addition, the college has contract with two apartment complexes across the street from the college. 60% of campus accessible to physically disabled. **Special Academic Facilities/Equipment:** Hoffman Gallery, Centrum Gallery, and 7 specialized studios for artmaking.

CAMPUS LIFE

Environment: Metropolis. **Activities:** student government, student newspaper 1 registered organization. **On-Campus Highlights:** Hands On Café, Centrum Art Gallery, Thesis Studios, Library, Computer Lab. **Environmental Initiatives:** Public Transportation; Campus-Wide Recycling; Storm Water Run-Off Retention.

ADMISSIONS

Freshman Academic Profile: Average high school GPA 3. 20% in top 10% of high school class, 20% in top 25% of high school class, 60% in top 50% of high school class. Minimum internet-based TOEFL 80. Minimum paper TOEFL 550. **Basis for Candidate Selection:** *Very important factors considered include:* application essay, academic GPA, level of applicant's interest, talent/ability. *Important factors considered include:* recommendation(s), rigor of secondary school record, character/personal qualities, interview. *Other factors considered include:* standardized test scores, alumni/ae relation, extracurricular activities, first generation, volunteer work, work experience. **Freshman Admission Requirements:** High school diploma is required and GED is accepted. **Freshman Admission Statistics:** 60 applied, 92% admitted, 47% enrolled. **Transfer Admission Requirements:** High school transcript, college transcript(s), essay or personal statement, Minimum college GPA of 2.0 required. Lowest grade transferable C. **General Admission Information:** Application Fee $35. Notification on a rolling basis, beginning on or about 1/1. Nonfall registration accepted. Admission may be deferred for a maximum of 1 year. Credit and/or placement offered for CEEB Advanced Placement tests.

COSTS AND FINANCIAL AID

Average book expense $1,000. **Required Forms and Deadlines:** FAFSA. **Notification of Awards:** Applicants will be notified of awards on a rolling basis beginning 3/15. **Types of Aid:** *Need-based scholarships/grants:* Federal Pell, SEOG, state scholarships/grants, private scholarships, the school's own gift aid. *Loans:* Subsidized Stafford, Unsubsidized Stafford, PLUS, state loans. *Student Employment:* Federal Work-Study Program available. Institutional employment available. **Financial Aid Statistics:** 100% freshmen, 84% undergrads receive need-based scholarship or grant aid. 88% freshmen, 82% undergrads receive non-need-based scholarship or grant aid. 94% freshmen, 95% undergrads receive need-based self-help aid. 0% freshmen, 0% undergrads receive athletic scholarships. 90% freshmen, 93% undergrads receive any aid. 0% undergrads borrow to pay for school. Average cumulative indebtedness $0. **Criteria for awarding institutional aid:** *Non-need-based:* academics, art.

OREGON HEALTH & SCIENCE UNIVERSITY

3181 SW Sam Jackson Park Rd, Portland, OR 97239
Phone: 503-494-2998 · **Financial Aid Phone:** 503-494-7800
E-mail: proginfo@ohsu.edu · **CEEB Code:** 4900
Fax: 503-494-3400 · **Website:** www.ohsu.edu

This public school was founded in 1867. It has a 120-acre campus.

RATINGS

Admissions Selectivity Rating: 60*   **Fire Safety Rating:** 60*

STUDENTS AND FACULTY

Enrollment: 591. **Student Body:** 84% female, 16% male, 10% out-of-state, 1% international. Asian 5%, African American 1%, Caucasian 79%, Hispanic 5%, Native American 2%
Faculty: 1,290 full-time faculty.

ACADEMICS

Degrees: associate, bachelor's, first professional, first professional certificate, master's, post-bachelor's certificate, post-master's certificate. **Majors with Highest Enrollment:** Registered Nursing/Registered Nurse; Clinical Laboratory Science/Medical Technology/Technologist; Emergency Medical Technology/Technician (EMT Paramedic). **Special Study Options:** Accelerated program, distance learning. **Combined degree programs:** MD/PhD, MD/MPH.

FACILITIES

Computers: Students can register for classes online.

CAMPUS LIFE

Environment: Metropolis. **Activities:** student government, student newspaper, yearbook. **On-Campus Highlights:** Portland Aerial Tram, Center for Health and Healing Café, Marquam Hill Hiking Trails.

ADMISSIONS

Freshman Admission Requirements: High school diploma is required and GED is accepted. **Transfer Admission Requirements:** college transcript(s), essay or personal statement, standardized test scores, statement of good standing from prior institution(s). Lowest grade transferable C. **General Admission Information:** Application Fee $120. Regular application deadline 1/15.

COSTS AND FINANCIAL AID

Types of Aid: *Need-based scholarships/grants:* Federal Pell, SEOG, state scholarships/grants, private scholarships, the school's own gift aid, Scholarship for Disadvantaged Student. *Loans:* Direct Subsidized Stafford, Direct Unsubsidized Stafford, Direct PLUS, Federal Perkins, Federal Nursing, college/university loans from institutional funds. *Student Employment:* Federal Work-Study Program available. Institutional employment available. Off-campus job opportunities are poor. **Financial Aid Statistics:**49% undergrads receive need-based scholarship or grant aid.1% undergrads receive non-need-based scholarship or grant aid.99% undergrads receive need-based self-help aid.0% undergrads receive athletic scholarships.70% undergrads receive any aid. **Criteria for awarding institutional aid:** *Non-need-based:* academics, minority status, state/district residency.

OREGON INSTITUTE OF TECHNOLOGY

3201 Campus Drive, Klamath Falls, OR 97601
Phone: 541-885-1150 · **Financial Aid Phone:** 541-885-1280
E-mail: oit@oit.edu · **CEEB Code:** 4587
Fax: 541-885-1115 · **ACT Code:** 3484

This public school was founded in 1947. It has a 173-acre campus.

RATINGS

Admissions Selectivity Rating: 79   **Fire Safety Rating:** 61

STUDENTS AND FACULTY

Enrollment: 2,663. **Student Body:** 44% female, 56% male, 15% out-of-state, 1% international (11 countries represented). Asian 5%, African American 1%, Caucasian 81%, Hispanic 4%, Native American 2%
Retention and Graduation: 69% freshmen return for sophomore year.
Faculty: 126 full-time faculty, 33% hold PhDs, 35% are members of minority groups, 6% are women.

ACADEMICS

Degrees: associate, bachelor's, certificate, master's. **Classes:** Most classes have 10–19 students. Most lab/discussion sessions have 10–19 students. **Majors with Highest Enrollment:** Mechanical Engineering/Mechanical Technology/Technician; Computer Engineering Technology/Technician; Computer Software Technology/Technician. **Special Study Options:** cooperative education program, cross-registration, distance learning, double major, dual enrollment, external degree program, internships, study abroad. **Disability Services:** Special programs offered to physically disabled students include note-taking services, reader services, tape recorders, tutors.

FACILITIES

Housing: Coed dorms **Special Academic Facilities/Equipment:** Shaw Historical library. **Computers:** Students can register for classes online. Administrative functions (other than registration) can be performed online.

CAMPUS LIFE

Environment: Town. **Activities:** Choral groups, pep band, radio station, student government, student newspaper, symphony orchestra, television station. 30 registered organizations, 5 honor societies, 1 religious organization. 1 fraternity, 1 sorority. **Athletics (Intercollegiate):** *Men:* baseball, basketball, cross-country, track/field (outdoor). *Women:* basketball, cross-country, soccer, softball, track/field (outdoor), volleyball. **On-Campus Highlights:** College Union Bistro, College Union Marketplace, Purvine Coffee Cart, Tech Fit, Fitness Center, Residnece Hall Lounge.

ADMISSIONS

Freshman Academic Profile: Average high school GPA 3.29. 25% in top 10% of high school class, 56% in top 25% of high school class, 92% in top 50% of high school class. SAT Math middle 50% range 480-600. SAT Critical Reading middle 50% range 460-570. ACT middle 50% range 21-26. Minimum paper TOEFL 520. **Basis for Candidate Selection:** *Very important factors considered include:* rigor of secondary school record, standardized test scores. *Other factors considered include:* Class rank, application essay, recommendation(s), character/personal qualities, interview, work experience. **Freshman Admission Requirements:** High school diploma is required and GED is accepted. *Academic units required:* 4 English, 3 mathematics, 2 science, (1 science labs), 2 foreign language, 3 social studies. **Freshman Admission Statistics:** 651 applied, 88% admitted, 46% enrolled. **Transfer Admission Requirements:** college transcript(s), Minimum college GPA of 2.0 required. Lowest grade transferable D. **General Admission Information:** Application Fee $50. Regular application deadline 10/1. Notification on a rolling basis, beginning on or about 10/15. Nonfall registration accepted. Admission may be deferred for a maximum of 2 years. Credit and/or placement offered for CEEB Advanced Placement tests.

COSTS AND FINANCIAL AID

Annual in-state tuition $4,590. Annual out-of-state tuition $14,760. Room and board $6,480. Required fees $1,329. Average book expense $1,000. **Required Forms and Deadlines:** FAFSA. **Notification of Awards:** Applicants will be notified of awards on a rolling basis beginning 4/1. **Types of Aid:** *Need-based scholarships/grants:* Federal Pell, SEOG, state scholarships/grants, private scholarships, the school's own gift aid. *Loans:* Subsidized Stafford, Unsubsidized Stafford, PLUS, Federal Perkins, college/university loans from institutional funds. **Financial Aid Statistics:** 37% freshmen, 48% undergrads receive need-based scholarship or grant aid. 7% freshmen, 5% undergrads receive non-need-based scholarship or grant aid. 60% freshmen, 72% undergrads receive need-based self-help aid. 0% freshmen, 1% undergrads receive athletic scholarships. 89% freshmen, 86% undergrads receive any aid. 7% undergrads borrow to pay for school. **Criteria for awarding institutional aid:** *Non-need-based:* academics, athletics, leadership, minority status.

OREGON STATE UNIVERSITY

104 Kerr Administration Building, Corvallis, OR 97331-2106
Phone: 541-737-4411 · **Financial Aid Phone:** 541-737-2241
E-mail: osuadmit@oregonstate.edu · **CEEB Code:** 3210
Fax: 541-737-2482 · **Website:** http://oregonstate.edu/ · **ACT Code:** 3482

This public school was founded in 1858. It has a 421-acre campus.

RATINGS
Admissions Selectivity Rating: 84   **Fire Safety Rating:** 87

STUDENTS AND FACULTY
Enrollment: 22,928. **Student Body:** 46% female, 54% male, 27% out-of-state, 6% international (71 countries represented). Asian 7%, African American 1%, Caucasian 68%, Hispanic 8%, Native American 1%
Retention and Graduation: 31% freshmen graduate within 4 years. 63% freshmen graduate within 6 years. **Faculty:** 1,111 full-time faculty, 85% hold PhDs, 36% are members of minority groups, 17% are women. 8.3% of classes are taught by teaching assistants.

ACADEMICS
Degrees: bachelor's, certificate, doctoral, master's, post-bachelor's certificate, post-master's certificate. **Classes:** Most classes have 20–29 students. Most lab/discussion sessions have 20–29 students. **Majors with Highest Enrollment:** Engineering; Business/Commerce; Human Development and Family Studies. **Special Study Options:** Accelerated program, cooperative education program, cross-registration, distance learning, double major, dual enrollment, English as a Second Language (ESL), exchange student program (domestic), external degree program, honors program, independent study, internships, liberal arts/career combination, student-designed major, study abroad, teacher certification program. **Combined degree programs:** 2-2 food science/technology program w/ U of Alaska. **Disability Services:** Special programs offered to physically disabled students include note-taking services, reader services, tape recorders, tutors. **Career services:** Alumni network, alumni services, career/job search classes, career assessment, internships, regional alumni.

FACILITIES
Housing: Coed dorms, special housing for disabled students, special housing for international students, fraternity/sorority housing, apartments for married students, cooperative housing, apartments for single students, Theme Housing. 86% of campus accessible to physically disabled. **Special Academic Facilities/Equipment:** Museums, galleries, collections, exhibits of cultural and scientific materials, language lab. **Computers:** 100% of classrooms, 2% of dorms, 100% of libraries, 50% of dining areas, 100% of student union, 2% of common outdoor areas have wireless network access. Students can register for classes online. Administrative functions (other than registration) can be performed online.

CAMPUS LIFE
Environment: Town. **Activities:** Choral groups, concert band, dance, drama/theater, jazz band, literary magazine, marching band, music ensembles, musical theater, opera, pep band, radio station, student government, student newspaper, student-run film society, symphony orchestra, television station, yearbook, Campus Ministries, International Student Organization, Model UN. 350 registered organizations, 29 honor societies, 23 religious organizations. 24 fraternities, 13 sororities. **Athletics (Intercollegiate):** *Men:* baseball, basketball, crew/rowing, football, golf, soccer, wrestling. *Women:* basketball, crew/rowing, cross-country, golf, gymnastics, soccer, softball, swimming, track/field (outdoor), volleyball. **On-Campus Highlights:** Memorial Union, Java II, Weatherford Hall, Dixon Recreation Center, Reser Stadium. **Environmental Initiatives:** OSU sustainability related research has impacts state- and nation-wide. Standout research occurs at the Oregon Climate Change Research Institute and within the colleges of Earth, Atmospheric and Oceanic Sciences, Agricultural Sciences and Engineering. More info at http://senergi.oregonstate.edu/home Degrees like ecological engineering offer a greener curriculum, and sustainability is becoming more embedded throughout the curriculum. OSUs new sustainability double degree program is available to students in all academic disciplines. The double degree requires that students complete 180 credits in an OSU major (or other from another baccalaureate degree institution) and can receive a second Bachelors degree in sustainability by completing an additional 36 credits. http://oregonstate.edu/sustainability/academics The Student Sustainability Initiative, a student fee funded organization, is a national model for student engagement and leadership development. It funds student employees and competitive grants open to all students that make campus more sustainable and expose students to sustainable practices. Four grant tracks include project grants, wage grants, travel grants and research grants. http://oregonstate.edu/ssi/

ADMISSIONS
Freshman Academic Profile: Average high school GPA 3.59. 27% in top 10% of high school class, 57% in top 25% of high school class, 89% in top 50% of high school class. SAT Math middle 50% range 500-620. SAT Critical Reading middle 50% range 480-610. SAT Writing middle 50% range 460-590. ACT middle 50% range 21-28. Minimum internet-based TOEFL 80. Minimum paper TOEFL 550. **Basis for Candidate Selection:** *Very important factors considered include:* application essay, academic GPA, rigor of secondary school record. *Important factors considered include:* Class rank, character/personal qualities, level of applicant's interest, talent/ability, volunteer work. *Other factors considered include:* recommendation(s), standardized test scores, extracurricular activities, first generation, interview, work experience. **Freshman Admission Requirements:** High school diploma is required and GED is accepted. *Academic units required:* 4 English, 3 mathematics, 2 science, (1 science labs), 2 foreign language, 3 social studies. **Freshman Admission Statistics:** 14,115 applied, 78% admitted, 34% enrolled. **Transfer Admission Requirements:** college transcript(s), essay or personal statement, statement of good standing from prior institution(s). Minimum college GPA of 2.25 required. Lowest grade transferable D. **General Admission Information:** Application Fee $50. Regular application deadline 9/1. Notification on a rolling basis, beginning on or about 10/1. Nonfall registration accepted. Admission may be deferred for a maximum of 1 year. Credit and/or placement offered for CEEB Advanced Placement tests.

COSTS AND FINANCIAL AID
Annual out-of-state tuition $24,822. Room and board $11,151. Required fees $1,472. Average book expense $1,965. **Required Forms and Deadlines:** FAFSA. **Notification of Awards:** Applicants will be notified of awards on a rolling basis beginning 4/1. **Types of Aid:** *Need-based scholarships/grants:* Federal Pell, SEOG, state scholarships/grants, private scholarships, the school's own gift aid. *Loans:* Direct Subsidized Stafford, Direct Unsubsidized Stafford, Direct PLUS, Federal Perkins, college/university loans from institutional funds. *Student Employment:* Federal Work-Study Program available. Institutional employment available. Off-campus job opportunities are good. **Financial Aid Statistics:** 81% freshmen, 76% undergrads receive need-based scholarship or grant aid. 1% freshmen, 1% undergrads receive non-need-based scholarship or grant aid. 96% freshmen, 97% undergrads receive need-based self-help aid. 2% freshmen, 1% undergrads receive athletic scholarships. 80% freshmen, 74% undergrads receive any aid. 58% undergrads borrow to pay for school. Average cumulative indebtedness $20,001. **Criteria for awarding institutional aid:** *Non-need-based:* academics, alumni affiliation, athletics, job skills, leadership, minority status, state/district residency.

OTIS COLLEGE OF ART AND DESIGN

9045 Lincoln Boulevard, Los Angeles, CA 90045
Phone: 310-665-6820 · **Financial Aid Phone:** 310-665-6880
E-mail: admissions@otis.edu · **CEEB Code:** 4394
Fax: 310-665-6821 · **Website:** www.otis.edu · **ACT Code:** 359

This private school was founded in 1918. It has a 5-acre campus.

RATINGS
Admissions Selectivity Rating: 82   **Fire Safety Rating:** 60*

STUDENTS AND FACULTY
Enrollment: 1,088. **Student Body:** 67% female, 33% male, 22% international. Asian 29%, African American 4%, Caucasian 24%, Hispanic 10%, Native American 1%
Retention and Graduation: 79% freshmen return for sophomore year. 52% freshmen graduate within 4 years. 62% freshmen graduate within 6 years. 80% grads pursue arts and sciences degrees. **Faculty:** 55 full-time faculty, 53% hold PhDs, 55% are members of minority groups, 20% are women. 0% of classes are taught by teaching assistants.

ACADEMICS
Degrees: bachelor's, master's. **Classes:** Most classes have 10–19 students. **Majors with Highest Enrollment:** Animation, Interactive Technology, Video Graphics and Special Effects; Fashion/Apparel Design; Graphic Design. **Special Study Options:** English as a Second Language (ESL), exchange student program (domestic), honors program, independent study, internships, study abroad. **Honors programs:** We have an honors program for qualified enrolled students. **Disability Services:** Special programs offered to physically disabled students include tape recorders, tutors. **Career services:** Alumni network, alumni services, career/job search classes, career assessment, internships. Career services highlights include a strong and growing network for students to experience real world work.

FACILITIES
Housing: apartments for single students. 100% of campus accessible to physically disabled. **Special Academic Facilities/Equipment:** Art gallery, student gallery, Woodshop, Metal Shop, Photo lab, Digital Media lab, Printmaking lab,

letterpress lab. **Computers:** Administrative functions (other than registration) can be performed online.

CAMPUS LIFE

Environment: Metropolis. **Activities:** literary magazine, student government, student newspaper. 7 registered organizations.

ADMISSIONS

Freshman Academic Profile: Average high school GPA 3.16. SAT Math middle 50% range 440-590. SAT Critical Reading middle 50% range 430-560. ACT middle 50% range 18-25. Minimum internet-based TOEFL 79. Minimum paper TOEFL 550. **Basis for Candidate Selection:** *Very important factors considered include:* rigor of secondary school record, talent/ability. *Important factors considered include:* application essay, standardized test scores. *Other factors considered include:* recommendation(s), alumni/ae relation, character/personal qualities, extracurricular activities, interview, volunteer work, work experience. **Freshman Admission Requirements:** High school diploma is required and GED is accepted. *Academic units required:* 4 English, 3 mathematics, 2 science, (1 science labs), 1 social studies, 2 history. **Freshman Admission Statistics:** 1,160 applied, 91% admitted, 27% enrolled. **Transfer Admission Requirements:** High school transcript, college transcript(s), essay or personal statement, statement of good standing from prior institution(s). Minimum college GPA of 2.5 required. Lowest grade transferable C. **General Admission Information:** Application Fee $50. Nonfall registration accepted. Credit offered for CEEB Advanced Placement tests.

COSTS AND FINANCIAL AID

Annual tuition $37,380. Room and board $11,800. Required fees $2,050. Average book expense $1,400. **Required Forms and Deadlines:** FAFSA, State aid form. **Notification of Awards:** Applicants will be notified of awards on a rolling basis beginning 3/1. **Types of Aid:** *Need-based scholarships/grants:* Federal Pell, SEOG, state scholarships/grants, private scholarships, the school's own gift aid. *Loans:* Subsidized Stafford, Unsubsidized Stafford, PLUS. *Student Employment:* Federal Work-Study Program available. Institutional employment available. Off-campus job opportunities are excellent. **Financial Aid Statistics:** 100% freshmen, 99% undergrads receive need-based scholarship or grant aid. 38% freshmen, 28% undergrads receive non-need-based scholarship or grant aid. 82% freshmen, 87% undergrads receive need-based self-help aid. 0% freshmen, 0% undergrads receive athletic scholarships. 68% undergrads borrow to pay for school. Average cumulative indebtedness $24,722. **Criteria for awarding institutional aid:** *Non-need-based:* academics, art.

OTTERBEIN COLLEGE

Office of Admission, Westerville, OH 43081
Phone: 614-823-1500 · **Financial Aid Phone:** 614-823-1502
E-mail: uotterb@otterbein.edu · **CEEB Code:** 1597
Fax: 614-823-1200 · **Website:** www.otterbein.edu · **ACT Code:** 3318

This private school, affiliated with the Methodist Church, was founded in 1847. It has a 140-acre campus.

RATINGS

Admissions Selectivity Rating: 82   **Fire Safety Rating:** 60*

STUDENTS AND FACULTY

Enrollment: 2,746. **Student Body:** 10% out-of-state, (12 countries represented).
Retention and Graduation: 92% freshmen return for sophomore year.
Faculty: 161 full-time faculty, 93% hold PhDs, 55% are members of minority groups, 11% are women. 0% of classes are taught by teaching assistants.

ACADEMICS

Degrees: bachelor's, master's. **Majors with Highest Enrollment:** Education; Business/Commerce; Registered Nursing/Registered Nurse. **Special Study Options:** Accelerated program, cooperative education program, cross-registration, double major, dual enrollment, exchange student program (domestic), honors program, independent study, internships, liberal arts/career combination, student-designed major, study abroad, teacher certification program, weekend college. **Honors programs:** The Honors Program at Otterbein College is designed to provide intellectual stimulation and challenge for students with high academic ability and motivation. The four-year program provides the opportunity to participate in a community of students and faculty who have shared scholarly and creative interests. As part of that community students develop and complete their own Honors research and creative projects. Through the Honors seminars and Honors project, students develop advanced knowledge in their disciplinary fields and acquire the skills for independent work in their own areas of academic and professional interest. The Honors Program at Ot-

terbein College is designed to provide intellectual stimulation and challenge for students with high academic ability and motivation. The four-year program provides the opportunity to participate in a community of students and faculty who have shared scholarly and creative interests. As part of that community students develop and complete their own Honors research and creative projects. Through the Honors seminars and Honors project, students develop advanced knowledge in their disciplinary fields and acquire the skills for independent work in their own areas of academic and professional interest. **Disability Services:** Special programs offered to physically disabled students include note-taking services, reader services, tape recorders, tutors. **Career services:** Alumni network, alumni services, career/job search classes, career assessment, internships, regional alumni.

FACILITIES

Housing: Coed dorms, men's dorms, women's dorms, fraternity/sorority housing, apartments for single students, Theme housing. **Special Academic Facilities/Equipment:** Language lab, horse stable, observatory and planetarium, Celestron 8-inch and 14-inch telescopes, 3 art galleries. **Computers:** Students can register for classes online. Administrative functions (other than registration) can be performed online.

CAMPUS LIFE

Environment: Town. **Activities:** Choral groups, concert band, dance, drama/theater, jazz band, literary magazine, marching band, music ensembles, musical theater, opera, pep band, radio station, student government, student newspaper, symphony orchestra, television station, yearbook, International Student Organization. 100 registered organizations, 7 fraternities, 6 sororities. **Athletics (Intercollegiate):** *Men:* baseball, basketball, cheerleading, cross-country, equestrian sports, football, golf, soccer, tennis, track/field (outdoor), track/field (indoor). *Women:* basketball, cheerleading, cross-country, equestrian sports, golf, soccer, softball, tennis, track/field (outdoor), track/field (indoor), volleyball. **On-Campus Highlights:** Clements Recreation Center, Cowen Hall- Theatre, Campus Center, Art Galleries/Art Building.

ADMISSIONS

Freshman Academic Profile: Average high school GPA 3.34. 24% in top 10% of high school class, 55% in top 25% of high school class, 85% in top 50% of high school class. SAT Math middle 50% range 480-590. SAT Critical Reading middle 50% range 470-600. SAT Writing middle 50% range 460-600. ACT middle 50% range 20-25. Minimum paper TOEFL 500. **Basis for Candidate Selection:** *Important factors considered include:* Class rank, rigor of secondary school record, standardized test scores. *Other factors considered include:* application essay, recommendation(s), alumni/ae relation, character/personal qualities, extracurricular activities, interview, racial/ethnic status, talent/ability, volunteer work, work experience. **Freshman Admission Requirements:** High school diploma is required and GED is accepted. **Freshman Admission Statistics:** 3,381 applied, 82% admitted, 24% enrolled. **Transfer Admission Requirements:** college transcript(s), Minimum college GPA of 2.5 required. Lowest grade transferable c-. **General Admission Information:** Application Fee $25. Notification on a rolling basis, beginning on or about 10/15. Nonfall registration accepted. Admission may be deferred for a maximum of 12. Credit and/or placement offered for CEEB Advanced Placement tests.

COSTS AND FINANCIAL AID

Annual tuition $26,319. Room and board $7,461. Average book expense $700. **Required Forms and Deadlines:** FAFSA. **Types of Aid:** *Need-based scholarships/grants:* Federal Pell, SEOG, state scholarships/grants, private scholarships, the school's own gift aid. *Loans:* Direct Subsidized Stafford, Direct Unsubsidized Stafford, Direct PLUS, Federal Perkins. *Student Employment:* Federal Work-Study Program available. Institutional employment available. Highest amount earned per year from on-campus jobs $1,800. Off-campus job opportunities are excellent. **Criteria for awarding institutional aid:** *Non-need-based:* academics, alumni affiliation, art, leadership, minority status, music/drama, religious affiliation.

OUACHITA BAPTIST UNIVERSITY

410 Ouachita St, Arkadelphia, AR 71998-0001
Phone: 870-245-5110 · **Financial Aid Phone:** 870-245-5587
E-mail: admissions@alpha.obu.edu · **CEEB Code:** 6549
Fax: 870-245-5500 · **Website:** www.obu.edu · **ACT Code:** 134

This private school, affiliated with the Southern Baptist Church, was founded in 1886. It has a 200-acre campus.

RATINGS

Admissions Selectivity Rating: 86   **Fire Safety Rating:** 90

STUDENTS AND FACULTY

Enrollment: 1,455. **Student Body:** 52% female, 48% male, 39% out-of-state, 2% international (36 countries represented). Asian 1%, African American 8%, Caucasian 84%, Hispanic 4%, Native American 1%

Retention and Graduation: 76% freshmen return for sophomore year. 50% freshmen graduate within 4 years. 58% freshmen graduate within 6 years. 44% grads go on to further study within 1 year. 22% grads pursue arts and sciences degrees. 2% grads pursue law degrees. 2% grads pursue business degrees. 13% grads pursue medical degrees. **Faculty:** 103 full-time faculty, 87% hold PhDs, 36% are members of minority groups, 4% are women. 0% of classes are taught by teaching assistants.

ACADEMICS

Degrees: bachelor's, terminal associate. **Classes:** Most classes have 10–19 students. Most lab/discussion sessions have fewer than 10 students. **Majors with Highest Enrollment:** Business Administration and Management; Biology/Biological Sciences; Mass Communication/Media Studies. **Special Study Options:** cross-registration, distance learning, double major, English as a Second Language (ESL), honors program, independent study, internships, study abroad, teacher certification program. **Disability Services:** Special programs offered to physically disabled students include note-taking services, reader services, tape recorders, tutors. **Career services:** Alumni network, alumni services, career/job search classes, career assessment, internships. Career services highlights include the Tiger Career Connection (online job postings and resources).

FACILITIES

Housing: special housing for disabled students, men's dorms, women's dorms, apartments for married students, apartments for single students. 95% of campus accessible to physically disabled. **Special Academic Facilities/Equipment:** Historical archives, Senator John McClellan collection, language lab, TV studio. **Computers:** 100% of classrooms, 100% of dorms, 100% of libraries, 100% of dining areas, 100% of student union, 50% of common outdoor areas have wireless network access. Administrative functions (other than registration) can be performed online.

CAMPUS LIFE

Environment: Village. **Activities:** Choral groups, concert band, dance, drama/theater, jazz band, literary magazine, marching band, music ensembles, musical theater, opera, pep band, student government, student newspaper, television station, yearbook, Campus Ministries, International Student Organization, Model UN. 60 registered organizations, 8 honor societies, 4 religious organizations. 5 fraternities, 5 sororities. **Athletics (Intercollegiate):** *Men:* baseball, basketball, diving, football, golf, soccer, swimming, tennis, wrestling. *Women:* basketball, cross-country, diving, golf, soccer, softball, swimming, tennis, volleyball. **On-Campus Highlights:** Starbuck's, Chick-fil-A, Commons (dining), Student Center, Sturgis Recreation Center. **Environmental Initiatives:** Employment of Energy Management Director; Faculty and staff initiatives for reduction of utility use; Re-cycling.

ADMISSIONS

Freshman Academic Profile: Average high school GPA 3.57. 27% in top 10% of high school class, 55% in top 25% of high school class, 81% in top 50% of high school class. 86% from public high schools. SAT Math middle 50% range 490-590. SAT Critical Reading middle 50% range 470-580. ACT middle 50% range 21-28. Minimum internet-based TOEFL 80. Minimum paper TOEFL 550. **Basis for Candidate Selection:** *Very important factors considered include:* academic GPA, rigor of secondary school record, standardized test scores. *Other factors considered include:* character/personal qualities, talent/ability. **Freshman Admission Requirements:** High school diploma is required and GED is accepted. *Academic units required:* 4 English, 2 mathematics, 2 science, 0 foreign language, 1 social studies, 2 history, 4 academic electives. **Freshman Admission Statistics:** 1,732 applied, 71% admitted, 34% enrolled. **Transfer Admission Requirements:** college transcript(s), statement of good standing from prior institution(s). Minimum college GPA of 2.0 required. Lowest grade transferable C. **General Admission Information:** Nonfall registration accepted. Admission may be deferred for a maximum of 1 year. Credit offered for CEEB Advanced Placement tests.

COSTS AND FINANCIAL AID

Annual tuition $23,600. Room and board $7,140. Required fees $520. Average book expense $1,100. **Required Forms and Deadlines:** FAFSA, State aid form. **Notification of Awards:** Applicants will be notified of awards on a rolling basis beginning 11/1. **Types of Aid:** *Need-based scholarships/grants:* Federal Pell, SEOG, state scholarships/grants, private scholarships, the school's own gift aid. *Loans:* Subsidized Stafford, Unsubsidized Stafford, PLUS, Federal Perkins, state loans, college/university loans from institutional funds, Alternative Loans. *Student Employment:* Federal Work-Study Program available. Highest amount earned per year from on-campus jobs $1,800. Off-campus job opportunities are fair. **Financial Aid Statistics:** 99% freshmen, 97% undergrads receive need-based scholarship or grant aid. 20% freshmen, 21% undergrads receive non-need-based scholarship or grant aid. 66% freshmen, 68% undergrads receive need-based self-help aid. 12% freshmen, 10% undergrads receive athletic scholarships. 98% freshmen, 96% undergrads receive any aid. 48% undergrads borrow to pay for school. Average cumulative indebtedness $25,823. **Criteria for awarding institutional aid:** *Non-need-based:* academics, alumni affiliation, art, athletics, leadership, minority status, music/drama, religious affiliation, state/district residency.

OUR LADY OF THE LAKE UNIVERSITY (OLLU)

Admissions Office, San Antonio, TX 78207-4689
Phone: 210-431-3961 • **Financial Aid Phone:** 800-324-4310
E-mail: webmaster@ollusa.edu • **CEEB Code:** 6550
Fax: 210-431-4036 • **Website:** www.ollusa.edu • **ACT Code:** 4140

This private school, affiliated with the Roman Catholic Church, was founded in 1895. It has a 75-acre campus.

RATINGS

Admissions Selectivity Rating: 84   **Fire Safety Rating:** 63

STUDENTS AND FACULTY

Enrollment: 1,554. **Student Body:** 73% female, 27% male, 2% out-of-state, 1% international. Asian 1%, African American 8%, Caucasian 17%, Hispanic 63%, Native American 1%

Retention and Graduation: 60% freshmen return for sophomore year. 14% freshmen graduate within 4 years. 32% freshmen graduate within 6 years. 30% grads go on to further study within 1 year. **Faculty:** 101 full-time faculty, 80% hold PhDs, 60% are members of minority groups, 35% are women. 0% of classes are taught by teaching assistants.

ACADEMICS

Degrees: bachelor's, master's. **Classes:** Most classes have fewer than 10 students. **Majors with Highest Enrollment:** Biology/Biological Sciences; Psychology; Business Administration and Management. **Special Study Options:** cooperative education program, cross-registration, distance learning, double major, dual enrollment, English as a Second Language (ESL), honors program, independent study, internships, liberal arts/career combination, study abroad, teacher certification program, weekend college, service learning. **Disability Services:** Special programs offered to physically disabled students include note-taking services, reader services, tape recorders, tutors. **Career services:** alumni services, career assessment.

FACILITIES

Housing: Coed dorms, special housing for disabled students, men's dorms, women's dorms, Wellness Housing. 99% of campus accessible to physically disabled. **Special Academic Facilities/Equipment:** Lab school for children with language and learning disabilities, elementary demonstration school, intercultural institute for training and research, language lab.

CAMPUS LIFE

Activities: Choral groups, dance, drama/theater, jazz band, music ensembles, musical theater, student government, student newspaper, symphony orchestra, television station, Campus Ministries.

ADMISSIONS

Freshman Academic Profile: Average high school GPA 3.3. 22% in top 10% of high school class, 49% in top 25% of high school class, 82% in top 50% of high school class. SAT Math middle 50% range 410-513. SAT Critical Reading middle 50% range 400-500. ACT middle 50% range 17-21. Minimum internet-based TOEFL 79. Minimum paper TOEFL 650. **Basis for Candidate Selection:** *Very important factors considered include:* academic GPA, rigor of secondary school record, standardized test scores. *Important factors considered include:* Class rank. *Other factors considered include:* application essay, recommendation(s), alumni/ae relation, character/personal qualities, extracurricular activities, first generation, interview, talent/ability, volunteer work, work experience. **Freshman Admission Requirements:** High school diploma is required and GED is accepted. *Academic units required:* 4 English, 2 mathematics, 2 science, (2 science labs), 3 foreign language, 3 social studies, 3 academic electives. **Freshman Admission Statistics:** 2,109 applied, 49% admitted, 29% enrolled. **Transfer Admission Requirements:** college transcript(s), Minimum college GPA of 2.0 required. Lowest grade transferable D. **General Admission Information:** Application Fee $25. Regular application deadline 7/15. Nonfall registration accepted. Admission may be deferred for a maximum of 1 year. Credit offered for CEEB Advanced Placement tests.

COSTS AND FINANCIAL AID

Annual tuition $22,256. Room and board $7,327. Required fees $581. Average book expense $1,200. **Required Forms and Deadlines:** FAFSA, Institution's own financial aid form. **Notification of Awards:** Applicants will be notified of awards on a rolling basis beginning 4/1. **Types of Aid:** *Need-based scholarships/ grants:* Federal Pell, SEOG, state scholarships/grants, private scholarships, the school's own gift aid. *Loans:* Subsidized Stafford, Unsubsidized Stafford, PLUS, Federal Perkins, state loans, Private Loans. *Student Employment:* Federal Work-Study Program available. Institutional employment available. Highest amount earned per year from on-campus jobs $1,206. Off-campus job opportunities are good. **Financial Aid Statistics:** 99% freshmen, 96% undergrads receive need-based scholarship or grant aid. 3% freshmen, 6% undergrads receive non-need-based scholarship or grant aid. 71% freshmen, 83% undergrads receive need-based self-help aid. 5% freshmen, 7% undergrads receive athletic scholarships. 91% freshmen, 89% undergrads receive any aid. 90% undergrads borrow to pay for school. Average cumulative indebtedness $23,334. **Criteria for awarding institutional aid:** *Non-need-based:* academics, alumni affiliation, art, music/drama.

PACE UNIVERSITY

1 Pace Plaza, New York, NY 10038
Phone: 212-346-1323 · **Financial Aid Phone:** 877-672-1830
E-mail: infoctr@pace.edu · **CEEB Code:** 2635
Fax: 212-346-1040 · **Website:** www.pace.edu · **ACT Code:** 2852

This private school was founded in 1906. It has a 1-acre campus.

RATINGS

Admissions Selectivity Rating: 77   Fire Safety Rating: 85

STUDENTS AND FACULTY
Enrollment: 8,163. **Student Body:** 59% female, 41% male, 41% out-of-state, 9% international (101 countries represented). Asian 9%, African American 11%, Caucasian 50%, Hispanic 15%, Native American <1%
Retention and Graduation: 76% freshmen return for sophomore year. 36% freshmen graduate within 4 years. 55% freshmen graduate within 6 years. 11% grads go on to further study within 1 year. **Faculty:** 471 full-time faculty, 90% hold PhDs, 48% are members of minority groups, 19% are women. 0% of classes are taught by teaching assistants.

ACADEMICS
Degrees: associate, bachelor's, certificate, first professional, first professional certificate, master's, post-bachelor's certificate, post-master's certificate. **Classes:** Most classes have 10–19 students. Most lab/discussion sessions have fewer than 10 students. **Majors with Highest Enrollment:** Finance; Accounting; Registered Nursing/Registered Nurse. **Special Study Options:** Accelerated program, cooperative education program, cross-registration, distance learning, double major, dual enrollment, English as a Second Language (ESL), honors program, independent study, internships, study abroad, teacher certification program, Evening and freshman studies programs, Pre-freshman summer program, Learning Communities and Service Learning. **Honors programs:** Pforzheimer Honors College for incoming freshmen. **Combined degree programs:** BA/JD, BA/MA, BBA/MBA; BA/MPA. **Disability Services:** Special programs offered to physically disabled students include note-taking services, reader services, tape recorders. **Career services:** Alumni network, alumni services, career/job search classes, career assessment, internships, regional alumni. Career services highlights include Cooperative Education/Internship Program.

FACILITIES
Housing: Coed dorms, apartments for single students, apartment style for 3-4 upperclassmen. 100% of campus accessible to physically disabled. **Special Academic Facilities/Equipment:** Laboratory Theatre, Communication Center, Language Center, Center for the Arts, Art Gallery, English Language Institute. **Computers:** 20% of classrooms, 10% of dorms, 100% of libraries, 100% of dining areas, 100% of student union, have wireless network access. Students can register for classes online. Administrative functions (other than registration) can be performed online.

CAMPUS LIFE
Environment: Metropolis. **Activities:** Choral groups, dance, drama/theater, literary magazine, musical theater, radio station, student government, student newspaper, student-run film society, television station, yearbook, International Student Organization, Model UN. 79 registered organizations, 25 honor societies, 4 religious organizations. 11 fraternity, 9 sororities. **Athletics (Intercollegiate):** *Men:* baseball, basketball, cross-country, football, golf, lacrosse, swimming, tennis, track/field (outdoor), track/field (indoor). *Women:* basketball, cheerleading, cross-country, equestrian sports, soccer, softball, swimming, tennis, track/field (outdoor), track/field (indoor), volleyball. **On-Campus Highlights:** Library, Fitness Center, Theater, Classrooms, Dormitories. **Environmental Initiatives:** Environmental Law Program—Pace Law School; Environ-

mental Sciences Program at Dyson College of Arts & Science; New York City Mayoral Challenge and participation with the Clinton Climate Initiative.

ADMISSIONS
Freshman Academic Profile: Average high school GPA 3.22. 14% in top 10% of high school class, 39% in top 25% of high school class, 75% in top 50% of high school class. 75% from public high schools. SAT Math middle 50% range 480-580. SAT Critical Reading middle 50% range 470-570. ACT middle 50% range 20-26. Minimum paper TOEFL 570. **Basis for Candidate Selection:** *Very important factors considered include:* rigor of secondary school record, standardized test scores. *Important factors considered include:* Class rank, academic GPA. *Other factors considered include:* application essay, recommendation(s), alumni/ae relation, character/personal qualities, extracurricular activities, talent/ability, volunteer work, work experience. **Freshman Admission Requirements:** High school diploma is required and GED is accepted. *Academic units required:* 4 English, 3 mathematics, 2 science, (2 science labs), 2 foreign language, 1 social studies, 2 history, 2 academic electives. **Freshman Admission Statistics:** 15,722 applied, 85% admitted, 15% enrolled. **Transfer Admission Requirements:** college transcript(s), statement of good standing from prior institution(s). Minimum college GPA of 2.5 required. Lowest grade transferable C. **General Admission Information:** Application Fee $45. Regular application deadline 3/1. Notification on a rolling basis, beginning on or about 12/15. Nonfall registration accepted. Admission may be deferred for a maximum of 12 months. Credit offered for CEEB Advanced Placement tests.

COSTS AND FINANCIAL AID
Annual tuition $38,200. Room and board $15,774. Required fees $1,497. Average book expense $800. **Required Forms and Deadlines:** FAFSA, State aid form. **Notification of Awards:** Applicants will be notified of awards on a rolling basis beginning 2/25. **Types of Aid:** *Need-based scholarships/grants:* Federal Pell, SEOG, state scholarships/grants, private scholarships, the school's own gift aid, Federal Nursing Scholarships., Endowed and Restricted scholarships and grants. *Loans:* Direct Subsidized Stafford, Direct Unsubsidized Stafford, Direct PLUS, Federal Perkins, Federal Nursing. *Student Employment:* Highest amount earned per year from on-campus jobs $1,564. Off-campus job opportunities are good. **Financial Aid Statistics:** 100% freshmen, 99% undergrads receive need-based scholarship or grant aid. 10% freshmen, 8% undergrads receive non-need-based scholarship or grant aid. 82% freshmen, 82% undergrads receive need-based self-help aid. 0% freshmen, 0% undergrads receive athletic scholarships. 92% freshmen, 85% undergrads receive any aid. 74% undergrads borrow to pay for school. Average cumulative indebtedness $28,084. **Criteria for awarding institutional aid:** *Non-need-based:* academics, athletics, music/drama.

PACIFIC LUTHERAN UNIVERSITY

Office of Admission, Tacoma, WA 98447
Phone: 253-535-7151 · **Financial Aid Phone:** 253-535-7134
E-mail: admissions@plu.edu · **CEEB Code:** 4597
Fax: 253-536-5136 · **Website:** www.plu.edu · **ACT Code:** 4597

This private school, affiliated with the Lutheran Church, was founded in 1890. It has a 126-acre campus.

RATINGS

Admissions Selectivity Rating: 86   Fire Safety Rating: 85

STUDENTS AND FACULTY
Enrollment: 2,907. **Student Body:** 63% female, 37% male, 20% out-of-state, 4% international (25 countries represented). Asian 7%, African American 3%, Caucasian 68%, Hispanic 8%, Native American 1%
Retention and Graduation: 82% freshmen return for sophomore year. 49% freshmen graduate within 4 years. 14% grads go on to further study within 1 year. **Faculty:** 216 full-time faculty, 92% hold PhDs, 50% are members of minority groups, 13% are women. 0% of classes are taught by teaching assistants.

ACADEMICS
Degrees: bachelor's, master's, post-bachelor's certificate, post-master's certificate. **Classes:** Most classes have 20–29 students. Most lab/discussion sessions have 10–19 students. **Majors with Highest Enrollment:** Business Administration and Management; Registered Nursing/Registered Nurse; Biology/Biological Sciences. **Special Study Options:** cooperative education program, cross-registration, double major, dual enrollment, English as a Second Language (ESL), exchange student program (domestic), honors program, independent study, internships, liberal arts/career combination, student-designed major, study abroad, teacher certification program. **Honors programs:** International Honors Program **Combined degree programs:** BA/MEng. **Disability**

Services: Special programs offered to physically disabled students include note-taking services, reader services, tape recorders, tutors. **Career services:** alumni services, career/job search classes, career assessment.

FACILITIES

Housing: Coed dorms, special housing for disabled students, special housing for international students, women's dorms, apartments for married students, apartments for single students, Foreign Languages Learning Housing. 90% of campus accessible to physically disabled. **Special Academic Facilities/Equipment:** Mary Baker Russell Music Center Wekell Art Gallery Keck Observatory Rieke Science Center Scandinavian Cultural Center Morken Center for Learning and Technology **Computers:** 25% of classrooms, 25% of dorms, 100% of libraries, 100% of dining areas, 100% of student union, 25% of common outdoor areas have wireless network access. Students can register for classes online.

CAMPUS LIFE

Environment: City. **Activities:** Choral groups, concert band, dance, drama/theater, jazz band, literary magazine, music ensembles, musical theater, opera, pep band, radio station, student government, student newspaper, student-run film society, symphony orchestra, television station, yearbook, Campus Ministries, International Student Organization. 67 registered organizations, 6 honor societies, 8 religious organizations. **Athletics (Intercollegiate):** *Men:* baseball, basketball, cheerleading, crew/rowing, cross-country, football, golf, soccer, swimming, tennis, track/field (outdoor), track/field (indoor). *Women:* basketball, cheerleading, crew/rowing, cross-country, golf, soccer, softball, swimming, tennis, track/field (outdoor), track/field (indoor), volleyball. **On-Campus Highlights:** Keck Observatory, Rieke Science Center, Mary Baker Russell Music Center, Wekell Art Gallery, Names Fitness Center, Morken Center for Learning and Technology, Scandinavian Cultural Center. **Environmental Initiatives:** Successfully building a community commitment to sustainability that encompasses students, faculty and staff in part through sustainability fellowships. Including environmental goals for waste diversion, reduction of water and electricity consumption, LEED building and carbon neutrality into the campus master plan. PLU is in the leadership circle for the President's Climate Commitment and is planning to meet all goals and deadlines of that commitment.

ADMISSIONS

Freshman Academic Profile: Average high school GPA 3.66. 30% in top 10% of high school class, 63% in top 25% of high school class, 96% in top 50% of high school class. SAT Math middle 50% range 490-600. SAT Critical Reading middle 50% range 490-610. SAT Writing middle 50% range 470-590. ACT middle 50% range 22-29. Minimum internet-based TOEFL 79. Minimum paper TOEFL 550. **Basis for Candidate Selection:** *Very important factors considered include:* application essay, rigor of secondary school record. *Important factors considered include:* Class rank, academic GPA, recommendation(s), standardized test scores, character/personal qualities, extracurricular activities, talent/ability, volunteer work. *Other factors considered include:* interview, work experience. **Freshman Admission Requirements:** High school diploma is required and GED is accepted. *Academic units required:* 2 mathematics, 2 foreign language. **Freshman Admission Statistics:** 3,438 applied, 75% admitted, 22% enrolled. **Transfer Admission Requirements:** High school transcript, college transcript(s), essay or personal statement, statement of good standing from prior institution(s). Minimum college GPA of 2.5 required. Lowest grade transferable C-. **General Admission Information:** Application Fee $40. Notification on a rolling basis, beginning on or about 10/1. Nonfall registration accepted. Admission may be deferred for a maximum of 2 years. Credit and/or placement offered for CEEB Advanced Placement tests.

COSTS AND FINANCIAL AID

Annual tuition $36,180. Room and board $10,230. Required fees $350. Average book expense $1,030. **Required Forms and Deadlines:** FAFSA. **Notification of Awards:** Applicants will be notified of awards on a rolling basis beginning 3/15. **Types of Aid:** *Need-based scholarships/grants:* Federal Pell, SEOG, state scholarships/grants, private scholarships, the school's own gift aid, Federal Nursing Scholarships. *Loans:* Subsidized Stafford, Unsubsidized Stafford, PLUS, Federal Perkins, Federal Nursing, state loans. *Student Employment:* Federal Work-Study Program available. Institutional employment available. Highest amount earned per year from on-campus jobs $13,754. Off-campus job opportunities are good. **Financial Aid Statistics:** 100% freshmen, 99% undergrads receive need-based scholarship or grant aid. 83% freshmen, 84% undergrads receive non-need-based scholarship or grant aid. 85% freshmen, 87% undergrads receive need-based self-help aid. 0% freshmen, 0% undergrads receive athletic scholarships. 99% freshmen, 97% undergrads receive any aid. 73% undergrads borrow to pay for school. Average cumulative indebtedness $27,497. **Criteria for awarding institutional aid:** *Non-need-based:* academics, alumni affiliation, art, leadership, music/drama, religious affiliation.

PACIFIC NORTHWEST COLLEGE OF ART

1241 NW Johnson Street, Portland, OR 97209
Phone: 503-821-8972
E-mail: admissions@pnca.edu • **CEEB Code:** 4504
Fax: 503-821-8978 • **Website:** www.pnca.edu • **ACT Code:** 3477

This private school was founded in 1909. It has a 1-acre campus.

RATINGS

Admissions Selectivity Rating: 73   **Fire Safety Rating:** 66

STUDENTS AND FACULTY

Enrollment: 288. **Student Body:** 59% female, 41% male, 24% out-of-state, 0% international. Asian 3%, African American 1%, Caucasian 92%, Hispanic 3%, Native American 1%
Retention and Graduation: 66% freshmen return for sophomore year. 18% freshmen graduate within 4 years. 33% freshmen graduate within 6 years.
Faculty: 13 full-time faculty, 85% hold PhDs, 38% are members of minority groups, 0% are women. 0% of classes are taught by teaching assistants.

ACADEMICS

Degrees: bachelor's. **Classes:** Most classes have 10–19 students. **Majors with Highest Enrollment:** Design and Visual Communications; Photography; Painting. **Special Study Options:** cross-registration, exchange student program (domestic), independent study, internships, student-designed major, study abroad. **Combined degree programs:** 5-year B.A./B.F.A. program with Reed College. **Career services:** career/job search classes, internships.

FACILITIES

Housing: apartments for single studentsHousing/student dorm available through College Housing Northwest in Portland, Oregon. 100% of campus accessible to physically disabled. **Special Academic Facilities/Equipment:** Student galleries, darkrooms, student painting studios, printmaking studio, computer labs. **Computers:** Administrative functions (other than registration) can be performed online.

CAMPUS LIFE

Environment: Metropolis. **Activities:** student government 2 registered organizations. **On-Campus Highlights:** Stevens Studios, Feldman Gallery.

ADMISSIONS

Freshman Academic Profile: Average high school GPA 2.98. 89% from public high schools. SAT Math middle 50% range 370-590. SAT Critical Reading middle 50% range 440-650. ACT middle 50% range 16-26. Minimum paper TOEFL 550. **Basis for Candidate Selection:** *Very important factors considered include:* academic GPA, talent/ability. *Important factors considered include:* application essay, rigor of secondary school record, extracurricular activities, interview. *Other factors considered include:* recommendation(s), standardized test scores, character/personal qualities, level of applicant's interest. **Freshman Admission Requirements:** High school diploma is required and GED is accepted. **Freshman Admission Statistics:** 120 applied, 73% admitted, 31% enrolled. **Transfer Admission Requirements:** college transcript(s), essay or personal statement, Minimum college GPA of 2.0 required. Lowest grade transferable C. **General Admission Information:** Application Fee $35. Notification on a rolling basis, beginning on or about 1/1. Nonfall registration accepted. Admission may be deferred for a maximum of 2 years. Credit and/or placement offered for CEEB Advanced Placement tests.

COSTS AND FINANCIAL AID

Annual tuition $16,490. Room and board $4,500. Required fees $806. Average book expense $98,500. **Required Forms and Deadlines:** FAFSA. **Notification of Awards:** Applicants will be notified of awards on a rolling basis beginning 4/1. **Types of Aid:** *Need-based scholarships/grants:* Federal Pell, SEOG, state scholarships/grants, private scholarships, the school's own gift aid. *Loans:* Subsidized Stafford, Unsubsidized Stafford, PLUS. *Student Employment:* Highest amount earned per year from on-campus jobs $1,000. **Financial Aid Statistics:** 77% freshmen, 97% undergrads receive need-based scholarship or grant aid. 0% freshmen, 12% undergrads receive non-need-based scholarship or grant aid. 77% freshmen, 97% undergrads receive need-based self-help aid. 0% freshmen, 0% undergrads receive athletic scholarships. 79% undergrads borrow to pay for school. **Criteria for awarding institutional aid:** *Non-need-based:* academics, art.

PACIFIC STATES UNIVERSITY

3450 Wilshire blvd, 5th floor, Los Angeles, CA 90010
Phone: 323-731-2383 EXT:203
E-mail: admissions@psuca.edu
Fax: 323-731-7276 · **Website:** www.psuca.edu

This private school was founded in 1928.

RATINGS

Admissions Selectivity Rating: 64   **Fire Safety Rating:** 60*

STUDENTS AND FACULTY

Enrollment: 14. **Student Body:** 29% female, 71% male, 5% out-of-state, 57% international. Asian 14%, African American 7%, Caucasian 7%, Hispanic 0%, Native American <1%
Retention and Graduation: 100% freshmen return for sophomore year. **Faculty:** 7 full-time faculty, 43% hold PhDs, 29% are members of minority groups.

ACADEMICS

Degrees: bachelor's, doctoral, master's, post-bachelor's certificate. **Special Study Options:** distance learning, double major, English as a Second Language (ESL), independent study.

FACILITIES

Housing: Coed dorms.

CAMPUS LIFE

Environment: Metropolis. **Activities:** television station.

ADMISSIONS

Basis for Candidate Selection: *Important factors considered include:* standardized test scores. *Other factors considered include:* application essay, academic GPA, rigor of secondary school record, level of applicant's interest. **Freshman Admission Requirements:** High school diploma is required and GED is accepted. **Freshman Admission Statistics:** 2 applied, 50% admitted, 100% enrolled. **Transfer Admission Requirements:** college transcript(s), Minimum college GPA of 2.5 required. Lowest grade transferable C. **General Admission Information:** Nonfall registration not accepted.

COSTS AND FINANCIAL AID

Annual tuition $14,055. Room and board $7,200. Required fees $540. Average book expense $1,800. **Required Forms and Deadlines:** FAFSA. **Types of Aid:** *Need-based scholarships/grants:* Federal Pell. *Loans:* Direct Subsidized Stafford, Direct Unsubsidized Stafford.

PACIFIC UNION COLLEGE

Enrollment Services, Angwin, CA 94508
Phone: 707-965-6336 · **Financial Aid Phone:** 707-965-7200
E-mail: enroll@puc.edu · **CEEB Code:** 4600
Fax: 707-965-6671 · **Website:** www.puc.edu · **ACT Code:** 362

This private school, affiliated with the Seventh Day Adventist Church, was founded in 1882. It has a 200-acre campus.

RATINGS

Admissions Selectivity Rating: 83   **Fire Safety Rating:** 82

STUDENTS AND FACULTY

Enrollment: 1,524. **Student Body:** 55% female, 45% male, 18% out-of-state, 3% international (21 countries represented). Asian 19%, African American 7%, Caucasian 29%, Hispanic 24%, Native American 1%
Retention and Graduation: 78% freshmen return for sophomore year. 23% freshmen graduate within 4 years. **Faculty:** 92 full-time faculty, 50% hold PhDs, 49% are members of minority groups, 33% are women. 0% of classes are taught by teaching assistants.

ACADEMICS

Degrees: associate, bachelor's, master's. **Classes:** Most classes have fewer than 10 students. Most lab/discussion sessions have fewer than 10 students. **Majors with Highest Enrollment:** Registered Nursing/Registered Nurse; Business/Commerce; Biology/Biological Sciences. **Special Study Options:** cooperative education program, double major, external degree program, honors program, independent study, internships, study abroad, teacher certification program.
Honors programs: The Honors Program offers an alternative general-education program for academically motivated students. There are no other general

education requirements. Students fulfilling the Honors Program graduate "With Honors." **Disability Services:** Special programs offered to physically disabled students include note-taking services, reader services, tape recorders, tutors. **Career services:** career/job search classes, career assessment, internships. Career services highlights include a Spring break externship program available to anyone that preregisters.

FACILITIES

Housing: men's dorms, women's dorms, apartments for married students. 80% of campus accessible to physically disabled. **Special Academic Facilities/Equipment:** Art gallery, natural history collection, Pitcairn Island studies center, on-campus elementary and high schools, airport, flight training facility, observatory. **Computers:** Students can register for classes online. Administrative functions (other than registration) can be performed online.

CAMPUS LIFE

Environment: Rural. **Activities:** Choral groups, concert band, drama/theater, jazz band, literary magazine, music ensembles, musical theater, radio station, student government, student newspaper, student-run film society, symphony orchestra, yearbook. 24 registered organizations, 8 honor societies. **Athletics (Intercollegiate):** *Men:* basketball, cross-country, volleyball. *Women:* basketball, cross-country, volleyball. **On-Campus Highlights:** Campus Center, Clark Hall/Museum, Pacific Auditorium (Gym), Paulin Auditorium (Music), 1500 acres of hiking/biking land. **Environmental Initiatives:** Buy Locally (50%); Water and Energy Conservation Efforts (clean co-generation power plant, landscaping water conservation system, etc.); Biology Club participation in Lake Berryessa Conservation Efforts.

ADMISSIONS

Freshman Academic Profile: Average high school GPA 3.33. 31% from public high schools. SAT Math middle 50% range 420–580. SAT Critical Reading middle 50% range 440–590. SAT Writing middle 50% range 440–560. ACT middle 50% range 18–24. Minimum internet-based TOEFL 70. Minimum paper TOEFL 525. **Basis for Candidate Selection:** *Very important factors considered include:* recommendation(s), rigor of secondary school record. *Important factors considered include:* academic GPA, character/personal qualities, level of applicant's interest. *Other factors considered include:* standardized test scores, extracurricular activities, interview, religious affiliation/commitment. **Freshman Admission Requirements:** High school diploma is required and GED is accepted. *Academic units required:* 4 English, 2 mathematics, 1 science, 1 history. **Freshman Admission Statistics:** 2,105 applied, 47% admitted, 29% enrolled. **Transfer Admission Requirements:** High school transcript, college transcript(s), Minimum college GPA of 2.0 required. Lowest grade transferable C-. **General Admission Information:** Application Fee $30. Notification on a rolling basis, beginning on or about 1/15. Nonfall registration accepted. Admission may be deferred for a maximum of 1 year. Credit offered for CEEB Advanced Placement tests.

COSTS AND FINANCIAL AID

Annual tuition $26,550. Room and board $7,485. Required fees $300. Average book expense $1,710. **Required Forms and Deadlines:** FAFSA, Institution's own financial aid form. **Types of Aid:** *Need-based scholarships/grants:* Federal Pell, SEOG, state scholarships/grants, the school's own gift aid. *Loans:* Subsidized Stafford, Unsubsidized Stafford, PLUS, Federal Perkins, college/university loans from institutional funds. *Student Employment:* Federal Work-Study Program available. Institutional employment available. Highest amount earned per year from on-campus jobs $3,000. Off-campus job opportunities are fair. **Financial Aid Statistics:** 100% freshmen, 100% undergrads receive need-based scholarship or grant aid. 23% freshmen, 36% undergrads receive non-need-based scholarship or grant aid. 96% freshmen, 97% undergrads receive need-based self-help aid. 2% freshmen, 0% undergrads receive athletic scholarships. 76% undergrads borrow to pay for school. Average cumulative indebtedness $22,897. **Criteria for awarding institutional aid:** *Non-need-based:* academics, leadership, religious affiliation.

PACIFIC UNIVERSITY

2043 College Way, Forest Grove, OR 97116
Phone: 503-352-2218 · **Financial Aid Phone:** 503-352-2222
E-mail: admissions@pacificu.edu · **CEEB Code:** 4601
Website: www.pacificu.edu

This private school was founded in 1849. It has a 60-acre campus.

RATINGS

Admissions Selectivity Rating: 87   **Fire Safety Rating:** 74

STUDENTS AND FACULTY

Enrollment: 1,555. **Student Body:** 58% female, 42% male, 47% out-of-state, 2% international (32 countries represented). Asian 14%, African American 2%, Caucasian 56%, Hispanic 8%, Native American 1%
Retention and Graduation: 75% freshmen return for sophomore year. 51% freshmen graduate within 4 years. 61% freshmen graduate within 6 years. 24% grads go on to further study within 1 year. 11% grads pursue arts and sciences degrees. 4% grads pursue law degrees. 2% grads pursue business degrees. 2% grads pursue medical degrees. **Faculty:** 216 full-time faculty, 87% hold PhDs, 51% are members of minority groups, 13% are women. 0% of classes are taught by teaching assistants.

ACADEMICS

Degrees: bachelor's, master's. **Classes:** Most classes have 10–19 students. Most lab/discussion sessions have 10–19 students. **Majors with Highest Enrollment:** Kinesiology and Exercise Science; Business Administration and Management; Biology/Biological Sciences. **Special Study Options:** cross-registration, double major, English as a Second Language (ESL), independent study, internships, liberal arts/career combination, study abroad, teacher certification program. **Combined degree programs:** 3-2 applied physics program and 4-1 computer scien. **Disability Services:** Special programs offered to physically disabled students include note-taking services, reader services, tape recorders, tutors. **Career services:** Alumni network, alumni services, career/job search classes, career assessment, internships, regional alumni. Career services highlights include internships.

FACILITIES

Housing: Coed dorms, special housing for disabled students, apartments for single students, Theme Housing1 wing designated female. **Special Academic Facilities/Equipment:** State history museum, performing arts center, media center, humanitarian center, Holocaust resource center, politics/law forum, Berglund Center for Internet Studies, electron microscopes. **Computers:** 100% of classrooms, 100% of dorms, 100% of libraries, 100% of dining areas, 100% of student union, 90% of common outdoor areas have wireless network access. Administrative functions (other than registration) can be performed online.

CAMPUS LIFE

Environment: Village. **Activities:** Choral groups, concert band, dance, drama/theater, jazz band, literary magazine, music ensembles, pep band, radio station, student government, student newspaper, student-run film society, Campus Ministries, International Student Organization. 58 registered organizations, 2 honor societies, 4 religious organizations. 3 fraternities, 4 sororities. **Athletics (Intercollegiate):** *Men:* baseball, basketball, cross-country, golf, soccer, swimming, tennis, track/field (outdoor), wrestling. *Women:* basketball, cross-country, golf, lacrosse, soccer, softball, swimming, tennis, track/field (outdoor), volleyball, wrestling. **On-Campus Highlights:** Pacific Athletic Center, Pacific Library (New Library), Marsh Hall, Old College Hall, New Bookstore/Vera's Café. **Environmental Initiatives:** Sustainability Committee; New LEED-certified buildings; B-Street Permaculture Project.

ADMISSIONS

Freshman Academic Profile: Average high school GPA 3.62. 34% in top 10% of high school class, 66% in top 25% of high school class, 92% in top 50% of high school class. 88% from public high schools. SAT Math middle 50% range 510-610. SAT Critical Reading middle 50% range 490-600. ACT middle 50% range 21-26. Minimum paper TOEFL 550. **Basis for Candidate Selection:** *Very important factors considered include:* academic GPA, recommendation(s), rigor of secondary school record, standardized test scores, character/personal qualities, extracurricular activities, level of applicant's interest, volunteer work. *Important factors considered include:* Class rank, application essay, talent/ability. *Other factors considered include:* alumni/ae relation, first generation, work experience. **Freshman Admission Requirements:** High school diploma is required and GED is accepted. **Freshman Admission Statistics:** 2,499 applied, 75% admitted, 20% enrolled. **Transfer Admission Requirements:** college transcript(s), essay or personal statement, statement of good standing from prior institution(s). Minimum college GPA of 2.70 required. Lowest grade transferable C-. **General Admission Information:** Application Fee $40. Regular application deadline 8/15. Notification on a rolling basis, beginning on or about 10/1. Nonfall registration accepted. Admission may be deferred for a maximum of 2 years. Credit and/or placement offered for CEEB Advanced Placement tests.

COSTS AND FINANCIAL AID

Annual tuition $34,460. Room and board $9,992. Required fees $800. Average book expense $1,050. **Required Forms and Deadlines:** FAFSA. **Notification of Awards:** Applicants will be notified of awards on a rolling basis beginning 3/1. **Types of Aid:** *Need-based scholarships/grants:* Federal Pell, SEOG, state scholarships/grants, private scholarships, the school's own gift aid. *Loans:* Subsidized Stafford, Unsubsidized Stafford, PLUS, Federal Perkins, Private Alternative Loans. *Student Employment:* Federal Work-Study Program available. Institutional employment available. **Financial Aid Statistics:** 97% freshmen, 94% undergrads receive need-based scholarship or grant aid. 8% freshmen, 7% undergrads receive non-need-based scholarship or grant aid. 86% freshmen,

88% undergrads receive need-based self-help aid. 0% freshmen, 0% undergrads receive athletic scholarships. 93% freshmen, 93% undergrads receive any aid. 74% undergrads borrow to pay for school. Average cumulative indebtedness $23,770. **Criteria for awarding institutional aid:** *Non-need-based:* academics, alumni affiliation, art, music/drama.

PALM BEACH ATLANTIC UNIVERSITY

PO Box 24708, West Palm Beach, FL 33416-4708
Phone: 561-803-2100 · **Financial Aid Phone:** 561-803-2126
E-mail: admit@pba.edu · **CEEB Code:** 5553
Fax: 561-803-2115 · **Website:** www.pba.edu · **ACT Code:** 739

This private school, affiliated with the Christian (Nondenominational) Church, was founded in 1968. It has a 25-acre campus.

RATINGS

Admissions Selectivity Rating: 71   **Fire Safety Rating:** 60*

STUDENTS AND FACULTY

Enrollment: 2,585. **Student Body:** 66% female, 34% male, 36% out-of-state, 4% international (28 countries represented). Asian 1%, African American 13%, Caucasian 61%, Hispanic 17%, Native American <1%
Retention and Graduation: 74% freshmen return for sophomore year. 43% freshmen graduate within 4 years. **Faculty:** 163 full-time faculty, 80% hold PhDs, 46% are members of minority groups, 18% are women. 0% of classes are taught by teaching assistants.

ACADEMICS

Degrees: associate, bachelor's, master's. **Classes:** Most classes have 10–19 students. Most lab/discussion sessions have 10–19 students. **Majors with Highest Enrollment:** Psychology; Accounting and Business/Management; Education. **Special Study Options:** Accelerated program, distance learning, double major, dual enrollment, honors program, independent study, internships, student-designed major, study abroad, teacher certification program. **Honors programs:** The Frederick M. Supper Honors Program exists to establish a community of scholars. The program encourages students to develop a thoughtful and insightful Christian worldview through enduring conversation to enable students to live the examined life and to facilitate character formation. **Combined degree programs:** BA/MA. **Career services:** alumni services, career/job search classes, career assessment, internships. Career services highlights include The Workship program, a distinctive service program at PBA which enables students to offer a Christian response to human needs by serving in nonprofit agencies, churches, and schools outside the university community.

FACILITIES

Housing: Coed dorms, men's dorms, women's dorms, apartments for married students, Theme Housing **Special Academic Facilities/Equipment:** DeSantis Family Chapel; Greene Sports Complex (Café); Helen K.Persson Recital Hall. **Computers:** Students can register for classes online. Administrative functions (other than registration) can be performed online.

CAMPUS LIFE

Environment: Metropolis. **Activities:** Choral groups, dance, drama/theater, jazz band, literary magazine, music ensembles, musical theater, pep band, radio station, student government, student newspaper, symphony orchestra, television station, yearbook, Campus Ministries, International Student Organization. 56 registered organizations, 29 honor societies, 6 religious organizations. **Athletics (Intercollegiate):** *Men:* baseball, basketball, cross-country, soccer, tennis. *Women:* basketball, cross-country, soccer, softball, tennis, volleyball. **On-Campus Highlights:** DeSantis Family Chapel, Greene Complex (athletics, snack shop), Vera Lea Rinker Music Building.

ADMISSIONS

Freshman Academic Profile: Average high school GPA 3.59. SAT Math middle 50% range 460-568. SAT Critical Reading middle 50% range 470-590. SAT Writing middle 50% range 450-560. ACT middle 50% range 21-27. Minimum paper TOEFL 550. Basis for Candidate Selection: Very important factors considered include: academic GPA, standardized test scores, character/personal qualities. Important factors considered include: application essay, recommendation(s), rigor of secondary school record, interview. Other factors considered include: Class rank, alumni/ae relation, extracurricular activities, religious affiliation/commitment, talent/ability, volunteer work. Freshman Admission Requirements: High school diploma is required and GED is accepted. Academic units required: 4 English, 3 mathematics, 4 science, (2 science labs), 0 foreign language. Freshman Admission Statistics: 1,564 applied, 95% admitted, 35% enrolled. Transfer Admission Requirements: college transcript(s), essay or personal statement, Minimum college GPA of 2.5 required. Lowest grade transferable C. General Admission Information: Notification on a rolling basis, beginning on or about 9/1. Nonfall registration accepted. Admission may be deferred for a maximum of 1 year. Credit offered for CEEB Advanced Placement tests. COSTS AND FINANCIAL AID Annual tuition $25,974. Room and board $8,600. Required fees $300. Average book expense $980. **Required Forms and Deadlines:** FAFSA, State aid form. **Notification of Awards:** Applicants will be notified of awards on a rolling basis beginning 2/15. **Types of Aid:** *Need-based scholarships/grants:* Federal Pell, SEOG, state scholarships/grants, private scholarships, the school's own gift aid. *Loans:* Subsidized Stafford, Unsubsidized Stafford, PLUS. *Student Employment:* Federal Work-Study Program available. Institutional employment available. Off-campus job opportunities are good. **Financial Aid Statistics:** 100% freshmen, 99% undergrads receive need-based scholarship or grant aid. 18% freshmen, 13% undergrads receive non-need-based scholarship or grant aid. 62% freshmen, 72% undergrads receive need-based self-help aid. 3% freshmen, 4% undergrads receive athletic scholarships. 100% freshmen, 100% undergrads receive any aid. 68% undergrads borrow to pay for school. Average cumulative indebtedness $23,775. **Criteria for awarding institutional aid:** *Non-need-based:* academics, alumni affiliation, athletics, minority status, music/drama, state/district residency.

PARK UNIVERSITY

8700 NW River Park Drive, Parkville, MO 64152
Phone: 816-584-6213 · **Financial Aid Phone:** 816-548-6290
E-mail: admissions@mail.park.edu · **CEEB Code:** 6574
Fax: 816-741-4462 · **ACT Code:** 2340

This private school was founded in 1875. It has a 700-acre campus.

RATINGS

Admissions Selectivity Rating: 77   **Fire Safety Rating:** 70

STUDENTS AND FACULTY

Enrollment: 1,672. **Student Body:** 56% female, 44% male, 20% out-of-state, 19% international (93 countries represented). Asian 0%, African American 10%, Caucasian 61%, Hispanic 5%, Native American 1%. **Retention and Graduation:** 61% freshmen return for sophomore year. 22% freshmen graduate within 4 years. 39% freshmen graduate within 6 years. 7% grads go on to further study within 1 year. 6% grads pursue arts and sciences degrees. 1% grads pursue business degrees. **Faculty:** 82 full-time faculty, 66% hold PhDs, 38% are members of minority groups, 4% are women. 0% of classes are taught by teaching assistants.

ACADEMICS

Degrees: associate, bachelor's, master's, post-bachelor's certificate. **Majors with Highest Enrollment:** Business Administration and Management; Education; Computer and Information Sciences. **Special Study Options:** Accelerated program, cross-registration, distance learning, double major, dual enrollment, English as a Second Language (ESL), honors program, independent study, internships, student-designed major, study abroad, teacher certification program, weekend college. **Disability Services:** Special programs offered to physically disabled students include note-taking services, reader services, tape recorders, tutors.

FACILITIES

Housing: Coed dorms, apartments for married students. 90% of campus accessible to physically disabled. **Computers:** Students can register for classes online. Administrative functions (other than registration) can be performed online.

CAMPUS LIFE

Environment: Town. **Activities:** Choral groups, drama/theater, literary magazine, radio station, student government, student newspaper, symphony orchestra, yearbook. 15 registered organizations, 4 honor societies, 13 religious organizations. **Athletics (Intercollegiate):** *Men:* baseball, basketball, cross-country, soccer, track/field (outdoor), track/field (indoor), volleyball. *Women:* basketball, cross-country, golf, soccer, softball, track/field (outdoor), track/field (indoor), volleyball. **On-Campus Highlights:** Gym, Cafeteria, Classrooms (Underground), Library, Bookstore.

ADMISSIONS

Freshman Academic Profile: Average high school GPA 3.3. 14% in top 10% of high school class, 37% in top 25% of high school class, 68% in top 50% of high school class. 80% from public high schools. ACT middle 50% range 17-23. Minimum paper TOEFL 500. **Basis for Candidate Selection:** *Very important factors considered include:* Class rank, rigor of secondary school record, standardized test scores. *Other factors considered include:* application essay, recommendation(s). **Freshman Admission Requirements:** High school diploma is required and GED is accepted. **Freshman Admission Statistics:** 778 applied, 69% admitted, 39% enrolled. **Transfer Admission Requirements:** High school transcript, college transcript(s), Minimum college GPA of

2.0 required. Lowest grade transferable C. **General Admission Information:** Application Fee $25. Regular application deadline 7/1. Nonfall registration accepted. Admission may be deferred for a maximum of Maximum of 1 year. Credit and/or placement offered for CEEB Advanced Placement tests.

COSTS AND FINANCIAL AID

Annual tuition $10,380. Room and board $7,045. Required fees $100. Average book expense $1,800. **Required Forms and Deadlines:** FAFSA, Institution's own financial aid form. **Types of Aid:** *Need-based scholarships/grants:* Federal Pell, SEOG, state scholarships/grants, private scholarships, the school's own gift aid. *Loans:* Subsidized Stafford, Unsubsidized Stafford, PLUS, Federal Perkins, college/university loans from institutional funds. *Student Employment:* Federal Work-Study Program available. **Financial Aid Statistics:** 78% freshmen, 73% undergrads receive need-based scholarship or grant aid. 75% freshmen, 52% undergrads receive non-need-based scholarship or grant aid. 56% freshmen, 70% undergrads receive need-based self-help aid. 17% freshmen, 11% undergrads receive athletic scholarships. 78% freshmen receive any aid. 41% undergrads borrow to pay for school. Average cumulative indebtedness $21,630. **Criteria for awarding institutional aid:** *Non-need-based:* academics, alumni affiliation, art, athletics, job skills, leadership, minority status, music/drama, religious affiliation.

PARSONS—THE NEW SCHOOL FOR DESIGN

72 Fifth Avenue, New York, NY 10011
Phone: 212-229-5150 · **Financial Aid Phone:** 212-229-8930
E-mail: thinkparsons@newschool.edu · **CEEB Code:** 2638
Website: www.parsons.edu · **ACT Code:** 2854

This private school was founded in 1896.

RATINGS

Admissions Selectivity Rating: 85   **Fire Safety Rating:** 79

STUDENTS AND FACULTY

Enrollment: 4,322. **Student Body:** 79% female, 21% male, 73% out-of-state, 41% international (95 countries represented). Asian 14%, African American 4%, Caucasian 27%, Hispanic 9%, Native American <1%. **Retention and Graduation:** 87% freshmen return for sophomore year. 55% freshmen graduate within 4 years. 12% grads go on to further study within 1 year. **Faculty:** Student/faculty ratio :1. 160 full-time faculty, 58% hold PhDs, 48% are are members of minority groups, 15% are women. % of classes are taught by teaching assistants.

ACADEMICS

Degrees: associate, bachelor's, certificate, master's. **Classes:** Most classes have 10-19 students. Most lab/discussion sessions have 20-29 students. **Special Study Options:** Accelerated program, cross-registration, distance learning, double major, dual enrollment, English as a Second Language (ESL), exchange student program (domestic), independent study, internships, liberal arts/career combination, student-designed major, study abroad, Five Year combined BA/BFA. **Combined degree programs:** BA/BFA, MA/ARC. **Disability Services:** Special programs offered to physically disabled students include note-taking services, reader services, tape recorders. **Career services:** Alumni network, alumni services, career/job search classes, career assessment, internships, regional alumni.

FACILITIES

Housing: Coed dorms, special housing for disabled students, apartments for single students 99% of campus accessible to physically disabled. **Special Academic Facilities/Equipment:** Fashion Education Center in New York's garment district with labs and studios for fashion design students. **Computers:** 95% of classrooms, 100% of libraries, 100% of dining areas, na% of student union, 100% of common outdoor areas have wireless network access. Students can register for classes online. Administrative functions (other than registration) can be performed online.

CAMPUS LIFE

Environment: Metropolis. **Activities:** Choral groups, dance, drama/theater, jazz band, literary magazine, music ensembles, radio station, student government, student newspaper, symphony orchestra, International Student Organization. 34 registered organizations. **On-Campus Highlights:** Sheila Johnson Design Center, Schwartz Fashion Center, University Welcome Center. **Environmental Initiatives:** In Fall 2010, The New School Facilities Management hired an engineering firm to conduct energy audits and to retro-commission five of the most energy-intensive owned buildings on campus. The New School Office for Sustainability hired a consultant to conduct a waste audit of the entire campus in Fall 2009. A waste reduction strategy is currently being finalized. Built in 1930, the university's founding building was upgraded to house two new steam dual-fuel boilers with a thermal efficiency of 86 percent and the option to burn #2 heating oil or, eventually, natural gas, the least carbon intensive fossil fuel in 2010.

ADMISSIONS

Freshman Academic Profile: Average high school GPA 3.24. 18% in top 10% of high school class, 41% in top 25% of high school class, 74% in top 50% of high school class. N/a% from public high schools. SAT Math middle 50% range 480-630. SAT Critical Reading middle 50% range 480-590. SAT Writing middle 50% range 470-610. ACT middle 50% range 21.5-26.5. Minimum internet-based TOEFL 79. **Basis for Candidate Selection:** *Very important factors considered include:* academic GPA, rigor of secondary school record, standardized test scores, level of applicant's interest, talent/ability. *Important factors considered include:* interview. *Other factors considered include:* Class rank, application essay, recommendation(s), extracurricular activities. **Freshman Admission Requirements:** High school diploma is required and GED is accepted. **Freshman Admission Statistics:** 2,501 applied, 61% admitted, 40% enrolled. **Transfer Admission Requirements:** college transcript(s), Minimum college GPA of 2.0 required. Lowest grade transferable C. **General Admission Information:** Application Fee $50. Notification on a rolling basis, beginning on or about 3/21. Nonfall registration accepted. Admission may be deferred for a maximum of 1 year. Neither credit nor placement offered for CEEB Advanced Placement tests.

COSTS AND FINANCIAL AID

Annual tuition $40,660. Room and board $18,490. Required fees $866. Average book expense $2,050. **Required Forms and Deadlines:** FAFSA, State aid form. **Notification of Awards:** Applicants will be notified of awards on a rolling basis beginning 3/1. **Types of Aid:** *Need-based scholarships/grants:* Federal Pell, SEOG, state scholarships/grants, private scholarships, the school's own gift aid. *Loans:* Subsidized Stafford, Unsubsidized Stafford, PLUS, Federal Perkins. *Student Employment:* Federal Work-Study Program available. Institutional employment available. Off-campus job opportunities are excellent. **Financial Aid Statistics:** 96% freshmen, 96% undergrads receive need-based scholarship or grant aid. 10% freshmen, 14% undergrads receive non-need-based scholarship or grant aid. 96% freshmen, 95% undergrads receive need-based self-help aid. 0% freshmen, 0% undergrads receive athletic scholarships. 57% undergrads borrow to pay for school. Average cumulative indebtedness $22,052. **Criteria for awarding institutional aid:** *Non-need-based:* academics, art.

PATRICK HENRY COLLEGE

10 Patrick Henry Circle, Purcellville, VA 20132
Financial Aid Phone: 540-441-8142
E-mail: admissions@phc.edu • **CEEB Code:** 2804
Fax: 540-441-8119 • **Website:** www.phc.edu • **ACT Code:** 4383

This private school, affiliated with the Christian (Nondenominational) Church, was founded in 2000. It has a 106-acre campus.

RATINGS

Admissions Selectivity Rating: 78   **Fire Safety Rating:** 83

STUDENTS AND FACULTY

Enrollment: 326. **Student Body:** 48% female, 52% male, 83% out-of-state. Asian 2%, African American 1%, Caucasian 84%, Hispanic 3%, Native American <1%
Retention and Graduation: 50% freshmen graduate within 4 years. 62% freshmen graduate within 6 years. 10% grads go on to further study within 1 year. 23% grads pursue law degrees. **Faculty:** 20 full-time faculty, 95% hold PhDs, 5% are members of minority groups. 0% of classes are taught by teaching assistants.

ACADEMICS

Degrees: bachelor's. **Classes:** Most classes have fewer than 10 students. **Majors with Highest Enrollment:** Political Science and Government; Journalism; Business/Managerial Economics. **Special Study Options:** distance learning, liberal arts/career combination. **Disability Services:** Special programs offered to physically disabled students include tutors. **Career services:** internships.

FACILITIES

Housing: men's dorms, women's dorms. 100% of campus accessible to physically disabled. **Computers:** 100% of classrooms, 100% of dorms, 100% of libraries, 100% of dining areas, 100% of student union, 100% of common outdoor areas have wireless network access. Students can register for classes online. Administrative functions (other than registration) can be performed online. Undergraduates are required to own a computer.

CAMPUS LIFE

Environment: Village. **Activities:** Choral groups, concert band, drama/theater, literary magazine, music ensembles, student government, student newspaper, student-run film society, yearbook, Campus Ministries, Model UN. **Athletics (Intercollegiate):** *Men:* basketball, soccer. *Women:* basketball, soccer. **On-Campus Highlights:** Student Coffee Lounge, Workout facilities, Raquetball courts. **Environmental Initiatives:** water conservation, energy management, recycling.

ADMISSIONS

Freshman Academic Profile: Average high school GPA 3.83. 20% from public high schools. SAT Math middle 50% range 550-660. SAT Critical Reading middle 50% range 630-740. SAT Writing middle 50% range 585-710. ACT middle 50% range 26-30. **Basis for Candidate Selection:** *Very important factors considered include:* application essay, academic GPA, recommendation(s), rigor of secondary school record, standardized test scores, character/personal qualities, extracurricular activities, interview, religious affiliation/commitment, talent/ability, volunteer work. *Important factors considered include:* level of applicant's interest. *Other factors considered include:* Class rank, alumni/ae relation, first generation, work experience. **Freshman Admission Requirements:** High school diploma is required and GED is accepted. *Academic units required:* 4 English, 3 mathematics, 2 science, 1 foreign language, 3 history, 5 academic electives. **Freshman Admission Statistics:** 227 applied, 95% admitted, 37% enrolled. **Transfer Admission Requirements:** High school transcript, college transcript(s), essay or personal statement, interview, standardized test scores, statement of good standing from prior institution(s). Lowest grade transferable C. **General Admission Information:** Application Fee $40. Regular application deadline 6/15. Notification on a rolling basis, beginning on or about 10/1. Nonfall registration accepted. Admission may be deferred for a maximum of one year. Credit and/or placement offered for CEEB Advanced Placement tests.

COSTS AND FINANCIAL AID

Annual tuition $26,848. Room and board $10,728. Required fees $200. Average book expense $1,000. **Required Forms and Deadlines:** CSS/Financial Aid PROFILE. **Types of Aid:** *Need-based scholarships/grants:* private scholarships, the school's own gift aid. *Loans:* private loans. *Student Employment:* Institutional employment available. Highest amount earned per year from on-campus jobs $2,880. Off-campus job opportunities are good. **Financial Aid Statistics:** 100% freshmen, 100% undergrads receive need-based scholarship or grant aid. 63% freshmen, 72% undergrads receive non-need-based scholarship or grant aid. 100% freshmen, 100% undergrads receive need-based self-help aid. 0% freshmen, 0% undergrads receive athletic scholarships. 94% freshmen, 94% undergrads receive any aid. 43% undergrads borrow to pay for school. Average cumulative indebtedness $0. **Criteria for awarding institutional aid:** *Non-need-based:* academics, leadership, music/drama.

THE PENNSYLVANIA ACADEMY OF THE FINE ARTS

128 North Broad Street, Philadelphia, PA 19102
Phone: 215-972-7625 • **Financial Aid Phone:** 215-972-2019
E-mail: admissions@pafa.edu
Fax: 215-569-0153 • **Website:** www.pafa.edu

This private school was founded in 1804.

RATINGS

Admissions Selectivity Rating: 60*   **Fire Safety Rating:** 60*

STUDENTS AND FACULTY

Student Body: 25% out-of-state, (19 countries represented).
Faculty: 0% of classes are taught by teaching assistants.

ACADEMICS

Degrees: bachelor's, certificate, master's, post-bachelor's certificate. **Majors with Highest Enrollment:** Painting; Fine/Studio Arts. **Special Study Options:** dual enrollment, exchange student program (domestic), independent study, internships. **Combined degree programs:** BFA in conjunction with the University of Pennsylvania.

FACILITIES

Housing: The Pennsylvania Academy has a housing arrangement with International House, Philadelphia. We do not offer our own on-campus housing opportunities.

CAMPUS LIFE

Environment: Metropolis. **Activities:** student government. 4 registered organizations. **On-Campus Highlights:** Museum of American Art, World Famous Cast Hall.

ADMISSIONS

Freshman Academic Profile: Minimum internet-based TOEFL 100. Minimum paper TOEFL 600. **Basis for Candidate Selection:** *Very important factors considered include:* application essay, academic GPA. *Important factors considered include:* interview. *Other factors considered include:* recommendation(s), standardized test scores. **Freshman Admission Requirements:** High school diploma is required and GED is accepted. **Transfer Admission Requirements:** High school transcript, essay or personal statement, Lowest grade transferable C. **General Admission Information:** Notification on a rolling basis, beginning on or about 9/15. Neither credit nor placement offered for CEEB Advanced Placement tests.

COSTS AND FINANCIAL AID

Annual tuition $28,930. Room and board $6,800. Required fees $1,450. Average book expense $1,314. **Required Forms and Deadlines:** FAFSA. **Types of Aid:** *Need-based scholarships/grants:* Federal Pell, SEOG, state scholarships/grants, private scholarships, the school's own gift aid. *Loans:* Subsidized Stafford, Unsubsidized Stafford, PLUS. *Student Employment:* Federal Work-Study Program available. Institutional employment available. Highest amount earned per year from on-campus jobs $5,000. Off-campus job opportunities are excellent. **Financial Aid Statistics:** 80% freshmen, 80% undergrads receive any aid. **Criteria for awarding institutional aid:** *Non-need-based:* academics.

PENNSYLVANIA COLLEGE OF TECHNOLOGY

One College Avenue, Williamsport, PA 17701
Phone: 570-327-4761 · **Financial Aid Phone:** 570-327-4766
E-mail: admissions@pct.edu
Fax: 570-321-5551 · **Website:** www.pct.edu

This public school was founded in 1989. It has a 984-acre campus.

RATINGS

Admissions Selectivity Rating: 60*   **Fire Safety Rating:** 76

STUDENTS AND FACULTY

Enrollment: 5,599. **Student Body:** 37% female, 63% male, 11% out-of-state, 1% international. Asian 1%, African American 4%, Caucasian 84%, Hispanic 3%, Native American <1%.
Retention and Graduation: 67% freshmen return for sophomore year. **Faculty:** 294 full-time faculty, 31% are members of minority groups, 6% are women. 0% of classes are taught by teaching assistants.

ACADEMICS

Degrees: associate, bachelor's, certificate, transfer associate. **Special Study Options:** Accelerated program, cooperative education program, cross-registration, distance learning, dual enrollment, exchange student program (domestic), honors program, independent study, internships, student-designed major, study abroad, weekend college. **Disability Services:** Special programs offered to physically disabled students include note-taking services, reader services, tape recorders, tutors. **Career services:** alumni services. For career services highlights see www.pct.edu/careerservices/.

FACILITIES

Housing: Coed dorms, apartments for single students, Wellness Housing. 100% of campus accessible to physically disabled. **Computers:** Students can register for classes online. Administrative functions (other than registration) can be performed online.

CAMPUS LIFE

Environment: Town. **Activities:** dance, radio station, student government, Campus Ministries. 50 registered organizations, 3 honor societies, 4 religious organizations. 3 fraternities. **Athletics (Intercollegiate):** *Men:* archery, baseball, basketball, bowling, cross-country, golf, soccer, tennis, volleyball. *Women:* archery, basketball, bowling, cross-country, golf, soccer, softball, tennis, volleyball. **On-Campus Highlights:** Academic Facilities, Madigan Library, Campus Center, Student & Administrative Services Center, Academic Center.

ADMISSIONS

Freshman Academic Profile: Minimum paper TOEFL 500. **Basis for Candidate Selection:** *Very important factors considered include:* academic GPA, standardized test scores. *Important factors considered include:* application essay. *Other factors considered include:* recommendation(s), rigor of secondary

school record. **Freshman Admission Requirements:** High school diploma is required and GED is accepted. **Freshman Admission Statistics:** 3,598 applied, 88% admitted, 38% enrolled. **Transfer Admission Requirements:** High school transcript, college transcript(s), Minimum college GPA of 2.5 required. Lowest grade transferable C. **General Admission Information:** Application Fee $50. Regular application deadline 8/1. Nonfall registration accepted. Admission may be deferred for a maximum of One year. Credit offered for CEEB Advanced Placement tests.

COSTS AND FINANCIAL AID

Annual in-state tuition $12,000. Annual out-of-state tuition $15,630. Room and board $10,500. Required fees $2,370. Average book expense $1,200. **Required Forms and Deadlines:** FAFSA, Institution's own financial aid form. **Notification of Awards:** Applicants will be notified of awards on a rolling basis beginning 3/1. **Types of Aid:** *Need-based scholarships/grants:* Federal Pell, state scholarships/grants, private scholarships, the school's own gift aid. *Loans:* Subsidized Stafford, Unsubsidized Stafford, PLUS. *Student Employment:* Institutional employment available. Highest amount earned per year from on-campus jobs $8,268. Off-campus job opportunities are good. **Criteria for awarding institutional aid:** *Non-need-based:* academics, alumni affiliation, leadership.

PENNSYLVANIA STATE UNIVERSITY— ABINGTON

1600 Woodland Rd, Abington, PA 19001
Phone: 215-881-7600
E-mail: abingtonadmissions@psu.edu
Fax: 215-881-7655 · **Website:** abington.psu.edu

This public school was founded in 1950. It has a 45-acre campus.

RATINGS

Admissions Selectivity Rating: 73   **Fire Safety Rating:** 60*

STUDENTS AND FACULTY

Enrollment: 3,505. **Student Body:** 51% female, 49% male, 7% out-of-state, 5% international. Asian 17%, African American 13%, Caucasian 50%, Hispanic 10%, Native American <1%.
Retention and Graduation: 23% freshmen graduate within 4 years. **Faculty:** 125 full-time faculty, 63% hold PhDs, 53% are members of minority groups, 14% are women.

ACADEMICS

Degrees: bachelor's, terminal associate, transfer associate. **Classes:** Most classes have 20–29 students. Most lab/discussion sessions have 20–29 students. **Special Study Options:** Accelerated program, cooperative education program, distance learning, double major, dual enrollment, English as a Second Language (ESL), exchange student program (domestic), external degree program, honors program, independent study, internships, liberal arts/career combination, student-designed major, study abroad.

CAMPUS LIFE

Environment: Village. **Activities:** dance, drama/theater, literary magazine, student government, student newspaper, student-run film society, Campus Ministries. **Athletics (Intercollegiate):** *Men:* basketball, soccer, softball, tennis. *Women:* basketball, field hockey, softball, tennis, volleyball.

ADMISSIONS

Freshman Academic Profile: Average high school GPA 3.18. 8.65% in top 10% of high school class, 30.19% in top 25% of high school class, 69.23% in top 50% of high school class. SAT Math middle 50% range 420-560. SAT Critical Reading middle 50% range 400-520. SAT Writing middle 50% range 400-520. ACT middle 50% range 18-23. Minimum paper TOEFL 550. **Basis for Candidate Selection:** *Very important factors considered include:* academic GPA, standardized test scores. *Important factors considered include:* rigor of secondary school record. *Other factors considered include:* Class rank, application essay, recommendation(s), alumni/ae relation, character/personal qualities, extracurricular activities, talent/ability, volunteer work, work experience. **Freshman Admission Requirements:** High school diploma is required and GED is accepted. *Academic units required:* 4 English, 3 mathematics, 3 science, (0 science labs), 2 foreign language, 3 social studies, 0 history, 0 academic electives. **Freshman Admission Statistics:** 3,906 applied, 79% admitted, 29% enrolled. **Transfer Admission Requirements:** High school transcript, college transcript(s), Lowest grade transferable C. **General Admission Information:** Application Fee $50. Notification on a rolling basis, beginning on or about 11/1. Nonfall registration accepted. Admission may be deferred for a maximum of 1 year.

COSTS AND FINANCIAL AID

Annual in-state tuition $13,012. Annual out-of-state tuition $19,848. Required fees $930. **Required Forms and Deadlines:** FAFSA. **Types of Aid:** *Need-based scholarships/grants:* Federal Pell, SEOG, state scholarships/grants, private scholarships, the school's own gift aid. *Loans:* Subsidized Stafford, Unsubsidized Stafford, PLUS, Federal Perkins, college/university loans from institutional funds, Private Loans. **Financial Aid Statistics:** 83% freshmen, 82% undergrads receive need-based scholarship or grant aid. 45% freshmen, 25% undergrads receive non-need-based scholarship or grant aid. 73% freshmen, 82% undergrads receive need-based self-help aid. 0% freshmen, 0% undergrads receive athletic scholarships. 63% undergrads borrow to pay for school. Average cumulative indebtedness $27,670. **Criteria for awarding institutional aid:** *Non-need-based:* academics, alumni affiliation, athletics, minority status.

PENNSYLVANIA STATE UNIVERSITY—ALTOONA

E108 Raymond Smith Building, Altoona, PA 16601-3760
Phone: 814-949-5466
E-mail: aaadmit@psu.edu
Fax: 814-949-5564 • **Website:** www.altoona.psu.edu

This public school was founded in 1929.

RATINGS

Admissions Selectivity Rating: 72   **Fire Safety Rating:** 60*

STUDENTS AND FACULTY

Enrollment: 3,829. **Student Body:** 45% female, 55% male, 19% out-of-state, 4% international. Asian 3%, African American 8%, Caucasian 76%, Hispanic 5%, Native American <1%
Retention and Graduation: 46% freshmen graduate within 4 years, 66% freshmen graduate within 6 years. **Faculty:** 190 full-time faculty, 68% hold PhDs, 49% are members of minority groups, 11% are women.

ACADEMICS

Degrees: bachelor's, terminal associate, transfer associate. **Classes:** Most classes have 20–29 students. Most lab/discussion sessions have 20–29 students. **Special Study Options:** cooperative education program, cross-registration, distance learning, double major, dual enrollment, English as a Second Language (ESL), exchange student program (domestic), honors program, independent study, internships, liberal arts/career combination, student-designed major, study abroad, teacher certification program.

FACILITIES

Housing: Coed dorms, special housing for disabled students, Suites, Special Interest Housing.

CAMPUS LIFE

Environment: Village. **Activities:** Choral groups, dance, drama/theater, jazz band, literary magazine, music ensembles, pep band, student government, student newspaper, student-run film society, yearbook, Campus Ministries, International Student Organization. **Athletics (Intercollegiate):** *Men:* basketball, diving, skiing (downhill/alpine), soccer, swimming, tennis, volleyball. *Women:* basketball, diving, skiing (downhill/alpine), swimming, tennis, volleyball.

ADMISSIONS

Freshman Academic Profile: Average high school GPA 3.08. 5.7% in top 10% of high school class, 26% in top 25% of high school class, 65.8% in top 50% of high school class. SAT Math middle 50% range 450-560. SAT Critical Reading middle 50% range 450-540. SAT Writing middle 50% range 430-530. ACT middle 50% range 19-24. **Basis for Candidate Selection:** *Very important factors considered include:* academic GPA, standardized test scores. *Important factors considered include:* rigor of secondary school record. *Other factors considered include:* Class rank, application essay, recommendation(s), alumni/ae relation, character/personal qualities, extracurricular activities, talent/ability, volunteer work, work experience. **Freshman Admission Requirements:** High school diploma is required and GED is accepted. *Academic units required:* 4 English, 3 mathematics, 3 science, (0 science labs), 2 foreign language, 3 social studies, 0 history, 0 academic electives. **Freshman Admission Statistics:** 5,630 applied, 88% admitted, 30% enrolled. **Transfer Admission Requirements:** High school transcript, college transcript(s), Lowest grade transferable C. **General Admission Information:** Application Fee $50. Notification on a rolling basis, beginning on or about 11/1. Nonfall registration accepted. Admission may be deferred for a maximum of One Year.

COSTS AND FINANCIAL AID

Annual in-state tuition $13,658. Annual out-of-state tuition $20,890. Room and board $10,520. Required fees $930. Average book expense $1,760. **Required**

Forms and Deadlines: FAFSA. **Types of Aid:** *Need-based scholarships/grants:* Federal Pell, SEOG, state scholarships/grants, private scholarships, the school's own gift aid. *Loans:* Subsidized Stafford, Unsubsidized Stafford, PLUS, Federal Perkins, college/university loans from institutional funds, Private Loans. **Financial Aid Statistics:** 60% freshmen, 62% undergrads receive need-based scholarship or grant aid. 61% freshmen, 43% undergrads receive non-need-based scholarship or grant aid. 80% freshmen, 84% undergrads receive need-based self-help aid. 0% freshmen, 0% undergrads receive athletic scholarships. 63% undergrads borrow to pay for school. Average cumulative indebtedness $27,670. **Criteria for awarding institutional aid:** *Non-need-based:* academics, alumni affiliation, athletics, minority status.

PENNSYLVANIA STATE UNIVERSITY—BEAVER

100 University Drive, 113 Student Union, Monaca, PA 15061-2799
Phone: 877-564-6778
E-mail: br-admissions@psu.edu
Fax: 724-773-3769 • **Website:** http://beaver.psu.edu

This is a public school.

RATINGS

Admissions Selectivity Rating: 72   **Fire Safety Rating:** 60*

STUDENTS AND FACULTY

Enrollment: 665. **Student Body:** 35% female, 65% male, 9% out-of-state, 3% international. Asian 3%, African American 10%, Caucasian 75%, Hispanic 5%, Native American <1%
Retention and Graduation: 21% freshmen graduate within 4 years. 41% freshmen graduate within 6 years. **Faculty:** 32 full-time faculty, 66% hold PhDs, 59% are members of minority groups, 22% are women.

ADMISSIONS

Freshman Academic Profile: Average high school GPA 3.07. 5.66% in top 10% of high school class, 27.67% in top 25% of high school class, 67.3% in top 50% of high school class. SAT Math middle 50% range 430-540. SAT Critical Reading middle 50% range 410-540. SAT Writing middle 50% range 380-520. ACT middle 50% range 17-21. **Freshman Admission Statistics:** 787 applied, 81% admitted, 34% enrolled.

COSTS AND FINANCIAL AID

Annual in-state tuition $12,718. Annual out-of-state tuition $19,404. Room and board $10,520. Required fees $918. Average book expense $1,760. **Required Forms and Deadlines:** FAFSA. **Financial Aid Statistics:** 70% freshmen, 74% undergrads receive need-based scholarship or grant aid. 71% freshmen, 53% undergrads receive non-need-based scholarship or grant aid. 80% freshmen, 85% undergrads receive need-based self-help aid. 0% freshmen, 0% undergrads receive athletic scholarships. 63% undergrads borrow to pay for school. Average cumulative indebtedness $27,670.

PENNSYLVANIA STATE UNIVERSITY—BERKS

Tulpehocken Road PO Box 7009, Reading, PA 19610-6009
Phone: 610-396-6060
E-mail: admissionsbk@psu.edu
Fax: 610-396-6077 • **Website:** http://berks.psu.edu

This public school was founded in 1924. It has a 241-acre campus.

RATINGS

Admissions Selectivity Rating: 71   **Fire Safety Rating:** 60*

STUDENTS AND FACULTY

Enrollment: 2,699. **Student Body:** 44% female, 56% male, 7% out-of-state, 3% international. Asian 4%, African American 10%, Caucasian 70%, Hispanic 11%, Native American <1%
Retention and Graduation: 33% freshmen graduate within 4 years. **Faculty:** 124 full-time faculty, 68% hold PhDs, 48% are members of minority groups, 15% are women.

ACADEMICS

Degrees: bachelor's, certificate, terminal associate, transfer associate. **Classes:** Most classes have 20–29 students. Most lab/discussion sessions have 10–19 students. **Special Study Options:** Accelerated program, cooperative education program, cross-registration, distance learning, dual enrollment, English as a

Second Language (ESL), honors program, independent study, internships, study abroad, teacher certification program.

FACILITIES
Housing: Coed dorms, special housing for disabled students, Honor Students, Suites, Special Interest Houses.

CAMPUS LIFE
Environment: Village. **Activities:** Choral groups, dance, drama/theater, pep band, radio station, student government, student newspaper, student-run film society, yearbook, Campus Ministries, International Student Organization. **Athletics (Intercollegiate):** *Men:* baseball, basketball, fencing, soccer, tennis, volleyball. *Women:* fencing, softball, tennis, volleyball.

ADMISSIONS
Freshman Academic Profile: Average high school GPA 3.01. 6.85% in top 10% of high school class, 25.12% in top 25% of high school class, 64.44% in top 50% of high school class. SAT Math middle 50% range 430-560. SAT Critical Reading middle 50% range 420-530. SAT Writing middle 50% range 400-520. ACT middle 50% range 18-25. Minimum paper TOEFL 550. **Basis for Candidate Selection:** *Very important factors considered include:* academic GPA, standardized test scores. *Important factors considered include:* rigor of secondary school record. *Other factors considered include:* Class rank, application essay, recommendation(s), alumni/ae relation, character/personal qualities, extracurricular activities, talent/ability, volunteer work, work experience. **Freshman Admission Requirements:** High school diploma is required and GED is accepted. *Academic units required:* 4 English, 3 mathematics, 3 science, (0 science labs), 2 foreign language, 3 social studies, 0 history, 0 academic electives. **Freshman Admission Statistics:** 2,398 applied, 89% admitted, 40% enrolled. **Transfer Admission Requirements:** High school transcript, college transcript(s), Lowest grade transferable C. **General Admission Information:** Application Fee $50. Notification on a rolling basis, beginning on or about 11/1. Nonfall registration accepted. Admission may be deferred for a maximum of 1 year.

COSTS AND FINANCIAL AID
Annual in-state tuition $13,658. Annual out-of-state tuition $20,890. Room and board $11,500. Required fees $930. Average book expense $1,760. **Required Forms and Deadlines:** FAFSA. **Types of Aid:** *Need-based scholarships/grants:* Federal Pell, SEOG, state scholarships/grants, private scholarships, the school's own gift aid. *Loans:* Direct Subsidized Stafford, Subsidized Stafford, Unsubsidized Stafford, PLUS, Federal Perkins, college/university loans from institutional funds, Private Loans. **Financial Aid Statistics:** 68% freshmen, 70% undergrads receive need-based scholarship or grant aid. 40% freshmen, 31% undergrads receive non-need-based scholarship or grant aid. 82% freshmen, 85% undergrads receive need-based self-help aid. 0% freshmen, 0% undergrads receive athletic scholarships. 63% undergrads borrow to pay for school. Average cumulative indebtedness $27,670. **Criteria for awarding institutional aid:** *Non-need-based:* academics, alumni affiliation, athletics, minority status.

PENNSYLVANIA STATE UNIVERSITY— BRANDYWINE

25 Yearsley Mill Road, Media, PA 19063
Phone: 610-892-1200
E-mail: bwadmissions@psu.edu
Fax: 610-892-1357 · **Website:** brandywine.psu.edu

This is a public school.

RATINGS
Admissions Selectivity Rating: 71   **Fire Safety Rating:** 60*

STUDENTS AND FACULTY
Enrollment: 1,334. **Student Body:** 41% female, 59% male, 6% out-of-state, 1% international. Asian 10%, African American 15%, Caucasian 65%, Hispanic 5%, Native American <1%
Retention and Graduation: 20% freshmen graduate within 4 years. 43% freshmen graduate within 6 years. **Faculty:** 68 full-time faculty, 69% hold PhDs, 56% are members of minority groups, 13% are women.

ADMISSIONS
Freshman Academic Profile: Average high school GPA 3.01. 3.95% in top 10% of high school class, 19.37% in top 25% of high school class, 58.89% in top 50% of high school class. SAT Math middle 50% range 440-550. SAT Critical Reading middle 50% range 410-530. SAT Writing middle 50% range 405-520. ACT middle 50% range 19-24. **Freshman Admission Statistics:** 1,182 applied, 85% admitted, 39% enrolled.

COSTS AND FINANCIAL AID
Annual in-state tuition $13,012. Annual out-of-state tuition $19,848. Required fees $930. **Required Forms and Deadlines:** FAFSA. **Financial Aid Statistics:** 75% freshmen, 75% undergrads receive need-based scholarship or grant aid. 51% freshmen, 34% undergrads receive non-need-based scholarship or grant aid. 69% freshmen, 80% undergrads receive need-based self-help aid. 0% freshmen, 0% undergrads receive athletic scholarships. 63% undergrads borrow to pay for school. Average cumulative indebtedness $27,670.

PENNSYLVANIA STATE UNIVERSITY— DELAWARE COUNTY

25 Yearsley Mill Road, Media, PA 19063-5596
Phone: 610-892-1200
E-mail: bwadmissions@psu.edu
Fax: 610-892-1320 · **Website:** ww.brandywine.psu.edu

This public school was founded in 1966. It has a 87-acre campus.

RATINGS
Admissions Selectivity Rating: 72   **Fire Safety Rating:** 60*

STUDENTS AND FACULTY
Enrollment: 1,403. **Student Body:** 44% female, 56% male, 4% out-of-state, 1% international. Asian 9%, African American 13%, Caucasian 68%, Hispanic 5%, Native American <1%
Retention and Graduation: 16% freshmen graduate within 4 years. **Faculty:** 61 full-time faculty, 57% hold PhDs, 51% are members of minority groups, 15% are women. 0% of classes are taught by teaching assistants.

ACADEMICS
Degrees: bachelor's, certificate, terminal associate, transfer associate. **Classes:** Most classes have 10–19 students. **Special Study Options:** distance learning, double major, dual enrollment, English as a Second Language (ESL), honors program, independent study, internships, study abroad, teacher certification program.

FACILITIES
Special Academic Facilities/Equipment: Culinary Archives and Museum.

CAMPUS LIFE
Environment: Village. **Activities:** Choral groups, dance, literary magazine, student government, student newspaper, student-run film society. **Athletics (Intercollegiate):** *Men:* baseball, basketball, ice hockey, riflery, soccer, tennis, volleyball. *Women:* basketball, ice hockey, riflery, soccer, tennis, volleyball.

ADMISSIONS
Freshman Academic Profile: Average high school GPA 3. 6.17% in top 10% of high school class, 23.87% in top 25% of high school class, 59.26% in top 50% of high school class. SAT Math middle 50% range 440-560. SAT Critical Reading middle 50% range 420-520. SAT Writing middle 50% range 410-530. ACT middle 50% range 17-23. Minimum paper TOEFL 550. **Basis for Candidate Selection:** *Very important factors considered include:* academic GPA, standardized test scores. *Important factors considered include:* rigor of secondary school record. *Other factors considered include:* Class rank, application essay, recommendation(s), alumni/ae relation, character/personal qualities, extracurricular activities, talent/ability, volunteer work, work experience. **Freshman Admission Requirements:** High school diploma is required and GED is accepted. *Academic units required:* 4 English, 3 mathematics, 3 science, (0 science labs), 2 foreign language, 3 social studies, 0 history, 0 academic electives. **Freshman Admission Statistics:** 1,279 applied, 79% admitted, 36% enrolled. **Transfer Admission Requirements:** High school transcript, college transcript(s), Lowest grade transferable C. **General Admission Information:** Application Fee $50. Notification on a rolling basis, beginning on or about 11/1. Nonfall registration accepted. Admission may be deferred for a maximum of 1 year.

COSTS AND FINANCIAL AID
Annual in-state tuition $10,454. Annual out-of-state tuition $15,954. Room and board $3,360. Required fees $552. Average book expense $1,168. **Required Forms and Deadlines:** FAFSA. **Types of Aid:** *Need-based scholarships/grants:* Federal Pell, SEOG, state scholarships/grants, private scholarships, the school's own gift aid. *Loans:* Subsidized Stafford, Unsubsidized Stafford, PLUS, Federal Perkins, college/university loans from institutional funds, Private Loans. **Financial Aid Statistics:** 76% freshmen, 77% undergrads receive need-based scholarship or grant aid. 48% freshmen, 29% undergrads receive non-need-based scholarship or grant aid. 73% freshmen, 79% undergrads receive need-based self-help aid. 0% freshmen, 0% undergrads receive athletic scholarships.

67% undergrads borrow to pay for school. Average cumulative indebtedness $19,600. **Criteria for awarding institutional aid:** *Non-need-based:* academics, alumni affiliation, athletics, minority status.

PENNSYLVANIA STATE UNIVERSITY—DUBOIS

Enrollment Services House, Dubois, PA 15801-3199
Phone: 814-375-4720
E-mail: duboisinfo@psu.edu
Fax: 814-375-4784 • **Website:** www.ds.psu.edu

This public school was founded in 1935. It has a 13-acre campus.

RATINGS
Admissions Selectivity Rating: 71   **Fire Safety Rating:** 60*

STUDENTS AND FACULTY
Enrollment: 724. **Student Body:** 51% female, 49% male, 1% out-of-state, 0% international. Asian 0%, African American 1%, Caucasian 99%, Hispanic 0%, Native American <1%
Retention and Graduation: 82% freshmen return for sophomore year.
Faculty: 43 full-time faculty, 65% hold PhDs, 44% are members of minority groups, 14% are women. 0% of classes are taught by teaching assistants.

ACADEMICS
Degrees: bachelor's, certificate, terminal associate, transfer associate. **Classes:** Most classes have 10–19 students. Most lab/discussion sessions have 10–19 students. **Special Study Options:** Accelerated program, cross-registration, distance learning, double major, dual enrollment, honors program, independent study, internships, student-designed major, study abroad.

FACILITIES
Housing: Indepently owned housing nearby.

CAMPUS LIFE
Environment: Village. **Activities:** Choral groups, drama/theater, literary magazine, student government, student newspaper, student-run film society. **Athletics (Intercollegiate):** *Men:* basketball. *Women:* volleyball.

ADMISSIONS
Freshman Academic Profile: Average high school GPA 2.91. 5.39% in top 10% of high school class, 21.08% in top 25% of high school class, 61.27% in top 50% of high school class. SAT Math middle 50% range 415-545. SAT Critical Reading middle 50% range 410-500. Minimum paper TOEFL 550. **Basis for Candidate Selection:** *Very important factors considered include:* academic GPA, standardized test scores. *Important factors considered include:* rigor of secondary school record. *Other factors considered include:* Class rank, application essay, recommendation(s), alumni/ae relation, character/personal qualities, extracurricular activities, talent/ability, volunteer work, work experience. **Freshman Admission Requirements:** High school diploma is required and GED is accepted. *Academic units required:* 4 English, 3 mathematics, 3 science, (0 science labs), 2 foreign language, 3 social studies, 0 history, 0 visual/performing arts, 0 computer science, 0 academic electives. **Freshman Admission Statistics:** 539 applied, 88% admitted, 48% enrolled. **Transfer Admission Requirements:** High school transcript, college transcript(s), Lowest grade transferable C. **General Admission Information:** Application Fee $50. Notification on a rolling basis, beginning on or about 11/1. Nonfall registration accepted. Admission may be deferred for a maximum of One Year.

COSTS AND FINANCIAL AID
Annual in-state tuition $10,454. Annual out-of-state tuition $15,954. Room and board $3,360. Required fees $542. Average book expense $1,168. **Required Forms and Deadlines:** FAFSA. **Notification of Awards:** Applicants will be notified of awards on a rolling basis beginning 3/1. **Types of Aid:** *Need-based scholarships/grants:* Federal Pell, SEOG, state scholarships/grants, private scholarships, the school's own gift aid. *Loans:* Subsidized Stafford, Unsubsidized Stafford, PLUS, Federal Perkins, college/university loans from institutional funds, Private Loans. **Financial Aid Statistics:** 84% freshmen, 88% undergrads receive need-based scholarship or grant aid. 41% freshmen, 33% undergrads receive non-need-based scholarship or grant aid. 83% freshmen, 89% undergrads receive need-based self-help aid. 0% freshmen, 0% undergrads receive athletic scholarships. 67% undergrads borrow to pay for school. Average cumulative indebtedness $19,600. **Criteria for awarding institutional aid:** *Non-need-based:* academics, alumni affiliation, athletics, minority status.

PENNSYLVANIA STATE UNIVERSITY— ERIE, THE BEHREND COLLEGE

Metzgar Admissions & Alumnia Ct, Erie, PA 16563-0105
Phone: 814-898-6100
E-mail: behrend.admissions@psu.edu
Fax: 814-898-6044 • **Website:** http://psbehrend.psu.edu/ • **ACT Code:** 3656

This public school was founded in 1948. It has a 732-acre campus.

RATINGS
Admissions Selectivity Rating: 75   **Fire Safety Rating:** 60*

STUDENTS AND FACULTY
Enrollment: 3,891. **Student Body:** 35% female, 65% male, 11% out-of-state, 7% international. Asian 3%, African American 4%, Caucasian 80%, Hispanic 3%, Native American <1%
Retention and Graduation: 44% freshmen graduate within 4 years. **Faculty:** 243 full-time faculty, 68% hold PhDs, 35% are members of minority groups, 13% are women. 0% of classes are taught by teaching assistants.

ACADEMICS
Degrees: bachelor's, certificate, master's, terminal associate, transfer associate. **Classes:** Most classes have 20–29 students. Most lab/discussion sessions have 10–19 students. **Special Study Options:** Accelerated program, cooperative education program, distance learning, double major, dual enrollment, honors program, independent study, internships, liberal arts/career combination, study abroad, teacher certification program. **Disability Services:** Special programs offered to physically disabled students include note-taking services, reader services, tape recorders, tutors. **Career services:** alumni services, career/job search classes, career assessment, internships.

FACILITIES
Housing: Coed dorms, special housing for disabled students, men's dorms, women's dorms, apartments for single students, Suites, Special Interest Housing. **Special Academic Facilities/Equipment:** Observatory, plastics lab. **Computers:** Students can register for classes online. Administrative functions (other than registration) can be performed online.

CAMPUS LIFE
Environment: Village. **Activities:** Choral groups, concert band, dance, drama/theater, jazz band, literary magazine, music ensembles, pep band, radio station, student government, student newspaper, student-run film society, Campus Ministries, International Student Organization. 75 registered organizations, 46 honor societies, 26 religious organizations. 6 fraternities, 4 sororities. **Athletics (Intercollegiate):** *Men:* baseball, basketball, cheerleading, cross-country, golf, soccer, swimming, tennis, track/field (outdoor), water polo, wrestling. *Women:* basketball, cheerleading, cross-country, golf, soccer, softball, swimming, tennis, track/field (outdoor), volleyball, water polo. **On-Campus Highlights:** Junker Athletic Center, Logan House, Smith Chapel and Carillon, Bruno's Caf, Reen Union Building, Historic Behrend Farmhouse.

ADMISSIONS
Freshman Academic Profile: Average high school GPA 3.27. 12.57% in top 10% of high school class, 39.57% in top 25% of high school class, 80% in top 50% of high school class. SAT Math middle 50% range 480-610. SAT Critical Reading middle 50% range 460-560. SAT Writing middle 50% range 430-540. ACT middle 50% range 19-26. Minimum paper TOEFL 550. **Basis for Candidate Selection:** *Very important factors considered include:* academic GPA, standardized test scores. *Important factors considered include:* rigor of secondary school record. *Other factors considered include:* Class rank, application essay, recommendation(s), alumni/ae relation, character/personal qualities, extracurricular activities, talent/ability, volunteer work, work experience. **Freshman Admission Requirements:** High school diploma is required and GED is accepted. *Academic units required:* 4 English, 3 mathematics, 3 science, (0 science labs), 2 foreign language, 3 social studies, 0 history, 0 visual/performing arts, 0 computer science, 0 academic electives. **Freshman Admission Statistics:** 4,054 applied, 87% admitted, 34% enrolled. **Transfer Admission Requirements:** High school transcript, college transcript(s), Lowest grade transferable C. **General Admission Information:** Application Fee $50. Notification on a rolling basis, beginning on or about 11/1. Nonfall registration accepted. Admission may be deferred for a maximum of One Year. Credit offered for CEEB Advanced Placement tests.

COSTS AND FINANCIAL AID
Annual in-state tuition $13,658. Annual out-of-state tuition $20,890. Room and board $10,520. Required fees $930. Average book expense $1,760. **Required Forms and Deadlines:** FAFSA. **Notification of Awards:** Applicants will be notified of awards on a rolling basis beginning 3/1. **Types of Aid:** *Need-based*

scholarships/grants: Federal Pell, SEOG, state scholarships/grants, private scholarships, the school's own gift aid. *Loans:* Subsidized Stafford, Unsubsidized Stafford, PLUS, Federal Perkins, college/university loans from institutional funds, Private Loans. *Student Employment:* Federal Work-Study Program available. Institutional employment available. Highest amount earned per year from on-campus jobs $656. Off-campus job opportunities are good. **Financial Aid Statistics:** 66% freshmen, 65% undergrads receive need-based scholarship or grant aid. 64% freshmen, 42% undergrads receive non-need-based scholarship or grant aid. 85% freshmen, 87% undergrads receive need-based self-help aid. 0% freshmen, 0% undergrads receive athletic scholarships. 63% undergrads borrow to pay for school. Average cumulative indebtedness $27,670. **Criteria for awarding institutional aid:** *Non-need-based:* academics, alumni affiliation, athletics, minority status.

PENNSYLVANIA STATE UNIVERSITY— FAYETTE, THE EBERLY CAMPUS

PO Box 519, Uniontown, PA 15401-0519
Phone: 724-430-4130
E-mail: feadm@psu.edu
Fax: 724-430-4175 • **Website:** www.fe.psu.edu

This public school was founded in 1934. It has a 193-acre campus.

RATINGS

Admissions Selectivity Rating: 73   Fire Safety Rating: 60*

STUDENTS AND FACULTY

Enrollment: 942. **Student Body:** 58% female, 42% male, 1% out-of-state, 0% international. Asian 0%, African American 7%, Caucasian 92%, Hispanic 1%, Native American <1%
Faculty: 55 full-time faculty, 51% hold PhDs, 36% are members of minority groups, 7% are women. 0% of classes are taught by teaching assistants.

ACADEMICS

Degrees: bachelor's, terminal associate, transfer associate. **Classes:** Most classes have 20–29 students. Most lab/discussion sessions have fewer than 10 students. **Special Study Options:** Accelerated program, cross-registration, distance learning, double major, dual enrollment, honors program, independent study, internships, student-designed major, study abroad, weekend classes.

FACILITIES

Housing: privately owned, off-campus housing.

CAMPUS LIFE

Environment: Village. **Activities:** drama/theater, musical theater, student government.

ADMISSIONS

Freshman Academic Profile: Average high school GPA 2.97. 8.11% in top 10% of high school class, 36.94% in top 25% of high school class, 77.03% in top 50% of high school class. SAT Math middle 50% range 400-520. SAT Critical Reading middle 50% range 400-510. Minimum paper TOEFL 550. **Basis for Candidate Selection:** *Very important factors considered include:* academic GPA, standardized test scores. *Important factors considered include:* rigor of secondary school record. *Other factors considered include:* Class rank, application essay, recommendation(s), alumni/ae relation, character/personal qualities, extracurricular activities, talent/ability, volunteer work, work experience. **Freshman Admission Requirements:** High school diploma is required and GED is accepted. *Academic units required:* 4 English, 3 mathematics, 3 science, (0 science labs), 2 foreign language, 3 social studies, 0 history, 0 visual/performing arts, 0 computer science, 0 academic electives. **Freshman Admission Statistics:** 605 applied, 90% admitted, 45% enrolled. **Transfer Admission Requirements:** High school transcript, college transcript(s), Lowest grade transferable C. **General Admission Information:** Application Fee $50. Notification on a rolling basis, beginning on or about 11/1. Nonfall registration accepted. Admission may be deferred for a maximum of One Year.

COSTS AND FINANCIAL AID

Annual in-state tuition $10,454. Annual out-of-state tuition $15,954. Room and board $3,360. Required fees $542. Average book expense $1,168. **Required Forms and Deadlines:** FAFSA. **Notification of Awards:** Applicants will be notified of awards on a rolling basis beginning 3/1. **Types of Aid:** *Need-based scholarships/grants:* Federal Pell, SEOG, state scholarships/grants, private scholarships, the school's own gift aid. *Loans:* Subsidized Stafford, Unsubsidized Stafford, PLUS, Federal Perkins, college/university loans from institutional funds, Private Loans. **Financial Aid Statistics:** 87% freshmen, 89% un-

dergrads receive need-based scholarship or grant aid. 36% freshmen, 33% undergrads receive non-need-based scholarship or grant aid. 78% freshmen, 87% undergrads receive need-based self-help aid. 0% freshmen, 0% undergrads receive athletic scholarships. 67% undergrads borrow to pay for school. Average cumulative indebtedness $19,600. **Criteria for awarding institutional aid:** *Non-need-based:* academics, alumni affiliation, athletics, minority status.

PENNSYLVANIA STATE UNIVERSITY— GREATER ALLEGHENY

101 Frable Bldg., 4000 University Drive, McKeesport, PA 15132-7698
Phone: 412-675-9010
E-mail: psuga@psu.edu
Fax: 412-675-9056 • **Website:** ga.psu.edu

This is a public school.

RATINGS

Admissions Selectivity Rating: 76   Fire Safety Rating: 60*

STUDENTS AND FACULTY

Enrollment: 554. **Student Body:** 44% female, 56% male, 10% out-of-state, 7% international. Asian 2%, African American 19%, Caucasian 61%, Hispanic 5%, Native American <1%
Retention and Graduation: 24% freshmen graduate within 4 years. 41% freshmen graduate within 6 years. **Faculty:** 35 full-time faculty, 71% hold PhDs, 54% are members of minority groups, 29% are women.

ADMISSIONS

Freshman Academic Profile: Average high school GPA 3.12. 13.39% in top 10% of high school class, 38.39% in top 25% of high school class, 71.43% in top 50% of high school class. SAT Math middle 50% range 420-560. SAT Critical Reading middle 50% range 420-530. SAT Writing middle 50% range 400-510. ACT middle 50% range 18-24. **Freshman Admission Statistics:** 741 applied, 76% admitted, 33% enrolled.

COSTS AND FINANCIAL AID

Annual in-state tuition $12,718. Annual out-of-state tuition $19,404. Room and board $10,520. Required fees $930. Average book expense $1,760. **Required Forms and Deadlines:** FAFSA. **Financial Aid Statistics:** 83% freshmen, 79% undergrads receive need-based scholarship or grant aid. 63% freshmen, 50% undergrads receive non-need-based scholarship or grant aid. 75% freshmen, 83% undergrads receive need-based self-help aid. 0% freshmen, 0% undergrads receive athletic scholarships. 63% undergrads borrow to pay for school. Average cumulative indebtedness $27,670.

PENNSYLVANIA STATE UNIVERSITY— HARRISBURG

Swatara Bldg., Middletown, PA 17057-4898
Phone: 717-948-6250
E-mail: hbgadmit@psu.edu
Fax: 717-948-6325 • **Website:** www.hbg.psu.edu

This public school was founded in 1966.

RATINGS

Admissions Selectivity Rating: 75   Fire Safety Rating: 60*

STUDENTS AND FACULTY

Enrollment: 3,595. **Student Body:** 40% female, 60% male, 16% out-of-state, 10% international. Asian 8%, African American 10%, Caucasian 59%, Hispanic 7%, Native American <1%
Retention and Graduation: 83% freshmen return for sophomore year. 43% freshmen graduate within 4 years. 67% freshmen graduate within 6 years. **Faculty:** 229 full-time faculty, 85% hold PhDs, 41% are members of minority groups, 19% are women.

ACADEMICS

Degrees: bachelor's, certificate, master's, post-bachelor's certificate, terminal associate, transfer associate. **Classes:** Most classes have 20–29 students. Most lab/discussion sessions have fewer than 10 students. **Special Study Options:**

cooperative education program, cross-registration, distance learning, double major, dual enrollment, honors program, independent study, internships, student-designed major, study abroad, teacher certification program.

FACILITIES
Housing: special housing for disabled students, apartments for single students, Special Interest Housing.

CAMPUS LIFE
Environment: Village. **Activities:** Choral groups, dance, drama/theater, literary magazine, music ensembles, radio station, student government, student newspaper 2 honor societies, 1 religious organization. **Athletics (Intercollegiate): Men:** basketball, skiing (downhill/alpine), soccer, tennis, track/field (outdoor), volleyball. **Women:** skiing (downhill/alpine), soccer, track/field (outdoor), volleyball.

ADMISSIONS
Freshman Academic Profile: Average high school GPA 3.15. 11.28% in top 10% of high school class, 35.11% in top 25% of high school class, 79.79% in top 50% of high school class. SAT Math middle 50% range 470-590. SAT Critical Reading middle 50% range 440-540. SAT Writing middle 50% range 430-540. ACT middle 50% range 20-26. **Basis for Candidate Selection:** *Very important factors considered include:* academic GPA, standardized test scores. *Important factors considered include:* rigor of secondary school record. *Other factors considered include:* Class rank, application essay, recommendation(s), alumni/ae relation, character/personal qualities, extracurricular activities, talent/ability, volunteer work, work experience. **Freshman Admission Requirements:** High school diploma is required and GED is accepted. *Academic units required:* 4 English, 3 mathematics, 3 science, (0 science labs), 2 foreign language, 3 social studies, 0 history, 0 visual/performing arts, 0 computer science, 0 academic electives. **Freshman Admission Statistics:** 3,404 applied, 82% admitted, 28% enrolled. **Transfer Admission Requirements:** High school transcript, college transcript(s), Lowest grade transferable C. **General Admission Information:** Application Fee $50. Notification on a rolling basis, beginning on or about 11/1. Nonfall registration accepted. Admission may be deferred for a maximum of 1 year.

COSTS AND FINANCIAL AID
Annual in-state tuition $13,658. Annual out-of-state tuition $20,890. Room and board $11,980. Required fees $930. Average book expense $1,760. **Required Forms and Deadlines:** FAFSA. **Notification of Awards:** Applicants will be notified of awards on a rolling basis beginning 3/1. **Types of Aid:** *Need-based scholarships/grants:* Federal Pell, SEOG, state scholarships/grants, private scholarships, the school's own gift aid. *Loans:* Subsidized Stafford, Unsubsidized Stafford, PLUS, Federal Perkins, college/university loans from institutional funds, Private Loans. **Financial Aid Statistics:** 61% freshmen, 67% undergrads receive need-based scholarship or grant aid. 72% freshmen, 41% undergrads receive non-need-based scholarship or grant aid. 75% freshmen, 83% undergrads receive need-based self-help aid. 0% freshmen, 0% undergrads receive athletic scholarships. 63% undergrads borrow to pay for school. Average cumulative indebtedness $27,670. **Criteria for awarding institutional aid:** *Non-need-based:* academics, alumni affiliation, athletics, minority status.

PENNSYLVANIA STATE UNIVERSITY— HAZLETON

110 Admin. Building, Hazleton, PA 18202-1291
Phone: 570-450-3142
E-mail: admissions-hn@psu.edu
Fax: 570-450-3182 • **Website:** www.hn.psu.edu

This public school was founded in 1934. It has a 73-acre campus.

RATINGS
Admissions Selectivity Rating: 72   Fire Safety Rating: 60*

STUDENTS AND FACULTY
Enrollment: 1,192. **Student Body:** 40% female, 60% male, 26% out-of-state, 0% international. Asian 4%, African American 8%, Caucasian 80%, Hispanic 7%, Native American <1%
Faculty: 51 full-time faculty, 65% hold PhDs, 41% are members of minority groups, 16% are women.

ACADEMICS
Degrees: bachelor's, terminal associate, transfer associate. **Classes:** Most classes have 20–29 students. **Special Study Options:** Accelerated program, cross-registration, distance learning, double major, dual enrollment, English as

a Second Language (ESL), honors program, independent study, internships, student-designed major, study abroad.

FACILITIES
Housing: Coed dorms, Townhouses, suites.

CAMPUS LIFE
Environment: Rural. **Activities:** Choral groups, dance, drama/theater, literary magazine, radio station, student government, student newspaper, Campus Ministries. **Athletics (Intercollegiate):** *Men:* baseball, basketball, soccer, tennis. *Women:* softball, tennis, volleyball.

ADMISSIONS
Freshman Academic Profile: Average high school GPA 2.91. 5.94% in top 10% of high school class, 24.36% in top 25% of high school class, 67.33% in top 50% of high school class. SAT Math middle 50% range 420-540. SAT Critical Reading middle 50% range 420-530. Minimum paper TOEFL 550. **Basis for Candidate Selection:** *Very important factors considered include:* academic GPA, standardized test scores. *Important factors considered include:* rigor of secondary school record. *Other factors considered include:* Class rank, application essay, recommendation(s), alumni/ae relation, character/personal qualities, extracurricular activities, talent/ability, volunteer work, work experience. **Freshman Admission Requirements:** High school diploma is required and GED is accepted. *Academic units required:* 4 English, 3 mathematics, 3 science, (0 science labs), 2 foreign language, 3 social studies, 0 history, 0 visual/performing arts, 0 computer science, 0 academic electives. **Freshman Admission Statistics:** 1,613 applied, 89% admitted, 40% enrolled. **Transfer Admission Requirements:** High school transcript, college transcript(s), Lowest grade transferable C. **General Admission Information:** Application Fee $50. Notification on a rolling basis, beginning on or about 11/1. Nonfall registration accepted. Admission may be deferred for a maximum of 1 year.

COSTS AND FINANCIAL AID
Annual in-state tuition $10,454. Annual out-of-state tuition $15,954. Room and board $7,180. Required fees $552. Average book expense $1,168. **Required Forms and Deadlines:** FAFSA. **Notification of Awards:** Applicants will be notified of awards on a rolling basis beginning 3/1. **Types of Aid:** *Need-based scholarships/grants:* Federal Pell, SEOG, state scholarships/grants, private scholarships, the school's own gift aid. *Loans:* Subsidized Stafford, Unsubsidized Stafford, PLUS, Federal Perkins, college/university loans from institutional funds, Private Loans. **Financial Aid Statistics:** 70% freshmen, 69% undergrads receive need-based scholarship or grant aid. 36% freshmen, 29% undergrads receive non-need-based scholarship or grant aid. 81% freshmen, 84% undergrads receive need-based self-help aid. 0% freshmen, 0% undergrads receive athletic scholarships. 67% undergrads borrow to pay for school. Average cumulative indebtedness $19,600. **Criteria for awarding institutional aid:** *Non-need-based:* academics, alumni affiliation, athletics, minority status.

PENNSYLVANIA STATE UNIVERSITY— LEHIGH VALLEY

2809 Saucon Valley Road, Center Valley, PA 18034-8447
Phone: 610-285-5035
E-mail: admissions-lv@psu.edu
Fax: 610-285-5220 • **Website:** www.lv.psu.edu

This public school was founded in 1912. It has a 42-acre campus.

RATINGS
Admissions Selectivity Rating: 73   Fire Safety Rating: 60*

STUDENTS AND FACULTY
Enrollment: 775. **Student Body:** 46% female, 54% male, 5% out-of-state, 1% international. Asian 8%, African American 5%, Caucasian 65%, Hispanic 18%, Native American <1%
Retention and Graduation: 30% freshmen graduate within 4 years. 54% freshmen graduate within 6 years. **Faculty:** 42 full-time faculty, 69% hold PhDs, 64% are members of minority groups, 14% are women.

ACADEMICS
Degrees: bachelor's, terminal associate, transfer associate. **Classes:** Most classes have 10–19 students. Most lab/discussion sessions have 10–19 students. **Special Study Options:** Accelerated program, cooperative education program, cross-registration, distance learning, dual enrollment, honors program, independent study, internships, study abroad.

CAMPUS LIFE

Activities: drama/theater, student government, student newspaper. **Athletics (Intercollegiate):** *Men:* basketball, cross-country, golf, soccer, tennis, volleyball. *Women:* basketball, golf, tennis, volleyball.

ADMISSIONS

Freshman Academic Profile: Average high school GPA 3. 8.39% in top 10% of high school class, 27.74% in top 25% of high school class, 69.03% in top 50% of high school class. SAT Math middle 50% range 430-590. SAT Critical Reading middle 50% range 430-555. SAT Writing middle 50% range 410-550. ACT middle 50% range 19-24. Minimum paper TOEFL 550. **Basis for Candidate Selection:** *Very important factors considered include:* academic GPA, standardized test scores. *Important factors considered include:* rigor of secondary school record. *Other factors considered include:* Class rank, application essay, recommendation(s), alumni/ae relation, character/personal qualities, extracurricular activities, talent/ability, volunteer work, work experience. **Freshman Admission Requirements:** High school diploma is required and GED is accepted. *Academic units required:* 4 English, 3 mathematics, 3 science, (0 science labs), 2 foreign language, 3 social studies, 0 history, 0 visual/performing arts, 0 computer science, 0 academic electives. **Freshman Admission Statistics:** 887 applied, 85% admitted, 28% enrolled. **Transfer Admission Requirements:** High school transcript, college transcript(s), Lowest grade transferable C. **General Admission Information:** Application Fee $50. Notification on a rolling basis, beginning on or about 11/1. Nonfall registration accepted. Admission may be deferred for a maximum of 1 year.

COSTS AND FINANCIAL AID

Annual in-state tuition $13,012. Annual out-of-state tuition $19,848. Required fees $918. **Required Forms and Deadlines:** FAFSA. **Types of Aid:** *Need-based scholarships/grants:* Federal Pell, SEOG, state scholarships/grants, private scholarships, the school's own gift aid. *Loans:* Subsidized Stafford, Unsubsidized Stafford, PLUS, Federal Perkins, college/university loans from institutional funds, Private Loans. **Financial Aid Statistics:** 74% freshmen, 77% undergrads receive need-based scholarship or grant aid. 50% freshmen, 32% undergrads receive non-need-based scholarship or grant aid. 79% freshmen, 83% undergrads receive need-based self-help aid. 0% freshmen, 0% undergrads receive athletic scholarships. 63% undergrads borrow to pay for school. Average cumulative indebtedness $27,670. **Criteria for awarding institutional aid:** *Non-need-based:* academics, alumni affiliation, athletics, minority status.

PENNSYLVANIA STATE UNIVERSITY— MONT ALTO

1 Campus Drive, Mont Alto, PA 17237-9703
Phone: 717-749-6130
E-mail: psuma@psu.edu
Fax: 717-749-6132 · **Website:** www.montalto.psu.edu

This public school was founded in 1929. It has a 62-acre campus.

RATINGS

Admissions Selectivity Rating: 75   Fire Safety Rating: 60*

STUDENTS AND FACULTY

Enrollment: 837. **Student Body:** 59% female, 41% male, 17% out-of-state, 0% international. Asian 1%, African American 8%, Caucasian 81%, Hispanic 4%, Native American <1%
Retention and Graduation: 75% freshmen return for sophomore year. 25% freshmen graduate within 4 years. 22% grads go on to further study within 1 year. **Faculty:** 58 full-time faculty, 48% hold PhDs, 53% are members of minority groups, 10% are women.

ACADEMICS

Degrees: bachelor's, terminal associate, transfer associate. **Classes:** Most classes have 10–19 students. Most lab/discussion sessions have 10–19 students. **Special Study Options:** Accelerated program, cross-registration, distance learning, double major, dual enrollment, honors program, independent study, internships, study abroad. **Honors programs:** The Schreyer Honors College is widely recognized as one of the best and most comprehensive undergraduate honors programs in the United States. http://www.scholars.psu.edu/index.cfm **Combined degree programs:** BA/MD, BA/MEng, Science/MBA Program; JD/MBA. **Disability Services:** Special programs offered to physically disabled students include note-taking services, reader services, tape recorders, tutors.

FACILITIES

Housing: Coed dorms, special housing for disabled students, Suites, Special Interest Housing, Townhouses. 99% of campus accessible to physically disabled.

CAMPUS LIFE

Environment: Village. **Activities:** dance, drama/theater, jazz band, student government, student newspaper, Campus Ministries. **Athletics (Intercollegiate):** *Men:* basketball, soccer, tennis. *Women:* basketball, tennis.

ADMISSIONS

Freshman Academic Profile: Average high school GPA 3.08. 9.46% in top 10% of high school class, 34.68% in top 25% of high school class, 73.42% in top 50% of high school class. SAT Math middle 50% range 420-530. SAT Critical Reading middle 50% range 410-530. SAT Writing middle 50% range 390-500. ACT middle 50% range 20-24. **Basis for Candidate Selection:** *Very important factors considered include:* academic GPA, standardized test scores. *Important factors considered include:* rigor of secondary school record. *Other factors considered include:* Class rank, application essay, recommendation(s), alumni/ae relation, character/personal qualities, extracurricular activities, talent/ability, volunteer work, work experience. **Freshman Admission Requirements:** High school diploma is required and GED is accepted. *Academic units required:* 4 English, 3 mathematics, 3 science, (0 science labs), 2 foreign language, 3 social studies, 0 history, 0 visual/performing arts, 0 computer science, 0 academic electives. **Freshman Admission Statistics:** 778 applied, 78% admitted, 45% enrolled. **Transfer Admission Requirements:** High school transcript, college transcript(s), Lowest grade transferable C. **General Admission Information:** Application Fee $50. Notification on a rolling basis, beginning on or about 11/1. Nonfall registration accepted. Admission may be deferred for a maximum of One Year.

COSTS AND FINANCIAL AID

Annual in-state tuition $12,718. Annual out-of-state tuition $19,404. Room and board $10,520. Required fees $930. Average book expense $1,760. **Required Forms and Deadlines:** FAFSA. **Notification of Awards:** Applicants will be notified of awards on a rolling basis beginning 3/1. **Types of Aid:** *Need-based scholarships/grants:* Federal Pell, SEOG, state scholarships/grants, private scholarships, the school's own gift aid. *Loans:* Subsidized Stafford, Unsubsidized Stafford, PLUS, Federal Perkins, college/university loans from institutional funds, Private Loans. **Financial Aid Statistics:** 71% freshmen, 73% undergrads receive need-based scholarship or grant aid. 55% freshmen, 48% undergrads receive non-need-based scholarship or grant aid. 82% freshmen, 86% undergrads receive need-based self-help aid. 0% freshmen, 0% undergrads receive athletic scholarships. 63% undergrads borrow to pay for school. Average cumulative indebtedness $27,670. **Criteria for awarding institutional aid:** *Non-need-based:* academics, alumni affiliation, athletics, minority status.

PENNSYLVANIA STATE UNIVERSITY— NEW KENSINGTON

3550 7th Street Road, Upper Barrell, PA 15068-1798
Phone: 724-334-5466
E-mail: nkadmissions@psu.edu
Fax: 724-334-6111

This public school was founded in 1958. It has a 71-acre campus.

RATINGS

Admissions Selectivity Rating: 72   Fire Safety Rating: 60*

STUDENTS AND FACULTY

Enrollment: 734. **Student Body:** 44% female, 56% male, 2% out-of-state, 0% international. Asian 1%, African American 3%, Caucasian 95%, Hispanic 1%, Native American <1%
Faculty: 38 full-time faculty, 61% hold PhDs, 45% are members of minority groups, 16% are women.

ACADEMICS

Degrees: bachelor's, certificate, terminal associate, transfer associate. **Classes:** Most classes have fewer than 10 students. Most lab/discussion sessions have 10–19 students. **Special Study Options:** cross-registration, distance learning, double major, dual enrollment, external degree program, honors program, independent study, internships, study abroad.

CAMPUS LIFE

Activities: Choral groups, dance, drama/theater, jazz band, literary magazine, musical theater, student government, student newspaper. **Athletics (Intercollegiate):** *Men:* baseball, basketball, ice hockey, tennis, volleyball. *Women:* basketball, ice hockey, tennis, volleyball.

ADMISSIONS

Freshman Academic Profile: Average high school GPA 3.01. 8.7% in top 10% of high school class, 28.8% in top 25% of high school class, 69.02% in top

50% of high school class. SAT Math middle 50% range 440-570. SAT Critical Reading middle 50% range 430-540. Minimum paper TOEFL 550. **Basis for Candidate Selection:** *Very important factors considered include:* academic GPA, standardized test scores. *Important factors considered include:* rigor of secondary school record. *Other factors considered include:* Class rank, application essay, recommendation(s), alumni/ae relation, character/personal qualities, extracurricular activities, talent/ability, volunteer work, work experience. **Freshman Admission Requirements:** High school diploma is required and GED is accepted. *Academic units required:* 4 English, 3 mathematics, 3 science, (0 science labs), 2 foreign language, 3 social studies, 0 history, 0 academic electives. **Freshman Admission Statistics:** 561 applied, 86% admitted, 44% enrolled. **Transfer Admission Requirements:** High school transcript, college transcript(s), Lowest grade transferable C. **General Admission Information:** Application Fee $50. Notification on a rolling basis, beginning on or about 11/1. Nonfall registration accepted. Admission may be deferred for a maximum of one year.

COSTS AND FINANCIAL AID

Annual in-state tuition $10,454. Annual out-of-state tuition $15,954. Room and board $3,360. Required fees $552. Average book expense $1,168. **Required Forms and Deadlines:** FAFSA. **Types of Aid:** *Need-based scholarships/ grants:* Federal Pell, SEOG, state scholarships/grants, private scholarships, the school's own gift aid. *Loans:* Subsidized Stafford, Unsubsidized Stafford, PLUS, Federal Perkins, college/university loans from institutional funds, Private Loans. **Financial Aid Statistics:** 72% freshmen, 80% undergrads receive need-based scholarship or grant aid. 52% freshmen, 32% undergrads receive non-need-based scholarship or grant aid. 73% freshmen, 84% undergrads receive need-based self-help aid. 0% freshmen, 0% undergrads receive athletic scholarships. 67% undergrads borrow to pay for school. Average cumulative indebtedness $19,600. **Criteria for awarding institutional aid:** *Non-need-based:* academics, alumni affiliation, athletics, minority status.

PENNSYLVANIA STATE UNIVERSITY— SCHUYLKILL

200 University Drive, Schuykill Haven, PA 17972-2208
Phone: 570-385-6252
E-mail: sl-admissions@psu.edu
Fax: 570-385-3672 • **Website:** sl.psu.edu

This public school was founded in 1934. It has a 42-acre campus.

RATINGS

Admissions Selectivity Rating: 72   Fire Safety Rating: 60*

STUDENTS AND FACULTY

Enrollment: 755. **Student Body:** 61% female, 39% male, 14% out-of-state, 2% international. Asian 1%, African American 20%, Caucasian 67%, Hispanic 6%, Native American <1%
Retention and Graduation: 75% freshmen return for sophomore year. 24% freshmen graduate within 4 years. 42% freshmen graduate within 6 years.
Faculty: 42 full-time faculty, 76% hold PhDs, 40% are members of minority groups, 2% are women.

ACADEMICS

Degrees: bachelor's, terminal associate, transfer associate. **Classes:** Most classes have 20–29 students. Most lab/discussion sessions have 10–19 students. **Special Study Options:** Accelerated program, cooperative education program, distance learning, double major, dual enrollment, honors program, independent study, internships, student-designed major, study abroad.

FACILITIES

Housing: special housing for disabled students, apartments for single students.

CAMPUS LIFE

Activities: Choral groups, dance, drama/theater, musical theater, student government, student newspaper, Campus Ministries. **Athletics (Intercollegiate):** *Men:* basketball, cross-country, softball, tennis, volleyball. *Women:* basketball, cross-country, softball, tennis, volleyball.

ADMISSIONS

Freshman Academic Profile: Average high school GPA 2.83. 6.11% in top 10% of high school class, 20.56% in top 25% of high school class, 56.67% in top 50% of high school class. SAT Math middle 50% range 400-500. SAT Critical Reading middle 50% range 400-500. SAT Writing middle 50% range 390-490. ACT middle 50% range 17-20. Minimum paper TOEFL 550. **Basis for Candidate Selection:** *Very important factors considered include:* academic

GPA, standardized test scores. *Important factors considered include:* rigor of secondary school record. *Other factors considered include:* Class rank, application essay, recommendation(s), alumni/ae relation, character/personal qualities, extracurricular activities, talent/ability, volunteer work, work experience. **Freshman Admission Requirements:** High school diploma is required and GED is accepted. *Academic units required:* 4 English, 3 mathematics, 3 science, (0 science labs), 2 foreign language, 3 social studies, 0 history, 0 academic electives. **Freshman Admission Statistics:** 686 applied, 75% admitted, 49% enrolled. **Transfer Admission Requirements:** High school transcript, college transcript(s), Lowest grade transferable C. **General Admission Information:** Application Fee $50. Notification on a rolling basis, beginning on or about 11/1. Nonfall registration accepted. Admission may be deferred for a maximum of 1 year.

COSTS AND FINANCIAL AID

Annual in-state tuition $13,012. Annual out-of-state tuition $19,848. Room and board $7,886. Required fees $858. Average book expense $1,760. **Required Forms and Deadlines:** FAFSA. **Types of Aid:** *Need-based scholarships/ grants:* Federal Pell, SEOG, state scholarships/grants, private scholarships, the school's own gift aid. *Loans:* Subsidized Stafford, Unsubsidized Stafford, PLUS, Federal Perkins, college/university loans from institutional funds, Private Loans. **Financial Aid Statistics:** 84% freshmen, 85% undergrads receive need-based scholarship or grant aid. 70% freshmen, 51% undergrads receive non-need-based scholarship or grant aid. 80% freshmen, 86% undergrads receive need-based self-help aid. 0% freshmen, 0% undergrads receive athletic scholarships. 63% undergrads borrow to pay for school. Average cumulative indebtedness $27,670. **Criteria for awarding institutional aid:** *Non-need-based:* academics, alumni affiliation, athletics, minority status.

PENNSYLVANIA STATE UNIVERSITY— SHENANGO

147 Shenango Ave, Sharon, PA 16146-1597
Phone: 724-983-2800
E-mail: psushenango@psu.edu
Fax: 724-983-2820

This public school was founded in 1965. It has a 14-acre campus.

RATINGS

Admissions Selectivity Rating: 70   Fire Safety Rating: 60*

STUDENTS AND FACULTY

Enrollment: 677. **Student Body:** 65% female, 35% male, 13% out-of-state, 0% international. Asian 1%, African American 8%, Caucasian 90%, Hispanic 1%, Native American <1%
Retention and Graduation: 71% freshmen return for sophomore year.
Faculty: 29 full-time faculty, 55% hold PhDs, 45% are members of minority groups, 10% are women. 0% of classes are taught by teaching assistants.

ACADEMICS

Degrees: bachelor's, certificate, terminal associate, transfer associate. **Classes:** Most classes have 10–19 students. Most lab/discussion sessions have 10–19 students. **Special Study Options:** Accelerated program, cross-registration, distance learning, double major, dual enrollment, honors program, independent study, internships, student-designed major, study abroad.

CAMPUS LIFE

Environment: Village. **Activities:** literary magazine, student government.

ADMISSIONS

Freshman Academic Profile: Average high school GPA 2.91. 2.48% in top 10% of high school class, 19383% in top 25% of high school class, 61.16% in top 50% of high school class. SAT Math middle 50% range 400-520. SAT Critical Reading middle 50% range 400-490. Minimum paper TOEFL 550. **Basis for Candidate Selection:** *Very important factors considered include:* academic GPA, standardized test scores. *Important factors considered include:* rigor of secondary school record. *Other factors considered include:* Class rank, application essay, recommendation(s), alumni/ae relation, character/personal qualities, extracurricular activities, talent/ability, volunteer work, work experience. **Freshman Admission Requirements:** High school diploma is required and GED is accepted. *Academic units required:* 4 English, 3 mathematics, 3 science, (0 science labs), 2 foreign language, 3 social studies, 0 history, 0 academic electives. **Freshman Admission Statistics:** 271 applied, 89% admitted, 61% enrolled. **Transfer Admission Requirements:** High school transcript, college transcript(s), Lowest grade transferable C. **General Admission Information:** Application Fee $50. Notification on a rolling basis, beginning on or about 11/1.

Nonfall registration accepted. Admission may be deferred for a maximum of one year.

COSTS AND FINANCIAL AID

Annual in-state tuition $10,454. Annual out-of-state tuition $15,954. Room and board $3,360. Required fees $552. Average book expense $1,168. **Required Forms and Deadlines:** FAFSA. **Types of Aid:** *Need-based scholarships/grants:* Federal Pell, SEOG, state scholarships/grants, private scholarships, the school's own gift aid. *Loans:* Subsidized Stafford, Unsubsidized Stafford, PLUS, Federal Perkins, college/university loans from institutional funds, Private Loans. **Financial Aid Statistics:** 88% freshmen, 89% undergrads receive need-based scholarship or grant aid. 54% freshmen, 38% undergrads receive non-need-based scholarship or grant aid. 85% freshmen, 91% undergrads receive need-based self-help aid. 0% freshmen, 0% undergrads receive athletic scholarships. 67% undergrads borrow to pay for school. Average cumulative indebtedness $19,600. **Criteria for awarding institutional aid:** *Non-need-based:* academics, alumni affiliation, athletics.

PENNSYLVANIA STATE UNIVERSITY— UNIVERSITY PARK

Best 380

201 Shields Building, University Park, PA 16802
Phone: 814-865-5471 · **Financial Aid Phone:** 814-865-6301
E-mail: admissions@psu.edu · **CEEB Code:** 2660
Fax: 814-863-7590 · **Website:** www.psu.edu · **ACT Code:** 3656

This public school was founded in 1855. It has a 7264-acre campus.

RATINGS

Admissions Selectivity Rating: 90   **Fire Safety Rating:** 99

STUDENTS AND FACULTY

Enrollment: 39,958. **Student Body:** 46% female, 54% male, 31% out-of-state, 10% international (107 countries represented). Asian 6%, African American 4%, Caucasian 71%, Hispanic 5%, Native American <1%
Retention and Graduation: 66% freshmen graduate within 4 years. 86% freshmen graduate within 6 years. 24% grads go on to further study within 1 year. **Faculty:** 2,659 full-time faculty, 79% hold PhDs, 38% are members of minority groups, 18% are women.

ACADEMICS

Degrees: associate, bachelor's, certificate, doctoral, master's, post-master's certificate, terminal associate, transfer associate. **Classes:** Most classes have 20–29 students. Most lab/discussion sessions have 20–29 students. **Special Study Options:** Accelerated program, cooperative education program, cross-registration, distance learning, double major, dual enrollment, English as a Second Language (ESL), exchange student program (domestic), external degree program, honors program, independent study, internships, liberal arts/career combination, student-designed major, study abroad, teacher certification program, weekend college. **Honors programs:** The Schreyer Honors College is widely recognized as one of the best and most comprehensive undergraduate honors programs in the United States. http://www.shc.psu.edu/ **Combined degree programs:** BA/MD, BA/MEng, Science/MBA Program; JD/MBA. **Disability Services:** Special programs offered to physically disabled students include note-taking services, reader services, tape recorders, tutors. **Career services:** Alumni network, alumni services, career/job search classes, career assessment, internships, regional alumni. Career services highlights include our e-ship programs, which are all based on problem-based learning and for which we have gained both national and international recognition. COurse modules are transferable and scalable and have been used by students at other US schools as well as majoe overseas Universities in Germany, Slovakia, Austria, etc.

FACILITIES

Housing: Coed dorms, special housing for disabled students, men's dorms, special housing for international students, women's dorms, fraternity/sorority housing, apartments for married students, apartments for single students, Suites, Special Interest Housing. 99% of campus accessible to physically disabled. **Special Academic Facilities/Equipment:** Museums, theatres, language labs, weather station, nuclear reactor. **Computers:** 83% of classrooms, 50% of dorms, 100% of libraries, 100% of dining areas, 100% of student union, 25% of common outdoor areas have wireless network access. Students can

register for classes online. Administrative functions (other than registration) can be performed online.

CAMPUS LIFE

Environment: Town. **Activities:** Choral groups, concert band, dance, drama/theater, jazz band, literary magazine, marching band, music ensembles, musical theater, opera, pep band, radio station, student government, student newspaper, student-run film society, symphony orchestra, television station, yearbook, Campus Ministries, International Student Organization, Model UN. 784 registered organizations, 34 honor societies, 49 religious organizations. 58 fraternities, 32 sororities. **Athletics (Intercollegiate):** *Men:* baseball, basketball, cheerleading, cross-country, diving, fencing, football, golf, gymnastics, lacrosse, soccer, swimming, tennis, track/field (outdoor), track/field (indoor), volleyball, wrestling. *Women:* basketball, cheerleading, cross-country, diving, fencing, field hockey, golf, gymnastics, lacrosse, soccer, softball, swimming, tennis, track/field (outdoor), track/field (indoor), volleyball. **On-Campus Highlights:** Hetzel Union Building, Pattee Paterno Library, The Creamery, Old Main, The Lion Shrine. **Environmental Initiatives:** To address the issue of climate change, Penn State established the goal of reducing greenhouse gas emissions by 17.5% below FY05/06 levels by 2012. This goal was achieved, and the university subsequently set a more ambitious goal of reducing emissions by an additional 17.5%, for a total 35% reduction by 2020, relative to the FY05/06 baseline. More information can be found at: www.ghg.psu.edu. In Fall 2013, the University began rollout of a new campus-wide program called M??bius, which will add organic waste collection to ALL recycling stations at University Park. This program is expected to increase the waste diversion rate from 65 percent in FY12/13 to 75 percent once fully implemented. The University is working to sustainably manage its growing transportation demands by switching to alternative fuels, reducing oil consumption, increasing the fuel efficiency of fleet vehicles, and encouraging the use of public and alternative modes of transportation. In December 2012, the League of American Bicyclists recognized Penn State University Park as a Bicycle Friendly University. The distinction honors the Universitys commitment to bicycling and initiatives that promote a safe and convenient biking environment on campus.

ADMISSIONS

Freshman Academic Profile: Average high school GPA 3.6. 40.12% in top 10% of high school class, 81.92% in top 25% of high school class, 98.5% in top 50% of high school class. SAT Math middle 50% range 560-670. SAT Critical Reading middle 50% range 530-620. SAT Writing middle 50% range 540-640. ACT middle 50% range 25-29. Minimum internet-based TOEFL 80. Minimum paper TOEFL 550. **Basis for Candidate Selection:** *Very important factors considered include:* academic GPA, standardized test scores. *Important factors considered include:* rigor of secondary school record. *Other factors considered include:* Class rank, application essay, recommendation(s), alumni/ae relation, character/personal qualities, extracurricular activities, talent/ability, volunteer work, work experience. **Freshman Admission Requirements:** High school diploma is required and GED is accepted. *Academic units required:* 4 English, 3 mathematics, 3 science, (0 science labs), 2 foreign language, 3 social studies, 0 history, 0 visual/performing arts, 0 computer science, 0 academic electives. **Freshman Admission Statistics:** 50,299 applied, 50% admitted, 32% enrolled. **Transfer Admission Requirements:** High school transcript, college transcript(s), Lowest grade transferable C. **General Admission Information:** Application Fee $50. Notification on a rolling basis, beginning on or about 11/1. Nonfall registration accepted. Admission may be deferred for a maximum of One Year. Credit and/or placement offered for CEEB Advanced Placement tests.

COSTS AND FINANCIAL AID

Annual in-state tuition $16,572. Annual out-of-state tuition $29,522. Room and board $10,520. Required fees $930. Average book expense $1,760. **Required Forms and Deadlines:** FAFSA. **Notification of Awards:** Applicants will be notified of awards on a rolling basis beginning 3/1. **Types of Aid:** *Need-based scholarships/grants:* Federal Pell, SEOG, state scholarships/grants, private scholarships, the school's own gift aid. *Loans:* Direct Subsidized Stafford, Direct Unsubsidized Stafford, Direct PLUS, Federal Perkins, college/university loans from institutional funds, Private Loans. *Student Employment:* Federal Work-Study Program available. Institutional employment available. Off-campus job opportunities are good. **Financial Aid Statistics:** 42% freshmen, 51% undergrads receive need-based scholarship or grant aid. 46% freshmen, 34% undergrads receive non-need-based scholarship or grant aid. 73% freshmen, 82% undergrads receive need-based self-help aid. 2% freshmen, 2% undergrads receive athletic scholarships. 69% freshmen, 68% undergrads receive any aid. 63% undergrads borrow to pay for school. Average cumulative indebtedness $27,670. **Criteria for awarding institutional aid:** *Non-need-based:* academics, alumni affiliation, athletics.

PENNSYLVANIA STATE UNIVERSITY— WILKES-BARRE

PO Box PSU, Lehman, PA 18627
Phone: 570-675-9238
E-mail: wbadmissions@psu.edu
Fax: 570-675-9113 · **Website:** www.wb.psu.edu

RATINGS

Admissions Selectivity Rating: 73   **Fire Safety Rating:** 60*

STUDENTS AND FACULTY

Enrollment: 563. **Student Body:** 29% female, 71% male, 4% out-of-state, 0% international. Asian 2%, African American 3%, Caucasian 93%, Hispanic 2%, Native American <1%
Faculty: 37 full-time faculty, 54% hold PhDs, 16% are members of minority groups, 16% are women.

ADMISSIONS

Freshman Academic Profile: Average high school GPA 3.03. 9.26% in top 10% of high school class, 35.19% in top 25% of high school class, 66.67% in top 50% of high school class. SAT Math middle 50% range 440-560. SAT Critical Reading middle 50% range 430-530. Minimum paper TOEFL 550. **Freshman Admission Statistics:** 630 applied, 84% admitted, 33% enrolled.

COSTS AND FINANCIAL AID

Annual in-state tuition $10,454. Annual out-of-state tuition $15,954. Room and board $3,360. Required fees $552. Average book expense $1,168. **Required Forms and Deadlines:** FAFSA. **Financial Aid Statistics:** 76% freshmen, 77% undergrads receive need-based scholarship or grant aid. 56% freshmen, 39% undergrads receive non-need-based scholarship or grant aid. 82% freshmen, 84% undergrads receive need-based self-help aid. 0% freshmen, 0% undergrads receive athletic scholarships. 67% undergrads borrow to pay for school. Average cumulative indebtedness $19,600.

PENNSYLVANIA STATE UNIVERSITY— WORTHINGTON SCRANTON

120 Ridge View Drive, Dunmore, PA 18512-1602
Phone: 570-963-2500
E-mail: wsadmissions@psu.edu
Fax: 570-963-2524 · **Website:** www.sn.psu.edu

This public school was founded in 1923. It has a 43-acre campus.

RATINGS

Admissions Selectivity Rating: 70   **Fire Safety Rating:** 60*

STUDENTS AND FACULTY

Enrollment: 1,185. **Student Body:** 50% female, 50% male, 1% out-of-state, 0% international. Asian 1%, African American 2%, Caucasian 93%, Hispanic 3%, Native American <1%
Faculty: 55 full-time faculty, 62% hold PhDs, 51% are members of minority groups, 13% are women.

ACADEMICS

Degrees: bachelor's, terminal associate, transfer associate. **Classes:** Most classes have 20–29 students. Most lab/discussion sessions have 20–29 students. **Special Study Options:** Accelerated program, cooperative education program, cross-registration, distance learning, double major, dual enrollment, honors program, independent study, internships, study abroad.

CAMPUS LIFE

Activities: Choral groups, drama/theater, jazz band, literary magazine, music ensembles, student government, student newspaper. **Athletics (Intercollegiate):** *Men:* baseball, basketball, cross-country, soccer. *Women:* volleyball.

ADMISSIONS

Freshman Academic Profile: Average high school GPA 2.84. 4.73% in top 10% of high school class, 18.91% in top 25% of high school class, 63.27% in top 50% of high school class. SAT Math middle 50% range 410-520. SAT Critical Reading middle 50% range 420-530. Minimum paper TOEFL 550. **Basis for**

Candidate Selection: *Very important factors considered include:* academic GPA, standardized test scores. *Important factors considered include:* rigor of secondary school record. *Other factors considered include:* Class rank, application essay, recommendation(s), alumni/ae relation, character/personal qualities, extracurricular activities, talent/ability, volunteer work, work experience. **Freshman Admission Requirements:** High school diploma is required and GED is accepted. *Academic units required:* 4 English, 3 mathematics, 3 science, (0 science labs), 2 foreign language, 3 social studies, 0 history, 0 academic electives. **Freshman Admission Statistics:** 903 applied, 86% admitted, 40% enrolled. **Transfer Admission Requirements:** High school transcript, college transcript(s), Lowest grade transferable C. **General Admission Information:** Application Fee $50. Notification on a rolling basis, beginning on or about 11/1. Nonfall registration accepted. Admission may be deferred for a maximum of 1 year.

COSTS AND FINANCIAL AID

Annual in-state tuition $10,454. Annual out-of-state tuition $15,954. Room and board $3,360. Required fees $532. Average book expense $1,168. **Required Forms and Deadlines:** FAFSA. **Types of Aid:** *Need-based scholarships/grants:* Federal Pell, SEOG, state scholarships/grants, private scholarships, the school's own gift aid. *Loans:* Subsidized Stafford, Unsubsidized Stafford, PLUS, Federal Perkins, college/university loans from institutional funds, Private Loans. **Financial Aid Statistics:** 77% freshmen, 80% undergrads receive need-based scholarship or grant aid. 24% freshmen, 21% undergrads receive non-need-based scholarship or grant aid. 78% freshmen, 85% undergrads receive need-based self-help aid. 0% freshmen, 0% undergrads receive athletic scholarships. 67% undergrads borrow to pay for school. Average cumulative indebtedness $19,600. **Criteria for awarding institutional aid:** *Non-need-based:* academics, alumni affiliation, athletics, minority status.

PENNSYLVANIA STATE UNIVERSITY—YORK

1031 Edgecomb Avenue, York, PA 17403-3398
Phone: 717-771-4040
E-mail: ykadmission@psu.edu
Fax: 717-771-4005 · **Website:** www.yk.psu.edu

This public school was founded in 1926. It has a 52-acre campus.

RATINGS

Admissions Selectivity Rating: 71   **Fire Safety Rating:** 60*

STUDENTS AND FACULTY

Enrollment: 1,070. **Student Body:** 44% female, 56% male, 5% out-of-state, 0% international. Asian 6%, African American 5%, Caucasian 83%, Hispanic 5%, Native American <1%
Retention and Graduation: 71% freshmen return for sophomore year.
Faculty: 59 full-time faculty, 61% hold PhDs, 36% are members of minority groups, 17% are women.

ACADEMICS

Degrees: bachelor's, terminal associate, transfer associate. **Classes:** Most classes have 10–19 students. Most lab/discussion sessions have fewer than 10 students. **Special Study Options:** Accelerated program, cross-registration, distance learning, double major, English as a Second Language (ESL), honors program, independent study, internships, student-designed major, study abroad.

FACILITIES

Housing: Nearby rooms, apartments, house rentals in the local community.

CAMPUS LIFE

Environment: Village. **Activities:** dance, drama/theater, literary magazine, student government, student newspaper, Campus Ministries, International Student Organization, Model UN. **Athletics (Intercollegiate):** *Men:* basketball, soccer, tennis. *Women:* tennis, volleyball.

ADMISSIONS

Freshman Academic Profile: Average high school GPA 2.81. 6% in top 10% of high school class, 24% in top 25% of high school class, 55% in top 50% of high school class. SAT Math middle 50% range 440-550. SAT Critical Reading middle 50% range 410-530. Minimum paper TOEFL 550. **Basis for Candidate Selection:** *Very important factors considered include:* academic GPA, standardized test scores. *Important factors considered include:* rigor of secondary school record. *Other factors considered include:* Class rank, application essay, recommendation(s), alumni/ae relation, character/personal qualities, extracurricular activities, talent/ability, volunteer work, work experience. **Freshman Admission Requirements:** High school diploma is required and GED is accepted. *Academic units required:* 4 English, 3 mathematics, 3 science, (0 science labs), 2 foreign language, 3 social studies, 0 history, 0 academic electives. **Freshman Admission Statistics:** 1,328 applied, 84% admitted, 30% enrolled. **Transfer Admission Requirements:** High school transcript, college transcript(s), Lowest grade transferable C. **General Admission Information:** Application Fee $50. Notification on a rolling basis, beginning on or about 11/1. Nonfall registration accepted. Admission may be deferred for a maximum of One year.

COSTS AND FINANCIAL AID
Annual in-state tuition $10,454. Annual out-of-state tuition $15,954. Room and board $3,360. Required fees $532. Average book expense $1,168. **Required Forms and Deadlines:** FAFSA. **Notification of Awards:** Applicants will be notified of awards on or about 3/1. **Types of Aid:** *Need-based scholarships/grants:* Federal Pell, SEOG, state scholarships/grants, private scholarships, the school's own gift aid. *Loans:* Subsidized Stafford, Unsubsidized Stafford, PLUS, Federal Perkins, college/university loans from institutional funds, Private Loans. **Financial Aid Statistics:** 66% freshmen, 75% undergrads receive need-based scholarship or grant aid. 39% freshmen, 35% undergrads receive non-need-based scholarship or grant aid. 79% freshmen, 81% undergrads receive need-based self-help aid. 0% freshmen, 0% undergrads receive athletic scholarships. 67% undergrads borrow to pay for school. Average cumulative indebtedness $19,600. **Criteria for awarding institutional aid:** *Non-need-based:* academics, alumni affiliation, athletics, minority status.

PEPPERDINE UNIVERSITY

Best 380

24255 Pacific Coast Highway, Malibu, CA 90263
Phone: 310-506-4392 • **Financial Aid Phone:** 310-506-4301
E-mail: admission-seaver@pepperdine.edu • **CEEB Code:** 4630
Fax: 310-506-4861 • **Website:** www.pepperdine.edu • **ACT Code:** 373

This private school, affiliated with the Church of Christ Church, was founded in 1937. It has a 830-acre campus.

RATINGS
Admissions Selectivity Rating: 93   **Fire Safety Rating:** 76

STUDENTS AND FACULTY
Enrollment: 3,434. **Student Body:** 59% female, 41% male, 41% out-of-state, 9% international (54 countries represented). Asian 0%, African American 0%, Caucasian 13%, Hispanic 13%, Native American 6%
Retention and Graduation: 75% freshmen graduate within 4 years. **Faculty:** 386 full-time faculty, 90% hold PhDs, 39% are members of minority groups, 18% are women. 0% of classes are taught by teaching assistants.

ACADEMICS
Degrees: bachelor's, master's. **Classes:** Most classes have 10–19 students. Most lab/discussion sessions have 20–29 students. **Majors with Highest Enrollment:** Business Administration and Management; Psychology; Political Science and Government. **Special Study Options:** double major, honors program, independent study, internships, student-designed major, study abroad, teacher certification program, weekend college, 3-2 programing engineering with University of Southern California, Washington University(MO), Boston University(MA). **Disability Services:** Special programs offered to physically disabled students include note-taking services, reader services, tape recorders, tutors. **Career services:** Alumni network, alumni services, career/job search classes, career assessment, internships, regional alumni. Career services highlights include a very active internship program that reaches into the local LA areas, Washington DC, nationally through our participation in the University Career Action Network, and internationally through an internship emphasis at our international campuses. Students at Pepperdine can receive academic credit for internships. Service-learning is employed as a teaching pedagogy by a variety of faculty members. One example the senior capstone business class "Service Leadership" where class members serve on a consulting team for a nonprofit.

FACILITIES
Housing: special housing for disabled students, men's dorms, women's dorms, apartments for married students, cooperative housing, apartments for single students, freshman and sophomores must live on campus or at home with parent or guardian if single and under age 21. **Special Academic Facilities/Equipment:** Weisman Art Museum. **Computers:** 100% of classrooms, 100% of dorms, 100% of libraries, 100% of dining areas, 100% of student union, 100%

of common outdoor areas have wireless network access. Students can register for classes online. Administrative functions (other than registration) can be performed online.

CAMPUS LIFE
Environment: City. **Activities:** Choral groups, concert band, dance, drama/theater, jazz band, literary magazine, music ensembles, musical theater, opera, pep band, radio station, student government, student newspaper, student-run film society, symphony orchestra, television station, yearbook, Campus Ministries, International Student Organization, Model UN. 50 registered organizations, 5 honor societies, 8 religious organizations. 5 fraternities, 7 sororities. **Athletics (Intercollegiate):** *Men:* baseball, basketball, cross-country, golf, tennis, volleyball, water polo. *Women:* basketball, cheerleading, cross-country, golf, soccer, swimming, tennis, track/field (outdoor), volleyball. **On-Campus Highlights:** Theme Tower, Smother'sTheatre, The Sandbar, Payson Library, Alumni Park. **Environmental Initiatives:** Pepperdine University conserves millions of gallons of drinking water annually dating back to 1972. Pepperdine uses recycled water to irrigate over 90% of the Universitys managed grounds. The University carefully monitors irrigation practices and uses an automated irrigation program based upon historical trends and current climactic conditions to conserve water and reduce runoff. Pepperdine University recycles all refuse disposed of on campus since 2000. The University has an average diversion rate of 78% meaning that 78% of all refuse gets reused. Pepperdine recycles high-tech equipment. All on-campus tree trimmings and brush clearance debris are either reused for grounds maintenance or turned into compost, which is used in many areas throughout campus. Pepperdine is committed to preserving the native environment in which the campus resides. 500 acres of the campus are set aside for conservation and 20% of the actively managed area is managed completely organically. Before the 50-acre Drescher Graduate Campus construction began, soil and seeds were collected on-site and were used to replant the slopes. In an effort to blend the Graduate Campus with the surrounding environment, the surrounding slopes contain approximately 99% native vegetation.

ADMISSIONS
Freshman Academic Profile: Average high school GPA 3.61. 46% in top 10% of high school class, 80% in top 25% of high school class, 96% in top 50% of high school class. SAT Math middle 50% range 570-680. SAT Critical Reading middle 50% range 550-650. SAT Writing middle 50% range 560-660. ACT middle 50% range 25-30. Minimum internet-based TOEFL 80. Minimum paper TOEFL 550. **Basis for Candidate Selection:** *Very important factors considered include:* application essay, academic GPA, recommendation(s), rigor of secondary school record, standardized test scores, character/personal qualities, extracurricular activities, talent/ability. *Important factors considered include:* religious affiliation/commitment, volunteer work. *Other factors considered include:* alumni/ae relation, first generation, racial/ethnic status, work experience. **Freshman Admission Requirements:** High school diploma is required and GED is accepted. **Freshman Admission Statistics:** 8,914 applied, 35% admitted, 21% enrolled. **Transfer Admission Requirements:** High school transcript, college transcript(s), essay or personal statement, Minimum college GPA of 3.00 required. Lowest grade transferable C. **General Admission Information:** Application Fee $65. Regular application deadline 1/15. Regular notification 4/1. Nonfall registration accepted. Credit and/or placement offered for CEEB Advanced Placement tests.

COSTS AND FINANCIAL AID
Required Forms and Deadlines: FAFSA. **Notification of Awards:** Applicants will be notified of awards on or about 4/15. **Types of Aid:** *Need-based scholarships/grants:* Federal Pell, SEOG, state scholarships/grants, private scholarships, the school's own gift aid, United Negro College Fund, ACG, SMART. *Loans:* Subsidized Stafford, Unsubsidized Stafford, PLUS, Federal Perkins, college/university loans from institutional funds. *Student Employment:* Federal Work-Study Program available. Institutional employment available. Off-campus job opportunities are good. **Financial Aid Statistics:** 99% freshmen, 97% undergrads receive need-based scholarship or grant aid. 0% freshmen, 0% undergrads receive non-need-based scholarship or grant aid. 73% freshmen, 81% undergrads receive need-based self-help aid. 4% freshmen, 3% undergrads receive athletic scholarships. 84% freshmen, 79% undergrads receive any aid. 63% undergrads borrow to pay for school. Average cumulative indebtedness $26,215. **Criteria for awarding institutional aid:** *Non-need-based:* academics, art, athletics, minority status, music/drama, religious affiliation.

PFEIFFER UNIVERSITY

P.O. Box 960, Misenheimer, NC 28109
Phone: 800-338-2060
E-mail: admissions@pfeiffer.edu • **CEEB Code:** 5536
Fax: 704-463-1363 • **Website:** www.pfeiffer.edu • **ACT Code:** 3140

This private school, affiliated with the Methodist Church, was founded in 1885.

RATINGS

Admissions Selectivity Rating: 76   **Fire Safety Rating:** 60*

STUDENTS AND FACULTY

Enrollment: 1,188. **Student Body:** 58% female, 42% male, 19% out-of-state, 5% international (13 countries represented). Asian 1%, African American 16%, Caucasian 59%, Hispanic 1%, Native American <1%. **Retention and Graduation:** 77% freshmen return for sophomore year. 41% freshmen graduate within 4 years. 60% freshmen graduate within 6 years. 23% grads go on to further study within 1 year. 15% grads pursue arts and sciences degrees. 5% grads pursue law degrees. 20% grads pursue business degrees. 2% grads pursue medical degrees. **Faculty:** 65 full-time faculty, 66% hold PhDs, 37% are members of minority groups, 11% are women. 0% of classes are taught by teaching assistants.

ACADEMICS

Degrees: bachelor's, master's, post-master's certificate. **Classes:** Most classes have fewer than 10 students. **Majors with Highest Enrollment:** Elementary Education and Teaching; Criminal Justice/Law Enforcement Administration; Business/Commerce. **Special Study Options:** Accelerated program, cross-registration, distance learning, double major, dual enrollment, honors program, independent study, internships, study abroad, teacher certification program, Capitol Hill Internship Program. **Honors programs:** Students who have demonstrated strong academic performance are invited to participate in the Honors Program. They enroll in honors-designated courses and are given expanded assignments or complete special projects. They live in honors housing and are invited to join the University Honors Association. Twelve students are chosen each year to serve as marshals at the graduation ceremony and the fall Academic Convocation. In addition, all Pfeiffer students are eligible to graduate cum laude, magna cum laude, and summa cum laude, depending on their grade point average. **Combined degree programs:** BA/MA. **Disability Services:** Special programs offered to physically disabled students include note-taking services, tutors. **Career services:** Alumni network, alumni services, career/job search classes, career assessment, internships, regional alumni.

FACILITIES

Housing: Coed dorms, men's dorms, women's dorms. **Special Academic Facilities/Equipment:** Beth Haltiwanger Retreat Center, Francis Center for Servant Leadership, new science building. **Computers:** Administrative functions (other than registration) can be performed online.

CAMPUS LIFE

Environment: Rural. **Activities:** Choral groups, concert band, drama/theater, jazz band, literary magazine, music ensembles, musical theater, pep band, student government, student newspaper, yearbook. 60 registered organizations, 6 honor societies, 1 religious organization. **Athletics (Intercollegiate):** *Men:* baseball, basketball, cheerleading, cross-country, golf, lacrosse, soccer, tennis. *Women:* basketball, cheerleading, cross-country, golf, lacrosse, soccer, softball, swimming, tennis, volleyball. **On-Campus Highlights:** Student Center, Merner Gymnasium, Chapel, Knapp Health and Fitness Center, Beth Haltiwanger Retreat Center, New science building.

ADMISSIONS

Freshman Academic Profile: Average high school GPA 3.1. 11% in top 10% of high school class, 30% in top 25% of high school class, 62% in top 50% of high school class. 90% from public high schools. SAT Math middle 50% range 450-570. SAT Critical Reading middle 50% range 430-540. ACT middle 50% range 18-24. Minimum paper TOEFL 500. **Basis for Candidate Selection:** *Very important factors considered include:* rigor of secondary school record, standardized test scores, character/personal qualities, volunteer work. *Important factors considered include:* recommendation(s), extracurricular activities, talent/ability. *Other factors considered include:* Class rank, application essay, alumni/ae relation, interview, religious affiliation/commitment, work experience. **Freshman Admission Requirements:** High school diploma is required and GED is accepted. *Academic units required:* 4 English, 3 mathematics, 2 science, (1 science labs), 2 social studies, 2 history. **Freshman Admission Statistics:** 586 applied, 72% admitted, 41% enrolled. **Transfer Admission Requirements:** college transcript(s), statement of good standing from prior institution(s). Minimum college GPA of 2.0 required. Lowest grade transferable

D. **General Admission Information:** Application Fee $25. Notification on a rolling basis, beginning on or about 9/1. Nonfall registration accepted. Credit offered for CEEB Advanced Placement tests.

COSTS AND FINANCIAL AID

Annual tuition $13,550. Room and board $5,430. Required fees $0. Average book expense $500. **Required Forms and Deadlines:** FAFSA. **Notification of Awards:** Applicants will be notified of awards on a rolling basis beginning 2/15. **Types of Aid:** *Need-based scholarships/grants:* Federal Pell, SEOG, state scholarships/grants, the school's own gift aid. *Loans:* Subsidized Stafford, Unsubsidized Stafford, PLUS, Federal Perkins. *Student Employment:* Federal Work-Study Program available. Off-campus job opportunities are good. **Financial Aid Statistics:** 99% freshmen, 99% undergrads receive need-based scholarship or grant aid. 32% freshmen, 16% undergrads receive non-need-based scholarship or grant aid. 85% freshmen, 87% undergrads receive need-based self-help aid. 0% freshmen, 0% undergrads receive athletic scholarships. 90% freshmen, 90% undergrads receive any aid. **Criteria for awarding institutional aid:** *Non-need-based:* academics, athletics, religious affiliation, state/district residency.

PHILADELPHIA UNIVERSITY

School House Lane and Henry Avenue, Philadelphia, PA 19144-5497
Phone: 215-951-2800 • **Financial Aid Phone:** 215-951-2940
E-mail: admissions@philau.edu • **CEEB Code:** 2666
Fax: 215-951-2907 • **Website:** www.PhilaU.edu • **ACT Code:** 3668

This private school was founded in 1884. It has a 100-acre campus.

RATINGS

Admissions Selectivity Rating: 85   **Fire Safety Rating:** 60*

STUDENTS AND FACULTY

Enrollment: 2,885. **Student Body:** 66% female, 34% male, 42% out-of-state, 4% international (30 countries represented). Asian 5%, African American 14%, Caucasian 59%, Hispanic 7%, Native American <1%. **Retention and Graduation:** 49% freshmen graduate within 4 years. 19% grads go on to further study within 1 year. 8% grads pursue arts and sciences degrees. 1% grads pursue law degrees. 10% grads pursue business degrees. 1% grads pursue medical degrees. **Faculty:** 123 full-time faculty, 76% hold PhDs, 46% are members of minority groups, 13% are women. 0% of classes are taught by teaching assistants.

ACADEMICS

Degrees: associate, bachelor's, certificate, master's, post-bachelor's certificate, post-master's certificate. **Classes:** Most classes have 10-19 students. Most lab/discussion sessions have 10-19 students. **Majors with Highest Enrollment:** Fashion/Apparel Design; Industrial and Product Design. **Special Study Options:** distance learning, double major, honors program, independent study, internships, liberal arts/career combination, study abroad. **Honors programs:** University Honors Program **Combined degree programs:** BS/MS, BS/MBA. **Disability Services:** Special programs offered to physically disabled students include note-taking services, reader services, tape recorders, tutors. **Career services:** alumni services, career/job search classes, career assessment, internships.

FACILITIES

Housing: Coed dorms, special housing for disabled students, women's dorms, apartments for single students, Townhouses. 63% of campus accessible to physically disabled. **Special Academic Facilities/Equipment:** The Design Center, Industrial Design Studios, Graphic Design Studios, Architecture Design Studios, CAD Labs in fashion design, interior design and architecture. **Computers:** Students can register for classes online. Administrative functions (other than registration) can be performed online.

CAMPUS LIFE

Environment: Metropolis. **Activities:** Choral groups, dance, drama/theater, student government, student newspaper, yearbook. 32 registered organizations, 3 religious organizations. 1 fraternity, 1 sorority. **Athletics (Intercollegiate):** *Men:* baseball, basketball, crew/rowing, cross-country, golf, soccer, tennis. *Women:* basketball, crew/rowing, cross-country, field hockey, lacrosse, soccer, softball, tennis, volleyball. **On-Campus Highlights:** Kanbar Campus Center, Athletic and Recreation Center, Gutman Library, Architecture and Design Building, The Design Center.

ADMISSIONS

Freshman Academic Profile: Average high school GPA 3.53. 17% in top 10% of high school class, 46% in top 25% of high school class, 78% in top 50% of

high school class. 80% from public high schools. SAT Math middle 50% range 490-600. SAT Critical Reading middle 50% range 480-580. SAT Writing middle 50% range 470-580. ACT middle 50% range 20-26. Minimum paper TOEFL 500. **Basis for Candidate Selection:** *Very important factors considered include:* academic GPA, rigor of secondary school record, standardized test scores. *Important factors considered include:* Class rank, recommendation(s), extracurricular activities, interview. *Other factors considered include:* application essay. **Freshman Admission Requirements:** High school diploma is required and GED is accepted. *Academic units required:* 4 English, 3 mathematics, 3 science, (2 science labs), 2 social studies, 1 history, 2 academic electives. **Freshman Admission Statistics:** 4,767 applied, 64% admitted, 22% enrolled. **Transfer Admission Requirements:** college transcript(s), Minimum college GPA of 2.5 required. Lowest grade transferable C. **General Admission Information:** Application Fee $35. Notification on a rolling basis, beginning on or about 11/1. Nonfall registration accepted. Admission may be deferred for a maximum of 1 year. Credit and/or placement offered for CEEB Advanced Placement tests.

COSTS AND FINANCIAL AID
Average book expense $1,600. **Required Forms and Deadlines:** FAFSA. **Notification of Awards:** Applicants will be notified of awards on a rolling basis beginning 2/10. **Types of Aid:** *Need-based scholarships/grants:* Federal Pell, SEOG, state scholarships/grants, private scholarships, the school's own gift aid, Gift scholarships from outside sources (non-endowed) for which University chooses recipient which may involve a need component. *Loans:* Subsidized Stafford, Unsubsidized Stafford, PLUS, Federal Perkins, Private Loan Programs. *Student Employment:* Federal Work-Study Program available. Institutional employment available. Off-campus job opportunities are good. **Financial Aid Statistics:** 100% freshmen, 100% undergrads receive need-based scholarship or grant aid. 24% freshmen, 10% undergrads receive non-need-based scholarship or grant aid. 77% freshmen, 88% undergrads receive need-based self-help aid. 1% freshmen, 3% undergrads receive athletic scholarships. 99% freshmen, 97% undergrads receive any aid. 79% undergrads borrow to pay for school. Average cumulative indebtedness $28,378. **Criteria for awarding institutional aid:** *Non-need-based:* academics, athletics.

PIEDMONT COLLEGE

P.O. Box 10, Demorest, GA 30535
Phone: 706-776-0103 · **Financial Aid Phone:** 706-778-3000
E-mail: ugrad@piedmont.edu · **CEEB Code:** 5537
Fax: 706-776-6635 · **Website:** www.piedmont.edu · **ACT Code:** 853

This private school, affiliated with the Congregational Church, was founded in 1897. It has a 115-acre campus.

RATINGS
Admissions Selectivity Rating: 81   Fire Safety Rating: 60*

STUDENTS AND FACULTY
Enrollment: 1,286. **Student Body:** 66% female, 34% male, 7% out-of-state, 0% international (8 countries represented). Asian 1%, African American 9%, Caucasian 73%, Hispanic 4%, Native American 1%
Retention and Graduation: 73% freshmen return for sophomore year. 37% freshmen graduate within 4 years. 50% freshmen graduate within 6 years. **Faculty:** 118 full-time faculty, 79% hold PhDs, 53% are members of minority groups. 0% of classes are taught by teaching assistants.

ACADEMICS
Degrees: bachelor's, master's, post-master's certificate. **Classes:** Most classes have fewer than 10 students. Most lab/discussion sessions have 10–19 students. **Majors with Highest Enrollment:** Elementary Education and Teaching; Business/Commerce; Nursing Practice. **Special Study Options:** Accelerated program, distance learning, double major, dual enrollment, honors program, independent study, internships, student-designed major, study abroad, teacher certification program. **Combined degree programs:** BA/MAT (Secondary Education). **Disability Services:** Special programs offered to physically disabled students include note-taking services, reader services, tape recorders, tutors. **Career services:** Alumni network, career/job search classes, career assessment, regional alumni.

FACILITIES
Housing: Coed dorms, special housing for disabled students, men's dorms, women's dorms, apartments for single students. 98% of campus accessible to physically disabled. **Special Academic Facilities/Equipment:** Art Gallery; 4 NE Georgia Youth and Tech Center; Botanical Center; Fitness Center. **Computers:** Administrative functions (other than registration) can be performed online.

CAMPUS LIFE
Environment: Rural. **Activities:** Choral groups, concert band, drama/theater, music ensembles, opera, radio station, student government, student newspaper, student-run film society, television station, yearbook. 20 registered organizations, 7 honor societies, 1 religious organization. **Athletics (Intercollegiate):** *Men:* baseball, basketball, cross-country, golf, soccer, tennis. *Women:* basketball, cross-country, golf, soccer, softball, tennis, volleyball. **On-Campus Highlights:** Johnny Mize Athletic Center, Lane Student Center, Stewart Hall, Center for Music and Worship, Arrendale Library.

ADMISSIONS
Freshman Academic Profile: Average high school GPA 3.4. 14% in top 10% of high school class, 37% in top 25% of high school class, 78% in top 50% of high school class. SAT Math middle 50% range 430-520. SAT Critical Reading middle 50% range 430-530. ACT middle 50% range 19-23. Minimum paper TOEFL 550. **Basis for Candidate Selection:** *Very important factors considered include:* academic GPA, rigor of secondary school record, standardized test scores. *Important factors considered include:* Class rank, application essay, recommendation(s), character/personal qualities, extracurricular activities, first generation, interview, talent/ability. *Other factors considered include:* alumni/ae relation, geographical residence, level of applicant's interest, state residency, volunteer work, work experience. **Freshman Admission Requirements:** High school diploma is required and GED is accepted. **Freshman Admission Statistics:** 994 applied, 58% admitted, 47% enrolled. **Transfer Admission Requirements:** college transcript(s), statement of good standing from prior institution(s). Minimum college GPA of 2.0 required. Lowest grade transferable C. **General Admission Information:** Regular application deadline 7/11. Regular notification 7/1. Nonfall registration accepted. Admission may be deferred for a maximum of 12 months. Neither credit nor placement offered for CEEB Advanced Placement tests.

COSTS AND FINANCIAL AID
Annual tuition $21,350. Room and board $8,786. Average book expense $700. **Required Forms and Deadlines:** FAFSA, Institution's own financial aid form, State aid form. **Types of Aid:** *Need-based scholarships/grants:* Federal Pell, SEOG, state scholarships/grants, private scholarships, the school's own gift aid. *Loans:* Direct Subsidized Stafford, Direct Unsubsidized Stafford, Direct PLUS. *Student Employment:* Federal Work-Study Program available. Institutional employment available. Highest amount earned per year from on-campus jobs $3,530. Off-campus job opportunities are good. **Financial Aid Statistics:** 100% freshmen, 99% undergrads receive need-based scholarship or grant aid. 18% freshmen, 12% undergrads receive non-need-based scholarship or grant aid. 63% freshmen, 74% undergrads receive need-based self-help aid. 0% freshmen, 0% undergrads receive athletic scholarships. 99% freshmen, 99% undergrads receive any aid. 84% undergrads borrow to pay for school. Average cumulative indebtedness $23,426. **Criteria for awarding institutional aid:** *Non-need-based:* academics, art, leadership, music/drama, religious affiliation, state/district residency.

PINE MANOR COLLEGE

400 Heath Street, Chestnut Hill, MA 02467-2332
Phone: 617-731-7104 · **Financial Aid Phone:** 800-762-1357
E-mail: admission@pmc.edu
Fax: 617-731-7102 · **Website:** www.pmc.edu

This is a private school.

RATINGS
Admissions Selectivity Rating: 71   Fire Safety Rating: 62

STUDENTS AND FACULTY
Enrollment: 477. **Student Body:** 100% female, 0% male, 24% out-of-state, 8% international. Asian 4%, African American 32%, Caucasian 25%, Hispanic 21%, Native American <1%
Retention and Graduation: 58% freshmen return for sophomore year. 31% freshmen graduate within 4 years. 39% freshmen graduate within 6 years. 27% grads go on to further study within 1 year. 11% grads pursue arts and sciences degrees. 1% grads pursue law degrees. 11% grads pursue business degrees. 4% grads pursue medical degrees. **Faculty:** 30 full-time faculty, 80% hold PhDs, 77% are members of minority groups, 10% are women. 0% of classes are taught by teaching assistants.

ACADEMICS
Degrees: associate, bachelor's, certificate, transfer associate. **Classes:** Most classes have 10–19 students. Most lab/discussion sessions have 10–19 students. **Majors with Highest Enrollment:** Communication and Media Studies;

Psychology; Business/Commerce. **Special Study Options:** cross-registration, double major, English as a Second Language (ESL), honors program, independent study, internships, liberal arts/career combination, student-designed major, study abroad, teacher certification program. **Disability Services:** Special programs offered to physically disabled students include reader services, tape recorders, tutors. **Career services:** alumni services, career/job search classes, career assessment, internships. Recognizing a fundamental link between a liberal arts education and the professional world, Pine Manor College integrates the internship experience heavily into the curriculum. Although all students are encouraged to participate in at least one internship before senior year, each Pine Manor student must complete a senior level internship during fall semester of senior year. The PMC Internship combines student's academic knowledge with practical experience in the workplace, while providing students with the opportunity to explore career options and develop the leadership skills employers seek. Many PMC interns are offered permanent positions at their sites. After working with top professionals at Boston's best corporations, hospitals, museums, laboratories, publications and social service agencies, PMC seniors feel prepared to make informed career choices.

FACILITIES

Housing: special housing for disabled students, women's dorms. 50% of campus accessible to physically disabled. **Special Academic Facilities/Equipment:** Hess Art Gallery, Annenberg Library and Communications Center, Ann Pappajohn Child Study Center. **Computers:** Administrative functions (other than registration) can be performed online.

CAMPUS LIFE

Activities: Choral groups, dance, drama/theater, literary magazine, radio station, student government, yearbook. 25 registered organizations, 1 honor society, 1 religious organization. **Athletics (Intercollegiate):** *Women:* basketball, cross-country, lacrosse, soccer, softball, tennis, volleyball.

ADMISSIONS

Freshman Academic Profile: Average high school GPA 2.4. 0% in top 10% of high school class, 23% in top 25% of high school class, 49% in top 50% of high school class. 89% from public high schools. SAT Math middle 50% range 340-450. SAT Critical Reading middle 50% range 360-480. ACT middle 50% range 15-19. Minimum paper TOEFL 475. **Basis for Candidate Selection:** *Very important factors considered include:* application essay, recommendation(s), rigor of secondary school record. *Important factors considered include:* standardized test scores, interview. *Other factors considered include:* Class rank, alumni/ae relation, character/personal qualities, extracurricular activities, talent/ability, volunteer work, work experience. **Freshman Admission Requirements:** High school diploma is required and GED is accepted. **Freshman Admission Statistics:** 478 applied, 75% admitted, 42% enrolled. **Transfer Admission Requirements:** college transcript(s), essay or personal statement, statement of good standing from prior institution(s). Minimum college GPA of 2.0 required. Lowest grade transferable C-. **General Admission Information:** Application Fee $25. Nonfall registration accepted. Admission may be deferred for a maximum of 1 year. Credit and/or placement offered for CEEB Advanced Placement tests.

COSTS AND FINANCIAL AID

Room and board $5,088. Required fees $826. Average book expense $900. **Required Forms and Deadlines:** FAFSA. **Notification of Awards:** Applicants will be notified of awards on a rolling basis beginning 3/1. **Types of Aid:** *Need-based scholarships/grants:* Federal Pell, SEOG, state scholarships/grants, private scholarships, the school's own gift aid. *Loans:* Subsidized Stafford, Unsubsidized Stafford, PLUS, state loans. *Student Employment:* Federal Work-Study Program available. Institutional employment available. Off-campus job opportunities are excellent. **Financial Aid Statistics:** 0% freshmen, 0% undergrads receive athletic scholarships. 84% freshmen, 85% undergrads receive any aid. **Criteria for awarding institutional aid:** *Non-need-based:* academics, alumni affiliation, leadership.

PITTSBURG STATE UNIVERSITY

1701 South Broadway, Pittsburg, KS 66762
Phone: 620-235-4251 · **Financial Aid Phone:** 800-854-7488
E-mail: psuadmit@pittstate.edu · **CEEB Code:** 6336
Fax: 620-235-6003 · **Website:** www.pittstate.edu · **ACT Code:** 1449

This public school was founded in 1903. It has a 443-acre campus.

RATINGS

Admissions Selectivity Rating: 76   Fire Safety Rating: 85

STUDENTS AND FACULTY

Enrollment: 5,842. **Student Body:** 48% female, 52% male, 27% out-of-state, 3% international (42 countries represented). Asian 1%, African American 4%, Caucasian 81%, Hispanic 5%, Native American 1%
Retention and Graduation: 28% freshmen graduate within 4 years. **Faculty:** 317 full-time faculty, 74% hold PhDs, 41% are members of minority groups, 9% are women. 2.2% of classes are taught by teaching assistants.

ACADEMICS

Degrees: associate, bachelor's, certificate, master's, post-master's certificate. **Classes:** Most classes have 20–29 students. Most lab/discussion sessions have 10–19 students. **Majors with Highest Enrollment:** Engineering Technology; Business Administration and Management; Education. **Special Study Options:** Accelerated program, distance learning, double major, dual enrollment, English as a Second Language (ESL), honors program, independent study, internships, student-designed major, study abroad, teacher certification program. **Honors programs:** Honors College. **Disability Services:** Special programs offered to physically disabled students include note-taking services, reader services, tape recorders. **Career services:** Alumni network, alumni services, career/job search classes, career assessment, internships.

FACILITIES

Housing: Coed dorms, special housing for disabled students, apartments for married students, substance free and academic excellence floors are available. 90% of campus accessible to physically disabled. **Special Academic Facilities/Equipment:** planetarium, observatory, field biology reserve, nature reach,herbarium, technology center, mammal collection, greenhouse, art gallery, polymer research center, cadaver lab, Veterans Memorial Amphitheater, broadcasting lab, public radio station. **Computers:** 100% of classrooms, 100% of dorms, 100% of libraries, 100% of dining areas, 100% of student union, 80% of common outdoor areas have wireless network access. Students can register for classes online. Administrative functions (other than registration) can be performed online.

CAMPUS LIFE

Environment: Village. **Activities:** Choral groups, concert band, dance, drama/theater, jazz band, literary magazine, marching band, music ensembles, pep band, radio station, student government, student newspaper, television station, yearbook, Campus Ministries, International Student Organization. 150 registered organizations, 8 fraternities, 3 sororities. **Athletics (Intercollegiate):** *Men:* baseball, basketball, cheerleading, cross-country, football, golf, track/field (outdoor), track/field (indoor). *Women:* basketball, cheerleading, cross-country, softball, track/field (outdoor), track/field (indoor), volleyball. **On-Campus Highlights:** Planetarium, Veterans Memorial Amphitheater, Gorilla Village, Brandenburg Field/Carnie Smith Stadium, Timmons Chapel, Russ Hall, Kansas Technology Center, Nature Reach, Centennial Mural, Centennial Bell Tower,herbarium, art gallery, broadcasting lab, cadaver lab, polymer research lab, mammal collection, ROTC & student fitness center. **Environmental Initiatives:** Addition of Sustainability as a goal in the university strategic plan. Completing a campus sustainability plan. AASHE STARS—Bronze Rating.

ADMISSIONS

Freshman Academic Profile: Average high school GPA 3.3. 13% in top 10% of high school class, 35% in top 25% of high school class, 67% in top 50% of high school class. ACT middle 50% range 19-24. Minimum internet-based TOEFL 68. Minimum paper TOEFL 520. **Basis for Candidate Selection:** *Very important factors considered include:* Class rank, academic GPA, rigor of secondary school record, standardized test scores. **Freshman Admission Requirements:** High school diploma is required and GED is accepted. **Freshman Admission Statistics:** 2,758 applied, 79% admitted, 47% enrolled. **Transfer Admission Requirements:** college transcript(s), Minimum college GPA of 2.0 required. Lowest grade transferable D. **General Admission Information:** Application Fee $30. Nonfall registration accepted. Credit and/or placement offered for CEEB Advanced Placement tests.

COSTS AND FINANCIAL AID

Room and board $6,734. Required fees $1,196. Average book expense $1,000. **Required Forms and Deadlines:** FAFSA, State aid form. **Notification of Awards:** Applicants will be notified of awards on a rolling basis beginning 3/1. **Types of Aid:** *Need-based scholarships/grants:* Federal Pell, SEOG, state scholarships/grants, private scholarships, the school's own gift aid. *Loans:* Direct Subsidized Stafford, Direct Unsubsidized Stafford, Direct PLUS, Subsidized Stafford, Unsubsidized Stafford, PLUS, Federal Perkins, Federal Nursing, college/university loans from institutional funds. *Student Employment:* Federal Work-Study Program available. Institutional employment available. Highest amount earned per year from on-campus jobs $5,100. Off-campus job opportunities are good. **Financial Aid Statistics:** 64% freshmen, 69% undergrads receive need-based scholarship or grant aid. 98% freshmen, 69% undergrads receive non-need-based scholarship or grant aid. 72% freshmen, 78% undergrads receive need-based self-help aid. 0% freshmen, 0% undergrads receive athletic scholarships. 91% freshmen, 85% undergrads receive any aid. 68% undergrads borrow to pay for school. Average cumulative indebtedness $23,204. **Criteria for awarding institutional aid:** *Non-need-based:* academics, alumni affiliation, art, athletics, leadership, minority status, music/drama.

PITZER COLLEGE

1050 North Mills Avenue, Claremont, CA 91711-6101
Phone: 909-621-8129 · **Financial Aid Phone:** 909-621-8208
E-mail: admission@pitzer.edu · **CEEB Code:** 4619
Fax: 909-621-8770 · **Website:** www.pitzer.edu · **ACT Code:** 363

This private school was founded in 1963. It has a 35-acre campus.

RATINGS

Admissions Selectivity Rating: 93   Fire Safety Rating: 80

STUDENTS AND FACULTY

Enrollment: 1,081. **Student Body:** 60% female, 40% male, 53% out-of-state, 5% international (15 countries represented). Asian 6%, African American 5%, Caucasian 49%, Hispanic 15%, Native American <1%
Retention and Graduation: 91% freshmen return for sophomore year. 72% freshmen graduate within 4 years. 81% freshmen graduate within 6 years. 17% grads go on to further study within 1 year. **Faculty:** 85 full-time faculty, 100% hold PhDs, 52% are members of minority groups, 31% are women. 0% of classes are taught by teaching assistants.

ACADEMICS

Degrees: bachelor's. **Classes:** Most classes have 10–19 students. **Majors with Highest Enrollment:** Psychology; Film/Cinema/Video Studies; Sociology. **Special Study Options:** cooperative education program, cross-registration, double major, English as a Second Language (ESL), exchange student program (domestic), honors program, independent study, internships, liberal arts/career combination, student-designed major, study abroad. **Combined degree programs:** BA/MA, B.A./D.O. (Doctor of Osteopathy); BA/MBA. **Disability Services:** Special programs offered to physically disabled students include note-taking services, reader services, tape recorders, tutors. **Career services:** Alumni network, career/job search classes, career assessment, internships. Career services highlights include an internship component in many of our classes, which provides students with practical experience as well as classroom learning.

FACILITIES

Housing: Coed dorms, special housing for disabled students, Theme Housing, Green housing. 95% of campus accessible to physically disabled. **Special Academic Facilities/Equipment:** Theatre arts center, Black, Asian American and Chicano Study centers; film, TV, and videotape studios; arboretum; biological field station; student health services, Gold Student Center **Computers:** 95% of classrooms, 100% of dorms, 95% of libraries, have wireless network access. Students can register for classes online. Administrative functions (other than registration) can be performed online.

CAMPUS LIFE

Environment: Town. **Activities:** Choral groups, dance, drama/theater, literary magazine, music ensembles, radio station, student government, student newspaper, symphony orchestra, Campus Ministries, International Student Organization, Model UN. 120 registered organizations, 1 honor society. **Athletics (Intercollegiate):** *Men:* baseball, basketball, cross-country, diving, football, golf, soccer, swimming, tennis, track/field (outdoor), water polo. *Women:* basketball, cross-country, diving, soccer, softball, swimming, tennis, track/field (outdoor), volleyball, water polo. **On-Campus Highlights:** Grove House, McConnell Center, Gloria and Peter Gold Student Center, Marquis Library, The Mounds, http://www.pitzer.edu/admission/campusvisit.aspThe Claremont Colleges Consortium Pitzer students may cross-register at any of The Claremont Colleges, and may utilize all Claremont facilities, including Honnold Library, the third-largest academic library in the state, with more than 2 million volumes; Huntley Bookstore; Baxter Medical Center; McAlister Center for Religious Activities and Monsour Counseling Center. Pitzer sponsors the Joint Science Program with Claremont McKenna and Scripps colleges, and the five undergraduate colleges offer a wide range of recreational facilities, student gathering places and dining areas. Pitzer combines with Pomona College for NCAA Division III sports. **Environmental Initiatives:** New "Green" dorms; Campus Climate challenge through Eco Center; Majors in Environmental Studies and Environmental Science; Class in Environmental Justice.

ADMISSIONS

Freshman Academic Profile: Average high school GPA 3.85. SAT Math middle 50% range 610-700. SAT Critical Reading middle 50% range 600-700. Minimum internet-based TOEFL 70. Minimum paper TOEFL 520. **Basis for Candidate Selection:** *Very important factors considered include:* Class rank, application essay, academic GPA, recommendation(s), rigor of secondary school record, character/personal qualities, extracurricular activities, racial/ethnic status. *Important factors considered include:* first generation, geographical residence, interview, level of applicant's interest, talent/ability, volunteer work. *Other factors considered include:* standardized test scores, alumni/ae relation, work experience. **Freshman Admission Requirements:** High school diploma is required and GED is accepted. *Academic units required:* 4 English, 3 mathematics, 3 science, (3 science labs), 3 foreign language, 3 social studies, 1 history, 1 visual/performing arts, 0 computer science. **Freshman Admission Statistics:** 4,115 applied, 15% admitted, 44% enrolled. **Transfer Admission Requirements:** college transcript(s), essay or personal statement, statement of good standing from prior institution(s). Minimum college GPA of 2.0 required. Lowest grade transferable C-. **General Admission Information:** Application Fee $60. Early decision application deadline 11/15. Regular application deadline 1/1. Regular notification 4/1. Nonfall registration not accepted. Admission may be deferred for a maximum of 1 year. Placement offered for CEEB Advanced Placement tests.

COSTS AND FINANCIAL AID

Annual tuition $46,720. Room and board $14,758. Required fees $272. Average book expense $1,000. **Required Forms and Deadlines:** FAFSA, CSS/Financial Aid PROFILE, State aid form, Noncustodial PROFILE. **Notification of Awards:** Applicants will be notified of awards on or about 4/1. **Types of Aid:** *Need-based scholarships/grants:* Federal Pell, SEOG, state scholarships/grants, private scholarships, the school's own gift aid, Federal ACG and National SMART. *Loans:* Subsidized Stafford, Unsubsidized Stafford, PLUS, Federal Perkins, college/university loans from institutional funds. *Student Employment:* Federal Work-Study Program available. Institutional employment available. Off-campus job opportunities are good. **Financial Aid Statistics:** 100% freshmen, 100% undergrads receive need-based scholarship or grant aid. 4% freshmen, 1% undergrads receive non-need-based scholarship or grant aid. 96% freshmen, 93% undergrads receive need-based self-help aid. 0% freshmen, 0% undergrads receive athletic scholarships. 34% freshmen, 40% undergrads receive any aid. 44% undergrads borrow to pay for school. Average cumulative indebtedness $15,002. **Criteria for awarding institutional aid:** *Non-need-based:* academics, leadership.

PLYMOUTH STATE UNIVERSITY

17 High Street, Plymouth, NH 3264
Phone: 603-535-2237 · **Financial Aid Phone:** 877-846-5755
E-mail: plymouthadmit@plymouth.edu · **CEEB Code:** 3690
Fax: 603-535-2714 · **Website:** www.plymouth.edu · **ACT Code:** 2518

This public school was founded in 1871. It has a 170-acre campus.

RATINGS

Admissions Selectivity Rating: 73   Fire Safety Rating: 99

STUDENTS AND FACULTY

Enrollment: 4,127. **Student Body:** 49% female, 51% male, 42% out-of-state, 1% international (34 countries represented). Asian 1%, African American 1%, Caucasian 79%, Hispanic 2%, Native American <1%
Retention and Graduation: 74% freshmen return for sophomore year. 40% freshmen graduate within 4 years. **Faculty:** 187 full-time faculty, 88% hold PhDs, 45% are members of minority groups, 8% are women. 0% of classes are taught by teaching assistants.

ACADEMICS

Degrees: bachelor's, doctoral, master's, post-bachelor's certificate, post-master's certificate. **Classes:** Most classes have 20–29 students. Most lab/discussion sessions have 10–19 students. **Majors with Highest Enrollment:** Business Administration and Management; Criminal Justice/Safety Studies; Psychology. **Special Study Options:** cross-registration, distance learning, double major, dual enrollment, English as a Second Language (ESL), exchange student program (domestic), external degree program, honors program, independent study, internships, student-designed major, study abroad, teacher certification program. **Honors programs:** First and Second Year Honors Program, Business Honors, Psychology Honors. **Disability Services:** Special programs offered to physically disabled students include note-taking services, reader services, tape recorders, tutors. **Career services:** Alumni network, alumni services, career/job search classes, career assessment, internships, regional alumni.

FACILITIES

Housing: Coed dorms, special housing for disabled students, fraternity/sorority housing, apartments for married students, apartments for single students, Wellness Housing, Theme HousingNon-traditional student apts. Quiet study/Academic. 80% of campus accessible to physically disabled. **Special Academic Facilities/Equipment:** Karl Drerup Art gallery, Silver Cultural Arts Center, Sylvestre Planetarium, Child Development and Family Center (NAEYC accredited lab school for children 2-6 years old), meteorology lab, Geographic Information System lab, psychology lab, graphic design computer lab. **Computers:** 75% of classrooms, 5% of dorms, 100% of libraries, 100% of dining areas, 100% of student union, 10% of common outdoor areas have wireless network access. Students can register for classes online. Administrative functions (other than registration) can be performed online.

CAMPUS LIFE

Environment: Village. **Activities:** Choral groups, concert band, dance, drama/theater, jazz band, literary magazine, music ensembles, musical theater, radio station, student government, student newspaper, student-run film society, yearbook, Campus Ministries, International Student Organization, Model UN. 80 registered organizations, 13 honor societies, 4 religious organizations. 3 sororities. **Athletics (Intercollegiate):** *Men:* baseball, basketball, football, ice hockey, lacrosse, skiing (downhill/alpine), soccer, wrestling. *Women:* basketball, cheerleading, diving, field hockey, ice hockey, lacrosse, skiing (downhill/alpine), soccer, softball, swimming, tennis, volleyball. **On-Campus Highlights:** Hartman Union Building, Silver Center for the Arts, PE Center-New-Fall '10 Ice Arena & Welcome Center, Prospect Dining Hall, Lamson Library—Information Commons. **Environmental Initiatives:** New degree program. All new campus construction must achieve LEED Silver Standard or the Equivalent Energy conservation projects

ADMISSIONS

Freshman Academic Profile: Average high school GPA 2.89. 3% in top 10% of high school class, 17% in top 25% of high school class, 55% in top 50% of high school class. SAT Math middle 50% range 440-540. SAT Critical Reading middle 50% range 440-520. SAT Writing middle 50% range 420-520. ACT middle 50% range 17-23. Minimum internet-based TOEFL 68. Minimum paper TOEFL 520. **Basis for Candidate Selection:** *Very important factors considered include:* rigor of secondary school record. *Important factors considered include:* Class rank, application essay, academic GPA, recommendation(s), standardized test scores, character/personal qualities, talent/ability. *Other factors considered include:* alumni/ae relation, extracurricular activities, racial/ethnic status, volunteer work, work experience. **Freshman Admission Requirements:** High school diploma is required and GED is accepted. *Academic units required:* 4 English, 3 mathematics, 2 science, (1 science labs), 0 foreign language, 2 social studies, 1 history, 0 academic electives. **Freshman Admission Statistics:** 4,940 applied, 76% admitted, 25% enrolled. **Transfer Admission Requirements:** High school transcript, college transcript(s), Minimum college GPA of 2.0 required. Lowest grade transferable C. **General Admission Information:** Application Fee $45. Regular application deadline 4/1. Notification on a rolling basis, beginning on or about 11/1. Nonfall registration accepted. Admission may be deferred for a maximum of 1 year. Credit offered for CEEB Advanced Placement tests.

COSTS AND FINANCIAL AID

Required Forms and Deadlines: FAFSA. **Notification of Awards:** Applicants will be notified of awards on a rolling basis beginning 3/1. **Types of Aid:** *Need-based scholarships/grants:* Federal Pell, SEOG, state scholarships/grants, private scholarships, the school's own gift aid. *Loans:* Direct Subsidized Stafford, Direct Unsubsidized Stafford, Direct PLUS, Federal Perkins. *Student Employment:* Federal Work-Study Program available. Institutional employment available. Highest amount earned per year from on-campus jobs $3,325. Off-campus job opportunities are good. **Financial Aid Statistics:** 60% freshmen, 62% undergrads receive need-based scholarship or grant aid. 39% freshmen, 31% undergrads receive non-need-based scholarship or grant aid. 94% freshmen, 95% undergrads receive need-based self-help aid. 0% freshmen, 0% undergrads receive athletic scholarships. 91% freshmen, 86% undergrads receive any aid. 82% undergrads borrow to pay for school. Average cumulative indebtedness $23,389. **Criteria for awarding institutional aid:** *Non-need-based:* academics, music/drama.

POINT LOMA NAZARENE UNIVERSITY

3900 Lomaland Drive, San Diego, CA 92106
Phone: 619-849-2273
E-mail: admissions@pointloma.edu • **CEEB Code:** 4605
Fax: 619-849-2601 • **ACT Code:** 370

This private school, affiliated with the Nazarene Church, was founded in 1902. It has a 90-acre campus.

RATINGS

Admissions Selectivity Rating: 88   **Fire Safety Rating:** 60*

STUDENTS AND FACULTY

Enrollment: 2,337. **Student Body:** 61% female, 39% male, 21% out-of-state, 0% international (17 countries represented). Asian 6%, African American 2%, Caucasian 78%, Hispanic 11%, Native American 1%
Retention and Graduation: 87% freshmen return for sophomore year. 60% freshmen graduate within 4 years. 70% freshmen graduate within 6 years. **Faculty:** 177 full-time faculty, 73% hold PhDs, 40% are members of minority groups, 10% are women. 0% of classes are taught by teaching assistants.

ACADEMICS

Degrees: bachelor's, master's. **Classes:** Most classes have 20–29 students. **Majors with Highest Enrollment:** Liberal Arts and Sciences/Liberal Studies; Psychology; Business/Commerce. **Special Study Options:** double major, honors program, independent study, internships, study abroad, teacher certification program. **Honors programs:** Honors Scholars Program.

FACILITIES

Housing: men's dorms, women's dorms, apartments for married students, apartments for single students. 100% of campus accessible to physically disabled. **Special Academic Facilities/Equipment:** Language lab, on-campus preschool, electron microscope. **Computers:** Students can register for classes online. Administrative functions (other than registration) can be performed online.

CAMPUS LIFE

Environment: Metropolis. **Activities:** Choral groups, concert band, drama/theater, jazz band, literary magazine, music ensembles, musical theater, radio station, student government, student newspaper, television station, yearbook, Campus Ministries, International Student Organization. 30 registered organizations, 2 honor societies, 7 religious organizations. 3 fraternities, 3 sororities. **Athletics (Intercollegiate):** *Men:* baseball, basketball, cross-country, golf, soccer, tennis, track/field (outdoor). *Women:* basketball, cross-country, softball, tennis, track/field (outdoor), volleyball. **On-Campus Highlights:** Point Break Café, Recreation Center, Ryan Library, Greek Ampitheatre, Golden Gymnasium.

ADMISSIONS

Freshman Academic Profile: Average high school GPA 3.72. 45% in top 10% of high school class, 72% in top 25% of high school class, 95% in top 50% of high school class. SAT Math middle 50% range 500-620. SAT Critical Reading middle 50% range 510-620. Minimum paper TOEFL 550. **Basis for Candidate Selection:** *Very important factors considered include:* academic GPA, rigor of secondary school record, standardized test scores, character/personal qualities, religious affiliation/commitment. *Important factors considered include:* Class rank, application essay, recommendation(s), interview. *Other factors considered include:* alumni/ae relation, extracurricular activities, first generation, level of applicant's interest, talent/ability. **Freshman Admission Requirements:** High school diploma is required and GED is accepted. **Freshman Admission Statistics:** 1,757 applied, 73% admitted, 41% enrolled. **Transfer Admission Requirements:** college transcript(s), essay or personal statement, interview, Minimum college GPA of 2.0 required. Lowest grade transferable D. **General Admission Information:** Application Fee $50. Regular notification 4/1. Nonfall registration not accepted. Credit and/or placement offered for CEEB Advanced Placement tests.

COSTS AND FINANCIAL AID

Annual tuition $24,580. Room and board $8,170. Required fees $540. Average book expense $1,566. **Required Forms and Deadlines:** FAFSA, Institution's own financial aid form. **Notification of Awards:** Applicants will be notified of awards on a rolling basis beginning 3/1. **Types of Aid:** *Need-based scholarships/grants:* Federal Pell, SEOG, state scholarships/grants, private scholarships, the school's own gift aid. *Loans:* Subsidized Stafford, Unsubsidized Stafford, PLUS, Federal Perkins, Federal Nursing. **Financial Aid Statistics:** 96% freshmen, 93% undergrads receive need-based scholarship or grant aid. 9% freshmen, 9% undergrads receive non-need-based scholarship or grant aid. 77% freshmen, 82% undergrads receive need-based self-help aid. 3% freshmen, 4% undergrads receive athletic scholarships. 86% undergrads borrow to pay for school. Average cumulative indebtedness $15,019.

POINT PARK UNIVERSITY

201 Wood Street, Pittsburgh, PA 15222
Phone: 412-392-3430 • **Financial Aid Phone:** 412-392-3930
E-mail: enroll@pointpark.edu • **CEEB Code:** 2676
Fax: 412-391-1980 • **ACT Code:** 3530

This private school was founded in 1960.

RATINGS

Admissions Selectivity Rating: 76   **Fire Safety Rating:** 95

STUDENTS AND FACULTY

Enrollment: 3,167. **Student Body:** 58% female, 42% male, 21% out-of-state, 2% international (38 countries represented). Asian 1%, African American 17%, Caucasian 73%, Hispanic 3%, Native American <1%
Retention and Graduation: 74% freshmen return for sophomore year. 39% freshmen graduate within 4 years. 50% freshmen graduate within 6 years. **Faculty:** 133 full-time faculty, 74% hold PhDs, 38% are members of minority groups, 10% are women. 0% of classes are taught by teaching assistants.

ACADEMICS

Degrees: associate, bachelor's, certificate, master's, post-bachelor's certificate. **Classes:** Most classes have 10–19 students. **Majors with Highest Enrollment:** Teacher Education and Professional Development, Specific Subject Areas; Dance; Drama and Dramatics/Theatre Arts. **Special Study Options:** Accelerated program, cooperative education program, cross-registration, distance learning, double major, dual enrollment, English as a Second Language (ESL), exchange student program (domestic), honors program, independent study, internships, liberal arts/career combination, student-designed major, study abroad, teacher certification program, weekend college. **Honors programs:** The Point Park Honors Program mission provides the foundation from which honors courses are developed. Honors courses will not be defined by more work but rather by a different kind of learning environment. Students will be introduced to the usual content and objectives of the course, but they will also develop in-depth understandings of topics. Students will be expected to use primary sources when possible and to develop appropriate research skills which should result in major documented papers or projects. Students will be encouraged to become adventurous, independent thinkers. Students should experience a variety of learning activities which may include collaborative learning, field experience, debates, documented projects, interviews, and presentations. Evaluation will be based on performance, creativity, imagination, critical thinking, and risk taking rather than on more assignments and tests. Honors students will be expected to participate in the quest for knowledge by being prepared and willing to contribute to all class activities. Honors students also may join our Honors Student Organization and participate in a variety of community service efforts and projects inside and outside the Point Park community. Students annually are offered the chance to travel for an alternative spring break, and they can present papers and research at national and regional honors conferences. Every effort is made to encourage all of them to assume leadership positions and propose their own activities and endeavors to complement their work in the classroom. Students who complete program requirements will be recognized in the program at graduation and will receive a separate certificate and notation on their transcript. **Disability Services:** Special programs offered to physically disabled students include note-taking services, reader services, tape recorders, tutors. **Career services:** Alumni network, alumni services, career/job search classes, career assessment, internships, regional alumni.

FACILITIES

Housing: Coed dorms, special housing for disabled students, women's dorms, apartments for single students, Theme HousingLiving & Learning Communities; Suite Style. 95% of campus accessible to physically disabled. **Special Academic Facilities/Equipment:** Theater, day care center and elementary school, engineering technology labs, television and radio studios, digital film editing suites, dance studios **Computers:** 100% of classrooms, 100% of libraries, 100% of dining areas, 100% of student union, 100% of common outdoor areas have wireless network access. Students can register for classes online. Administrative functions (other than registration) can be performed online.

CAMPUS LIFE

Environment: Metropolis. **Activities:** Choral groups, dance, drama/theater, literary magazine, musical theater, radio station, student government, student newspaper, student-run film society, television station, International Student Organization. 25 registered organizations, 3 honor societies, 2 religious organizations. **Athletics (Intercollegiate):** *Men:* baseball, basketball, cross-country, golf, soccer. *Women:* basketball, cross-country, golf, soccer, softball, volleyball. **On-Campus Highlights:** Point Café, Atrium Overlook, Recreation Center, Coffee Kiosk, Outdoor Patio. **Environmental Initiatives:** Recycling; LEED Building; Creating a greening committee with strategic plan.

ADMISSIONS

Freshman Academic Profile: Average high school GPA 3.21. 10% in top 10% of high school class, 30% in top 25% of high school class, 66% in top 50% of high school class. SAT Math middle 50% range 450-560. SAT Critical Reading middle 50% range 460-580. SAT Writing middle 50% range 450-560. ACT middle 50% range 20-26. Minimum paper TOEFL 500. **Basis for Candidate Selection:** *Other factors considered include:* Class rank, academic GPA, rigor of secondary school record, standardized test scores, talent/ability. **Freshman Admission Requirements:** High school diploma is required and GED is accepted. **Freshman Admission Statistics:** 3,673 applied, 76% admitted, 19% enrolled. **Transfer Admission Requirements:** college transcript(s), Minimum college GPA of 2.0 required. Lowest grade transferable C. **General Admission Information:** Application Fee $40. Notification on a rolling basis, beginning on or about 10/1. Nonfall registration accepted. Admission may be deferred for a maximum of 1 year. Neither credit nor placement offered for CEEB Advanced Placement tests.

COSTS AND FINANCIAL AID

Annual tuition $24,020. Room and board $9,920. Required fees $1,170. Average book expense $1,000. **Required Forms and Deadlines:** FAFSA. **Notification of Awards:** Applicants will be notified of awards on a rolling basis beginning 2/15. **Types of Aid:** *Need-based scholarships/grants:* Federal Pell, SEOG, state scholarships/grants, private scholarships, the school's own gift aid. *Loans:* Direct Subsidized Stafford, Direct Unsubsidized Stafford, Direct PLUS, Subsidized Stafford, Unsubsidized Stafford, PLUS, Federal Perkins. *Student Employment:* Federal Work-Study Program available. Institutional employment available. Highest amount earned per year from on-campus jobs $2,500. Off-campus job opportunities are good. **Financial Aid Statistics:** 100% freshmen, 99% undergrads receive need-based scholarship or grant aid. 11% freshmen, 9% undergrads receive non-need-based scholarship or grant aid. 87% freshmen, 87% undergrads receive need-based self-help aid. 1% freshmen, 2% undergrads receive athletic scholarships. 100% freshmen, 93% undergrads receive any aid. 79% undergrads borrow to pay for school. Average cumulative indebtedness $20,193. **Criteria for awarding institutional aid:** *Non-need-based:* academics, athletics, minority status.

POINT UNIVERSITY

507 West 10th Street, West Point, GA 31833
Phone: 706-385-1202 • **Financial Aid Phone:** 706-385-1045
E-mail: admissions@point.edu • **CEEB Code:** 5029
Fax: 706-645-9473 • **Website:** www.point.edu • **ACT Code:** 785

This private school, affiliated with the Christian (Nondenominational) Church, was founded in 1937. It has a 52-acre campus.

RATINGS

Admissions Selectivity Rating: 76   **Fire Safety Rating:** 68

STUDENTS AND FACULTY

Enrollment: 1,399. **Student Body:** 55% female, 45% male, 1% international (8 countries represented). Asian 1%, African American 40%, Caucasian 40%, Hispanic 4%, Native American <1%
Retention and Graduation: 52% freshmen return for sophomore year. 22% freshmen graduate within 4 years. **Faculty:** 34 full-time faculty, 56% hold PhDs, 56% are members of minority groups, 21% are women. 0% of classes are taught by teaching assistants.

ACADEMICS

Degrees: associate, bachelor's. **Majors with Highest Enrollment:** Business Administration and Management; Bible/Biblical Studies; Psychology. **Special Study Options:** double major, dual enrollment, independent study, internships. **Career services:** alumni services, career/job search classes, internships.

FACILITIES

Housing: men's dorms, women's dorms, apartments for married students, apartments for single students. 95% of campus accessible to physically disabled. **Computers:** Students can register for classes online.

CAMPUS LIFE

Environment: Village. **Activities:** Choral groups, music ensembles, student government, yearbook. 2 fraternities, 2 sororities. **Athletics (Intercollegiate):** *Men:* baseball, basketball, golf, soccer. *Women:* basketball, soccer, volleyball.

ADMISSIONS

Freshman Academic Profile: Average high school GPA 3.35. 5% in top 10% of high school class, 10% in top 25% of high school class, 58% in top 50% of high school class. 84% from public high schools. SAT Math middle 50% range

430-510. SAT Critical Reading middle 50% range 410-500. ACT middle 50% range 17-21. Minimum internet-based TOEFL 80. Minimum paper TOEFL 550. **Basis for Candidate Selection:** *Very important factors considered include:* recommendation(s), rigor of secondary school record, standardized test scores. *Important factors considered include:* character/personal qualities. **Freshman Admission Requirements:** High school diploma is required and GED is accepted. **Freshman Admission Statistics:** 954 applied, 52% admitted, 57% enrolled. **Transfer Admission Requirements:** college transcript(s), statement of good standing from prior institution(s). Minimum college GPA of 2.0 required. Lowest grade transferable C. **General Admission Information:** Application Fee $25. Early decision application deadline 11/15. Regular application deadline 8/1. Notification on a rolling basis, beginning on or about 8/20. Nonfall registration accepted. Admission may be deferred for a maximum of 1 semester. Credit and/or placement offered for CEEB Advanced Placement tests.

COSTS AND FINANCIAL AID
Annual tuition $16,700. Room and board $6,350. Required fees $950. Average book expense $2,000. *Student Employment:* Federal Work-Study Program available. Institutional employment available. Off-campus job opportunities are excellent. **Financial Aid Statistics:** 99% freshmen, 99% undergrads receive any aid.

POLYTECHNIC UNIVERSITY—BROOKLYN

6 Metrotech Center, Brooklyn, NY 11201-2999
Phone: 718-260-5955 · **Financial Aid Phone:** 718-260-3025
E-mail: uadmit@poly.edu · **CEEB Code:** 2668
Fax: 718-260-3446 · **Website:** www.poly.edu · **ACT Code:** 2860

This private school was founded in 1854. It has a 3-acre campus.

RATINGS
Admissions Selectivity Rating: 89   Fire Safety Rating: 74

STUDENTS AND FACULTY
Enrollment: 2,000. **Student Body:** 20% female, 80% male, 19% out-of-state, 10% international (34 countries represented). Asian 35%, African American 6%, Caucasian 30%, Hispanic 10%, Native American <1%
Retention and Graduation: 84% freshmen return for sophomore year. 31% freshmen graduate within 4 years. 54% freshmen graduate within 6 years. 15% grads go on to further study within 1 year. **Faculty:** 157 full-time faculty, 91% hold PhDs, 17% are members of minority groups, 29% are women. 0% of classes are taught by teaching assistants.

ACADEMICS
Degrees: bachelor's, certificate, doctoral, master's. **Classes:** Most classes have 10–19 students. Most lab/discussion sessions have 10–19 students. **Majors with Highest Enrollment:** Electrical and Electronics Engineering; Civil Engineering; Mechanical Engineering. **Special Study Options:** Accelerated program, cooperative education program, distance learning, double major, dual enrollment, honors program, independent study, internships. **Honors programs:** The Honors College serves as a magnet for attracting academically superior Undergraduates to the University. It accepts students of exceptional talent and promise from a variety of backgrounds. It offers outstanding Honors students the opportunity to earn a BS and possibly an MS degree in possibly as few as four years, including summers. Honors College students work one-on-one with faculty mentors, who, among other things, stress interdisciplinary research where appropriate, originality of thought, and active learning. Honors College students form a talented cadre of high-achievers who will become engineers, scientists, managers, and other professionals positioned for leadership roles in our emerging knowledge-based economy. They will also form a highly enthusiastic and supportive part of the University's alumni population and enhance the overall reputation of the University for delivering excellence in education. **Combined degree programs:** BA/MA, BA/MEng, 2-2 engineering program with CUNY Brooklyn Coll. **Disability Services:** Special programs offered to physically disabled students include note-taking services, tape recorders, tutors. **Career services:** Alumni network, alumni services, career/job search classes, career assessment, internships.

FACILITIES
Housing: Coed dorms, fraternity/sorority housing. 100% of campus accessible to physically disabled. **Special Academic Facilities/Equipment:** Electron microscope, supersonic wind tunnel. Art Displays in Student Center. **Computers:** 100% of classrooms, 100% of dorms, 100% of libraries, 100% of dining areas, 100% of student union, 100% of common outdoor areas have wireless network access. Students can register for classes online. Administrative functions (other

than registration) can be performed online. Undergraduates are required to own a computer.

CAMPUS LIFE
Environment: Metropolis. **Activities:** drama/theater, literary magazine, radio station, student government, student newspaper, student-run film society, yearbook. 36 registered organizations, 8 honor societies, 4 religious organizations. 3 fraternities, 1 sorority. **Athletics (Intercollegiate):** *Men:* baseball, basketball, cross-country, soccer, tennis, track/field (outdoor), volleyball. *Women:* basketball, cross-country, softball, tennis, track/field (outdoor), volleyball. **On-Campus Highlights:** Recreation Center—Wunsch Student Center, Fitness Center—Jacobs Building, Bern Dibner Library for Science and Technology, Jasper H. Kane Dining Hal—Rogers Hall, Gymnasium—Jacobs Building. **Environmental Initiatives:** Enhanced/expanded recycling. Signed Presidents' Climate Committment. Accepted Mayor's Challenge—30% in 10 years.

ADMISSIONS
Freshman Academic Profile: Average high school GPA 3.52. 46% in top 10% of high school class, 81% in top 25% of high school class, 95% in top 50% of high school class. 73% from public high schools. SAT Math middle 50% range 640-720. SAT Critical Reading middle 50% range 550-650. SAT Writing middle 50% range 540-650. ACT middle 50% range 26-30. Minimum internet-based TOEFL 80. Minimum paper TOEFL 550. **Basis for Candidate Selection:** *Very important factors considered include:* rigor of secondary school record, standardized test scores. *Important factors considered include:* Class rank. *Other factors considered include:* application essay, recommendation(s), interview. **Freshman Admission Requirements:** High school diploma is required and GED is accepted. *Academic units required:* 4 English, 4 mathematics, 4 science, 3 social studies, 2 academic electives. **Freshman Admission Statistics:** 3,284 applied, 75% admitted, 20% enrolled. **Transfer Admission Requirements:** college transcript(s), Minimum college GPA of 2.5 required. Lowest grade transferable c. **General Admission Information:** Application Fee $50. Nonfall registration accepted. Admission may be deferred for a maximum of 1. Credit and/or placement offered for CEEB Advanced Placement tests.

COSTS AND FINANCIAL AID
Annual tuition $40,060. Room and board $13,500. Required fees $1,268. Average book expense $1,500. **Required Forms and Deadlines:** FAFSA, Institution's own financial aid form, CSS/Financial Aid PROFILE, State aid form. **Notification of Awards:** Applicants will be notified of awards on a rolling basis beginning 2/15. **Types of Aid:** *Need-based scholarships/grants:* Federal Pell, SEOG, state scholarships/grants, private scholarships, the school's own gift aid, United Negro College Fund. *Loans:* Subsidized Stafford, Unsubsidized Stafford, PLUS, Federal Perkins, college/university loans from institutional funds, Alternative Loans. *Student Employment:* Highest amount earned per year from on-campus jobs $10,500. Off-campus job opportunities are excellent. **Financial Aid Statistics:** 93% freshmen, 93% undergrads receive need-based scholarship or grant aid. 88% freshmen, 59% undergrads receive non-need-based scholarship or grant aid. 85% freshmen, 86% undergrads receive need-based self-help aid. 0% freshmen, 0% undergrads receive athletic scholarships. 97% freshmen, 92% undergrads receive any aid. 68% undergrads borrow to pay for school. Average cumulative indebtedness $20,388. **Criteria for awarding institutional aid:** *Non-need-based:* academics, minority status, state/district residency.

POLYTECHNIC UNIVERSITY OF PUERTO RICO

PO BOX 192017, Hato Rey, PR 00919-2017
Phone: 787-622-8000 · **Financial Aid Phone:** 787-622-8000 · **CEEB Code:** 614
Fax: 787-764-8712 · **Website:** www.pupr.edu

This private school was founded in 1966.

RATINGS
Admissions Selectivity Rating: 60*   Fire Safety Rating: 60*

STUDENTS AND FACULTY
Enrollment: 3,759. **Student Body:** 20% female, 80% male, Asian 0%, African American 0%, Caucasian 0%, Hispanic 100%, Native American %
Retention and Graduation: 77% freshmen return for sophomore year. 1% freshmen graduate within 4 years. 18% freshmen graduate within 6 years. **Faculty:** 141 full-time faculty, 35% hold PhDs, 36% are members of minority groups. 3% of classes are taught by teaching assistants.

ACADEMICS
Degrees: bachelor's, master's. **Majors with Highest Enrollment:** Civil Engineering; Electrical and Electronics Engineering; Mechanical Engineering. **Special Study Options:** cooperative education program, distance learning, honors program. **Honors programs:** In a continuing effort to provide educational

opportunities consistent with the ability of the individual student, the University invites a select group of students to enroll in and benefit from the Honor Program and corresponding Scholarship. This program consists of honors seminars, special courses, and independent study. The special courses enable students who excel to be challenged to their full intellectual capacity. The program is designed both to broaden and deepen the student"s intellectual power. At the advanced level, honor students are encouraged to undertake faculty-guided independent research in their areas of special interest or competencies. These courses are conducted as seminars and involve topics at the forefront of current scientific interest. Students who excel in mathematics and physics, regardless of the major preference, are encouraged to enroll in these courses. The program also offers an opportunity for independent study for honor students whose interests lie beyond the topics ordinarily covered by the university program. **Disability Services:** Special programs offered to physically disabled students include note-taking services, tutors.

FACILITIES

Computers: 100% of classrooms, 100% of libraries, 100% of dining areas, 100% of student union, 100% of common outdoor areas have wireless network access.

CAMPUS LIFE

Environment: Metropolis. **Activities:** Choral groups, student government. 20 registered organizations, 1 honor society, 1 religious organization. **Athletics (Intercollegiate):** *Men:* basketball, cross-country, martial arts, table tennis, tennis, track/field (outdoor), volleyball, wrestling. *Women:* cross-country, martial arts, table tennis, tennis, track/field (outdoor), volleyball.

ADMISSIONS

Freshman Academic Profile: Average high school GPA 3.21. 39% from public high schools. **Freshman Admission Requirements:** High school diploma is required and GED is accepted. *Academic units required:* 3 English, 3 mathematics, 3 science, 3 foreign language, 3 social studies. **Freshman Admission Statistics:** 623 applied, 87% admitted, 81% enrolled. **Transfer Admission Requirements:** college transcript(s). **General Admission Information:** Application Fee $30. Placement offered for CEEB Advanced Placement tests.

COSTS AND FINANCIAL AID

Annual tuition $7,020. Required fees $780. Average book expense $2,342. **Required Forms and Deadlines:** FAFSA. *Student Employment:* Federal Work-Study Program available. **Financial Aid Statistics:** 97% freshmen, 96% undergrads receive need-based scholarship or grant aid. 59% freshmen, 30% undergrads receive non-need-based scholarship or grant aid. 12% freshmen, 18% undergrads receive need-based self-help aid. 57% freshmen, 29% undergrads receive athletic scholarships. 91% freshmen, 90% undergrads receive any aid. 57% undergrads borrow to pay for school. Average cumulative indebtedness $1,680.

POMONA COLLEGE

333 N. College Way, Claremont, CA 91711-6312
Phone: 909-621-8134 • **Financial Aid Phone:** 909-621-8205
E-mail: admissions@pomona.edu • **CEEB Code:** 4607
Fax: 909-621-8952 • **Website:** www.pomona.edu • **ACT Code:** 372

This private school was founded in 1887. It has a 140-acre campus.

RATINGS

Admissions Selectivity Rating: 98   Fire Safety Rating: 89

STUDENTS AND FACULTY

Enrollment: 1,587. **Student Body:** 52% female, 48% male, 67% out-of-state, 7% international (25 countries represented). Asian 12%, African American 6%, Caucasian 45%, Hispanic 15%, Native American <1%
Retention and Graduation: 97% freshmen return for sophomore year. 93% freshmen graduate within 4 years. 20% grads go on to further study within 1 year. **Faculty:** 190 full-time faculty, 99% hold PhDs, 45% are members of minority groups, 31% are women. 0% of classes are taught by teaching assistants.

ACADEMICS

Degrees: bachelor's. **Classes:** Most classes have 10–19 students. Most lab/discussion sessions have 10–19 students. **Special Study Options:** cross-registration, double major, exchange student program (domestic), independent

study, internships, student-designed major, study abroad, The college has a 3-2 combined Bachelors (BA & BS) in Engineering with Washington University in St. Louis and the California Institute of Technology. **Combined degree programs:** BA/MEng. **Disability Services:** Special programs offered to physically disabled students include note-taking services, reader services, tape recorders, tutors. **Career services:** Alumni network, alumni services, career/job search classes, career assessment, internships, regional alumni. Career services highlights include the Pomona College Internship Program (PCIP) Students receive school credit for having a part-time internship over the course of a semester, totaling at minimum 60 hours. They can choose from a list of local internship options coordinated through our Career Development Office. Students submit a written evaluation at the end of the semester.

FACILITIES

Housing: Coed dorms, Theme Housing, Language Residence Hall. 85% of campus accessible to physically disabled. **Special Academic Facilities/Equipment:** Oldenborg Center for Foreign Languages, Musuem of Art, Brackett Observatory. **Computers:** 75% of classrooms, 50% of dorms, 100% of libraries, 100% of dining areas, 100% of student union, 100% of common outdoor areas have wireless network access. Administrative functions (other than registration) can be performed online.

CAMPUS LIFE

Environment: Town. **Activities:** Choral groups, concert band, dance, drama/theater, jazz band, literary magazine, music ensembles, musical theater, pep band, radio station, student government, student newspaper, student-run film society, symphony orchestra, television station, yearbook, Campus Ministries, International Student Organization, Model UN. 280 registered organizations, 3 honor societies, 5 religious organizations. 3 fraternities. **Athletics (Intercollegiate):** *Men:* baseball, basketball, cross-country, diving, football, golf, soccer, swimming, tennis, track/field (outdoor), water polo. *Women:* basketball, cross-country, diving, golf, lacrosse, soccer, softball, swimming, tennis, track/field (outdoor), volleyball, water polo. **On-Campus Highlights:** Smith Campus Center, Sontag Greek Theater, Rains Center for Sports and Recreation, Brackett Observatory. **Environmental Initiatives:** Pomona's Environmental Analysis Program incorporates sustainability across the curriculum in a variety of disciplines. The program offers 11 tracks within its major and minor, allowing students to focus on sustainability in a variety of natural science, social science, and humanities subjects. Sustainability is well incorporated across the curriculum. Student programs and campus engagement efforts include a green office certification program, green living training for all RAs and student mentors, an annual sustainability film festival, a program where students can get free drying racks, CFL light bulbs, and compost buckets, and much more. All programming is focused on the educational experience for campus stakeholders, as well as the reduction of environmental impacts. Pomona's facilities are built with strict environmental standards dating back to 2003. All renovation, new construction, and remodel projects must develop sustainability goals and adhere to the campus' standard specifications for fixtures, furnishings, and building systems - including high-efficiency lighting and plumbing, non-toxic materials, and energy performance analysis. Lighting, HVAC, and other systems are systematically and regularly enhanced for energy performance, making buildings more efficient. All new construction must adhere to LEED standards for a Gold certification.

ADMISSIONS

Freshman Academic Profile: 92% in top 10% of high school class, 99% in top 25% of high school class, 100% in top 50% of high school class. 68% from public high schools. SAT Math middle 50% range 690-780. SAT Critical Reading middle 50% range 690-760. SAT Writing middle 50% range 690-780. ACT middle 50% range 31-34. Minimum internet-based TOEFL 100. Minimum paper TOEFL 600. **Basis for Candidate Selection:** *Very important factors considered include:* Class rank, application essay, academic GPA, recommendation(s), rigor of secondary school record, standardized test scores, character/personal qualities, extracurricular activities, talent/ability. *Important factors considered include:* interview. *Other factors considered include:* alumni/ae relation, first generation, geographical residence, racial/ethnic status, volunteer work, work experience. **Freshman Admission Requirements:** High school diploma or equivalent is not required. *Academic units required:* 4 English, 3 mathematics, 3 science, (2 science labs), 2 foreign language, 2 social studies, 3 history. **Freshman Admission Statistics:** 7,153 applied, 14% admitted, 40% enrolled. **Transfer Admission Requirements:** High school transcript, college transcript(s), essay or personal statement, standardized test scores, statement of good standing from prior institution(s). Lowest grade transferable C. **General Admission Information:** Application Fee $65. Early decision application deadline 11/1. Regular application deadline 1/2. Nonfall registration not accepted. Admission may be deferred for a maximum of 1 year. Credit and/or placement offered for CEEB Advanced Placement tests.

COSTS AND FINANCIAL AID

Average book expense $1,200. **Required Forms and Deadlines:** FAFSA, CSS/Financial Aid PROFILE, Noncustodial PROFILE, Business/Farm Supplement. **Notification of Awards:** Applicants will be notified of awards on or about 4/1. **Types of Aid:** *Need-based scholarships/grants:* Federal Pell, SEOG, state scholarships/grants, private scholarships, the school's own gift aid. *Loans:* Subsidized Stafford, Unsubsidized Stafford, PLUS, Federal Perkins, college/university loans from institutional funds. *Student Employment:* Federal Work-Study Program available. Institutional employment available. Off-campus job opportunities are good. **Financial Aid Statistics:** 100% freshmen, 100% undergrads receive need-based scholarship or grant aid. 0% freshmen, 0% undergrads receive non-need-based scholarship or grant aid. 100% freshmen, 100% undergrads receive need-based self-help aid. 0% freshmen, 0% undergrads receive athletic scholarships. 58% freshmen, 54% undergrads receive any aid. 33% undergrads borrow to pay for school. Average cumulative indebtedness $10,916.

PONTIFICAL COLLEGE JOSEPHINUM

7625 North High Street, Columbus, OH 43235-1498
Phone: 614-885-5585 · **Financial Aid Phone:** 614-885-5585
E-mail: admissions@pcj.edu
Fax: 614-885-2307

This private school, affiliated with the Roman Catholic Church,, affiliated with the Seminarian Church, was founded in 1888. It has a 100-acre campus.

RATINGS

Admissions Selectivity Rating: 79   **Fire Safety Rating:** 60*

STUDENTS AND FACULTY

Enrollment: 78. **Student Body:** 0% female, 100% male, 64% out-of-state, 8% international (15 countries represented). Asian 1%, African American 0%, Caucasian 79%, Hispanic 10%, Native American 1%
Retention and Graduation: 92% freshmen return for sophomore year. 63% freshmen graduate within 4 years. 62% freshmen graduate within 6 years. 95% grads go on to further study within 1 year. 5% grads pursue arts and sciences degrees. **Faculty:** 17 full-time faculty, 76% hold PhDs, 35% are members of minority groups, 0% are women. 0% of classes are taught by teaching assistants.

ACADEMICS

Degrees: bachelor's, master's. **Classes:** Most classes have 10–19 students. **Special Study Options:** cross-registration, double major, honors program, independent study.

FACILITIES

Housing: men's dorms.

CAMPUS LIFE

Environment: Metropolis. **Activities:** Choral groups 1 religious organization.

ADMISSIONS

Freshman Academic Profile: 25% in top 10% of high school class, 35% in top 25% of high school class, 60% in top 50% of high school class. SAT Math middle 50% range 360-610. SAT Critical Reading middle 50% range 380-600. SAT Writing middle 50% range 350-610. ACT middle 50% range 17-25. Minimum paper TOEFL 550. **Basis for Candidate Selection:** *Very important factors considered include:* recommendation(s), rigor of secondary school record, standardized test scores, religious affiliation/commitment. *Important factors considered include:* application essay, academic GPA, interview. *Other factors considered include:* Class rank, character/personal qualities, extracurricular activities, talent/ability, volunteer work. **Freshman Admission Requirements:** High school diploma is required and GED is accepted. *Academic units required:* 4 English, 2 mathematics, 1 science, 1 foreign language, 2 social studies. **Freshman Admission Statistics:** 8 applied, 75% admitted, 100% enrolled. **Transfer Admission Requirements:** High school transcript, college transcript(s), essay or personal statement, interview, standardized test scores, Lowest grade transferable C. **General Admission Information:** Application Fee $25. Notification on a rolling basis, beginning on or about 1/1. Nonfall registration not accepted.

COSTS AND FINANCIAL AID

Annual tuition $16,701. Room and board $7,908. Required fees $720. Average book expense $1,100. **Required Forms and Deadlines:** FAFSA, Institution's own financial aid form. **Types of Aid:** *Need-based scholarships/grants:* Federal Pell, SEOG, state scholarships/grants, private scholarships, the school's own gift aid. *Loans:* Subsidized Stafford, Unsubsidized Stafford, PLUS, Federal Perkins. *Student Employment:* Federal Work-Study Program available. Highest amount earned per year from on-campus jobs $1,200. **Financial Aid Statistics:** 0% freshmen, 83% undergrads receive need-based scholarship or grant aid. 0% freshmen, 0% undergrads receive non-need-based scholarship or grant

aid. 100% freshmen, 33% undergrads receive need-based self-help aid. 0% freshmen, 0% undergrads receive athletic scholarships. 20% undergrads borrow to pay for school. **Criteria for awarding institutional aid:** *Non-need-based:* academics.

PORTLAND STATE UNIVERSITY

Office of Admissions, Portland, OR 97207-0751
Phone: 503-725-3511 · **Financial Aid Phone:** 800-547-8887
E-mail: admissions@pdx.edu · **CEEB Code:** 4610
Fax: 503-725-5525 · **Website:** http://www.pdx.edu/ • **ACT Code:** 3492

This public school was founded in 1946. It has a 49-acre campus.

RATINGS

Admissions Selectivity Rating: 76   **Fire Safety Rating:** 67

STUDENTS AND FACULTY

Enrollment: 19,662. **Student Body:** 52% female, 48% male, 14% out-of-state, 5% international (94 countries represented). Asian 8%, African American 3%, Caucasian 60%, Hispanic 11%, Native American 1%
Retention and Graduation: 12% freshmen graduate within 4 years. **Faculty:** 843 full-time faculty, 73% hold PhDs, 46% are members of minority groups, 17% are women. 5% of classes are taught by teaching assistants.

ACADEMICS

Degrees: bachelor's, certificate, master's, post-bachelor's certificate. **Classes:** Most classes have 20–29 students. Most lab/discussion sessions have 20–29 students. **Majors with Highest Enrollment:** Psychology; Business/Commerce; Social Sciences. **Special Study Options:** Accelerated program, cooperative education program, cross-registration, distance learning, double major, English as a Second Language (ESL), exchange student program (domestic), honors program, independent study, internships, study abroad, teacher certification program, Haystack Summer Program in the Arts and Sciences. **Honors programs:** University Honors Program. **Disability Services:** Special programs offered to physically disabled students include note-taking services, reader services, tape recorders, tutors. **Career services:** Alumni network, alumni services, career/job search classes, career assessment, internships. Career services highlights include The Senior Capstone, the purpose of which is to further enhance student learning while cultivating crucial life abilities that are important both academically and professionally; establishing connections within the larger community, developing strategies for analyzing and addressing problems, and working with others trained in fields different from one's own. This 6-credit, community-based learning course is designed to provide students with the opportunity to apply, in a team context, what they have learned in the major and in their other University Studies courses to a real challenge emanating from the metropolitan community.

FACILITIES

Housing: Coed dorms, special housing for disabled students, special housing for international students, fraternity/sorority housing, apartments for married students, apartments for single students, Special housing for new students. Apartments for students with dependent children. 95% of campus accessible to physically disabled. **Special Academic Facilities/Equipment:** Art galleries, audiovisual resources, classroom multimedia computer systems, learning lab, child development center, native american center. **Computers:** 50% of dorms, 100% of libraries, 100% of dining areas, 100% of student union, have wireless network access. Students can register for classes online. Administrative functions (other than registration) can be performed online.

CAMPUS LIFE

Environment: Metropolis. **Activities:** Choral groups, concert band, dance, drama/theater, jazz band, literary magazine, music ensembles, musical theater, opera, pep band, radio station, student government, student newspaper, student-run film society, symphony orchestra, Campus Ministries, International Student Organization, Model UN. 200 registered organizations, 10 honor societies, 14 religious organizations. 4 fraternities, 4 sororities. **Athletics (Intercollegiate):** *Men:* basketball, cross-country, football, tennis, track/field (outdoor), track/field (indoor). *Women:* basketball, cross-country, golf, soccer, softball, tennis, track/field (outdoor), track/field (indoor), volleyball.
On-Campus Highlights: Park Blocks, Student Union Center **Environmental Initiatives:** Since 2002 PSU has focused on designing new buildings and

retrofitting and renovating older campus buildings with sustainability in mind. Several PSU buildings serve as models of these kinds of innovative sustainable design and construction projects. These include the new Engineering Building, Broadway Housing Building, Stephen Epler Hall, and Native American Student and Community Center. In all but the latter, the US Green Building Council's LEED certification program was used as the measuring stick and standard for sustainable design and construction. The Center for Sustainable Processes and Practices collaborates with public and private partners to study eco-roof efficiency. Graduate Sustainability Certificate—This graduate certificate (in process of approval) offers an integrated series of post-baccalaureate courses that comprise a multidisciplinary study of the environmental, social, and economic dimensions of sustainability.

ADMISSIONS

Freshman Academic Profile: Average high school GPA 3.39. 13% in top 10% of high school class, 40% in top 25% of high school class, 80% in top 50% of high school class. 85% from public high schools. SAT Math middle 50% range 450-570. SAT Critical Reading middle 50% range 460-590. SAT Writing middle 50% range 430-560. ACT middle 50% range 19-25. Minimum internet-based TOEFL 60. Minimum paper TOEFL 527. **Basis for Candidate Selection:** *Very important factors considered include:* academic GPA, rigor of secondary school record. *Other factors considered include:* standardized test scores. **Freshman Admission Requirements:** High school diploma is required and GED is accepted. *Academic units required:* 4 English, 3 mathematics, 2 science, 2 foreign language, 2 social studies, 1 history. **Freshman Admission Statistics:** 4,936 applied, 85% admitted, 39% enrolled. **Transfer Admission Requirements:** college transcript(s), Minimum college GPA of 2.25 required. Lowest grade transferable D-. **General Admission Information:** Application Fee $50. Notification on a rolling basis, beginning on or about 1/1. Nonfall registration accepted. Admission may be deferred for a maximum of One Year. Credit and/or placement offered for CEEB Advanced Placement tests.

COSTS AND FINANCIAL AID

Annual in-state tuition $6,525. Annual out-of-state tuition $2,250. Room and board $11,349. Required fees $1,269. Average book expense $2,028. **Required Forms and Deadlines:** FAFSA. **Types of Aid:** *Need-based scholarships/ grants:* Federal Pell, SEOG, state scholarships/grants, private scholarships, the school's own gift aid, United Negro College Fund. *Loans:* Direct Subsidized Stafford, Direct Unsubsidized Stafford, Direct PLUS, Subsidized Stafford, Unsubsidized Stafford, PLUS, Federal Perkins, state loans. *Student Employment:* Federal Work-Study Program available. Institutional employment available. Off-campus job opportunities are excellent. **Financial Aid Statistics:** 75% freshmen, 56% undergrads receive any aid. **Criteria for awarding institutional aid:** *Non-need-based:* academics, art, athletics, music/drama, state/ district residency.

POST UNIVERSITY

PO Box 2540, Waterbury, CT 6723
Phone: 203-596-4520 · **Financial Aid Phone:** 204-596-4526
E-mail: admissions@post.edu · **CEEB Code:** 3698
Fax: 203-756-5810 · **Website:** www.post.edu · **ACT Code:** 580

This proprietary school was founded in 1890. It has a 58-acre campus.

RATINGS

Admissions Selectivity Rating: 60*   **Fire Safety Rating:** 67

STUDENTS AND FACULTY

Enrollment: 1,055. **Student Body:** 61% female, 39% male, 13% out-of-state, 1% international (15 countries represented). Asian 1%, African American 15%, Caucasian 33%, Hispanic 7%, Native American <1%
Retention and Graduation: 25% grads go on to further study within 1 year. 20% grads pursue arts and sciences degrees. 5% grads pursue law degrees. 25% grads pursue business degrees. **Faculty:** 0% of classes are taught by teaching assistants.

ACADEMICS

Degrees: associate, bachelor's, certificate, master's, post-bachelor's certificate, terminal associate, transfer associate. **Majors with Highest Enrollment:** Criminal Justice/Law Enforcement Administration; Business/Commerce; Accounting. **Special Study Options:** Accelerated program, cooperative education program, cross-registration, distance learning, double major, honors program, independent study, internships, liberal arts/career combination, study abroad, weekend college. **Disability Services:** Special programs offered to physically disabled students include tape recorders, tutors. **Career services:** alumni services, career/job search classes, career assessment, internships.

FACILITIES

Housing: Coed dorms, apartments for single students, Inquire about learning communities. 75% of campus accessible to physically disabled. **Computers:** Students can register for classes online. Administrative functions (other than registration) can be performed online.

CAMPUS LIFE

Environment: City. **Activities:** Choral groups, drama/theater, literary magazine, musical theater, student government, student newspaper. 30 registered organizations. **Athletics (Intercollegiate):** *Men:* baseball, basketball, cross-country, equestrian sports, golf, soccer, tennis. *Women:* basketball, cross-country, equestrian sports, soccer, softball, tennis, volleyball. **On-Campus Highlights:** University Hall, Leever Student Center, Drubner Athletic Center.

ADMISSIONS

Freshman Academic Profile: Average high school GPA 2.7. 90% from public high schools. Minimum paper TOEFL 500. **Basis for Candidate Selection:** *Very important factors considered include:* academic GPA, interview, level of applicant's interest. *Important factors considered include:* standardized test scores, character/personal qualities, extracurricular activities, talent/ ability, volunteer work. *Other factors considered include:* application essay, recommendation(s), alumni/ae relation, first generation. **Freshman Admission Requirements:** High school diploma is required and GED is accepted. *Academic units required:* 4 English, 2 mathematics, 2 science, (1 science labs), 2 foreign language, 1 social studies, 2 history, 2 academic electives. **Transfer Admission Requirements:** college transcript(s), Minimum college GPA of 2.0 required. Lowest grade transferable C-. **General Admission Information:** Application Fee $40. Nonfall registration accepted. Admission may be deferred for a maximum of 1 year. Credit and/or placement offered for CEEB Advanced Placement tests.

COSTS AND FINANCIAL AID

Average book expense $1,000. **Required Forms and Deadlines:** FAFSA, Institution's own financial aid form. **Types of Aid:** *Need-based scholarships/ grants:* Federal Pell, SEOG, state scholarships/grants, private scholarships, the school's own gift aid. *Loans:* Subsidized Stafford, Unsubsidized Stafford, PLUS, Federal Perkins, state loans, college/university loans from institutional funds. *Student Employment:* Federal Work-Study Program available. Highest amount earned per year from on-campus jobs $2,100. **Financial Aid Statistics:** 80% freshmen, 75% undergrads receive any aid. **Criteria for awarding institutional aid:** *Non-need-based:* academics, alumni affiliation, athletics, job skills, leadership, minority status, state/district residency.

PRAIRIE VIEW A&M UNIVERSITY

PO Box 519, Prairie View, TX 77446
Phone: 936-261-3500 · **Financial Aid Phone:** 1-877-782-6830
E-mail: admissions@pvamu.edu · **CEEB Code:** 6580
Website: www.pvamu.edu • **ACT Code:** 4202

This public school was founded in 1876. It has a 1388-acre campus.

RATINGS

Admissions Selectivity Rating: 78   **Fire Safety Rating:** 74

STUDENTS AND FACULTY

Enrollment: 6,973. **Student Body:** 58% female, 42% male, 7% out-of-state, 1% international (40 countries represented). Asian 2%, African American 88%, Caucasian 3%, Hispanic 5%, Native American <1%
Retention and Graduation: 71% freshmen return for sophomore year. 12% freshmen graduate within 4 years. 32% freshmen graduate within 6 years. **Faculty:** 394 full-time faculty, 67% hold PhDs, 39% are are members of minority groups, 80% are women.

ACADEMICS

Degrees: bachelor's, doctoral, master's. **Majors with Highest Enrollment:** Multi-/Interdisciplinary Studies; Business Administration and Management. **Special Study Options:** Accelerated program, cooperative education program, distance learning, double major, dual enrollment, English as a Second Language (ESL), honors program, independent study, internships, liberal arts/career combination, study abroad, teacher certification program, weekend college. **Disability Services:** Special programs offered to physically disabled students include tape recorders, tutors. **Career services:** Alumni network, alumni services, career assessment, internships, regional alumni.

FACILITIES

Housing: Coed dorms, special housing for disabled students, apartments for single students. 90% of campus accessible to physically disabled. **Computers:**

100% of classrooms, 100% of dorms, 100% of libraries, 75% of dining areas, 75% of student union, 50% of common outdoor areas have wireless network access. Students can register for classes online.

CAMPUS LIFE

Environment: Rural. **Activities:** Choral groups, concert band, dance, drama/theater, jazz band, marching band, music ensembles, radio station, student government, student newspaper, symphony orchestra, television station, yearbook, Campus Ministries, International Student Organization. 100 registered organizations, 15 honor societies, 6 religious organizations. 9 fraternities, 9 sororities. **Athletics (Intercollegiate):** *Men:* baseball, basketball, cross-country, football, golf, tennis, track/field (outdoor), track/field (indoor). *Women:* basketball, cheerleading, cross-country, golf, soccer, softball, tennis, track/field (outdoor), track/field (indoor), volleyball. **On-Campus Highlights:** Purple Zone Student Sports Bar, Memorial Student Center, Baby Dome, J.B. Coleman Library, Jazzman Coffee Café, University College and University Village.

ADMISSIONS

Freshman Academic Profile: Average high school GPA 2.9. 5% in top 10% of high school class, 21.1% in top 25% of high school class, 55.84% in top 50% of high school class. SAT Math middle 50% range 380-440. SAT Critical Reading middle 50% range 370-450. SAT Writing middle 50% range 360-440. ACT middle 50% range 15-19. Minimum paper TOEFL 500. **Basis for Candidate Selection:** *Very important factors considered include:* Class rank, academic GPA, rigor of secondary school record, standardized test scores. *Other factors considered include:* character/personal qualities, extracurricular activities, first generation, volunteer work, work experience. **Freshman Admission Requirements:** High school diploma is required and GED is accepted. **Freshman Admission Statistics:** 7,931 applied, 42% admitted, 52% enrolled. **Transfer Admission Requirements:** college transcript(s), statement of good standing from prior institution(s). Minimum college GPA of 2.0 required. Lowest grade transferable C. **General Admission Information:** Application Fee $25. Regular application deadline 7/1. Nonfall registration accepted. Admission may be deferred for a maximum of 1 year. Credit and/or placement offered for CEEB Advanced Placement tests.

COSTS AND FINANCIAL AID

Annual out-of-state tuition $14,376. Room and board $7,064. Required fees $1,779. Average book expense $1,000. **Required Forms and Deadlines:** FAFSA, Institution's own financial aid form. **Notification of Awards:** Applicants will be notified of awards on or about 6/1. **Types of Aid:** *Need-based scholarships/grants:* Federal Pell, SEOG, state scholarships/grants, the school's own gift aid, United Negro College Fund. *Loans:* Direct Subsidized Stafford, Direct Unsubsidized Stafford, Direct PLUS, Subsidized Stafford, Unsubsidized Stafford, PLUS, Federal Perkins, college/university loans from institutional funds. **Financial Aid Statistics:** 69% freshmen, 63% undergrads receive need-based scholarship or grant aid. 26% freshmen, 13% undergrads receive non-need-based scholarship or grant aid. 69% freshmen, 63% undergrads receive need-based self-help aid. 1% freshmen, 4% undergrads receive athletic scholarships. 61% freshmen, 53% undergrads receive any aid. 76% undergrads borrow to pay for school. Average cumulative indebtedness $24,500. **Criteria for awarding institutional aid:** *Non-need-based:* academics, athletics.

PRATT INSTITUTE

200 Willoughby Avenue, Brooklyn, NY 11205
Phone: 718-636-3514 • **Financial Aid Phone:** 718-636-3599
E-mail: visit@pratt.edu • **CEEB Code:** 2669
Fax: 718-636-3670 • **Website:** http://www.pratt.edu • **ACT Code:** 2862

This private school was founded in 1887. It has a 25-acre campus.

RATINGS

Admissions Selectivity Rating: 82   **Fire Safety Rating:** 70

STUDENTS AND FACULTY

Enrollment: 3,098. **Student Body:** 68% female, 32% male, 70% out-of-state, 25% international (78 countries represented). Asian 17%, African American 4%, Caucasian 42%, Hispanic 10%, Native American <1%.
Retention and Graduation: 85% freshmen return for sophomore year. 42% freshmen graduate within 4 years. **Faculty:** 150 full-time faculty, 77% hold PhDs, 44% are are members of minority groups, 16% are women. 0% of classes are taught by teaching assistants.

ACADEMICS

Degrees: associate, bachelor's, master's, post-master's certificate, terminal associate, transfer associate. **Classes:** Most classes have 10-19 students. **Majors with Highest Enrollment:** Design and Visual Communications; Architecture;

Fine/Studio Arts. **Special Study Options:** English as a Second Language (ESL), exchange student program (domestic), independent study, internships, study abroad, teacher certification program. **Combined degree programs:** BA/MA, art history. **Disability Services:** Special programs offered to physically disabled students include note-taking services, reader services, tutors. **Career services:** Alumni network, alumni services, career/job search classes, career assessment, internships. As part of the intership program, students can become involved with community matters, contributing their design skills to a community program.

FACILITIES

Housing: Coed dorms, special housing for disabled students, special housing for international students, apartments for single students, Wellness Housing, Global Learning (for international and domestic students), Healthy Choice and Quiet Floors are available. **Special Academic Facilities/Equipment:** Five art galleries, fine arts center, printmaking center, computer graphics lab. **Computers:** Undergraduates are required to own a computer.

CAMPUS LIFE

Environment: Metropolis. **Activities:** literary magazine, music ensembles, radio station, student government, student newspaper, student-run film society, television station, yearbook, Campus Ministries, International Student Organization. 50 registered organizations, 4 honor societies, 3 religious organizations. 3 fraternities, 1 sorority. **Athletics (Intercollegiate):** *Men:* basketball, cross-country, soccer, tennis, track/field (outdoor), track/field (indoor). *Women:* basketball, cross-country, soccer, tennis, track/field (outdoor), volleyball. **On-Campus Highlights:** studios, galleries, three Cafeterias/coffee shops, athletic center, student union, Pratt is the only East Coast art school with a traditional campus (25 acres). **Environmental Initiatives:** Our new building, Myrtle Hall is LEED gold. We received a $475K FIPSE grant "Green by Design" to embed sustainable best practices into every program, create interdisciplinary programs that center around environmental projects and create a "living laboratory" that links greening our facilities with greening our academic programs and providing educational programs to our city. We have a new Center for Sustainable Design and Research that centers faculty and students from various programs around environmental projects and research.

ADMISSIONS

Freshman Academic Profile: Average high school GPA 3.64. 70% from public high schools. SAT Math middle 50% range 530-660. SAT Critical Reading middle 50% range 530-630. SAT Writing middle 50% range 540-640. ACT middle 50% range 24-28. Minimum paper TOEFL 550. **Basis for Candidate Selection:** *Very important factors considered include:* academic GPA, rigor of secondary school record, standardized test scores, talent/ability. *Important factors considered include:* application essay, recommendation(s), alumni/ae relation, character/personal qualities, level of applicant's interest. *Other factors considered include:* Class rank, extracurricular activities, interview, volunteer work, work experience. **Freshman Admission Requirements:** High school diploma is required and GED is accepted. **Freshman Admission Statistics:** 4,679 applied, 63% admitted, 22% enrolled. **Transfer Admission Requirements:** High school transcript, college transcript(s), essay or personal statement, statement of good standing from prior institution(s). Lowest grade transferable C. **General Admission Information:** Application Fee $50. Regular application deadline 1/5. Regular notification 4/1. Nonfall registration not accepted. Admission may be deferred for a maximum of one year. Credit and/or placement offered for CEEB Advanced Placement tests.

COSTS AND FINANCIAL AID

Annual tuition $44,580. Room and board $11,496. Required fees $2,006. Average book expense $1,750. **Required Forms and Deadlines:** FAFSA, State aid form. *Student Employment:* Federal Work-Study Program available. Institutional employment available. Highest amount earned per year from on-campus jobs $2,500. Off-campus job opportunities are excellent. **Financial Aid Statistics:** 88% freshmen, 73% undergrads receive need-based scholarship or grant aid. 70% freshmen, 83% undergrads receive non-need-based scholarship or grant aid. 100% freshmen, 91% undergrads receive need-based self-help aid. 0% freshmen, 0% undergrads receive athletic scholarships. 92% freshmen, 83% undergrads receive any aid.

PRESBYTERIAN COLLEGE

503 South Broad Street, Clinton, SC 29325
Phone: 864-833-8230 · **Financial Aid Phone:** 864-833-8287
E-mail: admissions@presby.edu · **CEEB Code:** 5540
Fax: 864-833-8195 · **Website:** www.presby.edu · **ACT Code:** 3874

This private school, affiliated with the Presbyterian Church,, affiliated with the Presbyterian USA Church, was founded in 1880. It has a 240-acre campus.

RATINGS

Admissions Selectivity Rating: 88 **Fire Safety Rating:** 95

STUDENTS AND FACULTY

Enrollment: 1,032. **Student Body:** 53% female, 47% male, 38% out-of-state, 1% international (23 countries represented). Asian 1%, African American 12%, Caucasian 81%, Hispanic 2%, Native American <1%
Retention and Graduation: 84% freshmen return for sophomore year. 58% freshmen graduate within 4 years. 65% freshmen graduate within 6 years. 28% grads go on to further study within 1 year. **Faculty:** 99 full-time faculty, 96% hold PhDs, 39% are are members of minority groups, 11% are women. 0% of classes are taught by teaching assistants.

ACADEMICS

Degrees: bachelor's. **Classes:** Most classes have 20-29 students. Most lab/discussion sessions have 20-29 students. **Majors with Highest Enrollment:** Business Administration and Management; Biology/Biological Sciences; Psychology. **Special Study Options:** double major, dual enrollment, exchange student program (domestic), honors program, independent study, internships, study abroad, teacher certification program, Program in forestry and environmental science, 3-2 engineering program. **Honors programs:** A variety of opportunities are available to highly motivated students with above average abilities through the normal programs of the College. These include research, internships, special projects, and directed studies. Presbyterian College also offers a special honors program for students who are chosen on the basis of their demonstrated ability. Students with a 3.20 GPA in all courses and a 3.40 GPA in all courses in the major field may, with the approval of departmental faculty, undertake an honors research program during the junior and/or senior years. Oral and written presentations of the results of the project will be required. Students who successfully complete the departmental honors research program will graduate with honors in the major field. **Disability Services:** Special programs offered to physically disabled students include tutors. **Career services:** Alumni network, alumni services, career/job search classes, career assessment, internships, regional alumni. Career services highlights include our Internship Program: Students of all disciplines are coordinated to participate in on-campus seminar sessions at the beginning, middle, and end of the semester to reflect/review, compare/contrast their internship experience as a group.

FACILITIES

Housing: Coed dorms, men's dorms, special housing for international students, women's dorms, fraternity/sorority housing, apartments for single students. Sorority housing is not available. 95% of campus accessible to physically disabled. **Special Academic Facilities/Equipment:** Art gallery, recital hall, media center, marine/ecological center, scanning and transmission electron microscopes, visible spectrophotometer. **Computers:** 95% of classrooms, 100% of dorms, 100% of libraries, 100% of dining areas, 100% of student union, 50% of common outdoor areas have wireless network access. Students can register for classes online. Administrative functions (other than registration) can be performed online.

CAMPUS LIFE

Environment: Village. **Activities:** Choral groups, concert band, dance, drama/theater, jazz band, literary magazine, music ensembles, musical theater, opera, pep band, radio station, student government, student newspaper, symphony orchestra, yearbook, Campus Ministries. 85 registered organizations, 11 honor societies, 6 religious organizations. 6 fraternities, 3 sororities. **Athletics (Intercollegiate):** *Men:* baseball, basketball, cheerleading, cross-country, football, golf, lacrosse, soccer, tennis. *Women:* basketball, cheerleading, cross-country, golf, lacrosse, soccer, softball, tennis, volleyball. **On-Campus Highlights:** Inklings Coffee House, Bailey Stadium, Springs Campus Center, Harrington Peachtree Academic Building, Thompson Library, Inklings—hot spot for open mics and up and coming bands, Springs Campus Center—workout facilities, Starbucks, WPCX, ping pong Harrington Peachtree Academic Building—commonly known as H-P it is an ideal study and gathering spot in the late night hours Thompson Library—with the new expansion and renovations to the existing facilities, the library has seen a Renaissance—comfy chairs and cozy corners offer students a relaxing atmosphere for studying and researching. **Environmental Initiatives:** Energy conservation; Use of alternative fuels; Recycling Center.

ADMISSIONS

Freshman Academic Profile: Average high school GPA 3.5. 29% in top 10% of high school class, 58% in top 25% of high school class, 90% in top 50% of high school class. SAT Math middle 50% range 490-610. SAT Critical Reading middle 50% range 480-600. ACT middle 50% range 21-26. Minimum internet-based TOEFL 80. Minimum paper TOEFL 550. **Basis for Candidate Selection:** *Very important factors considered include:* Class rank, application essay, academic GPA, rigor of secondary school record, standardized test scores. *Important factors considered include:* recommendation(s), character/personal qualities, extracurricular activities. *Other factors considered include:* alumni/ae relation, first generation, interview, level of applicant's interest, talent/ability, volunteer work, work experience. **Freshman Admission Requirements:** High school diploma is required and GED is accepted. *Academic units required:* 4 English, 4 mathematics, 2 science, (2 science labs), 2 foreign language, 2 social studies, 2 history, 2 academic electives. **Freshman Admission Statistics:** 1,506 applied, 54% admitted, 34% enrolled. **Transfer Admission Requirements:** High school transcript, college transcript(s), essay or personal statement, standardized test scores, statement of good standing from prior institution(s). Lowest grade transferable C. **General Admission Information:** Application Fee $40. Early decision application deadline 11/1. Regular application deadline 6/30. Regular notification 3/15. Nonfall registration accepted. Admission may be deferred for a maximum of 1 Year. Credit and/or placement offered for CEEB Advanced Placement tests.

COSTS AND FINANCIAL AID

Annual tuition $32,076. Room and board $9,344. Required fees $2,752. Average book expense $1,200. **Required Forms and Deadlines:** FAFSA. **Notification of Awards:** Applicants will be notified of awards on a rolling basis beginning 3/1. **Types of Aid:** *Need-based scholarships/grants:* Federal Pell, SEOG, state scholarships/grants, private scholarships, the school's own gift aid. *Loans:* Subsidized Stafford, Unsubsidized Stafford, PLUS, state loans, college/university loans from institutional funds, Private loans. *Student Employment:* Federal Work-Study Program available. Institutional employment available. Highest amount earned per year from on-campus jobs $1,800. Off-campus job opportunities are fair. **Financial Aid Statistics:** 100% freshmen, 100% undergrads receive need-based scholarship or grant aid. 33% freshmen, 34% undergrads receive non-need-based scholarship or grant aid. 47% freshmen, 49% undergrads receive need-based self-help aid. 19% freshmen, 18% undergrads receive athletic scholarships. 80% freshmen, 77% undergrads receive any aid. 61% undergrads borrow to pay for school. Average cumulative indebtedness $25,596. **Criteria for awarding institutional aid:** *Non-need-based:* academics, alumni affiliation, art, athletics, job skills, leadership, minority status, music/drama, religious affiliation, state/district residency.

PRESCOTT COLLEGE

220 Grove Avenue, Prescott, AZ 86301
Phone: 928-350-2100 x 2100 · **Financial Aid Phone:** 928-350-1112
E-mail: admissions@prescott.edu · **CEEB Code:** 9295
Fax: 928-776-5242 · **Website:** www.prescott.edu · **ACT Code:** 5022

This private school was founded in 1966. It has a 6-acre campus.

RATINGS

Admissions Selectivity Rating: 76 **Fire Safety Rating:** 71

STUDENTS AND FACULTY

Enrollment: 540. **Student Body:** 55% female, 45% male, 89% out-of-state, 1% international (11 countries represented). Asian 1%, African American 1%, Caucasian 73%, Hispanic 6%, Native American 2%
Retention and Graduation: 71% freshmen return for sophomore year. 23% freshmen graduate within 4 years. 37% freshmen graduate within 6 years. **Faculty:** 62 full-time faculty, 56% hold PhDs, 52% are are members of minority groups, 11% are women. 0% of classes are taught by teaching assistants.

ACADEMICS

Degrees: bachelor's, master's, post-bachelor's certificate, post-master's certificate. **Classes:** Most classes have 10-19 students. **Majors with Highest Enrollment:** Elementary Education and Teaching; Environmental Studies; Education. **Special Study Options:** cross-registration, double major, exchange student program (domestic), external degree program, independent study, internships, liberal arts/career combination, student-designed major, teacher certification program, Dual Credit. **Disability Services:** Special programs offered to physically disabled students include note-taking services, tape recorders, tutors. **Career services:** Alumni network, alumni services, career/job search classes, career assessment, regional alumni. Career services highlights include one on one career development counseling.

FACILITIES

Housing: Coed dorms. 90% of campus accessible to physically disabled. **Special Academic Facilities/Equipment:** Wolfberry Farm: An experimental agroecology farm Kino Bay Center, MX: A field station on the Gulf of CA. Sam Hill Warehouse: Our visual arts center GIS Lab (Geographic Information Systems) Several Computer Labs Multi-Media Center **Computers:** 50% of classrooms, 100% of dorms, 100% of libraries, 100% of dining areas, 75% of common outdoor areas have wireless network access.

CAMPUS LIFE

Environment: Town. **Activities:** dance, drama/theater, literary magazine, radio station, student government, student newspaper, student-run film society, International Student Organization. 18 registered organizations. **On-Campus Highlights:** Crossroads Café, Crossroads Library, HUB (Helping Understand Bikes), Sam Hill Visual Arts Building. **Environmental Initiatives:** ACUPCC commitment and Climate Action Plan Curriculum; Environmental awareness is an integral part of our curriculum, with social and environmental literacy as college-wide learning outcomes. Local food initiatives (campus Community Supported Agriculture, college farm and gardens).

ADMISSIONS

Freshman Academic Profile: Average high school GPA 3.11. 0% in top 10% of high school class, 0% in top 50% of high school class. 78% from public high schools. SAT Math middle 50% range 430-610. SAT Critical Reading middle 50% range 480-650. SAT Writing middle 50% range 490-580. ACT middle 50% range 20-26. Minimum internet-based TOEFL 61. Minimum paper TOEFL 550. **Basis for Candidate Selection:** *Very important factors considered include:* application essay, recommendation(s), rigor of secondary school record. *Important factors considered include:* academic GPA, standardized test scores, character/personal qualities, extracurricular activities, interview, level of applicant's interest, talent/ability, volunteer work, work experience. *Other factors considered include:* first generation. **Freshman Admission Requirements:** High school diploma is required and GED is accepted. **Freshman Admission Statistics:** 399 applied, 73% admitted, 17% enrolled. **Transfer Admission Requirements:** college transcript(s), essay or personal statement, Lowest grade transferable C. **General Admission Information:** Application Fee $25. Early decision application deadline 12/1. Regular application deadline 8/15. Notification on a rolling basis, beginning on or about 1/1. Nonfall registration accepted. Admission may be deferred for a maximum of 2 terms. Credit offered for CEEB Advanced Placement tests.

COSTS AND FINANCIAL AID

Annual tuition $24,960. Room and board $8,266. Average book expense $796. **Required Forms and Deadlines:** FAFSA. **Notification of Awards:** Applicants will be notified of awards on a rolling basis beginning 3/15. **Types of Aid:** *Need-based scholarships/grants:* Federal Pell, SEOG, state scholarships/grants, private scholarships, the school's own gift aid, ACT & SMART. *Loans:* Subsidized Stafford, Unsubsidized Stafford, PLUS. *Student Employment:* Federal Work-Study Program available. Institutional employment available. Highest amount earned per year from on-campus jobs $2,744. Off-campus job opportunities are good. **Financial Aid Statistics:** 93% freshmen, 95% undergrads receive need-based scholarship or grant aid. 3% freshmen, 3% undergrads receive non-need-based scholarship or grant aid. 93% freshmen, 95% undergrads receive need-based self-help aid. 0% freshmen, 0% undergrads receive athletic scholarships. 93% freshmen, 88% undergrads receive any aid. 93% undergrads borrow to pay for school. Average cumulative indebtedness $23,982. **Criteria for awarding institutional aid:** *Non-need-based:* academics, alumni affiliation, minority status, state/district residency.

PRINCETON UNIVERSITY

PO Box 430, Princeton, NJ 08544-0430
Phone: 609-258-3060 · **Financial Aid Phone:** 609-258-3330
E-mail: uaoffice@princeton.edu · **CEEB Code:** 2672
Fax: 609-258-6743 · **Website:** www.princeton.edu • **ACT Code:** 2588

This private school was founded in 1746. It has a 500-acre campus.

RATINGS

Admissions Selectivity Rating: 99   **Fire Safety Rating:** 90

STUDENTS AND FACULTY

Enrollment: 5,258. **Student Body:** 49% female, 51% male, 82% out-of-state, 11% international (92 countries represented). Asian 21%, African American 8%, Caucasian 46%, Hispanic 8%, Native American <1%
Retention and Graduation: 90% freshmen graduate within 4 years. **Faculty:** 902 full-time faculty, 93% hold PhDs, 31% are are members of minority groups, 21% are women. 0% of classes are taught by teaching assistants.

ACADEMICS

Degrees: bachelor's, master's. **Classes:** Most classes have 10-19 students. Most lab/discussion sessions have 10-19 students. **Majors with Highest Enrollment:** Computer Engineering; Public Administration; Economics. **Special Study Options:** cross-registration, exchange student program (domestic), independent study, student-designed major, study abroad, teacher certification program. **Disability Services:** Special programs offered to physically disabled students include note-taking services, reader services, tape recorders. **Career services:** Alumni network, alumni services, career/job search classes, career assessment, internships, regional alumni.

FACILITIES

Housing: Coed dorms, special housing for disabled students, apartments for married students. **Special Academic Facilities/Equipment:** Art Museum, Natural history museum, energy and environmental studies center, plasma physics lab, Center for Jewish Life, Center for Human Values, Woodrow WIlson School of Public and International Affairs, etc. **Computers:** 100% of classrooms, 100% of dorms, 70% of libraries, 100% of dining areas, 100% of student union, 20% of common outdoor areas have wireless network access. Students can register for classes online. Administrative functions (other than registration) can be performed online.

CAMPUS LIFE

Environment: Town. **Activities:** Choral groups, concert band, dance, drama/theater, jazz band, literary magazine, marching band, music ensembles, musical theater, opera, pep band, radio station, student government, student newspaper, student-run film society, symphony orchestra, yearbook, Campus Ministries, International Student Organization, Model UN. 250 registered organizations, 30 honor societies, 28 religious organizations. **Athletics (Intercollegiate):** *Men:* baseball, basketball, crew/rowing, cross-country, diving, fencing, football, golf, ice hockey, lacrosse, light weight football, soccer, squash, swimming, tennis, track/field (outdoor), track/field (indoor), volleyball, water polo, wrestling. *Women:* basketball, crew/rowing, cross-country, diving, fencing, field hockey, golf, ice hockey, lacrosse, soccer, softball, squash, swimming, tennis, track/field (outdoor), track/field (indoor), volleyball, water polo. **On-Campus Highlights:** Nassau Hall, Firestone Library, McCarter Theater, Princeton U. Art Museum, University Chapel, Frist Campus Center. **Environmental Initiatives:** Greenhouse Gas reduction goal: 1990 levels by 2020 through local verifiable action, while adding more than 1 million gross square feet of built area, and without the purchase of offsets. 5.3 megawatt solar PV installation to be installed on campus properaty by 2012. Sustainable Building Guidelines: requiring all new buildings and major renovations to be 50% more energy efficient than code requires, 95% demolition and construction debris recycling, major building systems life cycle costing, and use of sustainable materials. Implementation of transportation demand management program to reduce by 10% the number of cars coming to campus by 2020.

ADMISSIONS

Freshman Academic Profile: Average high school GPA 3.91. 96% in top 10% of high school class, 99% in top 25% of high school class, 100% in top 50% of high school class. 60% from public high schools. SAT Math middle 50% range 710-800. SAT Critical Reading middle 50% range 690-800. SAT Writing middle 50% range 700-800. ACT middle 50% range 31-35. Minimum paper TOEFL 600. **Basis for Candidate Selection:** *Very important factors considered* *include:* Class rank, application essay, academic GPA, recommendation(s), rigor of secondary school record, standardized test scores, character/personal qualities, talent/ability. *Important factors considered include:* extracurricular activities. *Other factors considered include:* alumni/ae relation, first generation, geographical residence, interview, racial/ethnic status, volunteer work, work experience. **Freshman Admission Requirements:** High school diploma or equivalent is not required. **Freshman Admission Statistics:** 26,641 applied, 7% admitted, 66% enrolled. **General Admission Information:** Application Fee $65. Regular application deadline 1/1. Regular notification 3/31. Nonfall registration not accepted. Admission may be deferred for a maximum of 1 year. Credit and/or placement offered for CEEB Advanced Placement tests.

COSTS AND FINANCIAL AID

Annual tuition $41,820. Room and board $13,620. Average book expense $1,050. **Required Forms and Deadlines:** FAFSA, Institution's own financial aid form. **Notification of Awards:** Applicants will be notified of awards on or about 4/1. **Types of Aid:** *Need-based scholarships/grants:* Federal Pell, SEOG, state scholarships/grants, private scholarships, the school's own gift aid. *Loans:* Subsidized Stafford, Unsubsidized Stafford, PLUS, Federal Perkins, college/university loans from institutional funds. *Student Employment:* Federal Work-Study Program available. Institutional employment available. Highest amount earned per year from on-campus jobs $3,500. Off-campus job opportunities are good. **Financial Aid Statistics:** 100% freshmen, 100% undergrads receive need-based scholarship or grant aid. 0% freshmen, 0% undergrads receive non-need-based scholarship or grant aid. 100% freshmen, 100% undergrads receive need-based self-help aid. 0% freshmen, 0% undergrads receive athletic scholarships. 59% freshmen, 59% undergrads receive any aid. 17% undergrads borrow to pay for school. Average cumulative indebtedness $7,132.

See page 1110.

PRINCIPIA COLLEGE

1 Maybeck Place, Elsah, IL 62028
Phone: 618-374-5181 · **Financial Aid Phone:** 800-218-7746 x3547
E-mail: collegeadmissions@principia.edu · **CEEB Code:** 1630
Fax: 618-374-4000 · **Website:** www.principiacollege.edu · **ACT Code:** 1118

This private school, affiliated with the Christian Science Church, was founded in 1898. It has a 2600-acre campus.

RATINGS

Admissions Selectivity Rating: 84   **Fire Safety Rating:** 86

STUDENTS AND FACULTY

Enrollment: 489. **Student Body:** 52% female, 48% male, 93% out-of-state, 18% international (28 countries represented). Asian 1%, African American 1%, Caucasian 69%, Hispanic 2%, Native American <1%
Retention and Graduation: 79% freshmen return for sophomore year. 76% freshmen graduate within 4 years. **Faculty:** 62 full-time faculty, 61% hold PhDs, 48% are are members of minority groups, 2% are women. 0% of classes are taught by teaching assistants.

ACADEMICS

Degrees: bachelor's. **Classes:** Most classes have 10-19 students. **Majors with Highest Enrollment:** Fine/Studio Arts; Business/Commerce; Digital Arts. **Special Study Options:** double major, independent study, internships, liberal arts/career combination, student-designed major, study abroad, teacher certification program, 3-2 Engineering with Washington University (St. Louis, MO), USC (Los Angeles), and Southern Illinois University (SIU) in Edwardsville, IL. **Honors programs:** One honors program of three courses is taught in conjunction with our First Year Experience Program (FYE). **Career services:** Alumni network, career/job search classes, career assessment, internships, regional alumni. Career services highlights include internships in San Fransisco as part of a school-sponsored program for students interested in practical internships in companies and businesses in the Bay Area.

FACILITIES

Housing: men's dorms, women's dorms, apartments for married students- Houses with single-sex wings (one side for men and one side for women) and a common living room. This is not really considered "coed" because there are no shared bathrooms or men and women living together on the same floor or on alternate floors. Cottages (for 8 people) are available for non-traditionally aged students, special programs, or theme houses. 75% of campus accessible to physically disabled. **Special Academic Facilities/Equipment:** Science Center with indoor aviary, School of Nations Museum and Classrooms, Voney Art Studio, School of Government, Merrick Wing for Performing Arts.

CAMPUS LIFE

Environment: Rural. **Activities:** Choral groups, dance, drama/theater, jazz band, music ensembles, musical theater, radio station, student government, student newspaper, television station, yearbook. 29 registered organizations, 1 honor society, 1 religous organization. **Athletics (Intercollegiate):** *Men:* baseball, basketball, cross-country, diving, football, soccer, swimming, tennis, track/field (outdoor), track/field (indoor). *Women:* basketball, cross-country, diving, soccer, swimming, tennis, track/field (outdoor), track/field (indoor), volleyball. **On-Campus Highlights:** Piasa Pub, Hay Field House, Planetarium, Science Center, Chapel, By January, 2007 a new 68,000 square foot athletic training center will be built. This includes two regulation-size basketball courts and 200 meter indoor track. Also part of the facility will be a 6-lane 25-meter natatorium with four diving boards and am adjacent well-appointed fitness center.

ADMISSIONS

Freshman Academic Profile: Average high school GPA 3.5. 23% in top 10% of high school class, 48% in top 25% of high school class, 68% in top 50% of high school class. 53% from public high schools. SAT Math middle 50% range 470-600. SAT Critical Reading middle 50% range 450-630. SAT Writing middle 50% range 430-595. ACT middle 50% range 20-29. Minimum internet-based TOEFL 79. **Basis for Candidate Selection:** *Very important factors considered include:* application essay, rigor of secondary school record, character/personal qualities, religious affiliation/commitment. *Important factors considered include:* Class rank, recommendation(s), standardized test scores, extracurricular activities, interview, talent/ability. *Other factors considered include:* alumni/ae relation, racial/ethnic status, volunteer work, work experience. **Freshman Admission Requirements:** High school diploma is required and GED is accepted. *Academic units required:* 4 English, 4 mathematics, 2 science, (2 science labs), 2 foreign language, 2 social studies, 1 history, 1 academic elective. **Freshman Admission Statistics:** 211 applied, 79% admitted, 72% enrolled. **Transfer Admission Requirements:** High school transcript, college transcript(s), essay or personal statement, Minimum college GPA of 2.0 required. Lowest grade transferable C-. **General Admission Information:** Regular application deadline 3/1. Notification on a rolling basis, beginning on or about 11/1. Nonfall registration accepted. Admission may be deferred for a maximum of 1 year. Credit and/or placement offered for CEEB Advanced Placement tests.

COSTS AND FINANCIAL AID

Annual tuition $26,940. Room and board $10,810. Required fees $500. Average book expense $1,000. **Required Forms and Deadlines:** CSS/Financial Aid PROFILE, Noncustodial PROFILE. **Notification of Awards:** Applicants will be notified of awards on a rolling basis beginning 3/15. **Types of Aid:** *Need-based scholarships/grants:* private scholarships, the school's own gift aid. *Loans:* college/university loans from institutional funds. *Student Employment:* Highest amount earned per year from on-campus jobs $1,310. **Financial Aid Statistics:** 100% freshmen, 100% undergrads receive need-based scholarship or grant aid. 64% freshmen, 50% undergrads receive non-need-based scholarship or grant aid. 100% freshmen, 100% undergrads receive need-based self-help aid. 0% freshmen, 0% undergrads receive athletic scholarships. 96% freshmen, 96% undergrads receive any aid. 55% undergrads borrow to pay for school. **Criteria for awarding institutional aid:** *Non-need-based:* academics, alumni affiliation.

PROVIDENCE COLLEGE

Harkins Hall 103, Providence, RI 2918
Phone: 401-865-2535 · **Financial Aid Phone:** 401-865-2286
E-mail: pcadmiss@providence.edu · **CEEB Code:** 3693
Fax: 401-865-2826 · **Website:** www.providence.edu · **ACT Code:** 3806

This private school, affiliated with the Roman Catholic Church, was founded in 1917. It has a 105-acre campus.

RATINGS

Admissions Selectivity Rating: 89   **Fire Safety Rating:** 96

STUDENTS AND FACULTY

Enrollment: 4,048. **Student Body:** 57% female, 43% male, 87% out-of-state, 2% international (27 countries represented). Asian 1%, African American 4%, Caucasian 77%, Hispanic 8%, Native American <1%
Retention and Graduation: 92% freshmen return for sophomore year. 83% freshmen graduate within 4 years. **Faculty:** 296 full-time faculty, 94% hold

PhDs, 41% are are members of minority groups, 11% are women. 0% of classes are taught by teaching assistants.

ACADEMICS

Degrees: associate, bachelor's, certificate, master's, terminal associate. **Classes:** Most classes have 20-29 students. Most lab/discussion sessions have 10-19 students. **Majors with Highest Enrollment:** Marketing/Marketing Management; Finance; Biology/Biological Sciences. **Special Study Options:** cross-registration, distance learning, double major, dual enrollment, exchange student program (domestic), honors program, independent study, internships, liberal arts/career combination, student-designed major, study abroad, teacher certification program. **Honors programs:** Liberal Arts Honors Program **Combined degree programs:** Comb-plan Bio/Opt w/ NE College of Optometry. **Disability Services:** Special programs offered to physically disabled students include note-taking services, reader services, tape recorders, tutors. **Career services:** Alumni network, alumni services, career/job search classes, career assessment, internships, regional alumni. Career services highlights include academic internships and field experience courses offered by over 20 departments. We also have the Friar Summer Internship Partner Program in which we pair students with high quality summer internships.

FACILITIES

Housing: Coed dorms, special housing for disabled students, men's dorms, women's dorms, Wellness Housing. 98% of campus accessible to physically disabled. **Special Academic Facilities/Equipment:** Hunt-Cavanagh Art Gallery, Blackfriar Theatre, Science Center Complex, Computer and Language Labs, Smith Center for the Arts. **Computers:** 100% of classrooms, 50% of dorms, 100% of libraries, 100% of dining areas, 100% of student union, 20% of common outdoor areas have wireless network access. Students can register for classes online. Administrative functions (other than registration) can be performed online.

CAMPUS LIFE

Environment: City. **Activities:** Choral groups, concert band, dance, drama/theater, jazz band, literary magazine, music ensembles, musical theater, pep band, radio station, student government, student newspaper, television station, yearbook, Campus Ministries, International Student Organization. 112 registered organizations, 18 honor societies, 2 religious organizations. **Athletics (Intercollegiate):** *Men:* basketball, cross-country, diving, ice hockey, lacrosse, soccer, swimming, track/field (outdoor), track/field (indoor). *Women:* basketball, cross-country, diving, field hockey, ice hockey, soccer, softball, swimming, tennis, track/field (outdoor), track/field (indoor), volleyball. **On-Campus Highlights:** McPhails- Student Activity Center, Peterson Center- Athletic Facility, Slavin Center- Student Center, Smith Center for the Arts, St. Dominic Chapel, Harkins Hall- Classrooms, Admin Offices; Blackfriars Theatre; Hunt-Cavanagh Art Gallery.

ADMISSIONS

Freshman Academic Profile: Average high school GPA 3.38. 34% in top 10% of high school class, 65% in top 25% of high school class, 94% in top 50% of high school class. 58% from public high schools. SAT Math middle 50% range 520-630. SAT Critical Reading middle 50% range 520-620. SAT Writing middle 50% range 530-640. ACT middle 50% range 23-28. Minimum internet-based TOEFL 90. **Basis for Candidate Selection:** *Very important factors considered include:* academic GPA, recommendation(s), rigor of secondary school record. *Important factors considered include:* application essay, character/personal qualities, extracurricular activities. *Other factors considered include:* Class rank, standardized test scores, alumni/ae relation, first generation, geographical residence, level of applicant's interest, racial/ethnic status, state residency, talent/ability, volunteer work, work experience. **Freshman Admission Requirements:** High school diploma is required and GED is not accepted. *Academic units required:* 4 English, 4 mathematics, 3 science, (2 science labs), 3 foreign language, 2 social studies, 2 history, 0 academic electives. **Freshman Admission Statistics:** 8,976 applied, 63% admitted, 18% enrolled. **Transfer Admission Requirements:** High school transcript, college transcript(s), essay or personal statement, statement of good standing from prior institution(s). Minimum college GPA of 3.0 required. Lowest grade transferable C. **General Admission Information:** Application Fee $55. Regular application deadline 1/15. Regular notification 4/1. Nonfall registration accepted. Admission may be deferred for a maximum of 12 months. Credit and/or placement offered for CEEB Advanced Placement tests.

COSTS AND FINANCIAL AID

Annual tuition $43,443. Room and board $13,060. Required fees $880. Average book expense $940. **Required Forms and Deadlines:** FAFSA, CSS/Financial Aid PROFILE. **Notification of Awards:** Applicants will be notified of awards on or about 4/1. **Types of Aid:** *Need-based scholarships/grants:* Federal Pell, SEOG, state scholarships/grants, private scholarships, the school's own gift aid, Federal Academic Competitive Grant/Smart Grant. *Loans:* Direct Subsidized Stafford, Direct Unsubsidized Stafford, Direct PLUS, Subsidized Stafford, Unsubsidized Stafford, PLUS, Federal Perkins. *Student Employment:* Federal

Work-Study Program available. Institutional employment available. Highest amount earned per year from on-campus jobs $6,500. Off-campus job opportunities are good. **Financial Aid Statistics:** 89% freshmen, 95% undergrads receive need-based scholarship or grant aid. 21% freshmen, 13% undergrads receive non-need-based scholarship or grant aid. 83% freshmen, 86% undergrads receive need-based self-help aid. 5% freshmen, 4% undergrads receive athletic scholarships. 81% freshmen, 80% undergrads receive any aid. 72% undergrads borrow to pay for school. Average cumulative indebtedness $22,866. **Criteria for awarding institutional aid:** *Non-need-based:* academics, athletics, minority status.

PURDUE UNIVERSITY—CALUMET

Office of Admissions, Hammond, IN 46323-2094
Phone: 219-989-2213 • **Financial Aid Phone:** 219-989-2301
E-mail: adms@purduecal.edu • **CEEB Code:** 1638
Fax: 219-989-2775 • **Website:** http://www.purduecal.edu/ • **ACT Code:** 1233

This public school was founded in 1946. It has a 194-acre campus.

RATINGS

Admissions Selectivity Rating: 74   **Fire Safety Rating:** 91

STUDENTS AND FACULTY

Enrollment: 8,403. **Student Body:** 55% female, 45% male, 11% out-of-state, 3% international (39 countries represented). Asian 1%, African American 19%, Caucasian 60%, Hispanic 15%, Native American <1%
Retention and Graduation: 69% freshmen return for sophomore year. 6% freshmen graduate within 4 years. 26% freshmen graduate within 6 years. **Faculty:** 268 full-time faculty, 69% hold PhDs, 48% are are members of minority groups, 21% are women.

ACADEMICS

Degrees: associate, bachelor's, certificate, master's, post-bachelor's certificate. **Classes:** Most classes have 20-29 students. Most lab/discussion sessions have 20-29 students. **Majors with Highest Enrollment:** Elementary Education and Teaching; Marketing/Marketing Management; Engineering. **Special Study Options:** Accelerated program, cooperative education program, distance learning, double major, dual enrollment, English as a Second Language (ESL), honors program, independent study, internships, study abroad, teacher certification program, weekend college. **Honors programs:** Purdue Calumet Honors Program **Combined degree programs:** 2-2 nursing program. **Disability Services:** Special programs offered to physically disabled students include note-taking services, reader services, tape recorders, tutors. **Career services:** career/job search classes, career assessment, internships.

FACILITIES

Housing: apartments for single students. 100% of campus accessible to physically disabled. **Special Academic Facilities/Equipment:** Audio-visual services, urban development institute. **Computers:** Students can register for classes online. Administrative functions (other than registration) can be performed online.

CAMPUS LIFE

Environment: City. **Activities:** Choral groups, dance, drama/theater, radio station, student government, student newspaper, Campus Ministries, International Student Organization. 56 registered organizations, 25 honor societies, 3 religious organizations. 2 fraternities, 3 sororities. **Athletics (Intercollegiate):** *Men:* basketball. *Women:* basketball. **On-Campus Highlights:** Physical Education and Recreation Building, Enrollment Services Center, Challenger Learning Center of Northwest Indiana. **Environmental Initiatives:** Campus-wide Recycling; WEP Energy Conservation Measures; Alternative Transportation including usage of electric vehicles.

ADMISSIONS

Freshman Academic Profile: Average high school GPA 2.58. 10% in top 10% of high school class, 28% in top 25% of high school class, 58% in top 50% of high school class. SAT Math middle 50% range 410-520. SAT Critical Reading middle 50% range 410-510. ACT middle 50% range 17-23. Minimum paper TOEFL 550. **Basis for Candidate Selection:** *Important factors considered include:* Class rank, academic GPA, rigor of secondary school record, standardized test scores. **Freshman Admission Requirements:** High school diploma is required and GED is accepted. *Academic units required:* 4 English, 2 mathematics, 1 science, (1 science labs), 2 foreign language, 1 social studies, 1 history. **Freshman Admission Statistics:** 5,884 applied, 69% admitted, 33% enrolled. **Transfer Admission Requirements:** High school transcript, Minimum college GPA of 2.0 required. Lowest grade transferable C. **General Admission Information:** Nonfall registration accepted. Admission may be deferred for a maximum of 1 semester. Credit offered for CEEB Advanced Placement tests.

COSTS AND FINANCIAL AID

Average book expense $1,125. **Required Forms and Deadlines:** FAFSA. **Notification of Awards:** Applicants will be notified of awards on a rolling basis beginning 4/15. **Types of Aid:** *Need-based scholarships/grants:* Federal Pell, SEOG, state scholarships/grants, the school's own gift aid. *Loans:* Direct Subsidized Stafford, Direct Unsubsidized Stafford, Direct PLUS, Federal Perkins. *Student Employment:* Federal Work-Study Program available. Off-campus job opportunities are fair. **Financial Aid Statistics:** 61% freshmen, 65% undergrads receive need-based scholarship or grant aid. 25% freshmen, 15% undergrads receive non-need-based scholarship or grant aid. 61% freshmen, 72% undergrads receive need-based self-help aid. 1% freshmen, 0% undergrads receive athletic scholarships. 62% undergrads borrow to pay for school. Average cumulative indebtedness $18,719. **Criteria for awarding institutional aid:** *Non-need-based:* academics, athletics, minority status, state/district residency.

PURDUE UNIVERSITY—WEST LAFAYETTE

Best 380

475 Stadium Mall Drive, West Lafayette, IN 47907-2050
Phone: 765-494-1776 • **Financial Aid Phone:** 765-494-0998
E-mail: admissions@purdue.edu • **CEEB Code:** 1631
Fax: 765-494-0544 • **Website:** www.purdue.edu • **ACT Code:** 1230

This public school was founded in 1869. It has a 2552-acre campus.

RATINGS

Admissions Selectivity Rating: 89   **Fire Safety Rating:** 91

STUDENTS AND FACULTY

Enrollment: 29,038. **Student Body:** 43% female, 57% male, 33% out-of-state, 18% international (123 countries represented). Asian 6%, African American 3%, Caucasian 65%, Hispanic 4%, Native American <1% **Faculty:** 2,063 full-time faculty, 98% hold PhDs, 32% are are members of minority groups, 22% are women. 29% of classes are taught by teaching assistants.

ACADEMICS

Degrees: bachelor's, certificate, doctoral, master's, terminal associate. **Classes:** Most classes have 20-29 students. Most lab/discussion sessions have 20-29 students. **Majors with Highest Enrollment:** Mechanical Engineering; Biology/Biological Sciences; Business Administration and Management. **Special Study Options:** Accelerated program, cooperative education program, cross-registration, distance learning, double major, dual enrollment, exchange student program (domestic), honors program, independent study, internships, liberal arts/career combination, study abroad, teacher certification program, weekend college. **Honors programs:** University Honors Program. **Disability Services:** Special programs offered to physically disabled students include note-taking services, reader services, tape recorders, tutors. **Career services:** Alumni network, alumni services, career/job search classes, career assessment, internships, regional alumni. Career services highlights include all of the above.

FACILITIES

Housing: Coed dorms, special housing for disabled students, men's dorms, women's dorms, fraternity/sorority housing, apartments for married students, cooperative housing, apartments for single students, Wellness Housing. 90% of campus accessible to physically disabled. **Special Academic Facilities/Equipment:** Hall of music, child development lab, speech and hearing clinic, small animal veterinary clinic, horticulture park, linear accelerator, tornado simulator, nuclear accelerator. **Computers:** 95% of classrooms, 5% of dorms, 95% of libraries, 90% of dining areas, 95% of student union, 5% of common outdoor areas have wireless network access. Students can register for classes online. Administrative functions (other than registration) can be performed online.

CAMPUS LIFE

Environment: Town. **Activities:** Choral groups, concert band, dance, drama/theater, jazz band, literary magazine, marching band, music ensembles, musical theater, opera, pep band, radio station, student government, student newspaper, student-run film society, symphony orchestra, television station, yearbook, Campus Ministries, International Student Organization, Model UN. 850 registered organizations, 25 honor societies, 66 religious organizations. 48 fraternities, 32 sororities. **Athletics (Intercollegiate):** *Men:* baseball, basketball, cross-country, diving, football, golf, swimming, tennis, track/field (outdoor), track/field (indoor), wrestling. *Women:* basketball, cross-country, diving, golf, soccer, softball, swimming, tennis, track/field (outdoor), track/field (indoor), volley-

ball. **On-Campus Highlights:** Pudue Memorial Union, Recreational Sports Center, Fountain areas, Libraries, Sporting events. **Environmental Initiatives:** Development and implementation of the Sustainability Strategic Plan. The Sustainability Strategic Plan also establishes eight program areas or pillars of sustainability focus on campus. These eight pillars are as follows: 1. Site Considerations 2. Water Resources 3. Energy and Built Environment 4. Materials Management 5. Food Systems 6. Academics and Research 7. Endowment / Development 8. Community Relationships. Within this plan, there are 56 short-term goals (to be achieved by 2014) and 85 long-term goals (to be achieved by 2025). Development of our Comprehensive Energy Master Plan. The purpose of the CEMP is to investigate the energy production, distribution and building demand on the West Lafayette Campus. The investigation analyzed the chilled water, steam and electrical production at the utility plants, modeled the chilled water and steam distribution systems and estimated the energy savings potential in the campus buildings. The result of this analysis is a fiscally and environmentally responsible Comprehensive Energy Master Plan that provides Purdue guidance in managing the energy production and consumption on the campus as it continues to grow and evolve. Academic / research leadership in sustainability. Examples include: Purdues Global Sustainability Initiative (GSI), led by Director Jon Harbor, focuses research and study within five major centers which include: Energy Center; Center for the Environment; Purdue Climate Change Research Center; Purdue Water Community; Purdue Center for Global Food Security. More information on GSIs programs and research activities can be found at the following website: www.purdue.edu/discoverypark/sustainability/index.php. The Purdue Solar Decathlon Team INhome (www.purdue.edu/inhome/) recently finished second in this international competition sponsored by the Department of Energy (www.solardecathlon.gov/). This was Purdues first foray into this competition, which was comprised of an extremely competitive group of international universities, many of which have been competing in the Solar Decathlon for years. Finishing in second place in our first attempt represents a stellar achievement for the INhome Team.

ADMISSIONS

Freshman Academic Profile: Average high school GPA 3.72. 42% in top 10% of high school class, 77% in top 25% of high school class, 97% in top 50% of high school class. SAT Math middle 50% range 560-700. SAT Critical Reading middle 50% range 520-630. SAT Writing middle 50% range 520-630. ACT middle 50% range 25-30. Minimum internet-based TOEFL 79. Minimum paper TOEFL 550. **Basis for Candidate Selection:** *Very important factors considered include:* application essay, rigor of secondary school record, standardized test scores. *Important factors considered include:* Class rank, academic GPA. *Other factors considered include:* recommendation(s), alumni/ae relation, character/personal qualities, extracurricular activities, first generation, state residency, volunteer work, work experience. **Freshman Admission Requirements:** High school diploma is required and GED is accepted. *Academic units required:* 4 English, 3 mathematics, 3 science, (3 science labs), 2 foreign language, 3 social studies. **Freshman Admission Statistics:** 39,706 applied, 59% admitted, 27% enrolled. **Transfer Admission Requirements:** college transcript(s), essay or personal statement, statement of good standing from prior institution(s). Minimum college GPA of 2.5 required. Lowest grade transferable C. **General Admission Information:** Application Fee $50. Regular application deadline 3/1. Notification on a rolling basis, beginning on or about 12/5. Nonfall registration accepted. Admission may be deferred for a maximum of 1 year. Credit and/or placement offered for CEEB Advanced Placement tests.

COSTS AND FINANCIAL AID

Required Forms and Deadlines: FAFSA. **Notification of Awards:** Applicants will be notified of awards on or about 4/15. **Types of Aid:** *Need-based scholarships/grants:* Federal Pell, SEOG, state scholarships/grants, private scholarships, the school's own gift aid, Federal Academic Competitiveness Grant (ACG) and National SMART Grant Program. *Loans:* Direct Subsidized Stafford, Direct Unsubsidized Stafford, Direct PLUS, Federal Perkins, college/university loans from institutional funds. *Student Employment:* Federal Work-Study Program available. Institutional employment available. Off-campus job opportunities are good. **Financial Aid Statistics:** 64% freshmen, 69% undergrads receive need-based scholarship or grant aid. 46% freshmen, 37% undergrads receive non-need-based scholarship or grant aid. 78% freshmen, 85% undergrads receive need-based self-help aid. 1% freshmen, 1% undergrads receive athletic scholarships. 74% freshmen, 77% undergrads receive any aid. 52% undergrads borrow to pay for school. Average cumulative indebtedness $22,765. **Criteria for awarding institutional aid:** *Non-need-based:* academics, athletics, leadership, music/drama, state/district residency.

QUEEN'S UNIVERSITY

Admission Services, Kingston, ON K7L3N6
Phone: 613-533-2218
E-mail: admission@queensu.ca • **CEEB Code:** 949
Fax: 613-533-6810 • **Website:** www.queensu.ca • **ACT Code:** 5236

This public school was founded in 1841. It has a 160-acre campus.

RATINGS
Admissions Selectivity Rating: 65   **Fire Safety Rating:** 60*

STUDENTS AND FACULTY
Enrollment: 14,130. **Student Body:** 59% female, 41% male, 18(129 countries represented).
Retention and Graduation: 93% freshmen graduate within 6 years. **Faculty:** 1,032 full-time faculty, 94% hold PhDs, 39% are are members of minority groups.

ACADEMICS
Degrees: bachelor's, master's. **Classes:** Most classes have 20-29 students. Most lab/discussion sessions have 20-29 students. **Majors with Highest Enrollment:** Sport and Fitness Administration/Management; Business/Commerce. **Special Study Options:** cooperative education program, distance learning, double major, dual enrollment, English as a Second Language (ESL), exchange student program (domestic), honors program, independent study, internships, study abroad, teacher certification program, The university owns and operates an International Study Centre (ISC) at Herstmonceux,East Sussex, England. **Disability Services:** Special programs offered to physically disabled students include note-taking services, reader services, tape recorders, tutors. **Career services:** career/job search classes, career assessment, internships.

FACILITIES
Housing: Coed dorms, men's dorms, special housing for international students, women's dorms, apartments for married students, cooperative housing, apartments for single students **Special Academic Facilities/Equipment:** Agnes Etherington Art Centre, Miller Museum of Geology. **Computers:** Students can register for classes online. Administrative functions (other than registration) can be performed online.

CAMPUS LIFE
Environment: City. **Activities:** Choral groups, concert band, dance, drama/theater, jazz band, literary magazine, marching band, music ensembles, musical theater, opera, pep band, radio station, student government, student newspaper, student-run film society, symphony orchestra, television station, yearbook 18 religious organizations. **Athletics (Intercollegiate):** *Men:* baseball, basketball, cheerleading, crew/rowing, cross-country, curling, fencing, football, golf, ice hockey, lacrosse, mountain biking, rodeo, rugby, sailing, skiing (nordic/cross-country), soccer, squash, swimming, tennis, track/field (outdoor), ultimate frisbee, volleyball, water polo, wrestling. *Women:* basketball, cheerleading, crew/rowing, cross-country, curling, fencing, field hockey, ice hockey, lacrosse, mountain biking, rodeo, rugby, sailing, skiing (nordic/cross-country), soccer, squash, swimming, synchronized swimming, tennis, track/field (outdoor), ultimate frisbee, volleyball, water polo, wrestling. **On-Campus Highlights:** Integrated Learning Centre (ILC), Agnes Etherington Art Centre, Stauffer Library, Biosciences Complex, Chernoff Hall.

ADMISSIONS
Freshman Academic Profile: Minimum paper TOEFL 580. **Basis for Candidate Selection:** *Very important factors considered include:* academic GPA, standardized test scores. *Important factors considered include:* rigor of secondary school record, extracurricular activities, talent/ability, volunteer work. *Other factors considered include:* Class rank, recommendation(s), work experience. **Freshman Admission Requirements:** High school diploma is required and GED is accepted. **Freshman Admission Statistics:** 25,403 applied, 42% admitted, 31% enrolled. **Transfer Admission Requirements:** High school transcript, college transcript(s). **General Admission Information:** Application Fee $135. Regular application deadline 2/16. Notification on a rolling basis, beginning on or about 1/2. Nonfall registration not accepted. Admission may be deferred for a maximum of 12 months.

COSTS AND FINANCIAL AID
Required Forms and Deadlines: Institution's own financial aid form. **Types of Aid:** *Need-based scholarships/grants:* private scholarships, the school's own gift aid. *Loans:* college/university loans from institutional funds. **Financial Aid Statistics:** 0% undergrads receive athletic scholarships. 30% undergrads borrow to pay for school. **Criteria for awarding institutional aid:** *Non-need-based:* academics, leadership, music/drama.

QUEENS UNIVERSITY OF CHARLOTTE

1900 Selwyn Avenue, Charlotte, NC 28274
Phone: 704-337-2212 • **Financial Aid Phone:** 704-337-2225
E-mail: admissions@queens.edu • **CEEB Code:** 5560
Fax: 704-337-2403 • **Website:** www.queens.edu • **ACT Code:** 3148

This private school, affiliated with the Presbyterian Church, was founded in 1857. It has a 30-acre campus.

RATINGS
Admissions Selectivity Rating: 79   **Fire Safety Rating:** 66

STUDENTS AND FACULTY
Enrollment: 1,911. **Student Body:** 76% female, 24% male, 8% international. Asian 2%, African American 16%, Caucasian 55%, Hispanic 3%, Native American 1%
Retention and Graduation: 70% freshmen return for sophomore year. 48% freshmen graduate within 4 years. 59% freshmen graduate within 6 years. **Faculty:** 123 full-time faculty, 72% hold PhDs, 68% are are members of minority groups, 7% are women. 0% of classes are taught by teaching assistants.

ACADEMICS
Degrees: associate, bachelor's, master's, post-bachelor's certificate, terminal associate. **Classes:** Most classes have 10-19 students. Most lab/discussion sessions have 10-19 students. **Majors with Highest Enrollment:** Business/Commerce; Communication and Media Studies; Adult Health Nurse/Nursing. **Special Study Options:** cross-registration, double major, dual enrollment, honors program, independent study, internships, liberal arts/career combination, student-designed major, study abroad, teacher certification program, weekend college. **Disability Services:** Special programs offered to physically disabled students include note-taking services, reader services, tape recorders, tutors. **Career services:** Alumni network, career/job search classes, internships. Career services highlights include an internship as a required component of the undergraduate degree here at Queens.

FACILITIES
Housing: Coed dorms, special housing for disabled studentsApartment style 2 bedroom suites for traditional-aged undergraduates 1/2 mile from campus. 60% of campus accessible to physically disabled. **Special Academic Facilities/Equipment:** Three art galleries, rare books museum.

CAMPUS LIFE
Environment: Metropolis. **Activities:** Choral groups, dance, drama/theater, literary magazine, music ensembles, musical theater, pep band, student government, student newspaper, yearbook, Campus Ministries, International Student Organization, Model UN. 38 registered organizations, 9 honor societies, 2 religious organizations. 2 fraternities, 4 sororities. **Athletics (Intercollegiate):** *Men:* basketball, cheerleading, cross-country, golf, lacrosse, soccer, tennis, track/field (outdoor). *Women:* basketball, cheerleading, cross-country, golf, lacrosse, soccer, softball, tennis, track/field (outdoor), volleyball. **On-Campus Highlights:** Fitness Center, The Lion's Den, Trexler Courtyard, Queens' Off-Campus Athletic Facility.

ADMISSIONS
Freshman Academic Profile: Average high school GPA 3.54. 14% in top 10% of high school class, 39% in top 25% of high school class, 78% in top 50% of high school class. 88% from public high schools. SAT Math middle 50% range 460-570. SAT Critical Reading middle 50% range 470-580. SAT Writing middle 50% range 460-560. ACT middle 50% range 20-25. Minimum internet-based TOEFL 80. Minimum paper TOEFL 550. **Basis for Candidate Selection:** *Very important factors considered include:* academic GPA, rigor of secondary school record, standardized test scores, character/personal qualities, extracurricular activities. *Important factors considered include:* Class rank, interview, volunteer work. *Other factors considered include:* application essay, recommendation(s), alumni/ae relation, first generation, talent/ability, work experience. **Freshman Admission Requirements:** High school diploma is required and GED is accepted. *Academic units required:* 4 English, 3 mathematics, 2 science, (1 science labs), 2 foreign language, 2 social studies. **Freshman Admission Statistics:** 2,199 applied, 74% admitted, 22% enrolled. **Transfer Admission Requirements:** High school transcript, college transcript(s), essay or personal statement, statement of good standing from prior institution(s). Minimum college GPA of 2.0 required. Lowest grade transferable C. **General Admission Information:** Application Fee $40. Notification on a rolling basis, beginning on or about 10/1. Nonfall registration accepted. Admission may be deferred for a maximum of 1 year. Credit and/or placement offered for CEEB Advanced Placement tests.

COSTS AND FINANCIAL AID
Required Forms and Deadlines: FAFSA, State aid form. **Notification of Awards:** Applicants will be notified of awards on a rolling basis beginning

3/15. **Types of Aid:** *Need-based scholarships/grants:* Federal Pell, SEOG, state scholarships/grants, private scholarships, the school's own gift aid. *Loans:* Subsidized Stafford, Unsubsidized Stafford, PLUS, Federal Perkins, state loans. *Student Employment:* Federal Work-Study Program available. Highest amount earned per year from on-campus jobs $1,500. Off-campus job opportunities are excellent. **Financial Aid Statistics:** 100% freshmen, 99% undergrads receive need-based scholarship or grant aid. 18% freshmen, 15% undergrads receive non-need-based scholarship or grant aid. 79% freshmen, 83% undergrads receive need-based self-help aid. 11% freshmen, 10% undergrads receive athletic scholarships. 83% freshmen, 86% undergrads borrow to pay for school. Average cumulative indebtedness $23,815. **Criteria for awarding institutional aid:** *Non-need-based:* academics, art, athletics, minority status, music/drama.

QUINCY UNIVERSITY

1800 College Avenue, Quincy, IL 62301-2699
Phone: 217-228-5210 • **Financial Aid Phone:** 217-228-5260
E-mail: admissions@quincy.edu • **CEEB Code:** 1645
Fax: 217-228-5479 • **Website:** www.quincy.edu • **ACT Code:** 1120

This private school, affiliated with the Roman Catholic Church, was founded in 1860. It has a 70-acre campus.

RATINGS

Admissions Selectivity Rating: 70   **Fire Safety Rating:** 72

STUDENTS AND FACULTY

Enrollment: 1,075. **Student Body:** 56% female, 44% male, 28(6 countries represented).
Retention and Graduation: 76% freshmen return for sophomore year. 33% freshmen graduate within 4 years. 49% freshmen graduate within 6 years. 22% grads go on to further study within 1 year. 11% grads pursue arts and sciences degrees. 2% grads pursue law degrees. 5% grads pursue business degrees. 2% grads pursue medical degrees. **Faculty:** 56 full-time faculty, 71% hold PhDs, 39% are are members of minority groups, 7% are women. 0% of classes are taught by teaching assistants.

ACADEMICS

Degrees: associate, bachelor's, master's. **Classes:** Most classes have 10-19 students. Most lab/discussion sessions have fewer than 10 students. **Majors with Highest Enrollment:** Elementary Education and Teaching; Registered Nursing/Registered Nurse; Management Science. **Special Study Options:** Accelerated program, distance learning, double major, dual enrollment, honors program, independent study, internships, student-designed major, study abroad, teacher certification program, 3-2 program in engineering with Washington University; 3-1 program in medical technology with various hospitals. **Honors programs:** The Honors Program provides a challenging course of study which adds an interdisciplinary dimension to a student's major field. The program promotes academic excellence through critical thinking, original research, exceptional writing, and public presentation of scholarship. **Combined degree programs:** Clinical Laboratory Science—B.S. **Disability Services:** Special programs offered to physically disabled students include note-taking services, reader services, tape recorders, tutors. **Career services:** Alumni network, alumni services, career/job search classes, career assessment, internships, regional alumni. The University, in cooperation with the state of Illinois and local businesses and social service agencies, provides early exploratory internships to first and second year students to aid in the career development/decision-making process.

FACILITIES

Housing: Coed dorms, men's dorms, women's dorms, fraternity/sorority housing, apartments for married students, apartments for single students, Theme Housing, Honors. 90% of campus accessible to physically disabled. **Special Academic Facilities/Equipment:** Reading center for student teachers, multimedia and graphic design labs, TV broadcast studio, temperature-controlled rare books Library archive, art gallery, 200-seat theater, environmental studies institute, hospital simulation lab, aviation facility with flight simulator, College-operated national public radio station. **Computers:** 100% of classrooms, 100% of dorms, 100% of libraries, 100% of dining areas, 100% of student union, 40% of common outdoor areas have wireless network access. Administrative functions (other than registration) can be performed online.

CAMPUS LIFE

Environment: Town. **Activities:** Choral groups, concert band, dance, drama/theater, jazz band, literary magazine, music ensembles, musical theater, opera, pep band, radio station, student government, student newspaper, symphony orchestra, television station, Campus Ministries. 40 registered organizations,

8 honor societies, 2 religious organizations. 1 fraternity, 2 sororities. **Athletics (Intercollegiate):** *Men:* baseball, basketball, cross-country, football, golf, soccer, tennis, volleyball. *Women:* basketball, cross-country, golf, soccer, softball, tennis, volleyball. **On-Campus Highlights:** Health and Fitness Center, Newly renovated University Center, QU Chapel, Francis Garden, Brenner Library. **Environmental Initiatives:** Residence hall renovation: Helein Hall renovations included use of recycled furniture and the installation of an energy-efficient VRV hvac system. New 36,000 sq.ft. suite-style residence hall constructed with high energy-efficient HVAC system and outdoor green area. On-going University-wide recycling program for paper, plastic, metal, and ink cartridges.

ADMISSIONS

Freshman Academic Profile: 76% from public high schools. SAT Math middle 50% range 410-490. SAT Critical Reading middle 50% range 460-490. ACT middle 50% range 19-25. Minimum internet-based TOEFL 61. Minimum paper TOEFL 500. **Basis for Candidate Selection:** *Very important factors considered include:* academic GPA, rigor of secondary school record. *Important factors considered include:* Class rank, application essay, recommendation(s), standardized test scores, character/personal qualities, extracurricular activities, level of applicant's interest, volunteer work, work experience. *Other factors considered include:* interview, talent/ability. **Freshman Admission Requirements:** High school diploma is required and GED is accepted. **Freshman Admission Statistics:** 903 applied, 89% admitted, 27% enrolled. **Transfer Admission Requirements:** college transcript(s), statement of good standing from prior institution(s). Minimum college GPA of 2.0 required. Lowest grade transferable D. **General Admission Information:** Application Fee $25. Notification on a rolling basis, beginning on or about 9/1. Nonfall registration accepted. Credit offered for CEEB Advanced Placement tests.

COSTS AND FINANCIAL AID

Annual tuition $25,598. Room and board $9,968. Required fees $974. Average book expense $1,250. **Required Forms and Deadlines:** FAFSA. **Notification of Awards:** Applicants will be notified of awards on a rolling basis beginning 2/15. **Types of Aid:** *Need-based scholarships/grants:* Federal Pell, SEOG, state scholarships/grants, private scholarships, the school's own gift aid. *Loans:* Subsidized Stafford, Unsubsidized Stafford, PLUS, Federal Perkins. *Student Employment:* Federal Work-Study Program available. Institutional employment available. Highest amount earned per year from on-campus jobs $2,000. Off-campus job opportunities are good. **Financial Aid Statistics:** 98% freshmen, 92% undergrads receive need-based scholarship or grant aid. 23% freshmen, 16% undergrads receive non-need-based scholarship or grant aid. 69% freshmen, 72% undergrads receive need-based self-help aid. 8% freshmen, 4% undergrads receive athletic scholarships. 100% freshmen, 93% undergrads receive any aid. 87% undergrads borrow to pay for school. Average cumulative indebtedness $26,280. **Criteria for awarding institutional aid:** *Non-need-based:* academics, alumni affiliation, art, athletics, music/drama.

QUINNIPIAC UNIVERSITY

Best 380

275 Mount Carmel Avenue, Hamden, CT 6518
Phone: 203-582-8600 • **Financial Aid Phone:** 203-582-8750
E-mail: admissions@quinnipiac.edu • **CEEB Code:** 3712
Fax: 203-582-8906 • **Website:** www.quinnipiac.edu • **ACT Code:** 582

This private school was founded in 1929. It has a 600-acre campus.

RATINGS

Admissions Selectivity Rating: 88   **Fire Safety Rating:** 97

STUDENTS AND FACULTY

Enrollment: 6,503. **Student Body:** 60% female, 40% male, 75% out-of-state, 2% international (43 countries represented). Asian 2%, African American 5%, Caucasian 75%, Hispanic 9%, Native American <1%
Retention and Graduation: 87% freshmen return for sophomore year. 72% freshmen graduate within 4 years. 76% freshmen graduate within 6 years. 37% grads go on to further study within 1 year. 18% grads pursue arts and sciences degrees. 2% grads pursue law degrees. 9% grads pursue business degrees. 2% grads pursue medical degrees. **Faculty:** 396 full-time faculty, 88% hold PhDs, 53% are are members of minority groups, 17% are women. 0% of classes are taught by teaching assistants.

ACADEMICS

Degrees: bachelor's, doctoral, master's, post-bachelor's certificate, post-master's certificate. **Classes:** Most classes have 10-19 students. Most lab/discussion sessions have 10-19 students. **Majors with Highest Enrollment:** Psychology; Physical Therapy/Therapist; Business/Commerce. **Special Study Options:** distance learning, double major, exchange student program (domestic), honors program, independent study, internships, liberal arts/career combination, student-designed major, study abroad, teacher certification program, Online option for summer course offerings Online degrees offered at the graduate level. **Honors programs:** The University Honors Program, limited to 60-70 freshmen who are selected following their acceptance,provides challenging coursework and opportunities for learning and service. BA/JD, BA/MA. **Career services:** Alumni network, alumni services, career/job search classes, career assessment, internships, regional alumni. Career services highlights include extensive internship programs in all business and communications fields. Clinical placements in all of the health science fields.

FACILITIES

Housing: Coed dorms, apartments for single students, Wellness HousingUniversity owned houses provide housing for about 100 seniors/juniors. 100% of campus accessible to physically disabled. **Special Academic Facilities/ Equipment:** Quinnipiac Polling Institute, Financial Technology Center, Motion Analysis Lab, Albert Schweitzer Institute, Critical Care Nursing Lab,Fully digital/high definition TV production studio,editing labs, news technology center. Lender family special collection room in Library on the Irish Famine, "An Gorta Mor". **Computers:** 100% of classrooms, 100% of dorms, 100% of libraries, 100% of dining areas, 100% of student union, 100% of common outdoor areas have wireless network access. Students can register for classes online. Administrative functions (other than registration) can be performed online. Undergraduates are required to own a computer.

CAMPUS LIFE

Environment: Town. **Activities:** Choral groups, dance, drama/theater, literary magazine, pep band, radio station, student government, student newspaper, television station, yearbook, Campus Ministries, International Student Organization. 78 registered organizations, 8 honor societies, 3 religious organizations. 2 fraternities, 3 sororities. **Athletics (Intercollegiate):** *Men:* baseball, basketball, cross-country, ice hockey, lacrosse, soccer, tennis. *Women:* basketball, cheerleading, cross-country, field hockey, ice hockey, lacrosse, soccer, softball, tennis, track/field (outdoor), track/field (indoor), volleyball. **On-Campus Highlights:** Arnold Bernhard Library, Recreation Center with suspended banked track, An Gorta Mor, Irish famine literature and art, Café Q with Zia/Starbucks, Bobcat Den/Coffee Bar, The nearby 250 acre 'York Hill' campus with the TD Bank Sports Center-twin 3500 seat arenas for ice hockey and basketball, includes residence halls with 1800 beds and a student/recreation center. About 5 miles away is the North Haven campus of 104 acres, home to the graduate programs in the School of Health Sciences. Upper division (juniors and seniors) students in Physical Therapy, Occupational Therapy, Nursing, Diagnostic Imaging and Physician Assistant programs also use this outstanding state-of-the-art facility. **Environmental Initiatives:** 100 percent of Quinnipiac electricity requirements on all three of its campuses have been purchased from renewable energy credits. 1,232 photovoltaic solar panels on the roof of the 475,000 square-foot Crescent residence hall, will convert energy from the sun to electricity and generate about 250,000kwh per year. A wind garden composed of 42 verticalaxis wind turbines will generate about 84,000 kilowatt hours per year on the York Hill campus—home to residence halls for 1800 students and the TD Bank Sports Center.

ADMISSIONS

Freshman Academic Profile: Average high school GPA 3.4. 27% in top 10% of high school class, 66% in top 25% of high school class, 93% in top 50% of high school class. 70% from public high schools. SAT Math middle 50% range 520-620. SAT Critical Reading middle 50% range 490-590. SAT Writing middle 50% range 500-590. ACT middle 50% range 22-27. Minimum internet-based TOEFL 81. Minimum paper TOEFL 550. **Basis for Candidate Selection:** *Very important factors considered include:* academic GPA, rigor of secondary school record. *Important factors considered include:* Class rank, application essay, standardized test scores. *Other factors considered include:* recommendation(s), alumni/ae relation, character/personal qualities, extracurricular activities, interview, level of applicant's interest, racial/ethnic status, talent/ability, volunteer work, work experience. **Freshman Admission Requirements:** High school diploma is required and GED is accepted. *Academic units required:* 4 English, 3 mathematics, 3 science, (2 science labs), 2 foreign language, 2 social studies, 4 4 years of Science and Math req. in PT,OT, Nursing and PA. **Freshman Admission Statistics:** 23,240 applied, 66% admitted, 11% enrolled. **Transfer Admission Requirements:** college transcript(s), essay or personal statement, Minimum college GPA of 2.5 required. Lowest grade transferable C. **General Admission Information:** Application Fee $45. Notification on a rolling basis, beginning on or about 12/15. Nonfall registration accepted. Admission may be deferred for a maximum of 12 months. Credit and/ or placement offered for CEEB Advanced Placement tests.

COSTS AND FINANCIAL AID

Annual tuition $40,720. Room and board $14,820. Required fees $1,550. Average book expense $800. **Required Forms and Deadlines:** FAFSA, CSS/ Financial Aid PROFILE. **Notification of Awards:** Applicants will be notified of awards on a rolling basis beginning 2/15. **Types of Aid:** *Need-based scholarships/grants:* Federal Pell, SEOG, state scholarships/grants, private scholarships, the school's own gift aid, Federal Nursing Scholarships. *Loans:* Direct Subsidized Stafford, Direct Unsubsidized Stafford, Direct PLUS, Subsidized Stafford, Unsubsidized Stafford, PLUS, Federal Perkins, Federal Nursing, state loans. *Student Employment:* Federal Work-Study Program available. Institutional employment available. Highest amount earned per year from on-campus jobs $2,100. Off-campus job opportunities are excellent. **Financial Aid Statistics:** 97% freshmen, 96% undergrads receive need-based scholarship or grant aid. 62% freshmen, 56% undergrads receive non-need-based scholarship or grant aid. 79% freshmen, 82% undergrads receive need-based self-help aid. 5% freshmen, 48% undergrads receive athletic scholarships. 88% freshmen, 83% undergrads receive any aid. 71% undergrads borrow to pay for school. Average cumulative indebtedness $25,906. **Criteria for awarding institutional aid:** *Non-need-based:* academics, athletics.

See page 1112.

RADFORD UNIVERSITY

PO Box 6903, Radford, VA 24142
Phone: 540-831-5371 · **Financial Aid Phone:** 540-831-5408
E-mail: admissions@radford.edu · **CEEB Code:** 5565
Fax: 540-831-5038 · **Website:** www.radford.edu · **ACT Code:** 4422

This public school was founded in 1910. It has a 191-acre campus.

RATINGS

Admissions Selectivity Rating: 72   **Fire Safety Rating:** 92

STUDENTS AND FACULTY

Enrollment: 8,843. **Student Body:** 56% female, 44% male, 5% out-of-state, 1% international (56 countries represented). Asian 1%, African American 12%, Caucasian 74%, Hispanic 5%, Native American <1%
Retention and Graduation: 43% freshmen graduate within 4 years. 20% grads go on to further study within 1 year. **Faculty:** 444 full-time faculty, 81% hold PhDs, 50% are are members of minority groups, 11% are women. 2.5% of classes are taught by teaching assistants.

ACADEMICS

Degrees: bachelor's, doctoral, master's, post-bachelor's certificate, post-master's certificate. **Classes:** Most classes have 20-29 students. Most lab/discussion sessions have 20-29 students. **Majors with Highest Enrollment:** Physical Education Teaching and Coaching; Multi-/Interdisciplinary Studies; Criminal Justice/Safety Studies. **Special Study Options:** Accelerated program, cross-registration, distance learning, double major, dual enrollment, honors program, independent study, internships, student-designed major, study abroad, teacher certification program. **Honors programs:** Student members of Honors Academy work toward graduating as Highlander Scholars. To graduate as a Highlander Scholar, one must complete 27 credit hours of Honors Coursework, present their Honors Capstone Project in a public forum, and have a cumulative GPA of 3.5 at the time of graduation. The 27 hours of honors coursework are completed as follows: 6-12 credits in the Core Curriculum as honors credits (usually earned by taking Honors Classes), 12-15 in one's major as honors credits (usually by contracting the course for honors credit and a 3-6 credit hour honors capstone project in one's major (a piece of scholarship completed under the supervision of a faculty member in one's department). There is also a residential/social component to the Honors Academy. Active members in the Honors Academy enjoy early registration, and their status as a Highlander Scholar Graduate is noted on their diploma and transcript. Students are also supported financially to present the results of their work at professional and undergraduate conferences. **Combined degree programs:** BA/MA. **Disability Services:** Special programs offered to physically disabled students include note-taking services, reader services, tape recorders, tutors. **Career services:** Alumni network, alumni services, career/job search classes, career assessment, internships, regional alumni. Career services highlights include strong job search classes and tools that now include the best software available in the field to assist students in career search training. RU makes available Optimal Resume & Optimal First Impressions software that assists with resume/business letter development; electronic portfolio construction; and virtual interview practice utilizing video and audio tape recording. Our students also have a job board of employer posted openings, a resume posting site, and interview scheduling software powered by CSO and called Hire a Highlander. In addition, each semester the career placement office provides a series of Internship Readiness Seminars and other programs developed to enhance interviewing, business protocol and confidence in the career transition process.

FACILITIES

Housing: Coed dorms, special housing for disabled students, special housing for international students, apartments for single students, Wellness Housing, Theme Housing. 100% of campus accessible to physically disabled. **Special Academic Facilities/Equipment:** Language Lab, Art Gallery with Sculpture Garden, Planetarium, Selu Conservancy, and on-campus speech/language/hearing clinic. **Computers:** 100% of classrooms, 100% of dorms, 100% of libraries, 100% of dining areas, 100% of student union, 100% of common outdoor areas have wireless network access. Students can register for classes online. Administrative functions (other than registration) can be performed online.

CAMPUS LIFE

Environment: Village. **Activities:** Choral groups, concert band, dance, drama/theater, jazz band, literary magazine, music ensembles, musical theater, pep band, radio station, student government, student newspaper, television station, yearbook, Campus Ministries, International Student Organization. 237 registered organizations, 14 honor societies, 10 religious organizations. 15 fraternities, 10 sororities. **Athletics (Intercollegiate):** *Men:* baseball, basketball, cheerleading, cross-country, golf, soccer, tennis, track/field (outdoor), track/field (indoor). *Women:* basketball, cheerleading, cross-country, diving, field hockey, golf, soccer, softball, swimming, tennis, track/field (outdoor), track/field (indoor), volleyball. **On-Campus Highlights:** Hurlburt Student Center— The Bonnie, Heth Hall- Students Services, Young Hall—High Tech Classrooms, Covington Center for Arts, Muse Hall—New River Grill.

ADMISSIONS

Freshman Academic Profile: Average high school GPA 3.2. 5% in top 10% of high school class, 20% in top 25% of high school class, 60% in top 50% of high school class. 94% from public high schools. SAT Math middle 50% range 440-530. SAT Critical Reading middle 50% range 450-530. SAT Writing middle 50% range 430-520. ACT middle 50% range 18-22. Minimum internet-based TOEFL 68. Minimum paper TOEFL 520. **Basis for Candidate Selection:** *Very important factors considered include:* rigor of secondary school record. *Important factors considered include:* academic GPA. *Other factors considered include:* Class rank, application essay, recommendation(s), standardized test scores, alumni/ae relation, character/personal qualities, extracurricular activities, first generation, geographical residence, level of applicant's interest, racial/ethnic status, state residency, talent/ability, volunteer work, work experience. **Freshman Admission Requirements:** High school diploma is required and GED is accepted. **Freshman Admission Statistics:** 7,737 applied, 79% admitted, 33% enrolled. **Transfer Admission Requirements:** college transcript(s), Minimum college GPA of 2.0 required. Lowest grade transferable C. **General Admission Information:** Application Fee $50. Regular application deadline 2/1. Regular notification 4/1. Nonfall registration accepted. Admission may be deferred for a maximum of 1 year. Credit and/or placement offered for CEEB Advanced Placement tests.

COSTS AND FINANCIAL AID

Annual in-state tuition $6,386. Annual out-of-state tuition $18,626. Room and board $8,406. Required fees $2,974. Average book expense $1,100. **Required Forms and Deadlines:** FAFSA. **Notification of Awards:** Applicants will be notified of awards on a rolling basis beginning 4/15. **Types of Aid:** *Need-based scholarships/grants:* Federal Pell, SEOG, state scholarships/grants, private scholarships, the school's own gift aid. *Loans:* Subsidized Stafford, Unsubsidized Stafford, PLUS, Federal Perkins, Federal Nursing, state loans, college/university loans from institutional funds. *Student Employment:* Federal Work-Study Program available. Institutional employment available. Highest amount earned per year from on-campus jobs $2,610. Off-campus job opportunities are good. **Financial Aid Statistics:** 60% freshmen, 63% undergrads receive need-based scholarship or grant aid. 26% freshmen, 20% undergrads receive non-need-based scholarship or grant aid. 78% freshmen, 82% undergrads receive need-based self-help aid. 1% freshmen, 1% undergrads receive athletic scholarships. 75% freshmen, 74% undergrads receive any aid. 62% undergrads borrow to pay for school. Average cumulative indebtedness $22,771. **Criteria for awarding institutional aid:** *Non-need-based:* academics, alumni affiliation, art, athletics, leadership, music/drama, state/district residency.

RAMAPO COLLEGE OF NEW JERSEY

505 Ramapo Valley Road-McBride House, Mahwah, NJ 07430-1680
Phone: 201-684-7300 · **Financial Aid Phone:** 201-684-7550
E-mail: admissions@ramapo.edu · **CEEB Code:** 2884
Fax: 201-684-7964 · **Website:** www.ramapo.edu · **ACT Code:** 2591

This public school was founded in 1971. It has a 300-acre campus.

RATINGS

Admissions Selectivity Rating: 81   **Fire Safety Rating:** 95

STUDENTS AND FACULTY

Enrollment: 5,447. **Student Body:** 55% female, 45% male, 5% out-of-state, 1% international (27 countries represented). Asian 6%, African American 6%, Caucasian 63%, Hispanic 14%, Native American <1%
Retention and Graduation: 58% freshmen graduate within 4 years. **Faculty:** 217 full-time faculty, 91% hold PhDs, 50% are are members of minority groups, 26% are women. 0% of classes are taught by teaching assistants.

ACADEMICS

Degrees: bachelor's, certificate, master's. **Classes:** Most classes have 20-29 students. Most lab/discussion sessions have 10-19 students. **Majors with Highest Enrollment:** Business Administration and Management; Psychology; Speech Communication and Rhetoric. **Special Study Options:** Accelerated program, cooperative education program, cross-registration, distance learning, double major, dual enrollment, exchange student program (domestic), external degree program, honors program, independent study, internships, liberal arts/career combination, student-designed major, study abroad, teacher certification program, The RCNJ Teacher's Education program is accredited by TEAC. Students with non-Business majors may enroll in courses to earn a Business Essentials Certificate. **Honors programs:** http://www.ramapo.edu/honors/ The Ramapo College Honors Program is designed for students who desire a scholarly environment and an opportunity to interact with challenging faculty members and like- minded students. The Honors Program provides expanded opportunities for learning and reflection. Other benefits of the College Honors Program include residence hall options, special seminars, and exciting trips. Graduation from the College Honors Program is one indicator of a highly motivated, highly skilled, self-initiating individual. Students may participate in the College Honors Program by completing three H-option courses and receiving an Honors Certificate or by completing three H-option courses and completing a senior project, in which case the student graduates with full college honors. Full college honors is indicated on the diploma. For more information, please log onto http://www.ramapo.edu/academics/honors/ **Combined degree programs:** BA/MD, BA/MA, BA/DDS, BS/DR- PT, Phys.Ast., Chiro., Optom., Osteo. **Disability Services:** Special programs offered to physically disabled students include note-taking services, reader services, tape recorders, tutors. **Career services:** Alumni network, alumni services, career/job search classes, career assessment, internships. Career services highlights include the College's Cooperative Education Program (created in the 1980-81 academic year), which has placed over 8,000 students and received more than $750,000 in grant awards from Federal, State, and private sources as well as nationwide recognition through U.S. Department of Education "national demonstration model" status.

FACILITIES

Housing: Coed dorms, special housing for disabled students, special housing for international students, cooperative housing, apartments for single students, Special arrangements are made from time to time. Disabled students live in same residence halls as non-disabled students. 100% of campus accessible to physically disabled. **Special Academic Facilities/Equipment:** Art museum, media center, international telecommunications center, electron microscope, astronomical observatory, Holocaust Studies Center, new sports/fitness complex. A new Center for Science, Education and Technology is underway, as well as a Sustainability Education Center, and a Spirituality Center. **Computers:** 100% of classrooms, 100% of dorms, 100% of libraries, 100% of dining areas, 100% of student union, 60% of common outdoor areas have wireless network access. Students can register for classes online. Administrative functions (other than registration) can be performed online.

CAMPUS LIFE

Environment: Town. **Activities:** Choral groups, dance, drama/theater, literary magazine, music ensembles, musical theater, radio station, student government, student newspaper, television station, yearbook, Campus Ministries, International Student Organization, Model UN. 80 registered organizations, 19 honor societies, 7 religious organizations. 10 fraternities, 11 sororities. **Athletics (Intercollegiate):** *Men:* baseball, basketball, cross-country, soccer, swimming, tennis, track/field (outdoor), track/field (indoor), volleyball. *Women:* basketball, cross-country, field hockey, lacrosse, soccer, softball, swimming, tennis, track/field (outdoor), track/field (indoor), volleyball. **On-Campus Highlights:** Berrie

Center for Performing and Visual Arts, The Pavilion, The Market Place at the Birch Tree Inn, J Lee's in the Student Center, The Bill Bradley Sports and Fitness center. **Environmental Initiatives:** Curriculum and a new building for the Sustainability Education Center.

ADMISSIONS

Freshman Academic Profile: Average high school GPA 3.21. 10.2% in top 10% of high school class, 25.6% in top 25% of high school class, 51.3% in top 50% of high school class. SAT Math middle 50% range 500-610. SAT Critical Reading middle 50% range 490-590. SAT Writing middle 50% range 480-580. ACT middle 50% range 20-26. Minimum internet-based TOEFL 90. Minimum paper TOEFL 550. **Basis for Candidate Selection:** *Very important factors considered include:* Class rank, academic GPA, rigor of secondary school record, standardized test scores. *Important factors considered include:* application essay, recommendation(s), extracurricular activities, talent/ability. *Other factors considered include:* alumni/ae relation, geographical residence, state residency, volunteer work, work experience. **Freshman Admission Requirements:** High school diploma is required and GED is accepted. *Academic units required:* 4 English, 3 mathematics, 3 science, (2 science labs), 2 foreign language, 3 social studies, 3 academic electives. **Freshman Admission Statistics:** 6,297 applied, 55% admitted, 26% enrolled. **Transfer Admission Requirements:** college transcript(s), essay or personal statement, Minimum college GPA of 2.5 required. Lowest grade transferable C. **General Admission Information:** Application Fee $60. Regular application deadline 3/1. Nonfall registration accepted. Admission may be deferred for a maximum of 12 months. Credit and/or placement offered for CEEB Advanced Placement tests.

COSTS AND FINANCIAL AID

Average book expense $1,400. **Required Forms and Deadlines:** FAFSA. **Notification of Awards:** Applicants will be notified of awards on a rolling basis beginning 4/1. **Types of Aid:** *Need-based scholarships/grants:* Federal Pell, SEOG, state scholarships/grants, private scholarships, the school's own gift aid, Federal Nursing Scholarships., Federal TRIO Grant. *Loans:* Direct Subsidized Stafford, Direct Unsubsidized Stafford, Direct PLUS, Federal Perkins, state loans. *Student Employment:* Federal Work-Study Program available. Institutional employment available. Highest amount earned per year from on-campus jobs $9,299. Off-campus job opportunities are good. **Financial Aid Statistics:** 41% freshmen, 49% undergrads receive need-based scholarship or grant aid. 94% freshmen, 25% undergrads receive non-need-based scholarship or grant aid. 79% freshmen, 87% undergrads receive need-based self-help aid. 0% freshmen, 0% undergrads receive athletic scholarships. 80% freshmen, 74% undergrads receive any aid. 69% undergrads borrow to pay for school. Average cumulative indebtedness $22,273.

See page 1114.

RANDOLPH COLLEGE

2500 Rivermont Avenue, Lynchburg, VA 24503-1555
Phone: 434-947-8100 · **Financial Aid Phone:** 434-947-8128
E-mail: admissions@randolphcollege.edu · **CEEB Code:** 5567
Fax: 434-947-8996 · **Website:** www.randolphcollege.com · **ACT Code:** 4388

This private school, affiliated with the Methodist Church, was founded in 1891. It has a 100-acre campus.

RATINGS

Admissions Selectivity Rating: 78   **Fire Safety Rating:** 89

STUDENTS AND FACULTY

Enrollment: 658. **Student Body:** 64% female, 36% male, 45% out-of-state, 10% international (21 countries represented). Asian 3%, African American 11%, Caucasian 67%, Hispanic 5%, Native American 1%
Retention and Graduation: 74% freshmen return for sophomore year. 36% freshmen graduate within 4 years. **Faculty:** 68 full-time faculty, 94% hold PhDs, 57% are are members of minority groups, 13% are women. 0% of classes are taught by teaching assistants.

ACADEMICS

Degrees: bachelor's, master's. **Classes:** Most classes have fewer than 10 students. Most lab/discussion sessions have fewer than 10 students. **Majors with Highest Enrollment:** Psychology; Biology/Biological Sciences; English Language and Literature. **Special Study Options:** Accelerated program, cross-registration, double major, dual enrollment, exchange student program (domestic), honors program, independent study, internships, liberal arts/career combination, student-designed major, study abroad, teacher certification program, 7-college exchange with Washington and Lee University, Hollins University, Hampden-Sydney College, Mary Baldwin College, Sweet Briar College, and Randolph-Macon College. Study abroad is encouraged and facilitated. The College currently offers a program for one or two semesters in Reading,England and affiliated programs in Greece, France, Denmark, Japan, Italy, Spain, N. Ireland, Mexico, and Czech Republic. Qualified students may elect to study abroad on a Randolph College or independent program. Endowed funds provide need-based assistance for study abroad to both American and international students. American Culture Program, a 1-Semester program that includes study on-site at key locations in and near Virginia, open to Randolph College students and students from other colleges who are accepted through a special application process. **Honors programs:** Juniors and seniors who have a cumulative 3.45 in all academic work and a 3.7 in the major are eligible to read for Honors in the Major. The Honors Program encourages students of exceptional ability to engage in independent and intensive study in their fields of interest. **Combined degree programs:** BA/MA, BA/MEng, BA/MS Nursing; BS/BS Engineering. **Disability Services:** Special programs offered to physically disabled students include note-taking services, reader services, tape recorders, tutors. **Career services:** Alumni network, alumni services, career assessment, internships, regional alumni. Career services highlights include our Experiential Learning opportunities made available to our students. The Career Development Center continues to provide all aspects of career services and is now within the Experiential Learning Center. The Center serves as a hub for all experiential activities and is responsible for coordination of those activities including service learning, study abroad, volunteerism and internships. The Experiential Learning Center empowers Randolph College students and faculty to creatively combine learning in the classroom with experiential opportunities within our campus and beyond. Through effective communication and collaboration, we help students make meaningful connections between their academic goals and life-long pursuits.

FACILITIES

Housing: Coed dorms, women's dorms, Special housing for non-traditional age students. 50% of campus accessible to physically disabled. **Special Academic Facilities/Equipment:** Maier Museum of American Art recognized as one of the most outstanding college collections in the nation, computer-equipped classrooms (including wireless computer networks and smart boards), 100-acre equestrian center, language lab, science and math resource center, learning resources center, writing lab, nursery school, nature preserves, observatory, electron microscope. **Computers:** 100% of classrooms, 100% of dorms, 100% of libraries, 100% of dining areas, 100% of student union, 100% of common outdoor areas have wireless network access. Students can register for classes online. Administrative functions (other than registration) can be performed online.

CAMPUS LIFE

Environment: City. **Activities:** Choral groups, dance, drama/theater, literary magazine, music ensembles, pep band, radio station, student government, student newspaper, student-run film society, yearbook, International Student Organization, Model UN. 40 registered organizations, 7 honor societies, 6 religious organizations. **Athletics (Intercollegiate):** *Men:* basketball, cross-country, equestrian sports, horseback riding, lacrosse, soccer, tennis. *Women:* basketball, cross-country, equestrian sports, horseback riding, lacrosse, soccer, softball, swimming, tennis, volleyball. **On-Campus Highlights:** The Maier Museum of Art, Macon Bookshop (on Rivermont Avenue), The Whiteside Amphitheater, Botanical Gardens, Main Hall and Main Grounds coffee bar, Randolph College Riding Center Skeller (in Main Hall), Houston Chapel.

ADMISSIONS

Freshman Academic Profile: Average high school GPA 3.49. 7% in top 10% of high school class, 36% in top 25% of high school class, 81% in top 50% of high school class. 78% from public high schools. SAT Math middle 50% range 470-600. SAT Critical Reading middle 50% range 480-600. SAT Writing middle 50% range 470-570. ACT middle 50% range 20-29. **Basis for Candidate Selection:** *Very important factors considered include:* academic GPA, rigor of secondary school record, character/personal qualities. *Important factors considered include:* Class rank, application essay, recommendation(s), standardized test scores, extracurricular activities. *Other factors considered include:* alumni/ae relation, first generation, interview, level of applicant's interest, talent/ability, volunteer work, work experience. **Freshman Admission Requirements:** High school diploma is required and GED is accepted. *Academic units required:* 4 English, 3 mathematics, 2 science, (2 science labs), 3 foreign language, 2 history, 2 academic electives. **Freshman Admission Statistics:** 1,353 applied, 81% admitted, 17% enrolled. **Transfer Admission Requirements:** High school transcript, college transcript(s), essay or personal statement, Lowest grade transferable C-. **General Admission Information:** Application Fee $50. Regular application deadline 4/1. Regular notification 4/15. Nonfall registration accepted. Admission may be deferred for a maximum of 1 year. Credit and/or placement offered for CEEB Advanced Placement tests.

COSTS AND FINANCIAL AID

Annual tuition $33,500. Room and board $11,650. Required fees $510. Average book expense $1,000. **Required Forms and Deadlines: Notification of Awards:** Applicants will be notified of awards on a rolling basis beginning 3/1. **Types of Aid:** *Need-based scholarships/grants:* Federal Pell, SEOG, state scholarships/grants, private scholarships, the school's own gift aid. *Loans:* Subsidized Stafford, Unsubsidized Stafford, PLUS, Federal Perkins, college/university loans from institutional funds, Private. *Student Employment:* Federal Work-Study Program available. Institutional employment available. Off-campus job opportunities are good. **Financial Aid Statistics:** 100% freshmen, 99% undergrads receive need-based scholarship or grant aid. 25% freshmen, 19% undergrads receive non-need-based scholarship or grant aid. 71% freshmen, 81% undergrads receive need-based self-help aid. 0% freshmen, 0% undergrads receive athletic scholarships. 99% freshmen, 99% undergrads receive any aid. 68% undergrads borrow to pay for school. Average cumulative indebtedness $29,352. **Criteria for awarding institutional aid:** *Non-need-based:* academics, alumni affiliation, art, leadership, minority status, music/drama, religious affiliation, state/district residency.

RANDOLPH-MACON COLLEGE

Best 380

P. O. Box 5005, Ashland, VA 23005
Phone: 804-752-7305 · **Financial Aid Phone:** 804-752-7259
E-mail: admissions@rmc.edu · **CEEB Code:** 5566
Fax: 804-752-4707 · **Website:** www.rmc.edu · **ACT Code:** 4386

This private school, affiliated with the Methodist Church, was founded in 1830. It has a 120-acre campus.

RATINGS

Admissions Selectivity Rating: 85   **Fire Safety Rating:** 85

STUDENTS AND FACULTY

Enrollment: 1,377. **Student Body:** 54% female, 46% male, 26% out-of-state, 2% international (25 countries represented). Asian 2%, African American 9%, Caucasian 77%, Hispanic 4%, Native American <1% **Retention and Graduation:** 77% freshmen return for sophomore year. 56% freshmen graduate within 4 years. 62% freshmen graduate within 6 years. 13% grads go on to further study within 1 year. 7% grads pursue arts and sciences degrees. 1% grads pursue law degrees. 2% grads pursue business degrees. 4% grads pursue medical degrees. **Faculty:** 96 full-time faculty, 96% hold PhDs, 46% are are members of minority groups, 10% are women. 0% of classes are taught by teaching assistants.

ACADEMICS

Degrees: bachelor's. **Classes:** Most classes have 10-19 students. **Majors with Highest Enrollment:** Biology/Biological Sciences; Psychology; Communication. **Special Study Options:** Accelerated program, cross-registration, double major, dual enrollment, exchange student program (domestic), honors program, independent study, internships, liberal arts/career combination, study abroad, teacher certification program, Member of Seven College Consortium, 3-2 program in engineering with Columbia University University of Virginia, 3-2 in forestry with Duke University, 4-1 in accounting with Virginia Commonwealth University. **Honors programs:** The Honors Program offers qualified students the opportunity to take special honors classes, participate in unique programs and events for honors students, and an Honors House for recreation and socializing. **Combined degree programs:** BA/MA, BA/MEng, 3:2 Forestry, 4:1 Accounting, 4:1 MBA. **Disability Services:** Special programs offered to physically disabled students include note-taking services, reader services, tape recorders, tutors. **Career services:** Alumni network, alumni services, career/job search classes, career assessment, internships, regional alumni. Career services highlights include outstanding internship opportunities to students of all class years and majors. Of greatest note is the Bassett Internship Program, open to seniors and juniors.

FACILITIES

Housing: Coed dorms, special housing for disabled students, men's dorms, special housing for international students, women's dorms, fraternity/sorority housing, apartments for single students, Honors House; Substance-free housing; Special Interest Housing. 50% of campus accessible to physically disabled. **Special Academic Facilities/Equipment:** Language lab, learning center, media center, greenhouse, observatory with telescope, electron microscopes, nuclear magnetic resonator, art gallery, fine arts center. **Computers:** 20% of classrooms, 100% of dorms, 100% of libraries, 100% of dining areas, 100% of student union, 25% of common outdoor areas have wireless network access. Students can register for classes online. Administrative functions (other than registration) can be performed online.

CAMPUS LIFE

Environment: Village. **Activities:** Choral groups, concert band, dance, drama/theater, jazz band, literary magazine, music ensembles, musical theater, pep band, radio station, student government, student newspaper, student-run film society, television station, yearbook, Campus Ministries, International Student Organization. 102 registered organizations, 18 honor societies, 4 religious organizations. 6 fraternities, 4 sororities. **Athletics (Intercollegiate):** *Men:* baseball, basketball, football, golf, lacrosse, soccer, tennis. *Women:* basketball, field hockey, lacrosse, soccer, softball, swimming, tennis, volleyball. **On-Campus Highlights:** Randolph-Macon Performing Arts Center, The Brock Sports and Recreation Center, Frank E. Brown Campus Center, Pace-Armistead Hall and Flippo Gallery, Washington and Franklin Hall, Campus is located on 120 acres in the suburban community of Ashland, Virginia. R-MC has six historic landmarks, including three academic buildings listed on the National Historic Register. **Environmental Initiatives:** Designing, Planning, Building and Operating a LEED-certified residence hall incorporating solar power, geothermal heat exchange, rainwater reclamation and other sustainable aspects Successfully achieving level E2 certification in the Virginia Department of Environmental Qualitys Virginia Environmental Excellence Program. R-MC was the second higher-ed institution (and the first residential college) to achieve this for their entire campus. Certification of Estes Dining Hall as a Virginia Green Restaurant through the DEQs Green Restaurant program.

ADMISSIONS

Freshman Academic Profile: Average high school GPA 3.57. 14% in top 10% of high school class, 48% in top 25% of high school class, 83% in top 50% of high school class. 77% from public high schools. SAT Math middle 50% range 490-590. SAT Critical Reading middle 50% range 490-600. SAT Writing middle 50% range 480-580. ACT middle 50% range 21-26. Minimum internet-based TOEFL 80. Minimum paper TOEFL 550. **Basis for Candidate Selection:** *Very important factors considered include:* academic GPA, rigor of secondary school record. *Important factors considered include:* Class rank, application essay, recommendation(s), standardized test scores. *Other factors considered include:* alumni/ae relation, character/personal qualities, extracurricular activities, first generation, interview, racial/ethnic status, talent/ability, volunteer work, work experience. **Freshman Admission Requirements:** High school diploma is required and GED is accepted. *Academic units required:* 4 English, 3 mathematics, 3 science, (2 science labs), 2 foreign language, 1 social studies, 2 history, 1 academic elective. **Freshman Admission Statistics:** 2,955 applied, 60% admitted, 24% enrolled. **Transfer Admission Requirements:** High school transcript, college transcript(s), essay or personal statement, statement of good standing from prior institution(s). Minimum college GPA of 2.0 required. Lowest grade transferable C-. **General Admission Information:** Application Fee $30. Early decision application deadline 11/15. Regular application deadline 3/1. Regular notification 4/1. Nonfall registration accepted. Admission may be deferred for a maximum of 1 year. Credit and/or placement offered for CEEB Advanced Placement tests.

COSTS AND FINANCIAL AID

Annual tuition $35,360. Room and board $10,750. Required fees $980. Average book expense $1,100. **Required Forms and Deadlines:** FAFSA, State aid form. **Notification of Awards:** Applicants will be notified of awards on or about 3/15. **Types of Aid:** *Need-based scholarships/grants:* Federal Pell, SEOG, state scholarships/grants, private scholarships, the school's own gift aid. *Loans:* Subsidized Stafford, Unsubsidized Stafford, PLUS, Federal Perkins, college/university loans from institutional funds. *Student Employment:* Federal Work-Study Program available. Institutional employment available. Highest amount earned per year from on-campus jobs $1,500. Off-campus job opportunities are excellent. **Financial Aid Statistics:** 100% freshmen, 100% undergrads receive need-based scholarship or grant aid. 23% freshmen, 21% undergrads receive non-need-based scholarship or grant aid. 75% freshmen, 78% undergrads receive need-based self-help aid. 0% freshmen, 0% undergrads receive athletic scholarships. 99% freshmen, 99% undergrads receive any aid. 68% undergrads borrow to pay for school. Average cumulative indebtedness $13,059. **Criteria for awarding institutional aid:** *Non-need-based:* academics, alumni affiliation, leadership, minority status, religious affiliation, state/district residency.

REED COLLEGE

3203 SE Woodstock Boulevard, Portland, OR 97202-8199
Phone: 503-777-7511 · **Financial Aid Phone:** 503-777-7223
E-mail: admission@reed.edu · **CEEB Code:** 4654
Fax: 503-777-7553 · **Website:** www.reed.edu · **ACT Code:** 3494

This private school was founded in 1908. It has a 116-acre campus.

RATINGS

Admissions Selectivity Rating: 95   **Fire Safety Rating:** 93

STUDENTS AND FACULTY

Enrollment: 1,351. **Student Body:** 52% female, 48% male, 88% out-of-state, 6% international (46 countries represented). Asian 5%, African American 2%, Caucasian 61%, Hispanic 11%, Native American <1%
Retention and Graduation: 94% freshmen return for sophomore year. 70% freshmen graduate within 4 years. 82% freshmen graduate within 6 years. 65% grads go on to further study within 1 year. 48% grads pursue arts and sciences degrees. 5% grads pursue law degrees. 3% grads pursue business degrees. 4% grads pursue medical degrees. **Faculty:** 153 full-time faculty, 96% hold PhDs, 43% are are members of minority groups, 8% are women. 0% of classes are taught by teaching assistants.

ACADEMICS

Degrees: bachelor's, master's. **Classes:** Most classes have 10-19 students. Most lab/discussion sessions have 10-19 students. **Majors with Highest Enrollment:** English Language and Literature; Anthropology; Psychology. **Special Study Options:** cross-registration, double major, dual enrollment, exchange student program (domestic), independent study, internships, liberal arts/career combination, study abroad, Computer Science By arrangement with the University of Washington, a student may obtain a bachelor of arts degree from Reed and a bachelor of science degree in computer science from the University of Washington. The program calls for three years at Reed, including completion of the general distribution requirements and major requirements in one department, the passing of the junior qualifying examination, the acquisition of a minimum of 22 Reed units (at least 20 of which, including the distribution requirements, must be earned at Reed), and two years at the University of Washington. The university will admit up to five students per year on the recommendation of Reed College. Recommended students must satisfy the university's GPA requirements for transfer students, which may differ from year to year and which are not necessarily the same for Washington residents and non-residents. Computer science degrees are also available under the engineering programs described later in this section. Course Requirements vary, depending upon the field of the Reed major—chemistry, mathematics, or physics. Consult the Reed dual degree coordinator for specific information. In special cases, an ad hoc program with the biology or economics department, or with another department, may be approved. Engineering By arrangement with the California Institute of Technology (Caltech), the Columbia University School of Engineering and Applied Sciences, or Rensselaer Polytechnic Institute, a student may obtain a bachelor's degree in engineering (alternatively, computer science or certain earth and planetary sciences) and a bachelor of arts degree from Reed. The program calls for three years at Reed, including the completion of the general college distribution requirements, completion of major requirements in one department (excluding thesis), the passing of the junior qualifying examination, the acquisition of a minimum of 22 Reed units (at least 20 of which, including all but two units of the distribution requirement, must be earned at Reed), and two years at the engineering school. Transfer students entering these programs should expect to spend no fewer than five semesters at Reed to meet this requirement. The two degrees will be awarded concurrently; all requirements for both degrees must be met before either is awarded. Admission to the engineering school is contingent on the college's recommendation and the student's having met certain course requirements of the engineering school while at Reed. Typical course requirements are two years of physics, one or two years of chemistry, and two years of mathematics, including differential equations. Normally, students with a G.P.A. less than 3.0 should not expect to be recommended. Admission to the specific field of engineering preferred by the student is not guaranteed; the student's academic record can be relevant. Admission to Caltech is not automatic upon recommendation, but is subject to review by Caltech and may depend upon factors that cannot be anticipated. Caltech does not guarantee financial aid to otherwise eligible students. While admission to the other programs is also subject to review by the participating school, admission can usually be expected upon

recommendation. Course Requirements During the freshman year: Mathematics 111/112 or 211/212; Physics 100. Consult with the Reed dual degree coordinator for information on other required courses. Forestry-Environmental Sciences By arrangement with the Nicholas School of the Environment of Duke University, a student may obtain a bachelor of arts degree at Reed and a professional master's degree from Duke (master of forestry or master of environmental management). Work at Duke emphasizes three aspects of study and research in forest and other renewable natural resources: management, science, and policy. The program calls for three years at Reed, including completion of the general college distribution and major requirements (excluding thesis), passing of the junior qualifying examination, the acquisition of a minimum of 22 Reed units (at least 20 of which, including the distribution requirements, must be earned at Reed), and two years at Duke. Students in all academic majors may qualify for the program. Course Requirements 1. Biology 101,102; Mathematics 111 or 112, and Mathematics 141; and Economics 201. 2. Successful completion of the junior qualifying exam before the end of the junior year. Students should plan to take the Graduate Record Examination and make formal application for admission to Duke during the third year at Reed. In the summer following the third year, the student should begin work at Duke. Additional information may be obtained from the faculty adviser for the forestry-environmental sciences program. Pre-Medical and Pre-Veterinary Medical schools value the breadth in educational programs offered by liberal arts colleges. Work in the humanities and social sciences, as well as non-academic factors are all very important. Students should choose a major according to their academic interests and include the following laboratory and other courses to fulfill the admission requirements of most medical schools: 1. General biology: Biology 101 and 102 2. General chemistry: Chemistry 101 and 102 3. Organic chemistry: Chemistry 201 and 202 4. General physics: Physics 100, with lab 5. English or humanities: Humanities 110 6. One year of mathematics, including calculus (Mathematics 111) Course prerequisites for veterinary school usually include the courses above plus additional specific courses, such as biochemistry or upper-level biology. Since there are more than 100 domestic medical schools and 30 veterinary schools, the student may encounter variation in the number and character of admission requirements. Students should be acquainted with the specific requirements and programs of the schools to which they apply. To prepare a competitive application portfolio, students considering medical or veterinary school are strongly encouraged to consult with health professions advisers and the career services office early in their undergraduate careers. In addition to offering advising, the career services office maintains a library of resources essential to the medical school planning process, such as Medical School Admission Requirements, a publication by the American Association of Medical Colleges. The guide Preparation for Medical School at Reed is available online, and includes important timelines, health care internship information, insight into letters of evaluation, and useful web links. It is strongly recommended that students take advantage of additional resources by attending informational seminars, seeking assistance with the application process, and using mock interviews. Graduating students who plan to take time off before applying to medical or veterinary school should discuss their plans with a health-profession adviser before graduation. Visual Arts The college has made arrangements for Reed students to participate in a variety of exchange programs and summer internships at other institutions. They may choose from programs in painting and sculpture, architecture, art history, archaeology, conservation, historic preservation, and museum work. A joint five-year program is also available with the Pacific Northwest College of Art. These programs are described in more detail in the art department section of the catalog. **Combined degree programs:** Computing: Univ. of Washington. **Disability Services:** Special programs offered to physically disabled students include note-taking services, reader services, tape recorders, tutors. **Career services:** Alumni network, alumni services, career/job search classes, career assessment, internships, regional alumni. For career services highlights see http://web.reed.edu/career/students.html.

FACILITIES

Housing: Coed dorms, special housing for disabled students, women's dorms, cooperative housing, apartments for single students, Wellness Housing, Theme Housing. Reed language houses accommodate upper-division students studying Chinese, French, German, Russian, and Spanish. First-year students required to live on campus; exceptions granted for unusual situations. 85% of campus accessible to physically disabled. **Special Academic Facilities/Equipment:** Art gallery, studio art building, language labs, computerized music listening lab, nuclear research reactor, 20 music practice rooms and midi lab, 760 seat auditorium, academic support center (quantitative skills, writing, math support), educational technology center. **Computers:** 100% of classrooms, 100% of dorms, 100% of libraries, 100% of dining areas, 100% of student union, 50% of common outdoor areas have wireless network access. Students can register for classes online. Administrative functions (other than registration) can be performed online.

CAMPUS LIFE

Environment: Metropolis. **Activities:** Choral groups, dance, drama/theater, literary magazine, music ensembles, radio station, student government, student newspaper, student-run film society, symphony orchestra, Campus Ministries, International Student Organization, Model UN. 130 registered organizations, 1 honor society, 5 religious organizations. **On-Campus Highlights:** Thesis Tower, Nuclear Research Reactor, Crystal Springs Canyon, Cerf Amphitheatre, The Paradox Café. **Environmental Initiatives:** LEED construction; recycling; installation for energy efficiency across campus, i.e., lighting, windows, heating.

ADMISSIONS

Freshman Academic Profile: Average high school GPA 3.9. 62% in top 10% of high school class, 88% in top 25% of high school class, 98% in top 50% of high school class. 59% from public high schools. SAT Math middle 50% range 620-720. SAT Critical Reading middle 50% range 660-750. SAT Writing middle 50% range 640-720. ACT middle 50% range 28-33. Minimum internet-based TOEFL 100. Minimum paper TOEFL 600. **Basis for Candidate Selection:** *Very important factors considered include:* application essay, academic GPA, rigor of secondary school record. *Important factors considered include:* Class rank, recommendation(s), standardized test scores, interview, level of applicant's interest. *Other factors considered include:* alumni/ae relation, character/personal qualities, extracurricular activities, first generation, geographical residence, racial/ethnic status, talent/ability, volunteer work, work experience. **Freshman Admission Requirements:** High school diploma is required and GED is accepted. **Freshman Admission Statistics:** 2,893 applied, 49% admitted, 25% enrolled. **Transfer Admission Requirements:** High school transcript, college transcript(s), essay or personal statement, standardized test scores, statement of good standing from prior institution(s). Lowest grade transferable C-. **General Admission Information:** Application Fee $50. Early decision application deadline 11/15. Regular application deadline 1/15. Regular notification 4/1. Nonfall registration not accepted. Admission may be deferred for a maximum of 1 year. Credit and/or placement offered for CEEB Advanced Placement tests.

COSTS AND FINANCIAL AID

Annual tuition $47,500. Room and board $12,200. Required fees $260. Average book expense $1,050. **Required Forms and Deadlines:** FAFSA, CSS/Financial Aid PROFILE, Noncustodial PROFILE, Business/Farm Supplement. **Notification of Awards:** Applicants will be notified of awards on or about 4/1. **Types of Aid:** *Need-based scholarships/grants:* Federal Pell, SEOG, state scholarships/grants, private scholarships, the school's own gift aid. *Loans:* Subsidized Stafford, Unsubsidized Stafford, PLUS, Federal Perkins. *Student Employment:* Federal Work-Study Program available. Institutional employment available. Highest amount earned per year from on-campus jobs $12,006. **Financial Aid Statistics:** 97% freshmen, 99% undergrads receive need-based scholarship or grant aid. 0% freshmen, 0% undergrads receive non-need-based scholarship or grant aid. 91% freshmen, 93% undergrads receive need-based self-help aid. 0% freshmen, 0% undergrads receive athletic scholarships. 53% freshmen, 54% undergrads receive any aid. 49% undergrads borrow to pay for school. Average cumulative indebtedness $17,467.

See page 1116.

REGENT UNIVERSITY

1000 Regent University Drive, Virginia Beach, VA 23464
Phone: 800-373-5504 · **Financial Aid Phone:** 757-352-4125
E-mail: admissions@regent.edu · **CEEB Code:** 30913
Fax: 757-352-4381 · **Website:** www.regent.edu · **ACT Code:** 6738

This private school, affiliated with the Christian (Nondenominational) Church, was founded in 1978. It has a 70-acre campus.

RATINGS

Admissions Selectivity Rating: 80   **Fire Safety Rating:** 84

STUDENTS AND FACULTY

Enrollment: 2,306. **Student Body:** 61% female, 39% male, 49% out-of-state, 1% international (73 countries represented). Asian 2%, African American 21%, Caucasian 59%, Hispanic 5%, Native American 1%
Retention and Graduation: 78% freshmen return for sophomore year. 29% freshmen graduate within 4 years. 53% freshmen graduate within 6 years. **Faculty:** 160 full-time faculty, 93% hold PhDs, 31% are are members of minority groups, 18% are women. 0% of classes are taught by teaching assistants.

ACADEMICS

Degrees: associate, bachelor's, doctoral, master's, post-master's certificate, terminal associate, transfer associate. **Classes:** Most classes have 20-29 students. **Majors with Highest Enrollment:** Religion/Religious Studies; Psychology; Business/Commerce. **Special Study Options:** distance learning, double major, dual enrollment, internships, study abroad, teacher certification program. **Disability Services:** Special programs offered to physically disabled students

include note-taking services, reader services, tape recorders, tutors. **Career services:** Alumni network, alumni services, career/job search classes, career assessment, internships, regional alumni.

FACILITIES

Housing: apartments for married students, apartments for single students. 100% of campus accessible to physically disabled. **Special Academic Facilities/Equipment:** The 31,000-square-foot Student Center on Regent's Virginia Beach Campus, opened in 2003, offers a central location for campus and student services. The building houses the University Bookstore, student organizations and meeting rooms, a Café/coffee shop, computer lab, student lounge and offices for the Registrar, Admissions and Financial Aid. The 135,000-square-foot Communication & Performing Arts Center, opened in 2002, includes film and animation studios, a state-of-the-art main theatre, screening rooms and editing suites in one of the most technologically advanced communication buildings on the east coast. **Computers:** 80% of classrooms, 100% of dorms, 100% of libraries, 100% of student union, 50% of common outdoor areas have wireless network access. Students can register for classes online. Administrative functions (other than registration) can be performed online.

CAMPUS LIFE

Environment: City. **Activities:** Choral groups, concert band, dance, drama/theater, student government, student newspaper, Campus Ministries, International Student Organization. 47 registered organizations, 4 honor societies. **On-Campus Highlights:** The Student Center, Communication & Performing Arts, The Ordinary Café and Coffee Shop, Robertson Hall, University Library. Robertson Hall is equipped with the latest technology in audio/video equipment and cameras for simultaneous broadcasting. The 132,000-square-foot building also boasts a 380-seat moot court/city council chamber. The 135,000-square-foot Communication & Performing Arts Center features a 750-seat theater and a 150-seat experimental theater, cinema-television production studio, film sound stage, screening theaters, technical studios and teaching labs. A back lot area offers space for sets for indoor and outdoor filming. Just opened in 2002, the 31,000-square-foot Student Center houses the University Bookstore, student organization offices, The Ordinary Café/coffee shop, a computer lab, student lounge and meeting rooms. **Environmental Initiatives:** Our investments in "cool storage" systems since our beginning in 1978 allows us to shave peak demand when the power company desires. This helps reduce the size of the power plant needed to support this area. This results in a major decrease in greenhouse emissions for this area. This fact is recognized by VA Dominion Power—our supplier of electricity. Our campus is one of the most beautiful campuses in Virginia because we have worked diligently to achieve the proper balance between "bricks and mortar" and the natural resources we have been blessed with. Our woods have diverse species of trees and plantings and we strive to enhance the wildlife habitat. For instance den trees are highly valued and preserved. Fruit bearing tree species are highly valued and retained whenever possible. The President and facilities director intensively manages the campus grounds to retain the nature setting. Branches are chipped and composted as are tree leaves and needles. Campus aquatic ecosystems are maintained with similar intensity. We have purposely changed locations for buildings, sidewalks, storm sewer, and other underground utilities in order to preserve natural resources. Additionally we resisted City of Virginia Beach directives to build additional parking lots which would "urbanize" our campus. We hired a lawyer, contested the directive and preserved our green campus. The investments we have made in energy saving devices has been remarkable and worthwhile as evidenced by usage reduction data. ALL building light fixtures have been renovated to T8 fixtures.A state of the art monitoring system is in place. All flat roofs were replaced with white TPO roofs. Most pumps were upgraded with variable frequency drives. All chillers and boilers are high efficiency models. There is much, much more.

ADMISSIONS

Freshman Academic Profile: Average high school GPA 3.52. 8% in top 10% of high school class, 51% in top 25% of high school class, 81% in top 50% of high school class. SAT Math middle 50% range 440-550. SAT Critical Reading middle 50% range 470-580. SAT Writing middle 50% range 450-570. ACT middle 50% range 19-25. Minimum internet-based TOEFL 90. Minimum paper TOEFL 577. **Freshman Admission Requirements:** High school diploma or equivalent is not required. **Freshman Admission Statistics:** 1,535 applied, 80% admitted, 17% enrolled. **Transfer Admission Requirements:** college transcript(s), Lowest grade transferable C. **General Admission Information:** Notification on a rolling basis, beginning on or about 1/1. Nonfall registration accepted. Admission may be deferred for a maximum of aslongasneed. Credit offered for CEEB Advanced Placement tests.

COSTS AND FINANCIAL AID

Annual tuition $16,350. Room and board $8,250. Required fees $800. Average book expense $1,000. **Required Forms and Deadlines:** FAFSA, Institution's own financial aid form, State aid form. **Notification of Awards:** Applicants will be notified of awards on a rolling basis beginning 5/1. **Types of Aid:** *Need-based scholarships/grants:* Federal Pell, SEOG, state scholarships/grants, private scholarships, the school's own gift aid. *Loans:* Subsidized Stafford, Unsubsidized Stafford, PLUS, state loans. *Student Employment:* Federal Work-Study Program available. Institutional employment available. Highest amount earned per year from on-campus jobs $3,000. Off-campus job opportunities are excellent. **Financial Aid Statistics:** 97% freshmen, 93% undergrads receive need-based scholarship or grant aid. 16% freshmen, 7% undergrads receive non-need-based scholarship or grant aid. 88% freshmen, 92% undergrads receive need-based self-help aid. 0% freshmen, 0% undergrads receive athletic scholarships. 94% freshmen, 90% undergrads receive any aid. 82% undergrads borrow to pay for school. Average cumulative indebtedness $35,755. **Criteria for awarding institutional aid:** *Non-need-based:* academics, alumni affiliation, art, athletics, leadership, minority status, music/drama, state/district residency.

REGIS COLLEGE

235 Wellesley Street, Weston, MA 02493-1571
Phone: 781-768-7100 · **Financial Aid Phone:** 781-768-7184
E-mail: admission@regiscollege.edu · **CEEB Code:** 3723
Fax: 781-768-7071 · **Website:** www.regiscollege.edu · **ACT Code:** 1886

This private school, affiliated with the Roman Catholic Church, was founded in 1927. It has a 131-acre campus.

RATINGS

Admissions Selectivity Rating: 75   **Fire Safety Rating:** 82

STUDENTS AND FACULTY

Enrollment: 1,188. **Student Body:** 76% female, 24% male, 14% out-of-state, 2% international (17 countries represented). Asian 6%, African American 20%, Caucasian 46%, Hispanic 11%, Native American <1%
Retention and Graduation: 77% freshmen return for sophomore year. 38% freshmen graduate within 4 years. 28% grads go on to further study within 1 year. 16% grads pursue arts and sciences degrees. 1% grads pursue law degrees. 2% grads pursue business degrees. 2% grads pursue medical degrees. **Faculty:** 80 full-time faculty, 75% hold PhDs, 78% are are members of minority groups, 10% are women. 0% of classes are taught by teaching assistants.

ACADEMICS

Degrees: associate, bachelor's, master's, post-master's certificate, transfer associate. **Classes:** Most classes have 10-19 students. **Majors with Highest Enrollment:** Registered Nursing/Registered Nurse; Business/Commerce; Biology/Biological Sciences. **Special Study Options:** Accelerated program, cross-registration, double major, English as a Second Language (ESL), exchange student program (domestic), honors program, independent study, internships, student-designed major, study abroad, teacher certification program. **Honors programs:** The Honors Program at Regis College offers qualified students a stimulating and challenging learning experience, and opportunities for distinguished scholarship. It prepares students to become leaders committed to the betterment of the human condition and our society, a goal that is central to the Regis College mission. **Combined degree programs:** BA/MSCO; BS/MSNU. **Disability Services:** Special programs offered to physically disabled students include note-taking services, tape recorders, tutors. **Career services:** Alumni network, alumni services, career/job search classes, career assessment, internships. Career services highlights include internships that offer students opportunities to apply classroom learning to the world of work while receiving academic credit.

FACILITIES

Housing: Coed dorms, women's dorms. 85% of campus accessible to physically disabled. **Special Academic Facilities/Equipment:** Fine arts center, philatelic museum. **Computers:** 30% of classrooms, 100% of dorms, 100% of libraries, 100% of dining areas, 100% of student union, 15% of common outdoor areas have wireless network access. Students can register for classes online. Administrative functions (other than registration) can be performed online.

CAMPUS LIFE

Environment: Village. **Activities:** Choral groups, dance, drama/theater, literary magazine, music ensembles, musical theater, radio station, student government, yearbook, Campus Ministries, Model UN. 36 registered organizations, 10 honor societies, 2 religious organizations. **Athletics (Intercollegiate):** *Men:* basketball, diving, soccer, swimming. *Women:* basketball, diving, field hockey, lacrosse, soccer, softball, swimming, tennis, track/field (outdoor), track/field (indoor), volleyball. **On-Campus Highlights:** College Hall, Student Union, Tower, Athletic Complex, Fine Arts Center. **Environmental Initiatives:** Replacement of steam boilers w/high efficiency designs; Replacement of mercury vapor and incandescent lighting with fluorescent; Elimination of the use of salt for snow/ice control.

ADMISSIONS

Freshman Academic Profile: Average high school GPA 3.02. 7% in top 10% of high school class, 32% in top 25% of high school class, 68% in top 50% of high school class. 75% from public high schools. SAT Math middle 50% range 420-540. SAT Critical Reading middle 50% range 420-520. SAT Writing middle 50% range 420-520. ACT middle 50% range 19-23. Minimum paper TOEFL 550. **Basis for Candidate Selection:** *Very important factors considered include:* application essay, academic GPA, recommendation(s), rigor of secondary school record, character/personal qualities. *Important factors considered include:* Class rank, standardized test scores, extracurricular activities, interview, talent/ability, volunteer work, work experience. *Other factors considered include:* alumni/ae relation, first generation, level of applicant's interest. **Freshman Admission Requirements:** High school diploma is required and GED is accepted. *Academic units required:* 4 English, 3 mathematics, 2 science, (1 science labs), 2 foreign language, 2 social studies, 3 academic electives. **Freshman Admission Statistics:** 2,158 applied, 72% admitted, 17% enrolled. **Transfer Admission Requirements:** High school transcript, college transcript(s), essay or personal statement, Minimum college GPA of 2.0 required. Lowest grade transferable C. **General Admission Information:** Application Fee $50. Notification on a rolling basis, beginning on or about 12/1. Nonfall registration accepted. Admission may be deferred for a maximum of 1 year. Credit and/or placement offered for CEEB Advanced Placement tests.

COSTS AND FINANCIAL AID

Annual tuition $34,380. Room and board $13,185. Average book expense $1,000. **Required Forms and Deadlines:** FAFSA, Institution's own financial aid form. **Notification of Awards:** Applicants will be notified of awards on a rolling basis beginning 3/15. **Types of Aid:** *Need-based scholarships/grants:* Federal Pell, SEOG, state scholarships/grants, private scholarships, the school's own gift aid, Federal Nursing Scholarships. *Loans:* Direct Subsidized Stafford, Direct Unsubsidized Stafford, Direct PLUS, Federal Perkins, Federal Nursing. *Student Employment:* Federal Work-Study Program available. Institutional employment available. Highest amount earned per year from on-campus jobs $5,355. Off-campus job opportunities are poor. **Financial Aid Statistics:** 86% freshmen, 84% undergrads receive need-based scholarship or grant aid. 79% freshmen, 76% undergrads receive non-need-based scholarship or grant aid. 96% freshmen, 95% undergrads receive need-based self-help aid. 0% freshmen, 0% undergrads receive athletic scholarships. 91% freshmen, 84% undergrads receive any aid. 88% undergrads borrow to pay for school. Average cumulative indebtedness $29,846. **Criteria for awarding institutional aid:** *Non-need-based:* academics, alumni affiliation, religious affiliation.

See page 1118.

REGIS UNIVERSITY

3333 Regis Boulevard, Denver, CO 80221-1099
Phone: 303-458-4900 · **Financial Aid Phone:** 303-458-4126
E-mail: regisadm@regis.edu · **CEEB Code:** 4656
Fax: 303-964-5534 · **Website:** www.regis.edu · **ACT Code:** 526

This private school, affiliated with the Roman Catholic Church, was founded in 1877. It has a 90-acre campus.

RATINGS

Admissions Selectivity Rating: 78   **Fire Safety Rating:** 82

STUDENTS AND FACULTY

Enrollment: 4,697. **Student Body:** 62% female, 38% male, 33% out-of-state, 1% international (11 countries represented). Asian 4%, African American 5%, Caucasian 61%, Hispanic 19%, Native American 1%
Retention and Graduation: 78% freshmen return for sophomore year. 43% freshmen graduate within 4 years. 60% freshmen graduate within 6 years. 17% grads go on to further study within 1 year. 44% grads pursue arts and sciences degrees. 8% grads pursue law degrees. 4% grads pursue business degrees. 40% grads pursue medical degrees. **Faculty:** 298 full-time faculty, 77% hold PhDs, 62% are are members of minority groups, 11% are women. 0% of classes are taught by teaching assistants.

ACADEMICS

Degrees: bachelor's, master's. **Classes:** Most classes have fewer than 10 students. Most lab/discussion sessions have 10-19 students. **Majors with Highest Enrollment:** Business Administration and Management; Registered Nursing/Registered Nurse; Computer Science. **Special Study Options:** Accelerated program, cooperative education program, cross-registration, distance learning, double major, dual enrollment, exchange student program (domestic), honors program, independent study, internships, liberal arts/career combination, student-designed major, study abroad, teacher certification program, weekend college. **Disability Services:** Special programs offered to physically disabled students include tutors. **Career services:** alumni services, career/job search classes, internships.

FACILITIES

Housing: Coed dorms, special housing for disabled students, apartments for single students. 90% of campus accessible to physically disabled. Language lab, wellness center, **Computers:** Administrative functions (other than registration) can be performed online.

CAMPUS LIFE

Environment: Metropolis. **Activities:** Choral groups, drama/theater, literary magazine, music ensembles, musical theater, radio station, student government, student newspaper, yearbook. 40 registered organizations, 1 honor society, 1 religous organization. **Athletics (Intercollegiate):** *Men:* baseball, basketball, cross-country, golf, soccer. *Women:* basketball, cross-country, lacrosse, soccer, softball, volleyball.

ADMISSIONS

Freshman Academic Profile: Average high school GPA 3.48. 21.83% in top 10% of high school class, 49.6% in top 25% of high school class, 78.57% in top 50% of high school class. SAT Math middle 50% range 470-590. SAT Critical Reading middle 50% range 480-600. SAT Writing middle 50% range 470-590. ACT middle 50% range 22-27. Minimum internet-based TOEFL 82. Minimum paper TOEFL 550. **Basis for Candidate Selection:** *Very important factors considered include:* rigor of secondary school record, standardized test scores. *Important factors considered include:* application essay, recommendation(s). *Other factors considered include:* Class rank, character/personal qualities, extracurricular activities, interview, talent/ability, volunteer work, work experience. **Freshman Admission Requirements:** High school diploma is required and GED is accepted. **Freshman Admission Statistics:** 2,422 applied, 96% admitted, 21% enrolled. **Transfer Admission Requirements:** college transcript(s), essay or personal statement, Minimum college GPA of 2.0 required. **General Admission Information:** Application Fee $40. Nonfall registration accepted. Credit and/or placement offered for CEEB Advanced Placement tests.

COSTS AND FINANCIAL AID

Annual tuition $33,110. Room and board $9,830. Required fees $600. Average book expense $1,800. **Required Forms and Deadlines:** FAFSA. **Notification of Awards:** Applicants will be notified of awards on a rolling basis beginning 3/15. **Types of Aid:** *Need-based scholarships/grants:* Federal Pell, SEOG, state scholarships/grants, private scholarships, the school's own gift aid, Federal Nursing Scholarships. *Loans:* Subsidized Stafford, Unsubsidized Stafford, PLUS, Federal Perkins, Federal Nursing. *Student Employment:* Federal Work-Study Program available. Highest amount earned per year from on-campus jobs $1,800. Off-campus job opportunities are good. **Financial Aid Statistics:** 97% freshmen, 81% undergrads receive need-based scholarship or grant aid. 13% freshmen, 7% undergrads receive non-need-based scholarship or grant aid. 75% freshmen, 82% undergrads receive need-based self-help aid. 7% freshmen, 5% undergrads receive athletic scholarships. 98% freshmen, 64% undergrads receive any aid. 68% undergrads borrow to pay for school. Average cumulative indebtedness $25,714. **Criteria for awarding institutional aid:** *Non-need-based:* academics, athletics.

REINHARDT UNIVERSITY

7300 Reinhardt Circle, Waleska, GA 30183
Phone: 770-720-5526 · **Financial Aid Phone:** 770-720-5667
E-mail: www.reinhardt.edu · **CEEB Code:**
Fax: 770-720-5899 · **Website:** www.reinhardt.edu · **ACT Code:** 856

This private school, affiliated with the Methodist Church, was founded in 1883. It has a 600-acre campus.

RATINGS

Admissions Selectivity Rating: 74   **Fire Safety Rating:** 96

STUDENTS AND FACULTY

Enrollment: 980. **Student Body:** 55% female, 45% male, 27% out-of-state, 0% international. Asian 1%, African American 13%, Caucasian 75%, Hispanic 4%, Native American 1%
Retention and Graduation: 23% freshmen graduate within 4 years. 35% grads go on to further study within 1 year. 20% grads pursue arts and sciences degrees. 5% grads pursue law degrees. 45% grads pursue business degrees. 5% grads pursue medical degrees. **Faculty:** 62 full-time faculty, 74% hold PhDs, 48% are are members of minority groups, 11% are women. 0% of classes are taught by teaching assistants.

ACADEMICS

Degrees: associate, bachelor's, master's, transfer associate. **Classes:** Most classes have 10-19 students. **Majors with Highest Enrollment:** Business Administration and Management; Elementary Education and Teaching; Music. **Special Study Options:** Accelerated program, double major, dual enrollment, external degree program, honors program, independent study, internships, study abroad, teacher certification program. **Honors programs:** The Honors Program is designed for students who are bright, curious and enjoy being challenged. Entering freshman with High Schjool GPA of at least 3.5 or a combined SAT of 1050 or higher, with verbal score of at least 580, will be invited to apply for admission to Reinhardt College's Honors Program. **Disability Services:** Special programs offered to physically disabled students include note-taking services, reader services, tape recorders, tutors. **Career services:** alumni services, career/job search classes, career assessment, internships, regional alumni. Career services highlights include internships for the Price School of Education.

FACILITIES

Housing: Coed dorms, special housing for disabled students, men's dorms, women's dorms, honors house. 93% of campus accessible to physically disabled. **Special Academic Facilities/Equipment:** Funk Heritage Center, Falany Performing Arts **Computers:** 100% of classrooms, 100% of dorms, 100% of libraries, 100% of student union, 5% of common outdoor areas have wireless network access. Students can register for classes online. Administrative functions (other than registration) can be performed online.

CAMPUS LIFE

Environment: Rural. **Activities:** Choral groups, concert band, drama/theater, jazz band, music ensembles, student government, student newspaper, student-run film society, television station, yearbook, Campus Ministries, International Student Organization. 40 registered organizations, 6 honor societies, 5 religious organizations. **Athletics (Intercollegiate):** *Men:* baseball, basketball, cheerleading, cross-country, golf, soccer, tennis. *Women:* basketball, cheerleading, cross-country, golf, soccer, softball, tennis, volleyball. **On-Campus Highlights:** Falany Performing Arts Center, Funk Heritage Center, Gordy Center, Library, Class room building. **Environmental Initiatives:** Recycle paper; RU Green; Follow EPA guidelines concerning hazardous waste; Continue to upgrade HVAC & electrical to conserve energy.

ADMISSIONS

Freshman Academic Profile: Average high school GPA 3.02. 63% in top 50% of high school class. 98% from public high schools. SAT Math middle 50% range 430-530. SAT Critical Reading middle 50% range 410-540. ACT middle 50% range 17-22. Minimum paper TOEFL 500. **Basis for Candidate Selection:** *Very important factors considered include:* academic GPA, standardized test scores. *Important factors considered include:* rigor of secondary school record. *Other factors considered include:* Class rank, recommendation(s), alumni/ae relation, character/personal qualities, extracurricular activities, first generation, geographical residence, level of applicant's interest, racial/ethnic status, religious affiliation/commitment, talent/ability, volunteer work, work experience. **Freshman Admission Requirements:** High school diploma is required and GED is accepted. *Academic units required:* 4 English, 4 mathematics, 3 science, 3 social studies. **Freshman Admission Statistics:** 1,310 applied, 59% admitted, 30% enrolled. **Transfer Admission Requirements:** college transcript(s), statement of good standing from prior institution(s). Minimum college GPA of 2.0 required. Lowest grade transferable C. **General Admission Information:** Application Fee $25. Nonfall registration accepted. Credit and/or placement offered for CEEB Advanced Placement tests.

COSTS AND FINANCIAL AID

Required Forms and Deadlines: FAFSA, State aid form. **Notification of Awards:** Applicants will be notified of awards on a rolling basis beginning 3/15. **Types of Aid:** *Need-based scholarships/grants:* Federal Pell, SEOG, state scholarships/grants, private scholarships, the school's own gift aid. *Loans:* Subsidized Stafford, Unsubsidized Stafford, PLUS. *Student Employment:* Federal Work-Study Program available. Highest amount earned per year from on-campus jobs $2,800. Off-campus job opportunities are good. **Financial Aid Statistics:** 99% freshmen, 98% undergrads receive need-based scholarship or grant aid. 7% freshmen, 7% undergrads receive non-need-based scholarship or grant aid. 76% freshmen, 74% undergrads receive need-based self-help aid. 9% freshmen, 7% undergrads receive athletic scholarships. 71% undergrads borrow to pay for school. Average cumulative indebtedness $19,936. **Criteria for awarding institutional aid:** *Non-need-based:* academics, art, athletics, leadership, music/drama, religious affiliation, state/district residency.

RENSSELAER POLYTECHNIC INSTITUTE

110 Eighth Street, Troy, NY 12180-3590
Phone: 518-276-6216 · **Financial Aid Phone:** 518-276-6813
E-mail: admissions@rpi.edu · **CEEB Code:** 2757
Fax: 518-276-4072 · **Website:** www.rpi.edu · **ACT Code:** 2866

This private school was founded in 1824. It has a 284-acre campus.

RATINGS

Admissions Selectivity Rating: 96   **Fire Safety Rating:** 89

STUDENTS AND FACULTY
Enrollment: 5,557. **Student Body:** 31% female, 69% male, 67% out-of-state, 9% international (33 countries represented). Asian 10%, African American 3%, Caucasian 62%, Hispanic 7%, Native American <1%. **Retention and Graduation:** 93% freshmen return for sophomore year. 61% freshmen graduate within 4 years. 82% freshmen graduate within 6 years. 24% grads go on to further study within 1 year. 5% grads pursue arts and sciences degrees. 2% grads pursue business degrees. 2% grads pursue medical degrees. **Faculty:** 411 full-time faculty, 96% hold PhDs, 23% are are members of minority groups, 31% are women. 0% of classes are taught by teaching assistants.

ACADEMICS
Degrees: bachelor's, certificate, master's. **Classes:** Most classes have 10-19 students. Most lab/discussion sessions have 10-19 students. **Majors with Highest Enrollment:** Computer Engineering; Electrical and Electronics Engineering; Business/Commerce. **Special Study Options:** Accelerated program, cooperative education program, cross-registration, double major, dual enrollment, exchange student program (domestic), honors program, independent study, internships, liberal arts/career combination, student-designed major, study abroad, The accelerated BS-Phd program in the School of Science is possible in all the science departments. Computer Science Physics Applied Physics Biology Biochemistry and Biophysics Geology Hydrogeology. **Honors programs:** The Rensselaer Medal Program, the Presidential Scholars Program **Combined degree programs:** BA/MEng, BS/MBA, BS/MS, BS/M.Eng, BS/MD, BS/JD, BS/Ph.D. **Disability Services:** Special programs offered to physically disabled students include note-taking services, reader services, tape recorders, tutors. **Career services:** Alumni network, alumni services, career/job search classes, career assessment, internships, regional alumni. Rensselaer has actively encouraged the translation of cutting edge academic research into new products and new businesses. Scientific and technological entrepreneurship is a significant part of "The Rensselaer Plan," a comprehensive strategic plan for the Institute. Historically and consistently, faculty, students, and alumni have successfully developed technologies, created innovations, and formed business ventures to bring ideas into practice to create value. Rensselaer's focus on entrepreneurship iscross-campus, interdisciplinary, and presents multiple perspectives. It involves creative thinking, and is not only ideas, but ideas to enterprise. Entrepreneurship at Rensselaer goes beyond curriculum, with a broad spectrum of technology presentations, lecture series, and mentor programs. It has a global focus, and is further focused as technology commercialization and entrepreneurship. The Lally School at Rensselaer has a strong tradition of developing entrepreneurs who create new ventures or bring their entrepreneurial management skills to established organizations. Theory and practice are combined in the classroom, and students interact with experienced entrepreneurs. The Severino Center for Technological Entrepreneurship is the focal point for both entrepreneurship scholarship and learning, and it serves as a bridge to the Rensselaer Incubator and Technology Park. Students participate in lectures and discussions, and events that include both the entire Rensselaer university community as well as professionals from successful startups and fast growth companies from the Tech Valley Region.

FACILITIES
Housing: Coed dorms, special housing for disabled students, fraternity/sorority housing, apartments for married students, apartments for single students, Theme Housing. 75% of campus accessible to physically disabled. **Special Academic Facilities/Equipment:** Shelnutt Art Gallery in the Student Union;The George M. Low Gallery (museum); Center for Terahertz Research; Nanoscale Science and Engineering Centers (NSEC); Center for Biotechnology and Interdisciplinary Studies; Gaerttner Linear Accelerator (LINAC) Laboratory; Hirsch Observatory; RPIdeaLab and Incubator Program (supports student business ventures); Rensselaer Technology Park; Darrin Fresh Water Institute at Lake George; Experimental Media and Performing Arts Center (EMPAC— under construction); Lighting Research Center; Social and Behavioral Research

Laboratory; O.T. Swanson Multidisciplinary Laboratory; and other research centers and laboratories as described at www.rpi.edu/research/research_centers. html,Computational Center for Nanotechnology Innovations (CCNI); http://www.rpi.edu/dept/ess/greening/EECbooks.html **Computers:** 75% of classrooms, 75% of dorms, 100% of libraries, 75% of dining areas, 100% of student union, 75% of common outdoor areas have wireless network access. Students can register for classes online. Administrative functions (other than registration) can be performed online. Undergraduates are required to own a computer.

CAMPUS LIFE
Environment: City. **Activities:** Choral groups, concert band, dance, drama/theater, jazz band, literary magazine, music ensembles, musical theater, pep band, radio station, student government, student newspaper, student-run film society, symphony orchestra, television station, yearbook, Campus Ministries, International Student Organization. 177 registered organizations, 40 honor societies, 11 religious organizations. 32 fraternities, 5 sororities. **Athletics (Intercollegiate):** *Men:* baseball, basketball, cross-country, diving, football, golf, ice hockey, lacrosse, soccer, swimming, tennis, track/field (outdoor), track/field (indoor). *Women:* basketball, cross-country, diving, field hockey, ice hockey, lacrosse, soccer, softball, swimming, tennis, track/field (outdoor), track/field (indoor). **On-Campus Highlights:** Rensselaer Union, Mueller Fitness Center, Experimental Media & Performing Arts Ctr, Houston Field House (hockey arena), ECAV, Quiet and parklike, yet full of all the conveniences of a self-contained city, Rensselaer's 275-acre campus is a blend of modern style and classic charm. The Institute is in a period of tremendous growth, building new facilities that greatly enhance the lives of our students and faculty. **Environmental Initiatives:** Student Sustainability Task Force; Energy Conservation Program; Purchase of Wind Certificates; Sustainability Initiatives in New Construction.

ADMISSIONS
Freshman Academic Profile: Average high school GPA 3.77. 69% in top 10% of high school class, 95% in top 25% of high school class, 99% in top 50% of high school class. 68% from public high schools. SAT Math middle 50% range 680-770. SAT Critical Reading middle 50% range 620-720. ACT middle 50% range 27-32. Minimum internet-based TOEFL 88. Minimum paper TOEFL 570. **Basis for Candidate Selection:** *Very important factors considered include:* Class rank, academic GPA, rigor of secondary school record, standardized test scores. *Important factors considered include:* application essay, recommendation(s), character/personal qualities, extracurricular activities, level of applicant's interest. *Other factors considered include:* alumni/ae relation, geographical residence, interview, racial/ethnic status, talent/ability, volunteer work, work experience. **Freshman Admission Requirements:** High school diploma is required and GED is accepted. *Academic units required:* 4 English, 4 mathematics, 3 science, 2 social studies. **Freshman Admission Statistics:** 18,602 applied, 38% admitted, 19% enrolled. **Transfer Admission Requirements:** college transcript(s), statement of good standing from prior institution(s). Minimum college GPA of 3.0 required. Lowest grade transferable C. **General Admission Information:** Application Fee $70. Early decision application deadline 11/2. Regular application deadline 1/15. Regular notification 3/13. Nonfall registration accepted. Admission may be deferred for a maximum of 1 year. Credit and/or placement offered for CEEB Advanced Placement tests.

COSTS AND FINANCIAL AID
Annual tuition $46,700. Room and board $13,620. Required fees $1,208. Average book expense $2,670. **Required Forms and Deadlines:** FAFSA, CSS/Financial Aid PROFILE. **Notification of Awards:** Applicants will be notified of awards on or about 3/25. **Types of Aid:** *Need-based scholarships/grants:* Federal Pell, SEOG, state scholarships/grants, private scholarships, the school's own gift aid, Gates Millennium Scholarship, ACG, Smart Grants. *Loans:* Subsidized Stafford, Unsubsidized Stafford, PLUS, Federal Perkins, state loans, college/university loans from institutional funds. *Student Employment:* Federal Work-Study Program available. Institutional employment available. Highest amount earned per year from on-campus jobs $2,000. Off-campus job opportunities are good. **Financial Aid Statistics:** 100% freshmen, 100% undergrads receive need-based scholarship or grant aid, 24% freshmen, 15% undergrads receive non-need-based scholarship or grant aid. 100% freshmen, 96% undergrads receive need-based self-help aid. 1% freshmen, 1% undergrads receive athletic scholarships. 90% freshmen, 91% undergrads receive any aid. 66% undergrads borrow to pay for school. **Criteria for awarding institutional aid:** *Non-need-based:* academics, alumni affiliation, art, athletics, leadership, minority status, music/drama.

RHODE ISLAND SCHOOL OF DESIGN

2 College Street, Providence, RI 2903
Phone: 401-454-6300 · **Financial Aid Phone:** 401-454-6636
E-mail: admissions@risd.edu · **CEEB Code:** 3726
Fax: 401-454-6309 · **Website:** www.risd.edu · **ACT Code:** 3812

This private school was founded in 1877. It has a 13-acre campus.

RATINGS

Admissions Selectivity Rating: 92   **Fire Safety Rating:** 71

STUDENTS AND FACULTY

Enrollment: 2,014. **Student Body:** 67% female, 33% male, 94% out-of-state, 26% international (56 countries represented). Asian 18%, African American 2%, Caucasian 32%, Hispanic 8%, Native American <1%
Retention and Graduation: 69% freshmen graduate within 4 years. **Faculty:** 155 full-time faculty, 70% hold PhDs, 44% are are members of minority groups, 10% are women.

ACADEMICS

Degrees: bachelor's, master's. **Majors with Highest Enrollment:** Illustration; Industrial and Product Design; Architecture. **Special Study Options:** cross-registration, exchange student program (domestic), independent study, internships, study abroad, Continuing Education program. 6-week precollege summer program for secondary school students. summer workshops for undergraduate credit. 6 week winter session study abroad courses. **Disability Services:** Special programs offered to physically disabled students include note-taking services, reader services, tape recorders.

FACILITIES

Housing: Coed dorms, apartments for single students **Special Academic Facilities/Equipment:** Art museum with over 45 galleries, extensive facilities for glassblowing, metalsmithing, lithography, sculpture, painting, and other art disciplines, nature lab. **Computers:** Administrative functions (other than registration) can be performed online.

CAMPUS LIFE

Environment: City. **Activities:** drama/theater, literary magazine, student government, student newspaper, student-run film society, yearbook. 35 registered organizations, 5 religious organizations. **On-Campus Highlights:** The RISD Museum, The Edna Lawrence Nature Lab, Metcalf 3 dimensional fine art building, 161 S. Main St.—Industrial Design Building, RISD Works.

ADMISSIONS

Freshman Academic Profile: Average high school GPA 3.4. 55% from public high schools. SAT Math middle 50% range 570-710. SAT Critical Reading middle 50% range 540-670. SAT Writing middle 50% range 570-690. ACT middle 50% range 27-32. Minimum internet-based TOEFL 93. Minimum paper TOEFL 580. **Basis for Candidate Selection:** *Very important factors considered include:* rigor of secondary school record, talent/ability. *Important factors considered include:* application essay, recommendation(s), standardized test scores, character/personal qualities. *Other factors considered include:* Class rank, alumni/ae relation, extracurricular activities, racial/ethnic status, volunteer work, work experience. **Freshman Admission Requirements:** High school diploma is required and GED is accepted. **Freshman Admission Statistics:** 2,408 applied, 41% admitted, 47% enrolled. **Transfer Admission Requirements:** college transcript(s), essay or personal statement, Lowest grade transferable C. **General Admission Information:** Application Fee $50. Regular application deadline 2/15. Regular notification 4/1. Nonfall registration accepted. Admission may be deferred for a maximum of 1 year. Credit and/or placement offered for CEEB Advanced Placement tests.

COSTS AND FINANCIAL AID

Annual tuition $44,284. Average book expense $2,700. **Required Forms and Deadlines:** FAFSA, CSS/Financial Aid PROFILE. **Notification of Awards:** Applicants will be notified of awards on or about 4/1. **Types of Aid:** *Need-based scholarships/grants:* Federal Pell, SEOG, state scholarships/grants, private scholarships, the school's own gift aid. *Loans:* Subsidized Stafford, Unsubsidized Stafford, PLUS, Federal Perkins. *Student Employment:* Federal Work-Study Program available. Institutional employment available. Highest amount earned per year from on-campus jobs $1,100. Off-campus job opportunities are good. **Financial Aid Statistics:** 73% freshmen, 80% undergrads receive need-based scholarship or grant aid. 3% freshmen, 3% undergrads receive non-need-based scholarship or grant aid. 100% freshmen, 100% undergrads receive need-based self-help aid. 0% freshmen, 0% undergrads receive athletic scholarships. 42% freshmen, 41% undergrads receive any aid. 48% undergrads borrow to pay for school. Average cumulative indebtedness $23,134. **Criteria for awarding institutional aid:** *Non-need-based:* academics, art.

RHODES COLLEGE

Best 380

2000 North Parkway, Memphis, TN 38112
Phone: 901-843-3700 · **Financial Aid Phone:** 901-843-3810
E-mail: adminfo@rhodes.edu · **CEEB Code:** 1730
Fax: 901-843-3631 · **Website:** http://www.rhodes.edu · **ACT Code:** 4008

This private school, affiliated with the Presbyterian Church, was founded in 1848. It has a 100-acre campus.

RATINGS

Admissions Selectivity Rating: 91   **Fire Safety Rating:** 79

STUDENTS AND FACULTY

Enrollment: 2,007. **Student Body:** 58% female, 42% male, 74% out-of-state, 2% international (15 countries represented). Asian 7%, African American 6%, Caucasian 76%, Hispanic 4%, Native American <1%
Retention and Graduation: 76% freshmen graduate within 4 years. 35% grads go on to further study within 1 year. **Faculty:** 174 full-time faculty, 96% hold PhDs, 49% are are members of minority groups, 10% are women. 0% of classes are taught by teaching assistants.

ACADEMICS

Degrees: bachelor's, master's. **Classes:** Most classes have 10-19 students. Most lab/discussion sessions have 10-19 students. **Majors with Highest Enrollment:** Biology/Biological Sciences; Business Administration and Management; English Language and Literature. **Special Study Options:** cooperative education program, cross-registration, double major, dual enrollment, exchange student program (domestic), honors program, independent study, internships, liberal arts/career combination, student-designed major, study abroad, duel degree: Master of Education; Master of Science in Nursing; Master of Science in Biomedical Engineering. **Honors programs:** The Honors program is a culminating experience in the major field, for seniors only. It is the principal means whereby a student may do more independent, intensive, and individual work than can be done in the regular degree programs. The Honors work offers an excellent introduction to graduate study as it employs the full resources of library and laboratory and encourages independent research and study. Honors is available in most majors. **Combined degree programs:** BA/MEd, BA/MSN, BS/MS Biomed Engineering. **Disability Services:** Special programs offered to physically disabled students include note-taking services, reader services, tape recorders, tutors. **Career services:** Alumni network, alumni services, career/job search classes, career assessment, internships, regional alumni. Career services highlights include The Rhodes St. Jude Summer Plus program, which typifies the integrated learning philosophy at Rhodes and through which students take classroom skills into the community where they connect knowledge with practice and learn effective leadership through service, internships, international travel and research. The approach also assures that students return to the classroom with the discoveries, problem-solving skills, contextualization, engagement and motivation gained through their experiences. John Sexton '04 describes his experience this way: "I was able to maintain close personal relationships with Rhodes faculty—the kind of relationships a student would be unlikely to have at a larger, research-oriented school—and also access the world-class facilities and experts at St. Jude—the kinds of resources not generally available to students at small liberal arts colleges." Clearly the Summer Plus program at St. Jude Children's Research Hospital provides the best of both worlds for the Rhodes science major who is ready to commit to two summers and a good deal of the school year working at a research hospital world renowned for its development of treatments for life-threatening diseases of childhood. In this program aspiring physicians and biomedical researchers have a unique opportunity to participate in every phase of the process in which basic research is translated into therapeutic interventions from bench to bedside. The intense and sustained challenge of work in this extraordinary environment fosters both scientific curiosity and humanitarian concern.

FACILITIES

Housing: Coed dorms, men's dorms, women's dorms, apartments for single students, learning communities; Substance free; quiet study; restricted visitation; non-smoking; special interest townhouses. 90% of campus accessible to physically disabled. **Special Academic Facilities/Equipment:** 136,000 square foot library; Art gallery; archaeology lab; astronomy observation domes with 14 and 31.5 inch telescopes; machine and woodworking shops; scanning electron microscopes; cell culture lab; nuclear magnetic resonance instrument; gas chromatography systems; UV, X-ray, infrared, and atomic absorption spectrophotometers. **Computers:** 100% of classrooms, 100% of dorms, 100% of libraries,

100% of dining areas, 50% of common outdoor areas have wireless network access. Students can register for classes online. Administrative functions (other than registration) can be performed online.

CAMPUS LIFE

Environment: Metropolis. **Activities:** Choral groups, dance, drama/theater, jazz band, literary magazine, music ensembles, musical theater, pep band, radio station, student government, student newspaper, student-run film society, symphony orchestra, television station, yearbook, Campus Ministries, International Student Organization, Model UN. 115 registered organizations, 14 honor societies, 8 religious organizations. 7 fraternities, 6 sororities. **Athletics (Intercollegiate):** *Men:* baseball, basketball, cross-country, football, golf, soccer, swimming, tennis, track/field (outdoor). *Women:* basketball, cross-country, field hockey, golf, soccer, softball, swimming, tennis, track/field (outdoor), volleyball. **On-Campus Highlights:** Barret Library (includes a Starbucks coffee shop), Burrow Center for Student Opportunity, Bryan Campus Life Center (home to the Ly, East Village (apartment-style dorms), McCoy Theater, The Burrow Center for Student Opportunity opened in Spring, 2008. It consolidates most student services under one roof, including a one-stop transaction center, enrolling and financing, student development and academic support, and out of class experiences. It also includes space for student organizations and is open to students 24x7. **Environmental Initiatives:** $500,000 Andrew W. Mellon Foundation grant to expand Environmental Studies initiatives through community partnerships; comprehensive campus-wide recycling program; centralized energy management system and Green Power Switch.

ADMISSIONS

Freshman Academic Profile: Average high school GPA 3.73. 48% in top 10% of high school class, 79% in top 25% of high school class, 96% in top 50% of high school class. 48% from public high schools. SAT Math middle 50% range 600-690. SAT Critical Reading middle 50% range 600-690. ACT middle 50% range 27-31. Minimum paper TOEFL 550. **Basis for Candidate Selection:** *Very important factors considered include:* Class rank, academic GPA, rigor of secondary school record. *Important factors considered include:* application essay, recommendation(s), standardized test scores, alumni/ae relation, character/personal qualities, racial/ethnic status. *Other factors considered include:* extracurricular activities, first generation, geographical residence, interview, level of applicant's interest, state residency, talent/ability, volunteer work, work experience. **Freshman Admission Requirements:** High school diploma is required and GED is accepted. *Academic units required:* 4 English, 3 mathematics, 2 science, (2 science labs), 2 foreign language, 2 social studies, 3 academic electives. **Freshman Admission Statistics:** 3,382 applied, 60% admitted, 25% enrolled. **Transfer Admission Requirements:** High school transcript, college transcript(s), essay or personal statement, standardized test scores, statement of good standing from prior institution(s). Lowest grade transferable C-. **General Admission Information:** Application Fee $45. Early decision application deadline 11/1. Regular notification 4/1. Nonfall registration accepted. Admission may be deferred for a maximum of 1 year. Credit and/or placement offered for CEEB Advanced Placement tests.

COSTS AND FINANCIAL AID

Annual tuition $41,262. Room and board $10,328. Required fees $310. Average book expense $1,125. **Required Forms and Deadlines:** FAFSA, CSS/Financial Aid PROFILE, Noncustodial PROFILE. **Types of Aid:** *Need-based scholarships/grants:* Federal Pell, SEOG, state scholarships/grants, private scholarships, the school's own gift aid. *Loans:* Direct Subsidized Stafford, Direct Unsubsidized Stafford, Direct PLUS, Subsidized Stafford, Unsubsidized Stafford, PLUS, Federal Perkins. **Student Employment:** Federal Work-Study Program available. Institutional employment available. Highest amount earned per year from on-campus jobs $5,140. Off-campus job opportunities are good. **Financial Aid Statistics:** 100% freshmen, 99% undergrads receive need-based scholarship or grant aid. 46% freshmen, 33% undergrads receive non-need-based scholarship or grant aid. 64% freshmen, 65% undergrads receive need-based self-help aid. 0% freshmen, 0% undergrads receive athletic scholarships. 95% freshmen, 94% undergrads receive any aid. 55% undergrads borrow to pay for school. Average cumulative indebtedness $25,317. **Criteria for awarding institutional aid:** *Non-need-based:* academics, art, minority status, music/drama, religious affiliation.

RICE UNIVERSITY

MS 17 PO Box 1892, Houston, TX 77251-1892
Phone: 713-348-7423 · **Financial Aid Phone:** 713-348-4958
E-mail: admi@rice.edu · **CEEB Code:** 6609
Fax: 713-348-5952 · **Website:** www.rice.edu · **ACT Code:** 4152

This private school was founded in 1912. It has a 300-acre campus.

RATINGS

Admissions Selectivity Rating: 97   **Fire Safety Rating:** 91

STUDENTS AND FACULTY

Enrollment: 3,920. **Student Body:** 49% female, 51% male, 49% out-of-state, 11% international (51 countries represented). Asian 21%, African American 6%, Caucasian 39%, Hispanic 15%, Native American <1%
Retention and Graduation: 79% freshmen graduate within 4 years. 91% freshmen graduate within 6 years. 48% grads go on to further study within 1 year. **Faculty:** 630 full-time faculty, 97% hold PhDs, 29% are are members of minority groups, 19% are women.

ACADEMICS

Degrees: bachelor's, master's. **Classes:** Most classes have 10-19 students. **Majors with Highest Enrollment:** Biology/Biological Sciences; Psychology; Economics. **Special Study Options:** cross-registration, double major, dual enrollment, English as a Second Language (ESL), honors program, independent study, internships, liberal arts/career combination, student-designed major, study abroad, teacher certification program, 8 year guaranteed medical school program with The Baylor College of Medicine. **Honors programs:** Honors programs through individual departments. **Combined degree programs:** guar.med.school program with Baylor College of Med. **Disability Services:** Special programs offered to physically disabled students include note-taking services, reader services, tape recorders. **Career services:** Alumni network, alumni services, career/job search classes, career assessment, internships, regional alumni. Career services highlights include our relationship with alumni and their support (in terms of professional advice as well as recruitment) of current undergraduate and graduate students.

FACILITIES

Housing: Coed dorms, special housing for disabled students, All undergraduate students are automatically assigned to one of nine (coed) residential colleges and keep affiliation regardless of whether they live on campus or not. 90% of campus accessible to physically disabled. **Special Academic Facilities/Equipment:** Art gallery, museum, media center, language labs, computer labs, civil engineering lab, observatory and NASA equipment for students in space physics courses. **Computers:** 100% of classrooms, 100% of dorms, 100% of libraries, 100% of dining areas, 100% of student union, 5% of common outdoor areas have wireless network access. Students can register for classes online. Administrative functions (other than registration) can be performed online.

CAMPUS LIFE

Environment: Metropolis. **Activities:** Choral groups, concert band, dance, drama/theater, jazz band, literary magazine, marching band, music ensembles, musical theater, opera, pep band, radio station, student government, student newspaper, student-run film society, symphony orchestra, television station, yearbook, Campus Ministries, International Student Organization, Model UN. 215 registered organizations, 11 honor societies, 14 religious organizations. **Athletics (Intercollegiate):** *Men:* baseball, basketball, cross-country, football, golf, tennis, track/field (outdoor), track/field (indoor). *Women:* basketball, cross-country, soccer, swimming, tennis, track/field (outdoor), track/field (indoor), volleyball. **On-Campus Highlights:** Rice Memorial Center, Baker Institute for Public Policy, Brochstein Pavilion (Café), Shepherd School of Music, Reckling Park—baseball stadium. **Environmental Initiatives:** 1. Green Building. At present, we have roughly 1,000,000 square feet of facilities on campus that are under construction that will receive some level of LEED certification, including the student dormitory Duncan College which is targeted for LEED-Gold. In addition, an off-campus child care center is pursuing LEED certification. Also, an off-campus graduate student apartment complex has been designed to LEED standards although it will not be formally submitted for certification. With this complex, we anticipate savings in energy of about 30% and water savings of 20%. Further, the complex was constructed in an area with excellent pedestrian access, and it includes extensive bicycle storage along with shuttle bus service to campus and to major nearby grocery stores. Our campus standard for on-campus LEED certification for new buildings is LEED-Silver as a minimum. The University has also enjoyed significant successes with construction waste recycling, with many of our largest projects to date logging diversion rates of 85-90% to recycling. 2. Energy Consumption and Prediction Reporting Application. Our campus energy managers have developed an application that provides in near real time a powerful building-level energy consumption and predictive analysis tool that takes into account variations in weather. For a given building, we can accurately model what that buildings energy consumption should be based on outdoor temperature, humidity, and past performance of the building. We then plot that versus actual consumption data from the meters. The difference between the two represents energy savings or losses. This tool allows us to see the immediate impact of energy conservation measures. To my knowledge, we are the only university with this capability to create our own weather-normalized predicted baselines. Our energy managers have partnered with Incuity Software to develop this tool into a campus energy management solution. Harvey Mudd College awarded this system with its first annual green engineering award in 2008. See http://www.incuity.com/HMC%20Award%20 News%20Release.pdf 3. Green Cleaning. The custodians of our Facilities Engineering and Planning Department provide the cleaning services for all of our non-residential buildings. Almost all of the cleaning is achieved with hot water, vapor, or a single environmentally-friendly cleaning chemical called H2Orange2 by Envirox. Disposable cleaning rags have been replaced by microfiber cloths, and string mops have been replaced with microfiber flat mops. FE&P custodians can attend optional English language training classes on-campus during work hours, which earns them credit through Houston Community College. They also can enroll in optional computer training, and are offered cross-training opportunities for positions such as plumbers and administrative assistants. Most of our custodians work daytime shifts (which saves building energy and improves customer services, while also being family-friendly and safer), and they receive full employee benefits.

ADMISSIONS

Freshman Academic Profile: 87% in top 10% of high school class, 97% in top 25% of high school class, 100% in top 50% of high school class. SAT Math middle 50% range 700-790. SAT Critical Reading middle 50% range 670-760. SAT Writing middle 50% range 670-770. ACT middle 50% range 31-34. Minimum internet-based TOEFL 100. Minimum paper TOEFL 600. **Basis for Candidate Selection:** *Very important factors considered include:* Class rank, application essay, academic GPA, recommendation(s), rigor of secondary school record, standardized test scores, character/personal qualities, extracurricular activities, talent/ability. *Other factors considered include:* alumni/ae relation, first generation, geographical residence, interview, level of applicant's interest, racial/ethnic status, state residency, volunteer work, work experience. **Freshman Admission Requirements:** High school diploma or equivalent is not required. *Academic units required:* 4 English, 3 mathematics, 2 science, (2 science labs), 2 foreign language, 2 social studies, 0 history, 3 academic electives, 0 History = Social Studies. Nat Sci and Eng div require trig or adv math courses and both chem and physics. May subst. a 2nd yr of chem or bio for phys. **Freshman Admission Statistics:** 15,415 applied, 17% admitted, 38% enrolled. **Transfer Admission Requirements:** High school transcript, college transcript(s), essay or personal statement, standardized test scores, statement of good standing from prior institution(s). Minimum college GPA of 3.2 required. Lowest grade transferable C-. **General Admission Information:** Application Fee $60. Early decision application deadline 11/1. Regular application deadline 1/2. Regular notification 4/1. Nonfall registration not accepted. Admission may be deferred for a maximum of 2 years. Credit and/or placement offered for CEEB Advanced Placement tests.

COSTS AND FINANCIAL AID

Annual tuition $38,260. Room and board $13,000. Required fees $681. Average book expense $800. **Required Forms and Deadlines:** FAFSA, CSS/Financial Aid PROFILE, Noncustodial PROFILE, Business/Farm Supplement. **Notification of Awards:** Applicants will be notified of awards on a rolling basis beginning 4/1. **Types of Aid:** *Need-based scholarships/grants:* Federal Pell, SEOG, state scholarships/grants, private scholarships, the school's own gift aid. *Loans:* Subsidized Stafford, Unsubsidized Stafford, PLUS, Federal Perkins. *Student Employment:* Federal Work-Study Program available. Institutional employment available. Off-campus job opportunities are excellent. **Financial Aid Statistics:** 100% freshmen, 100% undergrads receive need-based scholarship or grant aid. 5% freshmen, 5% undergrads receive non-need-based scholarship or grant aid. 61% freshmen, 57% undergrads receive need-based self-help aid. 6% freshmen, 7% undergrads receive athletic scholarships. 30% undergrads borrow to pay for school. Average cumulative indebtedness $13,791. **Criteria for awarding institutional aid:** *Non-need-based:* academics, art, athletics, leadership, minority status, music/drama, state/district residency.

RICHMOND, THE AMERICAN INTERNATIONAL UNIVERSITY IN LONDON

US Office of Admissions, Boston, MA 02210
Phone: 617-450-5617 • **Financial Aid Phone:** 011-44-20-8332-8244
E-mail: us_admissions@richmond.ac.uk • **CEEB Code:** 823
Fax: 617-450-5601 • **ACT Code:** 5244

This private school was founded in 1972. It has a 6-acre campus.

RATINGS

Admissions Selectivity Rating: 86   **Fire Safety Rating:** 67

STUDENTS AND FACULTY

Enrollment: 906. **Student Body:** 51% female, 49% male, 0% international. Asian 0%, African American 0%, Caucasian 0%, Hispanic 0%, Native American <1%

Retention and Graduation: 72% freshmen return for sophomore year. 35% grads go on to further study within 1 year. **Faculty:** 41 full-time faculty, 85% hold PhDs, 39% are are members of minority groups. 0% of classes are taught by teaching assistants.

ACADEMICS

Degrees: associate, bachelor's, master's, post-bachelor's certificate, terminal associate. **Classes:** Most classes have 10-19 students. **Majors with Highest Enrollment:** International Relations and Affairs; Business/Commerce. **Special Study Options:** English as a Second Language (ESL), independent study, internships, liberal arts/career combination, study abroad, Joint Engineering program with George Washington University.

FACILITIES

Housing: Coed dorms, men's dorms, women's dorms. **Computers:** Administrative functions (other than registration) can be performed online.

CAMPUS LIFE

Environment: Metropolis. **Activities:** Choral groups, dance, drama/theater, literary magazine, music ensembles, musical theater, student government, student newspaper, yearbook 1 honor society. **Athletics (Intercollegiate):** *Men:* rugby, soccer. *Women:* rugby. **On-Campus Highlights:** Caffe del Mondo Gourmet Coffee Shop, Wireless Computer Network, Student Common Room, Student Cafeteria.

ADMISSIONS

Freshman Academic Profile: Average high school GPA 3.25. 29% in top 10% of high school class, 40% in top 25% of high school class, 94% in top 50% of high school class. 60% from public high schools. SAT Math middle 50% range 488-610. SAT Critical Reading middle 50% range 495-625. ACT middle 50% range 24-28. Minimum paper TOEFL 550. **Basis for Candidate Selection:** *Very important factors considered include:* application essay, academic GPA, recommendation(s), rigor of secondary school record. *Important factors considered include:* extracurricular activities. *Other factors considered include:* standardized test scores, alumni/ae relation, character/personal qualities, interview, talent/ability. **Freshman Admission Requirements:** High school diploma is required and GED is accepted. *Academic units required:* 4 English, 3 mathematics, 3 science. **Freshman Admission Statistics:** 1,232 applied, 52% admitted, 32% enrolled. **Transfer Admission Requirements:** college transcript(s), essay or personal statement, statement of good standing from prior institution(s). Minimum college GPA of 2.5 required. Lowest grade transferable C. **General Admission Information:** Application Fee $50. Regular application deadline 8/1. Notification on a rolling basis, beginning on or about 11/1. Nonfall registration accepted. Admission may be deferred for a maximum of 1 year. Credit and/or placement offered for CEEB Advanced Placement tests.

COSTS AND FINANCIAL AID

Annual tuition $27,000. Room and board $12,900. Required fees $0. Average book expense $1,000. **Required Forms and Deadlines:** FAFSA. **Notification of Awards:** Applicants will be notified of awards on or about 3/15. **Types of Aid:** *Need-based scholarships/grants:* private scholarships, the school's own gift aid. *Loans:* Subsidized Stafford, Unsubsidized Stafford, PLUS, college/university loans from institutional funds. *Student Employment:* Highest amount earned per year from on-campus jobs $1,500. Off-campus job opportunities are good. **Financial Aid Statistics:** 80% freshmen, 70% undergrads receive any aid. 30% undergrads borrow to pay for school. **Criteria for awarding institutional aid:** *Non-need-based:* academics.

RIDER UNIVERSITY

2083 Lawrenceville Road, Lawrenceville, NJ 08648-3099
Phone: 609-896-5042 • **Financial Aid Phone:** 609-896-5360
E-mail: admissions@rider.edu • **CEEB Code:** 2758
Fax: 609-895-6645 • **Website:** www.rider.edu • **ACT Code:** 2590

This private school was founded in 1865. It has a 280-acre campus.

RATINGS

Admissions Selectivity Rating: 81   **Fire Safety Rating:** 75

STUDENTS AND FACULTY

Enrollment: 4,189. **Student Body:** 59% female, 41% male, 23% out-of-state, 3% international (64 countries represented). Asian 4%, African American 11%, Caucasian 64%, Hispanic 11%, Native American <1%
Retention and Graduation: 81% freshmen return for sophomore year. 52% freshmen graduate within 4 years. 63% freshmen graduate within 6 years. 23% grads go on to further study within 1 year. 4% grads pursue arts and sciences degrees. 2% grads pursue law degrees. 4% grads pursue business degrees. 2% grads pursue medical degrees. **Faculty:** 248 full-time faculty, 97% hold PhDs, 47% are are members of minority groups, 17% are women. 0% of classes are taught by teaching assistants.

ACADEMICS

Degrees: associate, bachelor's, master's, post-master's certificate. **Classes:** Most classes have 10-19 students. Most lab/discussion sessions have 10-19 students. **Majors with Highest Enrollment:** Accounting; Business Administration, Management and Operations; Elementary Education and Teaching. **Special Study Options:** cooperative education program, cross-registration, distance learning, double major, honors program, independent study, internships, liberal arts/career combination, study abroad, teacher certification program, weekend college, Learning Communities. **Honors programs:** The Baccalaureate Honors Program is designed to enrich the educational opportunities for Rider students of proven intellectual capability who choose to become Baccalaureate Scholars. Through a series of team-taught seminars, small classes, personal contact with faculty, colloquia and symposia, as well as independent study opportunities, the scholars extend their ability to think critically, coherently, and systematically about the great themes, ideals and movements of their human heritage. Students may apply, or be invited, as entering freshmen, as currently enrolled freshmen or sophomores, or as transfer freshmen or sophomores. To be considered for the program incoming freshmen must be in the top 10 percent of their high school class. **Combined degree programs:** BS/BA. **Disability Services:** Special programs offered to physically disabled students include reader services, tape recorders, tutors. **Career services:** Alumni network, alumni services, internships.

FACILITIES

Housing: Coed dorms, special housing for disabled students, women's dorms, fraternity/sorority housing, apartments for single students, Suites, Special interest areas: Wellness, Quite, First Year Experience, Science, Learning Community. 73% of campus accessible to physically disabled. **Special Academic Facilities/Equipment:** Art gallery, Holocaust/Genocide Resource Center. **Computers:** Students can register for classes online. Administrative functions (other than registration) can be performed online.

CAMPUS LIFE

Environment: Village. **Activities:** Choral groups, concert band, dance, drama/theater, literary magazine, music ensembles, musical theater, opera, pep band, radio station, student government, student newspaper, student-run film society, television station, yearbook, Campus Ministries, International Student Organization, Model UN. 84 registered organizations, 24 honor societies, 6 religious organizations. 4 fraternities, 8 sororities. **Athletics (Intercollegiate):** *Men:* baseball, basketball, cheerleading, cross-country, diving, golf, soccer, swimming, tennis, track/field (outdoor), wrestling. *Women:* basketball, cheerleading, cross-country, diving, field hockey, soccer, softball, swimming, tennis, track/field (outdoor), volleyball. **On-Campus Highlights:** Residence Hall Quad, Alumni Gym, Student Recreation Center, Daly's Dining Hall/Cranberry Café, Academic Quad. **Environmental Initiatives:** Signing the American College & University Presidents Climate Commitment and formation of the Energy and Sustainability Steering Committee in 2007 to implement strategic plan establishing sustainability initiatives for the university. Completion of a Greenhouse Gas Inventory for 2007-2008 and 2008-2009 and completion of a Carbon Neutrality Plan in 2010. Development of a student Eco-Rep program and currently employing 10 students. Building Silver LEED Certified new residence hall.

ADMISSIONS

Freshman Academic Profile: Average high school GPA 3.29. 17% in top 10% of high school class, 47% in top 25% of high school class, 82% in top 50% of high school class. SAT Math middle 50% range 470-570. SAT Critical Reading middle 50% range 460-550. SAT Writing middle 50% range 450-560. ACT middle 50% range 19-25. Minimum internet-based TOEFL 80. Minimum paper TOEFL 550. **Basis for Candidate Selection:** *Very important factors considered include:* application essay, academic GPA, recommendation(s), rigor of secondary school record, standardized test scores. *Important factors considered include:* level of applicant's interest. *Other factors considered include:* Class rank, alumni/ae relation, character/personal qualities, extracurricular activities, geographical residence, interview, state residency, talent/ability, volunteer work, work experience. **Freshman Admission Requirements:** High school diploma is required and GED is accepted. *Academic units required:* 4 English, 3 mathematics. **Freshman Admission Statistics:** 9,366 applied, 71% admitted, 15% enrolled. **Transfer Admission Requirements:** college transcript(s), essay or personal statement, Minimum college GPA of 2.5 required. Lowest grade transferable C. **General Admission Information:** Application Fee $50. Early decision application deadline 11/15. Notification on a rolling basis, beginning on or about 12/15. Nonfall registration accepted. Admission may be deferred for a maximum of 1 year. Credit and/or placement offered for CEEB Advanced Placement tests.

COSTS AND FINANCIAL AID

Annual tuition $36,120. Room and board $13,330. Required fees $710. Average book expense $1,500. **Required Forms and Deadlines:** FAFSA. **Notification of Awards:** Applicants will be notified of awards on a rolling basis beginning 2/20. **Types of Aid:** *Need-based scholarships/grants:* Federal Pell, SEOG, state scholarships/grants, private scholarships, the school's own gift aid. *Loans:* Subsidized Stafford, Unsubsidized Stafford, PLUS, Federal Perkins, state loans, college/university loans from institutional funds. *Student Employment:* Federal Work-Study Program available. Institutional employment available. Highest amount earned per year from on-campus jobs $6,195. Off-campus job opportunities are good. **Financial Aid Statistics:** 100% freshmen, 99% undergrads receive need-based scholarship or grant aid. 13% freshmen, 14% undergrads receive non-need-based scholarship or grant aid. 82% freshmen, 83% undergrads receive need-based self-help aid. 5% freshmen, 6% undergrads receive athletic scholarships. 73% undergrads borrow to pay for school. Average cumulative indebtedness $20,390. **Criteria for awarding institutional aid:** *Non-need-based:* academics, alumni affiliation, athletics, leadership, minority status, music/drama, state/district residency.

RINGLING COLLEGE OF ART AND DESIGN

2700 N. Tamiami Trail, Sarasota, FL 34234-5895
Phone: 941-351-5100 • **Financial Aid Phone:** 941-359-7534
E-mail: admissions@ringling.edu • **CEEB Code:** 5573
Fax: 941-359-7517 • **Website:** www.ringling.edu • **ACT Code:** 6724

This private school was founded in 1931. It has a 49-acre campus.

RATINGS

Admissions Selectivity Rating: 64   **Fire Safety Rating:** 78

STUDENTS AND FACULTY

Enrollment: 1,216. **Student Body:** 60% female, 40% male, 57% out-of-state, 16% international (53 countries represented). Asian 8%, African American 3%, Caucasian 55%, Hispanic 15%, Native American 1%
Retention and Graduation: 83% freshmen return for sophomore year. 55% freshmen graduate within 4 years. 66% freshmen graduate within 6 years. 5% grads go on to further study within 1 year. **Faculty:** 92 full-time faculty, 59% hold PhDs, 28% are are members of minority groups, 5% are women. 0% of classes are taught by teaching assistants.

ACADEMICS

Degrees: bachelor's, certificate. **Classes:** Most classes have 10-19 students. **Majors with Highest Enrollment:** Animation, Interactive Technology, Video Graphics and Special Effects; Illustration; Game and Interactive Media Design. **Special Study Options:** dual enrollment, exchange student program (domestic), independent study, internships, study abroad. **Disability Services:** Special programs offered to physically disabled students include note-taking services, reader services, tape recorders, tutors. **Career services:** Alumni network, alumni services, career/job search classes, career assessment, internships, regional alumni. Career services highlights include: Career/job search classes—direct approach to students on areas of interest, review of core approaches and resources; Alumni services—helping those who graduated, who, in turn, help us with recruiting, posting jobs, etc.; Regional alumni—help us with conference, workshops, visits to classes; Alumni network—same as above; Internships— growing opportunities especially in new majors and increasing success as full-time employees by those who interned at the company; Career assessment— help students (few) who need to determine best major for their goals.

FACILITIES

Housing: Coed dorms, men's dorms, women's dorms, apartments for married students, apartments for single students, Wellness HousingAll housing accommodations are ADA compliant. 98% of campus accessible to physically disabled. **Special Academic Facilities/Equipment:** William G. and Marie Selby Gallery, Crossley Gallery, Verman Kimbrough Memorial Library **Computers:** 60% of classrooms, 100% of dorms, 100% of libraries, 100% of dining areas, 100% of student union, 60% of common outdoor areas have wireless network access. Students can register for classes online. Administrative functions (other than registration) can be performed online.

CAMPUS LIFE

Environment: City. **Activities:** dance, drama/theater, student government, Campus Ministries, International Student Organization 22 registered organizations, 2 religious organizations. **On-Campus Highlights:** Student Center, Selby Gallery, Crossley Gallery, Verman Kimbrough Memorial Library, Hammond Commons. **Environmental Initiatives:** The College has an active sustainability committee comprised of staff, faculty and student members. the charge of the committee is to review current and proposed sustainability practices, provide oversight in the implementation of these practices and to raise awareness of sustainability practices. The College is a member of the Association for the Advancement of Sustainability in Higher Education (ASHE) and a participant of the Sustainability Tracking, Assessment and Rating system (STARS). The STARS program provides the College with framework to improve sustainability practices in education, operations and administrative categories. The College has two 80,000 sq ft LEED Gold certified buildings. A residents hall houses 228 students and an academic building provides teaching space to students from several majors.

ADMISSIONS

Freshman Academic Profile: Average high school GPA 3.2. Minimum internet-based TOEFL 61. Minimum paper TOEFL 500. **Basis for Candidate Selection:** *Very important factors considered include:* academic GPA, rigor of secondary school record, talent/ability. *Important factors considered include:* application essay, recommendation(s). *Other factors considered include:* alumni/ ae relation, extracurricular activities, geographical residence, interview, level of applicant's interest, volunteer work, work experience. **Freshman Admission Requirements:** High school diploma is required and GED is accepted. **Freshman Admission Statistics:** 1,409 applied, 70% admitted, 28% enrolled. **Transfer Admission Requirements:** High school transcript, college transcript(s), essay or personal statement, Minimum college GPA of 2.0 required. Lowest grade transferable C. **General Admission Information:** Application Fee $70. Notification on a rolling basis, beginning on or about 9/1. Nonfall registration not accepted. Admission may be deferred for a maximum of 2 years. Credit and/ or placement offered for CEEB Advanced Placement tests.

COSTS AND FINANCIAL AID

Required Forms and Deadlines: FAFSA. **Notification of Awards:** Applicants will be notified of awards on a rolling basis beginning 4/1. **Types of Aid:** *Need-based scholarships/grants:* Federal Pell, SEOG, state scholarships/grants, private scholarships, the school's own gift aid. *Loans:* Subsidized Stafford, Unsubsidized Stafford, PLUS. *Student Employment:* Federal Work-Study Program available. Institutional employment available. Highest amount earned per year from on-campus jobs $5,894. Off-campus job opportunities are good. **Financial Aid Statistics:** 99% freshmen, 97% undergrads receive need-based scholarship or grant aid. 5% freshmen, 3% undergrads receive non-need-based scholarship or grant aid. 86% freshmen, 88% undergrads receive need-based self-help aid. 0% freshmen, 0% undergrads receive athletic scholarships. 77% freshmen, 73% undergrads receive any aid. 67% undergrads borrow to pay for school. Average cumulative indebtedness $27,835. **Criteria for awarding institutional aid:** *Non-need-based:* academics, art.

RIPON COLLEGE

PO Box 248, Ripon, WI 54971
Phone: 920-748-8337 · **Financial Aid Phone:** 920-748-8301
E-mail: adminfo@ripon.edu · **CEEB Code:** 1664
Fax: 920-748-8335 · **Website:** www.ripon.edu · **ACT Code:** 4636

This private school was founded in 1851. It has a 250-acre campus.

RATINGS

Admissions Selectivity Rating: 85   Fire Safety Rating: 70

STUDENTS AND FACULTY

Enrollment: 820. **Student Body:** 54% female, 46% male, 27% out-of-state, 3% international (12 countries represented). Asian 1%, African American 2%, Caucasian 84%, Hispanic 5%, Native American <1%
Retention and Graduation: 86% freshmen return for sophomore year. 52% freshmen graduate within 4 years. 68% freshmen graduate within 6 years. 33% grads go on to further study within 1 year. 17% grads pursue arts and sciences degrees. 1% grads pursue law degrees. 3% grads pursue business degrees. 9% grads pursue medical degrees. **Faculty:** 66 full-time faculty, 97% hold PhDs, 38% are are members of minority groups, 9% are women. 0% of classes are taught by teaching assistants.

ACADEMICS

Degrees: bachelor's. **Classes:** Most classes have 10-19 students. Most lab/ discussion sessions have 10-19 students. **Majors with Highest Enrollment:** History; Business/Commerce; Health and Physical Education/Fitness. **Special Study Options:** double major, exchange student program (domestic), internships, student-designed major, study abroad, teacher certification program, Argonne Science Semester (Illinois). Newberry Library Program in the Humanities (Illinois). Urban Studies Program (Chicago). Wilderness Field Station Program (Minnesota). Other semester-away programs. **Disability Services:** Special programs offered to physically disabled students include tutors. **Career services:** Alumni network, career assessment, internships, regional alumni.

FACILITIES

Housing: Coed dorms, men's dorms, women's dorms, fraternity/sorority housing, apartments for single students **Special Academic Facilities/Equipment:** Art gallery, language labs. **Computers:** 2% of classrooms, 30% of libraries, 100% of dining areas, 60% of student union, have wireless network access.

CAMPUS LIFE

Environment: Village. **Activities:** Choral groups, concert band, dance, drama/ theater, jazz band, literary magazine, music ensembles, musical theater, radio station, student government, student newspaper, symphony orchestra, yearbook, Campus Ministries, International Student Organization. 45 registered organizations, 13 honor societies, 2 religious organizations. 5 fraternities, 3 sororities. **Athletics (Intercollegiate):** *Men:* baseball, basketball, cross-country, cycling, football, golf, soccer, swimming, tennis, track/field (outdoor), track/field (indoor). *Women:* basketball, cross-country, cycling, golf, soccer, softball, swimming, tennis, track/field (outdoor), track/field (indoor), volleyball. **On-Campus Highlights:** Ceresco Prairie Conservancy, Art Gallery, Storzer Athletic Center, Lane Library.

ADMISSIONS

Freshman Academic Profile: Average high school GPA 3.41. 25% in top 10% of high school class, 46% in top 25% of high school class, 71% in top 50% of high school class. 75% from public high schools. SAT Math middle 50% range 470-680. SAT Critical Reading middle 50% range 500-630. ACT middle 50% range 21-27. Minimum internet-based TOEFL 79. Minimum paper TOEFL 550. **Basis for Candidate Selection:** *Very important factors considered include:* rigor of secondary school record, interview. *Important factors considered include:* Class rank, academic GPA, recommendation(s), standardized test scores, character/personal qualities, extracurricular activities. *Other factors considered include:* application essay, talent/ability, volunteer work. **Freshman Admission Requirements:** High school diploma is required and GED is accepted. *Academic units required:* 4 English, 2 mathematics, 2 science, 2 social studies. **Freshman Admission Statistics:** 1,492 applied, 67% admitted, 21% enrolled. **Transfer Admission Requirements:** college transcript(s), essay or personal statement, statement of good standing from prior institution(s). Minimum college GPA of 2.0 required. Lowest grade transferable C. **General Admission Information:** Application Fee $30. Notification on a rolling basis, beginning on or about 9/15. Nonfall registration accepted. Admission may be deferred for a maximum of 1 year. Credit and/or placement offered for CEEB Advanced Placement tests.

COSTS AND FINANCIAL AID

Annual tuition $33,207. Room and board $9,085. Required fees $275. Average book expense $750. **Required Forms and Deadlines:** FAFSA. **Notification of Awards:** Applicants will be notified of awards on a rolling basis beginning 3/1. **Types of Aid:** *Need-based scholarships/grants:* Federal Pell, SEOG, state scholarships/grants, private scholarships, the school's own gift aid. *Loans:* Subsidized Stafford, Unsubsidized Stafford, PLUS, Federal Perkins. *Student Employment:* Federal Work-Study Program available. Institutional employment available. Highest amount earned per year from on-campus jobs $1,200. Off-campus job opportunities are good. **Financial Aid Statistics:** 100% freshmen, 100% undergrads receive need-based scholarship or grant aid. 14% freshmen, 13% undergrads receive non-need-based scholarship or grant aid. 85% freshmen, 85% undergrads receive need-based self-help aid. 0% freshmen, 0% undergrads receive athletic scholarships. 95% freshmen, 96% undergrads receive any aid. 83% undergrads borrow to pay for school. Average cumulative indebtedness $28,231. **Criteria for awarding institutional aid:** *Non-need-based:* academics, alumni affiliation, art, leadership, minority status, music/drama, religious affiliation, state/district residency.

See page 1120.

RIVIER COLLEGE

420 South Main Street, Nashua, NH 3060
Phone: 603-897-8219 · **Financial Aid Phone:** 603-897-8810
E-mail: rivadmit@rivier.edu · **CEEB Code:** 3728
Fax: 603-891-1799 · **Website:** www.rivier.edu · **ACT Code:** 2520

This private school, affiliated with the Roman Catholic Church, was founded in 1933. It has a 68-acre campus.

RATINGS

Admissions Selectivity Rating: 73   **Fire Safety Rating:** 83

STUDENTS AND FACULTY

Enrollment: 1,370. **Student Body:** 85% female, 15% male, 380% international (12 countries represented). Asian 2%, African American 2%, Caucasian 75%, Hispanic 5%, Native American 1%
Retention and Graduation: 78% freshmen return for sophomore year. 42% freshmen graduate within 4 years. 53% freshmen graduate within 6 years. **Faculty:** 68 full-time faculty, 75% hold PhDs, 65% are are members of minority groups. 0% of classes are taught by teaching assistants.

ACADEMICS

Degrees: associate, bachelor's, certificate, doctoral, master's, post-bachelor's certificate, post-master's certificate. **Classes:** Most classes have 10-19 students. Most lab/discussion sessions have fewer than 10 students. **Special Study Options:** cross-registration, double major, honors program, independent study, internships, liberal arts/career combination, student-designed major, teacher certification program. **Combined degree programs:** BA/MA. **Disability Services:** Special programs offered to physically disabled students include note-taking services, reader services, tape recorders, tutors.

FACILITIES

Housing: Coed dormsCoed wellness dorm (substance free). 75% of campus accessible to physically disabled. **Special Academic Facilities/Equipment:** Art gallery, Early Childhood Center/Laboratory School, language lab, TV microscope, video/laser disk system, photospectrometer, high-performance liquid chromatograph, digital imaging lab, several art studios including a photography darkroom. **Computers:** 100% of classrooms, 100% of dorms, 100% of libraries, 100% of dining areas, 100% of student union, 100% of common outdoor areas have wireless network access. Administrative functions (other than registration) can be performed online.

CAMPUS LIFE

Environment: City. **Activities:** Choral groups, dance, drama/theater, music ensembles, student government, student newspaper, television station, yearbook. 30 registered organizations, 2 honor societies, 2 religious organizations. **Athletics (Intercollegiate):** *Men:* baseball, basketball, cross-country, soccer, volleyball. *Women:* basketball, cross-country, soccer, softball, volleyball.

ADMISSIONS

Freshman Academic Profile: Average high school GPA 3. 5.8% in top 10% of high school class, 26.5% in top 25% of high school class, 71.4% in top 50% of high school class. SAT Math middle 50% range 410-510. SAT Critical Reading middle 50% range 410-510. SAT Writing middle 50% range 420-520. ACT middle 50% range 17-21. Minimum paper TOEFL 500. **Basis for Candidate Selection:** *Very important factors considered include:* academic GPA, rigor

of secondary school record. *Important factors considered include:* Class rank, application essay, standardized test scores, extracurricular activities, talent/ability, volunteer work, work experience. *Other factors considered include:* recommendation(s), character/personal qualities, interview. **Freshman Admission Requirements:** High school diploma is required and GED is accepted. **Freshman Admission Statistics:** 665 applied, 82% admitted, 36% enrolled. **Transfer Admission Requirements:** essay or personal statement, Minimum college GPA of 2.0 required. Lowest grade transferable C. **General Admission Information:** Application Fee $25. Notification on a rolling basis, beginning on or about 11/1. Nonfall registration not accepted. Admission may be deferred for a maximum of 1 year. Credit and/or placement offered for CEEB Advanced Placement tests.

COSTS AND FINANCIAL AID

Annual tuition $25,410. Room and board $9,798. Required fees $600. Average book expense $1,200. **Required Forms and Deadlines:** FAFSA. **Notification of Awards:** Applicants will be notified of awards on a rolling basis beginning 3/1. **Types of Aid:** *Need-based scholarships/grants:* Federal Pell, SEOG, state scholarships/grants, private scholarships, the school's own gift aid. *Loans:* Direct Subsidized Stafford, Direct Unsubsidized Stafford, Direct PLUS, Federal Perkins, college/university loans from institutional funds. *Student Employment:* Federal Work-Study Program available. Institutional employment available. Highest amount earned per year from on-campus jobs $4,500. Off-campus job opportunities are good. **Financial Aid Statistics:** 100% freshmen, 91% undergrads receive need-based scholarship or grant aid. 4% freshmen, 4% undergrads receive non-need-based scholarship or grant aid. 91% freshmen, 86% undergrads receive need-based self-help aid. 0% freshmen, 0% undergrads receive athletic scholarships. 82% freshmen, 89% undergrads receive any aid. 84% undergrads borrow to pay for school. Average cumulative indebtedness $24,327. **Criteria for awarding institutional aid:** *Non-need-based:* academics, alumni affiliation, leadership.

ROANOKE BIBLE COLLEGE

715 N. Poindexter St., Elizabeth City, NC 27909-4054
Phone: 252-334-2028 · **Financial Aid Phone:** 252-334-2020
E-mail: admissions@roanokebible.edu
Fax: 252-334-2064 · **ACT Code:** 3153

This private school was founded in 1948. It has a 20-acre campus.

RATINGS

Admissions Selectivity Rating: 78   **Fire Safety Rating:** 70

STUDENTS AND FACULTY

Enrollment: 166. **Student Body:** 1 country represented.
Retention and Graduation: 36% freshmen graduate within 4 years. 58% freshmen graduate within 6 years. **Faculty:** 9 full-time faculty, 56% hold PhDs, 33% are are members of minority groups, 0% are women. 0% of classes are taught by teaching assistants.

ACADEMICS

Degrees: associate, bachelor's, certificate. **Classes:** Most classes have fewer than 10 students. Most lab/discussion sessions have 10-19 students. **Majors with Highest Enrollment:** Bible/Biblical Studies. **Special Study Options:** distance learning, double major, dual enrollment, internships, Cross-cultural semester abroad. **Disability Services:** Special programs offered to physically disabled students include tape recorders, tutors.

FACILITIES

Housing: special housing for disabled students, men's dorms, women's dorms, apartments for married students, apartments for single students. 90% of campus accessible to physically disabled. **Computers:** 80% of classrooms, 100% of libraries, have wireless network access.

CAMPUS LIFE

Environment: Village. **Activities:** Choral groups, drama/theater, music ensembles, musical theater, student government, yearbook 1 honor society. **Athletics (Intercollegiate):** *Men:* basketball. *Women:* basketball, volleyball. **On-Campus Highlights:** On the Pasquotank River, New Married Housing apartments, New student life center. **Environmental Initiatives:** Geothermal heating & cooling; Solar hot water; Recycle program.

ADMISSIONS

Freshman Academic Profile: Average high school GPA 2.78. 2% in top 10% of high school class, 14% in top 25% of high school class, 36.6% in top 50% of high school class. 87% from public high schools. SAT Math middle 50% range 420-590. SAT Critical Reading middle 50% range 410-565. Minimum internet-based TOEFL 80. Minimum paper TOEFL 500. **Basis for Candidate Selection:** *Very important factors considered include:* Class rank, academic GPA, recommendation(s), standardized test scores, character/personal qualities, religious affiliation/commitment. *Important factors considered include:* application essay, rigor of secondary school record. *Other factors considered include:* extracurricular activities, interview, level of applicant's interest, talent/ability, volunteer work, work experience. **Freshman Admission Requirements:** High school diploma is required and GED is accepted. *Academic units required:* 4 English, 3 mathematics, 3 science, (2 science labs), 2 social studies, 2 history, 4 academic electives. **Freshman Admission Statistics:** 127 applied, 56% admitted, 58% enrolled. **Transfer Admission Requirements:** college transcript(s), essay or personal statement, statement of good standing from prior institution(s). Minimum college GPA of 2.0 required. Lowest grade transferable C. **General Admission Information:** Application Fee $50. Notification on a rolling basis, beginning on or about 9/1. Nonfall registration accepted. Admission may be deferred for a maximum of 1 semester. Credit and/or placement offered for CEEB Advanced Placement tests.

COSTS AND FINANCIAL AID

Required Forms and Deadlines: FAFSA, Institution's own financial aid form. **Notification of Awards:** Applicants will be notified of awards on a rolling basis beginning 5/1. **Types of Aid:** *Need-based scholarships/grants:* Federal Pell, SEOG, state scholarships/grants, private scholarships, the school's own gift aid. *Loans:* Subsidized Stafford, Unsubsidized Stafford, PLUS, Alternative Loans. *Student Employment:* Federal Work-Study Program available. Institutional employment available. Off-campus job opportunities are good. **Financial Aid Statistics:** 100% freshmen, 100% undergrads receive need-based scholarship or grant aid. 29% freshmen, 23% undergrads receive non-need-based scholarship or grant aid. 68% freshmen, 82% undergrads receive need-based self-help aid. 0% freshmen, 0% undergrads receive athletic scholarships. 88% freshmen, 90% undergrads receive any aid. 80% undergrads borrow to pay for school. Average cumulative indebtedness $19,451. **Criteria for awarding institutional aid:** *Non-need-based:* academics, alumni affiliation, art, athletics, leadership, music/drama, religious affiliation.

ROANOKE COLLEGE

221 College Lane, Salem, VA 24153-3794
Phone: 540-375-2270 · **Financial Aid Phone:** 540-375-2235
E-mail: admissions@roanoke.edu · **CEEB Code:** 5571
Fax: 540-375-2267 · **Website:** www.roanoke.edu · **ACT Code:** 4392

This private school, affiliated with the Lutheran Church, was founded in 1842. It has a 68-acre campus.

RATINGS

Admissions Selectivity Rating: 84   Fire Safety Rating: 82

STUDENTS AND FACULTY

Enrollment: 1,986. **Student Body:** 59% female, 41% male, 47% out-of-state, 2% international (33 countries represented). Asian 2%, African American 6%, Caucasian 83%, Hispanic 4%, Native American <1%
Retention and Graduation: 57% freshmen graduate within 4 years. 64% freshmen graduate within 6 years. 31% grads go on to further study within 1 year. **Faculty:** 164 full-time faculty, 85% hold PhDs, 48% are are members of minority groups, 10% are women. 0% of classes are taught by teaching assistants.

ACADEMICS

Degrees: bachelor's. **Classes:** Most classes have 10-19 students. Most lab/discussion sessions have 10-19 students. **Majors with Highest Enrollment:** Business Administration and Management; Psychology; Communication. **Special Study Options:** Accelerated program, cross-registration, double major, dual enrollment, English as a Second Language (ESL), honors program, independent study, internships, liberal arts/career combination, study abroad, teacher certification program. **Honors programs:** The Honors Program is designed for students with excellent academic performance, broad extracurricular interests, and leadership abilities. The Honors Program substitutes a coordinated sequence of interdisciplinary courses for a portion of the core requirements. A Plenary Enrichment Program of supplemental activities, a special scholarship, and a distinct recognition on the diploma and transcript are provided. **Disability Services:** Special programs offered to physically disabled students include

note-taking services, reader services, tape recorders, tutors. **Career services:** Alumni network, alumni services, career/job search classes, career assessment, internships, regional alumni. Career services highlights include Alumni Networking, which is offered to both students and alumni. Roanoke alumni are very open to helping students and fellow graduates in the career development area.

FACILITIES

Housing: Coed dorms, men's dorms, women's dorms, fraternity/sorority housing, apartments for single students, Theme Housing. 85% of campus accessible to physically disabled. **Special Academic Facilities/Equipment:** Fine arts center, community research center, language lab, church and society center. **Computers:** 100% of classrooms, 100% of libraries, 100% of dining areas, 100% of student union, 50% of common outdoor areas have wireless network access. Students can register for classes online. Administrative functions (other than registration) can be performed online.

CAMPUS LIFE

Environment: City. **Activities:** Choral groups, dance, drama/theater, jazz band, literary magazine, music ensembles, musical theater, pep band, radio station, student government, student newspaper, student-run film society, yearbook, Campus Ministries, International Student Organization, Model UN. 85 registered organizations, 30 honor societies, 7 religious organizations. 4 fraternities, 4 sororities. **Athletics (Intercollegiate):** *Men:* baseball, basketball, cross-country, golf, lacrosse, soccer, tennis, track/field (outdoor), track/field (indoor). *Women:* basketball, cross-country, field hockey, lacrosse, soccer, softball, tennis, track/field (outdoor), track/field (indoor), volleyball. **On-Campus Highlights:** Colket Student Center, Belk Fitness Center, Fintel Library, Bast Gymnasium & Kerr Stadium, Olin Hall (performing arts). **Environmental Initiatives:** Lucas Hall was renovated for the Fall of 2010. The Lucas renovation is LEED-Silver Certified. LEED stands for "Leadership in Energy and Environmental Design" and it means this construction project was environmentally sensitive in many different ways. A new residence hall opened in fall 2012 is also pending LEED certification. Campus recycling of plastics, aluminum, cardboard, and newspaper. RCycles is an initiative of the Office of the President, RCSustain, and Fintel Library with support from East Coasters Bicycle Shop that provides the free use of shared bicycles to the Roanoke College campus community.

ADMISSIONS

Freshman Academic Profile: Average high school GPA 3.5. 18% in top 10% of high school class, 43% in top 25% of high school class, 82% in top 50% of high school class. 80% from public high schools. SAT Math middle 50% range 490-600. SAT Critical Reading middle 50% range 490-610. SAT Writing middle 50% range 480-590. ACT middle 50% range 20-26. Minimum internet-based TOEFL 79. **Basis for Candidate Selection:** *Very important factors considered include:* Class rank, academic GPA, rigor of secondary school record, standardized test scores, character/personal qualities. *Important factors considered include:* recommendation(s), extracurricular activities, interview. *Other factors considered include:* application essay, alumni/ae relation, level of applicant's interest, racial/ethnic status, talent/ability, volunteer work, work experience. **Freshman Admission Requirements:** High school diploma is required and GED is accepted. *Academic units required:* 4 English, 3 mathematics, 2 science, (2 science labs), 2 social studies, 5 academic electives. **Freshman Admission Statistics:** 4,824 applied, 69% admitted, 17% enrolled. **Transfer Admission Requirements:** High school transcript, college transcript(s), statement of good standing from prior institution(s). Minimum college GPA of 2.2 required. Lowest grade transferable C-. **General Admission Information:** Application Fee $33. Early decision application deadline 12/1. Regular application deadline 3/15. Regular notification 4/1. Nonfall registration accepted. Admission may be deferred for a maximum of 2 years. Credit and/or placement offered for CEEB Advanced Placement tests.

COSTS AND FINANCIAL AID

Annual tuition $38,302. Room and board $12,370. Required fees $1,489. Average book expense $1,000. **Required Forms and Deadlines:** FAFSA, State aid form. **Notification of Awards:** Applicants will be notified of awards on a rolling basis beginning 11/1. **Types of Aid:** *Need-based scholarships/grants:* Federal Pell, SEOG, state scholarships/grants, private scholarships, the school's own gift aid. *Loans:* Subsidized Stafford, Unsubsidized Stafford, Federal Perkins, college/university loans from institutional funds, Alternative loans. *Student Employment:* Federal Work-Study Program available. Institutional employment available. Highest amount earned per year from on-campus jobs $2,000. Off-campus job opportunities are good. **Financial Aid Statistics:** 100% freshmen, 99% undergrads receive need-based scholarship or grant aid. 99% freshmen, 97% undergrads receive non-need-based scholarship or grant aid. 78% freshmen, 80% undergrads receive need-based self-help aid. 0% freshmen, 0% undergrads receive athletic scholarships. 99% freshmen, 98% undergrads receive any aid. 76% undergrads borrow to pay for school. Average cumulative indebtedness $26,243. **Criteria for awarding institutional aid:** *Non-need-based:* academics, minority status, music/drama, religious affiliation.

ROBERT MORRIS UNIVERSITY

6001 University Boulevard, Moon Township, PA 15108-1189
Phone: 412-397-5200 · **Financial Aid Phone:** 412-397-6250
E-mail: admissionsoffice@rmu.edu · **CEEB Code:** 2769
Fax: 412-397-2425 · **Website:** www.rmu.edu · **ACT Code:** 3674

This private school was founded in 1921. It has a 230-acre campus.

RATINGS

Admissions Selectivity Rating: 81   **Fire Safety Rating:** 87

STUDENTS AND FACULTY

Enrollment: 4,548. **Student Body:** 43% female, 57% male, 1310% international (24 countries represented). Asian 1%, African American 6%, Caucasian 75%, Hispanic 2%, Native American <1%
Retention and Graduation: 46% freshmen graduate within 4 years. 62% freshmen graduate within 6 years. 7% grads go on to further study within 1 year. **Faculty:** 214 full-time faculty, 87% hold PhDs, 44% are are members of minority groups, 17% are women. 0% of classes are taught by teaching assistants.

ACADEMICS

Degrees: bachelor's, certificate, master's, post-bachelor's certificate. **Classes:** Most classes have 20-29 students. **Majors with Highest Enrollment:** Accounting; Marketing/Marketing Management; Business Administration and Management. **Special Study Options:** cooperative education program, cross-registration, distance learning, double major, honors program, independent study, internships, study abroad, teacher certification program, weekend college, Evening, weekend and 5 week/8 week programs. **Honors programs:** International Honors Program **Combined degree programs:** BSBA/MS BS/MS. **Disability Services:** Special programs offered to physically disabled students include note-taking services, reader services, tape recorders, tutors. **Career services:** Alumni network, alumni services, career/job search classes, career assessment, internships, regional alumni. Career services highlights include an extensive internship and co-op placement program.

FACILITIES

Housing: Coed dorms, men's dorms, women's dorms, apartments for single students. 75% of campus accessible to physically disabled. **Computers:** 50% of classrooms, 75% of libraries, 100% of dining areas, 100% of student union, 25% of common outdoor areas have wireless network access. Students can register for classes online. Administrative functions (other than registration) can be performed online.

CAMPUS LIFE

Environment: Metropolis. **Activities:** Choral groups, drama/theater, literary magazine, marching band, musical theater, pep band, radio station, student government, student newspaper, television station, Campus Ministries, International Student Organization. 97 registered organizations, 6 honor societies, 5 religious organizations. 4 fraternities, 3 sororities. **Athletics (Intercollegiate):** *Men:* basketball, football, golf, ice hockey, lacrosse, soccer, tennis, track/field (outdoor), track/field (indoor). *Women:* basketball, crew/rowing, field hockey, golf, ice hockey, lacrosse, soccer, softball, tennis, track/field (outdoor), track/field (indoor), volleyball. **On-Campus Highlights:** Student Center, RMU Island Sports Center Complex, Computer Labs, Athletic Center, Health Club. **Environmental Initiatives:** Recycling paper, cardboard, plastic, bottles and cans, and florescent bulbs.

ADMISSIONS

Freshman Academic Profile: Average high school GPA 3.47. 19.1% in top 10% of high school class, 48.2% in top 25% of high school class, 79.5% in top 50% of high school class. 87% from public high schools. SAT Math middle 50% range 470-570. SAT Critical Reading middle 50% range 480-590. SAT Writing middle 50% range 440-540. ACT middle 50% range 20-24. Minimum internet-based TOEFL 61. Minimum paper TOEFL 500. **Basis for Candidate Selection:** *Very important factors considered include:* academic GPA, standardized test scores. *Important factors considered include:* Class rank, rigor of secondary school record, character/personal qualities, extracurricular activities, interview. *Other factors considered include:* application essay, recommendation(s), alumni/ae relation, level of applicant's interest, talent/ability, volunteer work, work experience. **Freshman Admission Requirements:** High school diploma is required and GED is accepted. *Academic units required:* 4 English, 3 mathematics, 2 science, 4 social studies, 3 academic electives. **Freshman Admission Statistics:** 6,064 applied, 76% admitted, 19% enrolled. **Transfer Admission Requirements:** college transcript(s), statement of good standing from prior institution(s). Minimum college GPA of 2.0 required. Lowest grade transferable C. **General Admission Information:** Application Fee $30. Regular application deadline 7/1. Notification on a rolling basis, beginning on or about 8/1. Nonfall registration accepted. Admission may be deferred for a maximum of 12 months. Credit and/or placement offered for CEEB Advanced Placement tests.

COSTS AND FINANCIAL AID

Room and board $11,810. Required fees $779. Average book expense $1,200. **Required Forms and Deadlines:** FAFSA. **Notification of Awards:** Applicants will be notified of awards on a rolling basis beginning 3/15. **Types of Aid:** *Need-based scholarships/grants:* Federal Pell, SEOG, state scholarships/grants, private scholarships, the school's own gift aid. *Loans:* Subsidized Stafford, Unsubsidized Stafford, PLUS, Federal Perkins, Alternative private loans. *Student Employment:* Federal Work-Study Program available. Institutional employment available. Off-campus job opportunities are good. **Financial Aid Statistics:** 100% freshmen, 97% undergrads receive need-based scholarship or grant aid. 10% freshmen, 9% undergrads receive non-need-based scholarship or grant aid. 89% freshmen, 88% undergrads receive need-based self-help aid. 2% freshmen, 2% undergrads receive athletic scholarships. 76% freshmen, 77% undergrads receive any aid. 85% undergrads borrow to pay for school. Average cumulative indebtedness $28,519. **Criteria for awarding institutional aid:** *Non-need-based:* academics, athletics.

See page 1122.

ROBERT MORRIS UNIVERSITY (IL)

401 South State Street, Chicago, IL 60605
Phone: 800-762-5960 · **Financial Aid Phone:** 312-935-4077
E-mail: enroll@robertmorris.edu · **CEEB Code:** 1670
Fax: 312-935-4440 · **ACT Code:** 1121

This is a private school.

RATINGS

Admissions Selectivity Rating: 80   **Fire Safety Rating:** 96

STUDENTS AND FACULTY

Enrollment: 3,196. **Student Body:** 53% female, 47% male, 81% international (27 countries represented). Asian 3%, African American 33%, Caucasian 38%, Hispanic 23%, Native American <1%
Retention and Graduation: 49% freshmen return for sophomore year. 69% freshmen graduate within 4 years. 73% freshmen graduate within 6 years. 16% grads go on to further study within 1 year. **Faculty:** 124 full-time faculty, 27% hold PhDs, 48% are are members of minority groups, 23% are women.

ACADEMICS

Degrees: associate, bachelor's, diploma, master's. **Classes:** Most classes have 20-29 students. **Majors with Highest Enrollment:** Business Administration and Management; Graphic Design; Information Technology. **Special Study Options:** Accelerated program, cooperative education program, distance learning, dual enrollment, honors program, internships, study abroad.

FACILITIES

Housing: Coed dorms.

CAMPUS LIFE

Activities: Choral groups, dance, drama/theater, literary magazine, student newspaper. **Environmental Initiatives:** The establishment of the RMU Sustainability Council, which is represented on our Academic Council and was issued a Proclamation for its work. The assessment of sustainability (along with diversity) as our Citizenship Assessment area in the College of Liberal Arts (also issued a Proclamation) The move away from mass use of printers.

ADMISSIONS

Freshman Academic Profile: Average high school GPA 2.7. 6% in top 10% of high school class, 19% in top 25% of high school class, 46% in top 50% of high school class. ACT middle 50% range 16-22. Minimum internet-based TOEFL 80. Minimum paper TOEFL 550. **Freshman Admission Requirements:** High school diploma is required and GED is accepted. **Freshman Admission Statistics:** 2,786 applied, 34% admitted, 124% enrolled. **General Admission Information:** Application Fee $75. Nonfall registration accepted. Admission may be deferred for a maximum of 1 year.

COSTS AND FINANCIAL AID

Annual tuition $22,800. Room and board $11,754. **Required Forms and Deadlines:** FAFSA. **Financial Aid Statistics:** 83% freshmen, 80% undergrads receive need-based scholarship or grant aid. 42% freshmen, 72% undergrads receive non-need-based scholarship or grant aid. 86% freshmen, 79% undergrads receive need-based self-help aid. 16% freshmen, 17% undergrads receive athletic scholarships. 92% freshmen, 92% undergrads receive any aid. 96% undergrads borrow to pay for school. Average cumulative indebtedness $26,569.

ROBERTS WESLEYAN COLLEGE

2301 Westside Drive, Rochester, NY 14624-1997
Phone: 585-594-6400 · **Financial Aid Phone:** 585-594-6150
E-mail: admissions@roberts.edu · **CEEB Code:** 2805
Fax: 585-594-6371 · **Website:** www.roberts.edu · **ACT Code:** 2868

This private school was founded in 1866. It has a 75-acre campus.

RATINGS

Admissions Selectivity Rating: 86   **Fire Safety Rating:** 68

STUDENTS AND FACULTY

Enrollment: 1,288. **Student Body:** 69% female, 31% male, 73% international (33 countries represented). Asian 1%, African American 12%, Caucasian 75%, Hispanic 5%, Native American <1%
Retention and Graduation: 48% freshmen graduate within 4 years. 59% freshmen graduate within 6 years. 24% grads go on to further study within 1 year. **Faculty:** 92 full-time faculty, 72% hold PhDs, 52% are are members of minority groups, 7% are women. 0% of classes are taught by teaching assistants.

ACADEMICS

Degrees: bachelor's, master's. **Classes:** Most classes have 10-19 students. Most lab/discussion sessions have 10-19 students. **Majors with Highest Enrollment:** Elementary Education and Teaching; Music Teacher Education. **Special Study Options:** cross-registration, distance learning, double major, English as a Second Language (ESL), honors program, independent study, internships, study abroad, teacher certification program. **Combined degree programs:** BA/MEng, Pharmacy. **Disability Services:** Special programs offered to physically disabled students include note-taking services, reader services, tape recorders, tutors. **Career services:** Alumni network, alumni services, career assessment, internships, regional alumni. Career services highlights include Alumni Networking and shadowing programs, Alumni Career Panels, Alumni Career Services Group on Linkedin.com, Mock Interviews.

FACILITIES

Housing: Coed dorms, special housing for disabled students, men's dorms, women's dorms, apartments for married students, apartments for single students. 71% of campus accessible to physically disabled. **Special Academic Facilities/Equipment:** Davison Art Gallery **Computers:** 100% of classrooms, 100% of dorms, 100% of libraries, 100% of dining areas, 100% of student union, 70% of common outdoor areas have wireless network access. Students can register for classes online. Administrative functions (other than registration) can be performed online.

CAMPUS LIFE

Environment: City. **Activities:** Choral groups, concert band, dance, drama/theater, jazz band, music ensembles, musical theater, opera, student government, student newspaper, symphony orchestra, yearbook, Campus Ministries, International Student Organization, Model UN. 28 registered organizations, 11 religious organizations. **Athletics (Intercollegiate):** *Men:* basketball, cross-country, golf, soccer, tennis, track/field (outdoor), track/field (indoor). *Women:* basketball, cross-country, soccer, tennis, track/field (outdoor), track/field (indoor), volleyball. **On-Campus Highlights:** Voller Athletic Center & Sports Complex, New B. Thomas Golisano Library, Rinker Community Service Center, BT's Café, Cultural Life Center.

ADMISSIONS

Freshman Academic Profile: Average high school GPA 3.4. 24% in top 10% of high school class, 49% in top 25% of high school class, 85% in top 50% of high school class. SAT Math middle 50% range 470-590. SAT Critical Reading middle 50% range 470-600. SAT Writing middle 50% range 440-580. ACT middle 50% range 20-27. Minimum internet-based TOEFL 75. Minimum paper TOEFL 540. **Basis for Candidate Selection:** *Very important factors considered include:* academic GPA, rigor of secondary school record, standardized test scores, character/personal qualities, interview, religious affiliation/commitment. *Important factors considered include:* application essay, recommendation(s), extracurricular activities. *Other factors considered include:* Class rank, alumni/ae relation, level of applicant's interest, talent/ability, volunteer work. **Freshman Admission Requirements:** High school diploma is required and GED is accepted. *Academic units required:* 4 English, 3 mathematics, 3 science, (1 science labs), 0 foreign language, 3 social studies. **Freshman Admission Statistics:** 1,928 applied, 47% admitted, 24% enrolled. **Transfer Admission Requirements:** college transcript(s), essay or personal statement, Minimum college GPA of 2.70 required. Lowest grade transferable C. **General Admission Information:** Application Fee $35. Notification on a rolling basis, beginning on or about 10/1. Nonfall registration accepted. Admission may be deferred for a maximum of 1 year. Credit and/or placement offered for CEEB Advanced Placement tests.

COSTS AND FINANCIAL AID

Annual tuition $25,350. Room and board $9,264. Required fees $1,349. Average book expense $1,000. **Required Forms and Deadlines:** FAFSA, State aid form. **Notification of Awards:** Applicants will be notified of awards on a rolling basis beginning 3/30. **Types of Aid:** *Need-based scholarships/grants:* Federal Pell, SEOG, state scholarships/grants, private scholarships, the school's own gift aid. *Loans:* Direct Subsidized Stafford, Direct Unsubsidized Stafford, Direct PLUS, Federal Perkins. *Student Employment:* Federal Work-Study Program available. Institutional employment available. Highest amount earned per year from on-campus jobs $3,000. Off-campus job opportunities are fair. **Financial Aid Statistics:** 100% freshmen, 98% undergrads receive need-based scholarship or grant aid. 12% freshmen, 7% undergrads receive non-need-based scholarship or grant aid. 86% freshmen, 89% undergrads receive need-based self-help aid. 6% freshmen, 3% undergrads receive athletic scholarships. 98% freshmen, 97% undergrads receive any aid. 90% undergrads borrow to pay for school. Average cumulative indebtedness $29,225. **Criteria for awarding institutional aid:** *Non-need-based:* academics, alumni affiliation, art, athletics, music/drama, religious affiliation.

ROCHESTER COLLEGE

800 West Avon Road, Rochester Hills, MI 48307
Phone: 248-218-2031
E-mail: admissions@rc.edu · **CEEB Code:** 1516
Fax: 248-218-2035 · **Website:** www.rc.edu · **ACT Code:** 2072

This private school, affiliated with the Church of Christ Church, was founded in 1959. It has a 83-acre campus.

RATINGS

Admissions Selectivity Rating: 60*   **Fire Safety Rating:** 60*

STUDENTS AND FACULTY

Enrollment: 1,059. **Student Body:** 14% out-of-state, (10 countries represented).
Retention and Graduation: 69% freshmen return for sophomore year. 8% freshmen graduate within 4 years. 12% freshmen graduate within 6 years. **Faculty:** 32 full-time faculty, 28% hold PhDs, 34% are are members of minority groups, 0% of classes are taught by teaching assistants.

ACADEMICS

Degrees: associate, bachelor's, master's, transfer associate. **Special Study Options:** Accelerated program, cross-registration, double major, dual enrollment, independent study, internships, liberal arts/career combination, study abroad, teacher certification program, weekend college. **Disability Services:** Special programs offered to physically disabled students include note-taking services, reader services. **Career services:** alumni services, career/job search classes, career assessment, internships.

FACILITIES

Housing: special housing for disabled students, men's dorms, women's dorms, apartments for married students.

CAMPUS LIFE

Environment: Village. **Activities:** Choral groups, drama/theater, jazz band, music ensembles, student government, student newspaper, yearbook. 19 registered organizations, 3 honor societies, 1 religous organization. **Athletics (Intercollegiate):** *Men:* baseball, basketball, cross-country, soccer, track/field (outdoor). *Women:* basketball, cross-country, softball, track/field (outdoor), volleyball.

ADMISSIONS

Freshman Academic Profile: Minimum paper TOEFL 500. **Basis for Candidate Selection:** *Important factors considered include:* rigor of secondary school record, standardized test scores. *Other factors considered include:* interview. **Freshman Admission Requirements:** High school diploma is required and GED is accepted. **Freshman Admission Statistics:** 277 applied, 83% admitted, 65% enrolled. **Transfer Admission Requirements:** High school transcript, college transcript(s), Minimum college GPA of 2.0 required. Lowest grade transferable C. **General Admission Information:** Application Fee $25. Notification on a rolling basis, beginning on or about 9/1. Nonfall registration accepted. Admission may be deferred for a maximum of 24 months. Credit and/or placement offered for CEEB Advanced Placement tests.

COSTS AND FINANCIAL AID

Average book expense $600. **Required Forms and Deadlines:** FAFSA, Institution's own financial aid form. **Notification of Awards:** Applicants will be notified of awards on a rolling basis beginning 6/1. **Types of Aid:** *Need-based* *scholarships/grants:* Federal Pell, SEOG, state scholarships/grants, private scholarships, the school's own gift aid. *Loans:* Direct Subsidized Stafford, Direct Unsubsidized Stafford, Direct PLUS, Federal Perkins. *Student Employment:* Federal Work-Study Program available. Institutional employment available. Off-campus job opportunities are excellent. **Financial Aid Statistics:** 87% freshmen receive need-based scholarship or grant aid. 79% freshmen receive non-need-based scholarship or grant aid. 84% freshmen receive need-based self-help aid. 29% receive athletic scholarships. 45% undergrads borrow to pay for school. **Criteria for awarding institutional aid:** *Non-need-based:* academics, alumni affiliation, athletics, leadership, music/drama.

ROCHESTER INSTITUTE OF TECHNOLOGY

60 Lomb Memorial Drive, Rochester, NY 14623-5604
Phone: 585-475-5502 · **Financial Aid Phone:** 585-475-5502
E-mail: admissions@rit.edu · **CEEB Code:** 2760
Fax: 585-475-7424 · **Website:** www.rit.edu · **ACT Code:** 2870

This private school was founded in 1829. It has a 1300-acre campus.

RATINGS

Admissions Selectivity Rating: 88   Fire Safety Rating: 81

STUDENTS AND FACULTY

Enrollment: 13,005. **Student Body:** 33% female, 67% male, 50% out-of-state, 5% international (107 countries represented). Asian 6%, African American 5%, Caucasian 61%, Hispanic 6%, Native American <1%
Retention and Graduation: 30% freshmen graduate within 4 years. 65% freshmen graduate within 6 years. 18% grads go on to further study within 1 year. **Faculty:** 996 full-time faculty, 68% hold PhDs, 34% are are members of minority groups, 18% are women. 0% of classes are taught by teaching assistants.

ACADEMICS

Degrees: associate, bachelor's, certificate, diploma, master's, post-bachelor's certificate, terminal associate, transfer associate. **Classes:** Most classes have 10-19 students. Most lab/discussion sessions have 10-19 students. **Majors with Highest Enrollment:** Photography; Mechanical Engineering; Information Technology. **Special Study Options:** Accelerated program, cooperative education program, cross-registration, distance learning, double major, English as a Second Language (ESL), exchange student program (domestic), honors program, independent study, internships, liberal arts/career combination, student-designed major, study abroad, weekend college. **Honors programs:** The RIT Honors Program provides a variety of curricular and extracurricular options, special Honors housing, and Honors scholarships. **Combined degree programs:** BA/MEng, BS/MS, BS/MBA. **Disability Services:** Special programs offered to physically disabled students include note-taking services, reader services, tape recorders, tutors. **Career services:** Alumni network, alumni services, career/job search classes, career assessment, internships, regional alumni. Every academic program at RIT offers some form of experiential education opportunity. Experiential education is designed to enrich the learning experience by providing students the opportunity to apply what they are learning in the lab and classroom to real-world problems, projects, and settings. Experiential education takes many forms including cooperative education, internships, study-abroad, undergraduate research, and industry sponsored project work. Experiential education requirements and opportunities vary among academic programs. Notable among these programs at RIT is cooperative education (co-op). The College of Applied Science and Technology, the E. Philip Saunders College of Business, the B. Thomas Golisano College of Computing and Information Sciences, and the Kate Gleason College of Engineering all require co-op for undergraduate students. It is available on an optional basis in other RIT colleges. Co-op students alternate periods of full-time study with periods of full-time paid work experience in business and industry directly related to their field of study and career interests. Last year more than 3,300 students completed work assignments with nearly 1,500 employers earning collectively in excess of $30 million.

FACILITIES

Housing: Coed dorms, special housing for disabled students, special housing for international students, fraternity/sorority housing, apartments for married students, apartments for single students, Special interest floors for selected majors/ groups. Men's floors Women's floors. 95% of campus accessible to physically disabled. **Special Academic Facilities/Equipment:** Art galleries, microelectronic engineering center, RIT Inn and Conference Center, observatory, student-managed restaurant, packaging testing facility, media resource center, Sunday 2000 printing press, Center for manufacturing studies, two OC3 connections to Internet and Internet2, laser optics laboratory, an observatory, an animal care facility, more than 100 color and black-and-white photography darkrooms, electronic prepress and publishing equipment, ceramic kilns, glass furnaces, a blacksmithing area, and computer graphics and robotic labs. **Computers:** 75% of classrooms, 25% of dorms, 100% of libraries, 100% of dining areas, 100% of student union, 100% of common outdoor areas have wireless network access. Students can register for classes online. Administrative functions (other than registration) can be performed online.

CAMPUS LIFE

Environment: City. **Activities:** Choral groups, concert band, dance, drama/theater, jazz band, literary magazine, music ensembles, musical theater, pep band, radio station, student government, student newspaper, student-run film society, symphony orchestra, yearbook, Campus Ministries, International Student Organization. 175 registered organizations, 9 honor societies, 5 religious organizations. 19 fraternities, 10 sororities. **Athletics (Intercollegiate):** *Men:* baseball, basketball, crew/rowing, cross-country, diving, ice hockey, lacrosse, soccer, swimming, tennis, track/field (outdoor), track/field (indoor), wrestling. *Women:* basketball, cheerleading, crew/rowing, cross-country, diving, ice hockey, lacrosse, soccer, softball, swimming, tennis, track/field (outdoor), track/field (indoor), volleyball. **On-Campus Highlights:** Java Wally's (Wallace Library coffee sho, Student Life Center/Field House/Ice Aren, ESPN Zone @ RIT Student Alumni Union, Ben and Jerry's (RIT Student Alumni Uni, The Café and Market at Crossroads. **Environmental Initiatives:** RIT has signed of the American College & University Presidents Climate Commitment (ACUPCC) and established 2030 as the target date for neutrality. A new senior level position of Sustainability Advisor to the President has been created to coordinate campus sustainable activity and connect with the sustainability-engaged communities. In addition, there are sustainability staff within Facilities Management, Auxiliary Services and the National Technical Institute for the Deaf (NTID) The University has completed the design stage for a $38 million building project designated to house the Golisano Institute for Sustainability (GIS). When completed, the GIS will become a national center of excellence in the areas of environmental science, and will position RIT in a leadership position in sustainable research and education. The GIS building is designed to make an enduring statement through its sustainable structure, energy efficiency, innovative technology applications and positive impact on its occupants and surrounding environment. The building is targeting LEED Platinum.

ADMISSIONS

Freshman Academic Profile: Average high school GPA 3.6. 32% in top 10% of high school class, 67% in top 25% of high school class, 95% in top 50% of high school class. 85% from public high schools. SAT Math middle 50% range 570-680. SAT Critical Reading middle 50% range 540-640. SAT Writing middle 50% range 520-630. ACT middle 50% range 26-31. Minimum internet-based TOEFL 79. Minimum paper TOEFL 550. **Basis for Candidate Selection:** *Very important factors considered include:* academic GPA, rigor of secondary school record. *Important factors considered include:* Class rank, standardized test scores. *Other factors considered include:* application essay, recommendation(s), alumni/ae relation, character/personal qualities, extracurricular activities, first generation, geographical residence, interview, level of applicant's interest, racial/ethnic status, talent/ability, volunteer work, work experience. **Freshman Admission Requirements:** High school diploma is required and GED is accepted. *Academic units required:* 4 English, 2 mathematics, 2 science, (1 science labs), 0 foreign language, 4 social studies, 10 academic electives. **Freshman Admission Statistics:** 17,936 applied, 57% admitted, 26% enrolled. **Transfer Admission Requirements:** college transcript(s), essay or personal statement, Minimum college GPA of 2.7 required. Lowest grade transferable C-. **General Admission Information:** Application Fee $50. Early decision application deadline 12/1. Regular application deadline 2/1. Notification on a rolling basis, beginning on or about 3/15. Nonfall registration accepted. Admission may be deferred for a maximum of 12 months. Credit and/or placement offered for CEEB Advanced Placement tests.

COSTS AND FINANCIAL AID

Annual tuition $35,256. Room and board $11,568. Required fees $512. Average book expense $1,050. **Required Forms and Deadlines:** FAFSA, Institution's own financial aid form, State aid form. **Notification of Awards:** Applicants will be notified of awards on a rolling basis beginning 3/15. **Types of Aid:** *Need-based scholarships/grants:* Federal Pell, SEOG, state scholarships/grants, private scholarships, the school's own gift aid, NACME. *Loans:* Direct Subsidized Stafford, Direct Unsubsidized Stafford, Direct PLUS, Federal Perkins, RIT Loan program; Alternative loans. *Student Employment:* Federal Work-Study Program available. Institutional employment available. Highest amount earned per year from on-campus jobs $2,500. Off-campus job opportunities are excellent. **Financial Aid Statistics:** 95% freshmen, 93% undergrads receive need-based scholarship or grant aid. 28% freshmen, 30% undergrads receive non-need-based scholarship or grant aid. 90% freshmen, 91% undergrads receive need-based self-help aid. 0% freshmen, 0% undergrads receive athletic scholarships. 87% freshmen, 77% undergrads receive any aid. 68% undergrads borrow to pay for school. **Criteria for awarding institutional aid:** *Non-need-based:* academics, art, leadership.

See page 1124.

ROCKFORD UNIVERSITY

Admission, Rockford, IL 61108-2393
Phone: 815-226-4050 · **Financial Aid Phone:** 815-226-4062
E-mail: RCAdmissions@rockford.edu · **CEEB Code:** 1665
Fax: 815-226-2822 · **Website:** www.rockford.edu • **ACT Code:** 1122

This private school was founded in 1847. It has a 130-acre campus.

RATINGS
Admissions Selectivity Rating: 84   **Fire Safety Rating:** 74

STUDENTS AND FACULTY
Enrollment: 857. **Student Body:** 61% female, 39% male, 10% out-of-state, 0% international. Asian 2%, African American 8%, Caucasian 69%, Hispanic 6%, Native American <1%
Faculty: 69 full-time faculty, 68% hold PhDs, 42% are are members of minority groups, 3% are women. 0% of classes are taught by teaching assistants.

ACADEMICS
Degrees: bachelor's, master's. **Classes:** Most classes have 10-19 students. Most lab/discussion sessions have fewer than 10 students. **Majors with Highest Enrollment:** Business/Commerce; Registered Nursing/Registered Nurse; Education. **Special Study Options:** Accelerated program, distance learning, double major, English as a Second Language (ESL), exchange student program (domestic), honors program, independent study, internships, study abroad, teacher certification program, Community-Based Learning, Tutorial Courses, Special Studies Courses. **Honors programs:** Honors program in Liberal Arts. **Disability Services:** Special programs offered to physically disabled students include note-taking services, reader services, tutors. **Career services:** career assessment, internships. Career services highlights include Community-Based Learning: Founded at Rockford College in the early 1990s, our community-based learning program is based on the conviction that Rockford College is a citizen of the community and that the community has a stake in Rockford College, as well. The work that the students perform serves the dual function of providing a defined need for the community while also fulfilling a specific learning objective determined by the professor.

FACILITIES
Housing: Coed dorms, special housing for disabled students, Theme Housing, Special housing for first-year students. We offer single rooms, double rooms, and suite style living options. **Special Academic Facilities/Equipment:** Language lab. Art Gallery. Sculpture Garden. **Computers:** Students can register for classes online. Administrative functions (other than registration) can be performed online.

CAMPUS LIFE
Environment: City. **Activities:** Choral groups, dance, drama/theater, literary magazine, music ensembles, musical theater, opera, pep band, student government, Campus Ministries, International Student Organization, Model UN. 25 registered organizations, 6 honor societies, 1 religious organization. **Athletics (Intercollegiate):** *Men:* baseball, basketball, cross-country, football, golf, soccer, tennis, track/field (outdoor), track/field (indoor). *Women:* basketball, cross-country, golf, soccer, softball, tennis, track/field (outdoor), track/field (indoor), volleyball. **On-Campus Highlights:** Residence Halls, Seaver Gym, Lion's Den-student gathering place, Football/Soccer Stadium, Clark Arts Center, Tour also highlights classroom buildings. **Environmental Initiatives:** Green Week; Trayless Tuesdays in the Cafeteria; Recycling options readily available.

ADMISSIONS
Freshman Academic Profile: Average high school GPA 3.07. 18% in top 10% of high school class, 33% in top 25% of high school class, 65% in top 50% of high school class. ACT middle 50% range 19-24. Minimum internet-based TOEFL 79. Minimum paper TOEFL 550. **Basis for Candidate Selection:** *Very important factors considered include:* academic GPA. *Important factors considered include:* application essay, rigor of secondary school record, standardized test scores. *Other factors considered include:* Class rank, recommendation(s). **Freshman Admission Requirements:** High school diploma is required and GED is accepted. *Academic units required:* 4 English,

3 mathematics, 3 science, (3 science labs), 3 social studies, 2 academic electives. **Freshman Admission Statistics:** 967 applied, 41% admitted, 23% enrolled. **Transfer Admission Requirements:** college transcript(s), statement of good standing from prior institution(s). Minimum college GPA of 2.3 required. Lowest grade transferable C. **General Admission Information:** Application Fee $35. Notification on a rolling basis, beginning on or about 9/15. Nonfall registration accepted. Admission may be deferred for a maximum of 1 year. Credit and/or placement offered for CEEB Advanced Placement tests.

COSTS AND FINANCIAL AID
Average book expense $1,200. **Required Forms and Deadlines:** FAFSA. **Notification of Awards:** Applicants will be notified of awards on a rolling basis beginning 3/1. **Types of Aid:** *Need-based scholarships/grants:* Federal Pell, SEOG, state scholarships/grants, private scholarships, the school's own gift aid. *Loans:* Subsidized Stafford, Unsubsidized Stafford, PLUS, Federal Perkins. *Student Employment:* Federal Work-Study Program available. Institutional employment available. Off-campus job opportunities are excellent. **Financial Aid Statistics:** 98% freshmen, 95% undergrads receive need-based scholarship or grant aid. 12% freshmen, 16% undergrads receive non-need-based scholarship or grant aid. 94% freshmen, 98% undergrads receive need-based self-help aid. 0% freshmen, 0% undergrads receive athletic scholarships. 99% freshmen, 99% undergrads receive any aid. 92% undergrads borrow to pay for school. Average cumulative indebtedness $22,830. **Criteria for awarding institutional aid:** *Non-need-based:* academics, alumni affiliation, leadership, minority status, music/drama, state/district residency.

ROCKHURST UNIVERSITY

1100 Rockhurst Road, Kansas City, MO 64110
Phone: 816-501-4100 · **Financial Aid Phone:** 816-501-4600
E-mail: admission@rockhurst.edu · **CEEB Code:** 6611
Fax: 816-501-4241 · **Website:** www.rockhurst.edu • **ACT Code:** 2342

This private school, affiliated with the Roman Catholic Church, was founded in 1910. It has a 55-acre campus.

RATINGS
Admissions Selectivity Rating: 86   **Fire Safety Rating:** 74

STUDENTS AND FACULTY
Enrollment: 1,652. **Student Body:** 58% female, 42% male, 32% out-of-state, 1% international (17 countries represented). Asian 3%, African American 4%, Caucasian 74%, Hispanic 6%, Native American <1%
Retention and Graduation: 62% freshmen graduate within 4 years. **Faculty:** 127 full-time faculty, 78% hold PhDs, 54% are are members of minority groups, 8% are women. 0% of classes are taught by teaching assistants.

ACADEMICS
Degrees: bachelor's, certificate, master's, post-bachelor's certificate. **Classes:** Most classes have 20-29 students. Most lab/discussion sessions have 10-19 students. **Majors with Highest Enrollment:** Psychology; Business/Commerce. **Special Study Options:** Accelerated program, cooperative education program, cross-registration, double major, dual enrollment, exchange student program (domestic), honors program, independent study, internships, study abroad, teacher certification program. **Honors programs:** The Rockhurst University Honors Program is for motivated and talented students, regardless of major, who want to be active participants in designing their education. Students find honors courses to be more innovative, personal, and challenging than other courses. The Benefits Beginning in the first year, honors students have specially designed core courses that are usually small in enrollment and are taught by some of the University's most creative faculty. During the sophomore through senior years, honors students may earn honors credit through "honors options"—individually designed projects that allow students to explore areas of their own interest under the mentorship of a professor. An honors option is typically an offshoot of a regular course, but an option can also be arranged as an independent study course. It is through the honors option that honors students shape their curriculum. **Combined degree programs:** BA/MOT, BA/DPT, BS/CSD, B/MBA. **Disability Services:** Special programs offered to physically disabled students include note-taking services, reader services, tape recorders, tutors. **Career services:** Alumni network, alumni services, career/job search classes, career assessment, internships, regional alumni. Career services highlights add to the experiential education programs at Rockhurst.

FACILITIES
Housing: Coed dorms, special housing for disabled students, men's dorms, women's dorms, apartments for single students, RU on-campus housing. 90% of campus accessible to physically disabled. **Special Academic Facilities/**

Equipment: Greenlease Art Gallery, Richardson Science Center. **Computers:** Students can register for classes online. Administrative functions (other than registration) can be performed online.

CAMPUS LIFE

Environment: Metropolis. **Activities:** Choral groups, drama/theater, literary magazine, musical theater, student government, student newspaper, yearbook. 44 registered organizations, 4 honor societies, 6 religious organizations. 3 fraternities, 3 sororities. **Athletics (Intercollegiate):** *Men:* baseball, basketball, golf, soccer, tennis. *Women:* basketball, golf, soccer, softball, tennis, volleyball. **On-Campus Highlights:** New Bell Tower and Fountains, Richardson Science Center / state-of-art facility, Business School / complete computer lab and classroom renovations, Career and Learning Center, The Old Gym (historic) plus the new.

ADMISSIONS

Freshman Academic Profile: Average high school GPA 3.6. 30% in top 10% of high school class, 58% in top 25% of high school class, 80% in top 50% of high school class. 41% from public high schools. SAT Math middle 50% range 485-650. SAT Critical Reading middle 50% range 510-640. ACT middle 50% range 23-28. Minimum paper TOEFL 550. **Basis for Candidate Selection:** *Very important factors considered include:* academic GPA, standardized test scores. *Important factors considered include:* Class rank, recommendation(s), rigor of secondary school record, character/personal qualities. *Other factors considered include:* alumni/ae relation, extracurricular activities, interview, level of applicant's interest, religious affiliation/commitment, talent/ability, volunteer work. **Freshman Admission Requirements:** High school diploma is required and GED is accepted. **Freshman Admission Statistics:** 2,494 applied, 77% admitted, 21% enrolled. **Transfer Admission Requirements:** college transcript(s), minimum college GPA of 2.5 required. Lowest grade transferable C-. **General Admission Information:** Application Fee $25. Regular notification 9/15. Nonfall registration accepted. Admission may be deferred for a maximum of 1 year. Credit and/or placement offered for CEEB Advanced Placement tests.

COSTS AND FINANCIAL AID

Annual tuition $32,075. Room and board $9,080. Required fees $790. Average book expense $1,485. **Required Forms and Deadlines:** FAFSA. **Notification of Awards:** Applicants will be notified of awards on a rolling basis beginning 1/30. **Types of Aid:** *Need-based scholarships/grants:* Federal Pell, SEOG, state scholarships/grants, private scholarships, the school's own gift aid. *Loans:* Subsidized Stafford, Unsubsidized Stafford, PLUS, Federal Perkins, Alternative Loans. *Student Employment:* Federal Work-Study Program available. Institutional employment available. Highest amount earned per year from on-campus jobs $1,650. Off-campus job opportunities are fair. **Financial Aid Statistics:** 80% freshmen, 86% undergrads receive need-based scholarship or grant aid. 99% freshmen, 99% undergrads receive non-need-based scholarship or grant aid. 75% freshmen, 82% undergrads receive need-based self-help aid. 14% freshmen, 14% undergrads receive athletic scholarships, 92% freshmen, 77% undergrads receive any aid. 70% undergrads borrow to pay for school. **Criteria for awarding institutional aid:** *Non-need-based:* academics, alumni affiliation, athletics, leadership, music/drama, state/district residency.

ROCKY MOUNTAIN COLLEGE

1511 Poly Drive, Billings, MT 59102-1796
Phone: 406-657-1026 • **Financial Aid Phone:** 406-657-1031
E-mail: admissions@rocky.edu • **CEEB Code:** 4660
Fax: 406-657-1189 • **Website:** www.rocky.edu • **ACT Code:** 2426

This private school was founded in 1878. It has a 60-acre campus.

RATINGS

Admissions Selectivity Rating: 81   **Fire Safety Rating:** 78

STUDENTS AND FACULTY

Enrollment: 984. **Student Body:** 49% female, 51% male, 44% out-of-state, 4% international (16 countries represented). Asian 1%, African American 3%, Caucasian 82%, Hispanic 4%, Native American 2%
Retention and Graduation: 67% freshmen return for sophomore year. 26% freshmen graduate within 4 years. 18% grads go on to further study within 1 year. 16% grads pursue arts and sciences degrees. 1% grads pursue law degrees. 1% grads pursue business degrees. **Faculty:** 65 full-time faculty, 77% hold PhDs, 40% are are members of minority groups. 0% of classes are taught by teaching assistants.

ACADEMICS

Degrees: associate, bachelor's, master's, terminal associate, transfer associate.

Classes: Most classes have 10-19 students. Most lab/discussion sessions have fewer than 10 students. **Majors with Highest Enrollment:** Biology/Biological Sciences; Airline/Commercial/Professional Pilot and Flight Crew; Business Administration and Management. **Special Study Options:** Accelerated program, distance learning, double major, dual enrollment, English as a Second Language (ESL), honors program, independent study, internships, student-designed major, study abroad, teacher certification program. **Honors programs:** Successful honors students find that participation in this program not only brings them closer to professionals in their chosen fields, but also grants them a substantial credential in their applications to graduate schools or employment opportunities. **Disability Services:** Special programs offered to physically disabled students include note-taking services, reader services, tape recorders, tutors. **Career services:** Alumni network, alumni services, career/job search classes, career assessment, internships, regional alumni.

FACILITIES

Housing: Coed dorms, apartments for married students, apartments for single students, Suites. 50% of campus accessible to physically disabled. **Special Academic Facilities/Equipment:** Billings Studio Theater, museum, studio, flight simulator/flight school, equestrian facilities, geology collection. **Computers:** Students can register for classes online. Administrative functions (other than registration) can be performed online.

CAMPUS LIFE

Environment: City. **Activities:** Choral groups, concert band, drama/theater, jazz band, literary magazine, music ensembles, musical theater, pep band, student government, student newspaper, yearbook. 28 registered organizations, 1 honor society, 4 religious organizations. **Athletics (Intercollegiate):** *Men:* basketball, cheerleading, football, golf, skiing (downhill/alpine). *Women:* basketball, cheerleading, golf, skiing (downhill/alpine), soccer, volleyball. **On-Campus Highlights:** Bair Family Student Center, Educational Resource Center, Fortin Center-Gymnasium, Herb Klindt Field-Football Stadium, Losekamp Hall-Music Theatre.

ADMISSIONS

Freshman Academic Profile: Average high school GPA 3.36. 10% in top 10% of high school class, 36% in top 25% of high school class, 70% in top 50% of high school class. SAT Math middle 50% range 450-550. SAT Critical Reading middle 50% range 440-540. SAT Writing middle 50% range 420-510. ACT middle 50% range 20-25. Minimum paper TOEFL 525. **Basis for Candidate Selection:** *Very important factors considered include:* academic GPA, rigor of secondary school record, standardized test scores. *Important factors considered include:* Class rank. *Other factors considered include:* application essay, recommendation(s), alumni/ae relation, character/personal qualities, extracurricular activities, interview, level of applicant's interest, talent/ability, volunteer work, work experience. **Freshman Admission Requirements:** High school diploma is required and GED is accepted. *Academic units required:* 4 English, 2 mathematics, 2 science, (1 science labs), 1 foreign language, 2 social studies, 2 history. **Freshman Admission Statistics:** 1,347 applied, 64% admitted, 31% enrolled. **Transfer Admission Requirements:** college transcript(s), Minimum college GPA of 2.0 required. Lowest grade transferable C-. **General Admission Information:** Application Fee $25. Notification on a rolling basis, beginning on or about 9/1. Nonfall registration accepted. Admission may be deferred for a maximum of 1 year. Credit and/or placement offered for CEEB Advanced Placement tests.

COSTS AND FINANCIAL AID

Annual tuition $22,442. Room and board $7,160. Required fees $450. Average book expense $1,300. **Required Forms and Deadlines:** FAFSA. **Notification of Awards:** Applicants will be notified of awards on a rolling basis beginning 2/1. **Types of Aid:** *Need-based scholarships/grants:* Federal Pell, SEOG, state scholarships/grants, private scholarships, the school's own gift aid. *Loans:* Subsidized Stafford, Unsubsidized Stafford, PLUS, Federal Perkins. *Student Employment:* Federal Work-Study Program available. Institutional employment available. Highest amount earned per year from on-campus jobs $3,985. Off-campus job opportunities are good. **Financial Aid Statistics:** 98% freshmen, 97% undergrads receive need-based scholarship or grant aid. 96% freshmen, 94% undergrads receive non-need-based scholarship or grant aid. 84% freshmen, 84% undergrads receive need-based self-help aid. 26% freshmen, 27% undergrads receive athletic scholarships. 90% freshmen, 90% undergrads receive any aid. 77% undergrads borrow to pay for school. Average cumulative indebtedness $26,364. **Criteria for awarding institutional aid:** *Non-need-based:* academics, alumni affiliation, art, athletics, leadership, minority status, music/drama, religious affiliation, state/district residency.

ROCKY MOUNTAIN COLLEGE OF ART + DESIGN

1600 Pierce St, Denver, CO 80214
Phone: 303-753-6046
E-mail: admissions@rmcad.edu
Fax: 303-567-7281 · **Website:** www.rmcad.edu · **ACT Code:** 5359

This proprietary school was founded in 1963. It has a 23-acre campus.

RATINGS

Admissions Selectivity Rating: 60*   Fire Safety Rating: 60*

STUDENTS AND FACULTY

Enrollment: 500. **Student Body:** 60% out-of-state.

ACADEMICS

Degrees: bachelor's. **Special Study Options:** independent study, internships, study abroad. **Career services:** Alumni network, alumni services, career/job search classes, career assessment, internships.

FACILITIES

Housing: Special Academic Facilities/Equipment: Philip Steele Gallery; Fine Arts Exhibit Space; Drive Up Gallery.

CAMPUS LIFE

Environment: Metropolis. **Activities:** dance, music ensembles, student government, student newspaper, Campus Ministries.

ADMISSIONS

Freshman Academic Profile: Minimum paper TOEFL 500. **Basis for Candidate Selection:** *Very important factors considered include:* extracurricular activities. *Important factors considered include:* academic GPA. **Freshman Admission Requirements:** High school diploma is required and GED is accepted. **Transfer Admission Requirements:** college transcript(s), Minimum college GPA of 2.0 required. **General Admission Information:** Nonfall registration accepted. Admission may be deferred for a maximum of one semester.

COSTS AND FINANCIAL AID

Average book expense $600. *Student Employment:* Federal Work-Study Program available. Off-campus job opportunities are good.

ROGER WILLIAMS UNIVERSITY

One Old Ferry Road, Bristol, RI 02809-2921
Phone: 401-254-3500 · **Financial Aid Phone:** 401-254-3100
E-mail: admit@rwu.edu · **CEEB Code:** 3729
Fax: 401-254-3557 · **Website:** www.rwu.edu · **ACT Code:** 3814

This private school was founded in 1956. It has a 140-acre campus.

RATINGS

Admissions Selectivity Rating: 74   Fire Safety Rating: 92

STUDENTS AND FACULTY

Enrollment: 4,370. **Student Body:** 49% female, 51% male, 83% out-of-state, 5% international (62 countries represented). Asian 1%, African American 2%, Caucasian 76%, Hispanic 5%, Native American <1%
Retention and Graduation: 83% freshmen return for sophomore year. 50% freshmen graduate within 4 years. **Faculty:** 203 full-time faculty, 90% hold PhDs, 43% are are members of minority groups, 11% are women. 0% of classes are taught by teaching assistants.

ACADEMICS

Degrees: associate, bachelor's, certificate, first professional, master's, post-bachelor's certificate, terminal associate. **Classes:** Most classes have 10-19 students. Most lab/discussion sessions have 10-19 students. **Majors with Highest Enrollment:** Criminal Justice/Law Enforcement Administration; Business/Commerce; Architecture. **Special Study Options:** cooperative education program, distance learning, double major, dual enrollment, English as a Second Language (ESL), exchange student program (domestic), external degree program, honors program, independent study, internships, liberal arts/career combination, student-designed major, study abroad, teacher certification program, weekend college. **Honors programs:** 1. Alpha Chi Honors Society-University-wide association for Juniors and Seniors; 2. Four-year Honors Program-For full-time students in any major which includes special sections of general education classes, a unique group service project for juniors and a required senior thesis. The program includes a variety of cultural and co-curricular activities, as well as

leadership opportunities; 3. Honors Society Associations-Department-level honors associations within various disciplines **Combined degree programs:** BA/JD, 3-3 law program. Dual Degree Architecture program. **Disability Services:** Special programs offered to physically disabled students include note-taking services, reader services, tape recorders, tutors.

FACILITIES

Housing: Coed dorms, special housing for disabled students, apartments for single students, Wellness Housing, Theme Housing, Special Interest, Academic Theme Housing, Honors, Wellness, Non-Smoking. **Special Academic Facilities/Equipment:** Marine and Natural Sciences Building, School of Law and Law Library, Main Library, Architecture Building and Architecture Library, Performing Arts Center, Thomas J. Paolino Recreation Center, Global Heritage Hall. **Computers:** 100% of classrooms, 100% of dorms, 100% of libraries, 100% of dining areas, 100% of student union, 20% of common outdoor areas have wireless network access. Students can register for classes online. Administrative functions (other than registration) can be performed online.

CAMPUS LIFE

Environment: Village. **Activities:** Choral groups, dance, drama/theater, literary magazine, musical theater, radio station, student government, student newspaper, student-run film society, yearbook, International Student Organization, Model UN. 93 registered organizations, 13 honor societies, 4 religious organizations. **Athletics (Intercollegiate):** *Men:* baseball, basketball, cross-country, diving, equestrian sports, lacrosse, sailing, soccer, swimming, tennis, track/field (outdoor), track/field (indoor), wrestling. *Women:* basketball, cross-country, diving, equestrian sports, lacrosse, sailing, soccer, softball, swimming, tennis, track/field (outdoor), track/field (indoor), volleyball. **On-Campus Highlights:** Recreation Center, Library, Dining Commons, Marine Science Wet Lab, Bookstore, Students are taken to any speficic place they would also like to see. Residence Halls are available for viewing with permission from occupants at certain points in the year. **Environmental Initiatives:** All renovation and new construction on campus meets LEED Silver standards Committed to reducing power consumption, reuse resources and recycle whenever possible Incorporating the idea of sustainability in all facets of the university

ADMISSIONS

Freshman Academic Profile: 85% from public high schools. SAT Math middle 50% range 500-600. SAT Critical Reading middle 50% range 480-580. SAT Writing middle 50% range 480-580. Minimum internet-based TOEFL 61. Minimum paper TOEFL 500. **Basis for Candidate Selection:** *Very important factors considered include:* application essay, academic GPA, recommendation(s), rigor of secondary school record, standardized test scores. *Important factors considered include:* Class rank, extracurricular activities. *Other factors considered include:* alumni/ae relation, first generation, level of applicant's interest, talent/ability, volunteer work, work experience. **Freshman Admission Requirements:** High school diploma is required and GED is accepted. *Academic units required:* 4 English, 3 mathematics, 2 science, (2 science labs), 0 foreign language, 2 social studies, 2 history, 2 academic electives. **Freshman Admission Statistics:** 9,021 applied, 81% admitted, 15% enrolled. **Transfer Admission Requirements:** college transcript(s), essay or personal statement, Minimum college GPA of 2.5 required. Lowest grade transferable C. **General Admission Information:** Application Fee $50. Regular application deadline 2/1. Regular notification 3/15. Nonfall registration accepted. Admission may be deferred for a maximum of 1 year. Credit and/or placement offered for CEEB Advanced Placement tests.

COSTS AND FINANCIAL AID

Annual tuition $29,976. Room and board $14,120. Required fees $1,692. Average book expense $900. **Required Forms and Deadlines:** FAFSA, CSS/Financial Aid PROFILE. **Notification of Awards:** Applicants will be notified of awards on a rolling basis beginning 3/20. **Types of Aid:** *Need-based scholarships/grants:* Federal Pell, SEOG, state scholarships/grants, private scholarships, the school's own gift aid. *Loans:* Subsidized Stafford, Unsubsidized Stafford, PLUS, Federal Perkins. *Student Employment:* Federal Work-Study Program available. Institutional employment available. Off-campus job opportunities are excellent. **Financial Aid Statistics:** 95% freshmen, 93% undergrads receive need-based scholarship or grant aid. 79% freshmen, 68% undergrads receive non-need-based scholarship or grant aid. 82% freshmen, 84% undergrads receive need-based self-help aid. 0% freshmen, 0% undergrads receive athletic scholarships. 81% freshmen, 82% undergrads receive any aid. 67% undergrads borrow to pay for school. Average cumulative indebtedness $23,965. **Criteria for awarding institutional aid:** *Non-need-based:* academics, leadership.

ROLLINS COLLEGE

Best 380

1000 Holt Avenue, Winter Park, FL 32789-4499
Phone: 407-646-2161 · **Financial Aid Phone:** 407-646-2395
E-mail: admission@rollins.edu · **CEEB Code:** 5572
Fax: 407-646-1502 · **Website:** http://www.rollins.edu · **ACT Code:** 748

This private school was founded in 1885. It has a 70-acre campus.

RATINGS

Admissions Selectivity Rating: 88   **Fire Safety Rating:** 96

STUDENTS AND FACULTY

Enrollment: 1,932. **Student Body:** 59% female, 41% male, 47% out-of-state, 8% international (54 countries represented). Asian 3%, African American 3%, Caucasian 67%, Hispanic 13%, Native American <1%
Retention and Graduation: 83% freshmen return for sophomore year. 63% freshmen graduate within 4 years. **Faculty:** 219 full-time faculty, 89% hold PhDs, 44% are are members of minority groups, 12% are women. 0% of classes are taught by teaching assistants.

ACADEMICS

Degrees: bachelor's, master's. **Classes:** Most classes have 10-19 students. **Majors with Highest Enrollment:** Psychology; Visual and Performing Arts; Communication and Media Studies. **Special Study Options:** Accelerated program, cross-registration, double major, dual enrollment, exchange student program (domestic), honors program, independent study, internships, student-designed major, study abroad, teacher certification program. **Combined degree programs:** BA/MBA. **Disability Services:** Special programs offered to physically disabled students include note-taking services, reader services, tape recorders, tutors. **Career services:** Alumni network, alumni services, career/job search classes, career assessment, internships.

FACILITIES

Housing: Coed dorms, special housing for disabled students, fraternity/sorority housing, apartments for single students, Theme Housing. 60% of campus accessible to physically disabled. **Special Academic Facilities/Equipment:** Art museum, theatres, fine arts center, language lab, skills development building, child development center, psychology center, "state-of-the-art" IT classroom. **Computers:** 100% of classrooms, 100% of dorms, 100% of libraries, 100% of dining areas, 100% of student union, have wireless network access. Students can register for classes online. Administrative functions (other than registration) can be performed online.

CAMPUS LIFE

Environment: Town. **Activities:** Choral groups, concert band, dance, drama/theater, jazz band, literary magazine, music ensembles, musical theater, pep band, radio station, student government, student newspaper, student-run film society, symphony orchestra, television station, yearbook, Campus Ministries, International Student Organization. 125 registered organizations, 5 honor societies, 5 religious organizations. 5 fraternities, 6 sororities. **Athletics (Intercollegiate):** *Men:* baseball, basketball, crew/rowing, cross-country, golf, lacrosse, sailing, soccer, swimming, tennis, water skiing. *Women:* basketball, crew/rowing, cross-country, golf, lacrosse, sailing, soccer, softball, swimming, tennis, volleyball, water skiing. **On-Campus Highlights:** Cornell Campus Center, Alfond Sports Center, Art Gallery, Cornell Fine Arts Museum, Olin Library, Rice Family Bookstore. **Environmental Initiatives:** Reuse existing buildings, renovating and updating to conform to LEED principles, but limited to and bound by LEED criteria; Planting of native and drought resistant foliage throughout the campus; Energy reduction initiatives including but not limited to centralized chilled water production and distribution.

ADMISSIONS

Freshman Academic Profile: Average high school GPA 3.33. 33% in top 10% of high school class, 64% in top 25% of high school class, 91% in top 50% of high school class. 51% from public high schools. SAT Math middle 50% range 550-640. SAT Critical Reading middle 50% range 550-640. SAT Writing middle 50% range 540-630. ACT middle 50% range 25-29. Minimum internet-based TOEFL 80. Minimum paper TOEFL 550. **Basis for Candidate Selection:** *Very important factors considered include:* academic GPA, rigor of secondary school record. *Important factors considered include:* application essay, recommendation(s), standardized test scores, extracurricular activities, talent/ability. *Other factors considered include:* Class rank, alumni/ae relation, character/personal qualities, first generation, interview, level of applicant's interest, volunteer work, work experience. **Freshman Admission Requirements:** High school diploma is required and GED is accepted. *Academic units required:* 4 English, 3 mathematics, 2 science, 2 foreign language, 2 social studies, 2 history, 2 academic electives. **Freshman Admission Statistics:** 4,858 applied, 57% admitted, 19% enrolled. **Transfer Admission Requirements:** High school transcript, college transcript(s), essay or personal statement, statement of good standing from prior institution(s). Lowest grade transferable C-. **General Admission Information:** Application Fee $40. Early decision application deadline 11/15. Regular application deadline 2/15. Regular notification 4/1. Nonfall registration accepted. Admission may be deferred for a maximum of one year. Credit and/or placement offered for CEEB Advanced Placement tests.

COSTS AND FINANCIAL AID

Average book expense $1,235. **Required Forms and Deadlines:** FAFSA. **Notification of Awards:** Applicants will be notified of awards on a rolling basis beginning 3/1. **Types of Aid:** *Need-based scholarships/grants:* Federal Pell, SEOG, state scholarships/grants, private scholarships, the school's own gift aid. *Loans:* Direct Subsidized Stafford, Direct Unsubsidized Stafford, Direct PLUS, Federal Perkins, college/university loans from institutional funds. *Student Employment:* Federal Work-Study Program available. Institutional employment available. **Financial Aid Statistics:** 99% freshmen, 99% undergrads receive need-based scholarship or grant aid. 13% freshmen, 11% undergrads receive non-need-based scholarship or grant aid. 67% freshmen, 70% undergrads receive need-based self-help aid. 4% freshmen, 5% undergrads receive athletic scholarships. 85% freshmen, 86% undergrads receive any aid. 56% undergrads borrow to pay for school. Average cumulative indebtedness $24,117. **Criteria for awarding institutional aid:** *Non-need-based:* academics, art, athletics, leadership, music/drama, state/district residency.

ROOSEVELT UNIVERSITY

430 South Michigan Avenue, Chicago, IL 60605
Phone: 877-277-5978 · **Financial Aid Phone:** 866-421-0935
E-mail: admission@roosevelt.edu · **CEEB Code:** 1666
Fax: 847-619-4216 · **Website:** http://www.roosevelt.edu/Home.aspx
ACT Code: 1124

This private school was founded in 1945. It has a 34-acre campus.

RATINGS

Admissions Selectivity Rating: 73   **Fire Safety Rating:** 92

STUDENTS AND FACULTY

Enrollment: 3,727. **Student Body:** 63% female, 37% male, 8% out-of-state, 3% international (63 countries represented). Asian 5%, African American 19%, Caucasian 45%, Hispanic 22%, Native American <1%
Retention and Graduation: 65% freshmen return for sophomore year. 18% freshmen graduate within 4 years. 30% freshmen graduate within 6 years. **Faculty:** 245 full-time faculty, 90% hold PhDs, 43% are are members of minority groups, 22% are women. 0% of classes are taught by teaching assistants.

ACADEMICS

Degrees: bachelor's, certificate, master's, post-master's certificate. **Classes:** Most classes have 10-19 students. **Majors with Highest Enrollment:** Psychology; Biology/Biological Sciences; Accounting. **Special Study Options:** Accelerated program, distance learning, double major, dual enrollment, English as a Second Language (ESL), exchange student program (domestic), honors program, independent study, internships, student-designed major, study abroad, teacher certification program. **Honors programs:** Roosevelt Scholars program offers an enriched academic program combining the students' area of interest with an interdisciplinary approach that includes internships, and research opportunities. Scholars are eligible to receive a special merit scholarship. The Scholars website is http://www.roosevelt.edu/scholars/default.htm **Combined degree programs:** BA/JD, MA/JD. **Disability Services:** Special programs offered to physically disabled students include note-taking services, reader services, tape recorders, tutors.

FACILITIES

Housing: Coed dorms, apartments for single students. 100% of campus accessible to physically disabled. **Special Academic Facilities/Equipment:** The Chicago campus is approx. 1 mile from the Museum of Natural History, Aquarium, Planetarium and Contemporary Art museums; and is 2 blocks from the Art Institute of Chicago **Computers:** Students can register for classes online. Administrative functions (other than registration) can be performed online.

CAMPUS LIFE

Environment: Metropolis. **Activities:** dance, literary magazine, radio station, student government, student newspaper, International Student Organization. 48

registered organizations, 3 honor societies, 4 religious organizations. 1 fraternity, 2 sororities. **Environmental Initiatives:** Roosevelt has achieved LEED certification for both of its new campus buildings in the heart of downtown Chicago—LEED Gold for Wabash Building and LEED Silver for the Goodman Center. The university has also achieved SERF (Society of Environmentally Responsible Facilities) certification for the Wabash Building. Roosevelt's suburban Schaumburg Campus underwent a major expansion of its community garden, as well as a restoration of over 70% of its landscape acreage to native Illinois prairie. Roosevelt University was recognized by the Illinois Governor's Campus Sustainability Compact at Silver Level, and the Sustainability Committee has started work on an institutional climate commitment and sustainability master plan.

ADMISSIONS

Freshman Academic Profile: Average high school GPA 3.3. 2.4% in top 10% of high school class, 8.5% in top 25% of high school class, 31.2% in top 50% of high school class. 80% from public high schools. SAT Math middle 50% range 460-560. SAT Critical Reading middle 50% range 480-600. SAT Writing middle 50% range 483-608. ACT middle 50% range 20-25. Minimum internet-based TOEFL 40. **Basis for Candidate Selection:** *Very important factors considered include:* academic GPA, rigor of secondary school record. *Important factors considered include:* standardized test scores. *Other factors considered include:* Class rank, application essay, recommendation(s), alumni/ae relation, character/personal qualities, extracurricular activities, first generation, interview, talent/ability. **Freshman Admission Requirements:** High school diploma is required and GED is accepted. *Academic units required:* 4 English, 3 mathematics, 2 science, (2 science labs), 0 foreign language, 2 social studies, 0 history, 0 visual/performing arts, 0 computer science, 0 academic electives. **Freshman Admission Statistics:** 5,409 applied, 76% admitted, 15% enrolled. **Transfer Admission Requirements:** college transcript(s), statement of good standing from prior institution(s). Minimum college GPA of 2.0 required. Lowest grade transferable D. **General Admission Information:** Application Fee $25. Notification on a rolling basis, beginning on or about 10/1. Nonfall registration accepted. Admission may be deferred for a maximum of 1 year. Credit and/or placement offered for CEEB Advanced Placement tests.

COSTS AND FINANCIAL AID

Annual tuition $27,300. Average book expense $1,200. **Required Forms and Deadlines:** FAFSA, Institution's own financial aid form. **Notification of Awards:** Applicants will be notified of awards on a rolling basis beginning 2/1. **Types of Aid:** *Need-based scholarships/grants:* Federal Pell, SEOG, state scholarships/grants, private scholarships, the school's own gift aid. *Loans:* Direct Subsidized Stafford, Direct Unsubsidized Stafford, Direct PLUS. **Financial Aid Statistics:** 94% undergrads receive need-based scholarship or grant aid. 79% freshmen, 81% undergrads receive need-based self-help aid. 0% freshmen, 0% undergrads receive athletic scholarships. 94% freshmen, 90% undergrads receive any aid. **Criteria for awarding institutional aid:** *Non-need-based:* academics, alumni affiliation, leadership, minority status, music/drama, state/district residency.

ROSE-HULMAN INSTITUTE OF TECHNOLOGY

5500 Wabash Avenue, Terre Haute, IN 47803-3999
Phone: 812-877-8213 • **Financial Aid Phone:** 812-877-8259
E-mail: admissions@rose-hulman.edu • **CEEB Code:** 1668
Fax: 812-877-8941 • **Website:** www.rose-hulman.edu • **ACT Code:** 1232

This private school was founded in 1874. It has a 200-acre campus.

RATINGS

Admissions Selectivity Rating: 93   **Fire Safety Rating:** 94

STUDENTS AND FACULTY

Enrollment: 2,208. **Student Body:** 22% female, 78% male, 64% out-of-state, 11% international (15 countries represented). Asian 4%, African American 2%, Caucasian 76%, Hispanic 3%, Native American <1%
Retention and Graduation: 62% freshmen graduate within 4 years. 78% freshmen graduate within 6 years. 21% grads go on to further study within 1 year. 19% grads pursue arts and sciences degrees. 2% grads pursue medical degrees. **Faculty:** 182 full-time faculty, 99% hold PhDs, 20% are members of minority groups, 13% are women. 0% of classes are taught by teaching assistants.

ACADEMICS

Degrees: bachelor's, master's. **Classes:** Most classes have 20-29 students. Most lab/discussion sessions have 20-29 students. **Majors with Highest Enrollment:** Chemical Engineering; Mechanical Engineering; Electrical and Electronics Engineering. **Special Study Options:** Accelerated program, cooperative education program, cross-registration, double major, independent study, internships, study abroad. **Combined degree programs:** MS/MD in Biomedical Engineering. **Disability Services:** Special programs offered to physically disabled students include reader services, tutors. **Career services:** Alumni network, alumni services, career/job search classes, career assessment, internships. Career services highlights include experiential learning that continually takes place during a student's college career. Whether it is through co-curricular activities, company projects brought to the classroom, or participation in degree related internship/co-op experiences. The Rose-Hulman graduate is fully prepared to enter the workforce running.

FACILITIES

Housing: Coed dorms, men's dorms, fraternity/sorority housing, apartments for single students. 95% of campus accessible to physically disabled. **Special Academic Facilities/Equipment:** Museums-none officially. Union Bldg-collection of British Watercolors. Moench Hall Section A-Western Sculpture. All Sections-Eclectic Art. Hadley Hall-Hadley Pottery and Salty Seamon Paintings. Other art in various offices. Oakley Observatory. **Computers:** 100% of classrooms, 5% of dorms, 100% of libraries, 100% of dining areas, 100% of student union, 25% of common outdoor areas have wireless network access. Students can register for classes online. Administrative functions (other than registration) can be performed online. Undergraduates are required to own a computer.

CAMPUS LIFE

Environment: Town. **Activities:** Choral groups, concert band, dance, drama/theater, jazz band, literary magazine, music ensembles, musical theater, pep band, radio station, student government, student newspaper, International Student Organization. 105 registered organizations, 7 honor societies, 2 religious organizations. 8 fraternities, 3 sororities. **Athletics (Intercollegiate):** *Men:* baseball, basketball, cross-country, diving, football, golf, riflery, soccer, swimming, tennis, track/field (outdoor), track/field (indoor). *Women:* basketball, cross-country, diving, golf, riflery, soccer, softball, swimming, tennis, track/field (outdoor), track/field (indoor), volleyball. **On-Campus Highlights:** Sports and Recreation Center, Hatfield Hall, White Chapel, Moench Hall, Chauncey's Place. **Environmental Initiatives:** Signing of the American College & University President's Climate Commitment; Formation of a Sustainability Team responsible for instilling a culture of sustainability; integrating sustainability with programs in education, operations, and community service; Serving as a pilot campus for the Sustainability Tracking and Assessment Rating System (STARS) Project through the Association for the Advancement of Sustainability in Higher Education.

ADMISSIONS

Freshman Academic Profile: Average high school GPA 3.96. 63% in top 10% of high school class, 93.8% in top 25% of high school class, 99.7% in top 50% of high school class. SAT Math middle 50% range 640-740. SAT Critical Reading middle 50% range 550-660. SAT Writing middle 50% range 540-640. ACT middle 50% range 27-32. Minimum internet-based TOEFL 80. Minimum paper TOEFL 550. **Basis for Candidate Selection:** *Very important factors considered include:* Class rank, rigor of secondary school record. *Important factors considered include:* academic GPA, recommendation(s), standardized test scores, character/personal qualities. *Other factors considered include:* application essay, alumni/ae relation, extracurricular activities, interview, talent/ability, volunteer work, work experience. **Freshman Admission Requirements:** High school diploma is required and GED is not accepted. *Academic units required:* 4 English, 4 mathematics, 2 science, (2 science labs), 2 social studies, 4 academic electives. **Freshman Admission Statistics:** 4,404 applied, 59% admitted, 22% enrolled. **Transfer Admission Requirements:** college transcript(s), essay or personal statement, statement of good standing from prior institution(s). Minimum college GPA of 3.0 required. Lowest grade transferable C. **General Admission Information:** Application Fee $40. Regular application deadline 3/1. Notification on a rolling basis, beginning on or about 10/1. Nonfall registration not accepted. Admission may be deferred for a maximum of 12 months. Credit and/or placement offered for CEEB Advanced Placement tests.

COSTS AND FINANCIAL AID

Annual tuition $40,449. Room and board $12,057. Required fees $834. Average book expense $1,500. **Required Forms and Deadlines:** FAFSA. **Notification of Awards:** Applicants will be notified of awards on or about 3/10. **Types of Aid:** *Need-based scholarships/grants:* Federal Pell, SEOG, state scholarships/grants, the school's own gift aid. *Loans:* Direct Subsidized Stafford, Direct Unsubsidized Stafford, Direct PLUS, Subsidized Stafford. *Student Employment:* Federal Work-Study Program available. Institutional employment available. Highest amount earned per year from on-campus jobs $1,500. **Financial Aid Statistics:** 88% freshmen, 87% undergrads receive need-based scholarship or grant aid. 100% freshmen, 99% undergrads receive non-need-based scholarship or grant aid. 92% freshmen, 89% undergrads receive need-based self-help aid. 0% freshmen, 0% undergrads receive athletic scholarships. 99% freshmen, 96% undergrads receive any aid. 64% undergrads borrow to pay for school. Average cumulative indebtedness $26,007. **Criteria for awarding institutional aid:** *Non-need-based:* academics, minority status.

ROSEMONT COLLEGE

1400 Montgomery Ave., Rosemont, PA 19010
Phone: 610-526-2966 · **Financial Aid Phone:** 610-527-0200
E-mail: admissions@rosemont.edu · **CEEB Code:** 2763
Fax: 610-520-4399 · **Website:** www.rosemont.edu · **ACT Code:** 3676

This private school, affiliated with the Roman Catholic Church, was founded in 1921. It has a 56-acre campus.

RATINGS

Admissions Selectivity Rating: 79 **Fire Safety Rating:** 75

STUDENTS AND FACULTY

Enrollment: 522. **Student Body:** 66% female, 34% male, 271% international (11 countries represented). Asian 5%, African American 38%, Caucasian 43%, Hispanic 6%, Native American <1%
Retention and Graduation: 67% freshmen return for sophomore year. 37% freshmen graduate within 4 years. 46% freshmen graduate within 6 years. 36% grads go on to further study within 1 year. 35% grads pursue arts and sciences degrees. 2% grads pursue law degrees. 5% grads pursue business degrees. 9% grads pursue medical degrees. **Faculty:** 26 full-time faculty, 96% hold PhDs, 54% are are members of minority groups, 12% are women. 0% of classes are taught by teaching assistants.

ACADEMICS

Degrees: bachelor's, master's, post-bachelor's certificate. **Classes:** Most classes have 10-19 students. **Majors with Highest Enrollment:** Art/Art Studies; Biology/Biological Sciences; Psychology. **Special Study Options:** Accelerated program, cross-registration, distance learning, double major, honors program, independent study, internships, liberal arts/career combination, student-designed major, study abroad, teacher certification program. **Combined degree programs:** BA/MA, BSN in conjunction with Drexel Univ. **Disability Services:** Special programs offered to physically disabled students include note-taking services, tape recorders, tutors. **Career services:** alumni services, career/job search classes, career assessment, internships. Career services highlights include an Internship or a form of Experiential Learning that all students partake in prior to graduation.

FACILITIES

Housing: women's dorms. Cornelia Connelly Hall located in the center of campus is totally redesigned. It is now a state of the art residence hall. Beginning with Fall 2009 Rosemont College welcomes men into the Undergraduate College. 45% of campus accessible to physically disabled. **Special Academic Facilities/Equipment:** McShain Performing Arts Center and Conwell Learning Center. **Computers:** 25% of classrooms, 25% of dorms, 50% of libraries, 15% of dining areas, 15% of student union, 10% of common outdoor areas have wireless network access. Students can register for classes online. Administrative functions (other than registration) can be performed online.

CAMPUS LIFE

Environment: Village. **Activities:** Choral groups, concert band, dance, drama/theater, jazz band, literary magazine, marching band, music ensembles, musical theater, opera, pep band, radio station, student government, student newspaper, yearbook, Campus Ministries. 23 registered organizations, 6 honor societies, 3 religious organizations. **Athletics (Intercollegiate):** *Men:* basketball, softball, tennis. *Women:* basketball, field hockey, lacrosse, softball, tennis, volleyball. **On-Campus Highlights:** Campus Grill, The Grind Coffee Shop, Fitness Center. **Environmental Initiatives:** Energy Star Procurement Policy. Waste Minimization Policy. Indoor Space Temperature Policy.

ADMISSIONS

Freshman Academic Profile: Average high school GPA 3.3. 70% from public high schools. SAT Math middle 50% range 390-525. SAT Critical Reading middle 50% range 410-538. ACT middle 50% range 18-22. Minimum internet-based TOEFL 61. Minimum paper TOEFL 500. **Basis for Candidate Selection:** *Very important factors considered include:* rigor of secondary school record, interview. *Important factors considered include:* Class rank, application essay, academic GPA, recommendation(s), standardized test scores, extracurricular activities, talent/ability, volunteer work. *Other factors considered include:* alumni/ae relation, character/personal qualities, work experience. **Freshman Admission Requirements:** High school diploma is required and GED is

accepted. *Academic units required:* 4 English, 3 mathematics, 3 science, (2 science labs), 0 foreign language, 1 social studies, 1 history, 7 academic electives. **Freshman Admission Statistics:** 800 applied, 58% admitted, 27% enrolled. **Transfer Admission Requirements:** college transcript(s), Minimum college GPA of 2.5 required. Lowest grade transferable C. **General Admission Information:** Application Fee $35. Regular application deadline 8/1. Regular notification 3/15. Notification on a rolling basis, beginning on or about 3/1. Nonfall registration accepted. Admission may be deferred for a maximum of 12 months. Credit and/or placement offered for CEEB Advanced Placement tests.

COSTS AND FINANCIAL AID

Annual tuition $30,600. Room and board $12,880. Required fees $980. Average book expense $1,500. **Required Forms and Deadlines:** FAFSA. **Notification of Awards:** Applicants will be notified of awards on a rolling basis beginning 2/15. **Types of Aid:** *Need-based scholarships/grants:* Federal Pell, SEOG, state scholarships/grants, private scholarships, the school's own gift aid. *Loans:* Subsidized Stafford, Unsubsidized Stafford, PLUS, Federal Perkins, Alternative loans offered, payment plans offered. *Student Employment:* Federal Work-Study Program available. Institutional employment available. Highest amount earned per year from on-campus jobs $2,000. Off-campus job opportunities are good. **Financial Aid Statistics:** 92% freshmen, 99% undergrads receive need-based scholarship or grant aid. 13% freshmen, 11% undergrads receive non-need-based scholarship or grant aid. 95% freshmen, 92% undergrads receive need-based self-help aid. 0% freshmen, 0% undergrads receive athletic scholarships. 92% freshmen, 92% undergrads receive any aid. 92% undergrads borrow to pay for school. Average cumulative indebtedness $34,039. **Criteria for awarding institutional aid:** *Non-need-based:* academics, art, leadership, religious affiliation.

ROWAN UNIVERSITY

Savitz Hall 201 Mullica Hill Road, Glassboro, NJ 08028-1701
Phone: 856-256-4200 · **Financial Aid Phone:** 856-256-5186
E-mail: admissions@rowan.edu · **CEEB Code:** 2515
Fax: 856-256-4430 · **Website:** www.rowan.edu · **ACT Code:** 2560

This public school was founded in 1923. It has a 800-acre campus.

RATINGS

Admissions Selectivity Rating: 80 **Fire Safety Rating:** 93

STUDENTS AND FACULTY

Enrollment: 11,819. **Student Body:** 47% female, 53% male, 5% out-of-state, 1% international (44 countries represented). Asian 6%, African American 9%, Caucasian 69%, Hispanic 9%, Native American <1%
Retention and Graduation: 86% freshmen return for sophomore year. 43% freshmen graduate within 4 years. **Faculty:** 95 full-time faculty, 333% hold PhDs, 195% are are members of minority groups, 112% are women. 0% of classes are taught by teaching assistants.

ACADEMICS

Degrees: bachelor's, master's. **Classes:** Most classes have 20-29 students. **Majors with Highest Enrollment:** Psychology; Elementary Education and Teaching; Biology/Biological Sciences. **Special Study Options:** cooperative education program, distance learning, double major, English as a Second Language (ESL), exchange student program (domestic), external degree program, honors program, independent study, internships, study abroad, teacher certification program, weekend college. **Honors programs:** The Thomas N. Bantavoglio Honors Concentration offers qualified students access to a variety of academic, enrichment, and service experiences including honors classes, the Honors Student Organization and the 45 activities sponsored by the HSO, as well as travel for cultural and enrichment activities along the eastern seaboard. **Combined degree programs:** BS/MA in Mathematics; BS/MS in Computer Science. **Disability Services:** Special programs offered to physically disabled students include note-taking services, reader services, tape recorders, tutors. **Career services:** Alumni network, alumni services, career/job search classes, career assessment, internships, regional alumni. Career services highlights include the Rowan University undergraduate Entrepreneurship program, which has been nationally ranked by The Princeton Review as a Top Program for Entrepreneurship.

FACILITIES

Housing: Coed dorms, special housing for disabled students, apartments for single students, Wellness Housing, Townhouses. 90% of campus accessible to physically disabled. **Special Academic Facilities/Equipment:** Concert hall, glass collection, student recreation center, on-campus early childhood demonstration center, greenhouse for biological studies, observatory, art gallery.

Computers: 100% of classrooms, 100% of dorms, 100% of libraries, 100% of dining areas, 100% of student union, 100% of common outdoor areas have wireless network access. Students can register for classes online. Administrative functions (other than registration) can be performed online.

CAMPUS LIFE

Environment: Town. **Activities:** Choral groups, concert band, dance, drama/theater, jazz band, literary magazine, music ensembles, musical theater, opera, pep band, radio station, student government, student newspaper, student-run film society, television station, yearbook, Campus Ministries. 135 registered organizations, 10 honor societies, 6 religious organizations. 10 fraternities, 10 sororities. **Athletics (Intercollegiate):** *Men:* baseball, basketball, cross-country, diving, football, soccer, swimming, track/field (outdoor), track/field (indoor). *Women:* basketball, cross-country, diving, field hockey, lacrosse, soccer, softball, swimming, track/field (outdoor), track/field (indoor), volleyball. **On-Campus Highlights:** Recreation Center, Student Center, Campbell Library, Savitz Hall (Student Services Building), Education Hall. **Environmental Initiatives:** Energy use has decreased 25% from fiscal year 13 to base year 11 because of the operation of the central utility plant and the co-generation. Cut energy usage from 700000 mmbtu's to 510000 mmbtu's over 2 years. Generating electricity in the co-generation plant avoids our purchase of coal generated electricity. Rowan University was the first institution of higher education in NJ to sign the American College and University Presidents Climate Commitment (ACUPCC). Rowan was among the first schools in NJ to convert to singe-stream recycling. This innovative program engages students, faculty and staff. The recycling program, coupled with other initiatives, has earned Rowan 9 major awards from federal and state agencies over the last 3 years.

ADMISSIONS

Freshman Academic Profile: Average high school GPA 3.46. SAT Math middle 50% range 520-630. SAT Critical Reading middle 50% range 490-590. SAT Writing middle 50% range 480-580. Minimum internet-based TOEFL 79. Minimum paper TOEFL 550. **Basis for Candidate Selection:** *Very important factors considered include:* rigor of secondary school record. *Important factors considered include:* Class rank, academic GPA, standardized test scores. *Other factors considered include:* recommendation(s), character/personal qualities, extracurricular activities, talent/ability, volunteer work, work experience. **Freshman Admission Requirements:** High school diploma is required and GED is accepted. *Academic units required:* 4 English, 3 mathematics, 2 science, (2 science labs), 2 social studies. **Freshman Admission Statistics:** 10,074 applied, 66% admitted, 29% enrolled. **Transfer Admission Requirements:** college transcript(s), Minimum college GPA of 2.0 required. Lowest grade transferable D. **General Admission Information:** Application Fee $50. Regular application deadline 3/1. Regular notification 4/15. Notification on a rolling basis, beginning on or about 10/1. Nonfall registration accepted. Admission may be deferred for a maximum of 1 semester. Credit and/or placement offered for CEEB Advanced Placement tests.

COSTS AND FINANCIAL AID

Annual in-state tuition $9,076. Annual out-of-state tuition $17,030. Room and board $11,406. Required fees $3,540. Average book expense $1,500. **Required Forms and Deadlines:** FAFSA. **Notification of Awards:** Applicants will be notified of awards on a rolling basis beginning 3/15. **Types of Aid:** *Need-based scholarships/grants:* Federal Pell, SEOG, state scholarships/grants, private scholarships, the school's own gift aid. *Loans:* Subsidized Stafford, Unsubsidized Stafford, PLUS. *Student Employment:* Federal Work-Study Program available. Institutional employment available. Highest amount earned per year from on-campus jobs $5,800. Off-campus job opportunities are good. **Financial Aid Statistics:** 45% freshmen receive need-based scholarship or grant aid. 48% freshmen, 22% undergrads receive non-need-based scholarship or grant aid. 71% freshmen, 80% undergrads receive need-based self-help aid. 0% freshmen, 0% undergrads receive athletic scholarships. 87% freshmen, 80% undergrads receive any aid. 73% undergrads borrow to pay for school. Average cumulative indebtedness $24,024. **Criteria for awarding institutional aid:** *Non-need-based:* academics, art, minority status, music/drama.

RUSH UNIVERSITY

600 South Paulina, Chicago, IL 60612-3878
Phone: 312-942-7100 • **Financial Aid Phone:** 312-942-6256
E-mail: Rush_Admissions@rush.edu • **CEEB Code:**
Fax: 312-942-2219 • **Website:** www.rushu.rush.edu • **ACT Code:** 1617

This private school was founded in 1972. It has a 35-acre campus.

RATINGS

Admissions Selectivity Rating: 60*   Fire Safety Rating: 71

STUDENTS AND FACULTY

Enrollment: 258. **Student Body:** 87% female, 13% male, 15% out-of-state, 2% international. Asian 18%, African American 7%, Caucasian 69%, Hispanic 3%, Native American <1%
Retention and Graduation: 25% grads go on to further study within 1 year. 5% grads pursue medical degrees. **Faculty:** 305 full-time faculty, 65% are are members of minority groups. 0% of classes are taught by teaching assistants.

ACADEMICS

Degrees: bachelor's, first professional, master's. **Classes:** Most classes have 10-19 students. **Majors with Highest Enrollment:** Audiology/Audiologist and Speech-Language Pathology/Pathologist; Medicine; Registered Nursing/Registered Nurse. **Special Study Options:** distance learning. **Combined degree programs:** MD/PhD. **Disability Services:** Special programs offered to physically disabled students include tape recorders, tutors. **Career services:** Alumni network, alumni services, career/job search classes, career assessment, internships, regional alumni.

FACILITIES

Housing: apartments for married students, apartments for single students. 85% of campus accessible to physically disabled.

CAMPUS LIFE

Environment: Metropolis. **Activities:** yearbook. 15 registered organizations, 2 honor societies, 1 religous organization. **On-Campus Highlights:** Student Lounge, Computer lab (100+ stations), Library, Au Bon Pain. **Environmental Initiatives:** Launched new recycling commitment and awareness campaign on Earth Day 2008.

ADMISSIONS

Freshman Academic Profile: 100% in top 50% of high school class. Minimum paper TOEFL 550. Freshman Admission Requirements. **Transfer Admission Requirements:** college transcript(s), essay or personal statement, Minimum college GPA of 2.7 required. Lowest grade transferable C. **General Admission Information:** Nonfall registration not accepted. Neither credit nor placement offered for CEEB Advanced Placement tests.

COSTS AND FINANCIAL AID

Required Forms and Deadlines: FAFSA, Institution's own financial aid form, Business/Farm Supplement. **Types of Aid:** *Need-based scholarships/grants:* Federal Pell, SEOG, state scholarships/grants, private scholarships, the school's own gift aid. *Loans:* Subsidized Stafford, Unsubsidized Stafford, PLUS, Federal Perkins, Federal Nursing, college/university loans from institutional funds, credit-based loans. *Student Employment:* Federal Work-Study Program available. Institutional employment available. Off-campus job opportunities are fair. **Financial Aid Statistics:** 74% undergrads receive need-based scholarship or grant aid. 13% undergrads receive non-need-based scholarship or grant aid. 84% undergrads receive need-based self-help aid. 0% undergrads receive athletic scholarships. 0% freshmen, 69% undergrads receive any aid. **Criteria for awarding institutional aid:** *Non-need-based:* academics, leadership, minority status.

RUSSELL SAGE COLLEGE

Office of Admissions, Troy, NY 12180
Phone: 518-244-2217 • **Financial Aid Phone:** 518-244-4525
E-mail: rscadm@sage.edu • **CEEB Code:** 2764
Fax: 518-244-6880 • **Website:** www.sage.edu/RSC • **ACT Code:** 2876

This private school was founded in 1916. It has a 8-acre campus.

RATINGS

Admissions Selectivity Rating: 84   Fire Safety Rating: 66

STUDENTS AND FACULTY

Enrollment: 801. **Student Body:** 100% female, 0% male, 9% out-of-state, 0% international. Asian 2%, African American 4%, Caucasian 77%, Hispanic 3%, Native American <1%
Retention and Graduation: 79% freshmen return for sophomore year. 46% freshmen graduate within 4 years. 62% freshmen graduate within 6 years. 48% grads go on to further study within 1 year. 24% grads pursue arts and sciences degrees. 5% grads pursue business degrees. **Faculty:** 61 full-time faculty, 87% hold PhDs, 61% are are members of minority groups, 7% are women. 0% of classes are taught by teaching assistants.

ACADEMICS

Degrees: bachelor's. **Classes:** Most classes have 10-19 students. Most lab/discussion sessions have fewer than 10 students. **Majors with Highest Enroll-**

ment: Education; Psychology. **Special Study Options:** Accelerated program, cooperative education program, cross-registration, distance learning, double major, honors program, independent study, internships, liberal arts/career combination, student-designed major, study abroad, teacher certification program. **Combined degree programs:** BA/JD, BA/MEng. **Disability Services:** Special programs offered to physically disabled students include tutors. **Career services:** alumni services, career/job search classes, career assessment, internships. Career services highlights include Women in the World Curriculum.

FACILITIES

Housing: women's dorms, Honors Housing, Over 21 Senior Housing, Spanish and French Housing, Returning Adult Housing. 70% of campus accessible to physically disabled. **Special Academic Facilities/Equipment:** Schacht fine arts center (home of NYS Theatre Institute), Robison Athletic and Recreational Ctr., State of the Art lab and research facilities in biology, Historic 19th Century Brownstones. **Computers:** Students can register for classes online. Administrative functions (other than registration) can be performed online.

CAMPUS LIFE

Environment: City. **Activities:** Choral groups, dance, drama/theater, literary magazine, music ensembles, musical theater, student government, student newspaper, yearbook. 40 registered organizations, 14 honor societies, 4 religious organizations. **Athletics (Intercollegiate):** *Women:* basketball, soccer, softball, tennis, volleyball. **On-Campus Highlights:** New York State Theatre Institute, Buchman Pavilion, Helen M. Upton Women's Center, Robison Athletic and Recreation Center, James L. Meader Little Theater.

ADMISSIONS

Freshman Academic Profile: Average high school GPA 3.4. 30% in top 10% of high school class, 67% in top 25% of high school class, 95% in top 50% of high school class. SAT Math middle 50% range 480-590. SAT Critical Reading middle 50% range 490-620. ACT middle 50% range 21-25. Minimum paper TOEFL 550. **Basis for Candidate Selection:** *Very important factors considered include:* rigor of secondary school record, standardized test scores. *Important factors considered include:* Class rank, recommendation(s), interview. *Other factors considered include:* application essay, academic GPA, alumni/ae relation, character/personal qualities, extracurricular activities, talent/ability, volunteer work, work experience. **Freshman Admission Requirements:** High school diploma is required and GED is accepted. *Academic units required:* 4 English, 3 mathematics, 3 science, (3 science labs), 2 foreign language, 4 social studies. **Freshman Admission Statistics:** 394 applied, 81% admitted, 36% enrolled. **Transfer Admission Requirements:** High school transcript, college transcript(s), statement of good standing from prior institution(s). Minimum college GPA of 2.5 required. Lowest grade transferable C-. **General Admission Information:** Application Fee $30. Early decision application deadline 12/1. Notification on a rolling basis, beginning on or about 12/15. Nonfall registration accepted. Admission may be deferred for a maximum of 1 year. Credit and/or placement offered for CEEB Advanced Placement tests.

COSTS AND FINANCIAL AID

Annual tuition $23,800. Room and board $8,370. Required fees $870. Average book expense $900. **Required Forms and Deadlines:** FAFSA, State aid form. **Notification of Awards:** Applicants will be notified of awards on a rolling basis beginning 3/12. **Types of Aid:** *Need-based scholarships/grants:* Federal Pell, SEOG, state scholarships/grants, private scholarships, the school's own gift aid, Federal Nursing Scholarships. *Loans:* Subsidized Stafford, Unsubsidized Stafford, PLUS, Federal Perkins. *Student Employment:* Highest amount earned per year from on-campus jobs $3,000. Off-campus job opportunities are good. **Financial Aid Statistics:** 64% freshmen, 61% undergrads receive need-based scholarship or grant aid. 64% freshmen, 57% undergrads receive non-need-based scholarship or grant aid. 100% freshmen, 99% undergrads receive need-based self-help aid. 0% freshmen, 0% undergrads receive athletic scholarships. 94% freshmen, 89% undergrads receive any aid. 91% undergrads borrow to pay for school. **Criteria for awarding institutional aid:** *Non-need-based:* academics, alumni affiliation.

RUST COLLEGE

150 Rust Avenue, Holly Springs, MS 38635

Phone: 662-252-8000 · **Financial Aid Phone:** 662-252-8000, x4062
E-mail: jb_mcdonald@rustcollege.edu
Fax: 662-252-8895 · **Website:** www.rustcollege.edu · **ACT Code:** 2240

This private school, affiliated with the Moravian Church, was founded in 1866. It has a 126-acre campus.

RATINGS

Admissions Selectivity Rating: 73   Fire Safety Rating: 60*

STUDENTS AND FACULTY

Enrollment: 922. **Student Body:** 63% female, 37% male, 5% international. Asian 0%, African American 93%, Caucasian 1%, Hispanic 0%, Native American <1%
Retention and Graduation: 53% freshmen return for sophomore year. 14% freshmen graduate within 4 years. 28% freshmen graduate within 6 years. **Faculty:** 48 full-time faculty, 40% are are members of minority groups, 90% are women. 0% of classes are taught by teaching assistants.

ACADEMICS

Degrees: associate, bachelor's. **Classes:** Most classes have 10-19 students. Most lab/discussion sessions have 10-19 students. **Majors with Highest Enrollment:** Computer and Information Sciences; Biology/Biological Sciences; Business/Commerce. **Special Study Options:** double major, honors program, independent study, internships, liberal arts/career combination, study abroad, teacher certification program, weekend college, Advanced Placement Program, Adult Pathway Program. Dual enrollment includes three Dual Degree Programs with other institutions and one Cooperative Program with another institution. **Disability Services:** Special programs offered to physically disabled students include tutors.

FACILITIES

Housing: men's dorms, women's dorms, Honors. 100% of campus accessible to physically disabled. **Special Academic Facilities/Equipment:** Dr. Ron Trojcak collection of African tribal art which includes fabrics, masks and statues used for religious ceremonies, weddings, ritual dance and funerals.

CAMPUS LIFE

Environment: Rural. **Activities:** Choral groups, concert band, dance, drama/theater, marching band, music ensembles, pep band, radio station, student government, student newspaper, television station, yearbook, International Student Organization. 35 registered organizations, 7 honor societies, 5 religious organizations. 3 fraternities, 4 sororities. **Athletics (Intercollegiate):** *Men:* baseball, basketball, cheerleading, cross-country, soccer, tennis, track/field (outdoor). *Women:* basketball, cheerleading, cross-country, softball, tennis, track/field (outdoor), volleyball. **On-Campus Highlights:** Leontyne Price Library Exhibits, James Elam Chapel, McDonald Science Building, David Beckley Conference Center, McMillan Multi-Purpose Center.

ADMISSIONS

Freshman Academic Profile: 98% from public high schools. ACT middle 50% range 14-21. Minimum paper TOEFL 540. **Basis for Candidate Selection:** *Very important factors considered include:* first generation. *Important factors considered include:* Class rank, application essay, academic GPA, recommendation(s), rigor of secondary school record, standardized test scores, alumni/ae relation, character/personal qualities, level of applicant's interest. *Other factors considered include:* talent/ability, volunteer work. **Freshman Admission Requirements:** High school diploma is required and GED is accepted. *Academic units required:* 4 English, 3 mathematics, 3 science, 3 social studies, 6 academic electives. **Freshman Admission Statistics:** 3,983 applied, 46% admitted, 15% enrolled. **Transfer Admission Requirements:** High school transcript, college transcript(s), statement of good standing from prior institution(s). Minimum college GPA of 2.0 required. Lowest grade transferable C. **General Admission Information:** Application Fee $10. Notification on a rolling basis, beginning on or about 7/15. Nonfall registration accepted. Admission may be deferred for a maximum of one year. Credit offered for CEEB Advanced Placement tests.

COSTS AND FINANCIAL AID

Annual tuition $8,100. Room and board $3,700. Average book expense $250. **Required Forms and Deadlines:** FAFSA, Institution's own financial aid form. **Notification of Awards:** Applicants will be notified of awards on a rolling basis beginning 6/9. **Types of Aid:** *Need-based scholarships/grants:* Federal Pell, SEOG, state scholarships/grants, private scholarships, United Negro College Fund. *Loans:* Subsidized Stafford, Unsubsidized Stafford, PLUS, United Methodist. *Student Employment:* Highest amount earned per year from on-campus jobs $1,600. **Financial Aid Statistics:** 86% freshmen, 87% undergrads receive need-based scholarship or grant aid. 43% freshmen, 29% undergrads receive non-need-based scholarship or grant aid. 87% freshmen, 89% undergrads receive need-based self-help aid. 0% freshmen, 0% undergrads receive athletic scholarships. 83% undergrads borrow to pay for school. Average cumulative indebtedness $18,389. **Criteria for awarding institutional aid:** *Non-need-based:* academics, leadership, music/drama, religious affiliation, state/district residency.

RUTGERS, THE STATE UNIVERSITY OF NEW JERSEY—CAMDEN

406 Penn Street, Camden, NJ 8102
Phone: 856-225-6104 · **Financial Aid Phone:** 732-932-7305
E-mail: admissions@ugadm.rutgers.edu · **CEEB Code:** 2765
Fax: 856-225-6498 · **Website:** Office of Institutional Research · **ACT Code:** 2592

This public school was founded in 1927. It has a 25-acre campus.

RATINGS

Admissions Selectivity Rating: 87   **Fire Safety Rating:** 74

STUDENTS AND FACULTY

Enrollment: 4,777. **Student Body:** 55% female, 45% male, 2% out-of-state, 1% international (20 countries represented). Asian 9%, African American 17%, Caucasian 56%, Hispanic 11%, Native American <1%
Retention and Graduation: 81% freshmen return for sophomore year. 27% freshmen graduate within 4 years. 52% freshmen graduate within 6 years. **Faculty:** 296 full-time faculty, 98% hold PhDs, 44% are are members of minority groups, 16% are women. 4% of classes are taught by teaching assistants.

ACADEMICS

Degrees: bachelor's, master's. **Majors with Highest Enrollment:** Psychology; Registered Nursing/Registered Nurse; Business Administration and Management. **Special Study Options:** Accelerated program, cooperative education program, cross-registration, distance learning, double major, dual enrollment, English as a Second Language (ESL), exchange student program (domestic), honors program, independent study, internships, liberal arts/career combination, student-designed major, study abroad, teacher certification program, weekend college, Cooperative baccalaureate program in engineering with School of Engineering (New Brunswick Campus). Interdisciplinary programs in African-American studies, general science. Cooperative baccalaureate in medical technology with approved hospital. B.A./M.A. in English, history, liberal studies or psychology; B.A./M.S. in biology, chemistry or mathematics (with the Graduate School-Camden). B.A. in economics or political science/Master of Public Administration (with the Graduate School-Camden). **Combined degree programs:** BA/MD, 2+4 Pharm. D. **Disability Services:** Special programs offered to physically disabled students include note-taking services, reader services, tape recorders, tutors.

FACILITIES

Housing: Coed dorms, special housing for disabled students, apartments for single students. **Computers:** Students can register for classes online. Administrative functions (other than registration) can be performed online.

CAMPUS LIFE

Environment: City. **Activities:** drama/theater, literary magazine, radio station, student government, yearbook, International Student Organization. 50 registered organizations, 11 honor societies, 4 fraternities, 4 sororities. **Athletics (Intercollegiate):** *Men:* baseball, basketball, cross-country, golf, soccer, track/field (outdoor). *Women:* basketball, cross-country, soccer, softball, track/field (outdoor), volleyball.

ADMISSIONS

Freshman Academic Profile: 38% in top 10% of high school class, 74% in top 25% of high school class, 96% in top 50% of high school class. 60% from public high schools. SAT Math middle 50% range 480-580. SAT Critical Reading middle 50% range 450-560. SAT Writing middle 50% range 460-560. Minimum internet-based TOEFL 79. Minimum paper TOEFL 550. **Basis for Candidate Selection:** *Very important factors considered include:* Class rank, academic GPA, rigor of secondary school record, standardized test scores. *Other factors considered include:* application essay, recommendation(s), extracurricular activities, first generation, geographical residence, racial/ethnic status, state residency, volunteer work, work experience. **Freshman Admission Requirements:** High school diploma is required and GED is accepted. *Academic units required:* 4 English, 3 mathematics, 2 science, 2 foreign language, 5 academic electives. **Freshman Admission Statistics:** 7,437 applied, 59% admitted, 11% enrolled. **Transfer Admission Requirements:** High school transcript, college transcript(s), Minimum college GPA of NA required. **General Admission Information:** Application Fee $65. Regular application deadline 12/1. Nonfall registration accepted. Credit and/or placement offered for CEEB Advanced Placement tests.

COSTS AND FINANCIAL AID

Average book expense $1,550. **Required Forms and Deadlines:** FAFSA. *Student Employment:* Federal Work-Study Program available. Institutional employment available. **Financial Aid Statistics:** 68% freshmen, 65% undergrads receive need-based scholarship or grant aid. 32% freshmen, 17% undergrads re-

ceive non-need-based scholarship or grant aid. 80% freshmen, 89% undergrads receive need-based self-help aid. 0% freshmen, 0% undergrads receive athletic scholarships. 70% freshmen, 72% undergrads receive any aid. 76% undergrads borrow to pay for school. Average cumulative indebtedness $22,212.

RUTGERS, THE STATE UNIVERSITY OF NEW JERSEY—NEW BRUNSWICK

Best 380

Rutgers Visitor Center, 100 Sutphen Road, Piscataway, NJ 08854-8097
Phone: 732-932-4636 · **Financial Aid Phone:** 732-932-7305
E-mail: admissions@ugadm.rutgers.edu · **CEEB Code:** 2765
Fax: 732-445-0237 · **Website:** www.rutgers.edu · **ACT Code:** 2592

This public school was founded in 1766. It has a 2695-acre campus.

RATINGS

Admissions Selectivity Rating: 86   **Fire Safety Rating:** 80

STUDENTS AND FACULTY

Enrollment: 25,951. **Student Body:** 50% female, 50% male, 6% out-of-state, 5% international (117 countries represented). Asian 33%, African American 10%, Caucasian 58%, Hispanic 16%, Native American <1%
Retention and Graduation: 91% freshmen return for sophomore year. 57% freshmen graduate within 4 years. 79% freshmen graduate within 6 years. **Faculty:** 1,964 full-time faculty, 99% hold PhDs, 46% are are members of minority groups, 18% are women. 20% of classes are taught by teaching assistants.

ACADEMICS

Degrees: bachelor's, master's, post-master's certificate. **Majors with Highest Enrollment:** Engineering; Biology/Biological Sciences. **Special Study Options:** Accelerated program, cooperative education program, cross-registration, distance learning, double major, dual enrollment, English as a Second Language (ESL), exchange student program (domestic), honors program, independent study, internships, liberal arts/career combination, student-designed major, study abroad, teacher certification program, 5-year B.A. or B.S./MBA program in Rutgers Business School; BS in business Discipline/MBA; BA or BS in Science Discipline/MBA; 8-year Bachelor/Medical Dual Degree program with UMDNJ-Robert Wood Johnson Medical School; 5-year BS/BS in Bioenvironmental Engineering with the School of Engineering; 5-year accelerated baccalaureate-M.B.A with Rutgers Business School.; Bureau of Engineering Research, supported by the university, industry, state and federal government, provides research opportunities for students and faculty; Continuing professional education; Exchange program between School of Engineering and the City University of London for qualified students majoring in civil, electrical, or mechanical engineering; 5-year (BA/BS degree) program in liberal arts and engineering; 5-year BA or BS/M.Ed. with the Graduate School of Education; Interdepartmental programs and certificate programs are available; Study Abroad in England, France, Italy,Ireland,Germany,Greece, Mexico, Israel, Australia, India, Japan, Netherlands, Scotland, South Africa, South Korea and Spain; Alumnae externship program; Language and Cultural House Program; 5-year BA/BS in cooperation with Rutgers Business School.; B.A./Master of communication and information studies (with SCILS); B.A./MLER (with School of Management and Labor Relations); Baccalaureate/M.C.R.P., M.P.H., or M.P.P with EJB School of Planning and Public Policy;Baccalaureate in Business major/Master of Human Resource Management (with School of Management and Labor Relations {SMLR}). **Combined degree programs:** BA/MD, 5-year BAor BS/MPP, 6-year Pharm.D., 6-year Bach. **Disability Services:** Special programs offered to physically disabled students include note-taking services, reader services, tape recorders, tutors. **Career services:** Alumni network, alumni services, career/job search classes, career assessment, internships, regional alumni.

FACILITIES

Housing: Coed dorms, men's dorms, special housing for international students, women's dorms, fraternity/sorority housing, apartments for married students, cooperative housing, apartments for single students, Theme HousingSpecial interest housing, language and cultural houses, substance-free house, Math/Science Engineering House for women, first-year residence, transfer center, residence for single mothers and children. **Special Academic Facilities/Equipment:** Geology Museum, Zimmerli Museum, Mason Gross Performing Arts Center; NJ Museum of Agriculture; NJ Film Festival/RU Film Co-op; Rutgers Gardens **Computers:** Students can register for classes online. Administrative functions (other than registration) can be performed online.

CAMPUS LIFE

Environment: Town. **Activities:** Choral groups, concert band, dance, drama/theater, jazz band, literary magazine, marching band, music ensembles, musical theater, opera, pep band, radio station, student government, student newspaper, student-run film society, symphony orchestra, television station, yearbook, Campus Ministries, International Student Organization. 400 registered organizations, 24 honor societies, 29 fraternities, 15 sororities. **Athletics (Intercollegiate):** *Men:* baseball, basketball, cheerleading, cross-country, diving, football, golf, lacrosse, soccer, track/field (outdoor), track/field (indoor), wrestling. *Women:* basketball, cheerleading, crew/rowing, cross-country, diving, field hockey, golf, gymnastics, lacrosse, soccer, softball, swimming, tennis, track/field (outdoor), track/field (indoor), volleyball. **On-Campus Highlights:** Geology Museum, Jane Voorhees Zimmereli Art Museum, Rutgers Display Gardens and Heylar Woods, Hutchenson Memorial Forest.

ADMISSIONS

Freshman Academic Profile: 22% in top 10% of high school class, 52% in top 25% of high school class, 88% in top 50% of high school class. SAT Math middle 50% range 570-690. SAT Critical Reading middle 50% range 520-640. SAT Writing middle 50% range 540-650. ACT middle 50% range 25-31. Minimum paper TOEFL 550. **Basis for Candidate Selection:** *Very important factors considered include:* Class rank, academic GPA, rigor of secondary school record, standardized test scores. *Other factors considered include:* application essay, recommendation(s), extracurricular activities, first generation, geographical residence, interview, racial/ethnic status, state residency, talent/ability, volunteer work, work experience. **Freshman Admission Requirements:** High school diploma is required and GED is accepted. *Academic units required:* 4 English, 3 mathematics, 2 science, 2 foreign language, 5 academic electives. **Freshman Admission Statistics:** 30,631 applied, 60% admitted, 35% enrolled. **Transfer Admission Requirements:** High school transcript, college transcript(s), Lowest grade transferable C. **General Admission Information:** Application Fee $65. Regular notification 3/1. Nonfall registration accepted. Credit and/or placement offered for CEEB Advanced Placement tests.

COSTS AND FINANCIAL AID

Annual out-of-state tuition $24,742. Room and board $11,578. Required fees $2,781. Average book expense $1,550. **Required Forms and Deadlines:** FAFSA. **Notification of Awards:** Applicants will be notified of awards on a rolling basis beginning 2/1. **Types of Aid:** *Need-based scholarships/grants:* Federal Pell, SEOG, state scholarships/grants, private scholarships, the school's own gift aid, Outside Scholarships. *Loans:* Direct Subsidized Stafford, Direct Unsubsidized Stafford, Direct PLUS, Federal Perkins, state loans, college/university loans from institutional funds, Other Educational Loans. *Student Employment:* Highest amount earned per year from on-campus jobs $1,374. **Financial Aid Statistics:** 63% freshmen, 64% undergrads receive need-based scholarship or grant aid. 26% freshmen, 20% undergrads receive non-need-based scholarship or grant aid. 87% freshmen, 86% undergrads receive need-based self-help aid. 2% freshmen, 1% undergrads receive athletic scholarships. 67% freshmen, 69% undergrads receive any aid. 57% undergrads borrow to pay for school. Average cumulative indebtedness $20,844. **Criteria for awarding institutional aid:** *Non-need-based:* academics, alumni affiliation, art, athletics, leadership, minority status, music/drama, religious affiliation.

RUTGERS, THE STATE UNIVERSITY OF NEW JERSEY—NEWARK CAMPUS

249 University Avenue, Newark, NJ 07102-1896
Phone: 973-353-5205 · **Financial Aid Phone:** 732-932-7305
E-mail: admissions@ugadm.rutgers.edu · **CEEB Code:** 2765
Fax: 973-353-1440 · **ACT Code:** 2592

This public school was founded in 1930. It has a 36-acre campus.

RATINGS

Admissions Selectivity Rating: 82   Fire Safety Rating: 75

STUDENTS AND FACULTY

Enrollment: 6,748. **Student Body:** 50% female, 50% male, 2% out-of-state, 3% international (84 countries represented). Asian 22%, African American 19%, Caucasian 26%, Hispanic 24%, Native American <1%
Retention and Graduation: 82% freshmen return for sophomore year. 32% freshmen graduate within 4 years. 67% freshmen graduate within 6 years. **Faculty:** 492 full-time faculty, 98% hold PhDs, 32% are are members of minority groups, 21% are women. 9% of classes are taught by teaching assistants.

ACADEMICS

Degrees: bachelor's, master's. **Majors with Highest Enrollment:** Biology/Biological Sciences; Registered Nursing/Registered Nurse; Business Administration and Management. **Special Study Options:** Accelerated program, cooperative education program, cross-registration, distance learning, double major, dual enrollment, English as a Second Language (ESL), exchange student program (domestic), honors program, independent study, internships, liberal arts/career combination, student-designed major, study abroad, teacher certification program, weekend college, 5-year baccalaureate-MBA with Rutgers Business School; Baccalaureate/M.A. in Criminal Justice with the School of Criminal Justice; Baccalaureate/MPA with the School of Public Affairs and Administration; Cooperative baccalaureate program with School of Engineering (New Brunswick campus); Cooperative baccalaureate in medical technology with affiliated hospitals; Interdisciplinary programs in archaeology, international affairs, legal studies, women's studies; continuing professional education; The College of Nursing offers a program on the New Brunswick Campus. Students are admitted in the fall semester only; Baccalaureate in Business Major/Master of Human Resource Management (with School of Management and Labor Relations in New Brunswick); Baccalaureate-master's dual degree programs with the School of Criminal Justice and Rutgers Business School. The Honors College of Rutgers University's Newark College of Arts and Sciences is a four-year program, a college within a college, providing its by-invitation-only students with opportunities for enrichment both in and outside of the classroom. Students invited to join the Honors College benefit from small classes with first-rate faculty, co-curricular internships in major corporations and other institutions, and other special options. Reserved dormitory space, a substantial scholarship program, and research assistantships with faculty members combine to make the RU-Newark Honors College experience unique. For additional information, visit the Honors College web site at http://honorsnewark.rutgers.edu or call 973-353-5860. BA/MD, BA/MA. **Disability Services:** Special programs offered to physically disabled students include note-taking services, reader services, tape recorders, tutors.

FACILITIES

Housing: Coed dorms, fraternity/sorority housing, apartments for single students. **Special Academic Facilities/Equipment:** Institute of Jazz Studies, TV/Radio media center, Institute of Animal Behavior, Center for Crime Prevention Studies, Center for Negotiation and Conflict Resolution, Center for Molecular and Behaviorial Neuroscience, Center for Nursing Research. **Computers:** Students can register for classes online. Administrative functions (other than registration) can be performed online.

CAMPUS LIFE

Activities: Choral groups, drama/theater, radio station, student government, student newspaper, yearbook, International Student Organization. 80 registered organizations, 16 honor societies, 7 fraternities, 7 sororities. **Athletics (Intercollegiate):** *Men:* baseball, basketball, soccer, tennis, volleyball. *Women:* basketball, softball, tennis, volleyball. **On-Campus Highlights:** The Arts at Rutgers Newark, Robeson Campus Center, Athletic Center, Bradley Hall/Bookstore, Dana Library.

ADMISSIONS

Freshman Academic Profile: 17% in top 10% of high school class, 43% in top 25% of high school class, 80% in top 50% of high school class. SAT Math middle 50% range 500-608. SAT Critical Reading middle 50% range 460-550. SAT Writing middle 50% range 480-560. Minimum paper TOEFL 550. **Basis for Candidate Selection:** *Very important factors considered include:* Class rank, academic GPA, rigor of secondary school record, standardized test scores. *Other factors considered include:* application essay, recommendation(s), extracurricular activities, first generation, geographical residence, racial/ethnic status, state residency, volunteer work, work experience. **Freshman Admission Requirements:** High school diploma is required and GED is accepted. *Academic units required:* 4 English, 3 mathematics, 2 science, 2 foreign language, 5 academic electives. **Freshman Admission Statistics:** 13,282 applied, 54% admitted, 15% enrolled. **Transfer Admission Requirements:** High school transcript, college transcript(s), Minimum college GPA of na required. **General Admission Information:** Application Fee $65. Regular notification 2/28. Nonfall registration accepted. Credit and/or placement offered for CEEB Advanced Placement tests.

COSTS AND FINANCIAL AID

Average book expense $1,550. **Required Forms and Deadlines:** FAFSA. **Notification of Awards:** Applicants will be notified of awards on a rolling basis beginning 2/1. **Types of Aid:** *Need-based scholarships/grants:* Federal Pell, SEOG, state scholarships/grants, private scholarships, the school's own gift aid, Outside Scholarships. *Loans:* Direct Subsidized Stafford, Direct Unsubsidized Stafford, Direct PLUS, Federal Perkins, state loans, college/university loans from institutional funds, Other Educational Loans. **Financial Aid Statistics:** 78% freshmen, 82% undergrads receive need-based scholarship or grant aid. 16% freshmen, 11% undergrads receive non-need-based scholarship or grant aid. 77% freshmen, 78% undergrads receive need-based self-help aid. 0%

freshmen, 0% undergrads receive athletic scholarships. 80% freshmen, 80% undergrads receive any aid. 52% undergrads borrow to pay for school. Average cumulative indebtedness $20,691. **Criteria for awarding institutional aid:** *Non-need-based:* academics, alumni affiliation, art, athletics, job skills, minority status, music/drama, religious affiliation, state/district residency.

SACRED HEART UNIVERSITY

5151 Park Avenue, Fairfield, CT 6825
Phone: 203-371-7880 · **Financial Aid Phone:** 203-371-7980
E-mail: enroll@sacredheart.edu · **CEEB Code:** 3780
Fax: 203-365-7607 · **Website:** www.sacredheart.edu · **ACT Code:** 589

This private school, affiliated with the Roman Catholic Church, was founded in 1963. It has a 67-acre campus.

RATINGS

Admissions Selectivity Rating: 79   **Fire Safety Rating:** 91

STUDENTS AND FACULTY

Enrollment: 4,904. **Student Body:** 64% female, 36% male, 60% out-of-state, 1% international (18 countries represented). Asian 2%, African American 4%, Caucasian 69%, Hispanic 7%, Native American <1%
Retention and Graduation: 82% freshmen return for sophomore year. 59% freshmen graduate within 4 years. 67% freshmen graduate within 6 years. 47% grads go on to further study within 1 year. **Faculty:** 261 full-time faculty, 77% hold PhDs, 54% are are members of minority groups, 11% are women. 0% of classes are taught by teaching assistants.

ACADEMICS

Degrees: associate, bachelor's, certificate, master's, post-bachelor's certificate, post-master's certificate. **Classes:** Most classes have 20-29 students. **Majors with Highest Enrollment:** Psychology; Nursing Science; Business Administration and Management. **Special Study Options:** Accelerated program, cooperative education program, cross-registration, distance learning, double major, English as a Second Language (ESL), exchange student program (domestic), honors program, independent study, internships, liberal arts/career combination, student-designed major, study abroad, teacher certification program, weekend college, Off-campus study: Summer program in Luxembourg, Summer, Winter Intercession, Spring Break, and Semester in Ireland. Sponsored and approved study abroad programs worldwide. **Combined degree programs:** combined degree programs in physical therapy (doctoral) and occupational therapy (masters). Accelerated 5th year M.B.A. program. Accelerated MSCIS (Computer Information Systems). **Honors programs:** The Thomas More School of Honors Studies offers a challenging curriculum of Honors-level courses. These studies will provide each student with the quest for the full meaning of our humanity exploring the following three components: (1) the cognitive, (2) the aesthetic and (3) the moral or ethical. The Program also includes advisement, cultural events, dinners with the University President and other events. **Combined degree programs:** BA/MA, BA/S/MBA; BA/S/DPT; BA/S/MSOT; BA/S/MAT; BS/MSCIS; BA/S/MACJ. **Disability Services:** Special programs offered to physically disabled students include note-taking services, reader services, tape recorders, tutors. **Career services:** Alumni network, alumni services, career/job search classes, career assessment, internships, regional alumni. The Office of Career Development works diligently to facilitate professional internship opportunities for students in all academic majors and career interests.

FACILITIES

Housing: Coed dorms, special housing for disabled students, apartments for single students, Wellness Housing, Thematic floors; living & learning communities for specific academic programs. 90% of campus accessible to physically disabled. **Special Academic Facilities/Equipment:** WHRT student radio station, WSHU National Public Radio, Edgerton Center for the Performing Arts, Gallery of Contemporary Art. **Computers:** 100% of classrooms, 100% of dorms, 100% of libraries, 100% of dining areas, 100% of student union, 100% of common outdoor areas have wireless network access. Students can register for classes online. Administrative functions (other than registration) can be performed online. Undergraduates are required to own a computer.

CAMPUS LIFE

Environment: Town. **Activities:** Choral groups, concert band, dance, drama/theater, jazz band, literary magazine, marching band, music ensembles, musi-

cal theater, pep band, radio station, student government, student newspaper, student-run film society, television station, yearbook, Campus Ministries, International Student Organization. 80 registered organizations, 14 honor societies, 4 religious organizations. 4 fraternities, 6 sororities. **Athletics (Intercollegiate):** *Men:* baseball, basketball, cross-country, fencing, football, golf, ice hockey, lacrosse, soccer, tennis, track/field (outdoor), track/field (indoor), volleyball, wrestling. *Women:* basketball, bowling, crew/rowing, cross-country, diving, equestrian sports, fencing, field hockey, golf, ice hockey, lacrosse, soccer, softball, swimming, tennis, track/field (outdoor), track/field (indoor), volleyball. **On-Campus Highlights:** Pitt Health and Recreation Center, Edgerton Center for Performing Arts, Holy Grounds Café, Ryan-Matura Library, Hawley Lounge, New University Chapel (Chapel of the Holy Spirit) opened in Fall 2009. **Environmental Initiatives:** Lighting renewal for all new construction and renovations, as well as low energy bulbs & motion detection systems. Transfer from 28 chemicals to 6 green chemicals for custodial work. Free shuttle service for students to reduce the number of cars traveling between campuses.

ADMISSIONS

Freshman Academic Profile: Average high school GPA 3.39. SAT Math middle 50% range 487-623. SAT Critical Reading middle 50% range 468-606. ACT middle 50% range 21-28. Minimum internet-based TOEFL 80. Minimum paper TOEFL 550. **Basis for Candidate Selection:** *Very important factors considered include:* academic GPA, rigor of secondary school record. *Important factors considered include:* Class rank, application essay, recommendation(s), character/personal qualities, extracurricular activities, interview, talent/ability, volunteer work, work experience. *Other factors considered include:* standardized test scores, alumni/ae relation, first generation, geographical residence, level of applicant's interest, racial/ethnic status, religious affiliation/commitment, state residency. **Freshman Admission Requirements:** High school diploma is required and GED is accepted. *Academic units required:* 4 English, 3 mathematics, 3 science, (1 science labs), 2 foreign language, 3 social studies, 3 history, 3 academic electives. **Freshman Admission Statistics:** 9,114 applied, 57% admitted, 27% enrolled. **Transfer Admission Requirements:** High school transcript, college transcript(s), essay or personal statement, Minimum college GPA of 2.5 required. Lowest grade transferable C-. **General Admission Information:** Application Fee $50. Early decision application deadline 12/1. Notification on a rolling basis, beginning on or about 1/1. Nonfall registration accepted. Admission may be deferred for a maximum of 1 year. Credit and/or placement offered for CEEB Advanced Placement tests.

COSTS AND FINANCIAL AID

Annual tuition $35,500. Room and board $13,514. Required fees $250. Average book expense $1,200. **Required Forms and Deadlines:** FAFSA, CSS/Financial Aid PROFILE, Noncustodial PROFILE. **Notification of Awards:** Applicants will be notified of awards on a rolling basis beginning 3/1. **Types of Aid:** *Need-based scholarships/grants:* Federal Pell, SEOG, state scholarships/grants, private scholarships, the school's own gift aid. *Loans:* Direct Subsidized Stafford, Direct Unsubsidized Stafford, Direct PLUS, Subsidized Stafford, Unsubsidized Stafford, PLUS, Federal Perkins, state loans, Alternative loans. *Student Employment:* Federal Work-Study Program available. Institutional employment available. Off-campus job opportunities are excellent. **Financial Aid Statistics:** 79% freshmen, 79% undergrads receive need-based scholarship or grant aid. 12% freshmen, 11% undergrads receive non-need-based scholarship or grant aid. 87% freshmen, 92% undergrads receive need-based self-help aid. 5% freshmen, 5% undergrads receive athletic scholarships. 73% freshmen, 67% undergrads receive any aid. 80% undergrads borrow to pay for school. Average cumulative indebtedness $24,576. **Criteria for awarding institutional aid:** *Non-need-based:* academics, alumni affiliation, art, athletics, leadership, minority status, music/drama.

SAGINAW VALLEY STATE UNIVERSITY

7400 Bay Road, University Center, MI 48710
Phone: 989-964-4200 · **Financial Aid Phone:** 989-964-4103
E-mail: admissions@svsu.edu · **CEEB Code:** 1766
Fax: 989-790-0180 · **Website:** www.svsu.edu · **ACT Code:** 2057

This public school was founded in 1963. It has a 782-acre campus.

RATINGS

Admissions Selectivity Rating: 78   **Fire Safety Rating:** 62

STUDENTS AND FACULTY

Enrollment: 8,453. **Student Body:** 58% female, 42% male, 1% out-of-state, 5% international (10 countries represented). Asian 1%, African American 11%, Caucasian 72%, Hispanic 4%, Native American <1%
Retention and Graduation: 9% freshmen graduate within 4 years. 20% grads go on to further study within 1 year. **Faculty:** 309 full-time faculty, 82% hold

PhDs, 44% are are members of minority groups. 0% of classes are taught by teaching assistants.

ACADEMICS
Degrees: bachelor's, master's, post-master's certificate. **Classes:** Most classes have 20-29 students. Most lab/discussion sessions have 10-19 students. **Majors with Highest Enrollment:** Registered Nursing/Registered Nurse; Social Work; Criminal Justice/Safety Studies. **Special Study Options:** Accelerated program, cooperative education program, distance learning, double major, dual enrollment, English as a Second Language (ESL), honors program, independent study, internships, student-designed major, study abroad, teacher certification program. **Honors programs:** The University Honors Program allows students to pursue their major and minor degree work, while providing enriched academic experiences in Honors courses, seminars, research projects, and social activities. The Honors experience enables students to work more intensively with active teacher/scholars and to participate in interdisciplinary courses. Honors students will have ample opportunity to develop as critical thinkers, active learners, and problem solvers. **Disability Services:** Special programs offered to physically disabled students include note-taking services, reader services, tutors. **Career services:** career assessment, internships.

FACILITIES
Housing: Coed dorms, special housing for disabled students, apartments for single students, Wellness Housing, Theme Housing. 95% of campus accessible to physically disabled. **Special Academic Facilities/Equipment:** Sculpture gallery, fine arts center, center for health and physical education, independent testing lab, center for economic and business research, applied technology research center. **Computers:** Students can register for classes online. Administrative functions (other than registration) can be performed online.

CAMPUS LIFE
Environment: City. **Activities:** Choral groups, concert band, dance, drama/theater, jazz band, literary magazine, marching band, music ensembles, musical theater, pep band, student government, student newspaper, student-run film society, Campus Ministries, International Student Organization, Model UN. 110 registered organizations, 8 honor societies, 9 religious organizations. 4 fraternities, 7 sororities. **Athletics (Intercollegiate):** *Men:* baseball, basketball, bowling, cheerleading, cross-country, football, golf, soccer, track/field (outdoor), track/field (indoor). *Women:* basketball, cheerleading, cross-country, soccer, softball, tennis, track/field (outdoor), track/field (indoor), volleyball. **On-Campus Highlights:** Student Center, Student Recreation Center (Ryder), Zahnow Library, Arbury Fine Arts Center, University Village. **Environmental Initiatives:** Building buildings with energy savings in mind for many years. Spending consistently through the years for energy and utility conservation measures. Recycling upgrades, cutting down on areas mowed, etc.

ADMISSIONS
Freshman Academic Profile: Average high school GPA 3.3. 21% in top 10% of high school class, 43% in top 25% of high school class, 75% in top 50% of high school class. ACT middle 50% range 19-25. Minimum internet-based TOEFL 61. Minimum paper TOEFL 500. **Basis for Candidate Selection:** *Very important factors considered include:* academic GPA, rigor of secondary school record, standardized test scores. *Other factors considered include:* recommendation(s). **Freshman Admission Requirements:** High school diploma is required and GED is accepted. *Academic units required:* 4 English, 3 mathematics, 2 science, 3 social studies. **Freshman Admission Statistics:** 6,266 applied, 79% admitted, 30% enrolled. **Transfer Admission Requirements:** college transcript(s), Minimum college GPA of 2.0 required. Lowest grade transferable C-. **General Admission Information:** Application Fee $25. Nonfall registration accepted. Admission may be deferred for a maximum of 1. Credit and/or placement offered for CEEB Advanced Placement tests.

COSTS AND FINANCIAL AID
Required Forms and Deadlines: FAFSA. **Notification of Awards:** Applicants will be notified of awards on a rolling basis beginning 3/20. **Types of Aid:** *Need-based scholarships/grants:* Federal Pell, SEOG, state scholarships/grants, private scholarships, the school's own gift aid. *Loans:* Direct Subsidized Stafford, Direct Unsubsidized Stafford, Direct PLUS, state loans, CitiAssist Loans; Signature Student Loans. *Student Employment:* Federal Work-Study Program available. Institutional employment available. Off-campus job opportunities are good. **Financial Aid Statistics:** 71% freshmen, 71% undergrads receive need-based scholarship or grant aid. 0% freshmen, 0% undergrads receive non-need-based scholarship or grant aid. 86% freshmen, 90% undergrads receive need-based self-help aid. 0% freshmen, 0% undergrads receive athletic scholarships. 94% freshmen, 95% undergrads receive any aid. **Criteria for awarding institutional aid:** *Non-need-based:* academics, art, athletics, leadership, minority status, music/drama.

SAINT ANSELM COLLEGE

100 Saint Anselm Drive, Manchester, NH 03102-1310
Phone: 603-641-7500 · **Financial Aid Phone:** 603-641-7110
E-mail: admission@anselm.edu · **CEEB Code:** 3748
Fax: 603-641-7550 · **Website:** www.anselm.edu · **ACT Code:** 2522

This private school, affiliated with the Roman Catholic Church, was founded in 1889. It has a 404-acre campus.

RATINGS
Admissions Selectivity Rating: 85   **Fire Safety Rating:** 77

STUDENTS AND FACULTY
Enrollment: 1,950. **Student Body:** 61% female, 39% male, 76% out-of-state, 1% international (6 countries represented). Asian 1%, African American 2%, Caucasian 80%, Hispanic 3%, Native American <1%
Retention and Graduation: 90% freshmen return for sophomore year. 70% freshmen graduate within 4 years. 75% freshmen graduate within 6 years. 16% grads go on to further study within 1 year. 11% grads pursue arts and sciences degrees. 3% grads pursue law degrees. 1% grads pursue business degrees. 2% grads pursue medical degrees. **Faculty:** 149 full-time faculty, 90% hold PhDs, 53% are are members of minority groups, 10% are women. 0% of classes are taught by teaching assistants.

ACADEMICS
Degrees: bachelor's, certificate. **Classes:** Most classes have 10-19 students. Most lab/discussion sessions have 10-19 students. **Majors with Highest Enrollment:** Registered Nursing/Registered Nurse; Biology; Psychology. **Special Study Options:** cross-registration, honors program, independent study, internships, liberal arts/career combination, study abroad, teacher certification program. **Honors programs:** Honors Program for Presidential Scholars. **Disability Services:** Special programs offered to physically disabled students include note-taking services, reader services, tape recorders, tutors. **Career services:** Alumni network, alumni services, career/job search classes, career assessment, internships, regional alumni.

FACILITIES
Housing: Coed dorms, special housing for disabled students, men's dorms, women's dorms, apartments for single students, Theme Housing, Substance Free Housing. 60% of campus accessible to physically disabled. **Special Academic Facilities/Equipment:** Chapel Art Center, New Hampshire Institute of Politics, Izart Observatory, Koonz Theatre, Comisky Studio (Fine Arts), Poisson Hall. **Computers:** 100% of classrooms, 100% of dorms, 100% of libraries, 100% of dining areas, 100% of student union, have wireless network access. Students can register for classes online. Administrative functions (other than registration) can be performed online.

CAMPUS LIFE
Environment: City. **Activities:** Choral groups, dance, drama/theater, jazz band, literary magazine, musical theater, radio station, student government, student newspaper, television station, yearbook, Campus Ministries, International Student Organization, Model UN. 120 registered organizations, 11 honor societies, 7 religious organizations. **Athletics (Intercollegiate):** *Men:* baseball, basketball, cross-country, football, golf, ice hockey, lacrosse, skiing (downhill/alpine), soccer, tennis. *Women:* basketball, cross-country, field hockey, golf, ice hockey, lacrosse, skiing (downhill/alpine), soccer, softball, tennis, volleyball. **On-Campus Highlights:** Joseph Hall Academic Building, Chapel Arts Center, Davidson Hall Dining Hall, Sullivan Ice Arena & Fitness Center, Abbey Church, Coffee Shop and Pub Cushing Student Center.

ADMISSIONS
Freshman Academic Profile: Average high school GPA 3.24. 27% in top 10% of high school class, 58% in top 25% of high school class, 90% in top 50% of high school class. 65% from public high schools. SAT Math middle 50% range 530-620. SAT Critical Reading middle 50% range 520-610. SAT Writing middle 50% range 520-610. ACT middle 50% range 23-28. Minimum internet-based TOEFL 80. Minimum paper TOEFL 550. **Basis for Candidate Selection:** *Very important factors considered include:* application essay, academic GPA, recommendation(s), rigor of secondary school record, standardized test scores. *Other factors considered include:* Class rank, alumni/ae relation, character/personal qualities, extracurricular activities, geographical residence, racial/ethnic status, state residency, talent/ability, volunteer work, work experience. **Freshman Admission Requirements:** High school diploma is required and GED

is accepted. *Academic units required:* 4 English, 3 mathematics, 3 science, (2 science labs), 2 foreign language, 2 social studies. **Freshman Admission Statistics:** 3,568 applied, 76% admitted, 19% enrolled. **Transfer Admission Requirements:** High school transcript, college transcript(s), essay or personal statement, standardized test scores, statement of good standing from prior institution(s). Minimum college GPA of 2.5 required. Lowest grade transferable C. **General Admission Information:** Application Fee $55. Early decision application deadline 11/15. Regular application deadline 3/1. Notification on a rolling basis, beginning on or about 1/1. Nonfall registration accepted. Admission may be deferred for a maximum of 1 year. Credit and/or placement offered for CEEB Advanced Placement tests.

COSTS AND FINANCIAL AID
Required Forms and Deadlines: FAFSA, CSS/Financial Aid PROFILE, Noncustodial PROFILE. **Notification of Awards:** Applicants will be notified of awards on a rolling basis beginning 3/1. **Types of Aid:** *Need-based scholarships/grants:* Federal Pell, SEOG, state scholarships/grants, private scholarships, the school's own gift aid. *Loans:* Subsidized Stafford, Unsubsidized Stafford, PLUS, Federal Perkins. *Student Employment:* Federal Work-Study Program available. Institutional employment available. Off-campus job opportunities are excellent. **Financial Aid Statistics:** 100% freshmen, 99% undergrads receive need-based scholarship or grant aid. 17% freshmen, 14% undergrads receive non-need-based scholarship or grant aid. 83% freshmen, 84% undergrads receive need-based self-help aid. 8% freshmen, 6% undergrads receive athletic scholarships. 96% freshmen, 98% undergrads receive any aid. 82% undergrads borrow to pay for school. Average cumulative indebtedness $26,813. **Criteria for awarding institutional aid:** *Non-need-based:* academics, alumni affiliation, athletics, state/district residency.

See page 1126.

SAINT ANTHONY COLLEGE OF NURSING

5658 East State Street, Rockford, IL 61108-2468
Phone: 815-227-2141 · **Financial Aid Phone:** 815-395-5089
E-mail: admissions@sacn.edu
Fax: 815-227-2730 · **Website:** www.sacn.edu

This private school, affiliated with the Roman Catholic Church, was founded in 1915.

RATINGS
Admissions Selectivity Rating: 60*   **Fire Safety Rating:** 60*

STUDENTS AND FACULTY
Enrollment: 233. **Student Body:** 88% female, 12% male, 8% out-of-state, 0% international (0 countries represented). Asian 5%, African American 6%, Caucasian 79%, Hispanic 8%, Native American <1%
Faculty: 20 full-time faculty, 15% hold PhDs, 95% are are members of minority groups, 10% are women. 0% of classes are taught by teaching assistants.

ACADEMICS
Degrees: bachelor's, master's. **Majors with Highest Enrollment:** Registered Nursing/Registered Nurse. **Special Study Options:** distance learning, independent study.

FACILITIES
Housing: Private apartments, student plan housing, private rooms.

CAMPUS LIFE
Environment: City. **Activities:** student government, student newspaper 1 registered organization.

ADMISSIONS
Freshman Academic Profile: Minimum paper TOEFL 550. **Basis for Candidate Selection:** *Important factors considered include:* application essay, recommendation(s), interview. *Other factors considered include:* extracurricular activities, volunteer work, work experience. **Freshman Admission Requirements:** High school diploma or equivalent is not required. **Transfer Admission Requirements:** college transcript(s), essay or personal statement, interview, Minimum college GPA of 2.5 required. Lowest grade transferable C. **General Admission Information:** Application Fee $50. Regular application deadline 1/15. Credit offered for CEEB Advanced Placement tests.

COSTS AND FINANCIAL AID
Required Forms and Deadlines: Types of Aid: *Need-based scholarships/grants:* Federal Pell, state scholarships/grants, private scholarships, the school's own gift aid. *Loans:* Subsidized Stafford, Unsubsidized Stafford, PLUS. **Financial Aid Statistics:** 64% undergrads receive need-based scholarship or

grant aid. 2% undergrads receive non-need-based scholarship or grant aid. 96% undergrads receive need-based self-help aid. 0% undergrads receive athletic scholarships. 0% freshmen, 86% undergrads receive any aid. **Criteria for awarding institutional aid:** *Non-need-based:* academics.

SAINT CLOUD STATE UNIVERSITY

720 South 4th Avenue, Saint Cloud, MN 56301-4498
Phone: 320-308-2244 · **Financial Aid Phone:** 320-308-2047
E-mail: scsu4u@stcloudstate.edu · **CEEB Code:** 6679
Fax: 320-308-2243 · **ACT Code:** 2144

This public school was founded in 1869. It has a 920-acre campus.

RATINGS
Admissions Selectivity Rating: 72   **Fire Safety Rating:** 60*

STUDENTS AND FACULTY
Enrollment: 13,120. **Student Body:** 53% female, 47% male, 8% out-of-state, 4% international (85 countries represented). Asian 2%, African American 2%, Caucasian 72%, Hispanic 1%, Native American 1%
Retention and Graduation: 71% freshmen return for sophomore year. **Faculty:** 650 full-time faculty, 80% hold PhDs, 41% are are members of minority groups, 18% are women. 0% of classes are taught by teaching assistants.

ACADEMICS
Degrees: associate, bachelor's, master's, post-bachelor's certificate, post-master's certificate. **Classes:** Most classes have 20-29 students. **Majors with Highest Enrollment:** Mass Communication/Media Studies; Elementary Education and Teaching; Marketing/Marketing Management. **Special Study Options:** Accelerated program, cooperative education program, cross-registration, distance learning, double major, dual enrollment, English as a Second Language (ESL), honors program, independent study, internships, student-designed major, study abroad, teacher certification program. **Disability Services:** Special programs offered to physically disabled students include note-taking services, reader services. **Career services:** Alumni network, alumni services, career/job search classes, career assessment, internships.

FACILITIES
Housing: Coed dorms, special housing for international students 86% of campus accessible to physically disabled. **Special Academic Facilities/Equipment:** Art and anthropology museums, electron microscope, planetarium, G.I.S. and weather labs. **Computers:** Students can register for classes online. Administrative functions (other than registration) can be performed online.

CAMPUS LIFE
Environment: Town. **Activities:** Choral groups, concert band, dance, drama/theater, music ensembles, musical theater, opera, radio station, student government, student newspaper, symphony orchestra, television station. 240 registered organizations, 6 honor societies, 12 religious organizations. 5 fraternities, 4 sororities. **Athletics (Intercollegiate):** *Men:* baseball, basketball, cheerleading, cross-country, diving, football, golf, ice hockey, rugby, swimming, tennis, track/field (outdoor), track/field (indoor), wrestling. *Women:* basketball, cheerleading, cross-country, diving, golf, ice hockey, rugby, skiing (downhill/alpine), soccer, softball, swimming, tennis, track/field (outdoor), track/field (indoor), volleyball. **On-Campus Highlights:** James W. Miller Learning Resource Center, National Hockey Center.

ADMISSIONS
Freshman Academic Profile: 7% in top 10% of high school class, 29% in top 25% of high school class, 76% in top 50% of high school class. 99% from public high schools. ACT middle 50% range 19-24. Minimum paper TOEFL 500. **Basis for Candidate Selection:** *Very important factors considered include:* Class rank, rigor of secondary school record. *Other factors considered include:* application essay, academic GPA, recommendation(s), standardized test scores, extracurricular activities, talent/ability. **Freshman Admission Requirements:** High school diploma is required and GED is accepted. *Academic units required:* 4 English, 3 mathematics, 3 science, (1 science labs), 2 foreign language, 3 social studies, 1 history, 1 Fine Arts. **Freshman Admission Statistics:** 5,912 applied, 78% admitted, 47% enrolled. **Transfer Admission Requirements:** college transcript(s), statement of good standing from prior institution(s). Minimum college GPA of 2.0 required. Lowest grade transferable C. **General Admission Information:** Application Fee $20. Regular application deadline 6/1. Notification on a rolling basis, beginning on or about 9/15. Nonfall registration accepted. Admission may be deferred for a maximum of 24 months. Credit offered for CEEB Advanced Placement tests.

COSTS AND FINANCIAL AID

Annual in-state tuition $4,760. Annual out-of-state tuition $10,332. Room and board $4,688. Required fees $562. Average book expense $1,000. **Required Forms and Deadlines:** FAFSA, Institution's own financial aid form. **Notification of Awards:** Applicants will be notified of awards on a rolling basis beginning 6/3. **Types of Aid:** *Need-based scholarships/grants:* Federal Pell, SEOG, state scholarships/grants, private scholarships, the school's own gift aid. *Loans:* Subsidized Stafford, Unsubsidized Stafford, PLUS, Federal Perkins, state loans. *Student Employment:* Federal Work-Study Program available. Institutional employment available. **Financial Aid Statistics:** 79% freshmen, 76% undergrads receive need-based scholarship or grant aid. 8% freshmen, 5% undergrads receive non-need-based scholarship or grant aid. 95% freshmen, 99% undergrads receive need-based self-help aid. 2% freshmen, 2% undergrads receive athletic scholarships. 52% undergrads borrow to pay for school. **Criteria for awarding institutional aid:** *Non-need-based:* academics, art, athletics, leadership, music/drama.

SAINT FRANCIS MEDICAL CENTER COLLEGE OF NURSING

511 NE. Greenleaf Street, Peoria, IL 61603
Phone: 309-624-8980
E-mail: janice.e.farquharson@osfhealthcare.org
Fax: 309-624-8973 · Website: http://www.sfmccon.edu/

This is a private school.

RATINGS

Admissions Selectivity Rating: 60*   **Fire Safety Rating:** 97

STUDENTS AND FACULTY

Enrollment: 402. **Student Body:** 89% female, 11% male, 0% international (2 countries represented). Asian 2%, African American 5%, Caucasian 89%, Hispanic 4%, Native American <1%
Faculty: 34 full-time faculty, 29% hold PhDs, 100% are are members of minority groups, 0% are women.

ACADEMICS

Degrees: bachelor's, doctoral, master's, post-master's certificate. **Classes:** Most classes have 40-49 students. Most lab/discussion sessions have fewer than 10 students. **Special Study Options:** Accelerated program, distance learning, independent study.

FACILITIES

Housing: Coed dorms.

CAMPUS LIFE

Activities: student government.

ADMISSIONS

Freshman Admission Requirements: High school diploma is required and GED is accepted. **Transfer Admission Requirements:** High school transcript, college transcript(s), essay or personal statement, statement of good standing from prior institution(s). Minimum college GPA of 2.50 required. Lowest grade transferable C. **General Admission Information:** Application Fee $50.

COSTS AND FINANCIAL AID

Average book expense $1,565. **Required Forms and Deadlines:** FAFSA, Institution's own financial aid form. **Notification of Awards:** Applicants will be notified of awards on a rolling basis beginning 5/15. **Types of Aid:** *Need-based scholarships/grants:* Federal Pell, state scholarships/grants. *Loans:* Subsidized Stafford, Unsubsidized Stafford, PLUS. **Financial Aid Statistics:** 72% undergrads receive need-based scholarship or grant aid. 0% undergrads receive non-need-based scholarship or grant aid. 89% undergrads receive need-based self-help aid. 0% undergrads receive athletic scholarships. **Criteria for awarding institutional aid:** *Non-need-based:* academics, alumni affiliation.

SAINT FRANCIS UNIVERSITY (PA)

PO Box 600, Loretto, PA 15940
Phone: 814-472-3000 · **Financial Aid Phone:** 814-472-3010
E-mail: admissions@francis.edu · **CEEB Code:** 2797
Fax: 814-472-3335 • **ACT Code:** 3682

This private school, affiliated with the Roman Catholic Church, was founded in 1847. It has a 600-acre campus.

RATINGS

Admissions Selectivity Rating: 84   **Fire Safety Rating:** 75

STUDENTS AND FACULTY

Enrollment: 1,650. **Student Body:** 63% female, 37% male, 20% out-of-state, 5% international (25 countries represented). Asian 1%, African American 6%, Caucasian 79%, Hispanic 2%, Native American <1%
Retention and Graduation: 63% freshmen graduate within 4 years. 72% freshmen graduate within 6 years. 29% grads go on to further study within 1 year. 5% grads pursue arts and sciences degrees. 3% grads pursue law degrees. 9% grads pursue business degrees. 3% grads pursue medical degrees. **Faculty:** 126 full-time faculty, 69% hold PhDs, 54% are are members of minority groups, 3% are women. 0% of classes are taught by teaching assistants.

ACADEMICS

Degrees: associate, bachelor's, master's, post-bachelor's certificate. **Classes:** Most classes have 10-19 students. Most lab/discussion sessions have 10-19 students. **Majors with Highest Enrollment:** Physician Assistant; Health Professions and Related Clinical Sciences; Business/Commerce. **Special Study Options:** cooperative education program, distance learning, double major, honors program, independent study, internships, liberal arts/career combination, student-designed major, study abroad, teacher certification program. **Honors programs:** Honors Program **Combined degree programs:** BA/MD, BA/DDS, BS/MPAS, BS/MOT, BS/DPT, 3-3 BS/PharmD, 2-3 PharmD. **Disability Services:** Special programs offered to physically disabled students include note-taking services, tape recorders, tutors. **Career services:** Alumni network, career/job search classes, career assessment, internships.

FACILITIES

Housing: Coed dorms, men's dorms, women's dorms, fraternity/sorority housing, apartments for single students, Special Housing for Honors Students Special Housing for Campus Ministry. 30% of campus accessible to physically disabled. **Special Academic Facilities/Equipment:** Art museum, elementary-level library for education majors, physician assistant practice facilities, cadaver lab, physical therapy lab, Center of Excellence for Remote and Medically Underserved Areas. **Computers:** Administrative functions (other than registration) can be performed online. Undergraduates are required to own a computer.

CAMPUS LIFE

Environment: Rural. **Activities:** Choral groups, dance, drama/theater, literary magazine, music ensembles, pep band, radio station, student government, student newspaper, student-run film society, television station, yearbook. 60 registered organizations, 9 honor societies, 10 religious organizations. 3 fraternities, 3 sororities. **Athletics (Intercollegiate):** *Men:* basketball, cross-country, football, golf, soccer, swimming, tennis, track/field (outdoor), track/field (indoor), volleyball. *Women:* basketball, cross-country, field hockey, golf, lacrosse, soccer, softball, swimming, tennis, track/field (outdoor), track/field (indoor), volleyball. **On-Campus Highlights:** Christian Hall—residence hall, JFK Student Center, Immaculate Conception Chapel, Stokes Athletics Facility, Mt. Assisi Gardens.

ADMISSIONS

Freshman Academic Profile: 24.41% in top 10% of high school class, 53.94% in top 25% of high school class, 81.5% in top 50% of high school class. 79% from public high schools. SAT Math middle 50% range 470-570. SAT Critical Reading middle 50% range 450-560. SAT Writing middle 50% range 440-560. ACT middle 50% range 20-25. Minimum paper TOEFL 500. **Basis for Candidate Selection:** *Very important factors considered include:* Class rank, academic GPA, rigor of secondary school record, standardized test scores, extracurricular activities. *Important factors considered include:* application essay, recommendation(s), character/personal qualities, interview, level of applicant's interest, talent/ability, volunteer work. *Other factors considered include:* alumni/ae relation, work experience. **Freshman Admission Requirements:** High school diploma is required and GED is accepted. *Academic units required:* 4 English, 2 mathematics, 1 science, (1 science labs), 2 social studies, 7 academic electives. **Freshman Admission Statistics:** 1,640 applied, 69% admitted, 35% enrolled. **Transfer Admission Requirements:** High school transcript, college transcript(s), standardized test scores, statement of good standing from prior institution(s). Minimum college GPA of 2.0 required. Lowest grade transferable C. **General Admission Information:** Application Fee $30. Notification on a rolling basis, beginning on or about 10/1. Nonfall registration accepted. Admission may be deferred for a maximum of 12. Credit offered for CEEB Advanced Placement tests.

COSTS AND FINANCIAL AID

Annual tuition $30,028. Room and board $10,760. Required fees $1,050. Average book expense $2,000. **Required Forms and Deadlines:** FAFSA. **Notification of Awards:** Applicants will be notified of awards on a rolling basis beginning 10/1. **Types of Aid:** *Need-based scholarships/grants:* Federal Pell, SEOG, state scholarships/grants, private scholarships, the school's own gift aid. *Loans:* Subsidized Stafford, Unsubsidized Stafford, PLUS, Federal Perkins. *Student Employment:* Federal Work-Study Program available. Institutional employment available. Highest amount earned per year from on-campus jobs $1,000. Off-campus job opportunities are fair. **Financial Aid Statistics:** 57% freshmen, 56% undergrads receive need-based scholarship or grant aid. 100% freshmen, 100% undergrads receive non-need-based scholarship or grant aid. 82% freshmen, 81% undergrads receive need-based self-help aid. 28% freshmen, 27% undergrads receive athletic scholarships. 98% freshmen, **Criteria for awarding institutional aid:** *Non-need-based:* academics, alumni affiliation, athletics, leadership, music/drama, religious affiliation.

See page 1128.

SAINT JOSEPH'S COLLEGE (IN)

P.O. Box 890, Rensselaer, IN 47978
Phone: 219-866-6170 · **Financial Aid Phone:** 219-866-6163
E-mail: admissions@saintjoe.edu · **CEEB Code:** 1697
Fax: 219-866-6122 · **Website:** www.saintjoe.edu • **ACT Code:** 1240

This private school, affiliated with the Roman Catholic Church, was founded in 1889. It has a 180-acre campus.

RATINGS

Admissions Selectivity Rating: 80   Fire Safety Rating: 76

STUDENTS AND FACULTY

Enrollment: 1,074. **Student Body:** 60% female, 40% male, 24% out-of-state, 1% international (3 countries represented). Asian 0%, African American 9%, Caucasian 81%, Hispanic 4%, Native American 1%
Retention and Graduation: 74% freshmen return for sophomore year. 40% freshmen graduate within 4 years. 45% freshmen graduate within 6 years. 16% grads go on to further study within 1 year. 8% grads pursue arts and sciences degrees. 1% grads pursue law degrees. 4% grads pursue business degrees. 1% grads pursue medical degrees. **Faculty:** 79 full-time faculty, 75% hold PhDs, 54% are are members of minority groups, 3% are women. 0% of classes are taught by teaching assistants.

ACADEMICS

Degrees: associate, bachelor's, certificate, diploma, master's, terminal associate. **Classes:** Most classes have 10-19 students. Most lab/discussion sessions have 10-19 students. **Majors with Highest Enrollment:** Business/Commerce; Elementary Education and Teaching; Biology/Biological Sciences. **Special Study Options:** Accelerated program, cross-registration, double major, dual enrollment, honors program, independent study, internships, liberal arts/career combination, student-designed major, study abroad, teacher certification program. **Disability Services:** Special programs offered to physically disabled students include note-taking services, reader services, tape recorders, tutors. **Career services:** Alumni network, career assessment, internships.

FACILITIES

Housing: Coed dorms, special housing for disabled students, men's dorms, women's dorms, apartments for single students. 74% of campus accessible to physically disabled. **Computers:** 100% of dorms, 100% of libraries, 100% of dining areas, have wireless network access.

CAMPUS LIFE

Environment: Village. **Activities:** Choral groups, concert band, dance, drama/theater, jazz band, literary magazine, marching band, music ensembles, musical theater, pep band, radio station, student government, student newspaper, student-run film society, television station. 41 registered organizations, 4 honor societies, 7 religious organizations. **Athletics (Intercollegiate):** *Men:* baseball, basketball, cross-country, football, golf, soccer, tennis, track/field (outdoor), track/field (indoor). *Women:* basketball, cross-country, golf, soccer, softball, tennis, track/field (outdoor), track/field (indoor), volleyball. **On-Campus Highlights:** Rev. Charles Banet, C.PP.S. Core Educati, Saint Joseph's Chapel, Lourdes Grotto, Hanson Recreation Center/Fitness Center, Lake Banet.

ADMISSIONS

Freshman Academic Profile: Average high school GPA 3.19. 15% in top 10% of high school class, 37% in top 25% of high school class, 68% in top 50% of high school class. 84% from public high schools. SAT Math middle 50% range 440-563. SAT Critical Reading middle 50% range 450-550. ACT middle 50% range 18-24. Minimum internet-based TOEFL 80. Minimum paper TOEFL 550. **Basis for Candidate Selection:** *Very important factors considered include:* academic GPA, rigor of secondary school record, standardized test scores. *Important factors considered include:* Class rank, character/personal qualities, extracurricular activities, volunteer work. *Other factors considered include:* application essay, recommendation(s), alumni/ae relation, interview, talent/ability, work experience. **Freshman Admission Requirements:** High school diploma is required and GED is accepted. **Freshman Admission Statistics:** 1,572 applied, 66% admitted, 21% enrolled. **Transfer Admission Requirements:** college transcript(s), Minimum college GPA of 2.0 required. Lowest grade transferable C-. **General Admission Information:** Application Fee $25. Notification on a rolling basis, beginning on or about 12/1. Nonfall registration accepted. Admission may be deferred for a maximum of 2. Credit offered for CEEB Advanced Placement tests.

COSTS AND FINANCIAL AID

Annual tuition $27,700. Room and board $8,610. Required fees $190. Average book expense $900. **Required Forms and Deadlines:** FAFSA. **Notification of Awards:** Applicants will be notified of awards on a rolling basis beginning 3/1. **Types of Aid:** *Need-based scholarships/grants:* Federal Pell, SEOG, state scholarships/grants, private scholarships, the school's own gift aid. *Loans:* Subsidized Stafford, Unsubsidized Stafford, PLUS, Federal Perkins. *Student Employment:* Federal Work-Study Program available. Institutional employment available. Highest amount earned per year from on-campus jobs $1,500. Off-campus job opportunities are poor. **Financial Aid Statistics:** 100% freshmen, 98% undergrads receive need-based scholarship or grant aid. 27% freshmen, 29% undergrads receive non-need-based scholarship or grant aid. 71% freshmen, 70% undergrads receive need-based self-help aid. 3% freshmen, 5% undergrads receive athletic scholarships. 99% freshmen, 99% undergrads receive any aid. 84% undergrads borrow to pay for school. Average cumulative indebtedness $28,143. **Criteria for awarding institutional aid:** *Non-need-based:* academics, alumni affiliation, athletics, minority status, music/drama.

SAINT JOSEPH'S COLLEGE OF MAINE

278 Whites Bridge Road, Standish, ME 04084-5263
Phone: 207-893-7746 · **Financial Aid Phone:** 207-893-6612
E-mail: admission@sjcme.edu · **CEEB Code:** 3755
Fax: 207-893-7862 · **Website:** www.sjcme.edu • **ACT Code:** 1659

This private school, affiliated with the Roman Catholic Church, was founded in 1912. It has a 350-acre campus.

RATINGS

Admissions Selectivity Rating: 70   Fire Safety Rating: 72

STUDENTS AND FACULTY

Enrollment: 1,034. **Student Body:** 65% female, 35% male, 44% out-of-state, 0% international (1 countries represented). Asian 0%, African American 2%, Caucasian 83%, Hispanic 1%, Native American <1%
Retention and Graduation: 78% freshmen return for sophomore year. 56% freshmen graduate within 4 years. 62% freshmen graduate within 6 years. 15% grads go on to further study within 1 year. 1% grads pursue arts and sciences degrees. 3% grads pursue business degrees. 2% grads pursue medical degrees. **Faculty:** 68 full-time faculty, 82% hold PhDs, 51% are are members of minority groups, 1% are women. 0% of classes are taught by teaching assistants.

ACADEMICS

Degrees: bachelor's. **Classes:** Most classes have 10-19 students. Most lab/discussion sessions have 10-19 students. **Majors with Highest Enrollment:** Elementary Education and Teaching; Registered Nursing/Registered Nurse; Business/Commerce. **Special Study Options:** cross-registration, distance learning, double major, dual enrollment, honors program, independent study, internships, student-designed major, study abroad, teacher certification program. **Honors programs:** 30-40 students per year are admitted for core curriculum Honors Program. **Disability Services:** Special programs offered to physically disabled students include note-taking services, reader services, tape recorders, tutors.

FACILITIES

Housing: Coed dorms, men's dorms, women's dorms, substance-free housing. 75% of campus accessible to physically disabled. **Special Academic Facilities/**

Equipment: radio studio, telescope **Computers:** Administrative functions (other than registration) can be performed online.

CAMPUS LIFE

Environment: Rural. **Activities:** Choral groups, dance, drama/theater, literary magazine, radio station, student government, student newspaper, yearbook. 25 registered organizations, 2 honor societies, 1 religous organization. **Athletics (Intercollegiate):** *Men:* baseball, basketball, cross-country, golf, lacrosse, soccer, swimming. *Women:* basketball, cross-country, field hockey, lacrosse, soccer, softball, swimming, volleyball. **On-Campus Highlights:** Harold Alford Center, Heffernan Center, Alfond Hall, Java Joe's Café, Mercy Hall.

ADMISSIONS

Freshman Academic Profile: 80% from public high schools. SAT Math middle 50% range 440-540. SAT Critical Reading middle 50% range 440-520. Minimum paper TOEFL 500. **Basis for Candidate Selection:** *Very important factors considered include:* application essay, recommendation(s), rigor of secondary school record, character/personal qualities. *Important factors considered include:* Class rank, academic GPA, standardized test scores, talent/ability, volunteer work. *Other factors considered include:* extracurricular activities, interview, level of applicant's interest, work experience. **Freshman Admission Requirements:** High school diploma is required and GED is accepted. **Freshman Admission Statistics:** 1,094 applied, 82% admitted, 41% enrolled. **Transfer Admission Requirements:** college transcript(s), essay or personal statement, statement of good standing from prior institution(s). Minimum college GPA of 2.0 required. Lowest grade transferable C. **General Admission Information:** Application Fee $50. Regular application deadline 8/1. Nonfall registration accepted. Admission may be deferred for a maximum of 1 year. Credit and/or placement offered for CEEB Advanced Placement tests.

COSTS AND FINANCIAL AID

Annual tuition $21,000. Room and board $9,030. Required fees $760. Average book expense $800. **Required Forms and Deadlines:** FAFSA, Institution's own financial aid form. **Notification of Awards:** Applicants will be notified of awards on a rolling basis beginning 3/1. **Types of Aid:** *Need-based scholarships/grants:* Federal Pell, SEOG, state scholarships/grants, private scholarships, the school's own gift aid, Federal Nursing Scholarships. *Loans:* Subsidized Stafford, Unsubsidized Stafford, PLUS, Federal Perkins, Federal Nursing, state loans. *Student Employment:* Federal Work-Study Program available. Institutional employment available. Highest amount earned per year from on-campus jobs $1,275. Off-campus job opportunities are good. **Financial Aid Statistics:** 100% freshmen, 100% undergrads receive need-based scholarship or grant aid. 13% freshmen, 12% undergrads receive non-need-based scholarship or grant aid. 86% freshmen, 87% undergrads receive need-based self-help aid. 0% freshmen, 0% undergrads receive athletic scholarships. 98% freshmen, 95% undergrads receive any aid. 84% undergrads borrow to pay for school. Average cumulative indebtedness $20,508. **Criteria for awarding institutional aid:** *Non-need-based:* academics, leadership.

SAINT JOSEPH'S UNIVERSITY (PA)

5600 City Avenue, Philadelphia, PA 19131
Phone: 610-660-1300 · **Financial Aid Phone:** 610-660-1556
E-mail: admit@sju.edu · **CEEB Code:** 2801
Fax: 610-660-1314 · **Website:** www.sju.edu · **ACT Code:** 3684

This private school, affiliated with the Roman Catholic-Jesuit Church,, affiliated with the Jesuit Church, was founded in 1851. It has a 103-acre campus.

RATINGS

Admissions Selectivity Rating: 84   **Fire Safety Rating:** 75

STUDENTS AND FACULTY

Enrollment: 5,378. **Student Body:** 54% female, 46% male, 53% out-of-state, 2% international (35 countries represented). Asian 3%, African American 7%, Caucasian 80%, Hispanic 6%, Native American <1%. **Retention and Graduation:** 67% freshmen graduate within 4 years. 73% freshmen graduate within 6 years. 21% grads go on to further study within 1 year. 31% grads pursue arts and sciences degrees. 16% grads pursue law degrees. 13% grads pursue business degrees. 18% grads pursue medical degrees. **Faculty:** 301 full-time faculty, 93% hold PhDs, 45% are are members of minority groups, 15% are women. 0% of classes are taught by teaching assistants.

ACADEMICS

Degrees: associate, bachelor's, certificate, master's, post-bachelor's certificate, post-master's certificate, transfer associate. **Classes:** Most classes have 20-29 students. Most lab/discussion sessions have 10-19 students. **Majors with High-**

est Enrollment: Special Products Marketing Operations; Marketing/Marketing Management; Finance. **Special Study Options:** Accelerated program, cooperative education program, distance learning, double major, dual enrollment, English as a Second Language (ESL), exchange student program (domestic), honors program, independent study, internships, student-designed major, study abroad, teacher certification program, weekend college, off campus study in Jesuit student exchange. **Honors programs:** There are distinctive benefits attached to belonging to the SJU Honors Program: Team-taught courses allow distinguished faculty members to share their knowledge and expertise with students in a challenging academic environment. Individual honors courses stress a detailed and thorough scholarly exploration of different fields of knowledge. Honors students register ahead of other students in their year. Honors suites in the residence halls allow like-minded students to live together, even as freshmen. Honors students are provided with free tickets and transportation to concerts and performances by world-renowned institutions such as the Arden Theater Company, the Curtis Institute of Music, the Philadelphia Orchestra, the Pennsylvania Ballet, the Academy of Vocal Arts, the Philadelphia Museum of Art, and the Franklin Science Institute. Receptions, concerts and lectures are regularly sponsored by the Honors Program for Honors Students. Students have access to Claver House, a quiet retreat where honors students can study, work with personal computers and attend receptions. Students have opportunities to present research and creative work at national conferences and seminars; they are also kept informed about scholarship and funding opportunities for graduate and professional work. **Combined degree programs:** BS/MS in Education, Psychology; 5th yr MA in Writing Studies. **Disability Services:** Special programs offered to physically disabled students include note-taking services, reader services, tape recorders, tutors. **Career services:** Alumni network, alumni services, career/job search classes, career assessment, internships, regional alumni. Career services highlights include Saint Joseph's University's Erivan K. Haub School of Business Cooperative Education (Co-op) Program allows students to engage in real-world applications of their academic pursuits. Through two full-time, professionally engaging and paid experiences (creating one year of full-time work experience within the four-year degree), students discover their professional passions and bring real-world experience back to the classroom. In addition, the Co-op Program offers students substantial earning potential. Co-op students earn an average of $8,400 during their four-month work term and $17,000 during their eight-month work term. Employers asked several of these students to continue as part-time employees following their formal Co-op assignment, adding to these earnings. Employers likewise have expressed significant satisfaction with Saint Joseph's Co-op students. Rating Co-op students on dependability, attitude, quality of work and overall performance, the collective rating of all Co-op students (since the Program's inception) is a 4.4 on a scale of 5.0, and 93% of employers would hire their Co-op student(s) full-time, if a full-time job were available.

FACILITIES

Housing: Coed dorms, men's dorms, women's dorms, apartments for single students, Theme Housing, Special accommodations upon need for disabled students. 85% of campus accessible to physically disabled. **Special Academic Facilities/Equipment:** Wall Street Trading Room, Claver House—Honors Program, Mandeville Hall, Moot Board Room, University Gallery. **Computers:** 100% of classrooms, 100% of dorms, 100% of libraries, 100% of dining areas, 100% of student union, 10% of common outdoor areas have wireless network access. Students can register for classes online. Administrative functions (other than registration) can be performed online.

CAMPUS LIFE

Environment: Metropolis. **Activities:** Choral groups, concert band, dance, drama/theater, jazz band, literary magazine, music ensembles, musical theater, pep band, radio station, student government, student newspaper, student-run film society, yearbook, Campus Ministries, International Student Organization 100. registered organizations, 20 honor societies, 4 fraternities, 4 sororities. **Athletics (Intercollegiate):** *Men:* baseball, basketball, crew/rowing, cross-country, golf, lacrosse, soccer, tennis, track/field (outdoor), track/field (indoor). *Women:* basketball, crew/rowing, cross-country, field hockey, lacrosse, soccer, softball, tennis, track/field (outdoor), track/field (indoor). **On-Campus Highlights:** Campion Student Center, Hagan Arena and Athletics Center, Chapel of St. Joseph, Mandeville Hall, Maguire Sports Complex, 2008 brought the expansion of the SJU campus through the acquisition of 38 acres of property adjacent to the University as well as the construction of a new parking and retail facility. **Environmental Initiatives:** We have a full-time office of Health, Safety and Environmental compliance. We have a full-time recycling program with full-time staff. We purchase whenever possible Green products and services.

ADMISSIONS

Freshman Academic Profile: Average high school GPA 3.46. 16.3% in top 10% of high school class, 44.1% in top 25% of high school class, 77.9% in top 50% of high school class. 50% from public high schools. SAT Math middle 50% range 520-620. SAT Critical Reading middle 50% range 510-600. SAT Writing middle 50% range 520-610. ACT middle 50% range 23-27. Minimum internet-based TOEFL 79. Minimum paper TOEFL 550. **Basis for Candidate Selection:** *Very important factors considered include:* academic GPA, rigor of secondary school record. *Important factors considered include:* application essay, recommendation(s), character/personal qualities. *Other factors considered include:* Class rank, standardized test scores, alumni/ae relation, extracurricular activities, first generation, level of applicant's interest, talent/ability, volunteer work, work experience. **Freshman Admission Requirements:** High school diploma is required and GED is not accepted. *Academic units required:* 4 English, 3 mathematics, 2 science, (1 science labs), 2 foreign language, 0 social studies, 1 history, 0 visual/performing arts, 0 computer science, 0 academic electives. **Freshman Admission Statistics:** 8,462 applied, 85% admitted, 19% enrolled. **Transfer Admission Requirements:** High school transcript, college transcript(s), statement of good standing from prior institution(s). Minimum college GPA of 2.5 required. Lowest grade transferable C. **General Admission Information:** Application Fee $60. Regular application deadline 2/1. Regular notification 3/15. Nonfall registration accepted. Admission may be deferred for a maximum of 1 year. Credit offered for CEEB Advanced Placement tests.

COSTS AND FINANCIAL AID
Annual tuition $40,420. Room and board $14,426. Required fees $160. Average book expense $825. **Required Forms and Deadlines:** FAFSA. **Notification of Awards:** Applicants will be notified of awards on a rolling basis beginning 3/1. **Types of Aid:** *Need-based scholarships/grants:* Federal Pell, SEOG, state scholarships/grants, private scholarships, the school's own gift aid. *Loans:* Direct Subsidized Stafford, Direct Unsubsidized Stafford, Direct PLUS, Subsidized Stafford, Unsubsidized Stafford, PLUS, Federal PerkinsThe Federal Direct Student Loan Program will be in effect beginning with the Fall 2010-11 academic year. *Student Employment:* Federal Work-Study Program available. Institutional employment available. Off-campus job opportunities are excellent. **Financial Aid Statistics:** 97% freshmen, 97% undergrads receive need-based scholarship or grant aid. 16% freshmen, 14% undergrads receive non-need-based scholarship or grant aid. 73% freshmen, 74% undergrads receive need-based self-help aid. 3% freshmen, 4% undergrads receive athletic scholarships. 100% freshmen, 96% undergrads receive any aid. **Criteria for awarding institutional aid:** *Non-need-based:* academics, alumni affiliation, art, athletics, minority status, music/drama.

SAINT JOSEPH SEMINARY COLLEGE

75376 River Road, St. Benedict, LA 70457
Phone: 985-867-2273 • **Financial Aid Phone:** 985-867-2229
E-mail: registrar@sjasc.edu • **CEEB Code:** 6689
Fax: 985-327-1085 • **ACT Code:** 1604

This private school, affiliated with the Roman Catholic Church, was founded in 1891. It has a 1200-acre campus.

RATINGS
Admissions Selectivity Rating: 60* **Fire Safety Rating:** 60*

STUDENTS AND FACULTY
Enrollment: 100. **Student Body:** 0% female, 100% male, 34% out-of-state. Asian 5%, Caucasian 69%, Hispanic 26%, Native American <1%
Faculty: 16 full-time faculty, 31% hold PhDs, 44% are are members of minority groups, 0% are women. 0% of classes are taught by teaching assistants.

ACADEMICS
Degrees: bachelor's. **Classes:** Most classes have 10-19 students. **Special Study Options:** distance learning, English as a Second Language (ESL), independent study, study abroad. **Disability Services:** Special programs offered to physically disabled students include tape recorders, tutors.

FACILITIES
Housing: men's dorms. 100% of campus accessible to physically disabled.

CAMPUS LIFE
Environment: Rural. **Activities:** Choral groups, drama/theater, literary magazine, student government, student newspaper, yearbook. 1 religous organization.

ADMISSIONS
Freshman Academic Profile: Minimum paper TOEFL 520. **Basis for Candidate Selection:** *Very important factors considered include:* rigor of secondary school record, character/personal qualities, religious affiliation/commitment. *Important factors considered include:* recommendation(s), standardized test scores. *Other factors considered include:* Class rank, extracurricular activities, interview, volunteer work. **Freshman Admission Requirements:** High school diploma is required and GED is accepted. *Academic units required:* 3 English,

2 mathematics, 2 science, (0 science labs), 2 foreign language, 0 social studies, 1 history, 0 academic electives. **Freshman Admission Statistics:** 11 applied, 100% admitted, 100% enrolled. **Transfer Admission Requirements:** High school transcript, college transcript(s), standardized test scores, Lowest grade transferable C. **General Admission Information:** Nonfall registration accepted. Neither credit nor placement offered for CEEB Advanced Placement tests.

COSTS AND FINANCIAL AID
Average book expense $1,000. **Required Forms and Deadlines:** FAFSA, Institution's own financial aid form, State aid form. **Notification of Awards:** Applicants will be notified of awards on a rolling basis beginning 8/3. **Types of Aid:** *Need-based scholarships/grants:* Federal Pell, SEOG, state scholarships/grants, private scholarships, the school's own gift aid. *Loans:* Subsidized Stafford, Unsubsidized Stafford, PLUS, Federal Perkins. **Financial Aid Statistics:** 100% freshmen, 100% undergrads receive need-based scholarship or grant aid. 100% freshmen, 20% undergrads receive non-need-based scholarship or grant aid. 100% freshmen, 100% undergrads receive need-based self-help aid. 0% freshmen, 0% undergrads receive athletic scholarships. 18% undergrads borrow to pay for school.

SAINT LEO UNIVERSITY

Office of Admission MC2008, Saint Leo, FL 33574-6665
Phone: (352)588-8283 • **Financial Aid Phone:** 800-240-7658
E-mail: admissions@saintleo.edu • **CEEB Code:** 5638
Fax: (352)588-8257 • **Website:** www.saintleo.edu • **ACT Code:** 755

This private school, affiliated with the Roman Catholic Church, was founded in 1889. It has a 186-acre campus.

RATINGS
Admissions Selectivity Rating: 77 **Fire Safety Rating:** 93

STUDENTS AND FACULTY
Enrollment: 2,282. **Student Body:** 52% female, 48% male, 28% out-of-state, 13% international (58 countries represented). Asian 1%, African American 13%, Caucasian 46%, Hispanic 17%, Native American <1%
Retention and Graduation: 27% freshmen graduate within 4 years. **Faculty:** 121 full-time faculty, 85% hold PhDs, 42% are are members of minority groups, 13% are women. 0% of classes are taught by teaching assistants.

ACADEMICS
Degrees: associate, bachelor's, certificate, master's, post-bachelor's certificate. **Classes:** Most classes have 20-29 students. Most lab/discussion sessions have 10-19 students. **Majors with Highest Enrollment:** Biology/Biological Sciences; Criminal Justice/Safety Studies; Business Administration and Management. **Special Study Options:** distance learning, double major, honors program, independent study, internships, liberal arts/career combination, study abroad, teacher certification program, weekend college. **Honors programs:** The Saint Leo University Honors Program consists of an integrated sequence of six interdisciplinary courses, spread over the first three years of college, and an extensive senior honors project carried out under the supervision of a distinguished faculty mentor. **Combined degree programs:** BA/DDS, BA/DO. **Disability Services:** Special programs offered to physically disabled students include note-taking services, reader services, tape recorders, tutors. **Career services:** Alumni network, alumni services, career/job search classes, career assessment, internships.

FACILITIES
Housing: Coed dorms, special housing for disabled students, men's dorms, women's dorms, apartments for single students, Wellness Housing, Theme Housing, Freshmen only housing. 95% of campus accessible to physically disabled. **Computers:** 95% of classrooms, 85% of dorms, 100% of libraries, 100% of dining areas, 100% of student union, 90% of common outdoor areas have wireless network access. Students can register for classes online. Administrative functions (other than registration) can be performed online.

CAMPUS LIFE
Environment: Rural. **Activities:** Choral groups, concert band, dance, drama/theater, literary magazine, music ensembles, musical theater, student government, student newspaper, television station, yearbook, Campus Ministries, International Student Organization. 58 registered organizations, 12 honor societies, 7 religious organizations. 6 fraternities, 4 sororities. **Athletics (Intercollegiate):** *Men:* baseball, basketball, cross-country, golf, lacrosse, soccer, swimming, tennis. *Women:* basketball, cross-country, golf, soccer, softball, swimming, tennis, volleyball. **On-Campus Highlights:** Student Community Center, Student Activities Building, Marion Bowman Activities Center, Swimming Pool, Lakefront.

ADMISSIONS

Freshman Academic Profile: Average high school GPA 3.39. 10% in top 10% of high school class, 26% in top 25% of high school class, 63% in top 50% of high school class. 78% from public high schools. SAT Math middle 50% range 460-550. SAT Critical Reading middle 50% range 440-540. SAT Writing middle 50% range 420-520. ACT middle 50% range 20-24. Minimum internet-based TOEFL 78. Minimum paper TOEFL 547. **Basis for Candidate Selection:** *Very important factors considered include:* academic GPA, recommendation(s), rigor of secondary school record, standardized test scores, character/personal qualities. *Important factors considered include:* alumni/ae relation, extracurricular activities, interview, level of applicant's interest, talent/ability, volunteer work. *Other factors considered include:* Class rank, application essay, first generation, racial/ethnic status, work experience. **Freshman Admission Requirements:** High school diploma is required and GED is accepted. **Freshman Admission Statistics:** 3,490 applied, 72% admitted, 25% enrolled. **Transfer Admission Requirements:** college transcript(s), essay or personal statement, statement of good standing from prior institution(s). Minimum college GPA of 2.0 required. Lowest grade transferable D. **General Admission Information:** Application Fee $35. Regular application deadline 8/15. Notification on a rolling basis, beginning on or about 10/15. Nonfall registration accepted. Admission may be deferred for a maximum of 1 year. Credit and/or placement offered for CEEB Advanced Placement tests.

COSTS AND FINANCIAL AID

Annual tuition $20,150. Room and board $9,870. Required fees $680. Average book expense $1,720. **Required Forms and Deadlines:** FAFSA. **Notification of Awards:** Applicants will be notified of awards on a rolling basis beginning 1/31. **Types of Aid:** *Need-based scholarships/grants:* Federal Pell, SEOG, state scholarships/grants, private scholarships, the school's own gift aid, United Negro College Fund. *Loans:* Direct Subsidized Stafford, Direct Unsubsidized Stafford, Direct PLUS, Federal Perkins, Private Loans Through Lenders. *Student Employment:* Federal Work-Study Program available. Institutional employment available. Highest amount earned per year from on-campus jobs $3,500. Off-campus job opportunities are good. **Financial Aid Statistics:** 100% freshmen, 100% undergrads receive need-based scholarship or grant aid. 4% freshmen, 8% undergrads receive non-need-based scholarship or grant aid. 93% freshmen, 89% undergrads receive need-based self-help aid. 4% freshmen, 5% undergrads receive athletic scholarships. 99% freshmen, 89% undergrads receive any aid. 70% undergrads borrow to pay for school. Average cumulative indebtedness $25,458. **Criteria for awarding institutional aid:** *Non-need-based:* academics, alumni affiliation, athletics, leadership, minority status, religious affiliation, state/district residency.

SAINT LOUIS UNIVERSITY

One North Grand Boulevard, Saint Louis, MO 63103
Phone: 314-977-2500 · **Financial Aid Phone:** 314-977-2350
E-mail: admission@slu.edu · **CEEB Code:** 6629
Fax: 314-977-7136 · **Website:** www.slu.edu · **ACT Code:** 2352

This private school, affiliated with the Roman Catholic Church, was founded in 1818. It has a 235-acre campus.

RATINGS

Admissions Selectivity Rating: 90   **Fire Safety Rating:** 85

STUDENTS AND FACULTY

Enrollment: 8,271. **Student Body:** 59% female, 41% male, 63% out-of-state, 7% international (78 countries represented). Asian 8%, African American 7%, Caucasian 66%, Hispanic 5%, Native American <1%
Retention and Graduation: 61% freshmen graduate within 4 years. 72% freshmen graduate within 6 years. 39% grads go on to further study within 1 year. **Faculty:** 740 full-time faculty, 89% hold PhDs, 48% are are members of minority groups, 16% are women. 3.9% of classes are taught by teaching assistants.

ACADEMICS

Degrees: bachelor's, certificate, doctoral, master's, post-bachelor's certificate, post-master's certificate. **Classes:** Most classes have 10-19 students. Most lab/discussion sessions have 10-19 students. **Majors with Highest Enrollment:** Business Administration and Management; Registered Nursing/Registered Nurse; Biology/Biological Sciences. **Special Study Options:** Accelerated program, cooperative education program, cross-registration, distance learning, double major, dual enrollment, English as a Second Language (ESL), honors program, independent study, internships, liberal arts/career combination, student-designed major, study abroad, teacher certification program. **Honors programs:** The Honors Program at Saint Louis University offers eligible students the opportunity to develop an individual course of study that complements their undergraduate major, leading to an Honors degree in that discipline. Undergraduates from any of the schools and colleges at Saint Louis University can successfully pursue an honors degree through the University Honors Program. The Saint Louis University Honors Program offers interdisciplinary programs and opportunities with reflective and expressive elements to students in the Honors Program. The Honors Program offers seminar courses with integrated collaborative learning experiences including service learning, internships, and research. The Honors Program offers Honors students study abroad opportunities. The Honors Program offers Honors courses at the Saint Louis University Madrid Campus. The Honors Program offers teaching assistant positions to undergraduate Honors students. The Honors Program offers a residential learning community and several Freshman Interest Groups. The Honors Program provides academic, cultural, and social opportunities. The Honors Program provides peer mentorship programs. **Combined degree programs:** BA/MA, BA/MSW, MD/MBA, MBA/MHA. **Disability Services:** Special programs offered to physically disabled students include note-taking services, reader services, tape recorders, tutors. **Career services:** Alumni network, alumni services, career/job search classes, career assessment, internships, regional alumni.

FACILITIES

Housing: Coed dorms, special housing for disabled students, men's dorms, women's dorms, fraternity/sorority housing, apartments for married students, apartments for single students, Theme Housing, Foreign Language Housing. 95% of campus accessible to physically disabled. **Special Academic Facilities/Equipment:** Saint Louis University Museum of Art (SLUMA), McNamee Gallery of Samuel Cupples House, Museum of Contemporary Religious Art (MOCRA). **Computers:** 100% of classrooms, 100% of dorms, 100% of libraries, 100% of dining areas, 100% of student union, 100% of common outdoor areas have wireless network access. Students can register for classes online. Administrative functions (other than registration) can be performed online.

CAMPUS LIFE

Environment: Metropolis. **Activities:** Choral groups, dance, drama/theater, jazz band, literary magazine, music ensembles, musical theater, pep band, radio station, student government, student newspaper, student-run film society, television station, yearbook, Campus Ministries, International Student Organization, Model UN. 170 registered organizations, 25 honor societies, 36 religious organizations. 11 fraternities, 6 sororities. **Athletics (Intercollegiate):** *Men:* baseball, basketball, cross-country, diving, soccer, swimming, tennis, track/field (outdoor), track/field (indoor). *Women:* basketball, cross-country, diving, field hockey, soccer, softball, swimming, tennis, track/field (outdoor), track/field (indoor), volleyball. **On-Campus Highlights:** St. Francis Xavier Church, Busch Student Center, St. Louis University Museum of Art, Simon Recreation Center, Robert R. Hermann Soccer Stadium, Chaifetz Arena. **Environmental Initiatives:** In 2010, Saint Louis University launched the Center for Sustainability. More than just another university office, department, or team, the Center for Sustainability is a dedicated degree-granting institution and the first of its kind of out 28 Jesuit colleges and universities in the United States. The Center for Sustainability was established by a $5 million grant from the Alberici Foundation, charitable arm of the Alberici Corporation. Alberici is recognized throughout the country as a leader in green building practices. With this grant they positioned SLU to become one of the nations leaders in the field of sustainability. Barely one-year old, the center has since received an additional $2 million in grant money from a separate source, further bolstering its mission to develop creative, collaborative solutions to the pressing environmental challenges facing society today. One way the center aims to achieve its mission is by educating the next generation of leaders in sustainability through its innovative Master of Sustainability (MOS) program. Launched in August of 2010, the MOS program is the first of its kind in the Midwest—a unique, interdisciplinary graduate degree focused entirely on sustainability. It is a collaborative effort between SLUs college of Arts and Sciences, College of Education and Public Service, John Cook School of Business, Parks College of Engineering, Aviation, and Technology, and the School of Public Health. As a university-wide effort, the program exposes students to sustainability-related instruction across multiple disciplines, including business, public policy, engineering, social work, public health, environmental science, and government. St. Louis University co-founded the St. Louis Regional Higher Education Sustainability Consortium (STL HESC), a formal network of over 20 colleges and universities working together to advance collective sustainability initiatives throughout the region. The mission of the St. Louis Regional Higher Education Sustainability Consortium is "to connect the strengths, resources, and knowledge of St. Louis area universities and colleges, to advance collective sustainable initiatives that cultivate innovation, to eliminate non-productive competition, and to create a network that is more than the sum of its parts." St. Louis was chosen to be a pilot region in the National Climate Prosperity Project along with Denver, Portland, and the Silicon Valley. Each of these regions is developing a climate prosperity strategy based on its unique comparative advantages and implementing it through regional public-private partnerships. In St. Louis, the pilot project is led by the St. Louis Regional Chamber and Growth Association (RCGA). The St. Louis Climate Prosperity Project engages area businesses, educational institutions, elected officials and governmental entities, and other civic organizations in the 16-county metropolitan region to broaden support around green savings, green opportunity, and green talent. Saint Louis Universitys Center for Sustainability has partnered with the RCGA to support and advance the goals of the Climate Prosperity Project. Saint Louis University joined the RCGAs St. Louis Green Business challenge as an inaugural member in January of 2010. The challenge was designed to encourage member institutions to adopt sustainable business practices that improve energy efficiency and indoor air quality, reduce waste and water consumption, as well as increase clean transportation options. The Center for Sustainability is also collaborating with the RCGA to help develop a regional Green Talent Strategy. The Green Talent Strategy aims to identify growth in green occupations in the St. Louis region, align job training providers with employers in green industries, and develop action plans to meet the growing talent needs of the regional green economy. In January of 2011 Saint Louis University hosted and helped organize the St. Louis Green Confluence to present the Green Talent Strategy to the St. Louis community and bring St. Louis area employers, educators, public policy makers and, citizens together to explore the future of the region's green economy. The two-day event was a collaborative effort between the Missouri Career Center, Illinois Work Net, the St. Louis Regional Chamber and Growth Association (RCGA), the St. Louis Higher Education Sustainability Consortium, St. Louis Green.com and SLU's Center for Sustainability. It featured a green economy symposium with expert speakers, a green career opportunity showcase with education workshops, and the unveiling of a new Web portal for green jobs. Climate Prosperity Project: http://www.climateprosperityproject.org/ St. Louis Green Economy Profile http://www.stlrcga.org/documents/mm/StLouis-GreenEconomy.pdf.

ADMISSIONS

Freshman Academic Profile: Average high school GPA 3.83. 43% in top 10% of high school class, 72% in top 25% of high school class, 91% in top 50% of high school class. SAT Math middle 50% range 550-670. SAT Critical Reading middle 50% range 540-660. ACT middle 50% range 25-30. Minimum internet-based TOEFL 80. Minimum paper TOEFL 550. **Basis for Candidate Selection:** *Very important factors considered include:* academic GPA, standardized test scores. *Important factors considered include:* application essay, rigor of secondary school record, character/personal qualities, extracurricular activities, talent/ability. *Other factors considered include:* recommendation(s), alumni/ae relation, first generation, interview, level of applicant's interest, volunteer work. **Freshman Admission Requirements:** High school diploma is required and GED is accepted. *Academic units required:* 4 English, 4 mathematics, 3 science, 3 foreign language, 3 social studies, 0 visual/performing arts, 0 computer science, 3 academic electives. **Freshman Admission Statistics:** 13,911 applied, 60% admitted, 19% enrolled. **Transfer Admission Requirements:** college transcript(s), Minimum college GPA of 2.0 required. Lowest grade transferable C. **General Admission Information:** Application Fee $25. Regular application deadline 8/1. Regular notification 8/1. Notification on a rolling basis, beginning on or about 10/1. Nonfall registration accepted. Admission may be deferred for a maximum of 1 Year. Credit and/or placement offered for CEEB Advanced Placement tests.

COSTS AND FINANCIAL AID

Annual tuition $37,350. Room and board $10,380. Required fees $616. Average book expense $1,500. **Required Forms and Deadlines:** FAFSA. **Notification of Awards:** Applicants will be notified of awards on a rolling basis beginning 3/1. **Types of Aid:** *Need-based scholarships/grants:* Federal Pell, SEOG, state scholarships/grants, private scholarships, the school's own gift aid, Federal Nursing Scholarships. *Loans:* Subsidized Stafford, Unsubsidized Stafford, PLUS, Federal Perkins, Federal Nursing, college/university loans from institutional funds. *Student Employment:* Federal Work-Study Program available. Institutional employment available. Highest amount earned per year from on-campus jobs $14,068. Off-campus job opportunities are good. **Financial Aid Statistics:** 97% freshmen, 95% undergrads receive need-based scholarship or grant aid. 13% freshmen, 10% undergrads receive non-need-based scholarship or grant aid. 69% freshmen, 75% undergrads receive need-based self-help aid. 2% freshmen, 2% undergrads receive athletic scholarships. 95% freshmen, 87% undergrads receive any aid. 61% undergrads borrow to pay for school. Average cumulative indebtedness $23,769. **Criteria for awarding institutional aid:** *Non-need-based:* academics, art, athletics, leadership, music/drama, religious affiliation.

See page 1132.

SAINT MARTIN'S UNIVERSITY

5000 Abbey Way SE, Lacey, WA 98503-7500
Phone: 360-438-4596
E-mail: admissions@stmartin.edu • **CEEB Code:** 4674
Fax: 360-412-6189 • **Website:** www.stmartin.edu • **ACT Code:** 4474

This private school, affiliated with the Roman Catholic Church, was founded in 1895. It has a 320-acre campus.

RATINGS

Admissions Selectivity Rating: 80   **Fire Safety Rating:** 60*

STUDENTS AND FACULTY

Enrollment: 1,275. **Student Body:** 51% female, 49% male, 27% out-of-state, 6% international (14 countries represented). Asian 5%, African American 5%, Caucasian 58%, Hispanic 12%, Native American 1%
Retention and Graduation: 31% freshmen graduate within 4 years. **Faculty:** 74 full-time faculty, 85% hold PhDs, 35% are are members of minority groups, 14% are women. 0% of classes are taught by teaching assistants.

ACADEMICS

Degrees: bachelor's, master's, post-bachelor's certificate, post-master's certificate. **Classes:** Most classes have fewer than 10 students. Most lab/discussion sessions have fewer than 10 students. **Majors with Highest Enrollment:** Business Administration and Management; Mechanical Engineering; Biology/Biological Sciences. **Special Study Options:** distance learning, double major, English as a Second Language (ESL), exchange student program (domestic), independent study, internships, study abroad, teacher certification program. **Combined degree programs:** BA/MEng. **Disability Services:** Special programs offered to physically disabled students include note-taking services, reader services, tape recorders, tutors. **Career services:** Alumni network, alumni services, career/job search classes, career assessment, regional alumni. Career services highlights include an invitation to our local alumni to participate in any and all of our career-related workshops and career advising sessions to which we have had a great turnout. The alumni have initiated an online mentor profile so that students may contact an alum with a question or ask advice. Many relationships can be formed by their participation in these two new activities.

FACILITIES

Housing: Coed dorms, special housing for disabled students, apartments for single students. 85% of campus accessible to physically disabled. **Special Academic Facilities/Equipment:** Cap Art Gallery, Waynick Museum **Computers:** 80% of classrooms, 10% of dorms, 100% of libraries, 100% of dining areas, 100% of student union, have wireless network access. Students can register for classes online. Administrative functions (other than registration) can be performed online.

CAMPUS LIFE

Environment: Town. **Activities:** Choral groups, concert band, dance, drama/theater, jazz band, musical theater, pep band, student government, student newspaper, Campus Ministries, International Student Organization, Model UN. 23 registered organizations, 3 honor societies, 3 religious organizations. **Athletics (Intercollegiate):** *Men:* baseball, basketball, cross-country, golf, track/field (outdoor), track/field (indoor). *Women:* basketball, cross-country, golf, softball, track/field (outdoor), track/field (indoor), volleyball. **On-Campus Highlights:** O'Grady Library, Student Union Building, Recreation and Fitness Center, Baran/Burton/Spangler Halls, Abbey Church, Dining Hall renovation completed in December 2009, Spangler Residence Hall opened Fall 2005. New residence hall and new academic building opened Fall 2008. New Recreation and fitness center opened in January 2010. **Environmental Initiatives:** FoodPlus recycling-for-compost program, growing garden.

ADMISSIONS

Freshman Academic Profile: Average high school GPA 3.46. 24% in top 10% of high school class, 58% in top 25% of high school class, 86% in top 50% of high school class. 95% from public high schools. SAT Math middle 50% range 475-590. SAT Critical Reading middle 50% range 460-565. SAT Writing middle 50% range 450-565. ACT middle 50% range 20-28. Minimum internet-based TOEFL 54. Minimum paper TOEFL 480. **Basis for Candidate Selection:** *Very important factors considered include:* academic GPA, rigor of secondary school record. *Important factors considered include:* application essay, recommendation(s), standardized test scores, character/personal qualities, extracurricular activities, volunteer work. *Other factors considered include:* Class rank, alumni/ae relation, interview, talent/ability, work experience. **Freshman Admission Requirements:** High school diploma is required and GED is accepted. **Freshman Admission Statistics:** 679 applied, 89% admitted, 25% enrolled. **Transfer Admission Requirements:** college transcript(s), essay or personal statement, Minimum college GPA of 2.25 required. Lowest grade transferable C-. **General Admission Information:** Application Fee $35. Notification on a rolling basis, beginning on or about 10/1. Nonfall registration accepted. Credit offered for CEEB Advanced Placement tests.

COSTS AND FINANCIAL AID

Annual tuition $31,300. Room and board $9,990. Required fees $388. Average book expense $1,000. **Required Forms and Deadlines:** FAFSA. **Notification of Awards:** Applicants will be notified of awards on a rolling basis beginning 2/15. **Types of Aid:** *Need-based scholarships/grants:* Federal Pell, SEOG, state scholarships/grants, private scholarships, the school's own gift aid. *Loans:* Subsidized Stafford, Unsubsidized Stafford, PLUS, Federal Perkins, state loans, college/university loans from institutional funds, Private, alternative educational loans. *Student Employment:* Federal Work-Study Program available. Institutional employment available. Highest amount earned per year from on-campus jobs $2,100. Off-campus job opportunities are good. **Financial Aid Statistics:** 100% freshmen, 99% undergrads receive need-based scholarship or grant aid. 22% freshmen, 13% undergrads receive non-need-based scholarship or grant aid. 77% freshmen, 82% undergrads receive need-based self-help aid. 14% freshmen, 6% undergrads receive athletic scholarships. 79% undergrads borrow to pay for school. Average cumulative indebtedness $24,008. **Criteria for awarding institutional aid:** *Non-need-based:* academics, alumni affiliation, art, athletics, leadership, minority status, music/drama, religious affiliation, state/district residency.

SAINT MARY'S COLLEGE (CA)

P.O. Box 4800, Moraga, CA 94575-4800
Phone: 925-631-4224 · **Financial Aid Phone:** 925-631-4370
E-mail: smcadmit@stmarys-ca.edu · **CEEB Code:** 4675
Fax: 925-376-7193 · **Website:** www.stmarys-ca.edu · **ACT Code:** 386

This private school, affiliated with the Roman Catholic Church, was founded in 1863. It has a 420-acre campus.

RATINGS

Admissions Selectivity Rating: 86   Fire Safety Rating: 88

STUDENTS AND FACULTY

Enrollment: 3,039. **Student Body:** 59% female, 41% male, 9% out-of-state, 2% international (26 countries represented). Asian 10%, African American 4%, Caucasian 43%, Hispanic 24%, Native American <1%
Retention and Graduation: 89% freshmen return for sophomore year. 50% freshmen graduate within 4 years. 60% freshmen graduate within 6 years. 27% grads go on to further study within 1 year. **Faculty:** 213 full-time faculty, 95% hold PhDs, 53% are are members of minority groups, 17% are women. 0% of classes are taught by teaching assistants.

ACADEMICS

Degrees: associate, bachelor's, doctoral, master's. **Classes:** Most classes have 10-19 students. **Majors with Highest Enrollment:** Business Administration, Management and Operations; Psychology; Communication and Media Studies. **Special Study Options:** double major, exchange student program (domestic), independent study, student-designed major, study abroad. **Disability Services:** Special programs offered to physically disabled students include note-taking services, reader services, tape recorders, tutors. **Career services:** Alumni network, alumni services, career/job search classes, career assessment, internships. Career services highlights include a Career Information Night Series plus our Career and Internship Fair.

FACILITIES

Housing: Coed dorms, special housing for disabled students, Theme Housing. 90% of campus accessible to physically disabled. **Special Academic Facilities/Equipment:** Hearst Art gallery, Brousseau Hall, Science Building, Geissberger Observatory. **Computers:** 100% of classrooms, 100% of libraries, 100% of dining areas, 100% of student union, 70% of common outdoor areas have wireless network access. Students can register for classes online. Administrative functions (other than registration) can be performed online.

CAMPUS LIFE

Environment: Village. **Activities:** Choral groups, dance, drama/theater, jazz band, music ensembles, musical theater, pep band, radio station, student government, student newspaper, Campus Ministries, International Student Organization. 56 registered organizations, 3 religious organizations. **Athletics**

(Intercollegiate): *Men:* baseball, basketball, cheerleading, cross-country, golf, soccer, tennis. *Women:* basketball, cheerleading, crew/rowing, cross-country, lacrosse, soccer, softball, tennis, volleyball. **On-Campus Highlights:** Br. Alfred Brousseau Hall, Cassin Student Union and LeFevre Quad, College Chapel, Hearst Art Gallery, Oliver Dining Hall, Power Plant (exercise facility), McKeon Pavilion, "St. Patty's Cathedral". **Environmental Initiatives:** 2007 Summer reading program for incoming students focuses on global warming; Energy conservation program (phase 2) reduces consumption by 71KW; Student-run organic vegetable garden: http://stmarys-ca.edu/about-smc/sustain-smc/for-students/vegetable-garden.html.

ADMISSIONS

Freshman Academic Profile: Average high school GPA 3.61. 31% in top 10% of high school class, 64% in top 25% of high school class, 92% in top 50% of high school class. 61% from public high schools. SAT Math middle 50% range 510-610. SAT Critical Reading middle 50% range 500-600. ACT middle 50% range 22-27. Minimum internet-based TOEFL 79. Minimum paper TOEFL 550. **Basis for Candidate Selection:** *Very important factors considered include:* academic GPA, rigor of secondary school record, standardized test scores. *Important factors considered include:* application essay, recommendation(s), first generation. *Other factors considered include:* Class rank, alumni/ae relation, character/personal qualities, extracurricular activities, geographical residence, interview, level of applicant's interest, racial/ethnic status, religious affiliation/commitment, talent/ability, volunteer work, work experience. **Freshman Admission Requirements:** High school diploma is required and GED is accepted. *Academic units required:* 4 English, 3 mathematics, 2 science, (1 science labs), 2 foreign language, 1 social studies, 1 history, 2 academic electives. **Freshman Admission Statistics:** 4,864 applied, 69% admitted, 18% enrolled. **Transfer Admission Requirements:** High school transcript, college transcript(s), essay or personal statement, Minimum college GPA of 2.3 required. Lowest grade transferable C-. **General Admission Information:** Application Fee $55. Regular application deadline 2/1. Regular notification 3/15. Nonfall registration accepted. Admission may be deferred for a maximum of 12 months. Credit and/or placement offered for CEEB Advanced Placement tests.

COSTS AND FINANCIAL AID

Annual tuition $41,230. Room and board $14,400. Required fees $150. Average book expense $1,107. **Required Forms and Deadlines:** FAFSA, State aid form. **Notification of Awards:** Applicants will be notified of awards on a rolling basis beginning 3/15. **Types of Aid:** *Need-based scholarships/grants:* Federal Pell, SEOG, state scholarships/grants, private scholarships, the school's own gift aid. *Loans:* Subsidized Stafford, Unsubsidized Stafford, PLUS, Federal Perkins. *Student Employment:* Federal Work-Study Program available. Institutional employment available. Highest amount earned per year from on-campus jobs $12,744. Off-campus job opportunities are good. **Financial Aid Statistics:** 98% freshmen, 95% undergrads receive need-based scholarship or grant aid. 50% freshmen, 39% undergrads receive non-need-based scholarship or grant aid. 82% freshmen, 90% undergrads receive need-based self-help aid. 4% freshmen, 3% undergrads receive athletic scholarships. 77% freshmen, 74% undergrads receive any aid. 75% undergrads borrow to pay for school. Average cumulative indebtedness $23,258. **Criteria for awarding institutional aid:** *Non-need-based:* academics, alumni affiliation, athletics, leadership.

SAINT MARY'S COLLEGE (IN)

Admission office, Notre Dame, IN 46556
Phone: 574-284-4587 · **Financial Aid Phone:** 574-284-4557
E-mail: admission@saintmarys.edu · **CEEB Code:** 1702
Fax: 574-284-4841 · **Website:** www.saintmarys.edu · **ACT Code:** 1244

This private school, affiliated with the Roman Catholic Church, was founded in 1844. It has a 275-acre campus.

RATINGS

Admissions Selectivity Rating: 87   Fire Safety Rating: 83

STUDENTS AND FACULTY

Enrollment: 1,508. **Student Body:** 100% female, 0% male, 74% out-of-state, 2% international (20 countries represented). Asian 2%, African American 1%, Caucasian 78%, Hispanic 11%, Native American <1%
Retention and Graduation: 78% freshmen graduate within 4 years. 81% freshmen graduate within 6 years. 28% grads go on to further study within 1 year. 4% grads pursue arts and sciences degrees. 2% grads pursue law degrees. 1% grads pursue business degrees. 2% grads pursue medical degrees. **Faculty:** 129 full-time faculty, 91% hold PhDs, 67% are are members of minority groups, 13% are women. 0% of classes are taught by teaching assistants.

ACADEMICS

Degrees: bachelor's. **Classes:** Most classes have 20-29 students. Most lab/discussion sessions have 10-19 students. **Majors with Highest Enrollment:** Registered Nursing, Nursing Administration, Nursing Research and Clinical Nursing; Elementary Education and Teaching; Communication Sciences and Disorders. **Special Study Options:** Accelerated program, cross-registration, double major, exchange student program (domestic), independent study, internships, liberal arts/career combination, student-designed major, study abroad, teacher certification program. **Disability Services:** Special programs offered to physically disabled students include note-taking services, reader services, tape recorders, tutors. **Career services:** Alumni network, alumni services, career/job search classes, career assessment, internships, regional alumni.

FACILITIES

Housing: special housing for disabled students, women's dorms, apartments for single students, Intercultural Living Floor. 100% of campus accessible to physically disabled. **Special Academic Facilities/Equipment:** Art gallery, early childhood development center, language lab, electron microscope. **Computers:** 80% of classrooms, 60% of dorms, 100% of libraries, 100% of dining areas, 100% of student union, have wireless network access. Students can register for classes online. Administrative functions (other than registration) can be performed online.

CAMPUS LIFE

Environment: City. **Activities:** Choral groups, dance, drama/theater, jazz band, literary magazine, marching band, music ensembles, musical theater, opera, pep band, radio station, student government, student newspaper, television station, yearbook, Campus Ministries, International Student Organization. 78 registered organizations, 14 honor societies, 8 religious organizations. **Athletics (Intercollegiate):** *Women:* basketball, cross-country, diving, golf, soccer, softball, swimming, tennis, volleyball. **On-Campus Highlights:** Student Center/Noble Family Dining hall, Dalloway's Coffee House, Angela Athletic Facility, Spes Unica, Moreau Center for the Arts / O'Laughlin. **Environmental Initiatives:** Campus Recycling Program Establishment of "Going Green Committee" to build on strategic plan goal of reducing carbon footprint. College Real Food Commitment to purchase 20% "real food" by 2020.

ADMISSIONS

Freshman Academic Profile: Average high school GPA 3.75. 35% in top 10% of high school class, 62% in top 25% of high school class, 94% in top 50% of high school class. 52% from public high schools. SAT Math middle 50% range 500-600. SAT Critical Reading middle 50% range 510-610. SAT Writing middle 50% range 500-610. ACT middle 50% range 23-28. Minimum internet-based TOEFL 80. Minimum paper TOEFL 550. **Basis for Candidate Selection:** *Important factors considered include:* academic GPA, rigor of secondary school record, standardized test scores, level of applicant's interest. *Other factors considered include:* Class rank, application essay, recommendation(s), alumni/ae relation, character/personal qualities, extracurricular activities, first generation, geographical residence, interview, racial/ethnic status, state residency, talent/ability, volunteer work, work experience. **Freshman Admission Requirements:** High school diploma is required and GED is accepted. *Academic units required:* 4 English, 3 mathematics, 2 science, (2 science labs), 2 foreign language, 2 history. **Freshman Admission Statistics:** 1,687 applied, 83% admitted, 27% enrolled. **Transfer Admission Requirements:** High school transcript, college transcript(s), essay or personal statement, standardized test scores, statement of good standing from prior institution(s). Minimum college GPA of 3.0 required. Lowest grade transferable C. **General Admission Information:** Application Fee $30. Early decision application deadline 11/15. Notification on a rolling basis, beginning on or about 1/1. Nonfall registration accepted. Credit and/or placement offered for CEEB Advanced Placement tests.

COSTS AND FINANCIAL AID

Annual tuition $35,210. Room and board $10,930. Required fees $760. Average book expense $1,000. **Required Forms and Deadlines:** FAFSA, CSS/Financial Aid PROFILE, Noncustodial PROFILE. **Notification of Awards:** Applicants will be notified of awards on a rolling basis beginning 3/15. **Types of Aid:** *Need-based scholarships/grants:* Federal Pell, SEOG, state scholarships/grants, private scholarships, the school's own gift aid. *Loans:* Subsidized Stafford, Unsubsidized Stafford, PLUS, Federal Perkins. *Student Employment:* Federal Work-Study Program available. Institutional employment available. Off-campus job opportunities are good. **Financial Aid Statistics:** 97% freshmen, 99% undergrads receive need-based scholarship or grant aid. 95% freshmen, 91% undergrads receive non-need-based scholarship or grant aid. 74% freshmen, 80% undergrads receive need-based self-help aid. 0% freshmen, 0% undergrads receive athletic scholarships. 100% freshmen, 97% undergrads receive any aid. 69% undergrads borrow to pay for school. Average cumulative indebtedness $23,140. **Criteria for awarding institutional aid:** *Non-need-based:* academics, art.

SAINT MARY'S UNIVERSITY OF MINNESOTA

700 Terrace Heights #2, Winona, MN 55987-1399
Phone: 507-457-1700 · **Financial Aid Phone:** 507-457-1438
E-mail: admission@smumn.edu · **CEEB Code:** 6632
Fax: 507-457-1722 · **Website:** www.smumn.edu · **ACT Code:** 2148

This private school, affiliated with the Roman Catholic Church, was founded in 1912. It has a 400-acre campus.

RATINGS

Admissions Selectivity Rating: 80   **Fire Safety Rating:** 90

STUDENTS AND FACULTY

Enrollment: 1,859. **Student Body:** 54% female, 46% male, 46% out-of-state, 2% international (38 countries represented). Asian 2%, African American 4%, Caucasian 55%, Hispanic 6%, Native American <1%
Retention and Graduation: 55% freshmen graduate within 4 years. 65% freshmen graduate within 6 years. 15% grads go on to further study within 1 year. 2% grads pursue arts and sciences degrees. 1% grads pursue law degrees. 1% grads pursue business degrees. 4% grads pursue medical degrees. **Faculty:** 101 full-time faculty, 90% hold PhDs, 41% are are members of minority groups, 2% are women. 0% of classes are taught by teaching assistants.

ACADEMICS

Degrees: bachelor's, certificate, diploma, doctoral, master's, post-bachelor's certificate, post-master's certificate. **Classes:** Most classes have 20-29 students. Most lab/discussion sessions have 10-19 students. **Majors with Highest Enrollment:** Marketing/Marketing Management; Biology/Biological Sciences; Elementary Education and Teaching. **Special Study Options:** cooperative education program, cross-registration, double major, dual enrollment, English as a Second Language (ESL), honors program, independent study, internships, student-designed major, study abroad, teacher certification program. **Honors programs:** The Lasallian Honors Program at Saint Mary's University is a general education program for motivated students who wish to engage in "shared inquiry" in small seminar classes. The hallmarks of the program are study of the Great Books, service learning, and participation in a community of learners who desire to grow intellectually and spiritually, together over four years. Great Books, Shared-Inquiry Seminars The Lasallian Honors Program is an interdisciplinary program of learning in the Great Books and other notable texts of Western and Eastern traditions. All of the courses are shared-inquiry seminars: the students and the professor discuss the works together in lively, interactive, and informed conversations about the most important ideas in human history. Working Smarter Honors courses do not necessarily require more work than other general education courses. What differs is the style of learning, in student-centered seminars. You have the opportunity to participate with other motivated students in small classes taught by professors committed to engaged learning and individualized attention. Streamlined General Education A practical advantage of the Honors program is that it streamlines course requirements. Because of our interdisciplinary 4-credit model, honors students take fewer general education courses. That leaves room for a second major, extracurricular activities, an internship, and/or studying abroad. Future Benefits Participation in the Lasallian Honors Program also has rewards after graduation. When it comes time to compete for a job, internship, or acceptance to graduate school, Honors students have a clear advantage. We have an enviable record (98%) of placing our students in some of the best graduate programs in the country. Personal Growth The most important reason to join the Lasallian Honors Program is the desire to extend yourself intellectually, spiritually, and creatively. We can help you do that in a supportive and challenging academic atmosphere. You will be part of a cohort group that shares your talents and interests—and likely will become your closest college friends. **Disability Services:** Special programs offered to physically disabled students include note-taking services, reader services, tape recorders, tutors. **Career services:** Alumni network, alumni services, career/job search classes, career assessment, internships.

FACILITIES

Housing: Coed dorms, special housing for disabled students, men's dorms, women's dorms, apartments for single students. 93% of campus accessible to physically disabled. **Special Academic Facilities/Equipment:** Art gallery, performance center, laboratories, observatory. **Computers:** 100% of dorms, 100% of libraries, 100% of dining areas, 100% of student union, have wireless network access. Students can register for classes online. Administrative functions (other than registration) can be performed online.

CAMPUS LIFE

Environment: Town. **Activities:** Choral groups, concert band, dance, drama/theater, jazz band, literary magazine, music ensembles, musical theater, radio station, student government, student newspaper, yearbook, Campus Ministries, International Student Organization. 80 registered organizations, 13 honor societies, 6 religious organizations. **Athletics (Intercollegiate):** *Men:* baseball, basketball, cross-country, diving, golf, ice hockey, skiing (nordic/cross-country), soccer, swimming, tennis, track/field (outdoor), track/field (indoor). *Women:* basketball, cross-country, diving, golf, ice hockey, skiing (nordic/cross-country), soccer, softball, swimming, tennis, track/field (outdoor), track/field (indoor), volleyball. **On-Campus Highlights:** Lillian Hogan Davis Galleries, Gostomski Fieldhouse, Page Theatre, Toner Student Center, Outdoor Track and Field Complex, Saint Mary's also offers an 18 hole disc golf course which runs through the bluffs surrounding the campus. Also, a network of trails run along the bluffs and into wooded valleys allowing for hiking, running, walking, and cross country skiing. **Environmental Initiatives:** ISO 14001 Certified Environmental Management System (EMS) Member of the Sustain Winona Collaboration Green Team—Sustainability Series

ADMISSIONS

Freshman Academic Profile: Average high school GPA 3.34. 16% in top 10% of high school class, 35% in top 25% of high school class, 69% in top 50% of high school class. 65% from public high schools. SAT Math middle 50% range 472.5-572.5. SAT Critical Reading middle 50% range 447.5-585. SAT Writing middle 50% range 460-562.5. ACT middle 50% range 20-26. Minimum internet-based TOEFL 79. Minimum paper TOEFL 520. **Basis for Candidate Selection:** *Very important factors considered include:* academic GPA, rigor of secondary school record, standardized test scores. *Important factors considered include:* Class rank, character/personal qualities, interview, talent/ability. *Other factors considered include:* application essay, recommendation(s), alumni/ae relation, extracurricular activities, level of applicant's interest, volunteer work. **Freshman Admission Requirements:** High school diploma is required and GED is accepted. *Academic units required:* 4 English, 3 mathematics, 3 science, (2 science labs), 0 foreign language, 2 social studies, 6 academic electives. **Freshman Admission Statistics:** 1,743 applied, 74% admitted, 26% enrolled. **Transfer Admission Requirements:** High school transcript, college transcript(s), statement of good standing from prior institution(s). Minimum college GPA of 2.0 required. Lowest grade transferable C. **General Admission Information:** Application Fee $25. Regular application deadline 5/1. Regular notification 5/1. Nonfall registration accepted. Admission may be deferred for a maximum of 1 year. Credit and/or placement offered for CEEB Advanced Placement tests.

COSTS AND FINANCIAL AID

Annual tuition $30,830. Room and board $8,240. Required fees $505. Average book expense $1,300. **Required Forms and Deadlines:** FAFSA. **Notification of Awards:** Applicants will be notified of awards on a rolling basis beginning 2/1. **Types of Aid:** *Need-based scholarships/grants:* Federal Pell, SEOG, state scholarships/grants, the school's own gift aid. *Loans:* Subsidized Stafford, Unsubsidized Stafford, PLUS, Federal Perkins, state loans. *Student Employment:* Federal Work-Study Program available. Institutional employment available. Highest amount earned per year from on-campus jobs $3,000. Off-campus job opportunities are good. **Financial Aid Statistics:** 100% freshmen, 98% undergrads receive need-based scholarship or grant aid. 0% freshmen, 0% undergrads receive non-need-based scholarship or grant aid. 72% freshmen, 80% undergrads receive need-based self-help aid. 0% freshmen, 0% undergrads receive athletic scholarships. 98% freshmen, 96% undergrads receive any aid. 81% undergrads borrow to pay for school. Average cumulative indebtedness $25,403. **Criteria for awarding institutional aid:** *Non-need-based:* academics, alumni affiliation, art, leadership, minority status, music/drama.

SAINT MARY-OF-THE-WOODS COLLEGE

Office of Admission, Saint Mary-of-the-Woods, IN 47876-0068
Phone: 812-535-5106 · **Financial Aid Phone:** 812-535-5100
E-mail: smwcadms@smwc.edu · **CEEB Code:** 1704
Fax: 812-535-5010 · **Website:** www.smwc.edu · **ACT Code:** 1242

This private school, affiliated with the Roman Catholic Church, was founded in 1840. It has a 67-acre campus.

RATINGS

Admissions Selectivity Rating: 73   **Fire Safety Rating:** 99

STUDENTS AND FACULTY

Enrollment: 1,176. **Student Body:** 97% female, 3% male, 30% out-of-state, (5 countries represented).
Retention and Graduation: 77% freshmen return for sophomore year. 35% freshmen graduate within 4 years. 42% freshmen graduate within 6 years. 18% grads go on to further study within 1 year. 15% grads pursue arts and sciences degrees. 1% grads pursue law degrees. 1% grads pursue business degrees. 1% grads pursue medical degrees. **Faculty:** 67 full-time faculty, 54% hold PhDs,

66% are are members of minority groups, 6% are women. 0% of classes are taught by teaching assistants.

ACADEMICS

Degrees: associate, bachelor's, certificate, master's, post-bachelor's certificate, post-master's certificate, transfer associate. **Classes:** Most classes have fewer than 10 students. **Majors with Highest Enrollment:** Elementary Education and Teaching; Biology/Biological Sciences; Equestrian/Equine Studies. **Special Study Options:** Accelerated program, cross-registration, distance learning, double major, external degree program, honors program, independent study, internships, student-designed major, study abroad, teacher certification program. **Disability Services:** Special programs offered to physically disabled students include tutors. **Career services:** Alumni network, alumni services, career/job search classes, career assessment, internships, regional alumni. Career services highlights include Experiential Learning: Externship, Supplemental Learning Experience, and Internship programs.

FACILITIES

Housing: special housing for disabled students, women's dorms. 100% of campus accessible to physically disabled. **Special Academic Facilities/Equipment:** Cecilian Auditorium and Conservatory of Music, SMWC Art Gallery. **Computers:** 100% of classrooms, 100% of dorms, 100% of libraries, 20% of dining areas, 15% of common outdoor areas have wireless network access. Students can register for classes online. Administrative functions (other than registration) can be performed online.

CAMPUS LIFE

Environment: Town. **Activities:** Choral groups, concert band, dance, drama/theater, jazz band, literary magazine, music ensembles, musical theater, student government, student newspaper, yearbook, Campus Ministries, International Student Organization. 30 registered organizations, 6 honor societies, 1 religous organization. **Athletics (Intercollegiate):** *Women:* basketball, equestrian sports, golf, soccer, softball, track/field (outdoor). **On-Campus Highlights:** Le Fer Hall (residence hall), Mari Hulman George School of Equine Studies, Softball/Soccer Fields, Cecilian Auditorium, Church of the Immaculate Conception. Saint Mary-of-the-Woods College is a 67-acre wooded campus located five miles northwest of Terre Haute, Indiana. The peaceful and beautiful campus features a fitness trail, lake and stables amid the stately academic buildings. Besides the College, Saint Mary-of-the-Woods is common ground for the Sisters of Providence, Woods Day Care/Pre-School, Providence Center and the White Violet Center for Eco-Justice. **Environmental Initiatives:** recycling, food service, decreasing waste, composting, use of local/organic foods, housekeeping services switched to green chemicals.

ADMISSIONS

Freshman Academic Profile: Average high school GPA 3.3. 85% from public high schools. SAT Math middle 50% range 410-520. SAT Critical Reading middle 50% range 430-540. SAT Writing middle 50% range 410-550. ACT middle 50% range 18-25. Minimum internet-based TOEFL 62. Minimum paper TOEFL 500. **Basis for Candidate Selection:** *Important factors considered include:* Class rank, application essay, academic GPA, recommendation(s), rigor of secondary school record, standardized test scores. *Other factors considered include:* character/personal qualities, interview, level of applicant's interest, talent/ability. **Freshman Admission Requirements:** High school diploma is required and GED is accepted. *Academic units required:* 8 English, 6 mathematics, 6 science, (2 science labs), 4 foreign language, 4 social studies, 2 history, 10 academic electives. **Freshman Admission Statistics:** 417 applied, 70% admitted, 44% enrolled. **Transfer Admission Requirements:** college transcript(s), essay or personal statement, Minimum college GPA of 2.0 required. Lowest grade transferable C. **General Admission Information:** Application Fee $30. Regular application deadline 8/8. Notification on a rolling basis, beginning on or about 10/1. Nonfall registration accepted. Admission may be deferred for a maximum of 1 year. Credit and/or placement offered for CEEB Advanced Placement tests.

COSTS AND FINANCIAL AID

Annual tuition $20,900. Room and board $7,890. Required fees $650. Average book expense $900. **Required Forms and Deadlines:** FAFSA. **Notification of Awards:** Applicants will be notified of awards on a rolling basis beginning 12/1. **Types of Aid:** *Need-based scholarships/grants:* Federal Pell, SEOG, state scholarships/grants, private scholarships, the school's own gift aid. *Loans:* Subsidized Stafford, Unsubsidized Stafford, PLUS, Federal Perkins. *Student Employment:* Federal Work-Study Program available. Institutional employment available. Highest amount earned per year from on-campus jobs $4,665. Off-campus job opportunities are good. **Financial Aid Statistics:** 77% freshmen, 92% undergrads receive need-based scholarship or grant aid. 76% freshmen, 12% undergrads receive non-need-based scholarship or grant aid. 49% freshmen, 82% undergrads receive need-based self-help aid. 10% freshmen, 4% undergrads receive athletic scholarships. 98% freshmen, 96% undergrads receive any aid. 89% undergrads borrow to pay for school. Average cumulative indebtedness $16,428. **Criteria for awarding institutional aid:** *Non-need-based:* academics, alumni affiliation, art, athletics, leadership, music/drama.

SAINT MICHAEL'S COLLEGE

One Winooski Park, Box 7, Colchester, VT 5439
Phone: 802-654-3000 · **Financial Aid Phone:** 802-654-3243
E-mail: admission@smcvt.edu · **CEEB Code:** 3757
Fax: 802-654-2906 · **Website:** www.smcvt.edu · **ACT Code:** 4312

This private school, affiliated with the Roman Catholic Church, was founded in 1904. It has a 440-acre campus.

RATINGS

Admissions Selectivity Rating: 85   **Fire Safety Rating:** 79

STUDENTS AND FACULTY

Enrollment: 2,039. **Student Body:** 55% female, 45% male, 81% out-of-state, 3% international (46 countries represented). Asian 2%, African American 2%, Caucasian 86%, Hispanic 5%, Native American <1%
Retention and Graduation: 73% freshmen graduate within 4 years. 79% freshmen graduate within 6 years. 16% grads go on to further study within 1 year. 9% grads pursue arts and sciences degrees. 4% grads pursue business degrees. 2% grads pursue medical degrees. **Faculty:** 146 full-time faculty, 86% hold PhDs, 45% are are members of minority groups, 5% are women. 0% of classes are taught by teaching assistants.

ACADEMICS

Degrees: bachelor's, master's, post-bachelor's certificate, post-master's certificate. **Classes:** Most classes have 10-19 students. Most lab/discussion sessions have 20-29 students. **Majors with Highest Enrollment:** Business/Commerce; Biology/Biological Sciences; Psychology. **Special Study Options:** cross-registration, distance learning, double major, dual enrollment, English as a Second Language (ESL), honors program, independent study, internships, liberal arts/career combination, student-designed major, study abroad, teacher certification program, Research for Academic Credit: Many majors require students to complete the equivalent of a senior thesis (sometimes called a Senior Seminar) for which they receive academic credit. Students work closely with an academic advisor on these capstone projects. Independent Research with **Faculty:** Independent research projects with faculty members—which are not-for-credit—often lead to peer-reviewed publications and presentations at major conferences. These projects are an exciting opportunity for students and faculty to work side-by-side, making important discoveries in their fields. For students, these opportunities not only provide excellent resume-building experience, but also the chance to work closely with a mentor. Some students may even qualify for grant-funded research stipends. **Honors programs:** The Honors Program at Saint Michael's provides additional challenges and opportunities to outstanding students through small group discussion, research and extra-curricular activities. Saint Michael's also has chapters of several national honors societies on campus including Phi Beta Kappa, and Delta Epsilon Sigma. **Combined degree programs:** BA/MA, 4+1 MBA w/Clarkson, (B.S., + D.Pharm.) with Albany College of Pharmacy. **Disability Services:** Special programs offered to physically disabled students include note-taking services, reader services, tape recorders, tutors. **Career services:** Alumni network, alumni services, career/job search classes, career assessment, internships, regional alumni. Career services highlights include an Internship Program that gives students the opportunity to integrate their academic studies with a supervised work experience. Internships enhance classroom learning by integrating academics with the world of business. This on-the-job experience assists students in their career decision-making process. Internships provide valuable work experiences that increase job opportunities after graduation. Through this process students learn valuable job search and career defining skills.

FACILITIES

Housing: Coed dorms, special housing for disabled students, men's dorms, special housing for international students, women's dorms, apartments for single students, Theme **Housing:** 1.Honors Housing, 2. Substance Free Housing. 75% of campus accessible to physically disabled. **Special Academic Facilities/Equipment:** Holcomb Observatory,McCarthy Arts Center Gallary. **Computers:** 90% of classrooms, 100% of dorms, 100% of libraries, 100% of dining areas, 100% of student union, have wireless network access. Students can register for classes online. Administrative functions (other than registration) can be performed online.

CAMPUS LIFE

Environment: City. **Activities:** Choral groups, concert band, dance, drama/theater, jazz band, literary magazine, music ensembles, musical theater, radio station, student government, student newspaper, yearbook, Campus Ministries, International Student Organization. 50 registered organizations, 11 honor societies, 1 religous organization. **Athletics (Intercollegiate):** *Men:* baseball, basketball, cross-country, diving, golf, ice hockey, lacrosse, skiing (downhill/alpine), skiing (nordic/cross-country), soccer, swimming, tennis. *Women:* basketball, cross-country, diving, field hockey, ice hockey, lacrosse, skiing (downhill/alpine), skiing (nordic/cross-country), soccer, softball, swimming, tennis, volleyball. **On-Campus Highlights:** Alliot Student Center, McCarthy Arts Center, Chapel of Saint Michael the Archangel, Vincent C. Ross Sports Center, Tarrant Student Recreational Center. **Environmental Initiatives:** Energy Efficiency Programs: "Three Degree Challenge" to further reduce campus wide building temperatures by turning down thermostats to reduce energy consumption (in addition to reducing energy consumption, all new major appliances must be energy star certified); new building aims for LEED certification; all campus buildings on an Energy Management System to ensure efficient use of energy; Creating a culture of sustainability with each First Year class: each first year student receives a green welcome package during their orientation: 2 reusable tote bags, reusable coffee mug, bus map. A Green Office Certification program just launched (Spring 2012) to encourage faculty and staff to be more sustainable. The Academic side of the college further supports creating a culture of sustainability by having just established a new major: Environmental Studies Local Food Program: The college has a 1/4 Organic Garden to give students hands on experience with sustainable agriculture and offers 2 paid positions during the summer; the college partners with the local Intervale Food Hub to offer CSA shares for faculty, staff and students that are delivered year round right to campus; a newly established Food Justice group was formed due to increased interests for local and fair trade food and the college has become a Fair Trade Certified university.

ADMISSIONS

Freshman Academic Profile: Average high school GPA 3.4. 22% in top 10% of high school class, 49% in top 25% of high school class, 79% in top 50% of high school class. 66% from public high schools. SAT Math middle 50% range 520-610. SAT Critical Reading middle 50% range 530-640. SAT Writing middle 50% range 520-620. ACT middle 50% range 24-28. Minimum paper TOEFL 550. **Basis for Candidate Selection:** *Very important factors considered include:* Class rank, academic GPA, rigor of secondary school record. *Important factors considered include:* application essay, recommendation(s), standardized test scores, character/personal qualities, extracurricular activities, talent/ability. *Other factors considered include:* alumni/ae relation, first generation, geographical residence, level of applicant's interest, racial/ethnic status, state residency, volunteer work, work experience. **Freshman Admission Requirements:** High school diploma is required and GED is accepted. *Academic units required:* 4 English, 3 mathematics, 3 science, (2 science labs), 3 foreign language, 3 social studies. **Freshman Admission Statistics:** 4,299 applied, 80% admitted, 17% enrolled. **Transfer Admission Requirements:** High school transcript, college transcript(s), essay or personal statement, standardized test scores, Minimum college GPA of 2.8 required, Lowest grade transferable C-. **General Admission Information:** Application Fee $50. Regular application deadline 2/1. Regular notification 4/1. Nonfall registration accepted. Admission may be deferred for a maximum of 1 year. Credit and/or placement offered for CEEB Advanced Placement tests.

COSTS AND FINANCIAL AID

Annual tuition $39,050. Room and board $10,600. Required fees $325. Average book expense $1,280. **Required Forms and Deadlines:** FAFSA. **Notification of Awards:** Applicants will be notified of awards on a rolling basis beginning 1/15. **Types of Aid:** *Need-based scholarships/grants:* Federal Pell, SEOG, state scholarships/grants, private scholarships, the school's own gift aid. *Loans:* Subsidized Stafford, Unsubsidized Stafford, PLUS, Federal Perkins. *Student Employment:* Federal Work-Study Program available. Institutional employment available. Highest amount earned per year from on-campus jobs $15,649. Off-campus job opportunities are excellent. **Financial Aid Statistics:** 100% freshmen, 100% undergrads receive need-based scholarship or grant aid. 25% freshmen, 21% undergrads receive non-need-based scholarship or grant aid. 75% freshmen, 78% undergrads receive need-based self-help aid. 0% freshmen, 1% undergrads receive athletic scholarships. 99% freshmen, 98% undergrads receive any aid. 75% undergrads borrow to pay for school. Average cumulative indebtedness $26,426. **Criteria for awarding institutional aid:** *Non-need-based:* academics, alumni affiliation, art, athletics, leadership, minority status, music/drama, state/district residency.

See page 1134.

SAINT PAUL'S COLLEGE

115 College Drive, Lawrenceville, VA 23868
Phone: 434-848-1856
E-mail: admissions@saintpauls.edu
Fax: 804-848-6407 • **Website:** www.saintpauls.edu • **ACT Code:** 4394

This private school, affiliated with the Episcopal Church, was founded in 1888. It has a 185-acre campus.

RATINGS

Admissions Selectivity Rating: 70   Fire Safety Rating: 69

STUDENTS AND FACULTY

Enrollment: 707. **Student Body:** 52% female, 48% male, 31% out-of-state, 0% international (6 countries represented). Asian 0%, African American 99%, Caucasian 2%, Hispanic 0%, Native American <1%
Retention and Graduation: 100% freshmen return for sophomore year. 16% freshmen graduate within 4 years. 10% grads go on to further study within 1 year. **Faculty:** 30 full-time faculty, 53% hold PhDs, 33% are are members of minority groups, 50% are women. 0% of classes are taught by teaching assistants.

ACADEMICS

Degrees: bachelor's. **Classes:** Most classes have fewer than 10 students. Most lab/discussion sessions have fewer than 10 students. **Majors with Highest Enrollment:** Criminal Justice/Police Science; Sociology; Business/Commerce. **Special Study Options:** Accelerated program, cooperative education program, double major, honors program, independent study, internships, liberal arts/career combination, study abroad, teacher certification program, U.S. Army ROTC. **Honors programs:** Alpha Kappa Mu Honor Society. **Disability Services:** Special programs offered to physically disabled students include tape recorders, tutors. **Career services:** Alumni network, alumni services, career/job search classes, career assessment, internships, regional alumni.

FACILITIES

Housing: men's dorms, women's dorms, apartments for single students **Special Academic Facilities/Equipment:** The Saul Building (1888) (the first classroom built on SPC campus).

CAMPUS LIFE

Environment: Rural. **Activities:** Choral groups, dance, drama/theater, student government, yearbook. 30 registered organizations, 2 honor societies, 2 religious organizations. 3 fraternities, 3 sororities. **Athletics (Intercollegiate):** *Men:* baseball, basketball, cross-country, golf, tennis, track/field (outdoor), track/field (indoor). *Women:* basketball, cross-country, golf, softball, tennis, track/field (outdoor), track/field (indoor), volleyball. **On-Campus Highlights:** Student Center, Gymnasium, Library, Cafeteria, Dorms.

ADMISSIONS

Freshman Academic Profile: Average high school GPA 2.5. 3% in top 10% of high school class, 8% in top 25% of high school class, 23% in top 50% of high school class. 95% from public high schools. SAT Math middle 50% range 330-410. SAT Critical Reading middle 50% range 330-410. ACT middle 50% range 13-17. **Basis for Candidate Selection:** *Important factors considered include:* Class rank, application essay, recommendation(s), rigor of secondary school record, standardized test scores, character/personal qualities, extracurricular activities, interview, talent/ability. *Other factors considered include:* volunteer work, work experience. **Freshman Admission Requirements:** High school diploma is required and GED is accepted. *Academic units required:* 4 English, 2 mathematics, 2 science. **Freshman Admission Statistics:** 641 applied, 71% admitted, 64% enrolled. **Transfer Admission Requirements:** High school transcript, college transcript(s), essay or personal statement, statement of good standing from prior institution(s). Minimum college GPA of 2 required. Lowest grade transferable C. **General Admission Information:** Application Fee $20. Nonfall registration accepted. Neither credit nor placement offered for CEEB Advanced Placement tests.

COSTS AND FINANCIAL AID

Annual tuition $10,400. Room and board $5,890. Required fees $681. Average book expense $600. **Required Forms and Deadlines:** FAFSA, State aid form. **Notification of Awards:** Applicants will be notified of awards on a rolling basis beginning 1/7. **Types of Aid:** *Need-based scholarships/grants:* Federal Pell, SEOG, state scholarships/grants, private scholarships, the school's own gift aid, United Negro College Fund. *Loans:* Direct Subsidized Stafford, Direct Unsubsidized Stafford, Direct PLUS, Federal Perkins. *Student Employment:* Federal Work-Study Program available. Highest amount earned per year from on-campus jobs $1,300. Off-campus job opportunities are fair. **Financial Aid Statistics:** 81% freshmen, 81% undergrads receive need-based scholarship or grant aid. 85% freshmen, 86% undergrads receive non-need-based scholarship

or grant aid. 89% freshmen, 88% undergrads receive need-based self-help aid. 4% freshmen, 11% undergrads receive athletic scholarships. 91% freshmen, 59% undergrads receive any aid. 80% undergrads borrow to pay for school. **Criteria for awarding institutional aid:** *Non-need-based:* academics, athletics, state/district residency.

SAINT PETER'S UNIVERSITY

2641 Kennedy Boulevard, Jersey City, NJ 7306
Phone: 201-761-7100 • **Financial Aid Phone:** 201-761-6071
E-mail: admissions@saintpeters.edu • **CEEB Code:** 2806
Fax: 201-761-7105 • **Website:** www.saintpeters.edu • **ACT Code:** 2604

This private school, affiliated with the Roman Catholic Church, was founded in 1872. It has a 10-acre campus.

RATINGS

Admissions Selectivity Rating: 73   Fire Safety Rating: 60*

STUDENTS AND FACULTY

Enrollment: 2,409. **Student Body:** 61% female, 39% male, 12% out-of-state, 2% international (56 countries represented). Asian 8%, African American 30%, Caucasian 22%, Hispanic 34%, Native American <1%
Retention and Graduation: 83% freshmen return for sophomore year. 37% freshmen graduate within 4 years. 27% grads go on to further study within 1 year. 9% grads pursue arts and sciences degrees. 5% grads pursue law degrees. 6% grads pursue business degrees. 7% grads pursue medical degrees. **Faculty:** 113 full-time faculty, 84% hold PhDs, 50% are are members of minority groups, 11% are women. 0% of classes are taught by teaching assistants.

ACADEMICS

Degrees: associate, bachelor's, diploma, master's. **Classes:** Most classes have 10-19 students. **Majors with Highest Enrollment:** Business Administration and Management; Biology/Biological Sciences; Registered Nursing/Registered Nurse. **Special Study Options:** Accelerated program, cooperative education program, double major, dual enrollment, exchange student program (domestic), honors program, independent study, internships, liberal arts/career combination, student-designed major, study abroad, teacher certification program, weekend college, Joint degree in clinical and laboratory sciences with the University of Medicine and Dentistry of New Jersey (UMDNJ); Joint degree in Pharmacy with Rutgers University. **Honors programs:** While Honors provides academic enrichment for highly motivated students, it is not a formal major or minor. Students enrolled in the program must complete a minimum of 30 credits designated as Honors courses, which include Honors core course seminars, Honors advanced electives, and 6 credits of Honors Thesis: research and independent study. Independent study projects must be approved by the Honors Program and the respective chairs of the student's major department. Independent study projects may carry departmental as well as Honors credit. **Combined degree programs:** BA/MD, BA/JD, Combined-Degree programs at Seton Hall and UMDNJ. **Disability Services:** Special programs offered to physically disabled students include note-taking services, reader services, tape recorders, tutors.

FACILITIES

Housing: Coed dorms, men's dorms, women's dorms, apartments for single students **Special Academic Facilities/Equipment:** TV production facilities, center for government affairs.

CAMPUS LIFE

Environment: City. **Activities:** Choral groups, drama/theater, literary magazine, radio station, student government, student newspaper, yearbook. 45 registered organizations, 11 honor societies. **Athletics (Intercollegiate):** *Men:* baseball, basketball, cheerleading, cross-country, diving, football, golf, soccer, swimming, tennis, track/field (outdoor). *Women:* basketball, bowling, cheerleading, cross-country, diving, soccer, softball, swimming, tennis, track/field (outdoor), volleyball. **Environmental Initiatives:** Use of solar and wind energy; Construction of Leed Silver Certified Student Center; Construction of cogeneration plant.

ADMISSIONS

Freshman Academic Profile: Average high school GPA 3.15. SAT Math middle 50% range 410-500. SAT Critical Reading middle 50% range 400-490. SAT Writing middle 50% range 400-490. ACT middle 50% range 16-21. Minimum internet-based TOEFL 79. Minimum paper TOEFL 550. **Basis for Candidate Selection:** *Very important factors considered include:* academic GPA, rigor of secondary school record, standardized test scores. *Important factors considered include:* Class rank, application essay, recommendation(s). *Other factors considered include:* character/personal qualities, extracurricular activities, interview, talent/ability, volunteer work, work experience. **Fresh-**

man **Admission Requirements:** High school diploma is required and GED is accepted. *Academic units required:* 4 English, 3 mathematics, 2 science, (1 science labs), 2 foreign language, 2 history, 3 academic electives. **Freshman Admission Statistics:** 5,993 applied, 57% admitted, 17% enrolled. **Transfer Admission Requirements:** college transcript(s), essay or personal statement, Minimum college GPA of 2.0 required. Lowest grade transferable C. **General Admission Information:** Notification on a rolling basis, beginning on or about 11/1. Nonfall registration accepted. Admission may be deferred for a maximum of 24. Credit offered for CEEB Advanced Placement tests.

COSTS AND FINANCIAL AID

Annual tuition $32,170. Room and board $13,996. Required fees $1,352. Average book expense $800. **Required Forms and Deadlines:** FAFSA, State aid form. **Notification of Awards:** Applicants will be notified of awards on a rolling basis beginning 2/15. **Types of Aid:** *Need-based scholarships/grants:* Federal Pell, SEOG, state scholarships/grants, the school's own gift aid. *Loans:* Subsidized Stafford, Unsubsidized Stafford, PLUS, Federal Perkins, state loans. *Student Employment:* Federal Work-Study Program available. Institutional employment available. Highest amount earned per year from on-campus jobs $1,500. Off-campus job opportunities are excellent. **Financial Aid Statistics:** 99% freshmen, 97% undergrads receive need-based scholarship or grant aid. 7% freshmen, 5% undergrads receive non-need-based scholarship or grant aid. 72% freshmen, 79% undergrads receive need-based self-help aid. 3% freshmen, 3% undergrads receive athletic scholarships. 76% undergrads borrow to pay for school. Average cumulative indebtedness $24,246.

SAINT VINCENT COLLEGE

Office of Admission and Financial Aid, Latrobe, PA 15650-2690
Phone: 724-537-4540 • **Financial Aid Phone:** 800-782-5549
E-mail: admission@stvincent.edu • **CEEB Code:** 2808
Fax: 724-532-5069 • **Website:** www.stvincent.edu • **ACT Code:** 3686

This private school, affiliated with the Roman Catholic Church, was founded in 1846. It has a 200-acre campus.

RATINGS

Admissions Selectivity Rating: 86   **Fire Safety Rating:** 65

STUDENTS AND FACULTY

Enrollment: 1,617. **Student Body:** 50% female, 50% male, 12% out-of-state, 1% international (15 countries represented). Asian 1%, African American 3%, Caucasian 90%, Hispanic 2%, Native American <1%.
Retention and Graduation: 60% freshmen graduate within 4 years, 70% freshmen graduate within 6 years. 30% grads go on to further study within 1 year. **Faculty:** 91 full-time faculty, 84% hold PhDs, 24% are are members of minority groups, 2% are women. 0% of classes are taught by teaching assistants.

ACADEMICS

Degrees: bachelor's, certificate, master's, post-bachelor's certificate. **Classes:** Most classes have 20-29 students. Most lab/discussion sessions have 10-19 students. **Majors with Highest Enrollment:** History; Biology/Biological Sciences; Psychology. **Special Study Options:** Accelerated program, cooperative education program, cross-registration, distance learning, double major, dual enrollment, external degree program, honors program, independent study, internships, liberal arts/career combination, study abroad, teacher certification program. **Honors programs:** Honors Classes Professors design Honors classes to challenge and reward students who seek substantial intellectual development in college. The quality, not the quantity of work, distinguishes Honors classes from other courses. Portfolio As part of their coursework in Honors classes, all students are required to submit a short reflective essay and sample of their work at the end of each Honors class. Honors Events Dinner and evening discussions based on a reading, or attendance of a play, a film, an art exhibit, etc., on campus provide a special, congenial setting for intellectual exchange as part of a course or an extracurricular event. Off-Campus Explorations All Honors students and faculty are regularly invited to attend a play, film, art exhibit, etc. Extended trips within the U.S. or abroad may be planned during breaks or the summer. Senior Capstone Projects Honors students in majors with a senior research or capstone project will be strongly encouraged to present their work in a special colloquium at Saint Vincent and at professional meetings in their research areas. **Combined degree programs:** BA/JD, BA/MEng, 3-3 JD, 4-1 MBA w/ Duquesne. **Disability Services:** Special programs offered to physically disabled students include note-taking services, tutors. **Career services:** Alumni network, alumni services, career assessment, internships, regional alumni. Career services highlights include an internship program that students can take for credit, though this is not required. Students are assisted in looking for internships in their field or industry of interest.

FACILITIES

Housing: Coed dorms, apartments for single students. 95% of campus accessible to physically disabled. **Special Academic Facilities/Equipment:** Art gallery, life sciences research center, spectrophotometer, spectrometer, physiograph work stations, data acquisition work station, planetarium, observatory, radio telescope, instructional technology resource center. **Computers:** 75% of libraries, 100% of student union, 25% of common outdoor areas have wireless network access. Students can register for classes online. Administrative functions (other than registration) can be performed online.

CAMPUS LIFE

Environment: Village. **Activities:** Choral groups, dance, drama/theater, literary magazine, music ensembles, musical theater, pep band, radio station, student government, student newspaper, television station, yearbook, Campus Ministries, International Student Organization. 43 registered organizations, 12 honor societies, 2 religious organizations. **Athletics (Intercollegiate):** *Men:* baseball, basketball, cross-country, football, golf, lacrosse, soccer, swimming, tennis, track/field (outdoor). *Women:* basketball, cross-country, field hockey, golf, lacrosse, soccer, softball, swimming, tennis, volleyball. **On-Campus Highlights:** Library, Carey Student Center, St. Benedict Hall, Basilica, Chuck Noll Field. **Environmental Initiatives:** New construction on campus, including a current building project, will be green; Environmental Education Center provides education opportunities to students.

ADMISSIONS

Freshman Academic Profile: Average high school GPA 3.55. 23.8% in top 10% of high school class, 53.9% in top 25% of high school class, 84.3% in top 50% of high school class. 67% from public high schools. SAT Math middle 50% range 490-600. SAT Critical Reading middle 50% range 480-590. SAT Writing middle 50% range 470-570. ACT middle 50% range 20-26. Minimum paper TOEFL 550. **Basis for Candidate Selection:** *Very important factors considered include:* Class rank, academic GPA, rigor of secondary school record. *Important factors considered include:* application essay, standardized test scores, character/personal qualities. *Other factors considered include:* recommendation(s), extracurricular activities, first generation, interview, talent/ability. **Freshman Admission Requirements:** High school diploma is required and GED is accepted. *Academic units required:* 4 English, 3 mathematics, 1 science, (1 science labs), 0 foreign language, 3 social studies, 0 history, 5 academic electives. **Freshman Admission Statistics:** 1,855 applied, 62% admitted, 37% enrolled. **Transfer Admission Requirements:** High school transcript, college transcript(s), essay or personal statement, statement of good standing from prior institution(s). Minimum college GPA of 2.5 required. Lowest grade transferable C-. **General Admission Information:** Application Fee $25. Regular application deadline 5/1. Notification on a rolling basis, beginning on or about 10/1. Nonfall registration accepted. Admission may be deferred for a maximum of 1 year. Credit and/or placement offered for CEEB Advanced Placement tests.

COSTS AND FINANCIAL AID

Annual tuition $22,350. Room and board $7,542. Required fees $650. Average book expense $650. **Required Forms and Deadlines:** FAFSA, State aid form. **Notification of Awards:** Applicants will be notified of awards on a rolling basis beginning 3/1. **Types of Aid:** *Need-based scholarships/grants:* Federal Pell, SEOG, state scholarships/grants, private scholarships, the school's own gift aid, United Negro College Fund. *Loans:* Subsidized Stafford, Unsubsidized Stafford, PLUS, Federal Perkins. *Student Employment:* Federal Work-Study Program available. Institutional employment available. Highest amount earned per year from on-campus jobs $2,432. Off-campus job opportunities are good. **Financial Aid Statistics:** 10% freshmen, 100% undergrads receive need-based scholarship or grant aid. 43% freshmen, 85% undergrads receive non-need-based scholarship or grant aid. 75% freshmen, 80% undergrads receive need-based self-help aid. 0% freshmen, 10% undergrads receive athletic scholarships. 99% freshmen, 96% undergrads receive any aid. **Criteria for awarding institutional aid:** *Non-need-based:* academics, alumni affiliation, leadership, minority status, music/drama.

SAINT XAVIER UNIVERSITY

3700 West 103rd Street., Chicago, IL 60655
Phone: 773-298-3050
E-mail: admissions@sxu.edu • **CEEB Code:** 1708
Fax: 773-298-3076 • **Website:** www.sxu.edu • **ACT Code:** 1134

This private school, affiliated with the Roman Catholic Church, was founded in 1847. It has a 70-acre campus.

RATINGS

Admissions Selectivity Rating: 80   **Fire Safety Rating:** 60*

STUDENTS AND FACULTY

Enrollment: 2,897. **Student Body:** 67% female, 33% male, 5% out-of-state, 0% international. Asian 3%, African American 16%, Caucasian 50%, Hispanic 23%, Native American <1%

Retention and Graduation: 75% freshmen return for sophomore year. 30% freshmen graduate within 4 years. 47% freshmen graduate within 6 years. 10% grads go on to further study within 1 year. **Faculty:** 168 full-time faculty, 86% hold PhDs, 57% are are members of minority groups, 13% are women. 0% of classes are taught by teaching assistants.

ACADEMICS

Degrees: bachelor's, certificate, master's, post-bachelor's certificate, post-master's certificate. **Classes:** Most classes have 20-29 students. Most lab/discussion sessions have 10-19 students. **Majors with Highest Enrollment:** Elementary Education and Teaching; Registered Nursing/Registered Nurse; Business/Commerce. **Special Study Options:** Accelerated program, cooperative education program, distance learning, double major, dual enrollment, English as a Second Language (ESL), external degree program, honors program, independent study, internships, liberal arts/career combination, student-designed major, study abroad, teacher certification program, weekend college. **Combined degree programs:** BS/RN RN/MS BS/LPN. **Disability Services:** Special programs offered to physically disabled students include note-taking services, reader services, tape recorders, tutors. **Career services:** alumni services, career/job search classes, career assessment, internships.

FACILITIES

Housing: Coed dorms, special housing for disabled students, apartments for single students. 98% of campus accessible to physically disabled. **Computers:** Students can register for classes online. Administrative functions (other than registration) can be performed online.

CAMPUS LIFE

Environment: Metropolis. **Activities:** Choral groups, concert band, jazz band, literary magazine, marching band, music ensembles, pep band, radio station, student government, student newspaper, student-run film society, symphony orchestra, yearbook, Campus Ministries, International Student Organization. 41 registered organizations, 2 honor societies, 2 religious organizations. **Athletics (Intercollegiate):** *Men:* baseball, basketball, football, soccer. *Women:* basketball, cross-country, soccer, softball, volleyball. **On-Campus Highlights:** Convocation and Athletic Center, McDonough Chapel and Mercy Ministry Center, McCarthy Hall, Speech language Pathology Clinic, Art Gallery.

ADMISSIONS

Freshman Academic Profile: 25% in top 10% of high school class, 54% in top 25% of high school class, 84% in top 50% of high school class. 55% from public high schools. SAT Math middle 50% range 440-545. SAT Critical Reading middle 50% range 455-570. SAT Writing middle 50% range 455-540. ACT middle 50% range 19-24. Minimum paper TOEFL 550. **Basis for Candidate Selection:** *Very important factors considered include:* application essay, academic GPA, standardized test scores. *Important factors considered include:* rigor of secondary school record. *Other factors considered include:* recommendation(s), character/personal qualities, extracurricular activities, interview, level of applicant's interest, talent/ability, volunteer work, work experience. **Freshman Admission Requirements:** High school diploma is required and GED is accepted. **Freshman Admission Statistics:** 6,693 applied, 79% admitted, 11% enrolled. **Transfer Admission Requirements:** college transcript(s), Minimum college GPA of 2.5 required. Lowest grade transferable C. **General Admission Information:** Application Fee $25. Nonfall registration accepted. Admission may be deferred for a maximum of not avail. Credit offered for CEEB Advanced Placement tests.

COSTS AND FINANCIAL AID

Average book expense $1,200. **Required Forms and Deadlines:** FAFSA. **Notification of Awards:** Applicants will be notified of awards on a rolling basis beginning 2/15. **Types of Aid:** *Need-based scholarships/grants:* Federal Pell, SEOG, state scholarships/grants, private scholarships, the school's own gift aid. *Loans:* Subsidized Stafford, Unsubsidized Stafford, PLUS, Federal Perkins. *Student Employment:* Federal Work-Study Program available. Institutional employment available. Off-campus job opportunities are excellent. **Financial Aid Statistics:** 100% freshmen, 99% undergrads receive need-based scholarship or grant aid. 98% freshmen, 92% undergrads receive non-need-based scholarship or grant aid. 84% freshmen, 87% undergrads receive need-based self-help aid. 12% freshmen, 9% undergrads receive athletic scholarships. 63% undergrads borrow to pay for school. **Criteria for awarding institutional aid:** *Non-need-based:* academics, athletics, music/drama.

See page 1136.

SALEM COLLEGE

PO Box 10548, Winston-Salem, NC 27108
Phone: 336-721-2621 • **Financial Aid Phone:** 336-721-2808
E-mail: admissions@salem.edu • **CEEB Code:** 5607
Fax: 336-917-5572 • **Website:** www.salem.edu • **ACT Code:** 3156

This private school, affiliated with the Moravian Church, was founded in 1772. It has a 57-acre campus.

RATINGS

Admissions Selectivity Rating: 88   **Fire Safety Rating:** 77

STUDENTS AND FACULTY

Enrollment: 741. **Student Body:** 98% female, 2% male, 23% out-of-state, 13% international (22 countries represented). Asian 1%, African American 19%, Caucasian 60%, Hispanic 4%, Native American <1%

Retention and Graduation: 78% freshmen return for sophomore year. 50% freshmen graduate within 4 years. 52% freshmen graduate within 6 years. 30% grads go on to further study within 1 year. 25% grads pursue arts and sciences degrees. 3% grads pursue law degrees. 5% grads pursue business degrees. **Faculty:** 57 full-time faculty, 86% hold PhDs, 61% are are members of minority groups, 9% are women. 0% of classes are taught by teaching assistants.

ACADEMICS

Degrees: bachelor's, master's. **Classes:** Most classes have 10-19 students. Most lab/discussion sessions have 10-19 students. **Majors with Highest Enrollment:** Sociology; Business/Commerce. **Special Study Options:** cross-registration, double major, dual enrollment, honors program, independent study, internships, liberal arts/career combination, student-designed major, study abroad, teacher certification program. **Career services:** Alumni network, internships.

FACILITIES

Housing: women's dorms, apartments for single students. 75% of campus accessible to physically disabled. **Special Academic Facilities/Equipment:** Art gallery, fine arts center, Center for Women Writers, videoconferencing center. **Computers:** Administrative functions (other than registration) can be performed online.

CAMPUS LIFE

Environment: City. **Activities:** Choral groups, dance, drama/theater, literary magazine, marching band, music ensembles, musical theater, student government, student newspaper, yearbook. 26 registered organizations, 14 honor societies, 7 religious organizations. **Athletics (Intercollegiate):** *Women:* basketball, cross-country, field hockey, swimming, tennis, volleyball. **On-Campus Highlights:** back porch of Main Hall, Salem Grille/Java City, residence hall basement lounges. **Environmental Initiatives:** Recylcle committment-all residence halls and academic buildings have paper, plastic and aluminum containers; Energy Conservation—1) systematically changing incandescent lights with CFL, 2)Limited installation of occupancy sensors, 3)Removal of lights in vending machines for energy conservation; EPA-self audit and self disclosure program.

ADMISSIONS

Freshman Academic Profile: Average high school GPA 3.7. 39% in top 10% of high school class, 67% in top 25% of high school class, 94% in top 50% of high school class. SAT Math middle 50% range 480-630. SAT Critical Reading middle 50% range 490-650. ACT middle 50% range 20-25. Minimum paper TOEFL 550. **Basis for Candidate Selection:** *Very important factors considered include:* academic GPA, rigor of secondary school record. *Important factors considered include:* Class rank, application essay, recommendation(s), standardized test scores, character/personal qualities, extracurricular activities, talent/ability. *Other factors considered include:* alumni/ae relation, first generation, interview, level of applicant's interest, volunteer work. **Freshman Admission Requirements:** High school diploma is required and GED is accepted. *Academic units required:* 4 English, 3 mathematics, 3 science, 2 foreign language, 2 history. **Freshman Admission Statistics:** 420 applied, 62% admitted, 46% enrolled. **Transfer Admission Requirements:** High school transcript, college transcript(s), essay or personal statement, statement of good standing from prior institution(s). Minimum college GPA of 2.0 required. Lowest grade transferable C-. **General Admission Information:** Application Fee $30. Notification on a rolling basis, beginning on or about 10/1. Nonfall registration accepted. Admission may be deferred for a maximum of 1 year. Credit and/or placement offered for CEEB Advanced Placement tests.

COSTS AND FINANCIAL AID

Annual tuition $18,850. Room and board $10,050. Required fees $340. Average book expense $900. **Required Forms and Deadlines:** FAFSA. **Notification of Awards:** Applicants will be notified of awards on a rolling basis beginning

3/1. **Types of Aid:** *Need-based scholarships/grants:* Federal Pell, SEOG, state scholarships/grants, private scholarships, the school's own gift aid. *Loans:* Subsidized Stafford, Unsubsidized Stafford, PLUS, Federal Perkins. **Financial Aid Statistics:** 80% freshmen, 71% undergrads receive need-based scholarship or grant aid. 96% freshmen, 95% undergrads receive non-need-based scholarship or grant aid. 88% freshmen, 83% undergrads receive need-based self-help aid. 0% freshmen, 0% undergrads receive athletic scholarships. 70% undergrads borrow to pay for school. Average cumulative indebtedness $17,125. **Criteria for awarding institutional aid:** *Non-need-based:* academics, alumni affiliation, leadership, minority status, music/drama, state/district residency.

SALEM INTERNATIONAL UNIVERSITY

223 West Main Street, Salem, WV 26426-0500
Phone: 304-782-5336
E-mail: admissions@salemiu.edu • **CEEB Code:** 5608
Fax: 304-782-5592 • **Website:** www.salemiu.edu • **ACT Code:** 4530

This private school was founded in 1888. It has a 300-acre campus.

RATINGS

Admissions Selectivity Rating: 69   Fire Safety Rating: 60*

STUDENTS AND FACULTY

Enrollment: 439. **Student Body:** 47% female, 53% male, 56% out-of-state, 39% international (20 countries represented). Asian 1%, African American 8%, Caucasian 46%, Hispanic 2%, Native American 1%
Retention and Graduation: 69% freshmen return for sophomore year. 3% grads go on to further study within 1 year. 2% grads pursue arts and sciences degrees. 1% grads pursue law degrees. 2% grads pursue business degrees. 1% grads pursue medical degrees. **Faculty:** 33 full-time faculty, 70% hold PhDs, 39% are are members of minority groups, 24% are women. 0% of classes are taught by teaching assistants.

ACADEMICS

Degrees: associate, bachelor's, master's, post-master's certificate. **Classes:** Most classes have fewer than 10 students. **Special Study Options:** distance learning, double major, English as a Second Language (ESL), independent study, internships, liberal arts/career combination, study abroad, undergrads may take grad level classes foreign exchange program(s): exchange programs abroad in Japan(Teikyo U, Hachioji)and Germany(Teikyo U Berlin). Combined Bachelor's/Graduate degree in molecular biology. **Disability Services:** Special programs offered to physically disabled students include tutors. **Career services:** career/job search classes, career assessment, internships,

FACILITIES

Housing: Coed dorms, men's dorms, women's dorms. 90% of campus accessible to physically disabled. **Special Academic Facilities/Equipment:** Living museum of culture and crafts of West Virginia settlers. Fort New Salem. Biotechnology labs, equestrian center.

CAMPUS LIFE

Environment: Rural. **Activities:** Choral groups, dance, student government, student newspaper, television station, yearbook. 20 registered organizations, 1 honor society, 2 religious organizations. 4 fraternities, 4 sororities. **Athletics (Intercollegiate):** *Men:* baseball, basketball, cheerleading, equestrian sports, golf, soccer, swimming, tennis, water polo. *Women:* basketball, cheerleading, equestrian sports, soccer, softball, swimming, tennis, volleyball, water polo. **On-Campus Highlights:** Barker Center, Cafeteria, Tiger's Den, Library, Computer Labs.

ADMISSIONS

Freshman Academic Profile: SAT Math middle 50% range 420-570. SAT Critical Reading middle 50% range 380-550. ACT middle 50% range 16-22. Minimum paper TOEFL 500. **Basis for Candidate Selection:** *Very important factors considered include:* rigor of secondary school record, standardized test scores. *Important factors considered include:* recommendation(s), extracurricular activities. *Other factors considered include:* application essay, alumni/ae relation, character/personal qualities, interview, talent/ability. **Freshman Admission Requirements:** High school diploma is required and GED is accepted. **Freshman Admission Statistics:** 251 applied, 99% admitted, 24% enrolled. **Transfer Admission Requirements:** High school transcript, college transcript(s), statement of good standing from prior institution(s). Minimum college GPA of 2.5 required. Lowest grade transferable C. **General Admission Information:** Application Fee $25. Nonfall registration accepted. Admission may be deferred for a maximum of 12 months. Credit and/or placement offered for CEEB Advanced Placement tests.

COSTS AND FINANCIAL AID

Average book expense $1,000. **Required Forms and Deadlines:** FAFSA, Institution's own financial aid form. **Notification of Awards:** Applicants will be notified of awards on a rolling basis beginning 2/15. **Types of Aid:** *Need-based scholarships/grants:* Federal Pell, SEOG, state scholarships/grants, private scholarships, the school's own gift aid. *Loans:* Direct Subsidized Stafford, Direct Unsubsidized Stafford, Direct PLUS, Subsidized Stafford, Unsubsidized Stafford, PLUS, Federal Perkins, college/university loans from institutional funds. *Student Employment:* Federal Work-Study Program available. Institutional employment available. Highest amount earned per year from on-campus jobs $2,000. Off-campus job opportunities are fair. **Financial Aid Statistics:** 67% freshmen, 63% undergrads receive need-based scholarship or grant aid. 9% freshmen, 37% undergrads receive non-need-based scholarship or grant aid. 94% freshmen, 87% undergrads receive need-based self-help aid. 31% freshmen, 6% undergrads receive athletic scholarships. 45% undergrads borrow to pay for school.

SALEM STATE UNIVERSITY

352 Lafayette Street, Salem, MA 1970
Phone: 978-542-6210 • **Financial Aid Phone:** 978-542-6112
E-mail: admissions@salemstate.edu • **CEEB Code:** 3522
Fax: 978-542-6893 • **Website:** www.salemstate.edu

This public school was founded in 1854. It has a 108-acre campus.

RATINGS

Admissions Selectivity Rating: 77   Fire Safety Rating: 71

STUDENTS AND FACULTY

Enrollment: 7,296. **Student Body:** 61% female, 39% male, 3% out-of-state, 3% international. Asian 3%, African American 9%, Caucasian 76%, Hispanic 7%, Native American <1%
Faculty: 333 full-time faculty, 54% are are members of minority groups, 10% are women. 0% of classes are taught by teaching assistants.

ACADEMICS

Degrees: bachelor's, master's, post-bachelor's certificate, post-master's certificate. **Classes:** Most classes have 10-19 students. Most lab/discussion sessions have 10-19 students. **Majors with Highest Enrollment:** Education; Criminal Justice/Law Enforcement Administration; Business/Commerce. **Special Study Options:** distance learning, double major, dual enrollment, English as a Second Language (ESL), honors program, independent study, internships, study abroad, teacher certification program. **Combined degree programs:** BS/MS Occupational Therapy. **Disability Services:** Special programs offered to physically disabled students include reader services, tape recorders.

FACILITIES

Housing: Coed dorms, Faculty in Residence. 100% of campus accessible to physically disabled. **Special Academic Facilities/Equipment:** Aquaculture center, On-campus elementary school, color TV studio, instructional media center.

CAMPUS LIFE

Environment: Village. **Activities:** Choral groups, concert band, dance, drama/theater, jazz band, literary magazine, music ensembles, musical theater, radio station, student government, student newspaper. 149 registered organizations, 13 honor societies, 3 religious organizations. **Athletics (Intercollegiate):** *Men:* baseball, basketball, cross-country, diving, golf, ice hockey, lacrosse, soccer, swimming, tennis, track/field (outdoor). *Women:* basketball, cross-country, diving, field hockey, lacrosse, soccer, softball, swimming, tennis, track/field (outdoor), volleyball.

ADMISSIONS

Freshman Academic Profile: SAT Math middle 50% range 450-540. SAT Critical Reading middle 50% range 440-550. Minimum paper TOEFL 500. **Basis for Candidate Selection:** *Very important factors considered include:* academic GPA, rigor of secondary school record, standardized test scores. *Other factors considered include:* recommendation(s), character/personal qualities, extracurricular activities, interview, level of applicant's interest, talent/ability, volunteer work, work experience. **Freshman Admission Requirements:** High school diploma is required and GED is accepted. *Academic units required:* 4 English, 3 mathematics, 3 science, (2 science labs), 2 foreign language, 2 social studies, 1 history, 1 visual/performing arts, 1 computer science, 2 academic electives. **Freshman Admission Statistics:** 5,697 applied, 57% admitted, 31% enrolled. **Transfer Admission Requirements:** college transcript(s), Minimum college GPA of 2.0 required. Lowest grade transferable C-. **General**

Admission Information: Application Fee $30. Notification on a rolling basis, beginning on or about 12/1. Nonfall registration accepted. Admission may be deferred for a maximum of 1 semester. Credit and/or placement offered for CEEB Advanced Placement tests.

COSTS AND FINANCIAL AID
Required Forms and Deadlines: FAFSA. **Notification of Awards:** Applicants will be notified of awards on a rolling basis beginning 6/1. **Financial Aid Statistics:** 73% freshmen, 75% undergrads receive any aid.

SALISBURY UNIVERSITY

Admissions Office, Salisbury, MD 21801
Phone: 410-543-6161 • **Financial Aid Phone:** 410-543-6165
E-mail: admissions@salisbury.edu • **CEEB Code:** 2091
Fax: 410-546-6016 • **Website:** www.salisbury.edu • **ACT Code:** 1716

This public school was founded in 1925. It has a 155-acre campus.

RATINGS
Admissions Selectivity Rating: 88   **Fire Safety Rating:** 94

STUDENTS AND FACULTY
Enrollment: 7,783. **Student Body:** 57% female, 43% male, 14% out-of-state, 1% international (67 countries represented). Asian 3%, African American 12%, Caucasian 73%, Hispanic 4%, Native American <1%
Retention and Graduation: 44% freshmen graduate within 4 years. 66% freshmen graduate within 6 years. 21% grads go on to further study within 1 year. 39% grads pursue arts and sciences degrees. 1% grads pursue law degrees. 8% grads pursue business degrees. **Faculty:** 417 full-time faculty, 85% hold PhDs, 49% are are members of minority groups, 15% are women. 4% of classes are taught by teaching assistants.

ACADEMICS
Degrees: bachelor's, certificate, master's, post-bachelor's certificate. **Classes:** Most classes have 20-29 students. Most lab/discussion sessions have 20-29 students. **Majors with Highest Enrollment:** Registered Nursing/Registered Nurse; Biology/Biological Sciences; Kinesiology and Exercise Science. **Special Study Options:** Accelerated program, cross-registration, distance learning, double major, dual enrollment, English as a Second Language (ESL), honors program, independent study, internships, liberal arts/career combination, student-designed major, study abroad, teacher certification program. **Honors programs:** The Thomas E. Bellavance Honors Program **Combined degree programs:** BASW/BA, BS/BS Biology/Envirn., Early Chidhood Educ/Elementary Educ. **Disability Services:** Special programs offered to physically disabled students include note-taking services, reader services, tutors. **Career services:** Alumni network, alumni services, career/job search classes, career assessment, internships, regional alumni.

FACILITIES
Housing: Coed dorms, men's dorms, women's dorms, apartments for single students, Wellness Housing, Theme Housing, Affiliated off-campus apartments, quiet/study housing available. World living/learning option-community of International and American students. 47% of campus accessible to physically disabled. **Special Academic Facilities/Equipment:** Arboretum, University Galleries, Delmarva History and Culture Research Center, Small Business Development Center, Ward Museum of Wildfowl Art. **Computers:** 100% of classrooms, 100% of dorms, 100% of libraries, 100% of dining areas, 100% of student union, have wireless network access. Students can register for classes online. Administrative functions (other than registration) can be performed online.

CAMPUS LIFE
Environment: Town. **Activities:** Choral groups, concert band, dance, drama/theater, jazz band, literary magazine, music ensembles, musical theater, pep band, radio station, student government, student newspaper, student-run film society, symphony orchestra, television station, Campus Ministries, International Student Organization. 126 registered organizations, 23 honor societies, 8 religious organizations. 8 fraternities, 4 sororities. **Athletics (Intercollegiate):** *Men:* baseball, basketball, cross-country, football, lacrosse, soccer, swimming, tennis, track/field (outdoor). *Women:* basketball, cross-country, field hockey, lacrosse, soccer, softball, swimming, tennis, track/field (outdoor), volleyball.
On-Campus Highlights: Commons (housing our Dining Hall and Bookstore),

Cool Beans Cyber Caf, Scarborough Leadership Center, Honors House, Maggs Physical Activities Center. **Environmental Initiatives:** 2013 winner of the Maryland Green Registry Leadership Award; Carbon neutral by 2050; Integration of sustainability into curriculum.

ADMISSIONS
Freshman Academic Profile: Average high school GPA 3.75. 23% in top 10% of high school class, 55% in top 25% of high school class, 91% in top 50% of high school class. SAT Math middle 50% range 530-620. SAT Critical Reading middle 50% range 540-610. SAT Writing middle 50% range 530-600. ACT middle 50% range 22-26. Minimum internet-based TOEFL 550. Minimum paper TOEFL 79. **Basis for Candidate Selection:** *Very important factors considered include:* academic GPA, rigor of secondary school record, extracurricular activities, talent/ability. *Important factors considered include:* Class rank, standardized test scores, alumni/ae relation, geographical residence, volunteer work. *Other factors considered include:* application essay, recommendation(s), character/personal qualities, racial/ethnic status, work experience. **Freshman Admission Requirements:** High school diploma is required and GED is accepted. *Academic units required:* 4 English, 3 mathematics, 3 science, (2 science labs), 2 foreign language, 3 social studies. **Freshman Admission Statistics:** 8,730 applied, 55% admitted, 24% enrolled. **Transfer Admission Requirements:** college transcript(s), Minimum college GPA of 2.0 required. Lowest grade transferable C. **General Admission Information:** Application Fee $45. Regular notification 3/15. Nonfall registration accepted. Credit offered for CEEB Advanced Placement tests.

COSTS AND FINANCIAL AID
Annual in-state tuition $6,268. Annual out-of-state tuition $14,614. Room and board $10,620. Required fees $2,292. Average book expense $1,300. **Required Forms and Deadlines:** FAFSA. **Notification of Awards:** Applicants will be notified of awards on a rolling basis beginning 3/15. **Types of Aid:** *Need-based scholarships/grants:* Federal Pell, SEOG, state scholarships/grants, private scholarships, the school's own gift aid. *Loans:* Direct Subsidized Stafford, Direct Unsubsidized Stafford, Federal Perkins. *Student Employment:* Federal Work-Study Program available. Institutional employment available. Off-campus job opportunities are fair. **Financial Aid Statistics:** 86% freshmen, 79% undergrads receive need-based scholarship or grant aid. 0% freshmen, 0% undergrads receive non-need-based scholarship or grant aid. 69% freshmen, 81% undergrads receive need-based self-help aid. 0% freshmen, 0% undergrads receive athletic scholarships. 85% freshmen, 77% undergrads receive any aid. 57% undergrads borrow to pay for school. Average cumulative indebtedness $21,641. **Criteria for awarding institutional aid:** *Non-need-based:* academics, alumni affiliation, art, leadership, music/drama, state/district residency.

SALVE REGINA UNIVERSITY

100 Ochre Point Avenue, Newport, RI 02840-4192
Phone: 401-341-2908 • **Financial Aid Phone:** 401-341-2901
E-mail: sruadmis@salve.edu • **CEEB Code:** 3759
Fax: 401-848-2823 • **Website:** www.salve.edu • **ACT Code:** 3816

This private school, affiliated with the Roman Catholic Church, was founded in 1947. It has a 81-acre campus.

RATINGS
Admissions Selectivity Rating: 83   **Fire Safety Rating:** 90

STUDENTS AND FACULTY
Enrollment: 2,081. **Student Body:** 70% female, 30% male, 77% out-of-state, 2% international (17 countries represented). Asian 1%, African American 2%, Caucasian 78%, Hispanic 7%, Native American <1%
Retention and Graduation: 64% freshmen graduate within 4 years. 67% freshmen graduate within 6 years. 19% grads go on to further study within 1 year. **Faculty:** 119 full-time faculty, 78% hold PhDs, 57% are are members of minority groups, 6% are women. 0% of classes are taught by teaching assistants.

ACADEMICS
Degrees: associate, bachelor's, certificate, doctoral, master's, post-bachelor's certificate, post-master's certificate. **Classes:** Most classes have 10-19 students. Most lab/discussion sessions have 20-29 students. **Majors with Highest Enrollment:** Criminal Justice/Law Enforcement Administration; Elementary Education and Teaching; Registered Nursing/Registered Nurse. **Special Study Options:** Accelerated program, distance learning, double major, dual enrollment, English as a Second Language (ESL), honors program, independent study, internships, liberal arts/career combination, study abroad, teacher certification program, Washington Semester. **Honors programs:** The Pell Honors Program is open to students from all majors who receive the Dean's,

Trustee's, or Presidential Scholarships, or who are nominated by Salve Regina faculty or the Admissions Office. The goal of the Pell Honors Program is to create a learning community of students from different disciplines. The honors education is an enhancement of the core curriculum with a focus in international relations and public policy emphasizing civic responsibility and action. Students are required to take classes together, participate in either an internship or study abroad experience, and write and publicly defend a senior thesis. **Combined degree programs:** BA/MA, 4-1 MA, 4-1 MS, BA,BS/MBA. **Disability Services:** Special programs offered to physically disabled students include note-taking services, reader services, tape recorders, tutors. **Career services:** Alumni network, alumni services, career/job search classes, career assessment, internships, regional alumni.

FACILITIES

Housing: Coed dorms, special housing for disabled students, men's dorms, women's dorms, apartments for single students, Wellness Housing. Both historic style housing and conventional style housing options are available on campus. Off-campus housing is available to upper class students. 85% of campus accessible to physically disabled. **Special Academic Facilities/Equipment:** Art gallery, theater, technology center. **Computers:** 98% of classrooms, 10% of dorms, 100% of libraries, 100% of dining areas, 100% of student union, 25% of common outdoor areas have wireless network access. Students can register for classes online. Administrative functions (other than registration) can be performed online. Undergraduates are required to own a computer.

CAMPUS LIFE

Environment: Town. **Activities:** Choral groups, concert band, dance, drama/ theater, jazz band, literary magazine, music ensembles, pep band, radio station, student government, student newspaper, student-run film society, yearbook, Campus Ministries, International Student Organization, Model UN. 42 registered organizations, 14 honor societies, 2 religious organizations. **Athletics (Intercollegiate):** *Men:* baseball, basketball, cross-country, football, ice hockey, lacrosse, soccer, tennis. *Women:* basketball, field hockey, ice hockey, lacrosse, soccer, softball, tennis, track/field (outdoor), volleyball. **On-Campus Highlights:** New Residence Hall, Athletic Center, O'Hare Academic & Antone Academic Cntrs, Library and Computer Labs, Historic Mansions on campus. **Environmental Initiatives:** Recycling; Energy conservation; Water conservation.

ADMISSIONS

Freshman Academic Profile: Average high school GPA 3.23. 16% in top 10% of high school class, 44% in top 25% of high school class, 79% in top 50% of high school class. 77% from public high schools. SAT Math middle 50% range 500-590. SAT Critical Reading middle 50% range 510-590. SAT Writing middle 50% range 500-590. ACT middle 50% range 22-27. Minimum internet-based TOEFL 80. Minimum paper TOEFL 500. **Basis for Candidate Selection:** *Very important factors considered include:* Class rank, academic GPA, rigor of secondary school record. *Important factors considered include:* application essay, recommendation(s), standardized test scores. *Other factors considered include:* alumni/ae relation, character/personal qualities, extracurricular activities, level of applicant's interest, racial/ethnic status, talent/ability, volunteer work, work experience. **Freshman Admission Requirements:** High school diploma is required and GED is accepted. *Academic units required:* 4 English, 3 mathematics, 2 science, (2 science labs), 2 foreign language, 1 social studies, 4 academic electives. **Freshman Admission Statistics:** 4,810 applied, 71% admitted, 18% enrolled. **Transfer Admission Requirements:** High school transcript, college transcript(s), essay or personal statement, statement of good standing from prior institution(s). Minimum college GPA of 2.7 required. Lowest grade transferable C. **General Admission Information:** Application Fee $50. Regular notification 4/1. Notification on a rolling basis, beginning on or about 12/15. Nonfall registration accepted. Admission may be deferred for a maximum of 12 months. Credit and/or placement offered for CEEB Advanced Placement tests.

COSTS AND FINANCIAL AID

Annual tuition $35,140. Room and board $12,860. Required fees $550. Average book expense $900. **Required Forms and Deadlines:** FAFSA. **Notification of Awards:** Applicants will be notified of awards on or about 4/1. **Types of Aid:** *Need-based scholarships/grants:* Federal Pell, SEOG, state scholarships/grants, private scholarships, the school's own gift aid. *Loans:* Subsidized Stafford, Unsubsidized Stafford, PLUS, Federal Perkins, Federal Nursing, private loans. *Student Employment:* Federal Work-Study Program available. Institutional employment available. Highest amount earned per year from on-campus jobs $1,200. Off-campus job opportunities are good. **Financial Aid Statistics:** 99% freshmen, 95% undergrads receive need-based scholarship or grant aid. 12% freshmen, 8% undergrads receive non-need-based scholarship or grant aid. 85% freshmen, 84% undergrads receive need-based self-help aid. 0% freshmen, 0% undergrads receive athletic scholarships, 90% freshmen, 85% undergrads receive any aid. 83% undergrads borrow to pay for school. Average cumulative indebtedness $26,728. **Criteria for awarding institutional aid:** *Non-need-based:* academics.

SAM HOUSTON STATE UNIVERSITY

Box 2418, Huntsville, TX 77341-2418
Phone: 936-294-1828 · **Financial Aid Phone:** 936-294-1774
E-mail: admissions@shsu.edu · **CEEB Code:** 6643
Website: www.shsu.edu • **ACT Code:** 4162

This public school was founded in 1879. It has a 272-acre campus.

RATINGS

Admissions Selectivity Rating: 78   **Fire Safety Rating:** 87

STUDENTS AND FACULTY

Enrollment: 15,611. **Student Body:** 58% female, 42% male, 1% out-of-state, 1% international (59 countries represented). Asian 1%, African American 17%, Caucasian 58%, Hispanic 17%, Native American <1%
Retention and Graduation: 27% freshmen graduate within 4 years. 49% freshmen graduate within 6 years. **Faculty:** 620 full-time faculty, 79% hold PhDs, 45% are are members of minority groups, 16% are women. 5.2% of classes are taught by teaching assistants.

ACADEMICS

Degrees: bachelor's, doctoral, master's. **Classes:** Most classes have 20-29 students. Most lab/discussion sessions have 20-29 students. **Majors with Highest Enrollment:** Multi-/Interdisciplinary Studies; Criminal Justice/Safety Studies; Business/Commerce. **Special Study Options:** distance learning, double major, dual enrollment, English as a Second Language (ESL), honors program, independent study, internships, teacher certification program. **Honors programs:** The Honors student earns Honors credit in a variety of specially designated classes, and works toward the distinction of graduating "With Honors" or "With Highest Honors." To qualify for graduation with honors, a student must have been a participant in the Honors Program and have completed 24 hours of Honors class credit, including participation in two interdisciplinary Honors seminars. To qualify for graduation "With Highest Honors" a student must, in addition, complete a senior thesis in an approved discipline under the direction of a faculty member of his/her choice. The student will receive 6 credit hours of departmental course credit when completing the senior thesis. **Disability Services:** Special programs offered to physically disabled students include note-taking services, reader services, tape recorders. **Career services:** Alumni network, alumni services, career/job search classes, career assessment, internships, regional alumni. Career services highlights include our close work with major public and private accounting firms as well as with a major retailer (Target) to promote their quality internship programs. We publicize, coordinate and host the interviews for these opportunities for our students and recent alumni.

FACILITIES

Housing: Coed dorms, men's dorms, women's dorms, fraternity/sorority housing, apartments for single students 85% of campus accessible to physically disabled. **Special Academic Facilities/Equipment:** Sam Houston Memorial Museum, on-campus elementary school, communications center for photography, radio, TV, and film, agricultural complex and university farm. **Computers:** Students can register for classes online. Administrative functions (other than registration) can be performed online.

CAMPUS LIFE

Environment: Town. **Activities:** Choral groups, concert band, dance, drama/ theater, jazz band, marching band, music ensembles, musical theater, pep band, radio station, student government, student newspaper, symphony orchestra, television station, yearbook, Campus Ministries, International Student Organization. 185 registered organizations, 12 honor societies, 17 religious organizations. 16 fraternities, 10 sororities. **Athletics (Intercollegiate):** *Men:* baseball, basketball, cheerleading, cross-country, equestrian sports, football, golf, rodeo, soccer, softball, tennis, track/field (outdoor), track/field (indoor). *Women:* basketball, cheerleading, cross-country, equestrian sports, golf, rodeo, soccer, softball, tennis, track/field (outdoor), track/field (indoor), volleyball. **On-Campus Highlights:** Lowman Student Center, Health and Kinesiology Center, Computer Labs, Mall Area, Old Main Pit. **Environmental Initiatives:** Hired an Energy Manager. Adopted green approach to new building design, but short of LEED certification. Recycling of all brush and organic material picked up on campus.

ADMISSIONS

Freshman Academic Profile: 13% in top 10% of high school class, 42% in top 25% of high school class, 85% in top 50% of high school class. SAT Math middle 50% range 470-550. SAT Critical Reading middle 50% range 450-540. ACT middle 50% range 19-23. Minimum paper TOEFL 550. **Basis for Candidate Selection:** *Very important factors considered include:* Class rank, standardized test scores. *Important factors considered include:* rigor of secondary school record. *Other factors considered include:* application essay, academic GPA, recommendation(s), character/personal qualities, extracurricular activities, talent/ability, volunteer work, work experience. **Freshman Admission Requirements:** High school diploma is required and GED is accepted. *Academic units required:* 4 English, 3 mathematics, 2 science, (0 science labs), 0 foreign language, 0 visual/performing arts, 1 computer science, 1 academic elective. **Freshman Admission Statistics:** 9,315 applied, 65% admitted, 40% enrolled. **Transfer Admission Requirements:** college transcript(s), statement of good standing from prior institution(s). Minimum college GPA of 2.0 required. Lowest grade transferable D. **General Admission Information:** Application Fee $40. Regular application deadline 8/1. Notification on a rolling basis, beginning on or about 9/1. Nonfall registration accepted. Credit and/or placement offered for CEEB Advanced Placement tests.

COSTS AND FINANCIAL AID

Annual in-state tuition $5,850. Annual out-of-state tuition $16,470. Room and board $8,324. Required fees $2,744. Average book expense $1,124. **Required Forms and Deadlines:** FAFSA. **Notification of Awards:** Applicants will be notified of awards on a rolling basis beginning 3/1. **Types of Aid:** *Need-based scholarships/grants:* Federal Pell, SEOG, state scholarships/grants, the school's own gift aid. *Loans:* Direct Subsidized Stafford, Direct Unsubsidized Stafford, Direct PLUS, Subsidized Stafford, Unsubsidized Stafford, PLUS, Federal Perkins, state loans, college/university loans from institutional funds. *Student Employment:* Federal Work-Study Program available. Highest amount earned per year from on-campus jobs $2,500. Off-campus job opportunities are excellent. **Financial Aid Statistics:** 86% freshmen, 80% undergrads receive need-based scholarship or grant aid. 3% freshmen, 1% undergrads receive non-need-based scholarship or grant aid. 75% freshmen, 81% undergrads receive need-based self-help aid. 2% freshmen, 2% undergrads receive athletic scholarships. 79% freshmen, 71% undergrads receive any aid. 62% undergrads borrow to pay for school. Average cumulative indebtedness $22,602. **Criteria for awarding institutional aid:** *Non-need-based:* academics, alumni affiliation, art, athletics, job skills, leadership, music/drama, religious affiliation, state/district residency.

SAMFORD UNIVERSITY

800 Lakeshore Drive, Birmingham, AL 35229
Phone: 205-726-3673 • **Financial Aid Phone:** 205-726-2905
E-mail: admission@samford.edu • **CEEB Code:** 1302
Fax: 205-726-2171 • **Website:** www.samford.edu • **ACT Code:** 16

This private school, affiliated with the Baptist Church, was founded in 1841. It has a 180-acre campus.

RATINGS

Admissions Selectivity Rating: 88   Fire Safety Rating: 91

STUDENTS AND FACULTY

Enrollment: 3,033. **Student Body:** 65% female, 35% male, 65% out-of-state, 3% international (24 countries represented). Asian 1%, African American 7%, Caucasian 82%, Hispanic 6%, Native American <1%
Retention and Graduation: 48% freshmen graduate within 4 years. 66% freshmen graduate within 6 years. **Faculty:** 300 full-time faculty, 85% hold PhDs, 47% are are members of minority groups, 11% are women. 0% of classes are taught by teaching assistants.

ACADEMICS

Degrees: associate, bachelor's, certificate, first professional, master's, post-master's certificate, terminal associate. **Classes:** Most classes have 10-19 students. Most lab/discussion sessions have 10-19 students. **Majors with Highest Enrollment:** Journalism; Registered Nursing/Registered Nurse; Biology/Biological Sciences. **Special Study Options:** Accelerated program, cooperative education program, distance learning, double major, dual enrollment, exchange student program (domestic), honors program, independent study, internships, liberal arts/career combination, study abroad, teacher certification program. **Honors programs:** Samford University Fellows program targets academically gifted high schools students for a highly-competitive program of innovative liberal arts courses, international study and undergraduate research. **Combined degree programs:** The Law School sponsors seven joint-degree program. **Disability Services:** Special programs offered to physically disabled students include note-taking services, reader services, tape recorders. **Career services:** career assessment, internships,

FACILITIES

Housing: special housing for disabled students, men's dorms, women's dorms, fraternity/sorority housing, Wellness Housing. 100% of campus accessible to physically disabled. **Special Academic Facilities/Equipment:** Language lab, reflective telescope, geographic information systems lab, global center, plan-

etarium, conservatory, Pete Hanna Sports Center. **Computers:** 100% of classrooms, 100% of libraries, 100% of dining areas, 100% of student union, have wireless network access. Students can register for classes online. Administrative functions (other than registration) can be performed online.

CAMPUS LIFE

Environment: Town. **Activities:** Choral groups, concert band, dance, drama/theater, jazz band, literary magazine, marching band, music ensembles, musical theater, radio station, student government, student newspaper, symphony orchestra, yearbook, Campus Ministries, International Student Organization, Model UN. 119 registered organizations, 25 honor societies, 16 religious organizations. 6 fraternities, 6 sororities. **Athletics (Intercollegiate):** *Men:* baseball, basketball, cross-country, football, golf, tennis, track/field (outdoor). *Women:* basketball, cross-country, golf, soccer, softball, tennis, track/field (outdoor), volleyball. **On-Campus Highlights:** Sciencenter, Pete Hanna Center, University Library, Wright Center Student Center, Beeson University Center, The Quad, Hodges Chapel, Harrison Theatre, and Jane Hollock Brock Recital Hall. **Environmental Initiatives:** Bike loan program; Installation of automatic towel dispensers; Only "green" products used by custodial.

ADMISSIONS

Freshman Academic Profile: Average high school GPA 3.6. 30% in top 10% of high school class, 56% in top 25% of high school class, 82% in top 50% of high school class. 48% from public high schools. SAT Math middle 50% range 500-615. SAT Critical Reading middle 50% range 510-620. SAT Writing middle 50% range 500-610. ACT middle 50% range 23-29. Minimum internet-based TOEFL 90. **Basis for Candidate Selection:** *Very important factors considered include:* application essay, academic GPA, recommendation(s), rigor of secondary school record, standardized test scores, character/personal qualities, religious affiliation/commitment. *Important factors considered include:* Class rank, alumni/ae relation, extracurricular activities, interview. *Other factors considered include:* geographical residence, level of applicant's interest, racial/ethnic status, state residency, talent/ability, volunteer work, work experience. **Freshman Admission Requirements:** High school diploma is required and GED is accepted. *Academic units required:* 4 English, 3 mathematics, 3 science, 2 foreign language, 2 social studies. **Freshman Admission Statistics:** 4,577 applied, 60% admitted, 27% enrolled. **Transfer Admission Requirements:** college transcript(s), essay or personal statement, statement of good standing from prior institution(s). Minimum college GPA of 2.5 required. Lowest grade transferable C-. **General Admission Information:** Application Fee $35. Notification on a rolling basis, beginning on or about 11/1. Nonfall registration accepted. Admission may be deferred for a maximum of 1 year. Credit and/or placement offered for CEEB Advanced Placement tests.

COSTS AND FINANCIAL AID

Annual tuition $26,524. Room and board $9,736. Required fees $800. Average book expense $1,000. **Required Forms and Deadlines:** FAFSA, State aid form. **Notification of Awards:** Applicants will be notified of awards on or about 4/1. **Types of Aid:** *Need-based scholarships/grants:* Federal Pell, SEOG, state scholarships/grants, private scholarships, the school's own gift aid. *Loans:* Direct Subsidized Stafford, Direct Unsubsidized Stafford, Direct PLUS, Subsidized Stafford, Unsubsidized Stafford, PLUS, Federal Perkins. *Student Employment:* Federal Work-Study Program available. Institutional employment available. Off-campus job opportunities are excellent. **Financial Aid Statistics:** 99% freshmen, 95% undergrads receive need-based scholarship or grant aid. 20% freshmen, 17% undergrads receive non-need-based scholarship or grant aid. 75% freshmen, 79% undergrads receive need-based self-help aid. 4% freshmen, 6% undergrads receive athletic scholarships. 96% freshmen, 89% undergrads receive any aid. 42% undergrads borrow to pay for school. Average cumulative indebtedness $23,450. **Criteria for awarding institutional aid:** *Non-need-based:* academics, athletics, leadership, religious affiliation, state/district residency.

SAN DIEGO STATE UNIVERSITY

5500 Campanile Drive, San Diego, CA 92182-7455
Phone: 619-594-6336 • **Financial Aid Phone:** 619-594-6323 • **CEEB Code:** 4682
Website: www.sdsu.edu • **ACT Code:** 398

This public school was founded in 1897. It has a 300-acre campus.

RATINGS

Admissions Selectivity Rating: 90   Fire Safety Rating: 79

STUDENTS AND FACULTY

Enrollment: 28,362. **Student Body:** 55% female, 45% male, 7% out-of-state, 6% international (119 countries represented). Asian 13%, African American 4%, Caucasian 35%, Hispanic 31%, Native American <1%

Retention and Graduation: 88% freshmen return for sophomore year. 30% freshmen graduate within 4 years. **Faculty:** 755 full-time faculty, 85% hold PhDs, 46% are are members of minority groups, 26% are women.

ACADEMICS

Degrees: bachelor's, master's, post-bachelor's certificate. **Classes:** Most classes have 20-29 students. Most lab/discussion sessions have 20-29 students. **Majors with Highest Enrollment:** Psychology; Criminal Justice/Safety Studies; Business Administration and Management. **Special Study Options:** distance learning, double major, English as a Second Language (ESL), exchange student program (domestic), external degree program, honors program, independent study, internships, liberal arts/career combination, study abroad, teacher certification program. **Combined degree programs:** MBA/JD, MSW/MPH, MSW/JD, MPH/MA. **Disability Services:** Special programs offered to physically disabled students include note-taking services, reader services, tape recorders, tutors. **Career services:** alumni services, career/job search classes, career assessment, internships.

FACILITIES

Housing: Coed dorms, special housing for international students, fraternity/sorority housing, apartments for single students, Extended Quiet Study Hours (more quiet study environment), Living/Learning Center, Housing Over the Break. 99% of campus accessible to physically disabled. **Special Academic Facilities/Equipment:** Art gallery, theatre, recital hall, research bureaus for labor economics, marine studies and social science, audiovisual center, electronic boardroom, multimedia interactive fine arts technology lab, Palomar Observatory (off-campus), field studies stations (off-campus). **Computers:** Students can register for classes online. Administrative functions (other than registration) can be performed online.

CAMPUS LIFE

Environment: City. **Activities:** Choral groups, concert band, dance, drama/theater, jazz band, literary magazine, marching band, music ensembles, musical theater, opera, pep band, radio station, student government, student newspaper, student-run film society, television station, Campus Ministries, International Student Organization. 264 registered organizations, 6 honor societies, 14 religious organizations. 21 fraternities, 23 sororities. **Athletics (Intercollegiate):** *Men:* baseball, basketball, football, golf, soccer, tennis. *Women:* basketball, crew/rowing, cross-country, diving, golf, soccer, softball, swimming, tennis, track/field (outdoor), track/field (indoor), volleyball, water polo. **Environmental Initiatives:** In spring 2012 SDSU opened a Student Sustainability Center in the Division of Undergraduate Studies, which is supported by a full-time staff member and is home to the Green Campus Interns program. Students can use the Center to access campus sustainability resources such as scholarships, internships, and courses; connect with faculty; work on green research projects, and utilize meeting space is available to green student organizations. The Student Center is a part of the SDSU Center for Regional Sustainability which provides faculty training and engagement opportunities on campus. SDSU has numerous green facilities upgrades, solar installations, and construction underway. The Aztec Student Union which is currently under construction and will be completed by fall 2013 is designed to LEED Platinum standards and will be the first student union in the world to seek a Platinum certification. http://as.sdsu.edu/aztec/ In fall 2011 the campus began an Energy Star building audit as a part of a campus-wide certification. Students with the SDSU Student USGBC chapter are assisting with the Energy Star certification process. Additionally the Storm and Nasatir Halls renovation and Plaza Linda Verde project, a pedestrian friendly, on-campus housing and retail complex project currently underway will be built to LEED Silver standards. http://newscenter.sdsu.edu/plazalindaverde/ SDSU is bike friendly! In 2011 the University adopted a campus area bike plan that created bike paths on major campus thoroughfares. The plan implemented a new bike policy that allows cyclists to bike on all campus streets and designated paths, giving cyclists greater access to campus and making it easy to commute by bike. New upgrades to buildings incorporate amenities for cyclists and skateboarders including facilities at the Aztec Recreation Center, transit station, and the new student union that make it easier for cyclists to get to campus and store bikes. At the weekly Farmers Market Student can learn about bike safety and maintenance at the Enviro Business booth, pick up a bike route map, and receive free printing by peddling on the Green Campus bike generator to power a printer with recycled paper.

ADMISSIONS

Freshman Academic Profile: Average high school GPA 3.69. 29% in top 10% of high school class, 77% in top 25% of high school class, 98% in top 50% of high school class. 92% from public high schools. SAT Math middle 50% range 510-620. SAT Critical Reading middle 50% range 490-600. SAT Writing middle 50% range 490-590. ACT middle 50% range 22-27. Minimum internet-based TOEFL 80. Minimum paper TOEFL 550. **Basis for Candidate Selection:** *Very important factors considered include:* academic GPA, rigor of secondary school record, standardized test scores. *Important factors considered include:* geographical residence, state residency. **Freshman Admission Requirements:** High school diploma is required and GED is accepted. *Academic units*

required: 4 English, 3 mathematics, 2 science, (2 science labs), 2 foreign language, 1 social studies, 1 history, 1 visual/performing arts, 1 academic elective. **Freshman Admission Statistics:** 56,921 applied, 34% admitted, 26% enrolled. **Transfer Admission Requirements:** college transcript(s), Lowest grade transferable D-. **General Admission Information:** Application Fee $55. Regular application deadline 11/30. Regular notification 3/1. Nonfall registration not accepted. Credit offered for CEEB Advanced Placement tests.

COSTS AND FINANCIAL AID

Annual in-state tuition $5,472. Annual out-of-state tuition $16,632. Room and board $14,745. Required fees $1,394. Average book expense $1,762. **Required Forms and Deadlines:** FAFSA, State aid form. **Notification of Awards:** Applicants will be notified of awards on a rolling basis beginning 2/14. **Types of Aid:** *Need-based scholarships/grants:* Federal Pell, SEOG, state scholarships/grants, private scholarships, the school's own gift aid, Federal Nursing Scholarships. *Loans:* Direct Subsidized Stafford, Direct Unsubsidized Stafford, Direct PLUS, Federal Perkins, college/university loans from institutional funds. *Student Employment:* Federal Work-Study Program available. Institutional employment available. Off-campus job opportunities are good. **Financial Aid Statistics:** 67% freshmen, 74% undergrads receive need-based scholarship or grant aid. 26% freshmen, 17% undergrads receive non-need-based scholarship or grant aid. 93% freshmen, 92% undergrads receive need-based self-help aid. 2% freshmen, 2% undergrads receive athletic scholarships. 59% freshmen, 63% undergrads receive any aid. 49% undergrads borrow to pay for school. Average cumulative indebtedness $18,400. **Criteria for awarding institutional aid:** *Non-need-based:* academics, alumni affiliation, art, athletics, leadership, music/drama, state/district residency.

SAN FRANCISCO STATE UNIVERSITY

1600 Holloway Avenue, San Francisco, CA 93132
Phone: 415-338-6486 • **Financial Aid Phone:** 415-338-7000
E-mail: ugadmit@sfsu.edu • **CEEB Code:** 4684
Fax: 415-338-3880 • **Website:** www.sfsu.edu

This public school was founded in 1899. It has a 142-acre campus.

RATINGS

Admissions Selectivity Rating: 76   **Fire Safety Rating:** 79

STUDENTS AND FACULTY

Enrollment: 25,170. **Student Body:** 56% female, 44% male, 1% out-of-state, 6% international (89 countries represented). Asian 28%, African American 5%, Caucasian 23%, Hispanic 22%, Native American <1%.
Retention and Graduation: 15% freshmen graduate within 4 years. 50% freshmen graduate within 6 years.

ACADEMICS

Degrees: bachelor's, certificate, master's, post-bachelor's certificate. **Classes:** Most classes have 20-29 students. Most lab/discussion sessions have 10-19 students. **Majors with Highest Enrollment:** Psychology; Marketing/Marketing Management; Communication. **Special Study Options:** cooperative education program, cross-registration, distance learning, double major, dual enrollment, English as a Second Language (ESL), honors program, independent study, internships, liberal arts/career combination, student-designed major, study abroad, teacher certification program. **Combined degree programs:** BA/MA. **Disability Services:** Special programs offered to physically disabled students include note-taking services, reader services, tape recorders, tutors. **Career services:** alumni services, career/job search classes, career assessment, internships.

FACILITIES

Housing: Coed dorms, special housing for disabled students, special housing for international students, apartments for married students, apartments for single students, Wellness Housing, Theme Housing, Women only floors. **Special Academic Facilities/Equipment:** Treganza Anthropology Museum, Moss Landing Marine Laboratories, Romberg Tiburon Center for Environmental Studies, Sierra Nevada Field Campus, Sutro Egyptian Collection. **Computers:** 100% of classrooms, 100% of dorms, 100% of libraries, 100% of dining areas, 100% of student union, 100% of common outdoor areas have wireless network access. Students can register for classes online. Administrative functions (other than registration) can be performed online.

CAMPUS LIFE

Environment: Metropolis. **Activities:** Choral groups, concert band, dance, drama/theater, jazz band, literary magazine, music ensembles, musical theater, opera, pep band, radio station, student government, student newspaper, student-run film society, symphony orchestra, television station, Campus Ministries, International Student Organization. 213 registered organizations, 6 honor societies, 13 religious organizations. 3 fraternities, 4 sororities. **Athletics (Intercollegiate):** *Men:* baseball, basketball, cross-country, soccer, wrestling. *Women:* basketball, cross-country, soccer, softball, track/field (outdoor), track/field (indoor), volleyball. **On-Campus Highlights:** Cesar Chavez Student Center, Cox Stadium, SFSU Fine Arts Gallery, Residential Theme Communities, J. Paul Leonard Library Annex, Malcolm X Plaza, The Village at Centennial Square, and McKenna Theatre. **Environmental Initiatives:** SF State is dedicated to reducing the campus' use of resources and its impact on climate change. Some of the projects that demonstrate that are: the Buy Recycled Campaign, purchasing 20% renewable energy, implementing a green cleaning program, hiring a Sustainability Programs Manager and a Sustainability Coordinator, offering alternative transportation incentives, pursuing LEED Gold for its new Rec and Wellness Center and diverting over 75% of the waste from the landfill. SF State completed its first Greenhouse Gas Emissions Inventory in May of 2008 and its second one in January 2010. The campus' Sustainability Committee completed a Climate Action Plan in May of 2010. It outlines the campus' goal of reducing emissions below 1990 levels; 25% by 2020 and 40% by 2050. The University is currently working on completing its third GHG inventory. SF State passed a sustainable literacy requirement for all students. SF State already incorporates sustainability into many of its departments. Students can receive an undergraduate degree in Environmental Studies, Geography, and Urban Planning. They can receive an MBA with an emphasis in Sustainable Business and conduct research at the Romburg Tiburon Center for Environmental Studies.

ADMISSIONS

Freshman Academic Profile: Average high school GPA 3.22. 88% from public high schools. SAT Math middle 50% range 440-560. SAT Critical Reading middle 50% range 430-550. ACT middle 50% range 18-24. Minimum internet-based TOEFL 61. Minimum paper TOEFL 500. **Basis for Candidate Selection:** *Very important factors considered include:* academic GPA, rigor of secondary school record, standardized test scores. *Important factors considered include:* state residency. *Other factors considered include:* recommendation(s), talent/ability. **Freshman Admission Requirements:** High school diploma is required and GED is accepted. *Academic units required:* 4 English, 3 mathematics, 2 science, (2 science labs), 2 foreign language, 1 social studies, 1 history, 1 visual/performing arts. **Freshman Admission Statistics:** 31,963 applied, 66% admitted, 18% enrolled. **Transfer Admission Requirements:** college transcript(s), statement of good standing from prior institution(s). Minimum college GPA of 2.0 required. Lowest grade transferable D. **General Admission Information:** Application Fee $55. Notification on a rolling basis, beginning on or about 10/1. Nonfall registration accepted. Credit offered for CEEB Advanced Placement tests.

COSTS AND FINANCIAL AID

Annual in-state tuition $5,472. Annual out-of-state tuition $16,632. Room and board $11,876. Required fees $996. Average book expense $1,826. **Required Forms and Deadlines:** FAFSA. **Notification of Awards:** Applicants will be notified of awards on a rolling basis beginning 2/1. **Types of Aid:** *Need-based scholarships/grants:* Federal Pell, SEOG, state scholarships/grants, private scholarships, the school's own gift aid. *Loans:* Direct Subsidized Stafford, Direct Unsubsidized Stafford, PLUS, Federal Perkins. *Student Employment:* Federal Work-Study Program available. Institutional employment available. **Financial Aid Statistics:** 95% freshmen, 95% undergrads receive need-based scholarship or grant aid. 7% freshmen, 4% undergrads receive non-need-based scholarship or grant aid. 95% freshmen, 94% undergrads receive need-based self-help aid. 0% freshmen, 1% undergrads receive athletic scholarships. 48% undergrads borrow to pay for school. Average cumulative indebtedness $21,702. **Criteria for awarding institutional aid:** *Non-need-based:* academics, athletics.

SAN JOSE STATE UNIVERSITY

One Washington Square, San Jose, CA 95192-0016
Phone: 408-283-7500 · **Financial Aid Phone:** 408-283-7500
E-mail: admissions@sjsu.edu · **CEEB Code:** 4687
Fax: 408-924-2050 · **Website:** www.sjsu.edu

This public school was founded in 1857. It has a 154-acre campus.

RATINGS

Admissions Selectivity Rating: 75   Fire Safety Rating: 60*

STUDENTS AND FACULTY

Enrollment: 26,664. **Student Body:** 48% female, 52% male, 0% out-of-state, 5% international (139 countries represented). Asian 35%, African American 3%, Caucasian 21%, Hispanic 25%, Native American <1%
Retention and Graduation: 83% freshmen return for sophomore year. 10% freshmen graduate within 4 years. **Faculty:** 630 full-time faculty, 47% are are

members of minority groups, 31% are women. 3.5% of classes are taught by teaching assistants.

ACADEMICS

Degrees: bachelor's, master's. **Classes:** Most classes have 20-29 students. Most lab/discussion sessions have 20-29 students. **Majors with Highest Enrollment:** Electrical and Electronics Engineering; Business Administration and Management; Art/Art Studies. **Special Study Options:** distance learning, double major, dual enrollment, honors program, independent study, internships, student-designed major, study abroad, teacher certification program. **Disability Services:** Special programs offered to physically disabled students include note-taking services, reader services, tutors. **Career services:** alumni services, career/job search classes, career assessment, internships. Career services highlights include our Neat Ideas Fair program, which was nominated for the 2008 USASBE innovative pedagogy award. The Fair is a venue for students from across the SJSU campus to display and pitch their business ideas and receive feedback from seasoned entrepreneurs, investors, lawyers, professors, and their peers.

FACILITIES

Housing: Coed dorms, special housing for disabled students, men's dorms, special housing for international students, women's dorms, fraternity/sorority housing, cooperative housing, apartments for single students. 100% of campus accessible to physically disabled. **Special Academic Facilities/Equipment:** Martin Luther King, Jr. Library (Joint with City) Child development lab, Chicano resource center, Beethoven studies center, John Steinbeck research center, art metal foundry, natural history living museum (science education), science resource center, deep-sea research ship, electro-acoustical/recording studios, nuclear science and engineering labs. **Computers:** Students can register for classes online. Administrative functions (other than registration) can be performed online.

CAMPUS LIFE

Environment: Metropolis. **Activities:** Choral groups, dance, drama/theater, literary magazine, marching band, music ensembles, musical theater, radio station, student government, student newspaper, student-run film society, symphony orchestra, Campus Ministries, International Student Organization. 283 registered organizations, 13 honor societies, 20 religious organizations. 20 fraternities, 15 sororities. **Athletics (Intercollegiate):** *Men:* baseball, basketball, cheerleading, cross-country, diving, football, golf, soccer, softball, swimming, volleyball, water polo. *Women:* basketball, cheerleading, cross-country, diving, golf, gymnastics, soccer, softball, swimming, tennis, volleyball, water polo. **On-Campus Highlights:** Martin Luther King, Jr. Library, Student Union, Art Quad, Market Café/Burger King/Sparro, Gym.

ADMISSIONS

Freshman Academic Profile: Average high school GPA 3.31. 77% from public high schools. SAT Math middle 50% range 450-600. SAT Critical Reading middle 50% range 450-600. SAT Writing middle 50% range 440-560. ACT middle 50% range 18-27. Minimum internet-based TOEFL 80. Minimum paper TOEFL 550. **Basis for Candidate Selection:** *Very important factors considered include:* academic GPA, rigor of secondary school record, standardized test scores. *Important factors considered include:* first generation. **Freshman Admission Requirements:** High school diploma is required and GED is accepted. *Academic units required:* 4 English, 3 mathematics, 2 science, (2 science labs), 2 foreign language, 1 social studies, 1 history, 1 visual/performing arts, 1 academic elective. **Freshman Admission Statistics:** 29,734 applied, 60% admitted, 20% enrolled. **Transfer Admission Requirements:** college transcript(s), statement of good standing from prior institution(s). Minimum college GPA of 2.0 required. Lowest grade transferable 2.0. **General Admission Information:** Application Fee $55. Regular application deadline 11/30. Notification on a rolling basis, beginning on or about 10/1. Nonfall registration accepted. Credit offered for CEEB Advanced Placement tests.

COSTS AND FINANCIAL AID

Annual out-of-state tuition $11,160. Room and board $11,810. Required fees $7,323. Average book expense $1,826. **Required Forms and Deadlines:** FAFSA. **Notification of Awards:** Applicants will be notified of awards on a rolling basis beginning 4/10. **Types of Aid:** *Need-based scholarships/grants:* Federal Pell, SEOG, state scholarships/grants, private scholarships, the school's own gift aid. *Loans:* Subsidized Stafford, Unsubsidized Stafford, PLUS, Federal Perkins, college/university loans from institutional funds. *Student Employment:* Federal Work-Study Program available. Institutional employment available. Off-campus job opportunities are excellent. **Financial Aid Statistics:** 69% freshmen, 71% undergrads receive need-based scholarship or grant aid. 1% freshmen, 1% undergrads receive non-need-based scholarship or grant aid. 50% freshmen, 49% undergrads receive need-based self-help aid. 0% freshmen, 0% undergrads receive athletic scholarships. 40% freshmen, 39% undergrads receive any aid. 45% undergrads borrow to pay for school. Average cumulative indebtedness $21,237. **Criteria for awarding institutional aid:** *Non-need-based:* academics, athletics.

SANTA CLARA UNIVERSITY

Best 380

500 El Camino Real, Santa Clara, CA 95053
Phone: 408-554-4700 · **Financial Aid Phone:** 408-554-4505
E-mail: Admission@scu.edu · **CEEB Code:** 4851
Fax: 408-554-5255 · **Website:** www.scu.edu

This private school, affiliated with the Roman Catholic Church, was founded in 1851. It has a 106-acre campus.

RATINGS

Admissions Selectivity Rating: 93   **Fire Safety Rating:** 86

STUDENTS AND FACULTY

Enrollment: 5,447. **Student Body:** 50% female, 50% male, 26% out-of-state, 3% international (44 countries represented). Asian 15%, African American 3%, Caucasian 48%, Hispanic 17%, Native American <1%
Retention and Graduation: 78% freshmen graduate within 4 years. 85% freshmen graduate within 6 years. 24% grads go on to further study within 1 year. 15% grads pursue arts and sciences degrees. 4% grads pursue law degrees. 2% grads pursue business degrees. 2% grads pursue medical degrees. **Faculty:** 518 full-time faculty, 93% hold PhDs, 45% are are members of minority groups, 25% are women. 0% of classes are taught by teaching assistants.

ACADEMICS

Degrees: bachelor's, master's, post-bachelor's certificate, post-master's certificate. **Classes:** Most classes have 20-29 students. Most lab/discussion sessions have 10-19 students. **Majors with Highest Enrollment:** Speech Communication and Rhetoric; Biology/Biological Sciences. **Special Study Options:** cooperative education program, double major, honors program, independent study, internships, student-designed major, study abroad, teacher certification program. **Honors programs:** The University Honors Program provides Santa Clara's most able students with intellectual opportunities based in small, seminar-style classes. With 14 to 17 students each, seminars emphasize analytical rigor, effective expression, and interaction among professors and students. The course of study combines broadly based, liberal learning with depth of specialization in a major field. Honors Program classes are designed to fit within the curricula of the humanities, natural and social sciences, business, and engineering. Possible majors include every undergraduate field in the University. **Combined degree programs:** BA/MEng. **Disability Services:** Special programs offered to physically disabled students include note-taking services, reader services, tape recorders, tutors. **Career services:** Alumni network, alumni services, career/job search classes, career assessment, internships, regional alumni. Career services highlights include access through the Career Center to quality internships on a local, national, and international level. Employers from all sectors recruit students for internships that emphasize intentional learning, professional development, real-world experience, skill-building, and networking. Almost 4,000 internships are posted each year that target our students on NACElink. Almost one-third of these are technical internships, reflecting our location in the heart of Silicon Valley. Students also have access to thousands of internships posted on over 100 internship databases through our online resources. In addition, we provide effective and successful co-curricular internship programming through which students effectively connect with employers; educate students, faculty/staff, and parents about all aspects of internships; offer a Freshmen/Sophomore Internship Fair each February; and educate employer organizations about developing substantive internship programs that are committed to intentional learning and provide quality, engaged supervision for the student. We also provide numerous internship-related workshops for students, clubs and organizations, classes, and parents during Parent Weekend.

FACILITIES

Housing: Coed dorms, apartments for single students, Theme Housing. 95% of campus accessible to physically disabled. **Special Academic Facilities/ Equipment:** Art and history museum (de Saisset), mission church, theatre, media lab, retail management institute, computer design center, engineering labs, Markkula Center for Applied Ethics, Center for Science, Technology, and Society, Ignatian Center for Jesuit Education. **Computers:** 100% of classrooms, 100% of dorms, 100% of libraries, 100% of dining areas, 100% of student union, 90% of common outdoor areas have wireless network access. Students can register for classes online. Administrative functions (other than registration) can be performed online.

CAMPUS LIFE

Environment: City. **Activities:** Choral groups, dance, drama/theater, jazz band, literary magazine, music ensembles, musical theater, opera, pep band, radio station, student government, student newspaper, symphony orchestra, yearbook, Campus Ministries, International Student Organization, Model UN. 86 registered organizations, 25 honor societies, 5 religious organizations. **Athletics (Intercollegiate):** *Men:* baseball, basketball, crew/rowing, cross-country, golf, soccer, tennis, track/field (outdoor), water polo. *Women:* basketball, crew/rowing, cross-country, golf, soccer, softball, tennis, track/field (outdoor), volleyball, water polo. **On-Campus Highlights:** Historic Mission Church; Mission gardens, Pat Malley Fitness Center, Harrington Learning Commons and Library, Benson Memorial Student Center, Leavey Activities Center, The palm tree dotted campus is gorgeous, with stunning gardens, walkways, Mission style buildings, and lots of greenery. At the heart of Santa Clara University is the historic Mission Santa Clara de Asis. Founded in 1777, it is the eighth oldest of the original 21 California missions. The current Mission Church was dedicated May 13, 1928. From then until now it has served as the University chapel, and is used by the University community for Masses, baptisms, weddings and funerals. The Mission Church is open to the public and welcomes visitors. The de Saisset Museum at Santa Clara University is the South Bay Area's free Museum of art and history. The 19,210 square foot facility was founded adjacent to the Mission Santa Clara de Asis on the Santa Clara University campus in 1955 and is currently one of only two museums in the South Bay accredited by the American Association of Museums. **Environmental Initiatives:** Santa Clara University strives to develop a culture of sustainability. Our Comprehensive Policy on Sustainability (adopted in 2004) targets our efforts toward stewardship, education, and outreach. We are a signatory of the ACUPCC in 2007, committing to transform SCU into a climate-neutral campus. The University's Sustainability Coordinator was hired in 2006. The Office of Sustainability was formally established in 2008 to support campus efforts, coordinate initiatives, serve as the "clearing-house" for campus sustainability data, and to showcase University sustainability programs to the public. The Sustainability Council was also formed at that time to guide the efforts of the Office of Sustainability. The University's Climate Neutrality Action Plan was adopted in 2010. SCU is a Charter STARS Participant, and achieved STARS Silver in 2011. Education: SCU is educating its students in and outside the classroom to help them develop a deeper understanding about sustainability and its environmental, economic, and social impact on the world. In 2009, the University launched a new core curriculum that engages students in sustainability, sustainable building design, and using the campus as a living lab. SCU created the Frugal Innovation Laboratory that fosters development and application of technologies in clean energy, clean water, public health, and mobile applications, in ways that meet the needs of marginalized communities worldwide. Justice and sustainability: SCU developed a half-acre education, demonstration, and community garden. The garden is used as a living laboratory and training facility for the Bronco Urban Gardens (BUG) Program. BUG helps communities and schools in low-income neighborhoods in San Jose build and utilize new gardens. Experiential Learning for Social Justice (ELSJ) is part of Santa Clara's new Undergraduate Core Curriculum. The ELSJ requirement, which must be completed by every undergraduate student at the University as part of their Core Curriculum, cultivates social justice, civic life, perspective, and civic engagement. ELSJ represents one of the ways that Santa Clara educates the whole person for a deeper understanding of the benefits of civic engagement and responsible citizenship.

ADMISSIONS

Freshman Academic Profile: Average high school GPA 3.67. 54% in top 10% of high school class, 86% in top 25% of high school class, 97% in top 50% of high school class. 45% from public high schools. SAT Math middle 50% range 620-710. SAT Critical Reading middle 50% range 590-680. ACT middle 50% range 27-32. Minimum internet-based TOEFL 90. Minimum paper TOEFL 575. **Basis for Candidate Selection:** *Very important factors considered include:* application essay, academic GPA, recommendation(s), rigor of secondary school record. *Important factors considered include:* standardized test scores, character/personal qualities, extracurricular activities, racial/ethnic status, talent/ability, volunteer work. *Other factors considered include:* Class rank, alumni/ ae relation, first generation, geographical residence, level of applicant's interest, religious affiliation/commitment, state residency, work experience. **Freshman Admission Requirements:** High school diploma is required and GED is not accepted. *Academic units required:* 4 English, 3 mathematics, 2 science, 2 foreign language, 3 social studies, 1 academic elective. **Freshman Admission Statistics:** 14,985 applied, 49% admitted, 18% enrolled. **Transfer Admission Requirements:** college transcript(s), essay or personal statement, Lowest grade transferable C. **General Admission Information:** Application Fee $55. Regular application deadline 1/7. Regular notification 4/1. Nonfall registration not accepted. Admission may be deferred for a maximum of 1 year. Credit and/ or placement offered for CEEB Advanced Placement tests.

COSTS AND FINANCIAL AID

Annual tuition $43,812. Room and board $12,921. Average book expense $1,746. **Required Forms and Deadlines:** FAFSA, CSS/Financial Aid PROFILE. **Notification of Awards:** Applicants will be notified of awards on or about 4/1. **Types of Aid:** *Need-based scholarships/grants:* Federal Pell, SEOG, state scholarships/grants, private scholarships, the school's own gift aid. *Loans:* Direct Subsidized Stafford, Direct Unsubsidized Stafford, Direct PLUS,

PLUS, Federal Perkins, Private alternative loans. *Student Employment:* Federal Work-Study Program available. Institutional employment available. Off-campus job opportunities are good. **Financial Aid Statistics:** 84% freshmen, 69% undergrads receive need-based scholarship or grant aid. 47% freshmen, 35% undergrads receive non-need-based scholarship or grant aid. 55% freshmen, 51% undergrads receive need-based self-help aid. 5% freshmen, 3% undergrads receive athletic scholarships. 72% freshmen, 83% undergrads receive any aid. 56% undergrads borrow to pay for school. Average cumulative indebtedness $22,084. **Criteria for awarding institutional aid:** *Non-need-based:* academics, alumni affiliation, athletics, music/drama.

SANTA FE UNIVERSITY OF ART AND DESIGN

1600 St. Michaels Drive, Santa Fe, NM 87505-7634
Phone: 505-473-6937 • **Financial Aid Phone:** 505-473-6318
E-mail: admissions@santafeuniversity.edu
Fax: 505-473-6127 • **Website:** www.santafeuniversity.edu

This private school was founded in 1874. It has a 100-acre campus.

RATINGS

Admissions Selectivity Rating: 60*   **Fire Safety Rating:** 97

STUDENTS AND FACULTY

Enrollment: 839. **Student Body:** 52% female, 48% male, 78% out-of-state, 5% international (21 countries represented). Asian 2%, African American 7%, Caucasian 45%, Hispanic 28%, Native American 3%
Retention and Graduation: 64% freshmen return for sophomore year. 17% freshmen graduate within 4 years. 21% freshmen graduate within 6 years.
Faculty:

ACADEMICS

Degrees: associate, bachelor's, master's, terminal associate. **Classes:** Most classes have 10-19 students. Most lab/discussion sessions have 40-49 students. **Majors with Highest Enrollment:** Film/Cinema/Video Studies; Graphic Design; Drama and Dramatics/Theatre Arts. **Special Study Options:** Accelerated program, cooperative education program, distance learning, double major, dual enrollment, exchange student program (domestic), independent study, internships, student-designed major, study abroad, teacher certification program. **Disability Services:** Special programs offered to physically disabled students include note-taking services, reader services, tape recorders, tutors. **Career services:** career assessment, internships, regional alumni.

FACILITIES

Housing: Coed dorms, special housing for disabled students, men's dorms, women's dorms, apartments for single studentsSubstance-free floors, quiet floors, smoking floors. 95% of campus accessible to physically disabled. **Special Academic Facilities/Equipment:** Thaw Art History Library, Marion Center Photographic Library, Garson Studios, Visual Art Center, Greer Garson Theatre Centre. **Computers:** Administrative functions (other than registration) can be performed online.

CAMPUS LIFE

Environment: Town. **Activities:** Choral groups, dance, drama/theater, literary magazine, music ensembles, musical theater, student government, student newspaper, television station. 14 registered organizations, 1 honor society. **Athletics (Intercollegiate):** *Men:* tennis. *Women:* tennis. **On-Campus Highlights:** Visual Arts Center, Garson Studios, Driscoll Fitness Center, Greer Garson Theatre Center, Fogelson Library.

ADMISSIONS

Freshman Academic Profile: Minimum internet-based TOEFL 79. Minimum paper TOEFL 550. **Basis for Candidate Selection:** *Very important factors considered include:* rigor of secondary school record, character/personal qualities, interview, talent/ability. *Important factors considered include:* Class rank, application essay, academic GPA, recommendation(s), standardized test scores, extracurricular activities, volunteer work. *Other factors considered include:* alumni/ae relation, geographical residence, racial/ethnic status, state residency, work experience. **Freshman Admission Requirements:** High school diploma is required and GED is accepted. *Academic units required:* 4 English, 2 mathematics, 2 science, (2 science labs), 0 foreign language, 2 social studies, 0 history, 6 academic electives. **Freshman Admission Statistics:** 608 applied, 100% admitted, 41% enrolled. **Transfer Admission Requirements:** High school transcript, college transcript(s), essay or personal statement, Lowest grade transferable C-. **General Admission Information:** Application Fee $35. Notification on a rolling basis, beginning on or about 1/15. Nonfall registration accepted. Admission may be deferred for a maximum of 1 year. Credit and/or placement offered for CEEB Advanced Placement tests.

COSTS AND FINANCIAL AID

Annual tuition $28,836. Room and board $8,984. Required fees $1,300. Average book expense $1,400. **Required Forms and Deadlines:** FAFSA. **Notification of Awards:** Applicants will be notified of awards on a rolling basis beginning 3/1. **Types of Aid:** *Need-based scholarships/grants:* Federal Pell, SEOG, state scholarships/grants, private scholarships, the school's own gift aid. *Loans:* Subsidized Stafford, Unsubsidized Stafford, PLUS, Federal Perkins, state loans, college/university loans from institutional funds. *Student Employment:* Federal Work-Study Program available. Institutional employment available. Off-campus job opportunities are excellent. **Financial Aid Statistics:** 100% freshmen, 100% undergrads receive need-based scholarship or grant aid. 4% freshmen, 4% undergrads receive non-need-based scholarship or grant aid. 94% freshmen, 91% undergrads receive need-based self-help aid. 0% freshmen, 0% undergrads receive athletic scholarships. 99% freshmen. **Criteria for awarding institutional aid:** *Non-need-based:* academics, alumni affiliation, art, athletics, leadership, minority status, music/drama.

SARAH LAWRENCE COLLEGE

Best 380

1 Mead Way, Bronxville, NY 10708-5999
Phone: 914-395-2510 • **Financial Aid Phone:** 914-395 2570
E-mail: slcadmit@sarahlawrence.edu • **CEEB Code:** 2810
Fax: 914-395-2515 • **Website:** www.slc.edu • **ACT Code:** 2904

This private school was founded in 1926. It has a 44-acre campus.

RATINGS

Admissions Selectivity Rating: 92   **Fire Safety Rating:** 93

STUDENTS AND FACULTY

Enrollment: 1,366. **Student Body:** 71% female, 29% male, 79% out-of-state, 13% international (52 countries represented). Asian 4%, African American 4%, Caucasian 57%, Hispanic 9%, Native American <1%
Retention and Graduation: 71% freshmen graduate within 4 years. 77% freshmen graduate within 6 years. **Faculty:** 107 full-time faculty, 91% hold PhDs, 48% are are members of minority groups, 18% are women. 0% of classes are taught by teaching assistants.

ACADEMICS

Degrees: bachelor's, certificate, master's, post-master's certificate. **Classes:** Most classes have 10-19 students. **Majors with Highest Enrollment:** Liberal Arts and Sciences/Liberal Studies. **Special Study Options:** double major, exchange student program (domestic), independent study, internships, student-designed major, study abroad, teacher certification program, Sarah Lawrence College has no formal majors. However students may concentrate in subject areas. All students design their own educational programs (with faculty advisement), so the equivalent of a "double major" is available. We have a 3-2 program where students can get their B.A. degree and M.S.Ed. in The Art of Teaching or M.A. in Women's History. We also have a 3-2 program in which the student receives a B.A. in the Liberal Arts from Sarah Lawrence and a B.S. in Engineering from Columbia. **Combined degree programs:** BA/MA, BA/MEng, B.A./M.A. Education, MSW/MA with NYU, MA/JD with Pace Law School. **Disability Services:** Special programs offered to physically disabled students include note-taking services, reader services, tape recorders, tutors. **Career services:** Alumni network, alumni services, career/job search classes, career assessment, internships. Career services highlights include both our Internship program as well as our Service Learning and Community Partnership program which offers experiential learning. The Internship Program provides high quality placements in work environments closely related to our students' career, personal, and academic interests. Since Sarah Lawrence College is a 25 minute train ride away from New York City, and NYC is the hub for so many career fields, our office has access to some of the most prestigious organizations available which consistently seek out our students. Our students' stellar performance in the workplace creates future internship opportunities for other students and full-time post-graduation employment.

FACILITIES

Housing: Coed dorms, men's dorms, women's dorms, Wellness Housing, Theme Housing. First year students required to live on campus unless living at home. 50% of campus accessible to physically disabled. **Special Academic Facilities/Equipment:** Performing arts center including a concert hall, dance studios,and theatres; visual arts center including studios, gallery, film theatre, sound stage, visual resources library; music building including music library; science center, early childhood center, greenhouse. **Computers:** 100% of classrooms, 30% of dorms, 100% of libraries, 100% of dining areas, 100% of common outdoor areas have wireless network access. Administrative functions (other than registration) can be performed online.

CAMPUS LIFE

Environment: Metropolis. **Activities:** Choral groups, dance, drama/theater, jazz band, literary magazine, music ensembles, musical theater, radio station, student government, student newspaper, student-run film society, symphony orchestra, yearbook, Campus Ministries, International Student Organization, Model UN. 30 registered organizations, 3 religious organizations. **Athletics (Intercollegiate):** *Men:* basketball, crew/rowing, cross-country, equestrian sports, soccer, tennis. *Women:* crew/rowing, cross-country, equestrian sports, softball, swimming, tennis, volleyball. **On-Campus Highlights:** Campbell Sports Center, Communitea House, Siegel Center, Library, Heimbold Visual Arts Center. **Environmental Initiatives:** A sustainable living residence and a green roof on another dorm; A LEED certified visual arts building; A campus-wide sustainability committee.

ADMISSIONS

Freshman Academic Profile: Average high school GPA 3.67. 41% in top 10% of high school class, 77% in top 25% of high school class, 96% in top 50% of high school class. SAT Math middle 50% range 560-660. SAT Critical Reading middle 50% range 600-720. SAT Writing middle 50% range 600-690. ACT middle 50% range 27-32. Minimum internet-based TOEFL 100. Minimum paper TOEFL 600. **Basis for Candidate Selection:** *Very important factors considered include:* application essay, recommendation(s), rigor of secondary school record. *Important factors considered include:* academic GPA, extracurricular activities, talent/ability. *Other factors considered include:* Class rank, alumni/ae relation, character/personal qualities, first generation, geographical residence, interview, level of applicant's interest, racial/ethnic status, volunteer work, work experience. **Freshman Admission Requirements:** High school diploma is required and GED is accepted. *Academic units required:* 4 English, 2 mathematics, 2 science, 2 foreign language, 2 history. **Freshman Admission Statistics:** 2,392 applied, 53% admitted, 28% enrolled. **Transfer Admission Requirements:** High school transcript, college transcript(s), essay or personal statement, statement of good standing from prior institution(s). Lowest grade transferable C. **General Admission Information:** Application Fee $60. Early decision application deadline 11/1. Regular application deadline 1/1. Regular notification 4/1. Nonfall registration not accepted. Admission may be deferred for a maximum of 1 year. Credit offered for CEEB Advanced Placement tests.

COSTS AND FINANCIAL AID

Annual tuition $49,680. Room and board $14,700. Required fees $1,100. **Required Forms and Deadlines:** FAFSA, CSS/Financial Aid PROFILE, State aid form, Noncustodial PROFILE. **Notification of Awards:** Applicants will be notified of awards on or about 4/1. **Types of Aid:** *Need-based scholarships/grants:* Federal Pell, SEOG, state scholarships/grants, private scholarships, the school's own gift aid. *Loans:* Subsidized Stafford, Unsubsidized Stafford, PLUS, Federal Perkins. *Student Employment:* Federal Work-Study Program available. Institutional employment available. Highest amount earned per year from on-campus jobs $1,500. Off-campus job opportunities are good. **Financial Aid Statistics:** 73% freshmen, 83% undergrads receive need-based scholarship or grant aid. 10% freshmen, 29% undergrads receive non-need-based scholarship or grant aid. 61% freshmen, 64% undergrads receive need-based self-help aid. 0% freshmen, 0% undergrads receive athletic scholarships. 79% freshmen, 78% undergrads receive any aid. 63% undergrads borrow to pay for school. Average cumulative indebtedness $16,494.

SAVANNAH COLLEGE OF ART AND DESIGN

PO Box 3146, Savannah, GA 31402-3146
Phone: 912-525-5100 · **Financial Aid Phone:** 800-869-7223
E-mail: admission@scad.edu · **CEEB Code:** 5631
Fax: 912-525-5986 · **Website:** www.scad.edu · **ACT Code:** 855

This private school was founded in 1978.

RATINGS

Admissions Selectivity Rating: 84   Fire Safety Rating: 73

STUDENTS AND FACULTY

Enrollment: 9,396. **Student Body:** 65% female, 35% male, 78% out-of-state, 14% international (107 countries represented). Asian 8%, African American 11%, Caucasian 53%, Hispanic 8%, Native American 1%
Retention and Graduation: 82% freshmen return for sophomore year. 51% freshmen graduate within 4 years. 65% freshmen graduate within 6 years. **Fac-**

ulty: 510 full-time faculty, 80% hold PhDs, 41% are are members of minority groups, 11% are women. 0% of classes are taught by teaching assistants.

ACADEMICS

Degrees: bachelor's, certificate, master's, post-bachelor's certificate. **Classes:** Most classes have 10-19 students. **Majors with Highest Enrollment:** Animation, Interactive Technology, Video Graphics and Special Effects; Graphic Design; Fashion/Apparel Design. **Special Study Options:** distance learning, double major, dual enrollment, English as a Second Language (ESL), independent study, internships, study abroad, teacher certification program, Summer quarter programs in New York City and Europe; apprenticeships with artists or designers and internships with museums, agencies, media production companies, architectural firms, and other companies in the U.S. or abroad. **Disability Services:** Special programs offered to physically disabled students include note-taking services, tape recorders, tutors. **Career services:** Alumni network, alumni services, career/job search classes, career assessment, internships, regional alumni.

FACILITIES

Housing: Coed dorms, women's dorms, apartments for single students, Learning communities. Accommodations for disabled students are handled on an individual basis. 85% of campus accessible to physically disabled. **Special Academic Facilities/Equipment:** Art galleries; computer, video, photography, and design labs; SCAD Museum of Art **Computers:** 80% of classrooms, 100% of dorms, 100% of libraries, 100% of dining areas, 100% of student union, 50% of common outdoor areas have wireless network access. Students can register for classes online. Administrative functions (other than registration) can be performed online.

CAMPUS LIFE

Environment: City. **Activities:** Choral groups, dance, drama/theater, music ensembles, musical theater, radio station, student government, student newspaper, television station, International Student Organization. 68 registered organizations, 2 honor societies, 3 religious organizations. **Athletics (Intercollegiate):** *Men:* baseball, basketball, cross-country, equestrian sports, golf, lacrosse, soccer, swimming, tennis. *Women:* basketball, cross-country, equestrian sports, golf, lacrosse, soccer, softball, swimming, tennis, volleyball. **On-Campus Highlights:** SCAD Museum of Art, Club SCAD, Jen Library, Café SCAD, Trustees Theatre.

ADMISSIONS

Freshman Academic Profile: Average high school GPA 3.44. 15.1% in top 10% of high school class, 40.7% in top 25% of high school class, 75.1% in top 50% of high school class. SAT Math middle 50% range 460-580. SAT Critical Reading middle 50% range 480-600. SAT Writing middle 50% range 460-580. ACT middle 50% range 20-27. Minimum internet-based TOEFL 85. Minimum paper TOEFL 550. **Basis for Candidate Selection:** *Very important factors considered include:* academic GPA, standardized test scores. *Important factors considered include:* rigor of secondary school record, level of applicant's interest. *Other factors considered include:* Class rank, application essay, recommendation(s), character/personal qualities, extracurricular activities, interview, talent/ability, volunteer work, work experience. **Freshman Admission Requirements:** High school diploma is required and GED is accepted. **Freshman Admission Statistics:** 9,656 applied, 66% admitted, 30% enrolled. **Transfer Admission Requirements:** college transcript(s), Minimum college GPA of 2.0 required. Lowest grade transferable C. **General Admission Information:** Application Fee $50. Regular application deadline 8/1. Nonfall registration accepted. Admission may be deferred for a maximum of 2 consec qtr. Credit and/or placement offered for CEEB Advanced Placement tests.

COSTS AND FINANCIAL AID

Annual tuition $33,795. Room and board $13,710. Required fees $500. Average book expense $2,586. **Required Forms and Deadlines:** FAFSA, State aid form. **Notification of Awards:** Applicants will be notified of awards on a rolling basis beginning 4/1. **Types of Aid:** *Need-based scholarships/grants:* Federal Pell, SEOG, state scholarships/grants, private scholarships, the school's own gift aid. *Loans:* Direct Subsidized Stafford, Direct Unsubsidized Stafford, Direct PLUS, state loans. *Student Employment:* Federal Work-Study Program available. Institutional employment available. Off-campus job opportunities are excellent. **Financial Aid Statistics:** 61% freshmen, 63% undergrads receive need-based scholarship or grant aid. 99% freshmen, 89% undergrads receive non-need-based scholarship or grant aid. 90% freshmen, 92% undergrads receive need-based self-help aid. 1% freshmen, 1% undergrads receive athletic scholarships. 61% undergrads borrow to pay for school. Average cumulative indebtedness $26,127. **Criteria for awarding institutional aid:** *Non-need-based:* academics, alumni affiliation, art, athletics, music/drama, state/district residency.

SAVANNAH STATE UNIVERSITY

College Station, Savannah, GA 31404
Phone: 912-356-2181
E-mail: SSUAdmissions@savstate.edu • **CEEB Code:** 5609
Fax: 912-356-2256 • **Website:** www.savstate.edu • **ACT Code:** 858

This public school was founded in 1890. It has a 165-acre campus.

RATINGS
Admissions Selectivity Rating: 60*   **Fire Safety Rating:** 60*

STUDENTS AND FACULTY
Enrollment: 2,635. **Student Body:** 15% out-of-state, (18 countries represented).
Retention and Graduation: 7% grads go on to further study within 1 year. 7% grads pursue arts and sciences degrees. **Faculty:**

ACADEMICS
Degrees: bachelor's, master's. **Special Study Options:** internships, study abroad, Undergrads may take grad level classes Off-campus study: summer quarter programs in New York City and Europe; apprenticeships with artists or designers and internships with musuems, agencies, media production companies, architectural firms, and other companies in the U.S. or abroad Foreign Exchange Program(s): study abroad in England, France, Germany, Italy, and Spain. **Career services:** internships.

FACILITIES
Housing: Coed dorms, men's dorms, women's dorms, fraternity/sorority housing.

CAMPUS LIFE
Activities: 8 honor societies, 3 religious organizations. 5 fraternities, 4 sororities.

ADMISSIONS
Freshman Academic Profile: 94% from public high schools. **Freshman Admission Requirements:** High school diploma is required and GED is accepted.High school diploma is required and GED is not accepted. **Transfer Admission Requirements:** Minimum college GPA of 2.0 required. Lowest grade transferable D. **General Admission Information:** Early decision application deadline 3/1. Regular application deadline 9/1. Nonfall registration accepted. Credit and/or placement offered for CEEB Advanced Placement tests.

COSTS AND FINANCIAL AID
Average book expense $750. **Required Forms and Deadlines:** FAFSA, Institution's own financial aid form. **Types of Aid:** *Need-based scholarships/grants:* state scholarships/grants. *Loans:* Subsidized Stafford, PLUS. *Student Employment:* Off-campus job opportunities are good.

SCHOOL OF THE ART INSTITUTE OF CHICAGO

36 South Wabash Avenue, Chicago, IL 60603
Phone: 312-629-6100 • **Financial Aid Phone:** 312-629-6600
E-mail: admiss@saic.edu • **CEEB Code:** 1713
Fax: 312-629-6101 • **Website:** www.saic.edu • **ACT Code:** 1136

This private school was founded in 1866.

RATINGS
Admissions Selectivity Rating: 74   **Fire Safety Rating:** 75

STUDENTS AND FACULTY
Enrollment: 2,782. **Student Body:** 71% female, 29% male, 70% out-of-state, 31% international (68 countries represented). Asian 13%, African American 3%, Caucasian 40%, Hispanic 7%, Native American <1%
Retention and Graduation: 82% freshmen return for sophomore year. 37% freshmen graduate within 4 years. 57% freshmen graduate within 6 years. **Faculty:** 153 full-time faculty, 90% hold PhDs, 43% are are members of minority groups, 18% are women.

ACADEMICS
Degrees: bachelor's, master's, post-bachelor's certificate. **Classes:** Most classes have 10-19 students. **Special Study Options:** cooperative education program, cross-registration, double major, English as a Second Language (ESL), exchange student program (domestic), independent study, internships, student-designed major, study abroad, teacher certification program, credit/no credit

grading option; multi-disciplinary curriculum; 6 credit off-campus requirement. **Disability Services:** Special programs offered to physically disabled students include note-taking services, reader services, tape recorders, tutors. **Career services:** Alumni network, alumni services, career/job search classes, career assessment, internships. Career services highlights include SAIC's Cooperative Education Program, which is the recipient of the National Society for Experiential Education (NSEE) Experiential Education Higher Education Program of the Year Award. The award recognizes an "outstanding educational institution that has demonstrated an exceptional commitment to experiential education in their classrooms or on their campuses."

FACILITIES
Housing: Coed dorms, special housing for disabled students. 99% of campus accessible to physically disabled. **Special Academic Facilities/Equipment:** The School is directly affiliated with the Art Institute of Chicago. Other resources include: The Gene Siskel Film Center; Fashion Resource Center, John M. Flaxman Library and Screening Room Galleries (Betty Rymer, Sullivan Galleries, Student Union Galleries, project space and Gallery X), Joan Flasch Artists' Book Collection,Poetry Center, Roger Brown Resources, Video Data Bank, The Poetry Center, Visiting Artists' Program, Media Center. **Computers:** Students can register for classes online. Administrative functions (other than registration) can be performed online. Undergraduates are required to own a computer.

CAMPUS LIFE
Environment: Metropolis. **Activities:** dance, drama/theater, literary magazine, radio station, student government, student newspaper, student-run film society, television station, Campus Ministries, International Student Organization. 43 registered organizations, 2 religious organizations. **On-Campus Highlights:** Studio Classrooms, Residence Halls, The Art Institute of Chicago, Gene Siskel Film Center, Galleries. **Environmental Initiatives:** Incandescent light bulbs in dorm rooms have been replaced with CFLs and new low-flow restrictions have been installed in all dorm room showers and sinks. Expected results are 206 Metric Tons of CO_2 not being release into the atmosphere and 1,7 Million Gallons of Water Saved annually. Fan drives in the MacLean Building were replaced with Variable Frequency Drives; it's like putting a dimmer switch on the fan that moves the air. Annual reduction of 183 metric tons of CO_2 SURPLUS is a system for material re-use at SAIC. SURPLUS is a service station where used and excess materials can be made available for other students to take and use for free. Students can bring anything they no longer need—materials, former art projects, etc., as long as they meet the material guidelines posted and take away stuff that they can use. SURPLUS provides a constantly changing resource for materials for artmaking, and it keeps quantities of used and excess materials that the school produces out of the landfills.

ADMISSIONS
Freshman Academic Profile: SAT Math middle 50% range 450-670. SAT Writing middle 50% range 450-670. ACT middle 50% range 18-28. Minimum internet-based TOEFL 79. Minimum paper TOEFL 550. **Basis for Candidate Selection:** *Very important factors considered include:* application essay, recommendation(s), rigor of secondary school record, standardized test scores, character/personal qualities, level of applicant's interest, talent/ability. *Important factors considered include:* Class rank, academic GPA, extracurricular activities, first generation, racial/ethnic status, volunteer work. *Other factors considered include:* alumni/ae relation, geographical residence, interview, state residency, work experience. **Freshman Admission Requirements:** High school diploma is required and GED is accepted. **Freshman Admission Statistics:** 3,737 applied, 69% admitted, 23% enrolled. **Transfer Admission Requirements:** High school transcript, college transcript(s), essay or personal statement, Lowest grade transferable C. **General Admission Information:** Application Fee $65. Regular application deadline 6/1. Notification on a rolling basis, beginning on or about 10/1. Nonfall registration accepted. Admission may be deferred for a maximum of 1 year. Credit offered for CEEB Advanced Placement tests.

COSTS AND FINANCIAL AID
Required Forms and Deadlines: FAFSA. **Notification of Awards:** Applicants will be notified of awards on a rolling basis beginning 3/1. **Types of Aid:** *Need-based scholarships/grants:* Federal Pell, SEOG, state scholarships/grants, private scholarships, the school's own gift aid. *Loans:* Subsidized Stafford, Unsubsidized Stafford, PLUS, Federal Perkins, Alternative/private. *Student Employment:* Off-campus job opportunities are fair. **Financial Aid Statistics:** 99% freshmen, 99% undergrads receive need-based scholarship or grant aid. 7% freshmen, 6% undergrads receive non-need-based scholarship or grant aid. 83% freshmen, 90% undergrads receive need-based self-help aid. 0% freshmen, 0% undergrads receive athletic scholarships. 98% freshmen, 99% undergrads receive any aid. 53% undergrads borrow to pay for school. Average cumulative indebtedness $28,312. **Criteria for awarding institutional aid:** *Non-need-based:* academics, art.

SCHOOL OF THE MUSEUM OF FINE ARTS

230 The Fenway, Boston, MA 2115
Phone: 617-369-3626 • **Financial Aid Phone:** 617-369-3684
E-mail: admissions@smfa.edu • **CEEB Code:** 3794
Fax: 617-369-4264 • **ACT Code:** 1895

This private school was founded in 1876. It has a 14-acre campus.

RATINGS

Admissions Selectivity Rating: 61   **Fire Safety Rating:** 83

STUDENTS AND FACULTY

Enrollment: 372. **Student Body:** 73% female, 27% male, 59% out-of-state, 10% international (45 countries represented). Asian 4%, African American 3%, Caucasian 50%, Hispanic 12%, Native American 1%
Retention and Graduation: 77% freshmen return for sophomore year. 38% freshmen graduate within 4 years. 51% freshmen graduate within 6 years. **Faculty:** 47 full-time faculty, 83% hold PhDs, 53% are are members of minority groups, 9% are women. 5% of classes are taught by teaching assistants.

ACADEMICS

Degrees: bachelor's, certificate, diploma, master's, post-bachelor's certificate. **Classes:** Most classes have 10-19 students. **Majors with Highest Enrollment:** Fine/Studio Arts; Fine Arts and Art Studies. **Special Study Options:** cross-registration, double major, English as a Second Language (ESL), exchange student program (domestic), independent study, internships, liberal arts/career combination, student-designed major, study abroad, teacher certification program, Combined Degree opportunity (BFA + BS or BA). All-studio elective program (Diploma). 5th Year study / Certificate for Diploma recipients. Joint BFA with Northeastern University. **Combined degree programs:** BA/BFA, BS/BFA, BFA/Diploma. **Disability Services:** Special programs offered to physically disabled students include reader services, tape recorders. **Career services:** Alumni network, alumni services, internships. Career services highlights include our internship program, which gives students the opportunity to earn studio credit, gain valuable experience, and make contacts in the local art scene. Students in the internship program receive extensive preparation, support and guidance throughout their internship.

FACILITIES

Housing: Coed dorms, Professional off-campus housing assistance. 100% of campus accessible to physically disabled. **Special Academic Facilities/Equipment:** Museum of Fine Arts, Boston; Art galleries; welding equipment; darkrooms; digital equipment; kilns; and more! **Computers:** 100% of classrooms, 100% of dorms, 100% of libraries, 100% of dining areas, 100% of student union, have wireless network access. Students can register for classes online. Administrative functions (other than registration) can be performed online.

CAMPUS LIFE

Environment: Metropolis. **Activities:** student government, student-run film society. 10 registered organizations. **On-Campus Highlights:** Classrooms and Studios, Museum of Fine Arts, Boston, Galleries and Exhibition Spaces, Museum and School Libraries, "Art in progress—everywhere you look." **Environmental Initiatives:** Migration from toxic (mostly wet photo and paint) to non-toxic art materials and solvents. Also disposal of hazardous waste. Re-use of supplies (where students swap or sell supplies to others). Installation of dense filters in the HVAC system.

ADMISSIONS

Freshman Academic Profile: Minimum internet-based TOEFL 79. Minimum paper TOEFL 550. **Basis for Candidate Selection:** *Very important factors considered include:* rigor of secondary school record, talent/ability. *Important factors considered include:* application essay, academic GPA, interview, level of applicant's interest. *Other factors considered include:* Class rank, recommendation(s), standardized test scores, alumni/ae relation, character/personal qualities, extracurricular activities, first generation, geographical residence, volunteer work, work experience. **Freshman Admission Requirements:** High school diploma is required and GED is accepted. **Freshman Admission Statistics:** 487 applied, 84% admitted, 19% enrolled, **Transfer Admission Requirements:** college transcript(s), essay or personal statement, Minimum college GPA of 1.75 required. Lowest grade transferable C-. **General Admission Information:** Application Fee $65. Notification on a rolling basis, beginning on or about 3/15. Nonfall registration accepted. Admission may be deferred for a maximum of 1 year. Neither credit nor placement offered for CEEB Advanced Placement tests.

COSTS AND FINANCIAL AID

Annual tuition $39,068. Room and board $14,850. Required fees $1,405. Average book expense $1,600. **Required Forms and Deadlines:** FAFSA. **Notification of Awards:** Applicants will be notified of awards on a rolling basis

beginning 4/15. **Types of Aid:** *Need-based scholarships/grants:* Federal Pell, SEOG, state scholarships/grants, private scholarships, the school's own gift aid. *Loans:* Subsidized Stafford, Unsubsidized Stafford, PLUS, state loans. *Student Employment:* Federal Work-Study Program available. Institutional employment available. Highest amount earned per year from on-campus jobs $3,500. Off-campus job opportunities are excellent. **Financial Aid Statistics:** 100% freshmen, 100% undergrads receive need-based scholarship or grant aid. 100% freshmen, 100% undergrads receive non-need-based scholarship or grant aid. 77% freshmen, 79% undergrads receive need-based self-help aid. 0% freshmen, 0% undergrads receive athletic scholarships. 94% freshmen, 97% undergrads receive any aid. 42% undergrads borrow to pay for school. Average cumulative indebtedness $26,130. **Criteria for awarding institutional aid:** *Non-need-based:* art.

SCHOOL OF VISUAL ARTS

209 East 23rd Street, New York, NY 10010
Phone: 212-592-2100 • **Financial Aid Phone:** 212-592-2030
E-mail: admissions@sva.edu • **CEEB Code:** 2835
Fax: 212-592-2116 • **Website:** www.sva.edu • **ACT Code:** 2895

This proprietary school was founded in 1947.

RATINGS

Admissions Selectivity Rating: 75   **Fire Safety Rating:** 98

STUDENTS AND FACULTY

Enrollment: 3,332. **Student Body:** 55% female, 45% male, 57% out-of-state, 15% international (55 countries represented). Asian 13%, African American 3%, Caucasian 49%, Hispanic 10%, Native American 1%
Retention and Graduation: 86% freshmen return for sophomore year. 60% freshmen graduate within 4 years. 67% freshmen graduate within 6 years. **Faculty:** 163 full-time faculty, 24% hold PhDs, 31% are are members of minority groups, 4% are women.

ACADEMICS

Degrees: bachelor's, master's. **Classes:** Most classes have 10-19 students. **Majors with Highest Enrollment:** Graphic Design; Photography; Film/Video and Photographic Arts. **Special Study Options:** English as a Second Language (ESL), exchange student program (domestic), honors program, internships, liberal arts/career combination, study abroad, teacher certification program. **Honors programs:** SVA offers an honors program for incoming freshmen; program involves a two year commitment, with an optional third year. **Disability Services:** Special programs offered to physically disabled students include note-taking services, reader services, tape recorders, tutors. **Career services:** Alumni network, alumni services, internships.

FACILITIES

Housing: Coed dorms, women's dorms. 100% of campus accessible to physically disabled. **Special Academic Facilities/Equipment:** Visual Art Museum, Milton Glaser Design Study Center and Archives, 8 student galleries. **Computers:** 100% of classrooms, 100% of libraries, 100% of student union, have wireless network access. Students can register for classes online. Administrative functions (other than registration) can be performed online.

CAMPUS LIFE

Environment: Metropolis. **Activities:** literary magazine, radio station, student government, student-run film society, yearbook. 23 registered organizations, 3 religious organizations. **On-Campus Highlights:** Visual Arts Gallery, Westside Gallery, Visual Arts Museum, Visual Arts Student Association, Student Lounge. **Environmental Initiatives:** Yes, we do recycle our trash, but we do it off site. Due to space limitations we dont have an area to collect and sort out recyclables from our trash, nor do we have the space to store the recyclables prior to shipment to an appropriate recycler. To accomplish this we rely on an outside contractor to collect our trash and sort it at their facilities. They ensure that anything that can be recycled from our trash finds its way to the recyclers. SVA recycles batteries used in electronic equipment as well as computers, monitors printers and other consumer electronics. We also recycle florescent light bulbs and electronic components. We monitor the waste water that comes from areas like the Photo Labs, Printmaking and the Sculpture Labs. The waste water is tested to make sure that it is in compliance with all city, state and federal regulations. We also do periodic air and water quality checks.

ADMISSIONS

Freshman Academic Profile: Average high school GPA 3.11. 60% from public high schools. SAT Math middle 50% range 460-590. SAT Critical Reading middle 50% range 450-580. SAT Writing middle 50% range 450-580. ACT middle 50% range 20-25. Minimum paper TOEFL 550. **Basis for Candi-**

date Selection: *Very important factors considered include:* application essay, academic GPA, rigor of secondary school record, interview, level of applicant's interest, talent/ability. *Other factors considered include:* recommendation(s), standardized test scores, alumni/ae relation, extracurricular activities, volunteer work, work experience. **Freshman Admission Requirements:** High school diploma is required and GED is accepted. **Freshman Admission Statistics:** 2,821 applied, 67% admitted, 35% enrolled. **Transfer Admission Requirements:** college transcript(s), essay or personal statement, statement of good standing from prior institution(s). Minimum college GPA of 2.0 required. Lowest grade transferable C. **General Admission Information:** Application Fee $50. Notification on a rolling basis, beginning on or about 2/1. Nonfall registration not accepted. Admission may be deferred for a maximum of 1 year. Credit offered for CEEB Advanced Placement tests.

COSTS AND FINANCIAL AID

Annual tuition $26,800. Room and board $12,700. Average book expense $3,150. **Required Forms and Deadlines:** FAFSA, State aid form. **Notification of Awards:** Applicants will be notified of awards on a rolling basis beginning 2/15. **Types of Aid:** *Need-based scholarships/grants:* Federal Pell, SEOG, state scholarships/grants, private scholarships, the school's own gift aid. Alternate loans. *Loans:* Subsidized Stafford, Unsubsidized Stafford, Federal Perkins. *Student Employment:* Federal Work-Study Program available. Off-campus job opportunities are fair. **Financial Aid Statistics:** 68% freshmen, 68% undergrads receive need-based scholarship or grant aid. 19% freshmen, 19% undergrads receive non-need-based scholarship or grant aid. 95% freshmen, 95% undergrads receive need-based self-help aid. 0% freshmen, 0% undergrads receive athletic scholarships. 60% freshmen, 55% undergrads receive any aid. 55% undergrads borrow to pay for school. Average cumulative indebtedness $6,933. **Criteria for awarding institutional aid:** *Non-need-based:* art.

SCHREINER UNIVERSITY

2100 Memorial Boulevard, Kerrville, TX 78028-5697
Phone: 830-792-7217 · **Financial Aid Phone:** 830-792-7217
E-mail: http://www.schreiner.edu/admission/index · **CEEB Code:** 6647
Fax: (830) 792-7226 · **Website:** www.schreiner.edu · **ACT Code:** 4168

This private school, affiliated with the Presbyterian Church, was founded in 1923. It has a 175-acre campus.

RATINGS

Admissions Selectivity Rating: 74   **Fire Safety Rating:** 62

STUDENTS AND FACULTY

Enrollment: 1,051. **Student Body:** 58% female, 42% male, 3% out-of-state, 0% international. Asian 1%, African American 3%, Caucasian 62%, Hispanic 29%, Native American <1%.
Retention and Graduation: 67% freshmen return for sophomore year. 35% freshmen graduate within 4 years. 41% freshmen graduate within 6 years. **Faculty:** 57 full-time faculty, 72% hold PhDs, 51% are are members of minority groups, 9% are women. 0% of classes are taught by teaching assistants.

ACADEMICS

Degrees: associate, bachelor's, certificate, master's, post-bachelor's certificate, post-master's certificate. **Classes:** Most classes have 20-29 students. Most lab/discussion sessions have 20-29 students. **Majors with Highest Enrollment:** Registered Nursing/Registered Nurse; Kinesiology and Exercise Science; Psychology. **Special Study Options:** Accelerated program, double major, dual enrollment, honors program, independent study, internships, liberal arts/career combination, student-designed major, study abroad, teacher certification program, weekend college. **Disability Services:** Special programs offered to physically disabled students include note-taking services, reader services, tape recorders, tutors. **Career services:** Alumni network, alumni services, career/job search classes, career assessment, internships, regional alumni.

FACILITIES

Housing: Coed dorms, special housing for disabled students, apartments for married students, apartments for single students. 95% of campus accessible to physically disabled. **Computers:** 100% of classrooms, 100% of dorms, 100% of libraries, 100% of dining areas, 100% of student union, 30% of common outdoor areas have wireless network access.

CAMPUS LIFE

Environment: Town. **Activities:** Choral groups, dance, drama/theater, literary magazine, music ensembles, musical theater, pep band, student government, student newspaper, symphony orchestra, Campus Ministries. 35 registered organizations, 5 honor societies, 7 religious organizations. 2 fraternities, 2 sororities. **Athletics (Intercollegiate):** *Men:* baseball, basketball, golf, soccer,

tennis. *Women:* basketball, cheerleading, golf, soccer, softball, tennis, volleyball.
On-Campus Highlights: Cailloux Campus Activity Center, Logan Library, Griffin Welcome Center, Deitert Auditorium, Gus Schreiner Student Center.

ADMISSIONS

Freshman Academic Profile: Average high school GPA 3.56. 11% in top 10% of high school class, 34% in top 25% of high school class, 73% in top 50% of high school class. SAT Math middle 50% range 450-550. SAT Critical Reading middle 50% range 430-540. SAT Writing middle 50% range 420-520. ACT middle 50% range 19-24. Minimum internet-based TOEFL 79. Minimum paper TOEFL 550. **Basis for Candidate Selection:** *Important factors considered include:* Class rank, application essay, academic GPA, rigor of secondary school record, standardized test scores, character/personal qualities, interview, level of applicant's interest, volunteer work, work experience. *Other factors considered include:* recommendation(s), extracurricular activities, talent/ability. **Freshman Admission Requirements:** High school diploma is required and GED is accepted. **Freshman Admission Statistics:** 894 applied, 93% admitted, 36% enrolled. **Transfer Admission Requirements:** college transcript(s), Minimum college GPA of 2.0 required. Lowest grade transferable D. **General Admission Information:** Application Fee $25. Regular application deadline 8/1. Nonfall registration accepted. Admission may be deferred for a maximum of 1 semester. Credit and/or placement offered for CEEB Advanced Placement tests.

COSTS AND FINANCIAL AID

Annual tuition $21,884. Room and board $10,250. Required fees $600. Average book expense $1,200. **Required Forms and Deadlines:** FAFSA. **Notification of Awards:** Applicants will be notified of awards on a rolling basis beginning 2/15. **Types of Aid:** *Need-based scholarships/grants:* Federal Pell, SEOG, state scholarships/grants, private scholarships, the school's own gift aid. *Loans:* Direct Subsidized Stafford, Direct Unsubsidized Stafford, Direct PLUS, Subsidized Stafford, Unsubsidized Stafford, PLUS, state loans. *Student Employment:* Federal Work-Study Program available. Institutional employment available. Off-campus job opportunities are good. **Financial Aid Statistics:** 100% freshmen, 99% undergrads receive need-based scholarship or grant aid. 11% freshmen, 10% undergrads receive non-need-based scholarship or grant aid. 81% freshmen, 82% undergrads receive need-based self-help aid. 0% freshmen, 0% undergrads receive athletic scholarships. 90% undergrads borrow to pay for school. Average cumulative indebtedness $24,539. **Criteria for awarding institutional aid:** *Non-need-based:* academics, art, leadership, music/drama, religious affiliation.

SCRIPPS COLLEGE

1030 Columbia Avenue, Claremont, CA 91711
Phone: 909-621-8149 · **Financial Aid Phone:** 909-621-8275
E-mail: admission@scrippscollege.edu · **CEEB Code:** 4693
Fax: 909-607-7508 · **Website:** www.scrippscollege.edu · **ACT Code:** 426

This private school was founded in 1926. It has a 37-acre campus.

RATINGS

Admissions Selectivity Rating: 97   **Fire Safety Rating:** 72

STUDENTS AND FACULTY

Enrollment: 962. **Student Body:** 100% female, 0% male, 50% out-of-state, 4% international (17 countries represented). Asian 19%, African American 3%, Caucasian 49%, Hispanic 9%, Native American <1%.
Retention and Graduation: 80% freshmen graduate within 4 years. 87% freshmen graduate within 6 years. **Faculty:** 89 full-time faculty, 99% hold PhDs, 55% are are members of minority groups, 24% are women. 0% of classes are taught by teaching assistants.

ACADEMICS

Degrees: bachelor's, post-bachelor's certificate. **Classes:** Most classes have 10-19 students. Most lab/discussion sessions have 10-19 students. **Majors with Highest Enrollment:** Political Science and Government; Psychology; Biology/Biological Sciences. **Special Study Options:** Accelerated program, cross-registration, double major, dual enrollment, exchange student program (domestic), independent study, internships, student-designed major, study abroad. **Honors programs:** Honors programs in all academic majors available. **Combined degree programs:** BA/MA, BA/MEng, BA/MBA. **Disability Services:** Special programs offered to physically disabled students include note-taking services, reader services, tape recorders, tutors. **Career services:** Alumni network, alumni services, career/job search classes, career assessment, internships, regional alumni. Career services highlights include a variety of internship resources to assist students in their internship search. Scripps is a member of the National Internship Consortium, with 16 schools across the country sharing over 9000 internship listings. CP&R is pleased to offer a number of internship grants, which allow students to pursue opportunities without having to worry about compensation.

FACILITIES

Housing: special housing for disabled students, women's dorms, apartments for single students, Small college owned houses. 85% of campus accessible to physically disabled. **Special Academic Facilities/Equipment:** Art center, music complex, dance studio, humanities museum and institute, science center, biological field station, field house **Computers:** 100% of classrooms, 100% of dorms, 100% of libraries, 100% of dining areas, 100% of common outdoor areas have wireless network access. Administrative functions (other than registration) can be performed online.

CAMPUS LIFE

Environment: Town. **Activities:** Choral groups, dance, drama/theater, literary magazine, music ensembles, radio station, student government, student newspaper, symphony orchestra, yearbook, Campus Ministries, International Student Organization, Model UN. 200 registered organizations, 5 honor societies, 7 religious organizations. **Athletics (Intercollegiate):** *Women:* basketball, cross-country, diving, golf, lacrosse, soccer, softball, swimming, tennis, track/field (outdoor), volleyball, water polo. **On-Campus Highlights:** Williamson Gallery, Rare book room, Denison Library, Margaret Fowler Garden, Malott Commons, Graffitti Wall, Sallie Tiernan Field House. **Environmental Initiatives:** Establishment of a sustainability committee to serve as an advisory counsel to president regarding campus operations. Requesting information from building contractors on sustainability practices/materials.

ADMISSIONS

Freshman Academic Profile: Average high school GPA 4.12. 83% in top 10% of high school class, 97% in top 25% of high school class, 100% in top 50% of high school class. SAT Math middle 50% range 620-710. SAT Critical Reading middle 50% range 640-750. SAT Writing middle 50% range 640-730. ACT middle 50% range 28-33. Minimum internet-based TOEFL 100. Minimum paper TOEFL 600. **Basis for Candidate Selection:** *Very important factors considered include:* Class rank, application essay, academic GPA, recommendation(s), rigor of secondary school record, standardized test scores, alumni/ae relation, character/personal qualities, extracurricular activities, first generation, interview, racial/ethnic status, talent/ability, volunteer work, work experience. *Important factors considered include:* geographical residence. **Freshman Admission Requirements:** High school diploma is required and GED is accepted. *Academic units required:* 4 English, 3 mathematics, 3 science, 3 foreign language, 3 social studies. **Freshman Admission Statistics:** 2,782 applied, 27% admitted, 33% enrolled. **Transfer Admission Requirements:** High school transcript, college transcript(s), essay or personal statement, standardized test scores, statement of good standing from prior institution(s). Minimum college GPA of 3.0 required. Lowest grade transferable C. **General Admission Information:** Application Fee $60. Early decision application deadline 11/1. Regular application deadline 1/1. Regular notification 4/1. Nonfall registration accepted. Admission may be deferred for a maximum of one year. Credit offered for CEEB Advanced Placement tests.

COSTS AND FINANCIAL AID

Annual tuition $47,164. Room and board $14,562. Required fees $214. Average book expense $800. **Required Forms and Deadlines:** FAFSA, CSS/Financial Aid PROFILE, State aid form, Noncustodial PROFILE, Business/Farm Supplement. **Notification of Awards:** Applicants will be notified of awards on or about 4/1. **Types of Aid:** *Need-based scholarships/grants:* Federal Pell, SEOG, state scholarships/grants, private scholarships, the school's own gift aid. *Loans:* Subsidized Stafford, Unsubsidized Stafford, PLUS, Federal Perkins, college/university loans from institutional funds. *Student Employment:* Federal Work-Study Program available. Institutional employment available. Off-campus job opportunities are good. **Financial Aid Statistics:** 100% freshmen, 100% undergrads receive need-based scholarship or grant aid. 8% freshmen, 3% undergrads receive non-need-based scholarship or grant aid. 81% freshmen, 89% undergrads receive need-based self-help aid. 0% freshmen, 0% undergrads receive athletic scholarships. 61% freshmen, 60% undergrads receive any aid. 50% undergrads borrow to pay for school. Average cumulative indebtedness $12,876. **Criteria for awarding institutional aid:** *Non-need-based:* academics, leadership.

SEATTLE PACIFIC UNIVERSITY

3307 3rd Avenue West, Seattle, WA 98119-1997
Phone: 206-281-2021 · **Financial Aid Phone:** 206-281-2061
E-mail: admissions@spu.edu · **CEEB Code:** 4694
Fax: 206-281-2669 · **Website:** www.spu.edu · **ACT Code:** 4476

This private school, affiliated with the Methodist Church, was founded in 1891. It has a 35-acre campus.

RATINGS

Admissions Selectivity Rating: 74   **Fire Safety Rating:** 60*

STUDENTS AND FACULTY

Enrollment: 3,248. **Student Body:** 67% female, 33% male, 39% out-of-state, 2% international (52 countries represented). Asian 11%, African American 4%, Caucasian 63%, Hispanic 7%, Native American <1%. **Retention and Graduation:** 85% freshmen return for sophomore year. 60% freshmen graduate within 4 years. 75% freshmen graduate within 6 years. **Faculty:** 202 full-time faculty, 82% hold PhDs, 46% are are members of minority groups, 11% are women. 0% of classes are taught by teaching assistants.

ACADEMICS

Degrees: bachelor's, doctoral, master's, post-master's certificate. **Classes:** Most classes have 10-19 students. Most lab/discussion sessions have fewer than 10 students. **Majors with Highest Enrollment:** Business/Commerce; Biology/Biological Sciences. **Special Study Options:** distance learning, double major, exchange student program (domestic), external degree program, honors program, independent study, internships, liberal arts/career combination, student-designed major, study abroad, teacher certification program. **Honors programs:** University Scholars. **Disability Services:** Special programs offered to physically disabled students include note-taking services, reader services, tape recorders. **Career services:** Alumni network, alumni services, career/job search classes, career assessment, internships. Career services highlights include a very strong internship program. Also great 1 & 2 credit classes offered as electives.

FACILITIES

Housing: Coed dorms, apartments for married students, apartments for single students, Theme Housing **Special Academic Facilities/Equipment:** Art gallery, theatre facilities **Computers:** 100% of classrooms, 90% of dorms, 100% of libraries, 100% of dining areas, 100% of student union, 50% of common outdoor areas have wireless network access. Students can register for classes online. Administrative functions (other than registration) can be performed online.

CAMPUS LIFE

Environment: Metropolis. **Activities:** Choral groups, drama/theater, jazz band, literary magazine, music ensembles, musical theater, pep band, radio station, student government, student newspaper, symphony orchestra, yearbook, Campus Ministries. 63 registered organizations, 1 honor society, 7 religious organizations. **Athletics (Intercollegiate):** *Men:* badminton, basketball, bowling, crew/rowing, cross-country, football, soccer, softball, table tennis, tennis, track/field (outdoor), track/field (indoor), volleyball, weight lifting. *Women:* badminton, basketball, bowling, crew/rowing, cross-country, football, gymnastics, soccer, softball, table tennis, tennis, track/field (outdoor), track/field (indoor), volleyball, weight lifting. **On-Campus Highlights:** Pura Vida Coffee Shop, Royal Brougham Pavilion, Weter Lounge, Student Union Building, The Science Building. **Environmental Initiatives:** 1. June 2010 completion of a solar photovoltaic installation atop our physics and engineering building. The installation was conceived as part of a senior honors project and returns to the grid the approximate amount of electricity consumed by our electric maintenance vehicles. A visible production meter in the second floor hallway allows students in the recently created Appropriate and Sustainable Engineering major to monitor its production. 2. New buildings on campus are required to meet a minimum LEED Silver standard. Beyond that, certain LEED credits focusing on energy efficiency, renewable energy, stormwater management, and habitat restoration are designated as priority credits for Seattle Pacific to achieve. 3. Spring 2010 completion of a climate action plan adopting a 2036 target for climate neutrality. The plan covers four distinct areas: planning and development, energy infrastructure, transportation options, and education for a sustainable future. The plan was assembled with input from a 20-person sustainability committee with representation from students, faculty, staff, and the administration.

ADMISSIONS

Freshman Academic Profile: Average high school GPA 3.55. 1% in top 10% of high school class, 3% in top 25% of high school class, 14% in top 50% of high school class. SAT Math middle 50% range 510-620. SAT Critical Reading middle 50% range 520-630. SAT Writing middle 50% range 500-610. ACT middle 50% range 23-28. Minimum internet-based TOEFL 79. Minimum paper TOEFL 550. **Basis for Candidate Selection:** *Very important factors considered include:* application essay, academic GPA, recommendation(s), rigor of secondary school record, standardized test scores. *Important factors considered include:* character/personal qualities, extracurricular activities, first generation, interview, level of applicant's interest, racial/ethnic status, religious affiliation/commitment, talent/ability, volunteer work, work experience. *Other factors considered include:* Class rank, alumni/ae relation, geographical residence. **Freshman Admission Requirements:** High school diploma is required and GED is accepted. **Freshman Admission Statistics:** 4,447 applied, 83% admitted, 18% enrolled. **Transfer Admission Requirements:** college transcript(s), essay or personal statement, Minimum college GPA of 2.5 required. Lowest grade transferable C. **General Admission Information:** Application Fee $45. Regular application deadline 2/1. Regular notification 3/1. Nonfall registration accepted. Credit offered for CEEB Advanced Placement tests.

COSTS AND FINANCIAL AID

Annual tuition $35,100. Room and board $10,086. Required fees $372. Average book expense $1,026. **Required Forms and Deadlines:** FAFSA. **Notification of Awards:** Applicants will be notified of awards on a rolling basis beginning 3/11. **Types of Aid:** *Need-based scholarships/grants:* Federal Pell, SEOG, state scholarships/grants, private scholarships, the school's own gift aid. *Loans:* Subsidized Stafford, Unsubsidized Stafford, PLUS, Federal Perkins, Federal Nursing, college/university loans from institutional funds. *Student Employment:* Federal Work-Study Program available. Institutional employment available. **Financial Aid Statistics:** 100% freshmen, 99% undergrads receive need-based scholarship or grant aid. 0% freshmen, 0% undergrads receive non-need-based scholarship or grant aid. 92% freshmen, 94% undergrads receive need-based self-help aid. 2% freshmen, 2% undergrads receive athletic scholarships. 71% undergrads borrow to pay for school. Average cumulative indebtedness $24,673. **Criteria for awarding institutional aid:** *Non-need-based:* academics, alumni affiliation, art, athletics, leadership, minority status, music/drama, religious affiliation.

SEATTLE UNIVERSITY

Admissions Office, Seattle, WA 98122-1090
Phone: 206-296-2000 • **Financial Aid Phone:** 206-296-8020
E-mail: admissions@seattleu.edu • **CEEB Code:** 4695
Fax: 206-296-5656 • **Website:** www.seattleu.edu • **ACT Code:** 4478

This private school, affiliated with the Roman Catholic-Jesuit Church, was founded in 1891. It has a 50-acre campus.

RATINGS

Admissions Selectivity Rating: 87   Fire Safety Rating: 96

STUDENTS AND FACULTY

Enrollment: 4,461. **Student Body:** 59% female, 41% male, 56% out-of-state, 11% international (79 countries represented). Asian 16%, African American 3%, Caucasian 45%, Hispanic 9%, Native American 1%
Retention and Graduation: 87% freshmen return for sophomore year. 61% freshmen graduate within 4 years. 78% freshmen graduate within 6 years. **Faculty:** 507 full-time faculty, 82% hold PhDs, 50% are members of minority groups, 18% are women. 0% of classes are taught by teaching assistants.

ACADEMICS

Degrees: bachelor's, master's, post-bachelor's certificate, post-master's certificate. **Classes:** Most classes have 10-19 students. Most lab/discussion sessions have 10-19 students. **Majors with Highest Enrollment:** Liberal Arts and Sciences Studies and Humanities; Registered Nursing/Registered Nurse; Business/Commerce. **Special Study Options:** cooperative education program, cross-registration, double major, English as a Second Language (ESL), honors program, independent study, internships, liberal arts/career combination, student-designed major, study abroad. **Honors programs:** The University Honors program provides students of high ability and motivation the opportunity to join a small, select, two-year-long learning community. The program is taken in the freshman and sophomore years and fulfills most of the University's Core Curriculum requirements. Honors programs are also offered within majors. **Combined degree programs:** BA/MBA. **Disability Services:** Special programs offered to physically disabled students include note-taking services, reader services, tape recorders, tutors. **Career services:** Alumni network, alumni services, career/job search classes, career assessment, internships.

FACILITIES

Housing: Coed dorms, special housing for disabled students, apartments for single students, Theme Housing. 95% of campus accessible to physically disabled. **Special Academic Facilities/Equipment:** Observatory, electron microscope, St. Ignatius Chapel **Computers:** 100% of classrooms, 20% of dorms, 100% of libraries, 100% of dining areas, 100% of student union, 95% of common outdoor areas have wireless network access. Students can register for classes online. Administrative functions (other than registration) can be performed online.

CAMPUS LIFE

Environment: Metropolis. **Activities:** Choral groups, drama/theater, jazz band, literary magazine, music ensembles, pep band, radio station, student government, student newspaper, Campus Ministries. 130 registered organizations. **Athletics (Intercollegiate):** *Men:* baseball, basketball, cross-country, golf, soccer, swimming, tennis, track/field (outdoor), track/field (indoor). *Women:* basketball, cross-country, golf, soccer, softball, swimming, tennis, track/field (outdoor), track/field (indoor), volleyball. **On-Campus Highlights:** Chapel of Saint Ignatius, Brand new Student Center, Award Winning Grounds and Open Space, Sullivan Hall, home of the School of Law **Environmental Initiatives:** Plastic bottled water is not sold anywhere on campus including: the bookstore, vending machines, athletics concession stands, restaurants, and catered events. Free, filtered water and bottle fillers are available at over 30 water fountains throughout campus. The Bookstore is selling a 27 ounce, steel water bottle at a discounted price to make owning a bottle affordable. Compost bins for collecting food waste are located in the restaurants, outside campus buildings, the library, a few staff offices, each residence hall residents room and each residence hall floors waste closet. All to-go ware from campus eateries is made from plant-based compostable materials. Our campus compost facility annually turns 52,000 pounds of food waste into compost—which is applied on our landscape. All new construction and major renovations must achieve LEED Gold certification. There are three completed LEED Gold buildings, a fourth is being built and one LEED Certified building. Two homes were renovated to a Built Green 3-Star rating out of three possible stars.

ADMISSIONS

Freshman Academic Profile: Average high school GPA 3.58. 27% in top 10% of high school class, 62% in top 25% of high school class, 92% in top 50% of high school class. 63% from public high schools. SAT Math middle 50% range 530-640. SAT Critical Reading middle 50% range 530-640. SAT Writing middle 50% range 530-630. ACT middle 50% range 24-29. Minimum internet-based TOEFL 68. Minimum paper TOEFL 520. **Basis for Candidate Selection:** *Very important factors considered include:* academic GPA, rigor of secondary school record, standardized test scores, character/personal qualities. *Important factors considered include:* application essay, recommendation(s), extracurricular activities, level of applicant's interest. *Other factors considered include:* Class rank, alumni/ae relation, first generation, geographical residence, interview, racial/ethnic status, religious affiliation/commitment, state residency, talent/ability, volunteer work, work experience. **Freshman Admission Requirements:** High school diploma is required and GED is accepted. *Academic units required:* 4 English, 3 mathematics, 2 science, (2 science labs), 2 foreign language, 2 social studies, 1 history, 2 academic electives. **Freshman Admission Statistics:** 7,392 applied, 73% admitted, 24% enrolled. **Transfer Admission Requirements:** college transcript(s), essay or personal statement, statement of good standing from prior institution(s). Minimum college GPA of 2.25 required. Lowest grade transferable C-. **General Admission Information:** Application Fee $50. Notification on a rolling basis, beginning on or about 2/1. Nonfall registration accepted. Admission may be deferred for a maximum of 1 year. Credit and/or placement offered for CEEB Advanced Placement tests.

COSTS AND FINANCIAL AID

Required Forms and Deadlines: FAFSA. **Notification of Awards:** Applicants will be notified of awards on a rolling basis beginning 3/21. **Types of Aid:** *Need-based scholarships/grants:* Federal Pell, SEOG, state scholarships/grants, private scholarships, the school's own gift aid, Federal Nursing Scholarships. *Loans:* Direct Subsidized Stafford, Direct Unsubsidized Stafford, Direct PLUS, Federal Perkins, Federal Nursing. **Financial Aid Statistics:** 90% freshmen, 92% undergrads receive need-based scholarship or grant aid. 59% freshmen, 44% undergrads receive non-need-based scholarship or grant aid. 71% freshmen, 74% undergrads receive need-based self-help aid. 7% freshmen, 5% undergrads receive athletic scholarships. 93% freshmen, 84% undergrads receive any aid. 73% undergrads borrow to pay for school. Average cumulative indebtedness $25,027. **Criteria for awarding institutional aid:** *Non-need-based:* academics, alumni affiliation, athletics, leadership, minority status, music/drama, state/district residency.

See page 1138.

SETON HALL UNIVERSITY

Best 380

Office of Admission, Seton Hall, South Orange, NJ 7079
Phone: 800-THE-HALL · **Financial Aid Phone:** 973-761-9332
E-mail: thehall@shu.edu · **CEEB Code:** 2811
Fax: 973-275-2339 · **Website:** www.shu.edu · **ACT Code:** 2606

This private school, affiliated with the Roman Catholic Church, was founded in 1856. It has a 58-acre campus.

RATINGS

Admissions Selectivity Rating: 84   Fire Safety Rating: 87

STUDENTS AND FACULTY
Enrollment: 5,295. **Student Body:** 59% female, 41% male, 22% out-of-state, 2% international (71 countries represented). Asian 8%, African American 13%, Caucasian 51%, Hispanic 16%, Native American <1%
Retention and Graduation: 30% grads go on to further study within 1 year. 9% grads pursue arts and sciences degrees. 7% grads pursue law degrees. 5% grads pursue business degrees. 9% grads pursue medical degrees. **Faculty:** 4% of classes are taught by teaching assistants.

ACADEMICS
Degrees: bachelor's, first professional, master's, post-master's certificate. **Classes:** Most classes have 10-19 students. Most lab/discussion sessions have 10-19 students. **Majors with Highest Enrollment:** Speech Communication and Rhetoric; Criminal Justice/Safety Studies; Communication, Journalism, and Related Programs. **Special Study Options:** Accelerated program, cooperative education program, cross-registration, distance learning, double major, dual enrollment, English as a Second Language (ESL), honors program, independent study, internships, study abroad, teacher certification program. **Honors programs:** University Honors Program fosters intellectual development through academic challenge. A structured sequence of colloquia and seminars helps to develop critical thinking abilities. Student study the great texts of the past and also have the opportunity to attend operas, theater, museums, concerts and other cultural events. **Combined degree programs:** BA/MA, BA/MEng, BS/MS Phys Asst or OT or Athl Trng, BS/D Phys Ther. **Disability Services:** Special programs offered to physically disabled students include note-taking services, reader services, tape recorders, tutors. **Career services:** Alumni network, career/job search classes, career assessment, internships, regional alumni. Career services highlights include internships.

FACILITIES
Housing: Coed dorms, special housing for disabled students, apartments for single students. 94% of campus is accessible to physically disabled. **Special Academic Facilities/Equipment:** Art, natural history, museums, theatre-in-the-round, archaeological research center, TV studio, radio station. **Computers:** 100% of classrooms, 100% of dorms, 100% of libraries, 100% of dining areas, 100% of student union, 100% of common outdoor areas have wireless network access. Students can register for classes online. Administrative functions (other than registration) can be performed online. Undergraduates are required to own a computer.

CAMPUS LIFE
Environment: Village. **Activities:** Choral groups, drama/theater, pep band, radio station, student government, television station. 100 registered organizations, 13 honor societies, 3 religious organizations. **Athletics (Intercollegiate):** *Men:* baseball, basketball, cross-country, diving, golf, soccer, swimming, track/field (outdoor). *Women:* basketball, cross-country, diving, soccer, softball, swimming, tennis, track/field (outdoor). **On-Campus Highlights:** Jubilee Hall, University Center, Walsh Library, Recreation Center, Chapel.

ADMISSIONS
Freshman Academic Profile: Average high school GPA 3.47. 37% in top 10% of high school class, 61% in top 25% of high school class, 86% in top 50% of high school class. 70% from public high schools. SAT Math middle 50% range 510-610. SAT Critical Reading middle 50% range 490-590. SAT Writing middle 50% range 490-600. ACT middle 50% range 22-27. Minimum paper TOEFL 550. **Freshman Admission Statistics:** 10,180 applied, 84% admitted, 17% enrolled.

COSTS AND FINANCIAL AID
Required Forms and Deadlines: FAFSA. **Financial Aid Statistics:** 97% freshmen, 97% undergrads receive any aid.

See page 1140.

SETON HILL UNIVERSITY

1 Seton Hill Drive, Greensburg, PA 15601
Phone: 724-838-4255 · **Financial Aid Phone:** 724-838-4293
E-mail: admit@setonhill.edu · **CEEB Code:** 2812
Fax: 724-830-1294 · **Website:** www.setonhill.edu · **ACT Code:** 3688

This private school, affiliated with the Roman Catholic Church, was founded in 1883. It has a 200-acre campus.

RATINGS

Admissions Selectivity Rating: 84   Fire Safety Rating: 80

STUDENTS AND FACULTY
Enrollment: 1,540. **Student Body:** 64% female, 36% male, 23% out-of-state, 3% international (13 countries represented). Asian 1%, African American 7%, Caucasian 71%, Hispanic 3%, Native American <1%
Retention and Graduation: 78% freshmen return for sophomore year. 49% freshmen graduate within 4 years. 30% grads go on to further study within 1 year. 20% grads pursue arts and sciences degrees. 1% grads pursue law degrees. 3% grads pursue business degrees. 1% grads pursue medical degrees. **Faculty:** 103 full-time faculty, 85% hold PhDs, 52% are are members of minority groups, 3% are women. 0% of classes are taught by teaching assistants.

ACADEMICS
Degrees: bachelor's, certificate, master's, post-bachelor's certificate, post-master's certificate. **Classes:** Most classes have 10-19 students. **Majors with Highest Enrollment:** Fine/Studio Arts; Business/Commerce; Psychology. **Special Study Options:** Accelerated program, cross-registration, distance learning, double major, dual enrollment, English as a Second Language (ESL), exchange student program (domestic), honors program, independent study, internships, liberal arts/career combination, student-designed major, study abroad, teacher certification program, weekend college. **Honors programs:** Honors Program has designated curriculum components. **Combined degree programs:** BA/JD, BS/DO, /DPharm with Lake Erie Coll of Osteopath Med, BA/Law with Duquesne U. **Disability Services:** Special programs offered to physically disabled students include note-taking services, reader services, tape recorders, tutors. **Career services:** Alumni network, alumni services, career assessment, internships, regional alumni. Career services highlights include internships that are encouraged or required in every major.

FACILITIES
Housing: Coed dorms, men's dorms, women's dorms, Special housing for honors students. 95% of campus accessible to physically disabled. **Special Academic Facilities/Equipment:** Art gallery, concert hall, theatre, Child Development Center, NEW- Performing Arts Center, Studio 215, smart classrooms. **Computers:** 100% of classrooms, 100% of dorms, 100% of libraries, 100% of dining areas, 100% of common outdoor areas have wireless network access. Students can register for classes online. Administrative functions (other than registration) can be performed online.

CAMPUS LIFE
Environment: Town. **Activities:** Choral groups, concert band, dance, drama/theater, jazz band, literary magazine, marching band, music ensembles, musical theater, pep band, student government, student newspaper, symphony orchestra, Campus Ministries, International Student Organization. 53 registered organizations, 4 honor societies, 7 religious organizations. **Athletics (Intercollegiate):** *Men:* baseball, basketball, cross-country, football, lacrosse, soccer, track/field (outdoor), track/field (indoor), wrestling. *Women:* basketball, cross-country, equestrian sports, field hockey, golf, lacrosse, soccer, softball, tennis, track/field (outdoor), track/field (indoor), volleyball. **On-Campus Highlights:** Griffin's Cove, McKenna Recreation Center, Sullivan Lounge, Residence Halls, Lowe Dining Hall, New additions to Seton Hill include the Center for Performing Arts and Visual Arts Center; both of these venues are located in downtown Greensburg within walking distance of campus. **Environmental Initiatives:** Association of Independent Colleges and Universities of Pennsylvania self/peer assessment program.

ADMISSIONS
Freshman Academic Profile: Average high school GPA 3.61. 27% in top 10% of high school class, 51% in top 25% of high school class, 83% in top 50% of high school class. SAT Math middle 50% range 470-600. SAT Critical Reading middle 50% range 470-580. SAT Writing middle 50% range 450-560. ACT middle 50% range 21-26. Minimum paper TOEFL 550. **Basis for Candidate Selection:** *Very important factors considered include:* academic GPA, rigor of secondary school record, interview. *Important factors considered include:* Class rank, standardized test scores, character/personal qualities, extracurricular activities, talent/ability. *Other factors considered include:* application essay, recommendation(s), alumni/ae relation, level of applicant's interest, volunteer

work, work experience. **Freshman Admission Requirements:** High school diploma is required and GED is accepted. *Academic units required:* 4 English, 2 mathematics, 1 science, (1 science labs), 0 foreign language, 2 social studies, 4 academic electives. **Freshman Admission Statistics:** 2,248 applied, 69% admitted, 21% enrolled. **Transfer Admission Requirements:** High school transcript, college transcript(s), statement of good standing from prior institution(s). Minimum college GPA of 2.0 required. Lowest grade transferable C-. **General Admission Information:** Application Fee $35. Regular application deadline 8/15. Notification on a rolling basis, beginning on or about 9/1. Nonfall registration accepted. Admission may be deferred for a maximum of 12 months. Credit and/or placement offered for CEEB Advanced Placement tests.

COSTS AND FINANCIAL AID
Annual tuition $31,037. Room and board $10,739. Required fees $1,000. Average book expense $1,200. **Required Forms and Deadlines:** FAFSA, Institution's own financial aid form, State aid form. **Notification of Awards:** Applicants will be notified of awards on a rolling basis beginning 11/15. **Types of Aid:** *Need-based scholarships/grants:* Federal Pell, SEOG, state scholarships/grants, private scholarships, the school's own gift aid. *Loans:* Subsidized Stafford, Unsubsidized Stafford, PLUS, Federal Perkins, college/university loans from institutional funds, Alternative. *Student Employment:* Federal Work-Study Program available. Institutional employment available. Highest amount earned per year from on-campus jobs $1,000. Off-campus job opportunities are good. **Financial Aid Statistics:** 100% freshmen, 99% undergrads receive need-based scholarship or grant aid. 19% freshmen, 14% undergrads receive non-need-based scholarship or grant aid. 78% freshmen, 83% undergrads receive need-based self-help aid. 15% freshmen, 11% undergrads receive athletic scholarships. 98% freshmen, 85% undergrads receive any aid. 85% undergrads borrow to pay for school. Average cumulative indebtedness $26,735. **Criteria for awarding institutional aid:** *Non-need-based:* academics, alumni affiliation, art, athletics, job skills, music/drama, religious affiliation.

SEWANEE—THE UNIVERSITY OF THE SOUTH

Best 380

735 University Avenue, Sewanee, TN 37383-1000
Phone: 931-598-1238 • **Financial Aid Phone:** 931-598-1312
E-mail: admiss@sewanee.edu • **CEEB Code:** 1842
Fax: 931-538-3248 • **Website:** www.sewanee.edu • **ACT Code:** 4924

This private school, affiliated with the Episcopal Church, was founded in 1857. It has a 13000-acre campus.

RATINGS
Admissions Selectivity Rating: 89   **Fire Safety Rating:** 85

STUDENTS AND FACULTY
Enrollment: 1,616. **Student Body:** 51% female, 49% male, 74% out-of-state, 3% international (24 countries represented). Asian 2%, African American 5%, Caucasian 82%, Hispanic 5%, Native American <1%.
Retention and Graduation: 76% freshmen graduate within 4 years. 24% grads go on to further study within 1 year. **Faculty:** 148 full-time faculty, 97% hold PhDs, 40% are are members of minority groups, 12% are women. 0% of classes are taught by teaching assistants.

ACADEMICS
Degrees: bachelor's, master's, post-bachelor's certificate, post-master's certificate. **Classes:** Most classes have 10-19 students. Most lab/discussion sessions have 20-29 students. **Majors with Highest Enrollment:** English Language and Literature; Economics; History. **Special Study Options:** double major, independent study, internships, student-designed major, study abroad. **Disability Services:** Special programs offered to physically disabled students include note-taking services, reader services, tape recorders. **Career services:** Alumni network, alumni services, career assessment, internships, regional alumni. Career services highlights include Sewanee's Internship Fund Program. Thanks to the help of alumni and the donors of Sewanee's 25 endowed internship funds, 150 students received a total of almost $300,000 in stipends or paid internships in 2007. Sewanee students interned in 20 states and 20 countries in 2007, and these endowed funds enabled the students to do meaningful internships that would otherwise have been unpaid.

FACILITIES
Housing: Coed dorms, special housing for disabled students, men's dorms, special housing for international students, women's dorms, fraternity/sorority housing, apartments for married students, cooperative housing, apartments for single students, Wellness Housing, Theme Housing, Substance-free housing & Living and Learning Communities. **Special Academic Facilities/Equipment:** Art gallery, observatory, keyboard collection, materials analysis lab with electron microscope. **Computers:** 80% of classrooms, 80% of dorms, 100% of libraries, 100% of dining areas, 100% of student union, 25% of common outdoor areas have wireless network access. Students can register for classes online. Administrative functions (other than registration) can be performed online.

CAMPUS LIFE
Environment: Rural. **Activities:** Choral groups, concert band, dance, drama/theater, jazz band, literary magazine, music ensembles, musical theater, radio station, student government, student newspaper, student-run film society, symphony orchestra, yearbook, Campus Ministries, International Student Organization, Model UN. 110 registered organizations, 9 honor societies, 11 religious organizations. 12 fraternities, 9 sororities. **Athletics (Intercollegiate):** *Men:* baseball, basketball, cross-country, diving, equestrian sports, football, golf, lacrosse, soccer, swimming, tennis, track/field (outdoor), track/field (indoor). *Women:* basketball, cheerleading, cross-country, diving, equestrian sports, field hockey, golf, lacrosse, soccer, softball, swimming, tennis, track/field (outdoor), track/field (indoor), volleyball. **On-Campus Highlights:** Outdoor recreation on Sewanee's 10,000 a, All Saints' Chapel, Abbo's Alley Ravine Garden, Memorial Cross and University View, University Golf and Tennis Club. **Environmental Initiatives:** In pursuit of a goal from our 2008 Strategic Planning Addendum, Sewanee's Sustainability Steering Committee developed a Sustainability Master Plan that has been formerly adopted. The plan, the first of its kind at Sewanee, is a blueprint for the institution's commitment to sustainability as we move forward, empowering Sewanee to teach and lead by example. We are in serious pursuit of a variety of energy conservation and renewable energy initiatives outlined in our Climate Action Plan, and have earned a STARS Silver rating. A Green Revolving Fund has been launched on campus to finance energy/water efficiency, renewable energy, and other sustainability projects that generate cost-savings.

ADMISSIONS
Freshman Academic Profile: Average high school GPA 3.69. 35% in top 10% of high school class, 68% in top 25% of high school class, 92% in top 50% of high school class. 44% from public high schools. SAT Math middle 50% range 560-670. SAT Critical Reading middle 50% range 570-690. SAT Writing middle 50% range 570-670. ACT middle 50% range 26-30. Minimum internet-based TOEFL 90. Minimum paper TOEFL 577. **Basis for Candidate Selection:** *Very important factors considered include:* academic GPA, recommendation(s), rigor of secondary school record. *Important factors considered include:* application essay, standardized test scores, character/personal qualities, extracurricular activities, volunteer work, work experience. *Other factors considered include:* Class rank, alumni/ae relation, first generation, geographical residence, interview, level of applicant's interest, racial/ethnic status, talent/ability. **Freshman Admission Requirements:** High school diploma is required and GED is not accepted. *Academic units required:* 4 English, 3 mathematics, 2 science, (2 science labs), 2 foreign language, 1 social studies, 1 history. **Freshman Admission Statistics:** 2,977 applied, 65% admitted, 24% enrolled. **Transfer Admission Requirements:** High school transcript, college transcript(s), essay or personal statement, standardized test scores, statement of good standing from prior institution(s). Minimum college GPA of 3.00 required. Lowest grade transferable C. **General Admission Information:** Application Fee $45. Early decision application deadline 11/15. Regular application deadline 2/1. Regular notification 3/17. Nonfall registration not accepted. Admission may be deferred for a maximum of 12 months. Credit and/or placement offered for CEEB Advanced Placement tests.

COSTS AND FINANCIAL AID
Annual tuition $38,428. Room and board $11,050. Required fees $272. Average book expense $900. **Required Forms and Deadlines:** FAFSA, CSS/Financial Aid PROFILE. **Notification of Awards:** Applicants will be notified of awards on or about 4/1. **Types of Aid:** *Need-based scholarships/grants:* Federal Pell, SEOG, state scholarships/grants, private scholarships, the school's own gift aid. *Loans:* Subsidized Stafford, Unsubsidized Stafford, PLUS, Federal Perkins, state loans, college/university loans from institutional funds, private alternative loans. *Student Employment:* Federal Work-Study Program available. Institutional employment available. Highest amount earned per year from on-campus jobs $1,500. Off-campus job opportunities are fair. **Financial Aid Statistics:** 99% freshmen, 98% undergrads receive need-based scholarship or grant aid. 34% freshmen, 28% undergrads receive non-need-based scholarship or grant aid. 80% freshmen, 76% undergrads receive need-based self-help aid. 0% freshmen, 0% undergrads receive athletic scholarships. 79% freshmen, 77% undergrads receive any aid. 39% undergrads borrow to pay for school. Average cumulative indebtedness $18,436. **Criteria for awarding institutional aid:** *Non-need-based:* academics, minority status, religious affiliation.

SHASTA BIBLE COLLEGE

2951 Goodwater Ave., Redding, CA 96002
Phone: 530-221-4275
E-mail: admissions@shasta.edu
Fax: 530-221-6929 • **Website:** www.shasta.edu • **ACT Code:** 427

This private school, affiliated with the Baptist Church, was founded in 1970. It has a 63-acre campus.

RATINGS

Admissions Selectivity Rating: 60*   **Fire Safety Rating:** 60*

STUDENTS AND FACULTY

Enrollment: 89. **Student Body:** 44% female, 56% male, 21% out-of-state, 3% international (5 countries represented). Asian 0%, African American 1%, Caucasian 73%, Hispanic 1%, Native American <1%
Retention and Graduation: 40% freshmen return for sophomore year. 100% freshmen graduate within 4 years. 100% grads go on to further study within 1 year. 20% grads pursue arts and sciences degrees. **Faculty:** 7 full-time faculty, 71% hold PhDs, 14% are are members of minority groups, 14% are women.

ACADEMICS

Degrees: associate, bachelor's, certificate, diploma, master's. **Classes:** Most classes have 10-19 students. **Majors with Highest Enrollment:** Electrical, Electronic and Communications Engineering Technology/Technician. **Special Study Options:** distance learning, double major, external degree program, independent study, teacher certification program, weekend college, Master's in School Administration. **Combined degree programs:** BA/MA. **Disability Services:** Special programs offered to physically disabled students include tutors.

FACILITIES

Housing: Coed dorms. 100% of campus accessible to physically disabled.

CAMPUS LIFE

Environment: Rural. **Activities:** radio station, student government, television station, yearbook.

ADMISSIONS

Freshman Academic Profile: 30% from public high schools. Minimum paper TOEFL 500. **Basis for Candidate Selection:** *Very important factors considered include:* application essay, recommendation(s), character/personal qualities, religious affiliation/commitment, volunteer work. *Important factors considered include:* extracurricular activities, work experience. *Other factors considered include:* Class rank, standardized test scores, alumni/ae relation, interview, talent/ability. **Freshman Admission Requirements:** High school diploma is required and GED is accepted. **Freshman Admission Statistics:** 38 applied, 100% admitted, 100% enrolled. **Transfer Admission Requirements:** High school transcript, college transcript(s), Minimum college GPA of 2.0 required. Lowest grade transferable C. **General Admission Information:** Application Fee $35. Nonfall registration accepted. Admission may be deferred for a maximum of 1 Semester. Neither credit nor placement offered for CEEB Advanced Placement tests.

COSTS AND FINANCIAL AID

Annual tuition $5,300. Room and board $1,200. Average book expense $250. **Required Forms and Deadlines: Notification of Awards:** Applicants will be notified of awards on a rolling basis beginning 1/2. **Types of Aid:** *Need-based scholarships/grants:* Federal Pell, state scholarships/grants. *Loans: Student Employment:* Federal Work-Study Program available. Highest amount earned per year from on-campus jobs $700. Off-campus job opportunities are excellent. **Financial Aid Statistics:** 0% freshmen, 0% undergrads receive athletic scholarships.

SHAW UNIVERSITY

118 East South Street, Raleigh, NC 27601
Phone: 919-546-8275 • **Financial Aid Phone:** 919-546-8565
E-mail: admissions@shawu.edu • **CEEB Code:** 5612
Fax: 919-546-8271 • **Website:** www.shawu.edu • **ACT Code:** 3158

This private school, affiliated with the Baptist Church, was founded in 1865. It has a 30-acre campus.

RATINGS

Admissions Selectivity Rating: 72   **Fire Safety Rating:** 60*

STUDENTS AND FACULTY

Enrollment: 2,027. **Student Body:** 58% female, 42% male, 30% out-of-state, 2% international (17 countries represented). Asian 0%, African American 85%, Caucasian 1%, Hispanic 0%, Native American <1%
Retention and Graduation: 13% freshmen graduate within 4 years. **Faculty:** 109 full-time faculty, 74% hold PhDs, 44% are are members of minority groups, 76% are women. 0% of classes are taught by teaching assistants.

ACADEMICS

Degrees: associate, bachelor's, first professional, master's. **Classes:** Most classes have fewer than 10 students. **Majors with Highest Enrollment:** Business Administration and Management; Social Work; Sociology. **Special Study Options:** Accelerated program, cross-registration, distance learning, double major, dual enrollment, honors program, independent study, internships, student-designed major, study abroad, teacher certification program, weekend college. **Disability Services:** Special programs offered to physically disabled students include tape recorders, tutors.

FACILITIES

Housing: men's dorms, women's dorms. **Special Academic Facilities/Equipment:** TV and film production facilities. Curriculum and Materials Center. **Computers:** Students can register for classes online. Administrative functions (other than registration) can be performed online.

CAMPUS LIFE

Environment: City. **Activities:** Choral groups, concert band, dance, drama/theater, jazz band, marching band, music ensembles, musical theater, pep band, radio station, student government, student newspaper, yearbook 4 honor societies, 4 fraternities, 4 sororities. **Athletics (Intercollegiate):** *Men:* baseball, basketball, cross-country, football, golf, tennis, track/field (outdoor), track/field (indoor). *Women:* basketball, bowling, cross-country, softball, tennis, track/field (outdoor), track/field (indoor), volleyball.

ADMISSIONS

Freshman Academic Profile: Average high school GPA 2.31. 1% in top 10% of high school class, 5% in top 25% of high school class, 25% in top 50% of high school class. 90% from public high schools. SAT Math middle 50% range 330-410. SAT Critical Reading middle 50% range 330-410. SAT Writing middle 50% range 310-390. ACT middle 50% range 13-16. **Basis for Candidate Selection:** *Very important factors considered include:* academic GPA, recommendation(s), first generation, geographical residence, level of applicant's interest. *Important factors considered include:* Class rank, application essay, rigor of secondary school record, standardized test scores, character/personal qualities, extracurricular activities, state residency, volunteer work, work experience. *Other factors considered include:* alumni/ae relation, talent/ability. **Freshman Admission Requirements:** High school diploma is required and GED is accepted. *Academic units required:* 3 English, 2 mathematics, 2 science, 2 social studies, 9 academic electives. **Freshman Admission Statistics:** 6,207 applied, 54% admitted, 15% enrolled. **Transfer Admission Requirements:** college transcript(s), Lowest grade transferable C. **General Admission Information:** Application Fee $25. Regular application deadline 7/30. Notification on a rolling basis, beginning on or about 8/1. Nonfall registration accepted. Admission may be deferred for a maximum of indefinite. Credit and/or placement offered for CEEB Advanced Placement tests.

COSTS AND FINANCIAL AID

Annual tuition $11,160. Room and board $7,844. Required fees $3,254. Average book expense $1,300. **Required Forms and Deadlines:** FAFSA, Institution's own financial aid form, State aid form. **Notification of Awards:** Applicants will be notified of awards on a rolling basis beginning 2/1. **Types of Aid:** *Need-based scholarships/grants:* Federal Pell, SEOG, state scholarships/grants, private scholarships, the school's own gift aid, United Negro College Fund. *Loans:* Subsidized Stafford, Unsubsidized Stafford, PLUS, Federal Perkins. *Student Employment:* Federal Work-Study Program available. Institutional employment available. Off-campus job opportunities are excellent. **Criteria for awarding institutional aid:** *Non-need-based:* academics, alumni affiliation, art, athletics, music/drama, religious affiliation.

SHAWNEE STATE UNIVERSITY

940 Second Street, Portsmouth, OH 45662
Phone: 740-351-4778 • **Financial Aid Phone:** 740-351-4357
E-mail: to_ssu@shawnee.edu • **CEEB Code:** 1790
Fax: 740-351-3111 • **Website:** www.shawnee.edu • **ACT Code:** 3336

This public school was founded in 1986. It has a 50-acre campus.

RATINGS

Admissions Selectivity Rating: 76   **Fire Safety Rating:** 91

STUDENTS AND FACULTY

Enrollment: 3,756. **Student Body:** 56% female, 44% male, 11% out-of-state, 1% international (20 countries represented). Asian 0%, African American 6%, Caucasian 87%, Hispanic 1%, Native American 1%
Retention and Graduation: 57% freshmen return for sophomore year. 13% freshmen graduate within 4 years. 27% freshmen graduate within 6 years. **Faculty:** 145 full-time faculty, 59% hold PhDs, 41% are are members of minority groups, 10% are women. 0% of classes are taught by teaching assistants.

ACADEMICS

Degrees: associate, bachelor's, certificate, master's. **Classes:** Most classes have 10-19 students. Most lab/discussion sessions have 20-29 students. **Majors with Highest Enrollment:** Psychology; Business Administration and Management; Biological and Biomedical Sciences. **Special Study Options:** cross-registration, distance learning, double major, dual enrollment, English as a Second Language (ESL), honors program, independent study, internships, student-designed major, study abroad, teacher certification program. **Disability Services:** Special programs offered to physically disabled students include note-taking services, reader services, tape recorders, tutors. **Career services:** alumni services, career/job search classes, career assessment, internships.

FACILITIES

Housing: Coed dorms, list of housing in community available. 100% of campus accessible to physically disabled. **Special Academic Facilities/Equipment:** Vern Riffe Center for the Arts. **Computers:** Students can register for classes online.

CAMPUS LIFE

Environment: Town. **Activities:** Choral groups, drama/theater, literary magazine, music ensembles, musical theater, student government, student newspaper, Campus Ministries. 36 registered organizations, 2 honor societies, 3 religious organizations. 1 fraternity, 1 sorority. **Athletics (Intercollegiate):** *Men:* baseball, basketball, cross-country, golf, soccer. *Women:* basketball, cross-country, soccer, softball, tennis, volleyball. **On-Campus Highlights:** Vern Riffe Center for the Arts, University Center. **Environmental Initiatives:** geothermal chiller plant for new building; single-stream recycle program; pulper for food waste in new kitchen.

ADMISSIONS

Freshman Academic Profile: 12% in top 10% of high school class, 33% in top 25% of high school class, 63% in top 50% of high school class. SAT Math middle 50% range 433-628. SAT Critical Reading middle 50% range 440-588. SAT Writing middle 50% range 405-548. ACT middle 50% range 18-24. Minimum internet-based TOEFL 60. Minimum paper TOEFL 500. **Freshman Admission Requirements:** High school diploma is required and GED is accepted. **Freshman Admission Statistics:** 3,686 applied, 74% admitted, 35% enrolled. **Transfer Admission Requirements:** High school transcript, college transcript(s), Minimum college GPA of 1.0 required. Lowest grade transferable D. **General Admission Information:** Nonfall registration accepted. Admission may be deferred for a maximum of one year. Credit and/or placement offered for CEEB Advanced Placement tests.

COSTS AND FINANCIAL AID

Annual in-state tuition $6,251. Annual out-of-state tuition $11,504. Room and board $9,552. Required fees $1,113. Average book expense $1,440. **Required Forms and Deadlines:** FAFSA. **Notification of Awards:** Applicants will be notified of awards on a rolling basis beginning 5/1. **Types of Aid:** *Need-based scholarships/grants:* Federal Pell, SEOG, state scholarships/grants, private scholarships, the school's own gift aid. *Loans:* Subsidized Stafford, Unsubsidized Stafford, PLUS, state loans. *Student Employment:* Off-campus job opportunities are fair. **Criteria for awarding institutional aid:** *Non-need-based:* academics, art, athletics, minority status, music/drama, state/district residency.

SHENANDOAH UNIVERSITY

1460 University Drive, Winchester, VA 22601-5195
Phone: 540.665.4581 • **Financial Aid Phone:** 540-665-4621
E-mail: admit@su.edu • **CEEB Code:** 5613
Fax: 540.665.4627 • **Website:** www.su.edu • **ACT Code:** 4396

This private school, affiliated with the Methodist Church, was founded in 1875. It has a 100-acre campus.

RATINGS

Admissions Selectivity Rating: 72   **Fire Safety Rating:** 84

STUDENTS AND FACULTY

Enrollment: 1,875. **Student Body:** 56% female, 44% male, 38% out-of-state, 5% international (55 countries represented). Asian 3%, African American 14%, Caucasian 65%, Hispanic 6%, Native American 2%
Retention and Graduation: 76% freshmen return for sophomore year. 36% freshmen graduate within 4 years. 18% grads go on to further study within 1 year. **Faculty:** 250 full-time faculty, 82% hold PhDs, 57% are are members of minority groups, 11% are women. 0% of classes are taught by teaching assistants.

ACADEMICS

Degrees: associate, bachelor's, certificate, first professional, master's, post-bachelor's certificate, post-master's certificate, terminal associate. **Classes:** Most classes have 10-19 students. Most lab/discussion sessions have fewer than 10 students. **Majors with Highest Enrollment:** Registered Nursing/Registered Nurse; Biology/Biological Sciences; Business Administration and Management. **Special Study Options:** Accelerated program, cooperative education program, distance learning, double major, English as a Second Language (ESL), independent study, internships, liberal arts/career combination, student-designed major, study abroad, teacher certification program, weekend college. **Combined degree programs:** Pharmacy/MBA; DPT/MBA; DPT/Athletic Training. **Disability Services:** Special programs offered to physically disabled students include note-taking services, reader services, tape recorders, tutors.

FACILITIES

Housing: Coed dorms, special housing for disabled students, special housing for international students. 91% of campus accessible to physically disabled. **Special Academic Facilities/Equipment:** None **Computers:** 100% of classrooms, 100% of dorms, 100% of libraries, 100% of dining areas, 100% of student union, 25% of common outdoor areas have wireless network access. Students can register for classes online. Administrative functions (other than registration) can be performed online.

CAMPUS LIFE

Environment: Town. **Activities:** Choral groups, concert band, dance, drama/theater, jazz band, music ensembles, musical theater, opera, radio station, student government, student newspaper, symphony orchestra, television station. 65 registered organizations, 2 honor societies, 2 religious organizations. 7 fraternities, 1 sorority. **Athletics (Intercollegiate):** *Men:* baseball, basketball, cross-country, football, golf, lacrosse, soccer, tennis. *Women:* basketball, cross-country, field hockey, lacrosse, soccer, softball, tennis, volleyball. **On-Campus Highlights:** Ohrstrom-Bryant Theatre, Aikens Athletic Center, Alson H. Smith, Jr. Library, Health Professions Building, Goodson Chapel/Recital Hall. **Environmental Initiatives:** Lighting Retrofits Residence hall recycling program. Beginning integrated pest management program.

ADMISSIONS

Freshman Academic Profile: Average high school GPA 3.39. SAT Math middle 50% range 440-560. SAT Critical Reading middle 50% range 440-550. SAT Writing middle 50% range 430-540. ACT middle 50% range 18-24. Minimum internet-based TOEFL 71. Minimum paper TOEFL 527. **Basis for Candidate Selection:** *Very important factors considered include:* academic GPA, rigor of secondary school record, interview, talent/ability. *Important factors considered include:* recommendation(s), standardized test scores, extracurricular activities, volunteer work. *Other factors considered include:* application essay, character/personal qualities, level of applicant's interest, work experience. **Freshman Admission Requirements:** High school diploma is required and GED is accepted. *Academic units required:* 4 English, 3 mathematics, 2 science, (1 science labs), 2 foreign language, 2 social studies, 2 history, 2 academic electives. **Freshman Admission Statistics:** 1,907 applied, 83% admitted, 26% enrolled. **Transfer Admission Requirements:** college transcript(s), statement of good standing from prior institution(s). Minimum college GPA of 2.0 required. Lowest grade transferable C. **General Admission Information:** Application Fee $30. Regular notification 8/7. Notification on a rolling basis, beginning on or about 10/6. Nonfall registration accepted. Admission may be deferred for a maximum of 12 months. Credit and/or placement offered for CEEB Advanced Placement tests.

COSTS AND FINANCIAL AID

Annual tuition $29,570. Room and board $9,920. Required fees $1,190. Average book expense $1,500. **Required Forms and Deadlines:** FAFSA, State aid form. **Notification of Awards:** Applicants will be notified of awards on a rolling basis beginning 3/15. **Types of Aid:** *Need-based scholarships/grants:* Federal Pell, SEOG, state scholarships/grants, private scholarships, the school's own gift aid, Federal Nursing Scholarships. *Loans:* Direct Subsidized Stafford, Direct Unsubsidized Stafford, Direct PLUS, Federal Perkins, Federal Nursing, college/university loans from institutional funds. *Student Employment:* Highest amount earned per year from on-campus jobs $1,500. **Financial Aid Statistics:** 43% freshmen, 43% undergrads receive need-based scholarship or grant aid. 100% freshmen, 100% undergrads receive non-need-based scholarship or grant aid. 73% freshmen, 75% undergrads receive need-based self-help aid. 0% freshmen, 0% undergrads receive athletic scholarships. 99% freshmen, 98% undergrads receive any aid. 85% undergrads borrow to pay for school. Average cumulative indebtedness $28,679. **Criteria for awarding institutional aid:** *Non-need-based:* academics, job skills, music/drama, religious affiliation, state/district residency.

SHEPHERD UNIVERSITY

Office of Admissions, Shepherdstown, WV 25443-5000
Phone: 304-876-5212 · **Financial Aid Phone:** 304-876-5470
E-mail: admissions@shepherd.edu · **CEEB Code:** 5615
Fax: 304-876-5165 · **Website:** www.shepherd.edu · **ACT Code:** 4532

This public school was founded in 1871. It has a 323-acre campus.

RATINGS

Admissions Selectivity Rating: 70   **Fire Safety Rating:** 80

STUDENTS AND FACULTY

Enrollment: 3,489. **Student Body:** 60% female, 40% male, 37% out-of-state, 0% international (15 countries represented). Asian 2%, African American 9%, Caucasian 83%, Hispanic 3%, Native American <1%.
Retention and Graduation: 68% freshmen return for sophomore year. 20% freshmen graduate within 4 years. 40% freshmen graduate within 6 years. **Faculty:** 139 full-time faculty, 87% hold PhDs, 46% are are members of minority groups, 12% are women. 0% of classes are taught by teaching assistants.

ACADEMICS

Degrees: bachelor's, master's. **Classes:** Most classes have 20-29 students. Most lab/discussion sessions have 20-29 students. **Majors with Highest Enrollment:** Business/Commerce; Teacher Education, Multiple Levels; Nursing Education. **Special Study Options:** cooperative education program, double major, dual enrollment, honors program, independent study, internships, study abroad, teacher certification program. **Honors programs:** See Honors Program on Web site www.shepherd.edu **Combined degree programs:** MedStep with WVU School of Medicine. **Disability Services:** Special programs offered to physically disabled students include note-taking services, reader services, tape recorders, tutors. **Career services:** Alumni network, alumni services, career/job search classes, career assessment, internships, regional alumni.

FACILITIES

Housing: Coed dorms, special housing for disabled students, apartments for single students, Theme Housing, Suites, first-year housing. 90% of campus accessible to physically disabled. **Special Academic Facilities/Equipment:** Nursery school, elementary education lab, art gallery, theaters, Fazioli Concert Grand Piano, George Tyler Moore Center for the Study of the Civil War, Robert C. Byrd Center for Legislative Studies. **Computers:** 90% of classrooms, 100% of libraries, 100% of dining areas, 100% of student union, 1% of common outdoor areas have wireless network access. Students can register for classes online. Administrative functions (other than registration) can be performed online.

CAMPUS LIFE

Environment: Village. **Activities:** Choral groups, concert band, drama/theater, jazz band, literary magazine, marching band, music ensembles, musical theater, pep band, radio station, student government, student newspaper, symphony orchestra, Campus Ministries, International Student Organization. 85 registered organizations, 9 honor societies, 4 religious organizations. 4 fraternities, 3 sororities. **Athletics (Intercollegiate):** *Men:* baseball, basketball, football, golf, soccer, tennis. *Women:* basketball, lacrosse, soccer, softball, tennis, volleyball. **On-Campus Highlights:** Butcher Athletic Center, Center for Contemporary Arts, Scarborough Library, Wellness Center, Student Center. **Environmental Initiatives:** Recycling; Upgrading HVAC equipment; Constructing new buildings to LEED standards.

ADMISSIONS

Freshman Academic Profile: Average high school GPA 3.33. 95% from public high schools. SAT Math middle 50% range 440-540. SAT Critical Reading middle 50% range 450-550. ACT middle 50% range 19-24. Minimum internet-based TOEFL 79. Minimum paper TOEFL 550. **Basis for Candidate Selection:** *Very important factors considered include:* academic GPA, rigor of secondary school record, standardized test scores. *Important factors considered include:* talent/ability. *Other factors considered include:* Class rank, application essay, recommendation(s), alumni/ae relation, character/personal qualities, extracurricular activities, interview, level of applicant's interest. **Freshman Admission Requirements:** High school diploma is required and GED is accepted. *Academic units required:* 4 English, 4 mathematics, 3 science, (3 science labs), 2 foreign language, 2 social studies, 1 history, 1 visual/performing arts, 5 academic electives. **Freshman Admission Statistics:** 1,817 applied, 98% admitted, 36% enrolled. **Transfer Admission Requirements:** college transcript(s), Minimum college GPA of 2.0 required. Lowest grade transferable D. **General Admission Information:** Application Fee $45. Regular application deadline 8/15. Notification on a rolling basis, beginning on or about 9/15. Nonfall registration accepted. Admission may be deferred for a maximum of 12 months. Credit and/or placement offered for CEEB Advanced Placement tests.

COSTS AND FINANCIAL AID

Average book expense $1,000. **Required Forms and Deadlines:** FAFSA, State aid form. **Notification of Awards:** Applicants will be notified of awards on a rolling basis beginning 3/15. **Types of Aid:** *Need-based scholarships/grants:* Federal Pell, SEOG, state scholarships/grants, private scholarships, the school's own gift aid. *Loans:* Direct Subsidized Stafford, Direct Unsubsidized Stafford, Direct PLUS, Federal Perkins. *Student Employment:* Federal Work-Study Program available. Institutional employment available. Highest amount earned per year from on-campus jobs $12,181. Off-campus job opportunities are good. **Financial Aid Statistics:** 64% freshmen, 67% undergrads receive need-based scholarship or grant aid. 54% freshmen, 34% undergrads receive non-need-based scholarship or grant aid. 64% freshmen, 71% undergrads receive need-based self-help aid. 10% freshmen, 7% undergrads receive athletic scholarships. 90% freshmen, 85% undergrads receive any aid. 68% undergrads borrow to pay for school. Average cumulative indebtedness $23,233. **Criteria for awarding institutional aid:** *Non-need-based:* academics, art, athletics, job skills, leadership, minority status, music/drama, state/district residency.

SHIMER COLLEGE

3424 S. State St, Chicago, IL 60616
Phone: 312-235-3555 · **Financial Aid Phone:** 312-235-3507
E-mail: admission@shimer.edu · **CEEB Code:** 1717
Fax: 888-808-3133 · **Website:** http://www.shimer.edu/ · **ACT Code:** 1142

This private school was founded in 1853. It has a 140-acre campus.

RATINGS

Admissions Selectivity Rating: 78   **Fire Safety Rating:** 60*

STUDENTS AND FACULTY

Enrollment: 74. **Student Body:** 47% female, 53% male, 50% out-of-state, 0% international (4 countries represented). Asian 7%, African American 9%, Caucasian 68%, Hispanic 12%, Native American <1%
Retention and Graduation: 19% freshmen graduate within 4 years. **Faculty:** 9 full-time faculty, 100% hold PhDs, 33% are are members of minority groups, 22% are women. 0% of classes are taught by teaching assistants.

ACADEMICS

Degrees: bachelor's. **Classes:** Most classes have 10-19 students. **Majors with Highest Enrollment:** Humanities/Humanistic Studies; Natural Sciences; Social Sciences. **Special Study Options:** cross-registration, double major, independent study, internships, liberal arts/career combination, study abroad, weekend college, one-on-one tutorials with faculty member for in depth study in any area of interest to the student. **Combined degree programs:** BA/JD. **Career services:** Alumni network, alumni services, career/job search classes, internships, regional alumni. Career services highlights include the opportunity to intern off campus during the program. Funded internships are available.

FACILITIES

Housing: Coed dorms, women's dorms, apartments for married students, apartments for single students. 100% of campus accessible to physically disabled. **Special Academic Facilities/Equipment:** The Galvin Library has over one million volumes and 120 digital databases. The MTCC (student center) is an amazing place to eat, play and hang out. **Computers:** 100% of classrooms, 100% of dorms, 100% of libraries, 100% of dining areas, 100% of student union, 100% of common outdoor areas have wireless network access.

CAMPUS LIFE

Environment: Metropolis. **Activities:** Choral groups, concert band, drama/theater, jazz band, literary magazine, music ensembles, radio station, student government, student newspaper, International Student Organization 10 religious organizations. **On-Campus Highlights:** The Shimer College space on the IIT Camp, The Galvin Library/Art Galery, McCormic Tribune Campus Center, Crown Hall, Keating Sports Center. Students are strongly encouraged to visit when classes are in session. The best way to know if Shimer is a good fit for you is if you sit in on a class.

ADMISSIONS

Freshman Academic Profile: Average high school GPA 2.99. 50% from public high schools. SAT Math middle 50% range 500-640. SAT Critical Reading middle 50% range 620-760. SAT Writing middle 50% range 500-620. Minimum paper TOEFL 625. **Basis for Candidate Selection:** *Very important factors considered include:* application essay, recommendation(s), interview, level of applicant's interest. *Important factors considered include:* rigor of secondary school record, character/personal qualities, talent/ability, volunteer work. *Other factors considered include:* Class rank, academic GPA, standardized test scores, alumni/ae relation, extracurricular activities, first generation, geographical residence, work experience. **Freshman Admission Requirements:** High school diploma or equivalent is not required. **Freshman Admission Statistics:** 31 applied, 84% admitted, 46% enrolled. **Transfer Admission Requirements:** college transcript(s), essay or personal statement, interview, Lowest grade transferable C. **General Admission Information:** Application Fee $25. Regular application deadline 8/1. Notification on a rolling basis, beginning on or about 9/15. Nonfall registration accepted. Admission may be deferred for a maximum of 2 years. Neither credit nor placement offered for CEEB Advanced Placement tests.

COSTS AND FINANCIAL AID

Annual tuition $26,510. Room and board $10,626. Required fees $4,720. Average book expense $800. **Required Forms and Deadlines:** FAFSA. **Notification of Awards:** Applicants will be notified of awards on a rolling basis beginning 2/1. **Types of Aid:** *Need-based scholarships/grants:* Federal Pell, SEOG, state scholarships/grants, private scholarships, the school's own gift aid. *Loans:* Subsidized Stafford, Unsubsidized Stafford, PLUS, Federal Perkins. *Student Employment:* Federal Work-Study Program available. Institutional employment available. Highest amount earned per year from on-campus jobs $1,500. Off-campus job opportunities are excellent. **Financial Aid Statistics:** 71% freshmen, 100% undergrads receive need-based scholarship or grant aid. 71% freshmen, 75% undergrads receive non-need-based scholarship or grant aid. 71% freshmen, 91% undergrads receive need-based self-help aid. 0% freshmen, 0% undergrads receive athletic scholarships. 74% freshmen, 84% undergrads receive any aid. 100% undergrads borrow to pay for school. Average cumulative indebtedness $25,125. **Criteria for awarding institutional aid:** *Non-need-based:* academics, alumni affiliation.

SHIPPENSBURG UNIVERSITY OF PENNSYLVANIA

Old Main 105, Shippensburg, PA 17257-2299
Phone: 717-477-1231 · **Financial Aid Phone:** 717-477-1131
E-mail: admiss@ship.edu · **CEEB Code:** 2657
Fax: 717-477-4016 · **Website:** www.ship.edu · **ACT Code:** 3714

This public school was founded in 1871. It has a 200-acre campus.

RATINGS

Admissions Selectivity Rating: 72   **Fire Safety Rating:** 89

STUDENTS AND FACULTY

Enrollment: 6,246. **Student Body:** 49% female, 51% male, 7% out-of-state, 0% international (29 countries represented). Asian 1%, African American 9%, Caucasian 79%, Hispanic 5%, Native American <1%
Retention and Graduation: 74% freshmen return for sophomore year. 37% freshmen graduate within 4 years. 55% freshmen graduate within 6 years. **Faculty:** 305 full-time faculty, 93% hold PhDs, 43% are are members of minority groups, 14% are women. 0% of classes are taught by teaching assistants.

ACADEMICS

Degrees: bachelor's, certificate, master's, post-bachelor's certificate, post-master's certificate. **Classes:** Most classes have 20-29 students. Most lab/discussion sessions have 10-19 students. **Majors with Highest Enrollment:** Psychology; Criminal Justice/Safety Studies; Business Administration and Management. **Special Study Options:** Accelerated program, cooperative education program,

distance learning, double major, dual enrollment, honors program, independent study, internships, study abroad, teacher certification program, Raider Plan. **Honors programs:** Program in General Education and Psychology **Combined degree programs:** 3-2 EngProg/PSU and U of Md; Chem and Bio/Med Tech. **Disability Services:** Special programs offered to physically disabled students include note-taking services, reader services, tape recorders, tutors. **Career services:** Alumni network, alumni services, career/job search classes, career assessment, internships, regional alumni. Pennsylvania has been working to transform itself from a manufacturing economy to a diversified service-based economy with strength in technology intensive industries. Pennsylvania's workforce development strategy seeks to align education and training to High Priority Occupations (HPOs), which are fields with identified skill needs and job openings. Internships are a vital link between education and employment. Shippensburg University, and each of the 14 Pennsylvania State System of Higher Education (PASSHE) Universities, received a $30,000 grant to increase internships in the Commonwealth during the 2007-2008 and 2008-2009 academic years. This Economic Development-Internships grant program is designed to help meet the Commonwealth goals to develop and retain employment in the state. The grant project will enhance resources for all stakeholders by increasing university-wide coordination and institutional capacity to manage and increase internships. Student teaching, practicuums, field experiences, and internships are offered by all three colleges at both the undergraduate and graduate levels. Students gain professional experience directly related to their major by working part- or full-time during the fall or spring semesters or during the summer. Students earn credit based upon the number of hours worked; they are supervised by a faculty advisor and are expected to develop a rapport with their employer to fully understand and satisfy the duties and responsibilities of their assignment. Students are expected to complete a variety of academic assignments related to their experience and in a number of programs, also participate in a seminar course associated with their experiential learning placement. Responsibility for assessment rests within the academic departments and is incorporated into departmental five-year program reviews.

FACILITIES

Housing: Coed dorms, Wellness Housing, Theme Housing, Suites, Apartment Complex Off-Campus. 91% of campus accessible to physically disabled. **Special Academic Facilities/Equipment:** art gallery, vertebrate museum, on-campus elementary school, planetarium, electron microscope, NMR spectrometer, greenhouse, herbarium, Fashion Archives, Women's Center, Closed Circuit TV. **Computers:** 95% of classrooms, 10% of dorms, 100% of libraries, 100% of dining areas, 95% of student union, 75% of common outdoor areas have wireless network access. Students can register for classes online. Administrative functions (other than registration) can be performed online.

CAMPUS LIFE

Environment: Village. **Activities:** Choral groups, concert band, dance, drama/theater, jazz band, literary magazine, marching band, music ensembles, musical theater, radio station, student government, student newspaper, television station, yearbook, Campus Ministries, International Student Organization. 200 registered organizations, 23 honor societies, 8 religious organizations. 12 fraternities, 15 sororities. **Athletics (Intercollegiate):** *Men:* baseball, basketball, cross-country, football, soccer, swimming, track/field (outdoor), track/field (indoor), wrestling. *Women:* basketball, cross-country, field hockey, lacrosse, soccer, softball, swimming, tennis, track/field (outdoor), track/field (indoor), volleyball. **On-Campus Highlights:** Ceddia Union Building, Heiges Field House, Student Recreation Center, Ritazza Coffee Shop, Student Fitness Center, Starbucks, Quiznos, Chick-fil-A, Dauphin Humanities Center, Lehman Library, Learning Assistant Center, Reisner Dining Hall.

ADMISSIONS

Freshman Academic Profile: Average high school GPA 3.2. 7.4% in top 10% of high school class, 24.7% in top 25% of high school class, 58.7% in top 50% of high school class. 90% from public high schools. SAT Math middle 50% range 450-550. SAT Critical Reading middle 50% range 440-540. SAT Writing middle 50% range 420-510. ACT middle 50% range 17-23. Minimum internet-based TOEFL 66. Minimum paper TOEFL 550. **Basis for Candidate Selection:** *Very important factors considered include:* Class rank, academic GPA, rigor of secondary school record, standardized test scores. *Other factors considered include:* application essay, recommendation(s), character/personal qualities, extracurricular activities, interview, level of applicant's interest, talent/ability, volunteer work, work experience. **Freshman Admission Requirements:** High school diploma is required and GED is accepted. **Freshman Admission Statistics:** 6,319 applied, 83% admitted, 28% enrolled. **Transfer Admission Requirements:** college transcript(s), statement of good standing from prior institution(s). Minimum college GPA of 2.2 required. Lowest grade transferable C. **General Admission Information:** Application Fee $30. Nonfall registration accepted. Admission may be deferred for a maximum of 1 year. Credit and/or placement offered for CEEB Advanced Placement tests.

COSTS AND FINANCIAL AID

Annual in-state tuition $6,820. Annual out-of-state tuition $15,346. Room and board $11,160. Required fees $2,954. Average book expense $1,200. **Required**

Forms and Deadlines: FAFSA. Types of Aid: *Need-based scholarships/ grants:* Federal Pell, SEOG, state scholarships/grants, private scholarships, the school's own gift aid, Academic Competitiveness Grant (ACG)and Smart Grant. *Loans:* Subsidized Stafford, Unsubsidized Stafford, PLUS, Federal Perkins, Alternative loans. *Student Employment:* Federal Work-Study Program available. Off-campus job opportunities are good. **Financial Aid Statistics:** 73% freshmen, 70% undergrads receive need-based scholarship or grant aid. 3% freshmen, 3% undergrads receive non-need-based scholarship or grant aid. 89% freshmen, 90% undergrads receive need-based self-help aid. 7% freshmen, 5% undergrads receive athletic scholarships. 89% freshmen, 86% undergrads receive any aid. 80% undergrads borrow to pay for school. Average cumulative indebtedness $24,327. **Criteria for awarding institutional aid:** *Non-need-based:* academics, athletics.

SHORTER UNIVERSITY

315 Shorter Avenue, Rome, GA 30165
Phone: 706-233-7319 · **Financial Aid Phone:** 706-233-7227
E-mail: admissions@shorter.edu · **CEEB Code:** 5616
Fax: 706-233-7224 · **Website:** www.shorter.edu · **ACT Code:** 860

This private school, affiliated with the Southern Baptist Church, was founded in 1873. It has a 150-acre campus.

RATINGS

Admissions Selectivity Rating: 82   **Fire Safety Rating:** 78

STUDENTS AND FACULTY

Enrollment: 1,581. **Student Body:** 55% female, 45% male, 12% out-of-state, 3% international (22 countries represented). Asian 1%, African American 17%, Caucasian 69%, Hispanic 4%, Native American <1%
Retention and Graduation: 68% freshmen return for sophomore year. 33% freshmen graduate within 4 years. 43% freshmen graduate within 6 years. 30% grads go on to further study within 1 year. **Faculty:** 92 full-time faculty, 70% hold PhDs, 50% are are members of minority groups, 9% are women. 0% of classes are taught by teaching assistants.

ACADEMICS

Degrees: bachelor's. **Classes:** Most classes have 10-19 students. Most lab/discussion sessions have 10-19 students. **Majors with Highest Enrollment:** Education; Visual and Performing Arts; Business Administration and Management. **Special Study Options:** cross-registration, double major, dual enrollment, honors program, independent study, internships, student-designed major, study abroad, teacher certification program, weekend college. **Honors programs:** Academy of Aristaeus: a four-year honors program featuring seminar discussions and a research project. **Disability Services:** Special programs offered to physically disabled students include note-taking services, reader services, tape recorders, tutors. **Career services:** career/job search classes, career assessment. Career services highlights include required internships for most majors.

FACILITIES

Housing: men's dorms, women's dorms, apartments for single students. 70% of campus accessible to physically disabled. **Special Academic Facilities/Equipment:** Shorter History Museum. **Computers:** Students can register for classes online. Administrative functions (other than registration) can be performed online.

CAMPUS LIFE

Environment: Town. **Activities:** Choral groups, concert band, dance, drama/theater, literary magazine, marching band, music ensembles, musical theater, opera, pep band, radio station, student government, student newspaper, student-run film society, yearbook, Campus Ministries, International Student Organization, Model UN. 34 registered organizations, 10 honor societies, 3 religious organizations. 3 fraternities, 3 sororities. **Athletics (Intercollegiate):** *Men:* baseball, basketball, cheerleading, cross-country, football, golf, soccer, tennis, track/field (outdoor). *Women:* basketball, cheerleading, cross-country, golf, lacrosse, soccer, softball, tennis, track/field (outdoor), volleyball. **On-Campus Highlights:** Fitton Student Union, Winthrop-King Activities Center, Brookes Chapel, Ledbetter Baseball Complex.

ADMISSIONS

Freshman Academic Profile: Average high school GPA 3.32. 21% in top 10% of high school class, 47% in top 25% of high school class, 77% in top 50% of high school class. 95% from public high schools. SAT Math middle 50% range 430-550. SAT Critical Reading middle 50% range 420-550. SAT Writing middle 50% range 410-530. ACT middle 50% range 18-24. Minimum paper TOEFL 500. **Basis for Candidate Selection:** *Very important factors considered include:* academic GPA, standardized test scores. *Important factors considered*

include: Class rank, application essay, rigor of secondary school record, talent/ability. *Other factors considered include:* recommendation(s), alumni/ae relation, character/personal qualities, extracurricular activities, first generation, interview, level of applicant's interest, volunteer work, work experience. **Freshman Admission Requirements:** High school diploma is required and GED is accepted. *Academic units required:* 4 English, 4 mathematics, 3 science, 2 foreign language, 3 history. **Freshman Admission Statistics:** 1,944 applied, 65% admitted, 32% enrolled. **Transfer Admission Requirements:** college transcript(s), statement of good standing from prior institution(s). Minimum college GPA of 2.0 required. Lowest grade transferable C. **General Admission Information:** Application Fee $25. Notification on a rolling basis, beginning on or about 11/1. Nonfall registration accepted. Admission may be deferred for a maximum of 2 years. Credit and/or placement offered for CEEB Advanced Placement tests.

COSTS AND FINANCIAL AID

Annual tuition $17,500. Room and board $8,600. Required fees $370. Average book expense $1,200. **Required Forms and Deadlines:** FAFSA, Institution's own financial aid form, State aid form. **Notification of Awards:** Applicants will be notified of awards on a rolling basis beginning 4/1. **Types of Aid:** *Need-based scholarships/grants:* Federal Pell, SEOG, state scholarships/grants, private scholarships, the school's own gift aid. *Loans:* Subsidized Stafford, Unsubsidized Stafford, PLUS, Federal Perkins, We have moved to using Direct Loans from the US Government. *Student Employment:* Federal Work-Study Program available. Institutional employment available. Highest amount earned per year from on-campus jobs $2,000. Off-campus job opportunities are good. **Financial Aid Statistics:** 99% freshmen, 99% undergrads receive need-based scholarship or grant aid. 16% freshmen, 15% undergrads receive non-need-based scholarship or grant aid. 79% freshmen, 75% undergrads receive need-based self-help aid. 15% freshmen, 11% undergrads receive athletic scholarships. 99% freshmen, 99% undergrads receive any aid. 93% undergrads borrow to pay for school. Average cumulative indebtedness $24,325. **Criteria for awarding institutional aid:** *Non-need-based:* academics, art, athletics, music/drama, religious affiliation.

SIENA COLLEGE

515 Loudon Road, Loudonville, NY 12211
Phone: 518-783-2423 · **Financial Aid Phone:** 888-287-4362
E-mail: admissions@siena.edu · **CEEB Code:** 2814
Fax: 518-783-2436 · **Website:** www.siena.edu · **ACT Code:** 2878

This private school, affiliated with the Roman Catholic Church, was founded in 1937. It has a 166-acre campus.

RATINGS

Admissions Selectivity Rating: 87   **Fire Safety Rating:** 77

STUDENTS AND FACULTY

Enrollment: 3,087. **Student Body:** 52% female, 48% male, 19% out-of-state, 2% international (17 countries represented). Asian 4%, African American 3%, Caucasian 80%, Hispanic 7%, Native American <1%
Retention and Graduation: 74% freshmen graduate within 4 years. 38% grads go on to further study within 1 year. **Faculty:** 231 full-time faculty, 90% hold PhDs, 44% are are members of minority groups, 11% are women. 0% of classes are taught by teaching assistants.

ACADEMICS

Degrees: bachelor's, certificate. **Classes:** Most classes have 20-29 students. Most lab/discussion sessions have 10-19 students. **Majors with Highest Enrollment:** Accounting; Biology; Psychology. **Special Study Options:** Accelerated program, cross-registration, double major, English as a Second Language (ESL), honors program, independent study, internships, liberal arts/career combination, study abroad, teacher certification program, Semester in Washington D.C., Gettysburg Semester. **Honors programs:** College-wide Honors program. **Combined degree programs:** BA/MD, BA/JD, BA/MA, BA/DDS, BA/MEng, BBA/MBA. **Disability Services:** Special programs offered to physically disabled students include note-taking services, reader services, tape recorders, tutors. **Career services:** Alumni network, alumni services, career/job search classes, career assessment, internships, regional alumni. Career services highlights include internships in almost every field.

FACILITIES

Housing: Coed dorms, special housing for disabled students, special housing for international students, apartments for single students, Quiet Living Area available; on-campus townhouses (men and women). 90% of campus accessible to physically disabled. **Special Academic Facilities/Equipment:** Hickey Financial Center **Computers:** 20% of classrooms, 40% of dorms, 100% of libraries, 100% of dining areas, 100% of student union, have wireless network access. Students can register for classes online. Administrative functions (other than registration) can be performed online.

CAMPUS LIFE

Environment: Town. **Activities:** Choral groups, dance, drama/theater, literary magazine, musical theater, opera, pep band, radio station, student government, student newspaper, symphony orchestra, television station, yearbook, Campus Ministries, Model UN. 70 registered organizations, 15 honor societies, 2 religious organizations. **Athletics (Intercollegiate):** *Men:* baseball, basketball, cross-country, golf, lacrosse, soccer, tennis. *Women:* basketball, cross-country, field hockey, golf, lacrosse, soccer, softball, swimming, tennis, volleyball, water polo. **On-Campus Highlights:** Sarazen Student Union, J. Spencer and Patricia Standish Library, MAC/ARC—Athletic Facilities, Siena Hall, Academic Quad, Hickey Financial Technical Center.

ADMISSIONS

Freshman Academic Profile: Average high school GPA 3.49. 22.9% in top 10% of high school class, 53.2% in top 25% of high school class, 87.3% in top 50% of high school class. SAT Math middle 50% range 520-620. SAT Critical Reading middle 50% range 500-600. SAT Writing middle 50% range 490-590. ACT middle 50% range 23-27. Minimum internet-based TOEFL 79. Minimum paper TOEFL 550. **Basis for Candidate Selection:** *Very important factors considered include:* academic GPA, rigor of secondary school record. *Important factors considered include:* recommendation(s), standardized test scores. *Other factors considered include:* Class rank, application essay, alumni/ae relation, character/personal qualities, extracurricular activities, first generation, interview, level of applicant's interest, racial/ethnic status, talent/ability, volunteer work, work experience. **Freshman Admission Requirements:** High school diploma is required and GED is accepted. *Academic units required:* 4 English, 3 mathematics, 3 science, (3 science labs), 0 foreign language, 1 social studies, 2 history, 0 visual/performing arts, 0 computer science, 0 academic electives. **Freshman Admission Statistics:** 8,647 applied, 58% admitted, 14% enrolled. **Transfer Admission Requirements:** college transcript(s), statement of good standing from prior institution(s). Minimum college GPA of 2.5 required. Lowest grade transferable C+. **General Admission Information:** Application Fee $50. Early decision application deadline 12/1. Regular application deadline 3/1. Regular notification 3/15. Nonfall registration accepted. Admission may be deferred for a maximum of 1 year. Credit and/or placement offered for CEEB Advanced Placement tests.

COSTS AND FINANCIAL AID

Annual tuition $33,165. Room and board $13,595. Required fees $810. Average book expense $1,282. **Required Forms and Deadlines:** FAFSA, State aid form. **Notification of Awards:** Applicants will be notified of awards on or about 4/1. **Types of Aid:** *Need-based scholarships/grants:* Federal Pell, SEOG, state scholarships/grants, private scholarships, the school's own gift aid. *Loans:* Subsidized Stafford, Unsubsidized Stafford, PLUS, Federal Perkins. *Student Employment:* Highest amount earned per year from on-campus jobs $1,000. **Financial Aid Statistics:** 100% freshmen, 100% undergrads receive need-based scholarship or grant aid. 92% freshmen, 92% undergrads receive non-need-based scholarship or grant aid. 78% freshmen, 81% undergrads receive need-based self-help aid. 9% freshmen, 8% undergrads receive athletic scholarships. 98% freshmen, 91% undergrads receive any aid. 77% undergrads borrow to pay for school. Average cumulative indebtedness $24,254. **Criteria for awarding institutional aid:** *Non-need-based:* academics, athletics, leadership, minority status, state/district residency.

SIERRA NEVADA COLLEGE

999 Tahoe Blvd., Incline Village, NV 89451
Phone: 775-831-1314 · **Financial Aid Phone:** 775-831-1314 x 7404
E-mail: admissions@sierraneveda.edu · **CEEB Code:** 9192
Fax: 775-831-6223 · **Website:** www.sierraneveda.edu · **ACT Code:** 2497

This private school was founded in 1969. It has a 25-acre campus.

RATINGS

Admissions Selectivity Rating: 73   **Fire Safety Rating:** 94

STUDENTS AND FACULTY

Enrollment: 516. **Student Body:** 41% female, 59% male, 84% out-of-state, 6% international (14 countries represented). Asian 1%, African American 1%, Caucasian 69%, Hispanic 1%, Native American 3% **Retention and Graduation:** 71% freshmen return for sophomore year. 33% freshmen graduate within 4 years. 45% freshmen graduate within 6 years. **Faculty:** 36 full-time faculty, 61% hold PhDs, 58% are are members of minority groups, 14% are women. 0% of classes are taught by teaching assistants.

ACADEMICS

Degrees: bachelor's, post-bachelor's certificate. **Majors with Highest Enrollment:** Business, Management, Marketing, and Related Support Services; Multi/Interdisciplinary Studies. **Special Study Options:** double major, honors program, internships, study abroad, teacher certification program. **Combined degree programs:** BA/Dr. Pharmacy. **Disability Services:** Special programs offered to physically disabled students include note-taking services, tutors. **Career services:** career/job search classes, career assessment, internships,

FACILITIES

Housing: Coed dorms. 50% of campus accessible to physically disabled. **Special Academic Facilities/Equipment:** McLean Observatory **Computers:**

CAMPUS LIFE

Environment: Village. **Activities:** literary magazine, student government, student newspaper. 10 registered organizations, 1 honor society, 2 religious organizations. **Athletics (Intercollegiate):** *Men:* equestrian sports, skiing (downhill/alpine). *Women:* equestrian sports, skiing (downhill/alpine). **Environmental Initiatives:** Sierra Nevada Colleges four Core Themes; Sustainability, Professional Preparedness, Entrepreneurship, Liberal Art Degrees and Programs to support Environmental Commitment: Interdisciplinary degree in Sustainability, Minor in Sustainability, Environmental Science+Ecology, Environmental Policy with options for several minors LEED Platinum Certified Building, Tahoe Center for Environmental Science

ADMISSIONS

Freshman Academic Profile: Average high school GPA 2.98. 0% in top 10% of high school class, 20% in top 25% of high school class, 50% in top 50% of high school class. 80% from public high schools. SAT Math middle 50% range 430-530. SAT Critical Reading middle 50% range 440-540. ACT middle 50% range 17-25. Minimum internet-based TOEFL 59. Minimum paper TOEFL 500. **Basis for Candidate Selection:** *Important factors considered include:* application essay, recommendation(s), rigor of secondary school record. *Other factors considered include:* Class rank, standardized test scores, alumni/ae relation, character/personal qualities, extracurricular activities, geographical residence, interview, racial/ethnic status, talent/ability, volunteer work, work experience. **Freshman Admission Requirements:** High school diploma is required and GED is accepted. **Freshman Admission Statistics:** 604 applied, 87% admitted, 17% enrolled. **Transfer Admission Requirements:** college transcript(s), essay or personal statement, Lowest grade transferable C. **General Admission Information:** Notification on a rolling basis, beginning on or about 12/15. Nonfall registration accepted. Admission may be deferred for a maximum of 1 year. Credit and/or placement offered for CEEB Advanced Placement tests.

COSTS AND FINANCIAL AID

Annual tuition $28,170. Room and board $12,066. Required fees $979. Average book expense $1,600. **Required Forms and Deadlines:** FAFSA. **Notification of Awards:** Applicants will be notified of awards on a rolling basis beginning 3/1. **Types of Aid:** *Need-based scholarships/grants:* Federal Pell, SEOG, state scholarships/grants, private scholarships, the school's own gift aid. *Loans:* Direct Subsidized Stafford, Direct PLUS. *Student Employment:* Federal Work-Study Program available. Institutional employment available. Off-campus job opportunities are excellent. **Financial Aid Statistics:** 100% freshmen, 100% undergrads receive need-based scholarship or grant aid. 100% freshmen, 100% undergrads receive non-need-based scholarship or grant aid. 100% freshmen, 100% undergrads receive need-based self-help aid. 0% freshmen, 1% undergrads receive athletic scholarships. 62% freshmen, 65% undergrads receive any aid. 50% undergrads borrow to pay for school. Average cumulative indebtedness $26,368. **Criteria for awarding institutional aid:** *Non-need-based:* academics, art, athletics, state/district residency.

SIMMONS COLLEGE

300 The Fenway, Boston, MA 2115
Phone: 617-521-2051 · **Financial Aid Phone:** 617-521-2001
E-mail: ugadm@simmons.edu · **CEEB Code:** 3761
Fax: 617-521-3190 · **Website:** www.simmons.edu · **ACT Code:** 1892

This private school was founded in 1899. It has a 12-acre campus.

RATINGS

Admissions Selectivity Rating: 88   Fire Safety Rating: 77

STUDENTS AND FACULTY

Enrollment: 1,598. **Student Body:** 100% female, 0% male, 39% out-of-state, 3% international (25 countries represented). Asian 10%, African American 6%, Caucasian 68%, Hispanic 6%, Native American <1%
Retention and Graduation: 86% freshmen return for sophomore year. 62% freshmen graduate within 4 years. 22% grads go on to further study within 1 year. 15% grads pursue arts and sciences degrees. 1% grads pursue law degrees. 2% grads pursue business degrees. 1% grads pursue medical degrees. **Faculty:** 209 full-time faculty, 72% are are members of minority groups, 21% are women.

ACADEMICS

Degrees: bachelor's, diploma, doctoral, master's, post-bachelor's certificate, post-master's certificate. **Classes:** Most classes have 10-19 students. **Majors with Highest Enrollment:** Nursing Practice. **Special Study Options:** Accelerated program, cross-registration, double major, dual enrollment, English as a Second Language (ESL), exchange student program (domestic), honors program, independent study, internships, liberal arts/career combination, student-designed major, study abroad, teacher certification program, Exhange program with Mills College (CA), Spellman College (GA), Fisk University (TN), American University (DC), Colleges of the Fenway exchange program, double-degree programs with Massachusetts College of Pharmacy and Health Sciences, and with Hebrew College. **Honors programs:** One Honors Program **Combined degree programs:** BA/MA, BA/MEng, BA/MAT BS/MS BA/MBA BA/MSW. **Disability Services:** Special programs offered to physically disabled students include note-taking services, reader services, tape recorders, tutors. **Career services:** Alumni network, alumni services, career/job search classes, career assessment, internships, regional alumni. Career services highlights include internships that lead to job placement.

FACILITIES

Housing: special housing for disabled students, women's dorms, Wellness Housing, Theme Housing. 99% of campus accessible to physically disabled. **Special Academic Facilities/Equipment:** Art gallery, media center, science center with dream/sleep analysis lab, physical therapy clinic areas, sports center with pool **Computers:** 100% of classrooms, 5% of dorms, 100% of libraries, 100% of dining areas, 100% of student union, have wireless network access. Students can register for classes online. Administrative functions (other than registration) can be performed online.

CAMPUS LIFE

Environment: City. **Activities:** Choral groups, dance, drama/theater, literary magazine, radio station, student government, student newspaper, student-run film society, symphony orchestra, yearbook. 91 registered organizations, 4 honor societies, 4 religious organizations. **Athletics (Intercollegiate):** *Women:* basketball, crew/rowing, diving, field hockey, lacrosse, soccer, softball, swimming, tennis, volleyball. **On-Campus Highlights:** Java City, Beatley Library, Park Science Center, Palace Road Building/Pottruck Technology, School of Management. **Environmental Initiatives:** Recycling and waste management program; Mechanical equipment upgrades to improve efficiency and performance; LEED certified new building.

ADMISSIONS

Freshman Academic Profile: Average high school GPA 3.25. 30% in top 10% of high school class, 64% in top 25% of high school class, 92% in top 50% of high school class. SAT Math middle 50% range 530-620. SAT Critical Reading middle 50% range 540-640. SAT Writing middle 50% range 540-650. ACT middle 50% range 24-28. Minimum internet-based TOEFL 83. Minimum paper TOEFL 83. **Basis for Candidate Selection:** *Very important factors considered include:* academic GPA, rigor of secondary school record. *Important factors considered include:* Class rank, application essay, recommendation(s), standardized test scores. *Other factors considered include:* extracurricular

activities, interview, talent/ability, volunteer work, work experience. **Freshman Admission Requirements:** High school diploma is required and GED is accepted. *Academic units required:* 4 English, 3 mathematics, 3 science, 3 foreign language, 3 social studies, 3 history. **Freshman Admission Statistics:** 3,999 applied, 52% admitted, 15% enrolled. **Transfer Admission Requirements:** High school transcript, college transcript(s), essay or personal statement, statement of good standing from prior institution(s). Minimum college GPA of 2.8 required. Lowest grade transferable C+. **General Admission Information:** Application Fee $55. Regular application deadline 2/1. Regular notification 4/15. Nonfall registration accepted. Admission may be deferred for a maximum of 1 Year. Credit and/or placement offered for CEEB Advanced Placement tests.

COSTS AND FINANCIAL AID

Required Forms and Deadlines: FAFSA, Institution's own financial aid form. **Notification of Awards:** Applicants will be notified of awards on a rolling basis beginning 3/15. **Types of Aid:** *Need-based scholarships/grants:* Federal Pell, SEOG, state scholarships/grants, private scholarships, the school's own gift aid. *Loans:* Direct Subsidized Stafford, Direct Unsubsidized Stafford, Direct PLUS, state loans, college/university loans from institutional funds. *Student Employment:* Federal Work-Study Program available. Institutional employment available. Highest amount earned per year from on-campus jobs $2,000. Off-campus job opportunities are excellent. **Financial Aid Statistics:** 100% freshmen, 99% undergrads receive need-based scholarship or grant aid. 10% freshmen, 5% undergrads receive non-need-based scholarship or grant aid. 85% freshmen, 91% undergrads receive need-based self-help aid. 0% freshmen, 0% undergrads receive athletic scholarships. 97% freshmen, 90% undergrads receive any aid. **Criteria for awarding institutional aid:** *Non-need-based:* academics, alumni affiliation, leadership, minority status.

See page 1142.

SIMPSON COLLEGE (IA)

701 North C Street, Indianola, IA 50125
Phone: 515-961-1624
E-mail: admiss@simpson.edu · **CEEB Code:** 6650
Fax: 515-961-1870 · **Website:** www.simpson.edu · **ACT Code:** 1354

This private school, affiliated with the Methodist Church, was founded in 1860. It has a 63-acre campus.

RATINGS

Admissions Selectivity Rating: 80   Fire Safety Rating: 60*

STUDENTS AND FACULTY

Enrollment: 1,758. **Student Body:** 60% female, 40% male, 10% out-of-state, 2% international (13 countries represented). Asian 1%, African American 1%, Caucasian 93%, Hispanic 1%, Native American <1%
Retention and Graduation: 78% freshmen return for sophomore year. 57% freshmen graduate within 4 years. 67% freshmen graduate within 6 years. 11% grads go on to further study within 1 year. 6% grads pursue arts and sciences degrees. 2% grads pursue law degrees. 1% grads pursue business degrees. 2% grads pursue medical degrees. **Faculty:** 84 full-time faculty, 87% hold PhDs, 29% are are members of minority groups, 6% are women. 0% of classes are taught by teaching assistants.

ACADEMICS

Degrees: bachelor's, post-bachelor's certificate. **Classes:** Most classes have 10-19 students. Most lab/discussion sessions have 10-19 students. **Special Study Options:** Accelerated program, cooperative education program, double major, English as a Second Language (ESL), honors program, independent study, internships, liberal arts/career combination, student-designed major, study abroad, teacher certification program, weekend college, International Program. **Disability Services:** Special programs offered to physically disabled students include note-taking services, reader services, tape recorders, tutors. **Career services:** alumni services, career/job search classes, career assessment, internships.

FACILITIES

Housing: Coed dorms, men's dorms, women's dorms, fraternity/sorority housing, apartments for single students. Simpson College owns several homes surrounding campus known as theme houses. Group of students petition for those houses on a yearly basis. **Special Academic Facilities/Equipment:** The biology department hosts a human cadaver lab while Dunn library boasts the Avery O'Craven Room which houses an extensive antebellum collection.

CAMPUS LIFE

Environment: Village. **Activities:** Choral groups, concert band, dance, drama/theater, jazz band, literary magazine, music ensembles, opera, pep band, radio station, student government, student newspaper, yearbook. 89 registered organizations, 15 honor societies, 17 religious organizations. 4 fraternities, 4 sororities. **Athletics (Intercollegiate):** *Men:* baseball, basketball, cheerleading, cross-country, football, golf, soccer, tennis, track/field (outdoor), track/field (indoor), wrestling. *Women:* basketball, cheerleading, cross-country, golf, soccer, softball, swimming, tennis, track/field (outdoor), track/field (indoor), volleyball. **On-Campus Highlights:** Carse Fitness Center, Blank Performing Arts Center, Carver Science Center and Open Atrium, Pfeiffer Dining Hall, Brenton Student Center.

ADMISSIONS

Freshman Academic Profile: 21% in top 10% of high school class, 57% in top 25% of high school class, 90% in top 50% of high school class. 96% from public high schools. ACT middle 50% range 22-27. Minimum paper TOEFL 550. **Basis for Candidate Selection:** *Very important factors considered include:* Class rank, rigor of secondary school record, standardized test scores. *Important factors considered include:* recommendation(s), character/personal qualities. *Other factors considered include:* alumni/ae relation, extracurricular activities, interview, volunteer work. **Freshman Admission Requirements:** High school diploma is required and GED is accepted. **Freshman Admission Statistics:** 1,442 applied, 76% admitted, 38% enrolled. **Transfer Admission Requirements:** High school transcript, college transcript(s), standardized test scores, Minimum college GPA of 2.5 required. Lowest grade transferable C-. **General Admission Information:** Nonfall registration accepted. Admission may be deferred for a maximum of 24 months. Credit and/or placement offered for CEEB Advanced Placement tests.

COSTS AND FINANCIAL AID

Annual tuition $17,908. Room and board $6,062. Required fees $189. Average book expense $800. **Required Forms and Deadlines:** FAFSA. **Notification of Awards:** Applicants will be notified of awards on a rolling basis beginning 3/15. **Types of Aid:** *Need-based scholarships/grants:* Federal Pell, SEOG, state scholarships/grants, private scholarships, the school's own gift aid. *Loans:* Subsidized Stafford, Unsubsidized Stafford, PLUS, Federal Perkins, state loans, college/university loans from institutional funds, Private Educational Loans. *Student Employment:* Federal Work-Study Program available. Institutional employment available. Highest amount earned per year from on-campus jobs $735. Off-campus job opportunities are fair. **Financial Aid Statistics:** 100% freshmen, 99% undergrads receive need-based scholarship or grant aid. 15% freshmen, 10% undergrads receive non-need-based scholarship or grant aid. 84% freshmen, 86% undergrads receive need-based self-help aid. 0% freshmen, 0% undergrads receive athletic scholarships. 91% undergrads borrow to pay for school. **Criteria for awarding institutional aid:** *Non-need-based:* academics, alumni affiliation, art, leadership, minority status, music/drama, religious affiliation, state/district residency.

SIMPSON UNIVERSITY

2211 College View Dr., Redding, CA 96003
Phone: 530-226-4606 · **Financial Aid Phone:** 530-224-5600
E-mail: admissions@simpsonuniversity.edu
Fax: 530-226-4861 · **Website:** www.simpsonuniversity.edu · **ACT Code:** 430

This private school, affiliated with the Christian & Missionary Alliance Church, was founded in 1921. It has a 92-acre campus.

RATINGS

Admissions Selectivity Rating: 81   Fire Safety Rating: 68

STUDENTS AND FACULTY

Enrollment: 964.
Retention and Graduation: 61% freshmen return for sophomore year. **Faculty:** 38 full-time faculty, 55% hold PhDs. 0% of classes are taught by teaching assistants.

ACADEMICS

Degrees: associate, bachelor's, certificate, master's. **Classes:** Most classes have 10-19 students. Most lab/discussion sessions have 10-19 students. **Majors with Highest Enrollment:** Elementary Education and Teaching; Psychology; Organizational Behavior Studies. **Special Study Options:** Accelerated program, distance learning, double major, honors program, independent study, internships, student-designed major, study abroad, teacher certification program, weekend college. **Honors programs:** Oxford Honours Programme through the CCCU (Coalition of Christian Colleges and Universities). **Disability Services:**

Special programs offered to physically disabled students include note-taking services, reader services, tutors. **Career services:** career/job search classes, career assessment.

FACILITIES

Housing: special housing for disabled students, men's dorms, special housing for international students, women's dorms, apartments for married students. 95% of campus accessible to physically disabled. **Computers:** Students can register for classes online. Administrative functions (other than registration) can be performed online.

CAMPUS LIFE

Environment: City. **Activities:** Choral groups, drama/theater, jazz band, music ensembles, pep band, student government, student newspaper, yearbook. 17 registered organizations, 1 honor society, 20 religious organizations. **Athletics (Intercollegiate):** *Men:* baseball, basketball. *Women:* basketball. **On-Campus Highlights:** Chapel (Heritage Student Life Center), Athletic Events (Heritage Student Life Center), Music Department (Heritage Student Life Center), Bible/Theology Classes (La-Baume Rudat Bldg.), AandB Coffee Shop and Bookstore (Owen Center).

ADMISSIONS

Freshman Academic Profile: Average high school GPA 3.32. 19% in top 10% of high school class, 47% in top 25% of high school class, 79% in top 50% of high school class. 63% from public high schools. SAT Math middle 50% range 430-560. SAT Critical Reading middle 50% range 450-590. ACT middle 50% range 18-23. Minimum paper TOEFL 500. **Basis for Candidate Selection:** *Very important factors considered include:* recommendation(s), rigor of secondary school record, standardized test scores, character/personal qualities, religious affiliation/commitment. *Important factors considered include:* Class rank, volunteer work. *Other factors considered include:* application essay, extracurricular activities, interview, talent/ability. **Freshman Admission Requirements:** High school diploma is required and GED is accepted. **Freshman Admission Statistics:** 938 applied, 59% admitted, 34% enrolled. **Transfer Admission Requirements:** High school transcript, college transcript(s), essay or personal statement, statement of good standing from prior institution(s). Minimum college GPA of 2.0 required. Lowest grade transferable C. **General Admission Information:** Application Fee $20. Nonfall registration accepted. Admission may be deferred for a maximum of 24 months. Credit and/or placement offered for CEEB Advanced Placement tests.

COSTS AND FINANCIAL AID

Annual tuition $17,000. Room and board $5,900. Average book expense $1,200. **Required Forms and Deadlines:** FAFSA, Institution's own financial aid form. **Notification of Awards:** Applicants will be notified of awards on a rolling basis beginning 3/16. **Types of Aid:** *Need-based scholarships/grants:* Federal Pell, SEOG, state scholarships/grants, private scholarships, the school's own gift aid. *Loans:* Subsidized Stafford, Unsubsidized Stafford, PLUS, Federal Perkins, Alternative Loans. *Student Employment:* Federal Work-Study Program available. Institutional employment available. Off-campus job opportunities are good. **Financial Aid Statistics:** 100% freshmen, 95% undergrads receive need-based scholarship or grant aid. 100% freshmen, 95% undergrads receive non-need-based scholarship or grant aid. 97% freshmen, 93% undergrads receive need-based self-help aid. 0% freshmen, 0% undergrads receive athletic scholarships. 96% freshmen, 96% undergrads receive any aid. 89% undergrads borrow to pay for school. **Criteria for awarding institutional aid:** *Non-need-based:* academics, alumni affiliation, leadership, minority status, music/drama, religious affiliation, state/district residency.

SKIDMORE COLLEGE

Best 380

815 North Broadway, Saratoga Springs, NY 12866-1632
Phone: 518-580-5570 · **Financial Aid Phone:** 518-580-5750
E-mail: admissions@skidmore.edu · **CEEB Code:** 2815
Fax: 518-580-5584 · **Website:** www.skidmore.edu · **ACT Code:** 2906

This private school was founded in 1903. It has a 750-acre campus.

RATINGS

Admissions Selectivity Rating: 92   Fire Safety Rating: 97

STUDENTS AND FACULTY

Enrollment: 2,612. **Student Body:** 59% female, 41% male, 67% out-of-state, 8% international (56 countries represented). Asian 6%, African American 4%, Caucasian 63%, Hispanic 8%, Native American <1%

Retention and Graduation: 85% freshmen graduate within 4 years. 87% freshmen graduate within 6 years. 12% grads go on to further study within 1 year. **Faculty:** 259 full-time faculty, 87% hold PhDs, 56% are are members of minority groups, 15% are women. 0% of classes are taught by teaching assistants.

ACADEMICS

Degrees: bachelor's, master's. **Classes:** Most classes have 10-19 students. Most lab/discussion sessions have 10-19 students. **Majors with Highest Enrollment:** Business/Commerce; Psychology; English Language and Literature. **Special Study Options:** Accelerated program, cross-registration, double major, dual enrollment, exchange student program (domestic), honors program, independent study, internships, liberal arts/career combination, student-designed major, study abroad, teacher certification program. **Honors programs:** Honors Forum. **Disability Services:** Special programs offered to physically disabled students include note-taking services, reader services, tape recorders, tutors. **Career services:** Alumni network, alumni services, career/job search classes, career assessment, internships, regional alumni. Career services highlights include our alumni network.

FACILITIES

Housing: Coed dorms, special housing for disabled students, special housing for international students, women's dorms, apartments for single students, gender neutral wing. 75% of campus accessible to physically disabled. **Special Academic Facilities/Equipment:** Tang Teaching Museum and Art Gallery, center for child study, art, music, dance, and theatre facilities, electron microscope, spectrometer. **Computers:** Students can register for classes online. Administrative functions (other than registration) can be performed online.

CAMPUS LIFE

Environment: Town. **Activities:** Choral groups, concert band, dance, drama/theater, jazz band, literary magazine, music ensembles, musical theater, opera, radio station, student government, student newspaper, symphony orchestra, television station, yearbook, Campus Ministries, International Student Organization, Model UN. 80 registered organizations, 10 honor societies, 3 religious organizations. **Athletics (Intercollegiate):** *Men:* baseball, basketball, crew/rowing, diving, golf, ice hockey, lacrosse, soccer, swimming, tennis. *Women:* basketball, crew/rowing, diving, equestrian sports, field hockey, lacrosse, soccer, softball, swimming, tennis, volleyball. **On-Campus Highlights:** Tang Teaching Museum, Lucy Scribner Library, Case Student Center, Woodlawn Village Apartments, Murray-Atkins Dining Hall.

ADMISSIONS

Freshman Academic Profile: 42.6% in top 10% of high school class, 78.1% in top 25% of high school class, 96.4% in top 50% of high school class. 62% from public high schools. SAT Math middle 50% range 570-680. SAT Critical Reading middle 50% range 560-670. SAT Writing middle 50% range 563-680. ACT middle 50% range 25-30. Minimum paper TOEFL 590. **Basis for Candidate Selection:** *Very important factors considered include:* rigor of secondary school record. *Important factors considered include:* Class rank, application essay, academic GPA, recommendation(s), character/personal qualities, extracurricular activities, talent/ability, volunteer work, work experience. *Other factors considered include:* standardized test scores, alumni/ae relation, first generation, geographical residence, interview, level of applicant's interest, racial/ethnic status. **Freshman Admission Requirements:** High school diploma is required and GED is accepted. *Academic units required:* 0 English, 0 mathematics, 0 science, (0 science labs), 0 foreign language, 0 social studies, 0 history, 0 academic electives. **Freshman Admission Statistics:** 8,669 applied, 37% admitted, 22% enrolled. **Transfer Admission Requirements:** High school transcript, college transcript(s), essay or personal statement, standardized test scores, statement of good standing from prior institution(s). Minimum college GPA of 2.7 required. Lowest grade transferable C. **General Admission Information:** Application Fee $60. Early decision application deadline 11/15. Regular application deadline 1/15. Regular notification 4/1. Nonfall registration not accepted. Admission may be deferred for a maximum of 2 years. Credit and/or placement offered for CEEB Advanced Placement tests.

COSTS AND FINANCIAL AID

Annual tuition $46,390. Room and board $12,628. Required fees $1,074. Average book expense $1,300. **Required Forms and Deadlines:** CSS/Financial Aid PROFILE, Noncustodial PROFILE. **Notification of Awards:** Applicants will be notified of awards on or about 4/1. **Types of Aid:** *Need-based scholarships/grants:* Federal Pell, SEOG, state scholarships/grants, the school's own gift aid. *Loans:* Subsidized Stafford, Unsubsidized Stafford, PLUS, Federal Perkins. *Student Employment:* Federal Work-Study Program available. Institutional employment available. Highest amount earned per year from on-campus jobs $2,300. Off-campus job opportunities are fair. **Financial Aid Statistics:** 100% freshmen, 99% undergrads receive need-based scholarship or grant aid. 7% freshmen, 9% undergrads receive non-need-based scholarship or grant aid. 67% freshmen, 72% undergrads receive need-based self-help aid. 0% freshmen, 0% undergrads receive athletic scholarships. 63% freshmen, 53% undergrads

receive any aid. 46% undergrads borrow to pay for school. Average cumulative indebtedness $19,400. **Criteria for awarding institutional aid:** *Non-need-based:* music/drama.

See page 1144.

SLIPPERY ROCK UNIVERSITY OF PENNSYLVANIA

1 Morrow Way, Slippery Rock, PA 16057
Phone: 724-738-2015 • **Financial Aid Phone:** 724-738-2044
E-mail: asktherock@sru.edu • **CEEB Code:** 2658
Fax: 724-738-2913 • **Website:** http://www.sru.edu • **ACT Code:** 3716

This public school was founded in 1889. It has a 600-acre campus.

RATINGS

Admissions Selectivity Rating: 79   **Fire Safety Rating:** 97

STUDENTS AND FACULTY

Enrollment: 7,526. **Student Body:** 57% female, 43% male, 10% out-of-state, 1% international (31 countries represented). Asian 1%, African American 5%, Caucasian 86%, Hispanic 2%, Native American <1%
Retention and Graduation: 49% freshmen graduate within 4 years. 23% grads go on to further study within 1 year. **Faculty:** 331 full-time faculty, 91% hold PhDs, 50% are are members of minority groups, 17% are women. 0% of classes are taught by teaching assistants.

ACADEMICS

Degrees: bachelor's, certificate, master's, post-bachelor's certificate. **Classes:** Most classes have 20-29 students. Most lab/discussion sessions have fewer than 10 students. **Majors with Highest Enrollment:** Kinesiology and Exercise Science; Business Administration and Management; Special Education and Teaching. **Special Study Options:** distance learning, double major, dual enrollment, exchange student program (domestic), honors program, independent study, internships, liberal arts/career combination, student-designed major, study abroad, teacher certification program. **Honors programs:** Undergraduate Honors Program **Combined degree programs:** Pre-Osteo 3+4 and Pre-Pharm 3+3 LECOM; Pre-Chiro 3+3 Logan; Pre-PT 3+3 SRU. **Disability Services:** Special programs offered to physically disabled students include note-taking services, reader services, tape recorders, tutors. **Career services:** alumni services, career/job search classes, career assessment, internships. Career services highlights include the opportunity to meet individually with career counselors.

FACILITIES

Housing: Coed dorms, special housing for disabled students, apartments for single students, Theme Housing. 80% of campus accessible to physically disabled. **Special Academic Facilities/Equipment:** Special education school for student teachers, physical therapy clinic, microvideo system, planetarium, electron microscope. Residence Halls have academic interest floors with special facilities for specific majors whereby students can interact with faculty and have academically related programs where they live. **Computers:** 80% of classrooms, 100% of dorms, 100% of libraries, 50% of dining areas, 100% of student union, 5% of common outdoor areas have wireless network access. Students can register for classes online. Administrative functions (other than registration) can be performed online.

CAMPUS LIFE

Environment: Rural. **Activities:** Choral groups, concert band, dance, drama/theater, jazz band, literary magazine, marching band, music ensembles, musical theater, radio station, student government, student newspaper, student-run film society, symphony orchestra, television station, Campus Ministries, International Student Organization, Model UN. 145 registered organizations, 37 honor societies, 4 religious organizations. 9 fraternities, 8 sororities. **Athletics (Intercollegiate):** *Men:* baseball, basketball, cheerleading, cross-country, football, soccer, track/field (outdoor), track/field (indoor). *Women:* basketball, cheerleading, cross-country, field hockey, lacrosse, soccer, softball, tennis, track/field (outdoor), track/field (indoor), volleyball. **On-Campus Highlights:** Aebersold Recreation Center, New Residential Suite Living Complexes, Bailey Library, Advanced Science and Technology Building, University Union. **Environmental Initiatives:** Energy conservation policy; LEED standards for building design and renovations; ESCO projects; Central heating plant and steam infrastructure improvements; Recycling.

ADMISSIONS

Freshman Academic Profile: Average high school GPA 3.42. 12% in top 10% of high school class, 36% in top 25% of high school class, 76% in top 50% of

high school class. 91% from public high schools. SAT Math middle 50% range 460-550. SAT Critical Reading middle 50% range 450-530. SAT Writing middle 50% range 430-520. ACT middle 50% range 19-24. Minimum internet-based TOEFL 61. Minimum paper TOEFL 500. **Basis for Candidate Selection:** *Important factors considered include:* Class rank, academic GPA, rigor of secondary school record, standardized test scores. *Other factors considered include:* application essay, recommendation(s), talent/ability. **Freshman Admission Requirements:** High school diploma is required and GED is accepted. **Freshman Admission Statistics:** 5,775 applied, 66% admitted, 42% enrolled. **Transfer Admission Requirements:** college transcript(s), Minimum college GPA of 2.0 required. Lowest grade transferable C. **General Admission Information:** Application Fee $30. Notification on a rolling basis, beginning on or about 6/15. Nonfall registration accepted. Admission may be deferred for a maximum of 1 year. Credit and/or placement offered for CEEB Advanced Placement tests.

COSTS AND FINANCIAL AID
Annual in-state tuition $6,820. Annual out-of-state tuition $10,230. Room and board $9,794. Required fees $2,489. Average book expense $1,517. **Required Forms and Deadlines:** FAFSA. **Notification of Awards:** Applicants will be notified of awards on a rolling basis beginning 3/15. **Types of Aid:** *Need-based scholarships/grants:* Federal Pell, SEOG, state scholarships/grants, private scholarships, the school's own gift aid. *Loans:* Subsidized Stafford, Unsubsidized Stafford, PLUS, Federal Perkins. *Student Employment:* Federal Work-Study Program available. Institutional employment available. Highest amount earned per year from on-campus jobs $4,000. Off-campus job opportunities are good. **Financial Aid Statistics:** 61% freshmen, 61% undergrads receive need-based scholarship or grant aid. 37% freshmen, 22% undergrads receive non-need-based scholarship or grant aid. 90% freshmen, 90% undergrads receive need-based self-help aid. 3% freshmen, 3% undergrads receive athletic scholarships. 93% freshmen, 86% undergrads receive any aid. 86% undergrads borrow to pay for school. Average cumulative indebtedness $25,379. **Criteria for awarding institutional aid:** *Non-need-based:* academics, alumni affiliation, art, athletics, job skills, leadership, minority status, music/drama, state/district residency.

SMITH COLLEGE

Best 380

7 College Lane, Northampton, MA 1063
Phone: 413-585-2500 • **Financial Aid Phone:** 413-585-2530
E-mail: admission@smith.edu • **CEEB Code:** 3762
Fax: 413-585-2527 • **Website:** www.smith.edu • **ACT Code:** 1894

This private school was founded in 1871. It has a 147-acre campus.

RATINGS
Admissions Selectivity Rating: 95   **Fire Safety Rating:** 76

STUDENTS AND FACULTY
Enrollment: 2,563. **Student Body:** 100% female, 0% male, 78% out-of-state, 14% international (59 countries represented). Asian 13%, African American 5%, Caucasian 46%, Hispanic 9%, Native American <1%
Retention and Graduation: 94% freshmen return for sophomore year. 82% freshmen graduate within 4 years. **Faculty:** 273 full-time faculty, 99% hold PhDs, 55% are are members of minority groups, 18% are women. 0% of classes are taught by teaching assistants.

ACADEMICS
Degrees: bachelor's, master's, post-bachelor's certificate, post-master's certificate. **Classes:** Most classes have 10-19 students. **Majors with Highest Enrollment:** Psychology; Political Science and Government; Economics. **Special Study Options:** Accelerated program, cross-registration, double major, exchange student program (domestic), honors program, independent study, internships, study abroad, teacher certification program. **Disability Services:** Special programs offered to physically disabled students include note-taking services, reader services, tape recorders, tutors. **Career services:** Alumni network, alumni services, career/job search classes, career assessment, internships, regional alumni. Career services highlights include Praxis internship program: guaranteed $2000 stipend per student for summer internship.

FACILITIES
Housing: women's dorms, cooperative housing. Apartment complex for limited number of juniors and seniors. Also,one senior house, french speaking house,

and Ada Comstock (non-traditional age) house. 85% of campus accessible to physically disabled. **Special Academic Facilities/Equipment:** Art museum, printing, darkroom, and sculpture facilities, dance, electronic music, television, and theatre studios, recital hall, rehearsal rooms, multimedia language lab, early childhood/elementary education campus school, two electronic classrooms, physiology and horticultural labs, animal care facilities, two electron microscopes, greenhouses, observatories. **Computers:** 85% of classrooms, 100% of dorms, 100% of libraries, 100% of dining areas, 100% of student union, 50% of common outdoor areas have wireless network access. Students can register for classes online. Administrative functions (other than registration) can be performed online.

CAMPUS LIFE
Environment: Town. **Activities:** Choral groups, concert band, dance, drama/theater, jazz band, literary magazine, music ensembles, musical theater, radio station, student government, student newspaper, television station, yearbook, Campus Ministries, International Student Organization, Model UN. 133 registered organizations, 3 honor societies, 9 religious organizations. **Athletics (Intercollegiate):** *Women:* basketball, crew/rowing, cross-country, diving, equestrian sports, field hockey, lacrosse, skiing (downhill/alpine), soccer, softball, squash, swimming, tennis, track/field (outdoor), track/field (indoor), volleyball. **On-Campus Highlights:** Smith Art Museum, The Botanical Gardens, Campus Center, Mendenhall Center for Performing Arts, Lyman Plant House. **Environmental Initiatives:** A new natural gas fired cogeneration facility went online in October 2008, which generates most campus electric use and schieves 80% efficiency with new absorption chillers. Constructed a LEED Gold Certified Science and Engineering facility. Implemented 18 energy efficiency projects and 7 conservation programs over past 4 years; these have generated substantial economic and environmental benefits and have reduced greenhouse gas emissions associated with electricity consumption by 18% and steam production by 15%. A recurring fund is being established to fund ongoing efficiency projects.

ADMISSIONS
Freshman Academic Profile: Average high school GPA 3.9. 62% in top 10% of high school class, 91% in top 25% of high school class, 100% in top 50% of high school class. 62% from public high schools. SAT Math middle 50% range 620-740. SAT Critical Reading middle 50% range 620-730. SAT Writing middle 50% range 630-720. ACT middle 50% range 28-31. Minimum internet-based TOEFL 90. Minimum paper TOEFL 600. **Basis for Candidate Selection:** *Very important factors considered include:* academic GPA, recommendation(s), rigor of secondary school record, character/personal qualities. *Important factors considered include:* Class rank, application essay, extracurricular activities, interview, talent/ability. *Other factors considered include:* standardized test scores, alumni/ae relation, first generation, racial/ethnic status, volunteer work, work experience. **Freshman Admission Requirements:** High school diploma or equivalent is not required. **Freshman Admission Statistics:** 4,466 applied, 42% admitted, 33% enrolled. **Transfer Admission Requirements:** High school transcript, college transcript(s), essay or personal statement, statement of good standing from prior institution(s). Lowest grade transferable C. **General Admission Information:** Application Fee $60. Early decision application deadline 11/15. Regular application deadline 1/15. Regular notification 4/1. Nonfall registration not accepted. Admission may be deferred for a maximum of 1 year. Credit and/or placement offered for CEEB Advanced Placement tests.

COSTS AND FINANCIAL AID
Annual tuition $42,840. Room and board $14,410. Required fees $274. Average book expense $800. **Required Forms and Deadlines:** FAFSA, Institution's own financial aid form, CSS/Financial Aid PROFILE, Noncustodial PROFILE. **Notification of Awards:** Applicants will be notified of awards on or about 4/1. **Types of Aid:** *Need-based scholarships/grants:* Federal Pell, SEOG, state scholarships/grants, the school's own gift aid. *Loans:* Direct Subsidized Stafford, Direct Unsubsidized Stafford, PLUS, Federal Perkins, state loans, college/university loans from institutional funds. *Student Employment:* Federal Work-Study Program available. Institutional employment available. Highest amount earned per year from on-campus jobs $2,558. Off-campus job opportunities are excellent. **Financial Aid Statistics:** 94% freshmen, 95% undergrads receive need-based scholarship or grant aid. 2% freshmen, 1% undergrads receive non-need-based scholarship or grant aid. 95% freshmen, 95% undergrads receive need-based self-help aid. 0% freshmen, 0% undergrads receive athletic scholarships. 70% freshmen, 71% undergrads receive any aid. 65% undergrads borrow to pay for school. Average cumulative indebtedness $20,195. **Criteria for awarding institutional aid:** *Non-need-based:* academics, state/district residency.

SOKA UNIVERSITY OF AMERICA

1 University Drive, Aliso Viejo, CA 92656-8081
Phone: 949-480-4150 · **Financial Aid Phone:** 949-480-4048
E-mail: admission@soka.edu · **CEEB Code:** 4066
Fax: 949-480-4151 · **Website:** www.soka.edu • **ACT Code:** 467

This private school was founded in 2001. It has a 103-acre campus.

RATINGS

Admissions Selectivity Rating: 90   **Fire Safety Rating:** 84

STUDENTS AND FACULTY

Enrollment: 412. **Student Body:** 60% female, 40% male, 20% out-of-state, 28% international (31 countries represented). Asian 14%, African American 4%, Caucasian 14%, Hispanic 7%, Native American 1%
Retention and Graduation: 95% freshmen return for sophomore year. 70% freshmen graduate within 4 years. 21% grads go on to further study within 1 year. 77% grads pursue arts and sciences degrees. 9% grads pursue law degrees. 5% grads pursue medical degrees. **Faculty:** 46 full-time faculty, 96% hold PhDs, 43% are are members of minority groups, 37% are women. 0% of classes are taught by teaching assistants.

ACADEMICS

Degrees: bachelor's, master's. **Classes:** Most classes have 10-19 students. Most lab/discussion sessions have 10-19 students. **Majors with Highest Enrollment:** Liberal Arts and Sciences/Liberal Studies. **Special Study Options:** English as a Second Language (ESL), independent study, internships, liberal arts/career combination, study abroad. **Disability Services:** Special programs offered to physically disabled students include note-taking services, reader services, tape recorders, tutors.

FACILITIES

Housing: Coed dorms, special housing for disabled students. 100% of campus accessible to physically disabled. **Special Academic Facilities/Equipment:** Art Gallery, Athenaeum (Reception Center). **Computers:** Students can register for classes online. Administrative functions (other than registration) can be performed online. Undergraduates are required to own a computer.

CAMPUS LIFE

Environment: Town. **Activities:** Choral groups, concert band, dance, drama/theater, jazz band, literary magazine, music ensembles, student government, student newspaper, student-run film society, symphony orchestra, yearbook. 38 registered organizations, 1 religous organization. **Athletics (Intercollegiate):** *Men:* cross-country, diving, soccer, swimming, track/field (outdoor). *Women:* cross-country, diving, soccer, swimming, track/field (outdoor). **On-Campus Highlights:** Founders Hall Art Gallery, Student Center Dining Hall, Student Center Bookstore, Recreation Center, Ikeda Library, Hiking trail along canyon rim surrounding campus.

ADMISSIONS

Freshman Academic Profile: Average high school GPA 3.82. 97% from public high schools. SAT Math middle 50% range 590-710. SAT Critical Reading middle 50% range 500-660. SAT Writing middle 50% range 530-650. ACT middle 50% range 24-29. **Basis for Candidate Selection:** *Very important factors considered include:* Class rank, application essay, academic GPA, recommendation(s), rigor of secondary school record, character/personal qualities, extracurricular activities, level of applicant's interest. *Important factors considered include:* standardized test scores, talent/ability, volunteer work. *Other factors considered include:* geographical residence, interview, racial/ethnic status, work experience. **Freshman Admission Requirements:** High school diploma is required and GED is accepted. **Freshman Admission Statistics:** 405 applied, 43% admitted, 57% enrolled. **General Admission Information:** Application Fee $45. Regular application deadline 1/6. Regular notification 3/15. Nonfall registration not accepted. Admission may be deferred for a maximum of 1 year. Neither credit nor placement offered for CEEB Advanced Placement tests.

COSTS AND FINANCIAL AID

Annual tuition $28,510. Room and board $11,134. Average book expense $1,570. **Required Forms and Deadlines:** FAFSA, State aid form. **Notification of Awards:** Applicants will be notified of awards on a rolling basis beginning 3/15. **Types of Aid:** *Need-based scholarships/grants:* Federal Pell, SEOG, state scholarships/grants, private scholarships, the school's own gift aid, Hispanic Educational Endowment Fund (HEEF). *Loans:* Subsidized Stafford, Unsubsidized Stafford, PLUS, college/university loans from institutional funds. *Student Employment:* Highest amount earned per year from on-campus jobs $5,400. **Financial Aid Statistics:** 99% freshmen, 101% undergrads receive need-based scholarship or grant aid. 100% freshmen, 101% undergrads receive non-need-based scholarship or grant aid. 29% freshmen, 31% undergrads receive need-

based self-help aid. 2% freshmen, 1% undergrads receive athletic scholarships. 100% freshmen, 100% undergrads receive any aid. 61% undergrads borrow to pay for school. Average cumulative indebtedness $18,388. **Criteria for awarding institutional aid:** *Non-need-based:* academics.

SONOMA STATE UNIVERSITY

1801 East Cotati Avenue, Rohnert Park, CA 94928
Phone: 707-664-2778 · **Financial Aid Phone:** 707-664-2389
E-mail: student.outreach@sonoma.edu · **CEEB Code:** 4723
Fax: 707-664-2060 · **Website:** www.sonoma.edu • **ACT Code:** 431

This public school was founded in 1960. It has a 269-acre campus.

RATINGS

Admissions Selectivity Rating: 70   **Fire Safety Rating:** 77

STUDENTS AND FACULTY

Enrollment: 8,406. **Student Body:** 62% female, 38% male, 1% out-of-state, 2% international (22 countries represented). Asian 5%, African American 3%, Caucasian 57%, Hispanic 21%, Native American 1%
Retention and Graduation: 80% freshmen return for sophomore year. 25% freshmen graduate within 4 years. **Faculty:** 225 full-time faculty, 92% hold PhDs, 49% are are members of minority groups, 20% are women. 1% of classes are taught by teaching assistants.

ACADEMICS

Degrees: bachelor's, master's. **Classes:** Most classes have 20-29 students. **Majors with Highest Enrollment:** Liberal Arts and Sciences Studies and Humanities; Business/Commerce. **Special Study Options:** Accelerated program, cooperative education program, cross-registration, distance learning, double major, dual enrollment, English as a Second Language (ESL), exchange student program (domestic), external degree program, honors program, independent study, internships, liberal arts/career combination, student-designed major, study abroad, teacher certification program, **Combined degree programs:** bachelors/MBA; bachelors/MPA. **Combined degree programs:** BA/MA. **Disability Services:** Special programs offered to physically disabled students include note-taking services, reader services, tape recorders, tutors. **Career services:** career/job search classes.

FACILITIES

Housing: Coed dorms, men's dorms, special housing for international students, women's dorms, apartments for single students, Housing for focused learning communities—freshman seminar dorms, healthy living dorms; women in math/science dorms. 99% of campus accessible to physically disabled. **Special Academic Facilities/Equipment:** Performing arts center, observatory, electron microscope, seismograph, information technology center, environmental technology center, high technology high school,nature preserve **Computers:** 95% of classrooms, 90% of dorms, 100% of libraries, 85% of dining areas, 100% of student union, 20% of common outdoor areas have wireless network access. Students can register for classes online. Administrative functions (other than registration) can be performed online. Undergraduates are required to own a computer.

CAMPUS LIFE

Environment: Town. **Activities:** Choral groups, dance, drama/theater, jazz band, literary magazine, music ensembles, musical theater, opera, pep band, radio station, student government, student newspaper, symphony orchestra 109. registered organizations, 2 honor societies, 4 religious organizations. 5 fraternities, 9 sororities. **Athletics (Intercollegiate):** *Men:* baseball, basketball, soccer, tennis. *Women:* basketball, cross-country, soccer, softball, tennis, track/field (outdoor), volleyball. **On-Campus Highlights:** Schultz Information Center, Environmental Technology Center, Charlie Brown's (coffee shop), Observatory, University Recreation Center. **Environmental Initiatives:** Energy efficiency; Recycling; Education.

ADMISSIONS

Freshman Academic Profile: Average high school GPA 3.21. 72% from public high schools. SAT Math middle 50% range 440-550. SAT Critical Reading middle 50% range 440-550. ACT middle 50% range 18-23. Minimum internet-based TOEFL 61. Minimum paper TOEFL 500. **Basis for Candidate Selection:** *Very important factors considered include:* academic GPA, rigor of secondary school record, standardized test scores. *Other factors* considered include: first generation, geographical residence, state residency. **Freshman Admission Requirements:** High school diploma is required and GED is accepted. *Academic units required:* 4 English, 3 mathematics, 2 science, (1 science labs), 2 foreign language, 2 history, 1 visual/performing arts, 1 academic elective, 1 US govt. **Freshman Admission Statistics:** 14,438 applied, 92% admitted, 16% enrolled. **Transfer Admission Requirements:** college transcript(s), Minimum college GPA of 2.0 required. Lowest grade transferable D. **General Admission Information:** Application Fee $55. Regular application deadline 11/30. Regular notification 3/1. Notification on a rolling basis, beginning on or about 11/1. Nonfall registration accepted. Credit and/or placement offered for CEEB Advanced Placement tests.

COSTS AND FINANCIAL AID

Annual out-of-state tuition $16,632. Room and board $11,799. Required fees $9,102. Average book expense $1,826. **Required Forms and Deadlines:** FAFSA. **Notification of Awards:** Applicants will be notified of awards on a rolling basis beginning 3/25. **Types of Aid:** *Need-based scholarships/grants:* Federal Pell, SEOG, state scholarships/grants, private scholarships, ACG, SMART. *Loans:* Direct Subsidized Stafford, Direct Unsubsidized Stafford, Direct PLUS, Federal Perkins. *Student Employment:* Federal Work-Study Program available. Institutional employment available. Highest amount earned per year from on-campus jobs $9,000. Off-campus job opportunities are good. **Financial Aid Statistics:** 65% freshmen, 66% undergrads receive need-based scholarship or grant aid. 20% freshmen, 14% undergrads receive non-need-based scholarship or grant aid. 67% freshmen, 64% undergrads receive need-based self-help aid. 1% freshmen, 1% undergrads receive athletic scholarships. 59% freshmen, 51% undergrads receive any aid. 65% undergrads borrow to pay for school. Average cumulative indebtedness $19,348. **Criteria for awarding institutional aid:** *Non-need-based:* academics, alumni affiliation, art, athletics, leadership, minority status, music/drama.

SOUTH DAKOTA SCHOOL OF MINES AND TECHNOLOGY

501 East St. Joseph Street, Rapid City, SD 57701-3995
Phone: 605-394-2414 · **Financial Aid Phone:** 605-394-2274
E-mail: admissions@sdsmt.edu · **CEEB Code:** 3470
Fax: 605-394-1979 · **Website:** www.sdsmt.edu · **ACT Code:** 3922

This public school was founded in 1885. It has a 118-acre campus.

RATINGS

Admissions Selectivity Rating: 81	Fire Safety Rating: 92

STUDENTS AND FACULTY

Enrollment: 2,335. **Student Body:** 20% female, 80% male, 50% out-of-state, 2% international (39 countries represented). Asian 2%, African American 2%, Caucasian 84%, Hispanic 4%, Native American 2%

Retention and Graduation: 77% freshmen return for sophomore year. 21% freshmen graduate within 4 years. 52% freshmen graduate within 6 years. 21% grads go on to further study within 1 year. 3% grads pursue arts and sciences degrees. 1% grads pursue law degrees. 1% grads pursue business degrees. 2% grads pursue medical degrees. **Faculty:** 151 full-time faculty, 9% hold PhDs, 25% are are members of minority groups, 17% are women.

ACADEMICS

Degrees: associate, bachelor's, master's, terminal associate. **Classes:** Most classes have 20-29 students. **Majors with Highest Enrollment:** Mechanical Engineering; Chemical Engineering; Civil Engineering. **Special Study Options:** cooperative education program, cross-registration, distance learning, dual enrollment, English as a Second Language (ESL), independent study, internships, liberal arts/career combination, study abroad, Distance Education—SDSMT offfers an M.S. degree in Technology Management via the internet. Dual Degrees—We do not offer double majors but students may graduate with more than one degree by completing a minimum of thirty (30) semester hours of credit in residence beyond the credit hours used for the first B.S. degree. **Disability Services:** Special programs offered to physically disabled students include note-taking services, reader services, tape recorders, tutors. **Career services:** Alumni network, alumni services, career/job search classes, career assessment, internships, regional alumni. Career services highlights include the cooperative/internship programs, both of which are very successful and usually lead to permanent employment for the students after graduation.

FACILITIES

Housing: Coed dorms, special housing for disabled students, fraternity/sorority housing, apartments for married students, apartments for single students, Well-

ness Housing. SDSM&T recently acquired apartments which can be rented by single students or groups of students or married students with families. 80% of campus accessible to physically disabled. **Special Academic Facilities/Equipment:** Museum of geology and paleontology, electron microscope, engineering/mining experiment station, supersonic wind tunnel, 3-D visualization lab, polymer processing lab, friction stir welding lab, high-frequency microwave lab, tech development lab, fluid computational dynamics lab, robotics lab, clean manufacturing lab, institute atmospheric science and other research institutes. **Computers:** 100% of classrooms, 100% of dorms, 100% of libraries, 100% of dining areas, 100% of student union, 100% of common outdoor areas have wireless network access. Students can register for classes online. Administrative functions (other than registration) can be performed online.

CAMPUS LIFE

Environment: Town. **Activities:** Choral groups, concert band, dance, drama/theater, jazz band, music ensembles, pep band, radio station, student government, student newspaper, Campus Ministries, International Student Organization. 67 registered organizations, 6 honor societies, 9 religious organizations. 4 fraternities, 2 sororities. **Athletics (Intercollegiate):** *Men:* basketball, cross-country, football, golf, track/field (outdoor), track/field (indoor). *Women:* basketball, cross-country, golf, track/field (outdoor), track/field (indoor), volleyball. **On-Campus Highlights:** O'Harra Stadium (football and track), King (Sports) Center—basketball, pool, exercise, Geology and Paleontology Museum, Surbeck Student Center, Apex Gallery. **Environmental Initiatives:** A minimun of LEED Silver is required on all new construction or renovation; Working on a Sustainable Engineering Minor; RecycleMania.

ADMISSIONS

Freshman Academic Profile: Average high school GPA 3.51. 20% in top 10% of high school class, 29% in top 25% of high school class, 82% in top 50% of high school class. SAT Math middle 50% range 560-657.5. SAT Critical Reading middle 50% range 510-650. SAT Writing middle 50% range 480-610. ACT middle 50% range 24-28. Minimum internet-based TOEFL 68. Minimum paper TOEFL 520. **Basis for Candidate Selection:** *Very important factors considered include:* Class rank, academic GPA, rigor of secondary school record, standardized test scores. *Other factors considered include:* character/personal qualities, extracurricular activities, talent/ability, volunteer work, work experience. **Freshman Admission Requirements:** High school diploma is required and GED is accepted. *Academic units required:* 4 English, 4 mathematics, 4 science, (3 science labs), 2 foreign language, 3 social studies, 1 visual/performing arts. **Freshman Admission Statistics:** 1,549 applied, 88% admitted, 42% enrolled. **Transfer Admission Requirements:** college transcript(s), statement of good standing from prior institution(s). Minimum college GPA of 2.0 required. Lowest grade transferable D. **General Admission Information:** Application Fee $20. Notification on a rolling basis, beginning on or about 11/1. Nonfall registration accepted. Admission may be deferred for a maximum of 12 months. Credit and/or placement offered for CEEB Advanced Placement tests.

COSTS AND FINANCIAL AID

Annual in-state tuition $4,170. Annual out-of-state tuition $7,000. Room and board $6,370. Required fees $5,870. Average book expense $1,800. **Required Forms and Deadlines:** FAFSA. **Notification of Awards:** Applicants will be notified of awards on a rolling basis beginning 5/1. **Types of Aid:** *Need-based scholarships/grants:* Federal Pell, SEOG, state scholarships/grants, private scholarships, the school's own gift aid, SMART grants, ACG grants. *Loans:* Subsidized Stafford, Unsubsidized Stafford, PLUS, Federal Perkins, Private alternative loans. *Student Employment:* Federal Work-Study Program available. Institutional employment available. Highest amount earned per year from on-campus jobs $2,000. Off-campus job opportunities are good. **Financial Aid Statistics:** 74% freshmen, 66% undergrads receive need-based scholarship or grant aid. 59% freshmen, 38% undergrads receive non-need-based scholarship or grant aid. 79% freshmen, 81% undergrads receive need-based self-help aid. 5% freshmen, 4% undergrads receive athletic scholarships. 90% freshmen, 79% undergrads receive any aid. 72% undergrads borrow to pay for school. Average cumulative indebtedness $26,309. **Criteria for awarding institutional aid:** *Non-need-based:* academics, athletics, leadership, minority status.

SOUTH DAKOTA STATE UNIVERSITY

SAD 200, Brookings, SD 57007-0649
Phone: 605-688-4121 · **Financial Aid Phone:** 605-688-4695
E-mail: sdsu.admissions@sdstate.edu · **CEEB Code:** 6653
Fax: 605-688-6891 · **Website:** www.sdstate.edu · **ACT Code:** 3924

This public school was founded in 1881. It has a 272-acre campus.

RATINGS

Admissions Selectivity Rating: 75	Fire Safety Rating: 82

STUDENTS AND FACULTY

Enrollment: 10,067. **Student Body:** 51% female, 49% male, 37% out-of-state. **Retention and Graduation:** 27% freshmen graduate within 4 years. 57% freshmen graduate within 6 years.

ACADEMICS

Degrees: associate, bachelor's, certificate, master's, post-bachelor's certificate, post-master's certificate, terminal associate. **Classes:** Most classes have 20-29 students. Most lab/discussion sessions have 20-29 students. **Special Study Options:** Accelerated program, cooperative education program, cross-registration, distance learning, double major, dual enrollment, exchange student program (domestic), honors program, independent study, internships, liberal arts/career combination, study abroad, teacher certification program, We offer help and courses in ESL but it is not an official program. **Honors programs:** For information about our Honors College, see: http://www3.sdstate.edu/Academics/HonorsCollege/ **Combined degree programs:** BS/MS in Economics. **Disability Services:** Special programs offered to physically disabled students include note-taking services, reader services, tape recorders, tutors. **Career services:** career/job search classes, career assessment, internships.

FACILITIES

Housing: Coed dorms, special housing for disabled students, special housing for international students, fraternity/sorority housing, apartments for married students, apartments for single students, Wellness Housing, Limited single rooms with optional meal plan for upperclassmen. Students out of high school less than 2 yrs are required to live in campus housing unless living with family. **Special Academic Facilities/Equipment:** SD Art Museum, SD Agricultural Heritage Museum, Northern Plains Bio-stress Laboratory, Animal Disease Research and Diagnostic Lab, McCrory Gardens, new Center for Infectious Disease Research and Vaccinology, EROS-SDSU GISc Center of Excellence. **Computers:** 30% of classrooms, 100% of dorms, 100% of libraries, 100% of dining areas, 100% of student union, 20% of common outdoor areas have wireless network access. Students can register for classes online. Administrative functions (other than registration) can be performed online.

CAMPUS LIFE

Environment: Village. **Activities:** Choral groups, concert band, dance, drama/theater, jazz magazine, literary magazine, marching band, music ensembles, musical theater, pep band, radio station, student government, student newspaper, symphony orchestra, yearbook. 200 registered organizations, 32 honor societies, 14 religious organizations. 6 fraternities, 4 sororities. **Athletics (Intercollegiate):** *Men:* baseball, basketball, cross-country, diving, football, golf, swimming, tennis, track/field (outdoor), track/field (indoor), wrestling. *Women:* basketball, cross-country, diving, equestrian sports, golf, soccer, softball, swimming, tennis, track/field (outdoor), track/field (indoor), volleyball. **On-Campus Highlights:** Performing Arts Center, Dairy Bar, University Student Union, Frost Arena, South Dakota Art Museum, Northern Plains Bio-Stress Laboratory Enterprise Institute SD Ag Heritage Museum. **Environmental Initiatives:** Establishment of environmental stewardship and sustainability shared governance committee. Reuse and recycle. Energy efficiency and effective building operations.

ADMISSIONS

Freshman Academic Profile: Average high school GPA 3.32. 13% in top 10% of high school class, 35% in top 25% of high school class, 69% in top 50% of high school class. SAT Math middle 50% range 460-600. SAT Critical Reading middle 50% range 440-590. ACT middle 50% range 20-25. Minimum internet-based TOEFL 61. Minimum paper TOEFL 550. **Basis for Candidate Selection:** *Very important factors considered include:* Class rank, academic GPA, standardized test scores. *Important factors considered include:* rigor of secondary school record. *Other factors considered include:* recommendation(s). **Freshman Admission Requirements:** High school diploma is required and GED is accepted. *Academic units required:* 4 English, 3 mathematics, 3 science, (3 science labs), 3 social studies, 1 Fine arts. **Freshman Admission Statistics:** 4,851 applied, 92% admitted, 52% enrolled. **Transfer Admission Requirements:** High school transcript, college transcript(s), statement of good standing from prior institution(s). Minimum college GPA of 2.0 required. Lowest grade transferable D. **General Admission Information:** Application Fee $20. Nonfall registration accepted. Admission may be deferred for a maximum of 12 Months. Credit and/or placement offered for CEEB Advanced Placement tests.

COSTS AND FINANCIAL AID

Average book expense $1,174. **Required Forms and Deadlines:** FAFSA. **Notification of Awards:** Applicants will be notified of awards on a rolling basis beginning 4/1. **Types of Aid:** *Need-based scholarships/grants:* Federal Pell, SEOG, state scholarships/grants, private scholarships, the school's own gift aid, United Negro College Fund, Federal Nursing Scholarships., Federal SMART grants; Federal Academic Comp Grants, TEACH Grants, TRIO. *Loans:* Subsidized Stafford, Unsubsidized Stafford, PLUS, Federal Perkins, Federal Nursing, college/university loans from institutional funds, Health Profession loans. Private alternative loans. *Student Employment:* Federal Work-Study Program

available. Institutional employment available. Highest amount earned per year from on-campus jobs $5,880. Off-campus job opportunities are good. **Financial Aid Statistics:** 57% freshmen, 54% undergrads receive need-based scholarship or grant aid. 70% freshmen, 44% undergrads receive non-need-based scholarship or grant aid. 84% freshmen, 87% undergrads receive need-based self-help aid. 5% freshmen, 4% undergrads receive athletic scholarships. 55% freshmen, 53% undergrads receive any aid. 67% undergrads borrow to pay for school. Average cumulative indebtedness $23,150. **Criteria for awarding institutional aid:** *Non-need-based:* academics, art, athletics, job skills, leadership, minority status, music/drama, state/district residency.

SOUTHEAST MISSOURI STATE UNIVERSITY

One University Plaza, Cape Girardeau, MO 63701
Phone: 573-651-2590 · **Financial Aid Phone:** 573-651-2253
E-mail: admissions@semo.edu · **CEEB Code:** 6655
Fax: 573-651-5936 · **Website:** www.semo.edu · **ACT Code:** 2366

This public school was founded in 1873. It has a 400-acre campus.

RATINGS

Admissions Selectivity Rating: 77   **Fire Safety Rating:** 82

STUDENTS AND FACULTY

Enrollment: 9,382. **Student Body:** 56% female, 44% male, 15% out-of-state, 7% international (54 countries represented). Asian 1%, African American 10%, Caucasian 78%, Hispanic 2%, Native American 1%
Retention and Graduation: 29% freshmen graduate within 4 years. 51% freshmen graduate within 6 years. **Faculty:** 397 full-time faculty, 75% hold PhDs, 53% are are members of minority groups, 15% are women. 3% of classes are taught by teaching assistants.

ACADEMICS

Degrees: associate, bachelor's, certificate, master's, post-master's certificate. **Classes:** Most classes have 20-29 students. **Majors with Highest Enrollment:** General Studies; Registered Nursing/Registered Nurse; Business Administration and Management. **Special Study Options:** Accelerated program, distance learning, double major, dual enrollment, English as a Second Language (ESL), honors program, independent study, internships, liberal arts/career combination, student-designed major, study abroad, teacher certification program. **Honors programs:** The Honors Program encourages intellectual perspective, addresses special needs of outstanding students and contributes to the general advancement of learning. **Disability Services:** Special programs offered to physically disabled students include note-taking services, reader services, tape recorders, tutors. **Career services:** Alumni network, alumni services, career/job search classes, career assessment, internships, regional alumni. Career services highlights include Career Linkages, which assists in locating experiential learning opportunities.

FACILITIES

Housing: Coed dorms, fraternity/sorority housing, Wellness Housing, Apartments for students with dependents. 100% of campus accessible to physically disabled. **Special Academic Facilities/Equipment:** River Campus at Southeast; Crisp Museum;Bedell Performance Hall; Center for Faulkner Studies; Center for Scholarship in Teaching and Learning; Missouri Statewide Early Literacy Intervention Program (MSELIP); Writing Center; University Demonstration Farm; 4 corporate video studios, 2 radio stations; Southeast Explorer; SHOW (Southeast Health on Wheels); Linda Godwin Center for Science and Math Education. **Computers:** 15% of dorms, 90% of libraries, 90% of dining areas, 90% of student union, 10% of common outdoor areas have wireless network access. Students can register for classes online. Administrative functions (other than registration) can be performed online.

CAMPUS LIFE

Environment: Town. **Activities:** Choral groups, concert band, dance, drama/theater, jazz band, literary magazine, marching band, music ensembles, musical theater, opera, pep band, radio station, student government, student newspaper, symphony orchestra, Campus Ministries, International Student Organization, Model UN. 136 registered organizations, 8 honor societies, 14 religious organizations. 11 fraternities, 7 sororities. **Athletics (Intercollegiate):** *Men:* baseball, basketball, cheerleading, cross-country, football, track/field (outdoor), track/field (indoor). *Women:* basketball, cheerleading, cross-country, gymnastics, soccer, softball, tennis, track/field (outdoor), track/field (indoor), volleyball. **On-Campus Highlights:** River Campus at Southeast, Recreation Center & Aquatic Center, Kent Library Information Commons, Otto and Della Seabaugh Polytechnic Bldg, Robert A. Dempster Hall, River Campus: Holland School of Visual adn Performing Arts,Bedell Performance Hall, Crisp Regional Museum,

Rust Flexible Theatre, Glenn Convocation Center, Shuck Music Recital Hall. **Environmental Initiatives:** Waste Management; Energy management—conduct energy savings workshops and energy audits for area companies; Green certified products.

ADMISSIONS

Freshman Academic Profile: Average high school GPA 3.36. 15% in top 10% of high school class, 41% in top 25% of high school class, 74% in top 50% of high school class. SAT Math middle 50% range 437.5-620. SAT Critical Reading middle 50% range 457.5-592.5. ACT middle 50% range 20-25. Minimum internet-based TOEFL 61. Minimum paper TOEFL 500. **Basis for Candidate Selection:** *Very important factors considered include:* academic GPA, rigor of secondary school record, standardized test scores. *Other factors considered include:* Class rank. **Freshman Admission Requirements:** High school diploma is required and GED is accepted. *Academic units required:* 4 English, 3 mathematics, 3 science, (1 science labs), 0 foreign language, 2 social studies, 1 history, 1 visual/performing arts, 3 academic electives. **Freshman Admission Statistics:** 4,750 applied, 85% admitted, 46% enrolled. **Transfer Admission Requirements:** college transcript(s), Minimum college GPA of 2.0 required. Lowest grade transferable D. **General Admission Information:** Application Fee $25. Regular application deadline 7/1. Notification on a rolling basis, beginning on or about 9/1. Nonfall registration accepted. Credit offered for CEEB Advanced Placement tests.

COSTS AND FINANCIAL AID

Annual in-state tuition $5,927. Annual out-of-state tuition $11,259. Room and board $8,432. Required fees $1,011. Average book expense $494. **Required Forms and Deadlines:** FAFSA. **Notification of Awards:** Applicants will be notified of awards on a rolling basis beginning 4/1. **Types of Aid:** *Need-based scholarships/grants:* Federal Pell, SEOG, state scholarships/grants, private scholarships, the school's own gift aid. *Loans:* Subsidized Stafford, Unsubsidized Stafford, PLUS, Federal Perkins, state loans. *Student Employment:* Federal Work-Study Program available. Institutional employment available. Off-campus job opportunities are fair. **Financial Aid Statistics:** 94% freshmen, 87% undergrads receive need-based scholarship or grant aid. 9% freshmen, 6% undergrads receive non-need-based scholarship or grant aid. 65% freshmen, 73% undergrads receive need-based self-help aid. 2% freshmen, 2% undergrads receive athletic scholarships. 84% freshmen, 81% undergrads receive any aid. 65% undergrads borrow to pay for school. Average cumulative indebtedness $25,145. **Criteria for awarding institutional aid:** *Non-need-based:* academics, alumni affiliation, art, athletics, job skills, leadership, minority status, music/drama, state/district residency.

SOUTHEASTERN BIBLE COLLEGE

2545 Valleydale Road, Birmingham, AL 35244
Phone: 205-970-9211
E-mail: info@sebc.edu
Fax: 205-970-9207 • **Website:** www.sebc.edu

This private school was founded in 1935. It has a 10-acre campus.

RATINGS

Admissions Selectivity Rating: 66   **Fire Safety Rating:** 60*

STUDENTS AND FACULTY

Enrollment: 170. **Student Body:** 45% female, 55% male, 7% out-of-state, 0% international. Asian 1%, African American 32%, Caucasian 62%, Hispanic 2%, Native American 1%
Retention and Graduation: 69% freshmen return for sophomore year. 15% freshmen graduate within 4 years. 15% freshmen graduate within 6 years. **Faculty:** 7 full-time faculty, 100% hold PhDs, 14% are are members of minority groups, 0% are women. 0% of classes are taught by teaching assistants.

ACADEMICS

Degrees: associate, bachelor's, diploma, terminal associate. **Classes:** Most classes have fewer than 10 students. **Majors with Highest Enrollment:** Bible/Biblical Studies. **Special Study Options:** independent study, internships. **Disability Services:** Special programs offered to physically disabled students include note-taking services, tape recorders.

FACILITIES

Housing: men's dorms, women's dorms, apartments for married students. 100% of campus accessible to physically disabled.

CAMPUS LIFE

Environment: Metropolis. **Activities:** Choral groups, music ensembles, student government. **On-Campus Highlights:** Gannett-Estes Library

ADMISSIONS

Freshman Academic Profile: ACT middle 50% range 18-21. **Basis for Candidate Selection:** *Very important factors considered include:* recommendation(s), rigor of secondary school record, standardized test scores, character/personal qualities, religious affiliation/commitment. *Important factors considered include:* application essay. *Other factors considered include:* alumni/ae relation, interview. **Freshman Admission Requirements:** High school diploma is required and GED is accepted. *Academic units required:* 4 English, 4 mathematics, 4 science. **Freshman Admission Statistics:** 27 applied, 100% admitted, 63% enrolled. **Transfer Admission Requirements:** High school transcript, college transcript(s), essay or personal statement, Minimum college GPA of 2.0 required. Lowest grade transferable C. **General Admission Information:** Application Fee $20. Regular application deadline 8/1. Notification on a rolling basis, beginning on or about 9/1. Nonfall registration accepted. Admission may be deferred for a maximum of 1 year. Credit offered for CEEB Advanced Placement tests.

COSTS AND FINANCIAL AID

Required Forms and Deadlines: FAFSA, Institution's own financial aid form. **Notification of Awards:** Applicants will be notified of awards on or about 6/1. **Types of Aid:** *Need-based scholarships/grants:* Federal Pell, SEOG, state scholarships/grants. *Loans:* Subsidized Stafford, Unsubsidized Stafford, PLUS. *Student Employment:* Federal Work-Study Program available. Highest amount earned per year from on-campus jobs $2,000. Off-campus job opportunities are excellent. **Financial Aid Statistics:** 77% undergrads borrow to pay for school. **Criteria for awarding institutional aid:** *Non-need-based:* academics, alumni affiliation, state/district residency.

SOUTHEASTERN LOUISIANA UNIVERSITY

SLU 10752, Hammond, LA 70402
Phone: 985-549-2066 • **Financial Aid Phone:** 985-549-2244
E-mail: admissions@selu.edu • **CEEB Code:** 6656
Fax: 985-549-5632 • **Website:** www.selu.edu • **ACT Code:** 1608

This public school was founded in 1925. It has a 365-acre campus.

RATINGS

Admissions Selectivity Rating: 73   **Fire Safety Rating:** 92

STUDENTS AND FACULTY

Enrollment: 11,191. **Student Body:** 62% female, 38% male, 4% out-of-state, 2% international (42 countries represented). Asian 1%, African American 16%, Caucasian 67%, Hispanic 7%, Native American <1%
Retention and Graduation: 62% freshmen return for sophomore year. **Faculty:** 496 full-time faculty, 67% hold PhDs, 55% are are members of minority groups, 14% are women. 0% of classes are taught by teaching assistants.

ACADEMICS

Degrees: associate, bachelor's, master's. **Classes:** Most classes have 20-29 students. Most lab/discussion sessions have 20-29 students. **Majors with Highest Enrollment:** Business Administration and Management; Registered Nursing/Registered Nurse; General Studies. **Special Study Options:** Accelerated program, cross-registration, distance learning, double major, dual enrollment, English as a Second Language (ESL), honors program, independent study, internships, liberal arts/career combination, study abroad, teacher certification program. **Honors programs:** reduced size classes, scholarships, honors residence hall, achievement awards, and honor academic credit shown on the transcript. **Disability Services:** Special programs offered to physically disabled students include note-taking services, tape recorders, tutors. **Career services:** alumni services, career assessment, internships. Career services highlights include a wide range of courses and curricula that address emerging regional, national and international priorities. The University embraces active partnerships that benefit students, faculty and the region we serve. Programs enable students to understand themselves and the world around them in a broad intellectual perspective. Such a perspective provides students the opportunity to live full, rich, balanced lives and to assume positions of leadership in the public and private sector. Graduates are prepared to think critically, communicate effectively and become lifelong learners. Emphasis is placed on preparation for careers or graduate study through undergraduate research in collaboration with faculty, "hands-on" internships, field experiences, work-study placements, cooperative education, service-learning, and opportunities to study abroad. Many of these opportunities earn college credit. Southeastern also has honors tracks in place for all degree programs. Undergraduate research programs such as Undergraduate Research and Creative Activities Grants Programs in the College of Arts, Humanities and Social Sciences, PROFIT (Preferred Research Option for Intensive Training) in the College of Business, SOAR (Student Opportunities for Achievement and Research) in the College of Nursing and Health Sciences, SURE (Student Undergraduate Research in Education) in the College of Education and Human Development, and STAR (Science and Technology Awards for Research) in the College of Science and Technology provide opportunities for undergraduate students to conduct research and engage in creative ventures with Southeastern faculty members.

FACILITIES

Housing: Coed dorms, women's dorms, fraternity/sorority housing, apartments for single students. 95% of campus accessible to physically disabled. **Special Academic Facilities/Equipment:** Contemporary Art Gallery, Radio Station, Television Station, Columbia Theatre, Maritime Museum **Computers:** 5% of classrooms, 100% of dorms, 100% of libraries, 50% of dining areas, 25% of student union, 25% of common outdoor areas have wireless network access. Students can register for classes online. Administrative functions (other than registration) can be performed online.

CAMPUS LIFE

Environment: Village. **Activities:** Choral groups, concert band, dance, drama/theater, jazz band, literary magazine, marching band, music ensembles, musical theater, opera, pep band, radio station, student government, student newspaper, student-run film society, symphony orchestra, television station, yearbook, Campus Ministries, International Student Organization. 105 registered organizations, 11 honor societies, 12 religious organizations. 7 fraternities, 8 sororities. **Athletics (Intercollegiate):** *Men:* baseball, basketball, cross-country, football, golf, track/field (outdoor), track/field (indoor). *Women:* basketball, cross-country, soccer, softball, tennis, track/field (outdoor), track/field (indoor), volleyball. **On-Campus Highlights:** Student Union, Student Recreation Center, Library, Bookstore, Campus Dining Complex. **Environmental Initiatives:** 1. Renewable Energy—investment in solar power, on site waste oil biodiesel fuel production, proactive energy usage reduction management. The university has focused on these areas to reduce both waste and the need for grid power. 2. Waste Reduction and Recycling—reduction of waste, reuse of waste and recycling of waste. 3. Sustainability Education—through the design and completion (in phases) of the Southeastern Sustainability Center the university has tied in sustainable practices with a physical location that serves to educate students, both in the university and regional K-12 students about sustainable solutions to todays problems

ADMISSIONS

Freshman Academic Profile: Average high school GPA 3.174. 11.1% in top 10% of high school class, 31.4% in top 25% of high school class, 65.6% in top 50% of high school class. ACT middle 50% range 20-24. Minimum internet-based TOEFL 61. Minimum paper TOEFL 500. **Basis for Candidate Selection:** *Very important factors considered include:* Class rank, academic GPA, rigor of secondary school record, standardized test scores. **Freshman Admission Requirements:** High school diploma is required and GED is accepted. *Academic units required:* 4 English, 3 mathematics, 3 science, 2 foreign language, 3 social studies, 1 visual/performing arts, 1 Mathematics or Science. **Freshman Admission Statistics:** 3,725 applied, 87% admitted, 75% enrolled. **Transfer Admission Requirements:** college transcript(s), statement of good standing from prior institution(s). Minimum college GPA of 2.0 required. Lowest grade transferable D. **General Admission Information:** Application Fee $20. Regular application deadline 8/1. Nonfall registration accepted. Admission may be deferred for a maximum of 1 year. Credit and/or placement offered for CEEB Advanced Placement tests.

COSTS AND FINANCIAL AID

Annual in-state tuition $4,798. Annual out-of-state tuition $17,362. Room and board $7,100. Required fees $1,749. Average book expense $1,200. **Required Forms and Deadlines:** FAFSA. **Notification of Awards:** Applicants will be notified of awards on a rolling basis beginning 3/1. **Types of Aid:** *Need-based scholarships/grants:* Federal Pell, SEOG, state scholarships/grants, private scholarships, the school's own gift aid, Federal Nursing Scholarships. *Loans:* Subsidized Stafford, Unsubsidized Stafford, PLUS, Federal Perkins, college/university loans from institutional funds. *Student Employment:* Federal Work-Study Program available. Institutional employment available. Highest amount earned per year from on-campus jobs $13,009. Off-campus job opportunities are good. **Financial Aid Statistics:** 64% freshmen, 67% undergrads receive need-based scholarship or grant aid. 67% freshmen, 50% undergrads receive non-need-based scholarship or grant aid. 51% freshmen, 59% undergrads receive need-based self-help aid. 2% freshmen, 3% undergrads receive athletic scholarships. 57% undergrads borrow to pay for school. Average cumulative indebtedness $18,637. **Criteria for awarding institutional aid:** *Non-need-based:* academics, athletics, job skills, leadership, music/drama, state/district residency.

SOUTHEASTERN OKLAHOMA STATE UNIVERSITY

1405 North 4th Avenue, Durant, OK 74701-0609
Phone: 580-745-2060 • **Financial Aid Phone:** 580-745-2186
E-mail: admissions@se.edu • **CEEB Code:** 6657
Fax: 580-745-4502 • **ACT Code:** 3438

This public school was founded in 1909. It has a 268-acre campus.

RATINGS

Admissions Selectivity Rating: 75   **Fire Safety Rating:** 79

STUDENTS AND FACULTY

Enrollment: 3,465. **Student Body:** 55% female, 45% male, 22% out-of-state, 1% international (28 countries represented). Asian 1%, African American 5%, Caucasian 59%, Hispanic 3%, Native American 31%
Retention and Graduation: 19% freshmen graduate within 4 years. **Faculty:** 143 full-time faculty, 74% hold PhDs, 41% are are members of minority groups, 17% are women. 0% of classes are taught by teaching assistants.

ACADEMICS

Degrees: bachelor's, master's, post-master's certificate. **Classes:** Most classes have 20-29 students. Most lab/discussion sessions have 20-29 students. **Majors with Highest Enrollment:** Elementary Education and Teaching; Occupational Safety and Health Technology/Technician; Psychology. **Special Study Options:** distance learning, double major, honors program, independent study, internships, teacher certification program. **Honors programs:** Our Honors program offers six different scholarships ranging in value from $6,400 to $26,400 over four years. **Disability Services:** Special programs offered to physically disabled students include note-taking services, reader services, tape recorders, tutors. **Career services:** Alumni network, career/job search classes, career assessment, internships.

FACILITIES

Housing: Coed dorms, apartments for single students. 100% of campus accessible to physically disabled. **Special Academic Facilities/Equipment:** Visual and Performing Arts Gallery **Computers:** 65% of classrooms, 50% of dorms, 100% of libraries, 100% of dining areas, 100% of student union, 50% of common outdoor areas have wireless network access. Students can register for classes online. Administrative functions (other than registration) can be performed online.

CAMPUS LIFE

Environment: Village. **Activities:** Choral groups, concert band, dance, drama/theater, jazz band, literary magazine, marching band, music ensembles, musical theater, opera, pep band, radio station, student government, student newspaper, yearbook, Campus Ministries, International Student Organization. 70 registered organizations, 12 honor societies, 8 religious organizations. 2 fraternities, 2 sororities. **Athletics (Intercollegiate):** *Men:* baseball, basketball, football, golf, tennis. *Women:* basketball, cross-country, softball, tennis, volleyball. **On-Campus Highlights:** Shearer Hall and Suites (New Apartments), New Student Union, Newly Renovated Football Stadium, New Basketball Arena, "Campus of a Thousand Magnolias."

ADMISSIONS

Freshman Academic Profile: Average high school GPA 3.29. 16% in top 10% of high school class, 40% in top 25% of high school class, 77% in top 50% of high school class. 99% from public high schools. ACT middle 50% range 18-23. Minimum paper TOEFL 500. **Basis for Candidate Selection:** *Very important factors considered include:* Class rank, academic GPA, standardized test scores. *Other factors considered include:* recommendation(s), rigor of secondary school record, character/personal qualities, interview, level of applicant's interest, state residency, talent/ability. **Freshman Admission Requirements:** High school diploma is required and GED is accepted. *Academic units required:* 4 English, 3 mathematics, 2 science, (2 science labs), 3 history, 2 academic electives. **Freshman Admission Statistics:** 916 applied, 82% admitted, 82% enrolled. **Transfer Admission Requirements:** college transcript(s), Minimum college GPA of 2.0 required. Lowest grade transferable D. **General Admission Information:** Application Fee $20. Nonfall registration accepted. Credit offered for CEEB Advanced Placement tests.

COSTS AND FINANCIAL AID

Average book expense $800. **Required Forms and Deadlines:** FAFSA, Institution's own financial aid form. **Notification of Awards:** Applicants will be notified of awards on a rolling basis beginning 4/15. **Types of Aid:** *Need-based scholarships/grants:* Federal Pell, SEOG, state scholarships/grants, private scholarships, the school's own gift aid. *Loans:* Subsidized Stafford, Unsubsidized Stafford, PLUS, Federal Perkins. *Student Employment:* Federal Work-Study

Program available. Institutional employment available. Highest amount earned per year from on-campus jobs $8,259. Off-campus job opportunities are good. **Financial Aid Statistics:** 71% freshmen, 81% undergrads receive need-based scholarship or grant aid. 44% freshmen, 32% undergrads receive non-need-based scholarship or grant aid. 36% freshmen, 58% undergrads receive need-based self-help aid. 10% freshmen, 7% undergrads receive athletic scholarships. 66% freshmen, 65% undergrads receive any aid. 37% undergrads borrow to pay for school. Average cumulative indebtedness $6,630. **Criteria for awarding institutional aid:** *Non-need-based:* academics, alumni affiliation, art, athletics, leadership, minority status, music/drama, state/district residency.

SOUTHERN ADVENTIST UNIVERSITY

P.O. Box 370, Collegedale, TN 37315
Phone: 423-236-2835 · **Financial Aid Phone:** 423-236-2894
E-mail: admissions@southern.edu · **CEEB Code:** 3518
Fax: 423-236-1835 · **ACT Code:** 4006

This private school, affiliated with the Seventh Day Adventist Church, was founded in 1892. It has a 1000-acre campus.

RATINGS

Admissions Selectivity Rating: 74   Fire Safety Rating: 84

STUDENTS AND FACULTY

Enrollment: 2,584. **Student Body:** 55% female, 45% male, 69% out-of-state, 5% international. Asian 6%, African American 12%, Caucasian 58%, Hispanic 19%, Native American <1%
Retention and Graduation: 72% freshmen return for sophomore year. 23% freshmen graduate within 4 years. 48% freshmen graduate within 6 years. 15% grads go on to further study within 1 year. 10% grads pursue arts and sciences degrees. 1% grads pursue business degrees. 3% grads pursue medical degrees. **Faculty:** 146 full-time faculty, 64% hold PhDs, 42% are are members of minority groups, 12% are women. 0% of classes are taught by teaching assistants.

ACADEMICS

Degrees: associate, bachelor's, certificate, master's, post-master's certificate. **Majors with Highest Enrollment:** Business/Commerce; Biology/Biological Sciences. **Special Study Options:** double major, dual enrollment, English as a Second Language (ESL), honors program, independent study, internships, study abroad, teacher certification program. **Honors programs:** Southern Scholars program includes special projects, inter-disciplinary studies, and designated honors courses to provide a challenging and intellectually stimulating educational experience. **Combined degree programs:** BA/MA, Nursing. **Disability Services:** Special programs offered to physically disabled students include note-taking services, reader services, tape recorders, tutors.

FACILITIES

Housing: men's dorms, women's dorms, apartments for married students, apartments for single students. 70% of campus accessible to physically disabled. **Special Academic Facilities/Equipment:** Near-Eastern archaeology teaching collection **Computers:** 100% of classrooms, 5% of dorms, 100% of libraries, 80% of dining areas, 10% of common outdoor areas have wireless network access. Students can register for classes online. Administrative functions (other than registration) can be performed online.

CAMPUS LIFE

Environment: Rural. **Activities:** Choral groups, concert band, drama/theater, jazz band, music ensembles, radio station, student government, student newspaper, student-run film society, symphony orchestra, television station, yearbook, Campus Ministries, International Student Organization. 30 registered organizations, 8 honor societies, 3 religious organizations. **On-Campus Highlights:** Student Center, Wellness Center, The Village Market, KRs Place, Library. **Environmental Initiatives:** Establishing environmental sustainability committee; Conducting a campus-wide chemical cleanout; Using green listed chemicals for cleaning.

ADMISSIONS

Freshman Academic Profile: Average high school GPA 3.4. 18% from public high schools. SAT Math middle 50% range 430-560. SAT Critical Reading middle 50% range 460-580. ACT middle 50% range 19-25. Minimum paper TOEFL 550. **Basis for Candidate Selection:** *Very important factors considered include:* academic GPA, rigor of secondary school record, standardized test scores. **Freshman Admission Requirements:** High school diploma is required and GED is accepted. *Academic units required:* 3 English, 2 mathematics, 2 science, 0 foreign language, 1 social studies, 1 history, 9 academic electives. **Freshman Admission Statistics:** 1,452 applied, 80% admitted, 54% enrolled. **Transfer Admission Requirements:** college transcript(s), Minimum

college GPA of 2 required. Lowest grade transferable D. **General Admission Information:** Application Fee $25. Regular application deadline 9/8. Nonfall registration accepted. Admission may be deferred for a maximum of 1 year. Credit and/or placement offered for CEEB Advanced Placement tests.

COSTS AND FINANCIAL AID

Annual tuition $17,534. Room and board $5,786. Required fees $790. Average book expense $1,100. **Required Forms and Deadlines:** FAFSA. **Notification of Awards:** Applicants will be notified of awards on a rolling basis beginning 2/15. **Types of Aid:** *Need-based scholarships/grants:* Federal Pell, SEOG, state scholarships/grants, private scholarships, the school's own gift aid. *Loans:* Subsidized Stafford, Unsubsidized Stafford, PLUS, Federal Perkins, Federal Nursing, college/university loans from institutional funds. *Student Employment:* Federal Work-Study Program available. Institutional employment available. Highest amount earned per year from on-campus jobs $2,000. Off-campus job opportunities are good. **Financial Aid Statistics:** 99% freshmen, 98% undergrads receive need-based scholarship or grant aid. 82% freshmen, 55% undergrads receive non-need-based scholarship or grant aid. 82% freshmen, 85% undergrads receive need-based self-help aid. 0% freshmen, 0% undergrads receive athletic scholarships. 95% undergrads receive any aid. 65% undergrads borrow to pay for school. Average cumulative indebtedness $23,078. **Criteria for awarding institutional aid:** *Non-need-based:* academics, alumni affiliation, art, leadership, music/drama.

SOUTHERN ARKANSAS UNIVERSITY

P. O. Box 9382, Magnolia, AR 71754
Phone: 870-235-4040 · **Financial Aid Phone:** 870-235-4023
E-mail: muleriders@saumag.edu · **CEEB Code:** 142
Fax: 870-235-5072 · **ACT Code:** 142

This public school was founded in 1909. It has a 1418-acre campus.

RATINGS

Admissions Selectivity Rating: 70   Fire Safety Rating: 60*

STUDENTS AND FACULTY

Enrollment: 2,671. **Student Body:** 57% female, 43% male, 21% out-of-state, 6% international (29 countries represented). Asian 1%, African American 29%, Caucasian 62%, Hispanic 1%, Native American 1%
Retention and Graduation: 62% freshmen return for sophomore year. 19% freshmen graduate within 4 years. 39% freshmen graduate within 6 years. **Faculty:** 148 full-time faculty, 38% are are members of minority groups. 0% of classes are taught by teaching assistants.

ACADEMICS

Degrees: associate, bachelor's, master's. **Classes:** Most classes have fewer than 10 students. Most lab/discussion sessions have 20-29 students. **Special Study Options:** cross-registration, distance learning, double major, dual enrollment, honors program, internships, teacher certification program. **Disability Services:** Special programs offered to physically disabled students include tape recorders, tutors.

FACILITIES

Housing: Coed dorms, men's dorms, women's dorms, apartments for married students, apartments for single students. 95% of campus accessible to physically disabled. **Computers:** Students can register for classes online. Administrative functions (other than registration) can be performed online.

CAMPUS LIFE

Environment: Rural. **Activities:** Choral groups, concert band, drama/theater, jazz band, marching band, music ensembles, musical theater, pep band, radio station, student government, student newspaper, yearbook. 80 registered organizations, 10 honor societies, 7 religious organizations. 5 fraternities, 6 sororities. **Athletics (Intercollegiate):** *Men:* baseball, basketball, cheerleading, cross-country, football, golf, rodeo, track/field (outdoor). *Women:* basketball, cheerleading, cross-country, rodeo, softball, tennis, track/field (outdoor), volleyball.

ADMISSIONS

Freshman Academic Profile: Average high school GPA 3.23. 38% in top 25% of high school class, 70% in top 50% of high school class. 99% from public high schools. ACT middle 50% range 17-23. Minimum paper TOEFL 500. **Basis for Candidate Selection:** *Very important factors considered include:* Class rank, rigor of secondary school record, standardized test scores. *Other factors considered include:* application essay, recommendation(s). **Freshman Admission Requirements:** High school diploma is required and GED is accepted. **Freshman Admission Statistics:** 1,417 applied, 100% admitted, 42% enrolled.

Transfer Admission Requirements: college transcript(s), statement of good standing from prior institution(s). Lowest grade transferable C. **General Admission Information:** Regular application deadline 8/27. Nonfall registration accepted. Admission may be deferred for a maximum of N/A. Credit offered for CEEB Advanced Placement tests.

COSTS AND FINANCIAL AID

Annual in-state tuition $4,260. Annual out-of-state tuition $6,450. Room and board $3,980. Required fees $630. Average book expense $1,000. **Required Forms and Deadlines:** FAFSA. **Notification of Awards:** Applicants will be notified of awards on a rolling basis beginning 4/15. **Types of Aid:** *Need-based scholarships/grants:* Federal Pell, SEOG, state scholarships/grants, private scholarships, the school's own gift aid. *Loans:* Subsidized Stafford, Unsubsidized Stafford, PLUS, Federal Perkins. *Student Employment:* Highest amount earned per year from on-campus jobs $4,900. **Financial Aid Statistics:** 65% freshmen, 93% undergrads receive need-based scholarship or grant aid. 92% freshmen, 58% undergrads receive non-need-based scholarship or grant aid. 80% freshmen, 82% undergrads receive need-based self-help aid. 0% freshmen, 0% undergrads receive athletic scholarships. 85% freshmen, 82% undergrads receive any aid. 61% undergrads borrow to pay for school. **Criteria for awarding institutional aid:** *Non-need-based:* academics, alumni affiliation, art, athletics, leadership, minority status, music/drama, state/district residency.

SOUTHERN CALIFORNIA INSTITUTE OF ARCHITECTURE

SCI-Arc Admissions Office, Los Angeles, CA 90013-1822
Phone: 213-356-5320 · **Financial Aid Phone:** 213-356-5346
E-mail: admissions@sciarc.edu
Fax: 213-613-2260 · **Website:** www.sciarc.edu

This private school was founded in 1972.

RATINGS

Admissions Selectivity Rating: 60*   Fire Safety Rating: 60*

STUDENTS AND FACULTY

Enrollment: 245. **Student Body:** 27% female, 73% male, 40% out-of-state, 20% international (45 countries represented). Asian 24%, African American 1%, Caucasian 30%, Hispanic 18%.
Retention and Graduation: 93% freshmen return for sophomore year. **Faculty:** 33 full-time faculty, 106% hold PhDs, 33% are are members of minority groups.

ACADEMICS

Degrees: bachelor's, master's. **Special Study Options:** internships, study abroad. **Career services:** Alumni network, internships.

FACILITIES

Housing: Special Academic Facilities/Equipment: SCI-Arc gallery, Wood/Metal Shop, Digital Fabrication shop **Computers:** Students can register for classes online.

CAMPUS LIFE

Environment: Metropolis. **Activities:** student government. **On-Campus Highlights:** SCI-Arc Gallery, Kappe Library, Wood/Metal Shop, Studios.

ADMISSIONS

Freshman Academic Profile: Minimum internet-based TOEFL 83. Minimum paper TOEFL 560. **Basis for Candidate Selection:** *Very important factors considered include:* application essay, academic GPA, recommendation(s), character/personal qualities, level of applicant's interest, talent/ability. *Important factors considered include:* rigor of secondary school record. *Other factors considered include:* standardized test scores, extracurricular activities, racial/ethnic status, volunteer work, work experience. **Freshman Admission Requirements:** High school diploma is required and GED is accepted. **Freshman Admission Statistics:** 70 applied, 91% admitted, 41% enrolled. **Transfer Admission Requirements:** college transcript(s), essay or personal statement, Lowest grade transferable C. **General Admission Information:** Application Fee $75. Regular application deadline 2/1. Regular notification 4/1. Nonfall registration not accepted. Admission may be deferred for a maximum of 1 year.

COSTS AND FINANCIAL AID

Required Forms and Deadlines: FAFSA, Institution's own financial aid form. **Types of Aid:** *Need-based scholarships/grants:* Federal Pell, SEOG, state scholarships/grants, the school's own gift aid. *Loans:* Subsidized Stafford, Unsubsidized Stafford, PLUS. *Student Employment:* Federal Work-Study

Program available. **Criteria for awarding institutional aid:** *Non-need-based:* academics, state/district residency.

SOUTHERN CONNECTICUT STATE UNIVERSITY

SCSU-Admissions House, New Haven, CT 06515-1202
Phone: 203-392-5644 · **CEEB Code:** 3662
Fax: 203-392-5727 · **Website:** www.southernct.edu

This public school was founded in 1893. It has a 168-acre campus.

RATINGS

Admissions Selectivity Rating: 72   Fire Safety Rating: 60*

STUDENTS AND FACULTY

Enrollment: 8,525. **Student Body:** 60% female, 40% male, 4% out-of-state, 0% international (39 countries represented). Asian 3%, African American 16%, Caucasian 62%, Hispanic 10%, Native American <1%
Retention and Graduation: 12% freshmen graduate within 4 years. 44% freshmen graduate within 6 years. 27% grads go on to further study within 1 year. **Faculty:** 403 full-time faculty, 90% hold PhDs, 45% are are members of minority groups, 14% are women.

ACADEMICS

Degrees: bachelor's, master's, post-master's certificate. **Classes:** Most classes have 20-29 students. Most lab/discussion sessions have 10-19 students. **Special Study Options:** Accelerated program, cooperative education program, cross-registration, distance learning, double major, exchange student program (domestic), external degree program, honors program, independent study, internships, liberal arts/career combination, student-designed major, study abroad, teacher certification program, Undergrads may take grad level classes Cooperative Education Programs: Arts, Business, Computer Science, Education, Health Professions, Humanities, Natural Science, Social/Behavioral Science, Technologies. Domestic Exchange Program(s): Exchange programs with other members of state university system. Foreign Exchange Program(s): Study abroad in England, France, and Spain. Evening division. **Disability Services:** Special programs offered to physically disabled students include note-taking services, reader services, tape recorders, tutors. **Career services:** career/job search classes, internships.

FACILITIES

Housing: Coed dorms, special housing for disabled students, apartments for single students, Freshmen have their own residence halls. Students must be 19 or older to live in upper-classman residence halls. 95% of campus accessible to physically disabled. **Special Academic Facilities/Equipment:** Art gallery, language lab, child development center, communication disorders center, planetarium and observatory, closed-circuit TV center.

CAMPUS LIFE

Environment: Village. **Activities:** Choral groups, concert band, drama/theater, literary magazine, marching band, music ensembles, pep band, radio station, student government, student newspaper, yearbook. 63 registered organizations, 3 religious organizations. 2 fraternities, 4 sororities. **Athletics (Intercollegiate):** *Men:* baseball, basketball, cross-country, football, golf, gymnastics, ice hockey, rugby, soccer, softball, swimming, track/field (outdoor), track/field (indoor), volleyball, wrestling. *Women:* basketball, cheerleading, cross-country, field hockey, golf, gymnastics, rugby, soccer, softball, swimming, track/field (outdoor), track/field (indoor), volleyball.

ADMISSIONS

Freshman Academic Profile: 5% in top 10% of high school class, 21% in top 25% of high school class, 60% in top 50% of high school class. 88% from public high schools. SAT Math middle 50% range 410-530. SAT Critical Reading middle 50% range 420-520. SAT Writing middle 50% range 420-530. ACT middle 50% range 17-22. Minimum paper TOEFL 525. **Basis for Candidate Selection:** *Very important factors considered include:* rigor of secondary school record. *Important factors considered include:* application essay, academic GPA, recommendation(s), standardized test scores. *Other factors considered include:* Class rank, alumni/ae relation, character/personal qualities, extracurricular activities, first generation, racial/ethnic status, talent/ability, volunteer work, work experience. **Freshman Admission Requirements:** High school diploma is required and GED is accepted. *Academic units required:* 4 English, 3 mathematics, 2 science, (1 science labs), 2 foreign language, 2 social studies, 2 history. **Freshman Admission Statistics:** 4,978 applied, 75% admitted, 37% enrolled. **Transfer Admission Requirements:** college transcript(s), essay or personal statement, statement of good standing from prior institution(s). Minimum college GPA of 2.0 required. Lowest grade transferable C-. **General Admission Information:** Application Fee $50. Regular application deadline

7/1. Notification on a rolling basis, beginning on or about 12/1. Nonfall registration accepted. Admission may be deferred for a maximum of 2 years. Credit offered for CEEB Advanced Placement tests.

COSTS AND FINANCIAL AID
Annual out-of-state tuition $15,137. Room and board $10,687. Required fees $4,256. Average book expense $1,400. **Required Forms and Deadlines:** FAFSA. **Types of Aid:** *Need-based scholarships/grants:* Federal Pell, SEOG, state scholarships/grants, the school's own gift aid. *Loans:* Subsidized Stafford, Unsubsidized Stafford, PLUS, Federal Perkins. *Student Employment:* Federal Work-Study Program available. Institutional employment available. Highest amount earned per year from on-campus jobs $1,400. Off-campus job opportunities are good. **Financial Aid Statistics:** 75% freshmen, 76% undergrads receive need-based scholarship or grant aid. 24% freshmen, 14% undergrads receive non-need-based scholarship or grant aid. 75% freshmen, 83% undergrads receive need-based self-help aid. 1% freshmen, 2% undergrads receive athletic scholarships. **Criteria for awarding institutional aid:** *Non-need-based:* academics, alumni affiliation, athletics.

SOUTHERN ILLINOIS UNIVERSITY CARBONDALE

Undergraduate Admissions, Mailcode 4710, Carbondale, IL 62901
Phone: 618-536-4405 • **Financial Aid Phone:** 618-453-4334
E-mail: admissions@siu.edu • **CEEB Code:** 1726
Website: www.siu.edu • **ACT Code:** 1144

This public school was founded in 1869. It has a 1136-acre campus.

RATINGS
Admissions Selectivity Rating: 77   **Fire Safety Rating:** 88

STUDENTS AND FACULTY
Enrollment: 13,171. **Student Body:** 46% female, 54% male, 15% out-of-state, 3% international (55 countries represented). Asian 2%, African American 20%, Caucasian 63%, Hispanic 8%, Native American <1%
Retention and Graduation: 68% freshmen return for sophomore year. 25% freshmen graduate within 4 years. 44% freshmen graduate within 6 years. **Faculty:** 829 full-time faculty, 79% hold PhDs, 37% are are members of minority groups, 21% are women. 30% of classes are taught by teaching assistants.

ACADEMICS
Degrees: associate, bachelor's, first professional, first professional certificate, master's, post-bachelor's certificate. **Classes:** Most classes have 10-19 students. Most lab/discussion sessions have 20-29 students. **Majors with Highest Enrollment:** Business Administration and Management; Elementary Education and Teaching; Health/Health Care Administration/Management. **Special Study Options:** cooperative education program, distance learning, double major, English as a Second Language (ESL), honors program, independent study, internships, student-designed major, study abroad, teacher certification program, ROTC: Army; Air Force. **Honors programs:** University Honors Program—to reward its best undergraduates for their high academic achievement, intended to give the Honors Student a taste of the private-college experience at a state-university price. Classes are small, intimate in character, and specially designed for University Honors Students by outstanding SIUC faculty. **Combined degree programs:** JD/MD, MA/MBA, MS/MBA, MBA/JD, MBA/MS, MSW/JD. **Disability Services:** Special programs offered to physically disabled students include note-taking services, reader services, tape recorders, tutors. **Career services:** alumni services, career/job search classes, career assessment, internships. Career services highlights include a job shadowing extern program. Business students typically comprise the largest number of participants of this campus-wide program, resulting in a 53+% job/internship offer rate.

FACILITIES
Housing: Coed dorms, special housing for disabled students, men's dorms, women's dorms, fraternity/sorority housing, apartments for married students, apartments for single students, Living Learning Communities; Residential College; General Living Learning; Freshman Interest Groups. 99% of campus accessible to physically disabled. **Special Academic Facilities/Equipment:** Art, natural history, and science museums, outdoor education center, center for crime studies, advertising and public relations agencies, child development lab, community human services center, airport training facility, archaeological research center, fisheries and wildlife research labs, coal research center, electron microscopy center. SIUC's two newest additions: Troutt-Wittmann Academic and Training Center; Student Health Center. **Computers:** 15% of classrooms, 100% of libraries, 95% of dining areas, 100% of student union, 70% of common outdoor areas have wireless network access. Students can register for classes online. Administrative functions (other than registration) can be performed online.

CAMPUS LIFE
Environment: Town. **Activities:** Choral groups, concert band, dance, drama/theater, jazz band, literary magazine, marching band, music ensembles, musical theater, opera, pep band, radio station, student government, student newspaper, student-run film society, symphony orchestra, television station, yearbook, Campus Ministries, International Student Organization. 408 registered organizations, 26 honor societies, 25 religious organizations. 20 fraternities, 8 sororities. **Athletics (Intercollegiate):** *Men:* baseball, basketball, cheerleading, cross-country, diving, football, golf, swimming, tennis, track/field (outdoor), track/field (indoor). *Women:* basketball, cheerleading, cross-country, diving, golf, softball, swimming, tennis, track/field (outdoor), track/field (indoor), volleyball. **On-Campus Highlights:** Morris Library, Student Center, Recreation Center, Campus Lake, Faner Museum. **Environmental Initiatives:** $4.0M campus-wide energy efficiency and conservation project to reduce purchased utilities. Vermicomposting facility to compost food waste from campus dining halls and turn it into fertilizer for campus plantings. The facility is heated by a clean-burning oil furnace fired with used motor oil from campus vehicles and is insulated with a soy-based foam product for energy conservation. New Transportation Education Center (currently in design phase) will be Certified under U.S. Green Building Council's LEED-NC 2.2 rating system.

ADMISSIONS
Freshman Academic Profile: Average high school GPA 2.91. 14% in top 10% of high school class, 34% in top 25% of high school class, 64% in top 50% of high school class. SAT Math middle 50% range 490-640. SAT Critical Reading middle 50% range 475-630. ACT middle 50% range 19-26. Minimum internet-based TOEFL 68. Minimum paper TOEFL 520. **Basis for Candidate Selection:** *Very important factors considered include:* Class rank, standardized test scores. *Important factors considered include:* academic GPA. *Other factors considered include:* recommendation(s), rigor of secondary school record, extracurricular activities, talent/ability, volunteer work, work experience. **Freshman Admission Requirements:** High school diploma is required and GED is accepted. *Academic units required:* 4 English, 3 mathematics, 3 science, 3 social studies, 2 academic electives. **Freshman Admission Statistics:** 10,877 applied, 82% admitted, 31% enrolled. **Transfer Admission Requirements:** college transcript(s), statement of good standing from prior institution(s). Minimum college GPA of 2.0 required. Lowest grade transferable D. **General Admission Information:** Application Fee $30. Notification on a rolling basis, beginning on or about 9/1. Nonfall registration accepted. Credit and/or placement offered for CEEB Advanced Placement tests.

COSTS AND FINANCIAL AID
Required Forms and Deadlines: FAFSA. **Notification of Awards:** Applicants will be notified of awards on a rolling basis beginning 3/21. **Types of Aid:** *Need-based scholarships/grants:* Federal Pell, SEOG, state scholarships/grants, private scholarships, the school's own gift aid. *Loans:* Direct Subsidized Stafford, Direct Unsubsidized Stafford, Direct PLUS, Federal Perkins, college/university loans from institutional funds. *Student Employment:* Federal Work-Study Program available. Institutional employment available. Highest amount earned per year from on-campus jobs $9,122. Off-campus job opportunities are good. **Financial Aid Statistics:** 70% freshmen receive need-based scholarship or grant aid. 39% freshmen, 28% undergrads receive non-need-based scholarship or grant aid. 84% freshmen, 83% undergrads receive need-based self-help aid. 3% freshmen, 3% undergrads receive athletic scholarships. 82% freshmen, 88% undergrads receive any aid. 70% undergrads borrow to pay for school. Average cumulative indebtedness $27,568. **Criteria for awarding institutional aid:** *Non-need-based:* academics, alumni affiliation, art, athletics, leadership, minority status, music/drama.

SOUTHERN ILLINOIS UNIVERSITY— EDWARDSVILLE

PO Box 1600, Edwardsville, IL 62026-1080
Phone: 618-650-3705 • **Financial Aid Phone:** 618-650-3880
E-mail: admissions@siue.edu • **CEEB Code:** 1759
Fax: 618-650-5013 • **Website:** www.siue.edu • **ACT Code:** 1147

This public school was founded in 1957. It has a 2660-acre campus.

RATINGS
Admissions Selectivity Rating: 75   **Fire Safety Rating:** 89

STUDENTS AND FACULTY
Enrollment: 11,371. **Student Body:** 53% female, 47% male, 1% international (48 countries represented). Asian 2%, African American 15%, Caucasian 74%, Hispanic 4%, Native American <1%

Retention and Graduation: 29% freshmen graduate within 4 years. 50% freshmen graduate within 6 years. **Faculty:** 623 full-time faculty, 81% hold PhDs, 49% are are members of minority groups, 20% are women. 3% of classes are taught by teaching assistants.

ACADEMICS

Degrees: bachelor's, first professional, first professional certificate, master's, post-bachelor's certificate, post-master's certificate. **Classes:** Most classes have 10-19 students. Most lab/discussion sessions have 10-19 students. **Majors with Highest Enrollment:** Business Administration and Management; Psychology; Registered Nursing/Registered Nurse. **Special Study Options:** Accelerated program, cooperative education program, cross-registration, distance learning, double major, English as a Second Language (ESL), honors program, independent study, internships, student-designed major, study abroad, teacher certification program, Independent Study; elementary and secondary teacher certificate programs in art, music, social studies, English,kinesiology, biology, chemistry, foreign languages, history, math, physics, speech communication. **Combined degree programs:** Econ and Finance; Chemistry; Biological Sciences. **Disability Services:** Special programs offered to physically disabled students include note-taking services, reader services, tape recorders, tutors. **Career services:** Alumni network, alumni services, career/job search classes, career assessment, internships, regional alumni. Career services highlights include the SIUE Co-op program, through which students work in professional assignments for employers throughout the U.S. and globally.

FACILITIES

Housing: Coed dorms, special housing for disabled students, fraternity/sorority housing, apartments for married students, apartments for single students, Focused Interest Communities. 100% of campus accessible to physically disabled. **Special Academic Facilities/Equipment:** Art gallery, anthropology museum, language lab, center for advanced manufacturing and production, technology commercialization center, electron microscope, psychomotorskills lab, new engineering building and lab. **Computers:** Administrative functions (other than registration) can be performed online.

CAMPUS LIFE

Environment: Village. **Activities:** Choral groups, concert band, dance, drama/theater, jazz band, literary magazine, music ensembles, musical theater, opera, pep band, radio station, student government, student newspaper, symphony orchestra, Campus Ministries. 140 registered organizations, 15 honor societies, 9 religious organizations. 10 fraternities, 7 sororities. **Athletics (Intercollegiate):** *Men:* baseball, basketball, cross-country, golf, soccer, tennis, track/field (outdoor), track/field (indoor), wrestling. *Women:* basketball, cross-country, golf, soccer, softball, tennis, track/field (outdoor), track/field (indoor), volleyball. **On-Campus Highlights:** Morris University Center, Starbucks Coffee, Auntie Anne's Pretzels, New School of Engineering Building, New School of Pharmacy Building, The SIUE campus sits on 2,660 acres of beautiful woodlands and lakes just 25 minutes from St. Louis, Missouri. Also, SIUE residence halls are among the newest in the state.

ADMISSIONS

Freshman Academic Profile: 19% in top 10% of high school class, 44.7% in top 25% of high school class, 77.8% in top 50% of high school class. N/A% from public high schools. SAT Math middle 50% range 480-570. SAT Critical Reading middle 50% range 440-600. SAT Writing middle 50% range 425-560. ACT middle 50% range 20-26. Minimum internet-based TOEFL 79. Minimum paper TOEFL 550. **Basis for Candidate Selection:** *Very important factors considered include:* Class rank, rigor of secondary school record, standardized test scores. **Freshman Admission Requirements:** High school diploma is required and GED is accepted. *Academic units required:* 4 English, 3 mathematics, 3 science, (3 science labs), 3 social studies, 2 academic electives. **Freshman Admission Statistics:** 7,594 applied, 87% admitted, 32% enrolled. **Transfer Admission Requirements:** college transcript(s), Minimum college GPA of 2 required. Lowest grade transferable D. **General Admission Information:** Application Fee $30. Regular application deadline 5/1. Notification on a rolling basis, beginning on or about 9/1. Nonfall registration accepted. Admission may be deferred for a maximum of 12 months. Credit and/or placement offered for CEEB Advanced Placement tests.

COSTS AND FINANCIAL AID

Annual out-of-state tuition $18,240. Room and board $8,531. Required fees $2,370. Average book expense $777. **Required Forms and Deadlines:** FAFSA. **Notification of Awards:** Applicants will be notified of awards on a rolling basis beginning 3/15. **Types of Aid:** *Need-based scholarships/grants:* Federal Pell, SEOG, state scholarships/grants, private scholarships, the school's own gift aid, Federal Nursing Scholarships., Presidential Scholars Program, Chancellor's Scholars Program, Johnetta Haley Scholarship Program, Provost Scholarship. *Loans:* Direct Subsidized Stafford, Direct Unsubsidized Stafford, Direct PLUS, Subsidized Stafford, Unsubsidized Stafford, PLUS, Federal Perkins, college/university loans from institutional funds, HPL. *Student Employment:* Highest amount earned per year from on-campus jobs $1,348. **Financial Aid Statistics:**

84% freshmen, 73% undergrads receive need-based scholarship or grant aid. 52% freshmen, 31% undergrads receive non-need-based scholarship or grant aid. 79% freshmen, 81% undergrads receive need-based self-help aid. 2% freshmen, 1% undergrads receive athletic scholarships. 75% freshmen, 67% undergrads receive any aid. Average cumulative indebtedness $30,209. **Criteria for awarding institutional aid:** *Non-need-based:* academics, art, athletics, leadership, minority status, music/drama.

SOUTHERN METHODIST UNIVERSITY

PO Box 750181, Dallas, TX 75275-0181
Phone: 214-768-2058 · **Financial Aid Phone:** 214-768-3417
E-mail: ugadmission@smu.edu · **CEEB Code:** 6660
Fax: 214-768-0103 · **Website:** www.smu.edu · **ACT Code:** 4171

This private school, affiliated with the Methodist Church, was founded in 1911. It has a 210-acre campus.

RATINGS

Admissions Selectivity Rating: 92   **Fire Safety Rating:** 96

STUDENTS AND FACULTY

Enrollment: 6,340. **Student Body:** 50% female, 50% male, 51% out-of-state, 7% international (101 countries represented). Asian 7%, African American 5%, Caucasian 66%, Hispanic 12%, Native American <1%
Retention and Graduation: 67% freshmen graduate within 4 years. 77% freshmen graduate within 6 years. **Faculty:** 736 full-time faculty, 84% hold PhDs, 39% are are members of minority groups, 19% are women.

ACADEMICS

Degrees: bachelor's, certificate, doctoral, master's, post-bachelor's certificate. **Classes:** Most classes have 10-19 students. Most lab/discussion sessions have 20-29 students. **Majors with Highest Enrollment:** Finance; Economics; Accounting. **Special Study Options:** Accelerated program, cooperative education program, distance learning, double major, English as a Second Language (ESL), exchange student program (domestic), honors program, independent study, internships, student-designed major, study abroad, teacher certification program. **Honors programs:** The University Honors Program is designed to prepare Honors students for a new millennium to ensure that they can cope with the challenges of rapid change while taking advantage of the possibilities such a volatile and versatile world presents. The BBA Honors Program, which is separate from the University Honors Program, is composed of special sections of courses in accounting, finance, statistics, operations management, marketing, and management. Advertising Honors Program: A student may apply for the Temerlin Advertising Institute Honors program after completion of his or her first semester as a declared Advertising major. **Combined degree programs:** BS/BA in Comp. Sci. and Music; 3-2 Bachelor's MBA. **Disability Services:** Special programs offered to physically disabled students include note-taking services, reader services, tape recorders, tutors. **Career services:** alumni services, career/job search classes, career assessment, internships.

FACILITIES

Housing: Coed dorms, fraternity/sorority housing, apartments for married students, apartments for single students, Wellness Housing, Theme Housing. 95% of campus accessible to physically disabled. **Special Academic Facilities/Equipment:** Art, natural history, and paleontology museums, southwest film/video archives, sculpture garden, performing arts theatres, pollen analysis and geothermal labs, electron microbe lab, microscopy lab, seismological observatory, institute of technology services, TV studio. **Computers:** 30% of classrooms, 100% of dorms, 100% of libraries, 100% of dining areas, 100% of student union, 10% of common outdoor areas have wireless network access. Students can register for classes online. Administrative functions (other than registration) can be performed online.

CAMPUS LIFE

Environment: Metropolis. **Activities:** Choral groups, concert band, dance, drama/theater, jazz band, literary magazine, marching band, music ensembles, musical theater, opera, pep band, radio station, student government, student newspaper, student-run film society, symphony orchestra, yearbook, Campus Ministries, International Student Organization. 180 registered organizations, 15 honor societies, 27 religious organizations. 15 fraternities, 13 sororities. **Athletics (Intercollegiate):** *Men:* basketball, diving, football, golf, soccer, swimming, tennis, volleyball, water polo. *Women:* basketball, crew/rowing, cross-country, diving, equestrian sports, golf, soccer, swimming, tennis, track/field (outdoor), volleyball, water polo. **On-Campus Highlights:** Gerald J Ford Stadium, Meadows Museum, Hughes Trigg Student Center, Dallas Hall, Fondren Library. **Environmental Initiatives:** Broad academic commitment: research from Geothermal Energy Lab has revealed widespread availability of green energy source. Geothermal Labs partnership with Google.org has resulted in sophisticated mapping of geothermal resources across North America. Lab hosts annual geothermal conference attended by the international community. Undergraduate and Graduate environmental degrees available through three portals: the Environmental Studies and Environmental Science programs in Dedman College of Science and Humanities, and the Environmental and Civil Engineering Department of the Lyle School of Engineering. 9 LEED Gold buildings: Embrey (engineering, first on-campus LEED building in Texas), Caruth (engineering), 7 casitas on SMU-in-Taos campus. 2 LEED-registered buildings: Simmons (education-expected to get LEED Gold) and Prothro (theology—expected to get LEED Silver). All new and major renovated buildings to be built to LEED Silver or comparable standard. Formal Sustainability Committee with wide-ranging commitment to education, outreach and campus sustainability best practices. Committee meets monthly, works with students, faculty and staff.

ADMISSIONS

Freshman Academic Profile: Average high school GPA 3.67. 46% in top 10% of high school class, 79% in top 25% of high school class, 95% in top 50% of high school class. 52% from public high schools. SAT Math middle 50% range 620-710. SAT Critical Reading middle 50% range 600-690. SAT Writing middle 50% range 600-695. ACT middle 50% range 28-31. Minimum internet-based TOEFL 80. Minimum paper TOEFL 550. **Basis for Candidate Selection:** *Very important factors considered include:* Class rank, application essay, academic GPA, recommendation(s), rigor of secondary school record, standardized test scores. *Important factors considered include:* character/personal qualities, extracurricular activities, talent/ability, volunteer work, work experience. *Other factors considered include:* alumni/ae relation, first generation, interview, level of applicant's interest. **Freshman Admission Requirements:** High school diploma is required and GED is not accepted. *Academic units required:* 4 English, 3 mathematics, 3 science, (2 science labs), 2 foreign language, 1 social studies, 2 history. **Freshman Admission Statistics:** 11,817 applied, 52% admitted, 24% enrolled. **Transfer Admission Requirements:** college transcript(s), essay or personal statement, Minimum college GPA of 2.7 required. Lowest grade transferable C-. **General Admission Information:** Application Fee $60. Regular application deadline 3/15. Notification on a rolling basis, beginning on or about 12/31. Nonfall registration accepted. Admission may be deferred for a maximum of 1 year. Credit and/or placement offered for CEEB Advanced Placement tests.

COSTS AND FINANCIAL AID

Average book expense $1,000. **Required Forms and Deadlines:** FAFSA, CSS/Financial Aid PROFILE, Noncustodial PROFILE. **Notification of Awards:** Applicants will be notified of awards on a rolling basis beginning 3/15. **Types of Aid:** *Need-based scholarships/grants:* Federal Pell, SEOG, state scholarships/grants, private scholarships, the school's own gift aid. *Loans:* Subsidized Stafford, Unsubsidized Stafford, PLUS, Federal Perkins, state loans, college/university loans from institutional funds. *Student Employment:* Off-campus job opportunities are good. **Financial Aid Statistics:** 69% freshmen, 75% undergrads receive need-based scholarship or grant aid. 75% freshmen, 64% undergrads receive non-need-based scholarship or grant aid. 74% freshmen, 80% undergrads receive need-based self-help aid. 5% freshmen, 5% undergrads receive athletic scholarships. 75% freshmen, 73% undergrads receive any aid. 42% undergrads borrow to pay for school. Average cumulative indebtedness $22,742. **Criteria for awarding institutional aid:** *Non-need-based:* academics, art, athletics, leadership, music/drama, religious affiliation, state/district residency.

SOUTHERN NEW HAMPSHIRE UNIVERSITY

2500 North River Road, Manchester, NH 03106-1045
Phone: 603-645-9611 · **Financial Aid Phone:** 603-645-9645
E-mail: admission@snhu.edu · **CEEB Code:** 3649
Fax: 603-645-9693 · **Website:** www.snhu.edu · **ACT Code:** 2514

This private school was founded in 1932. It has a 300-acre campus.

RATINGS

Admissions Selectivity Rating: 71   Fire Safety Rating: 95

STUDENTS AND FACULTY

Enrollment: 1,929. **Student Body:** 52% female, 48% male, 55% out-of-state, 5% international (79 countries represented). Asian 1%, African American 1%, Caucasian 75%, Hispanic 2%, Native American <1%
Retention and Graduation: 49% freshmen graduate within 4 years. 12% grads go on to further study within 1 year. **Faculty:** 120 full-time faculty, 76% hold PhDs, 38% are are members of minority groups, 12% are women. 0% of classes are taught by teaching assistants.

ACADEMICS

Degrees: associate, bachelor's, certificate, master's, post-bachelor's certificate, post-master's certificate. **Classes:** Most classes have 10-19 students. **Majors with Highest Enrollment:** Culinary Arts/Chef Training; Psychology; Business Administration and Management. **Special Study Options:** Accelerated program, cooperative education program, distance learning, double major, dual enrollment, English as a Second Language (ESL), honors program, independent study, internships, student-designed major, study abroad, teacher certification program, weekend college. **Honors programs:** Three-Year Honors Program (B.S. in Business Administration) and our traditional four-year honors program (available in conjunction with most majors) **Combined degree programs:** Three-Year Bachelor's Degree + 1-Year M.B.A. **Disability Services:** Special programs offered to physically disabled students include note-taking services, reader services, tape recorders, tutors. **Career services:** Alumni network, alumni services, career/job search classes, career assessment, internships. Career services highlights include an active internship program at the undergraduate and graduate level.

FACILITIES

Housing: Coed dorms, special housing for disabled students, apartments for single students, Wellness Housing, Theme Housing. 85% of campus accessible to physically disabled. **Special Academic Facilities/Equipment:** Art Gallery **Computers:** 100% of classrooms, 40% of dorms, 100% of libraries, 100% of dining areas, 100% of student union, have wireless network access. Students can register for classes online. Undergraduates are required to own a computer.

CAMPUS LIFE

Environment: City. **Activities:** Choral groups, concert band, dance, drama/theater, jazz band, literary magazine, musical theater, radio station, student government, student newspaper, television station, yearbook, Campus Ministries, International Student Organization, Model UN. 58 registered organizations, 7 honor societies, 1 religous organization. 3 fraternities, 3 sororities. **Athletics (Intercollegiate):** *Men:* baseball, basketball, cheerleading, cross-country, golf, ice hockey, lacrosse, soccer, tennis. *Women:* basketball, cheerleading, cross-country, lacrosse, soccer, softball, tennis, volleyball. **On-Campus Highlights:** Center for Financial Studies, Fitness Center / Athletic Complex, Robert Frost Hall (Academic Building), McIninch Art Gallery, Last Chapter Pub, In addition to our five most popular places on campus, we also have a gourmet restaurant on campus run by our culinary and hospitality students, a bakery and coffee shop. **Environmental Initiatives:** Renewable Energy Hedge from 2007-2022 based on 17,500 megawatt hours of wind power output with PPM Energy Inc. By a financial swap, the hedge will flat line SNHU energy budget, and 100% offset energy green house gas use in the voluntary market with RECs, and provide the wind developer a consistent stream of income to facilitate more wind construction. This represents a new sustainable model of utility cost control based on long-term agreements between energy users and renewable developers. The establishment of the SNHU School of Liberal Arts Bachelor of Arts in Environment, Ethics and Public Policy. This new degree program represents the effort by SNHU to provide an interdisciplinary approach to training the next generation of ecological leaders with a wide range of interests, backgrounds and skills, able to respond to the challenges posed by sustainability ion the 21st century. The development of campus sustainability energy plan based on development of initiatives for interconnected campus islands of sustainability. Under development are initiatives including use of sawdust for wood gasification for cogeneration units to supply electricity and heat; the use of geothermal systems based on innovative use of ground water near the Merrimack River for heat pumps; real time price control for optimization of energy use based on 5-minte ISO-NE price signals.

ADMISSIONS

Freshman Academic Profile: Average high school GPA 2.96. 88% from public high schools. SAT Math middle 50% range 440-540. SAT Critical Reading middle 50% range 440-520. SAT Writing middle 50% range 430-520. ACT middle 50% range 18-24. Minimum internet-based TOEFL 71. Minimum paper TOEFL 530. **Basis for Candidate Selection:** *Very important factors considered include:* academic GPA, rigor of secondary school record. *Important factors considered include:* application essay, recommendation(s), character/personal qualities, extracurricular activities, first generation, level of applicant's interest. *Other factors considered include:* Class rank, standardized test scores, alumni/ae relation, interview, talent/ability, volunteer work, work experience. **Freshman Admission Requirements:** High school diploma is required and GED is accepted. *Academic units required:* 4 English, (2 science labs). **Fresh-**

man **Admission Statistics:** 3,124 applied, 84% admitted, 18% enrolled. **Transfer Admission Requirements:** High school transcript, college transcript(s), essay or personal statement, Minimum college GPA of 2.50 required. Lowest grade transferable C-. **General Admission Information:** Application Fee $40. Nonfall registration accepted. Admission may be deferred for a maximum of 1 year. Credit and/or placement offered for CEEB Advanced Placement tests.

COSTS AND FINANCIAL AID

Required Forms and Deadlines: FAFSA. **Notification of Awards:** Applicants will be notified of awards on a rolling basis beginning 3/1. **Types of Aid:** *Need-based scholarships/grants:* Federal Pell, SEOG, state scholarships/grants, private scholarships, the school's own gift aid. *Loans:* Direct Subsidized Stafford, Direct Unsubsidized Stafford, Direct PLUS, Subsidized Stafford. *Student Employment:* Federal Work-Study Program available. Institutional employment available. Off-campus job opportunities are good. **Financial Aid Statistics:** 94% freshmen, 93% undergrads receive any aid. **Criteria for awarding institutional aid:** *Non-need-based:* academics, alumni affiliation, athletics, leadership, state/district residency.

SOUTHERN OREGON UNIVERSITY

Office of Admissions, Ashland, OR 97520-5032
Phone: 541-552-6411 · **Financial Aid Phone:** 541-552-6600
E-mail: admissions@sou.edu · **CEEB Code:** 4702
Fax: 541-552-8403 · **Website:** www.sou.edu · **ACT Code:** 3496

This public school was founded in 1926. It has a 175-acre campus.

RATINGS

Admissions Selectivity Rating: 70   Fire Safety Rating: 81

STUDENTS AND FACULTY

Enrollment: 4,120. **Student Body:** 57% female, 43% male, 34% out-of-state, 3% international (12 countries represented). Asian 2%, African American 3%, Caucasian 64%, Hispanic 10%, Native American 1%
Retention and Graduation: 23% freshmen graduate within 4 years. **Faculty:** 170 full-time faculty, 82% hold PhDs, 41% are are members of minority groups, 12% are women. 0% of classes are taught by teaching assistants.

ACADEMICS

Degrees: bachelor's, master's, post-bachelor's certificate. **Majors with Highest Enrollment:** Business Administration and Management; Psychology; Visual and Performing Arts. **Special Study Options:** Accelerated program, cooperative education program, cross-registration, distance learning, double major, dual enrollment, English as a Second Language (ESL), exchange student program (domestic), external degree program, honors program, independent study, internships, liberal arts/career combination, student-designed major, study abroad, teacher certification program, Undergrads may take grad level classes. Nursing programs with Oregon Health Sciences U. Exchange programs with Coll of the Redwoods, Coll of the Siskiyous, and Shasta Coll. Member of National Student Exchange(NSE). Exchange programs abroad in Korea(Dankook U) and Mexico(U of Guanajuato). Study abroad also in Asian, European, and South American countries. Concurrent enrollment with Rogue Community College. **Disability Services:** Special programs offered to physically disabled students include note-taking services, reader services, tape recorders, tutors. **Career services:** Alumni network, alumni services, career/job search classes, career assessment, internships, regional alumni.

FACILITIES

Housing: Coed dorms, special housing for disabled students, special housing for international students, apartments for married students, apartments for single students, Special quiet, substance free, nonsmoking, older students or freshman only residence halls. **Special Academic Facilities/Equipment:** Art and history museums, art galleries, on-campus preschool and kindergarten, National Guard armory, United States Wildlife Forensics Lab. **Computers:** Students can register for classes online. Administrative functions (other than registration) can be performed online.

CAMPUS LIFE

Environment: Village. **Activities:** Choral groups, concert band, dance, drama/theater, jazz band, literary magazine, music ensembles, musical theater, opera, pep band, radio station, student government, student newspaper, student-run film society, symphony orchestra, television station, International Student Organization. 52 registered organizations, 13 honor societies, 5 religious organizations. **Athletics (Intercollegiate):** *Men:* basketball, cross-country, football, track/field (outdoor), wrestling. *Women:* basketball, cross-country, soccer, softball, tennis, track/field (outdoor), volleyball. **On-Campus Highlights:** Hannon Library, Center for the Visual Arts, Student Union, Theatre Building,

Music Building. **Environmental Initiatives:** Through the student-initiated Green Energy Fee, SOU purchases Renewable Energy Certificates (RECs) to offset 100% of its electricity consumption and carbon offsets to offset 100% of its natural gas consumption. Among the 54 colleges and universities that are U. S. EPA Green Power Partners, SOU ranked #12 on the EPA's April 6, 2010 Top 20 College & University list. The Higher Education Center, jointly owned with Rogue Community College, received LEED Platinum certification in 2010, making it the first building in the Oregon University System to achieve the highest level of LEED certification. SOU has replaced two aging boilers in its Central Heat Plant with new boilers that can utilize biomass fuel.

ADMISSIONS

Freshman Academic Profile: Average high school GPA 3.31. 90% from public high schools. SAT Math middle 50% range 450-560. SAT Critical Reading middle 50% range 460-590. SAT Writing middle 50% range 430-550. ACT middle 50% range 20-25. Minimum paper TOEFL 520. **Basis for Candidate Selection:** *Very important factors considered include:* rigor of secondary school record, standardized test scores. *Other factors considered include:* application essay, recommendation(s), character/personal qualities, extracurricular activities, talent/ability, volunteer work, work experience. **Freshman Admission Requirements:** High school diploma is required and GED is accepted. *Academic units required:* 4 English, 3 mathematics, 2 science, 2 foreign language, 3 social studies. **Freshman Admission Statistics:** 2,209 applied, 93% admitted, 31% enrolled. **Transfer Admission Requirements:** college transcript(s), Minimum college GPA of 2.2 required. Lowest grade transferable D-. **General Admission Information:** Application Fee $50. Notification on a rolling basis, beginning on or about 9/1. Nonfall registration accepted. Admission may be deferred for a maximum of 1 year. Credit and/or placement offered for CEEB Advanced Placement tests.

COSTS AND FINANCIAL AID

Annual in-state tuition $6,307. Annual out-of-state tuition $19,883. Room and board $11,397. Required fees $1,413. Average book expense $960. **Required Forms and Deadlines:** FAFSA. **Notification of Awards:** Applicants will be notified of awards on a rolling basis beginning 4/1. **Types of Aid:** *Need-based scholarships/grants:* Federal Pell, SEOG, state scholarships/grants, private scholarships, the school's own gift aid. *Loans:* Direct Subsidized Stafford, Direct Unsubsidized Stafford, Direct PLUS, Federal Perkins, state loans, college/university loans from institutional funds. *Student Employment:* Federal Work-Study Program available. Institutional employment available. Off-campus job opportunities are excellent. **Financial Aid Statistics:** 83% freshmen, 85% undergrads receive need-based scholarship or grant aid. 6% freshmen, 3% undergrads receive non-need-based scholarship or grant aid. 88% freshmen, 90% undergrads receive need-based self-help aid. 2% freshmen, 2% undergrads receive athletic scholarships. 70% freshmen, 81% undergrads receive any aid. 88% undergrads borrow to pay for school. Average cumulative indebtedness $27,707. **Criteria for awarding institutional aid:** *Non-need-based:* academics, art, athletics, leadership, minority status, music/drama, state/district residency.

SOUTHERN POLYTECHNIC STATE UNIVERSITY

1100 South Marietta Parkway, Marietta, GA 30060-2896
Phone: 678-915-4188 · **Financial Aid Phone:** 678-915-7920
E-mail: admiss@spsu.edu · **CEEB Code:** 5626
Fax: 678-915-7292 · **Website:** http://www.spsu.edu/index.htm · **ACT Code:** 865

This public school was founded in 1948. It has a 198-acre campus.

RATINGS

Admissions Selectivity Rating: 78   Fire Safety Rating: 96

STUDENTS AND FACULTY

Enrollment: 5,324. **Student Body:** 18% female, 82% male, 2% out-of-state, 4% international (51 countries represented). Asian 6%, African American 22%, Caucasian 55%, Hispanic 8%, Native American <1%
Retention and Graduation: 7% freshmen graduate within 4 years. 37% freshmen graduate within 6 years. **Faculty:** 219 full-time faculty, 71% hold PhDs, 32% are are members of minority groups, 29% are women. 0% of classes are taught by teaching assistants.

ACADEMICS

Degrees: associate, bachelor's, certificate, master's, post-bachelor's certificate. **Classes:** Most classes have 20-29 students. Most lab/discussion sessions have 10-19 students. **Special Study Options:** cooperative education program, cross-registration, distance learning, double major, dual enrollment, honors program, independent study, internships, study abroad. **Honors programs:** The SPSU

Honors Program provides academically talented students the opportunity to develop their talents and skills in an expanded and enriched curriculum. It features seminar-size classes that demand intellectual rigor. The program provides students with a community of peers and ample opportunity for social interaction within the peer group and with Honors faculty. Students work closely with faculty and have opportunities to expand their learning through independent study, special projects, and research. **Disability Services:** Special programs offered to physically disabled students include note-taking services, reader services, tape recorders, tutors. **Career services:** alumni services, career/job search classes, career assessment, internships. Career services highlights include our co-op and internship programs. Industry actually seeks our students and value them greatly.

FACILITIES

Housing: Coed dorms, special housing for disabled students, men's dorms, apartments for single students. 100% of campus accessible to physically disabled. **Computers:** 100% of classrooms, 100% of libraries, 100% of dining areas, 100% of student union, 60% of common outdoor areas have wireless network access. Students can register for classes online. Administrative functions (other than registration) can be performed online.

CAMPUS LIFE

Environment: City. **Activities:** Choral groups, jazz band, pep band, radio station, student government, student newspaper, Campus Ministries, International Student Organization. 87 registered organizations, 3 honor societies, 8 fraternities, 3 sororities. **Athletics (Intercollegiate):** *Men:* baseball, basketball, cheerleading, soccer. *Women:* basketball, cheerleading. **On-Campus Highlights:** Student Activities Center, Health and Wellness Center, Library, Gym, Administration Building. **Environmental Initiatives:** Transportation Master Plan to reduce SOVs. Commitment to build all new and renovated buildings to LEED silver certification. Reducing the university's carbon footprint by using EMS, green building materials, and voluntary recycling.

ADMISSIONS

Freshman Academic Profile: Average high school GPA 3.28. 12.35% in top 10% of high school class, 41.79% in top 25% of high school class, 78.65% in top 50% of high school class. SAT Math middle 50% range 540-635. SAT Critical Reading middle 50% range 500-600. SAT Writing middle 50% range 470-570. ACT middle 50% range 21-26. Minimum internet-based TOEFL 79. Minimum paper TOEFL 550. **Basis for Candidate Selection:** *Very important factors considered include:* academic GPA, rigor of secondary school record, standardized test scores. **Freshman Admission Requirements:** High school diploma is required and GED is not accepted. *Academic units required:* 4 English, 4 mathematics, 3 science, (2 science labs), 2 foreign language, 3 social studies, 2 academic electives. **Freshman Admission Statistics:** 1,535 applied, 79% admitted, 65% enrolled. **Transfer Admission Requirements:** college transcript(s), Minimum college GPA of 2.0 required. Lowest grade transferable C. **General Admission Information:** Application Fee $20. Regular application deadline 8/1. Notification on a rolling basis, beginning on or about 9/1. Nonfall registration accepted. Admission may be deferred for a maximum of 1 term. Credit and/or placement offered for CEEB Advanced Placement tests.

COSTS AND FINANCIAL AID

Annual in-state tuition $5,256. Annual out-of-state tuition $18,704. Room and board $7,280. Required fees $1,422. Average book expense $1,700. **Required Forms and Deadlines:** FAFSA. **Notification of Awards:** Applicants will be notified of awards on a rolling basis beginning 6/1. **Types of Aid:** *Need-based scholarships/grants:* Federal Pell, SEOG, state scholarships/grants, private scholarships, the school's own gift aid. *Loans:* Subsidized Stafford, Unsubsidized Stafford, PLUS, state loans. *Student Employment:* Federal Work-Study Program available. Institutional employment available. Off-campus job opportunities are good. **Financial Aid Statistics:** 45% freshmen, 56% undergrads receive need-based scholarship or grant aid. 71% freshmen, 34% undergrads receive non-need-based scholarship or grant aid. 57% freshmen, 68% undergrads receive need-based self-help aid. 1% freshmen, 1% undergrads receive athletic scholarships. 93% freshmen, 77% undergrads receive any aid. 61% undergrads borrow to pay for school. Average cumulative indebtedness $6,927. **Criteria for awarding institutional aid:** *Non-need-based:* academics, athletics.

SOUTHERN UNIVERSITY AND A&M COLLEGE

P.O. Box 9901, Baton Rouge, LA 70813
Phone: 225-771-2430 • **Financial Aid Phone:** 225-771-2790
E-mail: admit@subr.edu • **CEEB Code:** 6663
Fax: 225-771-2500 • **Website:** subr.edu • **ACT Code:** 1610

This public school was founded in 1880. It has a 884-acre campus.

RATINGS

Admissions Selectivity Rating: 72   Fire Safety Rating: 71

STUDENTS AND FACULTY

Enrollment: 6,830. **Student Body:** 61% female, 39% male, 19% out-of-state, 2% international (48 countries represented). Asian 0%, African American 96%, Caucasian 3%, Hispanic 0%, Native American <1%
Retention and Graduation: 65% freshmen return for sophomore year. 7% freshmen graduate within 4 years. 29% freshmen graduate within 6 years. 16% grads go on to further study within 1 year. 15% grads pursue arts and sciences degrees. 1% grads pursue law degrees. **Faculty:** 405 full-time faculty, 66% hold PhDs, 47% are are members of minority groups, 85% are women. 0% of classes are taught by teaching assistants.

ACADEMICS

Degrees: associate, bachelor's, master's, post-master's certificate. **Classes:** Most classes have 20-29 students. Most lab/discussion sessions have 10-19 students. **Majors with Highest Enrollment:** Biology/Biological Sciences; Registered Nursing/Registered Nurse; Business Administration and Management. **Special Study Options:** cooperative education program, cross-registration, distance learning, double major, dual enrollment, exchange student program (domestic), honors program, independent study, internships, study abroad, teacher certification program, weekend college, Undergrads may take grad level classes. Cooperative Education Programs: Engineering Combined Degree Programs: Dual degree programs with Jackson State U and Xavier U. **Honors programs:** The Honors College provides an enhances educational experience for students who have a history of strong academic achievement and who have demonstrated exceptional creativity or talent. The College also provides cultural and intellectual opportunities that are designed to motivae students to perform at the highest level of excellence that they are capable of and through which they may become knowledgeable and effective leaders. **Disability Services:** Special programs offered to physically disabled students include note-taking services, tape recorders, tutors. **Career services:** career/job search classes, internships. Career services highlights include the 3.0 credit hour co-op education course.

FACILITIES

Housing: special housing for disabled students, men's dorms, women's dorms. 100% of campus accessible to physically disabled. **Special Academic Facilities/Equipment:** Jazz institute, Southern Museum of Art. **Computers:** 100% of classrooms, 20% of dorms, 100% of libraries, 50% of dining areas, 90% of student union, 25% of common outdoor areas have wireless network access. Students can register for classes online. Administrative functions (other than registration) can be performed online.

CAMPUS LIFE

Environment: Metropolis. **Activities:** Choral groups, concert band, dance, drama/theater, jazz band, literary magazine, marching band, music ensembles, musical theater, pep band, student government, student newspaper, yearbook. 88 registered organizations, 11 honor societies, 6 religious organizations. 4 fraternities, 4 sororities. **Athletics (Intercollegiate):** *Men:* baseball, basketball, cross-country, football, golf, tennis, track/field (outdoor). *Women:* basketball, cross-country, golf, softball, tennis, track/field (outdoor), volleyball. **On-Campus Highlights:** SUBR Museum of Art, Smith—Brown Student Union, Site of the original Red Stick for Baton, Bluff over the Mississippi River **Environmental Initiatives:** MS4-Stormwater Permit with the Parish of East Baton Rouge; Full-time Environmental, Safety and Health Director; Storm Water Plan (Debris Management).

ADMISSIONS

Freshman Academic Profile: Average high school GPA 2.8. 3% in top 10% of high school class, 13% in top 25% of high school class, 40% in top 50% of high school class. SAT Math middle 50% range 380-460. ACT middle 50% range 15-18. **Basis for Candidate Selection:** *Very important factors considered include:* Class rank, academic GPA, rigor of secondary school record, standardized test scores. *Other factors considered include:* talent/ability. **Freshman Admission Requirements:** High school diploma is required and GED is accepted. *Academic units required:* 4 English, 3 mathematics, 3 science, 2 foreign language, 2 social studies, 1 history, 1 Computer Science, Arts (1.5 credits). **Freshman Admission Statistics:** 2,179 applied, 56% admitted, 91% enrolled. **Transfer Admission Requirements:** High school transcript, college transcript(s), standardized test scores, statement of good standing from prior institution(s). Minimum college GPA of 2.0 required. Lowest grade transferable C. **General Admission Information:** Application Fee $20. Regular application deadline 7/1. Nonfall registration accepted. Admission may be deferred for a maximum of 2 semesters. Credit offered for CEEB Advanced Placement tests.

COSTS AND FINANCIAL AID

Annual in-state tuition $3,666. Annual out-of-state tuition $9,458. Room and board $5,784. Required fees $0. Average book expense $1,200. **Required Forms and Deadlines:** FAFSA, Institution's own financial aid form. **Notification of Awards:** Applicants will be notified of awards on a rolling basis beginning 6/30. **Types of Aid:** *Need-based scholarships/grants:* Federal Pell, SEOG, state scholarships/grants, private scholarships, the school's own gift aid. *Loans:* Direct Subsidized Stafford, Direct Unsubsidized Stafford, Direct PLUS, Subsidized Stafford, Unsubsidized Stafford, PLUS, college/university loans from institutional fundsTOPS TH Harris LEAP. *Student Employment:* Federal Work-Study Program available. Institutional employment available. Highest amount earned per year from on-campus jobs $1,000. Off-campus job opportunities are fair. **Financial Aid Statistics:** 80% freshmen, 77% undergrads receive need-based scholarship or grant aid. 21% freshmen, 18% undergrads receive non-need-based scholarship or grant aid. 79% freshmen, 87% undergrads receive need-based self-help aid. 5% freshmen, 3% undergrads receive athletic scholarships. 89% freshmen, 85% undergrads receive any aid. 85% undergrads borrow to pay for school. Average cumulative indebtedness $27,000. **Criteria for awarding institutional aid:** *Non-need-based:* academics, athletics.

SOUTHERN UTAH UNIVERSITY

S. Utah University, 351 W University Bvd, Cedar City, UT 84720
Phone: 435-586-7740 · **Financial Aid Phone:** 435-586-7735
E-mail: adminfo@suu.edu · **CEEB Code:** 4092
Fax: 435-865-8223 · **Website:** www.suu.edu · **ACT Code:** 4271

This public school was founded in 1897. It has a 113-acre campus.

RATINGS

Admissions Selectivity Rating: 83   Fire Safety Rating: 60*

STUDENTS AND FACULTY

Enrollment: 5,514. **Student Body:** 53% female, 47% male, 20% out-of-state, 5% international (26 countries represented). Asian 1%, African American 2%, Caucasian 79%, Hispanic 5%, Native American 1%
Retention and Graduation: 20% freshmen graduate within 4 years. 38% freshmen graduate within 6 years. **Faculty:** 281 full-time faculty, 69% hold PhDs, 33% are are members of minority groups, 7% are women. 0% of classes are taught by teaching assistants.

ACADEMICS

Degrees: associate, bachelor's, certificate, diploma, master's, terminal associate, transfer associate. **Classes:** Most classes have 20-29 students. Most lab/discussion sessions have 20-29 students. **Majors with Highest Enrollment:** General Studies; Elementary Education and Teaching; Physical Education Teaching and Coaching. **Special Study Options:** cooperative education program, distance learning, double major, English as a Second Language (ESL), honors program, independent study, internships, liberal arts/career combination, teacher certification program, weekend college. **Disability Services:** Special programs offered to physically disabled students include reader services, tape recorders, tutors. **Career services:** alumni services, career/job search classes, career assessment, internships.

FACILITIES

Housing: Coed dorms, special housing for disabled students, men's dorms, special housing for international students, women's dorms, fraternity/sorority housing, apartments for single students.

CAMPUS LIFE

Environment: Village. **Activities:** Choral groups, concert band, dance, drama/theater, jazz band, literary magazine, marching band, music ensembles, musical theater, opera, pep band, radio station, student government, student newspaper, symphony orchestra, television station, yearbook. **Athletics (Intercollegiate):** *Men:* baseball, basketball, cross-country, football, golf, track/field (outdoor). *Women:* basketball, cross-country, gymnastics, softball, tennis, track/field (outdoor).

ADMISSIONS

Freshman Academic Profile: Average high school GPA 3.4. 17.6% in top 10% of high school class, 42.7% in top 25% of high school class, 71.6% in top 50% of high school class. SAT Math middle 50% range 450-570. SAT Critical

Reading middle 50% range 460-570. SAT Writing middle 50% range 440-550. ACT middle 50% range 20-26. Minimum internet-based TOEFL 71. Minimum paper TOEFL 525. **Basis for Candidate Selection:** *Very important factors considered include:* academic GPA, standardized test scores. *Other factors considered include:* first generation, racial/ethnic status. **Freshman Admission Requirements:** High school diploma is required and GED is accepted. **Freshman Admission Statistics:** 8,268 applied, 61% admitted, 24% enrolled. **Transfer Admission Requirements:** college transcript(s), minimum college GPA of 2.25 required. Lowest grade transferable D. **General Admission Information:** Application Fee $40. Nonfall registration accepted. Credit and/or placement offered for CEEB Advanced Placement tests.

COSTS AND FINANCIAL AID

Annual in-state tuition $5,416. Annual out-of-state tuition $17,874. Room and board $6,890. Required fees $722. Average book expense $1,600. **Required Forms and Deadlines:** FAFSA. **Notification of Awards:** Applicants will be notified of awards on a rolling basis beginning 11/1. **Types of Aid:** *Need-based scholarships/grants:* Federal Pell, SEOG, state scholarships/grants, private scholarships, the school's own gift aid. *Loans:* Subsidized Stafford, Unsubsidized Stafford, PLUS, Federal Perkins. *Student Employment:* Federal Work-Study Program available. Institutional employment available. Highest amount earned per year from on-campus jobs $2,000. Off-campus job opportunities are good. **Financial Aid Statistics:** 98% freshmen, 97% undergrads receive need-based scholarship or grant aid. 37% freshmen, 18% undergrads receive non-need-based scholarship or grant aid. 53% freshmen, 59% undergrads receive need-based self-help aid. 4% freshmen, 5% undergrads receive athletic scholarships. 53% undergrads borrow to pay for school. Average cumulative indebtedness $14,425. **Criteria for awarding institutional aid:** *Non-need-based:* academics, alumni affiliation, art, athletics, job skills, leadership, minority status, music/drama, state/district residency.

SOUTHERN VERMONT COLLEGE

982 Mansion Drive, Bennington, VT 5201
Phone: 802-447-6304 · **Financial Aid Phone:** 800-660-3561
E-mail: admis@svc.edu · **CEEB Code:** 3796
Fax: 802-447-4695 · **Website:** www.svc.edu · **ACT Code:** 4310

This private school was founded in 1974. It has a 371-acre campus.

RATINGS

Admissions Selectivity Rating: 72   Fire Safety Rating: 60*

STUDENTS AND FACULTY

Enrollment: 464. **Student Body:** 64% female, 36% male, 66% out-of-state. Native American <1%
Retention and Graduation: 61% freshmen return for sophomore year. **Faculty:** 16 full-time faculty, 25% hold PhDs, 44% are are members of minority groups, 0% are women. 0% of classes are taught by teaching assistants.

ACADEMICS

Degrees: associate, bachelor's, terminal associate, transfer associate. **Special Study Options:** Accelerated program, cooperative education program, distance learning, double major, dual enrollment, honors program, independent study, internships, liberal arts/career combination, student-designed major, study abroad. **Disability Services:** Special programs offered to physically disabled students include note-taking services, tape recorders, tutors. **Career services:** Alumni network, alumni services, career/job search classes, career assessment, internships.

FACILITIES

Housing: Coed dorms, Quiet, substance-free and non-smoking, Freshmen and upper-classmen residence halls. 60% of campus accessible to physically disabled. **Special Academic Facilities/Equipment:** Mountaineers Field House and Fitness Center, Apartment style Resident Halls, courtyard Dining Hall, Student Center, Everett Mansion.

CAMPUS LIFE

Environment: Rural. **Activities:** drama/theater, literary magazine, music ensembles, radio station, student government, student newspaper, yearbook. 14 registered organizations, 1 honor society. **Athletics (Intercollegiate):** *Men:* baseball, basketball, cross-country, rugby, soccer, volleyball. *Women:* basketball, cross-country, rugby, soccer, softball, volleyball.

ADMISSIONS

Freshman Academic Profile: Average high school GPA 2.63. 0% in top 10% of high school class, 5% in top 25% of high school class, 35% in top 50% of high school class. 85% from public high schools. SAT Math middle 50% range 390-

490. SAT Critical Reading middle 50% range 420-510. Minimum paper TOEFL 500. **Basis for Candidate Selection:** *Very important factors considered include:* application essay, recommendation(s), rigor of secondary school record, interview. *Important factors considered include:* standardized test scores, character/personal qualities, extracurricular activities, volunteer work. *Other factors considered include:* Class rank, work experience. **Freshman Admission Requirements:** High school diploma is required and GED is accepted. *Academic units required:* 4 English, 2 mathematics. **Freshman Admission Statistics:** 373 applied, 71% admitted, 37% enrolled. **Transfer Admission Requirements:** High school transcript, college transcript(s), essay or personal statement, Minimum college GPA of 2.0 required. Lowest grade transferable C. **General Admission Information:** Application Fee $30. Notification on a rolling basis, beginning on or about 12/1. Nonfall registration accepted. Admission may be deferred for a maximum of 1 year. Credit offered for CEEB Advanced Placement tests.

COSTS AND FINANCIAL AID
Annual tuition $14,374. Room and board $6,948. Required fees $300. Average book expense $500. **Required Forms and Deadlines:** FAFSA, Institution's own financial aid form. **Notification of Awards:** Applicants will be notified of awards on or about 3/1. **Types of Aid:** *Need-based scholarships/grants:* Federal Pell, SEOG, state scholarships/grants, private scholarships, the school's own gift aid, Southern Vermont College Opportunity Grant Everett Scholarship Leadership Scholarship Vermont Resident Scholarship TRIO Scholarship. *Loans:* Direct Subsidized Stafford, Direct Unsubsidized Stafford, Direct PLUS. *Student Employment:* Federal Work-Study Program available. Off-campus job opportunities are good. **Financial Aid Statistics:** 89% freshmen, 90% undergrads receive need-based scholarship or grant aid. 0% freshmen, 0% undergrads receive non-need-based scholarship or grant aid. 94% freshmen, 94% undergrads receive need-based self-help aid. 0% freshmen, 0% undergrads receive athletic scholarships. 75% freshmen, 75% undergrads receive any aid. **Criteria for awarding institutional aid:** *Non-need-based:* academics, leadership.

SOUTHERN WESLEYAN UNIVERSITY

Wesleyan Drive, Central, SC 29630-1020
Phone: 864-644-5550 • **Financial Aid Phone:** 864-644-5500
E-mail: admissions@swu.edu • **CEEB Code:** 5896
Fax: 864-644-5972 • **Website:** www.swu.edu • **ACT Code:** 3837

This private school, affiliated with the Wesleyan Church, was founded in 1906. It has a 330-acre campus.

RATINGS
Admissions Selectivity Rating: 73   **Fire Safety Rating:** 70

STUDENTS AND FACULTY
Enrollment: 1,444. **Student Body:** 60% female, 40% male, 28% out-of-state, 1% international (9 countries represented). Asian 0%, African American 27%, Caucasian 61%, Hispanic 2%, Native American 1%
Retention and Graduation: 70% freshmen return for sophomore year. 33% freshmen graduate within 4 years. 39% freshmen graduate within 6 years. **Faculty:** 58 full-time faculty, 72% hold PhDs, 31% are are members of minority groups, 12% are women. 0% of classes are taught by teaching assistants.

ACADEMICS
Degrees: associate, bachelor's, master's. **Classes:** Most classes have 10-19 students. Most lab/discussion sessions have 20-29 students. **Majors with Highest Enrollment:** Elementary Education and Teaching; Religion/Religious Studies; Business/Commerce. **Special Study Options:** cross-registration, double major, dual enrollment, English as a Second Language (ESL), honors program, independent study, internships, student-designed major, study abroad, teacher certification program. **Honors programs:** The honors program consists of specialized coursework, non-credit academic experiences, and service opportunities. Honors students must complete a research-based Honors Major Project in their Junior or Senior years. **Disability Services:** Special programs offered to physically disabled students include note-taking services, reader services, tape recorders, tutors. **Career services:** career/job search classes, career assessment, internships. Career services highlights include career assessment.

FACILITIES
Housing: Coed dorms, special housing for disabled students, women's dorms, apartments for single students. 90% of campus accessible to physically disabled. **Special Academic Facilities/Equipment:** Freedom's Hill Historic Site, Clayton Genealogical Research library, Electron Microscope lab. **Computers:** 100% of classrooms, 50% of dorms, 100% of libraries, 100% of dining areas, 100% of student union, 25% of common outdoor areas have wireless network

access. Students can register for classes online. Administrative functions (other than registration) can be performed online.

CAMPUS LIFE
Environment: Town. **Activities:** Choral groups, concert band, drama/theater, jazz band, literary magazine, music ensembles, musical theater, student government, yearbook, Campus Ministries. 12 registered organizations, 2 honor societies, 3 religious organizations. **Athletics (Intercollegiate):** *Men:* baseball, basketball, cross-country, golf, soccer. *Women:* basketball, cross-country, soccer, softball, volleyball. **On-Campus Highlights:** Jennings Campus Center, Java City Coffee Shop, Historic Tysinger Gymnasium, Student Apartment Complex. **Environmental Initiatives:** Voluntary recycling of paper and plastic in residence halls and academic buildings. Materials are collected by the city.

ADMISSIONS
Freshman Academic Profile: Average high school GPA 3.5. 13% in top 10% of high school class, 34% in top 25% of high school class, 75% in top 50% of high school class. SAT Math middle 50% range 445-550. SAT Critical Reading middle 50% range 430-540. SAT Writing middle 50% range 420-520. ACT middle 50% range 18-22. Minimum paper TOEFL 500. **Basis for Candidate Selection:** *Very important factors considered include:* academic GPA, standardized test scores. *Other factors considered include:* Class rank, rigor of secondary school record, character/personal qualities, religious affiliation/commitment. **Freshman Admission Requirements:** High school diploma is required and GED is accepted. *Academic units required:* 4 English, 2 mathematics, 2 science, 2 social studies. **Transfer Admission Requirements:** college transcript(s), Minimum college GPA of 2.0 required. Lowest grade transferable C. **General Admission Information:** Application Fee $25. Regular application deadline 8/1. Nonfall registration accepted. Admission may be deferred for a maximum of 1 semester. Credit and/or placement offered for CEEB Advanced Placement tests.

COSTS AND FINANCIAL AID
Annual tuition $19,950. Room and board $8,410. Required fees $600. Average book expense $1,020. **Required Forms and Deadlines:** FAFSA, Institution's own financial aid form. **Notification of Awards:** Applicants will be notified of awards on a rolling basis beginning 2/1. **Types of Aid:** *Need-based scholarships/grants:* Federal Pell, SEOG, state scholarships/grants, private scholarships, the school's own gift aid. *Loans:* Subsidized Stafford, Unsubsidized Stafford, PLUS, Federal Perkins. *Student Employment:* Federal Work-Study Program available. Institutional employment available. Off-campus job opportunities are good. **Financial Aid Statistics:** 100% freshmen, 91% undergrads receive need-based scholarship or grant aid. 16% freshmen, 8% undergrads receive non-need-based scholarship or grant aid. 73% freshmen, 80% undergrads receive need-based self-help aid. 5% freshmen, 2% undergrads receive athletic scholarships. 100% freshmen, 99% undergrads receive any aid. 81% undergrads borrow to pay for school. Average cumulative indebtedness $24,059. **Criteria for awarding institutional aid:** *Non-need-based:* academics, athletics, music/drama, religious affiliation.

SOUTHWEST BAPTIST UNIVERSITY

1600 University Avenue, Bolivar, MO 65613-2597
Phone: 417-328-1810 • **Financial Aid Phone:** 417-328-1823
E-mail: admitme@sbuniv.edu • **CEEB Code:** 6664
Fax: 417-328-1808 • **ACT Code:** 2368

This private school, affiliated with the Southern Baptist Church, was founded in 1878. It has a 180-acre campus.

RATINGS
Admissions Selectivity Rating: 77   **Fire Safety Rating:** 70

STUDENTS AND FACULTY
Enrollment: 2,646. **Student Body:** 66% female, 34% male, 29% out-of-state, 1% international (16 countries represented). Asian 1%, African American 4%, Caucasian 86%, Hispanic 1%, Native American 1%
Retention and Graduation: 70% freshmen return for sophomore year. 38% freshmen graduate within 4 years. 48% freshmen graduate within 6 years. **Faculty:** 116 full-time faculty, 59% hold PhDs, 41% are are members of minority groups, 2% are women. 0% of classes are taught by teaching assistants.

ACADEMICS
Degrees: associate, bachelor's, certificate, master's, post-master's certificate. **Classes:** Most classes have fewer than 10 students. Most lab/discussion sessions have 10-19 students. **Majors with Highest Enrollment:** Elementary Education and Teaching; Psychology; Business Administration and Management. **Special Study Options:** cooperative education program, distance learning,

double major, dual enrollment, exchange student program (domestic), honors program, independent study, internships, student-designed major, study abroad, teacher certification program. **Honors programs:** Our academic honors program consists of the following components: academics, servant leadership, intercultural experiences, spiritual growth, and enrichment opportunities. **Disability Services:** Special programs offered to physically disabled students include note-taking services, reader services, tutors. **Career services:** career/job search classes, career assessment.

FACILITIES

Housing: special housing for disabled students, men's dorms, women's dorms, apartments for single students. 95% of campus accessible to physically disabled. **Special Academic Facilities/Equipment:** The Driskell Art Gallery, Jester Learning and Performance Center, Meyer Wellness and Sports Center. **Computers:** 100% of classrooms, 100% of dorms, 100% of libraries, 100% of dining areas, 100% of student union, 40% of common outdoor areas have wireless network access. Administrative functions (other than registration) can be performed online.

CAMPUS LIFE

Environment: Village. **Activities:** Choral groups, concert band, drama/theater, jazz band, music ensembles, musical theater, opera, pep band, student government, student newspaper, symphony orchestra, yearbook, Campus Ministries. 34 registered organizations, 8 honor societies, 10 religious organizations. **Athletics (Intercollegiate): Men:** baseball, basketball, cheerleading, cross-country, football, golf, tennis, track/field (outdoor), track/field (indoor). *Women:* basketball, cheerleading, cross-country, soccer, softball, tennis, track/field (outdoor), track/field (indoor), volleyball. **On-Campus Highlights:** Meyer Wellness and Sports Center, Jester Learning and Performance Center, Felix Goodson Student Union, Harriet K. Hutchens Library, Plaster Stadium.

ADMISSIONS

Freshman Academic Profile: Average high school GPA 3.47. 22% in top 10% of high school class, 41% in top 25% of high school class, 67% in top 50% of high school class. SAT Math middle 50% range 450-600. SAT Critical Reading middle 50% range 410-560. ACT middle 50% range 20-26. Minimum paper TOEFL 550. **Basis for Candidate Selection:** *Very important factors considered include:* Class rank, academic GPA, standardized test scores. *Important factors considered include:* application essay, recommendation(s), rigor of secondary school record. *Other factors considered include:* character/personal qualities, interview, talent/ability. **Freshman Admission Requirements:** High school diploma is required and GED is accepted. **Freshman Admission Statistics:** 1,617 applied, 92% admitted, 31% enrolled. **Transfer Admission Requirements:** High school transcript, college transcript, standardized test scores, Minimum college GPA of 2.0 required. Lowest grade transferable D. **General Admission Information:** Application Fee $30. Notification on a rolling basis, beginning on or about 9/1. Nonfall registration accepted. Admission may be deferred for a maximum of 1 year. Credit and/or placement offered for CEEB Advanced Placement tests.

COSTS AND FINANCIAL AID

Annual tuition $16,500. Room and board $5,720. Required fees $780. Average book expense $1,000. **Required Forms and Deadlines:** FAFSA, Institution's own financial aid form. **Notification of Awards:** Applicants will be notified of awards on a rolling basis beginning 3/1. **Types of Aid:** *Need-based scholarships/grants:* Federal Pell, SEOG, state scholarships/grants, private scholarships, the school's own gift aid. *Loans:* Subsidized Stafford, Unsubsidized Stafford, PLUS, Federal Perkins, Federal Nursing, Alternative loans. *Student Employment:* Federal Work-Study Program available. Institutional employment available. Off-campus job opportunities are good. **Financial Aid Statistics:** 66% freshmen, 68% undergrads receive need-based scholarship or grant aid. 93% freshmen, 80% undergrads receive non-need-based scholarship or grant aid. 80% freshmen, 84% undergrads receive need-based self-help aid. 16% freshmen, 12% undergrads receive athletic scholarships. 88% freshmen, 71% undergrads receive any aid. 69% undergrads borrow to pay for school. Average cumulative indebtedness $20,595. **Criteria for awarding institutional aid:** *Non-need-based:* academics, alumni affiliation, art, athletics, job skills, leadership, minority status, music/drama, religious affiliation, state/district residency.

SOUTHWEST MINNESOTA STATE UNIVERSITY

Admission Office, Marshall, MN 56258
Phone: 800-642-0684
E-mail: shearerr@southwest.msus.edu • **CEEB Code:** 6703
Fax: 507-537-7154 • **Website:** www.southwest.msus.edu • **ACT Code:** 2151

This public school was founded in 1963. It has a 216-acre campus.

RATINGS

Admissions Selectivity Rating: 67   Fire Safety Rating: 60*

STUDENTS AND FACULTY

Enrollment: 2,900. **Student Body:** 17% out-of-state.
Retention and Graduation: 66% freshmen return for sophomore year.
Faculty:

ACADEMICS

Degrees: associate, bachelor's, master's. **Special Study Options:** study abroad, Exchange program abroad in Japan. Study abroad also in Chile and China. **Disability Services:** Special programs offered to physically disabled students include note-taking services, reader services, tape recorders, tutors. **Career services:** alumni services, career/job search classes, career assessment, internships.

FACILITIES

Housing: apartments for single students. **Special Academic Facilities/Equipment:** Art gallery, natural history museum, science museum, planetarium, greenhouse, wildlife area.

CAMPUS LIFE

Environment: Rural. **Activities:** literary magazine, radio station, student government, student newspaper, television station, yearbook. 65 registered organizations, 1 honor society, 5 religious organizations. **Athletics (Intercollegiate): Men:** cross-country. *Women:* basketball, cross-country, softball, tennis, volleyball.

ADMISSIONS

Freshman Academic Profile: ACT middle 50% range 19-24. Minimum paper TOEFL 500. **Freshman Admission Requirements:** High school diploma is required and GED is accepted. High school diploma is required and GED is not accepted. Minimum college GPA of 2.0 required. Lowest grade transferable C. **General Admission Information:** Application Fee $20. Nonfall registration accepted. Credit offered for CEEB Advanced Placement tests.

COSTS AND FINANCIAL AID

Average book expense $800. **Required Forms and Deadlines:** FAFSA, Institution's own financial aid form. **Types of Aid:** *Need-based scholarships/grants:* Federal Pell, SEOG, state scholarships/grants, private scholarships, the school's own gift aid. *Loans:* Subsidized Stafford, Unsubsidized Stafford, PLUS, Federal Perkins, college/university loans from institutional funds. *Student Employment:* Federal Work-Study Program available. Institutional employment available. Highest amount earned per year from on-campus jobs $2,602. Off-campus job opportunities are excellent.

SOUTHWESTERN COLLEGE (KS)

100 College Street, Winfield, KS 67156
Phone: 620-229-6236 • **Financial Aid Phone:** 620-229-6215
E-mail: scadmit@sckans.edu • **CEEB Code:** 6670
Fax: 620-229-6344 • **Website:** www.sckans.edu • **ACT Code:** 1464

This private school, affiliated with the Methodist Church, was founded in 1885. It has a 85-acre campus.

RATINGS

Admissions Selectivity Rating: 76   Fire Safety Rating: 77

STUDENTS AND FACULTY

Enrollment: 1,471. **Student Body:** 48% female, 52% male, 34% out-of-state, 1% international (12 countries represented). Asian 2%, African American 8%, Caucasian 63%, Hispanic 6%, Native American 2%
Retention and Graduation: 70% freshmen return for sophomore year. 29% freshmen graduate within 4 years. 45% freshmen graduate within 6 years. **Faculty:** 47 full-time faculty, 60% hold PhDs, 38% are are members of minority groups, 6% are women. 0% of classes are taught by teaching assistants.

ACADEMICS

Degrees: bachelor's, master's, post-bachelor's certificate, post-master's certificate. **Classes:** Most classes have fewer than 10 students. Most lab/discussion sessions have fewer than 10 students. **Majors with Highest Enrollment:** Elementary Education and Teaching; Business Administration and Management; Registered Nursing/Registered Nurse. **Special Study Options:** Accelerated program, distance learning, double major, honors program, independent study, internships, student-designed major, teacher certification program. **Disability Services:** Special programs offered to physically disabled students include reader services, tape recorders, tutors.

FACILITIES

Housing: Coed dorms, men's dorms, women's dorms, apartments for married students, apartments for single students. 90% of campus accessible to physically disabled. **Special Academic Facilities/Equipment:** Ruth Warren Abbott Horticulture Lab, Floyd and Ethel Moore Biological Field Station, Norman E. Hege Education Center. **Computers:** 100% of classrooms, 100% of dorms, 100% of libraries, 100% of dining areas, 100% of student union, 100% of common outdoor areas have wireless network access. Students can register for classes online. Administrative functions (other than registration) can be performed online.

CAMPUS LIFE

Environment: Village. **Activities:** Choral groups, concert band, dance, drama/theater, jazz band, music ensembles, musical theater, pep band, radio station, student government, student newspaper, symphony orchestra, television station, yearbook, Campus Ministries, International Student Organization. 25 registered organizations, 2 honor societies, 7 religious organizations. 2 fraternities. **Athletics (Intercollegiate):** *Men:* basketball, cheerleading, cross-country, football, golf, soccer, tennis, track/field (outdoor), track/field (indoor). *Women:* basketball, cheerleading, cross-country, golf, soccer, softball, tennis, track/field (outdoor), track/field (indoor), volleyball. **On-Campus Highlights:** Brand new Women's residence hall, Beech Science Center, Historic Stewart Field House, Christy Administration Building, Roy L. Smith Student Center (Newly re-modeled Cafeteria and bookstore). **Environmental Initiatives:** Kansas Envirothon; RecyleMania; Encouraging students to recycle old cell phones.

ADMISSIONS

Freshman Academic Profile: Average high school GPA 3.33. 16% in top 10% of high school class, 44% in top 25% of high school class, 73% in top 50% of high school class. 95% from public high schools. SAT Math middle 50% range 430-550. SAT Critical Reading middle 50% range 380-540. SAT Writing middle 50% range 390-560. ACT middle 50% range 19-24. Minimum internet-based TOEFL 80. Minimum paper TOEFL 550. **Basis for Candidate Selection:** *Very important factors considered include:* academic GPA, rigor of secondary school record, standardized test scores. *Important factors considered include:* application essay. *Other factors considered include:* Class rank, recommendation(s), alumni/ae relation, character/personal qualities, extracurricular activities, interview, talent/ability. **Freshman Admission Requirements:** High school diploma is required and GED is accepted. *Academic units required:* 4 English, 3 mathematics, 2 science, (1 science labs), 1 history. **Freshman Admission Statistics:** 293 applied, 90% admitted, 45% enrolled. **Transfer Admission Requirements:** college transcript(s), essay or personal statement, Minimum college GPA of 2.25 required. Lowest grade transferable C. **General Admission Information:** Application Fee $25. Regular application deadline 8/25. Notification on a rolling basis, beginning on or about 9/15. Nonfall registration accepted. Credit offered for CEEB Advanced Placement tests.

COSTS AND FINANCIAL AID

Annual tuition $19,530. Room and board $5,750. Required fees $150. Average book expense $600. **Required Forms and Deadlines:** FAFSA. **Types of Aid:** *Need-based scholarships/grants:* Federal Pell, SEOG, state scholarships/grants, the school's own gift aid. *Loans:* Direct Subsidized Stafford, Direct Unsubsidized Stafford, Direct PLUS, Subsidized Stafford, Unsubsidized Stafford, PLUS, Federal Perkins. *Student Employment:* Federal Work-Study Program available. Institutional employment available. Off-campus job opportunities are fair. **Financial Aid Statistics:** 100% freshmen, 98% undergrads receive need-based scholarship or grant aid. 9% freshmen, 7% undergrads receive non-need-based scholarship or grant aid. 82% freshmen, 85% undergrads receive need-based self-help aid. 25% freshmen, 25% undergrads receive athletic scholarships. 100% freshmen, 99% undergrads receive any aid. 86% undergrads borrow to pay for school. Average cumulative indebtedness $25,416. **Criteria for awarding institutional aid:** *Non-need-based:* academics, athletics, leadership, minority status, music/drama.

SOUTHWESTERN OKLAHOMA STATE UNIVERSITY

100 Campus Drive, Weatherford, OK 73096
Phone: 580-774-3782
E-mail: admissions@swosu.edu • **CEEB Code:** 6673
Fax: 580-774-7131 • **Website:** www.swosu.edu • **ACT Code:** 3340

This public school was founded in 1901. It has a 73-acre campus.

RATINGS

Admissions Selectivity Rating: 75   **Fire Safety Rating:** 60*

STUDENTS AND FACULTY

Enrollment: 4,247. **Student Body:** 58% female, 42% male, 12% out-of-state, 3% international. Asian 1%, African American 5%, Caucasian 79%, Hispanic 4%, Native American 7%
Retention and Graduation: 65% freshmen return for sophomore year. **Faculty:** 211 full-time faculty, 59% hold PhDs, 43% are are members of minority groups, 8% are women. 5% of classes are taught by teaching assistants.

ACADEMICS

Degrees: associate, bachelor's, first professional, master's. **Classes:** Most classes have 10-19 students. Most lab/discussion sessions have 20-29 students. **Special Study Options:** Accelerated program, distance learning, double major, independent study, internships, student-designed major, teacher certification program, weekend college. **Career services:** alumni services, career/job search classes, career assessment.

FACILITIES

Housing: men's dorms, women's dorms, apartments for married students, apartments for single students. **Special Academic Facilities/Equipment:** Writing lab, museum.

CAMPUS LIFE

Environment: Village. **Activities:** Choral groups, concert band, drama/theater, jazz band, literary magazine, marching band, music ensembles, musical theater, pep band, student government, student newspaper, symphony orchestra, television station, yearbook 3 religious organizations. 3 fraternities, 3 sororities. **Athletics (Intercollegiate):** *Men:* baseball, basketball, football, golf, tennis, track/field (outdoor). *Women:* basketball, tennis.

ADMISSIONS

Freshman Academic Profile: Average high school GPA 3.39. 20% in top 10% of high school class, 43% in top 25% of high school class, 74% in top 50% of high school class. 98% from public high schools. ACT middle 50% range 18-24. Minimum paper TOEFL 500. **Basis for Candidate Selection:** *Very important factors considered include:* Class rank, academic GPA, standardized test scores. **Freshman Admission Requirements:** High school diploma is required and GED is accepted. *Academic units required:* 4 English, 3 mathematics, 2 science, (2 science labs), 1 social studies, 2 history, 3 Computer Science or Foreign Language. **Freshman Admission Statistics:** 1,301 applied, 89% admitted, 74% enrolled. **Transfer Admission Requirements:** college transcript(s), Minimum college GPA of 2.0 required. Lowest grade transferable D. **General Admission Information:** Application Fee $15. Nonfall registration accepted. Admission may be deferred for a maximum of 1 year. Credit and/or placement offered for CEEB Advanced Placement tests.

COSTS AND FINANCIAL AID

Annual in-state tuition $2,700. Annual out-of-state tuition $7,200. Room and board $3,550. Required fees $750. Average book expense $1,200. **Required Forms and Deadlines:** FAFSA, Institution's own financial aid form. **Notification of Awards:** Applicants will be notified of awards on or about 3/20. **Types of Aid:** *Need-based scholarships/grants:* Federal Pell, SEOG, state scholarships/grants, private scholarships, the school's own gift aid. *Loans:* Subsidized Stafford, Unsubsidized Stafford, PLUS, Alternative loans through various institutions. *Student Employment:* Federal Work-Study Program available. Institutional employment available. Off-campus job opportunities are fair. **Financial Aid Statistics:** 65% freshmen, 72% undergrads receive need-based scholarship or grant aid. 76% freshmen, 66% undergrads receive non-need-based scholarship or grant aid. 79% freshmen, 86% undergrads receive need-based self-help aid. 4% freshmen, 4% undergrads receive athletic scholarships. 58% undergrads borrow to pay for school. **Criteria for awarding institutional aid:** *Non-need-based:* academics, alumni affiliation, art, athletics, music/drama, state/district residency.

SOUTHWESTERN UNIVERSITY

Admission Office, Georgetown, TX 78627-0770
Phone: 512-863-1200 · **Financial Aid Phone:** 512-863-1259
E-mail: admission@southwestern.edu · **CEEB Code:** 6674
Fax: 512-863-9601 · **Website:** http://www.southwestern.edu · **ACT Code:** 4186

This private school, affiliated with the Methodist Church, was founded in 1840. It has a 703-acre campus.

RATINGS

Admissions Selectivity Rating: 89   **Fire Safety Rating:** 84

STUDENTS AND FACULTY

Enrollment: 1,536. **Student Body:** 58% female, 42% male, 86% out-of-state, 3% international (6 countries represented). Asian 5%, African American 5%, Caucasian 64%, Hispanic 19%, Native American <1%
Retention and Graduation: 65% freshmen graduate within 4 years. 30% grads go on to further study within 1 year. 17% grads pursue arts and sciences degrees. 3% grads pursue law degrees. 3% grads pursue medical degrees. **Faculty:** 113 full-time faculty, 97% hold PhDs, 48% are are members of minority groups, 18% are women. 0% of classes are taught by teaching assistants.

ACADEMICS

Degrees: bachelor's. **Classes:** Most classes have 10-19 students. Most lab/discussion sessions have 10-19 students. **Majors with Highest Enrollment:** Business/Commerce; Biology/Biological Sciences; Psychology. **Special Study Options:** double major, honors program, independent study, internships, liberal arts/career combination, student-designed major, study abroad, teacher certification program. **Disability Services:** Special programs offered to physically disabled students include note-taking services, reader services, tape recorders, tutors. **Career services:** Alumni network, alumni services, career assessment, internships, regional alumni.

FACILITIES

Housing: Coed dorms, special housing for disabled students, men's dorms, special housing for international students, women's dorms, fraternity/sorority housing, apartments for married students, apartments for single students. 100% of campus accessible to physically disabled. **Special Academic Facilities/Equipment:** Alma Thomas Fine Arts Center, Red and Charline McCombs Campus Center, Corbin J. Robertson Center for Fitness and Wellness, Fountainwood Astronomical Observatory. **Computers:** 100% of classrooms, 100% of dorms, 100% of libraries, 100% of dining areas, 100% of student union, 50% of common outdoor areas have wireless network access. Students can register for classes online. Administrative functions (other than registration) can be performed online.

CAMPUS LIFE

Environment: Town. **Activities:** Choral groups, concert band, dance, drama/theater, jazz band, literary magazine, music ensembles, musical theater, radio station, student government, student newspaper, student-run film society. 99 registered organizations, 14 honor societies, 10 religious organizations. 4 fraternities, 4 sororities. **Athletics (Intercollegiate):** *Men:* baseball, basketball, cross-country, diving, golf, lacrosse, soccer, swimming, tennis, track/field (outdoor). *Women:* basketball, cross-country, diving, golf, soccer, softball, swimming, tennis, track/field (outdoor), volleyball. **On-Campus Highlights:** Robertson Center-indoor olympic size pool, McCombs Center-Student Center, Fountainwood Observatory, Korovva Milkbar-student run coffee house, Academic Mall-grassy area in the middle of campus. **Environmental Initiatives:** 100% Green (wind) power; Gold Certification under the Leadership in Energy and Environmental Design (LEED); Green Building Rating System for New Admission Center in 2009; Second LEED certified buliding project opened in 2010.

ADMISSIONS

Freshman Academic Profile: 36% in top 10% of high school class, 66% in top 25% of high school class, 95% in top 50% of high school class. 75% from public high schools. SAT Math middle 50% range 530-630. SAT Critical Reading middle 50% range 520-630. ACT middle 50% range 23-28. Minimum internet-based TOEFL 88. Minimum paper TOEFL 570. **Basis for Candidate Selection:** *Very important factors considered include:* Class rank, application essay, academic GPA, recommendation(s), rigor of secondary school record, standardized test scores. *Important factors considered include:* alumni/ae relation, character/personal qualities, extracurricular activities, first generation, geographical residence, interview, level of applicant's interest, racial/ethnic status, talent/ability, volunteer work, work experience. **Freshman Admission Requirements:** High school diploma is required and GED is accepted. *Academic units required:* 4 English, 4 mathematics, 3 science, (2 science labs), 2 foreign language, 2 social studies, 1 history, 1 academic elective. **Freshman Admission Statistics:** 3,487 applied, 49% admitted, 23% enrolled. **Transfer Admission Requirements:** High school transcript, college transcript(s), essay or personal statement, statement of good standing from prior institution(s). Minimum college GPA of 3.0 required. Lowest grade transferable C. **General Admission Information:** Application Fee $40. Early decision application deadline 11/1. Regular notification 4/1. Nonfall registration accepted. Admission may be deferred for a maximum of 1 year. Credit offered for CEEB Advanced Placement tests.

COSTS AND FINANCIAL AID

Annual tuition $37,560. Room and board $11,498. Average book expense $1,200. **Required Forms and Deadlines:** FAFSA. **Notification of Awards:** Applicants will be notified of awards on a rolling basis beginning 3/1. **Types of Aid:** *Need-based scholarships/grants:* Federal Pell, SEOG, state scholarships/grants, private scholarships, the school's own gift aid. *Loans:* Direct Subsidized Stafford, Direct Unsubsidized Stafford, Direct PLUS, Federal Perkins, state loans, college/university loans from institutional funds. *Student Employment:* Federal Work-Study Program available. Institutional employment available. Off-campus job opportunities are good. **Financial Aid Statistics:** 100% freshmen, 99% undergrads receive need-based scholarship or grant aid. 99% freshmen, 96% undergrads receive non-need-based scholarship or grant aid. 83% freshmen, 85% undergrads receive need-based self-help aid. 0% freshmen, 0% undergrads receive athletic scholarships. 99% freshmen, 97% undergrads receive any aid. 60% undergrads borrow to pay for school. Average cumulative indebtedness $24,605. **Criteria for awarding institutional aid:** *Non-need-based:* academics, art, minority status, music/drama, religious affiliation.

SPELMAN COLLEGE

350 Spelman Lane, Atlanta, GA 30314-4399
Phone: 404-270-5193 · **Financial Aid Phone:** 404-270-5212
E-mail: admiss@spelman.edu · **CEEB Code:** 5628
Fax: 404-270-5201 · **Website:** www.spelman.edu · **ACT Code:** 794

This private school was founded in 1881. It has a 32-acre campus.

RATINGS

Admissions Selectivity Rating: 88   **Fire Safety Rating:** 91

STUDENTS AND FACULTY

Enrollment: 2,135. **Student Body:** 100% female, 0% male, 73% out-of-state, 1% international (13 countries represented). Asian 0%, African American 87%, Caucasian 0%, Hispanic 0%, Native American <1%
Retention and Graduation: 89% freshmen return for sophomore year. **Faculty:** 180 full-time faculty, 87% hold PhDs, 70% are are members of minority groups, 85% are women. 0% of classes are taught by teaching assistants.

ACADEMICS

Degrees: bachelor's. **Classes:** Most classes have 10-19 students. Most lab/discussion sessions have 20-29 students. **Majors with Highest Enrollment:** Political Science and Government; Psychology; Biology. **Special Study Options:** cross-registration, double major, exchange student program (domestic), honors program, independent study, internships, liberal arts/career combination, student-designed major, study abroad, teacher certification program. **Honors programs:** Ethel Waddell Githii Honors Program. **Disability Services:** Special programs offered to physically disabled students include note-taking services, reader services, tape recorders, tutors. **Career services:** Alumni network, alumni services, career/job search classes, career assessment, internships.

FACILITIES

Housing: women's dorms, apartments for single students. **Special Academic Facilities/Equipment:** Nursery-elementary school for child development majors, language lab, electron microscope. **Computers:** Students can register for classes online. Administrative functions (other than registration) can be performed online.

CAMPUS LIFE

Environment: Metropolis. **Activities:** Choral groups, dance, drama/theater, jazz band, student government, student newspaper, yearbook, Campus Ministries, International Student Organization. 17 registered organizations, 18 honor societies, 9 religious organizations. 4 sororities. **Athletics (Intercollegiate):** *Women:* basketball, cross-country, golf, soccer, softball, tennis, volleyball. **On-Campus Highlights:** Sister's Chapel, The Spelman College Art Museum, Camille Olivia Hanks-Cosby Academic Center, Albro, Falconer, Manley Science Center, The Oval and Alumni Arch. **Environmental Initiatives:** LEED Construction & Renovation; Recycling; Green Operations & Maintenance.

ADMISSIONS

Freshman Academic Profile: Average high school GPA 3.5. 25% in top 10% of high school class, 57% in top 25% of high school class, 86% in top 50% of high school class. SAT Math middle 50% range 440-540. SAT Critical Reading middle 50% range 460-560. ACT middle 50% range 19-24. Minimum internet-based TOEFL 120. Minimum paper TOEFL 550. **Basis for Candidate Selection:** *Very important factors considered include:* application essay, academic GPA, rigor of secondary school record, standardized test scores, character/ personal qualities. *Important factors considered include:* recommendation(s), extracurricular activities. *Other factors considered include:* Class rank, alumni/ ae relation, first generation, geographical residence, level of applicant's interest, volunteer work, work experience. **Freshman Admission Requirements:** High school diploma is required and GED is accepted. *Academic units required:* 4 English, 3 mathematics, 3 science, (2 science labs), 2 foreign language, 3 social studies, 2 history, 2 academic electives. **Freshman Admission Statistics:** 4,324 applied, 54% admitted, 24% enrolled. **Transfer Admission Requirements:** High school transcript, college transcript(s), Minimum college GPA of 2.0 required. Lowest grade transferable C. **General Admission Information:** Application Fee $35. Early decision application deadline 11/1. Regular application deadline 2/1. Regular notification 4/1. Nonfall registration not accepted. Admission may be deferred for a maximum of one year. Credit offered for CEEB Advanced Placement tests.

COSTS AND FINANCIAL AID

Annual tuition $22,055. Room and board $11,945. Required fees $3,441. Average book expense $2,000. **Required Forms and Deadlines:** FAFSA, State aid form. **Types of Aid:** *Need-based scholarships/grants:* Federal Pell, SEOG, state scholarships/grants, private scholarships, the school's own gift aid, United Negro College Fund. *Loans:* Subsidized Stafford, Unsubsidized Stafford, PLUS. *Student Employment:* Federal Work-Study Program available. Institutional employment available. Off-campus job opportunities are good. **Financial Aid Statistics:** 90% freshmen, 83% undergrads receive need-based scholarship or grant aid. 0% freshmen, 0% undergrads receive non-need-based scholarship or grant aid. 81% freshmen, 82% undergrads receive need-based self-help aid. 0% freshmen, 0% undergrads receive athletic scholarships. 94% freshmen, 97% undergrads receive any aid. 72% undergrads borrow to pay for school. Average cumulative indebtedness $27,729. **Criteria for awarding institutional aid:** *Non-need-based:* academics, alumni affiliation, leadership, music/drama, state/ district residency.

SPRING ARBOR UNIVERSITY

106 East Main Street, Spring Arbor, MI 49283-9799
Phone: 517-750-6458 · **Financial Aid Phone:** 800-968-0011
E-mail: admissions@admin.arbor.edu · **CEEB Code:** 1732
Fax: 517-750-6620 · **Website:** www.arbor.edu · **ACT Code:** 2056

This private school was founded in 1873. It has a 100-acre campus.

RATINGS

Admissions Selectivity Rating: 84   **Fire Safety Rating:** 75

STUDENTS AND FACULTY

Enrollment: 2,603. **Student Body:** 69% female, 31% male, 12% out-of-state, (10 countries represented).
Retention and Graduation: 78% freshmen return for sophomore year. 33% freshmen graduate within 4 years. 54% freshmen graduate within 6 years. 22% grads go on to further study within 1 year. 8% grads pursue arts and sciences degrees. 3% grads pursue business degrees. 8% grads pursue medical degrees. **Faculty:** 81 full-time faculty, 72% hold PhDs, 32% are are members of minority groups, 11% are women. 0% of classes are taught by teaching assistants.

ACADEMICS

Degrees: associate, bachelor's, master's, post-bachelor's certificate. **Classes:** Most classes have 10-19 students. Most lab/discussion sessions have 10-19 students. **Majors with Highest Enrollment:** Elementary Education and Teaching; Psychology; Secondary Education and Teaching. **Special Study Options:** Accelerated program, cross-registration, distance learning, double major, dual enrollment, English as a Second Language (ESL), honors program,

independent study, internships, student-designed major, study abroad, teacher certification program, weekend college. **Off-Campus Study:** Washington Journalism semester, Los Angeles Film Studies program, AuSable Inst of Environmental Studies Program (Michigan). Study abroad programs available: China, Latin America Middle East, Oxford Honors, Russian, Japan, Jerusalem Univ., Russia @ St. Petersburg, People's Republic of China @ Sichuan College. Other programs/destinations are available through petition. **Combined degree programs:** BA/MEng. **Disability Services:** Special programs offered to physically disabled students include note-taking services, reader services, tape recorders, tutors. **Career services:** Alumni network, alumni services, career/ job search classes, career assessment, internships, regional alumni.

FACILITIES

Housing: special housing for disabled students, men's dorms, special housing for international students, women's dorms, apartments for married students, apartments for single students. 80% of campus accessible to physically disabled. **Special Academic Facilities/Equipment:** State-of-the-art academic building (Poling Center); the Poling Center features the CP Federal Credit Union Trading Center and is equipped with some of the same technology that is used daily on Wall Street including: An electronic wrap-around ticker, large light emitting diode (LED) financial data board, Bloomberg terminal, and continuous financial news feeds. Radio and TV studios, commercial writing/computer graphics lab, science center, art gallery. **Computers:** 90% of classrooms, 100% of dorms, 100% of libraries, 100% of dining areas, 75% of common outdoor areas have wireless network access. Students can register for classes online. Administrative functions (other than registration) can be performed online.

CAMPUS LIFE

Environment: Rural. **Activities:** Choral groups, concert band, drama/theater, jazz band, literary magazine, music ensembles, musical theater, pep band, radio station, student government, student newspaper, student-run film society, symphony orchestra, television station, yearbook, Campus Ministries, International Student Organization. 50 registered organizations. **Athletics (Intercollegiate):** *Men:* baseball, basketball, cross-country, golf, soccer, tennis, track/field (outdoor), track/field (indoor). *Women:* basketball, cross-country, soccer, softball, tennis, track/field (outdoor), track/field (indoor), volleyball. **On-Campus Highlights:** Sacred Grounds (Starbucks), Ganton Art Gallery, Poling Center, University Plaza, McKenna Carillon Tower, State-of-the-Art Academic Building (Poling Center) houses a trading center that is equipped with some of the same technology used on Wall Street.

ADMISSIONS

Freshman Academic Profile: Average high school GPA 3.4. 22% in top 10% of high school class, 48% in top 25% of high school class, 77% in top 50% of high school class. 80% from public high schools. SAT Math middle 50% range 460-580. SAT Critical Reading middle 50% range 480-585. SAT Writing middle 50% range 480-550. ACT middle 50% range 20-26. Minimum paper TOEFL 525. **Basis for Candidate Selection:** *Very important factors considered include:* rigor of secondary school record, standardized test scores, character/ personal qualities. *Important factors considered include:* academic GPA. *Other factors considered include:* Class rank, application essay, recommendation(s), extracurricular activities, interview, religious affiliation/commitment, talent/ability. **Freshman Admission Requirements:** High school diploma is required and GED is accepted. *Academic units required:* 4 English, 3 mathematics, 3 science, (3 science labs), 3 history, 1 Physical Education or Health Related Course. **Freshman Admission Statistics:** 2,698 applied, 65% admitted, 21% enrolled. **Transfer Admission Requirements:** High school transcript, college transcript(s), essay or personal statement, Minimum college GPA of 2.0 required. Lowest grade transferable C. **General Admission Information:** Application Fee $30. Regular application deadline 8/1. Notification on a rolling basis, beginning on or about 9/1. Nonfall registration accepted. Admission may be deferred for a maximum of No Set Time. Credit offered for CEEB Advanced Placement tests.

COSTS AND FINANCIAL AID

Annual tuition $21,998. Room and board $7,900. Required fees $540. Average book expense $800. **Required Forms and Deadlines:** FAFSA. **Notification of Awards:** Applicants will be notified of awards on a rolling basis beginning 3/1. **Types of Aid:** *Need-based scholarships/grants:* Federal Pell, SEOG, state scholarships/grants, private scholarships, the school's own gift aid. *Loans:* Subsidized Stafford, Unsubsidized Stafford, PLUS, Federal Perkins, MI-Loan Program and Alternative Loans. *Student Employment:* Federal Work-Study Program available. Institutional employment available. Highest amount earned per year from on-campus jobs $1,550. Off-campus job opportunities are fair. **Financial Aid Statistics:** 100% freshmen, 99% undergrads receive need-based scholarship or grant aid. 10% freshmen, 10% undergrads receive non-need-based scholarship or grant aid. 83% freshmen, 84% undergrads receive need-based self-help aid. 22% freshmen, 19% undergrads receive athletic scholarships. 97% freshmen, 93% undergrads receive any aid. 84% undergrads borrow to pay for school. Average cumulative indebtedness $32,504. **Criteria for awarding institutional aid:** *Non-need-based:* academics, art, athletics, minority status, music/drama, religious affiliation.

SPRING HILL COLLEGE

4000 Dauphin Street, Mobile, AL 36608
Phone: 251-380-3030 • **Financial Aid Phone:** 251-380-3460
E-mail: admit@shc.edu • **CEEB Code:** 1733
Fax: 251-460-2186 • **Website:** www.shc.edu • **ACT Code:** 42

This private school, affiliated with the Roman Catholic Church, was founded in 1830. It has a 450-acre campus.

RATINGS

Admissions Selectivity Rating: 88   **Fire Safety Rating:** 76

STUDENTS AND FACULTY

Enrollment: 1,187. **Student Body:** 61% female, 39% male, 60% out-of-state, 1% international (9 countries represented). Asian 1%, African American 17%, Caucasian 65%, Hispanic 8%, Native American 1%
Retention and Graduation: 74% freshmen return for sophomore year. 55% freshmen graduate within 4 years. 62% freshmen graduate within 6 years. **Faculty:** 78 full-time faculty, 92% hold PhDs, 49% are are members of minority groups, 13% are women. 0% of classes are taught by teaching assistants.

ACADEMICS

Degrees: bachelor's, certificate, master's, post-bachelor's certificate, post-master's certificate. **Classes:** Most classes have 10-19 students. Most lab/discussion sessions have 20-29 students. **Majors with Highest Enrollment:** Business Administration and Management; Biology/Biological Sciences; Psychology. **Special Study Options:** Accelerated program, distance learning, double major, dual enrollment, honors program, independent study, internships, student-designed major, study abroad, teacher certification program, 3-2 engineering with Auburn University, University of Alabama Birmingham, Marquette University, University of Florida, and Texas A&M University. Marine biology classes at Dauphin Island Sea Lab in conjunction with the Marine Environmental Sciences Consortium. **Honors programs:** SHC's 4-year Honors Program offers a challenging and rewarding course of study to academically gifted and motivated students. It is comprised of academic courses; seminar experiences; and additional opportunities for service, leadership, cultural exploration, and social interaction both on and off campus. Honors courses cover material in greater depth, use primary materials when possible, stress student participation and responsibility, and encourage high individual achievement. **Disability Services:** Special programs offered to physically disabled students include tutors. **Career services:** Alumni network, alumni services, career/job search classes, career assessment, internships, regional alumni.

FACILITIES

Housing: Coed dorms, men's dorms, women's dorms, apartments for single students. 90% of campus accessible to physically disabled. **Special Academic Facilities/Equipment:** Public radio broadcasting station, theater. **Computers:** 50% of classrooms, 15% of dorms, 100% of libraries, 100% of dining areas, 100% of student union, 25% of common outdoor areas have wireless network access. Students can register for classes online. Administrative functions (other than registration) can be performed online.

CAMPUS LIFE

Environment: Metropolis. **Activities:** Choral groups, dance, drama/theater, literary magazine, student government, student newspaper, yearbook, Campus Ministries. 66 registered organizations, 16 honor societies, 5 religious organizations. 3 fraternities, 5 sororities. **Athletics (Intercollegiate):** *Men:* baseball, basketball, cross-country, golf, soccer, tennis. *Women:* basketball, cross-country, golf, soccer, softball, tennis, volleyball. **On-Campus Highlights:** Arthur Outlaw Recreation Center, Golf Course, Burke Library, Java City Coffee Shop, Dorn Field.

ADMISSIONS

Freshman Academic Profile: Average high school GPA 3.44. 20.1% in top 10% of high school class, 47.2% in top 25% of high school class, 80.5% in top 50% of high school class. SAT Math middle 50% range 483-600. SAT Critical Reading middle 50% range 480-620. SAT Writing middle 50% range 480-593. ACT middle 50% range 21-26. Minimum internet-based TOEFL 80. Minimum paper TOEFL 550. **Basis for Candidate Selection:** *Very important factors considered include:* academic GPA, rigor of secondary school record, standardized test scores. *Important factors considered include:* Class rank, recommendation(s), interview. *Other factors considered include:* application essay, alumni/ae relation, character/personal qualities, extracurricular activities, talent/ability, volunteer work. **Freshman Admission Requirements:** High school diploma is required and GED is accepted. **Freshman Admission Statistics:** 2,817 applied, 47% admitted, 10% enrolled. **Transfer Admission Requirements:** college transcript(s), statement of good standing from prior institution(s). Minimum college GPA of 2.5 required. Lowest grade transferable

C-. **General Admission Information:** Application Fee $25. Regular application deadline 7/15. Notification on a rolling basis, beginning on or about 11/1. Nonfall registration accepted. Admission may be deferred for a maximum of 1 year. Credit and/or placement offered for CEEB Advanced Placement tests.

COSTS AND FINANCIAL AID

Required Forms and Deadlines: FAFSA, State aid form. **Notification of Awards:** Applicants will be notified of awards on a rolling basis beginning 2/15. **Types of Aid:** *Need-based scholarships/grants:* Federal Pell, SEOG, state scholarships/grants, private scholarships, the school's own gift aid, ACG, SMART, and TEACH grants. *Loans:* Direct Subsidized Stafford, Direct Unsubsidized Stafford, Direct PLUS, Subsidized Stafford, Unsubsidized Stafford, PLUS, Federal Perkins, Alternative loans (Citiassist, Signature). *Student Employment:* Federal Work-Study Program available. Institutional employment available. Highest amount earned per year from on-campus jobs $1,759. Off-campus job opportunities are good. **Financial Aid Statistics:** 98% freshmen, 96% undergrads receive need-based scholarship or grant aid. 96% freshmen, 97% undergrads receive non-need-based scholarship or grant aid. 98% freshmen, 97% undergrads receive need-based self-help aid. 12% freshmen, 9% undergrads receive athletic scholarships, 71% undergrads borrow to pay for school. Average cumulative indebtedness $26,229. **Criteria for awarding institutional aid:** *Non-need-based:* academics, alumni affiliation, athletics, job skills, leadership, minority status, state/district residency.

SPRINGFIELD COLLEGE

263 Alden Street, Springfield, MA 1109
Phone: 413-748-3136
E-mail: admissions@spfldcol.edu • **CEEB Code:** 3763
Fax: 413-748-3694 • **Website:** www.spfldcol.edu

This private school was founded in 1885. It has a 80-acre campus.

RATINGS

Admissions Selectivity Rating: 76   **Fire Safety Rating:** 60*

STUDENTS AND FACULTY

Enrollment: 2,046. **Student Body:** (18 countries represented).
Retention and Graduation: 82% freshmen return for sophomore year. 58% freshmen graduate within 4 years. 68% freshmen graduate within 6 years. 20% grads go on to further study within 1 year. **Faculty:** 5% of classes are taught by teaching assistants.

ACADEMICS

Degrees: bachelor's, master's. **Special Study Options:** cooperative education program, cross-registration, distance learning, double major, English as a Second Language (ESL), independent study, internships, liberal arts/career combination, study abroad, teacher certification program, weekend college. **Career services:** alumni services, career/job search classes, career assessment.

FACILITIES

Housing: Coed dorms, special housing for disabled students, men's dorms, special housing for international students, women's dorms, apartments for married students, apartments for single students **Special Academic Facilities/Equipment:** International center, college-operated summer day camp, hypermedia lab, centers for allied health sciences, emergency medical services management, occupational therapy, and physician assistant.

CAMPUS LIFE

Activities: Choral groups, concert band, dance, drama/theater, jazz band, literary magazine, marching band, music ensembles, musical theater, opera, pep band, radio station, student government, student newspaper, student-run film society, symphony orchestra, yearbook. **Athletics (Intercollegiate):** *Men:* baseball, basketball, cross-country, diving, football, golf, gymnastics, lacrosse, soccer, swimming, tennis, track/field (outdoor), volleyball, wrestling. *Women:* basketball, cross-country, diving, field hockey, golf, gymnastics, lacrosse, soccer, softball, swimming, tennis, track/field (outdoor), volleyball. **On-Campus Highlights:** Cheney Hall-dining hall, Caf-dining hall, Wellness Center.

ADMISSIONS

Freshman Academic Profile: 84% from public high schools. SAT Math middle 50% range 450-550. SAT Critical Reading middle 50% range 440-550. Minimum paper TOEFL 525. Basis for Candidate Selection. *Other factors considered include:* Class rank, application essay, recommendation(s), rigor of secondary school record, alumni/ae relation, character/personal qualities, extracurricular activities, geographical residence, interview, racial/ethnic status, religious affiliation/commitment, talent/ability, volunteer work, work experience. **Freshman Admission Requirements:** High school diploma is required and

GED is accepted. **Freshman Admission Statistics:** 2,249 applied, 59% admitted, 38% enrolled. **Transfer Admission Requirements:** college transcript(s), essay or personal statement, interview, statement of good standing from prior institution(s). Minimum college GPA of 2.5 required. Lowest grade transferable C. **General Admission Information:** Application Fee $40. Early decision application deadline 12/1. Regular application deadline 4/11. Nonfall registration accepted. Admission may be deferred for a maximum of 12. Credit and/or placement offered for CEEB Advanced Placement tests.

COSTS AND FINANCIAL AID

Student Employment: Federal Work-Study Program available. Institutional employment available. Highest amount earned per year from on-campus jobs $1,100. Off-campus job opportunities are good.

ST. AMBROSE UNIVERSITY

518 West Locust Street, Davenport, IA 52803-2898
Phone: 563-333-6300 · **Financial Aid Phone:** 563-333-6314
E-mail: admit@sau.edu · **CEEB Code:** 6617
Fax: 563-333-6297 · **Website:** www.sau.edu · **ACT Code:** 1352

This private school, affiliated with the Roman Catholic Church, was founded in 1882. It has a 118-acre campus.

RATINGS

Admissions Selectivity Rating: 83   Fire Safety Rating: 78

STUDENTS AND FACULTY

Enrollment: 2,734. **Student Body:** 58% female, 42% male, 57% out-of-state, 1% international (14 countries represented). Asian 1%, African American 3%, Caucasian 83%, Hispanic 6%, Native American <1%
Retention and Graduation: 78% freshmen return for sophomore year. 48% freshmen graduate within 4 years. 63% freshmen graduate within 6 years. 23% grads go on to further study within 1 year. **Faculty:** 214 full-time faculty, 68% hold PhDs, 49% are are members of minority groups, 9% are women. 0% of classes are taught by teaching assistants.

ACADEMICS

Degrees: bachelor's, certificate, master's, post-bachelor's certificate, post-master's certificate. **Classes:** Most classes have 10-19 students. Most lab/discussion sessions have 20-29 students. **Majors with Highest Enrollment:** Business/Commerce; Nursing Science; Psychology. **Special Study Options:** Accelerated program, cooperative education program, distance learning, double major, independent study, internships, liberal arts/career combination, student-designed major, study abroad, teacher certification program, weekend college, We have overseas academic experiences in England, Ireland, Lithuania, and Ecuador. Our students can, also, take advantage of the overseas experiences thru Central College in Iowa. **Combined degree programs:** BS/D.Phys Therapy, BS/MOT, and BA/MED. **Disability Services:** Special programs offered to physically disabled students include note-taking services, reader services, tape recorders, tutors. **Career services:** Alumni network, alumni services, career/job search classes, career assessment, internships. Career services highlights include internships: 70% of our Business majors complete at least one internship.

FACILITIES

Housing: Coed dorms, special housing for disabled students, men's dorms, women's dorms, apartments for single students. The University owns several houses next to campus and will rent them out to graduate or married studens. 96% of campus accessible to physically disabled. **Special Academic Facilities/Equipment:** Art gallery, observatory, language lab, and distance learning classrooms (5). **Computers:** 1% of classrooms, 27% of dorms, 100% of libraries, 100% of student union, have wireless network access. Students can register for classes online. Administrative functions (other than registration) can be performed online.

CAMPUS LIFE

Environment: City. **Activities:** Choral groups, concert band, dance, drama/theater, jazz band, literary magazine, music ensembles, musical theater, opera, pep band, radio station, student government, student newspaper, symphony orchestra, television station, Campus Ministries, International Student Organization. 26 registered organizations, 12 honor societies, 3 religious organizations. **Athletics (Intercollegiate):** *Men:* baseball, basketball, bowling, cheerleading, cross-country, football, golf, soccer, tennis, track/field (outdoor), track/field (indoor), volleyball. *Women:* basketball, bowling, cheerleading, cross-country, golf, soccer, softball, tennis, track/field (outdoor), track/field (indoor), volleyball. **On-Campus Highlights:** Rogalski Center (Student Union), Cafeteria, Coffee Shop and Bookstore, Chapel, Galvin Fine Arts Building. **Environmental Initiatives:** Storm Water Detention. In order to minimize storm water flow

into underground storm sewers, the following areas have been developed to detain water during storm events and allow a slower release into the ground: Townhouse west, 2,154 gallons; University Center parking lot islands, 9,694 gallons; University Center west grounds, 71,808 gallons; Lombard Street at University Center, 10,771 gallons; LINK east entry, 1,212 gallons; Rohlman north, 2,100 gallons; Cosgrove north grounds, 8,617 gallons. TOTAL: 106,356 gallons of detention. Storm Water Retention Areas. In order to minimize underground storm water flows, the following areas have been developed to capture storm water and re-use the water for irrigation purposes: Franklin Hall west retention tanks, 12,000 gallons; Chapel east grounds retention tanks, 12,000 gallons; New Hall retention tanks, 21,000 gallons. We have changed cleaning products to use those products that are Green Sealed Certified. We use mirco fiber rags in glass and mirror cleaning and we use no glass cleaning chemical of any kind. We use compact fluorescent light bulbs everywhere they can be used for the last 11 years and as we replace old fixtures we replace them with new ones to accomodate the compact fluorescent bulbs. We no longer use paper or disposable rags or mops. We no longer use mop oil for our dust mops but instead we use them dry or we use pack vacuums to cut down on the dust.

ADMISSIONS

Freshman Academic Profile: Average high school GPA 3.28. 21% in top 10% of high school class, 44% in top 25% of high school class, 74% in top 50% of high school class. 70% from public high schools. ACT middle 50% range 20-26. Minimum paper TOEFL 500. **Basis for Candidate Selection:** *Very important factors considered include:* Class rank, academic GPA, rigor of secondary school record, standardized test scores. *Other factors considered include:* application essay, recommendation(s), alumni/ae relation, character/personal qualities, extracurricular activities, first generation, geographical residence, interview, racial/ethnic status, talent/ability, volunteer work. **Freshman Admission Requirements:** High school diploma is required and GED is accepted. **Freshman Admission Statistics:** 3,309 applied, 73% admitted, 24% enrolled. **Transfer Admission Requirements:** High school transcript, college transcript(s), standardized test scores, statement of good standing from prior institution(s). Minimum college GPA of 2.0 required. Lowest grade transferable D. **General Admission Information:** Application Fee $25. Notification on a rolling basis, beginning on or about 10/1. Nonfall registration accepted. Admission may be deferred for a maximum of 1 semester. Credit and/or placement offered for CEEB Advanced Placement tests.

COSTS AND FINANCIAL AID

Annual tuition $26,500. Room and board $9,016. Required fees $240. Average book expense $1,200. **Required Forms and Deadlines:** FAFSA. **Notification of Awards:** Applicants will be notified of awards on a rolling basis beginning 2/15. **Types of Aid:** *Need-based scholarships/grants:* Federal Pell, SEOG, state scholarships/grants, private scholarships, the school's own gift aid. *Loans:* Direct Subsidized Stafford, Direct Unsubsidized Stafford, Direct PLUS, Federal Perkins. *Student Employment:* Federal Work-Study Program available. Institutional employment available. Highest amount earned per year from on-campus jobs $6,128. Off-campus job opportunities are excellent. **Financial Aid Statistics:** 99% freshmen, 97% undergrads receive need-based scholarship or grant aid. 54% freshmen, 47% undergrads receive non-need-based scholarship or grant aid. 76% freshmen, 80% undergrads receive need-based self-help aid. 7% freshmen, 7% undergrads receive athletic scholarships. 99% freshmen, 88% undergrads receive any aid. 80% undergrads borrow to pay for school. Average cumulative indebtedness $25,520. **Criteria for awarding institutional aid:** *Non-need-based:* academics, art, athletics, music/drama.

ST. ANDREWS UNIVERSITY

1700 Dogwood Mile, Laurinburg, NC 28352
Phone: 910-277-5555 · **Financial Aid Phone:** 910-277-5560
E-mail: admissions@sapc.edu · **CEEB Code:** 5214
Fax: 910-277-5020 · **Website:** sapc.edu · **ACT Code:** 3146

This private school, affiliated with the Presbyterian Church, was founded in 1958. It has a 600-acre campus.

RATINGS

Admissions Selectivity Rating: 68   Fire Safety Rating: 60*

STUDENTS AND FACULTY

Enrollment: 601. **Student Body:** 54% female, 46% male, 59% out-of-state, 11% international (8 countries represented). African American 11%, Caucasian 58%,
Retention and Graduation: 59% freshmen return for sophomore year. 26% freshmen graduate within 4 years. 28% freshmen graduate within 6 years. 40% grads go on to further study within 1 year. **Faculty:** 30 full-time faculty, 73%

hold PhDs, 47% are are members of minority groups, 3% are women. 0% of classes are taught by teaching assistants.

ACADEMICS

Degrees: bachelor's, certificate. **Classes:** Most classes have 10-19 students. **Majors with Highest Enrollment:** Elementary Education and Teaching; English Language and Literature; Business/Commerce. **Special Study Options:** double major, honors program, independent study, internships, student-designed major, study abroad, teacher certification program, weekend college, online classes. **Disability Services:** Special programs offered to physically disabled students include note-taking services, reader services, tape recorders, tutors. **Career services:** Alumni network, alumni services, career/job search classes, career assessment, internships, regional alumni.

FACILITIES

Housing: Coed dorms, men's dorms, women's dorms. 90% of campus accessible to physically disabled. **Special Academic Facilities/Equipment:** Art gallery, anthropology museum, science lab, electron microscopy center with three electron microscopes, psychology lab, artronics graphics computer, Scottish Heritage Foundation. **Computers:** 100% of libraries, 50% of dining areas, 100% of student union, have wireless network access. Administrative functions (other than registration) can be performed online.

CAMPUS LIFE

Environment: Rural. **Activities:** Choral groups, drama/theater, literary magazine, student government, student newspaper, yearbook, Campus Ministries. 30 registered organizations, 3 honor societies, 1 religous organization. **Athletics (Intercollegiate):** *Men:* baseball, basketball, cross-country, equestrian sports, golf, horseback riding, lacrosse, soccer, track/field (outdoor), wrestling. *Women:* basketball, cross-country, equestrian sports, horseback riding, lacrosse, soccer, softball, track/field (outdoor), volleyball, wrestling. **On-Campus Highlights:** Equesterian Center, Morgan Jones Science Labs, Electronic and Fine Arts Center, Athletic Facilities, Art Studios.

ADMISSIONS

Freshman Academic Profile: Average high school GPA 3.2. 7% in top 10% of high school class, 30% in top 25% of high school class, 66% in top 50% of high school class. SAT Math middle 50% range 355-605. SAT Writing middle 50% range 330-590. Minimum paper TOEFL 550. **Basis for Candidate Selection:** *Important factors considered include:* academic GPA, standardized test scores, character/personal qualities, extracurricular activities. *Other factors considered include:* Class rank, application essay, recommendation(s), rigor of secondary school record, first generation, interview, talent/ability, volunteer work, work experience. **Freshman Admission Requirements:** High school diploma is required and GED is accepted. *Academic units required:* 3 English, 3 mathematics, 3 science, 1 foreign language, 3 social studies. **Freshman Admission Statistics:** 926 applied, 57% admitted, 29% enrolled. **Transfer Admission Requirements:** High school transcript, college transcript(s), statement of good standing from prior institution(s). Minimum college GPA of 2.5 required. Lowest grade transferable C-. **General Admission Information:** Application Fee $30. Notification on a rolling basis, beginning on or about 9/1. Nonfall registration accepted. Admission may be deferred for a maximum of one term. Credit offered for CEEB Advanced Placement tests.

COSTS AND FINANCIAL AID

Average book expense $1,800. **Required Forms and Deadlines: Notification of Awards:** Applicants will be notified of awards on a rolling basis beginning 10/1. **Types of Aid:** *Need-based scholarships/grants:* Federal Pell, SEOG, state scholarships/grants, private scholarships, the school's own gift aid. *Loans:* Subsidized Stafford, Unsubsidized Stafford, PLUS. *Student Employment:* Federal Work-Study Program available. Institutional employment available. Highest amount earned per year from on-campus jobs $2,000. **Financial Aid Statistics:** 99% freshmen, 98% undergrads receive need-based scholarship or grant aid. 9% freshmen, 8% undergrads receive non-need-based scholarship or grant aid. 85% freshmen, 84% undergrads receive need-based self-help aid. 17% freshmen, 17% undergrads receive athletic scholarships. 99% freshmen, 98% undergrads receive any aid. 76% undergrads borrow to pay for school. Average cumulative indebtedness $25,724. **Criteria for awarding institutional aid:** *Non-need-based:* academics, alumni affiliation, art, athletics, leadership, music/drama.

ST. BONAVENTURE UNIVERSITY

Best 380

3261 West State Road, St. Bonaventure, NY 14778
Phone: 716-375-2434 · **Financial Aid Phone:** 716-375-2528
E-mail: admissions@sbu.edu · **CEEB Code:** 2793
Fax: 716-375-4005 · **Website:** www.sbu.edu · **ACT Code:** 2882

This private school, affiliated with the Roman Catholic Church, was founded in 1858. It has a 500-acre campus.

RATINGS

Admissions Selectivity Rating: 82 **Fire Safety Rating:** 63

STUDENTS AND FACULTY

Enrollment: 1,733. **Student Body:** 50% female, 50% male, 25% out-of-state, 2% international (26 countries represented). Asian 4%, African American 5%, Caucasian 70%, Hispanic 7%, Native American <1%
Retention and Graduation: 84% freshmen return for sophomore year. 55% freshmen graduate within 4 years. 68% freshmen graduate within 6 years. 46% grads go on to further study within 1 year. **Faculty:** 145 full-time faculty, 78% hold PhDs, 39% are are members of minority groups, 8% are women.

ACADEMICS

Degrees: bachelor's, master's, post-bachelor's certificate, post-master's certificate. **Classes:** Most classes have 10-19 students. Most lab/discussion sessions have 10-19 students. **Majors with Highest Enrollment:** Biology/Biological Sciences; Journalism; Accounting. **Special Study Options:** Accelerated program, cross-registration, distance learning, double major, dual enrollment, exchange student program (domestic), honors program, independent study, internships, liberal arts/career combination, student-designed major, study abroad, teacher certification program, weekend college. **Combined degree programs:** BA/MA. **Disability Services:** Special programs offered to physically disabled students include note-taking services, reader services, tutors. **Career services:** Alumni network, career/job search classes, career assessment, internships, regional alumni.

FACILITIES

Housing: special housing for disabled students, men's dorms, women's dorms, apartments for single students. 93% of campus accessible to physically disabled. **Special Academic Facilities/Equipment:** Quick Center for the Arts, Digital Conferencing and Media Center, Franciscan Center for Social Concern, Franciscan Institute **Computers:** 100% of classrooms, have wireless network access. Students can register for classes online.

CAMPUS LIFE

Environment: Village. **Activities:** Choral groups, concert band, dance, drama/theater, jazz band, literary magazine, music ensembles, pep band, radio station, student government, student newspaper, television station, yearbook. 47 registered organizations, 7 honor societies, 6 religious organizations. **Athletics (Intercollegiate):** *Men:* baseball, basketball, cross-country, diving, golf, soccer, swimming, tennis. *Women:* basketball, cross-country, diving, lacrosse, soccer, softball, swimming, tennis. **On-Campus Highlights:** Reilly Center, Richter Center, Quick Arts Center, Allegany River Trail, Golf Course and Clubhouse, Several major construction projects are taking place between 2006 and 2008, including renovation and addition to Hickey Dining Hall, renovation of Shay-Loughlen Residence Hall and addition of rare books wing to Friedsam Library. **Environmental Initiatives:** New campus construction: St. Bonaventure's William F. Walsh Science Center and the Friedsam Memorial Library Rare Books addition use underground water for cooling systems, reducing the release of carbon dioxide. Fall 2010, Townhouse 23 was dedicated as a "green building." Students living in the 8-apartment complex will work toward sustainable living by composting, recycling and monitoring and limiting their energy use. In April 2010, SBU hosted a week long campus wide event called Eco-Fest. The celebration included a tree planting, a walking tour of the Allegany River Trail and a recycled craft fair.

ADMISSIONS

Freshman Academic Profile: Average high school GPA 3.4. 18% in top 10% of high school class, 43% in top 25% of high school class, 74% in top 50% of high school class. SAT Math middle 50% range 470-580. SAT Critical Reading middle 50% range 470-580. SAT Writing middle 50% range 450-562.5. ACT middle 50% range 21-27. Minimum paper TOEFL 550. **Basis for Candidate Selection:** *Very important factors considered include:* academic GPA, recommendation(s), rigor of secondary school record, character/personal qualities, interview. *Important factors considered include:* application essay, standardized test scores, extracurricular activities, level of applicant's interest, talent/ability, volunteer work. *Other factors considered include:* Class rank, alumni/ae relation, first generation, work experience. **Freshman Admission Requirements:** High school diploma is required and GED is accepted. *Academic units required:* 4 English, 3 mathematics, 3 science, 2 foreign language, 4 social studies. **Freshman Admission Statistics:** 2,682 applied, 70% admitted, 23% enrolled. **Transfer Admission Requirements:** High school transcript, college transcript(s), statement of good standing from prior institution(s). Minimum college GPA of 2.0 required. Lowest grade transferable C. **General Admission Information:** Application Fee $30. Regular application deadline 4/15. Notification on a rolling basis, beginning on or about 10/1. Nonfall registration accepted. Admission may be deferred for a maximum of 1 year. Credit and/or placement offered for CEEB Advanced Placement tests.

COSTS AND FINANCIAL AID

Annual tuition $29,510. Room and board $10,786. Required fees $965. Average book expense $800. **Required Forms and Deadlines:** FAFSA, State aid form. **Notification of Awards:** Applicants will be notified of awards on a rolling basis beginning 4/1. **Types of Aid:** *Need-based scholarships/grants:* Federal Pell, SEOG, state scholarships/grants, private scholarships, the school's own gift aid. *Loans:* Subsidized Stafford, Unsubsidized Stafford, PLUS, Federal Perkins, college/university loans from institutional funds. *Student Employment:* Highest amount earned per year from on-campus jobs $815. **Financial Aid Statistics:** 100% freshmen, 100% undergrads receive need-based scholarship or grant aid. 94% freshmen, 94% undergrads receive non-need-based scholarship or grant aid. 75% freshmen, 79% undergrads receive need-based self-help aid. 9% freshmen, 11% undergrads receive athletic scholarships. 99% freshmen, 99% undergrads receive any aid. 80% undergrads borrow to pay for school. Average cumulative indebtedness $26,491. **Criteria for awarding institutional aid:** *Non-need-based:* academics, art, athletics, minority status, music/drama, religious affiliation, state/district residency.

ST. CATHERINE UNIVERSITY

2004 Randolph Avenue, Saint Paul, MN 55105
Phone: 651-690-8850 · **Financial Aid Phone:** 651-690-6540
E-mail: admissions@stkate.edu · **CEEB Code:** 6105
Fax: 651-690-8868 · **Website:** www.stkate.edu · **ACT Code:** 2096

This private school, affiliated with the Roman Catholic Church, was founded in 1905. It has a 110-acre campus.

RATINGS

Admissions Selectivity Rating: 86   Fire Safety Rating: 81

STUDENTS AND FACULTY

Enrollment: 3,479. **Student Body:** 97% female, 3% male, 11% out-of-state, 1% international (34 countries represented). Asian 11%, African American 10%, Caucasian 66%, Hispanic 5%, Native American 1%
Retention and Graduation: 79% freshmen return for sophomore year. 38% freshmen graduate within 4 years. 61% freshmen graduate within 6 years. 28% grads go on to further study within 1 year. 2% grads pursue arts and sciences degrees. 4% grads pursue law degrees. 10% grads pursue business degrees. 2% grads pursue medical degrees. **Faculty:** 308 full-time faculty. 0% of classes are taught by teaching assistants.

ACADEMICS

Degrees: associate, bachelor's, certificate, master's, post-bachelor's certificate, post-master's certificate, terminal associate, transfer associate. **Classes:** Most classes have 10-19 students. Most lab/discussion sessions have 10-19 students. **Majors with Highest Enrollment:** Elementary Education and Teaching; Registered Nursing, Nursing Administration, Nursing Research and Clinical Nursing; Social Work. **Special Study Options:** cross-registration, double major, dual enrollment, exchange student program (domestic), honors program, independent study, internships, student-designed major, study abroad, weekend college. **Honors programs:** Antonian Scholars are students who exhibit exceptional academic performance in the University and who show promise as learners, researchers, writers, performers, campus or community leaders, and/or creative thinkers. Scholars possess both creativity and love of learning. Scholars are inquisitive and hard working. They love challenges. Scholars are also students who want to take an active role in "tailoring" their college experiences to their needs, interests and passions. Scholars complete a five-component program that includes interdisciplinary seminars, as well as optional honors sections of TRW and/or GSJ, optional study abroad experiences, and a required Senior Honors Project. Scholars participate in at least two and up to four Honors seminars specifically designed for their learning needs and offered

in an interdisciplinary format with two professors. All scholars as seniors are required to enroll in a four-credit independent study course in which they develop a senior project based on an interest, curiosity, or passion. Senior projects are completed with a faculty advisor and an interdisciplinary faculty committee who provide guidance and feedback on the project. Other privileges of membership in the Antonian Scholars Honors Program includes priority registration for courses each semester, special diplomas and commencement recognition, and leadership opportunities in the Honors Program Student Organization. Scholars also have opportunities on a regular basis to socialize, network, and converse with others in the Honors Program. Scholars have access to the Honor's Hub in Coeur de Catherine. The Hub is a quiet place to study when you need one and also a place where Scholars may gather for special activities or conversation. **Combined degree programs:** BA/DPT, BA/MA (Occupational Therapy). **Disability Services:** Special programs offered to physically disabled students include note-taking services, reader services, tape recorders, tutors. **Career services:** Alumni network, alumni services, career/job search classes, career assessment, internships.

FACILITIES

Housing: women's dorms, apartments for single students, Theme Housing, Housing for student-parents. 90% of campus accessible to physically disabled. **Special Academic Facilities/Equipment:** Art gallery, theatre, recital hall, experimental psychology lab, language lab, observatory. **Computers:** Students can register for classes online. Administrative functions (other than registration) can be performed online.

CAMPUS LIFE

Environment: Metropolis. **Activities:** Choral groups, drama/theater, literary magazine, music ensembles, musical theater, student government, student newspaper, Campus Ministries. 40 registered organizations, 24 honor societies, 4 religious organizations. 1 sorority. **Athletics (Intercollegiate):** *Women:* basketball, cross-country, diving, ice hockey, soccer, softball, swimming, tennis, track/field (outdoor), track/field (indoor), volleyball. **On-Campus Highlights:** Coeur de Catherine, English garden, Butler Center, Dew Drop Pond, Art Gallery. **Environmental Initiatives:** Retrofitted older building with green roof; energy-efficient design in new residence halls; sustainable landscaping.

ADMISSIONS

Freshman Academic Profile: Average high school GPA 3.61. 23% in top 10% of high school class, 52% in top 25% of high school class, 87% in top 50% of high school class. 86% from public high schools. SAT Math middle 50% range 490-560. SAT Critical Reading middle 50% range 490-630. ACT middle 50% range 22-26. Minimum paper TOEFL 500. **Basis for Candidate Selection:** *Very important factors considered include:* academic GPA, rigor of secondary school record. *Important factors considered include:* Class rank, application essay, recommendation(s), standardized test scores. *Other factors considered include:* interview. **Freshman Admission Requirements:** High school diploma is required and GED is accepted. **Freshman Admission Statistics:** 2,685 applied, 59% admitted, 24% enrolled. **Transfer Admission Requirements:** High school transcript, college transcript(s), statement of good standing from prior institution(s). Minimum college GPA of 2.0 required. Lowest grade transferable C-. **General Admission Information:** Credit offered for CEEB Advanced Placement tests.

COSTS AND FINANCIAL AID

Annual tuition $32,310. Room and board $8,568. Required fees $380. Average book expense $1,000. **Required Forms and Deadlines:** FAFSA, Institution's own financial aid form. **Notification of Awards:** Applicants will be notified of awards on a rolling basis beginning 3/15. **Types of Aid:** *Need-based scholarships/grants:* Federal Pell, SEOG, state scholarships/grants, private scholarships, the school's own gift aid. *Loans:* Direct Subsidized Stafford, Direct Unsubsidized Stafford, Direct PLUS, Federal Perkins, Federal Nursing, state loans. *Student Employment:* Federal Work-Study Program available. Institutional employment available. Highest amount earned per year from on-campus jobs $2,158. Off-campus job opportunities are excellent. **Financial Aid Statistics:** 84% freshmen, 87% undergrads receive need-based scholarship or grant aid. 90% freshmen, 78% undergrads receive non-need-based scholarship or grant aid. 86% freshmen, 88% undergrads receive need-based self-help aid. 0% freshmen, 0% undergrads receive athletic scholarships. 94% freshmen, 93% undergrads receive any aid. **Criteria for awarding institutional aid:** *Non-need-based:* academics, alumni affiliation, leadership, minority status, state/district residency.

ST. CHARLES BORROMENO SEMINARY

100 East Wynnewood Road, Wynnewood, PA 19096
Phone: 610-785-6271 • **Financial Aid Phone:** 610-785-6582
E-mail: dandrassy@adphila.org • **CEEB Code:** 2794
Fax: 610-617-9267 • **ACT Code:** 5923

This private school, affiliated with the Roman Catholic Church, was founded in 1832. It has a 77-acre campus.

RATINGS

Admissions Selectivity Rating: 76   Fire Safety Rating: 79

STUDENTS AND FACULTY

Enrollment: 53. **Student Body:** 0% female, 100% male, 42% out-of-state, 4% international (3 countries represented). Asian 4%, African American 0%, Caucasian 92%, Hispanic 0%, Native American <1%
Retention and Graduation: 75% freshmen return for sophomore year. 33% freshmen graduate within 4 years. 33% freshmen graduate within 6 years. 90% grads go on to further study within 1 year. **Faculty:** 21 full-time faculty, 67% hold PhDs, 14% are are members of minority groups, 0% are women. 0% of classes are taught by teaching assistants.

ACADEMICS

Degrees: bachelor's, first professional, master's. **Classes:** Most classes have 10-19 students. **Special Study Options:** Accelerated program, English as a Second Language (ESL), independent study.

FACILITIES

Housing: men's dorms, Men's and Women's dorms available during Summer sessions. 75% of campus accessible to physically disabled. **Computers:** Students can register for classes online.

CAMPUS LIFE

Environment: Town. **Activities:** Choral groups, drama/theater, music ensembles, student government, student newspaper. 3 registered organizations, 1 honor society, 2 religious organizations.

ADMISSIONS

Freshman Academic Profile: 22% in top 10% of high school class, 44% in top 25% of high school class, 67% in top 50% of high school class. 40% from public high schools. SAT Math middle 50% range 470-590. SAT Critical Reading middle 50% range 460-710. Minimum paper TOEFL 450. **Basis for Candidate Selection:** *Very important factors considered include:* application essay, recommendation(s), rigor of secondary school record, character/personal qualities, interview, religious affiliation/commitment. *Important factors considered include:* Class rank, standardized test scores. *Other factors considered include:* extracurricular activities, talent/ability, work experience. **Freshman Admission Requirements:** High school diploma is required and GED is accepted. **Freshman Admission Statistics:** 11 applied, 100% admitted, 91% enrolled. **Transfer Admission Requirements:** High school transcript, college transcript(s), essay or personal statement, Minimum college GPA of 2.0 required. Lowest grade transferable C. **General Admission Information:** Regular application deadline 7/15. Nonfall registration accepted. Credit and/or placement offered for CEEB Advanced Placement tests.

COSTS AND FINANCIAL AID

Required Forms and Deadlines: FAFSA, Institution's own financial aid form. *Student Employment:* Federal Work-Study Program available. Institutional employment available. Off-campus job opportunities are poor. **Financial Aid Statistics:** 100% freshmen, 100% undergrads receive any aid. 0% undergrads borrow to pay for school.

ST. EDWARD'S UNIVERSITY

3001 South Congress Avenue, Austin, TX 78704-6489
Phone: 512-448-8500 • **Financial Aid Phone:** 512-448-8523
E-mail: seu.admit@stedwards.edu • **CEEB Code:** 6619
Fax: 512-464-8877 • **Website:** www.stedwards.edu • **ACT Code:** 4156

This private school, affiliated with the Roman Catholic Church, was founded in 1885. It has a 160-acre campus.

RATINGS

Admissions Selectivity Rating: 81   Fire Safety Rating: 87

STUDENTS AND FACULTY

Enrollment: 3,991. **Student Body:** 61% female, 39% male, 12% out-of-state, 9% international (54 countries represented). Asian 3%, African American 4%, Caucasian 38%, Hispanic 40%, Native American <1%
Retention and Graduation: 83% freshmen return for sophomore year. 54% freshmen graduate within 4 years. **Faculty:** 202 full-time faculty, 89% hold PhDs, 50% are are members of minority groups, 12% are women. 0% of classes are taught by teaching assistants.

ACADEMICS

Degrees: bachelor's, master's, post-bachelor's certificate. **Classes:** Most classes have 20-29 students. **Majors with Highest Enrollment:** Psychology; Communication; International/Global Studies. **Special Study Options:** double major, honors program, internships, study abroad, teacher certification program. **Honors programs:** Honors Program. **Disability Services:** Special programs offered to physically disabled students include note-taking services, reader services, tutors. **Career services:** Alumni network, alumni services, career/job search classes, career assessment, internships, regional alumni. Career services highlights include service learning initiatives that are an integral part of many courses. Faculty receive training on how to integrate service learning into their courses, whereby learning outcomes are achieved while serving the community.

FACILITIES

Housing: Coed dorms, special housing for disabled students, women's dorms, apartments for single students, Community-style living (casas, casitas) and two living-learning communities: Global Understanding and Social Justice. 90% of campus accessible to physically disabled. **Special Academic Facilities/Equipment:** Fine arts facility with digital photography lab; natural sciences center including state-of-the-art labs, classrooms and seminar rooms; interdisciplinary research lab at Wild Basin Wilderness Preserve. **Computers:** 100% of classrooms, 100% of dorms, 100% of libraries, 100% of dining areas, 100% of student union, 100% of common outdoor areas have wireless network access. Students can register for classes online. Administrative functions (other than registration) can be performed online.

CAMPUS LIFE

Environment: Metropolis. **Activities:** Choral groups, dance, drama/theater, literary magazine, music ensembles, musical theater, student government, student newspaper, student-run film society, symphony orchestra, television station, Campus Ministries, International Student Organization. 95 registered organizations, 10 honor societies, 3 religious organizations. **Athletics (Intercollegiate):** *Men:* baseball, basketball, golf, soccer, tennis. *Women:* basketball, golf, soccer, softball, tennis, volleyball. **On-Campus Highlights:** Historic Main Building (view of Austin), Meadows Coffee House, New 119,000 sq ft residential villa 2009, John Brooks Williams Natural Sciences Center, Meditation and Prayer Grotto/Sorin Oak, Sorin Oak is the largest oak tree in Austin at 14.6 feet in circumference. **Environmental Initiatives:** Performance contract to reduce utility consumption across campus: lighting retrofit, thermal storage tank for chilled water supply, replaced steam system with individual building hot water boilers, installed low flow plumbing fixtures (toilets, urinals, showerheads, faucet aerators). John Brooks Williams South, our new science facility, is an Austin Green Energy Building 3-star facility. Lighting in the parking garage was replaced with LED lights in FY11/12. Over the past three summers, 178 water heaters have been replaced with higher efficiency units. 122 student apartments have had heat pumps replaced with higher efficiency units using more environmentally friendly refrigerants (R22 to R410A).

ADMISSIONS

Freshman Academic Profile: 23% in top 10% of high school class, 58% in top 25% of high school class, 85% in top 50% of high school class. 74% from public high schools. SAT Math middle 50% range 500-590. SAT Critical Reading middle 50% range 510-620. SAT Writing middle 50% range 490-600. ACT middle 50% range 22-27. Minimum internet-based TOEFL 61. Minimum paper TOEFL 500. **Basis for Candidate Selection:** *Very important factors considered include:* application essay, academic GPA, rigor of secondary school record, standardized test scores. *Important factors considered include:* Class rank, recommendation(s), extracurricular activities, volunteer work. *Other factors considered include:* alumni/ae relation, character/personal qualities, first generation, geographical residence, interview, level of applicant's interest, racial/ethnic status, religious affiliation/commitment, talent/ability, work experience. **Freshman Admission Requirements:** High school diploma is required and GED is accepted. *Academic units required:* 4 English, 3 mathematics, 2 science, (2 science labs), 2 foreign language, 1 social studies, 2 history, 0 visual/performing arts, 0 computer science, 0 academic electives. **Freshman Admission Statistics:** 4,423 applied, 78% admitted, 23% enrolled. **Transfer Admission Requirements:** High school transcript, college transcript(s), essay or personal statement, Minimum college GPA of 2.50 required. Lowest grade transferable C. **General Admission Information:** Application Fee $45. Regular application deadline 5/1. Notification on a rolling basis, beginning on or about 11/1. Nonfall registration accepted. Admission may be deferred for a maximum of One Year. Credit and/or placement offered for CEEB Advanced Placement tests.

COSTS AND FINANCIAL AID

Annual tuition $38,320. Room and board $11,664. Required fees $400. Average book expense $1,100. **Required Forms and Deadlines:** FAFSA. **Notification of Awards:** Applicants will be notified of awards on a rolling basis beginning 1/15. **Types of Aid:** *Need-based scholarships/grants:* Federal Pell, SEOG, state scholarships/grants, private scholarships, the school's own gift aid, Endowed scholarships. *Loans:* Direct PLUS, Subsidized Stafford, Unsubsidized Stafford, PLUS, Federal Perkins, state loans, Alternative educational loans. *Student Employment:* Federal Work-Study Program available. Institutional employment available. Highest amount earned per year from on-campus jobs $4,800. Off-campus job opportunities are good. **Financial Aid Statistics:** 93% freshmen, 91% undergrads receive need-based scholarship or grant aid. 67% freshmen, 66% undergrads receive non-need-based scholarship or grant aid. 71% freshmen, 77% undergrads receive need-based self-help aid. 3% freshmen, 5% undergrads receive athletic scholarships. 92% freshmen, 87% undergrads receive any aid. 66% undergrads borrow to pay for school. Average cumulative indebtedness $24,006. **Criteria for awarding institutional aid:** *Non-need-based:* academics, art, athletics, leadership, music/drama, state/district residency.

ST. FRANCIS COLLEGE (NY)

180 Remsen Street, Brooklyn Heights, NY 11201
Phone: 718-489-5200
E-mail: admissions@stfranciscollege.edu • **CEEB Code:** 2796
Fax: 718-522-1274 • **Website:** www.stfranciscollege.edu • **ACT Code:** 2884

This private school, affiliated with the Roman Catholic Church, was founded in 1884. It has a 1-acre campus.

RATINGS

Admissions Selectivity Rating: 68   **Fire Safety Rating:** 60*

STUDENTS AND FACULTY

Enrollment: 2,294. **Student Body:** 57% female, 43% male, 11% out-of-state, 3% international (52 countries represented). Asian 2%, African American 20%, Caucasian 49%, Hispanic 14%, Native American <1%
Retention and Graduation: 76% freshmen return for sophomore year. 21% freshmen graduate within 4 years. 44% freshmen graduate within 6 years. **Faculty:** 69 full-time faculty, 77% hold PhDs, 38% are are members of minority groups, 14% are women. 0% of classes are taught by teaching assistants.

ACADEMICS

Degrees: associate, bachelor's, master's. **Classes:** Most classes have 10-19 students. Most lab/discussion sessions have 20-29 students. **Special Study Options:** Accelerated program, cooperative education program, cross-registration, double major, dual enrollment, honors program, independent study, internships, study abroad, teacher certification program, Accelerated biomedical science program with New York Colllege of Podiatric Medicine; medical technology program with St. Vincent's Catholic Medical Centers of New York and New York Methodist Hospital; joint program in radiological sciences with St. Vincent's Catholic Medical Centers of New York; 7 year cooperative program with the New York University College of Dentistry; can complete B.A. at St. Francis and Master of Science in Computer Science from Polytechnic University. **Honors programs:** One college wide program that is not department specific. **Combined degree programs:** BA/DDS, MS/Computer Science. **Disability Services:** Special programs offered to physically disabled students include note-taking services, reader services, tape recorders, tutors. **Career services:** Alumni network, alumni services, career/job search classes, career assessment, internships, regional alumni.

FACILITIES

Housing: Students may apply for housing in the recently opened dormitory at Polytechnic University, a few minutes walk from St. Francis College. 100% of campus accessible to physically disabled.

CAMPUS LIFE

Environment: Metropolis. **Activities:** Choral groups, drama/theater, literary magazine, student government, student newspaper, yearbook. 25 registered organizations, 1 honor society, 1 religious organization. 1 fraternity, 1 sorority. **Athletics (Intercollegiate):** *Men:* basketball, cross-country, diving, golf, soccer, swimming, tennis, track/field (outdoor), track/field (indoor), water polo. *Women:* basketball, bowling, cross-country, diving, fencing, golf, swimming, tennis, track/field (outdoor), track/field (indoor), volleyball, water polo.

ADMISSIONS

Freshman Academic Profile: Average high school GPA 3.1. 44% from public high schools. SAT Math middle 50% range 400-550. SAT Critical Reading

middle 50% range 410-540. Minimum paper TOEFL 500. **Basis for Candidate Selection:** *Very important factors considered include:* rigor of secondary school record, standardized test scores. *Important factors considered include:* Class rank, application essay, recommendation(s), alumni/ae relation, character/personal qualities, interview, talent/ability. *Other factors considered include:* extracurricular activities, volunteer work. **Freshman Admission Requirements:** High school diploma is required and GED is accepted. *Academic units required:* 4 English, 3 mathematics, 2 science, (1 science labs), 2 foreign language, 4 social studies, 1 academic elective, 1 Music/art. **Freshman Admission Statistics:** 1,304 applied, 88% admitted, 38% enrolled. **Transfer Admission Requirements:** High school transcript, college transcript(s), essay or personal statement, statement of good standing from prior institution(s). Minimum college GPA of 2.0 required. Lowest grade transferable C. **General Admission Information:** Application Fee $35. Nonfall registration accepted. Admission may be deferred for a maximum of 12 months. Placement offered for CEEB Advanced Placement tests.

COSTS AND FINANCIAL AID

Required Forms and Deadlines: FAFSA, Institution's own financial aid form, State aid form. **Types of Aid:** *Need-based scholarships/grants:* Federal Pell, SEOG, state scholarships/grants, private scholarships, the school's own gift aid. *Loans:* Subsidized Stafford, Unsubsidized Stafford, PLUS, Federal Perkins. *Student Employment:* Federal Work-Study Program available. Institutional employment available. Off-campus job opportunities are good. **Financial Aid Statistics:** 100% undergrads receive need-based scholarship or grant aid. 34% undergrads receive non-need-based scholarship or grant aid. 56% undergrads receive need-based self-help aid. 0% freshmen, 7% undergrads receive athletic scholarships. **Criteria for awarding institutional aid:** *Non-need-based:* academics, athletics.

ST. JOHN FISHER COLLEGE

3690 East Avenue, Rochester, NY 14618-3597
Phone: 585-385-8064 • **Financial Aid Phone:** 585-385-8042
E-mail: admissions@sjfc.edu • **CEEB Code:** 2798
Fax: 585-385-8386 • **Website:** http://www.sjfc.edu/ • **ACT Code:** 2798

This private school, affiliated with the Roman Catholic Church,, affiliated with the The College is guided by its Catholic heritage. Church, was founded in 1948. It has a 154-acre campus.

RATINGS

Admissions Selectivity Rating: 85   **Fire Safety Rating:** 87

STUDENTS AND FACULTY

Enrollment: 2,844. **Student Body:** 60% female, 40% male, 3% out-of-state, 0% international (14 countries represented). Asian 3%, African American 4%, Caucasian 84%, Hispanic 4%, Native American <1%
Retention and Graduation: 88% freshmen return for sophomore year. 61% freshmen graduate within 4 years. 72% freshmen graduate within 6 years. **Faculty:** 226 full-time faculty, 89% hold PhDs, 53% are are members of minority groups, 17% are women. 0% of classes are taught by teaching assistants.

ACADEMICS

Degrees: bachelor's, master's, post-bachelor's certificate, post-master's certificate. **Classes:** Most classes have 20-29 students. Most lab/discussion sessions have 10-19 students. **Majors with Highest Enrollment:** Biology/Biological Sciences; Registered Nursing/Registered Nurse; Business Administration and Management. **Special Study Options:** Accelerated program, cross-registration, distance learning, double major, exchange student program (domestic), honors program, independent study, internships, liberal arts/career combination, student-designed major, study abroad, teacher certification program, weekend college. **Honors programs:** St John Fisher College Honors Program; Science Scholars Program. **Disability Services:** Special programs offered to physically disabled students include note-taking services, reader services, tape recorders, tutors. **Career services:** Alumni network, career/job search classes, career assessment, internships, regional alumni.

FACILITIES

Housing: Coed dorms, special housing for disabled students, women's dorms. 100% of campus accessible to physically disabled. **Special Academic Facilities/Equipment:** Student Campus Center, State-of-the-Art Laboratories, Two Electron Microscopes, Multimedia Computer Lab, TV Studio Childcare Center (for observation and development), Cyber Café, Skalny Welcome Center, Art Gallery. **Computers:** 25% of classrooms, 100% of libraries, 50% of dining areas, 100% of student union, 10% of common outdoor areas have wireless network access. Students can register for classes online. Administrative functions (other than registration) can be performed online.

CAMPUS LIFE

Environment: City. **Activities:** Choral groups, dance, drama/theater, literary magazine, musical theater, student government, student newspaper, television station, yearbook, Campus Ministries. 70 registered organizations, 10 honor societies, 4 religious organizations. **Athletics (Intercollegiate):** *Men:* baseball, basketball, football, golf, lacrosse, soccer, tennis. *Women:* basketball, golf, lacrosse, soccer, softball, tennis, volleyball. **On-Campus Highlights:** Campus Center, Cyber Café, Golisano Gateway, Growney Stadium, Student Life Center. **Environmental Initiatives:** Commitment to buying local, fresh, organic produce and foods (http://www.sjfc.edu/student-life/dining/about/green.dot); Commitment to Recycling (http://home.sjfc.edu/green/recycleGuide.asp); Commitment to Student Involvement (http://home.sjfc.edu/green/activities.asp#involved).

ADMISSIONS

Freshman Academic Profile: Average high school GPA 3.5. 18% in top 10% of high school class, 54% in top 25% of high school class, 92% in top 50% of high school class. 90% from public high schools. SAT Math middle 50% range 500-600. SAT Critical Reading middle 50% range 470-560. SAT Writing middle 50% range 450-550. ACT middle 50% range 23-27. Minimum internet-based TOEFL 80. Minimum paper TOEFL 550. **Basis for Candidate Selection:** *Very important factors considered include:* academic GPA, recommendation(s), rigor of secondary school record, alumni/ae relation, character/personal qualities. *Important factors considered include:* Class rank, application essay, standardized test scores, extracurricular activities, interview, level of applicant's interest, talent/ability, volunteer work, work experience. *Other factors considered include:* first generation, geographical residence, state residency. **Freshman Admission Requirements:** High school diploma is required and GED is not accepted. **Freshman Admission Statistics:** 3,836 applied, 68% admitted, 23% enrolled. **Transfer Admission Requirements:** college transcript(s), statement of good standing from prior institution(s). Minimum college GPA of 2.0 required. Lowest grade transferable C. **General Admission Information:** Application Fee $30. Early decision application deadline 12/1. Notification on a rolling basis, beginning on or about 12/1. Nonfall registration not accepted. Admission may be deferred for a maximum of 2 semesters. Credit offered for CEEB Advanced Placement tests.

COSTS AND FINANCIAL AID

Annual tuition $28,970. Room and board $11,158. Required fees $580. Average book expense $1,100. **Required Forms and Deadlines:** FAFSA, State aid form. **Notification of Awards:** Applicants will be notified of awards on a rolling basis beginning 3/22. **Types of Aid:** *Need-based scholarships/grants:* Federal Pell, SEOG, state scholarships/grants, private scholarships, the school's own gift aid, Federal Nursing Scholarships. *Loans:* Direct Subsidized Stafford, Direct Unsubsidized Stafford, Direct PLUS, Federal Perkins, Bureau of Indian Affairs; Adult Vocational; Federal College Work Study. *Student Employment:* Federal Work-Study Program available. Institutional employment available. Off-campus job opportunities are good. **Financial Aid Statistics:** 100% freshmen, 100% undergrads receive need-based scholarship or grant aid. 74% freshmen, 52% undergrads receive non-need-based scholarship or grant aid. 89% freshmen, 94% undergrads receive need-based self-help aid. 0% freshmen, 0% undergrads receive athletic scholarships. 99% freshmen, 99% undergrads receive any aid. 85% undergrads borrow to pay for school. Average cumulative indebtedness $26,606. **Criteria for awarding institutional aid:** *Non-need-based:* academics, leadership.

ST. JOHN'S COLLEGE (MD)

60 College Avenue, Annapolis, MD 21401
Phone: 410-626-2522 · **Financial Aid Phone:** 410-295-6932
E-mail: Annapolis.Admissions@sjc.edu · **CEEB Code:** 5598
Fax: 410-269-7916 · **Website:** www.sjc.edu • **ACT Code:** 1732

This private school was founded in 1696. It has a 36-acre campus.

RATINGS

Admissions Selectivity Rating: 83   Fire Safety Rating: 91

STUDENTS AND FACULTY

Enrollment: 443. **Student Body:** 45% female, 55% male, 72% out-of-state, 11% international (14 countries represented). Asian 2%, African American 2%, Caucasian 70%, Hispanic 6%, Native American <1%.

Retention and Graduation: 90% freshmen return for sophomore year. 52% freshmen graduate within 4 years. 13% grads go on to further study within 1 year. 12% grads pursue arts and sciences degrees. 1% grads pursue law degrees. **Faculty:** 72 full-time faculty, 79% hold PhDs, 28% are are members of minority groups, 0% are women. 0% of classes are taught by teaching assistants.

ACADEMICS

Degrees: bachelor's, master's. **Classes:** Most classes have 10-19 students. **Majors with Highest Enrollment:** Liberal Arts and Sciences/Liberal Studies. **Special Study Options:** internships, Students may spend one or more years at the college's Santa Fe, N.Mex., campus. **Disability Services:** Special programs offered to physically disabled students include reader services, tape recorders. **Career services:** alumni services, career assessment, internships, regional alumni. Career services highlights include Hodson Internships, allowing students to receive a stipend for internships which offer them a substantial opportunity to explore a career and learn related skills.

FACILITIES

Housing: Coed dorms, special housing for disabled students. 80% of campus accessible to physically disabled. **Special Academic Facilities/Equipment:** Art gallery, planetarium, pendulum, Ptolemy stone, Faraday cage, laboratories. **Computers:** 20% of dorms, 30% of common outdoor areas have wireless network access. Administrative functions (other than registration) can be performed online.

CAMPUS LIFE

Environment: Town. **Activities:** Choral groups, dance, drama/theater, literary magazine, music ensembles, student government, student newspaper, student-run film society, yearbook. 64 registered organizations, 3 religious organizations. **On-Campus Highlights:** Mitchell Art Gallery, Greenfiled Library, McDowell Hall, Caroll Barrister House, French Monument, The entire campus is a registered national landmark. **Environmental Initiatives:** purchasing renewable energy credits for 100% of our electric consumption installing a new central heating plant and distribution system that will reduce fossil fuel consumption for heating by approximately 25%, as well as smokestack emissions stabilization of 800'+ of waterfront with removal of bulkhead and installation/ restoration of natural wetland

ADMISSIONS

Freshman Academic Profile: 19% in top 10% of high school class, 37% in top 25% of high school class, 77% in top 50% of high school class. 60% from public high schools. SAT Math middle 50% range 550-690. SAT Critical Reading middle 50% range 600-720. ACT middle 50% range 27-30. Minimum internet-based TOEFL 100. Minimum paper TOEFL 600. **Basis for Candidate Selection:** *Very important factors considered include:* application essay. *Important factors considered include:* recommendation(s), rigor of secondary school record, character/personal qualities. *Other factors considered include:* Class rank, academic GPA, standardized test scores, alumni/ae relation, extracurricular activities, first generation, interview, racial/ethnic status, talent/ability. **Freshman Admission Requirements:** High school diploma is required and GED is accepted. *Academic units required:* 3 mathematics, 2 foreign language. **Freshman Admission Statistics:** 342 applied, 81% admitted, 45% enrolled. **Transfer Admission Requirements:** High school transcript, college transcript(s), essay or personal statement. **General Admission Information:** Nonfall registration accepted. Admission may be deferred for a maximum of 1 year. Neither credit nor placement offered for CEEB Advanced Placement tests.

COSTS AND FINANCIAL AID

Annual tuition $47,176. Room and board $11,270. Required fees $450. Average book expense $630. **Required Forms and Deadlines:** FAFSA. **Notification of Awards:** Applicants will be notified of awards on a rolling basis beginning 12/1. **Types of Aid:** *Need-based scholarships/grants:* Federal Pell, SEOG, state scholarships/grants, private scholarships, the school's own gift aid. *Loans:* Subsidized Stafford, Unsubsidized Stafford, PLUS, Federal Perkins, college/university loans from institutional funds. *Student Employment:* Federal Work-Study Program available. Institutional employment available. Highest amount earned per year from on-campus jobs $2,999. Off-campus job opportunities are good. **Financial Aid Statistics:** 100% freshmen, 97% undergrads receive need-based scholarship or grant aid. 23% freshmen, 9% undergrads receive non-need-based scholarship or grant aid. 99% freshmen, 98% undergrads receive need-based self-help aid. 0% freshmen, 0% undergrads receive athletic scholarships. 82% freshmen, 71% undergrads receive any aid. 78% undergrads borrow to pay for school. Average cumulative indebtedness $24,446.

ST. JOHN'S COLLEGE, DEPARTMENT OF NURSING (IL)

421 North Ninth Street, Springfield, IL 62702-5317
Phone: 217-525-5628
E-mail: College@st-johns.org
Fax: 217-757-6870 · **Website:** www.st-johns.org/collegeofnursing

This private school, affiliated with the Roman Catholic Church, was founded in 1992.

RATINGS

Admissions Selectivity Rating: 60*   **Fire Safety Rating:** 60*

STUDENTS AND FACULTY

Enrollment: 83. **Student Body:** 93% female, 7% male, 10% out-of-state, 1% international (1 countries represented). Asian 0%, African-American 1%, Caucasian 98%, Hispanic 0%, Native American <1%
Faculty: 12 full-time faculty, 17% hold PhDs, 100% are are members of minority groups, 0% are women. 0% of classes are taught by teaching assistants.

ACADEMICS

Degrees: bachelor's. **Classes:** Most classes have 30-39 students. Most lab/discussion sessions have fewer than 10 students. **Majors with Highest Enrollment:** Registered Nursing/Registered Nurse.

FACILITIES

Housing: Coed dorms, apartments for single students, Campus Apartments.

CAMPUS LIFE

Activities: Choral groups, drama/theater, literary magazine, student government, student newspaper, Campus Ministries. 1 registered organization.

ADMISSIONS

Freshman Academic Profile: 100% in top 50% of high school class. Minimum paper TOEFL 500. **Basis for Candidate Selection:** *Very important factors considered include:* Class rank, application essay, academic GPA, recommendation(s), rigor of secondary school record, standardized test scores, alumni/ae relation, character/personal qualities, extracurricular activities, interview, level of applicant's interest, volunteer work. *Other factors considered include:* talent/ability, work experience. **Freshman Admission Requirements:** High school diploma is required and GED is accepted. *Academic units required:* 4 English, 3 mathematics, 3 science, (3 science labs), 0 foreign language, 3 social studies, 0 history, 2 academic electives. **Transfer Admission Requirements:** High school transcript, college transcript(s), interview, statement of good standing from prior institution(s). Minimum college GPA of 2.5 required. Lowest grade transferable c. **General Admission Information:** Application Fee $50. Nonfall registration not accepted. Neither credit nor placement offered for CEEB Advanced Placement tests.

COSTS AND FINANCIAL AID

Annual tuition $11,708. Required fees $444. Average book expense $750.

ST. JOHN'S COLLEGE, SANTA FE

Best 380

1160 Camino Cruz Blanca, Santa Fe, NM 87505
Phone: 505-984-6060 · **Financial Aid Phone:** 505-984-6058
E-mail: SantaFe.Admissiosn@sjc.edu · **CEEB Code:** 4737
Fax: 505-984-6162 · **Website:** www.sjc.edu · **ACT Code:** 2649

This private school was founded in 1696. It has a 250-acre campus.

RATINGS

Admissions Selectivity Rating: 86   **Fire Safety Rating:** 63

STUDENTS AND FACULTY

Enrollment: 340. **Student Body:** 44% female, 56% male, 91% out-of-state, 16% international (27 countries represented). Asian 2%, African American 1%, Caucasian 61%, Hispanic 10%, Native American <1%

Retention and Graduation: 88% freshmen return for sophomore year. 42% freshmen graduate within 4 years. 14% grads go on to further study within 1 year. 4% grads pursue arts and sciences degrees. 3% grads pursue law degrees. 6% grads pursue medical degrees. **Faculty:** 59 full-time faculty, 80% hold PhDs, 25% are are members of minority groups, 2% are women. 0% of classes are taught by teaching assistants.

ACADEMICS

Degrees: bachelor's, master's. **Classes:** Most classes have 10-19 students. **Special Study Options:** Accelerated program, internships. **Career services:** Alumni network, alumni services, career/job search classes, internships, regional alumni. Career services highlights include the Ariel Internship Program, which provides stipends to undergraduates for a limited number of summer internship opportunities regardless of financial need. SJC recognizes that internships have become a significant component of modern academia, whether a student continues on to graduate school or enters the work force.

FACILITIES

Housing: Coed dorms, special housing for disabled students, men's dorms, women's dorms, apartments for married students, apartments for single students, Wellness Housing, Single-sex suites are available. 70% of campus accessible to physically disabled. **Special Academic Facilities/Equipment:** Art gallery. **Computers:** 75% of classrooms, 10% of dorms, 100% of dining areas, 100% of student union, 10% of common outdoor areas have wireless network access. Administrative functions (other than registration) can be performed online.

CAMPUS LIFE

Environment: City. **Activities:** Choral groups, concert band, dance, drama/theater, jazz band, literary magazine, music ensembles, musical theater, student government, student newspaper, student-run film society. 27 registered organizations. **On-Campus Highlights:** Placita/Fish Pond, Student Activities Center, Great Hall, Coffee Shop, Levan Hall (new building). **Environmental Initiatives:** Paper, glass, plastic, cardboard recycling; Compost food from Cafeteria; Rainwater collection from roofs.

ADMISSIONS

Freshman Academic Profile: 32% in top 10% of high school class, 46% in top 25% of high school class, 86% in top 50% of high school class. 59% from public high schools. SAT Math middle 50% range 590-700. SAT Critical Reading middle 50% range 620-750. SAT Writing middle 50% range 570-690. ACT middle 50% range 23-30. Minimum paper TOEFL 550. **Basis for Candidate Selection:** *Very important factors considered include:* application essay. *Important factors considered include:* recommendation(s), rigor of secondary school record, character/personal qualities, level of applicant's interest. *Other factors considered include:* Class rank, academic GPA, standardized test scores, alumni/ae relation, extracurricular activities, first generation, interview, racial/ethnic status, talent/ability, volunteer work, work experience. **Freshman Admission Requirements:** High school diploma is required and GED is accepted. *Academic units required:* 3 mathematics, 2 foreign language. **Freshman Admission Statistics:** 227 applied, 81% admitted, 42% enrolled. **Transfer Admission Requirements:** High school transcript, college transcript(s), essay or personal statement. **General Admission Information:** Nonfall registration accepted. Admission may be deferred for a maximum of 2 semesters. Neither credit nor placement offered for CEEB Advanced Placement tests.

COSTS AND FINANCIAL AID

Annual tuition $47,176. Room and board $10,582. Required fees $650. Average book expense $630. **Required Forms and Deadlines:** FAFSA. **Notification of Awards:** Applicants will be notified of awards on a rolling basis beginning 12/10. **Types of Aid:** *Need-based scholarships/grants:* Federal Pell, SEOG, state scholarships/grants, private scholarships, the school's own gift aid, Academic Competitiveness Grant/SMART Grants. *Loans:* Subsidized Stafford, Unsubsidized Stafford, PLUS, Federal Perkins, college/university loans from institutional funds. *Student Employment:* Federal Work-Study Program available. Institutional employment available. Highest amount earned per year from on-campus jobs $2,800. Off-campus job opportunities are excellent. **Financial Aid Statistics:** 80% freshmen, 100% undergrads receive need-based scholarship or grant aid. 20% freshmen, 9% undergrads receive non-need-based scholarship or grant aid. 93% freshmen, 103% undergrads receive need-based self-help aid. 25% freshmen, 6% undergrads receive athletic scholarships. 100% freshmen, 81% undergrads receive any aid. 80% undergrads borrow to pay for school. Average cumulative indebtedness $23,475.

ST. JOHN'S UNIVERSITY

Best 380

8000 Utopia Parkway, Queens, NY 11439
Phone: 718-990-2000 · **Financial Aid Phone:** 718-990-2000
E-mail: admission@stjohns.edu · **CEEB Code:** 2799
Fax: 718-990-2096 · **Website:** www.stjohns.edu · **ACT Code:** 2888

This private school, affiliated with the Roman Catholic Church, was founded in 1870. It has a 122-acre campus.

RATINGS

Admissions Selectivity Rating: 85   Fire Safety Rating: 90

STUDENTS AND FACULTY

Enrollment: 10,881. **Student Body:** 54% female, 46% male, 30% out-of-state, 5% international (98 countries represented). Asian 18%, African American 19%, Caucasian 34%, Hispanic 15%, Native American <1%
Retention and Graduation: 40% freshmen graduate within 4 years. 41% grads go on to further study within 1 year. 20% grads pursue arts and sciences degrees. 8% grads pursue law degrees. 5% grads pursue business degrees. 2% grads pursue medical degrees. **Faculty:** 614 full-time faculty, 92% hold PhDs, 44% are are members of minority groups, 25% are women. 0% of classes are taught by teaching assistants.

ACADEMICS

Degrees: associate, bachelor's, certificate, diploma, doctoral, master's, post-bachelor's certificate, post-master's certificate, terminal associate, transfer associate. **Classes:** Most classes have 20-29 students. Most lab/discussion sessions have 20-29 students. **Majors with Highest Enrollment:** Pharmacy; Biology/Biological Sciences; Psychology. **Special Study Options:** Accelerated program, cross-registration, distance learning, double major, dual enrollment, English as a Second Language (ESL), honors program, independent study, internships, liberal arts/career combination, study abroad, teacher certification program, weekend college. **Honors programs:** The University Honors Program is available to qualified incoming freshmen. The program primarily comprises honors versions of the courses which are part of the core curriculum. Honors students must complete 30 credits of honors-designated courses to complete the program. Additional options for obtaining honors credits are also available. The program also features a range of special activities and events. **Combined degree programs:** BA/JD, BA/MA, BS/MA, BS/MS, BS/MBA, BS/OD, BS/JD, MBA/JD. **Disability Services:** Special programs offered to physically disabled students include note-taking services, reader services, tape recorders, tutors. **Career services:** alumni services, career/job search classes, career assessment, internships.

FACILITIES

Housing: Coed dorms, apartments for single students, Theme Housing. Some off-campus apartments are available on a limited basis. 90% of campus accessible to physically disabled. **Special Academic Facilities/Equipment:** University Gallery; Instuctional Media Center; Institute of Asian Studies; Health Education Resource Center; Center for Psychological Services; TV Center; Speech and Hearing Center and Reading and Writing Education Center. **Computers:** 100% of classrooms, 90% of dorms, 100% of libraries, 100% of dining areas, 100% of student union, 100% of common outdoor areas have wireless network access. Students can register for classes online. Administrative functions (other than registration) can be performed online. Undergraduates are required to own a computer.

CAMPUS LIFE

Environment: Metropolis. **Activities:** Choral groups, dance, drama/theater, jazz band, literary magazine, music ensembles, musical theater, pep band, radio station, student government, student newspaper, television station, yearbook, Campus Ministries. 180 registered organizations. **Athletics (Intercollegiate):** *Men:* baseball, basketball, fencing, golf, lacrosse, soccer, softball, table tennis, tennis, volleyball, weight lifting. *Women:* basketball, cross-country, fencing, soccer, softball, table tennis, tennis, track/field (outdoor), track/field (indoor), volleyball, weight lifting. **On-Campus Highlights:** The Great Lawn, D'Angelo Center, The University Library. **Environmental Initiatives:** Senior management signed the NYC Mayoral Challenge committing to 30% reduction in carbon emissions by the year 2017. Senior management signed a Memorandum of Understanding with the EPA committing to continuous improvement in eight EPA Voluntary Partnership Programs. St. John's is a charter participant of STARS ("Sustainability Tracking, Assessment and Rating System"). Also, establishment of a Sustainability Office within the university's central administration for the purpose of advancing the university efforts for a sustainable future and hiring 17 student workers as Sustainability Coordinators.

ADMISSIONS

Freshman Academic Profile: Average high school GPA 3.4. 19% in top 10% of high school class, 43% in top 25% of high school class, 77% in top 50% of high school class. 59% from public high schools. SAT Math middle 50% range 500-620. SAT Critical Reading middle 50% range 490-590. ACT middle 50% range 22-28. Minimum internet-based TOEFL 80. Minimum paper TOEFL 550. **Basis for Candidate Selection:** *Very important factors considered include:* academic GPA, standardized test scores. *Important factors considered include:* rigor of secondary school record. *Other factors considered include:* Class rank, application essay, recommendation(s), alumni/ae relation, character/personal qualities, extracurricular activities, geographical residence, interview, level of applicant's interest, volunteer work, work experience. **Freshman Admission Requirements:** High school diploma is required and GED is accepted. *Academic units required:* 4 English. **Freshman Admission Statistics:** 44,597 applied, 63% admitted, 10% enrolled. **Transfer Admission Requirements:** college transcript(s), Lowest grade transferable C. **General Admission Information:** Application Fee $50. Notification on a rolling basis, beginning on or about 12/1. Nonfall registration accepted. Admission may be deferred for a maximum of 1 year. Credit and/or placement offered for CEEB Advanced Placement tests.

COSTS AND FINANCIAL AID

Annual tuition $37,870. Room and board $16,390. Required fees $810. Average book expense $600. **Required Forms and Deadlines:** FAFSA. **Notification of Awards:** Applicants will be notified of awards on a rolling basis beginning 3/15. **Types of Aid:** *Need-based scholarships/grants:* Federal Pell, SEOG, state scholarships/grants, private scholarships, the school's own gift aid. *Loans:* Direct Subsidized Stafford, Direct Unsubsidized Stafford, Direct PLUS, Federal Perkins. *Student Employment:* Federal Work-Study Program available. Institutional employment available. Highest amount earned per year from on-campus jobs $5,000. Off-campus job opportunities are good. **Financial Aid Statistics:** 86% freshmen, 87% undergrads receive need-based scholarship or grant aid. 95% freshmen, 85% undergrads receive non-need-based scholarship or grant aid. 98% freshmen, 97% undergrads receive need-based self-help aid. 2% freshmen, 2% undergrads receive athletic scholarships. 98% freshmen, 96% undergrads receive any aid. 75% undergrads borrow to pay for school. Average cumulative indebtedness $20,274. **Criteria for awarding institutional aid:** *Non-need-based:* academics, alumni affiliation, art, athletics, leadership, music/drama, religious affiliation.

ST. JOSEPH'S COLLEGE

245 Clinton Avenue, Brooklyn, NY 11205
Phone: 718-636-6868 · **Financial Aid Phone:** 631-447-3214
E-mail: www.sjcny.edu
Fax: 718-636-8303 · **Website:** www.sjcny.edu

This is a private school.

RATINGS

Admissions Selectivity Rating: 72   Fire Safety Rating: 60*

STUDENTS AND FACULTY

Enrollment: 1,037. **Student Body:** 76% female, 24% male, 1% out-of-state, 0% international. Asian 7%, African American 36%, Caucasian 38%, Hispanic 14%, Native American <1%
Retention and Graduation: 81% freshmen return for sophomore year. 70% freshmen graduate within 4 years. 73% freshmen graduate within 6 years. 61% grads go on to further study within 1 year. 5% grads pursue arts and sciences degrees. 2% grads pursue law degrees. 3% grads pursue business degrees. 1% grads pursue medical degrees. **Faculty:** 50 full-time faculty, 66% hold PhDs, 60% are are members of minority groups. 0% of classes are taught by teaching assistants.

ACADEMICS

Degrees: bachelor's, certificate, master's. **Classes:** Most classes have fewer than 10 students. Most lab/discussion sessions have fewer than 10 students. **Special Study Options:** Accelerated program, honors program, independent study, internships, teacher certification program, weekend college, Biomedical Program with New York College of Podiatric medicine. **Honors programs:** Freshman Honors Program provides enriched inter-disciplinary courses. Capstone course includes a travel or global studies component. Honors indicated on transcript. **Combined degree programs:** BS/MBA. **Disability Services:** Special programs offered to physically disabled students include note-taking services, reader services, tape recorders. **Career services:** alumni services, career/job search classes, career assessment, internships.

FACILITIES

Housing: 95% of campus accessible to physically disabled. **Special Academic Facilities/Equipment:** Clare Rose Playhouse. **Computers:** Students can register for classes online.

CAMPUS LIFE

Activities: Choral groups, dance, drama/theater, literary magazine, musical theater, student government, student newspaper, yearbook, Campus Ministries. 34 registered organizations, 8 honor societies, 2 religious organizations. 2 fraternities, 2 sororities. **On-Campus Highlights:** Athletic Center with pool, Eagles Nest Cafeteria, Student Lounge, Quad Area, Clare Rose Playhouse.

ADMISSIONS

Freshman Academic Profile: SAT Math middle 50% range 430-540. SAT Critical Reading middle 50% range 410-510. SAT Writing middle 50% range 400-500. Minimum internet-based TOEFL 100. Minimum paper TOEFL 600. **Basis for Candidate Selection:** *Very important factors considered include:* academic GPA, rigor of secondary school record, standardized test scores. *Important factors considered include:* Class rank, application essay, recommendation(s), extracurricular activities, interview. *Other factors considered include:* alumni/ae relation, talent/ability, volunteer work, work experience. **Freshman Admission Requirements:** High school diploma is required and GED is accepted. *Academic units required:* 4 English, 3 mathematics, 2 science, 2 foreign language, 4 social studies, 3 academic electives. **Freshman Admission Statistics:** 825 applied, 62% admitted, 25% enrolled. **Transfer Admission Requirements:** college transcript(s), interview, statement of good standing from prior institution(s). Minimum college GPA of 2.0 required. **General Admission Information:** Application Fee $25. Credit and/or placement offered for CEEB Advanced Placement tests.

COSTS AND FINANCIAL AID

Annual tuition $15,400. Required fees $563. **Required Forms and Deadlines:** FAFSA, Institution's own financial aid form, State aid form. **Notification of Awards:** Applicants will be notified of awards on a rolling basis beginning 3/15. **Types of Aid:** *Need-based scholarships/grants:* Federal Pell, SEOG, state scholarships/grants, private scholarships, the school's own gift aid. *Loans:* Subsidized Stafford, Unsubsidized Stafford, PLUS, Federal Perkins. *Student Employment:* Federal Work-Study Program available. Institutional employment available. Off-campus job opportunities are good. **Financial Aid Statistics:** 95% freshmen, 94% undergrads receive need-based scholarship or grant aid. 70% freshmen, 62% undergrads receive non-need-based scholarship or grant aid. 86% freshmen, 86% undergrads receive need-based self-help aid. 0% freshmen, 0% undergrads receive athletic scholarships. 48% undergrads borrow to pay for school. Average cumulative indebtedness $18,582. **Criteria for awarding institutional aid:** *Non-need-based:* academics.

See page 1130.

ST. JOSEPH'S COLLEGE, NEW YORK (PATCHOGUE)

155 West Roe Blvd, Patchogue, NY 11772
Phone: 631-447-3219 · **Financial Aid Phone:** 631-447-3214
E-mail: longislandas@sjcny.edu · **CEEB Code:** 2802
Fax: 631-447-1734 · **Website:** www.sjcny.edu · **ACT Code:** 2923

This private school was founded in 1916. It has a 30-acre campus.

RATINGS

Admissions Selectivity Rating: 73   **Fire Safety Rating:** 60*

STUDENTS AND FACULTY

Enrollment: 3,727. **Student Body:** 72% female, 28% male, 0% out-of-state, 0% international. Asian 1%, African American 4%, Caucasian 73%, Hispanic 6%, Native American <1%
Retention and Graduation: 83% freshmen return for sophomore year. 51% freshmen graduate within 4 years. 68% freshmen graduate within 6 years. 61% grads go on to further study within 1 year. 5% grads pursue arts and sciences degrees. 2% grads pursue law degrees. 3% grads pursue business degrees. 1% grads pursue medical degrees. **Faculty:** 111 full-time faculty, 68% hold PhDs, 59% are are members of minority groups. 0% of classes are taught by teaching assistants.

ACADEMICS

Degrees: bachelor's, certificate, master's. **Classes:** Most classes have 10-19 students. **Majors with Highest Enrollment:** Elementary Education and Teaching; Secondary Education and Teaching; Psychology. **Special Study Op-**

tions: Accelerated program, cross-registration, double major, honors program, internships, liberal arts/career combination, study abroad, teacher certification program, weekend college. **Honors programs:** Freshman Honors Program provides enriched inter-disciplinary courses. Capstone course includes a travel or global studies component. Honors indicated on transcript. **Combined degree programs:** BS/MBA. **Disability Services:** Special programs offered to physically disabled students include note-taking services, reader services, tape recorders. **Career services:** alumni services, career/job search classes, career assessment, internships.

FACILITIES

Housing: 95% of campus accessible to physically disabled. **Special Academic Facilities/Equipment:** Clare Rose Playhouse. **Computers:** Students can register for classes online.

CAMPUS LIFE

Environment: Town. **Activities:** Choral groups, dance, drama/theater, jazz band, literary magazine, music ensembles, musical theater, student government, student newspaper, yearbook, Campus Ministries. 34 registered organizations, 8 honor societies, 2 religious organizations. 2 fraternities, 2 sororities. **Athletics (Intercollegiate):** *Men:* baseball, basketball, cross-country, golf, soccer, tennis, track/field (outdoor). *Women:* basketball, cross-country, equestrian sports, soccer, softball, swimming, tennis, track/field (outdoor), volleyball. **On-Campus Highlights:** Athletic Center with pool, Eagles Nest Cafeteria, Student Lounge, Quad Area, Clare Rose Playhouse.

ADMISSIONS

Freshman Academic Profile: 88% from public high schools. SAT Math middle 50% range 490-590. SAT Critical Reading middle 50% range 480-560. SAT Writing middle 50% range 460-550. Minimum paper TOEFL 550. **Basis for Candidate Selection:** *Very important factors considered include:* Class rank, academic GPA, rigor of secondary school record, standardized test scores. *Important factors considered include:* application essay, recommendation(s), character/personal qualities, extracurricular activities, interview. *Other factors considered include:* alumni/ae relation, first generation, level of applicant's interest, talent/ability, volunteer work, work experience. **Freshman Admission Requirements:** High school diploma is required and GED is accepted. *Academic units required:* 4 English, 3 mathematics, 3 science, (3 science labs), 2 foreign language, 4 social studies, 2 academic electives. **Freshman Admission Statistics:** 1,375 applied, 74% admitted, 50% enrolled. **Transfer Admission Requirements:** college transcript(s), Minimum college GPA of 2.0 required. **General Admission Information:** Application Fee $25. Notification on a rolling basis, beginning on or about 11/15. Nonfall registration accepted. Admission may be deferred for a maximum of 2 years. Credit offered for CEEB Advanced Placement tests.

COSTS AND FINANCIAL AID

Annual tuition $15,400. Required fees $563. **Required Forms and Deadlines:** FAFSA, Institution's own financial aid form, State aid form. **Notification of Awards:** Applicants will be notified of awards on or about 3/15. **Types of Aid:** *Need-based scholarships/grants:* Federal Pell, SEOG, state scholarships/grants, private scholarships, the school's own gift aid. *Loans:* Subsidized Stafford, Unsubsidized Stafford, PLUS, Federal Perkins. *Student Employment:* Federal Work-Study Program available. Institutional employment available. Off-campus job opportunities are good. **Financial Aid Statistics:** 91% freshmen, 82% undergrads receive need-based scholarship or grant aid. 74% freshmen, 65% undergrads receive non-need-based scholarship or grant aid. 84% freshmen, 83% undergrads receive need-based self-help aid. 0% freshmen, 0% undergrads receive athletic scholarships. 69% undergrads borrow to pay for school. Average cumulative indebtedness $14,028. **Criteria for awarding institutional aid:** *Non-need-based:* academics.

ST. LAWRENCE UNIVERSITY

Payson Hall, Canton, NY 13617
Phone: 315-229-5261 · **Financial Aid Phone:** 315-229-5265
E-mail: admissions@stlawu.edu · **CEEB Code:** 2805
Fax: 315-229-5818 · **Website:** www.stlawu.edu · **ACT Code:** 2896

This private school was founded in 1856. It has a 1000-acre campus.

RATINGS

Admissions Selectivity Rating: 90   **Fire Safety Rating:** 80

STUDENTS AND FACULTY

Enrollment: 2,391. **Student Body:** 55% female, 45% male, 57% out-of-state, 8% international (46 countries represented). Asian 2%, African American 3%, Caucasian 80%, Hispanic 4%, Native American <1%
Retention and Graduation: 90% freshmen return for sophomore year. 77% freshmen graduate within 4 years. 80% freshmen graduate within 6 years. 22% grads go on to further study within 1 year. 6% grads pursue arts and sciences degrees. 2% grads pursue law degrees. 2% grads pursue business degrees. 3% grads pursue medical degrees. **Faculty:** 173 full-time faculty, 97% hold PhDs, 50% are are members of minority groups, 14% are women. 0% of classes are taught by teaching assistants.

ACADEMICS

Degrees: bachelor's, master's, post-master's certificate. **Classes:** Most classes have 10-19 students. Most lab/discussion sessions have 10-19 students. **Majors with Highest Enrollment:** Economics; Political Science and Government; Psychology. **Special Study Options:** cross-registration, double major, exchange student program (domestic), independent study, internships, student-designed major, study abroad, teacher certification program, Community-based learning. **Honors programs:** The University Fellows program offers a $3500 stipend plus room for summer research on campus. This is a competitive program for students who wish to undertake a serious, independent academic project as their summer employment. **Combined degree programs:** BA/MEng, 4 + 1 Business Program; 3-2 engineering programs. **Disability Services:** Special programs offered to physically disabled students include note-taking services, reader services, tape recorders, tutors. **Career services:** Alumni network, alumni services, career/job search classes, career assessment, internships. Career services highlights include our Alumni Network.

FACILITIES

Housing: Coed dorms, special housing for disabled students, special housing for international students, women's dorms, fraternity/sorority housing, apartments for single students, Theme Housing. 60% of campus accessible to physically disabled. **Special Academic Facilities/Equipment:** Art gallery, arts technology center, language lab, center for international education, environmental research facility, 76-acre forest preserve, two electron microscopes, microscopy and sleep labs, Neuroscience lab, sustainability lab **Computers:** 100% of classrooms, 100% of dorms, 100% of libraries, 100% of dining areas, 100% of student union, 100% of common outdoor areas have wireless network access. Students can register for classes online. Administrative functions (other than registration) can be performed online.

CAMPUS LIFE

Environment: Village. **Activities:** Choral groups, concert band, dance, drama/theater, jazz band, literary magazine, music ensembles, radio station, student government, student newspaper, student-run film society, yearbook, Campus Ministries, International Student Organization, Model UN. 117 registered organizations, 22 honor societies, 4 religious organizations. 2 fraternities, 4 sororities. **Athletics (Intercollegiate):** *Men:* baseball, basketball, crew/rowing, cross-country, equestrian sports, football, golf, ice hockey, lacrosse, skiing (downhill/alpine), skiing (nordic/cross-country), soccer, squash, swimming, tennis, track/field (outdoor), track/field (indoor). *Women:* basketball, crew/rowing, cross-country, equestrian sports, field hockey, golf, ice hockey, lacrosse, skiing (downhill/alpine), skiing (nordic/cross-country), soccer, softball, squash, swimming, tennis, track/field (outdoor), track/field (indoor), volleyball. **On-Campus Highlights:** Newell Field House, Brewer Bookstore, Johnson Hall of Science, Owen D. Young Library, Student Center, Student Center opened January 2004, Newell Center for Arts Technology opened 2007, LEED Gold Johnson Hall of Science opened fall 2007. **Environmental Initiatives:** Pledge of climate neutrality Energy audits of all on and off campus buildings and appropriate retrofits of energy and water efficiency measures. Beginning to re-source our electricity to renewable sources (15% currently) and analyzing a renewable source for our heat.

ADMISSIONS

Freshman Academic Profile: Average high school GPA 3.49. 34.3% in top 10% of high school class, 70.7% in top 25% of high school class, 95.4% in top 50% of high school class. 67% from public high schools. SAT Math middle 50% range 570-660. SAT Critical Reading middle 50% range 550-650. SAT Writing middle 50% range 550-650. ACT middle 50% range 25-30. Minimum internet-based TOEFL 82. Minimum paper TOEFL 600. **Basis for Candidate Selection:** *Very important factors considered include:* application essay, academic GPA, recommendation(s), character/personal qualities. *Important factors considered include:* Class rank, rigor of secondary school record, extracurricular activities, interview, racial/ethnic status. *Other factors considered include:* standardized test scores, alumni/ae relation, first generation, geographical residence, level of applicant's interest, talent/ability, volunteer work, work experience. **Freshman Admission Requirements:** High school diploma is required and GED is accepted. **Freshman Admission Statistics:** 4,424 applied, 46% admitted, 31% enrolled. **Transfer Admission Requirements:** High school transcript, college transcript(s), essay or personal statement, statement of

good standing from prior institution(s). Lowest grade transferable C. **General Admission Information:** Application Fee $60. Early decision application deadline 11/15. Regular application deadline 2/1. Nonfall registration accepted. Admission may be deferred for a maximum of 1 year. Credit offered for CEEB Advanced Placement tests.

COSTS AND FINANCIAL AID

Annual tuition $47,350. Room and board $12,286. Required fees $346. Average book expense $750. **Required Forms and Deadlines:** FAFSA, CSS/Financial Aid PROFILE, Noncustodial PROFILE. **Notification of Awards:** Applicants will be notified of awards on or about 3/30. **Types of Aid:** *Need-based scholarships/grants:* Federal Pell, SEOG, state scholarships/grants, private scholarships, the school's own gift aid. *Loans:* Direct Subsidized Stafford, Direct Unsubsidized Stafford, Direct PLUS, Federal Perkins, college/university loans from institutional funds. *Student Employment:* Federal Work-Study Program available. Institutional employment available. Highest amount earned per year from on-campus jobs $2,000. Off-campus job opportunities are poor. **Financial Aid Statistics:** 98% freshmen, 97% undergrads receive need-based scholarship or grant aid. 16% freshmen, 13% undergrads receive non-need-based scholarship or grant aid. 74% freshmen, 76% undergrads receive need-based self-help aid. 1% freshmen, 1% undergrads receive athletic scholarships. 97% freshmen, 93% undergrads receive any aid. 67% undergrads borrow to pay for school. Average cumulative indebtedness $26,832. **Criteria for awarding institutional aid:** *Non-need-based:* academics, alumni affiliation, athletics, leadership, minority status, state/district residency.

See page 1146.

ST. LOUIS COLLEGE OF PHARMACY

4588 Parkview Place, St. Louis, MO 63110
Phone: 314-367-8700
E-mail: connie.horrall@stlcop.edu • **CEEB Code:** 6626
Fax: 314-446-8310 • **Website:** www.stlcop.edu • **ACT Code:** 2346

This private school was founded in 1864. It has a 7-acre campus.

RATINGS

Admissions Selectivity Rating: 88	Fire Safety Rating: 70

STUDENTS AND FACULTY

Enrollment: 723. **Student Body:** 60% female, 40% male, 53% out-of-state, 1% international. Asian 14%, African American 3%, Caucasian 44%, Hispanic 0%, Native American <1%
Retention and Graduation: 92% freshmen return for sophomore year. 65% freshmen graduate within 6 years. **Faculty:** 91 full-time faculty, 100% hold PhDs, 47% are are members of minority groups, 9% are women.

ACADEMICS

Degrees: first professional, master's. **Career services:** alumni services, internships.

FACILITIES

Housing: Coed dorms, fraternity/sorority housing, apartments for single students.

CAMPUS LIFE

Activities: Choral groups, concert band, drama/theater, literary magazine, musical theater, student government, student newspaper, Campus Ministries. 2 honor societies, 6 religious organizations. 5 fraternities. **Athletics (Intercollegiate):** *Men:* basketball, cheerleading, cross-country. *Women:* cheerleading, cross-country, volleyball.

ADMISSIONS

Freshman Academic Profile: Average high school GPA 3.74. 50% in top 10% of high school class, 33% in top 25% of high school class, 17% in top 50% of high school class. SAT Math middle 50% range 640-730. SAT Critical Reading middle 50% range 570-660. ACT middle 50% range 25-29. Minimum paper TOEFL 550. **Basis for Candidate Selection:** *Very important factors considered include:* rigor of secondary school record, standardized test scores. *Important factors considered include:* Class rank. *Other factors considered include:* application essay, recommendation(s), alumni/ae relation, character/personal qualities, extracurricular activities, volunteer work, work experience. **Freshman Admission Requirements:** High school diploma is required and GED is accepted. *Academic units required:* 4 English, 3 mathematics, 2 science, (2 science labs). **Freshman Admission Statistics:** 555 applied, 62% admitted, 71% enrolled. **Transfer Admission Requirements:** college transcript(s), essay or personal statement, standardized test scores, Minimum college GPA of 3.0 required. Lowest grade transferable C. **General Admission Information:**

Application Fee $35. Regular application deadline 4/2. Notification on a rolling basis, beginning on or about 9/2. Nonfall registration accepted. Credit offered for CEEB Advanced Placement tests.

COSTS AND FINANCIAL AID
Average book expense $1,500. **Required Forms and Deadlines:** FAFSA. **Notification of Awards:** Applicants will be notified of awards on a rolling basis beginning 2/19. **Types of Aid:** *Need-based scholarships/grants:* Federal Pell, SEOG, state scholarships/grants, private scholarships, the school's own gift aid. *Loans:* Subsidized Stafford, Unsubsidized Stafford, PLUS, Federal Perkins, Health Professions Loan. *Student Employment:* Federal Work-Study Program available. Institutional employment available. Highest amount earned per year from on-campus jobs $800. Off-campus job opportunities are excellent. **Financial Aid Statistics:** 99% freshmen, 90% undergrads receive need-based scholarship or grant aid. 9% freshmen, 5% undergrads receive non-need-based scholarship or grant aid. 82% freshmen, 89% undergrads receive need-based self-help aid. 4% freshmen, 2% undergrads receive athletic scholarships. 89% undergrads borrow to pay for school. Average cumulative indebtedness $90,554. **Criteria for awarding institutional aid:** *Non-need-based:* job skills, state/district residency.

ST. MARY'S COLLEGE OF MARYLAND

Admissions Office—18952 E. Fisher Rd., St. Marys City, MD 20686-3001
Phone: 240-895-5000 • **Financial Aid Phone:** 240-895-3000
E-mail: admissions@smcm.edu • **CEEB Code:** 5601
Fax: 240-895-5001 • **Website:** www.smcm.edu • **ACT Code:** 1736

This public school was founded in 1840. It has a 319-acre campus.

RATINGS
Admissions Selectivity Rating: 80   **Fire Safety Rating:** 80

STUDENTS AND FACULTY
Enrollment: 1,751. **Student Body:** 57% female, 43% male, 9% out-of-state, 1% international (12 countries represented). Asian 3%, African American 8%, Caucasian 73%, Hispanic 7%, Native American <1%
Retention and Graduation: 72% freshmen graduate within 4 years. **Faculty:** 141 full-time faculty, 100% hold PhDs, 48% are are members of minority groups, 15% are women. 0% of classes are taught by teaching assistants.

ACADEMICS
Degrees: bachelor's, master's. **Classes:** Most classes have 10-19 students. Most lab/discussion sessions have 10-19 students. **Majors with Highest Enrollment:** English Language and Literature; Biology/Biological Sciences. **Special Study Options:** double major, dual enrollment, exchange student program (domestic), honors program, independent study, internships, student-designed major, study abroad, teacher certification program. **Honors programs:** Nitze Scholars Program. **Disability Services:** Special programs offered to physically disabled students include note-taking services, reader services, tape recorders, tutors. **Career services:** Alumni network, alumni services, career/job search classes, career assessment, internships, regional alumni. Career services highlights include our rigorous credit internship program, which supports students' academic and career goals through the availability of part- to full-time work-learning experiences in the local community and beyond.

FACILITIES
Housing: Coed dorms, special housing for disabled students, men's dorms, women's dorms, apartments for single students, Wellness Housing, Theme HousingThere are a variety of different housing options at SMCM. Townhouses for upper-class students as well as suites are offered. There is also special interest housing (ex. SAFE house which is substance and alcohol free housing) and living learning centers (ex. international house, Women in Science House (WiSH), eco-house). 95% of campus accessible to physically disabled. **Special Academic Facilities/Equipment:** Art gallery, archaeological sites, Historic St. Mary's City, historic state house of early Maryland settlers, electron microscope, freshwater and saltwater research facilities, research boat. **Computers:** 100% of classrooms, 20% of dorms, 100% of libraries, 100% of dining areas, 100% of student union, 100% of common outdoor areas have wireless network access. Students can register for classes online. Administrative functions (other than registration) can be performed online.

CAMPUS LIFE
Environment: Rural. **Activities:** Choral groups, dance, drama/theater, jazz band, literary magazine, music ensembles, musical theater, radio station, student government, student newspaper, symphony orchestra, television station, yearbook, Campus Ministries, International Student Organization. 117 registered organizations, 8 honor societies, 4 religious organizations. **Athletics (Intercollegiate):** *Men:* baseball, basketball, cross-country, lacrosse, sailing, soccer, swimming, tennis. *Women:* basketball, cross-country, field hockey, lacrosse, sailing, soccer, swimming, tennis, volleyball. **On-Campus Highlights:** Student Center, Library, Athletics and Recreation Center (ARC), Waterfront, Garden of Remembrance. **Environmental Initiatives:** In 2007, students voted overwhelmingly (94%) to increase student fees $25 to purchase renewable energy credits (RECs) to offset 100% of the Colleges annual purchased electrical consumption. In the last two years the College has been able to increase its purchase of renewable energy credits by 15% allowing the school to offset over 85% of GHG emissions from campus buildings. Last year, students also voted to begin "Meatless Mondays," a schoolwide effort to reduce carbon usage of students by encouraging vegetarianism and minimizing meat options on Mondays. From 2006-2008, the College completed a $2.8 million energy performance contract (EPC) which reduced the Colleges electricity consumption 16.5%, oil consumption 24%, and water consumption 35%. The College is currently reviewing the possibility of second EPC. In addition to these large projects, smaller in-house renovations and energy conservation programs have yielded large dividends for the campus and the environment. Most academic buildings have low-flow toilets and faucets and motion sensing lights. St. Mary's pioneered Maryland's first major public LEED certified building, Goodpastor Hall, which uses 40% less energy than a conventional building and saves over 300,000 gallons of water each year. The College Strategic Plan now mandates that all new building be at lease LEED Silver certifiable or equivalent. To date the College has consturcted 3 "green" buildings totaling over 54,000 NASF of space and has 1 additional 20,000 NASF green building currently in design. The new building, Anne Arundel Hall, will be LEED silver certified, and the Admissions building recently installed a geothermal heating unit.

ADMISSIONS
Freshman Academic Profile: Average high school GPA 3.39. 75% from public high schools. SAT Math middle 50% range 530-633. SAT Critical Reading middle 50% range 574-650. SAT Writing middle 50% range 515-640. ACT middle 50% range 23-28. Minimum internet-based TOEFL 90. Minimum paper TOEFL 550. **Basis for Candidate Selection:** *Very important factors considered include:* academic GPA, rigor of secondary school record. *Important factors considered include:* application essay, recommendation(s), standardized test scores, extracurricular activities, first generation, talent/ability, volunteer work. *Other factors considered include:* alumni/ae relation, geographical residence, interview, racial/ethnic status, state residency, work experience. **Freshman Admission Requirements:** High school diploma is required and GED is accepted. *Academic units required:* 4 English, 3 mathematics, 3 science, (2 science labs), 2 foreign language, 2 social studies, 1 history, 3. **Freshman Admission Statistics:** 1,874 applied, 79% admitted, 26% enrolled. **Transfer Admission Requirements:** college transcript(s), essay or personal statement, Minimum college GPA of 3.0 required. Lowest grade transferable C-. **General Admission Information:** Application Fee $50. Early decision application deadline 11/1. Regular application deadline 1/1. Regular notification 4/1. Nonfall registration accepted. Credit and/or placement offered for CEEB Advanced Placement tests.

COSTS AND FINANCIAL AID
Required Forms and Deadlines: FAFSA. **Notification of Awards:** Applicants will be notified of awards on or about 4/1. **Types of Aid:** *Need-based scholarships/grants:* Federal Pell, SEOG, state scholarships/grants, private scholarships, the school's own gift aid. *Loans:* Subsidized Stafford, Unsubsidized Stafford, PLUS, Federal Perkins. *Student Employment:* Federal Work-Study Program available. Institutional employment available. Highest amount earned per year from on-campus jobs $1,100. Off-campus job opportunities are good. **Financial Aid Statistics:** 89% freshmen, 79% undergrads receive need-based scholarship or grant aid. 44% freshmen, 46% undergrads receive non-need-based scholarship or grant aid. 61% freshmen, 68% undergrads receive need-based self-help aid. 0% freshmen, 0% undergrads receive athletic scholarships. 72% freshmen, 74% undergrads receive any aid. 53% undergrads borrow to pay for school. Average cumulative indebtedness $21,016. **Criteria for awarding institutional aid:** *Non-need-based:* academics, alumni affiliation.

See page 1148.

ST. MARY'S UNIVERSITY

One Camino Santa Maria, San Antonio, TX 78228-8503
Phone: 210-436-3126 · **Financial Aid Phone:** 210-436-3141
E-mail: uadm@stmarytx.edu · **CEEB Code:** 6637
Fax: 210-431-6742 · **Website:** http://www.stmarytx.edu/ · **ACT Code:** 4158

This private school, affiliated with the Roman Catholic Church, was founded in 1852. It has a 135-acre campus.

RATINGS

Admissions Selectivity Rating: 86   **Fire Safety Rating:** 78

STUDENTS AND FACULTY

Enrollment: 2,391. **Student Body:** 56% female, 44% male, 8% out-of-state, 3% international (35 countries represented). Asian 3%, African American 4%, Caucasian 14%, Hispanic 73%, Native American <1%
Retention and Graduation: 33% freshmen graduate within 4 years. 55% freshmen graduate within 6 years. **Faculty:** 212 full-time faculty, 93% hold PhDs, 36% are are members of minority groups, 20% are women. 0% of classes are taught by teaching assistants.

ACADEMICS

Degrees: bachelor's, master's. **Classes:** Most classes have 20-29 students. Most lab/discussion sessions have 20-29 students. **Majors with Highest Enrollment:** Psychology; Biology/Biological Sciences; Kinesiology and Exercise Science. **Special Study Options:** cross-registration, distance learning, double major, dual enrollment, English as a Second Language (ESL), exchange student program (domestic), honors program, independent study, internships, liberal arts/career combination, study abroad, teacher certification program, Evening Studies Program. **Honors programs:** The Honors Program offers an academically challenging and personally enriching course of study designed to cultivate critical analysis, clear oral and written expression, aesthetic awareness and ethical judgment. In and out of the classroom we seek to prepare our future graduates for lives of leadership and service to their communities. **Combined degree programs:** BA/MA, B.Phil/M.Div. **Disability Services:** Special programs offered to physically disabled students include note-taking services, reader services, tape recorders, tutors. **Career services:** Alumni network, alumni services, career/job search classes, career assessment, internships, regional alumni.

FACILITIES

Housing: Coed dorms, Science Learning, Living Community; Residence hall for students 22 years old or above/non traditional. 80% of campus accessible to physically disabled. **Computers:** 100% of classrooms, 100% of dorms, 100% of libraries, 100% of dining areas, 100% of student union, 80% of common outdoor areas have wireless network access. Students can register for classes online. Administrative functions (other than registration) can be performed online. Undergraduates are required to own a computer.

CAMPUS LIFE

Environment: Metropolis. **Activities:** Choral groups, concert band, dance, drama/theater, jazz band, literary magazine, music ensembles, musical theater, pep band, student government, student newspaper, Campus Ministries, International Student Organization. 91 registered organizations, 1 religous organization. 4 fraternities, 4 sororities. **Athletics (Intercollegiate):** *Men:* baseball, basketball, cheerleading, golf, soccer, tennis. *Women:* basketball, cheerleading, cross-country, golf, soccer, softball, tennis, volleyball. **On-Campus Highlights:** Alumni Athletics and Convocation Center, University Center, Java City Coffee Shop, The Quad, Barrett Memorial Bell Tower, Pecan Grove and the new 278-bed Founders Hall round out the list of popular campus spots. Founders Hall opened in fall 2009. Designed for freshmen, it provides spacious rooms, welcoming indoor and outdoor common spaces, and a cyber Café. **Environmental Initiatives:** Energy efficiency electric motors, chillers, lighting; Water conservation; Pilot program (Recycling).

ADMISSIONS

Freshman Academic Profile: Average high school GPA 3.4. 28.2% in top 10% of high school class, 56.8% in top 25% of high school class, 82.6% in top 50% of high school class. 68% from public high schools. SAT Math middle 50% range 480-580. SAT Critical Reading middle 50% range 470-570. SAT Writing middle 50% range 450-545. ACT middle 50% range 21-24. Minimum internet-based TOEFL 80. Minimum paper TOEFL 550. **Basis for Candidate Selection:** *Very important factors considered include:* academic GPA, rigor of secondary school record. *Important factors considered include:* Class rank, standardized test scores. *Other factors considered include:* application essay, recommendation(s), alumni/ae relation, character/personal qualities, extracurricular activities, geographical residence, interview, talent/ability, volunteer work, work experience. **Freshman Admission Requirements:** High school diploma is required and GED is accepted. *Academic units required:* 4 English, 3 mathematics, 3 science, 2 foreign language, 3 social studies, 1 academic elective. **Freshman Admission Statistics:** 5,147 applied, 58% admitted, 20% enrolled. **Transfer Admission Requirements:** college transcript(s), Minimum college GPA of 2.5 required. Lowest grade transferable C-. **General Admission Information:** Application Fee $30. Notification on a rolling basis, beginning on or about 10/20. Nonfall registration accepted. Admission may be deferred for a maximum of 1 year. Credit and/or placement offered for CEEB Advanced Placement tests.

COSTS AND FINANCIAL AID

Annual tuition $24,520. Room and board $8,666. Required fees $606. Average book expense $1,300. **Required Forms and Deadlines:** FAFSA. **Notification of Awards:** Applicants will be notified of awards on a rolling basis beginning 3/1. **Types of Aid:** *Need-based scholarships/grants:* Federal Pell, SEOG, state scholarships/grants, private scholarships, the school's own gift aid. *Loans:* Direct Subsidized Stafford, Direct Unsubsidized Stafford, Direct PLUS, Federal Perkins, state loans. *Student Employment:* Federal Work-Study Program available. Institutional employment available. Off-campus job opportunities are good. **Financial Aid Statistics:** 98% freshmen, 97% undergrads receive need-based scholarship or grant aid. 83% freshmen, 69% undergrads receive non-need-based scholarship or grant aid. 90% freshmen, 92% undergrads receive need-based self-help aid. 7% freshmen, 7% undergrads receive athletic scholarships. 96% freshmen, 91% undergrads receive any aid. 81% undergrads borrow to pay for school. Average cumulative indebtedness $15,891. **Criteria for awarding institutional aid:** *Non-need-based:* academics, alumni affiliation, athletics, leadership, minority status, music/drama, state/district residency.

ST. NORBERT COLLEGE

100 Grant Street, De Pere, WI 54115-2099
Phone: 920-403-3005 · **Financial Aid Phone:** 920-403-3071
E-mail: admit@snc.edu · **CEEB Code:** 1706
Fax: 920-403-4072 · **Website:** www.snc.edu · **ACT Code:** 4644

This private school, affiliated with the Roman Catholic Church, was founded in 1898. It has a 93-acre campus.

RATINGS

Admissions Selectivity Rating: 84   **Fire Safety Rating:** 84

STUDENTS AND FACULTY

Enrollment: 2,052. **Student Body:** 57% female, 43% male, 22% out-of-state, 2% international (16 countries represented). Asian 1%, African American 1%, Caucasian 90%, Hispanic 3%, Native American 1%
Retention and Graduation: 84% freshmen return for sophomore year. 63% freshmen graduate within 4 years. 70% freshmen graduate within 6 years. 12% grads go on to further study within 1 year. **Faculty:** 133 full-time faculty, 89% hold PhDs, 44% are are members of minority groups, 11% are women. 0% of classes are taught by teaching assistants.

ACADEMICS

Degrees: bachelor's, master's. **Classes:** Most classes have 10-19 students. Most lab/discussion sessions have 10-19 students. **Majors with Highest Enrollment:** Elementary Education and Teaching; Business/Commerce; Biology/Biological Sciences. **Special Study Options:** distance learning, double major, English as a Second Language (ESL), honors program, independent study, internships, student-designed major, study abroad, teacher certification program, Foundation for International Education (London)Internships; Washington Semester. **Honors programs:** The Honors Program at St. Norbert College offers a sophisticated and demanding program of studies and readings to provide the most academically talented students with an enriched academic curriculum that is stimulating and challenging. **Disability Services:** Special programs offered to physically disabled students include note-taking services, reader services, tape recorders, tutors. **Career services:** Alumni network, alumni services, career assessment, internships, regional alumni. Career services highlights include internships on campus or off campus, which students can begin after their freshmen year. Strong emphasis is placed on learning contracts.

FACILITIES

Housing: Coed dorms, special housing for disabled students, special housing for international students, women's dorms, fraternity/sorority housing, apartments for single students, Townhouses Off-campus college owned housing. 72% of campus accessible to physically disabled. **Special Academic Facilities/Equipment:** New state-of-the-art Mulva Library, Center for leadership and service, Bush Art Center with three art galleries, scanning electron microscope, visual and performing arts center, center for international education, riverfront campus center with marina, peace and justice center, career services, children's center in cooperation with early childhood education, center of economic education, survey center, Kress Inn, conference services, academic support services, St. Joseph Church, chapels in residence halls, women's center and Journey-Men (men's center). **Computers:** 100% of classrooms, 60% of dorms, 100% of libraries, 100% of dining areas, 100% of student union, have wireless network access. Students can register for classes online. Administrative functions (other than registration) can be performed online.

CAMPUS LIFE

Environment: Village. **Activities:** Choral groups, concert band, drama/theater, jazz band, literary magazine, music ensembles, musical theater, pep band, radio station, student government, student newspaper, student-run film society, television station, Campus Ministries, International Student Organization. 63 registered organizations, 10 honor societies, 3 religious organizations. 3 fraternities, 4 sororities. **Athletics (Intercollegiate):** *Men:* baseball, basketball, cross-country, football, golf, ice hockey, soccer, tennis, track/field (outdoor), track/field (indoor). *Women:* basketball, cross-country, golf, ice hockey, soccer, softball, tennis, track/field (outdoor), track/field (indoor), volleyball. **On-Campus Highlights:** The Ray Van Den Heuvel Campus Center, The Bush Fine Arts Center, The F.K. Bemis International Center, Austin E Cofrin Hall, New Mulva Library with Coffee Shop. **Environmental Initiatives:** Designed new Mulva Library with solar water heating system. Converting all campus outdoor lighting to meet "night sky" compliance. Plan and design of future science building will meet Gold standards of LEED certification.

ADMISSIONS

Freshman Academic Profile: Average high school GPA 3.5. 31% in top 10% of high school class, 61% in top 25% of high school class, 88% in top 50% of high school class. 75% from public high schools. ACT middle 50% range 22-27. Minimum internet-based TOEFL 80. Minimum paper TOEFL 550. **Basis for Candidate Selection:** *Very important factors considered include:* academic GPA, standardized test scores. *Important factors considered include:* rigor of secondary school record. *Other factors considered include:* Class rank, application essay, recommendation(s), alumni/ae relation, character/personal qualities, extracurricular activities, first generation, geographical residence, interview, level of applicant's interest, racial/ethnic status, religious affiliation/commitment, state residency, talent/ability, volunteer work, work experience. **Freshman Admission Requirements:** High school diploma is required and GED is accepted. **Freshman Admission Statistics:** 2,149 applied, 82% admitted, 31% enrolled. **Transfer Admission Requirements:** High school transcript, college transcript(s), essay or personal statement, standardized test scores, Minimum college GPA of 2.5 required. Lowest grade transferable C. **General Admission Information:** Application Fee $25. Notification on a rolling basis, beginning on or about 10/1. Nonfall registration accepted. Admission may be deferred for a maximum of 2 years. Credit and/or placement offered for CEEB Advanced Placement tests.

COSTS AND FINANCIAL AID

Annual tuition $32,408. Room and board $8,455. Required fees $615. Average book expense $950. **Required Forms and Deadlines:** FAFSA. **Notification of Awards:** Applicants will be notified of awards on a rolling basis beginning 3/15. **Types of Aid:** *Need-based scholarships/grants:* Federal Pell, SEOG, state scholarships/grants, private scholarships, the school's own gift aid. *Loans:* Direct Subsidized Stafford, Direct Unsubsidized Stafford, Direct PLUS, Federal Perkins, state loans, college/university loans from institutional funds. *Student Employment:* Federal Work-Study Program available. Institutional employment available. Off-campus job opportunities are good. **Financial Aid Statistics:** 98% freshmen, 98% undergrads receive need-based scholarship or grant aid. 3% freshmen, 4% undergrads receive non-need-based scholarship or grant aid. 79% freshmen, 81% undergrads receive need-based self-help aid. 0% freshmen, 0% undergrads receive athletic scholarships. 99% freshmen, 97% undergrads receive any aid. 78% undergrads borrow to pay for school. Average cumulative indebtedness $23,353. **Criteria for awarding institutional aid:** *Non-need-based:* academics, art, leadership, minority status, music/drama, state/district residency.

See page 1150.

ST. OLAF COLLEGE

1520 St. Olaf Avenue, Northfield, MN 55057
Phone: 507-786-3025 · **Financial Aid Phone:** 507-786-3019
E-mail: admissions@stolaf.edu · **CEEB Code:** 6638
Fax: 507-786-3832 · **Website:** http://wp.stolaf.edu · **ACT Code:** 2150

This private school, affiliated with the Lutheran Church, was founded in 1874. It has a 300-acre campus.

RATINGS

Admissions Selectivity Rating: 93   **Fire Safety Rating:** 72

STUDENTS AND FACULTY

Enrollment: 2,990. **Student Body:** 58% female, 42% male, 52% out-of-state, 7% international (73 countries represented). Asian 6%, African American 2%, Caucasian 77%, Hispanic 5%, Native American <1% **Retention and Graduation:** 86% freshmen graduate within 4 years. 26% grads go on to further study within 1 year. 8% grads pursue arts and sciences degrees. 1% grads pursue law degrees. 6% grads pursue medical degrees. **Faculty:** 215 full-time faculty, 93% hold PhDs, 46% are members of minority groups, 13% are women. 0% of classes are taught by teaching assistants.

ACADEMICS

Degrees: bachelor's. **Classes:** Most classes have 10-19 students. Most lab/discussion sessions have 20-29 students. **Majors with Highest Enrollment:** Biology/Biological Sciences; Economics; Psychology. **Special Study Options:** cross-registration, double major, dual enrollment, independent study, internships, student-designed major, study abroad, teacher certification program. **Combined degree programs:** Law w/Columbia University. **Disability Services:** Special programs offered to physically disabled students include note-taking services, reader services, tape recorders, tutors. **Career services:** Alumni network, alumni services, career/job search classes, career assessment, internships, regional alumni. Career services highlights include a comprehensive service offered by The Center for Experiential Learning that is linked to the academic program and offers many types of experiences to complement students' academic programs. THE CEL houses four programs: internships, service and civic leadership, entrepreneurial studies, and career services. The CEL has been bery successful in creating programming that meets the needs of students during their four years at St. Olaf. Some programs of which we are proud: entrepreneurial grants to start student-run businesses, service trips, civic engagement initiatives connected to specific courses, career-related seminars preseented in collaboration with academic departments, case study challenges created in conjunction with our corporate partners. Our academic internship program offers students an opportunity to receive credit for experiential learning. Since 2000, there have been over 900 Academic Internships completed by St. Olaf students at over 700 different organizations world wide.

FACILITIES

Housing: Coed dorms, special housing for disabled students, Theme Housing, Honor houses, language houses, quiet halls, first-year only dorms. Disabled students accommodated in dorm of their choice. 80% of campus accessible to physically disabled. **Special Academic Facilities/Equipment:** Finstad Program for Entrepreneurial Studies, Kierkegaard Library, Flaten Art Museum, Norwegian American Historical Association archives. **Computers:** 100% of classrooms, 100% of dorms, 100% of libraries, 100% of dining areas, 100% of student union, 100% of common outdoor areas have wireless network access. Students can register for classes online. Administrative functions (other than registration) can be performed online.

CAMPUS LIFE

Environment: Village. **Activities:** Choral groups, concert band, dance, drama/theater, jazz band, literary magazine, music ensembles, musical theater, opera, pep band, radio station, student government, student newspaper, student-run film society, symphony orchestra, television station, Campus Ministries, International Student Organization, Model UN. 193 registered organizations, 18 honor societies, 16 religious organizations. **Athletics (Intercollegiate):** *Men:* baseball, basketball, cross-country, diving, football, golf, ice hockey, skiing (downhill/alpine), skiing (nordic/cross-country), soccer, swimming, tennis, track/field (outdoor), track/field (indoor), wrestling. *Women:* basketball, cross-country, diving, golf, ice hockey, skiing (downhill/alpine), skiing (nordic/cross-country), soccer, softball, swimming, tennis, track/field (outdoor), track/field (indoor), volleyball. **On-Campus Highlights:** Regents Hall of Natural Science & Math, Buntrock Commons, Tostrud Recreation Center, The Lion's Pause, Dittman Art Museum, Beautiful 300 acre campus.

ADMISSIONS

Freshman Academic Profile: Average high school GPA 3.62. 52% in top 10% of high school class, 79% in top 25% of high school class, 97% in top 50% of high school class. 72% from public high schools. SAT Math middle 50% range 570-690. SAT Critical Reading middle 50% range 560-700. ACT middle 50% range 26-32. Minimum internet-based TOEFL 90. **Basis for Candidate Selection:** *Very important factors considered include:* application essay, academic GPA, rigor of secondary school record. *Important factors considered include:* Class rank, recommendation(s), standardized test scores, character/personal qualities, extracurricular activities. *Other factors considered include:* alumni/ae relation, first generation, geographical residence, interview, level of applicant's interest, racial/ethnic status, religious affiliation/commitment, state residency, talent/ability, volunteer work, work experience. **Freshman Admission Requirements:** High school diploma is required and GED is accepted. **Freshman Admission Statistics:** 4,875 applied, 51% admitted, 31% enrolled. **Transfer Admission Requirements:** High school transcript, college transcript(s), essay or personal statement, standardized test scores, statement of good standing from prior institution(s). Minimum college GPA of 2.50 required. Lowest grade transferable C. **General Admission Information:** Application Fee $40. Early decision application deadline 11/15. Regular notification 3/20. Nonfall registration not accepted. Admission may be deferred for a maximum of 1 year. Credit and/or placement offered for CEEB Advanced Placement tests.

COSTS AND FINANCIAL AID

Annual tuition $41,700. Room and board $9,500. Required fees $0. Average book expense $1,000. **Required Forms and Deadlines:** FAFSA, CSS/Financial Aid PROFILE, Noncustodial PROFILE, Business/Farm Supplement. **Notification of Awards:** Applicants will be notified of awards on a rolling basis beginning 3/1. **Types of Aid:** *Need-based scholarships/grants:* Federal Pell, SEOG, state scholarships/grants, private scholarships, the school's own gift aid. *Loans:* Subsidized Stafford, Unsubsidized Stafford, PLUS, Federal Perkins, Federal Nursing, state loans, college/university loans from institutional funds. *Student Employment:* Federal Work-Study Program available. Off-campus job opportunities are fair. **Financial Aid Statistics:** 100% freshmen, 99% undergrads receive need-based scholarship or grant aid. 26% freshmen, 24% undergrads receive non-need-based scholarship or grant aid. 100% freshmen, 100% undergrads receive need-based self-help aid. 0% freshmen, 0% undergrads receive athletic scholarships. 92% freshmen, 93% undergrads receive any aid. 60% undergrads borrow to pay for school. Average cumulative indebtedness $23,443. **Criteria for awarding institutional aid:** *Non-need-based:* academics, leadership, music/drama.

ST. THOMAS AQUINAS COLLEGE

125 Route 340, Sparkill, NY 10976
Phone: 845-398-4100 · **Financial Aid Phone:** 845-398-4098
E-mail: admissions@stac.edu · **CEEB Code:** 2807
Fax: 845-398-4372 · **Website:** www.stac.edu · **ACT Code:** 2897

This private school was founded in 1952. It has a 47-acre campus.

RATINGS

Admissions Selectivity Rating: 73   **Fire Safety Rating:** 87

STUDENTS AND FACULTY

Enrollment: 1,287. **Student Body:** 54% female, 46% male, 18% out-of-state, 2% international. Asian 2%, African American 8%, Caucasian 54%, Hispanic 18%, Native American <1%
Retention and Graduation: 81% freshmen return for sophomore year. 51% freshmen graduate within 6 years. 36% grads go on to further study within 1 year. 25% grads pursue arts and sciences degrees. 5% grads pursue law degrees. 5% grads pursue business degrees. 5% grads pursue medical degrees. **Faculty:** 59 full-time faculty. 75% hold PhDs. 51% are are members of minority groups, 7% are women. 0% of classes are taught by teaching assistants.

ACADEMICS

Degrees: associate, bachelor's, master's, post-master's certificate, terminal associate, transfer associate. **Classes:** Most classes have 20-29 students. **Majors with Highest Enrollment:** Elementary Education and Teaching; Criminal Justice/Law Enforcement Administration; Business/Commerce. **Special Study Options:** Accelerated program, cooperative education program, cross-registration, double major, dual enrollment, exchange student program (domestic), honors program, independent study, internships, liberal arts/career combination, study abroad, teacher certification program, Undergrads may take grad level classes—e.g. cooperative education programs: combined BS/MSW in social work in partnership with NYU; engineering combined degree programs: 3-2 engineering programs with George Washington U and Manhattan Coll

foreign exchange program(s): study abroad in England. **Honors programs:** Highly selective honors program with maximum 20 student each class. Honor students receive full scholarship. **Disability Services:** Special programs offered to physically disabled students include note-taking services, tape recorders, tutors. **Career services:** Alumni network, alumni services, career/job search classes, career assessment, internships, regional alumni.

FACILITIES

Housing: men's dorms, women's dorms, apartments for single students. 80% of campus accessible to physically disabled. **Special Academic Facilities/Equipment:** Azarian-McCullough Art Gallery, Sullivan Theatre, Spellman Technology Corridor, Costello Hall Science and Technology Center. **Computers:** Students can register for classes online.

CAMPUS LIFE

Environment: Village. **Activities:** Choral groups, dance, drama/theater, literary magazine, musical theater, opera, radio station, student government, student newspaper, yearbook. 35 registered organizations, 8 honor societies, 1 religious organization. **Athletics (Intercollegiate):** *Men:* baseball, basketball, cross-country, golf, soccer, tennis, track/field (outdoor), track/field (indoor). *Women:* basketball, cross-country, lacrosse, soccer, softball, tennis, track/field (outdoor). **On-Campus Highlights:** The College Commons, The Fitness Center, The Romano Alumni Center, The Art Gallery, The Techonology Corridor.

ADMISSIONS

Freshman Academic Profile: Average high school GPA 2.6. 5% in top 10% of high school class, 35% in top 25% of high school class, 50% in top 50% of high school class. 70% from public high schools. SAT Math middle 50% range 410-530. SAT Critical Reading middle 50% range 420-520. SAT Writing middle 50% range 410-510. ACT middle 50% range 17-20. Minimum paper TOEFL 530. **Basis for Candidate Selection:** *Very important factors considered include:* rigor of secondary school record. *Important factors considered include:* application essay, recommendation(s), standardized test scores, extracurricular activities, interview, talent/ability. *Other factors considered include:* alumni/ae relation, volunteer work, work experience. **Freshman Admission Requirements:** High school diploma is required and GED is accepted. *Academic units required:* 4 English, 3 mathematics, 3 science, (2 science labs), 3 foreign language, 4 social studies. **Freshman Admission Statistics:** 1,841 applied, 82% admitted, 22% enrolled. **Transfer Admission Requirements:** college transcript(s), statement of good standing from prior institution(s). Minimum college GPA of 2.0 required. Lowest grade transferable C. **General Admission Information:** Application Fee $30. Early decision application deadline 12/15. Notification on a rolling basis, beginning on or about 10/1. Nonfall registration accepted. Admission may be deferred for a maximum of one year. Credit and/or placement offered for CEEB Advanced Placement tests.

COSTS AND FINANCIAL AID

Annual tuition $27,130. Room and board $11,680. Required fees $500. Average book expense $1,000. **Required Forms and Deadlines:** FAFSA, State aid form. **Notification of Awards:** Applicants will be notified of awards on a rolling basis beginning 3/1. **Types of Aid:** *Need-based scholarships/grants:* Federal Pell, SEOG, state scholarships/grants, private scholarships, the school's own gift aid. *Loans:* Direct Subsidized Stafford, Direct Unsubsidized Stafford, Direct PLUS, Subsidized Stafford, Unsubsidized Stafford, PLUS, Federal Perkins, Private alternative loans from lending institutions. *Student Employment:* Federal Work-Study Program available. Institutional employment available. Off-campus job opportunities are good. **Financial Aid Statistics:** 89% freshmen, 105% undergrads receive need-based scholarship or grant aid. 29% freshmen, 33% undergrads receive non-need-based scholarship or grant aid. 86% freshmen, 102% undergrads receive need-based self-help aid. 12% freshmen, 8% undergrads receive athletic scholarships. 66% freshmen, 72% undergrads receive any aid. 78% undergrads borrow to pay for school. **Criteria for awarding institutional aid:** *Non-need-based:* academics, athletics.

ST. THOMAS UNIVERSITY

16401 Northwest 37th Avenue, Miami Gardens, FL 33054
Phone: 305-628-6546 • **Financial Aid Phone:** 305-628-6547
E-mail: signup@stu.edu • **CEEB Code:** 5076
Fax: 305-628-6591 • **Website:** www.stu.edu • **ACT Code:** 719

This private school, affiliated with the Roman Catholic Church, was founded in 1961. It has a 140-acre campus.

RATINGS

Admissions Selectivity Rating: 82   **Fire Safety Rating:** 70

STUDENTS AND FACULTY

Enrollment: 1,111. **Student Body:** 55% female, 45% male, 92% out-of-state, 12% international (57 countries represented). Asian 1%, African American 19%, Caucasian 10%, Hispanic 32%, Native American <1%
Retention and Graduation: 70% freshmen return for sophomore year. 22% freshmen graduate within 4 years. **Faculty:** 105 full-time faculty, 89% hold PhDs, 47% are are members of minority groups, 30% are women. 0% of classes are taught by teaching assistants.

ACADEMICS

Degrees: bachelor's, certificate, master's, post-bachelor's certificate, post-master's certificate. **Classes:** Most classes have 10-19 students. Most lab/discussion sessions have 10-19 students. **Majors with Highest Enrollment:** Psychology; Organizational Behavior Studies; Business Administration and Management. **Special Study Options:** distance learning, double major, dual enrollment, honors program, independent study, internships, liberal arts/career combination, teacher certification program. **Honors programs:** The St. Thomas University Honors Program is designed to provide an intensive and stimulating alternative for students who wish to enhance their college academic experience. Qualified students are offered the opportunity to take Honors courses in the subjects of their choice, and, if they desire, to work for an Honors degree. **Combined degree programs:** BA/JD. **Disability Services:** Special programs offered to physically disabled students include note-taking services, reader services, tape recorders, tutors. **Career services:** career/job search classes, career assessment, internships.

FACILITIES

Housing: men's dorms, women's dorms. 80% of campus accessible to physically disabled. **Special Academic Facilities/Equipment:** Multimedia computer equipment, TV studio, Art Atrium Gallery. **Computers:** 100% of libraries, 100% of dining areas, have wireless network access. Students can register for classes online. Administrative functions (other than registration) can be performed online.

CAMPUS LIFE

Environment: Metropolis. **Activities:** Choral groups, literary magazine, music ensembles, student government, television station, yearbook, Campus Ministries, International Student Organization. 26 registered organizations, 4 honor societies, 2 religious organizations. **Athletics (Intercollegiate):** *Men:* baseball, basketball, cross-country, golf, soccer, tennis. *Women:* basketball, cross-country, soccer, softball, tennis, volleyball. **On-Campus Highlights:** Campus Chapel, Library, Fernandez Family Center, Kennedy Hall.

ADMISSIONS

Freshman Academic Profile: Average high school GPA 2.97. 6% in top 10% of high school class, 17% in top 25% of high school class, 53% in top 50% of high school class. SAT Math middle 50% range 408-500. SAT Critical Reading middle 50% range 410-510. SAT Writing middle 50% range 400-490. ACT middle 50% range 16.25-20.75. Minimum paper TOEFL 525. **Basis for Candidate Selection:** *Very important factors considered include:* Class rank, academic GPA, standardized test scores. *Important factors considered include:* application essay, recommendation(s), rigor of secondary school record, alumni/ ae relation, level of applicant's interest. *Other factors considered include:* character/personal qualities, extracurricular activities, talent/ability, volunteer work, work experience. **Freshman Admission Requirements:** High school diploma is required and GED is accepted. *Academic units required:* 4 English, 3 mathematics, 2 science, 3 social studies, 6 academic electives. **Freshman Admission Statistics:** 727 applied, 46% admitted, 63% enrolled. **Transfer Admission Requirements:** college transcript(s), essay or personal statement, statement of good standing from prior institution(s). Minimum college GPA of 2.0 required. Lowest grade transferable C-. **General Admission Information:** Application Fee $40. Nonfall registration accepted. Admission may be deferred for a maximum of One year. Credit and/or placement offered for CEEB Advanced Placement tests.

COSTS AND FINANCIAL AID

Required Forms and Deadlines: FAFSA. **Notification of Awards:** Applicants will be notified of awards on a rolling basis beginning 3/1. **Types of Aid:**

Need-based scholarships/grants: Federal Pell, SEOG, state scholarships/grants, private scholarships, the school's own gift aid. *Loans:* Subsidized Stafford, Unsubsidized Stafford, PLUS, Federal Perkins. *Student Employment:* Federal Work-Study Program available. Institutional employment available. Off-campus job opportunities are good. **Financial Aid Statistics:** 77% freshmen, 76% undergrads receive need-based scholarship or grant aid. 72% freshmen, 71% undergrads receive need-based self-help aid. 12% freshmen, 15% undergrads receive athletic scholarships. **Criteria for awarding institutional aid:** *Non-need-based:* academics, athletics, leadership.

ST. THOMAS UNIVERSITY

Admissions Office, St. Thomas University, Fredericton, NB E3B 5G3
Phone: 506-452-0532
E-mail: admissions@stu.ca
Fax: 506-452-0617 • **Website:** http://www.stu.ca

This private school, affiliated with the Roman Catholic Church, was founded in 1910. It has a 21-acre campus.

RATINGS

Admissions Selectivity Rating: 61   **Fire Safety Rating:** 92

STUDENTS AND FACULTY

Enrollment: 2,475. **Student Body:** 66% female, 34% male, 27% out-of-state, 5% international (42 countries represented).
Retention and Graduation: 69% freshmen return for sophomore year. 41% freshmen graduate within 4 years. 54% freshmen graduate within 6 years. **Faculty:** 109 full-time faculty, 95% hold PhDs, 39% are are members of minority groups. 0% of classes are taught by teaching assistants.

ACADEMICS

Degrees: bachelor's, certificate, first professional, post-bachelor's certificate. **Classes:** Most classes have 10-19 students. **Majors with Highest Enrollment:** English Language and Literature; Psychology; Criminology. **Special Study Options:** Accelerated program, cross-registration, double major, English as a Second Language (ESL), exchange student program (domestic), honors program, independent study, student-designed major, study abroad, teacher certification program, Aquinas Program: Thematically linked courses from various disciplines. **Disability Services:** Special programs offered to physically disabled students include note-taking services, reader services, tape recorders, tutors. **Career services:** career/job search classes, career assessment, internships.

FACILITIES

Housing: Coed dorms, women's dorms. 80% of campus accessible to physically disabled. **Computers:** 100% of dorms, 100% of libraries, 100% of dining areas, have wireless network access. Students can register for classes online. Administrative functions (other than registration) can be performed online.

CAMPUS LIFE

Environment: Town. **Activities:** Choral groups, drama/theater, jazz band, music ensembles, musical theater, radio station, student government, student newspaper, student-run film society, yearbook, Campus Ministries, International Student Organization, Model UN 5 religious organizations. **Athletics (Intercollegiate):** *Men:* basketball, cross-country, golf, ice hockey, rugby, soccer, volleyball. *Women:* basketball, cross-country, golf, ice hockey, rugby, soccer, volleyball. **On-Campus Highlights:** Margaret Norrie McCain Hall, Lower courtyard, J.B. O'Keefe Fitness Centre, Sir James Dunn Hall, The Black Box Theatre. **Environmental Initiatives:** Recycle bins in all areas. Reduction of plastic and styrofoam products in Cafeteria. Promotion of reduced energy usage.

ADMISSIONS

Freshman Academic Profile: Average high school GPA 3.3. Minimum internet-based TOEFL 88. Minimum paper TOEFL 570. **Basis for Candidate Selection:** *Very important factors considered include:* academic GPA. *Other factors considered include:* application essay, recommendation(s), standardized test scores. **Freshman Admission Requirements:** High school diploma is required and GED is not accepted. **Freshman Admission Statistics:** 1,345 applied, 81% admitted, 58% enrolled. **Transfer Admission Requirements:** college transcript(s), statement of good standing from prior institution(s). Lowest grade transferable D. **General Admission Information:** Application Fee $35. Regular application deadline 8/31. Notification on a rolling basis, beginning on or about 10/15. Nonfall registration accepted. Admission may be deferred for a maximum of 1 year. Credit and/or placement offered for CEEB Advanced Placement tests.

COSTS AND FINANCIAL AID

Average book expense $1,000.

STANFORD UNIVERSITY

Undergraduate Admission, Stanford, CA 94305-6106
Phone: 650-723-2091 · **Financial Aid Phone:** 650-723-3058
E-mail: admission@stanford.edu · **CEEB Code:** 4704
Fax: 650-725-2846 · **Website:** www.stanford.edu · **ACT Code:** 434

This private school was founded in 1885. It has a 8180-acre campus.

RATINGS

Admissions Selectivity Rating: 99   Fire Safety Rating: 82

STUDENTS AND FACULTY

Enrollment: 7,018. **Student Body:** 47% female, 53% male, 59% out-of-state, 8% international (90 countries represented). Asian 20%, African American 6%, Caucasian 38%, Hispanic 16%, Native American 1%
Retention and Graduation: 98% freshmen return for sophomore year. 76% freshmen graduate within 4 years. 95% freshmen graduate within 6 years. 34% grads go on to further study within 1 year. 16% grads pursue arts and sciences degrees. 2% grads pursue law degrees. 1% grads pursue business degrees. 3% grads pursue medical degrees. **Faculty:** 1,559 full-time faculty, 99% hold PhDs. 26% are are members of minority groups, 22% are women. 6% of classes are taught by teaching assistants.

ACADEMICS

Degrees: bachelor's, master's. **Classes:** Most classes have 10-19 students. Most lab/discussion sessions have 10-19 students. **Majors with Highest Enrollment:** Computer Science; Human Biology; Engineering. **Special Study Options:** distance learning, double major, exchange student program (domestic), honors program, independent study, internships, student-designed major, study abroad, Marine research center, Bing Stanford in Washington program, exchange programs with Dartmouth, Howard, Morehouse and Spelman, undergraduate research opportunities, Bing Honors College, overseas study. **Honors programs:** About 100 student annually participate in Bing Honors College. About 25 percent of each graduating class earn departmental honors. **Combined degree programs:** BA/MA, Many bachelors/masters coterminal degree. **Disability Services:** Special programs offered to physically disabled students include note-taking services, reader services, tape recorders, tutors. **Career services:** Alumni network, alumni services, career/job search classes, career assessment, internships, regional alumni. Career services highlights include The Haas Center for Public Service at Stanford, which connects academic study with public service to strengthen communities and develop effective public leaders.

FACILITIES

Housing: Coed dorms, special housing for disabled students, women's dorms, fraternity/sorority housing, apartments for married students, cooperative housing, apartments for single students, Theme **Housing:** Academic, cross-cultural, language theme and ethnic theme houses. 98% of campus accessible to physically disabled. **Special Academic Facilities/Equipment:** Art museum, marine station, observatory, biological preserve, linear accelerator. **Computers:** 100% of classrooms, 100% of dorms, 100% of libraries, 100% of dining areas, 100% of student union, 75% of common outdoor areas have wireless network access. Students can register for classes online. Administrative functions (other than registration) can be performed online.

CAMPUS LIFE

Environment: City. **Activities:** Choral groups, concert band, dance, drama/theater, jazz band, literary magazine, marching band, music ensembles, musical theater, opera, pep band, radio station, student government, student newspaper, student-run film society, symphony orchestra, television station, yearbook, Campus Ministries, International Student Organization, Model UN. 600 registered organizations, 40 religious organizations. 17 fraternities, 11 sororities. **Athletics (Intercollegiate):** *Men:* baseball, basketball, crew/rowing, cross-country, diving, fencing, football, golf, gymnastics, sailing, soccer, swimming, tennis, track/field (outdoor), volleyball, water polo, wrestling. *Women:* basketball, crew/rowing, cross-country, diving, fencing, field hockey, golf, gymnastics, lacrosse, sailing, soccer, softball, squash, swimming, synchronized swimming, tennis, track/field (outdoor), volleyball, water polo. **On-Campus Highlights:** Cantor Center for the Visual Arts, Rodin Sculpture Garden, Memorial Church, Observation Deck at Hoover Tower, athletic facilities. The Stanford campus is among the most beautiful anywhere and is a popular destination for tourists and other visitors. **Environmental Initiatives:** (a) Significasnt commintment to sustainability project implementation: (1) The Stanford Energy System Innovations

(SESI) project is a $438 million major transformation of the campus district energy system from gas-fired combined heat and power with steam distribution to electrically-powered combined heat and cooling with hot water distribution. When completed, the new heat recovery system will be 52% more efficient than the existing cogeneration system; immediately cut Stanfords greenhouse gas emissions in half; save 18% of Stanfords drinking water supply; and save $303 million over the next 35 years compared to the existing system. Project additions with conceptual approval that are now under final feasibility study include the installation of 4 to 7 MW of on-site behind-the-meter photovoltaic (PV) power generation; installation of a Ground Source Heat Exchange system to augment the base heat recovery scheme; and the installation of a new 60kV high voltage transmission line connecting SLAC, Stanford, and the City of Palo Alto to strengthen the local transmission grid. http://sesi.stanford.edu (2) $433 million for the Initiative on Environment and Sustainability (research and teaching), a component of the Stanford Challenge http://thestanfordchallenge.stanford.edu/highlights-by-initiative/environment-sustainability/ (3) $70 million over the past ten years on energy retrofits, recommissioning, energy efficiency projects large and small, and water conservation measures?ùsince 2002, energy retrofits of older building shave resulted in an estimated savings of 176 million kilowatt-hours of electricity, about 8 months of Stanfords current electricity use. Water consumption has been reduced from 2.7 million gallons per day to 2.15 million since 2001. New constructions and major renovations have energy and water standards comparable to LEED-NC GOLD. http://sustainable.stanford.edu/climate_action http://sustainable.stanford.edu/energy_initiatives http://sustainable.stanford.edu/water_initiatives http://sustainable.stanford.edu/guidelines (b) collaborative governance & conservation campaigns (1) Starting in 2011, a consortium of senior faculty, operations staff, and student leaders in campus sustainability returned to the drawing board to develop Sustainability 3.0, a strategic plan to expand and enhance that sustainability over the next five to ten years. The goal was to outline a shared and actionable vision for making sustainability a core value through teaching, research, and action. The committee met with stakeholders across the university to examine its sustainability successes and identify opportunities for enhancement. The result was a blueprint for the future of sustainability at Stanford. Major goals include leading sustainability by example through on- and off-campus actions, and maintaining a global influence through sustainability in research, education, and operations. http://sustainable.stanford.edu/vision (2) Campus-wide Cardinal Green conservation campaigns and associated training continue to increase institutional awareness of programs to reduce resource consumption. Behavior-based conservation programs with pertinent messaging, relevant training, attractive incentives, and attainable goals have the potential to yield impressive results. Each campaign focuses on a single topic area and invites active community participation through hands-on training, online pledges, and results-based incentives. The two campaigns presented for the second time during the 2011-12 academic year exceeded their prior years performance and gained momentum through targeted promotion to the most relevant campus audiences. http://sustainable.stanford.edu/be_cardinal_green (3) Since 2000, Stanford has maintained detailed internal metrics and performance records in the key operational areas of energy, greenhouse gas (GHG) emissions, transportation, waste, and water. The campus has either maintained or lowered consumption per usable square foot (USF) in all areas, despite growth and the addition of nearly one million square feet of high-intensity research laboratory space. Based on its strong tradition of internal reporting and proven program success, national evaluating organizations continue to recognize Stanford as a leader in sustainability and a benchmark for the higher education community. Since 2008, Stanford has achieved top rankings in annual third-party sustainability evaluations such as Newsweeks Greenest Colleges (2nd place) Sustainable Endowments Institutes College Sustainability Report Card, and Sierra magazines Cool Schools (3rd place), and the AASHE STARS program (Gold Rating). (c) transportation demand management & waste management programs (1) Stanford's award-winning Transportation Demand Management program has been recognized by the EPA. It includes a free bus system powered by biodiesel and hybid buses; a commute club, free or pre-tax passes on public transportation; car rental options; commute planning assistance; charter services; and a bike program. In 2012, the employee drive-alone rate dropped to 47%, compared to 72% in 2002 at the inception of the formal TDM program. Commute-related emissions remain below 1990 levels. http://transportation.stanford.edu/ (2) Stanfords recycling program, started by students in the 1970s and recognized by the EPA, Stanford has increased its landfill diversion rate from 30% in 1994 to 62% in 2011, and reduced its landfilled tonnage to an all-time low. The university continues to work towards a 75% diversion rate en route to the ultimate goal of zero waste. http://recycling.stanford.edu

ADMISSIONS

Freshman Academic Profile: Average high school GPA 4.16. 95% in top 10% of high school class, 99% in top 25% of high school class, 100% in top 50% of high school class. 60% from public high schools. SAT Math middle 50% range 700-790. SAT Critical Reading middle 50% range 680-780. SAT Writing middle 50% range 690-790. ACT middle 50% range 31-34. **Basis for Candidate Selection:** *Very important factors considered include:* Class rank, application essay, academic GPA, recommendation(s), rigor of secondary school record, standardized test scores, character/personal qualities, extracurricular activities, talent/ability. *Other factors considered include:* alumni/ae relation, first generation, geographical residence, racial/ethnic status, volunteer work, work experience. **Freshman Admission Requirements:** High school diploma is required and GED is accepted. **Freshman Admission Statistics:** 42,167 applied, 5% admitted, 78% enrolled. **Transfer Admission Requirements:** High school transcript, college transcript(s), essay or personal statement, standardized test scores, statement of good standing from prior institution(s). Lowest grade transferable C-. **General Admission Information:** Application Fee $90. Regular application deadline 1/1. Regular notification 4/1. Nonfall registration not accepted. Admission may be deferred for a maximum of 2 years. Credit and/or placement offered for CEEB Advanced Placement tests.

COSTS AND FINANCIAL AID
Annual tuition $44,184. Room and board $13,631. Required fees $573. Average book expense $1,425. **Required Forms and Deadlines:** FAFSA, CSS/Financial Aid PROFILE. **Notification of Awards:** Applicants will be notified of awards on a rolling basis beginning 4/3. **Types of Aid:** *Need-based scholarships/grants:* Federal Pell, SEOG, state scholarships/grants, private scholarships, the school's own gift aid. *Loans:* Subsidized Stafford, Unsubsidized Stafford, PLUS, Federal Perkins. *Student Employment:* Federal Work-Study Program available. Institutional employment available. Off-campus job opportunities are good. **Financial Aid Statistics:** 99% freshmen, 98% undergrads receive need-based scholarship or grant aid. 3% freshmen, 3% undergrads receive non-need-based scholarship or grant aid. 69% freshmen, 77% undergrads receive need-based self-help aid. 6% freshmen, 7% undergrads receive athletic scholarships. 82% undergrads receive any aid. 23% undergrads borrow to pay for school. Average cumulative indebtedness $14,990.

STATE UNIVERSITY OF NEW YORK— ALFRED STATE COLLEGE

Huntington Administration Bldg., Alfred, NY 14802
Phone: 607-587-4215 • **Financial Aid Phone:** 607-587-4253
E-mail: admissions@alfredstate.edu • **CEEB Code:** 2522
Fax: 607-587-4299 • **Website:** www.alfredstate.edu • **ACT Code:** 2910

This public school was founded in 1908. It has a 840-acre campus.

RATINGS
Admissions Selectivity Rating: 74   **Fire Safety Rating:** 85

STUDENTS AND FACULTY
Enrollment: 3,607. **Student Body:** 39% female, 61% male, 6% out-of-state, 0% international (19 countries represented). Asian 2%, African American 8%, Caucasian 78%, Hispanic 6%, Native American <1%
Retention and Graduation: 45% freshmen graduate within 4 years. 56% freshmen graduate within 6 years. 38% grads go on to further study within 1 year. **Faculty:** 1,568 full-time faculty, 2% hold PhDs, 3% are members of minority groups, 1% are women. 0% of classes are taught by teaching assistants.

ACADEMICS
Degrees: associate, bachelor's, certificate, terminal associate, transfer associate. **Classes:** Most classes have 10-19 students. Most lab/discussion sessions have 10-19 students. **Majors with Highest Enrollment:** Construction Trades; Architectural Technology/Technician; Animal Sciences. **Special Study Options:** cooperative education program, cross-registration, distance learning, honors program, independent study, internships, student-designed major, study abroad, Internet courses. **Honors programs:** Participants complete a series of seminars, as well as a substantial honors project and 10 hours of volunteer community service. **Disability Services:** Special programs offered to physically disabled students include note-taking services, reader services, tape recorders, tutors. **Career services:** Alumni network, career/job search classes.

FACILITIES
Housing: Coed dorms, special housing for disabled students, Suite, corridor, singles, smoke-free, over 21 yrs, over 24 yrs, wellness living, quiet study, same curriculum housing, baccalaureate, single room options, and computer lifestyle, New upperclassmen apartment suite complex. 100% of campus accessible to physically disabled. **Computers:** 100% of classrooms, 100% of dorms, 100% of libraries, 100% of dining areas, 100% of common outdoor areas have wireless network access. Students can register for classes online. Administrative functions (other than registration) can be performed online.

CAMPUS LIFE
Environment: Rural. **Activities:** Choral groups, concert band, drama/theater, jazz band, literary magazine, music ensembles, musical theater, radio station,

student government, student newspaper, symphony orchestra, yearbook. 60 registered organizations, 4 honor societies, 3 fraternities, 2 sororities. **Athletics (Intercollegiate):** *Men:* baseball, basketball, cheerleading, cross-country, football, lacrosse, soccer, swimming, track/field (outdoor), wrestling. *Women:* basketball, cheerleading, cross-country, soccer, softball, swimming, track/field (outdoor), volleyball. **On-Campus Highlights:** Pioneer Center, Orvis (Athletic Center), Peach Pit, Central Dining Hall, Upperclassmen Apartment Suite Complex. **Environmental Initiatives:** Energy conservation, greenhouse gas inventory and shrinking our carbon footprint through renewable energy. Increase recycling and reduce what is going to the landfill. Composting and establishing a community garden.

ADMISSIONS
Freshman Academic Profile: Average high school GPA 85.11. SAT Math middle 50% range 430-560. SAT Critical Reading middle 50% range 410-530. ACT middle 50% range 19-25. Minimum internet-based TOEFL 61. Minimum paper TOEFL 500. **Basis for Candidate Selection:** *Very important factors considered include:* academic GPA, rigor of secondary school record. *Important factors considered include:* Class rank. *Other factors considered include:* application essay, recommendation(s), standardized test scores, alumni/ae relation, character/personal qualities, extracurricular activities, interview, talent/ability, volunteer work, work experience. **Freshman Admission Requirements:** High school diploma is required and GED is accepted. **Freshman Admission Statistics:** 6,034 applied, 54% admitted, 43% enrolled. **Transfer Admission Requirements:** High school transcript, college transcript(s), statement of good standing from prior institution(s). Minimum college GPA of 2.4 required. Lowest grade transferable C. **General Admission Information:** Application Fee $40. Notification on a rolling basis, beginning on or about 11/1. Nonfall registration accepted. Admission may be deferred for a maximum of 1 semester. Credit and/or placement offered for CEEB Advanced Placement tests.

COSTS AND FINANCIAL AID
Annual out-of-state tuition $9,740. Room and board $11,910. Required fees $1,476. Average book expense $1,200. **Required Forms and Deadlines:** FAFSA, State aid form. **Notification of Awards:** Applicants will be notified of awards on a rolling basis beginning 3/3. **Types of Aid:** *Need-based scholarships/grants:* Federal Pell, SEOG, state scholarships/grants, private scholarships, the school's own gift aid. *Loans:* Subsidized Stafford, Unsubsidized Stafford, PLUS, Federal Perkins, Federal Nursing. *Student Employment:* Federal Work-Study Program available. Institutional employment available. Off-campus job opportunities are fair. **Financial Aid Statistics:** 84% freshmen, 82% undergrads receive need-based scholarship or grant aid. 39% freshmen, 31% undergrads receive non-need-based scholarship or grant aid. 82% freshmen, 84% undergrads receive need-based self-help aid. 0% freshmen, 0% undergrads receive athletic scholarships. 82% freshmen, 82% undergrads receive any aid. 80% undergrads borrow to pay for school. Average cumulative indebtedness $25,495.

STATE UNIVERSITY OF NEW YORK AT BINGHAMTON (BINGHAMTON UNIVERSITY)

PO Box 6001, Binghamton, NY 13902-6001
Phone: 607-777-2171 • **Financial Aid Phone:** 607-777-2428
E-mail: admit@binghamton.edu • **CEEB Code:** 2535
Fax: 607-777-4445 • **Website:** www.binghamton.edu • **ACT Code:** 2956

This public school was founded in 1946. It has a 930-acre campus.

RATINGS
Admissions Selectivity Rating: 92   **Fire Safety Rating:** 87

STUDENTS AND FACULTY
Enrollment: 13,372. **Student Body:** 48% female, 52% male, 10% out-of-state, 10% international (115 countries represented). Asian 14%, African American 5%, Caucasian 55%, Hispanic 10%, Native American <1%
Retention and Graduation: 89% freshmen return for sophomore year. 68% freshmen graduate within 4 years. 81% freshmen graduate within 6 years. 45% grads go on to further study within 1 year. 17% grads pursue arts and sciences degrees. 4% grads pursue law degrees. 11% grads pursue business degrees. 9% grads pursue medical degrees. **Faculty:** 665 full-time faculty, 94% hold PhDs, 39% are members of minority groups, 23% are women. 6% of classes are taught by teaching assistants.

ACADEMICS

Degrees: bachelor's, master's, post-master's certificate. **Classes:** Most classes have 20-29 students. Most lab/discussion sessions have 20-29 students. **Majors with Highest Enrollment:** Business Administration and Management; Engineering; Psychology. **Special Study Options:** Accelerated program, cross-registration, distance learning, double major, dual enrollment, English as a Second Language (ESL), exchange student program (domestic), honors program, independent study, internships, liberal arts/career combination, student-designed major, study abroad, teacher certification program, Teacher Certification Program is graduate only. **Honors programs:** Binghamton University Scholars Program—See http://scholars.binghamton.edu Each academic department offers an honors program. Binghamton also has a PricewaterhouseCoopers Scholars program for students in the School of Management. **Combined degree programs:** BA/MA, >40 combined degrees for BA or BS with MBA/MPA/MAT/MA/MS. **Disability Services:** Special programs offered to physically disabled students include note-taking services, reader services, tape recorders. **Career services:** Alumni network, alumni services, career/job search classes, career assessment, internships, regional alumni. Career services highlights include Binghamton's Career Development Center, which has received numerous awards for excellence from the SUNY Career Development Organization in regard to programming, operations and recruitment.

FACILITIES

Housing: Coed dorms, special housing for disabled students, apartments for single students, Wellness Housing, Theme Housing. 90% of campus accessible to physically disabled. **Special Academic Facilities/Equipment:** Art gallery, performing arts center, indoor/outdoor theater, multi-climate and teaching greenhouse, sculpture foundry, 8,000-seat Events Center, Analytical and Diagnostics Laboratory, Electron Microscopy Facility, Public Archaeology Facility, 930-acre Nature Preserve. **Computers:** 95% of classrooms, 100% of dorms, 100% of libraries, 100% of dining areas, 100% of student union, 60% of common outdoor areas have wireless network access. Students can register for classes online. Administrative functions (other than registration) can be performed online.

CAMPUS LIFE

Environment: City. **Activities:** Choral groups, concert band, dance, drama/theater, jazz band, literary magazine, music ensembles, musical theater, opera, pep band, radio station, student government, student newspaper, student-run film society, symphony orchestra, television station, yearbook, Campus Ministries, International Student Organization, Model UN. 23 honor societies, 15 religious organizations. 23 fraternities, 23 sororities. **Athletics (Intercollegiate):** *Men:* baseball, basketball, cross-country, diving, golf, lacrosse, soccer, swimming, tennis, track/field (outdoor), track/field (indoor), wrestling. *Women:* basketball, cross-country, diving, lacrosse, soccer, softball, swimming, tennis, track/field (outdoor), track/field (indoor), volleyball. **On-Campus Highlights:** University Union, Fitspace, Nature Preserve, Events Center, Anderson Center for the Arts, Rosefsky Art Gallery, Libraries. **Environmental Initiatives:** Binghamton University's goal is to design, construct, operate and maintain all new buildings following guidelines set forth by the U.S. Green Building Council's LEED rating system. Since 2004, Binghamton has obtained multiple LEED certifications under the New Construction program including 2 LEED, 3 LEED Silver, 3 LEED Gold, and 1 LEED Platinum for a total of 966,000 square feet of building space. This represents 17% of total building space owned by Binghamton University. Energy Conservation: Since 2005, Binghamton University has continually invested in energy conservation projects such as installation of efficient lighting, occupancy sensors, variable speed drives on motors, free-cooling devices to take advantage of cooler outdoor temperatures, solar hot water heater and constant improvements to our energy management system. More recently the University added 135 kW of on-site photovoltaic systems and replaced roughly 20% of outdoor lighting with LED light fixtures. Waste Management Programs: Waste Management Program has made tremendous progress in areas such as recycling, waste reduction, composting and community outreach. The University's waste reduction rate has been steadily increased from 23.5% in 2010 to 29% in 2013, compost rate increased from 135 tons to 165 tons, and total solid waste was reduced by 200 tons in the same time frame even with increase campus population. Transportation: Binghamton University currently offers free public transportation to students, faculty and staff for commuting within the Broome County area. Additionally, campus fleet vehicles have been rapidly replaced by plug-in electric vehicles. The University also encourages car pooling through various programs such as offering preferred parking spaces for High Occupancy Vehicles, Broome-Tioga Green-Ride, and hourly car rentals on campus for car poolers convenience. Most recently the Student Association at Binghamton University successfully launched a bike-share program to offer free bicycle rental for on/off campus use. Nearly 70% of Binghamton Universitys 930-acre campus is in its natural state. The core of this undeveloped land is officially designated the Nature Preserve, encompassing 187 acres of land which includes a 20 acre wetland. Binghamton uses this large, valuable resource for teaching and learning, research, ecology, arts, literature and outdoor recreation. **·Website:** http://naturepreserve.binghamton.edu

ADMISSIONS

Freshman Academic Profile: Average high school GPA 3.6. 48% in top 10% of high school class, 83% in top 25% of high school class, 97% in top 50% of high school class. 88% from public high schools. SAT Math middle 50% range 620-700. SAT Critical Reading middle 50% range 590-670. SAT Writing middle 50% range 580-670. ACT middle 50% range 27-30. Minimum internet-based TOEFL 83. Minimum paper TOEFL 560. **Basis for Candidate Selection:** *Very important factors considered include:* academic GPA, rigor of secondary school record, standardized test scores. *Important factors considered include:* Class rank, application essay, recommendation(s), extracurricular activities, first generation. *Other factors considered include:* alumni/ae relation, character/personal qualities, geographical residence, level of applicant's interest, racial/ethnic status, state residency, talent/ability, volunteer work, work experience. **Freshman Admission Requirements:** High school diploma is required and GED is accepted. *Academic units required:* 4 English, 3 mathematics, 2 science, 3 foreign language, 2 social studies. **Freshman Admission Statistics:** 28,518 applied, 44% admitted, 21% enrolled. **Transfer Admission Requirements:** college transcript(s), Lowest grade transferable C-. **General Admission Information:** Application Fee $40. Regular notification 4/1. Nonfall registration accepted. Admission may be deferred for a maximum of 1 year. Credit offered for CEEB Advanced Placement tests.

COSTS AND FINANCIAL AID

Annual in-state tuition $6,170. Annual out-of-state tuition $17,810. Room and board $13,028. Required fees $2,450. Average book expense $1,000. **Required Forms and Deadlines:** FAFSA, State aid form. **Notification of Awards:** Applicants will be notified of awards on a rolling basis beginning 4/1. **Types of Aid:** *Need-based scholarships/grants:* Federal Pell, SEOG, state scholarships/grants, private scholarships, the school's own gift aid. *Loans:* Direct Subsidized Stafford, Direct Unsubsidized Stafford, Direct PLUS, Federal Perkins, Federal Nursing, college/university loans from institutional funds. *Student Employment:* Federal Work-Study Program available. Institutional employment available. Highest amount earned per year from on-campus jobs $5,700. Off-campus job opportunities are excellent. **Financial Aid Statistics:** 81% freshmen, 83% undergrads receive need-based scholarship or grant aid. 12% freshmen, 6% undergrads receive non-need-based scholarship or grant aid. 97% freshmen, 97% undergrads receive need-based self-help aid. 4% freshmen, 2% undergrads receive athletic scholarships. 81% freshmen, 70% undergrads receive any aid. 53% undergrads borrow to pay for school. Average cumulative indebtedness $21,539. **Criteria for awarding institutional aid:** *Non-need-based:* academics, art, athletics, leadership, minority status, music/drama, state/district residency.

STATE UNIVERSITY OF NEW YORK AT GENESEO

1 College Circle, Geneseo, NY 14454
Phone: 585-245-5571 · **Financial Aid Phone:** 585-245-5731
E-mail: admissions@geneseo.edu · **CEEB Code:** 2540
Fax: 585-245-5550 · **Website:** www.geneseo.edu · **ACT Code:** 2936

This public school was founded in 1871. It has a 220-acre campus.

RATINGS

Admissions Selectivity Rating: 89   **Fire Safety Rating:** 97

STUDENTS AND FACULTY

Enrollment: 5,497. **Student Body:** 58% female, 42% male, 2% out-of-state, 2% international (26 countries represented). Asian 6%, African American 3%, Caucasian 75%, Hispanic 7%, Native American <1%
Retention and Graduation: 66% freshmen graduate within 4 years. 25% grads go on to further study within 1 year. 32% grads pursue arts and sciences degrees. 9% grads pursue law degrees. 9% grads pursue business degrees. 22% grads pursue medical degrees. **Faculty:** 252 full-time faculty, 87% hold PhDs, 44% are are members of minority groups, 14% are women. 0% of classes are taught by teaching assistants.

ACADEMICS

Degrees: bachelor's, master's. **Classes:** Most classes have 20-29 students. Most lab/discussion sessions have 10-19 students. **Majors with Highest Enrollment:** Business Administration and Management; Biology; Psychology. **Special Study Options:** cross-registration, double major, dual enrollment, English as a Second Language (ESL), honors program, independent study, internships, study abroad, teacher certification program, Albany semester, Washington semester, 3/2 Engineering, 3-3 Engineering, 4/1 MBA, 3/4 Dentistry, 3/4 Optometry, 3/4 Osteopathic Medicine, 3/2 or 3/1 nursing, 3/3 physical therapy, pre-med and pre-law advisory program. **Combined degree programs:** BA/MA, BA/DDS, BA/DO; BA/OD. **Disability Services:** Special programs offered to physically disabled students include note-taking services, reader services, tape recorders. **Career services:** Alumni network, alumni services, career/job search classes, career assessment, internships. Career services highlights include a Career Partners Network.

FACILITIES

Housing: Coed dorms, special housing for disabled students, special housing for international students, Town houses and special interest housing is available. Some fraternities and sororities have housing independent of college. 95% of campus accessible to physically disabled. **Special Academic Facilities/Equipment:** Four theatres, electron microscopes. Integrated Science Center. **Computers:** 100% of classrooms, 60% of dorms, 100% of libraries, 100% of dining areas, 100% of student union, 10% of common outdoor areas have wireless network access. Students can register for classes online. Administrative functions (other than registration) can be performed online. Undergraduates are required to own a computer.

CAMPUS LIFE

Environment: Village. **Activities:** Choral groups, dance, drama/theater, jazz band, literary magazine, music ensembles, musical theater, pep band, radio station, student government, student newspaper, symphony orchestra, television station, Campus Ministries, International Student Organization, Model UN. 175 registered organizations, 12 honor societies, 7 religious organizations. 8 fraternities, 11 sororities. **Athletics (Intercollegiate):** *Men:* basketball, cross-country, diving, ice hockey, lacrosse, soccer, swimming, track/field (outdoor), track/field (indoor). *Women:* basketball, cross-country, diving, equestrian sports, field hockey, lacrosse, soccer, softball, swimming, tennis, track/field (outdoor), track/field (indoor), volleyball. **On-Campus Highlights:** MacVittie College Union, The Gazebo, Milne Library, Alumni Fieldhouse (Workout Center), College Green. **Environmental Initiatives:** Signing of the Presidents Climate Commitment. A final draft of the Climate Action Plan was released on July 2010. Establishment of Geneseo's Environmental Impact and Sustainability Task Force. Gold Lecture Series—Live Green Task Force Work/Initiatives.

ADMISSIONS

Freshman Academic Profile: Average high school GPA 3.67. 37.1% in top 10% of high school class, 76.1% in top 25% of high school class, 96.9% in top 50% of high school class. SAT Math middle 50% range 570-660. SAT Critical Reading middle 50% range 550-660. ACT middle 50% range 25.3-29. Minimum internet-based TOEFL 71. Minimum paper TOEFL 525. **Basis for Candidate Selection:** *Very important factors considered include:* rigor of secondary school record, standardized test scores. *Important factors considered include:* Class rank, application essay, academic GPA, recommendation(s), extracurricular activities, racial/ethnic status, talent/ability. *Other factors considered include:* alumni/ae relation, character/personal qualities, first generation, level of applicant's interest, volunteer work, work experience. **Freshman Admission Requirements:** High school diploma is required and GED is accepted. **Freshman Admission Statistics:** 9,305 applied, 59% admitted, 22% enrolled. **Transfer Admission Requirements:** High school transcript, college transcript(s), Minimum college GPA of 3.0 required. Lowest grade transferable D. **General Admission Information:** Application Fee $40. Early decision application deadline 11/15. Regular application deadline 1/1. Regular notification 3/1. Nonfall registration accepted. Admission may be deferred for a maximum of 1 year. Credit offered for CEEB Advanced Placement tests.

COSTS AND FINANCIAL AID

Required Forms and Deadlines: FAFSA, State aid form. **Notification of Awards:** Applicants will be notified of awards on a rolling basis beginning 3/15. **Types of Aid:** *Need-based scholarships/grants:* Federal Pell, SEOG, state scholarships/grants. *Loans:* Subsidized Stafford, Unsubsidized Stafford, PLUS, Federal Perkins. *Student Employment:* Federal Work-Study Program available. Institutional employment available. Highest amount earned per year from on-campus jobs $3,500. Off-campus job opportunities are poor. **Financial Aid Statistics:** 77% freshmen, 78% undergrads receive need-based scholarship or grant aid. 21% freshmen, 24% undergrads receive non-need-based scholarship or grant aid. 75% freshmen, 75% undergrads receive need-based self-help aid. 0% freshmen, 0% undergrads receive athletic scholarships. 71% freshmen, 66% undergrads receive any aid. 63% undergrads borrow to pay for school. Average cumulative indebtedness $22,900. **Criteria for awarding institutional aid:** *Non-need-based:* academics, art, leadership, minority status, music/drama, religious affiliation, state/district residency.

STATE UNIVERITY OF NEW YORK— THE COLLEGE AT BROCKPORT

350 New Campus Drive, Brockport, NY 14420
Phone: 585-395-2751 · **Financial Aid Phone:** 585-395-2501
E-mail: admit@brockport.edu · **CEEB Code:** 2537
Fax: 585-395-5452 · **Website:** www.brockport.edu · **ACT Code:** 2928

This public school was founded in 1835. It has a 464-acre campus.

RATINGS

Admissions Selectivity Rating: 60*   **Fire Safety Rating:** 60*

STUDENTS AND FACULTY

Enrollment: 6,952. **Student Body:** 54% female, 46% male, 99% out-of-state, 2% international (15 countries represented). Asian 2%, African American 9%, Caucasian 72%, Hispanic 5%, Native American <1%.
Retention and Graduation: 50% freshmen graduate within 4 years. **Faculty:** 332 full-time faculty, 86% hold PhDs, 53% are members of minority groups, 18% are women.

ACADEMICS

Degrees: bachelor's, master's, post-master's certificate. **Classes:** Most classes have 20–29 students. Most lab/discussion sessions have 10–19 students. **Majors with Highest Enrollment:** Health Services/Allied Health/Health Sciences; Criminal Justice/Safety Studies; Registered Nursing/Registered Nurse. **Special Study Options:** Accelerated program, cross-registration, distance learning, double major, dual enrollment, honors program, independent study, internships, student-designed major, study abroad, teacher certification program. **Honors programs:** 1) College Honors Program, which allows students to complete general education requirements in small classes; 2) Delta College, which is a time-variable degree program for highly-motivated students. **Disability Services:** Special programs offered to physically disabled students include note-taking services, reader services, tape recorders, tutors. **Career services:** Alumni network, alumni services, career/job search classes, career assessment, internships, regional alumni. Brockport has a 91% placement rate for recent graduates.

FACILITIES

Housing: Coed dorms, special housing for international students, apartments for single students, Wellness HousingExtended housing (open during college breaks-excludes summer). 95% of campus accessible to physically disabled. **Special Academic Facilities/Equipment:** aquaculture ponds, weather information system, high-resolution germanium detector, research vessel on Lake Ontario, electron microscope, low- temperature physics lab, vacuum deposition lab, computational; physics lab, 2 supercomputers, Doppler Radar system, ultramodern dance facilities including green room, hydrotherapy room, student learning center, academic computing center, and two theaters. **Computers:** 100% of classrooms, 100% of dorms, 100% of libraries, 100% of dining areas, 100% of student union, 80% of common outdoor areas have wireless network access. Students can register for classes online. Administrative functions (other than registration) can be performed online.

CAMPUS LIFE

Environment: Village. **Activities:** Choral groups, dance, drama/theater, literary magazine, music ensembles, musical theater, radio station, student government, student newspaper, television station, Campus Ministries, International Student Organization, Model UN. 71 registered organizations, 20 honor societies, 8 religious organizations. 6 fraternities, 3 sororities. **Athletics (Intercollegiate):** *Men:* baseball, basketball, cross-country, diving, football, ice hockey, lacrosse, soccer, swimming, track/field (outdoor), track/field (indoor), wrestling. *Women:* basketball, cross-country, diving, field hockey, gymnastics, lacrosse, soccer, softball, swimming, tennis, track/field (outdoor), track/field (indoor), volleyball. **On-Campus Highlights:** Seymour College Union, Drake Memorial Library, Hartwell Performance Center, Harrison Dining Hall, Tuttle Athletic Complex, Smith Hall Science Center, Dailey Hall, Computing Center Tower, Fine Arts Center. **Environmental Initiatives:** We received the 2010 Pollution Prevention Award from the Rochester Business Journal for our comprehensive programs and continuing efforts to improve our sustainability performance. Developed a comprehensive environmental management system and a Facilities Master Plan in order to continuously improve our environmental performanace. Invested over $50 million in several sustainable building projects (LEED Silver) that will reduce our impact on the environment and result in long term energy savings.

ADMISSIONS

Freshman Academic Profile: Average high school GPA 3.1. 14% in top 10% of high school class, 44% in top 25% of high school class, 83% in top 50% of high school class. SAT Math middle 50% range 480-580. SAT Critical Reading middle 50% range 470-570. SAT Writing middle 50% range 450-550. ACT middle 50% range 21-25. Minimum internet-based TOEFL 76. **Basis for Candidate Selection:** *Very important factors considered include:* academic GPA, rigor of secondary school record. *Important factors considered include:* Class rank, application essay, recommendation(s), standardized test scores, character/personal qualities, extracurricular activities, talent/ability, volunteer work, work experience. *Other factors considered include:* interview, level of applicant's interest, racial/ethnic status. **Freshman Admission Requirements:** High school diploma is required and GED is accepted. *Academic units required:* 4 English, 3 mathematics, 3 science, (1 science labs), 4 social studies, 3 academic electives. **Freshman Admission Statistics:** 9,769 applied, 49% admitted, 23% enrolled. **Transfer Admission Requirements:** college transcript(s), Minimum college GPA of 2.5 required. Lowest grade transferable D-. **General Admission Information:** Application Fee $40. Notification on a rolling basis, beginning on or about 11/15. Nonfall registration accepted. Admission may be deferred for a maximum of 1 year. Credit and/or placement offered for CEEB Advanced Placement tests.

COSTS AND FINANCIAL AID

Annual in-state tuition $6,170. Annual out-of-state tuition $15,820. Room and board $11,440. Required fees $1,392. Average book expense $1,100. **Required Forms and Deadlines:** FAFSA. **Notification of Awards:** Applicants will be notified of awards on a rolling basis beginning 3/15. **Types of Aid:** *Need-based scholarships/grants:* Federal Pell, SEOG, state scholarships/grants, private scholarships, the school's own gift aid. *Loans:* Direct Subsidized Stafford, Direct Unsubsidized Stafford, Direct PLUS, Federal Perkins, Federal Nursing, Private Alternative loans. *Student Employment:* Federal Work-Study Program available. Institutional employment available. Highest amount earned per year from on-campus jobs $14,059. Off-campus job opportunities are good. **Financial Aid Statistics:** 75% freshmen, 78% undergrads receive need-based scholarship or grant aid. 44% freshmen, 22% undergrads receive non-need-based scholarship or grant aid. 86% freshmen, 86% undergrads receive need-based self-help aid. 0% freshmen, 0% undergrads receive athletic scholarships. 90% freshmen, 83% undergrads receive any aid. 82% undergrads borrow to pay for school. Average cumulative indebtedness $24,521. **Criteria for awarding institutional aid:** *Non-need-based:* academics, alumni affiliation, art, athletics, leadership, minority status, music/drama.

STATE UNIVERSITY OF NEW YORK— BUFFALO STATE COLLEGE

1300 Elmwood Avenue, Buffalo, NY 14222
Phone: 716-878-4017 · **Financial Aid Phone:** 716-878-4902
E-mail: admissions@buffalostate.edu · **CEEB Code:** 2533
Fax: 716-878-6100 • **ACT Code:** 2930

This public school was founded in 1871. It has a 115-acre campus.

RATINGS

Admissions Selectivity Rating: 80   **Fire Safety Rating:** 70

STUDENTS AND FACULTY

Enrollment: 9,190. **Student Body:** 57% female, 43% male, 1% out-of-state, 1% international (52 countries represented). Asian 2%, African American 20%, Caucasian 63%, Hispanic 9%, Native American <1%
Retention and Graduation: 25% freshmen graduate within 4 years. 50% freshmen graduate within 6 years. 22% grads go on to further study within 1 year. 3% grads pursue arts and sciences degrees. 3% grads pursue law degrees. 7% grads pursue business degrees. **Faculty:** 415 full-time faculty, 87% hold PhDs, 47% are are members of minority groups, 14% are women. 0% of classes are taught by teaching assistants.

ACADEMICS

Degrees: bachelor's, master's, post-master's certificate. **Majors with Highest Enrollment:** Elementary Education and Teaching; Business/Commerce. **Special Study Options:** cooperative education program, cross-registration, distance learning, double major, dual enrollment, English as a Second Language (ESL), exchange student program (domestic), honors program, independent study, internships, liberal arts/career combination, study abroad, teacher certification program. **Disability Services:** Special programs offered to physically disabled students include note-taking services, reader services, tape recorders, tutors. **Career services:** Alumni network, alumni services, career/job search classes, career assessment, internships.

FACILITIES

Housing: Coed dorms, special housing for international students, Apartments for students with dependent children. 100% of campus accessible to physically disabled. **Special Academic Facilities/Equipment:** Burchfield Penney Art center, anthropology museum, concert hall with pipe organ, nature preserve. **Computers:** 10% of classrooms, 30% of libraries, 100% of dining areas, 50% of student union, 10% of common outdoor areas have wireless network access. Students can register for classes online. Administrative functions (other than registration) can be performed online.

CAMPUS LIFE

Environment: City. **Activities:** Choral groups, concert band, dance, drama/theater, jazz band, literary magazine, music ensembles, radio station, student government, student newspaper, student-run film society, television station, yearbook, International Student Organization. 75 registered organizations, 5 religious organizations. 10 fraternities, 10 sororities. **Athletics (Intercollegiate):** *Men:* basketball, cross-country, diving, football, ice hockey, soccer, swimming, track/field (outdoor), track/field (indoor). *Women:* basketball, cheerleading, cross-country, diving, ice hockey, lacrosse, soccer, softball, swimming, tennis, track/field (outdoor), track/field (indoor), volleyball. **On-Campus Highlights:** Burchfield Penny Art Center, Sports Arena, Houston Gymnasium/Fitness Center, Rockwell Hall/Performing Arts Center, Campus House. **Environmental Initiatives:** 1) Creation of a campus wide recycling program for plastic, glass, metal, paper, cardboard, light bulbs, electronics, electronic media (printer cartridges, dvds, cds, VHS, cassettes, etc), batteries, shrink wrap, bubble wrap, and many other misc items! This was applied to every building on campus including the residential halls. 2) "Don't Throw it Out Program"—Move out program for Residential students to bring unwanted furniture, food, clothing, shoes, appliances, etc to centrally located drop off stations. This reduces waste, and these items are then donated to nonprofit organizations. 3) Environmental Information Fair—20—30 organizations ranging from county depts. to coumminty organizations that congrigate on campus with the purpose of educating the campus population about environmental events and information that applies to their everyday life. It is a campus event that serves to create awareness among the campus and surrounding community. It is intended to promote and encourage a cleaner Western New York as we inform the community about going green.

ADMISSIONS

Freshman Academic Profile: Average high school GPA 3.1. 3% in top 10% of high school class, 32% in top 25% of high school class, 74% in top 50% of high school class. SAT Math middle 50% range 450-540. SAT Critical Reading middle 50% range 440-520. SAT Writing middle 50% range 420-510. ACT middle 50% range 19-23. Minimum paper TOEFL 500. **Basis for Candidate Selection:** *Very important factors considered include:* academic GPA, rigor of secondary school record, standardized test scores. *Important factors considered include:* Class rank. *Other factors considered include:* application essay, recommendation(s), character/personal qualities, extracurricular activities, first generation, interview, talent/ability, volunteer work, work experience. **Freshman Admission Requirements:** High school diploma is required and GED is accepted. *Academic units required:* 2 mathematics, 2 science. **Freshman Admission Statistics:** 11,251 applied, 49% admitted, 24% enrolled. **Transfer Admission Requirements:** college transcript(s), statement of good standing from prior institution(s). Minimum college GPA of 2.0 required. Lowest grade transferable C. **General Admission Information:** Application Fee $40. Early decision application deadline 11/15. Notification on a rolling basis, beginning on or about 12/15. Nonfall registration accepted. Admission may be deferred for a maximum of 1 year. Credit offered for CEEB Advanced Placement tests.

COSTS AND FINANCIAL AID

Annual in-state tuition $5,870. Annual out-of-state tuition $15,230. Room and board $11,288. Required fees $1,152. Average book expense $1,020. **Required Forms and Deadlines:** FAFSA. **Notification of Awards:** Applicants will be notified of awards on a rolling basis beginning 5/1. **Types of Aid:** *Need-based scholarships/grants:* Federal Pell, SEOG, state scholarships/grants. *Loans:* Subsidized Stafford, Unsubsidized Stafford, PLUS, Federal Perkins. **Financial Aid Statistics:** 84% freshmen, 81% undergrads receive need-based scholarship or grant aid. 10% freshmen, 6% undergrads receive non-need-based scholarship or grant aid. 62% freshmen, 65% undergrads receive need-based self-help aid. 0% freshmen, 0% undergrads receive athletic scholarships. 78% undergrads receive any aid. 78% undergrads borrow to pay for school. Average cumulative indebtedness $23,353. **Criteria for awarding institutional aid:** *Non-need-based:* academics, minority status.

STATE UNIVERSITY OF NEW YORK—CANTON

French Hall, Canton, NY 13617
Phone: 315-386-7123
E-mail: admissions@canton.edu • **CEEB Code:** 2523
Fax: 315-386-7929 • **Website:** www.canton.edu • **ACT Code:** 2912

This public school was founded in 1906. It has a 555-acre campus.

RATINGS

Admissions Selectivity Rating: 60*   **Fire Safety Rating:** 60*

STUDENTS AND FACULTY

Enrollment: 2,119. **Student Body:** 48% female, 52% male, 0% international (5 countries represented). Asian 0%, African American 8%, Caucasian 86%, Hispanic 3%, Native American 2%
Retention and Graduation: 81% freshmen return for sophomore year. 45% grads go on to further study within 1 year. **Faculty:** 83 full-time faculty, 20% hold PhDs, 66% are are members of minority groups, 2% are women. 0% of classes are taught by teaching assistants.

ACADEMICS

Degrees: associate, bachelor's, certificate, terminal associate, transfer associate. **Classes:** Most classes have 20-29 students. Most lab/discussion sessions have 10-19 students. **Special Study Options:** cooperative education program, cross-registration, distance learning, dual enrollment, internships, liberal arts/career combination, student-designed major. **Disability Services:** Special programs offered to physically disabled students include note-taking services, reader services, tape recorders, tutors. **Career services:** career/job search classes, career assessment, internships.

FACILITIES

Housing: Coed dormsSingle sex wings, Intensive Quiet Atmosphere, Relaxed Atmosphere, Suites, Private Rooms, Computer Floors, 21+ Floor, Grasse River Community (Pet floor), Umoja Ahora Community (multicultural), North Country Experience, Alcohol Free, Smoke Free. 100% of campus accessible to physically disabled. **Special Academic Facilities/Equipment:** Criminal Investigation Labs, radio station, distance learning classrooms.

CAMPUS LIFE

Environment: Rural. **Activities:** Choral groups, literary magazine, radio station, student government, student newspaper, yearbook. 50 registered organizations, 2 honor societies, 1 religous organization. 3 fraternities, 3 sororities. **Athletics (Intercollegiate):** *Men:* basketball, football, ice hockey, lacrosse, soccer. *Women:* basketball, soccer, softball, volleyball.

ADMISSIONS

Freshman Academic Profile: Minimum paper TOEFL 550. **Basis for Candidate Selection:** *Very important factors considered include:* rigor of secondary school record. *Other factors considered include:* Class rank, recommendation(s), standardized test scores, character/personal qualities, extracurricular activities, interview, talent/ability, work experience. **Freshman Admission Requirements:** High school diploma is required and GED is accepted. **Freshman Admission Statistics:** 1,830 applied, 98% admitted, 45% enrolled. **Transfer Admission Requirements:** High school transcript, college transcript(s), Lowest grade transferable c. **General Admission Information:** Application Fee $40. Notification on a rolling basis, beginning on or about 12/1. Nonfall registration accepted. Admission may be deferred for a maximum of 1 year.

COSTS AND FINANCIAL AID

Required Forms and Deadlines: FAFSA, State aid form. **Notification of Awards:** Applicants will be notified of awards on a rolling basis beginning 2/3. **Types of Aid:** *Need-based scholarships/grants:* Federal Pell, SEOG, private scholarships. *Loans:* Direct Subsidized Stafford, Direct Unsubsidized Stafford, Direct PLUS, Federal Perkins. *Student Employment:* Federal Work-Study Program available. Institutional employment available. Off-campus job opportunities are fair. **Financial Aid Statistics:** 0% freshmen, 0% undergrads receive athletic scholarships.

STATE UNIVERSITY OF NEW YORK— COBLESKILL

Knapp Hall, Cobleskill, NY 12043
Phone: 518-255-5525 • **Financial Aid Phone:** 518-255-5623
E-mail: admissions@cobleskill.edu • **CEEB Code:** 2524
Fax: 518-255-6769 • **Website:** www.cobleskill.edu • **ACT Code:** 2914

This public school was founded in 1916. It has a 750-acre campus.

RATINGS

Admissions Selectivity Rating: 72   **Fire Safety Rating:** 75

STUDENTS AND FACULTY

Enrollment: 2,421. **Student Body:** 52% female, 48% male, 10% out-of-state, 1% international (11 countries represented). Asian 1%, African American 12%, Caucasian 74%, Hispanic 7%, Native American <1%
Retention and Graduation: 74% freshmen return for sophomore year. 29% freshmen graduate within 4 years. 44% freshmen graduate within 6 years. 63% grads go on to further study within 1 year. **Faculty:** 100 full-time faculty, 46% hold PhDs, 33% are are members of minority groups, 7% are women. 0% of classes are taught by teaching assistants.

ACADEMICS

Degrees: associate, bachelor's, certificate, terminal associate, transfer associate. **Classes:** Most classes have 10-19 students. Most lab/discussion sessions have 10-19 students. **Majors with Highest Enrollment:** Animal Sciences; Business Administration and Management; Wildlife, Fish and Wildlands Science and Management. **Special Study Options:** cross-registration, distance learning, English as a Second Language (ESL), honors program, internships, study abroad, weekend college. **Disability Services:** Special programs offered to physically disabled students include note-taking services, reader services, tape recorders, tutors. **Career services:** alumni services, career/job search classes, career assessment, internships. Career services highlights include a 15-week internship required for nearly all of the baccalaureate programs. It is the capstone of our 4-year degrees.

FACILITIES

Housing: Coed dorms, special housing for disabled students, men's dorms, women's dorms, LIfestyle floors: designated quiet study lifestyle, wellness lifestyle, sustainability lifestyle, sophomore experience, upper class experience. **Special Academic Facilities/Equipment:** Art museum, 650 acre agricultural campus, distance learning classrooms, ski area, adult study center. **Computers:** Students can register for classes online. Administrative functions (other than registration) can be performed online.

CAMPUS LIFE

Environment: Rural. **Activities:** drama/theater, student government, student newspaper, Campus Ministries, International Student Organization. 40 registered organizations, 1 honor society, 1 religous organization. **Athletics (Intercollegiate):** *Men:* baseball, basketball, cross-country, diving, equestrian sports, golf, lacrosse, soccer, swimming, tennis, track/field (outdoor), volleyball. *Women:* basketball, cross-country, diving, equestrian sports, golf, soccer, softball, swimming, tennis, track/field (outdoor), volleyball. **On-Campus Highlights:** Bouck Hall/Student Union, Brickyard Point, American Heritage, Foundation Equestrian Center, Grosvenor Art Gallery. **Environmental Initiatives:** recycling—paper, plastics, metals, glass and cardboard box; waste reduction in dining halls, offices; "Taste Don't Waste" program; purchase of green cleaning supplies, recycled building products such as carpet—wear washing chemicals in dining halls.

ADMISSIONS

Freshman Academic Profile: Average high school GPA 82. 6% in top 10% of high school class, 22% in top 25% of high school class, 56% in top 50% of high school class. 98% from public high schools. SAT Math middle 50% range 380-500. SAT Critical Reading middle 50% range 380-500. ACT middle 50% range 17-22. Minimum paper TOEFL 500. **Basis for Candidate Selection:** *Important factors considered include:* academic GPA, rigor of secondary school record, standardized test scores. *Other factors considered include:* Class rank, application essay, recommendation(s), extracurricular activities, geographical residence, interview, level of applicant's interest, state residency, work experience. **Freshman Admission Requirements:** High school diploma is required and GED is accepted. *Academic units required:* 1 English, 2 mathematics, 1 science, 1 history, 1 academic elective. **Freshman Admission Statistics:** 2,765 applied, 73% admitted, 39% enrolled. **Transfer Admission Requirements:** college transcript(s), Minimum college GPA of 2.25 required. Lowest grade transferable D. **General Admission Information:** Application Fee $40. Notification on a rolling basis, beginning on or about 11/1. Nonfall registration accepted. Admission may be deferred for a maximum of 2 semesters. Credit offered for CEEB Advanced Placement tests.

COSTS AND FINANCIAL AID
Annual out-of-state tuition $15,320. Room and board $11,720. Required fees $1,279. Average book expense $1,200. **Required Forms and Deadlines:** FAFSA, State aid form. **Notification of Awards:** Applicants will be notified of awards on a rolling basis beginning 3/20. **Types of Aid:** *Need-based scholarships/grants:* Federal Pell, SEOG, state scholarships/grants, private scholarships, the school's own gift aid. *Loans:* Subsidized Stafford, Unsubsidized Stafford, PLUS, Federal Perkins. *Student Employment:* Federal Work-Study Program available. Institutional employment available. Highest amount earned per year from on-campus jobs $800. Off-campus job opportunities are fair. **Financial Aid Statistics:** 100% freshmen, 99% undergrads receive need-based scholarship or grant aid. 33% freshmen, 22% undergrads receive non-need-based scholarship or grant aid. 84% freshmen, 80% undergrads receive need-based self-help aid. 0% freshmen, 0% undergrads receive athletic scholarships. 81% freshmen, 75% undergrads receive any aid. 80% undergrads borrow to pay for school. Average cumulative indebtedness $19,918. **Criteria for awarding institutional aid:** *Non-need-based:* academics, alumni affiliation, leadership, state/district residency.

STATE UNIVERSITY OF NEW YORK— THE COLLEGE AT OLD WESTBURY

PO Box 307, Old Westbury, NY 11568-0307
Phone: 516-876-3073 · **Financial Aid Phone:** 516-876-3247
E-mail: enroll@oldwestbury.edu · **CEEB Code:** 2866
Fax: 516-876-3307 · **Website:** www.oldwestbury.edu · **ACT Code:** 2939

This public school was founded in 1968. It has a 605-acre campus.

RATINGS
Admissions Selectivity Rating: 76   **Fire Safety Rating:** 81

STUDENTS AND FACULTY
Enrollment: 4,176. **Student Body:** 58% female, 42% male, 2% out-of-state, 1% international (58 countries represented). Asian 10%, African American 31%, Caucasian 31%, Hispanic 21%, Native American <1%
Retention and Graduation: 84% freshmen return for sophomore year. 17% freshmen graduate within 4 years. 37% freshmen graduate within 6 years. **Faculty:** 151 full-time faculty, 86% hold PhDs, 54% are are members of minority groups, 40% are women. 0% of classes are taught by teaching assistants.

ACADEMICS
Degrees: bachelor's, certificate, master's. **Classes:** Most classes have 20-29 students. Most lab/discussion sessions have 20-29 students. **Majors with Highest Enrollment:** Accounting; Psychology; Biology/Biological Sciences. **Special Study Options:** cross-registration, distance learning, double major, English as a Second Language (ESL), exchange student program (domestic), honors program, independent study, internships, liberal arts/career combination, study abroad, teacher certification program, Disabled Student Services; Minority Access to Research Centers; Minority Biomedical Research. **Honors programs:** The Honors College teaches students to integrate learning methods by using in-depth primary source material and complex and intellectually challenging secondary sources. The program emphasizes critical thinking and experiential learning. **Combined degree programs:** BS/DO. **Disability Services:** Special programs offered to physically disabled students include note-taking services, reader services, tape recorders, tutors. **Career services:** Alumni network, alumni services, career/job search classes, career assessment, internships, regional alumni. Career services highlights include The Community Engagement and Partnership Center founded in 2006, and its First-Year Experience Program, which shares its resources with Old Westbury to support the programmatic efforts of non-profit organizations and to address issues of shared concern within various communities. The college, as a whole, is using its influential role as a regional employer and developer to contribute directly and tangibly to community revitalization efforts. Critical to this effort is the student community engagement component. Implemented by CEPC and the FYE, the College has initiated a voluntary course-embedded community-based learning and action program in which students engage in community service in areas related to their course of study.

FACILITIES
Housing: Coed dorms, Honors College residence. 90% of campus accessible to physically disabled. **Special Academic Facilities/Equipment:** Art gallery, language lab, TV studio, radio station, recital hall, physical recreation center and Maguire Theatre. **Computers:** 100% of classrooms, 60% of dorms, 100% of libraries, 100% of dining areas, 100% of student union, 30% of common outdoor areas have wireless network access. Students can register for classes online. Administrative functions (other than registration) can be performed online.

CAMPUS LIFE
Environment: Village. **Activities:** Choral groups, dance, drama/theater, radio station, student government, student newspaper, student-run film society, yearbook, Campus Ministries, International Student Organization. 55 registered organizations, 5 honor societies, 2 religious organizations. 6 fraternities, 4 sororities. **Athletics (Intercollegiate):** *Men:* baseball, basketball, cross-country, golf, soccer, swimming, ultimate frisbee, volleyball. *Women:* basketball, cross-country, soccer, softball, swimming, ultimate frisbee, volleyball. **On-Campus Highlights:** Student Union, Clark Center (athletic facility), Library, Theatre, Art Gallery. **Environmental Initiatives:** SEMPRA Energy Contract; One solar installation; Gas consortium; Energy STAR purchases; New building recently completed is Leeds Platinum.

ADMISSIONS
Freshman Academic Profile: Average high school GPA 3.1. 85% from public high schools. SAT Math middle 50% range 460-550. SAT Critical Reading middle 50% range 450-530. SAT Writing middle 50% range 430-530. Minimum internet-based TOEFL 65. Minimum paper TOEFL 513. **Basis for Candidate Selection:** *Very important factors considered include:* application essay, academic GPA, rigor of secondary school record. *Important factors considered include:* recommendation(s), standardized test scores. *Other factors considered include:* character/personal qualities, extracurricular activities, interview, talent/ability, volunteer work, work experience. **Freshman Admission Requirements:** High school diploma is required and GED is accepted. *Academic units required:* 4 English, 3 mathematics, 3 science, (2 science labs), 2 foreign language, 4 social studies, 2 academic electives. **Freshman Admission Statistics:** 3,490 applied, 62% admitted, 12% enrolled. **Transfer Admission Requirements:** college transcript(s), essay or personal statement, Minimum college GPA of 2.0 required. Lowest grade transferable C. **General Admission Information:** Application Fee $40. Notification on a rolling basis, beginning on or about 1/7. Nonfall registration accepted. Admission may be deferred for a maximum of one year. Credit and/or placement offered for CEEB Advanced Placement tests.

COSTS AND FINANCIAL AID
Annual in-state tuition $6,190. Annual out-of-state tuition $15,820. Room and board $10,390. Required fees $1,133. Average book expense $2,500. **Required Forms and Deadlines:** FAFSA, Institution's own financial aid form, State aid form. **Notification of Awards:** Applicants will be notified of awards on or about 4/15. **Types of Aid:** *Need-based scholarships/grants:* Federal Pell, SEOG, state scholarships/grants, private scholarships, the school's own gift aid. *Loans:* Subsidized Stafford, Unsubsidized Stafford, PLUS, Federal Perkins, Federal College Work Study Grants Federal Pell Grants Federal Supplemental Education Opportunity Grants State Educational Opportunity Program Grants Supplemental State Tuition Grants Aid for Part-time Study Grants Tuition Assistance Program Federal Parent Loans Alternative Loans. *Student Employment:* Federal Work-Study Program available. Institutional employment available. Off-campus job opportunities are good. **Financial Aid Statistics:** 85% freshmen, 83% undergrads receive need-based scholarship or grant aid. 4% freshmen, 1% undergrads receive non-need-based scholarship or grant aid. 49% freshmen, 55% undergrads receive need-based self-help aid. 0% freshmen, 0% undergrads receive athletic scholarships. 72% freshmen, 67% undergrads receive any aid. 60% undergrads borrow to pay for school. **Criteria for awarding institutional aid:** *Non-need-based:* academics, state/district residency.

STATE UNIVERSITY OF NEW YORK—COLLEGE OF ENVIRONMENTAL SCIENCE AND FORESTRY

Office of Undergraduate Admissions, Syracuse, NY 13210
Phone: 315-470-6600 · **Financial Aid Phone:** 315-470-6706
E-mail: esfinfo@esf.edu · **CEEB Code:** 2530
Fax: 315-470-6933 · **Website:** www.esf.edu · **ACT Code:** 2948

This public school was founded in 1911. It has a 25000-acre campus.

RATINGS
Admissions Selectivity Rating: 89   **Fire Safety Rating:** 98

STUDENTS AND FACULTY

Enrollment: 1,718. **Student Body:** 45% female, 55% male, 18% out-of-state, 1% international (37 countries represented). Asian 2%, African American 1%, Caucasian 69%, Hispanic 3%, Native American <1%
Retention and Graduation: 85% freshmen return for sophomore year. 47% freshmen graduate within 4 years. 68% freshmen graduate within 6 years. 20% grads go on to further study within 1 year. **Faculty:** 142 full-time faculty, 92% hold PhDs, 30% are are members of minority groups, 11% are women. 0% of classes are taught by teaching assistants.

ACADEMICS

Degrees: associate, bachelor's, master's, post-bachelor's certificate. **Classes:** Most classes have 10-19 students. Most lab/discussion sessions have 10-19 students. **Majors with Highest Enrollment:** Environmental Science; Environmental Biology; Landscape Architecture. **Special Study Options:** cooperative education program, cross-registration, distance learning, double major, English as a Second Language (ESL), honors program, independent study, internships, study abroad, teacher certification program, Associate degrees in forest technology & land surveying technology are offered at The Ranger School campus. Graduates of these degrees may then continue their studies at the Syracuse campus to complete bachelor degrees, usually in forest resources management or natural resources management. **Honors programs:** Lower Division Honors Program: freshmen & sophomores, all academic programs, highly selective, associated scholarship, mentoring, honors seminar, honors writing course. Upper Division Thesis Honors Program: juniors and seniors, 16 of 20 academic programs eligible, intensive research or creative projects guided by faculty mentors, thesis exploration seminar, related course work, Honors Thesis/Project course. **Combined degree programs:** BS/ Doctor of Physical Therapy. **Disability Services:** Special programs offered to physically disabled students include note-taking services, reader services, tape recorders, tutors. **Career services:** Alumni network, alumni services, career/job search classes, career assessment, internships, regional alumni. Career services highlights include experiential learning that is "built into" all aspects of learning at ESF. Service Learning is an integral part of an ESF education. Required and voluntary undergraduate research, internships and field experiences are components of every degree program. Learn more at http://www.esf.edu/students/servicelearning/.

FACILITIES

Housing: Coed dorms, special housing for disabled students, special housing for international students, fraternity/sorority housing, apartments for married students, apartments for single students, Theme Housing. 100% of campus accessible to physically disabled. **Special Academic Facilities/Equipment:** Museums, art galleries, plant growth and animal environmental simulation chambers, wildlife collection, electron microscope, paper making facility, photogrammetric and geodetic facilities, hydrology flumes. **Computers:** 50% of classrooms, 100% of dorms, 100% of libraries, 100% of dining areas, 100% of student union, 10% of common outdoor areas have wireless network access. Students can register for classes online. Administrative functions (other than registration) can be performed online.

CAMPUS LIFE

Environment: City. **Activities:** Choral groups, concert band, dance, drama/theater, jazz band, literary magazine, marching band, music ensembles, musical theater, pep band, radio station, student government, student newspaper, student-run film society, symphony orchestra, television station, yearbook, Campus Ministries, International Student Organization. 300 registered organizations, 1 honor society, 13 religious organizations. 26 fraternities, 21 sororities. **Athletics (Intercollegiate):** *Men:* cross-country, golf, soccer. *Women:* cross-country, golf, soccer. **On-Campus Highlights:** Library, Green houses, Wildlife collection, Labratories & Studios, Student lounge, snack bar, student store, SUNY-ESF is on the campus of Syracuse University. The most popular sites on that campus are the Carrier Dome, Crouse College (a historic building), Schine Student Center, Hendricks Chapel. **Environmental Initiatives:** (1)College uses a 250 kilowatt carbonate fuel cell to generate approximately 17% of electrical power. (2)photovoltaic arrays/green roof (3) College owns and manages 25,000 acres of forest (providing carbon offsets). Faculty at SUNY-ESF are conducting nationally recognized and government supported research in the development of ethanol and other renewable products from wood biomass. We have partnered with the NY State government and private industry to develop the state's first "biorefinery" aimed at producing ethanol and other chemical products from wood sugars. The College has also developed a genetically engineered species of fast growth willow that is being grown as an alternative to corn use in ethanol production. Forty percent of all College vehicles (cars, maintenance vehicles, buses, GEM, etc.) are powered with renewable fuels, electric or hybrid technologies. One fifth of all vehicles are powered with biodeisel, and a significant part of our biodeisel fuel is produced on campus from waste cooking oil.

ADMISSIONS

Freshman Academic Profile: Average high school GPA 3.65. 30% in top 10% of high school class, 66% in top 25% of high school class, 95% in top 50% of high school class. 90% from public high schools. SAT Math middle 50% range

550-630. SAT Critical Reading middle 50% range 530-630. ACT middle 50% range 22-26. Minimum internet-based TOEFL 79. Minimum paper TOEFL 550. **Basis for Candidate Selection:** *Very important factors considered include:* application essay, academic GPA, rigor of secondary school record, standardized test scores, level of applicant's interest. *Important factors considered include:* Class rank, recommendation(s), character/personal qualities, extracurricular activities, talent/ability, volunteer work, work experience. *Other factors considered include:* alumni/ae relation, first generation, geographical residence, interview, racial/ethnic status, state residency. **Freshman Admission Requirements:** High school diploma is required and GED is accepted. *Academic units required:* 4 English, 3 mathematics, 3 science, (3 science labs), 0 foreign language, 3 social studies, 0 history. **Freshman Admission Statistics:** 1,538 applied, 51% admitted, 37% enrolled. **Transfer Admission Requirements:** High school transcript, college transcript(s), Minimum college GPA of 2.25 required. Lowest grade transferable C. **General Admission Information:** Application Fee $40. Notification on a rolling basis, beginning on or about 2/1. Nonfall registration accepted. Admission may be deferred for a maximum of 1 year. Credit offered for CEEB Advanced Placement tests.

COSTS AND FINANCIAL AID

Annual in-state tuition $6,170. Annual out-of-state tuition $15,820. Room and board $15,120. Required fees $1,133. Average book expense $1,200. **Required Forms and Deadlines:** FAFSA, State aid form. **Notification of Awards:** Applicants will be notified of awards on a rolling basis beginning 3/15. **Types of Aid:** *Need-based scholarships/grants:* Federal Pell, SEOG, state scholarships/grants, private scholarships, the school's own gift aid Federal SMART Grants, Federal ACG Grants. *Loans:* Subsidized Stafford, Unsubsidized Stafford, PLUS, Federal Perkins. *Student Employment:* Federal Work-Study Program available. Institutional employment available. Highest amount earned per year from on-campus jobs $1,200. Off-campus job opportunities are excellent. **Financial Aid Statistics:** 91% freshmen, 96% undergrads receive need-based scholarship or grant aid. 60% freshmen, 50% undergrads receive non-need-based scholarship or grant aid. 100% freshmen, 91% undergrads receive need-based self-help aid. 0% freshmen, 0% undergrads receive athletic scholarships. 91% freshmen, 93% undergrads receive any aid. 80% undergrads borrow to pay for school. Average cumulative indebtedness $14,866. **Criteria for awarding institutional aid:** *Non-need-based:* academics, alumni affiliation, state/district residency.

STATE UNIVERSITY OF NEW YORK—CORTLAND

PO Box 2000, Cortland, NY 13045-0900
Phone: 607-753-4712 · **Financial Aid Phone:** 607-753-4717
E-mail: admissions@cortland.edu · **CEEB Code:** 2538
Fax: 607-753-5998 · **Website:** http://www2.cortland.edu/home/ · **ACT Code:** 2932

This public school was founded in 1868. It has a 191-acre campus.

RATINGS

Admissions Selectivity Rating: 85   **Fire Safety Rating:** 62

STUDENTS AND FACULTY

Enrollment: 6,316. **Student Body:** 57% female, 43% male, 4% out-of-state, 1% international (14 countries represented). Asian 1%, African American 5%, Caucasian 74%, Hispanic 11%, Native American <1%
Retention and Graduation: 81% freshmen return for sophomore year. 45% freshmen graduate within 4 years. **Faculty:** 287 full-time faculty, 76% hold PhDs, 52% are are members of minority groups, 14% are women. 0% of classes are taught by teaching assistants.

ACADEMICS

Degrees: bachelor's, master's, post-master's certificate. **Classes:** Most classes have 20-29 students. Most lab/discussion sessions have 20-29 students. **Special Study Options:** cooperative education program, cross-registration, distance learning, double major, dual enrollment, exchange student program (domestic), honors program, independent study, internships, liberal arts/career combination, student-designed major, study abroad, teacher certification program. **Disability Services:** Special programs offered to physically disabled students include note-taking services, reader services, tape recorders, tutors.

FACILITIES

Housing: Coed dorms, special housing for disabled students, special housing for international students, cooperative housing, apartments for single students, Wellness Housing, Leadership House, Transfer Floor, Quiet Atmosphere. 75% of campus accessible to physically disabled. **Special Academic Facilities/Equipment:** Natural science museum, greenhouse, center for speech and hearing disorders, classrooms with integrated technologies, specialized labs to support various program offerings. **Computers:** Students can register for classes online. Administrative functions (other than registration) can be performed online.

CAMPUS LIFE
Environment: Village. **Activities:** Choral groups, dance, drama/theater, literary magazine, music ensembles, musical theater, radio station, student government, student newspaper, student-run film society, symphony orchestra, television station, yearbook, Campus Ministries, International Student Organization, Model UN. 100 registered organizations, 16 honor societies, 3 religious organizations. 2 fraternities, 5 sororities. **Athletics (Intercollegiate):** *Men:* baseball, basketball, cheerleading, cross-country, diving, football, gymnastics, ice hockey, lacrosse, soccer, swimming, track/field (outdoor), track/field (indoor), wrestling. *Women:* basketball, cheerleading, cross-country, diving, field hockey, golf, gymnastics, ice hockey, lacrosse, soccer, softball, swimming, tennis, track/field (outdoor), track/field (indoor), volleyball. **On-Campus Highlights:** Corey Union, Stadium Complex, Fitness Facilities, Dining Halls, Library.

ADMISSIONS
Freshman Academic Profile: Average high school GPA 89.5. 14% in top 10% of high school class, 52% in top 25% of high school class, 95% in top 50% of high school class. 91% from public high schools. SAT Math middle 50% range 500-570. SAT Critical Reading middle 50% range 470-560. ACT middle 50% range 22-25. Minimum paper TOEFL 550. **Basis for Candidate Selection:** *Very important factors considered include:* rigor of secondary school record, standardized test scores. *Important factors considered include:* application essay, recommendation(s), extracurricular activities, talent/ability. *Other factors considered include:* Class rank, alumni/ae relation, geographical residence, interview, racial/ethnic status, state residency, volunteer work, work experience. **Freshman Admission Requirements:** High school diploma is required and GED is accepted. *Academic units required:* 4 English, 3 mathematics, 3 science, 3 foreign language, 4 social studies. **Freshman Admission Statistics:** 11,221 applied, 49% admitted, 22% enrolled. **Transfer Admission Requirements:** High school transcript, college transcript(s), Minimum college GPA of 2.5 required. Lowest grade transferable C-. **General Admission Information:** Application Fee $40. Early decision application deadline 11/15. Notification on a rolling basis, beginning on or about 1/2. Nonfall registration accepted. Admission may be deferred for a maximum of 1 year. Credit offered for CEEB Advanced Placement tests.

COSTS AND FINANCIAL AID
Annual in-state tuition $6,170. Annual out-of-state tuition $15,820. Room and board $12,040. Required fees $1,549. Average book expense $1,000. **Required Forms and Deadlines:** FAFSA, State aid form. **Notification of Awards:** Applicants will be notified of awards on a rolling basis beginning 3/15. **Types of Aid:** *Need-based scholarships/grants:* Federal Pell, SEOG, state scholarships/grants, private scholarships, the school's own gift aid. *Loans:* Subsidized Stafford, Unsubsidized Stafford, PLUS, Federal Perkins. **Financial Aid Statistics:** 64% freshmen, 69% undergrads receive need-based scholarship or grant aid. 36% freshmen, 24% undergrads receive non-need-based scholarship or grant aid. 84% freshmen, 84% undergrads receive need-based self-help aid. 0% freshmen, 0% undergrads receive athletic scholarships. 76% undergrads borrow to pay for school. Average cumulative indebtedness $24,040. **Criteria for awarding institutional aid:** *Non-need-based:* academics, art, leadership, minority status, music/drama, state/district residency.

STATE UNIVERSITY OF NEW YORK—DELHI

Bush Hall, Delhi, NY 13753
Phone: 607-746-4550
E-mail: enroll@Delhi.edu
Fax: 607-746-4104 · **Website:** www.delhi.edu

This is a public school.

RATINGS
Admissions Selectivity Rating: 60*   **Fire Safety Rating:** 60*

STUDENTS AND FACULTY
Enrollment: 1,791. **Student Body:** 44% female, 56% male, 4% out-of-state, 1% international. Asian 2%, African American 11%, Caucasian 84%, Hispanic 7%, Native American <1%

ACADEMICS
Degrees: associate, bachelor's, certificate, terminal associate, transfer associate. **Special Study Options:** distance learning, English as a Second Language (ESL), honors program, internships, student-designed major, weekend college.

FACILITIES
Housing: Coed dorms.

CAMPUS LIFE
Activities: Choral groups, dance, drama/theater, music ensembles, musical theater, radio station, student government, student newspaper, yearbook. **Athletics (Intercollegiate):** *Men:* basketball, cross-country, diving, golf, lacrosse, soccer, swimming, tennis, track/field (outdoor), track/field (indoor), wrestling. *Women:* basketball, cross-country, diving, golf, soccer, softball, swimming, tennis, track/field (outdoor), track/field (indoor), volleyball.

ADMISSIONS
Basis for Candidate Selection: *Very important factors considered include:* rigor of secondary school record. *Important factors considered include:* recommendation(s), character/personal qualities, talent/ability. *Other factors considered include:* Class rank, application essay, standardized test scores, alumni/ae relation, extracurricular activities, geographical residence, interview, state residency, volunteer work, work experience. **Freshman Admission Requirements:** High school diploma is required and GED is accepted. *Academic units required:* 4 English, 1 mathematics, 1 science, 3 social studies, 1 history. **Transfer Admission Requirements:** High school transcript, college transcript(s), Lowest grade transferable C. **General Admission Information:** Application Fee $30. Notification on a rolling basis, beginning on or about 11/1. Nonfall registration accepted. Admission may be deferred for a maximum of 12.

COSTS AND FINANCIAL AID
Financial Aid Statistics: 78% undergrads receive need-based scholarship or grant aid. 59% undergrads receive non-need-based scholarship or grant aid. 80% undergrads receive need-based self-help aid. 0% freshmen, 0% undergrads receive athletic scholarships. **Criteria for awarding institutional aid:** *Non-need-based:* academics, leadership, state/district residency.

STATE UNIVERSITY OF NEW YORK— EMPIRE STATE COLLEGE

Two Union Avenue, Saratoga, NY 12866
Phone: 518-587-2100 · **Financial Aid Phone:** 518-587-2100
E-mail: admissions@esc.edu · **CEEB Code:** 2214
Fax: 518-587-9759 · **Website:** esc.edu · **ACT Code:** 2737

This public school was founded in 1971.

RATINGS
Admissions Selectivity Rating: 61   **Fire Safety Rating:** 60*

STUDENTS AND FACULTY
Enrollment: 10,128. **Student Body:** 62% female, 38% male, 8% out-of-state, 0% international. Asian 2%, African American 18%, Caucasian 66%, Hispanic 5%, Native American 1%
Faculty: 202 full-time faculty, 96% hold PhDs, 64% are are members of minority groups, 19% are women. 0% of classes are taught by teaching assistants.

ACADEMICS
Degrees: associate, bachelor's, master's. **Majors with Highest Enrollment:** Business/Commerce; Community Organization and Advocacy; Physical Sciences. **Special Study Options:** cross-registration, distance learning, double major, dual enrollment, external degree program, independent study, internships, student-designed major, Student-designed courses of study. **Combined degree programs:** BA/MA, BS/MA; B.P.S./MA.

FACILITIES
Computers: Students can register for classes online. Administrative functions (other than registration) can be performed online.

CAMPUS LIFE
Environment: Village. **Activities:** literary magazine.

ADMISSIONS
Freshman Academic Profile: Minimum paper TOEFL 550. **Basis for Candidate Selection:** *Very important factors considered include:* application essay, character/personal qualities. *Other factors considered include:* recommendation(s), rigor of secondary school record, talent/ability. **Freshman Admission Requirements:** High school diploma is required and GED is accepted. **Freshman Admission Statistics:** 1,536 applied, 79% admitted, 72% enrolled. **Transfer Admission Requirements:** High school transcript, essay or personal statement, Lowest grade transferable C. **General Admission Information:** Nonfall registration accepted. Admission may be deferred for a maximum of 3 years.

COSTS AND FINANCIAL AID

Annual in-state tuition $5,570. Annual out-of-state tuition $14,820. Required fees $395. **Required Forms and Deadlines:** FAFSA, State aid form. **Types of Aid:** *Need-based scholarships/grants:* Federal Pell, SEOG, state scholarships/grants, private scholarships, the school's own gift aid. *Loans:* Subsidized Stafford, Unsubsidized Stafford, PLUS, Federal Perkins. *Student Employment:* Federal Work-Study Program available. **Financial Aid Statistics:** 63% undergrads receive any aid.

STATE UNIVERSITY OF NEW YORK— FASHION INSTITUTE OF TECHNOLOGY

Seventh Avenue at 27th Street, New York, NY 10001
Phone: 212-217-7675 · **Financial Aid Phone:** 212-217-3560
E-mail: fitinfo@fitsuny.edu · **CEEB Code:** 2257
Website: www.fitnyc.suny.edu · **ACT Code:** 2744

This public school was founded in 1944.

RATINGS

Admissions Selectivity Rating: 60*   **Fire Safety Rating:** 60*

STUDENTS AND FACULTY

Enrollment: 9,848 **Student Body:** 37% out-of-state, 13% international. Asian 10%, African American 9%, Caucasian 47%, Hispanic 15%, Native American <1%
Faculty: Student/faculty ratio 17:1.

ADMISSIONS

Freshman Admission Statistics: 4,449 applied, 45% admitted, 62% enrolled.

COSTS AND FINANCIAL AID

Annual in-state tuition $6,170. Annual out-of-state tuition $17,810. Required fees $720.

See page 1054.

STATE UNIVERSITY OF NEW YORK—FREDONIA

178 Central Avenue, Fredonia, NY 14063
Phone: 716-673-3251 · **Financial Aid Phone:** 716-673-3253
E-mail: admissions@fredonia.edu · **CEEB Code:** 2539
Fax: 716-673-3249 · **Website:** www.fredonia.edu · **ACT Code:** 2934

This public school was founded in 1826. It has a 249-acre campus.

RATINGS

Admissions Selectivity Rating: 84   **Fire Safety Rating:** 78

STUDENTS AND FACULTY

Enrollment: 4,904. **Student Body:** 54% female, 46% male, 2% out-of-state, 3% international (8 countries represented). Asian 1%, African American 6%, Caucasian 78%, Hispanic 6%, Native American <1%
Retention and Graduation: 48% freshmen graduate within 4 years. 67% freshmen graduate within 6 years. 44% grads go on to further study within 1 year. **Faculty:** 255 full-time faculty, 87% hold PhDs, 47% are are members of minority groups, 14% are women. 2% of classes are taught by teaching assistants.

ACADEMICS

Degrees: bachelor's, master's, post-master's certificate. **Classes:** Most classes have 10-19 students. Most lab/discussion sessions have 20-29 students. **Majors with Highest Enrollment:** Elementary Education and Teaching; Music; Business/Commerce. **Special Study Options:** Accelerated program, distance learning, double major, honors program, independent study, internships, student-designed major, study abroad, teacher certification program. **Combined degree programs:** BA/DDS, 3+4 Optometry with SUNY State College of Optometry. **Disability Services:** Special programs offered to physically disabled students include note-taking services, reader services, tape recorders, tutors. **Career services:** Alumni network, alumni services, career/job search classes, career assessment, internships.

FACILITIES

Housing: Coed dorms, special housing for disabled students, men's dorms, women's dorms, apartments for single students. 85% of campus accessible to physically disabled. **Special Academic Facilities/Equipment:** Art center, education and local history museums, teacher education research center, developmental reading center, Sheldon Communications Lab, SMART classrooms, greenhouse. **Computers:** 100% of classrooms, 100% of libraries, 100% of dining areas, 100% of student union, 85% of common outdoor areas have wireless network access. Students can register for classes online. Administrative functions (other than registration) can be performed online.

CAMPUS LIFE

Environment: Village. **Activities:** Choral groups, concert band, dance, drama/theater, jazz band, literary magazine, music ensembles, musical theater, opera, pep band, radio station, student government, student newspaper, symphony orchestra, television station, Campus Ministries, International Student Organization. 152 registered organizations, 22 honor societies, 5 religious organizations. 3 fraternities, 3 sororities. **Athletics (Intercollegiate):** *Men:* baseball, basketball, cross-country, diving, ice hockey, soccer, swimming, track/field (outdoor), track/field (indoor). *Women:* basketball, cheerleading, cross-country, diving, lacrosse, soccer, softball, swimming, tennis, track/field (outdoor), track/field (indoor), volleyball. **On-Campus Highlights:** University Commons, Michael C. Rockefeller Arts Center, Library, Natatorium-Swimming pool and diving area, Rosch Recital Hall. **Environmental Initiatives:** Campus owned gas well; Recycle Mania; Sustainability Committee.

ADMISSIONS

Freshman Academic Profile: Average high school GPA 3.25. 16% in top 10% of high school class, 39% in top 25% of high school class, 75% in top 50% of high school class. 95% from public high schools. SAT Math middle 50% range 470-570. SAT Critical Reading middle 50% range 470-570. ACT middle 50% range 22-26. Minimum internet-based TOEFL 62. Minimum paper TOEFL 500. **Basis for Candidate Selection:** *Very important factors considered include:* academic GPA, rigor of secondary school record. *Important factors considered include:* Class rank, recommendation(s), standardized test scores, extracurricular activities. *Other factors considered include:* application essay, alumni/ae relation, character/personal qualities, first generation, level of applicant's interest, racial/ethnic status, talent/ability, volunteer work, work experience. **Freshman Admission Requirements:** High school diploma is required and GED is accepted. *Academic units required:* 4 English, 3 mathematics, 3 science, 3 foreign language, 4 social studies. **Freshman Admission Statistics:** 6,095 applied, 53% admitted, 33% enrolled. **Transfer Admission Requirements:** college transcript(s), Minimum college GPA of 2.0 required. Lowest grade transferable D. **General Admission Information:** Application Fee $40. Early decision application deadline 11/1. Notification on a rolling basis, beginning on or about 12/1. Nonfall registration accepted. Admission may be deferred for a maximum of 1 year. Credit and/or placement offered for CEEB Advanced Placement tests.

COSTS AND FINANCIAL AID

Annual in-state tuition $6,170. Annual out-of-state tuition $15,820. Room and board $12,100. Required fees $1,571. Average book expense $1,000. **Required Forms and Deadlines:** FAFSA, State aid form. **Notification of Awards:** Applicants will be notified of awards on a rolling basis beginning 3/10. **Types of Aid:** *Need-based scholarships/grants:* Federal Pell, SEOG, state scholarships/grants, private scholarships, the school's own gift aid. *Loans:* Subsidized Stafford, Unsubsidized Stafford, PLUS, Federal Perkins. *Student Employment:* Federal Work-Study Program available. Highest amount earned per year from on-campus jobs $1,000. Off-campus job opportunities are good. **Financial Aid Statistics:** 75% freshmen, 75% undergrads receive need-based scholarship or grant aid. 40% freshmen, 24% undergrads receive non-need-based scholarship or grant aid. 85% freshmen, 85% undergrads receive need-based self-help aid. 0% freshmen, 0% undergrads receive athletic scholarships. 81% freshmen, 85% undergrads receive any aid. 86% undergrads borrow to pay for school. Average cumulative indebtedness $23,632. **Criteria for awarding institutional aid:** *Non-need-based:* academics, alumni affiliation, art, athletics, leadership, minority status, music/drama.

STATE UNIVERSITY OF NEW YORK— MARITIME COLLEGE

6 Pennyfield Ave, Throggs Neck, NY 10465
Phone: 718-409-7200 · **Financial Aid Phone:** 718-409-7268
E-mail: admissions@sunymaritime.edu
Fax: 718-409-7465 · **Website:** www.sunymaritime.edu · **ACT Code:** 2954

This public school was founded in 1874. It has a 56-acre campus.

RATINGS

Admissions Selectivity Rating: 84   **Fire Safety Rating:** 82

STUDENTS AND FACULTY

Enrollment: 1,624. **Student Body:** 10% female, 90% male, 26% out-of-state, 3% international (14 countries represented). Asian 4%, African American 4%, Caucasian 72%, Hispanic 10%, Native American <1%
Retention and Graduation: 85% freshmen return for sophomore year. 25% freshmen graduate within 4 years. 5% grads go on to further study within 1 year. **Faculty:** 89 full-time faculty, 46% hold PhDs, 24% are are members of minority groups, 9% are women. 0% of classes are taught by teaching assistants.

ACADEMICS

Degrees: associate, bachelor's, master's. **Classes:** Most classes have 20-29 students. Most lab/discussion sessions have 20-29 students. **Majors with Highest Enrollment:** Transportation/Mobility Management; Naval Architecture and Marine Engineering; Mechanical Engineering. **Special Study Options:** cooperative education program, distance learning, double major, dual enrollment, English as a Second Language (ESL), honors program, independent study, internships, United States Coast Guard-issued deck and engine license program. **Honors programs:** Honors Program **Combined degree programs:** BS/MS. **Disability Services:** Special programs offered to physically disabled students include note-taking services, reader services, tape recorders, tutors. **Career services:** Alumni network, alumni services, career/job search classes, career assessment, internships, regional alumni. SUNY Maritime Colleges undergraduate students achieve 99% career placement and earn the top average starting salaries in America. The average starting salary for the Class of 2008 was $61,000. Students who choose to participate in the Regiment of Cadets experience the benefits of a structured learning environment, along with opportunities to develop leadership ability and excel in leadership roles. Each summer, the Regiment of Cadets embarks on a Summer Sea Term onboard the Training Ship Empire State. The training ship is 565 feet long and 17,000 tons. While students reside and operate the Training Ship Empire State, they see the world, stopping in four our more international ports (i.e. Greece, Italy, Ireland, Turkey, etc).

FACILITIES

Housing: Coed dorms, special housing for disabled studentsMost undergraduates required to live in on-campus housing. 81% of campus accessible to physically disabled. **Special Academic Facilities/Equipment:** Maritime Industry Museum, Fort Schuyler(National Historic Landmark), Bridge Simulator, Liquid Cargo Simulator, 565 ft. Training Ship Empire State VI, Diesel Simulator, 2 Research Ships, State-of-the-Art Electrical Engineering Lab, NY State Strategic Center for Port and Maritime Security (224 ft USS Stalwart), Computerized Weather Station, Maritime College Waterfront Sailboat Fleet:20 Vanguard 420's, 6 Vanguard FJ's, 1 Laser, J-105, J-35, J-24, Colgate 26 **Computers:** 75% of classrooms, 30% of dorms, 100% of libraries, 50% of student union, have wireless network access. Students can register for classes online.

CAMPUS LIFE

Environment: Metropolis. **Activities:** Choral groups, jazz band, marching band, music ensembles, pep band, student government, yearbook, Campus Ministries, International Student Organization. 30 registered organizations, 4 religious organizations. **Athletics (Intercollegiate):** *Men:* baseball, basketball, cross-country, football, ice hockey, lacrosse, riflery, soccer, swimming. *Women:* basketball, crew/rowing, cross-country, lacrosse, riflery, soccer, softball, swimming, volleyball. **On-Campus Highlights:** Fort Schuyler, Empire State VI **Environmental Initiatives:** Energy Reduction Programs with NYPA; Building a green building with DASNY; Partnering with energy management companies.

ADMISSIONS

Freshman Academic Profile: Average high school GPA 86. 8% in top 10% of high school class, 44% in top 25% of high school class, 81% in top 50% of high school class. SAT Math middle 50% range 530-610. SAT Critical Reading middle 50% range 490-580. SAT Writing middle 50% range 470-560. ACT middle 50% range 22-26. Minimum internet-based TOEFL 79. Minimum paper TOEFL 550. **Basis for Candidate Selection:** *Very important factors considered include:* academic GPA, rigor of secondary school record, standardized test scores. *Important factors considered include:* recommendation(s), talent/ability, volunteer work, work experience. *Other factors considered include:* Class rank, application essay, alumni/ae relation, extracurricular activities, first generation, interview, level of applicant's interest. **Freshman Admission Requirements:** High school diploma is required and GED is accepted. *Academic units required:* 3 English, 3 mathematics, 3 science, (1 science labs), 1 foreign language, 3 social studies, 3 history. **Freshman Admission Statistics:** 1,795 applied, 53% admitted, 37% enrolled. **Transfer Admission Requirements:** High school transcript, college transcript(s), Minimum college GPA of 2.5 required. Lowest grade transferable 2. **General Admission Information:** Application Fee $40. Notification on a rolling basis, beginning on or about 9/15. Nonfall registration accepted. Credit offered for CEEB Advanced Placement tests.

COSTS AND FINANCIAL AID

Annual in-state tuition $6,170. Annual out-of-state tuition $15,820. Room and board $11,040. Required fees $1,276. Average book expense $1,464. **Required**

Forms and Deadlines: FAFSA. **Notification of Awards:** Applicants will be notified of awards on a rolling basis beginning 3/15. **Types of Aid:** *Need-based scholarships/grants:* Federal Pell, SEOG, state scholarships/grants, private scholarships, the school's own gift aid. *Loans:* Subsidized Stafford, Unsubsidized Stafford, PLUS, Federal Perkins, state loans. *Student Employment:* Federal Work-Study Program available. Institutional employment available. Highest amount earned per year from on-campus jobs $9,896. Off-campus job opportunities are fair. **Financial Aid Statistics:** 55% freshmen, 65% undergrads receive need-based scholarship or grant aid. 84% freshmen, 31% undergrads receive non-need-based scholarship or grant aid. 70% freshmen, 76% undergrads receive need-based self-help aid. 0% freshmen, 0% undergrads receive athletic scholarships. 83% freshmen, 78% undergrads receive any aid. **Criteria for awarding institutional aid:** *Non-need-based:* academics, leadership, state/district residency.

STATE UNIVERSITY OF NEW YORK—NEW PALTZ

100 Hawk Drive, New Paltz, NY 12561
Phone: 845-257-3200 • **Financial Aid Phone:** 845-257-3250
E-mail: admissions@newpaltz.edu • **CEEB Code:** 2541
Fax: 845-257-3209 • **Website:** www.newpaltz.edu • **ACT Code:** 2938

This public school was founded in 1828. It has a 216-acre campus.

RATINGS

Admissions Selectivity Rating: 89   **Fire Safety Rating:** 88

STUDENTS AND FACULTY

Enrollment: 6,464. **Student Body:** 62% female, 38% male, 3% out-of-state, 2% international (49 countries represented). Asian 5%, African American 6%, Caucasian 65%, Hispanic 16%, Native American <1%
Retention and Graduation: 55% freshmen graduate within 4 years. 27% grads go on to further study within 1 year. **Faculty:** 357 full-time faculty, 82% hold PhDs, 52% are are members of minority groups, 18% are women.

ACADEMICS

Degrees: bachelor's, master's, post-master's certificate. **Classes:** Most classes have 20-29 students. **Majors with Highest Enrollment:** Psychology; Elementary Education and Teaching; Visual and Performing Arts. **Special Study Options:** cooperative education program, cross-registration, distance learning, double major, dual enrollment, English as a Second Language (ESL), exchange student program (domestic), honors program, independent study, internships, liberal arts/career combination, student-designed major, study abroad, teacher certification program. **Honors programs:** The Honors Program exists to challenge New Paltz Students beyond what is usually expected of them. It was designed around the philosophy that intense and rigorous courses, taught by outstanding instructors and filled with motivated, focused students would create the optimal learning environment. The Honors Program is small, consisting of around 100 students. Once admitted to the Program, students take special Honors seminars, which are interdisciplinary and small in size (usually around 10 students). Unlike traditional lecture courses, Honors seminars emphasize dialogue and non-lecture based learning; students are expected to come to class with something to say and to actively participate in debate and discussion. **Combined degree programs:** BS/DO BS/OD BS/MS. **Disability Services:** Special programs offered to physically disabled students include note-taking services, reader services, tape recorders, tutors. **Career services:** alumni services, career/job search classes, career assessment, internships. Career services highlights include an internship stipend program that provides SUNY New Paltz students with scholarship stipends. These funds allow students to participate in career related experiences regardless of financial constraints.

FACILITIES

Housing: Coed dorms, special housing for disabled students, men's dorms, special housing for international students, women's dorms, The First-Year Initiative, Honors Housing, Art Program Housing. 90% of campus accessible to physically disabled. **Special Academic Facilities/Equipment:** Samuel Dorsky Museum of Art, Resnick Engineering Hall, Coykendall Media Center, Communication Disorders Training Center and Clinic; Music Therapy Training Center and Clinic; Shepherd Recital Hall, Honors Center; Martin Luther King, Jr. Study Center; Fournier Mass Spectrometer;Raymond Kurdt Theatre Collection; more **Computers:** 70% of classrooms, 45% of dorms, 100% of libraries, 90% of dining areas, 90% of student union, 10% of common outdoor areas have wireless network access. Students can register for classes online. Administrative functions (other than registration) can be performed online.

CAMPUS LIFE

Environment: Village. **Activities:** Choral groups, concert band, dance, drama/theater, jazz band, literary magazine, music ensembles, musical theater, radio station, student government, student newspaper, symphony orchestra, television station, Campus Ministries, International Student Organization, Model UN. 196 registered organizations, 12 honor societies, 10 religious organizations. 11 fraternities, 17 sororities. **Athletics (Intercollegiate):** Men: baseball, basketball, cross-country, diving, soccer, swimming, tennis, volleyball. Women: basketball, cross-country, diving, field hockey, lacrosse, soccer, softball, swimming, tennis, volleyball. **On-Campus Highlights:** Samuel Dorsky Museum of Art, Lenape and Esopus Residence Halls, Athletic and Wellness Center, Student Union, Hasbrouck Dining Hall. **Environmental Initiatives:** Investing $2 million in a campus wide submetering system for electricity, natural gas, high temp hot water, and domestic water. Initiating a zero waste initiative existing programs such as composting, recycling (single stream plus batteries, e-waste, light bulbs, ink cartridges, metal, etc.), and Recyclemania, and new programs including tracking recycling, composting, and landfill rates, improved signage, improved zero waste collection rooms in residence halls, and much behind-the-scenes coordination. Establishing an Office of Campus Sustainability with a Campus Sustainability Coordinator and an Energy Management Coordinator. The college has invested extensively in these two employees through professional developing trainings and conferences. Interns and student workers have worked on energy, food waste, recycling, and local food initiatives since establishing the office in May of 2014.

ADMISSIONS

Freshman Academic Profile: Average high school GPA 3.6. 33% in top 10% of high school class, 80% in top 25% of high school class, 98% in top 50% of high school class. SAT Math middle 50% range 520-600. SAT Critical Reading middle 50% range 510-600. SAT Writing middle 50% range 500-603. ACT middle 50% range 23-27. Minimum internet-based TOEFL 80. Minimum paper TOEFL 550. **Basis for Candidate Selection:** *Very important factors considered include:* academic GPA, rigor of secondary school record, standardized test scores. *Important factors considered include:* application essay, recommendation(s). *Other factors considered include:* Class rank, extracurricular activities, talent/ability, volunteer work, work experience. **Freshman Admission Requirements:** High school diploma is required and GED is accepted. *Academic units required:* 4 English, 3 mathematics, 3 science, (2 science labs), 2 foreign language, 4 social studies, 1 history. **Freshman Admission Statistics:** 13,726 applied, 42% admitted, 19% enrolled. **Transfer Admission Requirements:** college transcript(s), statement of good standing from prior institution(s). Minimum college GPA of 2.75 required. Lowest grade transferable C-. **General Admission Information:** Application Fee $40. Regular application deadline 4/1. Notification on a rolling basis, beginning on or about 1/1. Nonfall registration not accepted. Credit and/or placement offered for CEEB Advanced Placement tests.

COSTS AND FINANCIAL AID

Annual in-state tuition $6,170. Annual out-of-state tuition $15,820. Room and board $10,895. Required fees $1,238. Average book expense $1,500. **Required Forms and Deadlines:** FAFSA, State aid form. **Notification of Awards:** Applicants will be notified of awards on a rolling basis beginning 4/1. **Types of Aid:** *Need-based scholarships/grants:* Federal Pell, SEOG, state scholarships/grants, private scholarships, the school's own gift aid. *Loans:* Subsidized Stafford, Unsubsidized Stafford, PLUS, Federal Perkins. *Student Employment:* Federal Work-Study Program available. Institutional employment available. Highest amount earned per year from on-campus jobs $8,569. Off-campus job opportunities are good. **Financial Aid Statistics:** 58% freshmen, 58% undergrads receive need-based scholarship or grant aid. 11% freshmen, 6% undergrads receive non-need-based scholarship or grant aid. 86% freshmen, 88% undergrads receive need-based self-help aid. 0% freshmen, 0% undergrads receive athletic scholarships. 63% undergrads borrow to pay for school. Average cumulative indebtedness $24,864. **Criteria for awarding institutional aid:** *Non-need-based:* academics, alumni affiliation, art, music/drama.

STATE UNIVERSITY OF NEW YORK—OSWEGO

229 Sheldon Hall, Oswego, NY 13126-3599
Phone: 315-312-2250 · **Financial Aid Phone:** 315-312-2248
E-mail: admiss@oswego.edu · **CEEB Code:** 2543
Fax: 315-312-3260 · **Website:** www.oswego.edu · **ACT Code:** 2942

This public school was founded in 1861. It has a 696-acre campus.

RATINGS

Admissions Selectivity Rating: 86   **Fire Safety Rating:** 74

STUDENTS AND FACULTY

Enrollment: 7,102. **Student Body:** 51% female, 49% male, 2% out-of-state, 2% international (18 countries represented). Asian 2%, African American 7%, Caucasian 78%, Hispanic 9%, Native American <1%

Retention and Graduation: 44% freshmen graduate within 4 years. 63% freshmen graduate within 6 years. 19% grads go on to further study within 1 year. 22% grads pursue arts and sciences degrees. 4% grads pursue law degrees. 6% grads pursue business degrees. 5% grads pursue medical degrees. **Faculty:** 341 full-time faculty, 88% hold PhDs, 47% are are members of minority groups, 15% are women. 0% of classes are taught by teaching assistants.

ACADEMICS

Degrees: bachelor's, master's, post-master's certificate. **Classes:** Most classes have 10-19 students. Most lab/discussion sessions have 20-29 students. **Majors with Highest Enrollment:** Business Administration and Management; Mass Communication/Media Studies; Accounting. **Special Study Options:** Accelerated program, cross-registration, distance learning, double major, dual enrollment, English as a Second Language (ESL), exchange student program (domestic), external degree program, honors program, independent study, internships, liberal arts/career combination, study abroad, teacher certification program. **Honors programs:** Over 275 students participate in our campus wide Honors Program. Students will take smaller courses based on the program's core multidisciplinary courses in the social sciences, the natural sciences, the humanities, and philosophy, as well as several other courses in math, English, and a foreign language. The courses emphasize the interrelatedness of the disciplines, their historical and intellectual origins, their roles in modern society, and their impact on life in the future. **Combined degree programs:** BA/MA, BS/MBA—5 year accounting BS/MBA program. **Disability Services:** Special programs offered to physically disabled students include note-taking services, reader services, tape recorders, tutors. **Career services:** Alumni network, alumni services, career/job search classes, career assessment, internships, regional alumni. We currently have 133 student in our Internship Program, 43 male student and 90 female students, involving 78 organizations.

FACILITIES

Housing: Coed dorms, Wellness Housing, Theme HousingGlobal living and learning center, suites for upperclassmen, nontraditional student housing, first-year experience residence hall for incoming freshmen only, housing for 21 and over single suites, several rooms equipped with special equipment to meet needs of disabled students available. 85% of campus accessible to physically disabled. **Special Academic Facilities/Equipment:** Tyler Hall Art Galleries, Rice Creek Biological Field Station, curriculum materials center, electron microscopy lab, planetarium. **Computers:** 80% of classrooms, 10% of dorms, 100% of libraries, 100% of dining areas, 100% of student union, have wireless network access. Students can register for classes online. Administrative functions (other than registration) can be performed online.

CAMPUS LIFE

Environment: Village. **Activities:** Choral groups, concert band, dance, drama/theater, jazz band, literary magazine, music ensembles, musical theater, radio station, student government, student newspaper, student-run film society, symphony orchestra, television station, yearbook, International Student Organization. 148 registered organizations, 21 honor societies, 6 religious organizations. 13 fraternities, 10 sororities. **Athletics (Intercollegiate):** Men: baseball, basketball, cross-country, diving, golf, ice hockey, lacrosse, soccer, swimming, tennis, track/field (outdoor), track/field (indoor), wrestling. Women: basketball, cross-country, diving, field hockey, ice hockey, lacrosse, soccer, softball, swimming, tennis, track/field (outdoor), track/field (indoor), volleyball. **On-Campus Highlights:** Romney Fieldhouse/ Campus Ctr(Hockey and Conference), Hewitt Union; The Student Union, Rich Hall; The School of Business, Tyler Hall; The Fine Arts Building, Penfield Library and Café, Rice Creek Biological field station; The Sweete Shoppe in the Hewitt Union!; Laker Hall (Field House); Johnson Hall (1st Year Residence Hall). **Environmental Initiatives:** Commitment to LEED Gold for construction projects; President's Climate Commitment (ACUPCC); Actively pursuing on-site generation and geothermal sources.

ADMISSIONS

Freshman Academic Profile: Average high school GPA 3.5. 14.2% in top 10% of high school class, 53% in top 25% of high school class, 86% in top 50% of high school class. SAT Math middle 50% range 510-600. SAT Critical Reading middle 50% range 510-590. ACT middle 50% range 22-26. **Basis for Candidate Selection:** *Very important factors considered include:* academic GPA, rigor of secondary school record. *Important factors considered include:* Class rank, standardized test scores. *Other factors considered include:* application essay, recommendation(s), character/personal qualities, extracurricular activities, first generation, interview, level of applicant's interest, racial/ethnic status, talent/ability, volunteer work, work experience. **Freshman Admission Requirements:** High school diploma is required and GED is accepted. *Academic units required:* 4 English, 3 mathematics, 3 science, (2 science labs), 2 foreign language, 4 social studies. **Freshman Admission Statistics:** 11,022 applied, 48% admitted, 27% enrolled. **Transfer Admission Requirements:** college transcript(s), Minimum college GPA of 2.5 required. Lowest grade transferable D. **General Admission Information:** Application Fee $40. Early decision application deadline 11/15. Notification on a rolling basis, beginning on or about 1/15. Nonfall registration accepted. Admission may be deferred for a maximum of 12 months. Credit offered for CEEB Advanced Placement tests.

COSTS AND FINANCIAL AID

Annual in-state tuition $6,170. Annual out-of-state tuition $15,820. Room and board $12,690. Required fees $1,331. Average book expense $800. **Required Forms and Deadlines:** FAFSA, State aid form. **Notification of Awards:** Applicants will be notified of awards on a rolling basis beginning 3/1. **Types of Aid:** *Need-based scholarships/grants:* Federal Pell, SEOG, state scholarships/grants, private scholarships, the school's own gift aid. *Loans:* Subsidized Stafford, Unsubsidized Stafford, PLUS, Federal Perkins. *Student Employment:* Federal Work-Study Program available. Institutional employment available. Highest amount earned per year from on-campus jobs $2,000. **Financial Aid Statistics:** 94% freshmen, 86% undergrads receive need-based scholarship or grant aid. 69% freshmen, 34% undergrads receive non-need-based scholarship or grant aid. 93% freshmen, 94% undergrads receive need-based self-help aid. 0% freshmen, 0% undergrads receive athletic scholarships. 94% freshmen, 87% undergrads receive any aid. 77% undergrads borrow to pay for school. Average cumulative indebtedness $25,398. **Criteria for awarding institutional aid:** *Non-need-based:* academics, state/district residency.

STATE UNIVERSITY OF NEW YORK— PLATTSBURGH

1001 Kehoe Bldg., Plattsburgh, NY 12901
Phone: 518-564-2040
E-mail: admissions@plattsburgh.edu • **CEEB Code:** 2544
Fax: 518-564-2045 • **Website:** www.plattsburgh.edu • **ACT Code:** 2944

This public school was founded in 1889. It has a 300-acre campus.

RATINGS

Admissions Selectivity Rating: 78   **Fire Safety Rating:** 60*

STUDENTS AND FACULTY

Enrollment: 5,328. **Student Body:** 58% female, 42% male, 4% out-of-state, 7% international (56 countries represented). Asian 2%, African American 5%, Caucasian 76%, Hispanic 3%, Native American <1%
Retention and Graduation: 75% freshmen return for sophomore year. 37% freshmen graduate within 4 years. 59% freshmen graduate within 6 years. 34% grads go on to further study within 1 year. 31% grads pursue arts and sciences degrees. 1% grads pursue law degrees. 2% grads pursue business degrees. 1% grads pursue medical degrees. **Faculty:** 250 full-time faculty, 90% hold PhDs, 36% are are members of minority groups, 12% are women. 0% of classes are taught by teaching assistants.

ACADEMICS

Degrees: bachelor's, master's, post-bachelor's certificate, post-master's certificate. **Classes:** Most classes have 10-19 students. Most lab/discussion sessions have 20-29 students. **Majors with Highest Enrollment:** Special Education and Teaching; Early Childhood Education; Business/Commerce. **Special Study Options:** cooperative education program, cross-registration, distance learning, double major, dual enrollment, English as a Second Language (ESL), exchange student program (domestic), honors program, independent study, internships, liberal arts/career combination, student-designed major, study abroad, teacher certification program. **Honors programs:** The honors program is offered in two levels, General Honors and Advance Honors. Each seminar in General Honors program is limited to about 15 students and is taught by faculty who have a reputation of excellence in teaching. Occasionally distance-learning experiences are available which allow students to work with faculty at other colleges and universities in the US; Advance Honors' work continues the goals and ideals of General Honors, except the work is focused in student's major and requires that students design and carry out a project in research, in performance, in fieldwork, or whatever else would be appropriate to a particular major. **Combined degree programs:** 3-2 French, Spanish; 3-1 Medical Tech. and Cytote. **Disability Services:** Special programs offered to physically disabled students include note-taking services, reader services, tape recorders, tutors. **Career services:** Alumni network, alumni services, career/job search classes, career assessment, internships.

FACILITIES

Housing: Coed dorms, special housing for disabled students, special housing for international students, Wellness floor Substance free building and floors Quiet floors Men's floor Women's floors Extended logding. 95% of campus accessible to physically disabled. **Special Academic Facilities/Equipment:** Art galleries, sculpture courtyard, theatre and concert halls, communications/ lecture hall, interactive video for telecourses, radio and TV broadcasting facilities, planetarium, on-site research center for biotechnology and environmental science, enzymology lab, electron microscope, remote sensing lab,

NMR spectrophotometer, computer-operated infrared spectrophotometer, gas chromatograph, mass spectrometer, computerized liquid scintillation counter, facility for analysis of environmental pollutants in lake water, sediments and biota, lake research/sampling vesel with differential GPS navigation equipment, ubductively coupled plasma/mass spectrometer, ion chromatograph/high performance liquid chromatograph, mercury detector. **Computers:** Students can register for classes online. Administrative functions (other than registration) can be performed online.

CAMPUS LIFE

Environment: Village. **Activities:** Choral groups, concert band, drama/ theater, jazz band, literary magazine, music ensembles, radio station, student government, student newspaper, student-run film society, symphony orchestra, television station, yearbook. 97 registered organizations, 26 honor societies, 3 religious organizations. 6 fraternities, 7 sororities. **Athletics (Intercollegiate):** *Men:* basketball, cross-country, golf, ice hockey, lacrosse, rugby, soccer, track/ field (outdoor), track/field (indoor). *Women:* basketball, cross-country, golf, ice hockey, rugby, soccer, softball, tennis, track/field (outdoor), track/field (indoor), volleyball. **On-Campus Highlights:** Fitness Center, Art Museums, College Field House, Computer Labs, College Center.

ADMISSIONS

Freshman Academic Profile: Average high school GPA 3. 11% in top 10% of high school class, 33% in top 25% of high school class, 75% in top 50% of high school class. 98% from public high schools. SAT Math middle 50% range 480-560. SAT Critical Reading middle 50% range 480-560. ACT middle 50% range 19-24. Minimum paper TOEFL 450. **Basis for Candidate Selection:** *Very important factors considered include:* rigor of secondary school record, standardized test scores, interview. *Important factors considered include:* Class rank, application essay, recommendation(s), alumni/ae relation, character/ personal qualities, extracurricular activities, racial/ethnic status, talent/ability. *Other factors considered include:* volunteer work, work experience. **Freshman Admission Requirements:** High school diploma is required and GED is accepted. *Academic units required:* 4 English, 3 mathematics, 3 science, 3 foreign language, 3 social studies, 1 history. **Freshman Admission Statistics:** 6,798 applied, 62% admitted, 23% enrolled. **Transfer Admission Requirements:** college transcript(s), Minimum college GPA of 2.3 required. Lowest grade transferable D. **General Admission Information:** Application Fee $40. Early decision application deadline 11/15. Regular application deadline 8/1. Notification on a rolling basis, beginning on or about 1/15. Nonfall registration accepted. Admission may be deferred for a maximum of 1 year. Credit and/or placement offered for CEEB Advanced Placement tests.

COSTS AND FINANCIAL AID

Annual in-state tuition $4,350. Annual out-of-state tuition $10,300. Room and board $6,500. Required fees $850. Average book expense $850. **Required Forms and Deadlines:** FAFSA, State aid form. **Notification of Awards:** Applicants will be notified of awards on a rolling basis beginning 3/15. **Types of Aid:** *Need-based scholarships/grants:* Federal Pell, SEOG, state scholarships/grants, private scholarships, the school's own gift aid, Scholarships for disadvantaged students, State Educational Opportunity Program. *Loans:* Direct Subsidized Stafford, Direct Unsubsidized Stafford, Direct PLUS, Federal Perkins, Federal Nursing, Grace Appleton Loan, privately endowed administered by a Trust Company; Awarded by the College. *Student Employment:* Federal Work-Study Program available. Institutional employment available. Highest amount earned per year from on-campus jobs $1,540. Off-campus job opportunities are good. **Financial Aid Statistics:** 91% freshmen, 90% undergrads receive need-based scholarship or grant aid. 32% freshmen, 29% undergrads receive non-need-based scholarship or grant aid. 85% freshmen, 85% undergrads receive need-based self-help aid. 0% freshmen, 0% undergrads receive athletic scholarships. 73% undergrads borrow to pay for school. **Criteria for awarding institutional aid:** *Non-need-based:* academics, alumni affiliation, art, leadership, music/drama, state/district residency.

STATE UNIVERSITY OF NEW YORK POLYTECHNIC INSTITUTE

PO Box 3050, Utica, NY 13504
Phone: 315-792-7500 • **Financial Aid Phone:** 315-792-7210
E-mail: admissions@sunyit.edu • **CEEB Code:** 2896
Fax: 315-792-7837 • **Website:** www.sunyit.edu • **ACT Code:** 2953

This public school was founded in 1966. It has a 850-acre campus.

RATINGS

Admissions Selectivity Rating: 84   **Fire Safety Rating:** 60*

STUDENTS AND FACULTY

Enrollment: 1,893. **Student Body:** 38% female, 62% male, 1% out-of-state, 1% international (13 countries represented). Asian 3%, African American 8%, Caucasian 79%, Hispanic 7%, Native American <1%
Retention and Graduation: 84% freshmen return for sophomore year. 24% freshmen graduate within 4 years. 43% freshmen graduate within 6 years. **Faculty:** 131 full-time faculty, 87% hold PhDs, 32% are are members of minority groups, 22% are women.

ACADEMICS

Degrees: bachelor's, master's, post-master's certificate. **Classes:** Most classes have 10-19 students. Most lab/discussion sessions have 10-19 students. **Majors with Highest Enrollment:** Computer and Information Sciences; Business Administration and Management; Mechanical Engineering/Mechanical Technology/Technician. **Special Study Options:** Accelerated program, cross-registration, distance learning, double major, dual enrollment, English as a Second Language (ESL), independent study, internships, study abroad. **Combined degree programs:** Computer/Info Science—BS/MS, Nursing—BS/MS. **Disability Services:** Special programs offered to physically disabled students include note-taking services, reader services, tape recorders, tutors. **Career services:** alumni services, career/job search classes, career assessment, internships, regional alumni.

FACILITIES

Housing: Coed dorms, special housing for disabled students. 98% of campus accessible to physically disabled. **Special Academic Facilities/Equipment:** Gannett Gallery, New York State Telecommunications Museum. **Computers:** Students can register for classes online. Administrative functions (other than registration) can be performed online.

CAMPUS LIFE

Environment: Village. **Activities:** drama/theater, jazz band, music ensembles, radio station, student government, student newspaper, television station, yearbook, International Student Organization. 30 registered organizations, 4 honor societies, 1 religous organization. **Athletics (Intercollegiate):** *Men:* baseball, basketball, golf, lacrosse, soccer. *Women:* basketball, cross-country, golf, soccer, softball, volleyball.

ADMISSIONS

Freshman Academic Profile: Average high school GPA 88.99. 17% in top 10% of high school class, 43% in top 25% of high school class, 83% in top 50% of high school class. 98% from public high schools. SAT Math middle 50% range 460-650. SAT Critical Reading middle 50% range 460-610. ACT middle 50% range 22-28. Minimum internet-based TOEFL 79. Minimum paper TOEFL 550. **Basis for Candidate Selection:** *Very important factors considered include:* academic GPA, standardized test scores. *Important factors considered include:* rigor of secondary school record, extracurricular activities. *Other factors considered include:* application essay, recommendation(s), interview, talent/ability, volunteer work, work experience. **Freshman Admission Requirements:** High school diploma is required and GED is accepted. *Academic units required:* 4 English, 3 mathematics, 3 science, (3 science labs), 2 social studies, 2 history. **Freshman Admission Statistics:** 2,233 applied, 57% admitted, 27% enrolled. **Transfer Admission Requirements:** college transcript(s), statement of good standing from prior institution(s). Minimum college GPA of 2.5 required. Lowest grade transferable D. **General Admission Information:** Application Fee $40. Regular application deadline 8/1. Notification on a rolling basis, beginning on or about 1/15. Nonfall registration accepted. Admission may be deferred for a maximum of 1 year. Neither credit nor placement offered for CEEB Advanced Placement tests.

COSTS AND FINANCIAL AID

Annual in-state tuition $6,170. Annual out-of-state tuition $15,820. Room and board $12,250. Required fees $1,270. Average book expense $1,500. **Required Forms and Deadlines:** FAFSA, State aid form. **Notification of Awards:** Applicants will be notified of awards on a rolling basis beginning 3/17. **Types of Aid:** *Need-based scholarships/grants:* Federal Pell, SEOG, state scholarships/grants, private scholarships. *Loans:* Direct Subsidized Stafford, Direct Unsubsidized Stafford, Direct PLUS, Federal Perkins, Federal Nursing. *Student Employment:* Federal Work-Study Program available. Institutional employment available. Off-campus job opportunities are good. **Financial Aid Statistics:** 90% freshmen, 87% undergrads receive need-based scholarship or grant aid. 63% freshmen, 30% undergrads receive non-need-based scholarship or grant aid. 98% freshmen, 99% undergrads receive need-based self-help aid. 0% freshmen, 0% undergrads receive athletic scholarships. **Criteria for awarding institutional aid:** *Non-need-based:* academics.

STATE UNIVERSITY OF NEW YORK—POTSDAM

44 Pierrepont Avenue, Potsdam, NY 13676
Phone: 315-267-2180 • **Financial Aid Phone:** 315-267-2162
E-mail: admissions@potsdam.edu • **CEEB Code:** 2545
Fax: 315-267-2163 • **Website:** www.potsdam.edu • **ACT Code:** 2946

This public school was founded in 1816. It has a 240-acre campus.

RATINGS

Admissions Selectivity Rating: 78   Fire Safety Rating: 83

STUDENTS AND FACULTY

Enrollment: 3,669. **Student Body:** 56% female, 44% male, 3% out-of-state, 1% international (40 countries represented). Asian 2%, African American 8%, Caucasian 69%, Hispanic 10%, Native American 2%
Retention and Graduation: 36% freshmen graduate within 4 years. 54% freshmen graduate within 6 years. 33% grads go on to further study within 1 year. 16% grads pursue arts and sciences degrees. 1% grads pursue business degrees. 1% grads pursue medical degrees. **Faculty:** 249 full-time faculty, 84% hold PhDs, 44% are are members of minority groups, 12% are women.

ACADEMICS

Degrees: bachelor's, master's. **Classes:** Most classes have 10-19 students. Most lab/discussion sessions have 10-19 students. **Majors with Highest Enrollment:** Business Administration and Management; Elementary Education and Teaching; Music Teacher Education. **Special Study Options:** cross-registration, distance learning, double major, dual enrollment, exchange student program (domestic), honors program, independent study, internships, liberal arts/career combination, student-designed major, study abroad, teacher certification program, First-year students may enroll in interdisciplinary program to study art, literature, science, and sociology of the Adirondacks. Extension offers undergraduate and graduate courses with emphasis on teacher education. Combined degree options in engineering with Clarkson University and SUNY Binghamton; accounting, engineering or management with SUNY Institute of Technology. **Honors programs:** The Honors Program is designed to offer special curricular, co-curricular, and extra curricular opportunities for our college's most academically talented students. Benefits include priority registration, honors courses, field trips, mentoring, housing, and select study abroad options. **Combined degree programs:** BA/MA, BA/MST. **Disability Services:** Special programs offered to physically disabled students include note-taking services, reader services, tape recorders, tutors. **Career services:** Alumni network, alumni services, career/job search classes, career assessment.

FACILITIES

Housing: Coed dorms, special housing for disabled students, special housing for international students, apartments for single students, Wellness Housing, Theme Housing, First year experience, Quiet study, International House, Transfer student housing, Sustainability. 95% of campus accessible to physically disabled. **Special Academic Facilities/Equipment:** Art gallery, anthropology museum, ecology museum, three performance halls, theatre, synthesizer music studios, planetarium, electron microscope, nuclear magnetic resonator, seismograph. **Computers:** 20% of classrooms, 100% of dorms, 100% of libraries, 100% of dining areas, 100% of student union, 40% of common outdoor areas have wireless network access. Students can register for classes online. Administrative functions (other than registration) can be performed online.

CAMPUS LIFE

Environment: Village. **Activities:** Choral groups, concert band, dance, drama/theater, jazz band, literary magazine, music ensembles, musical theater, opera, radio station, student government, student newspaper, symphony orchestra, yearbook, Campus Ministries, International Student Organization. 100 registered organizations, 17 honor societies, 3 religious organizations. 4 fraternities, 7 sororities. **Athletics (Intercollegiate):** *Men:* basketball, cross-country, diving, equestrian sports, golf, ice hockey, lacrosse, soccer, swimming. *Women:* basketball, cross-country, diving, equestrian sports, ice hockey, lacrosse, soccer, softball, swimming, tennis, volleyball. **On-Campus Highlights:** Hosmer Concert Hall, Maxcy Athletic Complex, Townhouses, Gibson Art Gallery, Barrrington Student Union, Becky's Place (new dining facility) Minerva's Café. **Environmental Initiatives:** Increase recycle efforts; Increase purchase of green products and energy star equipment; Increase purchase of renewable energy.

ADMISSIONS

Freshman Academic Profile: Average high school GPA 87. 9.3% in top 10% of high school class, 32.4% in top 25% of high school class, 59.3% in top 50% of high school class. 94% from public high schools. SAT Math middle 50% range 450-570. SAT Critical Reading middle 50% range 450-570. ACT middle 50% range 20-27. Minimum internet-based TOEFL 79. Minimum paper TOEFL 550. **Basis for Candidate Selection:** *Very important factors considered* *include:* academic GPA, rigor of secondary school record. *Important factors considered include:* Class rank, application essay, recommendation(s), character/personal qualities, extracurricular activities, interview, talent/ability. *Other factors considered include:* standardized test scores, alumni/ae relation, level of applicant's interest, volunteer work, work experience. **Freshman Admission Requirements:** High school diploma is required and GED is accepted. *Academic units required:* 4 English, 2 mathematics, 2 science, (1 science labs), 0 foreign language, 4 social studies, 1 visual/performing arts. **Freshman Admission Statistics:** 5,155 applied, 68% admitted, 24% enrolled. **Transfer Admission Requirements:** college transcript(s), Minimum college GPA of 2.0 required. Lowest grade transferable D. **General Admission Information:** Application Fee $40. Notification on a rolling basis, beginning on or about 10/1. Nonfall registration accepted. Admission may be deferred for a maximum of 1 year. Credit and/or placement offered for CEEB Advanced Placement tests.

COSTS AND FINANCIAL AID
Average book expense $1,340. **Required Forms and Deadlines:** FAFSA, State aid form. **Notification of Awards:** Applicants will be notified of awards on a rolling basis beginning 2/1. **Types of Aid:** *Need-based scholarships/grants:* Federal Pell, SEOG, state scholarships/grants, private scholarships, the school's own gift aid, VESID, Veteran Benefits, BIA, Native American, Academic Achievement (ACG), SMART (National Math & Science Grant). *Loans:* Direct Subsidized Stafford, Direct Unsubsidized Stafford, Direct PLUS, Federal Perkins, college/university loans from institutional funds, Alternative Loans. *Student Employment:* Federal Work-Study Program available. Institutional employment available. Off-campus job opportunities are good. **Financial Aid Statistics:** 89% freshmen, 88% undergrads receive need-based scholarship or grant aid. 39% freshmen, 33% undergrads receive non-need-based scholarship or grant aid. 89% freshmen, 85% undergrads receive need-based self-help aid. 0% freshmen, 0% undergrads receive athletic scholarships. 88% freshmen, 88% undergrads receive any aid. 75% undergrads borrow to pay for school. Average cumulative indebtedness $20,047. **Criteria for awarding institutional aid:** *Non-need-based:* academics, art, leadership, minority status, music/drama.

STATE UNIVERSITY OF NEW YORK— STONY BROOK UNIVERSITY

Office of Admissions, Stony Brook, NY 11794-1901
Phone: 631-632-6868 · **Financial Aid Phone:** 631-632-6840
E-mail: enroll@stonybrook.edu · **CEEB Code:** 2548
Fax: 631-632-9898 · **Website:** www.stonybrook.edu/ · **ACT Code:** 2952

This public school was founded in 1957. It has a 1450-acre campus.

RATINGS
Admissions Selectivity Rating: 92   **Fire Safety Rating:** 75

STUDENTS AND FACULTY
Enrollment: 16,170. **Student Body:** 46% female, 54% male, 81% out-of-state, 1% international (125 countries represented). Asian 24%, African American 6%, Caucasian 38%, Hispanic 11%, Native American <1% **Retention and Graduation:** 89% freshmen return for sophomore year. 48% freshmen graduate within 4 years. 69% freshmen graduate within 6 years. 30% grads go on to further study within 1 year. 18% grads pursue arts and sciences degrees. 2% grads pursue law degrees. 1% grads pursue business degrees. 7% grads pursue medical degrees. **Faculty:** 1,138 full-time faculty, 91% hold PhDs, 36% are are members of minority groups, 22% are women.

ACADEMICS
Degrees: bachelor's, doctoral, master's, post-bachelor's certificate, post-master's certificate. **Classes:** Most classes have 20-29 students. Most lab/discussion sessions have 20-29 students. **Majors with Highest Enrollment:** Biology/Biological Sciences; Psychology; Health Services/Allied Health/Health Sciences. **Special Study Options:** cross-registration, distance learning, double major, English as a Second Language (ESL), exchange student program (domestic), honors program, independent study, internships, student-designed major, study abroad, teacher certification program, Albany Semester, Undergrads may take grad level courses BS/MS programs, BE/MS, BS/MA—Living Learning Centers in residence halls, Honors College, undergraduate research and creative activities program where undergraduates work with faculty on research projects, university learning communities and (WISE) Women in Science and Engineer-

ing. **Honors programs:** BA/MD **Combined degree programs:** BA/MA, MD/PhD. **Disability Services:** Special programs offered to physically disabled students include note-taking services, reader services, tape recorders, tutors. **Career services:** Alumni network, alumni services, career/job search classes, career assessment, internships, regional alumni. Career services highlights include Career services internship program modeled after successful corporate internship programs. Includes career counseling, marketing, graphics, human resources, and technology.

FACILITIES
Housing: Coed dorms, special housing for disabled students, apartments for married students, apartments for single students, Single sex floors in coed dorms, Living Learning Centers. First year resident members of each College are housed together in the same residential Quadrangle. 75% of campus accessible to physically disabled. **Special Academic Facilities/Equipment:** SAC Gallery, Staller Gallery, Wang Center, Tabler Center for the Arts. **Computers:** 50% of classrooms, 50% of dorms, 50% of libraries, 50% of dining areas, 50% of student union, 50% of common outdoor areas have wireless network access. Students can register for classes online. Administrative functions (other than registration) can be performed online.

CAMPUS LIFE
Environment: Town. **Activities:** Choral groups, concert band, dance, drama/theater, jazz band, literary magazine, marching band, music ensembles, musical theater, opera, pep band, radio station, student government, student newspaper, student-run film society, symphony orchestra, yearbook, Campus Ministries. 292 registered organizations, 6 honor societies, 25 religious organizations. 17 fraternities, 16 sororities. **Athletics (Intercollegiate):** *Men:* baseball, basketball, cross-country, diving, football, lacrosse, soccer, swimming, tennis, track/field (outdoor), track/field (indoor). *Women:* basketball, cross-country, diving, lacrosse, soccer, softball, swimming, tennis, track/field (outdoor), track/field (indoor), volleyball. **On-Campus Highlights:** Staller Center for the Arts, Sports Complex and Stadium, Student Activities Center, University Hospital, The Charles B. Wang Center, Building and Grounds: Main campus. 1,100 acres. Research and Development Campus, 246 acres adjacent to the main campus. Stony Brook Southampton, 82 acres. Stony Brook Manhattan. New buildings: Humanities Building, undergraduate apartments; Center for Excellence in Wireless and Information Technology under construction. **Environmental Initiatives:** Signing of ACUPCC. Commitment to obtain carbon nuetrality by 2050. Creation of Environmental Stewardship Department which focuses on energy reduction, waste reduction and all areas of sustainability for the campus. We have a Sustainability Task Force which meets routinely and works on projects each academic year.

ADMISSIONS
Freshman Academic Profile: Average high school GPA 3.78. 48% in top 10% of high school class, 82% in top 25% of high school class, 97% in top 50% of high school class. 90% from public high schools. SAT Math middle 50% range 610-710. SAT Critical Reading middle 50% range 540-640. SAT Writing middle 50% range 540-650. ACT middle 50% range 26-30. Minimum internet-based TOEFL 80. Minimum paper TOEFL 550. **Basis for Candidate Selection:** *Very important factors considered include:* academic GPA, rigor of secondary school record, standardized test scores. *Important factors considered include:* Class rank. *Other factors considered include:* application essay, recommendation(s), alumni/ae relation, character/personal qualities, extracurricular activities, first generation, interview, level of applicant's interest, state residency, talent/ability, volunteer work, work experience. **Freshman Admission Requirements:** High school diploma is required and GED is accepted. *Academic units required:* 4 English, 3 mathematics, 3 science, 2 foreign language, 4 social studies. **Freshman Admission Statistics:** 33,714 applied, 41% admitted, 20% enrolled. **Transfer Admission Requirements:** college transcript(s), Minimum college GPA of 3.0 required. Lowest grade transferable C. **General Admission Information:** Application Fee $40. Notification on a rolling basis, beginning on or about 2/1. Nonfall registration accepted. Admission may be deferred for a maximum of 2 semesters. Credit and/or placement offered for CEEB Advanced Placement tests.

COSTS AND FINANCIAL AID
Average book expense $900. **Required Forms and Deadlines:** FAFSA, State aid form. **Notification of Awards:** Applicants will be notified of awards on a rolling basis beginning 3/1. **Types of Aid:** *Need-based scholarships/grants:* Federal Pell, SEOG, state scholarships/grants, the school's own gift aid. *Loans:* Direct Subsidized Stafford, Direct Unsubsidized Stafford, Direct PLUS, Federal Perkins. *Student Employment:* Federal Work-Study Program available. Institutional employment available. Highest amount earned per year from on-campus jobs $12,638. Off-campus job opportunities are excellent. **Financial Aid Statistics:** 89% freshmen, 83% undergrads receive need-based scholarship or grant aid. 12% freshmen, 7% undergrads receive non-need-based scholarship or grant aid. 93% freshmen, 94% undergrads receive need-based self-help aid. 0% freshmen, 0% undergrads receive athletic scholarships. 78% freshmen, 69% undergrads receive any aid. 58% undergrads borrow to pay for school. Average

cumulative indebtedness $21,946. **Criteria for awarding institutional aid:** *Non-need-based:* academics, alumni affiliation, athletics, leadership, music/drama.

STATE UNIVERSITY OF NEW YORK— UNIVERSITY AT ALBANY

Office of Undergraduate Admissions, Albany, NY 12222
Phone: 518-442-5435 · **Financial Aid Phone:** 518-442-3202
E-mail: ugadmissions@albany.edu · **CEEB Code:** 2532
Fax: 518-442-5383 · **Website:** www.albany.edu · **ACT Code:** 2926

This public school was founded in 1844. It has a 795-acre campus.

RATINGS

Admissions Selectivity Rating: 60*   Fire Safety Rating: 60*

STUDENTS AND FACULTY

Enrollment: 12,659. **Student Body:** 48% female, 52% male, 6% out-of-state, 6% international (84 countries represented). Asian 8%, African American 15%, Caucasian 51%, Hispanic 14%, Native American <1%
Retention and Graduation: 80% freshmen return for sophomore year. 53% freshmen graduate within 4 years. **Faculty:** 606 full-time faculty, 93% hold PhDs, 39% are are members of minority groups, 24% are women. 10% of classes are taught by teaching assistants.

ACADEMICS

Degrees: bachelor's, master's, post-bachelor's certificate, post-master's certificate. **Classes:** Most classes have 20-29 students. Most lab/discussion sessions have 20-29 students. **Majors with Highest Enrollment:** English Language and Literature; Psychology; Business Administration and Management. **Special Study Options:** Accelerated program, cross-registration, distance learning, double major, dual enrollment, English as a Second Language (ESL), honors program, independent study, internships, liberal arts/career combination, student-designed major, study abroad, Accelerated 5 year Bachelors/Masters programs in 40 fields; Internships with New York State Legislature; Combined Bachelors/Law degree with Albany Law school; 3+2 Engineering Program with RPI, Clarkson, and others; Biology/Dental Program with Boston University Goldman School of Dental Medicine, Bachelors/Doctor of Optometry with SUNY State College; Early Assurance Program with Albany Medical College and SUNY Upstate Medical College. **Honors programs:** Our Presidential Scholars program combines merit scholarships, honors courses, priority registration, special housing, and faculty mentor opportunities. **Combined degree programs:** BA/JD, BA/MA, BA/MEng, Accelerated 5 yr Bachelors/Masters in 40 fields. **Disability Services:** Special programs offered to physically disabled students include note-taking services, reader services, tape recorders, tutors. **Career services:** Alumni network, alumni services, career/job search classes, career assessment, internships, regional alumni. Career services highlights include internships with New York State Legislature; On-Campus Recruiting for graduates and those seeking internships.

FACILITIES

Housing: Coed dorms, special housing for international students, apartments for married students, apartments for single students, Wellness Housing, Theme Housing. Disabled Student Services provides individualized services including information on accessible housing. 99% of campus accessible to physically disabled. **Special Academic Facilities/Equipment:** Performing Arts Center, Art Museum, art and dance studios, sculpture foundry, nuclear accelerator and advanced materials facilities, a peptide synthesis facility, recombinatnt DNA sequencing laboratories, and atmospheric science's Whiteface Mountain observational facility. **Computers:** 75% of classrooms, 100% of dorms, 100% of libraries, 75% of dining areas, 100% of student union, 75% of common outdoor areas have wireless network access. Students can register for classes online. Administrative functions (other than registration) can be performed online.

CAMPUS LIFE

Environment: City. **Activities:** Choral groups, concert band, dance, drama/theater, jazz band, literary magazine, music ensembles, musical theater, pep band, radio station, student government, student newspaper, student-run film society, symphony orchestra, television station, yearbook, Campus Ministries, International Student Organization. 200 registered organizations, 20 honor societies, 17 religious organizations. 11 fraternities, 18 sororities. **Athletics (Intercollegiate):** *Men:* baseball, basketball, cross-country, football, lacrosse, soccer, track/field (outdoor), track/field (indoor). *Women:* basketball, cross-country, field hockey, golf, lacrosse, soccer, softball, tennis, track/field (outdoor), track/field (indoor), volleyball. **On-Campus Highlights:** Campus Center with bookstore, Cafés, and lounges, SEFCU Arena, Science Library /Main Library, Performing Arts Center, University Art Museum, Students often find that a visit to the University at Albany helps them decide whether this is the university for them. Visitors can attend an information session and join a student-led tour during the academic year or the summer. The tour visits classrooms, academic and other facilities, a residence hall and a dining area. Information Sessions begin at 10:00 a.m. and 12:00 p.m. Your visit includes a Q&A session and campus tour. Please allow two hours for your visit. **Environmental Initiatives:** energy conservation; waste reduction; alternative transport.

ADMISSIONS

Freshman Academic Profile: Average high school GPA 3.5. 18% in top 10% of high school class, 49% in top 25% of high school class, 86% in top 50% of high school class. SAT Math middle 50% range 520-600. SAT Critical Reading middle 50% range 490-580. ACT middle 50% range 22-26. Minimum internet-based TOEFL 79. Minimum paper TOEFL 550. **Basis for Candidate Selection:** *Very important factors considered include:* Class rank, academic GPA, recommendation(s), rigor of secondary school record, standardized test scores, character/personal qualities. *Important factors considered include:* application essay. *Other factors considered include:* alumni/ae relation, extracurricular activities, first generation, geographical residence, talent/ability, volunteer work, work experience. **Freshman Admission Requirements:** High school diploma is required and GED is accepted. *Academic units required:* 4 English, 2 mathematics, 2 science, (2 science labs), 1 foreign language, 3 social studies, 2 history, 4 academic electives. **Freshman Admission Statistics:** 21,755 applied, 56% admitted, 32% enrolled. **Transfer Admission Requirements:** college transcript(s), essay or personal statement, statement of good standing from prior institution(s). Minimum college GPA of 2.5 required. Lowest grade transferable C. **General Admission Information:** Application Fee $50. Regular application deadline 3/1. Notification on a rolling basis, beginning on or about 1/1. Nonfall registration accepted. Admission may be deferred for a maximum of 1 year. Credit and/or placement offered for CEEB Advanced Placement tests.

COSTS AND FINANCIAL AID

Annual in-state tuition $6,170. Annual out-of-state tuition $17,810. Room and board $11,986. Required fees $2,357. Average book expense $1,200. **Required Forms and Deadlines:** FAFSA. **Notification of Awards:** Applicants will be notified of awards on a rolling basis beginning 3/20. **Types of Aid:** *Need-based scholarships/grants:* Federal Pell, SEOG, state scholarships/grants, private scholarships, the school's own gift aid, NY State residents should apply for TAP on-line at <http://www.tapweb.org>. *Loans:* Subsidized Stafford, Unsubsidized Stafford, PLUS, Federal Perkins. *Student Employment:* Federal Work-Study Program available. Institutional employment available. Highest amount earned per year from on-campus jobs $5,532. Off-campus job opportunities are good. **Financial Aid Statistics:** 85% freshmen, 82% undergrads receive need-based scholarship or grant aid. 3% freshmen, 2% undergrads receive non-need-based scholarship or grant aid. 81% freshmen, 83% undergrads receive need-based self-help aid. 2% freshmen, 2% undergrads receive athletic scholarships. 64% freshmen, 57% undergrads receive any aid. 69% undergrads borrow to pay for school. Average cumulative indebtedness $23,267. **Criteria for awarding institutional aid:** *Non-need-based:* academics, athletics, state/district residency.

STATE UNIVERSITY OF NEW YORK— UNIVERSITY AT BUFFALO

12 Capen Hall, Buffalo, NY 14260-1660
Phone: 716-645-6900 · **Financial Aid Phone:** 716-645-2450
E-mail: ub-admissions@buffalo.edu · **CEEB Code:** 2925
Fax: 716-645-6411 · **Website:** www.buffalo.edu · **ACT Code:** 2978

This public school was founded in 1846. It has a 1346-acre campus.

RATINGS

Admissions Selectivity Rating: 87   Fire Safety Rating: 62

STUDENTS AND FACULTY

Enrollment: 19,485. **Student Body:** 45% female, 55% male, 31% out-of-state, 6% international (110 countries represented). Asian 14%, African American 7%, Caucasian 49%, Hispanic 6%, Native American <1%
Retention and Graduation: 88% freshmen return for sophomore year. 53% freshmen graduate within 4 years. 72% freshmen graduate within 6 years. 40%

grads go on to further study within 1 year. **Faculty:** 1,220 full-time faculty, 95% hold PhDs, 36% are are members of minority groups, 24% are women. 10% of classes are taught by teaching assistants.

ACADEMICS
Degrees: bachelor's, doctoral, master's, post-master's certificate. **Classes:** Most classes have 20-29 students. Most lab/discussion sessions have 20-29 students. **Majors with Highest Enrollment:** Social Sciences; Business Administration and Management; Engineering. **Special Study Options:** Accelerated program, cooperative education program, cross-registration, distance learning, double major, dual enrollment, English as a Second Language (ESL), exchange student program (domestic), honors program, independent study, internships, liberal arts/career combination, student-designed major, study abroad, teacher certification program, Certificate programs, Combined Degree Programs, Early Assurance Program with School of Medicine & Dentistry, Honors College & Learning Communities. **Honors programs:** There is a University Honors College as well as honors programs within the majors. Undergraduate research is an option in a variety of disciplines and often affords the student an opportunity to participate in cutting-edge research activities. See • Website: http://honors.buffalo.edu **Combined degree programs:** BA/MA, BA/MS, BS/MS, BA/MBA, BS/MBA, BA/MA, BA/MSW, BS/DDS, BA/EDM, BA/MFA. **Disability Services:** Special programs offered to physically disabled students include note-taking services, reader services, tape recorders, tutors. **Career services:** Alumni network, alumni services, career/job search classes, internships.

FACILITIES
Housing: Coed dorms, special housing for disabled students, special housing for international students, apartments for married students, apartments for single students, Theme Housing, Honors Housing, Academic Interest Housing, Freshman Housing. See • Website: http://www.ub-housing.buffalo.edu/special. 90% of campus accessible to physically disabled. **Special Academic Facilities/Equipment:** UB Center for the Arts, Slee Concert Hall, Anthropology Research Museum, Multidisciplinary Center for Earthquake Engineering Research (MCEER), New York State Center of Excellence in Bioinformatics and Life Sciences, Center for Computational Research (CCR), Poetry and Rare Books Collection, Center of Excellence for Document Analysis and Recognition Center, New York State Center for Engineering Design and Industrial Innovation, Pharmacy Museum, The Virtual Site Museum, Electronic Poetry Center, Archeological Survey Center, Anderson Gallery, Alfiero Center and numerous research centers. **Computers:** Students can register for classes online. Administrative functions (other than registration) can be performed online.

CAMPUS LIFE
Environment: City. **Activities:** Choral groups, concert band, dance, drama/theater, jazz band, literary magazine, marching band, music ensembles, musical theater, pep band, radio station, student government, student newspaper, student-run film society, symphony orchestra, television station, Campus Ministries, International Student Organization. 215 registered organizations, 29 honor societies, 35 religious organizations. 22 fraternities, 17 sororities. **Athletics (Intercollegiate):** *Men:* baseball, basketball, cross-country, football, soccer, swimming, tennis, track/field (outdoor), wrestling. *Women:* basketball, crew/rowing, cross-country, soccer, softball, swimming, tennis, track/field (outdoor), volleyball. **On-Campus Highlights:** Center for the Arts, Alumni Arena and Athletic Stadium, Center for Computational Research, Apartment style student housing, The Commons (on-campus shopping).

ADMISSIONS
Freshman Academic Profile: Average high school GPA 3.2. 29.1% in top 10% of high school class, 63.2% in top 25% of high school class, 92.9% in top 50% of high school class. SAT Math middle 50% range 550-660. SAT Critical Reading middle 50% range 500-600. ACT middle 50% range 24-29. Minimum internet-based TOEFL 79. Minimum paper TOEFL 550. **Basis for Candidate Selection:** *Very important factors considered include:* academic GPA, rigor of secondary school record, standardized test scores. *Important factors considered include:* Class rank, recommendation(s), interview. *Other factors considered include:* application essay, character/personal qualities, extracurricular activities, first generation, geographical residence, racial/ethnic status, talent/ability, volunteer work, work experience. **Freshman Admission Requirements:** High school diploma is required and GED is accepted. **Freshman Admission Statistics:** 24,444 applied, 58% admitted, 25% enrolled. **Transfer Admission Requirements:** High school transcript, college transcript(s), essay or personal statement, Minimum college GPA of 2.5 required. Lowest grade transferable D. **General Admission Information:** Application Fee $40. Early decision application deadline 11/1. Notification on a rolling basis, beginning on or about 2/1. Nonfall registration accepted. Credit and/or placement offered for CEEB Advanced Placement tests.

COSTS AND FINANCIAL AID
Annual in-state tuition $6,170. Annual out-of-state tuition $19,590. Room and board $12,400. Required fees $2,701. Average book expense $1,164. **Required Forms and Deadlines:** FAFSA. **Notification of Awards:** Applicants will be

notified of awards on a rolling basis beginning 2/1. **Types of Aid:** *Need-based scholarships/grants:* Federal Pell, SEOG, state scholarships/grants, private scholarships, the school's own gift aid, Federal Nursing Scholarships. *Loans:* Direct Subsidized Stafford, Direct Unsubsidized Stafford, Direct PLUS, Federal Perkins, Federal Nursing, college/university loans from institutional funds. *Student Employment:* Federal Work-Study Program available. Institutional employment available. Off-campus job opportunities are good. **Financial Aid Statistics:** 86% freshmen, 67% undergrads receive need-based scholarship or grant aid. 19% freshmen, 28% undergrads receive non-need-based scholarship or grant aid. 79% freshmen, 72% undergrads receive need-based self-help aid. 2% freshmen, 2% undergrads receive athletic scholarships. 75% freshmen, 66% undergrads receive any aid. **Criteria for awarding institutional aid:** *Non-need-based:* academics, athletics, minority status, music/drama, state/district residency.

STATE UNIVERSITY OF NEW YORK— UPSTATE MEDICAL UNIVERSITY

766 Irving Avenue, Syracuse, NY 13210
Phone: 315-464-4570 • **Financial Aid Phone:** 315-464-4329
E-mail: admiss@upstate.edu • **CEEB Code:** 2547
Fax: 315-464-8867 • **ACT Code:** 2981

This public school was founded in 1850. It has a 25-acre campus.

RATINGS
Admissions Selectivity Rating: 60*   **Fire Safety Rating:** 73

STUDENTS AND FACULTY
Enrollment: 328. **Student Body:** 75% female, 25% male, 9% out-of-state. **Faculty:** 43 full-time faculty, 60% hold PhDs, 70% are are members of minority groups, 2% are women. 0% of classes are taught by teaching assistants.

ACADEMICS
Degrees: bachelor's, first professional, master's, post-master's certificate. **Classes:** Most classes have fewer than 10 students. **Disability Services:** Special programs offered to physically disabled students include note-taking services, reader services, tape recorders, tutors. **Career services:** Alumni network, regional alumni.

FACILITIES
Housing: Coed dorms, apartments for married students, apartments for single students. 100% of campus accessible to physically disabled. **Special Academic Facilities/Equipment:** 350 bed Tertiary Care Hospital. **Computers:** Administrative functions (other than registration) can be performed online.

CAMPUS LIFE
Environment: City. **Activities:** student government, International Student Organization. 51 registered organizations, 3 religious organizations. **On-Campus Highlights:** Weiskotten Hall, Silverman Hall, University Hospital, Institute for Human Performance, Campus Activities Building.

ADMISSIONS
Freshman Academic Profile: Minimum paper TOEFL 550. **Freshman Admission Requirements:** High school diploma is required and GED is accepted. **Transfer Admission Requirements:** High school transcript, college transcript(s), essay or personal statement, interview, Minimum college GPA of 2.0 required. Lowest grade transferable C-. **General Admission Information:** Application Fee $40. Nonfall registration not accepted. Admission may be deferred for a maximum of 1 Year.

COSTS AND FINANCIAL AID
Annual out-of-state tuition $13,380. Room and board $10,422. Required fees $575. Average book expense $1,070. **Required Forms and Deadlines:** FAFSA. **Notification of Awards:** Applicants will be notified of awards on a rolling basis beginning 6/1. **Types of Aid:** *Need-based scholarships/grants:* Federal Pell, SEOG, state scholarships/grants, the school's own gift aid. *Loans:* Subsidized Stafford, Unsubsidized Stafford, PLUS, Federal Perkins. *Student Employment:* Federal Work-Study Program available. Institutional employment available. Off-campus job opportunities are excellent. **Financial Aid Statistics:** 18% undergrads receive need-based scholarship or grant aid. 27% undergrads receive non-need-based scholarship or grant aid. 13% undergrads receive need-based self-help aid. 78% freshmen receive any aid.

STATE UNIVERSITY OF NEW YORK— PURCHASE COLLEGE

735 Anderson Hill Rd, Purchase, NY 10577
Phone: 914-251-6300
E-mail: admissions@purchase.edu • **CEEB Code:** 2878
Fax: 914-251-6314 • **Website:** www.purchase.edu • **ACT Code:** 2931

This public school was founded in 1967. It has a 550-acre campus.

RATINGS

Admissions Selectivity Rating: 83   **Fire Safety Rating:** 60*

STUDENTS AND FACULTY

Enrollment: 3,977. **Student Body:** 55% female, 45% male, 15% out-of-state, 2% international (39 countries represented). Asian 3%, African American 9%, Caucasian 56%, Hispanic 17%, Native American <1%
Retention and Graduation: 58% freshmen graduate within 4 years. **Faculty:** 173 full-time faculty, 52% hold PhDs, 51% are are members of minority groups, 12% are women. 1% of classes are taught by teaching assistants.

ACADEMICS

Degrees: bachelor's, master's, post-master's certificate. **Classes:** Most classes have 10-19 students. Most lab/discussion sessions have fewer than 10 students. **Majors with Highest Enrollment:** Visual and Performing Arts; Liberal Arts and Sciences/Liberal Studies. **Special Study Options:** cross-registration, distance learning, double major, English as a Second Language (ESL), independent study, internships, liberal arts/career combination, student-designed major, study abroad. **Disability Services:** Special programs offered to physically disabled students include note-taking services, reader services, tape recorders, tutors. **Career services:** alumni services, career/job search classes, career assessment, internships.

FACILITIES

Housing: Coed dorms, special housing for disabled students, special housing for international students, apartments for married students, apartments for single students, Wellness Housing, Theme Housing. 100% of campus accessible to physically disabled. **Special Academic Facilities/Equipment:** Museum, four-theatre performing arts center, visual arts facility, children's center, recording studio, electron microscopes. **Computers:** Students can register for classes online. Administrative functions (other than registration) can be performed online.

CAMPUS LIFE

Environment: Town. **Activities:** Choral groups, dance, drama/theater, jazz band, literary magazine, music ensembles, musical theater, radio station, student government, student newspaper, student-run film society, television station. 30 registered organizations. **Athletics (Intercollegiate):** *Men:* baseball, basketball, cross-country, golf, soccer, tennis, volleyball. *Women:* basketball, cross-country, soccer, softball, tennis, volleyball. **On-Campus Highlights:** The Performing Arts Center, The Neuberger Museum, State-of-the-Art Athletic Complex, Starbucks, Fort Awesome, New Student Services building. **Environmental Initiatives:** Committed to reduce GHG emissions by 80% by 2050 (Presidents Climate Commitment); Have campus policy that all new buildings constructed be LEED Silver Certified or better; Purchase biodegradable and recycled paper products for dining halls and 100% recycled copy paper.

ADMISSIONS

Freshman Academic Profile: Average high school GPA 3.24. SAT Math middle 50% range 490-590. SAT Critical Reading middle 50% range 500-620. ACT middle 50% range 19-25. Minimum paper TOEFL 550. **Basis for Candidate Selection:** *Very important factors considered include:* application essay, academic GPA, talent/ability. *Important factors considered include:* standardized test scores. *Other factors considered include:* Class rank, recommendation(s), rigor of secondary school record, character/personal qualities, extracurricular activities, interview. **Freshman Admission Requirements:** High school diploma is required and GED is accepted. **Freshman Admission Statistics:** 6,955 applied, 41% admitted, 27% enrolled. **Transfer Admission Requirements:** college transcript(s), Minimum college GPA of 3.0 required. Lowest grade transferable D. **General Admission Information:** Application Fee $40. Early decision application deadline 11/1. Regular application deadline 7/15. Regular notification 5/1. Nonfall registration accepted. Admission may be deferred for a maximum of 1 year. Credit and/or placement offered for CEEB Advanced Placement tests.

COSTS AND FINANCIAL AID

Annual out-of-state tuition $15,820. Room and board $12,232. Average book expense $1,207. **Required Forms and Deadlines:** FAFSA, State aid form. **Notification of Awards:** Applicants will be notified of awards on a rolling basis beginning 3/1. **Types of Aid:** *Need-based scholarships/grants:* Federal Pell, SEOG, state scholarships/grants, private scholarships, the school's own gift aid. *Loans:* Direct Subsidized Stafford, Direct Unsubsidized Stafford, Direct PLUS, Federal Perkins. *Student Employment:* Federal Work-Study Program available. Institutional employment available. Off-campus job opportunities are excellent. **Financial Aid Statistics:** 81% freshmen, 82% undergrads receive need-based scholarship or grant aid. 2% freshmen, 1% undergrads receive non-need-based scholarship or grant aid. 98% freshmen, 98% undergrads receive need-based self-help aid. 0% freshmen, 0% undergrads receive athletic scholarships. 60% undergrads borrow to pay for school. Average cumulative indebtedness $24,677. **Criteria for awarding institutional aid:** *Non-need-based:* academics, art, minority status, music/drama.

STATE UNIVERSITY OF NEW YORK— COLLEGE AT ONEONTA

116 Alumni Hall, Oneonta, NY 13820
Phone: 607-436-2524 • **Financial Aid Phone:** 607-436-2532
E-mail: admissions@oneonta.edu • **CEEB Code:** 2542
Fax: 607-436-3074 • **Website:** www.oneonta.edu • **ACT Code:** 2940

This public school was founded in 1889. It has a 250-acre campus.

RATINGS

Admissions Selectivity Rating: 89   **Fire Safety Rating:** 85

STUDENTS AND FACULTY

Enrollment: 5,804. **Student Body:** 60% female, 40% male, 1% out-of-state, 2% international (18 countries represented). Asian 1%, African American 3%, Caucasian 81%, Hispanic 4%, Native American <1%
Retention and Graduation: 84% freshmen return for sophomore year. 50% freshmen graduate within 4 years. 64% freshmen graduate within 6 years. **Faculty:** 259 full-time faculty, 86% hold PhDs, 43% are are members of minority groups, 17% are women. 0% of classes are taught by teaching assistants.

ACADEMICS

Degrees: bachelor's, master's, post-bachelor's certificate, post-master's certificate. **Classes:** Most classes have 10-19 students. **Majors with Highest Enrollment:** Elementary Education and Teaching; Family and Consumer Sciences/Home Economics Teacher Education; Secondary Education and Teaching. **Special Study Options:** cross-registration, distance learning, double major, English as a Second Language (ESL), honors program, independent study, internships, liberal arts/career combination, study abroad, teacher certification program, Variety of 3-1, 3-2, and 2-2 programs with other colleges and universities. **Honors programs:** Oneonta Honors Program. **Combined degree programs:** BA/MA, BA/MEng, acc't, bus. admin., mgmt., fashion, art, med. sci. **Disability Services:** Special programs offered to physically disabled students include note-taking services, reader services, tape recorders, tutors. **Career services:** Alumni network, alumni services, career/job search classes, career assessment, internships, regional alumni. Career services highlights include internships available in all academic majors.

FACILITIES

Housing: Coed dorms, Special interest wings in residence halls; apartment-style suites in new hall. 90% of campus accessible to physically disabled. **Special Academic Facilities/Equipment:** Science Discovery Center, Biological Field Station, digital planetarium, observatory, College Camp, children's center. **Computers:** 100% of classrooms, 100% of dorms, 100% of libraries, 100% of dining areas, 100% of student union, 100% of common outdoor areas have wireless network access. Students can register for classes online. Administrative functions (other than registration) can be performed online.

CAMPUS LIFE

Environment: Village. **Activities:** Choral groups, concert band, dance, drama/theater, jazz band, literary magazine, music ensembles, musical theater, opera, pep band, radio station, student government, student newspaper, student-run film society, symphony orchestra, television station, yearbook, Campus Ministries, International Student Organization, Model UN. 70 registered organizations, 14 honor societies, 4 religious organizations. 4 fraternities, 6 sororities. **Athletics (Intercollegiate):** *Men:* baseball, basketball, cross-country, diving, lacrosse, soccer, swimming, tennis, track/field (outdoor), track/field (indoor), wrestling. *Women:* basketball, cross-country, diving, field hockey, lacrosse, soccer, softball, swimming, tennis, track/field (outdoor), track/field (indoor), volleyball. **On-Campus Highlights:** Alumni Field House, Center for Multicultural Experiences, Hunt College Union, College Camp, Center for Social Responsibility and Community, Newly remodeled Science Building with state-of-the-art Digital Planetarium. **Environmental Initiatives:** Recycling program; Green construction standards; President's Advisory Council on Sustainability.

ADMISSIONS

Freshman Academic Profile: Average high school GPA 90.55. SAT Math middle 50% range 520-600. SAT Critical Reading middle 50% range 500-580. ACT middle 50% range 22-26. Minimum internet-based TOEFL 61. Minimum paper TOEFL 500. **Basis for Candidate Selection:** *Very important factors considered include:* rigor of secondary school record. *Important factors considered include:* application essay, academic GPA, standardized test scores, extracurricular activities, interview, talent/ability, volunteer work. *Other factors considered include:* recommendation(s), alumni/ae relation, level of applicant's interest, racial/ethnic status, work experience. **Freshman Admission Requirements:** High school diploma is required and GED is accepted. *Academic units required:* 4 English, 2 mathematics, 2 science, (2 science labs), 2 foreign language, 3 social studies. **Freshman Admission Statistics:** 12,031 applied, 43% admitted, 22% enrolled. **Transfer Admission Requirements:** college transcript(s), Minimum college GPA of 2.5 required. Lowest grade transferable C-. **General Admission Information:** Application Fee $40. Notification on a rolling basis, beginning on or about 11/15. Nonfall registration accepted. Admission may be deferred for a maximum of 12 months. Credit offered for CEEB Advanced Placement tests.

COSTS AND FINANCIAL AID

Required Forms and Deadlines: FAFSA, Noncustodial PROFILE. **Notification of Awards:** Applicants will be notified of awards on a rolling basis beginning 3/1. **Types of Aid:** *Need-based scholarships/grants:* Federal Pell, SEOG, state scholarships/grants, private scholarships, the school's own gift aid. *Loans:* Subsidized Stafford, Unsubsidized Stafford, PLUS, Federal Perkins. *Student Employment:* Federal Work-Study Program available. Institutional employment available. Highest amount earned per year from on-campus jobs $1,800. Off-campus job opportunities are good. **Financial Aid Statistics:** 73% freshmen, 95% undergrads receive need-based scholarship or grant aid. 26% freshmen, 0% undergrads receive non-need-based scholarship or grant aid. 84% freshmen, 81% undergrads receive need-based self-help aid. 0% freshmen, 0% undergrads receive athletic scholarships. 83% freshmen, 66% undergrads receive any aid. 66% undergrads borrow to pay for school. Average cumulative indebtedness $12,562. **Criteria for awarding institutional aid:** *Non-need-based:* academics, alumni affiliation, leadership, minority status, music/drama, state/district residency.

STEPHEN F. AUSTIN STATE UNIVERSITY

P. O. Box 13051, Nacogdoches, TX 75962
Phone: 936-468-2504 · **Financial Aid Phone:** 936-468-2403
E-mail: admissions@sfasu.edu · **CEEB Code:** 6682
Fax: 936-468-3849 · **Website:** www.sfasu.edu · **ACT Code:** 4188

This public school was founded in 1923. It has a 401-acre campus.

RATINGS

Admissions Selectivity Rating: 77   Fire Safety Rating: 68

STUDENTS AND FACULTY

Enrollment: 9,568. **Student Body:** 59% female, 41% male, 2% out-of-state, 1% international (42 countries represented). Asian 1%, African American 16%, Caucasian 74%, Hispanic 7%, Native American 1%
Retention and Graduation: 66% freshmen return for sophomore year. 17% freshmen graduate within 4 years. 35% freshmen graduate within 6 years. **Faculty:** 434 full-time faculty, 76% hold PhDs, 41% are are members of minority groups, 7% are women.

ACADEMICS

Degrees: bachelor's, master's. **Classes:** Most classes have 20-29 students. Most lab/discussion sessions have 10-19 students. **Majors with Highest Enrollment:** Multi-/Interdisciplinary Studies; Health and Physical Education/Fitness; Registered Nursing/Registered Nurse. **Special Study Options:** Accelerated program, distance learning, double major, dual enrollment, honors program, independent study, internships, liberal arts/career combination, student-designed major, study abroad, teacher certification program. **Honors programs:** www.sfasu.edu/honors/ **Combined degree programs:** BBA(Accounting)/MPAC(Professional Accountancy). **Disability Services:** Special programs offered to physically disabled students include note-taking services, reader services, tape recorders, tutors.

FACILITIES

Housing: Coed dorms, special housing for disabled students, men's dorms, women's dorms, fraternity/sorority housing, apartments for married students, apartments for single students, Apartments for students with dependent children. 99% of campus accessible to physically disabled. **Special Academic Facilities/Equipment:** Stone Fort Museum, Planetarium, Arboretum, Observatory, GIS Lab, Forest Resources Institute, Soils Analysis Lab, East Texas Historical Assoc., East Texas Research Center, Science Research Center, Research Feed Mill. **Computers:** Students can register for classes online. Administrative functions (other than registration) can be performed online.

CAMPUS LIFE

Environment: Town. **Activities:** Choral groups, concert band, dance, drama/theater, jazz band, literary magazine, marching band, music ensembles, musical theater, opera, pep band, radio station, student government, student newspaper, student-run film society, symphony orchestra, television station, yearbook. 21 registered organizations, 15 honor societies, 25 religious organizations. 25 fraternities, 14 sororities. **Athletics (Intercollegiate):** *Men:* basketball, cross-country, football, golf, track/field (outdoor), track/field (indoor). *Women:* basketball, cross-country, soccer, softball, tennis, track/field (outdoor), track/field (indoor), volleyball. **On-Campus Highlights:** Stone Fort Museum, University Center, Art Galleries—Art Center, Griffith Gallery, Library, Arboretum.

ADMISSIONS

Freshman Academic Profile: 16% in top 10% of high school class, 44% in top 25% of high school class, 83% in top 50% of high school class. 90% from public high schools. SAT Math middle 50% range 450-550. SAT Critical Reading middle 50% range 450-560. ACT middle 50% range 18-23. Minimum paper TOEFL 550. **Basis for Candidate Selection:** *Very important factors considered include:* Class rank, rigor of secondary school record, standardized test scores. *Other factors considered include:* extracurricular activities, geographical residence, talent/ability, volunteer work, work experience. **Freshman Admission Requirements:** High school diploma is required and GED is accepted. *Academic units required:* 4 English, 3 mathematics, 3 science, 2 foreign language. **Freshman Admission Statistics:** 5,873 applied, 75% admitted, 38% enrolled. **Transfer Admission Requirements:** college transcript(s), Minimum college GPA of 2.0 required. Lowest grade transferable D. **General Admission Information:** Application Fee $25. Notification on a rolling basis, beginning on or about 9/1. Nonfall registration accepted. Credit and/or placement offered for CEEB Advanced Placement tests.

COSTS AND FINANCIAL AID

Annual in-state tuition $3,360. Annual out-of-state tuition $11,100. Room and board $5,012. Required fees $938. Average book expense $905. **Required Forms and Deadlines:** FAFSA. **Notification of Awards:** Applicants will be notified of awards on a rolling basis beginning 5/1. **Types of Aid:** *Need-based scholarships/grants:* Federal Pell, SEOG, state scholarships/grants, private scholarships, the school's own gift aid. *Loans:* Subsidized Stafford, Unsubsidized Stafford, PLUS, Federal Perkins, state loans, college/university loans from institutional funds, Alternative loans. *Student Employment:* Highest amount earned per year from on-campus jobs $4,100. **Financial Aid Statistics:** 76% freshmen, 79% undergrads receive need-based scholarship or grant aid. 53% freshmen, 43% undergrads receive non-need-based scholarship or grant aid. 72% freshmen, 81% undergrads receive need-based self-help aid. 3% freshmen, 3% undergrads receive athletic scholarships. 46% freshmen, 47% undergrads receive any aid. 62% undergrads borrow to pay for school. **Criteria for awarding institutional aid:** *Non-need-based:* academics, alumni affiliation, art, athletics, leadership, music/drama, state/district residency.

STEPHENS COLLEGE

1200 East Broadway, Columbia, MO 65215
Phone: 573-876-7207 · **Financial Aid Phone:** 573-876-7106
E-mail: apply@stephens.edu · **CEEB Code:** 6683
Fax: 573-876-7237 · **Website:** http://www.stephens.edu/ · **ACT Code:** 2374

This private school was founded in 1833. It has a 86-acre campus.

RATINGS

Admissions Selectivity Rating: 87   Fire Safety Rating: 76

STUDENTS AND FACULTY

Enrollment: 668. **Student Body:** 99% female, 1% male, 45% out-of-state, 0% international (2 countries represented). Asian 2%, African American 16%, Caucasian 68%, Hispanic 5%, Native American <1%
Retention and Graduation: 61% freshmen return for sophomore year. 34% freshmen graduate within 4 years. 34% freshmen graduate within 6 years. **Faculty:** 54 full-time faculty, 59% hold PhDs, 76% are are members of minority groups, 4% are women. 0% of classes are taught by teaching assistants.

ACADEMICS

Degrees: associate, bachelor's, master's, post-bachelor's certificate. **Classes:** Most classes have 10-19 students. Most lab/discussion sessions have 10-19 students. **Majors with Highest Enrollment:** Fashion/Apparel Design; Film/Cinema/Video Studies. **Special Study Options:** cross-registration, distance learning, double major, dual enrollment, external degree program, independent study, internships, liberal arts/career combination, student-designed major, study abroad, teacher certification program. **Combined degree programs:** BA/JD, BA/MA, Occupational Therapy with Washington University. **Disability Services:** Special programs offered to physically disabled students include note-taking services, tutors. **Career services:** Alumni network, alumni services, career/job search classes, career assessment, internships, regional alumni. Career services highlights include internships.

FACILITIES

Housing: special housing for disabled students, women's dorms, fraternity/sorority housing, apartments for single students, Pet Friendly Residence. 80% of campus accessible to physically disabled. **Special Academic Facilities/Equipment:** Art gallery and historical costume collections, on-campus pre-school, kindergarten, and elementary school, language lab. **Computers:** 100% of classrooms, 100% of dorms, 100% of libraries, 100% of dining areas, 100% of student union, have wireless network access. Students can register for classes online. Administrative functions (other than registration) can be performed online.

CAMPUS LIFE

Environment: City. **Activities:** Choral groups, dance, drama/theater, literary magazine, music ensembles, musical theater, radio station, student government, student newspaper, student-run film society, television station. 28 registered organizations, 11 honor societies, 3 religious organizations. 2 sororities. **Athletics (Intercollegiate):** *Women:* basketball, cross-country, softball, swimming, tennis, volleyball. **On-Campus Highlights:** Equestrian Stables, The Commons, Senior Hall, The Quad, Residence Halls. **Environmental Initiatives:** Recycling; Decreased energy usage; Meeting LEED criteria on building projects and operations.

ADMISSIONS

Freshman Academic Profile: Average high school GPA 3.3. 16% in top 10% of high school class, 41% in top 25% of high school class, 77% in top 50% of high school class. 80% from public high schools. ACT middle 50% range 26-29. Minimum paper TOEFL 550. **Basis for Candidate Selection:** *Very important factors considered include:* application essay, rigor of secondary school record, standardized test scores. *Important factors considered include:* academic GPA, recommendation(s), extracurricular activities. *Other factors considered include:* Class rank, character/personal qualities, interview, level of applicant's interest, talent/ability, volunteer work, work experience. **Freshman Admission Requirements:** High school diploma is required and GED is accepted. *Academic units required:* 4 English, 3 mathematics, 2 science, 2 foreign language, 1 social studies. **Freshman Admission Statistics:** 1,153 applied, 54% admitted, 30% enrolled. **Transfer Admission Requirements:** High school transcript, college transcript(s), essay or personal statement, Minimum college GPA of 2.0 required. Lowest grade transferable C-. **General Admission Information:** Application Fee $25. Notification on a rolling basis, beginning on or about 9/15. Nonfall registration accepted. Admission may be deferred for a maximum of 1 year. Credit offered for CEEB Advanced Placement tests.

COSTS AND FINANCIAL AID

Average book expense $900. **Required Forms and Deadlines:** FAFSA. **Notification of Awards:** Applicants will be notified of awards on a rolling basis beginning 3/1. **Types of Aid:** *Need-based scholarships/grants:* Federal Pell, SEOG, state scholarships/grants, private scholarships, the school's own gift aid, Federal ACG Federal SMART Grant. *Loans:* Subsidized Stafford, Unsubsidized Stafford, PLUS, Federal Perkins. *Student Employment:* Federal Work-Study Program available. Institutional employment available. Highest amount earned per year from on-campus jobs $1,600. Off-campus job opportunities are good. **Financial Aid Statistics:** 100% freshmen, 100% undergrads receive need-based scholarship or grant aid. 65% freshmen, 75% undergrads receive non-need-based scholarship or grant aid. 91% freshmen, 93% undergrads receive need-based self-help aid. 20% freshmen, 14% undergrads receive athletic scholarships. 100% freshmen, 99% undergrads receive any aid. 75% undergrads borrow to pay for school. Average cumulative indebtedness $26,942. **Criteria for awarding institutional aid:** *Non-need-based:* academics, alumni affiliation, athletics, leadership, music/drama, state/district residency.

STERLING COLLEGE

125 W. Cooper, Sterling, KS 67579
Phone: 620-278-4275 • **Financial Aid Phone:** 620-278-4207
E-mail: admissions@sterling.edu • **CEEB Code:** 6684
Fax: 620-278-4416 • **Website:** www.sterlingcollege.edu • **ACT Code:** 1466

This private school, affiliated with the Presbyterian Church, was founded in 1887. It has a 42-acre campus.

RATINGS

Admissions Selectivity Rating: 80   **Fire Safety Rating:** 66

STUDENTS AND FACULTY

Enrollment: 693. **Student Body:** 50% female, 50% male, 49% out-of-state, 1% international (6 countries represented). Asian 2%, African American 8%, Caucasian 79%, Hispanic 7%, Native American 2%
Retention and Graduation: 62% freshmen return for sophomore year. 35% freshmen graduate within 4 years. 41% freshmen graduate within 6 years. **Faculty:** 41 full-time faculty, 46% hold PhDs, 27% are are members of minority groups, 10% are women. 0% of classes are taught by teaching assistants.

ACADEMICS

Degrees: bachelor's. **Classes:** Most classes have fewer than 10 students. Most lab/discussion sessions have 20-29 students. **Majors with Highest Enrollment:** Elementary Education and Teaching; Health and Physical Education/Fitness; Business/Commerce. **Special Study Options:** distance learning, double major, dual enrollment, external degree program, honors program, independent study, internships, student-designed major, study abroad, teacher certification program. **Honors programs:** The honors program is still being developed. At this point honors level general education classes are offered in interdisciplinary history and literature. **Disability Services:** Special programs offered to physically disabled students include tutors. **Career services:** Alumni network, alumni services, career assessment, internships.

FACILITIES

Housing: men's dorms, women's dorms. 80% of campus accessible to physically disabled. **Special Academic Facilities/Equipment:** History/cultural museum. **Computers:** Administrative functions (other than registration) can be performed online.

CAMPUS LIFE

Environment: Rural. **Activities:** Choral groups, concert band, drama/theater, jazz band, literary magazine, music ensembles, musical theater, radio station, student government, student newspaper, television station, yearbook, Campus Ministries. 16 registered organizations, 4 honor societies, 2 religious organizations. **Athletics (Intercollegiate):** *Men:* baseball, basketball, cross-country, football, golf, soccer, track/field (outdoor). *Women:* basketball, cheerleading, cross-country, golf, soccer, softball, track/field (outdoor), volleyball. **On-Campus Highlights:** Gleason Phy. Educ. Center, Student Union, Cooper Hall, Evan's Hall, Campbell Hall.

ADMISSIONS

Freshman Academic Profile: Average high school GPA 3.18. 7% in top 10% of high school class, 14% in top 25% of high school class, 54% in top 50% of high school class. 80% from public high schools. SAT Math middle 50% range 420-530. SAT Critical Reading middle 50% range 410-500. SAT Writing middle 50% range 410-490. ACT middle 50% range 19-24. Minimum internet-based TOEFL 70. Minimum paper TOEFL 525. **Basis for Candidate Selection:** *Very important factors considered include:* rigor of secondary school record, standardized test scores, character/personal qualities. *Important factors considered include:* application essay, academic GPA, recommendation(s), extracurricular activities, interview, level of applicant's interest, religious affiliation/commitment, volunteer work. *Other factors considered include:* Class rank, alumni/ae relation, first generation, talent/ability, work experience. **Freshman Admission Requirements:** High school diploma is required and GED is accepted. **Freshman Admission Statistics:** 821 applied, 50% admitted, 36% enrolled. **Transfer Admission Requirements:** college transcript(s), essay or personal statement, Minimum college GPA of 2.2 required. Lowest grade transferable C-. **General Admission Information:** Application Fee $25. Notification on a rolling basis, beginning on or about 9/15. Nonfall registration accepted. Admission may be deferred for a maximum of 1 semester. Credit offered for CEEB Advanced Placement tests.

COSTS AND FINANCIAL AID

Annual tuition $19,950. Room and board $7,166. Required fees $100. Average book expense $700. **Required Forms and Deadlines:** FAFSA. **Notification of Awards:** Applicants will be notified of awards on a rolling basis beginning 1/1. **Types of Aid:** *Need-based scholarships/grants:* Federal Pell, SEOG, state scholarships/grants, private scholarships, the school's own gift aid. *Loans:*

Subsidized Stafford, Unsubsidized Stafford, PLUS, Federal Perkins. *Student Employment:* Federal Work-Study Program available. Institutional employment available. Highest amount earned per year from on-campus jobs $1,100. Off-campus job opportunities are fair. **Financial Aid Statistics:** 0% freshmen, 0% undergrads receive athletic scholarships. 100% freshmen, 96% undergrads receive any aid. **Criteria for awarding institutional aid:** *Non-need-based:* academics, art, athletics, leadership, music/drama.

STERLING COLLEGE (VT)

PO Box 72, Craftsbury Common, VT 5827
Phone: 802-586-7711 · **Financial Aid Phone:** 802-586-7711 x 103
E-mail: admission@sterlingcollege.edu · **CEEB Code:** 3752
Fax: 802-586-2596 · **Website:** www.sterlingcollege.edu · **ACT Code:** 6946

This private school was founded in 1958. It has a 430-acre campus.

RATINGS

Admissions Selectivity Rating: 64   Fire Safety Rating: 90

STUDENTS AND FACULTY
Enrollment: 121. **Student Body:** 49% female, 51% male, 77% out-of-state, 2% international (4 countries represented). Asian 1%, African American 4%, Caucasian 83%, Hispanic 2%, Native American <1%
Retention and Graduation: 85% freshmen return for sophomore year. 33% freshmen graduate within 4 years. 52% freshmen graduate within 6 years. 23% grads go on to further study within 1 year. 8% grads pursue arts and sciences degrees. 3% grads pursue law degrees. **Faculty:** 17 full-time faculty, 24% hold PhDs, 47% are are members of minority groups, 0% are women. 0% of classes are taught by teaching assistants.

ACADEMICS
Degrees: bachelor's. **Classes:** Most classes have 10-19 students. **Majors with Highest Enrollment:** Agroecology and Sustainable Agriculture; Ecology; Outdoor Education. **Special Study Options:** double major, dual enrollment, exchange student program (domestic), independent study, internships, student-designed major, study abroad, Global Field Studies to Japan, Scandinavia, Belize, Alaska, Sierra Nevada, Newfoundland, Iceland, James Bay, and more. **Disability Services:** Special programs offered to physically disabled students include tutors. **Career services:** Alumni network, alumni services, career/job search classes, career assessment, internships. Career services highlights include The Internship, a ten-week experience (working full time) and two courses prior to and after the experience. It is a total of 8 credits and a requirement of all second year students. Past Internship sites have included: 58 federal agencies, including National Forests, National Parks, and National Wildlife Refuges, 18 state agencies, 94 educational organizations including environmental, outdoor adventure, classroom, and interpretative centers,112 agricultural producers, 24 environmental advocacy organizations, 21 wildlife rehabilitation, veterinary medicine, and animal shelter organizations, 30 for-profit green businesses, 36 research institutions, and several national organizations including The Sierra Club, National Audubon Society, PETA, Heifer Project International, The Nature Conservancy, Outward Bound, and NOLS.

FACILITIES
Housing: Coed dorms, Wellness Housing. **Special Academic Facilities/ Equipment:** Library serves as art gallery. There is a 6—8 week rotation of Vermont artist displays. Campus also includes wind and solar-powered barns that serves as an instructional facility and lab, a greenhouse provides a working lab for plant and soil studies. Other facilities include: a woodshop, logging shop, sugarhouse, root cellar, darkroom, certified organic gardens, and a 32' tall climbing wall provides students with the ability to develop leadership and technical rock-climbing skills. The Center for Northern Studies at Sterling College includes a 300 acre boreal forest. **Computers:** 100% of classrooms, 100% of dorms, 100% of libraries, 100% of dining areas, 100% of student union, 100% of common outdoor areas have wireless network access. Administrative functions (other than registration) can be performed online.

CAMPUS LIFE
Environment: Rural. **Activities:** Choral groups, dance, drama/theater, music ensembles, student government, student-run film society, yearbook. **On-Campus Highlights:** Challenge Course and Climbing Wall, Organic Gardens and Livestock Farm, Dining Hall serves local, organic food, 300-acre Boreal Forest, Wind and Solar Powered Barns, Student Lounge, Dancing Goat Café, Recreation Room, Lean-tos, XC ski trails, nature trails, Computer labs, common areas in dorms, front porch.

ADMISSIONS
Freshman Academic Profile: Average high school GPA 3.1. 18% in top 10% of high school class, 35% in top 25% of high school class, 71% in top 50% of

high school class. 68% from public high schools. Minimum internet-based TOEFL 61. Minimum paper TOEFL 500. **Basis for Candidate Selection:** *Very important factors considered include:* academic GPA, recommendation(s), rigor of secondary school record, level of applicant's interest. *Important factors considered include:* Class rank, application essay, character/personal qualities, extracurricular activities, interview, talent/ability, volunteer work. *Other factors considered include:* standardized test scores, alumni/ae relation, geographical residence, work experience. **Freshman Admission Requirements:** High school diploma is required and GED is accepted. *Academic units required:* 4 English, 3 mathematics, 2 science, (2 science labs), 0 foreign language, 2 social studies, 2 history. **Freshman Admission Statistics:** 68 applied, 99% admitted, 31% enrolled. **Transfer Admission Requirements:** High school transcript, college transcript(s), essay or personal statement, Minimum college GPA of 2.0 required. Lowest grade transferable C. **General Admission Information:** Application Fee $35. Regular application deadline 2/15. Regular notification 4/1. Nonfall registration accepted. Admission may be deferred for a maximum of One year. Credit and/or placement offered for CEEB Advanced Placement tests.

COSTS AND FINANCIAL AID
Annual tuition $29,992. Room and board $8,796. Required fees $3,650. Average book expense $900. **Required Forms and Deadlines:** FAFSA, Institution's own financial aid form, State aid form. **Notification of Awards:** Applicants will be notified of awards on a rolling basis beginning 2/1. **Types of Aid:** *Need-based scholarships/grants:* Federal Pell, SEOG, state scholarships/grants, private scholarships, the school's own gift aid. *Loans:* Subsidized Stafford, Unsubsidized Stafford, PLUS. *Student Employment:* Federal Work-Study Program available. Institutional employment available. Highest amount earned per year from on-campus jobs $1,500. Off-campus job opportunities are fair. **Financial Aid Statistics:** 100% freshmen, 100% undergrads receive need-based scholarship or grant aid. 0% freshmen, 22% undergrads receive non-need-based scholarship or grant aid. 100% freshmen, 100% undergrads receive need-based self-help aid. 0% freshmen, 0% undergrads receive athletic scholarships. 100% freshmen, 98% undergrads receive any aid. 91% undergrads borrow to pay for school. Average cumulative indebtedness $35,937. **Criteria for awarding institutional aid:** *Non-need-based:* academics, leadership, state/district residency.

STETSON UNIVERSITY

Best 380

421 N. Woodland Blvd, DeLand, FL 32723
Phone: 386-822-7100 · **Financial Aid Phone:** 800-688-7120
E-mail: admissions@stetson.edu · **CEEB Code:** 5630
Fax: 386-822-7112 · **Website:** stetson.edu · **ACT Code:** 756

This private school was founded in 1883. It has a 175-acre campus.

RATINGS

Admissions Selectivity Rating: 88   Fire Safety Rating: 81

STUDENTS AND FACULTY
Enrollment: 2,821. **Student Body:** 57% female, 43% male, 28% out-of-state, 5% international (49 countries represented). Asian 2%, African American 8%, Caucasian 65%, Hispanic 14%, Native American <1%
Retention and Graduation: 79% freshmen return for sophomore year. 56% freshmen graduate within 4 years. 27% grads go on to further study within 1 year. 25% grads pursue arts and sciences degrees. 5% grads pursue law degrees. 18% grads pursue business degrees. 6% grads pursue medical degrees. **Faculty:** 262 full-time faculty, 94% hold PhDs, 46% are are members of minority groups, 16% are women. 0% of classes are taught by teaching assistants.

ACADEMICS
Degrees: bachelor's, master's. **Classes:** Most classes have 10-19 students. Most lab/discussion sessions have 10-19 students. **Majors with Highest Enrollment:** Psychology; Finance; Business Administration and Management. **Special Study Options:** Accelerated program, double major, honors program, independent study, internships, liberal arts/career combination, student-designed major, study abroad, teacher certification program, weekend college. **Combined degree programs:** BA/JD, Cooperative Program in Forestry and Environ. Studies. **Disability Services:** Special programs offered to physically disabled students include note-taking services, reader services, tape recorders, tutors. **Career services:** Alumni network, alumni services, career/job search classes, career assessment, internships, regional alumni.

FACILITIES

Housing: Coed dorms, men's dorms, women's dorms, fraternity/sorority housing, apartments for single students, Wellness Housing, Theme Housing, "Pet" Dorm (pets allowed), Foreign Language House, French House, The Service Station (community service house). **Special Academic Facilities/Equipment:** Language lab, art gallery, greenhouse with growth chambers, mineral museum, electron microscopes. **Computers:** 90% of classrooms, 100% of dorms, 100% of libraries, 95% of dining areas, 100% of student union, 30% of common outdoor areas have wireless network access. Students can register for classes online. Administrative functions (other than registration) can be performed online.

CAMPUS LIFE

Environment: Town. **Activities:** Choral groups, concert band, dance, drama/theater, jazz band, literary magazine, music ensembles, musical theater, opera, pep band, radio station, student government, student newspaper, student-run film society, symphony orchestra, Campus Ministries, International Student Organization, Model UN. 125 registered organizations, 24 honor societies, 8 religious organizations. 6 fraternities, 5 sororities. **Athletics (Intercollegiate):** *Men:* baseball, basketball, crew/rowing, cross-country, golf, soccer, tennis. *Women:* basketball, crew/rowing, cross-country, golf, soccer, softball, tennis, volleyball. **On-Campus Highlights:** Lynn Business Center, DuPont-Ball Library, Homer and Dolly Hand Art Center, Hollis Center, Sage Hall. **Environmental Initiatives:** The Stetson College of Law is home to the Institute for Biodiversity Law and Policy. The Institute serves as an interdisciplinary focal point for education, research and service activities related to biodiversity issues, and is committed to environmental education and service from the local to the global scale. Each semester, the Institute sponsors several biodiversity lectures. Stetson has recycled more than 1 million lbs. of paper and 42,000 lbs. of plastic. In the 2008-2009 year alone, 106 tons of paper, 7,790 pounds of plastic and 1,060 pounds of aluminum were recycled at the DeLand campus. Other items that are recycled include metals when possible, concrete and construction materials. Stetson University uses LEED system as design criteria for all new projects. Stetsons Eugene M. and Christine Lynn Business Center was the first LEED-certified building in the state of Florida (2003).

ADMISSIONS

Freshman Academic Profile: Average high school GPA 3.79. 26% in top 10% of high school class, 58% in top 25% of high school class, 90% in top 50% of high school class. 78% from public high schools. SAT Math middle 50% range 530-625. SAT Critical Reading middle 50% range 540-650. SAT Writing middle 50% range 520-620. ACT middle 50% range 24-28. Minimum internet-based TOEFL 79. Minimum paper TOEFL 550. **Basis for Candidate Selection:** *Very important factors considered include:* academic GPA, rigor of secondary school record. *Important factors considered include:* Class rank, application essay, recommendation(s), standardized test scores, character/personal qualities, extracurricular activities, interview, talent/ability, volunteer work, work experience. *Other factors considered include:* alumni/ae relation, geographical residence, racial/ethnic status, state residency. **Freshman Admission Requirements:** High school diploma is required and GED is accepted. *Academic units required:* 4 English, 3 mathematics, 3 science, 2 foreign language, 2 social studies. **Freshman Admission Statistics:** 10,986 applied, 61% admitted, 11% enrolled. **Transfer Admission Requirements:** High school transcript, college transcript(s), essay or personal statement, standardized test scores, statement of good standing from prior institution(s). Minimum college GPA of 2.0 required. Lowest grade transferable C. **General Admission Information:** Application Fee $40. Early decision application deadline 11/1. Notification on a rolling basis, beginning on or about 12/1. Nonfall registration accepted. Admission may be deferred for a maximum of 1. Credit and/or placement offered for CEEB Advanced Placement tests.

COSTS AND FINANCIAL AID

Average book expense $1,200. **Required Forms and Deadlines:** FAFSA, Institution's own financial aid form. **Notification of Awards:** Applicants will be notified of awards on a rolling basis beginning 2/15. **Types of Aid:** *Need-based scholarships/grants:* Federal Pell, SEOG, state scholarships/grants, private scholarships, the school's own gift aid. *Loans:* Subsidized Stafford, Unsubsidized Stafford, PLUS, Federal Perkins. *Student Employment:* Federal Work-Study Program available. Institutional employment available. Highest amount earned per year from on-campus jobs $4,000. Off-campus job opportunities are good. **Financial Aid Statistics:** 100% freshmen, 99% undergrads receive need-based scholarship or grant aid. 20% freshmen, 17% undergrads receive non-need-based scholarship or grant aid. 71% freshmen, 74% undergrads receive need-based self-help aid. 4% freshmen, 3% undergrads receive athletic scholarships. 100% freshmen, 99% undergrads receive any aid. 70% undergrads borrow to pay for school. Average cumulative indebtedness $27,491. **Criteria for awarding institutional aid:** *Non-need-based:* academics, alumni affiliation, art, athletics, leadership, minority status, music/drama, religious affiliation, state/district residency.

STEVENS INSTITUTE OF TECHNOLOGY

One Castle Point Terrace, Hoboken, NJ 7030
Phone: 201-216-5194 · **Financial Aid Phone:** 201-216-5555
E-mail: admissions@stevens.edu · **CEEB Code:** 2819
Fax: 201-216-8348 · **Website:** http://www.stevens.edu/princetonreview
ACT Code: 2610

This private school was founded in 1870. It has a 55-acre campus.

RATINGS

Admissions Selectivity Rating: 93   **Fire Safety Rating:** 98

STUDENTS AND FACULTY

Enrollment: 2,369. **Student Body:** 27% female, 73% male, 40% out-of-state, 4% international (40 countries represented). Asian 9%, African American 2%, Caucasian 42%, Hispanic 7%, Native American <1%
Retention and Graduation: 90% freshmen return for sophomore year. 30% freshmen graduate within 4 years. 75% freshmen graduate within 6 years. 24% grads go on to further study within 1 year. 5% grads pursue arts and sciences degrees. 2% grads pursue law degrees. 1% grads pursue business degrees. 4% grads pursue medical degrees. **Faculty:** 226 full-time faculty, 20% are members of minority groups, 25% are women. 0% of classes are taught by teaching assistants.

ACADEMICS

Degrees: bachelor's, doctoral, master's, post-bachelor's certificate. **Majors with Highest Enrollment:** Mechanical Engineering; Bioengineering and Biomedical Engineering; Civil Engineering. **Special Study Options:** Accelerated program, cooperative education program, cross-registration, distance learning, double major, dual enrollment, honors program, independent study, internships, study abroad, Dual enrollment program with NYU. **Honors programs:** The Scholars Program allows high-achieving students to participate in research over the summer or take up to four tuition-free courses each summer. Scholars students may also complete their Bachelor's in three years or a combined bachelor's and Master's in four years at no extra cost. **Combined degree programs:** BA/MD, BA/JD, BA/DDS, BS/MS; BS/DMD; BS/JD; BS/MD. **Disability Services:** Special programs offered to physically disabled students include note-taking services, tutors. **Career services:** Alumni network, alumni services, career/job search classes, career assessment, internships, regional alumni. Our educational philosophy encourages experience with real-world practitioners in business, science and engineering, therefore, 100% of Stevens students participate in co-ops, research or internships; 40% of students participate in co-ops.

FACILITIES

Housing: Coed dorms, women's dorms, fraternity/sorority housing, apartments for married students, apartments for single students. Freshmen not living at home must live on campus. 100% of campus accessible to physically disabled. **Special Academic Facilities/Equipment:** Art museum, electron microscope, ocean engineering lab, HDTV research facility, advanced telecommunications institute, environmental lab, design/manufacturing institute, wind tunnel, robotics lab, product management center, polymer processing institute. DeBaun Theater, a multi-media facility, wireless campus network. **Computers:** 95% of classrooms, 100% of dorms, 100% of libraries, 100% of dining areas, 100% of student union, 99% of common outdoor areas have wireless network access. Students can register for classes online. Administrative functions (other than registration) can be performed online. Undergraduates are required to own a computer.

CAMPUS LIFE

Environment: Town. **Activities:** Choral groups, concert band, dance, drama/theater, jazz band, literary magazine, music ensembles, musical theater, pep band, radio station, student government, student newspaper, student-run film society, symphony orchestra, television station, yearbook, Campus Ministries, International Student Organization. 120 registered organizations, 12 honor societies, 6 religious organizations. 10 fraternities, 3 sororities. **Athletics (Intercollegiate):** *Men:* baseball, basketball, cross-country, fencing, lacrosse, soccer, swimming, tennis, track/field (outdoor), track/field (indoor), volleyball, wrestling. *Women:* basketball, cross-country, equestrian sports, fencing, field hockey, lacrosse, soccer, swimming, tennis, track/field (outdoor), track/field (indoor), volleyball. **On-Campus Highlights:** Schaefer Athletic Center, DeBaun Auditorium, Castle Point, overlooking Manhattan, Babbio Center, Wesley J. Howe Center. **Environmental Initiatives:** Green minor; Green Book Award.

ADMISSIONS

Freshman Academic Profile: Average high school GPA 3.83. 58% in top 10% of high school class, 88% in top 25% of high school class, 98% in top 50% of high school class. 72% from public high schools. SAT Math middle 50% range 620-700. SAT Critical Reading middle 50% range 560-640. SAT Writing middle 50% range 550-650. ACT middle 50% range 25-30. Minimum internet-based TOEFL 82. Minimum paper TOEFL 550. **Basis for Candidate Selection:** *Very important factors considered include:* application essay, academic GPA, recommendation(s), rigor of secondary school record, standardized test scores, character/personal qualities, extracurricular activities, interview, volunteer work, work experience. *Important factors considered include:* Class rank, talent/ability. *Other factors considered include:* alumni/ae relation. **Freshman Admission Requirements:** High school diploma is required and GED is not accepted. *Academic units required:* 4 English, 4 mathematics, 3 science, (3 science labs), 0 foreign language, 0 social studies, 0 history, 0 academic electives. **Freshman Admission Statistics:** 3,239 applied, 47% admitted, 36% enrolled. **Transfer Admission Requirements:** High school transcript, college transcript(s), essay or personal statement, interview, Minimum college GPA of 3.0 required. Lowest grade transferable C. **General Admission Information:** Application Fee $55. Early decision application deadline 11/15. Regular application deadline 2/1. Regular notification 3/15. Nonfall registration accepted. Admission may be deferred for a maximum of 1 year. Credit and/or placement offered for CEEB Advanced Placement tests.

COSTS AND FINANCIAL AID

Average book expense $950. **Required Forms and Deadlines:** FAFSA. **Notification of Awards:** Applicants will be notified of awards on a rolling basis beginning 3/30. **Types of Aid:** *Need-based scholarships/grants:* Federal Pell, SEOG, state scholarships/grants, private scholarships, the school's own gift aid. *Loans:* Direct Subsidized Stafford, Direct Unsubsidized Stafford, Direct PLUS, Subsidized Stafford, Federal Perkins, state loans, Signature Loans, TERI Loans, NJ CLASS, CitiAssist. *Student Employment:* Federal Work-Study Program available. Institutional employment available. Highest amount earned per year from on-campus jobs $1,300. Off-campus job opportunities are excellent. **Financial Aid Statistics:** 83% freshmen, 67% undergrads receive need-based scholarship or grant aid. 78% freshmen, 68% undergrads receive non-need-based scholarship or grant aid. 82% freshmen, 71% undergrads receive need-based self-help aid. 0% freshmen, 0% undergrads receive athletic scholarships. 82% freshmen, 75% undergrads receive any aid. 66% undergrads borrow to pay for school. Average cumulative indebtedness $17,885. **Criteria for awarding institutional aid:** *Non-need-based:* academics, leadership, minority status, music/drama.

See page 1152.

STEVENSON UNIVERSITY

1525 Greenspring Valley Road, Stevenson, MD 21153-0641
Phone: 410-486-7001 · **Financial Aid Phone:** 443-352-4369
E-mail: admissions@stevenson.edu · **CEEB Code:** 2107
Fax: 443-352-4440 · **Website:** http://www.stevenson.edu · **ACT Code:** 1753

This private school was founded in 1947. It has a 150-acre campus.

RATINGS

Admissions Selectivity Rating: 80   Fire Safety Rating: 71

STUDENTS AND FACULTY

Enrollment: 3,826. **Student Body:** 65% female, 35% male, 21% out-of-state, (7 countries represented). Asian 3%, African American 29%, Caucasian 57%, Hispanic 4%, Native American <1%
Retention and Graduation: 17% grads go on to further study within 1 year. **Faculty:** 130 full-time faculty, 74% hold PhDs, 54% are are members of minority groups, 15% are women. 0% of classes are taught by teaching assistants.

ACADEMICS

Degrees: bachelor's, master's. **Classes:** Most classes have 10-19 students. **Majors with Highest Enrollment:** Legal Assistant/Paralegal; Business Administration and Management; Registered Nursing/Registered Nurse. **Special Study Options:** Accelerated program, cooperative education program, cross-registration, distance learning, double major, dual enrollment, honors program, independent study, internships, liberal arts/career combination, student-designed major, study abroad, teacher certification program. **Honors programs:** Consistent with its mission, the Stevenson University Honors Program seeks to admit academically outstanding students who are interested in challenging themselves through a unique and stimulating curriculum that extends beyond traditional academic boundaries. **Disability Services:** Special programs offered to physically disabled students include note-taking services, reader services, tape recorders, tutors. **Career services:** Alumni network, alumni services, career assessment, internships.

FACILITIES

Housing: apartments for single students, suite style (2 bedrooms share 1 bath); accommodations made for students with disabilities. 100% of campus accessible to physically disabled. **Special Academic Facilities/Equipment:** Art gallery and theatre. **Computers:** Students can register for classes online. Administrative functions (other than registration) can be performed online.

CAMPUS LIFE

Environment: Village. **Activities:** Choral groups, dance, drama/theater, jazz band, literary magazine, music ensembles, pep band, student government, student newspaper, symphony orchestra, Campus Ministries, International Student Organization. 40 registered organizations, 10 honor societies, 4 religious organizations. 2 sororities. **Athletics (Intercollegiate):** *Men:* baseball, basketball, cheerleading, cross-country, golf, lacrosse, soccer, tennis, track/field (indoor), volleyball. *Women:* basketball, cheerleading, cross-country, field hockey, lacrosse, soccer, softball, tennis, track/field (indoor), volleyball. **On-Campus Highlights:** Rockland Center (Dining Hall/Student Ce), Avalon Community Center, The Wellness Center/Caves, Garrison Hall, Theater.

ADMISSIONS

Freshman Academic Profile: Average high school GPA 3.2. 11% in top 10% of high school class, 31% in top 25% of high school class, 58% in top 50% of high school class. 70% from public high schools. SAT Math middle 50% range 450-560. SAT Critical Reading middle 50% range 440-540. SAT Writing middle 50% range 450-540. ACT middle 50% range 18-23. Minimum paper TOEFL 550. **Basis for Candidate Selection:** *Very important factors considered include:* academic GPA, rigor of secondary school record. *Important factors considered include:* application essay, standardized test scores, extracurricular activities, talent/ability. *Other factors considered include:* Class rank, recommendation(s), alumni/ae relation, character/personal qualities, geographical residence, interview, level of applicant's interest, volunteer work, work experience. **Freshman Admission Requirements:** High school diploma is required and GED is accepted. *Academic units required:* 4 English, 3 mathematics, 3 science, (2 science labs), 0 foreign language, 2 social studies, 1 history, 0 visual/performing arts, 0 computer science, 4 academic electives. **Freshman Admission Statistics:** 5,318 applied, 60% admitted, 24% enrolled. **Transfer Admission Requirements:** college transcript(s), statement of good standing from prior institution(s). Minimum college GPA of 2.5 required. Lowest grade transferable C. **General Admission Information:** Application Fee $40. Notification on a rolling basis, beginning on or about 12/1. Nonfall registration accepted. Admission may be deferred for a maximum of 1 year. Credit and/or placement offered for CEEB Advanced Placement tests.

COSTS AND FINANCIAL AID

Annual tuition $25,210. Room and board $11,894. Required fees $1,872. Average book expense $1,250. **Required Forms and Deadlines:** FAFSA. **Notification of Awards:** Applicants will be notified of awards on a rolling basis beginning 3/15. **Types of Aid:** *Need-based scholarships/grants:* Federal Pell, SEOG, state scholarships/grants, private scholarships, the school's own gift aid. *Loans:* Direct Subsidized Stafford, Direct Unsubsidized Stafford, Direct PLUS, Federal Perkins. *Student Employment:* Federal Work-Study Program available. Institutional employment available. Off-campus job opportunities are excellent. **Financial Aid Statistics:** 99% freshmen, 96% undergrads receive need-based scholarship or grant aid. 9% freshmen, 8% undergrads receive non-need-based scholarship or grant aid. 78% freshmen, 78% undergrads receive need-based self-help aid. 0% freshmen, 0% undergrads receive athletic scholarships. 69% undergrads borrow to pay for school. Average cumulative indebtedness $20,667. **Criteria for awarding institutional aid:** *Non-need-based:* academics, art, leadership, music/drama.

STOCKTON UNIVERSITY

101 Vera King Farris Drive, Galloway, NJ 8205
Phone: 609-652-4261 · **Financial Aid Phone:** 609-652-4203
E-mail: admissions@stockton.edu · **CEEB Code:** 2889
Fax: 609-748-5541 · **Website:** www.stockton.edu

This public school was founded in 1969. It has a 1600-acre campus.

RATINGS

Admissions Selectivity Rating: 83   Fire Safety Rating: 94

STUDENTS AND FACULTY

Enrollment: 7,679. **Student Body:** 59% female, 41% male, 1% out-of-state, 0% international (11 countries represented). Asian 5%, African American 6%, Caucasian 73%, Hispanic 10%, Native American <1%

Retention and Graduation: 51% freshmen graduate within 4 years. 67% freshmen graduate within 6 years. 33% grads go on to further study within 1 year. 71% grads pursue arts and sciences degrees. 5% grads pursue law degrees. 6% grads pursue business degrees. 4% grads pursue medical degrees. **Faculty:** 304 full-time faculty, 96% hold PhDs, 51% are are members of minority groups, 26% are women. 0% of classes are taught by teaching assistants.

ACADEMICS

Degrees: bachelor's, certificate, master's, post-bachelor's certificate, post-master's certificate. **Classes:** Most classes have 30-39 students. Most lab/discussion sessions have 10-19 students. **Majors with Highest Enrollment:** Psychology; Business Administration and Management; Biology/Biological Sciences. **Special Study Options:** Accelerated program, distance learning, double major, English as a Second Language (ESL), honors program, independent study, internships, liberal arts/career combination, study abroad, teacher certification program, Dual degree bachelor's program in engineering with Rutger's University and New Jersey Institute of Technology, preceptorial advising, opportunities for specialized research, Washington Internship available, and Service-Learning. **Honors programs:** Stockton Honors Program. **Combined degree programs:** BA/MD, BA/MA, BA/DDS, BA/MEng, BA/MA Criminal Justice, BS/PSM Environmental Science, BS/DPT. **Disability Services:** Special programs offered to physically disabled students include note-taking services, reader services, tape recorders, tutors. **Career services:** Alumni network, alumni services, career/job search classes, career assessment, internships, regional alumni. Career services highlights include our internship and experiential learning opportunities.

FACILITIES

Housing: Coed dorms, special housing for disabled students, apartments for single students, Wellness Housing, Theme Housing, Academic units. Living/Learning Communities include themes of Diversity, Global Citizenship, Sustainability, and Wellness. 100% of campus accessible to physically disabled. **Special Academic Facilities/Equipment:** Observatory, Nacote Creek field station, Holocaust Resource Center. **Computers:** 100% of classrooms, 5% of dorms, 100% of libraries, 100% of dining areas, 10% of common outdoor areas have wireless network access. Students can register for classes online. Administrative functions (other than registration) can be performed online.

CAMPUS LIFE

Environment: Town. **Activities:** Choral groups, concert band, dance, drama/theater, literary magazine, music ensembles, musical theater, radio station, student government, student newspaper, television station, yearbook, Campus Ministries, International Student Organization. 130 registered organizations, 6 honor societies, 5 religious organizations. 11 fraternities, 9 sororities. **Athletics (Intercollegiate):** *Men:* baseball, basketball, cheerleading, cross-country, lacrosse, soccer, track/field (outdoor), track/field (indoor). *Women:* basketball, cheerleading, crew/rowing, cross-country, field hockey, soccer, softball, tennis, track/field (outdoor), track/field (indoor), volleyball. **On-Campus Highlights:** Performing Arts Center, Library, Housing options, Osprey's Nest, Marine Field Station. **Environmental Initiatives:** Alternative Energy: A. Solar electrical generation: 1200 KW capacity arrays operating on campus. This includes rooftop installations and shade canopies over parking lots. An additional 700 KW is under construction, expected to be operational in June of 2012. B. The Geothermal Project provides up to 1650 tons of cooling capacity and allows portions of the building to be heated and cooled using the same equipment. C. Solar hot water heating has been installed on the roof of the newest residential facility, which accommodates 390 students. The Richard Stockton College Coastal Research Center, located on Nacote Creek in Port Republic, is housed at the College's Nacote Creek Marine and Environmental Science Field Station, which functions as a teaching and training facility for Stockton students. The CRC conducts about 20 research projects a year. The CRC is at the forefront of research groups at Richard Stockton College, and is a leader in coastal geoscience and resource studies in the Mid-Atlantic region. A Sustainability Living Learning Community supports residential students interested in and committed to sustainability. Faculty presents lectures, students engage in community service to protect the environment and staff provide additional learning opportunities and links to local, regional and national bodies of knowledge.

ADMISSIONS

Freshman Academic Profile: 23% in top 10% of high school class, 54% in top 25% of high school class, 91% in top 50% of high school class. 88% from public high schools. SAT Math middle 50% range 500-600. SAT Critical Reading middle 50% range 480-600. SAT Writing middle 50% range 470-580. ACT middle 50% range 18-24. Minimum internet-based TOEFL 80. Minimum paper TOEFL 550. **Basis for Candidate Selection:** *Very important factors considered include:* Class rank, academic GPA, rigor of secondary school record. *Important factors considered include:* standardized test scores. *Other factors considered include:* application essay, recommendation(s), alumni/ae relation, character/personal qualities, extracurricular activities, level of applicant's interest, talent/ability, volunteer work, work experience. **Freshman Admission Requirements:** High school diploma is required and GED is accepted. *Academic*

units required: 4 English, 3 mathematics, 2 science, (2 science labs), 2 social studies, 5 academic electives. **Freshman Admission Statistics:** 5,229 applied, 65% admitted, 35% enrolled. Minimum college GPA of 2.5 required. Lowest grade transferable C. **General Admission Information:** Application Fee $50. Regular application deadline 5/1. Notification on a rolling basis, beginning on or about 10/1. Nonfall registration accepted. Credit and/or placement offered for CEEB Advanced Placement tests.

COSTS AND FINANCIAL AID

Annual in-state tuition $8,107. Annual out-of-state tuition $14,628. Room and board $11,164. Required fees $4,461. Average book expense $1,562. **Required Forms and Deadlines:** FAFSA, State aid form. **Notification of Awards:** Applicants will be notified of awards on a rolling basis beginning 4/1. **Types of Aid:** *Need-based scholarships/grants:* Federal Pell, SEOG, state scholarships/grants, the school's own gift aid. *Loans:* Direct Subsidized Stafford, Direct Unsubsidized Stafford, Direct PLUS, Federal Perkins, state loans. *Student Employment:* Federal Work-Study Program available. Institutional employment available. Highest amount earned per year from on-campus jobs $1,643. Off-campus job opportunities are excellent. **Financial Aid Statistics:** 68% freshmen, 57% undergrads receive need-based scholarship or grant aid. 38% freshmen, 27% undergrads receive non-need-based scholarship or grant aid. 77% freshmen, 78% undergrads receive need-based self-help aid. 0% freshmen, 0% undergrads receive athletic scholarships. 86% freshmen, 84% undergrads receive any aid. 76% undergrads borrow to pay for school. Average cumulative indebtedness $24,886. **Criteria for awarding institutional aid:** *Non-need-based:* academics, art, leadership, minority status, music/drama, state/district residency.

STONEHILL COLLEGE

Best 380

320 Washington Street, Easton, MA 02357-5610
Phone: 508-565-1373 • **Financial Aid Phone:** 508-565-1088
E-mail: admission@stonehill.edu • **CEEB Code:** 3770
Fax: 508-565-1545 • **Website:** www.stonehill.edu • **ACT Code:** 1918

This private school, affiliated with the Roman Catholic Church, was founded in 1948. It has a 375-acre campus.

RATINGS

Admissions Selectivity Rating: 85   **Fire Safety Rating:** 95

STUDENTS AND FACULTY

Enrollment: 2,390. **Student Body:** 60% female, 40% male, 44% out-of-state, 1% international (9 countries represented). Asian 2%, African American 4%, Caucasian 84%, Hispanic 5%, Native American <1%
Retention and Graduation: 90% freshmen return for sophomore year. 79% freshmen graduate within 4 years. 29% grads go on to further study within 1 year. 13% grads pursue arts and sciences degrees. 2% grads pursue law degrees. 5% grads pursue business degrees. 3% grads pursue medical degrees. **Faculty:** 160 full-time faculty, 88% hold PhDs, 39% are are members of minority groups, 11% are women. 0% of classes are taught by teaching assistants.

ACADEMICS

Degrees: bachelor's. **Classes:** Most classes have 20-29 students. Most lab/discussion sessions have 10-19 students. **Majors with Highest Enrollment:** Psychology; Accounting; Communication. **Special Study Options:** cross-registration, double major, dual enrollment, honors program, independent study, internships, liberal arts/career combination, student-designed major, study abroad, teacher certification program. **Honors programs:** The Honors Program, which requires 5 honors courses and a Senior Honors Experience. **Disability Services:** Special programs offered to physically disabled students include note-taking services, reader services, tape recorders, tutors. **Career services:** Alumni network, alumni services, career/job search classes, career assessment, internships. Career services highlights include the fact that 79% of our senior class has completed some type of internship-related experience.

FACILITIES

Housing: Coed dorms, special housing for disabled students, women's dorms, Wellness Housing, Special interest housing. 80% of campus accessible to physically disabled. **Special Academic Facilities/Equipment:** Institute for law and society, observatory, Stonehill Industrial History Center, shovel museum. **Computers:** 30% of classrooms, 80% of dorms, 100% of libraries, 100% of dining areas, 50% of student union, 20% of common outdoor areas have wireless network access. Students can register for classes online. Administrative functions (other than registration) can be performed online.

CAMPUS LIFE

Environment: Village. **Activities:** Choral groups, dance, drama/theater, literary magazine, music ensembles, musical theater, pep band, radio station, student government, student newspaper, student-run film society, yearbook, Campus Ministries. 76 registered organizations, 19 honor societies, 3 religious organizations. **Athletics (Intercollegiate):** *Men:* baseball, basketball, cross-country, football, ice hockey, soccer, tennis, track/field (outdoor), track/field (indoor). *Women:* basketball, cross-country, equestrian sports, field hockey, lacrosse, soccer, softball, tennis, track/field (outdoor), track/field (indoor), volleyball. **On-Campus Highlights:** The Hill (entertainment/dining social space), The MacPhaidin Library, The Roche Dining Commons, The Residence Courts (housing/social space), The Sally Blair Ames Sports Complex. **Environmental Initiatives:** Joined AASHE (Association for the Advancement of Sustainability in Higher Education) and will participate in the STARS survey. Zip Cars—the College has two zip cars to provide a community car sharing program. Thinking Outside the Bottle proposal was implemented. The College has eliminated the majority of bottled water.

ADMISSIONS

Freshman Academic Profile: Average high school GPA 3.3. 29% in top 10% of high school class, 62% in top 25% of high school class, 89% in top 50% of high school class. 67% from public high schools. SAT Math middle 50% range 510-620. SAT Critical Reading middle 50% range 500-600. SAT Writing middle 50% range 510-610. ACT middle 50% range 23-28. Minimum internet-based TOEFL 90. Minimum paper TOEFL 575. **Basis for Candidate Selection:** *Very important factors considered include:* Class rank, academic GPA, rigor of secondary school record, character/personal qualities, talent/ability. *Important factors considered include:* application essay, recommendation(s), extracurricular activities, level of applicant's interest, volunteer work, work experience. *Other factors considered include:* standardized test scores, alumni/ae relation, first generation, geographical residence, interview, racial/ethnic status, religious affiliation/commitment. **Freshman Admission Requirements:** High school diploma is required and GED is accepted. *Academic units required:* 4 English, 3 mathematics, 1 science, (1 science labs), 2 foreign language, 3 history, 3 academic electives. **Freshman Admission Statistics:** 6,006 applied, 77% admitted, 13% enrolled. **Transfer Admission Requirements:** High school transcript, college transcript(s), essay or personal statement, statement of good standing from prior institution(s). Minimum college GPA of 2.0 required. Lowest grade transferable C. **General Admission Information:** Application Fee $60. Early decision application deadline 11/1. Regular application deadline 1/15. Regular notification 3/15. Nonfall registration accepted. Admission may be deferred for a maximum of 1 year. Credit and/or placement offered for CEEB Advanced Placement tests.

COSTS AND FINANCIAL AID

Annual tuition $37,426. Room and board $14,190. Average book expense $893. **Required Forms and Deadlines:** FAFSA, CSS/Financial Aid PROFILE, Noncustodial PROFILE. **Notification of Awards:** Applicants will be notified of awards on or about 4/1. **Types of Aid:** *Need-based scholarships/grants:* Federal Pell, SEOG, state scholarships/grants, private scholarships, the school's own gift aid. *Loans:* Direct Subsidized Stafford, Direct Unsubsidized Stafford, Direct PLUS, Federal Perkins, state loans. *Student Employment:* Federal Work-Study Program available. Institutional employment available. Highest amount earned per year from on-campus jobs $2,505. Off-campus job opportunities are good. **Financial Aid Statistics:** 98% freshmen, 95% undergrads receive need-based scholarship or grant aid. 20% freshmen, 18% undergrads receive non-need-based scholarship or grant aid. 77% freshmen, 81% undergrads receive need-based self-help aid. 3% freshmen, 3% undergrads receive athletic scholarships. 98% freshmen, 94% undergrads receive any aid. 78% undergrads borrow to pay for school. Average cumulative indebtedness $23,756. **Criteria for awarding institutional aid:** *Non-need-based:* academics, athletics, job skills, leadership, minority status, music/drama.

SUFFOLK UNIVERSITY

8 Ashburton Place, Boston, MA 2108
Phone: 617-573-8480 · **Financial Aid Phone:** 617-573-8470
E-mail: admission@suffolk.edu · **CEEB Code:** 3771
Fax: 617-573-1574 · **Website:** www.suffolk.edu · **ACT Code:** 1920

This private school was founded in 1906.

RATINGS

Admissions Selectivity Rating: 79   **Fire Safety Rating:** 98

STUDENTS AND FACULTY

Enrollment: 5,361. **Student Body:** 55% female, 45% male, 29% out-of-state, 22% international (108 countries represented). Asian 8%, African American 6%, Caucasian 39%, Hispanic 12%, Native American <1%
Retention and Graduation: 39% freshmen graduate within 4 years. 55% freshmen graduate within 6 years. 30% grads go on to further study within 1 year. 4% grads pursue arts and sciences degrees. 4% grads pursue law degrees. 7% grads pursue business degrees. 1% grads pursue medical degrees. **Faculty:** 336 full-time faculty, 90% hold PhDs, 43% are are members of minority groups, 21% are women.

ACADEMICS

Degrees: associate, bachelor's, certificate, diploma, master's, post-bachelor's certificate, post-master's certificate. **Classes:** Most classes have 10-19 students. Most lab/discussion sessions have 10-19 students. **Special Study Options:** Accelerated program, cooperative education program, cross-registration, distance learning, double major, English as a Second Language (ESL), honors program, independent study, internships, liberal arts/career combination, study abroad, weekend college. **Honors programs:** A Community of Scholars Suffolk University honors students work in collaboration with their school's program director and advisory committee to plan events that bring the honors community together on a regular basis outside of the classroom. Lectures by Suffolk University scholars or by noted intellectuals outside of the University, a variety of social events, visits to cultural and historical sites, and public service projects offer intellectual challenge, promote leadership, and develop networking skills with faculty, alumni, community, business, and government leaders. The program provides honors scholars with a broader context for their academic pursuits, while strengthening their sense of community. Special Benefits and Recognition for Honors Scholars: Honors scholars are eligible for a full tuition scholarship. In addition, honors scholars enjoy the following benefits and recognition: Guaranteed housing in University residence halls through the sophomore year; Priority course registration; Special honors program advisors; Application assistance, when applicable, for Fulbright, Marshall, Rhodes, and other post-graduate academic and scholarship programs; Honors Program designation on official academic transcript; and Special listing in commencement program. http://www.suffolk.edu/admission/gchonors.htm **Combined degree programs:** BA/JD, BA/MA. **Disability Services:** Special programs offered to physically disabled students include note-taking services, reader services, tape recorders, tutors. **Career services:** Alumni network, alumni services, career/job search classes, career assessment, internships, regional alumni. Career services highlights include the Co-op Program, which offers both part-time and full-time work options and is available to full-time undergraduate and graduate students. By combining relevant work experience with academic studies, students have the best opportunity for personal, professional and career development. Additionally, students are able to subsidize their education costs while building their resumes in preparation for their professional lives. Students can work either part-time (the most popular option) or full-time. Part-time co-ops usually involve working 15-25 hours per week while continuing to take a full load of courses. Students working full-time must have completed a full load of courses the previous semester and then must return to school for the semester after their co-op placement. Co-ops are available for all majors. Most positions are located in businesses and organizations within easy commuting distance of campus, so that students can balance their work and academic schedules. Some of the employers who have participated in the Suffolk Co-op Program include: 96.9 FM Biogen Boston Globe Cape Cod Potato Chips Commonwealth of Massachusetts EF Education Ernst and Young, LLP Fidelity Investments Greater Boston Convention and Visitors Bureau Investors Bank and Trust Mass General Hospital Massport North Suffolk Mental Health Association PricewaterhouseCoopers Eligibility for participation in Co-op Program: Undergraduates must have a minimum 2.5 GPA Undergraduates have completed their freshman year Transfer students must have completed one semester at Suffolk University Full-time graduate students are eligible upon enrollment in their degree program. Student interested in Co-op must call the office at 617-573-8480 to schedule an appointment with a counselor.

FACILITIES

Housing: Coed dorms, apartments for single students **Special Academic Facilities/Equipment:** Marine biology field station in Maine, NESAD art gallery, Adams art gallery, C. Walsh Theatre and 10 West Street Theatre. **Computers:** 100% of classrooms, 100% of dorms, 100% of libraries, 100% of dining areas, 100% of student union, 20% of common outdoor areas have wireless network access. Students can register for classes online. Administrative functions (other than registration) can be performed online.

CAMPUS LIFE

Environment: Metropolis. **Activities:** Choral groups, dance, drama/theater, literary magazine, music ensembles, musical theater, radio station, student government, student newspaper, television station, yearbook, Campus Ministries, International Student Organization. 75 registered organizations, 11 honor societies, 3 religious organizations. 1 fraternity, 1 sorority. **Athletics (Intercollegiate):** *Men:* baseball, basketball, cross-country, golf, ice hockey, soccer, tennis. *Women:* basketball, cross-country, softball, tennis, volleyball. **On-Campus Highlights:** Donahue Student Lounge, Donahue Café, Sawyer Library, NESAD Gallery, Alumni Park, Sawyer Computer Lab, Donahue Computer Lab, Sawyer Lounge, 150 Tremont St Dining Room. **Environmental Initiatives:** Energy efficiency and conservation; Green Building Practices; Waste Reduction; and Recycling.

ADMISSIONS

Freshman Academic Profile: Average high school GPA 3.12. 16% in top 10% of high school class, 41% in top 25% of high school class, 76% in top 50% of high school class. 60% from public high schools. SAT Math middle 50% range 450-560. SAT Critical Reading middle 50% range 440-570. SAT Writing middle 50% range 440-570. ACT middle 50% range 20-25. Minimum internet-based TOEFL 77. Minimum paper TOEFL 550. **Basis for Candidate Selection:** *Very important factors considered include:* rigor of secondary school record. *Important factors considered include:* Class rank, application essay, academic GPA, standardized test scores, character/personal qualities. *Other factors considered include:* recommendation(s), alumni/ae relation, extracurricular activities, first generation, geographical residence, interview, level of applicant's interest, talent/ability, volunteer work, work experience. **Freshman Admission Requirements:** High school diploma is required and GED is accepted. *Academic units required:* 4 English, 3 mathematics, 2 science, (1 science labs), 2 foreign language, 1 history, 4 academic electives. **Freshman Admission Statistics:** 9,917 applied, 75% admitted, 15% enrolled. **Transfer Admission Requirements:** High school transcript, college transcript(s), essay or personal statement, Minimum college GPA of 2.5 required. Lowest grade transferable C. **General Admission Information:** Application Fee $50. Regular application deadline 3/1. Notification on a rolling basis, beginning on or about 2/5. Nonfall registration accepted. Admission may be deferred for a maximum of 1 year. Credit and/or placement offered for CEEB Advanced Placement tests.

COSTS AND FINANCIAL AID

Required Forms and Deadlines: FAFSA. **Notification of Awards:** Applicants will be notified of awards on a rolling basis beginning 2/5. **Types of Aid:** *Need-based scholarships/grants:* Federal Pell, SEOG, state scholarships/grants, private scholarships, the school's own gift aid. *Loans:* Direct Subsidized Stafford, Direct Unsubsidized Stafford, Direct PLUS, Federal Perkins, state loans, college/university loans from institutional funds. *Student Employment:* Federal Work-Study Program available. Institutional employment available. Highest amount earned per year from on-campus jobs $8,217. Off-campus job opportunities are excellent. **Financial Aid Statistics:** 82% freshmen, 89% undergrads receive need-based scholarship or grant aid. 92% freshmen, 55% undergrads receive non-need-based scholarship or grant aid. 95% freshmen, 95% undergrads receive need-based self-help aid. 0% freshmen, 0% undergrads receive athletic scholarships. 94% freshmen, 73% undergrads receive any aid. 75% undergrads borrow to pay for school. Average cumulative indebtedness $22,215. **Criteria for awarding institutional aid:** *Non-need-based:* academics, alumni affiliation.

SUSQUEHANNA UNIVERSITY

514 University Avenue, Selinsgrove, PA 17870
Phone: 570-372-4260 • **Financial Aid Phone:** 570-372-4450
E-mail: suadmiss@susqu.edu • **CEEB Code:** 2820
Fax: 570-372-2722 • **Website:** www.susqu.edu • **ACT Code:** 3720

This private school, affiliated with the Lutheran Church, was founded in 1858. It has a 306-acre campus.

RATINGS

Admissions Selectivity Rating: 84   **Fire Safety Rating:** 99

STUDENTS AND FACULTY

Enrollment: 2,022. **Student Body:** 55% female, 45% male, 51% out-of-state, 2% international (12 countries represented). Asian 2%, African American 5%, Caucasian 83%, Hispanic 6%, Native American <1% **Retention and Graduation:** 71% freshmen graduate within 4 years. 18% grads go on to further study within 1 year. **Faculty:** 140 full-time faculty, 92% hold PhDs, 46% are are members of minority groups, 19% are women. 0% of classes are taught by teaching assistants.

ACADEMICS

Degrees: bachelor's. **Classes:** Most classes have 10-19 students. Most lab/discussion sessions have 10-19 students. **Majors with Highest Enrollment:** Business Administration and Management; Psychology; Speech Communication and Rhetoric. **Special Study Options:** Accelerated program, cross-registration, distance learning, double major, dual enrollment, exchange student program (domestic), honors program, independent study, internships, student-designed major, study abroad, teacher certification program. **Honors programs:** Recognized as a model for similar programs throughout the country, the Honors Program at Susquehanna offers a challenging curriculum to students interested in a more self-directed and interdisciplinary approach at the undergraduate level. The program is well suited to the aggressively curious, active learner who values breadth of study and multiple perspectives. Discussion groups, lectures, off-campus visits and residential programs complement Honors Program courses. **Combined degree programs:** BA/DDS, BA/M.E.M. or BA/M.F. with Duke Universit. **Disability Services:** Special programs offered to physically disabled students include note-taking services, reader services, tape recorders, tutors. **Career services:** Alumni network, alumni services, career/job search classes, career assessment, internships, regional alumni. Susquehanna University and the Center for Career Services support and encourage student participation in credit internships. Gundaker Enrichment Fund Grants provide qualifying students with supplemental support for internships or volunteer activities. Awards from the funds are intended to provide a range of experiential learning opportunities for students. In addition, Susquehanna University has partnerships with several programs offering students opportunities to combine internships and academic coursework for university credit.

FACILITIES

Housing: Coed dorms, special housing for disabled students, special housing for international students, fraternity/sorority housing, apartments for single students, Theme Housing. 90% of campus accessible to physically disabled. **Special Academic Facilities/Equipment:** Art gallery, electronic music lab, child development center, foreign language broadcast system, teaching theatre, greenhouse, rare book room, ecological field station, electron microscope, reflecting telescope, fluorescent microscopes, video conference center, and the new Business and Communications Building featuring three multimedia classrooms, three computer laboratories/classrooms, conference and seminar rooms, student team study rooms and alcoves, two video studios, seminar/observation rooms and a room for faculty instructional development. The building facilitates use of laptop computers by offering informational technology dataports for every seat in the classrooms, team study areas and student lounges and faculty offices. **Computers:** 90% of classrooms, 10% of dorms, 100% of libraries, 100% of dining areas, 100% of student union, 30% of common outdoor areas have wireless network access. Students can register for classes online. Administrative functions (other than registration) can be performed online.

CAMPUS LIFE

Environment: Town. **Activities:** Choral groups, concert band, dance, drama/theater, jazz band, literary magazine, music ensembles, musical theater, opera, pep band, radio station, student government, student newspaper, student-run film society, symphony orchestra, television station, yearbook, Campus Ministries, International Student Organization. 120 registered organizations, 24 honor societies, 12 religious organizations, 4 fraternities, 5 sororities. **Athletics (Intercollegiate):** *Men:* baseball, basketball, crew/rowing, cross-country, football, golf, lacrosse, soccer, swimming, tennis, track/field (outdoor), track/field (indoor). *Women:* basketball, crew/rowing, cross-country, field hockey, golf, lacrosse, soccer, softball, swimming, tennis, track/field (outdoor), track/field (indoor), volleyball. **On-Campus Highlights:** Sports and Fitness Complex, Business and Communications Center, Blough-Weis Library, Trax (campus nightclub), Java City in the Campus Center. **Environmental Initiatives:** New science facility and new student housing are LEED certified. This housing and two units built in 2010 utilize geo-thermal energy for heating and cooling. Actively pursuing alternative sources of fuel to replace coal-fired power plant. Cut fuel usage 25% last year by installing highly-efficient insulated steam lines. Susquehanna University is a flagship member of the Graduation Pledge Alliance, a national student organization whose mission is to promote socially and environmentally responsible actions by graduating seniors. Commitments include participation in a recycling cooperative with the borough.

ADMISSIONS

Freshman Academic Profile: Average high school GPA 3.38. 28% in top 10% of high school class, 54% in top 25% of high school class, 85% in top 50% of high school class. 79% from public high schools. SAT Math middle 50% range 520-610. SAT Critical Reading middle 50% range 500-600. SAT Writing middle 50% range 490-600. ACT middle 50% range 22-28. Minimum internet-based TOEFL 81. Minimum paper TOEFL 550. **Basis for Candidate Selection:** *Very important factors considered include:* academic GPA, rigor of secondary school record. *Important factors considered include:* Class rank, application essay, recommendation(s), standardized test scores, alumni/ae relation, character/personal qualities, extracurricular activities, interview, level of applicant's interest, racial/ethnic status, talent/ability, volunteer work, work experience. *Other factors considered include:* first generation, geographical residence, religious affiliation/commitment, state residency. **Freshman Admission Requirements:** High school diploma is required and GED is accepted. *Academic units required:* 4 English, 3 mathematics, 3 science, (2 science labs), 2 foreign language, 2 social studies, 2 history, 2 academic electives. **Freshman Admission Statistics:** 4,510 applied, 78% admitted, 16% enrolled. **Transfer Admission Requirements:** High school transcript, college transcript(s), essay or personal statement, statement of good standing from prior institution(s). Minimum college GPA of 2.0 required. Lowest grade transferable C-. **General Admission Information:** Application Fee $35. Early decision application deadline 11/15. Regular application deadline 3/1. Notification on a rolling basis, beginning on or about 12/15. Nonfall registration accepted. Admission may be deferred for a maximum of one year. Credit and/or placement offered for CEEB Advanced Placement tests.

COSTS AND FINANCIAL AID

Required Forms and Deadlines: FAFSA, CSS/Financial Aid PROFILE, Business/Farm Supplement. **Notification of Awards:** Applicants will be notified of awards on or about 3/1. **Types of Aid:** *Need-based scholarships/grants:* Federal Pell, SEOG, state scholarships/grants, private scholarships, the school's own gift aid. *Loans:* Subsidized Stafford, Unsubsidized Stafford, PLUS, Federal Perkins, college/university loans from institutional funds. *Student Employment:* Federal Work-Study Program available. Institutional employment available. Highest amount earned per year from on-campus jobs $8,337. Off-campus job opportunities are good. **Financial Aid Statistics:** 98% freshmen, 100% undergrads receive need-based scholarship or grant aid. 19% freshmen, 14% undergrads receive non-need-based scholarship or grant aid. 77% freshmen, 83% undergrads receive need-based self-help aid. 0% freshmen, 0% undergrads receive athletic scholarships. 98% freshmen, 98% undergrads receive any aid. 55% undergrads borrow to pay for school. Average cumulative indebtedness $23,903. **Criteria for awarding institutional aid:** *Non-need-based:* academics, alumni affiliation, leadership, minority status, music/drama.

SWARTHMORE COLLEGE

Best 380

500 College Avenue, Swarthmore, PA 19081
Phone: 610-328-8300 · **Financial Aid Phone:** 610-328-8358
E-mail: admissions@swarthmore.edu · **CEEB Code:** 2821
Fax: 610-328-8580 · **Website:** www.swarthmore.edu · **ACT Code:** 3722

This private school was founded in 1864. It has a 399-acre campus.

RATINGS

Admissions Selectivity Rating: 98	**Fire Safety Rating:** 85

STUDENTS AND FACULTY

Enrollment: 1,524. **Student Body:** 51% female, 49% male, 87% out-of-state, 9% international (64 countries represented). Asian 15%, African American 6%, Caucasian 43%, Hispanic 14%, Native American <1%
Retention and Graduation: 96% freshmen return for sophomore year. 89% freshmen graduate within 4 years. 93% freshmen graduate within 6 years. 26% grads go on to further study within 1 year. 10% grads pursue arts and sciences degrees. 2% grads pursue law degrees. 1% grads pursue business degrees. 2% grads pursue medical degrees. **Faculty:** 178 full-time faculty, 98% hold PhDs, 42% are are members of minority groups, 16% are women. 0% of classes are taught by teaching assistants.

ACADEMICS

Degrees: bachelor's. **Classes:** Most classes have 10-19 students. Most lab/discussion sessions have fewer than 10 students. **Majors with Highest Enrollment:** Economics; Biology/Biological Sciences; Political Science and Government. **Special Study Options:** Accelerated program, cross-registration, double major, exchange student program (domestic), honors program, independent study, internships, student-designed major, study abroad, teacher certification program, Swarthmore offers cooperative exchange programs with Rice and Tufts universities and Harvey Mudd, Pomona, Mills and Middlebury colleges. **Honors programs:** Swarthmore's Honors Program features faculty working with small groups of dedicated and accomplished students; an emphasis on independent learning; students entering into a dialogue with peers, teachers, and examiners; a demanding program of study in major and minor fields; and an examination at the end of two years' study by outside scholars. **Combined degree programs:** BA/BS in engineering and another major. **Disability Services:** Special programs offered to physically disabled students include note-taking services, reader services, tape recorders, tutors. **Career services:** Alumni network, alumni services, career/job search classes, career assessment, internships, regional alumni. Career services highlights include Swarthmore's externship program, which matches 200 students annually with over 300 alumni sponsors in diverse career fields and locations nationwide.

FACILITIES

Housing: Coed dorms, men's dorms, women's dorms, Gender Neutral housing (students of any gender may share rooms and/or share bathrooms). 85% of campus accessible to physically disabled. **Special Academic Facilities/Equipment:** The Campus is a 399-acre, nationally registered arboretum. The Lang Performing Arts Center's resources include an art gallery, dance studios, cinema, and theater performance space. Highlights of Swarthmore's library facilities include the Friends Historical Library and the Peace Collection. The athletics facilities include a lighted stadium complex, a 400-meter dual durometer track, and synthetic grass playing field, state-of-the-art fitness center and three indoor tennis courts with Rebound Ace surface. The Science Center has been recognized by the U.S. Green Building Council for "leadership in energy and environmental design." The College's two newest residence halls feature loft-style rooms and environmentally friendly green roofs. **Computers:** 100% of classrooms, 100% of dorms, 100% of libraries, 100% of dining areas, 100% of student union, 100% of common outdoor areas have wireless network access. Students can register for classes online. Administrative functions (other than registration) can be performed online.

CAMPUS LIFE

Environment: Village. **Activities:** Choral groups, dance, drama/theater, jazz band, literary magazine, music ensembles, opera, student government, student newspaper, student-run film society, symphony orchestra, yearbook, Campus Ministries, International Student Organization. 138 registered organizations, 3 honor societies, 12 religious organizations. 2 fraternities. **Athletics (Intercollegiate):** *Men:* baseball, basketball, cross-country, golf, lacrosse, soccer, swimming, tennis, track/field (outdoor), track/field (indoor). *Women:* badminton, basketball, cross-country, field hockey, lacrosse, soccer, softball, swimming, tennis, track/field (outdoor), track/field (indoor), volleyball. **On-Campus Highlights:** Kohlberg & Eldridge Commons Coffee Bars, Parrish Beach (the central campus lawn), Scott Outdoor Amphitheater, Mullan Tennis & Fitness Center, Paces (student-run Café). Recent years have seen an exciting array of student projects and student spaces develop at Swarthmore. Among them: The acclaimed War News Radio (www.warnewsradio.org), the nation's only student-run national radio program focusing on the wars in Iraq and Afghanistan, now carried by more than 60 stations worldwide; the Genocide Intervention Network (www.genocideintervention.net), a student-founded group that is raising hundreds of thousands of dollars to support peace-keeping in Darfur; two new dormitories, whose student-influenced integrative design features loft-style doubles, wide halls, generous lounge and community kitchens'—all aimed at promoting robust hall social life; and the Lang Center for Civic and Social Responsibility (www.swarthmore.edu/langcenter) which prepares students for leadership in civic engagement, public service, advocacy, and social action. **Environmental Initiatives:** 100% of the Colleges electrical demands are met by renewable energy credits and the College has made the decision to burn natural gas as it's primary fuel and convert the heat plant from #6 fuel oil to #2 fuel oil as it's back-up reserve. The College has more than doubled its 14,300 sq. feet of green roof by adding an additional 31,000 sq.ft. of green roof on the Eugene and Teresa Lang Performing Arts Center The College with the urging of the Board of Managers has formed a new committee of Board members, alums, staff construction and maintenance professionals and members of the sustainability committee to establish energy and sustainability standards for new construction and renovation.

ADMISSIONS

Freshman Academic Profile: 89% in top 10% of high school class, 99% in top 25% of high school class, 100% in top 50% of high school class. 57% from public high schools. SAT Math middle 50% range 670-770. SAT Critical Reading middle 50% range 680-760. SAT Writing middle 50% range 680-770. ACT middle 50% range 31-34. **Basis for Candidate Selection:** *Very important factors considered include:* Class rank, application essay, academic GPA, recommendation(s), rigor of secondary school record, character/personal qualities. *Important factors considered include:* standardized test scores, extracurricular activities. *Other factors considered include:* alumni/ae relation, first generation, geographical residence, interview, level of applicant's interest, racial/ethnic status, talent/ability, volunteer work, work experience. **Freshman Admission Requirements:** High school diploma or equivalent is not required. **Freshman Admission Statistics:** 6,615 applied, 14% admitted, 41% enrolled. **Transfer Admission Requirements:** High school transcript, college transcript(s), essay or personal statement, standardized test scores, statement of good standing from prior institution(s). Lowest grade transferable C. **General Admission Information:** Application Fee $60. Early decision application deadline 11/15. Regular application deadline 1/2. Regular notification 4/1. Nonfall registration not accepted. Admission may be deferred for a maximum of 1 Year. Credit and/or placement offered for CEEB Advanced Placement tests.

COSTS AND FINANCIAL AID

Annual tuition $45,700. Room and board $13,550. Required fees $360. Average book expense $1,230. **Required Forms and Deadlines:** FAFSA, Institution's own financial aid form, CSS/Financial Aid PROFILE, State aid form, Non-custodial PROFILE, Business/Farm Supplement. **Notification of Awards:** Applicants will be notified of awards on or about 4/1. **Types of Aid:** *Need-based scholarships/grants:* Federal Pell, SEOG, state scholarships/grants, private scholarships, the school's own gift aid. *Loans:* Subsidized Stafford, Unsubsidized Stafford, PLUS, Federal Perkins, state loans, college/university loans from institutional funds. *Student Employment:* Federal Work-Study Program available. Institutional employment available. Highest amount earned per year from on-campus jobs $1,760. Off-campus job opportunities are good. **Financial Aid Statistics:** 100% freshmen, 100% undergrads receive need-based scholarship or grant aid. 0% freshmen, 0% undergrads receive non-need-based scholarship or grant aid. 99% freshmen, 98% undergrads receive need-based self-help aid. 0% freshmen, 0% undergrads receive athletic scholarships. 52% freshmen, 50% undergrads receive any aid. 36% undergrads borrow to pay for school. Average cumulative indebtedness $17,323. **Criteria for awarding institutional aid:** *Non-need-based:* academics, leadership, state/district residency.

See page 1154.

SYRACUSE UNIVERSITY

100 Crouse-Hinds Hall, Syracuse, NY 13244-2130
Phone: 315-443-3611 · **Financial Aid Phone:** 315-443-1513
E-mail: orange@syr.edu · **CEEB Code:** 2823
Fax: 315-443-4226 · **Website:** www.syr.edu · **ACT Code:** 2968

This private school was founded in 1870. It has a 200-acre campus.

RATINGS

Admissions Selectivity Rating: 89   Fire Safety Rating: 92

STUDENTS AND FACULTY

Enrollment: 14,768. **Student Body:** 55% female, 45% male, 57% out-of-state, 11% international (84 countries represented). Asian 8%, African American 9%, Caucasian 55%, Hispanic 11%, Native American 1%
Retention and Graduation: 92% freshmen return for sophomore year. 69% freshmen graduate within 4 years. 21% grads go on to further study within 1 year. 1% grads pursue arts and sciences degrees. 1% grads pursue law degrees. 2% grads pursue business degrees. 1% grads pursue medical degrees. **Faculty:** 1,058 full-time faculty, 89% hold PhDs, 37% are are members of minority groups, 19% are women.

ACADEMICS

Degrees: associate, bachelor's, certificate, master's, post-bachelor's certificate, post-master's certificate. **Classes:** Most classes have 10-19 students. Most lab/discussion sessions have 20-29 students. **Majors with Highest Enrollment:** Information Science/Studies; Psychology; Architecture. **Special Study Options:** Accelerated program, cooperative education program, distance learning, double major, dual enrollment, English as a Second Language (ESL), honors program, independent study, internships, liberal arts/career combination, student-designed major, study abroad, teacher certification program, SU offers many undergraduate research opportunities, pre-professional programs, and minors. **Honors programs:** The University Honors program combines the benefits of a small intimate community with the advantages of diversity and opportunity found only at larger institutions. Students enjoy provocative coursework in small classes taught by some of the University's most able and experienced faculty, as well as some of the nation's leading research scholars. In the Honors Thesis Project upper class students are closely guided by faculty to pursue intensive research on a topic of their choice. **Combined degree programs:** BA/JD, BA/MEng. **Disability Services:** Special programs offered to physically disabled students include note-taking services, reader services, tape recorders, tutors. **Career services:** Alumni network, alumni services, career/job search classes, career assessment, internships, regional alumni. Career services highlights include Syracuse University's South Side Entrepreneurial Connect Project (SSECP), launched in June of 2004, which works with the challenged inner city neighborhoods on the south side of Syracuse to create sustainable small business ventures. The goal of the SSECP is to foster the development of an entrepreneurial community within the south side through increasing the number of new start ups and developing a supportive infrastructure that ensures the long-term sustainability of existing small businesses within the community. In this comprehensive initiative, students are intimately involved in all facets of SSECP management and implementation, including: consultation teams with faculty and students from other disciplines that work closely with entrepreneurs in creating and growing ventures; management of a microcredit fund for inner city entrepreneurs; organizing community functions; legal counseling for entrepreneurs from Law School students; youth mentoring and empowerment programs; assistance in coordinating our South Side Entrepreneurs Association; resource mapping and connecting; involvement in the cross-marketing program; and research projects that provide insights that enable the sustainability of the inner city entrepreneurial development model that guides our efforts. Our students intern and work in the SSIC, and it has become the nerve center for a wide range of entrepreneurial initiatives and activities involving the inner city of Syracuse.

FACILITIES

Housing: Coed dorms, special housing for disabled students, special housing for international students, fraternity/sorority housing, apartments for married students, apartments for single students, Wellness Housing, Theme Housing, International living center, single-sex floors and wings of residence halls, numerous learning communities, and interest housing available. 92% of campus accessible to physically disabled. **Special Academic Facilities/Equipment:** SUArt Galleries; The Warehouse Gallery; digital media convergence center; Syracuse Center of Excellence in Environmental and Energy Systems; Fidelity MOTUS 622i flight simulator for aerospace engineering; Ballentine Investment Institute; community darkrooms; Syracuse Stage professional equity theater; Bernice M. Wright Child Development Laboratory School; Belfer Audio Laboratory and Archive; Gebbie Speech, Language, and Hearing Clinic; Life Sciences Complex; SU Library Special Collections Research Center; UPSTATE: A Center for Design, Research and Real Estate at the SU School of Architecture; Center on Human Policy; Center for Emerging Network Technologies; JPMorgan Chase Technology Center. **Computers:** 75% of classrooms, 100% of dorms, 100% of libraries, 100% of dining areas, 100% of student union, 75% of common outdoor areas have wireless network access. Students can register for classes online. Administrative functions (other than registration) can be performed online.

CAMPUS LIFE

Environment: Metropolis. **Activities:** Choral groups, concert band, dance, drama/theater, jazz band, literary magazine, marching band, music ensembles, musical theater, pep band, radio station, student government, student newspaper, student-run film society, symphony orchestra, television station, yearbook, Campus Ministries, International Student Organization. 347 registered organizations, 43 honor societies, 30 religious organizations. 29 fraternities, 19 sororities. **Athletics (Intercollegiate):** *Men:* basketball, cheerleading, crew/rowing, cross-country, diving, football, lacrosse, soccer, swimming, track/field (outdoor). *Women:* basketball, cheerleading, crew/rowing, cross-country, diving, field hockey, ice hockey, lacrosse, soccer, softball, swimming, tennis, track/field (outdoor), volleyball. **On-Campus Highlights:** Schine Student Center, Bird Library Café, Hendricks Chapel, Whitman School, Archbold Athletic Complex. **Environmental Initiatives:** SU has established a target date of 2040 for carbon neutrality, at least a decade earlier than most ACUPCC signatories. At present, we are ahead of schedule for attaining that target. SU has created a comprehensive set of services which encourage students, faculty and staff to live on or near campus, and to either walk to campus or use public transportation. SU has taken operating control of the University's steam and chilled water plant from an under-performing contractor, and substantially redesigned plant operations to improve operating efficiency significantly (empirical measurement is currently underway). Through partnership arrangements, heating and cooling efficiency improvements accrue not only to SU, but also to SUNY-ESF, SUNY Upstate Medical University, and two local hospitals.

ADMISSIONS

Freshman Academic Profile: Average high school GPA 3.6. 37% in top 10% of high school class, 71% in top 25% of high school class, 93% in top 50% of high school class. 67% from public high schools. SAT Math middle 50% range 550-660. SAT Critical Reading middle 50% range 520-620. SAT Writing middle 50% range 530-630. ACT middle 50% range 24-29. Minimum internet-based TOEFL 85. Minimum paper TOEFL 550. **Basis for Candidate Selection:** *Very important factors considered include:* Class rank, application essay, academic GPA, recommendation(s), rigor of secondary school record, standardized test scores, character/personal qualities, extracurricular activities, interview, level of applicant's interest, talent/ability. *Important factors considered include:* alumni/ae relation, first generation, geographical residence, state residency, volunteer work, work experience. *Other factors considered include:* racial/ethnic status. **Freshman Admission Requirements:** High school diploma is required and GED is accepted. *Academic units required:* 4 English, 4 mathematics, 4 science, (4 science labs), 3 foreign language, 4 social studies. **Freshman Admission Statistics:** 26,790 applied, 53% admitted, 24% enrolled. **Transfer Admission Requirements:** college transcript(s), essay or personal statement, statement of good standing from prior institution(s). Lowest grade transferable C. **General Admission Information:** Application Fee $70. Early decision application deadline 11/1. Regular application deadline 1/1. Notification on a rolling basis, beginning on or about 3/15. Nonfall registration accepted. Admission may be deferred for a maximum of 1 year. Credit and/or placement offered for CEEB Advanced Placement tests.

COSTS AND FINANCIAL AID

Annual tuition $40,380. Room and board $14,460. Required fees $1,506. Average book expense $1,376. **Required Forms and Deadlines:** FAFSA, CSS/Financial Aid PROFILE, Noncustodial PROFILE. **Notification of Awards:** Applicants will be notified of awards on or about 3/21. **Types of Aid:** *Need-based scholarships/grants:* Federal Pell, SEOG, state scholarships/grants, private scholarships, the school's own gift aid. *Loans:* Direct Subsidized Stafford, Direct Unsubsidized Stafford, Direct PLUS, Federal Perkins. *Student Employment:* Federal Work-Study Program available. Institutional employment available. Off-campus job opportunities are good. **Financial Aid Statistics:** 92% freshmen, 91% undergrads receive need-based scholarship or grant aid. 9% freshmen, 6% undergrads receive non-need-based scholarship or grant aid. 91% freshmen, 92% undergrads receive need-based self-help aid. 2% freshmen, 2% undergrads receive athletic scholarships. 73% freshmen, 74% undergrads receive any aid. 66% undergrads borrow to pay for school. Average cumulative indebtedness $27,477. **Criteria for awarding institutional aid:** *Non-need-based:* academics, art, athletics, music/drama, state/district residency.

TALLADEGA COLLEGE

627 West Battle Street, Talladega, AL 35160
Phone: 205-761-6235 · **Financial Aid Phone:** 256-761-6341
E-mail: admissions@talladega.edu
Fax: 205-362-0274 · **Website:** www.talladega.edu • **ACT Code:** 26

This private school, affiliated with the United Church of Christ Church, was founded in 1867. It has a 50-acre campus.

RATINGS

| Admissions Selectivity Rating: 76 | Fire Safety Rating: 86 |

STUDENTS AND FACULTY

Enrollment: 601. **Student Body:** 58% female, 42% male, 48% out-of-state, 0% international. Asian 0%, African American 95%, Caucasian 0%, Hispanic 4%, Native American <1%.
Retention and Graduation: 43% freshmen return for sophomore year. 27% freshmen graduate within 4 years. 41% freshmen graduate within 6 years. 25% grads go on to further study within 1 year. 25% grads pursue arts and sciences degrees. 25% grads pursue law degrees. 25% grads pursue business degrees. 25% grads pursue medical degrees. **Faculty:** 29 full-time faculty, 62% hold PhDs, 45% are members of minority groups, 66% are women. 0% of classes are taught by teaching assistants.

ACADEMICS

Degrees: bachelor's. **Classes:** Most classes have fewer than 10 students. Most lab/discussion sessions have fewer than 10 students. **Majors with Highest**

Enrollment: Biology/Biological Sciences; Psychology; Business/Commerce. **Special Study Options:** double major, dual enrollment, independent study, internships, teacher certification program. **Disability Services:** Special programs offered to physically disabled students include note-taking services, tape recorders, tutors. **Career services:** Alumni network, alumni services, career assessment, internships.

FACILITIES

Housing: men's dorms, women's dorms. 100% of campus accessible to physically disabled. **Special Academic Facilities/Equipment:** Savery Library, Home of the famous Amistad Murals, historic Swayne Hall, which is listed on the National Register; DeForest Chapel, which has the stained glass windows by famous artist, David Driskell; Goodnow Art Building **Computers:** 100% of libraries, 50% of common outdoor areas have wireless network access. Administrative functions (other than registration) can be performed online.

CAMPUS LIFE

Environment: Rural. **Activities:** Choral groups, concert band, dance, drama/theater, jazz band, student government, student newspaper, yearbook. 40 registered organizations, 8 honor societies, 1 religous organization. 4 fraternities, 4 sororities. **Athletics (Intercollegiate):** *Men:* baseball, basketball, golf. *Women:* basketball, cheerleading, volleyball. **On-Campus Highlights:** Savery Library, DeForest Chapel, Swayne Hall, Callanan Hall, Fanning Hall.

ADMISSIONS

Freshman Academic Profile: Average high school GPA 2.71. 90% from public high schools. SAT Math middle 50% range 340-410. SAT Critical Reading middle 50% range 320-460. ACT middle 50% range 16-19. Minimum paper TOEFL 500. **Basis for Candidate Selection:** *Very important factors considered include:* application essay, recommendation(s), rigor of secondary school record, standardized test scores, character/personal qualities, extracurricular activities, talent/ability, volunteer work, work experience. *Important factors considered include:* Class rank. *Other factors considered include:* interview. **Freshman Admission Requirements:** High school diploma is required and GED is accepted. *Academic units required:* 4 English, 2 mathematics, 2 science, (0 science labs), 0 foreign language, 3 social studies, 0 history, 2 Physical Education or Health. **Freshman Admission Statistics:** 2,000 applied, 40% admitted, 38% enrolled. **Transfer Admission Requirements:** High school transcript, college transcript(s), essay or personal statement, standardized test scores, statement of good standing from prior institution(s). Minimum college GPA of 2.0 required. Lowest grade transferable C. **General Admission Information:** Application Fee $25. Nonfall registration accepted. Admission may be deferred for a maximum of 2 years. Credit and/or placement offered for CEEB Advanced Placement tests.

COSTS AND FINANCIAL AID

Annual tuition $6,720. Room and board $4,290. Required fees $608. Average book expense $1,000. **Required Forms and Deadlines:** FAFSA, Institution's own financial aid form, CSS/Financial Aid PROFILE, State aid form. **Notification of Awards:** Applicants will be notified of awards on or about 4/1. **Types of Aid:** *Need-based scholarships/grants:* Federal Pell, SEOG, state scholarships/grants, private scholarships, the school's own gift aid, United Negro College Fund. *Loans:* Subsidized Stafford, Unsubsidized Stafford, PLUS, Federal Perkins. *Student Employment:* Highest amount earned per year from on-campus jobs $1,200. Off-campus job opportunities are good. **Financial Aid Statistics:** 45% freshmen, 26% undergrads receive need-based scholarship or grant aid. 45% freshmen, 26% undergrads receive non-need-based scholarship or grant aid. 0% freshmen, 0% undergrads receive need-based self-help aid. 0% freshmen, 0% undergrads receive athletic scholarships. 90% freshmen, 90% undergrads receive any aid. 80% undergrads borrow to pay for school. Average cumulative indebtedness $5,000. **Criteria for awarding institutional aid:** *Non-need-based:* academics, alumni affiliation, art, athletics, music/drama.

TARLETON STATE UNIVERSITY

PO Box T-0030, Stephenville, TX 76402
Phone: 254-968-9125 · **Financial Aid Phone:** 254-968-9070
E-mail: uadm@tarleton.edu · **CEEB Code:** 6817
Fax: 254-968-9951 • **ACT Code:** 4204

This public school was founded in 1899. It has a 125-acre campus.

RATINGS

| Admissions Selectivity Rating: 72 | Fire Safety Rating: 90 |

STUDENTS AND FACULTY

Enrollment: 8,856. **Student Body:** 59% female, 41% male, 2% out-of-state, 1% international (22 countries represented). Asian 1%, African American 6%,

Caucasian 76%, Hispanic 14%, Native American 1%
Retention and Graduation: 67% freshmen return for sophomore year. 18% freshmen graduate within 4 years. 40% freshmen graduate within 6 years. **Faculty:** 311 full-time faculty, 49% are are members of minority groups, 9% are women. 2% of classes are taught by teaching assistants.

ACADEMICS

Degrees: associate, bachelor's, master's. **Classes:** Most classes have 20-29 students. Most lab/discussion sessions have 10-19 students. **Majors with Highest Enrollment:** Multi-/Interdisciplinary Studies; Kinesiology and Exercise Science; Psychology. **Special Study Options:** Accelerated program, distance learning, double major, dual enrollment, honors program, internships, study abroad, teacher certification program, Undergrads may take grad level classes. **Honors programs:** Offer honors classes in core curriculum subjects, including English, history, political science, chemistry, biology, geology, and speech. Courses offer intellectually challenging material, innovative approaches to the subject, increased opportunities for honing critical thinking and writing skills, and the opportunity to interact closely with similarly motivated students and with outstanding faculty. **Disability Services:** Special programs offered to physically disabled students include note-taking services, reader services, tutors. **Career services:** career/job search classes, career assessment, internships. Career services highlights include the Education Department and Student Teaching opportunities.

FACILITIES

Housing: Coed dorms, special housing for disabled students, men's dorms, special housing for international students, women's dorms, fraternity/sorority housing, apartments for married students, cooperative housing, apartments for single students, 20. **Special Academic Facilities/Equipment:** Planetarium in Science Bldg., W.K. Gordon Center for Industrial History of Texas. **Computers:** 100% of classrooms, 100% of dorms, 100% of libraries, 100% of student union, have wireless network access. Students can register for classes online. Administrative functions (other than registration) can be performed online.

CAMPUS LIFE

Environment: Village. **Activities:** Choral groups, concert band, dance, drama/theater, jazz band, literary magazine, marching band, music ensembles, musical theater, opera, pep band, radio station, student government, student newspaper, student-run film society, symphony orchestra, television station, yearbook, Campus Ministries, International Student Organization. 117 registered organizations, 13 honor societies, 13 religious organizations. 7 fraternities, 8 sororities. **Athletics (Intercollegiate):** *Men:* baseball, basketball, cheerleading, cross-country, football, rodeo, track/field (outdoor). *Women:* basketball, cheerleading, cross-country, golf, rodeo, softball, tennis, track/field (outdoor), volleyball. **On-Campus Highlights:** Barry B. Thompson Student Center, New Recreational Sports Facility, Dick Smith Library, Wisdom Gym, Science Bldg with Planetarium. **Environmental Initiatives:** 15% Electric from wind; In compliance with SB12.

ADMISSIONS

Freshman Academic Profile: 9% in top 10% of high school class, 23% in top 25% of high school class, 76% in top 50% of high school class. 97% from public high schools. SAT Math middle 50% range 450-550. SAT Critical Reading middle 50% range 430-530. SAT Writing middle 50% range 410-500. ACT middle 50% range 19-23. Minimum internet-based TOEFL 190. Minimum paper TOEFL 520. **Basis for Candidate Selection:** *Very important factors considered include:* Class rank, rigor of secondary school record, standardized test scores. *Important factors considered include:* academic GPA. **Freshman Admission Requirements:** High school diploma is required and GED is accepted. *Academic units required:* 4 English, 3 mathematics, 2 science, (2 science labs), 2 social studies, 1 history, 2 academic electives. **Freshman Admission Statistics:** 4,643 applied, 76% admitted, 49% enrolled. **Transfer Admission Requirements:** college transcript(s), Minimum college GPA of 2.0 required. Lowest grade transferable D. **General Admission Information:** Application Fee $25. Regular application deadline 8/1. Nonfall registration accepted. Credit offered for CEEB Advanced Placement tests.

COSTS AND FINANCIAL AID

Annual in-state tuition $3,696. Annual out-of-state tuition $12,120. Room and board $7,633. Required fees $1,826. Average book expense $1,174. **Required Forms and Deadlines:** FAFSA. **Notification of Awards:** Applicants will be notified of awards on a rolling basis beginning 2/1. **Types of Aid:** *Need-based scholarships/grants:* Federal Pell, SEOG, state scholarships/grants, private scholarships, the school's own gift aid. *Loans:* Subsidized Stafford, Unsubsidized Stafford, PLUS, state loans, college/university loans from institutional funds. **Financial Aid Statistics:** 64% freshmen, 64% undergrads receive need-based scholarship or grant aid. 26% freshmen, 21% undergrads receive non-need-based scholarship or grant aid. 55% freshmen, 56% undergrads receive need-based self-help aid. 0% freshmen, 0% undergrads receive athletic scholarships. 57% freshmen, 37% undergrads receive any aid. 56% undergrads borrow to pay for school. Average cumulative indebtedness $18,500. **Criteria for awarding institutional aid:** *Non-need-based:* academics, alumni affiliation, art, athletics, leadership, music/drama.

TAYLOR UNIVERSITY

236 West Reade Avenue, Upland, IN 46989-1001
Phone: 765-998-5134 • **Financial Aid Phone:** 765-998-5358
E-mail: admissions@tayloru.edu • **CEEB Code:** 1802
Fax: 765-998-4925 • **Website:** www.taylor.edu • **ACT Code:** 1248

This private school was founded in 1846. It has a 952-acre campus.

RATINGS

Admissions Selectivity Rating: 86   **Fire Safety Rating:** 91

STUDENTS AND FACULTY

Enrollment: 1,856. **Student Body:** 55% female, 45% male, 61% out-of-state, 5% international (30 countries represented). Asian 2%, African American 3%, Caucasian 86%, Hispanic 3%, Native American <1%
Retention and Graduation: 88% freshmen return for sophomore year. 67% freshmen graduate within 4 years. 74% freshmen graduate within 6 years. 19% grads go on to further study within 1 year. 4% grads pursue arts and sciences degrees. 1% grads pursue law degrees. 2% grads pursue business degrees. 1% grads pursue medical degrees. **Faculty:** 127 full-time faculty, 89% hold PhDs, 25% are are members of minority groups, 6% are women. 0% of classes are taught by teaching assistants.

ACADEMICS

Degrees: associate, bachelor's, certificate, diploma, master's. **Classes:** Most classes have 10-19 students. Most lab/discussion sessions have 10-19 students. **Majors with Highest Enrollment:** Biology/Biological Sciences; Elementary Education and Teaching; Kinesiology and Exercise Science. **Special Study Options:** cooperative education program, distance learning, double major, dual enrollment, exchange student program (domestic), honors program, independent study, internships, student-designed major, study abroad, teacher certification program. **Honors programs:** Honors Program emphasizes to a greater extent than the general curriculum, integration of faith and learning, ideas and values in content and discussion and student initiative in format. Also offer Freshmen Irish Studies Program in Ireland. **Combined degree programs:** BA/MA, BA and MA in Environmental Science. **Disability Services:** Special programs offered to physically disabled students include note-taking services, reader services, tape recorders, tutors. **Career services:** Alumni network, alumni services, career assessment, internships, regional alumni.

FACILITIES

Housing: men's dorms, women's dorms, apartments for married students, apartments for single students, some off-campus apartments available to upperclassmen with special permission. 85% of campus accessible to physically disabled. **Special Academic Facilities/Equipment:** Compton Art Gallery, Edwin W. Brown Collection/CS Lewis and Friends. **Computers:** 100% of classrooms, 100% of dorms, 100% of libraries, 100% of dining areas, 100% of student union, 50% of common outdoor areas have wireless network access. Students can register for classes online. Administrative functions (other than registration) can be performed online.

CAMPUS LIFE

Environment: Rural. **Activities:** Choral groups, concert band, drama/theater, jazz band, literary magazine, music ensembles, musical theater, opera, pep band, radio station, student government, student newspaper, student-run film society, symphony orchestra, television station, yearbook, Campus Ministries, International Student Organization, Model UN. 87 registered organizations, 7 honor societies, 23 religious organizations. **Athletics (Intercollegiate):** *Men:* baseball, basketball, cross-country, football, golf, soccer, tennis, track/field (outdoor), track/field (indoor). *Women:* basketball, cross-country, soccer, softball, tennis, track/field (outdoor), track/field (indoor), volleyball. **On-Campus Highlights:** The Jumping Bean (Student coffee shop), Kesler Student Activities Center, Modelle Metcalf Visual Arts Center, Rediger Chapel and Auditorium, Mitchell Theater. **Environmental Initiatives:** The 127,000 sq. ft. Euler Science Complex, scheduled to be completed in the summer of 2012, is designed to LEED specifications and includes innovative sustainability features. This includes two 50kW wind turbines and a 10kW photovoltaic system. Students are engaged in sustainability through various initiatives including the national RecycleMania competition and Campus Conservation Nationals (residence hall electricity and water conservation competition). Taylor hired its first Coordinator of Sustainability and Stewardship in 2010 to help lead the campus on the path to environmental, social, and economic sustainability.

ADMISSIONS

Freshman Academic Profile: Average high school GPA 3.65. 34% in top 10% of high school class, 66% in top 25% of high school class, 90% in top 50% of high school class. 80% from public high schools. SAT Math middle 50% range 500-630. SAT Critical Reading middle 50% range 490-630. SAT Writing middle 50% range 490-610. ACT middle 50% range 24-30. Minimum paper TOEFL 550. **Basis for Candidate Selection:** *Very important factors considered in-*

clude: application essay, academic GPA, recommendation(s), rigor of secondary school record, standardized test scores, character/personal qualities, religious affiliation/commitment. *Important factors considered include:* Class rank, extracurricular activities, interview, volunteer work. *Other factors considered include:* alumni/ae relation, first generation, geographical residence, racial/ethnic status, state residency, talent/ability, work experience. **Freshman Admission Requirements:** High school diploma is required and GED is accepted. *Academic units required:* 4 English, 3 mathematics, 3 science, (3 science labs), 2 social studies, 3 academic electives. **Freshman Admission Statistics:** 1,496 applied, 88% admitted, 33% enrolled. **Transfer Admission Requirements:** High school transcript, college transcript(s), essay or personal statement, standardized test scores, statement of good standing from prior institution(s). Minimum college GPA of 2.5 required. Lowest grade transferable C+. **General Admission Information:** Application Fee $25. Regular application deadline 8/1. Notification on a rolling basis, beginning on or about 10/1. Nonfall registration accepted. Admission may be deferred for a maximum of 2 years. Credit and/or placement offered for CEEB Advanced Placement tests.

COSTS AND FINANCIAL AID

Annual tuition $29,298. Room and board $8,283. Required fees $240. Average book expense $3,000. **Required Forms and Deadlines:** FAFSA. **Notification of Awards:** Applicants will be notified of awards on a rolling basis beginning 3/1. **Types of Aid:** *Need-based scholarships/grants:* Federal Pell, SEOG, state scholarships/grants, private scholarships, the school's own gift aid. *Loans:* Direct Subsidized Stafford, Direct Unsubsidized Stafford, Direct PLUS, Federal Perkins, college/university loans from institutional funds. *Student Employment:* Federal Work-Study Program available. Institutional employment available. Highest amount earned per year from on-campus jobs $3,500. Off-campus job opportunities are poor. **Financial Aid Statistics:** 100% freshmen, 99% undergrads receive need-based scholarship or grant aid. 18% freshmen, 15% undergrads receive non-need-based scholarship or grant aid. 82% freshmen, 84% undergrads receive need-based self-help aid. 5% freshmen, 6% undergrads receive athletic scholarships. 99% freshmen, 96% undergrads receive any aid. 63% undergrads borrow to pay for school. Average cumulative indebtedness $23,260. **Criteria for awarding institutional aid:** *Non-need-based:* academics, alumni affiliation, art, athletics, leadership, minority status, music/drama, religious affiliation, state/district residency.

TEMPLE UNIVERSITY

Best 380

1801 North Broad Street (041-09), Philadelphia, PA 19122-6096
Phone: 215-204-7200 · **Financial Aid Phone:** 215-204-2244
E-mail: TUADM@TEMPLE.EDU · **CEEB Code:** 2906
Fax: 215-204-5694 · **Website:** www.temple.edu · **ACT Code:** 3724

This public school was founded in 1888. It has a 330-acre campus.

RATINGS

Admissions Selectivity Rating: 86   **Fire Safety Rating:** 85

STUDENTS AND FACULTY

Enrollment: 27,748. **Student Body:** 51% female, 49% male, 22% out-of-state, 5% international (107 countries represented). Asian 10%, African American 13%, Caucasian 58%, Hispanic 6%, Native American <1%
Retention and Graduation: 89% freshmen return for sophomore year. 41% freshmen graduate within 4 years. **Faculty:** 1,407 full-time faculty, 41% are are members of minority groups, 17% are women.

ACADEMICS

Degrees: associate, bachelor's, certificate, diploma, doctoral, master's, post-bachelor's certificate, post-master's certificate, terminal associate, transfer associate. **Classes:** Most classes have 20-29 students. Most lab/discussion sessions have 20-29 students. **Majors with Highest Enrollment:** Psychology; Accounting; Marketing/Marketing Management. **Special Study Options:** cooperative education program, cross-registration, distance learning, double major, dual enrollment, English as a Second Language (ESL), exchange student program (domestic), honors program, independent study, internships, liberal arts/career combination, study abroad, teacher certification program, Programs are offered in a number of foreign countries: Japan, Italy, Costa Rica, France,Germany, Ghana, India, Spain, Turkey, United Kingdom and Brazil. **Honors programs:** 1) Honors Certificate Program 2) Honors Scholars Program **Combined degree programs:** BA/MA, M.B.A./M.A and M.B.A./M.S. and B.F.A with Teach-

ing Certification. **Disability Services:** Special programs offered to physically disabled students include note-taking services, reader services, tape recorders, tutors. **Career services:** Alumni network, alumni services, career/job search classes, career assessment, internships, regional alumni.

FACILITIES

Housing: Coed dorms, special housing for disabled students, apartments for single students, Living/Learning Centers are available. 100% of campus accessible to physically disabled. **Special Academic Facilities/Equipment:** Blockson Collection, Urban Archieves, observatory. **Computers:** 40% of classrooms, 30% of dorms, 80% of libraries, 90% of dining areas, 100% of student union, 40% of common outdoor areas have wireless network access. Students can register for classes online. Administrative functions (other than registration) can be performed online.

CAMPUS LIFE

Environment: Metropolis. **Activities:** Choral groups, concert band, dance, drama/theater, jazz band, literary magazine, marching band, music ensembles, musical theater, opera, pep band, radio station, student government, student newspaper, student-run film society, symphony orchestra, television station, yearbook, Campus Ministries, International Student Organization. 232 registered organizations, 12 honor societies, 24 religious organizations. 11 fraternities, 9 sororities. **Athletics (Intercollegiate):** *Men:* baseball, basketball, cheerleading, crew/rowing, cross-country, football, golf, gymnastics, soccer, table tennis, tennis, track/field (outdoor), track/field (indoor). *Women:* basketball, cheerleading, crew/rowing, cross-country, fencing, field hockey, gymnastics, lacrosse, soccer, softball, table tennis, tennis, track/field (outdoor), track/field (indoor), volleyball. **On-Campus Highlights:** The Tech Center, Howard Gittis Student Center, Liacouras Center (athletic/convocation center), The Shops at Liacouras Walk, Bell Tower, Independence Blue Cross Student Recreation Center, Alumni Circle, Rock Hall, Student Pavilion, Campus mall. **Environmental Initiatives:** President Hart signed the American College and University Presidents Climate Commitment in April 2008. The Office of Sustainability was established July 2008. Completion of Climate Action Plan in May 2010.

ADMISSIONS

Freshman Academic Profile: Average high school GPA 3.47. 20.5% in top 10% of high school class, 51% in top 25% of high school class, 87.4% in top 50% of high school class. SAT Math middle 50% range 510-620. SAT Critical Reading middle 50% range 500-610. SAT Writing middle 50% range -603. ACT middle 50% range 22-28. Minimum internet-based TOEFL 79. **Basis for Candidate Selection:** *Very important factors considered include:* academic GPA, rigor of secondary school record. *Important factors considered include:* Class rank, standardized test scores. *Other factors considered include:* application essay, recommendation(s), alumni/ae relation, character/personal qualities, extracurricular activities, talent/ability, volunteer work, work experience. **Freshman Admission Requirements:** High school diploma is required and GED is accepted. *Academic units required:* 4 English, 3 mathematics, 2 science, (1 science labs), 2 foreign language, 2 social studies, 1 history, 1 academic elective. **Freshman Admission Statistics:** 26,496 applied, 62% admitted, 27% enrolled. **Transfer Admission Requirements:** High school transcript, college transcript(s), essay or personal statement, Minimum college GPA of 2.50 required. Lowest grade transferable C. **General Admission Information:** Application Fee $50. Regular application deadline 3/1. Notification on a rolling basis, beginning on or about 10/15. Nonfall registration accepted. Admission may be deferred for a maximum of 1 year. Credit and/or placement offered for CEEB Advanced Placement tests.

COSTS AND FINANCIAL AID

Annual in-state tuition $14,406. Annual out-of-state tuition $24,432. Room and board $10,738. Required fees $690. Average book expense $1,000. **Required Forms and Deadlines:** FAFSA. **Notification of Awards:** Applicants will be notified of awards on a rolling basis beginning 2/15. **Types of Aid:** *Need-based scholarships/grants:* Federal Pell, SEOG, state scholarships/grants, private scholarships, the school's own gift aid, Federal Nursing Scholarships. *Loans:* Subsidized Stafford, Unsubsidized Stafford, PLUS, Federal Perkins, Federal Nursing, state loans, college/university loans from institutional funds. *Student Employment:* Federal Work-Study Program available. Institutional employment available. Off-campus job opportunities are excellent. **Financial Aid Statistics:** 85% freshmen, 85% undergrads receive need-based scholarship or grant aid. 53% freshmen, 37% undergrads receive non-need-based scholarship or grant aid. 78% freshmen, 85% undergrads receive need-based self-help aid. 2% freshmen, 2% undergrads receive athletic scholarships. 83% undergrads receive any aid. 77% undergrads borrow to pay for school. Average cumulative indebtedness $26,359. **Criteria for awarding institutional aid:** *Non-need-based:* academics, art, athletics, music/drama.

See page 1156.

TENNESSEE STATE UNIVERSITY

3500 John Merritt Boulevard, Nashville, 37209-1561
Phone: 615-963-3101
E-mail: jcade@tnstate.edu
Fax: 615-963-5108 · **Website:** www.tnstate.edu

This is a public school.

RATINGS

Admissions Selectivity Rating: 87   Fire Safety Rating: 60*

STUDENTS AND FACULTY

Enrollment: 7,000. **Student Body:** 63% female, 37% male, 49% out-of-state, 1% international. Asian 1%, African American 83%, Caucasian 15%, Hispanic 1%, Native American <1%. **Retention and Graduation:** 77% freshmen return for sophomore year. **Faculty:** 383 full-time faculty, 74% hold PhDs, 42% are are members of minority groups, 37% are women.

ACADEMICS

Degrees: associate, bachelor's, master's. **Classes:** Most classes have fewer than 10 students. Most lab/discussion sessions have 10-19 students. **Special Study Options:** cooperative education program, cross-registration, double major, exchange student program (domestic), honors program, independent study, internships, liberal arts/career combination, teacher certification program, On-line Degree (courses offered via computer approved by Tennessee Board of Regents).

FACILITIES

Housing: Coed dorms, men's dorms, women's dorms, apartments for single students.

CAMPUS LIFE

Activities: Choral groups, drama/theater, jazz band, marching band, music ensembles, radio station, student government, student newspaper, yearbook.

ADMISSIONS

Freshman Academic Profile: Average high school GPA 2.99. 90% from public high schools. SAT Math middle 50% range 430-510. SAT Critical Reading middle 50% range 430-510. ACT middle 50% range 18-21. Minimum paper TOEFL 500. **Basis for Candidate Selection:** *Very important factors considered include:* standardized test scores, state residency. *Important factors considered include:* Class rank, recommendation(s), rigor of secondary school record, geographical residence. *Other factors considered include:* alumni/ae relation, character/personal qualities, extracurricular activities, talent/ability. **Freshman Admission Requirements:** High school diploma is required and GED is accepted. *Academic units required:* 4 English, 3 mathematics, 2 science, (1 science labs), 2 foreign language, 1 social studies, 1 history, 1 academic elective. **Freshman Admission Statistics:** 6,344 applied, 35% admitted, 59% enrolled. **Transfer Admission Requirements:** college transcript(s), Minimum college GPA of 2.9 required. Lowest grade transferable C. **General Admission Information:** Application Fee $15. Regular application deadline 8/1. Credit and/or placement offered for CEEB Advanced Placement tests.

COSTS AND FINANCIAL AID

Annual in-state tuition $3,272. Annual out-of-state tuition $10,230. Room and board $3,060. Required fees $150. Average book expense $850. **Required Forms and Deadlines:** FAFSA, CSS/Financial Aid PROFILE, Noncustodial PROFILE. **Types of Aid:** *Need-based scholarships/grants:* Federal Pell, SEOG. *Loans:* Direct Subsidized Stafford, Direct Unsubsidized Stafford, Direct PLUS, Subsidized Stafford, Unsubsidized Stafford, PLUS, Federal Perkins. **Financial Aid Statistics:** 66% freshmen, 64% undergrads receive need-based scholarship or grant aid. 24% freshmen, 23% undergrads receive non-need-based scholarship or grant aid. 75% freshmen, 75% undergrads receive need-based self-help aid. 1% freshmen receive any aid.

TENNESSEE TECHNOLOGICAL UNIVERSITY

PO Box 5006, Cookeville, TN 38505
Phone: 931-372-3888 · **Financial Aid Phone:** 931-372-3073
E-mail: admissions@tntech.edu · **CEEB Code:** 1804
Fax: 931-372-6250 · **Website:** www.tntech.edu · **ACT Code:** 4012

This public school was founded in 1915. It has a 235-acre campus.

RATINGS

Admissions Selectivity Rating: 78   Fire Safety Rating: 72

STUDENTS AND FACULTY

Enrollment: 9,647. **Student Body:** 45% female, 55% male, 3% out-of-state, 6% international. Asian 1%, African American 4%, Caucasian 84%, Hispanic 2%, Native American <1%. **Retention and Graduation:** 70% freshmen return for sophomore year. 20% freshmen graduate within 4 years. **Faculty:** 389 full-time faculty, 72% hold PhDs, 40% are are members of minority groups, 13% are women. 1% of classes are taught by teaching assistants.

ACADEMICS

Degrees: bachelor's, master's, post-master's certificate. **Classes:** Most classes have 20-29 students. Most lab/discussion sessions have 20-29 students. **Majors with Highest Enrollment:** Elementary Education and Teaching; Mechanical Engineering; Business/Commerce. **Special Study Options:** cooperative education program, distance learning, double major, dual enrollment, honors program, internships, study abroad, teacher certification program. **Disability Services:** Special programs offered to physically disabled students include note-taking services, reader services, tape recorders, tutors. **Career services:** Alumni network, alumni services, career/job search classes, internships, regional alumni.

FACILITIES

Housing: Coed dorms, special housing for disabled students, men's dorms, special housing for international students, women's dorms, apartments for married students, apartments for single students. 99% of campus accessible to physically disabled. **Special Academic Facilities/Equipment:** 300-acre farm lab, electric power center, water resources center, manufacturing center. **Computers:** Students can register for classes online. Administrative functions (other than registration) can be performed online.

CAMPUS LIFE

Environment: Rural. **Activities:** Choral groups, concert band, dance, drama/theater, jazz band, literary magazine, marching band, music ensembles, musical theater, opera, pep band, radio station, student government, student newspaper, symphony orchestra, television station, yearbook. 182 registered organizations, 26 honor societies, 16 religious organizations. 12 fraternities, 8 sororities. **Athletics (Intercollegiate):** *Men:* baseball, basketball, cheerleading, cross-country, football, golf, riflery, tennis. *Women:* basketball, cheerleading, cross-country, golf, riflery, soccer, softball, tennis, track/field (outdoor), track/field (indoor), volleyball. **On-Campus Highlights:** Recreation/ Fitness Center, Barnes and Noble Bookstore, Joan Derryberry Art Gallery, New Residence Halls, Bryan Fine Arts Music Auditorium.

ADMISSIONS

Freshman Academic Profile: Average high school GPA 3.37. 24% in top 10% of high school class, 50% in top 25% of high school class, 82% in top 50% of high school class. 80% from public high schools. SAT Math middle 50% range 490-640. SAT Critical Reading middle 50% range 480-600. ACT middle 50% range 20-26. Minimum paper TOEFL 500. **Basis for Candidate Selection:** *Very important factors considered include:* academic GPA, rigor of secondary school record, standardized test scores. *Other factors considered include:* application essay, recommendation(s), alumni/ae relation, character/personal qualities, extracurricular activities, interview. **Freshman Admission Requirements:** High school diploma is required and GED is accepted. *Academic units required:* 4 English, 3 mathematics, 2 science, (1 science labs), 2 foreign language, 1 social studies, 1 history, 1 visual / performing art. **Freshman Admission Statistics:** 4,553 applied, 94% admitted, 45% enrolled. **Transfer Admission Requirements:** college transcript(s), Minimum college GPA of 2.0 required. Lowest grade transferable D. **General Admission Information:** Application Fee $15. Regular application deadline 8/1. Nonfall registration accepted. Admission may be deferred for a maximum of 1 semester. Credit and/or placement offered for CEEB Advanced Placement tests.

COSTS AND FINANCIAL AID

Annual in-state tuition $5,004. Annual out-of-state tuition $18,000. Room and board $7,382. Required fees $1,034. Average book expense $1,500. **Required Forms and Deadlines:** FAFSA. **Notification of Awards:** Applicants will be notified of awards on a rolling basis beginning 3/15. **Types of Aid:** *Need-based scholarships/grants:* Federal Pell, SEOG, state scholarships/grants, private scholarships, the school's own gift aid, United Negro College Fund. *Loans:* Direct Subsidized Stafford, Direct Unsubsidized Stafford, PLUS, Federal Perkins, state loans, college/university loans from institutional funds. **Financial Aid Statistics:** 61% freshmen, 63% undergrads receive need-based scholarship or grant aid. 91% freshmen, 67% undergrads receive non-need-based scholarship or grant aid. 49% freshmen, 57% undergrads receive need-based self-help aid. 2% freshmen, 2% undergrads receive athletic scholarships. 91% freshmen, 89% undergrads receive any aid. 44% undergrads borrow to pay for school. Average cumulative indebtedness $9,107. **Criteria for awarding institutional aid:** *Non-need-based:* academics, alumni affiliation, art, athletics, leadership, minority status, music/drama.

TENNESSEE WESLEYAN COLLEGE

P.O. Box 40, Athens, TN 37371-0040
Phone: 423-745-7504 • **Financial Aid Phone:** 423-746-5209
E-mail: twilliams@twcnet.edu • **CEEB Code:**
Fax: 423-745-9335 • **Website:** www.twcnet.edu • **ACT Code:** 4014

This private school was founded in 1857. It has a 40-acre campus.

RATINGS

Admissions Selectivity Rating: 70   **Fire Safety Rating:** 78

STUDENTS AND FACULTY

Enrollment: 847. **Student Body:** 68% female, 32% male, 6% out-of-state, 3% international (13 countries represented). Asian 1%, African American 3%, Caucasian 75%, Hispanic 2%, Native American <1%
Retention and Graduation: 65% freshmen return for sophomore year. 16% freshmen graduate within 4 years. 32% freshmen graduate within 6 years. **Faculty:** 46 full-time faculty, 59% hold PhDs, 50% are are members of minority groups, 2% are women. 0% of classes are taught by teaching assistants.

ACADEMICS

Degrees: bachelor's. **Classes:** Most classes have 10-19 students. Most lab/discussion sessions have 10-19 students. **Majors with Highest Enrollment:** Education; Registered Nursing/Registered Nurse; Business/Commerce. **Special Study Options:** Accelerated program, double major, honors program, independent study, internships, student-designed major, study abroad, teacher certification program. **Disability Services:** Special programs offered to physically disabled students include note-taking services, tape recorders, tutors. **Career services:** alumni services, internships. Career services highlights include Cyber and Sounds Café.

FACILITIES

Housing: men's dorms, women's dorms, apartments for single studentsResidency Exemption Policy: All students are required to live on campus unless they: are married; have custody of a child; is a military veteran eligible for benefits under Public Law 358, GI Bill effective 6/66; is a resident in the home of parents or legal guardian who live within the commuting area; is an independent student as defined by financial aid criteria; established residency in the commuting area for 6 months immediately prior to making application to Tennessee Wesleyan College; or enrolled as a senior. 56% of campus accessible to physically disabled. **Special Academic Facilities/Equipment:** Old College—building is on historical register.

CAMPUS LIFE

Environment: Town. **Activities:** Choral groups, drama/theater, literary magazine, musical theater, student government, student newspaper, yearbook. 19 registered organizations, 5 honor societies, 3 religious organizations. 2 sororities. **Athletics (Intercollegiate):** *Men:* baseball, basketball, cheerleading, cross-country, golf, soccer, tennis. *Women:* basketball, cheerleading, cross-country, golf, soccer, softball, tennis, volleyball. **On-Campus Highlights:** Student Activity Center, Student Theatre, Athletic Events (intramural sports), J. Wesley Grill and Starbucks Coffee House, Merner-Pfeiffer Library (book signings, special ev, College Quad.

ADMISSIONS

Freshman Academic Profile: Average high school GPA 3.21. 96% from public high schools. ACT middle 50% range 18-24. Minimum paper TOEFL 500. **Basis for Candidate Selection:** *Very important factors considered include:* academic GPA, rigor of secondary school record, standardized test scores. *Important factors considered include:* application essay, recommendation(s), level of applicant's interest. *Other factors considered include:* Class rank, alumni/ae relation, extracurricular activities, first generation, interview. **Freshman Admission Requirements:** High school diploma is required and GED is accepted. **Freshman Admission Statistics:** 515 applied, 77% admitted, 42% enrolled. **Transfer Admission Requirements:** college transcript(s), Minimum college GPA of 2.0 required. Lowest grade transferable D. **General Admission Information:** Application Fee $25. Regular application deadline 8/20. Nonfall registration accepted. Admission may be deferred for a maximum of 1 semester. Credit and/or placement offered for CEEB Advanced Placement tests.

COSTS AND FINANCIAL AID

Annual tuition $14,000. Room and board $5,500. Required fees $550. Average book expense $1,000. **Required Forms and Deadlines:** FAFSA, Institution's own financial aid form. **Notification of Awards:** Applicants will be notified of awards on a rolling basis beginning 2/1. **Types of Aid:** *Need-based scholarships/grants:* Federal Pell, SEOG, state scholarships/grants, private scholarships, the school's own gift aid. *Loans:* Subsidized Stafford, Unsubsidized Stafford, PLUS, Federal Perkins, United Methodist. *Student Employment:* Highest amount earned per year from on-campus jobs $2,800. **Financial Aid Statistics:**

100% freshmen, 99% undergrads receive need-based scholarship or grant aid. 17% freshmen, 12% undergrads receive non-need-based scholarship or grant aid. 66% freshmen, 75% undergrads receive need-based self-help aid. 20% freshmen, 13% undergrads receive athletic scholarships. 99% freshmen, 99% undergrads receive any aid. 81% undergrads borrow to pay for school. **Criteria for awarding institutional aid:** *Non-need-based:* academics, alumni affiliation, art, athletics, job skills, leadership, minority status, music/drama, religious affiliation, state/district residency.

TEXAS A&M UNIVERSITY AT GALVESTON

Admissions Office, Galveston, TX 77553
Phone: 409-740-4414 • **Financial Aid Phone:** 409-740-4418
E-mail: seaaggie@tamug.edu • **CEEB Code:** 6835
Fax: 409-740-4731 • **Website:** www.tamug.edu • **ACT Code:** 6592

This public school was founded in 1963. It has a 150-acre campus.

RATINGS

Admissions Selectivity Rating: 82   **Fire Safety Rating:** 87

STUDENTS AND FACULTY

Enrollment: 2,045. **Student Body:** 37% female, 63% male, 13% out-of-state, 0% international (19 countries represented). Asian 2%, African American 2%, Caucasian 77%, Hispanic 15%, Native American <1%
Retention and Graduation: 24% freshmen graduate within 4 years. 53% freshmen graduate within 6 years. **Faculty:** 105 full-time faculty, 61% hold PhDs, 33% are are members of minority groups, 21% are women. 3% of classes are taught by teaching assistants.

ACADEMICS

Degrees: bachelor's, master's. **Classes:** Most classes have 10-19 students. **Majors with Highest Enrollment:** Naval Architecture and Marine Engineering; Marine Biology and Biological Oceanography. **Special Study Options:** Accelerated program, cooperative education program, double major, dual enrollment, independent study, internships, study abroad, teacher certification program, Merchant Marine Certification NROTC Naval Sciences. **Combined degree programs:** BS/License Option and BA/License Option. **Disability Services:** Special programs offered to physically disabled students include note-taking services, reader services, tutors. **Career services:** Alumni network, career assessment, internships, regional alumni. For career services highlights see: http://www.tamug.edu/career/.

FACILITIES

Housing: Coed dorms, special housing for disabled students, women's dorms, Privatized apartment housing available next to campus. 90% of campus accessible to physically disabled. **Special Academic Facilities/Equipment:** USTS Texas Clipper II, Radar School/Ship Bridge Simulator, Engineering Laboratory Building, Sea Camp, Center for Bioacoustics, Center for Marine Training and Safety/TEEX, Laboratory for Oceanographic and Environmental Research, Galveston Bay Information Center, Center for Ports and Waterways, Coastal Zone Laboratory, GulfCet, Marine Mammal Research Program, Naval Science, Texas State Maritime Academy, Texas Institute of Oceanography, Texas Marine Mammal Stranding Network, Sea Turtle/Fisheries Ecology Lab. **Computers:** Students can register for classes online. Administrative functions (other than registration) can be performed online.

CAMPUS LIFE

Environment: Town. **Activities:** Choral groups, dance, drama/theater, literary magazine, student government, student newspaper, television station, yearbook. 45 registered organizations, 16 honor societies, 4 religious organizations. **Athletics (Intercollegiate):** *Men:* crew/rowing, sailing. *Women:* crew/rowing, sailing. **On-Campus Highlights:** Mary Moody Northen Student Center, P.E. Facility, Small Boat Basin, Training Ship—Sirius, Jack K. Williams Library.

ADMISSIONS

Freshman Academic Profile: 9% in top 10% of high school class, 36% in top 25% of high school class, 78% in top 50% of high school class. 81% from public high schools. SAT Math middle 50% range 510-600. SAT Critical Reading middle 50% range 480-580. SAT Writing middle 50% range 470-560. ACT middle 50% range 22-26. Minimum internet-based TOEFL 80. Minimum paper TOEFL 550. **Basis for Candidate Selection:** *Very important factors considered include:* Class rank, rigor of secondary school record, standardized test scores. *Important factors considered include:* application essay, academic GPA, recommendation(s), character/personal qualities, extracurricular activities, talent/ability, volunteer work, work experience. *Other factors considered include:* alumni/ae relation, first generation, interview, level of applicant's interest. **Freshman Admission Requirements:** High school diploma is required and GED is accepted. *Academic units required:* 4 English, 3 mathematics, 3 science, (2 science labs), 3 social studies, 1 computer. **Freshman Admission Statistics:** 1,329 applied, 56% admitted, 61% enrolled. **Transfer Admission Requirements:** High school transcript, college transcript(s), essay or personal statement, Minimum college GPA of 2.5 required. Lowest grade transferable C. **General Admission Information:** Application Fee $45. Nonfall registration accepted. Admission may be deferred for a maximum of 1 Semester. Credit offered for CEEB Advanced Placement tests.

COSTS AND FINANCIAL AID
Average book expense $1,246. **Required Forms and Deadlines:** FAFSA. **Notification of Awards:** Applicants will be notified of awards on or about 3/15. **Types of Aid:** *Need-based scholarships/grants:* Federal Pell, SEOG, state scholarships/grants, private scholarships, the school's own gift aid. *Loans:* Direct Subsidized Stafford, Direct Unsubsidized Stafford, Direct PLUS, Subsidized Stafford, Unsubsidized Stafford, PLUS, Federal Perkins, college/university loans from institutional funds. *Student Employment:* Federal Work-Study Program available. Institutional employment available. Highest amount earned per year from on-campus jobs $2,100. Off-campus job opportunities are good. **Financial Aid Statistics:** 75% freshmen, 74% undergrads receive need-based scholarship or grant aid. 35% freshmen, 28% undergrads receive non-need-based scholarship or grant aid. 72% freshmen, 76% undergrads receive need-based self-help aid. 0% freshmen, 0% undergrads receive athletic scholarships. 45% freshmen, 56% undergrads receive any aid. 57% undergrads borrow to pay for school. Average cumulative indebtedness $25,739. **Criteria for awarding institutional aid:** *Non-need-based:* academics, leadership, state/district residency.

TEXAS A&M UNIVERSITY—COLLEGE STATION

Best 380

P.O. Box 30014, College Station, TX 77843-3014
Phone: 979-845-1060 • **Financial Aid Phone:** 979-845-3236
E-mail: admissions@tamu.edu • **CEEB Code:** 6003
Fax: 979-458-1808 • **Website:** www.tamu.edu • **ACT Code:** 4198

This public school was founded in 1876. It has a 5200-acre campus.

RATINGS
Admissions Selectivity Rating: 89   **Fire Safety Rating:** 94

STUDENTS AND FACULTY
Enrollment: 46,941. **Student Body:** 49% female, 51% male, 4% out-of-state, 1% international (81 countries represented). Asian 5%, African American 3%, Caucasian 66%, Hispanic 21%, Native American <1%
Retention and Graduation: 90% freshmen return for sophomore year. 50% freshmen graduate within 4 years. 79% freshmen graduate within 6 years. **Faculty:** 2,714 full-time faculty, 89% hold PhDs, 33% are are members of minority groups, 22% are women. 15.3% of classes are taught by teaching assistants.

ACADEMICS
Degrees: bachelor's, master's, post-bachelor's certificate. **Classes:** Most classes have 20-29 students. Most lab/discussion sessions have 20-29 students. **Majors with Highest Enrollment:** Psychology; Accounting; Biomedical Sciences. **Special Study Options:** Accelerated program, cooperative education program, cross-registration, distance learning, double major, dual enrollment, English as a Second Language (ESL), exchange student program (domestic), honors program, independent study, internships, study abroad, teacher certification program. **Disability Services:** Special programs offered to physically disabled students include note-taking services, reader services, tape recorders, tutors. **Career services:** Alumni network, alumni services, career/job search classes, internships.

FACILITIES
Housing: Coed dorms, special housing for disabled students, men's dorms, women's dorms, fraternity/sorority housing, apartments for married students, cooperative housing, apartments for single students, Theme Housing, Honors Dorm. 65% of campus accessible to physically disabled. **Special Academic Facilities/Equipment:** Bush Library/Museum; Jordan International Collection; Corps of Cadets Center/Museum; Forsyth Center Gallery; MSC Visual Arts Gallery; J.Wayne Stark University Center Galleries; Oran W. Nicks Low Speed Wind Tunnel; Astronomical Observatory; Ocean Drilling Program Building. **Computers:** 100% of classrooms, 10% of dorms, 100% of libraries, 100% of

dining areas, 100% of student union, have wireless network access. Students can register for classes online. Administrative functions (other than registration) can be performed online.

CAMPUS LIFE
Environment: City. **Activities:** Choral groups, concert band, dance, drama/theater, jazz band, literary magazine, marching band, music ensembles, musical theater, radio station, student government, student newspaper, student-run film society, symphony orchestra, television station, yearbook, Campus Ministries, International Student Organization. 725 registered organizations, 34 honor societies, 77 religious organizations. 33 fraternities, 23 sororities. **Athletics (Intercollegiate):** *Men:* baseball, basketball, cross-country, diving, football, golf, riflery, swimming, tennis, track/field (outdoor), track/field (indoor). *Women:* basketball, cross-country, diving, equestrian sports, golf, riflery, soccer, softball, swimming, tennis, track/field (outdoor), track/field (indoor), volleyball. **On-Campus Highlights:** Student Recreation Center, Kyle Field, Corps of Cadets, George Bush Presidential Library/Museum, Research Park. **Environmental Initiatives:** Energy Stewardship Program; Paper Recycling; Transportation Fuel.

ADMISSIONS
Freshman Academic Profile: 64.6% in top 10% of high school class, 90.09% in top 25% of high school class, 98.54% in top 50% of high school class. SAT Math middle 50% range 550-670. SAT Critical Reading middle 50% range 510-640. SAT Writing middle 50% range 480-610. ACT middle 50% range 23-30. Minimum internet-based TOEFL 80. Minimum paper TOEFL 550. **Basis for Candidate Selection:** *Very important factors considered include:* Class rank, academic GPA, rigor of secondary school record, standardized test scores, extracurricular activities, talent/ability. *Important factors considered include:* application essay, first generation, geographical residence, state residency, volunteer work, work experience. *Other factors considered include:* recommendation(s), character/personal qualities. **Freshman Admission Requirements:** High school diploma is required and GED is accepted. *Academic units required:* 4 English, 3 mathematics, 3 science, (2 science labs), 2 foreign language, 2 social studies, 1 history, 0 visual/performing arts, 0 computer science, 0 academic electives. **Freshman Admission Statistics:** 32,190 applied, 71% admitted, 47% enrolled. **Transfer Admission Requirements:** High school transcript, college transcript(s), Minimum college GPA of 2.5 required. Lowest grade transferable D. **General Admission Information:** Application Fee $60. Regular application deadline 1/15. Notification on a rolling basis, beginning on or about 4/1. Nonfall registration accepted. Credit offered for CEEB Advanced Placement tests.

COSTS AND FINANCIAL AID
Annual in-state tuition $5,971. Annual out-of-state tuition $23,147. Room and board $9,522. Required fees $3,209. Average book expense $1,000. **Required Forms and Deadlines:** FAFSA. **Notification of Awards:** Applicants will be notified of awards on a rolling basis beginning 4/1. **Types of Aid:** *Need-based scholarships/grants:* Federal Pell, SEOG, state scholarships/grants, private scholarships, the school's own gift aid. *Loans:* Subsidized Stafford, Unsubsidized Stafford, PLUS, Federal Perkins, state loans, college/university loans from institutional funds. *Student Employment:* Federal Work-Study Program available. Institutional employment available. Highest amount earned per year from on-campus jobs $2,639. Off-campus job opportunities are excellent. **Financial Aid Statistics:** 93% freshmen, 85% undergrads receive need-based scholarship or grant aid. 16% freshmen, 10% undergrads receive non-need-based scholarship or grant aid. 42% freshmen, 58% undergrads receive need-based self-help aid. 1% freshmen, 1% undergrads receive athletic scholarships. 75% freshmen, 71% undergrads receive any aid. 52% undergrads borrow to pay for school. Average cumulative indebtedness $20,086. **Criteria for awarding institutional aid:** *Non-need-based:* academics, alumni affiliation, art, athletics, job skills, leadership, music/drama, state/district residency.

TEXAS A&M UNIVERSITY—COMMERCE

P.O. Box 3011, Commerce, TX 75429
Phone: 903-886-5106
E-mail: admissions@tamu-commerce.edu
Fax: 903-886-5888 • **ACT Code:** 6188

This public school was founded in 1889. It has a 140-acre campus.

RATINGS
Admissions Selectivity Rating: 80   **Fire Safety Rating:** 60*

STUDENTS AND FACULTY
Enrollment: 5,205. **Student Body:** 4% out-of-state.

Retention and Graduation: 35% freshmen graduate within 6 years. **Faculty:** 294 full-time faculty, 64% hold PhDs, 37% are are members of minority groups, 14% are women. 10% of classes are taught by teaching assistants.

ACADEMICS

Degrees: bachelor's, master's. **Classes:** Most classes have 10-19 students. **Majors with Highest Enrollment:** Computer and Information Sciences; Criminal Justice/Safety Studies; Business/Commerce. **Special Study Options:** cooperative education program, distance learning, double major, dual enrollment, honors program, independent study, internships, study abroad, teacher certification program, weekend college, Week-end classes for graduate students only. Selected courses available online. **Combined degree programs:** BA/MD. **Disability Services:** Special programs offered to physically disabled students include reader services, tape recorders, tutors. **Career services:** career/job search classes, internships.

FACILITIES

Housing: Coed dorms, special housing for disabled students, men's dorms, special housing for international students, women's dorms, fraternity/sorority housing, apartments for married students, apartments for single students. 35% of campus accessible to physically disabled. **Computers:** Students can register for classes online. Administrative functions (other than registration) can be performed online.

CAMPUS LIFE

Environment: Rural. **Activities:** Choral groups, concert band, dance, drama/theater, jazz band, literary magazine, marching band, music ensembles, musical theater, pep band, radio station, student government, student newspaper, student-run film society, television station, yearbook. 110 registered organizations, 12 honor societies, 10 religious organizations. 9 fraternities, 9 sororities. **Athletics (Intercollegiate):** *Men:* basketball, cheerleading, cross-country, football, golf, track/field (outdoor). *Women:* basketball, cheerleading, cross-country, golf, soccer, track/field (outdoor), volleyball.

ADMISSIONS

Freshman Academic Profile: Average high school GPA 3.35. 13% in top 10% of high school class, 26% in top 25% of high school class, 33% in top 50% of high school class. 98% from public high schools. SAT Math middle 50% range 460-560. SAT Critical Reading middle 50% range 440-560. ACT middle 50% range 17-23. Minimum paper TOEFL 500. **Basis for Candidate Selection:** *Very important factors considered include:* Class rank, rigor of secondary school record, standardized test scores. *Other factors considered include:* work experience. **Freshman Admission Requirements:** High school diploma is required and GED is accepted. *Academic units required:* 4 English, 3 mathematics, 2 science, 2 History and Social Studies. **Freshman Admission Statistics:** 1,899 applied, 51% admitted, 58% enrolled. **Transfer Admission Requirements:** college transcript(s), standardized test scores, statement of good standing from prior institution(s). Minimum college GPA of 2.0 required. Lowest grade transferable D. **General Admission Information:** Application Fee $25. Regular application deadline 8/1. Notification on a rolling basis, beginning on or about 10/1. Nonfall registration accepted. Admission may be deferred for a maximum of 1 year. Credit and/or placement offered for CEEB Advanced Placement tests.

COSTS AND FINANCIAL AID

Average book expense $1,010. **Required Forms and Deadlines:** FAFSA. **Notification of Awards:** Applicants will be notified of awards on a rolling basis beginning 6/1. **Types of Aid:** *Need-based scholarships/grants:* Federal Pell, SEOG, state scholarships/grants, private scholarships, the school's own gift aid. *Loans:* Direct Subsidized Stafford, Direct Unsubsidized Stafford, Subsidized Stafford, Unsubsidized Stafford, PLUS, Federal Perkins. *Student Employment:* Federal Work-Study Program available. Institutional employment available. Highest amount earned per year from on-campus jobs $2,500. Off-campus job opportunities are good. **Financial Aid Statistics:** 98% freshmen, 95% undergrads receive need-based scholarship or grant aid. 0% freshmen, 0% undergrads receive non-need-based scholarship or grant aid. 76% freshmen, 83% undergrads receive need-based self-help aid. 3% freshmen, 2% undergrads receive athletic scholarships. 63% undergrads borrow to pay for school. Average cumulative indebtedness $20,585. **Criteria for awarding institutional aid:** *Non-need-based:* academics, art, athletics, minority status.

TEXAS A&M UNIVERSITY—KINGSVILLE

MSC 105, Kingsville, TX 78363
Phone: 361-593-2315
E-mail: ksossrx@tamuk.edu
Fax: 361-593-2195 • **Website:** www.tamuk.edu

This is a public school.

RATINGS

Admissions Selectivity Rating: 60*   **Fire Safety Rating:** 60*

STUDENTS AND FACULTY

Enrollment: 5,087. **Student Body:** 47% female, 53% male, 2% out-of-state, 1% international. Asian 1%, African American 4%, Caucasian 23%, Hispanic 57%, Native American <1%
Retention and Graduation: 59% freshmen return for sophomore year. **Faculty:** 276 full-time faculty, 70% hold PhDs, 35% are are members of minority groups, 24% are women.

ACADEMICS

Degrees: bachelor's, master's, post-bachelor's certificate, post-master's certificate. **Classes:** Most classes have 10-19 students. Most lab/discussion sessions have 20-29 students. **Special Study Options:** Accelerated program, cooperative education program, distance learning, double major, English as a Second Language (ESL), honors program, internships, study abroad, teacher certification program.

FACILITIES

Housing: Coed dorms, men's dorms, women's dorms, apartments for married students.

CAMPUS LIFE

Activities: Choral groups, concert band, dance, drama/theater, jazz band, marching band, music ensembles, musical theater, pep band, radio station, student government, student newspaper, television station.

ADMISSIONS

Basis for Candidate Selection: *Important factors considered include:* Class rank, rigor of secondary school record, standardized test scores. **Freshman Admission Statistics:** 2,105 applied, 99% admitted, 43% enrolled. Minimum college GPA of 2.0 required. **General Admission Information:** Application Fee $15. Nonfall registration not accepted. Admission may be deferred for a maximum of varies.

COSTS AND FINANCIAL AID

Annual in-state tuition $1,380. Annual out-of-state tuition $7,590. Room and board $3,966. Required fees $1,602. Average book expense $614. **Required Forms and Deadlines:** FAFSA. **Financial Aid Statistics:** 92% freshmen, 100% undergrads receive need-based scholarship or grant aid. 31% freshmen, 71% undergrads receive non-need-based scholarship or grant aid. 87% freshmen, 82% undergrads receive need-based self-help aid. 0% freshmen, 0% undergrads receive athletic scholarships. 46% undergrads borrow to pay for school.

TEXAS A&M UNIVERSITY—TEXARKANA

P.O. Box 5518, Texarkana, TX 75505
Phone: 903-223-3069
E-mail: admissions@tamut.edu
Fax: 903-223-3140

This public school was founded in 1971. It has a 1-acre campus.

RATINGS

Admissions Selectivity Rating: 60*   **Fire Safety Rating:** 60*

STUDENTS AND FACULTY

Enrollment: 1,030. **Student Body:** 71% female, 29% male, 0% international. Asian 1%, African American 16%, Caucasian 78%, Hispanic 6%, Native American 1%
Faculty: 59 full-time faculty, 41% are are members of minority groups, 15% are women.

ACADEMICS

Degrees: bachelor's, master's. **Majors with Highest Enrollment:** General Studies; Multi-/Interdisciplinary Studies; Accounting. **Special Study Options:**

cross-registration, distance learning, independent study, internships, liberal arts/career combination, study abroad, teacher certification program. **Disability Services:** Special programs offered to physically disabled students include note-taking services, tape recorders. **Career services:** career/job search classes.

FACILITIES
Housing: 100% of campus accessible to physically disabled. **Computers:** Students can register for classes online. Administrative functions (other than registration) can be performed online.

CAMPUS LIFE
Environment: Village. **Activities:** student government, student newspaper. 20 registered organizations, 5 honor societies, 1 religous organization.

ADMISSIONS
Freshman Academic Profile: Minimum paper TOEFL 550. **Transfer Admission Requirements:** college transcript(s), Minimum college GPA of 2.0 required. Lowest grade transferable D. **General Admission Information:** Nonfall registration not accepted. Credit offered for CEEB Advanced Placement tests.

COSTS AND FINANCIAL AID
Average book expense $0. **Required Forms and Deadlines:** FAFSA, Institution's own financial aid form. **Notification of Awards:** Applicants will be notified of awards on or about 6/1. **Types of Aid:** *Need-based scholarships/grants:* Federal Pell, SEOG, state scholarships/grants, private scholarships, the school's own gift aid. *Loans:* Subsidized Stafford, Unsubsidized Stafford, PLUS, college/university loans from institutional funds. *Student Employment:* Federal Work-Study Program available. Off-campus job opportunities are good. **Financial Aid Statistics:** 0% undergrads receive athletic scholarships. **Criteria for awarding institutional aid:** *Non-need-based:* academics, alumni affiliation, leadership, state/district residency.

TEXAS CHRISTIAN UNIVERSITY

Office of Admissions, Fort Worth, TX 76129
Phone: 817-257-7490 • **Financial Aid Phone:** 817-257-7858
E-mail: frogmail@tcu.edu • **CEEB Code:** 6820
Fax: 817-257-7268 • **Website:** www.tcu.edu • **ACT Code:** 4206

This private school, affiliated with the Disciples of Christ Church, was founded in 1873. It has a 300-acre campus.

RATINGS
Admissions Selectivity Rating: 89   **Fire Safety Rating:** 88

STUDENTS AND FACULTY
Enrollment: 8,600. **Student Body:** 60% female, 40% male, 43% out-of-state, 5% international (74 countries represented). Asian 3%, African American 5%, Caucasian 74%, Hispanic 11%, Native American 1%
Retention and Graduation: 90% freshmen return for sophomore year. 59% freshmen graduate within 4 years. 29% grads go on to further study within 1 year. **Faculty:** 613 full-time faculty, 83% hold PhDs, 45% are are members of minority groups, 13% are women. 1.3% of classes are taught by teaching assistants.

ACADEMICS
Degrees: bachelor's, certificate, first professional, first professional certificate, master's, post-bachelor's certificate. **Classes:** Most classes have 10-19 students. Most lab/discussion sessions have 20-29 students. **Majors with Highest Enrollment:** Registered Nursing/Registered Nurse; Public Relations, Advertising, and Applied Communication; Psychology. **Special Study Options:** Accelerated program, cross-registration, distance learning, double major, dual enrollment, English as a Second Language (ESL), honors program, independent study, internships, liberal arts/career combination, study abroad, teacher certification program. **Honors programs:** John V. Roach Honors College The Honors College offers programs for students of all majors and complements all areas of study on campus. Entering freshmen who complete the Honors College requirements will graduate with a John V. Roach Honors College Diploma, as well as a specialized degree from the college of their chosen major(s). **Combined degree programs:** BSE/MED. **Disability Services:** Special programs offered to physically disabled students include note-taking services. **Career services:** Alumni network, alumni services, career/job search classes, career assessment,

internships, regional alumni. Career services highlights include career services and entrepreneurship.

FACILITIES
Housing: Coed dorms, men's dorms, women's dorms, fraternity/sorority housing, apartments for married students, apartments for single students, Wellness Housing, Theme Housing, Designated rooms available for ADA needs. 97% of campus accessible to physically disabled. **Special Academic Facilities/Equipment:** Art exhibition hall, Tandy film library, speech/hearing clinic, TV studios, computer labs, observatory, Moncrief Meteorite, special collections, alumni and visitors center, cable TV, radio station, performance hall, variety of athletic facilities. **Computers:** 100% of classrooms, 100% of dorms, 100% of libraries, 100% of dining areas, 100% of student union, 100% of common outdoor areas have wireless network access. Students can register for classes online. Administrative functions (other than registration) can be performed online.

CAMPUS LIFE
Environment: Metropolis. **Activities:** Choral groups, concert band, dance, drama/theater, jazz band, literary magazine, marching band, music ensembles, musical theater, opera, pep band, radio station, student government, student newspaper, television station, yearbook, Campus Ministries, International Student Organization, Model UN. 200 registered organizations, 29 honor societies, 17 religious organizations. 15 fraternities, 18 sororities. **Athletics (Intercollegiate):** *Men:* baseball, basketball, cross-country, diving, football, golf, swimming, tennis, track/field (outdoor), track/field (indoor). *Women:* basketball, cross-country, diving, equestrian sports, golf, riflery, soccer, swimming, tennis, track/field (outdoor), track/field (indoor), volleyball. **On-Campus Highlights:** Amon Carter Stadium, University Recreation Center, Monnig Meteorite Collection, Brown-Lupton University Union, Campus Commons/Frog Fountain. **Environmental Initiatives:** American Colleges and Universities President's Climate Commitment Climate Commitment; Curriculum Committee—planning how to integrate concepts of climate neutrality and sustainability into the curriculum of all TCU students; Academic research initiatives in areas such as green roofs, wind energy, and alternative fuels.

ADMISSIONS
Freshman Academic Profile: 42% in top 10% of high school class, 73% in top 25% of high school class, 96% in top 50% of high school class. 61% from public high schools. SAT Math middle 50% range 550-650. SAT Critical Reading middle 50% range 530-630. SAT Writing middle 50% range 540-650. ACT middle 50% range 24-30. Minimum internet-based TOEFL 80. Minimum paper TOEFL 550. **Basis for Candidate Selection:** *Very important factors considered include:* Class rank, application essay, academic GPA, recommendation(s), rigor of secondary school record, standardized test scores, character/personal qualities. *Important factors considered include:* extracurricular activities, first generation, geographical residence, level of applicant's interest, racial/ethnic status, religious affiliation/commitment, talent/ability, volunteer work, work experience. *Other factors considered include:* alumni/ae relation, interview. **Freshman Admission Requirements:** High school diploma is required and GED is not accepted. *Academic units required:* 4 English, 3 mathematics, 3 science, 2 foreign language, 3 social studies, 2 academic electives. **Freshman Admission Statistics:** 17,029 applied, 49% admitted, 23% enrolled. **Transfer Admission Requirements:** college transcript(s), essay or personal statement, Minimum college GPA of 2.0 required. Lowest grade transferable C. **General Admission Information:** Application Fee $40. Regular application deadline 2/15. Regular notification 4/1. Nonfall registration accepted. Admission may be deferred for a maximum of 1 year. Credit offered for CEEB Advanced Placement tests.

COSTS AND FINANCIAL AID
Annual tuition $36,500. Room and board $10,980. Required fees $90. Average book expense $1,050. **Required Forms and Deadlines:** FAFSA, CSS/Financial Aid PROFILE, Noncustodial PROFILE. **Notification of Awards:** Applicants will be notified of awards on a rolling basis beginning 3/15. **Types of Aid:** *Need-based scholarships/grants:* Federal Pell, SEOG, state scholarships/grants, private scholarships, the school's own gift aid. *Loans:* Subsidized Stafford, Unsubsidized Stafford, PLUS, Federal Perkins, Federal Nursing, state loans. *Student Employment:* Federal Work-Study Program available. Institutional employment available. Highest amount earned per year from on-campus jobs $12,750. Off-campus job opportunities are excellent. **Financial Aid Statistics:** 92% freshmen, 92% undergrads receive need-based scholarship or grant aid. 62% freshmen, 57% undergrads receive non-need-based scholarship or grant aid. 70% freshmen, 74% undergrads receive need-based self-help aid. 3% freshmen, 3% undergrads receive athletic scholarships. 77% freshmen, 74% undergrads receive any aid. 43% undergrads borrow to pay for school. Average cumulative indebtedness $21,769. **Criteria for awarding institutional aid:** *Non-need-based:* academics, alumni affiliation, art, minority status, music/drama, religious affiliation, state/district residency.

TEXAS COLLEGE

2404 North Grand Ave., Tyler, TX 75702
Phone: 903-593-8311
E-mail: afrancis@texascollege.edu
Fax: 903-593-0588 • **Website:** www.texascollege.edu • **ACT Code:** 4210

This private school, affiliated with the Methodist Church, was founded in 1894. It has a 25-acre campus.

RATINGS

Admissions Selectivity Rating: 60*   **Fire Safety Rating:** 63

STUDENTS AND FACULTY

Enrollment: 1,035. **Student Body:** 49% female, 51% male, 15% out-of-state, 0% international (2 countries represented). Asian 0%, African American 95%, Caucasian 2%, Hispanic 2%, Native American <1%
Retention and Graduation: 5% grads go on to further study within 1 year. 5% grads pursue arts and sciences degrees. 2% grads pursue business degrees. 1% grads pursue medical degrees. **Faculty:** 28 full-time faculty, 46% hold PhDs, 46% are are members of minority groups, 79% are women. 0% of classes are taught by teaching assistants.

ACADEMICS

Degrees: associate, bachelor's. **Classes:** Most classes have 30-39 students. **Majors with Highest Enrollment:** Social Work; Sociology; Business/Commerce. **Special Study Options:** Accelerated program, distance learning, dual enrollment, independent study, internships, teacher certification program. **Honors programs:** None **Combined degree programs:** NA. **Career services:** alumni services, career assessment, internships

FACILITIES

Housing: men's dorms, women's dorms, apartments for single students. 80% of campus accessible to physically disabled. **Special Academic Facilities/Equipment:** Moody Science-Business Center; D. R. Glass Library; Willie Lee Glass Community Development Services Center.

CAMPUS LIFE

Environment: City. **Activities:** Choral groups, jazz band, marching band, student government, yearbook. 31 registered organizations, 3 religious organizations. 3 fraternities, 3 sororities. **Athletics (Intercollegiate):** *Men:* baseball, basketball, cheerleading, football, track/field (outdoor). *Women:* basketball, cheerleading, softball, track/field (outdoor), volleyball. **On-Campus Highlights:** Gus F. Taylor Gymnasium, Student Union, D. R. Glass Library, Moody Science-Business Center, Mattie Fair Hall (women's residence hall).

ADMISSIONS

Freshman Academic Profile: 98% from public high schools. Minimum paper TOEFL 500. **Basis for Candidate Selection:** *Very important factors considered include:* rigor of secondary school record. **Freshman Admission Requirements:** High school diploma is required and GED is accepted. *Academic units required:* 4 English, 2 mathematics, 2 science, 2 social studies, 2 history, 4 academic electives. **Freshman Admission Statistics:** 1,066 applied, 98% admitted, 32% enrolled. **Transfer Admission Requirements:** college transcript(s), statement of good standing from prior institution(s). Lowest grade transferable C. **General Admission Information:** Application Fee $20. Regular notification 8/15. Notification on a rolling basis, beginning on or about 4/1. Nonfall registration accepted. Admission may be deferred for a maximum of 1 year.

COSTS AND FINANCIAL AID

Annual tuition $7,680. Room and board $4,730. Required fees $20. Average book expense $800. **Required Forms and Deadlines:** FAFSA, Institution's own financial aid form. **Notification of Awards:** Applicants will be notified of awards on a rolling basis beginning 4/15. **Types of Aid:** *Need-based scholarships/grants:* Federal Pell, SEOG, state scholarships/grants, private scholarships, the school's own gift aid, United Negro College Fund. *Loans:* state loans. *Student Employment:* Federal Work-Study Program available. Off-campus job opportunities are good. **Financial Aid Statistics:** 100% freshmen, 100% undergrads receive need-based scholarship or grant aid. 0% freshmen, 0% undergrads receive non-need-based scholarship or grant aid. 100% freshmen, 104% undergrads receive need-based self-help aid. 15% freshmen, 14% undergrads receive athletic scholarships. 100% freshmen, 90% undergrads receive any aid. 90% undergrads borrow to pay for school. **Criteria for awarding institutional aid:** *Non-need-based:* academics, athletics.

TEXAS LUTHERAN UNIVERSITY

1000 West Court Street, Seguin, TX 78155
Phone: 830-372-8050 • **Financial Aid Phone:** 830-372-8078
E-mail: admissions@tlu.edu • **CEEB Code:**
Fax: 830-372-8096 • **Website:** www.tlu.edu

This private school, affiliated with the Lutheran Church, was founded in 1891. It has a 184-acre campus.

RATINGS

Admissions Selectivity Rating: 85   **Fire Safety Rating:** 79

STUDENTS AND FACULTY

Enrollment: 1,270. **Student Body:** 52% female, 48% male, 3% out-of-state, 0% international (7 countries represented). Asian 1%, African American 8%, Caucasian 54%, Hispanic 31%, Native American <1%
Retention and Graduation: 70% freshmen return for sophomore year. 31% freshmen graduate within 4 years. 44% freshmen graduate within 6 years. **Faculty:** 81 full-time faculty, 84% hold PhDs, 49% are are members of minority groups, 12% are women. 0% of classes are taught by teaching assistants.

ACADEMICS

Degrees: bachelor's. **Classes:** Most classes have 10-19 students. **Majors with Highest Enrollment:** Education; Business/Commerce; Accounting. **Special Study Options:** double major, dual enrollment, exchange student program (domestic), honors program, independent study, internships, study abroad, teacher certification program, senior seminars. **Disability Services:** Special programs offered to physically disabled students include note-taking services, reader services, tutors. **Career services:** Alumni network, alumni services, career/job search classes, internships.

FACILITIES

Housing: Coed dorms, men's dorms, women's dorms, apartments for married students, apartments for single students. 95% of campus accessible to physically disabled. **Special Academic Facilities/Equipment:** Mexican-American studies center, geological museum. **Computers:** 100% of classrooms, 100% of dorms, 100% of libraries, 100% of dining areas, 100% of student union, 100% of common outdoor areas have wireless network access. Students can register for classes online. Administrative functions (other than registration) can be performed online.

CAMPUS LIFE

Environment: Town. **Activities:** Choral groups, concert band, dance, drama/theater, jazz band, literary magazine, music ensembles, musical theater, pep band, student government, student newspaper, symphony orchestra, Campus Ministries, International Student Organization. 53 registered organizations, 10 honor societies, 3 religious organizations. 5 fraternities, 4 sororities. **Athletics (Intercollegiate):** *Men:* baseball, basketball, football, golf, soccer, tennis. *Women:* basketball, cross-country, golf, soccer, softball, tennis, track/field (outdoor), track/field (indoor), volleyball. **On-Campus Highlights:** Lucky's Snack Shack, Fitness Center, Alumni Student Center, Residence Halls, Hein Dining Hall. **Environmental Initiatives:** Installation of more efficient HVAC system campus wide; Installation of rainwater collection system; Creation of a sustainability committee and recycling program.

ADMISSIONS

Freshman Academic Profile: Average high school GPA 3.65. 20% in top 10% of high school class, 50% in top 25% of high school class, 83% in top 50% of high school class. 95% from public high schools. SAT Math middle 50% range 470-580. SAT Critical Reading middle 50% range 450-550. SAT Writing middle 50% range 420-530. ACT middle 50% range 19-24. Minimum internet-based TOEFL 80. Minimum paper TOEFL 550. **Basis for Candidate Selection:** *Very important factors considered include:* Class rank, application essay, academic GPA, recommendation(s), rigor of secondary school record, standardized test scores. *Important factors considered include:* character/personal qualities, interview, talent/ability, volunteer work. *Other factors considered include:* extracurricular activities, level of applicant's interest, work experience. **Freshman Admission Requirements:** High school diploma is required and GED is accepted. *Academic units required:* 4 English, 3 mathematics, 3 science, (2 science labs), 2 foreign language, 3 social studies, 0 history, 0 computer science, 0 Speech. **Freshman Admission Statistics:** 1,516 applied, 56% admitted, 36% enrolled. **Transfer Admission Requirements:** High school transcript, college transcript(s), essay or personal statement, statement of good standing from prior institution(s). Minimum college GPA of 2.25 required. Lowest grade transferable C. **General Admission Information:** Application Fee $25. Regular application deadline 8/1. Notification on a rolling basis, beginning on or about 10/1. Nonfall registration accepted. Admission may be deferred for a maximum of 1 year. Credit and/or placement offered for CEEB Advanced Placement tests.

COSTS AND FINANCIAL AID

Annual tuition $26,670. Room and board $9,240. Required fees $130. Average book expense $950. **Required Forms and Deadlines:** FAFSA. **Notification of Awards:** Applicants will be notified of awards on a rolling basis beginning 3/1. **Types of Aid:** *Need-based scholarships/grants:* Federal Pell, SEOG, state scholarships/grants, the school's own gift aid. *Loans:* Subsidized Stafford, Unsubsidized Stafford, PLUS, Federal Perkins, state loans. *Student Employment:* Federal Work-Study Program available. Institutional employment available. Off-campus job opportunities are good. **Financial Aid Statistics:** 96% freshmen, 97% undergrads receive need-based scholarship or grant aid. 14% freshmen, 21% undergrads receive non-need-based scholarship or grant aid. 60% freshmen, 70% undergrads receive need-based self-help aid. 0% freshmen, 0% undergrads receive athletic scholarships. 99% freshmen, 98% undergrads receive any aid. 82% undergrads borrow to pay for school. Average cumulative indebtedness $26,767. **Criteria for awarding institutional aid:** *Non-need-based:* academics, alumni affiliation, leadership, music/drama, religious affiliation.

TEXAS STATE UNIVERSITY

429 North Guadalupe St., San Marcos, TX 78666
Phone: 512-245-2364 · **Financial Aid Phone:** 512-245 2315
E-mail: admissions@txstate.edu · **CEEB Code:** 6667
Fax: 512-245-8044 · **Website:** www.txstate.edu · **ACT Code:** 4178

This public school was founded in 1899. It has a 455-acre campus.

RATINGS

Admissions Selectivity Rating: 77   **Fire Safety Rating:** 79

STUDENTS AND FACULTY

Enrollment: 32,177. **Student Body:** 56% female, 44% male, 2% out-of-state, 0% international (66 countries represented). Asian 2%, African American 8%, Caucasian 51%, Hispanic 33%, Native American <1%
Retention and Graduation: 76% freshmen return for sophomore year. 27% freshmen graduate within 4 years. 55% freshmen graduate within 6 years. 22% grads go on to further study within 1 year. 1% grads pursue arts and sciences degrees. 2% grads pursue law degrees. 4% grads pursue business degrees. 1% grads pursue medical degrees. **Faculty:** 1,231 full-time faculty, 79% hold PhDs, 48% are are members of minority groups, 22% are women. 4% of classes are taught by teaching assistants.

ACADEMICS

Degrees: bachelor's, doctoral, master's, post-bachelor's certificate. **Classes:** Most classes have 20-29 students. Most lab/discussion sessions have 20-29 students. **Majors with Highest Enrollment:** Multi-/Interdisciplinary Studies; Business Administration and Management; Psychology. **Special Study Options:** Accelerated program, distance learning, double major, dual enrollment, English as a Second Language (ESL), exchange student program (domestic), honors program, independent study, internships, study abroad, teacher certification program, weekend college, English as a Second Language is offered to international students or any students for that matter, who wish to improve their command of the English language. But it is not offered as a degree program. **Honors programs:** To graduate in the University Honors Program, a student must complete at least five Honors Classes (which includes the Honors Thesis course) and maintain a minimum GPA of 3.25. Honors courses substitute for certain general education core curriculum and inidividual departmental requirements and thus become integral parts of the degree program. **Combined degree programs:** BA/MD, BA/DDS, See 2008-2010 undgrad catalog page 63 and 64. **Disability Services:** Special programs offered to physically disabled students include note-taking services, reader services, tape recorders, tutors. **Career services:** Alumni network, alumni services, career/job search classes, career assessment Career services highlights include experiential learning through the College of Education. All teacher education majors participate on practice teaching with a supervising teacher mentoring.

FACILITIES

Housing: Coed dorms, special housing for disabled students, men's dorms, women's dorms, fraternity/sorority housing, apartments for married students, apartments for single students, Non-smoking, honors, access for the disabled, but not separate housing. 88% of campus accessible to physically disabled. **Special Academic Facilities/Equipment:** Child development center, aquifer research center, two demonstration farms, physical anthropology and archaeology laboratories. Southwestern Writer's Collection. Observatory with a 17 inch telescope. **Computers:** 100% of classrooms, 100% of dorms, 100% of libraries, 100% of dining areas, 100% of student union, 100% of common outdoor areas have wireless network access. Students can register for classes online. Administrative functions (other than registration) can be performed online.

CAMPUS LIFE

Environment: Town. **Activities:** Choral groups, concert band, dance, drama/theater, jazz band, literary magazine, marching band, music ensembles, musical theater, opera, pep band, radio station, student government, student newspaper, student-run film society, symphony orchestra, yearbook, Campus Ministries, International Student Organization, Model UN. 254 registered organizations, 16 honor societies, 27 religious organizations. 18 fraternities, 14 sororities. **Athletics (Intercollegiate):** *Men:* baseball, basketball, cheerleading, cross-country, football, golf, track/field (outdoor). *Women:* basketball, cheerleading, cross-country, golf, soccer, softball, tennis, track/field (outdoor), volleyball. **On-Campus Highlights:** LBJ Student Center, Alkek Library, Student Recreation Center, The Quad, Sewell Park, The Quad is a walk way that runs the length of the campus which most academic buildings open on to. Student gather here to socialize between classes. Sewell Park is a general recreational park where students gather to swim, sun bathe, throw frisbees, and play ball. The San Marcos river runs through the park. **Environmental Initiatives:** Established the Texas Rivers Systems Institute. Our programs and projects demonstrate our deep commitment to the careful stewardship of the world's freshwater resources. Through collaborative research, public advocacy, and education on river systems, the Institute affirms the unique role of water in our lives. As one of the earth's most remarkable resources, we are dedicated to preserving and protecting this irreplaceable gift—water. The James and Marilyn Lovell Center for Environmental Geography and Hazards Research located within Texas State University' Department of Geography (one of the largest such departments in the United States), the JMLC provides a focal point around which its scholars can gather to share ideas and mentor students. Faculty Scholars seek to better understand Earths environment, to analyze and reduce the impacts of natural and technological hazards, and through their work to improve policies directed toward Earth's environment and its hazards. Full-time position of coordinator of recycling and waste management for a campus wide recycling program.

ADMISSIONS

Freshman Academic Profile: 11% in top 10% of high school class, 43% in top 25% of high school class, 88% in top 50% of high school class. 98% from public high schools. SAT Math middle 50% range 470-570. SAT Critical Reading middle 50% range 460-560. SAT Writing middle 50% range 440-530. ACT middle 50% range 20-25. Minimum internet-based TOEFL 78. Minimum paper TOEFL 550. **Basis for Candidate Selection:** *Very important factors considered include:* Class rank, standardized test scores. *Other factors considered include:* application essay, rigor of secondary school record, talent/ability. **Freshman Admission Requirements:** High school diploma is required and GED is accepted. *Academic units required:* 4 English, 3 mathematics, 3 science, (2 science labs), 2 foreign language, 1 visual/performing arts, 1 computer science, 3 PE 1.5, Eco.0.5, Health Ed. 0.5, Speech 0.5. **Freshman Admission Statistics:** 18,413 applied, 73% admitted, 40% enrolled. **Transfer Admission Requirements:** college transcript(s), statement of good standing from prior institution(s). Minimum college GPA of 2.2 required. Lowest grade transferable D. **General Admission Information:** Application Fee $60. Regular application deadline 5/1. Notification on a rolling basis, beginning on or about 9/1. Nonfall registration accepted. Admission may be deferred for a maximum of indefinite, fee req. Credit offered for CEEB Advanced Placement tests.

COSTS AND FINANCIAL AID

Annual in-state tuition $7,160. Annual out-of-state tuition $18,020. Room and board $7,612. Required fees $2,356. Average book expense $810. **Required Forms and Deadlines:** FAFSA. **Notification of Awards:** Applicants will be notified of awards on a rolling basis beginning 5/1. **Types of Aid:** *Need-based scholarships/grants:* Federal Pell, SEOG, state scholarships/grants, private scholarships, the school's own gift aid. *Loans:* Direct Subsidized Stafford, Direct Unsubsidized Stafford, Direct PLUS, Subsidized Stafford, Unsubsidized Stafford, PLUS, Federal Perkins, state loans, college/university loans from institutional funds, Alternative Loans, Emergency tuition loans. *Student Employment:* Federal Work-Study Program available. Institutional employment available. Highest amount earned per year from on-campus jobs $9,264. Off-campus job opportunities are good. **Financial Aid Statistics:** 79% freshmen, 81% undergrads receive need-based scholarship or grant aid. 16% freshmen, 8% undergrads receive non-need-based scholarship or grant aid. 74% freshmen, 77% undergrads receive need-based self-help aid. 1% freshmen, 1% undergrads receive athletic scholarships. 85% freshmen, 73% undergrads receive any aid. 64% undergrads borrow to pay for school. Average cumulative indebtedness $24,447. **Criteria for awarding institutional aid:** *Non-need-based:* academics, art, athletics, leadership, music/drama, state/district residency.

TEXAS TECH UNIVERSITY

Box 45005, Lubbock, TX 79409-5005
Phone: 806-742-1480 · **Financial Aid Phone:** 806-742-3681
E-mail: admissions@ttu.edu · **CEEB Code:** 6827
Fax: 806-742-0062 · **Website:** www.ttu.edu · **ACT Code:** 4220

This public school was founded in 1923. It has a 1839-acre campus.

RATINGS

Admissions Selectivity Rating: 82   **Fire Safety Rating:** 95

STUDENTS AND FACULTY

Enrollment: 28,278. **Student Body:** 45% female, 55% male, 6% out-of-state, 4% international (72 countries represented). Asian 3%, African American 6%, Caucasian 61%, Hispanic 22%, Native American <1%
Retention and Graduation: 33% freshmen graduate within 4 years. **Faculty:** 1,412 full-time faculty, 38% are are members of minority groups, 13% are women. 15.01% of classes are taught by teaching assistants.

ACADEMICS

Degrees: bachelor's, first professional, master's, post-bachelor's certificate. **Classes:** Most classes have 10-19 students. Most lab/discussion sessions have 20-29 students. **Majors with Highest Enrollment:** Kinesiology and Exercise Science; Psychology; Biology/Biological Sciences. **Special Study Options:** Accelerated program, cooperative education program, distance learning, double major, dual enrollment, English as a Second Language (ESL), external degree program, honors program, independent study, internships, liberal arts/career combination, student-designed major, study abroad, teacher certification program. **Honors programs:** Honors Studies is a special program under our Honors College for highly motivated and academically talented students who want to maximize their college education. It is designed to provide such students with a unique and broadly integrated intellectual experience that is complementary to virtually every major and career path. **Combined degree programs:** BA/MA, MBA/JD; MBA/MD; MPA/JD; MBA/M.Arch; MBA/MS;MS/MS;MBA/MA;JD/MSA;JD/MS;MPA/MA. **Disability Services:** Special programs offered to physically disabled students include note-taking services, reader services, tape recorders, tutors. **Career services:** alumni services, career/job search classes, internships, regional alumni.

FACILITIES

Housing: Coed dorms, special housing for disabled students, men's dorms, women's dorms, apartments for single students. 100% of campus accessible to physically disabled. **Special Academic Facilities/Equipment:** Museum, child development center, textile research center, agricultural research center, planetarium, ranching heritage center, semi-arid land studies center, ranching heritage center, seismological observatory. **Computers:** Students can register for classes online. Administrative functions (other than registration) can be performed online.

CAMPUS LIFE

Environment: City. **Activities:** Choral groups, concert band, dance, drama/theater, jazz band, marching band, music ensembles, musical theater, pep band, radio station, student government, student newspaper, symphony orchestra, television station, yearbook, Campus Ministries, International Student Organization. 399 registered organizations, 33 honor societies, 35 religious organizations. 25 fraternities, 18 sororities. **Athletics (Intercollegiate):** *Men:* baseball, basketball, cross-country, football, golf, tennis, track/field (outdoor), track/field (indoor). *Women:* basketball, cross-country, golf, soccer, softball, tennis, track/field (outdoor), track/field (indoor), volleyball. **On-Campus Highlights:** Student Union Building, Student Recreation Center, Library, Classrooms, United Spirit Arena, Jones AT&T Stadium, Museums, National Ranching and Heritage Center. Reduction of waste hauled to landfill.

ADMISSIONS

Freshman Academic Profile: 20% in top 10% of high school class, 54% in top 25% of high school class, 85% in top 50% of high school class. SAT Math middle 50% range 510-610. SAT Critical Reading middle 50% range 490-590. SAT Writing middle 50% range 470-560. ACT middle 50% range 22-27. Minimum internet-based TOEFL 79. Minimum paper TOEFL 550. **Basis for Candidate Selection:** *Very important factors considered include:* Class rank, academic GPA, rigor of secondary school record, standardized test scores. *Important factors considered include:* application essay, alumni/ae relation, character/personal qualities, extracurricular activities, talent/ability, volunteer work, work experience. *Other factors considered include:* recommendation(s), first generation, level of applicant's interest, racial/ethnic status. **Freshman Admission Requirements:** High school diploma is required and GED is accepted. *Academic units required:* 4 English, 3 mathematics, 2 science, (2 science labs), 2 foreign language, 0 social studies, 0 history, 0 visual/perform-

ing arts, 0 computer science, 0 academic electives. **Freshman Admission Statistics:** 21,873 applied, 66% admitted, 39% enrolled. **Transfer Admission Requirements:** college transcript(s), statement of good standing from prior institution(s). Minimum college GPA of 2.25 required. Lowest grade transferable D-. **General Admission Information:** Application Fee $50. Regular application deadline 5/1. Nonfall registration accepted. Credit offered for CEEB Advanced Placement tests.

COSTS AND FINANCIAL AID

Annual in-state tuition $6,388. Annual out-of-state tuition $17,248. Room and board $8,405. Required fees $2,920. Average book expense $1,200. **Required Forms and Deadlines:** FAFSA. **Types of Aid:** *Need-based scholarships/grants:* Federal Pell, SEOG, state scholarships/grants, private scholarships, the school's own gift aid. *Loans:* Subsidized Stafford, Unsubsidized Stafford, PLUS, Federal Perkins, state loans, college/university loans from institutional funds. *Student Employment:* Federal Work-Study Program available. Institutional employment available. Highest amount earned per year from on-campus jobs $5,017. Off-campus job opportunities are excellent. **Financial Aid Statistics:** 50% freshmen, 63% undergrads receive any aid. **Criteria for awarding institutional aid:** *Non-need-based:* academics, art, athletics, job skills, leadership, music/drama.

TEXAS WOMAN'S UNIVERSITY

P.O. Box 425589, Denton, TX 76204-5589
Phone: 940-898-3188 · **Financial Aid Phone:** 940-898-3050
E-mail: admissions@twu.edu · **CEEB Code:** 6826
Fax: 940-898-3081 · **Website:** www.twu.edu · **ACT Code:** 4224

This public school was founded in 1901. It has a 270-acre campus.

RATINGS

Admissions Selectivity Rating: 80   **Fire Safety Rating:** 99

STUDENTS AND FACULTY

Enrollment: 7,389. **Student Body:** 93% female, 7% male, 1% out-of-state, 2% international (62 countries represented). Asian 8%, African American 21%, Caucasian 51%, Hispanic 18%, Native American 1%
Retention and Graduation: 71% freshmen return for sophomore year. 22% freshmen graduate within 4 years. 44% freshmen graduate within 6 years. 4% grads go on to further study within 1 year. **Faculty:** 306 full-time faculty, 71% are are members of minority groups, 17% are women.

ACADEMICS

Degrees: bachelor's, master's, post-bachelor's certificate, post-master's certificate. **Classes:** Most classes have 10-19 students. **Special Study Options:** cross-registration, distance learning, double major, dual enrollment, honors program, independent study, internships, study abroad, teacher certification program. **Honors programs:** Honors Scholars Program www.twu.edu/honors/index.html **Combined degree programs:** BA/MEng, 3-2 program with UNT. **Disability Services:** Special programs offered to physically disabled students include note-taking services, reader services, tape recorders, tutors. **Career services:** internships.

FACILITIES

Housing: Coed dorms, special housing for disabled students, special housing for international students, women's dorms, apartments for married students, apartments for single students, Wellness Housing, Theme Housing. 100% of campus accessible to physically disabled. **Special Academic Facilities/Equipment:** Museum, radiation lab, language lab, Texas First Ladies' Gown Collection, Texas Women's Hall of Fame. **Computers:** Students can register for classes online. Administrative functions (other than registration) can be performed online.

CAMPUS LIFE

Environment: City. **Activities:** Choral groups, dance, drama/theater, jazz band, music ensembles, musical theater, opera, student government, student newspaper, television station, International Student Organization. 94 registered organizations, 16 honor societies, 10 religious organizations. 9 sororities. **Athletics (Intercollegiate):** *Women:* basketball, gymnastics, soccer, softball, volleyball. **On-Campus Highlights:** Student Union, Pioneer Hall, Mega Computer Lab, Guinn/Stark High Rise Resident Halls, Little Chapel-in-the-Woods, TWU has four campuses—two in Dallas, one in Houston and the 270 acre main campus in Denton. The Denton Campus houses the Texas Women's Hall of Fame and the Gowns of Texas First Ladies Collection; The Houston Campus is located in the Houston Medical Center and recently opened the new facility; The Dallas campuses have begun construction on a new multi-million dollar facility.

ADMISSIONS

Freshman Academic Profile: Average high school GPA 3.2. 18% in top 10% of high school class, 29% in top 25% of high school class, 77% in top 50% of high school class. 93% from public high schools. SAT Math middle 50% range 420-530. SAT Critical Reading middle 50% range 420-520. ACT middle 50% range 18-22. Minimum paper TOEFL 550. **Basis for Candidate Selection:** *Very important factors considered include:* Class rank, rigor of secondary school record, standardized test scores. *Important factors considered include:* academic GPA. **Freshman Admission Requirements:** High school diploma is required and GED is accepted. *Academic units required:* 4 English, 3 mathematics, 2 science, 0 foreign language, 2 social studies, 3 academic electives. **Freshman Admission Statistics:** 3,649 applied, 56% admitted, 41% enrolled. **Transfer Admission Requirements:** college transcript(s), Minimum college GPA of 2.0 required. Lowest grade transferable D. **General Admission Information:** Application Fee $30. Notification on a rolling basis, beginning on or about 10/1. Nonfall registration accepted. Admission may be deferred for a maximum of 2 years. Credit and/or placement offered for CEEB Advanced Placement tests.

COSTS AND FINANCIAL AID

Average book expense $930. **Required Forms and Deadlines:** FAFSA. **Notification of Awards:** Applicants will be notified of awards on a rolling basis beginning 3/1. **Types of Aid:** *Need-based scholarships/grants:* Federal Pell, SEOG, state scholarships/grants, private scholarships, the school's own gift aid, Federal Nursing Scholarships., Leaveraging Educational Assistance Partnership Grant. *Loans:* Subsidized Stafford, Unsubsidized Stafford, PLUS, Federal Perkins, Federal Nursing, state loans, college/university loans from institutional funds, Alternative non-federal loans. *Student Employment:* Highest amount earned per year from on-campus jobs $5,120. **Financial Aid Statistics:** 66% freshmen, 72% undergrads receive need-based scholarship or grant aid. 67% freshmen, 34% undergrads receive non-need-based scholarship or grant aid. 92% freshmen, 94% undergrads receive need-based self-help aid. 0% freshmen, 1% undergrads receive athletic scholarships. 77% freshmen, 85% undergrads receive any aid. 58% undergrads borrow to pay for school. Average cumulative indebtedness $19,409. **Criteria for awarding institutional aid:** *Non-need-based:* academics, art, athletics, music/drama.

THIEL COLLEGE

75 College Avenue, Greenville, PA 16125
Phone: 724-589-2345 · **Financial Aid Phone:** 724-589-2178
E-mail: admissions@thiel.edu · **CEEB Code:** 2910
Fax: 724-589-2013 · **Website:** www.thiel.edu · **ACT Code:** 3730

This private school, affiliated with the Lutheran Church, was founded in 1866. It has a 135-acre campus.

RATINGS

Admissions Selectivity Rating: 76	Fire Safety Rating: 80

STUDENTS AND FACULTY

Enrollment: 1,019. **Student Body:** 43% female, 57% male, 37% out-of-state, 3% international (14 countries represented). Asian 0%, African American 6%, Caucasian 69%, Hispanic 2%, Native American <1%
Retention and Graduation: 67% freshmen return for sophomore year. 30% freshmen graduate within 4 years. 13% grads go on to further study within 1 year. 86% grads pursue arts and sciences degrees. 1% grads pursue law degrees. 12% grads pursue business degrees. 1% grads pursue medical degrees. **Faculty:** 64 full-time faculty, 73% hold PhDs, 41% are are members of minority groups, 8% are women. 0% of classes are taught by teaching assistants.

ACADEMICS

Degrees: associate, bachelor's. **Classes:** Most classes have 10-19 students. Most lab/discussion sessions have 20-29 students. **Majors with Highest Enrollment:** Elementary Education and Teaching; Biology/Biological Sciences; Business/Commerce. **Special Study Options:** cooperative education program, distance learning, double major, dual enrollment, English as a Second Language (ESL), honors program, independent study, internships, liberal arts/career combination, study abroad, teacher certification program. **Honors programs:** Four year Honors Program with special courses for honors students. **Disability Services:** Special programs offered to physically disabled students include note-taking services, reader services, tape recorders, tutors. **Career services:** Alumni network, career/job search classes, career assessment, internships.

FACILITIES

Housing: Coed dorms, fraternity/sorority housing, apartments for single students. 90% of campus accessible to physically disabled. **Special Academic Facilities/Equipment:** Art Gallery, Blackbox Theater, Starbucks Bistro. **Com-**

puters: Students can register for classes online. Undergraduates are required to own a computer.

CAMPUS LIFE

Environment: Rural. **Activities:** Choral groups, concert band, dance, drama/ theater, literary magazine, musical theater, pep band, radio station, student government, student newspaper, symphony orchestra, television station, yearbook, Campus Ministries. 40 registered organizations, 8 honor societies, 4 religious organizations. 3 fraternities, 4 sororities. **Athletics (Intercollegiate):** *Men:* baseball, basketball, cheerleading, cross-country, football, golf, soccer, track/ field (outdoor), track/field (indoor), wrestling. *Women:* basketball, cheerleading, cross-country, soccer, softball, track/field (outdoor), track/field (indoor), volleyball. **On-Campus Highlights:** Howard Miller Student Center, Robinson Black Box Theater, New Student Appartments, Alumni Stadium, Paul Bush Memorial Fitness Center.

ADMISSIONS

Freshman Academic Profile: Average high school GPA 3.02. 12% in top 10% of high school class, 25% in top 25% of high school class, 46% in top 50% of high school class. 88% from public high schools. SAT Math middle 50% range 420-520. SAT Critical Reading middle 50% range 410-510. ACT middle 50% range 18-23. Minimum paper TOEFL 450. **Basis for Candidate Selection:** *Very important factors considered include:* application essay, academic GPA, recommendation(s), rigor of secondary school record, standardized test scores, interview, level of applicant's interest. *Important factors considered include:* Class rank, character/personal qualities. *Other factors considered include:* extracurricular activities, talent/ability, volunteer work, work experience. **Freshman Admission Requirements:** High school diploma is required and GED is accepted. **Freshman Admission Statistics:** 1,856 applied, 68% admitted, 28% enrolled. **Transfer Admission Requirements:** High school transcript, college transcript(s), essay or personal statement, interview, standardized test scores, statement of good standing from prior institution(s). Minimum college GPA of 2.0 required. Lowest grade transferable C. **General Admission Information:** Application Fee $35. Regular application deadline 6/30. Notification on a rolling basis, beginning on or about 9/15. Nonfall registration accepted. Admission may be deferred for a maximum of 1 year. Credit and/or placement offered for CEEB Advanced Placement tests.

COSTS AND FINANCIAL AID

Required Forms and Deadlines: FAFSA, State aid form. **Notification of Awards:** Applicants will be notified of awards on a rolling basis beginning 2/15. **Types of Aid:** *Need-based scholarships/grants:* Federal Pell, SEOG, state scholarships/grants, private scholarships, the school's own gift aid. *Loans:* Subsidized Stafford, Unsubsidized Stafford, PLUS, Federal Perkins, college/ university loans from institutional funds. *Student Employment:* Federal Work-Study Program available. Institutional employment available. Off-campus job opportunities are fair. **Financial Aid Statistics:** 100% undergrads receive need-based scholarship or grant aid. 0% undergrads receive non-need-based scholarship or grant aid. 100% undergrads receive need-based self-help aid. 0% freshmen, 0% undergrads receive athletic scholarships. **Criteria for awarding institutional aid:** *Non-need-based:* academics, alumni affiliation, leadership, religious affiliation, state/district residency.

THOMAS AQUINAS COLLEGE

10000 Ojai Road, Santa Paula, CA 93060
Phone: 805-525-4417 · **Financial Aid Phone:** 800-634-9797
E-mail: admissions@thomasaquinas.edu · **CEEB Code:** 4828
Fax: 805-421-5905 · **Website:** www.thomasaquinas.edu · **ACT Code:** 425

This private school, affiliated with the Roman Catholic Church, was founded in 1971. It has a 131-acre campus.

RATINGS

Admissions Selectivity Rating: 88	Fire Safety Rating: 90

STUDENTS AND FACULTY

Enrollment: 378. **Student Body:** 49% female, 51% male, 57% out-of-state, 4% international (10 countries represented). Asian 1%, African American 0%, Caucasian 71%, Hispanic 15%, Native American 1%
Retention and Graduation: 97% freshmen return for sophomore year. 63% freshmen graduate within 4 years. 72% freshmen graduate within 6 years. 16%

grads go on to further study within 1 year. 3% grads pursue arts and sciences degrees. **Faculty:** 32 full-time faculty, 84% hold PhDs, 13% are are members of minority groups. 0% of classes are taught by teaching assistants.

ACADEMICS

Degrees: bachelor's. **Classes:** Most classes have 10-19 students. **Majors with Highest Enrollment:** Liberal Arts and Sciences/Liberal Studies. **Special Study Options:** The sole academic program offered: a "cross-disciplinary" curriculum of liberal education through reading and analyzing the "Great Books," with special emphasis on philosophy, theology, mathematics, science, and literature. **Career services:** Alumni network, alumni services, career/job search classes, career assessment, internships, regional alumni. Career services highlights include Career Assessment: We work directly with our students, one on one, in order to help them determine their strengths. We then talk with them about their various interests, and advise them on possible options, given their strengths and interests. We encourage them to talk to people within those fields, including networking with our alumni. We also have guest speakers and discernment classes that help as well.

FACILITIES

Housing: men's dorms, women's dorms, Students living with their families may live off campus. 100% of campus accessible to physically disabled. **Special Academic Facilities/Equipment:** St. Bernardine Library.

CAMPUS LIFE

Environment: Rural. **Activities:** Choral groups, dance, drama/theater, music ensembles, musical theater. 2 registered organizations, 4 religious organizations. **On-Campus Highlights:** St. Joseph Commons, The Dumb Ox Coffee Shop, Dorm Commons, St. Bernardine Library, Student Lounge. **Environmental Initiatives:** The College recycles recyclable material. 100% of the campus landscape waste is made into either mulch or wood chips for further use. Green products are used for some cleaning applications.

ADMISSIONS

Freshman Academic Profile: Average high school GPA 3.75. 36% in top 10% of high school class, 71% in top 25% of high school class, 93% in top 50% of high school class. 13% from public high schools. SAT Math middle 50% range 560-640. SAT Critical Reading middle 50% range 620-710. SAT Writing middle 50% range 590-690. ACT middle 50% range 24-31. Minimum paper TOEFL 570. **Basis for Candidate Selection:** *Very important factors considered include:* application essay, recommendation(s), rigor of secondary school record, standardized test scores, character/personal qualities, level of applicant's interest. *Important factors considered include:* academic GPA. *Other factors considered include:* Class rank, extracurricular activities, interview, religious affiliation/commitment, talent/ability, volunteer work, work experience. **Freshman Admission Requirements:** High school diploma is required and GED is accepted. *Academic units required:* 4 English, 3 mathematics, 2 science, 2 foreign language, 2 history. **Freshman Admission Statistics:** 185 applied, 83% admitted, 58% enrolled. **General Admission Information:** Notification on a rolling basis, beginning on or about 10/1. Nonfall registration not accepted. Admission may be deferred for a maximum of 1 year. Neither credit nor placement offered for CEEB Advanced Placement tests.

COSTS AND FINANCIAL AID

Annual tuition $24,500. Room and board $7,950. Required fees $0. Average book expense $50. **Required Forms and Deadlines:** FAFSA, Institution's own financial aid form, State aid form. **Notification of Awards:** Applicants will be notified of awards on a rolling basis beginning 1/1. **Types of Aid:** *Need-based scholarships/grants:* Federal Pell, state scholarships/grants, private scholarships, the school's own gift aid. *Loans:* Subsidized Stafford, Unsubsidized Stafford, PLUS, college/university loans from institutional funds, Canadian student Loans. *Student Employment:* Off-campus job opportunities are fair. **Financial Aid Statistics:** 93% freshmen, 92% undergrads receive need-based scholarship or grant aid. 0% freshmen, 0% undergrads receive non-need-based scholarship or grant aid. 100% freshmen, 99% undergrads receive need-based self-help aid. 0% freshmen, 0% undergrads receive athletic scholarships. 74% freshmen, 80% undergrads receive any aid. 85% undergrads borrow to pay for school. Average cumulative indebtedness $16,414.

THOMAS COLLEGE

180 West River Road, Waterville, ME 4901
Phone: 207-859-1101 · **Financial Aid Phone:** 207-859-1105
E-mail: admiss@thomas.edu · **CEEB Code:** 2052
Fax: 207-859-1114 · **Website:** www.thomas.edu · **ACT Code:** 1663

This private school was founded in 1894. It has a 120-acre campus.

RATINGS

Admissions Selectivity Rating: 71 **Fire Safety Rating:** 92

STUDENTS AND FACULTY

Enrollment: 739. **Student Body:** 49% female, 51% male, 20% out-of-state, 0% international. Asian 1%, African American 2%, Caucasian 88%, Hispanic 1%, Native American <1% **Retention and Graduation:** 51% freshmen graduate within 6 years. 7% grads go on to further study within 1 year. 7% grads pursue business degrees. **Faculty:** 21 full-time faculty, 48% hold PhDs, 38% are are members of minority groups, 0% are women. 0% of classes are taught by teaching assistants.

ACADEMICS

Degrees: associate, bachelor's, master's, terminal associate, transfer associate. **Classes:** Most classes have 20-29 students. **Majors with Highest Enrollment:** Accounting; Accounting and Business/Management; Sport and Fitness Administration/Management. **Special Study Options:** cross-registration, distance learning, double major, internships, study abroad, teacher certification program. **Combined degree programs:** BS/MBA. **Career services:** career assessment, internships.

FACILITIES

Housing: Coed dorms, Residence halls are designated coed—male or female by floor or suite, not by building. 71% of campus accessible to physically disabled. **Computers:** Students can register for classes online. Administrative functions (other than registration) can be performed online.

CAMPUS LIFE

Environment: Rural. **Activities:** Choral groups, dance, drama/theater, student government, student newspaper, yearbook. 26 registered organizations, 3 honor societies, 1 fraternity, 1 sorority. **Athletics (Intercollegiate):** *Men:* baseball, basketball, golf, lacrosse, soccer, tennis. *Women:* basketball, field hockey, lacrosse, soccer, softball, volleyball.

ADMISSIONS

Freshman Academic Profile: Average high school GPA 2.7. 7% in top 10% of high school class, 19% in top 25% of high school class, 54% in top 50% of high school class. SAT Math middle 50% range 390-510. SAT Critical Reading middle 50% range 400-500. SAT Writing middle 50% range 380-500. ACT middle 50% range 13-22. Minimum paper TOEFL 530. **Basis for Candidate Selection:** *Very important factors considered include:* Class rank, application essay, academic GPA, recommendation(s), rigor of secondary school record, standardized test scores. *Important factors considered include:* character/personal qualities, extracurricular activities, interview. *Other factors considered include:* alumni/ae relation, first generation, level of applicant's interest, talent/ability, volunteer work, work experience. **Freshman Admission Requirements:** High school diploma is required and GED is accepted. **Freshman Admission Statistics:** 668 applied, 81% admitted, 45% enrolled. **Transfer Admission Requirements:** High school transcript, college transcript(s), essay or personal statement, Minimum college GPA of 2.0 required. Lowest grade transferable C. **General Admission Information:** Application Fee $50. Notification on a rolling basis, beginning on or about 12/1. Nonfall registration accepted. Admission may be deferred for a maximum of 2 years. Credit and/or placement offered for CEEB Advanced Placement tests.

COSTS AND FINANCIAL AID

Annual tuition $17,280. Room and board $7,430. Required fees $450. Average book expense $800. **Required Forms and Deadlines:** FAFSA. **Notification of Awards:** Applicants will be notified of awards on a rolling basis beginning 3/15. **Types of Aid:** *Need-based scholarships/grants:* Federal Pell, SEOG, state scholarships/grants, private scholarships, the school's own gift aid. *Loans:* Direct Subsidized Stafford, Direct Unsubsidized Stafford, Direct PLUS, Federal Perkins. *Student Employment:* Federal Work-Study Program available. Institutional employment available. Off-campus job opportunities are excellent. **Financial Aid Statistics:** 100% freshmen, 98% undergrads receive need-based scholarship or grant aid. 31% freshmen, 19% undergrads receive non-need-based scholarship or grant aid. 90% freshmen, 89% undergrads receive need-based self-help aid. 0% freshmen, 0% undergrads receive athletic scholarships. 95% freshmen, 90% undergrads receive any aid. 75% undergrads borrow to pay for school. Average cumulative indebtedness $25,329. **Criteria for awarding institutional aid:** *Non-need-based:* academics.

THOMAS EDISON STATE COLLEGE

101 West State Street, Trenton, NJ 08608-1176
Phone: 888-442-8372 · **Financial Aid Phone:** 609-633-9658
E-mail: admissions@tesc.edu · **CEEB Code:** 2612
Fax: 609-984-8447 · **Website:** www.tesc.edu · **ACT Code:** 274872

This public school was founded in 1972. It has a 2-acre campus.

RATINGS

Admissions Selectivity Rating: 60*   **Fire Safety Rating:** 60*

STUDENTS AND FACULTY

Enrollment: 19,404. **Student Body:** 45% female, 55% male, 59% out-of-state, 1% international (68 countries represented). Asian 4%, African American 16%, Caucasian 60%, Hispanic 8%, Native American 1%
Faculty:

ACADEMICS

Degrees: associate, bachelor's, certificate, master's, post-bachelor's certificate, post-master's certificate. **Majors with Highest Enrollment:** Nuclear Engineering Technology/Technician; Liberal Arts and Sciences/Liberal Studies; Registered Nursing/Registered Nurse. **Special Study Options:** distance learning, dual enrollment, external degree program, independent study, Joint degree program with the University of Medicine and Dentistry of New Jersey for Bachelor of Science in Health Sciences. Graduates of associate degree and diploma programs of nursing may enroll for a BSN degree only (RN-BSN program), or both a BSN and a MSN degree (RN-BSN/MSN program) with preparation as a Nurse Educator at the Master's level. **Combined degree programs:** BSN/MSN. **Career services:** Alumni network.

FACILITIES

Housing: Thomas Edison State College serves adult students at a distance. The College doesn't own/operate any housing units and/or dorms. 97% of campus accessible to physically disabled. **Computers:** Students can register for classes online. Administrative functions (other than registration) can be performed online.

CAMPUS LIFE

Environment: City. **Activities:** 3 honor societies. **On-Campus Highlights:** Prudence Townsend Kelsey Memorial Room. **Environmental Initiatives:** Solar panels installed on 2 facilities. Purchased hybrid vehicle for Vice Presidents to use. Adopted recycling programs.

ADMISSIONS

Freshman Academic Profile: Minimum internet-based TOEFL 79. Minimum paper TOEFL 550. **Freshman Admission Requirements:** High school diploma is required and GED is accepted. **Transfer Admission Requirements:** college transcript(s), Lowest grade transferable D. **General Admission Information:** Application Fee $75. Credit offered for CEEB Advanced Placement tests.

COSTS AND FINANCIAL AID

Required Forms and Deadlines: FAFSA, Institution's own financial aid form. **Types of Aid:** *Need-based scholarships/grants:* Federal Pell, state scholarships/grants, private scholarships. *Loans:* Subsidized Stafford, Unsubsidized Stafford, PLUS, state loans, Private Educational Loans. **Financial Aid Statistics:** 17% undergrads receive any aid.

THOMAS JEFFERSON UNIVERSITY

130 South 9th Street, Philadelphia, PA 19107
Phone: 215-503-8890 · **Financial Aid Phone:** 215-955-2867
E-mail: jchp@jefferson.edu · **CEEB Code:** 2903
Fax: 215-503-7241 · **Website:** www.jefferson.edu/jchp

This private school was founded in 1967.

RATINGS

Admissions Selectivity Rating: 60*   **Fire Safety Rating:** 71

STUDENTS AND FACULTY

Enrollment: 827. **Student Body:** 83% female, 17% male, 27% out-of-state, 1% international. Asian 8%, African American 9%, Caucasian 71%, Hispanic 3%, Native American <1%
Faculty: 82 full-time faculty, 43% hold PhDs, 85% are are members of minority groups, 12% are women.

ACADEMICS

Degrees: associate, bachelor's, master's, post-bachelor's certificate, post-master's certificate, transfer associate. **Majors with Highest Enrollment:** Registered Nursing/Registered Nurse; Clinical Laboratory Science/Medical Technology/Technologist; Health Services/Allied Health/Health Sciences. **Special Study Options:** Accelerated program, distance learning, double major, independent study, internships, study abroad. **Disability Services:** Special programs offered to physically disabled students include note-taking services, reader services, tutors. **Career services:** Alumni network, alumni services, career/job search classes, career assessment, regional alumni.

FACILITIES

Housing: Coed dorms, special housing for disabled students, apartments for married students, apartments for single students. 80% of campus accessible to physically disabled. **Special Academic Facilities/Equipment:** Copy of the famous Gross Clinic, New building with simulation labs. Located in the heart of Center City close to all historical sights as well as cultural events and museums. **Computers:** 100% of classrooms, 100% of dorms, 100% of libraries, have wireless network access. Students can register for classes online. Administrative functions (other than registration) can be performed online.

CAMPUS LIFE

Environment: Metropolis. **Activities:** Choral groups, student government, yearbook, International Student Organization. **On-Campus Highlights:** New Education and Research Building, Famous painting called the Gross Clinic, Close to Historic Sites, Close to famous museums, Many fine restaurants and theaters, Jefferson is located in Center City Philadelphia, near the Convention Center with many fine restaurants, shops and other cultural sights.

ADMISSIONS

Freshman Admission Requirements: High school diploma is required and GED is accepted. **Transfer Admission Requirements:** college transcript(s), essay or personal statement, statement of good standing from prior institution(s). Minimum college GPA of 2.5 required. Lowest grade transferable C. **General Admission Information:** Application Fee $50. Notification on a rolling basis, beginning on or about 11/1. Nonfall registration accepted.

COSTS AND FINANCIAL AID

Annual tuition $23,685. Room and board $8,280. Required fees $400. Average book expense $1,495. **Required Forms and Deadlines:** FAFSA, Institution's own financial aid form. **Types of Aid:** *Need-based scholarships/grants:* Federal Pell, SEOG, state scholarships/grants, private scholarships, the school's own gift aid, Federal Nursing Scholarships. *Loans:* Direct Subsidized Stafford, Direct Unsubsidized Stafford, Subsidized Stafford, Unsubsidized Stafford, PLUS, Federal Perkins, Federal Nursing, state loans, college/university loans from institutional funds. *Student Employment:* Federal Work-Study Program available. Institutional employment available. Off-campus job opportunities are excellent. **Criteria for awarding institutional aid:** *Non-need-based:* academics, leadership, state/district residency.

THOMAS MORE COLLEGE

333 Thomas More Pkwy., Crestview Hill, KY 41017-3495
Phone: 859-344-3332 · **Financial Aid Phone:** 859-344-3319
E-mail: admissions@thomasmore.edu · **CEEB Code:** 3892
Fax: 859-344-3444 · **Website:** www.thomasmore.edu · **ACT Code:** 1560

This private school, affiliated with the Roman Catholic Church, was founded in 1921. It has a 100-acre campus.

RATINGS

Admissions Selectivity Rating: 80   **Fire Safety Rating:** 62

STUDENTS AND FACULTY

Enrollment: 1,371. **Student Body:** 51% female, 49% male, 66% out-of-state, 1% international. Asian 1%, African American 5%, Caucasian 79%, Hispanic 0%, Native American <1%
Retention and Graduation: 62% freshmen return for sophomore year. 39% freshmen graduate within 4 years. 55% freshmen graduate within 6 years. 25% grads go on to further study within 1 year. 44% grads pursue arts and sciences degrees. 6% grads pursue law degrees. 5% grads pursue business degrees. 5% grads pursue medical degrees. **Faculty:** 71 full-time faculty, 66% hold PhDs, 39% are are members of minority groups, 7% are women. 0% of classes are taught by teaching assistants.

ACADEMICS

Degrees: associate, bachelor's, certificate, master's, terminal associate. **Classes:** Most classes have 10-19 students. Most lab/discussion sessions have 10-19 students. **Majors with Highest Enrollment:** Teacher Education and Professional Development, Specific Subject Areas; Business/Commerce. **Special Study Options:** Accelerated program, cooperative education program, cross-registration, double major, dual enrollment, English as a Second Language (ESL), honors program, independent study, internships, liberal arts/career combination, student-designed major, study abroad, teacher certification program, weekend college. **Honors programs:** Thomas More Honors Program. **Disability Services:** Special programs offered to physically disabled students include note-taking services, reader services, tape recorders, tutors.

FACILITIES

Housing: Coed dorms, men's dorms, women's dorms. 99% of campus accessible to physically disabled. **Special Academic Facilities/Equipment:** See www2.thomasmore.edu/undergrad_admissions/resources.cfm?group=Resources. **Computers:** Students can register for classes online. Administrative functions (other than registration) can be performed online.

CAMPUS LIFE

Environment: Village. **Activities:** Choral groups, drama/theater, literary magazine, student government, yearbook. 29 registered organizations, 5 honor societies, 1 religous organization. 1 fraternity. **Athletics (Intercollegiate):** *Men:* baseball, basketball, cross-country, football, golf, soccer, tennis. *Women:* basketball, cross-country, golf, soccer, softball, tennis, volleyball. **On-Campus Highlights:** Steigerwald Student Center, Connor Convocation Center (Athletic Center), Bank of KY Observatory at Thomas More College, Biology Field Station on the Ohio River, Murphy Hall.

ADMISSIONS

Freshman Academic Profile: Average high school GPA 2.88. 7% in top 10% of high school class, 31% in top 25% of high school class, 85% in top 50% of high school class. 69% from public high schools. SAT Math middle 50% range 460-600. SAT Critical Reading middle 50% range 460-580. ACT middle 50% range 19-24. Minimum paper TOEFL 515. **Basis for Candidate Selection:** *Very important factors considered include:* rigor of secondary school record, standardized test scores. *Important factors considered include:* Class rank. *Other factors considered include:* application essay, recommendation(s), character/personal qualities, extracurricular activities, interview, talent/ability, volunteer work. **Freshman Admission Requirements:** High school diploma is required and GED is accepted. *Academic units required:* 4 English, 3 mathematics, 3 science, (1 science labs), 2 foreign language, 3 social studies. **Freshman Admission Statistics:** 1,363 applied, 61% admitted, 31% enrolled. **Transfer Admission Requirements:** college transcript(s), statement of good standing from prior institution(s). Minimum college GPA of 2.0 required. Lowest grade transferable C. **General Admission Information:** Application Fee $25. Notification on a rolling basis, beginning on or about 3/15. Nonfall registration accepted. Admission may be deferred for a maximum of 1 year. Credit and/or placement offered for CEEB Advanced Placement tests.

COSTS AND FINANCIAL AID

Annual tuition $19,500. Room and board $5,400. Required fees $450. Average book expense $800. **Required Forms and Deadlines:** FAFSA, Institution's own financial aid form. **Notification of Awards:** Applicants will be notified of awards on a rolling basis beginning 3/1. **Types of Aid:** *Need-based scholarships/grants:* Federal Pell, SEOG, private scholarships, the school's own gift aid, United Negro College Fund. *Loans:* Subsidized Stafford, Unsubsidized Stafford, PLUS, Federal Perkins, Federal Nursing, college/university loans from institutional funds. *Student Employment:* Highest amount earned per year from on-campus jobs $1,400. **Financial Aid Statistics:** 96% freshmen, 90% undergrads receive need-based scholarship or grant aid. 66% freshmen, 61% undergrads receive need-based self-help aid. 0% freshmen, 0% undergrads receive athletic scholarships. 90% freshmen, 74% undergrads receive any aid. 62% undergrads borrow to pay for school. **Criteria for awarding institutional aid:** *Non-need-based:* academics, alumni affiliation, art, job skills, leadership, minority status, music/drama, religious affiliation.

THOMAS MORE COLLEGE OF LIBERAL ARTS

6 Manchester Street, Merrimack, NH 03054-4818
Phone: 603-880-8308
E-mail: admissions@thomasmorecollege.edu
Fax: 603-880-9280 • **Website:** www.thomasmorecollege.edu • **ACT Code:** 3892

This private school, affiliated with the Roman Catholic Church, was founded in 1978. It has a 13-acre campus.

RATINGS

Admissions Selectivity Rating: 65   **Fire Safety Rating:** 60*

STUDENTS AND FACULTY

Enrollment: 92. **Student Body:** 48% female, 52% male, 84% out-of-state, 4% international. Asian 0%, African American 0%, Caucasian 52%, Hispanic 1%, Native American <1%
Retention and Graduation: 60% freshmen return for sophomore year. 52% grads go on to further study within 1 year. 48% grads pursue arts and sciences degrees. 8% grads pursue law degrees. 2% grads pursue business degrees. 2% grads pursue medical degrees. **Faculty:** 5 full-time faculty, 100% hold PhDs, 20% are are members of minority groups. 0% of classes are taught by teaching assistants.

ACADEMICS

Degrees: bachelor's. **Classes:** Most classes have 10-19 students. **Majors with Highest Enrollment:** Computer and Information Sciences; Biology; Business/Commerce. **Special Study Options:** internships, study abroad, Spring semester in Rome for all sophomores.

FACILITIES

Housing: men's dorms, women's dorms. 70% of campus accessible to physically disabled.

CAMPUS LIFE

Environment: Village. **Activities:** Choral groups, drama/theater.

ADMISSIONS

Freshman Academic Profile: 12% from public high schools. **Basis for Candidate Selection:** *Very important factors considered include:* application essay, recommendation(s), character/personal qualities, interview. *Important factors considered include:* talent/ability. *Other factors considered include:* Class rank, academic GPA, rigor of secondary school record, standardized test scores, extracurricular activities, level of applicant's interest, religious affiliation/commitment. **Freshman Admission Requirements:** High school diploma is required and GED is accepted. *Academic units required:* 4 English, 3 mathematics, 2 science, (2 science labs), 2 foreign language, 2 social studies, 2 history. **Freshman Admission Statistics:** 75 applied, 55% admitted, 63% enrolled. **Transfer Admission Requirements:** college transcript(s), essay or personal statement, Lowest grade transferable C. **General Admission Information:** Notification on a rolling basis, beginning on or about 1/6. Nonfall registration accepted. Admission may be deferred for a maximum of n/a. Neither credit nor placement offered for CEEB Advanced Placement tests.

COSTS AND FINANCIAL AID

Annual tuition $11,100. Room and board $8,000. Average book expense $525. **Required Forms and Deadlines:** FAFSA. **Notification of Awards:** Applicants will be notified of awards on a rolling basis beginning 3/15. **Types of Aid:** *Need-based scholarships/grants:* Federal Pell, SEOG, state scholarships/grants, private scholarships, the school's own gift aid. *Loans:* Subsidized Stafford, Unsubsidized Stafford, PLUS. *Student Employment:* Off-campus job opportunities are good. **Financial Aid Statistics:** 100% freshmen, 100% undergrads receive need-based scholarship or grant aid. 70% freshmen, 62% undergrads receive need-based self-help aid. 0% freshmen, 0% undergrads receive athletic scholarships. 79% undergrads borrow to pay for school. Average cumulative indebtedness $19,119. **Criteria for awarding institutional aid:** *Non-need-based:* academics.

THOMPSON RIVERS UNIVERISTY

TRU Admissions, Kamloops, BC V2C 5N3
Phone: 250-828-5071
E-mail: admissions@tru.ca
Fax: 250-371-5513 • **Website:** www.tru.ca

This public school was founded in 1970. It has a 200-acre campus.

RATINGS

Admissions Selectivity Rating: 60*   **Fire Safety Rating:** 60*

STUDENTS AND FACULTY

Enrollment: 4,497. **Student Body:** 61% female, 39% male, 15% out-of-state, (43 countries represented).
Faculty: 375 full-time faculty, 28% hold PhDs. 0% of classes are taught by teaching assistants.

ACADEMICS

Degrees: associate, bachelor's, certificate, diploma, master's, post-bachelor's certificate, terminal associate, transfer associate. **Classes:** Most classes have 20-29 students. Most lab/discussion sessions have 10-19 students. **Special Study Options:** Accelerated program, cooperative education program, distance learning, double major, English as a Second Language (ESL), external degree program, honors program, independent study, internships, liberal arts/career combination, study abroad, teacher certification program. **Disability Services:** Special programs offered to physically disabled students include note-taking services, reader services, tape recorders, tutors. **Career services:** Alumni network, career/job search classes, career assessment.

FACILITIES

Housing: 95% of campus accessible to physically disabled. **Computers:** Students can register for classes online. Administrative functions (other than registration) can be performed online.

CAMPUS LIFE

Activities: literary magazine, student government 5 religious organizations. **Athletics (Intercollegiate):** *Men:* baseball, basketball, soccer, volleyball. *Women:* basketball, soccer, volleyball.

ADMISSIONS

Freshman Academic Profile: 95% from public high schools. **Basis for Candidate Selection:** *Very important factors considered include:* rigor of secondary school record. *Important factors considered include:* standardized test scores. *Other factors considered include:* recommendation(s), character/personal qualities, interview, racial/ethnic status, talent/ability, volunteer work, work experience. Freshman Admission Requirements. **Transfer Admission Requirements:** High school transcript, college transcript(s). **General Admission Information:** Application Fee $60. Regular application deadline 3/1, Notification on a rolling basis, beginning on or about 10/1. Nonfall registration accepted. Admission may be deferred for a maximum of 1 Year. Neither credit nor placement offered for CEEB Advanced Placement tests.

COSTS AND FINANCIAL AID

Room and board $2,100. Required fees $200. Average book expense $1,000. *Student Employment:* Off-campus job opportunities are good.

TIFFIN UNIVERSITY

155 Miami Street, Tiffin, OH 44883
Phone: 419-448-3423 · **Financial Aid Phone:** 419-448-3415
E-mail: admiss@tiffin.edu · **CEEB Code:** 1817
Fax: 419-443-5006 · **Website:** www.tiffin.edu/ • **ACT Code:** 3334

This private school was founded in 1888. It has a 110-acre campus.

RATINGS

Admissions Selectivity Rating: 84   Fire Safety Rating: 79

STUDENTS AND FACULTY

Enrollment: 2,595. **Student Body:** 53% female, 47% male, 34% out-of-state, 7% international (34 countries represented). Asian 0%, African American 17%, Caucasian 44%, Hispanic 3%, Native American <1%
Retention and Graduation: 62% freshmen return for sophomore year. 34% freshmen graduate within 4 years. 25% grads go on to further study within 1 year. **Faculty:** 72 full-time faculty, 61% hold PhDs, 46% are are members of minority groups, 4% are women. 0% of classes are taught by teaching assistants.

ACADEMICS

Degrees: associate, bachelor's, certificate, master's, post-bachelor's certificate. **Classes:** Most classes have fewer than 10 students. Most lab/discussion sessions have fewer than 10 students. **Majors with Highest Enrollment:** Marketing/Marketing Management; Business Administration and Management; Forensic Science and Technology. **Special Study Options:** Accelerated program, cross-registration, distance learning, double major, dual enrollment, English as a Second Language (ESL), honors program, independent study, internships, study abroad, teacher certification program. **Honors programs:** We offer a Freshman Honors Program. **Career services:** Alumni network, alumni services, career/job search classes, career assessment, internships, regional alumni.

FACILITIES

Housing: Coed dorms, special housing for disabled students, men's dorms, special housing for international students, women's dorms, fraternity/sorority housing, apartments for married students, Theme Housing. 85% of campus accessible to physically disabled. **Special Academic Facilities/Equipment:** University Art Gallery, Multi-Media Lab. **Computers:** 100% of classrooms, 25% of dorms, 100% of libraries, 100% of dining areas, 100% of student union, have wireless network access. Students can register for classes online. Administrative functions (other than registration) can be performed online.

CAMPUS LIFE

Environment: Village. **Activities:** Choral groups, concert band, dance, drama/theater, jazz band, literary magazine, marching band, music ensembles, musical

theater, pep band, student government, student newspaper, Campus Ministries, International Student Organization. 32 registered organizations, 1 honor society, 2 religious organizations. 3 fraternities, 3 sororities. **Athletics (Intercollegiate):** *Men:* baseball, basketball, cheerleading, cross-country, equestrian sports, football, golf, soccer, tennis, track/field (outdoor), track/field (indoor). *Women:* basketball, cheerleading, cross-country, equestrian sports, golf, lacrosse, soccer, softball, tennis, track/field (outdoor), track/field (indoor), volleyball. **On-Campus Highlights:** Gillmor Student Center, Hayes Center for the Arts, Hertzer Technology Center, Main Classroom Building, Franks Hall. **Environmental Initiatives:** Establishment of a Green Committee and formation of a Green Technologies Minor and Concentration; All future buildings will be considered for LEED certification (silver level); Paper recycling program has been implemented at the University along with a trayless program in the dining hall.

ADMISSIONS

Freshman Academic Profile: Average high school GPA 2.99. 75% from public high schools. SAT Math middle 50% range 400-500. SAT Critical Reading middle 50% range 420-500. ACT middle 50% range 17-22. Minimum internet-based TOEFL 61. Minimum paper TOEFL 500. **Basis for Candidate Selection:** *Very important factors considered include:* academic GPA, rigor of secondary school record, standardized test scores. *Important factors considered include:* Class rank, application essay, recommendation(s), extracurricular activities, geographical residence, state residency. *Other factors considered include:* alumni/ae relation, character/personal qualities, first generation, interview, level of applicant's interest, racial/ethnic status, talent/ability, volunteer work. **Freshman Admission Requirements:** High school diploma is required and GED is accepted. *Academic units required:* 4 English, 3 mathematics, 3 science, 3 social studies. **Freshman Admission Statistics:** 4,384 applied, 54% admitted, 21% enrolled. **Transfer Admission Requirements:** High school transcript, college transcript(s), Minimum college GPA of 2.0 required. Lowest grade transferable C. **General Admission Information:** Application Fee $20. Notification on a rolling basis, beginning on or about 9/15. Nonfall registration accepted. Credit offered for CEEB Advanced Placement tests.

COSTS AND FINANCIAL AID

Annual tuition $21,510. Room and board $9,870. Average book expense $2,000. **Required Forms and Deadlines:** FAFSA. **Notification of Awards:** Applicants will be notified of awards on a rolling basis beginning 1/15. **Types of Aid:** *Need-based scholarships/grants:* Federal Pell, SEOG, state scholarships/grants, private scholarships, the school's own gift aid. *Loans:* Direct Subsidized Stafford, Direct Unsubsidized Stafford, Direct PLUS, Subsidized Stafford, Unsubsidized Stafford, PLUS, Federal Perkins, college/university loans from institutional funds. *Student Employment:* Federal Work-Study Program available. Institutional employment available. Highest amount earned per year from on-campus jobs $1,600. Off-campus job opportunities are good. **Financial Aid Statistics:** 100% freshmen, 97% undergrads receive need-based scholarship or grant aid. 7% freshmen, 8% undergrads receive non-need-based scholarship or grant aid. 93% freshmen, 91% undergrads receive need-based self-help aid. 4% freshmen, 4% undergrads receive athletic scholarships. 95% freshmen, 95% undergrads receive any aid. 88% undergrads borrow to pay for school. Average cumulative indebtedness $27,834. **Criteria for awarding institutional aid:** *Non-need-based:* academics, alumni affiliation, athletics, music/drama, state/district residency.

TOCCOA FALLS COLLEGE

Toccoa Falls College, Toccoa Falls, GA 30598
Phone: 888-785-5624 · **Financial Aid Phone:** 706-886-6831
E-mail: admissions@tfc.edu
Fax: 706-282-6012 · **Website:** www.tfc.edu • **ACT Code:** 868

This private school, affiliated with the Christian & Missionary Allianc Church, was founded in 1907. It has a 1100-acre campus.

RATINGS

Admissions Selectivity Rating: 86   Fire Safety Rating: 65

STUDENTS AND FACULTY

Enrollment: 858. **Student Body:** 54% female, 46% male, 46% out-of-state, 1% international. Asian 8%, African American 3%, Caucasian 86%, Hispanic 2%, Native American <1%
Retention and Graduation: 60% freshmen return for sophomore year. 46% freshmen graduate within 4 years. 55% freshmen graduate within 6 years. **Faculty:** 47 full-time faculty, 57% hold PhDs, 21% are are members of minority groups, 4% are women. 0% of classes are taught by teaching assistants.

ACADEMICS

Degrees: associate, bachelor's, certificate. **Classes:** Most classes have fewer than 10 students. **Majors with Highest Enrollment:** Missions/Missionary

Studies and Missiology; Elementary Education and Teaching. **Special Study Options:** distance learning, double major, dual enrollment, independent study, internships, teacher certification program. **Disability Services:** Special programs offered to physically disabled students include note-taking services, reader services, tutors. **Career services:** career assessment.

FACILITIES

Housing: men's dorms, special housing for international students, women's dorms, apartments for married students, Mobile home court living available for married students. 70% of campus accessible to physically disabled. **Computers:** 40% of classrooms, 50% of dorms, 100% of libraries, 100% of dining areas, 50% of student union, 1% of common outdoor areas have wireless network access. Students can register for classes online. Administrative functions (other than registration) can be performed online.

CAMPUS LIFE

Environment: Rural. **Activities:** Choral groups, concert band, drama/theater, jazz band, music ensembles, radio station, student government, student newspaper, yearbook, Campus Ministries. **Athletics (Intercollegiate):** *Men:* baseball, basketball, cross-country, golf, soccer, tennis. *Women:* basketball, cheerleading, cross-country, golf, soccer, tennis, volleyball. **On-Campus Highlights:** The Waterfall, Student Center, Gymnatorium, Eagle's Nest, Grace Chapel & Performing Arts Center.

ADMISSIONS

Freshman Academic Profile: Average high school GPA 3.4. 12% in top 10% of high school class, 38% in top 25% of high school class, 70% in top 50% of high school class. 57% from public high schools. SAT Math middle 50% range 430-550. SAT Critical Reading middle 50% range 460-570. ACT middle 50% range 18-25. Minimum paper TOEFL 500. **Basis for Candidate Selection:** *Very important factors considered include:* application essay, academic GPA, recommendation(s), rigor of secondary school record, standardized test scores, character/personal qualities, religious affiliation/commitment. *Other factors considered include:* extracurricular activities, interview, level of applicant's interest, talent/ability, volunteer work, work experience. **Freshman Admission Requirements:** High school diploma is required and GED is accepted. **Freshman Admission Statistics:** 1,188 applied, 45% admitted, 31% enrolled. **Transfer Admission Requirements:** college transcript(s), essay or personal statement, Minimum college GPA of 2.0 required. Lowest grade transferable C-. **General Admission Information:** Application Fee $20. Regular application deadline 8/1. Regular notification 3/1. Nonfall registration accepted. Admission may be deferred for a maximum of 2 years. Credit and/or placement offered for CEEB Advanced Placement tests.

COSTS AND FINANCIAL AID

Average book expense $1,000. **Required Forms and Deadlines:** FAFSA, Institution's own financial aid form, State aid form. **Notification of Awards:** Applicants will be notified of awards on a rolling basis beginning 3/1. **Types of Aid:** *Need-based scholarships/grants:* Federal Pell, SEOG, state scholarships/grants, private scholarships, the school's own gift aid. *Loans:* Subsidized Stafford, Unsubsidized Stafford, PLUS, Federal Perkins, state loans, college/university loans from institutional funds. *Student Employment:* Highest amount earned per year from on-campus jobs $6,000. **Financial Aid Statistics:** 44% freshmen, 52% undergrads receive need-based scholarship or grant aid. 95% freshmen, 100% undergrads receive non-need-based scholarship or grant aid. 20% freshmen, 16% undergrads receive need-based self-help aid. 0% freshmen, 0% undergrads receive athletic scholarships. 100% freshmen, 98% undergrads receive any aid. 78% undergrads borrow to pay for school. Average cumulative indebtedness $4,864. **Criteria for awarding institutional aid:** *Non-need-based:* academics, alumni affiliation, leadership, music/drama, religious affiliation, state/district residency.

TOUGALOO COLLEGE

500 West Country Line Road, Tougaloo, MS 39174
Phone: 888-424-2566 · **Financial Aid Phone:** 601-977-7769
E-mail: jjacobs@mail.tougaloo.edu
Fax: 601-977-6185 · **Website:** tougaloo.edu

This private school, affiliated with the Church of Christ Church, was founded in 1869. It has a 500-acre campus.

RATINGS

Admissions Selectivity Rating: 66   Fire Safety Rating: 84

STUDENTS AND FACULTY

Enrollment: 967. **Student Body:** 72% female, 28% male, 18% out-of-state, 0% international (3 countries represented). Asian 0%, African American 99%, Caucasian 0%, Hispanic 0%, Native American <1%

Retention and Graduation: 70% freshmen return for sophomore year. 63% freshmen graduate within 4 years. 100% freshmen graduate within 6 years. 69% grads go on to further study within 1 year. 50% grads pursue arts and sciences degrees. 20% grads pursue law degrees. 10% grads pursue business degrees. 20% grads pursue medical degrees. **Faculty:** 78 full-time faculty, 60% hold PhDs, 51% are are members of minority groups, 55% are women. 0% of classes are taught by teaching assistants.

ACADEMICS

Degrees: associate, bachelor's, certificate, terminal associate, transfer associate. **Classes:** Most classes have 20-29 students. Most lab/discussion sessions have 10-19 students. **Special Study Options:** cooperative education program, cross-registration, double major, dual enrollment, exchange student program (domestic), honors program, independent study, internships, liberal arts/career combination, study abroad, teacher certification program. **Honors programs:** There is a general Honors Program **Combined degree programs:** Nursing with Univ. of MS Medical School. **Disability Services:** Special programs offered to physically disabled students include tape recorders, tutors. **Career services:** Alumni network, alumni services, career/job search classes, career assessment, internships.

FACILITIES

Housing: men's dorms, women's dorms. 70% of campus accessible to physically disabled. **Special Academic Facilities/Equipment:** Tougaloo Art Collections Bailey-Ward Black Collection **Computers:** Students can register for classes online. Administrative functions (other than registration) can be performed online.

CAMPUS LIFE

Environment: City. **Activities:** Choral groups, dance, drama/theater, jazz band, literary magazine, music ensembles, student government, student newspaper, television station, yearbook. 50 registered organizations, 2 honor societies, 7 religious organizations. 4 fraternities, 4 sororities. **Athletics (Intercollegiate):** *Men:* baseball, basketball, cross-country, golf, tennis, track/field (outdoor). *Women:* basketball, cross-country, golf, softball, tennis, track/field (outdoor). **On-Campus Highlights:** Woodworth Chapel, L. Zenobia Coleman Library and Archives, Warren Hall Student Center, Owens Health and Wellness Center, Blackmon Administration Center.

ADMISSIONS

Freshman Academic Profile: Average high school GPA 3.2. 95% from public high schools. ACT middle 50% range 16-21. Minimum paper TOEFL 500. **Basis for Candidate Selection:** *Important factors considered include:* recommendation(s), rigor of secondary school record, standardized test scores, character/personal qualities, talent/ability. *Other factors considered include:* Class rank, application essay, alumni/ae relation, extracurricular activities, interview. **Freshman Admission Requirements:** High school diploma is required and GED is accepted. *Academic units required:* 3 English, 2 mathematics, 2 science, 0 foreign language, 1 social studies, 1 history, 7 academic electives, 0. **Transfer Admission Requirements:** college transcript(s), standardized test scores, statement of good standing from prior institution(s). Minimum college GPA of 2.0 required. Lowest grade transferable C. **General Admission Information:** Application Fee $25. Notification on a rolling basis, beginning on or about 10/15. Nonfall registration accepted. Admission may be deferred for a maximum of 1 semester. Credit and/or placement offered for CEEB Advanced Placement tests.

COSTS AND FINANCIAL AID

Average book expense $1,200. **Required Forms and Deadlines:** FAFSA, Institution's own financial aid form, CSS/Financial Aid PROFILE. **Notification of Awards:** Applicants will be notified of awards on a rolling basis beginning 10/15. **Types of Aid:** *Need-based scholarships/grants:* Federal Pell, SEOG, state scholarships/grants, private scholarships, the school's own gift aid, United Negro College Fund. *Loans:* Direct Subsidized Stafford, Direct PLUS, Unsubsidized Stafford, Federal Perkins, Federal Nursing. *Student Employment:* Federal Work-Study Program available. Highest amount earned per year from on-campus jobs $2,800. Off-campus job opportunities are excellent. **Financial Aid Statistics:** 96% freshmen, 96% undergrads receive need-based scholarship or grant aid. 0% freshmen, 17% undergrads receive non-need-based scholarship or grant aid. 0% freshmen, 22% undergrads receive need-based self-help aid. 0% freshmen, 1% undergrads receive athletic scholarships. 95% freshmen, 95% undergrads receive any aid. 85% undergrads borrow to pay for school. Average cumulative indebtedness $8,000. **Criteria for awarding institutional aid:** *Non-need-based:* academics, art, athletics, leadership, music/drama.

TOWSON UNIVERSITY

8000 York Road, Towson, MD 21252-0001
Phone: 410-704-2113 • **Financial Aid Phone:** 410-704-6242
E-mail: admissions@towson.edu • **CEEB Code:** 5404
Fax: 410-704-3030 • **Website:** www.towson.edu • **ACT Code:** 1718

This public school was founded in 1866. It has a 328-acre campus.

RATINGS

Admissions Selectivity Rating: 85   **Fire Safety Rating:** 75

STUDENTS AND FACULTY

Enrollment: 18,546. **Student Body:** 60% female, 40% male, 15% out-of-state, 2% international (74 countries represented). Asian 5%, African American 16%, Caucasian 63%, Hispanic 6%, Native American <1%
Retention and Graduation: 85% freshmen return for sophomore year. 43% freshmen graduate within 4 years. 68% freshmen graduate within 6 years. 32% grads go on to further study within 1 year. **Faculty:** 872 full-time faculty, 79% hold PhDs, 54% are are members of minority groups, 19% are women. 0% of classes are taught by teaching assistants.

ACADEMICS

Degrees: bachelor's, master's, post-bachelor's certificate, post-master's certificate. **Classes:** Most classes have 20-29 students. Most lab/discussion sessions have 10-19 students. **Majors with Highest Enrollment:** Psychology; Business Administration and Management; Biology/Biological Sciences. **Special Study Options:** cooperative education program, cross-registration, distance learning, double major, dual enrollment, English as a Second Language (ESL), exchange student program (domestic), honors program, independent study, internships, liberal arts/career combination, student-designed major, study abroad, teacher certification program. **Honors programs:** Honors College. **Disability Services:** Special programs offered to physically disabled students include note-taking services, reader services. **Career services:** Alumni network, alumni services, career/job search classes, career assessment, internships, regional alumni. Career services highlights include internships.
FACILITIES **Housing:** Coed dorms, special housing for disabled students, special housing for international students, apartments for single students. 80% of campus accessible to physically disabled. **Special Academic Facilities/Equipment:** Art galleries, animal museum, Asian art collection, elementary school, media center, speech/language clinic, planetarium/observatory, herbarium, electron microscope, argon laser. **Computers:** 100% of classrooms, 100% of dorms, 100% of libraries, 100% of dining areas, 100% of student union, 100% of common outdoor areas have wireless network access. Students can register for classes online. Administrative functions (other than registration) can be performed online.

CAMPUS LIFE

Environment: Metropolis. **Activities:** Choral groups, concert band, dance, drama/theater, jazz band, literary magazine, marching band, music ensembles, musical theater, pep band, radio station, student government, student newspaper, symphony orchestra, television station, yearbook, Campus Ministries, International Student Organization. 198 registered organizations, 15 honor societies, 12 religious organizations. 12 fraternities, 10 sororities. **Athletics (Intercollegiate):** *Men:* baseball, basketball, cheerleading, cross-country, diving, football, golf, lacrosse, soccer, swimming, tennis. *Women:* basketball, cheerleading, cross-country, diving, field hockey, gymnastics, lacrosse, soccer, softball, swimming, tennis, track/field (outdoor), volleyball. **On-Campus Highlights:** Johnny Unitas Stadium, University Union, Burdick Hall-athletic facilities, The Den, Towson Center-events. **Environmental Initiatives:** Sign the American College and University President's Climate Committment (ACUPCC) in 2007 pledging to become/achieve climate neutrality RecycleMania Partcipate in B-CaUSE which is comprised of 12 institutions of higher education from the Baltimore region

ADMISSIONS

Freshman Academic Profile: Average high school GPA 3.61. 19% in top 10% of high school class, 49% in top 25% of high school class, 86% in top 50% of high school class. SAT Math middle 50% range 500-590. SAT Critical Reading middle 50% range 500-580. SAT Writing middle 50% range 490-580. ACT middle 50% range 21-25. Minimum internet-based TOEFL 61. Minimum paper TOEFL 500. **Basis for Candidate Selection:** *Very important factors considered include:* academic GPA. *Important factors considered include:* rigor of secondary school record, standardized test scores. *Other factors considered include:* Class rank, application essay, recommendation(s), first generation, talent/ability. **Freshman Admission Requirements:** High school diploma is required and GED is accepted. *Academic units required:* 4 English, 3 mathematics, 3 science, (2 science labs), 2 foreign language, 3 social studies, 6 academic electives. **Freshman Admission Statistics:** 18,134 applied, 59% admitted,

25% enrolled. **Transfer Admission Requirements:** college transcript(s), Minimum college GPA of 2.0 required. Lowest grade transferable D. **General Admission Information:** Application Fee $45. Regular application deadline 2/15. Notification on a rolling basis, beginning on or about 10/15. Nonfall registration accepted. Admission may be deferred for a maximum of Up to 1 year. Credit and/or placement offered for CEEB Advanced Placement tests.

COSTS AND FINANCIAL AID

Annual in-state tuition $6,004. Annual out-of-state tuition $17,682. Room and board $11,260. Required fees $2,586. Average book expense $1,080. **Required Forms and Deadlines:** FAFSA. **Notification of Awards:** Applicants will be notified of awards on a rolling basis beginning 3/21. **Types of Aid:** *Need-based scholarships/grants:* Federal Pell, SEOG, state scholarships/grants, private scholarships, the school's own gift aid. *Loans:* Direct Subsidized Stafford, Direct Unsubsidized Stafford, Direct PLUS, Federal Perkins. *Student Employment:* Federal Work-Study Program available. Institutional employment available. Off-campus job opportunities are excellent. **Financial Aid Statistics:** 51% freshmen, 64% undergrads receive need-based scholarship or grant aid. 35% freshmen, 24% undergrads receive non-need-based scholarship or grant aid. 68% freshmen, 69% undergrads receive need-based self-help aid. 2% freshmen, 1% undergrads receive athletic scholarships. 75% freshmen, 73% undergrads receive any aid. 63% undergrads borrow to pay for school. Average cumulative indebtedness $20,785. **Criteria for awarding institutional aid:** *Non-need-based:* academics, art, athletics, music/drama.

TRANSYLVANIA UNIVERSITY

300 North Broadway, Lexington, KY 40508-1797
Phone: 859-233-8242 • **Financial Aid Phone:** 859-233-8239
E-mail: admissions@transy.edu • **CEEB Code:** 1808
Fax: 859-281-3649 • **Website:** www.transy.edu • **ACT Code:** 1550

This private school, affiliated with the Christian (Nondenominational) Church, was founded in 1780. It has a 36-acre campus.

RATINGS

Admissions Selectivity Rating: 88   **Fire Safety Rating:** 88

STUDENTS AND FACULTY

Enrollment: 1,014. **Student Body:** 58% female, 42% male, 23% out-of-state, 4% international (7 countries represented). Asian 2%, African American 3%, Caucasian 80%, Hispanic 5%, Native American <1%
Retention and Graduation: 83% freshmen return for sophomore year. 63% freshmen graduate within 4 years. 70% freshmen graduate within 6 years. 39% grads go on to further study within 1 year. 8% grads pursue arts and sciences degrees. 4% grads pursue law degrees. 3% grads pursue business degrees. 3% grads pursue medical degrees. **Faculty:** 87 full-time faculty, 97% hold PhDs, 45% are are members of minority groups, 7% are women. 0% of classes are taught by teaching assistants.

ACADEMICS

Degrees: bachelor's. **Classes:** Most classes have 10-19 students. Most lab/discussion sessions have 10-19 students. **Majors with Highest Enrollment:** Biology/Biological Sciences; Business/Commerce; Accounting. **Special Study Options:** double major, independent study, internships, liberal arts/career combination, student-designed major, study abroad, teacher certification program. **Disability Services:** Special programs offered to physically disabled students include note-taking services, reader services, tape recorders, tutors. **Career services:** Alumni network, alumni services, career/job search classes, career assessment, internships, regional alumni. Career services highlights include Internship Programs.

FACILITIES

Housing: Coed dorms, special housing for disabled students, men's dorms, women's dorms, apartments for single students, Theme HousingEfficiency apartment option for upperclassmen. Units with facilities for disabled students. 90% of campus accessible to physically disabled. **Special Academic Facilities/Equipment:** Art gallery, museum of early scientific apparatus, medical museum, language lab, transmission electron microscope. **Computers:** 20% of classrooms, 20% of dorms, 75% of libraries, 20% of dining areas, 100% of student union, 10% of common outdoor areas have wireless network access. Administrative functions (other than registration) can be performed online.

CAMPUS LIFE

Environment: City. **Activities:** Choral groups, concert band, dance, drama/theater, jazz band, literary magazine, music ensembles, musical theater, opera, pep band, radio station, student government, student newspaper, yearbook. 55 registered organizations, 10 honor societies, 7 religious organizations. 4 fraternities, 4 sororities. **Athletics (Intercollegiate):** *Men:* baseball, basketball, cheerleading, cross-country, diving, golf, soccer, swimming, tennis, track/field (outdoor). *Women:* basketball, cheerleading, cross-country, diving, field hockey, golf, soccer, softball, swimming, tennis, track/field (outdoor), volleyball. **On-Campus Highlights:** Beck Athletic and Recreation Center, William T. Young Campus Center, Mitchell Fine Arts Center, Little Theater, 1780 Café. **Environmental Initiatives:** Developing a comprehensive sustainability master plan. Comprehensive environmental policy including commitment to build to LEED silver. Ongoing outreach to faculty, staff, and students on a variety of sustainability issues.

ADMISSIONS

Freshman Academic Profile: Average high school GPA 3.74. 51% in top 10% of high school class, 76% in top 25% of high school class, 94% in top 50% of high school class. 78% from public high schools. SAT Math middle 50% range 530-660. SAT Critical Reading middle 50% range 510-640. ACT middle 50% range 25-30. Minimum internet-based TOEFL 80. Minimum paper TOEFL 550. **Basis for Candidate Selection:** *Very important factors considered include:* academic GPA, rigor of secondary school record, standardized test scores. *Important factors considered include:* application essay, recommendation(s), extracurricular activities. *Other factors considered include:* Class rank, alumni/ae relation, character/personal qualities, first generation, geographical residence, interview, talent/ability, volunteer work, work experience. **Freshman Admission Requirements:** High school diploma is required and GED is accepted. *Academic units required:* 4 English, 3 mathematics, 3 science, 0 foreign language, 2 social studies, 0 history, 0 academic electives. **Freshman Admission Statistics:** 1,444 applied, 83% admitted, 22% enrolled. **Transfer Admission Requirements:** High school transcript, college transcript(s), essay or personal statement, Minimum college GPA of 2.75 required. Lowest grade transferable C-. **General Admission Information:** Application Fee $30. Regular application deadline 2/1. Regular notification 3/1. Nonfall registration accepted. Admission may be deferred for a maximum of 12 months. Credit and/or placement offered for CEEB Advanced Placement tests.

COSTS AND FINANCIAL AID

Annual tuition $32,010. Room and board $9,300. Required fees $1,350. Average book expense $1,000. **Required Forms and Deadlines:** FAFSA. **Notification of Awards:** Applicants will be notified of awards on a rolling basis beginning 3/15. **Types of Aid:** *Need-based scholarships/grants:* Federal Pell, SEOG, state scholarships/grants, private scholarships, the school's own gift aid. *Loans:* Subsidized Stafford, Unsubsidized Stafford, PLUS, Federal Perkins, college/university loans from institutional funds. *Student Employment:* Federal Work-Study Program available. Institutional employment available. Off-campus job opportunities are excellent. **Financial Aid Statistics:** 100% freshmen, 100% undergrads receive need-based scholarship or grant aid. 20% freshmen, 17% undergrads receive non-need-based scholarship or grant aid. 74% freshmen, 75% undergrads receive need-based self-help aid. 0% freshmen, 0% undergrads receive athletic scholarships. 99% freshmen, 98% undergrads receive any aid. 70% undergrads borrow to pay for school. Average cumulative indebtedness $25,165. **Criteria for awarding institutional aid:** *Non-need-based:* academics, art, leadership, minority status, music/drama, religious affiliation, state/district residency.

See page 1158.

TREVECCA NAZARENE UNIVERSITY

333 Murfreesboro Road, Nashville, TN 37210
Phone: 615-248-1320 • **Financial Aid Phone:** 615-248-1242
E-mail: admissions_und@trevecca.edu
Fax: 615-248-7406 • **Website:** www.trevecca.edu • **ACT Code:** 4016

This private school, affiliated with the Nazarene Church, was founded in 1901. It has a 65-acre campus.

RATINGS

Admissions Selectivity Rating: 75   **Fire Safety Rating:** 60*

STUDENTS AND FACULTY

Enrollment: 1,609. **Student Body:** 56% female, 44% male, 38% out-of-state, 1% international (11 countries represented). Asian 1%, African American 9%, Caucasian 71%, Hispanic 4%, Native American 1%

Retention and Graduation: 39% freshmen graduate within 4 years. **Faculty:** 80 full-time faculty, 90% hold PhDs, 34% are are members of minority groups, 9% are women.

ACADEMICS

Degrees: associate, bachelor's, master's. **Classes:** Most classes have 10-19 students. **Majors with Highest Enrollment:** Biology/Biological Sciences; Business Administration and Management; Psychology. **Special Study Options:** double major, internships, study abroad, teacher certification program, Four adult degree-completion programs offer non-traditional class schedules (night/on-line). **Disability Services:** Special programs offered to physically disabled students include note-taking services, reader services, tutors. **Career services:** career/job search classes, internships.

FACILITIES

Housing: men's dorms, women's dorms, apartments for married students, apartments for single students. **Computers:** 100% of classrooms, 100% of dorms, 100% of libraries, 100% of dining areas, 100% of student union, 100% of common outdoor areas have wireless network access. Administrative functions (other than registration) can be performed online.

CAMPUS LIFE

Environment: Metropolis. **Activities:** Choral groups, concert band, drama/theater, jazz band, literary magazine, marching band, music ensembles, musical theater, pep band, radio station, student government, student newspaper, symphony orchestra, television station, yearbook, Campus Ministries, International Student Organization. **Athletics (Intercollegiate):** *Men:* baseball, basketball, golf, soccer. *Women:* basketball, golf, soccer, softball, volleyball. **On-Campus Highlights:** Library, Student Center.

ADMISSIONS

Freshman Academic Profile: Average high school GPA 3.41. SAT Math middle 50% range 450-590. SAT Critical Reading middle 50% range 470-590. ACT middle 50% range 20-26. Minimum internet-based TOEFL 173. Minimum paper TOEFL 500. **Basis for Candidate Selection:** *Very important factors considered include:* academic GPA, standardized test scores, character/personal qualities. *Important factors considered include:* level of applicant's interest. *Other factors considered include:* Class rank, application essay, recommendation(s), extracurricular activities, interview, talent/ability. **Freshman Admission Requirements:** High school diploma is required and GED is accepted. **Freshman Admission Statistics:** 1,029 applied, 73% admitted, 43% enrolled. **Transfer Admission Requirements:** college transcript(s), Lowest grade transferable D. **General Admission Information:** Application Fee $25. Regular application deadline 8/1. Nonfall registration accepted. Credit offered for CEEB Advanced Placement tests.

COSTS AND FINANCIAL AID

Required Forms and Deadlines: FAFSA. **Notification of Awards:** Applicants will be notified of awards on a rolling basis beginning 3/1. **Types of Aid:** *Need-based scholarships/grants:* Federal Pell, SEOG, state scholarships/grants, private scholarships, the school's own gift aid. *Loans:* Subsidized Stafford, Unsubsidized Stafford, PLUS, Federal Perkins. *Student Employment:* Federal Work-Study Program available. Institutional employment available. Off-campus job opportunities are good. **Financial Aid Statistics:** 94% undergrads receive any aid. 76% undergrads borrow to pay for school. **Criteria for awarding institutional aid:** *Non-need-based:* academics, alumni affiliation, art, athletics, leadership, minority status, music/drama, religious affiliation.

TRINE UNIVERSITY

1 University Avenue, Angola, IN 46703
Phone: 260-665-4100 • **Financial Aid Phone:** 260-664-4158
E-mail: admit@trine.edu • **CEEB Code:** 1811
Fax: 260-665-4578 • **Website:** www.trine.edu • **ACT Code:** 1250

This private school was founded in 1884. It has a 400-acre campus.

RATINGS

Admissions Selectivity Rating: 84   **Fire Safety Rating:** 88

STUDENTS AND FACULTY

Enrollment: 1,653. **Student Body:** 28% female, 72% male, 39% out-of-state, 8% international (13 countries represented). Asian 0%, African American 2%, Caucasian 78%, Hispanic 4%, Native American <1%
Retention and Graduation: 35% freshmen graduate within 4 years. 51% freshmen graduate within 6 years. 25% grads go on to further study within 1 year. 10% grads pursue arts and sciences degrees. 5% grads pursue law degrees. 10% grads pursue business degrees. **Faculty:** 107 full-time faculty, 60% hold

PhDs, 32% are are members of minority groups, 13% are women. 0% of classes are taught by teaching assistants.

ACADEMICS

Degrees: associate, bachelor's, master's. **Classes:** Most classes have 20-29 students. Most lab/discussion sessions have 10-19 students. **Majors with Highest Enrollment:** Civil Engineering; Mechanical Engineering; Criminal Justice/Safety Studies. **Special Study Options:** cooperative education program, distance learning, double major, dual enrollment, English as a Second Language (ESL), honors program, internships, liberal arts/career combination, study abroad, teacher certification program. **Honors programs:** Honors program began with Fall 2006 entering class of freshmen. **Combined degree programs:** BA/MEng. **Disability Services:** Special programs offered to physically disabled students include tutors. **Career services:** Alumni network, alumni services, career/job search classes, career assessment, internships, regional alumni. Career services highlights includecooperative education (Co-op) that students may elect to incorporate as a part of their academic curriculum. Co-op students alternate semesters of employment with semesters of full-time study, that provides both academic knowledge,relevant work experience, and a salary or stipend. A Co-op background is highly regarded by prospective employers; seniors seeking full-time employment with the cooperative education credential are consistently selected over candidates without this major-related experience.

FACILITIES

Housing: Coed dorms, men's dorms, women's dorms, apartments for single students, Honors housing. 95% of campus accessible to physically disabled. **Special Academic Facilities/Equipment:** Lewis Hershey Museum; Wells Gallery of Engravings; Zollner Golf Course **Computers:** 100% of classrooms, 100% of dorms, 100% of libraries, 100% of dining areas, 100% of student union, have wireless network access. Students can register for classes online. Administrative functions (other than registration) can be performed online.

CAMPUS LIFE

Environment: Village. **Activities:** Choral groups, dance, drama/theater, music ensembles, pep band, radio station, student government, student newspaper, yearbook. 35 registered organizations, 13 honor societies, 3 religious organizations. 8 fraternities, 6 sororities. **Athletics (Intercollegiate):** *Men:* baseball, basketball, cross-country, football, golf, lacrosse, soccer, tennis, track/field (outdoor), track/field (indoor), wrestling. *Women:* basketball, cross-country, golf, lacrosse, soccer, softball, tennis, track/field (outdoor), track/field (indoor), volleyball. **On-Campus Highlights:** University Center/Ctr for online Technol, Fawick Hall of Engineering, Taylor Hall of Humanities, Zollner Golf Course (on campus), Hershey Hall (Recreational Facilities). **Environmental Initiatives:** IDEM—MS4 Storm Water Program; Erosion control best management practices; public outreach; World Wide Water Sampling Day; Water retention projects; water gardens; storm water inlet identification; Audubon Certification—green chemicals on golf course, campus, and athletic fields, water-based paints; Green Cleaning chemicals and floor scrubbing equipment that reduces water consumption.

ADMISSIONS

Freshman Academic Profile: Average high school GPA 3.47. 31% in top 10% of high school class, 57% in top 25% of high school class, 84% in top 50% of high school class. 85% from public high schools. SAT Math middle 50% range 490-600. SAT Critical Reading middle 50% range 455-560. ACT middle 50% range 21-27. Minimum internet-based TOEFL 80. Minimum paper TOEFL 550. **Basis for Candidate Selection:** *Very important factors considered include:* Class rank, academic GPA, rigor of secondary school record, standardized test scores. *Important factors considered include:* application essay, recommendation(s), extracurricular activities, interview. *Other factors considered include:* alumni/ae relation, character/personal qualities, talent/ability, volunteer work, work experience. **Freshman Admission Requirements:** High school diploma is required and GED is accepted. *Academic units required:* 4 English, 3 mathematics, 3 science, (2 science labs), 3 social studies, 2 history, 3 academic electives. **Freshman Admission Statistics:** 2,890 applied, 76% admitted, 24% enrolled. **Transfer Admission Requirements:** High school transcript, college transcript(s), statement of good standing from prior institution(s). Minimum college GPA of 2.0 required. Lowest grade transferable C. **General Admission Information:** Regular application deadline 8/1. Nonfall registration accepted. Admission may be deferred for a maximum of 12 months. Credit and/or placement offered for CEEB Advanced Placement tests.

COSTS AND FINANCIAL AID

Annual tuition $29,300. Room and board $9,800. Required fees $300. Average book expense $1,200. **Required Forms and Deadlines:** FAFSA. **Notification of Awards:** Applicants will be notified of awards on a rolling basis beginning 2/15. **Types of Aid:** *Need-based scholarships/grants:* Federal Pell, SEOG, state scholarships/grants, private scholarships, the school's own gift aid. *Loans:* Subsidized Stafford, Unsubsidized Stafford, PLUS. *Student Employment:* Federal Work-Study Program available. Highest amount earned per year from on-campus jobs $2,420. Off-campus job opportunities are good. **Financial Aid**

Statistics: 81% freshmen, 89% undergrads receive need-based scholarship or grant aid. 13% freshmen, 17% undergrads receive non-need-based scholarship or grant aid. 100% freshmen, 100% undergrads receive need-based self-help aid. 0% freshmen, 0% undergrads receive athletic scholarships. 99% freshmen, 98% undergrads receive any aid. 86% undergrads borrow to pay for school. Average cumulative indebtedness $22,349. **Criteria for awarding institutional aid:** *Non-need-based:* academics, music/drama.

TRINITY BIBLE COLLEGE

50 South 6th Avenue, Ellendale, ND 58436-7150
Phone: 701-349-5403
E-mail: admissions@trinitybiblecollege.edu
Fax: 701-349-5443 • **Website:** www.trinitybiblecollege.edu

This is a private school.

RATINGS

Admissions Selectivity Rating: 60*   **Fire Safety Rating:** 60*

STUDENTS AND FACULTY

Enrollment: 305. **Student Body:** 54% female, 46% male, 60% out-of-state, 0% international. Asian 1%, African American 3%, Caucasian 91%, Hispanic 2%, Native American 4%
Retention and Graduation: 77% freshmen return for sophomore year. 44% freshmen graduate within 6 years.

ACADEMICS

Degrees: associate, bachelor's, certificate. **Special Study Options:** distance learning, double major, dual enrollment, independent study, teacher certification program.

FACILITIES

Housing: apartments for married students, apartments for single students.

CAMPUS LIFE

Activities: student government.

ADMISSIONS

Basis for Candidate Selection: *Very important factors considered include:* recommendation(s), standardized test scores, character/personal qualities. *Important factors considered include:* application essay. *Other factors considered include:* rigor of secondary school record, religious affiliation/commitment. **Freshman Admission Requirements:** High school diploma is required and GED is accepted. **Transfer Admission Requirements:** High school transcript, college transcript(s), essay or personal statement, statement of good standing from prior institution(s). Lowest grade transferable C. **General Admission Information:** Application Fee $25. Notification on a rolling basis, beginning on or about 9/2. Nonfall registration accepted. Admission may be deferred indefinitely.

COSTS AND FINANCIAL AID

Annual tuition $9,680. Room and board $4,370. Required fees $1,478. Average book expense $700. **Required Forms and Deadlines:** FAFSA. **Notification of Awards:** Applicants will be notified of awards on a rolling basis beginning 3/1. **Types of Aid:** *Need-based scholarships/grants:* Federal Pell, SEOG, state scholarships/grants, private scholarships, the school's own gift aid. *Loans:* Subsidized Stafford, Unsubsidized Stafford, PLUS, Federal Perkins. **Financial Aid Statistics:** 100% freshmen, 100% undergrads receive need-based scholarship or grant aid. 0% freshmen, 0% undergrads receive non-need-based scholarship or grant aid. 99% freshmen, 98% undergrads receive need-based self-help aid. 0% freshmen, 0% undergrads receive athletic scholarships. **Criteria for awarding institutional aid:** *Non-need-based:* academics, alumni affiliation, art, leadership, music/drama, religious affiliation.

TRINITY CHRISTIAN COLLEGE

6601 West College Drive, Palos Heights, IL 60463
Phone: 708-239-4708 · **Financial Aid Phone:** 708-239-4872
E-mail: admissions@trnty.edu · **CEEB Code:** 1820
Fax: 708-239-4826 · **Website:** www.trnty.edu · **ACT Code:** 1165

This private school was founded in 1959. It has a 60-acre campus.

RATINGS

Admissions Selectivity Rating: 81   **Fire Safety Rating:** 81

STUDENTS AND FACULTY

Enrollment: 1,237. **Student Body:** 65% female, 35% male, 35% out-of-state, 4% international (8 countries represented). Asian 2%, African American 10%, Caucasian 69%, Hispanic 11%, Native American <1%
Retention and Graduation: 84% freshmen return for sophomore year. 45% freshmen graduate within 4 years. 58% freshmen graduate within 6 years. 12% grads go on to further study within 1 year. 4% grads pursue arts and sciences degrees. 1% grads pursue law degrees. 1% grads pursue business degrees. 2% grads pursue medical degrees. **Faculty:** 85 full-time faculty, 65% hold PhDs, 52% are are members of minority groups, 13% are women. 0% of classes are taught by teaching assistants.

ACADEMICS

Degrees: bachelor's. **Classes:** Most classes have 10-19 students. Most lab/discussion sessions have 10-19 students. **Majors with Highest Enrollment:** Elementary Education and Teaching; Business/Commerce; Registered Nursing/Registered Nurse. **Special Study Options:** cooperative education program, double major, English as a Second Language (ESL), honors program, independent study, internships, liberal arts/career combination, study abroad, teacher certification program. **Honors programs:** The Trinity Honors Program challenges and academically supports gifted students through seminars, unique opportunities within the major program, and participation in co-curricular activities. **Disability Services:** Special programs offered to physically disabled students include reader services, tape recorders, tutors. **Career services:** Alumni network, alumni services, career assessment, internships, regional alumni. Career services highlights include Chicago Semester Internships.

FACILITIES

Housing: Coed dorms, apartments for married students, apartments for single students 98% of campus accessible to physically disabled. **Special Academic Facilities/Equipment:** Dutch Heritage Center. **Computers:** 100% of classrooms, 100% of dorms, 100% of libraries, 100% of dining areas, 100% of student union, 15% of common outdoor areas have wireless network access. Students can register for classes online. Administrative functions (other than registration) can be performed online.

CAMPUS LIFE

Environment: Metropolis. **Activities:** Choral groups, concert band, dance, drama/theater, jazz band, music ensembles, musical theater, student government, student newspaper, yearbook, Campus Ministries 15 registered organizations, 2 honor societies, 1 religous organization. **Athletics (Intercollegiate):** *Men:* baseball, basketball, cross-country, soccer, track/field (outdoor), track/field (indoor). *Women:* basketball, cross-country, soccer, softball, track/field (outdoor), track/field (indoor), volleyball. **On-Campus Highlights:** Bootsma Bookstore/Café, West Hall Rec, Chapel, South Hall Lobby. **Environmental Initiatives:** Recycling of paper, aluminum, and glass; Maintenance of a nature trail on campus; Recycling of all electronics.

ADMISSIONS

Freshman Academic Profile: Average high school GPA 3.5. 20% in top 10% of high school class, 42% in top 25% of high school class, 70% in top 50% of high school class. 54% from public high schools. SAT Math middle 50% range 460-620. SAT Critical Reading middle 50% range 450-560. ACT middle 50% range 20-27. Minimum internet-based TOEFL 79. Minimum paper TOEFL 550. **Basis for Candidate Selection:** *Very important factors considered include:* academic GPA, rigor of secondary school record, standardized test scores. *Important factors considered include:* Class rank, application essay, recommendation(s), character/personal qualities, extracurricular activities, interview, level of applicant's interest, religious affiliation/commitment, talent/ability. *Other factors considered include:* alumni/ae relation, first generation, geographical residence, racial/ethnic status, state residency, volunteer work, work experience. **Freshman Admission Requirements:** High school diploma is required and GED is accepted. *Academic units required:* 3 English, 3 mathematics, 2 science, 2 social studies. *Academic units recommended:* 3 English, 3 mathematics, 2 science, 2 social studies. **Freshman Admission Statistics:** 805 applied, 78% admitted, 30% enrolled. **Transfer Admission Requirements:** college transcript(s), essay or personal statement, interview, statement of good

standing from prior institution(s). Minimum college GPA of 2.0 required. Lowest grade transferable C. **General Admission Information:** Application Fee $20. Notification on a rolling basis, beginning on or about 9/1. Nonfall registration accepted. Admission may be deferred for a maximum of 2 semesters. Credit and/or placement offered for CEEB Advanced Placement tests.

COSTS AND FINANCIAL AID

Annual tuition $17,920. Room and board $7,010. Required fees $195. Average book expense $925. **Required Forms and Deadlines:** FAFSA. **Notification of Awards:** Applicants will be notified of awards on or about 3/15. **Types of Aid:** *Need-based scholarships/grants:* Federal Pell, SEOG, state scholarships/grants, private scholarships, the school's own gift aid. *Loans:* Subsidized Stafford, Unsubsidized Stafford, PLUS, Federal Perkins, Federal Nursing. *Student Employment:* Federal Work-Study Program available. Institutional employment available. Highest amount earned per year from on-campus jobs $10,905. Off-campus job opportunities are good. **Financial Aid Statistics:** 100% freshmen, 97% undergrads receive need-based scholarship or grant aid. 12% freshmen, 8% undergrads receive non-need-based scholarship or grant aid. 84% freshmen, 85% undergrads receive need-based self-help aid. 3% freshmen, 4% undergrads receive athletic scholarships. 97% freshmen, 91% undergrads receive any aid. 83% undergrads borrow to pay for school. Average cumulative indebtedness $25,529. **Criteria for awarding institutional aid:** *Non-need-based:* academics, alumni affiliation, art, athletics, leadership, minority status, music/drama, religious affiliation, state/district residency.

TRINITY COLLEGE (CT)

300 Summit Street, Hartford, CT 6016
Phone: 860-297-2180 · **Financial Aid Phone:** 860-297-2047
E-mail: admissions.office@trincoll.edu · **CEEB Code:** 3899
Fax: 860-297-2287 · **Website:** www.trincoll.edu · **ACT Code:** 598

This private school was founded in 1823. It has a 100-acre campus.

RATINGS

Admissions Selectivity Rating: 92   **Fire Safety Rating:** 90

STUDENTS AND FACULTY

Enrollment: 2,308. **Student Body:** 48% female, 52% male, 85% out-of-state, 8% international (48 countries represented). Asian 5%, African American 6%, Caucasian 65%, Hispanic 7%, Native American <1%
Retention and Graduation: 81% freshmen graduate within 4 years. 86% freshmen graduate within 6 years. 19% grads go on to further study within 1 year. 10% grads pursue arts and sciences degrees. 4% grads pursue law degrees. 1% grads pursue business degrees. 1% grads pursue medical degrees. **Faculty:** 198 full-time faculty, 92% hold PhDs, 46% are are members of minority groups, 20% are women. 0% of classes are taught by teaching assistants.

ACADEMICS

Degrees: bachelor's, master's. **Classes:** Most classes have 10-19 students. Most lab/discussion sessions have 10-19 students. **Majors with Highest Enrollment:** Economics; Political Science and Government; English Language and Literature. **Special Study Options:** Accelerated program, cross-registration, double major, exchange student program (domestic), honors program, independent study, internships, liberal arts/career combination, student-designed major, study abroad, teacher certification program, 5-year BS/MS in Electrical Engineering or Mechanical Engineering with Rensselaer Polytechnic Institute, Community Learning Initiative. **Combined degree programs:** BA/MEng, BA/MS in Elect, Engg,or Mech Engg. with RPI. **Disability Services:** Special programs offered to physically disabled students include note-taking services, reader services, tape recorders, tutors. **Career services:** Alumni network, alumni services, career/job search classes, career assessment, internships, regional alumni. Career services highlights include our academic internships, which provide real-life experiences within the framework of an academic analysis. They range from internships in for-profit governmental to non-profit organizations. Over half of our students take courses with a community-based experiential component also linking community engagement with an academic course.

FACILITIES

Housing: Coed dorms, special housing for disabled students, fraternity/sorority housing, Community service dorm, quiet dorm, wellness and substance-free,

21+ only, cooking. All dorms are non-smoking. 60% of campus accessible to physically disabled. **Special Academic Facilities/Equipment:** Watkinson Library; Austin Arts Center **Computers:** 95% of classrooms, 85% of dorms, 100% of libraries, 100% of dining areas, 100% of student union, 90% of common outdoor areas have wireless network access. Students can register for classes online. Administrative functions (other than registration) can be performed online.

CAMPUS LIFE

Environment: Metropolis. **Activities:** Choral groups, dance, drama/theater, jazz band, literary magazine, music ensembles, musical theater, radio station, student government, student newspaper, student-run film society, yearbook, Campus Ministries, International Student Organization, Model UN 105 registered organizations, 5 honor societies, 5 religious organizations. 7 fraternities, 3 sororities. **Athletics (Intercollegiate):** *Men:* baseball, basketball, crew/rowing, cross-country, diving, football, golf, ice hockey, lacrosse, soccer, squash, swimming, tennis, track/field (outdoor), track/field (indoor), wrestling. *Women:* basketball, crew/rowing, cross-country, diving, field hockey, ice hockey, lacrosse, soccer, softball, squash, swimming, tennis, track/field (outdoor), track/field (indoor), volleyball. **On-Campus Highlights:** The Learning Corridor, Library, The Science/Engineering Labs, Summit Suites (newest residence hall), The Chapel. **Environmental Initiatives:** Reduced energy consumption in the dining halls through automated lighting and low-draw fume hoods as well as a new Building Automation System to increase control of temperatures on campus. Contracted a new facilities management company, ARAMARK, and included a 10% energy reduction in 10 years as part of the contract. A renewed focus on recycling including the switch to single stream collection, additional bins and signs, education, and participation in Recyclemania.

ADMISSIONS

Freshman Academic Profile: 23% in top 10% of high school class, 59% in top 25% of high school class, 99% in top 50% of high school class. 40% from public high schools. SAT Math middle 50% range 580-670. SAT Critical Reading middle 50% range 570-660. SAT Writing middle 50% range 590-673. ACT middle 50% range 25-29. **Basis for Candidate Selection:** *Very important factors considered include:* rigor of secondary school record. *Important factors considered include:* Class rank, application essay, academic GPA, recommendation(s), standardized test scores, character/personal qualities, extracurricular activities, interview, racial/ethnic status, talent/ability. *Other factors considered include:* alumni/ae relation, first generation, geographical residence, level of applicant's interest, volunteer work, work experience. **Freshman Admission Requirements:** High school diploma is required and GED is accepted. *Academic units required:* 4 English, 3 mathematics, 2 science, (2 science labs), 3 foreign language, 2 history. 4 English, 3 mathematics, 2 science, (2 science labs), 3 foreign language, 2 history, **Freshman Admission Statistics:** 7,652 applied, 32% admitted, 25% enrolled. **Transfer Admission Requirements:** High school transcript, college transcript(s), essay or personal statement, standardized test scores, statement of good standing from prior institution(s). Minimum college GPA of 3.0 required. Lowest grade transferable C-. **General Admission Information:** Application Fee $60. Early decision application deadline 11/15. Regular application deadline 1/1. Regular notification 4/1. Nonfall registration not accepted. Admission may be deferred for a maximum of 12 months. Credit and/or placement offered for CEEB Advanced Placement tests.

COSTS AND FINANCIAL AID

Annual tuition $46,796. Room and board $12,700. Required fees $2,260. Average book expense $1,000. **Required Forms and Deadlines:** FAFSA, CSS/Financial Aid PROFILE, Noncustodial PROFILE, Business/Farm Supplement. **Notification of Awards:** Applicants will be notified of awards on or about 4/1. **Types of Aid:** *Need-based scholarships/grants:* Federal Pell, SEOG, state scholarships/grants, private scholarships, the school's own gift aid. *Loans:* Direct Subsidized Stafford, Direct Unsubsidized Stafford, Direct PLUS, Subsidized Stafford, Unsubsidized Stafford, PLUS, Federal Perkins, college/university loans from institutional funds. *Student Employment:* Federal Work-Study Program available. Institutional employment available. Highest amount earned per year from on-campus jobs $6,000. Off-campus job opportunities are good. **Financial Aid Statistics:** 96% freshmen, 95% undergrads receive need-based scholarship or grant aid. 15% freshmen, 6% undergrads receive non-need-based scholarship or grant aid. 70% freshmen, 76% undergrads receive need-based self-help aid. 0% freshmen, 0% undergrads receive athletic scholarships. 40% freshmen, 39% undergrads receive any aid. 45% undergrads borrow to pay for school. Average cumulative indebtedness $19,317. **Criteria for awarding institutional aid:** *Non-need-based:* academics, leadership.

See page 1160.

TRINITY COLLEGE DUBLIN

Academic Registry, Watts Building, Dublin 2, Ireland
Phone: 35318964500 · **Email:** academic.registry@tcd.ie
Website: www.tcd.ie

This is a public school.

RATINGS

Admissions Selectivity Rating: 70   **Fire Safety Rating:** 83

STUDENTS AND FACULTY

Enrollment: 11,839. **Student Body:** 60% female, 40% male, 15% out-of-state, (122 countries represented).
Retention and Graduation: 91% freshmen return for sophomore year. **Faculty:** 864 full-time faculty. 10% of classes are taught by teaching assistants.

COSTS AND FINANCIAL AID

Required Forms and Deadlines: FAFSA. **Financial Aid Statistics:** 25% undergrads borrow to pay for school.

TRINITY COLLEGE OF FLORIDA

2430 Welbilt Boulevard, Trinity, FL 34655
Phone: 727-569-1411 · **Financial Aid Phone:** 727-569-1413
E-mail: admissions@trinitycollege.edu · **CEEB Code:**
Fax: 727-569-1410 · **Website:** www.trinitycollege.edu   •   **ACT Code:** 4876

This private school was founded in 1932. It has a 40-acre campus.

RATINGS

Admissions Selectivity Rating: 70   **Fire Safety Rating:** 77

STUDENTS AND FACULTY

Enrollment: 210. **Student Body:** 39% female, 61% male, 28% out-of-state, 1% international (2 countries represented). Asian 0%, African American 18%, Caucasian 64%, Hispanic 16%, Native American <1%
Retention and Graduation: 67% freshmen return for sophomore year. 30% freshmen graduate within 4 years. 14% grads go on to further study within 1 year. **Faculty:** 6 full-time faculty, 83% hold PhDs, 17% are are members of minority groups, 0% are women. 0% of classes are taught by teaching assistants.

ACADEMICS

Degrees: associate, bachelor's, certificate, terminal associate. **Classes:** Most classes have fewer than 10 students. **Majors with Highest Enrollment:** Pastoral Studies/Counseling; Youth Ministry; Pre-Theology/Pre-Ministerial Studies. **Special Study Options:** Accelerated program, double major, dual enrollment, honors program, independent study, internships, weekend college. **Honors programs:** Our honors program consists of 4 Great Books Seminars. **Disability Services:** Special programs offered to physically disabled students include tutors. **Career services:** career assessment, internships,

FACILITIES

Housing: special housing for disabled students, men's dorms, women's dorms, Apartments available for double occupancy or more. 100% of campus accessible to physically disabled. **Computers:** 100% of classrooms, 100% of dorms, 100% of libraries, 100% of dining areas, 100% of student union, have wireless network access.

CAMPUS LIFE

Environment: City. **Activities:** Choral groups, drama/theater, student government, yearbook, Campus Ministries 4 religious organizations. **Athletics (Intercollegiate):** *Men:* basketball. *Women:* volleyball. **On-Campus Highlights:** Epiphanies Coffee Shop, Library, Lounge Areas, Outdoor Gazebo, Horseshoe Pits.

ADMISSIONS

Freshman Academic Profile: Average high school GPA 2.8. SAT Math middle 50% range 370-480. SAT Critical Reading middle 50% range 460-550. ACT middle 50% range 19-23. Minimum paper TOEFL 500. **Basis for Candidate Selection:** *Very important factors considered include:* application essay, academic GPA, recommendation(s), standardized test scores, religious affiliation/commitment. *Important factors considered include:* character/personal qualities. *Other factors considered include:* extracurricular activities. **Freshman Admission Requirements:** High school diploma is required and GED is accepted. *Academic units required:* 4 English, 4 mathematics, 4 science, (0 science labs), 2 foreign language, 2 social studies, 2 history, 0 visual/performing arts, 0 computer science, 0 academic electives, 0 0. *Academic units recommended:* 4 English, 4 mathematics, 4 science, (0 science labs), 2 foreign language, 2 social studies, 2 history, 0 visual/performing arts, 0 computer science, 0 academic electives, 0 0 **Freshman Admission Statistics:** 79 applied, 85% admitted, 49% enrolled. **Transfer Admission Requirements:** High school transcript, college transcript(s), essay or personal statement, Minimum college GPA of 2.0 required. Lowest grade transferable C. **General Admission Information:** Application Fee $25. Regular application deadline 8/2. Nonfall registration accepted. Admission may be deferred for a maximum of 1 year. Credit and/or placement offered for CEEB Advanced Placement tests.

COSTS AND FINANCIAL AID

Annual tuition $11,024. Room and board $6,656. Required fees $800. Average book expense $1,185. **Required Forms and Deadlines:** FAFSA, Institution's own financial aid form. **Types of Aid:** *Need-based scholarships/grants:* Federal Pell, SEOG, state scholarships/grants, private scholarships, the school's own gift aid. *Loans:* Subsidized Stafford, Unsubsidized Stafford, PLUS, Private Loans. *Student Employment:* Federal Work-Study Program available. Institutional employment available. Highest amount earned per year from on-campus jobs $4,350. Off-campus job opportunities are excellent. **Financial Aid Statistics:** 100% freshmen, 86% undergrads receive need-based scholarship or grant aid. 100% freshmen, 74% undergrads receive non-need-based scholarship or grant aid. 75% freshmen, 79% undergrads receive need-based self-help aid. 0% freshmen, 0% undergrads receive athletic scholarships. 99% freshmen, 99% undergrads receive any aid. 80% undergrads borrow to pay for school. Average cumulative indebtedness $20,523. **Criteria for awarding institutional aid:** *Non-need-based:* academics, music/drama.

TRINITY INTERNATIONAL UNIVERSITY

2065 Half Day Road, Deerfield, IL 60015
Phone: 847-317-7000 • **Financial Aid Phone:** 847-317-7033
E-mail: tcadmissions@tiu.edu • **CEEB Code:** 1810
Fax: 847-317-8097 • **Website:** www.tiu.edu • **ACT Code:** 1150

This private school was founded in 1897. It has a 111-acre campus.

RATINGS

Admissions Selectivity Rating: 86   Fire Safety Rating: 74

STUDENTS AND FACULTY

Enrollment: 950. **Student Body:** 57% female, 43% male, 41% out-of-state, 1% international (38 countries represented). Asian 5%, African American 17%, Caucasian 63%, Hispanic 4%, Native American <1%
Retention and Graduation: 66% freshmen return for sophomore year. 40% freshmen graduate within 4 years. 52% freshmen graduate within 6 years. 32% grads go on to further study within 1 year. **Faculty:** 43 full-time faculty, 84% hold PhDs, 42% are are members of minority groups, 14% are women. 0% of classes are taught by teaching assistants.

ACADEMICS

Degrees: bachelor's, certificate, first professional, master's, post-bachelor's certificate. **Classes:** Most classes have 20-29 students. Most lab/discussion sessions have 10-19 students. **Majors with Highest Enrollment:** Elementary Education and Teaching; Theology and Religious Vocations; Business/Commerce. **Special Study Options:** cross-registration, double major, dual enrollment, honors program, independent study, internships, study abroad, teacher certification program, REACH (for nontraditional students with previous college credit), Graduate courses. **Honors programs:** Trinity has adopted a model for an Honors Program that is intended to enhance the breadth and depth of your liberal-arts learning, but without the burden of many additional requirements. Hence, you will do honors work in the areas of your disciplinary major, general education, and special interdisciplinary classes, but virtually all of your honors work will also fulfill regular Trinity requirements. **Combined degree programs:** BA/MA. **Disability Services:** Special programs offered to physically disabled students include note-taking services, reader services, tape recorders, tutors. **Career services:** alumni services, career/job search classes, career assessment, internships. Career services highlights include Students in Trinity International University's Athletic Training Education Program have benefited through Trinity's partnership with Condell Health Network in Libertyville, Illinois. Condell's internship opportunities provide our students with necessary clinical experience while they work under the supervision of certified athletic trainers.

FACILITIES

Housing: special housing for disabled students, men's dorms, women's dorms, apartments for married students, apartments for single students 75% of campus accessible to physically disabled. **Special Academic Facilities/Equipment:** None **Computers:** 100% of classrooms, 50% of dorms, 100% of libraries, 100% of student union, have wireless network access. Students can register for classes online. Administrative functions (other than registration) can be performed online.

CAMPUS LIFE

Environment: Village. **Activities:** Choral groups, concert band, drama/theater, jazz band, music ensembles, musical theater, pep band, student government, student newspaper, symphony orchestra, yearbook, Campus Ministries 33 registered organizations, 2 honor societies. **Athletics (Intercollegiate):** *Men:* baseball, basketball, football, soccer. *Women:* basketball, soccer, softball, volleyball. **On-Campus Highlights:** Lew Student Center, Trinity Hall, McLennan Academic Building, Rodine Global Ministry Building, Melton Dining Hall.

ADMISSIONS

Freshman Academic Profile: Average high school GPA 3.26. 37% in top 10% of high school class, 43% in top 25% of high school class, 68% in top 50% of high school class. 69% from public high schools. SAT Math middle 50% range 440-600. SAT Critical Reading middle 50% range 445-610. ACT middle 50% range 19-26. Minimum paper TOEFL 530. **Basis for Candidate Selection:** *Very important factors considered include:* Class rank, application essay, academic GPA, recommendation(s), standardized test scores, character/personal qualities, religious affiliation/commitment. *Other factors considered include:* rigor of secondary school record, extracurricular activities, first generation, talent/ability. **Freshman Admission Requirements:** High school diploma is required and GED is accepted. *Academic units required:* 4 English, 2 mathematics, 2 science, (1 science labs), 2 foreign language, 2 social studies, 2 history, 2 visual/performing arts, 0 academic electives, 0. 4 English, 2 mathematics, 2 science, (1 science labs), 2 foreign language, 2 social studies, 2 history, 2 visual/performing arts, 0 academic electives, 0 **Freshman Admission Statistics:** 548 applied, 63% admitted, 39% enrolled. **Transfer Admission Requirements:** High school transcript, college transcript(s), essay or personal statement, statement of good standing from prior institution(s). Minimum college GPA of 2.0 required. Lowest grade transferable C-. **General Admission Information:** Application Fee $25. Notification on a rolling basis, beginning on or about 9/1. Nonfall registration accepted. Admission may be deferred for a maximum of 12 months. Credit and/or placement offered for CEEB Advanced Placement tests.

COSTS AND FINANCIAL AID

Annual tuition $21,980. Room and board $7,430. Required fees $390. **Required Forms and Deadlines:** FAFSA. **Notification of Awards:** Applicants will be notified of awards on a rolling basis beginning 2/15. **Types of Aid:** *Need-based scholarships/grants:* Federal Pell, SEOG, state scholarships/grants, private scholarships, the school's own gift aid. *Loans:* Subsidized Stafford, Unsubsidized Stafford, PLUS, Federal Perkins. *Student Employment:* Federal Work-Study Program available. Institutional employment available. Off-campus job opportunities are excellent. **Financial Aid Statistics:** 95% freshmen, 95% undergrads receive need-based scholarship or grant aid. 95% freshmen, 95% undergrads receive non-need-based scholarship or grant aid. 82% freshmen, 78% undergrads receive need-based self-help aid. 0% freshmen, 0% undergrads receive athletic scholarships. 90% freshmen, 86% undergrads receive any aid. 79% undergrads borrow to pay for school. Average cumulative indebtedness $18,937. **Criteria for awarding institutional aid:** *Non-need-based:* academics, alumni affiliation, athletics, minority status, music/drama, religious affiliation.

TRINITY LUTHERAN COLLEGE

4221 228th Avenue SE, Issaquah, WA 98029
Phone: 425-961-5510 • **Financial Aid Phone:** 425-961-5514
E-mail: admission@tlc.edu • **CEEB Code:**
Fax: 425-392-0404 • **Website:** www.tlc.edu

This private school, affiliated with the Lutheran Church, was founded in 1944.

RATINGS

Admissions Selectivity Rating: 61   Fire Safety Rating: 74

STUDENTS AND FACULTY

Enrollment: 91. **Student Body:** 53% female, 47% male, 35% out-of-state, 0% international. Asian 4%, African American 1%, Caucasian 112%, Hispanic 4%, Native American 1%

Retention and Graduation: 78% freshmen return for sophomore year. **Faculty:** 13 full-time faculty.

ACADEMICS
Degrees: associate, bachelor's, diploma, post-bachelor's certificate, terminal associate, transfer associate. **Majors with Highest Enrollment:** Bible/Biblical Studies; Youth Ministry; Music. **Special Study Options:** double major, independent study, internships, liberal arts/career combination, student-designed major, study abroad, teacher certification program. **Disability Services:** Special programs offered to physically disabled students include note-taking services, reader services, tape recorders, tutors. **Career services:** Alumni network, alumni services, career assessment, internships, regional alumni. Career services highlights include 10 week internships are a graduation requirement for all students.

FACILITIES
Housing: Coed dorms, special housing for disabled students, men's dorms, women's dorms, apartments for married students, apartments for single students, Special housing for married students and non-traditional age students. **Computers:** Administrative functions (other than registration) can be performed online.

CAMPUS LIFE
Environment: Village. **Activities:** Choral groups, drama/theater, music ensembles, musical theater, student government, student newspaper, yearbook. **Athletics (Intercollegiate):** *Men:* basketball, softball. *Women:* softball. **On-Campus Highlights:** Student Center, The Running Cup, Chapel, YMCA, Bookstore.

ADMISSIONS
Freshman Academic Profile: 0% in top 10% of high school class, 33% in top 25% of high school class, 60% in top 50% of high school class. Minimum paper TOEFL 525. **Basis for Candidate Selection:** *Very important factors considered include:* recommendation(s), character/personal qualities. *Important factors considered include:* academic GPA, rigor of secondary school record, standardized test scores, religious affiliation/commitment, volunteer work. *Other factors considered include:* alumni/ae relation, extracurricular activities, first generation, level of applicant's interest, talent/ability, work experience. **Freshman Admission Requirements:** High school diploma is required and GED is accepted. **Transfer Admission Requirements:** college transcript(s), Minimum college GPA of 2.0 required. Lowest grade transferable C-. **General Admission Information:** Application Fee $30. Regular application deadline 8/15. Nonfall registration accepted. Admission may be deferred for a maximum of 2 years. Credit and/or placement offered for CEEB Advanced Placement tests.

COSTS AND FINANCIAL AID
Average book expense $500. **Required Forms and Deadlines:** FAFSA, Institution's own financial aid form. **Notification of Awards:** Applicants will be notified of awards on a rolling basis beginning 1/1. **Types of Aid:** *Need-based scholarships/grants:* Federal Pell, SEOG, private scholarships, the school's own gift aid. *Loans:* Direct Subsidized Stafford, Direct Unsubsidized Stafford, Direct PLUS, Subsidized Stafford, PLUS. *Student Employment:* Federal Work-Study Program available. Institutional employment available. Off-campus job opportunities are excellent. **Financial Aid Statistics: Criteria for awarding institutional aid:** *Non-need-based:* academics, alumni affiliation, art, leadership, music/drama, religious affiliation.

TRINITY UNIVERSITY

One Trinity Place, San Antonio, TX 78212-7200
Phone: 210-999-7207 · **Financial Aid Phone:** 210-999-8898
E-mail: admissions@trinity.edu · **CEEB Code:** 6831
Fax: 210-999-8164 · **Website:** www.trinity.edu · **ACT Code:** 4226

This private school was founded in 1869. It has a 117-acre campus.

RATINGS
Admissions Selectivity Rating: 90   **Fire Safety Rating:** 78

STUDENTS AND FACULTY
Enrollment: 2,279. **Student Body:** 52% female, 48% male, 25% out-of-state, 7% international (47 countries represented). Asian 6%, African American 4%, Caucasian 57%, Hispanic 18%, Native American <1%.
Retention and Graduation: 88% freshmen return for sophomore year. 72%

---

freshmen graduate within 4 years. 25% grads go on to further study within 1 year. 4% grads pursue law degrees. 3% grads pursue medical degrees. **Faculty:** 226 full-time faculty, 99% hold PhDs, 42% are are members of minority groups, 22% are women. 0% of classes are taught by teaching assistants.

ACADEMICS
Degrees: bachelor's, master's. **Classes:** Most classes have 10-19 students. Most lab/discussion sessions have 10-19 students. **Majors with Highest Enrollment:** Communication; Engineering Science; Accounting. **Special Study Options:** Accelerated program, double major, honors program, independent study, internships, liberal arts/career combination, student-designed major, study abroad, teacher certification program. **Honors programs:** Honors Program **Combined degree programs:** BA/MA, BA/MA-education, BS/MS-accounting. **Disability Services:** Special programs offered to physically disabled students include note-taking services, reader services, tutors. **Career services:** Alumni network, career assessment, internships. Career services highlights include The Alumni Network is an amazing program. With over 500 alumni in our Career Network making themselves available for networking with students and fellow graduates.

FACILITIES
Housing: Coed dorms, Wellness Housing, Theme Housing. **Special Academic Facilities/Equipment:** Steiren Theatre, Richardson Communication Center, Ruth Taylor Arts Complex including art gallery, Laurie Auditorium. **Computers:** 100% of classrooms, 100% of dorms, 100% of libraries, 100% of dining areas, 100% of student union, 100% of common outdoor areas have wireless network access. Students can register for classes online. Administrative functions (other than registration) can be performed online.

CAMPUS LIFE
Environment: Metropolis. **Activities:** Choral groups, concert band, dance, drama/theater, jazz band, literary magazine, music ensembles, musical theater, opera, pep band, radio station, student government, student newspaper, student-run film society, symphony orchestra, television station, yearbook, Campus Ministries, International Student Organization, Model UN 130 registered organizations, 24 honor societies, 4 religious organizations. 7 fraternities, 6 sororities. **Athletics (Intercollegiate):** *Men:* baseball, basketball, cross-country, diving, football, golf, soccer, swimming, tennis, track/field (outdoor). *Women:* basketball, cross-country, diving, golf, soccer, softball, swimming, tennis, track/field (outdoor), volleyball. **On-Campus Highlights:** Stieren Theatre, Laurie Auditorium, Coates Library, Bell Athletic Center, Coates University Center, Northrup Hall.

ADMISSIONS
Freshman Academic Profile: Average high school GPA 3.48. 39% in top 10% of high school class, 71% in top 25% of high school class, 93% in top 50% of high school class. 63% from public high schools. SAT Math middle 50% range 590-680. SAT Critical Reading middle 50% range 580-680. SAT Writing middle 50% range 560-650. ACT middle 50% range 27-31. **Basis for Candidate Selection:** *Very important factors considered include:* Class rank, academic GPA, rigor of secondary school record. *Important factors considered include:* application essay, recommendation(s), standardized test scores, character/personal qualities, extracurricular activities, interview, talent/ability. *Other factors considered include:* alumni/ae relation, first generation, geographical residence, level of applicant's interest, racial/ethnic status, volunteer work, work experience. **Freshman Admission Requirements:** High school diploma is required and GED is accepted. *Academic units required:* 4 English, 3 mathematics, 3 science, (2 science labs), 2 foreign language, 3 social studies. *Academic units recommended:* 4 English, 3 mathematics, 3 science, (2 science labs), 2 foreign language, 3 social studies. **Freshman Admission Statistics:** 5,502 applied, 48% admitted, 25% enrolled. **Transfer Admission Requirements:** High school transcript, college transcript(s), essay or personal statement, statement of good standing from prior institution(s). Minimum college GPA of 3.0 required. Lowest grade transferable C-. **General Admission Information:** Application Fee $50. Early decision application deadline 11/1. Regular application deadline 2/1. Regular notification 4/1. Nonfall registration not accepted. Admission may be deferred for a maximum of 1 year. Credit and/or placement offered for CEEB Advanced Placement tests.

COSTS AND FINANCIAL AID
Required Forms and Deadlines: FAFSA, CSS/Financial Aid PROFILE. **Notification of Awards:** Applicants will be notified of awards on or about 4/1. **Types of Aid:** *Need-based scholarships/grants:* Federal Pell, SEOG, state scholarships/grants, private scholarships, the school's own gift aid. *Loans:* Subsidized Stafford, Unsubsidized Stafford, PLUS, Federal Perkins, state loans, college/university loans from institutional funds. *Student Employment:* Federal Work-Study Program available. Institutional employment available. Off-campus job opportunities are good. **Financial Aid Statistics:** 100% freshmen, 99% undergrads receive need-based scholarship or grant aid. 61% freshmen, 25% undergrads receive non-need-based scholarship or grant aid. 70% freshmen, 79% undergrads receive need-based self-help aid. 0% freshmen, 0% undergrads receive athletic scholarships. 97% freshmen, 95% undergrads receive any aid. 50% undergrads borrow to pay for school. Average cumulative indebtedness

$23,559. **Criteria for awarding institutional aid:** *Non-need-based:* academics, leadership, music/drama.

TRINITY (WASHINGTON) UNIVERSITY

125 Michigan Avenue, NE, Washington, DC 20017
Phone: 202-884-9400 • **Financial Aid Phone:** 202-884-9530
E-mail: admissions@trinitydc.edu • **CEEB Code:** 5796
Fax: 202-884-9403 • **Website:** www.trinitydc.edu • **ACT Code:** 696

This private school was founded in 1897. It has a 26-acre campus.

RATINGS

Admissions Selectivity Rating: 60*   **Fire Safety Rating:** 60*

STUDENTS AND FACULTY

Enrollment: 962. **Student Body:** 98% female, 2% male, 48% out-of-state, 1% international (42 countries represented). Asian 2%, African American 68%, Caucasian 7%, Hispanic 11%, Native American 1%
Retention and Graduation: 66% freshmen return for sophomore year. 29% freshmen graduate within 4 years. 44% freshmen graduate within 6 years. **Faculty:** 61 full-time faculty, 100% hold PhDs, 72% are are members of minority groups, 30% are women. 0% of classes are taught by teaching assistants.

ACADEMICS

Degrees: bachelor's, master's, post-bachelor's certificate. **Classes:** Most classes have 10-19 students. **Majors with Highest Enrollment:** Speech Communication and Rhetoric Business Administration and Management. **Special Study Options:** Accelerated program, cross-registration, distance learning, double major, dual enrollment, honors program, independent study, internships, student-designed major, study abroad, teacher certification program, weekend college. **Honors programs:** The Honors Program at Trinity encourages students to take advantage of small, seminar-style classes with the rich cultural benefits of our location in the nation's capital. It provides academically motivated students with the intellectual stimulation that comes not only from courses designed specifically for them by faculty members but also from intensive debate and discussion with their peers. **Combined degree programs:** BA/BS—with GWU or Univ. Maryland. **Disability Services:** Special programs offered to physically disabled students include note-taking services, reader services, tape recorders, tutors. **Career services:** Alumni network, alumni services, career/job search classes, career assessment, internships, regional alumni. Career services highlights include a service learning component of a required first year seminar.

FACILITIES

Housing: women's dorms **Special Academic Facilities/Equipment:** Art Gallery, Media Technology Center, Writing Center, Marilley Computer Classroom. **Computers:** Students can register for classes online.

CAMPUS LIFE

Activities: Choral groups, dance, drama/theater, literary magazine, student government, student newspaper, student-run film society, yearbook. 34 registered organizations, 5 honor societies, 2 religious organizations. **Athletics (Intercollegiate):** *Women:* basketball, field hockey, lacrosse, soccer, softball, swimming, tennis, volleyball. **On-Campus Highlights:** Trinity Center for Women and Girls in Sports, University Chapel, Main Hall.

ADMISSIONS

Freshman Academic Profile: Average high school GPA 2.8. SAT Math middle 50% range 330-480. SAT Critical Reading middle 50% range 360-482. ACT middle 50% range 13-18. Minimum paper TOEFL 550. **Basis for Candidate Selection:** *Very important factors considered include:* rigor of secondary school record, character/personal qualities. *Important factors considered include:* application essay, recommendation(s), alumni/ae relation, extracurricular activities, talent/ability, volunteer work. *Other factors considered include:* Class rank, standardized test scores, geographical residence, interview, work experience. **Freshman Admission Requirements:** High school diploma is required and GED is accepted. *Academic units required:* 4 English, 3 mathematics, 2 science, (1 science labs), 2 foreign language, 3 social studies, 2 history. **Freshman Admission Statistics:** 441 applied, 86% admitted, 39% enrolled. **Transfer Admission Requirements:** college transcript(s), essay or personal statement, Minimum college GPA of 2.5 required. Lowest grade transferable C. **General Admission Information:** Application Fee $40. Nonfall registration accepted. Admission may be deferred for a maximum of 1 year. Credit and/or placement offered for CEEB Advanced Placement tests.

COSTS AND FINANCIAL AID

Annual tuition $17,200. Room and board $7,574. Required fees $160. Average book expense $1,000. **Required Forms and Deadlines:** FAFSA. **Notification**

of Awards: Applicants will be notified of awards on a rolling basis beginning 2/1. **Types of Aid:** *Need-based scholarships/grants:* Federal Pell, SEOG, state scholarships/grants, private scholarships, the school's own gift aid. *Loans:* Subsidized Stafford, Unsubsidized Stafford, PLUS, Federal Perkins. *Student Employment:* Federal Work-Study Program available. Institutional employment available. Highest amount earned per year from on-campus jobs $2,000. Off-campus job opportunities are excellent. **Financial Aid Statistics:** 100% freshmen, 97% undergrads receive need-based scholarship or grant aid. 8% freshmen, 4% undergrads receive non-need-based scholarship or grant aid. 81% freshmen, 83% undergrads receive need-based self-help aid. 0% freshmen, 0% undergrads receive athletic scholarships. 97% freshmen, 94% undergrads receive any aid. 78% undergrads borrow to pay for school. **Criteria for awarding institutional aid:** *Non-need-based:* academics, alumni affiliation, leadership.

TRINITY WESTERN UNIVERSITY

P.O Box 1409, Blaine, WA 98231
Phone: 604-513-2019
E-mail: admissions@twu.ca • **CEEB Code:** 876
Fax: 604-513-2064 • **Website:** www.twu.ca • **ACT Code:** 5242

This private school was founded in 1962. It has a 100-acre campus.

RATINGS

Admissions Selectivity Rating: 61   **Fire Safety Rating:** 60*

STUDENTS AND FACULTY

Enrollment: 1,968. **Student Body:** 57% female, 43% male, 3% out-of-state. **Retention and Graduation:** 80% freshmen return for sophomore year. 15% grads go on to further study within 1 year. 3% grads pursue law degrees. 3% grads pursue medical degrees. **Faculty:** 77 full-time faculty, 90% hold PhDs, 18% are are members of minority groups, 4% are women. 0% of classes are taught by teaching assistants.

ACADEMICS

Degrees: bachelor's, certificate, diploma, first professional, master's. **Majors with Highest Enrollment:** Electrical, Electronic and Communications Engineering Technology/Technician. **Special Study Options:** cooperative education program, double major, English as a Second Language (ESL), honors program, internships, study abroad. **Career services:** alumni services, career/job search classes, career assessment, internships.

FACILITIES

Housing: 95% of campus accessible to physically disabled. **Special Academic Facilities/Equipment:** Museum of Biblical History. **Computers:** Administrative functions (other than registration) can be performed online.

CAMPUS LIFE

Environment: Town. **Activities:** drama/theater, literary magazine, student government, student newspaper, student-run film society 33 registered organizations. **Athletics (Intercollegiate):** *Men:* basketball, cross-country, ice hockey, rugby, soccer, track/field (outdoor), volleyball. *Women:* basketball, cross-country, rugby, soccer, track/field (outdoor), volleyball.

ADMISSIONS

Freshman Academic Profile: 80% from public high schools. Minimum paper TOEFL 570. **Basis for Candidate Selection:** *Very important factors considered include:* recommendation(s), rigor of secondary school record, standardized test scores. *Important factors considered include:* application essay. *Other factors considered include:* Class rank, character/personal qualities, extracurricular activities, religious affiliation/commitment, talent/ability. **Freshman Admission Requirements:** High school diploma is required and GED is accepted. *Academic units required:* 4 English, 3 mathematics, 2 science, (1 science labs), 2 social studies, 2 academic electives. 4 English, 3 mathematics, 2 science, (1 science labs), 2 social studies, 2 academic electives, **Freshman Admission Statistics:** 1,371 applied, 78% admitted, 39% enrolled. **Transfer Admission Requirements:** High school transcript, college transcript(s), essay or personal statement, Minimum college GPA of 2.0 required. Lowest grade transferable D. **General Admission Information:** Application Fee $35. Regular application deadline 6/15. Notification on a rolling basis, beginning on or about 10/15. Nonfall registration accepted. Admission may be deferred for a maximum of 3 semesters. Credit and/or placement offered for CEEB Advanced Placement tests.

COSTS AND FINANCIAL AID

Annual tuition $10,350. Room and board $5,990. Required fees $120. Average book expense $800. **Required Forms and Deadlines:** Institution's own financial aid form. **Notification of Awards:** Applicants will be notified of awards on a rolling basis beginning 4/1. **Types of Aid:** *Need-based scholarships/grants:* state scholarships/grants, private scholarships, the school's own gift aid. *Loans:* Direct Subsidized Stafford, Direct Unsubsidized Stafford, Direct PLUS. *Student Employment:* Institutional employment available. Highest amount earned per year from on-campus jobs $1,000. Off-campus job opportunities are good. **Financial Aid Statistics:** 2% freshmen, 18% undergrads receive need-based scholarship or grant aid. 2% freshmen, 3% undergrads receive non-need-based scholarship or grant aid. 34% freshmen, 35% undergrads receive need-based self-help aid. 0% freshmen, 0% undergrads receive athletic scholarships. 65% undergrads borrow to pay for school. **Criteria for awarding institutional aid:** *Non-need-based:* academics, athletics, leadership, music/drama.

TROY UNIVERSITY—TROY
(FORMERLY TROY STATE UNIVERSITY)

111 Adams Administration, Troy, AL 36082
Phone: 334-670-3179 • **Financial Aid Phone:** 334-670-3186
E-mail: admit@troy.edu • **CEEB Code:** 1738
Fax: 334-670-3733 • **Website:** www.troy.edu • **ACT Code:** 48

This public school was founded in 1887. It has a 512-acre campus.

RATINGS

Admissions Selectivity Rating: 79   Fire Safety Rating: 90

STUDENTS AND FACULTY

Enrollment: 15,026. **Student Body:** 61% female, 39% male, 32% out-of-state, 3% international. Asian 1%, African American 34%, Caucasian 51%, Hispanic 3%, Native American 1%
Retention and Graduation: 76% freshmen return for sophomore year. 15% freshmen graduate within 4 years. 36% freshmen graduate within 6 years. **Faculty:** 538 full-time faculty, 74% hold PhDs, 47% are are members of minority groups, 17% are women. 1% of classes are taught by teaching assistants.

ACADEMICS

Degrees: associate, bachelor's, doctoral, master's, post-master's certificate. **Classes:** Most classes have 10-19 students. Most lab/discussion sessions have 20-29 students. **Majors with Highest Enrollment:** Liberal Arts and Sciences Studies and Humanities; Criminal Justice/Safety Studies; Business Administration and Management. **Special Study Options:** Accelerated program, cross-registration, distance learning, double major, dual enrollment, English as a Second Language (ESL), external degree program, honors program, independent study, internships, study abroad, teacher certification program, weekend college. **Honors programs:** The University Honors Program, open to students in all undergraduate divisions of the university, is administered by the Honors Council and the director of university honors. The purpose of the University Honors Program is to offer the academically superior student a specially designed program, within a supportive community, that fosters critical thinking, intellectual development and social responsibility. This enhanced program is designed to provide a balance of common experience and flexibility addressed to individual achievement as well as a comprehensive framework on which to build disciplinary studies. The Honors Program also has an honors house on campus which houses both male and female students. Students should consult with the director of the University Honors Program and the director of University Housing for availabilities and stipulations. The house serves as a residence and a focal point for meetings and activities with the Honors Alliance, faculty and staff in the Honors Program. The official student voice within the program is the University Honors Alliance. Membership to the University Honors Alliance is offered to any student with a 3.3 grade point average or higher. There is an annual membership fee of $5. **Disability Services:** Special programs offered to physically disabled students include note-taking services, reader services, tape recorders, tutors.

FACILITIES

Housing: Coed dorms, men's dorms, special housing for international students, women's dorms, fraternity/sorority housing, apartments for married students, apartments for single students, Substance Free Housing Honor Student Housing. 95% of campus accessible to physically disabled. **Special Academic Facilities/Equipment:** Art museum, recording studio. **Computers:** Students can register for classes online.

CAMPUS LIFE

Environment: Town. **Activities:** Choral groups, concert band, dance, drama/ theater, jazz band, marching band, music ensembles, musical theater, opera, pep band, radio station, student government, student newspaper, symphony orchestra, television station, yearbook 125 registered organizations, 22 honor societies, 7 religious organizations. 12 fraternities, 9 sororities. **Athletics (Intercollegiate):** *Men:* baseball, basketball, cheerleading, cross-country, football, golf, rodeo, tennis, track/field (outdoor). *Women:* basketball, cheerleading, cross-country, golf, rodeo, soccer, softball, tennis, track/field (outdoor), volleyball. **On-Campus Highlights:** Movie Gallery Veterans Stadium, Malone Art Gallery, Hall of Honor/National Band Hall of Fame, Trojan Center, Rosa Parks Museum—Montgomery Campus. **Environmental Initiatives:** recycling; alternative fuel sources; landscaping.

ADMISSIONS

Freshman Academic Profile: Average high school GPA 3.339. 54% in top 25% of high school class, 85% in top 50% of high school class. ACT middle 50% range 18.9-25.6. Minimum internet-based TOEFL 80. Minimum paper TOEFL 500. **Basis for Candidate Selection:** *Very important factors considered include:* academic GPA, rigor of secondary school record, standardized test scores. *Other factors considered include:* application essay, recommendation(s), alumni/ae relation, character/personal qualities, extracurricular activities, interview, talent/ability. **Freshman Admission Requirements:** High school diploma is required and GED is accepted. *Academic units required:* 4 English, 4 mathematics, 4 science, 4 social studies. *Academic units recommended:* 4 English, 4 mathematics, 4 science, 4 social studies. **Freshman Admission Statistics:** 5,646 applied, 72% admitted, 47% enrolled. **Transfer Admission Requirements:** college transcript(s), Minimum college GPA of 2.0 required. Lowest grade transferable D. **General Admission Information:** Application Fee $30. Nonfall registration accepted. Admission may be deferred for a maximum of 2 years. Credit and/or placement offered for CEEB Advanced Placement tests.

COSTS AND FINANCIAL AID

Annual in-state tuition $6,528. Annual out-of-state tuition $13,056. Room and board $6,498. Required fees $1,036. Average book expense $1,105. **Required Forms and Deadlines:** FAFSA, Institution's own financial aid form. **Notification of Awards:** Applicants will be notified of awards on a rolling basis beginning 5/1. **Types of Aid:** *Need-based scholarships/grants:* Federal Pell, SEOG, state scholarships/grants, private scholarships, the school's own gift aid. *Loans:* Subsidized Stafford, Unsubsidized Stafford, PLUS, Federal Perkins. **Financial Aid Statistics:** 33% freshmen, 66% undergrads receive need-based scholarship or grant aid. 63% freshmen, 37% undergrads receive non-need-based scholarship or grant aid. 99% freshmen, 99% undergrads receive need-based self-help aid. 2% freshmen, 3% undergrads receive athletic scholarships. **Criteria for awarding institutional aid:** *Non-need-based:* academics, athletics, leadership, music/drama.

TRUMAN STATE UNIVERSITY

100 E. Normal Ave., Kirksville, MO 63501
Phone: 660-785-4114 • **Financial Aid Phone:** 660-785-4130
E-mail: admissions@truman.edu • **CEEB Code:** 6483
Fax: 660-785-7456 • **Website:** http://www.truman.edu • **ACT Code:** 2336

This public school was founded in 1867. It has a 140-acre campus.

RATINGS

Admissions Selectivity Rating: 89   Fire Safety Rating: 92

STUDENTS AND FACULTY

Enrollment: 5,394. **Student Body:** 58% female, 42% male, 197% international (50 countries represented). Asian 2%, African American 4%, Caucasian 81%, Hispanic 3%, Native American <1%
Retention and Graduation: 88% freshmen return for sophomore year. 5% out-of-state, 7% freshmen graduate within 4 years. 71% freshmen graduate within 6 years. 46% grads go on to further study within 1 year. **Faculty:** 318 full-time faculty, 87% hold PhDs, 41% are are members of minority groups, 11% are women. 1% of classes are taught by teaching assistants.

ACADEMICS

Degrees: bachelor's, master's. **Classes:** Most classes have 20-29 students. Most lab/discussion sessions have 20-29 students. **Majors with Highest Enrollment:** Business Administration, Management and Operations; Biology/ Biological Sciences; Psychology. **Special Study Options:** double major, dual enrollment, honors program, independent study, internships, student-designed major, study abroad, teacher certification program. **Honors programs:** General Honors Program: Students must complete five upper-level courses in math, social science, science and humanities with a 3.5 GPA in these 5 courses. Departmental honors are also available in some disciplines. **Disability Services:** Special programs offered to physically disabled students include note-taking services, reader services, tape recorders, tutors. **Career services:** Alumni network, alumni services, career assessment, internships, regional alumni. Career services highlights include a wide variety of experiential internships through the "Truman in Washington" program in Washington, D.C. Included are work-experience opportunities in such areas as foreign affairs/diplomacy, government affairs, criminal justice, international relations, health and human services, and communications as well as other areas.

FACILITIES

Housing: Coed dorms, special housing for disabled students, special housing for international students, apartments for married students, apartments for single students, Theme Housing, sorority housing, French language housing, and Spanish language housing. 98% of campus accessible to physically disabled. **Special Academic Facilities/Equipment:** Art gallery, local history and artifacts museum, human performance lab, greenhouse, observatory, IR and NMR instrumentation, and convergent media center (TV studio, newspaper, and radio station). **Computers:** 100% of classrooms, 100% of dorms, 100% of libraries, 75% of dining areas, 100% of student union, 90% of common outdoor areas have wireless network access. Students can register for classes online. Administrative functions (other than registration) can be performed online.

CAMPUS LIFE

Environment: Village. **Activities:** Choral groups, concert band, dance, drama/theater, jazz band, literary magazine, marching band, music ensembles, musical theater, opera, pep band, radio station, student government, student newspaper, student-run film society, symphony orchestra, television station, Campus Ministries, International Student Organization, Model UN. 282 registered organizations, 18 honor societies, 16 religious organizations. 16 fraternities, 11 sororities. **Athletics (Intercollegiate):** *Men:* baseball, basketball, cross-country, football, golf, soccer, swimming, tennis, track/field (outdoor), track/field (indoor), wrestling. *Women:* basketball, cross-country, golf, soccer, softball, swimming, tennis, track/field (outdoor), track/field (indoor), volleyball. **On-Campus Highlights:** Student Recreation Center, Pickler Memorial Library, Student Union Building, The Quadrangle, Jazzman's Coffee Shop. **Environmental Initiatives:** Energy Plan: committed to achieve at least a 5% reduction in total energy used on campus by the year 2015. Compost Program: all waste from the residence halls and Cafeterias is composted and used in landscaping and farm projects (including the community garden) on campus. Local foods coordination: grant received that pays for a local food coordinator to work on initiatives begun by Truman students, faculty and Sodexo food staff members.

ADMISSIONS

Freshman Academic Profile: Average high school GPA 3.76. 48.8% in top 10% of high school class, 79.8% in top 25% of high school class, 97.7% in top 50% of high school class. 79% from public high schools. SAT Math middle 50% range 560-680. SAT Critical Reading middle 50% range 570-690. ACT middle 50% range 24-30. Minimum internet-based TOEFL 79. Minimum paper TOEFL 550. **Basis for Candidate Selection:** *Very important factors considered include:* Class rank, academic GPA, rigor of secondary school record, standardized test scores. *Important factors considered include:* application essay. *Other factors considered include:* recommendation(s), alumni/ae relation, character/personal qualities, extracurricular activities, first generation, geographical residence, racial/ethnic status, state residency, talent/ability, volunteer work, work experience. **Freshman Admission Requirements:** High school diploma is required and GED is accepted. *Academic units required:* 4 English, 3 mathematics, 3 science, (1 science labs), 2 foreign language, 2 social studies, 1 history, 1 visual/performing arts. **Freshman Admission Statistics:** 4,095 applied, 74% admitted, 43% enrolled. **Transfer Admission Requirements:** college transcript(s), essay or personal statement. **General Admission Information:** Nonfall registration accepted. Admission may be deferred for a maximum of 12 months. Credit and/or placement offered for CEEB Advanced Placement tests.

COSTS AND FINANCIAL AID

Annual in-state tuition $7,096. Annual out-of-state tuition $13,160. Room and board $8,167. Required fees $278. Average book expense $1,000. **Required Forms and Deadlines:** FAFSA. **Notification of Awards:** Applicants will be notified of awards on a rolling basis beginning 3/1. **Types of Aid:** *Need-based scholarships/grants:* Federal Pell, SEOG, state scholarships/grants, private scholarships, the school's own gift aid, Federal ACG, SMART and TEACH Grants. *Loans:* Subsidized Stafford, Unsubsidized Stafford, PLUS, Federal Perkins, Federal Nursing, college/university loans from institutional funds, Alternative loans. *Student Employment:* Federal Work-Study Program available. Institutional employment available. Highest amount earned per year from on-campus jobs $4,208. Off-campus job opportunities are good. **Financial Aid Statistics:** 100% freshmen, 94% undergrads receive need-based scholarship or

grant aid. 98% freshmen, 79% undergrads receive non-need-based scholarship or grant aid. 70% freshmen, 80% undergrads receive need-based self-help aid. 6% freshmen, 6% undergrads receive athletic scholarships. 99% freshmen, 87% undergrads receive any aid. 54% undergrads borrow to pay for school. Average cumulative indebtedness $22,146. **Criteria for awarding institutional aid:** *Non-need-based:* academics, alumni affiliation, art, athletics, leadership, minority status, music/drama, state/district residency.

See page 1162.

TUFTS UNIVERSITY

Bendetson Hall, Medford, MA 2155
Phone: 617-627-3170 · **Financial Aid Phone:** 617-627-2000
E-mail: admissions.inquiry@ase.tufts.edu · **CEEB Code:** 3901
Fax: 617-627-3860 · **Website:** www.tufts.edu · **ACT Code:** 1922

This private school was founded in 1852. It has a 150-acre campus.

RATINGS

Admissions Selectivity Rating: 98   **Fire Safety Rating:** 77

STUDENTS AND FACULTY

Enrollment: 5,146. **Student Body:** 51% female, 49% male, 77% out of state, 8% international (93 countries represented). Asian 11%, African American 4%, Caucasian 56%, Hispanic 6%, Native American <1%
Retention and Graduation: 96% freshmen return for sophomore year. 8% out-of-state, 7% freshmen graduate within 4 years. 92% freshmen graduate within 6 years. 18% grads go on to further study within 1 year. **Faculty:** 710 full-time faculty, 94% hold PhDs, 40% are are members of minority groups, 19% are women. 1% of classes are taught by teaching assistants.

ACADEMICS

Degrees: bachelor's, master's, post-bachelor's certificate, post-master's certificate. **Classes:** Most classes have 10-19 students. Most lab/discussion sessions have 10-19 students. **Majors with Highest Enrollment:** Economics; International Relations and Affairs; Biology/Biological Sciences. **Special Study Options:** cross-registration, double major, exchange student program (domestic), honors program, independent study, internships, liberal arts/career combination, student-designed major, study abroad, teacher certification program. **Combined degree programs:** BA/MD, BA/MA, BA/DDS, 5-yr BA/BFA with museum school of Fine Arts; 5-yr. **Disability Services:** Special programs offered to physically disabled students include note-taking services, reader services, tape recorders, tutors. **Career services:** Alumni network, alumni services, career/job search classes, career assessment, internships, regional alumni. Thanks to our proximity to Boston, most of our students are able to pursue an internship during their 4 years, many for academic credit. Tufts also has a program geared at providing a stipend to students who pursue an internship with non-profit or public sector organizations.

FACILITIES

Housing: Coed dorms, special housing for disabled students, women's dorms, fraternity/sorority housing, cooperative housing, Special Interest Housing. **Special Academic Facilities/Equipment:** Language lab, nutrition institute, research lab for physical electronics, bioelectrical and biochemical labs, computer-aided design (CAD) facility, electro-optics technology and environmental management centers. **Computers:** 50% of classrooms, 20% of dorms, 100% of libraries, 75% of dining areas, 100% of student union, 75% of common outdoor areas have wireless network access. Students can register for classes online. Administrative functions (other than registration) can be performed online.

CAMPUS LIFE

Environment: Town. **Activities:** Choral groups, concert band, dance, drama/theater, jazz band, literary magazine, marching band, music ensembles, musical theater, opera, pep band, radio station, student government, student newspaper, student-run film society, symphony orchestra, television station, yearbook, Campus Ministries, International Student Organization, Model UN. 160 registered organizations, 4 honor societies, 6 religious organizations. 11 fraternities, 3 sororities. **Athletics (Intercollegiate):** *Men:* baseball, basketball, crew/rowing, cross-country, diving, football, golf, ice hockey, lacrosse, sailing, soccer, squash, swimming, tennis, track/field (outdoor), track/field (indoor). *Women:* basketball, cheerleading, crew/rowing, cross-country, diving, fencing, field hockey, golf, lacrosse, sailing, soccer, softball, squash, swimming, tennis, track/field (outdoor), track/field (indoor), volleyball. **On-Campus Highlights:** The Aidekman Arts Center, Tisch Library, Edwin Ginn Library, Cousens Gymnasium, Ellis Oval, Meyer Campus Center. **Environmental Initiatives:** Reduced green house gas emissions to below 1998 levels; LEED Gold building and comprehensive energy efficiency efforts; Comprehensive recycling and green purchasing and green dining initiatives.

ADMISSIONS
Freshman Academic Profile: 91% in top 10% of high school class, 99% in top 25% of high school class, 100% in top 50% of high school class. 56% from public high schools. SAT Math middle 50% range 690-770. SAT Critical Reading middle 50% range 680-750. SAT Writing middle 50% range 680-770. ACT middle 50% range 30-33. Minimum internet-based TOEFL 100. Minimum paper TOEFL 600. **Basis for Candidate Selection:** *Very important factors considered include:* application essay, academic GPA, rigor of secondary school record, character/personal qualities. *Important factors considered include:* Class rank, recommendation(s), standardized test scores, extracurricular activities, talent/ability, volunteer work, work experience. *Other factors considered include:* alumni/ae relation, first generation, geographical residence, interview, racial/ethnic status. **Freshman Admission Requirements:** High school diploma is required and GED is accepted. **Freshman Admission Statistics:** 18,406 applied, 19% admitted, 38% enrolled. **Transfer Admission Requirements:** High school transcript, college transcript(s), essay or personal statement, standardized test scores, statement of good standing from prior institution(s). Lowest grade transferable C. **General Admission Information:** Application Fee $70. Early decision application deadline 11/1. Regular application deadline 1/1. Regular notification 4/1. Nonfall registration not accepted. Admission may be deferred for a maximum of 12 Months. Credit and/or placement offered for CEEB Advanced Placement tests.

COSTS AND FINANCIAL AID
Annual tuition $47,596. Room and board $12,634. Required fees $1,047. Average book expense $800. **Required Forms and Deadlines:** FAFSA, CSS/Financial Aid PROFILE, Noncustodial PROFILE. **Notification of Awards:** Applicants will be notified of awards on or about 4/1. **Types of Aid:** *Need-based scholarships/grants:* Federal Pell, SEOG, state scholarships/grants, the school's own gift aid. *Loans:* Direct Subsidized Stafford, Direct Unsubsidized Stafford, Federal Perkins, college/university loans from institutional funds. *Student Employment:* Federal Work-Study Program available. Institutional employment available. Off-campus job opportunities are good. **Financial Aid Statistics:** 93% freshmen, 93% undergrads receive need-based scholarship or grant aid. 7% freshmen, 4% undergrads receive non-need-based scholarship or grant aid. 88% freshmen, 92% undergrads receive need-based self-help aid. 0% freshmen, 0% undergrads receive athletic scholarships. 41% freshmen, 40% undergrads receive any aid. 41% undergrads borrow to pay for school. Average cumulative indebtedness $18,019. **Criteria for awarding institutional aid:** *Non-need-based:* academics.

TULANE UNIVERSITY

Best 380

6823 St. Charles Avenue, New Orleans, LA 70118
Phone: 504-865-5731 · **Financial Aid Phone:** 504-865-5723
E-mail: undergrad.admission@tulane.edu · **CEEB Code:** 6832
Fax: 504-862-8715 · **Website:** www.tulane.edu · **ACT Code:** 1614

This private school was founded in 1834. It has a 110-acre campus.

RATINGS
Admissions Selectivity Rating: 95   **Fire Safety Rating:** 91

STUDENTS AND FACULTY
Enrollment: 8,284. **Student Body:** 58% female, 42% male, 743% international (40 countries represented). Asian 3%, African American 9%, Caucasian 72%, Hispanic 6%, Native American <1%
Retention and Graduation: 70% freshmen graduate within 4 years. 8% out-of-state, 3% freshmen graduate within 6 years. **Faculty:** 689 full-time faculty, 95% hold PhDs, 40% are are members of minority groups, 18% are women.

ACADEMICS
Degrees: associate, bachelor's, certificate, doctoral, master's, post-bachelor's certificate. **Classes:** Most classes have 10-19 students. **Special Study Options:** Accelerated program, cross-registration, distance learning, double major,

English as a Second Language (ESL), exchange student program (domestic), honors program, independent study, internships, liberal arts/career combination, student-designed major, study abroad, teacher certification program. **Honors programs:** Tulane Honors Program **Combined degree programs:** BA/MD, BA/JD, BA/MA, Integrated Graduate Studies 4+1 programs. **Disability Services:** Special programs offered to physically disabled students include note-taking services, reader services, tape recorders, tutors. **Career services:** Alumni network, alumni services, career/job search classes, career assessment, internships, regional alumni.

FACILITIES
Housing: Coed dorms, special housing for disabled students, special housing for international students, women's dorms, apartments for married students, apartments for single students, Wellness Housing. 60% of campus accessible to physically disabled. **Special Academic Facilities/Equipment:** Newcomb Art Gallery, Amistad Research Center, Latin American Library, Maxwell Music Library, Hogan Jazz Archives, Louisiana Special Collection, Manuscripts Department, Koch Herbarium, Tulane Museum of Natural History, Government Documents. **Computers:** 100% of classrooms, 100% of dorms, 100% of libraries, 100% of dining areas, 100% of student union, 100% of common outdoor areas have wireless network access. Students can register for classes online. Administrative functions (other than registration) can be performed online.

CAMPUS LIFE
Environment: City. **Activities:** Choral groups, concert band, dance, drama/theater, jazz band, literary magazine, marching band, music ensembles, musical theater, pep band, radio station, student government, student newspaper, student-run film society, television station, yearbook. 250 registered organizations, 43 honor societies, 16 religious organizations. 15 fraternities, 11 sororities. **Athletics (Intercollegiate):** *Men:* baseball, basketball, cross-country, football, tennis, track/field (outdoor). *Women:* basketball, cross-country, diving, golf, swimming, tennis, track/field (outdoor), track/field (indoor), volleyball. **On-Campus Highlights:** Amistad Research Center, Newcomb Art Gallery, Reily Recreation Center, Howard Tilton Memorial Library, PJ's Coffee Shop. **Environmental Initiatives:** Almost every school within the university offers undergraduates or graduates an environmental major or focus. These include a top-ranked Environmental Law program, Environmental Health Sciences degrees at the graduate and undergraduate levels, an Environmental Science degree, an interdisciplinary Environmental Studies degree and studios that focus on sustainable design in the School of Architecture. In addition, the Ecology and Evolutionary Biology and Earth and Environmental Sciences departments have strong programs that address coastal sustainability and global environmental change. Tulanes Center for Public Service and the public service requirement ensures that academic inquiry is integrated with active civic engagement, largely within the context of helping New Orleans rebuild as a more sustainable community. Tulane has a number of green building projects on campus, and since Hurricane Katrina many Tulane students, staff and faculty have been engaged in sustainable building, design, and neighborhood planning projects in the larger community. Most recently on campus, the renovation of the Lavin-Bernick Center for University Life included the installation of natural ventilation and daylighting features, including solar chimneys, extensive fans, exterior sunshades, and lighting systems that adjust to daylight. Off-campus, projects such as a Tulane-facilitated energy efficient neighborhood plan and green, affordable homes designed and constructed by Tulane architecture students have advanced sustainable rebuilding efforts in New Orleans. Tulane is currently implementing numerous energy efficiency and water conservation measures that will reduce annual uptown campus greenhouse gas emissions by a projected 10%. In addition to heating, cooling, lighting and water conversation improvements, the university has student-led energy savings education programs, such the countrys first Energy Star Showcase Dorm Room. To further this effort to reduce energy use and carbon emissions, Tulane has joined the Presidents Climate Commitment.

ADMISSIONS
Freshman Academic Profile: Average high school GPA 3.49. 55.7% in top 10% of high school class, 84.21% in top 25% of high school class, 97% in top 50% of high school class. SAT Math middle 50% range 620-700. SAT Critical Reading middle 50% range 610-710. SAT Writing middle 50% range 640-720. ACT middle 50% range 29-32. Minimum paper TOEFL 550. **Basis for Candidate Selection:** *Very important factors considered include:* Class rank, academic GPA, rigor of secondary school record, standardized test scores. *Important factors considered include:* application essay, recommendation(s), character/personal qualities. *Other factors considered include:* alumni/ae relation, extracurricular activities, first generation, interview, talent/ability, volunteer work, work experience. **Freshman Admission Requirements:** High school diploma is required and GED is accepted. **Freshman Admission Statistics:** 28,901 applied, 28% admitted, 20% enrolled. **Transfer Admission Requirements:** High school transcript, college transcript(s), essay or personal statement, Minimum college GPA of 2.5 required. Lowest grade transferable C. **General Admission Information:** Regular application deadline 1/15. Regular

notification 4/1. Nonfall registration accepted. Admission may be deferred for a maximum of 1 year. Credit and/or placement offered for CEEB Advanced Placement tests.

COSTS AND FINANCIAL AID
Average book expense $1,200. **Required Forms and Deadlines:** FAFSA, CSS/Financial Aid PROFILE, Noncustodial PROFILE, Business/Farm Supplement. **Notification of Awards:** Applicants will be notified of awards on a rolling basis beginning 3/15. **Types of Aid:** *Need-based scholarships/ grants:* Federal Pell, SEOG, state scholarships/grants, private scholarships, the school's own gift aid, Academic Competitiveness Grant, SMART Grant. *Loans:* Subsidized Stafford, Unsubsidized Stafford, PLUS, Federal Perkins. *Student Employment:* Federal Work-Study Program available. Institutional employment available. Highest amount earned per year from on-campus jobs $2,500. Off-campus job opportunities are good. **Financial Aid Statistics:** 97% freshmen, 96% undergrads receive need-based scholarship or grant aid. 36% freshmen, 25% undergrads receive non-need-based scholarship or grant aid. 62% freshmen, 71% undergrads receive need-based self-help aid. 3% freshmen, 3% undergrads receive athletic scholarships. 45% undergrads borrow to pay for school. Average cumulative indebtedness $26,602. **Criteria for awarding institutional aid:** *Non-need-based:* academics, athletics, leadership, music/ drama, state/district residency.

TUSCULUM COLLEGE

PO Box 5051, Greenville, TN 37743
Phone: 423-636-7300 · **Financial Aid Phone:** 800-729-0256
E-mail: admissions@tusculum.edu · **CEEB Code:** 1812
Fax: 423-638-7166 • **ACT Code:** 4018

This private school, affiliated with the Presbyterian Church, was founded in 1794. It has a 142-acre campus.

RATINGS
Admissions Selectivity Rating: 74   **Fire Safety Rating:** 71

STUDENTS AND FACULTY
Enrollment: 2,600. **Student Body:** 60% female, 40% male, 182% international (8 countries represented). Asian 0%, African American 11%, Caucasian 83%, Hispanic 2%, Native American <1%
Retention and Graduation: 62% freshmen return for sophomore year. 2% out-of-state, 6% freshmen graduate within 4 years. 42% freshmen graduate within 6 years. 10% grads go on to further study within 1 year. 12% grads pursue arts and sciences degrees. 1% grads pursue law degrees. 5% grads pursue business degrees. 2% grads pursue medical degrees. **Faculty:** 75 full-time faculty, 63% hold PhDs, 44% are are members of minority groups, 3% are women. 0% of classes are taught by teaching assistants.

ACADEMICS
Degrees: bachelor's, master's. **Classes:** Most classes have 10-19 students. **Majors with Highest Enrollment:** Elementary Education and Teaching; Biology/Biological Sciences; Business Administration and Management. **Special Study Options:** double major, honors program, independent study, internships, student-designed major, study abroad, teacher certification program, 16 month accelerated evening program for non-traditional students. **Honors programs:** Honors program for those students meeting gpa and act standards—available after the first semester. **Disability Services:** Special programs offered to physically disabled students include tutors. **Career services:** Alumni network, alumni services, career assessment, internships, regional alumni. Career services highlights include Service-Learning.

FACILITIES
Housing: Coed dorms, men's dorms, women's dorms, apartments for single students. 80% of campus accessible to physically disabled. **Special Academic Facilities/Equipment:** The Andrew Johnson Presidential Museum and Library. The College Archives. The Charles Coffin Collection. **Computers:** Administrative functions (other than registration) can be performed online.

CAMPUS LIFE
Environment: Village. **Activities:** dance, drama/theater, radio station, student government, student newspaper, yearbook. 12 registered organizations, 1 honor society, 2 religious organizations. 1 fraternity, 1 sorority. **Athletics (Intercollegiate):** *Men:* baseball, basketball, cheerleading, cross-country, football, golf, soccer, tennis. *Women:* basketball, cheerleading, cross-country, golf, soccer, softball, tennis, volleyball. **On-Campus Highlights:** Niswonger Commons Center, Perk Coffee House, Indoor Athletic Facility.

ADMISSIONS
Freshman Academic Profile: Average high school GPA 2.85. 16% in top 10% of high school class, 42% in top 25% of high school class, 78% in top 50% of high school class. SAT Math middle 50% range 410-540. SAT Critical Reading middle 50% range 410-540. ACT middle 50% range 18-23. Minimum paper TOEFL 550. **Basis for Candidate Selection:** *Very important factors considered include:* rigor of secondary school record, standardized test scores. *Important factors considered include:* application essay. *Other factors considered include:* Class rank, recommendation(s), character/personal qualities, extracurricular activities, interview, talent/ability, volunteer work. **Freshman Admission Requirements:** High school diploma is required and GED is accepted. *Academic units required:* 4 English, 3 mathematics, 2 science, 3 social studies. **Freshman Admission Statistics:** 1,456 applied, 81% admitted, 24% enrolled. **Transfer Admission Requirements:** college transcript(s), statement of good standing from prior institution(s). Minimum college GPA of 2.0 required. Lowest grade transferable D. **General Admission Information:** Notification on a rolling basis, beginning on or about 1/3. Nonfall registration accepted. Admission may be deferred for a maximum of 12 months. Credit offered for CEEB Advanced Placement tests.

COSTS AND FINANCIAL AID
Average book expense $0. **Required Forms and Deadlines:** FAFSA. **Notification of Awards:** Applicants will be notified of awards on a rolling basis beginning 3/15. **Types of Aid:** *Need-based scholarships/grants:* Federal Pell, SEOG, state scholarships/grants, private scholarships, the school's own gift aid. *Loans:* Subsidized Stafford, Unsubsidized Stafford, PLUS, Federal Perkins. *Student Employment:* Federal Work-Study Program available. Institutional employment available. Off-campus job opportunities are good. **Financial Aid Statistics:** 75% freshmen, 62% undergrads receive need-based scholarship or grant aid. 91% freshmen, 58% undergrads receive non-need-based scholarship or grant aid. 77% freshmen, 80% undergrads receive need-based self-help aid. 15% freshmen, 14% undergrads receive athletic scholarships. 90% freshmen, 85% undergrads receive any aid. **Criteria for awarding institutional aid:** *Non-need-based:* academics, athletics, leadership, music/drama, state/district residency.

TUSKEGEE UNIVERSITY

Best 380

Margaret Murray Washington Hall, Tuskegee, AL 36088
Phone: 334-727-8500 · **Financial Aid Phone:** 334-727-8500
E-mail: admissions@mytu.tuskegee.edu · **CEEB Code:** 1813
Fax: 334-727-5750 · **Website:** www.tuskegee.edu • **ACT Code:** 50

This private school was founded in 1881. It has a 5200-acre campus.

RATINGS
Admissions Selectivity Rating: 88   **Fire Safety Rating:** 76

STUDENTS AND FACULTY
Enrollment: 2,598. **Student Body:** 57% female, 43% male, 69% out-of-state, 2% international (19 countries represented). Asian 0%, African American 82%, Caucasian 0%, Hispanic 0%, Native American <1%
Retention and Graduation: 73% freshmen return for sophomore year. 17% freshmen graduate within 4 years. 23% grads go on to further study within 1 year. 11% grads pursue arts and sciences degrees. 2% grads pursue law degrees. 4% grads pursue business degrees. 3% grads pursue medical degrees. **Faculty:** 271 full-time faculty, 77% hold PhDs, 35% are are members of minority groups, 66% are women. 0% of classes are taught by teaching assistants.

ACADEMICS
Degrees: bachelor's, doctoral, master's. **Classes:** Most classes have 10-19 students. **Majors with Highest Enrollment:** Electrical and Electronics Engineering; Veterinary Medicine. **Special Study Options:** cooperative education program, double major, dual enrollment, honors program, independent study, internships, teacher certification program. **Career services:** Alumni network, career/job search classes, career assessment, internships, regional alumni.

FACILITIES
Housing: Coed dorms, men's dorms, women's dorms, apartments for married students, apartments for single students. **Special Academic Facilities/ Equipment:** Agricultural and natural history museum, electron microscopes, two nursery schools. **Computers:** 100% of classrooms, 100% of dorms, 100%

of libraries, 100% of dining areas, 100% of student union, 100% of common outdoor areas have wireless network access. Students can register for classes online.

CAMPUS LIFE

Environment: Rural. **Activities:** Choral groups, drama/theater, marching band, student government, student newspaper, yearbook, Campus Ministries, International Student Organization. 36 registered organizations, 22 honor societies, 6 religious organizations. 5 fraternities, 6 sororities. **Athletics (Intercollegiate):** *Men:* baseball, basketball, cheerleading, cross-country, diving, fencing, football, golf, gymnastics, riflery, soccer, swimming, tennis, track/field (outdoor), track/field (indoor), volleyball. *Women:* basketball, cheerleading, cross-country, diving, fencing, golf, gymnastics, riflery, soccer, swimming, tennis, track/field (outdoor), track/field (indoor), volleyball. **On-Campus Highlights:** George Washington Carver Museum, Kellogg Conference Center, Tuskegee Chapel, The Tuskegee Cemetery, General Daniel.

ADMISSIONS

Freshman Academic Profile: Average high school GPA 3.24. 20% in top 10% of high school class, 60% in top 25% of high school class, 100% in top 50% of high school class. SAT Math middle 50% range 400-520. SAT Critical Reading middle 50% range 400-510. ACT middle 50% range 18-22. Minimum paper TOEFL 500. **Basis for Candidate Selection:** *Very important factors considered include:* Class rank, academic GPA, recommendation(s), rigor of secondary school record, standardized test scores, talent/ability. *Important factors considered include:* alumni/ae relation, character/personal qualities. *Other factors considered include:* application essay, extracurricular activities, first generation, geographical residence, interview, state residency, volunteer work, work experience. **Freshman Admission Requirements:** High school diploma is required and GED is accepted. *Academic units required:* 4 English, 3 mathematics, 2 science, 3 social studies, 4 academic electives. **Freshman Admission Statistics:** 10,022 applied, 35% admitted, 18% enrolled. **Transfer Admission Requirements:** college transcript(s), Minimum college GPA of 2.0 required. Lowest grade transferable C. **General Admission Information:** Application Fee $25. Regular application deadline 7/15. Regular notification 3/15. Notification on a rolling basis, beginning on or about 3/1. Nonfall registration accepted. Credit and/or placement offered for CEEB Advanced Placement tests.

COSTS AND FINANCIAL AID

Annual tuition $18,100. Room and board $8,510. Required fees $1,425. Average book expense $1,282. **Required Forms and Deadlines:** FAFSA, Institution's own financial aid form, CSS/Financial Aid PROFILE. **Types of Aid:** *Need-based scholarships/grants:* Federal Pell, SEOG, state scholarships/grants, private scholarships, the school's own gift aid, United Negro College Fund, Federal Nursing Scholarships. *Loans:* Direct Subsidized Stafford, Direct Unsubsidized Stafford, Direct PLUS, Subsidized Stafford, Unsubsidized Stafford, PLUS, Federal Perkins, Federal Nursing, state loans, college/university loans from institutional funds. *Student Employment:* Federal Work-Study Program available. Institutional employment available. Highest amount earned per year from on-campus jobs $1,540. Off-campus job opportunities are good. **Financial Aid Statistics:** 84% freshmen, 86% undergrads receive need-based scholarship or grant aid. 47% freshmen, 41% undergrads receive non-need-based scholarship or grant aid. 49% freshmen, 53% undergrads receive need-based self-help aid. 8% freshmen, 5% undergrads receive athletic scholarships. 80% freshmen, 92% undergrads receive any aid. 91% undergrads borrow to pay for school. Average cumulative indebtedness $21,000. **Criteria for awarding institutional aid:** *Non-need-based:* academics, athletics, state/district residency.

UNION COLLEGE

310 College Street, Barbourville, KY 40906
Phone: 606-546-1229 · **Financial Aid Phone:** 606-546-1224
E-mail: enrollme@unionky.edu
Fax: 606-546-1667 · **Website:** www.unionky.edu · **ACT Code:** 15520

This private school, affiliated with the Methodist Church, was founded in 1879.

RATINGS

Admissions Selectivity Rating: 88   **Fire Safety Rating:** 68

STUDENTS AND FACULTY

Enrollment: 811. **Student Body:** 46% female, 54% male, 25% out-of-state, 3% international (9 countries represented). Asian 0%, African American 12%, Caucasian 79%, Hispanic 1%, Native American <1%.
Retention and Graduation: 14% freshmen graduate within 4 years. 28% freshmen graduate within 6 years. **Faculty:** 61 full-time faculty, 72% hold

PhDs, 44% are are members of minority groups, 10% are women. 0% of classes are taught by teaching assistants.

ACADEMICS

Degrees: bachelor's, master's, post-bachelor's certificate, post-master's certificate. **Classes:** Most classes have 10-19 students. Most lab/discussion sessions have 10-19 students. **Majors with Highest Enrollment:** Business Administration and Management; Psychology; Special Education and Teaching. **Special Study Options:** distance learning, double major, honors program, independent study, internships, liberal arts/career combination, student-designed major, study abroad, teacher certification program. **Disability Services:** Special programs offered to physically disabled students include reader services, tape recorders, tutors. **Career services:** Alumni network, career/job search classes, career assessment, internships, regional alumni.

FACILITIES

Housing: men's dorms, women's dorms, apartments for married students, apartments for single students. 50% of campus accessible to physically disabled. **Computers:** 100% of classrooms, 100% of dorms, 100% of libraries, 100% of dining areas, 100% of student union, 50% of common outdoor areas have wireless network access. Students can register for classes online. Administrative functions (other than registration) can be performed online.

CAMPUS LIFE

Environment: Rural. **Activities:** Choral groups, drama/theater, literary magazine, pep band, student government, television station, yearbook. 23 registered organizations, 2 honor societies, 2 religious organizations. **Athletics (Intercollegiate):** *Men:* baseball, basketball, bowling, cheerleading, cross-country, cycling, football, golf, soccer, swimming, tennis, track/field (outdoor). *Women:* basketball, bowling, cheerleading, cross-country, cycling, golf, soccer, softball, swimming, tennis, track/field (outdoor), volleyball. **On-Campus Highlights:** Student Center, Sharp Center Coffee Shop, Fitness Center.

ADMISSIONS

Freshman Academic Profile: Average high school GPA 2.91. SAT Math middle 50% range 438-508. SAT Critical Reading middle 50% range 415-455. ACT middle 50% range 17-21. Minimum paper TOEFL 550. **Basis for Candidate Selection:** *Important factors considered include:* Class rank, academic GPA, rigor of secondary school record, standardized test scores, level of applicant's interest. *Other factors considered include:* recommendation(s), alumni/ae relation, character/personal qualities, extracurricular activities, first generation, geographical residence, talent/ability, volunteer work. **Freshman Admission Requirements:** High school diploma is required and GED is accepted. **Freshman Admission Statistics:** 1,226 applied, 28% admitted, 55% enrolled. **Transfer Admission Requirements:** college transcript(s), Minimum college GPA of 2.0 required. Lowest grade transferable 2. **General Admission Information:** Application Fee $10. Nonfall registration accepted.

COSTS AND FINANCIAL AID

Annual tuition $18,244. Room and board $5,950. Required fees $605. Average book expense $1,400. **Required Forms and Deadlines:** FAFSA. **Notification of Awards:** Applicants will be notified of awards on a rolling basis beginning 3/1. **Types of Aid:** *Need-based scholarships/grants:* Federal Pell, SEOG, state scholarships/grants, private scholarships, the school's own gift aid. *Loans:* Subsidized Stafford, Unsubsidized Stafford, PLUS, college/university loans from institutional funds. *Student Employment:* Federal Work-Study Program available. Institutional employment available. Off-campus job opportunities are fair. **Financial Aid Statistics:** 93% freshmen, 96% undergrads receive need-based scholarship or grant aid. 10% freshmen, 12% undergrads receive non-need-based scholarship or grant aid. 86% freshmen, 87% undergrads receive need-based self-help aid. 0% freshmen, 0% undergrads receive athletic scholarships. 73% undergrads borrow to pay for school. Average cumulative indebtedness $22,388. **Criteria for awarding institutional aid:** *Non-need-based:* academics, athletics, job skills, religious affiliation, state/district residency.

UNION COLLEGE

Grant Hall, Schenectady, NY 12308
Phone: 518-388-6112 · **Financial Aid Phone:** 518-388-6123
E-mail: admissions@union.edu · **CEEB Code:** 2920
Fax: 518-388-6986 · **Website:** www.union.edu · **ACT Code:** 2970

This private school was founded in 1795. It has a 100-acre campus.

RATINGS

Admissions Selectivity Rating: 94   **Fire Safety Rating:** 92

STUDENTS AND FACULTY

Enrollment: 2,204. **Student Body:** 46% female, 54% male, 70% out-of-state, 7% international (35 countries represented). Asian 6%, African American 4%, Caucasian 75%, Hispanic 7%, Native American <1%
Retention and Graduation: 90% freshmen return for sophomore year. 80% freshmen graduate within 4 years. 86% freshmen graduate within 6 years. 35% grads go on to further study within 1 year. 10% grads pursue arts and sciences degrees. 3% grads pursue law degrees. 3% grads pursue business degrees. 4% grads pursue medical degrees. **Faculty:** 206 full-time faculty, 98% hold PhDs, 41% are are members of minority groups, 12% are women. 0% of classes are taught by teaching assistants.

ACADEMICS

Degrees: bachelor's. **Classes:** Most classes have 10-19 students. Most lab/discussion sessions have 10-19 students. **Majors with Highest Enrollment:** Economics; Psychology; Biology/Biological Sciences. **Special Study Options:** Accelerated program, cross-registration, double major, dual enrollment, honors program, independent study, internships, liberal arts/career combination, student-designed major, study abroad, teacher certification program. **Honors programs:** The Union Scholars program offers selected students the opportunity to take full advantage of the diverse intellectual experiences at Union. Specific features of the program are an enriched two-term version of First-Year Preceptorial; a sophomore independent study project with a professor of the student's choosing; the option to participate as a junior in a program in which students take a leadership role in the College's intellectual and social life; and a Scholars Colloquium run by students for presenting faculty and student research, in the senior year. Union Scholars use their extra courses to create an enriched program that meets their specific needs and interests. **Combined degree programs:** BA/JD, BS/MS or MBA/MD; BS/MS;BA or BS/MBA(joint pgms). **Disability Services:** Special programs offered to physically disabled students include note-taking services, reader services, tape recorders. **Career services:** Alumni network, alumni services, career/job search classes, career assessment, internships, regional alumni. Career services highlights include faculty, alumni, and athletics involvement in student career planning.

FACILITIES

Housing: Coed dorms, fraternity/sorority housing, apartments for single students, Theme HousingMinerva Houses. Up to 45 students live in each. All students and faculty members have (Minerva) house affiliations. Each house contributes intellectual, cultural, and social events to the campus. **Special Academic Facilities/Equipment:** The Nott Memorial and its Mandeville Gallery; Yulman Theater; Burns Arts Atrium; Taylor Music Center and its Emerson Auditorium; Special Collections at Schaffer Library; Memorial Chapel; Jackson's Garden, an eight-acre formal garden and woodland. Academic facilities include the F.W. Olin Center, with high technology classrooms and laboratories, a multi-media auditorium, collaborative computer classrooms, and a 20-inch remote-controlled telescope. Science and engineering facilities include superconducting nuclear magnetic resonance spectrometer, two electron microscopes, tandem pelletron positive ion accelerator, a fully accessible machine lab, and Aerogel fabrication and analysis lab. **Computers:** 100% of classrooms, 75% of dorms, 100% of libraries, 100% of dining areas, 100% of student union, 100% of common outdoor areas have wireless network access. Students can register for classes online. Administrative functions (other than registration) can be performed online.

CAMPUS LIFE

Environment: Town. **Activities:** Choral groups, concert band, dance, drama/theater, jazz band, literary magazine, music ensembles, radio station, student government, student newspaper, student-run film society, symphony orchestra, television station, yearbook, Campus Ministries, International Student Organization, Model UN. 100 registered organizations, 13 honor societies, 7 religious organizations. 12 fraternities, 5 sororities. **Athletics (Intercolle-**

giate): *Men:* baseball, basketball, crew/rowing, cross-country, diving, football, ice hockey, lacrosse, soccer, swimming, tennis, track/field (outdoor), track/field (indoor). *Women:* basketball, crew/rowing, cross-country, diving, field hockey, ice hockey, lacrosse, soccer, softball, swimming, tennis, track/field (outdoor), track/field (indoor), volleyball. **On-Campus Highlights:** The Nott Memorial, Schaffer Library, Reamer Campus Center, Jackson's Garden, Memorial Chapel. **Environmental Initiatives:** Incorporation of Sustainability into Union College's Strategic Plan. Performance of extensive Energy Audit resulting in $1.5M in energy projects. Funding Sustainability: 1) Presidential Green Grants: up to $2,000 is available to students/faculty/staff for a sustainability related project. 2) The Union College Green Fee: $5 is taken from each student's Student Activities Fees and placed in a fund for projects that will reduce the college's carbon footprint.

ADMISSIONS

Freshman Academic Profile: Average high school GPA 3.41. 70% in top 10% of high school class, 87% in top 25% of high school class, 98% in top 50% of high school class. 68% from public high schools. SAT Math middle 50% range 620-720. SAT Critical Reading middle 50% range 590-680. SAT Writing middle 50% range 590-670. ACT middle 50% range 28-31. Minimum internet-based TOEFL 90. Minimum paper TOEFL 600. **Basis for Candidate Selection:** *Very important factors considered include:* Class rank, academic GPA, rigor of secondary school record. *Important factors considered include:* recommendation(s), standardized test scores, character/personal qualities, extra-curricular activities, talent/ability. *Other factors considered include:* application essay, alumni/ae relation, first generation, geographical residence, interview, level of applicant's interest, racial/ethnic status, state residency, volunteer work, work experience. **Freshman Admission Requirements:** High school diploma is required and GED is not accepted. *Academic units required:* 4 English, 3 mathematics, 2 science, (2 science labs), 2 foreign language, 1 social studies, 1 history. **Freshman Admission Statistics:** 5,406 applied, 41% admitted, 26% enrolled. **Transfer Admission Requirements:** High school transcript, college transcript(s), essay or personal statement, statement of good standing from prior institution(s). Minimum college GPA of 3.0 required. Lowest grade transferable C. **General Admission Information:** Application Fee $50. Early decision application deadline 11/15. Regular application deadline 1/15. Regular notification 4/1. Nonfall registration not accepted. Admission may be deferred for a maximum of one year. Credit and/or placement offered for CEEB Advanced Placement tests.

COSTS AND FINANCIAL AID

Required Forms and Deadlines: FAFSA, CSS/Financial Aid PROFILE, State aid form, Noncustodial PROFILE. **Types of Aid:** *Need-based scholarships/grants:* Federal Pell, SEOG, state scholarships/grants, private scholarships, the school's own gift aid. *Loans:* Direct Subsidized Stafford, Direct Unsubsidized Stafford, Direct PLUS, Federal Perkins, college/university loans from institutional funds. *Student Employment:* Federal Work-Study Program available. Institutional employment available. Highest amount earned per year from on-campus jobs $3,800. Off-campus job opportunities are good. **Financial Aid Statistics:** 96% freshmen, 97% undergrads receive need-based scholarship or grant aid. 7% freshmen, 9% undergrads receive non-need-based scholarship or grant aid. 94% freshmen, 94% undergrads receive need-based self-help aid. 0% freshmen, 0% undergrads receive athletic scholarships. 81% freshmen, 77% undergrads receive any aid. 69% undergrads borrow to pay for school. Average cumulative indebtedness $22,221. **Criteria for awarding institutional aid:** *Non-need-based:* academics.

See page 1164.

UNION COLLEGE (NE)

3800 South 48th Street, Lincoln, NE 68506-4300
Phone: 402-486-2504 · **Financial Aid Phone:** 402-426-2505
E-mail: ucenroll@ucollege.edu
Fax: 402-486-2566 · **Website:** www.ucollege.edu · **ACT Code:** 2480

This private school, affiliated with the Seventh Day Adventist Church, was founded in 1891.

RATINGS

Admissions Selectivity Rating: 85   **Fire Safety Rating:** 62

STUDENTS AND FACULTY

Enrollment: 845. **Student Body:** 56% female, 44% male, 79% out-of-state, 11% international (34 countries represented). Asian 2%, African American 2%, Caucasian 75%, Hispanic 6%, Native American 1%
Retention and Graduation: 69% freshmen return for sophomore year. 21%

grads go on to further study within 1 year. 8% grads pursue arts and sciences degrees. 2% grads pursue law degrees. 5% grads pursue business degrees. 6% grads pursue medical degrees. **Faculty:** 54 full-time faculty, 54% hold PhDs, 35% are members of minority groups, 13% are women. 0% of classes are taught by teaching assistants.

ACADEMICS

Degrees: associate, bachelor's, master's. **Classes:** Most classes have fewer than 10 students. **Majors with Highest Enrollment:** Physician Assistant; Registered Nursing/Registered Nurse; Business/Commerce. **Special Study Options:** cross-registration, distance learning, double major, dual enrollment, English as a Second Language (ESL), honors program, independent study, internships, student-designed major, study abroad, teacher certification program. **Honors programs:** The honors program is available for students who have demonstrated superior scholastic ability. **Disability Services:** Special programs offered to physically disabled students include note-taking services, reader services, tape recorders, tutors. **Career services:** career assessment, internships.

FACILITIES

Housing: men's dorms, women's dorms, apartments for married students, apartments for single students. 75% of campus accessible to physically disabled. **Computers:** Administrative functions (other than registration) can be performed online.

CAMPUS LIFE

Environment: Village. **Activities:** Choral groups, concert band, drama/theater, literary magazine, music ensembles, student government, student newspaper, yearbook. 1 honor society, 3 religious organizations. **Athletics (Intercollegiate):** *Men:* basketball, volleyball. *Women:* basketball, volleyball. **On-Campus Highlights:** Cafeteria, The Ortner Center, The Arboretum, Dick Administration Bldg., Larson Life Style Center.

ADMISSIONS

Freshman Academic Profile: 17% in top 10% of high school class, 14% in top 25% of high school class, 57% in top 50% of high school class. 10% from public high schools. ACT middle 50% range 19-25. Minimum paper TOEFL 550. **Basis for Candidate Selection:** *Very important factors considered include:* recommendation(s), rigor of secondary school record, standardized test scores, character/personal qualities. *Important factors considered include:* Class rank, extracurricular activities, interview, religious affiliation/commitment. *Other factors considered include:* application essay, alumni/ae relation, geographical residence, state residency, talent/ability. **Freshman Admission Requirements:** High school diploma is required and GED is accepted. *Academic units required:* 3 English, 2 mathematics, 2 science, (1 science labs), 1 social studies, 1 history, 3 academic electives. **Freshman Admission Statistics:** 635 applied, 43% admitted, 66% enrolled. **Transfer Admission Requirements:** High school transcript, college transcript(s), Minimum college GPA of 2.0 required. Lowest grade transferable C-. **General Admission Information:** Nonfall registration accepted. Credit and/or placement offered for CEEB Advanced Placement tests.

COSTS AND FINANCIAL AID

Average book expense $950. **Required Forms and Deadlines:** FAFSA. **Notification of Awards:** Applicants will be notified of awards on a rolling basis beginning 5/1. **Types of Aid:** *Need-based scholarships/grants:* Federal Pell, SEOG, state scholarships/grants, private scholarships, the school's own gift aid. *Loans:* Subsidized Stafford, Unsubsidized Stafford, PLUS, Federal Perkins, Federal Nursing, college/university loans from institutional funds. *Student Employment:* Highest amount earned per year from on-campus jobs $1,300. **Financial Aid Statistics:** 100% freshmen, 100% undergrads receive need-based scholarship or grant aid. 14% freshmen, 11% undergrads receive non-need-based scholarship or grant aid. 85% freshmen, 88% undergrads receive need-based self-help aid. 0% freshmen, 0% undergrads receive athletic scholarships. 100% freshmen, 58% undergrads receive any aid. **Criteria for awarding institutional aid:** *Non-need-based:* academics, leadership, religious affiliation.

UNION INSTITUTE & UNIVERSITY

440 East McMillan Street, Cincinnati, OH 45206
Phone: 513-861-6400 · **Financial Aid Phone:** 800-486-3116
E-mail: admissions@myunion.edu
Fax: 513-861-3238 · **Website:** www.myunion.edu

This private school was founded in 1964.

RATINGS

Admissions Selectivity Rating: 60*   **Fire Safety Rating:** 60*

STUDENTS AND FACULTY

Enrollment: 1,101. **Student Body:** 53% female, 47% male, 16% out-of-state, 0% international (24 countries represented). Asian 1%, African American 27%, Caucasian 35%, Hispanic 14%, Native American 1%
Retention and Graduation: 90% freshmen return for sophomore year. 9% freshmen graduate within 4 years. 9% freshmen graduate within 6 years. **Faculty:** 31 full-time faculty, 84% hold PhDs, 52% are members of minority groups, 19% are women. 0% of classes are taught by teaching assistants.

ACADEMICS

Degrees: bachelor's, doctoral, master's, post-bachelor's certificate, post-master's certificate. **Majors with Highest Enrollment:** Criminal Justice/Law Enforcement Administration; Liberal Arts and Sciences Studies and Humanities; Child Development. **Special Study Options:** cross-registration, distance learning, external degree program, independent study, internships, teacher certification program. **Career services:** alumni services, career assessment.

FACILITIES

Housing: Housing (not university-owned) available for learners participating in brief on-campus residencies at Montpelier, Vermont center (applicable to BA and MEd programs only). 100% of campus accessible to physically disabled. **Computers:** Students can register for classes online. Administrative functions (other than registration) can be performed online.

CAMPUS LIFE

Environment: Metropolis.

ADMISSIONS

Basis for Candidate Selection: *Very important factors considered include:* application essay, recommendation(s), interview. *Important factors considered include:* level of applicant's interest. *Other factors considered include:* character/personal qualities, extracurricular activities, talent/ability, volunteer work, work experience. **Freshman Admission Requirements:** High school diploma is required and GED is accepted. **Transfer Admission Requirements:** college transcript(s), essay or personal statement, interview, Lowest grade transferable D. **General Admission Information:** Application Fee $35. Nonfall registration accepted. Admission may be deferred for a maximum of 12 months. Credit offered for CEEB Advanced Placement tests.

COSTS AND FINANCIAL AID

Required Forms and Deadlines: FAFSA, Institution's own financial aid form. **Notification of Awards:** Applicants will be notified of awards on a rolling basis beginning 5/1. **Types of Aid:** *Need-based scholarships/grants:* Federal Pell, SEOG, state scholarships/grants, private scholarships, the school's own gift aid. *Loans:* Subsidized Stafford, Unsubsidized Stafford, PLUS, Federal Perkins. *Student Employment:* Federal Work-Study Program available. Off-campus job opportunities are good. **Financial Aid Statistics: Criteria for awarding institutional aid:** *Non-need-based:* academics, state/district residency.

UNION UNIVERSITY

1050 Union University Drive, Jackson, TN 38305-3697
Phone: 731-661-5000 · **Financial Aid Phone:** 731-661-5015
E-mail: rgrimm@uu.edu · **CEEB Code:** 1826
Fax: 731-661-5017 · **ACT Code:** 4020

This private school, affiliated with the Southern Baptist Church, was founded in 1823. It has a 360-acre campus.

RATINGS

Admissions Selectivity Rating: 87   **Fire Safety Rating:** 77

STUDENTS AND FACULTY

Enrollment: 2,567. **Student Body:** 62% female, 38% male, 31% out-of-state, 1% international (36 countries represented). Asian 1%, African American 12%, Caucasian 65%, Hispanic 2%, Native American <1%
Retention and Graduation: 93% freshmen return for sophomore year. 51% freshmen graduate within 4 years. 40% grads go on to further study within 1 year. **Faculty:** 229 full-time faculty, 83% hold PhDs, 49% are members of minority groups, 10% are women. 0% of classes are taught by teaching assistants.

ACADEMICS

Degrees: associate, bachelor's, diploma, doctoral, master's, post-master's certificate, transfer associate. **Classes:** Most classes have 10-19 students. Most lab/discussion sessions have 10-19 students. **Majors with Highest Enrollment:** Elementary Education and Teaching; Christian Studies; Registered Nursing/Registered Nurse. **Special Study Options:** Accelerated program, cross-registration, distance learning, double major, dual enrollment, English as a Second

Language (ESL), exchange student program (domestic), honors program, independent study, internships, study abroad, teacher certification program. **Disability Services:** Special programs offered to physically disabled students include note-taking services, reader services, tape recorders, tutors. **Career services:** Alumni network, alumni services, career/job search classes, career assessment, internships, regional alumni. Career services highlights include the career development and recruitment opportunities that are discpline-specific (What Can I Do With a Major In...? workshops) and recruitment-specific (College to Career, professional development and prep; Career "U"niversity, internship opportunities; the Job Market, career recruitment, and Teacher Expo, education recruitment).

FACILITIES

Housing: special housing for disabled students, men's dorms, women's dorms, apartments for married students. 98% of campus accessible to physically disabled. **Special Academic Facilities/Equipment:** Elementary education lab, 21st-century classroom, TV communications truck, nursing/health assessment labs, health and wellness center, art gallery. **Computers:** 75% of classrooms, 100% of dorms, 100% of libraries, 50% of dining areas, 100% of student union, have wireless network access. Administrative functions (other than registration) can be performed online.

CAMPUS LIFE

Environment: City. **Activities:** Choral groups, concert band, drama/theater, jazz band, literary magazine, music ensembles, pep band, student government, student newspaper, student-run film society, yearbook, Campus Ministries, International Student Organization. 67 registered organizations, 12 honor societies, 4 religious organizations. 3 fraternities, 3 sororities. **Athletics (Intercollegiate):** *Men:* baseball, basketball, cheerleading, cross-country, golf, soccer. *Women:* basketball, cheerleading, cross-country, soccer, softball, volleyball. **On-Campus Highlights:** Bowld Commons, New Residence Life Complexes, Pharmacy Building, White Hall, Jennings Hall, Athletic Facility, Penick Academic Complex, Barefoot's Joe Coffee Shop. **Environmental Initiatives:** Campus-wide recycling campaign for aluminum, plastics and paper. This includes pick up from all student residential areas as well as all buildings/offices. Particpation in recyclemania.org; organizing new student sustainability organization to help with consistent and active marketing of the program. Working towards environmental stewardship through the creation of the on-campus garden, the composting program, and sustainability events.

ADMISSIONS

Freshman Academic Profile: Average high school GPA 3.67. 33% in top 10% of high school class, 62% in top 25% of high school class, 85% in top 50% of high school class. 57% from public high schools. SAT Math middle 50% range 520-670. SAT Critical Reading middle 50% range 500-680. ACT middle 50% range 22-29. Minimum internet-based TOEFL 80. Minimum paper TOEFL 550. **Basis for Candidate Selection:** *Very important factors considered include:* academic GPA, rigor of secondary school record, character/personal qualities, level of applicant's interest. *Important factors considered include:* Class rank, standardized test scores, extracurricular activities, interview, religious affiliation/commitment, talent/ability. *Other factors considered include:* application essay, recommendation(s), alumni/ae relation, first generation, volunteer work, work experience. **Freshman Admission Requirements:** High school diploma is required and GED is accepted. *Academic units required:* 4 English, 3 mathematics, 3 science, (2 science labs), 1 foreign language, 2 social studies, 1 history, 0 visual/performing arts, 0 computer science, 1 academic elective. enrolled. **Transfer Admission Requirements:** college transcript(s), statement of good standing from prior institution(s). Minimum college GPA of 2.3 required. Lowest grade transferable C. **General Admission Information:** Application Fee $35. Regular application deadline 8/1. Notification on a rolling basis, beginning on or about 10/1. Nonfall registration accepted. Admission may be deferred for a maximum of 1 year. Credit offered for CEEB Advanced Placement tests.

COSTS AND FINANCIAL AID

Annual tuition $26,160. Room and board $8,430. Required fees $720. Average book expense $1,220. **Required Forms and Deadlines:** FAFSA, Institution's own financial aid form. **Notification of Awards:** Applicants will be notified of awards on a rolling basis beginning 12/1. **Types of Aid:** *Need-based scholarships/grants:* Federal Pell, SEOG, state scholarships/grants, private scholarships, the school's own gift aid. *Loans:* Direct Subsidized Stafford, Direct Unsubsidized Stafford, Direct PLUS, Federal Perkins, Alternative Loans. *Student Employment:* Federal Work-Study Program available. Institutional employment available. Highest amount earned per year from on-campus jobs $1,500. Off-campus job opportunities are excellent. **Financial Aid Statistics:** 76% freshmen, 70% undergrads receive need-based scholarship or grant aid. 99% freshmen, 77% undergrads receive non-need-based scholarship or grant aid. 58% freshmen, 69% undergrads receive need-based self-help aid. 7% freshmen, 7% undergrads receive athletic scholarships. 99% freshmen, 99% undergrads receive any aid. 56% undergrads borrow to pay for school. Average cumulative indebtedness $23,169. **Criteria for awarding institutional aid:** *Non-need-based:* academics, alumni affiliation, art, athletics, leadership, minority status, music/drama, religious affiliation.

UNITED STATES AIR FORCE ACADEMY

HQ USAFA/ RRS, USAF Academy, CO 80840-5025
Phone: 719-333-2520
E-mail: rr_webmail@usafa.edu
Fax: 719-333-3012 · **Website:** www.academyadmissions.com • **ACT Code:** 530

This public school was founded in 1954. It has a 18000-acre campus.

RATINGS

Admissions Selectivity Rating: 97   **Fire Safety Rating:** 85

STUDENTS AND FACULTY

Enrollment: 3,952. **Student Body:** 22% female, 78% male, 87% out-of-state, 1% international (35 countries represented). Asian 4%, African American 6%, Caucasian 65%, Hispanic 10%, Native American <1%
Retention and Graduation: 94% freshmen return for sophomore year. 83% freshmen graduate within 4 years. 84% freshmen graduate within 6 years. 12% grads go on to further study within 1 year. 10% grads pursue arts and sciences degrees. 2% grads pursue medical degrees. **Faculty:** 505 full-time faculty, 57% hold PhDs, 19% are are members of minority groups, 11% are women. 0% of classes are taught by teaching assistants.

ACADEMICS

Degrees: bachelor's. **Classes:** Most classes have 10-19 students. Most lab/discussion sessions have 10-19 students. **Majors with Highest Enrollment:** Business/Commerce; Social Sciences; Aerospace, Aeronautical and Astronautical/Space Engineering. **Special Study Options:** double major, English as a Second Language (ESL), exchange student program (domestic), honors program, independent study, internships, student-designed major, study abroad, Academically At-Risk Program, Hospital Instruction Program, Extra Instruction Program, Summer Programs.

FACILITIES

Housing: Coed dormsAll students are required to live on campus all four years. **Special Academic Facilities/Equipment:** Language learning center, laser and optics research center, USAFA observatory, Dept. of Engineering Mechanics Lab, US Air Force Academy visitor's center, consolidated educational training facility, Air Force Academy cadet chapel, American Legion Memorial Tower, Clune area athletic and speaking events (seats 6,000), air garden, Falcon Stadium, Aeronautics Lab, Meterology Lab, Arnold Hall Broadway Theater, ballroom and conference rooms, and historical displays. **Computers:** 100% of classrooms, 100% of libraries, 100% of student union, have wireless network access. Students can register for classes online. Administrative functions (other than registration) can be performed online. Undergraduates are required to own a computer.

CAMPUS LIFE

Environment: Metropolis. **Activities:** Choral groups, dance, drama/theater, marching band, musical theater, pep band, radio station, yearbook, Campus Ministries, Model UN. 77 registered organizations, 2 honor societies, 14 religious organizations. **Athletics (Intercollegiate):** *Men:* baseball, basketball, boxing, cheerleading, cross-country, diving, fencing, football, golf, gymnastics, ice hockey, lacrosse, riflery, soccer, swimming, tennis, track/field (outdoor), track/field (indoor), water polo, wrestling. *Women:* basketball, cheerleading, cross-country, diving, fencing, gymnastics, riflery, soccer, swimming, tennis, track/field (outdoor), track/field (indoor), volleyball. **On-Campus Highlights:** USAF Academy Chapel, Thunderbird Lookout and Air Field, Falcon Stadium, Cadet Sports Complex, Visitor Center. **Environmental Initiatives:** Solar Power; Hydro Geo Thermal (Ground-Source Heat Pumps).

ADMISSIONS

Freshman Academic Profile: Average high school GPA 3.85. 56% in top 10% of high school class, 85% in top 25% of high school class, 98% in top 50% of high school class. SAT Math middle 50% range 620-710. SAT Critical Reading middle 50% range 590-680. ACT middle 50% range 28.25-32.25. **Basis for Candidate Selection:** *Very important factors considered include:* Class rank, application essay, academic GPA, recommendation(s), rigor of secondary school record, standardized test scores, character/personal qualities, interview. *Important factors considered include:* extracurricular activities, talent/ability, volunteer work, work experience. *Other factors considered include:* alumni/ae relation, first generation, geographical residence, racial/ethnic status, state residency. **Freshman Admission Requirements:** High school diploma is required and GED is accepted. **Freshman Admission Statistics:** 9,050 applied, 17% admitted, 81% enrolled. **Transfer Admission Requirements:** High school transcript, college transcript(s), essay or personal statement, interview, standardized test scores, Minimum college GPA of 2.0 required. **General Admission Information:** Regular application deadline 2/15. Notification on a rolling basis, beginning on or about 11/15. Nonfall registration not accepted. Credit and/or placement offered for CEEB Advanced Placement tests.

COSTS AND FINANCIAL AID
Required fees $0. Average book expense $0.

UNITED STATES COAST GUARD ACADEMY

31 Mohegan Avenue, New London, CT 06320-8103
Phone: 860-444-8500
E-mail: USCGA.Admissions@uscga.edu • **CEEB Code:** 5807
Fax: 860-701-6700 • **Website:** www.uscga.edu • **ACT Code:** 600

This public school was founded in 1876. It has a 120-acre campus.

RATINGS
Admissions Selectivity Rating: 95   **Fire Safety Rating:** 86

STUDENTS AND FACULTY
Enrollment: 896. **Student Body:** 35% female, 65% male, 94% out-of-state, 3% international (15 countries represented). Asian 6%, African American 4%, Caucasian 65%, Hispanic 12%, Native American 1%
Retention and Graduation: 91% freshmen return for sophomore year. 84% freshmen graduate within 4 years. **Faculty:** 118 full-time faculty, 52% hold PhDs, 30% are are members of minority groups, 13% are women. 0% of classes are taught by teaching assistants.

ACADEMICS
Degrees: bachelor's. **Classes:** Most classes have 10-19 students. Most lab/discussion sessions have fewer than 10 students. **Majors with Highest Enrollment:** Oceanography, Chemical and Physical; Political Science and Government; Business Administration and Management. **Special Study Options:** double major, exchange student program (domestic), honors program, independent study, internships. **Career services:** Alumni network, career assessment, regional alumni. All graduates are "employed" and assigned to operational field units upon graduation.

FACILITIES
Housing: Coed dorms. 95% of campus accessible to physically disabled. **Special Academic Facilities/Equipment:** CG Museum; Library; Visitors Center; Alumni Center. **Computers:** 100% of classrooms, 65% of dorms, 100% of libraries, 50% of dining areas, 100% of student union, 50% of common outdoor areas have wireless network access. Students can register for classes online. Administrative functions (other than registration) can be performed online. Undergraduates are required to own a computer.

CAMPUS LIFE
Environment: City. **Activities:** Choral groups, concert band, dance, drama/theater, jazz band, marching band, pep band, yearbook, Campus Ministries 2 honor societies, 7 religious organizations. **Athletics (Intercollegiate):** *Men:* baseball, basketball, crew/rowing, cross-country, diving, football, pistol, riflery, sailing, soccer, swimming, tennis, track/field (outdoor), track/field (indoor), wrestling. *Women:* basketball, cheerleading, crew/rowing, cross-country, diving, pistol, riflery, sailing, soccer, softball, swimming, track/field (outdoor), track/field (indoor), volleyball. **On-Campus Highlights:** Coast Guard Barque EAGLE, Coast Guard Museum, Sailing Center and Waterfront, Souvenier Shop (Military Exchange), Coast Guard Academy Chapel and Crown Park. **Environmental Initiatives:** Federal Electronic Recycling Challenge Participant and winner 2008 and 2009. Recyclemania (http://www.campusdish.com/en-US/csne/uscga/Sustainability). Federal electronics challenge facility partner 2009 and 2010.

ADMISSIONS
Freshman Academic Profile: Average high school GPA 3.87. 40% in top 10% of high school class, 76% in top 25% of high school class, 97% in top 50% of high school class. 77% from public high schools. SAT Math middle 50% range 600-680. SAT Critical Reading middle 50% range 570-660. SAT Writing middle 50% range 570-650. ACT middle 50% range 26-30. Minimum paper TOEFL 560. **Basis for Candidate Selection:** *Very important factors considered include:* Class rank, academic GPA, rigor of secondary school record,

---

standardized test scores, character/personal qualities, extracurricular activities. *Important factors considered include:* application essay, recommendation(s), talent/ability. *Other factors considered include:* alumni/ae relation, interview, level of applicant's interest, volunteer work, work experience. **Freshman Admission Requirements:** High school diploma is required and GED is accepted. *Academic units required:* 4 English, 4 mathematics, 3 science, (3 science labs). **Freshman Admission Statistics:** 2,096 applied, 18% admitted, 66% enrolled. **Transfer Admission Requirements:** High school transcript, essay or personal statement, standardized test scores, statement of good standing from prior institution(s). **General Admission Information:** Regular application deadline 2/1. Notification on a rolling basis, beginning on or about 12/15. Nonfall registration not accepted. Placement offered for CEEB Advanced Placement tests.

COSTS AND FINANCIAL AID
Required fees $942. Average book expense $1,358. **Financial Aid Statistics:** 0% freshmen, 0% undergrads receive athletic scholarships. 0% freshmen, 0% undergrads receive any aid.

UNITED STATES MERCHANT MARINE ACADEMY

Office of Admissions, Kings Point, NY 11024-1699
Phone: 516-773-5391 • **Financial Aid Phone:** 516-773-5295
E-mail: admissions@usmma.edu • **CEEB Code:** 2923
Fax: 516-773-5390 • **Website:** www.usmma.edu • **ACT Code:** 2974

This public school was founded in 1943. It has a 82-acre campus.

RATINGS
Admissions Selectivity Rating: 92   **Fire Safety Rating:** 60*

STUDENTS AND FACULTY
Enrollment: 958. **Student Body:** 15% female, 85% male, 87% out-of-state, 1% international (4 countries represented). Asian 6%, African American 3%, Caucasian 80%, Hispanic 9%, Native American 1%
Retention and Graduation: 97% freshmen return for sophomore year. 62% freshmen graduate within 4 years. **Faculty:** 120 full-time faculty, 34% hold PhDs, 13% are are members of minority groups, 8% are women.

ACADEMICS
Degrees: bachelor's, master's. **Classes:** Most classes have 10-19 students. Most lab/discussion sessions have 10-19 students. **Majors with Highest Enrollment:** Engineering; Naval Architecture and Marine Engineering; Transportation and Materials Moving. **Special Study Options:** honors program, independent study, internships. **Career services:** Alumni network, alumni services, career/job search classes, career assessment, internships.

FACILITIES
Housing: Coed dormsAll students required to live on campus in dormitories provided. **Special Academic Facilities/Equipment:** American Merchant Marine Museum. **Computers:** Students can register for classes online. Administrative functions (other than registration) can be performed online. Undergraduates are required to own a computer.

CAMPUS LIFE
Environment: Village. **Activities:** Choral groups, concert band, drama/theater, marching band, student government, student newspaper, yearbook, Campus Ministries 3 religious organizations. **Athletics (Intercollegiate):** *Men:* baseball, basketball, crew/rowing, cross-country, diving, football, golf, lacrosse, riflery, sailing, soccer, swimming, tennis, track/field (outdoor), volleyball, water polo, wrestling. *Women:* basketball, crew/rowing, cross-country, diving, golf, riflery, sailing, softball, swimming, tennis, track/field (outdoor), volleyball.

ADMISSIONS
Freshman Academic Profile: Average high school GPA 3.6. 33% in top 10% of high school class, 57% in top 25% of high school class, 92% in top 50% of high school class. 75% from public high schools. SAT Math middle 50% range 613-688. SAT Critical Reading middle 50% range 570-663. ACT middle 50% range 26-30. Minimum internet-based TOEFL 73. Minimum paper TOEFL 533. **Basis for Candidate Selection:** *Very important factors considered include:* rigor of secondary school record, standardized test scores, character/personal qualities. *Important factors considered include:* Class rank, application

essay, academic GPA, recommendation(s), extracurricular activities, level of applicant's interest, talent/ability. *Other factors considered include:* geographical residence, interview, racial/ethnic status, state residency, volunteer work, work experience. **Freshman Admission Requirements:** High school diploma is required and GED is accepted. *Academic units required:* 4 English, 3 mathematics, 3 science, (1 science labs), 8 academic electives. **Freshman Admission Statistics:** 2,252 applied, 18% admitted, 58% enrolled. **Transfer Admission Requirements:** High school transcript, college transcript(s), essay or personal statement, standardized test scores, statement of good standing from prior institution(s). Minimum college GPA of 2.5 required. **General Admission Information:** Regular application deadline 3/1. Notification on a rolling basis, beginning on or about 11/1. Nonfall registration not accepted. Credit offered for CEEB Advanced Placement tests.

COSTS AND FINANCIAL AID

Required fees $9,768. Average book expense $2,887. **Required Forms and Deadlines:** FAFSA, Institution's own financial aid form. **Notification of Awards:** Applicants will be notified of awards on a rolling basis beginning 1/31. **Types of Aid:** *Need-based scholarships/grants:* Federal Pell, private scholarships, Federal SMART Grants & Federal Academic Competitiveness Grants. *Loans:* Direct PLUS, Subsidized Stafford, Unsubsidized Stafford, PLUS. *Student Employment:* Off-campus job opportunities are poor.

UNITED STATES MILITARY ACADEMY

646 Swift Road, West Point, NY 10996-1905
Phone: 845-938-4041
E-mail: admissions@usma.edu • **CEEB Code:** 2924
Fax: 845-938-3021 • **Website:** www.westpoint.edu • **ACT Code:** 2976

This public school was founded in 1802. It has a 16080-acre campus.

RATINGS

Admissions Selectivity Rating: 95   **Fire Safety Rating:** 86

STUDENTS AND FACULTY

Enrollment: 4,414. **Student Body:** 17% female, 83% male, 93% out-of-state, 1% international (33 countries represented). Asian 6%, African American 9%, Caucasian 67%, Hispanic 11%, Native American 1%. **Retention and Graduation:** 94% freshmen return for sophomore year. 79% freshmen graduate within 4 years. 81% freshmen graduate within 6 years. 38% grads go on to further study within 1 year. 1% grads pursue arts and sciences degrees. 2% grads pursue medical degrees. **Faculty:** 612 full-time faculty, 46% hold PhDs, 18% are are members of minority groups, 11% are women. 0% of classes are taught by teaching assistants.

ACADEMICS

Degrees: bachelor's. **Classes:** Most classes have 10-19 students. Most lab/discussion sessions have 10-19 students. **Majors with Highest Enrollment:** Economics; Business Administration and Management; Engineering/Industrial Management. **Special Study Options:** double major, exchange student program (domestic), honors program, independent study, internships, study abroad, Opportunities to attend Army Schools (Airborne, Air Assault, etc.) to learn special skills.

FACILITIES

Housing: Coed dorms, Coed dorms are called barracks. **Special Academic Facilities/Equipment:** West Point Museum.(oldest of U.S. army museums. The athletic facilities rate as highly as the academic plant. Arvin gymnasium, featuring swimming pools, wrestling, squash, racquetball, handball, and volleyball courts has undergone a major renovation to modernize and improve its contribution to the physical development of the corps of cadets. Michie Stadium, home of the Army football team, is considered one of America's most picturesque stadiums to watch a college football game. Holleder Center houses Tate Rink for the Army hockey team and Christl Arena is the home of the Army men and women's basketball teams. Additionally, the Shea Stadium outdoor track facility and Gillis Field House indoor practice facility are newly renovated to include an all-weather track, an astroturf football field and new lighting. There is also a redesigned 18-hole golf course and a new indoor tennis facility. Eisenhower Hall, the modern "student union," contains a 4,500- seat auditorium, a 1,000-seat snack bar and Cafeteria, a large ballroom, and other social and recreational rooms. About 60 major productions, to include Broadway shows,

musicals, popular rock, jazz, country/western, and alternative music concerts are staged annually in the theater. The new cadet library, Jefferson Hall opened this year. **Computers:** 100% of classrooms, 100% of libraries, 100% of student union, have wireless network access. Students can register for classes online. Administrative functions (other than registration) can be performed online. Undergraduates are required to own a computer.

CAMPUS LIFE

Environment: Village. **Activities:** Choral groups, drama/theater, jazz band, music ensembles, pep band, radio station, student government, student newspaper, television station, yearbook, Campus Ministries, International Student Organization, Model UN. 105 registered organizations, 7 honor societies, 13 religious organizations. **Athletics (Intercollegiate):** *Men:* baseball, basketball, cross-country, football, golf, gymnastics, ice hockey, lacrosse, riflery, soccer, swimming, tennis, track/field (outdoor), track/field (indoor), wrestling. *Women:* basketball, cross-country, riflery, soccer, softball, swimming, tennis, track/field (outdoor), track/field (indoor), volleyball. **On-Campus Highlights:** Cadet Chapel, West Point Museum, Eisenhower Hall, Michie Stadium, Trophy Point, Fort Putnam, West Point Cemetery.

ADMISSIONS

Freshman Academic Profile: 52% in top 10% of high school class, 78% in top 25% of high school class, 95% in top 50% of high school class. 78% from public high schools. SAT Math middle 50% range 590-700. SAT Critical Reading middle 50% range 570-690. SAT Writing middle 50% range 550-660. ACT middle 50% range 26-31. Minimum internet-based TOEFL 75. Minimum paper TOEFL 500. **Basis for Candidate Selection:** *Very important factors considered include:* Class rank, application essay, academic GPA, recommendation(s), rigor of secondary school record, standardized test scores, character/personal qualities, extracurricular activities, talent/ability. *Important factors considered include:* geographical residence, interview, level of applicant's interest, racial/ethnic status, volunteer work. *Other factors considered include:* alumni/ae relation, state residency, work experience. **Freshman Admission Requirements:** High school diploma is required and GED is accepted. **Freshman Admission Statistics:** 14,977 applied, 9% admitted, 85% enrolled. **General Admission Information:** Regular application deadline 2/28. Notification on a rolling basis, beginning on or about 11/15. Nonfall registration not accepted. Placement offered for CEEB Advanced Placement tests.

COSTS AND FINANCIAL AID

Required fees $0. Average book expense $0. **Required Forms and Deadlines: Types of Aid:** *Need-based scholarships/grants:* All students receive an annual salary of approximately $10,148. Room and board, medical and dental care is provided by the institution. A one-time deposit of $2,900 is required upon admission to pay for the initial issue of uniforms, books, supplies, equipment and fees. If needed, loans for the deposit are available for $100 to $2,400. *Loans:* All students receive an annual salary of approximately $10,148. Room and board, medical and dental care is provided by the institution. A one-time deposit of $2,900 is required upon admission to pay for the initial issue of uniforms, books, supplies, equipment and fees. If needed, loans for the deposit are available for $100 to $2,400. **Financial Aid Statistics:** 0% freshmen, 0% undergrads receive athletic scholarships. 0% undergrads borrow to pay for school. Average cumulative indebtedness $0.

See page 1166.

UNITED STATES NAVAL ACADEMY

52 King George Street, Annapolis, MD 21402
Phone: 410-293-4361
E-mail: webmail@usna.edu • **CEEB Code:** 5809
Fax: 410-293-1815 • **Website:** www.usna.edu • **ACT Code:** 1742

This public school was founded in 1845. It has a 330-acre campus.

RATINGS

Admissions Selectivity Rating: 97   **Fire Safety Rating:** 71

STUDENTS AND FACULTY

Enrollment: 4,511. **Student Body:** 23% female, 77% male, 93% out-of-state, 1% international (31 countries represented). Asian 7%, African American 7%, Caucasian 65%, Hispanic 11%, Native American <1%
Retention and Graduation: 97% freshmen return for sophomore year. 90% freshmen graduate within 4 years. 90% freshmen graduate within 6 years. 6%

grads go on to further study within 1 year. 1% grads pursue medical degrees. **Faculty:** 549 full-time faculty, 64% hold PhDs, 28% are are members of minority groups, 11% are women. 0% of classes are taught by teaching assistants.

ACADEMICS

Degrees: bachelor's. **Classes:** Most classes have 10-19 students. **Majors with Highest Enrollment:** Economics; Political Science and Government; Systems Engineering. **Special Study Options:** double major, exchange student program (domestic), honors program, independent study, Voluntary Graduate Education Program. **Honors programs:** Voluntary Graduate Education Program—second semester seniors may enroll in graduate school at a nearby college or university. Career services highlights include The United States Navy and the United States Marine Corps hiring all our graduates.

FACILITIES

Housing: Coed dormsNo options. All midshipmen live in same dormitory. **Special Academic Facilities/Equipment:** Naval history museum, Naval Institute Proceedings, propulsion lab, wind tunnels, flight simulator, ship tow tanks, satellite dish, coastal chamber facilities, fleet of small training craft (power and sail), oceanographic research vessel. **Computers:** Students can register for classes online. Administrative functions (other than registration) can be performed online. Undergraduates are required to own a computer.

CAMPUS LIFE

Environment: Town. **Activities:** Choral groups, concert band, drama/theater, jazz band, literary magazine, marching band, musical theater, pep band, radio station, student government, yearbook, Campus Ministries, International Student Organization. 70 registered organizations, 10 honor societies, 8 religious organizations. **Athletics (Intercollegiate):** *Men:* baseball, basketball, crew/rowing, cross-country, diving, football, golf, gymnastics, lacrosse, light weight football, riflery, sailing, soccer, squash, swimming, tennis, track/field (outdoor), track/field (indoor), water polo, wrestling. *Women:* basketball, crew/rowing, cross-country, diving, lacrosse, riflery, sailing, soccer, swimming, tennis, track/field (outdoor), track/field (indoor), volleyball. **On-Campus Highlights:** Bancroft Hall, U.S. Naval Academy Museum, Armel-Leftwich Visitor Center, U.S. Naval Academy Chapel, Lejeune Hall.

ADMISSIONS

Freshman Academic Profile: 59% in top 10% of high school class, 81% in top 25% of high school class, 95% in top 50% of high school class. 60% from public high schools. SAT Math middle 50% range 610-710. SAT Critical Reading middle 50% range 560-670. **Basis for Candidate Selection:** *Very important factors considered include:* Class rank, application essay, academic GPA, recommendation(s), rigor of secondary school record, character/personal qualities, extracurricular activities, interview, level of applicant's interest. *Important factors considered include:* standardized test scores, talent/ability. *Other factors considered include:* alumni/ae relation, first generation, geographical residence, racial/ethnic status, state residency, volunteer work, work experience. **Freshman Admission Requirements:** High school diploma or equivalent is not required. **Freshman Admission Statistics:** 17,618 applied, 8% admitted, 85% enrolled. **General Admission Information:** Regular application deadline 1/31. Regular notification 4/15. Notification on a rolling basis, beginning on or about 9/1. Nonfall registration not accepted. Credit and/or placement offered for CEEB Advanced Placement tests.

COSTS AND FINANCIAL AID

Required fees $0. Average book expense $0. **Financial Aid Statistics:** 0% freshmen, 0% undergrads receive athletic scholarships. 0% freshmen, 0% undergrads receive any aid. 0% undergrads borrow to pay for school. Average cumulative indebtedness $0.

UNITY COLLEGE

PO Box 532, Unity, ME 4988
Phone: 800.624.1024 • **Financial Aid Phone:** 207-948-3131 ext 235
E-mail: admissions@unity.edu • **CEEB Code:** 6858
Fax: 207.948.9776 • **Website:** www.unity.edu • **ACT Code:** 3925

This is a private school.

RATINGS

Admissions Selectivity Rating: 83   **Fire Safety Rating:** 88

STUDENTS AND FACULTY

Enrollment: 574. **Student Body:** 55% female, 45% male, 75% out-of-state, 0% international. Asian 1%, African American 1%, Caucasian 93%, Hispanic 2%, Native American 2%
Retention and Graduation: 83% freshmen return for sophomore year. 37% freshmen graduate within 4 years. 46% freshmen graduate within 6 years. 24%

grads go on to further study within 1 year. 22% grads pursue arts and sciences degrees. 1% grads pursue law degrees. **Faculty:** 37 full-time faculty, 89% hold PhDs, 54% are are members of minority groups, 0% are women.

ACADEMICS

Degrees: associate, bachelor's. **Majors with Highest Enrollment:** Wildlife Biology; Natural Resources Law Enforcement and Protective Services; Marine Biology and Biological Oceanography.

CAMPUS LIFE

Environmental Initiatives: We only offer environmental degree programs and every student studies sustainability through our Environmental Stewardship Core curriculum. Campus sustainability efforts are an outgrowth of our academic focus. Charter signatory to the ACUPCC and active leaders in the higher education sustainability community. Unity's TerraHaus is the nation's first student residence built to strict Passive House energy performance standards. Our campus also boasts the net-zero energy, LEED Platinum president's home, Unity House.

ADMISSIONS

Freshman Academic Profile: Average high school GPA 3.27. 14% in top 10% of high school class, 33% in top 25% of high school class, 55% in top 50% of high school class. SAT Math middle 50% range 490-560. SAT Critical Reading middle 50% range 480-560. SAT Writing middle 50% range 450-520. ACT middle 50% range 22-25. Minimum paper TOEFL 550. Freshman Admission Requirements. **Freshman Admission Statistics:** 737 applied, 61% admitted, 38% enrolled. **General Admission Information:** Credit and/or placement offered for CEEB Advanced Placement tests.

COSTS AND FINANCIAL AID

Annual tuition $22,440. Room and board $8,380. Required fees $800. Average book expense $500. **Required Forms and Deadlines:** FAFSA. **Financial Aid Statistics:** 100% freshmen, 100% undergrads receive need-based scholarship or grant aid. 8% freshmen, 3% undergrads receive non-need-based scholarship or grant aid. 91% freshmen, 95% undergrads receive need-based self-help aid. 0% freshmen, 0% undergrads receive athletic scholarships. 98% freshmen, 98% undergrads receive any aid.

UNIVERSITÉ LAVAL—FACULTÉ DES SCIENCES DE L'ADMINISTRATION

2345 Allée des bibliothèques, local 2440, Québec, Qc G1V 0A6
Phone: 418-656-3080 • **Financial Aid Phone:** 418-656-3332
E-mail: reg@reg.ulaval.ca
Fax: 418-656-5216 • **Website:** www.fsa.ulaval.ca

This public school was founded in 1924.

RATINGS

Admissions Selectivity Rating: 60*   **Fire Safety Rating:** 60*

STUDENTS AND FACULTY

Enrollment: 2,009. **Student Body:** 43% female, 57% male, 3% international. **Retention and Graduation:** 75% freshmen return for sophomore year. 65% freshmen graduate within 4 years. 68% freshmen graduate within 6 years.

ACADEMICS

Degrees: bachelor's, certificate, diploma, master's, post-bachelor's certificate. **Special Study Options:** cooperative education program, exchange student program (domestic), internships, student-designed major, study abroad. **Disability Services:** Special programs offered to physically disabled students include note-taking services, reader services, tape recorders. **Career services:** Alumni network, alumni services, career/job search classes, internships.

FACILITIES

Housing: Coed dorms, men's dorms, women's dorms. 100% of campus accessible to physically disabled. **Computers:** 100% of classrooms, 100% of dorms, 100% of libraries, 100% of dining areas, 100% of student union, 100% of common outdoor areas have wireless network access. Students can register for classes online. Administrative functions (other than registration) can be performed online. Undergraduates are required to own a computer.

CAMPUS LIFE

Environment: Metropolis. **Activities:** Choral groups, concert band, dance, drama/theater, jazz band, literary magazine, music ensembles, radio station, student government, student newspaper, International Student Organization, Model UN. 200 registered organizations. **Athletics (Intercollegiate):** *Men:* badminton, basketball, diving, golf, rugby, skiing (downhill/alpine), skiing (nordic/cross-country), soccer, swimming, track/field (outdoor), track/field (indoor), volleyball. *Women:* badminton, basketball, diving, golf, rugby, skiing (downhill/

alpine), skiing (nordic/cross-country), soccer, swimming, track/field (outdoor), track/field (indoor), volleyball. **Environmental Initiatives:** Table de concertation sur le développement durabla, See http://www.developpementdurable. ulaval.ca/agir/la_table_de_concertation_sur_le_developpement_durable/. Fonds de développement durable/Sustainable Developement: 2M$ in 5 years to support on-campus sustainable development projects. All other initiatives: http://www.developpementdurable.ulaval.ca/agir/

ADMISSIONS

Basis for Candidate Selection: *Very important factors considered include:* academic GPA, rigor of secondary school record. *Other factors considered include:* standardized test scores, extracurricular activities, work experience. **Freshman Admission Requirements:** High school diploma is required and GED is not accepted. **Freshman Admission Statistics:** 1,377 applied, 71% admitted, 57% enrolled. **General Admission Information:** Application Fee $30. Nonfall registration accepted.

COSTS AND FINANCIAL AID

Annual in-state tuition $2,500. Annual out-of-state tuition $5,956. Room and board $2,232. Average book expense $2,000. *Student Employment:* Off-campus job opportunities are good.

UNIVERSITY OF ADVANCING TECHNOLOGY (UAT)

2625 W. Baseline Rd., Tempe, AZ 85283-1056
Phone: 602-383-8228 · **Financial Aid Phone:** 602-383-8228
E-mail: admissions@uat.edu
Fax: 602-383-8222 · **Website:** www.uat.edu

This proprietary school was founded in 1983.

RATINGS

Admissions Selectivity Rating: 60*   Fire Safety Rating: 60*

STUDENTS AND FACULTY

Enrollment: 1,090. **Student Body:** 10% female, 90% male, 6% out-of-state, 0% international. Asian 4%, African American 7%, Caucasian 61%, Hispanic 6%, Native American 1%
Faculty: 31 full-time faculty, 16% hold PhDs, 35% are are members of minority groups. 0% of classes are taught by teaching assistants.

ACADEMICS

Degrees: associate, bachelor's, diploma, master's. **Classes:** Most classes have 20-29 students. **Special Study Options:** Accelerated program, cooperative education program, distance learning, double major, independent study, internships, student-designed major. **Career services:** Alumni network, alumni services, career/job search classes, career assessment, internships, regional alumni. Career services highlights include internship opportunities for all of our majors. For example, many of our game design students are currently interns at Rainbow Studios, Buena Vista Games and many other prominent game development companies. Internships are also a graduation requirements for all UAT students.

FACILITIES

Housing: 100% of campus accessible to physically disabled. **Computers:** Administrative functions (other than registration) can be performed online.

CAMPUS LIFE

Environment: Metropolis. **Activities:** student government. 1 religous organization. **On-Campus Highlights:** Cuban Pete's Café, UAT Library, Computer Commons, Campus Game Stations.

ADMISSIONS

Freshman Academic Profile: Minimum paper TOEFL 550. **Basis for Candidate Selection:** *Very important factors considered include:* character/personal qualities, interview, level of applicant's interest, talent/ability. *Important factors considered include:* rigor of secondary school record. *Other factors considered include:* academic GPA, standardized test scores, volunteer work. **Freshman Admission Requirements:** High school diploma is required and GED is accepted. **Transfer Admission Requirements:** High school transcript, college transcript(s), Minimum college GPA of 2.0 required. Lowest grade transferable C. **General Admission Information:** Nonfall registration accepted. Admission may be deferred for a maximum of 1 year.

COSTS AND FINANCIAL AID

Annual tuition $19,400. Average book expense $1,000. **Required Forms and Deadlines:** FAFSA. **Types of Aid:** *Need-based scholarships/grants:* Federal Pell, SEOG, private scholarships, the school's own gift aid. *Loans:* Subsidized Stafford, Unsubsidized Stafford, PLUS. **Financial Aid Statistics:** 72% undergrads borrow to pay for school.

THE UNIVERSITY OF AKRON

The University of Akron, Akron, OH 44325-2001
Phone: 330-972-7100 · **Financial Aid Phone:** 800-621-3847
E-mail: admissions@uakron.edu · **CEEB Code:** 1829
Fax: 330-972-7022 · **Website:** www.uakron.edu · **ACT Code:** 3338

This public school was founded in 1870. It has a 223-acre campus.

RATINGS

Admissions Selectivity Rating: 72   Fire Safety Rating: 86

STUDENTS AND FACULTY

Enrollment: 19,016. **Student Body:** 47% female, 53% male, 3% out-of-state, 1% international (57 countries represented). Asian 2%, African American 14%, Caucasian 74%, Hispanic 2%, Native American <1%
Retention and Graduation: 66% freshmen return for sophomore year. **Faculty:** 779 full-time faculty, 80% hold PhDs, 43% are are members of minority groups, 20% are women. 4% of classes are taught by teaching assistants.

ACADEMICS

Degrees: associate, bachelor's, certificate, doctoral, master's, post-bachelor's certificate, post-master's certificate. **Classes:** Most classes have 20-29 students. Most lab/discussion sessions have 10-19 students. **Majors with Highest Enrollment:** Mechanical Engineering; Biology/Biological Sciences; Marketing/Marketing Management. **Special Study Options:** Accelerated program, cooperative education program, distance learning, double major, English as a Second Language (ESL), external degree program, honors program, independent study, internships, student-designed major, study abroad, teacher certification program, weekend college, Undergraduates may take graduate level courses. Co-Op Programs: Arts, Business, Computer Science, Engineering, Family and Consumer Sciences, Humanities, Natural Science, Technologies. Dual Enrollment offered for select graduate level programs. **Honors programs:** Honors Delegates, Engineering Program, Emerging Leaders Program **Combined degree programs:** BA/MD, RN/MSN in Nursing, BS/MS in Accounting and Math. **Disability Services:** Special programs offered to physically disabled students include note-taking services, reader services, tape recorders, tutors. **Career services:** alumni services, career/job search classes, career assessment, internships. Career services highlights include our placement as one of two finalists for the "Most innovative Pedagogy for Entrepreneurship Education Award" at the United States Assocatiation for Small Business and Entrepreneurship (USASBE) annual conference, 2009.

FACILITIES

Housing: Coed dorms, special housing for disabled students, men's dorms, special housing for international students, women's dorms, fraternity/sorority housing, Honors student dormitory. 90% of campus accessible to physically disabled. Performing arts hall, nursery center, language lab, speech and hearing center, nursing learning resource labs, institute of polymer science and engineering, chemical lab, institute for health and social policy, Bliss Institute of Applied Politics. **Computers:** 100% of classrooms, 100% of dorms, 100% of libraries, 100% of dining areas, 100% of student union, 100% of common outdoor areas have wireless network access. Students can register for classes online. Administrative functions (other than registration) can be performed online.

CAMPUS LIFE

Environment: City. **Activities:** Choral groups, concert band, dance, drama/theater, jazz band, marching band, music ensembles, musical theater, pep band, radio station, student government, student newspaper, symphony orchestra, television station, yearbook, Campus Ministries, International Student Organization. 216 registered organizations, 30 honor societies, 12 religious organizations. 15 fraternities, 8 sororities. **Athletics (Intercollegiate):** *Men:* baseball, basketball, cheerleading, cross-country, football, golf, riflery, soccer, track/field (outdoor), track/field (indoor). *Women:* basketball, cheerleading, cross-country, diving, riflery, soccer, softball, swimming, tennis, track/field (outdoor), track/field (indoor), volleyball. **On-Campus Highlights:** Recreation Center, Student Union (includes food court, Starbucks), E.J. Thomas Performing Arts Hall, James A. Rhodes Arena, Robertson Café, Student Recreation and Wellness Center, which features a 56-foot rock-climbing wall, recreation pool, "lazy river", spa, ball courts and fitness facilities; Student Union with a movie theatre, bowling and billiards, a food court and a Starbucks Café.

ADMISSIONS

Freshman Academic Profile: Average high school GPA 3.1. 13% in top 10% of high school class, 33% in top 25% of high school class, 62% in top 50% of high school class. SAT Math middle 50% range 470-610. SAT Critical Reading middle 50% range 450-590. ACT middle 50% range 18-25. Minimum internet-based TOEFL 71. Minimum paper TOEFL 550. **Basis for Candidate Selection:** *Very important factors considered include:* Class rank, academic GPA, rigor of secondary school record, standardized test scores. **Freshman Admission Requirements:** High school diploma is required and GED is accepted. **Freshman Admission Statistics:** 10,575 applied, 96% admitted, 37% enrolled. **Transfer Admission Requirements:** college transcript(s), statement of good standing from prior institution(s). Lowest grade transferable D-. **General Admission Information:** Application Fee $30. Regular application deadline 8/10. Notification on a rolling basis, beginning on or about 9/15. Nonfall registration accepted. Admission may be deferred for a maximum of 2 Semesters. Credit offered for CEEB Advanced Placement tests.

COSTS AND FINANCIAL AID

Annual in-state tuition $8,449. Annual out-of-state tuition $16,813. Room and board $10,382. Required fees $1,605. Average book expense $1,000. **Required Forms and Deadlines:** FAFSA, Institution's own financial aid form. **Notification of Awards:** Applicants will be notified of awards on a rolling basis beginning 4/1. **Types of Aid:** *Need-based scholarships/grants:* Federal Pell, SEOG. *Loans:* Subsidized Stafford, Unsubsidized Stafford, PLUS, Federal Perkins, Federal Nursing. *Student Employment:* Federal Work-Study Program available. Institutional employment available. Highest amount earned per year from on-campus jobs $5,800. Off-campus job opportunities are excellent. **Financial Aid Statistics:** 63% freshmen, 61% undergrads receive need-based scholarship or grant aid. 60% freshmen, 53% undergrads receive non-need-based scholarship or grant aid. 80% freshmen, 82% undergrads receive need-based self-help aid. 1% freshmen, 1% undergrads receive athletic scholarships. 78% freshmen, 81% undergrads receive any aid. 72% undergrads borrow to pay for school. Average cumulative indebtedness $19,479. **Criteria for awarding institutional aid:** *Non-need-based:* academics, art, athletics, leadership, music/drama, state/district residency.

THE UNIVERSITY OF ALABAMA AT BIRMINGHAM

Office of Undergraduate Admissions, Birmingham, AL 35294-4412
Phone: 205-934-8221 · **Financial Aid Phone:** 205-934-8223
E-mail: chooseuab@uab.edu · **CEEB Code:** 1856
Fax: 205-975-7114 · **Website:** www.uab.edu · **ACT Code:** 56

This public school was founded in 1969. It has a 183-acre campus.

RATINGS

Admissions Selectivity Rating: 81   Fire Safety Rating: 86

STUDENTS AND FACULTY

Enrollment: 11,679. **Student Body:** 58% female, 42% male, 9% out-of-state, 2% international (53 countries represented). Asian 5%, African American 25%, Caucasian 58%, Hispanic 3%, Native American <1%
Retention and Graduation: 33% freshmen graduate within 4 years. 56% freshmen graduate within 6 years. **Faculty:** 865 full-time faculty, 86% hold PhDs, 46% are are members of minority groups, 24% are women.

ACADEMICS

Degrees: bachelor's, certificate, doctoral, master's, post-bachelor's certificate, post-master's certificate. **Classes:** Most classes have 10-19 students. Most lab/discussion sessions have 20-29 students. **Majors with Highest Enrollment:** Biology/Biological Sciences; Psychology; Speech Communication and Rhetoric. **Special Study Options:** Accelerated program, cooperative education program, cross-registration, distance learning, double major, dual enrollment, English as a Second Language (ESL), honors program, independent study, internships, student-designed major, study abroad, teacher certification program. **Honors programs:** The University Honors Program is designed for students who want to satisfy their intellectual curiosity both inside and outside the classroom. The program is limited in size to 200 students who represent a wide variety of disciplines, backgrounds and interests. Without delaying progress toward a degree, the Honors Program provides students an opportunity to participate in a community of committed scholars, to form close relationships with faculty, to explore new ideas, and to share their ideas, interests, and lives on a daily basis in the Honors House. Students have opportunities to work on independent projects, to travel, and to participate in special extracurricular activities. Those who complete the program are recognized with the designation "With University Honors" on their transcripts and in the graduation program. Please visit our Univeristy Honors website for more information: http://main.uab.edu/show.

asp?durki=80738 **Combined degree programs:** BA/MD, BA/MA, Fifth Year BS/MS in Biology Program; EMSAP. **Disability Services:** Special programs offered to physically disabled students include note-taking services, reader services, tape recorders. **Career services:** alumni services, career/job search classes, career assessment, regional alumni.

FACILITIES

Housing: Coed dorms, special housing for disabled students, special housing for international students, apartments for married students, apartments for single students, Theme Housing. 100% of campus accessible to physically disabled. **Special Academic Facilities/Equipment:** Museum of health sciences. **Computers:** Students can register for classes online. Administrative functions (other than registration) can be performed online.

CAMPUS LIFE

Environment: Metropolis. **Activities:** Choral groups, concert band, dance, drama/theater, jazz band, literary magazine, marching band, music ensembles, musical theater, opera, pep band, radio station, student government, student newspaper, Campus Ministries, International Student Organization. 150 registered organizations, 45 honor societies, 9 religious organizations. 9 fraternities, 8 sororities. **Athletics (Intercollegiate):** *Men:* baseball, basketball, football, golf, soccer, tennis. *Women:* basketball, cross-country, golf, riflery, soccer, softball, synchronized swimming, tennis, track/field (outdoor), track/field (indoor), volleyball. **On-Campus Highlights:** Student Rec Center, Commons Dining Hall, Hill University Center, Blazer Hall, Heritage Hall. **Environmental Initiatives:** Recycling; Air Handler; Condensate Recovery System; Building Energy Set-backs.

ADMISSIONS

Freshman Academic Profile: Average high school GPA 3.59. 28.3% in top 10% of high school class, 55.2% in top 25% of high school class, 82.5% in top 50% of high school class. ACT middle 50% range 21-27. Minimum internet-based TOEFL 77. **Basis for Candidate Selection:** *Very important factors considered include:* academic GPA, rigor of secondary school record, standardized test scores. **Freshman Admission Requirements:** High school diploma is required and GED is accepted. *Academic units required:* 4 English, 3 mathematics, 3 science, (2 science labs), 1 foreign language, 3 social studies, 3 academic electives. **Freshman Admission Statistics:** 5,710 applied, 86% admitted, 36% enrolled. **Transfer Admission Requirements:** college transcript(s), Minimum college GPA of 2.0 required. **General Admission Information:** Application Fee $35. Regular application deadline 3/1. Nonfall registration accepted. Admission may be deferred for a maximum of 1 year. Credit offered for CEEB Advanced Placement tests.

COSTS AND FINANCIAL AID

Annual in-state tuition $9,280. Annual out-of-state tuition $21,220. Room and board $9,810. Required fees $0. Average book expense $1,200. **Required Forms and Deadlines:** FAFSA. **Notification of Awards:** Applicants will be notified of awards on a rolling basis beginning 4/1. **Types of Aid:** *Need-based scholarships/grants:* Federal Pell, SEOG, state scholarships/grants, private scholarships, the school's own gift aid, United Negro College Fund. *Loans:* Direct Subsidized Stafford, Direct Unsubsidized Stafford, Direct PLUS, Federal Perkins, state loans, college/university loans from institutional funds. *Student Employment:* Federal Work-Study Program available. Institutional employment available. Off-campus job opportunities are excellent. **Financial Aid Statistics:** 56% freshmen, 64% undergrads receive need-based scholarship or grant aid. 63% freshmen, 36% undergrads receive non-need-based scholarship or grant aid. 67% freshmen, 76% undergrads receive need-based self-help aid. 3% freshmen, 3% undergrads receive athletic scholarships. 58% undergrads borrow to pay for school. Average cumulative indebtedness $25,954. **Criteria for awarding institutional aid:** *Non-need-based:* academics, alumni affiliation, art, athletics, leadership, minority status, music/drama.

THE UNIVERSITY OF ALABAMA IN HUNTSVILLE

UAH Office of Admissions, Huntsville, AL 35899
Phone: 256-824-2773 · **Financial Aid Phone:** 256-824-2761
E-mail: uahadmissions@uah.edu · **CEEB Code:** 1854
Fax: 256-824-4539 · **Website:** www.uah.edu · **ACT Code:** 53

This public school was founded in 1950. It has a 400-acre campus.

RATINGS

Admissions Selectivity Rating: 83   Fire Safety Rating: 93

STUDENTS AND FACULTY

Enrollment: 5,525. **Student Body:** 44% female, 56% male, 10% out-of-state, 3% international (75 countries represented). Asian 4%, African American 18%, Caucasian 70%, Hispanic 3%, Native American 1%

Retention and Graduation: 81% freshmen return for sophomore year. 16% freshmen graduate within 4 years. 48% freshmen graduate within 6 years. **Faculty:** 309 full-time faculty, 86% hold PhDs, 39% are are members of minority groups, 22% are women. 3% of classes are taught by teaching assistants.

ACADEMICS

Degrees: bachelor's, doctoral, master's, post-bachelor's certificate, post-master's certificate. **Classes:** Most classes have 20-29 students. Most lab/discussion sessions have fewer than 10 students. **Majors with Highest Enrollment:** Mechanical Engineering; Biology/Biological Sciences; Registered Nursing/Registered Nurse. **Special Study Options:** cooperative education program, cross-registration, distance learning, double major, dual enrollment, English as a Second Language (ESL), honors program, independent study, internships, study abroad, teacher certification program, Intensive English Program. **Honors programs:** The Honors Program at UAH provides academically talented undergraduate students with opportunities to develop their special talents and skills within an expanded and enriched version of the curriculum leading to an Honors Diploma. Honors coursework parallels regular offerings in all majors and programs. The courses include special interdisciplinary seminars, and opportunities for independent study and research/creative work, including the opportunity to work closely with faculty on special student projects. Students may participate in an Honors internship that offers active involvement in a business enterprise, professional organization, or government agency that has particular interest and relevance to the student's course of study. Participating students also benefit from the interaction the Honors Program affords with other talented and highly motivated students. See honors.uah.edu for more information. **Combined degree programs:** BA/MA, Biological Sciences, Physics, Computer Science. **Disability Services:** Special programs offered to physically disabled students include note-taking services, reader services, tape recorders, tutors. **Career services:** alumni services, career/job search classes, career assessment, internships. Career services highlights include our Coop program, one of the largest in the state of Alabama and accredited by the Accreditation Council for Cooperative Education.

FACILITIES

Housing: Coed dorms, special housing for disabled students, fraternity/sorority housing, apartments for married students, cooperative housing, apartments for single students, Theme Housing, Athletic Teammates. 98% of campus accessible to physically disabled. **Special Academic Facilities/Equipment:** Art museum and galleries, observatory with a Solar Magnetometer, optics building, centers for applied optics, micro-gravity research, robotics, solar research, space plasma, and aeronomic research. **Computers:** 25% of classrooms, 30% of dorms, 100% of libraries, 100% of dining areas, 100% of student union, 90% of common outdoor areas have wireless network access. Students can register for classes online. Administrative functions (other than registration) can be performed online.

CAMPUS LIFE

Environment: City. **Activities:** Choral groups, concert band, dance, drama/theater, jazz band, literary magazine, music ensembles, pep band, student government, student newspaper, Campus Ministries, International Student Organization. 52 registered organizations, 24 honor societies, 5 religious organizations. 7 fraternities, 4 sororities. **Athletics (Intercollegiate):** *Men:* baseball, basketball, cheerleading, cross-country, ice hockey, soccer, tennis, track/field (outdoor), track/field (indoor). *Women:* basketball, cheerleading, cross-country, soccer, softball, tennis, track/field (outdoor), track/field (indoor), volleyball. **On-Campus Highlights:** University Fitness Center, Shelby Center, Salmon Library, University Center, Central Campus Residence Hall. **Environmental Initiatives:** A hazard chemical waste and waste minimization program has been in effect for over 15 years. Improved environmental awareness communications and training/learning opportunities will soon be available on the OEHS web site. The energy conservation program included the upgrade of the Central Plant boilers which are now among the most energy efficient and environmentally friendly in the state of Alabama. A recycling program that has been in place for over 20 years.

ADMISSIONS

Freshman Academic Profile: Average high school GPA 3.64. 28% in top 10% of high school class, 50% in top 25% of high school class, 83% in top 50% of high school class. 90% from public high schools. SAT Math middle 50% range 510-650. SAT Critical Reading middle 50% range 510-640. ACT middle 50% range 23-29. Minimum internet-based TOEFL 62. Minimum paper TOEFL 500. **Basis for Candidate Selection:** *Very important factors considered include:* academic GPA, rigor of secondary school record, standardized test scores. *Other factors considered include:* Class rank, application essay, recommendation(s), level of applicant's interest. **Freshman Admission Requirements:** High school diploma is required and GED is accepted. *Academic units required:* 4 English, 3 mathematics, 3 science, (0 science labs), 0 foreign language, 4 social studies, 6 academic electives. **Freshman Admission Statistics:** 2,054 applied, 81% admitted, 39% enrolled. **Transfer Admission Requirements:** college transcript(s), statement of good standing from prior

institution(s). Minimum college GPA of 2.0 required. Lowest grade transferable D. **General Admission Information:** Application Fee $30. Regular application deadline 8/19. Nonfall registration accepted. Admission may be deferred for a maximum of 1 year. Credit and/or placement offered for CEEB Advanced Placement tests.

COSTS AND FINANCIAL AID

Annual in-state tuition $9,192. Annual out-of-state tuition $21,506. Room and board $8,265. Average book expense $1,592. **Required Forms and Deadlines:** FAFSA. **Notification of Awards:** Applicants will be notified of awards on a rolling basis beginning 4/1. **Types of Aid:** *Need-based scholarships/grants:* Federal Pell, SEOG, state scholarships/grants, private scholarships, the school's own gift aid, Federal Nursing Scholarships. *Loans:* Direct Subsidized Stafford, Direct Unsubsidized Stafford, Direct PLUS. *Student Employment:* Federal Work-Study Program available. Institutional employment available. Off-campus job opportunities are fair. **Financial Aid Statistics:** 87% freshmen, 77% undergrads receive need-based scholarship or grant aid. 12% freshmen, 5% undergrads receive non-need-based scholarship or grant aid. 79% freshmen, 87% undergrads receive need-based self-help aid. 7% freshmen, 4% undergrads receive athletic scholarships. 88% freshmen, 78% undergrads receive any aid. 58% undergrads borrow to pay for school. Average cumulative indebtedness $26,116. **Criteria for awarding institutional aid:** *Non-need-based:* academics, art, athletics, leadership, minority status, music/drama.

THE UNIVERSITY OF ALABAMA AT TUSCALOOSA

 Best 380

Box 870132, Tuscaloosa, AL 35487-0132
Phone: 205-348-5666 • **Financial Aid Phone:** 205-348-7949
E-mail: admissions@ua.edu • **CEEB Code:** 1830
Fax: 205-348-9046 • **Website:** www.ua.edu • **ACT Code:** 52

This public school was founded in 1831. It has a 1000-acre campus.

RATINGS

Admissions Selectivity Rating: 89   **Fire Safety Rating:** 73

STUDENTS AND FACULTY

Enrollment: 29,851. **Student Body:** 54% female, 46% male, 50% out-of-state, 3% international (56 countries represented). Asian 1%, African American 11%, Caucasian 78%, Hispanic 3%, Native American <1%
Retention and Graduation: 39% freshmen graduate within 4 years. 66% freshmen graduate within 6 years. 26% grads go on to further study within 1 year. 3% grads pursue law degrees. 2% grads pursue medical degrees. **Faculty:** 1,244 full-time faculty, 83% hold PhDs, 43% are are members of minority groups, 18% are women. 14% of classes are taught by teaching assistants.

ACADEMICS

Degrees: bachelor's, doctoral, master's, post-master's certificate. **Classes:** Most classes have 10-19 students. Most lab/discussion sessions have 20-29 students. **Majors with Highest Enrollment:** Business Administration and Management; Mechanical Engineering; Accounting. **Special Study Options:** Accelerated program, cooperative education program, cross-registration, distance learning, double major, dual enrollment, English as a Second Language (ESL), exchange student program (domestic), external degree program, honors program, independent study, internships, liberal arts/career combination, student-designed major, study abroad, teacher certification program, weekend college. **Honors programs:** University Honors College is composed of the University Honors Program, Computer-Based Honors Program and the International Honors Program. There is also a program called the University Fellows Experience. **Combined degree programs:** BS-MBA. **Disability Services:** Special programs offered to physically disabled students include note-taking services, reader services, tape recorders, tutors. **Career services:** Alumni network, alumni services, career/job search classes, career assessment, internships, regional alumni. Career services highlights include Cooperative Education, a special academic program at The University of Alabama. In order to promote, encourage, and improve the education of students and to provide maximum service to industry, business, and government agencies, The University of Alabama offers qualified students and approved employers the opportunity to participate in Cooperative Education (Co-op) where students alternate periods of full-time study with periods of full-time employment.

FACILITIES

Housing: Coed dorms, special housing for disabled students, men's dorms, special housing for international students, women's dorms, fraternity/sorority housing, apartments for married students, apartments for single students, Theme Housing, Apartments for visiting scholars. 98% of campus accessible to physically disabled. **Special Academic Facilities/Equipment:** Art gallery, natural history museum, concert hall, archaeologic site and museum, arboretum, observatory, simulated coal mine, robotics lab, wind tunnel, artificial intelligence lab, jet propulsion engine mini-lab, special collections building. **Computers:** 55% of classrooms, 100% of dorms, 100% of libraries, 75% of dining areas, 100% of student union, 22% of common outdoor areas have wireless network access. Students can register for classes online. Administrative functions (other than registration) can be performed online.

CAMPUS LIFE

Environment: City. **Activities:** Choral groups, concert band, dance, drama/ theater, jazz band, literary magazine, marching band, music ensembles, musical theater, opera, pep band, radio station, student government, student newspaper, student-run film society, symphony orchestra, television station, yearbook, Campus Ministries, International Student Organization, Model UN. 294 registered organizations, 66 honor societies, 30 religious organizations. 31 fraternities, 23 sororities. **Athletics (Intercollegiate):** *Men:* baseball, basketball, cross-country, diving, football, golf, swimming, tennis, track/field (outdoor), track/field (indoor). *Women:* basketball, crew/rowing, cross-country, diving, golf, gymnastics, soccer, softball, swimming, tennis, track/field (outdoor), track/field (indoor), volleyball. **On-Campus Highlights:** University of Alabama Museum of Natural History, Amelia Gayle Gorgas Library, Bryant-Denny Stadium, The Gorgas House Museum (built in 1829), Paul W. Bryant Museum, Located right on campus is a wonderful blend of cultures and ethnic foods. Interesting shops, a new shopping center, great coffee shops, local and visiting musical talent—all located on University Blvd. **Environmental Initiatives:** Recycling has increased by 181% over fiscal year 2008. Currently we are recycling over 1,300 tons of recyclable material. Community Recycling after the tornados of April 2011. As a result of an aggressive energy reduction program, The Univeristy of Alabama uses 27% less energy per square foot than the national average for universities.

ADMISSIONS

Freshman Academic Profile: Average high school GPA 3.65. 41.4% in top 10% of high school class, 61.1% in top 25% of high school class, 83.4% in top 50% of high school class. SAT Math middle 50% range 500-630. SAT Critical Reading middle 50% range 490-620. SAT Writing middle 50% range 480-600. ACT middle 50% range 22-31. Minimum internet-based TOEFL 71. Minimum paper TOEFL 527. **Basis for Candidate Selection:** *Very important factors considered include:* academic GPA, rigor of secondary school record, standardized test scores. *Important factors considered include:* Class rank. *Other factors considered include:* application essay, recommendation(s), alumni/ae relation, character/personal qualities, extracurricular activities, first generation, interview, talent/ability, volunteer work, work experience. **Freshman Admission Requirements:** High school diploma is required and GED is accepted. *Academic units required:* 4 English, 3 mathematics, 3 science, (2 science labs), 1 foreign language, 4 social studies, 1 history, 5 academic electives. **Freshman Admission Statistics:** 33,736 applied, 51% admitted, 40% enrolled. **Transfer Admission Requirements:** college transcript(s), Minimum college GPA of 2.0 required. Lowest grade transferable D. **General Admission Information:** Application Fee $40. Notification on a rolling basis, beginning on or about 8/1. Nonfall registration accepted. Credit and/or placement offered for CEEB Advanced Placement tests.

COSTS AND FINANCIAL AID

Annual out-of-state tuition $24,950. Room and board $8,866. Required fees $0. Average book expense $1,200. **Required Forms and Deadlines:** FAFSA, Institution's own financial aid form, CSS/Financial Aid PROFILE, State aid form, Noncustodial PROFILE, Business/Farm Supplement. **Notification of Awards:** Applicants will be notified of awards on a rolling basis beginning 4/1. **Types of Aid:** *Need-based scholarships/grants:* Federal Pell, SEOG, state scholarships/grants, private scholarships, the school's own gift aid, Federal Nursing Scholarships. *Loans:* Direct Subsidized Stafford, Direct Unsubsidized Stafford, Direct PLUS, Federal Perkins, college/university loans from institutional funds. *Student Employment:* Federal Work-Study Program available. Institutional employment available. Highest amount earned per year from on-campus jobs $2,466. Off-campus job opportunities are good. **Financial Aid Statistics:** 76% freshmen, 71% undergrads receive need-based scholarship or grant aid. 58% freshmen, 43% undergrads receive non-need-based scholarship or grant aid. 67% freshmen, 80% undergrads receive need-based self-help aid. 2% freshmen, 2% undergrads receive athletic scholarships. 76% freshmen, 71% undergrads receive any aid. 45% undergrads borrow to pay for school. Average cumulative indebtedness $23,479. **Criteria for awarding institutional aid:** *Non-need-based:* academics, alumni affiliation, art, athletics, leadership, minority status, music/drama, state/district residency.

UNIVERSITY OF ALASKA ANCHORAGE

3211 Providence Drive, Anchorage, AK 99508-8046
Phone: 907-786-1480
E-mail: enroll@uaa.alaska.edu • **CEEB Code:** 4896
Fax: 907-786-4888 • **Website:** www.uaa.alaska.edu/ • **ACT Code:** 137

This public school was founded in 1954. It has a 384-acre campus.

RATINGS

Admissions Selectivity Rating: 76   **Fire Safety Rating:** 69

STUDENTS AND FACULTY

Enrollment: 13,390. **Student Body:** 58% female, 42% male, 10% out-of-state, 0% international (35 countries represented). Asian 7%, African American 4%, Caucasian 58%, Hispanic 7%, Native American 12%
Retention and Graduation: 73% freshmen return for sophomore year. **Faculty:** 680 full-time faculty, 53% hold PhDs, 52% are are members of minority groups, 12% are women. 0% of classes are taught by teaching assistants.

ACADEMICS

Degrees: associate, bachelor's, certificate, master's, post-bachelor's certificate, post-master's certificate. **Classes:** Most classes have fewer than 10 students. Most lab/discussion sessions have 10-19 students. **Special Study Options:** cooperative education program, cross-registration, distance learning, double major, dual enrollment, English as a Second Language (ESL), exchange student program (domestic), honors program, independent study, internships, liberal arts/career combination, student-designed major, study abroad, teacher certification program. **Honors programs:** University Honors Program. **Disability Services:** Special programs offered to physically disabled students include note-taking services, reader services, tape recorders. **Career services:** alumni services, career/job search classes, career assessment, internships.

FACILITIES

Housing: Coed dorms, special housing for disabled students, special housing for international students, apartments for single students, Wellness HousingSeparate floors for: Alaska natives studying engineering, nursing students, honor students, language and cultures, first-year students under age 20, healthy lifestyle, quiet lifestyle, WWAMI program, Far East exchange program. 95% of campus accessible to physically disabled. **Special Academic Facilities/ Equipment:** Kimura and student Center Galleries. **Computers:** Students can register for classes online. Administrative functions (other than registration) can be performed online.

CAMPUS LIFE

Environment: City. **Activities:** Choral groups, dance, drama/theater, jazz band, literary magazine, music ensembles, musical theater, opera, radio station, student government, student newspaper, student-run film society, Campus Ministries, International Student Organization, Model UN. 70 registered organizations, 5 honor societies, 5 religious organizations. 1 fraternity, 2 sororities. **Athletics (Intercollegiate):** *Men:* basketball, cross-country, ice hockey, skiing (downhill/alpine), skiing (nordic/cross-country). *Women:* basketball, cross-country, gymnastics, skiing (downhill/alpine), skiing (nordic/cross-country), volleyball. **On-Campus Highlights:** Campus Center, Wells Fargo Sports Center, Creakside Eatery, Cuddy Center, Student Health Center, The University of Alaska Anchorage campus has covered walkways across much of the campus as well as bike trails that connect the camus to the town's bike trail system. Student Housing is adjacent to the campus with shuttle buses running every 15 minutes throughout the main campus and University Center area of campus.

ADMISSIONS

Freshman Academic Profile: 13% in top 10% of high school class, 32% in top 25% of high school class, 62% in top 50% of high school class. 95% from public high schools. SAT Math middle 50% range 440-570. SAT Critical Reading middle 50% range 430-580. Minimum paper TOEFL 450. **Basis for Candidate Selection:** *Very important factors considered include:* rigor of secondary school record. *Other factors considered include:* Class rank, standardized test scores, talent/ability. **Freshman Admission Requirements:** High school diploma is required and GED is accepted. **Freshman Admission Statistics:** 3,924 applied, 76% admitted, 43% enrolled. **Transfer Admission Requirements:** college transcript(s), statement of good standing from prior institution(s). Minimum college GPA of 2.0 required. Lowest grade transferable C. **General Admission Information:** Application Fee $50. Regular application deadline 7/1. Nonfall registration accepted. Admission may be deferred for a maximum of 1 year. Credit offered for CEEB Advanced Placement tests.

COSTS AND FINANCIAL AID

Average book expense $1,575. **Required Forms and Deadlines:** FAFSA, Institution's own financial aid form. **Notification of Awards:** Applicants will be notified of awards on a rolling basis beginning 3/15. **Types of Aid:** *Need-based* scholarships/grants: Federal Pell, SEOG, state scholarships/grants, private scholarships, the school's own gift aid, Federal Work Study. *Loans:* Subsidized Stafford, Unsubsidized Stafford, PLUS, state loans. *Student Employment:* Federal Work-Study Program available. Institutional employment available. Off-campus job opportunities are good. **Financial Aid Statistics:** 84% freshmen, 74% undergrads receive need-based scholarship or grant aid. 10% freshmen, 3% undergrads receive non-need-based scholarship or grant aid. 63% freshmen, 71% undergrads receive need-based self-help aid. 2% freshmen, 1% undergrads receive athletic scholarships. 49% undergrads borrow to pay for school. Average cumulative indebtedness $22,813. **Criteria for awarding institutional aid:** *Non-need-based:* academics, athletics.

UNIVERSITY OF ALASKA FAIRBANKS

PO Box 757480, Fairbanks, AK 99775-7480
Phone: 907-474-7500 · **Financial Aid Phone:** 888-474-7256
E-mail: admissions@uaf.edu · **CEEB Code:** 4866
Fax: 907-474-5379 · **Website:** www.uaf.edu · **ACT Code:** 64

This public school was founded in 1917. It has a 2250-acre campus.

RATINGS

Admissions Selectivity Rating: 79   **Fire Safety Rating:** 87

STUDENTS AND FACULTY

Enrollment: 5,737. **Student Body:** 56% female, 44% male, 12% out-of-state, 1% international (54 countries represented). Asian 1%, African American 2%, Caucasian 45%, Hispanic 5%, Native American 14%
Retention and Graduation: 77% freshmen return for sophomore year. 14% freshmen graduate within 4 years. 38% freshmen graduate within 6 years. **Faculty:** 375 full-time faculty, 61% hold PhDs, 44% are are members of minority groups, 22% are women.

ACADEMICS

Degrees: associate, bachelor's, certificate, master's, post-bachelor's certificate, terminal associate, transfer associate. **Majors with Highest Enrollment:** Biology/Biological Sciences; Business Administration and Management; Mechanical Engineering. **Special Study Options:** Accelerated program, cooperative education program, distance learning, double major, dual enrollment, exchange student program (domestic), external degree program, honors program, independent study, internships, student-designed major, study abroad, teacher certification program, Legislative Aide Intern Program; Undergraduate Research Opportunities. **Honors programs:** The Honors Program at UAF provides superior undergraduate students with intellectual opportunities greater than those generally found in university lecture halls. Honors students experience small classes, direct contact with top faculty members, a flexible curriculum and great encouragement to pursue their own intellectual interests. **Combined degree programs:** BS/MS Computer Science, BS/MS Mechanical Engineering. **Disability Services:** Special programs offered to physically disabled students include note-taking services, reader services, tape recorders, tutors. **Career services:** Alumni network, alumni services, career/job search classes, career assessment, internships,

FACILITIES

Housing: Coed dorms, special housing for disabled students, apartments for married students, apartments for single students, Wellness HousingAlaska Native cultural housing. 90% of campus accessible to physically disabled. **Special Academic Facilities/Equipment:** Museum of natural/cultural history of Alaska and the North, Cray Super Computer, extensive telecommunication network, Geophysical Institute, NASA earth station, Poker Flat Research Range, electron microscope, microprobe, International Arctic Research Center, Institute of Arctic Biology, Institute of Northern Engineering, Arctic Region Supercomputing Center, Institute of Marine Biology, Agriculture and Forestry Experiment Station, Office of Electronic Miniaturization, Alaska Native Language Center, Georgeson Botanical Gardens, Cold Climate Housing Research Center, Large Animal Research Station. **Computers:** 100% of classrooms, 100% of dorms, 100% of libraries, 100% of dining areas, 100% of student union, 50% of common outdoor areas have wireless network access. Students can register for classes online. Administrative functions (other than registration) can be performed online.

CAMPUS LIFE

Environment: City. **Activities:** Choral groups, concert band, dance, drama/theater, jazz band, literary magazine, music ensembles, pep band, radio station, student government, student newspaper, symphony orchestra, television station, Campus Ministries, International Student Organization, Model UN. 122 registered organizations, 11 honor societies, 10 religious organizations. 1 fraternity,

1 sorority. **Athletics (Intercollegiate):** *Men:* basketball, cross-country, ice hockey, riflery, skiing (nordic/cross-country). *Women:* basketball, cross-country, riflery, skiing (nordic/cross-country), volleyball. **On-Campus Highlights:** Wood Center (includes food court), Student Recreation Center (SRC), Rasmuson Library, Groomed cross-country ski trails on campus, Hess Recreation Center, Wood Center (includes food court, coffee shop, bowling alley and pool tables, Outdoor Adventures, the Pub and various spaces for groups to gather or hold meetings) The 2,250 acre Fairbanks campus includes two lakes and 17 miles of ski and hiking trails as well as a major student recreation complex. We often refer to UAF as having a 360-million-acre campus because research and field work might take you anywhere in Alaska.

ADMISSIONS

Freshman Academic Profile: Average high school GPA 3.19. 18% in top 10% of high school class, 39% in top 25% of high school class, 67% in top 50% of high school class. SAT Math middle 50% range 470-610. SAT Critical Reading middle 50% range 470-600. SAT Writing middle 50% range 440-560. ACT middle 50% range 18-25. Minimum internet-based TOEFL 79. Minimum paper TOEFL 550. **Basis for Candidate Selection:** *Very important factors considered include:* academic GPA, standardized test scores. **Freshman Admission Requirements:** High school diploma is required and GED is not accepted. *Academic units required:* 4 English, 3 mathematics, 3 science, (1 science labs), 3 social studies. **Freshman Admission Statistics:** 1,529 applied, 80% admitted, 73% enrolled. **Transfer Admission Requirements:** college transcript(s), Minimum college GPA of 2.0 required. Lowest grade transferable C. **General Admission Information:** Application Fee $50. Regular application deadline 7/1. Regular notification 9/1. Notification on a rolling basis, beginning on or about 1/1. Nonfall registration accepted. Admission may be deferred for a maximum of 1 calendar year. Credit and/or placement offered for CEEB Advanced Placement tests.

COSTS AND FINANCIAL AID

Annual out-of-state tuition $18,540. Room and board $7,450. Required fees $962. Average book expense $1,400. **Required Forms and Deadlines:** FAFSA. **Notification of Awards:** Applicants will be notified of awards on a rolling basis beginning 3/1. **Types of Aid:** *Need-based scholarships/grants:* Federal Pell, SEOG, state scholarships/grants, private scholarships, the school's own gift aid. *Loans:* Subsidized Stafford, Unsubsidized Stafford, PLUS, state loans. *Student Employment:* Federal Work-Study Program available. Institutional employment available. Highest amount earned per year from on-campus jobs $5,320. Off-campus job opportunities are good. **Financial Aid Statistics:** 84% freshmen, 83% undergrads receive need-based scholarship or grant aid. 18% freshmen, 12% undergrads receive non-need-based scholarship or grant aid. 47% freshmen, 63% undergrads receive need-based self-help aid. 2% freshmen, 3% undergrads receive athletic scholarships. 83% freshmen, 76% undergrads receive any aid. 48% undergrads borrow to pay for school. Average cumulative indebtedness $23,217. **Criteria for awarding institutional aid:** *Non-need-based:* academics, art, athletics, leadership, minority status, music/drama, state/district residency.

UNIVERSITY OF ARIZONA

PO Box 210040, Tucson, AZ 85721-0073
Phone: 520-621-3237 · **Financial Aid Phone:** 520-626-6809
E-mail: admissions@arizona.edu · **CEEB Code:** 4832
Fax: 520-621-9799 · **Website:** http://www.arizona.edu · **ACT Code:** 96

This public school was founded in 1885. It has a 378-acre campus.

RATINGS

Admissions Selectivity Rating: 85   **Fire Safety Rating:** 85

STUDENTS AND FACULTY

Enrollment: 32,646. **Student Body:** 52% female, 48% male, 28% out-of-state, 6% international (112 countries represented). Asian 6%, African American 4%, Caucasian 53%, Hispanic 25%, Native American 1%
Retention and Graduation: 40% freshmen graduate within 4 years. **Faculty:** 1,583 full-time faculty, 38% are are members of minority groups, 19% are women.

ACADEMICS

Degrees: bachelor's, master's, post-bachelor's certificate, post-master's certificate. **Classes:** Most classes have 20-29 students. Most lab/discussion sessions have 20-29 students. **Majors with Highest Enrollment:** Psychology; Political Science and Government; Cell/Cellular and Molecular Biology. **Special Study Options:** Accelerated program, cooperative education program, cross-registration, distance learning, double major, dual enrollment, English as a Second Language (ESL), exchange student program (domestic), external degree program, independent study, internships, liberal arts/career combination, study abroad, teacher certification program, weekend college. **Honors programs:** For information on our Honors College, visit: http://www.honors.arizona.edu/. **Disability Services:** Special programs offered to physically disabled students include note-taking services, reader services, tape recorders, tutors. **Career services:** alumni services, career/job search classes, career assessment, internships.

FACILITIES

Housing: Coed dorms, special housing for disabled students, special housing for international students, women's dorms, fraternity/sorority housing, apartments for single students. 85% of campus accessible to physically disabled. **Special Academic Facilities/Equipment:** Art, photography, and natural history museums, tree-ring lab, planetarium, optical sciences center, nuclear reactor. **Computers:** 100% of classrooms, 100% of dorms, 100% of libraries, 100% of dining areas, 100% of student union, 75% of common outdoor areas have wireless network access. Students can register for classes online. Administrative functions (other than registration) can be performed online.

CAMPUS LIFE

Environment: Metropolis. **Activities:** Choral groups, concert band, dance, drama/theater, jazz band, literary magazine, marching band, music ensembles, musical theater, opera, pep band, radio station, student government, student newspaper, symphony orchestra, television station, yearbook, Campus Ministries, International Student Organization, Model UN. 504 registered organizations, 13 honor societies, 13 religious organizations. 25 fraternities, 20 sororities. **Athletics (Intercollegiate):** *Men:* baseball, basketball, cross-country, diving, football, golf, swimming, tennis, track/field (outdoor). *Women:* basketball, cross-country, diving, golf, gymnastics, soccer, softball, swimming, tennis, track/field (outdoor), track/field (indoor), volleyball. **On-Campus Highlights:** Flandrau Science Center, Center for Creative Photography, UA Museum of Art, Athletics Events, Arizona State Museum. **Environmental Initiatives:** The University of Arizonas top environmental commitments are conducting comprehensive research on environmental issues ranging from biodiversity, management, and global change. Research and advocacy for the development and adoption of solar energy sources. By the pursuing operating procedures that promote energy efficiency and lower environmental impact while providing world class service.

ADMISSIONS

Freshman Academic Profile: Average high school GPA 3.37. 31% in top 10% of high school class, 60% in top 25% of high school class, 88% in top 50% of high school class. 90% from public high schools. SAT Math middle 50% range 490-620. SAT Critical Reading middle 50% range 480-600. SAT Writing middle 50% range 470-590. ACT middle 50% range 21-27. Minimum internet-based TOEFL 70. **Basis for Candidate Selection:** *Very important factors considered include:* academic GPA, rigor of secondary school record. *Other factors considered include:* Class rank, application essay, recommendation(s), standardized test scores, character/personal qualities, extracurricular activities, first generation, geographical residence, interview, racial/ethnic status, state residency, talent/ability, volunteer work, work experience. **Freshman Admission Requirements:** High school diploma is required and GED is accepted. *Academic units required:* 4 English, 3 mathematics, 3 science, (3 science labs), 2 foreign language, 1 social studies, 1 history, 1 Fine Art. **Freshman Admission Statistics:** 32,723 applied, 75% admitted, 32% enrolled. **Transfer Admission Requirements:** college transcript(s), Lowest grade transferable C. **General Admission Information:** Application Fee $50. Regular application deadline 5/1. Notification on a rolling basis, beginning on or about 11/1. Nonfall registration accepted. Credit offered for CEEB Advanced Placement tests.

COSTS AND FINANCIAL AID

Annual in-state tuition $9,952. Annual out-of-state tuition $28,416. Room and board $9,700. Required fees $1,005. Average book expense $1,200. **Required Forms and Deadlines:** FAFSA. **Types of Aid:** *Need-based scholarships/grants:* Federal Pell, SEOG, state scholarships/grants, private scholarships, the school's own gift aid, Federal Nursing Scholarships. *Loans:* Subsidized Stafford, Unsubsidized Stafford, PLUS, Federal Perkins, Federal Nursing, college/university loans from institutional funds. *Student Employment:* Federal Work-Study Program available. Institutional employment available. Off-campus job opportunities are good. **Financial Aid Statistics:** 91% freshmen, 88% undergrads receive need-based scholarship or grant aid. 13% freshmen, 8% undergrads receive non-need-based scholarship or grant aid. 53% freshmen, 62% undergrads receive need-based self-help aid. 1% freshmen, 1% undergrads receive athletic scholarships. 49% undergrads borrow to pay for school. **Criteria for awarding institutional aid:** *Non-need-based:* academics, art, music/drama.

UNIVERSITY OF ARKANSAS AT PINE BLUFF

1200 N. University Drive, Pine Bluff, AR 71601
Phone: 870-575-8492
E-mail: fultone@uapb.edu
Fax: 870-575-4608 • **Website:** http://www.uapb.edu

This is a public school.

RATINGS

Admissions Selectivity Rating: 60*   **Fire Safety Rating:** 60*

STUDENTS AND FACULTY

Enrollment: 3,048. **Student Body:** 58% female, 42% male, 330% international. Asian 0%, African American 96%, Caucasian 3%, Hispanic 0%, Native American <1%
Retention and Graduation: 57% freshmen return for sophomore year. 14% freshmen graduate within 4 years. 32% freshmen graduate within 6 years. **Faculty:** 164 full-time faculty, 54% are are members of minority groups, 46% are women.

ACADEMICS

Degrees: associate, bachelor's, certificate, master's. **Classes:** Most classes have fewer than 10 students. **Special Study Options:** cooperative education program, distance learning, double major, dual enrollment, honors program, internships, study abroad, teacher certification program.

FACILITIES

Housing: men's dorms, women's dorms.

CAMPUS LIFE

Activities: Choral groups, concert band, drama/theater, jazz band, marching band, radio station, student government, student newspaper, television station, yearbook.

ADMISSIONS

Freshman Academic Profile: 93% from public high schools. SAT Math middle 50% range 350-450. SAT Critical Reading middle 50% range 350-440. ACT middle 50% range 14-18. Minimum paper TOEFL 500. **Basis for Candidate Selection:** *Very important factors considered include:* rigor of secondary school record, standardized test scores. *Important factors considered include:* academic GPA. **Freshman Admission Requirements:** High school diploma is required and GED is accepted. *Academic units required:* 4 English, 3 mathematics, 3 science, (2 science labs), 2 foreign language, 1 social studies, 2 history, 4 academic electives. **Freshman Admission Statistics:** 2,169 applied, 64% admitted, 59% enrolled. **Transfer Admission Requirements:** High school transcript, college transcript(s). **General Admission Information:** Nonfall registration accepted. Credit offered for CEEB Advanced Placement tests.

COSTS AND FINANCIAL AID

Annual out-of-state tuition $7,710. Room and board $6,070. Required fees $1,199. Average book expense $1,000. **Required Forms and Deadlines:** FAFSA. Notification of Awards. **Types of Aid:** *Need-based scholarships/grants:* Federal Pell, SEOG, state scholarships/grants, private scholarships, the school's own gift aid. *Loans:* Subsidized Stafford, Unsubsidized Stafford, Federal Perkins.

UNIVERSITY OF ARKANSAS—FAYETTEVILLE

Best 380

232 Silas Hunt Hall, Fayetteville, AR 72701
Phone: 479-575-5346 • **Financial Aid Phone:** 479-575-3806
E-mail: uofa@uark.edu • **CEEB Code:** 6866
Fax: 479-575-7515 • **Website:** http://www.uark.edu • **ACT Code:** 144

This public school was founded in 1871. It has a 410-acre campus.

RATINGS

Admissions Selectivity Rating: 87   **Fire Safety Rating:** 86

STUDENTS AND FACULTY

Enrollment: 21,405. **Student Body:** 52% female, 48% male, 39% out-of-state, 3% international (121 countries represented). Asian 3%, African American 5%, Caucasian 78%, Hispanic 7%, Native American 1%

Retention and Graduation: 83% freshmen return for sophomore year. 37% freshmen graduate within 4 years. 33% grads go on to further study within 1 year. 9% grads pursue arts and sciences degrees. 2% grads pursue law degrees. 1% grads pursue business degrees. 6% grads pursue medical degrees. **Faculty:** 1,108 full-time faculty, 84% hold PhDs, 38% are are members of minority groups, 15% are women. 19% of classes are taught by teaching assistants.

ACADEMICS

Degrees: bachelor's, master's, post-bachelor's certificate, post-master's certificate. **Classes:** Most classes have 20-29 students. Most lab/discussion sessions have 20-29 students. **Majors with Highest Enrollment:** Health and Physical Education/Fitness; Biology/Biological Sciences; Marketing/Marketing Management. **Special Study Options:** Accelerated program, cooperative education program, distance learning, double major, dual enrollment, English as a Second Language (ESL), honors program, independent study, internships, liberal arts/career combination, student-designed major, study abroad, teacher certification program. **Honors programs:** The Honors College provides exceptional opportunities for outstanding undergraduates. The College incorporates 4 areas of responsiblity: recruitment, administration of honors fellowships, coordination of honors program and curricula, and coordination of related services. **Combined degree programs:** BA/MD, BA/JD, BA/DDS, MBA/JD. **Disability Services:** Special programs offered to physically disabled students include note-taking services, reader services, tape recorders, tutors. **Career services:** Alumni network, alumni services, career assessment, internships.

FACILITIES

Housing: Coed dorms, women's dorms, fraternity/sorority housing, apartments for single students, Suites with private bedrooms. Special interest floors. Enhanced learning centers. First year experience program area. Adaptable housing for disabled students. Several residences remain open over holiday and winter breaks. Honors housing. Sophmore and beyond program area. 100% of campus accessible to physically disabled. **Special Academic Facilities/Equipment:** Public Radio-KUAF, High Density Electronics Center, Reynolds Center for Enterprise Development, Center for Excellence in Poultry Science, Genesis Small Business Incubation Center, Chemical Hazards Research Center (NEW), Honors College. **Computers:** Students can register for classes online. Administrative functions (other than registration) can be performed online.

CAMPUS LIFE

Environment: Town. **Activities:** Choral groups, concert band, dance, drama/theater, jazz band, literary magazine, marching band, music ensembles, musical theater, opera, pep band, radio station, student government, student newspaper, student-run film society, symphony orchestra, television station, yearbook, Campus Ministries, International Student Organization. 340 registered organizations, 39 honor societies, 32 religious organizations. 16 fraternities, 11 sororities. **Athletics (Intercollegiate):** *Men:* baseball, basketball, cross-country, football, golf, tennis, track/field (outdoor), track/field (indoor). *Women:* basketball, cross-country, diving, golf, gymnastics, soccer, softball, swimming, tennis, track/field (outdoor), track/field (indoor), volleyball. **On-Campus Highlights:** Bud Walton Arena, Old Main, Reynolds Razorback Stadium, Greek AmphiTheater, Senior Walk (every graduate's name engraved). **Environmental Initiatives:** ACUPCC Signatory, GHG inventory, climate action plan, $52 million investment in conservation on campus, Razorback Recycling.

ADMISSIONS

Freshman Academic Profile: Average high school GPA 3.63. 26% in top 10% of high school class, 55% in top 25% of high school class, 86% in top 50% of high school class. 83% from public high schools. SAT Math middle 50% range 510-620. SAT Critical Reading middle 50% range 500-610. ACT middle 50% range 23-28. Minimum internet-based TOEFL 79. Minimum paper TOEFL 550. **Basis for Candidate Selection:** *Very important factors considered include:* Class rank, academic GPA, rigor of secondary school record, standardized test scores. *Other factors considered include:* application essay, recommendation(s), alumni/ae relation, character/personal qualities, extracurricular activities, first generation, geographical residence, racial/ethnic status, state residency, talent/ability, volunteer work, work experience. **Freshman Admission Requirements:** High school diploma is required and GED is accepted. *Academic units required:* 4 English, 4 mathematics, 3 science, (2 science labs), 3 social studies, 2 academic electives. **Freshman Admission Statistics:** 18,984 applied, 62% admitted, 39% enrolled. **Transfer Admission Requirements:** college transcript(s), Minimum college GPA of 2.0 required. Lowest grade transferable C-. **General Admission Information:** Application Fee $40. Regular application deadline 8/1. Notification on a rolling basis, beginning on or about 9/15. Nonfall registration accepted. Credit and/or placement offered for CEEB Advanced Placement tests.

COSTS AND FINANCIAL AID

Annual in-state tuition $6,824. Annual out-of-state tuition $18,914. Room and board $9,454. Required fees $1,386. Average book expense $1,400. **Required Forms and Deadlines:** FAFSA. **Notification of Awards:** Applicants will be notified of awards on a rolling basis beginning 4/1. **Types of Aid:** *Need-based*

scholarships/grants: Federal Pell, SEOG, state scholarships/grants, private scholarships, the school's own gift aid. *Loans:* Subsidized Stafford, Unsubsidized Stafford, PLUS, Federal Perkins, state loans, college/university loans from institutional funds, Alternative Loans. *Student Employment:* Federal Work-Study Program available. Institutional employment available. Highest amount earned per year from on-campus jobs $3,000. **Financial Aid Statistics:** 81% freshmen, 77% undergrads receive need-based scholarship or grant aid. 11% freshmen, 9% undergrads receive non-need-based scholarship or grant aid. 67% freshmen, 70% undergrads receive need-based self-help aid. 2% freshmen, 2% undergrads receive athletic scholarships. 79% freshmen, 73% undergrads receive any aid. 48% undergrads borrow to pay for school. Average cumulative indebtedness $22,043. **Criteria for awarding institutional aid:** *Non-need-based:* academics, alumni affiliation, art, athletics, leadership, minority status, music/drama, state/district residency.

UNIVERSITY OF THE ARTS

320 South Broad Street, Philadelphia, PA 19102
Phone: 215-717-6049 • **Financial Aid Phone:** 215-717-6170
E-mail: admissions@uarts.edu • **CEEB Code:** 2664
Fax: 215-717-6045 • **Website:** www.uarts.edu • **ACT Code:** 3664

This private school was founded in 1876. It has a 18-acre campus.

RATINGS

Admissions Selectivity Rating: 73   **Fire Safety Rating:** 60*

STUDENTS AND FACULTY

Enrollment: 1,865. **Student Body:** 58% female, 42% male, 62% out-of-state, 5% international (19 countries represented). Asian 3%, African American 13%, Caucasian 62%, Hispanic 9%, Native American <1%
Retention and Graduation: 82% freshmen return for sophomore year. 57% freshmen graduate within 4 years. **Faculty:** 113 full-time faculty. 0% of classes are taught by teaching assistants.

ACADEMICS

Degrees: bachelor's, certificate, diploma, master's, post-bachelor's certificate. **Classes:** Most classes have 10-19 students. **Majors with Highest Enrollment:** Graphic Design; Dance; Illustration. **Special Study Options:** Accelerated program, cross-registration, double major, dual enrollment, English as a Second Language (ESL), exchange student program (domestic), independent study, internships, study abroad, teacher certification program. **Combined degree programs:** BFA/MAT Teaching Visual Arts, BM/MAT Music Ed. **Disability Services:** Special programs offered to physically disabled students include note-taking services, reader services, tape recorders, tutors. **Career services:** alumni services, career/job search classes, career assessment, internships.

FACILITIES

Housing: Coed dorms, apartments for single students. 85% of campus accessible to physically disabled. **Special Academic Facilities/Equipment:** Rosenwald-Wolf Gallery, Merriam Theater, Arts Bank, Borowsky Center for Publication arts, Gershman Y.

CAMPUS LIFE

Environment: Metropolis. **Activities:** Choral groups, concert band, dance, drama/theater, jazz band, music ensembles, musical theater, radio station, student government. 5 registered organizations, 1 religous organization.

ADMISSIONS

Freshman Academic Profile: SAT Math middle 50% range 440-550. SAT Critical Reading middle 50% range 450-580. SAT Writing middle 50% range 440-560. ACT middle 50% range 18-25. Minimum internet-based TOEFL 80. Minimum paper TOEFL 550. **Basis for Candidate Selection:** *Very important factors considered include:* rigor of secondary school record, interview, talent/ability. *Important factors considered include:* Class rank, application essay, standardized test scores, character/personal qualities, extracurricular activities. *Other factors considered include:* recommendation(s), alumni/ae relation, racial/ethnic status, volunteer work, work experience. **Freshman Admission Requirements:** High school diploma is required and GED is accepted. *Academic units required:* 4 English. **Freshman Admission Statistics:** 1,479 applied, 75% admitted, 41% enrolled. **Transfer Admission Requirements:** High school transcript, college transcript(s), essay or personal statement, standardized test scores, Minimum college GPA of 2.0 required. Lowest grade transferable C. **General Admission Information:** Application Fee $60. Notification on a rolling basis, beginning on or about 11/1. Nonfall registration accepted. Admission may be deferred for a maximum of 12 months. Credit and/or placement offered for CEEB Advanced Placement tests.

COSTS AND FINANCIAL AID

Required Forms and Deadlines: FAFSA. **Notification of Awards:** Applicants will be notified of awards on a rolling basis beginning 3/15. **Types of Aid:** *Need-based scholarships/grants:* Federal Pell, SEOG, state scholarships/grants, private scholarships, the school's own gift aid, merit scholarships. *Loans:* Subsidized Stafford, Unsubsidized Stafford, PLUS, Federal Perkinsalternative loans. *Student Employment:* Federal Work-Study Program available. Institutional employment available. Highest amount earned per year from on-campus jobs $1,200. Off-campus job opportunities are excellent. **Financial Aid Statistics:** 95% freshmen, 94% undergrads receive need-based scholarship or grant aid. 10% freshmen, 5% undergrads receive non-need-based scholarship or grant aid. 99% freshmen, 98% undergrads receive need-based self-help aid. 0% freshmen, 0% undergrads receive athletic scholarships. 80% undergrads receive any aid. **Criteria for awarding institutional aid:** *Non-need-based:* academics, art, music/drama.

UNIVERSITY OF BALTIMORE

1420 North Charles Street, Baltimore, MD 21201
Phone: 410-837-4777 • **Financial Aid Phone:** 410-837-4763
E-mail: admissions@ubmall.ubalt.edu • **CEEB Code:** 5810
Fax: 410-837-4793 • **Website:** http://www.ubalt.edu/admission/

This public school was founded in 1925. It has a 47-acre campus.

RATINGS

Admissions Selectivity Rating: 72   **Fire Safety Rating:** 60*

STUDENTS AND FACULTY

Enrollment: 3,526. **Student Body:** 57% female, 43% male, 4% out-of-state, 5% international. Asian 8%, African American 71%, Caucasian 78%, Hispanic 8%, Native American 1%
Retention and Graduation: 18% grads go on to further study within 1 year. 10% grads pursue arts and sciences degrees. 2% grads pursue law degrees. 9% grads pursue business degrees. **Faculty:** 182 full-time faculty, 85% hold PhDs, 45% are are members of minority groups, 23% are women. 0% of classes are taught by teaching assistants.

ACADEMICS

Degrees: bachelor's, master's, post-bachelor's certificate. **Classes:** Most classes have 20-29 students. **Majors with Highest Enrollment:** Criminal Justice/Law Enforcement Administration; Business Administration and Management; Digital Communication and Media/Multimedia. **Special Study Options:** Accelerated program, cooperative education program, distance learning, honors program, independent study, internships, student-designed major, study abroad. **Combined degree programs:** BA/JD, BA/MA, MBA/JD. **Disability Services:** Special programs offered to physically disabled students include note-taking services, reader services, tape recorders, tutors. **Career services:** Alumni network, alumni services, career/job search classes, career assessment, internships, regional alumni. Career services highlights include the internship program, which serves students who do not have experimental learning built into their academic units.

FACILITIES

Housing: The University works with several apartment complexes in the area to provide direct leases to students. 100% of campus accessible to physically disabled. **Computers:** Students can register for classes online. Administrative functions (other than registration) can be performed online.

CAMPUS LIFE

Environment: Metropolis. **Activities:** drama/theater, literary magazine, student government, student newspaper, International Student Organization. 26 registered organizations, 11 honor societies, 2 religious organizations. **On-Campus Highlights:** Student Union **Environmental Initiatives:** 30% energy reduction contract with Energy Systems Group Single steam recycling Certificate of Sustainabilty (MBA Program) Creation of Human Ecology and Sustainabilty Minor in 2010 and major in 2011.

ADMISSIONS

Freshman Academic Profile: Average high school GPA 2.95. SAT Math middle 50% range 410-540. SAT Critical Reading middle 50% range 420-560. SAT Writing middle 50% range 420-530. ACT middle 50% range 17-21. Minimum paper TOEFL 550. **Basis for Candidate Selection:** *Important factors considered include:* Class rank, academic GPA, rigor of secondary school record, standardized test scores. *Other factors considered include:* application essay, recommendation(s), alumni/ae relation, character/personal qualities, extracurricular activities, first generation, talent/ability, volunteer work, work experi-

ence. **Freshman Admission Requirements:** High school diploma is required and GED is accepted. *Academic units required:* 4 English, 3 mathematics, 3 science, (2 science labs), 3 social studies, 4 academic electives. **Freshman Admission Statistics:** 730 applied, 64% admitted, 51% enrolled. **Transfer Admission Requirements:** college transcript(s), Minimum college GPA of 2.0 required. Lowest grade transferable D. **General Admission Information:** Application Fee $30. Regular notification 4/1. Nonfall registration accepted. Admission may be deferred for a maximum of 1 year. Credit and/or placement offered for CEEB Advanced Placement tests.

COSTS AND FINANCIAL AID

Annual in-state tuition $5,992. Annual out-of-state tuition $16,550. Required fees $1,846. **Required Forms and Deadlines:** FAFSA. **Types of Aid:** *Need-based scholarships/grants:* Federal Pell, SEOG, state scholarships/grants, private scholarships, the school's own gift aid. *Loans:* Direct Subsidized Stafford, Direct Unsubsidized Stafford, Direct PLUS. *Student Employment:* Federal Work-Study Program available. Institutional employment available. **Financial Aid Statistics:** 90% freshmen, 91% undergrads receive need-based scholarship or grant aid. 0% freshmen, 0% undergrads receive non-need-based scholarship or grant aid. 65% freshmen, 72% undergrads receive need-based self-help aid. 0% freshmen, 0% undergrads receive athletic scholarships. 97% freshmen, 86% undergrads receive any aid. 55% undergrads borrow to pay for school. **Criteria for awarding institutional aid:** *Non-need-based:* academics, state/district residency.

UNIVERSITY OF BRIDGEPORT

126 Park Avenue, Bridgeport, CT 6604
Phone: 203-576-4552 • **Financial Aid Phone:** 203-576-4568
E-mail: admit@.bridgeport.edu • **CEEB Code:** 3914
Fax: 203-576-4941 • **ACT Code:** 602

This private school was founded in 1927. It has a 86-acre campus.

RATINGS

Admissions Selectivity Rating: 76   **Fire Safety Rating:** 85

STUDENTS AND FACULTY

Enrollment: 2,688. **Student Body:** 68% female, 32% male, 38% out-of-state, 11% international (74 countries represented). Asian 3%, African American 37%, Caucasian 27%, Hispanic 18%, Native American 1%
Retention and Graduation: 62% freshmen return for sophomore year. 23% freshmen graduate within 4 years. 32% freshmen graduate within 6 years. 15% grads go on to further study within 1 year. 5% grads pursue arts and sciences degrees. 10% grads pursue law degrees. 10% grads pursue business degrees. 5% grads pursue medical degrees. **Faculty:** 121 full-time faculty, 79% hold PhDs, 38% are are members of minority groups, 19% are women. 0% of classes are taught by teaching assistants.

ACADEMICS

Degrees: associate, bachelor's, certificate, master's, post-master's certificate. **Classes:** Most classes have 10-19 students. **Majors with Highest Enrollment:** Dental Hygiene/Hygienist; Business/Commerce; Psychology. **Special Study Options:** Accelerated program, cooperative education program, cross-registration, distance learning, double major, English as a Second Language (ESL), honors program, independent study, internships, liberal arts/career combination, student-designed major, study abroad, teacher certification program, weekend college. **Combined degree programs:** BS/DC, BS/MBA. **Disability Services:** Special programs offered to physically disabled students include note-taking services, reader services, tape recorders, tutors. **Career services:** Alumni network, alumni services, career/job search classes, career assessment, internships, regional alumni.

FACILITIES

Housing: Coed dorms, Mens, Womens floors. 80% of campus accessible to physically disabled. **Computers:** 80% of classrooms, 100% of dorms, 100% of libraries, 30% of dining areas, 50% of student union, have wireless network access. Students can register for classes online. Administrative functions (other than registration) can be performed online.

CAMPUS LIFE

Environment: City. **Activities:** Choral groups, dance, literary magazine, music ensembles, student government, student newspaper, yearbook, International Student Organization. 30 registered organizations, 11 honor societies, 6 religious organizations. 2 fraternities, 4 sororities. **Athletics (Intercollegiate):** *Men:* baseball, basketball, cross-country, soccer, swimming. *Women:* basketball, cross-country, gymnastics, lacrosse, soccer, softball, swimming, volleyball. **On-Campus Highlights:** Arnold Bernhard Center, Wheeler Recreation Center, John J. Cox Student Center, The University Gallery, Hubbell Gymnasium.

ADMISSIONS

Freshman Academic Profile: Average high school GPA 2.98. 1% in top 10% of high school class, 32% in top 25% of high school class, 69% in top 50% of high school class. 90% from public high schools. SAT Math middle 50% range 410-500. SAT Critical Reading middle 50% range 410-490. SAT Writing middle 50% range 410-490. ACT middle 50% range 18-21. Minimum internet-based TOEFL 61. Minimum paper TOEFL 500. **Basis for Candidate Selection:** *Very important factors considered include:* rigor of secondary school record, standardized test scores. *Important factors considered include:* Class rank, application essay, academic GPA, recommendation(s), talent/ability. *Other factors considered include:* alumni/ae relation, character/personal qualities, extracurricular activities, interview, level of applicant's interest, volunteer work, work experience. **Freshman Admission Requirements:** High school diploma is required and GED is accepted. *Academic units required:* 4 English, 3 mathematics, 2 science, (2 science labs), 2 social studies, 5 academic electives. **Freshman Admission Statistics:** 5,736 applied, 63% admitted, 16% enrolled. **Transfer Admission Requirements:** college transcript(s), essay or personal statement, Minimum college GPA of 2.0 required. Lowest grade transferable C-. **General Admission Information:** Application Fee $25. Notification on a rolling basis, beginning on or about 10/1. Nonfall registration accepted. Admission may be deferred for a maximum of 1 year. Credit and/or placement offered for CEEB Advanced Placement tests.

COSTS AND FINANCIAL AID

Annual tuition $25,950. Room and board $12,050. Required fees $2,190. Average book expense $1,500. **Required Forms and Deadlines:** FAFSA. **Notification of Awards:** Applicants will be notified of awards on a rolling basis beginning 3/1. **Types of Aid:** *Need-based scholarships/grants:* Federal Pell, SEOG, state scholarships/grants, private scholarships, the school's own gift aid. *Loans:* Direct Subsidized Stafford, Direct Unsubsidized Stafford, Direct PLUS, Subsidized Stafford, Unsubsidized Stafford, PLUS, Federal Perkins. *Student Employment:* Federal Work-Study Program available. Institutional employment available. Highest amount earned per year from on-campus jobs $2,000. Off-campus job opportunities are good. **Financial Aid Statistics:** 85% freshmen, 87% undergrads receive need-based scholarship or grant aid. 95% freshmen, 88% undergrads receive non-need-based scholarship or grant aid. 85% freshmen, 87% undergrads receive need-based self-help aid. 3% freshmen, 8% undergrads receive athletic scholarships. 98% freshmen, 98% undergrads receive any aid. 86% undergrads borrow to pay for school. Average cumulative indebtedness $25,252. **Criteria for awarding institutional aid:** *Non-need-based:* academics, athletics, leadership, music/drama, state/district residency.

THE UNIVERSITY OF BRITISH COLUMBIA

Room 2016, Vancouver, BC V6T 1Z1
Phone: 604-822-3014 · **Financial Aid Phone:** 604-822-5111
E-mail: askme@interchange.ubc.ca · **CEEB Code:**
Fax: 604-822-3599 · **Website:** www.ubc.ca

This public school was founded in 1908. It has a 1000-acre campus.

RATINGS

Admissions Selectivity Rating: 60*   Fire Safety Rating: 71

STUDENTS AND FACULTY

Enrollment: 29,717. **Student Body:** 54% female, 46% male, (144 countries represented).
Retention and Graduation: 31% freshmen graduate within 4 years. 50% grads go on to further study within 1 year. **Faculty:**

ACADEMICS

Degrees: bachelor's, certificate, diploma, doctoral, master's. **Classes:** Most classes have 50-59 students. Most lab/discussion sessions have 20-29 students. **Majors with Highest Enrollment:** Computer and Information Sciences; Biological and Physical Sciences; Psychology. **Special Study Options:** cooperative education program, distance learning, double major, dual enrollment, English as a Second Language (ESL), exchange student program (domestic), honors program, internships, liberal arts/career combination, student-designed major, study abroad, teacher certification program, Cross-disciplinary first year options. **Honors programs:** UBC offers many honours programs for academically strong undergraduates **Combined degree programs:** BA/BSc. **Disability Services:** Special programs offered to physically disabled students include note-taking services, reader services, tape recorders, tutors. **Career services:** Alumni network, alumni services, career/job search classes, career assessment, internships, regional alumni. Career services highlights include Outstanding Coop (Work Learn) programs in six major Faculties.

FACILITIES

Housing: Coed dorms, special housing for disabled students, men's dorms, special housing for international students, women's dorms, fraternity/sorority housing, apartments for married students, apartments for single students, Theme HousingNational theme housing in association with partner universities in Japan, Mexico, Korea, and Hong Kong SAR. 90% of campus accessible to physically disabled. **Special Academic Facilities/Equipment:** Museum of Anthropology Barber Learning Centre Beaty Biodiversity Museum Geological Museum TRIUMF, sub-atomic particle research Botanical Gardens Nitobe Garden Belkin Art Gallery Chan Centre for Performing Arts Liu International Studies Centre St.John's College (Graduate College) Pulp and Paper Centre Centre for Intergrated Systems Research Wall Centre for Interdisciplinary Studies **Computers:** 100% of classrooms, 100% of dorms, 100% of libraries, 100% of dining areas, 100% of student union, 100% of common outdoor areas have wireless network access. Students can register for classes online. Administrative functions (other than registration) can be performed online.

CAMPUS LIFE

Environment: Metropolis. **Activities:** Choral groups, concert band, dance, drama/theater, literary magazine, music ensembles, musical theater, opera, radio station, student government, student newspaper, student-run film society, symphony orchestra, International Student Organization. 250 registered organizations, 1 honor society, 7 religious organizations. 9 fraternities, 8 sororities. **Athletics (Intercollegiate):** *Men:* baseball, basketball, crew/rowing, cross-country, field hockey, football, golf, ice hockey, rugby, soccer, swimming, track/field (outdoor), volleyball. *Women:* basketball, crew/rowing, cross-country, field hockey, golf, ice hockey, rugby, soccer, swimming, track/field (outdoor), volleyball. **On-Campus Highlights:** Koerner Library, Museum of Anthropology, Chan Centre, Student Union Building, Barber Learning Centre. **Environmental Initiatives:** UBC is a signatory to the Talloires Declaration. It has integrated sustainability into its vision statement and strategic plan and formed a Presidents Advisory Council on Sustainability. The UBC Sustainability Office opened in 1998 the first of its kind in a Canadian university. UBC has created an advisory committee of faculty, staff, students and alumni on socially responsible investing. The committee advises the Board of Governors on issues of transparency, proxy votes, and socially responsible investment practices. UBC met 2012 Kyoto Protocol targets in 2006, having reduced over the past 16 years greenhouse gas emissions by 25 per cent. UBC has one of the most ambitious plans for reduction of GHG emissions of any institution of its size in the world, with a target emissions reduction from 2007 levels of 33% by 2015, 67% by 2020, and 100% by 2050. http://www.sustain.ubc.ca/climate-action In 2011, the Centre for Interactive Research on Sustainability was opened on the Vancouver campus. The CIRS building is a remarkable demonstration of sustainability in construction, functioning, and use and will form a living laboratory and focal centre for examination of sustainability concerns. http://www.sustain.ubc.ca/ubc-opens-north-americas-greenest-building Numerous other initiatives: Initiatives such as the Student Ambassadors Initiative, Sustainability Pledge Program and Student Environment Centre fully engage students in sustainable living. UBCs dining services exclusively serves local eggs, poultry and milk. UBC currently offers more than 300 sustainability-related courses. UBC Okanagan heating energy is projected to come from fully sustainable resources (ground source) within the next two to three years. For other commitments see: http://www.sustain.ubc.ca/

ADMISSIONS

Basis for Candidate Selection: *Very important factors considered include:* academic GPA, rigor of secondary school record. *Other factors considered include:* application essay, recommendation(s), standardized test scores, character/personal qualities, extracurricular activities, level of applicant's interest, talent/ability, volunteer work, work experience. **Freshman Admission Requirements:** High school diploma is required and GED is not accepted. *Academic units required:* 4 English, 3 mathematics, 12 academic electives. **Transfer Admission Requirements:** college transcript(s), statement of good standing from prior institution(s). **General Admission Information:** Application Fee $100. Regular application deadline 2/28. Notification on a rolling basis, beginning on or about 2/15. Nonfall registration accepted. Admission may be deferred for a maximum of up to one year. Credit and/or placement offered for CEEB Advanced Placement tests.

COSTS AND FINANCIAL AID

Required Forms and Deadlines: Institution's own financial aid form. **Types of Aid:** *Need-based scholarships/grants:* Provincial scholarships and grants are available for Canadian citizens permanent residents of Canada. International students are eligible for modest merit awards. No application is necessary for merit-based awards. International students of outstanding academic merit and personal accomplishment who would otherwise not have the means to attend university may be nominated for awards, of which a limited number are awarded annually of between $15,000 and $35,000, depending on means. These awards are by nomination only (deadline for nominations February 1). Athletic scholarships are available for outstanding athletes, at head coach discretion in accordance with CIS rules. *Loans:* Direct Subsidized Stafford, Direct Unsubsidized Stafford, Direct PLUS, Subsidized Stafford, Unsubsidized Stafford, PLUS. *Student Employment:* Institutional employment available. Off-campus job opportunities are good. **Financial Aid Statistics: Criteria for awarding institutional aid:** *Non-need-based:* academics, athletics, leadership.

UNIVERSITY OF CALIFORNIA—BERKELEY

110 Sproul Hall, Berkeley, CA 94720-5800
CEEB Code: 4833
Website: www.berkeley.edu • **ACT Code:** 444

This public school was founded in 1868. It has a 1232-acre campus.

RATINGS

Admissions Selectivity Rating: 98   **Fire Safety Rating:** 86

STUDENTS AND FACULTY

Enrollment: 25,951. **Student Body:** 52% female, 48% male, 14% out-of-state, 13% international. Asian 35%, African American 2%, Caucasian 29%, Hispanic 13%, Native American <1%
Retention and Graduation: 97% freshmen return for sophomore year. 72% freshmen graduate within 4 years. 91% freshmen graduate within 6 years. **Faculty:** 1,620 full-time faculty, 99% hold PhDs, 35% are are members of minority groups, 21% are women. 0% of classes are taught by teaching assistants.

ACADEMICS

Degrees: bachelor's, master's, post-bachelor's certificate. **Majors with Highest Enrollment:** Computer Engineering; English Language and Literature; Political Science and Government. **Special Study Options:** Accelerated program, cross-registration, double major, dual enrollment, English as a Second Language (ESL), exchange student program (domestic), honors program, independent study, internships, student-designed major, study abroad, teacher certification program. **Combined degree programs:** 10 Engineering Double Majors BS Degree. **Disability Services:** Special programs offered to physically disabled students include note-taking services, reader services, tape recorders, tutors. **Career services:** alumni services, career/job search classes, career assessment, internships.

FACILITIES

Housing: Coed dorms, special housing for disabled students, men's dorms, special housing for international students, women's dorms, fraternity/sorority housing, apartments for married students, cooperative housing, apartments for single students, Theme Housing. 95% of campus accessible to physically disabled. **Special Academic Facilities/Equipment:** Lawrence Berkeley National Lab, Pacific Film Archive, Earthquake Data Center, Museums of art, anthropology, natural history, paleontology, Botanical Garden. **Computers:** Students can register for classes online. Administrative functions (other than registration) can be performed online.

CAMPUS LIFE

Activities: Choral groups, concert band, dance, drama/theater, jazz band, literary magazine, marching band, music ensembles, musical theater, pep band, radio station, student government, student newspaper, student-run film society, symphony orchestra, television station, yearbook, International Student Organization, Model UN. 300 registered organizations, 6 honor societies, 28 religious organizations. 38 fraternities, 19 sororities. **Athletics (Intercollegiate):** *Men:* baseball, basketball, crew/rowing, cross-country, diving, football, golf, gymnastics, rugby, sailing, soccer, swimming, tennis, track/field (outdoor), water polo. *Women:* basketball, crew/rowing, cross-country, diving, field hockey, golf, gymnastics, lacrosse, sailing, soccer, softball, swimming, tennis, track/field (outdoor), volleyball, water polo. **On-Campus Highlights:** Botanical Gardens, Lawrence Hall of Science, Museum of Anthropology, Museum of Art. **Environmental Initiatives:** Climate and Energy: Six years ago the campus set out to reduce its carbon footprint by one-third to bring Berkeleys greenhouse gas emissions from campus operations back to the levels they were in 1990. Our most recent emissions inventory reveals that Berkeley has met this target, two years ahead of schedule. Ambitious at the outset, this voluntary target to reduce greenhouse gas emissions (GHG) to 1990 levels by 2014 puts Berkeley ahead of UC Policy and State of California guidelines which call for this level of reduction by the year 2020. We have reduced our emissions and met our first target by: Investing in energy efficiency and sustainable transportation practices. Since 2006, the campus has saved 20 million kWh of electricity through building retrofits and reduced fuel use by more than 1 million gallons by increasing the number of bicycle, pedestrian and mass-transit commuters. Buying Greener Power. The campus is using electricity that includes more solar and wind energy and less coal through purchases from Pacific Gas & Electric, a utility that is required by state law to provide power that by 2020 will include 33 percent renewable energy. Improving Data and Methods. UC Berkeley has improved the accuracy of its emissions inventory profile by using the best data available about campus energy use and by staying current with the best reporting methods. Planning and Reporting: Berkeley works to find solutions to these pressing issues and to make the world a better place. We ask difficult questions and find answers to them. By setting ambitious goals and working to accelerate the achievement of these goals, we strive to cultivate a dynamic, energized community of sustainability and to integrate cutting edge sustainability practices into our operations. UC Berkeley has published six previous Campus Sustainability Reports, each more comprehensive than the one before it and each with a goal of being accountable for the progress made toward our sustainability and environmental goals. In the past year, we have seen significant success this year, especially on greenhouse gas reductions, and have met many of our goals and are on track to achieve others. We have also added two new sections to the Report, Economic and Social Sustainability, as part of the process to prepare the report in accordance with the Global Reporting Initiative (GRI) Guidelines (Core). In 2013, the Office of Sustainability partnered with a student team from Net Impact Berkeley, who provided recommendations and content aimed at improving campus sustainability reporting and achieving compliance with the reporting guidelines published by GRI. Why the Global Reporting Initiative (GRI) standard? Rather than solely reporting on environmental data, UC Berkeley feels that its stakeholders deserve transparent accounts of our economic, social, and environmental performance indicators. Through the integrative reporting of the GRI standards, we are able to hold ourselves more accountable and publicize our commitment to reducing and improving our impacts. By driving transparent accounting of our operations, GRI and specifically the new G4 standard is the medium chosen by UC Berkeley for reporting on sustainability. The Green Initiative Fund: TGIF is a student fee funded grant program for projects that reduce UC Berkeley's negative impact on the environment and make the campus more sustainable. In five years, it has awarded over $1.5 million to 96 different projects, which have resulted in 195 paid student internships. The Green Initiative Fund was created via a referendum in 2007, where 69% of students voted for the Fund. TGIF allocates funds to projects that promote sustainable modes of transportation, increase energy and water efficiency, restore habitat, promote environmental and food justice, and reduce the amount of waste created by UC Berkeley. Portions of the fund also support education and behaviour change initiatives, student financial aid. Students, faculty, and staff may submit project proposals, which are selected for funding by an annually appointed grant-making committee, consisting of students, faculty, and staff, on which the students have the majority vote.

ADMISSIONS

Freshman Academic Profile: Average high school GPA 3.86. 98% in top 10% of high school class, 100% in top 25% of high school class, 100% in top 50% of high school class. SAT Math middle 50% range 650-770. SAT Critical Reading middle 50% range 600-730. SAT Writing middle 50% range 620-740. ACT middle 50% range 27-33. Minimum internet-based TOEFL 80. Minimum paper TOEFL 550. **Basis for Candidate Selection:** *Very important factors considered include:* application essay, academic GPA, rigor of secondary school record, state residency. *Important factors considered include:* standardized test scores, character/personal qualities, extracurricular activities, talent/ability, volunteer work, work experience. *Other factors considered include:* first generation, geographical residence. **Freshman Admission Requirements:** High school diploma is required and GED is accepted. *Academic units required:* 4 English, 3 mathematics, 2 science, (2 science labs), 2 foreign language, 2 history, 1 visual/performing arts, 1 academic elective. **Freshman Admission Statistics:** 66,794 applied, 18% admitted, 40% enrolled. **Transfer Admission Requirements:** essay or personal statement, Minimum college GPA of 2.4 required. Lowest grade transferable D. **General Admission Information:** Application Fee $60. Regular application deadline 11/30. Nonfall registration accepted. Neither credit nor placement offered for CEEB Advanced Placement tests.

COSTS AND FINANCIAL AID

Annual out-of-state tuition $34,098. Room and board $15,180. Required fees $1,644. Average book expense $1,226. **Required Forms and Deadlines:** FAFSA, State aid form. **Notification of Awards:** Applicants will be notified of awards on or about 4/15. **Types of Aid:** *Need-based scholarships/grants:* Federal Pell, SEOG, state scholarships/grants, private scholarships, the school's own gift aid. *Loans:* Direct Subsidized Stafford, Direct Unsubsidized Stafford, Direct PLUS, Federal Perkins. *Student Employment:* Federal Work-Study Program available. Institutional employment available. Off-campus job opportunities are excellent. **Financial Aid Statistics:** 91% freshmen, 96% undergrads receive need-based scholarship or grant aid. 21% freshmen, 16% undergrads receive non-need-based scholarship or grant aid. 82% freshmen, 86% undergrads receive need-based self-help aid. 3% freshmen, 2% undergrads receive athletic scholarships. 43% undergrads borrow to pay for school. Average cumulative indebtedness $16,530. **Criteria for awarding institutional aid:** *Non-need-based:* academics.

UNIVERSITY OF CALIFORNIA—DAVIS

178 Mrak Hall, One Shields Ave, Davis, CA 95616
Phone: 530-752-2971 · **Financial Aid Phone:** 530-752-2396
E-mail: undergraduateadmissions@ucdavis.edu · **CEEB Code:** 4834
Fax: 530-752-1280 · **Website:** www.ucdavis.edu · **ACT Code:** 454

This public school was founded in 1908. It has a 5200-acre campus.

RATINGS

Admissions Selectivity Rating: 90   **Fire Safety Rating:** 88

STUDENTS AND FACULTY

Enrollment: 27,547. **Student Body:** 58% female, 42% male, 3% out-of-state, 8% international (121 countries represented). Asian 34%, African American 2%, Caucasian 29%, Hispanic 18%, Native American <1%
Retention and Graduation: 93% freshmen return for sophomore year. 54% freshmen graduate within 4 years. 83% freshmen graduate within 6 years. 40% grads go on to further study within 1 year. 23% grads pursue arts and sciences degrees. 4% grads pursue law degrees. 1% grads pursue business degrees. 12% grads pursue medical degrees. **Faculty:** 1,605 full-time faculty, 98% hold PhDs, 36% are are members of minority groups, 24% are women.

ACADEMICS

Degrees: bachelor's, doctoral, master's, post-bachelor's certificate, post-master's certificate. **Classes:** Most classes have 20-29 students. Most lab/discussion sessions have 20-29 students. **Majors with Highest Enrollment:** Biology/Biological Sciences; Psychology; Economics. **Special Study Options:** Accelerated program, cross-registration, double major, dual enrollment, English as a Second Language (ESL), honors program, independent study, internships, student-designed major, study abroad, teacher certification program, Washington DC Center. **Honors programs:** The Davis Honors Challenge (DHC) is an innovative, open-application, campuswide honors program for highly motivated students. In addition to a mentor program and a residential living-learning option for first-year students, DHC offers students the opportunity to participate in an honors program for four years. Integrated Studies Honors Program (ISHP), the oldest continuous residential learning community in the UC system, is an invitational, residential honors program for first-year students. ISHP provides an academic residential community similar to those of the best small colleges and helps students integrate knowledge from the arts and humanities, natural sciences and engineering, and social sciences. **Disability Services:** Special programs offered to physically disabled students include note-taking services, reader services, tape recorders, tutors.

FACILITIES

Housing: Coed dorms, special housing for disabled students, women's dorms, apartments for married students, cooperative housing, apartments for single students, Wellness Housing, Theme Housing, Special Interest Communities: Davis Honors Challenge, Hammarskjöld International Relations, Integrated Studies, Multiethnic Program, Music, Arts & Performance, Quiet Program, Rainbow House, Women's Community. **Special Academic Facilities/Equipment:** Art galleries, 150-acre university arboretum, equestrian center, craft center, student experimental farm, nuclear lab, human performance lab, natural reserves, early childhood lab, raptor center, primate research center. **Computers:** Students can register for classes online. Administrative functions (other than registration) can be performed online.

CAMPUS LIFE

Environment: Town. **Activities:** Choral groups, concert band, dance, drama/theater, jazz band, literary magazine, marching band, music ensembles, musical theater, pep band, radio station, student government, student newspaper, student-run film society, symphony orchestra, television station, yearbook, Campus Ministries, International Student Organization, Model UN. 364 registered organizations, 1 honor society, 50 religious organizations. 28 fraternities, 21 sororities. **Athletics (Intercollegiate):** *Men:* baseball, basketball, cross-country, diving, football, golf, soccer, swimming, tennis, track/field (outdoor), track/field (indoor), water polo, wrestling. *Women:* basketball, crew/rowing, cross-country, diving, field hockey, golf, gymnastics, lacrosse, soccer, softball, swimming, ten-

nis, track/field (outdoor), track/field (indoor), volleyball, water polo. **On-Campus Highlights:** Mondavi Center for the Performing Arts, Memorial Union/Coffee House, Activities and Recreation Center (The ARC), Sciences Laboratory Building, The UC Davis Arboretum, http://daviswiki.org/. **Environmental Initiatives:** UC Davis is taking action to reduce greenhouse gas emissions and energy use on campus through programs like the Strategic Energy Partnership Program, which is improving energy conservation and energy efficiency on campus and has identified retrofit and recommissioning projects that will save more than 28 million kilowatt-hours and 2 million therms. The campus installed a 756kW solar photovoltaic system, which generates over 1 million kilowatt-hours a year. UC Davis has also embarked on an ambitious initiative to reduce lighting energy use by 60% in five years, which will reduce energy use and greenhouse gas emissions (www.sustainability.ucdavis.edu/news/2010/november/smart_lighting.html) and is pursuing a project to build an on-campus anaerobic biodigester that will generate about 2 million kilowatt-hours a year of clean, renewable electricity from campus organic wastes (news.ucdavis.edu/search/news_detail.lasso?id=10202). Work on climate issues at UC Davis includes everything from studying pollution in the Arctic atmosphere and building global climate models to the campus Climate Action Plan (CAP) and energy use reduction. UC Davis faculty and student research on climate change spans a wide range of investigation from basic inquiry to solution-based engineering work (climatechange.ucdavis.edu/). The CAP analyzes campus issues around greenhouse gas emissions reductions, energy use and energy sourcing (www.sustainability.ucdavis.edu/progress/climate/index.html). The bike is boss at UC Davis, which is one of only two campuses to achieve the Gold level designation for a Bicycle Friendly University from the League of American Bicyclists. On any given day, up to 20,000 bikes are on campus, there are about 21,000 bike parking spaces, 42 miles of bike paths and 10 bike tool stations around campus (http://campusmap.ucdavis.edu/sustainability/). The Bike Barn helps on-campus cyclists with over 10,000 repairs per year at their shop and also provides tools for the Bike Garage, a do-it-yourself bike maintenance workshop on campus. UC Davis students run Unitrans, the community bus system (www.unitrans.ucdavis.edu), which has a fleet of clean busses that runs on compressed natural gas, and provides more than 3,000,000 rides per year. And, the campus has partnered with ZipCar to make hourly car rentals available to the campus community to reduce the need for a car on campus. UC Davis is a leader in green building design. Four projects at UC Davis have been awarded LEED Platinum, the highest rating given by the US Green Building Council, and five projects have been awarded LEED Gold. For the Davis campus, new buildings must be at least 25% more efficient than required by Californias strict energy code. New buildings must also be designed to meet LEED Silver as a minimum and they typically achieve LEED Gold or Platinum. The Winery, Brewery and Food Science Laboratory is the first such facility in the world to be awarded LEED Platinum, and features on-site solar power generation, extensive daylighting, a large capacity rainwater capture system and is designed as a test bed for innovative production processes to capture carbon dioxide, re-use process water and dramatically reduce energy use. Valley Hall Veterinary Medicine Instructional Facility earned LEED Platinum and is designed to optimize daylight harvesting and use natural ventilation in order to achieve deep energy savings. The Gallagher Hall Graduate School of Management and Conference Center also earned LEED Platinum certification and employs a radiant heating and cooling system coupled with a ground source heat pump and on-site photovoltaic panels. The UC Davis Tahoe Environmental Research Center was one of the very first laboratory buildings in the world to be awarded LEED Platinum. Wall, Campbell and Potter Halls in the Tercero Student Housing complex achieved LEED Gold certification with solar thermal panels, night-time ventilation, a green cleaning policy, and an active education program that informs residents about green building practices.

ADMISSIONS

Freshman Academic Profile: Average high school GPA 4. 84% from public high schools. SAT Math middle 50% range 560-700. SAT Critical Reading middle 50% range 520-650. SAT Writing middle 50% range 540-660. ACT middle 50% range 25-31. Minimum internet-based TOEFL 60. Minimum paper TOEFL 550. **Basis for Candidate Selection:** *Very important factors considered include:* academic GPA, rigor of secondary school record, standardized test scores. *Important factors considered include:* application essay, character/personal qualities, extracurricular activities, first generation, talent/ability. *Other factors considered include:* state residency, volunteer work, work experience. **Freshman Admission Requirements:** High school diploma is required and GED is accepted. *Academic units required:* 4 English, 3 mathematics, 2 science, (2 science labs), 2 foreign language, 2 social studies, 1 visual/performing arts, 1 academic elective. **Freshman Admission Statistics:** 60,506 applied, 41% admitted, 22% enrolled. **Transfer Admission Requirements:** High school transcript, college transcript(s), essay or personal statement, statement of good standing from prior institution(s). Lowest grade transferable D-. **General Admission Information:** Application Fee $60. Regular application deadline 11/30. Regular notification 3/15. Nonfall registration not accepted. Credit and/or placement offered for CEEB Advanced Placement tests.

COSTS AND FINANCIAL AID

Annual out-of-state tuition $34,098. Room and board $14,218. Required fees $2,676. Average book expense $1,560. **Required Forms and Deadlines:** FAFSA, State aid form. **Notification of Awards:** Applicants will be notified of awards on a rolling basis beginning 3/12. **Types of Aid:** *Need-based scholarships/grants:* Federal Pell, SEOG, state scholarships/grants, private scholarships, the school's own gift aid, specify):Academic Competitiveness Grant (ACG) and National Science and Mathematics Access to Retain Talent Grant (SMART). *Loans:* Direct Subsidized Stafford, Direct Unsubsidized Stafford, Direct PLUS, Federal Perkins, college/university loans from institutional funds. *Student Employment:* Highest amount earned per year from on-campus jobs $7,280. **Financial Aid Statistics:** 97% freshmen, 97% undergrads receive need-based scholarship or grant aid. 1% freshmen, 1% undergrads receive non-need-based scholarship or grant aid. 69% freshmen, 67% undergrads receive need-based self-help aid. 1% freshmen, 1% undergrads receive athletic scholarships. 55% undergrads receive any aid. 52% undergrads borrow to pay for school. Average cumulative indebtedness $15,681. **Criteria for awarding institutional aid:** *Non-need-based:* academics, athletics.

UNIVERSITY OF CALIFORNIA—IRVINE

Office of Admissions and Relations with Schools, Irvine, CA 92697-1075
Phone: 949-824-6703 · **Financial Aid Phone:** 949-824-2004
E-mail: admissions@uci.edu · **CEEB Code:** 4859
Fax: 949-824-2951 · **Website:** www.uci.edu

This public school was founded in 1965. It has a 1500-acre campus.

RATINGS

Admissions Selectivity Rating: 95   **Fire Safety Rating:** 80

STUDENTS AND FACULTY

Enrollment: 24,489. **Student Body:** 54% female, 46% male, 2% out-of-state, 12% international (72 countries represented). Asian 41%, African American 2%, Caucasian 14%, Hispanic 24%, Native American <1%
Retention and Graduation: 92% freshmen return for sophomore year. 68% freshmen graduate within 4 years. 87% freshmen graduate within 6 years. **Faculty:** 1,172 full-time faculty, 98% hold PhDs, 36% are are members of minority groups, 29% are women.

ACADEMICS

Degrees: bachelor's, master's, post-bachelor's certificate. **Classes:** Most classes have 20-29 students. Most lab/discussion sessions have fewer than 10 students. **Majors with Highest Enrollment:** Biology/Biological Sciences; Social Psychology; Business/Managerial Economics. **Special Study Options:** Accelerated program, distance learning, double major, dual enrollment, English as a Second Language (ESL), honors program, independent study, internships, liberal arts/career combination, study abroad, teacher certification program. **Honors programs:** Campuswide Honors Program (CHP). **Combined degree programs:** 3-2 MBA. **Disability Services:** Special programs offered to physically disabled students include note-taking services, reader services, tape recorders. **Career services:** Alumni network, alumni services, career/job search classes, career assessment, internships.

FACILITIES

Housing: Coed dorms, special housing for disabled students, men's dorms, special housing for international students, women's dorms, fraternity/sorority housing, apartments for married students, cooperative housing, apartments for single students, Theme Housing. 95% of campus accessible to physically disabled. **Special Academic Facilities/Equipment:** Museum of systemic biology, freshwater marsh reserve, electron microscope, nuclear reactor, laser institute, research facilities. **Computers:** 90% of classrooms, 100% of libraries, 100% of dining areas, 100% of student union, have wireless network access. Students can register for classes online. Administrative functions (other than registration) can be performed online.

CAMPUS LIFE

Environment: City. **Activities:** Choral groups, concert band, dance, drama/theater, jazz band, literary magazine, music ensembles, musical theater, opera, pep band, radio station, student government, student newspaper, student-run film society, symphony orchestra, yearbook, International Student Organization, Model UN. 484 registered organizations, 18 honor societies, 51 religious organizations. 21 fraternities, 23 sororities. **Athletics (Intercollegiate):** *Men:* baseball, basketball, cross-country, golf, sailing, soccer, tennis, track/field (outdoor), volleyball, water polo. *Women:* basketball, cross-country, golf, sailing, soccer, tennis, track/field (outdoor), volleyball, water polo. **On-Campus Highlights:** Anteater Recreation Center, Bren Events Center, Cross-Cultural Center,

Beall Center for Art and Technology, Arts Plaza. **Environmental Initiatives:** Better Buildings Challenge: The University of California, Irvine accepted the Obama administrations invitation to become an inaugural partner in the U.S. Department of Energys Better Buildings Challenge shortly after the program was launched in December 2011. In doing so, UC Irvine committed to reducing electricity use on the main campus 20 percent by the year 2020, as measured against a baseline established in 2008. The commitment includes 7 million square feet of the campus most energy-intensive building space, including more than 180 buildings housing instruction, office, complex laboratory space, and recreational and patient care facilities. We are on track to meet the stated goal. Smart Labs Initiative: UC Irvines Smart Labs Initiative safely reduces energy use in laboratories by as much as 60 percent using sensors and software to control lab and building systems (ventilation, HVAC, exhaust, illumination) precisely rather than rely on massive safety margins for ventilation rates, exhaust airspeeds, and other design criteria. UC Irvine continues to share its methods, learnings, and results with audiences around the world. This is the UC Irvines showcase project in the Obama administrations Better Buildings Challenge (see above) and has been recognized with the following awards: Californias highest environmental honor, the Governors Environmental & Economic Leadership Award (2013); S-Lab Conference Award for International Laboratory Operations (Liverpool; 2013); Green California Leadership Award (2013); Inaugural APPA Sustainability Award (2012); APPAs Effective & Innovative Practices Award (2011) Summer Institute for Sustainability Leadership (SISL): The Institute—the first of its kind in the University of California system—seeks to cultivate a campus culture of sustainability by developing leadership skills in a cadre of first-year and transfer college students interested in a range of sustainability issues. The idea is to help grow the next generation of sustainability leaders, for our campus and society at large. The inaugural Institute was held July 21-23, 2013. This program was initiated by the Vice Chancellor for Student Affairs and is a collaboration among Student Government; the Global Sustainability Resource Center (GSRC) in Academic Affairs, which serves as a hub for student leadership and sustainability education; Student Life and Leadership; and The Green Initiative Fund, a student-led fee referendum designed to empower undergraduate students with the financial resources to fund sustainability projects on campus. These entities collaborate with Administrative and Business Services, and in particular, the Director of Environmental Planning and Sustainability. The opportunity to participate in the 2013 Institute was made available to all incoming students. The 20 who were selected will work with more senior student mentors and staff who will help them advance their leadership and networking skills, as well as their knowledge of sustainability practices at UC Irvine. This program will be repeated in 2014.

ADMISSIONS

Freshman Academic Profile: Average high school GPA 3.94. 96% in top 10% of high school class, 100% in top 25% of high school class, 100% in top 50% of high school class. 75% from public high schools. SAT Math middle 50% range 550-690. SAT Critical Reading middle 50% range 490-620. SAT Writing middle 50% range 510-620. Minimum internet-based TOEFL 80. Minimum paper TOEFL 550. **Basis for Candidate Selection:** *Very important factors considered include:* application essay, academic GPA, rigor of secondary school record, standardized test scores, extracurricular activities, level of applicant's interest, talent/ability, volunteer work, work experience. *Important factors considered include:* character/personal qualities. *Other factors considered include:* first generation, state residency. **Freshman Admission Requirements:** High school diploma is required and GED is accepted. *Academic units required:* 4 English, 3 mathematics, 2 science, (2 science labs), 2 foreign language, 0 social studies, 2 history, 1 visual/performing arts, 1 academic elective. **Freshman Admission Statistics:** 66,505 applied, 37% admitted, 22% enrolled. **Transfer Admission Requirements:** High school transcript, college transcript(s), essay or personal statement, Minimum college GPA of 2.0 required. Lowest grade transferable C. **General Admission Information:** Application Fee $60. Regular application deadline 11/30. Regular notification 3/31. Nonfall registration not accepted. Credit offered for CEEB Advanced Placement tests.

COSTS AND FINANCIAL AID

Annual in-state tuition $11,220. Annual out-of-state tuition $34,098. Room and board $12,638. Required fees $3,357. Average book expense $1,732. **Required Forms and Deadlines:** FAFSA, State aid form. **Notification of Awards:** Applicants will be notified of awards on a rolling basis beginning 4/1. **Types of Aid:** *Need-based scholarships/grants:* Federal Pell, SEOG, state scholarships/grants, private scholarships, the school's own gift aid. *Loans:* Direct Subsidized Stafford, Direct Unsubsidized Stafford, Direct PLUS, Subsidized Stafford, Unsubsidized Stafford, PLUS, Federal Perkins, college/university loans from institutional funds, Private Loans. *Student Employment:* Federal Work-Study Program available. Institutional employment available. **Financial Aid Statistics:** 94% freshmen, 92% undergrads receive need-based scholarship or grant aid. 1% freshmen, 1% undergrads receive non-need-based scholarship or grant aid. 77% freshmen, 68% undergrads receive need-based self-help aid. 0% freshmen, 1% undergrads receive athletic scholarships. 55% undergrads borrow to pay for school. Average cumulative indebtedness $19,459. **Criteria**

for awarding institutional aid: *Non-need-based:* academics, art, athletics, job skills, leadership, music/drama, state/district residency.

UNIVERSITY OF CALIFORNIA—LOS ANGELES

1147 Murphy Hall, Los Angeles, CA 90095-1436
Phone: 310-825-3101 • **Financial Aid Phone:** 310-206-0400
E-mail: ugadm@saonet.ucla.edu • **CEEB Code:** 4837
Fax: 310-206-1206 • **Website:** www.ucla.edu • **ACT Code:** 448

This public school was founded in 1919. It has a 419-acre campus.

RATINGS

Admissions Selectivity Rating: 98   **Fire Safety Rating:** 88

STUDENTS AND FACULTY

Enrollment: 29,625. **Student Body:** 56% female, 44% male, 91% out-of-state, 3% international (138 countries represented). Asian 30%, African American 3%, Caucasian 28%, Hispanic 20%, Native American <1%. **Retention and Graduation:** 97% freshmen return for sophomore year. 73% freshmen graduate within 4 years. 91% freshmen graduate within 6 years. **Faculty:** 2,001 full-time faculty, 98% hold PhDs, 33% are are members of minority groups, 26% are women. 0% of classes are taught by teaching assistants.

ACADEMICS

Degrees: bachelor's, first professional, master's. **Classes:** Most classes have 10-19 students. Most lab/discussion sessions have 20-29 students. **Majors with Highest Enrollment:** Biology/Biological Sciences; Psychology; Business/Managerial Economics. **Special Study Options:** Accelerated program, double major, English as a Second Language (ESL), honors program, independent study, internships, liberal arts/career combination, student-designed major, study abroad. **Honors programs:** The College Honors Program. **Disability Services:** Special programs offered to physically disabled students include note-taking services, reader services, tape recorders, tutors. **Career services:** Alumni network, alumni services, career/job search classes, career assessment, internships, regional alumni. Based at the UC Washington Center, CAPPP students carry out a research project on a topic of their own choosing, and complete a challenging, substantive internship at one of DC's hundreds of government agencies, think tanks, NGOs, non-profits, media outlets, advocacy, trade, and business organizations. Program participants earn up to 16 upper division units while remaining full-time UCLA students.

FACILITIES

Housing: Coed dorms, special housing for disabled students, fraternity/sorority housing, apartments for married students, apartments for single students, Wellness Housing, Theme Housing. 100% of campus accessible to physically disabled. **Special Academic Facilities/Equipment:** Art gallery, cultural history museum, sculpture garden, graphic arts center, numerous study centers, research institutes, UCLA Armand Hammer Museum of Art and Cultural Center, Murphy Sculpture Garden, Fowler Museum of Cultural History **Computers:** Students can register for classes online. Administrative functions (other than registration) can be performed online.

CAMPUS LIFE

Environment: Metropolis. **Activities:** Choral groups, concert band, dance, drama/theater, jazz band, literary magazine, marching band, music ensembles, musical theater, opera, pep band, radio station, student government, student newspaper, student-run film society, symphony orchestra, television station, yearbook, Campus Ministries, International Student Organization, Model UN. 870 registered organizations, 21 honor societies, 38 religious organizations. 36 fraternities, 28 sororities. **Athletics (Intercollegiate):** *Men:* baseball, basketball, cross-country, football, golf, soccer, tennis, track/field (outdoor), track/field (indoor), volleyball, water polo. *Women:* basketball, crew/rowing, cross-country, diving, golf, gymnastics, soccer, softball, swimming, tennis, track/field (outdoor), track/field (indoor), volleyball, water polo. **On-Campus Highlights:** The UCLA Library, UCLA Fowler Museum of Cultural History, UCLA Book Store, DeNeve Plaza, Kerckhoff Coffee House. **Environmental Initiatives:** The University of California and state legislation set a target of reducing greenhouse gas emissions to 1990 levels by 2020. UCLA's greenhouse gas emissions come from mobile sources like the campus fleet and commutes, as well as buildings and energy. Sustainable transportation efforts at UCLA began before the term was coined. UCLA's been greening its transportation since 1984, when the campus had to address transportation issues in preparation for the olympics. Due to its location within the Los Angeles Basin and the South Coast Air Qual-

ity Management District, the campus has long endured traffic congestion and focused on reducing emissions. In the 1990s UCLA began a well developed transportation program that included vanpools, carpools and a campus shuttle. 2010 the new UCLA Police Station won a green building award from the Los Angeles Business Council during their 40th Annual Architectural Awards. The Police Station was the third building on campus to achieve LEED Certification from the US Green Building Council. Green buildings use less energy and water and generate less waste than standard buildings. The Leadership in Energy and Environmental Design (LEED) Green Building Rating System recognizes buildings that meet strict environmental criteria and addresses a variety of building features including energy use, water efficiency, GHG emissions, building materials, site and landscaping, and transportation infrastructure. UCLA, along with the other campuses in the UC System, requires all new construction and major renovations to achieve LEED Silver or higher certification. This policy is part of a comprehensive Sustainable Practices Policy, developed by the 10 campuses of the UC system, which covers clean energy, climate, waste, purchasing, and food, in addition to green buildings.

ADMISSIONS

Freshman Academic Profile: Average high school GPA 4.31. 97% in top 10% of high school class, 100% in top 25% of high school class, 100% in top 50% of high school class. 68% from public high schools. SAT Math middle 50% range 600-750. SAT Critical Reading middle 50% range 570-710. SAT Writing middle 50% range 590-730. ACT middle 50% range 25-32. Minimum internet-based TOEFL 83. Minimum paper TOEFL 550. **Basis for Candidate Selection:** *Very important factors considered include:* application essay, academic GPA, rigor of secondary school record, standardized test scores. *Important factors considered include:* character/personal qualities, extracurricular activities, talent/ability, volunteer work, work experience. *Other factors considered include:* first generation, geographical residence. **Freshman Admission Requirements:** High school diploma is required and GED is accepted. *Academic units required:* 4 English, 3 mathematics, 2 science, (2 science labs), 2 foreign language, 2 history, 1 academic elective, 1 Visual and Performing Arts. **Freshman Admission Statistics:** 86,548 applied, 19% admitted, 36% enrolled. **Transfer Admission Requirements:** college transcript(s), essay or personal statement, statement of good standing from prior institution(s). Minimum college GPA of 2.4 required. Lowest grade transferable D. **General Admission Information:** Application Fee $60. Regular application deadline 11/30. Notification on a rolling basis, beginning on or about 3/31. Nonfall registration not accepted. Credit and/or placement offered for CEEB Advanced Placement tests.

COSTS AND FINANCIAL AID

Annual in-state tuition $11,220. Annual out-of-state tuition $34,098. Room and board $12,895. Required fees $1,642. Average book expense $1,536. **Required Forms and Deadlines:** FAFSA. **Notification of Awards:** Applicants will be notified of awards on a rolling basis beginning 3/15. **Types of Aid:** *Need-based scholarships/grants:* Federal Pell, SEOG, state scholarships/grants, private scholarships, the school's own gift aid, United Negro College Fund, Federal Nursing Scholarships. *Loans:* Subsidized Stafford, Unsubsidized Stafford, PLUS, Federal Perkins, Federal Nursing, state loans, college/university loans from institutional funds. *Student Employment:* Federal Work-Study Program available. Institutional employment available. Off-campus job opportunities are good. **Financial Aid Statistics:** 96% freshmen, 95% undergrads receive need-based scholarship or grant aid. 1% freshmen, 1% undergrads receive non-need-based scholarship or grant aid. 63% freshmen, 65% undergrads receive need-based self-help aid. 1% freshmen, 1% undergrads receive athletic scholarships. 56% freshmen, 54% undergrads receive any aid. 49% undergrads borrow to pay for school. Average cumulative indebtedness $18,629. **Criteria for awarding institutional aid:** *Non-need-based:* academics, alumni affiliation, athletics.

UNIVERSITY OF CALIFORNIA—RIVERSIDE

3106 Student Services Building, Riverside, CA 92521
Phone: 951-827-3411 • **Financial Aid Phone:** 951-827-7249
E-mail: admit@ucr.edu • **CEEB Code:** 4839
Fax: 951-827-6344 • **Website:** www.ucr.edu

This public school was founded in 1954. It has a 1200-acre campus.

RATINGS

Admissions Selectivity Rating: 93   **Fire Safety Rating:** 90

STUDENTS AND FACULTY

Enrollment: 18,612. **Student Body:** 51% female, 49% male, 0% out-of-state, 3% international (100 countries represented). Asian 36%, African American 5%, Caucasian 14%, Hispanic 36%, Native American <1%
Retention and Graduation: 41% freshmen graduate within 4 years. 69% freshmen graduate within 6 years. **Faculty:** 763 full-time faculty, 98% hold PhDs, 33% are are members of minority groups, 34% are women. 0% of classes are taught by teaching assistants.

ACADEMICS

Degrees: bachelor's, master's, post-bachelor's certificate. **Classes:** Most classes have 20-29 students. Most lab/discussion sessions have 20-29 students. **Majors with Highest Enrollment:** Psychology; Business Administration and Management; Biological and Biomedical Sciences. **Special Study Options:** Accelerated program, cross-registration, double major, English as a Second Language (ESL), honors program, independent study, internships, student-designed major, study abroad, teacher certification program. **Disability Services:** Special programs offered to physically disabled students include note-taking services, reader services, tape recorders, tutors. **Career services:** Alumni network, alumni services, career/job search classes, career assessment, internships. Today's students do not always have the time to come to the brinks and mortar home of the traditional Career Center. The UCR Career Center has responded by developing state-of-the-art best practices to deliver services whether this is job search, internships, or career counseling. These new alternatives and virtual services range from a highly interactive website using podcast and YouTube features to providing workshops either in the classroom or in a virtual environment.

FACILITIES

Housing: Coed dorms, special housing for disabled students, special housing for international students, apartments for married students, apartments for single students, Theme Housing. **Special Academic Facilities/Equipment:** Art gallery, photography museum, botanical gardens, audio-visual resource center/studios, media resource center, statistical consulting center, citrus research center and agricultural experiment station, air pollution research center, center for environmental research and technology, water resources center, geophysics and planetary physics institute, center for bibliographical studies, center for family studies, center for crime and justice studies, natural reserve system, water resources center, salinity lab. **Computers:** 100% of classrooms, 15% of dorms, 100% of libraries, 100% of dining areas, 100% of student union, 100% of common outdoor areas have wireless network access. Students can register for classes online. Administrative functions (other than registration) can be performed online.

CAMPUS LIFE

Environment: City. **Activities:** Choral groups, concert band, dance, drama/theater, jazz band, literary magazine, music ensembles, musical theater, pep band, radio station, student government, student newspaper, student-run film society, International Student Organization. 264 registered organizations, 9 honor societies, 27 religious organizations. 20 fraternities, 20 sororities. **Athletics (Intercollegiate):** *Men:* baseball, basketball, cross-country, golf, soccer, tennis, track/field (outdoor), track/field (indoor). *Women:* basketball, cross-country, golf, soccer, softball, tennis, track/field (outdoor), track/field (indoor), volleyball. **On-Campus Highlights:** Basketball Games, Student Recreation Center and intramural sports, The Barn (music and comedy acts), Coffee Bean and Tea Leaf, The Highlander Union Building (HUB). **Environmental Initiatives:** UCR has a funded non-restrictive Office of Sustainability charged with coordinating sustainability initiatives throughout the campus supported by the Chancellor's Committee on Sustainability with the Chancellor serving as chair. UCR has an active engagement with the community including continuing education training courses on sustainability, a year long themed seminar on sustainability, and the development of a sustainability focused community garden. UCR takes a systems thinking approach to developing the built environment of the campus; integrating transportation, research, academics, design, energy, water and waste conservation into all projects.

ADMISSIONS

Freshman Academic Profile: Average high school GPA 3.6. 94% in top 10% of high school class, 100% in top 25% of high school class, 100% in top 50% of high school class. 90% from public high schools. SAT Math middle 50% range 510-630. SAT Critical Reading middle 50% range 480-580. SAT Writing middle 50% range 480-590. ACT middle 50% range 20-26. Minimum internet-based TOEFL 80. Minimum paper TOEFL 550. **Basis for Candidate Selection:** *Very important factors considered include:* academic GPA, rigor of secondary school record, standardized test scores, state residency. *Important factors considered include:* application essay. *Other factors considered include:* first generation. **Freshman Admission Requirements:** High school diploma is required and GED is accepted. *Academic units required:* 4 English, 3 mathematics, 2 science, (2 science labs), 2 foreign language, 2 history, 1 visual/performing arts, 1 academic elective. **Freshman Admission Statistics:** 34,816 applied, 60% admitted, 20% enrolled. **Transfer Admission Requirements:** college

transcript(s), essay or personal statement, statement of good standing from prior institution(s). Minimum college GPA of 2.4 required. Lowest grade transferable D-. **General Admission Information:** Application Fee $60. Regular application deadline 11/30. Notification on a rolling basis, beginning on or about 2/1. Nonfall registration not accepted. Credit and/or placement offered for CEEB Advanced Placement tests.

COSTS AND FINANCIAL AID

Annual in-state tuition $11,220. Annual out-of-state tuition $34,098. Room and board $15,000. Required fees $3,850. Average book expense $1,700. **Required Forms and Deadlines:** FAFSA, State aid form. **Notification of Awards:** Applicants will be notified of awards on a rolling basis beginning 3/1. **Types of Aid:** *Need-based scholarships/grants:* Federal Pell, SEOG, state scholarships/grants, private scholarships, the school's own gift aid. *Loans:* Direct Subsidized Stafford, Direct Unsubsidized Stafford, Direct PLUS, Federal Perkins, college/university loans from institutional funds. *Student Employment:* Federal Work-Study Program available. Institutional employment available. Off-campus job opportunities are excellent. **Financial Aid Statistics:** 94% freshmen, 94% undergrads receive need-based scholarship or grant aid. 1% freshmen, 1% undergrads receive non-need-based scholarship or grant aid. 79% freshmen, 72% undergrads receive need-based self-help aid. 1% freshmen, 0% undergrads receive athletic scholarships. 89% freshmen, 85% undergrads receive any aid. 70% undergrads borrow to pay for school. Average cumulative indebtedness $20,242. **Criteria for awarding institutional aid:** *Non-need-based:* academics, art, athletics, job skills, leadership, music/drama, state/district residency.

UNIVERSITY OF CALIFORNIA—SAN DIEGO

9500 Gilman Drive, La Jolla, CA 92093-0021
Phone: 858-534-4831 • **Financial Aid Phone:** 858-534-4480
E-mail: admissionsinfo@ucsd.edu • **CEEB Code:** 4836
Fax: 858-534-5723 • **Website:** www.ucsd.edu

This public school was founded in 1960. It has a 1976-acre campus.

RATINGS

Admissions Selectivity Rating: 97   **Fire Safety Rating:** 87

STUDENTS AND FACULTY

Enrollment: 24,810. **Student Body:** 48% female, 52% male, 20% out-of-state, 20% international (87 countries represented). Asian 35%, African American 2%, Caucasian 20%, Hispanic 15%, Native American <1%
Retention and Graduation: 96% freshmen return for sophomore year. 57% freshmen graduate within 4 years. 86% freshmen graduate within 6 years. 40% grads go on to further study within 1 year. 34% grads pursue arts and sciences degrees. 15% grads pursue law degrees. 8% grads pursue business degrees. 16% grads pursue medical degrees. **Faculty:** 1,001 full-time faculty, 99% hold PhDs, 28% are are members of minority groups, 24% are women. 0% of classes are taught by teaching assistants.

ACADEMICS

Degrees: bachelor's, master's. **Classes:** Most classes have 10-19 students. Most lab/discussion sessions have 20-29 students. **Majors with Highest Enrollment:** Economics; Biology/Biological Sciences. **Special Study Options:** Accelerated program, cooperative education program, cross-registration, double major, English as a Second Language (ESL), exchange student program (domestic), honors program, independent study, internships, liberal arts/career combination, student-designed major, study abroad, teacher certification program, Summer sessions for credit; special services for students with learning disabilities; Research programs, freshman honors program, in-depth academic assignments working in small groups or one-to-one with faculty. **Honors programs:** Each of UCSD's six colleges offers an honors program. Honors programs differ from college to college and year to year. Honors programs at John Muir College have been established to provide outstanding students with enhanced educational experiences through close interaction with faculty and other honors students. The Muir 90 Honors Seminar is by invitation and focuses primarily on entering freshmen. Please consult the Muir Academic Advising Office for details on the honors program. During the fall quarter of their freshman year, entering freshmen with outstanding high school records are invited to enroll in the Muir 90 Honors Seminar, which is noted on the UC San Diego transcript for one unit and P/NP. Students meet with a variety of faculty members from different disciplines to learn more about their research and about academic enrichment opportunities at UC San Diego. The format consists of eight meetings for Fall Quarters. The program includes discussions about a particular current issue, with professors providing insight based upon their areas of expertise. On the basis of outstanding high school grade point averages and College Board Scholastic Aptitude Test scores, a number of entering students are invited to participate in the ERC First-Year Honors Seminar. These weekly seminars are led by Provost Ann Craig, and she invites a variety of faculty colleagues and other knowledgeable individuals to discuss their own career development and research interests. The group also goes on field trips and takes advantage of additional educational opportunities on campus. Second-year honors students have the opportunity to select topics from MMW courses and to pursue independent study with individual faculty members. Projects may extend for one to three quarters. Honors projects are often selected for presentation at the UCSD Undergraduate Research Conference held each spring. Cultural and social events such as lectures, plays, and visits to museums are also an important component of the honors programs. The Sixth College Honors Program nurtures high-achieving students academically, intellectually, and socially; increases students' awareness about opportunities of academic, social, and cultural engagement; motivates students to become community leaders at Sixth College, at UCSD, and in communities outside the University. The Sixth College provost and Sixth College associated faculty mentor and guide honors students through seminars, research, social, and cultural events, introducing students to the academic, cultural, artistic, and social richness of the campus. Participants in the Honors Program include: New freshmen who have distinguished themselves academically in their high schools; New freshmen who complete at least 12 graded units with a 3.7 cumulative GPA during their first quarter at UCSD; Second-year honors students who maintain a minimum cumulative GPA of 3.5 Students must maintain a 3.5 cumulative GPA to remain in the Honors Program. **Combined degree programs:** BA/MD, BA/MA, Psychology, Experimental Psychology, Chemistry, Biochemistry, Cognitive Sci. **Disability Services:** Special programs offered to physically disabled students include note-taking services, reader services, tape recorders, tutors. **Career services:** Alumni network, alumni services, career/job search classes, career assessment, internships, regional alumni. Career services highlights include the CalIT2 Undergraduate Research program. This program, which began the summer of 2001, provides talented undergraduates with hands-on research experience to help them better define their career goals and help them sort out what options to pursue after graduation. Students conduct 10 weeks of research under the guidance of CalIT2- affiliated faculty and participate in a series of meetings focused on topics of interest to them. The program typically ends with a formal scholarly poster session to in which the students present their work to their peers, advisors, and often the larger campus and industry communities. UCSD students (including students graduating in the spring) are eligible to apply to this program, which typically is advertised in the early spring. CalIT2 also hires undergraduate students as employees to work on specific tasks associated with administrative, communications, and technical needs. Interested student can apply for such positions through the UCSD Career Services Center, and open jobs are also listed at http://www.calit2.net/recruitment.html. CalIT2 is also committed to bringing new project and mentorship opportunities to various campus initiatives. The UCSD division regularly sponsors student projects in conjunction with existing student design courses in the ECE and MAE departments. Student teams sponsored by CalIT2 work under the supervision of CalIT2 researchers or technical professionals on real-world engineering projects. This core space for undergraduate research space is intended to support collaboration among students involved in the various CalIT2 programs. This shared space, on the sixth floor of the CalIT2 building, can be used for experimentation and developing proofs of concept to enhance the competitiveness of grant applications. The UCSD division of CalIT2 sponsors undergraduate students involved in the new Teams in Engineering Service program launched by the UCSD Jacobs School of Engineering (http://www.jacobsschool.ucsd.edu/TIES/). Through TIES, multi-disciplinary teams of UCSD students design, build and deploy projects that solve technology-based problems for local community organizations. The UCSD division provides support to various initiatives aimed at improving the undergraduate bioinformatics education at UCSD. The program includes a structure for students to identify research opportunities and join bioinformatics research labs across campus, a mentoring program with graduate students, research symposia, a CalIT2 Bioinformatics Scholar Award, and travel support to conferences to present research findings. CalIT2 also values programs that enhance the quality of undergraduate experience through opportunities for research or collaborative experience, particularly in other countries. PRIME (Pacific Rim Undergraduate Experiences Program) provides project-based, international experience for undergraduate students, leveraging several UCSD programs and NSF's investment in the Pacific Rim Application Grid Middleware Assembly (PRAGMA). During the initial phase of funding, the program is targeting science and engineering students from Sixth College, which is focused on the integration of culture, arts, and technology. Students will work on cyberinfrastructure projects with dual mentors, one at UCSD and one in another country spend the summer at an institution outside the US, and participate in an international meeting to present the results of the project.

FACILITIES

Housing: Coed dorms, special housing for disabled students, men's dorms, special housing for international students, women's dorms, fraternity/sorority housing, apartments for married students, cooperative housing, apartments for single students, International House for international students and others interested in international living. 100% of campus accessible to physically disabled. **Special Academic Facilities/Equipment:** Art galleries, center for U.S. -Mexican studies, music recording studio, audiovisual center, center for music experimentation, aquarium, structural lab, San Diego supercomputer center,electron microscopes lab, the UC San Diego Medical Center, Scripps Institution of Oceanography, California Institute for Telecommunications and Information Technology (CalIT2), Institute on Global Conflict and Cooperation, Institute of the Americas. **Computers:** 100% of classrooms, 100% of dorms, 100% of libraries, 100% of dining areas, 100% of student union, 30% of common outdoor areas have wireless network access. Students can register for classes online. Administrative functions (other than registration) can be performed online.

CAMPUS LIFE

Environment: Metropolis. **Activities:** Choral groups, concert band, dance, drama/theater, jazz band, literary magazine, marching band, music ensembles, musical theater, opera, pep band, radio station, student government, student newspaper, student-run film society, symphony orchestra, television station, yearbook, Campus Ministries, International Student Organization, Model UN. 406 registered organizations, 5 honor societies, 46 religious organizations. 19 fraternities, 14 sororities. **Athletics (Intercollegiate):** *Men:* baseball, basketball, crew/rowing, cross-country, diving, fencing, golf, soccer, swimming, tennis, track/field (outdoor), volleyball, water polo. *Women:* basketball, crew/rowing, cross-country, diving, fencing, soccer, softball, swimming, tennis, track/field (outdoor), volleyball, water polo. **On-Campus Highlights:** Geisel Library, Stuart Art (sculpture) Gallery, Sun God Statue, Ocean Cliffs, Stephen Birch Aquarium and Museum, Price Center Expansion. **Environmental Initiatives:** The LEED Gold Certified Sustainability Resource Center (SRC) Campus Housing, Dining, & Hospitality (HDH) sustainability staff have made amazing strides in establishing a culture of sustainability in residence halls and dining facilities.

ADMISSIONS

Freshman Academic Profile: Average high school GPA 4. 100% in top 10% of high school class, 100% in top 25% of high school class, 100% in top 50% of high school class. SAT Math middle 50% range 620-750. SAT Critical Reading middle 50% range 560-670. SAT Writing middle 50% range 580-690. ACT middle 50% range 26-32. Minimum paper TOEFL 550. **Basis for Candidate Selection:** *Very important factors considered include:* application essay, academic GPA, rigor of secondary school record, standardized test scores, character/personal qualities, state residency, talent/ability. *Important factors considered include:* extracurricular activities, volunteer work. *Other factors considered include:* first generation, work experience. **Freshman Admission Requirements:** High school diploma is required and GED is accepted. **Academic units required:** 4 English, 3 mathematics, 2 science, (2 science labs), 2 foreign language, 2 history, 1 visual/performing arts, 1 academic elective. **Freshman Admission Statistics:** 73,440 applied, 33% admitted, 20% enrolled. **Transfer Admission Requirements:** college transcript(s), essay or personal statement, statement of good standing from prior institution(s). Minimum college GPA of 2.4 required. Lowest grade transferable D. **General Admission Information:** Application Fee $60. Regular application deadline 11/30. Regular notification 3/31. Notification on a rolling basis, beginning on or about 3/15. Nonfall registration accepted. Credit and/or placement offered for CEEB Advanced Placement tests.

COSTS AND FINANCIAL AID

Annual out-of-state tuition $36,334. Room and board $12,254. Required fees $1,413. Average book expense $1,509. **Required Forms and Deadlines:** FAFSA, State aid form. **Notification of Awards:** Applicants will be notified of awards on a rolling basis beginning 3/15. **Types of Aid:** *Need-based scholarships/grants:* Federal Pell, SEOG, state scholarships/grants, private scholarships, the school's own gift aid, Federal Academic Competitive Grant Federal National SMART Grant. *Loans:* Subsidized Stafford, Unsubsidized Stafford, PLUS, Federal Perkins, college/university loans from institutional funds, Alternative Loans. *Student Employment:* Federal Work-Study Program available. Institutional employment available. Highest amount earned per year from on-campus jobs $15,840. Off-campus job opportunities are good. **Financial Aid Statistics:** 92% freshmen, 94% undergrads receive need-based scholarship or grant aid. 1% freshmen, 0% undergrads receive non-need-based scholarship or grant aid. 82% freshmen, 83% undergrads receive need-based self-help aid. 2% freshmen, 1% undergrads receive athletic scholarships. 77% freshmen, 63% undergrads receive any aid. 56% undergrads borrow to pay for school. Average cumulative indebtedness $18,987. **Criteria for awarding institutional aid:** *Non-need-based:* academics, art, athletics, leadership, minority status, music/drama.

UNIVERSITY OF CALIFORNIA— SANTA BARBARA

Office of Admissions, Santa Barbara, CA 93106-2014
Phone: 805-893-2881 · **Financial Aid Phone:** 805-893-8209-2432
E-mail: admissions@sa.ucsb.edu · **CEEB Code:** 4835
Fax: 805-893-2676 · **Website:** www.ucsb.edu

This public school was founded in 1909. It has a 989-acre campus.

RATINGS

Admissions Selectivity Rating: 96   **Fire Safety Rating:** 92

STUDENTS AND FACULTY

Enrollment: 20,238. **Student Body:** 53% female, 47% male, 46% international (79 countries represented). Asian 21%, African American 2%, Caucasian 38%, Hispanic 25%, Native American <1% **Retention and Graduation:** 92% freshmen return for sophomore year. 69% freshmen graduate within 4 years. 81% freshmen graduate within 6 years. **Faculty:** 899 full-time faculty, 100% hold PhDs, 36% are are members of minority groups, 20% are women.

ACADEMICS

Degrees: bachelor's, master's, post-bachelor's certificate, post-master's certificate. **Classes:** Most classes have fewer than 10 students. Most lab/discussion sessions have 20-29 students. **Majors with Highest Enrollment:** Biology/Biological Sciences; Economics; Psychology. **Special Study Options:** Accelerated program, cross-registration, double major, dual enrollment, English as a Second Language (ESL), exchange student program (domestic), honors program, independent study, internships, student-designed major, study abroad, teacher certification program, Undergrads may take grad level classes. **Off-Campus Study:** Washington, DC. Freshman Seminars, pre-professional programs and advising, academic minors, and undergraduate research. **Honors programs:** The College Honors Program is designed to give students in the College of Letters and Science the opportunity to pursue their interests as part of a small community of scholars. The program connects such students to the resources of a large university, while providing an intimate collegiate atmosphere where students work closely with peers and professors in small classes, research laboratories, and special program and activities. **Combined degree programs:** BA/MA, BS/MS. **Disability Services:** Special programs offered to physically disabled students include note-taking services, reader services, tape recorders, tutors. **Career services:** career/job search classes, career assessment, internships.

FACILITIES

Housing: Coed dorms, fraternity/sorority housing, apartments for married students, cooperative housing, apartments for single students, Wellness Housing, Theme Housing. **Special Academic Facilities/Equipment:** Art museum, centers for black studies, Chicano studies, and study of developing nations, institutes for applied behavioral sciences, community/organizational research, marine science, and theoretical physics, Channel Islands field station. **Computers:** 100% of dorms, 100% of dining areas, 100% of student union, have wireless network access. Students can register for classes online. Administrative functions (other than registration) can be performed online.

CAMPUS LIFE

Environment: City. **Activities:** Choral groups, concert band, dance, drama/theater, jazz band, literary magazine, music ensembles, musical theater, opera, pep band, radio station, student government, student newspaper, student-run film society, symphony orchestra, television station, yearbook, Campus Ministries, International Student Organization, Model UN. 508 registered organizations, 5 honor societies, 19 religious organizations. 17 fraternities, 18 sororities. **Athletics (Intercollegiate):** *Men:* baseball, basketball, cross-country, diving, golf, gymnastics, soccer, swimming, tennis, track/field (outdoor), volleyball, water polo. *Women:* basketball, cross-country, diving, gymnastics, soccer, softball, swimming, tennis, track/field (outdoor), volleyball, water polo. **On-Campus Highlights:** Storke Tower Plaza/University Center, University Art Museum, UCSB Davidson Library, Recreation Center, Career and Counseling Services Center. **Environmental Initiatives:** *Green buildings:* minimum silver and strive for gold LEED certification Energy: through HVAC and lighting retrofits, delamping (removing unnecessary lights), Flex Your Power campaigns, etc., the campus has decreased its per-square-footage electrical consumption by 31% and its natural gas consumption by 23% since 1998. Creation of a high-level Sustainability Committee that includes administration, deans, Nobel laureates, senior faculty, staff and students in charge of making recommendations for sustainability projects to the Chancellor.

ADMISSIONS

Freshman Academic Profile: Average high school GPA 3.98. 100% in top 10% of high school class, 100% in top 25% of high school class, 100% in top 50% of high school class. 84% from public high schools. SAT Math middle 50% range 570-710. SAT Critical Reading middle 50% range 550-670. SAT Writing middle 50% range 570-690. ACT middle 50% range 24-30. Minimum internet-based TOEFL 80. Minimum paper TOEFL 550. **Basis for Candidate Selection:** *Very important factors considered include:* application essay, academic GPA, rigor of secondary school record, standardized test scores. *Other factors considered include:* Class rank, character/personal qualities, extracurricular activities, first generation, state residency, talent/ability, volunteer work, work experience. **Freshman Admission Requirements:** High school diploma is required and GED is accepted. **Academic units required:** 4 English, 3 mathematics, (2 science labs), 2 foreign language, 2 history, 1 visual/performing arts, 1 academic elective. **Freshman Admission Statistics:** 66,813 applied, 36% admitted, 20% enrolled. **Transfer Admission Requirements:** High school transcript, college transcript(s), essay or personal statement, Minimum college GPA of 2.4 required. Lowest grade transferable D. **General Admission Information:** Application Fee $60. Regular application deadline 11/30. Regular notification 3/1. Nonfall registration not accepted. Credit and/or placement offered for CEEB Advanced Placement tests.

COSTS AND FINANCIAL AID

Annual out-of-state tuition $35,070. Room and board $13,805. Required fees $1,554. Average book expense $1,444. **Required Forms and Deadlines:** FAFSA. **Notification of Awards:** Applicants will be notified of awards on a rolling basis beginning 3/15. **Types of Aid:** *Need-based scholarships/grants:* Federal Pell, SEOG, state scholarships/grants, private scholarships, the school's own gift aid, Work Study is also available as need-based aid. *Loans:* Direct Subsidized Stafford, Direct Unsubsidized Stafford, Direct PLUS, Federal Perkins. *Student Employment:* Federal Work-Study Program available. Institutional employment available. Off-campus job opportunities are good. **Financial Aid Statistics:** 88% freshmen, 89% undergrads receive need-based scholarship or grant aid. 1% freshmen, 1% undergrads receive non-need-based scholarship or grant aid. 78% freshmen, 81% undergrads receive need-based self-help aid. 1% freshmen, 1% undergrads receive athletic scholarships. 67% undergrads receive any aid. 56% undergrads borrow to pay for school. Average cumulative indebtedness $19,548. **Criteria for awarding institutional aid:** *Non-need-based:* academics, athletics.

UNIVERSITY OF CALIFORNIA—SANTA CRUZ

Office of Admissions, Cook House, Santa Cruz, CA 95064
Phone: 831-459-4008 · **Financial Aid Phone:** 831-459-2963
E-mail: admissions@ucsc.edu · **CEEB Code:** 4860
Fax: 831-459-4452 · **Website:** www.ucsc.edu

This public school was founded in 1965. It has a 2000-acre campus.

RATINGS

Admissions Selectivity Rating: 93   **Fire Safety Rating:** 80

STUDENTS AND FACULTY

Enrollment: 17,553. **Student Body:** 92% male, 3% out-of-state, 0% international (89 countries represented). Asian 14%, African American 1%, Caucasian 29%, Hispanic 18%, Native American <1% **Faculty:** 557 full-time faculty, 37% are are members of minority groups, 25% are women. 0% of classes are taught by teaching assistants.

ACADEMICS

Degrees: bachelor's, doctoral, master's, post-bachelor's certificate. **Classes:** Most classes have 10-19 students. Most lab/discussion sessions have 10-19 students. **Majors with Highest Enrollment:** Business/Commerce; Art/Art Studies; Ecology, Evolution, Systematics and Population Biology. **Special Study Options:** cooperative education program, cross-registration, double major, exchange student program (domestic), independent study, internships, student-designed major, study abroad, teacher certification program. **Combined degree programs:** BA/MA, Economics/Applied Economics, Business Management Economics, Global Economic. **Disability Services:** Special programs offered to physically disabled students include note-taking services, reader services, tape recorders, tutors. **Career services:** Alumni network, alumni services, career/job search classes, career assessment, internships. Career services highlights include the Chancellor's Undergraduate Internship Program (CUIP), which provides professional level on-campus internships in administrative departments throughout campus. Interns work with a mentor to develop personal and professional skills and take a lead role in producing a product or result in thir one-year internship. Interns receive a scholarship equivalent to their registration fees for a year in exchange for 450 hours of work. Students attend a 2-unit leadership seminar led by the Dean of Undergraduate Education during both Fall and Spring quarters. This program places an average of 35 students per year. Professions Training Program and Bonner Leaders (PTP/BL) is a service-learning program provides internships in local non-profit organizations along with an academic component focused on leadership development. Students receive a $1000 scholarship for 300 hours of work. This program is a partnership with the Bonner Foundation and AmeriCorps and places 15-20 students each year.

FACILITIES

Housing: Coed dorms, men's dorms, special housing for international students, women's dorms, apartments for married students, apartments for single students, Theme Housing, University-sponsored off-campus housing, RV Park, University Inn and Conference Center. **Special Academic Facilities/Equipment:** Eloise Pickard Smith Gallery Mary Porter Sesnon Gallery Center for Agroecology Wellness Center Long Marine Laboratory. **Computers:** 100% of classrooms, 100% of dorms, 100% of libraries, 100% of dining areas, 100% of student union, have wireless network access. Students can register for classes online. Administrative functions (other than registration) can be performed online.

CAMPUS LIFE

Environment: City. **Activities:** Choral groups, dance, drama/theater, jazz band, literary magazine, music ensembles, musical theater, opera, radio station, student government, student newspaper, student-run film society, symphony orchestra, television station, Campus Ministries, International Student Organization, Model UN. 138 registered organizations, 3 honor societies, 19 religious organizations. 9 fraternities, 11 sororities. **Athletics (Intercollegiate):** *Men:* basketball, diving, soccer, swimming, tennis, volleyball. *Women:* basketball, cross-country, diving, golf, soccer, swimming, tennis, volleyball. **On-Campus Highlights:** Arboretum, Farm and Garden, East Field House, Bay Tree Bookstore/Grad Student Commons, Pogonip Open Area Reserve. **Environmental Initiatives:** Climate Action Plan—Achieve 2000 levels of emissions by 2014 Achieve Zero Waste by 2020 (and 75% diversion by 2012); Campus Sustainability Plan—with specific environmental targets in 8 topic areas including increasing water conservation, already at 40% lower per capita than 20 years ago.

ADMISSIONS

Freshman Academic Profile: Average high school GPA 3.62. 96% in top 10% of high school class, 100% in top 25% of high school class, 100% in top 50% of high school class. 87% from public high schools. ACT middle 50% range 20-27. Minimum internet-based TOEFL 83. Minimum paper TOEFL 550. **Basis for Candidate Selection:** *Very important factors considered include:* application essay, academic GPA, rigor of secondary school record, standardized test scores, state residency. *Important factors considered include:* Class rank, character/personal qualities, extracurricular activities, first generation, geographical residence, talent/ability. *Other factors considered include:* volunteer work, work experience. **Freshman Admission Requirements:** High school diploma is required and GED is accepted. **Academic units required:** 4 English, 3 mathematics, 2 science, (2 science labs), 2 foreign language, 1 social studies, 1 history, 1 visual/performing arts, 1 academic elective. **Freshman Admission Statistics:** 33,142 applied, 61% admitted, 19% enrolled. **Transfer Admission Requirements:** college transcript(s), essay or personal statement, statement of good standing from prior institution(s). Minimum college GPA of 2.4 required. Lowest grade transferable D. **General Admission Information:** Application Fee $60. Regular application deadline 11/30. Regular notification 3/31. Notification on a rolling basis, beginning on or about 3/15. Nonfall registration accepted. Neither credit nor placement offered for CEEB Advanced Placement tests.

COSTS AND FINANCIAL AID

Annual in-state tuition $12,192. Annual out-of-state tuition $35,070. Room and board $14,856. Required fees $1,224. Average book expense $1,407. **Required Forms and Deadlines:** FAFSA, State aid form. **Notification of Awards:** Applicants will be notified of awards on a rolling basis beginning 4/1. **Types of Aid:** *Need-based scholarships/grants:* Federal Pell, SEOG, state scholarships/grants, private scholarships, the school's own gift aid. *Loans:* Direct Subsidized Stafford, Direct Unsubsidized Stafford, Direct PLUS, Federal Perkins. *Student Employment:* Federal Work-Study Program available. Institutional employment available. Off-campus job opportunities are excellent. **Financial Aid Statistics:** 87% freshmen, 88% undergrads receive need-based scholarship or grant aid. 1% freshmen, 1% undergrads receive non-need-based scholarship or grant aid. 86% freshmen, 86% undergrads receive need-based self-help aid. 0% freshmen, 0% undergrads receive athletic scholarships. 59% freshmen, 56% undergrads receive any aid. 53% undergrads borrow to pay for school. Average cumulative indebtedness $14,683. **Criteria for awarding institutional aid:** *Non-need-based:* academics, alumni affiliation, art, leadership, music/drama.

UNIVERSITY OF CENTRAL ARKANSAS

201 Donaghey Avenue, Conway, AR 72035
Phone: 501-450-3128 • **Financial Aid Phone:** 501-450-3140
E-mail: admissions@uca.edu • **CEEB Code:** 6012
Fax: 501-450-5228 • **Website:** www.uca.edu/ • **ACT Code:** 118

This public school was founded in 1907. It has a 262-acre campus.

RATINGS

Admissions Selectivity Rating: 74   **Fire Safety Rating:** 62

STUDENTS AND FACULTY

Enrollment: 9,232. **Student Body:** 59% female, 41% male, 9% out-of-state, 4% international (59 countries represented). Asian 2%, African American 20%, Caucasian 65%, Hispanic 4%, Native American <1%
Faculty: 0% of classes are taught by teaching assistants.

ACADEMICS

Degrees: associate, bachelor's, certificate, master's, post-bachelor's certificate, post-master's certificate. **Classes:** Most classes have 20-29 students. **Special Study Options:** Accelerated program, cooperative education program, distance learning, double major, dual enrollment, English as a Second Language (ESL), honors program, independent study, internships, liberal arts/career combination, study abroad, teacher certification program, 5 year professional program in Physical and Occupational Therapy. **Disability Services:** Special programs offered to physically disabled students include note-taking services, reader services, tape recorders. **Career services:** internships.

FACILITIES

Housing: Coed dorms, special housing for disabled students, men's dorms, special housing for international students, women's dorms, fraternity/sorority housing, apartments for married students, apartments for single students, Residential colleges are offered, as well as Honors housing. **Special Academic Facilities/Equipment:** Greenhouse, Baum Gellery, HPER Center, Planetarium, Technology Plaza, Smartboards, H.L. Minton Center for Geospatial Analysis and Research. **Computers:** 100% of classrooms, 100% of dorms, 100% of libraries, 100% of dining areas, 100% of student union, 100% of common outdoor areas have wireless network access. Students can register for classes online. Administrative functions (other than registration) can be performed online.

CAMPUS LIFE

Environment: Town. **Activities:** Choral groups, concert band, dance, drama/theater, jazz band, literary magazine, marching band, music ensembles, pep band, radio station, student government, student newspaper, student-run film society, symphony orchestra, television station, yearbook, Campus Ministries, International Student Organization, Model UN. 158 registered organizations, 11 honor societies, 16 religious organizations. 12 fraternities, 8 sororities. **Athletics (Intercollegiate):** *Men:* baseball, basketball, cheerleading, cross-country, football, golf, soccer, tennis, track/field (outdoor), track/field (indoor). *Women:* basketball, cheerleading, cross-country, golf, soccer, softball, tennis, track/field (outdoor), track/field (indoor), volleyball. **On-Campus Highlights:** Student Center, HPER Center, Baum Gallery, Estes Stadium, Farris Center.

ADMISSIONS

Freshman Academic Profile: Average high school GPA 3.36. 17% in top 10% of high school class, 43% in top 25% of high school class, 75% in top 50% of high school class. SAT Math middle 50% range 450-580. SAT Critical Reading middle 50% range 430-550. SAT Writing middle 50% range 420-530. ACT middle 50% range 19-26. Minimum internet-based TOEFL 61. Minimum paper TOEFL 500. **Basis for Candidate Selection:** *Very important factors considered include:* academic GPA, standardized test scores. *Important factors considered include:* Class rank. **Freshman Admission Requirements:** High school diploma is required and GED is accepted. **Freshman Admission Statistics:** 5,160 applied, 94% admitted, 46% enrolled. **Transfer Admission Requirements:** college transcript(s), statement of good standing from prior institution(s). Minimum college GPA of 2.0 required. Lowest grade transferable C. **General Admission Information:** Notification on a rolling basis, beginning on or about 10/1. Nonfall registration accepted. Credit and/or placement offered for CEEB Advanced Placement tests.

COSTS AND FINANCIAL AID

Notification of Awards: Applicants will be notified of awards on a rolling basis beginning 5/4. **Types of Aid:** *Need-based scholarships/grants:* Federal Pell, SEOG, state scholarships/grants, private scholarships, the school's own gift aid, Federal Nursing Scholarships. *Loans:* Subsidized Stafford, Unsubsidized Stafford, PLUS, Federal Perkins, Federal Nursing, state loans, External Loans. *Student Employment:* Federal Work-Study Program available. Institutional employment available. **Financial Aid Statistics:** 83% freshmen, 80% undergrads receive any aid. **Criteria for awarding institutional aid:** *Non-need-based:* academics, art, athletics, leadership, minority status, music/drama, state/district residency.

UNIVERSITY OF CENTRAL FLORIDA

P.O. Box 160111, Orlando, FL 32816-0111
Phone: 407-823-3000 · **Financial Aid Phone:** 407-823-2827
E-mail: admission@ucf.edu · **CEEB Code:** 5233
Fax: 407-823-5625 · **Website:** www.ucf.edu · **ACT Code:** 735

This public school was founded in 1963. It has a 1415-acre campus.

RATINGS

Admissions Selectivity Rating: 89   **Fire Safety Rating:** 92

STUDENTS AND FACULTY

Enrollment: 52,296. **Student Body:** 55% female, 45% male, 5% out-of-state, 1% international (143 countries represented). Asian 6%, African American 11%, Caucasian 55%, Hispanic 23%, Native American <1%
Retention and Graduation: 40% freshmen graduate within 4 years. 70% freshmen graduate within 6 years. **Faculty:** 1,330 full-time faculty, 79% hold PhDs, 42% are are members of minority groups, 24% are women. 6% of classes are taught by teaching assistants.

ACADEMICS

Degrees: associate, bachelor's, certificate, master's, post-bachelor's certificate. **Classes:** Most classes have 20-29 students. Most lab/discussion sessions have 30-39 students. **Majors with Highest Enrollment:** Marketing/Marketing Management; Psychology; Health Services/Allied Health/Health Sciences. **Special Study Options:** cooperative education program, distance learning, double major, dual enrollment, English as a Second Language (ESL), honors program, internships, study abroad, teacher certification program. **Honors programs:** The Burnett Honors College combines the intimacy of a small liberal arts college with the benefits of a large, metropolitan research university. The college fosters an atmosphere of intellectual excitement and a passion for learning; offers cutting-edge courses and innovative teaching methods; provides academic and professional advisement, mentoring, select co-curricular activities to Honors students; and develops sound values of social responsibility, inclusiveness, and good citizenship. The Burnett Honors College offers two main tracks, University Honors and Honors in the Major, and a special accelerated Medical School program in partnership with University of South Florida. University Honors targets primarily incoming freshmen and comprises a special freshman symposium, General Education Program (GEP) courses, and upper-division seminars and disciplinary core courses. Honors GEP courses are taught across the curriculum and are limited to enrollments of 20 students for all courses except English Composition, which is limited to 15 students. Honors English Composition also differs from regular Composition offerings that follow a standardized curriculum in that each Honors section is "themed." Upper division University Honors students take 9-15 hours of special interdisciplinary, team-taught seminars or, in the case of the professional colleges, a combination of core courses in their fields and interdisciplinary seminars. In addition, students participating in University Honors enroll in a well-respected and established first-year experience course, the Honors Symposium. lt;brgt;lt;brgt; Honors in the Major is a senior thesis Honors program. Honors in the Major students engage in a two-semester course of study consisting of preparing a research proposal, conducting original research, and writing a thesis. The student selects a three-member faculty committee to oversee the thesis process that culminates in the thesis defense. UCF/USF Early Acceptance/Accelerated Medical Program: This unique program offers qualified UCF Honors students the opportunity to complete the baccalaureate and Doctor in Medicine degrees in seven years. Through a special partnership with the College of Medicine at the University of South Florida, UCF Honors students are guaranteed admission to the USF medical school once they have successfully completed the program requirements. **Combined degree programs:** BA/MD, BA/MA, BA/MEng, BS/MS. **Disability Services:** Special programs offered to physically disabled students include note-taking services, reader services, tape recorders, tutors. **Career services:** career/job search classes, career assessment

FACILITIES

Housing: Coed dorms, men's dorms, women's dorms, fraternity/sorority housing, apartments for single students, Wellness Housing, Theme Housing, Affiliated student residences available across street from campus with university resident assistants. On-campus: Honors Center, Living Learning Communities, Lead Scholars Center. 97% of campus accessible to physically disabled. **Special Academic Facilities/Equipment:** Center for research and education in optics and lasers, arboretum, observatory, New student union, student recreation center. **Computers:** 100% of classrooms, 100% of dorms, 100% of libraries, 90% of dining areas, 100% of student union, 90% of common outdoor areas have wireless network access. Students can register for classes online. Administrative functions (other than registration) can be performed online.

CAMPUS LIFE

Environment: City. **Activities:** Choral groups, concert band, drama/theater, jazz band, literary magazine, marching band, music ensembles, musical theater, pep band, radio station, student government, student newspaper, student-run film society, symphony orchestra, Campus Ministries, International Student Organization, Model UN. 361 registered organizations, 36 honor societies, 29 religious organizations. 21 fraternities, 18 sororities. **Athletics (Intercollegiate):** *Men:* baseball, basketball, cheerleading, cross-country, football, golf, soccer, tennis. *Women:* basketball, cheerleading, crew/rowing, cross-country, golf, soccer, softball, tennis, track/field (outdoor), track/field (indoor), volleyball. **On-Campus Highlights:** Student Union, Recreation and Wellness Center, Bookstore (Barnes and Noble caf), Reflecting Pond, New Arena and Football Stadium. **Environmental Initiatives:** In House Building Commisssioning Team; Full Time Sustainability Marketing; and Outreach Goal to get all major educational buildings Energy Star and LEED certified.

ADMISSIONS

Freshman Academic Profile: Average high school GPA 3.86. 31% in top 10% of high school class, 71% in top 25% of high school class, 96% in top 50% of high school class. SAT Math middle 50% range 550-640. SAT Critical Reading middle 50% range 540-640. SAT Writing middle 50% range 510-610. ACT middle 50% range 24-28. Minimum internet-based TOEFL 80. Minimum paper TOEFL 550. **Basis for Candidate Selection:** *Very important factors considered include:* academic GPA, rigor of secondary school record, standardized test scores. *Important factors considered include:* application essay, recommendation(s). *Other factors considered include:* Class rank, alumni/ae relation, character/personal qualities, extracurricular activities, first generation, geographical residence, interview, level of applicant's interest, state residency, talent/ability, volunteer work, work experience. **Freshman Admission Requirements:** High school diploma is required and GED is accepted. **Academic units required:** 4 English, 4 mathematics, 3 science, (2 science labs), 2 foreign language, 3 social studies, 2 academic electives. **Freshman Admission Statistics:** 33,226 applied, 50% admitted, 39% enrolled. **Transfer Admission Requirements:** college transcript(s), Minimum college GPA of 2.0 required. Lowest grade transferable D. **General Admission Information:** Application Fee $30. Regular application deadline 5/1. Notification on a rolling basis, beginning on or about 10/1. Nonfall registration accepted. Credit offered for CEEB Advanced Placement tests.

COSTS AND FINANCIAL AID

Annual in-state tuition $6,368. Annual out-of-state tuition $22,467. Room and board $9,300. Required fees $0. Average book expense $1,146. **Required Forms and Deadlines:** FAFSA. **Notification of Awards:** Applicants will be notified of awards on a rolling basis beginning 3/15. **Types of Aid:** *Need-based scholarships/grants:* Federal Pell, SEOG, state scholarships/grants, private scholarships, the school's own gift aid, University scholarships and grants. *Loans:* Subsidized Stafford, Unsubsidized Stafford, PLUS, Federal Perkins. *Student Employment:* Federal Work-Study Program available. Institutional employment available. **Financial Aid Statistics:** 65% freshmen, 72% undergrads receive need-based scholarship or grant aid. 88% freshmen, 55% undergrads receive non-need-based scholarship or grant aid. 50% freshmen, 59% undergrads receive need-based self-help aid. 1% freshmen, 1% undergrads receive athletic scholarships. 88% freshmen, 80% undergrads receive any aid. 50% undergrads borrow to pay for school. Average cumulative indebtedness $22,526. **Criteria for awarding institutional aid:** *Non-need-based:* academics, alumni affiliation, athletics, leadership, state/district residency.

See page 1168.

UNIVERSITY OF CENTRAL MISSOURI

Office of Admissions, Warrensburg, MO 64093
Phone: 660-543-4290 · **Financial Aid Phone:** 660-543-4040
E-mail: admit@ucmovmb.edu · **CEEB Code:** 6090
Fax: 660-543-8517 · **Website:** www.cmsu.edu · **ACT Code:** 2272

This public school was founded in 1871. It has a 1561-acre campus.

RATINGS

Admissions Selectivity Rating: 74   **Fire Safety Rating:** 73

STUDENTS AND FACULTY

Enrollment: 8,441. **Student Body:** 56% female, 44% male, 7% out-of-state, 2% international (53 countries represented). Asian 1%, African American 5%, Caucasian 76%, Hispanic 2%, Native American <1%

Retention and Graduation: 68% freshmen return for sophomore year. 23% freshmen graduate within 4 years. 50% freshmen graduate within 6 years. **Faculty:** 449 full-time faculty, 73% hold PhDs, 40% are are members of minority groups, 7% are women. 4% of classes are taught by teaching assistants.

ACADEMICS

Degrees: associate, bachelor's, master's, post-bachelor's certificate, post-master's certificate. **Classes:** Most classes have 20-29 students. **Majors with Highest Enrollment:** Education; Criminal Justice/Law Enforcement Administration; Marketing/Marketing Management. **Special Study Options:** Accelerated program, cooperative education program, cross-registration, distance learning, double major, dual enrollment, English as a Second Language (ESL), honors program, internships, student-designed major, study abroad, teacher certification program, weekend college. **Disability Services:** Special programs offered to physically disabled students include note-taking services, reader services, tape recorders, tutors.

FACILITIES

Housing: Coed dorms, special housing for disabled students, special housing for international students, women's dorms, fraternity/sorority housing, apartments for married students, apartments for single students, Economy Suites and Townhouses. 95% of campus accessible to physically disabled. **Special Academic Facilities/Equipment:** Art gallery,Nance Museum and Library of Antiquities, natural history museum, English language center, child development lab, speech and hearing lab, 260-acre farm, Missouri Safety center, National Police Institute, driving/safety range, center for technology and business research,airport for aviation program, Extended campus, Lee's Summit, MO, KCMW-FM, KMOS-TV, Public Broadcasting Stations. **Computers:** Students can register for classes online. Administrative functions (other than registration) can be performed online.

CAMPUS LIFE

Environment: Rural. **Activities:** Choral groups, concert band, dance, drama/theater, jazz band, literary magazine, marching band, music ensembles, musical theater, opera, pep band, radio station, student government, student newspaper, student-run film society, symphony orchestra, television station, yearbook. 150 registered organizations, 24 honor societies, 14 religious organizations. 9 fraternities, 10 sororities. **Athletics (Intercollegiate):** *Men:* baseball, basketball, bowling, cross-country, football, golf, soccer, track/field (outdoor), wrestling. *Women:* basketball, bowling, cross-country, soccer, softball, track/field (outdoor), volleyball. **On-Campus Highlights:** Union Commons, Library, Pertle Springs, Multi-purpose building.

ADMISSIONS

Freshman Academic Profile: Average high school GPA 3.29. 12% in top 10% of high school class, 36% in top 25% of high school class, 71% in top 50% of high school class. 90% from public high schools. ACT middle 50% range 20-24. Minimum paper TOEFL 500. **Basis for Candidate Selection:** *Very important factors considered include:* Class rank, rigor of secondary school record, standardized test scores. *Other factors considered include:* recommendation(s), alumni/ae relation, character/personal qualities, extracurricular activities, talent/ability. **Freshman Admission Requirements:** High school diploma is required and GED is accepted. **Academic units required:** 4 English, 3 mathematics, 2 science, (1 science labs), 3 social studies, 3 academic electives, 1 arts. **Freshman Admission Statistics:** 3,631 applied, 84% admitted, 52% enrolled. **Transfer Admission Requirements:** college transcript(s), Minimum college GPA of 2.0 required. Lowest grade transferable C. **General Admission Information:** Application Fee $30. Regular application deadline 8/18. Notification on a rolling basis, beginning on or about 9/3. Nonfall registration accepted. Admission may be deferred for a maximum of 3 semesters. Credit offered for CEEB Advanced Placement tests.

COSTS AND FINANCIAL AID

Required Forms and Deadlines: FAFSA. **Notification of Awards:** Applicants will be notified of awards on or about 3/1. **Types of Aid:** *Need-based scholarships/grants:* Federal Pell, SEOG, state scholarships/grants, private scholarships, the school's own gift aid. *Loans:* Direct Subsidized Stafford, Direct Unsubsidized Stafford, Direct PLUS, Federal Perkins, state loans. *Student Employment:* Highest amount earned per year from on-campus jobs $2,000. **Financial Aid Statistics:** 50% freshmen, 58% undergrads receive need-based scholarship or grant aid. 67% freshmen, 52% undergrads receive non-need-based scholarship or grant aid. 81% freshmen, 88% undergrads receive need-based self-help aid. 5% freshmen, 5% undergrads receive athletic scholarships. 51% freshmen, 61% undergrads receive any aid. 68% undergrads borrow to pay for school. Average cumulative indebtedness $12,633. **Criteria for awarding institutional aid:** *Non-need-based:* academics, alumni affiliation, art, athletics, leadership, minority status, music/drama, state/district residency.

UNIVERSITY OF CENTRAL OKLAHOMA

100 North University Drive, Edmond, OK 73034
Phone: 405-974-2338 · **Financial Aid Phone:** 405-974-3334
E-mail: admituco@uco.edu · **CEEB Code:** 6091
Fax: 405-341-4964 · **ACT Code:** 3390

This public school was founded in 1890. It has a 200-acre campus.

RATINGS

Admissions Selectivity Rating: 76   **Fire Safety Rating:** 81

STUDENTS AND FACULTY

Enrollment: 14,019. **Student Body:** 58% female, 42% male, 3% out-of-state, 6% international (75 countries represented). Asian 3%, African American 9%, Caucasian 60%, Hispanic 4%, Native American 5%
Retention and Graduation: 61% freshmen return for sophomore year. **Faculty:** 441 full-time faculty, 68% hold PhDs, 48% are are members of minority groups, 13% are women.

ACADEMICS

Degrees: bachelor's, certificate, master's. **Classes:** Most classes have 20-29 students. Most lab/discussion sessions have 10-19 students. **Majors with Highest Enrollment:** Elementary Education and Teaching; Registered Nursing/Registered Nurse; Business Administration and Management. **Special Study Options:** Accelerated program, distance learning, double major, dual enrollment, English as a Second Language (ESL), honors program, independent study, internships, teacher certification program. **Disability Services:** Special programs offered to physically disabled students include note-taking services, reader services, tape recorders, tutors. **Career services:** alumni services, career/job search classes, career assessment, internships.

FACILITIES

Housing: Coed dorms, men's dorms, women's dorms, fraternity/sorority housing, apartments for married students, apartments for single students. 95% of campus accessible to physically disabled. **Special Academic Facilities/Equipment:** Art and history museums, archives. **Computers:** 100% of classrooms, 100% of dorms, 100% of libraries, 100% of dining areas, 100% of student union, 50% of common outdoor areas have wireless network access. Students can register for classes online. Administrative functions (other than registration) can be performed online.

CAMPUS LIFE

Environment: Metropolis. **Activities:** Choral groups, concert band, dance, drama/theater, jazz band, marching band, music ensembles, musical theater, pep band, radio station, student government, student newspaper, symphony orchestra, television station, yearbook. 150 registered organizations, 27 honor societies, 16 religious organizations. 9 fraternities, 10 sororities. **Athletics (Intercollegiate):** *Men:* baseball, basketball, football, golf, wrestling. *Women:* basketball, cross-country, golf, soccer, softball, tennis, volleyball. **On-Campus Highlights:** Starbucks, Wellness Center, University Center **Environmental Initiatives:** Use 100% wind power; Waterless Urinals; Motion sensor lighting.

ADMISSIONS

Freshman Academic Profile: Average high school GPA 3.28. 12% in top 10% of high school class, 35% in top 25% of high school class, 72% in top 50% of high school class. ACT middle 50% range 19-23. Minimum internet-based TOEFL 83. Minimum paper TOEFL 560. **Basis for Candidate Selection:** *Very important factors considered include:* Class rank, academic GPA, rigor of secondary school record, standardized test scores. *Other factors considered include:* extracurricular activities, talent/ability. **Freshman Admission Requirements:** High school diploma is required and GED is accepted. **Academic units required:** 4 English, 3 mathematics, 2 science, (2 science labs), 0 foreign language, 1 social studies, 2 history, 0 visual/performing arts, 0 computer science, 0 academic electives. **Freshman Admission Statistics:** 4,614 applied, 69% admitted, 67% enrolled. **Transfer Admission Requirements:** college transcript(s), statement of good standing from prior institution(s). Minimum college GPA of 2.0 required. Lowest grade transferable D. **General Admission Information:** Application Fee $25. Notification on a rolling basis, beginning on or about 4/1. Nonfall registration accepted. Admission may be deferred for a maximum of 1 semester. Credit and/or placement offered for CEEB Advanced Placement tests.

COSTS AND FINANCIAL AID

Annual in-state tuition $3,681. Annual out-of-state tuition $10,110. Room and board $7,468. Required fees $542. Average book expense $1,000. **Required Forms and Deadlines:** FAFSA, Institution's own financial aid form. **Notification of Awards:** Applicants will be notified of awards on a rolling basis beginning 5/1. **Types of Aid:** *Need-based scholarships/grants:* Federal Pell, SEOG, state scholarships/grants, private scholarships, the school's own gift aid.

Loans: Subsidized Stafford, Unsubsidized Stafford, PLUS, Federal Perkins. *Student Employment:* Federal Work-Study Program available. Institutional employment available. Highest amount earned per year from on-campus jobs $7,200. Off-campus job opportunities are excellent. **Financial Aid Statistics:** 88% freshmen, 89% undergrads receive need-based scholarship or grant aid. 2% freshmen, 3% undergrads receive non-need-based scholarship or grant aid. 90% freshmen, 92% undergrads receive need-based self-help aid. 2% freshmen, 2% undergrads receive athletic scholarships. 66% freshmen, 75% undergrads receive any aid. 48% undergrads borrow to pay for school. Average cumulative indebtedness $16,943. **Criteria for awarding institutional aid:** *Non-need-based:* academics, alumni affiliation, art, athletics, leadership, minority status, music/drama, state/district residency.

UNIVERSITY OF CHARLESTON

2300 MacCorkle Ave SE, Charleston, WV 25304
Phone: 304-357-4750 · **Financial Aid Phone:** 304-357-4950
E-mail: admissions@ucwv.edu · **CEEB Code:** 5419
Fax: 304-357-4781 · **Website:** http://www.ucwv.edu/ · **ACT Code:** 4528

This private school was founded in 1888. It has a 24-acre campus.

RATINGS

Admissions Selectivity Rating: 75   **Fire Safety Rating:** 77

STUDENTS AND FACULTY

Enrollment: 1,527. **Student Body:** 57% female, 43% male, 27% out-of-state, 8% international (44 countries represented). Asian 1%, African American 10%, Caucasian 66%, Hispanic 3%, Native American 1%. **Retention and Graduation:** 61% freshmen return for sophomore year. 26% freshmen graduate within 4 years. 36% freshmen graduate within 6 years. **Faculty:** 101 full-time faculty, 50% hold PhDs, 68% are are members of minority groups.

ACADEMICS

Degrees: associate, bachelor's, master's. **Classes:** Most classes have 10-19 students. Most lab/discussion sessions have fewer than 10 students. **Majors with Highest Enrollment:** Business Administration and Management; Biology/Biological Sciences; Registered Nursing/Registered Nurse. **Special Study Options:** double major, English as a Second Language (ESL), independent study, internships, liberal arts/career combination, study abroad. **Disability Services:** Special programs offered to physically disabled students include note-taking services, reader services, tape recorders, tutors.

FACILITIES

Housing: Coed dorms, special housing for disabled students, apartments for single students **Special Academic Facilities/Equipment:** Erma Byrd Art Gallery **Computers:** 75% of classrooms, 100% of dorms, 100% of libraries, 100% of dining areas, 100% of student union, 50% of common outdoor areas have wireless network access. Students can register for classes online. Administrative functions (other than registration) can be performed online.

CAMPUS LIFE

Environment: City. **Activities:** Choral groups, dance, drama/theater, music ensembles, pep band, student government, student newspaper, yearbook, Campus Ministries, International Student Organization, Model UN. 39 registered organizations, 7 honor societies, 2 religious organizations. 2 fraternities, 3 sororities. **Athletics (Intercollegiate):** *Men:* baseball, basketball, football, golf, soccer, tennis. *Women:* basketball, crew/rowing, cross-country, golf, soccer, softball, tennis, track/field (outdoor), volleyball. **On-Campus Highlights:** New Fitness Center, School of Pharmacy, Coffee Tavern, University of Charleston Stadium, Graduate School of Business. **Environmental Initiatives:** Recycling on campus; Planting trees; Energy conservation specifically electricity.

ADMISSIONS

Freshman Academic Profile: Average high school GPA 3.3. SAT Math middle 50% range 450-550. SAT Critical Reading middle 50% range 430-538. ACT middle 50% range 19-23. Minimum internet-based TOEFL 61. Minimum paper TOEFL 500. **Basis for Candidate Selection:** *Very important factors considered include:* academic GPA, standardized test scores. *Important factors considered include:* Class rank, rigor of secondary school record, alumni/ae relation, extracurricular activities. *Other factors considered include:* application essay, recommendation(s), character/personal qualities, first generation, interview, level of applicant's interest, talent/ability, volunteer work, work experience. **Freshman Admission Requirements:** High school diploma is required and GED is accepted. **Academic units required:** 1 Algebra for BS Nursing. **Freshman Admission Statistics:** 1,787 applied, 61% admitted, 31% enrolled. **Transfer Admission Requirements:** college transcript(s), Minimum college

GPA of 2.25 required. Lowest grade transferable C. **General Admission Information:** Application Fee $25. Notification on a rolling basis, beginning on or about 10/1. Nonfall registration accepted. Credit and/or placement offered for CEEB Advanced Placement tests.

COSTS AND FINANCIAL AID

Annual tuition $19,500. Room and board $9,000. Required fees $200. Average book expense $1,500. **Required Forms and Deadlines:** FAFSA, Institution's own financial aid form, State aid form. **Notification of Awards:** Applicants will be notified of awards on a rolling basis beginning 3/1. **Types of Aid:** *Need-based scholarships/grants:* Federal Pell, SEOG, state scholarships/grants, private scholarships, the school's own gift aid, TEACH/Academic Competitiveness/SMART. *Loans:* Subsidized Stafford, Unsubsidized Stafford, PLUS, Federal Perkins, Federal Nursing. *Student Employment:* Federal Work-Study Program available. Off-campus job opportunities are good. **Financial Aid Statistics:** 100% freshmen, 86% undergrads receive any aid. **Criteria for awarding institutional aid:** *Non-need-based:* academics, alumni affiliation, athletics, leadership, music/drama.

THE UNIVERSITY OF CHICAGO

Best 380

1101 E 58th Street, Chicago, IL 60637
Phone: 773-702-8650 · **Financial Aid Phone:** 773-702-8666
E-mail: collegeadmissions@uchicago.edu · **CEEB Code:** 1832
Fax: 773-702-4199 · **Website:** collegeadmissions@uchicago.edu · **ACT Code:** 1152

This private school was founded in 1890. It has a 211-acre campus.

RATINGS

Admissions Selectivity Rating: 99   **Fire Safety Rating:** 91

STUDENTS AND FACULTY

Enrollment: 5,672. **Student Body:** 47% female, 53% male, 83% out-of-state, 10% international (72 countries represented). Asian 17%, African American 5%, Caucasian 45%, Hispanic 9%, Native American <1%. **Retention and Graduation:** 99% freshmen return for sophomore year. 87% freshmen graduate within 4 years. 93% freshmen graduate within 6 years. **Faculty:** 1,303 full-time faculty, 100% hold PhDs, 30% are are members of minority groups, 20% are women.

ACADEMICS

Degrees: bachelor's, doctoral, master's. **Classes:** Most classes have fewer than 10 students. Most lab/discussion sessions have 10-19 students. **Majors with Highest Enrollment:** Economics; Biology/Biological Sciences; Political Science and Government. **Special Study Options:** Accelerated program, cross-registration, double major, dual enrollment, English as a Second Language (ESL), exchange student program (domestic), honors program, independent study, internships, student-designed major, study abroad, teacher certification program. **Combined degree programs:** BA/MA. **Career services:** Alumni network, alumni services, career/job search classes, career assessment, internships, regional alumni. Career services highlights include the internship program: Jeff Metcalf Fellows Program provides outstanding opportunities for both students and hosting organizations. It has grown dramatically since its creation in 1997, and this year placed 210 students in internships across the US. We are particularly proud of the relationships this program has built with alumni.

FACILITIES

Housing: Coed dorms, special housing for disabled students, special housing for international students, fraternity/sorority housing, apartments for married students, cooperative housing. **Special Academic Facilities/Equipment:** Smart Museum, Renaissance Society, Oriental Institute, Business and Economics Resource Center, D'Angelo Law Library, Echhart Library, John Crerar Library, Joseph Regenstein Library, Special Collections Research Center, Social Services Administration Library, Yerkes Obsevatory Library, On Campus Lab School(PreK-12), Argonne National Laboratory, Enrico Fermi Institute, Court Theater, Observatory, Two Telescopes, Fermi National Accelerator Laboratory. **Computers:** 100% of classrooms, 100% of dorms, 100% of libraries, 100% of dining areas, 100% of student union, 100% of common outdoor areas have wireless network access. Students can register for classes online.

CAMPUS LIFE

Environment: Metropolis. **Activities:** Choral groups, concert band, dance, drama/theater, jazz band, literary magazine, music ensembles, musical theater, pep band, radio station, student government, student newspaper, student-run film society, symphony orchestra, yearbook, Campus Ministries, International Student Organization, Model UN. 400 registered organizations, 5 honor societies, 36 religious organizations. 10 fraternities, 3 sororities. **Athletics (Intercollegiate):** *Men:* baseball, basketball, cross-country, diving, football, soccer, swimming, tennis, track/field (outdoor), track/field (indoor), volleyball, wrestling. *Women:* basketball, cross-country, diving, soccer, softball, swimming, tennis, track/field (outdoor), track/field (indoor), volleyball. **On-Campus Highlights:** Gerald Ratner Athletics Center, Joseph Regenstein Library, Robie House, Court Theatre, Rockefeller Memorial Chapel, Food on Campus—UChicago boasts over a dozen on-campus coffee shops and three residential dining halls, as well as a host of delis and snack shops. Of note, Bartlett Dining Commons, once an athletic field house, is a large dining hall that offers excellent a la carte options and a kosher deli and Hallowed Grounds, a student-run lounge that offers international food from neighborhood restaurants, two pool tables, and popular open-mic nights. Books on Campus Seminary Co-op Bookstore (58th Street and University Avenue) One of the best academic bookstores in the world, the Co-Op also has a veritable maze of fiction, poetry, drama, and everything in-between. It also carries the textbooks for most social sciences and humanities courses. University of Chicago Bookstore (Barnes and Noble) (58th Street and Ellis Ave)—University t-shirts, pennants, and math and science textbooks. Also contains a Starbucks. O'Gara and Wilson, Chicago's 'oldest' bookstore, specializing in rare and used books. Arts and Music on campus Professional companies and artists in residence include Court Theatre, one of the top reparatory theater companies in the city; the critically acclaimed (and Grammy award winning) Pacifica Quartet; the Newberry Consort, famed for their performances of medieval and Renaissance music on period instruments; the Saint Paul Chamber Orchestra; and the modern ensemble 'eighth blackbird.' The University of Chicago Presents series brings musicians from all over the world to Mandel Hall in the Reynolds Club (the main student center.). **Environmental Initiatives:** Formation of the Program on the Global Environment. Facilities Services has increased University attention in this area by leading the construction of energy efficient central utilities plants to provide steam and chilled water, aggressive program promoting alternative transportation, green roof initiatives, and silver LEED certification pursuit on renovation project. Support of the Sustainability Council to engage students, faculty and staff in sustainability issues and hiring of a full-time sustainability officer.

ADMISSIONS

Freshman Academic Profile: Average high school GPA 4.16. 98% in top 10% of high school class, 99% in top 25% of high school class, 100% in top 50% of high school class. 59% from public high schools. SAT Math middle 50% range 710-790. SAT Critical Reading middle 50% range 720-800. SAT Writing middle 50% range 710-780. ACT middle 50% range 32-35. Minimum internet-based TOEFL 104. Minimum paper TOEFL 600. **Basis for Candidate Selection:** *Very important factors considered include:* application essay, recommendation(s), rigor of secondary school record, character/personal qualities, talent/ability. *Important factors considered include:* Class rank, academic GPA, extracurricular activities, volunteer work. *Other factors considered include:* standardized test scores, alumni/ae relation, first generation, interview, level of applicant's interest, racial/ethnic status, work experience. **Freshman Admission Requirements:** High school diploma or equivalent is not required. **Freshman Admission Statistics:** 27,500 applied, 9% admitted, 60% enrolled. **Transfer Admission Requirements:** High school transcript, college transcript(s), essay or personal statement, standardized test scores, statement of good standing from prior institution(s). Minimum college GPA of 3.0 required. Lowest grade transferable 2. **General Admission Information:** Application Fee $65. Regular application deadline 1/2. Regular notification 4/1. Nonfall registration not accepted. Admission may be deferred for a maximum of 1 year. Credit and/or placement offered for CEEB Advanced Placement tests.

COSTS AND FINANCIAL AID

Required Forms and Deadlines: FAFSA, Institution's own financial aid form. **Notification of Awards:** Applicants will be notified of awards on or about 4/15. **Types of Aid:** *Need-based scholarships/grants:* Federal Pell, SEOG, state scholarships/grants, private scholarships, the school's own gift aid. *Loans:* Subsidized Stafford, Unsubsidized Stafford, PLUS, Federal Perkins. **Financial Aid Statistics:** 99% freshmen, 99% undergrads receive need-based scholarship or grant aid. 0% freshmen, 0% undergrads receive non-need-based scholarship or grant aid. 40% freshmen, 58% undergrads receive need-based self-help aid. 0% freshmen, 0% undergrads receive athletic scholarships. 61% freshmen, 62% undergrads receive any aid. 41% undergrads borrow to pay for school. Average cumulative indebtedness $19,206. **Criteria for awarding institutional aid:** *Non-need-based:* academics, leadership.

See page 1170.

UNIVERSITY OF CINCINNATI

P.O. Box 210091, Cincinnati, OH 45221-0091
Phone: 513-556-1100 · **Financial Aid Phone:** 513-556-3511
E-mail: admissions@uc.edu · **CEEB Code:** 1833
Fax: 513-556-1105 · **Website:** www.uc.edu · **ACT Code:** 3340

This public school was founded in 1819. It has a 392-acre campus.

RATINGS

Admissions Selectivity Rating: 82   **Fire Safety Rating:** 94

STUDENTS AND FACULTY

Enrollment: 23,902. **Student Body:** 50% female, 50% male, 11% out-of-state, 4% international (127 countries represented). Asian 3%, African American 7%, Caucasian 76%, Hispanic 3%, Native American <1%
Retention and Graduation: 86% freshmen return for sophomore year. 28% freshmen graduate within 4 years. **Faculty:** 1,192 full-time faculty, 76% hold PhDs, 42% are are members of minority groups, 16% are women.

ACADEMICS

Degrees: associate, bachelor's, certificate, first professional, master's, post-bachelor's certificate, terminal associate, transfer associate. **Classes:** Most classes have 20-29 students. **Majors with Highest Enrollment:** Marketing/Marketing Management; Psychology; Criminal Justice/Safety Studies. **Special Study Options:** Accelerated program, cooperative education program, distance learning, double major, English as a Second Language (ESL), honors program, independent study, internships, liberal arts/career combination, study abroad, teacher certification program, weekend college. **Honors programs:** www.uc.edu/honors. **Disability Services:** Special programs offered to physically disabled students include note-taking services, reader services, tape recorders, tutors. **Career services:** Alumni network, alumni services, career/job search classes, career assessment, internships, regional alumni. Career services highlights include Cooperative Learning: UC Professional Practice Program has over 100 years of service.

FACILITIES

Housing: Coed dorms, men's dorms, women's dorms, fraternity/sorority housing, apartments for married students, apartments for single students. **Special Academic Facilities/Equipment:** Art museum, language lab, observatory. **Computers:** 50% of classrooms, 75% of libraries, 75% of dining areas, 55% of student union, 75% of common outdoor areas have wireless network access. Students can register for classes online. Administrative functions (other than registration) can be performed online.

CAMPUS LIFE

Environment: Metropolis. **Activities:** Choral groups, concert band, dance, drama/theater, jazz band, marching band, music ensembles, musical theater, opera, pep band, radio station, student government, student newspaper, student-run film society, symphony orchestra, yearbook. 250 registered organizations, 16 honor societies, 23 religious organizations. 23 fraternities, 10 sororities. **Athletics (Intercollegiate):** *Men:* baseball, basketball, cheerleading, cross-country, diving, football, golf, soccer, swimming, track/field (outdoor). *Women:* basketball, cheerleading, cross-country, diving, golf, lacrosse, soccer, swimming, tennis, track/field (outdoor), track/field (indoor), volleyball. **Environmental Initiatives:** UC has commited to a policy that all new construction and major renovations on campus will be built to LEED standards, striving for at least Silver certification levels. UC has invested significant resources in energy efficiency projects, including a thermal storage project for chilled water and lighting upgrades throughout campus. These projects have been recognized several times, earning UC the EPA's Combined Heat and Power Award and Duke Energy's Power Partner of the Year Award among others. UC's commitment to the environment includes waste reduction and diversion initiatives. Since 2005, total waste generated on campus has been reduced by nearly 40%, while at the same time campus population and size has increased.

ADMISSIONS

Freshman Academic Profile: Average high school GPA 3.46. 20% in top 10% of high school class, 48% in top 25% of high school class, 83% in top 50% of high school class. SAT Math middle 50% range 530-660. SAT Critical Reading middle 50% range 510-630. SAT Writing middle 50% range 490-610. ACT middle 50% range 23-28. Minimum internet-based TOEFL 66. Minimum paper TOEFL 517. **Basis for Candidate Selection:** *Very important factors considered include:* Class rank, academic GPA, rigor of secondary school record, standardized test scores. *Other factors considered include:* application essay, extracurricular activities. **Freshman Admission Requirements:** High school diploma is required and GED is accepted. **Academic units required:** 4 English, 3 mathematics, 2 science, 2 foreign language, 2 social studies, 2 academic electives. **Freshman Admission Statistics:** 16,593 applied, 76% admitted, 36% enrolled. **General Admission Information:** Application Fee $40. Regular application deadline 9/1. Nonfall registration accepted. Admission may be deferred for a maximum of one year. Credit and/or placement offered for CEEB Advanced Placement tests.

COSTS AND FINANCIAL AID

Annual in-state tuition $9,322. Annual out-of-state tuition $24,656. Room and board $10,496. Required fees $1,678. Average book expense $1,480. **Required Forms and Deadlines:** FAFSA. **Notification of Awards:** Applicants will be notified of awards on a rolling basis beginning 3/10. **Types of Aid:** *Need-based scholarships/grants:* Federal Pell, SEOG, state scholarships/grants, private scholarships, the school's own gift aid, United Negro College Fund, Federal Nursing Scholarships, ACG, SMART, TEACH. *Loans:* Subsidized Stafford, Unsubsidized Stafford, PLUS, Federal Perkins, Federal Nursing, state loans, college/university loans from institutional funds. *Student Employment:* Federal Work-Study Program available. Institutional employment available. Off-campus job opportunities are excellent. **Financial Aid Statistics:** 38% freshmen, 43% undergrads receive need-based scholarship or grant aid. 51% freshmen, 36% undergrads receive non-need-based scholarship or grant aid. 70% freshmen, 75% undergrads receive need-based self-help aid. 1% freshmen, 1% undergrads receive athletic scholarships. 83% freshmen, 78% undergrads receive any aid. 66% undergrads borrow to pay for school. Average cumulative indebtedness $25,395. **Criteria for awarding institutional aid:** *Non-need-based:* academics, alumni affiliation, art, athletics, leadership, minority status, music/drama, state/district residency.

UNIVERSITY OF COLORADO AT COLORADO SPRINGS

1420 Austin Bluffs Parkway, Colorado Springs, CO 80918
Phone: 719-255-3084 · **Financial Aid Phone:** 719-262-3460
E-mail: go@uccs.edu · **CEEB Code:** 4874
Website: www.uccs.edu · **ACT Code:** 535

This public school was founded in 1965. It has a 504-acre campus.

RATINGS

Admissions Selectivity Rating: 75   Fire Safety Rating: 60*

STUDENTS AND FACULTY

Enrollment: 8,868. **Student Body:** 53% female, 47% male, 11% out-of-state, 1% international (35 countries represented). Asian 3%, African American 4%, Caucasian 69%, Hispanic 14%, Native American 1%
Retention and Graduation: 71% freshmen return for sophomore year. 26% freshmen graduate within 4 years. **Faculty:** 371 full-time faculty, 73% hold PhDs, 51% are are members of minority groups, 14% are women.

ACADEMICS

Degrees: bachelor's, certificate, master's, post-bachelor's certificate, post-master's certificate. **Classes:** Most classes have 10-19 students. Most lab/discussion sessions have 20-29 students. **Special Study Options:** Accelerated program, cooperative education program, cross-registration, distance learning, double major, dual enrollment, English as a Second Language (ESL), exchange student program (domestic), independent study, internships, liberal arts/career combination, student-designed major, study abroad, teacher certification program. **Disability Services:** Special programs offered to physically disabled students include note-taking services, reader services, tape recorders, tutors.

FACILITIES

Housing: Coed dorms, special housing for disabled students, men's dorms, women's dorms, apartments for single students. 100% of campus accessible to physically disabled. **Special Academic Facilities/Equipment:** Gallery of contemporary art. **Computers:** Students can register for classes online.

CAMPUS LIFE

Environment: Metropolis. **Activities:** Choral groups, dance, drama/theater, jazz band, literary magazine, music ensembles, musical theater, radio station, student government, student newspaper, student-run film society. 55 registered organizations, 7 religious organizations. 1 sorority. **Athletics (Intercollegiate):** *Men:* basketball, cross-country, golf, soccer, tennis, track/field (outdoor). *Women:* basketball, cross-country, softball, tennis, track/field (outdoor), volleyball. **On-Campus Highlights:** El Pomar Center (Kramer family Library), University Center, The Lodge, Gallery of Contemporary Art.

ADMISSIONS

Freshman Academic Profile: Average high school GPA 3.31. 13% in top 10% of high school class, 36% in top 25% of high school class, 70% in top 50% of high school class. SAT Math middle 50% range 472-600. SAT Critical Reading middle 50% range 470-590. SAT Writing middle 50% range 450-560. ACT middle 50% range 21-25. Minimum paper TOEFL 550. **Basis for Candidate Selection:** *Very important factors considered include:* Class rank, academic GPA, rigor of secondary school record, standardized test scores. *Important factors considered include:* recommendation(s), level of applicant's interest. *Other factors considered include:* application essay, alumni/ae relation, character/personal qualities, extracurricular activities, geographical residence, state residency, talent/ability, volunteer work. **Freshman Admission Requirements:** High school diploma is required and GED is accepted. **Academic units required:** 4 English, 3 mathematics, 3 science, (2 science labs), 2 foreign language, 2 social studies, 0 history, 1 academic elective. **Freshman Admission Statistics:** 7,352 applied, 89% admitted, 25% enrolled. **Transfer Admission Requirements:** High school transcript, college transcript(s), Minimum college GPA of 2.0 required. Lowest grade transferable C. **General Admission Information:** Application Fee $50. Regular application deadline 7/1. Notification on a rolling basis, beginning on or about 10/1. Nonfall registration accepted. Admission may be deferred for a maximum of 12 months. Neither credit nor placement offered for CEEB Advanced Placement tests.

COSTS AND FINANCIAL AID

Average book expense $1,800. **Required Forms and Deadlines:** FAFSA. **Notification of Awards:** Applicants will be notified of awards on a rolling basis beginning 4/15. **Types of Aid:** *Need-based scholarships/grants:* Federal Pell, SEOG, state scholarships/grants, private scholarships, the school's own gift aid, Federal Nursing Scholarships. *Loans:* Subsidized Stafford, Unsubsidized Stafford, PLUS, Federal Perkins, college/university loans from institutional funds. **Financial Aid Statistics:** 58% freshmen, 65% undergrads receive need-based scholarship or grant aid. 35% freshmen, 23% undergrads receive non-need-based scholarship or grant aid. 70% freshmen, 78% undergrads receive need-based self-help aid. 2% freshmen, 2% undergrads receive athletic scholarships. 41% undergrads borrow to pay for school. **Criteria for awarding institutional aid:** *Non-need-based:* academics, athletics, leadership, state/district residency.

UNIVERSITY OF COLORADO AT DENVER

P.O. Box 173364, Denver, CO 80217
Phone: 303-556-2704 · **Financial Aid Phone:** 303-556-2886
E-mail: admissions@cudenver.edu · **CEEB Code:** 4875
Fax: 303-556-4838 · **Website:** www.cudenver.edu · **ACT Code:** 533

This public school was founded in 1912. It has a 127-acre campus.

RATINGS

Admissions Selectivity Rating: 82   Fire Safety Rating: 60*

STUDENTS AND FACULTY

Enrollment: 8,327. **Student Body:** 55% female, 45% male, 4% out-of-state, 1% international (57 countries represented). Asian 10%, African American 5%, Caucasian 63%, Hispanic 12%, Native American 1%
Retention and Graduation: 71% freshmen return for sophomore year. 7% grads go on to further study within 1 year. 19% grads pursue arts and sciences degrees. 8% grads pursue business degrees. **Faculty:** 2,186 full-time faculty, 81% hold PhDs, 47% are are members of minority groups, 11% are women.

ACADEMICS

Degrees: bachelor's, first professional, master's, post-master's certificate. **Classes:** Most classes have 20-29 students. Most lab/discussion sessions have 20-29 students. **Majors with Highest Enrollment:** Biology/Biological Sciences; Psychology; Business/Commerce. **Special Study Options:** Accelerated program, cooperative education program, cross-registration, distance learning, double major, English as a Second Language (ESL), honors program, independent study, internships, student-designed major, study abroad, teacher certification program, weekend college. **Combined degree programs:** BS/MBA. **Disability Services:** Special programs offered to physically disabled students include note-taking services, reader services, tape recorders, tutors. **Career services:** alumni services, career assessment, internships.

FACILITIES

Housing: Coed dorms. 100% of campus accessible to physically disabled. **Special Academic Facilities/Equipment:** Emmanual Gallery. **Computers:** Students can register for classes online. Administrative functions (other than registration) can be performed online.

CAMPUS LIFE

Environment: Metropolis. **Activities:** Choral groups, dance, drama/theater, jazz band, music ensembles, musical theater, student government, student newspaper. 77 registered organizations, 5 honor societies, 4 religious organizations. **On-Campus Highlights:** PE/Events Center and Emmanuel Gallery, The Auraria Library, Tivoli Student Union, St. Elizabeth's Church, King Academic and Performing Arts Center.

ADMISSIONS

Freshman Academic Profile: Average high school GPA 3.3. 17% in top 10% of high school class, 43% in top 25% of high school class, 78% in top 50% of high school class. SAT Math middle 50% range 490-590. SAT Critical Reading middle 50% range 490-600. ACT middle 50% range 19-25. Minimum internet-based TOEFL 71. Minimum paper TOEFL 525. **Basis for Candidate Selection:** *Very important factors considered include:* Class rank, academic GPA, rigor of secondary school record, standardized test scores. *Important factors considered include:* application essay, recommendation(s), level of applicant's interest. *Other factors considered include:* character/personal qualities, extracurricular activities, talent/ability. **Freshman Admission Requirements:** High school diploma is required and GED is accepted. **Academic units required:** 4 English, 3 mathematics, 3 science, 2 foreign language, 2 social studies, 1 academic elective. **Freshman Admission Statistics:** 3,521 applied, 68% admitted, 45% enrolled. **Transfer Admission Requirements:** college transcript(s), statement of good standing from prior institution(s). Minimum college GPA of 2.4 required. Lowest grade transferable C-. **General Admission Information:** Application Fee $50. Nonfall registration accepted. Admission may be deferred for a maximum of 12 months. Credit and/or placement offered for CEEB Advanced Placement tests.

COSTS AND FINANCIAL AID

Annual in-state tuition $5,054. Annual out-of-state tuition $17,010. Room and board $9,990. Required fees $878. Average book expense $1,700. **Required Forms and Deadlines:** FAFSA, Institution's own financial aid form. **Notification of Awards:** Applicants will be notified of awards on a rolling basis beginning 5/1. **Types of Aid:** *Need-based scholarships/grants:* Federal Pell, SEOG, state scholarships/grants, private scholarships, the school's own gift aid, Federal Nursing Scholarships. *Loans:* Direct Subsidized Stafford, Direct Unsubsidized Stafford, Direct PLUS, Subsidized Stafford, Unsubsidized Stafford, PLUS, Federal Perkins, Federal Nursing. *Student Employment:* Federal Work-Study Program available. Off-campus job opportunities are good. **Financial Aid Statistics:** 97% freshmen, 86% undergrads receive need-based scholarship or grant aid. 12% freshmen, 5% undergrads receive non-need-based scholarship or grant aid. 72% freshmen, 85% undergrads receive need-based self-help aid. 0% freshmen, 0% undergrads receive athletic scholarships. 44% undergrads borrow to pay for school. Average cumulative indebtedness $15,775. **Criteria for awarding institutional aid:** *Non-need-based:* academics, art, leadership, music/drama.

UNIVERSITY OF COLORADO AT DENVER AND HEALTH SCIENCES CENTER— HEALTH SCIENCES PROGRAM

4200 E. 9th Ave, Denver, CO 80262
Phone: 303-315-7676 · **Financial Aid Phone:** 303-315-8364
E-mail: student.services@uchsc.edu
Fax: 303-315-3358 · **Website:** www.uchsc.edu

This public school was founded in 1883.

RATINGS

Admissions Selectivity Rating: 60*   **Fire Safety Rating:** 60*

STUDENTS AND FACULTY

Enrollment: 359. **Student Body:** 90% female, 10% male, 1% international. Asian 5%, African American 2%, Caucasian 79%, Hispanic 6%, Native American 1%
Faculty: 1,342 full-time faculty, 97% hold PhDs.

ACADEMICS

Degrees: bachelor's, first professional, master's, post-master's certificate. **Special Study Options:** cross-registration, distance learning, independent study, internships.

FACILITIES

Housing: 90% of campus accessible to physically disabled. **Computers:** Students can register for classes online. Administrative functions (other than registration) can be performed online.

CAMPUS LIFE

Environment: Metropolis. **Activities:** dance, drama/theater, musical theater, student government, student newspaper, yearbook.

ADMISSIONS

Freshman Academic Profile: Minimum paper TOEFL 550. **Transfer Admission Requirements:** college transcript(s), essay or personal statement, Minimum college GPA of 2.0 required. Lowest grade transferable C. **General Admission Information:** Nonfall registration not accepted.

COSTS AND FINANCIAL AID

Types of Aid: *Need-based scholarships/grants:* Federal Pell, SEOG, state scholarships/grants, private scholarships, the school's own gift aid. *Loans:* Direct Subsidized Stafford, Direct Unsubsidized Stafford, Direct PLUS, Federal Perkins, Federal Nursing, college/university loans from institutional funds. **Financial Aid Statistics:** 26% undergrads receive need-based scholarship or grant aid. 16% undergrads receive non-need-based scholarship or grant aid. 96% undergrads receive need-based self-help aid. 0% undergrads receive athletic scholarships. 93% undergrads borrow to pay for school.

UNIVERSITY OF COLORADO BOULDER

Best 380

552 UCB, Boulder, CO 80309-0552
Phone: 303-492-6301 · **Financial Aid Phone:** 303-492-5091 · **CEEB Code:** 4841
Fax: 303-735-2501 · **Website:** www.colorado.edu/ · **ACT Code:** 532

This public school was founded in 1876. It has a 600-acre campus.

RATINGS

Admissions Selectivity Rating: 85   **Fire Safety Rating:** 90

STUDENTS AND FACULTY

Enrollment: 25,859. **Student Body:** 44% female, 56% male, 38% out-of-state, 5% international (107 countries represented). Asian 5%, African American 2%, Caucasian 72%, Hispanic 10%, Native American <1%
Retention and Graduation: 84% freshmen return for sophomore year. 46% freshmen graduate within 4 years. 70% freshmen graduate within 6 years. 20% grads go on to further study within 1 year. 5% grads pursue arts and sciences degrees. 2% grads pursue law degrees. 2% grads pursue business degrees. 1% grads pursue medical degrees. **Faculty:** 1,417 full-time faculty, 91% hold PhDs, 37% are are members of minority groups, 18% are women. 12% of classes are taught by teaching assistants.

ACADEMICS

Degrees: bachelor's, master's, post-master's certificate. **Classes:** Most classes have 10-19 students. Most lab/discussion sessions have 20-29 students. **Majors with Highest Enrollment:** Physiology; Psychology; Speech Communication and Rhetoric. **Special Study Options:** Accelerated program, cooperative education program, cross-registration, distance learning, double major, dual enrollment, English as a Second Language (ESL), exchange student program (domestic), honors program, independent study, internships, liberal arts/career combination, student-designed major, study abroad, teacher certification program, °Research and combined BA/MA include Undergraduate Research Opportunities and Concurrent Bachelor's/Master's Programs. °°Small Group Academic Programs include Residence Hall Academic Programs, FallFEST, and Presidents Leadership Class. **Honors programs:** The CU Honors Program provides special educational opportunities for academically prepared, highly motivated undergraduate students. The Honors Program offers a wide-ranging curriculum supported by thoughtful advising and close contact with faculty. The program aspires to provide the best education possible for the leaders of the future. The Honors Residential Academic Program (HRAP) is a residential academic program within the general Honors Program. Qualified first-year students who are invited to participate in the Honors Program may elect to live in an honors part of the Kittredge residence hall complex. In this living and learning environment, students experience all of the advantages of a small liberal arts college while also enjoying the diverse resources of a major university. We offer incoming students the opportunity to associate with other bright, highly motivated students and to become part of a special community of peers and faculty. The Norlin Scholars Program is a community of students with a broad, synthetic view of education that embraces active learning, creativity, and interdisciplinary scholarship. Norlin Scholars participate in small, specialized courses and other small-group experiences emphasizing critical thinking, collaboration, and written and oral communications skills. They also engage in research or creative work with faculty mentors. The Presidents Leadership

Class (PLC) offers a unique opportunity to those students who want to make a difference for themselves and their community. The core of PLC is an academic program focusing on leadership, service, ethics, American communities, and global challenges. PLC scholars receive a four-year scholarship. **Combined degree programs:** BA/MA, BS/MS. **Disability Services:** Special programs offered to physically disabled students include note-taking services, reader services, tape recorders, tutors. **Career services:** Alumni network, alumni services, career/job search classes, career assessment, internships, regional alumni. Career services highlights include International and National Voluntary Service Training (INVST) Based on service learning principles, INVST is a two-year leadership-training program in community service. It offers a unique educational experience to all majors in the College of Arts and Sciences. Aspects of the program include small innovative classes, a community-building experience in the mountains, two summer programs of service in the US and abroad, and supervised community service positions during the fall and spring semesters. Issues of global development, nonviolent social change, interpersonal conflict and conflict resolution, community development, and solving community problems are all addressed, with focus on poverty, racism, and other manifestations of social inequality and injustice.

FACILITIES

Housing: Coed dorms, special housing for disabled students, fraternity/sorority housing, apartments for married students, apartments for single students, Wellness Housing, Theme Housing, Residential academic programs within specific dorms. 80% of campus accessible to physically disabled. **Special Academic Facilities/Equipment:** Art galleries, natural history museum, heritage center, observatory, planetarium and science center, electron microscopes, outdoor theater, video interactive foreign language laboratory, mountain research station, centrifuge, hands-on teaching and learning laboratory for engineering, multipurpose cultural/athletics/educational events and conference center, a premier concert hall, and an innovative multi-disciplinary Information Technology center. **Computers:** 100% of classrooms, 65% of dorms, 100% of libraries, 100% of dining areas, 100% of student union, 50% of common outdoor areas have wireless network access. Students can register for classes online. Administrative functions (other than registration) can be performed online.

CAMPUS LIFE

Environment: City. **Activities:** Choral groups, concert band, dance, drama/theater, jazz band, literary magazine, marching band, music ensembles, musical theater, opera, pep band, radio station, student government, student newspaper, student-run film society, symphony orchestra, television station, Campus Ministries, International Student Organization, Model UN. 300 registered organizations, 26 honor societies, 35 religious organizations. 20 fraternities, 19 sororities. **Athletics (Intercollegiate):** *Men:* basketball, cross-country, football, golf, skiing (downhill/alpine), skiing (nordic/cross-country), track/field (outdoor), track/field (indoor). *Women:* basketball, cross-country, golf, skiing (downhill/alpine), skiing (nordic/cross-country), soccer, tennis, track/field (outdoor), track/field (indoor), volleyball. **On-Campus Highlights:** University Memorial Center (UMC), Student Recreation Center, Norlin Library, ATLAS Building, Farrand Field, CU-Boulder's Outdoor Program, at the Recreation Center, offers many opportunities to explore the wonderful backcountry regions of Colorado and other unique locations. The program provides recreational experiences emphasizing adventure, skill acquisition, environmental awareness, safety, challenge, a sense of community, and fun. **Environmental Initiatives:** Education and Research: Campus commitment to environmental education and research has helped CU-Boulder become one of the nations top environmental research universities. CU-Boulders reputation and performance as a national leader in environmental issues and sustainability helps recruit and retain faculty with the recognized expertise to win leading-edge research awards, to contribute to the global sustainability knowledge base, and to enhance an already respected environmental studies department—one with integrated environmental content across the campus. Environmental Studies is an interdisciplinary program that draws from curricula in the earth and natural sciences as well as the social sciences. Undergraduate students have the opportunity to participate in three residential academic programs (RAPs) that emphasize environmental studies and sustainability. All offer smaller courses in the residences halls. The Baker RAP consists of a cohort of students with interest in the environment and in future careers in working on environmental problems, such as sustainable use of our resources. The Sustainable by Design RAP includes students with an interest in resource-efficient design, renewable energy, and environmental and social impacts of community development. The Social Entrepreneurship for Equitable Development & Sustainability RAP guides students in developing innovative, self-sustaining solutions for addressing critical social and environmental issues around the globe. Student Engagement: CU-Boulder students have a decades-long legacy of leadership in environmental action. On Earth Day 1970, students founded the Environmental Center, now the nations oldest, largest, and most accomplished student-led center of its kind. In 1974, CU-Boulder students founded the nations first campus recycling program; in 1991, students voted to raise student fees to purchase pre-paid bus passes for all students; in 2000, students on our campus became the nations first to raise student fees to buy wind energy credits for student buildings; and in 2007, the student government became the nations first to sign the ACUPCC commitment for student buildings. Campus Greening: An aggressive campus operational greening campaign has produced consistently reduced energy and potable water consumption trends since 2001 in spite of ongoing growth in student population and in research funding that leads to increased lab activity. Overall, electricity usage has fallen from 14.6 KWh/SqFt to 12.19 KWh/SqFt. Steam use decreased from 75.19 lbs/SqFt to 51.95 lbs/SqFt. Potable water consumption has declined from 61.69 Gal/SqFt to 25.09 Gal/SqFt for over 10.8 million square feet of campus buildings. These reductions are direct results of a large number of energy conservation projects such as: HVAC recommissioning, weather-stripping, IR scanning of buildings to add insulation, lighting and lighting controls upgrade, energy audits of campus buildings, computer/desktop energy management, building scheduling improvements, water conservation in research labs, ditch water for irrigation, etc. Also, the campus has engaged in numerous educational and behavioral initiatives including Buff Energy Star competition, campus pledge card, stickers/posters, and ongoing outreach/public events.

ADMISSIONS

Freshman Academic Profile: Average high school GPA 3.58. 27% in top 10% of high school class, 54% in top 25% of high school class, 87% in top 50% of high school class. 90% from public high schools. SAT Math middle 50% range 540-660. SAT Critical Reading middle 50% range 520-630. ACT middle 50% range 24-30. Minimum internet-based TOEFL 75. Minimum paper TOEFL 537. **Basis for Candidate Selection:** *Very important factors considered include:* Class rank, application essay, academic GPA, recommendation(s), rigor of secondary school record. *Important factors considered include:* standardized test scores, character/personal qualities, first generation, state residency. *Other factors considered include:* alumni/ae relation, extracurricular activities, geographical residence, level of applicant's interest, talent/ability, volunteer work, work experience. **Freshman Admission Requirements:** High school diploma is required and GED is accepted. **Academic units required:** 4 English, 4 mathematics, 3 science, (2 science labs), 3 foreign language, 3 social studies, 1 history, 1 geography. **Freshman Admission Statistics:** 28,768 applied, 84% admitted, 24% enrolled. **Transfer Admission Requirements:** High school transcript, college transcript(s), essay or personal statement, Lowest grade transferable C-. **General Admission Information:** Application Fee $50. Regular application deadline 1/15. Regular notification 4/1. Nonfall registration accepted. Admission may be deferred for a maximum of 12 months. Credit and/or placement offered for CEEB Advanced Placement tests.

COSTS AND FINANCIAL AID

Annual out-of-state tuition $31,410. Room and board $12,810. Required fees $1,741. Average book expense $1,800. **Required Forms and Deadlines:** FAFSA. **Notification of Awards:** Applicants will be notified of awards on a rolling basis beginning 3/1. **Types of Aid:** *Need-based scholarships/grants:* Federal Pell, SEOG, state scholarships/grants, private scholarships, the school's own gift aid. *Loans:* Direct Subsidized Stafford, Direct Unsubsidized Stafford, Direct PLUS, Federal Perkins, college/university loans from institutional funds, Private lenders. *Student Employment:* Federal Work-Study Program available. Institutional employment available. Highest amount earned per year from on-campus jobs $12,050. Off-campus job opportunities are excellent. **Financial Aid Statistics:** 76% freshmen, 75% undergrads receive need-based scholarship or grant aid. 4% freshmen, 3% undergrads receive non-need-based scholarship or grant aid. 0% freshmen, 86% undergrads receive need-based self-help aid. 1% freshmen, 1% undergrads receive athletic scholarships. 71% freshmen, 58% undergrads receive any aid. 46% undergrads borrow to pay for school. Average cumulative indebtedness $19,500. **Criteria for awarding institutional aid:** *Non-need-based:* academics, alumni affiliation, art, athletics, leadership, music/drama, state/district residency.

UNIVERSITY OF CONNECTICUT

2131 Hillside Road, Storrs, CT 06268-3088
Phone: 860-486-3137 · **Financial Aid Phone:** 860-486-2819
E-mail: beahusky@uconn.edu · **CEEB Code:** 3915
Fax: 860-486-1476 · **Website:** www.uconn.edu · **ACT Code:** 604

This public school was founded in 1881. It has a 4104-acre campus.

RATINGS

Admissions Selectivity Rating: 90   Fire Safety Rating: 85

STUDENTS AND FACULTY

Enrollment: 18,016. **Student Body:** 50% female, 50% male, 22% out-of-state, 4% international (113 countries represented). Asian 10%, African American 5%, Caucasian 62%, Hispanic 8%, Native American <1%

Retention and Graduation: 93% freshmen return for sophomore year. 19% freshmen graduate within 4 years. 32% grads go on to further study within 1 year. 19% grads pursue arts and sciences degrees. 2% grads pursue law degrees. 3% grads pursue business degrees. 1% grads pursue medical degrees. **Faculty:** 20% of classes are taught by teaching assistants.

ACADEMICS

Degrees: associate, bachelor's, doctoral, master's, post-bachelor's certificate, post-master's certificate, terminal associate, transfer associate. **Classes:** Most classes have 10-19 students. Most lab/discussion sessions have 10-19 students. **Majors with Highest Enrollment:** Psychology; Biology/Biological Sciences; Economics. **Special Study Options:** Accelerated program, cooperative education program, distance learning, double major, dual enrollment, English as a Second Language (ESL), exchange student program (domestic), honors program, independent study, internships, liberal arts/career combination, student-designed major, study abroad, teacher certification program, Winter inter-session, summer session, and urban semester. **Honors programs:** Honors Scholar Program for all Undergraduates. **Combined degree programs:** BA/MD, BA/MA, BA/DDS, Pharm.D. **Disability Services:** Special programs offered to physically disabled students include note-taking services, reader services, tape recorders, tutors.

FACILITIES

Housing: Coed dorms, special housing for disabled students, men's dorms, special housing for international students, women's dorms, fraternity/sorority housing, apartments for married students, apartments for single students, Wellness Housing, Theme Housing: Special Interests, Honors, Foreign Languages, Older-Student Housing, Freshman Year Experience Housing, "Global House," Women in Math, Science, and Engineering, Other learning communities. 90% of campus accessible to physically disabled. **Special Academic Facilities/Equipment:** Art and natural history museums, child development labs, national undersea research center, arboretum, institute for social inquiry, institute of materials science, electron microscope labs. **Computers:** 90% of libraries, 5% of dining areas, 25% of student union, have wireless network access. Students can register for classes online. Administrative functions (other than registration) can be performed online.

CAMPUS LIFE

Environment: Town. **Activities:** Choral groups, concert band, dance, drama/theater, jazz band, literary magazine, marching band, music ensembles, musical theater, opera, pep band, radio station, student government, student newspaper, student-run film society, symphony orchestra, television station, yearbook, Campus Ministries, International Student Organization, Model UN. 303 registered organizations, 29 honor societies, 17 religious organizations. 14 fraternities, 12 sororities. **Athletics (Intercollegiate):** *Men:* baseball, basketball, cross-country, diving, football, golf, ice hockey, soccer, swimming, tennis, track/field (outdoor), track/field (indoor). *Women:* basketball, crew/rowing, cross-country, diving, field hockey, ice hockey, lacrosse, soccer, softball, swimming, tennis, track/field (outdoor), track/field (indoor), volleyball. **On-Campus Highlights:** William Benton Museum of Art, Dairy Product Salesroom, Puppetry Museum, Green Houses, Jorgensen Auditorium and Connecticut Repertory Theater. **Environmental Initiatives:** Signed ACUPCC and began developing Climate Action Plan and, in 2010, began implementing several of its more than 200 strategies related to energy, transportation, sustainable development and environmental literacy. Adopted Sustainable Design & Construction Policy (March 2007) setting LEED Silver rating as minimum performance standard for all new construction and major renovation projects especially significant because UConn has 8 years and $1 billion remaining on a 20-year, $2.3 billion, state bond-funded capital improvement program. Developed Academic Plan for 2008-2013 which includes the environment as one of three areas of excellence has already resulted in corresponding investment in academic programs and research infrastructure focused on environmental sustainability, e.g., start-up of EcoHouse (Environmental Living and Learning Community) in Fall 2009, which now houses 130 students; creation of Spring Valley Farm, a year-long student experiential learning residence located on UConn farm property and devoted to organic agriculture and sustainable living; hiring of numerous faculty with expertise in sustainable energy, climate and atmosphere, and consideration of ways to improve environmental literacy at UConn, such as new environmental majors, courses, and certification programs.

ADMISSIONS

Freshman Academic Profile: 50% in top 10% of high school class, 85% in top 25% of high school class, 98% in top 50% of high school class. 88% from public high schools. SAT Math middle 50% range 590-690. SAT Critical Reading middle 50% range 560-660. SAT Writing middle 50% range 550-660. ACT middle 50% range 26-30. Minimum internet-based TOEFL 79. Minimum paper TOEFL 550. **Basis for Candidate Selection:** *Very important factors considered include:* Class rank, academic GPA, rigor of secondary school record, standardized test scores. *Important factors considered include:* application essay, recommendation(s), character/personal qualities, extracurricular activities, first generation, racial/ethnic status, talent/ability, volunteer work. *Other factors considered include:* alumni/ae relation, geographical residence, level of

applicant's interest, state residency, work experience. **Freshman Admission Requirements:** High school diploma is required and GED is accepted. **Academic units required:** 4 English, 3 mathematics, 2 science, (2 science labs), 2 foreign language, 2 social studies, 3 academic electives. **Freshman Admission Statistics:** 31,280 applied, 50% admitted, 23% enrolled. **Transfer Admission Requirements:** High school transcript, college transcript(s), essay or personal statement, Minimum college GPA of 2.7 required. Lowest grade transferable C. **General Admission Information:** Application Fee $70. Regular application deadline 2/1. Notification on a rolling basis, beginning on or about 1/1. Nonfall registration accepted. Admission may be deferred for a maximum of 1 year. Credit and/or placement offered for CEEB Advanced Placement tests.

COSTS AND FINANCIAL AID

Annual in-state tuition $9,858. Annual out-of-state tuition $30,038. Room and board $12,074. Required fees $2,842. Average book expense $850. **Required Forms and Deadlines:** FAFSA. **Notification of Awards:** Applicants will be notified of awards on a rolling basis beginning 3/1. **Types of Aid:** *Need-based scholarships/grants:* Federal Pell, SEOG, state scholarships/grants, private scholarships, the school's own gift aid. *Loans:* Subsidized Stafford, Unsubsidized Stafford, PLUS, Federal Perkins. *Student Employment:* Federal Work-Study Program available. Institutional employment available. Highest amount earned per year from on-campus jobs $3,500. Off-campus job opportunities are good. **Financial Aid Statistics:** 66% freshmen, 72% undergrads receive need-based scholarship or grant aid. 48% freshmen, 34% undergrads receive non-need-based scholarship or grant aid. 68% freshmen, 72% undergrads receive need-based self-help aid. 3% freshmen, 2% undergrads receive athletic scholarships. 49% freshmen, 48% undergrads receive any aid. 62% undergrads borrow to pay for school. Average cumulative indebtedness $21,207. **Criteria for awarding institutional aid:** *Non-need-based:* academics, art, athletics, leadership, minority status, music/drama.

UNIVERSITY OF THE CUMBERLANDS

6178 College Station Drive, Williamsburg, KY 40769
Phone: 606-539-4241 · **Financial Aid Phone:** 606-539-4220
E-mail: admiss@ucumberlands.edu · **CEEB Code:** 1145
Fax: 606-539-4303 · **ACT Code:** 1510

This private school was founded in 1888. It has a 50-acre campus.

RATINGS

Admissions Selectivity Rating: 78   **Fire Safety Rating:** 91

STUDENTS AND FACULTY

Enrollment: 1,389. **Student Body:** 53% female, 47% male, 38% out-of-state, 2% international (22 countries represented). Asian 1%, African American 5%, Caucasian 65%, Hispanic 1%, Native American <1%
Retention and Graduation: 62% freshmen return for sophomore year. 22% freshmen graduate within 4 years. 42% freshmen graduate within 6 years. 7% grads go on to further study within 1 year. 3% grads pursue arts and sciences degrees. 1% grads pursue law degrees. 2% grads pursue business degrees. 3% grads pursue medical degrees. **Faculty:** 85 full-time faculty, 74% hold PhDs, 36% are are members of minority groups, 6% are women. 0% of classes are taught by teaching assistants.

ACADEMICS

Degrees: bachelor's, master's. **Classes:** Most classes have 10-19 students. Most lab/discussion sessions have fewer than 10 students. **Majors with Highest Enrollment:** Elementary Education and Teaching; Biology/Biological Sciences; Business/Commerce. **Special Study Options:** Accelerated program, cooperative education program, distance learning, double major, dual enrollment, English as a Second Language (ESL), honors program, independent study, internships, liberal arts/career combination, student-designed major, study abroad, teacher certification program. **Disability Services:** Special programs offered to physically disabled students include tutors. **Career services:** Alumni network, alumni services, career/job search classes, career assessment, internships, regional alumni. Career services highlights include Internships with Rollins Corporation.

FACILITIES

Housing: men's dorms, women's dorms. 55% of campus accessible to physically disabled. **Special Academic Facilities/Equipment:** Natural Science History, distance learning lab, and student art museums. **Computers:** Students can register for classes online. Administrative functions (other than registration) can be performed online.

CAMPUS LIFE

Environment: Rural. **Activities:** Choral groups, concert band, dance, drama/theater, jazz band, marching band, music ensembles, musical theater, pep band, radio station, student government, student newspaper, television station. 45 registered organizations, 11 honor societies, 18 religious organizations. **Athletics (Intercollegiate):** *Men:* baseball, basketball, cheerleading, cross-country, football, golf, soccer, swimming, tennis, track/field (outdoor), wrestling. *Women:* basketball, cheerleading, cross-country, golf, soccer, softball, swimming, tennis, track/field (outdoor), volleyball, wrestling. **On-Campus Highlights:** Cumberland Inn and Museum, Wayne Rollins Center, Rollins Fine Arts Center, Taylor Stadium, Boswell Campus Center.

ADMISSIONS

Freshman Academic Profile: Average high school GPA 3.4. 20% in top 10% of high school class, 44% in top 25% of high school class, 79% in top 50% of high school class. 90% from public high schools. SAT Math middle 50% range 410-570. SAT Critical Reading middle 50% range 410-560. ACT middle 50% range 19-24. Minimum paper TOEFL 550. **Basis for Candidate Selection:** *Very important factors considered include:* rigor of secondary school record. *Other factors considered include:* Class rank, application essay, academic GPA, recommendation(s), standardized test scores, character/personal qualities, extracurricular activities, first generation, interview, level of applicant's interest, talent/ability, volunteer work. **Freshman Admission Requirements:** High school diploma is required and GED is accepted. **Academic units required:** 4 English, 3 mathematics, 2 science, 1 social studies. **Freshman Admission Statistics:** 849 applied, 83% admitted, 50% enrolled. **Transfer Admission Requirements:** college transcript(s), essay or personal statement, statement of good standing from prior institution(s). Minimum college GPA of 2.0 required. Lowest grade transferable C. **General Admission Information:** Application Fee $30. Regular notification 8/15. Notification on a rolling basis, beginning on or about 9/1. Nonfall registration accepted. Admission may be deferred for a maximum of 1 semester. Credit offered for CEEB Advanced Placement tests.

COSTS AND FINANCIAL AID

Annual tuition $13,298. Room and board $6,626. Required fees $360. Average book expense $1,000. **Required Forms and Deadlines:** FAFSA. **Notification of Awards:** Applicants will be notified of awards on a rolling basis beginning 2/1. **Types of Aid:** *Need-based scholarships/grants:* Federal Pell, SEOG, state scholarships/grants, private scholarships, the school's own gift aid. *Loans:* Subsidized Stafford, Unsubsidized Stafford, PLUS, Federal Perkins, college/university loans from institutional funds. *Student Employment:* Federal Work-Study Program available. Institutional employment available. Highest amount earned per year from on-campus jobs $2,400. Off-campus job opportunities are fair. **Financial Aid Statistics:** 100% freshmen, 100% undergrads receive need-based scholarship or grant aid. 100% freshmen, 100% undergrads receive non-need-based scholarship or grant aid. 77% freshmen, 69% undergrads receive need-based self-help aid. 4% freshmen, 3% undergrads receive athletic scholarships. 94% freshmen, 92% undergrads receive any aid. 72% undergrads borrow to pay for school. Average cumulative indebtedness $19,497. **Criteria for awarding institutional aid:** *Non-need-based:* academics, alumni affiliation, art, athletics, leadership, music/drama, religious affiliation, state/district residency.

See page 1172.

UNIVERSITY OF DALLAS

1845 East Northgate Drive, Irving, TX 75062
Phone: 972-721-5266 · **Financial Aid Phone:** 972-721-5266
E-mail: crusader@udallas.edu · **CEEB Code:** 6868
Fax: 972-721-5017 · **Website:** www.udallas.edu · **ACT Code:** 4234

This private school, affiliated with the Roman Catholic Church, was founded in 1956. It has a 450-acre campus.

RATINGS

Admissions Selectivity Rating: 83   **Fire Safety Rating:** 78

STUDENTS AND FACULTY

Enrollment: 1,325. **Student Body:** 55% female, 45% male, 55% out-of-state, 3% international (19 countries represented). Asian 4%, African American 2%, Caucasian 66%, Hispanic 19%, Native American <1% **Retention and Graduation:** 80% freshmen return for sophomore year. 63% freshmen graduate within 4 years. 70% freshmen graduate within 6 years. **Faculty:** 140 full-time faculty, 89% hold PhDs, 36% are are members of minority groups, 8% are women. 0% of classes are taught by teaching assistants.

ACADEMICS

Degrees: bachelor's, master's, post-bachelor's certificate, post-master's certificate. **Classes:** Most classes have 20-29 students. Most lab/discussion sessions have 10-19 students. **Majors with Highest Enrollment:** English Language and Literature; Biology/Biological Sciences; History. **Special Study Options:** double major, dual enrollment, independent study, internships, liberal arts/career combination, student-designed major, study abroad, teacher certification program. **Combined degree programs:** BA/MA, BA/MBA BA/M-Psy BA/MA Philosophy. **Disability Services:** Special programs offered to physically disabled students include note-taking services, reader services, tape recorders, tutors. **Career services:** Alumni network, alumni services, career/job search classes, career assessment, internships. Career services highlights include a recruiting program for graduating students.

FACILITIES

Housing: Coed dorms, men's dorms, women's dorms, apartments for single students 50% of campus accessible to physically disabled. **Special Academic Facilities/Equipment:** Art gallery, theater, language science, and computer labs, observatory. **Computers:** 50% of classrooms, 100% of dorms, 100% of libraries, 20% of dining areas, 100% of student union, 50% of common outdoor areas have wireless network access. Students can register for classes online. Administrative functions (other than registration) can be performed online.

CAMPUS LIFE

Environment: City. **Activities:** Choral groups, dance, drama/theater, literary magazine, music ensembles, musical theater, radio station, student government, student newspaper, student-run film society, yearbook, Campus Ministries, International Student Organization. 35 registered organizations, 4 honor societies, 5 religious organizations. **Athletics (Intercollegiate):** *Men:* baseball, basketball, cross-country, golf, lacrosse, soccer, track/field (outdoor). *Women:* basketball, cross-country, lacrosse, soccer, softball, track/field (outdoor), volleyball. **On-Campus Highlights:** Church of the Incarnation, Capp Bar, The Mall, The Rathskeller, Art Village. **Environmental Initiatives:** Student Government recycling committee and Environmental Alliance Club. SG provides recycling receptacles for cans and papers. Replacing all water faucets with reduction flow fixtures (low flow). Energy survey of all buildings to determine current efficiency and needed improvements. Upgraded HVAC systems in many buildings.

ADMISSIONS

Freshman Academic Profile: Average high school GPA 3.81. 50% from public high schools. SAT Math middle 50% range 530-640. SAT Critical Reading middle 50% range 550-680. SAT Writing middle 50% range 520-640. ACT middle 50% range 24-30. Minimum internet-based TOEFL 79. **Basis for Candidate Selection:** *Very important factors considered include:* application essay, academic GPA, recommendation(s), rigor of secondary school record, standardized test scores, character/personal qualities. *Important factors considered include:* Class rank, talent/ability. *Other factors considered include:* alumni/ae relation, extracurricular activities, first generation, interview, level of applicant's interest, volunteer work, work experience. **Freshman Admission Requirements:** High school diploma is required and GED is accepted. **Academic units required:** 4 English, 3 mathematics, 3 science, 2 foreign language, 3 social studies, 3 history, 2 visual/performing arts, 4 academic electives. **Freshman Admission Statistics:** 1,432 applied, 85% admitted, 28% enrolled. **Transfer Admission Requirements:** college transcript(s), essay or personal statement, statement of good standing from prior institution(s). Minimum college GPA of 2.5 required. Lowest grade transferable C-. **General Admission Information:** Application Fee $40. Regular application deadline 8/1. Notification on a rolling basis, beginning on or about 3/1. Nonfall registration accepted. Admission may be deferred for a maximum of 1 year. Credit and/or placement offered for CEEB Advanced Placement tests.

COSTS AND FINANCIAL AID

Annual tuition $33,360. Room and board $11,300. Required fees $2,440. Average book expense $1,200. **Required Forms and Deadlines:** FAFSA. **Notification of Awards:** Applicants will be notified of awards on a rolling basis beginning 3/30. **Types of Aid:** *Need-based scholarships/grants:* Federal Pell, SEOG, state scholarships/grants, the school's own gift aid. *Loans:* Subsidized Stafford, Unsubsidized Stafford, PLUS, state loans. *Student Employment:* Federal Work-Study Program available. Institutional employment available. Highest amount earned per year from on-campus jobs $1,500. Off-campus job opportunities are fair. **Financial Aid Statistics:** 100% freshmen, 99% undergrads receive need-based scholarship or grant aid. 20% freshmen, 17% undergrads receive non-need-based scholarship or grant aid. 71% freshmen, 74% undergrads receive need-based self-help aid. 0% freshmen, 0% undergrads receive athletic scholarships. 96% freshmen, 94% undergrads receive any aid. 61% undergrads borrow to pay for school. Average cumulative indebtedness $26,924. **Criteria for awarding institutional aid:** *Non-need-based:* academics, art, leadership, music/drama.

UNIVERSITY OF DAYTON

Best 380

300 College Park, Dayton, OH 45469-1310
Phone: 937-229-4411 · **Financial Aid Phone:** 800-427-5029
E-mail: admission@udayton.edu · **CEEB Code:** 1834
Fax: 937-229-4729 · **Website:** www.udayton.edu · **ACT Code:** 3342

This private school, affiliated with the Roman Catholic Church, was founded in 1850. It has a 259-acre campus.

RATINGS

Admissions Selectivity Rating: 88   **Fire Safety Rating:** 73

STUDENTS AND FACULTY

Enrollment: 7,793. **Student Body:** 48% female, 52% male, 43% out-of-state, 6% international (70 countries represented). Asian 1%, African American 3%, Caucasian 84%, Hispanic 2%, Native American <1%
Retention and Graduation: 88% freshmen return for sophomore year. 60% freshmen graduate within 4 years. 78% freshmen graduate within 6 years. 26% grads go on to further study within 1 year. **Faculty:** 508 full-time faculty, 89% hold PhDs, 37% are are members of minority groups, 16% are women. 3.4% of classes are taught by teaching assistants.

ACADEMICS

Degrees: bachelor's, master's, post-master's certificate. **Classes:** Most classes have 20-29 students. Most lab/discussion sessions have 10-19 students. **Majors with Highest Enrollment:** Speech Communication and Rhetoric; Marketing/ Marketing Management; Psychology. **Special Study Options:** Accelerated program, cooperative education program, cross-registration, distance learning, double major, dual enrollment, English as a Second Language (ESL), exchange student program (domestic), honors program, independent study, internships, liberal arts/career combination, student-designed major, study abroad, teacher certification program, Distance learning courses are offered, but not programs; domestic exchange only among other Marianist institutions; student-designed major is general studies. **Honors programs:** The University Honors Program offers courses, programming, fellowship advising, funding, guidance and benefits to undergraduates who have superior academic records, culminating in an Honors-designated diploma. Through the Honors Program, students can develop their academic talents, explore the world, undertake extensive, self-directed research, and apply their knowledge for the benefit of others. **Combined degree programs:** BA/MA, ACC/MBA. **Disability Services:** Special programs offered to physically disabled students include note-taking services, reader services, tape recorders, tutors. **Career services:** Alumni network, alumni services, career/job search classes, career assessment, internships, regional alumni.

FACILITIES

Housing: Coed dorms, special housing for disabled students, men's dorms, special housing for international students, women's dorms, fraternity/sorority housing, apartments for single students, Wellness Housing, Theme HousingUniversity-owned houses. 95% of campus accessible to physically disabled.
Special Academic Facilities/Equipment: UD Research Institute, Bombeck Family Learning Center, Learning Teaching Center, Davis Center for Portfolio Management, Marian Library, ArtStreet living-learning complex, RecPlex.
Computers: 100% of classrooms, 100% of dorms, 100% of libraries, 100% of dining areas, 100% of student union, 100% of common outdoor areas have wireless network access. Students can register for classes online. Administrative functions (other than registration) can be performed online. Undergraduates are required to own a computer.

CAMPUS LIFE

Environment: City. **Activities:** Choral groups, concert band, dance, drama/ theater, jazz band, literary magazine, marching band, music ensembles, musical theater, opera, pep band, radio station, student government, student newspaper, symphony orchestra, television station, yearbook, Campus Ministries, International Student Organization, Model UN. 200 registered organizations, 14 honor societies, 30 religious organizations. 13 fraternities, 9 sororities.
Athletics (Intercollegiate): *Men:* baseball, basketball, cheerleading, crosscountry, football, golf, soccer, tennis. *Women:* basketball, cheerleading, crew/ rowing, cross-country, golf, soccer, softball, tennis, track/field (outdoor), track/ field (indoor), volleyball. **On-Campus Highlights:** John F. Kennedy Memorial Union, Ryan C. Harris Learning-Teaching Center, University of Dayton Arena, University of Dayton Science Center, Kettering Laboratories; UDRI, ArtStreet, an innovative living-learning complex, combines student residential quarters with performance and visual arts spaces, a recording studio, radio station and

Café. Mariant Hall, a multifunctional facility consisting of student housing, a book store, post office, credit union, food emporium, worship space and learning center, was completed in fall 2004. A $22 million addition to and renovation of Sherman and Wohlleben Halls, home to UD science programs, connects them and provides close to 55,000 square feet for new laboratories, classrooms, offices and gathering spaces. A fitness and recreation complex, or RecPlex, opened in January 2006. It consists of three levels and totals 129,540 square feet. **Environmental Initiatives:** Composting program that has eliminated ~90% of waste from all campus dining halls complete with a total conversion to compostable disposable products for takeout and washable service ware for dine-in customers. A commingle single-stream recycling program for plastic, steel and aluminum cans, cardboard and paper, with additional recycling of ink and toner, electronics, scrap metal, batteries, and construction and renovation debris. Coupled with a program to divert usable items to charity during student move out, we have reduced waste leaving campus by 40% in 5 years. To reduce energy use, the following measures have been taken: efficient equipment including tankless hot water heaters and 92% efficient furnaces are standard when upgrading the houses in the student neighborhood; campus buildings have been set to 74 in summer and 68 in winter; building HVAC equipment has been optimized and control systems installed to reduce over-conditioning; boiler controls have increased efficiency of the central boiler plant by 15%; a demand reduction program implemented this past summer resulted in 10%+ savings each month and has been continued permanently; a student behavior change campaign culminated with a dorm energy competition in which the winning dorm reduced energy use by over 20% compared to the same period last year.

ADMISSIONS

Freshman Academic Profile: Average high school GPA 3.64. 26% in top 10% of high school class, 57% in top 25% of high school class, 88% in top 50% of high school class. 43% from public high schools. SAT Math middle 50% range 503-640. SAT Critical Reading middle 50% range 510-620. ACT middle 50% range 24-29. Minimum internet-based TOEFL 70. Minimum paper TOEFL 523. **Basis for Candidate Selection:** *Very important factors considered include:* academic GPA. *Important factors considered include:* Class rank, rigor of secondary school record, standardized test scores, talent/ability. *Other factors considered include:* application essay, recommendation(s), alumni/ae relation, character/personal qualities, extracurricular activities, first generation, interview, racial/ethnic status, volunteer work, work experience. **Freshman Admission Requirements:** High school diploma is required and GED is accepted. **Academic units required:** 2 units of foreign language are required for admission to the College of Arts and Sciences. **Freshman Admission Statistics:** 15,101 applied, 55% admitted, 25% enrolled. **Transfer Admission Requirements:** High school transcript, college transcript(s), essay or personal statement, Minimum college GPA of 2.0 required. Lowest grade transferable C-. **General Admission Information:** Regular application deadline 3/1. Nonfall registration accepted. Admission may be deferred for a maximum of 2 years. Credit and/or placement offered for CEEB Advanced Placement tests.

COSTS AND FINANCIAL AID

Annual tuition $32,000. Room and board $10,350. Required fees $1,400. Average book expense $1,000. **Required Forms and Deadlines:** FAFSA. **Notification of Awards:** Applicants will be notified of awards on a rolling basis beginning 3/15. **Types of Aid:** *Need-based scholarships/grants:* Federal Pell, SEOG, state scholarships/grants, private scholarships, the school's own gift aid, ACG, SMART. *Loans:* Subsidized Stafford, Unsubsidized Stafford, PLUS, Federal Perkins. *Student Employment:* Federal Work-Study Program available. Institutional employment available. Off-campus job opportunities are good. **Financial Aid Statistics:** 100% freshmen, 100% undergrads receive need-based scholarship or grant aid. 23% freshmen, 22% undergrads receive non-need-based scholarship or grant aid. 80% freshmen, 83% undergrads receive need-based self-help aid. 2% freshmen, 2% undergrads receive athletic scholarships. 98% freshmen, 94% undergrads receive any aid. 62% undergrads borrow to pay for school. Average cumulative indebtedness $23,306. **Criteria for awarding institutional aid:** *Non-need-based:* academics, alumni affiliation, art, athletics, leadership, music/drama, state/district residency.

UNIVERSITY OF DELAWARE

Best 380

210 South College Ave., Newark, DE 19716
Phone: 302-831-8123 · **Financial Aid Phone:** 302-831-0520
E-mail: admissions@udel.edu · **CEEB Code:** 5811
Fax: 302-831-6905 · **Website:** http://www.udel.edu · **ACT Code:** 634

This public school was founded in 1743. It has a 1000-acre campus.

RATINGS

Admissions Selectivity Rating: 89   **Fire Safety Rating:** 97

STUDENTS AND FACULTY

Enrollment: 16,871. **Student Body:** 58% female, 42% male, 60% out-of-state, 4% international (55 countries represented). Asian 4%, African American 5%, Caucasian 76%, Hispanic 7%, Native American <1% **Retention and Graduation:** 68% freshmen graduate within 4 years. 82% freshmen graduate within 6 years. 24% grads go on to further study within 1 year. 19% grads pursue arts and sciences degrees. 9% grads pursue law degrees. 6% grads pursue business degrees. 9% grads pursue medical degrees. **Faculty:** 1,176 full-time faculty, 86% hold PhDs, 40% are are members of minority groups, 19% are women. 5% of classes are taught by teaching assistants.

ACADEMICS

Degrees: associate, bachelor's, master's. **Classes:** Most classes have 20-29 students. Most lab/discussion sessions have 10-19 students. **Majors with Highest Enrollment:** Registered Nursing/Registered Nurse; Finance. **Special Study Options:** Accelerated program, cooperative education program, distance learning, double major, dual enrollment, English as a Second Language (ESL), honors program, independent study, internships, liberal arts/career combination, student-designed major, study abroad, teacher certification program. **Honors programs:** University Honors Program, http://honors.udel.edu/ **Combined degree programs:** 4+1 BS Hotel Restaurant and Inst. Mgmt./MBA. **Disability Services:** Special programs offered to physically disabled students include note-taking services, reader services, tape recorders, tutors. **Career services:** Alumni network, alumni services, career/job search classes, career assessment, internships. Career services highlights include an extensive web-based career workshop series. Strong relationships with academic departments and colleges to deliver services to students. Discovery Learning: internships, study abroad, undergraduate research, and service learning.

FACILITIES

Housing: Coed dorms, special housing for disabled students, women's dorms, fraternity/sorority housing, apartments for married students, apartments for single students, Theme Housing, Special-interest housing. 95% of campus accessible to physically disabled. **Special Academic Facilities/Equipment:** $20 million Lammont du Pont Laboratory, $11 million Biotechnology Center, $1,8 million Fischer Greenhouse Laboratory, 23,000-seat Delaware Football Stadium, 350-acre Agricultural Teachning and Research Complex, 35-acre Woodlot harboring numerous wild species of animals and birds, 28 micro-computing sites, 6-acre Morris Library containing pver 2.8 million books and over 270 networked databases, 2 student/University centers, art coservation laboratories at Winterthur Museum and Gardens, Bob Carpenter Sports/Convocation Center, livestock arena and working farm, composites manufacturing science laboratory, Delaware Field House, Fred P. Rullo Stadium, Gerald Culley foreign language media center, historic costume and textile collection, laboratory for the analysis of cultural materials, medical technology laboratories, the mineralogical museum, nursing practice practice laboratories, orthopedic and biomechanical engineering center, Rust and Gold ice skating arenas, textiles, botanical gardens, the University gallery, University honors center, University laboratory preschool, Vita Nova, 40+ research centers and institutes, Center for the Arts. **Computers:** 100% of classrooms, 100% of dorms, 100% of libraries, 100% of dining areas, 100% of student union, 50% of common outdoor areas have wireless network access. Students can register for classes online. Administrative functions (other than registration) can be performed online.

CAMPUS LIFE

Environment: Town. **Activities:** Choral groups, concert band, dance, drama/theater, jazz band, literary magazine, marching band, music ensembles, musical theater, opera, pep band, radio station, student government, student newspaper, student-run film society, symphony orchestra, television station, Campus Ministries, International Student Organization, Model UN. 250 registered organizations, 23 honor societies, 24 religious organizations. 22 fraternities, 15 sororities. **Athletics (Intercollegiate):** *Men:* baseball, basketball, cross-country, diving, football, golf, lacrosse, soccer, swimming, tennis, track/field (outdoor). *Women:*

basketball, crew/rowing, cross-country, diving, field hockey, lacrosse, soccer, softball, swimming, tennis, track/field (outdoor), track/field (indoor), volleyball. **On-Campus Highlights:** Trabant University Center, Gore Hall, Memorial Hall, Morris Library, Delaware Stadium/Bob Carpenter Center. **Environmental Initiatives:** The University of Delaware is launching a revolving energy loan fund dedicated to increase energy efficiency of campus buildings. Expanding Renewable Energy Use The University of Delaware installed a 2MW wind turbine that produced over 5 million kilowatt hours. See: http://www.ceoe.udel.edu/LewesTurbine/ In addition to pursuing the use of wind power, the University also installed 870kw solar system that is projected to generate over 1 million kilowatt hours annually. Creation of the University of Delaware Sustainability Task Force. The Task Force comprised of students, staff and faculty stimulates networking; educates the University community; raises awareness of existing practices at the University; and encourages education, research, service, and operations to build a more sustainable community. See: http://www.udel.edu/sustainability/taskforce/

ADMISSIONS

Freshman Academic Profile: Average high school GPA 3.5. 37% in top 10% of high school class, 72% in top 25% of high school class, 96% in top 50% of high school class. 80% from public high schools. SAT Math middle 50% range 550-660. SAT Critical Reading middle 50% range 540-640. SAT Writing middle 50% range 540-640. ACT middle 50% range 24-29. Minimum internet-based TOEFL 90. Minimum paper TOEFL 570. **Basis for Candidate Selection:** *Very important factors considered include:* academic GPA, rigor of secondary school record, state residency. *Important factors considered include:* application essay, recommendation(s), standardized test scores, character/personal qualities, extracurricular activities, talent/ability, volunteer work, work experience. *Other factors considered include:* Class rank, alumni/ae relation, first generation, geographical residence, interview, level of applicant's interest, racial/ethnic status. **Freshman Admission Requirements:** High school diploma is required and GED is accepted. **Academic units required:** 4 English, 3 mathematics, 3 science, (2 science labs), 2 foreign language, 2 social studies, 2 history, 2 academic electives. **Freshman Admission Statistics:** 24,657 applied, 63% admitted, 24% enrolled. **Transfer Admission Requirements:** High school transcript, college transcript(s), essay or personal statement, statement of good standing from prior institution(s). Minimum college GPA of 2.5 required. Lowest grade transferable C. **General Admission Information:** Application Fee $75. Regular application deadline 1/15. Regular notification 3/15. Nonfall registration accepted. Admission may be deferred for a maximum of 1 year. Credit offered for CEEB Advanced Placement tests.

COSTS AND FINANCIAL AID

Annual in-state tuition $10,900. Annual out-of-state tuition $29,250. Room and board $11,868. Required fees $1,442. Average book expense $800. **Required Forms and Deadlines:** FAFSA. **Notification of Awards:** Applicants will be notified of awards on a rolling basis beginning 3/15. **Types of Aid:** *Need-based scholarships/grants:* Federal Pell, SEOG, state scholarships/grants, private scholarships, the school's own gift aid. *Loans:* Direct Subsidized Stafford, Direct Unsubsidized Stafford, Direct PLUS, Federal Perkins, Federal Nursing, college/university loans from institutional funds. *Student Employment:* Federal Work-Study Program available. Institutional employment available. Highest amount earned per year from on-campus jobs $2,000. Off-campus job opportunities are excellent. **Financial Aid Statistics:** 91% freshmen, 77% undergrads receive need-based scholarship or grant aid. 42% freshmen, 28% undergrads receive non-need-based scholarship or grant aid. 75% freshmen, 80% undergrads receive need-based self-help aid. 3% freshmen, 3% undergrads receive athletic scholarships. 56% freshmen, 49% undergrads receive any aid. 62% undergrads borrow to pay for school. Average cumulative indebtedness $22,846. **Criteria for awarding institutional aid:** *Non-need-based:* academics, alumni affiliation, art, athletics, leadership, minority status, music/drama, state/district residency.

See page 1174.

UNIVERSITY OF DENVER

Best 380

Office of Admission, Denver, CO 80208
Phone: 303-871-2036 · **Financial Aid Phone:** 303-871-4020
E-mail: admission@du.edu · **CEEB Code:** 4842
Fax: 303-871-3301 · **Website:** http://www.du.edu · **ACT Code:** 534

This private school was founded in 1864. It has a 125-acre campus.

RATINGS

Admissions Selectivity Rating: 88   **Fire Safety Rating:** 63

STUDENTS AND FACULTY

Enrollment: 5,629. **Student Body:** 54% female, 46% male, 57% out-of-state, 10% international (43 countries represented). Asian 4%, African American 3%, Caucasian 68%, Hispanic 9%, Native American <1%. **Retention and Graduation:** 66% freshmen graduate within 4 years. **Faculty:** 696 full-time faculty, 90% hold PhDs, 44% are are members of minority groups, 15% are women. 2% of classes are taught by teaching assistants.

ACADEMICS

Degrees: bachelor's, certificate, doctoral, master's, post-bachelor's certificate, post-master's certificate. **Classes:** Most classes have 10-19 students. Most lab/discussion sessions have 20-29 students. **Majors with Highest Enrollment:** International Relations and Affairs; Finance; Psychology. **Special Study Options:** Accelerated program, cooperative education program, distance learning, double major, dual enrollment, English as a Second Language (ESL), honors program, independent study, internships, student-designed major, study abroad, teacher certification program, weekend college, Learning disabilities services. **Honors programs:** The University of Denver offers a challenging Honors Program for talented students who seek an advanced liberal education, lively dialogue with their peers and faculty on important issues, study abroad in first-rate universities, and inspiring in-depth work in their majors. The aim of the program is to challenge students to cultivate strong habits of critical thinking, creativity, and scholarship and to offer close support for advanced work. Students in the Honors Program have the best of both worlds: the small classes and close community of a liberal arts college and the opportunities and resources of a research university. **Combined degree programs:** BA/MA, BA/MPP, BSBA/MBA, BA or BS and MSW, BS/MS in Engineering, others. **Disability Services:** Special programs offered to physically disabled students include note-taking services, reader services, tape recorders, tutors. **Career services:** Alumni network, alumni services, career/job search classes, career assessment, internships, regional alumni. Career services highlights include the Backpacks to Briefcases program, which guides and supports students from their first year at Daniels College of Business through their transition to the working world. To symbolize this important time of growth, Daniels students receive a complimentary backpack when they enroll and briefcases embossed with the Daniels logo when they graduate. The mission of Backpacks to Briefcases is two-fold: Help students get the most of out of their college experience; Prepare students to realize their full potential when transitioning to the business world. This mission is accomplished through fun and informative workshops, professional development programs, networking opportunities and other memorable experiences. Past events have included a "Fashion your Future" fashion show and seminar of business attire and etiquette, a Career Conference on "Negotiating your Career Path in a Difficult Economy" with specialized breakout sessions for everyone from first-year students to graduating seniors, and a workshop on "The Art of Small Talk" to help you make a great first impression at networking receptions, job fairs and other events.

FACILITIES

Housing: Coed dorms, fraternity/sorority housing, apartments for married students, apartments for single students, Wellness Housing, Theme Housing. 85% of campus accessible to physically disabled. **Special Academic Facilities/Equipment:** Art gallery, performing arts center, centers for Judaic and Latin American studies, Anthropology Museum, center for child study, center for gifted and talented children, regional conservation center, high altitude research lab, law enforcement technology center, observatory. **Computers:** 75% of classrooms, 10% of dorms, 100% of libraries, 100% of dining areas, 100% of student union, 50% of common outdoor areas have wireless network access. Students can register for classes online. Administrative functions (other than registration) can be performed online. Undergraduates are required to own a computer.

CAMPUS LIFE

Environment: Metropolis. **Activities:** Choral groups, concert band, dance, drama/theater, jazz band, literary magazine, music ensembles, musical theater, opera, pep band, radio station, student government, student newspaper, student-run film society, symphony orchestra, Campus Ministries, International Student Organization, Model UN. 160 registered organizations, 19 honor societies, 14 religious organizations. 9 fraternities, 6 sororities. **Athletics (Intercollegiate):** *Men:* basketball, diving, golf, ice hockey, lacrosse, skiing (downhill/alpine), skiing (nordic/cross-country), soccer, swimming, tennis. *Women:* basketball, diving, golf, gymnastics, lacrosse, skiing (downhill/alpine), skiing (nordic/cross-country), soccer, swimming, tennis, volleyball. **On-Campus Highlights:** Campus Green (Driscoll Lawn), Ritchie Center (athletic facility), Newman Center (performing arts), Daniels College of Business building, Jazzman's Café (located inside Driscoll Center). **Environmental Initiatives:** The University of Denver expanded from single stream recycling to outdoor bins and composting in two campus dining halls. The University of Denver established the Reserve Energy Fund in 2009, a regenerate funding mechanism in which current savings from energy conservation projects fund future conservation initiatives. The University of Denver hosted the Rocky Mountain Sustainability Summit February 17-18, 2011. Summit sessions and keynote speakers will focus on sustainability issues in higher education, making the business case for sustainability, educating on environmental justice issues, moving from talk to action in the area of sustainability on campus, and focusing on regional sustainability issues.

ADMISSIONS

Freshman Academic Profile: Average high school GPA 3.68. 42% in top 10% of high school class, 74% in top 25% of high school class, 95% in top 50% of high school class. SAT Math middle 50% range 560-660. SAT Critical Reading middle 50% range 550-640. SAT Writing middle 50% range 510-620. ACT middle 50% range 25-30. Minimum internet-based TOEFL 80. Minimum paper TOEFL 550. **Basis for Candidate Selection:** *Very important factors considered include:* academic GPA, rigor of secondary school record, standardized test scores, character/personal qualities. *Important factors considered include:* application essay, recommendation(s), extracurricular activities, interview, level of applicant's interest, talent/ability, volunteer work, work experience. **Freshman Admission Requirements:** High school diploma is required and GED is accepted. **Freshman Admission Statistics:** 13,670 applied, 76% admitted, 14% enrolled. **Transfer Admission Requirements:** college transcript(s), essay or personal statement, statement of good standing from prior institution(s). Lowest grade transferable C. **General Admission Information:** Application Fee $50. Regular application deadline 1/15. Regular notification 3/15. Nonfall registration accepted. Admission may be deferred for a maximum of 12 months. Credit and/or placement offered for CEEB Advanced Placement tests.

COSTS AND FINANCIAL AID

Annual tuition $41,112. Room and board $11,307. Required fees $978. Average book expense $1,800. **Required Forms and Deadlines:** FAFSA, CSS/Financial Aid PROFILE, Noncustodial PROFILE. **Notification of Awards:** Applicants will be notified of awards on or about 4/1. **Types of Aid:** *Need-based scholarships/grants:* Federal Pell, SEOG, state scholarships/grants, private scholarships, the school's own gift aid. *Loans:* Direct Subsidized Stafford, Direct Unsubsidized Stafford, Direct PLUS, Subsidized Stafford, Unsubsidized Stafford, PLUS, Federal Perkins, college/university loans from institutional funds. *Student Employment:* Off-campus job opportunities are excellent. **Financial Aid Statistics:** 98% freshmen, 98% undergrads receive need-based scholarship or grant aid. 26% freshmen, 24% undergrads receive non-need-based scholarship or grant aid. 66% freshmen, 70% undergrads receive need-based self-help aid. 3% freshmen, 4% undergrads receive athletic scholarships. 85% freshmen, 83% undergrads receive any aid. 45% undergrads borrow to pay for school. Average cumulative indebtedness $22,848. **Criteria for awarding institutional aid:** *Non-need-based:* academics, art, athletics, leadership, music/drama, state/district residency.

UNIVERSITY OF DETROIT MERCY

4001 W McNichols Rd, Detroit, MI 48221-3038
Phone: 313-993-1245
E-mail: admissions@udmercy.edu · **CEEB Code:** 1835
Fax: 313-993-3326 · **Website:** www.udmercy.edu · **ACT Code:** 2060

This private school, affiliated with the Roman Catholic-Jesuit Church, was founded in 1877. It has a 70-acre campus.

RATINGS

Admissions Selectivity Rating: 76   **Fire Safety Rating:** 60*

STUDENTS AND FACULTY

Enrollment: 2,986. **Student Body:** 68% female, 32% male, 4% out-of-state, 3% international. Asian 2%, African American 32%, Caucasian 52%, Hispanic 2%, Native American 1%

Retention and Graduation: 76% freshmen return for sophomore year. 33% freshmen graduate within 4 years. 54% freshmen graduate within 6 years. 20% grads go on to further study within 1 year. 5% grads pursue arts and sciences degrees. 4% grads pursue law degrees. 8% grads pursue business degrees. 3% grads pursue medical degrees. **Faculty:** 270 full-time faculty, 85% hold PhDs, 44% are are members of minority groups, 14% are women. 0% of classes are taught by teaching assistants.

ACADEMICS

Degrees: associate, bachelor's, certificate, first professional, first professional certificate, master's, post-bachelor's certificate, post-master's certificate, terminal associate, transfer associate. **Special Study Options:** Accelerated program, cooperative education program, double major, dual enrollment, English as a Second Language (ESL), honors program, independent study, internships, liberal arts/career combination, study abroad, teacher certification program, weekend college. **Combined degree programs:** BA/DDS. **Disability Services:** Special programs offered to physically disabled students include note-taking services. **Career services:** alumni services, career/job search classes, career assessment, internships.

FACILITIES

Housing: Coed dorms, fraternity/sorority housing, apartments for married students, Peace and Justice Floor Honors Floors WISE (Women in Science and Engineering) floor. **Computers:**

CAMPUS LIFE

Activities: dance, drama/theater, literary magazine, pep band, radio station, student government, student newspaper. 55 registered organizations, 1 honor society, 7 fraternities, 3 sororities. **Athletics (Intercollegiate):** *Men:* baseball, basketball, cheerleading, cross-country, fencing, golf, soccer, track/field (outdoor), track/field (indoor). *Women:* basketball, cheerleading, cross-country, fencing, soccer, softball, tennis, track/field (outdoor), track/field (indoor).

ADMISSIONS

Freshman Academic Profile: Average high school GPA 3.33. 22% in top 10% of high school class, 50% in top 25% of high school class, 83% in top 50% of high school class. ACT middle 50% range 19-25. **Basis for Candidate Selection:** *Very important factors considered include:* rigor of secondary school record, standardized test scores. *Other factors considered include:* Class rank, application essay, recommendation(s), alumni/ae relation, extracurricular activities, interview, volunteer work. **Freshman Admission Requirements:** High school diploma is required and GED is accepted. **Academic units required:** 4 English, 3 mathematics, 2 science, (1 science labs), 1 social studies, 1 history. **Freshman Admission Statistics:** 2,181 applied, 81% admitted, 27% enrolled. **Transfer Admission Requirements:** college transcript(s), Minimum college GPA of 2.0 required. Lowest grade transferable C. **General Admission Information:** Application Fee $25. Regular application deadline 7/1. Notification on a rolling basis, beginning on or about 9/1. Nonfall registration accepted. Admission may be deferred for a maximum of 12. Credit and/or placement offered for CEEB Advanced Placement tests.

COSTS AND FINANCIAL AID

Annual tuition $20,400. Room and board $7,040. Required fees $570. Average book expense $1,300. **Required Forms and Deadlines:** FAFSA. **Notification of Awards:** Applicants will be notified of awards on or about 3/1. **Types of Aid:** *Need-based scholarships/grants:* Federal Pell, SEOG, state scholarships/grants, private scholarships, the school's own gift aid, Federal Nursing Scholarships. *Loans:* Subsidized Stafford, Unsubsidized Stafford, PLUS, Federal Perkins, Federal Nursing, college/university loans from institutional funds. *Student Employment:* Federal Work-Study Program available. Institutional employment available. Off-campus job opportunities are good. **Financial Aid Statistics:** 83% freshmen, 92% undergrads receive need-based scholarship or grant aid. 83% undergrads receive non-need-based scholarship or grant aid. 74% freshmen, 89% undergrads receive need-based self-help aid. 2% freshmen, 1% undergrads receive athletic scholarships. **Criteria for awarding institutional aid:** *Non-need-based:* academics, athletics, leadership, minority status, music/drama, religious affiliation.

UNIVERSITY OF THE DISTRICT OF COLUMBIA

4200 Connecticut Avenue Northwest, Washington, DC 20008
Phone: 202-274-6110
E-mail: lflannagan@udc.edu • **CEEB Code:** 5929
Fax: 202-274-5552 • **Website:** www.udc.edu • **ACT Code:** 695

This public school was founded in 1976. It has a 23-acre campus.

RATINGS

Admissions Selectivity Rating: 60*   **Fire Safety Rating:** 60*

STUDENTS AND FACULTY

Enrollment: 5,300. **Student Body:** 60% female, 40% male, 27% out-of-state, 0% international. Asian 2%, African American 73%, Caucasian 6%, Hispanic 5%, Native American <1%
Retention and Graduation: 6% grads go on to further study within 1 year. 1% grads pursue arts and sciences degrees. 1% grads pursue law degrees. 3% grads pursue business degrees. 1% grads pursue medical degrees. **Faculty:** 215 full-time faculty, 66% hold PhDs, 47% are are members of minority groups, 60% are women. 0% of classes are taught by teaching assistants.

ACADEMICS

Degrees: associate, bachelor's, master's. **Classes:** Most classes have 30-39 students. Most lab/discussion sessions have 20-29 students. **Special Study Options:** cooperative education program, English as a Second Language (ESL), honors program, independent study, teacher certification program, weekend college, Business, Computer Science, Home Economics, Technologies. **Disability Services:** Special programs offered to physically disabled students include reader services, tape recorders, tutors.

FACILITIES

Housing: The University of the District of Columbia is a Commuter School with an open-admission policy. 100% of campus accessible to physically disabled. **Special Academic Facilities/Equipment:** Theatre, greenhouse.

CAMPUS LIFE

Activities: Choral groups, concert band, dance, drama/theater, jazz band, literary magazine, music ensembles, opera, pep band, student government, student newspaper, symphony orchestra, television station, yearbook. 28 registered organizations, 8 honor societies, 3 fraternities, 3 sororities. **Athletics (Intercollegiate):** *Men:* basketball, cross-country, soccer, tennis. *Women:* basketball, tennis, track/field (outdoor), volleyball. **On-Campus Highlights:** Library, Recruitment Office, Office of Admission, Gym.

ADMISSIONS

Freshman Academic Profile: 90% from public high schools. Minimum paper TOEFL 550. **Basis for Candidate Selection:** *Very important factors considered include:* rigor of secondary school record. *Other factors considered include:* recommendation(s), character/personal qualities, extracurricular activities, state residency, talent/ability. **Freshman Admission Requirements:** High school diploma is required and GED is accepted. **Academic units required:** 4 English, 2 mathematics, 2 science, (2 science labs), 2 foreign language, 2 social studies, 2 history, 0 academic electives. **Transfer Admission Requirements:** college transcript(s), Minimum college GPA of 2.0 required. Lowest grade transferable C. **General Admission Information:** Application Fee $20. Regular application deadline 6/14. Nonfall registration accepted. Admission may be deferred for a maximum of 1 semester. Placement offered for CEEB Advanced Placement tests.

COSTS AND FINANCIAL AID

Annual in-state tuition $2,160. Annual out-of-state tuition $4,800. Required fees $510. Average book expense $900. **Required Forms and Deadlines:** FAFSA, Institution's own financial aid form. **Notification of Awards:** Applicants will be notified of awards on a rolling basis beginning 5/5. **Types of Aid:** *Need-based scholarships/grants:* Federal Pell, SEOG, state scholarships/grants, private scholarships, the school's own gift aid. *Loans:* Subsidized Stafford, Unsubsidized Stafford, PLUS, Federal Perkins. *Student Employment:* Federal Work-Study Program available. Institutional employment available. Highest amount earned per year from on-campus jobs $1,950. Off-campus job opportunities are good. **Financial Aid Statistics:** 87% freshmen, 81% undergrads receive need-based scholarship or grant aid. 32% freshmen, 2% undergrads receive non-need-based scholarship or grant aid. 15% freshmen, 14% undergrads receive need-based self-help aid. 5% freshmen, 5% undergrads receive athletic scholarships. 63% undergrads borrow to pay for school. **Criteria for awarding institutional aid:** *Non-need-based:* academics, alumni affiliation, athletics.

UNIVERSITY OF DUBUQUE

2000 University Avenue, Dubuque, IA 52001-5050
Phone: 319-589-3200 • **Financial Aid Phone:** 563-589-3396
E-mail: admssns@dbq.edu • **CEEB Code:** 6869
Fax: 319-589-3690 • **Website:** www.dbq.edu • **ACT Code:** 1358

This private school, affiliated with the Presbyterian Church, was founded in 1852. It has a 56-acre campus.

RATINGS

Admissions Selectivity Rating: 75   **Fire Safety Rating:** 94

STUDENTS AND FACULTY

Enrollment: 1,542. **Student Body:** 44% female, 56% male, 53% out-of-state, 1% international. Asian 2%, African American 12%, Caucasian 73%, Hispanic 3%, Native American 1%
Retention and Graduation: 68% freshmen return for sophomore year. 21% freshmen graduate within 4 years. 38% freshmen graduate within 6 years. 20% grads go on to further study within 1 year. 10% grads pursue arts and sciences degrees. 2% grads pursue law degrees. 3% grads pursue business degrees. 2% grads pursue medical degrees. **Faculty:** 87 full-time faculty, 56% hold PhDs, 39% are are members of minority groups, 6% are women. 0% of classes are taught by teaching assistants.

ACADEMICS

Degrees: associate, bachelor's, master's. **Classes:** Most classes have 10-19 students. Most lab/discussion sessions have fewer than 10 students. **Majors with Highest Enrollment:** Animation, Interactive Technology, Video Graphics and Special Effects; Airline/Commercial/Professional Pilot and Flight Crew; Business/Commerce. **Special Study Options:** cooperative education program, cross-registration, distance learning, double major, dual enrollment, independent study, internships, liberal arts/career combination, student-designed major, study abroad, teacher certification program, Undergrads may take grad level classes. **Off-Campus Study:** Semester-away programs. **Combined degree programs:** BA/MA, 3-3. M.Div. program, BBA/MBA (4+1). **Disability Services:** Special programs offered to physically disabled students include note-taking services, reader services, tape recorders, tutors. **Career services:** Alumni network, alumni services, career/job search classes, career assessment, internships, regional alumni.

FACILITIES

Housing: Coed dorms, special housing for disabled students, apartments for married students, apartments for single students, Houses and Townhouses and Suites. 50% of campus accessible to physically disabled. **Special Academic Facilities/Equipment:** Art gallery, language labs, electron microscope, gas chromatograph/mass spectrometer, floating science lab on the Mississippi River, computer graphics/interactive media stduios, multimedia project production studio in the new Charles C. Myers Library **Computers:** 20% of classrooms, 100% of libraries, 100% of student union, have wireless network access. Students can register for classes online. Administrative functions (other than registration) can be performed online.

CAMPUS LIFE

Environment: Town. **Activities:** Choral groups, dance, drama/theater, jazz band, literary magazine, music ensembles, musical theater, pep band, student government, student newspaper, student-run film society, yearbook, Campus Ministries, International Student Organization. 50 registered organizations, 2 honor societies, 3 religious organizations. 7 fraternities, 4 sororities. **Athletics (Intercollegiate)**: *Men:* baseball, basketball, cross-country, football, golf, soccer, tennis, track/field (outdoor), track/field (indoor), wrestling. *Women:* basketball, cross-country, golf, soccer, softball, tennis, track/field (outdoor), track/field (indoor), volleyball. **On-Campus Highlights:** Coffee Shop, Stoltz Sports Center, Library, Student Union, Chlapaty Recreation & Wellness Center. **Environmental Initiatives:** Campus-wide recycling; Heating, cooling, recycling, etc. standards.

ADMISSIONS

Freshman Academic Profile: Average high school GPA 2.96. 7% in top 10% of high school class, 24% in top 25% of high school class, 54% in top 50% of high school class. 85% from public high schools. SAT Math middle 50% range 420-550. SAT Critical Reading middle 50% range 440-550. ACT middle 50% range 18-23. Minimum paper TOEFL 500. **Basis for Candidate Selection:** *Very important factors considered include:* Class rank, application essay, recommendation(s), rigor of secondary school record, standardized test scores, character/personal qualities. *Other factors considered include:* alumni/ae relation, extracurricular activities, interview, talent/ability, volunteer work, work experience. **Freshman Admission Requirements:** High school diploma is required and GED is accepted. **Academic units required:** 4 English, 3 mathematics, 3 science, (0 science labs), 0 foreign language, 3 social studies,

0 history, 0 visual/performing arts, 0 computer science, 3 academic electives. **Freshman Admission Statistics:** 1,288 applied, 76% admitted, 42% enrolled. **Transfer Admission Requirements:** college transcript(s), Minimum college GPA of 2.0 required. Lowest grade transferable C. **General Admission Information:** Application Fee $25. Notification on a rolling basis, beginning on or about 9/1. Nonfall registration accepted. Admission may be deferred for a maximum of 1 year. Credit offered for CEEB Advanced Placement tests.

COSTS AND FINANCIAL AID

Annual tuition $21,000. Room and board $7,370. Required fees $590. Average book expense $950. **Required Forms and Deadlines:** FAFSA. **Notification of Awards:** Applicants will be notified of awards on a rolling basis beginning 3/1. **Types of Aid:** *Need-based scholarships/grants:* Federal Pell, SEOG, state scholarships/grants, private scholarships, the school's own gift aid. *Loans:* Direct Subsidized Stafford, Direct Unsubsidized Stafford, Direct PLUS, Subsidized Stafford, Unsubsidized Stafford, PLUS, Federal Perkins, state loans, college/university loans from institutional funds. *Student Employment:* Federal Work-Study Program available. Institutional employment available. Highest amount earned per year from on-campus jobs $1,500. Off-campus job opportunities are excellent. **Financial Aid Statistics:** 99% freshmen, 98% undergrads receive need-based scholarship or grant aid. 16% freshmen, 12% undergrads receive non-need-based scholarship or grant aid. 80% freshmen, 83% undergrads receive need-based self-help aid. 0% freshmen, 0% undergrads receive athletic scholarships. 85% freshmen, 85% undergrads receive any aid. 95% undergrads borrow to pay for school. Average cumulative indebtedness $24,006. **Criteria for awarding institutional aid:** *Non-need-based:* academics, alumni affiliation, leadership, music/drama, state/district residency.

UNIVERSITY OF EVANSVILLE

1800 Lincoln Avenue, Evansville, IN 47722
Phone: 812-488-2468 • **Financial Aid Phone:** 812-488-2364
E-mail: admission@evansville.edu • **CEEB Code:** 1208
Fax: 812-488-4076 • **Website:** www.evansville.edu • **ACT Code:** 1188

This private school, affiliated with the Methodist Church, was founded in 1854. It has a 75-acre campus.

RATINGS

Admissions Selectivity Rating: 85   **Fire Safety Rating:** 63

STUDENTS AND FACULTY

Enrollment: 2,339. **Student Body:** 55% female, 45% male, 41% out-of-state, 14% international (52 countries represented). Asian 1%, African American 3%, Caucasian 74%, Hispanic 3%, Native American <1%
Retention and Graduation: 53% freshmen graduate within 4 years. 64% freshmen graduate within 6 years. 18% grads go on to further study within 1 year. **Faculty:** 176 full-time faculty, 86% hold PhDs, 44% are are members of minority groups, 10% are women. 0% of classes are taught by teaching assistants.

ACADEMICS

Degrees: associate, bachelor's, master's. **Classes:** Most classes have 10-19 students. Most lab/discussion sessions have 20-29 students. **Majors with Highest Enrollment:** Drama and Dramatics/Theatre Arts; Kinesiology and Exercise Science; Registered Nursing/Registered Nurse. **Special Study Options:** Accelerated program, cooperative education program, double major, dual enrollment, English as a Second Language (ESL), external degree program, honors program, independent study, internships, student-designed major, study abroad, teacher certification program. **Honors programs:** The Honors Program incorporates unique courses with distinct learning environments to provide enhanced educational learning experiences for exceptional students. Students openly discuss different viewpoints in small, seminar-style classes offered in various academic disciplines. Intellectually curious students who desire academic challenges will enjoy the collaborative learning atmosphere of the Honors Program, as well as the opportunity to engage in advanced independent study, a senior project, and special social programs. **Combined degree programs:** BS/MS in health services administration. **Disability Services:** Special programs offered to physically disabled students include note-taking services, tutors. **Career services:** Alumni network, alumni services, career/job search classes, career assessment, internships, regional alumni.

FACILITIES

Housing: Coed dorms, men's dorms, women's dorms, fraternity/sorority housing, apartments for single students, Theme Housing. 87% of campus accessible to physically disabled. **Computers:** 100% of classrooms, 100% of dorms, 100% of libraries, 100% of dining areas, 100% of student union, 100% of common outdoor areas have wireless network access. Students can register for classes online. Administrative functions (other than registration) can be performed online.

CAMPUS LIFE

Environment: City. **Activities:** Choral groups, concert band, dance, drama/theater, jazz band, literary magazine, music ensembles, musical theater, opera, pep band, radio station, student government, student newspaper, student-run film society, symphony orchestra, yearbook, Campus Ministries, International Student Organization, Model UN. 154 registered organizations, 11 honor societies, 10 religious organizations. 6 fraternities, 5 sororities. **Athletics (Intercollegiate):** *Men:* baseball, basketball, cross-country, diving, golf, soccer, swimming. *Women:* basketball, cross-country, diving, golf, soccer, softball, swimming, tennis, volleyball. **On-Campus Highlights:** Koch Center, Fitness Center, School of Business Administration, Ridgway Student Center, Jazzman's Café. The library and Memorial Plaza are also popular places on campus.

ADMISSIONS

Freshman Academic Profile: Average high school GPA 3.62. 30% in top 10% of high school class, 62% in top 25% of high school class, 93% in top 50% of high school class. SAT Math middle 50% range 510-620. SAT Critical Reading middle 50% range 510-610. SAT Writing middle 50% range 480-590. ACT middle 50% range 23-28. Minimum internet-based TOEFL 61. Minimum paper TOEFL 500. **Basis for Candidate Selection:** *Very important factors considered include:* academic GPA, rigor of secondary school record. *Important factors considered include:* standardized test scores, extracurricular activities. *Other factors considered include:* Class rank, recommendation(s), alumni/ae relation, character/personal qualities, level of applicant's interest, racial/ethnic status, talent/ability, volunteer work, work experience. **Freshman Admission Requirements:** High school diploma is required and GED is accepted. **Academic units required:** 4 English, 3 mathematics, 2 science, (2 science labs), 1 social studies, 1 history. **Freshman Admission Statistics:** 2,762 applied, 83% admitted, 23% enrolled. **Transfer Admission Requirements:** High school transcript, college transcript(s), statement of good standing from prior institution(s). Minimum college GPA of 2.0 required. Lowest grade transferable C. **General Admission Information:** Application Fee $35. Regular application deadline 2/1. Regular notification 2/15. Nonfall registration accepted. Admission may be deferred for a maximum of 1 year. Credit and/or placement offered for CEEB Advanced Placement tests.

COSTS AND FINANCIAL AID

Required Forms and Deadlines: FAFSA. **Notification of Awards:** Applicants will be notified of awards on a rolling basis beginning 3/25. **Types of Aid:** *Need-based scholarships/grants:* Federal Pell, SEOG, state scholarships/grants, the school's own gift aid. *Loans:* Direct Subsidized Stafford, Direct Unsubsidized Stafford, Direct PLUS, Federal Perkins, Federal Nursing, college/university loans from institutional funds. *Student Employment:* Federal Work-Study Program available. Institutional employment available. Highest amount earned per year from on-campus jobs $1,300. Off-campus job opportunities are good. **Financial Aid Statistics:** 100% freshmen, 99% undergrads receive need-based scholarship or grant aid. 100% freshmen, 96% undergrads receive non-need-based scholarship or grant aid. 65% freshmen, 67% undergrads receive need-based self-help aid. 2% freshmen, 4% undergrads receive athletic scholarships. 95% freshmen, 94% undergrads receive any aid. 75% undergrads borrow to pay for school. Average cumulative indebtedness $25,731. **Criteria for awarding institutional aid:** *Non-need-based:* academics, alumni affiliation, art, athletics, leadership, minority status, music/drama, religious affiliation, state/district residency.

THE UNIVERSITY OF FINDLAY

1000 North Main Street, Findlay, OH 45840
Phone: 419-434-4732
E-mail: admissions@findlay.edu • **CEEB Code:** 1223
Fax: 419-434-4898 • **ACT Code:** 3272

This private school was founded in 1882. It has a 175-acre campus.

RATINGS

Admissions Selectivity Rating: 84   Fire Safety Rating: 60*

STUDENTS AND FACULTY

Enrollment: 3,381. **Student Body:** 57% female, 43% male, 20% out-of-state, 1% international. Asian 4%, African American 4%, Caucasian 72%, Hispanic 2%, Native American <1%.
Retention and Graduation: 72% freshmen return for sophomore year. 32% freshmen graduate within 4 years. 53% freshmen graduate within 6 years. 18% grads go on to further study within 1 year. 3% grads pursue arts and sciences degrees. 4% grads pursue law degrees. 3% grads pursue business degrees. 1% grads pursue medical degrees. **Faculty:** 160 full-time faculty, 51% hold PhDs, 40% are are members of minority groups, 41% are women. 0% of classes are taught by teaching assistants.

ACADEMICS

Degrees: associate, bachelor's, master's. **Classes:** Most classes have 10-19 students. **Special Study Options:** Accelerated program, cooperative education program, distance learning, double major, dual enrollment, English as a Second Language (ESL), external degree program, honors program, independent study, internships, liberal arts/career combination, student-designed major, study abroad, teacher certification program, weekend college, BS in nursing with Mount Carmel College of Nursing, 3-1 arrangement with Art Institute Consortium. **Combined degree programs:** 3-1 medical technology and nuclear medicine tech. **Disability Services:** Special programs offered to physically disabled students include note-taking services, tutors. **Career services:** alumni services, career/job search classes, career assessment, internships.

FACILITIES

Housing: special housing for disabled students, men's dorms, special housing for international students, women's dorms, fraternity/sorority housing, apartments for single students, Honors house, Special Interest houses. 90% of campus accessible to physically disabled. **Special Academic Facilities/Equipment:** Fine arts pavilion, planetarium. Mazza Gallery (Children's Book Illustrations).

CAMPUS LIFE

Environment: Village. **Activities:** Choral groups, concert band, drama/theater, jazz band, literary magazine, marching band, music ensembles, musical theater, pep band, radio station, student government, student newspaper, student-run film society, television station, yearbook. 40 registered organizations, 1 honor society, 1 religous organization. 3 fraternities, 2 sororities. **Athletics (Intercollegiate):** *Men:* baseball, basketball, cross-country, diving, equestrian sports, football, golf, ice hockey, soccer, swimming, tennis, track/field (outdoor), track/field (indoor), volleyball, wrestling. *Women:* basketball, cross-country, diving, equestrian sports, golf, ice hockey, soccer, softball, swimming, tennis, track/field (outdoor), track/field (indoor), volleyball.

ADMISSIONS

Freshman Academic Profile: Average high school GPA 3.38. 26% in top 10% of high school class, 54% in top 25% of high school class, 80% in top 50% of high school class. 92% from public high schools. SAT Math middle 50% range 470-580. SAT Critical Reading middle 50% range 470-580. SAT Writing middle 50% range 460-590. ACT middle 50% range 20-25. Minimum paper TOEFL 500. **Basis for Candidate Selection:** *Very important factors considered include:* application essay, academic GPA, recommendation(s), rigor of secondary school record, standardized test scores. *Important factors considered include:* interview. *Other factors considered include:* Class rank, alumni/ae relation, character/personal qualities, extracurricular activities, religious affiliation/commitment, talent/ability, volunteer work. **Freshman Admission Requirements:** High school diploma is required and GED is accepted. **Freshman Admission Statistics:** 2,708 applied, 72% admitted, 37% enrolled. **Transfer Admission Requirements:** college transcript(s), Minimum college GPA of 2.0 required. Lowest grade transferable C. **General Admission Information:** Regular application deadline 7/1. Notification on a rolling basis, beginning on or about 9/1. Nonfall registration accepted. Admission may be deferred for a maximum of 1 year. Credit and/or placement offered for CEEB Advanced Placement tests.

COSTS AND FINANCIAL AID

Required Forms and Deadlines: FAFSA. **Notification of Awards:** Applicants will be notified of awards on a rolling basis beginning 3/1. **Types of Aid:** *Need-based scholarships/grants:* Federal Pell, SEOG, state scholarships/grants, private scholarships, the school's own gift aid. *Loans:* Direct Subsidized Stafford, Direct Unsubsidized Stafford, Direct PLUS, Federal Perkins, college/university loans from institutional funds. *Student Employment:* Federal Work-Study Program available. Institutional employment available. Highest amount earned per year from on-campus jobs $600. Off-campus job opportunities are excellent. **Financial Aid Statistics:** 94% freshmen, 86% undergrads receive need-based scholarship or grant aid. 23% freshmen, 23% undergrads receive non-need-based scholarship or grant aid. 97% freshmen, 86% undergrads receive need-based self-help aid. 15% freshmen, 10% undergrads receive athletic scholarships. 85% undergrads borrow to pay for school. **Criteria for awarding institutional aid:** *Non-need-based:* academics, alumni affiliation, athletics, music/drama, religious affiliation, state/district residency.

See page 1176.

UNIVERSITY OF FLORIDA

Best 380

201 Criser Hall, Gainesville, FL 32611-4000
Phone: 352-392-1365 · **Financial Aid Phone:** 352-392-1271
E-mail: webrequests@admissions.ufl.edu · **CEEB Code:** 5812
Fax: 352-392-2115 · **Website:** www.ufl.edu

This public school was founded in 1853. It has a 2000-acre campus.

RATINGS

Admissions Selectivity Rating: 94   **Fire Safety Rating:** 60*

STUDENTS AND FACULTY

Enrollment: 32,758. **Student Body:** 55% female, 45% male, 3% out-of-state, 1% international (152 countries represented). Asian 8%, African American 7%, Caucasian 58%, Hispanic 20%, Native American <1%
Faculty: 3,468 full-time faculty, 80% hold PhDs, 35% are are members of minority groups, 25% are women. 34% of classes are taught by teaching assistants.

ACADEMICS

Degrees: bachelor's, first professional, master's. **Classes:** Most classes have 10-19 students. Most lab/discussion sessions have 10-19 students. **Majors with Highest Enrollment:** Psychology; Biology/Biological Sciences; Mechanical Engineering. **Special Study Options:** Accelerated program, cooperative education program, cross-registration, distance learning, double major, dual enrollment, English as a Second Language (ESL), exchange student program (domestic), external degree program, honors program, independent study, internships, liberal arts/career combination, student-designed major, study abroad, teacher certification program, weekend college, Adult/Continuing Education, TV-delivered credit-bearing courses, Honors Program, and distance learning courses. **Honors programs:** The University of Florida Honors Program blends the vast resources of a research university with the individualized attention often available only at small liberal arts colleges. With small classes taught by the top faculty at the university, the program offers students the opportunity to make the most of their education al experience. Close interaction with faculty often leads to undergraduate research projects, and students are encouraged to pursue such activities. Students in the Honors Program have the opportunity to live in the Honors Residential College at Hume Hall, the university's newest and most modern dormitory, where they will be surrounded by like-minded individuals and engage in a unique living-learning community. **Combined degree programs:** http://www.registrar.ufl.edu/catalog/programs/combined.html. **Disability Services:** Special programs offered to physically disabled students include note-taking services, reader services, tape recorders. **Career services:** alumni services, career/job search classes, career assessment, internships. Career services highlights include a major Career Showcase conducted each semester—one of the largest fairs of its type nationally. Number one Career Center in U.S. for 2010.

FACILITIES

Housing: Coed dorms, special housing for disabled students, special housing for international students, fraternity/sorority housing, apartments for married students, apartments for single students, Honors Residential College at Hume Hall, International House at Weaver Hall, Career Exploration Community at Graham Hall, Wellness Communities at Springs and Beaty Towers, Faculty-In-Residence Program, First-Year Experience Program, No-Visitation by Opposite Sex Floor available by request, East Hall Engineering Community, Community Service Floor in Fletcher, Fine Arts Living-Learning Community in Reid hall, Global Learning Community in Yulee. 98% of campus accessible to physically disabled. **Special Academic Facilities/Equipment:** Natural history museum, art museum, art gallery, center for the performing arts, Aeolian Skinner organ, cast-bell carillon, citrus research center, coastal engineering wave tank, 100-kilowatt training and research reactor, academic computing center, microkelvin lab, self-contained intensive care hyperbaric chamber. **Computers:** 80% of classrooms, 100% of dorms, 100% of libraries, 100% of dining areas, 100% of student union, 100% of common outdoor areas have wireless network access. Students can register for classes online. Administrative functions (other than registration) can be performed online.

CAMPUS LIFE

Environment: City. **Activities:** Choral groups, concert band, dance, drama/theater, jazz band, literary magazine, marching band, music ensembles, musical theater, pep band, radio station, student government, student newspaper, student-run film society, symphony orchestra, television station, yearbook. 853 registered organizations. **Athletics (Intercollegiate):** *Men:* baseball, basketball, cross-country, diving, football, golf, swimming, tennis, track/field (outdoor),

track/field (indoor). *Women:* basketball, cross-country, diving, golf, gymnastics, lacrosse, soccer, softball, swimming, tennis, track/field (outdoor), track/field (indoor), volleyball. **On-Campus Highlights:** Center for Performing Arts, Florida Museum of Natural History, Cancer & Genetic Research Complex, Brain Institute, Lake Alice Wildlife Reserve. **Environmental Initiatives:** Zero Waste by 2015: As a result of Dr. Machens goal for Zero Waste by 2015, UF now recycles over 6,500 tons of material annually, approximately 43% of the waste stream. Additionally, UF strives to recycle at least 75% of its deconstruction debris and has instituted an Electronics Reuse/Recycling Policy and accompanying step-by-step guide for disposal and recycling. Indoor collection of paper, cans & bottles is institution-wide. UF initiated a Tail-gator recycling program for home game days in 2006 and the program has diverted more than 350,000 pounds of recyclables from the landfill since then. This program continues to grow through self-service stations and other outreach on campus and within the stadium. In 2013, UF began composting efforts on campus by taking the stadium "zero waste" through the football season- diverting an additional 50,000 pounds of organic waste from the landfill. UF researchers recycle Helium on campus and the Veterinary Medical Center repurposes animal waste through a composting partnership with the Forestry Service. Carbon Neutrality by 2025: UF completed its first greenhouse gas inventory and assessment in 2004. In October 2006, UF President J. Bernard Machen, was the first to sign the American College and University Presidents Climate Commitment, which committed UF to creating an action plan for becoming carbon neutral and to adding the impacts of air travel and commuting to its original greenhouse gas inventory. In 2009, UF completed a carbon inventory and developed a carbon action plan in accordance with the ACUPCC. UF hosted the first-ever carbon neutral college football game against FSU in 2007. The game inspired a Gator alumnus and his family to start a non-profit that generated all of the carbon offsets required for a fully carbon neutral 2008 home football season the first of its kind in the NCAA, and in 2009, this partnership continued to work on carbon emissions in athletics, taking the entire athletic program carbon neutral. This commitment continued through the 2012 season. LEED Gold certification is required for all new construction: In 2001, UF adopted the Leadership in Energy and Environmental Design (LEED) standards for all major new construction and renovation projects. In 2006, this commitment was re-confirmed and strengthened by requiring LEED-Gold criteria for design and construction of all major new construction and renovation projects to deliver high performance and sustainable building design. To date, the campus boasts 3 Platinum certified building, 26 Gold certified buildings, 11 Silver certified buildings, and 14 certified buildings. The first Platinum and Gold certified buildings in the state were on the UF campus. The Facilities, Planning, and Construction Department, which administers this program, has undertaken a LEED portfolio program for existing buildings; UF was selected by the US Green Building Council as one of 12 entities to pursue this portfolio approach. The Campus Historic District is listed on the National Register of Historic Places; the university is committed to preservation of the campus in a manner that meets its goals for energy efficiency. UF built its first green roof atop the Charles R. Perry Construction Yard building this year. The roof, which contains soil and live plants, helps reduce storm water runoff and insulates the building against heat and sound. In support of the indoor health of the built environment, Green Seal-certified cleaning products are used by custodial staff whenever possible.

ADMISSIONS

Freshman Academic Profile: 75% in top 10% of high school class, 97% in top 25% of high school class, 100% in top 50% of high school class. 73% from public high schools. SAT Math middle 50% range 590-690. SAT Critical Reading middle 50% range 580-670. SAT Writing middle 50% range 580-670. ACT middle 50% range 26-31. **Basis for Candidate Selection:** *Very important factors considered include:* academic GPA, rigor of secondary school record. *Important factors considered include:* application essay, character/personal qualities, extracurricular activities, first generation, talent/ability. *Other factors considered include:* Class rank, standardized test scores, alumni/ae relation, geographical residence, level of applicant's interest, state residency, volunteer work, work experience. **Freshman Admission Requirements:** High school diploma is required and GED is accepted. **Academic units required:** 4 English, 3 mathematics, 3 science, (2 science labs), 2 foreign language, 3 social studies, 0 history, 3 academic electives. **Freshman Admission Statistics:** 27,852 applied, 47% admitted, 50% enrolled. **Transfer Admission Requirements:** High school transcript, college transcript(s), standardized test scores, Minimum college GPA of 2.0 required. **General Admission Information:** Application Fee $30. Regular application deadline 11/1. Nonfall registration accepted. Credit and/or placement offered for CEEB Advanced Placement tests.

COSTS AND FINANCIAL AID

Annual in-state tuition $6,313. Annual out-of-state tuition $28,590. Room and board $9,630. Average book expense $1,290. **Required Forms and Deadlines:** FAFSA. **Notification of Awards:** Applicants will be notified of awards on a rolling basis beginning 4/1. **Types of Aid:** *Need-based scholarships/grants:* Federal Pell, SEOG, state scholarships/grants, private scholarships, the school's own gift aid State, Academic, Creative arts/performance, Special achievements/

activities, Special characteristics, Athletic and ROTC. *Loans:* Direct Subsidized Stafford, Direct Unsubsidized Stafford, Direct PLUS, Federal Perkins, college/university loans from institutional funds. *Student Employment:* Federal Work-Study Program available. Institutional employment available. Highest amount earned per year from on-campus jobs $19,744. Off-campus job opportunities are fair. **Financial Aid Statistics:** 58% freshmen, 60% undergrads receive need-based scholarship or grant aid. 95% freshmen, 81% undergrads receive non-need-based scholarship or grant aid. 41% freshmen, 48% undergrads receive need-based self-help aid. 2% undergrads receive athletic scholarships. 95% freshmen, 89% undergrads receive any aid. 43% undergrads borrow to pay for school. Average cumulative indebtedness $20,100. **Criteria for awarding institutional aid:** *Non-need-based:* academics, art, athletics, leadership, minority status, music/drama, state/district residency.

THE UNIVERSITY OF GEORGIA

Terrell Hall, 210 South Jackson Street, Athens, GA 30602-1633
Phone: 706-542-8776 · **Financial Aid Phone:** 706-542-6147
E-mail: admproc@uga.edu · **CEEB Code:** 5813
Fax: 706-542-1466 · **Website:** www.uga.edu · **ACT Code:** 872

This public school was founded in 1785. It has a 324-acre campus.

RATINGS

Admissions Selectivity Rating: 92   **Fire Safety Rating:** 77

STUDENTS AND FACULTY

Enrollment: 26,120. **Student Body:** 57% female, 43% male, 8% out-of-state, 1% international (122 countries represented). Asian 9%, African American 7%, Caucasian 73%, Hispanic 5%, Native American <1%
Retention and Graduation: 58% freshmen graduate within 4 years. 20% grads go on to further study within 1 year. **Faculty:** 1,892 full-time faculty, 94% hold PhDs, 38% are are members of minority groups, 21% are women. 18% of classes are taught by teaching assistants.

ACADEMICS

Degrees: bachelor's, certificate, doctoral, master's, post-bachelor's certificate, post-master's certificate. **Classes:** Most classes have 20-29 students. **Majors with Highest Enrollment:** Biology/Biological Sciences; Psychology; Finance. **Special Study Options:** Accelerated program, cooperative education program, cross-registration, distance learning, double major, dual enrollment, exchange student program (domestic), external degree program, honors program, independent study, internships, liberal arts/career combination, student-designed major, study abroad, teacher certification program. **Honors programs:** General Honors Program (university-wide), Foundation Fellows, Center for Undergraduate Research Summer Research Fellows, CURO Apprentice Program. **Disability Services:** Special programs offered to physically disabled students include note-taking services, reader services, tape recorders, tutors. **Career services:** Alumni network, alumni services, career/job search classes, career assessment, internships, regional alumni. Career services highlights include Career Academy: Approximately 200 students participated. This event is scheduled the day "before" classes start at UGA and is dedicated to help students begin their job search. The University of Georgia Career Academy is a one-day, intensive career conference that jump starts the career skills of participating students so that they can immediately launch a successful job search campaign. During the event, students heard from employers representing McKesson, Eli Lilly, Altria, Target, FBI, Sherwin Williams, Liberty Mutual, State Department, Unum, E & J Gallo, and PWC.

FACILITIES

Housing: Coed dorms, special housing for disabled students, special housing for international students, women's dorms, fraternity/sorority housing, apartments for married students, apartments for single students, Theme Housing, Honors and Language focused dorms are available. 90% of campus accessible to physically disabled. **Special Academic Facilities/Equipment:** Miller Learning Center, Georgia Museum of Art, Georgia Museum of Natural History, Ramsey Student Center for Physical Activities, Performing Arts Center, Tate Student Center **Computers:** 90% of classrooms, 15% of dorms, 100% of libraries, 100% of dining areas, 100% of student union, 100% of common outdoor areas have wireless network access. Students can register for classes online. Administrative functions (other than registration) can be performed online.

CAMPUS LIFE

Environment: City. **Activities:** Choral groups, concert band, dance, drama/theater, jazz band, literary magazine, marching band, music ensembles, musical theater, opera, pep band, radio station, student government, student newspaper, student-run film society, symphony orchestra, television station, yearbook, Campus Ministries, International Student Organization, Model UN. 597 registered organizations, 22 honor societies, 35 religious organizations. 34 fraternities, 25 sororities. **Athletics (Intercollegiate):** *Men:* baseball, basketball, cross-country, diving, football, golf, swimming, tennis, track/field (outdoor), track/field (indoor). *Women:* basketball, cross-country, diving, equestrian sports, golf, gymnastics, soccer, softball, swimming, tennis, track/field (outdoor), track/field (indoor), volleyball. **On-Campus Highlights:** Zell B. Miller Learning Center, Sanford Stadium, Ramsey Student Center for Physical Activ, Performing and Visual Arts Complex, Tate Student Center. **Environmental Initiatives:** Inclusion of sustainability as a hallmark of the 2020 Strategic Plan, campus sustainability specifically included in Strategic Direction VII, and woven through all other strategic directions. Hallmarks of the 2020 Strategic Plan: "Two other themes emerge in the 2020 Plan, sustainability and diversity. First, a comprehensive set of recommendations will allow UGA, which was after all the home of the pioneering ecologist Gene Odum, to emerge as a model institution and national leader in research and implementation in this important area. These, then, are the hallmarks of the UGA 2020 Strategic Plan: a clarion call to improving research and graduate education, while preserving and enhancing recent gains in undergraduate education; increasing interdisciplinary efforts across campus as well as local-to-global education and outreach experiences as keys to expanding opportunities for both research and education; establishing a leadership position in sustainability as a major theme for research, education, and service; and ensuring the future relevance of our missions by diversifying the UGA community to better reflect the demographics of Georgia." Strategic Direction 7—Improving Stewardship of Natural Resources and Advancing Campus Sustainability Because the University of Georgia is committed by its land- and sea-grant mission to serve people living and working in Georgia along with our vision to be a leading university internationally, it is incumbent upon the University to provide leadership concerning unprecedented environmental challenges. It is equally important for the University to manage financial and human resources with the greatest of care and respect and to the maximum benefit of the state. A sustainable university is one that meets the needs of the present without compromising the ability of future generations to meet their needs. It also creates opportunities for students, faculty, and staff to enhance the quality of life throughout their communities (Working Group on Sustainability, 2009; World Commission on Environment and Development). A sustainable university acts as a living laboratory where sustainability is researched, taught, tested, and constantly refined. UGA must demonstrate and promote leadership in sustainable living and learning, contextualizing the local as part of the global in sustainability. Over the next decade, the Universitys campuses should be examples to others in reducing their environmental footprints to the greatest extent possible. This includes efforts to reduce energy use significantly, and intelligently, and carefully use and reuse scarce water resources, improve air and water quality, provide sustainable food and transportation options, purchase environmentally responsible products and equipment, increase recycling, and drastically reduce waste. Second, in the effort to prepare students for effective leadership on campus and beyond, sustainability should be infused into formal and informal educational opportunities throughout the University. Campus buildings and landscapes should be incorporated as teaching opportunities, which through design and functional interpretation will reveal innovative practices with the potential to enlighten and inform students and citizens about sound approaches to sustainable living. Third, research generated by UGA faculty and students as well as advances from the global community will be used to reduce dependency on fossil fuels, increase the reuse of materials, and continue the search for other methods that will reduce human impacts on the environment. A priority for the University at large is to design and construct buildings, plaza spaces, hardscapes, and other landscapes that embody the latest in environmental advances and to incorporate the increasing social nature of learning today by creating ample spaces for people to interact. To accomplish these goals, the University should establish a formal coordinating body to work with the UGA Office of Sustainability to develop and implement a comprehensive sustainability plan for the University. 1. Strategic Priority: Annually evaluate and update the Universitys sustainability performance in instruction, research, public service, campus development, and operations activities. Benchmark: Stages for developing a systematic evaluation of the Universitys sustainability performance in instruction, research, public service, campus development, and operations activities. Goal: An annual report on the status of and progress in sustainability performance in instruction, research, public service, campus development, and operations activities by 2020. 2. Strategic Priority: Demonstrate a commitment to reducing fossil fuel use, thereby reducing the Universitys carbon emissions. Pre-benchmark Activity: Calculate the Universitys carbon footprint. Benchmark: The Universitys carbon footprint when calculated. Goals: By 2020: Reduce carbon emissions by 20 percent. Reduce University consumption of energy by 25 percent. Increase purchase of energy from renewable sources by 10 percent. Increase generation of energy from renewable sources by 10 percent. 3. Strategic Priority: Update UGA Guidelines for Design and Construction to incorporate, implement, and monitor current sustainable design strategies, including Leadership in Energy and Environmental Design (LEED) and Sustainable Sites Initiative standards when appropriate. Benchmark: Stages of completion of drafting, gaining support for, and implementing the guidelines. Goal: Updated Guidelines for Design and Construction by 2020. 4. Strategic Priority: Integrate sustainability into the student experience through curricular and co-curricular activities both in the classroom and beyond. Pre-benchmark Activity: Develop a system for identifying and designating courses with a curricular sustainability component. Benchmark: The number of courses with curricular sustainability component when system is implemented. Goal: Increase number of courses with curricular sustainability component by10 percent by 2020. Pre-benchmark Activity: Develop a system for identifying and designating co-curricular experiences with a sustainability component. Benchmark: The number of available co-curricular experiences with sustainability components when system is implemented. Goal: Increase number of available co-curricular experiences with sustainability components by 10 percent by 2020. 5. Strategic Priority: Enhance the coordination, support, and awareness of the Universitys sustainability efforts by establishing a coordinating body to lead efforts, increasing endowments for sustainable activities and promoting campus sustainability efforts. Benchmark: Stages for establishing and charging a coordinating body to oversee sustainability efforts. Goal: A functioning coordinating body to oversee sustainability efforts by 2020. Benchmark: The level of endowment funds for sustainable activities in 2010-2011. Goal: Increase the endowment for sustainable activities by 25 percent by 2020. Benchmark: Stages of action to identify, develop, fund, and install interpretive signs for key campus sustainability efforts. Goal: Interpretive signs installed by 2020. 6. Strategic Priority: Encourage the further development and use of mass transportation to and on campus. Benchmark: The number of campus bus passengers in 2010-2011. Goal: Increase the number of campus bus passengers by 2020. Benchmark: The number of faculty, staff, and students who commute to campus who use alternate modes of transportation such as mass transit, bicycles, or walking in 2010-2011. Goal: Increase by 20 percent the number of faculty, staff, and students who commute to campus using alternate modes of transportation such as mass transit, bicycles, or walking by 2020. Benchmark: The number of Alternative Transportation Permits in 2010-2011(2,100). Goal: Increase the number of Alternative Transportat UAGrden Learning & Demonstration Farm UGArden seeks to promote the social, environmental, and nutritional benefits of sustainable gardening through the creation of a student-run community garden. Such a unique outdoor learning experience encourages engagement with the natural world, fosters interdisciplinary pursuits at UGA, and offers a meaningful sense of place to a largely transitory student body. http://ugarden.uga.edu/ugarden3/Welcome.html UGA Campus Sustianability Grants Program In spring 2014, UGA Office of Sustainability awarded $28,000 in sustainability grants to fund 9 student-initiated projects, and a total of 26 projects and $87,000 in the last four years. The UGA Campus Sustainability Grants Program provides competitive funding for student-proposed projects and initiatives designed to advance sustainability through education, research, service / social entrepreneurship, and campus operations. Successful projects will address priorities outlined in UGAs 2020 Strategic Plan to actively conserve resources, educate the campus community, influence positive action for people and the environment, and provide useful research data to inform future campus sustainability efforts. Interdisciplinary projects designed to inspire, beautify and uplift as well as to inform and conserve—are encouraged. http://sustainability.uga.edu/get-involved/students/sustainability_grants/

ADMISSIONS

Freshman Academic Profile: Average high school GPA 3.86. 53% in top 10% of high school class, 91% in top 25% of high school class, 99% in top 50% of high school class. 81% from public high schools. SAT Math middle 50% range 580-670. SAT Critical Reading middle 50% range 570-660. SAT Writing middle 50% range 560-670. ACT middle 50% range 26-30. Minimum internet-based TOEFL 80. Minimum paper TOEFL 550. **Basis for Candidate Selection:** *Very important factors considered include:* academic GPA, rigor of secondary school record. *Important factors considered include:* standardized test scores. *Other factors considered include:* application essay, recommendation(s), character/personal qualities, extracurricular activities, first generation, talent/ability, volunteer work, work experience. **Freshman Admission Requirements:** High school diploma is required and GED is accepted. **Academic units required:** 4 English, 4 mathematics, 3 science, (2 science labs), 2 foreign language, 3 social studies. **Freshman Admission Statistics:** 20,045 applied, 55% admitted, 48% enrolled. **Transfer Admission Requirements:** college transcript(s), Lowest grade transferable D. **General Admission Information:** Application Fee $60. Regular application deadline 1/15. Nonfall registration accepted. Admission may be deferred for a maximum of one year. Credit and/or placement offered for CEEB Advanced Placement tests.

COSTS AND FINANCIAL AID

Annual out-of-state tuition $26,800. Room and board $9,246. Required fees $2,246. Average book expense $800. **Required Forms and Deadlines:**

FAFSA. **Notification of Awards:** Applicants will be notified of awards on a rolling basis beginning 5/15. **Types of Aid:** *Need-based scholarships/grants:* Federal Pell, SEOG, state scholarships/grants, private scholarships, the school's own gift aid. *Loans:* Direct Subsidized Stafford, Direct Unsubsidized Stafford, Direct PLUS, Federal Perkins, state loans, college/university loans from institutional funds. **Financial Aid Statistics:** 98% freshmen, 91% undergrads receive need-based scholarship or grant aid. 16% freshmen, 11% undergrads receive non-need-based scholarship or grant aid. 62% freshmen, 70% undergrads receive need-based self-help aid. 2% freshmen, 2% undergrads receive athletic scholarships. 45% freshmen, 46% undergrads receive any aid. 48% undergrads borrow to pay for school. Average cumulative indebtedness $19,155. **Criteria for awarding institutional aid:** *Non-need-based:* academics, athletics, state/district residency.

UNIVERSITY OF GREAT FALLS

1301 20th Street South, Great Falls, MT 59405
Phone: 406-791-5200 · **Financial Aid Phone:** 406-791-5235
E-mail: enroll@ugf.edu · **CEEB Code:** 4058
Fax: 406-791-5209 · **Website:** www.ugf.edu · **ACT Code:** 2410

This private school, affiliated with the Roman Catholic Church, was founded in 1932. It has a 44-acre campus.

RATINGS

Admissions Selectivity Rating: 74   **Fire Safety Rating:** 60*

STUDENTS AND FACULTY

Enrollment: 612. **Student Body:** 63% female, 37% male, 20% out-of-state. **Retention and Graduation:** 59% freshmen return for sophomore year. 20% grads pursue arts and sciences degrees. 100% grads pursue medical degrees. **Faculty:** 33 full-time faculty, 61% hold PhDs, 33% are are members of minority groups, 6% are women. 0% of classes are taught by teaching assistants.

ACADEMICS

Degrees: associate, bachelor's, master's, terminal associate, transfer associate. **Classes:** Most classes have fewer than 10 students. **Majors with Highest Enrollment:** Elementary Education and Teaching; Psychology; Criminal Justice/Safety Studies. **Special Study Options:** cooperative education program, distance learning, double major, independent study, internships, liberal arts/career combination, teacher certification program. **Disability Services:** Special programs offered to physically disabled students include note-taking services, reader services, tape recorders, tutors. **Career services:** Alumni network, alumni services, career/job search classes, internships.

FACILITIES

Housing: Coed dorms, apartments for married students, apartments for single students. 85% of campus accessible to physically disabled. **Special Academic Facilities/Equipment:** Art museum; Dr. Hong Herbarium. **Computers:** 70% of classrooms, 100% of dorms, 100% of libraries, 100% of student union, have wireless network access. Students can register for classes online.

CAMPUS LIFE

Environment: Town. **Activities:** Choral groups, concert band, dance, drama/theater, jazz band, music ensembles, musical theater, pep band, radio station, student government, student newspaper, symphony orchestra, Campus Ministries. 10 registered organizations, 2 honor societies, 1 religous organization. **Athletics (Intercollegiate):** *Men:* basketball, cheerleading, cross-country, golf, track/field (outdoor), wrestling. *Women:* basketball, cheerleading, cross-country, golf, soccer, softball, track/field (outdoor), volleyball. **On-Campus Highlights:** Student Center, Wellness Center, Athletic Facility, Art Gallery.

ADMISSIONS

Freshman Academic Profile: Average high school GPA 3.37. 87% from public high schools. SAT Math middle 50% range 360-490. SAT Critical Reading middle 50% range 330-430. ACT middle 50% range 18-24. Minimum paper TOEFL 500. **Basis for Candidate Selection:** *Important factors considered include:* application essay, academic GPA, rigor of secondary school record, standardized test scores, character/personal qualities, interview, level of applicant's interest, religious affiliation/commitment. *Other factors considered include:* Class rank, recommendation(s), extracurricular activities, first generation, racial/ethnic status, talent/ability, volunteer work, work experience. **Freshman Admission Requirements:** High school diploma is required and GED is accepted. **Academic units required:** 4 English, 3 mathematics, 3 science, (1 science labs), 0 foreign language, 1 social studies, 3 history, 5 academic electives. **Freshman Admission Statistics:** 351 applied, 57% admitted, 74% enrolled. **Transfer Admission Requirements:** college transcript(s), essay or personal statement, Minimum college GPA of 2.0 required. Lowest grade transferable

C. General Admission Information: Application Fee $35. Regular application deadline 8/30. Notification on a rolling basis, beginning on or about 10/1. Nonfall registration accepted. Admission may be deferred for a maximum of 2 Semesters. Credit and/or placement offered for CEEB Advanced Placement tests.

COSTS AND FINANCIAL AID

Annual tuition $15,500. Room and board $6,490. Required fees $900. Average book expense $500. **Required Forms and Deadlines:** FAFSA. **Notification of Awards:** Applicants will be notified of awards on a rolling basis beginning 3/1. **Types of Aid:** *Need-based scholarships/grants:* Federal Pell, SEOG, state scholarships/grants, private scholarships, the school's own gift aid. *Loans:* Subsidized Stafford, Unsubsidized Stafford, PLUS, Federal Perkins. *Student Employment:* Federal Work-Study Program available. Institutional employment available. Highest amount earned per year from on-campus jobs $2,000. Off-campus job opportunities are fair. **Financial Aid Statistics:** 69% freshmen, 73% undergrads receive need-based scholarship or grant aid. 92% freshmen, 92% undergrads receive non-need-based scholarship or grant aid. 90% freshmen, 93% undergrads receive need-based self-help aid. 47% freshmen, 38% undergrads receive athletic scholarships. 46% freshmen, 50% undergrads receive any aid. 83% undergrads borrow to pay for school. **Criteria for awarding institutional aid:** *Non-need-based:* academics, alumni affiliation, art, athletics, job skills, leadership, minority status, music/drama, religious affiliation, state/district residency.

UNIVERSITY OF HARTFORD

200 Bloomfield Avenue, West Hartford, CT 6117
Phone: 860-768-4296 • **Financial Aid Phone:** 800-947-4303
E-mail: admissions@mail.hartford.edu • **CEEB Code:** 3436
Fax: 860-768-4961 • **Website:** www.hartford.edu • **ACT Code:** 606

This private school was founded in 1877. It has a 320-acre campus.

RATINGS

Admissions Selectivity Rating: 76   **Fire Safety Rating:** 71

STUDENTS AND FACULTY

Enrollment: 5,318. **Student Body:** 51% female, 49% male, 61% out-of-state, 3% international (65 countries represented). Asian 3%, African American 10%, Caucasian 67%, Hispanic 5%, Native American <1%
Retention and Graduation: 78% freshmen return for sophomore year. 45% freshmen graduate within 4 years. 54% freshmen graduate within 6 years. 22% grads go on to further study within 1 year. 39% grads pursue arts and sciences degrees. 2% grads pursue law degrees. 14% grads pursue business degrees. 2% grads pursue medical degrees. **Faculty:** 325 full-time faculty, 72% hold PhDs, 36% are are members of minority groups, 11% are women. 0% of classes are taught by teaching assistants.

ACADEMICS

Degrees: associate, bachelor's, certificate, diploma, master's, post-bachelor's certificate, post-master's certificate. **Classes:** Most classes have 10-19 students. Most lab/discussion sessions have fewer than 10 students. **Majors with Highest Enrollment:** Speech Communication and Rhetoric; Architectural Engineering Technology/Technician; Psychology. **Special Study Options:** cooperative education program, cross-registration, distance learning, double major, dual enrollment, English as a Second Language (ESL), exchange student program (domestic), honors program, independent study, internships, liberal arts/career combination, student-designed major, study abroad, teacher certification program. **Combined degree programs:** BS Health Science/MS Physical Therapy. **Disability Services:** Special programs offered to physically disabled students include note-taking services, reader services, tutors.

FACILITIES

Housing: Coed dorms, special housing for disabled students, women's dorms, apartments for single students, Honors Housing. **Special Academic Facilities/Equipment:** Museum of presidential memorabilia, Art Gallery, off-campus child care center for student teaching, learning skills and language lab, audiovisual aids center, 8,000-acre environmental center. **Computers:** Students can register for classes online. Administrative functions (other than registration) can be performed online.

CAMPUS LIFE

Environment: Metropolis. **Activities:** Choral groups, concert band, dance, drama/theater, jazz band, literary magazine, music ensembles, musical theater, opera, pep band, radio station, student government, student newspaper, symphony orchestra, television station, yearbook. 93 registered organizations, 22 honor societies, 7 religious organizations. 16 fraternities, 14 sororities. **Athletics**

(Intercollegiate): *Men:* baseball, basketball, cross-country, golf, lacrosse, soccer, tennis, track/field (outdoor), track/field (indoor). *Women:* basketball, cross-country, golf, soccer, softball, tennis, track/field (outdoor), track/field (indoor), volleyball. **On-Campus Highlights:** Museum of American Political Life, Art Gallery, Sports Center, Java City Coffee House, Hawk's Nest.

ADMISSIONS

Freshman Academic Profile: 76% from public high schools. SAT Math middle 50% range 490-590. SAT Critical Reading middle 50% range 480-580. ACT middle 50% range 21-25. Minimum paper TOEFL 550. **Basis for Candidate Selection:** *Very important factors considered include:* rigor of secondary school record. *Important factors considered include:* Class rank, standardized test scores. *Other factors considered include:* application essay, recommendation(s), character/personal qualities, extracurricular activities, interview, talent/ability. **Freshman Admission Requirements:** High school diploma is required and GED is accepted. **Academic units required:** 4 English, 2 mathematics, 2 science, 2 social studies, 2 history, 4 academic electives. **Freshman Admission Statistics:** 12,065 applied, 66% admitted, 19% enrolled. **Transfer Admission Requirements:** college transcript(s), Minimum college GPA of 2.2 required. Lowest grade transferable C-. **General Admission Information:** Application Fee $35. Notification on a rolling basis, beginning on or about 10/1. Nonfall registration accepted. Admission may be deferred for a maximum of 1 year. Credit and/or placement offered for CEEB Advanced Placement tests.

COSTS AND FINANCIAL AID

Annual tuition $24,576. Room and board $9,922. Required fees $1,190. Average book expense $860. **Required Forms and Deadlines:** FAFSA, Institution's own financial aid form. **Notification of Awards:** Applicants will be notified of awards on a rolling basis beginning 3/1. **Types of Aid:** *Need-based scholarships/grants:* Federal Pell, SEOG, state scholarships/grants, private scholarships, the school's own gift aid. *Loans:* Subsidized Stafford, Unsubsidized Stafford, PLUS, Federal Perkins. **Financial Aid Statistics:** 97% freshmen, 95% undergrads receive need-based scholarship or grant aid. 96% freshmen, 94% undergrads receive non-need-based scholarship or grant aid. 90% freshmen, 92% undergrads receive need-based self-help aid. 2% freshmen, 3% undergrads receive athletic scholarships. 97% freshmen, 95% undergrads receive any aid. 66% undergrads borrow to pay for school. **Criteria for awarding institutional aid:** *Non-need-based:* academics, art, athletics, music/drama.

See page 1178.

UNIVERSITY OF HAWAII—HILO

200 West Kawili Street, Hilo, HI 96720-4091
Phone: 808-974-7414 • **Financial Aid Phone:** 808-974-7323
E-mail: uhhadm@hawaii.edu
Fax: 808-933-0861 • **ACT Code:** 904

This public school was founded in 1970. It has a 225-acre campus.

RATINGS

Admissions Selectivity Rating: 81   **Fire Safety Rating:** 60*

STUDENTS AND FACULTY

Enrollment: 3,385. **Student Body:** 59% female, 41% male, 35% out-of-state, 5% international. Asian 19%, African American 1%, Caucasian 24%, Hispanic 10%, Native American 1%
Retention and Graduation: 12% freshmen graduate within 4 years. 36% freshmen graduate within 6 years. **Faculty:** 227 full-time faculty, 44% are members of minority groups. 0% of classes are taught by teaching assistants.

ACADEMICS

Degrees: bachelor's, certificate, first professional, master's, post-bachelor's certificate. **Classes:** Most classes have 10-19 students. **Majors with Highest Enrollment:** Psychology; Business, Management, Marketing, and Related Support Services. **Special Study Options:** cross-registration, distance learning, double major, dual enrollment, English as a Second Language (ESL), exchange student program (domestic), honors program, independent study, internships, student-designed major, study abroad, teacher certification program. **Disability Services:** Special programs offered to physically disabled students include note-taking services, reader services, tape recorders, tutors. **Career services:** Alumni network, alumni services, career assessment, internships. Career services highlights include Service Learning opportunities.

FACILITIES

Housing: Coed dorms, special housing for disabled students, apartments for married students, apartments for single students. 90% of campus accessible to physically disabled. **Computers:** Students can register for classes online. Administrative functions (other than registration) can be performed online.

CAMPUS LIFE

Environment: Town. **Activities:** Choral groups, dance, drama/theater, jazz band, literary magazine, music ensembles, radio station, student government, student newspaper. 43 registered organizations, 4 religious organizations. **Athletics (Intercollegiate):** *Men:* baseball, basketball, cross-country, golf, tennis. *Women:* cross-country, softball, tennis, volleyball. **On-Campus Highlights:** University Classroom Building (opened Fall '02), University Campus Center Plaza (opening Sp '04), University Lava Landing (Student Cyber Lounge), University Mo`okini Library, University Theatre, Student Life Center Facilities (Opening Spr 08).

ADMISSIONS

Freshman Academic Profile: Average high school GPA 3.3. 17% in top 10% of high school class, 47% in top 25% of high school class, 82% in top 50% of high school class. SAT Math middle 50% range 440-600. SAT Critical Reading middle 50% range 440-560. ACT middle 50% range 17-24. Minimum paper TOEFL 500. **Basis for Candidate Selection:** *Very important factors considered include:* rigor of secondary school record. *Important factors considered include:* Class rank, standardized test scores. *Other factors considered include:* application essay, recommendation(s), extracurricular activities, talent/ability. **Freshman Admission Requirements:** High school diploma is required and GED is accepted. **Academic units required:** 4 English, 3 mathematics, 3 science, (3 science labs), 7 academic electives. **Freshman Admission Statistics:** 1,500 applied, 72% admitted, 44% enrolled. **Transfer Admission Requirements:** college transcript(s), Minimum college GPA of 2.0 required. Lowest grade transferable C. **General Admission Information:** Application Fee $50. Regular application deadline 7/1. Notification on a rolling basis, beginning on or about 10/1. Nonfall registration accepted. Admission may be deferred for a maximum of 1 semester. Credit offered for CEEB Advanced Placement tests.

COSTS AND FINANCIAL AID

Average book expense $1,017. **Required Forms and Deadlines:** FAFSA. **Notification of Awards:** Applicants will be notified of awards on a rolling basis beginning 4/12. **Types of Aid:** *Need-based scholarships/grants:* Federal Pell, SEOG, state scholarships/grants, private scholarships, the school's own gift aid. *Loans:* Subsidized Stafford, Unsubsidized Stafford, PLUS, Federal Perkins, state loans. *Student Employment:* Federal Work-Study Program available. Institutional employment available. Highest amount earned per year from on-campus jobs $1,832. **Financial Aid Statistics:** 78% freshmen, 79% undergrads receive need-based scholarship or grant aid. 15% freshmen, 17% undergrads receive non-need-based scholarship or grant aid. 56% freshmen, 65% undergrads receive need-based self-help aid. 3% freshmen, 3% undergrads receive athletic scholarships. 53% undergrads borrow to pay for school. Average cumulative indebtedness $16,462. **Criteria for awarding institutional aid:** *Non-need-based:* academics, art, athletics, leadership, minority status, music/drama.

UNIVERSITY OF HAWAII—MANOA

2600 Campus Road, Honolulu, HI 96822
Phone: 808-956-8975 · **Financial Aid Phone:** 808-956-7251
E-mail: ar-info@hawaii.edu · **CEEB Code:** 4867
Fax: 808-956-4148 · **Website:** http://manoa.hawaii.edu · **ACT Code:** 902

This public school was founded in 1907. It has a 320-acre campus.

RATINGS

Admissions Selectivity Rating: 83   Fire Safety Rating: 83

STUDENTS AND FACULTY

Enrollment: 14,097. **Student Body:** 54% female, 46% male, 24% out-of-state, 2% international (98 countries represented). Asian 41%, African American 1%, Caucasian 20%, Hispanic 2%, Native American <1%
Faculty: 1,209 full-time faculty, 87% hold PhDs, 45% are are members of minority groups, 41% are women.

ACADEMICS

Degrees: bachelor's, master's, post-bachelor's certificate. **Classes:** Most classes have 10-19 students. Most lab/discussion sessions have 20-29 students. **Majors with Highest Enrollment:** Biology/Biological Sciences; Art/Art Studies; Hospitality Administration/Management. **Special Study Options:** cooperative education program, distance learning, double major, English as a Second Language (ESL), exchange student program (domestic), honors program, independent study, internships, student-designed major, study abroad, teacher certification program. **Honors programs:** Selected Studies Program **Combined degree**

programs: Architecture. **Disability Services:** Special programs offered to physically disabled students include note-taking services, reader services, tape recorders. **Career services:** alumni services, career/job search classes, career assessment, internships. Research has shown that out of classroom experiences are positively linked to academic persistence and educational attainment. Work-based experiences can contribute to students finding meaning in their academic pursuits, and vice versa. As a result, a partnership with the Colleges of Arts and Sciences was implemented The Arts & Sciences Internship Program (ASIP) supports the mission of the Center for Career Development and Student Employment (CCDSE) at UH, to empower students to engage in career life planning through awareness, exploration, experience, and reflection.

FACILITIES

Housing: Coed dorms, special housing for disabled students, apartments for married students, apartments for single students. 40% of campus accessible to physically disabled. **Special Academic Facilities/Equipment:** UH Art and Commons Galleries, John Young Museum, John F. Kennedy Theatre, Lyon Arboretum, Waikiki Aquarium, Sunset (travel industry) Library, Chuck Gee Technology Learning Center, Advanced Computing Research Laboratory, Environmental Engineering Lab, Hawaii Center for Advanced Communications, Coral Reef Science Laboratory, traditionally designed Korean Studies Building, Coconut Island marine biology labs, Wong Audio-Visual Center, language lab, speech and hearing and dental hygiene clinics, law library, Hawaiian lo'i(garden), electron microscope and laser laboratories, ship and submersible research fleet, and Maui Super Computer, Jakuan Tea House. **Computers:** Students can register for classes online. Administrative functions (other than registration) can be performed online.

CAMPUS LIFE

Environment: Metropolis. **Activities:** Choral groups, concert band, dance, drama/theater, jazz band, literary magazine, marching band, music ensembles, musical theater, pep band, radio station, student government, student newspaper, student-run film society, symphony orchestra, Campus Ministries, International Student Organization. 161 registered organizations, 7 honor societies, 24 religious organizations. 3 fraternities, 2 sororities. **Athletics (Intercollegiate):** *Men:* baseball, basketball, cheerleading, diving, football, golf, sailing, swimming, tennis, volleyball. *Women:* basketball, cheerleading, cross-country, diving, golf, sailing, soccer, softball, swimming, tennis, track/field (outdoor), track/field (indoor), volleyball, water polo. **On-Campus Highlights:** Campus Center, Queen Lili'uokalani Ctr for Student Svcs, Quad Courtyard, Sinclair Library, Hamilton Library. **Environmental Initiatives:** Creation & convening of Manoa Sustainability Corps; Manoa Green Days—our energy reduction program to consolidate building uses & completely shut down buildings; Sustainable UH—a student run sustainability organization.

ADMISSIONS

Freshman Academic Profile: Average high school GPA 3.46. 27.3% in top 10% of high school class, 57.8% in top 25% of high school class, 89.4% in top 50% of high school class. 66% from public high schools. SAT Math middle 50% range 500-620. SAT Critical Reading middle 50% range 470-580. SAT Writing middle 50% range 470-570. ACT middle 50% range 20-26. Minimum internet-based TOEFL 61. Minimum paper TOEFL 500. **Basis for Candidate Selection:** *Very important factors considered include:* academic GPA, rigor of secondary school record, standardized test scores. *Important factors considered include:* Class rank, state residency. *Other factors considered include:* application essay, recommendation(s), extracurricular activities, geographical residence, interview, talent/ability. **Freshman Admission Requirements:** High school diploma is required and GED is accepted. **Academic units required:** 4 English, 3 mathematics, 3 science, 3 social studies, 5 academic electives, 4 College Prep Courses. **Freshman Admission Statistics:** 7,361 applied, 80% admitted, 34% enrolled. **Transfer Admission Requirements:** college transcript(s), Minimum college GPA of 2.5 required. Lowest grade transferable D. **General Admission Information:** Application Fee $50. Regular application deadline 5/1. Notification on a rolling basis, beginning on or about 12/1. Nonfall registration accepted. Credit and/or placement offered for CEEB Advanced Placement tests.

COSTS AND FINANCIAL AID

Annual in-state tuition $9,840. Annual out-of-state tuition $28,632. Room and board $10,218. Required fees $740. Average book expense $1,246. **Required Forms and Deadlines:** FAFSA. **Notification of Awards:** Applicants will be notified of awards on a rolling basis beginning 4/1. **Types of Aid:** *Need-based scholarships/grants:* Federal Pell, SEOG, state scholarships/grants, private scholarships, the school's own gift aid. *Loans:* Subsidized Stafford, Unsubsidized Stafford, PLUS, Federal Perkins, Federal Nursing, state loans. *Student Employment:* Federal Work-Study Program available. Institutional employment available. Highest amount earned per year from on-campus jobs $5,897. Off-campus job opportunities are good. **Financial Aid Statistics:** 97% freshmen, 92% undergrads receive need-based scholarship or grant aid. 26% freshmen, 16% undergrads receive non-need-based scholarship or grant aid. 55% freshmen, 63% undergrads receive need-based self-help aid. 2% freshmen, 2% undergrads receive athletic scholarships. 62% freshmen, 59% undergrads receive any aid.

43% undergrads borrow to pay for school. Average cumulative indebtedness $19,388. **Criteria for awarding institutional aid:** *Non-need-based:* academics, alumni affiliation, art, athletics, leadership, music/drama.

UNIVERSITY OF HAWAII—WEST OAHU

91-1001 Farrington Hwy, Kapolei, HI 96707
Phone: 808-689-2900 · **Financial Aid Phone:** 808-454-4700
E-mail: uhwo.admissions@hawaii.edu · **CEEB Code:** 1042
Fax: 808-689-2901 · **Website:** www.uhwo.hawaii.edu · **ACT Code:** 6465

This public school was founded in 1976.

RATINGS

Admissions Selectivity Rating: 64   Fire Safety Rating: 60*

STUDENTS AND FACULTY

Enrollment: 1,950. **Student Body:** 67% female, 33% male, 2% out-of-state, 0% international (16 countries represented). Asian 41%, African American 1%, Caucasian 14%, Hispanic 1%, Native American <1%
Faculty: 51 full-time faculty, 92% hold PhDs, 41% are are members of minority groups, 51% are women. 0% of classes are taught by teaching assistants.

ACADEMICS

Degrees: bachelor's, certificate. **Classes:** Most classes have 10-19 students. Most lab/discussion sessions have 20-29 students. **Majors with Highest Enrollment:** Psychology; Business/Commerce; Elementary Education and Teaching. **Special Study Options:** distance learning, double major, teacher certification program. **Disability Services:** Special programs offered to physically disabled students include note-taking services, reader services.

FACILITIES

Housing: 100% of campus accessible to physically disabled. **Computers:** 10% of classrooms, 30% of common outdoor areas have wireless network access. Students can register for classes online.

CAMPUS LIFE

Environment: Town. **Activities:** student government. 12 registered organizations, 1 honor society. **Environmental Initiatives:** All buildings being constructed at new campus are LEED Silver Certified or above. Engagement with community farming programs to develop sustainable food sources and uses. Engagement with community programs, partners, and organizations to develop sustainable approaches and practices in education.

ADMISSIONS

Freshman Academic Profile: 74% from public high schools. Minimum internet-based TOEFL 79. Minimum paper TOEFL 550. **Basis for Candidate Selection:** *Very important factors considered include:* academic GPA. *Important factors considered include:* rigor of secondary school record. *Other factors considered include:* application essay, recommendation(s), standardized test scores, extracurricular activities, first generation, geographical residence, state residency. **Freshman Admission Requirements:** High school diploma is required and GED is accepted. **Academic units required:** 4 English, 3 mathematics, 3 science, 3 social studies, 5 academic electives, 4 College prepatory courses. **Freshman Admission Statistics:** 908 applied, 51% admitted, 64% enrolled. Minimum college GPA of 2.0 required. Lowest grade transferable D. **General Admission Information:** Application Fee $50. Regular application deadline 8/1. Notification on a rolling basis, beginning on or about 2/1. Nonfall registration accepted. Admission may be deferred for a maximum of 1 semester. Credit and/or placement offered for CEEB Advanced Placement tests.

COSTS AND FINANCIAL AID

Annual out-of-state tuition $16,656. **Required Forms and Deadlines:** FAFSA. **Notification of Awards:** Applicants will be notified of awards on a rolling basis beginning 4/1. **Types of Aid:** *Need-based scholarships/grants:* Federal Pell, SEOG, state scholarships/grants, private scholarships, the school's own gift aid. *Loans:* Subsidized Stafford, Unsubsidized Stafford, PLUS. *Student Employment:* Federal Work-Study Program available. Institutional employment available. Highest amount earned per year from on-campus jobs $8,000. Off-campus job opportunities are good. **Financial Aid Statistics:** 40% freshmen, 69% undergrads receive need-based scholarship or grant aid. 70% freshmen, 10% undergrads receive non-need-based scholarship or grant aid. 20% freshmen, 62% undergrads receive need-based self-help aid. 0% freshmen, 0% undergrads receive athletic scholarships.

UNIVERSITY OF HOUSTON

Office of Admissions, Houston, TX 77204-2023
Phone: 713-743-1010 · **Financial Aid Phone:** 713-743-9051
E-mail: admissions@uh.edu · **CEEB Code:** 6870
Fax: 713-743-7542 · **Website:** www.uh.edu · **ACT Code:** 4236

This public school was founded in 1927. It has a 551-acre campus.

RATINGS

Admissions Selectivity Rating: 86   Fire Safety Rating: 89

STUDENTS AND FACULTY

Enrollment: 31,722. **Student Body:** 49% female, 51% male, 2% out-of-state, 5% international (105 countries represented). Asian 22%, African American 11%, Caucasian 27%, Hispanic 31%, Native American <1%
Retention and Graduation: 86% freshmen return for sophomore year. 18% freshmen graduate within 4 years. 48% freshmen graduate within 6 years. **Faculty:** 1,456 full-time faculty, 85% hold PhDs, 38% are are members of minority groups, 27% are women. 2.8% of classes are taught by teaching assistants.

ACADEMICS

Degrees: bachelor's, first professional, master's. **Classes:** Most classes have 20-29 students. Most lab/discussion sessions have 20-29 students. **Majors with Highest Enrollment:** Business Administration and Management; Biology/Biological Sciences; Psychology. **Special Study Options:** Accelerated program, cooperative education program, cross-registration, distance learning, double major, dual enrollment, English as a Second Language (ESL), exchange student program (domestic), honors program, independent study, internships, study abroad, teacher certification program, weekend college, Academic Enrichment programs, certification programs, affiliated studies, and continuing education. **Honors programs:** The Honors College at the University of Houston is a nationally recognized, intellectually stimulating learning community. As a vibrant, leading presence within the university, The Honors College attracts highly talented and motivated students and educators to a collegial environment where tradition is honored and possibilities are both realized and created. **Combined degree programs:** JD/MBA, MBA/MA, MBA/MIE, MBA/MSW. **Disability Services:** Special programs offered to physically disabled students include note-taking services, reader services, tape recorders, tutors. **Career services:** Alumni network, alumni services, career/job search classes, career assessment, internships. Career services highlights include The Campus Recruitment program.

FACILITIES

Housing: Coed dorms, special housing for disabled students, fraternity/sorority housing, apartments for married students, apartments for single students, Special housing for honors students, upper level and graduate students. Cambridge Oaks and Cullen Oaks Apartments. 98% of campus accessible to physically disabled. **Special Academic Facilities/Equipment:** Art gallery, language lab, human development lab school, University Hilton (staffed in part by students in Coll. of Hotel and Restaurant Management), opera studio. **Computers:** 100% of classrooms, 25% of dorms, 100% of libraries, 25% of dining areas, 100% of student union, 25% of common outdoor areas have wireless network access. Students can register for classes online. Administrative functions (other than registration) can be performed online.

CAMPUS LIFE

Environment: Metropolis. **Activities:** Choral groups, concert band, dance, drama/theater, jazz band, literary magazine, marching band, music ensembles, musical theater, opera, pep band, radio station, student government, student newspaper, student-run film society, symphony orchestra, television station, yearbook, Campus Ministries, International Student Organization. 350 registered organizations, 25 honor societies, 39 religious organizations. 21 fraternities, 19 sororities. **Athletics (Intercollegiate):** *Men:* baseball, basketball, cross-country, football, golf, track/field (outdoor), track/field (indoor). *Women:* basketball, cross-country, diving, soccer, softball, swimming, tennis, track/field (outdoor), track/field (indoor), volleyball. **On-Campus Highlights:** University Center, Campus Recreation and Wellness Center, University Center Satellite, Blaffer Gallery, Campus Activities. **Environmental Initiatives:** Energy conservation/retro commissioning of existing buildings; clean energy; Sustainable Transportation; Recycling/waste minimization.

ADMISSIONS

Freshman Academic Profile: 32% in top 10% of high school class, 63% in top 25% of high school class, 89% in top 50% of high school class. 93% from public high schools. SAT Math middle 50% range 540-640. SAT Critical

Reading middle 50% range 500-610. ACT middle 50% range 22-27. Minimum internet-based TOEFL 79. Minimum paper TOEFL 550. **Basis for Candidate Selection:** *Very important factors considered include:* Class rank, rigor of secondary school record. *Important factors considered include:* academic GPA, standardized test scores. *Other factors considered include:* recommendation(s), character/personal qualities, extracurricular activities, first generation, talent/ability, volunteer work, work experience. **Freshman Admission Requirements:** High school diploma is required and GED is accepted. **Freshman Admission Statistics:** 17,328 applied, 63% admitted, 37% enrolled. **Transfer Admission Requirements:** college transcript(s), Minimum college GPA of 2.0 required. Lowest grade transferable C-. **General Admission Information:** Application Fee $50. Regular application deadline 4/1. Nonfall registration accepted. Admission may be deferred for a maximum of 12 months. Credit and/or placement offered for CEEB Advanced Placement tests.

COSTS AND FINANCIAL AID

Annual in-state tuition $9,000. Annual out-of-state tuition $22,860. Room and board $9,278. Required fees $954. Average book expense $1,200. **Required Forms and Deadlines:** FAFSA. **Notification of Awards:** Applicants will be notified of awards on a rolling basis beginning 5/1. **Types of Aid:** *Need-based scholarships/grants:* Federal Pell, SEOG, state scholarships/grants, private scholarships, the school's own gift aid. *Loans:* Subsidized Stafford, Unsubsidized Stafford, PLUS, Federal Perkins, state loans. *Student Employment:* Federal Work-Study Program available. Institutional employment available. Off-campus job opportunities are good. **Financial Aid Statistics:** 88% freshmen, 80% undergrads receive need-based scholarship or grant aid. 8% freshmen, 3% undergrads receive non-need-based scholarship or grant aid. 50% freshmen, 62% undergrads receive need-based self-help aid. 1% freshmen, 1% undergrads receive athletic scholarships. 85% freshmen, 76% undergrads receive any aid. 48% undergrads borrow to pay for school. **Criteria for awarding institutional aid:** *Non-need-based:* academics, alumni affiliation, art, athletics, job skills, leadership, music/drama, state/district residency.

UNIVERSITY OF HOUSTON—CLEAR LAKE

2700 Bay Area Boulevard, Houston, TX 77058-1098
Phone: 281-283-2500 · **Financial Aid Phone:** 281-283-2480
E-mail: admissions@uhcl.edu · **CEEB Code:** 6916
Fax: 281-283-2522

This public school was founded in 1974. It has a 524-acre campus.

RATINGS

Admissions Selectivity Rating: 60*   **Fire Safety Rating:** 60*

STUDENTS AND FACULTY

Enrollment: 4,689. **Student Body:** 68% female, 32% male, 0% out-of-state, 2% international (45 countries represented). Asian 6%, African American 9%, Caucasian 49%, Hispanic 32%, Native American <1%
Faculty: 247 full-time faculty, 86% hold PhDs, 46% are are members of minority groups, 27% are women.

ACADEMICS

Degrees: bachelor's, certificate, doctoral, master's, post-bachelor's certificate, post-master's certificate. **Classes:** Most classes have 10-19 students. **Majors with Highest Enrollment:** Accounting; Psychology; Multi-/Interdisciplinary Studies. **Special Study Options:** cooperative education program, distance learning, double major, dual enrollment, independent study, internships, student-designed major, study abroad, teacher certification program, weekend college. **Combined degree programs:** BS/MS, BS/MHBA. **Disability Services:** Special programs offered to physically disabled students include note-taking services, reader services, tape recorders, tutors. **Career services:** Alumni network, alumni services, career/job search classes, career assessment, internships.

FACILITIES

Housing: Privatized Housing Apartments. 100% of campus accessible to physically disabled. **Special Academic Facilities/Equipment:** Student Art Gallery, Fitness Center/Fitness Zone. **Computers:** 100% of classrooms, 100% of libraries, 100% of dining areas, 100% of student union, 100% of common outdoor areas have wireless network access. Students can register for classes online. Administrative functions (other than registration) can be performed online.

CAMPUS LIFE

Environment: Metropolis. **Activities:** literary magazine, student government, student newspaper, student-run film society, International Student Organization. 70 registered organizations, 16 honor societies, 5 religious organizations. **On-Campus Highlights:** Student Serivce Building, Bayou Building, Library, Delta Building, Computer Labs.

ADMISSIONS

Freshman Academic Profile: Minimum internet-based TOEFL 79. Minimum paper TOEFL 550. **Transfer Admission Requirements:** college transcript(s), standardized test scores, statement of good standing from prior institution(s). Minimum college GPA of 2.0 required. Lowest grade transferable D-. **General Admission Information:** Application Fee $35. Regular application deadline 8/1. Nonfall registration accepted. Admission may be deferred for a maximum of 1 year.

COSTS AND FINANCIAL AID

Types of Aid: *Need-based scholarships/grants:* Federal Pell, SEOG, state scholarships/grants, private scholarships, the school's own gift aid. *Loans:* Direct Subsidized Stafford, Direct Unsubsidized Stafford, Direct PLUS, Federal Perkins, state loans. *Student Employment:* Federal Work-Study Program available. Institutional employment available. Off-campus job opportunities are good. **Financial Aid Statistics:** 41% undergrads receive any aid.

UNIVERSITY OF HOUSTON—DOWNTOWN

One Main Street, Office of Admissions, Houston, TX 77002-1001
Phone: 713-221-8522 · **Financial Aid Phone:** 713-221-8041
E-mail: uhdadmit@uhd.edu
Fax: 713-221-8157 · **Website:** www.uhd.edu

This public school was founded in 1974.

RATINGS

Admissions Selectivity Rating: 71   **Fire Safety Rating:** 60*

STUDENTS AND FACULTY

Enrollment: 13,662. **Student Body:** 60% female, 40% male, 1% out-of-state, 5% international (65 countries represented). Asian 9%, African American 24%, Caucasian 17%, Hispanic 41%, Native American <1%
Retention and Graduation: 3% freshmen graduate within 4 years. **Faculty:** 336 full-time faculty, 84% hold PhDs, 50% are are members of minority groups, 34% are women. 0% of classes are taught by teaching assistants.

ACADEMICS

Degrees: bachelor's, master's. **Classes:** Most classes have 20-29 students. Most lab/discussion sessions have 20-29 students. **Majors with Highest Enrollment:** Psychology; Multi-/Interdisciplinary Studies; Accounting. **Special Study Options:** cooperative education program, distance learning, double major, dual enrollment, English as a Second Language (ESL), honors program, independent study, internships, study abroad, teacher certification program, weekend college.

FACILITIES

Computers: Students can register for classes online. Administrative functions (other than registration) can be performed online.

CAMPUS LIFE

Environment: Metropolis. **Activities:** drama/theater, jazz band, literary magazine, student government, student newspaper. 52 registered organizations, 3 honor societies, 2 religious organizations. 4 fraternities, 4 sororities. **Athletics (Intercollegiate):** *Men:* badminton, basketball, bowling, football, soccer, softball, tennis, volleyball, weight lifting. *Women:* badminton, basketball, bowling, soccer, softball, tennis, volleyball, weight lifting. **On-Campus Highlights:** Special Events Center, O' Kane Gallery, Food court and adjoining Coffee House, Jesse H. Jones Student Life Center, O' Kane Theatre.

ADMISSIONS

Freshman Academic Profile: 9% in top 10% of high school class, 35% in top 25% of high school class, 74% in top 50% of high school class. 86% from public high schools. SAT Math middle 50% range 430-510. SAT Critical Reading middle 50% range 390-470. SAT Writing middle 50% range 380-480. ACT middle 50% range 16-20. Minimum internet-based TOEFL 80. Minimum paper TOEFL 550. **Freshman Admission Requirements:** High school diploma is required and GED is accepted. **Freshman Admission Statistics:** 3,235 applied, 84% admitted, 36% enrolled. **Transfer Admission Requirements:** college transcript(s), Lowest grade transferable C. **General Admission Information:** Application Fee $35. Regular application deadline 7/1. Nonfall registration accepted. Admission may be deferred for a maximum of text. Credit offered for CEEB Advanced Placement tests.

COSTS AND FINANCIAL AID

Annual in-state tuition $5,490. Annual out-of-state tuition $16,350. Required fees $1,124. **Required Forms and Deadlines:** FAFSA. **Notification of Awards:** Applicants will be notified of awards on a rolling basis beginning 4/1. **Types of Aid:** *Need-based scholarships/grants:* Federal Pell, SEOG, state scholarships/grants, private scholarships, the school's own gift aid. *Loans:* Subsidized Stafford, Unsubsidized Stafford, PLUS, state loans. **Financial Aid Statistics:** 86% freshmen, 85% undergrads receive need-based scholarship or grant aid. 25% freshmen, 9% undergrads receive non-need-based scholarship or grant aid. 33% freshmen, 58% undergrads receive need-based self-help aid. 0% freshmen, 0% undergrads receive athletic scholarships. 81% freshmen, 78% undergrads receive any aid. 57% undergrads borrow to pay for school. Average cumulative indebtedness $23,019. **Criteria for awarding institutional aid:** *Non-need-based:* academics, leadership, state/district residency.

UNIVERSITY OF HOUSTON—VICTORIA

Admissions and Records, Victoria, TX 77901-4450
Phone: 361-570-4110 · **Financial Aid Phone:** 316-570-4131
E-mail: admissions@uhv.edu
Fax: 361-580-5500 · **Website:** www.uhv.edu

This public school was founded in 1973.

RATINGS

Admissions Selectivity Rating: 76   Fire Safety Rating: 60*

STUDENTS AND FACULTY

Enrollment: 2,879. **Student Body:** 66% female, 34% male, 1% international (43 countries represented). Asian 7%, African American 17%, Caucasian 40%, Hispanic 31%, Native American <1%
Retention and Graduation: 48% freshmen return for sophomore year. **Faculty:** 125 full-time faculty, 90% hold PhDs, 50% are are members of minority groups, 35% are women. 0% of classes are taught by teaching assistants.

ACADEMICS

Degrees: bachelor's, master's, post-bachelor's certificate, post-master's certificate. **Classes:** Most classes have 20-29 students. **Majors with Highest Enrollment:** Education; Multi-/Interdisciplinary Studies; Business/Commerce. **Special Study Options:** distance learning, double major, honors program, independent study, internships, study abroad, teacher certification program. **Disability Services:** Special programs offered to physically disabled students include note-taking services, tutors. **Career services:** alumni services, career/job search classes, career assessment, internships.

FACILITIES

Housing: Coed dorms. 100% of campus accessible to physically disabled. **Special Academic Facilities/Equipment:** Museum of Coastal Bend. **Computers:** Students can register for classes online. Administrative functions (other than registration) can be performed online.

CAMPUS LIFE

Environment: City. **Activities:** student government, International Student Organization. **Athletics (Intercollegiate):** *Men:* baseball. *Women:* softball.

ADMISSIONS

Freshman Academic Profile: 7% in top 10% of high school class, 23% in top 25% of high school class, 68% in top 50% of high school class. SAT Math middle 50% range 420-515. SAT Critical Reading middle 50% range 390-490. ACT middle 50% range 16-21. Minimum paper TOEFL 79. **Freshman Admission Requirements:** High school diploma is required and GED is accepted. **Freshman Admission Statistics:** 2,873 applied, 52% admitted, 19% enrolled. **Transfer Admission Requirements:** college transcript(s), standardized test scores, Minimum college GPA of 2.0 required. Lowest grade transferable C. **General Admission Information:** Nonfall registration accepted.

COSTS AND FINANCIAL AID

Annual in-state tuition $6,528. Annual out-of-state tuition $13,056. Room and board $6,498. Required fees $1,036. Average book expense $1,105. **Required Forms and Deadlines:** FAFSA, Institution's own financial aid form. **Notification of Awards:** Applicants will be notified of awards on a rolling basis beginning 5/1. **Types of Aid:** *Need-based scholarships/grants:* Federal Pell, SEOG, state scholarships/grants, private scholarships, the school's own gift aid. *Loans:* Subsidized Stafford, Unsubsidized Stafford, PLUS, Federal Nursing, state loans. *Student Employment:* Federal Work-Study Program available. Institutional employment available. Off-campus job opportunities are good. **Financial Aid Statistics:** 84% undergrads receive any aid. **Criteria for awarding institutional aid:** *Non-need-based:* academics, athletics, leadership, state/district residency.

UNIVERSITY OF IDAHO

UI Admissions Office, Moscow, ID 83844-4264
Phone: 208-885-6326 · **Financial Aid Phone:** 208-885-6312
E-mail: admappl@uidaho.edu · **CEEB Code:** 4843
Fax: 208-885-9119 · **Website:** http://www.uidaho.edu/ · **ACT Code:** 928

This public school was founded in 1889. It has a 12500-acre campus.

RATINGS

Admissions Selectivity Rating: 83   Fire Safety Rating: 83

STUDENTS AND FACULTY

Enrollment: 8,162. **Student Body:** 46% female, 54% male, 23% out-of-state, 4% international (77 countries represented). Asian 1%, African American 1%, Caucasian 77%, Hispanic 9%, Native American 1%
Retention and Graduation: 28% freshmen graduate within 4 years. 14% grads go on to further study within 1 year. **Faculty:** 559 full-time faculty, 80% hold PhDs, 36% are are members of minority groups, 14% are women. 9% of classes are taught by teaching assistants.

ACADEMICS

Degrees: bachelor's, certificate, master's, post-bachelor's certificate, post-master's certificate. **Classes:** Most classes have 20-29 students. Most lab/discussion sessions have 10-19 students. **Majors with Highest Enrollment:** Mechanical Engineering; Psychology; Marketing/Marketing Management. **Special Study Options:** Accelerated program, cooperative education program, cross-registration, distance learning, double major, dual enrollment, English as a Second Language (ESL), exchange student program (domestic), honors program, independent study, internships, student-designed major, study abroad, teacher certification program. **Honors programs:** Established in 1983, the University Honors Program offers a stimulating course of study and the advantages of an enriched learning community for over 500 students from all colleges and majors. The UHP's diverse curriculum, including special topic courses and innovative seminars, serves a variety of needs and interests. Beyond the classroom, the program's extracurricular opportunities include concerts, plays, films, lectures and other off-campus excursions that foster cultural enrichment, friendship, and learning. Honors classes offer opportunities to explore subjects and methods in significant depth— students find that their education and their academic performance are enhanced by strong mentoring relationships with faculty devoted to enabling each student to fulfill his or her potential, and by the lively, participation-based modes of learning in small classes. Lower-division honors core courses enable students to learn with their peers in small classes taught by honors faculty. Moreover, each year the program offers innovative upper-division seminars, with each class limited to fifteen students. Honors students are frequently interested in and encouraged to apply for exchanges to other American universities or to universities abroad. As part of a dynamic, broad-based education, members are also encouraged to participate in domestic or international exchange programs, and to take advantage of opportunities to engage in laboratory or field-based research programs as well as internships and other forms of cooperative education. **Disability Services:** Special programs offered to physically disabled students include note-taking services, reader services, tape recorders, tutors. **Career services:** Alumni network, alumni services, career/job search classes, career assessment, internships, regional alumni. Career services highlights include internships.

FACILITIES

Housing: Coed dorms, special housing for disabled students, men's dorms, special housing for international students, women's dorms, fraternity/sorority housing, apartments for married students, apartments for single students. 85% of campus accessible to physically disabled. **Special Academic Facilities/Equipment:** On-campus preschool, experimental forest, electron microscope. **Computers:** 100% of classrooms, 100% of dorms, 100% of libraries, 100% of dining areas, 100% of student union, have wireless network access. Students can register for classes online. Administrative functions (other than registration) can be performed online.

CAMPUS LIFE

Environment: Town. **Activities:** Choral groups, concert band, dance, drama/theater, jazz band, marching band, music ensembles, musical theater, opera, pep band, radio station, student government, student newspaper, student-run film society, symphony orchestra, television station, Campus Ministries, International Student Organization. 190 registered organizations, 13 honor societies, 20 religious organizations. 18 fraternities, 9 sororities. **Athletics (Intercolle-**

giate): *Men:* basketball, cross-country, football, golf, track/field (outdoor), track/field (indoor). *Women:* basketball, cross-country, golf, soccer, swimming, track/field (outdoor), track/field (indoor), volleyball. **On-Campus Highlights:** Idaho Commons—food and meeting rooms, 18 hole golf course, Kibbie Dome—athletics, Student Recreation Center, Borah Theater, Rec Center/Outdoors Program, Frisbee Golf Course, Religious Centers. See our campus live with web cams at http://www.uidaho.edu/webcams. **Environmental Initiatives:** $35 mil ESCO for energy conservation projects currently underway; Built institutional infrastructure; launched a Sustainability Center, formed committees, task forces, passed a student fee of $5/semester to support sustainability, etc. to assess and develop long-term plans for sustainability issues; Converted steam plant to a biomass boiler.

ADMISSIONS

Freshman Academic Profile: Average high school GPA 3.41. 20% in top 10% of high school class, 45% in top 25% of high school class, 73% in top 50% of high school class. 90% from public high schools. SAT Math middle 50% range 460-590. SAT Critical Reading middle 50% range 450-580. SAT Writing middle 50% range 450-560. ACT middle 50% range 20-27. Minimum internet-based TOEFL 70. Minimum paper TOEFL 525. **Basis for Candidate Selection:** *Very important factors considered include:* academic GPA, standardized test scores. *Other factors considered include:* recommendation(s). **Freshman Admission Requirements:** High school diploma is required and GED is accepted. **Academic units required:** 4 English, 3 mathematics, 3 science, (1 science labs), 1 foreign language. **Freshman Admission Statistics:** 8,515 applied, 67% admitted, 28% enrolled. **Transfer Admission Requirements:** college transcript(s), Minimum college GPA of 2.0 required. Lowest grade transferable D. **General Admission Information:** Application Fee $40. Regular application deadline 8/1. Nonfall registration accepted. Credit and/or placement offered for CEEB Advanced Placement tests.

COSTS AND FINANCIAL AID

Annual in-state tuition $4,784. Annual out-of-state tuition $18,314. Room and board $8,022. Required fees $2,000. Average book expense $1,232. **Required Forms and Deadlines:** FAFSA. **Notification of Awards:** Applicants will be notified of awards on a rolling basis beginning 3/30. **Types of Aid:** *Need-based scholarships/grants:* Federal Pell, SEOG, state scholarships/grants, private scholarships, the school's own gift aid. *Loans:* Direct Subsidized Stafford, Direct Unsubsidized Stafford, Direct PLUS, Federal Perkins, college/university loans from institutional funds. *Student Employment:* Federal Work-Study Program available. Institutional employment available. Off-campus job opportunities are good. **Financial Aid Statistics:** 73% freshmen, 76% undergrads receive need-based scholarship or grant aid. 89% freshmen, 59% undergrads receive non-need-based scholarship or grant aid. 72% freshmen, 77% undergrads receive need-based self-help aid. 4% freshmen, 3% undergrads receive athletic scholarships. 90% freshmen, 80% undergrads receive any aid. 68% undergrads borrow to pay for school. Average cumulative indebtedness $24,595. **Criteria for awarding institutional aid:** *Non-need-based:* academics, alumni affiliation, art, athletics, leadership, minority status, music/drama, state/district residency.

UNIVERSITY OF ILLINOIS AT CHICAGO

Suite 100, SSB, 1200 W. Harrison St., Chicago, IL 60607-7161
Phone: 312-996-4350 · **Financial Aid Phone:** 312-996-3126
E-mail: uicadmit@uic.edu · **CEEB Code:** 1851
Fax: 312-413-7628 · **Website:** http://www.uic.edu · **ACT Code:** 1155

This public school was founded in 1965. It has a 218-acre campus.

RATINGS

Admissions Selectivity Rating: 84   **Fire Safety Rating:** 98

STUDENTS AND FACULTY

Enrollment: 16,635. **Student Body:** 50% female, 50% male, 2% out-of-state, 2% international (55 countries represented). Asian 23%, African American 8%, Caucasian 36%, Hispanic 26%, Native American <1%
Retention and Graduation: 33% freshmen graduate within 4 years. 23% grads go on to further study within 1 year. **Faculty:** 1,357 full-time faculty, 87% hold PhDs, 51% are are members of minority groups, 26% are women.

ACADEMICS

Degrees: bachelor's, doctoral, master's, post-bachelor's certificate, post-master's certificate. **Classes:** Most classes have 20-29 students. Most lab/discussion sessions have 20-29 students. **Majors with Highest Enrollment:** Psychology; Biology/Biological Sciences. **Special Study Options:** Accelerated program, cooperative education program, distance learning, double major, dual enrollment, exchange student program (domestic), honors program, independent

study, internships, student-designed major, study abroad, teacher certification program. **Combined degree programs:** BA/MD, BA/DDS. **Disability Services:** Special programs offered to physically disabled students include note-taking services, reader services, tape recorders, tutors. **Career services:** Alumni network, alumni services, career/job search classes, career assessment, internships, regional alumni. Career services highlights include The Entrepreneurship Consulting Program provides an opportunity for teams of students to work with a professional consultant to solve real business problems for entrepreneurial firms. Also, we are equally proud because this year we received a National Award for Excellence from the National (Global) Consortium of Entrepreneurship Centers, held at Syracuse University. It was for founding (1997) and growing the national Collegiate Entrepreneurs' Organization (CEO), one of our UIC programs. We have student entrepreneurship clubs on more than 140 university campuses and the Annual CEO Conference attracted 1300 students (and faculty).

FACILITIES

Housing: Coed dorms, special housing for disabled students, apartments for single students, honors floor, Presidential Awards House. 80% of campus accessible to physically disabled. **Computers:** 95% of classrooms, 100% of dorms, 100% of libraries, 100% of dining areas, 100% of student union, have wireless network access. Students can register for classes online. Administrative functions (other than registration) can be performed online.

CAMPUS LIFE

Environment: Metropolis. **Activities:** Choral groups, concert band, drama/theater, jazz band, literary magazine, music ensembles, pep band, radio station, student government, student newspaper, International Student Organization. 370 registered organizations, 10 honor societies, 33 religious organizations. 13 fraternities, 15 sororities. **Athletics (Intercollegiate):** *Men:* baseball, basketball, cross-country, diving, gymnastics, soccer, swimming, tennis, track/field (outdoor). *Women:* basketball, cross-country, diving, gymnastics, softball, swimming, tennis, track/field (outdoor), volleyball. **On-Campus Highlights:** Student Center East, Student Center West, UIC Pavilion, Student Services Building, Student Recreation Facility. **Environmental Initiatives:** Establishment of Office of Sustainability; Preparation of a climate action plan and work to improve energy efficiency and test new green technologies; Undertaking a Sustainability Strategic Thinking and Planning Process.

ADMISSIONS

Freshman Academic Profile: Average high school GPA 3.306. 24.4% in top 10% of high school class, 61.5% in top 25% of high school class, 92.1% in top 50% of high school class. 59% from public high schools. SAT Math middle 50% range 530-660. SAT Critical Reading middle 50% range 460-580. SAT Writing middle 50% range 480-580. ACT middle 50% range 22-27. Minimum internet-based TOEFL 80. Minimum paper TOEFL 550. **Basis for Candidate Selection:** *Very important factors considered include:* Class rank, application essay, academic GPA, rigor of secondary school record, standardized test scores. *Other factors considered include:* recommendation(s), character/personal qualities, extracurricular activities. **Freshman Admission Requirements:** High school diploma is required and GED is accepted. **Academic units required:** 4 English, 3 mathematics, 3 science, 2 foreign language, 3 social studies. **Freshman Admission Statistics:** 15,949 applied, 73% admitted, 26% enrolled. **Transfer Admission Requirements:** college transcript(s), Minimum college GPA of 2.5 required. **General Admission Information:** Application Fee $40. Regular application deadline 1/15. Notification on a rolling basis, beginning on or about 11/30. Nonfall registration not accepted. Credit and/or placement offered for CEEB Advanced Placement tests.

COSTS AND FINANCIAL AID

Annual in-state tuition $10,584. Annual out-of-state tuition $22,976. Room and board $10,871. Required fees $3,050. Average book expense $1,400. **Required Forms and Deadlines:** FAFSA. **Notification of Awards:** Applicants will be notified of awards on a rolling basis beginning 3/15. **Types of Aid:** *Need-based scholarships/grants:* Federal Pell, SEOG, state scholarships/grants, private scholarships, the school's own gift aid. *Loans:* Direct Subsidized Stafford, Direct Unsubsidized Stafford, Direct PLUS, Federal Perkins, Federal Nursing, state loans, college/university loans from institutional funds, Alternative Loans. *Student Employment:* Federal Work-Study Program available. Institutional employment available. Off-campus job opportunities are good. **Financial Aid Statistics:** 82% freshmen, 80% undergrads receive need-based scholarship or grant aid. 4% freshmen, 2% undergrads receive non-need-based scholarship or grant aid. 60% freshmen, 68% undergrads receive need-based self-help aid. 1% freshmen, 1% undergrads receive athletic scholarships. 75% freshmen, 74% undergrads receive any aid. 65% undergrads borrow to pay for school. Average cumulative indebtedness $20,431. **Criteria for awarding institutional aid:** *Non-need-based:* academics, art, music/drama.

UNIVERSITY OF ILLINOIS AT SPRINGFIELD

One University Plaza, Springfield, IL 62703-5407
Phone: 217-206-4847 • **Financial Aid Phone:** 217-206-6724
E-mail: admissions@uis.edu • **CEEB Code:** 834
Fax: 217-206-6620 • **Website:** www.uis.edu • **ACT Code:** 1137

This public school was founded in 1969. It has a 746-acre campus.

RATINGS

Admissions Selectivity Rating: 83   **Fire Safety Rating:** 82

STUDENTS AND FACULTY

Enrollment: 2,969. **Student Body:** 51% female, 49% male, 14% out-of-state, 4% international (17 countries represented). Asian 4%, African American 15%, Caucasian 66%, Hispanic 6%, Native American <1%
Retention and Graduation: 33% freshmen graduate within 4 years. 49% freshmen graduate within 6 years. **Faculty:** 214 full-time faculty, 85% hold PhDs, 45% are are members of minority groups, 17% are women.

ACADEMICS

Degrees: bachelor's, master's, post-bachelor's certificate, post-master's certificate. **Classes:** Most classes have 20-29 students. Most lab/discussion sessions have 10-19 students. **Majors with Highest Enrollment:** Business Administration and Management; Computer Science; Psychology. **Special Study Options:** distance learning, double major, English as a Second Language (ESL), honors program, independent study, internships, study abroad, teacher certification program. **Honors programs:** Interdisciplinary four-year baccalaureate experience for highly qualified freshman. **Combined degree programs:** BA/MA. **Disability Services:** Special programs offered to physically disabled students include note-taking services, reader services, tape recorders. **Career services:** Alumni network, alumni services, career/job search classes, career assessment, internships, regional alumni.

FACILITIES

Housing: Coed dorms, special housing for disabled students, special housing for international students, apartments for married students, apartments for single students, Wellness Housing, Theme Housing, Family Housing. 99% of campus accessible to physically disabled. **Special Academic Facilities/Equipment:** Norris L. Brookens Library, Sangamon Auditorium, Observatory **Computers:** 100% of classrooms, 100% of dorms, 100% of libraries, 100% of dining areas, 100% of student union, 100% of common outdoor areas have wireless network access. Students can register for classes online. Administrative functions (other than registration) can be performed online.

CAMPUS LIFE

Environment: City. **Activities:** Choral groups, concert band, dance, drama/theater, jazz band, music ensembles, pep band, student government, student newspaper, student-run film society, Campus Ministries, International Student Organization, Model UN. 76 registered organizations. **Athletics (Intercollegiate):** *Men:* basketball, golf, soccer, tennis. *Women:* basketball, cheerleading, golf, soccer, softball, tennis, volleyball. **On-Campus Highlights:** University Hall, Public Affairs Center **Environmental Initiatives:** Construction of a residence hall with a "green roof." With the support of a grant from the State of Illinois, the university has expanded the recycling program from only academic buildings to include housing. The university has committed 1.95 million dollars to retrofit old single glazed windows in one campus building with double-glazed windows for energy conservation.

ADMISSIONS

Freshman Academic Profile: Average high school GPA 3.42. 21.4% in top 10% of high school class, 43.4% in top 25% of high school class, 77% in top 50% of high school class. 84% from public high schools. ACT middle 50% range 20-27. Minimum paper TOEFL 500. **Basis for Candidate Selection:** *Very important factors considered include:* application essay, academic GPA, rigor of secondary school record. *Important factors considered include:* standardized test scores. *Other factors considered include:* Class rank, recommendation(s), extracurricular activities, first generation, level of applicant's interest, work experience. **Freshman Admission Requirements:** High school diploma is required and GED is accepted. **Academic units required:** 4 English, 3 mathematics, 3 science, (2 science labs), 2 foreign language, 2 social studies, 2 history, 2 visual/performing arts. **Freshman Admission Statistics:** 1,460 applied, 62% admitted, 34% enrolled. **Transfer Admission Requirements:** college transcript(s), Minimum college GPA of 2.0 required. Lowest grade transferable D. **General Admission Information:** Application Fee $40. Nonfall registration not accepted. Admission may be deferred for a maximum of 1 year. Credit and/or placement offered for CEEB Advanced Placement tests.

COSTS AND FINANCIAL AID

Annual out-of-state tuition $18,930. Room and board $11,550. Required fees $2,008. **Required Forms and Deadlines:** FAFSA. **Notification of Awards:**

Applicants will be notified of awards on a rolling basis beginning 1/1. **Types of Aid:** *Need-based scholarships/grants:* Federal Pell, SEOG, state scholarships/grants, private scholarships, the school's own gift aid. *Loans:* Direct Subsidized Stafford, Direct Unsubsidized Stafford, Direct PLUS, Federal Perkins, college/university loans from institutional funds. **Financial Aid Statistics:** 98% freshmen, 88% undergrads receive need-based scholarship or grant aid. 20% freshmen, 11% undergrads receive non-need-based scholarship or grant aid. 79% freshmen, 86% undergrads receive need-based self-help aid. 2% freshmen, 2% undergrads receive athletic scholarships. 70% undergrads borrow to pay for school. Average cumulative indebtedness $21,939. **Criteria for awarding institutional aid:** *Non-need-based:* academics, alumni affiliation, art, athletics, job skills, leadership, minority status, music/drama, state/district residency.

UNIVERSITY OF ILLINOIS AT URBANA-CHAMPAIGN

901 West Illinois Street, Urbana, IL 61801-3028
Phone: 217-333-0302 • **Financial Aid Phone:** 217-333-0100
E-mail: http://admissions.illinois.edu/contact_u • **CEEB Code:** 4607
Fax: 217-244-4614 • **Website:** illinois.edu • **ACT Code:** 1154

This public school was founded in 1867. It has a 4724-acre campus.

RATINGS

Admissions Selectivity Rating: 90   **Fire Safety Rating:** 70

STUDENTS AND FACULTY

Enrollment: 31,663. **Student Body:** 44% female, 56% male, 11% out-of-state, 15% international (123 countries represented). Asian 15%, African American 6%, Caucasian 53%, Hispanic 8%, Native American <1%
Retention and Graduation: 93% freshmen return for sophomore year. 68% freshmen graduate within 4 years. 26% grads go on to further study within 1 year. 18% grads pursue arts and sciences degrees. 3% grads pursue law degrees. 2% grads pursue business degrees. 3% grads pursue medical degrees. **Faculty:** 1,893 full-time faculty, 92% hold PhDs, 33% are are members of minority groups, 26% are women. 26% of classes are taught by teaching assistants.

ACADEMICS

Degrees: bachelor's, certificate, first professional, master's, post-bachelor's certificate, post-master's certificate. **Classes:** Most classes have 20-29 students. Most lab/discussion sessions have 20-29 students. **Majors with Highest Enrollment:** Cell/Cellular and Molecular Biology; Psychology; Political Science and Government. **Special Study Options:** Accelerated program, cooperative education program, cross-registration, distance learning, double major, dual enrollment, English as a Second Language (ESL), exchange student program (domestic), honors program, independent study, internships, liberal arts/career combination, student-designed major, study abroad, teacher certification program, Jonathan Baldwin Turner Honors program, Campus Honors, Illinois Leadership & Entrepreneurial Programs. **Honors programs:** Campus Honors Program, James Scholars Program **Combined degree programs:** BA/MEng, MD/Ph.D. **Disability Services:** Special programs offered to physically disabled students include note-taking services, reader services, tape recorders, tutors. **Career services:** Alumni network, alumni services, career/job search classes, career assessment, internships, regional alumni. Career services highlights include Illinois'"elementhouse," placed ninth overall (out of 20 entries) in the U.S. Department of Energy's Solar Decathlon competition. The 8-day event culminated with an awards ceremony on Friday, October 19 on the National Mall in Washington, D.C.

FACILITIES

Housing: Coed dorms, special housing for disabled students, men's dorms, special housing for international students, women's dorms, fraternity/sorority housing, apartments for married students, cooperative housing, apartments for single students, Living and Learning Communities housed within the residence halls; Private Certified Housing. 100% of campus accessible to physically disabled. **Special Academic Facilities/Equipment:** Art, cultural and natural history museums, performing arts center, National Center for Supercomputing Applications, Beckman Institute, Siebel Computer Science Center, University Library (37 separate libraries and centers on campus), Japan House and Gardens, Assembly Hall for large concerts, Allerton Park and Conference Center, Arboretum, and the Illini Student Union **Computers:** 85% of classrooms, 100% of dorms, 100% of libraries, 100% of dining areas, 100% of student union, 1% of common outdoor areas have wireless network access. Students can register for classes online. Administrative functions (other than registration) can be performed online.

CAMPUS LIFE

Environment: City. **Activities:** Choral groups, concert band, dance, drama/theater, jazz band, literary magazine, marching band, music ensembles, musical theater, opera, pep band, radio station, student government, student newspaper, student-run film society, symphony orchestra, television station, yearbook, Campus Ministries, International Student Organization, Model UN. 1000 registered organizations, 30 honor societies, 95 religious organizations. 60 fraternities, 36 sororities. **Athletics (Intercollegiate):** *Men:* baseball, basketball, cheerleading, cross-country, football, golf, gymnastics, tennis, track/field (outdoor), wrestling. *Women:* basketball, cheerleading, cross-country, diving, golf, gymnastics, soccer, softball, swimming, tennis, track/field (outdoor), volleyball. **On-Campus Highlights:** Campus Town restaurants and shops, Krannert Center for Performing Arts, Assembly Hall, Multiple Campus Recreation Centers, Illini Student Union, On-campus Arboretum; The Japan House; extensive athletic facilities; historic round barns; Siebel Computer Science Center; spacious green space at the Central and Bardeen Quads; Papa Dels Pizza and Za's Italian Cafe. **Environmental Initiatives:** The state-of-the-art Business Instructional Facility at the University of Illinois has earned the world's highest honor for sustainable, environmentally friendly construction and design. The year-old building is the first business facility at a public university anywhere in the world to earn platinum certification. Illinois has recently completed a Sustainability Vision process and is now implementing steps that will infuse sustainability into education, research, outreach and operations. The University's retrocommissioning team has completed nearly 2 million square feet of upgrades to campus buildings, resulting in ~10% energy reduction in 2 years.

ADMISSIONS

Freshman Academic Profile: 55% in top 10% of high school class, 87% in top 25% of high school class, 99% in top 50% of high school class. 75% from public high schools. SAT Math middle 50% range 700-780. SAT Critical Reading middle 50% range 560-670. SAT Writing middle 50% range 580-670. ACT middle 50% range 26-31. Minimum internet-based TOEFL 79. Minimum paper TOEFL 550. **Basis for Candidate Selection:** *Very important factors considered include:* Class rank, application essay, academic GPA, rigor of secondary school record, standardized test scores. *Important factors considered include:* character/personal qualities, extracurricular activities, first generation, talent/ability, volunteer work, work experience. *Other factors considered include:* geographical residence, racial/ethnic status, state residency. **Freshman Admission Requirements:** High school diploma is required and GED is accepted. **Academic units required:** 4 English, 3 mathematics, 2 science, (2 science labs), 2 foreign language, 2 social studies, 0 history, 2 academic electives. 3.5 years of mathematics including trigonometry are required in the following programs: Agricultural. **Freshman Admission Statistics:** 33,171 applied, 62% admitted, 35% enrolled. **Transfer Admission Requirements:** college transcript(s), essay or personal statement, Lowest grade transferable D. **General Admission Information:** Application Fee $40. Regular application deadline 1/2. Regular notification 12/14. Nonfall registration not accepted. Admission may be deferred for a maximum of 12 months. Credit and/or placement offered for CEEB Advanced Placement tests.

COSTS AND FINANCIAL AID

Annual in-state tuition $12,036. Annual out-of-state tuition $26,662. Room and board $10,848. Required fees $3,566. Average book expense $1,200. **Required Forms and Deadlines:** FAFSA. **Notification of Awards: Types of Aid:** *Need-based scholarships/grants:* Federal Pell, SEOG, state scholarships/grants, private scholarships, the school's own gift aid, United Negro College Fund. *Loans:* Direct Subsidized Stafford, Direct Unsubsidized Stafford, Direct PLUS, Federal Perkins, college/university loans from institutional funds. *Student Employment:* Federal Work-Study Program available. Institutional employment available. Highest amount earned per year from on-campus jobs $13,377. Off-campus job opportunities are excellent. **Financial Aid Statistics:** 78% freshmen, 77% undergrads receive need-based scholarship or grant aid. 18% freshmen, 10% undergrads receive non-need-based scholarship or grant aid. 78% freshmen, 82% undergrads receive need-based self-help aid. 1% freshmen, 1% undergrads receive athletic scholarships. 69% freshmen, 72% undergrads receive any aid. 52% undergrads borrow to pay for school. Average cumulative indebtedness $21,455. **Criteria for awarding institutional aid:** *Non-need-based:* academics, alumni affiliation, art, athletics, leadership, music/drama, state/district residency.

See page 1180.

See page 1180.

UNIVERSITY OF THE INCARNATE WORD

4301 Broadway, San Antonio, TX 78209-6397
Phone: 210-829-6005 • **Financial Aid Phone:** 210-829-6008
E-mail: admis@uiwtx.edu • **CEEB Code:** 6303
Fax: 210-829-3921 • **Website:** www.uiw.edu • **ACT Code:** 4106

This private school, affiliated with the Roman Catholic Church, was founded in 1881. It has a 154-acre campus.

RATINGS

Admissions Selectivity Rating: 73   **Fire Safety Rating:** 88

STUDENTS AND FACULTY

Enrollment: 6,325. **Student Body:** 61% female, 39% male, 6% out-of-state, 4% international (41 countries represented). Asian 2%, African American 8%, Caucasian 19%, Hispanic 60%, Native American <1%. **Retention and Graduation:** 74% freshmen return for sophomore year. 19% freshmen graduate within 4 years. 42% freshmen graduate within 6 years. **Faculty:** 278 full-time faculty, 62% hold PhDs, 53% are are members of minority groups, 31% are women.

ACADEMICS

Degrees: associate, bachelor's, first professional, master's, post-bachelor's certificate. **Classes:** Most classes have 20-29 students. Most lab/discussion sessions have 10-19 students. **Majors with Highest Enrollment:** Biology/Biological Sciences; Registered Nursing/Registered Nurse; Business Administration and Management. **Special Study Options:** Accelerated program, cross-registration, distance learning, double major, dual enrollment, English as a Second Language (ESL), honors program, independent study, internships, student-designed major, study abroad, teacher certification program, weekend college. **Honors programs:** UIW Honors Program **Combined degree programs:** BBA/MS—Accounting. **Disability Services:** Special programs offered to physically disabled students include note-taking services, reader services, tape recorders, tutors. **Career services:** alumni services, career/job search classes, career assessment, internships.

FACILITIES

Housing: Coed dorms, special housing for disabled students, men's dorms, women's dorms, apartments for single students. 95% of campus accessible to physically disabled. **Computers:** 100% of classrooms, 100% of dorms, 100% of libraries, 100% of dining areas, 100% of student union, 100% of common outdoor areas have wireless network access. Students can register for classes online. Administrative functions (other than registration) can be performed online. Undergraduates are required to own a computer.

CAMPUS LIFE

Environment: Metropolis. **Activities:** Choral groups, dance, drama/theater, jazz band, literary magazine, music ensembles, musical theater, radio station, student government, student newspaper, symphony orchestra, Campus Ministries, International Student Organization. 58 registered organizations, 8 honor societies, 2 religious organizations. 2 fraternities, 4 sororities. **Athletics (Intercollegiate):** *Men:* baseball, basketball, cross-country, football, golf, soccer, swimming, tennis, track/field (outdoor). *Women:* basketball, cross-country, golf, soccer, softball, swimming, synchronized swimming, tennis, track/field (outdoor), volleyball. **On-Campus Highlights:** Student Center, Chick-Fil-A, Library, Wellness Center, Dubuis Lawn.

ADMISSIONS

Freshman Academic Profile: Average high school GPA 3.47. 14% in top 10% of high school class, 37% in top 25% of high school class, 69% in top 50% of high school class. SAT Math middle 50% range 430-540. SAT Critical Reading middle 50% range 420-530. SAT Writing middle 50% range 413-510. ACT middle 50% range 18-23. Minimum internet-based TOEFL 79. Minimum paper TOEFL 650. **Basis for Candidate Selection:** *Very important factors considered include:* academic GPA, rigor of secondary school record. *Important factors considered include:* Class rank, standardized test scores. *Other factors considered include:* application essay, recommendation(s), alumni/ae relation, character/personal qualities, extracurricular activities, geographical residence, interview, level of applicant's interest, talent/ability, volunteer work, work experience. **Freshman Admission Requirements:** High school diploma is required and GED is accepted. **Academic units required:** 4 English, 3 mathematics, 3 science, 2 foreign language, 3 social studies, 1 visual/performing arts. **Freshman Admission Statistics:** 4,257 applied, 93% admitted, 24% enrolled. **Transfer Admission Requirements:** college transcript(s), Minimum college GPA of 2.50 required. Lowest grade transferable C. **General Admission Information:** Application Fee $20. Nonfall registration accepted. Admission may be deferred for a maximum of 1 term. Credit offered for CEEB Advanced Placement tests.

COSTS AND FINANCIAL AID

Annual tuition $25,900. Room and board $11,364. Required fees $1,898. Average book expense $1,200. **Required Forms and Deadlines:** FAFSA. **Notification of Awards:** Applicants will be notified of awards on a rolling basis beginning 2/15. **Types of Aid:** *Need-based scholarships/grants:* Federal Pell, SEOG, state scholarships/grants, private scholarships, the school's own gift aid, United Negro College Fund, Federal Nursing Scholarships. *Loans:* Subsidized Stafford, Unsubsidized Stafford, PLUS, Federal Perkins, Federal Nursing, state loans. *Student Employment:* Federal Work-Study Program available. Institutional employment available. Off-campus job opportunities are good. **Financial Aid Statistics:** 96% freshmen, 97% undergrads receive need-based scholarship or grant aid. 5% freshmen, 5% undergrads receive non-need-based scholarship or grant aid. 38% freshmen, 83% undergrads receive need-based self-help aid. 2% freshmen, 3% undergrads receive athletic scholarships. 99% freshmen, 82% undergrads borrow to pay for school. Average cumulative indebtedness $21,491. **Criteria for awarding institutional aid:** *Non-need-based:* academics, alumni affiliation, art, athletics, leadership, music/drama, religious affiliation, state/district residency.

UNIVERSITY OF INDIANAPOLIS

1400 East Hanna Avenue, Indianapolis, IN 46227-3697
Phone: 317-788-3216 • **Financial Aid Phone:** 317-788-3217
E-mail: admissions@uindy.edu • **CEEB Code:** 1321
Fax: 317-788-3300 • **Website:** www.uindy.edu • **ACT Code:** 1204

This private school, affiliated with the Methodist Church, was founded in 1902. It has a 65-acre campus.

RATINGS

Admissions Selectivity Rating: 81   **Fire Safety Rating:** 67

STUDENTS AND FACULTY

Enrollment: 4,138. **Student Body:** 68% female, 32% male, 9% out-of-state, 5% international (47 countries represented). Asian 1%, African American 13%, Caucasian 73%, Hispanic 2%, Native American <1%
Retention and Graduation: 74% freshmen return for sophomore year. 36% freshmen graduate within 4 years. 52% freshmen graduate within 6 years. **Faculty:** 218 full-time faculty, 76% hold PhDs, 57% are are members of minority groups, 6% are women. 0% of classes are taught by teaching assistants.

ACADEMICS

Degrees: associate, bachelor's, master's. **Classes:** Most classes have 10-19 students. Most lab/discussion sessions have 20-29 students. **Majors with Highest Enrollment:** Business/Commerce; Registered Nursing/Registered Nurse; Psychology. **Special Study Options:** Accelerated program, cross-registration, double major, dual enrollment, English as a Second Language (ESL), honors program, independent study, internships, liberal arts/career combination, student-designed major, study abroad, teacher certification program, Spring Term Session (4-4-1). **Disability Services:** Special programs offered to physically disabled students include note-taking services, reader services, tape recorders, tutors.

FACILITIES

Housing: Coed dorms, women's dorms, apartments for married students, apartments for single students. 90% of campus accessible to physically disabled. **Special Academic Facilities/Equipment:** Developmental preschool, art gallery, observatory. **Computers:** 100% of classrooms, 100% of dorms, 100% of libraries, 100% of dining areas, 100% of student union, 100% of common outdoor areas have wireless network access.

CAMPUS LIFE

Environment: Metropolis. **Activities:** Choral groups, concert band, dance, drama/theater, jazz band, literary magazine, music ensembles, musical theater, opera, pep band, radio station, student government, student newspaper, television station, yearbook, Campus Ministries, International Student Organization. 53 registered organizations, 14 honor societies, 4 religious organizations. **Athletics (Intercollegiate):** *Men:* baseball, basketball, cross-country, diving, football, golf, soccer, swimming, tennis, track/field (outdoor), wrestling. *Women:* basketball, cross-country, diving, golf, soccer, softball, swimming, tennis, track/field (outdoor), volleyball. **On-Campus Highlights:** Ruth Lilly Fitness Center, Schwitzer Center, Krannert Memorial Library, Christel Dehaan Fine Arts Center, Martin Hall.

ADMISSIONS

Freshman Academic Profile: Average high school GPA 3.42. 27% in top 10% of high school class, 56% in top 25% of high school class, 88% in top 50% of high school class. SAT Math middle 50% range 460-570. SAT Critical Reading middle 50% range 450-560. SAT Writing middle 50% range 440-550. ACT middle 50% range 19-25. Minimum paper TOEFL 500. **Basis for Candidate Selection:** *Very important factors considered include:* academic GPA, rigor of secondary school record. *Important factors considered include:* Class rank, standardized test scores. *Other factors considered include:* recommendation(s), extracurricular activities, interview. **Freshman Admission Requirements:** High school diploma is required and GED is accepted. **Academic units required:** 4 English, 3 mathematics, 3 science, (2 science labs), 2 foreign language, 1 social studies, 1 history, 1 academic elective. **Freshman Admission Statistics:** 5,396 applied, 79% admitted, 19% enrolled. **Transfer Admission Requirements:** High school transcript, college transcript(s), standardized test scores, statement of good standing from prior institution(s). Minimum college GPA of 2.0 required. Lowest grade transferable C-. **General Admission Information:** Application Fee $25. Notification on a rolling basis, beginning on or about 9/1. Nonfall registration accepted. Credit offered for CEEB Advanced Placement tests.

COSTS AND FINANCIAL AID

Annual tuition $23,590. Room and board $9,090. Required fees $240. Average book expense $1,076. **Required Forms and Deadlines:** FAFSA, Institution's own financial aid form. **Notification of Awards:** Applicants will be notified of awards on a rolling basis beginning 3/1. **Types of Aid:** *Need-based scholarships/grants:* Federal Pell, SEOG, state scholarships/grants, private scholarships, the school's own gift aid. *Loans:* Subsidized Stafford, Unsubsidized Stafford, PLUS, Federal Perkins. *Student Employment:* Federal Work-Study Program available. Institutional employment available. Off-campus job opportunities are good. **Financial Aid Statistics:** 57% freshmen, 68% undergrads receive need-based scholarship or grant aid. 99% freshmen, 69% undergrads receive non-need-based scholarship or grant aid. 78% freshmen, 78% undergrads receive need-based self-help aid. 8% freshmen, 8% undergrads receive athletic scholarships. 99% freshmen, 98% undergrads receive any aid. 79% undergrads borrow to pay for school. Average cumulative indebtedness $22,735. **Criteria for awarding institutional aid:** *Non-need-based:* academics, alumni affiliation, art, athletics, job skills, leadership, music/drama, religious affiliation, state/district residency.

UNIVERSITY OF IOWA

107 Calvin Hall, Iowa City, IA 52242
Phone: 319-335-3847 • **Financial Aid Phone:** 319-335-1450
E-mail: admissions@uiowa.edu • **CEEB Code:** 6681
Fax: 319-333-1535 • **Website:** www.uiowa.edu • **ACT Code:** 1356

This public school was founded in 1847. It has a 1900-acre campus.

RATINGS

Admissions Selectivity Rating: 85   **Fire Safety Rating:** 84

STUDENTS AND FACULTY

Enrollment: 21,486. **Student Body:** 52% female, 48% male, 34% out-of-state, 11% international (98 countries represented). Asian 3%, African American 3%, Caucasian 68%, Hispanic 6%, Native American <1%
Retention and Graduation: 86% freshmen return for sophomore year. 48% freshmen graduate within 4 years. 70% freshmen graduate within 6 years. **Faculty:** 1,484 full-time faculty, 97% hold PhDs, 32% are are members of minority groups, 19% are women.

ACADEMICS

Degrees: bachelor's, certificate, master's, post-master's certificate. **Classes:** Most classes have 10-19 students. Most lab/discussion sessions have 20-29 students. **Majors with Highest Enrollment:** Business/Commerce; Engineering; Pre-Medicine/Pre-Medical Studies. **Special Study Options:** Accelerated program, cooperative education program, distance learning, double major, dual enrollment, English as a Second Language (ESL), exchange student program (domestic), external degree program, honors program, independent study, internships, liberal arts/career combination, student-designed major, study abroad, teacher certification program. **Honors programs:** The University of Iowa Honors Program is dedicated to the academic and personal enrichment of its students. This enrichment is accomplished through special academic opportunities and programs that are sponsored by the Honors Program and open to all Honors students. **Combined degree programs:** BA/MA, BA/DDS, BA/MEng, BBA/BA,BS BSE/BA, BS BSN/BA,BS. **Disability Services:** Special programs offered to physically disabled students include note-taking services, reader services, tape recorders, tutors. **Career services:** Alumni network, alumni services, career/job search classes, career assessment, internships, regional alumni. Career services highlights include The University of Iowa Pomerantz Career Center, a world-class facility with a national reputation for excellence. The Center directly serves more than 20,000 students from the Henry B. Tippie College of Business, the College of Engineering, and the College of Liberal Arts and Sciences.

FACILITIES

Housing: Coed dorms, special housing for disabled students, fraternity/sorority housing, apartments for married students, apartments for single students, Wellness Housing, Theme HousingQuiet Houses available. Living-Learning Communities for the following interests: Honors; Iowa Writers; Health Sciences; Business and Entrepreneurship, Women in Science and Engineering; Men in Engineering; performing arts; international interests; citizenship and service; Law Study and Legal Careers, Sustainability, Career Leadership Academy, Healthy Living Network, Hispanic Culture and Language. 98% of campus accessible to physically disabled. **Special Academic Facilities/Equipment:** National Advanced Driving Simulator, electron microscope, laser facility, Oakdale Research park, UI Hygienic Lab, UI Center for Biocatalysis & Bioprocessing, UI Research Foundation, survey research facilities natural history museum, Medical Museum, Old Capitol Museum, Main Library and 10 departmental libraries, information arcade, newspaper production lab, TV lab, UI Technology Innovation Center, and Project Art. **Computers:** 100% of classrooms, 25% of dorms, 100% of libraries, 25% of dining areas, 90% of student union, 15% of common outdoor areas have wireless network access. Students can register for classes online. Administrative functions (other than registration) can be performed online.

CAMPUS LIFE

Environment: City. **Activities:** Choral groups, concert band, dance, drama/theater, jazz band, literary magazine, marching band, music ensembles, musical theater, opera, pep band, radio station, student government, student newspaper, student-run film society, symphony orchestra, television station, Campus Ministries, International Student Organization. 488 registered organizations, 21 honor societies, 24 religious organizations. 18 fraternities, 18 sororities. **Athletics (Intercollegiate):** *Men:* baseball, basketball, cheerleading, cross-country, diving, football, golf, gymnastics, swimming, tennis, track/field (outdoor), track/field (indoor), wrestling. *Women:* basketball, cheerleading, crew/rowing, cross-country, diving, field hockey, golf, gymnastics, soccer, softball, swimming, tennis, track/field (outdoor), track/field (indoor), volleyball. **On-Campus Highlights:** Kinnick Stadium/Carver Hawkeye Arena, The University of Iowa Museum of Natural History, UI Recreational Services, Hawkeye Hall of Fame, UIHC Project Art. **Environmental Initiatives:** The University of Iowa has established seven 2020 Sustainability Targets that include goals for energy conservation, renewable energy, waste diversion, reduced carbon impact of transportation, increasing student opportunities to learn and practice sustainability principles, support sustainability research and develop partnerships to advance collaborative initiatives. The UI was the first certified Tree Campus in Iowa.The number of LEED-Accredited Professionals on staff in Facilities Management tripled to total 17. The University of Iowa has established a sustainability partnership with EPA Region 7 to "address climate change, as well as sustain air, water and land resources." The UI is recognized by the US EPA as one of the Top 20 on-site green power producers (for both 2009 and 2010), the only university to be listed in the top 20. The University of Iowa is integrating sustainability into its academic and research mission through the creation of ten new interdisciplinary faculty positions and the development of a sustainability studies certificate. Over 130 studeents are now enrolled in the certificate program. A new sustainable living/learning community has been established.

ADMISSIONS

Freshman Academic Profile: Average high school GPA 3.63. 29% in top 10% of high school class, 56% in top 25% of high school class, 90% in top 50% of high school class. 91% from public high schools. SAT Math middle 50% range 540-700. SAT Critical Reading middle 50% range 460-620. ACT middle 50% range 23-28. Minimum internet-based TOEFL 80. Minimum paper TOEFL 530. **Basis for Candidate Selection:** *Very important factors considered include:* Class rank, academic GPA, rigor of secondary school record, standardized test scores. *Other factors considered include:* recommendation(s), character/personal qualities, state residency, talent/ability. **Freshman Admission Requirements:** High school diploma is required and GED is accepted. **Academic units required:** 4 English, 3 mathematics, 3 science, 2 foreign language, 3 social studies. **Freshman Admission Statistics:** 24,097 applied, 81% admitted, 98% enrolled. **Transfer Admission Requirements:** High school transcript, college transcript(s), Minimum college GPA of 2.5 required. Lowest grade transferable D. **General Admission Information:** Application Fee $40. Regular application deadline 4/1. Notification on a rolling basis, beginning on or about 9/15. Nonfall registration accepted. Admission may be deferred for a maximum of 12. Credit and/or placement offered for CEEB Advanced Placement tests.

COSTS AND FINANCIAL AID

Annual in-state tuition $6,678. Annual out-of-state tuition $26,464. Room and board $9,728. Required fees $1,426. Average book expense $1,240. **Required Forms and Deadlines:** FAFSA, Institution's own financial aid form. **Notification of Awards:** Applicants will be notified of awards on a rolling basis beginning 3/15. **Types of Aid:** *Need-based scholarships/grants:* Federal Pell, SEOG, state scholarships/grants, private scholarships, the school's own gift aid. *Loans:* Direct Subsidized Stafford, Direct Unsubsidized Stafford, Direct PLUS, Federal Perkins, Federal Nursing, college/university loans from institutional funds, Short term. *Student Employment:* Federal Work-Study Program available. Institutional employment available. Highest amount earned per year from on-campus jobs $7,200. Off-campus job opportunities are good. **Financial Aid Statistics:** 72% freshmen, 68% undergrads receive need-based scholarship or grant aid. 67% freshmen, 46% undergrads receive non-need-based scholarship or grant aid. 85% freshmen, 89% undergrads receive need-based self-help aid. 3% freshmen, 3% undergrads receive athletic scholarships. 79% freshmen, 72% undergrads receive any aid. 56% undergrads borrow to pay for school. Average cumulative indebtedness $23,808. **Criteria for awarding institutional aid:** *Non-need-based:* academics, alumni affiliation, art, athletics, leadership, minority status, music/drama.

UNIVERSITY OF JAMESTOWN

6081 College Lane, Jamestown, ND 58405-0001
Phone: 701-252-3467 • **Financial Aid Phone:** 701-252-3467
E-mail: admissions@uj.edu
Fax: 701-253-4318 • **Website:** www.uj.edu • **ACT Code:** 3200

This private school, affiliated with the Presbyterian Church, was founded in 1883. It has a 110-acre campus.

RATINGS

Admissions Selectivity Rating: 83   **Fire Safety Rating:** 70

STUDENTS AND FACULTY

Enrollment: 917. **Student Body:** 52% female, 48% male, 55% out-of-state, 6% international (15 countries represented). Asian 1%, African American 3%, Caucasian 83%, Hispanic 5%, Native American 1%
Retention and Graduation: 61% freshmen return for sophomore year. 34% freshmen graduate within 4 years. 52% freshmen graduate within 6 years. 14% grads go on to further study within 1 year. 9% grads pursue arts and sciences degrees. 2% grads pursue law degrees. 2% grads pursue medical degrees. **Faculty:** 60 full-time faculty, 55% hold PhDs, 50% are are members of minority groups, 5% are women. 0% of classes are taught by teaching assistants.

ACADEMICS

Degrees: bachelor's. **Classes:** Most classes have 10-19 students. Most lab/discussion sessions have fewer than 10 students. **Majors with Highest Enrollment:** Elementary Education and Teaching; Business/Commerce; Registered Nursing/Registered Nurse. **Special Study Options:** cooperative education program, double major, dual enrollment, English as a Second Language (ESL), exchange student program (domestic), honors program, independent study, internships, liberal arts/career combination, student-designed major, study abroad, teacher certification program. **Honors programs:** Character and Leadership Program. The heart of the Character in Leadership program is its academic core. Each student who participates will receive a minor in leadership. Jamestown College values its reputation for quality education and therefore is committed through its Character in Leadership Program to providing a broad and sound intellectual foundation that will enable its students to provide ethical leadership in an ever-changing world. **Disability Services:** Special programs offered to physically disabled students include note-taking services, reader services, tape recorders, tutors. **Career services:** Alumni network, alumni services, career/job search classes, internships.

FACILITIES

Housing: Coed dorms, special housing for disabled students, apartments for married students, apartments for single students. 80% of campus accessible to physically disabled. **Computers:** 95% of classrooms, 100% of dorms, 100% of libraries, 100% of dining areas, 100% of student union, 50% of common outdoor areas have wireless network access. Students can register for classes online. Administrative functions (other than registration) can be performed online.

CAMPUS LIFE

Environment: Village. **Activities:** Choral groups, concert band, dance, drama/theater, jazz band, literary magazine, music ensembles, musical theater, pep band, student government, student newspaper, television station, Campus Ministries, International Student Organization. 35 registered organizations, 6 honor societies, 5 religious organizations. **Athletics (Intercollegiate):** *Men:* baseball, basketball, cross-country, football, golf, track/field (outdoor), track/field (indoor), wrestling. *Women:* basketball, cross-country, golf, soccer, softball, track/field (outdoor), track/field (indoor), volleyball, wrestling. **On-Campus Highlights:** Library lobby, Lounge/tv room outside of Cafeteria, Larson Center (athletic center)/Foss Wellness Center, Residence Hall lounges, Level 2 (campus nightclub).

ADMISSIONS

Freshman Academic Profile: Average high school GPA 3.37. 12% in top 10% of high school class, 35.7% in top 25% of high school class, 68.6% in top 50% of high school class. SAT Math middle 50% range 430-530. SAT Critical Reading middle 50% range 430-570. ACT middle 50% range 20-24. Minimum internet-based TOEFL 70. Minimum paper TOEFL 525. **Basis for Candidate Selection:** *Important factors considered include:* academic GPA, recommendation(s), standardized test scores. *Other factors considered include:* rigor of secondary school record, character/personal qualities, extracurricular activities, level of applicant's interest, talent/ability, volunteer work, work experience. **Freshman Admission Requirements:** High school diploma is required and GED is accepted. **Freshman Admission Statistics:** 1,088 applied, 57% admitted, 42% enrolled. **Transfer Admission Requirements:** High school transcript, college transcript(s), statement of good standing from prior institution(s). Minimum college GPA of 2.5 required. Lowest grade transferable c. **General Admission Information:** Application Fee $35. Notification on a rolling basis, beginning on or about 7/1. Nonfall registration accepted. Admission may be deferred for a maximum of 1. Credit offered for CEEB Advanced Placement tests.

COSTS AND FINANCIAL AID

Annual tuition $18,650. Room and board $6,430. Required fees $520. Average book expense $1,000. **Required Forms and Deadlines:** FAFSA. **Notification of Awards:** Applicants will be notified of awards on a rolling basis beginning 2/1. **Types of Aid:** *Need-based scholarships/grants:* Federal Pell, SEOG, state scholarships/grants, private scholarships, the school's own gift aid, Federal Nursing Scholarships. *Loans:* Subsidized Stafford, Unsubsidized Stafford, PLUS, Federal Perkins, college/university loans from institutional funds, Alternative Loans (Private). *Student Employment:* Federal Work-Study Program available. Institutional employment available. Highest amount earned per year from on-campus jobs $2,262. Off-campus job opportunities are good. **Financial Aid Statistics:** 100% freshmen, 100% undergrads receive need-based scholarship or grant aid. 18% freshmen, 16% undergrads receive non-need-based scholarship or grant aid. 78% freshmen, 80% undergrads receive need-based self-help aid. 23% freshmen, 23% undergrads receive athletic scholarships. 100% freshmen, 98% undergrads receive any aid. 78% undergrads borrow to pay for school. Average cumulative indebtedness $27,258. **Criteria for awarding institutional aid:** *Non-need-based:* academics, alumni affiliation, art, athletics, job skills, leadership, music/drama, religious affiliation.

UNIVERSITY OF KANSAS

Office of Admissions, Lawrence, KS 66045-7576
Phone: 785-864-3911 · **Financial Aid Phone:** 785-864-4700
E-mail: adm@ku.edu · **CEEB Code:** 6871
Fax: 785-864-5006 · **Website:** http://www.ku.edu/ · **ACT Code:** 1470

This public school was founded in 1866. It has a 1100-acre campus.

RATINGS

Admissions Selectivity Rating: 82   **Fire Safety Rating:** 89

STUDENTS AND FACULTY

Enrollment: 18,802. **Student Body:** 50% female, 50% male, 24% out-of-state, 5% international (73 countries represented). Asian 4%, African American 5%, Caucasian 73%, Hispanic 7%, Native American <1%. **Retention and Graduation:** 80% freshmen return for sophomore year. 37% freshmen graduate within 4 years. 60% freshmen graduate within 6 years. 29% grads go on to further study within 1 year. **Faculty:** 1,386 full-time faculty, 92% hold PhDs, 40% are are members of minority groups, 20% are women. 20% of classes are taught by teaching assistants.

ACADEMICS

Degrees: bachelor's, master's, post-master's certificate. **Classes:** Most classes have 20-29 students. Most lab/discussion sessions have 10-19 students. **Majors with Highest Enrollment:** Business/Commerce; Biology/Biological Sciences;

Journalism. **Special Study Options:** Accelerated program, cooperative education program, distance learning, double major, dual enrollment, English as a Second Language (ESL), honors program, independent study, internships, liberal arts/career combination, study abroad, teacher certification program, Off Campus Study: Washington DC semester; Study abroad in over 60 countries. **Honors programs:** The University Honors Program gives outstanding and creative students opportunities for intellectual growth and achievement through its small, challenging classes. web site at www.honors.ku.edu. **Disability Services:** Special programs offered to physically disabled students include note-taking services, reader services, tape recorders, tutors. **Career services:** career/job search classes, career assessment, internships. Career services highlights include Alternative Breaks, In the Streets Week, Center for Community Outreach.

FACILITIES

Housing: Coed dorms, women's dorms, fraternity/sorority housing, apartments for married students, cooperative housing, apartments for single students. 95% of campus accessible to physically disabled. **Special Academic Facilities/Equipment:** 12 libraries (including art and architecture, engineering, law, medical, music and dance, rare research materials, special collections, and science), performing arts center, organ recital hall, museums (art, anthropology, classical, entomology, invertebrate paleontology, and natural history), film studio, student operated radio and television stations, public radio station, herbarium, space technology center, observatory, Robert J. Dole Institute for Politics, Hall Center for the Humanities, Center for International Business Education and Research, ecological reserves, Biological Survey, Geological Survey, Information and Telecommunication Technology Center, energy research center, flight research lab, Transportation Research Center, 400+ bed hospital for clinical learning, Hoglund Brain Imaging Center, Center on Aging.

CAMPUS LIFE

Environment: City. **Activities:** Choral groups, concert band, dance, drama/theater, jazz band, literary magazine, marching band, music ensembles, musical theater, opera, pep band, radio station, student government, student newspaper, symphony orchestra, television station, International Student Organization. 476 registered organizations, 14 honor societies, 39 religious organizations. 27 fraternities, 16 sororities. **Athletics (Intercollegiate):** *Men:* baseball, basketball, cross-country, football, golf, track/field (outdoor), track/field (indoor). *Women:* basketball, crew/rowing, cross-country, diving, golf, soccer, softball, swimming, tennis, track/field (outdoor), track/field (indoor), volleyball. **On-Campus Highlights:** Spencer Museum of Art, Kansas Union and Bookstore, Natural History Museum, Athletic Hall of Fame, Robert J. Dole Institute of Politics, Beautiful campus to walk around. **Environmental Initiatives:** In fall 2011, the University of Kansas released its campus sustainability plan, Building Sustainable Traditions, which establishes a vision for a more sustainable campus and outlines specific strategies for achieving the goals of the plan. Action steps are focused in 9 key areas: administration, research & curriculum, student life, energy, built environment, campus grounds, procurement, waste, and transportation. (http://www.sustainability.ku.edu/Plan/). Three of four research initiatives included in the strategic plan, Bold Aspirations, have a sustainability connection: "Sustaining the Planet, Powering the World", "Promoting Well-Being, Fining Cures", and "Building Communities, Expanding Opportunities". These themes represent the highest priorities for research investment for the next 5 years. Summits on each of the themes were held in 2011 and 2012 to help form research networks, identify funding opportunities and faculty leaders, strategize about needed infrastructure, and inform priorities for future faculty hiring. In 2011, KU opened its Center for Design Research, an incubator for design innovation, in what will likely be the first commercial certified passive building in North America. It is also the fourth LEED Platinum building completed by Studio 804, an architecture design-build course that focuses on sustainable design and construction. The building features solar panels and a wind turbine, a green roof and living wall, an electrochromic curtainwall that controls the amount of sunlight—and therefore heat—entering the windows, and bricks that were hand-cut by students from limestone tailings.

ADMISSIONS

Freshman Academic Profile: Average high school GPA 3.5. 26% in top 10% of high school class, 56% in top 25% of high school class, 87% in top 50% of high school class. ACT middle 50% range 22-28. **Basis for Candidate Selection:** *Very important factors considered include:* Class rank, academic GPA, standardized test scores. **Freshman Admission Requirements:** High school diploma is required and GED is accepted. **Academic units required:** 4 English, 3 mathematics, 3 science, 3 social studies. **Freshman Admission Statistics:** 15,767 applied, 91% admitted, 28% enrolled. **Transfer Admission Requirements:** college transcript(s), Minimum college GPA of 2.5 required. Lowest grade transferable C. **General Admission Information:** Application Fee $30. Regular application deadline 4/1. Notification on a rolling basis, beginning on or about 9/1. Nonfall registration accepted. Credit and/or placement offered for CEEB Advanced Placement tests.

COSTS AND FINANCIAL AID

Annual out-of-state tuition $24,831. Room and board $7,896. Required fees $900. Average book expense $950. **Required Forms and Deadlines:** FAFSA.

Notification of Awards: Applicants will be notified of awards on a rolling basis beginning 4/1. **Types of Aid:** *Need-based scholarships/grants:* Federal Pell, SEOG, state scholarships/grants, private scholarships, the school's own gift aid. *Loans:* Direct Subsidized Stafford, Direct Unsubsidized Stafford, Direct PLUS, Subsidized Stafford, Unsubsidized Stafford, PLUS, Federal Perkins, college/university loans from institutional funds. *Student Employment:* Federal Work-Study Program available. Institutional employment available. Highest amount earned per year from on-campus jobs $4,800. Off-campus job opportunities are excellent. **Financial Aid Statistics:** 55% freshmen, 59% undergrads receive need-based scholarship or grant aid. 48% freshmen, 32% undergrads receive non-need-based scholarship or grant aid. 67% freshmen, 76% undergrads receive need-based self-help aid. 2% freshmen, 2% undergrads receive athletic scholarships. 73% freshmen, 59% undergrads receive any aid. 53% undergrads borrow to pay for school. Average cumulative indebtedness $22,358. **Criteria for awarding institutional aid:** *Non-need-based:* academics, alumni affiliation, art, athletics, leadership, minority status, music/drama, state/district residency.

UNIVERSITY OF KENTUCKY

100 Funkhouser Building, Lexington, KY 40506
Phone: 859-257-2000 · **Financial Aid Phone:** 859-257-3172
E-mail: admissions@uky.edu · **CEEB Code:** 1837
Fax: 859-257-3823 · **Website:** www.uky.edu · **ACT Code:** 1554

This public school was founded in 1865. It has a 687-acre campus.

RATINGS

Admissions Selectivity Rating: 87   **Fire Safety Rating:** 84

STUDENTS AND FACULTY
Enrollment: 20,436. **Student Body:** 51% female, 49% male, 21% out-of-state, 2% international (117 countries represented). Asian 2%, African American 8%, Caucasian 80%, Hispanic 3%, Native American <1%
Retention and Graduation: 81% freshmen return for sophomore year. 34% freshmen graduate within 4 years. **Faculty:** 1,365 full-time faculty, 93% hold PhDs, 36% are are members of minority groups, 18% are women. 20% of classes are taught by teaching assistants.

ACADEMICS
Degrees: bachelor's, certificate, first professional, master's. **Classes:** Most classes have 20-29 students. Most lab/discussion sessions have 20-29 students. **Special Study Options:** Accelerated program, cooperative education program, distance learning, double major, English as a Second Language (ESL), exchange student program (domestic), honors program, independent study, internships, study abroad, teacher certification program, weekend college. **Combined degree programs:** BA/MA, JD/MBA. **Disability Services:** Special programs offered to physically disabled students include note-taking services, reader services.

FACILITIES
Housing: Coed dorms, special housing for disabled students, men's dorms, special housing for international students, women's dorms, fraternity/sorority housing, apartments for married students, apartments for single students. 95% of campus accessible to physically disabled. **Special Academic Facilities/Equipment:** Anthropology and art museums, center for the humanities, centers for equine research, cancer research, and robotics, pharmacy manufacturing lab. **Computers:** 30% of classrooms, 10% of dorms, 100% of libraries, 80% of dining areas, 70% of student union, 50% of common outdoor areas have wireless network access. Students can register for classes online. Administrative functions (other than registration) can be performed online.

CAMPUS LIFE
Environment: City. **Activities:** Choral groups, concert band, dance, drama/theater, jazz band, literary magazine, marching band, music ensembles, musical theater, opera, pep band, radio station, student government, student newspaper, symphony orchestra, yearbook, International Student Organization. 348 registered organizations, 28 honor societies, 20 religious organizations. 19 fraternities, 16 sororities. **Athletics (Intercollegiate):** *Men:* baseball, basketball, cheerleading, cross-country, diving, football, golf, riflery, soccer, swimming, tennis, track/field (outdoor), track/field (indoor). *Women:* basketball, cheerleading, cross-country, diving, golf, gymnastics, riflery, soccer, softball, swimming, tennis, track/field (outdoor), track/field (indoor), volleyball. **On-Campus Highlights:** W.T. Young Library, Johnson Fitness Center, Memorial Coliseum, Arboretum, Memorial Hall.

ADMISSIONS
Freshman Academic Profile: Average high school GPA 3.46. 32% in top 10% of high school class, 61% in top 25% of high school class, 88% in top 50% of high school class. SAT Math middle 50% range 510-630. SAT Critical Reading middle 50% range 500-620. SAT Writing middle 50% range 480-600. ACT middle 50% range 23-28. Minimum paper TOEFL 527. **Basis for Candidate Selection:** *Very important factors considered include:* academic GPA, rigor of secondary school record, standardized test scores. *Other factors considered include:* Class rank, application essay, recommendation(s), alumni/ae relation, character/personal qualities, extracurricular activities, first generation, geographical residence, interview, racial/ethnic status, talent/ability, volunteer work. **Freshman Admission Requirements:** High school diploma is required and GED is accepted. **Academic units required:** 4 English, 3 mathematics, 3 science, 2 foreign language, 3 social studies, 5 academic electives, 2 Fine or Performing Arts (1), Health (.5), and Physical Ed. (.5). **Freshman Admission Statistics:** 18,802 applied, 67% admitted, 37% enrolled. **Transfer Admission Requirements:** college transcript(s), Minimum college GPA of 2.0 required. Lowest grade transferable D. **General Admission Information:** Application Fee $50. Regular application deadline 2/15. Notification on a rolling basis, beginning on or about 10/1. Nonfall registration accepted. Admission may be deferred for a maximum of 1 year. Credit and/or placement offered for CEEB Advanced Placement tests.

COSTS AND FINANCIAL AID
Annual out-of-state tuition $18,798. Room and board $10,192. Required fees $1,066. Average book expense $800. **Required Forms and Deadlines:** FAFSA. **Notification of Awards:** Applicants will be notified of awards on a rolling basis beginning 4/1. **Types of Aid:** *Need-based scholarships/grants:* Federal Pell, SEOG, state scholarships/grants, private scholarships, the school's own gift aid. *Loans:* Direct Subsidized Stafford, Direct Unsubsidized Stafford, Direct PLUS, Subsidized Stafford, Unsubsidized Stafford, PLUS, Federal Perkins, state loans, college/university loans from institutional funds. *Student Employment:* Federal Work-Study Program available. **Financial Aid Statistics:** 46% freshmen, 49% undergrads receive need-based scholarship or grant aid. 89% freshmen, 71% undergrads receive non-need-based scholarship or grant aid. 59% freshmen, 68% undergrads receive need-based self-help aid. 3% freshmen, 3% undergrads receive athletic scholarships. 40% freshmen, 38% undergrads receive any aid. 40% undergrads borrow to pay for school. Average cumulative indebtedness $16,374. **Criteria for awarding institutional aid:** *Non-need-based:* academics, alumni affiliation, art, athletics, job skills, leadership, minority status, music/drama, state/district residency.

UNIVERSITY OF KING'S COLLEGE

Registrars Office, Halifax, NS B3H 2A1
Phone: 902-422-1271
E-mail: admissions@ukings.ns.ca
Fax: 902-423-3357 · **Website:** www.ukings.ca

This public school was founded in 1789. It has a 3-acre campus.

RATINGS

Admissions Selectivity Rating: 66   **Fire Safety Rating:** 60*

STUDENTS AND FACULTY
Enrollment: 1,137. **Student Body:** 57% female, 43% male, 53% out-of-state, (6 countries represented).
Faculty: 51 full-time faculty, 71% hold PhDs, 31% are are members of minority groups. 0% of classes are taught by teaching assistants.

ACADEMICS
Degrees: bachelor's. **Majors with Highest Enrollment:** Sociology; English Language and Literature; Psychology. **Special Study Options:** cooperative education program, double major, honors program, internships, study abroad. **Career services:** career/job search classes, career assessment.

FACILITIES
Housing: Coed dorms, men's dorms, women's dorms. **Computers:** Students can register for classes online. Administrative functions (other than registration) can be performed online.

CAMPUS LIFE
Environment: Metropolis. **Activities:** Choral groups, dance, drama/theater, literary magazine, radio station, student government, student newspaper, student-run film society, yearbook. **Athletics (Intercollegiate):** *Men:* badminton, basketball, soccer, volleyball. *Women:* badminton, basketball, soccer, volleyball. **On-Campus Highlights:** The Pit, The Wardroom, The Manning Room, The Library, The Quad.

ADMISSIONS

Freshman Academic Profile: Minimum paper TOEFL 580. **Basis for Candidate Selection:** *Very important factors considered include:* rigor of secondary school record, standardized test scores. **Freshman Admission Requirements:** High school diploma is required and GED is not accepted. **Freshman Admission Statistics:** 1,043 applied, 41% admitted, 83% enrolled. **Transfer Admission Requirements:** college transcript(s), Lowest grade transferable C. **General Admission Information:** Application Fee $45. Regular application deadline 6/1. Notification on a rolling basis, beginning on or about 3/1. Nonfall registration not accepted. Admission may be deferred for a maximum of 1 year.

COSTS AND FINANCIAL AID

Average book expense $1,000. *Student Employment:* Off-campus job opportunities are good.

UNIVERSITY OF LA VERNE

1950 Third Street, La Verne, CA 91750
Phone: 800-876-4858 · **Financial Aid Phone:** 1-800-649-0160
E-mail: admission@laverne.edu · **CEEB Code:** 4381
Fax: 909-392-2714 · **Website:** www.laverne.edu · **ACT Code:** 295

This private school was founded in 1891. It has a 38-acre campus.

RATINGS

Admissions Selectivity Rating: 86   **Fire Safety Rating:** 88

STUDENTS AND FACULTY

Enrollment: 2,706. **Student Body:** 59% female, 41% male, 4% out-of-state, 5% international (21 countries represented). Asian 6%, African American 5%, Caucasian 25%, Hispanic 52%, Native American <1%
Retention and Graduation: 86% freshmen return for sophomore year. 41% freshmen graduate within 4 years. 59% freshmen graduate within 6 years. **Faculty:** 218 full-time faculty, 80% hold PhDs, 50% are are members of minority groups, 24% are women. 0% of classes are taught by teaching assistants.

ACADEMICS

Degrees: associate, bachelor's, certificate, master's, post-bachelor's certificate. **Classes:** Most classes have 10-19 students. Most lab/discussion sessions have fewer than 10 students. **Majors with Highest Enrollment:** Business Administration and Management; Psychology; Liberal Arts and Sciences/Liberal Studies. **Special Study Options:** distance learning, double major, English as a Second Language (ESL), exchange student program (domestic), honors program, independent study, internships, liberal arts/career combination, student-designed major, study abroad, teacher certification program, weekend college. **Honors programs:** For students who have demonstrated exceptional academic achievement and motivation, the ULV Honors Program offers increased opportunities for intellectual and personal growth. Participants in the Honors Program can enrich their undergraduate experience through a special Honors curriculum that emphasizes critical thinking skills and the integration of knowledge from various disciplines, through individualized attention from faculty mentors, and through community outreach activities and cultural programs. All eligible undergraduate students, regardless of major, are invited to apply, but participation in the program is completely voluntary. Students who complete the entire program receive the designation "Honors Program Graduate" on their diplomas and transcripts. Students who complete a minimum of two Interdisciplinary Seminars and a total of at least 10 units in Honors receive the designation "Honors Program Participant" on their transcripts. Besides these benefits, students in the program also receive specialized academic advising, greater opportunities for original research and study, and additional enrichment activities, including guest lectures. They may also be eligible for Honors Scholarships. The Honors Center, available to Honors Program students, offers a study lounge, computer laboratory, and a seminar room. **Combined degree programs:** JD/MBA. **Disability Services:** Special programs offered to physically disabled students include note-taking services, reader services, tape recorders, tutors. **Career services:** career/job search classes, career assessment, internships. Career services highlights include numerous internship listings in all career fields.

FACILITIES

Housing: Coed dorms, special housing for disabled students, women's dorms. 95% of campus accessible to physically disabled. **Special Academic Facilities/Equipment:** Greenhouse and Animal Care Facility; Montana Field Station—Magpie Ranch; Jeagar science specimen Museum; Photography and Art galleries. **Computers:** 100% of classrooms, 100% of dorms, 100% of libraries, 100% of dining areas, 100% of student union, 100% of common outdoor areas have wireless network access. Students can register for classes online. Administrative functions (other than registration) can be performed online.

CAMPUS LIFE

Environment: Town. **Activities:** Choral groups, dance, drama/theater, literary magazine, music ensembles, musical theater, radio station, student government, student newspaper, student-run film society, television station, Campus Ministries, International Student Organization, Model UN. 40 registered organizations, 2 honor societies, 1 religous organization. 3 fraternities, 6 sororities. **Athletics (Intercollegiate):** *Men:* baseball, basketball, cross-country, diving, football, golf, soccer, swimming, tennis, track/field (outdoor), water polo. *Women:* basketball, cross-country, diving, soccer, softball, swimming, tennis, track/field (outdoor), volleyball, water polo. **On-Campus Highlights:** Campus Center, Sneaky Park (outdoor events), Davenport Dining Hall, Dailey Theater (Fine Arts Performances), University Quad. **Environmental Initiatives:** Total Recycling Program; Energy Management: dual Central Chillers for HVAC, Lighting Fixture replacement; Water Conservation: Plumbing Fixtures, Irrigation, Xeriscaping.

ADMISSIONS

Freshman Academic Profile: Average high school GPA 3.43. 19.7% in top 10% of high school class, 51.6% in top 25% of high school class, 86.1% in top 50% of high school class. SAT Math middle 50% range 470-550. SAT Critical Reading middle 50% range 460-550. SAT Writing middle 50% range 450-540. ACT middle 50% range 20-23. Minimum internet-based TOEFL 80. Minimum paper TOEFL 550. **Basis for Candidate Selection:** *Very important factors considered include:* application essay, academic GPA, recommendation(s), rigor of secondary school record, standardized test scores, character/personal qualities. *Important factors considered include:* Class rank, extracurricular activities. *Other factors considered include:* alumni/ae relation, first generation, interview, level of applicant's interest, racial/ethnic status, talent/ability, volunteer work, work experience. **Freshman Admission Requirements:** High school diploma is required and GED is accepted. **Academic units required:** 4 English, 3 mathematics, 2 science, (1 science labs), 0 foreign language, 2 social studies, 3 history, 0 visual/performing arts, 0 computer science, 0 academic electives. **Freshman Admission Statistics:** 8,233 applied, 47% admitted, 15% enrolled. **Transfer Admission Requirements:** college transcript(s), essay or personal statement, Minimum college GPA of 2.7 required. Lowest grade transferable C-. **General Admission Information:** Application Fee $50. Notification on a rolling basis, beginning on or about 12/1. Nonfall registration accepted. Admission may be deferred for a maximum of 1 Year. Credit and/or placement offered for CEEB Advanced Placement tests.

COSTS AND FINANCIAL AID

Annual tuition $35,300. Room and board $12,200. Required fees $1,444. Average book expense $1,746. **Required Forms and Deadlines:** FAFSA, State aid form. **Notification of Awards:** Applicants will be notified of awards on a rolling basis beginning 3/17. **Types of Aid:** *Need-based scholarships/grants:* Federal Pell, SEOG, state scholarships/grants, private scholarships, the school's own gift aid. *Loans:* Subsidized Stafford, Unsubsidized Stafford, PLUS, Federal Perkins, college/university loans from institutional funds, Private Alternative Loans. *Student Employment:* Federal Work-Study Program available. **Financial Aid Statistics:** 98% freshmen, 88% undergrads receive need-based scholarship or grant aid. 99% freshmen, 99% undergrads receive non-need-based scholarship or grant aid. 93% freshmen, 93% undergrads receive need-based self-help aid. 0% freshmen, 0% undergrads receive athletic scholarships. 87% freshmen, 82% undergrads receive any aid. 80% undergrads borrow to pay for school. Average cumulative indebtedness $25,201. **Criteria for awarding institutional aid:** *Non-need-based:* academics, alumni affiliation, art, leadership, minority status, music/drama, religious affiliation.

THE UNIVERSITY OF LETHBRIDGE

4401 University Drive, Lethbridge, AB T1K 3M4
Phone: 403-382-7134 · **Financial Aid Phone:** 403-329-2585
E-mail: admissions@uleth.ca
Fax: 403-329-5159 · **Website:** www.uleth.ca · **ACT Code:** 5202

This public school was founded in 1967. It has a 568-acre campus.

RATINGS

Admissions Selectivity Rating: 60*   **Fire Safety Rating:** 60*

STUDENTS AND FACULTY

Enrollment: 7,498. **Student Body:** 11% out-of-state.

ACADEMICS

Degrees: bachelor's, certificate, diploma, doctoral, master's, post-bachelor's certificate. **Classes:** Most classes have 10-19 students. Most lab/discussion sessions have 10-19 students. **Majors with Highest Enrollment:** Accounting;

Business Administration and Management; Kinesiology and Exercise Science. **Special Study Options:** Accelerated program, cooperative education program, double major, English as a Second Language (ESL), exchange student program (domestic), honors program, independent study, internships, student-designed major, study abroad, teacher certification program, Applied Studies. **Combined degree programs:** B.A.or B.Sc./B.Ed.,B.A.or B.Sc./B.Mgt.,B.Mgt./B.Ed. **Disability Services:** Special programs offered to physically disabled students include note-taking services, reader services, tape recorders, tutors. **Career services:** alumni services, career/job search classes, career assessment, internships.

FACILITIES
Housing: Coed dorms, special housing for disabled students, apartments for married students, apartments for single students, Townhouses for single and married students and students with families. 100% of campus accessible to physically disabled. **Special Academic Facilities/Equipment:** Art Gallery, Theatres. **Computers:** 100% of classrooms, 100% of libraries, 100% of dining areas, 100% of student union, have wireless network access. Students can register for classes online. Administrative functions (other than registration) can be performed online.

CAMPUS LIFE
Environment: City. **Activities:** Choral groups, dance, drama/theater, jazz band, literary magazine, music ensembles, musical theater, radio station, student government, student newspaper, student-run film society, symphony orchestra, International Student Organization. 1 fraternity, 1 sorority. **Athletics (Intercollegiate):** *Men:* basketball, ice hockey, soccer, swimming, track/field (outdoor). *Women:* basketball, ice hockey, rugby, soccer, swimming, track/field (outdoor).

ADMISSIONS
Freshman Academic Profile: Minimum internet-based TOEFL 80. Minimum paper TOEFL 550. **Basis for Candidate Selection:** *Very important factors considered include:* rigor of secondary school record. *Other factors considered include:* Class rank, standardized test scores. **Freshman Admission Requirements:** High school diploma is required and GED is not accepted. **Transfer Admission Requirements:** college transcript(s). **General Admission Information:** Application Fee $75. Regular application deadline 6/1. Nonfall registration accepted. Admission may be deferred for a maximum of 1 semester.

COSTS AND FINANCIAL AID
Required Forms and Deadlines: Institution's own financial aid form. *Student Employment:* Institutional employment available. Off-campus job opportunities are good.

UNIVERSITY OF LOUISIANA AT LAFAYETTE

P.O. Drawer 41210, Lafayette, LA 70504
Phone: 337-482-6553 · **Financial Aid Phone:** 337-482-6506
E-mail: enroll@louisiana.edu · **CEEB Code:** 6672
Fax: 337-482-1112 · **Website:** www.louisiana.edu · **ACT Code:** 1612

This public school was founded in 1898. It has a 1375-acre campus.

RATINGS
Admissions Selectivity Rating: 85   Fire Safety Rating: 88

STUDENTS AND FACULTY
Enrollment: 14,667. **Student Body:** 56% female, 44% male, 8% out-of-state, 2% international (101 countries represented). Asian 2%, African American 21%, Caucasian 68%, Hispanic 3%, Native American <1%
Retention and Graduation: 76% freshmen return for sophomore year. 15% freshmen graduate within 4 years. 48% freshmen graduate within 6 years. **Faculty:** 598 full-time faculty, 62% hold PhDs, 45% are are members of minority groups, 20% are women.

ACADEMICS
Degrees: bachelor's, doctoral, master's, post-master's certificate. **Classes:** Most classes have 20-29 students. **Majors with Highest Enrollment:** Business Administration and Management; Registered Nursing/Registered Nurse; Biology/Biological Sciences. **Special Study Options:** Accelerated program, cooperative education program, cross-registration, distance learning, double major, dual enrollment, exchange student program (domestic), honors program, independent study, internships, student-designed major, study abroad, teacher

certification program. **Honors programs:** Honors Baccalaureate degree is available. **Disability Services:** Special programs offered to physically disabled students include note-taking services, reader services, tape recorders, tutors. **Career services:** career/job search classes, career assessment.

FACILITIES
Housing: men's dorms, women's dorms, fraternity/sorority housing, apartments for married students, apartments for single students. 85% of campus accessible to physically disabled. **Special Academic Facilities/Equipment:** Art museum, experimental farm, primate center, CAD/CAM laboratory, marine research facility, on campus restaurant and hotel with instructional facilities, 2 nuclear accelerators, 2 electron microscopes, radio station and television production studio, nursery school laboratory, Louisiana Emersive Technologies Enterprise. **Computers:** Students can register for classes online. Administrative functions (other than registration) can be performed online.

CAMPUS LIFE
Environment: City. **Activities:** Choral groups, concert band, dance, drama/theater, jazz band, literary magazine, marching band, music ensembles, musical theater, opera, radio station, student government, student newspaper, symphony orchestra, yearbook, Campus Ministries, International Student Organization. 155 registered organizations, 14 honor societies, 8 religious organizations. 11 fraternities, 9 sororities. **Athletics (Intercollegiate):** *Men:* baseball, basketball, cheerleading, cross-country, football, golf, tennis, track/field (outdoor), track/field (indoor). *Women:* basketball, cheerleading, cross-country, soccer, softball, tennis, track/field (outdoor), track/field (indoor), volleyball. **On-Campus Highlights:** University Museum, Student Center, Cajun Field, Cajundome, Dupre Library.

ADMISSIONS
Freshman Academic Profile: Average high school GPA 3.3. 19% in top 10% of high school class, 43% in top 25% of high school class, 74% in top 50% of high school class. SAT Math middle 50% range 490-590. SAT Critical Reading middle 50% range 470-590. ACT middle 50% range 21-25. Minimum paper TOEFL 525. **Basis for Candidate Selection:** *Very important factors considered include:* Class rank, academic GPA, rigor of secondary school record, standardized test scores. *Other factors considered include:* state residency. **Freshman Admission Requirements:** High school diploma is required and GED is accepted. **Academic units required:** 4 English, 4 mathematics, 3 science, (0 science labs), 2 foreign language, 1 social studies, 2 history, 1 visual/performing arts, 1 Computer Science/Literacy. **Freshman Admission Statistics:** 9,386 applied, 56% admitted, 56% enrolled. **Transfer Admission Requirements:** college transcript(s), Lowest grade transferable D. **General Admission Information:** Application Fee $25. Nonfall registration accepted. Admission may be deferred for a maximum of 1 semester. Credit and/or placement offered for CEEB Advanced Placement tests.

COSTS AND FINANCIAL AID
Annual in-state tuition $4,916. Annual out-of-state tuition $17,316. Room and board $8,566. Required fees $2,033. Average book expense $1,200. **Required Forms and Deadlines:** FAFSA. **Notification of Awards:** Applicants will be notified of awards on a rolling basis beginning 4/1. **Types of Aid:** *Need-based scholarships/grants:* Federal Pell, SEOG, state scholarships/grants, private scholarships, the school's own gift aid, Federal Nursing Scholarships. *Loans:* Subsidized Stafford, Unsubsidized Stafford, PLUS, Federal Perkins, Federal Nursing. *Student Employment:* Federal Work-Study Program available. Institutional employment available. Off-campus job opportunities are good. **Financial Aid Statistics:** 96% freshmen, 88% undergrads receive need-based scholarship or grant aid. 15% freshmen, 9% undergrads receive non-need-based scholarship or grant aid. 48% freshmen, 59% undergrads receive need-based self-help aid. 2% freshmen, 3% undergrads receive athletic scholarships. 87% freshmen, 72% undergrads receive any aid.

THE UNIVERSITY OF LOUISIANA AT MONROE

700 University Avenue, Monroe, LA 71209
Phone: 318-342-5252
E-mail: hood@ulm.edu · **CEEB Code:** 6482
Fax: 318-342-5274 · **Website:** www.ulm.edu · **ACT Code:** 1598

This public school was founded in 1931. It has a 238-acre campus.

RATINGS
Admissions Selectivity Rating: 67   Fire Safety Rating: 60*

STUDENTS AND FACULTY
Enrollment: 8,542. **Student Body:** 61% female, 39% male, 7% out-of-state, 1% international (47 countries represented). Asian 3%, African American 27%, Caucasian 95%, Hispanic 1%, Native American <1%

Retention and Graduation: 8% freshmen graduate within 4 years. 29% freshmen graduate within 6 years.

ACADEMICS

Degrees: associate, bachelor's, certificate, master's, post-master's certificate. **Special Study Options:** Accelerated program, cooperative education program, distance learning, English as a Second Language (ESL), honors program, internships, teacher certification program. **Disability Services:** Special programs offered to physically disabled students include note-taking services, reader services, tape recorders. **Career services:** career/job search classes.

FACILITIES

Housing: Coed dorms, men's dorms, women's dorms, fraternity/sorority housing. 95% of campus accessible to physically disabled. **Special Academic Facilities/Equipment:** Agricultural farm lab, soil/plant analysis lab, climatic research center, herbarium, pre-school child lab, educational media center, cancer research center.

CAMPUS LIFE

Environment: Village. **Activities:** Choral groups, concert band, dance, drama/theater, jazz band, literary magazine, marching band, music ensembles, musical theater, pep band, radio station, student government, student newspaper, television station, yearbook. 128 registered organizations, 22 honor societies, 11 religious organizations. 8 fraternities, 8 sororities. **Athletics (Intercollegiate):** *Men:* baseball, basketball, cross-country, soccer, tennis. *Women:* basketball, cross-country, soccer, softball, tennis, volleyball.

ADMISSIONS

Freshman Academic Profile: ACT middle 50% range 16-22. **Freshman Admission Statistics:** 2,657 applied, 92% admitted, 74% enrolled. **Transfer Admission Requirements:** High school transcript, college transcript(s). **General Admission Information:** Application Fee $15. Notification on a rolling basis, beginning on or about 4/1. Nonfall registration accepted.

COSTS AND FINANCIAL AID

Average book expense $668. **Required Forms and Deadlines:** FAFSA. **Types of Aid:** *Need-based scholarships/grants:* Federal Pell, private scholarships, the school's own gift aid. *Student Employment:* Federal Work-Study Program available. Highest amount earned per year from on-campus jobs $1,000. Off-campus job opportunities are good.

UNIVERSITY OF LOUISVILLE

Admissions Office, Louisville, KY 40292
Phone: 502-852-6531 · **Financial Aid Phone:** 502-852-5511
E-mail: admitme@louisville.edu
Fax: 502-852-4776 · **Website:** www.louisville.edu · **ACT Code:** 1556

This public school was founded in 1798. It has a 274-acre campus.

RATINGS

Admissions Selectivity Rating: 79   **Fire Safety Rating:** 89

STUDENTS AND FACULTY

Enrollment: 15,038. **Student Body:** 51% female, 49% male, 15% out-of-state, 1% international (94 countries represented). Asian 3%, African American 11%, Caucasian 76%, Hispanic 4%, Native American <1%
Retention and Graduation: 25% freshmen graduate within 4 years. 26% grads go on to further study within 1 year. 20% grads pursue arts and sciences degrees. 8% grads pursue law degrees. 11% grads pursue business degrees. 14% grads pursue medical degrees. **Faculty:** 808 full-time faculty, 88% hold PhDs, 45% are are members of minority groups, 20% are women. 8.87% of classes are taught by teaching assistants.

ACADEMICS

Degrees: associate, bachelor's, certificate, diploma, doctoral, master's, post-bachelor's certificate, post-master's certificate, terminal associate, transfer associate. **Classes:** Most classes have 20-29 students. **Majors with Highest Enrollment:** Registered Nursing/Registered Nurse; Biology/Biological Sciences; Speech Communication and Rhetoric. **Special Study Options:** Accelerated program, cooperative education program, cross-registration, distance learning, double major, dual enrollment, English as a Second Language (ESL), honors program, independent study, internships, student-designed major, study abroad, teacher certification program. **Combined degree programs:** BS-BA/MBA.

Disability Services: Special programs offered to physically disabled students include note-taking services, reader services, tape recorders, tutors.

FACILITIES

Housing: Coed dorms, special housing for disabled students, fraternity/sorority housing, apartments for married students, cooperative housing, apartments for single students, Theme Housing. 100% of campus accessible to physically disabled. **Special Academic Facilities/Equipment:** Natural history and art museums, planetarium, numerous institutes and centers. **Computers:** Administrative functions (other than registration) can be performed online.

CAMPUS LIFE

Environment: Metropolis. **Activities:** Choral groups, concert band, dance, drama/theater, jazz band, literary magazine, marching band, music ensembles, musical theater, opera, pep band, radio station, student government, student newspaper, symphony orchestra, Campus Ministries, International Student Organization. 237 registered organizations, 7 honor societies, 18 religious organizations. 13 fraternities, 10 sororities. **Athletics (Intercollegiate):** *Men:* baseball, basketball, cheerleading, cross-country, diving, football, golf, soccer, swimming, tennis, track/field (outdoor). *Women:* basketball, cheerleading, crew/rowing, cross-country, diving, field hockey, golf, lacrosse, soccer, softball, swimming, tennis, track/field (outdoor), volleyball. **On-Campus Highlights:** Student Activity Center, J.B. Speed Art Museum **Environmental Initiatives:** Unlimited free public transit ride contract for all UofL students, staff and faculty and Commute Green campaign: http://louisville.edu/parking/commute-green.html Local food purchasing and promotion: New campus garden; Community Supported Agriculture (CSA) program on campus; campus Farmers Market (Gray Street); Minimum 15% local requirement in dining contract with Sodexo; Promoting catering services offering local foods. Brownfield redevelopment: Smart campus growth through the redevelopment of surrounding brownfields has helped enhance environmental quality, revitalize neighborhoods, and reduce vehicle miles traveled by creating a campus environment where people want to live. UofL has been involved in the remediation and reclamation of over 200 acres of brownfields in Louisville.

ADMISSIONS

Freshman Academic Profile: Average high school GPA 3.55. 79% from public high schools. SAT Math middle 50% range 510-630. SAT Critical Reading middle 50% range 500-620. ACT middle 50% range 22-28. Minimum paper TOEFL 550. **Basis for Candidate Selection:** *Very important factors considered include:* academic GPA, rigor of secondary school record, standardized test scores. *Other factors considered include:* Class rank, recommendation(s), extracurricular activities, racial/ethnic status, state residency, talent/ability, volunteer work, work experience. **Freshman Admission Requirements:** High school diploma is required and GED is accepted. **Academic units required:** 4 English, 3 mathematics, 3 science, (1 science labs), 2 foreign language, 3 social studies, 1 visual/performing arts, 5 academic electives, 5 electives must be rigorous; History is included in Social Studies. **Freshman Admission Statistics:** 10,604 applied, 54% admitted, 50% enrolled. **Transfer Admission Requirements:** college transcript(s), Minimum college GPA of 2.0 required. Lowest grade transferable D. **General Admission Information:** Application Fee $40. Regular application deadline 8/25. Nonfall registration accepted. Credit and/or placement offered for CEEB Advanced Placement tests.

COSTS AND FINANCIAL AID

Annual out-of-state tuition $24,124. Room and board $7,710. Average book expense $1,000. **Required Forms and Deadlines:** FAFSA. **Financial Aid Statistics:** 97% freshmen, 88% undergrads receive need-based scholarship or grant aid. 18% freshmen, 11% undergrads receive non-need-based scholarship or grant aid. 55% freshmen, 62% undergrads receive need-based self-help aid. 4% freshmen, 3% undergrads receive athletic scholarships. 97% freshmen, 79% undergrads receive any aid. 55% undergrads borrow to pay for school. Average cumulative indebtedness $20,681.

UNIVERSITY OF MAINE

5713 Chadbourne Hall, Orono, ME 04469-5713
Phone: 207-581-1561 · **Financial Aid Phone:** 207-581-1324
E-mail: um-admit@maine.edu · **CEEB Code:** 3916
Fax: 207-581-1213 · **Website:** www.umaine.edu · **ACT Code:** 1664

This public school was founded in 1865. It has a 660-acre campus.

RATINGS

Admissions Selectivity Rating: 80   **Fire Safety Rating:** 97

STUDENTS AND FACULTY

Enrollment: 8,682. **Student Body:** 47% female, 53% male, 24% out-of-state, 2% international (41 countries represented). Asian 1%, African American 2%, Caucasian 82%, Hispanic 2%, Native American 1% **Retention and Graduation:** 77% freshmen return for sophomore year. 37% freshmen graduate within 4 years. **Faculty:** 488 full-time faculty, 85% hold PhDs, 34% are are members of minority groups, 8% are women. 10% of classes are taught by teaching assistants.

ACADEMICS

Degrees: bachelor's, doctoral, master's, post-master's certificate. **Classes:** Most classes have 10-19 students. Most lab/discussion sessions have 10-19 students. **Majors with Highest Enrollment:** Psychology; Business Administration and Management; Registered Nursing/Registered Nurse. **Special Study Options:** Accelerated program, cooperative education program, distance learning, double major, dual enrollment, English as a Second Language (ESL), honors program, independent study, internships, liberal arts/career combination, study abroad, teacher certification program. **Honors programs:** The Honors College at The University of Maine provides a unique opportunity for a community of five hundred motivated students to investigate diverse academic areas of the University, to be challenged in a supportive intellectual environment, and to critically engage fellow students and enthusiastic, distinguished faculty in thoughtful, provocative discussion. The benefits and rewards are substantial, and the program is flexible enough to be tailored precisely to the individual student's needs and interests. **Combined degree programs:** BA/MD, BA/MA, BA/DO. **Disability Services:** Special programs offered to physically disabled students include note-taking services, reader services, tape recorders, tutors. **Career services:** Alumni network, alumni services, career/job search classes, career assessment, internships, regional alumni. For career services highlights visit us at http://www.umaine.edu/career/coop.html.

FACILITIES

Housing: Coed dorms, special housing for disabled students, special housing for international students, fraternity/sorority housing, apartments for married students, apartments for single students, Wellness Housing, Theme Housing: Honor's College Housing; Graduate Student Housing; Smoke free; chem free; clusters for engineering and science majors. First Year Residential Experience (FYRE). 90% of campus accessible to physically disabled. **Special Academic Facilities/Equipment:** Laboratory for Advanced Surface Science and Technology (LASST), Advanced Manufacturing Center, Anthropology museum, Digital Media Lab, folklore and oral history museum, art museum, Canadian-American center, social sciences research institute, exceptional child research lab, preschool, experimental farms, land/water resources center, center for marine studies, planetarium/observatory, electron microscopes, farm museum, papermaking machine, aquaculture production facility, woodland preserve, botanical garden, arts center, Franco-American Center. **Computers:** 100% of classrooms, 10% of dorms, 100% of libraries, 100% of dining areas, 100% of student union, 50% of common outdoor areas have wireless network access. Students can register for classes online. Administrative functions (other than registration) can be performed online.

CAMPUS LIFE

Environment: Village. **Activities:** Choral groups, concert band, dance, drama/theater, jazz band, literary magazine, marching band, music ensembles, musical theater, opera, pep band, radio station, student government, student newspaper, student-run film society, symphony orchestra, television station, yearbook, Campus Ministries, International Student Organization. 224 registered organizations, 42 honor societies, 7 religious organizations. 13 fraternities, 6 sororities. **Athletics (Intercollegiate):** *Men:* baseball, basketball, cross-country, diving, football, ice hockey, soccer, swimming, track/field (outdoor), track/field (indoor). *Women:* basketball, cross-country, diving, field hockey, ice hockey, soccer, softball, swimming, track/field (outdoor), track/field (indoor), volleyball. **On-Campus Highlights:** Collins Center for the Arts, Alfond Arena, Market Place—Memorial Union, Student Recreation Center, The Mall. **Environmental Initiatives:** UMaine has developed a master plan centered on sustainability, restoring habitat, avoiding sprawl, maximizing solar orientation, and reducing carbon emissions. Major efficiency upgrades and fuel switching (No. 6 fuel oil replaced with natural gas) at the university's central heating plant, including the installation of a back-pressure turbine and a new high-efficiency boiler. These improvements have resulted in a 20% decrease in campus GHG emissions (relative to 2005 levels). An institutional commitment (including a $300,000 Green Loan Fund supported by the University of Maine Foundation) to support sustainability, energy efficiency and renewable energy projects on campus. The institution has a huge research focus on renewable energy and sustainability programs, including the Advanced Structures & Composites Center's DeepCWind project, the Climate Change Institute, Sustainability Solutions Initiative, Forest Bioproducts Research Initiative, and interdisciplinary tidal power research. There has also been a push to add curriculum, including UMaine's new renewable energy minors; a sustainability track in the M.B.A. program; an M.A. in global policy with a concentration in international environmental policy; and a planned major in climate change and culture.

ADMISSIONS

Freshman Academic Profile: Average high school GPA 3.27. 20% in top 10% of high school class, 46% in top 25% of high school class, 81% in top 50% of high school class. N/A% from public high schools. SAT Math middle 50% range 480-600. SAT Critical Reading middle 50% range 480-590. SAT Writing middle 50% range 460-570. ACT middle 50% range 21-27. Minimum internet-based TOEFL 79. Minimum paper TOEFL 550. **Basis for Candidate Selection:** *Very important factors considered include:* Class rank, academic GPA, rigor of secondary school record, standardized test scores. *Important factors considered include:* application essay, recommendation(s). *Other factors considered include:* character/personal qualities, extracurricular activities, geographical residence, interview, talent/ability, volunteer work, work experience. **Freshman Admission Requirements:** High school diploma is required and GED is accepted. **Academic units required:** 4 English, 3 mathematics, 2 science, (2 science labs), 2 foreign language, 2 social studies, 0 history, 4 academic electives, 1 Physical education for Education Majors. **Freshman Admission Statistics:** 11,552 applied, 83% admitted, 22% enrolled. **Transfer Admission Requirements:** High school transcript, college transcript(s), essay or personal statement, Minimum college GPA of 2.0 required. Lowest grade transferable C-. **General Admission Information:** Application Fee $40. Notification on a rolling basis, beginning on or about 2/1. Nonfall registration accepted. Admission may be deferred for a maximum of 2 semesters. Credit offered for CEEB Advanced Placement tests.

COSTS AND FINANCIAL AID

Annual in-state tuition $8,370. Annual out-of-state tuition $26,250. Room and board $9,296. Required fees $2,236. Average book expense $1,000. **Required Forms and Deadlines:** FAFSA. **Notification of Awards:** Applicants will be notified of awards on a rolling basis beginning 3/15. *Types of Aid: Need-based scholarships/grants:* Federal Pell, SEOG, state scholarships/grants, private scholarships, the school's own gift aid. *Loans:* Subsidized Stafford, Unsubsidized Stafford, PLUS, Federal Perkins, state loans. *Student Employment:* Federal Work-Study Program available. Institutional employment available. Highest amount earned per year from on-campus jobs $4,000. Off-campus job opportunities are good. **Financial Aid Statistics:** 96% freshmen, 85% undergrads receive need-based scholarship or grant aid. 8% freshmen, 5% undergrads receive non-need-based scholarship or grant aid. 84% freshmen, 86% undergrads receive need-based self-help aid. 1% freshmen, 1% undergrads receive athletic scholarships. 93% freshmen, 83% undergrads receive any aid. 77% undergrads borrow to pay for school. Average cumulative indebtedness $26,468. **Criteria for awarding institutional aid:** *Non-need-based:* academics, alumni affiliation, art, athletics, job skills, leadership, minority status, music/drama, religious affiliation, state/district residency.

See page 1182.

UNIVERSITY OF MAINE AT AUGUSTA

46 University Drive, Augusta, ME 4330
Phone: 207-621-3465 · **Financial Aid Phone:** 207-621-3455
E-mail: umaadm@maine.edu · **CEEB Code:** 3929
Fax: 207-621-3333 · **Website:** www.uma.edu · **ACT Code:** 1641

This public school was founded in 1965. It has a 159-acre campus.

RATINGS

Admissions Selectivity Rating: 60*   **Fire Safety Rating:** 60*

STUDENTS AND FACULTY

Enrollment: 4,523. **Student Body:** 73% female, 27% male, 3% out-of-state, 0% international (5 countries represented). Asian 1%, African American 1%, Caucasian 85%, Hispanic 1%, Native American 2%
Retention and Graduation: 53% freshmen return for sophomore year. 4% freshmen graduate within 4 years. 40% grads go on to further study within 1 year. **Faculty:** 103 full-time faculty, 56% hold PhDs, 58% are are members of minority groups, 0% are women. 0% of classes are taught by teaching assistants.

ACADEMICS

Degrees: associate, bachelor's, certificate, post-bachelor's certificate, terminal associate, transfer associate. **Classes:** Most classes have 10-19 students. Most lab/discussion sessions have 10-19 students. **Majors with Highest Enrollment:** Social Sciences; Health Services/Allied Health/Health Sciences; Business/Commerce. **Special Study Options:** cross-registration, distance learning, double major, dual enrollment, honors program, independent study, internships, liberal arts/career combination, student-designed major, study abroad. **Honors programs:** UMA Honors Program—augments a student's academic and co-curricular experience. **Disability Services:** Special programs offered to physically disabled students include note-taking services. **Career services:** career/job search classes, career assessment.

FACILITIES

Housing: 99% of campus accessible to physically disabled. **Special Academic Facilities/Equipment:** Jewett Gallery, Katz Library, Student Center. **Computers:** 100% of classrooms, 100% of libraries, 100% of dining areas, 100% of student union, 100% of common outdoor areas have wireless network access. Students can register for classes online. Administrative functions (other than registration) can be performed online.

CAMPUS LIFE

Environment: Village. **Activities:** drama/theater, jazz band, music ensembles, pep band, student government, student newspaper, International Student Organization. 23 registered organizations, 1 honor society, 1 religous organization. **Athletics (Intercollegiate):** *Men:* basketball, golf, soccer. *Women:* basketball, golf, soccer. **On-Campus Highlights:** Katz Library, Student Center, Campus Center at UCB, Huskins Lounge at UCB. **Environmental Initiatives:** Reduce—Reuse—Recycle program in place since 1990. Energy policy states UMA will purchase at least 15% of its electicity from renewable sources. All new facilities over 5000 sq. ft. and major capital renovations over 50% of building replacement value will seek LEED silver rating or equivalent.

ADMISSIONS

Freshman Academic Profile: 95% from public high schools. Minimum paper TOEFL 500. **Basis for Candidate Selection:** *Important factors considered include:* Class rank, academic GPA, rigor of secondary school record. *Other factors considered include:* application essay, recommendation(s), standardized test scores, character/personal qualities, interview, level of applicant's interest, talent/ability, volunteer work, work experience. **Freshman Admission Requirements:** High school diploma is required and GED is accepted. **Freshman Admission Statistics:** 875 applied, 93% admitted, 63% enrolled. **Transfer Admission Requirements:** college transcript(s), Minimum college GPA of 2.0 required. Lowest grade transferable C. **General Admission Information:** Application Fee $40. Regular application deadline 8/30. Nonfall registration accepted. Admission may be deferred for a maximum of 12 months. Credit offered for CEEB Advanced Placement tests.

COSTS AND FINANCIAL AID

Annual in-state tuition $6,510. Annual out-of-state tuition $15,750. Required fees $938. **Required Forms and Deadlines:** FAFSA. **Notification of Awards:** Applicants will be notified of awards on a rolling basis beginning 3/15. **Types of Aid:** *Need-based scholarships/grants:* Federal Pell, SEOG, state scholarships/grants, private scholarships, the school's own gift aid. *Loans:* Direct Subsidized Stafford, Direct Unsubsidized Stafford, Subsidized Stafford, Unsubsidized Stafford, PLUS, Federal Perkins, Federal Nursing, state loans. *Student Employment:* Federal Work-Study Program available. Institutional employment available. Highest amount earned per year from on-campus jobs $3,800. Off-campus job opportunities are fair. **Financial Aid Statistics:** 87% freshmen, 86% undergrads receive need-based scholarship or grant aid. 0% freshmen, 1% undergrads receive non-need-based scholarship or grant aid. 79% freshmen, 89% undergrads receive need-based self-help aid. 0% freshmen, 0% undergrads receive athletic scholarships. 64% freshmen, 72% undergrads receive any aid. 76% undergrads borrow to pay for school. Average cumulative indebtedness $23,769. **Criteria for awarding institutional aid:** *Non-need-based:* academics, athletics, leadership, music/drama, state/district residency.

UNIVERSITY OF MAINE AT FARMINGTON

246 Main Street, Farmington, ME 4938
Phone: 207-778-7050 · **Financial Aid Phone:** 207-778-7100
E-mail: umfadmit@maine.edu · **CEEB Code:** 3506
Fax: 207-778-8182 · **Website:** www.umf.maine.edu · **ACT Code:** 1640

This public school was founded in 1863. It has a 55-acre campus.

RATINGS

Admissions Selectivity Rating: 74   Fire Safety Rating: 88

STUDENTS AND FACULTY

Enrollment: 1,738. **Student Body:** 65% female, 35% male, 16% out-of-state, 0% international (7 countries represented). Asian 1%, African American 2%, Caucasian 86%, Hispanic 1%, Native American 1% **Retention and Graduation:** 75% freshmen return for sophomore year. 36% freshmen graduate within 4 years. **Faculty:** 116 full-time faculty, 89% hold PhDs, 55% are are members of minority groups, 6% are women. 0% of classes are taught by teaching assistants.

ACADEMICS

Degrees: bachelor's, master's. **Classes:** Most classes have 10-19 students. Most lab/discussion sessions have 10-19 students. **Majors with Highest**

Enrollment: Elementary Education and Teaching; Secondary Education and Teaching; Psychology. **Special Study Options:** cooperative education program, cross-registration, double major, dual enrollment, exchange student program (domestic), honors program, independent study, internships, liberal arts/career combination, student-designed major, study abroad, teacher certification program, SALT, Documentary Field Study in Portland,ME, National Student Exchange, Service Learning. **Honors programs:** UMF Honors Program. **Disability Services:** Special programs offered to physically disabled students include note-taking services, reader services. **Career services:** career assessment. Career services highlights include Student Teaching programs.

FACILITIES

Housing: Coed dorms, special housing for international students, women's dorms, Wellness Housing, Theme HousingHousing for students maintaining a certain GPA, medical rooms, quiet floors, wellness community, international community, independent living environment housing available. 75% of campus accessible to physically disabled. **Special Academic Facilities/Equipment:** Art gallery, health and fitness center, computer center, Mantor Library, Alumni theater, Nordica Auditorium, observatory. **Computers:** 100% of classrooms, 100% of dorms, 100% of libraries, 100% of dining areas, 100% of student union, 100% of common outdoor areas have wireless network access. Students can register for classes online. Administrative functions (other than registration) can be performed online.

CAMPUS LIFE

Environment: Village. **Activities:** Choral groups, concert band, dance, drama/theater, literary magazine, music ensembles, musical theater, radio station, student government, student newspaper, yearbook, International Student Organization. 52 registered organizations, 3 honor societies, 3 religious organizations. **Athletics (Intercollegiate):** *Men:* baseball, basketball, cross-country, golf, soccer. *Women:* basketball, cross-country, field hockey, soccer, softball, volleyball. **On-Campus Highlights:** Recreation and Fitness Center, Landing, Computer Center, Education Center, Student Center. **Environmental Initiatives:** Completion of two LEED-certified buildings and commitment to new construction and major renovations at the LEED silver level. ACUPCC signatory with completion of GHG inventory and Climate Action Plan as of January 2010. Energy conservation resulting in an energy footprint 20% below national average for comparable colleges.

ADMISSIONS

Freshman Academic Profile: Average high school GPA 2.95. 10% in top 10% of high school class, 37% in top 25% of high school class, 75% in top 50% of high school class. 91% from public high schools. SAT Math middle 50% range 430-540. SAT Critical Reading middle 50% range 440-560. SAT Writing middle 50% range 420-550. Minimum internet-based TOEFL 79. Minimum paper TOEFL 550. **Basis for Candidate Selection:** *Very important factors considered include:* Class rank, rigor of secondary school record, extracurricular activities. *Important factors considered include:* application essay, academic GPA, recommendation(s), character/personal qualities, interview, talent/ability, volunteer work, work experience. *Other factors considered include:* alumni/ae relation, first generation, geographical residence, level of applicant's interest, racial/ethnic status, state residency. **Freshman Admission Requirements:** High school diploma is required and GED is accepted. **Academic units required:** 4 English, 3 mathematics, 2 science, (2 science labs), 2 foreign language, 2 social studies. **Freshman Admission Statistics:** 1,463 applied, 85% admitted, 33% enrolled. **Transfer Admission Requirements:** High school transcript, college transcript(s), essay or personal statement, Minimum college GPA of 2.5 required. Lowest grade transferable C. **General Admission Information:** Application Fee $40. Notification on a rolling basis, beginning on or about 12/15. Nonfall registration accepted. Admission may be deferred for a maximum of one year. Credit and/or placement offered for CEEB Advanced Placement tests.

COSTS AND FINANCIAL AID

Annual in-state tuition $8,352. Annual out-of-state tuition $17,440. Room and board $8,970. Required fees $865. Average book expense $840. **Required Forms and Deadlines:** FAFSA. **Notification of Awards:** Applicants will be notified of awards on a rolling basis beginning 3/15. **Types of Aid:** *Need-based scholarships/grants:* Federal Pell, SEOG, state scholarships/grants, private scholarships, the school's own gift aid, Native American scholarships and waivers. *Loans:* Direct Subsidized Stafford, Direct Unsubsidized Stafford, Direct PLUS, Subsidized Stafford, Unsubsidized Stafford, PLUS, Federal Perkins, state loans, college/university loans from institutional funds, Teachers for Maine *Student Employment:* Federal Work-Study Program available. Institutional employment available. Highest amount earned per year from on-campus jobs $5,530. Off-campus job opportunities are fair. **Financial Aid Statistics:** 96% freshmen, 90% undergrads receive need-based scholarship or grant aid. 4% freshmen, 1% undergrads receive non-need-based scholarship or grant aid. 92% freshmen, 95% undergrads receive need-based self-help aid. 0% freshmen, 0% undergrads receive athletic scholarships. 92% freshmen, 83% undergrads receive any aid. 86% undergrads borrow to pay for school. Average cumulative indebtedness $27,009. **Criteria for awarding institutional aid:** *Non-need-based:* academics, leadership, minority status, state/district residency.

UNIVERSITY OF MAINE AT FORT KENT

23 University Drive, Fort Kent, ME 4774
Phone: 888-879-8635 · **Financial Aid Phone:** 207-834-7607
E-mail: umfkadm@maine.maine.edu · **CEEB Code:** 3393
Fax: 207-834-7609 · **Website:** www.umfk.maine.edu · **ACT Code:** 1642

This public school was founded in 1878. It has a 52-acre campus.

RATINGS
Admissions Selectivity Rating: 77   **Fire Safety Rating:** 99

STUDENTS AND FACULTY
Enrollment: 913. **Student Body:** 71% female, 29% male, 7% out-of-state, 9% international. Asian 0%, African American 2%, Caucasian 65%, Hispanic 1%, Native American 1%
Retention and Graduation: 59% freshmen return for sophomore year. 34% freshmen graduate within 4 years. 44% freshmen graduate within 6 years. 5% grads go on to further study within 1 year. 3% grads pursue arts and sciences degrees. **Faculty:** 35 full-time faculty, 49% hold PhDs, 46% are are members of minority groups, 9% are women. 0% of classes are taught by teaching assistants.

ACADEMICS
Degrees: associate, bachelor's. **Classes:** Most classes have 10-19 students. Most lab/discussion sessions have fewer than 10 students. **Majors with Highest Enrollment:** Elementary Education and Teaching; Business/Commerce. **Special Study Options:** cross-registration, distance learning, double major, English as a Second Language (ESL), honors program, independent study, internships, liberal arts/career combination, student-designed major, teacher certification program, Distance learning within entire UMaine system. **Disability Services:** Special programs offered to physically disabled students include note-taking services, reader services, tape recorders, tutors. **Career services:** alumni services, career/job search classes, career assessment, internships.

FACILITIES
Housing: Coed dorms, special housing for disabled students, men's dorms, women's dorms. 80% of campus accessible to physically disabled. **Computers:** 100% of classrooms, 100% of dorms, 100% of libraries, 100% of dining areas, 100% of student union, 100% of common outdoor areas have wireless network access. Students can register for classes online. Administrative functions (other than registration) can be performed online.

CAMPUS LIFE
Environment: Rural. **Activities:** Choral groups, drama/theater, student government. 25 registered organizations, 1 honor society, 1 religous organization. 1 sorority. **Athletics (Intercollegiate):** *Men:* basketball, cross-country, golf, skiing (downhill/alpine), skiing (nordic/cross-country), soccer. *Women:* basketball, cross-country, golf, skiing (downhill/alpine), skiing (nordic/cross-country), soccer, volleyball. **On-Campus Highlights:** Bengal's Lair, The Lodge (res hall), Library.

ADMISSIONS
Freshman Academic Profile: Average high school GPA 3.1. 7% in top 25% of high school class, 23% in top 50% of high school class. 96% from public high schools. SAT Math middle 50% range 410-500. SAT Critical Reading middle 50% range 408-500. SAT Writing middle 50% range 400-500. ACT middle 50% range 18-. Minimum paper TOEFL 500. **Basis for Candidate Selection:** *Very important factors considered include:* level of applicant's interest. *Important factors considered include:* Class rank, application essay, academic GPA, recommendation(s), rigor of secondary school record, character/personal qualities, first generation, geographical residence, state residency, talent/ability, volunteer work. *Other factors considered include:* standardized test scores, alumni/ae relation, extracurricular activities, interview, work experience. **Freshman Admission Requirements:** High school diploma is required and GED is accepted. **Academic units required:** 4 English, 2 mathematics, 2 science, (2 science labs). **Freshman Admission Statistics:** 464 applied, 44% admitted, 80% enrolled. **Transfer Admission Requirements:** High school transcript, college transcript(s), essay or personal statement, Lowest grade transferable C-. **General Admission Information:** Application Fee $40. Notification on a rolling basis, beginning on or about 12/1. Nonfall registration accepted. Credit and/or placement offered for CEEB Advanced Placement tests.

COSTS AND FINANCIAL AID
Average book expense $1,000. **Required Forms and Deadlines:** FAFSA, Institution's own financial aid form, CSS/Financial Aid PROFILE, State aid form. **Types of Aid:** *Need-based scholarships/grants:* Federal Pell, SEOG, state scholarships/grants, private scholarships, the school's own gift aid, Federal Nursing Scholarships. *Loans:* Direct Subsidized Stafford, Direct Unsubsidized Stafford, Direct PLUS, Subsidized Stafford, Unsubsidized Stafford, PLUS, Federal Perkins, Federal Nursing, state loans, college/university loans from institutional funds. *Student Employment:* Federal Work-Study Program available. Institutional employment available. Highest amount earned per year from on-campus jobs $1,500. Off-campus job opportunities are good. **Financial Aid Statistics:** 98% freshmen, 95% undergrads receive need-based scholarship or grant aid. 2% freshmen, 1% undergrads receive non-need-based scholarship or grant aid. 84% freshmen, 84% undergrads receive need-based self-help aid. 0% freshmen, 0% undergrads receive athletic scholarships. 97% freshmen, 55% undergrads receive any aid. 72% undergrads borrow to pay for school. Average cumulative indebtedness $19,530. **Criteria for awarding institutional aid:** *Non-need-based:* academics, alumni affiliation, job skills, leadership, state/district residency.

UNIVERSITY OF MAINE AT MACHIAS

Office of Admissions, Machias, ME 4654
Phone: 207-255-1318 · **Financial Aid Phone:** 207-255-1203
E-mail: ummadmissions@maine.edu · **CEEB Code:** 3956
Fax: 207-255-1363 · **Website:** www.umm.maine.edu · **ACT Code:** 1666

This public school was founded in 1909. It has a 42-acre campus.

RATINGS
Admissions Selectivity Rating: 71   **Fire Safety Rating:** 70

STUDENTS AND FACULTY
Enrollment: 554. **Student Body:** 65% female, 35% male, 24% out-of-state, 4% international (18 countries represented). Asian 1%, African American 1%, Caucasian 88%, Hispanic 2%, Native American 4%
Retention and Graduation: 12% freshmen graduate within 4 years. 42% freshmen graduate within 6 years. **Faculty:** 30 full-time faculty, 73% hold PhDs, 33% are are members of minority groups, 3% are women. 0% of classes are taught by teaching assistants.

ACADEMICS
Degrees: bachelor's. **Classes:** Most classes have 10-19 students. Most lab/discussion sessions have 10-19 students. **Majors with Highest Enrollment:** Marine Biology and Biological Oceanography; Parks, Recreation and Leisure Facilities Management; Elementary Education and Teaching. **Special Study Options:** cooperative education program, distance learning, double major, dual enrollment, honors program, independent study, internships, student-designed major, study abroad, teacher certification program. **Disability Services:** Special programs offered to physically disabled students include reader services, tape recorders, tutors. **Career services:** career assessment, internships.

FACILITIES
Housing: Coed dorms. 85% of campus accessible to physically disabled. **Special Academic Facilities/Equipment:** Art Gallery Book Arts Print Shop Geographic Information Systems Laboratory and Service Center **Computers:** 100% of classrooms, 100% of dorms, 100% of libraries, 100% of dining areas, 100% of student union, 100% of common outdoor areas have wireless network access. Students can register for classes online. Administrative functions (other than registration) can be performed online.

CAMPUS LIFE
Environment: Rural. **Activities:** Choral groups, dance, drama/theater, literary magazine, music ensembles, musical theater, pep band, radio station, student government, Campus Ministries. 38 registered organizations, 2 religious organizations. 5 fraternities, 4 sororities. **Athletics (Intercollegiate):** *Men:* basketball, soccer. *Women:* basketball, soccer, volleyball. **On-Campus Highlights:** Aquatics/Fitness Center/Gymnasium, Residence Halls, Wireless Computer Lab/Classroom, Performing Arts Center, Early Care and Education Center, The Portal—multi-media center, Marine Biology lab facilities, Campus Radio Station, Art Studios and Gallery, Bookstore, Book Arts Print Shop, Kilburn Commons, The Galley. **Environmental Initiatives:** Green Council; Recycle-Mania.

ADMISSIONS
Freshman Academic Profile: 12.8% in top 10% of high school class, 24.4% in top 25% of high school class, 62.8% in top 50% of high school class. SAT Math middle 50% range 400-530. SAT Critical Reading middle 50% range 440-530. ACT middle 50% range 15-25. Minimum paper TOEFL 500. **Basis for Candidate Selection:** *Very important factors considered include:* application essay, recommendation(s), rigor of secondary school record, interview. *Important factors considered include:* Class rank, standardized test scores, extracurricular activities. *Other factors considered include:* character/personal qualities, talent/ability, volunteer work, work experience. **Freshman Admission Requirements:** High school diploma is required and GED is accepted. **Academic units required:** 4 English, 3 mathematics, 2 science, (2 science labs), 2 social studies. **Freshman Admission Statistics:** 381 applied, 92% admitted, 32% enrolled. **Transfer Admission Requirements:** High school transcript, college transcript(s), statement of good standing from prior institution(s). Minimum

college GPA of 2.0 required. Lowest grade transferable C-. **General Admission Information:** Application Fee $40. Regular application deadline 8/15. Nonfall registration accepted. Admission may be deferred for a maximum of 1 year. Credit offered for CEEB Advanced Placement tests.

COSTS AND FINANCIAL AID
Annual out-of-state tuition $16,550. Room and board $6,574. Average book expense $650. **Required Forms and Deadlines:** FAFSA. **Notification of Awards:** Applicants will be notified of awards on a rolling basis beginning 3/1. **Types of Aid:** *Need-based scholarships/grants:* Federal Pell, SEOG, state scholarships/grants, private scholarships, the school's own gift aid. *Loans:* Subsidized Stafford, Unsubsidized Stafford, PLUS, Federal Perkins. *Student Employment:* Federal Work-Study Program available. Institutional employment available. Highest amount earned per year from on-campus jobs $1,200. Off-campus job opportunities are good. **Financial Aid Statistics:** 97% freshmen, 87% undergrads receive need-based scholarship or grant aid. 9% freshmen, 5% undergrads receive non-need-based scholarship or grant aid. 81% freshmen, 79% undergrads receive need-based self-help aid. 0% freshmen, 0% undergrads receive athletic scholarships. 82% freshmen, 74% undergrads receive any aid. 69% undergrads borrow to pay for school. **Criteria for awarding institutional aid:** *Non-need-based:* academics, alumni affiliation, art, leadership, minority status, music/drama, state/district residency.

UNIVERSITY OF MAINE AT PRESQUE ISLE

Office of Admissions, Presque Isle, ME 4769
Phone: 207-768-9532 • **Financial Aid Phone:** 207-768-9510
E-mail: admissions@umpi.edu • **CEEB Code:** 3008
Fax: 207-768-9777 • **Website:** www.umpi.edu

This public school was founded in 1903. It has a 150-acre campus.

RATINGS
Admissions Selectivity Rating: 74   **Fire Safety Rating:** 76

STUDENTS AND FACULTY
Enrollment: 847. **Student Body:** 61% female, 39% male, 4% out-of-state, 8% international (3 countries represented). Asian 0%, African American 1%, Caucasian 80%, Hispanic 1%, Native American 3%
Retention and Graduation: 61% freshmen return for sophomore year. 26% freshmen graduate within 4 years. 46% freshmen graduate within 6 years. **Faculty:** 44 full-time faculty, 66% hold PhDs, 50% are are members of minority groups, 7% are women. 0% of classes are taught by teaching assistants.

ACADEMICS
Degrees: associate, bachelor's, certificate. **Classes:** Most classes have 10-19 students. Most lab/discussion sessions have 10-19 students. **Majors with Highest Enrollment:** Elementary Education and Teaching; Liberal Arts and Sciences/Liberal Studies; Business/Commerce. **Special Study Options:** Accelerated program, cooperative education program, cross-registration, distance learning, double major, exchange student program (domestic), honors program, independent study, internships, student-designed major, study abroad, teacher certification program. **Honors programs:** HON 300 Honors Seminar, HON/HTY 401 Oral History, HON 421 Honors Senior Year Project. **Disability Services:** Special programs offered to physically disabled students include note-taking services, reader services, tape recorders, tutors. **Career services:** alumni services, career/job search classes, career assessment, internships.

FACILITIES
Housing: Coed dorms, apartments for married students. 100% of campus accessible to physically disabled. **Special Academic Facilities/Equipment:** Museumn and Art Gallery, Gentile Hall **Computers:** Students can register for classes online. Administrative functions (other than registration) can be performed online.

CAMPUS LIFE
Environment: Village. **Activities:** drama/theater, radio station, student government, student newspaper. 27 registered organizations, 1 honor society, 1 religous organization. 1 fraternity, 1 sorority. **Athletics (Intercollegiate):** *Men:* baseball, basketball, cross-country, golf, skiing (nordic/cross-country), soccer. *Women:* basketball, cross-country, skiing (nordic/cross-country), soccer, softball, volleyball. **On-Campus Highlights:** Caroline D. Gentile Hall, Campus Center, Library, Fitness Center, Owl's Nest, Caroline D. Gentile Hall, the newest building at the University of Maine at Presque Isle, will officially open to the public on January 21, 2006. Named in honor of the University's longest serving faculty member, Gentile Hall features a large multipurpose court, fitness center, pool, elevated track, and climbing wall. The facility will support the University's academic programs and student body, but the community will also be welcomed and encouraged to use its resources.

ADMISSIONS
Freshman Academic Profile: Average high school GPA 2.91. 7% in top 10% of high school class, 19% in top 25% of high school class, 46% in top 50% of high school class. SAT Math middle 50% range 391-534. SAT Critical Reading middle 50% range 402-528. SAT Writing middle 50% range 395-510. ACT middle 50% range 17-. Minimum internet-based TOEFL 71. Minimum paper TOEFL 530. **Basis for Candidate Selection:** *Very important factors considered include:* Class rank, application essay, academic GPA, recommendation(s), rigor of secondary school record. *Important factors considered include:* interview. *Other factors considered include:* standardized test scores, alumni/ae relation, character/personal qualities, extracurricular activities, racial/ethnic status, state residency, talent/ability, volunteer work, work experience. **Freshman Admission Requirements:** High school diploma is required and GED is accepted. **Freshman Admission Statistics:** 580 applied, 66% admitted, 52% enrolled. **Transfer Admission Requirements:** High school transcript, college transcript(s), essay or personal statement, statement of good standing from prior institution(s). Minimum college GPA of 2.0 required. Lowest grade transferable C-. **General Admission Information:** Application Fee $40. Nonfall registration accepted. Admission may be deferred for a maximum of up to 1 year. Credit offered for CEEB Advanced Placement tests.

COSTS AND FINANCIAL AID
Annual in-state tuition $6,600. Annual out-of-state tuition $9,900. Room and board $7,656. Required fees $836. Average book expense $900. **Required Forms and Deadlines:** FAFSA. **Notification of Awards:** Applicants will be notified of awards on a rolling basis beginning 3/1. **Types of Aid:** *Need-based scholarships/grants:* Federal Pell, SEOG, state scholarships/grants, private scholarships, the school's own gift aid. *Loans:* Direct Subsidized Stafford, Direct Unsubsidized Stafford, Direct PLUS, Federal Perkins, state loans, college/university loans from institutional funds. **Financial Aid Statistics:** 100% freshmen, 98% undergrads receive need-based scholarship or grant aid. 6% freshmen, 4% undergrads receive non-need-based scholarship or grant aid. 79% freshmen, 80% undergrads receive need-based self-help aid. 0% freshmen, 0% undergrads receive athletic scholarships. 83% freshmen, 76% undergrads receive any aid. 80% undergrads borrow to pay for school. Average cumulative indebtedness $22,713. **Criteria for awarding institutional aid:** *Non-need-based:* academics, alumni affiliation, art, job skills, leadership, minority status, music/drama, state/district residency.

UNIVERSITY OF MARY

7500 University Drive, Bismarck, ND 58504
Phone: 701-255-7500
E-mail: sueroo@umary.edu • **CEEB Code:** 6428
Fax: 701-255-7687 • **Website:** www.umary.edu • **ACT Code:** 3201

This private school, affiliated with the Roman Catholic Church, was founded in 1959. It has a 107-acre campus.

RATINGS
Admissions Selectivity Rating: 68   **Fire Safety Rating:** 60*

STUDENTS AND FACULTY
Enrollment: 1,722. **Student Body:** 62% female, 38% male, 0% out-of-state, 0% international. Asian 0%, African American 0%, Caucasian 11%, Hispanic 0%, Native American <1%
Retention and Graduation: 70% freshmen return for sophomore year. 1% grads pursue arts and sciences degrees. 2% grads pursue law degrees. 4% grads pursue business degrees. **Faculty:** 0% of classes are taught by teaching assistants.

ACADEMICS
Degrees: associate, bachelor's, master's. **Majors with Highest Enrollment:** Health Services/Allied Health/Health Sciences; Registered Nursing/Registered Nurse; Business/Commerce. **Special Study Options:** Accelerated program, cooperative education program, distance learning, double major, dual enrollment, external degree program, honors program, independent study, internships, study abroad, teacher certification program. **Combined degree programs:** BA/MA. **Disability Services:** Special programs offered to physically disabled students include tape recorders, tutors. **Career services:** alumni services, career/job search classes, career assessment, internships.

FACILITIES
Housing: men's dorms, women's dorms, apartments for single students. 75% of campus accessible to physically disabled. **Special Academic Facilities/Equipment:** Art gallery.

CAMPUS LIFE

Environment: Village. **Activities:** Choral groups, concert band, drama/theater, jazz band, literary magazine, music ensembles, musical theater, pep band, radio station, student government, student newspaper, television station, yearbook. 50 registered organizations, 5 honor societies, 6 religious organizations. **Athletics (Intercollegiate):** *Men:* baseball, basketball, cross-country, football, golf, soccer, tennis, track/field (outdoor), track/field (indoor), wrestling. *Women:* basketball, cheerleading, cross-country, golf, soccer, softball, tennis, track/field (outdoor), track/field (indoor), volleyball.

ADMISSIONS

Freshman Academic Profile: ACT middle 50% range 19-24. Minimum paper TOEFL 500. **Basis for Candidate Selection:** *Very important factors considered include:* standardized test scores. *Important factors considered include:* Class rank, recommendation(s), rigor of secondary school record. *Other factors considered include:* application essay, character/personal qualities, interview. **Freshman Admission Requirements:** High school diploma is required and GED is accepted. **Freshman Admission Statistics:** 943 applied, 95% admitted, 48% enrolled. **Transfer Admission Requirements:** college transcript(s), Minimum college GPA of 2.0 required. Lowest grade transferable D. **General Admission Information:** Application Fee $15. Regular application deadline 8/23. Notification on a rolling basis, beginning on or about 9/2. Nonfall registration accepted. Admission may be deferred for a maximum of 12. Credit and/or placement offered for CEEB Advanced Placement tests.

COSTS AND FINANCIAL AID

Annual tuition $9,200. Room and board $3,540. Required fees $300. Average book expense $610. **Required Forms and Deadlines:** FAFSA. **Types of Aid:** *Need-based scholarships/grants:* Federal Pell, SEOG, state scholarships/grants, private scholarships, the school's own gift aid. *Loans:* Subsidized Stafford, Unsubsidized Stafford, PLUS, Federal Perkins, Federal Nursing. *Student Employment:* Federal Work-Study Program available. Institutional employment available. Highest amount earned per year from on-campus jobs $1,000. Off-campus job opportunities are good. **Financial Aid Statistics:** 100% freshmen, 100% undergrads receive need-based scholarship or grant aid. 100% freshmen, 61% undergrads receive non-need-based scholarship or grant aid. 100% freshmen, 100% undergrads receive need-based self-help aid. 0% freshmen, 0% undergrads receive athletic scholarships. 77% undergrads borrow to pay for school.

UNIVERSITY OF MARY HARDIN—BAYLOR

UMHB Box 8004, Belton, TX 76513
Phone: 254-295-4520 · **Financial Aid Phone:** 254-295-4517
E-mail: admissions@umhb.edu · **CEEB Code:** 3588
Fax: 254-295-5049 · **Website:** www.umhb.edu · **ACT Code:** 4128

This private school, affiliated with the Baptist Church, was founded in 1845. It has a 170-acre campus.

RATINGS

Admissions Selectivity Rating: 72   **Fire Safety Rating:** 72

STUDENTS AND FACULTY

Enrollment: 3,039. **Student Body:** 61% female, 39% male, 2% out-of-state, 2% international (12 countries represented). Asian 1%, African American 15%, Caucasian 58%, Hispanic 19%, Native American 1%. **Retention and Graduation:** 68% freshmen return for sophomore year. 29% freshmen graduate within 4 years. 48% freshmen graduate within 6 years. **Faculty:** 155 full-time faculty, 74% hold PhDs, 57% are are members of minority groups, 13% are women. 0% of classes are taught by teaching assistants.

ACADEMICS

Degrees: bachelor's, doctoral, master's. **Classes:** Most classes have 10-19 students. Most lab/discussion sessions have 10-19 students. **Majors with Highest Enrollment:** Elementary Education and Teaching; Registered Nursing/Registered Nurse. **Special Study Options:** Accelerated program, double major, dual enrollment, English as a Second Language (ESL), honors program, independent study, internships, student-designed major, study abroad, teacher certification program, Tuition exchange program with other participating universities. Undergrads may take grad level classes. Military degree completion programs. Servicemember Opportunity Colleges (SOCS) programs. **Honors programs:** Lower Level Honors Program—approximately the top 10% of UMHB's entering freshman class. Freshman year offerings include English and religion, and sophomore year offerings are interdisciplinary courses in the humanities and social sciences. Upper Level Honors Program—Minimum requirements for completion of this program is the completion of three upper

level courses designated as honors level and the completion of HNRS 3110 "Great Books and Ideas" and HNRS 3120 "living Issues." Successful completion of these requirements will allow the student to graduate with the cum laude designation. To receive the higher designations of magna cum laude or summa cum laude, the student must also successfully complete an Honors Research Project. This project must include original research and both written and oral presentations of that research to the Honors Committee. **Combined degree programs:** BBA/MBA; 3-1 Clinical Lab Science with local hospital. **Disability Services:** Special programs offered to physically disabled students include note-taking services, reader services, tape recorders, tutors. **Career services:** Alumni network, alumni services, career/job search classes, career assessment, internships, regional alumni. Career services highlights include The UMHB Career Development Center, which offers an array of self assessments, exploration, document preparation, and career planning opportunities. The most used and results-generated career program is the one-on-one Résumé Clinic which involves an interactive session with our students drafting a successful career document. Many times this is their first résumé, and the new confidence that is reflective by the student after completing this document is most exciting. Additional popular programs and workshops include, Show Me the Money: salary negotiations; Facebook, My Space and My Future Employer; and the President's Senior Etiquette Dinner Program.

FACILITIES

Housing: special housing for disabled students, men's dorms, women's dorms, apartments for single students. 85% of campus accessible to physically disabled. **Special Academic Facilities/Equipment:** Language lab **Computers:** 100% of classrooms, 100% of dorms, 100% of libraries, 100% of dining areas, 100% of student union, 80% of common outdoor areas have wireless network access. Students can register for classes online. Administrative functions (other than registration) can be performed online.

CAMPUS LIFE

Environment: City. **Activities:** Choral groups, concert band, drama/theater, jazz band, literary magazine, marching band, music ensembles, musical theater, opera, pep band, student government, student newspaper, symphony orchestra, yearbook, Campus Ministries, International Student Organization. 51 registered organizations, 5 honor societies, 7 religious organizations. **Athletics (Intercollegiate):** *Men:* baseball, basketball, football, golf, soccer, tennis. *Women:* basketball, golf, soccer, softball, tennis, volleyball. **On-Campus Highlights:** SUB (Student Union Building), Sportsplex or ANY sporting event, Millennium Oaks Park (gazebo, pond), Mayborn Center exercise/fitness facilities, Quad area.

ADMISSIONS

Freshman Academic Profile: Average high school GPA 3.49. SAT Math middle 50% range 480-570. SAT Critical Reading middle 50% range 470-570. SAT Writing middle 50% range 420-530. ACT middle 50% range 21-26. **Basis for Candidate Selection:** *Very important factors considered include:* Class rank, standardized test scores. *Important factors considered include:* academic GPA, level of applicant's interest. *Other factors considered include:* application essay, recommendation(s), rigor of secondary school record, alumni/ae relation, character/personal qualities, extracurricular activities, first generation, geographical residence, interview, racial/ethnic status, religious affiliation/commitment, state residency, talent/ability, volunteer work, work experience. **Freshman Admission Requirements:** High school diploma is required and GED is accepted. **Academic units required:** 4 English, 3 mathematics, 3 science, 2 foreign language, 3 social studies. **Freshman Admission Statistics:** 7,037 applied, 80% admitted, 13% enrolled. **Transfer Admission Requirements:** college transcript(s), Minimum college GPA of 2.0 required. Lowest grade transferable C. **General Admission Information:** Application Fee $35. Nonfall registration accepted. Admission may be deferred for a maximum of no set limit. Credit offered for CEEB Advanced Placement tests.

COSTS AND FINANCIAL AID

Annual tuition $23,400. Room and board $6,750. Required fees $2,250. Average book expense $1,300. **Required Forms and Deadlines:** FAFSA. **Notification of Awards:** Applicants will be notified of awards on a rolling basis beginning 2/1. **Types of Aid:** *Need-based scholarships/grants:* Federal Pell, SEOG, state scholarships/grants, private scholarships, the school's own gift aid, Federal Nursing Scholarships, federal work study, Texas state work study, UMHB work duty. *Loans:* Direct Subsidized Stafford, Direct Unsubsidized Stafford, Subsidized Stafford, Unsubsidized Stafford, PLUS, Federal Perkins, state loans, college/university loans from institutional funds. *Student Employment:* Federal Work-Study Program available. Institutional employment available. Highest amount earned per year from on-campus jobs $3,500. Off-campus job opportunities are good. **Financial Aid Statistics:** 100% freshmen, 98% undergrads receive need-based scholarship or grant aid. 8% freshmen, 5% undergrads receive non-need-based scholarship or grant aid. 81% freshmen, 83% undergrads receive need-based self-help aid. 0% freshmen, 0% undergrads receive athletic scholarships. 84% freshmen, 87% undergrads receive any aid. 80% undergrads borrow to pay for school. Average cumulative indebtedness $31,825. **Criteria for awarding institutional aid:** *Non-need-based:* academics, art, leadership, music/drama, religious affiliation.

UNIVERSITY OF MARY WASHINGTON

1301 College Avenue, Fredericksburg, VA 22401
Phone: 540-654-2000 · **Financial Aid Phone:** 540-654-2468
E-mail: admit@umw.edu · **CEEB Code:** 5398
Fax: 540-654-1857 · **Website:** www.umw.edu · **ACT Code:** 4414

This public school was founded in 1908. It has a 176-acre campus.

RATINGS

Admissions Selectivity Rating: 81   **Fire Safety Rating:** 89

STUDENTS AND FACULTY

Enrollment: 4,101. **Student Body:** 65% female, 35% male, 11% out-of-state, 1% international (27 countries represented). Asian 4%, African American 6%, Caucasian 69%, Hispanic 7%, Native American <1%
Retention and Graduation: 78% freshmen return for sophomore year. 61% freshmen graduate within 4 years. 70% freshmen graduate within 6 years. 17% grads go on to further study within 1 year. 10% grads pursue arts and sciences degrees. 1% grads pursue law degrees. 1% grads pursue business degrees. 1% grads pursue medical degrees. **Faculty:** 250 full-time faculty, 88% hold PhDs, 47% are are members of minority groups, 16% are women. 0% of classes are taught by teaching assistants.

ACADEMICS

Degrees: bachelor's, certificate, master's, post-bachelor's certificate. **Classes:** Most classes have 20-29 students. Most lab/discussion sessions have 20-29 students. **Majors with Highest Enrollment:** Biology/Biological Sciences; Business Administration and Management; Psychology. **Special Study Options:** Accelerated program, distance learning, double major, independent study, internships, student-designed major, study abroad, teacher certification program. **Combined degree programs:** BA/BS & M.S. elementary education, BS computer science & MSMIS, MBA/MSMIS. **Disability Services:** Special programs offered to physically disabled students include note-taking services, reader services, tape recorders. **Career services:** Alumni network, alumni services, career/job search classes, career assessment, internships, regional alumni. Career services highlights include our academic credit internship program, which allows students to take up to 12 experiential credits toward graduation. Most experiences are graded and in many cases count toward the major.

FACILITIES

Housing: Coed dorms, special housing for disabled students, men's dorms, special housing for international students, women's dorms, apartments for single students, Wellness Housing, Theme Housing, Substance-Free. 63% of campus accessible to physically disabled. **Special Academic Facilities/Equipment:** Two art galleries, Center for Historic Preservation, language labs, Leidecker Center for Asian Studies, cartography lab, greenhouse. **Computers:** 100% of classrooms, 100% of dorms, 100% of libraries, 100% of dining areas, 100% of student union, 5% of common outdoor areas have wireless network access. Students can register for classes online. Administrative functions (other than registration) can be performed online.

CAMPUS LIFE

Environment: City. **Activities:** Choral groups, concert band, dance, drama/theater, jazz band, literary magazine, music ensembles, musical theater, opera, radio station, student government, student newspaper, student-run film society, symphony orchestra, yearbook, Campus Ministries, International Student Organization, Model UN, 120 registered organizations, 23 honor societies, 10 religious organizations. **Athletics (Intercollegiate):** *Men:* baseball, basketball, crew/rowing, cross-country, equestrian sports, lacrosse, soccer, swimming, tennis, track/field (outdoor), track/field (indoor). *Women:* basketball, crew/rowing, cross-country, equestrian sports, field hockey, lacrosse, soccer, softball, swimming, tennis, track/field (outdoor), track/field (indoor), volleyball. **On-Campus Highlights:** Woodard Campus Center, Battleground Athletic facilities/Fitness Center, Palmieri Plaza Fountain, Ball Circle, Lee Hall. **Environmental Initiatives:** In July 2010, UMW adopted sustainability policies and practices committing to reducing solid waste, conserving energy and water,encouraging the purchasing of products to promote sustainability and promote alternative methods of transportation. In 2009, the President's Council on Sustainability was formed as an advisory committee to the University's President and Cabinet on how the university can best act and articulate the institutions commitment to sustainability and environmental stewardship as outlined in the Strategic Plan. The committee is directly responsible to the Executive Vice President for Administration and Finance and the Provost. UMW has a significant University-wide recycling program in place for aluminum, paper, newspaper, cardboard, plastic, motor oil, oil filters, printer cartridges, antifreeze, tires, auto parts, refrigerators, freon, latex paint, computer monitors, CPUs without hard drives, printers and fluorescent tubes. Waste reduction includes composting of yard waste and re-use of wood chips from tree removal. Learn about the second annual RECYCLEMANIA at http://sustainability.umw.edu/recycling/umw-recyclemania/.

ADMISSIONS

Freshman Academic Profile: Average high school GPA 3.54. 16% in top 10% of high school class, 45% in top 25% of high school class, 86% in top 50% of high school class. 82% from public high schools. SAT Math middle 50% range 500-590. SAT Critical Reading middle 50% range 520-610. SAT Writing middle 50% range 500-600. ACT middle 50% range 22-26. Minimum internet-based TOEFL 88. Minimum paper TOEFL 570. **Basis for Candidate Selection:** *Very important factors considered include:* academic GPA, rigor of secondary school record. *Important factors considered include:* Class rank, application essay, recommendation(s), standardized test scores, extracurricular activities. *Other factors considered include:* alumni/ae relation, character/personal qualities, first generation, geographical residence, racial/ethnic status, state residency, talent/ability, volunteer work, work experience. **Freshman Admission Requirements:** High school diploma is required and GED is accepted. **Academic units required:** 4 English, 3 mathematics, 3 science, (3 science labs), 2 foreign language, 2 social studies, 1 history, 0 visual/performing arts, 0 computer science, 0 academic electives. **Freshman Admission Statistics:** 5,336 applied, 77% admitted, 21% enrolled. **Transfer Admission Requirements:** High school transcript, college transcript(s), essay or personal statement, statement of good standing from prior institution(s). Minimum college GPA of 2.0 required. Lowest grade transferable C. **General Admission Information:** Application Fee $50. Regular application deadline 2/1. Regular notification 4/1. Nonfall registration accepted. Admission may be deferred for a maximum of 2 semesters. Credit offered for CEEB Advanced Placement tests.

COSTS AND FINANCIAL AID

Annual in-state tuition $7,146. Annual out-of-state tuition $20,432. Room and board $9,430. Required fees $3,106. Average book expense $1,100. **Required Forms and Deadlines:** FAFSA. **Notification of Awards:** Applicants will be notified of awards on or about 4/15. **Types of Aid:** *Need-based scholarships/grants:* Federal Pell, SEOG, state scholarships/grants, private scholarships, the school's own gift aid, Unendowed gifts. *Loans:* Subsidized Stafford, Unsubsidized Stafford, PLUS, Federal Perkins. *Student Employment:* Federal Work-Study Program available. Institutional employment available. Highest amount earned per year from on-campus jobs $5,200. Off-campus job opportunities are good. **Financial Aid Statistics:** 41% freshmen, 45% undergrads receive need-based scholarship or grant aid. 21% freshmen, 19% undergrads receive non-need-based scholarship or grant aid. 72% freshmen, 78% undergrads receive need-based self-help aid. 0% freshmen, 0% undergrads receive athletic scholarships. 67% freshmen, 63% undergrads receive any aid. 48% undergrads borrow to pay for school. Average cumulative indebtedness $14,946. **Criteria for awarding institutional aid:** *Non-need-based:* academics, alumni affiliation, art, leadership, music/drama, state/district residency.

UNIVERSITY OF MARYLAND, BALTIMORE COUNTY

1000 Hilltop Circle, Baltimore, MD 21250
Phone: 410-455-2291 · **Financial Aid Phone:** 410-455-2387
E-mail: admissions@umbc.edu · **CEEB Code:** 5835
Fax: 410-455-1094 · **Website:** www.umbc.edu · **ACT Code:** 1751

This public school was founded in 1966. It has a 530-acre campus.

RATINGS

Admissions Selectivity Rating: 88   **Fire Safety Rating:** 95

STUDENTS AND FACULTY

Enrollment: 10,838. **Student Body:** 45% female, 55% male, 6% out-of-state, 4% international (96 countries represented). Asian 20%, African American 16%, Caucasian 47%, Hispanic 5%, Native American <1%
Retention and Graduation: 49% grads go on to further study within 1 year. 30% grads pursue arts and sciences degrees. 1% grads pursue law degrees. 2%

grads pursue business degrees. 5% grads pursue medical degrees. **Faculty:** 497 full-time faculty, 86% hold PhDs, 44% are are members of minority groups, 22% are women. 1.5% of classes are taught by teaching assistants.

ACADEMICS

Degrees: bachelor's, master's, post-bachelor's certificate. **Classes:** Most classes have 20-29 students. Most lab/discussion sessions have 10-19 students. **Majors with Highest Enrollment:** Computer and Information Sciences; Biology/Biological Sciences; Mechanical Engineering. **Special Study Options:** Accelerated program, cooperative education program, cross-registration, double major, dual enrollment, English as a Second Language (ESL), exchange student program (domestic), honors program, independent study, internships, student-designed major, study abroad, teacher certification program. **Honors programs:** UMBC Honors College, Merehoff (Science, Technology, Engineering, and Mathematics), Scholars Program, Sherman Teacher Education Scholars Program, Sondheim Scholars Programs, Center for Women and Information Technology (CWIT) Scholars Program, Humanities Scholars Program, Lineman Scholars Program. **Combined degree programs:** BA/MA, BA/MEng, biochemistry, chemistry, economics, info. systems. **Disability Services:** Special programs offered to physically disabled students include note-taking services, reader services, tape recorders, tutors. **Career services:** Alumni network, alumni services, career/job search classes, career assessment, internships, regional alumni. UMBC Career Services is proud of many of the programs and stellar customer service that it delivers to multiple constituents. Collaboration is high with internal and external partners and a primary example of this type of collaboration is demonstrated by the development of Career Path, a website that is intended to help students understand what they can do with their major within a variety of industries, access current jobs and hear the stories of UMBC alumni. We are also extremely proud of consistent and continual employer recruitment activities and presence on campus despite a downturn in the economy. Our graduates continue to report very good job offers.

FACILITIES

Housing: Coed dorms, special housing for disabled students, apartments for single students, Theme Housing, Same sex floors, honors floors, quiet lifestyle, Substance-free, and living-learning communities: Center for Women and Information Technology, Emergency Health Services, Exploratory Majors, Honors College, Humanities Floor, Intercultural Living Exchange, Shriver Living Learning Center, Visual and Performing Arts Floor, and Women Involved in Learning and Leadership, gender neutral. 95% of campus accessible to physically disabled. **Special Academic Facilities/Equipment:** Albin O. Kuhn Library and Gallery, Center for Art and Visual Culture, Women's Center, Center for Environmental Science, Center for Photonics Technology, Center for Women and Information Technology, Center on Research and Teaching in Social Work, Howard Hughes Medical Institute at UMBC, Imaging Research Center, Institute for Global Electronic Commerce, Joint Center for Earth Systems Technology, Laboratory for Healthcare Informatics, Maryland Center for Telecommunications Research, Maryland Institute for Policy Analysis and Research, bwtech@umbc Research and Technology Park and Incubator and Accelerator, Shriver Center, UMBC Technology Center, Goddard Earth Science and Technology Center. **Computers:** 100% of classrooms, 80% of dorms, 100% of libraries, 100% of dining areas, 100% of student union, 40% of common outdoor areas have wireless network access. Students can register for classes online. Administrative functions (other than registration) can be performed online.

CAMPUS LIFE

Environment: Metropolis. **Activities:** Choral groups, dance, drama/theater, jazz band, literary magazine, music ensembles, musical theater, pep band, radio station, student government, student newspaper, student-run film society, symphony orchestra, Campus Ministries, International Student Organization, Model UN. 230 registered organizations, 8 honor societies, 20 religious organizations. 11 fraternities, 12 sororities. **Athletics (Intercollegiate):** *Men:* baseball, basketball, cheerleading, cross-country, diving, lacrosse, soccer, swimming, tennis, track/field (outdoor), track/field (indoor). *Women:* basketball, cheerleading, cross-country, diving, lacrosse, soccer, softball, swimming, tennis, track/field (outdoor), track/field (indoor), volleyball. **On-Campus Highlights:** Albin O. Kuhn Library and Gallery, The Commons (Student Center), Center for Art , Design and Visual Cultu, Howard Hughes Medical Institute Lab, Retriever Activities Center, Students attend, and take part in, a world of excellent theatre, music and dance performances on campus. They go to art openings and lectures, start clubs and exchange ideas through the campus paper and literary magazines. **Environmental Initiatives:** Climate Commitment Task Force (students, faculty, staff) will commence implementation of its Climate Action Plan and reduce our carbon footprint. Implement energy performance contract. Pursuing a minimum of LEED Silver certification for all new construction and major renovations, including the new Performing Arts and Humanities Building and the Patapsco Hall Addition.

ADMISSIONS

Freshman Academic Profile: Average high school GPA 3.71. 29% in top 10% of high school class, 56% in top 25% of high school class, 85% in top 50% of high school class. NA% from public high schools. SAT Math middle 50% range 580-670. SAT Critical Reading middle 50% range 550-650. SAT Writing middle 50% range 530-640. ACT middle 50% range 24-29. Minimum internet-based TOEFL 48. Minimum paper TOEFL 460. **Basis for Candidate Selection:** *Very important factors considered include:* academic GPA, rigor of secondary school record, standardized test scores. *Important factors considered include:* Class rank, application essay, recommendation(s), talent/ability. *Other factors considered include:* character/personal qualities, extracurricular activities. **Freshman Admission Requirements:** High school diploma is required and GED is accepted. **Academic units required:** 4 English, 3 mathematics, 3 science, 2 foreign language, 3 social studies, 3 Social Studies & History. **Freshman Admission Statistics:** 8,514 applied, 60% admitted, 30% enrolled. **Transfer Admission Requirements:** college transcript(s), statement of good standing from prior institution(s). Minimum college GPA of 2.5 required. Lowest grade transferable D. **General Admission Information:** Application Fee $50. Regular application deadline 2/1. Notification on a rolling basis, beginning on or about 12/15. Nonfall registration accepted. Admission may be deferred for a maximum of one year. Credit and/or placement offered for CEEB Advanced Placement tests.

COSTS AND FINANCIAL AID

Annual in-state tuition $9,764. Annual out-of-state tuition $20,825. Room and board $10,866. Average book expense $1,200. **Required Forms and Deadlines:** FAFSA. **Notification of Awards:** Applicants will be notified of awards on a rolling basis beginning 3/15. **Types of Aid:** *Need-based scholarships/grants:* Federal Pell, SEOG, state scholarships/grants, private scholarships, the school's own gift aid. *Loans:* Direct Subsidized Stafford, Direct Unsubsidized Stafford, Direct PLUS, Federal Perkins. *Student Employment:* Federal Work-Study Program available. Institutional employment available. Off-campus job opportunities are excellent. **Financial Aid Statistics:** 72% freshmen, 75% undergrads receive need-based scholarship or grant aid. 22% freshmen, 9% undergrads receive non-need-based scholarship or grant aid. 56% freshmen, 69% undergrads receive need-based self-help aid. 3% freshmen, 2% undergrads receive athletic scholarships. 70% freshmen, 64% undergrads receive any aid. 53% undergrads borrow to pay for school. Average cumulative indebtedness $18,643. **Criteria for awarding institutional aid:** *Non-need-based:* academics, alumni affiliation, art, athletics, music/drama.

See page 1184.

UNIVERSITY OF MARYLAND—COLLEGE PARK

Best 380

Mitchell Building, College Park, MD 20742-5235
Phone: 301-314-8385 · **Financial Aid Phone:** 301-314-9000
E-mail: um-admit@uga.umd.edu · **CEEB Code:** 5814
Fax: 301-314-9693 · **Website:** http://www.umd.edu · **ACT Code:** 1746

This public school was founded in 1856. It has a 1382-acre campus.

RATINGS

Admissions Selectivity Rating: 94	Fire Safety Rating: 81

STUDENTS AND FACULTY

Enrollment: 26,532. **Student Body:** 46% female, 54% male, 20% out-of-state, 3% international (79 countries represented). Asian 16%, African American 13%, Caucasian 53%, Hispanic 9%, Native American <1%
Retention and Graduation: 67% freshmen graduate within 4 years. 85% freshmen graduate within 6 years. 17% grads go on to further study within 1 year. 2% grads pursue law degrees. 1% grads pursue business degrees. 2% grads pursue medical degrees. **Faculty:** 1,756 full-time faculty, 92% hold PhDs, 18% are are members of minority groups, 22% are women. 12% of classes are taught by teaching assistants.

ACADEMICS

Degrees: bachelor's, certificate, master's, post-bachelor's certificate, post-master's certificate. **Classes:** Most classes have 20-29 students. Most lab/discussion sessions have 20-29 students. **Majors with Highest Enrollment:** Biology/Biological Sciences; Criminology; Economics. **Special Study Options:** Accelerated program, cooperative education program, cross-registration, distance learning, double major, dual enrollment, English as a Second Language (ESL), exchange student program (domestic), external degree program, honors program, independent study, internships, liberal arts/career combination, student-designed major, study abroad, teacher certification program, Living-Learning programs including Gemstone Program, Honors, First-Year Focus,

Jiminez-Porter Writers House, Civicus, College Park Scholars, and others. **Honors programs:** Gemstones, Honors, Honors Humanities. **Combined degree programs:** BA/JD, BA/MA, BA/MBA. **Disability Services:** Special programs offered to physically disabled students include note-taking services, reader services, tape recorders, tutors. **Career services:** internships.

FACILITIES

Housing: Coed dorms, special housing for disabled students, special housing for international students, women's dorms, fraternity/sorority housing, cooperative housing, apartments for single students, Wellness Housing, Theme HousingLiving/Learning program housing includes Gemstone program, College Park Scholars, Language House, Beyond the Classroom, Civicus, Hinman CEOs, Global Communities, Jimenz-Porter Writer's House, Honors, International House, Honors Humanities, SmokFree/Alcohol-Free. **Special Academic Facilities/Equipment:** Aerospace buoyancy lab, art gallery, international piano archives, center for architectural design and research, model nuclear reactor, wind tunnel. **Computers:** 100% of classrooms, 100% of dorms, 100% of libraries, 100% of dining areas, 100% of student union, 100% of common outdoor areas have wireless network access. Students can register for classes online. Administrative functions (other than registration) can be performed online.

CAMPUS LIFE

Environment: Metropolis. **Activities:** Choral groups, concert band, dance, drama/theater, jazz band, literary magazine, marching band, music ensembles, musical theater, opera, pep band, radio station, student government, student newspaper, student-run film society, symphony orchestra, television station, yearbook, Campus Ministries, International Student Organization, Model UN. 574 registered organizations, 53 honor societies, 55 religious organizations. 36 fraternities, 27 sororities. **Athletics (Intercollegiate):** *Men:* baseball, basketball, cross-country, football, golf, lacrosse, soccer, swimming, tennis, track/field (outdoor), track/field (indoor), wrestling. *Women:* basketball, cheerleading, cross-country, field hockey, golf, gymnastics, lacrosse, soccer, softball, swimming, tennis, track/field (outdoor), track/field (indoor), volleyball, water polo. **On-Campus Highlights:** Clarice Smith Performing Arts Center, Adele H. Stamp Student Union, Eppley Recreation Center, Chevy Chase Bank Field at Byrd Stadium, Comcast Center, Memorial Chapel, Riggs Alumni Center. **Environmental Initiatives:** The Green Office Program engages staff, faculty and students in a voluntary, self-guided initiative that promotes best environmental practices at the University of Maryland. The program supports and promotes offices that are taking steps toward reducing their environmental footprint. Learn more at http://www.sustainability.umd.edu/content/culture/green_offices. php. The University of Maryland has made great strides in the area of energy management, both by working to reduce energy consumption through energy performance contracts and installation of energy-saving technologies around campus, and by collaborating with other public agencies and universities in Maryland to ramp up renewable energy supply. UMD completed a $20,000,000 energy performance contract with Johnson Controls Inc. that is designed to save nearly $2,000,000 a year in energy and reduce the CO_2 emissions by over 4,200 tons per year. A new $2,200,000 contract has been awarded to Pepco Energy Services to implement a series of energy conservation measures at various athletic facilities on campus which will result in $190,000 in utility savings annually. UMD is also working to add more Power Purchase Agreements for renewable energy in addition to those described under the Renewable Energy Credit above. The University Sustainability Fund provides funding for projects that promote environmental sustainability, and positively impact and enhance the student experience at UMD. $300,000 is available this year. The Fund allocates funds to projects that increase the use of renewable energy on campus and/or in the local community, increase the energy efficiency of our facilities, reduce the amount of waste created and material resources used on campus, encourage sustainable behaviors, and integrate sustainability into teaching, research, and service at UMD. The Fund is supported by student fees and administered through a student-majority subcommittee of the University Sustainability Council. Learn about funded projects and more at http://sustainability.umd.edu/content/about/fund.php.

ADMISSIONS

Freshman Academic Profile: Average high school GPA 4.15. 71% in top 10% of high school class, 88% in top 25% of high school class, 98% in top 50% of high school class. SAT Math middle 50% range 620-730. SAT Critical Reading middle 50% range 590-690. Minimum internet-based TOEFL 100. **Basis for Candidate Selection:** *Very important factors considered include:* academic GPA, rigor of secondary school record, standardized test scores. *Important factors considered include:* Class rank, application essay, recommendation(s), first generation, state residency, talent/ability. *Other factors considered include:* alumni/ae relation, character/personal qualities, extracurricular activities, geographical residence, racial/ethnic status, volunteer work, work experience. **Freshman Admission Requirements:** High school diploma is required and GED is accepted. **Academic units required:** 4 English, 3 mathematics, 3 science, (2 science labs), 2 foreign language, 3 social studies. **Freshman Admission Statistics:** 26,268 applied, 48% admitted, 33% enrolled. **Transfer**

Admission Requirements: college transcript(s), essay or personal statement, statement of good standing from prior institution(s). Lowest grade transferable C. **General Admission Information:** Application Fee $55. Regular application deadline 1/20. Nonfall registration accepted. Admission may be deferred for a maximum of 1 year. Credit and/or placement offered for CEEB Advanced Placement tests.

COSTS AND FINANCIAL AID

Annual in-state tuition $7,612. Annual out-of-state tuition $27,905. Room and board $10,633. Required fees $1,815. Average book expense $1,130. **Required Forms and Deadlines:** FAFSA. **Notification of Awards:** Applicants will be notified of awards on a rolling basis beginning 4/1. **Types of Aid:** *Need-based scholarships/grants:* Federal Pell, SEOG, state scholarships/grants, private scholarships, the school's own gift aid. *Loans:* Subsidized Stafford, Unsubsidized Stafford, PLUS, Federal Perkins. *Student Employment:* Federal Work-Study Program available. Institutional employment available. Off-campus job opportunities are good. **Financial Aid Statistics:** 84% freshmen, 83% undergrads receive need-based scholarship or grant aid. 12% freshmen, 6% undergrads receive non-need-based scholarship or grant aid. 86% freshmen, 92% undergrads receive need-based self-help aid. 1% freshmen, 1% undergrads receive athletic scholarships. 86% freshmen, 71% undergrads receive any aid. 45% undergrads borrow to pay for school. Average cumulative indebtedness $19,894. **Criteria for awarding institutional aid:** *Non-need-based:* academics, art, athletics.

UNIVERSITY OF MARYLAND
UNIVERSITY COLLEGE

3501 University Blvd. East, Adelphi, MD 20783
Phone: 301-985-7000
E-mail: umucinfo@nova.umuc.edu
Fax: 301-985-7364 • **Website:** www.umuc.edu • **ACT Code:** 20097

This public school was founded in 1947.

RATINGS

Admissions Selectivity Rating: 60*   **Fire Safety Rating:** 60*

STUDENTS AND FACULTY

Enrollment: 17,527. **Student Body:** 58% female, 42% male, 31% out-of-state. **Faculty:** 119 full-time faculty, 66% hold PhDs, 38% are are members of minority groups.

ACADEMICS

Degrees: associate, bachelor's, certificate, master's, post-bachelor's certificate. **Classes:** Most classes have 20-29 students. **Majors with Highest Enrollment:** Information Science/Studies; Multi-/Interdisciplinary Studies; Business/Commerce. **Special Study Options:** Accelerated program, cooperative education program, cross-registration, distance learning, double major, dual enrollment, external degree program, teacher certification program, weekend college. **Disability Services:** Special programs offered to physically disabled students include note-taking services, reader services, tape recorders, tutors. **Career services:** alumni services, career/job search classes, career assessment,

FACILITIES

Housing: 85% of campus accessible to physically disabled. **Computers:** Students can register for classes online. Administrative functions (other than registration) can be performed online.

CAMPUS LIFE

Environment: Village.

ADMISSIONS

Freshman Academic Profile: Minimum paper TOEFL 550. **Freshman Admission Requirements:** High school diploma is required and GED is accepted. **Freshman Admission Statistics:** 994 applied, 100% admitted, 53% enrolled. **Transfer Admission Requirements:** High school transcript, college transcript(s), Minimum college GPA of 2.0 required. Lowest grade transferable D. **General Admission Information:** Application Fee $30. Nonfall registration accepted. Admission may be deferred for a maximum of 24 months. Credit and/or placement offered for CEEB Advanced Placement tests.

COSTS AND FINANCIAL AID

Annual in-state tuition $5,208. Annual out-of-state tuition $9,576. Required fees $120. Average book expense $1,362. **Required Forms and Deadlines:** FAFSA, Institution's own financial aid form. **Notification of Awards:** Applicants will be notified of awards on a rolling basis beginning 5/1. **Types of Aid:** *Need-based scholarships/grants:* Federal Pell, SEOG, state scholarships/grants, private scholarships, the school's own gift aid. *Loans:* Direct Subsidized Stafford, Direct Unsubsidized Stafford, Direct PLUS, Federal Perkins. *Student*

Employment: Off-campus job opportunities are good. **Financial Aid Statistics:** 50% freshmen, 60% undergrads receive need-based scholarship or grant aid. 0% freshmen, 3% undergrads receive non-need-based scholarship or grant aid. 62% freshmen, 80% undergrads receive need-based self-help aid. 0% freshmen, 0% undergrads receive athletic scholarships. **Criteria for awarding institutional aid:** *Non-need-based:* academics, leadership.

UNIVERSITY OF MASSACHUSETTS AMHERST

University Admissions Center, Amherst, MA 01003-9291
Phone: 413-545-0222 · **Financial Aid Phone:** 413-545-0801
E-mail: mail@admissions.umass.edu · **CEEB Code:** 3917
Fax: 413-545-4312 · **Website:** www.umass.edu · **ACT Code:** 1924

This public school was founded in 1863. It has a 1463-acre campus.

RATINGS

Admissions Selectivity Rating: 89   Fire Safety Rating: 88

STUDENTS AND FACULTY

Enrollment: 21,864. **Student Body:** 49% female, 51% male, 21% out-of-state, 3% international (74 countries represented). Asian 8%, African American 4%, Caucasian 68%, Hispanic 5%, Native American <1%
Retention and Graduation: 63% freshmen graduate within 4 years. 21% grads go on to further study within 1 year. 1% grads pursue law degrees. 3% grads pursue business degrees. 2% grads pursue medical degrees. **Faculty:** 1,277 full-time faculty, 94% hold PhDs, 42% are are members of minority groups, 21% are women.

ACADEMICS

Degrees: associate, bachelor's, certificate, doctoral, master's, post-bachelor's certificate, post-master's certificate. **Classes:** Most classes have 20-29 students. Most lab/discussion sessions have 20-29 students. **Majors with Highest Enrollment:** Psychology; Hospitality Administration/Management; Biology/Biological Sciences. **Special Study Options:** cooperative education program, cross-registration, distance learning, double major, dual enrollment, English as a Second Language (ESL), exchange student program (domestic), honors program, independent study, internships, liberal arts/career combination, student-designed major, study abroad, teacher certification program. **Honors programs:** Commonwealth Honors College offers the advantages of a small honors college, but also the wide-ranging opportunities of a nationally recognized research university. There are approximately 2,800 academically talented students in the Commonwealth College, all experiencing the challenges of a dynamic curriculum that includes interdisciplinary seminars, enriched honors courses, colloquia, independent study, service learning, a "culminating experience" and an honors thesis or project, as well as the option of special living-learning accommodations. **Disability Services:** Special programs offered to physically disabled students include note-taking services, reader services, tape recorders, tutors. **Career services:** Alumni network, alumni services, career/job search classes, career assessment, internships, regional alumni. Career services highlights include the comprehensive career planning services we provide to the students at the University.

FACILITIES

Housing: Coed dorms, special housing for disabled students, men's dorms, special housing for international students, women's dorms, fraternity/sorority housing, apartments for married students, apartments for single students, Wellness Housing, Theme Housing, first year housing. **Special Academic Facilities/Equipment:** Computer Science Complex, Polymer Research Institute, Herter (Art) Gallery, University Art Gallery, Natural History Museum, Fine Arts Center, Mullins Center (sports and entertainment arena, Learning Commons. **Computers:** 97% of classrooms, 10% of dorms, 100% of libraries, 100% of dining areas, 100% of student union, 20% of common outdoor areas have wireless network access. Students can register for classes online. Administrative functions (other than registration) can be performed online.

CAMPUS LIFE

Environment: Town. **Activities:** Choral groups, concert band, dance, drama/theater, jazz band, literary magazine, marching band, music ensembles, musical theater, opera, pep band, radio station, student government, student newspaper, student-run film society, symphony orchestra, television station, Campus Ministries, International Student Organization, Model UN. 291 registered organiza-

tions, 30 honor societies, 14 religious organizations. 21 fraternities, 15 sororities. **Athletics (Intercollegiate):** *Men:* baseball, basketball, cross-country, diving, football, ice hockey, lacrosse, soccer, swimming, track/field (outdoor), track/field (indoor). *Women:* basketball, crew/rowing, cross-country, diving, field hockey, lacrosse, soccer, softball, swimming, tennis, track/field (outdoor), track/field (indoor). **On-Campus Highlights:** The Campus Center / Student Union, The Learning Commons, Recreation Center, The Mullins Center, The Fine Arts Center, http://www.umass.edu/umhome/visit_campus/. **Environmental Initiatives:** Central Heating Plant: Our new Central Heating Plant now allows us to produce roughly 70% of our campus' energy through co-generation. The Central Heating Plant is fueled by mostly natural gas with some oil in the winter time and has won national awards. *Climate Action Plan:* The development of our campus' Climate Action Plan is our most recent success that will help UMass Amherst move toward a more sustainable future. Our Climate Action Plan not only lists what UMass Amherst has done, but how we plan to recude our greenhouse gas emissions and other negative environmental impacts in important areas such as energy conservation, green building, transportation, etc. The first Update to the Climate Action Plan is currently being assembled and published by the Environmental Performance Advisory Committee to the Chancellor (EPAC). Student Involvement: UMass Amherst is dedicated to not only reducing our greenhouse gas emissions and other environmental impacts through infrastructural changes, but also through actively involving student sin all parts of its sustainability initiative. The UMass Amherst Eco-Rep Program is one of the largest in the country with upwards of 70 Eco-Reps working to educate their peers about environmental issues that they can have a positive impact on as college students. The Initiative employs Sustainability Interns to aid the campus Sustainability Manager and our Environmental Performance Advisory Committee in carrying out the Climate Action Plan. Students have been instrumental in launching the UMass Bike Share Program, participation and placing top 5 nationwide in the EPA Gameday Challenge, and was just recognized by the White House for the UMass Permaculture Initiative. Aside from the Campus Sustainability Manager who works in the Physical Plant, Auxiliary Services employs 3 Sustainability employees, all UMass alumni and University Relations is currently in the process of hiring a Sustainability Communications and Marketing Manager to carry out a green visibility campaign for campus.

ADMISSIONS

Freshman Academic Profile: Average high school GPA 3.78. 33% in top 10% of high school class, 72% in top 25% of high school class, 98% in top 50% of high school class. SAT Math middle 50% range 570-670. SAT Critical Reading middle 50% range 550-640. ACT middle 50% range 24-30. Minimum internet-based TOEFL 80. **Basis for Candidate Selection:** *Very important factors considered include:* academic GPA, rigor of secondary school record. *Important factors considered include:* Class rank, standardized test scores. *Other factors considered include:* application essay, recommendation(s), character/personal qualities, extracurricular activities, first generation, geographical residence, level of applicant's interest, racial/ethnic status, state residency, talent/ability, volunteer work, work experience. **Freshman Admission Requirements:** High school diploma is required and GED is accepted. **Academic units required:** 4 English, 3 mathematics, 3 science, (2 science labs), 2 foreign language, 2 social studies, 2 academic electives. **Freshman Admission Statistics:** 37,183 applied, 61% admitted, 20% enrolled. **Transfer Admission Requirements:** college transcript(s), essay or personal statement, Minimum college GPA of 2.5 required. Lowest grade transferable C-. **General Admission Information:** Regular application deadline 1/15. Nonfall registration accepted. Admission may be deferred for a maximum of 1 year. Credit and/or placement offered for CEEB Advanced Placement tests.

COSTS AND FINANCIAL AID

Annual in-state tuition $13,443. Annual out-of-state tuition $28,998. Room and board $11,457. Average book expense $1,000. **Required Forms and Deadlines:** FAFSA. **Notification of Awards:** Applicants will be notified of awards on a rolling basis beginning 3/1. **Types of Aid:** *Need-based scholarships/grants:* Federal Pell, SEOG, state scholarships/grants, private scholarships, the school's own gift aid. *Loans:* Direct Subsidized Stafford, Direct Unsubsidized Stafford, Direct PLUS, Federal Perkins, state loans. *Student Employment:* Federal Work-Study Program available. Institutional employment available. Off-campus job opportunities are good. **Financial Aid Statistics:** 89% freshmen, 85% undergrads receive need-based scholarship or grant aid. 8% freshmen, 5% undergrads receive non-need-based scholarship or grant aid. 76% freshmen, 82% undergrads receive need-based self-help aid. 1% freshmen, 1% undergrads receive athletic scholarships. 89% freshmen, 84% undergrads receive any aid. 72% undergrads borrow to pay for school. Average cumulative indebtedness $23,848. **Criteria for awarding institutional aid:** *Non-need-based:* academics, art, athletics, music/drama, state/district residency.

UNIVERSITY OF MASSACHUSETTS BOSTON

100 Morrissey Boulevard, Boston, MA 02125-3393
Phone: 617-287-6000 • **Financial Aid Phone:** 617-287-6300
E-mail: enrollment.info@umb.edu • **CEEB Code:** 3924
Fax: 617-287-5999 • **Website:** www.umb.edu

This public school was founded in 1964. It has a 177-acre campus.

RATINGS

Admissions Selectivity Rating: 73   **Fire Safety Rating:** 60*

STUDENTS AND FACULTY

Enrollment: 12,108. **Student Body:** 55% female, 45% male, 51% out-of-state, 2% international (150 countries represented). Asian 12%, African American 16%, Caucasian 39%, Hispanic 13%, Native American <1%
Retention and Graduation: 80% freshmen return for sophomore year. 16% freshmen graduate within 4 years. **Faculty:** 650 full-time faculty, 98% hold PhDs, 50% are are members of minority groups, 20% are women. 0% of classes are taught by teaching assistants.

ACADEMICS

Degrees: bachelor's, certificate, master's, post-bachelor's certificate, post-master's certificate. **Classes:** Most classes have 20-29 students. Most lab/discussion sessions have fewer than 10 students. **Majors with Highest Enrollment:** Management Science. **Special Study Options:** cooperative education program, cross-registration, distance learning, double major, dual enrollment, English as a Second Language (ESL), exchange student program (domestic), honors program, independent study, internships, liberal arts/career combination, student-designed major, study abroad, teacher certification program. **Honors programs:** The University Honors Program seeks to meet the needs of students who thrive on intellectual challenge by offering special interdisciplinary academic opportunities outside the major. **Combined degree programs:** BA/MA, BA/MBA BA/MA Applied Science BA/MA Sociology. **Disability Services:** Special programs offered to physically disabled students include note-taking services, reader services, tape recorders, tutors. **Career services:** Alumni network, alumni services, career/job search classes, career assessment, internships, regional alumni.

FACILITIES

Housing: University housing referral service. 100% of campus accessible to physically disabled. **Special Academic Facilities/Equipment:** Art gallery, tropical greenhouse, observatory, adaptive computer lab. **Computers:** 100% of classrooms, 100% of libraries, 100% of dining areas, 100% of student union, have wireless network access. Students can register for classes online. Administrative functions (other than registration) can be performed online.

CAMPUS LIFE

Environment: Metropolis. **Activities:** Choral groups, concert band, dance, drama/theater, jazz band, literary magazine, music ensembles, radio station, student government, student newspaper, student-run film society, symphony orchestra, yearbook, Campus Ministries, International Student Organization, Model UN. 75 registered organizations, 1 honor society. **Athletics (Intercollegiate):** *Men:* baseball, basketball, cross-country, ice hockey, lacrosse, soccer, tennis, track/field (outdoor), track/field (indoor). *Women:* basketball, cross-country, ice hockey, soccer, softball, tennis, track/field (outdoor), track/field (indoor), volleyball. **On-Campus Highlights:** New Campus Center, Clark Athletic Center, Waterfront area and weekly boat tours, Greenhouse, Healey Library. **Environmental Initiatives:** 1. Comprehensive sustainability program, toxics use reduction program, energy conservation and management efforts, master planning. UMB awarded MA Sustainable Campus of the Year in 2004. 2. Signing Tailories and ACUPCC commitments—only public university in Boston to do so. Academic program with environmental focus in both graduate and undergraduate levels—in many colleges within the university.

ADMISSIONS

Freshman Academic Profile: Average high school GPA 3.19. SAT Math middle 50% range 490-580. SAT Critical Reading middle 50% range 460-570. Minimum internet-based TOEFL 79. **Basis for Candidate Selection:** *Very important factors considered include:* academic GPA, rigor of secondary school record, standardized test scores, character/personal qualities. *Important factors considered include:* application essay, recommendation(s). *Other factors considered include:* extracurricular activities, first generation, interview, level of applicant's interest, talent/ability, volunteer work, work experience. **Freshman Admission Requirements:** High school diploma is required and GED is accepted. **Academic units required:** 4 English, 3 mathematics, 3 science, (2 science labs), 2 foreign language, 1 social studies, 1 history, 2 academic electives. **Freshman Admission Statistics:** 8,453 applied, 71% admitted, 26% enrolled. **Transfer Admission Requirements:** college transcript(s), essay or personal statement, statement of good standing from prior institution(s). Minimum college GPA of 2.5 required. Lowest grade transferable C-. **General Admission Information:** Application Fee $40. Regular application deadline 6/1. Nonfall registration accepted. Admission may be deferred for a maximum of 1 year. Credit offered for CEEB Advanced Placement tests.

COSTS AND FINANCIAL AID

Annual in-state tuition $1,714. Annual out-of-state tuition $9,758. Required fees $10,252. **Required Forms and Deadlines:** FAFSA. **Notification of Awards:** Applicants will be notified of awards on a rolling basis beginning 3/21. **Types of Aid:** *Need-based scholarships/grants:* Federal Pell, SEOG, state scholarships/grants, private scholarships, the school's own gift aid, Federal Nursing Scholarships. *Loans:* Direct Subsidized Stafford, Direct Unsubsidized Stafford, Direct PLUS, Federal Perkins. *Student Employment:* Off-campus job opportunities are excellent. **Financial Aid Statistics:** 93% freshmen, 91% undergrads receive need-based scholarship or grant aid. 5% freshmen, 2% undergrads receive non-need-based scholarship or grant aid. 92% freshmen, 96% undergrads receive need-based self-help aid. 0% freshmen, 0% undergrads receive athletic scholarships. 68% undergrads borrow to pay for school. Average cumulative indebtedness $24,352. **Criteria for awarding institutional aid:** *Non-need-based:* academics, leadership, state/district residency.

UNIVERSITY OF MASSACHUSETTS DARTMOUTH

285 Old Westport Road, N Dartmouth, MA 02747-2300
Phone: (508) 999-8605 • **Financial Aid Phone:** 508-999-8643
E-mail: admissions@umassd.edu • **CEEB Code:** 3786
Fax: (508) 999-8755 • **Website:** http://www.umassd.edu/ • **ACT Code:** 1906

This public school was founded in 1895. It has a 710-acre campus.

RATINGS

Admissions Selectivity Rating: 71   **Fire Safety Rating:** 77

STUDENTS AND FACULTY

Enrollment: 7,185. **Student Body:** 48% female, 52% male, 5% out-of-state, 1% international (52 countries represented). Asian 3%, African American 13%, Caucasian 66%, Hispanic 8%, Native American <1%
Retention and Graduation: 27% freshmen graduate within 4 years. 47% freshmen graduate within 6 years. **Faculty:** 378 full-time faculty, 88% hold PhDs, 44% are are members of minority groups, 22% are women. 3% of classes are taught by teaching assistants.

ACADEMICS

Degrees: bachelor's, doctoral, master's, post-bachelor's certificate, post-master's certificate. **Classes:** Most classes have 20-29 students. Most lab/discussion sessions have 20-29 students. **Majors with Highest Enrollment:** Psychology; Liberal Arts and Sciences Studies and Humanities; Registered Nursing, Nursing Administration, Nursing Research and Clinical Nursing. **Special Study Options:** cooperative education program, cross-registration, distance learning, double major, dual enrollment, exchange student program (domestic), honors program, independent study, internships, student-designed major, study abroad, teacher certification program. **Honors programs:** Honors Program **Combined degree programs:** BA/JD, BA/MA, B.S./M.S. chemistry, biology, engineering, and Nursing;BS/MAT and BA/MAT. **Disability Services:** Special programs offered to physically disabled students include note-taking services, reader services, tape recorders, tutors. **Career services:** Alumni network, career/job search classes, internships.

FACILITIES

Housing: Coed dorms, special housing for disabled students, apartments for single students, Apartments for upperclassmen and graduate students. Program dedicated suites. 97% of campus accessible to physically disabled. **Special Academic Facilities/Equipment:** Art gallery, language center, center for Jewish culture, Robert F. Kennedy assassination archives, electron microscope, observatory, marine research vessels, Advanced Manufacturing and Technology Center, School of Marine Science and Technology. **Computers:** 100% of classrooms, 100% of dorms, 100% of libraries, 100% of dining areas, 100% of student union, 100% of common outdoor areas have wireless network access. Students can register for classes online. Administrative functions (other than registration) can be performed online.

CAMPUS LIFE

Environment: Town. **Activities:** Choral groups, concert band, dance, drama/theater, jazz band, literary magazine, music ensembles, musical theater, pep band, radio station, student government, student newspaper, symphony orchestra, yearbook, International Student Organization. 103 registered organizations, 5 honor societies, 6 religious organizations. 5 fraternities, 3 sororities. **Athletics (Intercollegiate):** *Men:* baseball, basketball, cross-country, diving, football, golf, ice hockey, lacrosse, soccer, swimming, tennis, track/field (outdoor), track/field (indoor). *Women:* basketball, cheerleading, cross-country, diving, equestrian sports, field hockey, golf, lacrosse, soccer, softball, swimming, tennis, track/field (outdoor), track/field (indoor), volleyball. **On-Campus Highlights:** Underground Café, Tripp Athletic Center, Woodlawn Commons, MacLean Campus Center, Observatory. **Environmental Initiatives:** Large scale energy performance. Lighting,heating, AC, water, sewer LEED Silver Library Forest Stewardship FSC.

ADMISSIONS

Freshman Academic Profile: Average high school GPA 3.15. 88% from public high schools. SAT Math middle 50% range 470-570. SAT Critical Reading middle 50% range 450-560. SAT Writing middle 50% range 440-540. ACT middle 50% range 19-25. Minimum internet-based TOEFL 68. Minimum paper TOEFL 520. **Basis for Candidate Selection:** *Very important factors considered include:* academic GPA, rigor of secondary school record, standardized test scores. *Other factors considered include:* Class rank, application essay, recommendation(s), alumni/ae relation, character/personal qualities, extracurricular activities, first generation, talent/ability, volunteer work, work experience. **Freshman Admission Requirements:** High school diploma is required and GED is accepted. **Academic units required:** 4 English, 3 mathematics, 3 science, (2 science labs), 2 foreign language, 1 social studies, 1 history, 2 academic electives. **Freshman Admission Statistics:** 7,472 applied, 77% admitted, 26% enrolled. **Transfer Admission Requirements:** college transcript(s), essay or personal statement, Minimum college GPA of 2.5 required. Lowest grade transferable C-. **General Admission Information:** Application Fee $40. Early decision application deadline 11/15. Notification on a rolling basis, beginning on or about 12/15. Nonfall registration accepted. Admission may be deferred for a maximum of 2 semesters. Credit and/or placement offered for CEEB Advanced Placement tests.

COSTS AND FINANCIAL AID

Notification of Awards: Applicants will be notified of awards on a rolling basis beginning 3/25. **Types of Aid:** *Need-based scholarships/grants:* Federal Pell, SEOG, state scholarships/grants, private scholarships, the school's own gift aid. *Loans:* Direct Subsidized Stafford, Direct Unsubsidized Stafford, Direct PLUS, Federal Perkins, Federal Nursing, state loans. *Student Employment:* Federal Work-Study Program available. Institutional employment available. Off-campus job opportunities are excellent. **Financial Aid Statistics:** 77% freshmen, 73% undergrads receive any aid. **Criteria for awarding institutional aid:** *Non-need-based:* academics, minority status, state/district residency.

UNIVERSITY OF MASSACHUSETTS LOWELL

University Crossing Suite 420, Lowell, MA 01854-5104
Phone: 978-934-3931 · **Financial Aid Phone:** 978-934-4220
E-mail: admissions@uml.edu · **CEEB Code:** 3911
Website: www.uml.edu · **ACT Code:** 1854

This public school was founded in 1894. It has a 150-acre campus.

RATINGS

Admissions Selectivity Rating: 85   **Fire Safety Rating:** 95

STUDENTS AND FACULTY

Enrollment: 12,196. **Student Body:** 38% female, 62% male, 14% out-of-state, 2% international (58 countries represented). Asian 8%, African American 6%, Caucasian 66%, Hispanic 9%, Native American <1%
Retention and Graduation: 84% freshmen return for sophomore year. 27% freshmen graduate within 4 years. 54% freshmen graduate within 6 years. **Faculty:** 549 full-time faculty, 91% hold PhDs, 41% are are members of minority groups, 22% are women. 0% of classes are taught by teaching assistants.

ACADEMICS

Degrees: associate, bachelor's, master's, post-master's certificate. **Classes:** Most classes have 20-29 students. Most lab/discussion sessions have 10-19 students. **Majors with Highest Enrollment:** Business Administration and Management; Criminal Justice/Law Enforcement Administration; Psychology. **Special Study Options:** Accelerated program, cooperative education program, cross-registration, distance learning, double major, dual enrollment, honors program, internships, liberal arts/career combination, study abroad, teacher certification program, Teacher Certification program for Education is Graduate only. **Honors programs:** The Honors Program at UMass Lowell offers high-achieving students individualized instruction in small groups, often in seminar format; opportunities for undergraduate research; special "Commonwealth Honors Program Scholar" designation on transcripts and diplomas—upon completion of program requirements; opportunity to live on one of the Honors floors in the residence halls; and Honors Program social events. LEARN PROGRAM— With the Fall 2004 entering class, all first year students will participate in the LEARN Program. LEARN, which stands for Living Education and Resource

Networking, links academic, residential and personal development experiences by clustering offices, labs and classrooms among residence hall rooms, and offering a year-long schedule of programs that address a range of pertinent social and personal issues. BA/MA, BA/MEng. **Disability Services:** Special programs offered to physically disabled students include note-taking services, reader services, tape recorders, tutors. **Career services:** Alumni network, alumni services, career/job search classes, career assessment, internships, regional alumni.

FACILITIES

Housing: Coed dorms, special housing for disabled students, apartments for married students, cooperative housing, apartments for single students. 80% of campus accessible to physically disabled. **Special Academic Facilities/Equipment:** Language lab, media center, audio-visual department, Centers for Learning, Center for field studies, Center for Performing and Visual Arts, Center for Health Promotion, Research Nuclear Reactor. New $19.5 million recreation center which includes multi court gymnasium, 1/8 mile indoor elevated track, aerobics room, game rooms, locker rooms, and a sauna. Also included are meeting rooms and an indoor/outdoor food court. **Computers:** 50% of classrooms, 90% of dorms, 100% of libraries, 100% of dining areas, 100% of student union, 75% of common outdoor areas have wireless network access. Students can register for classes online. Administrative functions (other than registration) can be performed online.

CAMPUS LIFE

Environment: City. **Activities:** Choral groups, concert band, dance, drama/theater, jazz band, literary magazine, marching band, music ensembles, pep band, radio station, student government, student newspaper, student-run film society, symphony orchestra, yearbook, International Student Organization. 100 registered organizations, 16 honor societies, 4 religious organizations. **Athletics (Intercollegiate):** *Men:* baseball, basketball, crew/rowing, cross-country, golf, ice hockey, soccer, track/field (outdoor), track/field (indoor). *Women:* basketball, crew/rowing, cross-country, field hockey, soccer, softball, track/field (outdoor), track/field (indoor), volleyball. **On-Campus Highlights:** Campus Recreation Center, South Campus Quad, McGauvran Student Center, Fox Multi-purpose Room, Southwick Lounge, New updated state of the art dining facility in the Southwick Lounge. **Environmental Initiatives:** Focus on reduction of GHG emissions by implementation of energy conservation projects of electrical and thermal utilities. Also add solar power panels and other renewables. Increase percentage of students residing at University in residence halls by building new residence halls. Institute a campus transportation plan to reduce vehicle miles travelled.

ADMISSIONS

Freshman Academic Profile: Average high school GPA 3.43. 23% in top 10% of high school class, 52% in top 25% of high school class, 83% in top 50% of high school class. 87% from public high schools. SAT Math middle 50% range 540-640. SAT Critical Reading middle 50% range 510-600. SAT Writing middle 50% range 490-590. ACT middle 50% range 22-28. Minimum internet-based TOEFL 213. Minimum paper TOEFL 550. **Basis for Candidate Selection:** *Very important factors considered include:* application essay, academic GPA, rigor of secondary school record, standardized test scores. *Important factors considered include:* recommendation(s), first generation, level of applicant's interest. *Other factors considered include:* Class rank, character/personal qualities, extracurricular activities, interview, talent/ability, volunteer work, work experience. **Freshman Admission Requirements:** High school diploma is required and GED is accepted. **Academic units required:** 4 English, 3 mathematics, 3 science, (2 science labs), 2 foreign language, 2 social studies, 2 academic electives. **Freshman Admission Statistics:** 9,394 applied, 62% admitted, 28% enrolled. **Transfer Admission Requirements:** college transcript(s), Minimum college GPA of 2.0 required. Lowest grade transferable C-. **General Admission Information:** Application Fee $60. Notification on a rolling basis, beginning on or about 12/1. Nonfall registration accepted. Admission may be deferred for a maximum of 12 months. Credit offered for CEEB Advanced Placement tests.

COSTS AND FINANCIAL AID

Required Forms and Deadlines: FAFSA. **Notification of Awards:** Applicants will be notified of awards on a rolling basis beginning 3/25. **Types of Aid:** *Need-based scholarships/grants:* Federal Pell, SEOG, state scholarships/grants, private scholarships. *Loans:* Direct Subsidized Stafford, Direct Unsubsidized Stafford, Direct PLUS, Federal Perkins. *Student Employment:* Federal Work-Study Program available. Institutional employment available. Highest amount earned per year from on-campus jobs $4,000. Off-campus job opportunities are good. **Financial Aid Statistics:** 93% freshmen, 88% undergrads receive need-based scholarship or grant aid. 6% freshmen, 4% undergrads receive non-need-based scholarship or grant aid. 92% freshmen, 94% undergrads receive need-based self-help aid. 3% freshmen, 2% undergrads receive athletic scholarships. 72% freshmen, 72% undergrads receive any aid. 81% undergrads borrow to pay for school. Average cumulative indebtedness $26,185. **Criteria for awarding institutional aid:** *Non-need-based:* academics, alumni affiliation, art, athletics, job skills, leadership, minority status, music/drama, religious affiliation, state/district residency.

See page 1186.

THE UNIVERSITY OF MEMPHIS

101 Wilder Tower, Memphis, TN 38152
Phone: 901-678-2111 · **Financial Aid Phone:** 901-678-4825
E-mail: recruitment@memphis.edu · **CEEB Code:** 1459
Fax: 901-678-3053 · **Website:** www.memphis.edu · **ACT Code:** 3992

This public school was founded in 1912. It has a 1160-acre campus.

RATINGS

Admissions Selectivity Rating: 79   **Fire Safety Rating:** 80

STUDENTS AND FACULTY

Enrollment: 16,741. **Student Body:** 61% female, 39% male, 10% out-of-state, 1% international (53 countries represented). Asian 3%, African American 40%, Caucasian 49%, Hispanic 3%, Native American <1% **Retention and Graduation:** 76% freshmen return for sophomore year. 13% freshmen graduate within 4 years. **Faculty:** 136 full-time faculty, 59% hold PhDs, 57% are are members of minority groups, 14% are women.

ACADEMICS

Degrees: bachelor's, master's, post-bachelor's certificate, post-master's certificate. **Classes:** Most classes have 20-29 students. Most lab/discussion sessions have 10-19 students. **Majors with Highest Enrollment:** General Studies; Psychology; Biology/Biological Sciences. **Special Study Options:** Accelerated program, cooperative education program, cross-registration, distance learning, double major, dual enrollment, English as a Second Language (ESL), exchange student program (domestic), external degree program, honors program, independent study, internships, liberal arts/career combination, student-designed major, study abroad, teacher certification program. **Honors programs:** The Honors Program offers students the opportunity to take small classes and interdisciplinary seminars with the University's most outstanding faculty. The program also includes many wonderful opportunities beyond the classroom such as study abroad, independent research, and co-curricular activities. Honors students also have the chance to participate in nationally recognized undergraduate research conferences and extend their learning through internships and public service. **Disability Services:** Special programs offered to physically disabled students include note-taking services, reader services, tape recorders. **Career services:** Alumni network, alumni services, career/job search classes, career assessment, internships, regional alumni. Career services highlights include Fresh Connections, learning communities that use clusters of courses to connect different disciplines to a common theme. Students in the Learning Communitites take these courses together to develop a deeper understanding of the material.

FACILITIES

Housing: Coed dorms, special housing for disabled students, men's dorms, women's dorms, fraternity/sorority housing, apartments for married students, apartments for single students, Living-Learning communities. 95% of campus accessible to physically disabled. **Special Academic Facilities/Equipment:** Center for Earthquake Research & Information Institute of Egyptian Art & Archaeology Bureau of Business and Economic Research **Computers:** 100% of classrooms, 55% of dorms, 100% of libraries, 100% of dining areas, 100% of student union, 10% of common outdoor areas have wireless network access. Students can register for classes online. Administrative functions (other than registration) can be performed online.

CAMPUS LIFE

Environment: Metropolis. **Activities:** Choral groups, concert band, dance, drama/theater, jazz band, literary magazine, marching band, music ensembles, musical theater, opera, pep band, radio station, student government, student newspaper, symphony orchestra, Campus Ministries, International Student Organization. 140 registered organizations, 20 honor societies, 12 religious organizations. 14 fraternities, 11 sororities. **Athletics (Intercollegiate):** *Men:* baseball, basketball, cross-country, football, golf, riflery, soccer, tennis, track/field (outdoor). *Women:* basketball, cross-country, golf, riflery, soccer, softball, tennis, track/field (outdoor), volleyball. **On-Campus Highlights:** Rose Theater Lecture Hall, FedEx Institute of Technology, Finch Recreation Facility, Harris Concert Hall, Institute of Egyptian Art & Archaeology. **Environmental Initiatives:** Energy Conservation; Recycling; University of Memphis Campus Sustainability Strategic Plan.

ADMISSIONS

Freshman Academic Profile: Average high school GPA 3.33. 1% in top 10% of high school class, 42% in top 25% of high school class, 79% in top 50% of high school class. SAT Math middle 50% range 440-590. SAT Critical Reading middle 50% range 440-570. SAT Writing middle 50% range 410-560. ACT middle 50% range 20-25. Minimum paper TOEFL 550. **Basis for Candidate Selection:** *Very important factors considered include:* academic GPA, rigor of secondary school record, standardized test scores. *Other factors considered include:* application essay, recommendation(s), character/personal qualities,

talent/ability, work experience. **Freshman Admission Requirements:** High school diploma is required and GED is accepted. **Academic units required:** 4 English, 3 mathematics, 2 science, (1 science labs), 2 foreign language, 2 social studies, 1 history, 1 visual/performing arts. **Freshman Admission Statistics:** 6,798 applied, 62% admitted, 53% enrolled. **Transfer Admission Requirements:** college transcript(s), standardized test scores, Lowest grade transferable C. **General Admission Information:** Application Fee $25. Regular application deadline 7/1. Nonfall registration accepted. Credit and/or placement offered for CEEB Advanced Placement tests.

COSTS AND FINANCIAL AID

Required Forms and Deadlines: FAFSA. **Notification of Awards:** Applicants will be notified of awards on a rolling basis beginning 3/1. **Types of Aid:** *Need-based scholarships/grants:* Federal Pell, SEOG, state scholarships/grants, private scholarships, the school's own gift aid. *Loans:* Direct Subsidized Stafford, Direct Unsubsidized Stafford, Direct PLUS, Federal Perkins, state loans, college/university loans from institutional funds. *Student Employment:* Federal Work-Study Program available. Institutional employment available. Off-campus job opportunities are excellent. **Financial Aid Statistics:** 67% freshmen, 71% undergrads receive need-based scholarship or grant aid. 46% freshmen, 54% undergrads receive non-need-based scholarship or grant aid. 56% freshmen, 72% undergrads receive need-based self-help aid. 3% freshmen, 2% undergrads receive athletic scholarships. 95% freshmen, 91% undergrads receive any aid. 46% undergrads borrow to pay for school. Average cumulative indebtedness $26,413. **Criteria for awarding institutional aid:** *Non-need-based:* academics, alumni affiliation, art, athletics, leadership, minority status, music/drama, state/district residency.

UNIVERSITY OF MIAMI

P.O. Box 248025, Coral Gables, FL 33124-4616
Phone: 305-284-4323 · **Financial Aid Phone:** 305-284-5212
E-mail: admission@miami.edu · **CEEB Code:** 5815
Fax: 305-284-6605 · **Website:** www.miami.edu · **ACT Code:** 760

This private school was founded in 1925. It has a 260-acre campus.

RATINGS

Admissions Selectivity Rating: 95   **Fire Safety Rating:** 85

STUDENTS AND FACULTY

Enrollment: 10,917. **Student Body:** 51% female, 49% male, 55% out-of-state, 14% international (102 countries represented). Asian 6%, African American 7%, Caucasian 43%, Hispanic 21%, Native American <1% **Retention and Graduation:** 93% freshmen return for sophomore year. 68% freshmen graduate within 4 years. 81% freshmen graduate within 6 years. 33% grads go on to further study within 1 year. 10% grads pursue arts and sciences degrees. 5% grads pursue law degrees. 2% grads pursue business degrees. 6% grads pursue medical degrees. **Faculty:** 1,087 full-time faculty, 89% hold PhDs, 40% are are members of minority groups, 32% are women. 7% of classes are taught by teaching assistants.

ACADEMICS

Degrees: bachelor's, certificate, master's, post-bachelor's certificate, post-master's certificate. **Classes:** Most classes have 10-19 students. Most lab/discussion sessions have 10-19 students. **Special Study Options:** Accelerated program, distance learning, double major, dual enrollment, English as a Second Language (ESL), honors program, independent study, internships, liberal arts/career combination, student-designed major, study abroad, teacher certification program, weekend college. **Honors programs:** Honors Program in Medicine (HPM) BA/MD, BA/JD, BA/MEng. **Disability Services:** Special programs offered to physically disabled students include note-taking services, reader services, tutors. **Career services:** Alumni network, alumni services, career/job search classes, career assessment, internships, regional alumni.

FACILITIES

Housing: Coed dorms, special housing for disabled students, fraternity/sorority housing, apartments for single students, Theme Housing. **Special Academic Facilities/Equipment:** Lowe Art Museum, Gusman Concert Hall, Jerry Herman Ring Theatre, Bill Cosford Cinema, Convocation Center, Wellness Center. **Computers:** 100% of classrooms, 100% of dorms, 100% of libraries, 100% of dining areas, 100% of student union, 100% of common outdoor areas have wireless network access. Students can register for classes online. Administrative functions (other than registration) can be performed online.

CAMPUS LIFE

Environment: Town. **Activities:** Choral groups, concert band, dance, drama/theater, jazz band, literary magazine, marching band, music ensembles, musical theater, opera, pep band, radio station, student government, student newspaper, student-run film society, symphony orchestra, television station, yearbook, Campus Ministries, International Student Organization, Model UN. **Athletics (Intercollegiate): Men:** baseball, basketball, cheerleading, cross-country, football, tennis, track/field (outdoor), track/field (indoor). **Women:** basketball, cheerleading, crew/rowing, cross-country, diving, golf, soccer, swimming, tennis, track/field (outdoor), track/field (indoor), volleyball. **On-Campus Highlights:** Lowe Art Museum, Jerry Herman Ring Theater, Bank United Center, Mark Light Stadium (Baseball), Gusman Concert Hall & Recording Studio, University Center Breezeway/ Student Union, The Rock (free speech area). **Environmental Initiatives:** The President signed the ACUPCC and the Talloires Declaration. The University has implemented new building standards for new construction and major renovations to meet or exceed USGBC LEED Silver certification. The University has signed the Panama Pact: a collaboration on a world-class education and research facility addressing present and 22nd century challenges focusing on technologies that are sustainable.

ADMISSIONS

Freshman Academic Profile: Average high school GPA 4.3. 66% in top 10% of high school class, 87% in top 25% of high school class, 95% in top 50% of high school class. 68% from public high schools. SAT Math middle 50% range 620-730. SAT Critical Reading middle 50% range 600-690. SAT Writing middle 50% range 590-690. ACT middle 50% range 28-32. Minimum internet-based TOEFL 80. Minimum paper TOEFL 550. **Basis for Candidate Selection:** *Very important factors considered include:* Class rank, application essay, academic GPA, recommendation(s), rigor of secondary school record, standardized test scores, extracurricular activities. *Important factors considered include:* volunteer work. *Other factors considered include:* alumni/ae relation, character/personal qualities, first generation, geographical residence, racial/ethnic status, talent/ability, work experience. **Freshman Admission Requirements:** High school diploma is required and GED is accepted. **Freshman Admission Statistics:** 31,607 applied, 38% admitted, 17% enrolled. **Transfer Admission Requirements:** college transcript(s), statement of good standing from prior institution(s). Lowest grade transferable C. **General Admission Information:** Application Fee $65. Early decision application deadline 11/1. Regular application deadline 1/15. Regular notification 4/15. Nonfall registration accepted. Admission may be deferred for a maximum of 1 year. Credit and/or placement offered for CEEB Advanced Placement tests.

COSTS AND FINANCIAL AID

Required Forms and Deadlines: FAFSA, CSS/Financial Aid PROFILE, Noncustodial PROFILE, Business/Farm Supplement. **Notification of Awards:** Applicants will be notified of awards on a rolling basis beginning 3/1. **Types of Aid:** *Need-based scholarships/grants:* Federal Pell, SEOG, state scholarships/grants, private scholarships, the school's own gift aid, Federal Nursing Scholarships, Federal Academic Competitiveness Grant Federal SMART Grant. *Loans:* Subsidized Stafford, Unsubsidized Stafford, PLUS, Federal Perkins, Federal Nursing, college/university loans from institutional funds, Private Alternative Education Loans. *Student Employment:* Federal Work-Study Program available. Institutional employment available. Highest amount earned per year from on-campus jobs $3,000. Off-campus job opportunities are excellent. **Financial Aid Statistics:** 98% freshmen, 94% undergrads receive need-based scholarship or grant aid. 24% freshmen, 27% undergrads receive non-need-based scholarship or grant aid. 69% freshmen, 76% undergrads receive need-based self-help aid. 2% freshmen, 2% undergrads receive athletic scholarships. 78% freshmen, 73% undergrads receive any aid. 43% undergrads borrow to pay for school. Average cumulative indebtedness $26,586. **Criteria for awarding institutional aid:** *Non-need-based:* academics, athletics, music/drama.

UNIVERSITY OF MICHIGAN—ANN ARBOR

515 E. Jefferson St, Ann Arbor, MI 48109-1316
Phone: 734-764-7433 · **Financial Aid Phone:** 313-593-5300 · **CEEB Code:** 1839
Fax: 734-936-0740 · **Website:** umich.edu · **ACT Code:** 2062

This public school was founded in 1817. It has a 3177-acre campus.

RATINGS

Admissions Selectivity Rating: 95   Fire Safety Rating: 80

STUDENTS AND FACULTY

Enrollment: 28,217. **Student Body:** 49% female, 51% male, 37% out-of-state, 7% international (121 countries represented). Asian 13%, African American 4%, Caucasian 62%, Hispanic 4%, Native American <1%
Retention and Graduation: 97% freshmen return for sophomore year. 76% freshmen graduate within 4 years. 91% freshmen graduate within 6 years. **Faculty:** 2,660 full-time faculty, 90% hold PhDs, 40% are are members of minority groups, 23% are women. 38% of classes are taught by teaching assistants.

ACADEMICS

Degrees: bachelor's, doctoral, master's, post-bachelor's certificate, post-master's certificate. **Classes:** Most classes have 10-19 students. Most lab/discussion sessions have 20-29 students. **Majors with Highest Enrollment:** Experimental Psychology; Economics; Business Administration and Management. **Special Study Options:** Accelerated program, cooperative education program, cross-registration, distance learning, double major, dual enrollment, English as a Second Language (ESL), exchange student program (domestic), external degree program, honors program, independent study, internships, liberal arts/career combination, student-designed major, study abroad, teacher certification program, weekend college. **Honors programs:** LSA Honors Program; departmental honors programs **Combined degree programs:** BA/MA, BA/MEng, BA/M. Arch.; BS/M.S.B.E.; BA Ling/M.A. Info; BS/M.P.H. **Disability Services:** Special programs offered to physically disabled students include note-taking services, reader services, tape recorders, tutors. **Career services:** Alumni network, alumni services, career/job search classes, career assessment, internships. Career services highlights include all of the cooperative, experiential, and internship learning opportunities.

FACILITIES

Housing: Coed dorms, special housing for disabled students, women's dorms, fraternity/sorority housing, apartments for married students, cooperative housing, apartments for single students, Wellness Housing, Theme Housing, Living/learning communities; substance free dorms. 97% of campus accessible to physically disabled. **Special Academic Facilities/Equipment:** Anthropology, archaeology, art, natural science, paleontology, and zoology museums; audiovisual center, planetarium, electron microscope, biology station, geology camp, athletic campus, medical center, nuclear lab, botanical garden, herbarium, arboretum. **Computers:** 85% of classrooms, 40% of dorms, 80% of libraries, 95% of dining areas, 80% of student union, 10% of common outdoor areas have wireless network access. Students can register for classes online. Administrative functions (other than registration) can be performed online.

CAMPUS LIFE

Environment: City. **Activities:** Choral groups, concert band, dance, drama/theater, jazz band, literary magazine, marching band, music ensembles, musical theater, opera, pep band, radio station, student government, student newspaper, student-run film society, symphony orchestra, television station, yearbook, Campus Ministries, International Student Organization, Model UN. 1000 registered organizations, 13 honor societies, 67 religious organizations. 39 fraternities, 27 sororities. **Athletics (Intercollegiate): Men:** baseball, basketball, cheerleading, cross-country, diving, football, golf, gymnastics, ice hockey, swimming, tennis, track/field (outdoor), track/field (indoor), wrestling. **Women:** basketball, cheerleading, crew/rowing, cross-country, diving, field hockey, golf, gymnastics, soccer, softball, swimming, tennis, track/field (outdoor), track/field (indoor), volleyball, water polo. **On-Campus Highlights:** Michigan Stadium, Museum of Natural History, Museum of Art, Margaret Dow Towsley Sports Museum. **Environmental Initiatives:** Formal announcement of Campus Sustainability goals (http://sustainability.umich.edu/news/leadership-voice-president-coleman-speech-about-going-green-staying-blue-sustainability-michig), Campus Sustainability Integrated Assessment (http://sustainability.umich.edu/news/campus-sustainability-integrated-assessment-principles-and-goals), Planet Blue Operations Teams—a comprehensive campus energy reduction program that combines intensive technical assessment and building occupant involvement (http://opsteams.plantops.umich.edu/).

ADMISSIONS

Freshman Academic Profile: Average high school GPA 3.81. SAT Math middle 50% range 660-760. SAT Critical Reading middle 50% range 620-720. SAT Writing middle 50% range 640-730. ACT middle 50% range 29-33. Minimum internet-based TOEFL 88. Minimum paper TOEFL 570. **Basis for Candidate Selection:** *Very important factors considered include:* rigor of secondary school record. *Important factors considered include:* application essay, academic GPA, recommendation(s), standardized test scores, character/personal qualities, first generation. *Other factors considered include:* Class rank, alumni/ae relation, extracurricular activities, geographical residence, level of applicant's interest, state residency, talent/ability, volunteer work, work experience. **Freshman Admission Requirements:** High school diploma is required and GED is accepted. **Academic units required:** 4 English, (1 science labs), 3 social studies, 3 history, 1 academic elective. **Freshman Admission Statistics:** 49,776 applied, 32% admitted, 41% enrolled. **Transfer Admission Requirements:** High school transcript, college transcript(s), essay or personal statement, statement of good standing from prior institution(s). Minimum college GPA of 3.0

required. Lowest grade transferable C. **General Admission Information:** Application Fee $40. Regular application deadline 2/1. Notification on a rolling basis, beginning on or about 11/1. Nonfall registration accepted. Admission may be deferred for a maximum of 1 year. Credit and/or placement offered for CEEB Advanced Placement tests.

COSTS AND FINANCIAL AID
Required Forms and Deadlines: FAFSA, CSS/Financial Aid PROFILE. **Notification of Awards:** Applicants will be notified of awards on a rolling basis beginning 3/14. **Types of Aid:** *Need-based scholarships/grants:* Federal Pell, SEOG, state scholarships/grants, private scholarships, the school's own gift aid, Academic Competitive Grant (ACG); National SMART; DC Tag Program; Byrd; Teach Grant. *Loans:* Direct Subsidized Stafford, Direct Unsubsidized Stafford, Direct PLUS, Federal Perkins, Federal Nursing, college/university loans from institutional funds, Direct Loan Grad Plus; Health Professional Student Loans. *Student Employment:* Federal Work-Study Program available. Institutional employment available. Off-campus job opportunities are excellent. **Financial Aid Statistics:** 75% freshmen, 78% undergrads receive need-based scholarship or grant aid. 77% freshmen, 64% undergrads receive non-need-based scholarship or grant aid. 82% freshmen, 86% undergrads receive need-based self-help aid. 3% freshmen, 2% undergrads receive athletic scholarships. 90% freshmen, 81% undergrads receive any aid. 45% undergrads borrow to pay for school. Average cumulative indebtedness $21,744. **Criteria for awarding institutional aid:** *Non-need-based:* academics, alumni affiliation, art, athletics, leadership, music/drama, religious affiliation, state/district residency.

UNIVERSITY OF MICHIGAN—DEARBORN

4901 Evergreen Road, Dearborn, MI 48128-1491
Phone: 313-593-5100 · **Financial Aid Phone:** 313-593-5300
E-mail: admissions@umd.umich.edu · **CEEB Code:** 1861
Fax: 313-436-9167 · **Website:** umdearborn.edu · **ACT Code:** 2074

This is a public school.

RATINGS
Admissions Selectivity Rating: 70   Fire Safety Rating: 60*

STUDENTS AND FACULTY
Enrollment: 6,906. **Student Body:** 49% female, 51% male, 0% out-of-state, 1% international (27 countries represented). Asian 6%, African American 10%, Caucasian 70%, Hispanic 6%, Native American <1% **Retention and Graduation:** 16% freshmen graduate within 4 years. 50% freshmen graduate within 6 years. 27% grads go on to further study within 1 year. 10% grads pursue arts and sciences degrees. 3% grads pursue law degrees. 4% grads pursue business degrees. 1% grads pursue medical degrees. **Faculty:** 332 full-time faculty, 86% hold PhDs, 40% are are members of minority groups, 32% are women. 0% of classes are taught by teaching assistants.

ACADEMICS
Degrees: bachelor's, master's, post-bachelor's certificate. **Classes:** Most classes have 20-29 students. Most lab/discussion sessions have 10-19 students. **Majors with Highest Enrollment:** Psychology; Mechanical Engineering; Biology/Biological Sciences. **Special Study Options:** Accelerated program, cooperative education program, cross-registration, distance learning, double major, dual enrollment, honors program, independent study, internships, liberal arts/career combination, student-designed major, study abroad, teacher certification program.

FACILITIES
Housing: fraternity/sorority housing.

CAMPUS LIFE
Activities: drama/theater, literary magazine, radio station, student government, student newspaper, student-run film society, television station.

ADMISSIONS
Freshman Academic Profile: 28% in top 10% of high school class, 57.9% in top 25% of high school class, 89.5% in top 50% of high school class. Minimum internet-based TOEFL 80. Minimum paper TOEFL 550. **Basis for Candidate Selection:** *Very important factors considered include:* rigor of secondary school record, standardized test scores. *Other factors considered include:* Class rank, application essay, recommendation(s), interview. **Freshman Admission Requirements:** High school diploma is required and GED is accepted. **Freshman Admission Statistics:** 5,174 applied, 64% admitted, 29% enrolled. **Transfer Admission Requirements:** High school transcript, college transcript(s), Lowest grade transferable C. **General Admission Information:** Application Fee $30. Nonfall registration accepted. Admission may be deferred for a maximum of no limit. Credit and/or placement offered for CEEB Advanced Placement tests.

COSTS AND FINANCIAL AID
Required Forms and Deadlines: FAFSA. **Notification of Awards:** Applicants will be notified of awards on a rolling basis beginning 5/1. **Types of Aid:** *Need-based scholarships/grants:* Federal Pell, SEOG, state scholarships/grants, private scholarships, the school's own gift aid. *Loans:* Direct Subsidized Stafford, Direct Unsubsidized Stafford, Direct PLUS, Federal Perkins, state loans, college/university loans from institutional funds. *Student Employment:* Federal Work-Study Program available. Institutional employment available. Off-campus job opportunities are excellent. **Financial Aid Statistics:** 73% freshmen, 74% undergrads receive need-based scholarship or grant aid. 58% freshmen, 35% undergrads receive non-need-based scholarship or grant aid. 79% freshmen, 86% undergrads receive need-based self-help aid. 3% freshmen, 2% undergrads receive athletic scholarships. 90% freshmen, 81% undergrads receive any aid. 58% undergrads borrow to pay for school. Average cumulative indebtedness $21,167. **Criteria for awarding institutional aid:** *Non-need-based:* academics, alumni affiliation, art, athletics, job skills, leadership, minority status, music/drama, state/district residency.

UNIVERSITY OF MICHIGAN—FLINT

303 E. Kearsley St., Flint, MI 48502
Phone: 810-762-3300 · **Financial Aid Phone:** 810-762-3444
E-mail: admissions@umflint.edu · **CEEB Code:** 1853
Fax: 810-762-3272 · **Website:** www.umflint.edu · **ACT Code:** 2063

This public school was founded in 1956. It has a 72-acre campus.

RATINGS
Admissions Selectivity Rating: 79   Fire Safety Rating: 92

STUDENTS AND FACULTY
Enrollment: 6,565. **Student Body:** 60% female, 40% male, 2% out-of-state, 6% international (50 countries represented). Asian 2%, African American 13%, Caucasian 68%, Hispanic 4%, Native American 1% **Retention and Graduation:** 72% freshmen return for sophomore year. 9% freshmen graduate within 4 years. 34% freshmen graduate within 6 years. **Faculty:** 315 full-time faculty, 69% hold PhDs, 52% are are members of minority groups, 23% are women. 0.01% of classes are taught by teaching assistants.

ACADEMICS
Degrees: bachelor's, master's. **Classes:** Most classes have 20-29 students. Most lab/discussion sessions have 20-29 students. **Majors with Highest Enrollment:** Registered Nursing/Registered Nurse; Business Administration and Management; Health/Health Care Administration/Management. **Special Study Options:** cooperative education program, distance learning, double major, dual enrollment, English as a Second Language (ESL), honors program, independent study, internships, student-designed major, study abroad, teacher certification program. **Honors programs:** 4-yr University Honors Scholar Program, 2-yr Junior/Senior University Honors Scholar Program. **Combined degree programs:** BBA/MBA. **Disability Services:** Special programs offered to physically disabled students include note-taking services, reader services, tape recorders, tutors. **Career services:** career/job search classes, career assessment, internships.

FACILITIES
Housing: Coed dorms. 97% of campus accessible to physically disabled. **Special Academic Facilities/Equipment:** Frances Willson Thompson Library **Computers:** 100% of classrooms, 100% of dorms, 100% of libraries, 100% of dining areas, 100% of student union, have wireless network access. Students can register for classes online. Administrative functions (other than registration) can be performed online.

CAMPUS LIFE
Environment: City. **Activities:** Choral groups, concert band, dance, drama/theater, jazz band, literary magazine, music ensembles, musical theater, student government, student newspaper, television station, International Student Organization. 99 registered organizations, 7 honor societies, 6 religious organizations. 4 fraternities, 5 sororities. **On-Campus Highlights:** Recreation Center, University Center/Student Union, University Pavilion/Food Court/Bookstore, Resident's Hall, Frances Willson Thompson Library. **Environmental Initiatives:** Recycling and Waste Minimization; Energy Conservation and use of biodegradable paper dining products; Protecton of Campus' Natural Resources.

ADMISSIONS
Freshman Academic Profile: Average high school GPA 3.22. 17% in top 10% of high school class, 41% in top 25% of high school class, 77% in top 50% of high school class. 95% from public high schools. SAT Math middle 50% range 523-680. SAT Critical Reading middle 50% range 468-583. SAT Writing middle 50% range 500-583. ACT middle 50% range 18-24. Minimum internet-based

TOEFL 61. Minimum paper TOEFL 560. **Basis for Candidate Selection:** *Very important factors considered include:* academic GPA, rigor of secondary school record, standardized test scores. *Important factors considered include:* extracurricular activities. *Other factors considered include:* Class rank, application essay, recommendation(s), interview, talent/ability. **Freshman Admission Requirements:** High school diploma is required and GED is accepted. **Academic units required:** 4 English, 3 mathematics, 2 science, 3 social studies. **Freshman Admission Statistics:** 3,160 applied, 79% admitted, 27% enrolled. **Transfer Admission Requirements:** High school transcript, college transcript(s), Minimum college GPA of 2.0 required. Lowest grade transferable 2. **General Admission Information:** Application Fee $30. Notification on a rolling basis, beginning on or about 12/1. Nonfall registration accepted. Admission may be deferred for a maximum of 1 Year. Credit and/or placement offered for CEEB Advanced Placement tests.

COSTS AND FINANCIAL AID

Annual in-state tuition $9,720. Annual out-of-state tuition $18,942. Room and board $7,911. Required fees $418. Average book expense $1,000. **Required Forms and Deadlines:** FAFSA, Institution's own financial aid form. **Notification of Awards:** Applicants will be notified of awards on a rolling basis beginning 3/15. **Types of Aid:** *Need-based scholarships/grants:* Federal Pell, SEOG, state scholarships/grants, private scholarships, the school's own gift aid. *Loans:* Direct Subsidized Stafford, Direct Unsubsidized Stafford, Direct PLUS, Federal Perkins, state loans. *Student Employment:* Federal Work-Study Program available. Institutional employment available. Off-campus job opportunities are poor. **Financial Aid Statistics:** 73% freshmen, 74% undergrads receive need-based scholarship or grant aid. 29% freshmen, 19% undergrads receive non-need-based scholarship or grant aid. 75% freshmen, 81% undergrads receive need-based self-help aid. 0% freshmen, 0% undergrads receive athletic scholarships. 67% freshmen, 67% undergrads receive any aid. 68% undergrads borrow to pay for school. Average cumulative indebtedness $30,127. **Criteria for awarding institutional aid:** *Non-need-based:* academics, art, leadership, minority status, music/drama.

UNIVERSITY OF MINNESOTA, CROOKSTON

University of Minnesota, Crookston, Crookston, MN 56716-5001
Phone: 218-281-8569 · **Financial Aid Phone:** 218-281-8563
E-mail: UMCinfo@umn.edu · **CEEB Code:** 6893
Fax: 218-281-8575 · **Website:** http://www1.crk.umn.edu/ · **ACT Code:** 2129

This public school was founded in 1966. It has a 237-acre campus.

RATINGS
Admissions Selectivity Rating: 77   Fire Safety Rating: 99

STUDENTS AND FACULTY
Enrollment: 1,876. **Student Body:** 50% female, 50% male, 28% out-of-state, 4% international (35 countries represented). Asian 2%, African American 7%, Caucasian 80%, Hispanic 3%, Native American <1%
Retention and Graduation: 66% freshmen return for sophomore year. 33% freshmen graduate within 4 years. 48% freshmen graduate within 6 years. 12% grads go on to further study within 1 year. **Faculty:** 66 full-time faculty, 53% hold PhDs, 41% are are members of minority groups, 6% are women. 0% of classes are taught by teaching assistants.

ACADEMICS
Degrees: bachelor's, certificate. **Classes:** Most classes have 10-19 students. Most lab/discussion sessions have 10-19 students. **Majors with Highest Enrollment:** Business Administration and Management; Natural Resources/Conservation; Animal Sciences. **Special Study Options:** cross-registration, distance learning, double major, dual enrollment, English as a Second Language (ESL), honors program, independent study, internships, student-designed major, study abroad, teacher certification program. **Honors programs:** The University of Minnesota, Crookston Honor's Program was developed to inspire and transform the students' writing, discussion and critical thinking skills that reflect high expectations for academically successful students. Students will be nurtured and challenged to explore ideas, assess values and develop leadership skills. Honors coursework will address the diverse and global atmosphere in which we live. In addition, students in the Honors Program will have the opportunity for various social outings outside of the normal campus experience: Designed for academically highly-motivated students who want more than a degree; Small class sizes ensure one-on-one time with faculty, who invest in your success; Flexible curriculum helps you meet career goals while meeting discipline and honors specific requirements; Innovative program structure involves honor courses, student led discussion groups and individual studies in discipline specific

courses; You will develop and conduct an original scholarly project as a senior to satisfy final program requirements; Exposure to culturally-rich experiences will enable you to develop a global perspective and leadership skills. **Disability Services:** Special programs offered to physically disabled students include note-taking services, reader services, tape recorders, tutors. **Career services:** alumni services, career/job search classes, career assessment, internships. Career services highlights include internships that provide experiential learning and on-the-job training for all students.

FACILITIES
Housing: Coed dorms, special housing for disabled students, apartments for single students, Theme Housing. 90% of campus accessible to physically disabled. **Special Academic Facilities/Equipment:** Red River Valley Natural History Area; Northwest Research and Outreach Center; UMC Horse Riding Arena; Valley Technology Park **Computers:** 20% of classrooms, 100% of dorms, 100% of libraries, 75% of dining areas, 100% of student union, 25% of common outdoor areas have wireless network access. Students can register for classes online. Administrative functions (other than registration) can be performed online.

CAMPUS LIFE
Environment: Village. **Activities:** Choral groups, drama/theater, pep band, radio station, student government, Campus Ministries, International Student Organization. 38 registered organizations, 1 honor society, 2 religious organizations. 1 fraternity, 1 sorority. **Athletics (Intercollegiate):** *Men:* baseball, basketball, football, golf, ice hockey. *Women:* basketball, equestrian sports, golf, soccer, softball, tennis, volleyball. **On-Campus Highlights:** Sargeant Student Center, University Teaching and Outreach Center, Sports Center, Bergland Laboratory, Centennial Hall Student Apartments, Campus Mall, Dairy Barns, Kiehle Auditorium. **Environmental Initiatives:** Evaluate the reduction of coal as a primary feedstock for the campus energy and supplement with renewable fuels. Increase the amount of local food grown on campus and served in campus dining facilities. Increased behaviour modification of campus community towards energy use which includes increased monitoring.

ADMISSIONS
Freshman Academic Profile: Average high school GPA 3.15. 12% in top 10% of high school class, 31% in top 25% of high school class, 65% in top 50% of high school class. SAT Math middle 50% range 470-510. SAT Critical Reading middle 50% range 430-480. SAT Writing middle 50% range 390-470. ACT middle 50% range 19-24. Minimum internet-based TOEFL 68. Minimum paper TOEFL 520. **Basis for Candidate Selection:** *Very important factors considered include:* Class rank, academic GPA, rigor of secondary school record, standardized test scores. *Other factors considered include:* application essay, recommendation(s). **Freshman Admission Requirements:** High school diploma is required and GED is accepted. **Academic units required:** 4 English, 3 mathematics, 3 science, (2 science labs), 3 social studies. **Freshman Admission Statistics:** 927 applied, 71% admitted, 41% enrolled. **Transfer Admission Requirements:** college transcript(s), Minimum college GPA of 2.0 required. Lowest grade transferable D. **General Admission Information:** Application Fee $30. Notification on a rolling basis, beginning on or about 9/1. Nonfall registration accepted. Admission may be deferred for a maximum of 1 year. Credit and/or placement offered for CEEB Advanced Placement tests.

COSTS AND FINANCIAL AID
Annual in-state tuition $10,034. Annual out-of-state tuition $10,034. Room and board $7,018. Required fees $1,402. Average book expense $1,000. **Required Forms and Deadlines:** FAFSA. **Notification of Awards:** Applicants will be notified of awards on a rolling basis beginning 3/1. **Types of Aid:** *Need-based scholarships/grants:* Federal Pell, SEOG, state scholarships/grants, private scholarships, the school's own gift aid, Federal Academic Competitiveness Grant and SMART Grant. *Loans:* Direct Subsidized Stafford, Direct Unsubsidized Stafford, Direct PLUS, Federal Perkins, state loans, Private Loans. *Student Employment:* Federal Work-Study Program available. Institutional employment available. Highest amount earned per year from on-campus jobs $2,000. Off-campus job opportunities are fair. **Financial Aid Statistics:** 96% freshmen, 91% undergrads receive need-based scholarship or grant aid. 10% freshmen, 6% undergrads receive non-need-based scholarship or grant aid. 78% freshmen, 78% undergrads receive need-based self-help aid. 3% freshmen, 2% undergrads receive athletic scholarships. 88% freshmen, 48% undergrads receive any aid. 77% undergrads borrow to pay for school. Average cumulative indebtedness $20,572. **Criteria for awarding institutional aid:** *Non-need-based:* academics, alumni affiliation, athletics, leadership, minority status, music/drama, state/district residency.

UNIVERSITY OF MINNESOTA, DULUTH

25 Solon Campus Center, Duluth, MN 55812-3000
Phone: 218-726-7171 · Financial Aid Phone: 218-726-8000
E-mail: umdadmis@d.umn.edu · CEEB Code: 6873
Fax: 218-726-7040 · Website: www.d.umn.edu · ACT Code: 2157

This public school was founded in 1947. It has a 247-acre campus.

RATINGS

Admissions Selectivity Rating: 79   Fire Safety Rating: 89

STUDENTS AND FACULTY

Enrollment: 9,422. **Student Body:** 47% female, 53% male, 11% out-of-state, 1% international (42 countries represented). Asian 3%, African American 1%, Caucasian 90%, Hispanic 1%, Native American 1%
Retention and Graduation: 81% freshmen return for sophomore year. 16% grads go on to further study within 1 year. **Faculty:** 463 full-time faculty, 75% hold PhDs, 43% are are members of minority groups, 19% are women.

ACADEMICS

Degrees: bachelor's, master's, post-bachelor's certificate. **Classes:** Most classes have 20-29 students. Most lab/discussion sessions have 10-19 students. **Majors with Highest Enrollment:** Business Administration and Management; Elementary Education and Teaching; Biology/Biological Sciences. **Special Study Options:** Accelerated program, cross-registration, distance learning, double major, dual enrollment, exchange student program (domestic), honors program, independent study, internships, liberal arts/career combination, study abroad, teacher certification program, weekend college. **Honors programs:** The Honors Program offers motivated students who are serious about their intellectual and personal growth a variety of special classes enhanced by cultural events and activities, as well as leadership and research opportunities. **Disability Services:** Special programs offered to physically disabled students include note-taking services, reader services, tape recorders, tutors. **Career services:** alumni services, career/job search classes, career assessment, internships.

FACILITIES

Housing: Coed dorms, special housing for disabled students, men's dorms, women's dorms. 100% of campus accessible to physically disabled. **Special Academic Facilities/Equipment:** Art museum, planetarium, music performance hall, theatre. **Computers:** 100% of classrooms, 100% of libraries, 100% of dining areas, 100% of student union, have wireless network access. Students can register for classes online. Administrative functions (other than registration) can be performed online.

CAMPUS LIFE

Environment: Village. **Activities:** Choral groups, concert band, dance, drama/theater, jazz band, literary magazine, marching band, music ensembles, musical theater, opera, pep band, radio station, student government, student newspaper, student-run film society, symphony orchestra, Campus Ministries, International Student Organization, Model UN. 150 registered organizations, 10 honor societies, 7 religious organizations. 2 fraternities, 2 sororities. **Athletics (Intercollegiate):** *Men:* baseball, basketball, cross-country, football, ice hockey, track/field (outdoor), track/field (indoor). *Women:* basketball, cross-country, ice hockey, soccer, softball, tennis, track/field (outdoor), track/field (indoor), volleyball. **On-Campus Highlights:** Solon Campus Center, Library, Residence Halls, Kirby Student Center Food Court, Sports and Health Center. **Environmental Initiatives:** LEED; Stormwater Management Plan; Energy Conservation Projects.

ADMISSIONS

Freshman Academic Profile: 16.49% in top 10% of high school class, 41.75% in top 25% of high school class, 85.14% in top 50% of high school class. 94% from public high schools. SAT Math middle 50% range 480-620. SAT Critical Reading middle 50% range 480-590. SAT Writing middle 50% range 460-580. ACT middle 50% range 20-26. Minimum internet-based TOEFL 80. Minimum paper TOEFL 550. **Basis for Candidate Selection:** *Very important factors considered include:* Class rank, standardized test scores. *Important factors considered include:* rigor of secondary school record. *Other factors considered include:* application essay, academic GPA, recommendation(s), alumni/ae relation, extracurricular activities, first generation, geographical residence, racial/ethnic status, state residency, talent/ability. **Freshman Admission Requirements:** High school diploma is required and GED is accepted. **Academic units required:** 4 English, 3 mathematics, 3 science, 2 foreign language, 2 social studies, 1 history. **Freshman Admission Statistics:** 7,936 applied, 71% admitted, 37% enrolled. **Transfer Admission Requirements:** High school transcript, college transcript(s), Minimum college GPA of 2.0 required. Lowest grade transferable D. **General Admission Information:** Application Fee $35. Regular application deadline 8/1. Notification on a rolling basis, beginning on

or about 9/17. Nonfall registration accepted. Admission may be deferred for a maximum of 3 semesters. Credit and/or placement offered for CEEB Advanced Placement tests.

COSTS AND FINANCIAL AID

Annual in-state tuition $8,230. Annual out-of-state tuition $10,230. Room and board $6,078. Required fees $2,030. Average book expense $1,248. **Required Forms and Deadlines:** FAFSA. **Notification of Awards:** Applicants will be notified of awards on or about 3/1. **Types of Aid:** *Need-based scholarships/grants:* Federal Pell, SEOG, state scholarships/grants, private scholarships, the school's own gift aid. *Loans:* Direct Subsidized Stafford, Direct Unsubsidized Stafford, Direct PLUS, Federal Perkins, state loans, college/university loans from institutional funds. *Student Employment:* Federal Work-Study Program available. Institutional employment available. Off-campus job opportunities are excellent. **Financial Aid Statistics:** 100% freshmen, 97% undergrads receive need-based scholarship or grant aid. 25% freshmen, 27% undergrads receive non-need-based scholarship or grant aid. 84% freshmen, 87% undergrads receive need-based self-help aid. 0% freshmen, 0% undergrads receive athletic scholarships. 85% freshmen, 81% undergrads receive any aid. 72% undergrads borrow to pay for school. Average cumulative indebtedness $16,851. **Criteria for awarding institutional aid:** *Non-need-based:* academics, alumni affiliation, art, athletics, leadership, minority status, music/drama, state/district residency.

UNIVERSITY OF MINNESOTA, MORRIS

600 E 4th St, Morris, MN 56267
Phone: 320-589-6035 · Financial Aid Phone: 800-992-8863
E-mail: http://admissions.morris.umn.edu/contact · CEEB Code: 6890
Website: www.morris.umn.edu · ACT Code: 2155

This public school was founded in 1959. It has a 130-acre campus.

RATINGS

Admissions Selectivity Rating: 85   Fire Safety Rating: 99

STUDENTS AND FACULTY

Enrollment: 1,803. **Student Body:** 54% female, 46% male, 14% out-of-state, 10% international (16 countries represented). Asian 3%, African American 1%, Caucasian 64%, Hispanic 4%, Native American 7%
Retention and Graduation: 79% freshmen return for sophomore year. 54% freshmen graduate within 4 years. 22% grads go on to further study within 1 year. 11% grads pursue arts and sciences degrees. 2% grads pursue law degrees. 2% grads pursue business degrees. 3% grads pursue medical degrees. **Faculty:** 119 full-time faculty, 85% hold PhDs, 40% are are members of minority groups, 9% are women. 0% of classes are taught by teaching assistants.

ACADEMICS

Degrees: bachelor's, certificate. **Classes:** Most classes have 10-19 students. Most lab/discussion sessions have 10-19 students. **Majors with Highest Enrollment:** Biology/Biological Sciences; Business Administration and Management; Psychology. **Special Study Options:** Accelerated program, cooperative education program, distance learning, double major, exchange student program (domestic), honors program, independent study, internships, student-designed major, study abroad, teacher certification program. **Honors programs:** The purpose of the Honors Program is to provide a distinctive, academically challenging, intellectual experience that amplifies and complements the liberal arts mission of UMM for motivated and high-achieving students. It does this by relying upon an interdisciplinary curriculum that is team-taught by UMM's finest faculty. The program consists of a core course, "Traditions in Human Thought." This course explores significant works from history, literature, philosophy, and science from an interdiscplinary perspective. Following the core course, students choose from a variety of interdisciplinary honors courses, participate in service learning and volunteer programs, and complete a senior honors project. **Disability Services:** Special programs offered to physically disabled students include note-taking services, reader services, tape recorders, tutors. **Career services:** alumni services, career/job search classes, career assessment, internships. Career services highlights include The Undergraduate Research Opportunities Program (UROP), a competitive, merit-based program that provides student stipends and expense allowances for students to partner with a faculty member on research, scholarly, or creative projects in laboratories, studios, libraries, and field sites. Students develop detailed knowledge of research methods and may choose to work with faculty members from UMM or from other University of Minnesota campuses, thus giving students access to the University's wide range of faculty and research facilities.

FACILITIES

Housing: Coed dorms, special housing for disabled students, men's dorms, women's dorms, apartments for single students. 70% of campus accessible to physically disabled. **Special Academic Facilities/Equipment:** HFA Art Gallery, conservatory, observatory. **Computers:** Students can register for classes online. Administrative functions (other than registration) can be performed online.

CAMPUS LIFE

Environment: Rural. **Activities:** Choral groups, concert band, dance, drama/theater, jazz band, literary magazine, music ensembles, musical theater, radio station, student government, student newspaper, symphony orchestra, television station. 90 registered organizations, 5 honor societies, 12 religious organizations. **Athletics (Intercollegiate):** *Men:* baseball, basketball, football, golf, tennis, track/field (outdoor), track/field (indoor). *Women:* basketball, cross-country, diving, golf, soccer, softball, swimming, tennis, track/field (outdoor), track/field (indoor), volleyball. **On-Campus Highlights:** Student Center—KUMM, Café, Louis' Lower Level, Regional Fitness Center—Outdoor Center, pools, Science Center—completed '02, Humanities Fine Arts Center—gallery, recitals, The Mall—outdoor recreation area. **Environmental Initiatives:** 1. Morris is actively working to become a sustainable and low-carbon community, and renewable energy research and demonstration is a big part of that effort. Morris receives power from two 1.65 MW University of Minnesota wind turbines. We receive 60% of our annual electricity from wind. We have an on-campus biomass gasification research and demonstration platform. We have solar thermal and solar PV projects on campus. And we have completed a multi-million dollar energy service contract to retrofit the campus for conservation. 2. Morris has a commitment to developing healthy, local and sustainable food systems. We are a founding partner in Pride of the Prairie. Our student are actively engaged in food projects and research on campus, including a small organic garden. Morris is leads the Morris Healthy Eating initiative, a community-wide program working to improve access and knowledge about healthy foods. 3. Morris supports the evolving campus sustainability movement and sustainability reporting initiatives. We are members of ACUPCC, AASHE STARS. Through these efforts, Morris works hard to cultivate student leadership.

ADMISSIONS

Freshman Academic Profile: 27% in top 10% of high school class, 55% in top 25% of high school class, 90% in top 50% of high school class. 92% from public high schools. SAT Math middle 50% range 510-650. SAT Critical Reading middle 50% range 530-680. SAT Writing middle 50% range 490-580. ACT middle 50% range 22-28. Minimum internet-based TOEFL 79. Minimum paper TOEFL 550. **Basis for Candidate Selection:** *Very important factors considered include:* Class rank, rigor of secondary school record, standardized test scores. *Important factors considered include:* application essay, recommendation(s), character/personal qualities, extracurricular activities, talent/ability, volunteer work, work experience. *Other factors considered include:* alumni/ae relation, interview, racial/ethnic status. **Freshman Admission Requirements:** High school diploma is required and GED is accepted. **Academic units required:** 4 English, 3 mathematics, 3 science, (2 science labs), 2 foreign language, 4 social studies, 4 history. **Freshman Admission Statistics:** 2,867 applied, 64% admitted, 23% enrolled. **Transfer Admission Requirements:** college transcript(s), essay or personal statement, statement of good standing from prior institution(s). Minimum college GPA of 2.5 required. Lowest grade transferable D. **General Admission Information:** Application Fee $35. Regular application deadline 3/15. Regular notification 4/1. Notification on a rolling basis, beginning on or about 9/1. Nonfall registration accepted. Admission may be deferred for a maximum of 1 year. Credit and/or placement offered for CEEB Advanced Placement tests.

COSTS AND FINANCIAL AID

Required Forms and Deadlines: FAFSA. **Notification of Awards:** Applicants will be notified of awards on a rolling basis beginning 3/15. **Types of Aid:** *Need-based scholarships/grants:* Federal Pell, SEOG, state scholarships/grants, private scholarships, the school's own gift aid. *Loans:* Direct Subsidized Stafford, Direct Unsubsidized Stafford, Direct PLUS, Federal Perkins, state loans. *Student Employment:* Federal Work-Study Program available. Institutional employment available. Highest amount earned per year from on-campus jobs $2,343. Off-campus job opportunities are good. **Financial Aid Statistics:** 95% freshmen, 94% undergrads receive need-based scholarship or grant aid. 8% freshmen, 8% undergrads receive non-need-based scholarship or grant aid. 68465% freshmen, 69% undergrads receive need-based self-help aid. 0% freshmen, 0% undergrads receive athletic scholarships. 95% freshmen, 91% undergrads receive any aid. 68% undergrads borrow to pay for school. Average cumulative indebtedness $19,255. **Criteria for awarding institutional aid:** *Non-need-based:* academics, alumni affiliation, leadership, minority status, music/drama, state/district residency.

UNIVERSITY OF MINNESOTA—
TWIN CITIES CAMPUS

240 Williamson Hall, Minneapolis, MN 55455-0213
Phone: 612-625-2008 • **Financial Aid Phone:** 612-624-1111 • **CEEB Code:** 6874
Fax: 612-626-1693 • **Website:** www.umn.edu • **ACT Code:** 2156

This public school was founded in 1851. It has a 2000-acre campus.

RATINGS

Admissions Selectivity Rating: 91   **Fire Safety Rating:** 80

STUDENTS AND FACULTY

Enrollment: 30,135. **Student Body:** 51% female, 49% male, 27% out-of-state, 9% international (134 countries represented). Asian 9%, African American 4%, Caucasian 70%, Hispanic 3%, Native American <1%
Retention and Graduation: 92% freshmen return for sophomore year. 58% freshmen graduate within 4 years. 78% freshmen graduate within 6 years. **Faculty:** 1,942 full-time faculty, 79% hold PhDs, 42% are are members of minority groups, 17% are women.

ACADEMICS

Degrees: bachelor's, certificate, diploma, master's, post-bachelor's certificate, post-master's certificate. **Classes:** Most classes have 20-29 students. Most lab/discussion sessions have 10-19 students. **Majors with Highest Enrollment:** Psychology; Journalism; Rhetoric and Composition. **Special Study Options:** Accelerated program, cooperative education program, cross-registration, distance learning, double major, dual enrollment, English as a Second Language (ESL), exchange student program (domestic), external degree program, honors program, independent study, internships, liberal arts/career combination, student-designed major, study abroad, teacher certification program, Minors offered in most majors. Students may register in the College of Continuing Education and take courses in any division for B.A. or B.S. degrees. Programs in Foreign Service and pre-social work. Phi Beta Kappa. Pass/fail grading option. Internships. Qualified undergraduates may take graduate level classes. Pre-professional programs in law, medicine, veterinary science, pharmacy, dentistry, architecture, biology, education, journalism, landscape architecture, management, medical technology, mortuary science, nursing, and occupational/physical therapy. **Honors programs:** Honors, Undergraduate Research Opportunities Program. **Disability Services:** Special programs offered to physically disabled students include note-taking services, reader services, tape recorders, tutors. **Career services:** Alumni network, alumni services, career/job search classes, career assessment, internships, regional alumni. Career services highlights include very unique experiential classes, an intern program, and a new business hatchery in which 17 undergraduate students receive pro bono legal support, advice from entrepreneurs-in-residence and access to seed funding.

FACILITIES

Housing: Coed dorms, special housing for disabled students, special housing for international students, fraternity/sorority housing, apartments for married students, cooperative housing, apartments for single students, Honors housing, residential college (academic programs in residence). Eight conventional residence halls, plus three new apartment style residence halls. Housing application, $25 non-refundable residence hall application fee, and $100 residence hall advance payment (refundable), required by May 1 for guaranteed freshman housing. Off-campus housing office provides off-campus housing listings. **Special Academic Facilities/Equipment:** Frederick R. Weisman Art Museum, Bell Museum of Natural History, Ted Mann Concert Hall, Recreational Sports Center, Civil Engineering Building, Basic Sciences/Biomedical Engineering Building, Coffman Memorial Union, West Bank Arts Quarter, Goldstein Gallery, Arboretum. **Computers:** Students can register for classes online. Administrative functions (other than registration) can be performed online.

CAMPUS LIFE

Environment: Metropolis. **Activities:** Choral groups, concert band, dance, drama/theater, jazz band, literary magazine, marching band, music ensembles, musical theater, opera, pep band, radio station, student government, student newspaper, student-run film society, symphony orchestra, television station, International Student Organization. 600 registered organizations, 10 religious organizations. 22 fraternities, 12 sororities. **Athletics (Intercollegiate):** *Men:* baseball, basketball, cross-country, diving, football, golf, gymnastics, ice hockey, swimming, tennis, track/field (outdoor), track/field (indoor), wrestling. *Women:* basketball, cheerleading, cross-country, diving, golf, gymnastics, ice hockey, soccer, softball, swimming, tennis, track/field (outdoor), track/field (indoor), volleyball. **On-Campus Highlights:** Weisman Art Museum, McNamara Alumni Center, TCF Bank Stadium, Goldstein Gallery, Northrup Memorial Auditorium, Coffman Memorial Union, Mariucci Arena, University Theater, Rarig Center. **Environmental Initiatives:** The University of Minnesota adopted a systemwide sustainability and energy efficiency policy in 2004 founded on earlier waste abatement and energy policies. The University established goals to implement the policy, including one of the most important undertakings as a systemwide signatory of the American College and University Presidents Climate Commitment (2008). The commitment and Climate Action Plan (CAP) include reducing our carbon footprint but also integrating climate science into the fiber of the university—curriculum, research, outreach and engagement. The University of Minnesota engages its students and faculty in various ways. The It All Adds Up campaign strives to raise awareness within the campus community about energy use and to encourage the community to use energy more efficiently. It All Adds Up has resulted in over 14,000 individual pledges campus wide to conserve energy. When combined with other energy conservation efforts, they helped the University avoid more than $6.8 million (cumulatively about $15 Million) in energy costs, and resulted in the release of nearly 112,000 fewer tons of $CO2$ into the atmosphere annually. Greenhouse gas emissions from energy sources dropped by 22% compared to the 2008 baseline. The University also received the Xcel Energys Platinum award in 2013 for its long term commitment to energy conservation. In collaboration between It All Adds Up and Housing and Residential Life, the Live Green Games Program was created with the ultimate goal of encouraging students to participate in energy conservation to help the University meet it's goals. In 2013, a new gaming feature was piloted in order to make sustainability fun and effortless. A list of green acts was promoted among students, showing how they could help create a more sustainable campus, community and world. The pilot resulted in over 7000 acts of green saving 125 tons of carbon, over 97,000 gallons of water and 252,000kWh electricity. The University Services Sustainability Office collaborates with faculty to raise awareness of the campus CAP. For example, the Sustainability Director presented on the CAP, which was featured in Architecture 5750—Planning and Design of the University, a course offered through College of Design. The Sustainability Office participated on the steering committee and work teams to update the City of Minneapolis Climate Action Plan, which provides a roadmap to guide Minneapolis towards greenhouse gas emissions reduction targets. The Twin Cities and Morris campuses, Twin Cities Sustainability Education program and Institute on the Environmental provided space and some support for the Next Generation Congress a group of students who developed long term environmental policy recommendations and delivered them to the Governors Environmental Congress. The recommendations included addressing climate impacts by supporting renewable energy and sustainable energy and building practices. Some of these students connected through programs and education the University offered to raised awareness about energy and climate, such as It All Adds Up and the Sustainability Minor. The student leaders who helped organize the efforts received the Assn. for the Advancement of Sustainability in Higher Education (AASHE) Student Leadership Award. (Links: http://italladdsup.umn. edu/news/platinum.award_03132013.php, http://ow.ly/tDUAt http://ow.ly/ tDUWF.) The University of Minnesota Twin Cities (UMTC) campus has over 80,000 visitors per day to classes, facilities, events and hospital. Sustainability Goals include: Use lower impact transportation alternatives that increase fuel efficiency, provide more sustainable fuel options, and help reduce the miles traveled on campus, to campus, and as part of the University of Minnesota (U of MN) enterprise. One important undertaking is supporting a vibrant and active biking community helping connect the university to the greater Twin Cities area. Biking programs at the University of Minnesota are essential to campus life. The Twin Cities campus was awarded the Gold designation award as a Bicycle Friendly University (BFU), one of the four gold awards nationwide, by the League of American Bicyclists in November 2013. The numbers of cyclist on campus rose 13%, or 1000 bikes in 2013. Many UMTC cyclists participate in Dero ZAP. This partnership with DERO, came to be because the University of Minnesota wanted to be able to track its bike commuters automatically, so it could reward those bicycling to/from campus. The program has spread throughout the Twin Cities and also at U of MN campuses across the state. It tagged its 2,500th Gopher ZAP at the end of 2013. Users were estimated to log nearly two million miles. Thats an estimated 1,368,379 lb $CO2$ reduction and 61,224,398 calories burned by ZAP participants on their commutes. Using bicycles to commute allowed nearly 600 employees to earn healthy insurance premium reductions. Students receive incentives by participating. UMTC has an on-campus bike-center, bike-sharing program (Nice Ride) that connects across the Twin Cities, and new pedestrian/biking/transit mall to make it a more convenient lifestyle. (https://www.dero.com/blog/?p=728, http://www.derozap. com/gopherzap/, http://www1.umn.edu/pts/bike/index.html.) One major undertaking by the university where progress is being made is Strengthening Sustainability Education, infusing sustainability throughout the curriculum. This has been done through the work of individual faculty members creating classes, but also by connecting faculty and finding creative ways to build a broader foundation of environmental and sustainability awareness. 1. The University of Minnesota Sustainability Faculty Network: The University of Minnesota Sustainability Faculty Network (the Network) includes faculty and staff members from nearly all colleges and schools across the Twin Cities campus. Network members share a common interest in sharing the expertise in sustainability education and building new opportunities to serve students across the University: Build community and enhance communication among faculty members; Better coordination and dissemination of information about the wide range of sustainability education efforts across U of MN—Maintaining awareness of courses, programs, international travel, and other opportunities. One project of the Network is the Resilient Communities Project (RCP): Building Community-University Partnerships for Sustainability. The Resilient Communities Project (RCP) was developed with the mission of connecting communities in Minnesota with the wide-ranging expertise of UMTC faculty and students to address pressing local issues in ways that advance sustainability and resilience. Various opportunities are provided to students and faculty, allowing them to apply their knowledge, training, and innovative approaches to address difficult, persistent problems. Their participation plays a major role in helping communities achieve their goals in many aspects: architecture, planning, engineering, business, environmental sciences, and humanities. This year will partner with a city to complete 21 projects, with the help of nine colleges and schools and over hundreds of students from UMTC. 2. Sustainability focused Workshops and Programs. a. The Institute on the Environment sponsors faculty workshops to improve sustainability education for faculty. These workshops allow faculty to hear success stories from faculty colleagues across disciplines who have infused sustainability into their courses and programs, connect with community experts in sustainability, enjoy outdoor place-based experiences, and benefit from activities and dialogue to help write or adapt a syllabus, create new course activities and envision learning outcomes for future sustainability students. b. Art and Science combine for Education: Sustainability is an issue that affects everyone, and it is important that everyone can learn more and become engaged. The Institute on the Environment unrolled a series of sustainability-related art exhibits in 2013. This is an opportunity to learn more about sustainability in all its forms and to teach others. 3. Individual Classes?à on a global scale Sustainability of Food System: A Global Life Cycle Perspective, with over 20,000 registrations in June 2013, was one of the first five massive open online courses (MOOCs) offered at UMTC for free. Such an impressive number of registrations reflected the surge of interest in food systems and the challenges society would face in meeting increasing food demand in a sustainable way. (Links: http://www.susteducation.umn.edu/, http:// rcp.umn.edu/, http://www.cura.umn.edu/RCP, http://discover.umn.edu/news/ teaching-education/moocs-u-m.)

ADMISSIONS

Freshman Academic Profile: 47.3% in top 10% of high school class, 85.8% in top 25% of high school class, 99.4% in top 50% of high school class. SAT Math middle 50% range 620-750. SAT Critical Reading middle 50% range 560-690. SAT Writing middle 50% range 570-680. ACT middle 50% range 26-30. Minimum paper TOEFL 550. **Basis for Candidate Selection:** *Very important factors considered include:* Class rank, academic GPA, rigor of secondary school record, standardized test scores. *Other factors considered include:* alumni/ae relation, character/personal qualities, extracurricular activities, first generation, geographical residence, racial/ethnic status, talent/ability, volunteer work, work experience. **Freshman Admission Requirements:** High school diploma is required and GED is accepted. **Academic units required:** 4 English, 3 mathematics, 3 science, 2 foreign language, 3 social studies, 1 history. **Freshman Admission Statistics:** 44,761 applied, 45% admitted, 27% enrolled. **Transfer Admission Requirements:** college transcript(s), Minimum college GPA of 2.0 required. Lowest grade transferable D. **General Admission Information:** Application Fee $45. Nonfall registration accepted. Admission may be deferred for a maximum of 1 Year. Neither credit nor placement offered for CEEB Advanced Placement tests.

COSTS AND FINANCIAL AID

Required Forms and Deadlines: FAFSA, Institution's own financial aid form. **Notification of Awards:** Applicants will be notified of awards on a rolling basis beginning 2/15. **Types of Aid:** *Need-based scholarships/grants:* Federal Pell, SEOG, state scholarships/grants, private scholarships, the school's own gift aid, Federal Nursing Scholarships. *Loans:* Direct Subsidized Stafford, Direct Unsubsidized Stafford, Direct PLUS, Federal Perkins, Federal Nursing, state loans, college/university loans from institutional funds. *Student Employment:* Federal Work-Study Program available. Institutional employment available. **Financial Aid Statistics:** 85% freshmen, 85% undergrads receive need-based scholarship or grant aid. 10% freshmen, 7% undergrads receive non-need-based scholarship or grant aid. 79% freshmen, 80% undergrads receive need-based self-help aid. 0% freshmen, 0% undergrads receive athletic scholarships. 61% undergrads borrow to pay for school. Average cumulative indebtedness $21,600. **Criteria for awarding institutional aid:** *Non-need-based:* academics, art, athletics, job skills, leadership, minority status, music/drama, state/district residency.

UNIVERSITY OF MISSISSIPPI

145 Martindale, University, MS 38677
Phone: 662-915-7226 · **Financial Aid Phone:** 800-891-4596
E-mail: admissions@olemiss.edu · **CEEB Code:** 1840
Fax: 662-915-5869 · **Website:** www.olemiss.edu · **ACT Code:** 2250

This public school was founded in 1844. It has a 2500-acre campus.

RATINGS

Admissions Selectivity Rating: 80   Fire Safety Rating: 60*

STUDENTS AND FACULTY

Enrollment: 17,809. **Student Body:** 56% female, 44% male, 1% international. Asian 2%, African American 15%, Caucasian 77%, Hispanic 3%, Native American <1%
Retention and Graduation: 37% freshmen graduate within 4 years. 61% freshmen graduate within 6 years. **Faculty:** 823 full-time faculty, 84% hold PhDs, 43% are are members of minority groups, 20% are women.

ACADEMICS

Degrees: bachelor's, certificate, master's. **Classes:** Most classes have 10-19 students. Most lab/discussion sessions have 20-29 students. **Majors with Highest Enrollment:** Elementary Education and Teaching; Accounting; Marketing/ Marketing Management. **Special Study Options:** Accelerated program, cooperative education program, distance learning, double major, dual enrollment, English as a Second Language (ESL), honors program, independent study, internships, study abroad, teacher certification program. **Honors programs:** Sally McDonnell-Barksdale Honors College. **Disability Services:** Special programs offered to physically disabled students include note-taking services, reader services, tape recorders.

FACILITIES

Housing: men's dorms, special housing for international students, women's dorms, fraternity/sorority housing, apartments for married students, apartments for single students, Graduate/Older Students, intensive study floors, special interest, substance free, environmental interest housing available. **Special Academic Facilities/Equipment:** Sally McDonnell-Barksdale Honors College, Croft Institute for International Studies, National Food Service Management Institute, Mississippi Center for Supercomputing Research, Art and archaeology museums, women's studies center, Center for Study of Southern Culture, William Faulkner home, Marine Minerals Research Institute, National Center for Physical Acoustics, National Center for Natural Products Research, Biological Field Station, Barksdale Reading Institute, Ford Center for the Performing Arts, William Winter Institutue for Racial Reconciliation, Paris-Yates Chapel, Trent Lott Leadership Institute, Living Blues Archive, Student Media Center. **Computers:** 30% of classrooms, 100% of dorms, 100% of libraries, 80% of dining areas, 100% of student union, 30% of common outdoor areas have wireless network access. Students can register for classes online. Administrative functions (other than registration) can be performed online.

CAMPUS LIFE

Environment: Village. **Activities:** Choral groups, concert band, dance, drama/ theater, jazz band, marching band, music ensembles, musical theater, opera, pep band, radio station, student government, student newspaper, symphony orchestra, television station, yearbook, Campus Ministries, International Student Organization. 250 registered organizations, 25 honor societies, 21 religious organizations. 18 fraternities, 13 sororities. **Athletics (Intercollegiate): Men:** baseball, basketball, cheerleading, cross-country, football, golf, tennis, track/ field (outdoor), track/field (indoor). *Women:* basketball, cheerleading, cross-country, golf, riflery, soccer, softball, tennis, track/field (outdoor), track/field (indoor), volleyball. **On-Campus Highlights:** Lyceum, Gertrude C. Ford Center for the Performing Arts, Intramural Sports Practice Facility, Student Union, Business School, INFORMATION SESSIONS at 9 am, 11 am, 1pm, 2 pm; TOURS-10 am, and 3 pm (Please register by phone, email, or online); RED/BLUE PREVIEWS-select Saturdays 8:30-1:00 pm (Register online); Fall and Spring Visit Days-8 am to noon (No advanced registration required). **Environmental Initiatives:** UM is installing SmartMeters on the majority of campus buildings. All new construction on campus must be built to meet LEED Silver certification. UM is in the process of major improvements to its recycling infrastructure.

ADMISSIONS

Freshman Academic Profile: Average high school GPA 3.49. 22% in top 10% of high school class, 47% in top 25% of high school class, 75% in top 50% of high school class. SAT Math middle 50% range 490-590. SAT Critical Reading middle 50% range 480-590. ACT middle 50% range 21-27. Minimum paper TOEFL 550. **Basis for Candidate Selection:** *Very important factors considered include:* academic GPA, rigor of secondary school record. *Important factors considered include:* Class rank, standardized test scores. *Other factors considered include:* alumni/ae relation, state residency, talent/ability. **Freshman Admission Requirements:** High school diploma is required and GED is accepted. **Academic units required:** 4 English, 3 mathematics, 3 science, (2 science labs), 1 foreign language, 1 social studies, 2 history, 1 academic elective. **Freshman Admission Statistics:** 16,101 applied, 81% admitted, 29% enrolled. **Transfer Admission Requirements:** college transcript(s), Minimum college GPA of 2.0 required. Lowest grade transferable D. **General Admission Information:** Application Fee $25. Regular application deadline 7/20. Notification on a rolling basis, beginning on or about 10/1. Nonfall registration accepted. Credit offered for CEEB Advanced Placement tests.

COSTS AND FINANCIAL AID

Annual in-state tuition $6,996. Annual out-of-state tuition $19,044. Room and board $9,908. Required fees $100. Average book expense $1,200. **Required Forms and Deadlines:** FAFSA. **Notification of Awards:** Applicants will be notified of awards on a rolling basis beginning 4/1. **Types of Aid:** *Need-based scholarships/grants:* Federal Pell, SEOG, state scholarships/grants, private scholarships, the school's own gift aid. *Loans:* Subsidized Stafford, Unsubsidized Stafford, PLUS, Federal Perkins, college/university loans from institutional funds. *Student Employment:* Federal Work-Study Program available. Institutional employment available. Off-campus job opportunities are fair. **Financial Aid Statistics:** 89% freshmen, 84% undergrads receive need-based scholarship or grant aid. 15% freshmen, 9% undergrads receive non-need-based scholarship or grant aid. 70% freshmen, 76% undergrads receive need-based self-help aid. 2% freshmen, 1% undergrads receive athletic scholarships. 83% freshmen, 78% undergrads receive any aid. 49% undergrads borrow to pay for school. Average cumulative indebtedness $24,160. **Criteria for awarding institutional aid:** *Non-need-based:* academics, alumni affiliation, art, athletics, leadership, minority status, music/drama, state/district residency.

UNIVERSITY OF MISSOURI

230 Jesse Hall, Columbia, MO 65211
Phone: 573-882-7786 · **Financial Aid Phone:** 573-882-7506
E-mail: MU4U@missouri.edu · **CEEB Code:** 260735
Fax: 573-882-7887 · **Website:** www.missouri.edu · **ACT Code:** 2382

This public school was founded in 1839. It has a 1372-acre campus.

RATINGS

Admissions Selectivity Rating: 76   Fire Safety Rating: 91

STUDENTS AND FACULTY

Enrollment: 27,276. **Student Body:** 52% female, 48% male, 25% out-of-state, 3% international (120 countries represented). Asian 2%, African American 8%, Caucasian 79%, Hispanic 3%, Native American <1%
Retention and Graduation: 47% freshmen graduate within 4 years. 70% freshmen graduate within 6 years. **Faculty:** 1,379 full-time faculty, 91% hold PhDs, 38% are are members of minority groups, 20% are women.

ACADEMICS

Degrees: bachelor's, doctoral, master's, post-master's certificate. **Classes:** Most classes have 10-19 students. Most lab/discussion sessions have 20-29 students. **Majors with Highest Enrollment:** Business/Commerce; Biological and Biomedical Sciences; Journalism. **Special Study Options:** Accelerated program, cooperative education program, cross-registration, distance learning, double major, dual enrollment, English as a Second Language (ESL), exchange student program (domestic), external degree program, honors program, independent study, internships, student-designed major, study abroad, teacher certification program, Evening College, MU Direct. **Honors programs:** Honors College **Combined degree programs:** BA/MA, Accounting. **Disability Services:** Special programs offered to physically disabled students include note-taking services, reader services, tape recorders, tutors. **Career services:** Alumni network, alumni services, career/job search classes, career assessment, internships, regional alumni. Career services highlights include our new recruitment website: www.HireMizzouGrads.com.

FACILITIES

Housing: Coed dorms, men's dorms, women's dorms, fraternity/sorority housing, apartments for married students, Freshmen Interest Groups and unique learning communities allow students to live in coed residence halls and share in exploring the same academic area of interest. 100% of campus accessible to physically disabled. **Special Academic Facilities/Equipment:** Life Sciences Center for Research TigerPlace—licensed care facility, Department of Nursing; James B Nutter Family Information Commons; Ellis Library; Museum of Anthropology; Museum of Art and Archeology; World's most powerful univesity research reactor for Nuclear Medicine; one of 15 European Union Centers on college campuses. **Computers:** 100% of classrooms, 10% of dorms, 100% of libraries, 100% of dining areas, 100% of student union, 10% of common outdoor areas have wireless network access. Students can register for classes online. Administrative functions (other than registration) can be performed online.

CAMPUS LIFE

Environment: City. **Activities:** Choral groups, concert band, dance, drama/theater, jazz band, literary magazine, marching band, music ensembles, musical theater, opera, pep band, radio station, student government, student newspaper, student-run film society, symphony orchestra, television station, yearbook, Campus Ministries, International Student Organization, Model UN. 598 registered organizations, 25 honor societies, 47 religious organizations. 32 fraternities, 19 sororities. **Athletics (Intercollegiate):** *Men:* baseball, basketball, cross-country, diving, football, golf, swimming, track/field (outdoor), track/field (indoor), wrestling. *Women:* basketball, cheerleading, cross-country, diving, golf, gymnastics, soccer, softball, swimming, tennis, track/field (outdoor), track/field (indoor), volleyball. **On-Campus Highlights:** Student Recreation Center, Mizzou Arena—home of Tiger Basketball, Memorial Stadium—home of Tiger Football, Jesse Hall, Life Sciences Center, Renovation and construction on campus: Life Sciences Center, Mizzou Arena, James B Nutter Family Infomration Center in Ellis Library, Virginia Avenue Housing, and Dining Expansion. **Environmental Initiatives:** Signatory to ACUPCC climate change commitment. Recent purchase of 100% biomass boiler that will reduce greenhouse gas emissions by up to 30% by 2016. Major commitment to energy conservation for the past 20 years, currently saves MU over six million dollars annually. We have an ongoing goal to save an additional 1% cost each year.

ADMISSIONS

Freshman Academic Profile: 27.4% in top 10% of high school class, 86.7% in top 50% of high school class. SAT Math middle 50% range 530-660. SAT Critical Reading middle 50% range 520-650. ACT middle 50% range 23-28. Minimum internet-based TOEFL 61. Minimum paper TOEFL 500. **Basis for Candidate Selection:** *Very important factors considered include:* Class rank, academic GPA, standardized test scores. *Important factors considered include:* rigor of secondary school record. *Other factors considered include:* application essay, recommendation(s), first generation, level of applicant's interest, racial/ethnic status, talent/ability, volunteer work, work experience. **Freshman Admission Requirements:** High school diploma is required and GED is accepted. **Academic units required:** 4 English, 4 mathematics, 3 science, (1 science labs), 2 foreign language, 3 social studies, 1 fine arts. **Freshman Admission Statistics:** 21,163 applied, 78% admitted, 40% enrolled. **Transfer Admission Requirements:** college transcript(s), Minimum college GPA of 2.5 required. **General Admission Information:** Application Fee $45. Notification on a rolling basis, beginning on or about 1/15. Nonfall registration accepted. Admission may be deferred for a maximum of 1 year. Credit and/or placement offered for CEEB Advanced Placement tests.

COSTS AND FINANCIAL AID

Annual in-state tuition $8,220. Annual out-of-state tuition $23,247. Room and board $9,386. Required fees $1,213. Average book expense $1,114. **Required Forms and Deadlines:** FAFSA. **Notification of Awards:** Applicants will be notified of awards on a rolling basis beginning 4/1. **Types of Aid:** *Need-based scholarships/grants:* Federal Pell, SEOG, state scholarships/grants, private scholarships, the school's own gift aid, outside. *Loans:* Direct Subsidized Stafford, Direct Unsubsidized Stafford, Direct PLUS, PLUS, Federal Perkins, Federal Nursing, state loans, college/university loans from institutional funds, outside or 3rd party loans. *Student Employment:* Federal Work-Study Program available. Institutional employment available. Off-campus job opportunities are excellent. **Financial Aid Statistics:** 84% freshmen, 81% undergrads receive need-based scholarship or grant aid. 6% freshmen, 4% undergrads receive non-need-based scholarship or grant aid. 73% freshmen, 76% undergrads receive need-based self-help aid. 1% freshmen, 1% undergrads receive athletic scholarships. 55% undergrads borrow to pay for school. Average cumulative indebtedness $22,167. **Criteria for awarding institutional aid:** *Non-need-based:* academics, alumni affiliation, art, athletics, leadership, minority status, music/drama, state/district residency.

UNIVERSITY OF MISSOURI—KANSAS CITY

5100 Rockhill Road, Kansas City, mo 64114
Phone: 816-235-1111 · **Financial Aid Phone:** 816-235-1154
E-mail: admit@umkc.edu · **CEEB Code:** 6872
Fax: 816-235-5544 · **Website:** www.umkc.edu · **ACT Code:** 2380

This private school was founded in 1929. It has a 191-acre campus.

RATINGS

Admissions Selectivity Rating: 87   **Fire Safety Rating:** 74

STUDENTS AND FACULTY

Enrollment: 8,127. **Student Body:** 57% female, 43% male, 22% out-of-state, 4% international (68 countries represented). Asian 6%, African American 16%, Caucasian 57%, Hispanic 7%, Native American <1%
Retention and Graduation: 25% freshmen graduate within 4 years. 51% freshmen graduate within 6 years. **Faculty:** 727 full-time faculty, 82% hold PhDs, 46% are are members of minority groups, 21% are women. 0% of classes are taught by teaching assistants.

ACADEMICS

Degrees: bachelor's, master's, post-master's certificate. **Classes:** Most classes have 10-19 students. Most lab/discussion sessions have 10-19 students. **Majors with Highest Enrollment:** Business/Commerce; Psychology; Registered Nursing/Registered Nurse. **Special Study Options:** Accelerated program, distance learning, double major, dual enrollment, English as a Second Language (ESL), honors program, independent study, internships, liberal arts/career combination, student-designed major, study abroad, teacher certification program. **Honors programs:** UMKC Honors Program. **Combined degree programs:** BA/MD, BA/JD, BA/DDS, BLA/MD, BA/MPA, BBA/MBA. **Disability Services:** Special programs offered to physically disabled students include note-taking services, reader services, tape recorders, tutors. **Career services:** Alumni network, alumni services, career/job search classes, career assessment, internships. Career services highlights include Cooperative Learning Programs.

FACILITIES

Housing: Coed dorms, special housing for disabled students, fraternity/sorority housing, apartments for married students, apartments for single students, University owned houses. 98% of campus accessible to physically disabled. **Special Academic Facilities/Equipment:** Art gallery, professional theater, geosciences museums, language lab, observatory. **Computers:** 90% of classrooms, 100% of dorms, 100% of libraries, 100% of dining areas, 100% of student union, have wireless network access. Students can register for classes online. Administrative functions (other than registration) can be performed online.

CAMPUS LIFE

Environment: Metropolis. **Activities:** Choral groups, concert band, dance, drama/theater, jazz band, literary magazine, music ensembles, musical theater, opera, pep band, student government, student newspaper, symphony orchestra, Campus Ministries, International Student Organization, Model UN. 200 registered organizations, 32 honor societies, 13 religious organizations. 6 fraternities, 7 sororities. **Athletics (Intercollegiate):** *Men:* basketball, cheerleading, cross-country, golf, riflery, soccer, tennis, track/field (outdoor). *Women:* basketball, cheerleading, cross-country, golf, riflery, softball, tennis, track/field (outdoor), volleyball. **On-Campus Highlights:** Muddy's Coffee Shop, Nelson Atkins Museum, Sweeney Recreation Center, Minsky's restaurant, Planet Sub restaurant. **Environmental Initiatives:** Recycling; Energy Management; Building Design.

ADMISSIONS

Freshman Academic Profile: Average high school GPA 3.32. 29% in top 10% of high school class, 57% in top 25% of high school class, 84% in top 50% of high school class. SAT Math middle 50% range 500-680. SAT Critical Reading middle 50% range 480-680. ACT middle 50% range 27-27. Minimum internet-based TOEFL 61. Minimum paper TOEFL 500. **Basis for Candidate Selection:** *Very important factors considered include:* Class rank, academic GPA, rigor of secondary school record, standardized test scores. *Other factors considered include:* application essay, recommendation(s), character/personal qualities, extracurricular activities, first generation, interview, talent/ability, volunteer work, work experience. **Freshman Admission Requirements:** High school diploma is required and GED is accepted. **Academic units required:** 4 English, 4 mathematics, 3 science, (1 science labs), 2 foreign language, 3 social studies, 1 Fine Arts. **Freshman Admission Statistics:** 4,377 applied, 64% admitted, 39% enrolled. **Transfer Admission Requirements:** college transcript(s), Minimum college GPA of 2.0 required. Lowest grade transferable D. **General Admission Information:** Application Fee $45. Nonfall registration accepted. Admission may be deferred for a maximum of 2 semesters. Credit offered for CEEB Advanced Placement tests.

COSTS AND FINANCIAL AID

Required Forms and Deadlines: FAFSA. **Notification of Awards:** Applicants will be notified of awards on a rolling basis beginning 4/15. **Types of Aid:** *Need-based scholarships/grants:* Federal Pell, SEOG, state scholarships/grants, private scholarships, the school's own gift aid, United Negro College Fund, Federal Nursing Scholarships. *Loans:* Direct Subsidized Stafford, Direct Unsubsidized Stafford, Direct PLUS, Federal Perkins, Federal Nursing, state loans, college/university loans from institutional funds. *Student Employment:* Federal Work-Study Program available. Institutional employment available. Highest amount earned per year from on-campus jobs $5,700. Off-campus job opportunities are excellent. **Financial Aid Statistics:** 92% freshmen, 83% undergrads receive need-based scholarship or grant aid. 5% freshmen, 2% undergrads receive non-need-based scholarship or grant aid. 59% freshmen, 74% undergrads receive need-based self-help aid. 2% freshmen, 2% undergrads receive athletic scholarships. 94% freshmen, 67% undergrads receive any aid. 58% undergrads borrow to pay for school. Average cumulative indebtedness $25,029. **Criteria for awarding institutional aid:** *Non-need-based:* academics, alumni affiliation, art, athletics, leadership, minority status, music/drama, state/district residency.

UNIVERSITY OF MISSOURI—ST. LOUIS

351 Millenium Student Center, St. Louis, MO 63121-4400
Phone: 314-516-5451 · **Financial Aid Phone:** 314-516-5526
E-mail: admissions@umsl.edu · **CEEB Code:** 6889
Fax: 314-516-5310 · **Website:** www.umsl.edu · **ACT Code:** 2383

This public school was founded in 1963. It has a 475-acre campus.

RATINGS

Admissions Selectivity Rating: 84   **Fire Safety Rating:** 73

STUDENTS AND FACULTY

Enrollment: 8,936. **Student Body:** 57% female, 43% male, 11% out-of-state, 3% international (53 countries represented). Asian 5%, African American 19%, Caucasian 62%, Hispanic 3%, Native American <1%
Retention and Graduation: 79% freshmen return for sophomore year. 17% grads go on to further study within 1 year. 37% grads pursue arts and sciences degrees. 4% grads pursue law degrees. 27% grads pursue business degrees. **Faculty:** 475 full-time faculty, 73% hold PhDs, 53% are are members of minority groups, 20% are women. 12% of classes are taught by teaching assistants.

ACADEMICS

Degrees: bachelor's, doctoral, master's, post-bachelor's certificate, post-master's certificate. **Classes:** Most classes have 10-19 students. Most lab/discussion sessions have 10-19 students. **Majors with Highest Enrollment:** Business/Commerce; Registered Nursing/Registered Nurse; Criminology. **Special Study Options:** Accelerated program, cooperative education program, cross-registration, distance learning, double major, dual enrollment, English as a Second Language (ESL), exchange student program (domestic), honors program, independent study, internships, student-designed major, study abroad, teacher certification program, Engineering UMSL/WU, 2+3 B.S./M.A. Program in Economics, 2+3 B.A./B.S.-Ed and M.A. Program in History, 2+3 B.A./M.A. Program in Philosophy, 2+3 B.A./M.A. Program in Political Science, 2+3 B.A. in Psychology and M.S. in Gerontology Program, 2+3 B.A./M.A. Program in Sociology, Art and Art History 3+4 Program for School of Architecture at Washington University, Biology 3+4 Program for UMSL College of Optometry, Physics and Astronomy 3+4 Program for UMSL College of Optometry, Biology 3+3 Program for Logan Chiropractic College. **Honors programs:** Pierre Laclede Honors College offers a four-year (for freshmen) and a two-year (for internal and external transfers) honors program through which students can meet their General Education and some other graduation requirements (e.g., advanced composition, global awareness, cultural diversity). Most instruction is in small seminars (average enrollment is 13). There is a six-hour independent study requirement, and a writing program engages all students. **Combined degree programs:** BA/MA, BA/DOPT; BS/DOPT. **Disability Services:** Special programs offered to physically disabled students include note-taking services, reader services, tape recorders. **Career services:** alumni services, career assessment, internships. Career services highlights include experiential learning, including our Internship and Cooperative Education programs.

FACILITIES

Housing: Coed dorms, special housing for disabled students, special housing for international students, fraternity/sorority housing, apartments for married students, apartments for single students, Theme Housing, Housing for graduate students and students over 21 in apartments; other themed communities. 100% of campus accessible to physically disabled. **Special Academic Facilities/**

Equipment: Art galleries, language, writing labs, math labs Mercantile Library, and observatory, radio station. **Computers:** 68% of classrooms, 90% of dorms, 90% of libraries, 100% of dining areas, 90% of student union, 60% of common outdoor areas have wireless network access. Students can register for classes online. Administrative functions (other than registration) can be performed online.

CAMPUS LIFE

Environment: Metropolis. **Activities:** Choral groups, dance, drama/theater, jazz band, literary magazine, music ensembles, musical theater, opera, pep band, radio station, student government, student newspaper, student-run film society, Campus Ministries, International Student Organization, Model UN. 125 registered organizations, 24 honor societies, 9 religious organizations. 3 fraternities, 3 sororities. **Athletics (Intercollegiate):** *Men:* baseball, basketball, golf, soccer, tennis. *Women:* basketball, golf, soccer, softball, tennis, volleyball. **On-Campus Highlights:** Millennium Student Center, Touhill Performing Arts Center, Mark Twain Athletic Complex, Gallery 210, Pilot House. **Environmental Initiatives:** Energy Conservation; Waste Management and Recycling; Pollution Prevention.

ADMISSIONS

Freshman Academic Profile: Average high school GPA 3.446. 29% in top 10% of high school class, 59% in top 25% of high school class, 86% in top 50% of high school class. 80% from public high schools. SAT Math middle 50% range 490-660. SAT Critical Reading middle 50% range 440-550. SAT Writing middle 50% range 430-520. ACT middle 50% range 21-27. Minimum paper TOEFL 500. **Basis for Candidate Selection:** *Very important factors considered include:* Class rank, academic GPA, rigor of secondary school record, standardized test scores. *Other factors considered include:* application essay, recommendation(s). **Freshman Admission Requirements:** High school diploma is required and GED is accepted. **Academic units required:** 4 English, 4 mathematics, 3 science, (1 science labs), 2 foreign language, 3 social studies, 1 Fine Arts. **Freshman Admission Statistics:** 1,733 applied, 76% admitted, 39% enrolled. **Transfer Admission Requirements:** college transcript(s), Minimum college GPA of 2.0 required. Lowest grade transferable D. **General Admission Information:** Application Fee $35. Regular application deadline 8/23. Notification on a rolling basis, beginning on or about 10/1. Nonfall registration accepted. Credit and/or placement offered for CEEB Advanced Placement tests.

COSTS AND FINANCIAL AID

Required Forms and Deadlines: FAFSA. **Notification of Awards:** Applicants will be notified of awards on a rolling basis beginning 4/1. **Types of Aid:** *Need-based scholarships/grants:* Federal Pell, SEOG, state scholarships/grants, private scholarships, the school's own gift aid, Federal Nursing Scholarships, Federal ACG and SMART grants. *Loans:* Subsidized Stafford, Unsubsidized Stafford, PLUS, Federal Perkins, Federal Nursing, Federal Teach Grants. *Student Employment:* Federal Work-Study Program available. Institutional employment available. Highest amount earned per year from on-campus jobs $8,000. Off-campus job opportunities are good. **Financial Aid Statistics:** 96% freshmen, 86% undergrads receive need-based scholarship or grant aid. 16% freshmen, 6% undergrads receive non-need-based scholarship or grant aid. 65% freshmen, 84% undergrads receive need-based self-help aid. 3% freshmen, 1% undergrads receive athletic scholarships. 90% freshmen, 77% undergrads receive any aid. 66% undergrads borrow to pay for school. Average cumulative indebtedness $24,069. **Criteria for awarding institutional aid:** *Non-need-based:* academics, alumni affiliation, art, athletics, music/drama, state/district residency.

UNIVERSITY OF MOBILE

5735 College Parkway, Mobile, AL 36613-2842
Phone: 251-442-2273 · **Financial Aid Phone:** 251-442-2222
E-mail: adminfo@mail.umobile.edu · **CEEB Code:** 1515
Fax: 251-442-2498 · **Website:** www.umobile.edu · **ACT Code:** 29

This private school, affiliated with the Southern Baptist Church, was founded in 1961. It has a 830-acre campus.

RATINGS

Admissions Selectivity Rating: 84   **Fire Safety Rating:** 85

STUDENTS AND FACULTY

Enrollment: 1,462. **Student Body:** 65% female, 35% male, 26% out-of-state, 4% international (23 countries represented). Asian 0%, African American 21%, Caucasian 65%, Hispanic 2%, Native American 2%
Retention and Graduation: 77% freshmen return for sophomore year. 26% freshmen graduate within 4 years. **Faculty:** 84 full-time faculty, 62% hold PhDs, 55% are are members of minority groups, 7% are women. 0% of classes are taught by teaching assistants.

ACADEMICS

Degrees: associate, bachelor's, master's. **Classes:** Most classes have 10-19 students. Most lab/discussion sessions have 10-19 students. **Majors with Highest Enrollment:** Elementary Education and Teaching; Business Administration and Management; Registered Nursing/Registered Nurse. **Special Study Options:** Accelerated program, double major, honors program, independent study, internships, teacher certification program. **Honors programs:** Exploring the great books and the enduring questions; join a community of enthusiastic students like yourself; take courses designed not to make you do more work, but do the kind of work that will help you become a thinking leader; earn the "Honors Scholar" designation and seal on your diploma and transcript; participate in special events, such as an annual honor dinner hosted by President Foley; have frequent access to honors faculty; benefit from honors roundtable designed to help students prepare for and apply to graduate school, seek grants and scholarships, and pursue post-graduate career opportunities. **Combined degree programs:** BS/MBA. **Disability Services:** Special programs offered to physically disabled students include tutors. **Career services:** alumni services, career/job search classes, career assessment, internships.

FACILITIES

Housing: men's dorms, women's dorms. 100% of campus accessible to physically disabled. **Special Academic Facilities/Equipment:** Art gallery, forest learning center **Computers:** 10% of classrooms, 100% of dorms, 100% of libraries, 50% of dining areas, 100% of student union, 20% of common outdoor areas have wireless network access. Students can register for classes online. Administrative functions (other than registration) can be performed online.

CAMPUS LIFE

Environment: City. **Activities:** Choral groups, concert band, jazz band, music ensembles, musical theater, opera, pep band, student government, Campus Ministries. 52 registered organizations, 12 honor societies, 3 religious organizations. **Athletics (Intercollegiate):** *Men:* baseball, basketball, cross-country, golf, soccer, tennis. *Women:* basketball, cheerleading, cross-country, golf, soccer, softball, tennis, volleyball. **On-Campus Highlights:** Ram Hall-State of the Art Auditorium, Newly renovated dining hall, Martin Hall, Donald Art Gallery, New Dorms—Faulkner and Samford Halls, Baseball Field/Swimming Pool. **Environmental Initiatives:** Recycling; Wildlife conservation; Green Energy; Sanitary Underground Injection System.

ADMISSIONS

Freshman Academic Profile: Average high school GPA 3.3. 18% in top 10% of high school class, 48% in top 25% of high school class, 76% in top 50% of high school class. SAT Math middle 50% range 420-510. SAT Critical Reading middle 50% range 410-530. ACT middle 50% range 20-24. Minimum internet-based TOEFL 61. Minimum paper TOEFL 500. **Basis for Candidate Selection:** *Very important factors considered include:* academic GPA, standardized test scores. *Other factors considered include:* Class rank, recommendation(s), rigor of secondary school record, character/personal qualities, extracurricular activities, level of applicant's interest, talent/ability. **Freshman Admission Requirements:** High school diploma is required and GED is accepted. **Freshman Admission Statistics:** 1,009 applied, 58% admitted, 47% enrolled. **Transfer Admission Requirements:** college transcript(s), Minimum college GPA of 2.75 required. Lowest grade transferable C. **General Admission Information:** Application Fee $50. Regular application deadline 8/1. Nonfall registration accepted. Admission may be deferred for a maximum of 1 year. Credit offered for CEEB Advanced Placement tests.

COSTS AND FINANCIAL AID

Required Forms and Deadlines: FAFSA, Institution's own financial aid form, State aid form. **Types of Aid:** *Need-based scholarships/grants:* Federal Pell, SEOG, state scholarships/grants, private scholarships, the school's own gift aid, Federal Nursing Scholarships. *Loans:* Subsidized Stafford, Unsubsidized Stafford, PLUS, Federal Perkins. *Student Employment:* Federal Work-Study Program available. Institutional employment available. Highest amount earned per year from on-campus jobs $1,855. Off-campus job opportunities are fair. **Financial Aid Statistics:** 70% freshmen, 61% undergrads receive need-based scholarship or grant aid. 100% freshmen, 94% undergrads receive non-need-based scholarship or grant aid. 44% freshmen, 7% undergrads receive need-based self-help aid. 2% freshmen, 2% undergrads receive athletic scholarships. 90% freshmen, 90% undergrads receive any aid. 90% undergrads borrow to pay for school. Average cumulative indebtedness $26,950. **Criteria for awarding institutional aid:** *Non-need-based:* academics, alumni affiliation, athletics, music/drama, religious affiliation.

THE UNIVERSITY OF MONTANA

Lommasson Center 103, Missoula, MT 59812
Phone: 406-243-6266 • **Financial Aid Phone:** 406-243-5373
E-mail: admiss@umontana.edu • **CEEB Code:** 4489
Fax: 406-243-5711 • **Website:** www.umontana.edu • **ACT Code:** 2422

This public school was founded in 1893. It has a 220-acre campus.

RATINGS

Admissions Selectivity Rating: 76   **Fire Safety Rating:** 83

STUDENTS AND FACULTY

Enrollment: 12,071. **Student Body:** 54% female, 46% male, 19% out-of-state, 2% international (71 countries represented). Asian 1%, African American 1%, Caucasian 79%, Hispanic 4%, Native American 3%
Retention and Graduation: 73% freshmen return for sophomore year. 24% freshmen graduate within 4 years. 48% freshmen graduate within 6 years. 26% grads go on to further study within 1 year. **Faculty:** 579 full-time faculty, 80% hold PhDs, 37% are are members of minority groups, 9% are women. 9% of classes are taught by teaching assistants.

ACADEMICS

Degrees: associate, bachelor's, certificate, first professional, master's, post-master's certificate, terminal associate. **Classes:** Most classes have 10-19 students. Most lab/discussion sessions have 20-29 students. **Majors with Highest Enrollment:** Business Administration and Management; Psychology; Forest Management/Forest Resources Management. **Special Study Options:** cooperative education program, cross-registration, distance learning, double major, English as a Second Language (ESL), exchange student program (domestic), external degree program, honors program, independent study, internships, study abroad, teacher certification program, Bachelor of Nursing in Missoula in cooperation with Montana State Univeristy-Bozeman. **Honors programs:** The Davidson Honors College offers talented and motivated students an academic and social community as an important part of their undergraduate experience at The University of Montana, regardless of their major disciplines. Honors courses are taught by many of the best scholars on campus and are generally limited to twenty students. The Honors College encourages its students to participate in community service activities, international educational experiences and undergraduate research. **Combined degree programs:** JD/MBA, MBA/PharmD, JD/MPA. **Disability Services:** Special programs offered to physically disabled students include note-taking services, reader services, tape recorders, tutors. **Career services:** Alumni network, alumni services, career/job search classes, career assessment, internships, regional alumni.

FACILITIES

Housing: Coed dorms, special housing for disabled students, men's dorms, special housing for international students, women's dorms, fraternity/sorority housing, apartments for married students, apartments for single students, Theme Housing, Apartments for students and families; Honors floors, International floors, and quiet floors in dorms; activity dorms; personal development housing. **Special Academic Facilities/Equipment:** On main campus: clinical psychology center; environmental studies lab; geology field camp; several biological, biomedical, kinesiology, physiology, forestry-related, and other research labs or centers; art galleries; broadcast media center (public radio and television) and performing arts-radio-television building; practical ethics center; extensive presentation technology equipment and services, and others. Other locations: biological station, experimental forest, two-year college of technology (two locations), Fort Missoula field research center, and others. **Computers:** 20% of classrooms, 100% of libraries, 60% of dining areas, 100% of student union, 5% of common outdoor areas have wireless network access. Students can register for classes online. Administrative functions (other than registration) can be performed online.

CAMPUS LIFE

Environment: City. **Activities:** Choral groups, concert band, dance, drama/theater, jazz band, literary magazine, marching band, music ensembles, musical theater, opera, pep band, radio station, student government, student newspaper, symphony orchestra, television station. 150 registered organizations, 5 fraternities, 4 sororities. **Athletics (Intercollegiate):** *Men:* basketball, cheerleading, cross-country, football, tennis, track/field (outdoor), track/field (indoor). *Women:* basketball, cheerleading, cross-country, golf, soccer, tennis, track/field (outdoor), track/field (indoor), volleyball. **On-Campus Highlights:** Adams Event Center (basketball, shows, etc.), Washington-Grizzly Stadium (football, other), Campus Recreation Center (student recreation), University Center (student center, movie theater), Performing Arts-RadioTV Center (public radio-TV), 2. Washington-Grizzly Stadium also used for MAJOR events, like Pearl Jam concert a few years ago (kicking off their annual tour), the Rolling Stones concert Oct 2006, and Elton John concerts (2007 and 2008). **Environmental Initiatives:** Climate Action Plan to reach carbon neutrality by 2020 and biannual Greenhouse Gas Inventories are completed by a full-time Sustainability Coordinator and the Sustainable Campus Committee. Students have created the Smart Buildings Initiative to drive deep energy efficiency retrofits in existing buildings. This initiative is a statewide effort and has already accomplished real-time energy monitoring in some buildings and a full-time energy manager for the Missoula campus. Farm to College Program provides locally sourced food for on-campus dining services and at events. (http://ordway.umt.edu/sa/UDS/index.cfm/name/Overview)

ADMISSIONS

Freshman Academic Profile: Average high school GPA 3.3. 18% in top 10% of high school class, 40% in top 25% of high school class, 70% in top 50% of high school class. SAT Math middle 50% range 480-590. SAT Critical Reading middle 50% range 490-620. SAT Writing middle 50% range 470-590. ACT middle 50% range 21-26. Minimum paper TOEFL 500. **Basis for Candidate Selection:** *Very important factors considered include:* Class rank, academic GPA, rigor of secondary school record, standardized test scores. *Important factors considered include:* extracurricular activities, talent/ability. *Other factors considered include:* application essay, recommendation(s). **Freshman Admission Requirements:** High school diploma is required and GED is accepted. **Academic units required:** 4 English, 3 mathematics, 2 science, (2 science labs), 3 social studies, 2 history. **Freshman Admission Statistics:** 4,820 applied, 94% admitted, 43% enrolled. **Transfer Admission Requirements:** college transcript(s), Minimum college GPA of 2.0 required. Lowest grade transferable D. **General Admission Information:** Application Fee $30. Notification on a rolling basis, beginning on or about 9/15. Nonfall registration accepted. Admission may be deferred for a maximum of 1 year. Credit and/or placement offered for CEEB Advanced Placement tests.

COSTS AND FINANCIAL AID

Annual in-state tuition $4,373. Annual out-of-state tuition $20,646. Room and board $8,006. Required fees $1,726. Average book expense $950. **Required Forms and Deadlines:** FAFSA. **Notification of Awards:** Applicants will be notified of awards on a rolling basis beginning 4/1. **Types of Aid:** *Need-based scholarships/grants:* Federal Pell, SEOG, state scholarships/grants, private scholarships, the school's own gift aid. *Loans:* Subsidized Stafford, Unsubsidized Stafford, PLUS, Federal Perkins. *Student Employment:* Federal Work-Study Program available. Institutional employment available. Off-campus job opportunities are good. **Financial Aid Statistics:** 100% freshmen, 71% undergrads receive need-based scholarship or grant aid. 64% freshmen, 32% undergrads receive non-need-based scholarship or grant aid. 100% freshmen, 99% undergrads receive need-based self-help aid. 3% freshmen, 3% undergrads receive athletic scholarships. 62% freshmen, 59% undergrads receive any aid. 62% undergrads borrow to pay for school. Average cumulative indebtedness $30,135. **Criteria for awarding institutional aid:** *Non-need-based:* academics, alumni affiliation, athletics, leadership, music/drama, state/district residency.

THE UNIVERSITY OF MONTANA—WESTERN

710 South Atlantic, Dillon, MT 59725
Phone: 406-683-7331
E-mail: admissions@umwestern.edu · **CEEB Code:** 4945
Fax: 406-683-7493 · **Website:** www.umwestern.edu · **ACT Code:** 2428

This public school was founded in 1893. It has a 34-acre campus.

RATINGS

Admissions Selectivity Rating: 69   Fire Safety Rating: 60*

STUDENTS AND FACULTY

Enrollment: 1,159. **Student Body:** 59% female, 41% male, 15% out-of-state, 0% international (5 countries represented). Asian 0%, African American 0%, Caucasian 0%, Hispanic 0%, Native American <1%
Retention and Graduation: 62% freshmen return for sophomore year. 8% freshmen graduate within 4 years. 24% freshmen graduate within 6 years. 50% grads go on to further study within 1 year. **Faculty:** 50 full-time faculty, 74% hold PhDs, 44% are are members of minority groups, 8% are women. 0% of classes are taught by teaching assistants.

ACADEMICS

Degrees: associate, bachelor's. **Classes:** Most classes have 10-19 students. **Majors with Highest Enrollment:** Environmental Studies; Elementary Education and Teaching; Business/Commerce. **Special Study Options:** coop-

erative education program, distance learning, double major, dual enrollment, honors program, independent study, internships, teacher certification program. **Disability Services:** Special programs offered to physically disabled students include note-taking services, reader services, tape recorders, tutors. **Career services:** alumni services, career/job search classes, career assessment, internships.

FACILITIES

Housing: Coed dorms, special housing for disabled students, men's dorms, women's dorms, apartments for married students, apartments for single students, Students with fewer than 30 credits not living w/ family required to live in dorm. Transfer students under 21 w/ less than 30 credits not living with parents must live in dorm. 90% of campus accessible to physically disabled. **Special Academic Facilities/Equipment:** Art gallery, outdoor education center, learning center. **Computers:** Students can register for classes online. Administrative functions (other than registration) can be performed online.

CAMPUS LIFE

Environment: Rural. **Activities:** Choral groups, concert band, drama/theater, jazz band, literary magazine, music ensembles, radio station, student government, student newspaper, yearbook. 25 registered organizations, 2 honor societies, 2 religious organizations. **Athletics (Intercollegiate):** *Men:* basketball, cheerleading, football, golf, rodeo. *Women:* basketball, cheerleading, golf, rodeo, volleyball. **On-Campus Highlights:** SUB (Sudent Union Building), Straugh Arena, The Cup, STC Tech Building, Bark'n Bite.

ADMISSIONS

Freshman Academic Profile: Average high school GPA 2.99. 5% in top 10% of high school class, 18% in top 25% of high school class, 49% in top 50% of high school class. 96% from public high schools. SAT Math middle 50% range 430-520. SAT Critical Reading middle 50% range 410-510. ACT middle 50% range 16-22. Minimum paper TOEFL 500. **Basis for Candidate Selection:** *Very important factors considered include:* Class rank, rigor of secondary school record, standardized test scores. *Other factors considered include:* alumni/ae relation, extracurricular activities, racial/ethnic status, state residency, talent/ability. **Freshman Admission Requirements:** High school diploma is required and GED is accepted. **Academic units required:** 4 English, 3 mathematics, 2 science, (2 science labs), 3 social studies, 4 academic electives. **Freshman Admission Statistics:** 428 applied, 99% admitted, 57% enrolled. **Transfer Admission Requirements:** college transcript(s), Minimum college GPA of 2.0 required. Lowest grade transferable c. **General Admission Information:** Application Fee $30. Regular application deadline 7/1. Notification on a rolling basis, beginning on or about 9/1. Nonfall registration accepted. Admission may be deferred for a maximum of 18. Credit and/or placement offered for CEEB Advanced Placement tests.

COSTS AND FINANCIAL AID

Average book expense $850. **Required Forms and Deadlines:** FAFSA. **Notification of Awards:** Applicants will be notified of awards on a rolling basis beginning 3/1. **Types of Aid:** *Need-based scholarships/grants:* Federal Pell, SEOG, state scholarships/grants, the school's own gift aid. *Loans:* Subsidized Stafford, Unsubsidized Stafford, PLUS, Federal Perkins. *Student Employment:* Federal Work-Study Program available. Institutional employment available. Highest amount earned per year from on-campus jobs $1,350. Off-campus job opportunities are good. **Financial Aid Statistics:** 85% freshmen, 85% undergrads receive need-based scholarship or grant aid. 3% freshmen, 3% undergrads receive non-need-based scholarship or grant aid. 86% freshmen, 87% undergrads receive need-based self-help aid. 10% freshmen, 17% undergrads receive athletic scholarships. 84% undergrads borrow to pay for school. **Criteria for awarding institutional aid:** *Non-need-based:* academics, alumni affiliation, art, athletics, job skills, leadership, minority status, music/drama, religious affiliation, state/district residency.

UNIVERSITY OF MONTEVALLO

Station 6030, Montevallo, AL 35115
Phone: 205-665-6030 · **Financial Aid Phone:** 205-665-6050
E-mail: admissions@montevallo.edu · **CEEB Code:** 1004
Fax: 205-665-6032 · **Website:** http://www.montevallo.edu/ · **ACT Code:** 4

This public school was founded in 1896. It has a 160-acre campus.

RATINGS

Admissions Selectivity Rating: 74   Fire Safety Rating: 74

STUDENTS AND FACULTY

Enrollment: 2,644. **Student Body:** 67% female, 33% male, 8% out-of-state, 1% international (23 countries represented). Asian 1%, African American 14%, Caucasian 73%, Hispanic 3%, Native American 1%

Retention and Graduation: 79% freshmen return for sophomore year. 21% freshmen graduate within 4 years. 44% freshmen graduate within 6 years. **Faculty:** 141 full-time faculty, 96% hold PhDs, 50% are are members of minority groups, 8% are women. 0% of classes are taught by teaching assistants.

ACADEMICS

Degrees: bachelor's, master's, post-master's certificate. **Classes:** Most classes have 10-19 students. Most lab/discussion sessions have 20-29 students. **Majors with Highest Enrollment:** Elementary Education and Teaching; Business Administration and Management; Health and Physical Education/Fitness. **Special Study Options:** Accelerated program, cross-registration, double major, dual enrollment, exchange student program (domestic), honors program, independent study, internships, study abroad, teacher certification program, Advanced placement credit; Academic remediation; and Learning disabilities services. **Honors programs:** Honors History; Honors Composition; Honors Literature; Honors Thesis **Combined degree programs:** 3-2 engineering program with U of Alabama at Birmi. **Disability Services:** Special programs offered to physically disabled students include note-taking services, reader services, tape recorders, tutors. **Career services:** alumni services, career assessment Career services highlights include assistance for students through all aspects of the career-planning process. Career counseling, including career assessments is available to all enrolled students. Other services include employability skills training, job postings, internship information, on-campus interviewing, career events and seminars and graduate school information.

FACILITIES

Housing: Coed dorms, men's dorms, women's dorms, fraternity/sorority housing, apartments for married students. **Special Academic Facilities/Equipment:** Art gallery, child development, speech and hearing, traffic safety, and undergraduate liberal studies centers, mass communications center with cable TV broadcasting capabilities. **Computers:** 98% of classrooms, 85% of dorms, 100% of libraries, 100% of dining areas, 100% of student union, 75% of common outdoor areas have wireless network access. Students can register for classes online. Administrative functions (other than registration) can be performed online.

CAMPUS LIFE

Environment: Rural. **Activities:** Choral groups, concert band, dance, drama/theater, jazz band, literary magazine, music ensembles, musical theater, student government, student newspaper, television station, yearbook. 93 registered organizations, 26 honor societies, 8 religious organizations. 7 fraternities, 8 sororities. **Athletics (Intercollegiate):** *Men:* baseball, basketball, golf, soccer. *Women:* basketball, cross-country, golf, soccer, tennis, volleyball. **On-Campus Highlights:** Cafeteria, Student Activity Center, Main Quad, University of Montevallo Student Lake, Intramural Fields. **Environmental Initiatives:** Campus lighting retrofit to energy saving bulbs. Campus-wide retrofit of all toilets, showers and faucets to low use fixtures. An aggressive energy management program. Installed new high efficient 800 ton chiller. Re-designed chilled water loop operation, including VFD's.

ADMISSIONS

Freshman Academic Profile: Average high school GPA 3.41. 90% from public high schools. SAT Math middle 50% range 460-595. SAT Critical Reading middle 50% range 495-600. SAT Writing middle 50% range 480-585. ACT middle 50% range 20-26. Minimum internet-based TOEFL 71. Minimum paper TOEFL 525. **Basis for Candidate Selection:** *Very important factors considered include:* rigor of secondary school record, standardized test scores. *Other factors considered include:* Class rank, recommendation(s), alumni/ae relation, character/personal qualities, extracurricular activities, interview, talent/ability, work experience. **Freshman Admission Requirements:** High school diploma is required and GED is accepted. **Academic units required:** 4 English, 2 mathematics, 2 science, 2 social studies, 2 history, 4 academic electives. **Freshman Admission Statistics:** 1,821 applied, 74% admitted, 40% enrolled. **Transfer Admission Requirements:** college transcript(s), Minimum college GPA of 2.0 required. Lowest grade transferable D. **General Admission Information:** Application Fee $25. Regular application deadline 8/1. Notification on a rolling basis, beginning on or about 9/1. Nonfall registration accepted. Admission may be deferred for a maximum of 2 years.

COSTS AND FINANCIAL AID

Annual in-state tuition $9,990. Annual out-of-state tuition $20,550. Room and board $6,400. Required fees $670. Average book expense $2,050. **Required Forms and Deadlines:** FAFSA. **Notification of Awards:** Applicants will be notified of awards on a rolling basis beginning 4/20. **Types of Aid:** *Need-based scholarships/grants:* Federal Pell, SEOG, state scholarships/grants, private scholarships, the school's own gift aid. *Loans:* Subsidized Stafford, Unsubsidized Stafford, PLUS, Federal Perkins. *Student Employment:* Federal Work-Study Program available. Institutional employment available. Highest amount earned per year from on-campus jobs $3,100. Off-campus job opportunities are good. **Financial Aid Statistics:** 85% freshmen, 84% undergrads receive need-based scholarship or grant aid. 18% freshmen, 10% undergrads receive non-need-based scholarship or grant aid. 77% freshmen, 84% undergrads receive need-

based self-help aid. 4% freshmen, 4% undergrads receive athletic scholarships. 87% freshmen, 77% undergrads receive any aid. 61% undergrads borrow to pay for school. Average cumulative indebtedness $27,034. **Criteria for awarding institutional aid:** *Non-need-based:* academics, art, athletics, leadership, minority status, music/drama.

UNIVERSITY OF MOUNT UNION

1972 Clark Avenue, Alliance, OH 44601-3993
Phone: 330-823-2590 • **Financial Aid Phone:** 877-543-9185
E-mail: admission@mountunion.edu • **CEEB Code:** 1492
Fax: 330-823-5097 • **Website:** www.mountunion.edu

This private school, affiliated with the Methodist Church, was founded in 1846. It has a 115-acre campus.

RATINGS

Admissions Selectivity Rating: 80	**Fire Safety Rating:** 83

STUDENTS AND FACULTY

Enrollment: 2,144. **Student Body:** 49% female, 51% male, 15% out-of-state, 3% international (16 countries represented). Asian 1%, African American 6%, Caucasian 83%, Hispanic 2%, Native American <1% **Retention and Graduation:** 78% freshmen return for sophomore year. 51% freshmen graduate within 4 years. 63% freshmen graduate within 6 years. 26% grads go on to further study within 1 year. 14% grads pursue arts and sciences degrees. 7% grads pursue law degrees. 9% grads pursue business degrees. 34% grads pursue medical degrees. **Faculty:** 129 full-time faculty, 87% hold PhDs, 45% are are members of minority groups, 16% are women. 0% of classes are taught by teaching assistants.

ACADEMICS

Degrees: bachelor's, master's. **Classes:** Most classes have 10-19 students. Most lab/discussion sessions have fewer than 10 students. **Majors with Highest Enrollment:** Business Administration and Management; Early Childhood Education and Teaching; Sport and Fitness Administration/Management. **Special Study Options:** cooperative education program, double major, dual enrollment, English as a Second Language (ESL), honors program, independent study, internships, liberal arts/career combination, student-designed major, study abroad, teacher certification program. **Honors programs:** Four honors programs are offered. Honors in Liberal Arts, Honors in the Major, First Year in Honors and Latin Honors. A qualified student may participate in any program and may discontinue honors study without penalty. Students must declare their intent to participate in an honors program no later than the first semester of their junior year. **Disability Services:** Special programs offered to physically disabled students include note-taking services, reader services, tape recorders, tutors. **Career services:** Alumni network, alumni services, career/job search classes, career assessment, internships, regional alumni. Career services highlights include employment success results/report.

FACILITIES

Housing: Coed dorms, special housing for disabled students, men's dorms, special housing for international students, women's dorms, fraternity/sorority housing, apartments for single students, Theme Housing, Small, single-sex, college-owned residential homes converted to college housing. 85% of campus accessible to physically disabled. **Special Academic Facilities/Equipment:** Art gallery, ecological center, observatory, educational media center. **Computers:** 100% of classrooms, 90% of dorms, 100% of libraries, 100% of dining areas, 100% of student union, 50% of common outdoor areas have wireless network access. Students can register for classes online. Administrative functions (other than registration) can be performed online.

CAMPUS LIFE

Environment: Village. **Activities:** Choral groups, concert band, dance, drama/theater, jazz band, literary magazine, marching band, music ensembles, musical theater, pep band, radio station, student government, student newspaper, television station, yearbook, Campus Ministries, International Student Organization, Model UN. 80 registered organizations, 16 honor societies, 10 religious organizations. 4 fraternities, 4 sororities. **Athletics (Intercollegiate):** *Men:* baseball, basketball, cross-country, diving, football, golf, soccer, swimming, tennis, track/field (outdoor), track/field (indoor), wrestling. *Women:* basketball, cheerleading, cross-country, diving, golf, soccer, softball, swimming, tennis, track/field (outdoor), track/field (indoor), volleyball. **On-Campus Highlights:** Hoover Price Campus Center, Kolenbrander Harter Information Center, McPherson Athletic Building, Dewald Chapel, Bracy Hall Science Building, Welcome Center. **Environmental Initiatives:** Sustainability (Climate Action) Plan; 54 KW Solar Panel; LEED certified welcome center.

ADMISSIONS

Freshman Academic Profile: Average high school GPA 3.4. 18% in top 10% of high school class, 44% in top 25% of high school class, 77% in top 50% of high school class. 75% from public high schools. SAT Math middle 50% range 450-580. SAT Critical Reading middle 50% range 440-550. ACT middle 50% range 21-25. Minimum internet-based TOEFL 80. Minimum paper TOEFL 550. **Basis for Candidate Selection:** *Very important factors considered include:* Class rank, academic GPA, rigor of secondary school record, standardized test scores. *Important factors considered include:* recommendation(s). *Other factors considered include:* application essay, alumni/ae relation, character/personal qualities, extracurricular activities, racial/ethnic status, talent/ability, volunteer work, work experience. **Freshman Admission Requirements:** High school diploma is required and GED is accepted. **Freshman Admission Statistics:** 2,529 applied, 74% admitted, 34% enrolled. **Transfer Admission Requirements:** High school transcript, college transcript(s), essay or personal statement, statement of good standing from prior institution(s). Minimum college GPA of 2.0 required. Lowest grade transferable C. **General Admission Information:** Notification on a rolling basis, beginning on or about 10/1. Nonfall registration accepted. Admission may be deferred for a maximum of one semester. Credit and/or placement offered for CEEB Advanced Placement tests.

COSTS AND FINANCIAL AID

Annual tuition $27,060. Room and board $8,780. Required fees $320. Average book expense $1,100. **Required Forms and Deadlines:** FAFSA. **Types of Aid:** *Need-based scholarships/grants:* Federal Pell, SEOG, state scholarships/grants, the school's own gift aid. *Loans:* Subsidized Stafford, Unsubsidized Stafford, PLUS, Federal Perkins, college/university loans from institutional funds. *Student Employment:* Federal Work-Study Program available. Institutional employment available. Highest amount earned per year from on-campus jobs $2,600. Off-campus job opportunities are fair. **Financial Aid Statistics:** 100% freshmen, 99% undergrads receive need-based scholarship or grant aid. 10% freshmen, 9% undergrads receive non-need-based scholarship or grant aid. 90% freshmen, 89% undergrads receive need-based self-help aid. 0% freshmen, 0% undergrads receive athletic scholarships. 89% freshmen, 90% undergrads receive any aid. 93% undergrads borrow to pay for school. Average cumulative indebtedness $27,862. **Criteria for awarding institutional aid:** *Non-need-based:* academics, alumni affiliation, art, job skills, minority status, music/drama, state/district residency.

UNIVERSITY OF NEBRASKA AT KEARNEY

905 West 25th, Kearney, NE 68849
Phone: 800-532-7639
E-mail: admissionsug@unk.edu · **CEEB Code:** 6467
Fax: 308-865-8987 · **Website:** www.unk.edu · **ACT Code:** 2468

This public school was founded in 1903. It has a 235-acre campus.

RATINGS

Admissions Selectivity Rating: 60*   **Fire Safety Rating:** 60*

STUDENTS AND FACULTY

Enrollment: 5,886. **Student Body:** 56% female, 44% male, 6% out-of-state, 3% international. Asian 1%, African American 1%, Caucasian 88%, Hispanic 2%, Native American <1%
Faculty:

ACADEMICS

Degrees: bachelor's, master's. **Special Study Options:** distance learning, double major, English as a Second Language (ESL), exchange student program (domestic), external degree program, honors program, internships, study abroad, teacher certification program. **Combined degree programs:** 3-1 Medical technology program. **Disability Services:** Special programs offered to physically disabled students include note-taking services, reader services, tape recorders, tutors. **Career services:** career assessment, internships.

FACILITIES

Housing: Coed dorms, men's dorms, women's dorms, fraternity/sorority housing, apartments for married students, apartments for single students. **Special Academic Facilities/Equipment:** Art gallery, language lab, museum of Nebraska art.

CAMPUS LIFE

Environment: Village. **Activities:** Choral groups, concert band, dance, drama/theater, jazz band, literary magazine, marching band, music ensembles, musical theater, opera, pep band, radio station, student government, student newspaper,

symphony orchestra, television station 1 religous organization. 10 fraternities, 6 sororities. **Athletics (Intercollegiate):** *Men:* baseball, basketball, cross-country, diving, football, golf, soccer, softball, swimming, tennis, volleyball. *Women:* basketball, cross-country, diving, football, golf, soccer, softball, swimming, tennis, volleyball.

ADMISSIONS

Freshman Academic Profile: 90% from public high schools. Minimum paper TOEFL 520. **Basis for Candidate Selection:** *Very important factors considered include:* Class rank, rigor of secondary school record, standardized test scores. *Other factors considered include:* religious affiliation/commitment, talent/ability. **Freshman Admission Requirements:** High school diploma is required and GED is accepted. **Academic units required:** 4 English, 3 mathematics, 3 science, (1 science labs), 2 foreign language, 1 social studies, 2 history, 1 academic elective. **Freshman Admission Statistics:** 2,672 applied. **Transfer Admission Requirements:** High school transcript, college transcript(s), Minimum college GPA of 2.0 required. Lowest grade transferable C. **General Admission Information:** Application Fee $25. Regular application deadline 8/1. Notification on a rolling basis, beginning on or about 10/1. Nonfall registration accepted. Credit and/or placement offered for CEEB Advanced Placement tests.

COSTS AND FINANCIAL AID

Annual in-state tuition $2,715. Annual out-of-state tuition $5,550. Room and board $4,156. Required fees $498. Average book expense $700. **Required Forms and Deadlines:** FAFSA, Institution's own financial aid form. **Notification of Awards:** Applicants will be notified of awards on or about 5/1. **Types of Aid:** *Need-based scholarships/grants:* Federal Pell, SEOG, state scholarships/grants, private scholarships, the school's own gift aid. *Loans:* Subsidized Stafford, Unsubsidized Stafford, PLUS, Federal Perkins. *Student Employment:* Federal Work-Study Program available. Institutional employment available. Off-campus job opportunities are excellent. **Financial Aid Statistics:** 43% undergrads borrow to pay for school. **Criteria for awarding institutional aid:** *Non-need-based:* academics, art, athletics, leadership, music/drama.

UNIVERSITY OF NEBRASKA AT OMAHA

Office of Admissions, Omaha, NE 68182
Phone: 402-554-2393 · **Financial Aid Phone:** 402-554-2327
E-mail: unoadmissions@unomaha.edu · **CEEB Code:** 6420
Fax: 402-554-3472 · **Website:** www.unomaha.edu · **ACT Code:** 2464

This public school was founded in 1908. It has a 472-acre campus.

RATINGS

Admissions Selectivity Rating: 79   **Fire Safety Rating:** 96

STUDENTS AND FACULTY

Enrollment: 12,153. **Student Body:** 52% female, 48% male, 7% out-of-state, 3% international (62 countries represented). Asian 3%, African American 7%, Caucasian 72%, Hispanic 9%, Native American <1%
Retention and Graduation: 75% freshmen return for sophomore year. 14% freshmen graduate within 4 years. 42% freshmen graduate within 6 years. 21% grads go on to further study within 1 year. **Faculty:** 520 full-time faculty, 83% hold PhDs, 44% are are members of minority groups, 18% are women. 4% of classes are taught by teaching assistants.

ACADEMICS

Degrees: bachelor's, master's, post-bachelor's certificate, post-master's certificate. **Classes:** Most classes have 20-29 students. Most lab/discussion sessions have 20-29 students. **Majors with Highest Enrollment:** Business Administration and Management; Criminal Justice/Safety Studies. **Special Study Options:** cooperative education program, cross-registration, distance learning, double major, dual enrollment, English as a Second Language (ESL), exchange student program (domestic), honors program, independent study, internships, student-designed major, study abroad, teacher certification program, Business; Engineering. **Honors programs:** UNO Honors Program includes many opportunities such as Early Registration, Honors-only courses, Honors-priority Housing, Honors domestic and international semesters, Honors internships, and a Washington Center affiliation. **Combined degree programs:** MPA/MSW in Public Administration and Social Work. **Disability Services:** Special programs offered to physically disabled students include note-taking services, reader services, tape recorders, tutors. **Career services:** career/job search classes, career assessment, internships. Career services highlights include internships, a UNO strength.

FACILITIES

Housing: Coed dorms, Leased Apartment dwellings. 99% of campus accessible to physically disabled. **Special Academic Facilities/Equipment:** Center for

Afghanistan studies, physical education facility, Strauss Performing Arts Center, Speech Center, Writing Center, Math/Science Center, Peter Kiewit Information Technology Building, and Career Center. **Computers:** 100% of classrooms, 100% of dorms, 100% of libraries, 100% of dining areas, 100% of student union, 85% of common outdoor areas have wireless network access. Students can register for classes online. Administrative functions (other than registration) can be performed online.

CAMPUS LIFE

Environment: Metropolis. **Activities:** Choral groups, concert band, dance, drama/theater, jazz band, literary magazine, marching band, music ensembles, musical theater, opera, pep band, radio station, student government, student newspaper, student-run film society, symphony orchestra, television station, Campus Ministries, International Student Organization, Model UN. 127 registered organizations, 23 honor societies, 14 religious organizations. 6 fraternities, 8 sororities. **Athletics (Intercollegiate):** *Men:* baseball, basketball, football, ice hockey, wrestling. *Women:* basketball, cross-country, diving, golf, soccer, softball, swimming, tennis, track/field (outdoor), track/field (indoor), volleyball. **On-Campus Highlights:** University Library, Strauss Performing Arts Center, Milo Bail Student Center, Durham Science Center, Peter Kiewit Institute. **Environmental Initiatives:** To identify sustainability opportunities and to develop a recommended action plan for each; To integrate sustainability with campus operations, education and outreach, wherever and whenever prudence dictates; To engage the campus in an ongoing dialogue about sustainability.

ADMISSIONS

Freshman Academic Profile: Average high school GPA 3.4. 15% in top 10% of high school class, 40% in top 25% of high school class, 75% in top 50% of high school class. 90% from public high schools. ACT middle 50% range 20-26. Minimum internet-based TOEFL 61. Minimum paper TOEFL 500. **Basis for Candidate Selection:** *Very important factors considered include:* Class rank, rigor of secondary school record, standardized test scores. *Other factors considered include:* character/personal qualities. **Freshman Admission Requirements:** High school diploma is required and GED is accepted. **Academic units required:** 4 English, 3 mathematics, 3 science, (1 science labs), 2 foreign language, 1 social studies, 2 history, 1 academic elective. **Freshman Admission Statistics:** 4,955 applied, 71% admitted, 54% enrolled. **Transfer Admission Requirements:** college transcript(s), statement of good standing from prior institution(s). Minimum college GPA of 2.0 required. Lowest grade transferable C-. **General Admission Information:** Application Fee $45. Regular application deadline 8/1. Nonfall registration accepted.

COSTS AND FINANCIAL AID

Annual out-of-state tuition $15,520. Room and board $8,090. Required fees $1,370. Average book expense $1,000. **Required Forms and Deadlines:** FAFSA. **Notification of Awards:** Applicants will be notified of awards on a rolling basis beginning 4/15. **Types of Aid:** *Need-based scholarships/grants:* Federal Pell, SEOG, state scholarships/grants, private scholarships, the school's own gift aid. *Loans:* Subsidized Stafford, Unsubsidized Stafford, PLUS, Federal Perkins, college/university loans from institutional funds. *Student Employment:* Federal Work-Study Program available. Institutional employment available. Highest amount earned per year from on-campus jobs $15,600. Off-campus job opportunities are excellent. **Financial Aid Statistics:** 60% freshmen, 64% undergrads receive need-based scholarship or grant aid. 12% freshmen, 13% undergrads receive non-need-based scholarship or grant aid. 52% freshmen, 65% undergrads receive need-based self-help aid. 3% freshmen, 2% undergrads receive athletic scholarships. 80% freshmen, 81% undergrads receive any aid. 64% undergrads borrow to pay for school. Average cumulative indebtedness $25,674. **Criteria for awarding institutional aid:** *Non-need-based:* academics, alumni affiliation, art, athletics, leadership, minority status, music/drama, state/district residency.

UNIVERSITY OF NEBRASKA—LINCOLN

1410 Q Street, Lincoln, NE 68588-0417
Phone: 402-472-2023 · **Financial Aid Phone:** 402-472-2030
E-mail: admissions@unl.edu · **CEEB Code:** 6877
Fax: 402-472-0670 · **Website:** http://www.unl.edu · **ACT Code:** 2482

This public school was founded in 1869. It has a 617-acre campus.

RATINGS

Admissions Selectivity Rating: 85   Fire Safety Rating: 75

STUDENTS AND FACULTY

Enrollment: 19,376. **Student Body:** 46% female, 54% male, 19% out-of-state, 6% international (107 countries represented). Asian 2%, African American 2%, Caucasian 80%, Hispanic 5%, Native American <1%
Retention and Graduation: 84% freshmen return for sophomore year. 32% freshmen graduate within 4 years. 23% grads go on to further study within 1 year. **Faculty:** 1,075 full-time faculty, 94% hold PhDs, 30% are are members of minority groups, 18% are women.

ACADEMICS

Degrees: associate, bachelor's, first professional, master's, post-bachelor's certificate, post-master's certificate, terminal associate. **Classes:** Most classes have 20-29 students. Most lab/discussion sessions have 20-29 students. **Majors with Highest Enrollment:** Psychology; Business Administration and Management; Foods, Nutrition, and Wellness Studies. **Special Study Options:** Accelerated program, cooperative education program, cross-registration, distance learning, double major, dual enrollment, English as a Second Language (ESL), exchange student program (domestic), honors program, independent study, internships, liberal arts/career combination, student-designed major, study abroad, teacher certification program. **Honors programs:** University Honors Program: Acceptance into the program is based on a comprehensive evaluation of student's potential by the Honors Program Faculty Committee. A special notation is made on the transcript and diploma upon graduation. J.D. Edwards Honors Program: Purpose is to produce top quality graduates who combine business knowledge and computing fundamentals for enterprise information and software systems. **Disability Services:** Special programs offered to physically disabled students include note-taking services, reader services, tape recorders, tutors. **Career services:** alumni services, career/job search classes, career assessment.

FACILITIES

Housing: Coed dorms, special housing for disabled students, men's dorms, special housing for international students, women's dorms, fraternity/sorority housing, apartments for married students, cooperative housing, apartments for single students. 85% of campus accessible to physically disabled. **Special Academic Facilities/Equipment:** Art gallery, performing arts center, food industries complex, planetarium, center for mass spectrometry, natural science museum, animal science complex, veterinary animal research/diagnosis center.

CAMPUS LIFE

Environment: City. **Activities:** Choral groups, concert band, dance, drama/theater, jazz band, literary magazine, marching band, music ensembles, musical theater, opera, pep band, radio station, student government, student newspaper, student-run film society, symphony orchestra, television station, yearbook, Campus Ministries, International Student Organization, Model UN. 335 registered organizations, 57 honor societies, 25 religious organizations. 27 fraternities, 18 sororities. **Athletics (Intercollegiate):** *Men:* baseball, basketball, cross-country, football, golf, gymnastics, rodeo, tennis, track/field (outdoor), track/field (indoor), wrestling. *Women:* basketball, bowling, cross-country, diving, golf, gymnastics, riflery, rodeo, soccer, softball, swimming, tennis, track/field (outdoor), track/field (indoor), volleyball. **On-Campus Highlights:** Student Union, Student Recreation, Library, Memorial Stadium and Hewitt Center, Residence Halls. **Environmental Initiatives:** Recycling of paper, plastic, aluminum and many other materials; "Green" new construction—must meet LEED Silver standards; Energy conservation measures.

ADMISSIONS

Freshman Academic Profile: 26% in top 10% of high school class, 52% in top 25% of high school class, 83% in top 50% of high school class. SAT Math middle 50% range 520-670. SAT Critical Reading middle 50% range 490-660. ACT middle 50% range 22-28. Minimum internet-based TOEFL 70. **Basis for Candidate Selection:** *Very important factors considered include:* Class rank, standardized test scores. *Important factors considered include:* rigor of secondary school record. *Other factors considered include:* academic GPA, recommendation(s), first generation, talent/ability. **Freshman Admission Requirements:** High school diploma is required and GED is accepted. **Academic units required:** 4 English, 4 mathematics, 3 science, (1 science labs), 2 foreign language, 3 social studies. **Freshman Admission Statistics:** 10,929 applied, 64% admitted, 63% enrolled. **Transfer Admission Requirements:** High school transcript, college transcript(s), Minimum college GPA of 2.0 required. Lowest grade transferable D. **General Admission Information:** Application Fee $45. Regular application deadline 5/1. Notification on a rolling basis, beginning on or about 9/1. Nonfall registration accepted. Neither credit nor placement offered for CEEB Advanced Placement tests.

COSTS AND FINANCIAL AID

Annual in-state tuition $6,480. Annual out-of-state tuition $20,400. Room and board $9,961. Required fees $1,590. Average book expense $1,050. **Required Forms and Deadlines:** FAFSA. **Notification of Awards:** Applicants will be notified of awards on a rolling basis beginning 4/1. **Types of Aid:** *Need-based scholarships/grants:* Federal Pell, SEOG, state scholarships/grants, private scholarships, the school's own gift aid. *Loans:* Direct Subsidized Stafford, Direct Unsubsidized Stafford, Direct PLUS, Subsidized Stafford, Unsubsidized Stafford, PLUS, Federal Perkins, college/university loans from institutional funds. *Student Employment:* Federal Work-Study Program available. Institutional employment available. Off-campus job opportunities are excellent. **Financial Aid Statistics:** 80% freshmen, 76% undergrads receive need-based scholarship or grant aid. 7% freshmen, 6% undergrads receive non-need-based scholarship or grant aid. 70% freshmen, 73% undergrads receive need-based self-help aid. 4% freshmen, 3% undergrads receive athletic scholarships. 86% freshmen, 70% undergrads receive any aid. 59% undergrads borrow to pay for school. Average cumulative indebtedness $22,132. **Criteria for awarding institutional aid:** *Non-need-based:* academics, alumni affiliation, art, athletics, leadership, minority status, music/drama, state/district residency.

UNIVERSITY OF NEBRASKA MEDICAL CENTER

984230 Nebr Med Ctr, Omaha, NE 68198-4230
Phone: 402-559-6864 · **Financial Aid Phone:** 402-559-4109
E-mail: ttonjes@unmc.edu
Fax: 402-559-6796 · **Website:** http://www.unmc.edu/

This public school was founded in 1902.

RATINGS

Admissions Selectivity Rating: 60*   Fire Safety Rating: 60*

STUDENTS AND FACULTY

Enrollment: 812. **Student Body:** 88% female, 12% male, 12% out-of-state, 1% international. Asian 1%, African American 1%, Caucasian 93%, Hispanic 3%, Native American 1%
Faculty: 768 full-time faculty, 90% hold PhDs, 39% are are members of minority groups, 14% are women.

ACADEMICS

Degrees: bachelor's, first professional, master's, post-bachelor's certificate, post-master's certificate. **Majors with Highest Enrollment:** Medicine; Registered Nursing/Registered Nurse; Pharmacy. **Special Study Options:** Accelerated program, distance learning, honors program, independent study. **Disability Services:** Special programs offered to physically disabled students include note-taking services, tutors.

CAMPUS LIFE

Environment: Metropolis. **Activities:** student government, student newspaper.

ADMISSIONS

Freshman Academic Profile: Minimum paper TOEFL 551. **Transfer Admission Requirements:** college transcript(s), Lowest grade transferable C. **General Admission Information:** Nonfall registration not accepted.

COSTS AND FINANCIAL AID

Average book expense $950. **Required Forms and Deadlines:** FAFSA, Institution's own financial aid form. **Notification of Awards:** Applicants will be notified of awards on or about 4/1. **Types of Aid:** *Need-based scholarships/ grants:* Federal Pell, SEOG, state scholarships/grants, private scholarships, the school's own gift aid. *Loans:* Subsidized Stafford, Unsubsidized Stafford, PLUS, Federal Perkins, Federal Nursing, state loans. *Student Employment:* Federal Work-Study Program available. Institutional employment available. Off-campus job opportunities are fair. **Financial Aid Statistics:** 79% undergrads receive need-based scholarship or grant aid. 4% undergrads receive non-need-based scholarship or grant aid. 88% undergrads receive need-based self-help aid. 0% undergrads receive athletic scholarships. **Criteria for awarding institutional aid:** *Non-need-based:* academics, leadership, minority status.

UNIVERSITY OF NEVADA—LAS VEGAS

4505 Maryland Parkway, Las Vegas, NV 89154-1021
Phone: 702-774-8658
E-mail: Undergraduate.Recruitment@ccmail.nevada.edu · **CEEB Code:** 4861
Fax: 702-774-8008 · **Website:** www.unlv.edu · **ACT Code:** 2496

This public school was founded in 1957. It has a 337-acre campus.

RATINGS

Admissions Selectivity Rating: 77   Fire Safety Rating: 60*

STUDENTS AND FACULTY

Enrollment: 20,607. **Student Body:** 56% female, 44% male, 22% out-of-state, 4% international (84 countries represented). Asian 14%, African American 8%, Caucasian 53%, Hispanic 11%, Native American 1%
Retention and Graduation: 73% freshmen return for sophomore year. 12% freshmen graduate within 4 years. 42% freshmen graduate within 6 years. **Faculty:** 776 full-time faculty, 90% hold PhDs, 33% are are members of minority groups, 18% are women. 11% of classes are taught by teaching assistants.

ACADEMICS

Degrees: bachelor's, certificate, first professional, master's, post-bachelor's certificate, post-master's certificate. **Classes:** Most classes have 20-29 students. Most lab/discussion sessions have 20-29 students. **Majors with Highest Enrollment:** Elementary Education and Teaching; Psychology; Hospitality Administration/Management. **Special Study Options:** Accelerated program, cooperative education program, cross-registration, distance learning, double major, dual enrollment, English as a Second Language (ESL), exchange student program (domestic), honors program, independent study, internships, student-designed major, study abroad, teacher certification program. **Combined degree programs:** interdisciplinary program in environmental science. **Disability Services:** Special programs offered to physically disabled students include note-taking services, reader services, tape recorders, tutors. **Career services:** Alumni network, alumni services, career/job search classes, career assessment, internships, regional alumni.

FACILITIES

Housing: Coed dorms **Special Academic Facilities/Equipment:** Art galleries, national supercomputing center for energy and environment, natural history museum, arboretum, 3 theaters, concert hall, law school, dental school, international gaming institute, professional practice school for teachers. **Computers:** Students can register for classes online. Administrative functions (other than registration) can be performed online.

CAMPUS LIFE

Environment: Metropolis. **Activities:** Choral groups, concert band, dance, drama/theater, jazz band, literary magazine, marching band, music ensembles, musical theater, opera, pep band, radio station, student government, student newspaper, student-run film society, symphony orchestra, television station 24 honor societies, 14 religious organizations. 8 fraternities, 6 sororities. **Athletics (Intercollegiate):** *Men:* baseball, basketball, football, golf, soccer, swimming, tennis. *Women:* basketball, cross-country, equestrian sports, golf, soccer, softball, swimming, tennis, track/field (outdoor), volleyball. **On-Campus Highlights:** Lied Library, Artemus W. Ham Concert Hall, Moyer Student Union, Judy Bailey Theatre, Student Services Complex, Thomas and Mack and Cox Pavilion Event Centers, Lied Athletic Complex, Tonopah Residence Complex.

ADMISSIONS

Freshman Academic Profile: Average high school GPA 3.34. 18% in top 10% of high school class, 47% in top 25% of high school class, 82% in top 50% of high school class. SAT Math middle 50% range 450-580. SAT Critical Reading middle 50% range 440-560. ACT middle 50% range 18-24. Minimum paper TOEFL 500. **Basis for Candidate Selection:** *Very important factors considered include:* rigor of secondary school record, standardized test scores. *Other factors considered include:* recommendation(s). **Freshman Admission Requirements:** High school diploma is required and GED is accepted. **Academic units required:** 4 English, 3 mathematics, 3 science, (2 science labs), 3 social studies. **Freshman Admission Statistics:** 7,042 applied, 81% admitted, 58% enrolled. **Transfer Admission Requirements:** college transcript(s), Minimum college GPA of 2.0 required. Lowest grade transferable D-. **General Admission Information:** Application Fee $60. Regular application deadline 4/1. Notification on a rolling basis, beginning on or about 11/1. Nonfall registration accepted. Admission may be deferred for a maximum of 1 year. Credit and/ or placement offered for CEEB Advanced Placement tests.

COSTS AND FINANCIAL AID

Required Forms and Deadlines: FAFSA, Institution's own financial aid form. **Notification of Awards:** Applicants will be notified of awards on a rolling basis beginning 4/1. **Types of Aid:** *Need-based scholarships/grants:* Federal Pell, SEOG, state scholarships/grants, private scholarships, the school's own gift aid. *Loans:* Direct Subsidized Stafford, Direct Unsubsidized Stafford, Direct PLUS, Federal Perkins, state loans, college/university loans from institutional funds. *Student Employment:* Federal Work-Study Program available. Institutional employment available. Highest amount earned per year from on-campus jobs $3,680. Off-campus job opportunities are excellent. **Financial Aid Statistics:** 42% freshmen, 57% undergrads receive need-based scholarship or grant aid. 58% freshmen, 33% undergrads receive non-need-based scholarship or grant aid. 32% freshmen, 47% undergrads receive need-based self-help aid. 4% freshmen, 3% undergrads receive athletic scholarships. 39% undergrads borrow to pay for school. **Criteria for awarding institutional aid:** *Non-need-based:* academics, alumni affiliation, art, athletics, job skills, leadership, minority status, music/drama, state/district residency.

UNIVERSITY OF NEVADA—RENO

Mail Stop 120, Reno, NV 89557
Phone: 775-784-4700
E-mail: asknevada@unr.edu · **CEEB Code:** 4844
Fax: 775-784-4283 · **Website:** www.unr.edu · **ACT Code:** 2497

This public school was founded in 1864. It has a 200-acre campus.

RATINGS

Admissions Selectivity Rating: 70   **Fire Safety Rating:** 60*

STUDENTS AND FACULTY

Enrollment: 11,605. **Student Body:** 55% female, 45% male, 18% out-of-state, 3% international (56 countries represented). Asian 7%, African American 2%, Caucasian 73%, Hispanic 7%, Native American 1% **Retention and Graduation:** 76% freshmen return for sophomore year. 15% freshmen graduate within 4 years. 47% freshmen graduate within 6 years. **Faculty:** 682 full-time faculty, 88% hold PhDs, 35% are are members of minority groups, 14% are women.

ACADEMICS

Degrees: bachelor's, first professional, first professional certificate, master's, post-bachelor's certificate, post-master's certificate. **Classes:** Most classes have 20-29 students. Most lab/discussion sessions have 20-29 students. **Special Study Options:** distance learning, double major, dual enrollment, English as a Second Language (ESL), exchange student program (domestic), honors program, independent study, internships, study abroad, teacher certification program. **Disability Services:** Special programs offered to physically disabled students include note-taking services, reader services, tutors. **Career services:** alumni services, career/job search classes, career assessment, internships.

FACILITIES

Housing: Coed dorms, special housing for disabled students, men's dorms, women's dorms, apartments for married students, apartments for single students.

CAMPUS LIFE

Activities: Choral groups, concert band, dance, drama/theater, jazz band, literary magazine, marching band, music ensembles, musical theater, opera, pep band, radio station, student government, student newspaper, yearbook. **Athletics (Intercollegiate):** *Men:* basketball, cross-country, diving, softball, swimming, tennis, track/field (outdoor), volleyball. *Women:* basketball, cross-country, diving, soccer, softball, swimming, tennis, track/field (outdoor), volleyball.

ADMISSIONS

Freshman Academic Profile: Average high school GPA 3.36. SAT Math middle 50% range 480-600. SAT Critical Reading middle 50% range 470-590. ACT middle 50% range 20-25. **Basis for Candidate Selection:** *Very important factors considered include:* rigor of secondary school record. *Other factors considered include:* standardized test scores. **Freshman Admission Requirements:** High school diploma is required and GED is not accepted. **Academic units required:** 4 English, 3 mathematics, 3 science, (2 science labs), 0 foreign language, 3 social studies. **Freshman Admission Statistics:** 4,024 applied, 88% admitted, 59% enrolled. **Transfer Admission Requirements:** college transcript(s), Minimum college GPA of 2.0 required. Lowest grade transferable D-. **General Admission Information:** Application Fee $60. Nonfall registration accepted. Admission may be deferred for a maximum of 1 year. Credit and/or placement offered for CEEB Advanced Placement tests.

COSTS AND FINANCIAL AID

Required Forms and Deadlines: FAFSA. **Notification of Awards:** Applicants will be notified of awards on a rolling basis beginning 4/1. **Types of Aid:** *Need-based scholarships/grants:* Federal Pell, SEOG, private scholarships, the school's own gift aid. *Loans:* Subsidized Stafford, Unsubsidized Stafford, PLUS, Federal Perkins, college/university loans from institutional funds. *Student Employment:* Federal Work-Study Program available. Institutional employment available. Highest amount earned per year from on-campus jobs $3,000. Off-campus job opportunities are excellent. **Financial Aid Statistics:** 44% freshmen, 53% undergrads receive need-based scholarship or grant aid. 87% freshmen, 60% undergrads receive non-need-based scholarship or grant aid. 44% freshmen, 63% undergrads receive need-based self-help aid. 3% freshmen, 4% undergrads receive athletic scholarships. 44% undergrads borrow to pay for school.

UNIVERSITY OF NEW ENGLAND

11 Hills Beach Road, Biddeford, ME 04005-9599
Phone: 207-602-2297 · **Financial Aid Phone:** 207-602-2342
E-mail: admissions@une.edu · **CEEB Code:** 3751
Fax: 207-602-5900 · **Website:** www.une.edu · **ACT Code:** 3751

This private school was founded in 1831. It has a 550-acre campus.

RATINGS

Admissions Selectivity Rating: 72   **Fire Safety Rating:** 82

STUDENTS AND FACULTY

Enrollment: 2,217. **Student Body:** 70% female, 30% male, 67% out-of-state, 1% international (11 countries represented). Asian 3%, African American 1%, Caucasian 74%, Hispanic 0%, Native American <1% **Retention and Graduation:** 53% freshmen graduate within 4 years. 61% freshmen graduate within 6 years. **Faculty:** 265 full-time faculty, 54% are are members of minority groups, 5% are women. 0% of classes are taught by teaching assistants.

ACADEMICS

Degrees: associate, bachelor's, certificate, diploma, first professional, master's, post-bachelor's certificate, post-master's certificate, terminal associate. **Classes:** Most classes have 20-29 students. Most lab/discussion sessions have 10-19 students. **Majors with Highest Enrollment:** Biomedical Sciences; Marine Biology and Biological Oceanography; Athletic Training/Trainer. **Special Study Options:** cross-registration, distance learning, double major, English as a Second Language (ESL), honors program, independent study, internships, student-designed major, study abroad, teacher certification program, Advanced standing options are available for qualified undergraduates to both our Physician Assistant and Doctor of Osteopathic Medicine graduate programs. **Honors programs:** The College of Arts and Sciences offers and honors program to qualified applicants. **Combined degree programs:** DO/MPH and DO/PhD. **Disability Services:** Special programs offered to physically disabled students include note-taking services, reader services, tutors. **Career services:** Alumni network, career/job search classes, career assessment, internships.

FACILITIES

Housing: Coed dorms, women's dorms. 85% of campus accessible to physically disabled. **Special Academic Facilities/Equipment:** Payson Art Gallery; Maine Women Writers Collection; Marine Science Education and Research Center; Marine Animal Rehabilitation Center (MARC); Performance Enhancement and Evaluation Center for health sciences (PEEC); Center for Health Ethics, Law and Policy; Center for Transcultural Health; and New England Institute of Cognitive Science and Evolutionary Psychology. **Computers:** Students can register for classes online.

CAMPUS LIFE

Environment: Village. **Activities:** Choral groups, dance, literary magazine, music ensembles, student government, student newspaper, yearbook. 36 registered organizations, 3 honor societies, 1 religous organization. **Athletics (Intercollegiate):** *Men:* basketball, cross-country, golf, lacrosse, soccer. *Women:* basketball, cross-country, field hockey, golf, lacrosse, soccer, softball, swimming, volleyball. **On-Campus Highlights:** Marine Science and Research Center, Alfond Health Science Center, UNE Beach (on Atlantic Ocean and Saco River), The Point Picnic Area, Campus Center.

ADMISSIONS

Freshman Academic Profile: Average high school GPA 3.3. SAT Math middle 50% range 490-590. SAT Critical Reading middle 50% range 480-580. Minimum paper TOEFL 550. **Basis for Candidate Selection:** *Very important factors considered include:* academic GPA, rigor of secondary school record. *Important factors considered include:* Class rank, interview. *Other factors considered include:* application essay, recommendation(s), standardized test scores, alumni/ae relation, character/personal qualities, extracurricular activities, geographical residence, level of applicant's interest, talent/ability, volunteer work, work experience. **Freshman Admission Requirements:** High school diploma is required and GED is accepted. **Academic units required:** 4 English, 3 mathematics, 3 science, (2 science labs), 2 social studies, 2 history. **Transfer Admission Requirements:** college transcript(s), Minimum college GPA of 2.0 required. Lowest grade transferable C-. **General Admission Information:** Application Fee $40. Notification on a rolling basis, beginning on or about 12/15. Nonfall registration accepted. Admission may be deferred for a maximum of 12. Credit and/or placement offered for CEEB Advanced Placement tests.

COSTS AND FINANCIAL AID

Average book expense $1,400. **Required Forms and Deadlines:** FAFSA. **Notification of Awards:** Applicants will be notified of awards on a rolling basis beginning 3/15. **Types of Aid:** *Need-based scholarships/grants:* Federal Pell, SEOG, state scholarships/grants, private scholarships, the school's own gift aid. *Loans:* Subsidized Stafford, Unsubsidized Stafford, PLUS, Federal Perkins, Federal Nursing. *Student Employment:* Federal Work-Study Program available. Institutional employment available. Highest amount earned per year from on-campus jobs $2,000. Off-campus job opportunities are good. **Financial Aid Statistics:** 98% freshmen, 98% undergrads receive any aid. **Criteria for awarding institutional aid:** *Non-need-based:* academics, alumni affiliation, leadership.

See page 1188.

UNIVERSITY OF NEW HAMPSHIRE

UNH Office of Admissions, Durham, NH 3824
Phone: 603-862-1360 · **Financial Aid Phone:** 603-862-3600
E-mail: admissions@unh.edu · **CEEB Code:** 3918
Fax: 603-862-0077 · **Website:** www.unh.edu · **ACT Code:** 2524

This public school was founded in 1866. It has a 2600-acre campus.

RATINGS

Admissions Selectivity Rating: 80   **Fire Safety Rating:** 97

STUDENTS AND FACULTY

Enrollment: 12,591. **Student Body:** 54% female, 46% male, 49% out-of-state, 2% international (35 countries represented). Asian 2%, African American 1%, Caucasian 81%, Hispanic 3%, Native American <1%
Retention and Graduation: 86% freshmen return for sophomore year. 66% freshmen graduate within 4 years. 77% freshmen graduate within 6 years. 30% grads go on to further study within 1 year. 26% grads pursue arts and sciences degrees. 1% grads pursue law degrees. 14% grads pursue business degrees. 1% grads pursue medical degrees. **Faculty:** 610 full-time faculty, 89% hold PhDs, 43% are are members of minority groups, 12% are women. 1% of classes are taught by teaching assistants.

ACADEMICS

Degrees: associate, bachelor's, doctoral, master's, post-bachelor's certificate, post-master's certificate, terminal associate. **Classes:** Most classes have 20-29 students. Most lab/discussion sessions have 20-29 students. **Majors with Highest Enrollment:** Psychology; Business Administration and Management; Biomedical Sciences. **Special Study Options:** Accelerated program, cooperative education program, cross-registration, distance learning, double major, English as a Second Language (ESL), exchange student program (domestic), honors program, independent study, internships, student-designed major, study abroad, teacher certification program, weekend college, Research/Creative Projects, Learning Communities, Experiential Learning, Senior Capstone, Service Learning, Work Study, Honors. **Honors programs:** The UNH honors program offers small and dynamic classes, opportunities for research and study overseas, individualized advising and a close and supportive community. **Combined degree programs:** BA/MA, BS/MS OT, BA/BS and MBA, BS/MS Account,BA/ BS and MEduc, BS/MS in biochem. **Disability Services:** Special programs offered to physically disabled students include note-taking services, reader services, tape recorders, tutors. **Career services:** Alumni network, alumni services, career/job search classes, career assessment, internships, regional alumni. Career services highlights include UNH's Washington Internship Program, which allows UNH students to earn academic credit while working and living in Washington, DC. Recent internships for UNH students have included the US Senate, State Department, US Attorney Generals Office, Environmental Protection Agency, Smithsonian Museum, public interest law firms, lobbyists, and non-profit organizations.

FACILITIES

Housing: Coed dorms, special housing for international students, fraternity/sorority housing, apartments for married students, apartments for single students, Theme HousingThere are 11 theme dorms for only freshman and 11 others for all students. Four "small halls" of 45 to 50 people in mostly single rooms are also available. 85% of campus accessible to physically disabled. **Special Academic Facilities/Equipment:** Journalism laboratory, Milne Special Collections Archives and Museum, optical observatory, marine research laboratory,

experiential learning center, child development center,language lab, art gallery, agricultural and equine facilities, electron microscope, sawmill, nature preserves and trails, survey center, radio station **Computers:** 5% of classrooms, 100% of dorms, 100% of libraries, 100% of student union, 2% of common outdoor areas have wireless network access. Students can register for classes online. Administrative functions (other than registration) can be performed online.

CAMPUS LIFE

Environment: Village. **Activities:** Choral groups, concert band, dance, drama/ theater, jazz band, literary magazine, marching band, music ensembles, musical theater, pep band, radio station, student government, student newspaper, student-run film society, symphony orchestra, television station, yearbook, Campus Ministries, International Student Organization, Model UN. 187 registered organizations, 18 honor societies, 10 religious organizations. 10 fraternities, 7 sororities. **Athletics (Intercollegiate):** *Men:* basketball, cross-country, football, ice hockey, skiing (downhill/alpine), skiing (nordic/cross-country), soccer, track/ field (outdoor), track/field (indoor). *Women:* basketball, cross-country, diving, field hockey, gymnastics, ice hockey, lacrosse, skiing (downhill/alpine), skiing (nordic/cross-country), soccer, swimming, track/field (outdoor), track/field (indoor), volleyball. **On-Campus Highlights:** Dimond Library, Whittemore Center, Hamel Recreation Center, Student Union/Holloway Commons, College Woods, Other spots include Dairy Bar/Train Station, Art Gallery, Thompson Hall, Morse Hall. **Environmental Initiatives:** 1. The UNH USustainability Academy (UNHSA) is the oldest endowed sustainability program in higher education in the U.S. and has worked with the larger campus community over nearly 15 years to develop UNHs unique sustainable learning community model and to foster sustainability locally, statewide, and regionally. www.sustainableunh.unh.edu Under our comprehensive Climate Education Initiative and as a key component of its climate action plan, WildCAP and signature to the American College and University Presidents Climate Commitment, UNH has committed to cut its greenhouse gas emission 50% by 2020 and 80% by 2050 on the road to carbon neutrality by 2100. We also use processed landfill gas from the EcoLine project, a landfill gas-to-energy project that uses methane gas from a nearby landfill, as the primary fuel for our on-campus cogeneration plan. By selling the renewable energy credits associate with EcoLine we are able to help finance this project and invest in more energy efficiency on campus via a new revolving energy efficiency fund. More info at www.sustainableunh.unh.edu/ ecoline, www.sustainableunh.unh.edu/cei and http://www.sustainableunh.unh. edu/wildcap. Responding to a need by farmers for scientific research to support organic dairy efforts, UNH is the first land grant university to have an organic dairy farm and education/research center. The organic dairy is a research center for organic production and management and an education center for organic dairy farmers, farmers considering the transition to organic, and students of sustainable agriculture. The organic dairy research farm is part of UNHs broader Food & Society Initiative (FAS) through which UNH meets its commitment to being a sustainable food community. Other efforts include a Dual Major in EcoGastronomy for undergraduate students and a Local Harvest Initiative in the dining halls. More info at www.sustainableunh.unh.edu/fas

ADMISSIONS

Freshman Academic Profile: 17% in top 10% of high school class, 48% in top 25% of high school class, 87% in top 50% of high school class. 81% from public high schools. SAT Math middle 50% range 510-610. SAT Critical Reading middle 50% range 490-590. SAT Writing middle 50% range 500-600. ACT middle 50% range 22-27. Minimum internet-based TOEFL 80. Minimum paper TOEFL 550. **Basis for Candidate Selection:** *Very important factors considered include:* Class rank, rigor of secondary school record. *Important factors considered include:* academic GPA, recommendation(s). *Other factors considered include:* application essay, standardized test scores, alumni/ae relation, character/personal qualities, extracurricular activities, first generation, geographical residence, racial/ethnic status, state residency, talent/ability, volunteer work, work experience. **Freshman Admission Requirements:** High school diploma is required and GED is accepted. **Academic units required:** 4 English, 3 mathematics, 3 science, (2 science labs), 2 foreign language, 3 social studies. **Freshman Admission Statistics:** 18,420 applied, 80% admitted, 22% enrolled. **Transfer Admission Requirements:** High school transcript, college transcript(s), essay or personal statement, interview, standardized test scores, Minimum college GPA of 2.8 required. Lowest grade transferable C. **General Admission Information:** Application Fee $50. Regular application deadline 2/1. Notification on a rolling basis, beginning on or about 2/1. Nonfall registration accepted. Admission may be deferred for a maximum of 1 year. Credit and/ or placement offered for CEEB Advanced Placement tests.

COSTS AND FINANCIAL AID

Annual in-state tuition $13,670. Annual out-of-state tuition $26,650. Room and board $10,360. Required fees $2,882. Average book expense $1,200. **Required Forms and Deadlines:** FAFSA. **Notification of Awards:** Applicants will be notified of awards on a rolling basis beginning 3/1. **Types of Aid:** *Need-based scholarships/grants:* Federal Pell, SEOG, state scholarships/grants, private scholarships, the school's own gift aid, Veterans Educational Benefits. *Loans:* Subsidized Stafford, Unsubsidized Stafford, PLUS, Federal Perkins, college/ university loans from institutional funds. *Student Employment:* Federal Work-

Study Program available. Institutional employment available. Highest amount earned per year from on-campus jobs $25,487. Off-campus job opportunities are excellent. **Financial Aid Statistics:** 75% freshmen, 69% undergrads receive need-based scholarship or grant aid. 5% freshmen, 4% undergrads receive non-need-based scholarship or grant aid. 94% freshmen, 95% undergrads receive need-based self-help aid. 1% freshmen, 1% undergrads receive athletic scholarships. 85% freshmen, 81% undergrads receive any aid. 79% undergrads borrow to pay for school. Average cumulative indebtedness $26,714. **Criteria for awarding institutional aid:** *Non-need-based:* academics, art, athletics, leadership, music/drama, religious affiliation.

UNIVERSITY OF NEW HAMPSHIRE AT MANCHESTER

400 Commercial Street, Manchester, NH 3101
Phone: 603-641-4150
E-mail: unhm.admissions@unh.edu · **CEEB Code:** 2094
Fax: 603-641-4125 · **Website:** http://www.unh.edu/unhm/

This public school was founded in 1985.

RATINGS

Admissions Selectivity Rating: 71   Fire Safety Rating: 60*

STUDENTS AND FACULTY

Enrollment: 704. **Student Body:** 64% female, 36% male, 1% out-of-state, 1% international (5 countries represented). Asian 1%, African American 2%, Caucasian 94%, Hispanic 1%, Native American <1%
Faculty: 23 full-time faculty, 78% hold PhDs, 52% are are members of minority groups. 3% of classes are taught by teaching assistants.

ACADEMICS

Degrees: associate, bachelor's. **Classes:** Most classes have 10-19 students. **Special Study Options:** cross-registration, double major, English as a Second Language (ESL), exchange student program (domestic), independent study, internships, study abroad, teacher certification program. **Disability Services:** Special programs offered to physically disabled students include note-taking services, reader services, tape recorders, tutors. **Career services:** alumni services, career/job search classes, career assessment, internships.

FACILITIES

Housing: 85% of campus accessible to physically disabled.

CAMPUS LIFE

Activities: student government.

ADMISSIONS

Freshman Academic Profile: SAT Math middle 50% range 440-550. SAT Critical Reading middle 50% range 460-550. Minimum internet-based TOEFL 75. Minimum paper TOEFL 550. **Basis for Candidate Selection:** *Very important factors considered include:* rigor of secondary school record. *Important factors considered include:* Class rank, application essay, recommendation(s), standardized test scores. *Other factors considered include:* alumni/ae relation, character/personal qualities, extracurricular activities, interview, racial/ethnic status, state residency, talent/ability, volunteer work, work experience. **Freshman Admission Requirements:** High school diploma is required and GED is accepted. **Academic units required:** 4 English, 3 mathematics, (3 science labs), 2 foreign language, 2 social studies. **Freshman Admission Statistics:** 218 applied, 74% admitted, 66% enrolled. **Transfer Admission Requirements:** High school transcript, college transcript(s), essay or personal statement, statement of good standing from prior institution(s). Minimum college GPA of 2.5 required. Lowest grade transferable C. **General Admission Information:** Application Fee $50. Regular application deadline 6/15. Notification on a rolling basis, beginning on or about 1/31. Nonfall registration accepted. Admission may be deferred for a maximum of 2 Semesters. Credit offered for CEEB Advanced Placement tests.

COSTS AND FINANCIAL AID

Annual out-of-state tuition $12,190. Required fees $54. Average book expense $700. **Required Forms and Deadlines:** FAFSA, Noncustodial PROFILE, Business/Farm Supplement. **Notification of Awards:** Applicants will be notified of awards on a rolling basis beginning 4/1. **Types of Aid:** *Need-based scholarships/grants:* Federal Pell, SEOG, state scholarships/grants, private scholarships, the school's own gift aid. *Loans:* Subsidized Stafford, Unsubsidized Stafford, PLUS, Federal Perkins, Outside Loans. *Student Employment:* Federal Work-Study Program available. Institutional employment available. Off-campus job opportunities are excellent. **Criteria for awarding institutional aid:** *Non-need-based:* academics, minority status.

UNIVERSITY OF NEW HAVEN

300 Boston Post Road, West Haven, CT 6516
Phone: 203-932-7319 · **Financial Aid Phone:** 203-932-7315
E-mail: admission@newhaven.edu · **CEEB Code:** 3663
Fax: 203-931-6093 · **Website:** www.newhaven.edu · **ACT Code:** 576

This private school was founded in 1920. It has a 78-acre campus.

RATINGS

Admissions Selectivity Rating: 82   Fire Safety Rating: 60*

STUDENTS AND FACULTY

Enrollment: 4,974. **Student Body:** 50% female, 50% male, 58% out-of-state, 8% international (30 countries represented). Asian 2%, African American 9%, Caucasian 59%, Hispanic 10%, Native American <1%
Retention and Graduation: 39% freshmen graduate within 4 years. **Faculty:** 263 full-time faculty, 82% hold PhDs, 33% are are members of minority groups, 23% are women.

ACADEMICS

Degrees: associate, bachelor's, certificate, master's, post-bachelor's certificate. **Classes:** Most classes have 10-19 students. Most lab/discussion sessions have 10-19 students. **Majors with Highest Enrollment:** Criminal Justice/Law Enforcement Administration; Forensic Science and Technology; Psychology. **Special Study Options:** Accelerated program, cooperative education program, cross-registration, double major, dual enrollment, English as a Second Language (ESL), honors program, independent study, internships, student-designed major, study abroad. **Combined degree programs:** BS/MS in environmental science. **Disability Services:** Special programs offered to physically disabled students include note-taking services, reader services, tape recorders, tutors. **Career services:** Alumni network, alumni services, career/job search classes, career assessment, internships.

FACILITIES

Housing: Coed dorms, apartments for single students. 82% of campus accessible to physically disabled. **Special Academic Facilities/Equipment:** Art gallery, forensic science lab, radio station, tv station, theater, Orchestra New England, music and sound recording studio.

CAMPUS LIFE

Environment: Village. **Activities:** Choral groups, dance, drama/theater, music ensembles, musical theater, pep band, radio station, student government, student newspaper, television station, yearbook. 50 registered organizations, 5 honor societies, 1 religous organization. 2 fraternities, 3 sororities. **Athletics (Intercollegiate):** *Men:* baseball, basketball, cross-country, golf, lacrosse, soccer, track/field (outdoor), track/field (indoor), volleyball. *Women:* basketball, cheerleading, cross-country, lacrosse, soccer, softball, tennis, volleyball. **On-Campus Highlights:** Bartel's Student Union, Student Run Dance Hall, Coffe Shop.

ADMISSIONS

Freshman Academic Profile: Average high school GPA 3.4. 17% in top 10% of high school class, 50% in top 25% of high school class, 82% in top 50% of high school class. SAT Math middle 50% range 480-590. SAT Critical Reading middle 50% range 470-570. SAT Writing middle 50% range 470-570. ACT middle 50% range 21-26. Minimum internet-based TOEFL 80. **Basis for Candidate Selection:** *Very important factors considered include:* rigor of secondary school record, standardized test scores. *Important factors considered include:* Class rank, application essay, recommendation(s). *Other factors considered include:* alumni/ae relation, character/personal qualities, extracurricular activities, interview, talent/ability, volunteer work, work experience. **Freshman Admission Requirements:** High school diploma is required and GED is accepted. **Academic units required:** 4 English, 3 mathematics, 2 science, 2 history, 3 academic electives. **Freshman Admission Statistics:** 9,006 applied, 81% admitted, 17% enrolled. **Transfer Admission Requirements:** High school transcript, college transcript(s), Minimum college GPA of 2.5 required. Lowest grade transferable C. **General Admission Information:** Application Fee $50. Notification on a rolling basis, beginning on or about 9/15. Nonfall registration accepted. Admission may be deferred for a maximum of 1 year. Credit and/or placement offered for CEEB Advanced Placement tests.

COSTS AND FINANCIAL AID

Required Forms and Deadlines: FAFSA. **Notification of Awards:** Applicants will be notified of awards on a rolling basis beginning 3/15. **Types of Aid:** *Need-based scholarships/grants:* Federal Pell, SEOG, state scholarships/grants, private scholarships, the school's own gift aid. *Loans:* Subsidized Stafford, Unsubsidized Stafford, PLUS, Federal Perkins. *Student Employment:* Federal Work-Study Program available. Institutional employment available. Highest amount earned per year from on-campus jobs $900. Off-campus job opportunities are excellent. **Financial Aid Statistics:** 100% freshmen, 100% undergrads receive need-based scholarship or grant aid. 11% freshmen, 12% undergrads receive non-need-based scholarship or grant aid. 83% freshmen, 82% undergrads receive need-based self-help aid. 1% freshmen, 0% undergrads receive athletic scholarships. 84% undergrads borrow to pay for school. Average cumulative indebtedness $26,700. **Criteria for awarding institutional aid:** *Non-need-based:* academics, athletics.

UNIVERSITY OF NEW MEXICO

Office of Admissions, Albuquerque, NM 87196-4895
Phone: 505-277-2446 · **Financial Aid Phone:** 505-277-8900
E-mail: apply@unm.edu · **CEEB Code:** 4845
Fax: 505-277-6686 · **Website:** www.unm.edu · **ACT Code:** 2650

This public school was founded in 1889. It has a 769-acre campus.

RATINGS

Admissions Selectivity Rating: 77   **Fire Safety Rating:** 72

STUDENTS AND FACULTY

Student Body: 10% out-of-state, (92 countries represented).
Retention and Graduation: 74% freshmen return for sophomore year. **Faculty:** 949 full-time faculty, 82% hold PhDs, 46% are are members of minority groups, 24% are women.

ACADEMICS

Degrees: associate, bachelor's, certificate, first professional, master's, post-master's certificate. **Classes:** Most classes have 20-29 students. Most lab/discussion sessions have 10-19 students. **Majors with Highest Enrollment:** Biology/Biological Sciences; Psychology; Business Administration and Management. **Special Study Options:** Accelerated program, cooperative education program, distance learning, double major, dual enrollment, English as a Second Language (ESL), exchange student program (domestic), honors program, independent study, internships, student-designed major, study abroad, teacher certification program, weekend college. **Honors programs:** The University Honors Program offers the chance to explore major contemporary ideas and values in small interdisciplinary seminars with the additional benefits of personal interaction with outstanding UNM faculty, opportunities for upper-division independent research, social and cultural events, lecture series, and opportunities to participate in regional and national honors conferences. UHP students do not major in University Honors. They graduate with a degree from one of UNM's degree-granting colleges or schools. **Combined degree programs:** BA/MD, 3-2 Latin American Studies/mba. **Disability Services:** Special programs offered to physically disabled students include note-taking services, reader services, tape recorders, tutors. **Career services:** Alumni network, alumni services, career/job search classes, career assessment, internships, regional alumni.

FACILITIES

Housing: Coed dorms, fraternity/sorority housing, apartments for married students, apartments for single students, Special living options include graduate and senior housing, academic floors, scholars wing, and outdoor/wellness units. Computer Science and Engineering unit also available. 100% of campus accessible to physically disabled. **Special Academic Facilities/Equipment:** Museums of art, anthropology, geology, and Southwestern biology, lithography institute, meteoritics institute, electron and electron scanning microscopes, nuclear reactor, robotics lab, observatory, planetarium, Science and Technology Park. **Computers:** 100% of classrooms, 100% of dorms, 100% of libraries, 100% of dining areas, 100% of student union, 85% of common outdoor areas have wireless network access. Students can register for classes online. Administrative functions (other than registration) can be performed online.

CAMPUS LIFE

Environment: Metropolis. **Activities:** Choral groups, concert band, dance, drama/theater, jazz band, literary magazine, marching band, music ensembles, musical theater, opera, pep band, radio station, student government, student newspaper, student-run film society, symphony orchestra, television station. 375 registered organizations, 20 honor societies, 23 religious organizations. 9 fraternities, 10 sororities. **Athletics (Intercollegiate):** *Men:* baseball, basketball, cross-country, football, golf, skiing (downhill/alpine), skiing (nordic/cross-country), soccer, tennis, track/field (outdoor), track/field (indoor). *Women:* basketball, cross-country, diving, golf, skiing (downhill/alpine), skiing (nordic/cross-country), soccer, softball, swimming, tennis, track/field (outdoor), track/

field (indoor), volleyball. **On-Campus Highlights:** SUB (Student Union Building), Duck Pond, Zimmerman Library, Popejoy Hall—Performing Arts Center, Residency Halls, Maxwell Museum, Trolly Tour of Campus for new and prospective students. **Environmental Initiatives:** In November 2009 UNM submitted its first Climate Action Plan to the American College and University Presidents Climate Commitment website and set a climate neutrality target date of year 2050. UNM will use a multi-tiered approach to reducing our greenhouse gas emissions. The tiers are behavior- based energy conservation, technological improvements in utilities production and consumption, renewable energy, and alternative transportation. UNM has won two Energy Star awards from the U. S. Environmental Protection Agency. In November 2007 the Physical Plant Department received the Energy Star Combined Heat and Power award for the Ford Utilities Center cogeneration unit, which met the criteria for energy efficiency and fuel savings. In November 2009 University Hospital became the first academic hospital to be presented with an Energy Star award. In collaboration with over 100 community partners, the Research Service Learning Program (RSLP) under the direction of Dr. Dan Young has offered UNM students 31 courses related to sustainability, food security, and social development since the summer of 2006. During the fall 2009 semester RSLP students in wrote a Guide to Green Living at UNM and developed an Eco Rep Program for the resident halls. The Eco Reps serve as sustainability advocates to their peers in each dorm providing guidance and leadership in recycling, energy conservation, alternative transportation, and purchasing locally grown, organic foods. In fall 2010, the RSLP will partner with Sustainability Studies on a Sustainability Living and Learning Center for 12—20 freshmen in the dorms.

ADMISSIONS

Freshman Academic Profile: Average high school GPA 3.29. SAT Math middle 50% range 470-590. SAT Critical Reading middle 50% range 470-600. ACT middle 50% range 19-25. Minimum internet-based TOEFL 68. Minimum paper TOEFL 520. **Basis for Candidate Selection:** *Very important factors considered include:* academic GPA, rigor of secondary school record. *Important factors considered include:* Class rank, standardized test scores. *Other factors considered include:* application essay, recommendation(s), character/personal qualities, extracurricular activities, first generation, volunteer work, work experience. **Freshman Admission Requirements:** High school diploma is required and GED is accepted. **Academic units required:** 4 English, 3 mathematics, 2 science, (1 science labs), 2 foreign language, 1 social studies, 1 history. **Freshman Admission Statistics:** 11,410 applied, 64% admitted, 46% enrolled. **Transfer Admission Requirements:** college transcript(s). Minimum college GPA of 2.0 required. Lowest grade transferable C. **General Admission Information:** Application Fee $20. Regular application deadline 6/15. Nonfall registration accepted. Admission may be deferred for a maximum of 1 year. Credit and/or placement offered for CEEB Advanced Placement tests.

COSTS AND FINANCIAL AID

Average book expense $958. **Required Forms and Deadlines:** FAFSA. **Notification of Awards:** Applicants will be notified of awards on a rolling basis beginning 4/15. **Types of Aid:** *Need-based scholarships/grants:* Federal Pell, SEOG, state scholarships/grants, private scholarships, the school's own gift aid, United Negro College Fund, Federal Nursing Scholarships. *Loans:* Direct Subsidized Stafford, Direct Unsubsidized Stafford, Direct PLUS, Federal Perkins, Federal Nursing, state loans, college/university loans from institutional funds. *Student Employment:* Federal Work-Study Program available. **Criteria for awarding institutional aid:** *Non-need-based:* academics, alumni affiliation, art, athletics, job skills, leadership, minority status, music/drama, religious affiliation, state/district residency.

UNIVERSITY OF NEW ORLEANS

University of New Orleans PEC, New Orleans, LA 70148
Phone: 504-280-6595 · **Financial Aid Phone:** 504-280-6603
E-mail: pecuno.edu · **CEEB Code:** 6379
Fax: 504-280-3973 · **Website:** www.uno.edu · **ACT Code:** 1591

This public school was founded in 1956. It has a 195-acre campus.

RATINGS

Admissions Selectivity Rating: 87   **Fire Safety Rating:** 75

STUDENTS AND FACULTY

Enrollment: 6,742. **Student Body:** 50% female, 50% male, 5% out-of-state, 4% international (60 countries represented). Asian 8%, African American 16%,

Caucasian 55%, Hispanic 10%, Native American <1%. **Retention and Graduation:** 69% freshmen return for sophomore year. 13% freshmen graduate within 4 years. 34% freshmen graduate within 6 years. **Faculty:** 281 full-time faculty, 80% hold PhDs, 39% are are members of minority groups, 20% are women.

ACADEMICS

Degrees: bachelor's, master's, post-bachelor's certificate. **Classes:** Most classes have 20-29 students. **Majors with Highest Enrollment:** Business Administration and Management; Multi-/Interdisciplinary Studies; Biology/Biological Sciences. **Special Study Options:** cooperative education program, cross-registration, distance learning, double major, dual enrollment, English as a Second Language (ESL), exchange student program (domestic), honors program, independent study, internships, student-designed major, study abroad, teacher certification program, weekend college. **Disability Services:** Special programs offered to physically disabled students include note-taking services, reader services, tape recorders, tutors. **Career services:** alumni services, career assessment, internships.

FACILITIES

Housing: Coed dorms, special housing for disabled students, apartments for married students, apartments for single students. 100% of campus accessible to physically disabled. **Special Academic Facilities/Equipment:** Performing arts center, audiovisual center, TV studio, Eisenhower leadership studies center, child care center, Louisiana collection. **Computers:** 100% of libraries, 100% of student union, have wireless network access. Students can register for classes online. Administrative functions (other than registration) can be performed online.

CAMPUS LIFE

Environment: Metropolis. **Activities:** Choral groups, concert band, dance, drama/theater, jazz band, literary magazine, music ensembles, musical theater, opera, pep band, radio station, student government, student newspaper, student-run film society, Campus Ministries, International Student Organization. 120 registered organizations, 7 religious organizations. 9 fraternities, 8 sororities. **Athletics (Intercollegiate):** *Men:* baseball, basketball, diving, golf, swimming, tennis. *Women:* basketball, diving, swimming, tennis, volleyball. **On-Campus Highlights:** Recreation and Fitness Center, The University Center, The Homer L. Hitt Alumni and Visitors Ce, Earl K. Long Library.

ADMISSIONS

Freshman Academic Profile: Average high school GPA 3.25. 16% in top 10% of high school class, 39% in top 25% of high school class, 67% in top 50% of high school class. 63% from public high schools. SAT Math middle 50% range 500-670. SAT Critical Reading middle 50% range 500-630. ACT middle 50% range 21-25. Minimum internet-based TOEFL 213. Minimum paper TOEFL 550. **Basis for Candidate Selection:** *Very important factors considered include:* Class rank, academic GPA, rigor of secondary school record, standardized test scores. *Other factors considered include:* recommendation(s), geographical residence, state residency. **Freshman Admission Requirements:** High school diploma is required and GED is accepted. **Academic units required:** 4 English, 3 mathematics, 3 science, 2 foreign language, 1 social studies, 2 history, 1 visual/performing arts. **Freshman Admission Statistics:** 3,828 applied, 44% admitted, 52% enrolled. **Transfer Admission Requirements:** college transcript(s), Minimum college GPA of 2.25 required. Lowest grade transferable D. **General Admission Information:** Application Fee $40. Regular application deadline 8/20. Notification on a rolling basis, beginning on or about 10/1. Nonfall registration accepted. Admission may be deferred for a maximum of 1 year. Credit and/or placement offered for CEEB Advanced Placement tests.

COSTS AND FINANCIAL AID

Required Forms and Deadlines: FAFSA. **Notification of Awards:** Applicants will be notified of awards on a rolling basis beginning 4/20. **Types of Aid:** *Need-based scholarships/grants:* Federal Pell, SEOG, state scholarships/grants, private scholarships, the school's own gift aid. *Loans:* Direct Subsidized Stafford, Direct Unsubsidized Stafford, Direct PLUS, Subsidized Stafford, Unsubsidized Stafford, PLUS, Federal Perkins, college/university loans from institutional funds. *Student Employment:* Federal Work-Study Program available. Institutional employment available. Highest amount earned per year from on-campus jobs $23,920. **Financial Aid Statistics:** 76% freshmen, 67% undergrads receive need-based scholarship or grant aid. 67% freshmen, 40% undergrads receive non-need-based scholarship or grant aid. 35% freshmen, 44% undergrads receive need-based self-help aid. 3% freshmen, 2% undergrads receive athletic scholarships. 68% freshmen, 64% undergrads receive any aid. 53% undergrads borrow to pay for school. Average cumulative indebtedness $18,111. **Criteria for awarding institutional aid:** *Non-need-based:* academics, athletics.

UNIVERSITY OF NORTH ALABAMA

UNA Box 5011, Florence, AL 35632-0001
Phone: 256-765-4318 · **Financial Aid Phone:** 256-765-4278
E-mail: admissions@una.edu · **CEEB Code:**
Fax: 256-765-4329 · **Website:** http://www.una.edu/ · **ACT Code:** 14

This public school was founded in 1830. It has a 130-acre campus.

RATINGS

Admissions Selectivity Rating: 73   **Fire Safety Rating:** 67

STUDENTS AND FACULTY

Enrollment: 5,235. **Student Body:** 57% female, 43% male, 19% out-of-state, 9% international (67 countries represented). Asian 1%, African American 10%, Caucasian 70%, Hispanic 1%, Native American 1%. **Retention and Graduation:** 68% freshmen return for sophomore year. 55% freshmen graduate within 6 years. **Faculty:** 247 full-time faculty, 63% hold PhDs, 47% are are members of minority groups, 14% are women. 0% of classes are taught by teaching assistants.

ACADEMICS

Degrees: bachelor's, master's, post-master's certificate. **Classes:** Most classes have fewer than 10 students. Most lab/discussion sessions have 20-29 students. **Majors with Highest Enrollment:** Secondary Education and Teaching; Registered Nursing/Registered Nurse; Business/Commerce. **Special Study Options:** Accelerated program, cooperative education program, distance learning, double major, dual enrollment, English as a Second Language (ESL), honors program, independent study, internships, student-designed major, teacher certification program, weekend college. **Disability Services:** Special programs offered to physically disabled students include tutors.

FACILITIES

Housing: Coed dorms, men's dorms, special housing for international students, women's dorms, fraternity/sorority housing, apartments for married students, apartments for single students. 99% of campus accessible to physically disabled. **Special Academic Facilities/Equipment:** On-campus lab school (N-6), planetarium, observatory, art gallery. **Computers:** Students can register for classes online.

CAMPUS LIFE

Environment: Town. **Activities:** Choral groups, concert band, drama/theater, jazz band, literary magazine, marching band, music ensembles, musical theater, pep band, radio station, student government, student newspaper, yearbook. 98 registered organizations. **Athletics (Intercollegiate):** *Men:* baseball, basketball, cross-country, football, golf, tennis. *Women:* basketball, cross-country, soccer, softball, tennis, volleyball. **On-Campus Highlights:** Guillot University Center, Academic Resource Center, Entertainment Industry Center, Recreation Center, Flowers Hall.

ADMISSIONS

Freshman Academic Profile: Average high school GPA 2.97. 44% in top 25% of high school class, 76% in top 50% of high school class. 99% from public high schools. ACT middle 50% range 18-24. Minimum paper TOEFL 500. **Basis for Candidate Selection:** *Very important factors considered include:* Class rank, academic GPA, standardized test scores. *Important factors considered include:* rigor of secondary school record, character/personal qualities. **Freshman Admission Requirements:** High school diploma is required and GED is accepted. **Academic units required:** 4 English, 2 mathematics, 2 science, 2 foreign language, 3 social studies. **Freshman Admission Statistics:** 2,227 applied, 84% admitted, 54% enrolled. **Transfer Admission Requirements:** college transcript(s), Minimum college GPA of 2.0 required. Lowest grade transferable C. **General Admission Information:** Application Fee $25. Notification on a rolling basis, beginning on or about 6/15. Nonfall registration accepted. Admission may be deferred for a maximum of 1 semester. Credit offered for CEEB Advanced Placement tests.

COSTS AND FINANCIAL AID

Annual out-of-state tuition $7,536. Room and board $4,372. Required fees $883. Average book expense $830. **Required Forms and Deadlines:** FAFSA. **Notification of Awards:** Applicants will be notified of awards on a rolling basis beginning 5/31. **Types of Aid:** *Need-based scholarships/grants:* Federal Pell, SEOG, state scholarships/grants, private scholarships, the school's own gift aid. *Loans:* Subsidized Stafford, Unsubsidized Stafford, PLUS, Federal Perkins. **Financial Aid Statistics:** 63% freshmen, 61% undergrads receive need-based scholarship or grant aid. 79% freshmen, 54% undergrads receive non-need-based scholarship or grant aid. 60% freshmen, 73% undergrads receive need-based self-help aid. 5% freshmen, 5% undergrads receive athletic scholarships. 47% undergrads borrow to pay for school. **Criteria for awarding institutional aid:** *Non-need-based:* academics, art, athletics, leadership, minority status, music/drama, state/district residency.

THE UNIVERSITY OF NORTH CAROLINA AT ASHEVILLE

Best 380

CPO #1320, Asheville, NC 28804-8502
Phone: 828-251-6481 · **Financial Aid Phone:** 828-251-6481
E-mail: admissions@unca.edu · **CEEB Code:** 5013
Fax: 828-251-6482 · **Website:** www.unca.edu · **ACT Code:** 3064

This public school was founded in 1927. It has a 265-acre campus.

RATINGS

Admissions Selectivity Rating: 86   **Fire Safety Rating:** 96

STUDENTS AND FACULTY

Enrollment: 3,323. **Student Body:** 57% female, 43% male, 12% out-of-state, 0% international (32 countries represented). Asian 1%, African American 3%, Caucasian 83%, Hispanic 4%, Native American <1%
Retention and Graduation: 80% freshmen return for sophomore year. 37% freshmen graduate within 4 years. 60% freshmen graduate within 6 years. **Faculty:** 219 full-time faculty, 85% hold PhDs, 45% are are members of minority groups, 15% are women. 0% of classes are taught by teaching assistants.

ACADEMICS

Degrees: bachelor's, master's, post-bachelor's certificate. **Classes:** Most classes have 10-19 students. Most lab/discussion sessions have 20-29 students. **Majors with Highest Enrollment:** Psychology; English Language and Literature; Environmental Studies. **Special Study Options:** cross-registration, distance learning, double major, dual enrollment, exchange student program (domestic), honors program, independent study, internships, liberal arts/career combination, student-designed major, study abroad, teacher certification program.
Honors programs: University Honors Program—Designed for talented and motivated students, the Honors curriculum complements the General Education and major curricula. Successful completion of the Honors Program enables the student to graduate with Distinction as a University Scholar. (See http://www.unca.edu/honors/ for further information.) Undergraduate Research Program—The Undergraduate Research Program at UNCA seeks to encourage the establishment of faculty/student research pairs who work together on a project of mutual interest. Research may be performed in any discipline on campus. Students who have made oral presentations at symposia and have had their work reviewed and published can receive recognition as University Research Scholars. (See http://www.unca.edu/urp/ for more information.). **Disability Services:** Special programs offered to physically disabled students include note-taking services, reader services, tape recorders, tutors. **Career services:** Alumni network, alumni services, career/job search classes, career assessment, internships, regional alumni.

FACILITIES

Housing: Coed dorms, special housing for disabled students, men's dorms, women's dorms, substance-free dorms, 24 hour quiet dorms. 95% of campus accessible to physically disabled. **Special Academic Facilities/Equipment:** Undergraduate Research Center, Steelcase Teleconference Center, Music Recording Center, Asheville Botanical Gardens, NC Arboretum, Center for Creative Retirement. **Computers:** 1% of classrooms, 100% of libraries, 100% of dining areas, 90% of student union, have wireless network access. Students can register for classes online. Administrative functions (other than registration) can be performed online.

CAMPUS LIFE

Environment: Town. **Activities:** Choral groups, concert band, dance, drama/theater, jazz band, literary magazine, music ensembles, musical theater, pep band, radio station, student government, student newspaper, Campus Ministries, International Student Organization. 82 registered organizations, 14 honor societies, 10 religious organizations. 1 fraternity, 2 sororities. **Athletics (Intercollegiate):** *Men:* baseball, basketball, cheerleading, cross-country, soccer, tennis, track/field (outdoor). *Women:* basketball, cheerleading, cross-country, soccer, tennis, track/field (outdoor), volleyball. **On-Campus Highlights:** Health and Fitness Center, Main Campus Quadrangle, Highsmith University Union, Asheville Botanical Gardens, Café Ramsey in Ramsey Library. **Environmental Initiatives:** Sustainability is the priority in all campus renovation and new construction:Between 2004 and 2012, the university added four different geothermal systems for heating and cooling which serve three classroom and office buildings and the newest residence hall, while contributing to the needs of six older nearby residence halls. A ground-source heat pump system has been installed to serve another building. A solar thermal system now serves the heating/cooling and hot water systems in one office building, and the university is awaiting approval of funding to add solar panels that will serve two residence halls. Rainwater harvesting is now taking place on three locations, serving campus gardens, and toilets in three buildings. To reduce energy use in its new buildings, UNC Asheville employed designs that maximize natural light, and also installed occupancy sensors and daylighting controls. UNC Asheville follows the University of Buffalo Green Design Guidelines, with new construction stressing a high-performance building envelope and use of high-recycled-content materials. The university has opted to renovate rather than replace older buildings wherever possible, conserving embedded energy, maximizing reuse and recycling of building materials, and adding energy efficiency design features. The university has designed new buildings and renovation to LEED standards, but has not sought certification. Student Initiatives: In 2012, UNC Ashevilles Student Government Association (SGA) continued the tradition of participation and funding of green projects on and around campus. The SGA voted to recommend that student fees help fund construction of a portion of a new greenway linking campus to downtown. The one-time $10 fee, a student initiative then approved by the university's Board of Trustees, will generate roughly $34,000 for the greenway project, complementing contributions by the university, neighborhood and environmental groups, government and grant funding. Students were also a key part of the preliminary clean-up and land-scaping work done to this point on the greenway land. The universitys Student Environmental Center (SEC) is also supported by a student-initiated green fee that funds sustainable technologies, educational displays and campaigns. SEC projects include participation in the national Flip the Switch campaign in 2012 and the Eco-Reps program which oversees sustainability-related projects in the residence halls. The SEC leads recycling projects such as the FreeStore and campus wide ink-cartridge and battery recycling. The student sustainability fee has also funded the purchase of electric vehicles for use by Campus Parking Enforcement and bikes to enlarge the campus loaner-bike fleet. The green fee has also been used for installation of dual-flush valves throughout campus restrooms and occupancy sensors in office spaces, as well as instituting post-consumer composting in the dining hall. Students have used the fee proceeds to start and maintain a campus garden, and to sponsor environmental films and conferences. Transportation: UNC Asheville opened two electric vehicle charging stations on campus in 2012, continuing its work to encourage more green transportation. The university has reduced petroleum usage by its own fleet by more than 30% since 2005 with use of electric and biodiesel vehicles and reducing overall miles traveled, while still providing regular free shuttle service that allows students living near campus to leave their cars at home. UNC Asheville also encourages mass transit use by funding weekend service to campus by City of Asheville buses, and funds free access to those buses for the campus community. The university has added bike lanes and bike parking while student green fees have funded a larger loaner-bike fleet for students.

ADMISSIONS

Freshman Academic Profile: Average high school GPA 3.98. 21.8% in top 10% of high school class, 53.6% in top 25% of high school class, 90.2% in top 50% of high school class. 87% from public high schools. SAT Math middle 50% range 540-630. SAT Critical Reading middle 50% range 560-660. SAT Writing middle 50% range 530-630. ACT middle 50% range 24-27. Minimum internet-based TOEFL 79. Minimum paper TOEFL 550. **Basis for Candidate Selection:** *Very important factors considered include:* Class rank, academic GPA, rigor of secondary school record. *Important factors considered include:* application essay, recommendation(s), standardized test scores. *Other factors considered include:* alumni/ae relation, extracurricular activities, first generation, geographical residence, interview, level of applicant's interest, racial/ethnic status, state residency, talent/ability, volunteer work, work experience. **Freshman Admission Requirements:** High school diploma is required and GED is not accepted. **Academic units required:** 4 English, 4 mathematics, 3 science, (1 science labs), 2 foreign language, 1 social studies, 1 history. **Freshman Admission Statistics:** 3,173 applied, 69% admitted, 27% enrolled. **Transfer Admission Requirements:** college transcript(s), Minimum college GPA of 2.50 required. Lowest grade transferable C. **General Admission Information:** Application Fee $50. Regular application deadline 2/15. Regular notification 4/1. Nonfall registration accepted. Admission may be deferred for a maximum of One Year. Credit and/or placement offered for CEEB Advanced Placement tests.

COSTS AND FINANCIAL AID

Annual in-state tuition $3,817. Annual out-of-state tuition $18,688. Room and board $8,332. Required fees $2,575. Average book expense $1,200. **Required Forms and Deadlines:** FAFSA. **Notification of Awards:** Applicants will be notified of awards on a rolling basis beginning 3/15. **Types of Aid:** *Need-based scholarships/grants:* Federal Pell, SEOG, state scholarships/grants, private scholarships, the school's own gift aid. *Loans:* Direct Subsidized Stafford, Direct Unsubsidized Stafford, Direct PLUS, Federal Perkins, state loans, college/university loans from institutional funds. *Student Employment:* Federal Work-Study Program available. Institutional employment available. Off-campus job opportunities are good. **Financial Aid Statistics:** 96% freshmen, 90% undergrads receive need-based scholarship or grant aid. 11% freshmen, 12%

undergrads receive non-need-based scholarship or grant aid. 65% freshmen, 73% undergrads receive need-based self-help aid. 5% freshmen, 3% undergrads receive athletic scholarships. 71% freshmen, 72% undergrads receive any aid. 58% undergrads borrow to pay for school. Average cumulative indebtedness $17,554. **Criteria for awarding institutional aid:** *Non-need-based:* academics, alumni affiliation, art, athletics, job skills, leadership, minority status, music/drama, state/district residency.

THE UNIVERSITY OF NORTH CAROLINA AT CHAPEL HILL

Best 380

Chapel Hill, NC
Financial Aid Phone: 919-962-8396 • **CEEB Code:** 5816
Website: www.unc.edu

This public school was founded in 1789. It has a 729-acre campus.

RATINGS

Admissions Selectivity Rating: 96   **Fire Safety Rating:** 93

STUDENTS AND FACULTY

Enrollment: 17,908. **Student Body:** 58% female, 42% male, 17% out-of-state, 2% international (86 countries represented). Asian 9%, African American 8%, Caucasian 65%, Hispanic 7%, Native American 1%
Retention and Graduation: 81% freshmen graduate within 4 years. 90% freshmen graduate within 6 years. 24% grads go on to further study within 1 year. 14% grads pursue arts and sciences degrees. 4% grads pursue law degrees. 1% grads pursue business degrees. 2% grads pursue medical degrees. **Faculty:** 1,814 full-time faculty, 87% hold PhDs, 45% are are members of minority groups, 24% are women. 20.2% of classes are taught by teaching assistants.

ACADEMICS

Degrees: bachelor's, certificate, doctoral, master's, post-bachelor's certificate, post-master's certificate. **Classes:** Most classes have 10-19 students. Most lab/discussion sessions have 10-19 students. **Majors with Highest Enrollment:** Biology/Biological Sciences; Psychology; Economics. **Special Study Options:** cross-registration, distance learning, double major, dual enrollment, honors program, independent study, internships, student-designed major, study abroad, teacher certification program. **Honors programs:** see http://www.honors.unc.edu/. **Disability Services:** Special programs offered to physically disabled students include note-taking services, reader services, tape recorders. **Career services:** Alumni network, alumni services, career/job search classes, career assessment, internships, regional alumni. Career services highlights include the eight networking nights we do each year. For each night we bring in 20-30 professionals deep in one career area that is very difficult to break into for internships and full-time jobs. This gives students multiple opportunities to make contacts that they can follow up with to gain a "foot in the door" in fields/industries where it is hard to find an internship/job.

FACILITIES

Housing: Coed dorms, special housing for disabled students, men's dorms, special housing for international students, women's dorms, fraternity/sorority housing, apartments for married students, apartments for single students, Wellness Housing, Theme Housing, Special Options in Housing—Learning Communities such as RELIC—Religion as Explorative Learning Integrated in our Community, Language Houses, The Carolina Experience, Men@Carolina, W.E.L.L.—Women's Experiences: Learning and Leadership, Connected Learning Program, Service and Leadership, Substance Free Environments, Sustainability, UNITAS. 98% of campus accessible to physically disabled. **Special Academic Facilities/Equipment:** Art museum, Folklore council, Institute of Folk Music, communications center, Basketball Museum, Institute of Latin American Studies, Institute of fisheries research, Sitterson Hall Computer Museum, Institute of Natural Science, Research Laboratory of Anthropology, Hayden Planetarium, Paul Green Theatre, Playmakers Theater, Memorial Hall. **Computers:** 75% of classrooms, 15% of dorms, 100% of libraries, 100% of dining areas, 100% of student union, 50% of common outdoor areas have wireless network access. Students can register for classes online. Administrative functions (other than registration) can be performed online. Undergraduates are required to own a computer.

CAMPUS LIFE

Environment: Town. **Activities:** Choral groups, concert band, dance, drama/theater, jazz band, literary magazine, marching band, music ensembles, musical theater, opera, pep band, radio station, student government, student newspaper, student-run film society, symphony orchestra, television station, yearbook, Campus Ministries, International Student Organization, Model UN. 635 registered organizations, 19 honor societies, 42 religious organizations. 35 fraternities, 23 sororities. **Athletics (Intercollegiate):** *Men:* baseball, basketball, cross-country, diving, fencing, football, golf, lacrosse, soccer, swimming, tennis, track/field (outdoor), track/field (indoor), wrestling. *Women:* basketball, crew/rowing, cross-country, diving, fencing, field hockey, golf, gymnastics, lacrosse, soccer, softball, swimming, tennis, track/field (outdoor), track/field (indoor), volleyball. **On-Campus Highlights:** The Pit, McCorkle Place, Polk Place, Dean Smith Center, Student Union, Old Well, Coker Arboretum, Morehead Planetarium, Ackland Art Museum, Kenan Stadium. **Environmental Initiatives:** Partnered with Orange (County) Water and Sewer Authority (OWASA) to install a water reclamation and reuse system that replaced 175 million gallons of potable water in FY 2013. This system reduces total daily water demand in the OWASA service territory by ~10%. Started in summer 2009, the system provides makeup water at campus cooling towers, irrigates athletic fields and grounds, and flushes toilets in new buildings adjacent to the distribution network. 32 MW Cogeneration Facility, district heating and cooling, and 5 million gallon thermal storage facility. Currently testing biomass fuel sources. Constructed a I MW generator to produce electricity from landfill gas. Real-time, online energy dashboards monitor steam, electricity, and chilled water use in more than 200 campus buildings. Fare Free Transit and Commuter Alternatives Program. More than 7 million free bus rides provided annually. UNC contributes more than $7 million annually to fund Chapel Hill Transit.

ADMISSIONS

Freshman Academic Profile: Average high school GPA 4.59. 78% in top 10% of high school class, 96% in top 25% of high school class, 99% in top 50% of high school class. 82% from public high schools. SAT Math middle 50% range 610-710. SAT Critical Reading middle 50% range 600-690. SAT Writing middle 50% range 590-700. ACT middle 50% range 27-32. Minimum internet-based TOEFL 100. Minimum paper TOEFL 600. **Basis for Candidate Selection:** *Very important factors considered include:* Class rank, application essay, academic GPA, recommendation(s), rigor of secondary school record, standardized test scores, character/personal qualities, extracurricular activities, state residency, talent/ability. *Important factors considered include:* alumni/ae relation, first generation, racial/ethnic status, volunteer work, work experience. **Freshman Admission Requirements:** High school diploma is required and GED is not accepted. **Academic units required:** 4 English, 4 mathematics, 3 science, (1 science labs), 2 foreign language, 1 social studies, 1 history. **Freshman Admission Statistics:** 31,332 applied, 28% admitted, 45% enrolled. **Transfer Admission Requirements:** High school transcript, college transcript(s), essay or personal statement, statement of good standing from prior institution(s). Minimum college GPA of 2.0 required. Lowest grade transferable C. **General Admission Information:** Application Fee $70. Regular application deadline 1/15. Nonfall registration not accepted. Admission may be deferred for a maximum of 1 year. Credit and/or placement offered for CEEB Advanced Placement tests.

COSTS AND FINANCIAL AID

Annual in-state tuition $6,423. Annual out-of-state tuition $31,505. Room and board $10,592. Required fees $1,913. Average book expense $1,484. **Required Forms and Deadlines:** FAFSA, CSS/Financial Aid PROFILE. **Notification of Awards:** Applicants will be notified of awards on a rolling basis beginning 3/15. **Types of Aid:** *Need-based scholarships/grants:* Federal Pell, SEOG, state scholarships/grants, private scholarships, the school's own gift aid, State Grants. *Loans:* Subsidized Stafford, Unsubsidized Stafford, PLUS, Federal Perkins, state loans, college/university loans from institutional funds, Alternative Loans. *Student Employment:* Federal Work-Study Program available. Institutional employment available. Off-campus job opportunities are good. **Financial Aid Statistics:** 93% freshmen, 95% undergrads receive need-based scholarship or grant aid. 8% freshmen, 5% undergrads receive non-need-based scholarship or grant aid. 65% freshmen, 72% undergrads receive need-based self-help aid. 2% freshmen, 2% undergrads receive athletic scholarships. 68% freshmen, 65% undergrads receive any aid. 41% undergrads borrow to pay for school. Average cumulative indebtedness $17,113. **Criteria for awarding institutional aid:** *Non-need-based:* academics, alumni affiliation, art, athletics, leadership, music/drama, religious affiliation, state/district residency.

THE UNIVERSITY OF NORTH CAROLINA
AT CHARLOTTE

9201 University City Boulevard, Charlotte, NC 28223-0001
Phone: 704-687-5507 • **Financial Aid Phone:** 704-687-5504
E-mail: admissions@uncc.edu • **CEEB Code:** 5105
Fax: 704-687-6483 • **Website:** www.uncc.edu/ • **ACT Code:** 3163

This public school was founded in 1946. It has a 1000-acre campus.

RATINGS

Admissions Selectivity Rating: 86   **Fire Safety Rating:** 95

STUDENTS AND FACULTY
Enrollment: 22,120. **Student Body:** 48% female, 52% male, 6% out-of-state, 2% international (59 countries represented). Asian 5%, African American 17%, Caucasian 60%, Hispanic 8%, Native American <1%
Retention and Graduation: 82% freshmen return for sophomore year. 26% freshmen graduate within 4 years. 55% freshmen graduate within 6 years. 20% grads go on to further study within 1 year. **Faculty:** 1,076 full-time faculty, 83% hold PhDs, 45% are are members of minority groups, 18% are women. 2.33% of classes are taught by teaching assistants.

ACADEMICS
Degrees: bachelor's, master's, post-master's certificate. **Classes:** Most classes have 20-29 students. Most lab/discussion sessions have 10-19 students. **Majors with Highest Enrollment:** Social Sciences; Business Administration and Management; Engineering. **Special Study Options:** Accelerated program, cooperative education program, cross-registration, distance learning, double major, dual enrollment, English as a Second Language (ESL), honors program, independent study, internships, study abroad, teacher certification program, weekend college, Wilderness Exploration Program. **Disability Services:** Special programs offered to physically disabled students include note-taking services, reader services, tape recorders, tutors. **Career services:** career/job search classes, career assessment, internships.

FACILITIES
Housing: Coed dorms, special housing for disabled students, special housing for international students, women's dorms, fraternity/sorority housing, apartments for single students, Rooms for students with disabilities limited, apply early. Graduate and older non-traditional student housing and substance free housing available upon request. 95% of campus accessible to physically disabled. **Special Academic Facilities/Equipment:** Urban studies and community service institute, mock court room, applied research center, language lab, 63-acre ecological reserve, botanical and horticultural complex, tropical rainforest conservatory. **Computers:** 10% of classrooms, 10% of dorms, 30% of libraries, 70% of dining areas, 30% of student union, 10% of common outdoor areas have wireless network access. Students can register for classes online. Administrative functions (other than registration) can be performed online.

CAMPUS LIFE
Environment: Metropolis. **Activities:** Choral groups, concert band, dance, drama/theater, jazz band, literary magazine, music ensembles, musical theater, opera, pep band, student government, student newspaper, television station, yearbook, Campus Ministries. 222 registered organizations, 25 honor societies, 22 religious organizations. 14 fraternities, 10 sororities. **Athletics (Intercollegiate):** *Men:* baseball, basketball, cross-country, golf, soccer, tennis, track/field (outdoor). *Women:* basketball, cross-country, soccer, softball, tennis, track/field (outdoor), volleyball. **On-Campus Highlights:** Bonnie E. Cone University Center, James H. Barnhardt Student Activity Center, J. Murrey Atkins Library, UNCC Botanical Gardens and Greenhouse, Ritazza Coffee Shop, After Hours at the Rathskeller, Robinson Hall Theatre. **Environmental Initiatives:** Energy and Water Conservation initiatives led by a full-time Energy Manager. Development of multiple research institutes focused on environmental sustainability. Waste Management initiatives that provide a model for the region.

ADMISSIONS
Freshman Academic Profile: Average high school GPA 3.86. 23% in top 10% of high school class, 56% in top 25% of high school class, 88% in top 50% of high school class. SAT Math middle 50% range 510-600. SAT Critical Reading middle 50% range 490-570. SAT Writing middle 50% range 480-560. ACT middle 50% range 21-25. Minimum internet-based TOEFL 64. Minimum paper TOEFL 507. **Basis for Candidate Selection:** *Very important factors considered include:* academic GPA, rigor of secondary school record, standardized test scores. *Other factors considered include:* character/personal qualities, extracurricular activities, geographical residence, level of applicant's interest, state residency, talent/ability. **Freshman Admission Requirements:** High school diploma is required and GED is accepted. **Academic units required:** 4 English, 4 mathematics, 3 science, (1 science labs), 2 foreign language, 2 social studies. **Freshman Admission Statistics:** 15,610 applied, 64% admitted, 33%

enrolled. **Transfer Admission Requirements:** High school transcript, college transcript(s), statement of good standing from prior institution(s). Minimum college GPA of 2.0 required. Lowest grade transferable C. **General Admission Information:** Application Fee $50. Regular application deadline 7/1. Notification on a rolling basis, beginning on or about 11/1. Nonfall registration accepted. Credit and/or placement offered for CEEB Advanced Placement tests.

COSTS AND FINANCIAL AID
Annual in-state tuition $3,522. Annual out-of-state tuition $16,693. Room and board $4,460. Required fees $2,755. Average book expense $1,200. **Required Forms and Deadlines:** FAFSA. **Notification of Awards:** Applicants will be notified of awards on a rolling basis beginning 3/15. **Types of Aid:** *Need-based scholarships/grants:* Federal Pell, SEOG, state scholarships/grants, private scholarships, the school's own gift aid. *Loans:* Subsidized Stafford, Unsubsidized Stafford, PLUS, Federal Perkins, college/university loans from institutional funds. *Student Employment:* Highest amount earned per year from on-campus jobs $2,000. Off-campus job opportunities are good. **Financial Aid Statistics:** 75% freshmen, 79% undergrads receive need-based scholarship or grant aid. 17% freshmen, 11% undergrads receive non-need-based scholarship or grant aid. 80% freshmen, 80% undergrads receive need-based self-help aid. 0% freshmen, 0% undergrads receive athletic scholarships. 75% freshmen, 72% undergrads receive any aid. 71% undergrads borrow to pay for school. Average cumulative indebtedness $24,009. **Criteria for awarding institutional aid:** *Non-need-based:* academics, athletics, leadership, music/drama.

THE UNIVERSITY OF NORTH CAROLINA
AT GREENSBORO

1400 Spring Garden Street, Greensboro, NC 27402-6170
Phone: 336-334-5243 • **Financial Aid Phone:** 336-334-5702
E-mail: admissions@uncg.edu • **CEEB Code:** 5913
Fax: 336-334-4180 • **Website:** www.uncg.edu • **ACT Code:** 3166

This public school was founded in 1891. It has a 357-acre campus.

RATINGS

Admissions Selectivity Rating: 83   **Fire Safety Rating:** 73

STUDENTS AND FACULTY
Enrollment: 14,497. **Student Body:** 66% female, 34% male, 6% out-of-state, 2% international (12 countries represented). Asian 5%, African American 27%, Caucasian 55%, Hispanic 7%, Native American <1%
Retention and Graduation: 78% freshmen return for sophomore year. 31% freshmen graduate within 4 years. **Faculty:** 754 full-time faculty, 55% are are members of minority groups, 21% are women.

ACADEMICS
Degrees: bachelor's, master's, post-bachelor's certificate, post-master's certificate. **Classes:** Most classes have 20-29 students. Most lab/discussion sessions have 20-29 students. **Majors with Highest Enrollment:** Business Administration and Management; Biology/Biological Sciences. **Special Study Options:** Accelerated program, cross-registration, distance learning, double major, dual enrollment, honors program, independent study, internships, study abroad, teacher certification program, Evening University. **Combined degree programs:** BA/MA, Accounting, Mathematics, Chem, various BA and MBA. **Disability Services:** Special programs offered to physically disabled students include note-taking services, reader services, tape recorders, tutors. **Career services:** alumni services, career/job search classes, career assessment, internships.

FACILITIES
Housing: Coed dorms, special housing for international students, women's dorms, apartments for single students **Special Academic Facilities/Equipment:** 42-acre recreational site, art gallery, 45,000 sq.ft. Student Center, New Music Building, New Science Building. **Computers:** 90% of dorms, 35% of libraries, have wireless network access. Students can register for classes online. Administrative functions (other than registration) can be performed online.

CAMPUS LIFE
Environment: City. **Activities:** Choral groups, concert band, dance, drama/theater, jazz band, literary magazine, music ensembles, musical theater, opera, pep band, radio station, student government, student newspaper, student-run

film society, symphony orchestra, International Student Organization. 200 registered organizations, 23 honor societies, 13 religious organizations. 11 fraternities, 11 sororities. **Athletics (Intercollegiate): Men:** baseball, basketball, cross-country, golf, soccer, tennis, wrestling. *Women:* basketball, cross-country, golf, soccer, softball, tennis, volleyball. **On-Campus Highlights:** Elliott University Center, Student Rec Center, Weatherspoon Art Museum, Peabody Park, UNCG Theatre.

ADMISSIONS

Freshman Academic Profile: Average high school GPA 3.66. 16% in top 10% of high school class, 43% in top 25% of high school class, 82% in top 50% of high school class. 95% from public high schools. SAT Math middle 50% range 470-550. SAT Critical Reading middle 50% range 470-550. SAT Writing middle 50% range 440-530. ACT middle 50% range 19-24. Minimum internet-based TOEFL 79. Minimum paper TOEFL 550. **Basis for Candidate Selection:** *Very important factors considered include:* academic GPA, rigor of secondary school record. *Important factors considered include:* standardized test scores. *Other factors considered include:* recommendation(s). **Freshman Admission Requirements:** High school diploma is required and GED is not accepted. **Academic units required:** 4 English, 4 mathematics, 3 science, (1 science labs), 2 foreign language, 2 social studies. **Freshman Admission Statistics:** 9,852 applied, 60% admitted, 41% enrolled. **Transfer Admission Requirements:** High school transcript, college transcript(s), standardized test scores, statement of good standing from prior institution(s). Minimum college GPA of 2.0 required. Lowest grade transferable 2. **General Admission Information:** Application Fee $45. Regular application deadline 3/1. Notification on a rolling basis, beginning on or about 12/15. Nonfall registration accepted. Admission may be deferred for a maximum of 1 semester. Credit and/or placement offered for CEEB Advanced Placement tests.

COSTS AND FINANCIAL AID

Annual in-state tuition $3,932. Annual out-of-state tuition $18,794. Room and board $7,688. Required fees $2,453. Average book expense $1,300. **Required Forms and Deadlines:** FAFSA. **Notification of Awards:** Applicants will be notified of awards on a rolling basis beginning 3/15. **Types of Aid:** *Need-based scholarships/grants:* Federal Pell, SEOG, state scholarships/grants, private scholarships, the school's own gift aid. *Loans:* Direct Subsidized Stafford, Direct Unsubsidized Stafford, Direct PLUS, Subsidized Stafford, Unsubsidized Stafford, PLUS, Federal Perkins, college/university loans from institutional funds. *Student Employment:* Federal Work-Study Program available. Institutional employment available. Off-campus job opportunities are good. **Financial Aid Statistics:** 89% freshmen, 81% undergrads receive need-based scholarship or grant aid. 74% freshmen, 60% undergrads receive non-need-based scholarship or grant aid. 79% freshmen, 79% undergrads receive need-based self-help aid. 1% freshmen, 1% undergrads receive athletic scholarships. 90% freshmen, 82% undergrads receive any aid. 88% undergrads borrow to pay for school. Average cumulative indebtedness $24,408. **Criteria for awarding institutional aid:** *Non-need-based:* academics, alumni affiliation, art, athletics, music/drama, state/district residency.

THE UNIVERSITY OF NORTH CAROLINA AT PEMBROKE

One University Drive, Pembroke, NC 28372
Phone: 910-521-6262 · **Financial Aid Phone:** 910-521-6255
E-mail: admissions@uncp.edu · **CEEB Code:** 5534
Fax: 910-521-6497 · **Website:** www.uncp.edu · **ACT Code:** 3138

This public school was founded in 1887. It has a 161-acre campus.

RATINGS

Admissions Selectivity Rating: 71   **Fire Safety Rating:** 96

STUDENTS AND FACULTY

Enrollment: 5,303. **Student Body:** 60% female, 40% male, 4% out-of-state, 1% international (18 countries represented). Asian 2%, African American 36%, Caucasian 38%, Hispanic 5%, Native American 15%
Retention and Graduation: 68% freshmen return for sophomore year. 15% freshmen graduate within 4 years. **Faculty:** 320 full-time faculty, 69% hold PhDs, 48% are are members of minority groups, 23% are women. 0% of classes are taught by teaching assistants.

ACADEMICS

Degrees: bachelor's, certificate, master's. **Classes:** Most classes have 20-29 students. Most lab/discussion sessions have fewer than 10 students. **Majors with Highest Enrollment:** Business Administration and Management; Biology/Biological Sciences; Criminal Justice/Safety Studies. **Special Study Options:** Accelerated program, cooperative education program, cross-registration,

distance learning, double major, dual enrollment, English as a Second Language (ESL), exchange student program (domestic), external degree program, honors program, independent study, internships, study abroad, teacher certification program. **Honors programs:** The Esther G. Maynor Honors College began in 2001 to attract top scholars to UNCP, and provide an environment that stimulates academic and personal growth. **Combined degree programs:** BA/MA. **Disability Services:** Special programs offered to physically disabled students include note-taking services, reader services, tape recorders, tutors. **Career services:** Alumni network, alumni services, career/job search classes, career assessment, internships. Career services highlights include the opportunities for experiential learning/internships that we offer. This is something we believe is very important and we encourage students to seek out these opportunities.

FACILITIES

Housing: Coed dorms, special housing for disabled students, men's dorms, women's dorms, apartments for single students. 99% of campus accessible to physically disabled. **Special Academic Facilities/Equipment:** Native American Resources Center and Museum **Computers:** 100% of classrooms, 50% of dorms, 100% of libraries, 100% of dining areas, 100% of student union, 30% of common outdoor areas have wireless network access. Students can register for classes online. Administrative functions (other than registration) can be performed online. Undergraduates are required to own a computer.

CAMPUS LIFE

Environment: Rural. **Activities:** Choral groups, concert band, dance, drama/theater, jazz band, literary magazine, marching band, music ensembles, musical theater, pep band, student government, student newspaper, student-run film society, television station, yearbook, Campus Ministries, International Student Organization, Model UN. 70 registered organizations, 11 honor societies, 5 religious organizations. 10 fraternities, 11 sororities. **Athletics (Intercollegiate): Men:** baseball, basketball, cheerleading, cross-country, football, golf, soccer, track/field (outdoor), wrestling. *Women:* basketball, cheerleading, cross-country, golf, soccer, softball, tennis, track/field (outdoor), volleyball. **On-Campus Highlights:** Newly renovated athletic facility, Native American Resource Center/Museum, Givens Performing Arts Center, Newly renovated Bookstore, Higher Ground Ropes Course. **Environmental Initiatives:** Planning & Construction Dept. mandates all new facilities to be LEED certified. Campus wide single-stream recycling program. Housekeeping staff utilize "green" cleaning products.

ADMISSIONS

Freshman Academic Profile: Average high school GPA 3.38. 1% in top 10% of high school class, 5% in top 25% of high school class, 28% in top 50% of high school class. 95% from public high schools. SAT Math middle 50% range 510-430. SAT Critical Reading middle 50% range 500-420. SAT Writing middle 50% range 470-390. ACT middle 50% range 17-21. Minimum internet-based TOEFL 68. Minimum paper TOEFL 520. **Basis for Candidate Selection:** *Very important factors considered include:* Class rank, academic GPA, rigor of secondary school record, standardized test scores. *Other factors considered include:* application essay, recommendation(s), character/personal qualities, interview, talent/ability. **Freshman Admission Requirements:** High school diploma is required and GED is accepted. **Academic units required:** 4 English, 4 mathematics, 3 science, (1 science labs), 2 foreign language, 1 social studies, 1 history. **Freshman Admission Statistics:** 4,035 applied, 73% admitted, 36% enrolled. **Transfer Admission Requirements:** High school transcript, college transcript(s), statement of good standing from prior institution(s). Minimum college GPA of 2.0 required. Lowest grade transferable C. **General Admission Information:** Application Fee $40. Regular application deadline 7/31. Notification on a rolling basis, beginning on or about 9/15. Nonfall registration accepted. Admission may be deferred for a maximum of 1 year. Credit offered for CEEB Advanced Placement tests.

COSTS AND FINANCIAL AID

Annual in-state tuition $3,211. Annual out-of-state tuition $13,162. Room and board $8,101. Required fees $2,076. Average book expense $1,440. **Required Forms and Deadlines:** FAFSA. **Notification of Awards:** Applicants will be notified of awards on a rolling basis beginning 4/15. **Types of Aid:** *Need-based scholarships/grants:* Federal Pell, SEOG, state scholarships/grants, private scholarships, the school's own gift aid. *Loans:* Subsidized Stafford, Unsubsidized Stafford, PLUS, Federal Perkins, college/university loans from institutional funds. *Student Employment:* Federal Work-Study Program available. Off-campus job opportunities are fair. **Financial Aid Statistics:** 84% freshmen, 83% undergrads receive need-based scholarship or grant aid. 17% freshmen, 15% undergrads receive non-need-based scholarship or grant aid. 84% freshmen, 84% undergrads receive need-based self-help aid. 2% freshmen, 1% undergrads receive athletic scholarships. 79% freshmen, 75% undergrads receive any aid. 81% undergrads borrow to pay for school. Average cumulative indebtedness $22,847. **Criteria for awarding institutional aid:** *Non-need-based:* academics, alumni affiliation, art, athletics, music/drama, state/district residency.

THE UNIVERSITY OF NORTH CAROLINA AT WILMINGTON

601 South College Rd, Wilmington, NC 28403-5904
Phone: 910-962-3243 · **Financial Aid Phone:** 910-962-3177
E-mail: admissions@uncw.edu · **CEEB Code:** 5907
Fax: 910-962-3038 · **Website:** www.uncw.edu · **ACT Code:** 3174

This public school was founded in 1947. It has a 656-acre campus.

RATINGS

Admissions Selectivity Rating: 88   **Fire Safety Rating:** 91

STUDENTS AND FACULTY

Enrollment: 12,178. **Student Body:** 60% female, 40% male, 14% out-of-state, 1% international (62 countries represented). Asian 2%, African American 5%, Caucasian 80%, Hispanic 6%, Native American <1%. **Retention and Graduation:** 52% freshmen graduate within 4 years. 71% freshmen graduate within 6 years. **Faculty:** 641 full-time faculty, 91% hold PhDs, 48% are are members of minority groups, 19% are women.

ACADEMICS

Degrees: bachelor's, certificate, master's, post-bachelor's certificate, post-master's certificate. **Classes:** Most classes have 20-29 students. Most lab/discussion sessions have 20-29 students. **Majors with Highest Enrollment:** Business/Managerial Economics; Elementary Education and Teaching; Psychology. **Special Study Options:** Accelerated program, cooperative education program, cross-registration, distance learning, double major, dual enrollment, English as a Second Language (ESL), exchange student program (domestic), honors program, independent study, internships, study abroad, teacher certification program, 2+2 Pre-Engineering Program. **Honors programs:** The Honors Scholars Program at UNCW is designed to offer academically talented students challenging and exciting experiences both in and out of the classroom. A student may begin with general honors in the first two years, and then go on to departmental honors in their major. In their freshman and sophomore years, students take special interdisciplinary honors seminars and honors sections of basic studies courses. Honors classes are small—generally not over 20 students to encourage discussion and faculty-student interaction. **Disability Services:** Special programs offered to physically disabled students include note-taking services, reader services, tape recorders, tutors. **Career services:** Alumni network, alumni services, career assessment, internships, regional alumni. Career services highlights include The UNCW Virtual Career Center, which is nationally recognized for it's comprehensive website.

FACILITIES

Housing: Coed dorms, special housing for international students, women's dorms, apartments for single students, Wellness Housing, Theme Housing. 95% of campus accessible to physically diasbled. **Special Academic Facilities/Equipment:** Upperman African American Cultural Arts Center, N.C. Teachers Legacy Hall, Ev-Henwood Nature Preserve, Center for Marine Science at Myrtle Grove, Almkuist-Nixon Sports Medicine Building, Museum of World Cultures, Claude Howell Gallery, UNCW Library Archives and Special Collections. **Computers:** 100% of classrooms, 100% of dorms, 100% of libraries, 100% of dining areas, 100% of student union, 50% of common outdoor areas have wireless network access. Students can register for classes online. Administrative functions (other than registration) can be performed online.

CAMPUS LIFE

Environment: City. **Activities:** Choral groups, concert band, dance, drama/theater, jazz band, literary magazine, music ensembles, pep band, radio station, student government, student newspaper, student-run film society, symphony orchestra, television station, Campus Ministries, International Student Organization, Model UN. 173 registered organizations, 8 honor societies, 14 religious organizations. 11 fraternities, 11 sororities. **Athletics (Intercollegiate):** *Men:* baseball, basketball, cheerleading, cross-country, diving, golf, soccer, swimming, tennis, track/field (outdoor). *Women:* basketball, cheerleading, cross-country, diving, golf, soccer, softball, swimming, tennis, track/field (outdoor), volleyball. **On-Campus Highlights:** Fisher Student Center, William Randall Library, UNCW Student Recreation Center, Trask Coliseum, Cultural Arts Building. **Environmental Initiatives:** All vegetable oil in Hawk's Nest is recycled as bio-diesel. Trayless dining and recyclable to-go containers at campus dining facilities. UNCW Carpool Program LEED certification for new housing and parking development. Current residence halls going green with students turning in regular lightbulbs for energy efficient ones and conserving water. Dining services—using biopak containers, going trayless, offering free trade coffee, using reusable clean cloths.

ADMISSIONS

Freshman Academic Profile: Average high school GPA 4.06. 26.6% in top 10% of high school class, 65.4% in top 25% of high school class, 96% in top 50% of high school class. % from public high schools. SAT Math middle 50% range 560-640. SAT Critical Reading middle 50% range 550-630. SAT Writing middle 50% range 530-620. ACT middle 50% range 23-27. Minimum internet-based TOEFL 71. Minimum paper TOEFL 525. **Basis for Candidate Selection:** *Very important factors considered include:* application essay, academic GPA, recommendation(s), rigor of secondary school record, standardized test scores. *Important factors considered include:* Class rank. *Other factors considered include:* alumni/ae relation, character/personal qualities, extracurricular activities, first generation, geographical residence, level of applicant's interest, racial/ethnic status, state residency, talent/ability, volunteer work, work experience. **Freshman Admission Requirements:** High school diploma is required and GED is accepted. **Academic units required:** 4 English, 4 mathematics, 3 science, (1 science labs), 2 foreign language, 2 social studies, 1 history. **Freshman Admission Statistics:** 10,838 applied, 57% admitted, 31% enrolled. **Transfer Admission Requirements:** High school transcript, college transcript(s), essay or personal statement, Minimum college GPA of 2.5 required. Lowest grade transferable C. **General Admission Information:** Application Fee $60. Regular application deadline 2/1. Regular notification 4/1. Nonfall registration accepted. Admission may be deferred for a maximum of 1 year. Credit and/or placement offered for CEEB Advanced Placement tests.

COSTS AND FINANCIAL AID

Annual in-state tuition $4,026. Annual out-of-state tuition $16,163. Room and board $8,624. Required fees $2,317. Average book expense $1,030. **Required Forms and Deadlines:** FAFSA. **Notification of Awards:** Applicants will be notified of awards on a rolling basis beginning 4/1. **Types of Aid:** *Need-based scholarships/grants:* Federal Pell, SEOG, state scholarships/grants, private scholarships, the school's own gift aid. *Loans:* Direct Subsidized Stafford, Direct Unsubsidized Stafford, Direct PLUS, Subsidized Stafford, Unsubsidized Stafford, PLUS, Federal Perkins, state loans, college/university loans from institutional funds. *Student Employment:* Federal Work-Study Program available. Institutional employment available. Off-campus job opportunities are good. **Financial Aid Statistics:** 88% freshmen, 87% undergrads receive need-based scholarship or grant aid. 19% freshmen, 12% undergrads receive non-need-based scholarship or grant aid. 96% freshmen, 97% undergrads receive need-based self-help aid. 3% freshmen, 1% undergrads receive athletic scholarships. 73% freshmen, 73% undergrads receive any aid. 57% undergrads borrow to pay for school. Average cumulative indebtedness $21,901. **Criteria for awarding institutional aid:** *Non-need-based:* academics, alumni affiliation, art, athletics, leadership, music/drama, state/district residency.

THE UNIVERSITY OF NORTH DAKOTA

3501 University Avenue Stop 8357, Grand Forks, ND 58202
Phone: 701-777-3000 · **Financial Aid Phone:** 701-777-3121
E-mail: UND.admissions@UND.edu · **CEEB Code:** 6878
Fax: 701-777-2721 · **Website:** UND.edu/admissions/undergraduate · **ACT Code:** 3218

This public school was founded in 1883. It has a 549-acre campus.

RATINGS

Admissions Selectivity Rating: 79   **Fire Safety Rating:** 79

STUDENTS AND FACULTY

Enrollment: 10,979. **Student Body:** 43% female, 57% male, 60% out-of-state, 5% international (84 countries represented). Asian 1%, African American 2%, Caucasian 82%, Hispanic 3%, Native American 2%. **Retention and Graduation:** 80% freshmen return for sophomore year. 13% grads go on to further study within 1 year. 1% grads pursue law degrees. 2% grads pursue medical degrees. **Faculty:** 701 full-time faculty, 75% hold PhDs, 43% are are members of minority groups, 7% are women.

ACADEMICS

Degrees: bachelor's, certificate, diploma, master's, post-bachelor's certificate. **Classes:** Most classes have 20-29 students. Most lab/discussion sessions have fewer than 10 students. **Majors with Highest Enrollment:** General Studies; Registered Nursing/Registered Nurse; Psychology. **Special Study Options:** Accelerated program, cooperative education program, cross-registration, distance learning, double major, dual enrollment, English as a Second Language (ESL), exchange student program (domestic), external degree program, honors program, independent study, internships, liberal arts/career combination, student-designed major, study abroad, teacher certification program, weekend college. **Honors programs:** Students may participate in the Honors

Program throughout their undergraduate career. Students in any college of the University may enroll in the Honors Program. Most students graduate from the Program as "Scholars in the Honors Program" while also fulfilling a major in the Colleges, but the Honors Program also offers the option of creating an individually designed program of study through Honors. This option may result in either a B.A. or a B.S. degree earned through the College of Arts and Sciences. **Combined degree programs:** http://www.und.edu/dept/registrar/catalogs/catalog. **Disability Services:** Special programs offered to physically disabled students include note-taking services, reader services, tape recorders. **Career services:** Alumni network, alumni services, career/job search classes, career assessment, internships. Career services highlights include Cooperative Learning, Internships, and the opportunity for students to work closely with entrepreneur practitioners.

FACILITIES

Housing: Coed dorms, special housing for disabled students, men's dorms, women's dorms, fraternity/sorority housing, apartments for married students, apartments for single students, Wellness Housing, Theme Housing. 99% of campus accessible to physically disabled. **Special Academic Facilities/Equipment:** Hughes Fine Arts Center, Burtness Theatre, North Dakota Museum of Art, Chester Fritz Auditorium, mining/mineral resources research institute/energy research center, remote sensing institute, aviation facilities, meteorology data center, Ralph Engelstad Arena. **Computers:** 70% of classrooms, 100% of dorms, 100% of libraries, 50% of dining areas, 100% of student union, have wireless network access. Students can register for classes online. Administrative functions (other than registration) can be performed online.

CAMPUS LIFE

Environment: Town. **Activities:** Choral groups, concert band, dance, drama/theater, jazz band, literary magazine, marching band, music ensembles, musical theater, opera, pep band, radio station, student government, student newspaper, student-run film society, symphony orchestra, television station, Campus Ministries, International Student Organization. 230 registered organizations, 42 honor societies, 3 religious organizations. 13 fraternities, 7 sororities. **Athletics (Intercollegiate):** *Men:* baseball, basketball, cross-country, diving, football, golf, ice hockey, swimming, track/field (outdoor), track/field (indoor). *Women:* basketball, cross-country, diving, golf, ice hockey, soccer, softball, swimming, tennis, track/field (outdoor), track/field (indoor), volleyball. **On-Campus Highlights:** Engelstad Arena, Memorial Union, Archives Coffee shop, International Centre, North Dakota Museum of Art. **Environmental Initiatives:** Energy Conservation Programs; Presidential Climate Committment; Recycling.

ADMISSIONS

Freshman Academic Profile: Average high school GPA 3.4. 17% in top 10% of high school class, 39% in top 25% of high school class, 36% in top 50% of high school class. 92% from public high schools. ACT middle 50% range 21-26. Minimum internet-based TOEFL 76. Minimum paper TOEFL 550. **Basis for Candidate Selection:** *Very important factors considered include:* academic GPA, standardized test scores. *Other factors considered include:* Class rank, rigor of secondary school record. **Freshman Admission Requirements:** High school diploma is required and GED is accepted. **Academic units required:** 4 English, 3 mathematics, 3 science, (3 science labs), 3 social studies. **Freshman Admission Statistics:** 4,642 applied, 86% admitted, 48% enrolled. **Transfer Admission Requirements:** college transcript(s), Minimum college GPA of 2.0 required. **General Admission Information:** Application Fee $35. Notification on a rolling basis, beginning on or about 9/1. Nonfall registration accepted. Admission may be deferred for a maximum of 1 Semester. Credit and/or placement offered for CEEB Advanced Placement tests.

COSTS AND FINANCIAL AID

Annual out-of-state tuition $17,056. Room and board $6,810. Required fees $1,353. Average book expense $1,000. **Notification of Awards:** Applicants will be notified of awards on a rolling basis beginning 5/15. **Types of Aid:** *Need-based scholarships/grants:* Federal Pell, SEOG, state scholarships/grants, private scholarships, the school's own gift aid, Federal Nursing Scholarships. *Loans:* Subsidized Stafford, Unsubsidized Stafford, PLUS, Federal Perkins, Federal Nursing, Alternative Commercial *Student Employment:* Federal Work-Study Program available. Institutional employment available. Highest amount earned per year from on-campus jobs $2,071. Off-campus job opportunities are excellent. **Criteria for awarding institutional aid:** *Non-need-based:* academics, alumni affiliation, art, athletics, job skills, leadership, music/drama, religious affiliation.

UNIVERSITY OF NORTH FLORIDA

1 UNF Drive, Jacksonville, FL 32224-7699
Phone: 904-620-5555 • **Financial Aid Phone:** 904-620-2698
E-mail: admissions@unf.edu • **CEEB Code:** 9841
Fax: 904-620-2414 • **Website:** www.unf.edu • **ACT Code:** 5490

This public school was founded in 1965. It has a 1300-acre campus.

RATINGS

Admissions Selectivity Rating: 88   Fire Safety Rating: 72

STUDENTS AND FACULTY

Enrollment: 14,124. **Student Body:** 56% female, 44% male, 2% out-of-state, 1% international (116 countries represented). Asian 4%, African American 10%, Caucasian 71%, Hispanic 9%, Native American <1%
Retention and Graduation: 20% freshmen graduate within 4 years. 48% freshmen graduate within 6 years. **Faculty:** 539 full-time faculty, 80% hold PhDs, 45% are are members of minority groups, 12% are women. 0% of classes are taught by teaching assistants.

ACADEMICS

Degrees: associate, bachelor's, master's, post-bachelor's certificate, post-master's certificate, terminal associate, transfer associate. **Classes:** Most classes have 20-29 students. Most lab/discussion sessions have 20-29 students. **Majors with Highest Enrollment:** Mass Communication/Media Studies; Psychology; Business Administration and Management. **Special Study Options:** Accelerated program, cooperative education program, distance learning, double major, dual enrollment, English as a Second Language (ESL), exchange student program (domestic), honors program, independent study, internships, student-designed major, study abroad, teacher certification program, weekend college, Learning Communities. **Honors programs:** The Honors Program at the University of North Florida offers talented and ambitious students a unique approach to higher education. Honors Classes are limited to 20 students, combining active and experiential learning in an interdisciplinary setting. The goal is to build a community of learners who have the ability to take their learning outside the classroom and into the real world helping to bridge the gap between education and experience. The honors program is a limited access program and spaces are filled on a first-come-first-serve basis. **Disability Services:** Special programs offered to physically disabled students include note-taking services, reader services, tape recorders. **Career services:** alumni services, career/job search classes, internships.

FACILITIES

Housing: Coed dorms, special housing for disabled students, apartments for single students, Suite style housing. **Special Academic Facilities/Equipment:** Art gallery, bird sanctuary, Fine Arts Center. **Computers:** 100% of classrooms, 50% of dorms, 100% of libraries, 50% of dining areas, 100% of student union, 100% of common outdoor areas have wireless network access. Students can register for classes online. Administrative functions (other than registration) can be performed online.

CAMPUS LIFE

Environment: Metropolis. **Activities:** Choral groups, concert band, dance, drama/theater, jazz band, literary magazine, music ensembles, pep band, radio station, student government, student newspaper, television station, Campus Ministries, International Student Organization. 140 registered organizations, 8 honor societies, 29 religious organizations. 14 fraternities, 10 sororities. **Athletics (Intercollegiate):** *Men:* baseball, basketball, cheerleading, cross-country, golf, soccer, tennis, track/field (outdoor), track/field (indoor). *Women:* basketball, cheerleading, cross-country, diving, soccer, softball, swimming, tennis, track/field (outdoor), track/field (indoor), volleyball. **On-Campus Highlights:** Student Union, Bookstore, Art Gallery, Nature Trails, Campus skate park, Greek Affairs, Earth Music Festival, Athletics NCAA I, Free movies on Campus, Jazz Program (nationally recognized), Division I sports. **Environmental Initiatives:** Requiring LEED Silver or comparable compliance; Establishing sustainability committee and programs through Environmental Center, including Recyclemania and Garbage on the Green; A three-hundred acre natural area on campus was designated as a preserve in May 2006 by UNF President John Delaney.

ADMISSIONS

Freshman Academic Profile: Average high school GPA 3.72. 24% in top 10% of high school class, 56% in top 25% of high school class, 87% in top 50% of high school class. SAT Math middle 50% range 540-620. SAT Critical Reading middle 50% range 530-620. ACT middle 50% range 23-26. Minimum internet-based TOEFL 61. Minimum paper TOEFL 500. **Basis for Candidate Selection:** *Very important factors considered include:* academic GPA, rigor of secondary school record, standardized test scores. *Other factors considered include:* Class rank, application essay, recommendation(s), extracurricular activities, level of applicant's interest, talent/ability, volunteer work, work experience.

Freshman Admission Requirements: High school diploma is required and GED is accepted. **Academic units required:** 4 English, 3 mathematics, 3 science, (1 science labs), 2 foreign language, 3 social studies, 4 academic electives. **Freshman Admission Statistics:** 10,412 applied, 52% admitted, 30% enrolled. **Transfer Admission Requirements:** college transcript(s), Minimum college GPA of 2.0 required. Lowest grade transferable D. **General Admission Information:** Application Fee $30. Regular application deadline 6/11. Regular notification 12/11. Notification on a rolling basis, beginning on or about 11/13. Nonfall registration accepted. Admission may be deferred for a maximum of 2 Semesters. Credit offered for CEEB Advanced Placement tests.

COSTS AND FINANCIAL AID
Annual in-state tuition $4,281. Annual out-of-state tuition $17,999. Room and board $9,165. Required fees $2,072. Average book expense $1,200. **Required Forms and Deadlines:** FAFSA. **Notification of Awards:** Applicants will be notified of awards on a rolling basis beginning 3/15. **Types of Aid:** *Need-based scholarships/grants:* Federal Pell, SEOG, state scholarships/grants, private scholarships, the school's own gift aid, 2-2 Scholarships jointly sponsored with Florida Community College at Jacksonville. *Loans:* Subsidized Stafford, Unsubsidized Stafford, PLUS, Federal Perkins. *Student Employment:* Federal Work-Study Program available. Institutional employment available. Highest amount earned per year from on-campus jobs $3,750. Off-campus job opportunities are good. **Financial Aid Statistics:** 56% freshmen, 59% undergrads receive need-based scholarship or grant aid. 88% freshmen, 52% undergrads receive non-need-based scholarship or grant aid. 47% freshmen, 54% undergrads receive need-based self-help aid. 3% freshmen, 2% undergrads receive athletic scholarships. 93% freshmen, 77% undergrads receive any aid. 42% undergrads borrow to pay for school. Average cumulative indebtedness $16,268. **Criteria for awarding institutional aid:** *Non-need-based:* academics, athletics, leadership, minority status, music/drama, state/district residency.

UNIVERSITY OF NORTH GEORGIA

Office of Undergraduate Admissions, Dahlonega, GA 30597
Phone: 706-864-1800 · **Financial Aid Phone:** 706-864-1412
E-mail: admissions@ung.edu · **CEEB Code:** 5497
Fax: 706-864-1478 · **Website:** www.ung.edu · **ACT Code:** 848

This public school was founded in 1873. It has a 120-acre campus.

RATINGS
Admissions Selectivity Rating: 83   **Fire Safety Rating:** 92

STUDENTS AND FACULTY
Enrollment: 14,977. **Student Body:** 55% female, 45% male, 3% out-of-state, 1% international (94 countries represented). Asian 3%, African American 4%, Caucasian 78%, Hispanic 9%, Native American <1%
Retention and Graduation: 26% freshmen graduate within 4 years. 52% freshmen graduate within 6 years. **Faculty:** 507 full-time faculty, 78% hold PhDs, 50% are are members of minority groups, 19% are women. 0% of classes are taught by teaching assistants.

ACADEMICS
Degrees: associate, bachelor's, certificate, master's, post-bachelor's certificate, post-master's certificate. **Classes:** Most classes have 20-29 students. Most lab/discussion sessions have fewer than 10 students. **Majors with Highest Enrollment:** Biology/Biological Sciences; Business Administration and Management; Registered Nursing/Registered Nurse. **Special Study Options:** cooperative education program, distance learning, double major, dual enrollment, external degree program, honors program, independent study, internships, study abroad, teacher certification program, Dual degree in Engineering with GA Institute of Technology and Clemson University. **Disability Services:** Special programs offered to physically disabled students include note-taking services, reader services, tape recorders, tutors.

FACILITIES
Housing: Coed dorms, men's dorms, women's dorms, apartments for single students. 90% of campus accessible to physically disabled. **Special Academic Facilities/Equipment:** Planetarium; 2 Art galleries; Hall of fame; NGCSU museum. **Computers:** Students can register for classes online. Administrative functions (other than registration) can be performed online.

CAMPUS LIFE
Environment: Rural. **Activities:** Choral groups, drama/theater, jazz band, literary magazine, marching band, music ensembles, pep band, student government, student newspaper, symphony orchestra, yearbook. 60 registered organizations, 8 honor societies, 5 religious organizations. 6 fraternities, 4 sororities. **Athletics (Intercollegiate):** *Men:* baseball, basketball, cross-country,

football, golf, riflery, soccer, table tennis, tennis, track/field (outdoor), volleyball, water polo. *Women:* basketball, cheerleading, cross-country, golf, riflery, soccer, softball, table tennis, tennis, track/field (outdoor), volleyball, water polo.
On-Campus Highlights: Canteen, Commuter Lounge, Game Room, Uniform Store, Lounge Areas.

ADMISSIONS
Freshman Academic Profile: Average high school GPA 3.25. SAT Math middle 50% range 500-600. SAT Critical Reading middle 50% range 510-600. SAT Writing middle 50% range 480-570. ACT middle 50% range 22-26. Minimum paper TOEFL 550. **Basis for Candidate Selection:** *Very important factors considered include:* rigor of secondary school record, standardized test scores. *Other factors considered include:* Class rank, recommendation(s), alumni/ae relation, character/personal qualities, extracurricular activities, talent/ability, volunteer work, work experience. **Freshman Admission Requirements:** High school diploma is required and GED is accepted. **Academic units required:** 4 English, 4 mathematics, 3 science, (1 science labs), 2 foreign language, 3 social studies, 0 history, 0 academic electives. **Freshman Admission Statistics:** 4,904 applied, 65% admitted, 47% enrolled. **Transfer Admission Requirements:** college transcript(s), statement of good standing from prior institution(s). Minimum college GPA of 2.0 required. Lowest grade transferable C. **General Admission Information:** Application Fee $25. Regular application deadline 7/1. Nonfall registration accepted. Credit offered for CEEB Advanced Placement tests.

COSTS AND FINANCIAL AID
Average book expense $1,390. **Required Forms and Deadlines:** FAFSA. **Notification of Awards:** Applicants will be notified of awards on a rolling basis beginning 5/15. **Types of Aid:** *Need-based scholarships/grants:* Federal Pell, SEOG, state scholarships/grants, private scholarships, the school's own gift aid. *Loans:* Subsidized Stafford, Unsubsidized Stafford, PLUS, Federal Perkins, state loans, college/university loans from institutional funds. **Financial Aid Statistics:** 59% freshmen, 58% undergrads receive need-based scholarship or grant aid. 68% undergrads receive non-need-based scholarship or grant aid. 84% freshmen, 91% undergrads receive need-based self-help aid. 2% freshmen, 2% undergrads receive athletic scholarships. 51% undergrads borrow to pay for school. Average cumulative indebtedness $11,995. **Criteria for awarding institutional aid:** *Non-need-based:* academics, alumni affiliation, art, athletics, leadership, music/drama, state/district residency.

UNIVERSITY OF NORTH TEXAS

1155 Union Circle #311277, Denton, TX 76203-5017
Phone: 940-565-2681 · **Financial Aid Phone:** 940-565-3901
E-mail: undergrad@unt.edu · **CEEB Code:** 6481
Fax: 940-565-2408 · **Website:** www.unt.edu · **ACT Code:** 4136

This public school was founded in 1890. It has a 850-acre campus.

RATINGS
Admissions Selectivity Rating: 83   **Fire Safety Rating:** 89

STUDENTS AND FACULTY
Enrollment: 29,481. **Student Body:** 52% female, 48% male, 4% out-of-state, 3% international (164 countries represented). Asian 6%, African American 13%, Caucasian 53%, Hispanic 20%, Native American 1%
Retention and Graduation: 23% freshmen graduate within 4 years. **Faculty:** 963 full-time faculty, 81% hold PhDs, 40% are are members of minority groups, 30% are women. 11% of classes are taught by teaching assistants.

ACADEMICS
Degrees: bachelor's, master's, post-bachelor's certificate. **Classes:** Most classes have 20-29 students. Most lab/discussion sessions have 20-29 students. **Majors with Highest Enrollment:** Business/Commerce; Multi-/Interdisciplinary Studies; Biology/Biological Sciences. **Special Study Options:** Accelerated program, cooperative education program, cross-registration, distance learning, double major, dual enrollment, English as a Second Language (ESL), honors program, independent study, internships, study abroad, teacher certification program, weekend college. **Honors programs:** University of North Texas Honors College **Combined degree programs:** BA/MD, BA/JD, BA/MA, BA/DDS, BA/MEng. **Disability Services:** Special programs offered to physically disabled students include note-taking services, reader services, tape recorders, tutors. **Career services:** Alumni network, alumni services, career/job search classes, career assessment, internships, regional alumni. Career services highlights include Alumni Services to our alumni at no cost (very important in these times especially), and have developed some very strong programs for the alumni to help them in their tranisition.

FACILITIES

Housing: Coed dorms, special housing for disabled students, women's dorms, fraternity/sorority housing, apartments for married students, cooperative housing, apartments for single students, Theme Housing. 90% of campus accessible to physically disabled. **Special Academic Facilities/Equipment:** laser, observatory, accelerators, recreational facility, music facilities, environmental sciences, planetarium, art galleries **Computers:** 75% of classrooms, 30% of dorms, 100% of libraries, 100% of dining areas, 100% of student union, 10% of common outdoor areas have wireless network access. Students can register for classes online. Administrative functions (other than registration) can be performed online.

CAMPUS LIFE

Environment: City. **Activities:** Choral groups, concert band, dance, drama/theater, jazz band, literary magazine, marching band, music ensembles, musical theater, opera, pep band, radio station, student government, student newspaper, student-run film society, symphony orchestra, television station, Campus Ministries, International Student Organization. 330 registered organizations, 40 honor societies, 34 religious organizations. 23 fraternities, 16 sororities. **Athletics (Intercollegiate):** *Men:* basketball, cross-country, football, golf, softball, track/field (indoor). *Women:* basketball, cross-country, diving, golf, soccer, softball, swimming, tennis, track/field (indoor), volleyball. **On-Campus Highlights:** University Union, Student Recreation Center, Library Mall and pavilion, Murchison Performing Arts Center, Eagle Student Services Center, Chestnut Hall. **Environmental Initiatives:** In 2011 UNT completed construction on three community sized wind turbines located at the universitys Eagle Point. The project was funded through a 2.2 million dollar grant awarded by the State Energy Conservation Office. Since their completion the wind turbines have generated 284,182 kWh of energy. The university has partnered with Schneider Electric to further improve many of the universitys current energy and water systems. UNT previously worked with Schneider on a 10-year energy savings project that began in 1997, and has allowed the university to save $1.2 million a year in energy costs. The new project will increase that savings to an estimated $3.2 million a year, and guarantee at least $42 million in savings over the next 20 years. The University of North Texas has in the last three years completed construction on three LEED certified Gold buildings and a LEED certified Platinum football stadium. The Life Science complex, Business Leadership Building and Highland Street parking garage have all received LEED Gold certifications, and UNTs Apogee Stadium has received LEED Platinum certification.

ADMISSIONS

Freshman Academic Profile: 20% in top 10% of high school class, 52% in top 25% of high school class, 90% in top 50% of high school class. 95% from public high schools. SAT Math middle 50% range 510-610. SAT Critical Reading middle 50% range 490-600. SAT Writing middle 50% range 460-570. ACT middle 50% range 20-26. Minimum internet-based TOEFL 79. Minimum paper TOEFL 550. **Basis for Candidate Selection:** *Very important factors considered include:* Class rank, academic GPA, standardized test scores. *Important factors considered include:* application essay, recommendation(s), rigor of secondary school record. *Other factors considered include:* character/personal qualities, extracurricular activities, first generation, geographical residence, level of applicant's interest, talent/ability, volunteer work, work experience. **Freshman Admission Requirements:** High school diploma is required and GED is accepted. **Academic units required:** 4 English, 3 mathematics, 3 science, (3 science labs), 2 foreign language, 2 social studies, 2 history, 3 academic electives. **Freshman Admission Statistics:** 16,326 applied, 61% admitted, 44% enrolled. **Transfer Admission Requirements:** college transcript(s), statement of good standing from prior institution(s). Minimum college GPA of 2.5 required. Lowest grade transferable D. **General Admission Information:** Application Fee $40. Regular application deadline 8/1. Notification on a rolling basis, beginning on or about 10/15. Nonfall registration accepted. Credit and/or placement offered for CEEB Advanced Placement tests.

COSTS AND FINANCIAL AID

Annual in-state tuition $6,834. Annual out-of-state tuition $17,364. Room and board $7,356. Required fees $2,590. Average book expense $1,000. **Required Forms and Deadlines:** FAFSA. **Notification of Awards:** Applicants will be notified of awards on a rolling basis beginning 4/1. **Types of Aid:** *Need-based scholarships/grants:* Federal Pell, SEOG, state scholarships/grants, private scholarships, the school's own gift aid. *Loans:* Direct Subsidized Stafford, Direct Unsubsidized Stafford, Direct PLUS, Federal Perkins, state loans. *Student Employment:* Federal Work-Study Program available. Institutional employment available. Highest amount earned per year from on-campus jobs $8,726. Off-campus job opportunities are excellent. **Financial Aid Statistics:** 82% freshmen, 74% undergrads receive need-based scholarship or grant aid. 49% freshmen, 26% undergrads receive non-need-based scholarship or grant aid. 78% freshmen, 81% undergrads receive need-based self-help aid. 0% freshmen, 1% undergrads receive athletic scholarships. 88% freshmen, 71% undergrads receive any aid. **Criteria for awarding institutional aid:** *Non-need-based:* academics.

UNIVERSITY OF NORTHERN COLORADO

UNC Admissions Office, Greeley, CO 80639
Phone: 970-351-2881 • **Financial Aid Phone:** 970-351-2502
E-mail: admissions@unco.edu • **CEEB Code:** 4074
Fax: 970-351-2984 • **Website:** www.unco.edu • **ACT Code:** 502

This public school was founded in 1890. It has a 243-acre campus.

RATINGS

Admissions Selectivity Rating: 75   **Fire Safety Rating:** 92

STUDENTS AND FACULTY

Enrollment: 9,975. **Student Body:** 62% female, 38% male, 10% out-of-state, 1% international (49 countries represented). Asian 2%, African American 4%, Caucasian 70%, Hispanic 12%, Native American 1%
Retention and Graduation: 70% freshmen return for sophomore year.
Faculty: 498 full-time faculty, 50% are are members of minority groups, 10% are women.

ACADEMICS

Degrees: bachelor's, master's, post-master's certificate. **Classes:** Most classes have 20-29 students. Most lab/discussion sessions have 20-29 students. **Majors with Highest Enrollment:** Multi-/Interdisciplinary Studies; Kinesiology and Exercise Science; Business Administration and Management. **Special Study Options:** cooperative education program, cross-registration, distance learning, double major, English as a Second Language (ESL), exchange student program (domestic), external degree program, honors program, independent study, internships, student-designed major, study abroad, teacher certification program. **Honors programs:** The University Honors Program is designed to offer exceptional students both the resources of a comprehensive university and the individual attention traditionally associated with a small college. It asks that they be alive to the life of the mind and pushes them to raise the expectations they have for themselves and their education. It seeks to involve them in learning, heighten their critical awareness, and encourage their independent thinking and research. **Disability Services:** Special programs offered to physically disabled students include note-taking services, reader services, tape recorders, tutors. **Career services:** alumni services, career/job search classes, career assessment, internships.

FACILITIES

Housing: Coed dorms, special housing for disabled students, women's dorms, fraternity/sorority housing, apartments for married students, apartments for single students. 100% of campus accessible to physically disabled. **Special Academic Facilities/Equipment:** Art Museum, Music Library, James A. Michener Collection **Computers:** 100% of classrooms, 100% of dorms, 100% of libraries, 100% of dining areas, 100% of student union, 5% of common outdoor areas have wireless network access. Students can register for classes online. Administrative functions (other than registration) can be performed online.

CAMPUS LIFE

Environment: City. **Activities:** Choral groups, concert band, dance, drama/theater, jazz band, literary magazine, marching band, music ensembles, musical theater, opera, pep band, radio station, student government, student newspaper, student-run film society, symphony orchestra, television station, Campus Ministries, International Student Organization. 137 registered organizations, 9 honor societies, 18 religious organizations. 9 fraternities, 8 sororities. **Athletics (Intercollegiate):** *Men:* baseball, basketball, football, golf, tennis, track/field (outdoor), wrestling. *Women:* basketball, cross-country, diving, golf, soccer, softball, swimming, tennis, track/field (outdoor), volleyball. **On-Campus Highlights:** University Center, James Michener Library, Recreation Center, Cultural Centers **Environmental Initiatives:** Performance Contracting; Recycling; Non-Potable Water Usage for Irrigation.

ADMISSIONS

Freshman Academic Profile: Average high school GPA 3.22. 13.8% in top 10% of high school class, 37.9% in top 25% of high school class, 70.3% in top 50% of high school class. SAT Math middle 50% range 450-580. SAT Critical Reading middle 50% range 460-580. ACT middle 50% range 19-25. Minimum internet-based TOEFL 80. Minimum paper TOEFL 550. **Basis for Candidate Selection:** *Very important factors considered include:* Class rank, academic GPA, standardized test scores. *Important factors considered include:* recommendation(s). *Other factors considered include:* rigor of secondary school record, character/personal qualities, extracurricular activities, interview, racial/ethnic status, state residency, talent/ability, work experience. **Freshman Admission Requirements:** High school diploma is required and GED is accepted. **Academic units required:** 4 English, 3 mathematics, 3 science, (2 science labs), 3 social studies, 2 academic electives. **Freshman Admission Statistics:** 6,410 applied, 88% admitted, 40% enrolled. **Transfer Admission**

Requirements: college transcript(s), statement of good standing from prior institution(s). Minimum college GPA of 2.4 required. Lowest grade transferable C. **General Admission Information:** Application Fee $45. Nonfall registration accepted. Admission may be deferred for a maximum of 3 semesters. Credit offered for CEEB Advanced Placement tests.

COSTS AND FINANCIAL AID

Annual in-state tuition $5,300. Annual out-of-state tuition $16,822. Room and board $9,750. Required fees $1,323. Average book expense $1,325. **Required Forms and Deadlines:** FAFSA. **Notification of Awards:** Applicants will be notified of awards on a rolling basis beginning 4/15. **Types of Aid:** *Need-based scholarships/grants:* Federal Pell, SEOG, state scholarships/grants, private scholarships, the school's own gift aid. *Loans:* Subsidized Stafford, Unsubsidized Stafford, PLUS, Federal Perkins, college/university loans from institutional funds. *Student Employment:* Federal Work-Study Program available. Institutional employment available. Highest amount earned per year from on-campus jobs $4,726. Off-campus job opportunities are fair. **Financial Aid Statistics:** 71% freshmen, 67% undergrads receive need-based scholarship or grant aid. 70% freshmen, 45% undergrads receive non-need-based scholarship or grant aid. 89% freshmen, 90% undergrads receive need-based self-help aid. 2% freshmen, 2% undergrads receive athletic scholarships. **Criteria for awarding institutional aid:** *Non-need-based:* academics, athletics, music/drama.

UNIVERSITY OF NORTHERN IOWA

1227 West 27th Street, Cedar Falls, IA 50614-0018
Phone: 319-273-2281 · **Financial Aid Phone:** 319-273-2701
E-mail: admissions@uni.edu · **CEEB Code:** 6307
Fax: 319-273-2885 · **Website:** www.uni.edu · **ACT Code:** 1322

This public school was founded in 1876. It has a 910-acre campus.

RATINGS

Admissions Selectivity Rating: 85   **Fire Safety Rating:** 83

STUDENTS AND FACULTY

Enrollment: 9,882. **Student Body:** 56% female, 44% male, 6% out-of-state, 4% international (63 countries represented). Asian 1%, African American 3%, Caucasian 85%, Hispanic 3%, Native American <1%
Retention and Graduation: 38% freshmen graduate within 4 years. 64% freshmen graduate within 6 years. 16% grads go on to further study within 1 year. 8% grads pursue arts and sciences degrees. 2% grads pursue business degrees. 2% grads pursue medical degrees. **Faculty:** 569 full-time faculty, 75% hold PhDs, 47% are are members of minority groups, 16% are women. 2% of classes are taught by teaching assistants.

ACADEMICS

Degrees: bachelor's, doctoral, master's. **Classes:** Most classes have 20-29 students. Most lab/discussion sessions have 10-19 students. **Majors with Highest Enrollment:** Elementary Education and Teaching; Biology/Biological Sciences; Psychology. **Special Study Options:** Accelerated program, cooperative education program, distance learning, double major, dual enrollment, English as a Second Language (ESL), exchange student program (domestic), external degree program, honors program, independent study, internships, liberal arts/career combination, student-designed major, study abroad, teacher certification program, weekend college, Combined Bachelors/Masters degree programs (BA/MA, BS/MS, BA/MS); undergraduate Dual Degree Majors; 2+2 Programs; undergraduate and graduate certificates. **Honors programs:** University Honors Program—includes all 5 colleges and is open to all majors. www.uni.edu/honors **Combined degree programs:** BA/MA, BA/MS, BA/MAcc, Biology, Chemistry, Technlgy. **Disability Services:** Special programs offered to physically disabled students include note-taking services, reader services, tape recorders, tutors. **Career services:** alumni services, career/job search classes, career assessment, internships. UNI has had over 10,000 students conduct internships for credit over the past 30 years, with thousands more participating in an internship for no credit.

FACILITIES

Housing: Coed dorms, men's dorms, women's dorms, fraternity/sorority housing, apartments for married students, apartments for single students, Facilities accessible by persons with disabilities. 90% of campus accessible to physically disabled. **Special Academic Facilities/Equipment:** Natural history museum, art gallery, greenhouse and biological preserves, Lakeside biology lab and field lab for conservation problems, Tallgrass Prairie Center, Educational Technology Center, curriculum lab, on-campus school for student teachers, NASA Regional Teacher Resource Center, speech and hearing clinic, Small Business Development Center, Iowa Waste Reduction Center, Center for Applied Research in Metal Casting. Iowa Communications Network provides two-way audio/video

link between classrooms across the state. Satellite video production truck with three cameras. Performing Arts Center. **Computers:** 80% of classrooms, 75% of libraries, 100% of dining areas, 100% of student union, have wireless network access. Students can register for classes online. Administrative functions (other than registration) can be performed online.

CAMPUS LIFE

Environment: Town. **Activities:** Choral groups, concert band, dance, drama/theater, jazz band, literary magazine, marching band, music ensembles, musical theater, opera, pep band, radio station, student government, student newspaper, symphony orchestra, yearbook, Campus Ministries, International Student Organization, Model UN. 278 registered organizations, 18 honor societies, 21 religious organizations. 5 fraternities, 4 sororities. **Athletics (Intercollegiate):** *Men:* basketball, cross-country, football, golf, track/field (outdoor), track/field (indoor), wrestling. *Women:* basketball, cross-country, diving, golf, soccer, softball, swimming, tennis, track/field (outdoor), track/field (indoor), volleyball. **On-Campus Highlights:** Wellness Recreation Center, Gallagher-Bluedorn Performing Arts Center, Piazza and Rialto Dining Centers, Maucker University Union, UNI-DOME and McLeod Center. **Environmental Initiatives:** During the last year, UNI has had a theme for the year of "Food Matters". This theme has focused on many things related to sustainable food systems and a more sustainable campus. UNI had 2965 students participate in a campus candle light dinner for Campus Sustainability Day. Students decided to eat with the lights off to reduce their energy demands in on-campus residences. Nearly 80% of students at UNI experience learning outcomes directly related to sustainability.

ADMISSIONS

Freshman Academic Profile: Average high school GPA 3.48. 17% in top 10% of high school class, 47% in top 25% of high school class, 83% in top 50% of high school class. ACT middle 50% range 20-25. Minimum internet-based TOEFL 79. Minimum paper TOEFL 550. **Basis for Candidate Selection:** *Very important factors considered include:* Class rank, academic GPA, rigor of secondary school record, standardized test scores. *Other factors considered include:* application essay, recommendation(s), first generation, interview, talent/ability. **Freshman Admission Requirements:** High school diploma is required and GED is accepted. **Academic units required:** 4 English, 3 mathematics, 3 science, 3 social studies, 2 academic electives. **Freshman Admission Statistics:** 5,509 applied, 54% admitted, 61% enrolled. **Transfer Admission Requirements:** college transcript(s), Lowest grade transferable D. **General Admission Information:** Application Fee $40. Regular application deadline 8/15. Notification on a rolling basis, beginning on or about 9/1. Nonfall registration accepted. Admission may be deferred for a maximum of indefinitely. Credit and/or placement offered for CEEB Advanced Placement tests.

COSTS AND FINANCIAL AID

Annual in-state tuition $6,648. Annual out-of-state tuition $16,546. Room and board $8,046. Required fees $1,101. Average book expense $900. **Required Forms and Deadlines:** FAFSA. **Notification of Awards:** Applicants will be notified of awards on a rolling basis beginning 3/1. **Types of Aid:** *Need-based scholarships/grants:* Federal Pell, SEOG, state scholarships/grants, private scholarships, the school's own gift aid. *Loans:* Direct Subsidized Stafford, Direct Unsubsidized Stafford, Direct PLUS, Federal Perkins, Private, Alternative Loans. *Student Employment:* Federal Work-Study Program available. Institutional employment available. Highest amount earned per year from on-campus jobs $5,872. Off-campus job opportunities are good. **Financial Aid Statistics:** 54% freshmen, 57% undergrads receive need-based scholarship or grant aid. 67% freshmen, 41% undergrads receive non-need-based scholarship or grant aid. 76% freshmen, 78% undergrads receive need-based self-help aid. 3% freshmen, 2% undergrads receive athletic scholarships. 91% freshmen, 87% undergrads receive any aid. 75% undergrads borrow to pay for school. Average cumulative indebtedness $21,602. **Criteria for awarding institutional aid:** *Non-need-based:* academics, alumni affiliation, art, athletics, leadership, minority status, music/drama, state/district residency.

UNIVERSITY OF NOTRE DAME

220 Main Building, Notre Dame, IN 46556
Phone: 574-631-7505 · **Financial Aid Phone:** 574-631-6436
E-mail: admissions@nd.edu · **CEEB Code:** 1841
Fax: 574-631-8865 · **Website:** www.nd.edu · **ACT Code:** 1252

This private school, affiliated with the Roman Catholic Church, was founded in 1842. It has a 1250-acre campus.

RATINGS

Admissions Selectivity Rating: 98   **Fire Safety Rating:** 97

STUDENTS AND FACULTY

Enrollment: 8,427. **Student Body:** 48% female, 52% male, 92% out-of-state, 5% international (87 countries represented). Asian 6%, African American 4%, Caucasian 71%, Hispanic 10%, Native American <1%
Retention and Graduation: 98% freshmen return for sophomore year. 90% freshmen graduate within 4 years. 95% freshmen graduate within 6 years. 29% grads go on to further study within 1 year. **Faculty:** 1,119 full-time faculty, 91% hold PhDs, 30% are are members of minority groups, 17% are women. 9% of classes are taught by teaching assistants.

ACADEMICS

Degrees: bachelor's, first professional, master's. **Classes:** Most classes have 10-19 students. Most lab/discussion sessions have 10-19 students. **Majors with Highest Enrollment:** Finance; Psychology; Political Science and Government. **Special Study Options:** Accelerated program, cross-registration, double major, dual enrollment, exchange student program (domestic), honors program, independent study, internships, liberal arts/career combination, student-designed major, study abroad, teacher certification program, Teacher Certification only available through Cross Registration with St. Mary's College. **Combined degree programs:** B.S. Engr./MBA. **Disability Services:** Special programs offered to physically disabled students include note-taking services, reader services, tape recorders. **Career services:** Alumni network, alumni services, career/job search classes, career assessment, internships. Career services highlights include Employer Development and Alumni Networking: To continue forming and growing relationships with employers during difficult economic times, The Career Center has increased it efforts and outreach to employers to identify career opportunities for students. The importance of networking continues to grow given the current state of the economy. Also recognizing that building and maintaining professional networking relationships will be critical to the hiring process this year. The Career Center has several programs planned for the spring semester that will help students network. ° The Career Center sent emails to 24,000 alumni in select industries to identify opportunities for Notre Dame students. As a result, employers including IBM, Skanska USA, SwitchFast, Radio Flyer, Fidelity, Bristol Myers Squibb, Lockheed Martin, Draftfcb, and Societe Generale registered for the Winter Career Fair and/or posted job opportunities for our students. Career Counselors have received additional training on searching for jobs within the federal government and public service, a key sector of employment opportunities. The Career Center has successfully developed recruiting relationships with small, mid-sized, and family-owned companies to post jobs and internships. The Career Center will host a special program in NYC with ND alumni working in private equity and banking, to expand placement opportunities and internships on Wall Street. Also arranging two-week unpaid externships on Wall Street to help students gain experience in a very tough job market. The Career Center has added DirectEmployers Association to its Employer Advisory Board and gained instant access to 420 Fortune 500 employers. The Career Center is working with Alumni Clubs to help seniors find jobs in or near their hometowns. The Career Center is networking with GradStaff.com, CityStaff.com, Adecco and other professional organizations to help students connect to short-term, paid, professional jobs to gain experience with Fortune 500 companies. The Career Center has also implemented distance interviewing with Skype, and Polycam technology as an additional service for employers who cannot travel to campus to interview. A Notre Dame Alumni Group has been established on LinkedIn and currently has over 8,200 members. The Career Center launched a Job Shadow Program in Fall 2008 with over 1,200 alumni volunteering to host students at their companies for a one day networking visit. The Career Center also has an agreement with the ND Alumni Association to grant seniors access to Irish Online, the online community of the Notre Dame Alumni Association. Senior students can create an account on this website before graduation and find alumni contacts. Additionally, networking workshops are being offered, providing students with access to Irish Online that will enable them to find key contacts for career de-

velopment. Additional programs and information: Confirmed 1,475 internships for ND students documented in the Intern Survey for the Summer of 2008; Raised funding to reimburse students $200 for travel to the Big East Career Fair in March 2008 and March 2009.

FACILITIES

Housing: men's dorms, women's dorms. 95% of campus accessible to physically disabled. **Special Academic Facilities/Equipment:** Art Museum, Theater, Germ-free research facility, Radiation laboratory. **Computers:** Students can register for classes online. Administrative functions (other than registration) can be performed online.

CAMPUS LIFE

Environment: City. **Activities:** Choral groups, concert band, dance, drama/theater, jazz band, literary magazine, marching band, music ensembles, musical theater, opera, pep band, radio station, student government, student newspaper, student-run film society, symphony orchestra, yearbook, Campus Ministries, International Student Organization, Model UN. 299 registered organizations, 10 honor societies, 11 religious organizations. **Athletics (Intercollegiate):** *Men:* baseball, basketball, cross-country, diving, fencing, football, golf, ice hockey, lacrosse, soccer, swimming, tennis, track/field (outdoor). *Women:* basketball, crew/rowing, cross-country, diving, fencing, golf, lacrosse, soccer, softball, swimming, tennis, track/field (outdoor), volleyball. **On-Campus Highlights:** Grotto, The Dome (Main Building), Basilica of the Sacred Heart, Notre Dame Stadium, Eck Center. **Environmental Initiatives:** Expansion of Office of Sustainability to include 3 full time staff and 7 interns; development of metrics and quantitative goals in 7 key sustainability areas; Investment of $4 million this year to improve lighting and/or HVAC efficiency in 24 campus buildings; Continuous utilization of $2 million Green Loan Fund to support capital projects that save energy and natural resources.

ADMISSIONS

Freshman Academic Profile: 90% in top 10% of high school class, 97% in top 25% of high school class, 100% in top 50% of high school class. 40% from public high schools. SAT Math middle 50% range 680-770. SAT Critical Reading middle 50% range 660-750. SAT Writing middle 50% range 660-760. ACT middle 50% range 32-34. Minimum internet-based TOEFL 100. Minimum paper TOEFL 560. **Basis for Candidate Selection:** *Very important factors considered include:* rigor of secondary school record. *Important factors considered include:* Class rank, application essay, academic GPA, recommendation(s), standardized test scores, alumni/ae relation, character/personal qualities, extracurricular activities, talent/ability, volunteer work. *Other factors considered include:* first generation, level of applicant's interest, racial/ethnic status, religious affiliation/commitment, work experience. **Freshman Admission Requirements:** High school diploma is required and GED is not accepted. **Academic units required:** 4 English, 3 mathematics, 2 science, (2 science labs), 2 foreign language, 2 history, 3 academic electives. **Freshman Admission Statistics:** 17,901 applied, 21% admitted, 53% enrolled. **Transfer Admission Requirements:** High school transcript, college transcript(s), essay or personal statement, standardized test scores, statement of good standing from prior institution(s). Minimum college GPA of 3.0 required. Lowest grade transferable C. **General Admission Information:** Application Fee $65. Regular application deadline 12/31. Regular notification 4/10. Nonfall registration accepted. Admission may be deferred for a maximum of 12 months.

COSTS AND FINANCIAL AID

Annual tuition $45,730. Room and board $13,224. Required fees $507. Average book expense $1,050. **Required Forms and Deadlines:** FAFSA, CSS/Financial Aid PROFILE, Noncustodial PROFILE, Business/Farm Supplement. **Notification of Awards:** Applicants will be notified of awards on or about 4/1. **Types of Aid:** *Need-based scholarships/grants:* Federal Pell, SEOG, state scholarships/grants, private scholarships, the school's own gift aid, Federal ACG and SMART Grants. *Loans:* Subsidized Stafford, Unsubsidized Stafford, PLUS, Federal Perkins, Private Student *Student Employment:* Highest amount earned per year from on-campus jobs $6,300. Off-campus job opportunities are fair. **Financial Aid Statistics:** 93% freshmen, 95% undergrads receive need-based scholarship or grant aid. 49% freshmen, 48% undergrads receive non-need-based scholarship or grant aid. 75% freshmen, 81% undergrads receive need-based self-help aid. 5% freshmen, 5% undergrads receive athletic scholarships. 66% freshmen, 77% undergrads receive any aid. 50% undergrads borrow to pay for school. Average cumulative indebtedness $21,534. **Criteria for awarding institutional aid:** *Non-need-based:* athletics.

UNIVERSITY OF OKLAHOMA

1000 Asp Aveune, Norman, OK 73019
Phone: 405-325-2252 · **Financial Aid Phone:** 405-325-5505
E-mail: admrec@ou.edu · **CEEB Code:** 6879
Fax: 405-325-7124 · **Website:** www.ou.edu · **ACT Code:** 3442

This public school was founded in 1890. It has a 3914-acre campus.

RATINGS

Admissions Selectivity Rating: 87   **Fire Safety Rating:** 84

STUDENTS AND FACULTY

Enrollment: 21,372. **Student Body:** 50% female, 50% male, 32% out-of-state, 4% international (111 countries represented). Asian 6%, African American 5%, Caucasian 63%, Hispanic 9%, Native American 4%
Retention and Graduation: 37% freshmen graduate within 4 years. 67% freshmen graduate within 6 years. **Faculty:** 1,479 full-time faculty, 83% hold PhDs, 44% are are members of minority groups, 21% are women. 12.6% of classes are taught by teaching assistants.

ACADEMICS

Degrees: bachelor's, certificate, master's, post-bachelor's certificate, post-master's certificate. **Classes:** Most classes have 10-19 students. Most lab/discussion sessions have 20-29 students. **Majors with Highest Enrollment:** Registered Nursing/Registered Nurse; Psychology; Accounting. **Special Study Options:** Accelerated program, cooperative education program, distance learning, double major, dual enrollment, English as a Second Language (ESL), external degree program, honors program, independent study, internships, liberal arts/career combination, student-designed major, study abroad, teacher certification program, weekend college. **Honors programs:** Honors at Oxford: This summer program enables students to study at Oxford (while living at Brasenose College). While there, students work in private tutorials with distinguished Oxford dons. Students can earn up to 6 hours of honors credit in one of our four classes that are offered. Honors in Italy: Honors in Italy is built around a three-hours course called "Imagining Italy" which is taught in the Tuscan town of Arezzo and includes side trips to Florence, Venice, and Rome where students are led on walking tours of the art and history of Italy. The focus is on how Italian culture has influenced writers, filmmakers, and artists from John Adams to Henry James and from Mark Twain to Martin Scorsese. Honors in Germany (new for summer 2010): Honors students and other OU students travel to Leipzig, Germany in June, live at the University of Leipzig, study German, and take a course on German-American literary relations (American writers who wrote in Germany about German culture.) Additionally, students focus on experiencing and exploring major sites for the history and memory of WWII in Germany by taking day trips from Leipzig to major WWII-related sites in Germany. The course will be for six hours credit and will be offered each summer. Honors Undergraduate Research Assistant Program: Honors Undergraduate Research Assistant Program provides undergraduates the opportunity to work with professors as research assistants on specific projects. Student assistants are expected to work 10 hours a week for 10 weeks for $6 an hour. Honors College students with at least 15 hours of college credit and a 3.4+ GPA are eligible to apply. Medical Humanities Scholars Program: The Honors College and the University of Oklahoma College of Medicine have created a special pathway (through a bachelor of arts degree leading to a medical doctorate) for up to five high school students each year who wish to study the humanistic aspects of medicine as undergraduates. Through a special admissions process, the Medical Humanities Scholars are accepted at the medical school as part of their application to OU's undergraduate honors program. The Honors College has also created a Medical Humanities Minor open to all honors students wishing to study medicine from the perspectives of history, sociology, anthropology, bioethics, literature, and economics. Honors Undergraduate Writing Assistant Program: The Honors Undergraduate Writing Assistant Program includes assistants who receive a stipend to work as writing assistants for the required freshman American Perspectives courses. Students who wish to be writing assistants apply to the program and, if they are selected, participate in a required upper-division preparatory course that focuses on composition pedagogy, research and writing skills, and strategies for commenting and conferencing on students writing. Honors Undergraduate Research Opportunities Program: The Undergraduate Research Opportunities Program is open to all undergraduates at OU. Each semester the Honors College awards more than $12,500 to undergraduate students and their faculty mentors for research and creative activity. Undergraduate Research Day: Each spring the college hosts an Undergraduate Research Day, in which

scholars, Honors students or not, share their research with the peers. The Honors College, Phi Beta Kappa and Phi Kappa Phi give cash awards to the best presentations in various categories. Conversations with the Dean: Each week the Dean of the Honors College has in a distinguished professor, author, diplomat, politician, or some other important community or intellectual figure to discuss world events. With the Dean as moderator, students are encouraged to participate in vibrant discussion with the week's important guest. Honors College Reading Groups: The Dean and Honors College faculty assign a book of their individual choosing to students who voluntarily join an Honors College Reading Group. Limited to 15 students per group, the books are provided free of charge to participants who then meet as a group, one hour a week, to discuss the assigned pages with the professor. There is no charge for this activity, there are no grades, and students may come and go as they please. The aim is to encourage students to read, think, and discuss with other Honors College students important topics of mutual interest, whether fiction or non-fiction. The Honors Undergraduate Research Journal: The Honors Undergraduate Research Journal is a forum in which Honors students of all majors have the opportunity to have their work published. A panel of Honors College professors who annually appoint an editorial board of about eight Honors students advises THURJ. The board accepts research papers, poetry, and short stories of which the top submissions are published every spring. Freshman Summer Reading Series: Each summer all incoming freshmen receive a free, theme-based book chosen by the faculty. The students are encouraged to actively engage the material (the book arrives at the student's home in late June), which provides the incoming class with a common intellectual experience that the faculty and students can build on during their first semester in order to develop and nurture a collective intellectual community. **Combined degree programs:** BA/MA, BA/MEng, BAC/ MAC. **Disability Services:** Special programs offered to physically disabled students include note-taking services, reader services, tutors. **Career services:** Alumni network, alumni services, career/job search classes, career assessment, internships. Career services highlights include our Alumni Network. Alumni provide career mentoring to currently enrolled students.

FACILITIES

Housing: Coed dorms, special housing for disabled students, men's dorms, special housing for international students, women's dorms, fraternity/sorority housing, apartments for married students, apartments for single students, Honors House, Cultural Housing, National Merit, and Scholastics floors. 92% of campus accessible to physically disabled. **Special Academic Facilities/ Equipment:** Fred Jones Museum of Art, Sam Noble Museum of Natural History, National Weather Center, National Severe Storms Library, OU Biological Station, History of Science Collection, Western History Collection, Oklahoma Geological Survey. **Computers:** 60% of classrooms, 80% of dorms, 100% of libraries, 75% of dining areas, 100% of student union, 80% of common outdoor areas have wireless network access. Students can register for classes online. Administrative functions (other than registration) can be performed online.

CAMPUS LIFE

Environment: City. **Activities:** Choral groups, concert band, dance, drama/ theater, jazz band, literary magazine, marching band, music ensembles, musical theater, opera, pep band, radio station, student government, student newspaper, student-run film society, symphony orchestra, television station, yearbook, Campus Ministries, International Student Organization, Model UN. 388 registered organizations, 17 honor societies, 39 religious organizations. 30 fraternities, 20 sororities. **Athletics (Intercollegiate):** *Men:* baseball, basketball, cross-country, football, golf, gymnastics, tennis, track/field (outdoor), track/field (indoor), wrestling. *Women:* basketball, crew/rowing, cross-country, golf, gymnastics, soccer, softball, tennis, track/field (outdoor), track/field (indoor), volleyball. **On-Campus Highlights:** Fred Jones Jr. Museum of Art, The Gaylord Family Oklahoma Memorial Sta, Sam Noble Ok. Museum of Natural History, Oklahoma Memorial Union, Lloyd Noble Center. **Environmental Initiatives:** Membership in the Chicago Climate Exchange; Joining with the University Presidents' Campus Climate Challenge Operation of the Academic Department for Interdisciplinary Perspectives on the Environment; and creation of the Department of Geography and Environmental Sustainability.

ADMISSIONS

Freshman Academic Profile: Average high school GPA 3.59. 35% in top 10% of high school class, 65% in top 25% of high school class, 91% in top 50% of high school class. SAT Math middle 50% range 540-670. SAT Critical Reading middle 50% range 520-670. ACT middle 50% range 23-29. Minimum internet-based TOEFL 79. Minimum paper TOEFL 550. **Basis for Candidate Selection:** *Very important factors considered include:* Class rank, academic GPA, rigor of secondary school record, standardized test scores. *Other factors considered include:* application essay, recommendation(s), state residency. **Freshman Admission Requirements:** High school diploma is required and GED is accepted. **Academic units required:** 4 English, 3 mathematics, 3 science, (3 science labs), 2 social studies, 1 history, 2 academic electives. **Freshman Admission Statistics:** 11,331 applied, 81% admitted, 45% enrolled. **Transfer Admission Requirements:** college transcript(s), Lowest grade transferable D. **General Admission Information:** Application Fee $40. Regular application deadline 4/1. Nonfall registration accepted. Credit and/or placement offered for CEEB Advanced Placement tests.

COSTS AND FINANCIAL AID
Required Forms and Deadlines: FAFSA. **Notification of Awards:** Applicants will be notified of awards on a rolling basis beginning 3/15. **Types of Aid:** *Need-based scholarships/grants:* Federal Pell, SEOG, state scholarships/grants, private scholarships, the school's own gift aid, United Negro College Fund. *Loans:* Subsidized Stafford, Unsubsidized Stafford, PLUS, Federal Perkins, Federal Nursing, college/university loans from institutional funds. *Student Employment:* Federal Work-Study Program available. Institutional employment available. Highest amount earned per year from on-campus jobs $3,108. Off-campus job opportunities are excellent. **Financial Aid Statistics:** 53% freshmen, 62% undergrads receive need-based scholarship or grant aid. 72% freshmen, 57% undergrads receive non-need-based scholarship or grant aid. 63% freshmen, 71% undergrads receive need-based self-help aid. 2% freshmen, 1% undergrads receive athletic scholarships. 87% freshmen, 89% undergrads receive any aid. 49% undergrads borrow to pay for school. Average cumulative indebtedness $21,774. **Criteria for awarding institutional aid:** *Non-need-based:* academics, alumni affiliation, art, athletics, leadership, music/drama, religious affiliation.

UNIVERSITY OF OREGON

1217 University of Oregon, Eugene, OR 97403-1217
Phone: 541-346-3201 · **Financial Aid Phone:** 800-760-6953
E-mail: uoadmit@uoregon.edu · **CEEB Code:** 4846
Fax: 541-346-5815 · **Website:** www.uoregon.edu

This public school was founded in 1876. It has a 295-acre campus.

RATINGS
Admissions Selectivity Rating: 86   **Fire Safety Rating:** 77

STUDENTS AND FACULTY
Enrollment: 20,252. **Student Body:** 52% female, 48% male, 41% out-of-state, 13% international (74 countries represented). Asian 5%, African American 2%, Caucasian 62%, Hispanic 9%, Native American 1%
Retention and Graduation: 87% freshmen return for sophomore year. 46% freshmen graduate within 4 years. 69% freshmen graduate within 6 years. **Faculty:** 1,049 full-time faculty, 98% hold PhDs, 43% are are members of minority groups, 17% are women. 15% of classes are taught by teaching assistants.

ACADEMICS
Degrees: bachelor's, master's, post-bachelor's certificate. **Classes:** Most classes have 20-29 students. Most lab/discussion sessions have 20-29 students. **Majors with Highest Enrollment:** Business/Commerce; Psychology; Social Sciences. **Special Study Options:** cross-registration, distance learning, double major, English as a Second Language (ESL), exchange student program (domestic), honors program, independent study, internships, liberal arts/career combination, student-designed major, study abroad, teacher certification program, Semester at Sea program; Professional distinctions program, a certificate program in which students gain direct professional preparation through internships, special courses, a professional mentor program, and the development of an electronic resume and portfolio. There is also a dual enrollment program that allows you to enroll in both UO and Lane Community College or UO and Southwestern Oregon Community College (differs from CDS definition in that it is not a high school dual enrollment program). **Honors programs:** Robert D. Clark Honors College, College of Arts and Sciences Society of College Scholars, Professional Distinctions program, Dean's List, Junior Scholars. **Disability Services:** Special programs offered to physically disabled students include note-taking services, reader services, tape recorders, tutors. **Career services:** Alumni network, alumni services, career/job search classes, career assessment, internships, regional alumni. Career services highlights include the Career Assessment Program: This is a free opportunity available to all students that assists them in assessing values, interests, preferences and strengths. Through this process students gain confidence and self direction which helps them gain insight in major selection and career direction.

FACILITIES
Housing: Coed dorms, fraternity/sorority housing, apartments for married students, cooperative housing, apartments for single students, Wellness Housing, Theme Housing. Most residence halls have separate men's and women's floors.

Graduate Student Housing. 95% of campus accessible to physically disabled. **Special Academic Facilities/Equipment:** Jordan Schnitzer Museum of Art; Museum of Natural and Cultural History; James Warsaw Sports Marketing Center; Lundquist Center for Entrepreneurship; University of Oregon Many Nations Longhouse; Green Chemistry Laboratory and Alice C. Tyler Instrumentation Center; Future Music Oregon, a computer music center in the School of Music; Pine Mountain Observatory (Bend, Oregon); Oregon Institute of Marine Biology (Oregon Coast); Central Oregon programs affiliated with the Oregon University System Cascades Campus (Bend, Oregon); Urban Architecture program and BetterBricks Daylighting Laboratory at the University of Oregon Portland Center (Portland, Oregon). **Computers:** 95% of classrooms, 35% of dorms, 100% of libraries, 100% of dining areas, 100% of student union, 30% of common outdoor areas have wireless network access. Students can register for classes online. Administrative functions (other than registration) can be performed online.

CAMPUS LIFE
Environment: City. **Activities:** Choral groups, concert band, dance, drama/theater, jazz band, literary magazine, marching band, music ensembles, musical theater, opera, pep band, radio station, student government, student newspaper, student-run film society, symphony orchestra, Campus Ministries, International Student Organization. 250 registered organizations, 22 honor societies, 20 religious organizations. 12 fraternities, 10 sororities. **Athletics (Intercollegiate):** *Men:* baseball, basketball, cross-country, football, golf, tennis, track/field (outdoor). *Women:* basketball, cross-country, golf, gymnastics, lacrosse, soccer, softball, tennis, track/field (outdoor), volleyball. **On-Campus Highlights:** University of Oregon Duckstore, Knight Library, Erb Memorial Union, Laverne Krauss Gallery in Lawrence Hall, Watch sports at Autzen, Hayward, or Mac Court, The University of Oregon's 295-acre, park-like campus is home to more than 500 varieties of trees, various private spots to study or simply stare at the sky, and tons of quick stops where you can grab a bite between classes. With a wealth of campus resources to make your life as a student easier, the UO campus feeds the mind, body, and spirit. On average, each course you take at the UO will have a person from another country, six people from different states, and several people with religious, cultural, and ethnic heritage different from your own. You'll thrive because this diversity pushes you to see the world differently. You'll listen to new ideas, and maybe even change the world because you changed your mind. **Environmental Initiatives:** Created the Oregon Model for Sustainable Development which puts a cap on building energy consumption. Massive energy efficiency upgrades; lighting retrofits, building upgrades Sustainable Cities Initiative is a unique service-learning program. Twenty-five faculty teach 500 students across twenty-eight courses which results in 80,000 hours of service for an Oregon city working to improve its sustainability performance.

ADMISSIONS
Freshman Academic Profile: Average high school GPA 3.58. 23% in top 10% of high school class, 66% in top 25% of high school class, 93% in top 50% of high school class. SAT Math middle 50% range 500-620. SAT Critical Reading middle 50% range 490-610. SAT Writing middle 50% range 490-600. ACT middle 50% range 22-27. Minimum internet-based TOEFL 61. Minimum paper TOEFL 500. **Basis for Candidate Selection:** *Very important factors considered include:* academic GPA, rigor of secondary school record. *Other factors considered include:* Class rank, application essay, recommendation(s), standardized test scores, extracurricular activities, first generation, geographical residence, racial/ethnic status, state residency, talent/ability, volunteer work, work experience. **Freshman Admission Requirements:** High school diploma is required and GED is accepted. **Academic units required:** 4 English, 3 mathematics, 2 science, 2 foreign language, 3 social studies. **Freshman Admission Statistics:** 21,359 applied, 75% admitted, 25% enrolled. **Transfer Admission Requirements:** college transcript(s), Minimum college GPA of 2.25 required. Lowest grade transferable D-. **General Admission Information:** Application Fee $50. Regular application deadline 1/15. Notification on a rolling basis, beginning on or about 12/15. Nonfall registration accepted. Credit and/or placement offered for CEEB Advanced Placement tests.

COSTS AND FINANCIAL AID
Annual in-state tuition $8,190. Annual out-of-state tuition $29,160. Room and board $11,442. Required fees $1,728. Average book expense $1,050. **Required Forms and Deadlines:** FAFSA. **Notification of Awards:** Applicants will be notified of awards on a rolling basis beginning 4/15. **Types of Aid:** *Need-based scholarships/grants:* Federal Pell, SEOG, state scholarships/grants, private scholarships, the school's own gift aid. *Loans:* Direct Subsidized Stafford, Direct Unsubsidized Stafford, Direct PLUS, Federal Perkins, college/university loans from institutional funds. *Student Employment:* Federal Work-Study Program available. Institutional employment available. Off-campus job opportunities are good. **Financial Aid Statistics:** 71% freshmen, 72% undergrads receive need-based scholarship or grant aid. 8% freshmen, 3% undergrads receive non-need-based scholarship or grant aid. 67% freshmen, 76% undergrads receive need-based self-help aid. 2% freshmen, 2% undergrads receive athletic scholarships. 85% freshmen, 91% undergrads receive any aid. 50% undergrads borrow to pay for school. Average cumulative indebtedness $22,174. **Criteria for awarding**

institutional aid: *Non-need-based:* academics, art, athletics, leadership, minority status, music/drama, state/district residency.

UNIVERSITY OF THE OZARKS

415 N College Avenue, Clarksville, AR 72830
Phone: 479-979-1227 · **Financial Aid Phone:** 479-979-1221
E-mail: admiss@ozarks.edu · **CEEB Code:** 6111
Fax: 479-979-1417 · **Website:** www.ozarks.edu · **ACT Code:** 120

This private school, affiliated with the Presbyterian Church, was founded in 1834. It has a 56-acre campus.

RATINGS
Admissions Selectivity Rating: 84   **Fire Safety Rating:** 73

STUDENTS AND FACULTY
Enrollment: 615. **Student Body:** 55% female, 45% male, 29% out-of-state, 14% international (21 countries represented). Asian 1%, African American 4%, Caucasian 71%, Hispanic 6%, Native American 2%
Retention and Graduation: 64% freshmen return for sophomore year. 33% freshmen graduate within 4 years. 53% freshmen graduate within 6 years. **Faculty:** 49 full-time faculty, 69% hold PhDs, 37% are are members of minority groups, 8% are women. 0% of classes are taught by teaching assistants.

ACADEMICS
Degrees: bachelor's. **Classes:** Most classes have 10-19 students. **Majors with Highest Enrollment:** Biology/Biological Sciences; Business Administration and Management; Marketing/Marketing Management. **Special Study Options:** cooperative education program, double major, dual enrollment, independent study, internships, liberal arts/career combination, study abroad, teacher certification program. **Disability Services:** Special programs offered to physically disabled students include note-taking services, reader services, tape recorders, tutors. **Career services:** Alumni network, alumni services, career assessment, internships, regional alumni.

FACILITIES
Housing: Coed dorms, men's dorms, women's dorms, apartments for married students, apartments for single students, University owned housing. 100% of campus accessible to physically disabled. **Special Academic Facilities/Equipment:** Walton Fine Arts Center; Stephens Gallery; Smith-Broyles Science Center; Walker Hall Teacher Education and Communications Center **Computers:** 100% of libraries, have wireless network access.

CAMPUS LIFE
Environment: Village. **Activities:** Choral groups, drama/theater, literary magazine, music ensembles, radio station, student government, student-run film society, television station, yearbook, Campus Ministries, International Student Organization. 40 registered organizations, 5 honor societies, 6 religious organizations. **Athletics (Intercollegiate):** *Men:* baseball, basketball, cheerleading, cross-country, soccer, tennis. *Women:* basketball, cheerleading, cross-country, soccer, softball, tennis. **On-Campus Highlights:** Seay Student Center, Walton Fine Arts Center, Walker Education and Communications Building, Robson Library, Gilbert's Park.

ADMISSIONS
Freshman Academic Profile: Average high school GPA 3.31. 18% in top 10% of high school class, 44% in top 25% of high school class, 76% in top 50% of high school class. 92% from public high schools. SAT Math middle 50% range 443-560. SAT Critical Reading middle 50% range 450-570. ACT middle 50% range 19-25. Minimum paper TOEFL 500. **Basis for Candidate Selection:** *Important factors considered include:* standardized test scores. *Other factors considered include:* application essay, academic GPA, recommendation(s), rigor of secondary school record, alumni/ae relation, character/personal qualities, extracurricular activities, interview, level of applicant's interest, talent/ability, volunteer work, work experience. **Freshman Admission Requirements:** High school diploma is required and GED is accepted. **Freshman Admission Statistics:** 1,372 applied, 59% admitted, 25% enrolled. **Transfer Admission Requirements:** college transcript(s), Minimum college GPA of 2.0 required. Lowest grade transferable C. **General Admission Information:** Application Fee $30. Nonfall registration accepted. Credit and/or placement offered for CEEB Advanced Placement tests.

COSTS AND FINANCIAL AID
Annual tuition $21,450. Room and board $6,500. Required fees $600. Average book expense $800. **Required Forms and Deadlines:** FAFSA. **Notification of Awards:** Applicants will be notified of awards on a rolling basis beginning 3/1. **Types of Aid:** *Need-based scholarships/grants:* Federal Pell, SEOG, state scholarships/grants, private scholarships, the school's own gift aid, United Negro

College Fund, Federal Nursing Scholarships. *Loans:* Subsidized Stafford, Unsubsidized Stafford, PLUS, Federal Perkins, college/university loans from institutional funds. *Student Employment:* Federal Work-Study Program available. Institutional employment available. Highest amount earned per year from on-campus jobs $5,726. Off-campus job opportunities are fair. **Financial Aid Statistics:** 97% freshmen, 97% undergrads receive need-based scholarship or grant aid. 0% freshmen, 0% undergrads receive non-need-based scholarship or grant aid. 82% freshmen, 85% undergrads receive need-based self-help aid. 0% freshmen, 0% undergrads receive athletic scholarships. 95% freshmen, 94% undergrads receive any aid. 56% undergrads borrow to pay for school. Average cumulative indebtedness $15,164. **Criteria for awarding institutional aid:** *Non-need-based:* academics, alumni affiliation, art, leadership, minority status, music/drama, religious affiliation, state/district residency.

UNIVERSITY OF THE PACIFIC

Best 380

3601 Pacific Avenue, Stockton, CA 95211
Phone: 209-946-2211 · **Financial Aid Phone:** 209-946-2421
E-mail: admissions@pacific.edu · **CEEB Code:** 4065
Fax: 209-946-4213 · **Website:** www.pacific.edu · **ACT Code:** 240

This private school was founded in 1851. It has a 175-acre campus.

RATINGS
Admissions Selectivity Rating: 86   **Fire Safety Rating:** 88

STUDENTS AND FACULTY
Enrollment: 3,802. **Student Body:** 52% female, 48% male, 7% out-of-state, 7% international (66 countries represented). Asian 33%, African American 2%, Caucasian 30%, Hispanic 18%, Native American 1%
Retention and Graduation: 86% freshmen return for sophomore year. 43% freshmen graduate within 4 years. **Faculty:** 437 full-time faculty, 94% hold PhDs, 42% are are members of minority groups, 19% are women.

ACADEMICS
Degrees: bachelor's, master's. **Classes:** Most classes have fewer than 10 students. Most lab/discussion sessions have 10-19 students. **Majors with Highest Enrollment:** Engineering; Biology/Biological Sciences; Business/Commerce. **Special Study Options:** Accelerated program, double major, dual enrollment, English as a Second Language (ESL), exchange student program (domestic), honors program, independent study, internships, liberal arts/career combination, student-designed major, study abroad, teacher certification program, minors, practicum, thematic minors, undergraduate research, ethnic studies, environmental science, gender studies, service learning. **Combined degree programs:** BA/DDS, BA or BS/MBA, BA or BS/DDS, BS/Pharm.D. **Disability Services:** Special programs offered to physically disabled students include note-taking services, reader services, tape recorders, tutors. **Career services:** Alumni network, alumni services, career/job search classes, career assessment, internships.

FACILITIES
Housing: Coed dorms, fraternity/sorority housing, apartments for single students. 90% of campus accessible to physically disabled. **Special Academic Facilities/Equipment:** John Muir Collection, Dave and Iola Brubeck Collection, Brubeck Institute for Jazz Studies, Reynolds Art Gallery **Computers:** 100% of classrooms, 90% of dorms, 100% of libraries, 100% of dining areas, 100% of student union, 30% of common outdoor areas have wireless network access. Students can register for classes online. Administrative functions (other than registration) can be performed online.

CAMPUS LIFE
Environment: City. **Activities:** Choral groups, concert band, dance, drama/theater, jazz band, literary magazine, music ensembles, musical theater, opera, pep band, radio station, student government, student newspaper, student-run film society, symphony orchestra, yearbook, Campus Ministries, International Student Organization, Model UN. 100 registered organizations, 14 honor societies, 10 religious organizations. 8 fraternities, 7 sororities. **Athletics (Intercollegiate):** *Men:* baseball, basketball, golf, swimming, tennis, volleyball, water polo. *Women:* basketball, cross-country, field hockey, soccer, softball, swimming, tennis, volleyball, water polo. **On-Campus Highlights:** Brubeck Istitute for Jazz Studies, John Muir Collection and Center, Alex Spanos Center, Reynolds Art Gallery, Pharmacy and Health Sciences Bldg. **Environmental Initiatives:** Natural Resource Institute; Calaveras River Restoration Project; LEED Certification of New Student Center.

The Princeton Review's Complete Book of Colleges

ADMISSIONS

Freshman Academic Profile: Average high school GPA 3.49. 37% in top 10% of high school class, 62% in top 25% of high school class, 89% in top 50% of high school class. 82% from public high schools. SAT Math middle 50% range 530-683. SAT Critical Reading middle 50% range 508-630. SAT Writing middle 50% range 510-640. ACT middle 50% range 23-30. Minimum internet-based TOEFL 52. Minimum paper TOEFL 475. **Basis for Candidate Selection:** *Very important factors considered include:* rigor of secondary school record. *Important factors considered include:* application essay, academic GPA, recommendation(s), standardized test scores, extracurricular activities, first generation. *Other factors considered include:* Class rank, alumni/ae relation, character/personal qualities, geographical residence, level of applicant's interest, talent/ability, volunteer work, work experience. **Freshman Admission Requirements:** High school diploma is required and GED is accepted. **Freshman Admission Statistics:** 11,197 applied, 74% admitted, 11% enrolled. **Transfer Admission Requirements:** college transcript(s), statement of good standing from prior institution(s). Minimum college GPA of 3.0 required. Lowest grade transferable C. **General Admission Information:** Application Fee $60. Regular application deadline 1/15. Notification on a rolling basis, beginning on or about 3/15. Nonfall registration accepted. Admission may be deferred for a maximum of 1 year. Credit and/or placement offered for CEEB Advanced Placement tests.

COSTS AND FINANCIAL AID

Annual tuition $40,822. Room and board $12,582. Required fees $520. Average book expense $1,746. **Required Forms and Deadlines:** FAFSA. **Notification of Awards:** Applicants will be notified of awards on a rolling basis beginning 3/15. **Types of Aid:** *Need-based scholarships/grants:* Federal Pell, SEOG, state scholarships/grants, private scholarships, the school's own gift aid, ACG, SMART. *Loans:* Direct Subsidized Stafford, Direct Unsubsidized Stafford, Direct PLUS, Subsidized Stafford, Unsubsidized Stafford, PLUS, Federal Perkins, Direct Graduate/Professional PLUS Loans. **Financial Aid Statistics:** 98% freshmen, 97% undergrads receive need-based scholarship or grant aid. 0% freshmen, 0% undergrads receive non-need-based scholarship or grant aid. 86% freshmen, 92% undergrads receive need-based self-help aid. 3% freshmen, 4% undergrads receive athletic scholarships. 91% freshmen, 83% undergrads receive any aid. **Criteria for awarding institutional aid:** *Non-need-based:* academics, athletics, leadership, music/drama, religious affiliation.

UNIVERSITY OF PENNSYLVANIA

1 College Hall, Philadelphia, PA 19104
Phone: 215-898-7507 · **Financial Aid Phone:** 215-898-1988
E-mail: info@admissions.upenn.edu · **CEEB Code:** 2926
Fax: 215-898-9670 · **Website:** www.upenn.edu · **ACT Code:** 3732

This private school was founded in 1740. It has a 279-acre campus.

RATINGS

Admissions Selectivity Rating: 99   **Fire Safety Rating:** 75

STUDENTS AND FACULTY

Enrollment: 9,682. **Student Body:** 50% female, 50% male, 53% out-of-state, 11% international (126 countries represented). Asian 19%, African American 7%, Caucasian 44%, Hispanic 9%, Native American <1%
Retention and Graduation: 63% freshmen graduate within 4 years. 96% freshmen graduate within 6 years. 20% grads go on to further study within 1 year. 5% grads pursue arts and sciences degrees. 4% grads pursue law degrees. 1% grads pursue business degrees. 5% grads pursue medical degrees. **Faculty:** 1,437 full-time faculty, 100% hold PhDs, 37% are members of minority groups, 19% are women. 5% of classes are taught by teaching assistants.

ACADEMICS

Degrees: associate, bachelor's, certificate, first professional, first professional certificate, master's, post-bachelor's certificate, post-master's certificate, terminal associate. **Classes:** Most classes have 10-19 students. **Majors with Highest Enrollment:** Finance; Economics; Registered Nursing/Registered Nurse. **Special Study Options:** Accelerated program, cross-registration, double major, dual enrollment, English as a Second Language (ESL), exchange student program (domestic), honors program, independent study, internships, liberal arts/career combination, student-designed major, study abroad, teacher certification program, Joint degree programs among schools. Accelerated degree programs. Opportunities for preprofessional programs in predentistry, prelaw, premedi-

cine, and preveterinary studies (not actual majors). Washington semester.
Honors programs: Penn's general honors program is called the Benjamin Franklin Scholars program, although the honors program for students in business is called Joseph Wharton Scholars. There are specialized honors programs including Fisher Program in Management and Technology, the Huntsman Program in International Studies and Business, the Vagelos Scholars Program in Molecular Life Sciences, and the Civic Scholars Program which offers opportunities to integrate community service and academics. The University Scholars Program is open to already matriculated students who are interested in engaging in high-level research. **Combined degree programs:** BA/JD, BA/MA, BA/DDS, BA/MEng, 4-yr. BSE/BS, BSE/MBA, BA/MS Ed., BAS/MS Ed. **Disability Services:** Special programs offered to physically disabled students include note-taking services, reader services, tape recorders, tutors. **Career services:** Alumni network, alumni services, career assessment, internships, regional alumni. In addition to a full on-campus recruiting program (over 13,000 interviews conducted annually), Career Services sponsors the following career days for undergraduates: CareerLink (business fair), Engineering Career Day, Government and Public Policy Career Day, International Opportunities Fair, Nursing Career Day, and a Spring Career Fair for non-profits and just in time opportunities as well as internships.

FACILITIES

Housing: Coed dorms, special housing for disabled students, fraternity/sorority housing, apartments for married students, apartments for single students, Wellness Housingprivate off-campus. 92% of campus accessible to physically disabled. **Special Academic Facilities/Equipment:** Art gallery, anthropology museum, institute for contemporary art, language lab, large animal research center, primate research center, arboretum, observatory, wind tunnel, electron microscope. **Computers:** 85% of classrooms, 100% of dorms, 100% of libraries, 85% of dining areas, 100% of student union, 25% of common outdoor areas have wireless network access. Students can register for classes online. Administrative functions (other than registration) can be performed online.

CAMPUS LIFE

Environment: Metropolis. **Activities:** Choral groups, concert band, dance, drama/theater, jazz band, literary magazine, marching band, music ensembles, musical theater, opera, pep band, radio station, student government, student newspaper, student-run film society, symphony orchestra, television station, yearbook, Campus Ministries, International Student Organization, Model UN. 350 registered organizations, 9 honor societies, 29 religious organizations. 35 fraternities, 13 sororities. **Athletics (Intercollegiate):** *Men:* baseball, basketball, crew/rowing, cross-country, diving, fencing, football, golf, lacrosse, light weight football, soccer, squash, swimming, tennis, track/field (outdoor), track/field (indoor), wrestling. *Women:* basketball, crew/rowing, cross-country, diving, fencing, field hockey, golf, gymnastics, lacrosse, soccer, softball, squash, swimming, tennis, track/field (outdoor), track/field (indoor), volleyball. **On-Campus Highlights:** University of Pennsylvania Museum, Institute of Contemporary Art, Walnut Street shops and restuarants, Annenberg Center, Franklin Field. **Environmental Initiatives:** Building optimization implementation, a program to optimize building systems in high-energy-use buildings to reduce their utility use and carbon footprint. This effort is enhanced by Penn's comprehensive building metering program. The Penn Eco-Reps program has successfully connected grassroots sustainability advocates to policy-makers and influenced real change at the University. In addition to the 100-plus students who are members of the College House, Greek Chapter, and Hillel Eco-Reps programs, over 80 representatives from buildings and departments across campus now volunteer as Staff/Faculty Eco-Reps. Committed to renewable energy, Penn currently purchases 200,000 wind RECs annually, and is the largest purchaser among all colleges and universities in the US. Penn has been the largest purchaser of RECs among higher institutions in the US since 2008.

ADMISSIONS

Freshman Academic Profile: Average high school GPA 3.9. 94% in top 10% of high school class, 99% in top 25% of high school class, 100% in top 50% of high school class. 60% from public high schools. SAT Math middle 50% range 690-780. SAT Critical Reading middle 50% range 660-760. SAT Writing middle 50% range 680-770. ACT middle 50% range 30-34. **Basis for Candidate Selection:** *Very important factors considered include:* recommendation(s), rigor of secondary school record, character/personal qualities. *Important factors considered include:* Class rank, application essay, academic GPA, standardized test scores, extracurricular activities, work experience. *Other factors considered include:* alumni/ae relation, first generation, geographical residence, interview, racial/ethnic status, talent/ability, volunteer work. **Freshman Admission Requirements:** High school diploma or equivalent is not required. **Academic units required:** 4 English, 4 mathematics, 3 science, (3 science labs), 4 foreign language, 3 history. **Freshman Admission Statistics:** 31,218 applied, 13% admitted, 65% enrolled. **Transfer Admission Requirements:** High school transcript, college transcript(s), essay or personal statement, standardized test scores, statement of good standing from prior institution(s). Lowest grade transferable C. **General Admission Information:** Application Fee $75. Early decision application deadline 11/1. Regular application deadline 1/1. Regular notification 4/1. Nonfall registration not accepted. Admission may be deferred for a maximum of 1 year. Credit and/or placement offered for CEEB Advanced Placement tests.

COSTS AND FINANCIAL AID
Average book expense $1,190. **Required Forms and Deadlines:** FAFSA, Institution's own financial aid form, CSS/Financial Aid PROFILE, Noncustodial PROFILE, Business/Farm Supplement. **Notification of Awards:** Applicants will be notified of awards on or about 4/1. **Types of Aid:** *Need-based scholarships/grants:* Federal Pell, SEOG, state scholarships/grants, private scholarships, the school's own gift aid. *Loans:* Subsidized Stafford, Unsubsidized Stafford, PLUS, Federal Perkins, Federal Nursing, college/university loans from institutional funds, Supplemental 3rd Party Loans guaranteed by institution. *Student Employment:* Federal Work-Study Program available. Institutional employment available. Off-campus job opportunities are excellent. **Financial Aid Statistics:** 97% freshmen, 98% undergrads receive need-based scholarship or grant aid. 0% freshmen, 0% undergrads receive non-need-based scholarship or grant aid. 100% freshmen, 100% undergrads receive need-based self-help aid. 0% freshmen, 0% undergrads receive athletic scholarships. 47% freshmen, 45% undergrads receive any aid. 38% undergrads borrow to pay for school. Average cumulative indebtedness $19,197.

UNIVERSITY OF PHOENIX

4035 S. Riverpoint Parkway, Phoenix, AZ 85040
Phone: 480-446-4600 · **Financial Aid Phone:** 1-800-921-1904
Website: www.phoenix.edu

This proprietary school was founded in 1976.

RATINGS
Admissions Selectivity Rating: 60*   **Fire Safety Rating:** 60*

STUDENTS AND FACULTY
Enrollment: 332,377. **Student Body:** 69% female, 31% male, 3% international. Asian 2%, African American 17%, Caucasian 36%, Hispanic 8%, Native American 1%
Retention and Graduation: 1% freshmen graduate within 4 years. 9% freshmen graduate within 6 years. **Faculty:** 1,410 full-time faculty, 23% hold PhDs, 46% are are members of minority groups, 19% are women. 0% of classes are taught by teaching assistants.

ACADEMICS
Degrees: associate, bachelor's, certificate, master's, post-bachelor's certificate, post-master's certificate, transfer associate. **Majors with Highest Enrollment:** Health/Health Care Administration/Management; Business Administration and Management; Accounting. **Special Study Options:** Accelerated program, distance learning, independent study, Evening courses meeting 4 hours per night, one night per week for 5 weeks at the bachelor level and 6 weeks at the master level. **Disability Services:** Special programs offered to physically disabled students include tape recorders. **Career services:** Alumni network,

FACILITIES
Housing: 100% of campus accessible to physically disabled. **Computers:** Students can register for classes online. Administrative functions (other than registration) can be performed online.

CAMPUS LIFE
Environment: Metropolis. **Activities:** 2 honor societies.

ADMISSIONS
Freshman Academic Profile: Minimum paper TOEFL 550. **Basis for Candidate Selection:** *Very important factors considered include:* work experience. *Other factors considered include:* recommendation(s). **Freshman Admission Requirements:** High school diploma is required and GED is accepted. **Transfer Admission Requirements:** college transcript(s). **General Admission Information:** Nonfall registration accepted. Neither credit nor placement offered for CEEB Advanced Placement tests.

UNIVERSITY OF PIKEVILLE

Admissions Office, Pikeville, KY 41501
Phone: 606-218-5251 · **Financial Aid Phone:** 606-218-5247
E-mail: wewantyou@upike.edu · **CEEB Code:** 1980
Fax: 606-218-5255 · **Website:** http://www.upike.edu/ · **ACT Code:** 1540

This private school, affiliated with the Presbyterian Church, was founded in 1889. It has a 25-acre campus.

RATINGS
Admissions Selectivity Rating: 71   **Fire Safety Rating:** 78

STUDENTS AND FACULTY
Enrollment: 1,329. **Student Body:** 50% female, 50% male, 20% out-of-state, 3% international (23 countries represented). Asian 0%, African American 12%, Caucasian 82%, Hispanic 2%, Native American <1%
Retention and Graduation: 55% freshmen return for sophomore year. 25% freshmen graduate within 4 years. 38% freshmen graduate within 6 years. 32% grads go on to further study within 1 year. 75% grads pursue business degrees. **Faculty:** 67 full-time faculty, 60% hold PhDs, 49% are are members of minority groups, 4% are women. 0% of classes are taught by teaching assistants.

ACADEMICS
Degrees: associate, bachelor's, post-bachelor's certificate, terminal associate, transfer associate. **Classes:** Most classes have 10-19 students. **Majors with Highest Enrollment:** Business/Commerce; Biology; Criminal Justice/Safety Studies. **Special Study Options:** double major, dual enrollment, independent study, internships, liberal arts/career combination, student-designed major, study abroad, teacher certification program. **Disability Services:** Special programs offered to physically disabled students include tape recorders, tutors.

FACILITIES
Housing: Coed dorms, men's dorms, women's dorms. 90% of campus accessible to physically disabled.

CAMPUS LIFE
Environment: Village. **Activities:** Choral groups, dance, literary magazine, pep band, student government, student newspaper, yearbook, Campus Ministries. 40 registered organizations, 6 honor societies, 2 religious organizations. **Athletics (Intercollegiate):** *Men:* baseball, basketball, bowling, cheerleading, cross-country, football, golf, soccer, tennis. *Women:* basketball, bowling, cheerleading, cross-country, golf, soccer, softball, tennis, volleyball. **On-Campus Highlights:** Administration Building, Armington Hall, Allara Library, Record Hall, Kinzer Hall.

ADMISSIONS
Freshman Academic Profile: Average high school GPA 3.14. 14% in top 10% of high school class, 32% in top 25% of high school class, 61% in top 50% of high school class. 99% from public high schools. SAT Math middle 50% range 410-500. SAT Writing middle 50% range 380-480. ACT middle 50% range 18-23. Minimum internet-based TOEFL 78. **Freshman Admission Requirements:** High school diploma is required and GED is accepted. **Freshman Admission Statistics:** 2,278 applied, 100% admitted, 15% enrolled. **Transfer Admission Requirements:** High school transcript, college transcript(s), standardized test scores, statement of good standing from prior institution(s). Lowest grade transferable C. **General Admission Information:** Regular application deadline 8/15. Notification on a rolling basis, beginning on or about 9/15. Nonfall registration accepted. Credit and/or placement offered for CEEB Advanced Placement tests.

COSTS AND FINANCIAL AID
Annual tuition $18,840. Room and board $7,210. Required fees $0. Average book expense $2,500. **Required Forms and Deadlines:** FAFSA. **Notification of Awards:** Applicants will be notified of awards on a rolling basis beginning 2/1. **Types of Aid:** *Need-based scholarships/grants:* Federal Pell, SEOG, state scholarships/grants, private scholarships, the school's own gift aid. *Loans:* Subsidized Stafford, Unsubsidized Stafford, PLUS, Federal Perkins, college/university loans from institutional funds. *Student Employment:* Federal Work-Study Program available. Off-campus job opportunities are good. **Financial Aid Statistics:** 100% freshmen, 100% undergrads receive need-based scholarship or grant aid. 53% freshmen, 47% undergrads receive non-need-based scholarship or grant aid. 87% freshmen, 83% undergrads receive need-based self-help aid. 0% freshmen, 0% undergrads receive athletic scholarships. 100% freshmen, 97% undergrads receive any aid. 70% undergrads borrow to pay for school. Average cumulative indebtedness $18,767.

UNIVERSITY OF PITTSBURGH—BRADFORD

Office of Admissions–Hanley Library, Bradford, PA 16701
Phone: 814-362-7555 · **Financial Aid Phone:** 814-362-7550
E-mail: Admissions@upb.pitt.edu · **CEEB Code:** 2935
Fax: 814-362-5150 · **Website:** www.upb.pitt.edu · **ACT Code:** 3731

This public school was founded in 1963. It has a 317-acre campus.

RATINGS

Admissions Selectivity Rating: 79   **Fire Safety Rating:** 89

STUDENTS AND FACULTY

Enrollment: 1,472. **Student Body:** 54% female, 46% male, 16% out-of-state, 4% international (11 countries represented). Asian 2%, African American 10%, Caucasian 73%, Hispanic 5%, Native American <1%
Retention and Graduation: 72% freshmen return for sophomore year. 36% freshmen graduate within 4 years. 53% freshmen graduate within 6 years. 23% grads go on to further study within 1 year. 18% grads pursue arts and sciences degrees. 1% grads pursue law degrees. 1% grads pursue business degrees. 1% grads pursue medical degrees. **Faculty:** 69 full-time faculty, 71% hold PhDs, 38% are members of minority groups, 14% are women. 0% of classes are taught by teaching assistants.

ACADEMICS

Degrees: associate, bachelor's, terminal associate, transfer associate. **Classes:** Most classes have 20-29 students. Most lab/discussion sessions have 10-19 students. **Majors with Highest Enrollment:** Criminal Justice/Law Enforcement Administration; Business/Commerce; Athletic Training/Trainer. **Special Study Options:** cross-registration, distance learning, double major, dual enrollment, external degree program, honors program, independent study, internships, study abroad, teacher certification program. **Honors programs:** The University of Pittsburgh at Bradford offers the Scholars Program which is designed to create a learning community for outstanding students at Pitt-Bradford. **Disability Services:** Special programs offered to physically disabled students include note-taking services, reader services, tape recorders, tutors. **Career services:** Alumni network, alumni services, career assessment, internships, regional alumni. Career services highlights include Career Messenger, a monthly newsletter that will be distributed via e-mail. To receive this newsletter you must subscribe.

FACILITIES

Housing: Coed dorms, special housing for disabled students, apartments for single students. 99% of campus accessible to physically disabled. **Special Academic Facilities/Equipment:** Ceramics Studio, Biodiesal Lab, Television and Radio Broadcast Labs. **Computers:** 100% of classrooms, 100% of dorms, 90% of libraries, 90% of dining areas, 100% of student union, 50% of common outdoor areas have wireless network access. Students can register for classes online. Administrative functions (other than registration) can be performed online.

CAMPUS LIFE

Environment: Village. **Activities:** Choral groups, dance, drama/theater, literary magazine, radio station, student government, student newspaper, Campus Ministries. 54 registered organizations, 8 honor societies, 1 religous organization. 3 fraternities, 3 sororities. **Athletics (Intercollegiate):** *Men:* baseball, basketball, cross-country, golf, soccer, swimming, tennis. *Women:* basketball, cross-country, golf, soccer, softball, swimming, tennis, volleyball. **On-Campus Highlights:** Sport and Fitness Center, The Commons, Student apartments, Blaisdell Hall (Fine Arts Building), Smart classrooms. **Environmental Initiatives:** Installation of a 2.6 kW solar array to power a sustainability information center in the student commons which connects to energy monitors that were installed on every building on campus. Implementation of a no-sort recycling program and on-site trash compactor to increase waste diversion and minimize collection trips. Conducting a tree inventory to become a member of Tree Campus USA.

ADMISSIONS

Freshman Academic Profile: Average high school GPA 3.24. 12% in top 10% of high school class, 32% in top 25% of high school class, 67% in top 50% of high school class. 89% from public high schools. SAT Math middle 50% range 450-560. SAT Critical Reading middle 50% range 430-530. SAT Writing middle 50% range 400-510. ACT middle 50% range 19-24. Minimum paper TOEFL 550. **Basis for Candidate Selection:** *Very important factors considered include:* level of applicant's interest. *Important factors considered include:* academic GPA, rigor of secondary school record, standardized test scores, interview. *Other factors considered include:* Class rank, application essay, recommendation(s), character/personal qualities, extracurricular activities, talent/ability, volunteer work, work experience. **Freshman Admission Requirements:** High school diploma is required and GED is accepted. **Academic

units required: 4 English, 2 mathematics, 1 science, (1 science labs), 2 foreign language, 0 social studies, 1 history, 0 visual/performing arts, 0 computer science, 5 academic electives. **Freshman Admission Statistics:** 1,720 applied, 62% admitted, 37% enrolled. **Transfer Admission Requirements:** college transcript(s), statement of good standing from prior institution(s). Minimum college GPA of 2.0 required. Lowest grade transferable C-. **General Admission Information:** Application Fee $45. Notification on a rolling basis, beginning on or about 11/1. Nonfall registration accepted. Admission may be deferred for a maximum of 1 year. Credit and/or placement offered for CEEB Advanced Placement tests.

COSTS AND FINANCIAL AID

Annual in-state tuition $12,452. Annual out-of-state tuition $23,268. Room and board $8,480. Required fees $870. Average book expense $1,170. **Required Forms and Deadlines:** FAFSA. **Notification of Awards:** Applicants will be notified of awards on a rolling basis beginning 4/1. **Types of Aid:** *Need-based scholarships/grants:* Federal Pell, SEOG, state scholarships/grants, private scholarships, the school's own gift aid. *Loans:* Subsidized Stafford, Unsubsidized Stafford, PLUS, Federal Perkins. *Student Employment:* Federal Work-Study Program available. Institutional employment available. Off-campus job opportunities are fair. **Financial Aid Statistics:** 93% freshmen, 92% undergrads receive need-based scholarship or grant aid. 4% freshmen, 5% undergrads receive non-need-based scholarship or grant aid. 92% freshmen, 91% undergrads receive need-based self-help aid. 0% freshmen, 0% undergrads receive athletic scholarships. 87% freshmen, 84% undergrads receive any aid. 89% undergrads borrow to pay for school. Average cumulative indebtedness $30,779. **Criteria for awarding institutional aid:** *Non-need-based:* academics, alumni affiliation, state/district residency.

See page 1190.

UNIVERSITY OF PITTSBURGH—GREENSBURG

150 Finoli Drive, Greensburg, PA 15601
Phone: 724-836-9880 · **Financial Aid Phone:** 724-836-9881
E-mail: upgadmit@pitt.edu · **CEEB Code:** 2936
Fax: 724-836-7471 · **Website:** www.greensburg.pitt.edu · **ACT Code:** 3733

This public school was founded in 1963. It has a 217-acre campus.

RATINGS

Admissions Selectivity Rating: 77   **Fire Safety Rating:** 60*

STUDENTS AND FACULTY

Enrollment: 1,578. **Student Body:** 52% female, 48% male, 2% out-of-state, 1% international. Asian 4%, African American 6%, Caucasian 79%, Hispanic 4%, Native American <1%
Retention and Graduation: 76% freshmen return for sophomore year. 33% freshmen graduate within 4 years. 53% freshmen graduate within 6 years. 26% grads go on to further study within 1 year. 11% grads pursue arts and sciences degrees. 1% grads pursue law degrees. 2% grads pursue business degrees. 1% grads pursue medical degrees. **Faculty:** 76 full-time faculty, 83% hold PhDs, 57% are are members of minority groups, 13% are women. 0% of classes are taught by teaching assistants.

ACADEMICS

Degrees: bachelor's, certificate. **Classes:** Most classes have 30-39 students. Most lab/discussion sessions have 20-29 students. **Majors with Highest Enrollment:** Management Information Systems; Biology/Biological Sciences; Psychology. **Special Study Options:** cross-registration, double major, dual enrollment, exchange student program (domestic), independent study, internships, liberal arts/career combination, student-designed major, study abroad. **Disability Services:** Special programs offered to physically disabled students include note-taking services, reader services, tape recorders, tutors. **Career services:** Alumni network, alumni services, career/job search classes, career assessment, internships, regional alumni.

FACILITIES

Housing: Coed dorms, Theme Housing. 95% of campus accessible to physically disabled. **Computers:** 100% of libraries, 100% of dining areas, 100% of student union, have wireless network access. Students can register for classes online. Administrative functions (other than registration) can be performed online.

CAMPUS LIFE

Environment: Village. **Activities:** Choral groups, dance, drama/theater, literary magazine, musical theater, radio station, student government, student newspaper, Campus Ministries, International Student Organization. 25

registered organizations, 8 honor societies, 3 religious organizations. **Athletics (Intercollegiate):** *Men:* baseball, basketball, cross-country, golf, soccer, tennis. *Women:* basketball, cross-country, golf, soccer, softball, volleyball. **On-Campus Highlights:** Academic Villages, Exchange—Coffee House, Fireside Lounge, Wagner Dining Hall, Ferguson Theater.

ADMISSIONS

Freshman Academic Profile: Average high school GPA 3.51. 15% in top 10% of high school class, 47% in top 25% of high school class, 84% in top 50% of high school class. 95% from public high schools. SAT Math middle 50% range 460-560. SAT Critical Reading middle 50% range 460-550. SAT Writing middle 50% range 440-540. ACT middle 50% range 18-24. Minimum internet-based TOEFL 80. Minimum paper TOEFL 550. **Basis for Candidate Selection:** *Very important factors considered include:* Class rank, academic GPA, rigor of secondary school record, standardized test scores. *Other factors considered include:* application essay, recommendation(s), character/personal qualities, extracurricular activities, interview, level of applicant's interest, talent/ability, volunteer work. **Freshman Admission Requirements:** High school diploma is required and GED is accepted. **Academic units required:** 4 English, 2 mathematics, 1 science, (1 science labs), 3 foreign language, 2 social studies, 2 history, 1 academic elective. **Freshman Admission Statistics:** 1,538 applied, 81% admitted, 35% enrolled. **Transfer Admission Requirements:** High school transcript, college transcript(s), statement of good standing from prior institution(s). Minimum college GPA of 2.0 required. Lowest grade transferable C. **General Admission Information:** Application Fee $45. Notification on a rolling basis, beginning on or about 9/15. Nonfall registration accepted. Admission may be deferred for a maximum of 12 months. Credit and/or placement offered for CEEB Advanced Placement tests.

COSTS AND FINANCIAL AID

Annual in-state tuition $12,452. Annual out-of-state tuition $23,268. Room and board $9,490. Required fees $920. **Required Forms and Deadlines:** FAFSA, State aid form. **Notification of Awards:** Applicants will be notified of awards on a rolling basis beginning 3/15. **Types of Aid:** *Need-based scholarships/grants:* Federal Pell, SEOG, state scholarships/grants, private scholarships, the school's own gift aid, United Negro College Fund. *Loans:* Subsidized Stafford, Unsubsidized Stafford, PLUS, Federal Perkins, college/university loans from institutional funds. *Student Employment:* Federal Work-Study Program available. Institutional employment available. Off-campus job opportunities are good. **Financial Aid Statistics:** 83% freshmen, 79% undergrads receive need-based scholarship or grant aid. 8% freshmen, 4% undergrads receive non-need-based scholarship or grant aid. 81% freshmen, 85% undergrads receive need-based self-help aid. 0% freshmen, 0% undergrads receive athletic scholarships. 82% undergrads borrow to pay for school. Average cumulative indebtedness $27,630. **Criteria for awarding institutional aid:** *Non-need-based:* academics, leadership, minority status.

UNIVERSITY OF PITTSBURGH—JOHNSTOWN

157 Blackington Hall, Johnstown, PA 15904
Phone: 814-269-7050 · **Financial Aid Phone:** 814-269-7045
E-mail: upjadmit@pitt.edu · **CEEB Code:** 2934
Fax: 814-269-7044 · **Website:** www.upj.pitt.edu

This public school was founded in 1927. It has a 650-acre campus.

RATINGS

Admissions Selectivity Rating: 74	Fire Safety Rating: 79

STUDENTS AND FACULTY

Enrollment: 2,956. **Student Body:** 46% female, 54% male, 2% out-of-state, 1% international (20 countries represented). Asian 1%, African American 3%, Caucasian 90%, Hispanic 2%, Native American <1%.
Retention and Graduation: 74% freshmen return for sophomore year. 39% freshmen graduate within 4 years. 60% freshmen graduate within 6 years. 8% grads pursue arts and sciences degrees. 1% grads pursue law degrees. 1% grads pursue business degrees. 2% grads pursue medical degrees. **Faculty:** 0% of classes are taught by teaching assistants.

ACADEMICS

Degrees: associate, bachelor's, certificate. **Classes:** Most classes have 20-29 students. Most lab/discussion sessions have 10-19 students. **Special Study Options:** Accelerated program, cooperative education program, cross-registration, distance learning, double major, dual enrollment, independent study, internships, liberal arts/career combination, student-designed major, study abroad, teacher certification program. **Honors programs:** President's Scholars Program. **Disability Services:** Special programs offered to physically disabled students include tutors. **Career services:** Alumni network, alumni services, internships.

FACILITIES

Housing: Coed dorms, special housing for disabled students, fraternity/sorority housing, apartments for single students, Theme Housing, Townhouses, Lodges, Single-sex residence upon request. 100% of campus accessible to physically disabled. **Special Academic Facilities/Equipment:** Art museum, performing arts center, language lab. **Computers:** 75% of classrooms, 100% of libraries, 50% of dining areas, 100% of student union, 50% of common outdoor areas have wireless network access. Administrative functions (other than registration) can be performed online.

CAMPUS LIFE

Environment: City. **Activities:** Choral groups, concert band, dance, drama/theater, literary magazine, music ensembles, musical theater, pep band, radio station, student government, student newspaper, television station, yearbook, Campus Ministries, Model UN. 70 registered organizations, 11 honor societies, 3 religious organizations. 5 fraternities, 3 sororities. **Athletics (Intercollegiate):** *Men:* baseball, basketball, golf, soccer, wrestling. *Women:* basketball, cheerleading, cross-country, golf, soccer, track/field (outdoor), volleyball. **On-Campus Highlights:** Student Union Building, Sports Center, Cafeteria, Living/Learning Center, Performing Arts Center.

ADMISSIONS

Freshman Academic Profile: Average high school GPA 3.38. 11% in top 10% of high school class, 34% in top 25% of high school class, 71% in top 50% of high school class. SAT Math middle 50% range 460-560. SAT Critical Reading middle 50% range 450-540. SAT Writing middle 50% range 430-530. ACT middle 50% range 20-24. Minimum internet-based TOEFL 80. Minimum paper TOEFL 550. **Basis for Candidate Selection:** *Very important factors considered include:* Class rank, academic GPA, rigor of secondary school record. *Important factors considered include:* application essay, recommendation(s), standardized test scores, extracurricular activities, interview, level of applicant's interest, talent/ability, volunteer work, work experience. *Other factors considered include:* character/personal qualities, racial/ethnic status. **Freshman Admission Requirements:** High school diploma is required and GED is accepted. **Academic units required:** 4 English, 2 mathematics, 2 science, (1 science labs), 2 foreign language, 4 social studies. **Freshman Admission Statistics:** 1,613 applied, 88% admitted, 53% enrolled. **Transfer Admission Requirements:** High school transcript, college transcript(s), Minimum college GPA of 2.0 required. Lowest grade transferable C. **General Admission Information:** Application Fee $45. Notification on a rolling basis, beginning on or about 9/1. Nonfall registration accepted. Admission may be deferred for a maximum of 12 months. Credit and/or placement offered for CEEB Advanced Placement tests.

COSTS AND FINANCIAL AID

Average book expense $1,030. **Required Forms and Deadlines:** FAFSA. **Notification of Awards:** Applicants will be notified of awards on a rolling basis beginning 3/15. **Types of Aid:** *Need-based scholarships/grants:* Federal Pell, SEOG, state scholarships/grants, private scholarships, the school's own gift aid. *Loans:* Subsidized Stafford, Unsubsidized Stafford, PLUS, Federal Perkins. *Student Employment:* Federal Work-Study Program available. Institutional employment available. Off-campus job opportunities are good. **Financial Aid Statistics:** 72% freshmen, 69% undergrads receive need-based scholarship or grant aid. 34% freshmen, 30% undergrads receive non-need-based scholarship or grant aid. 89% freshmen, 86% undergrads receive need-based self-help aid. 5% freshmen, 5% undergrads receive athletic scholarships. 80% freshmen, 80% undergrads receive any aid. 83% undergrads borrow to pay for school. Average cumulative indebtedness $21,142. **Criteria for awarding institutional aid:** *Non-need-based:* academics, athletics, leadership, minority status, state/district residency.

UNIVERSITY OF PITTSBURGH— PITTSBURGH CAMPUS

Best 380

4227 Fifth Avenue, Pittsburgh, PA 15260
Phone: 412-624-7488 · **Financial Aid Phone:** 412-624-7488
E-mail: oafa@pitt.edu · **CEEB Code:** 2927
Fax: 412-648-8815 · **Website:** www.pitt.edu · **ACT Code:** 3734

This public school was founded in 1787. It has a 132-acre campus.

RATINGS

Admissions Selectivity Rating: 92   **Fire Safety Rating:** 86

STUDENTS AND FACULTY

Enrollment: 18,474. **Student Body:** 50% female, 50% male, 11% out-of-state, 4% international (45 countries represented). Asian 8%, African American 5%, Caucasian 76%, Hispanic 3%, Native American <1%

Retention and Graduation: 93% freshmen return for sophomore year. 65% freshmen graduate within 4 years. 82% freshmen graduate within 6 years. 32% grads go on to further study within 1 year. 45% grads pursue arts and sciences degrees. 7% grads pursue law degrees. 6% grads pursue business degrees. 14% grads pursue medical degrees. **Faculty:** 1,621 full-time faculty, 94% hold PhDs, 43% are are members of minority groups, 17% are women.

ACADEMICS

Degrees: bachelor's, certificate, doctoral, master's, post-bachelor's certificate, post-master's certificate. **Classes:** Most classes have 10-19 students. Most lab/discussion sessions have 20-29 students. **Majors with Highest Enrollment:** Psychology; Finance; Registered Nursing/Registered Nurse. **Special Study Options:** Accelerated program, cooperative education program, cross-registration, distance learning, double major, dual enrollment, English as a Second Language (ESL), exchange student program (domestic), external degree program, honors program, independent study, internships, liberal arts/career combination, student-designed major, study abroad, teacher certification program, weekend college. **Honors programs:** University Honors College **Combined degree programs:** BA/MD, BA/DMD. **Disability Services:** Special programs offered to physically disabled students include note-taking services, reader services, tape recorders. **Career services:** Alumni network, alumni services, career/job search classes, career assessment, internships, regional alumni. Career services highlights include The Pitt Career Network, an extremely valuable tool to which Pitt students have access. This is a database of over 6,000 alumni volunteers worldwide searchable by students. They also provide job shadowing opportunities nationwide. The Office of Student Employment and Placement Assistance (SEPA) hosted its first Career Kickoff event this past fall. The theme for this event was "On the Road With SEPA", since this was an event that would be held in multiple locations and the tag line was "Amp Up Your Career" to tie into the road/concert theme. Career Kickoff was created as a weeklong event held in various locations throughout campus making it convenient for students to stop by in between classes. The goal of this event was to provide students with valuable information before the career fair. We gave seniors and juniors a CD filled with valuabe information such as resume templates, sample cover letters, and acceptance letters. We also gave students a long-sleeved American Eagle t-shirt that listed every career-related event and date on the back of the shirt (similar to a concert t-shirt to tie into the "On the Road" theme.), magnets with the dates of the career-related events, networking tips, career fair tips, and an opportunity to win a pair of donated Cirque du Soleil tickets. Several components made this event unique. While most schools host a career week prior to their career fairs in their offices, we were in a different location each day making it convenient for students to attend. We also invited various regional employers to participate reviewing student resumes, discussing career opportunities in their companies, and providing students tips on networking with employers. Students had the opportunity to hear first hand from an employer tips on improving their resume. Students also had the opportunity to discuss possible positions with employers prior to the career fair, giving them a competitive edge in their job search. This event was extremely successful attacting over 2,300 students, making this the largest non-career fair event in our office.

FACILITIES

Housing: Coed dorms, special housing for disabled students, women's dorms, fraternity/sorority housing, apartments for single students, Wellness Housing, Theme Housing. 90% of campus accessible to physically disabled. **Special Academic Facilities/Equipment:** Stephen Foster Memorial, observatory. **Computers:** 100% of classrooms, 25% of dorms, 100% of libraries, 100% of dining areas, 100% of student union, 50% of common outdoor areas have wireless network access. Students can register for classes online. Administrative functions (other than registration) can be performed online.

CAMPUS LIFE

Environment: Metropolis. **Activities:** Choral groups, concert band, dance, drama/theater, jazz band, literary magazine, marching band, music ensembles, pep band, radio station, student government, student newspaper, student-run film society, television station, yearbook, Campus Ministries, International Student Organization, Model UN. 395 registered organizations, 17 honor societies, 20 fraternities, 16 sororities. **Athletics (Intercollegiate):** *Men:* baseball, basketball, cross-country, diving, football, soccer, swimming, track/field (outdoor), wrestling. *Women:* basketball, cross-country, diving, gymnastics, soccer, softball, swimming, tennis, track/field (outdoor), volleyball. **On-Campus Highlights:** Cathedral of Learning, William Pitt Union, Heinz Chapel, Peterson Event Center, Sennott Square. **Environmental Initiatives:** Energy Center: The Facilities Management Division recently consolidated all energy-related operations to a single location. The newly constructed Energy Center space is designed to increase collaboration among energy managers, engineers, utility analysts, and energy management system personnel. These personnel will use new and existing controls and diagnostic tools to place an even greater focus on ensuring optimal building operations and incorporating new technologies into building system designs to further energy conservation on campus. A new command center provides technicians and managers with consolidated access to the building automation system and other diagnostic tools. Energy Conservation and Green Construction: The University has invested extensively in energy conservation and green construction. Pitt's comprehensive building automation/energy management system provides automated control of building temperatures and operating schedules, allowing for setbacks during unoccupied periods and automated curtailment during peak periods. Significant investments have been made in energy conservation measures, including lighting upgrades, occupancy sensors, sub-metering of electric, steam, and chilled water consumption, upgrades and retrocommissioning of HVAC systems, and the expansion of the University's central steam and chilled water infrastructure. Pitt has also converted selected buildings from constant volume to variable air volume systems and has installed heat recovery systems in recent laboratory upgrades. Over the past 17 years, an estimated cost avoidance of over $44 million has been achieved via energy management and conservation projects. The University pursues LEED certification for most large construction and renovation projects. The McGowan Institute for Regenerative Medicine was the first laboratory building in Pennsylvanie to achieve LEED Gold certification. Two new projects achieved LEED Gold certification in December, 2011—the Benedum Hall Phase I Renovation and the Addition/Renovation to Benedum Hall for the Mascaro Center for Sustainable Innovation. In February, 2013, the University was notified that the Addition to the Chevron Science Center has also achieved LEED Gold certification. An additional ten projects currently in design or construction are pursuing LEED certification. The University has incorporated many sustainable design standards into its Professional Design Manual. Examples include occupancy sensors, direct digital controls, energy efficient lighting, premium efficiency motors, carpet with recycled content, low or no VOC paints and adhesives and VAV controls, among many others (www.facmgmt.pitt.edu/Sustainability.html). Mascaro Center For Sustainable Innovation: The Mascaro Center for Sustainable Innovation at the University of Pittsburgh is a center of excellence in sustainable engineering focusing on the design of sustainable neighborhoods. The Center encourages and nurtures new collaborative projects based on strong and innovative research, translating the fundamental science of sustainability into real products and processes. MCSI's goal is to create innovations that positively impact the environment and improve quality of life. Research includes projects on greening the built environment, more sustainable use of water, and the design of distributed power systems. Other specific areas of interest include Green Building Design and Construction, infrastructure, and sustainable materials (www.mascarocenter.pitt.edu/research/).

ADMISSIONS

Freshman Academic Profile: Average high school GPA 3.99. 54% in top 10% of high school class, 87% in top 25% of high school class, 99% in top 50% of high school class. SAT Math middle 50% range 600-690. SAT Critical Reading middle 50% range 580-670. SAT Writing middle 50% range 570-670. ACT middle 50% range 26-31. Minimum internet-based TOEFL 100. Minimum paper TOEFL 600. **Basis for Candidate Selection:** *Very important factors considered include:* academic GPA, rigor of secondary school record. *Important factors considered include:* standardized test scores. *Other factors considered include:* Class rank, application essay, recommendation(s), character/personal qualities, extracurricular activities, first generation, geographical residence, interview, level of applicant's interest, racial/ethnic status, talent/ability, volunteer work, work experience. **Freshman Admission Requirements:** High school diploma is required and GED is not accepted. **Academic units required:** 4 English, 3 mathematics, 3 science, (3 science labs), 2 foreign language, 2 social studies, 0 history, 0 visual/performing arts, 0 computer science, 3 academic electives. **Freshman Admission Statistics:** 30,629 applied, 53% admitted, 24% enrolled. **Transfer Admission Requirements:** High school transcript, college transcript(s), essay or personal statement, Lowest grade transferable

C. **General Admission Information:** Application Fee $45. Notification on a rolling basis, beginning on or about 10/1. Nonfall registration accepted. Credit offered for CEEB Advanced Placement tests.

COSTS AND FINANCIAL AID
Annual in-state tuition $16,872. Annual out-of-state tuition $27,268. Room and board $10,800. Required fees $900. Average book expense $1,170. **Required Forms and Deadlines:** FAFSA. **Notification of Awards:** Applicants will be notified of awards on a rolling basis beginning 3/15. **Types of Aid:** *Need-based scholarships/grants:* Federal Pell, SEOG, state scholarships/grants, private scholarships, the school's own gift aid, Federal Nursing Scholarships. *Loans:* Subsidized Stafford, Unsubsidized Stafford, PLUS, Federal Perkins, Federal Nursing, college/university loans from institutional funds. *Student Employment:* Federal Work-Study Program available. Institutional employment available. Off-campus job opportunities are excellent. **Financial Aid Statistics:** 77% freshmen, 68% undergrads receive need-based scholarship or grant aid. 7% freshmen, 4% undergrads receive non-need-based scholarship or grant aid. 81% freshmen, 55% undergrads receive need-based self-help aid. 2% freshmen, 2% undergrads receive athletic scholarships. 64% freshmen, 58% undergrads receive any aid. 67% undergrads borrow to pay for school. Average cumulative indebtedness $25,244. **Criteria for awarding institutional aid:** *Non-need-based:* academics, athletics.

UNIVERSITY OF PORTLAND

5000 North Willamette Blvd., Portland, OR 97203-7147
Phone: 503-943-7147 · **Financial Aid Phone:** 503-943-7311
E-mail: admissions@up.edu · **CEEB Code:** 4847
Fax: 503-943-7315 · **Website:** www.up.edu · **ACT Code:** 3500

This private school, affiliated with the Roman Catholic Church, was founded in 1901. It has a 130-acre campus.

RATINGS
Admissions Selectivity Rating: 89   **Fire Safety Rating:** 87

STUDENTS AND FACULTY
Enrollment: 3,654. **Student Body:** 59% female, 41% male, 68% out-of-state, 3% international (32 countries represented). Asian 10%, African American 1%, Caucasian 62%, Hispanic 11%, Native American <1%
Retention and Graduation: 73% freshmen graduate within 4 years. 80% freshmen graduate within 6 years. 15% grads go on to further study within 1 year. **Faculty:** 211 full-time faculty, 88% hold PhDs, 48% are are members of minority groups, 8% are women. 0% of classes are taught by teaching assistants.

ACADEMICS
Degrees: bachelor's, master's, post-master's certificate. **Classes:** Most classes have 20-29 students. Most lab/discussion sessions have 10-19 students. **Majors with Highest Enrollment:** Registered Nursing, Nursing Administration, Nursing Research and Clinical Nursing; Biology/Biological Sciences; Mechanical Engineering. **Special Study Options:** cross-registration, double major, honors program, independent study, internships, liberal arts/career combination, study abroad, teacher certification program. **Honors programs:** The honors program provides an exciting intellectual challenge for highly motivated students whit above average high school records. The program is designed to facilitate learning through special small classes which permit a high level of student-faculty interaction. Honors students may be enrolled in any major. **Disability Services:** Special programs offered to physically disabled students include note-taking services, reader services, tutors. **Career services:** Alumni network, alumni services, career/job search classes, career assessment, internships, regional alumni.

FACILITIES
Housing: Coed dorms, men's dorms, women's dorms, Theme Housing, Rental housing. 80% of campus accessible to physically disabled. **Special Academic Facilities/Equipment:** Art gallery, observatory. **Computers:** 100% of classrooms, 100% of dorms, 100% of libraries, 100% of dining areas, 100% of student union, 100% of common outdoor areas have wireless network access. Students can register for classes online. Administrative functions (other than registration) can be performed online.

CAMPUS LIFE
Environment: Metropolis. **Activities:** Choral groups, concert band, dance, drama/theater, jazz band, literary magazine, music ensembles, musical theater, pep band, radio station, student government, student newspaper, student-run film society, symphony orchestra, yearbook, Campus Ministries, International Student Organization. 40 registered organizations, 15 honor societies, 9 religious organizations. **Athletics (Intercollegiate):** *Men:* baseball, basketball,

cross-country, golf, soccer, tennis, track/field (outdoor). *Women:* basketball, cross-country, golf, soccer, tennis, track/field (outdoor), volleyball. **On-Campus Highlights:** The Cove, St. Mary's Lounge, Howard Recreation Hall. **Environmental Initiatives:** Food for Thought (with Michael Pollan), April 2011; Confluences, Water and Justice (with Maude Barlow), May 2010; Portland host and active participant of Focus the Nation, January 30, 2008; LEED Platinum Engineering building, 2 Leed Gold Dorms; First university or college on west coast to prohibit sale of platic water bottles on campus (2010).

ADMISSIONS
Freshman Academic Profile: Average high school GPA 3.63. 35% in top 10% of high school class, 73% in top 25% of high school class, 94% in top 50% of high school class. 60% from public high schools. SAT Math middle 50% range 540-650. SAT Critical Reading middle 50% range 540-660. Minimum internet-based TOEFL 71. Minimum paper TOEFL 525. **Basis for Candidate Selection:** *Very important factors considered include:* academic GPA, rigor of secondary school record, standardized test scores. *Important factors considered include:* Class rank, application essay, recommendation(s), extracurricular activities, talent/ability, volunteer work. *Other factors considered include:* alumni/ae relation, character/personal qualities, first generation, geographical residence, interview, level of applicant's interest, racial/ethnic status, religious affiliation/commitment, work experience. **Freshman Admission Requirements:** High school diploma is required and GED is accepted. **Academic units required:** 3 English, 2 mathematics, 2 science, 2 social studies, 2 history, 7 academic electives. **Freshman Admission Statistics:** 11,099 applied, 63% admitted, 15% enrolled. **Transfer Admission Requirements:** college transcript(s), essay or personal statement, Minimum college GPA of 2.5 required. Lowest grade transferable C. **General Admission Information:** Application Fee $50. Regular application deadline 6/1. Notification on a rolling basis, beginning on or about 10/1. Nonfall registration accepted. Credit and/or placement offered for CEEB Advanced Placement tests.

COSTS AND FINANCIAL AID
Annual tuition $38,350. Room and board $11,444. Required fees $170. Average book expense $1,080. **Required Forms and Deadlines:** FAFSA. **Notification of Awards:** Applicants will be notified of awards on a rolling basis beginning 3/15. **Types of Aid:** *Need-based scholarships/grants:* Federal Pell, SEOG, state scholarships/grants, private scholarships, the school's own gift aid. *Loans:* Subsidized Stafford, Unsubsidized Stafford, PLUS, Federal Perkins, Federal Nursing, college/university loans from institutional funds. *Student Employment:* Federal Work-Study Program available. Highest amount earned per year from on-campus jobs $1,377. Off-campus job opportunities are good. **Financial Aid Statistics:** 81% freshmen, 81% undergrads receive need-based scholarship or grant aid. 95% freshmen, 91% undergrads receive non-need-based scholarship or grant aid. 75% freshmen, 77% undergrads receive need-based self-help aid. 3% freshmen, 3% undergrads receive athletic scholarships. 98% freshmen, 95% undergrads receive any aid. 68% undergrads borrow to pay for school. Average cumulative indebtedness $23,419. **Criteria for awarding institutional aid:** *Non-need-based:* academics, alumni affiliation, athletics, music/drama, religious affiliation.

UNIVERSITY OF PRINCE EDWARD ISLAND

Office of the Registrar, Charlottetown, PE C1A 4P3
Phone: 902-566-0439 · **Financial Aid Phone:** 902-566-0358
E-mail: registrar@upei.ca
Fax: 902-566-0795 · **Website:** www.upei.ca

This public school was founded in 1969. It has a 130-acre campus.

RATINGS
Admissions Selectivity Rating: 63   **Fire Safety Rating:** 60*

STUDENTS AND FACULTY
Enrollment: 3,449. **Student Body:** 15% out-of-state, (50 countries represented).
Faculty: 244 full-time faculty. 0% of classes are taught by teaching assistants.

ACADEMICS
Degrees: bachelor's, certificate, diploma, first professional, master's. **Classes:** Most classes have 20-29 students. Most lab/discussion sessions have fewer than 10 students. **Special Study Options:** Accelerated program, cooperative education program, distance learning, double major, English as a Second Language (ESL), exchange student program (domestic), honors program, internships, study abroad, teacher certification program. **Disability Services:** Special programs offered to physically disabled students include tutors.

FACILITIES

Housing: Coed dorms, special housing for disabled students, men's dorms, women's dorms, apartments for single students. **Computers:** Students can register for classes online. Administrative functions (other than registration) can be performed online.

CAMPUS LIFE

Environment: Town. **Activities:** Choral groups, concert band, drama/theater, music ensembles, radio station, student government, student newspaper, yearbook. 25 registered organizations, 3 religious organizations. **Athletics (Intercollegiate):** *Men:* basketball, ice hockey, soccer. *Women:* basketball, field hockey, ice hockey, rugby, soccer, volleyball. **On-Campus Highlights:** Chi-Wan Young Sports Centre, W.A. Murphy Student Centre, MacLauchlan Arena and Aquatic Centre, Atlantic Veterinary College, Robertson Library.

ADMISSIONS

Freshman Academic Profile: 90% from public high schools. Minimum paper TOEFL 550. **Basis for Candidate Selection:** *Very important factors considered include:* academic GPA, rigor of secondary school record. *Important factors considered include:* Class rank, recommendation(s). *Other factors considered include:* standardized test scores. **Freshman Admission Statistics:** 1,044 applied, 61% admitted, 91% enrolled. **Transfer Admission Requirements:** college transcript(s), statement of good standing from prior institution(s). **General Admission Information:** Application Fee $50. Regular application deadline 8/1. Regular notification 8/31. Nonfall registration accepted. Admission may be deferred for a maximum of one semester. Neither credit nor placement offered for CEEB Advanced Placement tests.

COSTS AND FINANCIAL AID

Average book expense $500.

UNIVERSITY OF PUGET SOUND

1500 North Warner Street CMB 1062, Tacoma, WA 98416-1062
Phone: 253-879-3211 · **Financial Aid Phone:** 253-879-3214
E-mail: admission@pugetsound.edu · **CEEB Code:** 4067
Fax: 253-879-3993 · **Website:** www.pugetsound.edu · **ACT Code:** 4450

This private school was founded in 1888. It has a 97-acre campus.

RATINGS

Admissions Selectivity Rating: 83   **Fire Safety Rating:** 76

STUDENTS AND FACULTY

Enrollment: 2,539. **Student Body:** 57% female, 43% male, 76% out-of-state, 0% international (9 countries represented). Asian 7%, African American 1%, Caucasian 75%, Hispanic 7%, Native American <1% **Retention and Graduation:** 87% freshmen return for sophomore year. 68% freshmen graduate within 4 years. **Faculty:** 231 full-time faculty, 90% hold PhDs, 47% are are members of minority groups, 8% are women. 0% of classes are taught by teaching assistants.

ACADEMICS

Degrees: bachelor's, first professional, master's, post-master's certificate. **Classes:** Most classes have 10-19 students. Most lab/discussion sessions have 10-19 students. **Majors with Highest Enrollment:** Psychology; Business/Commerce; Biology/Biological Sciences. **Special Study Options:** cooperative education program, double major, honors program, independent study, internships, student-designed major, study abroad, teacher certification program, 1 year of study in Asia, 3-2 engineering program, Business Leadership Program. **Honors programs:** Business Leadership Program; Honors Program. **Disability Services:** Special programs offered to physically disabled students include note-taking services, reader services, tape recorders, tutors. **Career services:** Alumni network, alumni services, career/job search classes, career assessment, internships, regional alumni. Career services highlights include an Internship Seminar. In this seminar students examine issues related to work and its meaning in individual and collective life. Among the requirements are the completion of 120 hours of field experience at a site prearranged in consultation with the internship coordinator. The seminar provides the context to reflect on concrete experiences at the site and link them to political, psychological, social, economic and intellectual forces that shape our views on work and its meaning.

FACILITIES

Housing: Coed dorms, special housing for disabled students, women's dorms, fraternity/sorority housing, Small residential houses, theme floors in halls. 85% of campus accessible to physically disabled. **Special Academic Facilities/Equipment:** Art gallery, natural history museum, concert hall, transmission and scanning electron microscopes, spectrometers, exercise science lab, observatory, paleomagnetic and X-ray lab, physiology labs, and DNA Sequencer. **Computers:** 30% of classrooms, 30% of dorms, 95% of libraries, 95% of dining areas, 85% of student union, 10% of common outdoor areas have wireless network access. Students can register for classes online. Administrative functions (other than registration) can be performed online.

CAMPUS LIFE

Environment: City. **Activities:** Choral groups, concert band, dance, drama/theater, jazz band, literary magazine, music ensembles, musical theater, opera, radio station, student government, student newspaper, student-run film society, symphony orchestra, yearbook. 77 registered organizations, 2 honor societies, 12 religious organizations. 4 fraternities, 4 sororities. **Athletics (Intercollegiate):** *Men:* baseball, basketball, crew/rowing, cross-country, football, golf, soccer, swimming, tennis, track/field (outdoor), track/field (indoor). *Women:* basketball, crew/rowing, cross-country, golf, lacrosse, soccer, softball, swimming, tennis, track/field (outdoor), track/field (indoor), volleyball. **On-Campus Highlights:** 3-story Dale Chihuly glass sculpture in Wyatt Hall, Harned Hall, new state-of-the-art science facility, Diversions Caf, 97 acres of rolling lawns, native fir groves, and Tudor Gothic architecture, Music and theater productions directed by faculty and students on campus. **Environmental Initiatives:** In 2005, President Thomas established the Sustainability Advisory Committee (SAC), which reports to the president through the Vice President of Student Affairs and the Vice President for Finance and Administration. The president empowered the committee to advise on and implement sustainability policies and programs on campus and collaboratively with our regional community. The committee addresses sustainability across the institution and in partnership with external organizations. It also uniquely engages students, faculty, and staff in comprehensive, collaborative, and strategic sustainability endeavors. In 2010, the Sustainability Advisory Committee (SAC) reorganized itself around the Sustainability Tracking, Assessment, and Rating System (STARS) to facilitate comprehensive sustainability assessment and management. The SAC created subcommittees structured under STARS to assess Puget Sounds sustainability status, identify priorities, and establish objectives. In 2012, Puget Sound earned a gold STARS rating that evidences our commitment to sustainability. Relatively few institutions have a gold rating. Puget Sound has intentionally embedded sustainability across its curriculum and in its research. We conducted workshops for faculty to incorporate sustainability into many courses. We offer a broad range of sustainability related and focused courses. This engages virtually all students in all disciplines with environmental education. The Association for the Advancement of Sustainability in Higher Education (AASHE) operated a sustainability learning objectives group that established a rubric of seven sustainability principles for courses. Sustainability-related courses incorporate sustainability as a distinct course component or module, or concentrate on, a single sustainability principle or issue. A sustainability-focused course concentrates on the concept of sustainability or uses sustainability as a lens if it engages at least three of the seven sustainability principles in this rubric (using educational goals and learning outcomes in the rubric that match course content to determine "engaging the principles"). A sustainability related course engages at least one but not more than two of the seven principles (using educational goals and learning outcomes in the rubric that match course content to determine "engaging the principles"). Based upon a 2010 comprehensive course survey, Puget Sound offered 923 total courses, 98 of which were sustainability focused and 307 of which were sustainability related. Of 34 academic departments, 32 offered at least one sustainability related or focused course. Sustainability research focuses on a key principle of sustainability (such as social equity or environmental stewardship); addresses a sustainability challenge (such as climate change or poverty); or furthers understanding of the interconnectedness of societal and environmental challenges. Sustainability research leads toward solutions that support economic prosperity, social well-being, and ecological health. We use the rubric of seven sustainability principles adopted by the AASHE Sustainability Learning Objective Group to inform analysis of research focus. Based upon a 2010 survey, 353 faculty members were involved in research, 153 of whom engaged in sustainability research. Of 33 departments engaged in research, 32 had at least one faculty member involved in sustainability research.

ADMISSIONS

Freshman Academic Profile: 26% in top 10% of high school class, 51% in top 25% of high school class, 89% in top 50% of high school class. 73% from public high schools. SAT Math middle 50% range 550-660. SAT Critical Reading middle 50% range 570-670. SAT Writing middle 50% range 550-670. ACT middle 50% range 25-30. Minimum internet-based TOEFL 79. Minimum paper TOEFL 550. **Basis for Candidate Selection:** *Very important factors considered include:* academic GPA, rigor of secondary school record, standardized test scores. *Important factors considered include:* application essay, recommendation(s), alumni/ae relation, character/personal qualities, extracurricular activities, racial/ethnic status, talent/ability. *Other factors considered include:* Class rank, first generation, interview, level of applicant's interest, volunteer work, work experience. **Freshman Admission Requirements:** High school diploma is required and GED is accepted. **Freshman Admission Statistics:** 4,588 applied, 85% admitted, 17% enrolled. **Transfer Admission Requirements:** college transcript(s), essay or personal statement, statement of good standing from prior institution(s). Minimum college GPA of 2.0 required. Lowest grade transferable D. **General Admission Information:** Application Fee $40. Early decision application deadline 11/15. Regular application deadline 2/15. Regular notification 4/1. Nonfall registration accepted. Admission may be deferred for a maximum of 1 year. Credit and/or placement offered for CEEB Advanced Placement tests.

COSTS AND FINANCIAL AID

Annual tuition $43,200. Room and board $11,180. Required fees $228. Average book expense $1,000. **Required Forms and Deadlines:** FAFSA. **Notification of Awards:** Applicants will be notified of awards on a rolling basis beginning 3/15. **Types of Aid:** *Need-based scholarships/grants:* Federal Pell, SEOG, state scholarships/grants, private scholarships, the school's own gift aid. *Loans:* Subsidized Stafford, Unsubsidized Stafford, PLUS, Federal Perkins. *Student Employment:* Federal Work-Study Program available. Institutional employment available. Highest amount earned per year from on-campus jobs $2,650. Off-campus job opportunities are excellent. **Financial Aid Statistics:** 99% freshmen, 99% undergrads receive need-based scholarship or grant aid. 22% freshmen, 11% undergrads receive non-need-based scholarship or grant aid. 66% freshmen, 77% undergrads receive need-based self-help aid. 0% freshmen, 0% undergrads receive athletic scholarships. 96% freshmen, 94% undergrads receive any aid. 61% undergrads borrow to pay for school. Average cumulative indebtedness $26,466. **Criteria for awarding institutional aid:** *Non-need-based:* academics, alumni affiliation, art, leadership, music/drama, religious affiliation.

UNIVERSITY OF REDLANDS

1200 E. Colton Avenue, Redlands, CA 92373
Phone: 909-748-8074 · **Financial Aid Phone:** 909-748-8047
E-mail: admissions@redlands.edu · **CEEB Code:** 4848
Fax: 909-335-4089 · **Website:** www.redlands.edu · **ACT Code:** 464

This private school was founded in 1907. It has a 160-acre campus.

RATINGS

Admissions Selectivity Rating: 87	**Fire Safety Rating:** 78

STUDENTS AND FACULTY

Enrollment: 2,673. **Student Body:** 57% female, 43% male, 24% out-of-state, 1% international (17 countries represented). Asian 3%, African American 2%, Caucasian 41%, Hispanic 18%, Native American <1%
Retention and Graduation: 63% freshmen graduate within 4 years. 73% freshmen graduate within 6 years. 19% grads go on to further study within 1 year. 5% grads pursue law degrees. 20% grads pursue business degrees. 2% grads pursue medical degrees. **Faculty:** 161 full-time faculty, 88% hold PhDs, 51% are are members of minority groups, 16% are women. 0% of classes are taught by teaching assistants.

ACADEMICS

Degrees: associate, bachelor's, certificate, master's, post-bachelor's certificate, post-master's certificate. **Classes:** Most classes have 10-19 students. **Majors with Highest Enrollment:** Business/Commerce; Psychology; Liberal Arts and Sciences/Liberal Studies. **Special Study Options:** cross-registration, double major, dual enrollment, exchange student program (domestic), honors program, independent study, internships, liberal arts/career combination, student-designed major, study abroad, teacher certification program. **Honors programs:** The Johnston Center for Integrative Studies allows students to design their own majors in consultation with faculty advisors. Students write contracts for their courses and receive narrative evaluations in lieu of traditional grades. The center has received national acclaim for its innovative approaches to education. **Disability Services:** Special programs offered to physically disabled students include note-taking services, reader services, tutors. **Career services:** alumni services, career/job search classes, regional alumni.

FACILITIES

Housing: Coed dorms, special housing for disabled students, men's dorms, women's dorms, fraternity/sorority housing, apartments for single students, Abroad Programming. Apartments for students with dependent children. 75% of campus accessible to physically disabled. **Special Academic Facilities/Equipment:** Art gallery, Far East art collection, Southwest collection, center for communicative disorders, language lab, Helen and Vernon Farquar Anthropology Lab, Physics Laser Photonics Lab, Irvine Map Library, Geographic Information System lab. **Computers:** 100% of classrooms, 100% of dorms, 100% of libraries, 100% of dining areas, 100% of student union, 100% of common outdoor areas have wireless network access. Students can register for classes online. Administrative functions (other than registration) can be performed online.

CAMPUS LIFE

Environment: Town. **Activities:** Choral groups, concert band, dance, drama/theater, jazz band, literary magazine, music ensembles, musical theater, opera, radio station, student government, student newspaper, student-run film society, symphony orchestra, yearbook. 105 registered organizations, 8 honor societies, 8 religious organizations. 5 fraternities, 5 sororities. **Athletics (Intercollegiate):** *Men:* baseball, basketball, cross-country, diving, football, golf, soccer, swimming, tennis, track/field (outdoor), water polo. *Women:* basketball, cross-country, diving, golf, lacrosse, soccer, softball, swimming, tennis, track/field (outdoor), volleyball, water polo. **On-Campus Highlights:** Armacost Library, Peppers Art Center, Currier Gymnasium/Fitness Center, Chapel, Post Office, Other popular places on campus: Math and Physics Building, Aquatic Center, Football Stadium, Jasper's Corner, and Plaza Café. **Environmental Initiatives:** Co-Generation facility to provide power to much of the campus; Lewis Hall—a high performance earth-sheltered green building that houses the department of Environmental Studies, the GIS program, and the Resdlands Institute Art & Theater Center LEED (green) building.

ADMISSIONS

Freshman Academic Profile: Average high school GPA 3.66. 34.8% in top 10% of high school class, 65.2% in top 25% of high school class, 95.6% in top 50% of high school class. SAT Math middle 50% range 520-620. SAT Critical Reading middle 50% range 510-610. ACT middle 50% range 23-27. Minimum paper TOEFL 550. **Basis for Candidate Selection:** *Very important factors considered include:* academic GPA, recommendation(s), rigor of secondary school record, character/personal qualities, talent/ability. *Important factors considered include:* application essay, standardized test scores. *Other factors considered include:* alumni/ae relation, extracurricular activities, first generation, geographical residence, interview, racial/ethnic status, volunteer work, work experience. **Freshman Admission Requirements:** High school diploma is required and GED is accepted. **Academic units required:** 4 English, 3 mathematics, 2 science, (1 science labs), 2 foreign language, 2 social studies, 0 history, 0 academic electives, 0. **Freshman Admission Statistics:** 4,668 applied, 67% admitted, 21% enrolled. **Transfer Admission Requirements:** High school transcript, college transcript(s), essay or personal statement, Minimum college GPA of 2.5 required. Lowest grade transferable C. **General Admission Information:** Application Fee $30. Regular application deadline 6/1. Notification on a rolling basis, beginning on or about 11/1. Nonfall registration accepted. Admission may be deferred for a maximum of 12 months. Credit and/or placement offered for CEEB Advanced Placement tests.

COSTS AND FINANCIAL AID

Annual tuition $42,836. Room and board $12,710. Required fees $350. Average book expense $1,746. **Required Forms and Deadlines:** FAFSA, State aid form. **Notification of Awards:** Applicants will be notified of awards on a rolling basis beginning 2/28. **Types of Aid:** *Need-based scholarships/grants:* Federal Pell, SEOG, state scholarships/grants, private scholarships, the school's own gift aid. *Loans:* Subsidized Stafford, Unsubsidized Stafford, PLUS, Federal Perkins, college/university loans from institutional funds. *Student Employment:* Federal Work-Study Program available. Highest amount earned per year from on-campus jobs $2,000. Off-campus job opportunities are fair. **Financial Aid Statistics:** 100% freshmen, 99% undergrads receive need-based scholarship or grant aid. 74% freshmen, 57% undergrads receive non-need-based scholarship or grant aid. 84% freshmen, 91% undergrads receive need-based self-help aid. 0% freshmen, 0% undergrads receive athletic scholarships. 94% freshmen, 94% undergrads receive any aid. 71% undergrads borrow to pay for school. Average cumulative indebtedness $25,585. **Criteria for awarding institutional aid:** *Non-need-based:* academics, art, music/drama.

UNIVERSITY OF RHODE ISLAND

Newman Hall, Kingston, RI 2881
Phone: 401-874-7100 · **Financial Aid Phone:** 401-874-7530
E-mail: admission@uri.edu · **CEEB Code:** 3919
Fax: 401-874-5523 · **Website:** www.uri.edu · **ACT Code:** 3818

This public school was founded in 1892. It has a 1300-acre campus.

RATINGS

Admissions Selectivity Rating: 83   **Fire Safety Rating:** 82

STUDENTS AND FACULTY

Enrollment: 13,205. **Student Body:** 54% female, 46% male, 44% out-of-state, 1% international (49 countries represented). Asian 3%, African American 5%, Caucasian 70%, Hispanic 9%, Native American <1%
Retention and Graduation: 82% freshmen return for sophomore year. 39% freshmen graduate within 4 years. 59% freshmen graduate within 6 years. **Faculty:** 704 full-time faculty, 83% hold PhDs, 46% are are members of minority groups, 17% are women. 4% of classes are taught by teaching assistants.

ACADEMICS

Degrees: bachelor's, first professional, master's, post-bachelor's certificate. **Classes:** Most classes have 20-29 students. Most lab/discussion sessions have 10-19 students. **Majors with Highest Enrollment:** Registered Nursing, Nursing Administration, Nursing Research and Clinical Nursing; Speech Communication and Rhetoric; Psychology. **Special Study Options:** distance learning, double major, dual enrollment, exchange student program (domestic), honors program, independent study, internships, study abroad, teacher certification program, weekend college. **Honors programs:** The Honors Program at URI features small classes, a nationally renowned Honors Colloquium, National Scholarship for upper class students, advising and honors housing for upper class students. **Combined degree programs:** MCP/JD, MPA/MDS, PH.D/MMA, MS/JD, MA/MLIS, MMA/JD, PharmD/MBA, MPA/MLIS, MP. **Disability Services:** Special programs offered to physically disabled students include note-taking services, tape recorders. **Career services:** Alumni network, alumni services, career assessment, internships, regional alumni. Career services highlights include career assessments and job search assistance.

FACILITIES

Housing: Coed dorms, special housing for disabled students, fraternity/sorority housing, apartments for married students, cooperative housing, apartments for single students, Wellness Housing, Theme Housing, Learning communities for undecided majors, honor program, health sciences, engineering, college environment and health sciences majors, and nursing. 100% of campus accessible to physically disabled. **Special Academic Facilities/Equipment:** Center for robotic research, animal science farm, planetarium, Watson House Museum, Narragansett Bay Campus for Marine Sciences, American historic textiles museum, aquaculture center, fisheries and marine technology laboratory, center for biotechnology and life sciences, human performance laboratory. **Computers:** 50% of classrooms, 100% of dorms, 100% of libraries, 75% of dining areas, 100% of student union, 25% of common outdoor areas have wireless network access. Students can register for classes online. Administrative functions (other than registration) can be performed online.

CAMPUS LIFE

Environment: Village. **Activities:** Choral groups, concert band, dance, drama/theater, jazz band, literary magazine, marching band, music ensembles, musical theater, pep band, radio station, student government, student newspaper, student-run film society, television station, yearbook, Campus Ministries, International Student Organization. 100 registered organizations, 40 honor societies, 5 religious organizations. 11 fraternities, 9 sororities. **Athletics (Intercollegiate):** *Men:* baseball, basketball, cheerleading, cross-country, football, golf, soccer, track/field (outdoor), track/field (indoor). *Women:* basketball, cheerleading, crew/rowing, cross-country, diving, soccer, softball, swimming, tennis, track/field (outdoor), track/field (indoor), volleyball. **On-Campus Highlights:** Ryan Center and Boss Ice Arena, Ballentine Hall (Business building), Memorial Student Union, Multi-Cultural Center in heart of campus, Hope Dining Commons, Center for Biotechnology and Life Sciences—LEED certified and the focal point of a statewide effort to build a new, knowledge-based economy for Rhode Island. Green Hall—historic building houses Registrar, Financial Aid and Bursar, as well as Administrative Offices. **Environmental Initiatives:** Development of a sustainability component to the general education requirements for all undergraduate students Reduction of energy use through staff/faculty/student behavior change program Reduction of single-occupancy vehicles driven to/from campus via increasing public transportation awareness, promoting biking/walking, car share and car pooling.

ADMISSIONS

Freshman Academic Profile: Average high school GPA 3.4. 19% in top 10% of high school class, 49% in top 25% of high school class, 86% in top 50% of high school class. SAT Math middle 50% range 510-610. SAT Critical Reading middle 50% range 500-590. SAT Writing middle 50% range 490-590. ACT middle 50% range 22-26. Minimum internet-based TOEFL 79. Minimum paper TOEFL 550. **Basis for Candidate Selection:** *Very important factors considered include:* rigor of secondary school record. *Important factors considered include:* Class rank, application essay, academic GPA, standardized test scores. *Other factors considered include:* recommendation(s), alumni/ae relation, character/personal qualities, extracurricular activities, first generation, geographical residence, level of applicant's interest, racial/ethnic status, state residency, talent/ability, volunteer work, work experience. **Freshman Admission Requirements:** High school diploma is required and GED is accepted. **Academic units required:** 4 English, 3 mathematics, 2 science, (1 science labs), 2 foreign language, 2 social studies, 5 academic electives. 4 English, 3 mathematics, 2 science, (1 science labs), 2 foreign language, 2 social studies, 5 academic electives. **Freshman Admission Statistics:** 20,928 applied, 76% admitted, 22% enrolled. **Transfer Admission Requirements:** college transcript(s), essay or personal statement, statement of good standing from prior institution(s). Minimum college GPA of 2.5 required. Lowest grade transferable C. **General Admission Information:** Application Fee $65. Regular application deadline 2/1. Regular notification 3/31. Notification on a rolling basis, beginning on or about 12/1. Nonfall registration accepted. Credit and/or placement offered for CEEB Advanced Placement tests.

COSTS AND FINANCIAL AID

Annual in-state tuition $10,878. Annual out-of-state tuition $26,444. Room and board $11,160. Required fees $1,628. Average book expense $1,200. **Required Forms and Deadlines:** FAFSA. **Notification of Awards:** Applicants will be notified of awards on a rolling basis beginning 3/31. **Types of Aid:** *Need-based scholarships/grants:* Federal Pell, SEOG, state scholarships/grants, private scholarships, the school's own gift aid. *Loans:* Direct Subsidized Stafford, Direct Unsubsidized Stafford, Direct PLUS, Federal Perkins, Federal Nursing, state loans, college/university loans from institutional funds. *Student Employment:* Federal Work-Study Program available. Institutional employment available. Highest amount earned per year from on-campus jobs $2,000. Off-campus job opportunities are good. **Financial Aid Statistics:** 84% freshmen, 80% undergrads receive need-based scholarship or grant aid. 16% freshmen, 9% undergrads receive non-need-based scholarship or grant aid. 79% freshmen, 75% undergrads receive need-based self-help aid. 0% freshmen, 0% undergrads receive athletic scholarships. 91% freshmen, 90% undergrads receive any aid. 70% undergrads borrow to pay for school. Average cumulative indebtedness $26,894. **Criteria for awarding institutional aid:** *Non-need-based:* academics, alumni affiliation, art, athletics, music/drama.

UNIVERSITY OF RICHMOND

Brunet Memorial Hall: 28 Westhampton Way, University of Richmond, VA 23173
Phone: 804-289-8640 · **Financial Aid Phone:** 804-289-8438
E-mail: admission@richmond.edu · **CEEB Code:** 5569
Fax: 804-287-6003 · **Website:** www.richmond.edu · **ACT Code:** 4410

This private school was founded in 1830. It has a 350-acre campus.

RATINGS

Admissions Selectivity Rating: 94   **Fire Safety Rating:** 87

STUDENTS AND FACULTY

Enrollment: 2,881. **Student Body:** 51% female, 49% male, 80% out-of-state, 9% international (69 countries represented). Asian 7%, African American 6%, Caucasian 58%, Hispanic 8%, Native American <1%
Retention and Graduation: 94% freshmen return for sophomore year. 80% freshmen graduate within 4 years. 84% freshmen graduate within 6 years. 20% grads go on to further study within 1 year. 6% grads pursue arts and sciences degrees. 3% grads pursue law degrees. 1% grads pursue business degrees. 2% grads pursue medical degrees. **Faculty:** 323 full-time faculty, 93% hold PhDs, 41% are are members of minority groups, 13% are women. 0% of classes are taught by teaching assistants.

ACADEMICS

Degrees: associate, bachelor's, certificate, diploma, master's, post-bachelor's certificate. **Classes:** Most classes have 10-19 students. Most lab/discussion sessions have 10-19 students. **Majors with Highest Enrollment:** Business Administration and Management; Organizational Behavior Studies; Accounting. **Special Study Options:** Accelerated program, cross-registration, distance learning, double major, English as a Second Language (ESL), exchange student program (domestic), honors program, independent study, internships, student-designed major, study abroad, teacher certification program, Notes on above: Summer English Language Institute is for accepted International Students only. Distance Learning offered through School of Continuing Studies. **Career services:** Alumni network, alumni services, career/job search classes, career assessment, internships. Career services highlights include Spider Road Trips. Trips include Spiders on Wall Street to visit Wall Street firms; Spiders in Media and Communications to New York City; Spiders for the Common Good to public service organizations in Washington D.C. and day trips to selected organizations in the Richmond area. Accompanied by staff, groups of approximately 25 students are given the opportunity to see the operations and hear speakers in different organizations.

FACILITIES

Housing: Coed dorms, special housing for disabled students, men's dorms, women's dorms, apartments for single students, Theme Housing: Global House, Outdoor House, and Civic Engagement represent co-ed housing. Other housing options include: Spinning your Web (for first-year males) and Ready for Moore (for first-year females). 90% of campus accessible to physically disabled. **Special Academic Facilities/Equipment:** Art gallery, mineral museum, Virginia Baptist archives, language lab, Neuroscience lab, Speech Center, Music Technology lab, Jepson School of Leadership, Center for Civic Engagement. **Computers:** 100% of classrooms, 100% of dorms, 100% of libraries, 100% of dining areas, 100% of student union, 100% of common outdoor areas have wireless network access. Students can register for classes online. Administrative functions (other than registration) can be performed online.

CAMPUS LIFE

Environment: Metropolis. **Activities:** Choral groups, concert band, dance, drama/theater, jazz band, literary magazine, music ensembles, musical theater, pep band, radio station, student government, student newspaper, student-run film society, symphony orchestra, Campus Ministries, International Student Organization, Model UN. 208 registered organizations, 28 honor societies, 17 religious organizations. 6 fraternities, 8 sororities. **Athletics (Intercollegiate):** *Men:* baseball, basketball, cross-country, football, golf, soccer, tennis, track/field (outdoor), track/field (indoor). *Women:* basketball, cross-country, diving, field hockey, golf, lacrosse, soccer, swimming, tennis, track/field (outdoor), track/field (indoor). **On-Campus Highlights:** Tyler Haynes Commons, Robins Center (Athletic Center), Boatwright Memorial Library and Coffee Shop, Stern Plaza (Weinstein Hall, Jepson Hall, etc.), Westhampton Green (Modlin Center for the Arts). **Environmental Initiatives:** Signing the ACUPCC and completing the Climate Action Plan in December 2010. Initiated a LEED Silver minimum requirement on all new construction. Continuing waste diversion initiatives. Energy conservation and efficiency projects.

ADMISSIONS

Freshman Academic Profile: 59% in top 10% of high school class, 87% in top 25% of high school class, 98% in top 50% of high school class. 60% from public high schools. SAT Math middle 50% range 620-720. SAT Critical Reading middle 50% range 600-710. SAT Writing middle 50% range 600-703. ACT middle 50% range 29-32. Minimum internet-based TOEFL 80. Minimum paper TOEFL 550. **Basis for Candidate Selection:** *Very important factors considered include:* academic GPA, rigor of secondary school record. *Important factors considered include:* Class rank, application essay, standardized test scores, character/personal qualities, first generation, talent/ability. *Other factors considered include:* recommendation(s), alumni/ae relation, extracurricular activities, geographical residence, interview, racial/ethnic status, state residency, volunteer work, work experience. **Freshman Admission Requirements:** High school diploma is required and GED is accepted. **Academic units required:** 4 English, 3 mathematics, 2 science, (2 science labs), 2 foreign language, 2 history. **Freshman Admission Statistics:** 9,921 applied, 32% admitted, 26% enrolled. **Transfer Admission Requirements:** High school transcript, college transcript(s), essay or personal statement, statement of good standing from prior institution(s). Minimum college GPA of 2.0 required. Lowest grade transferable C. **General Admission Information:** Application Fee $50. Early decision application deadline 11/15. Regular application deadline 1/15. Regular notification 4/1. Nonfall registration not accepted. Admission may be deferred for a maximum of 12 months. Credit and/or placement offered for CEEB Advanced Placement tests.

COSTS AND FINANCIAL AID

Annual tuition $46,680. Room and board $10,790. Required fees $0. Average book expense $1,100. **Required Forms and Deadlines:** FAFSA, CSS/Financial Aid PROFILE, Noncustodial PROFILE. **Notification of Awards:** Applicants will be notified of awards on or about 4/1. **Types of Aid:** *Need-based*

scholarships/grants: Federal Pell, SEOG, state scholarships/grants, private scholarships, the school's own gift aid. *Loans:* Direct Subsidized Stafford, Direct Unsubsidized Stafford, Direct PLUS, Federal Perkins. *Student Employment:* Federal Work-Study Program available. Institutional employment available. Off-campus job opportunities are excellent. **Financial Aid Statistics:** 98% freshmen, 98% undergrads receive need-based scholarship or grant aid. 24% freshmen, 17% undergrads receive non-need-based scholarship or grant aid. 75% freshmen, 82% undergrads receive need-based self-help aid. 8% freshmen, 7% undergrads receive athletic scholarships. 64% freshmen, 67% undergrads receive any aid. 44% undergrads borrow to pay for school. Average cumulative indebtedness $18,850. **Criteria for awarding institutional aid:** *Non-need-based:* academics, art, athletics, leadership, minority status, music/drama.

UNIVERSITY OF RIO GRANDE

218 North College Avenue, Rio Grande, OH 45774
Phone: 740-245-7206 · **Financial Aid Phone:** 740-245-7219
E-mail: admissions@rio.edu · **CEEB Code:** 1663
Fax: 740-245-7260 · **Website:** rio.edu · **ACT Code:** 3324

This private school was founded in 1876. It has a 68-acre campus.

RATINGS

Admissions Selectivity Rating: 63	Fire Safety Rating: 79

STUDENTS AND FACULTY

Enrollment: 1,322. **Student Body:** 64% female, 36% male, 4% out-of-state, 1% international. Asian 0%, African American 6%, Caucasian 84%, Hispanic 1%, Native American <1%
Retention and Graduation: 54% freshmen return for sophomore year. 27% freshmen graduate within 4 years. 39% freshmen graduate within 6 years. **Faculty:** 86 full-time faculty, 52% hold PhDs, 48% are are members of minority groups, 5% are women. 0% of classes are taught by teaching assistants.

ACADEMICS

Degrees: associate, bachelor's, certificate, master's. **Classes:** Most classes have fewer than 10 students. Most lab/discussion sessions have 20-29 students. **Majors with Highest Enrollment:** Elementary Education and Teaching; Business/Office Automation/Technology/Data Entry. **Special Study Options:** Accelerated program, cooperative education program, distance learning, double major, dual enrollment, English as a Second Language (ESL), honors program, independent study, internships, liberal arts/career combination, student-designed major, study abroad, teacher certification program. **Combined degree programs:** 2-2 programs: nursing, business, industrial tech. **Disability Services:** Special programs offered to physically disabled students include note-taking services, reader services, tape recorders, tutors. **Career services:** alumni services, career assessment, internships.

FACILITIES

Housing: Coed dorms, special housing for disabled students, men's dorms, women's dorms, Wellness HousingPrivate housing owned and operated by university available to responsible students. 75% of campus accessible to physically disabled. **Special Academic Facilities/Equipment:** Archives of local and college history, art museum, fine woodworking, theater, art annex. **Computers:** 75% of classrooms, 100% of dorms, 100% of libraries, 100% of dining areas, 100% of student union, 25% of common outdoor areas have wireless network access. Students can register for classes online. Administrative functions (other than registration) can be performed online.

CAMPUS LIFE

Environment: Rural. **Activities:** Choral groups, concert band, dance, drama/theater, jazz band, literary magazine, music ensembles, musical theater, pep band, radio station, student government, student newspaper, television station. 34 registered organizations, 4 honor societies, 3 religious organizations. 4 fraternities, 5 sororities. **Athletics (Intercollegiate):** *Men:* baseball, basketball, cross-country, soccer, track/field (outdoor), track/field (indoor). *Women:* basketball, cheerleading, cross-country, soccer, softball, track/field (outdoor), track/field (indoor), volleyball. **On-Campus Highlights:** Food Court, Red Zone, Basketball Court **Environmental Initiatives:** Recycling program, some solar powered equipment, energy usage reduction program, trayless Tuesdays in the Cafeteria.

ADMISSIONS

Freshman Academic Profile: Average high school GPA 2.94. 5% in top 10% of high school class, 20% in top 25% of high school class, 49% in top 50% of high school class. 95% from public high schools. Minimum paper TOEFL 400. **Basis for Candidate Selection:** *Other factors considered include:* Class rank, academic GPA, standardized test scores. **Freshman Admission Requirements:** High school diploma is required and GED is accepted. **Academic**

units required: 4 English, 3 mathematics, 3 science, (1 science labs), 0 foreign language, 3 social studies, 7 academic electives. **Freshman Admission Statistics:** 1,754 applied, 73% admitted, 36% enrolled. **Transfer Admission Requirements:** High school transcript, college transcript(s), statement of good standing from prior institution(s). Minimum college GPA of 0 required. Lowest grade transferable D. **General Admission Information:** Application Fee $25. Nonfall registration accepted. Credit and/or placement offered for CEEB Advanced Placement tests.

COSTS AND FINANCIAL AID

Annual tuition $21,540. Room and board $9,450. Required fees $450. Average book expense $1,200. **Required Forms and Deadlines:** FAFSA, Institution's own financial aid form. **Notification of Awards:** Applicants will be notified of awards on a rolling basis beginning 1/15. **Types of Aid:** *Need-based scholarships/grants:* Federal Pell, SEOG, state scholarships/grants, private scholarships, the school's own gift aid. *Loans:* Direct Subsidized Stafford, Direct Unsubsidized Stafford, Direct PLUS, Subsidized Stafford, PLUS, Federal Perkins, Federal Nursing, college/university loans from institutional funds. *Student Employment:* Off-campus job opportunities are fair. **Financial Aid Statistics:** 68% freshmen, 70% undergrads receive need-based scholarship or grant aid. 64% freshmen, 70% undergrads receive non-need-based scholarship or grant aid. 70% freshmen, 71% undergrads receive need-based self-help aid. 56% freshmen, 20% undergrads receive athletic scholarships. 78% freshmen, 77% undergrads receive any aid. 86% undergrads borrow to pay for school. Average cumulative indebtedness $26,531. **Criteria for awarding institutional aid:** *Non-need-based:* academics, alumni affiliation, athletics, leadership, music/drama, state/district residency.

UNIVERSITY OF ROCHESTER

300 Wilson Blvd, Rochester, NY 14627
Phone: 585-275-3221 · **Financial Aid Phone:** 585-275-3226
E-mail: admit@admissions.rochester.edu · **CEEB Code:** 2928
Fax: 585-461-4595 · **Website:** www.rochester.edu · **ACT Code:** 2980

This private school was founded in 1850. It has a 655-acre campus.

RATINGS

Admissions Selectivity Rating: 95   **Fire Safety Rating:** 89

STUDENTS AND FACULTY

Enrollment: 6,074. **Student Body:** 51% female, 49% male, 59% out-of-state, 17% international (89 countries represented). Asian 11%, African American 5%, Caucasian 51%, Hispanic 6%, Native American <1%
Retention and Graduation: 97% freshmen return for sophomore year. 73% freshmen graduate within 4 years. 84% freshmen graduate within 6 years. 34% grads go on to further study within 1 year. 64% grads pursue arts and sciences degrees. 7% grads pursue law degrees. 5% grads pursue business degrees. 15% grads pursue medical degrees. **Faculty:** 583 full-time faculty, 94% hold PhDs.

ACADEMICS

Degrees: bachelor's, master's, post-bachelor's certificate, post-master's certificate. **Classes:** Most classes have 10-19 students. **Majors with Highest Enrollment:** Economics; Biology/Biological Sciences; Psychology. **Special Study Options:** Accelerated program, cooperative education program, cross-registration, double major, dual enrollment, English as a Second Language (ESL), honors program, independent study, internships, liberal arts/career combination, student-designed major, study abroad, teacher certification program, "Take 5" a fifth year tuition free to supplement regular requirements; Washington Semester Program; Rochester Curriculum (clusters); Quest Courses. **Combined degree programs:** BA/MD, BA/MA, Medicine, Business, Education, Engineering. **Disability Services:** Special programs offered to physically disabled students include note-taking services, reader services, tape recorders, tutors. **Career services:** Alumni network, alumni services, career assessment, internships. Rochester students pursue internship, externship, research and volunteer experiences at a high rate. Many are involved in programs directed by other organizations, including 67 study abroad programs in which the University is a partner. The campus career center guides individualized plans for student career development and enjoys extraordinary success.

FACILITIES

Housing: Coed dorms, special housing for disabled students, men's dorms, special housing for international students, women's dorms, fraternity/sorority housing, apartments for married students, apartments for single students, Wellness Housing, Theme Housing, Freshman housing, Special interest housing, Suite style living. 90% of campus accessible to physically disabled. **Special Academic Facilities/Equipment:** Art center and gallery, African and African-American studies institute, center for women's studies, visual science and space science centers, institute of optics, observatory, laser energetics and nuclear structure research labs, electron microscopes. Judaic studies center, political economy institute, sign language research center, biomedical ultrasound center, Polish and central European studies center, electronic imaging systems center, center for future health. **Computers:** 100% of classrooms, 30% of dorms, 100% of libraries, 100% of dining areas, 100% of student union, have wireless network access. Students can register for classes online. Administrative functions (other than registration) can be performed online.

CAMPUS LIFE

Environment: Metropolis. **Activities:** Choral groups, concert band, dance, drama/theater, jazz band, literary magazine, music ensembles, musical theater, opera, pep band, radio station, student government, student newspaper, student-run film society, symphony orchestra, television station, International Student Organization, Model UN. 224 registered organizations, 6 honor societies, 14 religious organizations. 17 fraternities, 13 sororities. **Athletics (Intercollegiate): Men:** baseball, basketball, cross-country, diving, football, golf, soccer, squash, swimming, tennis, track/field (outdoor), track/field (indoor). *Women:* basketball, crew/rowing, cross-country, diving, field hockey, golf, lacrosse, soccer, softball, swimming, tennis, track/field (outdoor), track/field (indoor), volleyball. **On-Campus Highlights:** Eastman Theater, Memorial Art Gallery, Rush Rhees Library, Interfaith Chapel, Robert B. Goergen Athletic Center, Recent New Buildings on Campus: Robert B. Goergen Hall for Biomedical Engineering and Optics—A five-story facility that pairs biomedical engineering and optics in an environment of teaching laboratories, high-tech demonstration areas, and gathering spaces for collaboration. The Gleason Library—A collaborative study space, designed with student input, which features an open floor plan and lightweight furniture that students are encouraged to reconfigure. Riverview Student Apartments—A five-building, 120-unit dormitory complex. The waterfront building features fully furnished apartments and offers amenities not found in other on-campus housing, including air conditioning, kitchens and separate living rooms. Each of the three- and four-story buildings is equipped with laundry and vending facilities. University Health Services Building -The new facility brings together UHS medical care services, physical therapy, health promotion, administrative offices, and the University Counseling Center. The UHS building is the primary health-care stop for Arts, Sciences & Engineering students, as well as faculty, staff, and other members of the University community. **Environmental Initiatives:** The Universitys first LEED certified building opened its doors in May. The Universitys newly dedicated Saunders Research Building, which houses the Clinical and Translational Science Institute, is the first on campus to formally receive LEED (Leadership in Energy and Environmental Design) status. Built to facilitate collaboration between researchers in community and preventive medicine, neurological disorders, cancer, pediatrics, cardiovascular disease, emergency medicine, biostatistics , bioinformatics, and experimental therapeutics, its designers and construction teams have labored to create a working environment both ideal for interaction and certifiably green. That beauty can accompany energy efficiency and cost savings in a green building is immediately apparent on entering the Saunders open and spacious atrium, with its rich Forest Stewardship Council certified wood panels and soaring glass windows. This blending of natural aesthetics and advanced technologies in service to sustainability is a theme of the building throughout. The large windows that line the building are energy efficient, brightening the rooms of its open layout floor plan naturally, reducing need for artificial lighting. Sensors dim the lighting system when daylight is sufficient and shut it off when offices are unoccupied. Heating and cooling system s are also built for efficiency. One of the buildings four air handlers uses Heat Wheel technology, a system which recovers and re-circulates heat from the exhaust side to the supply side, rather than releasing it into the air as waste. Ducts and piping were sealed during the construction phase to prevent contaminants from entering the system prior to start-up. These features are projected to lead to system performance 15% over and above American Society of Heating, Refrigerating, and Air Conditioning Engineers requirements. Sustainable building methods also figure prominently on Saunders exterior. Sections of the roof were constructed with a highly reflective white surface to reduce the buildings and Universitys overall heat island effect. Parking areas are built of porous pavement with underlying drainage systems that direct storm water runoff to a rain garden. The rain garden filters the water then directs it to the native plant species that enhance the buildings north and south entries, eliminating the need for irrigation. Over the two years of the project, the building process reflected sustainable methods: crews diverted 75% of construction waste away from landfills by grinding up drywall to use as soil, recycling metal, paper and cardboard, and recycling concrete and brick. The commitment to sustainability does not cease with constructions end. Efforts to promote mindfulness among Saunders occupants are also part of the long-term plan. For openers, preferred parking spaces located nearest the buildings entry will be allocated for those driving low emission, fuel efficient vehicles. Ongoing initiatives to enhance features and shape behavior make it likely that Saunders will eventually receive LEED Silver (possibly Gold) Certification for consistent effort to construct and maintain a sustainable building. The Clinical and Translational Research Institute will provide hundreds of new jobs, housing more than 600 scientists, physicians, nurses, statisticians, research administrators, and support staff when fully occupied. The Center for Governmental Research projects that it will bring $30 million per year from grants and research activity to Rochester. For its economic contribution, its mission to speed the movement of health care research from the lab to the bedside, and for its commitment to sustainable living, the Institute can truly be called a leader for a better tomorrow. For more information, please visit: www.urmc.rochester.edu/news/saunders-research-building/elements.cfm. The College of Arts, Sciences & Engineering introduces a minor in sustainability. In Fall 2010, Dean of the College Richard Feldman convened a multidisciplinary committee of College faculty from the sciences, social sciences and humanities, and charged them with developing a sustainability minor, an addition to the undergraduate curriculum eagerly anticipated by students seeking to pursue studies and careers in environmental science and policy. By graduation 2011, the group had completed its charge and secured approval from the College Curriculum Committee for an interdisciplinary minor including courses from nine different departments. Set to enroll its first students in Fall 2011, the Minor in Sustainability will prepare students to explore, communicate, and solve problems in sustainability and global change that span disciplinary boundaries and carry far-reaching implications for society. The structure of the program roots the minor in environmental science, provides philosophical and historical context from which to view the interrelationships of environment and society and explores the mechanisms of economics and politics that impact environmental policy. The Wilson Commons makeover: good looking, good tasting, and green! Step into the Wilson Commons space formerly known as the Pit, and it is immediately clear that sweeping change came to the Universitys central dining center over the summer of 2010. The steep and austere tiles that line the 30-foot walls and have dominated the view remain, but the eye is now drawn to the human level, the feeling of entering a vast empty space replaced by a sense of coming into a hub of activity?uinviting seating options, for eating and hanging with friends at terrace level tables, or sitting cozily apart with coffee and books in overstuffed chairs, in the light of the upper atriums glass tower. Food choices and displays have expanded from serviceable?usandwiches, pizza, a carry-out market?uto a range of beautifully presented selections reflecting international tastes, local farms and healthy eating. Behind the beauty and the bounty of the Commons renovation, less visible to the eye but no less ubiquitous, is a commitment to sustainability that took root in 2004 with a decision to begin purchasing from local suppliers (Upstate Dairy) and has blossomed into the most creative and comprehensive approach to green practice on campus. Continuing a focus on green building that began with the 2007 construction of the Connections Caf?? in Rush Rhees Library (and will extend to the renovations of the Danforth and Douglass dining centers) the greening of the Commons is marked by the use of sustainable materials, energy efficiency and waste reduction. Low VOC paint and mastic products were used throughout the dining and kitchen spaces. Hand-formed, sun-baked adobe tiles form the facing on the service counter in the Mexican food venue and counter tops in the seating area are made from recycled glass. Pursuit of energy efficiency was relentless: variable frequency drives power the mechanical equipment, allowing units to supply just what air is needed throughout the space; fluorescent lighting with electronic ballasts and occupancy sensors serve the back-of-house areas and the dining areas lights are dimmable; a zoned lighting system in the Hive provides different levels of light depending on time of day and lights in the serving areas separate venues can be turned off when any one is closed for business. Other energy savers: self-closing doors on reach-in refrigerators and freezers; automatic defrost cycles; gas versus less efficient electric appliances wherever possible; an Eco-smart combi-oven that automatically modulates energy consumption to reduce power and water usage; back-load coolers to avoid energy waste during product loading. And paper waste was reduced to near zero by substituting digital menu and message boards for printed marketing materials. Recipient of a grade of A in Food & Recycling in the Sustainable Endowments Institutes national report card for college campuses for two years running, UR Dining Services sustainability leadership is fueled by the energy of a 5five-student intern group hired each spring, Team Green, who leave no stone unturned in pursuit of sustainable foods, waste elimination and environmental education. The A is well earned. An extensive program in waste reduction is in place and keeps expanding: Styrofoam is banned; dining trays have been eliminated; grease is converted to biodiesel; reusable mugs and to-go cartons are promoted and sold; 100% of recyclable metals, plastic, and glass used in dining center kitchens gets recycled, compost is generated and sent to a local food supplier. A commitment to local foods is strong and growing: the UR was the first campus in the state to join the Pride of New York Program, supporting food raised and processed in New York; thirty-two local vendors supply Dining Services kitchens; organic, fair trade, locally roasted coffee is served throughout campus; a week each semester is devoted to themed dinners, speakers and farmers markets, in celebration of local foods.

ADMISSIONS

Freshman Academic Profile: Average high school GPA 3.8. 72% in top 10% of high school class, 93% in top 25% of high school class, 100% in top 50% of high school class. 74% from public high schools. SAT Math middle 50% range 640-760. SAT Critical Reading middle 50% range 600-700. SAT Writing middle 50% range 610-710. ACT middle 50% range 29-33. Minimum internet-based TOEFL 100. Minimum paper TOEFL 600. **Basis for Candidate Selection:** *Very important factors considered include:* recommendation(s), rigor of secondary school record, character/personal qualities. *Important factors considered include:* application essay, academic GPA, standardized test scores, extracurricular activities, interview, talent/ability. *Other factors considered include:* Class rank, alumni/ae relation, first generation, geographical residence, level of applicant's interest, racial/ethnic status, volunteer work, work experience. **Freshman Admission Requirements:** High school diploma is required and GED is accepted. **Freshman Admission Statistics:** 17,410 applied, 36% admitted, 23% enrolled. **Transfer Admission Requirements:** college transcript(s), essay or personal statement, Lowest grade transferable C. **General Admission Information:** Application Fee $60. Early decision application deadline 11/1. Regular application deadline 1/1. Regular notification 4/1. Nonfall registration accepted. Admission may be deferred for a maximum of 1 year. Credit and/or placement offered for CEEB Advanced Placement tests.

COSTS AND FINANCIAL AID

Annual tuition $46,150. Room and board $13,708. Required fees $810. Average book expense $1,310. **Required Forms and Deadlines:** FAFSA, CSS/Financial Aid PROFILE, State aid form, Noncustodial PROFILE. **Notification of Awards:** Applicants will be notified of awards on or about 4/1. **Types of Aid:** *Need-based scholarships/grants:* Federal Pell, SEOG, state scholarships/grants, the school's own gift aid. *Loans:* Direct Subsidized Stafford, Direct Unsubsidized Stafford, Direct PLUS, Federal Perkins, Federal Nursing, college/university loans from institutional funds. *Student Employment:* Federal Work-Study Program available. Institutional employment available. Off-campus job opportunities are excellent. **Criteria for awarding institutional aid:** *Non-need-based:* academics, alumni affiliation, leadership, music/drama.

UNIVERSITY OF SAINT JOSEPH

1678 Asylum Avenue, West Hartford, CT 6117
Phone: 860-231-5216 · **Financial Aid Phone:** 860-231-5223
E-mail: admissions@usj.edu
Fax: 860-231-5744 · **Website:** www.usj.edu

This private school, affiliated with the Roman Catholic Church, was founded in 1932. It has a 84-acre campus.

RATINGS

Admissions Selectivity Rating: 76   **Fire Safety Rating:** 99

STUDENTS AND FACULTY

Enrollment: 930. **Student Body:** 99% female, 1% male, 5% out-of-state, 0% international. Asian 2%, African American 16%, Caucasian 54%, Hispanic 15%, Native American <1%
Retention and Graduation: 79% freshmen return for sophomore year. 41% freshmen graduate within 4 years. 51% freshmen graduate within 6 years. **Faculty:** 122 full-time faculty, 84% hold PhDs, 70% are are members of minority groups, 22% are women. 0% of classes are taught by teaching assistants.

ACADEMICS

Degrees: bachelor's, certificate, master's, post-bachelor's certificate. **Classes:** Most classes have 10-19 students. Most lab/discussion sessions have 10-19 students. **Majors with Highest Enrollment:** Social Work; Registered Nursing/Registered Nurse; Psychology. **Special Study Options:** Accelerated program, cross-registration, distance learning, double major, honors program, independent study, internships, liberal arts/career combination, student-designed major, study abroad, teacher certification program, weekend college. **Combined degree programs:** BA/MA. **Career services:** alumni services, career/job search classes, career assessment, internships.

FACILITIES

Housing: special housing for disabled students, women's dorms, Suite living (double rooms with shared common area and kitchen). **Computers:** Students can register for classes online.

CAMPUS LIFE

Environment: Town. **Activities:** Choral groups, dance, drama/theater, music ensembles, student government, student newspaper, yearbook, Campus Ministries, International Student Organization. **Athletics (Intercollegiate):** *Women:* basketball, cross-country, diving, lacrosse, soccer, softball, swimming, tennis, volleyball.

ADMISSIONS

Freshman Academic Profile: Average high school GPA 3.21. 14% in top 10% of high school class, 43% in top 25% of high school class, 57% in top 50% of high school class. SAT Math middle 50% range 440-530. SAT Critical Reading middle 50% range 430-530. ACT middle 50% range 19-23. Minimum paper TOEFL 550. **Basis for Candidate Selection:** *Very important factors considered include:* academic GPA, standardized test scores. *Other factors considered include:* Class rank, application essay, recommendation(s), rigor of secondary school record, alumni/ae relation, character/personal qualities, extracurricular activities, first generation, geographical residence, interview, level of applicant's interest, racial/ethnic status, religious affiliation/commitment, state residency, talent/ability, volunteer work, work experience. **Freshman Admission Requirements:** High school diploma is required and GED is accepted. **Academic units required:** 4 English, 3 mathematics, 3 science, 3 foreign language, 3 social studies. **Freshman Admission Statistics:** 724 applied, 80% admitted, 26% enrolled. **Transfer Admission Requirements:** High school transcript, college transcript(s), Lowest grade transferable C. **General Admission Information:** Application Fee $50. Notification on a rolling basis, beginning on or about 10/1. Nonfall registration accepted.

COSTS AND FINANCIAL AID

Required Forms and Deadlines: FAFSA. **Notification of Awards:** Applicants will be notified of awards on a rolling basis beginning 3/1. **Types of Aid:** *Need-based scholarships/grants:* Federal Pell, SEOG, state scholarships/grants, private scholarships, the school's own gift aid, Federal Nursing Scholarships. *Loans:* Direct Subsidized Stafford, Direct Unsubsidized Stafford, Direct PLUS, Subsidized Stafford, Unsubsidized Stafford, PLUS, Federal Perkins, state loans. *Student Employment:* Off-campus job opportunities are good. **Financial Aid Statistics:** 99% freshmen, 96% undergrads receive need-based scholarship or grant aid. 9% freshmen, 7% undergrads receive non-need-based scholarship or grant aid. 96% freshmen, 90% undergrads receive need-based self-help aid. 0% freshmen, 0% undergrads receive athletic scholarships. 90% undergrads borrow to pay for school. Average cumulative indebtedness $28,509. **Criteria for awarding institutional aid:** *Non-need-based:* academics.

See page 1192.

UNIVERSITY OF SAINT MARY (KS)

4100 South Fourth Street Trafficway, Leavenworth, KS 66048
Phone: 913-758-6118
E-mail: admissions@stmary.edu • **CEEB Code:** 6630
Fax: 913-758-6140 • **Website:** www.stmary.edu • **ACT Code:** 1455

This private school, affiliated with the Roman Catholic Church, was founded in 1923. It has a 240-acre campus.

RATINGS

Admissions Selectivity Rating: 79   **Fire Safety Rating:** 60*

STUDENTS AND FACULTY

Enrollment: 819. **Student Body:** 65% female, 35% male, 42% out-of-state, 1% international. Asian 1%, African American 10%, Caucasian 60%, Hispanic 11%, Native American 1%
Retention and Graduation: 27% freshmen graduate within 4 years. 35% freshmen graduate within 6 years. **Faculty:** 61 full-time faculty, 75% hold PhDs, 52% are members of minority groups, 10% are women. 0% of classes are taught by teaching assistants.

ACADEMICS

Degrees: associate, bachelor's, master's, transfer associate. **Classes:** Most classes have fewer than 10 students. **Majors with Highest Enrollment:** Registered Nursing/Registered Nurse; Biology/Biological Sciences; Sport and Fitness Administration/Management. **Special Study Options:** Accelerated program, distance learning, double major, dual enrollment, honors program, independent study, internships, student-designed major, study abroad, teacher certification program, Semester-away programs available. **Disability Services:** Special programs offered to physically disabled students include note-taking services, tutors.

FACILITIES

Housing: Coed dorms **Special Academic Facilities/Equipment:** Lincoln Library Collection, Art Gallery, Bible Collection. **Computers:** Students can register for classes online. Administrative functions (other than registration) can be performed online.

CAMPUS LIFE

Environment: Town. **Activities:** Choral groups, concert band, drama/theater, literary magazine, music ensembles, musical theater, pep band, student govern-

ment, Campus Ministries. 22 registered organizations, 2 honor societies, 2 religious organizations. **Athletics (Intercollegiate):** *Men:* baseball, basketball, football, soccer. *Women:* basketball, soccer, softball, volleyball.

ADMISSIONS

Freshman Academic Profile: Average high school GPA 3.32. 0% in top 10% of high school class, 6.7% in top 25% of high school class, 18.9% in top 50% of high school class. 80% from public high schools. SAT Math middle 50% range 420-525. SAT Critical Reading middle 50% range 430-530. ACT middle 50% range 19-24. Minimum paper TOEFL 500. **Basis for Candidate Selection:** *Very important factors considered include:* academic GPA, rigor of secondary school record, character/personal qualities. *Important factors considered include:* standardized test scores, extracurricular activities, interview, talent/ability, volunteer work. *Other factors considered include:* Class rank, application essay, recommendation(s), alumni/ae relation, work experience. **Freshman Admission Requirements:** High school diploma is required and GED is accepted. **Academic units required:** 4 English, 2 mathematics, 2 science, 2 history. **Freshman Admission Statistics:** 737 applied, 47% admitted, 31% enrolled. **Transfer Admission Requirements:** college transcript(s), Minimum college GPA of 2.0 required. Lowest grade transferable C. **General Admission Information:** Application Fee $25. Nonfall registration accepted. Admission may be deferred for a maximum of 1 semester. Credit and/or placement offered for CEEB Advanced Placement tests.

COSTS AND FINANCIAL AID

Required Forms and Deadlines: FAFSA. **Notification of Awards:** Applicants will be notified of awards on a rolling basis beginning 2/1. **Types of Aid:** *Need-based scholarships/grants:* Federal Pell, SEOG, state scholarships/grants, private scholarships, the school's own gift aid. *Loans:* Subsidized Stafford, Unsubsidized Stafford, PLUS, Federal Perkins. *Student Employment:* Highest amount earned per year from on-campus jobs $1,500. **Financial Aid Statistics:** 89% undergrads borrow to pay for school. Average cumulative indebtedness $23,332. **Criteria for awarding institutional aid:** *Non-need-based:* academics, art, athletics, leadership, music/drama.

UNIVERSITY OF SAINT THOMAS (MN)

2115 Summit Avenue, St. Paul, MN 55105
Phone: 651-962-6150 • **Financial Aid Phone:** 651-962-6550
E-mail: admissions@stthomas.edu • **CEEB Code:** 6110
Fax: 651-962-6160 • **Website:** www.stthomas.edu • **ACT Code:** 2102

This private school, affiliated with the Roman Catholic Church, was founded in 1885. It has a 78-acre campus.

RATINGS

Admissions Selectivity Rating: 80   **Fire Safety Rating:** 92

STUDENTS AND FACULTY

Enrollment: 6,234. **Student Body:** 46% female, 54% male, 20% out-of-state, 3% international. Asian 0%, African American 4%, Caucasian 81%, Hispanic 4%, Native American <1%
Retention and Graduation: 85% freshmen return for sophomore year. 60% freshmen graduate within 4 years. **Faculty:** 0% of classes are taught by teaching assistants.

ACADEMICS

Degrees: bachelor's, certificate, master's, post-bachelor's certificate, post-master's certificate. **Classes:** Most classes have 20-29 students. Most lab/discussion sessions have 10-19 students. **Special Study Options:** cross-registration, double major, English as a Second Language (ESL), exchange student program (domestic), honors program, independent study, internships, student-designed major, study abroad, teacher certification program. **Honors programs:** The Aquinas Scholars Program is the undergraduate honors program. Its purpose is to provide opportunities for motivated and curious students to deepen and enrich their undergraduate education. **Combined degree programs:** BA/MEng. **Disability Services:** Special programs offered to physically disabled students include note-taking services, reader services, tape recorders, tutors. **Career services:** Alumni network, alumni services, career assessment, internships, regional alumni.

FACILITIES

Housing: men's dorms, special housing for international students, women's dorms, apartments for single studentsChemical-free lifestyle, women in science house, first year experience houses, Catholic women's and Catholic men's communities. **Special Academic Facilities/Equipment:** Seminary **Computers:** 100% of classrooms, 100% of dorms, 100% of libraries, 100% of dining areas, 100% of student union, 100% of common outdoor areas have wireless network access. Students can register for classes online. Administrative functions (other than registration) can be performed online.

CAMPUS LIFE

Environment: Metropolis. **Activities:** Choral groups, concert band, dance, drama/theater, jazz band, literary magazine, music ensembles, pep band, radio station, student government, student newspaper, television station, yearbook, Campus Ministries, International Student Organization, Model UN. 114 registered organizations, 7 religious organizations. 1 fraternity. **Athletics (Intercollegiate):** *Men:* baseball, basketball, cross-country, diving, football, golf, ice hockey, soccer, swimming, tennis, track/field (outdoor), track/field (indoor). *Women:* basketball, cross-country, diving, golf, ice hockey, soccer, softball, swimming, tennis, track/field (outdoor), track/field (indoor), volleyball. **On-Campus Highlights:** O'Shaughnessy—Frey Library, Scooters non-alcoholic pub and restaurant, Koch Commons (workout facility residence hall area), Frey Science and Engineering Center, Chapel of St. Thomas Aquinas. **Environmental Initiatives:** Climate Action Plan approved by President's Staff June 24, 2010; Anderson Student Center opened 17 Jan 2012; LEED Silver status certification application submitted (www.stthomas.edu/openingdoors/studentCenter); Campus Sustainability Fund established awarding in the initial year $50,000 to three on-campus sustainability projects Nov 2011.

ADMISSIONS

Freshman Academic Profile: Average high school GPA 3.6. 29% in top 10% of high school class, 58% in top 25% of high school class, 92% in top 50% of high school class. 66% from public high schools. SAT Math middle 50% range 430-530. SAT Critical Reading middle 50% range 380-540. ACT middle 50% range 16-24. Minimum internet-based TOEFL 80. Minimum paper TOEFL 550. **Basis for Candidate Selection:** *Very important factors considered include:* academic GPA, rigor of secondary school record, standardized test scores. *Important factors considered include:* Class rank, application essay. *Other factors considered include:* recommendation(s), alumni/ae relation, character/personal qualities, extracurricular activities, geographical residence, racial/ethnic status, talent/ability, volunteer work. **Freshman Admission Requirements:** High school diploma is required and GED is accepted. **Academic units required:** 3 mathematics, 2 science. **Freshman Admission Statistics:** 5,540 applied, 86% admitted, 29% enrolled. **Transfer Admission Requirements:** High school transcript, college transcript(s), essay or personal statement, statement of good standing from prior institution(s). Minimum college GPA of 2.3 required. Lowest grade transferable C-. **General Admission Information:** Notification on a rolling basis, beginning on or about 10/1. Nonfall registration accepted. Credit and/or placement offered for CEEB Advanced Placement tests.

COSTS AND FINANCIAL AID

Annual tuition $35,872. Room and board $9,200. Required fees $810. Average book expense $1,000. **Required Forms and Deadlines:** FAFSA. **Notification of Awards:** Applicants will be notified of awards on a rolling basis beginning 3/1. **Types of Aid:** *Need-based scholarships/grants:* Federal Pell, SEOG, state scholarships/grants, private scholarships, the school's own gift aid. *Loans:* Direct Subsidized Stafford, Direct Unsubsidized Stafford, Direct PLUS, Federal Perkins, state loans, private loans. *Student Employment:* Federal Work-Study Program available. Institutional employment available. Off-campus job opportunities are fair. **Financial Aid Statistics:** 98% freshmen, 137% undergrads receive need-based scholarship or grant aid. 19% freshmen, 17% undergrads receive non-need-based scholarship or grant aid. 77% freshmen. 0% freshmen, 0% undergrads receive athletic scholarships. 99% freshmen, 94% undergrads receive any aid. 65% undergrads borrow to pay for school. Average cumulative indebtedness $24,435. **Criteria for awarding institutional aid:** *Non-need-based:* academics, music/drama.

UNIVERSITY OF SAN DIEGO

Best 380

5998 Alcala Park, San Diego, CA 92110-2492
Phone: 619-260-4506 · **Financial Aid Phone:** 619-260-4514
E-mail: admissions@sandiego.edu · **CEEB Code:** 4849
Fax: 619-260-6836 · **Website:** www.sandiego.edu · **ACT Code:** 394

This private school, affiliated with the Roman Catholic Church, was founded in 1949. It has a 180-acre campus.

RATINGS

Admissions Selectivity Rating: 92   Fire Safety Rating: 81

STUDENTS AND FACULTY

Enrollment: 5,656. **Student Body:** 55% female, 45% male, 37% out-of-state, 7% international (61 countries represented). Asian 6%, African American 3%, Caucasian 54%, Hispanic 19%, Native American <1%
Retention and Graduation: 90% freshmen return for sophomore year. 67% freshmen graduate within 4 years. 76% freshmen graduate within 6 years. 11% grads go on to further study within 1 year. 36% grads pursue arts and sciences degrees. 28% grads pursue law degrees. 22% grads pursue business degrees. 9% grads pursue medical degrees. **Faculty:** 406 full-time faculty, 97% hold PhDs, 47% are are members of minority groups, 21% are women. 0% of classes are taught by teaching assistants.

ACADEMICS

Degrees: bachelor's, master's, post-bachelor's certificate, post-master's certificate. **Classes:** Most classes have 30-39 students. Most lab/discussion sessions have 10-19 students. **Majors with Highest Enrollment:** Business Administration and Management; Communication; Finance. **Special Study Options:** double major, English as a Second Language (ESL), honors program, independent study, internships, liberal arts/career combination, study abroad, teacher certification program. **Honors programs:** Phi Beta Kappa, Honors Program. **Combined degree programs:** BS/MSN, MBA/JD. **Career services:** Alumni network, alumni services, career/job search classes, career assessment, internships, regional alumni.

FACILITIES

Housing: Coed dorms, special housing for disabled students, men's dorms, women's dorms, apartments for married students, apartments for single students, Wellness Housing, Theme Housing. 85% of campus accessible to physically disabled. **Special Academic Facilities/Equipment:** Art gallery, peace and justice institute, child development center, language labs. **Computers:** 100% of classrooms, 100% of dorms, 100% of libraries, 100% of dining areas, 100% of student union, 100% of common outdoor areas have wireless network access. Students can register for classes online. Administrative functions (other than registration) can be performed online.

CAMPUS LIFE

Environment: Metropolis. **Activities:** Choral groups, dance, drama/theater, jazz band, literary magazine, music ensembles, musical theater, pep band, radio station, student government, student newspaper, symphony orchestra, television station, yearbook, Campus Ministries, International Student Organization, Model UN. 129 registered organizations, 20 honor societies, 2 religious organizations. 5 fraternities, 6 sororities. **Athletics (Intercollegiate):** *Men:* baseball, basketball, crew/rowing, cross-country, football, golf, soccer, tennis. *Women:* basketball, cheerleading, crew/rowing, cross-country, diving, soccer, softball, swimming, tennis, track/field (outdoor), volleyball. **On-Campus Highlights:** Aromas Coffee House, Donald P. Shiley Center for Science and Technology, Jenny Craig Pavilion (Sporting/concert venue), Joan B. Kroc Institute for Peace and Justice, Student Life Pavilion. **Environmental Initiatives:** 1. USD opened a full time electronic waste collection center, the first of its kind on a college campus. The E-waste Collection Center educates the public on the importance of proper e-waste recycling, offering a necessary service to the entire San Diego for free complete e-waste recycling. 2. The university is committed to climate change awareness and education. Several initiatives support this commitment. Namely, a $5 million grant from the National Science Foundation to establish the Climate Education Partnership with the primary goal of understanding how best to communicate the causes of climate change, and its impacts, and how to adapt to or prevent those impacts on our region (www.sandiego.edu/climate). The university is also active in helping create and establish other regoional Climate initiatives with local governments to highlight work being done on climate issues (http://www.sdclimatecollaborative.org/). We've also had several students help create Climate Action Plans for local cities throughout the region through our partnerships with local governments. USD's commitment to sustainability is highlighted by our conservation efforts. Since our baseline year° (2005) we have seen the following reductions: MTC02: reduction of 3897 Tons (12% reduction); kWh: reduction of 7,816,014 kWh (22% reduction); Water: 55,789,665 gallons (39% reduction); Waste Diversion: increased diversion rate from 34% to 60% (Increased diversion rate by 75%). Note: °2009 was used as the baseline year for electricity due to increases in square footage.

ADMISSIONS

Freshman Academic Profile: Average high school GPA 3.9. 45% in top 10% of high school class, 78% in top 25% of high school class, 94% in top 50% of high school class. 57% from public high schools. SAT Math middle 50% range 570-670. SAT Critical Reading middle 50% range 560-650. SAT Writing middle 50% range 560-660. ACT middle 50% range 26-30. Minimum internet-based TOEFL 80. Minimum paper TOEFL 550. **Basis for Candidate Selection:** *Very important factors considered include:* academic GPA, rigor of secondary school record, standardized test scores, religious affiliation/commitment. *Important factors considered include:* Class rank, application essay, recommendation(s), character/personal qualities, extracurricular activities, talent/ability, volunteer work. *Other factors considered include:* alumni/ae relation, first generation, geographical residence, level of applicant's interest, racial/ethnic status, work experience. **Freshman Admission Requirements:** High school diploma is required and GED is accepted. **Academic units required:** 4 English, 3 mathematics, 3 science, (2 science labs), 2 foreign language, 3 social studies. **Freshman Admission Statistics:** 14,247 applied, 46% admitted, 17% enrolled. **Transfer Admission Requirements:** High school transcript, college transcript(s), essay or personal statement, Minimum college GPA of 3.0 required. Lowest grade transferable C. **General Admission Information:** Application Fee $55. Regular application deadline 3/1. Regular notification 4/15. Nonfall registration accepted. Admission may be deferred for a maximum of one year. Credit and/or placement offered for CEEB Advanced Placement tests.

COSTS AND FINANCIAL AID

Annual tuition $42,330. Room and board $11,910. Required fees $578. Average book expense $1,752. **Required Forms and Deadlines:** FAFSA. **Notification of Awards:** Applicants will be notified of awards on a rolling basis beginning 3/1. **Types of Aid:** *Need-based scholarships/grants:* Federal Pell, SEOG, state scholarships/grants, private scholarships, the school's own gift aid, Federal Nursing Scholarships. *Loans:* Subsidized Stafford, Unsubsidized Stafford, PLUS, Federal Perkins, college/university loans from institutional funds. *Student Employment:* Federal Work-Study Program available. Institutional employment available. Off-campus job opportunities are good. **Financial Aid Statistics:** 98% freshmen, 95% undergrads receive need-based scholarship or grant aid. 57% freshmen, 46% undergrads receive non-need-based scholarship or grant aid. 70% freshmen, 77% undergrads receive need-based self-help aid. 2% freshmen, 2% undergrads receive athletic scholarships. 81% freshmen, 72% undergrads receive any aid. 54% undergrads borrow to pay for school. Average cumulative indebtedness $22,671. **Criteria for awarding institutional aid:** *Non-need-based:* academics, athletics, leadership, music/drama, religious affiliation.

UNIVERSITY OF SAN FRANCISCO

Best 380

2130 Fulton Street, San Francisco, CA 94117
Phone: 415-422-6563 • **Financial Aid Phone:** 415-422-2020
E-mail: admission@usfca.edu • **CEEB Code:** 1325
Fax: 415-422-2217 • **Website:** www.usfca.edu • **ACT Code:** 466

This private school, affiliated with the Roman Catholic Church and the Jesuit Church, was founded in 1855. It has a 55-acre campus.

RATINGS
Admissions Selectivity Rating: 86   **Fire Safety Rating:** 60*

STUDENTS AND FACULTY
Enrollment: 6,308. **Student Body:** 62% female, 38% male, 18% out-of-state, 18% international (63 countries represented). Asian 19%, African American 3%, Caucasian 31%, Hispanic 19%, Native American <1%. **Retention and Graduation:** 55% freshmen graduate within 4 years. 69% freshmen graduate within 6 years. **Faculty:** 0% of classes are taught by teaching assistants.

ACADEMICS
Degrees: bachelor's, certificate, first professional, master's, post-master's certificate. **Classes:** Most classes have 10-19 students. Most lab/discussion sessions have 10-19 students. **Majors with Highest Enrollment:** Psychology; Registered Nursing/Registered Nurse; Business/Commerce. **Special Study Options:** Accelerated program, cross-registration, distance learning, double major, English as a Second Language (ESL), exchange student program (domestic), external degree program, honors program, independent study, internships, liberal arts/career combination, student-designed major, study abroad, teacher certification program. **Combined degree programs:** BA/JD, BA/MA, BA/MEng. **Disability Services:** Special programs offered to physically disabled students include note-taking services, reader services, tape recorders, tutors. **Career services:** career/job search classes, career assessment, internships.

FACILITIES
Housing: Coed dorms, women's dorms, apartments for single students, Several off campus buildings with flats have been purchased and converted into multiple student housing units. 100% of campus accessible to physically disabled. **Special Academic Facilities/Equipment:** Rare Book Room, Ricci Institute for Chinese-Western Cultural History **Computers:** 25% of classrooms, 25% of dorms, 25% of dining areas, 75% of student union, 25% of common outdoor

areas have wireless network access. Students can register for classes online. Administrative functions (other than registration) can be performed online.

CAMPUS LIFE
Environment: Metropolis. **Activities:** Choral groups, dance, drama/theater, literary magazine, music ensembles, musical theater, pep band, radio station, student government, student newspaper, television station, yearbook. 90 registered organizations, 14 honor societies, 4 fraternities, 4 sororities. **Athletics (Intercollegiate):** *Men:* baseball, basketball, cross-country, golf, riflery, soccer, tennis, track/field (outdoor). *Women:* basketball, cross-country, golf, riflery, soccer, tennis, track/field (outdoor), volleyball. **On-Campus Highlights:** Koret Health and Recreation Center, War Memorial Gym, St. Ignatius Church, Geschke Learning Resourse Center, Loan Mountain Campus. **Environmental Initiatives:** Sustainability. Placed 5th in National competition in Recyclemania. Currently, USF's co-generation plant produces about half of lower campus' peak energy needs. Located in the basement of Gleeson Library, the plant converts natural gas into electricity. Although the conversion of natural gas to energy does produce some emissions, natural gas is considered the cleanest of the fossil fuels. The plant gets its co-generation designation because it also captures heat lost during the conversion process and uses that to provide some of the heat lower campus uses. The plant provides about 38 percent of lower campus' heating needs. Additionally, the university uses thermal panels on top of Phelan, Gillson, and Hayes-Healy halls. The panels differ from solar panels in that they heat water directly rather than producing electricity, providing some of the hot water needed in those halls. LEED Goals on new projects Incorporation of "green" building practices in construction, including the renovation of Kalmanovitz Hall (formerly Campion Hall). London said USF will try to achieve LEED certification for the new Integrated Science Center, currently being designed. Awarded by the U.S. Green Building Council, LEED provides a suite of standards for environmentally sustainable construction. If the Integrated Science Center receives the certification, it would be the first such building on campus. Installation of Photo voltaic panels. As part of that process, USF is installing new solar panels on top of the Koret Health and Recreation Center, University Center, Cowell Hall, and Kalmanovitz Hall. Together with the solar panels already on Gleeson Library, the panels will produce about 16 percent of lower campus' peak electricity needs.

ADMISSIONS
Freshman Academic Profile: Average high school GPA 3.6. 26% in top 10% of high school class, 59% in top 25% of high school class, 91% in top 50% of high school class. SAT Math middle 50% range 530-630. SAT Critical Reading middle 50% range 510-620. SAT Writing middle 50% range 520-620. ACT middle 50% range 22-27. Minimum internet-based TOEFL 79. **Basis for Candidate Selection:** *Very important factors considered include:* academic GPA, recommendation(s), rigor of secondary school record, standardized test scores. *Important factors considered include:* Class rank, application essay. *Other factors considered include:* alumni/ae relation, character/personal qualities, extracurricular activities, interview, talent/ability, volunteer work. **Freshman Admission Requirements:** High school diploma is required and GED is accepted. **Freshman Admission Statistics:** 11,223 applied, 69% admitted, 17% enrolled. **Transfer Admission Requirements:** college transcript(s), essay or personal statement, Minimum college GPA of 2.5 required. Lowest grade transferable C. **General Admission Information:** Application Fee $55. Regular notification 4/1. Nonfall registration accepted. Admission may be deferred for a maximum of 1 semester. Credit offered for CEEB Advanced Placement tests.

COSTS AND FINANCIAL AID
Annual tuition $40,996. Room and board $13,320. Required fees $454. Average book expense $1,600. **Required Forms and Deadlines:** FAFSA. **Notification of Awards:** Applicants will be notified of awards on a rolling basis beginning 4/1. **Types of Aid:** *Need-based scholarships/grants:* Federal Pell, SEOG, state scholarships/grants, private scholarships, the school's own gift aid, Federal Nursing Scholarships. *Loans:* Direct Subsidized Stafford, Direct Unsubsidized Stafford, Direct PLUS, Subsidized Stafford, Unsubsidized Stafford, PLUS, Federal Perkins, Federal Nursing, college/university loans from institutional funds, Note: Loans are for Graduate students only. *Student Employment:* Federal Work-Study Program available. Institutional employment available. Highest amount earned per year from on-campus jobs $2,000. Off-campus job opportunities are excellent. **Financial Aid Statistics:** 93% freshmen, 89% undergrads receive need-based scholarship or grant aid. 72% freshmen, 45% undergrads receive non-need-based scholarship or grant aid. 86% freshmen, 87% undergrads receive need-based self-help aid. 3% freshmen, 3% undergrads receive athletic scholarships. 63% undergrads receive any aid. 65% undergrads borrow to pay for school. Average cumulative indebtedness $24,622. **Criteria for awarding institutional aid:** *Non-need-based:* academics, athletics.

See page 1194.

UNIVERSITY OF SCIENCE & ARTS OF OKLAHOMA

1727 West Alabama, Chickasha, OK 73018
Phone: 405-574-1357 · **Financial Aid Phone:** 405-574-1240
E-mail: usao-admissions@usao.edu · **CEEB Code:** 6544
Fax: 405-574-1220 · **Website:** www.usao.edu · **ACT Code:** 3418

This public school was founded in 1908. It has a 75-acre campus.

RATINGS

Admissions Selectivity Rating: 82   **Fire Safety Rating:** 94

STUDENTS AND FACULTY

Enrollment: 908. **Student Body:** 64% female, 36% male, 10% out-of-state, 6% international (19 countries represented). Asian 1%, African American 4%, Caucasian 69%, Hispanic 6%, Native American 13%
Retention and Graduation: 78% freshmen return for sophomore year. 27% freshmen graduate within 4 years. 40% freshmen graduate within 6 years. **Faculty:** 52 full-time faculty, 87% hold PhDs, 48% are are members of minority groups, 15% are women. 0% of classes are taught by teaching assistants.

ACADEMICS

Degrees: bachelor's. **Classes:** Most classes have 10-19 students. Most lab/discussion sessions have 10-19 students. **Majors with Highest Enrollment:** Business Administration and Management; Psychology; Elementary Education and Teaching. **Special Study Options:** Accelerated program, double major, dual enrollment, honors program, independent study, internships, student-designed major, study abroad, teacher certification program. **Disability Services:** Special programs offered to physically disabled students include note-taking services, tutors. **Career services:** career/job search classes, career assessment, internships.

FACILITIES

Housing: Coed dorms, apartments for single students. 95% of campus accessible to physically disabled. **Special Academic Facilities/Equipment:** Language labs, speech and hearing clinic, multiple computer labs, herbarium. **Computers:** 100% of classrooms, 85% of dorms, 100% of libraries, 100% of dining areas, 100% of student union, 100% of common outdoor areas have wireless network access.

CAMPUS LIFE

Environment: Village. **Activities:** Choral groups, concert band, drama/theater, jazz band, literary magazine, music ensembles, musical theater, pep band, student government, student newspaper, television station, Campus Ministries. 24 registered organizations, 7 honor societies, 4 religious organizations. 1 fraternity, 1 sorority. **Athletics (Intercollegiate):** *Men:* baseball, basketball, cheerleading, soccer. *Women:* basketball, cheerleading, soccer, softball. **On-Campus Highlights:** Lawson Court, Nash Library, Student Center, Bill Smith Ballpark, Scooter's Grill.

ADMISSIONS

Freshman Academic Profile: Average high school GPA 3.43. 20% in top 10% of high school class, 43% in top 25% of high school class, 66% in top 50% of high school class. 90% from public high schools. SAT Math middle 50% range 530-430. SAT Critical Reading middle 50% range 545-475. ACT middle 50% range 24-19. Minimum internet-based TOEFL 61. Minimum paper TOEFL 500. **Basis for Candidate Selection:** *Very important factors considered include:* Class rank, academic GPA, rigor of secondary school record, standardized test scores. *Important factors considered include:* talent/ability. *Other factors considered include:* recommendation(s), character/personal qualities. **Freshman Admission Requirements:** High school diploma is required and GED is accepted. **Academic units required:** 4 English, 3 mathematics, 3 science, (3 science labs), 2 social studies, 1 history, 2 academic electives. **Freshman Admission Statistics:** 594 applied, 62% admitted, 41% enrolled. **Transfer Admission Requirements:** college transcript(s), Minimum college GPA of 2.0 required. Lowest grade transferable D. **General Admission Information:** Application Fee $25. Regular application deadline 9/1. Notification on a rolling basis, beginning on or about 2/10. Nonfall registration accepted. Admission may be deferred for a maximum of NA. Credit offered for CEEB Advanced Placement tests.

COSTS AND FINANCIAL AID

Annual out-of-state tuition $12,660. Room and board $5,310. Required fees $1,170. Average book expense $1,200. **Required Forms and Deadlines:** FAFSA. **Notification of Awards:** Applicants will be notified of awards on a rolling basis beginning 3/15. **Types of Aid:** *Need-based scholarships/grants:* Federal Pell, SEOG, state scholarships/grants, private scholarships, the school's own gift aid. *Loans:* Subsidized Stafford, Unsubsidized Stafford, PLUS, Federal Perkins, college/university loans from institutional funds. *Student Employment:* Federal Work-Study Program available. Institutional employment available.

Highest amount earned per year from on-campus jobs $8,600. Off-campus job opportunities are good. **Financial Aid Statistics:** 98% freshmen, 92% undergrads receive need-based scholarship or grant aid. 17% freshmen, 9% undergrads receive non-need-based scholarship or grant aid. 54% freshmen, 61% undergrads receive need-based self-help aid. 13% freshmen, 12% undergrads receive athletic scholarships. 93% freshmen, 89% undergrads receive any aid. 53% undergrads borrow to pay for school. Average cumulative indebtedness $23,964. **Criteria for awarding institutional aid:** *Non-need-based:* academics, art, athletics, leadership, music/drama, state/district residency.

UNIVERSITY OF THE SCIENCES IN PHILADELPHIA

600 South 43rd Street, Philadelphia, PA 19104-4495
Phone: 215-596-8810 · **Financial Aid Phone:** 215-596-8894
E-mail: admit@usciences.edu · **CEEB Code:** 2663
Fax: 215-596-8821 · **ACT Code:** 3671

This private school was founded in 1821. It has a 35-acre campus.

RATINGS

Admissions Selectivity Rating: 89   **Fire Safety Rating:** 72

STUDENTS AND FACULTY

Enrollment: 2,427. **Student Body:** 61% female, 39% male, 59% out-of-state, 2% international (20 countries represented). Asian 36%, African American 5%, Caucasian 46%, Hispanic 2%, Native American <1%
Retention and Graduation: 88% freshmen return for sophomore year. 67% freshmen graduate within 4 years. 72% freshmen graduate within 6 years. **Faculty:** 191 full-time faculty, 82% hold PhDs, 52% are are members of minority groups, 20% are women. 0% of classes are taught by teaching assistants.

ACADEMICS

Degrees: bachelor's, master's, post-bachelor's certificate, post-master's certificate. **Classes:** Most classes have 20-29 students. Most lab/discussion sessions have 20-29 students. **Majors with Highest Enrollment:** Biology/Biological Sciences; Pharmacy; Physical Therapy/Therapist. **Special Study Options:** distance learning, double major, English as a Second Language (ESL), honors program, internships, liberal arts/career combination, teacher certification program, academic remediation, advanced placement credit, learning disabilities services, off-campus study. **Honors programs:** The Honors Program at University of the Sciences offers exceptional students the opportunity for specialized, intensive learning experiences both inside and outside the classroom. As an honors student, you will take part in special honors classes and recitations. The workload for these classes is not harder than others at University of the Sciences, but different. For example you may do smaller, more advanced experiments in a lab course. You may tour historic sites for a history class, or meet with a visiting author in your writing class. You will work in smaller classes and have more independent and group projects. **Combined degree programs:** PharmD/MBA;BSHS/MOT;BSHS/MPT;BSHS/DPT. **Disability Services:** Special programs offered to physically disabled students include note-taking services, reader services, tape recorders, tutors. **Career services:** alumni services, career/job search classes, career assessment, internships. Career services highlights include USP Alumni Career Panels.

FACILITIES

Housing: Coed dorms, fraternity/sorority housing, apartments for single students, Wellness Housing, honor halls in certain dormitories, upper level floor for upper level students. 90% of campus accessible to physically disabled. **Special Academic Facilities/Equipment:** Pharmacy museum, electron microscope. **Computers:** 80% of classrooms, 100% of dorms, 100% of libraries, 100% of dining areas, 40% of common outdoor areas have wireless network access. Students can register for classes online. Administrative functions (other than registration) can be performed online.

CAMPUS LIFE

Environment: Metropolis. **Activities:** Choral groups, concert band, dance, drama/theater, literary magazine, musical theater, student government, student newspaper, yearbook. 66 registered organizations, 6 honor societies, 6 religious organizations. 2 fraternities, 2 sororities. **Athletics (Intercollegiate):** *Men:* baseball, basketball, cross-country, golf, riflery, tennis. *Women:* basketball, cross-country, golf, riflery, softball, tennis, volleyball. **On-Campus Highlights:** McNeil Science and Technology Center, Athletic Recreation Center, Wilson Hall, Marvin Sampson Museum, Griffith Hall, More than 80 state-of-the-art laboratories, including the Center for Advanced Pharmacy Studies (CAPS), the first laboratory of its kind at any college of pharmacy nationwide. In September 2003, USP opened a new 78,000-square-foot athletic/recreation center that provides exercise and practice space for varsity and intramural sports as well as general recreational facilities. The new building, part of a $30 million campus expansion and beautification project, contains a 3,500-square-foot, three-lane swimming pool; additional classrooms and faculty offices; and space for student organizations to meet and for students to gather informally. In August 2006, USP opened the McNeil Science and Technology Center, a three-story, 77,000-square-foot leading edge facility that reflects the University's commitment to its innovative curriculum. The Center's research laboratories and state-of-the-art-equipped support spaces will accommodate more undergraduate, graduate, post-doctoral, and faculty researchers in biology, microbiology, physics, and other scientific fields. The Center features a 400-seat auditorium, classrooms, computer workrooms and other flexible space that supports innovative teaching and learning through multi-media technology. The Center's two-story, light-filled commons provides a comfortable space for students to relax and study. **Environmental Initiatives:** All "On the Go" containers are fully recyclable. Five meal periods a week are trayless to conserve water and reduce chemical use. We have an Eco-Clam Shell program where a guest can purchase a re-usable fully recyclable clam shell and trade it in for a clean one at each meal period.

ADMISSIONS

Freshman Academic Profile: Average high school GPA 3.6. 45% in top 10% of high school class, 80% in top 25% of high school class, 98% in top 50% of high school class. SAT Math middle 50% range 550-650. SAT Critical Reading middle 50% range 520-590. SAT Writing middle 50% range 520-610. ACT middle 50% range 22-27. Minimum paper TOEFL 550. **Basis for Candidate Selection:** *Very important factors considered include:* Class rank, academic GPA, rigor of secondary school record, standardized test scores. *Important factors considered include:* character/personal qualities, level of applicant's interest. *Other factors considered include:* application essay, recommendation(s), alumni/ae relation, extracurricular activities, interview, talent/ability, volunteer work, work experience. **Freshman Admission Requirements:** High school diploma is required and GED is accepted. **Academic units required:** 4 English, 3 mathematics, 3 science, (3 science labs), 1 foreign language, 1 social studies, 1 history, 4 academic electives. **Freshman Admission Statistics:** 4,099 applied, 61% admitted, 18% enrolled. **Transfer Admission Requirements:** college transcript(s), standardized test scores, Minimum college GPA of 3.0 required. Lowest grade transferable C. **General Admission Information:** Application Fee $45. Notification on a rolling basis, beginning on or about 10/1. Nonfall registration not accepted. Admission may be deferred for a maximum of 12 months. Credit offered for CEEB Advanced Placement tests.

COSTS AND FINANCIAL AID

Annual tuition $34,336. Room and board $14,108. Required fees $1,760. Average book expense $1,050. **Required Forms and Deadlines:** FAFSA. **Notification of Awards:** Applicants will be notified of awards on a rolling basis beginning 1/15. **Types of Aid:** *Need-based scholarships/grants:* Federal Pell, SEOG, state scholarships/grants, private scholarships, the school's own gift aid. *Loans:* Subsidized Stafford, Unsubsidized Stafford, PLUS, Federal Perkins, college/university loans from institutional funds. *Student Employment:* Federal Work-Study Program available. Institutional employment available. Highest amount earned per year from on-campus jobs $4,899. **Financial Aid Statistics:** 81% freshmen, 82% undergrads receive need-based scholarship or grant aid. 97% freshmen, 89% undergrads receive non-need-based scholarship or grant aid. 77% freshmen, 84% undergrads receive need-based self-help aid. 1% freshmen, 7% undergrads receive athletic scholarships. 100% freshmen, 89% undergrads receive any aid. 41% undergrads borrow to pay for school. Average cumulative indebtedness $39,665. **Criteria for awarding institutional aid:** *Non-need-based:* academics, athletics.

THE UNIVERSITY OF SCRANTON

Best 380

800 Linden Street, Scranton, PA 18510
Phone: 570-941-7540 • **Financial Aid Phone:** 570-941-7701
E-mail: admissions@scranton.edu • **CEEB Code:** 2929
Fax: 570-941-5928 • **Website:** www.scranton.edu • **ACT Code:** 3736

This private school, affiliated with the Roman Catholic-Jesuit Church, was founded in 1888. It has a 50-acre campus.

RATINGS

Admissions Selectivity Rating: 85   Fire Safety Rating: 91

STUDENTS AND FACULTY

Enrollment: 3,909. **Student Body:** 57% female, 43% male, 60% out-of-state, 0% international (15 countries represented). Asian 2%, African American 2%, Caucasian 82%, Hispanic 8%, Native American <1%
Retention and Graduation: 89% freshmen return for sophomore year. 74% freshmen graduate within 4 years. 80% freshmen graduate within 6 years. 41% grads go on to further study within 1 year. 13% grads pursue arts and sciences degrees. 2% grads pursue law degrees. 4% grads pursue business degrees. 6% grads pursue medical degrees. **Faculty:** 291 full-time faculty, 88% hold PhDs, 40% are are members of minority groups, 7% are women. 0% of classes are taught by teaching assistants.

ACADEMICS

Degrees: associate, bachelor's, certificate, master's, post-bachelor's certificate, post-master's certificate. **Classes:** Most classes have 10-19 students. Most lab/discussion sessions have 10-19 students. **Majors with Highest Enrollment:** Biology/Biological Sciences; Registered Nursing/Registered Nurse; Human Services. **Special Study Options:** Accelerated program, cross-registration, distance learning, double major, dual enrollment, English as a Second Language (ESL), exchange student program (domestic), honors program, independent study, internships, study abroad, teacher certification program, Baccalaureate/masters degree program. **Combined degree programs:** BA/MA, BS/MA, MS/MHA, BS/MS, BS/MBA. **Disability Services:** Special programs offered to physically disabled students include note-taking services, reader services, tape recorders, tutors.

FACILITIES

Housing: Coed dorms, men's dorms, women's dorms, apartments for single students, Theme Housing. 100% of campus accessible to physically disabled. **Special Academic Facilities/Equipment:** Art gallery, fine arts facility, theatre, center for music groups, language lab, microbiology institute, electron microscope, greenhouse. **Computers:** 40% of classrooms, 100% of dorms, 100% of libraries, 100% of dining areas, 100% of student union, 90% of common outdoor areas have wireless network access. Students can register for classes online. Administrative functions (other than registration) can be performed online.

CAMPUS LIFE

Environment: City. **Activities:** Choral groups, concert band, dance, drama/theater, jazz band, literary magazine, music ensembles, radio station, student government, student newspaper, television station, yearbook, Campus Ministries, International Student Organization. 50 registered organizations, 32 honor societies, 14 religious organizations. **Athletics (Intercollegiate):** *Men:* baseball, basketball, cross-country, golf, ice hockey, lacrosse, soccer, swimming, tennis, wrestling. *Women:* basketball, cross-country, field hockey, lacrosse, soccer, softball, swimming, tennis, volleyball. **On-Campus Highlights:** Brennan Hall (Home of the Kania School of Management), DeNaples Campus Center, The Harry and Jeanette Weiberg Memorial Library, The Murray Room (workout facility). **Environmental Initiatives:** We have incorporated energy efficient technology in our new construction and renovations over the past 20 years. We have One LEED Silver buiding, one pending LEED Gold building, and new building under construction committed to LEED Silver at a minimum. In addition we have a long standing and internationally known program/commitment to Green (sustainable) chemistry: http://academic.scranton.edu/faculty/CANNM1/greenchemistry.html. The ongoing infusion of sustainability across the curriculum via our annual Faculty Workshop on Sustainability (http://www.scranton.edu/sustainability/done_so_far_academics.shtml). Over 70 faulty members have participated in this program. Earth Day Celebration events on campus continue to grow. In 2014 we will have 14 events spread out over the month of April with most events occurring during the week of Earth Day. The events will include guest lectures, Earth Day Fair, Environmental 5K Run/Walk, Art Shows, K-12 local school Art and Essay contest, and Spring Symposium on our 2014 topic, "Water: our most precious resource."

ADMISSIONS

Freshman Academic Profile: Average high school GPA 3.38. 24% in top 10% of high school class, 57% in top 25% of high school class, 86% in top 50% of high school class. SAT Math middle 50% range 520-610. SAT Critical Reading middle 50% range 520-600. ACT middle 50% range 22-27. Minimum internet-based TOEFL 61. Minimum paper TOEFL 550. **Basis for Candidate Selection:** *Very important factors considered include:* Class rank, academic GPA, rigor of secondary school record, standardized test scores. *Important factors considered include:* extracurricular activities. *Other factors considered include:* application essay, recommendation(s), alumni/ae relation, character/personal qualities, interview, level of applicant's interest, talent/ability, volunteer work, work experience. **Freshman Admission Requirements:** High school diploma is required and GED is accepted. **Academic units required:** 4 English, 3 mathematics, 3 science, (1 science labs), 2 foreign language, 2 social studies, 2 history, 4 academic electives. **Freshman Admission Statistics:** 9,404 applied, 77% admitted, 15% enrolled. **Transfer Admission Requirements:** High school transcript, college transcript(s), Minimum college GPA of 2.75 required. Lowest grade transferable C. **General Admission Information:** Regular application deadline 3/1. Notification on a rolling basis, beginning on or about 12/15. Nonfall registration accepted. Admission may be deferred for a maximum of 12 months. Credit and/or placement offered for CEEB Advanced Placement tests.

COSTS AND FINANCIAL AID
Average book expense $1,200. **Required Forms and Deadlines:** FAFSA. **Notification of Awards:** Applicants will be notified of awards on a rolling basis beginning 3/15. **Types of Aid:** *Need-based scholarships/grants:* Federal Pell, SEOG, state scholarships/grants, private scholarships, the school's own gift aid. *Loans:* Direct Subsidized Stafford, Direct Unsubsidized Stafford, Direct PLUS, Federal Perkins, Federal Nursing. *Student Employment:* Federal Work-Study Program available. Institutional employment available. Off-campus job opportunities are good. **Financial Aid Statistics:** 98% freshmen, 96% undergrads receive need-based scholarship or grant aid. 10% freshmen, 7% undergrads receive non-need-based scholarship or grant aid. 83% freshmen, 87% undergrads receive need-based self-help aid. 0% freshmen, 0% undergrads receive athletic scholarships. 93% freshmen, 95% undergrads receive any aid. 75% undergrads borrow to pay for school. Average cumulative indebtedness $26,460. **Criteria for awarding institutional aid:** *Non-need-based:* academics.

UNIVERSITY OF SOUTH ALABAMA

Meisler Hall, Suite 2500, Mobile, AL 36688-0002
Phone: 251-460-6141 · **Financial Aid Phone:** 800-305-6828
E-mail: admiss@usouthal.edu · **CEEB Code:** 1880
Fax: 251-460-7876 · **Website:** www.usouthal.edu · **ACT Code:** 59

This public school was founded in 1963. It has a 1215-acre campus.

RATINGS
Admissions Selectivity Rating: 71   **Fire Safety Rating:** 63

STUDENTS AND FACULTY
Enrollment: 11,267. **Student Body:** 56% female, 44% male, 18% out-of-state, 4% international (76 countries represented). Asian 3%, African American 24%, Caucasian 61%, Hispanic 3%, Native American 1%
Retention and Graduation: 71% freshmen return for sophomore year. 15% freshmen graduate within 4 years. **Faculty:** 546 full-time faculty, 77% hold PhDs, 49% are are members of minority groups, 14% are women.

ACADEMICS
Degrees: bachelor's, certificate, master's, post-bachelor's certificate, post-master's certificate. **Majors with Highest Enrollment:** Elementary Education and Teaching; Registered Nursing/Registered Nurse; Speech Communication and Rhetoric. **Special Study Options:** Accelerated program, cooperative education program, distance learning, double major, dual enrollment, English as a Second Language (ESL), honors program, independent study, internships, student-designed major, study abroad, teacher certification program, weekend college. **Honors programs:** Honor Program. **Disability Services:** Special programs offered to physically disabled students include note-taking services, reader services, tape recorders, tutors.

FACILITIES
Housing: Coed dorms, special housing for disabled students, men's dorms, women's dorms, fraternity/sorority housing, apartments for married students, apartments for single students **Special Academic Facilities/Equipment:** Museum/gallery complex, three hospitals, center for clinical education in health programs, engineering labs. **Computers:** Students can register for classes online. Administrative functions (other than registration) can be performed online. Undergraduates are required to own a computer.

CAMPUS LIFE
Environment: City. **Activities:** Choral groups, concert band, dance, drama/theater, jazz band, literary magazine, marching band, music ensembles, musical theater, opera, student government, student newspaper, student-run film society, symphony orchestra, television station, Campus Ministries. 185 registered organizations, 2 honor societies, 1 religous organization. 8 fraternities, 8 sororities. **Athletics (Intercollegiate):** *Men:* baseball, basketball, cross-country, football, golf, tennis, track/field (outdoor). *Women:* basketball, cross-country, golf, soccer, softball, tennis, track/field (outdoor), volleyball. **On-Campus Highlights:** Mitchell Center (arena), Stanky Field, John W. Laidlaw Performing Arts Center, Intramural Field Complex.

ADMISSIONS
Freshman Academic Profile: Average high school GPA 3.41. 88% from public high schools. SAT Math middle 50% range 450-585. SAT Critical Reading middle 50% range 450-570. SAT Writing middle 50% range 430-540. ACT middle 50% range 20-25. Minimum internet-based TOEFL 61. Minimum paper TOEFL 500. **Basis for Candidate Selection:** *Very important factors*

considered include: rigor of secondary school record, standardized test scores. **Freshman Admission Requirements:** High school diploma is required and GED is accepted. **Freshman Admission Statistics:** 5,614 applied, 84% admitted, 44% enrolled. **Transfer Admission Requirements:** college transcript(s), Minimum college GPA of 2.0 required. Lowest grade transferable D. **General Admission Information:** Application Fee $35. Regular application deadline 9/10. Nonfall registration accepted. Admission may be deferred for a maximum of N/A. Credit and/or placement offered for CEEB Advanced Placement tests.

COSTS AND FINANCIAL AID
Annual out-of-state tuition $17,220. Room and board $7,100. Average book expense $1,200. **Required Forms and Deadlines:** FAFSA, Institution's own financial aid form. **Notification of Awards:** Applicants will be notified of awards on a rolling basis beginning 5/15. **Types of Aid:** *Need-based scholarships/grants:* Federal Pell, SEOG, state scholarships/grants, private scholarships, the school's own gift aid. *Loans:* Subsidized Stafford, Unsubsidized Stafford, PLUS, Federal Perkins, college/university loans from institutional funds. *Student Employment:* Federal Work-Study Program available. **Financial Aid Statistics:** 90% freshmen, 81% undergrads receive need-based scholarship or grant aid. 90% freshmen, 81% undergrads receive non-need-based scholarship or grant aid. 93% freshmen, 95% undergrads receive need-based self-help aid. 4% freshmen, 4% undergrads receive athletic scholarships. 59% freshmen, 80% undergrads receive any aid. **Criteria for awarding institutional aid:** *Non-need-based:* academics, alumni affiliation, art, athletics, minority status, music/drama.

UNIVERSITY OF SOUTH CAROLINA AIKEN

471 University Parkway, Aiken, SC 29801
Phone: 803-641-3366 · **Financial Aid Phone:** 803-641-3476
E-mail: admit@usca.edu · **CEEB Code:** 5840
Fax: 803-641-3727 · **Website:** web.usca.edu · **ACT Code:** 3879

This public school was founded in 1961. It has a 453-acre campus.

RATINGS
Admissions Selectivity Rating: 81   **Fire Safety Rating:** 90

STUDENTS AND FACULTY
Enrollment: 3,004. **Student Body:** 63% female, 37% male, 12% out-of-state, 3% international (23 countries represented). Asian 1%, African American 26%, Caucasian 59%, Hispanic 4%, Native American <1%
Retention and Graduation: 67% freshmen return for sophomore year. 19% freshmen graduate within 4 years. 39% freshmen graduate within 6 years. **Faculty:** 149 full-time faculty, 76% hold PhDs, 48% are are members of minority groups, 18% are women. 0% of classes are taught by teaching assistants.

ACADEMICS
Degrees: bachelor's, master's. **Classes:** Most classes have 20-29 students. Most lab/discussion sessions have 20-29 students. **Majors with Highest Enrollment:** Business Administration and Management; Registered Nursing/Registered Nurse; Kinesiology and Exercise Science. **Special Study Options:** cooperative education program, distance learning, double major, dual enrollment, English as a Second Language (ESL), honors program, independent study, internships, student-designed major, study abroad, teacher certification program. **Honors programs:** The USCA Honors Program is designed to increase the educational opportunities for the academically well qualified and highly motivated student. Designed in accordance with the principles of the National Collegiate Honors Council, the USC Aiken Honors Program provides an enriched academic experience, both in and out of the classroom, for outstanding students committed to reaching their highest potential as scholars and creative thinkers. For details on our Honors Program or the other high quality academic opportunities awaiting you at USC Aiken, please call on our Office of Admissions toll free at 888.WOW.USCA or locally at 803.641.3366. The Honors Director may be reached at 803.641.3226. **Disability Services:** Special programs offered to physically disabled students include note-taking services, reader services, tape recorders. **Career services:** Alumni network, alumni services, career/job search classes, career assessment, internships, regional alumni.

FACILITIES
Housing: Coed dorms, special housing for disabled students, apartments for single students, Wellness Housing, Theme Housing. 100% of campus accessible to physically disabled. **Special Academic Facilities/Equipment:** Ruth Patrick Science Education Center, Etherredge Center (Fine Arts Center), Wellness Center, Planetarium. **Computers:** 100% of classrooms, 100% of dorms, 100% of libraries, 100% of dining areas, 100% of student union, 100% of common outdoor areas have wireless network access. Students can register for classes online. Administrative functions (other than registration) can be performed online.

CAMPUS LIFE

Environment: Town. **Activities:** concert band, dance, drama/theater, music ensembles, musical theater, pep band, student government, student newspaper, symphony orchestra, yearbook, Campus Ministries, International Student Organization. 89 registered organizations, 12 honor societies, 7 religious organizations. 5 fraternities, 7 sororities. **Athletics (Intercollegiate):** *Men:* baseball, basketball, cheerleading, golf, soccer, tennis. *Women:* basketball, cheerleading, cross-country, soccer, softball, tennis, volleyball. **On-Campus Highlights:** DuPont Planetarium in the Ruth Patrick Science Education Center, The Etherredge Center for Visual and Performing Arts, The Wellness Center and Natatorium, The Alan B. Miller Nursing Building, Pacer Commons Student Housing, Roberto Hernandez Baseball Stadium USC Aiken Convocation Center. **Environmental Initiatives:** Obtain State Energy Department stimulus funding approval to jump start significant energy conservation actions with a goal of completion by 2012. The energy conservation projects will reduce each building's energy use (kWh) by 18%—reducing the carbon footprint from purchased electricity by at least 20%. Expand energy management system to include all main campus heating/cooling units and monitor energy usage continuously in 15 minute intervals using SCE&G usage monitoring software. The goal is to keep usage below 22 KW and significantly reduce the August/September KW peak for main campus by using load shedding and energy alert usage reduction campus-wide. Educate and involve students, faculty and staff in sustainability and carbon footprint reduction actions with training and planned USCA carbon footprint reduction web site. Continue to inform, challenge and involve everyone in carbon footprint reduction (ongoing).

ADMISSIONS

Freshman Academic Profile: Average high school GPA 3.66. 14% in top 10% of high school class, 43% in top 25% of high school class, 78% in top 50% of high school class. 91% from public high schools. SAT Math middle 50% range 430-540. SAT Critical Reading middle 50% range 430-540. SAT Writing middle 50% range 420-510. ACT middle 50% range 18-23. Minimum internet-based TOEFL 80. Minimum paper TOEFL 550. **Basis for Candidate Selection:** *Very important factors considered include:* Class rank, academic GPA, rigor of secondary school record, standardized test scores. **Freshman Admission Requirements:** High school diploma is required and GED is accepted. **Academic units required:** 4 English, 4 mathematics, 3 science, (3 science labs), 2 foreign language, 2 social studies, 1 history, 4 academic electives, 1 elective must be PE or ROTC. **Freshman Admission Statistics:** 2,091 applied, 66% admitted, 47% enrolled. **Transfer Admission Requirements:** college transcript(s), statement of good standing from prior institution(s). Minimum college GPA of 2.0 required. Lowest grade transferable C. **General Admission Information:** Application Fee $45. Regular application deadline 8/1. Notification on a rolling basis, beginning on or about 9/1. Nonfall registration accepted. Credit and/or placement offered for CEEB Advanced Placement tests.

COSTS AND FINANCIAL AID

Annual out-of-state tuition $18,636. Room and board $7,110. Required fees $290. Average book expense $1,320. **Required Forms and Deadlines:** FAFSA. **Notification of Awards:** Applicants will be notified of awards on a rolling basis beginning 4/20. **Types of Aid:** *Need-based scholarships/grants:* Federal Pell, SEOG, state scholarships/grants, private scholarships, the school's own gift aid. *Loans:* Direct Subsidized Stafford, Direct Unsubsidized Stafford, Direct PLUS, Subsidized Stafford, Unsubsidized Stafford, PLUS, Federal Perkins, state loans. *Student Employment:* Federal Work-Study Program available. Institutional employment available. Off-campus job opportunities are fair. **Financial Aid Statistics:** 83% freshmen, 68% undergrads receive need-based scholarship or grant aid. 36% freshmen, 35% undergrads receive non-need-based scholarship or grant aid. 45% freshmen, 51% undergrads receive need-based self-help aid. 2% freshmen, 4% undergrads receive athletic scholarships. 66% freshmen, 56% undergrads receive any aid. 67% undergrads borrow to pay for school. Average cumulative indebtedness $26,346. **Criteria for awarding institutional aid:** *Non-need-based:* academics, alumni affiliation, art, athletics, leadership, minority status, music/drama, state/district residency.

UNIVERSITY OF SOUTH CAROLINA BEAUFORT

1 University Boulevard, Bluffton, SC 29909
Phone: 843-208-8000 • **Financial Aid Phone:** 843-521-3104
E-mail: admissions@uscb.edu • **CEEB Code:** 5845
Fax: 843-208-8290 • **Website:** www.uscb.edu • **ACT Code:** 3835

This public school was founded in 1959. It has a 213-acre campus.

RATINGS

Admissions Selectivity Rating: 60*   **Fire Safety Rating:** 60*

STUDENTS AND FACULTY

Enrollment: 1,773. **Student Body:** 63% female, 37% male, 22% out-of-state, (14 countries represented).
Faculty: 59 full-time faculty, 76% hold PhDs, 47% are are members of minority groups, 15% are women.

ACADEMICS

Degrees: associate, bachelor's, post-bachelor's certificate, transfer associate. **Classes:** Most classes have 10-19 students. **Majors with Highest Enrollment:** Business Administration and Management; Hospitality Administration/Management; Registered Nursing, Nursing Administration, Nursing Research and Clinical Nursing. **Special Study Options:** cooperative education program, cross-registration, distance learning, dual enrollment, independent study, internships, study abroad, teacher certification program, weekend college. **Disability Services:** Special programs offered to physically disabled students include note-taking services, reader services, tape recorders, tutors. **Career services:** career/job search classes, internships.

FACILITIES

Housing: Coed dorms, special housing for disabled students, apartments for single students. **Computers:** Students can register for classes online. Administrative functions (other than registration) can be performed online.

CAMPUS LIFE

Environment: Village. **Activities:** Choral groups, drama/theater, literary magazine, musical theater, student government, student newspaper. 11 registered organizations. **Athletics (Intercollegiate):** *Men:* baseball, cross-country, golf, track/field (outdoor). **On-Campus Highlights:** Sandbar Café, Campus Center Gym, Library.

ADMISSIONS

Freshman Academic Profile: Minimum paper TOEFL 550. **Basis for Candidate Selection:** *Very important factors considered include:* academic GPA, standardized test scores. *Important factors considered include:* Class rank, rigor of secondary school record. **Freshman Admission Requirements:** High school diploma is required and GED is accepted. **Academic units required:** 4 English, 3 mathematics, 3 science, (3 science labs), 2 foreign language, 2 social studies, 1 history, 4 academic electives, 1 Physical Education. **Transfer Admission Requirements:** college transcript(s), Minimum college GPA of 2.0 required. Lowest grade transferable C-. **General Admission Information:** Application Fee $40. Notification on a rolling basis, beginning on or about 2/1. Nonfall registration accepted. Credit offered for CEEB Advanced Placement tests.

COSTS AND FINANCIAL AID

Required Forms and Deadlines: FAFSA. **Notification of Awards:** Applicants will be notified of awards on a rolling basis beginning 5/31. **Types of Aid:** *Need-based scholarships/grants:* Federal Pell, SEOG, state scholarships/grants, private scholarships, the school's own gift aid. *Loans:* Subsidized Stafford, Unsubsidized Stafford, PLUS, state loans. **Financial Aid Statistics:** 35% freshmen, 65% undergrads receive any aid. **Criteria for awarding institutional aid:** *Non-need-based:* academics, state/district residency.

UNIVERSITY OF SOUTH CAROLINA—COLUMBIA

Best 380

Office of Undergraduate Admissions, Columbia, SC 29208
Phone: 803-777-7700 • **Financial Aid Phone:** 803-777-8134
E-mail: admissions-ugrad@sc.edu • **CEEB Code:** 5818
Fax: 803-777-0101 • **Website:** www.sc.edu • **ACT Code:** 3880

This public school was founded in 1801. It has a 384-acre campus.

RATINGS

Admissions Selectivity Rating: 88   **Fire Safety Rating:** 93

STUDENTS AND FACULTY

Enrollment: 23,987. **Student Body:** 54% female, 46% male, 30% out-of-state, 1% international (115 countries represented). Asian 2%, African American 10%, Caucasian 77%, Hispanic 4%, Native American <1%
Retention and Graduation: 54% freshmen graduate within 4 years. 73% freshmen graduate within 6 years. **Faculty:** 1,560 full-time faculty, 83% hold PhDs, 43% are are members of minority groups, 18% are women.

ACADEMICS

Degrees: associate, bachelor's, doctoral, master's, post-bachelor's certificate, post-master's certificate. **Classes:** Most classes have 20-29 students. Most lab/discussion sessions have 20-29 students. **Majors with Highest Enrollment:** Experimental Psychology; Registered Nursing, Nursing Administration, Nursing Research and Clinical Nursing; Criminal Justice/Law Enforcement Administration. **Special Study Options:** Accelerated program, cooperative education program, cross-registration, distance learning, double major, dual enrollment, English as a Second Language (ESL), exchange student program (domestic), external degree program, honors program, independent study, internships, student-designed major, study abroad, teacher certification program, weekend college, Alternative Spring Break, Dobson Internship Program, Volunteer Service Program, International Program for Students, Undergraduate Research. **Honors programs:** The Honors College is a small college of about 1,000 students, all of whom excel in academics. What makes the Honors College different is its ability to weave engaging, exciting course offerings into any undergraduate major. You choose your major and set up your course schedule just like any other student at the University. But your choices include classes especially for Honors College students over 100 courses each semester. **Combined degree programs:** BA/MEng. **Disability Services:** Special programs offered to physically disabled students include note-taking services, reader services, tape recorders. **Career services:** alumni services, career/job search classes, career assessment, internships. Career services highlights include Experiential learning through consulting with and assisting with startup of new businesses.

FACILITIES

Housing: Coed dorms, special housing for disabled students, men's dorms, special housing for international students, women's dorms, fraternity/sorority housing, apartments for married students, apartments for single students, Wellness HousingHonors housing (first year freshman and upperclass), Preston Residential College, Pre-Medical (first year and upperclass), Pre-Law, Engineering and Computing Community, Athletic, Greek, Teaching Fellows, Global, Green, Magellan Explorers, Capstone Scholars, Bridge Community, Journalism, Music, French House, Spanish Language, other Special Interest. 95% of campus accessible to physically disabled. **Special Academic Facilities/Equipment:** Art gallery, movie theater, McKissick Museum, South Caroliniana Library, Melton Observatory, Gibbes Planetarium, Melton Observatory, Filtration Research Engineering Demonstration Unit, Belser Arboretum, A.C. Moore Gardens. **Computers:** Students can register for classes online. Administrative functions (other than registration) can be performed online.

CAMPUS LIFE

Environment: City. **Activities:** Choral groups, concert band, dance, drama/theater, jazz band, literary magazine, marching band, music ensembles, musical theater, opera, pep band, radio station, student government, student newspaper, symphony orchestra. 300 registered organizations, 25 honor societies, 32 religious organizations. 20 fraternities, 14 sororities. **Athletics (Intercollegiate):** *Men:* baseball, basketball, diving, football, golf, racquetball, soccer, softball, swimming, tennis, track/field (outdoor). *Women:* basketball, cross-country, diving, equestrian sports, golf, racquetball, soccer, softball, swimming, tennis, track/field (outdoor), volleyball. **On-Campus Highlights:** Strom Thurmond Wellness & Fitness Center, Russell House, Greek Village, Williams Brice Stadium, Historic Horseshoe. **Environmental Initiatives:** Sustainable Carolina represents all the sustainability efforts on campus and utilizes over 40 student interns to implement the campus sustainability plan. The program is based on leadership development and allows students to apply sustainability practices on campus. Last year students put in nearly 20,000 hours working, learning and training on sustainability issues. Campus has committed to converting 100% of its fleet to alternative fuel vehicles by 2015, which will eliminate 2,000 tons of CO_2 emissions/year. The new Darla Moore School of Business is being designed as the largest net zero energy building in the country. Additionally, the campus efficiency upgrades have reduced energy and water consumption in over 2/3rds of the campus buildings. The campus energy consumption has been reduced by 33% and water consumption by 44% since 2004 producing upto $5 million/year in savings.

ADMISSIONS

Freshman Academic Profile: Average high school GPA 4.15. 30% in top 10% of high school class, 66% in top 25% of high school class, 94% in top 50% of high school class. SAT Math middle 50% range 550-650. SAT Critical Reading middle 50% range 540-630. ACT middle 50% range 24-29. Minimum internet-based TOEFL 77. Minimum paper TOEFL 550. **Basis for Candidate Selection:** *Very important factors considered include:* academic GPA, rigor of secondary school record, standardized test scores. *Important factors considered include:* Class rank. *Other factors considered include:* application essay, recommendation(s), alumni/ae relation, character/personal qualities, extracurricular activities, first generation, racial/ethnic status, state residency, talent/ability, volunteer work, work experience. **Freshman Admission Requirements:** High school diploma is required and GED is accepted. **Academic units required:** 4 English, 4 mathematics, 3 science, (3 science labs), 2 foreign language, 2 social studies, 1 history, 1 academic elective, 2 PE or ROTC and Fine Arts. **Freshman Admission Statistics:** 23,035 applied,

64% admitted, 30% enrolled. **Transfer Admission Requirements:** college transcript(s), Minimum college GPA of 2.25 required. Lowest grade transferable C-. **General Admission Information:** Application Fee $50. Regular application deadline 12/1. Notification on a rolling basis, beginning on or about 3/15. Nonfall registration accepted. Credit and/or placement offered for CEEB Advanced Placement tests.

COSTS AND FINANCIAL AID

Annual in-state tuition $10,416. Annual out-of-state tuition $28,128. Room and board $8,459. Required fees $400. Average book expense $994. **Required Forms and Deadlines:** FAFSA. **Notification of Awards:** Applicants will be notified of awards on a rolling basis beginning 1/4. **Types of Aid:** *Need-based scholarships/grants:* Federal Pell, SEOG, state scholarships/grants, private scholarships, the school's own gift aid, United Negro College Fund, Federal Nursing Scholarships, USC Opportunity Grant—Institutional Gamecock Guarantee. *Loans:* Subsidized Stafford, Unsubsidized Stafford, PLUS, Federal Perkins, Federal Nursing. *Student Employment:* Federal Work-Study Program available. Institutional employment available. Off-campus job opportunities are good. **Financial Aid Statistics:** 42% freshmen, 51% undergrads receive need-based scholarship or grant aid. 89% freshmen, 63% undergrads receive non-need-based scholarship or grant aid. 90% freshmen, 91% undergrads receive need-based self-help aid. 3% freshmen, 3% undergrads receive athletic scholarships. 96% freshmen, 87% undergrads receive any aid. 45% undergrads borrow to pay for school. Average cumulative indebtedness $21,789. **Criteria for awarding institutional aid:** *Non-need-based:* academics, alumni affiliation, art, athletics, job skills, leadership, minority status, music/drama, religious affiliation, state/district residency.

UNIVERSITY OF SOUTH CAROLINA UPSTATE

800 University Way, Spartanburg, SC 29303
Phone: 864-503-5246
E-mail: dstewart@uscs.edu • **CEEB Code:** 5850
Fax: 864-503-5727 • **Website:** www.uscs.edu • **ACT Code:** 3889

This public school was founded in 1967. It has a 298-acre campus.

RATINGS

Admissions Selectivity Rating: 60*   **Fire Safety Rating:** 60*

STUDENTS AND FACULTY

Enrollment: 4,237. **Student Body:** 65% female, 35% male, 7% out-of-state, 2% international (30 countries represented). Asian 3%, African American 26%, Caucasian 64%, Hispanic 1%, Native American <1%. **Retention and Graduation:** 67% freshmen return for sophomore year. 17% freshmen graduate within 4 years. 37% freshmen graduate within 6 years. 20% grads go on to further study within 1 year. **Faculty:** 179 full-time faculty, 79% hold PhDs, 54% are are members of minority groups. 0% of classes are taught by teaching assistants.

ACADEMICS

Degrees: associate, bachelor's, master's, terminal associate. **Classes:** Most classes have 20-29 students. Most lab/discussion sessions have 20-29 students. **Majors with Highest Enrollment:** Education; Registered Nursing/Registered Nurse; Business/Commerce. **Special Study Options:** Accelerated program, cross-registration, distance learning, double major, exchange student program (domestic), honors program, independent study, internships, student-designed major, study abroad, teacher certification program. **Disability Services:** Special programs offered to physically disabled students include note-taking services, reader services, tape recorders, tutors. **Career services:** alumni services, career/job search classes, career assessment, internships.

FACILITIES

Housing: Coed dorms, apartments for single students. 100% of campus accessible to physically disabled. **Special Academic Facilities/Equipment:** Campus Life Center; performing arts building, including 450 seat theater; arts studies film theater; recital hall; language laboratory; Quality Institute. **Computers:** Students can register for classes online. Administrative functions (other than registration) can be performed online.

CAMPUS LIFE

Activities: Choral groups, dance, drama/theater, jazz band, literary magazine, music ensembles, musical theater, student government, student newspaper. 61 registered organizations, 5 religious organizations. 2 fraternities, 3 sororities. **Athletics (Intercollegiate):** *Men:* baseball, basketball, cross-country, soccer, tennis. *Women:* basketball, cross-country, soccer, softball, tennis, volleyball. **On-Campus Highlights:** Campus Life Center, Aboretum.

ADMISSIONS

Freshman Academic Profile: Average high school GPA 3.4. 11% in top 10% of high school class, 37% in top 25% of high school class, 68% in top 50% of high school class. SAT Math middle 50% range 450-540. SAT Critical Reading middle 50% range 440-530. ACT middle 50% range 18-21. Minimum paper TOEFL 500. **Basis for Candidate Selection:** *Very important factors considered include:* rigor of secondary school record, standardized test scores. **Freshman Admission Requirements:** High school diploma is required and GED is accepted. **Academic units required:** 4 English, 3 mathematics, 3 science, (2 science labs), 2 foreign language, 2 social studies, 1 history, 4 academic electives, 1 physical education or ROTC. **Freshman Admission Statistics:** 1,904 applied, 49% admitted, 75% enrolled. **Transfer Admission Requirements:** college transcript(s), statement of good standing from prior institution(s). Minimum college GPA of 2.0 required. Lowest grade transferable C. **General Admission Information:** Application Fee $35. Notification on a rolling basis, beginning on or about 9/15. Nonfall registration accepted. Admission may be deferred for a maximum of 1 year. Credit offered for CEEB Advanced Placement tests.

COSTS AND FINANCIAL AID

Annual in-state tuition $5,310. Annual out-of-state tuition $10,936. Room and board $4,940. Required fees $226. Average book expense $700. **Required Forms and Deadlines:** FAFSA. **Types of Aid:** *Need-based scholarships/grants:* Federal Pell, SEOG, state scholarships/grants, private scholarships, the school's own gift aid, Non-need-based (college-administered): Academic merit Athletic State scholarships/grants ROTC scholarships. *Loans:* Subsidized Stafford, Unsubsidized Stafford, PLUS, Federal Perkins, Federal Nursing, state loans. *Student Employment:* Federal Work-Study Program available. Institutional employment available. Off-campus job opportunities are excellent. **Financial Aid Statistics:** 59% freshmen, 63% undergrads receive need-based scholarship or grant aid. 67% freshmen, 24% undergrads receive non-need-based scholarship or grant aid. 56% freshmen, 78% undergrads receive need-based self-help aid. 3% freshmen, 3% undergrads receive athletic scholarships. 64% undergrads borrow to pay for school. **Criteria for awarding institutional aid:** *Non-need-based:* academics, athletics, minority status, state/district residency.

THE UNIVERSITY OF SOUTH DAKOTA

414 East Clark, Vermillion, SD 57069
Phone: 605-677-5434 · **Financial Aid Phone:** 605-677-5446
E-mail: admissions@usd.edu · **CEEB Code:** 6881
Fax: 605-677-6323 · **Website:** www.usd.edu · **ACT Code:** 3928

This public school was founded in 1862. It has a 273-acre campus.

RATINGS

Admissions Selectivity Rating: 75   **Fire Safety Rating:** 97

STUDENTS AND FACULTY

Enrollment: 6,331. **Student Body:** 63% female, 37% male, 33% out-of-state, 2% international (46 countries represented). Asian 1%, African American 2%, Caucasian 87%, Hispanic 3%, Native American 2%
Retention and Graduation: 75% freshmen return for sophomore year. 33% freshmen graduate within 4 years. 57% freshmen graduate within 6 years. 48% grads go on to further study within 1 year. 26% grads pursue arts and sciences degrees. 9% grads pursue law degrees. 9% grads pursue business degrees. 9% grads pursue medical degrees. **Faculty:** 453 full-time faculty, 83% hold PhDs, 49% are are members of minority groups, 15% are women. 8% of classes are taught by teaching assistants.

ACADEMICS

Degrees: associate, bachelor's, certificate, doctoral, master's, post-bachelor's certificate, post-master's certificate, terminal associate. **Classes:** Most classes have 10-19 students. Most lab/discussion sessions have 20-29 students. **Majors with Highest Enrollment:** Psychology; Business/Commerce; Education. **Special Study Options:** Accelerated program, cross-registration, distance learning, double major, dual enrollment, English as a Second Language (ESL), exchange student program (domestic), external degree program, honors program, independent study, internships, liberal arts/career combination, student-designed major, study abroad, teacher certification program. **Honors programs:** University Honors Program. The program has its own core curriculum that replaces the University's general education requirements. Thesis Scholars Program, Alumni Student Scholars Program, Law Honors Scholars Program **Combined degree programs:** BA/MA. **Disability Services:** Special programs offered to physically disabled students include note-taking services, reader services, tape recorders, tutors. **Career services:** Alumni network, alumni services, career/job search classes, career assessment, internships. USD, as the flagship liberal arts institution in the state, provides the framework for an extraordinary education and includes the Interdisciplinary Education & Action or "IdEA" Program. The U. has purposefully designed a contemporary liberal arts education that includes a solid foundation of knowledge, exposure to many different academic disciplines, immersion in interdisciplinary and diverse ways of thinkingt, and understanding of service and citizenship. All students at the U. follow a flexible course of study that first exposes them to great ideas, but ultimately challenges them to integrate their knowledge in ways that serve their own careers and other citizens. (http://catalog.usd.edu/content.php?catoid=3&navoid=34). The integration component of this education is found in the IdEA Program, which invites USD students to explore interdisciplinary approaches to questions that matter in a global, contemporary society. It occurs when juniors and seniors are experiencing the conclusion of their academic careers at USD and at a time when individuals are moving beyond their immediate and personal identities and defining their roles and responsibilities in a wider social, political, economic and physical environments. It provides key liberal learning outcomes such as critical thinking, integrative approaches and active citizenship.

FACILITIES

Housing: Coed dorms, special housing for disabled students, fraternity/sorority housing, apartments for married students, apartments for single students, Apartments for students with dependent children. Brand new state of the art apartment style housing currently under construction with a new wellness center being constructed due to open in 2010. 98% of campus accessible to physically disabled. **Special Academic Facilities/Equipment:** W.H. Over Museum, The National Music Museum, Oscar Howe Art Gallery, Center for Instructional Design and Delivery, Institute of American Indian Studies, Native American Cultural Center, Disaster Mental Health Institute, Neuharth Center for Excellence in Journalism, Missouri Rive Institute. **Computers:** 60% of classrooms, 100% of libraries, 100% of dining areas, 100% of student union, have wireless network access. Students can register for classes online. Administrative functions (other than registration) can be performed online.

CAMPUS LIFE

Environment: Village. **Activities:** Choral groups, concert band, dance, drama/theater, jazz band, literary magazine, marching band, music ensembles, musical theater, opera, pep band, radio station, student government, student newspaper, symphony orchestra, television station, Campus Ministries, International Student Organization. 120 registered organizations, 6 honor societies, 6 religious organizations. 8 fraternities, 3 sororities. **Athletics (Intercollegiate):** *Men:* basketball, cross-country, diving, football, golf, swimming, track/field (outdoor), track/field (indoor). *Women:* basketball, cross-country, diving, golf, soccer, softball, swimming, tennis, track/field (outdoor), track/field (indoor), volleyball. **On-Campus Highlights:** Al Neuharth Media Center, The National Music Museum, The Dakota Dome, Belbus Student Service Center, Coyote Student Center. **Environmental Initiatives:** Creation of the Sustainability Task Force for evaluation, monitoring and policy creation. Facility Management efforts to increase efficiency and decrease energy use. All new construction buildings comply with LEED Silver standards. Faculty, student and administration involvement in sustainability projects including recycling, climate commitment and public outreach.

ADMISSIONS

Freshman Academic Profile: Average high school GPA 3.37. 15% in top 10% of high school class, 37% in top 25% of high school class, 72% in top 50% of high school class. 75% from public high schools. SAT Math middle 50% range 470-610. SAT Critical Reading middle 50% range 400-440. SAT Writing middle 50% range 410-510. ACT middle 50% range 20-25. Minimum internet-based TOEFL 81. Minimum paper TOEFL 550. **Basis for Candidate Selection:** *Very important factors considered include:* Class rank, academic GPA, rigor of secondary school record, standardized test scores. *Important factors considered include:* alumni/ae relation. *Other factors considered include:* application essay, recommendation(s), character/personal qualities, extracurricular activities, geographical residence, racial/ethnic status, state residency, talent/ability, volunteer work, work experience. **Freshman Admission Requirements:** High school diploma is required and GED is accepted. **Academic units required:** 4 English, 3 mathematics, 3 science, (3 science labs), 3 social studies, 1 Fine Arts. **Freshman Admission Statistics:** 3,542 applied, 89% admitted, 40% enrolled. **Transfer Admission Requirements:** High school transcript, college transcript(s), Minimum college GPA of 2.0 required. Lowest grade transferable D. **General Admission Information:** Application Fee $20. Notification on a rolling basis, beginning on or about 9/10. Nonfall registration accepted. Admission may be deferred for a maximum of 1 Semester. Credit and/or placement offered for CEEB Advanced Placement tests.

COSTS AND FINANCIAL AID

Annual in-state tuition $4,164. Annual out-of-state tuition $6,246. Room and board $7,089. Required fees $3,858. Average book expense $1,100. **Required Forms and Deadlines:** FAFSA. **Notification of Awards:** Applicants will be notified of awards on a rolling basis beginning 3/1. **Types of Aid:** *Need-based* scholarships/grants: Federal Pell, SEOG, private scholarships, the school's own gift aid, Federal Nursing Scholarships. Loans: Subsidized Stafford, Unsubsidized Stafford, PLUS, Federal Perkins, Federal Nursing, college/university loans from institutional funds. Student Employment: Federal Work-Study Program available. Institutional employment available. Highest amount earned per year from on-campus jobs $3,300. Off-campus job opportunities are good. **Financial Aid Statistics:** 47% freshmen, 50% undergrads receive need-based scholarship or grant aid. 77% freshmen, 54% undergrads receive non-need-based scholarship or grant aid. 80% freshmen, 86% undergrads receive need-based self-help aid. 6% freshmen, 6% undergrads receive athletic scholarships. 94% freshmen, 81% undergrads receive any aid. 75% undergrads borrow to pay for school. Average cumulative indebtedness $25,554. **Criteria for awarding institutional aid:** Non-need-based: academics, art, athletics, leadership, minority status, music/drama.

UNIVERSITY OF SOUTH FLORIDA

Best 380

4202 East Fowler Avenue, Tampa, FL 33620-9951
Phone: 813-974-3350 · **Financial Aid Phone:** 813-974-4700
E-mail: admissions@admin.usf.edu · **CEEB Code:** 5828
Fax: 813-974-9689 · **Website:** www.usf.edu · **ACT Code:** 761

This public school was founded in 1956. It has a 1797-acre campus.

RATINGS

Admissions Selectivity Rating: 89   Fire Safety Rating: 72

STUDENTS AND FACULTY

Enrollment: 30,376. **Student Body:** 55% female, 45% male, 7% out-of-state, 3% international (155 countries represented). Asian 6%, African American 11%, Caucasian 55%, Hispanic 20%, Native American <1%
Retention and Graduation: 89% freshmen return for sophomore year. 20% grads go on to further study within 1 year. **Faculty:** 12,006 full-time faculty, 8% hold PhDs, 4% are are members of minority groups, 4% are women. 17% of classes are taught by teaching assistants.

ACADEMICS

Degrees: associate, bachelor's, master's. **Classes:** Most classes have 20-29 students. Most lab/discussion sessions have 20-29 students. **Majors with Highest Enrollment:** Psychology; Business/Commerce; Microbiology. **Special Study Options:** Accelerated program, cooperative education program, cross-registration, distance learning, double major, dual enrollment, exchange student program (domestic), honors program, internships, study abroad, teacher certification program, weekend college, Honors undergraduate research majors. **Honors programs:** Honors College: http://honors.usf.edu/ **Combined degree programs:** BA/MD, BA/MA, BA/MEng. **Disability Services:** Special programs offered to physically disabled students include note-taking services, reader services, tutors. **Career services:** alumni services, career/job search classes, career assessment, internships.

FACILITIES

Housing: Coed dorms, special housing for disabled students, men's dorms, special housing for international students, women's dorms, fraternity/sorority housing, apartments for married students, cooperative housing, apartments for single students, Grad students only; Medical students only. 100% of campus accessible to physically disabled. **Special Academic Facilities/Equipment:** Art museum and galleries, contemporary art museum, graphic studio, anthropology museum, fitness center, par course. **Computers:** 80% of classrooms, 35% of dorms, 100% of libraries, 50% of dining areas, 100% of student union, 50% of common outdoor areas have wireless network access. Students can register for classes online. Administrative functions (other than registration) can be performed online.

CAMPUS LIFE

Environment: Metropolis. **Activities:** Choral groups, concert band, dance, drama/theater, jazz band, literary magazine, marching band, music ensembles, musical theater, opera, pep band, radio station, student government, student newspaper, student-run film society, symphony orchestra, television station. 507 registered organizations, 33 honor societies, 42 religious organizations. 16 fraternities, 22 sororities. **Athletics (Intercollegiate):** Men: baseball, basketball, cheerleading, cross-country, football, golf, sailing, soccer, tennis, track/field (outdoor), track/field (indoor). Women: basketball, cheerleading, cross-country, golf, sailing, soccer, softball, tennis, track/field (outdoor), track/field (indoor), volley-

ball. **On-Campus Highlights:** Marshall Center, The Tampa Campus Library, Contemporary Art Museum, Botanical Gardens, Sun Dome. **Environmental Initiatives:** USFs 2008 Going Green Tampa Bay sustainability EXPO which drew over 3,000 visitors; Our USF Sustainability Initiative and 14 subcommittees; Our rapidly expanding Recycling program; Our Campus Transportation program; We have incorporated sustainability into our USF Strategic Plan.

ADMISSIONS

Freshman Academic Profile: Average high school GPA 3.86. 35.68% in top 10% of high school class, 65.47% in top 25% of high school class, 76.03% in top 50% of high school class. 95% from public high schools. SAT Math middle 50% range 550-640. SAT Critical Reading middle 50% range 530-620. SAT Writing middle 50% range 510-610. ACT middle 50% range 23-28. Minimum internet-based TOEFL 80. **Basis for Candidate Selection:** Very important factors considered include: academic GPA, rigor of secondary school record. Important factors considered include: standardized test scores, first generation. Other factors considered include: Class rank, application essay, recommendation(s), character/personal qualities, extracurricular activities, geographical residence, state residency, talent/ability, volunteer work, work experience. **Freshman Admission Requirements:** High school diploma is required and GED is accepted. **Academic units required:** 4 English, 4 mathematics, 3 science, (2 science labs), 2 foreign language, 3 social studies, 3 academic electives. **Freshman Admission Statistics:** 28,512 applied, 45% admitted, 29% enrolled. **Transfer Admission Requirements:** college transcript(s), statement of good standing from prior institution(s). Minimum college GPA of 2.3 required. Lowest grade transferable D. **General Admission Information:** Application Fee $30. Regular application deadline 4/15. Regular notification 4/15. Notification on a rolling basis, beginning on or about 10/1. Nonfall registration accepted. Credit and/or placement offered for CEEB Advanced Placement tests.

COSTS AND FINANCIAL AID

Annual in-state tuition $4,559. Annual out-of-state tuition $15,474. Room and board $9,400. Required fees $1,851. Average book expense $1,000. **Required Forms and Deadlines:** FAFSA. **Notification of Awards:** Applicants will be notified of awards on a rolling basis beginning 3/15. **Types of Aid:** Need-based scholarships/grants: Federal Pell, SEOG, state scholarships/grants, private scholarships, the school's own gift aid. Loans: Subsidized Stafford, Unsubsidized Stafford, PLUS, Federal Perkins, college/university loans from institutional funds. Student Employment: Federal Work-Study Program available. Institutional employment available. Off-campus job opportunities are good. **Financial Aid Statistics:** 68% freshmen, 67% undergrads receive need-based scholarship or grant aid. 92% freshmen, 65% undergrads receive non-need-based scholarship or grant aid. 49% freshmen, 61% undergrads receive need-based self-help aid. 2% freshmen, 2% undergrads receive athletic scholarships. 76% freshmen, 69% undergrads receive any aid. 59% undergrads borrow to pay for school. Average cumulative indebtedness $21,393. **Criteria for awarding institutional aid:** Non-need-based: academics, alumni affiliation, art, athletics, job skills, leadership, minority status, music/drama, religious affiliation, state/district residency.

UNIVERSITY OF SOUTHERN CALIFORNIA

Best 380

Office of Admission/ John Hubbard Hall, Los Angeles, CA 90089-0911
Phone: 213-740-1111 · **Financial Aid Phone:** 213-740-4444
E-mail: admitusc@usc.edu · **CEEB Code:** 4852
Fax: 213-821-0200 · **Website:** www.usc.edu · **ACT Code:** 470

This private school was founded in 1880. It has a 155-acre campus.

RATINGS

Admissions Selectivity Rating: 98   Fire Safety Rating: 96

STUDENTS AND FACULTY

Enrollment: 18,392. **Student Body:** 51% female, 49% male, 32% out-of-state, 13% international (112 countries represented). Asian 22%, African American 4%, Caucasian 36%, Hispanic 14%, Native American <1%
Retention and Graduation: 97% freshmen return for sophomore year. 76% freshmen graduate within 4 years. 91% freshmen graduate within 6 years. **Faculty:** 1,869 full-time faculty, 90% hold PhDs, 37% are are members of minority groups, 29% are women.

ACADEMICS

Degrees: bachelor's, doctoral, master's, post-bachelor's certificate, post-master's certificate. **Classes:** Most classes have 10-19 students. Most lab/discussion sessions have 20-29 students. **Special Study Options:** cooperative education program, distance learning, double major, English as a Second Language (ESL), exchange student program (domestic), honors program, independent study, internships, liberal arts/career combination, student-designed major, study abroad, Learning communities, Thematic Option, Undergraduate Research, and Freshman Seminars. **Honors programs:** Thematic Option Program Multimedia Scholarship **Combined degree programs:** BA/MD, BA/MA, BA/MEng, BS/MA, BS/MS. **Disability Services:** Special programs offered to physically disabled students include note-taking services, reader services, tape recorders, tutors. **Career services:** Alumni network, alumni services, career assessment, internships, regional alumni. Career services highlights include the Joint Educational Project, a service learning program that provides an interface between USC and the local community.

FACILITIES
Housing: Coed dorms, special housing for disabled students, special housing for international students, fraternity/sorority housing, apartments for married students, apartments for single students, Wellness Housing, Theme Housing, Special interest floors. 97% of campus accessible to physically disabled. **Special Academic Facilities/Equipment:** USC Fisher Museum of Art; Hancock Memorial Museum; specialized architecture and fine arts galleries, studios and labs; media labs; cinema scoring sound stage; recording studios; theatres and recital halls; exercise physiology lab; specialized engineering laboratories; biomedical imaging labs; Center for Electron Microscopy and Microanalysis; genomic research facilities; GIS research lab; USC Shoah Foundation Institute visual history archive; Archival Research Center; High-Performance Computing Center; public computing centers and labs; extensive wireless access to the USC network; classrooms outfitted with multiple webcams and microphones. **Computers:** 15% of classrooms, 10% of dorms, 100% of libraries, 100% of dining areas, 100% of student union, 90% of common outdoor areas have wireless network access. Students can register for classes online. Administrative functions (other than registration) can be performed online.

CAMPUS LIFE
Environment: Metropolis. **Activities:** Choral groups, concert band, dance, drama/theater, jazz band, literary magazine, marching band, music ensembles, musical theater, opera, pep band, radio station, student government, student newspaper, student-run film society, symphony orchestra, television station, yearbook, Campus Ministries, International Student Organization, Model UN. 676 registered organizations, 49 honor societies, 74 religious organizations. 41 fraternities, 23 sororities. **Athletics (Intercollegiate):** *Men:* baseball, basketball, diving, football, golf, swimming, tennis, track/field (outdoor), volleyball, water polo. *Women:* basketball, crew/rowing, cross-country, diving, golf, soccer, swimming, tennis, track/field (outdoor), volleyball, water polo. **On-Campus Highlights:** USC Fisher Museum of Art, Galen Center (event & training pavilion), Leavey Library (open 24 hours), Heritage Hall (athletic awards), Tutor Campus Center (opens fall 2010), USC's University Park campus—located three miles south of downtown Los Angeles, adjacent to the museums and recreational facilities of historic Exposition Park—is an urban oasis, offering a park-like atmosphere and rich architectural history. **Environmental Initiatives:** Energy Efficiency & Innovation: USC employs a full time Director of Energy Services to manage energy programs including lighting retrofits, equipment upgrades, and a recent retrofit of chillers, cooling towers, and pumps throughout the University, including a three million gallon centralized thermal energy storage tank installed below ground. The 3 million-gallon thermal energy water storage (TES) system was built 40 feet below ground. It is estimated that the new system conserves about 4,500 megawatt-hours of electricity a year by circulating chilled water to air conditioning systems throughout the University Park Campus, significantly expanding the capacity of the campus' existing chilled-water system while reducing utility use. The warmer water coming back through pipes has a chance to chill overnight before it is recirculated which allows USC to shift much of the kilowatt-hour usage to off-peak hours when electricity is more available. The entire system was conceived in 2001 and completed in 2005. Transportation Initiatives: USC counts on the services of a full time Rideshare Coordinator to ensure that transportation programs are available to all members of the University community. In 2006 USC achieved an Average Vehicle Ridership (AVR) of 1.69, exceeding the target of 1.50 established by the South Coast Air Quality Management District (SCAQMD). Seventeen strategies are used to achieve this AVR, most notably: a carpool/vanpool program; transit and parking charge subsidies; telecommuting; various incentives and raffles; availability of compressed work weeks; bicycle accessibility; and various support strategies like providing transit information and ridesharing assistance. There are five primary ride sharing options available to the USC community. Students, Staff, and Faculty are encouraged to ride the MTA Bus Lines, DASH Bus Lines, Metrolink Trains, or participate in carpools and vanpools. Eligible full time employees of USC who participate in the programs receive a subsidy of $30 as a benefit for not purchasing a parking pass. The subsidies provided to employees may be applied to the purchase of monthly passes for Metro (light rail or bus), LADOT, Metrolink, or other services not sold through the Transportation Office. In order to facilitate participation in the carpool program,

employees are encouraged to participate in L.A. Countys ridematch program to find potential carpool partners. The online database matches potential rideshare partners from the five county regions of Los Angeles, San Bernardino, Orange, Ventura, and Riverside. In addition, USCs Rideshare Office conducts an annual rideshare survey to generate a customized rideguide to match potential carpoolers in a given area. Trojan Transportation has three alternative fuel trams that run on biodiesel which provide service to off-campus housing, between campuses, and to Union Train Station. Recently purchased electric-powered, three-wheeled vehicles and bicycles are now used daily to patrol the campus by the Department of Public Safety. Eight of the three wheeled carts are used daily and offer a green alternative to gasoline powered patrol cars. In addition, the Facilities Management Services organization counts on a fleet of electric and hybrid vehicles for campus use. Also of note, USC has partnered with Flexcar, a unique car-sharing service that offers members affordable hourly access to vehicles, thus reducing the need for vehicles on campus. The service is available to everyone in the USC community. Sustainability Steering Committee: The Sustainability Steering Committees core intent is to help USC maintain its current needs without compromising the ability of future generations to do the same. Specific responsibilities of this oversight committee include: a. Benchmarking trends in institutional sustainability and identifying the best economic, social, environmental opportunities on which USC can act; b. Identifying USCs strengths and opportunities relative to advancing sustainability in the areas of campus operations, and community outreach; c. Communicating USCs sustainability initiatives and their benefits to the university community; and d. Making recommendations to the Senior Vice President of Administration detailing specific actions and resources required to best allow USC administrative functions to operationalize sustainable practices. The Sustainability Steering Committee consists of at least 12 voting members appointed by the Senior Vice President, Administration and General Counsel. Members are drawn from a group of senior level administrators, staff, students, and faculty representatives who are knowledgeable of and/or play a potentially large role in the area of sustainability. Sub-committees (such as the Operations Sustainability Steering Committee, which is overseen by the Sustainability Steering Committee) are used as needed to carry out individual initiatives. Committee created the sustainability program manager position to launch new program and has guided the recent establishment of the Sustainability Office. Beginning in 2009, USC's Sustainability Steering Committee set forth to develop a greenhouse gas emissions report that would establish a baseline for the university. This commitment was a significant milestone for the many students, faculty, and staff who have dedicated efforts to promote sustainability initiatives on campus. The completed report establishes USC's greenhouse gas emissions baseline for the years 2001 through 2009, accounting for emissions generated from USCs consumption of electricity, natural gas, refrigerants, and gasoline/diesel fuels. The report can be accessed, along with building-specific energy dashboards, on the USC Sustainability web page located at: http://green.usc.edu/ghg.

ADMISSIONS
Freshman Academic Profile: Average high school GPA 3.73. 88% in top 10% of high school class, 97% in top 25% of high school class, 100% in top 50% of high school class. 54% from public high schools. SAT Math middle 50% range 660-760. SAT Critical Reading middle 50% range 620-720. SAT Writing middle 50% range 640-740. ACT middle 50% range 29-33. **Basis for Candidate Selection:** *Very important factors considered include:* application essay, academic GPA, recommendation(s), rigor of secondary school record, standardized test scores. *Important factors considered include:* extracurricular activities, talent/ability. *Other factors considered include:* Class rank, alumni/ae relation, character/personal qualities, first generation, interview, racial/ethnic status, volunteer work, work experience. **Freshman Admission Requirements:** High school diploma is required and GED is not accepted. **Academic units required:** 4 English, 3 mathematics, 2 science, (2 science labs), 2 foreign language, 2 social studies, 3 academic electives. **Freshman Admission Statistics:** 51,920 applied, 18% admitted, 33% enrolled. **Transfer Admission Requirements:** High school transcript, college transcript(s), essay or personal statement, Lowest grade transferable C-. **General Admission Information:** Application Fee $65. Regular application deadline 1/10. Regular notification 4/1. Nonfall registration accepted. Credit and/or placement offered for CEEB Advanced Placement tests.

COSTS AND FINANCIAL AID
Required Forms and Deadlines: FAFSA, CSS/Financial Aid PROFILE, Noncustodial PROFILE, Business/Farm Supplement. **Notification of Awards:** Applicants will be notified of awards on a rolling basis beginning 3/15. **Types of Aid:** *Need-based scholarships/grants:* Federal Pell, SEOG, state scholarships/grants, private scholarships, the school's own gift aid. *Loans:* Subsidized Stafford, Unsubsidized Stafford, PLUS, Federal Perkins, "Credit Ready" and Credit Based *Student Employment:* Federal Work-Study Program available. Institutional employment available. Off-campus job opportunities are excellent. **Financial Aid Statistics:** 100% freshmen, 100% undergrads receive need-based scholarship or grant aid. 63% freshmen, 45% undergrads receive non-need-based scholarship or grant aid. 87% freshmen, 90% undergrads

receive need-based self-help aid. 3% freshmen, 2% undergrads receive athletic scholarships. 71% freshmen, 67% undergrads receive any aid. 45% undergrads borrow to pay for school. Average cumulative indebtedness $24,034. **Criteria for awarding institutional aid:** *Non-need-based:* academics, alumni affiliation, art, athletics, leadership, music/drama.

UNIVERSITY OF SOUTHERN INDIANA

8600 University Boulevard, Evansville, IN 47712
Phone: 812-464-1765 · **Financial Aid Phone:** 812-464-1767
E-mail: enroll@usi.edu · **CEEB Code:** 1335
Fax: 812-465-7154 · **Website:** www.usi.edu · **ACT Code:** 1207

This public school was founded in 1965. It has a 330-acre campus.

RATINGS

Admissions Selectivity Rating: 78   Fire Safety Rating: 76

STUDENTS AND FACULTY

Enrollment: 8,253. **Student Body:** 60% female, 40% male, 11% out-of-state, 2% international (26 countries represented). Asian 1%, African American 4%, Caucasian 86%, Hispanic 2%, Native American <1%
Retention and Graduation: 17% freshmen graduate within 4 years. 13% grads go on to further study within 1 year. **Faculty:** 352 full-time faculty, 69% hold PhDs, 54% are are members of minority groups, 7% are women. 0% of classes are taught by teaching assistants.

ACADEMICS

Degrees: associate, bachelor's, certificate, master's, post-bachelor's certificate, terminal associate, transfer associate. **Classes:** Most classes have 20-29 students. Most lab/discussion sessions have 20-29 students. **Majors with Highest Enrollment:** Registered Nursing/Registered Nurse; Health/Health Care Administration/Management; Business Administration and Management. **Special Study Options:** cooperative education program, distance learning, double major, dual enrollment, English as a Second Language (ESL), honors program, independent study, internships, study abroad, teacher certification program. **Combined degree programs:** RN/MSN. **Disability Services:** Special programs offered to physically disabled students include note-taking services, reader services, tape recorders, tutors. **Career services:** Alumni network, alumni services, career/job search classes, career assessment, internships.

FACILITIES

Housing: Coed dorms, special housing for disabled students, fraternity/sorority housing, apartments for married students, apartments for single students, Wellness Housing, Theme Housing. 95% of campus accessible to physically disabled. **Computers:** 100% of classrooms, 100% of dorms, 100% of libraries, 100% of dining areas, 100% of student union, 100% of common outdoor areas have wireless network access. Students can register for classes online. Administrative functions (other than registration) can be performed online.

CAMPUS LIFE

Environment: City. **Activities:** Choral groups, dance, drama/theater, jazz band, literary magazine, pep band, radio station, student government, student newspaper, Campus Ministries, International Student Organization, Model UN. 102 registered organizations, 6 honor societies, 7 religious organizations. 7 fraternities, 4 sororities. **Athletics (Intercollegiate):** *Men:* baseball, basketball, cross-country, golf, soccer, tennis, track/field (outdoor), track/field (indoor). *Women:* basketball, cross-country, golf, soccer, softball, tennis, track/field (outdoor), track/field (indoor), volleyball. **On-Campus Highlights:** Eagle's Nest, The Loft, Recreation and Fitness Center, Rice Library. **Environmental Initiatives:** Established environmental stewardship committee Being more conscious of sustainable materials such as CFL lighting and reducing energy consumption Highlight starter program to recycle materials from new construction and renovation projects. To dovetail with our ongoing recycling of paper, cardboard, plastic, aluminum, and metals recycling.

ADMISSIONS

Freshman Academic Profile: Average high school GPA 3.27. 12% in top 10% of high school class, 37% in top 25% of high school class, 74% in top 50% of high school class. SAT Math middle 50% range 450-550. SAT Critical Reading middle 50% range 440-550. SAT Writing middle 50% range 430-520. ACT middle 50% range 19-24. Minimum internet-based TOEFL 71. Minimum paper TOEFL 525. **Basis for Candidate Selection:** *Important factors considered include:* Class rank, academic GPA, standardized test scores. *Other factors considered include:* application essay, recommendation(s), rigor of secondary school record, alumni/ae relation, character/personal qualities, extracurricular activities, interview, talent/ability, work experience. **Freshman Admission Requirements:** High school diploma is required and GED is accepted. **Fresh-**

man **Admission Statistics:** 5,831 applied, 71% admitted, 39% enrolled. **Transfer Admission Requirements:** High school transcript, college transcript(s), Minimum college GPA of 2.0 required. Lowest grade transferable C-. **General Admission Information:** Application Fee $25. Regular application deadline 8/15. Notification on a rolling basis, beginning on or about 7/1. Nonfall registration accepted. Credit and/or placement offered for CEEB Advanced Placement tests.

COSTS AND FINANCIAL AID

Annual in-state tuition $6,637. Annual out-of-state tuition $15,977. Room and board $7,928. Required fees $569. Average book expense $1,100. **Required Forms and Deadlines:** FAFSA. **Notification of Awards:** Applicants will be notified of awards on a rolling basis beginning 4/1. **Types of Aid:** *Need-based scholarships/grants:* Federal Pell, SEOG, state scholarships/grants, private scholarships, the school's own gift aid, Federal Nursing Scholarships. *Loans:* Direct Subsidized Stafford, Direct Unsubsidized Stafford, Direct PLUS. *Student Employment:* Federal Work-Study Program available. Institutional employment available. Off-campus job opportunities are good. **Financial Aid Statistics:** 62% freshmen, 61% undergrads receive need-based scholarship or grant aid. 39% freshmen, 32% undergrads receive non-need-based scholarship or grant aid. 85% freshmen, 86% undergrads receive need-based self-help aid. 1% freshmen, 1% undergrads receive athletic scholarships. 89% freshmen, 91% undergrads receive any aid. 69% undergrads borrow to pay for school. Average cumulative indebtedness $23,448. **Criteria for awarding institutional aid:** *Non-need-based:* academics, art, athletics, leadership, music/drama, state/district residency.

UNIVERSITY OF SOUTHERN MAINE

PO Box 9300, Portland, ME 4104
Phone: 207-780-5670 · **Financial Aid Phone:** 207-780-5250
E-mail: usmadm@usm.maine.edu · **CEEB Code:** 9762
Fax: 207-780-5640 · **Website:** www.usm.maine.edu · **ACT Code:** 1644

This public school was founded in 1878. It has a 144-acre campus.

RATINGS

Admissions Selectivity Rating: 73   Fire Safety Rating: 76

STUDENTS AND FACULTY

Enrollment: 5,783. **Student Body:** 57% female, 43% male, 8% out-of-state, 1% international (19 countries represented). Asian 2%, African American 3%, Caucasian 81%, Hispanic 2%, Native American 1%
Retention and Graduation: 12% freshmen graduate within 4 years. 31% freshmen graduate within 6 years. **Faculty:** 311 full-time faculty, 87% hold PhDs, 46% are are members of minority groups, 5% are women. 0% of classes are taught by teaching assistants.

ACADEMICS

Degrees: bachelor's, certificate, master's, post-master's certificate. **Majors with Highest Enrollment:** Registered Nursing/Registered Nurse; Biology/Biological Sciences; Business Administration and Management. **Special Study Options:** Accelerated program, cooperative education program, cross-registration, distance learning, double major, English as a Second Language (ESL), exchange student program (domestic), honors program, independent study, internships, liberal arts/career combination, student-designed major, study abroad, teacher certification program, weekend college, Preengineering program with University of Maine at Orono, living/learning scholars program, Greater Portland Alliance—cross registration with University of New England, St. Joseph's (Maine), Southern Maine Technical College, and Maine College of Art. **Honors programs:** Russell Scholars—living/learning community, USM honors program. **Disability Services:** Special programs offered to physically disabled students include note-taking services, tape recorders, tutors. **Career services:** career/job search classes, internships.

FACILITIES

Housing: Coed dorms, special housing for disabled students, fraternity/sorority housing, apartments for married students, apartments for single students, Fine Arts House, Russell Scholars (living/learning), Chemical Free Floor 24 Hour Quiet Floor, Community Living program. 100% of campus accessible to physically disabled. **Special Academic Facilities/Equipment:** Southworth Planetarium, Osher Map Collection and Smith Center for Cartographic Education, WMPG (radio station), GTV (cable t.v. station), Free Press (campus newspaper), various art galleries on all three campuses. **Computers:** Students can register for classes online. Administrative functions (other than registration) can be performed online.

CAMPUS LIFE

Environment: Town. **Activities:** Choral groups, concert band, dance, drama/theater, jazz band, literary magazine, music ensembles, musical theater, opera, radio station, student government, student newspaper, symphony orchestra, television station, yearbook, International Student Organization. 100 registered organizations, 2 honor societies, 3 religious organizations. 4 fraternities, 4 sororities. **Athletics (Intercollegiate):** *Men:* baseball, basketball, cheerleading, cross-country, golf, ice hockey, lacrosse, soccer, tennis, track/field (outdoor), track/field (indoor), wrestling. *Women:* basketball, cheerleading, cross-country, field hockey, golf, ice hockey, lacrosse, soccer, softball, tennis, track/field (outdoor), track/field (indoor), volleyball. **On-Campus Highlights:** Art Gallery, Costello Sports Complex, Russell Theater and Concert Hall, Southworth Planetarium, TV/Radio Station.

ADMISSIONS

Freshman Academic Profile: Average high school GPA 3.04. 7% in top 10% of high school class, 30% in top 25% of high school class, 67% in top 50% of high school class. SAT Math middle 50% range 440-550. SAT Critical Reading middle 50% range 440-560. SAT Writing middle 50% range 420-530. ACT middle 50% range 20-24. Minimum internet-based TOEFL 80. **Basis for Candidate Selection:** *Very important factors considered include:* Class rank, rigor of secondary school record, standardized test scores. *Important factors considered include:* application essay, recommendation(s). *Other factors considered include:* academic GPA, alumni/ae relation, character/personal qualities, extracurricular activities, geographical residence, interview, level of applicant's interest, racial/ethnic status, state residency, talent/ability, volunteer work, work experience. **Freshman Admission Requirements:** High school diploma is required and GED is accepted. **Academic units required:** 4 English, 3 mathematics, 2 science, (2 science labs), 2 foreign language, 2 social studies, 2 history. **Freshman Admission Statistics:** 3,781 applied, 84% admitted, 23% enrolled. **Transfer Admission Requirements:** High school transcript, college transcript(s), essay or personal statement, Minimum college GPA of 2.0 required. Lowest grade transferable C-. **General Admission Information:** Application Fee $40. Notification on a rolling basis, beginning on or about 1/1. Nonfall registration accepted. Admission may be deferred for a maximum of 1 year. Credit and/or placement offered for CEEB Advanced Placement tests.

COSTS AND FINANCIAL AID

Annual in-state tuition $7,590. Annual out-of-state tuition $19,950. Room and board $9,150. Required fees $1,330. Average book expense $1,346. **Required Forms and Deadlines:** FAFSA. **Notification of Awards:** Applicants will be notified of awards on a rolling basis beginning 3/15. **Types of Aid:** *Need-based scholarships/grants:* Federal Pell, SEOG, state scholarships/grants, private scholarships, the school's own gift aid. *Loans:* Subsidized Stafford, Unsubsidized Stafford, PLUS, Federal Perkins, Federal Nursing, state loans. *Student Employment:* Federal Work-Study Program available. Off-campus job opportunities are excellent. **Financial Aid Statistics:** 75% freshmen, 76% undergrads receive need-based scholarship or grant aid. 41% freshmen, 26% undergrads receive non-need-based scholarship or grant aid. 84% freshmen, 89% undergrads receive need-based self-help aid. 0% freshmen, 0% undergrads receive athletic scholarships. 74% undergrads borrow to pay for school. **Criteria for awarding institutional aid:** *Non-need-based:* academics, music/drama, state/district residency.

UNIVERSITY OF SOUTHERN MISSISSIPPI

118 College Drive #5166, Hattiesburg, MS 39406
Phone: 601-266-5000 · **Financial Aid Phone:** 601-266-4774
E-mail: admissions@usm.edu · **CEEB Code:** 1479
Fax: 601-266-5148 · **Website:** www.usm.edu · **ACT Code:** 2218

This public school was founded in 1910. It has a 1090-acre campus.

RATINGS

Admissions Selectivity Rating: 74   **Fire Safety Rating:** 84

STUDENTS AND FACULTY

Enrollment: 11,906. **Student Body:** 64% female, 36% male, 16% out-of-state, 1% international. Asian 1%, African American 30%, Caucasian 61%, Hispanic 3%, Native American <1%
Retention and Graduation: 74% freshmen return for sophomore year. 25% freshmen graduate within 4 years. 48% freshmen graduate within 6 years. **Faculty:** 712 full-time faculty, 78% hold PhDs, 48% are are members of minority groups, 16% are women.

ACADEMICS

Degrees: bachelor's, certificate, doctoral, master's, post-master's certificate.
Classes: Most classes have 10-19 students. Most lab/discussion sessions have 10-19 students. **Majors with Highest Enrollment:** Elementary Education

and Teaching; Psychology; Registered Nursing/Registered Nurse. **Special Study Options:** distance learning, double major, dual enrollment, honors program, independent study, internships, study abroad, teacher certification program. **Disability Services:** Special programs offered to physically disabled students include note-taking services, reader services, tape recorders, tutors. **Career services:** alumni services, career/job search classes, career assessment, internships. Career services highlights include Career Assesment, Individualized counselors, and 24/7 online career center.

FACILITIES

Housing: special housing for disabled students, men's dorms, women's dorms, fraternity/sorority housing, apartments for married students, Theme Housing. **Special Academic Facilities/Equipment:** Museum of Art **Computers:** 100% of classrooms, 100% of dorms, 100% of libraries, 100% of dining areas, 100% of student union, 30% of common outdoor areas have wireless network access. Students can register for classes online. Administrative functions (other than registration) can be performed online.

CAMPUS LIFE

Environment: City. **Activities:** Choral groups, concert band, dance, drama/theater, jazz band, literary magazine, marching band, music ensembles, musical theater, opera, pep band, radio station, student government, student newspaper, student-run film society, symphony orchestra, yearbook, Campus Ministries, International Student Organization 8 honor societies, 20 religious organizations. 15 fraternities, 11 sororities. **Athletics (Intercollegiate):** *Men:* baseball, basketball, football, golf, tennis, track/field (outdoor), track/field (indoor). *Women:* basketball, cross-country, golf, soccer, softball, tennis, track/field (outdoor), track/field (indoor), volleyball. **On-Campus Highlights:** Starbucks, Thad Cochran Center, Barnes & Nobles Bookstore **Environmental Initiatives:** Recycling (12+ years); Energy Conservation; LEED certification on new buildings; Pursuing use of green seal cleaning products and organic grounds maintenance.

ADMISSIONS

Freshman Academic Profile: Average high school GPA 3.26. 88% from public high schools. SAT Math middle 50% range 460-555. SAT Critical Reading middle 50% range 450-560. ACT middle 50% range 19-25. Minimum internet-based TOEFL 71. Minimum paper TOEFL 525. **Basis for Candidate Selection:** *Very important factors considered include:* academic GPA, standardized test scores. *Other factors considered include:* Class rank. **Freshman Admission Requirements:** High school diploma is required and GED is accepted. **Academic units required:** 4 English, 3 mathematics, 3 science, (0 science labs), 0 foreign language, 3 social studies, 0 history, 0 visual/performing arts, 2 academic electives. **Freshman Admission Statistics:** 5,850 applied, 67% admitted, 41% enrolled. **Transfer Admission Requirements:** college transcript(s), statement of good standing from prior institution(s). Minimum college GPA of 2.0 required. Lowest grade transferable D. **General Admission Information:** Application Fee $35. Notification on a rolling basis, beginning on or about 9/1. Nonfall registration accepted. Credit and/or placement offered for CEEB Advanced Placement tests.

COSTS AND FINANCIAL AID

Annual out-of-state tuition $16,094. Room and board $7,640. Required fees $0. Average book expense $1,400. **Required Forms and Deadlines:** FAFSA. **Notification of Awards:** Applicants will be notified of awards on a rolling basis beginning 4/1. **Types of Aid:** *Need-based scholarships/grants:* Federal Pell, SEOG, state scholarships/grants, private scholarships, the school's own gift aid. *Loans:* Direct Subsidized Stafford, Direct Unsubsidized Stafford, Direct PLUS, Subsidized Stafford. *Student Employment:* Federal Work-Study Program available. Institutional employment available. Highest amount earned per year from on-campus jobs $3,668. Off-campus job opportunities are good. **Financial Aid Statistics:** 67% freshmen, 67% undergrads receive need-based scholarship or grant aid. 70% freshmen, 51% undergrads receive non-need-based scholarship or grant aid. 74% freshmen, 77% undergrads receive need-based self-help aid. 6% freshmen, 4% undergrads receive athletic scholarships. 62% freshmen, 63% undergrads receive any aid. 67% undergrads borrow to pay for school. Average cumulative indebtedness $17,806.

UNIVERSITY OF THE SOUTHWEST

6610 Lovington Highway, Hobbs, NM 88240
Phone: 505-392-6563 · **Financial Aid Phone:** 505-392-6561
E-mail: admissions@csw.edu · **CEEB Code:** 4116
Fax: 505-392-6006 · **Website:** www.csw.edu · **ACT Code:** 2633

This private school was founded in 1962. It has a 162-acre campus.

RATINGS

Admissions Selectivity Rating: 82   **Fire Safety Rating:** 82

STUDENTS AND FACULTY

Enrollment: 430. **Student Body:** 64% female, 36% male, 39% out-of-state, 1% international (12 countries represented). Asian 1%, African American 4%, Caucasian 52%, Hispanic 39%, Native American 2%

Retention and Graduation: 32% freshmen return for sophomore year. 10% freshmen graduate within 4 years. 29% freshmen graduate within 6 years. 30% grads go on to further study within 1 year. 30% grads pursue arts and sciences degrees. **Faculty:** 20 full-time faculty, 60% hold PhDs, 45% are are members of minority groups, 10% are women. 0% of classes are taught by teaching assistants.

ACADEMICS

Degrees: bachelor's, master's. **Classes:** Most classes have fewer than 10 students. Most lab/discussion sessions have fewer than 10 students. **Majors with Highest Enrollment:** Elementary Education and Teaching; Criminal Justice/Police Science; Business/Commerce. **Special Study Options:** distance learning, double major, internships, teacher certification program. **Disability Services:** Special programs offered to physically disabled students include tutors.

FACILITIES

Housing: men's dorms, women's dorms. 90% of campus accessible to physically disabled.

CAMPUS LIFE

Environment: Town. **Activities:** Choral groups, drama/theater, literary magazine, student government, student newspaper 3 honor societies, 1 religous organization. **Athletics (Intercollegiate):** *Men:* baseball, cross-country, golf, rodeo, soccer, track/field (outdoor). *Women:* cross-country, golf, rodeo, soccer, softball, track/field (outdoor), volleyball. **On-Campus Highlights:** Residential Halls-East and West, Scarborough Memorial Library, Mabee Southwest Heritage Center, Jack Williams Baseball Field, Joan M. Tucker Center for Business Leadership, The Mabee Teaching and Learning Center, Fadke Arts and Science Building, Bill Danies Campus Center.

ADMISSIONS

Freshman Academic Profile: Average high school GPA 3.11. 1% in top 10% of high school class, 16% in top 25% of high school class, 69% in top 50% of high school class. SAT Math middle 50% range 340-500. SAT Critical Reading middle 50% range 340-470. SAT Writing middle 50% range 330-460. ACT middle 50% range 14-20. Minimum paper TOEFL 550. **Basis for Candidate Selection:** *Very important factors considered include:* Class rank, academic GPA, standardized test scores. **Freshman Admission Requirements:** High school diploma is required and GED is accepted. **Freshman Admission Statistics:** 2,207 applied, 23% admitted, 10% enrolled. **Transfer Admission Requirements:** college transcript(s), Minimum college GPA of 2.0 required. Lowest grade transferable D. **General Admission Information:** Application Fee $25. Notification on a rolling basis, beginning on or about 10/5. Nonfall registration accepted. Credit offered for CEEB Advanced Placement tests.

COSTS AND FINANCIAL AID

Annual tuition $11,700. Room and board $5,400. Required fees $0. Average book expense $800. **Required Forms and Deadlines:** FAFSA, Institution's own financial aid form. **Notification of Awards:** Applicants will be notified of awards on or about 4/2. *Types of Aid: Need-based scholarships/grants:* Federal Pell, SEOG, state scholarships/grants, private scholarships, the school's own gift aid. *Loans:* Subsidized Stafford, Unsubsidized Stafford, PLUS. *Student Employment:* Highest amount earned per year from on-campus jobs $3,000. **Financial Aid Statistics:** 36% freshmen, 77% undergrads receive need-based scholarship or grant aid. 5% freshmen, 74% undergrads receive non-need-based scholarship or grant aid. 5% freshmen, 18% undergrads receive need-based self-help aid. 12% freshmen, 26% undergrads receive athletic scholarships. 75% freshmen, 77% undergrads receive any aid. 85% undergrads borrow to pay for school. **Criteria for awarding institutional aid:** *Non-need-based:* academics, athletics, job skills, leadership, music/drama, religious affiliation, state/district residency.

UNIVERSITY OF ST. FRANCIS

500 Wilcox Street, Joliet, IL 60435
Phone: 815-740-2270 · **Financial Aid Phone:** 866-890-8331
E-mail: admissions@stfrancis.edu · **CEEB Code:** 1130
Fax: 815-740-5078 · **Website:** www.stfrancis.edu · **ACT Code:** 1000

This private school, affiliated with the Roman Catholic Church, was founded in 1920. It has a 22-acre campus.

RATINGS

Admissions Selectivity Rating: 84   Fire Safety Rating: 91

STUDENTS AND FACULTY

Enrollment: 1,359. **Student Body:** 64% female, 36% male, 5% out-of-state, 2% international (16 countries represented). Asian 2%, African American 8%, Caucasian 68%, Hispanic 17%, Native American <1%

Retention and Graduation: 81% freshmen return for sophomore year. 38% freshmen graduate within 4 years. 56% freshmen graduate within 6 years. 14% grads go on to further study within 1 year. **Faculty:** 102 full-time faculty, 70% hold PhDs, 61% are are members of minority groups, 15% are women. 0% of classes are taught by teaching assistants.

ACADEMICS

Degrees: bachelor's, master's, post-master's certificate. **Classes:** Most classes have 10-19 students. Most lab/discussion sessions have 10-19 students. **Majors with Highest Enrollment:** Business/Commerce; Registered Nursing/Registered Nurse; Biology/Biological Sciences. **Special Study Options:** cross-registration, distance learning, double major, honors program, independent study, internships, student-designed major, study abroad, teacher certification program. **Honors programs:** Duns Scotus Fellow/Scholars Program is designed to create a learning community of motivated students who are challenged to excel academically. **Combined degree programs:** BBA/MBA. **Disability Services:** Special programs offered to physically disabled students include note-taking services, reader services, tape recorders, tutors. **Career services:** Alumni network, alumni services, career/job search classes, career assessment, internships, regional alumni.

FACILITIES

Housing: Coed dorms, apartments for single students, Wellness Housing. 100% of campus accessible to physically disabled. **Special Academic Facilities/Equipment:** Rialto City Center Campus, new home of the Art & Design Department; Student Center/Bistro in the Motherhouse; Abbey in Marian Residence Hall; Moser Performing Arts Center. **Computers:** 100% of classrooms, 100% of dorms, 100% of libraries, 100% of dining areas, 100% of student union, 100% of common outdoor areas have wireless network access. Students can register for classes online. Administrative functions (other than registration) can be performed online.

CAMPUS LIFE

Environment: City. **Activities:** Choral groups, dance, drama/theater, literary magazine, music ensembles, musical theater, opera, radio station, student government, student newspaper, symphony orchestra, television station, Campus Ministries, International Student Organization. 29 registered organizations, 13 honor societies, 1 religous organization. **Athletics (Intercollegiate):** *Men:* baseball, basketball, cross-country, football, golf, soccer, tennis, track/field (outdoor), track/field (indoor). *Women:* basketball, cheerleading, cross-country, golf, soccer, softball, tennis, track/field (outdoor), track/field (indoor), volleyball. **On-Campus Highlights:** Rialto City Center Campus, Student Center/Bistro in Motherhouse, Abbey (in Marian Residence Hall), Moser Performing Arts Center. **Environmental Initiatives:** Campus-wide recycling; Energy efficient lighting; Water conservation.

ADMISSIONS

Freshman Academic Profile: Average high school GPA 3.4. 10% in top 10% of high school class, 44% in top 25% of high school class, 77% in top 50% of high school class. 92% from public high schools. SAT Math middle 50% range 460-530. SAT Critical Reading middle 50% range 460-520. SAT Writing middle 50% range 430-530. ACT middle 50% range 21-25. Minimum internet-based TOEFL 79. Minimum paper TOEFL 550. **Basis for Candidate Selection:** *Very important factors considered include:* Class rank, academic GPA, rigor of secondary school record, standardized test scores. *Other factors considered include:* application essay, recommendation(s), interview. **Freshman Admission Requirements:** High school diploma is required and GED is accepted. **Academic units required:** 4 English, 3 mathematics, 2 science, (1 science labs), 2 social studies, 3 academic electives, 3 3 units from 2 areas: language, computer science, music or art. **Freshman Admission Statistics:** 1,509 applied, 51% admitted, 28% enrolled. **Transfer Admission Requirements:** college transcript(s), statement of good standing from prior institution(s). Minimum college GPA of 2.5 required. **General Admission Information:** Application Fee $30. Regular application deadline 8/1. Notification on a rolling basis, beginning on or about 9/15. Nonfall registration accepted. Admission may be deferred for a maximum of 12 months. Credit and/or placement offered for CEEB Advanced Placement tests.

COSTS AND FINANCIAL AID

Required Forms and Deadlines: FAFSA, Institution's own financial aid form. **Notification of Awards:** Applicants will be notified of awards on a rolling basis beginning 2/15. *Types of Aid: Need-based scholarships/grants:* Federal Pell, SEOG, state scholarships/grants, private scholarships, the school's own gift aid, Federal Nursing Scholarships, Federal ACG and SMART funds. *Loans:* Direct Subsidized Stafford, Direct Unsubsidized Stafford, Direct PLUS, Federal Perkins. *Student Employment:* Federal Work-Study Program available. Institutional employment available. Highest amount earned per year from on-campus jobs

$9,350. Off-campus job opportunities are good. **Financial Aid Statistics:** 69% freshmen, 73% undergrads receive need-based scholarship or grant aid, 94% freshmen, 97% undergrads receive non-need-based scholarship or grant aid. 72% freshmen, 78% undergrads receive need-based self-help aid. 7% freshmen, 6% undergrads receive athletic scholarships. 100% freshmen, 92% undergrads receive any aid. 78% undergrads borrow to pay for school. Average cumulative indebtedness $27,367. **Criteria for awarding institutional aid:** *Non-need-based:* academics, alumni affiliation, art, athletics, leadership, music/drama, religious affiliation, state/district residency.

UNIVERSITY OF ST. THOMAS

3800 Montrose Boulevard, Houston, TX 77006-4696
Phone: 713-525-3500 · **Financial Aid Phone:** 713-525-2151
E-mail: admissions@stthom.edu · **CEEB Code:** 6880
Fax: 713-525-3558 · **Website:** www.stthom.edu · **ACT Code:** 4238

This private school, affiliated with the Roman Catholic Church, was founded in 1947. It has a 20-acre campus.

RATINGS

Admissions Selectivity Rating: 82   Fire Safety Rating: 92

STUDENTS AND FACULTY

Enrollment: 1,568. **Student Body:** 61% female, 39% male, 41% out-of-state, 0% international (50 countries represented). Asian 12%, African American 7%, Caucasian 29%, Hispanic 38%, Native American <1%
Retention and Graduation: 88% freshmen return for sophomore year. 34% freshmen graduate within 4 years. 52% freshmen graduate within 6 years. **Faculty:** 177 full-time faculty, 93% hold PhDs, 45% are are members of minority groups, 28% are women. 0% of classes are taught by teaching assistants.

ACADEMICS

Degrees: bachelor's, diploma, master's. **Classes:** Most classes have 10-19 students. Most lab/discussion sessions have 10-19 students. **Majors with Highest Enrollment:** Finance; Psychology; Biology/Biological Sciences. **Special Study Options:** Accelerated program, distance learning, double major, dual enrollment, honors program, independent study, internships, liberal arts/career combination, student-designed major, study abroad, teacher certification program, weekend college. **Honors programs:** The Honors Program at the University of St. Thomas is a four-year interdisciplinary program for students of exceptional intellectual ability, motivation, and curiosity. It is designed not simply to provoke students to master specific disciplines such as philosophy, history, mathematics, and natural science but to offer an experience which integrates, on the deepest and most profound level, the intellectual, cultural and spiritual foundations of a liberal arts education. **Combined degree programs:** BBA/MBA. **Disability Services:** Special programs offered to physically disabled students include note-taking services, reader services, tape recorders, tutors. **Career services:** career/job search classes, career assessment, internships.

FACILITIES

Housing: Coed dorms, apartments for single students **Special Academic Facilities/Equipment:** Learning and Writing Center, Chapel of St. Basil, Doherty Library **Computers:** 100% of classrooms, 100% of libraries, 100% of dining areas, 100% of common outdoor areas have wireless network access. Students can register for classes online. Administrative functions (other than registration) can be performed online.

CAMPUS LIFE

Environment: Metropolis. **Activities:** Choral groups, dance, drama/theater, jazz band, literary magazine, music ensembles, musical theater, student government, student newspaper, Campus Ministries, International Student Organization. 69 registered organizations, 22 honor societies, 5 religious organizations. **Athletics (Intercollegiate):** *Men:* basketball, soccer. *Women:* volleyball. **On-Campus Highlights:** Jerabeck Activity and Athletic Center, Crooker Student Center, Chapel of St. Basil, The Lounge, Academic Mall. **Environmental Initiatives:** Campus Recycling of glass, aluminum, plastic & paper.

ADMISSIONS

Freshman Academic Profile: Average high school GPA 3.54. 28% in top 10% of high school class, 49% in top 25% of high school class, 80% in top 50% of high school class. 80% from public high schools. SAT Math middle 50% range 500-620. SAT Critical Reading middle 50% range 490-600. SAT Writing middle 50% range 480-580. ACT middle 50% range 22-27. Minimum internet-based TOEFL 79. Minimum paper TOEFL 550. **Basis for Candidate Selection:** *Very important factors considered include:* Class rank, application essay, academic GPA, rigor of secondary school record, standardized test scores. *Other factors considered include:* recommendation(s), character/personal qualities,

extracurricular activities, interview, level of applicant's interest, talent/ability, volunteer work, work experience. **Freshman Admission Requirements:** High school diploma is required and GED is accepted. **Academic units required:** 4 English, 3 mathematics, 3 science, (2 science labs), 2 foreign language, 2 social studies, 1 history, 3 Electives in college preparatory classes. **Freshman Admission Statistics:** 795 applied, 79% admitted, 36% enrolled. **Transfer Admission Requirements:** college transcript(s), Minimum college GPA of 2.50 required. Lowest grade transferable C. **General Admission Information:** Application Fee $25. Regular application deadline 5/1. Notification on a rolling basis, beginning on or about 11/15. Nonfall registration accepted. Admission may be deferred for a maximum of 1 year. Credit and/or placement offered for CEEB Advanced Placement tests.

COSTS AND FINANCIAL AID

Annual tuition $29,100. Room and board $8,250. Required fees $340. Average book expense $1,094. **Required Forms and Deadlines:** FAFSA. **Notification of Awards:** Applicants will be notified of awards on a rolling basis beginning 3/22. **Types of Aid:** *Need-based scholarships/grants:* Federal Pell, SEOG, state scholarships/grants, private scholarships, the school's own gift aid, ACG Grant, SMART grant. *Loans:* Subsidized Stafford, Unsubsidized Stafford, PLUS, Federal Perkins, state loans. *Student Employment:* Federal Work-Study Program available. Off-campus job opportunities are excellent. **Financial Aid Statistics:** 96% freshmen, 98% undergrads receive need-based scholarship or grant aid. 11% freshmen, 5% undergrads receive non-need-based scholarship or grant aid. 61% freshmen, 69% undergrads receive need-based self-help aid. 7% freshmen, 5% undergrads receive athletic scholarships. 90% freshmen, 74% undergrads receive any aid. 57% undergrads borrow to pay for school. Average cumulative indebtedness $30,484. **Criteria for awarding institutional aid:** *Non-need-based:* academics, athletics.

UNIVERSITY OF TAMPA

Best 380

401 West Kennedy Boulevard, Tampa, FL 33606-1490
Phone: 813-253-6211 · **Financial Aid Phone:** 813-253-6219
E-mail: admissions@ut.edu · **CEEB Code:** 5819
Fax: 813-258-7398 · **Website:** www.ut.edu · **ACT Code:** 762

This private school was founded in 1931. It has a 100-acre campus.

RATINGS

Admissions Selectivity Rating: 87   Fire Safety Rating: 97

STUDENTS AND FACULTY

Enrollment: 6,811. **Student Body:** 56% female, 44% male, 67% out-of-state, 10% international (114 countries represented). Asian 1%, African American 5%, Caucasian 59%, Hispanic 12%, Native American <1%
Retention and Graduation: 52% freshmen graduate within 4 years. 62% freshmen graduate within 6 years. 27% grads go on to further study within 1 year. 9% grads pursue arts and sciences degrees. 2% grads pursue law degrees. 4% grads pursue business degrees. 3% grads pursue medical degrees. **Faculty:** 283 full-time faculty, 90% hold PhDs, 59% are are members of minority groups, 13% are women. 0% of classes are taught by teaching assistants.

ACADEMICS

Degrees: associate, bachelor's, certificate, master's, post-master's certificate. **Classes:** Most classes have 20-29 students. Most lab/discussion sessions have 10-19 students. **Majors with Highest Enrollment:** Business Administration and Management; Communication; Marketing/Marketing Management. **Special Study Options:** double major, dual enrollment, exchange student program (domestic), honors program, independent study, internships, liberal arts/career combination, study abroad, teacher certification program, Certificate in International Studies program. **Honors programs:** UT's Honors Program offers special classes that are developed to enhance creative thinking processes while meeting general distribution requirements. **Combined degree programs:** MSN-MBA; BS Chemistry-MBA; RN-MSN. **Disability Services:** Special programs offered to physically disabled students include note-taking services, reader services, tutors. **Career services:** Alumni network, alumni services, career/job search classes, career assessment, internships. From their first day on campus, students are supported and involved. They are rewarded with an unlimited array of opportunities that take them to the edge of their imaginations and beyond. All students have opportunities to balance "learning by thinking" with "learning by doing." Both in-class hands on projects and out-of-classroom learning activities help students integrate classroom theory with real world practices. Interactive learning activities such as case studies, behavioral and computer simulations, internships, performances, exhibitions, research, service learning, study abroad, etc., are offered across the curriculum.

FACILITIES
Housing: Coed dorms, special housing for disabled students, apartments for single students, Theme Housing. 100% of campus accessible to physically disabled. **Special Academic Facilities/Equipment:** Victorian art and furniture museum, theatres, studios, music center, language lab, fully equipped research vessel for marine science, H.B. Plant Museum, marine science research center on Tampa Bay. **Computers:** 50% of classrooms, 25% of dorms, 100% of libraries, 80% of dining areas, 100% of student union, 80% of common outdoor areas have wireless network access. Students can register for classes online. Administrative functions (other than registration) can be performed online.

CAMPUS LIFE
Environment: Metropolis. **Activities:** Choral groups, concert band, dance, drama/theater, jazz band, literary magazine, music ensembles, musical theater, pep band, radio station, student government, student newspaper, student-run film society, symphony orchestra, television station, yearbook, Campus Ministries, International Student Organization, Model UN. 145 registered organizations, 13 honor societies, 8 religious organizations. 9 fraternities, 10 sororities. **Athletics (Intercollegiate):** *Men:* baseball, basketball, cross-country, golf, soccer, swimming. *Women:* basketball, crew/rowing, cross-country, soccer, softball, swimming, tennis, volleyball. **On-Campus Highlights:** Vaughn Student Center, Plant Hall, Stadium Center, Vaughn Center Courtyard, Martinez Sports Center.

ADMISSIONS
Freshman Academic Profile: Average high school GPA 3.3. 20.37% in top 10% of high school class, 48.05% in top 25% of high school class, 82.84% in top 50% of high school class. 73% from public high schools. SAT Math middle 50% range 500-580. SAT Critical Reading middle 50% range 490-580. SAT Writing middle 50% range 490-570. ACT middle 50% range 22-27. Minimum internet-based TOEFL 79. Minimum paper TOEFL 550. **Basis for Candidate Selection:** *Very important factors considered include:* academic GPA, rigor of secondary school record, standardized test scores. *Important factors considered include:* application essay, recommendation(s), talent/ability. *Other factors considered include:* Class rank, alumni/ae relation, character/personal qualities, extracurricular activities, first generation, interview, level of applicant's interest, volunteer work, work experience. **Freshman Admission Requirements:** High school diploma is required and GED is accepted. **Academic units required:** 4 English, 3 mathematics, 3 science, (2 science labs), 2 foreign language, 3 social studies, 3 academic electives. **Freshman Admission Statistics:** 17,208 applied, 52% admitted, 20% enrolled. **Transfer Admission Requirements:** college transcript(s), Minimum college GPA of 2.2 required. Lowest grade transferable C. **General Admission Information:** Application Fee $40. Notification on a rolling basis, beginning on or about 10/1. Nonfall registration accepted. Admission may be deferred for a maximum of 1 term. Credit and/or placement offered for CEEB Advanced Placement tests.

COSTS AND FINANCIAL AID
Annual tuition $24,528. Room and board $9,624. Required fees $1,802. Average book expense $1,200. **Required Forms and Deadlines:** State aid form. **Notification of Awards:** Applicants will be notified of awards on a rolling basis beginning 2/1. **Types of Aid:** *Need-based scholarships/grants:* Federal Pell, SEOG, state scholarships/grants, private scholarships, the school's own gift aid. *Loans:* Subsidized Stafford, Unsubsidized Stafford, PLUS, Federal Perkins, college/university loans from institutional funds. *Student Employment:* Federal Work-Study Program available. Institutional employment available. Off-campus job opportunities are fair. **Financial Aid Statistics:** 100% freshmen, 98% undergrads receive need-based scholarship or grant aid. 100% freshmen, 98% undergrads receive non-need-based scholarship or grant aid. 81% freshmen, 80% undergrads receive need-based self-help aid. 3% freshmen, 4% undergrads receive athletic scholarships. 92% freshmen, 90% undergrads receive any aid. 61% undergrads borrow to pay for school. Average cumulative indebtedness $25,930. **Criteria for awarding institutional aid:** *Non-need-based:* academics, alumni affiliation, art, athletics, leadership, music/drama, state/district residency.

See page 1196.

UNIVERSITY OF TENNESSEE AT CHATTANOOGA

615 McCallie Avenue, Chattanooga, TN 37403
Phone: 423-425-4662 • **Financial Aid Phone:** 423-425-4677
E-mail: utcmocs@utc.edu • **CEEB Code:** 1831
Fax: 423-425-4157 • **Website:** www.utc.edu • **ACT Code:** 4022

This public school was founded in 1886. It has a 120-acre campus.

RATINGS
Admissions Selectivity Rating: 77   **Fire Safety Rating:** 93

STUDENTS AND FACULTY
Enrollment: 10,213. **Student Body:** 56% female, 44% male, 6% out-of-state, 1% international (37 countries represented). Asian 2%, African American 11%, Caucasian 74%, Hispanic 3%, Native American <1%
Retention and Graduation: 70% freshmen return for sophomore year. 16% freshmen graduate within 4 years. **Faculty:** 469 full-time faculty, 75% hold PhDs, 45% are are members of minority groups, 16% are women. 5% of classes are taught by teaching assistants.

ACADEMICS
Degrees: bachelor's, certificate, master's, post-bachelor's certificate, post-master's certificate. **Classes:** Most classes have 20-29 students. Most lab/discussion sessions have 20-29 students. **Majors with Highest Enrollment:** Business Administration and Management; Biology/Biological Sciences; Health and Physical Education/Fitness. **Special Study Options:** cooperative education program, cross-registration, distance learning, double major, dual enrollment, English as a Second Language (ESL), honors program, independent study, internships, study abroad, teacher certification program. **Honors programs:** The University Honors curriculum is a 37-hour sequence of specially designed and enhanced seminar courses in the humanities, the fine arts, cultural perspectives, the history of science, and the social sciences, culminating in a senior-year departmental honors project. These seminars fulfill all of the student's general education course requirements except mathematics and laboratory science (http://www.utc.edu/Academic/UniversityHonors/). **Disability Services:** Special programs offered to physically disabled students include note-taking services, reader services, tape recorders, tutors. **Career services:** Alumni network, alumni services, internships.

FACILITIES
Housing: Coed dorms, fraternity/sorority housing, apartments for married students, apartments for single students. 95% of campus accessible to physically disabled. **Special Academic Facilities/Equipment:** Walker Teaching Resource Center; Jones Observatory; Institute of Archaeology; Odor Research Center; SIM Center; Challenger Center; Center for Applied Social Research; The Ochs Center for Metropolitan Studies. **Computers:** 90% of classrooms, 100% of libraries, 100% of dining areas, 100% of student union, 60% of common outdoor areas have wireless network access. Students can register for classes online. Administrative functions (other than registration) can be performed online.

CAMPUS LIFE
Environment: City. **Activities:** Choral groups, concert band, dance, drama/theater, jazz band, literary magazine, marching band, music ensembles, opera, pep band, radio station, student government, student newspaper, student-run film society, symphony orchestra, television station, Campus Ministries, International Student Organization, Model UN. 130 registered organizations, 34 honor societies, 8 religious organizations. 7 fraternities, 7 sororities. **Athletics (Intercollegiate):** *Men:* basketball, cross-country, football, golf, tennis, track/field (outdoor), wrestling. *Women:* basketball, cross-country, golf, soccer, softball, tennis, track/field (outdoor), volleyball. **On-Campus Highlights:** Challenger Center, University Center, The Aquatic and Recreation Center (ARC), The Crossroads. **Environmental Initiatives:** Central Plan Improvements; HVAC and lighting energy-efficient upgrades; LEED Certified Building Design (Bretske Hall; Engineer, Math and Computer Science Buildling; new UTC Library).

ADMISSIONS
Freshman Academic Profile: Average high school GPA 3.42. 46.5% in top 25% of high school class, 85.2% in top 50% of high school class. 75% from public high schools. SAT Math middle 50% range 460-580. SAT Critical Reading middle 50% range 460-600. ACT middle 50% range 21-26. Minimum internet-based TOEFL 61. Minimum paper TOEFL 500. **Basis for Candidate Selection:** *Very important factors considered include:* academic GPA, rigor of secondary school record, standardized test scores. *Important factors considered include:* character/personal qualities. *Other factors considered include:* application essay, recommendation(s), extracurricular activities, talent/ability, volunteer work, work experience. **Freshman Admission Requirements:** High school diploma is required and GED is accepted. **Academic units required:** 4

English, 3 mathematics, 2 science, (2 science labs), 2 foreign language, 1 social studies, 1 history, 1 visual/performing arts. **Freshman Admission Statistics:** 7,399 applied, 77% admitted, 38% enrolled. **Transfer Admission Requirements:** college transcript(s), Minimum college GPA of 2.0 required. Lowest grade transferable D. **General Admission Information:** Application Fee $30. Regular application deadline 8/1. Nonfall registration accepted. Admission may be deferred for a maximum of 1 semester. Credit and/or placement offered for CEEB Advanced Placement tests.

COSTS AND FINANCIAL AID

Annual in-state tuition $6,430. Annual out-of-state tuition $22,548. Room and board $8,110. Required fees $1,708. Average book expense $1,400. **Required Forms and Deadlines:** FAFSA. **Notification of Awards:** Applicants will be notified of awards on a rolling basis beginning 3/1. **Types of Aid:** *Need-based scholarships/grants:* Federal Pell, SEOG, state scholarships/grants, private scholarships, the school's own gift aid, United Negro College Fund. *Loans:* Subsidized Stafford, Unsubsidized Stafford, PLUS, Federal Perkins, college/university loans from institutional funds. *Student Employment:* Federal Work-Study Program available. Institutional employment available. Highest amount earned per year from on-campus jobs $19,500. Off-campus job opportunities are good. **Financial Aid Statistics:** 95% freshmen, 85% undergrads receive need-based scholarship or grant aid. 2% freshmen, 3% undergrads receive non-need-based scholarship or grant aid. 71% freshmen, 75% undergrads receive need-based self-help aid. 2% freshmen, 1% undergrads receive athletic scholarships. 65% freshmen, 63% undergrads receive any aid. 57% undergrads borrow to pay for school. Average cumulative indebtedness $20,906. **Criteria for awarding institutional aid:** *Non-need-based:* academics, alumni affiliation, art, athletics, job skills, leadership, minority status, music/drama, religious affiliation, state/district residency.

UNIVERSITY OF TENNESSEE AT KNOXVILLE

Best 380

320 Student Service Building, Knoxville, TN 37996-0230
Phone: 865-974-2184 · **Financial Aid Phone:** 865-974-3131
E-mail: admissions@utk.edu · **CEEB Code:** 1843
Website: http://www.utk.edu · **ACT Code:** 4026

This public school was founded in 1794. It has a 520-acre campus.

RATINGS

Admissions Selectivity Rating: 89   **Fire Safety Rating:** 91

STUDENTS AND FACULTY

Enrollment: 21,396. **Student Body:** 50% female, 50% male, 10% out-of-state, 1% international (113 countries represented). Asian 3%, African American 7%, Caucasian 80%, Hispanic 3%, Native American <1%
Retention and Graduation: 40% freshmen graduate within 4 years. 69% freshmen graduate within 6 years. **Faculty:** 1,773 full-time faculty, 86% hold PhDs, 43% are are members of minority groups, 18% are women.

ACADEMICS

Degrees: bachelor's, doctoral, master's, post-master's certificate. **Classes:** Most classes have 20-29 students. Most lab/discussion sessions have 20-29 students. **Majors with Highest Enrollment:** Biology/Biological Sciences; Psychology; Kinesiology and Exercise Science. **Special Study Options:** Accelerated program, cooperative education program, cross-registration, distance learning, double major, dual enrollment, English as a Second Language (ESL), exchange student program (domestic), external degree program, honors program, independent study, internships, liberal arts/career combination, student-designed major, study abroad, teacher certification program. **Honors programs:** 1. Chancellor's Honors Program 2. Haslam Scholars Program 3. College Scholars Program 4. Global Leadership Scholars Program 5. College of Engineering Honors Program 6. College of Agricultural and Natural Resources Honors Program 7. College of Social Work Honors Program 8. Howard H. Baker Jr. Center for Public Policy's Baker Scholars Program 9. The Math Honors Program 10. Additional departmental honors programs. **Combined degree programs:** JD/MBA, JD/MPA. **Disability Services:** Special programs offered to physically disabled students include note-taking services, reader services, tape recorders, tutors. **Career services:** Alumni network, alumni services, career/job search classes, career assessment, internships. Career services highlights include the Office of Professional Practice in Engineering's Cooperative Education Program. This program matches students with employers to ensure a real world

work experience that significantly enhances the students chances for quality work opportunities at graduation. Approximately 250 students participate in this program annually.

FACILITIES

Housing: Coed dorms, special housing for disabled students, men's dorms, special housing for international students, women's dorms, fraternity/sorority housing, apartments for married students, apartments for single students, Theme Housing, Transfer student floors. 95% of campus accessible to physically disabled. **Special Academic Facilities/Equipment:** Comprehensive museum of anthropology, archaeology, art, geology, natural history, and medicine, theatre-in-the-round, livestock farms, robotics research center, electron microscope, McClung Museum. **Computers:** 100% of classrooms, 100% of dorms, 100% of libraries, 100% of dining areas, 100% of student union, 25% of common outdoor areas have wireless network access. Students can register for classes online.

CAMPUS LIFE

Environment: City. **Activities:** Choral groups, concert band, dance, drama/theater, jazz band, literary magazine, marching band, music ensembles, musical theater, opera, pep band, radio station, student government, student newspaper, student-run film society, symphony orchestra, television station, yearbook, Campus Ministries, International Student Organization, Model UN. 450 registered organizations, 90 honor societies, 30 religious organizations. 23 fraternities, 18 sororities. **Athletics (Intercollegiate):** *Men:* baseball, basketball, cheerleading, cross-country, diving, football, golf, swimming, tennis, track/field (outdoor), track/field (indoor). *Women:* basketball, cheerleading, crew/rowing, cross-country, diving, golf, soccer, softball, swimming, tennis, track/field (outdoor), track/field (indoor), volleyball. **On-Campus Highlights:** Ayres Hall and the Hill, Neyland Stadium, Hodges Library, Rec Sports Center, Howard Baker, Jr. Ctr. for Public Policy, McClung Museum, Alumni Memorial Building and Cox Auditorium, Thompson-Boling Arena. **Environmental Initiatives:** Climate Action Plan; Sustainable Cities Initiative; Sustainability Major.

ADMISSIONS

Freshman Academic Profile: Average high school GPA 3.79. 50% in top 10% of high school class, 90% in top 25% of high school class, 100% in top 50% of high school class. SAT Math middle 50% range 530-640. SAT Critical Reading middle 50% range 520-630. ACT middle 50% range 24-29. Minimum internet-based TOEFL 70. Minimum paper TOEFL 523. **Basis for Candidate Selection:** *Very important factors considered include:* academic GPA, rigor of secondary school record, standardized test scores. *Other factors considered include:* Class rank, application essay, recommendation(s), alumni/ae relation, character/personal qualities, extracurricular activities, first generation, geographical residence, level of applicant's interest, racial/ethnic status, state residency, talent/ability, volunteer work, work experience. **Freshman Admission Requirements:** High school diploma is required and GED is accepted. **Academic units required:** 4 English, 3 mathematics, 2 science, (1 science labs), 2 foreign language, 1 social studies, 1 history, 1 visual/performing arts. **Freshman Admission Statistics:** 15,442 applied, 75% admitted, 41% enrolled. **Transfer Admission Requirements:** High school transcript, college transcript(s), statement of good standing from prior institution(s). Minimum college GPA of 2.0 required. Lowest grade transferable C. **General Admission Information:** Application Fee $30. Regular application deadline 12/1. Regular notification 3/15. Nonfall registration accepted. Credit offered for CEEB Advanced Placement tests.

COSTS AND FINANCIAL AID

Annual in-state tuition $10,366. Annual out-of-state tuition $28,556. Room and board $10,296. Required fees $1,510. Average book expense $1,582. **Required Forms and Deadlines:** FAFSA. **Notification of Awards:** Applicants will be notified of awards on a rolling basis beginning 3/15. **Types of Aid:** *Need-based scholarships/grants:* Federal Pell, SEOG, state scholarships/grants, private scholarships, the school's own gift aid, Federal Nursing Scholarships. *Loans:* Subsidized Stafford, Unsubsidized Stafford, PLUS, Federal Perkins, college/university loans from institutional funds. *Student Employment:* Federal Work-Study Program available. Off-campus job opportunities are fair. **Financial Aid Statistics:** 95% freshmen, 89% undergrads receive need-based scholarship or grant aid. 0% freshmen, 0% undergrads receive non-need-based scholarship or grant aid. 99% freshmen, 99% undergrads receive need-based self-help aid. 3% freshmen, 3% undergrads receive athletic scholarships. 61% freshmen, 60% undergrads receive any aid. 51% undergrads borrow to pay for school. Average cumulative indebtedness $21,602. **Criteria for awarding institutional aid:** *Non-need-based:* academics, art, athletics, leadership, minority status, music/drama, state/district residency.

UNIVERSITY OF TENNESSEE AT MARTIN

200 Hall-Moody, Martin, TN 38238
Phone: 731-881-7020 · **Financial Aid Phone:** 731-881-7031
E-mail: admitme@utm.edu
Fax: 731-881-7029 · **Website:** www.utm.edu · **ACT Code:** 4032

This public school was founded in 1900. It has a 930-acre campus.

RATINGS

Admissions Selectivity Rating: 83   **Fire Safety Rating:** 79

STUDENTS AND FACULTY

Enrollment: 6,387. **Student Body:** 58% female, 42% male, 5% out-of-state, 3% international (20 countries represented). Asian 1%, African American 16%, Caucasian 76%, Hispanic 2%, Native American <1%
Retention and Graduation: 71% freshmen return for sophomore year. 20% freshmen graduate within 4 years. 47% freshmen graduate within 6 years. 21% grads go on to further study within 1 year. **Faculty:** 295 full-time faculty, 73% hold PhDs, 44% are are members of minority groups, 10% are women. 0% of classes are taught by teaching assistants.

ACADEMICS

Degrees: bachelor's, master's. **Classes:** Most classes have 10-19 students. Most lab/discussion sessions have 10-19 students. **Majors with Highest Enrollment:** Agricultural Business and Management; Registered Nursing/Registered Nurse; Health and Physical Education/Fitness. **Special Study Options:** Accelerated program, cooperative education program, cross-registration, distance learning, double major, dual enrollment, English as a Second Language (ESL), exchange student program (domestic), honors program, independent study, internships, student-designed major, study abroad, teacher certification program, 3-1 programs in pharmacy, veterinary medicine, dentistry, medicine, optometry, podiatry and chiropractory. **Honors programs:** University Scholars Honors Seminar. **Disability Services:** Special programs offered to physically disabled students include note-taking services, reader services, tape recorders, tutors. **Career services:** Alumni network, alumni services, career/job search classes, internships, regional alumni. Career services highlights include erecruiting.com, which allows our students faster and more significant information on employers and job openings from their computers.

FACILITIES

Housing: Coed dorms, special housing for disabled students, men's dorms, special housing for international students, women's dorms, fraternity/sorority housing, apartments for married students, apartments for single students, Theme Housing. 100% of campus accessible to physically disabled. **Special Academic Facilities/Equipment:** Paul Meek Library, contains Houston Gordon University Museum. **Computers:** 100% of classrooms, 50% of dorms, 100% of libraries, 100% of dining areas, 100% of student union, 100% of common outdoor areas have wireless network access. Students can register for classes online. Administrative functions (other than registration) can be performed online.

CAMPUS LIFE

Environment: Rural. **Activities:** Choral groups, concert band, dance, drama/theater, jazz band, literary magazine, marching band, music ensembles, opera, pep band, radio station, student government, student newspaper, television station, yearbook, Campus Ministries, International Student Organization. 100 registered organizations, 27 honor societies, 11 religious organizations. 12 fraternities, 8 sororities. **Athletics (Intercollegiate):** *Men:* baseball, basketball, cross-country, football, golf, riflery, rodeo. *Women:* basketball, cheerleading, cross-country, equestrian sports, riflery, rodeo, soccer, softball, tennis, volleyball. **On-Campus Highlights:** Boling University Center, Paul Meek Library, Fitness Center, Elam Center and Intramural facilities, Quad, Captain's Coffee in Paul Meek Library Student Life Center. **Environmental Initiatives:** Establishing a Recycling Facility to collect campus and community recyclables. The campus recycles its paper, cardboard, cans and plastic bottles. Purchasing green products such as carpet made from recycled materials and recycled paper products. Retrofit lighting with new, more energy-efficient lamps and ballasts, updating HVAC controls, and installing low flush toilets and urinals and occupancy lighting sensors.

ADMISSIONS

Freshman Academic Profile: Average high school GPA 3.52. 28% in top 10% of high school class, 62% in top 25% of high school class, 90% in top 50% of high school class. 94% from public high schools. ACT middle 50% range 20-25. Minimum internet-based TOEFL 61. Minimum paper TOEFL 500. **Basis for Candidate Selection:** *Very important factors considered include:* academic GPA, rigor of secondary school record, standardized test scores. **Freshman Admission Requirements:** High school diploma is required and GED is accepted. **Academic units required:** 4 English, 3 mathematics, 2 science, (1 science labs), 2 foreign language, 0 social studies, 2 history, 1 visual/perform-

ing arts. **Freshman Admission Statistics:** 3,526 applied, 73% admitted, 46% enrolled. **Transfer Admission Requirements:** High school transcript, college transcript(s), Minimum college GPA of 2.0 required. Lowest grade transferable D. **General Admission Information:** Application Fee $30. Regular application deadline 8/1. Notification on a rolling basis, beginning on or about 9/1. Nonfall registration accepted. Admission may be deferred for a maximum of rolling. Credit and/or placement offered for CEEB Advanced Placement tests.

COSTS AND FINANCIAL AID

Annual in-state tuition $6,716. Annual out-of-state tuition $20,660. Room and board $5,786. Required fees $1,308. Average book expense $1,600. **Required Forms and Deadlines:** FAFSA. **Notification of Awards:** Applicants will be notified of awards on a rolling basis beginning 4/1. **Types of Aid:** *Need-based scholarships/grants:* Federal Pell, SEOG, state scholarships/grants, private scholarships, the school's own gift aid. *Loans:* Subsidized Stafford, Unsubsidized Stafford, PLUS, Federal Perkins. *Student Employment:* Federal Work-Study Program available. Institutional employment available. Highest amount earned per year from on-campus jobs $9,668. Off-campus job opportunities are fair. **Financial Aid Statistics:** 67% freshmen, 70% undergrads receive need-based scholarship or grant aid. 91% freshmen, 55% undergrads receive non-need-based scholarship or grant aid. 53% freshmen, 65% undergrads receive need-based self-help aid. 8% freshmen, 4% undergrads receive athletic scholarships. 77% freshmen, 73% undergrads receive any aid. 63% undergrads borrow to pay for school. Average cumulative indebtedness $26,060. **Criteria for awarding institutional aid:** *Non-need-based:* academics, art, athletics, leadership, music/drama, state/district residency.

THE UNIVERSITY OF TEXAS AT ARLINGTON

Office of Admissions, Arlington, TX 76019-0111
Phone: 817-272-6287 · **Financial Aid Phone:** 817-272-3561
E-mail: admissions@uta.edu · **CEEB Code:** 6013
Fax: 817-272-3435 · **Website:** www.uta.edu · **ACT Code:** 4200

This public school was founded in 1895. It has a 394-acre campus.

RATINGS

Admissions Selectivity Rating: 86   **Fire Safety Rating:** 94

STUDENTS AND FACULTY

Enrollment: 25,414. **Student Body:** 56% female, 44% male, 3% out-of-state, 4% international (123 countries represented). Asian 12%, African American 15%, Caucasian 40%, Hispanic 26%, Native American <1%
Retention and Graduation: 74% freshmen return for sophomore year. 18% freshmen graduate within 4 years. 44% freshmen graduate within 6 years. **Faculty:** 941 full-time faculty, 42% are are members of minority groups, 28% are women. 16% of classes are taught by teaching assistants.

ACADEMICS

Degrees: bachelor's, master's, post-bachelor's certificate, post-master's certificate. **Classes:** Most classes have 20-29 students. **Majors with Highest Enrollment:** Business Administration and Management; Registered Nursing/Registered Nurse. **Special Study Options:** cross-registration, distance learning, double major, dual enrollment, English as a Second Language (ESL), honors program, independent study, internships, student-designed major, study abroad, teacher certification program. **Honors programs:** We have the only Honors College in N. Texas. Freshmen interest groups, honors study abroad. **Combined degree programs:** BA/MD, BS/MBA. **Disability Services:** Special programs offered to physically disabled students include note-taking services, reader services, tape recorders, tutors. **Career services:** alumni services, career/job search classes, career assessment, internships.

FACILITIES

Housing: Coed dorms, men's dorms, women's dorms, fraternity/sorority housing, apartments for married students, apartments for single students, Family housing (priority given to students with dependent children). 95% of campus accessible to physically disabled. **Special Academic Facilities/Equipment:** Cartographic history library, maps collection, minority cultures collection, library of Texana and Mexican war. Continuing Education Work Force Development Center. material, planetarium, Automation and Robotics Research institute, Wave Scattering Research Center. **Computers:** Students can register for classes online. Administrative functions (other than registration) can be performed online.

CAMPUS LIFE

Environment: Metropolis. **Activities:** Choral groups, concert band, dance, drama/theater, jazz band, literary magazine, marching band, music ensembles, opera, radio station, student government, student newspaper, student-run film society, symphony orchestra, Campus Ministries, International Student Organization 459 registered organizations, 30 honor societies, 27 religious organizations. 12 fraternities, 13 sororities. **Athletics (Intercollegiate):** *Men:* baseball, basketball, cross-country, golf, tennis, track/field (outdoor). *Women:* basketball, cross-country, softball, tennis, track/field (outdoor), volleyball. **On-Campus Highlights:** Click Café in Library, E. H. Herford University Center, Activities Bldg., Library Mall/Free speech area, Architectue courtyard. **Environmental Initiatives:** Transportation programs like car sharing, ride share, bike program; Energy Conservation Outreach; Education and Collaboration with other entities.

ADMISSIONS

Freshman Academic Profile: 28% in top 10% of high school class, 75% in top 25% of high school class, 98% in top 50% of high school class. SAT Math middle 50% range 500-620. SAT Critical Reading middle 50% range 460-580. SAT Writing middle 50% range 450-560. ACT middle 50% range 20-26. Minimum internet-based TOEFL 79. Minimum paper TOEFL 550. **Basis for Candidate Selection:** *Very important factors considered include:* Class rank, academic GPA, standardized test scores. *Important factors considered include:* rigor of secondary school record. *Other factors considered include:* application essay, recommendation(s), character/personal qualities, extracurricular activities, first generation, level of applicant's interest, talent/ability, volunteer work, work experience. **Freshman Admission Requirements:** High school diploma is required and GED is not accepted. **Academic units required:** 4 English, 3 mathematics, 3 science, (0 science labs), 2 foreign language, 3 social studies, 0 history, 0 visual/performing arts, 0 computer science, 5 academic electives: Physical Education 1.5; Health 0.5; Computer proficiency 1; Fine Arts 1; Music, Theater, Art 1. **Freshman Admission Statistics:** 10,679 applied, 60% admitted, 42% enrolled. **Transfer Admission Requirements:** High school transcript, college transcript(s), Minimum college GPA of 2.25 required. Lowest grade transferable C. **General Admission Information:** Application Fee $35. Nonfall registration accepted. Admission may be deferred for a maximum of 1 year. Credit offered for CEEB Advanced Placement tests.

COSTS AND FINANCIAL AID

Annual in-state tuition $8,878. Annual out-of-state tuition $19,497. Room and board $7,864. Average book expense $1,160. **Required Forms and Deadlines:** FAFSA. **Notification of Awards:** Applicants will be notified of awards on a rolling basis beginning 4/1. **Types of Aid:** *Need-based scholarships/grants:* Federal Pell, SEOG, state scholarships/grants, private scholarships, the school's own gift aid, United Negro College Fund. *Loans:* Subsidized Stafford, Unsubsidized Stafford, PLUS, Federal Perkins, college/university loans from institutional funds. *Student Employment:* Federal Work-Study Program available. Institutional employment available. Off-campus job opportunities are excellent. **Financial Aid Statistics:** 74% freshmen, 80% undergrads receive need-based scholarship or grant aid. 50% freshmen, 31% undergrads receive non-need-based scholarship or grant aid. 94% freshmen, 95% undergrads receive need-based self-help aid. 0% freshmen, 0% undergrads receive athletic scholarships. 65% freshmen, 68% undergrads receive any aid. 58% undergrads borrow to pay for school. Average cumulative indebtedness $21,314.

THE UNIVERSITY OF TEXAS AT AUSTIN

Best 380

P.O. Box 8058, Austin, TX 78713-8058
Phone: 512-475-7399 · **Financial Aid Phone:** 512-475-6282
E-mail: http://bealonghorn.utexas.edu/ask/contac · **CEEB Code:** 6882
Fax: 512-475-7478 · **Website:** http://www.utexas.edu · **ACT Code:** 4240

This public school was founded in 1883. It has a 350-acre campus.

RATINGS

Admissions Selectivity Rating: 93   Fire Safety Rating: 76

STUDENTS AND FACULTY

Enrollment: 39,323. **Student Body:** 52% female, 48% male, 5% out-of-state, 5% international (98 countries represented). Asian 18%, African American 4%, Caucasian 48%, Hispanic 22%, Native American <1%
Retention and Graduation: 51% freshmen graduate within 4 years. **Faculty:** 2,752 full-time faculty, 90% hold PhDs, 38% are are members of minority groups, 20% are women.

ACADEMICS

Degrees: bachelor's, first professional, master's. **Classes:** Most classes have 10-19 students. Most lab/discussion sessions have 10-19 students. **Majors with Highest Enrollment:** Liberal Arts and Sciences/Liberal Studies; Biology/

Biological Sciences; Business/Commerce. **Special Study Options:** Accelerated program, cooperative education program, distance learning, double major, dual enrollment, English as a Second Language (ESL), honors program, independent study, internships, liberal arts/career combination, student-designed major, study abroad, teacher certification program. **Disability Services:** Special programs offered to physically disabled students include note-taking services, reader services. **Career services:** Alumni network, career/job search classes, career assessment, internships, regional alumni. Career services highlights include Internships. All BBA students must complete at least one internship in order to graduate. Our internship programs allow our BBAs to compete on a national level.

FACILITIES

Housing: Coed dorms, men's dorms, women's dorms, apartments for married students, apartments for single students, Honors Residence, Living Learning Centers (First-time Freshmen). 98% of campus accessible to physically disabled. **Special Academic Facilities/Equipment:** Blanton Museun of Art, Lyndon Baines Johnson Presidential Library/Museum, Performing Arts Center, Texas Memorial Museum, Harry Ransom Humanities Research Center. **Computers:** Students can register for classes online. Administrative functions (other than registration) can be performed online.

CAMPUS LIFE

Environment: Metropolis. **Activities:** Choral groups, concert band, dance, drama/theater, jazz band, literary magazine, marching band, music ensembles, musical theater, opera, pep band, radio station, student government, student newspaper, student-run film society, symphony orchestra, television station, yearbook, Campus Ministries, International Student Organization. 900 registered organizations, 15 honor societies, 95 religious organizations. 26 fraternities, 22 sororities. **Athletics (Intercollegiate):** *Men:* baseball, basketball, cross-country, diving, football, golf, swimming, tennis, track/field (outdoor). *Women:* basketball, crew/rowing, cross-country, diving, golf, soccer, softball, swimming, tennis, track/field (outdoor), volleyball. **On-Campus Highlights:** Texas Union, Frank Erwin Special Events Center, Performing Arts Center, Harry Ransom Humanities Research Center, Blanton Museum of Art. **Environmental Initiatives:** Incorporation of sustainability principles throughout the institution's approved Campus Master Plan (May 2013). Creation of the Academic Sustainability Directory, an interactive website dedicated to organizing and presenting sustainability-related education and research at UT Austin. The Directory inventories sustainability-related faculty/staff, research/initiatives, courses, degree plans & curriculum, and centers/institutes across campus. Adoption of the student green fee—$503,000 per year allocated by a majority student committee. Fee was passed via student referendum in 2010 and the first fees were collected in Fall 2011. The current referendum has a five-year cycle.

ADMISSIONS

Freshman Academic Profile: 75.3% in top 10% of high school class, 90.5% in top 25% of high school class, 97.7% in top 50% of high school class. SAT Math middle 50% range 590-710. SAT Critical Reading middle 50% range 550-670. SAT Writing middle 50% range 550-680. ACT middle 50% range 25-31. Minimum internet-based TOEFL 79. Minimum paper TOEFL 550. **Basis for Candidate Selection:** *Very important factors considered include:* Class rank, rigor of secondary school record. *Important factors considered include:* application essay, standardized test scores, extracurricular activities, talent/ability, volunteer work, work experience. *Other factors considered include:* recommendation(s), character/personal qualities, first generation, level of applicant's interest, racial/ethnic status, state residency. **Freshman Admission Requirements:** High school diploma is required and GED is accepted. **Academic units required:** 4 English, 3 mathematics, 2 science, (2 science labs), 2 foreign language, 3 social studies. **Freshman Admission Statistics:** 38,161 applied, 40% admitted, 47% enrolled. **Transfer Admission Requirements:** college transcript(s), essay or personal statement, Minimum college GPA of 3.0 required. Lowest grade transferable C. **General Admission Information:** Application Fee $60. Regular application deadline 12/15. Nonfall registration accepted. Credit and/or placement offered for CEEB Advanced Placement tests.

COSTS AND FINANCIAL AID

Annual in-state tuition $9,798. Annual out-of-state tuition $34,722. Room and board $11,456. Required fees $0. Average book expense $760. **Required Forms and Deadlines:** FAFSA, Institution's own financial aid form. **Notification of Awards:** Applicants will be notified of awards on a rolling basis beginning 3/15. **Types of Aid:** *Need-based scholarships/grants:* Federal Pell, SEOG, state scholarships/grants, private scholarships, the school's own gift aid. *Loans:* Subsidized Stafford, Unsubsidized Stafford, PLUS, Federal Perkins, state loans. *Student Employment:* Federal Work-Study Program available. Off-campus job opportunities are fair. **Financial Aid Statistics:** 91% freshmen, 81% undergrads receive need-based scholarship or grant aid. 46% freshmen, 26% undergrads receive non-need-based scholarship or grant aid. 62% freshmen, 73% undergrads receive need-based self-help aid. 0% freshmen, 0% undergrads receive athletic scholarships. 45% undergrads receive any aid. 50% undergrads borrow to pay for school. Average cumulative indebtedness $22,295. **Criteria for awarding institutional aid:** *Non-need-based:* academics, art, athletics, leadership, music/drama, state/district residency.

THE UNIVERSITY OF TEXAS AT BROWNSVILLE

80 Fort Brown, Brownsville, TX 78520
Phone: 956-882-8295 · **Financial Aid Phone:** 956-882-8814
E-mail: admissions@utb.edu · **CEEB Code:** 6825
Fax: 956-882-7810 · **Website:** www.utb.edu

This public school was founded in 1926.

RATINGS

Admissions Selectivity Rating: 61   **Fire Safety Rating:** 60*

STUDENTS AND FACULTY

Enrollment: 10,145. **Student Body:** 60% female, 40% male, 4% out-of-state, 4% international (21 countries represented). Asian 0%, African American 0%, Caucasian 5%, Hispanic 90%, Native American <1%
Faculty: 366 full-time faculty, 59% hold PhDs, 43% are are members of minority groups, 46% are women. 0% of classes are taught by teaching assistants.

ACADEMICS

Degrees: associate, bachelor's, certificate, master's, terminal associate, transfer associate. **Majors with Highest Enrollment:** Multi-/Interdisciplinary Studies; Psychology; Business/Commerce. **Special Study Options:** cooperative education program, distance learning, double major, dual enrollment, English as a Second Language (ESL), independent study, internships, teacher certification program. **Disability Services:** Special programs offered to physically disabled students include note-taking services, reader services, tape recorders, tutors.

FACILITIES

Housing: Coed dorms, special housing for disabled students, men's dorms, women's dorms, apartments for single students. **Computers:** Students can register for classes online. Administrative functions (other than registration) can be performed online.

CAMPUS LIFE

Environment: City. **Activities:** Choral groups, concert band, dance, drama/theater, jazz band, music ensembles, opera, radio station, student government, student newspaper. 56 registered organizations, 6 honor societies. **Athletics (Intercollegiate):** *Men:* baseball, golf. *Women:* golf, volleyball.

ADMISSIONS

Freshman Academic Profile: Average high school GPA 2.61. 10% in top 10% of high school class, 27% in top 25% of high school class, 57% in top 50% of high school class. 95% from public high schools. **Freshman Admission Requirements:** High school diploma or equivalent is not required. **Academic units required:** 4 English, 2 mathematics, 2 science, (2 science labs), 2 foreign language, 4 social studies, 2 history, 1 academic elective. **Freshman Admission Statistics:** 3,174 applied, 100% admitted, 57% enrolled. **Transfer Admission Requirements:** High school transcript, college transcript(s), Minimum college GPA of 2.0 required. Lowest grade transferable C. **General Admission Information:** Regular application deadline 7/1. Nonfall registration accepted. Admission may be deferred for a maximum of 1 year. Credit offered for CEEB Advanced Placement tests.

COSTS AND FINANCIAL AID

Average book expense $615. **Required Forms and Deadlines:** FAFSA. **Notification of Awards:** Applicants will be notified of awards on or about 5/1. **Types of Aid:** *Need-based scholarships/grants:* Federal Pell, SEOG, state scholarships/grants, private scholarships, the school's own gift aid. *Loans:* Subsidized Stafford, Unsubsidized Stafford, PLUS, college/university loans from institutional funds. **Criteria for awarding institutional aid:** *Non-need-based:* academics, art, athletics, leadership, music/drama.

THE UNIVERSITY OF TEXAS AT DALLAS

| Best 380 |

Admission & Enrollment, 800 W Campbell R, Richardson, TX 75080-3021
Phone: 972-883-2270 · **Financial Aid Phone:** 972-883-2941
E-mail: interest@utdallas.edu · **CEEB Code:** 6897
Fax: 972-883-2599 · **Website:** www.utdallas.edu · **ACT Code:** 4243

This public school was founded in 1969. It has a 500-acre campus.

RATINGS

Admissions Selectivity Rating: 88   **Fire Safety Rating:** 89

STUDENTS AND FACULTY

Enrollment: 14,033. **Student Body:** 43% female, 57% male, 4% out-of-state, 4% international (109 countries represented). Asian 28%, African American 6%, Caucasian 39%, Hispanic 18%, Native American <1%
Retention and Graduation: 87% freshmen return for sophomore year. 51% freshmen graduate within 4 years. 71% freshmen graduate within 6 years. **Faculty:** 792 full-time faculty, 93% hold PhDs, 30% are are members of minority groups, 27% are women. 3% of classes are taught by teaching assistants.

ACADEMICS

Degrees: bachelor's, master's, post-bachelor's certificate. **Classes:** Most classes have 10-19 students. Most lab/discussion sessions have 20-29 students. **Majors with Highest Enrollment:** Biology/Biological Sciences; Accounting; Computer and Information Sciences. **Special Study Options:** Accelerated program, cooperative education program, cross-registration, distance learning, double major, dual enrollment, English as a Second Language (ESL), honors program, independent study, internships, liberal arts/career combination, student-designed major, study abroad, teacher certification program, 3-2 Engineering programs, 2-2 Transfer programs. **Honors programs:** Collegium V offers small classes, innovative instruction, world class faculty, bright and inquisitive colleagues, and an array of extracurricular events to provide special opportunities for professional and personal growth. **Combined degree programs:** BA/MA, BS/MS, BA/MPA, BS/MPA, MS/PhD. **Disability Services:** Special programs offered to physically disabled students include note-taking services, reader services, tape recorders, tutors. **Career services:** career/job search classes, career assessment, internships.

FACILITIES

Housing: Coed dorms, apartments for married students, apartments for single students, Living Learning communities for freshmen. 100% of campus accessible to physically disabled. **Special Academic Facilities/Equipment:** McDermott Library Special Collections which includes History of Aviation Collection, Wineburgh Philatelic Research Library and Louise B. Belsterling Botanical Library. **Computers:** 80% of classrooms, 100% of dorms, 100% of libraries, 100% of student union, 5% of common outdoor areas have wireless network access. Students can register for classes online.

CAMPUS LIFE

Environment: Metropolis. **Activities:** Choral groups, concert band, dance, drama/theater, jazz band, literary magazine, music ensembles, musical theater, pep band, radio station, student government, student newspaper, student-run film society, symphony orchestra, television station, International Student Organization. 142 registered organizations, 8 honor societies, 9 religious organizations. 9 fraternities, 6 sororities. **Athletics (Intercollegiate):** *Men:* baseball, basketball, cross-country, golf, soccer, tennis. *Women:* basketball, cross-country, golf, soccer, softball, tennis, volleyball. **On-Campus Highlights:** The Pub (coffeehouse), Comet Café, Student Union, Activity Center, University Village clubhouses. **Environmental Initiatives:** Campus recycling program; DART shuttle program. Free DART passes for students, discounted passes for faculty, staff.

ADMISSIONS

Freshman Academic Profile: 38% in top 10% of high school class, 70% in top 25% of high school class, 92% in top 50% of high school class. 91% from public high schools. SAT Math middle 50% range 590-700. SAT Critical Reading middle 50% range 550-670. SAT Writing middle 50% range 530-650. ACT middle 50% range 25-31. Minimum internet-based TOEFL 80. Minimum paper TOEFL 550. **Basis for Candidate Selection:** *Very important factors considered include:* Class rank, academic GPA, rigor of secondary school record, standardized test scores. *Important factors considered include:* application essay, extracurricular activities. *Other factors considered include:* recommendation(s), character/personal qualities, first generation, geographical residence, level of applicant's interest, state residency, talent/ability, volunteer work, work experience. **Freshman Admission Requirements:** High school diploma is required and GED is accepted. **Academic units required:** 4 English, 4 mathematics, 3 science, (3 science labs), 2 foreign language, 3 social studies, 0 Health, PE. **Freshman Admission Statistics:** 9,587 applied, 62% admitted, 42% enrolled. **Transfer Admission Requirements:** college transcript(s), Minimum college GPA of 2.5 required. Lowest grade transferable C. **General Admission Information:** Application Fee $50. Regular application deadline 7/1. Nonfall registration accepted. Admission may be deferred for a maximum of One year. Credit and/or placement offered for CEEB Advanced Placement tests.

COSTS AND FINANCIAL AID

Annual in-state tuition $11,806. Annual out-of-state tuition $31,328. Room and board $9,542. Average book expense $1,200. **Required Forms and Deadlines:** FAFSA. **Notification of Awards:** Applicants will be notified of awards on a rolling basis beginning 3/1. **Types of Aid:** *Need-based scholarships/grants:* Federal Pell, SEOG, state scholarships/grants, private scholarships, the school's own gift aid. *Loans:* Subsidized Stafford, Unsubsidized Stafford, PLUS, Federal Perkins, state loans, college/university loans from institutional funds. *Student Employment:* Federal Work-Study Program available. Institutional employment available. Highest amount earned per year from on-campus jobs $15,318. Off-campus job opportunities are excellent. **Financial Aid Statistics:** 89% freshmen, 86% undergrads receive need-based scholarship or grant aid. 18% freshmen, 7% undergrads receive non-need-based scholarship or grant aid. 75% freshmen, 86% undergrads receive need-based self-help aid. 0% freshmen, 0% undergrads receive athletic scholarships. 80% freshmen, 70% undergrads receive any aid. 48% undergrads borrow to pay for school. Average cumulative indebtedness $19,675. **Criteria for awarding institutional aid:** *Non-need-based:* academics.

See page 1198.

THE UNIVERSITY OF TEXAS AT EL PASO

Mike Loya Academic Services Bldg., #102, El Paso, TX 79968-0510
Phone: 915-747-5890
E-mail: www.academics.utep.edu • **CEEB Code:** 6829
Fax: 915-747-8893 • **Website:** http://www.utep.edu/ • **ACT Code:** 4223

This public school was founded in 1913. It has a 330-acre campus.

RATINGS

Admissions Selectivity Rating: 71   **Fire Safety Rating:** 69

STUDENTS AND FACULTY

Enrollment: 19,078. **Student Body:** 54% female, 46% male, 3% out-of-state, 5% international (65 countries represented). Asian 1%, African American 3%, Caucasian 8%, Hispanic 81%, Native American <1%
Retention and Graduation: 72% freshmen return for sophomore year. **Faculty:** 2% of classes are taught by teaching assistants.

ACADEMICS

Degrees: bachelor's, master's. **Classes:** Most classes have 20-29 students. Most lab/discussion sessions have 10-19 students. **Majors with Highest Enrollment:** Multi-/Interdisciplinary Studies; Psychology; Criminal Justice/Safety Studies. **Special Study Options:** Accelerated program, cooperative education program, cross-registration, distance learning, double major, dual enrollment, English as a Second Language (ESL), exchange student program (domestic), honors program, independent study, internships, study abroad, teacher certification program, weekend college. **Combined degree programs:** BA/MA. **Disability Services:** Special programs offered to physically disabled students include note-taking services, reader services, tape recorders. **Career services:** alumni services, career assessment, internships.

FACILITIES

Housing: special housing for disabled students, apartments for single students. 90% of campus accessible to physically disabled. **Special Academic Facilities/Equipment:** Cross-cultural ethnic study center, natural history and cultural museum, solar pond and solar house, electron microscope, atmospheric and acoustic research lab, seismic observatory. **Computers:** Students can register for classes online. Administrative functions (other than registration) can be performed online.

CAMPUS LIFE

Environment: Metropolis. **Activities:** Choral groups, concert band, dance, drama/theater, jazz band, literary magazine, marching band, music ensembles, musical theater, opera, pep band, radio station, student government, student newspaper, student-run film society, symphony orchestra. 1 honor society, 1 religous organization. 6 fraternities, 4 sororities. **Athletics (Intercollegiate):** *Men:* basketball, cross-country, football, golf, track/field (outdoor), track/field (indoor). *Women:* basketball, cross-country, golf, riflery, soccer, softball, tennis, track/field (outdoor), track/field (indoor), volleyball.

ADMISSIONS

Freshman Academic Profile: Average high school GPA 3.15. 17% in top 10% of high school class, 40% in top 25% of high school class, 69% in top 50% of high school class. 94% from public high schools. SAT Math middle 50% range 420-530. SAT Critical Reading middle 50% range 390-500. ACT middle 50% range 17-22. **Basis for Candidate Selection:** *Very important factors considered include:* Class rank, rigor of secondary school record. *Important factors considered include:* standardized test scores, state residency. *Other factors considered include:* recommendation(s), alumni/ae relation, character/personal qualities, extracurricular activities, geographical residence, interview, talent/ability, volunteer work, work experience. **Freshman Admission Requirements:** High school diploma is required and GED is accepted. **Freshman Admission Statistics:** 6,240 applied, 100% admitted, 70% enrolled. **Transfer Admission Requirements:** college transcript(s), Minimum college GPA of 2.0 required. Lowest grade transferable D. **General Admission Information:** Regular application deadline 7/31. Nonfall registration accepted. Admission may be deferred for a maximum of 1 semester.

COSTS AND FINANCIAL AID

Annual in-state tuition $5,565. Annual out-of-state tuition $16,095. Room and board $8,924. Required fees $1,649. Average book expense $1,160. **Notification of Awards:** Applicants will be notified of awards on or about 6/30. **Types of Aid:** *Need-based scholarships/grants:* Federal Pell, SEOG, state scholarships/grants, private scholarships, the school's own gift aid, United Negro College Fund, Federal Nursing Scholarships. *Loans:* Subsidized Stafford, Unsubsidized Stafford, PLUS, Federal Perkins, state loans, college/university loans from institutional funds. *Student Employment:* Federal Work-Study Program available. Institutional employment available. Off-campus job opportunities are good. **Financial Aid Statistics:** 88% freshmen, 88% undergrads receive need-based scholarship or grant aid. 25% freshmen, 14% undergrads receive non-need-based scholarship or grant aid. 81% freshmen, 85% undergrads receive need-based self-help aid. 1% freshmen, 1% undergrads receive athletic scholarships. 77% freshmen, 65% undergrads receive any aid. 61% undergrads borrow to pay for school. Average cumulative indebtedness $21,173. **Criteria for awarding institutional aid:** *Non-need-based:* academics, alumni affiliation, art, athletics, job skills, leadership, minority status, music/drama, religious affiliation, state/district residency.

THE UNIVERSITY OF TEXAS AT SAN ANTONIO

One UTSA Circle, San Antonio, TX 78249-0617
Phone: 210-458-8000 • **Financial Aid Phone:** 210-458-8000
E-mail: prospects@utsa.edu • **CEEB Code:** 6919
Fax: 210-458-7857 • **Website:** http://www.utsa.edu/ • **ACT Code:** 4239

This public school was founded in 1969. It has a 600-acre campus.

RATINGS

Admissions Selectivity Rating: 78   **Fire Safety Rating:** 62

STUDENTS AND FACULTY

Enrollment: 23,815. **Student Body:** 48% female, 52% male, 3% out-of-state, 4% international (63 countries represented). Asian 5%, African American 9%, Caucasian 26%, Hispanic 51%, Native American <1%
Retention and Graduation: 64% freshmen return for sophomore year. 11% freshmen graduate within 4 years.

ACADEMICS

Degrees: bachelor's, doctoral, master's, post-bachelor's certificate. **Classes:** Most classes have 20-29 students. Most lab/discussion sessions have 10-19 students. **Majors with Highest Enrollment:** Kinesiology and Exercise Science; Psychology; Multi-/Interdisciplinary Studies. **Special Study Options:** Accelerated program, cooperative education program, distance learning, double major, dual enrollment, English as a Second Language (ESL), exchange student program (domestic), honors program, independent study, internships, study abroad, teacher certification program. **Honors programs:** The mission of the Honors College is to provide enhanced educational opportunities for selected, motivated, enthusiastic, diverse, and inquisitive students and to foster the pursuit of excellence in undergraduate, higher education. The underlying philosophy of the program is that well-educated individuals should understand broad, interdisciplinary perspectives while demonstrating expertise in their chosen field. The Honors College is open to students from all academic disciplines. Members of the Honors College pursue a rigorous academic program which satisfies all requirements of their academic departments and Colleges and goes beyond those requirements to provide the basis for outstanding achievement and appropriate recognition for that achievement. The Honors College offers small classes with greater opportunities for student participation, increased student-faculty contact, greater individual attention, lively discussions of important issues, special interdisciplinary seminars, community service opportunities, and supervised research experiences, all designed to challenge talented students. **Disability Services:** Special programs offered to physically disabled students include note-taking services, reader services, tape recorders.

FACILITIES

Housing: Coed dorms, special housing for disabled students, apartments for married students, apartments for single students. 100% of campus accessible to physically disabled. **Special Academic Facilities/Equipment:** Art gallery, audiovisual center, Institute of Texan Cultures Museum. **Computers:** Students can register for classes online. Administrative functions (other than registration) can be performed online.

CAMPUS LIFE

Environment: Metropolis. **Activities:** Choral groups, concert band, dance, drama/theater, jazz band, literary magazine, music ensembles, opera, pep band, student government, student newspaper, symphony orchestra, yearbook, Campus Ministries, International Student Organization. 140 registered organizations, 40 honor societies, 9 religious organizations. 10 fraternities, 9 sororities. **Athletics (Intercollegiate):** *Men:* baseball, basketball, cross-country, golf, tennis, track/field (outdoor), track/field (indoor). *Women:* basketball, cross-country, soccer, softball, tennis, track/field (outdoor), track/field (indoor), volleyball.

ADMISSIONS

Freshman Academic Profile: 19.3% in top 10% of high school class, 63.5% in top 25% of high school class, 92.3% in top 50% of high school class. SAT Math middle 50% range 480-490. SAT Critical Reading middle 50% range 450-560. SAT Writing middle 50% range 430-540. ACT middle 50% range 19-25. Minimum internet-based TOEFL 79. Minimum paper TOEFL 550. **Basis for Candidate Selection:** *Very important factors considered include:* Class rank, academic GPA, standardized test scores. *Other factors considered include:* recommendation(s). **Freshman Admission Requirements:** High school diploma is required and GED is accepted. **Freshman Admission Statistics:** 14,933 applied, 76% admitted, 45% enrolled. **Transfer Admission Requirements:** college transcript(s), Minimum college GPA of 2.0 required. Lowest grade transferable D. **General Admission Information:** Application Fee $40. Regular application deadline 7/1. Regular notification 9/1. Nonfall registration accepted. Credit and/or placement offered for CEEB Advanced Placement tests.

COSTS AND FINANCIAL AID

Annual in-state tuition $5,982. Annual out-of-state tuition $17,295. Room and board $7,624. Required fees $2,755. Average book expense $1,000. **Required Forms and Deadlines:** FAFSA, Institution's own financial aid form. **Notification of Awards:** Applicants will be notified of awards on a rolling basis beginning 4/1. **Types of Aid:** *Need-based scholarships/grants:* Federal Pell, SEOG, state scholarships/grants, private scholarships, the school's own gift aid. *Loans:* Direct Subsidized Stafford, Direct Unsubsidized Stafford, Direct PLUS, Subsidized Stafford, Unsubsidized Stafford, PLUS, Federal Perkins, state loans, college/university loans from institutional funds. **Criteria for awarding institutional aid:** *Non-need-based:* academics, alumni affiliation, art, athletics, job skills, leadership, music/drama, state/district residency.

THE UNIVERSITY OF TEXAS AT TYLER

3900 University Blvd., Tyler, TX 75799
Phone: 903-566-7202 · **Financial Aid Phone:** 903-566-7180
E-mail: admissions@mail.uttyl.edu · **CEEB Code:**
Fax: 903-566-7068 · **Website:** www.uttyler.edu

This public school was founded in 1971. It has a 204-acre campus.

RATINGS

Admissions Selectivity Rating: 71	Fire Safety Rating: 87

STUDENTS AND FACULTY

Enrollment: 4,700. **Student Body:** 60% female, 40% male, 2% out-of-state, 1% international (45 countries represented). Asian 2%, African American 10%, Caucasian 79%, Hispanic 6%, Native American 1%
Retention and Graduation: 59% freshmen return for sophomore year. 41% freshmen graduate within 6 years. 14% grads go on to further study within 1 year. **Faculty:** 234 full-time faculty, 70% hold PhDs, 49% are are members of minority groups, 12% are women.

ACADEMICS

Degrees: bachelor's, master's. **Classes:** Most classes have 20-29 students. **Majors with Highest Enrollment:** Multi-/Interdisciplinary Studies; Registered Nursing/Registered Nurse; Business/Managerial Economics. **Special Study Options:** cooperative education program, distance learning, double major, English as a Second Language (ESL), exchange student program (domestic), independent study, internships, student-designed major, study abroad, teacher certification program, weekend college. **Disability Services:** Special programs offered to physically disabled students include note-taking services, reader services. **Career services:** career/job search classes, career assessment.

FACILITIES

Housing: Coed dorms, apartments for married students, apartments for single students, Univ Pines Apts-384 beds, Patriot Village Apts—200 beds. Residence Hall Project underway, will be five stories with 268 beds, expected to open in fall 2006. http://www.uttyler.edu/housing. **Computers:** Students can register for classes online. Administrative functions (other than registration) can be performed online.

CAMPUS LIFE

Environment: City. **Activities:** Choral groups, concert band, drama/theater, jazz band, literary magazine, music ensembles, musical theater, opera, pep band, student government, student newspaper, student-run film society. 73 registered organizations, 6 honor societies, 4 fraternities, 4 sororities. **Athletics (Intercollegiate):** *Men:* baseball, basketball, cheerleading, cross-country, golf, soccer, tennis. *Women:* basketball, cheerleading, cross-country, golf, soccer, tennis, volleyball. **On-Campus Highlights:** Herrington Patriot Center, Riter Tower and Plaza, Cowan Fine and Performing Art Center, Bill Ratliff Engineering and Science Complex, University Center.

ADMISSIONS

Freshman Academic Profile: SAT Math middle 50% range 480-580. SAT Critical Reading middle 50% range 470-570. ACT middle 50% range 20-25. Minimum paper TOEFL 550. **Basis for Candidate Selection:** *Very important factors considered include:* Class rank, academic GPA, standardized test scores. *Important factors considered include:* rigor of secondary school record, extracurricular activities, first generation, volunteer work, work experience. **Freshman Admission Requirements:** High school diploma is required and GED is accepted. **Academic units required:** 4 English, 3 mathematics, 3 science, (1 science labs), 2 foreign language, 3 social studies. **Freshman Admission Statistics:** 1,823 applied, 76% admitted, 46% enrolled. **Transfer Admission Requirements:** college transcript(s), Minimum college GPA of 2.0 required. Lowest grade transferable C. **General Admission Information:** Application Fee $25. Notification on a rolling basis, beginning on or about 9/1. Nonfall registration accepted. Admission may be deferred for a maximum of 1 year.

COSTS AND FINANCIAL AID

Required Forms and Deadlines: FAFSA, Institution's own financial aid form. **Notification of Awards:** Applicants will be notified of awards on a rolling basis beginning 4/15. **Types of Aid:** *Need-based scholarships/grants:* Federal Pell, SEOG, state scholarships/grants, private scholarships, the school's own gift aid, Texas Grant Program, Teach for Texas Conditional Program. *Loans:* Subsidized Stafford, Unsubsidized Stafford, PLUS, Federal Perkins, state loans. **Financial Aid Statistics:** 84% freshmen, 81% undergrads receive need-based scholarship or grant aid. 14% freshmen, 6% undergrads receive non-need-based scholarship or grant aid. 84% freshmen, 91% undergrads receive need-based self-help aid. 0% freshmen, 0% undergrads receive athletic scholarships. 44% undergrads borrow to pay for school. Average cumulative indebtedness $11,286. **Criteria for awarding institutional aid:** *Non-need-based:* academics, art, music/drama.

THE UNIVERSITY OF TEXAS HEALTH SCIENCE CENTER AT HOUSTON

PO Box 20036, Houston, TX 77225
Phone: 713-500-3361
E-mail: admissions@uth.tmc.edu
Fax: 713-500-3356 · **Website:** www.uth.tmc.edu

This public school was founded in 1972.

RATINGS

Admissions Selectivity Rating: 60*	Fire Safety Rating: 60*

STUDENTS AND FACULTY

Enrollment: 381. **Student Body:** 88% female, 12% male, 2% international. Asian 17%, African American 7%, Caucasian 58%, Hispanic 15%, Native American 1%
Faculty: 985 full-time faculty, 41% are are members of minority groups.

ACADEMICS

Degrees: bachelor's, certificate, first professional, master's, post-master's certificate.

FACILITIES

Housing: University owns an apartment complex which is located approximately 1 1/2 miles from campus. It is competivtively priced with other apartment complexes in the area and does not cater exclusively to students. 100% of campus accessible to physically disabled. **Special Academic Facilities/ Equipment:** The student's learning experience takes place in the heart of the Texas Medical Center. Among state of the art hospitals and research facilites. **Computers:** Students can register for classes online. Administrative functions (other than registration) can be performed online. Undergraduates are required to own a computer.

CAMPUS LIFE

Activities: student government.

ADMISSIONS

Freshman Academic Profile: Minimum paper TOEFL 565. **Transfer Admission Requirements:** college transcript(s), interview, standardized test scores, statement of good standing from prior institution(s). Minimum college GPA of 2.8 required. Lowest grade transferable C. **General Admission Information:** Application Fee $30. Regular application deadline 1/1. Nonfall registration not accepted.

COSTS AND FINANCIAL AID

Required Forms and Deadlines: FAFSA, Institution's own financial aid form. **Types of Aid:** *Need-based scholarships/grants:* Federal Pell, SEOG, state scholarships/grants, the school's own gift aid, Federal Nursing Scholarships, outside Scholarships. *Loans:* Subsidized Stafford, Unsubsidized Stafford, PLUS, Federal Perkins, Federal Nursing, college/university loans from institutional funds, Outside Loans. *Student Employment:* Off-campus job opportunities are excellent. **Financial Aid Statistics:** 71% undergrads receive need-based scholarship or grant aid. 0% undergrads receive non-need-based scholarship or grant aid. 78% undergrads receive need-based self-help aid. 0% undergrads receive athletic scholarships. 90% undergrads borrow to pay for school.

THE UNIVERSITY OF TEXAS MEDICAL BRANCH

301 University Boulevard, Galveston, TX 77555-1305
Phone: 409-772-1215 • **Financial Aid Phone:** 409-772-1215
E-mail: enrollment.services@utmb.edu • **CEEB Code:** 6887
Fax: 409-772-4466 • **Website:** www.utmb.edu

This public school was founded in 1891. It has a 85-acre campus.

RATINGS

Admissions Selectivity Rating: 60*   **Fire Safety Rating:** 60*

STUDENTS AND FACULTY

Enrollment: 492. **Student Body:** 80% female, 20% male, 1% out-of-state, 2% international (34 countries represented). Asian 18%, African American 18%, Caucasian 42%, Hispanic 14%, Native American 1%
Faculty:

ACADEMICS

Degrees: bachelor's, master's, post-master's certificate. **Majors with Highest Enrollment:** Registered Nursing/Registered Nurse; Clinical Laboratory Science/Medical Technology/Technologist; Respiratory Care Therapy/Therapist. **Special Study Options:** distance learning, independent study, internships. **Combined degree programs:** MD/PhD. **Disability Services:** Special programs offered to physically disabled students include note-taking services, reader services, tape recorders, tutors. **Career services:** Alumni network, alumni services, internships.

FACILITIES

Housing: Coed dorms, fraternity/sorority housing, apartments for married students, apartments for single students. 100% of campus accessible to physically disabled. **Special Academic Facilities/Equipment:** Moody Medical Library. **Computers:** Students can register for classes online. Administrative functions (other than registration) can be performed online.

CAMPUS LIFE

Environment: Town. **Activities:** student government, student newspaper, yearbook. 94 registered organizations, 4 honor societies, 7 religious organizations. 5 fraternities. **On-Campus Highlights:** Joe Jamail Student Center, Rosenberg House, Ashbel Smith Building, Alumni Field House, Moody Medical Library.

ADMISSIONS

Freshman Academic Profile: Minimum paper TOEFL 550. **Transfer Admission Requirements:** college transcript(s), Minimum college GPA of 2.0 required. Lowest grade transferable C. **General Admission Information:** Neither credit nor placement offered for CEEB Advanced Placement tests.

COSTS AND FINANCIAL AID

Required Forms and Deadlines: FAFSA. **Types of Aid:** *Need-based scholarships/grants:* Federal Pell, SEOG, state scholarships/grants, private scholarships, the school's own gift aid. *Loans:* Direct Subsidized Stafford, Direct Unsubsidized Stafford, Direct PLUS, Federal Perkins, Federal Nursing, college/university loans from institutional funds. *Student Employment:* Federal Work-Study Program available. Institutional employment available. Off-campus job opportunities are good. **Criteria for awarding institutional aid:** *Non-need-based:* academics, minority status, state/district residency.

THE UNIVERSITY OF TEXAS—PAN AMERICAN

1201 West University Drive, Edinburg, TX 78539-2999
Phone: 956-665-2999 • **Financial Aid Phone:** 956-665-2501
E-mail: admissions@utpa.edu • **CEEB Code:** 6570
Fax: 956-665-2687 • **Website:** www.utpa.edu • **ACT Code:** 4142

This public school was founded in 1927. It has a 330-acre campus.

RATINGS

Admissions Selectivity Rating: 81   **Fire Safety Rating:** 71

STUDENTS AND FACULTY

Enrollment: 17,994. **Student Body:** 56% female, 44% male, 0% out-of-state, 2% international (25 countries represented). Asian 1%, African American 1%, Caucasian 3%, Hispanic 91%, Native American <1%
Retention and Graduation: 17% freshmen graduate within 4 years. 43% freshmen graduate within 6 years. **Faculty:** 708 full-time faculty, 77% hold PhDs, 40% are are members of minority groups, 52% are women.

ACADEMICS

Degrees: bachelor's, master's, post-bachelor's certificate. **Classes:** Most classes have 30-39 students. Most lab/discussion sessions have 20-29 students. **Majors with Highest Enrollment:** Multi-/Interdisciplinary Studies; Business Administration and Management; Biology/Biological Sciences. **Special Study Options:** Accelerated program, cooperative education program, distance learning, double major, dual enrollment, English as a Second Language (ESL), exchange student program (domestic), honors program, independent study, internships, study abroad, teacher certification program, weekend college. **Honors programs:** PRE-MEDICAL HONORS COLLEGE with Baylor College of Medicine. **Disability Services:** Special programs offered to physically disabled students include note-taking services, reader services, tape recorders, tutors. **Career services:** alumni services, career assessment, internships.

FACILITIES

Housing: Coed dorms, men's dorms, women's dorms, apartments for married students, apartments for single students. 100% of campus accessible to physically disabled. **Computers:** Students can register for classes online. Administrative functions (other than registration) can be performed online.

CAMPUS LIFE

Environment: Town. **Activities:** Choral groups, concert band, dance, drama/theater, jazz band, music ensembles, musical theater, pep band, student government, student newspaper, symphony orchestra, Campus Ministries, International Student Organization. 80 registered organizations, 9 honor societies, 7 religious organizations. 4 fraternities, 1 sorority. **Athletics (Intercollegiate):** *Men:* baseball, basketball, cross-country, golf, tennis, track/field (outdoor). *Women:* basketball, cross-country, golf, tennis, track/field (outdoor), volleyball. **On-Campus Highlights:** Visitors Center, Science Courtyard, Residence Halls, Student Union. **Environmental Initiatives:** The direction of disposal of hazardous waste streams toward recycling or reuse. The use of environmentally friendly (low water) landscaping materials The upgrade of lighting fixtures, energy management system components, and chiller systems for energy reduction and emissions friendlier to the environment.

ADMISSIONS

Freshman Academic Profile: 22% in top 10% of high school class, 53% in top 25% of high school class, 83% in top 50% of high school class. 99% from public high schools. SAT Math middle 50% range 440-540. SAT Critical Reading middle 50% range 420-520. SAT Writing middle 50% range 410-510. ACT middle 50% range 18-22. Minimum internet-based TOEFL 63. Minimum paper TOEFL 500. **Basis for Candidate Selection:** *Very important factors considered include:* standardized test scores. *Important factors considered* include: Class rank, academic GPA, rigor of secondary school record. **Freshman Admission Requirements:** High school diploma is required and GED is accepted. **Academic units required:** 4 English, 3 mathematics, 3 science, 2 foreign language. **Freshman Admission Statistics:** 10,679 applied, 63% admitted, 52% enrolled. **Transfer Admission Requirements:** college transcript(s), Minimum college GPA of 2.0 required. Lowest grade transferable D. **General Admission Information:** Regular application deadline 8/11. Nonfall registration accepted. Credit and/or placement offered for CEEB Advanced Placement tests.

COSTS AND FINANCIAL AID

Required Forms and Deadlines: FAFSA. **Notification of Awards:** Applicants will be notified of awards on or about 3/15. **Types of Aid:** *Need-based scholarships/grants:* Federal Pell, SEOG, state scholarships/grants, private scholarships, the school's own gift aid. *Loans:* Subsidized Stafford, Unsubsidized Stafford, PLUS, Federal Perkins, state loans. *Student Employment:* Federal Work-Study Program available. Institutional employment available. Off-campus job opportunities are good. **Financial Aid Statistics:** 98% freshmen, 95% undergrads receive need-based scholarship or grant aid. 1% freshmen, 1% undergrads receive non-need-based scholarship or grant aid. 26% freshmen, 48% undergrads receive need-based self-help aid. 1% freshmen, 1% undergrads receive athletic scholarships. 61% undergrads borrow to pay for school. Average cumulative indebtedness $14,700. **Criteria for awarding institutional aid:** *Non-need-based:* academics, alumni affiliation, art, athletics, leadership, music/drama.

THE UNIVERSITY OF TOLEDO

2801 West Bancroft, Toledo, OH 43606
Phone: 419-530-8700 · **Financial Aid Phone:** 419-530-8700
E-mail: enroll@utnet.utoledo.edu · **CEEB Code:** 1845
Fax: 419-530-5713 · **Website:** www.utoledo.edu · **ACT Code:** 3344

This public school was founded in 1872. It has a 400-acre campus.

RATINGS

Admissions Selectivity Rating: 77   **Fire Safety Rating:** 60*

STUDENTS AND FACULTY

Enrollment: 15,288. **Student Body:** 49% female, 51% male, 8% out-of-state, 1% international (108 countries represented). Asian 2%, African American 13%, Caucasian 76%, Hispanic 3%, Native American <1%
Retention and Graduation: 69% freshmen return for sophomore year. 17% freshmen graduate within 4 years. 43% freshmen graduate within 6 years. **Faculty:** 813 full-time faculty, 73% hold PhDs, 35% are are members of minority groups, 17% are women.

ACADEMICS

Degrees: associate, bachelor's, certificate, first professional, master's, post-bachelor's certificate, post-master's certificate. **Majors with Highest Enrollment:** Education; Engineering; Marketing/Marketing Management. **Special Study Options:** Accelerated program, cooperative education program, cross-registration, distance learning, double major, dual enrollment, exchange student program (domestic), honors program, independent study, internships, liberal arts/career combination, student-designed major, study abroad, teacher certification program, weekend college. **Disability Services:** Special programs offered to physically disabled students include note-taking services, reader services, tutors.

FACILITIES

Housing: Coed dorms, special housing for disabled students, men's dorms, special housing for international students, women's dorms, fraternity/sorority housing. 95% of campus accessible to physically disabled. **Special Academic Facilities/Equipment:** Language lab, arboretum, planetariums, two observatories, electron microscope. **Computers:** Students can register for classes online.

CAMPUS LIFE

Environment: City. **Activities:** Choral groups, concert band, dance, drama/theater, jazz band, literary magazine, marching band, music ensembles, musical theater, opera, pep band, radio station, student government, student newspaper, student-run film society, symphony orchestra, television station. 200 registered organizations, 14 fraternities, 13 sororities. **Athletics (Intercollegiate):** *Men:* baseball, basketball, cheerleading, cross-country, diving, football, golf, lacrosse, softball, swimming, tennis, track/field (outdoor), track/field (indoor), volleyball. *Women:* basketball, cheerleading, cross-country, diving, golf, lacrosse, softball, swimming, tennis, track/field (outdoor), track/field (indoor), volleyball.

ADMISSIONS

Freshman Academic Profile: Average high school GPA 3.08. 16% in top 10% of high school class, 37% in top 25% of high school class, 64% in top

50% of high school class. SAT Math middle 50% range 460-600. SAT Critical Reading middle 50% range 450-570. ACT middle 50% range 19-25. Minimum paper TOEFL 500. **Basis for Candidate Selection:** *Very important factors considered include:* rigor of secondary school record, standardized test scores, state residency. **Freshman Admission Requirements:** High school diploma is required and GED is accepted. **Academic units required:** 4 English, 3 mathematics, 3 science, 3 social studies. **Freshman Admission Statistics:** 8,126 applied, 80% admitted, 49% enrolled. **Transfer Admission Requirements:** college transcript(s), statement of good standing from prior institution(s). Minimum college GPA of 2.0 required. Lowest grade transferable C. **General Admission Information:** Application Fee $40. Notification on a rolling basis, beginning on or about 10/1. Nonfall registration accepted. Admission may be deferred for a maximum of 12 months. Credit and/or placement offered for CEEB Advanced Placement tests.

COSTS AND FINANCIAL AID

Average book expense $690. **Required Forms and Deadlines:** FAFSA. **Notification of Awards:** Applicants will be notified of awards on a rolling basis beginning 4/1. **Types of Aid:** *Need-based scholarships/grants:* Federal Pell, SEOG, state scholarships/grants, private scholarships, the school's own gift aid. *Loans:* Direct Subsidized Stafford, Direct Unsubsidized Stafford, Direct PLUS, Federal Perkins, state loans. *Student Employment:* Federal Work-Study Program available. **Financial Aid Statistics:** 70% freshmen, 70% undergrads receive need-based scholarship or grant aid. 21% freshmen, 25% undergrads receive non-need-based scholarship or grant aid. 77% freshmen, 81% undergrads receive need-based self-help aid. 55% undergrads receive any aid. 65% undergrads borrow to pay for school. **Criteria for awarding institutional aid:** *Non-need-based:* academics, art, athletics, minority status, music/drama, state/district residency.

UNIVERSITY OF TORONTO

Best 380

172 St. George Street, Toronto, ON M5R 0A3
Phone: 416-978-2190
E-mail: admissions.help@utoronto.ca · **CEEB Code:** 982
Fax: 416-978-7022 · **Website:** www.utoronto.ca

This public school was founded in 1827. It has a 1767-acre campus.

RATINGS

Admissions Selectivity Rating: 61   **Fire Safety Rating:** 71

STUDENTS AND FACULTY

Enrollment: 64,962. **Student Body:** 56% female, 44% male, 81% out-of-state, 3% international (166 countries represented). Asian 0%, African American 0%, Caucasian 0%, Hispanic 0%, Native American <1%
Retention and Graduation: 82% freshmen graduate within 6 years. **Faculty:** 5,381 full-time faculty.

ACADEMICS

Degrees: bachelor's, certificate, diploma, master's. **Special Study Options:** cooperative education program, double major, English as a Second Language (ESL), exchange student program (domestic), honors program, internships, study abroad, teacher certification program. **Combined degree programs:** JD/MBA, JD/MA, JD/PhD/, JD/MISt, JD/MSW. **Disability Services:** Special programs offered to physically disabled students include note-taking services, reader services, tape recorders, tutors. **Career services:** career/job search classes.

FACILITIES

Housing: Coed dorms, men's dorms, women's dorms, apartments for married students, cooperative housing. **Computers:** Students can register for classes online. Administrative functions (other than registration) can be performed online.

CAMPUS LIFE

Environment: Metropolis. **Activities:** Choral groups, concert band, dance, drama/theater, jazz band, literary magazine, music ensembles, opera, radio station, student government, student newspaper, student-run film society, symphony orchestra. 200 registered organizations, 49 religious organizations. **Athletics (Intercollegiate):** *Men:* badminton, baseball, basketball, crew/rowing, cross-country, curling, fencing, football, golf, ice hockey, lacrosse, mountain biking, rugby, skiing (nordic/cross-country), soccer, squash, swimming, tennis, track/field (outdoor), track/field (indoor), volleyball, water polo, wrestling.

Women: badminton, basketball, crew/rowing, cross-country, curling, fencing, field hockey, ice hockey, lacrosse, mountain biking, rugby, skiing (nordic/cross-country), soccer, squash, swimming, tennis, track/field (outdoor), track/field (indoor), volleyball, water polo, wrestling. **On-Campus Highlights:** Hart House, The Athletic Centre, Justine Barnike Gallery, Thomas Fisher Rare Book Library, Convocation Hall.

ADMISSIONS

Freshman Academic Profile: Minimum paper TOEFL 600. **Basis for Candidate Selection:** *Very important factors considered include:* academic GPA, standardized test scores. **Freshman Admission Requirements:** High school diploma is required and GED is accepted. **Freshman Admission Statistics:** 67,955 applied, 69% admitted, 18% enrolled. **Transfer Admission Requirements:** High school transcript, college transcript(s), standardized test scores. **General Admission Information:** Application Fee $80. Regular application deadline 3/1. Notification on a rolling basis, beginning on or about 3/15. Nonfall registration not accepted.

THE UNIVERSITY OF TULSA

Best 380

800 South Tucker Drive, Tulsa, OK 74104
Phone: 918-631-2307 • **Financial Aid Phone:** 918-631-2526
E-mail: admission@utulsa.edu • **CEEB Code:** 6883
Fax: 918-631-5003 • **Website:** www.utulsa.edu • **ACT Code:** 3444

This private school, affiliated with the Presbyterian Church, was founded in 1894. It has a 209-acre campus.

RATINGS

Admissions Selectivity Rating: 95   **Fire Safety Rating:** 92

STUDENTS AND FACULTY

Enrollment: 3,441. **Student Body:** 42% female, 58% male, 45% out-of-state, 27% international (56 countries represented). Asian 3%, African American 4%, Caucasian 55%, Hispanic 4%, Native American 4%
Retention and Graduation: 89% freshmen return for sophomore year. 52% freshmen graduate within 4 years. 70% freshmen graduate within 6 years. 33% grads go on to further study within 1 year. 28% grads pursue arts and sciences degrees. 18% grads pursue law degrees. 18% grads pursue business degrees. 9% grads pursue medical degrees. **Faculty:** 343 full-time faculty, 97% hold PhDs, 32% are are members of minority groups, 17% are women. 4% of classes are taught by teaching assistants.

ACADEMICS

Degrees: bachelor's, master's, post-bachelor's certificate. **Classes:** Most classes have 10-19 students. Most lab/discussion sessions have 10-19 students. **Majors with Highest Enrollment:** Petroleum Engineering; Psychology; Finance. **Special Study Options:** Accelerated program, double major, English as a Second Language (ESL), honors program, independent study, internships, liberal arts/career combination, student-designed major, study abroad, teacher certification program. **Honors programs:** The Honors Program is a four-year course of study consisting of 21 hours of academic credit. In small classes and individual tutorials, students pursue a critical examination of the moral and political commitments, scientific achievments, and artistic sensibilities that have shaped the modern world. The program culminates in the senior year with students designing and executing individual research projects. The Tulsa Undergraduate Research Challenge (TURC) is an innovative program that enables undergraduates to take challenging courses and conduct advanced research with the guidance of top professors. Its aim is to create leaders in scholarship, research, and public life. The centerpiece of the program is research; the goal of such research may be to deliver papers at academic conferences, to produce publishable articles, or to initiate meaningful community projects. **Combined degree programs:** BA/JD, Bachelor's and MBA. **Disability Services:** Special programs offered to physically disabled students include note-taking services, reader services, tape recorders, tutors. **Career services:** Alumni network, alumni services, career/job search classes, career assessment, internships, regional alumni. Career services highlights include internships that provide students with the opportunity to supplement classroom training with real-world experience in a position related to their major or career goals. Students may be paid or may receive academic credit or a combination of pay and credit.

FACILITIES

Housing: Coed dorms, special housing for disabled students, men's dorms, women's dorms, fraternity/sorority housing, apartments for married students,

apartments for single students, Honors House. 80% of campus accessible to physically disabled. **Special Academic Facilities/Equipment:** Alexandre Hogue Art Gallery, Biotechnology Institute, Center for Communicative Disorders, Charge-Coupled Camera Microscope, Donald W. Reynolds Center (site of a state-of-the-art athletic training program), Education Technology Lab, Electron Microscopes, Kendall Theatre, McFarlin Library Special Collections (focus on American, British, and Irish Literature of the late 19th and early 20th centuries, and on Native American History and Law), Multimedia "boardroom" style classrooms (3), ONEOK Multimedia Auditorium, Sadie Adwan Communication Lab, Sidney Born Technical Library (contains an outstanding collection concerning energy, most notably petroleum), Sun Computer Work Stations, World's largest research flow-loop in Petroleum Engr. **Computers:** 100% of classrooms, 100% of dorms, 100% of libraries, 100% of dining areas, 100% of student union, 100% of common outdoor areas have wireless network access. Students can register for classes online. Administrative functions (other than registration) can be performed online.

CAMPUS LIFE

Environment: Metropolis. **Activities:** Choral groups, concert band, dance, drama/theater, jazz band, literary magazine, marching band, music ensembles, musical theater, opera, pep band, radio station, student government, student newspaper, symphony orchestra, television station, yearbook, Campus Ministries, International Student Organization, Model UN. 245 registered organizations, 40 honor societies, 21 religious organizations. 7 fraternities, 9 sororities. **Athletics (Intercollegiate):** *Men:* basketball, cheerleading, cross-country, football, golf, soccer, tennis, track/field (outdoor), track/field (indoor). *Women:* basketball, cheerleading, crew/rowing, cross-country, golf, soccer, softball, tennis, track/field (outdoor), track/field (indoor), volleyball. **On-Campus Highlights:** Collins Fitness Center, Reynolds Center, McFarlin Library, Allen Chapman Activity Center, Fraternity/Sorority Row, Collins College of Business, The College of Engineering and Natural Sciences, Chapman Hall—The College of Arts and Sciences, Phillips Hall—School of Art, Kendall Hall Theatre, Collins Hall—Visitors Center and Office of Admission, H.A. Chapman Stadium. **Environmental Initiatives:** All campus shuttles run on compressed natural gas; Paperless reduction efforts such as direct deposit, student tuition billing, enrollment, and the launching of our campus connection portal are some of the ways that TU promotes paper reduction within the institution; TU also maintains a full recycling program for all buildings including paper, cardboard, glass, plastic and aluminum and single stream recycling; Earth Day Week—trayless meals in dining halls, and distribution of recycling bags and totes to students and campus organizations.

ADMISSIONS

Freshman Academic Profile: Average high school GPA 3.9. 75% in top 10% of high school class, 92% in top 25% of high school class, 98% in top 50% of high school class. 73% from public high schools. SAT Math middle 50% range 570-700. SAT Critical Reading middle 50% range 560-710. ACT middle 50% range 26-32. Minimum internet-based TOEFL 80. Minimum paper TOEFL 550. **Basis for Candidate Selection:** *Very important factors considered include:* Class rank, academic GPA, rigor of secondary school record, standardized test scores, interview, level of applicant's interest. *Important factors considered include:* application essay, recommendation(s), character/personal qualities, extracurricular activities, talent/ability. *Other factors considered include:* alumni/ae relation, first generation, racial/ethnic status, volunteer work, work experience. **Freshman Admission Requirements:** High school diploma is required and GED is accepted. **Freshman Admission Statistics:** 7,636 applied, 40% admitted, 25% enrolled. **Transfer Admission Requirements:** college transcript(s), essay or personal statement, statement of good standing from prior institution(s). Minimum college GPA of 2.5 required. Lowest grade transferable C. **General Admission Information:** Application Fee $35. Notification on a rolling basis, beginning on or about 10/1. Nonfall registration accepted. Admission may be deferred for a maximum of 1 year. Credit and/or placement offered for CEEB Advanced Placement tests.

COSTS AND FINANCIAL AID

Annual tuition $38,556. Room and board $10,680. Required fees $965. Average book expense $1,200. **Required Forms and Deadlines:** FAFSA. **Notification of Awards:** Applicants will be notified of awards on a rolling basis beginning 3/1. **Types of Aid:** *Need-based scholarships/grants:* Federal Pell, SEOG, state scholarships/grants, private scholarships, the school's own gift aid. *Loans:* Subsidized Stafford, Unsubsidized Stafford, PLUS, Federal Perkins. *Student Employment:* Federal Work-Study Program available. Institutional employment available. Highest amount earned per year from on-campus jobs $4,700. Off-campus job opportunities are good. **Financial Aid Statistics:** 30% freshmen, 36% undergrads receive need-based scholarship or grant aid. 95% freshmen, 89% undergrads receive non-need-based scholarship or grant aid. 64% freshmen, 54% undergrads receive need-based self-help aid. 12% freshmen, 10% undergrads receive athletic scholarships. 90% freshmen, 86% undergrads receive any aid. 49% undergrads borrow to pay for school. Average cumulative indebtedness $24,625. **Criteria for awarding institutional aid:** *Non-need-based:* academics, alumni affiliation, art, athletics, leadership, minority status, music/drama, religious affiliation.

See page 1200.

UNIVERSITY OF UTAH

Best 380

201 South 1460 East, Salt Lake City, UT 84112
Phone: 801-581-7281 • **Financial Aid Phone:** 801-581-6211
E-mail: admissions@sa.utah.edu • **CEEB Code:** 4853
Fax: 801-585-7864 • **Website:** www.utah.edu • **ACT Code:** 4274

This public school was founded in 1850. It has a 1535-acre campus.

RATINGS

Admissions Selectivity Rating: 83   **Fire Safety Rating:** 75

STUDENTS AND FACULTY

Enrollment: 23,795. **Student Body:** 45% female, 55% male, 20% out-of-state, 6% international (120 countries represented). Asian 5%, African American 1%, Caucasian 68%, Hispanic 10%, Native American <1%
Retention and Graduation: 89% freshmen return for sophomore year. 24% freshmen graduate within 4 years. 62% freshmen graduate within 6 years. **Faculty:** 1,416 full-time faculty, 87% hold PhDs, 38% are are members of minority groups, 15% are women. 28.2% of classes are taught by teaching assistants.

ACADEMICS

Degrees: bachelor's, doctoral, master's, post-bachelor's certificate, post-master's certificate. **Classes:** Most classes have 20-29 students. Most lab/discussion sessions have 10-19 students. **Majors with Highest Enrollment:** Psychology; Economics. **Special Study Options:** Accelerated program, cooperative education program, cross-registration, distance learning, double major, dual enrollment, English as a Second Language (ESL), exchange student program (domestic), honors program, independent study, internships, liberal arts/career combination, student-designed major, study abroad, teacher certification program. **Honors programs:** The Honors Program promotes an enriched academic environment for talented and highly motivated students. We foster values of social responsibility, inclusiveness and academic quality—in short a community of excellence. The Honors Program provides talented students with an enhanced undergraduate experience through a number of opportunities. Honors students typically enroll in one or two Honors classes each semester during their first two years. This will put students in contact with other students who set high goals for themselves, like to be challenged and are highly motivated. Rather than the large auditorium classes so many freshmen or sophomore students take, honors classes will be small and students will get to know their professors well. Students will have personal, intense advising at key moments in the next four years that will help them plan for graduation with the Honors degree at each step along the way. **Combined degree programs:** BA/MEng, Neuroscience MD/Phd. **Disability Services:** Special programs offered to physically disabled students include note-taking services, reader services, tape recorders, tutors. **Career services:** Alumni network, alumni services, career/job search classes, career assessment, internships.

FACILITIES

Housing: Coed dorms, special housing for disabled students, special housing for international students, fraternity/sorority housing, apartments for married students, Theme Housing, Limited Visitation, 24-hour Quiet, First Year Students only. 100% of campus accessible to physically disabled. **Special Academic Facilities/Equipment:** Museums of natural history and fine arts, government institute, environmental biological research facilities, human genetics lab. **Computers:** 100% of classrooms, 100% of dorms, 100% of libraries, 100% of dining areas, 100% of student union, 60% of common outdoor areas have wireless network access. Students can register for classes online. Administrative functions (other than registration) can be performed online.

CAMPUS LIFE

Environment: Metropolis. **Activities:** Choral groups, concert band, dance, drama/theater, jazz band, literary magazine, marching band, music ensembles, musical theater, opera, pep band, radio station, student government, student newspaper, student-run film society, symphony orchestra, television station, Campus Ministries, International Student Organization, Model UN. 238 registered organizations, 41 honor societies, 9 religious organizations. 7 fraternities, 6 sororities. **Athletics (Intercollegiate):** *Men:* baseball, basketball, cheerleading, diving, football, golf, skiing (downhill/alpine), skiing (nordic/cross-country), swimming, tennis. *Women:* basketball, cheerleading, cross-country, diving, gymnastics, skiing (downhill/alpine), skiing (nordic/cross-country), soccer, softball, swimming, tennis, track/field (outdoor), track/field (indoor), volleyball. **On-Campus Highlights:** Rice Eccles Stadium, Jon M. Huntsman Center, Huntsman Cancer Institute, Utah Museum of Fine Arts, Utah Museum of Natural History, Marriott Library Red Butte Gardens Olympic Cauldron Park

Fort Douglas Museum and Cemetery Kingsbury Hall/Gardner Hall. **Environmental Initiatives:** Transportation: Free public transportation (Ed-Pass) for all students, staff and faculty; gas-electric hybrid, biodiesel, and natural gas-powered campus vehicles. Energy Initiatives: Offset more than 10% of our electricity consumption with windpower purchases; new co-generation plant under construction will cut outside energy purchases by another 10%, ongoing building retrofits for lighting, HVAC, and other efficiency gains. Student Involvement: campus as a sustainability learning lab for courses; numerous on-campus green groups; environmental service opportunities with Bennion Community Service Center, student internships available through the Office of Sustainability, and also the greater community through Environmental Studies and Masters in Science and Technology programs.

ADMISSIONS

Freshman Academic Profile: Average high school GPA 3.57. 22% in top 10% of high school class, 49% in top 25% of high school class, 82% in top 50% of high school class. 91% from public high schools. SAT Math middle 50% range 520-650. SAT Critical Reading middle 50% range 500-640. SAT Writing middle 50% range 490-610. ACT middle 50% range 21-28. Minimum internet-based TOEFL 80. Minimum paper TOEFL 550. **Basis for Candidate Selection:** *Very important factors considered include:* academic GPA, rigor of secondary school record, standardized test scores. *Important factors considered include:* talent/ability. *Other factors considered include:* Class rank, recommendation(s), extracurricular activities, interview, racial/ethnic status. **Freshman Admission Requirements:** High school diploma is required and GED is accepted. **Academic units required:** 4 English, 2 mathematics, 3 science, (1 science labs), 2 foreign language, 1 history, 4 academic electives. **Freshman Admission Statistics:** 10,991 applied, 81% admitted, 35% enrolled. **Transfer Admission Requirements:** college transcript(s), statement of good standing from prior institution(s). Minimum college GPA of 2.6 required. Lowest grade transferable D-. **General Admission Information:** Application Fee $45. Regular application deadline 4/1. Nonfall registration accepted. Credit and/or placement offered for CEEB Advanced Placement tests.

COSTS AND FINANCIAL AID

Annual out-of-state tuition $24,261. Room and board $8,528. Required fees $1,006. Average book expense $1,280. **Required Forms and Deadlines:** FAFSA, Institution's own financial aid form. **Notification of Awards:** Applicants will be notified of awards on a rolling basis beginning 4/15. **Types of Aid:** *Need-based scholarships/grants:* Federal Pell, SEOG, state scholarships/grants, private scholarships, the school's own gift aid, Federal Nursing Scholarships, ACG, National SMART Grant, and TEACH Grant. *Loans:* Subsidized Stafford, Unsubsidized Stafford, PLUS, Federal Perkins, Federal Nursing, college/university loans from institutional funds, Private Alternative Loans. *Student Employment:* Federal Work-Study Program available. Institutional employment available. Highest amount earned per year from on-campus jobs $8,800. Off-campus job opportunities are excellent. **Financial Aid Statistics:** 86% freshmen, 83% undergrads receive need-based scholarship or grant aid. 10% freshmen, 4% undergrads receive non-need-based scholarship or grant aid. 85% freshmen, 94% undergrads receive need-based self-help aid. 2% freshmen, 1% undergrads receive athletic scholarships. 62% freshmen, 61% undergrads receive any aid. 39% undergrads borrow to pay for school. Average cumulative indebtedness $19,112. **Criteria for awarding institutional aid:** *Non-need-based:* academics, alumni affiliation, art, athletics, leadership, minority status, music/drama, state/district residency.

THE UNIVERSITY OF VERMONT

Best 380

University of Vermont Admissions, Burlington, VT 05401-3596
Phone: 802-656-3370 • **Financial Aid Phone:** 802-656-5700
E-mail: admissions@uvm.edu • **CEEB Code:** 3920
Fax: 802-656-8611 • **Website:** www.uvm.edu • **ACT Code:** 4322

This public school was founded in 1791. It has a 460-acre campus.

RATINGS

Admissions Selectivity Rating: 87   **Fire Safety Rating:** 95

STUDENTS AND FACULTY

Enrollment: 9,958. **Student Body:** 55% female, 45% male, 69% out-of-state, 3% international (40 countries represented). Asian 2%, African American 1%, Caucasian 83%, Hispanic 4%, Native American <1%

Retention and Graduation: 67% freshmen graduate within 4 years. 24% grads go on to further study within 1 year. 6% grads pursue arts and sciences degrees. 2% grads pursue law degrees. 1% grads pursue business degrees. 1% grads pursue medical degrees. **Faculty:** 608 full-time faculty, 88% hold PhDs, 47% are are members of minority groups, 16% are women. 2% of classes are taught by teaching assistants.

ACADEMICS

Degrees: bachelor's, master's, post-bachelor's certificate, post-master's certificate. **Classes:** Most classes have fewer than 10 students. Most lab/discussion sessions have 20-29 students. **Majors with Highest Enrollment:** Business Administration and Management; Psychology; Biology/Biological Sciences. **Special Study Options:** cooperative education program, distance learning, double major, dual enrollment, exchange student program (domestic), honors program, independent study, internships, liberal arts/career combination, student-designed major, study abroad, teacher certification program, Evening University option in several programs. **Honors programs:** University wide Honors College, a residential learning community where students live together and take classes in one of UVM's newest residence halls. Honors College students are simultaneously enrolled in one of seven other UVM undergraduate colleges or schools. Honors College courses comprise approximately 20% of a students overall coursework and include a year-long common first year seminar, a choice of a variety of sophomore seminars, a junior year thesis prep course, and a senior year thesis, creative project or practicum. Upon graduation program completers are designated as Honors College Scholars. **Combined degree programs:** BA/JD, BS/DVM with Tufts University, BA/BS-DPT. **Disability Services:** Special programs offered to physically disabled students include note-taking services, reader services, tape recorders, tutors. **Career services:** alumni services, career assessment, internships. Career services highlights include Dollar Enterprise, an award winning service learning activity in which students are provided with $1 of working capital and develop and run a campus based entrepreneurial activity for one week. The activity is done for one week. All profits are donated to a charity of the group's choice.

FACILITIES

Housing: Coed dorms, fraternity/sorority housing, apartments for married students, apartments for single students, Wellness Housing, Theme Housing. 90% of campus accessible to physically disabled. **Special Academic Facilities/Equipment:** Art/ethnography museum, chemistry/physics library, medical library, on-campus preschool, government research and world affairs centers, agricultural experiment station, horse farm, multinuclear magnetic resonance spectrometers, mass spectrometer. **Computers:** 10% of classrooms, 15% of dorms, 100% of libraries, 100% of dining areas, 100% of student union, 5% of common outdoor areas have wireless network access. Students can register for classes online. Administrative functions (other than registration) can be performed online.

CAMPUS LIFE

Environment: Town. **Activities:** Choral groups, concert band, dance, drama/theater, jazz band, literary magazine, music ensembles, musical theater, pep band, radio station, student government, student newspaper, student-run film society, symphony orchestra, television station, Campus Ministries, International Student Organization. 140 registered organizations, 30 honor societies, 10 religious organizations. 9 fraternities, 6 sororities. **Athletics (Intercollegiate):** *Men:* basketball, cross-country, ice hockey, lacrosse, skiing (downhill/alpine), skiing (nordic/cross-country), soccer, track/field (outdoor), track/field (indoor). *Women:* basketball, cross-country, diving, field hockey, ice hockey, lacrosse, skiing (downhill/alpine), skiing (nordic/cross-country), soccer, swimming, track/field (outdoor), track/field (indoor). **On-Campus Highlights:** Davis Student Center, Fleming Museum, Campus Green, Athletic Complex/Fitness Center, Spear Street Research Farm and Equine Center. **Environmental Initiatives:** Reporting jointly to the Provost and the VP of Finance & Administration, the Office of Sustainability supports the infusion of sustainability into operations, student life, curriculum, and communications, managing University commitments for energy, food, and sustainability education Eco-Reps Program provides peer education in residence halls, supports campus-wide events, develops student leaders, and connects them with key administrative, faculty, and community leaders Climate Action Plan goals for climate neutral electricity by 2015, thermal energy by 2020, all other emissions by 2025. Related activities: LEED Silver minimum for new buildings: Clean Energy Fund for renewable energy research and education; $13M Energy Revolving Fund continues energy efficiency investments that have yielded millions of dollars in avoided costs.

ADMISSIONS

Freshman Academic Profile: Average high school GPA 3.49. 29% in top 10% of high school class, 68% in top 25% of high school class, 94% in top 50% of high school class. 70% from public high schools. SAT Math middle 50% range 540-650. SAT Critical Reading middle 50% range 540-640. SAT Writing middle 50% range 540-640. ACT middle 50% range 24-29. Minimum internet-based TOEFL 79. Minimum paper TOEFL 550. **Basis for Candidate Selection:** *Very important factors considered include:* rigor of secondary school record. *Important factors considered include:* Class rank, application essay, academic GPA,

standardized test scores, character/personal qualities, state residency. *Other factors considered include:* recommendation(s), alumni/ae relation, extracurricular activities, first generation, geographical residence, interview, level of applicant's interest, racial/ethnic status, talent/ability, volunteer work, work experience. **Freshman Admission Requirements:** High school diploma is required and GED is accepted. **Academic units required:** 4 English, 3 mathematics, 2 science, (1 science labs), 2 foreign language, 3 social studies. **Freshman Admission Statistics:** 24,051 applied, 74% admitted, 13% enrolled. **Transfer Admission Requirements:** High school transcript, college transcript(s), essay or personal statement, Minimum college GPA of 2.5 required. Lowest grade transferable C. **General Admission Information:** Application Fee $45. Regular application deadline 1/15. Regular notification 3/31. Nonfall registration accepted. Admission may be deferred for a maximum of 12 months. Credit and/or placement offered for CEEB Advanced Placement tests.

COSTS AND FINANCIAL AID

Annual in-state tuition $14,184. Annual out-of-state tuition $35,832. Room and board $10,780. Required fees $2,042. Average book expense $1,200. **Required Forms and Deadlines:** FAFSA. **Notification of Awards:** Applicants will be notified of awards on a rolling basis beginning 3/15. **Types of Aid:** *Need-based scholarships/grants:* Federal Pell, SEOG, state scholarships/grants, private scholarships, the school's own gift aid, Federal Nursing Scholarships. *Loans:* Subsidized Stafford, Unsubsidized Stafford, PLUS, Federal Perkins, Federal Nursing, college/university loans from institutional funds. *Student Employment:* Federal Work-Study Program available. Institutional employment available. Off-campus job opportunities are good. **Financial Aid Statistics:** 97% freshmen, 97% undergrads receive need-based scholarship or grant aid. 12% freshmen, 8% undergrads receive non-need-based scholarship or grant aid. 71% freshmen, 74% undergrads receive need-based self-help aid. 2% freshmen, 2% undergrads receive athletic scholarships. 93% freshmen, 83% undergrads receive any aid. 63% undergrads borrow to pay for school. Average cumulative indebtedness $21,821. **Criteria for awarding institutional aid:** *Non-need-based:* academics, art, athletics.

UNIVERSITY OF VIRGINIA

Office of Admission, Charlottesville, VA 22906
Phone: 434-982-3200 · **Financial Aid Phone:** 434-924-4241
E-mail: undergradadmission@virginia.edu · **CEEB Code:** 5820
Fax: 434-924-3587 · **Website:** www.virginia.edu · **ACT Code:** 4412

This public school was founded in 1819. It has a 1167-acre campus.

RATINGS

Admissions Selectivity Rating: 97   **Fire Safety Rating:** 80

STUDENTS AND FACULTY

Enrollment: 15,430. **Student Body:** 55% female, 45% male, 28% out-of-state, 5% international (121 countries represented). Asian 12%, African American 6%, Caucasian 61%, Hispanic 6%, Native American <1%
Retention and Graduation: 87% freshmen graduate within 4 years. 94% freshmen graduate within 6 years. **Faculty:** 1,332 full-time faculty, 91% hold PhDs, 36% are are members of minority groups, 15% are women. 7.5% of classes are taught by teaching assistants.

ACADEMICS

Degrees: bachelor's, master's, post-master's certificate. **Classes:** Most classes have 10-19 students. Most lab/discussion sessions have 20-29 students. **Majors with Highest Enrollment:** Business/Commerce; Psychology; Economics. **Special Study Options:** Accelerated program, cooperative education program, double major, English as a Second Language (ESL), exchange student program (domestic), honors program, independent study, internships, liberal arts/career combination, student-designed major, study abroad, teacher certification program, Special January term (during Winter Break) where students can take one course. Semester at Sea option of spending an academic semester on board a ship travelling to multiple countries. **Honors programs:** Jefferson Scholars: Full scholarship given to approximately 30 students per year. Special lectures and discussions with distinguished University faculty; all first year Jefferson Scholars take part in an outdoor leadership experience; all rising-second year Jefferson Scholars, prior to the beginning of school, participate in a two-week Institute for Leadership and Citizenship designed to foster a deeper understanding of the art of leadership and the importance of citizenship. Additionally, all Jefferson Scholars are granted an opportunity to travel and study abroad between their second and third year. Scholars may elect to spend three weeks of study at either Regent's College in England or the Erasmus Institute in Tuscany, Italy. Following the structured tutorial, each Scholar designs and completes two weeks of travel and independent inquiry. Echols Scholars-School of Arts and Sciences. Separate dormitory, with Rodman Scholars, for first-year students. Flexible degree requirements; exemption from some requirements; preference for courses. Rodman Scholars-School of Engineering and Applied Sciences. Separate dormitory, with Echols Scholars, for first-year students. Special courses designed only for Rodman Scholars in first two years. **Combined degree programs:** 5-year B.A./M.Teaching. **Disability Services:** Special programs offered to physically disabled students include note-taking services, reader services, tape recorders, tutors. **Career services:** Alumni network, alumni services, career/job search classes, career assessment, internships, regional alumni. Career services highlights include our on-grounds interviewing programming which is, for our size school, an exceedingly robust program (7,000 to 10,000 individual student interviews per year; and most of the top tier organizations you'd find listed in the Fortune 100), with student interviews very often evenly distributed among the College, Commerce, and SEAS (Engineering School). We are equally proud of the dramatic growth and popularity of our internship programs among our students—not only corporate internships, but also non-profit/public policy/community service internships, an initiative you rarely find on a large public university campus.

FACILITIES
Housing: Coed dorms, special housing for international students, fraternity/sorority housing, apartments for married students, apartments for single students, Theme Housing, French, German, Spanish and Russian houses, a multi-lingual house, and three residential colleges. 100% of campus accessible to physically disabled. **Special Academic Facilities/Equipment:** 15 libraries, art museum, experimental farm, biological station, observatory/planetarium, nuclear information center, media center (multimedia editing). **Computers:** 100% of classrooms, 100% of dorms, 100% of libraries, 100% of dining areas, 100% of student union, 26-50% of common outdoor areas have wireless network access. Students can register for classes online. Administrative functions (other than registration) can be performed online.

CAMPUS LIFE
Environment: City. **Activities:** Choral groups, concert band, dance, drama/theater, jazz band, literary magazine, marching band, music ensembles, musical theater, opera, pep band, radio station, student government, student newspaper, student-run film society, symphony orchestra, television station, Campus Ministries, International Student Organization, Model UN. 7 honor societies, 44 religious organizations. 28 fraternities, 15 sororities. **Athletics (Intercollegiate):** *Men:* baseball, basketball, cross-country, diving, football, golf, lacrosse, soccer, swimming, tennis, track/field (outdoor), track/field (indoor), wrestling. *Women:* basketball, crew/rowing, cross-country, diving, field hockey, golf, lacrosse, soccer, softball, swimming, tennis, track/field (outdoor), track/field (indoor), volleyball. **On-Campus Highlights:** Rotunda/Academical Village (orig campus), Alderman and Clemons Libraries, John Paul Jones Arena, Football and Soccer Stadiums, Aquatic and Fitness Center, Location of the future "arts precinct;" new library housing original rare and early American manuscripts; Birdwood Golf Course; Observatory; Old Cabell Hall (music performances); Culbreth Theatre (drama); Newcomb Hall (student services building); University of Virginia Bookstore. **Environmental Initiatives:** Academics: The University of Virginia offers 70+ courses in 8 different schools with significant focus on sustainability, including a global sustainability course, a new course model cross listed and taught jointly by faculty from Engineering, Architecture, and Commerce. In Spring 2011, the University created the interdisciplinary Global Sustainability minor. Sustainable Design and Construction: The Universitys policy to achieve LEED certification on all new buildings and major renovations has led to 30 projects registered with the US Green Building Council, with 10 of these complete and certified (3 Gold, 4 Silver, 3 Certified). Ongoing efficiency and conservation efforts, including: award winning recycling and stormwater management program, extensive building retro-commissioning team, Environmental Management System implementation across multiple departments, and Green Dining that include composting, reusable to-go containers, and local farm relationships.

ADMISSIONS
Freshman Academic Profile: Average high school GPA 4.23. 89% in top 10% of high school class, 98% in top 25% of high school class, 99% in top 50% of high school class. 72% from public high schools. SAT Math middle 50% range 630-740. SAT Critical Reading middle 50% range 620-720. SAT Writing middle 50% range 620-720. ACT middle 50% range 28-33. **Basis for Candidate Selection:** *Very important factors considered include:* Class rank, academic GPA, recommendation(s), rigor of secondary school record, alumni/ae relation, first generation, racial/ethnic status, state residency. *Important factors considered include:* application essay, standardized test scores, character/personal qualities, extracurricular activities, talent/ability. *Other factors considered include:* geographical residence, volunteer work, work experience. **Freshman Admis-**

sion Requirements: High school diploma is required and GED is accepted. **Academic units required:** 4 English, 4 mathematics, 2 science, 2 foreign language, 1 social studies. **Freshman Admission Statistics:** 31,021 applied, 29% admitted, 41% enrolled. **Transfer Admission Requirements:** High school transcript, college transcript(s), essay or personal statement, standardized test scores, statement of good standing from prior institution(s). Minimum college GPA of 2.0 required. Lowest grade transferable C. **General Admission Information:** Application Fee $60. Regular application deadline 1/1. Regular notification 4/1. Nonfall registration not accepted. Admission may be deferred for a maximum of 1 year. Credit and/or placement offered for CEEB Advanced Placement tests.

COSTS AND FINANCIAL AID
Annual in-state tuition $10,484. Annual out-of-state tuition $38,988. Room and board $9,717. Required fees $2,724. Average book expense $1,260. **Required Forms and Deadlines:** FAFSA, CSS/Financial Aid PROFILE. **Notification of Awards:** Applicants will be notified of awards on or about 4/5. **Types of Aid:** *Need-based scholarships/grants:* Federal Pell, SEOG, state scholarships/grants, private scholarships, the school's own gift aid, Federal Nursing Scholarships. *Loans:* Subsidized Stafford, Unsubsidized Stafford, PLUS, Federal Perkins, Federal Nursing, college/university loans from institutional funds, Alternative/Private Loans. *Student Employment:* Federal Work-Study Program available. Institutional employment available. **Financial Aid Statistics:** 82% freshmen, 81% undergrads receive need-based scholarship or grant aid. 10% freshmen, 7% undergrads receive non-need-based scholarship or grant aid. 65% freshmen, 63% undergrads receive need-based self-help aid. 3% freshmen, 3% undergrads receive athletic scholarships. 56% freshmen, 51% undergrads receive any aid. 36% undergrads borrow to pay for school. Average cumulative indebtedness $20,029. **Criteria for awarding institutional aid:** *Non-need-based:* academics, athletics, leadership, minority status, music/drama, state/district residency.

UNIVERSITY OF VIRGINIA'S COLLEGE AT WISE

1 College Avenue, Wise, VA 24293
Phone: 276-328-0102
E-mail: admissions@uvawise.edu • **CEEB Code:** 5124
Fax: 276-328-0251 • **Website:** www.uvawise.edu • **ACT Code:** 4343

This public school was founded in 1954. It has a 367-acre campus.

RATINGS
Admissions Selectivity Rating: 76   **Fire Safety Rating:** 60*

STUDENTS AND FACULTY
Enrollment: 1,629. **Student Body:** 52% female, 48% male, 5% out-of-state, 0% international. Asian 1%, African American 7%, Caucasian 90%, Hispanic 2%, Native American <1%
Retention and Graduation: 73% freshmen return for sophomore year. 25% freshmen graduate within 4 years. 44% freshmen graduate within 6 years. 14% grads go on to further study within 1 year. 7% grads pursue arts and sciences degrees. 6% grads pursue law degrees. 4% grads pursue business degrees. 1% grads pursue medical degrees. **Faculty:** 91 full-time faculty, 29% hold PhDs, 41% are are members of minority groups, 13% are women. 0% of classes are taught by teaching assistants.

ACADEMICS
Degrees: bachelor's. **Classes:** Most classes have 10-19 students. Most lab/discussion sessions have 10-19 students. **Special Study Options:** Accelerated program, cooperative education program, distance learning, double major, dual enrollment, honors program, independent study, internships, student-designed major, study abroad, teacher certification program. **Disability Services:** Special programs offered to physically disabled students include note-taking services, reader services, tape recorders, tutors. **Career services:** alumni services, career/job search classes, career assessment, internships.

FACILITIES
Housing: Coed dorms, special housing for disabled students, men's dorms, women's dorms, apartments for single students. 95% of campus accessible to physically disabled. **Computers:** Administrative functions (other than registration) can be performed online.

CAMPUS LIFE
Environment: Rural. **Activities:** Choral groups, concert band, dance, drama/theater, literary magazine, music ensembles, musical theater, pep band, radio station, student government, student newspaper, television station, yearbook. 40 registered organizations. 3 honor societies, 3 religious organizations. 3 fraternities, 2 sororities. **Athletics (Intercollegiate):** *Men:* baseball, basketball, cross-country, football, golf, tennis, track/field (outdoor). *Women:* basketball, cross-country, softball, tennis, track/field (outdoor), volleyball.

ADMISSIONS

Freshman Academic Profile: Average high school GPA 3.3. 18% in top 10% of high school class, 40% in top 25% of high school class, 78% in top 50% of high school class. 99% from public high schools. SAT Math middle 50% range 430-530. SAT Critical Reading middle 50% range 420-530. ACT middle 50% range 16-21. Minimum paper TOEFL 550. **Basis for Candidate Selection:** *Very important factors considered include:* Class rank, rigor of secondary school record. *Important factors considered include:* standardized test scores, talent/ability. *Other factors considered include:* application essay, recommendation(s), character/personal qualities, extracurricular activities, interview, racial/ethnic status, volunteer work, work experience. **Freshman Admission Requirements:** High school diploma is required and GED is accepted. **Academic units required:** 4 English, 3 mathematics, 2 science, (2 science labs), 2 foreign language, 1 social studies, 1 history, 5 academic electives. **Freshman Admission Statistics:** 1,084 applied, 81% admitted, 45% enrolled. **Transfer Admission Requirements:** college transcript(s), Minimum college GPA of 2.3 required. Lowest grade transferable C-. **General Admission Information:** Application Fee $25. Regular application deadline 8/1. Notification on a rolling basis, beginning on or about 9/15. Nonfall registration accepted. Admission may be deferred for a maximum of 1 year. Credit and/or placement offered for CEEB Advanced Placement tests.

COSTS AND FINANCIAL AID

Required Forms and Deadlines: FAFSA. **Notification of Awards:** Applicants will be notified of awards on a rolling basis beginning 4/1. **Types of Aid:** *Need-based scholarships/grants:* Federal Pell, SEOG, state scholarships/grants, private scholarships, the school's own gift aid. *Loans:* Subsidized Stafford, Unsubsidized Stafford, PLUS, Federal Perkins, state loans, college/university loans from institutional funds. *Student Employment:* Federal Work-Study Program available. Institutional employment available. Highest amount earned per year from on-campus jobs $900. Off-campus job opportunities are fair. **Criteria for awarding institutional aid:** *Non-need-based:* academics, alumni affiliation, art, athletics, job skills, leadership, music/drama, state/district residency.

UNIVERSITY OF THE VIRGIN ISLANDS

2 John Brewers Bay, St. Thomas, VI 00802-9990
Phone: 340-693-1150
E-mail: admissions@uvi.edu · **CEEB Code:** 879
Fax: 340-693-1220 · **Website:** www.uvi.edu

This public school was founded in 1962.

RATINGS

Admissions Selectivity Rating: 70   **Fire Safety Rating:** 60*

STUDENTS AND FACULTY

Enrollment: 1,972. **Student Body:** 80% female, 20% male, 36% out-of-state, 7% international. Asian 1%, African American 71%, Caucasian 2%, Hispanic 3%, Native American <1%
Faculty: 99 full-time faculty, 68% hold PhDs, 44% are are members of minority groups, 53% are women.

ACADEMICS

Degrees: associate, master's. **Special Study Options:** cooperative education program, distance learning, dual enrollment, exchange student program (domestic), independent study, internships, teacher certification program.

FACILITIES

Housing: men's dorms, women's dorms. **Computers:** Administrative functions (other than registration) can be performed online.

CAMPUS LIFE

Environment: Village. **Activities:** Choral groups, concert band, dance, drama/theater, jazz band, music ensembles, student government, student newspaper, yearbook. 27 registered organizations, 2 honor societies, 2 religious organizations. 1 fraternity, 3 sororities. **Athletics (Intercollegiate):** *Men:* basketball, soccer, swimming, tennis, volleyball. *Women:* basketball, swimming, tennis, volleyball.

ADMISSIONS

Freshman Academic Profile: SAT Math middle 50% range 330-450. SAT Critical Reading middle 50% range 360-470. **Basis for Candidate Selection:** *Very important factors considered include:* rigor of secondary school record. *Other factors considered include:* standardized test scores, state residency. **Freshman Admission Requirements:** High school diploma is required and GED is accepted. **Freshman Admission Statistics:** 854 applied, 73% admitted, 45% enrolled. **Transfer Admission Requirements:** High school transcript, college transcript(s), statement of good standing from prior institution(s).

Minimum college GPA of 2.0 required. Lowest grade transferable C. **General Admission Information:** Application Fee $20. Regular application deadline 4/30. Nonfall registration accepted. Admission may be deferred for a maximum of not specific.

COSTS AND FINANCIAL AID

Annual in-state tuition $1,500. Annual out-of-state tuition $4,500. Room and board $2,715. Required fees $208. Average book expense $400. **Types of Aid:** *Need-based scholarships/grants:* Federal Pell.

UNIVERSITY OF WASHINGTON

Best 380

1410 NE Campus Parkway, Seattle, WA 98195-5852
Phone: 206-543-9686 · **Financial Aid Phone:** 206-543-6101 · **CEEB Code:** 4854
Fax: 206-685-3655 · **Website:** www.washington.edu · **ACT Code:** 4484

This public school was founded in 1861. It has a 700-acre campus.

RATINGS

Admissions Selectivity Rating: 92   **Fire Safety Rating:** 94

STUDENTS AND FACULTY

Enrollment: 29,468. **Student Body:** 52% female, 48% male, 16% out-of-state, 7% international (107 countries represented). Asian 12%, African American 1%, Caucasian 25%, Hispanic 3%, Native American <1%
Retention and Graduation: 94% freshmen return for sophomore year. 61% freshmen graduate within 4 years. 84% freshmen graduate within 6 years. **Faculty:** 3,308 full-time faculty, 89% hold PhDs, 40% are are members of minority groups, 23% are women.

ACADEMICS

Degrees: bachelor's, first professional, first professional certificate, master's, post-master's certificate. **Classes:** Most classes have 20-29 students. Most lab/discussion sessions have 20-29 students. **Majors with Highest Enrollment:** Bioengineering and Biomedical Engineering; Business/Commerce; Computer Science. **Special Study Options:** cooperative education program, distance learning, double major, English as a Second Language (ESL), exchange student program (domestic), honors program, independent study, internships, student-designed major, study abroad, teacher certification program, Friday Harbor Labs. **Honors programs:** We have a University Honors Program, as well as departmental honors options. **Disability Services:** Special programs offered to physically disabled students include note-taking services, reader services, tape recorders, tutors. **Career services:** Alumni network, alumni services, career/job search classes, career assessment, internships, regional alumni.

FACILITIES

Housing: Coed dorms, special housing for disabled students, special housing for international students, fraternity/sorority housing, apartments for married students, apartments for single students, Theme Housing. 100% of campus accessible to physically disabled. **Special Academic Facilities/Equipment:** Multiple art galleries, an anthropology and natural history museum, arboretum, closed-circuit TV studio. **Computers:** 100% of dorms, 100% of libraries, 100% of student union, have wireless network access. Students can register for classes online. Administrative functions (other than registration) can be performed online.

CAMPUS LIFE

Environment: Metropolis. **Activities:** Choral groups, concert band, dance, drama/theater, jazz band, literary magazine, marching band, music ensembles, musical theater, opera, pep band, radio station, student government, student newspaper, student-run film society, symphony orchestra, television station, Campus Ministries, International Student Organization, Model UN. 711 registered organizations, 13 honor societies, 52 religious organizations. 31 fraternities, 16 sororities. **Athletics (Intercollegiate):** *Men:* baseball, basketball, crew/rowing, cross-country, football, golf, soccer, tennis, track/field (outdoor). *Women:* basketball, crew/rowing, cross-country, golf, gymnastics, soccer, softball, tennis, track/field (outdoor), volleyball. **On-Campus Highlights:** Henry Art Gallery, Burke Museum, Meany Hall for Performing Arts, football games at Husky Stadium, Waterfront Activities Center (WAC). **Environmental Initiatives:** College of the Environment (http://coenv.washington.edu/); Environmental Stewardship and Sustainability Office; F2 Administration/Strategy Management Finance and Facilities (http://green.washington.edu); Campus Sustainability Fund, a student-led fee for sustainability projects (http://csf. washington.edu); This office supports the Environmental Stewardship Committee (ESAC) (http://f2.washington.edu/ess/inform/esac); Charter signatory of the American College & University Presidents Climate Commitment (ACUPCC); development and submission of a Climate Action Plan (http://f2.washington.edu/ess/inform/uw-climate-action-plan).

ADMISSIONS
Freshman Academic Profile: Average high school GPA 3.76. 73% from public high schools. SAT Math middle 50% range 580-700. SAT Critical Reading middle 50% range 530-650. SAT Writing middle 50% range 520-640. ACT middle 50% range 25-31. Minimum internet-based TOEFL 76. Minimum paper TOEFL 540. **Basis for Candidate Selection:** *Very important factors considered include:* application essay, academic GPA, rigor of secondary school record. *Important factors considered include:* standardized test scores, character/personal qualities, extracurricular activities, first generation, talent/ability, volunteer work, work experience. *Other factors considered include:* state residency. **Freshman Admission Requirements:** High school diploma or equivalent is not required. **Academic units required:** 4 English, 3 mathematics, 2 science, (1 science labs), 2 foreign language, 3 social studies, 0 history, 0 computer science, 0 academic electives. **Freshman Admission Statistics:** 31,611 applied, 55% admitted, 36% enrolled. **Transfer Admission Requirements:** High school transcript, college transcript(s), essay or personal statement, Minimum college GPA of 2.5 required. Lowest grade transferable.7. **General Admission Information:** Application Fee $50. Regular application deadline 1/15. Regular notification 4/15. Notification on a rolling basis, beginning on or about 11/1. Nonfall registration accepted. Credit and/or placement offered for CEEB Advanced Placement tests.

COSTS AND FINANCIAL AID
Average book expense $1,206. **Required Forms and Deadlines:** FAFSA. **Notification of Awards:** Applicants will be notified of awards on or about 3/31. **Types of Aid:** *Need-based scholarships/grants:* Federal Pell, SEOG, state scholarships/grants, private scholarships, the school's own gift aid. *Loans:* Direct Subsidized Stafford, Direct Unsubsidized Stafford, Direct PLUS, Federal Perkins, Federal Nursing, college/university loans from institutional funds. *Student Employment:* Federal Work-Study Program available. Institutional employment available. Off-campus job opportunities are excellent. **Financial Aid Statistics:** 74% freshmen, 73% undergrads receive need-based scholarship or grant aid. 11% freshmen, 5% undergrads receive non-need-based scholarship or grant aid. 70% freshmen, 71% undergrads receive need-based self-help aid. 1% freshmen, 1% undergrads receive athletic scholarships. 50% freshmen, 50% undergrads receive any aid. 46% undergrads borrow to pay for school. Average cumulative indebtedness $20,500. **Criteria for awarding institutional aid:** *Non-need-based:* academics, alumni affiliation, art, athletics, leadership, music/drama.

UNIVERSITY OF WEST ALABAMA

Station 4, Livingston, AL 35470
Phone: 205-652-3578 · **Financial Aid Phone:** 205-652-3576
E-mail: admissions@uwa.edu
Fax: 205-652-3522 · **Website:** http://www.uwa.edu/ · **ACT Code:** 24

This public school was founded in 1835. It has a 600-acre campus.

RATINGS
Admissions Selectivity Rating: 71   Fire Safety Rating: 84

STUDENTS AND FACULTY
Enrollment: 1,916. **Student Body:** 56% female, 44% male, 21% out-of-state, 6% international (17 countries represented). Asian 0%, African American 41%, Caucasian 44%, Hispanic 2%, Native American <1%
Retention and Graduation: 64% freshmen return for sophomore year. 13% freshmen graduate within 4 years. 32% freshmen graduate within 6 years. **Faculty:** 122 full-time faculty, 84% hold PhDs, 53% are are members of minority groups, 23% are women. 0% of classes are taught by teaching assistants.

ACADEMICS
Degrees: associate, bachelor's, master's. **Classes:** Most classes have fewer than 10 students. Most lab/discussion sessions have 10-19 students. **Majors with Highest Enrollment:** Elementary Education and Teaching; Business Administration and Management; Accounting. **Special Study Options:** Accelerated program, cooperative education program, distance learning, double major, dual enrollment, exchange student program (domestic), honors program, independent study, internships, teacher certification program. **Combined degree programs:** BA/MEng, 2-yr transfer program in fisheries and wildlife ma. **Disability Services:** Special programs offered to physically disabled students include tutors. **Career services:** alumni services, career assessment.

FACILITIES
Housing: Coed dorms, men's dorms, women's dorms, apartments for married students, apartments for single students. 100% of campus accessible to physically disabled. **Computers:** Administrative functions (other than registration) can be performed online.

CAMPUS LIFE
Environment: Rural. **Activities:** Choral groups, concert band, dance, drama/theater, marching band, student government, student newspaper, television station, yearbook, Campus Ministries, International Student Organization. 30 registered organizations, 8 honor societies, 5 religious organizations. 7 fraternities, 6 sororities. **Athletics (Intercollegiate):** *Men:* baseball, basketball, cheerleading, cross-country, football, rodeo. *Women:* basketball, cheerleading, cross-country, rodeo, softball, volleyball.

ADMISSIONS
Freshman Academic Profile: 84% from public high schools. ACT middle 50% range 19-23. Minimum internet-based TOEFL 61. Minimum paper TOEFL 500. **Basis for Candidate Selection:** *Very important factors considered include:* rigor of secondary school record, standardized test scores. **Freshman Admission Requirements:** High school diploma is required and GED is accepted. **Academic units required:** 3 English, 3 mathematics, 3 science, 3 social studies, 3 academic electives. **Freshman Admission Statistics:** 1,014 applied, 72% admitted, 48% enrolled. **Transfer Admission Requirements:** college transcript(s), statement of good standing from prior institution(s). Minimum college GPA of 2.0 required. Lowest grade transferable C. **General Admission Information:** Application Fee $50. Nonfall registration accepted. Admission may be deferred for a maximum of 1 year. Credit and/or placement offered for CEEB Advanced Placement tests.

COSTS AND FINANCIAL AID
Annual out-of-state tuition $13,736. Room and board $6,256. Required fees $1,150. Average book expense $1,120. **Required Forms and Deadlines:** FAFSA. **Notification of Awards:** Applicants will be notified of awards on a rolling basis beginning 6/1. **Types of Aid:** *Need-based scholarships/grants:* Federal Pell, SEOG, state scholarships/grants, the school's own gift aid. *Loans:* Subsidized Stafford, Unsubsidized Stafford, PLUS, Federal Perkins, Stafford Federal Loan Teacher Loan Forgiveness. *Student Employment:* Federal Work-Study Program available. Highest amount earned per year from on-campus jobs $1,317. Off-campus job opportunities are good. **Financial Aid Statistics:** 73% freshmen, 73% undergrads receive need-based scholarship or grant aid. 57% freshmen, 40% undergrads receive non-need-based scholarship or grant aid. 7% freshmen, 11% undergrads receive need-based self-help aid. 12% freshmen, 14% undergrads receive athletic scholarships. 89% freshmen, 73% undergrads receive any aid. 73% undergrads borrow to pay for school. Average cumulative indebtedness $31,740. **Criteria for awarding institutional aid:** *Non-need-based:* academics, alumni affiliation, athletics, leadership, music/drama, state/district residency.

UNIVERSITY OF WEST FLORIDA

11000 University Parkway, Pensacola, FL 32514-5750
Phone: 850-474-2230 · **Financial Aid Phone:** 850-474-2400
E-mail: admissions@uwf.edu · **CEEB Code:** 5833
Fax: 850-474-3360 · **Website:** http://uwf.edu · **ACT Code:** 771

This public school was founded in 1963. It has a 1600-acre campus.

RATINGS
Admissions Selectivity Rating: 78   Fire Safety Rating: 84

STUDENTS AND FACULTY
Enrollment: 9,948. **Student Body:** 57% female, 43% male, 10% out-of-state, 1% international (97 countries represented). Asian 3%, African American 12%, Caucasian 70%, Hispanic 8%, Native American 1%
Retention and Graduation: 23% freshmen graduate within 4 years. 48% freshmen graduate within 6 years. **Faculty:** 298 full-time faculty, 43% are members of minority groups, 15% are women. 3.6% of classes are taught by teaching assistants.

ACADEMICS
Degrees: associate, bachelor's, doctoral, master's, post-master's certificate. **Classes:** Most classes have 20-29 students. Most lab/discussion sessions have 20-29 students. **Majors with Highest Enrollment:** Psychology; Biology/Biological Sciences; Accounting. **Special Study Options:** cooperative education program, distance learning, dual enrollment, exchange student program (domestic), honors program, independent study, internships, study abroad, teacher certification program, Learning disability services. **Combined degree pro-**

grams: BS/MS Biology, Chemistry—called Fast Track. **Disability Services:** Special programs offered to physically disabled students include note-taking services, reader services, tape recorders, tutors. **Career services:** career assessment. UWF is an accredited cooperative education school. We offer the Myers Briggs Type Indicator and Strong Interest Inventory as career assessments.

FACILITIES

Housing: Coed dorms, fraternity/sorority housing, apartments for married students, apartments for single students, Special dorm rooms for disabled students. 80% of campus accessible to physically disabled. **Special Academic Facilities/Equipment:** Archeology museum,instructional media center, biology, chemistry, physics, and psychology labs, property on the Gulf of Mexico for marine and ecology research. **Computers:** 100% of classrooms, 100% of libraries, 100% of dining areas, 100% of student union, 100% of common outdoor areas have wireless network access. Students can register for classes online. Administrative functions (other than registration) can be performed online.

CAMPUS LIFE

Environment: City. **Activities:** Choral groups, concert band, dance, drama/theater, jazz band, music ensembles, musical theater, radio station, student government, student newspaper, symphony orchestra, television station. 157 registered organizations, 15 honor societies, 17 religious organizations. 10 fraternities, 7 sororities. **Athletics (Intercollegiate):** *Men:* baseball, basketball, cross-country, golf, soccer, tennis. *Women:* basketball, cross-country, golf, soccer, softball, tennis, volleyball. **On-Campus Highlights:** The Commons (has Cafeteria and bookstore), Fitness Facilities, Center for Fine and Performing Arts, Nature Trails, Library, Archeology Institute Artifact Display. **Environmental Initiatives:** All new buildings must be at least L.E.E.D Silver Certified; Energy Reduction Program; Environmentally Friendly/Green Purchasing Initiative; Recycling.

ADMISSIONS

Freshman Academic Profile: 9.4% in top 10% of high school class, 35.09% in top 25% of high school class, 76% in top 50% of high school class. 93% from public high schools. SAT Math middle 50% range 450-540. SAT Critical Reading middle 50% range 450-550. SAT Writing middle 50% range 430-530. ACT middle 50% range 20-25. Minimum paper TOEFL 550. **Basis for Candidate Selection:** *Very important factors considered include:* academic GPA, rigor of secondary school record, standardized test scores, state residency. *Other factors considered include:* Class rank, application essay, recommendation(s), alumni/ae relation, character/personal qualities, extracurricular activities, first generation, geographical residence, level of applicant's interest, talent/ability, volunteer work, work experience. **Freshman Admission Requirements:** High school diploma is required and GED is accepted. **Academic units required:** 4 English, 3 mathematics, 3 science, (2 science labs), 2 foreign language, 3 social studies, 4 academic electives. **Freshman Admission Statistics:** 5,744 applied, 63% admitted, 37% enrolled. **Transfer Admission Requirements:** college transcript(s), Minimum college GPA of 2.0 required. Lowest grade transferable D. **General Admission Information:** Application Fee $30. Regular application deadline 6/30. Notification on a rolling basis, beginning on or about 10/1. Nonfall registration accepted. Admission may be deferred for a maximum of one year. Credit offered for CEEB Advanced Placement tests.

COSTS AND FINANCIAL AID

Annual in-state tuition $3,742. Annual out-of-state tuition $16,010. Room and board $8,574. Required fees $1,683. Average book expense $1,200. **Required Forms and Deadlines:** FAFSA, Institution's own financial aid form. **Notification of Awards:** Applicants will be notified of awards on a rolling basis beginning 2/1. **Types of Aid:** *Need-based scholarships/grants:* Federal Pell, SEOG, state scholarships/grants, private scholarships, the school's own gift aid. *Loans:* Direct Subsidized Stafford, Direct Unsubsidized Stafford, Federal Perkins, college/university loans from institutional funds. *Student Employment:* Federal Work-Study Program available. Institutional employment available. Off-campus job opportunities are good. **Criteria for awarding institutional aid:** *Non-need-based:* academics, alumni affiliation, art, athletics, minority status, music/drama.

UNIVERSITY OF WEST GEORGIA

1601 Maple Street, Carrollton, GA 30118
Phone: 678-839-5600 • **Financial Aid Phone:** 678-839-6421
E-mail: admiss@westga.edu • **CEEB Code:** 5900
Fax: 678-839-4747 • **Website:** www.westga.edu • **ACT Code:** 878

This public school was founded in 1906. It has a 645-acre campus.

RATINGS

Admissions Selectivity Rating: 76   **Fire Safety Rating:** 93

STUDENTS AND FACULTY

Enrollment: 10,249. **Student Body:** 63% female, 37% male, 3% out-of-state, 1% international (76 countries represented). Asian 1%, African American 36%, Caucasian 51%, Hispanic 4%, Native American <1%
Retention and Graduation: 16% freshmen graduate within 4 years. 41% freshmen graduate within 6 years. **Faculty:** 413 full-time faculty, 76% hold PhDs, 57% are are members of minority groups, 21% are women. 1% of classes are taught by teaching assistants.

ACADEMICS

Degrees: bachelor's, certificate, doctoral, master's, post-bachelor's certificate, post-master's certificate. **Classes:** Most classes have 20-29 students. Most lab/discussion sessions have 20-29 students. **Majors with Highest Enrollment:** Biology; Journalism; Criminology. **Special Study Options:** Accelerated program, cooperative education program, distance learning, double major, dual enrollment, external degree program, honors program, independent study, internships, study abroad, teacher certification program. **Disability Services:** Special programs offered to physically disabled students include note-taking services, reader services, tape recorders, tutors. **Career services:** alumni services, internships.

FACILITIES

Housing: Coed dorms, special housing for disabled students, women's dorms, fraternity/sorority housing. 85% of campus accessible to physically disabled. **Special Academic Facilities/Equipment:** Archaelolgical laboratory, art gallery, electron microscope, observatory, preschool, performing arts center, TV studio. **Computers:** 20% of classrooms, 10% of dorms, 100% of libraries, 100% of dining areas, 100% of student union, 80% of common outdoor areas have wireless network access. Students can register for classes online. Administrative functions (other than registration) can be performed online.

CAMPUS LIFE

Environment: City. **Activities:** Choral groups, concert band, dance, drama/theater, jazz band, literary magazine, marching band, music ensembles, musical theater, opera, pep band, radio station, student government, student newspaper, television station, Campus Ministries, International Student Organization. 131 registered organizations, 32 honor societies, 17 religious organizations. 14 fraternities, 8 sororities. **Athletics (Intercollegiate):** *Men:* baseball, basketball, cheerleading, cross-country, football, golf. *Women:* basketball, cheerleading, cross-country, golf, soccer, softball, volleyball. **On-Campus Highlights:** Technology Learning Center (TLC), Bookstore, Ingram Library, Football Stadium, Campus Recreation Center, University Community Center, Coliseum, and Campus Visitor's Center.

ADMISSIONS

Freshman Academic Profile: Average high school GPA 3.13. 95% from public high schools. SAT Math middle 50% range 430-510. SAT Critical Reading middle 50% range 440-520. SAT Writing middle 50% range 420-500. ACT middle 50% range 18-22. Minimum internet-based TOEFL 69. Minimum paper TOEFL 523. **Basis for Candidate Selection:** *Very important factors considered include:* academic GPA, rigor of secondary school record, standardized test scores. **Freshman Admission Requirements:** High school diploma is required and GED is not accepted. **Academic units required:** 4 English, 4 mathematics, 3 science, (2 science labs), 2 foreign language, 1 social studies, 2 history. **Freshman Admission Statistics:** 7,868 applied, 49% admitted, 58% enrolled. **Transfer Admission Requirements:** college transcript(s), Minimum college GPA of 2.0 required. Lowest grade transferable D. **General Admission Information:** Application Fee $30. Regular application deadline 6/1. Notification on a rolling basis, beginning on or about 8/1. Nonfall registration accepted. Credit and/or placement offered for CEEB Advanced Placement tests.

COSTS AND FINANCIAL AID

Annual in-state tuition $5,098. Annual out-of-state tuition $17,994. Room and board $8,532. Required fees $1,858. Average book expense $1,500. **Required Forms and Deadlines:** FAFSA. **Notification of Awards:** Applicants will be notified of awards on a rolling basis beginning 6/1. **Types of Aid:** *Need-based scholarships/grants:* Federal Pell, SEOG, state scholarships/grants, private scholarships, the school's own gift aid, United Negro College Fund, Federal Nursing Scholarships. *Loans:* Direct Subsidized Stafford, Direct Unsubsidized Stafford, Direct PLUS, Federal Perkins, state loans, college/university loans from institutional funds. *Student Employment:* Federal Work-Study Program available. Institutional employment available. Highest amount earned per year from on-campus jobs $5,220. **Financial Aid Statistics:** 66% freshmen, 68% undergrads receive need-based scholarship or grant aid. 17% freshmen, 12% undergrads receive non-need-based scholarship or grant aid. 89% freshmen, 90% undergrads receive need-based self-help aid. 2% freshmen, 2% undergrads receive athletic scholarships. 76% undergrads borrow to pay for school. Average cumulative indebtedness $25,923. **Criteria for awarding institutional aid:** *Non-need-based:* academics, alumni affiliation, art, athletics, leadership, minority status, music/drama, religious affiliation, state/district residency.

UNIVERSITY OF WINDSOR

Office of the Registrar, Windsor, ON N9B3P4
Phone: 519-253-3000 · **Financial Aid Phone:** 519-253-3000
E-mail: registrar@uwindsor.ca
Fax: 519-971-3653 · **Website:** www.uwindsor.ca

This public school was founded in 1857. It has a 125-acre campus.

RATINGS

Admissions Selectivity Rating: 62   Fire Safety Rating: 81

STUDENTS AND FACULTY

Enrollment: 13,230. **Student Body:** 52% female, 48% male, (99 countries represented).
Faculty: 559 full-time faculty, 85% hold PhDs, 39% are are members of minority groups.

ACADEMICS

Degrees: bachelor's, certificate, master's. **Majors with Highest Enrollment:** Engineering; Social Sciences; Business/Commerce. **Special Study Options:** cooperative education program, distance learning, double major, English as a Second Language (ESL), exchange student program (domestic), honors program, independent study, internships, study abroad, teacher certification program, MBA for Managers and Professionals, which is offered on weekends (Centre for Executive Education). **Honors programs:** As a comprehensive university we have distinguished ourselves at many levels. **Combined degree programs:** BA (French)/BEd, BA/BEd/ECE, BScBEd, BMath/BEd, BCS/BEd, JD/LLB. **Disability Services:** Special programs offered to physically disabled students include note-taking services, reader services, tape recorders, tutors. **Career services:** career/job search classes, career assessment, internships. Career services highlights include The Centre for Career Education, which contributes to the holistic education of students and complements academic programs of study by supporting a wide range of career-related programs and resources with an emphasis on excellence in learning from experience. We guide students through the career development process including the exploration of personal workplace preferences and strengths, the development of career competencies, and the construction of a career plan.

FACILITIES

Housing: Coed dorms, special housing for disabled students, special housing for international students, fraternity/sorority housing, apartments for married students, cooperative housing, apartments for single students, off campus housing lists for tenants and landlords. 100% of campus accessible to physically disabled. **Special Academic Facilities/Equipment:** Centre for Engineering Innovation (completion date 2011,) C.A.R.E. (Centre for Automotive Research and Education), GLIER (Great Lakes Institute for Environemntal Research), Jackman Dramatic Art Centre (Theatrical space), Bio-Learning Centre (BLC), Biotechnology Laboratory. **Computers:** 100% of classrooms, 100% of dorms, 100% of libraries, 100% of dining areas, 100% of student union, 100% of common outdoor areas have wireless network access. Students can register for classes online. Administrative functions (other than registration) can be performed online.

CAMPUS LIFE

Environment: City. **Activities:** Choral groups, dance, drama/theater, jazz band, literary magazine, music ensembles, musical theater, radio station, student government, student newspaper, student-run film society, Campus Ministries, International Student Organization. 116 registered organizations, 1 honor society, 13 religious organizations. 3 fraternities, 3 sororities. **Athletics (Intercollegiate):** *Men:* basketball, cross-country, football, ice hockey, soccer, track/field (outdoor), track/field (indoor), volleyball. *Women:* basketball, cross-country, ice hockey, soccer, track/field (outdoor), track/field (indoor), volleyball. **On-Campus Highlights:** CAW Student Centre, Forge Fitness facility, The Basement Pub, St. Denis Athletic Centre/University Sta, Leddy Library, Odette Sculpture Garden which includes a scenic 5km waterfront trail. Many students will exercise or study/relax by the water. **Environmental Initiatives:** In January 2013, the Environmental Advocate was appointed, the University of Windsor Joined AASHE, and the sustainability website was created. The Environmental Advocate is also a member of the Ontario College and University Sustainability Professionals. In October of 2012 the Ed Lumley Centre for Engineering Innovation became fully occupied. This is a LEEDs gold-designed building. In January 2013, the University of Windsor received the Essex Regional Conservation Authority 2012 Conservation Award for biology teaching related to the environment, and opening the CEI.

ADMISSIONS

Basis for Candidate Selection: *Very important factors considered include:* academic GPA, rigor of secondary school record. *Other factors considered include:* recommendation(s), standardized test scores, extracurricular activities,

geographical residence, interview. **Freshman Admission Requirements:** High school diploma is required and GED is not accepted. **Freshman Admission Statistics:** 10,991 applied, 66% admitted, 35% enrolled. **Transfer Admission Requirements:** college transcript(s). **General Admission Information:** Application Fee $75. Notification on a rolling basis, beginning on or about 1/1. Nonfall registration accepted.

COSTS AND FINANCIAL AID

Required Forms and Deadlines: FAFSA, Institution's own financial aid form. **Notification of Awards:** Applicants will be notified of awards on a rolling basis beginning 6/1. **Types of Aid:** *Need-based scholarships/grants:* the school's own gift aid. *Loans:* Ontario Student Assistance Program (OSAP). *Student Employment:* Off-campus job opportunities are good. **Criteria for awarding institutional aid:** *Non-need-based:* academics, art, athletics, leadership, minority status, music/drama, state/district residency.

UNIVERSITY OF WISCONSIN—EAU CLAIRE

105 Garfield Avenue, Eau Claire, WI 54701
Phone: 715-836-5415 · **Financial Aid Phone:** 715-836-3373
E-mail: admissions@uwec.edu · **CEEB Code:** 1913
Fax: 715-836-2409 · **Website:** www.uwec.edu · **ACT Code:** 4670

This public school was founded in 1916. It has a 333-acre campus.

RATINGS

Admissions Selectivity Rating: 77   Fire Safety Rating: 78

STUDENTS AND FACULTY

Enrollment: 9,910. **Student Body:** 59% female, 41% male, 26% out-of-state, 2% international (36 countries represented). Asian 3%, African American 1%, Caucasian 71%, Hispanic 2%, Native American <1%
Retention and Graduation: 83% freshmen return for sophomore year. 29% freshmen graduate within 4 years. 69% freshmen graduate within 6 years. 21% grads go on to further study within 1 year. 29% grads pursue arts and sciences degrees. 11% grads pursue law degrees. 5% grads pursue business degrees. 5% grads pursue medical degrees. **Faculty:** 443 full-time faculty, 82% hold PhDs, 48% are are members of minority groups, 17% are women. 0% of classes are taught by teaching assistants.

ACADEMICS

Degrees: associate, bachelor's, certificate, master's, post-bachelor's certificate, post-master's certificate, terminal associate, transfer associate. **Classes:** Most classes have 20-29 students. Most lab/discussion sessions have 20-29 students. **Majors with Highest Enrollment:** Registered Nursing, Nursing Administration, Nursing Research and Clinical Nursing; Biology/Biological Sciences; Kinesiology and Exercise Science. **Special Study Options:** Accelerated program, cooperative education program, cross-registration, distance learning, double major, dual enrollment, English as a Second Language (ESL), exchange student program (domestic), external degree program, honors program, independent study, internships, student-designed major, study abroad, teacher certification program, Collaborative programs in Early Childhood Education. **Disability Services:** Special programs offered to physically disabled students include note-taking services, reader services, tutors. **Career services:** Alumni network, alumni services, career/job search classes, career assessment, internships, regional alumni.

FACILITIES

Housing: Coed dorms, men's dorms, women's dorms, apartments for single students. 80% of campus accessible to physically disabled. **Special Academic Facilities/Equipment:** Art gallery, human development center, bird museum, field station, planetarium. **Computers:** 50% of classrooms, 10% of dorms, 100% of libraries, 100% of dining areas, 100% of student union, 100% of common outdoor areas have wireless network access. Students can register for classes online. Administrative functions (other than registration) can be performed online.

CAMPUS LIFE

Environment: Town. **Activities:** Choral groups, concert band, dance, drama/theater, jazz band, literary magazine, marching band, music ensembles, musical theater, opera, pep band, radio station, student government, student newspaper, student-run film society, symphony orchestra, television station, Campus Ministries, International Student Organization, Model UN. 240 registered organizations, 30 honor societies, 16 religious organizations. 2 fraternities, 3 sororities. **Athletics (Intercollegiate):** *Men:* basketball, cross-country, diving, football, golf, ice hockey, swimming, tennis, track/field (outdoor), track/field (indoor), wrestling. *Women:* basketball, cross-country, diving, golf, gymnastics, ice hockey, soccer, softball, swimming, tennis, track/field (outdoor), track/field (indoor), volleyball. **On-Campus Highlights:** Chippewa River Footbridge, Davies Center (Student Center/Union), McPhee Center (Athletic Facility), Hass Fine Arts Center, Higher Ground (Recreational Facility). **Environmental Initiatives:** Creation of an energy performance contract to provide $3.4 million in energy conservation measures across campus, including heating and ventilation, lighting, water conservation, etc. Initiation of a "green fee" and organization of the Student Office of Sustainability to administer it, with an annual budget of approximately $220,000 for sustainability initiatives on campus. Approval for hiring of two new faculty members into the interdisciplinary Watershed Institute for Collaborative Environmental Studies; they will develop new courses in sustainability and environmental studies for general education, for environmental studies minors and will develop a major.

ADMISSIONS

Freshman Academic Profile: 17% in top 10% of high school class, 47% in top 25% of high school class, 92% in top 50% of high school class. SAT Math middle 50% range 480-610. SAT Critical Reading middle 50% range 480-560. ACT middle 50% range 22-26. Minimum internet-based TOEFL 79. Minimum paper TOEFL 550. **Basis for Candidate Selection:** *Very important factors considered include:* Class rank, rigor of secondary school record. *Important factors considered include:* standardized test scores. *Other factors considered include:* application essay, academic GPA, recommendation(s), character/personal qualities, extracurricular activities, first generation, interview, level of applicant's interest, racial/ethnic status, talent/ability, volunteer work, work experience. **Freshman Admission Requirements:** High school diploma is required and GED is accepted. **Academic units required:** 4 English, 3 mathematics, 3 science, 2 foreign language, 3 social studies, 2 academic electives. **Freshman Admission Statistics:** 5,441 applied, 84% admitted, 44% enrolled. **Transfer Admission Requirements:** High school transcript, college transcript(s), statement of good standing from prior institution(s). Minimum college GPA of 2.0 required. Lowest grade transferable D-. **General Admission Information:** Application Fee $44. Notification on a rolling basis, beginning on or about 9/15. Nonfall registration accepted. Credit and/or placement offered for CEEB Advanced Placement tests.

COSTS AND FINANCIAL AID

Annual in-state tuition $7,361. Annual out-of-state tuition $14,934. Room and board $6,986. Required fees $1,383. Average book expense $400. **Required Forms and Deadlines:** FAFSA. **Notification of Awards:** Applicants will be notified of awards on a rolling basis beginning 4/15. **Types of Aid:** *Need-based scholarships/grants:* Federal Pell, SEOG, state scholarships/grants, private scholarships, the school's own gift aid, Federal Nursing Scholarships, Academic Competetiveness Grant, SMART Grant, BIA Excellence in Math/Comp. Science, EMAC, Student Support Services Grant. *Loans:* Direct Subsidized Stafford, Direct Unsubsidized Stafford, Direct PLUS, Federal Perkins, state loans, college/university loans from institutional funds, Private Loans. *Student Employment:* Federal Work-Study Program available. Institutional employment available. Highest amount earned per year from on-campus jobs $10,023. Off-campus job opportunities are fair. **Financial Aid Statistics:** 79% freshmen, 76% undergrads receive need-based scholarship or grant aid. 3% freshmen, 2% undergrads receive non-need-based scholarship or grant aid. 93% freshmen, 94% undergrads receive need-based self-help aid. 0% freshmen, 0% undergrads receive athletic scholarships. 80% freshmen, 70% undergrads receive any aid. 68% undergrads borrow to pay for school. Average cumulative indebtedness $23,515. **Criteria for awarding institutional aid:** *Non-need-based:* academics, art, leadership, minority status, music/drama, state/district residency.

UNIVERSITY OF WISCONSIN—GREEN BAY

2420 Nicolet Drive, Green Bay, WI 53411-7001
Phone: 920-465-2111 · **Financial Aid Phone:** 920-465-2075
E-mail: admissions@uwgb.edu · **CEEB Code:** 1859
Fax: 920-465-5754 · **Website:** http://www.uwgb.edu/ · **ACT Code:** 4688

This public school was founded in 1965. It has a 700-acre campus.

RATINGS

Admissions Selectivity Rating: 73   **Fire Safety Rating:** 74

STUDENTS AND FACULTY

Enrollment: 5,661. **Student Body:** 66% female, 34% male, 7% out-of-state, 1% international (38 countries represented). Asian 3%, African American 1%, Caucasian 86%, Hispanic 4%, Native American 1%
Retention and Graduation: 77% freshmen return for sophomore year. 24% freshmen graduate within 4 years. 51% freshmen graduate within 6 years. 15% grads go on to further study within 1 year. 7% grads pursue arts and sciences degrees. 1% grads pursue law degrees. 3% grads pursue business degrees. 1%

grads pursue medical degrees. **Faculty:** 190 full-time faculty, 87% hold PhDs, 47% are are members of minority groups, 18% are women. 0% of classes are taught by teaching assistants.

ACADEMICS

Degrees: associate, bachelor's, master's, post-bachelor's certificate. **Classes:** Most classes have 20-29 students. Most lab/discussion sessions have 20-29 students. **Majors with Highest Enrollment:** Psychology; Business Administration and Management; Multi-/Interdisciplinary Studies. **Special Study Options:** cross-registration, distance learning, double major, exchange student program (domestic), external degree program, independent study, internships, liberal arts/career combination, student-designed major, study abroad, teacher certification program. **Combined degree programs:** BS/MS Environmental Science/Env Science & Policy. **Disability Services:** Special programs offered to physically disabled students include note-taking services, reader services, tape recorders. **Career services:** Alumni network, alumni services, career/job search classes, internships.

FACILITIES

Housing: Coed dorms, apartments for single students, Suites w/ private bedrooms. 99% of campus accessible to physically disabled. **Special Academic Facilities/Equipment:** 290-acre arboretum, Herbarium, regional Performing Arts Center **Computers:** 75% of classrooms, 100% of dorms, 100% of libraries, 100% of dining areas, 100% of student union, 10% of common outdoor areas have wireless network access. Students can register for classes online. Administrative functions (other than registration) can be performed online.

CAMPUS LIFE

Environment: City. **Activities:** Choral groups, concert band, dance, drama/theater, jazz band, literary magazine, music ensembles, musical theater, pep band, radio station, student government, student newspaper, student-run film society, television station, Campus Ministries, International Student Organization. 100 registered organizations, 7 honor societies, 5 religious organizations. 2 fraternities, 2 sororities. **Athletics (Intercollegiate):** *Men:* basketball, cheerleading, cross-country, diving, golf, skiing (nordic/cross-country), soccer, swimming, tennis. *Women:* basketball, cheerleading, cross-country, diving, golf, skiing (nordic/cross-country), soccer, softball, swimming, tennis, volleyball. **On-Campus Highlights:** Mary Ann Cofrin Hall—State-of-the-art academic bldg., Kress Event Center—recently remodeled, Weidner Center for Performing Arts, Lambeau Cottage on the shores of Green B, Student Union-recently remodeled. **Environmental Initiatives:** Building integrated photovoltaics in Mary Ann Cofrin Hall (http://www.buildingsolar.com/index.html) Historically strong academic programs in environmental science and environmental policy and planning at both bachelor's and master's level. Campus design connects buildings with energy efficient underground tunnels.

ADMISSIONS

Freshman Academic Profile: Average high school GPA 3.33. 95% from public high schools. ACT middle 50% range 20-25. Minimum internet-based TOEFL 61. Minimum paper TOEFL 500. **Basis for Candidate Selection:** *Very important factors considered include:* academic GPA, rigor of secondary school record, standardized test scores, extracurricular activities. *Important factors considered include:* application essay, level of applicant's interest, volunteer work, work experience. *Other factors considered include:* recommendation(s), character/personal qualities, geographical residence, interview, racial/ethnic status, state residency, talent/ability. **Freshman Admission Requirements:** High school diploma is required and GED is accepted. **Academic units required:** 4 English, 3 mathematics, 3 science, (1 science labs), 0 foreign language, 3 social studies, 0 history, 4 academic electives. **Freshman Admission Statistics:** 2,483 applied, 68% admitted, 45% enrolled. **Transfer Admission Requirements:** college transcript(s), Minimum college GPA of 2.0 required. Lowest grade transferable D. **General Admission Information:** Application Fee $44. Notification on a rolling basis, beginning on or about 9/15. Nonfall registration accepted. Admission may be deferred for a maximum of 1 year. Credit and/or placement offered for CEEB Advanced Placement tests.

COSTS AND FINANCIAL AID

Annual in-state tuition $6,298. Annual out-of-state tuition $13,871. Room and board $7,224. Required fees $1,460. Average book expense $800. **Required Forms and Deadlines:** FAFSA. **Notification of Awards:** Applicants will be notified of awards on a rolling basis beginning 1/1. **Types of Aid:** *Need-based scholarships/grants:* Federal Pell, SEOG, state scholarships/grants, private scholarships, the school's own gift aid. *Loans:* Subsidized Stafford, Unsubsidized Stafford, PLUS, Federal Perkins. *Student Employment:* Federal Work-Study Program available. Institutional employment available. Off-campus job opportunities are good. **Financial Aid Statistics:** 75% freshmen, 72% undergrads receive need-based scholarship or grant aid. 3% freshmen, 2% undergrads receive non-need-based scholarship or grant aid. 76% freshmen, 78% undergrads receive need-based self-help aid. 3% freshmen, 1% undergrads receive athletic scholarships. 69% freshmen, 69% undergrads receive any aid. 78% undergrads borrow to pay for school. Average cumulative indebtedness $25,297. **Criteria** for awarding institutional aid: *Non-need-based:* academics, art, athletics, leadership, minority status, music/drama.

UNIVERSITY OF WISCONSIN—LA CROSSE

1725 State Street, La Crosse, WI 54601-3742
Phone: 608-785-8939 · **Financial Aid Phone:** 608-785-8604
E-mail: admissions@uwlax.edu · **CEEB Code:** 1914
Fax: 608-785-8940 · **Website:** www.uwlax.edu · **ACT Code:** 4672

This public school was founded in 1909. It has a 120-acre campus.

RATINGS

Admissions Selectivity Rating: 83   **Fire Safety Rating:** 62

STUDENTS AND FACULTY

Enrollment: 9,466. **Student Body:** 57% female, 43% male, 17% out-of-state, 2% international (23 countries represented). Asian 2%, African American 1%, Caucasian 90%, Hispanic 3%, Native American <1%.
Retention and Graduation: 86% freshmen return for sophomore year. 33% freshmen graduate within 4 years. **Faculty:** 502 full-time faculty, 84% hold PhDs, 51% are are members of minority groups, 12% are women.

ACADEMICS

Degrees: associate, bachelor's, certificate, master's, post-bachelor's certificate. **Classes:** Most classes have 20-29 students. Most lab/discussion sessions have 20-29 students. **Majors with Highest Enrollment:** Biology/Biological Sciences; Kinesiology and Exercise Science; Psychology. **Special Study Options:** cooperative education program, cross-registration, distance learning, double major, dual enrollment, English as a Second Language (ESL), honors program, independent study, internships, liberal arts/career combination, study abroad, teacher certification program, Weekend college: grad only. **Honors programs:** University Honors Program, see http://www.uwlax.edu/honors/gt; **Combined degree programs:** BS/MSPT; BS/MSOT. **Disability Services:** Special programs offered to physically disabled students include note-taking services, reader services, tape recorders, tutors.

FACILITIES

Housing: Coed dorms, special housing for international students, Wellness Housing, First Year Experience. 98% of campus accessible to physically disabled. **Special Academic Facilities/Equipment:** Greenhouse, planetarium, Health Science Center, Mississippi Valley Archaeology Center, River Studies center, Business Development Center, La Crosse Exercise and Health Program. **Computers:** Students can register for classes online. Administrative functions (other than registration) can be performed online.

CAMPUS LIFE

Environment: City. **Activities:** Choral groups, concert band, drama/theater, jazz band, marching band, music ensembles, pep band, radio station, student government, student newspaper, symphony orchestra, International Student Organization. 180 registered organizations, 13 honor societies, 10 religious organizations. 4 fraternities, 2 sororities. **Athletics (Intercollegiate):** *Men:* baseball, basketball, cross-country, diving, football, swimming, tennis, track/field (outdoor), track/field (indoor), wrestling. *Women:* basketball, cross-country, diving, gymnastics, soccer, softball, swimming, tennis, track/field (outdoor), track/field (indoor), volleyball. **On-Campus Highlights:** Recreation Eagle Center, Cyber Café, Archaeology Museum, Murphy Library, Wing Technology Computer Lab. The 119 acre campus has 32 buildings, including 19 used for instruction, academic support and administrative purposes, 10 residence halls and three student centers.

ADMISSIONS

Freshman Academic Profile: 24% in top 10% of high school class, 65% in top 25% of high school class, 98% in top 50% of high school class. SAT Math middle 50% range 477.5-615. SAT Critical Reading middle 50% range 487.5-612.5. SAT Writing middle 50% range 465-562.5. ACT middle 50% range 23-27. Minimum internet-based TOEFL 73. Minimum paper TOEFL 550. **Basis for Candidate Selection:** *Very important factors considered include:* Class rank, academic GPA, rigor of secondary school record, standardized test scores. *Important factors considered include:* application essay, extracurricular activities, level of applicant's interest, volunteer work. *Other factors considered include:* recommendation(s), alumni/ae relation, character/personal qualities, first generation, geographical residence, interview, racial/ethnic status, state residency, talent/ability, work experience. **Freshman Admission Requirements:** High school diploma is required and GED is accepted. **Academic units required:** 4 English, 3 mathematics, 3 science, (2 science labs), 3 social studies, 4 academic electives. **Freshman Admission Statistics:** 6,030 applied, 76% admitted, 43% enrolled. **Transfer Admission Requirements:** college transcript(s), statement of good standing from prior institution(s). Minimum college GPA of

3.0 required. Lowest grade transferable D-. **General Admission Information:** Application Fee $44. Notification on a rolling basis, beginning on or about 9/15. Nonfall registration accepted. Credit and/or placement offered for CEEB Advanced Placement tests.

COSTS AND FINANCIAL AID

Required Forms and Deadlines: FAFSA. **Notification of Awards:** Applicants will be notified of awards on a rolling basis beginning 4/1. **Types of Aid:** *Need-based scholarships/grants:* Federal Pell, SEOG, state scholarships/grants, private scholarships, the school's own gift aid. *Loans:* Subsidized Stafford, Unsubsidized Stafford, PLUS, Federal Perkins. *Student Employment:* Highest amount earned per year from on-campus jobs $7,020. **Financial Aid Statistics:** 41% freshmen, 48% undergrads receive need-based scholarship or grant aid. 61% freshmen, 35% undergrads receive non-need-based scholarship or grant aid. 77% freshmen, 84% undergrads receive need-based self-help aid. 0% freshmen, 0% undergrads receive athletic scholarships. 88% freshmen, 77% undergrads receive any aid. 67% undergrads borrow to pay for school. Average cumulative indebtedness $23,004. **Criteria for awarding institutional aid:** *Non-need-based:* academics, art, athletics, leadership, music/drama.

UNIVERSITY OF WISCONSIN—MADISON

702 West Johnson Street, Suite 101, Madison, WI 53715?û1007
Phone: 608-262-3961 · **Financial Aid Phone:** 608-262-3060
E-mail: onwisconsin@admissions.wisc.edu · **CEEB Code:** 1846
Fax: 608-262-7706 · **Website:** www.wisc.edu · **ACT Code:** 4656

This public school was founded in 1848. It has a 933-acre campus.

RATINGS

Admissions Selectivity Rating: 93   **Fire Safety Rating:** 74

STUDENTS AND FACULTY

Enrollment: 29,302. **Student Body:** 51% female, 49% male, 33% out-of-state, 7% international (144 countries represented). Asian 5%, African American 2%, Caucasian 77%, Hispanic 5%, Native American <1%
Retention and Graduation: 56% freshmen graduate within 4 years. 85% freshmen graduate within 6 years. **Faculty:** 2,386 full-time faculty, 90% hold PhDs, 37% are are members of minority groups, 18% are women.

ACADEMICS

Degrees: bachelor's, doctoral, master's, post-master's certificate. **Classes:** Most classes have 10-19 students. Most lab/discussion sessions have 20-29 students. **Majors with Highest Enrollment:** Political Science and Government; Biology/Biological Sciences; Economics. **Special Study Options:** Accelerated program, cooperative education program, distance learning, double major, dual enrollment, English as a Second Language (ESL), exchange student program (domestic), honors program, independent study, internships, liberal arts/career combination, student-designed major, study abroad, teacher certification program. **Disability Services:** Special programs offered to physically disabled students include note-taking services, reader services, tape recorders, tutors. **Career services:** Alumni network, career/job search classes, career assessment, internships. Career services highlights include multiple career placement centers for different schools and colleges. Futhermore, we have all of the services above, offered through various departments and organizations. For example, internships are generally organized through academic departments and alumni services are provided through our alumni association.

FACILITIES

Housing: Coed dorms, men's dorms, special housing for international students, women's dorms, fraternity/sorority housing, apartments for married students, cooperative housing, apartments for single students, Theme Housing, Residential Learning Communities. 80% of campus accessible to physically disabled. **Special Academic Facilities/Equipment:** Art, physics, and geology museums, nuclear reactor, arboretum, botanical gardens, observatory, campus dairy store (campus-made ice cream and cheese), american indian burial mounds **Computers:** 100% of classrooms, 25% of dorms, 100% of libraries, 100% of dining areas, 100% of student union, 100% of common outdoor areas have wireless network access. Students can register for classes online. Administrative functions (other than registration) can be performed online.

CAMPUS LIFE

Environment: City. **Activities:** Choral groups, concert band, dance, drama/theater, jazz band, literary magazine, marching band, music ensembles, musical theater, opera, pep band, radio station, student government, student newspaper, student-run film society, symphony orchestra, television station, yearbook, International Student Organization. 685 registered organizations, 27 honor societies, 26 fraternities, 11 sororities. **Athletics (Intercollegiate):** *Men:* basketball, cheerleading, crew/rowing, cross-country, football, golf, ice hockey, soccer, swimming, tennis, track/field (outdoor), wrestling. *Women:* basketball, cheerleading, crew/rowing, cross-country, golf, ice hockey, soccer, softball, swimming, tennis, track/field (outdoor), volleyball. **On-Campus Highlights:** Allen Centennial Gardens, Kohl Center, Memorial Union Terrace, Chazen Museum of Art, Babcock Hall Dairy Plant and Store, http://www.visit.wisc.edu/todo.html. **Environmental Initiatives:** Our conservation efforts in the last four years have reduced campus energy consumption by over 1 trillion BTUs and water consumption by 178,000,000 gallons annually. Investment of over $70 million in energy conservation since 2001. Integrating research, teaching, and operations arms of the University to maximize sustainability culture change in the university.

ADMISSIONS

Freshman Academic Profile: Average high school GPA 3.83. 52% in top 10% of high school class, 90% in top 25% of high school class, 100% in top 50% of high school class. SAT Math middle 50% range 630-740. SAT Critical Reading middle 50% range 570-670. SAT Writing middle 50% range 590-680. ACT middle 50% range 26-31. Minimum internet-based TOEFL 80. Minimum paper TOEFL 550. **Basis for Candidate Selection:** *Very important factors considered include:* Class rank, academic GPA, rigor of secondary school record. *Important factors considered include:* application essay, standardized test scores, state residency. *Other factors considered include:* recommendation(s), alumni/ae relation, character/personal qualities, extracurricular activities, first generation, level of applicant's interest, racial/ethnic status, talent/ability, volunteer work, work experience. **Freshman Admission Requirements:** High school diploma is required and GED is accepted. **Academic units required:** 4 English, 3 mathematics, 3 science, 2 foreign language, 3 social studies, 2 academic electives. **Freshman Admission Statistics:** 30,464 applied, 50% admitted, 41% enrolled. **Transfer Admission Requirements:** High school transcript, college transcript(s), essay or personal statement, Lowest grade transferable D. **General Admission Information:** Application Fee $44. Regular application deadline 2/1. Notification on a rolling basis, beginning on or about 10/1. Nonfall registration accepted. Admission may be deferred for a maximum of 1 year. Credit and/or placement offered for CEEB Advanced Placement tests.

COSTS AND FINANCIAL AID

Average book expense $1,200. **Required Forms and Deadlines:** FAFSA. **Notification of Awards:** Applicants will be notified of awards on a rolling basis beginning 4/1. **Types of Aid:** *Need-based scholarships/grants:* Federal Pell, SEOG, state scholarships/grants, private scholarships, the school's own gift aid. *Loans:* Subsidized Stafford, Unsubsidized Stafford, PLUS, Federal Perkins, Federal Nursing, state loansWe are transitioning to direct lending within the next year. *Student Employment:* Federal Work-Study Program available. Institutional employment available. Off-campus job opportunities are excellent. **Financial Aid Statistics:** 79% freshmen, 77% undergrads receive need-based scholarship or grant aid. 7% freshmen, 7% undergrads receive non-need-based scholarship or grant aid. 76% freshmen, 56% undergrads receive need-based self-help aid. 2% freshmen, 1% undergrads receive athletic scholarships. 51% undergrads borrow to pay for school. Average cumulative indebtedness $23,152. **Criteria for awarding institutional aid:** *Non-need-based:* academics, alumni affiliation, art, athletics, job skills, leadership, minority status, music/drama, religious affiliation, state/district residency.

UNIVERSITY OF WISCONSIN—MILWAUKEE

Department of Admissions and Recruitment, Milwaukee, WI 53211
Phone: 414-229-2222 · **Financial Aid Phone:** 414-229-4541
E-mail: uwmlook@uwm.edu · **CEEB Code:** 1473
Fax: 414-229-6940 · **Website:** www4.uwm.edu · **ACT Code:** 4658

This public school was founded in 1956. It has a 93-acre campus.

RATINGS

Admissions Selectivity Rating: 72   **Fire Safety Rating:** 97

STUDENTS AND FACULTY

Enrollment: 21,729. **Student Body:** 50% female, 50% male, 7% out-of-state, 3% international (81 countries represented). Asian 6%, African American 8%, Caucasian 72%, Hispanic 8%, Native American <1%
Faculty: 1,093 full-time faculty, 76% hold PhDs, 47% are are members of minority groups, 25% are women.

ACADEMICS

Degrees: bachelor's, certificate, master's, post-bachelor's certificate, post-master's certificate. **Classes:** Most classes have 20-29 students. Most lab/discussion sessions have 20-29 students. **Majors with Highest Enrollment:** Education. **Special Study Options:** Accelerated program, cooperative education program, cross-registration, distance learning, double major, dual enrollment, English as a Second Language (ESL), external degree program, honors program, independent study, internships, liberal arts/career combination, student-designed major, study abroad, teacher certification program. **Disability Services:** Special programs offered to physically disabled students include note-taking services, reader services, tape recorders, tutors. **Career services:** career assessment, internships. Career services highlights include LaMacchia Enterprises Entrepreneur Internship.

FACILITIES

Housing: Coed dorms, special housing for disabled students, apartments for single students. **Special Academic Facilities/Equipment:** Art and geology museums, childhood education center, foreign language resource center, Great Lakes research facility and environmental studies field station, planetarium.

CAMPUS LIFE

Activities: Choral groups, concert band, dance, drama/theater, jazz band, literary magazine, marching band, music ensembles, musical theater, pep band, radio station, student government, student newspaper, student-run film society, symphony orchestra, Campus Ministries, International Student Organization, Model UN. 250 registered organizations, 1 honor society, 4 religious organizations. 8 fraternities, 4 sororities. **Athletics (Intercollegiate):** *Men:* baseball, basketball, cross-country, diving, soccer, swimming, track/field (outdoor). *Women:* basketball, cross-country, soccer, swimming, tennis, track/field (outdoor), volleyball. **Environmental Initiatives:** Performance Contracting—Energy Matters is UWM's energy efficiency project with a goal to achieve an energy reduction of 25% by 2013, reduce campus use of fossil fuels, and provide comfortable study and work space. With more than 50% of the project complete, results are showing an even faster rate of return with a 42% savings. Implementation of campus-wide stormwater management plan—In 2006, UWM began work on a campus-wide stormwater master plan. James Wasley of UWM's School of Architecture and Urban Planning, in conjunction with the Metropolitan Milwaukee Sewerage District authored a document envisioning "UWM as a Zero Discharge Zone." The master plan served as the framework for completed projects such as new green roofs at Sanburg Residence Hall and Golda Meir Library, as well as Parking Lot 18's transformation into a stormwater demonstration project. The plan is currently approaching campus-wide implementation. Campus community gardens adjacent to Sandburg residence hall were built in Spring 2012. Community gardens include: Restaurant Operations plots; fruit and nut trees; and vegetables and herbs available for campus consumption.

ADMISSIONS

Freshman Academic Profile: Average high school GPA 3.05. 9% in top 10% of high school class, 28% in top 25% of high school class, 63% in top 50% of high school class. ACT middle 50% range 19-24. Minimum internet-based TOEFL 68. Minimum paper TOEFL 520. **Basis for Candidate Selection:** *Very important factors considered include:* academic GPA, rigor of secondary school record. *Important factors considered include:* Class rank, standardized test scores, talent/ability. *Other factors considered include:* application essay, recommendation(s), character/personal qualities, extracurricular activities, first generation, geographical residence, interview, level of applicant's interest, racial/ethnic status, state residency, volunteer work, work experience. **Freshman Admission Requirements:** High school diploma is required and GED is accepted. **Academic units required:** 4 English, 3 mathematics, 3 science, (1 science labs), 0 foreign language, 3 social studies, 2 academic electives, 2 From the above areas, computer science, fine arts, or other appropriate courses. **Freshman Admission Statistics:** 8,311 applied, 88% admitted, 44% enrolled. **Transfer Admission Requirements:** High school transcript, college transcript(s), Minimum college GPA of 2.0 required. Lowest grade transferable D-. **General Admission Information:** Application Fee $44. Regular application deadline 7/1. Notification on a rolling basis, beginning on or about 9/15. Nonfall registration accepted. Admission may be deferred for a maximum of 1 semester. Credit offered for CEEB Advanced Placement tests.

COSTS AND FINANCIAL AID

Annual in-state tuition $8,091. Annual out-of-state tuition $17,820. Room and board $9,136. Required fees $1,209. Average book expense $700. **Required Forms and Deadlines:** FAFSA. **Notification of Awards:** Applicants will be notified of awards on a rolling basis beginning 3/10. **Types of Aid:** *Need-based scholarships/grants:* Federal Pell, SEOG, state scholarships/grants, private scholarships, the school's own gift aid, Federal Nursing Scholarships. *Loans:* Subsidized Stafford, Unsubsidized Stafford, PLUS, Federal Perkins, Federal Nursing, state loans, Alternative Loans. *Student Employment:* Federal Work-Study Program available. Institutional employment available. Off-campus job opportunities are good. **Financial Aid Statistics:** 59% freshmen, 56%

undergrads receive need-based scholarship or grant aid. 26% freshmen, 16% undergrads receive non-need-based scholarship or grant aid. 82% freshmen, 69% undergrads receive need-based self-help aid. 1% freshmen, 4% undergrads receive athletic scholarships. 73% undergrads borrow to pay for school. Average cumulative indebtedness $25,317. **Criteria for awarding institutional aid:** *Non-need-based:* academics, art, athletics, music/drama.

UNIVERSITY OF WISCONSIN—OSHKOSH

Dempsey Hall 135, Oshkosh, WI 54901
Phone: 920-424-0202 · **Financial Aid Phone:** 920-424-4025
E-mail: oshadmuw@uwosh.edu · **CEEB Code:** 1916
Fax: 920-424-1098 · **Website:** http://www.uwosh.edu/home · **ACT Code:** 4674

This public school was founded in 1871. It has a 192-acre campus.

RATINGS
Admissions Selectivity Rating: 77   Fire Safety Rating: 60*

STUDENTS AND FACULTY
Enrollment: 10,771. **Student Body:** 57% female, 43% male, 3% out-of-state, 1% international (32 countries represented). Asian 4%, African American 2%, Caucasian 88%, Hispanic 3%, Native American 1%
Retention and Graduation: 75% freshmen return for sophomore year. 13% freshmen graduate within 4 years. **Faculty:** 416 full-time faculty, 84% hold PhDs, 47% are are members of minority groups, 12% are women. 0% of classes are taught by teaching assistants.

ACADEMICS
Degrees: associate, bachelor's, certificate, master's. **Classes:** Most classes have 20-29 students. Most lab/discussion sessions have 20-29 students. **Majors with Highest Enrollment:** Elementary Education and Teaching; Business/Commerce; Registered Nursing, Nursing Administration, Nursing Research and Clinical Nursing. **Special Study Options:** Accelerated program, cooperative education program, cross-registration, distance learning, double major, dual enrollment, English as a Second Language (ESL), exchange student program (domestic), honors program, independent study, internships, liberal arts/career combination, student-designed major, study abroad, teacher certification program, weekend college. **Disability Services:** Special programs offered to physically disabled students include note-taking services, reader services, tape recorders, tutors.

FACILITIES
Housing: Coed dorms, special housing for disabled students, men's dorms, women's dorms, fraternity/sorority housing. **Special Academic Facilities/Equipment:** Art gallery, ceramics lab, electron microscope. **Computers:** Students can register for classes online.

CAMPUS LIFE
Environment: Village. **Activities:** Choral groups, concert band, dance, drama/theater, jazz band, literary magazine, music ensembles, pep band, radio station, student government, student newspaper, student-run film society, television station, Campus Ministries, International Student Organization, Model UN. 175 registered organizations, 15 honor societies, 6 religious organizations. 8 fraternities, 5 sororities. **Athletics (Intercollegiate):** *Men:* baseball, basketball, cross-country, diving, football, soccer, swimming, tennis, track/field (outdoor), track/field (indoor), wrestling. *Women:* basketball, cross-country, diving, golf, gymnastics, soccer, softball, swimming, tennis, track/field (outdoor), track/field (indoor), volleyball. **Environmental Initiatives:** Leadership in adopting renewable energy, from 2003 as the largest purchaser of renewable electricity in the State of Wisconsin to the recent construction of the first commercial-scale dry anerobic biodigester in the Western Hemisphere. Adopting LEED Gold as the goal for future construction and renovation; 2 buildings are in review for certification and a third is under construction. General education reform listing an essential learning outcome of understanding sustainability and its applications.

ADMISSIONS
Freshman Academic Profile: Average high school GPA 3.3. 10% in top 10% of high school class, 37% in top 25% of high school class, 84% in top 50% of high school class. 90% from public high schools. ACT middle 50% range 20-24. Minimum internet-based TOEFL 70. Minimum paper TOEFL 525. **Basis for Candidate Selection:** *Very important factors considered include:* rigor of secondary school record. *Important factors considered include:* Class rank, academic GPA, standardized test scores. *Other factors considered include:* application essay, recommendation(s), alumni/ae relation, character/personal qualities, extracurricular activities, first generation, racial/ethnic status, talent/ability, volunteer work, work experience. **Freshman Admission Requirements:** High school diploma is required and GED is accepted. **Academic units required:** 4 English, 3 mathematics, 3 science, (3 science labs), 3 social studies, 4 academic

electives. **Freshman Admission Statistics:** 6,052 applied, 68% admitted, 44% enrolled. **Transfer Admission Requirements:** college transcript(s), Minimum college GPA of 2.50 required. Lowest grade transferable D. **General Admission Information:** Application Fee $44. Regular application deadline 8/1. Notification on a rolling basis, beginning on or about 9/15. Nonfall registration accepted. Admission may be deferred for a maximum of 12. Credit offered for CEEB Advanced Placement tests.

COSTS AND FINANCIAL AID
Annual in-state tuition $7,360. Annual out-of-state tuition $14,934. Room and board $6,926. Average book expense $1,000. **Required Forms and Deadlines:** FAFSA. **Notification of Awards:** Applicants will be notified of awards on or about 4/15. **Types of Aid:** *Need-based scholarships/grants:* Federal Pell, SEOG, state scholarships/grants, private scholarships, the school's own gift aid, Federal Nursing Scholarships. *Loans:* Subsidized Stafford, Unsubsidized Stafford, PLUS, Federal Perkins, Federal Nursing, state loans, college/university loans from institutional funds. *Student Employment:* Federal Work-Study Program available. Institutional employment available. **Financial Aid Statistics:** 53% freshmen, 55% undergrads receive need-based scholarship or grant aid. 34% freshmen, 20% undergrads receive non-need-based scholarship or grant aid. 28% freshmen, 20% undergrads receive need-based self-help aid. 0% freshmen, 0% undergrads receive athletic scholarships. 66% undergrads borrow to pay for school. Average cumulative indebtedness $22,414. **Criteria for awarding institutional aid:** *Non-need-based:* academics, art, job skills, leadership, minority status, music/drama, state/district residency.

UNIVERSITY OF WISCONSIN—PARKSIDE

Box 2000, Kenosha, WI 53141-2000
Phone: 262-595-2355 · **Financial Aid Phone:** 262-595-2574
E-mail: matthew.jensen@uwp.edu · **CEEB Code:** 1860
Fax: 262-595-2008 · **Website:** www.uwp.edu · **ACT Code:** 4690

This public school was founded in 1968. It has a 700-acre campus.

RATINGS
Admissions Selectivity Rating: 70   Fire Safety Rating: 64

STUDENTS AND FACULTY
Enrollment: 4,590. **Student Body:** 57% female, 43% male, 7% out-of-state, 1% international (28 countries represented). Asian 3%, African American 8%, Caucasian 69%, Hispanic 6%, Native American 1%
Retention and Graduation: 65% freshmen return for sophomore year. 9% freshmen graduate within 4 years. 28% freshmen graduate within 6 years. **Faculty:** 181 full-time faculty, 74% hold PhDs, 45% are are members of minority groups, 22% are women. 0% of classes are taught by teaching assistants.

ACADEMICS
Degrees: bachelor's, certificate, master's. **Classes:** Most classes have fewer than 10 students. Most lab/discussion sessions have 20-29 students. **Majors with Highest Enrollment:** Criminal Justice/Law Enforcement Administration; Sociology; Business/Commerce. **Special Study Options:** Accelerated program, distance learning, double major, dual enrollment, exchange student program (domestic), honors program, independent study, internships, liberal arts/career combination, study abroad, teacher certification program, weekend college, Cooperative nursing program with University of Wisconsin: Milwaukee. **Disability Services:** Special programs offered to physically disabled students include note-taking services, reader services, tape recorders. **Career services:** alumni services, career/job search classes, career assessment, internships.

FACILITIES
Housing: Coed dorms, special housing for disabled students, special housing for international students, apartments for single students. 99% of campus accessible to physically disabled. **Special Academic Facilities/Equipment:** Language lab, electron microscope. **Computers:** Students can register for classes online. Administrative functions (other than registration) can be performed online.

CAMPUS LIFE
Environment: City. **Activities:** Choral groups, concert band, dance, drama/theater, jazz band, literary magazine, music ensembles, musical theater, pep band, radio station, student government, student newspaper, symphony orchestra. 48 registered organizations, 5 honor societies, 1 religous organization. 3 fraternities, 3 sororities. **Athletics (Intercollegiate):** *Men:* baseball, basketball, cross-country, golf, soccer, track/field (outdoor), track/field (indoor), wrestling. *Women:* basketball, cross-country, soccer, softball, track/field (outdoor), track/field (indoor), volleyball. **On-Campus Highlights:** Wyllie Library/Main Place, Communication Arts Building, Student Union, Student Activities Center, Molinaro Hall.

ADMISSIONS

Freshman Academic Profile: 5% in top 10% of high school class, 23% in top 25% of high school class, 56% in top 50% of high school class. 92% from public high schools. ACT middle 50% range 18-22. Minimum paper TOEFL 525. **Basis for Candidate Selection:** *Very important factors considered include:* Class rank, academic GPA, rigor of secondary school record, standardized test scores. *Other factors considered include:* application essay, recommendation(s), alumni/ae relation, character/personal qualities, extracurricular activities, first generation, interview, level of applicant's interest, racial/ethnic status, talent/ability, volunteer work, work experience. **Freshman Admission Requirements:** High school diploma is required and GED is accepted. **Academic units required:** 4 English, 3 mathematics, 3 science, (0 science labs), 0 foreign language, 3 social studies, 0 history, 4 academic electives. **Freshman Admission Statistics:** 1,868 applied, 92% admitted, 51% enrolled. **Transfer Admission Requirements:** High school transcript, college transcript(s), statement of good standing from prior institution(s). Minimum college GPA of 2.0 required. Lowest grade transferable D-. **General Admission Information:** Application Fee $35. Regular application deadline 8/1. Notification on a rolling basis, beginning on or about 9/15. Nonfall registration accepted. Admission may be deferred for a maximum of 1 year. Credit and/or placement offered for CEEB Advanced Placement tests.

COSTS AND FINANCIAL AID

Annual in-state tuition $4,277. Annual out-of-state tuition $14,323. Room and board $5,550. Required fees $720. Average book expense $784. **Required Forms and Deadlines:** FAFSA. **Notification of Awards:** Applicants will be notified of awards on a rolling basis beginning 4/1. **Types of Aid:** *Need-based scholarships/grants:* Federal Pell, SEOG, state scholarships/grants, private scholarships, the school's own gift aid, Federal Nursing Scholarships. *Loans:* Subsidized Stafford, Unsubsidized Stafford, PLUS, Federal Perkins, state loans. *Student Employment:* Federal Work-Study Program available. Institutional employment available. Off-campus job opportunities are excellent. **Financial Aid Statistics:** 81% freshmen, 79% undergrads receive need-based scholarship or grant aid. 33% freshmen, 15% undergrads receive non-need-based scholarship or grant aid. 77% freshmen, 63% undergrads receive need-based self-help aid. 0% freshmen, 0% undergrads receive athletic scholarships. 56% undergrads borrow to pay for school. **Criteria for awarding institutional aid:** *Non-need-based:* academics, art, athletics, minority status, music/drama, state/district residency.

UNIVERSITY OF WISCONSIN—PLATTEVILLE

1 University Plaza, Platteville, WI 53818
Phone: 608-342-1125 · **Financial Aid Phone:** 608-342-1836
E-mail: admit@uwplatt.edu · **CEEB Code:** 1917
Fax: 608-342-1122 · **Website:** www.uwplatt.edu · **ACT Code:** 4676

This public school was founded in 1866. It has a 820-acre campus.

RATINGS

Admissions Selectivity Rating: 73   **Fire Safety Rating:** 71

STUDENTS AND FACULTY

Enrollment: 5,631. **Student Body:** 38% female, 62% male, 10% out-of-state, 0% international (20 countries represented). Asian 1%, African American 1%, Caucasian 95%, Hispanic 1%, Native American <1%
Retention and Graduation: 76% freshmen return for sophomore year. **Faculty:** 249 full-time faculty, 83% hold PhDs, 31% are are members of minority groups, 16% are women. 0% of classes are taught by teaching assistants.

ACADEMICS

Degrees: associate, bachelor's, certificate, diploma, master's, transfer associate. **Classes:** Most classes have fewer than 10 students. Most lab/discussion sessions have 20-29 students. **Majors with Highest Enrollment:** Mechanical Engineering; Criminal Justice/Safety Studies; Business Administration and Management. **Special Study Options:** cooperative education program, distance learning, double major, dual enrollment, English as a Second Language (ESL), exchange student program (domestic), external degree program, honors program, independent study, internships, liberal arts/career combination, student-designed major, study abroad, teacher certification program. **Honors programs:** UW-Platteville has a University Honors Program that provides exceptional students with opportunities to study the problems, ideas, and methods of the liberal arts with an intensity, depth, and perspective that cannot usually be achieved in regular courses. **Disability Services:** Special programs offered to physically disabled students include note-taking services, reader services, tape recorders, tutors.

FACILITIES

Housing: Coed dorms, men's dorms, women's dorms, fraternity/sorority housing. 100% of campus accessible to physically disabled. **Special Academic Facilities/Equipment:** Electron microscope, Nohr Art Gallery, The Wisconsin Room. **Computers:** Students can register for classes online. Administrative functions (other than registration) can be performed online.

CAMPUS LIFE

Environment: Village. **Activities:** Choral groups, concert band, drama/theater, jazz band, literary magazine, marching band, music ensembles, musical theater, pep band, radio station, student government, student newspaper, symphony orchestra, television station. 180 registered organizations, 15 honor societies, 9 religious organizations. 9 fraternities, 5 sororities. **Athletics (Intercollegiate):** *Men:* baseball, basketball, cross-country, football, soccer, track/field (outdoor), track/field (indoor), wrestling. *Women:* basketball, cross-country, golf, soccer, softball, track/field (outdoor), track/field (indoor), volleyball. **On-Campus Highlights:** Pioneer Student Center, Resident Halls, Field House, Ullrich Hall, New Athletic Fields, Check out our virtual tour at http://www.uwplatt.edu/university/vtour/.

ADMISSIONS

Freshman Academic Profile: 12% in top 10% of high school class, 35% in top 25% of high school class, 77% in top 50% of high school class. 94% from public high schools. ACT middle 50% range 20-25. Minimum paper TOEFL 550. **Basis for Candidate Selection:** *Very important factors considered include:* Class rank, rigor of secondary school record, standardized test scores. *Important factors considered include:* geographical residence, state residency. *Other factors considered include:* academic GPA, recommendation(s), extracurricular activities, interview, talent/ability. **Freshman Admission Requirements:** High school diploma is required and GED is accepted. **Academic units required:** 4 English, 3 mathematics, 3 science, (2 science labs), 3 social studies, 4 academic electives. **Freshman Admission Statistics:** 3,075 applied, 85% admitted, 46% enrolled. **Transfer Admission Requirements:** college transcript(s), statement of good standing from prior institution(s). Minimum college GPA of 2.0 required. Lowest grade transferable D. **General Admission Information:** Application Fee $35. Notification on a rolling basis, beginning on or about 9/15. Nonfall registration accepted. Admission may be deferred for a maximum of 1 semester. Credit offered for CEEB Advanced Placement tests.

COSTS AND FINANCIAL AID

Annual in-state tuition $4,277. Annual out-of-state tuition $14,323. Room and board $4,654. Required fees $848. Average book expense $320. **Required Forms and Deadlines:** FAFSA. **Notification of Awards:** Applicants will be notified of awards on a rolling basis beginning 4/15. **Types of Aid:** *Need-based scholarships/grants:* state scholarships/grants. *Loans:* Subsidized Stafford, Unsubsidized Stafford, PLUS, Federal Perkins. **Financial Aid Statistics:** 0% freshmen, 0% undergrads receive athletic scholarships. 60% undergrads borrow to pay for school. **Criteria for awarding institutional aid:** *Non-need-based:* academics, leadership.

UNIVERSITY OF WISCONSIN—RIVER FALLS

410 South Third Street, River Falls, WI 54022
Phone: 715-425-3500 · **Financial Aid Phone:** 715-425-4111
E-mail: admit@uwrf.edu · **CEEB Code:** 3923
Website: www.uwrf.edu · **ACT Code:** 1918

This public school was founded in 1874. It has a 225-acre campus.

RATINGS

Admissions Selectivity Rating: 78   **Fire Safety Rating:** 75

STUDENTS AND FACULTY

Enrollment: 5,351. **Student Body:** 61% female, 39% male, 53% out-of-state, 1% international (21 countries represented). Asian 2%, African American 2%, Caucasian 89%, Hispanic 3%, Native American <1%
Retention and Graduation: 18% grads go on to further study within 1 year. 23% grads pursue arts and sciences degrees. 10% grads pursue business degrees. **Faculty:** 204 full-time faculty, 34% are are members of minority groups, 5% are women. 0% of classes are taught by teaching assistants.

ACADEMICS

Degrees: bachelor's, master's, post-bachelor's certificate, post-master's certificate. **Classes:** Most classes have 20-29 students. Most lab/discussion sessions have 10-19 students. **Majors with Highest Enrollment:** Business Administration and Management; Animal Sciences; Elementary Education and Teaching. **Special Study Options:** Accelerated program, cooperative education program, (domestic), honors program, independent study, internships, student-designed major, study abroad, teacher certification program. **Honors programs:** The UW-River Falls Honors Program is designed to meet the educational needs of students who have an outstanding record of academic achievement and a true sense of intellectual adventure. It allows students to experience a variety of course types and educationally related experiences while gaining academic credit. Students enrolled in the program may choose Honors sections of many general education classes, take introductory and advanced Honors seminars, participate in Honors colloquia, complete an Honors thesis/project, enroll in a service-learning experience for credit and receive credits for participation in the intellectual and creative life of the UW-RF community and elsewhere. All of these experiences are gained while still keeping within the major and minor requirements of an Honors student's academic program. **Disability Services:** Special programs offered to physically disabled students include note-taking services, reader services, tape recorders, tutors. **Career services:** Alumni network, alumni services, career/job search classes, career assessment, internships, regional alumni. Career services highlights include professional staff available for one hour appointments to help you with placement, resume writing, portfolio help, licensing, etc.

FACILITIES

Housing: Coed dorms, women's dorms, fraternity/sorority housing, apartments for single students. 95% of campus accessible to physically disabled. **Special Academic Facilities/Equipment:** Local history museum, 20-inch reflecting telescope, observatory, electron microscope, greenhouse, lab farms, educational technology center. **Computers:** Students can register for classes online. Administrative functions (other than registration) can be performed online.

CAMPUS LIFE

Environment: Village. **Activities:** Choral groups, concert band, dance, drama/theater, jazz band, literary magazine, music ensembles, musical theater, pep band, radio station, student government, student newspaper, symphony orchestra, television station. 120 registered organizations, 9 honor societies, 12 religious organizations. 5 fraternities, 4 sororities. **Athletics (Intercollegiate):** *Men:* basketball, cross-country, football, ice hockey, swimming, track/field (outdoor), track/field (indoor). *Women:* basketball, cross-country, golf, ice hockey, soccer, softball, swimming, tennis, track/field (outdoor), track/field (indoor), volleyball. **On-Campus Highlights:** University Student Center, Leadership Center, Knowles/Hunt Recreation Complex, Chalmer Davee Library, Educational Technology Center, Swenson Sundial (world's largest), Carillon, Fine Arts performing complex, Two campus laboratory farms, and Kansas City Chiefs summer camp.

ADMISSIONS

Freshman Academic Profile: Average high school GPA 3.31. 10% in top 10% of high school class, 33% in top 25% of high school class, 74% in top 50% of high school class. 86% from public high schools. SAT Math middle 50% range 425-510. SAT Critical Reading middle 50% range 450-580. SAT Writing middle 50% range 475-560. ACT middle 50% range 20-25. Minimum paper TOEFL 500. **Basis for Candidate Selection:** *Very important factors considered include:* Class rank, rigor of secondary school record, standardized test scores. *Other factors considered include:* academic GPA, recommendation(s). **Freshman Admission Requirements:** High school diploma is required and GED is accepted. **Academic units required:** 4 English, 3 mathematics, 3 science, 0 foreign language, 3 social studies, 4 academic electives. **Freshman Admission Statistics:** 2,684 applied, 78% admitted, 49% enrolled. **Transfer Admission Requirements:** college transcript(s), statement of good standing from prior institution(s). Minimum college GPA of 2.6 required. Lowest grade transferable D. **General Admission Information:** Application Fee $44. Notification on a rolling basis, beginning on or about 9/15. Nonfall registration accepted. Admission may be deferred for a maximum of 12 months. Credit and/or placement offered for CEEB Advanced Placement tests.

COSTS AND FINANCIAL AID

Annual in-state tuition $6,428. Annual out-of-state tuition $14,001. Room and board $6,435. Required fees $1,323. Average book expense $360. **Required Forms and Deadlines:** FAFSA. **Notification of Awards:** Applicants will be notified of awards on a rolling basis beginning 4/1. **Types of Aid:** *Need-based scholarships/grants:* Federal Pell, SEOG, state scholarships/grants, private scholarships, the school's own gift aid. *Loans:* Subsidized Stafford, Unsubsidized Stafford, PLUS, Federal Perkins. *Student Employment:* Federal Work-Study Program available. Institutional employment available. Off-campus job opportunities are good. **Financial Aid Statistics:** 53% freshmen, 53% undergrads receive need-based scholarship or grant aid. 18% freshmen, 17% undergrads receive non-need-based scholarship or grant aid. 79% freshmen, 81% undergrads receive need-based self-help aid. 0% freshmen, 0% undergrads receive athletic scholarships. 80% freshmen, 73% undergrads receive any aid. 76% undergrads borrow to pay for school. Average cumulative indebtedness $23,570.

UNIVERSITY OF WISCONSIN—STEVENS POINT

1108 Fremont St., Stevens Point, WI 54481
Phone: 715-346-2441 • **Financial Aid Phone:** 715-346-4771
E-mail: admiss@uwsp.edu • **CEEB Code:** 1919
Fax: 715-346-3296 • **Website:** www.uwsp.edu • **ACT Code:** 4680

This public school was founded in 1894. It has a 335-acre campus.

RATINGS

Admissions Selectivity Rating: 81   **Fire Safety Rating:** 72

STUDENTS AND FACULTY

Enrollment: 9,213. **Student Body:** 52% female, 48% male, 9% out-of-state, 2% international (30 countries represented), Asian 2%, African American 1%, Caucasian 89%, Hispanic 3%, Native American <1%
Retention and Graduation: 79% freshmen return for sophomore year. 23% freshmen graduate within 4 years. 58% freshmen graduate within 6 years. 14% grads go on to further study within 1 year. 20% grads pursue arts and sciences degrees. 1% grads pursue business degrees. **Faculty:** 412 full-time faculty, 89% hold PhDs, 44% are are members of minority groups, 8% are women. 0% of classes are taught by teaching assistants.

ACADEMICS

Degrees: associate, bachelor's, master's, terminal associate. **Classes:** Most classes have 20-29 students. Most lab/discussion sessions have 20-29 students. **Majors with Highest Enrollment:** Business/Commerce; Biological and Physical Sciences; Natural Resources/Conservation. **Special Study Options:** Accelerated program, distance learning, double major, dual enrollment, English as a Second Language (ESL), independent study, internships, student-designed major, study abroad, teacher certification program. **Disability Services:** Special programs offered to physically disabled students include note-taking services, reader services, tape recorders, tutors. **Career services:** Alumni network, career/job search classes, career assessment, internships.

FACILITIES

Housing: Coed dorms, men's dorms, women's dorms, Wellness Housing, Theme HousingFreshman Interest Groups. 100% of campus accessible to physically disabled. **Special Academic Facilities/Equipment:** Art galleries, costume and goblet collections, museum of natural history, early childhood study institute, communicative disorders center, map center, observatory, planetarium, Foucault pendulum, nature preserve, environmental station, groundwater center, herbarium, aviary, wellness institute. **Computers:** 100% of classrooms, 10% of dorms, 100% of libraries, 100% of dining areas, 100% of student union, have wireless network access. Students can register for classes online. Administrative functions (other than registration) can be performed online.

CAMPUS LIFE

Environment: Town. **Activities:** Choral groups, concert band, dance, drama/theater, jazz band, literary magazine, music ensembles, musical theater, opera, pep band, radio station, student government, student newspaper, student-run film society, symphony orchestra, television station, Campus Ministries, International Student Organization, Model UN. 185 registered organizations, 12 honor societies, 9 religious organizations. 4 fraternities, 3 sororities. **Athletics (Intercollegiate):** *Men:* baseball, basketball, cross-country, diving, football, ice hockey, swimming, track/field (outdoor), wrestling. *Women:* basketball, cross-country, diving, golf, ice hockey, soccer, softball, swimming, tennis, track/field (outdoor), volleyball. **On-Campus Highlights:** University Center/Brewhouse, Schmeeckle Reserve/Wisconsin Conservation Hall of, Health Enhancement Center, Allen Recreation Center, Fine Arts Building, The University Center houses the Information Center, Student Activities and Involvement Center, the university bookstore, meeting rooms, study lounges, Multicultural Center, and several dining options. The Schmeeckle Reserve is a 265-acre reserve available for educational and recreational use by students and community alike. The reserve includes a 24-acre lake and a 2 1/2 mile trail system used for recreational purposes. The Health Enhancement Center houses athletics, facilities for physical education programs, an Olympic-sized swimming pool, 7,500 square foot weight room, state-of-the-art training room, 8-lane indoor track with an infield for 6 tennis courts or 4 full-sized basketball courts, a fieldhouse and the Berg Gym. Allen Recreation Center provides a cardio-fitness facility, massage rooms, and a recreation center with rental equipment available for students. The Fine Arts Center houses the departments of Art and Design, Music, and Theatre and Dance. Concerts and drama productions are scheduled throughout the year in its two theatres. The Carlsten Art Gallery is also located here. Other highlights on campus include a huge mosaic on the outer, south wall of the College of Natural Resources building; a plenetarium located in the Science Building; the Learning Resources Center which contains Instructional Media Services, the library, and the Museum of Natural History; and the Communication Arts Center which houses the student radio station, student newspaper and several television studios. **Environmental Initiatives:** In December 2012, UWSP hired an energy service company (ESCO) through the WI Performance Contracting Program. The ESCO will audit, identify and evaluate energy savings opportunities. Web-based building dashboards will be included in the project to display energy, water, and other environmental variables on kiosks. In 2012, we received LEED-NC Gold for a residence hall and LEED-EB Silver for another. Remodeling for any residence halls will seek LEED certification. We are in the planning stages of a science building seeking LEED-Gold. We are in pre-design of a Health & Wellness Center seeking LEED-Gold. We are in pre-design of a Parking Garage that will have sustainable attributes and we make seek LEED certification if those standards exist when we build in 2014. All new building construction and remodeling will consider sustainable attributes and may seek LEED certification. UWSP recently added a Sustainable Energy minor to its Human Dimensions of Natural Resource Management program. The minor includes courses on sustainable energy and energy policy and law.

ADMISSIONS

Freshman Academic Profile: Average high school GPA 3.45. 18% in top 10% of high school class, 45% in top 25% of high school class, 88% in top 50% of high school class. SAT Math middle 50% range 467.5-605. SAT Critical Reading middle 50% range 497.5-595. SAT Writing middle 50% range 460-595. ACT middle 50% range 21-25. Minimum internet-based TOEFL 70. **Basis for Candidate Selection:** *Very important factors considered include:* Class rank, academic GPA, rigor of secondary school record, standardized test scores. *Important factors considered include:* application essay, recommendation(s). *Other factors considered include:* character/personal qualities, extracurricular activities, first generation, level of applicant's interest, racial/ethnic status, talent/ability, volunteer work, work experience. **Freshman Admission Requirements:** High school diploma is required and GED is accepted. **Academic units required:** 4 English, 3 mathematics, 3 science, 0 foreign language, 3 social studies, 4 academic electives, 4 Additional: 2 units from English, mathematics, social sciences, sciences, or foreign language and 2 units from above areas or other academic areas. **Freshman Admission Statistics:** 4,915 applied, 75% admitted, 45% enrolled. **Transfer Admission Requirements:** High school transcript, college transcript(s), statement of good standing from prior institution(s). Minimum college GPA of 2.25 required. Lowest grade transferable D. **General Admission Information:** Application Fee $44. Nonfall registration accepted. Admission may be deferred for a maximum of 1 semester. Credit and/or placement offered for CEEB Advanced Placement tests.

COSTS AND FINANCIAL AID

Annual in-state tuition $6,298. Annual out-of-state tuition $13,781. Room and board $6,714. Required fees $1,279. Average book expense $500. **Required Forms and Deadlines:** FAFSA. **Notification of Awards:** Applicants will be notified of awards on a rolling basis beginning 5/1. **Types of Aid:** *Need-based scholarships/grants:* Federal Pell, SEOG, state scholarships/grants, private scholarships, the school's own gift aid. *Loans:* Subsidized Stafford, Unsubsidized Stafford, PLUS, Federal Perkins. *Student Employment:* Federal Work-Study Program available. Institutional employment available. Off-campus job opportunities are good. **Financial Aid Statistics:** 52% freshmen, 57% undergrads receive need-based scholarship or grant aid. 44% freshmen, 49% undergrads receive non-need-based scholarship or grant aid. 85% freshmen, 87% undergrads receive need-based self-help aid. 0% freshmen, 0% undergrads receive athletic scholarships. 74% freshmen, 74% undergrads receive any aid. 74% undergrads borrow to pay for school. Average cumulative indebtedness $24,046. **Criteria for awarding institutional aid:** *Non-need-based:* academics, alumni affiliation, art, music/drama.

UNIVERSITY OF WISCONSIN—STOUT

Admissions UW-Stout, Menomonie, WI 54751
Phone: 715-232-1411 · **Financial Aid Phone:** 715-232-1363
E-mail: admissions@uwstout.edu · **CEEB Code:** 1740
Fax: 715-232-1667 · **Website:** www.uwstout.edu · **ACT Code:** 4652

This public school was founded in 1891. It has a 110-acre campus.

RATINGS

Admissions Selectivity Rating: 75   **Fire Safety Rating:** 62

STUDENTS AND FACULTY

Enrollment: 8,062. **Student Body:** 46% female, 54% male, 32% out-of-state, 3% international (28 countries represented). Asian 3%, African American 2%, Caucasian 88%, Hispanic 1%, Native American <1%
Retention and Graduation: 19% freshmen graduate within 4 years. 9% grads go on to further study within 1 year. **Faculty:** 406 full-time faculty, 75% hold

PhDs, 44% are are members of minority groups, 12% are women. 0% of classes are taught by teaching assistants.

ACADEMICS

Degrees: bachelor's, certificate, master's, post-bachelor's certificate, post-master's certificate. **Classes:** Most classes have 20-29 students. Most lab/discussion sessions have 20-29 students. **Majors with Highest Enrollment:** Design and Applied Arts; Business/Commerce; Hospitality Administration/Management. **Special Study Options:** Accelerated program, cooperative education program, cross-registration, distance learning, double major, dual enrollment, exchange student program (domestic), external degree program, honors program, independent study, internships, study abroad, teacher certification program. **Honors programs:** The University Honors Program (UHP) is designed to enhance the education of students challenging them to think in more depth and detail and to provide the opportunity to meet other students while doing so. **Disability Services:** Special programs offered to physically disabled students include note-taking services, reader services, tutors. **Career services:** alumni services, career/job search classes, internships. Career services highlights include our Co-op Program, which now exceeds 676 co-op students per year.

FACILITIES

Housing: Coed dorms, special housing for disabled students, apartments for single students, freshmen housing, smoke-free housing, upperclass/graduate housing, alcohol-free housing. 100% of campus accessible to physically disabled. **Special Academic Facilities/Equipment:** Specialized labs support degree programs throughout the campus. Furlong Art Gallery in Micheal's Hall. **Computers:** Students can register for classes online. Administrative functions (other than registration) can be performed online. Undergraduates are required to own a computer.

CAMPUS LIFE

Environment: Village. **Activities:** Choral groups, concert band, dance, drama/theater, jazz band, literary magazine, marching band, music ensembles, musical theater, pep band, radio station, student government, student newspaper, student-run film society, Campus Ministries, International Student Organization, Model UN. 120 registered organizations, 1 honor society, 12 religious organizations. 5 fraternities, 3 sororities. **Athletics (Intercollegiate):** *Men:* baseball, basketball, cross-country, football, ice hockey, track/field (outdoor). *Women:* basketball, cross-country, gymnastics, soccer, softball, tennis, track/field (outdoor), volleyball. **On-Campus Highlights:** Millenium Hall, Athletic Complex, Ropes Course, Climbing Wall, In-line Skating, Student Center, Micheels Hall.

ADMISSIONS

Freshman Academic Profile: Average high school GPA 3.3. 8.6% in top 10% of high school class, 28.7% in top 25% of high school class, 69.4% in top 50% of high school class. ACT middle 50% range 20-24. Minimum paper TOEFL 500. **Basis for Candidate Selection:** *Very important factors considered include:* Class rank, standardized test scores. *Important factors considered include:* application essay, rigor of secondary school record. *Other factors considered include:* academic GPA, recommendation(s), alumni/ae relation, character/personal qualities, extracurricular activities, first generation, interview, level of applicant's interest, racial/ethnic status, talent/ability, volunteer work, work experience. **Freshman Admission Requirements:** High school diploma is required and GED is accepted. **Academic units required:** 4 English, 3 mathematics, 3 science, (0 science labs), 0 foreign language, 3 social studies, 0 history, 4 academic electives. **Freshman Admission Statistics:** 3,352 applied, 82% admitted, 53% enrolled. **Transfer Admission Requirements:** college transcript(s), statement of good standing from prior institution(s). Minimum college GPA of 2.5 required. Lowest grade transferable D-. **General Admission Information:** Application Fee $44. Notification on a rolling basis, beginning on or about 9/15. Nonfall registration accepted. Credit offered for CEEB Advanced Placement tests.

COSTS AND FINANCIAL AID

Annual in-state tuition $7,014. Annual out-of-state tuition $14,760. Room and board $6,434. Required fees $2,011. Average book expense $396. **Required Forms and Deadlines:** FAFSA. **Notification of Awards:** Applicants will be notified of awards on a rolling basis beginning 4/1. **Types of Aid:** *Need-based scholarships/grants:* Federal Pell, SEOG, state scholarships/grants, private scholarships, the school's own gift aid. *Loans:* Subsidized Stafford, Unsubsidized Stafford, PLUS, Federal Perkins, Alternative Educational Loans. *Student Employment:* Federal Work-Study Program available. Institutional employment available. Highest amount earned per year from on-campus jobs $948. Off-campus job opportunities are good. **Financial Aid Statistics:** 52% freshmen, 56% undergrads receive need-based scholarship or grant aid. 42% freshmen, 26% undergrads receive non-need-based scholarship or grant aid. 89% freshmen, 91% undergrads receive need-based self-help aid. 0% freshmen, 0% undergrads receive athletic scholarships. 71% freshmen, 74% undergrads receive any aid. 76% undergrads borrow to pay for school. Average cumulative indebtedness $23,547. **Criteria for awarding institutional aid:** *Non-need-based:* academics.

UNIVERSITY OF WISCONSIN—SUPERIOR

Belknap and Catlin, P.O. Box 2000, Superior, WI 54880-4500
Phone: 715-394-8230 • Financial Aid Phone: 715-394-8200
E-mail: admissions@uwsuper.edu • CEEB Code: 1920
Fax: 715-394-8407 • Website: www.uwsuper.edu • ACT Code: 4682

This public school was founded in 1893. It has a 230-acre campus.

RATINGS

Admissions Selectivity Rating: 76   Fire Safety Rating: 76

STUDENTS AND FACULTY
Enrollment: 2,339. **Student Body:** 60% female, 40% male, 43% out-of-state, 6% international (38 countries represented). Asian 1%, African American 2%, Caucasian 83%, Hispanic 2%, Native American 3%
Retention and Graduation: 72% freshmen return for sophomore year. 19% freshmen graduate within 4 years. 43% freshmen graduate within 6 years. **Faculty:** 126 full-time faculty, 70% hold PhDs, 49% are are members of minority groups, 14% are women. 0% of classes are taught by teaching assistants.

ACADEMICS
Degrees: associate, bachelor's, certificate, master's, post-master's certificate. **Classes:** Most classes have 10-19 students. Most lab/discussion sessions have 10-19 students. **Majors with Highest Enrollment:** Business Administration and Management; Elementary Education and Teaching; Communication. **Special Study Options:** cooperative education program, cross-registration, distance learning, double major, dual enrollment, English as a Second Language (ESL), exchange student program (domestic), external degree program, independent study, internships, liberal arts/career combination, student-designed major, study abroad, teacher certification program. **Combined degree programs:** 3-2 Forestry program w/ Michigan Tech U. **Disability Services:** Special programs offered to physically disabled students include note-taking services, tape recorders, tutors. **Career services:** Alumni network, career/job search classes, career assessment, internships.

FACILITIES
Housing: Coed dorms, special housing for disabled students, women's dorms, apartments for married students, apartments for single students. 90% of campus accessible to physically disabled. **Special Academic Facilities/Equipment:** TV, radio, and film facilities,observatory, greenhouse,two art galleries, recital hall, four theaters, modern health and wellness center. Major Library renovations to be completed and major student center renovation in works. **Computers:** 40% of classrooms, 100% of libraries, 100% of dining areas, 100% of student union, 20% of common outdoor areas have wireless network access. Students can register for classes online. Administrative functions (other than registration) can be performed online.

CAMPUS LIFE
Environment: City. **Activities:** Choral groups, concert band, dance, drama/theater, jazz band, literary magazine, music ensembles, musical theater, pep band, radio station, student government, student newspaper, student-run film society, symphony orchestra, television station, Campus Ministries, International Student Organization. 70 registered organizations, 1 honor society, 5 religious organizations. 1 sorority. **Athletics (Intercollegiate):** *Men:* baseball, basketball, cross-country, ice hockey, soccer, track/field (outdoor), track/field (indoor). *Women:* basketball, cross-country, golf, ice hockey, soccer, softball, track/field (outdoor), track/field (indoor), volleyball. **On-Campus Highlights:** New Health and Wellness Center, Coffee Nook, Snack Bar, Rothwell Student Center Student Lounge, Multicultural Center, Health and Wellness Center is a new $17 million facility complete with running track, climbing wall, raquetball courts and much more. Library renovations underway, new student center renovations starting soon. **Environmental Initiatives:** LEED certification for new buildings that are now in the planning/construction process.

ADMISSIONS
Freshman Academic Profile: Average high school GPA 3.17. 7% in top 10% of high school class, 17% in top 25% of high school class, 62% in top 50% of high school class. 90% from public high schools. ACT middle 50% range 19-24. Minimum internet-based TOEFL 61. Minimum paper TOEFL 500. **Basis for Candidate Selection:** *Very important factors considered include:* rigor of secondary school record. *Important factors considered include:* Class rank, standardized test scores. *Other factors considered include:* application essay, recommendation(s), character/personal qualities, extracurricular activities, first generation, interview, level of applicant's interest, racial/ethnic status, talent/ability, volunteer work, work experience. **Freshman Admission Requirements:** High school diploma is required and GED is accepted. **Academic units required:** 4 English, 3 mathematics, 3 science, 3 social studies, 4 academic electives. **Freshman Admission Statistics:** 877 applied, 68% admitted, 55% enrolled. **Transfer Admission Requirements:** college transcript(s), Minimum college GPA of 2.0 required. Lowest grade transferable D. **General**

Admission Information: Application Fee $44. Notification on a rolling basis, beginning on or about 10/1. Nonfall registration accepted. Admission may be deferred for a maximum of 1 year. Credit offered for CEEB Advanced Placement tests.

COSTS AND FINANCIAL AID
Annual in-state tuition $6,535. Annual out-of-state tuition $14,108. Room and board $6,320. Required fees $1,459. Average book expense $800. **Required Forms and Deadlines:** FAFSA. **Notification of Awards:** Applicants will be notified of awards on a rolling basis beginning 3/15. **Types of Aid:** *Need-based scholarships/grants:* Federal Pell, SEOG, state scholarships/grants, private scholarships, the school's own gift aid. *Loans:* Direct Subsidized Stafford, Direct Unsubsidized Stafford, Direct PLUS, Federal Perkins, state loans, college/university loans from institutional funds. *Student Employment:* Federal Work-Study Program available. Institutional employment available. Highest amount earned per year from on-campus jobs $11,000. Off-campus job opportunities are good. **Financial Aid Statistics:** 54% freshmen, 68% undergrads receive need-based scholarship or grant aid. 50% freshmen, 26% undergrads receive non-need-based scholarship or grant aid. 84% freshmen, 85% undergrads receive need-based self-help aid. 0% freshmen, 0% undergrads receive athletic scholarships. 64% freshmen, 68% undergrads receive any aid. 72% undergrads borrow to pay for school. Average cumulative indebtedness $26,472. **Criteria for awarding institutional aid:** *Non-need-based:* academics, alumni affiliation, art, leadership, minority status, music/drama, state/district residency.

UNIVERSITY OF WISCONSIN—WHITEWATER

800 West Main Street, Whitewater, WI 53190-1791
Phone: 262-472-1440 • Financial Aid Phone: 262-472-1130
E-mail: uwwadmit@uww.edu • CEEB Code: 1921
Fax: 262-472-1515 • Website: http://www.uww.edu/ • ACT Code: 4684

This public school was founded in 1868. It has a 385-acre campus.

RATINGS

Admissions Selectivity Rating: 71   Fire Safety Rating: 76

STUDENTS AND FACULTY
Enrollment: 8,999. **Student Body:** 50% female, 50% male, 4% out-of-state, 0% international (69 countries represented). Asian 2%, African American 4%, Caucasian 90%, Hispanic 2%, Native American <1%
Retention and Graduation: 74% freshmen return for sophomore year. 21% freshmen graduate within 4 years. **Faculty:** 392 full-time faculty, 85% hold PhDs, 44% are are members of minority groups, 18% are women. 0% of classes are taught by teaching assistants.

ACADEMICS
Degrees: associate, bachelor's, master's. **Classes:** Most classes have 30-39 students. **Majors with Highest Enrollment:** Journalism; Elementary Education and Teaching; Physical Education Teaching and Coaching. **Special Study Options:** Accelerated program, cooperative education program, cross-registration, distance learning, double major, dual enrollment, English as a Second Language (ESL), exchange student program (domestic), external degree program, honors program, independent study, internships, liberal arts/career combination, student-designed major, study abroad, teacher certification program, weekend college. **Honors programs:** General academic honors program. **Disability Services:** Special programs offered to physically disabled students include note-taking services, reader services, tape recorders, tutors. **Career services:** career/job search classes, career assessment, internships. Career services highlights include internships.

FACILITIES
Housing: Coed dorms, special housing for disabled students, special housing for international students, women's dorms. 100% of campus accessible to physically disabled. **Special Academic Facilities/Equipment:** Two electron microscopes, State of the Art Theater/Auditorium. **Computers:** Students can register for classes online. Administrative functions (other than registration) can be performed online.

CAMPUS LIFE
Environment: Village. **Activities:** Choral groups, concert band, dance, drama/theater, jazz band, literary magazine, marching band, music ensembles, musical theater, opera, radio station, student government, student newspaper, symphony orchestra, television station 130 registered organizations, 4 honor societies, 8 religious organizations. 9 fraternities, 8 sororities. **Athletics (Intercollegiate):** *Men:* baseball, basketball, cross-country, diving, football, soccer, swimming, tennis, track/field (outdoor), track/field (indoor), wrestling. *Women:* basketball, bowling, cross-country, diving, golf, gymnastics, soccer, softball, swimming, tennis, track/field (outdoor), track/field (indoor), volleyball. **On-Campus High-**

lights: New Kachel Field House, University Center, Underground Dance Club, Ritazza Coffee Shop, Warhawk Room.

ADMISSIONS

Freshman Academic Profile: 9% in top 10% of high school class, 32% in top 25% of high school class, 77% in top 50% of high school class. 90% from public high schools. SAT Math middle 50% range 480-600. SAT Writing middle 50% range 470-610. ACT middle 50% range 20-24. Minimum paper TOEFL 500. **Basis for Candidate Selection:** *Very important factors considered include:* Class rank, rigor of secondary school record, standardized test scores. *Other factors considered include:* application essay, academic GPA, recommendation(s), character/personal qualities, extracurricular activities, first generation, geographical residence, interview, level of applicant's interest, racial/ethnic status, state residency, talent/ability, volunteer work, work experience. **Freshman Admission Requirements:** High school diploma is required and GED is accepted. **Academic units required:** 4 English, 3 mathematics, 3 science, (1 science labs), 0 foreign language, 3 social studies, 4 academic electives. **Transfer Admission Requirements:** High school transcript, college transcript(s), Minimum college GPA of 2.0 required. Lowest grade transferable D-. **General Admission Information:** Application Fee $35. Notification on a rolling basis, beginning on or about 9/15. Nonfall registration accepted. Admission may be deferred for a maximum of 3 terms or 1. Credit offered for CEEB Advanced Placement tests.

COSTS AND FINANCIAL AID

Annual in-state tuition $5,568. Annual out-of-state tuition $13,042. Room and board $4,322. Required fees $710. Average book expense $170. **Required Forms and Deadlines:** FAFSA. **Notification of Awards:** Applicants will be notified of awards on a rolling basis beginning 4/1. **Types of Aid:** *Need-based scholarships/grants:* Federal Pell, SEOG, state scholarships/grants, private scholarships, the school's own gift aid. *Loans:* Direct Subsidized Stafford, Direct Unsubsidized Stafford, Direct PLUS, Federal Perkins, college/university loans from institutional funds, Alternative Loans. *Student Employment:* Highest amount earned per year from on-campus jobs $3,000. **Financial Aid Statistics:** 38% freshmen, 44% undergrads receive need-based scholarship or grant aid. 27% freshmen, 13% undergrads receive non-need-based scholarship or grant aid. 85% freshmen, 84% undergrads receive need-based self-help aid. 0% freshmen, 0% undergrads receive athletic scholarships. 52% freshmen, 42% undergrads receive any aid. 65% undergrads borrow to pay for school. Average cumulative indebtedness $14,512. **Criteria for awarding institutional aid:** *Non-need-based:* academics, alumni affiliation, art, leadership, minority status, music/drama, state/district residency.

UNIVERSITY OF WYOMING

Dept 3435, Laramie, WY 82071
Phone: 307-766-5160 · **Financial Aid Phone:** 307-766-2116
E-mail: admissions@uwyo.edu · **CEEB Code:** 4855
Fax: 307-766-4042 · **Website:** www.uwyo.edu · **ACT Code:** 5006

This public school was founded in 1886. It has a 785-acre campus.

RATINGS

Admissions Selectivity Rating: 77   **Fire Safety Rating:** 85

STUDENTS AND FACULTY

Enrollment: 9,910. **Student Body:** 52% female, 48% male, 31% out-of-state, 4% international (91 countries represented). Asian 1%, African American 1%, Caucasian 78%, Hispanic 7%, Native American 1%
Retention and Graduation: 75% freshmen return for sophomore year. 24% freshmen graduate within 4 years. 54% freshmen graduate within 6 years. **Faculty:** 747 full-time faculty, 81% hold PhDs, 41% are are members of minority groups, 11% are women. 10% of classes are taught by teaching assistants.

ACADEMICS

Degrees: bachelor's, certificate, doctoral, master's, post-bachelor's certificate, post-master's certificate. **Classes:** Most classes have 20-29 students. Most lab/discussion sessions have 20-29 students. **Majors with Highest Enrollment:** Registered Nursing/Registered Nurse; Elementary Education and Teaching; Psychology. **Special Study Options:** Accelerated program, distance learning, double major, English as a Second Language (ESL), exchange student program (domestic), external degree program, honors program, independent study, internships, student-designed major, study abroad. **Honors programs:** The University Honors Program provides highly motivated students a series of curricular and extracurricular opportunities. Most students are selected for the program prior to their freshman year, although the program welcomes UW and transfer students up to the beginning of the junior year. Each year the Honors Program awards scholarships to qualifying students who are beginning their undergraduate education or who are entering the University as transfer students. The honors students organize extracurricular activities, have a student lounge and computers for their use, and have the option of living on one of the honors floors in the residence halls or in the Honors House. Courses offered in the honors program are restricted to honors program students; exceptions must be approved by the Honors program office. **Disability Services:** Special programs offered to physically disabled students include note-taking services, reader services, tape recorders, tutors. **Career services:** Alumni network, alumni services, career/job search classes, career assessment, internships, regional alumni.

FACILITIES

Housing: Coed dorms, special housing for disabled students, fraternity/sorority housing, apartments for married students, apartments for single students, Floor specific living plans in the residence halls; Health Sciences Living house. 95% of campus accessible to physically disabled. **Special Academic Facilities/Equipment:** Art gallery, Geology museum, American Heritage Center, Rocky Mountain Herbarium, Solheim Mycology Herbarium, art museum, planetarium, environmental biology lab, anthropology museum, on-site elementary school, state veterinary lab, infrared telescope observatory, lysimeter lab, insect museum and gallery room, Wyoming Geographic Information Science Center, Writing Center, Wyoming Cooperative Fishery and Wildlife Research Unit **Computers:** 75% of classrooms, 20% of dorms, 100% of libraries, 5% of dining areas, 100% of student union, 10% of common outdoor areas have wireless network access. Students can register for classes online. Administrative functions (other than registration) can be performed online.

CAMPUS LIFE

Environment: Town. **Activities:** Choral groups, concert band, dance, drama/theater, jazz band, literary magazine, marching band, music ensembles, musical theater, opera, pep band, radio station, student government, student newspaper, symphony orchestra, television station, Campus Ministries, International Student Organization, Model UN. 223 registered organizations, 41 honor societies, 17 religious organizations. 8 fraternities, 6 sororities. **Athletics (Intercollegiate):** *Men:* basketball, cheerleading, cross-country, diving, football, golf, swimming, track/field (outdoor), track/field (indoor), wrestling. *Women:* basketball, cheerleading, cross-country, diving, golf, soccer, swimming, tennis, track/field (outdoor), track/field (indoor), volleyball. **On-Campus Highlights:** Student Union, American Heritage Center and Art Museum, Geology Museum, Fine Arts Center, Half-Acre Gym. **Environmental Initiatives:** Campus Sustainability Committee; College of Business Sustainable Business Program; Presidents Climate Commitment.

ADMISSIONS

Freshman Academic Profile: Average high school GPA 3.46. 19.4% in top 10% of high school class, 47.6% in top 25% of high school class, 78.8% in top 50% of high school class. SAT Math middle 50% range 470-610. SAT Critical Reading middle 50% range 470-600. ACT middle 50% range 22-27. Minimum internet-based TOEFL 76. Minimum paper TOEFL 540. **Basis for Candidate Selection:** *Very important factors considered include:* academic GPA, rigor of secondary school record, standardized test scores. *Important factors considered include:* level of applicant's interest. *Other factors considered include:* application essay, recommendation(s), character/personal qualities, extracurricular activities, interview, state residency, talent/ability. **Freshman Admission Requirements:** High school diploma is required and GED is accepted. **Academic units required:** 4 English, 3 mathematics, 3 science, (3 science labs), 3 Cultural Context Electives—Recomended—3 behavioral or social sciences, 3 visual or performing arts, 3 humanities or earth/space sciences. **Freshman Admission Statistics:** 4,187 applied, 98% admitted, 38% enrolled. **Transfer Admission Requirements:** college transcript(s), Minimum college GPA of 2.0 required. Lowest grade transferable D. **General Admission Information:** Application Fee $40. Regular application deadline 8/10. Nonfall registration accepted. Admission may be deferred for a maximum of 1 year. Credit and/or placement offered for CEEB Advanced Placement tests.

COSTS AND FINANCIAL AID

Annual in-state tuition $3,390. Annual out-of-state tuition $13,620. Room and board $9,755. Required fees $1,256. Average book expense $1,200. **Required Forms and Deadlines:** FAFSA. **Notification of Awards:** Applicants will be notified of awards on a rolling basis beginning 3/15. **Types of Aid:** *Need-based scholarships/grants:* Federal Pell, SEOG, state scholarships/grants, private scholarships, the school's own gift aid. *Loans:* Subsidized Stafford, Unsubsidized Stafford, PLUS, Federal Perkins. *Student Employment:* Federal Work-Study Program available. Institutional employment available. Off-campus job opportunities are good. **Financial Aid Statistics:** 61% freshmen, 69% undergrads receive need-based scholarship or grant aid. 83% freshmen, 69% undergrads receive non-need-based scholarship or grant aid. 52% freshmen, 61% undergrads receive need-based self-help aid. 2% freshmen, 2% undergrads receive athletic scholarships. 48% undergrads borrow to pay for school. Average cumulative indebtedness $21,230. **Criteria for awarding institutional aid:** *Non-need-based:* academics, alumni affiliation, art, athletics, leadership, minority status, music/drama, religious affiliation, state/district residency.

UPPER IOWA UNIVERSITY

Parker Fox Hall Box 1859, Fayette, IA 52142-1859
Phone: 800-553-4150 · **Financial Aid Phone:** 563-425-5276
E-mail: admission@uiu.edu
Fax: 563-425-5277 · **ACT Code:** 1360

This private school was founded in 1857. It has a 80-acre campus.

RATINGS

Admissions Selectivity Rating: 83	Fire Safety Rating: 76

STUDENTS AND FACULTY
Enrollment: 4,513. **Student Body:** 60% female, 40% male, 55% out-of-state, 3% international (30 countries represented). Asian 1%, African American 19%, Caucasian 66%, Hispanic 4%, Native American <1%
Retention and Graduation: 24% freshmen graduate within 4 years. 40% freshmen graduate within 6 years. 23% grads go on to further study within 1 year. 17% grads pursue arts and sciences degrees. 3% grads pursue law degrees. 25% grads pursue business degrees. 1% grads pursue medical degrees. **Faculty:** 78 full-time faculty, 72% hold PhDs, 54% are are members of minority groups, 3% are women. 0% of classes are taught by teaching assistants.

ACADEMICS
Degrees: associate, bachelor's, certificate, master's, terminal associate, transfer associate. **Classes:** Most classes have 10-19 students. Most lab/discussion sessions have 10-19 students. **Majors with Highest Enrollment:** Psychology; Human Services; Human Resources Management/Personnel Administration. **Special Study Options:** Accelerated program, distance learning, double major, dual enrollment, English as a Second Language (ESL), external degree program, independent study, internships, liberal arts/career combination, student-designed major, study abroad, teacher certification program. **Disability Services:** Special programs offered to physically disabled students include reader services, tape recorders, tutors. **Career services:** alumni services, career/job search classes, career assessment, internships.

FACILITIES
Housing: Coed dorms, men's dorms, women's dorms, Apartment-style housing. 70% of campus accessible to physically disabled. **Computers:** 100% of classrooms, 100% of dorms, 100% of libraries, 100% of dining areas, 100% of student union, 33% of common outdoor areas have wireless network access. Students can register for classes online. Administrative functions (other than registration) can be performed online.

CAMPUS LIFE
Environment: Rural. **Activities:** Choral groups, pep band, student government, student newspaper, Campus Ministries, International Student Organization. 40 registered organizations, 1 honor society, 1 religous organization. 4 fraternities, 5 sororities. **Athletics (Intercollegiate):** *Men:* baseball, basketball, cross-country, football, golf, soccer, wrestling. *Women:* basketball, cross-country, golf, soccer, softball, tennis, volleyball. **On-Campus Highlights:** Rec Center, Grill 151, Dorman Gym, Andres Center for Business and Education, Cafeteria, We have 3 new buildings that will be opening in 2010. A new student center, liberal arts building and new housing unit. **Environmental Initiatives:** Geothermal Heating/Cooling; Lighting Retrofit; Daylight Harvesting.

ADMISSIONS
Freshman Academic Profile: Average high school GPA 3.21. 16% in top 10% of high school class, 35% in top 25% of high school class, 65% in top 50% of high school class. ACT middle 50% range 19-25. Minimum internet-based TOEFL 61. Minimum paper TOEFL 500. **Basis for Candidate Selection:** *Very important factors considered include:* standardized test scores. *Important factors considered include:* academic GPA. *Other factors considered include:* Class rank, recommendation(s), rigor of secondary school record, alumni/ae relation, first generation. **Freshman Admission Requirements:** High school diploma is required and GED is accepted. **Freshman Admission Statistics:** 1,229 applied, 58% admitted, 33% enrolled. **Transfer Admission Requirements:** High school transcript, college transcript(s), Lowest grade transferable D-. **General Admission Information:** Application Fee $15. Regular application deadline 8/23. Nonfall registration accepted. Admission may be deferred for a maximum of one term. Credit and/or placement offered for CEEB Advanced Placement tests.

COSTS AND FINANCIAL AID
Annual tuition $24,400. Room and board $7,510. Required fees $0. Average book expense $1,400. **Required Forms and Deadlines:** FAFSA. **Types of**

Aid: *Need-based scholarships/grants:* Federal Pell, SEOG, state scholarships/grants, private scholarships, the school's own gift aid. *Loans:* Subsidized Stafford, Unsubsidized Stafford, PLUS, Federal Perkins, Alternative Loans. *Student Employment:* Federal Work-Study Program available. Highest amount earned per year from on-campus jobs $1,860. Off-campus job opportunities are fair. **Financial Aid Statistics:** 99% freshmen, 86% undergrads receive need-based scholarship or grant aid. 53% freshmen, 12% undergrads receive non-need-based scholarship or grant aid. 66% freshmen, 82% undergrads receive need-based self-help aid. 0% freshmen, 0% undergrads receive athletic scholarships. 97% freshmen, 90% undergrads receive any aid. 73% undergrads borrow to pay for school. Average cumulative indebtedness $30,029. **Criteria for awarding institutional aid:** *Non-need-based:* academics, alumni affiliation, athletics.

URSINUS COLLEGE

Best 380

Ursinus College, Collegeville, PA 19426
Phone: 610-409-3200 · **Financial Aid Phone:** 610-409-3600
E-mail: admission@ursinus.edu · **CEEB Code:** 2931
Fax: 610-409-3197 · **Website:** www.ursinus.edu · **ACT Code:** 3738

This private school was founded in 1869. It has a 170-acre campus.

RATINGS

Admissions Selectivity Rating: 82	Fire Safety Rating: 81

STUDENTS AND FACULTY
Enrollment: 1,656. **Student Body:** 52% female, 48% male, 46% out-of-state, 2% international (16 countries represented). Asian 5%, African American 6%, Caucasian 75%, Hispanic 6%, Native American <1%
Retention and Graduation: 79% freshmen graduate within 4 years. 81% freshmen graduate within 6 years. 27% grads go on to further study within 1 year. 40% grads pursue arts and sciences degrees. 14% grads pursue law degrees. 3% grads pursue business degrees. 36% grads pursue medical degrees. **Faculty:** 123 full-time faculty, 92% hold PhDs, 49% are are members of minority groups, 14% are women. 0% of classes are taught by teaching assistants.

ACADEMICS
Degrees: bachelor's. **Classes:** Most classes have fewer than 10 students. Most lab/discussion sessions have 10-19 students. **Majors with Highest Enrollment:** Economics; Biology/Biological Sciences; Psychology. **Special Study Options:** double major, dual enrollment, English as a Second Language (ESL), honors program, independent study, internships, student-designed major, study abroad, teacher certification program, Howard University Semester. **Honors programs:** The Ursinus Summer Fellows program provides stipends to rising juniors and seniors to live on campus and do faculty-mentored research over the summer months. Fellows' projects often lead to senior honors projects. **Combined degree programs:** BA/MD, BA/MEng, Early Assurance-Drexel Univ. College of Medicine. **Disability Services:** Special programs offered to physically disabled students include note-taking services, reader services, tape recorders, tutors. **Career services:** Alumni network, alumni services, career/job search classes, career assessment, internships, regional alumni. Career services highlights include our internship opportunities, which are exceptional and numerous and have taken our students on all sorts of adventures: to nearby pharmaceutical labs, to U.S. embassies overseas, to the summer stock stages of the Berkshires, and to a marine mammal rescue station at the Jersey Shore. Internships are available to students in every major, and even to those studying abroad. With a full range of staffing and Internet resources to find, match and place students in internships that are right for them, Ursinus has a high percentage of students who participate in these experiences.

FACILITIES
Housing: Coed dorms, men's dorms, special housing for international students, women's dorms, Ursinus features the Residential Village, a cluster of 25 restored Victorian-era houses. Theme houses include: Musser International, Unity, Wellness, Language, Biology, Service, Zwingli Literary House and Wicks Honors House. 40 percent of Ursinus students reside in these houses. 95% of campus accessible to physically disabled. **Special Academic Facilities/Equipment:** The Kaleidoscope (performing arts center), New field house, new 143-bed dormitory, Berman Museum of Art, 6 new telescopes, scanning electron microscope, Bruker 300 MHz NMR, Perkin Elmer Spectrum 1000 FTIR, LKB Isothermal Calorimeter, an assortment of spectrometers and an HPLC, recently-renovated Pfahler Hall of Science. **Computers:** 100% of class-

rooms, 100% of libraries, 100% of dining areas, 100% of student union, 50% of common outdoor areas have wireless network access. Students can register for classes online. Administrative functions (other than registration) can be performed online. Undergraduates are required to own a computer.

CAMPUS LIFE

Environment: City. **Activities:** Choral groups, concert band, dance, drama/theater, jazz band, literary magazine, music ensembles, musical theater, pep band, radio station, student government, student newspaper, student-run film society, television station, yearbook. 88 registered organizations, 27 honor societies, 4 religious organizations. 7 fraternities, 7 sororities. **Athletics (Intercollegiate):** *Men:* baseball, basketball, cross-country, football, golf, lacrosse, soccer, swimming, tennis, track/field (outdoor), track/field (indoor), wrestling. *Women:* basketball, cross-country, field hockey, golf, gymnastics, lacrosse, soccer, softball, swimming, tennis, track/field (outdoor), track/field (indoor), volleyball. **On-Campus Highlights:** The Kaleidoscope Performing Arts Centerl, Berman Museum of Art lt;brgt;, Pfahler Hall of Science, Richter-North Hall (new dormitory), Bakes Center (field house and fitness center), Wismer Center houses campus bookstore and dining facilities. Victorian dormitories along Main Street and traditional campus buildings give Ursinus a classic college ambience. **Environmental Initiatives:** Energy efficient enhancements and Energy Dashboard; Food waste recycling; UCGreen Fellows; student sustainability leadership and professional development program.

ADMISSIONS

Freshman Academic Profile: 24% in top 10% of high school class, 54% in top 25% of high school class, 88% in top 50% of high school class. 69% from public high schools. SAT Math middle 50% range 530-630. SAT Critical Reading middle 50% range 520-630. SAT Writing middle 50% range 500-620. ACT middle 50% range 23-28. Minimum internet-based TOEFL 80. **Basis for Candidate Selection:** *Very important factors considered include:* Class rank, rigor of secondary school record, extracurricular activities. *Important factors considered include:* application essay, academic GPA, recommendation(s), standardized test scores, alumni/ae relation, racial/ethnic status, talent/ability, volunteer work, work experience. *Other factors considered include:* character/personal qualities, first generation, geographical residence, interview, level of applicant's interest. **Freshman Admission Requirements:** High school diploma is required and GED is accepted. **Academic units required:** 4 English, 3 mathematics, 1 science, (1 science labs), 2 foreign language, 1 social studies. **Freshman Admission Statistics:** 2,672 applied, 83% admitted, 22% enrolled. **Transfer Admission Requirements:** High school transcript, college transcript(s), essay or personal statement, standardized test scores, Minimum college GPA of 3.0 required. Lowest grade transferable C. **General Admission Information:** Application Fee $50. Early decision application deadline 1/15. Regular application deadline 2/15. Regular notification 4/1. Nonfall registration accepted. Admission may be deferred for a maximum of 1 year. Credit and/or placement offered for CEEB Advanced Placement tests.

COSTS AND FINANCIAL AID

Required Forms and Deadlines: FAFSA, CSS/Financial Aid PROFILE. **Notification of Awards:** Applicants will be notified of awards on or about 4/1. **Types of Aid:** *Need-based scholarships/grants:* Federal Pell, SEOG, state scholarships/grants, private scholarships, the school's own gift aid. *Loans:* Subsidized Stafford, Unsubsidized Stafford, PLUS, Federal Perkins. *Student Employment:* Federal Work-Study Program available. Institutional employment available. Highest amount earned per year from on-campus jobs $1,200. Off-campus job opportunities are excellent. **Financial Aid Statistics:** 100% freshmen, 100% undergrads receive need-based scholarship or grant aid. 21% freshmen, 16% undergrads receive non-need-based scholarship or grant aid. 77% freshmen, 81% undergrads receive need-based self-help aid. 0% freshmen, 0% undergrads receive athletic scholarships. 79% undergrads borrow to pay for school. Average cumulative indebtedness $25,612. **Criteria for awarding institutional aid:** *Non-need-based:* academics, alumni affiliation, art, music/drama.

URSULINE COLLEGE

2550 Lander Road, Pepper Pike, OH 44124-4398
Phone: 440-449-4203 · **Financial Aid Phone:** 440-646-8309
E-mail: admission@ursuline.edu · **CEEB Code:** 1848
Fax: 440-684-6138 · **Website:** www.ursuline.edu

This private school, affiliated with the Roman Catholic Church, was founded in 1871. It has a 110-acre campus.

RATINGS

Admissions Selectivity Rating: 80   **Fire Safety Rating:** 81

STUDENTS AND FACULTY

Enrollment: 697. **Student Body:** 92% female, 8% male, 8% out-of-state, 1% international (23 countries represented). Asian 1%, African American 26%, Caucasian 65%, Hispanic 3%, Native American <1%. **Retention and Graduation:** 73% freshmen return for sophomore year. 26% freshmen graduate within 4 years. 47% freshmen graduate within 6 years. **Faculty:** 75 full-time faculty, 63% hold PhDs, 84% are are members of minority groups, 8% are women. 0% of classes are taught by teaching assistants.

ACADEMICS

Degrees: bachelor's, certificate, master's, post-bachelor's certificate, post-master's certificate. **Classes:** Most classes have 10-19 students. Most lab/discussion sessions have 10-19 students. **Majors with Highest Enrollment:** Early Childhood Education and Teaching; Health Services/Allied Health/Health Sciences; Art Therapy/Therapist. **Special Study Options:** Accelerated program, cooperative education program, cross-registration, double major, independent study, internships, teacher certification program. **Disability Services:** Special programs offered to physically disabled students include note-taking services, reader services, tape recorders, tutors. **Career services:** career assessment, internships. Career services highlights include our e-recruiting program that assists students in their search.

FACILITIES

Housing: Coed dorms, women's dorms. 98% of campus accessible to physically disabled. **Special Academic Facilities/Equipment:** Fritsche Gallery (Art) Fitness Center Swimming Pool **Computers:** 100% of classrooms, 100% of libraries, 100% of dining areas, have wireless network access.

CAMPUS LIFE

Environment: City. **Activities:** Choral groups, drama/theater, literary magazine, student government, Campus Ministries. 21 registered organizations, 4 honor societies. **Athletics (Intercollegiate):** *Women:* basketball, bowling, cross-country, golf, soccer, softball, swimming, tennis, track/field (outdoor), volleyball. **On-Campus Highlights:** Bishop Anthony M. Pilla Student Learning Center, Florence O'Donnell Wasmer Gallery, Matthew J. O'Brien Campus Center, Joseph J. Mullen Academic Center, Ralph M. Besse Library. **Environmental Initiatives:** Increased Recycling; Energy Conservation; Renewable Energy.

ADMISSIONS

Freshman Academic Profile: Average high school GPA 3.3. 12% in top 10% of high school class, 31% in top 25% of high school class, 76% in top 50% of high school class. 80% from public high schools. SAT Math middle 50% range 450-590. SAT Critical Reading middle 50% range 440-580. SAT Writing middle 50% range 400-570. ACT middle 50% range 18-25. Minimum internet-based TOEFL 60. Minimum paper TOEFL 500. **Basis for Candidate Selection:** *Very important factors considered include:* academic GPA, standardized test scores. *Important factors considered include:* application essay, recommendation(s). *Other factors considered include:* Class rank, rigor of secondary school record, alumni/ae relation, interview. **Freshman Admission Requirements:** High school diploma is required and GED is accepted. **Freshman Admission Statistics:** 374 applied, 66% admitted, 38% enrolled. **Transfer Admission Requirements:** college transcript(s), essay or personal statement, Minimum college GPA of 2.5 required. Lowest grade transferable c. **General Admission Information:** Application Fee $25. Nonfall registration accepted. Admission may be deferred for a maximum of 1 year. Credit and/or placement offered for CEEB Advanced Placement tests.

COSTS AND FINANCIAL AID

Average book expense $1,200. **Required Forms and Deadlines:** FAFSA. **Notification of Awards:** Applicants will be notified of awards on a rolling basis beginning 2/20. **Types of Aid:** *Need-based scholarships/grants:* Federal Pell, SEOG, state scholarships/grants, private scholarships, the school's own gift aid, Federal Nursing Scholarships. *Loans:* Subsidized Stafford, Unsubsidized Stafford, PLUS, Federal Perkins, state loans, college/university loans from institutional funds. *Student Employment:* Federal Work-Study Program available. Off-campus job opportunities are good. **Financial Aid Statistics:** 100% freshmen, 90% undergrads receive need-based scholarship or grant aid. 18% freshmen, 10% undergrads receive non-need-based scholarship or grant aid. 85% freshmen, 90% undergrads receive need-based self-help aid. 20% freshmen, 11% undergrads receive athletic scholarships. 99% freshmen, 86% undergrads receive any aid. 87% undergrads borrow to pay for school. Average cumulative indebtedness $25,253. **Criteria for awarding institutional aid:** *Non-need-based:* academics, alumni affiliation, art, athletics, leadership, religious affiliation.

UTAH STATE UNIVERSITY

0160 Old Main Hill, Logan, UT 84322-0160
Phone: 435-797-1079 · **Financial Aid Phone:** 435-797-0173
E-mail: admit@usu.edu
Fax: 435-797-3708 · **Website:** www.usu.edu · **ACT Code:** 4276

This public school was founded in 1888. It has a 400-acre campus.

RATINGS

Admissions Selectivity Rating: 75   **Fire Safety Rating:** 74

STUDENTS AND FACULTY

Enrollment: 21,087. **Student Body:** 53% female, 47% male, 25% out-of-state, 2% international (88 countries represented). Asian 1%, African American 1%, Caucasian 81%, Hispanic 6%, Native American 2%
Retention and Graduation: 71% freshmen return for sophomore year. 23% freshmen graduate within 4 years. 49% freshmen graduate within 6 years. 32% grads go on to further study within 1 year. **Faculty:** 878 full-time faculty, 81% hold PhDs, 36% are are members of minority groups, 10% are women. 7% of classes are taught by teaching assistants.

ACADEMICS

Degrees: associate, bachelor's, certificate, master's, post-bachelor's certificate, post-master's certificate, terminal associate, transfer associate. **Classes:** Most classes have 20-29 students. Most lab/discussion sessions have 10-19 students. **Majors with Highest Enrollment:** Communication Sciences and Disorders; Economics; Physical Education Teaching and Coaching. **Special Study Options:** Accelerated program, cooperative education program, cross-registration, distance learning, double major, dual enrollment, English as a Second Language (ESL), exchange student program (domestic), honors program, independent study, internships, liberal arts/career combination, student-designed major, study abroad, teacher certification program, weekend college. **Honors programs:** The Honors Program is a community of scholars whose curiosity, creativity, and enthusiasm for learning foster educational achievement and personal growth. Our students are going places—graduate school, professional school, terrific jobs. Honors offers undergraduate students intensive seminars, experimental and interdisciplinary courses, writing projects, leadership opportunities, artistic and social activities. Our classes are smaller, allowing students to get to know professors and encouraging classroom interaction and discussion. We allow students to define their own interests and pursue them through "contracts" with professors, fostering close contact with professors. Other advantages include priority registration, an Honors-only computer lab, the Honors lounge and study areas. Starting in Fall 2005, Honors expects to offer housing. **Disability Services:** Special programs offered to physically disabled students include reader services, tape recorders. **Career services:** Alumni network, career/job search classes, career assessment, internships.

FACILITIES

Housing: Coed dorms, special housing for disabled students, men's dorms, special housing for international students, women's dorms, fraternity/sorority housing, apartments for married students, apartments for single students, Theme Housing, Mobile Home Park. 96% of campus accessible to physically disabled. **Special Academic Facilities/Equipment:** Art gallery, agricultural and engineering experiment station, water research lab, wildlife and fishery research unit, on-campus school, intermountain herbarium, electron microscope, space dynamics lab. **Computers:** 99% of classrooms, 95% of dorms, 99% of libraries, 99% of dining areas, 99% of student union, 50% of common outdoor areas have wireless network access. Students can register for classes online. Administrative functions (other than registration) can be performed online.

CAMPUS LIFE

Environment: Town. **Activities:** Choral groups, concert band, dance, drama/theater, jazz band, marching band, music ensembles, musical theater, opera, pep band, radio station, student government, student newspaper, student-run film society, symphony orchestra, television station, Campus Ministries, International Student Organization. 194 registered organizations, 32 honor societies, 8 religious organizations. 5 fraternities, 3 sororities. **Athletics (Intercollegiate):** *Men:* basketball, cross-country, football, golf, tennis, track/field (outdoor), track/field (indoor). *Women:* basketball, cross-country, gymnastics, soccer, softball, tennis, track/field (outdoor), track/field (indoor), volleyball. **On-Campus Highlights:** Outdoor Recreation Center, Nora Eccles Jones Art Museum, Fieldhouse athletic facility, Taggart Student Center, The quad. **Environmental Initiatives:** Increased efficiency All the new buildings on campus on USU campus are LEED Silver or higher, and projects must achieve EA Credit 3, enhanced commissioning. According to LEED, this can result in 5%–10% improvements in energy efficiency, ensure personnel know how to operate key building systems, and catch mistakes like incorrectly installed equipment. Many buildings have been retro-commiensed to ensure existing buildings are operating efficiently. Non-potable water is used for irrigation. Irrigation systems use

central computer controls to maximize efficiency, and water lines are regularly inspected for leaks. Campus housing has installed 6500 LEDs and water efficient shower heads. Resource Use and Recycling A purchasing committee on campus is exploring ways to increase the awareness and practice of using environmental criteria in purchasing decisions. Currently, 98.8% of expenditures on computers are for EPEAT (Preference for Electronic Product Environmental Assessment Tool) Silver or higher machines. Green cleaning and paper purchases are other areas of focus. "In December of 1990, the official program of USU Recycling began. With a $50,000 initial grant, the program consisted of one vehicle for retrieval, containers for each building on campus, one student employee, and one part-time supervisor." "USU recycles all grades of paper products and cardboard. Other items that are recycled include: glass bottles, aluminum and steel (tin) cans, plastic milk and pop containers, wood pallets, batteries, and scrap metal.In addition to serving all campus buildings and housing dorms, USU also provides convenient drop-off centers for those who wish to bring items from home." University departments send unwanted property Surplus Property Sales. Items include, electronics, furniture, sporting goods, and vehicles. Alternative Transportation Aggie Blue Bikes "Our mission is to get more people on more bikes, more often. This is achieved through bicycle lending, education and advocacy. We believe that cycling promotes healthy and sustainable communities, better air quality in Cache Valley and a reduction of on-campus congestion and motor accidents." Aggie Shuttle "The Aggie Shuttle is a fare free service provided to the Utah State University community. It uses Natural Gas to provide a cleaner and more environmentally friendly way to transport students, faculty, staff and visitors." All buses are equipped with bike racks. Cache Valley transit District "The mission of the Cache Valley Transit District is to become the premier public transportation agency serving the Cache Valley Region, with excellence and the highest quality of service. Transit services began fare-free services for citizens and visitors of Logan on April 27, 1992." All buses are equipped with bike racks. USU Rideshare USU hosts a page for students to find others with matching trips. Carshare Parking and Transportation will have a carshare program on campus before next fall.

ADMISSIONS

Freshman Academic Profile: Average high school GPA 3.46. 18.6% in top 10% of high school class, 42% in top 25% of high school class, 73.6% in top 50% of high school class. SAT Math middle 50% range 450-590. SAT Critical Reading middle 50% range 470-590. ACT middle 50% range 20-26. Minimum internet-based TOEFL 71. **Basis for Candidate Selection:** *Very important factors considered include:* academic GPA, standardized test scores. *Important factors considered include:* rigor of secondary school record. *Other factors considered include:* Class rank, recommendation(s). **Freshman Admission Requirements:** High school diploma is required and GED is accepted. **Academic units required:** 4 English, 3 mathematics, 3 science, (1 science labs), 1 history, 4 academic electives. **Freshman Admission Statistics:** 12,835 applied, 98% admitted, 32% enrolled. **Transfer Admission Requirements:** college transcript(s), Minimum college GPA of 2.2 required. Lowest grade transferable D. **General Admission Information:** Application Fee $40. Nonfall registration accepted. Admission may be deferred for a maximum of 2 years+ one semeste. Credit and/or placement offered for CEEB Advanced Placement tests.

COSTS AND FINANCIAL AID

Annual out-of-state tuition $17,561. Room and board $5,680. Required fees $930. Average book expense $1,260. **Required Forms and Deadlines:** FAFSA. **Notification of Awards:** Applicants will be notified of awards on a rolling basis beginning 4/1. **Types of Aid:** *Need-based scholarships/grants:* Federal Pell, SEOG, state scholarships/grants, private scholarships, the school's own gift aid. *Loans:* Subsidized Stafford, Unsubsidized Stafford, PLUS, Federal Perkins, college/university loans from institutional funds. *Student Employment:* Federal Work-Study Program available. Institutional employment available. Highest amount earned per year from on-campus jobs $10,200. Off-campus job opportunities are excellent. **Financial Aid Statistics:** 89% freshmen, 87% undergrads receive need-based scholarship or grant aid. 10% freshmen, 5% undergrads receive non-need-based scholarship or grant aid. 61% freshmen, 66% undergrads receive need-based self-help aid. 1% freshmen, 1% undergrads receive athletic scholarships. 81% freshmen, 80% undergrads receive any aid. 49% undergrads borrow to pay for school. Average cumulative indebtedness $18,990. **Criteria for awarding institutional aid:** *Non-need-based:* academics, alumni affiliation, art, athletics, leadership, minority status, music/drama, religious affiliation, state/district residency.

UTICA COLLEGE

1600 Burrstone Road, Utica, NY 13502-4892
Phone: 315-792-3006 · **Financial Aid Phone:** 315-792-3179
E-mail: admiss@utica.edu · **CEEB Code:** 2932
Fax: 315-792-3003 · **Website:** www.utica.edu · **ACT Code:** 2932

This private school was founded in 1946. It has a 128-acre campus.

RATINGS

Admissions Selectivity Rating: 73   **Fire Safety Rating:** 81

STUDENTS AND FACULTY

Enrollment: 2,857. **Student Body:** 61% female, 39% male, 10% out-of-state, 3% international (28 countries represented). Asian 3%, African American 11%, Caucasian 66%, Hispanic 8%, Native American 1%
Retention and Graduation: 30% freshmen graduate within 4 years. 44% freshmen graduate within 6 years. 46% grads go on to further study within 1 year. 1% grads pursue medical degrees. **Faculty:** 141 full-time faculty, 51% are are members of minority groups, 9% are women. 0% of classes are taught by teaching assistants.

ACADEMICS

Degrees: bachelor's, certificate, master's, post-bachelor's certificate. **Classes:** Most classes have 10-19 students. Most lab/discussion sessions have 10-19 students. **Majors with Highest Enrollment:** Corrections and Criminal Justice; Health Services/Allied Health/Health Sciences; Business/Commerce. **Special Study Options:** Accelerated program, cooperative education program, cross-registration, distance learning, double major, dual enrollment, exchange student program (domestic), honors program, independent study, internships, liberal arts/career combination, study abroad, teacher certification program, weekend college, BS Health Studies/ MS OT weekend program; ECI online program for undergraduate transfer students. **Honors programs:** http://www.utica.edu/academic/opportunities/honors.cfm **Combined degree programs:** BS(Health Studies)/MS OT; BS(Health Stud. **Disability Services:** Special programs offered to physically disabled students include note-taking services, reader services, tape recorders, tutors. **Career services:** Alumni network, alumni services, career/job search classes, career assessment, internships.

FACILITIES

Housing: Coed dorms, special housing for disabled students, apartments for single students, Women's floors, Men's floors. 85% of campus accessible to physically disabled. **Special Academic Facilities/Equipment:** Edith Langley Barrett Art Gallery. **Computers:** 95% of classrooms, 10% of dorms, 100% of libraries, 100% of dining areas, 100% of student union, have wireless network access. Students can register for classes online. Administrative functions (other than registration) can be performed online.

CAMPUS LIFE

Environment: City. **Activities:** Choral groups, concert band, dance, drama/theater, literary magazine, radio station, student government, student newspaper, student-run film society, yearbook. 80 registered organizations, 8 honor societies, 4 religious organizations. 5 fraternities, 4 sororities. **Athletics (Intercollegiate):** *Men:* baseball, basketball, cross-country, diving, football, golf, ice hockey, lacrosse, soccer, swimming, tennis, track/field (outdoor). *Women:* basketball, cross-country, diving, field hockey, ice hockey, lacrosse, soccer, softball, swimming, tennis, track/field (outdoor), volleyball, water polo. **On-Campus Highlights:** Strebel Student Center and Lounge, Pioneer Café, Clark Athletic Center, Romano Hall Lounge, Library Café. **Environmental Initiatives:** Committee on sustainability formed in 2007. Extensive recycling program. Partnership in co-generation electrical generation plant.

ADMISSIONS

Freshman Academic Profile: Average high school GPA 2.86. 9% in top 10% of high school class, 30% in top 25% of high school class, 63% in top 50% of high school class. SAT Math middle 50% range 440-550. SAT Critical Reading middle 50% range 430-520. SAT Writing middle 50% range 420-510. ACT middle 50% range 19-24. Minimum paper TOEFL 525. **Basis for Candidate Selection:** *Very important factors considered include:* academic GPA, rigor of secondary school record. *Important factors considered include:* application essay, recommendation(s), character/personal qualities, extracurricular activities, interview, talent/ability, volunteer work, work experience. *Other factors considered include:* Class rank, standardized test scores, alumni/ae relation, first generation, level of applicant's interest. **Freshman Admission Requirements:** High school diploma is required and GED is accepted. **Academic units required:** 4 English, 3 mathematics, 3 science, 2 foreign language, 3 social studies, 1 academic elective. **Freshman Admission Statistics:** 3,677 applied, 82% admitted, 16% enrolled. **Transfer Admission Requirements:** college transcript(s), essay or personal statement, Minimum college GPA of 2.50 required. Lowest grade transferable C. **General Admission Informa-**

tion: Application Fee $40. Notification on a rolling basis, beginning on or about 9/1. Nonfall registration accepted. Admission may be deferred for a maximum of one year. Credit and/or placement offered for CEEB Advanced Placement tests.

COSTS AND FINANCIAL AID

Annual tuition $33,216. Room and board $11,934. Required fees $520. Average book expense $1,308. **Required Forms and Deadlines:** FAFSA, State aid form. **Notification of Awards:** Applicants will be notified of awards on a rolling basis beginning 2/1. **Types of Aid:** *Need-based scholarships/grants:* Federal Pell, SEOG, state scholarships/grants, private scholarships, the school's own gift aid, Federal Nursing Scholarships. *Loans:* Direct Subsidized Stafford, Direct Unsubsidized Stafford, Direct PLUS, Federal Perkins, Alternative Loans. *Student Employment:* Federal Work-Study Program available. Institutional employment available. Off-campus job opportunities are good. **Financial Aid Statistics:** 100% freshmen, 96% undergrads receive need-based scholarship or grant aid. 3% freshmen, 5% undergrads receive non-need-based scholarship or grant aid. 94% freshmen, 93% undergrads receive need-based self-help aid. 0% freshmen, 0% undergrads receive athletic scholarships. 96% freshmen, 95% undergrads receive any aid. 93% undergrads borrow to pay for school. Average cumulative indebtedness $29,779. **Criteria for awarding institutional aid:** *Non-need-based:* academics.

VALDOSTA STATE UNIVERSITY

1500 North Patterson Street, Valdosta, GA 31698
Phone: 229-333-5791 · **Financial Aid Phone:** 229-333-5935
E-mail: admissions@valdosta.edu · **CEEB Code:** 5855
Fax: 229-333-5482 · **Website:** http://www.valdosta.edu/ · **ACT Code:** 874

This public school was founded in 1906. It has a 178-acre campus.

RATINGS

Admissions Selectivity Rating: 77   **Fire Safety Rating:** 62

STUDENTS AND FACULTY

Enrollment: 10,638. **Student Body:** 60% female, 40% male, 4% out-of-state, 1% international (73 countries represented). Asian 1%, African American 34%, Caucasian 54%, Hispanic 4%, Native American <1%
Retention and Graduation: 67% freshmen return for sophomore year. 17% freshmen graduate within 4 years. 43% freshmen graduate within 6 years. **Faculty:** 489 full-time faculty, 77% hold PhDs, 48% are are members of minority groups, 15% are women. 1.8% of classes are taught by teaching assistants.

ACADEMICS

Degrees: associate, bachelor's, master's, post-master's certificate. **Classes:** Most classes have 20-29 students. Most lab/discussion sessions have 20-29 students. **Majors with Highest Enrollment:** Biology/Biological Sciences; Registered Nursing/Registered Nurse; Psychology. **Special Study Options:** cooperative education program, distance learning, double major, dual enrollment, English as a Second Language (ESL), external degree program, honors program, independent study, internships, study abroad, teacher certification program, weekend college. **Honors programs:** Honors Program. **Disability Services:** Special programs offered to physically disabled students include note-taking services, reader services, tape recorders, tutors. **Career services:** alumni services, career/job search classes, career assessment, internships.

FACILITIES

Housing: Coed dorms, special housing for disabled students, men's dorms, special housing for international students, women's dorms, apartments for married students, apartments for single studentsWellness floors and honors floors. 100% of campus accessible to physically disabled. **Special Academic Facilities/Equipment:** Planetarium; Herbarium; Art Gallery; VSU Archives. **Computers:** Students can register for classes online. Administrative functions (other than registration) can be performed online.

CAMPUS LIFE

Environment: City. **Activities:** Choral groups, concert band, dance, drama/theater, jazz band, literary magazine, marching band, music ensembles, pep band, radio station, student government, student newspaper, symphony orchestra, television station. 140 registered organizations, 22 honor societies, 11 religious organizations. 12 fraternities, 10 sororities. **Athletics (Intercollegiate):** *Men:* baseball, basketball, cross-country, football, golf, tennis. *Women:* basketball, cheerleading, cross-country, softball, tennis, volleyball. **On-Campus Highlights:** Student Recreation Center, Game Room, Internet Café, The Loop, Palms Dining Center and quad. **Environmental Initiatives:** Recycling; Faculty and Student Environmental Advocacy Groups.

ADMISSIONS

Freshman Academic Profile: Average high school GPA 3.07. SAT Math middle 50% range 460-540. SAT Critical Reading middle 50% range 470-540. SAT Writing middle 50% range 450-530. ACT middle 50% range 20-23. Minimum paper TOEFL 523. **Basis for Candidate Selection:** *Very important factors considered include:* standardized test scores. *Important factors considered include:* Class rank, academic GPA, rigor of secondary school record. **Freshman Admission Requirements:** High school diploma is required and GED is not accepted. **Academic units required:** 4 English, 4 mathematics, 3 science, (2 science labs), 2 foreign language, 3 social studies. **Freshman Admission Statistics:** 7,950 applied, 58% admitted, 48% enrolled. **Transfer Admission Requirements:** college transcript(s), Minimum college GPA of 2.0 required. Lowest grade transferable D. **General Admission Information:** Application Fee $40. Regular application deadline 7/1. Notification on a rolling basis, beginning on or about 8/1. Nonfall registration accepted. Admission may be deferred for a maximum of 2 years. Credit and/or placement offered for CEEB Advanced Placement tests.

COSTS AND FINANCIAL AID

Annual in-state tuition $3,787. Annual out-of-state tuition $13,368. Room and board $6,850. Required fees $1,910. Average book expense $1,200. **Required Forms and Deadlines:** FAFSA. **Notification of Awards:** Applicants will be notified of awards on a rolling basis beginning 5/15. **Types of Aid:** *Need-based scholarships/grants:* Federal Pell, SEOG, state scholarships/grants, private scholarships, the school's own gift aid, LEAP, ACG SMART Grant. *Loans:* Direct Subsidized Stafford, Direct Unsubsidized Stafford, Direct PLUS, Subsidized Stafford, Unsubsidized Stafford, PLUS. *Student Employment:* Federal Work-Study Program available. Institutional employment available. Highest amount earned per year from on-campus jobs $4,000. Off-campus job opportunities are good. **Financial Aid Statistics:** 89% freshmen, 82% undergrads receive need-based scholarship or grant aid. 6% freshmen, 5% undergrads receive non-need-based scholarship or grant aid. 87% freshmen, 76% undergrads receive need-based self-help aid. 1% freshmen, 0% undergrads receive athletic scholarships. 76% freshmen, 70% undergrads receive any aid. 66% undergrads borrow to pay for school. Average cumulative indebtedness $20,410. **Criteria for awarding institutional aid:** *Non-need-based:* academics, art, athletics, leadership, music/drama, state/district residency.

VALLEY CITY STATE UNIVERSITY

101 College St. SW, Valley City, ND 58072
Phone: 701-845-7101 · **Financial Aid Phone:** 701-845-7412
E-mail: enrollment.services@vcsu.edu
Fax: 701-845-7299 · **Website:** www.vcsu.edu · **ACT Code:** 3216

This public school was founded in 1890. It has a 55-acre campus.

RATINGS

Admissions Selectivity Rating: 71   Fire Safety Rating: 66

STUDENTS AND FACULTY

Enrollment: 1,013. **Student Body:** 53% female, 47% male, 28% out-of-state, 5% international (7 countries represented). Asian 0%, African American 2%, Caucasian 89%, Hispanic 1%, Native American 2%
Retention and Graduation: 64% freshmen return for sophomore year. **Faculty:** 55 full-time faculty, 36% hold PhDs, 51% are are members of minority groups, 0% are women. 0% of classes are taught by teaching assistants.

ACADEMICS

Degrees: bachelor's, master's. **Majors with Highest Enrollment:** Computer and Information Sciences and Support Services; Elementary Education and Teaching. **Special Study Options:** Accelerated program, cooperative education program, distance learning, double major, dual enrollment, internships, liberal arts/career combination, student-designed major, teacher certification program. **Disability Services:** Special programs offered to physically disabled students include note-taking services, reader services, tape recorders, tutors. **Career services:** career/job search classes, career assessment, internships.

FACILITIES

Housing: Coed dorms, special housing for disabled students, men's dorms, women's dorms, fraternity/sorority housing, apartments for married students, Apts. for students with dependant children. 85% of campus accessible to physically disabled. **Special Academic Facilities/Equipment:** Planetarium. **Computers:** Students can register for classes online. Administrative functions (other than registration) can be performed online.

CAMPUS LIFE

Environment: Rural. **Activities:** Choral groups, concert band, drama/theater, jazz band, music ensembles, musical theater, pep band, student government,

---

student newspaper, yearbook. 16 registered organizations, 5 honor societies, 3 religious organizations. 1 fraternity, 1 sorority. **Athletics (Intercollegiate):** *Men:* baseball, basketball, football. *Women:* basketball, cheerleading, softball, volleyball. **On-Campus Highlights:** Planetarium, Medicine Wheel, Fieldhouse, Vangstad Auditorium, Student Center.

ADMISSIONS

Freshman Academic Profile: Average high school GPA 3. 6% in top 10% of high school class, 22% in top 25% of high school class, 54% in top 50% of high school class. 98% from public high schools. SAT Math middle 50% range 450-570. SAT Critical Reading middle 50% range 450-580. ACT middle 50% range 18-23. Minimum paper TOEFL 525. **Basis for Candidate Selection:** *Very important factors considered include:* rigor of secondary school record. *Other factors considered include:* Class rank, standardized test scores. **Freshman Admission Requirements:** High school diploma is required and GED is accepted. **Academic units required:** 4 English, 3 mathematics, 3 science, (3 science labs), 3 social studies. **Freshman Admission Statistics:** 256 applied, 94% admitted, 73% enrolled. **Transfer Admission Requirements:** college transcript(s), statement of good standing from prior institution(s). Minimum college GPA of 2.0 required. Lowest grade transferable D. **General Admission Information:** Application Fee $35. Nonfall registration accepted. Admission may be deferred for a maximum of indefinete. Neither credit nor placement offered for CEEB Advanced Placement tests.

COSTS AND FINANCIAL AID

Average book expense $700. **Required Forms and Deadlines:** FAFSA. **Notification of Awards:** Applicants will be notified of awards on a rolling basis beginning 1/15. **Types of Aid:** *Need-based scholarships/grants:* Federal Pell, SEOG, state scholarships/grants. *Loans:* Subsidized Stafford, Unsubsidized Stafford, PLUS, Federal Perkins. **Financial Aid Statistics:** 51% freshmen, 55% undergrads receive need-based scholarship or grant aid. 74% freshmen, 54% undergrads receive non-need-based scholarship or grant aid. 87% freshmen, 89% undergrads receive need-based self-help aid. 6% freshmen, 5% undergrads receive athletic scholarships. 93% freshmen, 86% undergrads receive any aid. 36% undergrads borrow to pay for school. **Criteria for awarding institutional aid:** *Non-need-based:* academics, alumni affiliation, athletics, leadership, minority status, music/drama.

VALPARAISO UNIVERSITY

Duesenberg Welcome Center, Valparaiso, IN 46383
Phone: 219-464-5011 · **Financial Aid Phone:** 219-464-5015
E-mail: undergrad.admission@valpo.edu · **CEEB Code:** 1874
Fax: 219-464-6898 · **Website:** http://www.valpo.edu · **ACT Code:** 1256

This private school, affiliated with the Lutheran Church, was founded in 1859. It has a 320-acre campus.

RATINGS

Admissions Selectivity Rating: 87   Fire Safety Rating: 76

STUDENTS AND FACULTY

Enrollment: 3,219. **Student Body:** 52% female, 48% male, 59% out-of-state, 8% international (33 countries represented). Asian 2%, African American 5%, Caucasian 73%, Hispanic 8%, Native American <1%
Retention and Graduation: 60% freshmen graduate within 4 years. 67% freshmen graduate within 6 years. 18% grads go on to further study within 1 year. 12% grads pursue arts and sciences degrees. 1% grads pursue law degrees. 2% grads pursue business degrees. 1% grads pursue medical degrees. **Faculty:** 279 full-time faculty, 85% hold PhDs, 43% are are members of minority groups, 10% are women. 0% of classes are taught by teaching assistants.

ACADEMICS

Degrees: associate, bachelor's, certificate, master's, post-bachelor's certificate, post-master's certificate, terminal associate. **Classes:** Most classes have 10-19 students. Most lab/discussion sessions have 10-19 students. **Majors with Highest Enrollment:** Registered Nursing/Registered Nurse; Psychology; Mechanical Engineering. **Special Study Options:** Accelerated program, cooperative education program, cross-registration, distance learning, double major, English as a Second Language (ESL), exchange student program (domestic), honors program, independent study, internships, liberal arts/career combination, student-designed major, study abroad, teacher certification program. **Honors programs:** Christ College, VU's honors college, provides an honors-level liberal arts curriculum dedicated to the study and practice of the basic arts of inquiry and committed to educational processes that enable students to achieve a measure of intellectual independence. **Combined degree programs:** BA/JD, BA/MA, JD/MA, JD/MBA, JD/MALS, JD/MS, BSN/MSN, BA/EdS. **Disability Services:** Special programs offered to physically disabled students include note-taking services, reader services, tape recorders, tutors. **Career services:** Alumni network, alumni services, career/job search classes, career assessment, internships, regional alumni.

FACILITIES

Housing: Coed dorms, women's dorms, fraternity/sorority housing, apartments for single students, Theme Housing, Residence hall for German language students. 86% of campus accessible to physically disabled. **Special Academic Facilities/Equipment:** Art museum, galleries, language lab, planetarium, electron microscope, observatory, TV Studio, weather station, Virtual Nursing Learning Center, VisBox, non-linear video editing, Christopher Center for Learning and Information Resources, Doppler Radar faciltiy **Computers:** 60% of classrooms, 100% of dorms, 100% of libraries, 100% of dining areas, 100% of student union, 15% of common outdoor areas have wireless network access. Students can register for classes online. Administrative functions (other than registration) can be performed online.

CAMPUS LIFE

Environment: Town. **Activities:** Choral groups, concert band, dance, drama/theater, jazz band, literary magazine, music ensembles, musical theater, pep band, radio station, student government, student newspaper, symphony orchestra, yearbook, Campus Ministries, International Student Organization. 94 registered organizations, 33 honor societies, 7 religious organizations. 9 fraternities, 7 sororities. **Athletics (Intercollegiate):** *Men:* baseball, basketball, cross-country, diving, football, golf, soccer, swimming, tennis, track/field (outdoor), track/field (indoor). *Women:* basketball, bowling, cross-country, diving, golf, soccer, softball, swimming, tennis, track/field (outdoor), track/field (indoor), volleyball. **On-Campus Highlights:** Harre Union, Christopher Center for Library & Infor., VU Center for the Arts, Brauer Art Museum, Athletics-Recreation Center, Kallay-Christopher Hall Kade Duesenberg German House Grinder's Café. **Environmental Initiatives:** In addition to previous years, this year the College of Engineering received partial funding from the Dept. of Energy to construct a solar furnace. In addition to previous years, an addition to the College of Engineering completed & seeking LEED platinum certification. A new building nearly complete & seeking LEED Silver certification. Sustainability subcommittee worked with 3 student groups to provide programming for Earthweek (awareness, collection of electronics, batteries, and clothing). The battery recycling program has now been extended on an ongoing basis to a number of buildings. For 2012, we are launching the US Energy Stars Checklist completion program.

ADMISSIONS

Freshman Academic Profile: Average high school GPA 3.67. 34.8% in top 10% of high school class, 64.2% in top 25% of high school class, 94% in top 50% of high school class. SAT Math middle 50% range 500-620. SAT Critical Reading middle 50% range 500-600. SAT Writing middle 50% range 480-580. ACT middle 50% range 23-29. Minimum internet-based TOEFL 80. Minimum paper TOEFL 550. **Basis for Candidate Selection:** *Very important factors considered include:* academic GPA, rigor of secondary school record. *Important factors considered include:* Class rank, standardized test scores, alumni/ae relation, character/personal qualities, extracurricular activities, talent/ability. *Other factors considered include:* application essay, recommendation(s), first generation, interview, level of applicant's interest, racial/ethnic status, religious affiliation/commitment, volunteer work. **Freshman Admission Requirements:** High school diploma is required and GED is accepted. **Academic units required:** 4 English, 3 mathematics, 2 science, (2 science labs), 2 foreign language, 2 history, 3 academic electives. **Freshman Admission Statistics:** 6,491 applied, 82% admitted, 13% enrolled. **Transfer Admission Requirements:** college transcript(s), essay or personal statement, statement of good standing from prior institution(s). Minimum college GPA of 2.0 required. Lowest grade transferable C-. **General Admission Information:** Application Fee $30. Regular application deadline 8/15. Notification on a rolling basis, beginning on or about 10/1. Nonfall registration accepted. Admission may be deferred for a maximum of 1 year. Credit and/or placement offered for CEEB Advanced Placement tests.

COSTS AND FINANCIAL AID

Annual tuition $33,680. Room and board $10,180. Required fees $1,080. Average book expense $1,200. **Required Forms and Deadlines:** FAFSA. **Notification of Awards:** Applicants will be notified of awards on a rolling basis beginning 3/1. **Types of Aid:** *Need-based scholarships/grants:* Federal Pell, SEOG, state scholarships/grants, private scholarships, the school's own gift aid. *Loans:* Direct Subsidized Stafford, Direct Unsubsidized Stafford, Direct PLUS, Federal Perkins, college/university loans from institutional funds, Private/alternative education loans if credit standards are met. *Student Employment:* Federal Work-Study Program available. Institutional employment available. Highest amount earned per year from on-campus jobs $5,481. Off-campus job opportunities are good. **Financial Aid Statistics:** 99% freshmen, 99% undergrads receive need-based scholarship or grant aid. 15% freshmen, 12% undergrads receive non-need-based scholarship or grant aid. 76% freshmen, 84% undergrads receive need-based self-help aid. 2% freshmen, 3% undergrads receive athletic scholarships. 95% freshmen, 94% undergrads receive any aid.

74% undergrads borrow to pay for school. Average cumulative indebtedness $27,312. **Criteria for awarding institutional aid:** *Non-need-based:* academics, alumni affiliation, art, athletics, leadership, music/drama, religious affiliation, state/district residency.

VANDERBILT UNIVERSITY

Best 380

2305 West End Avenue, Nashville, TN 37203
Phone: 615-322-2561 · **Financial Aid Phone:** 800-288-0204
E-mail: admissions@vanderbilt.edu · **CEEB Code:** 1871
Fax: 615-343-7765 · **Website:** www.vanderbilt.edu · **ACT Code:** 4036

This private school was founded in 1873. It has a 323-acre campus.

RATINGS

Admissions Selectivity Rating: 98   **Fire Safety Rating:** 98

STUDENTS AND FACULTY

Enrollment: 6,818. **Student Body:** 50% female, 50% male, 89% out-of-state, 6% international (49 countries represented). Asian 10%, African American 8%, Caucasian 58%, Hispanic 8%, Native American <1%
Retention and Graduation: 97% freshmen return for sophomore year. 88% freshmen graduate within 4 years. 31% grads go on to further study within 1 year. 13% grads pursue arts and sciences degrees. 11% grads pursue law degrees. 3% grads pursue business degrees. 27% grads pursue medical degrees. **Faculty:** 912 full-time faculty, 37% are are members of minority groups, 14% are women.

ACADEMICS

Degrees: bachelor's, doctoral, master's. **Classes:** Most classes have 10-19 students. Most lab/discussion sessions have 10-19 students. **Majors with Highest Enrollment:** Engineering Science; Social Sciences; Multi-/Interdisciplinary Studies. **Special Study Options:** Accelerated program, cooperative education program, cross-registration, distance learning, double major, dual enrollment, English as a Second Language (ESL), honors program, independent study, internships, liberal arts/career combination, student-designed major, study abroad, teacher certification program. **Honors programs:** Psychology, Child Development, Cognitive Studies, and Child Studies, Biomedical Engineering, Biological Sciences **Combined degree programs:** BA/MBA, MBA/JD, MBA/MD, JD/MDIV, JD/MTS. **Disability Services:** Special programs offered to physically disabled students include note-taking services, reader services, tape recorders, tutors. **Career services:** Alumni network, alumni services, career/job search classes, career assessment, internships, regional alumni.

FACILITIES

Housing: Coed dorms, special housing for disabled students, men's dorms, special housing for international students, women's dorms, apartments for married students, apartments for single students, Theme Housing. The Commons is a community of first-year students, residential faculty, and professional staff. 95% of campus accessible to physically disabled. **Special Academic Facilities/Equipment:** Art galleries, center for research on education and human development, multimedia classrooms, teaching center, observatories, free-electron laser, electron microscope. **Computers:** 100% of classrooms, 100% of dorms, 100% of libraries, 100% of dining areas, 100% of student union, 100% of common outdoor areas have wireless network access. Students can register for classes online. Administrative functions (other than registration) can be performed online.

CAMPUS LIFE

Environment: Metropolis. **Activities:** Choral groups, concert band, dance, drama/theater, jazz band, literary magazine, marching band, music ensembles, musical theater, opera, pep band, radio station, student government, student newspaper, student-run film society, symphony orchestra, television station, yearbook, Campus Ministries, International Student Organization, Model UN. 329 registered organizations, 20 honor societies, 18 religious organizations. 19 fraternities, 12 sororities. **Athletics (Intercollegiate):** *Men:* baseball, basketball, cross-country, football, golf, tennis. *Women:* basketball, cross-country, golf, lacrosse, soccer, tennis, track/field (outdoor). **On-Campus Highlights:** The Commons, Jean and Alexander Heard Library, Student Recreation Center, Student Life Center, Sarratt Student Center. **Environmental Initiatives:** 1. Greenhouse gas emissions reduction—Overall greenhouse gas emissions from Vanderbilts campus and medical center decreased by 12 percent from an all-time high reached in 2008?ùand by 7 percent from 2005 to 2011?ùeven though Vanderbilt has seen significant growth in square footage, staff, students and research dollars over the last four years. GHG emissions per square foot have gone down 21 percent over the past seven years, which reflects a lot of hard work to improve the energy efficiency of existing buildings, some that are very old, as well as new construction and renovation projects that have incorporated excellent energy efficiency. GHG emissions per person, per student, per research dollar, per inpatient day and per ambulatory visit also have trended significantly in a positive direction since 2005. Most university greenhouse gas inventory reports do not include research and/or patient care activity, making Vanderbilts report more comprehensive than most and also more comprehensive than what is now required by the Environmental Protection Agency. 2. Environmental and Sustainability Studies minor In Fall 2012, Vanderbilt University launched a new minor in environmental and sustainability studies. This minor is focused on the humanities and social sciences, but it also includes exposure to the natural sciences. The minor in Earth and Environmental Sciences is also available for students who wish to pursue a more natural science-oriented curriculum. 3. Recycling—In 2012, VU achieved a 57% increase in the recycling of traditional materials such as cardboard, plastic, paper, confidential paper, aluminum, compost and scrap metal, resulting in the diversion of 2,488 tons of material from the landfill. Additionally, an 83% increase in cardboard recycling was seen just during the 2012 student move-in from numbers recorded in 2011 almost a 400% increase since 2008. Vanderbilt also partnered with Waste Management in early 2012 to expand plastics recycling to accept plastics #1-7 and to implement a scrap metal recycling program. Recycling containers are also readily available at home football, basketball, and baseball games, move-in, move-out, and Commencement. For the 2012 EPA sponsored Game Day Challenge, Vanderbilt improved our recycling rate by 84% and excelled in the waste minimization category, ranking 1st out of the Southeastern Conference schools, 8th in the Division I Football Bowl Subdivision (FBS), and 22nd out of 63 participating colleges and universities, including Division II and Division III schools. The community is also encouraged to utilize Vandy FreeSwap, an online, Vanderbilt-hosted forum for the trading of free items among VU employees and students: http://www.vanderbilt.edu/sustainvu/vandy-freeswap/. For more information about recycling at Vanderbilt visit http://www.vanderbilt.edu/sustainvu/what-we-do/waste-and-recycling/.

ADMISSIONS

Freshman Academic Profile: Average high school GPA 3.78. 91% in top 10% of high school class, 96.7% in top 25% of high school class, 99.5% in top 50% of high school class. 65% from public high schools. SAT Math middle 50% range 720-800. SAT Critical Reading middle 50% range 710-780. SAT Writing middle 50% range 680-770. ACT middle 50% range 32-34. Minimum internet-based TOEFL 100. Minimum paper TOEFL 570. **Basis for Candidate Selection:** *Very important factors considered include:* Class rank, application essay, academic GPA, rigor of secondary school record, standardized test scores, character/personal qualities, extracurricular activities. *Important factors considered include:* recommendation(s), talent/ability. *Other factors considered include:* alumni/ae relation, first generation, geographical residence, interview, racial/ethnic status, state residency, volunteer work, work experience. **Freshman Admission Requirements:** High school diploma is required and GED is accepted. **Academic units required:** 4 English, 3 mathematics, 3 science, (2 science labs), 2 foreign language, 2 social studies, 1 history, 0 visual/performing arts, 0 computer science, 3 academic electives. **Freshman Admission Statistics:** 29,518 applied, 13% admitted, 42% enrolled. **Transfer Admission Requirements:** college transcript(s), essay or personal statement, statement of good standing from prior institution(s). Lowest grade transferable C. **General Admission Information:** Application Fee $50. Early decision application deadline 11/1. Regular application deadline 1/3. Regular notification 4/1. Nonfall registration not accepted. Admission may be deferred for a maximum of 1 year. Credit and/or placement offered for CEEB Advanced Placement tests.

COSTS AND FINANCIAL AID

Annual tuition $42,768. Room and board $14,382. Required fees $1,774. Average book expense $1,370. **Required Forms and Deadlines:** FAFSA, CSS/Financial Aid PROFILE. **Notification of Awards:** Applicants will be notified of awards on or about 4/1. **Types of Aid:** *Need-based scholarships/grants:* Federal Pell, SEOG, state scholarships/grants, private scholarships, the school's own gift aid. *Loans:* Subsidized Stafford, Unsubsidized Stafford, PLUS, Federal Perkins, Federal Nursing, college/university loans from institutional funds, Undergrad Education Loan. *Student Employment:* Federal Work-Study Program available. Institutional employment available. Highest amount earned per year from on-campus jobs $2,000. Off-campus job opportunities are excellent. **Financial Aid Statistics:** 90% freshmen, 92% undergrads receive need-based scholarship or grant aid. 56% freshmen, 42% undergrads receive non-need-based scholarship or grant aid. 40% freshmen, 48% undergrads receive need-based self-help aid. 4% freshmen, 4% undergrads receive athletic scholarships. 69% freshmen, 65% undergrads receive any aid. 24% undergrads borrow to pay for school. Average cumulative indebtedness $15,330. **Criteria for awarding institutional aid:** *Non-need-based:* academics, athletics, leadership, minority status, music/drama, state/district residency.

See page 1202.

VANDERCOOK COLLEGE OF MUSIC

3140 South Federal Street, Chicago, IL 60616-3731
Phone: 312-788-1120 • **Financial Aid Phone:** 312-788-1146
E-mail: admissions@vandercook.edu • **CEEB Code:** 1872
Fax: 312-225-5211 • **Website:** www.vandercook.edu • **ACT Code:** 1156

This private school was founded in 1909. It has a 1-acre campus.

RATINGS

Admissions Selectivity Rating: 83   **Fire Safety Rating:** 74

STUDENTS AND FACULTY

Enrollment: 108. **Student Body:** 49% female, 51% male, 24% out-of-state, 2% international (4 countries represented). Asian 1%, African American 6%, Caucasian 66%, Hispanic 21%, Native American <1%
Retention and Graduation: 87% freshmen return for sophomore year. 60% freshmen graduate within 4 years. 73% freshmen graduate within 6 years. **Faculty:** 9 full-time faculty, 67% hold PhDs, 56% are are members of minority groups, 33% are women. 0% of classes are taught by teaching assistants.

ACADEMICS

Degrees: bachelor's, master's. **Special Study Options:** independent study, teacher certification program.

FACILITIES

Housing: Coed dorms, men's dorms, women's dorms, fraternity/sorority housing.

CAMPUS LIFE

Environment: Metropolis. **Activities:** Choral groups, concert band, jazz band, music ensembles, musical theater, student newspaper. 5 registered organizations, 1 fraternity.

ADMISSIONS

Freshman Academic Profile: Average high school GPA 3.68. 10% in top 10% of high school class, 60% in top 25% of high school class, 85% in top 50% of high school class. SAT Math middle 50% range 540-620. SAT Critical Reading middle 50% range 532-577. SAT Writing middle 50% range 525-575. ACT middle 50% range 20-28. Minimum internet-based TOEFL 70. Minimum paper TOEFL 500. **Basis for Candidate Selection:** *Very important factors considered include:* interview, talent/ability. *Important factors considered include:* application essay, rigor of secondary school record, extracurricular activities. *Other factors considered include:* Class rank, recommendation(s), standardized test scores, alumni/ae relation, character/personal qualities, volunteer work, work experience. **Freshman Admission Requirements:** High school diploma is required and GED is accepted. **Academic units required:** 3 English, 2 mathematics, 2 science, 2 foreign language, 3 social studies, 3 academic electives. **Freshman Admission Statistics:** 46 applied, 76% admitted, 71% enrolled. **Transfer Admission Requirements:** High school transcript, college transcript(s), essay or personal statement, interview, standardized test scores, Minimum college GPA of 2.5 required. Lowest grade transferable C. **General Admission Information:** Application Fee $35. Regular application deadline 5/1. Nonfall registration accepted. Admission may be deferred for a maximum of case by case. Credit offered for CEEB Advanced Placement tests.

COSTS AND FINANCIAL AID

Annual tuition $24,150. Room and board $11,180. Required fees $1,540. Average book expense $1,900. **Required Forms and Deadlines:** FAFSA. **Types of Aid:** *Need-based scholarships/grants:* state scholarships/grants. *Loans:* Subsidized Stafford, PLUS. **Financial Aid Statistics:** 100% freshmen, 100% undergrads receive need-based scholarship or grant aid. 100% freshmen, 99% undergrads receive non-need-based scholarship or grant aid. 92% freshmen, 97% undergrads receive need-based self-help aid. 0% freshmen, 0% undergrads receive athletic scholarships. 100% freshmen, 100% undergrads receive any aid. 71% undergrads borrow to pay for school. Average cumulative indebtedness $25,623.

VANGUARD UNIVERSITY
OF SOUTHERN CALIFORNIA

55 Fair Drive, Costa Mesa, CA 92626
Phone: 714-556-3610 · **Financial Aid Phone:** 714-556-3610
E-mail: admissions@vanguard.edu · **CEEB Code:** 4701
Fax: 714-966-5471 · **Website:** www.vanguard.edu · **ACT Code:** 432

This private school, affiliated with the Assemblies of God Church, was founded in 1920. It has a 38-acre campus.

RATINGS

Admissions Selectivity Rating: 79   **Fire Safety Rating:** 81

STUDENTS AND FACULTY

Enrollment: 1,847. **Student Body:** 63% female, 37% male, 14% out-of-state, 1% international (17 countries represented). Asian 4%, African American 3%, Caucasian 66%, Hispanic 17%, Native American 1%
Retention and Graduation: 76% freshmen return for sophomore year. 37% freshmen graduate within 4 years. 49% freshmen graduate within 6 years. **Faculty:** 66 full-time faculty, 77% hold PhDs, 39% are are members of minority groups, 14% are women. 0% of classes are taught by teaching assistants.

ACADEMICS

Degrees: bachelor's, master's. **Classes:** Most classes have 10-19 students. Most lab/discussion sessions have fewer than 10 students. **Majors with Highest Enrollment:** Education; Psychology; Business/Commerce. **Special Study Options:** Accelerated program, cooperative education program, cross-registration, double major, dual enrollment, external degree program, independent study, internships, study abroad, teacher certification program. **Disability Services:** Special programs offered to physically disabled students include note-taking services, tutors.

FACILITIES

Housing: special housing for disabled students, men's dorms, women's dorms, apartments for married students, apartments for single students, One dorm is coed (Floors 1, 2, 4 for males; floor 3 for females). 95% of campus accessible to physically disabled. **Special Academic Facilities/Equipment:** Lyceum Theater; Computer Lab; Communications Lab. **Computers:** Students can register for classes online. Administrative functions (other than registration) can be performed online.

CAMPUS LIFE

Environment: City. **Activities:** Choral groups, concert band, dance, drama/theater, jazz band, music ensembles, musical theater, opera, pep band, student government, student newspaper, symphony orchestra, yearbook. 50 registered organizations, 5 honor societies, 25 religious organizations. **Athletics (Intercollegiate):** *Men:* baseball, basketball, cross-country, soccer, tennis, track/field (outdoor), track/field (indoor). *Women:* basketball, cross-country, soccer, softball, tennis, track/field (outdoor), track/field (indoor), volleyball. **On-Campus Highlights:** Cove-Student Union, The Library, The Pit-our gymnasium, Heath Academic Center, The Dining Commons.

ADMISSIONS

Freshman Academic Profile: Average high school GPA 3.35. 22% in top 10% of high school class, 49% in top 25% of high school class, 78% in top 50% of high school class. 73% from public high schools. SAT Math middle 50% range 430-560. SAT Critical Reading middle 50% range 450-570. ACT middle 50% range 19-24. Minimum paper TOEFL 550. **Basis for Candidate Selection:** *Very important factors considered include:* application essay, academic GPA, recommendation(s), rigor of secondary school record, character/personal qualities. *Important factors considered include:* standardized test scores, religious affiliation/commitment. *Other factors considered include:* extracurricular activities, interview, level of applicant's interest, talent/ability, volunteer work, work experience. **Freshman Admission Requirements:** High school diploma is required and GED is accepted. **Freshman Admission Statistics:** 899 applied, 83% admitted, 53% enrolled. **Transfer Admission Requirements:** college transcript(s), essay or personal statement, Minimum college GPA of 2.0 required. Lowest grade transferable C-. **General Admission Information:** Application Fee $45. Notification on a rolling basis, beginning on or about 1/15. Nonfall registration accepted. Credit offered for CEEB Advanced Placement tests.

COSTS AND FINANCIAL AID

Annual tuition $22,466. Room and board $7,270. Required fees $520. Average book expense $1,314. **Required Forms and Deadlines:** FAFSA, State aid form. **Notification of Awards:** Applicants will be notified of awards on a rolling basis beginning 4/1. **Types of Aid:** *Need-based scholarships/grants:* Federal Pell, SEOG, state scholarships/grants, private scholarships, the school's own gift aid. *Loans:* Subsidized Stafford, Unsubsidized Stafford, PLUS, Federal Perkins. *Student Employment:* Federal Work-Study Program available. Institutional employment available. Highest amount earned per year from on-campus jobs $6,000. Off-campus job opportunities are excellent. **Financial Aid Statistics:** 80% freshmen, 67% undergrads receive need-based scholarship or grant aid. 90% freshmen, 85% undergrads receive non-need-based scholarship or grant aid. 81% freshmen, 91% undergrads receive need-based self-help aid. 2% freshmen, 2% undergrads receive athletic scholarships. 94% freshmen, 99% undergrads receive any aid. 76% undergrads borrow to pay for school. Average cumulative indebtedness $4,632. **Criteria for awarding institutional aid:** *Non-need-based:* academics, athletics, music/drama.

VASSAR COLLEGE

Box 10, 124 Raymond Avenue, Poughkeepsie, NY 12604
Phone: 845-437-7300 · **Financial Aid Phone:** 845-437-5320
E-mail: admissions@vassar.edu · **CEEB Code:** 2956
Fax: 845-437-7063 · **Website:** www.vassar.edu · **ACT Code:** 2982

This private school was founded in 1861. It has a 1000-acre campus.

RATINGS

Admissions Selectivity Rating: 96   **Fire Safety Rating:** 85

STUDENTS AND FACULTY

Enrollment: 2,386. **Student Body:** 56% female, 44% male, 73% out-of-state, 7% international (44 countries represented). Asian 11%, African American 6%, Caucasian 59%, Hispanic 11%, Native American <1%
Retention and Graduation: 94% freshmen return for sophomore year. 88% freshmen graduate within 4 years. 92% freshmen graduate within 6 years. 20% grads go on to further study within 1 year. 11% grads pursue arts and sciences degrees. 2% grads pursue law degrees. 1% grads pursue business degrees. 4% grads pursue medical degrees. **Faculty:** 277 full-time faculty, 87% hold PhDs, 46% are are members of minority groups, 24% are women. 0% of classes are taught by teaching assistants.

ACADEMICS

Degrees: bachelor's, master's. **Classes:** Most classes have 10-19 students. Most lab/discussion sessions have 10-19 students. **Majors with Highest Enrollment:** Psychology; Political Science and Government; Economics. **Special Study Options:** cooperative education program, cross-registration, double major, exchange student program (domestic), independent study, internships, liberal arts/career combination, student-designed major, study abroad, teacher certification program. **Combined degree programs:** BA/MA. **Disability Services:** Special programs offered to physically disabled students include note-taking services, reader services, tape recorders. **Career services:** Alumni network, alumni services, career/job search classes, career assessment, internships, regional alumni.

FACILITIES

Housing: Coed dorms, special housing for disabled students, special housing for international students, women's dorms, apartments for married students, cooperative housing, apartments for single students, Wellness Housing, Quiet Housing. 69% of campus accessible to physically disabled. **Special Academic Facilities/Equipment:** Art center, theatres, nursery school, environmental field station, geology museum, electron microscope, observatory, Skinner Music Hall, Fitness Center. **Computers:** 100% of classrooms, 100% of dorms, 100% of libraries, 100% of dining areas, 100% of student union, 80% of common outdoor areas have wireless network access. Students can register for classes online. Administrative functions (other than registration) can be performed online.

CAMPUS LIFE

Environment: Town. **Activities:** Choral groups, concert band, dance, drama/theater, jazz band, literary magazine, marching band, music ensembles, musical theater, opera, radio station, student government, student newspaper, student-run film society, symphony orchestra, television station, yearbook, Campus Ministries, International Student Organization, Model UN. 105 registered organizations, 2 honor societies, 11 religious organizations. **Athletics (Intercollegiate):** *Men:* baseball, basketball, crew/rowing, cross-country, diving, fencing, lacrosse, soccer, squash, swimming, tennis, track/field (outdoor), volleyball. *Women:* basketball, crew/rowing, cross-country, diving, fencing, field hockey, golf, lacrosse, soccer, squash, swimming, tennis, track/field (outdoor), volleyball. **On-Campus Highlights:** Library, Shakespeare Garden, Class of 1951 Observatory, Frances Lehman Loeb Art Center, Center for Drama and Film. **Environmental Initiatives:** Tree Campus USA & Landscaping choices in 2012/13 CCS and B&G worked together to phase out the use of harmful pesticides on campus to more environmentally friendly products. Concurrently, we have just been certified by Tree Campus USA, approved a formal tree care plan and seek to transition 3+ acres of lawn to naturalized habitat areas in spring 2013. During Winter 12/13 we have switched to a salt water brine solution, that has cut our total usage of salt on campus by 50%. Student & Community Engagement We believe that collaboration is a key tenant of Sustainability and so strive to engage as many people as possible in our initiatives, programming and decisions. The College Committee on Sustainability includes representatives from most Departments on campus. Our robust intern program hires 7 students each year to spearhead efforts on campus, providing them with valuable leadership skills. The annual move-out program, SWAPR, has been running for over 12 years and provides more than 14 local charities and non-profits with donations that would have otherwise been tossed. Our new EcoLeader program selects 13 students to be green liaisons to their dorms; they participate in training monthly and organize a green initiative for their residence halls. The RCF (Resource Conservation Fund) is our campus green revolving fund that enables students, faculty and staff to submit proposals for energy saving projects on campus. A key goal for the program is applicant participation, so we have worked to make the application process as streamlined and accessible as possible and work with applicants throughout the process with research, calculations, and guidance. We received 10 applications in 2012 and 17 applications in 2013. To date, the RCF has funded LED lighting upgrades, behavior modification efforts, investigations into landscape naturalization and the phasing out of bottled water.

ADMISSIONS

Freshman Academic Profile: 68.9% in top 10% of high school class, 95.1% in top 25% of high school class, 99.5% in top 50% of high school class. 68% from public high schools. SAT Math middle 50% range 650-740. SAT Critical Reading middle 50% range 670-750. SAT Writing middle 50% range 660-750. ACT middle 50% range 30-33. Minimum internet-based TOEFL 100. Minimum paper TOEFL 600. **Basis for Candidate Selection:** *Very important factors considered include:* rigor of secondary school record. *Important factors considered include:* Class rank, application essay, academic GPA, recommendation(s), standardized test scores, extracurricular activities, talent/ability. *Other factors considered include:* alumni/ae relation, character/personal qualities, first generation, geographical residence, interview, level of applicant's interest, racial/ethnic status, volunteer work, work experience. **Freshman Admission Requirements:** High school diploma is required and GED is accepted. **Academic units required:** 4 English, 4 mathematics, 4 science, (3 science labs), 3 foreign language, 2 social studies, 2 history, 4 academic electives. **Freshman Admission Statistics:** 7,784 applied, 24% admitted, 36% enrolled. **Transfer Admission Requirements:** High school transcript, college transcript(s), essay or personal statement, standardized test scores, statement of good standing from prior institution(s). Minimum college GPA of 3.0 required. Lowest grade transferable C. **General Admission Information:** Application Fee $60. Early decision application deadline 11/15. Regular application deadline 1/1. Regular notification 4/1. Nonfall registration not accepted. Admission may be deferred for a maximum of 12 months. Credit and/or placement offered for CEEB Advanced Placement tests.

COSTS AND FINANCIAL AID

Annual tuition $48,840. Room and board $11,570. Required fees $810. Average book expense $900. **Required Forms and Deadlines:** FAFSA, CSS/Financial Aid PROFILE, Noncustodial PROFILE. **Notification of Awards:** Applicants will be notified of awards on or about 3/30. **Types of Aid:** *Need-based scholarships/grants:* Federal Pell, SEOG, state scholarships/grants, private scholarships, the school's own gift aid. *Loans:* Direct Subsidized Stafford, Direct Unsubsidized Stafford, Direct PLUS, Federal Perkins, Loans for Non-citizens with need. *Student Employment:* Federal Work-Study Program available. Institutional employment available. Highest amount earned per year from on-campus jobs $4,350. Off-campus job opportunities are fair. **Financial Aid Statistics:** 99% freshmen, 99% undergrads receive need-based scholarship or grant aid. 0% freshmen, 0% undergrads receive non-need-based scholarship or grant aid. 100% freshmen, 100% undergrads receive need-based self-help aid. 0% freshmen, 0% undergrads receive athletic scholarships. 61% freshmen, 58% undergrads receive any aid. 57% undergrads borrow to pay for school. Average cumulative indebtedness $15,091.

VAUGHN COLLEGE OF AERONAUTICS AND TECHNOLOGY

86-01 23rd Avenue, Flushing, NY 11369
Phone: 718-429-6600 · **Financial Aid Phone:** 718-429-6600
E-mail: admitme@vaughn.edu · **CEEB Code:** 2001
Fax: 718-779-2231 · **Website:** www.vaughn.edu

This private school was founded in 1932. It has a 6-acre campus.

RATINGS
Admissions Selectivity Rating: 72   **Fire Safety Rating:** 94

STUDENTS AND FACULTY
Enrollment: 1,605. **Student Body:** 13% female, 87% male, 11% out-of-state, 2% international. Asian 12%, African American 22%, Caucasian 13%, Hispanic 38%, Native American <1%
Retention and Graduation: 26% freshmen graduate within 4 years. **Faculty:** 41 full-time faculty, 49% hold PhDs, 20% are are members of minority groups, 37% are women. 0% of classes are taught by teaching assistants.

ACADEMICS
Degrees: associate, bachelor's, certificate, master's. **Classes:** Most classes have 20-29 students. Most lab/discussion sessions have 20-29 students. **Majors with Highest Enrollment:** Airframe Mechanics and Aircraft Maintenance Technology/Technician; Aeronautics/Aviation/Aerospace Science and Technology; Airline/Commercial/Professional Pilot and Flight Crew. **Special Study Options:** Accelerated program, distance learning, double major, independent study, internships, liberal arts/career combination. **Career services:** Alumni network, alumni services, career/job search classes, career assessment, internships. Career services highlights include our internship program.

FACILITIES
Housing: Coed dorms **Computers:** 100% of classrooms, 100% of dorms, 100% of libraries, 100% of dining areas, 100% of common outdoor areas have wireless network access. Administrative functions (other than registration) can be performed online.

CAMPUS LIFE
Environment: City. **Activities:** dance, drama/theater, student government, yearbook, International Student Organization 21 registered organizations, 1 honor society. **Athletics (Intercollegiate):** *Men:* basketball, soccer. *Women:* tennis. **On-Campus Highlights:** Complex of six flight simulators, Laboratories, Observation Tower, Cafeteria, Library.

ADMISSIONS
Freshman Academic Profile: Average high school GPA 86. SAT Math middle 50% range 459-560. SAT Critical Reading middle 50% range 432-533. ACT middle 50% range 19-24. Minimum internet-based TOEFL 80. Minimum paper TOEFL 580. **Basis for Candidate Selection:** *Very important factors considered include:* rigor of secondary school record. *Important factors considered include:* academic GPA, standardized test scores, level of applicant's interest. *Other factors considered include:* application essay, recommendation(s), character/personal qualities, extracurricular activities, first generation, interview, talent/ability, volunteer work, work experience. **Freshman Admission Requirements:** High school diploma is required and GED is accepted. **Academic units required:** 4 English, 3 mathematics, 2 science, (2 science labs), 0 foreign language, 1 social studies, 0 history, 0 academic electives. **Freshman Admission Statistics:** 813 applied, 75% admitted, 51% enrolled. **Transfer Admission Requirements:** college transcript(s), Minimum college GPA of 2.0 required. Lowest grade transferable C. **General Admission Information:** Application Fee $40. Notification on a rolling basis, beginning on or about 10/1. Nonfall registration accepted. Admission may be deferred for a maximum of 1 year. Credit and/or placement offered for CEEB Advanced Placement tests.

COSTS AND FINANCIAL AID
Annual tuition $20,840. Room and board $12,365. Required fees $960. Average book expense $2,160. **Required Forms and Deadlines:** FAFSA, State aid form. **Notification of Awards:** Applicants will be notified of awards on a rolling basis beginning 4/15. **Types of Aid:** *Need-based scholarships/grants:* Federal Pell, SEOG, state scholarships/grants, private scholarships, the school's own gift aid. *Loans:* Subsidized Stafford, Unsubsidized Stafford, PLUS. *Student Employment:* Federal Work-Study Program available. Institutional employment available. Off-campus job opportunities are excellent. **Financial Aid Statistics:** 99% freshmen, 91% undergrads receive need-based scholarship or grant aid. 29% freshmen, 23% undergrads receive non-need-based scholarship or grant aid. 96% freshmen, 76% undergrads receive need-based self-help aid. 0% freshmen, 0% undergrads receive athletic scholarships. 94% freshmen, 95% undergrads receive any aid. 94% undergrads borrow to pay for school. Average

cumulative indebtedness $32,500. **Criteria for awarding institutional aid:** *Non-need-based:* academics, alumni affiliation, job skills, leadership.

See page 1204.

VERMONT TECHNICAL COLLEGE

PO Box 500, Randolph Center, VT 5061
Phone: 802-728-1242
E-mail: Admissions@vtc.edu
Fax: 802-728-1321 · **Website:** http://www.vtc.edu/

This is a public school.

RATINGS

Admissions Selectivity Rating: 78   **Fire Safety Rating:** 60*

STUDENTS AND FACULTY
Enrollment: 1,378. **Student Body:** 40% female, 60% male, 21% out-of-state. **Retention and Graduation:** 65% freshmen return for sophomore year. **Faculty:** 79 full-time faculty, 80% hold PhDs, 47% are are members of minority groups.

ACADEMICS
Degrees: associate, bachelor's, certificate, diploma. **Classes:** Most classes have 10-19 students. Most lab/discussion sessions have 10-19 students. **Special Study Options:** distance learning, double major, dual enrollment, internships.

FACILITIES
Housing: Coed dorms.

CAMPUS LIFE
Activities: radio station, student government, television station, yearbook.

ADMISSIONS
Freshman Academic Profile: 8% in top 10% of high school class, 27% in top 25% of high school class, 60% in top 50% of high school class. SAT Math middle 50% range 450-560. SAT Critical Reading middle 50% range 410-520. SAT Writing middle 50% range 410-520. **Basis for Candidate Selection:** *Very important factors considered include:* academic GPA, rigor of secondary school record. *Important factors considered include:* recommendation(s), standardized test scores, interview. *Other factors considered include:* application essay, alumni/ae relation, character/personal qualities, extracurricular activities, first generation, volunteer work, work experience. **Freshman Admission Requirements:** High school diploma is required and GED is accepted. **Academic units required:** 4 English, 3 mathematics, 2 science, (1 science labs), 2 social studies, 2 history. **Freshman Admission Statistics:** 920 applied, 58% admitted, 54% enrolled. **Transfer Admission Requirements:** college transcript(s), statement of good standing from prior institution(s). Lowest grade transferable C-. **General Admission Information:** Application Fee $36. Notification on a rolling basis, beginning on or about 10/1. Nonfall registration accepted.

COSTS AND FINANCIAL AID
Financial Aid Statistics: 80% freshmen, 74% undergrads receive need-based scholarship or grant aid. 3% freshmen, 5% undergrads receive non-need-based scholarship or grant aid. 84% freshmen, 82% undergrads receive need-based self-help aid. 0% freshmen, 0% undergrads receive athletic scholarships.

VILLA MARIA COLLEGE OF BUFFALO

240 Pine Ridge Road, Buffalo, NY 14225
Phone: 716-961-1805 · **Financial Aid Phone:** 716-961-1850
E-mail: admissions@villa.edu
Fax: 716-896-0705 · **ACT Code:** 2983

This private school, affiliated with the Roman Catholic Church, was founded in 1960. It has a 9-acre campus.

RATINGS

Admissions Selectivity Rating: 70   **Fire Safety Rating:** 60*

STUDENTS AND FACULTY
Enrollment: 456. **Student Body:** 66% female, 34% male, 3% out-of-state, 0% international (0 countries represented). Asian 1%, African American 24%, Caucasian 65%, Hispanic 5%, Native American 1%

Retention and Graduation: 59% freshmen return for sophomore year. 25% freshmen graduate within 4 years. 33% freshmen graduate within 6 years. **Faculty:** 29 full-time faculty, 52% hold PhDs, 55% are are members of minority groups. 0% of classes are taught by teaching assistants.

ACADEMICS
Degrees: associate, bachelor's. **Classes:** Most classes have 10-19 students. Most lab/discussion sessions have 10-19 students. **Majors with Highest Enrollment:** Visual and Performing Arts; Physical Therapy Technician/Assistant. **Special Study Options:** cooperative education program, cross-registration, dual enrollment, internships, liberal arts/career combination, study abroad, Selected courses are offered in evening modules primarily with non-traditional students in mind. These offerings are limited. **Disability Services:** Special programs offered to physically disabled students include tutors. **Career services:** alumni services, career/job search classes, career assessment, internships.

FACILITIES
Housing: apartments for married students, apartments for single students- Housing is available at Collegiate Village (college affiliated) which is a mile off-campus; however van service to campus is available. There is no on-campus housing. 100% of campus accessible to physically disabled. **Special Academic Facilities/Equipment:** Art Gallery, Music Building, Recording Studio, Student Center, Athletic Center, Art Shop **Computers:** 100% of libraries, 100% of dining areas, have wireless network access. Students can register for classes online. Administrative functions (other than registration) can be performed online.

CAMPUS LIFE
Environment: City. **Activities:** Choral groups, jazz band, literary magazine, music ensembles, student government, student newspaper, Campus Ministries 1 honor society. **On-Campus Highlights:** Athletic/Student Center, Recording Studio.

ADMISSIONS
Freshman Academic Profile: Average high school GPA 2.96. 5% in top 10% of high school class, 11% in top 25% of high school class, 41% in top 50% of high school class. 93% from public high schools. SAT Math middle 50% range 300-500. SAT Critical Reading middle 50% range 350-500. ACT middle 50% range 17-26. Minimum internet-based TOEFL 133. Minimum paper TOEFL 450. **Basis for Candidate Selection:** *Very important factors considered include:* application essay, academic GPA, interview, talent/ability. *Important factors considered include:* level of applicant's interest. *Other factors considered include:* recommendation(s), rigor of secondary school record, standardized test scores, volunteer work, work experience. **Freshman Admission Requirements:** High school diploma is required and GED is accepted. **Freshman Admission Statistics:** 243 applied, 81% admitted, 38% enrolled. **Transfer Admission Requirements:** college transcript(s), interview, Lowest grade transferable C. **General Admission Information:** Nonfall registration accepted. Admission may be deferred for a maximum of 2 semesters. Credit and/or placement offered for CEEB Advanced Placement tests.

COSTS AND FINANCIAL AID
Required Forms and Deadlines: FAFSA. **Notification of Awards:** Applicants will be notified of awards on a rolling basis beginning 2/15. **Types of Aid:** *Need-based scholarships/grants:* Federal Pell, SEOG, state scholarships/grants, private scholarships, the school's own gift aid. *Loans:* Subsidized Stafford, Unsubsidized Stafford, PLUS. *Student Employment:* Federal Work-Study Program available. Off-campus job opportunities are fair. **Financial Aid Statistics:** 98% freshmen, 99% undergrads receive need-based scholarship or grant aid. 49% freshmen, 78% undergrads receive non-need-based scholarship or grant aid. 19% freshmen, 15% undergrads receive need-based self-help aid. 0% freshmen, 0% undergrads receive athletic scholarships. 99% freshmen, 92% undergrads receive any aid. **Criteria for awarding institutional aid:** *Non-need-based:* academics, alumni affiliation, art, leadership, minority status, music/drama.

VILLANOVA UNIVERSITY

Austin Hall, 800 Lancaster Avenue, Villanova, PA 19085
Phone: 610-519-4000 · **Financial Aid Phone:** 610-519-4010
E-mail: gotovu@villanova.edu · **CEEB Code:** 2959
Fax: 610-519-6450 · **Website:** www.villanova.edu · **ACT Code:** 3744

This private school, affiliated with the Roman Catholic Church, was founded in 1842. It has a 254-acre campus.

RATINGS

Admissions Selectivity Rating: 94   **Fire Safety Rating:** 94

STUDENTS AND FACULTY

Enrollment: 6,895. **Student Body:** 52% female, 48% male, 81% out-of-state, 2% international (71 countries represented). Asian 7%, African American 5%, Caucasian 76%, Hispanic 7%, Native American <1%
Retention and Graduation: 85% freshmen graduate within 4 years. 23% grads go on to further study within 1 year. 7% grads pursue arts and sciences degrees. 5% grads pursue law degrees. 1% grads pursue business degrees. 2% grads pursue medical degrees. **Faculty:** 619 full-time faculty, 88% hold PhDs, 39% are are members of minority groups, 15% are women. 1% of classes are taught by teaching assistants.

ACADEMICS

Degrees: associate, bachelor's, master's, post-bachelor's certificate, post-master's certificate. **Classes:** Most classes have 10-19 students. Most lab/discussion sessions have 10-19 students. **Majors with Highest Enrollment:** Finance; Registered Nursing/Registered Nurse; Mass Communication/Media Studies. **Special Study Options:** Accelerated program, cooperative education program, cross-registration, distance learning, double major, dual enrollment, English as a Second Language (ESL), exchange student program (domestic), honors program, independent study, internships, liberal arts/career combination, study abroad, teacher certification program. **Honors programs:** Honors at Villanova is a comprehensive four-year program that offers challenging seminars, research opportunities, service projects, and cultural and social events designed to bring together superior students and dedicated faculty. Honors courses and co-curricular activities enrich and complement the academic experience inherent in a Villanova education. The Honors Program also works closely with the University's Center for Undergraduate Grants and Awards, which administers the Presidential Scholarship program for incoming students; Connelly-Delouvrier International Scholarships for study abroad; and Villanova's support for students pursuing prestigious national fellowships. The Villanova University Honors Program is an active member of both the National Collegiate Honors Council and the Northeast Region of the National Collegiate Honors Council. **Combined degree programs:** BS/MD, BS/OD, BS/MS, BS/DDM. **Disability Services:** Special programs offered to physically disabled students include note-taking services, reader services, tape recorders, tutors. **Career services:** Alumni network, alumni services, career/job search classes, career assessment, internships, regional alumni. Career services highlights include recruitment of students by hundreds of companies for internships—either on campus or via job boards—each year. Many internships ultimately lead to full-time job offers.

FACILITIES

Housing: Coed dorms, men's dorms, women's dorms, apartments for single students, Wellness Housing, Theme Housing, Learning Communities. 100% of campus accessible to physically disabled. **Special Academic Facilities/Equipment:** Driscoll Hall, home of the Villanova College of Nursing; the Villanova School of Business Applied Finance Lab; the Structural Engineering Teaching and Research Laboratory; the Augustinian Historical Museum, and the Villanova Observatory. **Computers:** 90% of classrooms, 90% of dorms, 100% of libraries, 100% of dining areas, 100% of student union, 10% of common outdoor areas have wireless network access. Students can register for classes online. Administrative functions (other than registration) can be performed online. Undergraduates are required to own a computer.

CAMPUS LIFE

Environment: Village. **Activities:** Choral groups, concert band, dance, drama/theater, jazz band, literary magazine, marching band, music ensembles, musical theater, pep band, radio station, student government, student newspaper, student-run film society, symphony orchestra, television station, yearbook, Campus Ministries, International Student Organization, Model UN. 250 registered organizations, 34 honor societies, 15 religious organizations. 9 fraternities, 9 sororities. **Athletics (Intercollegiate):** *Men:* baseball, basketball, cheerleading, cross-country, diving, football, golf, lacrosse, soccer, swimming, tennis, track/field (outdoor), track/field (indoor). *Women:* basketball, cheerleading, crew/rowing, cross-country, diving, field hockey, lacrosse, soccer, softball, swimming, tennis, track/field (outdoor), track/field (indoor), volleyball, water polo. **On-Campus Highlights:** St. Thomas of Villanova Church, Davis Center for Athletics and Fitness, Villanova University Shop, Connelly Center and Cinema, Bartley Hall Exchange. **Environmental Initiatives:** Academic programs: The masters degree in sustainable engineering; the first-year environmental leadership learning community; bachelors degrees in environmental science and environmental studies; an undergraduate minor in sustainability; a biology masters degree, graduate certificate, and advanced graduate certificate with a concentration in ecology, evolution, and organismal biology; a masters degree in water resources and environmental engineering, and a graduate certificate in urban water resources design. Non-academic programs: In addition to the contributions of academic departments, several groups of students, faculty, and staff are working together to strengthen Villanova's commitment to the environment. These groups include the Presidents Environmental Sustainability Committee, the Villanova Environmental Group, the Villanova Ecological Society, Business Without Borders, Engineers Without Borders, and Engineers for a Sustainable World. In Fall 2010, the Student Government Association (SGA) at Villanova established a sustainability subcommittee designed to promote sustainable practices on campus. Villanova has a green dorm, as well as an ongoing dorm energy conservation competition. The Sustainable Endowments Institute awarded Villanova an "A" in several categories in its most recent Green Report Card, including Food & Recycling. The Institute also considers Villanova to be an "Endowment Sustainability Leader," a title given to only a few colleges that earned an average grade of A- or better on three endowment management categories: transparency, investment priorities, and shareholder engagement. Lastly, the University implements green building practices, with features that include green roofs, extensive natural lighting and other energy-conserving building features, efficient plumbing, and a 90% construction waste diversion rate. Villanova has committed to achieving a minimum of LEED Silver, and is especially pleased to have received LEED Gold for the two buildings most recently constructed. Dining services: Villanova has implemented a comprehensive composting initiative, and has transitioned one of its locations into a green facility, reducing its trash volume by two thirds. In addition, Villanova Dining Services (VDS) purchases a large percentage of its food from local and organic sources. Since August 2006, VDS has been purchasing and serving organic produce, organic fruits and organic groceries. VDS, through its partnership with Primo Produce, is purchasing local produce and vegetables from approximately 63 farms located in Pennsylvania, New York, New Jersey, Maryland, and Delaware. Primo Produce contracts with local farmers throughout New Jersey and Pennsylvania to purchase fruits, vegetables and herbs in season; their total purchases in local produce (PA, NJ, NY, MD, DE, and OH) are 27% of their total produce purchases. Primo Produce is dedicated to supplying produce grown with good stewardship. Primo has dedicated to partner with growers whose mission as good stewards is to grow the finest quality fruits and vegetables, using the natural resources entrusted to them, without compromising the ability of future generations to do the same. Finally, VDS supports local dairies by purchasing all University dairy products exclusively from a local dairy. The largest retail food outlet on campus operated by VDS, the Belle Air Terrace, features a totally organic salad bar. On the operations side, VDS offers a large selection and variety of organic groceries and healthy products (including Chelten House products, United Natural Food products, and Earth Bound Organic products) in convenience stores on campus, and serves organic and fair-trade coffee. Villanova Dining Services partnered with local consortia to bring a farmers market to campus on Earth Day in both April 2010 and 2011. Villanova partners with the Monterey Bay Aquarium, following the Seafood Watch program (exclusively purchasing and serving seafood which is abundant, and caught or farmed in environmentally-friendly ways). Finally, 100% of the resident dining halls are trayless and have complete vegetarian options available.

ADMISSIONS

Freshman Academic Profile: Average high school GPA 3.87. 55% in top 10% of high school class, 87% in top 25% of high school class, 98% in top 50% of high school class. 53% from public high schools. SAT Math middle 50% range 620-710. SAT Critical Reading middle 50% range 600-690. SAT Writing middle 50% range 600-700. ACT middle 50% range 28-31. Minimum paper TOEFL 550. **Basis for Candidate Selection:** *Very important factors considered include:* Class rank, academic GPA, rigor of secondary school record, standardized test scores. *Important factors considered include:* application essay, recommendation(s), character/personal qualities, extracurricular activities, talent/ability, volunteer work, work experience. *Other factors considered include:* alumni/ae relation, first generation, geographical residence, level of applicant's interest, racial/ethnic status, state residency. **Freshman Admission Requirements:** High school diploma is required and GED is accepted. **Academic units required:** 4 English, 4 mathematics, 4 science, (2 science labs), 2 foreign language, 2 academic electives. **Freshman Admission Statistics:** 15,705 applied, 49% admitted, 22% enrolled. **Transfer Admission Requirements:** High school transcript, college transcript(s), essay or personal statement, standardized test scores, statement of good standing from prior institution(s). Lowest grade transferable C. **General Admission Information:** Application Fee $75. Regular application deadline 1/7. Regular notification 4/1. Nonfall registration not accepted. Admission may be deferred for a maximum of 1 year. Credit and/or placement offered for CEEB Advanced Placement tests.

COSTS AND FINANCIAL AID
Annual tuition $45,376. Room and board $12,278. Required fees $740. Average book expense $950. **Required Forms and Deadlines:** FAFSA, CSS/Financial Aid PROFILE, Noncustodial PROFILE. **Notification of Awards:** Applicants will be notified of awards on or about 4/1. **Types of Aid:** *Need-based scholarships/grants:* Federal Pell, SEOG, state scholarships/grants, private scholarships, the school's own gift aid. *Loans:* Subsidized Stafford, Unsubsidized Stafford, PLUS, Federal Perkins, Federal Nursing. *Student Employment:* Federal Work-Study Program available. Institutional employment available. Off-campus job opportunities are excellent. **Financial Aid Statistics:** 93% freshmen, 89% undergrads receive need-based scholarship or grant aid. 15% freshmen, 25% undergrads receive non-need-based scholarship or grant aid. 86% freshmen, 93% undergrads receive need-based self-help aid. 2% freshmen, 3% undergrads receive athletic scholarships. 67% freshmen, 70% undergrads receive any aid. 51% undergrads borrow to pay for school. Average cumulative indebtedness $23,785. **Criteria for awarding institutional aid:** *Non-need-based:* academics, alumni affiliation, athletics, leadership, minority status, religious affiliation.

VIRGINIA COMMONWEALTH UNIVERSITY

821 West Franklin Street, Richmond, VA 23284
Phone: 804-828-1222 · **Financial Aid Phone:** 804-828-7372
E-mail: upgrad@vcu.edu · **CEEB Code:** 5570
Fax: 804-828-1899 · **Website:** www.vcu.edu

This public school was founded in 1838. It has a 143-acre campus.

RATINGS
Admissions Selectivity Rating: 83   **Fire Safety Rating:** 87

STUDENTS AND FACULTY
Enrollment: 22,335. **Student Body:** 57% female, 43% male, 7% out-of-state, 3% international (106 countries represented). Asian 12%, African American 18%, Caucasian 50%, Hispanic 8%, Native American <1%
Faculty: 2,229 full-time faculty, % hold PhDs, 43% are are members of minority groups, 22% are women.

ACADEMICS
Degrees: bachelor's, certificate, master's, post-bachelor's certificate, post-master's certificate. **Classes:** Most classes have 10-19 students. Most lab/discussion sessions have 20-29 students. **Majors with Highest Enrollment:** Mass Communication/Media Studies; Biology/Biological Sciences; Psychology. **Special Study Options:** Accelerated program, cooperative education program, distance learning, double major, dual enrollment, English as a Second Language (ESL), honors program, independent study, internships, liberal arts/career combination, student-designed major, study abroad, teacher certification program. **Honors programs:** Mentorship Programs—All first year students are invited to participate in this program. In this program upper classmen volunteer to serve as mentors offering support and assistance to new honors students during their first semester. **Combined degree programs:** BA/MD, BA/DDS, Pharmacy (PharmD) as a part of Honors Program. **Disability Services:** Special programs offered to physically disabled students include note-taking services, reader services, tape recorders, tutors. **Career services:** Alumni network, alumni services, career/job search classes, career assessment, internships.

FACILITIES
Housing: Coed dorms, special housing for disabled students, apartments for single students. 90% of campus accessible to physically diasbled. **Special Academic Facilities/Equipment:** Anderson Gallery, Student Art Gallery, Larrick Student Center, Shafer Ct. Dining Facilities, Student Commons, Siegel Center, Cabell Library, Biotech Research Bldgs., Tompkins McCaw Library and VCU Bookstores. **Computers:** 75% of classrooms, 100% of dorms, 100% of libraries, 100% of dining areas, 100% of student union, 25% of common outdoor areas have wireless network access. Students can register for classes online. Administrative functions (other than registration) can be performed online. Undergraduates are required to own a computer.

CAMPUS LIFE
Environment: Metropolis. **Activities:** Choral groups, concert band, dance, drama/theater, jazz band, literary magazine, musical theater, pep band, radio station, student government, student newspaper, television station, yearbook, Campus Ministries, International Student Organization. 377 registered organizations, 30 religious organizations. 22 fraternities, 13 sororities. **Athletics**

(Intercollegiate): *Men:* baseball, basketball, cross-country, golf, soccer, tennis, track/field (outdoor). *Women:* basketball, cross-country, field hockey, soccer, tennis, track/field (outdoor), volleyball. **On-Campus Highlights:** Student Commons, Cabell Library, Siegel Center, Anderson Gallery, Shafer Court Dining Facility, Cary Street Recreation Complex. **Environmental Initiatives:** GHG reduction goal of 3,000 to 4,000 MTCDE to achieve climate neutrality by 2050; VCU successfully secured $3.1 million in federal funds for solar energy projects; Completion of two VCU mobility hubs consisting of bicycle racks, air compressors, ZipCars, in proximity to GRTC/VCU Campus Connector bus stops and L2 electric vehicle charging stations.

ADMISSIONS
Freshman Academic Profile: Average high school GPA 3.59. 18.78% in top 10% of high school class, 47.37% in top 25% of high school class, 84.6% in top 50% of high school class. SAT Math middle 50% range 500-600. SAT Critical Reading middle 50% range 500-610. SAT Writing middle 50% range 480-590. ACT middle 50% range 21-27. Minimum internet-based TOEFL 80. Minimum paper TOEFL 550. **Basis for Candidate Selection:** *Very important factors considered include:* academic GPA, rigor of secondary school record. *Important factors considered include:* standardized test scores, talent/ability. *Other factors considered include:* Class rank, application essay, recommendation(s), extracurricular activities, first generation, volunteer work, work experience. **Freshman Admission Requirements:** High school diploma is required and GED is accepted. **Academic units required:** 4 English, 3 mathematics, 3 science, (1 science labs), 2 foreign language, 1 social studies, 2 history, 0 visual/performing arts, 0 computer science. **Freshman Admission Statistics:** 15,126 applied, 69% admitted, 34% enrolled. **Transfer Admission Requirements:** college transcript(s), Minimum college GPA of 2.25 required. Lowest grade transferable C. **General Admission Information:** Application Fee $40. Notification on a rolling basis, beginning on or about 12/1. Nonfall registration accepted. Admission may be deferred for a maximum of 1 semester. Credit offered for CEEB Advanced Placement tests.

COSTS AND FINANCIAL AID
Required Forms and Deadlines: FAFSA. **Notification of Awards:** Applicants will be notified of awards on a rolling basis beginning 4/1. **Types of Aid:** *Need-based scholarships/grants:* Federal Pell, SEOG, state scholarships/grants, private scholarships, the school's own gift aid. *Loans:* Direct Subsidized Stafford, Direct Unsubsidized Stafford, Direct PLUS, Federal Perkins, Federal Nursing. *Student Employment:* Federal Work-Study Program available. Institutional employment available. Off-campus job opportunities are good. **Financial Aid Statistics:** 82% freshmen, 78% undergrads receive need-based scholarship or grant aid. 28% freshmen, 17% undergrads receive non-need-based scholarship or grant aid. 76% freshmen, 82% undergrads receive need-based self-help aid. 1% freshmen, 1% undergrads receive athletic scholarships. 73% freshmen, 65% undergrads receive any aid. 66% undergrads borrow to pay for school. Average cumulative indebtedness $28,391. **Criteria for awarding institutional aid:** *Non-need-based:* academics, alumni affiliation, art, athletics, leadership, music/drama.

VIRGINIA INTERMONT COLLEGE

1013 Moore Street, Bristol, VA 24201-4298
Phone: 276-466-7856 · **Financial Aid Phone:** 276-466-7872
E-mail: viadmit@vic.edu · **CEEB Code:** 5857
Fax: 276-466-7855 · **ACT Code:** 4416

This private school, affiliated with the Baptist Church, was founded in 1884. It has a 27-acre campus.

RATINGS
Admissions Selectivity Rating: 80   **Fire Safety Rating:** 82

STUDENTS AND FACULTY
Enrollment: 885. **Student Body:** 69% female, 31% male, 68% out-of-state, 8% international. Asian 1%, African American 7%, Caucasian 78%, Hispanic 2%, Native American 1%
Retention and Graduation: 74% freshmen return for sophomore year. 10% grads go on to further study within 1 year. 3% grads pursue arts and sciences degrees. 1% grads pursue law degrees. 2% grads pursue business degrees. 1% grads pursue medical degrees. **Faculty:** 44 full-time faculty, 61% hold PhDs, 41% are are members of minority groups, 5% are women. 0% of classes are taught by teaching assistants.

ACADEMICS
Degrees: associate, bachelor's. **Classes:** Most classes have fewer than 10 students. Most lab/discussion sessions have fewer than 10 students. **Majors with Highest Enrollment:** Equestrian/Equine Studies; Photography; Business/

Commerce. **Special Study Options:** Accelerated program, cross-registration, distance learning, double major, English as a Second Language (ESL), honors program, independent study, internships, study abroad, teacher certification program. **Honors programs:** Honors program available for students who meet the necessary academic requirements. **Disability Services:** Special programs offered to physically disabled students include note-taking services, reader services, tape recorders, tutors. **Career services:** alumni services, career/job search classes, internships.

FACILITIES

Housing: Coed dorms, special housing for disabled students, men's dorms, women's dorms, apartments for married students, apartments for single students. 25% of campus accessible to physically disabled. **Special Academic Facilities/Equipment:** Museum/gallery, 129-acre riding center for equestrian program, Newly constructed Fine Arts Center. **Computers:** Students can register for classes online. Administrative functions (other than registration) can be performed online.

CAMPUS LIFE

Environment: Town. **Activities:** Choral groups, dance, drama/theater, musical theater, student government, yearbook. 26 registered organizations, 4 honor societies, 2 religious organizations. **Athletics (Intercollegiate):** *Men:* baseball, basketball, cross-country, equestrian sports, golf, soccer, tennis, track/field (outdoor), track/field (indoor). *Women:* basketball, cheerleading, cross-country, equestrian sports, soccer, softball, tennis, track/field (outdoor), track/field (indoor), volleyball. **On-Campus Highlights:** Fine Arts Gallery, Van Dyke Davis Alumni House, President's Home, Equestrian Center, Bell Tower.

ADMISSIONS

Freshman Academic Profile: Average high school GPA 3.2. 8% in top 10% of high school class, 20% in top 25% of high school class, 58% in top 50% of high school class. 85% from public high schools. SAT Math middle 50% range 410-540. SAT Critical Reading middle 50% range 410-530. ACT middle 50% range 17-25. Minimum paper TOEFL 500. **Basis for Candidate Selection:** *Very important factors considered include:* academic GPA, rigor of secondary school record, standardized test scores. *Other factors considered include:* Class rank, application essay, recommendation(s), alumni/ae relation, character/personal qualities, extracurricular activities, first generation, interview, level of applicant's interest, talent/ability, work experience. **Freshman Admission Requirements:** High school diploma is required and GED is accepted. **Academic units required:** 4 English, 2 mathematics, 1 science, (1 science labs), 0 foreign language, 2 social studies, 0 history, 6 academic electives. **Freshman Admission Statistics:** 624 applied, 55% admitted, 44% enrolled. **Transfer Admission Requirements:** college transcript(s), essay or personal statement, statement of good standing from prior institution(s). Minimum college GPA of 2.0 required. Lowest grade transferable C. **General Admission Information:** Application Fee $25. Nonfall registration accepted. Admission may be deferred for a maximum of 2 terms. Credit and/or placement offered for CEEB Advanced Placement tests.

COSTS AND FINANCIAL AID

Annual tuition $16,895. Room and board $6,095. Required fees $950. Average book expense $900. **Required Forms and Deadlines:** FAFSA, State aid form. **Notification of Awards:** Applicants will be notified of awards on a rolling basis beginning 2/15. **Types of Aid:** *Need-based scholarships/grants:* Federal Pell, SEOG, state scholarships/grants, private scholarships, the school's own gift aid. *Loans:* Subsidized Stafford, Unsubsidized Stafford, PLUS, Federal Perkins. *Student Employment:* Federal Work-Study Program available. Highest amount earned per year from on-campus jobs $1,500. Off-campus job opportunities are good. **Financial Aid Statistics:** 98% freshmen, 93% undergrads receive need-based scholarship or grant aid. 8% freshmen, 5% undergrads receive non-need-based scholarship or grant aid. 76% freshmen, 86% undergrads receive need-based self-help aid. 14% freshmen, 10% undergrads receive athletic scholarships. 65% freshmen, 73% undergrads receive any aid. 79% undergrads borrow to pay for school. Average cumulative indebtedness $19,129. **Criteria for awarding institutional aid:** *Non-need-based:* academics, alumni affiliation, art, athletics, minority status, music/drama, religious affiliation, state/district residency.

VIRGINIA MILITARY INSTITUTE

VMI Office of Admissions, Lexington, VA 24450-0304
Phone: 540-464-7211 · **Financial Aid Phone:** 540-464-7208
E-mail: admissions@vmi.edu · **CEEB Code:** 5858
Fax: 540-464-7746 · **Website:** www.vmi.edu · **ACT Code:** 4418

This public school was founded in 1839. It has a 140-acre campus.

RATINGS

Admissions Selectivity Rating: 85 **Fire Safety Rating:** 71

STUDENTS AND FACULTY

Enrollment: 1,428. **Student Body:** 8% female, 92% male, 41% out-of-state, 2% international (9 countries represented). Asian 4%, African American 6%, Caucasian 84%, Hispanic 4%, Native American <1%. **Retention and Graduation:** 8% grads go on to further study within 1 year. 3% grads pursue arts and sciences degrees. 2% grads pursue law degrees. 1% grads pursue business degrees. 1% grads pursue medical degrees. **Faculty:** 120 full-time faculty, 98% hold PhDs, 19% are are members of minority groups, 7% are women. 0% of classes are taught by teaching assistants.

ACADEMICS

Degrees: bachelor's. **Classes:** Most classes have 10-19 students. **Majors with Highest Enrollment:** Mechanical Engineering; Business/Managerial Economics; History. **Special Study Options:** Accelerated program, double major, exchange student program (domestic), honors program, independent study, internships, study abroad, teacher certification program, Summer Transition Program: Optional for incoming freshman. **Honors programs:** Institute Honors Program, departmental honors programs. **Career services:** Alumni network, career/job search classes, career assessment, internships.

FACILITIES

Housing: Barracks (3-5 students/room). 50% of campus accessible to physically disabled. **Special Academic Facilities/Equipment:** VMI Museum George C. Marshall Museum **Computers:** Students can register for classes online. Administrative functions (other than registration) can be performed online.

CAMPUS LIFE

Environment: Village. **Activities:** Choral groups, concert band, drama/theater, jazz band, literary magazine, marching band, music ensembles, musical theater, pep band, student government, student newspaper, yearbook. 50 registered organizations, 11 honor societies, 3 religious organizations. **Athletics (Intercollegiate):** *Men:* baseball, basketball, cross-country, football, golf, lacrosse, riflery, soccer, swimming, track/field (outdoor), track/field (indoor), wrestling. *Women:* cross-country, riflery, soccer, swimming, track/field (outdoor), track/field (indoor). **On-Campus Highlights:** VMI Museum, George C. Marshall Museum.

ADMISSIONS

Freshman Academic Profile: Average high school GPA 3.351. 9.9% in top 10% of high school class, 39.9% in top 25% of high school class, 81.5% in top 50% of high school class. 84% from public high schools. SAT Math middle 50% range 530-620. SAT Critical Reading middle 50% range 510-620. SAT Writing middle 50% range 480-590. ACT middle 50% range 21-26. Minimum paper TOEFL 500. **Basis for Candidate Selection:** *Very important factors considered include:* Class rank, rigor of secondary school record, standardized test scores, character/personal qualities. *Important factors considered include:* extracurricular activities, interview, racial/ethnic status, state residency, volunteer work. *Other factors considered include:* recommendation(s), alumni/ae relation, geographical residence, talent/ability. **Freshman Admission Requirements:** High school diploma is required and GED is not accepted. **Academic units required:** 4 English, 3 mathematics, 3 science, (3 science labs), 3 foreign language. **Freshman Admission Statistics:** 1,600 applied, 54% admitted, 48% enrolled. **Transfer Admission Requirements:** High school transcript, college transcript(s), standardized test scores, Minimum college GPA of 2.0 required. Lowest grade transferable C. **General Admission Information:** Application Fee $35. Early decision application deadline 11/15. Regular application deadline 2/15. Notification on a rolling basis, beginning on or about 1/1. Nonfall registration not accepted. Credit and/or placement offered for CEEB Advanced Placement tests.

COSTS AND FINANCIAL AID

Required Forms and Deadlines: FAFSA, Institution's own financial aid form. **Notification of Awards:** Applicants will be notified of awards on a rolling basis beginning 3/15. **Types of Aid:** *Need-based scholarships/grants:* Federal Pell, SEOG, state scholarships/grants, private scholarships, the school's own gift aid. *Loans:* Direct Subsidized Stafford, Direct Unsubsidized Stafford, Direct PLUS, Federal Perkins. *Student Employment:* Highest amount earned per year from on-campus jobs $850. **Financial Aid Statistics:** 75% freshmen, 75% undergrads receive need-based scholarship or grant aid. 27% freshmen, 28%

undergrads receive non-need-based scholarship or grant aid. 43% freshmen, 47% undergrads receive need-based self-help aid. 11% freshmen, 7% undergrads receive athletic scholarships. 85% freshmen, 82% undergrads receive any aid. 52% undergrads borrow to pay for school. Average cumulative indebtedness $14,068. **Criteria for awarding institutional aid:** *Non-need-based:* academics, alumni affiliation, athletics, leadership, music/drama.

VIRGINIA POLYTECHNIC INSTITUTE AND STATE UNIVERSITY

Undergraduate Admissions, Blacksburg, VA 24061
Phone: 540-231-6267 · **Financial Aid Phone:** 540-231-5179
E-mail: admissions@vt.edu · **CEEB Code:** 5859
Fax: 540-231-3242 · **Website:** www.vt.edu · **ACT Code:** 4420

This public school was founded in 1872. It has a 2600-acre campus.

RATINGS

Admissions Selectivity Rating: 89   **Fire Safety Rating:** 78

STUDENTS AND FACULTY

Enrollment: 23,928. **Student Body:** 41% female, 59% male, 24% out-of-state, 4% international (113 countries represented). Asian 8%, African American 3%, Caucasian 72%, Hispanic 5%, Native American <1%
Retention and Graduation: 83% freshmen graduate within 6 years. 27% grads go on to further study within 1 year. **Faculty:** 1,427 full-time faculty, 90% hold PhDs, 33% are are members of minority groups, 18% are women.

ACADEMICS

Degrees: associate, bachelor's, master's, post-master's certificate. **Classes:** Most classes have 20-29 students. Most lab/discussion sessions have 20-29 students. **Majors with Highest Enrollment:** Engineering; Biology/Biological Sciences. **Special Study Options:** Accelerated program, cooperative education program, distance learning, double major, dual enrollment, English as a Second Language (ESL), honors program, independent study, internships, study abroad, teacher certification program. **Combined degree programs:** BA/MA. **Disability Services:** Special programs offered to physically disabled students include note-taking services, reader services, tape recorders, tutors. **Career services:** Alumni network, alumni services, career/job search classes, career assessment, internships.

FACILITIES

Housing: Coed dorms, special housing for disabled students, men's dorms, special housing for international students, women's dorms, fraternity/sorority housing, Wellness Housing, Theme Housing, Housing for Corps of Cadets and athletes. The World—a cross cultural environment The W.E.L.L.—a personal health/development community. Foreign language hall and academic success hall available. The Wing—a transitional/orientation community for freshmen. Residential Leadership Community, Biological and Life Sciences Learning Community, Virginia Tech Design Collaborative. 60% of campus accessible to physically disabled. **Special Academic Facilities/Equipment:** Art gallery, digital music facilities, multimedia labs, Black Cultural Center, television studio, anaerobic lab, CAD-CAM labs, observatory, wind tunnel, farms, Math Emporium, the CAVE (virtual reality learning facility). **Computers:** Students can register for classes online. Administrative functions (other than registration) can be performed online. Undergraduates are required to own a computer.

CAMPUS LIFE

Environment: Town. **Activities:** Choral groups, concert band, dance, drama/theater, jazz band, literary magazine, marching band, music ensembles, musical theater, pep band, radio station, student government, student newspaper, yearbook. 600 registered organizations, 32 honor societies, 53 religious organizations. 31 fraternities, 12 sororities. **Athletics (Intercollegiate):** *Men:* baseball, basketball, cheerleading, cross-country, diving, football, golf, soccer, swimming, tennis, track/field (outdoor), track/field (indoor), ultimate frisbee, water polo. *Women:* basketball, cheerleading, cross-country, diving, lacrosse, soccer, softball, swimming, tennis, track/field (outdoor), track/field (indoor), ultimate frisbee, volleyball, water polo. **Environmental Initiatives:** I. The Virginia Tech Climate Action Commitment And Sustainability Plan Implementation: On June 1, 2009 the Virginia Tech Board of Visitors unanimously approved The Virginia Tech Climate Action Commitment and accepted the

accompanying Sustainability Plan. See: http://www.facilities.vt.edu/documents/sustainability/sustPlan.pdf .The Sustainability Plan contains six topical areas: administrative structure and governance, facilities infrastructure, facilities operations, transportation, behavior and campus life, and academic programs. Each topical area identifies actions and measures to be conducted in the immediate term (2009-2012), in the midterm (2013-2025), or in the long term (2026-2050). The Office of Energy and Sustainability has the responsibility for overseeing the implementation of the Sustainability Plan and reporting progress. The Virginia Tech Climate Action Commitment and Sustainability Plan Status Report contains over 80 sustainability actions and measures in the immediate term. See: http://www.facilities.vt.edu/documents/sustainability/vtcac_status.pdf Virginia Techs Sustainability Plan Implementation was the recipient of the 2011 Governors Environmental Excellence Gold Award in the Environmental Program Category which was presented at the 22nd Annual Environment Virginia Symposium at the Virginia Military Institute in Lexington. See: http://www.vtnews.vt.edu/articles/2011/04/040811-facilities-excellenceaward.html Virginia Tech achieved a Silver Rating from the Association for the Advancement of Sustainability in Higher Education (AASHE) for sustainability performance in the Sustainability Tracking, Assessment & Rating System (STARS) program. The STARS program provides a common standard of measurement for 135 separate sustainability topics which are organized into three primary categories: Education & Research; Operations; and Planning, Administration and Engagement. The STARS program serves as an excellent framework for universities to objectively and transparently assess their sustainability efforts. STARS has been a very useful tool in benchmarking our progress towards a more sustainable campus. Virginia Tech earned a Silver Rating for sustainability performance in the STARS program, with an overall score of 61.94 points (just 3.06 points shy of the 65 points needed for gold rating). To view Virginia Techs STARS submission, please visit: https://stars.aashe.org/institutions/virginia-tech-va/report/2011-08-02/. II. Energy Reduction, Efficiency and Conservation Measures: 1. In accordance with the Campus Energy and Water Policy 5505, significant energy reduction has been achieved through the implementation of temperature settings (68 degrees Fahrenheit for the heating season and 74 degrees Fahrenheit for the cooling season). These measures have resulted in substantial energy savings, cost savings, and reductions in greenhouse gas emissions. 2. Significant energy reduction has been achieved through the select shutdown of building air handlers during periods of reduced occupancy using the Building Automation System. Substantial energy savings, cost savings, and reductions in greenhouse gas emissions have been realized. 3. Implementation of the use of the free cooling during the winter months for campus chilled water systems has provided energy savings, cost savings, and reductions in greenhouse gas emissions. 4. Completion of a $28 million capital project significantly enhanced the Central Steam Plant efficiency and campus-wide steam distribution infrastructure. 5. A $5.3 million Energy Performance Contract was recently executed for Energy Service Company (ESCO) Pepco Energy Services, Inc. to complete an energy conservation measure package for five major buildings to include: the Central Steam Plant, Cassell Coliseum (Athletics), Dietrick Dining Hall, McBryde Hall (Academic), and Hahn Hall-South (Research). Implementation is scheduled to begin in January 2012, and is expected to be completed by the end of calendar year 2012. 6. The Virginia Tech Climate Action Commitment Resolution point #6 states the university will pursue LEED Silver Certification or better for all new buildings and major renovations. Fifteen new construction and major renovation capital projects totaling 1,050,222 gross square feet (GSF) are registered in the Leadership in Energy and Environmental Design (LEED) program with the U.S. Green Building Council. Recently certified buildings include the Henderson Hall Renovation & Theatre 101 Addition LEED Gold (38,750 GSF), Addition to the Football Locker Room LEED Silver (42,145 GSF), and the Institute for Critical Technology & Applied Sciences II LEED Gold (42,190 GSF). 7. The Energy and Sustainability Committee recently revised campus policies on energy and water to incorporate additional energy use, water use, waste reduction, transportation, and travel guidelines and directives. The revision to the campus policy is entitled, University Policy 5505 Campus Energy, Water, and Waste Reduction. In accordance with Policy 5505, the Office of Energy and Sustainability successfully developed the Comprehensive Waste Management Plan for Virginia Tech. The plan was completed on July 15, 2011 and included stakeholders from all major campus units. See: http://facilities.vt.edu/documents/sustainability/unlinked/Comprehensive_Waste_Mangement_Plan_Virginia_Tech_7_15_2011_Final.pdf. III. Student Sustainability Intern Program: Developed and coordinated by the first sustainability intern in the Office of Energy and Sustainability, an extremely innovative student sustainability internship program is being implemented at Virginia Tech with a focus on student development. What makes this program unique is the emphasis on interdisciplinary collaboration between all of the layers of the university and its focus on the synergy between project based and classroom based learning outcomes. The projects chosen for the program allow interns to apply the concepts and skills learned in the classroom to real world challenges that exist right here on campus to gain experience working with their peers in different career fields. Students are charged to develop creative solutions to on campus sustainability challenges while being provided with structure to understand the project itself and skills based workshops that offer individual and professional development opportunities. Started in the spring of 2010, this program just completed its third cohort and will be expanding to a year-long program starting in the fall of 2012. Program Mission & Vision: Our current undergraduate and graduate students are the sustainability professionals of tomorrow. They will enter the working world with a new set of challenges and parameters that will define the work that they can and will do, regardless of their field. Because of this, it is critical that we, as an institution of higher education, prepare our students for the world that they will soon be leading by providing them with the critical skills and a learning environment that will prepare them to be the inventors of a sustainable future. With the foundations in collaborative research and interdisciplinary teamwork to tackle campus sustainability, this project and classroom based learning experience will train students to be able to understand and address societys most pressing challenges. Examples of Current and Past Projects: a. Campus Sustainability Web Portal Development The purpose of this project is to create an information portal for the Virginia Tech community to streamline, connect, and organize all sustainability related activities. Interns will focus on the development and coding of a dynamic web portal, in collaboration with the existing Ensemble CMS framework, to organize existing information and details gathered (including all STARS credits data) to facilitate communication and collaboration on sustainability projects on campus. The portal will continually evolve each year and can be accessed at www.sustainability.vt.edu b. Football Game Best Practices Toolkit Student interns conducted original research in collaboration with a panel of technical experts from across the country and major national campus sustainability organizations. The findings were presented in a toolkit outlining best practices and case studies of some of the most successful programs in the nation. The toolkit was extremely well received and can be downloaded from the College and University Recycling Coalition (CURC) website: http://curc3r.org/images/pdfs/collegiate_football_smm_guide_final.pdf. See toolkit article: http://www.vtnews.vt.edu/articles/2011/10/102111-facilities-toolkit.html.

ADMISSIONS

Freshman Academic Profile: 41.46% in top 10% of high school class, 83.45% in top 25% of high school class, 98.38% in top 50% of high school class. SAT Math middle 50% range 580-680. SAT Critical Reading middle 50% range 540-640. SAT Writing middle 50% range 540-640. Minimum paper TOEFL 550. **Basis for Candidate Selection:** *Very important factors considered include:* academic GPA, rigor of secondary school record, standardized test scores. *Other factors considered include:* recommendation(s), alumni/ae relation, character/personal qualities, extracurricular activities, first generation, geographical residence, racial/ethnic status, state residency, talent/ability, volunteer work, work experience. **Freshman Admission Requirements:** High school diploma is required and GED is accepted. **Academic units required:** 4 English, 3 mathematics, 2 science, (2 science labs), 1 social studies, 1 history, 4 academic electives. **Freshman Admission Statistics:** 19,112 applied, 70% admitted, 40% enrolled. **Transfer Admission Requirements:** High school transcript, college transcript(s), Minimum college GPA of 3.0 required. Lowest grade transferable C. **General Admission Information:** Application Fee $50. Early decision application deadline 11/1. Regular application deadline 1/15. Regular notification 4/1. Nonfall registration accepted. Admission may be deferred for a maximum of 1 year. Credit and/or placement offered for CEEB Advanced Placement tests.

COSTS AND FINANCIAL AID

Average book expense $1,120. **Required Forms and Deadlines:** FAFSA. **Notification of Awards:** Applicants will be notified of awards on a rolling basis beginning 3/30. **Types of Aid:** *Need-based scholarships/grants:* Federal Pell, SEOG, state scholarships/grants, private scholarships, the school's own gift aid, cadet scholarships/grants. *Loans:* Direct Subsidized Stafford, Direct Unsubsidized Stafford, Direct PLUS, Federal Perkins, college/university loans from institutional funds. *Student Employment:* Federal Work-Study Program available. Off-campus job opportunities are excellent. **Financial Aid Statistics:** 67% freshmen, 70% undergrads receive need-based scholarship or grant aid. 49% freshmen, 37% undergrads receive non-need-based scholarship or grant aid. 67% freshmen, 74% undergrads receive need-based self-help aid. 1% freshmen, 1% undergrads receive any athletic scholarships. 77% freshmen, 75% undergrads receive any aid. 55% undergrads borrow to pay for school. Average cumulative indebtedness $22,884. **Criteria for awarding institutional aid:** *Non-need-based:* academics, art, athletics, leadership, minority status, music/drama, state/district residency.

VIRGINIA STATE UNIVERSITY

One Hayden Drive, Petersburg, VA 23806
Phone: 804-524-5902 • **Financial Aid Phone:** 804-524-5990
E-mail: admiss@vsu.edu • **CEEB Code:** 5860
Fax: 804-524-5055 • **Website:** www.vsu.edu • **ACT Code:** 4424

This public school was founded in 1882. It has a 246-acre campus.

RATINGS

Admissions Selectivity Rating: 71   **Fire Safety Rating:** 60*

STUDENTS AND FACULTY

Enrollment: 4,481. **Student Body:** 60% female, 40% male, 32% out-of-state, 0% international (29 countries represented). Asian 0%, African American 85%, Caucasian 3%, Hispanic 2%, Native American <1%
Retention and Graduation: 61% freshmen return for sophomore year. 23% freshmen graduate within 4 years. 43% freshmen graduate within 6 years. **Faculty:** 296 full-time faculty, 42% are are members of minority groups. 0% of classes are taught by teaching assistants.

ACADEMICS

Degrees: associate, bachelor's, certificate, master's, post-master's certificate. **Majors with Highest Enrollment:** Physical Education Teaching and Coaching; Liberal Arts and Sciences/Liberal Studies; Sociology. **Special Study Options:** cooperative education program, double major, dual enrollment, exchange student program (domestic), honors program, independent study, internships, teacher certification program. **Disability Services:** Special programs offered to physically disabled students include note-taking services, reader services, tutors. **Career services:** Alumni network, internships.

FACILITIES

Housing: Coed dorms, men's dorms, women's dorms, apartments for single studentsNote:Coed dorm—students required to have a 3.0 GPA and a record of leadership and service. (Honors Co-educational Residence Facility). 90% of campus accessible to physically disabled. **Computers:** Administrative functions (other than registration) can be performed online.

CAMPUS LIFE

Environment: Town. **Activities:** Choral groups, concert band, dance, drama/theater, jazz band, literary magazine, marching band, music ensembles, pep band, radio station, student government, student newspaper, television station, yearbook, Campus Ministries. 70 registered organizations, 6 honor societies, 4 religious organizations. 5 fraternities, 4 sororities. **Athletics (Intercollegiate):** *Men:* baseball, basketball, cheerleading, cross-country, football, golf, tennis, track/field (outdoor), track/field (indoor), *Women:* basketball, bowling, cheerleading, cross-country, golf, softball, tennis, track/field (outdoor), track/field (indoor), volleyball.

ADMISSIONS

Freshman Academic Profile: Average high school GPA 2.85. 3% in top 10% of high school class, 17% in top 25% of high school class, 53% in top 50% of high school class. SAT Math middle 50% range 380-460. SAT Critical Reading middle 50% range 380-460. SAT Writing middle 50% range 370-440. ACT middle 50% range 15-19. Minimum paper TOEFL 500. **Basis for Candidate Selection:** *Very important factors considered include:* application essay, recommendation(s), rigor of secondary school record, standardized test scores. *Important factors considered include:* academic GPA. *Other factors considered include:* Class rank, alumni/ae relation, character/personal qualities, extracurricular activities, geographical residence, state residency, talent/ability, volunteer work, work experience. **Freshman Admission Requirements:** High school diploma is required and GED is accepted. **Academic units required:** 4 English, 3 mathematics, 2 science, (1 science labs), 2 social studies. **Freshman Admission Statistics:** 5,923 applied, 80% admitted, 19% enrolled. **Transfer Admission Requirements:** college transcript(s), essay or personal statement, statement of good standing from prior institution(s). Minimum college GPA of 2.0 required. Lowest grade transferable C. **General Admission Information:** Application Fee $25. Regular application deadline 5/1. Notification on a rolling basis, beginning on or about 11/1. Nonfall registration accepted. Credit offered for CEEB Advanced Placement tests.

COSTS AND FINANCIAL AID

Average book expense $1,300. **Required Forms and Deadlines:** FAFSA, Institution's own financial aid form. **Notification of Awards:** Applicants will be notified of awards on a rolling basis beginning 5/1. **Types of Aid:** *Need-based scholarships/grants:* Federal Pell, SEOG, state scholarships/grants, private scholarships, the school's own gift aid. *Loans:* Direct Subsidized Stafford, Direct Unsubsidized Stafford, Direct PLUS, PLUS, Federal Perkins, college/university loans from institutional funds. *Student Employment:* Federal Work-Study Program available. Institutional employment available. **Financial Aid**

Statistics: 80% freshmen, 80% undergrads receive need-based scholarship or grant aid. 22% freshmen, 22% undergrads receive non-need-based scholarship or grant aid. 72% freshmen, 72% undergrads receive need-based self-help aid. 3% freshmen, 3% undergrads receive athletic scholarships. 90% undergrads borrow to pay for school. Average cumulative indebtedness $25,750. **Criteria for awarding institutional aid:** *Non-need-based:* academics, alumni affiliation, art, job skills, leadership, music/drama, religious affiliation.

VIRGINIA WESLEYAN COLLEGE

1584 Wesleyan Drive, Norfolk/Virginia Beach, VA 23502-5599
Phone: 757-455-3208 · **Financial Aid Phone:** 757-455-3345
E-mail: admissions@vwc.edu · **CEEB Code:** 5867
Fax: 757-461-5238 · **Website:** www.vwc.edu · **ACT Code:** 4429

This private school, affiliated with the Methodist Church, was founded in 1961. It has a 300-acre campus.

RATINGS

Admissions Selectivity Rating: 74   Fire Safety Rating: 72

STUDENTS AND FACULTY

Enrollment: 1,493. **Student Body:** 62% female, 38% male, 25% out-of-state, 1% international (7 countries represented). Asian 1%, African American 23%, Caucasian 56%, Hispanic 8%, Native American <1%
Retention and Graduation: 42% freshmen graduate within 4 years. 48% freshmen graduate within 6 years. 32% grads go on to further study within 1 year. 1% grads pursue law degrees. 1% grads pursue business degrees. **Faculty:** 92 full-time faculty, 91% hold PhDs, 48% are are members of minority groups, 11% are women. 0% of classes are taught by teaching assistants.

ACADEMICS

Degrees: bachelor's. **Classes:** Most classes have 10-19 students. **Majors with Highest Enrollment:** Business Administration and Management; Criminal Justice/Safety Studies; Social Sciences. **Special Study Options:** double major, honors program, independent study, internships, liberal arts/career combination, student-designed major, study abroad, teacher certification program, Externships; PORTfolio, a 4-year competitive program designed to integrate liberal arts and experiential learning. **Honors programs:** Wesleyan Scholars is an honors program which is designed for applicants with superior high school achievement records. The Honors and Scholars program, including Wesleyan Scholars, offers academically challenging honors courses and stimulating co-curricular experiences. Program enhancement is also offered through PORTfolio, a selective program designed to integrate the liberal arts with experiential learning opportunities available in Hampton Roads. **Combined degree programs:** 2-2 program in business/accounting with Tidewater. **Disability Services:** Special programs offered to physically disabled students include note-taking services, reader services, tape recorders, tutors. **Career services:** Alumni network, career/job search classes, internships, regional alumni.

FACILITIES

Housing: Coed dorms, special housing for disabled students, special housing for international students, women's dorms, fraternity/sorority housing, apartments for single students, Wellness Housing, Townhouses, Honors and Scholars Hall, Wellness Hall—a substance free hall which provides special programs focusing on social, physical, spiritual, emotional, and intellectual wellness. 90% of campus accessible to physically disabled. **Special Academic Facilities/Equipment:** Greenhouse, language lab, teleconferencing facility, social science teach. and learn. lab, radio station, TV studio, Barclay Sheaks Art Gallery, computerized classrooms, Internet access all classrooms, 24-hr. computer lab, Lambuth M. Clarke Hall with state-of-the-art teaching technologies, three academic villages combining residences and campus offices and services. **Computers:** 20% of classrooms, 100% of libraries, 100% of student union, have wireless network access. Students can register for classes online. Administrative functions (other than registration) can be performed online.

CAMPUS LIFE

Environment: Metropolis. **Activities:** Choral groups, dance, drama/theater, literary magazine, music ensembles, musical theater, radio station, student government, student newspaper, yearbook, Campus Ministries, International Student Organization, Model UN. 60 registered organizations, 19 honor societies, 4 religious organizations. 3 fraternities, 4 sororities. **Athletics (Intercollegiate):**

Men: baseball, basketball, cross-country, golf, lacrosse, soccer, tennis, track/field (outdoor), track/field (indoor). *Women:* basketball, cheerleading, cross-country, field hockey, lacrosse, soccer, softball, tennis, track/field (outdoor), track/field (indoor), volleyball. **On-Campus Highlights:** The Marlin Restaurant, Jane P. Batten Student Center, Village III, Trinder Athletic Center **Environmental Initiatives:** Green Roof, Recycling, Composting, Sustainable Purchasing.

ADMISSIONS

Freshman Academic Profile: Average high school GPA 3.3. 13% in top 10% of high school class, 38% in top 25% of high school class, 74% in top 50% of high school class. 86% from public high schools. SAT Math middle 50% range 430-550. SAT Critical Reading middle 50% range 440-550. SAT Writing middle 50% range 425-530. ACT middle 50% range 18-25. Minimum paper TOEFL 550. **Basis for Candidate Selection:** *Very important factors considered include:* academic GPA, rigor of secondary school record, level of applicant's interest. *Important factors considered include:* application essay, recommendation(s), standardized test scores, extracurricular activities. *Other factors considered include:* alumni/ae relation, character/personal qualities, first generation, interview, talent/ability, volunteer work, work experience. **Freshman Admission Requirements:** High school diploma is required and GED is accepted. **Academic units required:** 4 English, 3 mathematics, 2 science, (2 science labs), 2 foreign language, 1 history, 1 computer science. science labs), 2 foreign language, 1 history, 1 computer science, **Freshman Admission Statistics:** 2,072 applied, 89% admitted, 22% enrolled. **Transfer Admission Requirements:** High school transcript, college transcript(s), essay or personal statement, statement of good standing from prior institution(s). Minimum college GPA of 2.5 required. Lowest grade transferable C. **General Admission Information:** Application Fee $40. Notification on a rolling basis, beginning on or about 9/15. Nonfall registration accepted. Credit and/or placement offered for CEEB Advanced Placement tests.

COSTS AND FINANCIAL AID

Annual tuition $32,636. Room and board $8,594. Required fees $650. Average book expense $1,500. **Required Forms and Deadlines:** FAFSA, State aid form. **Notification of Awards:** Applicants will be notified of awards on a rolling basis beginning 2/1. **Types of Aid:** *Need-based scholarships/grants:* Federal Pell, SEOG, state scholarships/grants, private scholarships, the school's own gift aid, Virginia Coalition for Independent Colleges; United Methodist Greater Higher Education Board. *Loans:* Subsidized Stafford, Unsubsidized Stafford, PLUS, Federal Perkins, state loans, Private Alternative Loan Program. *Student Employment:* Federal Work-Study Program available. Institutional employment available. Highest amount earned per year from on-campus jobs $1,200. Off-campus job opportunities are good. **Financial Aid Statistics:** 100% freshmen, 100% undergrads receive need-based scholarship or grant aid. 19% freshmen, 17% undergrads receive non-need-based scholarship or grant aid. 78% freshmen, 78% undergrads receive need-based self-help aid. 0% freshmen, 0% undergrads receive athletic scholarships. 99% freshmen, 98% undergrads receive any aid. **Criteria for awarding institutional aid:** *Non-need-based:* academics, alumni affiliation, leadership, religious affiliation, state/district residency.

VITERBO UNIVERSITY

900 Viterbo Drive, La Crosse, WI 54601
Phone: 608-796-3010 · **Financial Aid Phone:** 608-496-3900
E-mail: admission@viterbo.edu · **CEEB Code:** 1878
Fax: 608-796-3020 · **ACT Code:** 4662

This private school, affiliated with the Roman Catholic Church, was founded in 1890. It has a 25-acre campus.

RATINGS

Admissions Selectivity Rating: 74   Fire Safety Rating: 68

STUDENTS AND FACULTY

Enrollment: 1,922. **Student Body:** 71% female, 29% male, 19% out-of-state, 1% international (15 countries represented). Asian 1%, African American 1%, Caucasian 93%, Hispanic 1%, Native American 1%
Retention and Graduation: 74% freshmen return for sophomore year. 30% freshmen graduate within 4 years. 48% freshmen graduate within 6 years. 7% grads go on to further study within 1 year. 4% grads pursue arts and sciences degrees. 1% grads pursue law degrees. 2% grads pursue medical degrees. **Faculty:** 110 full-time faculty, 56% hold PhDs, 56% are are members of minority groups, 4% are women. 0% of classes are taught by teaching assistants.

ACADEMICS

Degrees: associate, bachelor's, master's, post-bachelor's certificate, terminal associate, transfer associate. **Classes:** Most classes have 10-19 students. Most lab/discussion sessions have 10-19 students. **Majors with Highest Enrollment:** Elementary Education and Teaching; Registered Nursing/Registered Nurse; Business Administration and Management. **Special Study Options:** Accelerated program, cross-registration, distance learning, double major, dual enrollment, honors program, independent study, internships, liberal arts/career combination, student-designed major, study abroad, teacher certification program, weekend college, Weekend college is basically for our Master's level programs. **Honors programs:** The mission of the Viterbo University Honors Program is to provide a supportive, enriched learning environment responsive to the educational needs of highly able and exceptionally motivated undergraduate students who are committed to achieving academic excellence. The program provides honors sections of regular, general education courses, honors credit within regular sections, interdisciplinary Honors Capstone courses, oversight of senior honors projects, and increased opportunity for undergraduate research and creative activity. The program complements and enhances the Liberal Arts mission of the university. Together, honors students and faculty constitute a community of scholars. **Combined degree programs:** chiropractic. **Disability Services:** Special programs offered to physically disabled students include note-taking services, reader services, tape recorders, tutors. **Career services:** Alumni network, alumni services, career/job search classes, career assessment, internships, regional alumni. Career services highlights include successful placement of our students in internships that have not only assisted the student but the larger La Crosse community.

FACILITIES

Housing: Coed dorms, apartments for single students, Theme floors in dorms and university owned theme houses. 90% of campus accessible to physically disabled. **Special Academic Facilities/Equipment:** Fine Arts Center; Center for Ethics, Science and Technology with distance education labs and video conferencing; Nursing center with labs and simulated equipment; new recreation and education center co-sponsored by Viterbo University and the Boys and Girls Club. **Computers:** Students can register for classes online. Administrative functions (other than registration) can be performed online.

CAMPUS LIFE

Environment: Town. **Activities:** Choral groups, dance, drama/theater, literary magazine, music ensembles, musical theater, opera, pep band, student government, student newspaper. 22 registered organizations, 2 honor societies, 2 religious organizations. **Athletics (Intercollegiate):** *Men:* baseball, basketball, golf, soccer. *Women:* basketball, golf, soccer, softball, volleyball. **On-Campus Highlights:** Reinhart Center for Ethics, Science and Technology, Fine Arts Center, Amie Mathy Center for Recreation and Education, Student Activity Center, Dancing Francis, Center for Ethics, Science and Technology opened the Fall of 2003. Center for Recreation and Wellness opened Fall 2005, co-sponsored by Viterbo and the Boys/Girls club. Dancing Francis is a bronze sculpture of Francis of Assisi by Paul Granland. Fine Arts Center is home of performing arts in the region. Student Activity Center is home to the V-Hawks as well as fitness center for all students.

ADMISSIONS

Freshman Academic Profile: Average high school GPA 3.3. 12.6% in top 10% of high school class, 38.8% in top 25% of high school class, 72.9% in top 50% of high school class. 97% from public high schools. ACT middle 50% range 20-24. Minimum paper TOEFL 550. **Basis for Candidate Selection:** *Very important factors considered include:* academic GPA, rigor of secondary school record, standardized test scores, character/personal qualities, level of applicant's interest. *Important factors considered include:* Class rank, interview, talent/ability. *Other factors considered include:* application essay, recommendation(s), alumni/ae relation, extracurricular activities, first generation, volunteer work. **Freshman Admission Requirements:** High school diploma is required and GED is accepted. **Academic units required:** 3 English, 2 mathematics, 2 science, 2 social studies, 5 academic electives. **Freshman Admission Statistics:** 1,148 applied, 88% admitted, 36% enrolled. **Transfer Admission Requirements:** High school transcript, college transcript(s), statement of good standing from prior institution(s). Minimum college GPA of 2.0 required. Lowest grade transferable C-. **General Admission Information:** Application Fee $25. Nonfall registration accepted. Admission may be deferred for a maximum of 2 years. Credit offered for CEEB Advanced Placement tests.

COSTS AND FINANCIAL AID

Annual tuition $18,170. Room and board $6,140. Required fees $420. Average book expense $800. **Required Forms and Deadlines:** FAFSA, Institution's own financial aid form. **Notification of Awards:** Applicants will be notified of awards on a rolling basis beginning 4/1. **Types of Aid:** *Need-based scholarships/grants:* Federal Pell, SEOG, state scholarships/grants, private scholarships, the school's own gift aid. *Loans:* Subsidized Stafford, Unsubsidized Stafford, PLUS, Federal Perkins, Federal Nursing, state loans. *Student Employment:* Federal Work-Study Program available. Institutional employment available. Highest amount earned per year from on-campus jobs $2,500. Off-campus job opportunities are good. **Financial Aid Statistics:** 98% freshmen, 97% undergrads receive need-based scholarship or grant aid. 6% freshmen, 6% undergrads receive non-need-based scholarship or grant aid. 94% freshmen, 93% undergrads receive need-based self-help aid. 0% freshmen, 1% undergrads receive athletic scholarships. 98% freshmen, 89% undergrads receive any aid. 86% undergrads borrow to pay for school. **Criteria for awarding institutional aid:** *Non-need-based:* academics, alumni affiliation, art, athletics, leadership, minority status, music/drama.

VOORHEES COLLEGE

P.O. BOX 678, Denmark, SC 29042
Phone: 803-703-7111
E-mail: white@voorhees.edu • **CEEB Code:** 5863
Fax: 803-793-1117 • **Website:** www.voorhees.edu • **ACT Code:** 3882

This private school, affiliated with the Episcopal Church, was founded in 1897. It has a 350-acre campus.

RATINGS

Admissions Selectivity Rating: 80	**Fire Safety Rating:** 63

STUDENTS AND FACULTY

Enrollment: 738. **Student Body:** 64% female, 36% male, 30% out-of-state, 1% international. Asian 0%, African American 98%, Caucasian 1%, Hispanic 0%, Native American <1%
Retention and Graduation: 70% freshmen return for sophomore year. 100% freshmen graduate within 4 years. 25% grads go on to further study within 1 year. 17% grads pursue arts and sciences degrees. 2% grads pursue law degrees. 5% grads pursue business degrees. 4% grads pursue medical degrees. **Faculty:** 43 full-time faculty, 44% hold PhDs, 37% are are members of minority groups, 91% are women. 0% of classes are taught by teaching assistants.

ACADEMICS

Degrees: bachelor's, terminal associate. **Special Study Options:** cooperative education program, honors program, internships, weekend college. **Disability Services:** Special programs offered to physically disabled students include tape recorders, tutors. **Career services:** Alumni network, career/job search classes, internships.

FACILITIES

Housing: men's dorms, women's dorms, fraternity/sorority housing, Faculty + Staff Apartments, Housing for Single Mothers. **Computers:** Administrative functions (other than registration) can be performed online.

CAMPUS LIFE

Environment: Rural. **Activities:** Choral groups, drama/theater, literary magazine, pep band, radio station, student government, student newspaper, yearbook. 33 registered organizations, 2 honor societies, 3 religious organizations. 4 fraternities, 4 sororities. **Athletics (Intercollegiate):** *Men:* baseball, basketball, cheerleading, cross-country. *Women:* basketball, cheerleading, cross-country, softball, volleyball.

ADMISSIONS

Freshman Academic Profile: Average high school GPA 2. 1% in top 10% of high school class, 44% in top 25% of high school class, 50% in top 50% of high school class. 95% from public high schools. SAT Math middle 50% range 390-410. SAT Critical Reading middle 50% range 300-400. ACT middle 50% range 11-18. Minimum paper TOEFL 500. **Basis for Candidate Selection:** *Very important factors considered include:* Class rank, rigor of secondary school record, standardized test scores. *Important factors considered include:* recommendation(s), alumni/ae relation, character/personal qualities, talent/ability. *Other factors considered include:* extracurricular activities. **Freshman Admission Requirements:** High school diploma is required and GED is accepted. **Academic units required:** 4 English, 3 mathematics, 2 science, 2 foreign language, 1 social studies, 1 history, 7 academic electives. **Freshman Admission Statistics:** 3,511 applied, 37% admitted, 19% enrolled. **Transfer Admission Requirements:** college transcript(s), statement of good standing from prior institution(s). Minimum college GPA of 2.0 required. Lowest grade transferable C. **General Admission Information:** Application Fee $25. Notification on a rolling basis, beginning on or about 1/1. Nonfall registration accepted. Admission may be deferred for a maximum of 2 years. Credit offered for CEEB Advanced Placement tests.

COSTS AND FINANCIAL AID

Annual tuition $6,460. Room and board $3,516. Average book expense $2,500. **Required Forms and Deadlines:** FAFSA, Institution's own financial aid form. **Notification of Awards:** Applicants will be notified of awards on a rolling basis beginning 5/1. **Types of Aid:** *Need-based scholarships/grants:* Federal Pell, SEOG, state scholarships/grants, private scholarships, the school's own gift aid, United Negro College Fund. *Loans:* Subsidized Stafford, Unsubsidized Stafford, PLUS, Federal Perkins. *Student Employment:* Federal Work-Study Program available. Institutional employment available. Off-campus job opportunities are poor. **Financial Aid Statistics:** 93% freshmen, 89% undergrads receive need-based scholarship or grant aid. 1% freshmen, 1% undergrads receive non-need-based scholarship or grant aid. 90% freshmen, 92% undergrads receive need-based self-help aid. 0% freshmen, 0% undergrads receive athletic scholarships. 70% undergrads borrow to pay for school. **Criteria for awarding institutional aid:** *Non-need-based:* academics, art, athletics, leadership.

WABASH COLLEGE

PO Box 352, Crawfordsville, IN 47933
Phone: 765-361-6225 • **Financial Aid Phone:** 765-361-6370
E-mail: admissions@wabash.edu • **CEEB Code:** 1895
Fax: 765-361-6437 • **Website:** www.wabash.edu • **ACT Code:** 1260

This private school was founded in 1832. It has a 60-acre campus.

RATINGS

Admissions Selectivity Rating: 87   **Fire Safety Rating:** 86

STUDENTS AND FACULTY

Enrollment: 923. **Student Body:** 0% female, 100% male, 25% out-of-state, 7% international (8 countries represented). Asian 1%, African American 6%, Caucasian 75%, Hispanic 6%, Native American 1%
Retention and Graduation: 89% freshmen return for sophomore year. 68% freshmen graduate within 4 years. 73% freshmen graduate within 6 years. 24% grads go on to further study within 1 year. 10% grads pursue arts and sciences degrees. 6% grads pursue law degrees. 7% grads pursue medical degrees. **Faculty:** 85 full-time faculty, 99% hold PhDs, 35% are are members of minority groups, 12% are women. 0% of classes are taught by teaching assistants.

ACADEMICS

Degrees: bachelor's. **Classes:** Most classes have 10-19 students. Most lab/discussion sessions have fewer than 10 students. **Majors with Highest Enrollment:** Biology; History; Psychology. **Special Study Options:** double major, independent study, internships, liberal arts/career combination, study abroad, teacher certification program, Student designed majors, minors, or areas of concentration. Immersion Learning courses are offered, which involve travel domestically and abroad. **Combined degree programs:** BA/JD, BA/MEng, Columbia University School of Law. **Disability Services:** Special programs offered to physically disabled students include note-taking services, reader services, tape recorders, tutors. **Career services:** Alumni network, alumni services, career/job search classes, career assessment, internships, regional alumni. Career services highlights include our Wabash Business Leaders Program: Co-curricular program, designed to provide a comprehensive background in business, regardless of major. Couples our Business Sequence with experiential learning through internships, immersion programs, case studies, and speaker events.

FACILITIES

Housing: special housing for disabled students, men's dorms, fraternity/sorority housing, College-owned houses and apartments. 80% of campus accessible to physically disabled. **Special Academic Facilities/Equipment:** Malcolm X Institute of Black Studies, two art galleries, language lab, electron microscope, atomic absorption, nuclear and infrared spectrometers, Beowulf Supercomputer, Center of Inquiry in the Liberal Arts, Wabash Center for Teaching and Learning in Theology and Religion, Ramsey Archival Center. **Computers:** 100% of classrooms, 100% of dorms, 100% of libraries, 100% of dining areas, 100% of student union, 100% of common outdoor areas have wireless network access. Administrative functions (other than registration) can be performed online.

CAMPUS LIFE

Environment: Village. **Activities:** Choral groups, concert band, drama/theater, jazz band, literary magazine, music ensembles, pep band, radio station, student government, student newspaper, student-run film society, symphony orchestra, yearbook, Campus Ministries, International Student Organization, Model UN. 65 registered organizations, 7 honor societies, 5 religious organizations, 9 fraternities. **Athletics (Intercollegiate):** *Men:* baseball, basketball, cross-country, diving, football, golf, soccer, swimming, tennis, track/field (outdoor), track/field (indoor), wrestling. **On-Campus Highlights:** Allen Athletics and Recreation Center, Wabash Chapel, New Science Building, Hays Hall, Trippet Hall, Lilly Library, Malcolm X Institute of Black Studies. **Environmental Initiatives:** Printing Quota that saved 240,000 sheets of paper in the first semester (among 900 students); New, state-of-the-art, energy efficient boilers; A commitment to purchasing locally grown and raised food for use by our food service partner, and the establishment of a Community Garden.

ADMISSIONS

Freshman Academic Profile: Average high school GPA 3.6. 29% in top 10% of high school class, 66% in top 25% of high school class, 90% in top 50% of high school class. 92% from public high schools. SAT Math middle 50% range 520-640. SAT Critical Reading middle 50% range 500-600. SAT Writing middle 50% range 460-590. ACT middle 50% range 22-27. Minimum internet-based TOEFL 80. Minimum paper TOEFL 550. **Basis for Candidate Selection:** *Very important factors considered include:* Class rank, academic GPA, rigor of secondary school record. *Important factors considered include:* recommendation(s), standardized test scores, extracurricular activities, interview, level of applicant's interest, talent/ability. *Other factors considered include:* application essay, alumni/ae relation, character/personal qualities, first generation, geographical residence, racial/ethnic status, volunteer work, work experience. **Freshman Admission Requirements:** High school diploma is required and GED is accepted. **Freshman Admission Statistics:** 1,259 applied, 70% admitted, 29% enrolled. **Transfer Admission Requirements:** High school transcript, college transcript(s), essay or personal statement, standardized test scores, statement of good standing from prior institution(s). Lowest grade transferable C. **General Admission Information:** Application Fee $40. Early decision application deadline 11/15. Notification on a rolling basis, beginning on or about 11/15. Nonfall registration accepted. Admission may be deferred for a maximum of 1 year. Credit and/or placement offered for CEEB Advanced Placement tests.

COSTS AND FINANCIAL AID

Annual tuition $37,100. Room and board $9,130. Required fees $650. Average book expense $1,000. **Required Forms and Deadlines:** FAFSA, CSS/Financial Aid PROFILE. **Notification of Awards:** Applicants will be notified of awards on or about 3/31. **Types of Aid:** *Need-based scholarships/grants:* Federal Pell, state scholarships/grants, private scholarships, the school's own gift aid. *Loans:* Direct Subsidized Stafford, Direct Unsubsidized Stafford, Direct PLUS, college/university loans from institutional funds. *Student Employment:* Institutional employment available. Highest amount earned per year from on-campus jobs $3,000. Off-campus job opportunities are good. **Financial Aid Statistics:** 100% freshmen, 98% undergrads receive need-based scholarship or grant aid. 18% freshmen, 14% undergrads receive non-need-based scholarship or grant aid. 80% freshmen, 85% undergrads receive need-based self-help aid. 0% freshmen, 0% undergrads receive athletic scholarships. 98% freshmen, 96% undergrads receive any aid. 92% undergrads borrow to pay for school. Average cumulative indebtedness $21,776. **Criteria for awarding institutional aid:** *Non-need-based:* academics, art, job skills, music/drama.

WAGNER COLLEGE

1 Campus Rd, Staten Island, NY 10301
Phone: 718-390-3411 • **Financial Aid Phone:** 718-390-3183
E-mail: adm@wagner.edu • **CEEB Code:** 2966
Fax: 718-390-3105 • **Website:** www.wagner.edu • **ACT Code:** 2984

This private school was founded in 1883. It has a 110-acre campus.

RATINGS

Admissions Selectivity Rating: 87   **Fire Safety Rating:** 98

STUDENTS AND FACULTY

Enrollment: 1,800. **Student Body:** 63% female, 37% male, 52% out-of-state, 3% international (31 countries represented). Asian 3%, African American 7%, Caucasian 67%, Hispanic 10%, Native American <1%
Retention and Graduation: 87% freshmen return for sophomore year. 61% freshmen graduate within 4 years. 31% grads go on to further study within 1 year. 18% grads pursue arts and sciences degrees. 4% grads pursue law degrees. 30% grads pursue business degrees. 6% grads pursue medical degrees. **Faculty:** 98 full-time faculty, 82% hold PhDs, 50% are are members of minority groups, 9% are women. 0% of classes are taught by teaching assistants.

ACADEMICS

Degrees: bachelor's, master's, post-bachelor's certificate. **Classes:** Most classes have 10-19 students. Most lab/discussion sessions have 10-19 students. **Majors with Highest Enrollment:** Business/Commerce; Visual and Performing Arts; Nursing Science. **Special Study Options:** double major, exchange student program (domestic), honors program, independent study, internships, study abroad, teacher certification program, Learning Communities. **Combined degree programs:** BA/DDS, 7-year dental program with New York University. **Disability Services:** Special programs offered to physically disabled students include note-taking services, reader services, tape recorders, tutors. **Career services:** Alumni network, alumni services, internships. Career services highlights include The Wagner Plan for the Practical Liberal Arts. involves both alumni services and internships.

FACILITIES

Housing: Coed dorms, fraternity/sorority housing, apartments for single students, Theme Housing. **Special Academic Facilities/Equipment:** Art gallery, early childhood center, nursing resource center, planetarium, two electron microscopes, solar energy project. **Computers:** 90% of classrooms, 100% of dorms, 100% of libraries, 100% of dining areas, 100% of student union, 50% of common outdoor areas have wireless network access. Students can register for classes online. Administrative functions (other than registration) can be performed online.

CAMPUS LIFE

Environment: Metropolis. **Activities:** Choral groups, dance, drama/theater, jazz band, literary magazine, music ensembles, musical theater, pep band, radio station, student government, student newspaper, yearbook, Campus Ministries, International Student Organization, Model UN. 66 registered organizations, 11 honor societies, 4 religious organizations. 5 fraternities, 4 sororities. **Athletics (Intercollegiate):** *Men:* baseball, basketball, cross-country, football, golf, lacrosse, tennis, track/field (outdoor), track/field (indoor). *Women:* basketball, cross-country, golf, lacrosse, soccer, softball, swimming, tennis, track/field (outdoor), track/field (indoor), water polo. **On-Campus Highlights:** Coffee House, Spiro Sports Center, Wagner Student Union, Main Hall Theatre, Foundation Hall, Hawk's Nest. **Environmental Initiatives:** competing in Recylemania, trayless dining in all venues.

ADMISSIONS

Freshman Academic Profile: Average high school GPA 89.3. 16% in top 10% of high school class, 73% in top 25% of high school class, 92% in top 50% of high school class. 67% from public high schools. SAT Math middle 50% range 520-640. SAT Critical Reading middle 50% range 540-630. SAT Writing middle 50% range 520-630. ACT middle 50% range 22-27. Minimum internet-based TOEFL 79. Minimum paper TOEFL 550. **Basis for Candidate Selection:** *Very important factors considered include:* Class rank, academic GPA, rigor of secondary school record. *Important factors considered include:* application essay, recommendation(s), standardized test scores, extracurricular activities, interview. *Other factors considered include:* character/personal qualities, geographical residence, level of applicant's interest, talent/ability, volunteer work, work experience. **Freshman Admission Requirements:** High school diploma is required and GED is accepted. **Academic units required:** 4 English, 3 mathematics, 2 science, (1 science labs), 2 foreign language, 1 social studies, 3 history, 6 academic electives. **Freshman Admission Statistics:** 2,764 applied, 72% admitted, 22% enrolled. **Transfer Admission Requirements:** college transcript(s), essay or personal statement, statement of good standing from prior institution(s). Minimum college GPA of 3.0 required. Lowest grade transferable C. **General Admission Information:** Application Fee $50. Early decision application deadline 1/1. Regular application deadline 2/15. Regular notification 3/1. Nonfall registration accepted. Admission may be deferred for a maximum of 1 year. Credit offered for CEEB Advanced Placement tests.

COSTS AND FINANCIAL AID

Annual tuition $40,450. Room and board $12,450. Required fees $300. Average book expense $809. **Required Forms and Deadlines:** FAFSA, State aid form. **Notification of Awards:** Applicants will be notified of awards on a rolling basis beginning 3/1. **Types of Aid:** *Need-based scholarships/grants:* Federal Pell, SEOG, state scholarships/grants, private scholarships. *Loans:* Subsidized Stafford, Unsubsidized Stafford, PLUS, Federal Perkins, Federal Nursing, Alternative Loans. *Student Employment:* Federal Work-Study Program available. Institutional employment available. Highest amount earned per year from on-campus jobs $1,000. Off-campus job opportunities are good. **Financial Aid Statistics:** 100% freshmen, 99% undergrads receive need-based scholarship or grant aid. 0% freshmen, 0% undergrads receive non-need-based scholarship or grant aid. 70% freshmen, 76% undergrads receive need-based self-help aid. 5% freshmen, 7% undergrads receive athletic scholarships. 98% freshmen, 93% undergrads receive any aid. **Criteria for awarding institutional aid:** *Non-need-based:* academics, athletics, music/drama.

WAKE FOREST UNIVERSITY

Best 380

P.O. Box 7305, Winston Salem, NC 27109
Phone: 336-758-5201 · **Financial Aid Phone:** 336-758-5154
E-mail: admissions@wfu.edu · **CEEB Code:** 5885
Fax: 336-758-4324 · **Website:** www.wfu.edu · **ACT Code:** 3168

This private school was founded in 1834. It has a 340-acre campus.

RATINGS

Admissions Selectivity Rating: 93   **Fire Safety Rating:** 92

STUDENTS AND FACULTY

Enrollment: 4,812. **Student Body:** 52% female, 48% male, 77% out-of-state, 4% international (27 countries represented). Asian 5%, African American 7%, Caucasian 76%, Hispanic 6%, Native American <1%
Retention and Graduation: 82% freshmen graduate within 4 years. 32% grads go on to further study within 1 year. 28% grads pursue arts and sciences degrees. 16% grads pursue law degrees. 36% grads pursue business degrees. 17% grads pursue medical degrees. **Faculty:** 550 full-time faculty, 92% hold PhDs, 41% are are members of minority groups, 13% are women. 0% of classes are taught by teaching assistants.

ACADEMICS

Degrees: first professional, master's, post-bachelor's certificate. **Classes:** Most classes have 10-19 students. Most lab/discussion sessions have 10-19 students. **Majors with Highest Enrollment:** Political Science and Government; Business/Commerce; Psychology. **Special Study Options:** cross-registration, double major, dual enrollment, honors program, independent study, internships, study abroad, teacher certification program. **Honors programs:** For highly qualified students, a series of interdisciplinary honors courses are offered. Additionally, for students especially talented in individual areas of study, most departments in the College offer special studies leading to graduation with honors in a particular discipline. **Combined degree programs:** BS/MS in accountancy. **Disability Services:** Special programs offered to physically disabled students include note-taking services, reader services, tape recorders, tutors. **Career services:** Alumni network, alumni services, career/job search classes, career assessment, internships, regional alumni.

FACILITIES

Housing: Coed dorms, fraternity/sorority housing, apartments for single students, Wellness Housing, Theme Housing, Wellness = Substance Free. **Special Academic Facilities/Equipment:** Museum of Anthropology; Charlotte and Philip Hanes Art Gallery; Scales Fine Arts Center; Reynolda House, Museum of American Art; Laser and Electron Microscope Labs. **Computers:** 100% of classrooms, 100% of dorms, 100% of libraries, 100% of dining areas, 100% of student union, 5% of common outdoor areas have wireless network access. Students can register for classes online. Administrative functions (other than registration) can be performed online. Undergraduates are required to own a computer.

CAMPUS LIFE

Environment: City. **Activities:** Choral groups, concert band, dance, drama/theater, jazz band, literary magazine, marching band, music ensembles, pep band, radio station, student government, student newspaper, student-run film society, symphony orchestra, television station, yearbook, Campus Ministries, International Student Organization, Model UN. 168 registered organizations, 16 honor societies, 16 religious organizations. 14 fraternities, 9 sororities. **Athletics (Intercollegiate):** *Men:* baseball, basketball, cheerleading, cross-country, football, golf, soccer, tennis, track/field (outdoor), track/field (indoor). *Women:* basketball, cheerleading, cross-country, field hockey, golf, soccer, tennis, track/field (outdoor), track/field (indoor), volleyball. **On-Campus Highlights:** Charlotte and Philip Hanes Art Gallery, Museum of Anthropology, The Z. Smith Reynolds Library, Wait Chapel, Benson University Center. **Environmental Initiatives:** Campus Master Plan: Wake Forest has completed a new campus master plan that will guide development over the next 50 years. Heavily integrated into that plan are tenents for sustainable design (e.g. LEED) as well as stormwater management and biohabitat protection. This new master plan will guide the campus in integrating sustainability within the built and natural environments for the years ahead. Energy management: the university has a robust Energy Management software system to conserve energy during normal operating periods and to cycle down energy use to minimal levels during low- or no-occupancy periods. Also, energy reduction projects are underway in FY09—lighting retrofits, motor replacements, central plant upgrades, etc. Also, new capital projects are designed to achieve energy savings in excess of 30% greater than ASHRAE requirements. Recycling: Approximately 30 percent of the WFU waste stream is diverted from the landfill as either recycled or reused. A renewed emphasis on recycling—to include deskside capture and more functional campus collection containers—is seeing significant success.

ADMISSIONS

Freshman Academic Profile: 93% in top 25% of high school class, 99% in top 50% of high school class. 65% from public high schools. SAT Math middle 50% range 630-720. SAT Critical Reading middle 50% range 600-700. ACT middle 50% range 28-31. Minimum paper TOEFL 600. **Basis for Candidate Selection:** *Very important factors considered include:* Class rank, application essay, academic GPA, rigor of secondary school record, character/personal qualities. *Important factors considered include:* recommendation(s), extracurricular activities, interview, talent/ability. *Other factors considered include:* standardized test scores, alumni/ae relation, first generation, geographical residence, level of applicant's interest, racial/ethnic status, religious affiliation/commitment, state residency, volunteer work. **Freshman Admission Requirements:** High school diploma is required and GED is accepted. **Academic units required:** 4 English, 3 mathematics, 1 science, 2 foreign language, 2 social studies. **Freshman Admission Statistics:** 11,121 applied, 35% admitted, 31% enrolled. **Transfer Admission Requirements:** High school transcript, college transcript(s), essay or personal statement, statement of good standing from prior institution(s). Minimum college GPA of 2.0 required. Lowest grade transferable C. **General Admission Information:** Application Fee $50. Early decision application deadline 11/15. Regular application deadline 1/15. Regular notification 4/1. Nonfall registration not accepted. Admission may be deferred for a maximum of 1 year. Credit and/or placement offered for CEEB Advanced Placement tests.

COSTS AND FINANCIAL AID

Annual tuition $45,638. Room and board $12,638. Required fees $562. Average book expense $1,300. **Required Forms and Deadlines:** FAFSA, CSS/Financial Aid PROFILE, State aid form, Noncustodial PROFILE. **Notification of Awards:** Applicants will be notified of awards on a rolling basis beginning 4/1. **Types of Aid:** *Need-based scholarships/grants:* Federal Pell, SEOG, state scholarships/grants, private scholarships, the school's own gift aid. *Loans:* Subsidized Stafford, Unsubsidized Stafford, PLUS, Federal Perkins, state loans, college/university loans from institutional funds. *Student Employment:* Federal Work-Study Program available. Institutional employment available. Highest amount earned per year from on-campus jobs $2,495. Off-campus job opportunities are excellent. **Financial Aid Statistics:** 83% freshmen, 93% undergrads receive need-based scholarship or grant aid. 49% freshmen, 69% undergrads receive non-need-based scholarship or grant aid. 66% freshmen, 87% undergrads receive need-based self-help aid. 6% freshmen, 4% undergrads receive athletic scholarships. 39% freshmen, 34% undergrads receive any aid. 47% undergrads borrow to pay for school. Average cumulative indebtedness $23,858. **Criteria for awarding institutional aid:** *Non-need-based:* academics, alumni affiliation, art, athletics, leadership, music/drama, religious affiliation, state/district residency.

WALDORF COLLEGE

106 South 6th St., Forest City, IA 50436
Phone: 641-585-8112
E-mail: admissions@waldorf.edu
Fax: 641-585-8125 · **Website:** www.waldorf.edu · **ACT Code:** 1895

This private school, affiliated with the Lutheran Church, was founded in 1903. It has a 40-acre campus.

RATINGS

Admissions Selectivity Rating: 62   **Fire Safety Rating:** 62

STUDENTS AND FACULTY

Enrollment: 573. **Student Body:** 53% female, 47% male, 17% out-of-state, 6% international. Asian 1%, African American 4%, Caucasian 99%, Hispanic 1%, Native American <1%
Faculty: 64 full-time faculty, 25% hold PhDs. 0% of classes are taught by teaching assistants.

ACADEMICS

Degrees: associate, bachelor's. **Classes:** Most classes have 10-19 students. Most lab/discussion sessions have fewer than 10 students. **Majors with Highest Enrollment:** Communication, Journalism, and Related Programs; Computer and Information Sciences and Support Services; Business, Management, Marketing, and Related Support Services. **Special Study Options:** Accelerated program, cooperative education program, double major, English as a Second

Language (ESL), honors program, internships, student-designed major, study abroad, teacher certification program. **Combined degree programs:** BA/MD. **Disability Services:** Special programs offered to physically disabled students include note-taking services, reader services, tutors. **Career services:** Alumni network, alumni services, career/job search classes, career assessment, internships. Career services highlights include internships.

FACILITIES

Housing: Coed dorms, special housing for disabled students, Suites, Special Interest Housing, Townhouses. **Computers:** Administrative functions (other than registration) can be performed online.

CAMPUS LIFE

Environment: Rural. **Activities:** dance, drama/theater, jazz band, student government, student newspaper, Campus Ministries. **Athletics (Intercollegiate):** *Men:* baseball, basketball, football, golf, soccer, wrestling. *Women:* basketball, cheerleading, golf, soccer, softball, volleyball. **On-Campus Highlights:** Walucks (coffee/snacks), Wellness Center, Video-Production Studio, Library (new), Breen Hall.

ADMISSIONS

Freshman Academic Profile: Average high school GPA 3.01. 95% from public high schools. Minimum paper TOEFL 500. **Basis for Candidate Selection:** *Very important factors considered include:* recommendation(s), rigor of secondary school record, standardized test scores. *Important factors considered include:* extracurricular activities, talent/ability. *Other factors considered include:* Class rank, alumni/ae relation, character/personal qualities, interview, racial/ethnic status, religious affiliation/commitment. **Freshman Admission Requirements:** High school diploma is required and GED is accepted. **Freshman Admission Statistics:** 584 applied, 67% admitted, 50% enrolled. **Transfer Admission Requirements:** High school transcript, college transcript(s), standardized test scores, statement of good standing from prior institution(s). Minimum college GPA of 2.0 required. Lowest grade transferable C-. **General Admission Information:** Notification on a rolling basis, beginning on or about 10/4. Nonfall registration not accepted. Admission may be deferred for a maximum of 1 year.

WALLA WALLA UNIVERSITY

Office of Admissions, College Place, WA 99324-1198
Phone: 509-527-2615 · **Financial Aid Phone:** 509-527-2815
E-mail: info@wallawalla.edu · **CEEB Code:** 4940
Fax: 509-527-2253 · **Website:** www.wallawalla.edu · **ACT Code:** 4486

This private school, affiliated with the Seventh Day Adventist Church, was founded in 1892. It has a 77-acre campus.

RATINGS

Admissions Selectivity Rating: 61   **Fire Safety Rating:** 62

STUDENTS AND FACULTY

Enrollment: 1,549. **Student Body:** 50% female, 50% male, 59% out-of-state, 2% international (30 countries represented). African American 2%, Caucasian 60%, Hispanic 8%, Native American 1%
Retention and Graduation: 78% freshmen return for sophomore year. 23% freshmen graduate within 4 years. **Faculty:** 112 full-time faculty, 69% hold PhDs, 39% are are members of minority groups, 6% are women. 0% of classes are taught by teaching assistants.

ACADEMICS

Degrees: associate, bachelor's, master's. **Classes:** Most classes have fewer than 10 students. Most lab/discussion sessions have fewer than 10 students. **Majors with Highest Enrollment:** Engineering; Social Work; Business/Commerce. **Special Study Options:** cooperative education program, distance learning, double major, honors program, independent study, internships, liberal arts/career combination, study abroad, teacher certification program. **Disability Services:** Special programs offered to physically disabled students include note-taking services, reader services, tape recorders, tutors. **Career services:** Alumni network, career/job search classes, career assessment, internships. Career services highlights include internships that all of our accounting and management students participate in.

FACILITIES

Housing: special housing for disabled students, men's dorms, women's dorms, apartments for married students, apartments for single students, Wellness Housing. 75% of campus accessible to physically disabled. **Special Academic Facilities/Equipment:** Marine station on the Rosario Strait of the Puget Sound in Washington state. **Computers:** Students can register for classes online.

CAMPUS LIFE

Environment: Town. **Activities:** Choral groups, concert band, drama/theater, literary magazine, music ensembles, radio station, student government, student newspaper, symphony orchestra, television station, yearbook, Campus Ministries, International Student Organization. 33 registered organizations, 7 honor societies, 6 religious organizations. **Athletics (Intercollegiate):** *Men:* basketball, golf, soccer, volleyball. *Women:* basketball, softball, volleyball. **On-Campus Highlights:** The Dairy Express, Peterson Memorial Library, The Student Association Center, Winter Educational Complex: gym/climbing wall/pool, The College Store, Clyde and Mary Harris Gallery.

ADMISSIONS

Freshman Academic Profile: 9% from public high schools. Minimum paper TOEFL 550. **Basis for Candidate Selection:** *Very important factors considered include:* academic GPA, recommendation(s), rigor of secondary school record. *Important factors considered include:* character/personal qualities, level of applicant's interest. *Other factors considered include:* Class rank, standardized test scores, extracurricular activities, talent/ability. **Freshman Admission Requirements:** High school diploma is required and GED is accepted. **Academic units required:** 4 English, 3 mathematics, 2 science, (2 science labs), 2 history. **Freshman Admission Statistics:** 626 applied, 89% admitted, 54% enrolled. **Transfer Admission Requirements:** college transcript(s), Minimum college GPA of 2.0 required. Lowest grade transferable D-. **General Admission Information:** Application Fee $40. Notification on a rolling basis, beginning on or about 9/25. Nonfall registration accepted. Admission may be deferred for a maximum of 1 year. Credit and/or placement offered for CEEB Advanced Placement tests.

COSTS AND FINANCIAL AID

Annual tuition $23,670. Room and board $5,655. Required fees $528. Average book expense $1,068. **Required Forms and Deadlines:** FAFSA, Institution's own financial aid form. **Notification of Awards:** Applicants will be notified of awards on a rolling basis beginning 3/15. **Types of Aid:** *Need-based scholarships/grants:* Federal Pell, SEOG, state scholarships/grants, private scholarships, the school's own gift aid, Federal Nursing Scholarships. *Loans:* Subsidized Stafford, Unsubsidized Stafford, PLUS, Federal Perkins, Federal Nursing, college/university loans from institutional funds. *Student Employment:* Federal Work-Study Program available. Institutional employment available. Off-campus job opportunities are good. **Financial Aid Statistics:** 79% freshmen, 79% undergrads receive need-based scholarship or grant aid. 99% freshmen, 80% undergrads receive non-need-based scholarship or grant aid. 89% freshmen, 93% undergrads receive need-based self-help aid. 0% freshmen, 0% undergrads receive athletic scholarships. 84% freshmen, 83% undergrads receive any aid. 70% undergrads borrow to pay for school. Average cumulative indebtedness $22,873. **Criteria for awarding institutional aid:** *Non-need-based:* academics, leadership, music/drama.

WALSH COLLEGE OF ACCOUNTANCY AND BUSINESS ADMINISTRATION

3838 Livernois Road, Troy, MI 48007-7006
Phone: 248-689-8282 · **Financial Aid Phone:** 248-823-1285
E-mail: admissions@walshcollege.edu
Fax: 248-689-0938

This private school was founded in 1922. It has a 20-acre campus.

RATINGS

Admissions Selectivity Rating: 60*   **Fire Safety Rating:** 60*

STUDENTS AND FACULTY

Enrollment: 984. **Student Body:** 55% female, 45% male, 1% out-of-state, 4% international (46 countries represented). Asian 3%, African American 5%, Caucasian 65%, Hispanic 1%, Native American <1%
Faculty: 18 full-time faculty, 72% hold PhDs, 44% are are members of minority groups, 6% are women. 0% of classes are taught by teaching assistants.

ACADEMICS

Degrees: bachelor's, master's, post-bachelor's certificate, post-master's certificate. **Classes:** Most classes have 20-29 students. **Majors with Highest Enrollment:** Pharmacy; Biology/Biological Sciences; Psychology. **Special Study Options:** distance learning, double major, dual enrollment, independent study, internships. **Disability Services:** Special programs offered to physically disabled students include note-taking services, reader services, tape recorders, tutors. **Career services:** Alumni network, alumni services, career/job search classes, career assessment, internships.

FACILITIES

Housing: 100% of campus accessible to physically disabled. **Computers:** 100% of classrooms, 100% of libraries, 100% of dining areas, have wireless network access. Students can register for classes online. Administrative functions (other than registration) can be performed online.

CAMPUS LIFE

Environment: City. **Activities:** student government, student newspaper, student-run film society. 6 registered organizations, 1 honor society. **On-Campus Highlights:** Barry Center.

ADMISSIONS

Freshman Academic Profile: Minimum internet-based TOEFL 79. Minimum paper TOEFL 550. **Transfer Admission Requirements:** college transcript(s), Minimum college GPA of 2.0 required. Lowest grade transferable C. **General Admission Information:** Application Fee $25.

COSTS AND FINANCIAL AID

Required Forms and Deadlines: FAFSA. **Types of Aid:** *Need-based scholarships/grants:* Federal Pell, SEOG, state scholarships/grants, the school's own gift aid. *Loans:* Subsidized Stafford, Unsubsidized Stafford, state loans. *Student Employment:* Federal Work-Study Program available. Off-campus job opportunities are fair. **Financial Aid Statistics:** 64% undergrads receive need-based scholarship or grant aid. 18% undergrads receive non-need-based scholarship or grant aid. 100% undergrads receive need-based self-help aid. 0% undergrads receive athletic scholarships. 61% undergrads borrow to pay for school. **Criteria for awarding institutional aid:** *Non-need-based:* academics.

WALSH UNIVERSITY

2020 East Maple St, North Canton, OH 44720-3396
Phone: 330-490-7172 · **Financial Aid Phone:** 330-490-7367
E-mail: admissions@walsh.edu · **CEEB Code:** 1926
Fax: 330-490-7165 · **Website:** www.walsh.edu · **ACT Code:** 3349

This private school, affiliated with the Roman Catholic Church, was founded in 1958. It has a 140-acre campus.

RATINGS

Admissions Selectivity Rating: 77   **Fire Safety Rating:** 86

STUDENTS AND FACULTY

Enrollment: 2,264. **Student Body:** 62% female, 38% male, 6% out-of-state, 3% international (31 countries represented). Asian 0%, African American 6%, Caucasian 78%, Hispanic 2%, Native American <1%
Retention and Graduation: 76% freshmen return for sophomore year. 44% freshmen graduate within 4 years. 55% freshmen graduate within 6 years. 23% grads go on to further study within 1 year. 17% grads pursue arts and sciences degrees. 1% grads pursue law degrees. 3% grads pursue business degrees. 1% grads pursue medical degrees. **Faculty:** 133 full-time faculty, 66% hold PhDs, 55% are are members of minority groups, 7% are women. 0% of classes are taught by teaching assistants.

ACADEMICS

Degrees: associate, bachelor's, master's. **Classes:** Most classes have 10-19 students. Most lab/discussion sessions have fewer than 10 students. **Majors with Highest Enrollment:** Business Administration and Management; Biology/Biological Sciences; Nursing Practice. **Special Study Options:** Accelerated program, double major, dual enrollment, English as a Second Language (ESL), exchange student program (domestic), external degree program, honors program, independent study, internships, liberal arts/career combination, study abroad, teacher certification program, Combined bachelor's/master's degree programs CCSA College Consortium for Study Abroad Rome Experience. **Honors programs:** Honors Program students may pursue any major and have opportunity annually to attend the national honors conference, where Walsh students frequently present their research. **Combined degree programs:** BA/MA, 3-1 med-tech, 3-4 dentistry. **Disability Services:** Special programs offered to physically disabled students include reader services, tape recorders, tutors. **Career services:** Alumni network, alumni services, career assessment, internships, regional alumni.

FACILITIES

Housing: Coed dorms, special housing for disabled students, special housing for international students, apartments for single students, Wellness Housing-Apartment-style residence hall with kitchens. 100% of campus accessible to physically disabled. **Special Academic Facilities/Equipment:** bioinformatics lab, Hoover Museum, human cadaver lab (prosection for undergrad), Gathering Garden for Education activities with schoolchildren, Religious Education Center **Computers:** 10% of classrooms, 12% of dorms, 100% of libraries, 100%

of dining areas, 100% of student union, 5% of common outdoor areas have wireless network access. Students can register for classes online. Administrative functions (other than registration) can be performed online.

CAMPUS LIFE

Environment: City. **Activities:** Choral groups, dance, drama/theater, literary magazine, music ensembles, pep band, radio station, student government, student newspaper, Campus Ministries, International Student Organization. 30 registered organizations, 10 honor societies, 3 religious organizations. **Athletics (Intercollegiate):** *Men:* baseball, basketball, cheerleading, cross-country, football, golf, soccer, tennis, track/field (outdoor), track/field (indoor). *Women:* basketball, cheerleading, cross-country, golf, soccer, softball, tennis, track/field (outdoor), track/field (indoor), volleyball. **On-Campus Highlights:** David Campus Center, Alumni Arena, University Apartments, Barrette Business and Community Center, Wellness Center. **Environmental Initiatives:** HVAC & electrical managament system; recycling program for paper, plastic, and aluminum; ink cartridge recycle system.

ADMISSIONS

Freshman Academic Profile: Average high school GPA 3.37. 16% in top 10% of high school class, 45% in top 25% of high school class, 76% in top 50% of high school class. 71% from public high schools. SAT Math middle 50% range 460-560. SAT Critical Reading middle 50% range 440-550. ACT middle 50% range 20-25. Minimum internet-based TOEFL 61. Minimum paper TOEFL 500. **Basis for Candidate Selection:** *Very important factors considered include:* academic GPA, rigor of secondary school record, standardized test scores. *Important factors considered include:* recommendation(s), character/personal qualities. *Other factors considered include:* Class rank, application essay, interview, volunteer work. **Freshman Admission Requirements:** High school diploma is required and GED is accepted. **Freshman Admission Statistics:** 1,480 applied, 81% admitted, 37% enrolled. **Transfer Admission Requirements:** High school transcript, college transcript(s), Minimum college GPA of 2.0 required. Lowest grade transferable C. **General Admission Information:** Application Fee $25. Regular application deadline 8/15. Notification on a rolling basis, beginning on or about 10/1. Nonfall registration accepted. Admission may be deferred for a maximum of 1 year. Credit offered for CEEB Advanced Placement tests.

COSTS AND FINANCIAL AID

Annual tuition $25,350. Room and board $9,580. Required fees $1,320. Average book expense $1,104. **Required Forms and Deadlines:** FAFSA. **Notification of Awards:** Applicants will be notified of awards on a rolling basis beginning 2/15. **Types of Aid:** *Need-based scholarships/grants:* Federal Pell, SEOG, state scholarships/grants, private scholarships, the school's own gift aid. *Loans:* Direct Subsidized Stafford, Direct Unsubsidized Stafford, Direct PLUS, Federal Perkins, state loans. *Student Employment:* Federal Work-Study Program available. Institutional employment available. Highest amount earned per year from on-campus jobs $3,000. **Financial Aid Statistics:** 98% freshmen, 92% undergrads receive need-based scholarship or grant aid. 123% freshmen, 100% undergrads receive non-need-based scholarship or grant aid. 98% freshmen, 89% undergrads receive need-based self-help aid. 18% freshmen, 16% undergrads receive athletic scholarships. 99% freshmen, 89% undergrads receive any aid. 81% undergrads borrow to pay for school. Average cumulative indebtedness $22,134. **Criteria for awarding institutional aid:** *Non-need-based:* academics, alumni affiliation, athletics, music/drama, religious affiliation, state/district residency.

WARNER PACIFIC COLLEGE

Office of Admissions, Portland, OR 97215
Phone: 503-517-1020 · **Financial Aid Phone:** 503-517-1091
E-mail: admissions@warnerpacific.edu · **CEEB Code:** 4595
Fax: 503-517-1540 · **Website:** http://www.warnerpacific.edu/

This private school, affiliated with the Church of God Church, was founded in 1937. It has a 15-acre campus.

RATINGS

Admissions Selectivity Rating: 81   **Fire Safety Rating:** 63

STUDENTS AND FACULTY

Enrollment: 501. **Student Body:** 56% female, 44% male, 35% out-of-state, (12 countries represented). Asian 3%, African American 5%, Caucasian 47%, Hispanic 7%, Native American <1%
Retention and Graduation: 32% freshmen return for sophomore year. 28% freshmen graduate within 4 years. 7% grads go on to further study within 1 year. 2% grads pursue arts and sciences degrees. 2% grads pursue business degrees. 1% grads pursue medical degrees. **Faculty:** 31 full-time faculty, 68% hold PhDs, 35% are are members of minority groups, 10% are women. 0% of classes are taught by teaching assistants.

ACADEMICS

Degrees: associate, bachelor's, certificate, master's. **Classes:** Most classes have 10-19 students. **Majors with Highest Enrollment:** Human Development and Family Studies; Business Administration, Management and Operations; Biology/Biological Sciences. **Special Study Options:** cooperative education program, double major, independent study, internships, student-designed major, study abroad, teacher certification program, weekend college, Adult Degree Program. **Disability Services:** Special programs offered to physically disabled students include note-taking services, reader services, tape recorders, tutors. **Career services:** career assessment, internships.

FACILITIES

Housing: men's dorms, women's dorms, apartments for married students, apartments for single students. 50% of campus accessible to physically disabled. **Special Academic Facilities/Equipment:** Early learning center, electron microscopes. **Computers:** 100% of classrooms, 10% of dorms, 100% of libraries, 100% of dining areas, 100% of student union, 50% of common outdoor areas have wireless network access.

CAMPUS LIFE

Environment: Metropolis. **Activities:** Choral groups, concert band, dance, drama/theater, jazz band, literary magazine, music ensembles, musical theater, student government, student newspaper, yearbook, Campus Ministries, International Student Organization. 20 registered organizations, 2 religious organizations. **Athletics (Intercollegiate):** *Men:* basketball, cross-country, golf, soccer, track/field (outdoor), track/field (indoor). *Women:* basketball, cross-country, golf, soccer, track/field (outdoor), track/field (indoor), volleyball. **On-Campus Highlights:** Tabor Grind Coffee Shop, Dining Hall, Student Union Building, Otto F. Linn Library, A.F. Gray lawn.

ADMISSIONS

Freshman Academic Profile: Average high school GPA 3.17. 8% in top 10% of high school class, 25% in top 25% of high school class, 77% in top 50% of high school class. SAT Math middle 50% range 410-550. SAT Critical Reading middle 50% range 420-550. SAT Writing middle 50% range 350-530. ACT middle 50% range 16-22. Minimum internet-based TOEFL 71. Minimum paper TOEFL 525. **Basis for Candidate Selection:** *Important factors considered include:* application essay, academic GPA, standardized test scores. *Other factors considered include:* Class rank, recommendation(s), rigor of secondary school record. **Freshman Admission Requirements:** High school diploma is required and GED is accepted. **Freshman Admission Statistics:** 948 applied, 53% admitted, 15% enrolled. **Transfer Admission Requirements:** college transcript(s), essay or personal statement, Minimum college GPA of 2.5 required. Lowest grade transferable d. **General Admission Information:** Application Fee $50. Early decision application deadline 6/1. Nonfall registration accepted. Admission may be deferred for a maximum of 1 year. Credit offered for CEEB Advanced Placement tests.

COSTS AND FINANCIAL AID

Room and board $7,690. Required fees $660. Average book expense $1,300. **Required Forms and Deadlines:** FAFSA. **Notification of Awards:** Applicants will be notified of awards on a rolling basis beginning 3/1. **Types of Aid:** *Need-based scholarships/grants:* Federal Pell, SEOG, state scholarships/grants, private scholarships, the school's own gift aid. *Loans:* Direct Subsidized Stafford, Direct Unsubsidized Stafford, Direct PLUS, Subsidized Stafford, Unsubsidized Stafford, PLUS, Federal Perkins. *Student Employment:* Federal Work-Study Program available. Institutional employment available. Highest amount earned per year from on-campus jobs $4,000. **Financial Aid Statistics:** 97% freshmen, 93% undergrads receive need-based scholarship or grant aid. 95% freshmen, 89% undergrads receive non-need-based scholarship or grant aid. 94% freshmen, 91% undergrads receive need-based self-help aid. 9% freshmen, 5% undergrads receive athletic scholarships. 99% freshmen, 99% undergrads receive any aid. 83% undergrads borrow to pay for school. Average cumulative indebtedness $25,904. **Criteria for awarding institutional aid:** *Non-need-based:* academics, alumni affiliation, athletics, leadership, music/drama, religious affiliation.

WARNER SOUTHERN COLLEGE

13985 Hwy. 27, Lake Wales, FL 33859
Phone: 863-638-7212 · **Financial Aid Phone:** 863-638-7203
E-mail: admissions@warner.edu · **CEEB Code:** 5883
Fax: 863-638-7290 · **ACT Code:** 777

This private school, affiliated with the Church of God Church, was founded in 1968. It has a 320-acre campus.

RATINGS

Admissions Selectivity Rating: 75   **Fire Safety Rating:** 72

STUDENTS AND FACULTY

Enrollment: 937. **Student Body:** 58% female, 42% male, 1% international (20 countries represented). Asian 1%, African American 17%, Caucasian 56%, Hispanic 8%, Native American <1%
Retention and Graduation: 26% freshmen graduate within 4 years. 34% freshmen graduate within 6 years. **Faculty:** 34 full-time faculty, 59% hold PhDs, 38% are are members of minority groups, 12% are women. 0% of classes are taught by teaching assistants.

ACADEMICS

Degrees: associate, bachelor's, certificate, master's, terminal associate. **Classes:** Most classes have 10-19 students. **Majors with Highest Enrollment:** Education; Pastoral Studies/Counseling; Business/Commerce. **Special Study Options:** Accelerated program, distance learning, double major, dual enrollment, English as a Second Language (ESL), independent study, internships, study abroad, teacher certification program.

FACILITIES

Housing: men's dorms, women's dorms. 80% of campus accessible to physically disabled.

CAMPUS LIFE

Environment: Rural. **Activities:** Choral groups, music ensembles, student government, student newspaper. 2 registered organizations, 6 honor societies, 1 religous organization. 2 fraternities, 2 sororities. **Athletics (Intercollegiate):** *Men:* baseball, basketball, cheerleading, cross-country, golf, soccer, tennis, track/field (outdoor), track/field (indoor). *Women:* basketball, cheerleading, cross-country, golf, soccer, softball, tennis, track/field (outdoor), track/field (indoor), volleyball. **On-Campus Highlights:** Lion's Den, Turner Athletic Center, Pontious Learning Resource Center, Caffe Cristiano.

ADMISSIONS

Freshman Academic Profile: Average high school GPA 3. 11% in top 10% of high school class, 23% in top 25% of high school class, 66% in top 50% of high school class. 90% from public high schools. SAT Math middle 50% range 351-613. SAT Critical Reading middle 50% range 342-580. ACT middle 50% range 15-24. Minimum paper TOEFL 500. **Basis for Candidate Selection:** *Important factors considered include:* Class rank, academic GPA, recommendation(s), standardized test scores, level of applicant's interest. *Other factors considered include:* application essay, rigor of secondary school record, alumni/ae relation, character/personal qualities, extracurricular activities, interview, talent/ability, volunteer work. **Freshman Admission Requirements:** High school diploma is required and GED is accepted. **Freshman Admission Statistics:** 363 applied, 66% admitted, 47% enrolled. **Transfer Admission Requirements:** college transcript(s), essay or personal statement, statement of good standing from prior institution(s). Minimum college GPA of 2.0 required. Lowest grade transferable D. **General Admission Information:** Application Fee $20. Notification on a rolling basis, beginning on or about 9/1. Nonfall registration accepted. Admission may be deferred for a maximum of No time set. Neither credit nor placement offered for CEEB Advanced Placement tests.

COSTS AND FINANCIAL AID

Annual tuition $13,600. Room and board $5,730. Required fees $150. Average book expense $1,000. **Required Forms and Deadlines:** FAFSA, State aid form. **Notification of Awards:** Applicants will be notified of awards on a rolling basis beginning 1/15. **Types of Aid:** *Need-based scholarships/grants:* Federal Pell, SEOG, state scholarships/grants, private scholarships, the school's own gift aid. *Loans:* Subsidized Stafford, Unsubsidized Stafford, PLUS, Federal Perkins, Alternative Loans. *Student Employment:* Federal Work-Study Program available. Institutional employment available. Highest amount earned per year from on-campus jobs $1,200. Off-campus job opportunities are good. **Financial Aid Statistics:** 79% freshmen, 66% undergrads receive need-based scholarship or grant aid. 100% freshmen, 98% undergrads receive non-need-based scholarship or grant aid. 81% freshmen, 89% undergrads receive need-based self-help aid. 66% freshmen, 34% undergrads receive athletic scholarships. 100% freshmen, 93% undergrads receive any aid. **Criteria for awarding institutional aid:** *Non-need-based:* academics, alumni affiliation, athletics, leadership, minority status, music/drama, religious affiliation, state/district residency.

WARREN WILSON COLLEGE

PO Box 9000, Asheville, NC 28815-9000
Phone: 828-771-2073 · **Financial Aid Phone:** 828-771-2082
E-mail: admit@warren-wilson.edu · **CEEB Code:** 5886
Fax: 828-298-1440 · **Website:** www.warren-wilson.edu · **ACT Code:** 3170

This private school, affiliated with the Presbyterian Church, was founded in 1894. It has a 1100-acre campus.

RATINGS

Admissions Selectivity Rating: 87   **Fire Safety Rating:** 65

STUDENTS AND FACULTY

Enrollment: 819. **Student Body:** 62% female, 38% male, 77% out-of-state, (15 countries represented).
Retention and Graduation: 66% freshmen return for sophomore year. 42% freshmen graduate within 4 years. **Faculty:** 67 full-time faculty, 93% hold PhDs, 48% are are members of minority groups, 12% are women. 0% of classes are taught by teaching assistants.

ACADEMICS

Degrees: bachelor's, master's. **Classes:** Most classes have 10-19 students. Most lab/discussion sessions have 10-19 students. **Majors with Highest Enrollment:** Environmental Studies; Psychology; Creative Writing. **Special Study Options:** cross-registration, double major, dual enrollment, English as a Second Language (ESL), exchange student program (domestic), honors program, independent study, internships, liberal arts/career combination, student-designed major, study abroad. **Disability Services:** Special programs offered to physically disabled students include tape recorders. **Career services:** career assessment, internships, regional alumni.

FACILITIES

Housing: Coed dorms, men's dorms, women's dorms, apartments for married students, cooperative housing, apartments for single students. 100% of campus accessible to physically disabled. **Special Academic Facilities/Equipment:** 300-acre farm,700-acre forest, community gardens, archaeological dig on campus, organically managed garden, GIS lab, photomicroscopy lab.

CAMPUS LIFE

Environment: Village. **Activities:** Choral groups, dance, drama/theater, jazz band, literary magazine, music ensembles, musical theater, student government, student newspaper, yearbook. 25 registered organizations, 5 religious organizations. **Athletics (Intercollegiate):** *Men:* basketball, cross-country, diving, kayaking, mountain biking, soccer, swimming, ultimate frisbee. *Women:* basketball, cross-country, diving, kayaking, mountain biking, soccer, swimming, ultimate frisbee. **On-Campus Highlights:** Sage Caf, Pond, Witherspoon/Morse Science Center, Dogwood-a short hike to this great view, Cow Pie Caf. **Environmental Initiatives:** Climate Action Plan to achieve 80% reduction in emissions campus wide by 2020 includes our formal climate change partnership with city of Asheville; quarterly emissions reports to support changes; college solar array KW's sold to NC Green Power for sustainability outreach to community to influence reduction in GHG's; 100% renewable energy wind credits purchased each year equal to total campus electric use; INSULATE! weatherization program in region for people in poverty where faculty/students and staff to do a house a weekend to provide assistance and reduce regional GHG emissions. Curriculum of our Triad of academics, work and service: Environmental studies largest major on campus (since '70's)with 6 concentrations using on campus living laboratory of farm, garden and forest; new inter-disciplinary sustainability curriculum focusing on energy; service learning curriculum focused on regional study of food security for the academic year; work crew supervisors (all students work 15 hours a week to run the campus) now evaluate students on adherence to sustainability principles; Sustainability Recognition Program established for programs that engage Triad in environmental sustainability education; the Sustainability Speaker Series for the campus has hosted Bill McKibben, Lester Brown, Peter Raven, Wendell Berry, and others over the past 3 semesters. Built environment: more than 30% of core campus buildings are either LEED Gold(4), LEED EB platinum(1) or green (1); 3 existing buildings (dorm, office and classroom) have undergone energy efficient retrofits that have included installation of geothermal HVAC systems; Campus energy usage measured monthly for all buildings; use of digital controls underway to reduce energy use; one campus building serves as case study for sustainable practices for rest of campus.

ADMISSIONS

Freshman Academic Profile: Average high school GPA 3.6. 28% in top 10% of high school class, 52% in top 25% of high school class, 80% in top 50% of high school class. 81% from public high schools. SAT Math middle 50% range 480-580. SAT Critical Reading middle 50% range 530-640. SAT Writing middle 50% range 480-610. ACT middle 50% range 23-28. Minimum internet-based TOEFL 80. **Basis for Candidate Selection:** *Very important factors considered include:* application essay, rigor of secondary school record, standardized test scores, character/personal qualities, interview, volunteer work, work experience. *Important factors considered include:* Class rank, recommendation(s). *Other factors considered include:* alumni/ae relation, extracurricular activities, state residency, talent/ability. **Freshman Admission Requirements:** High school diploma is required and GED is accepted. **Academic units required:** 4 English, 3 mathematics, 2 science, (2 science labs), 3 history. **Freshman Admission Statistics:** 1,176 applied, 72% admitted, 28% enrolled. **Transfer Admission Requirements:** High school transcript, college transcript(s), standardized test scores, Minimum college GPA of 3.0 required. Lowest grade transferable C. **General Admission Information:** Early decision application deadline 11/15. Regular application deadline 2/15. Nonfall registration accepted. Admission may be deferred for a maximum of 1 year. Credit and/or placement offered for CEEB Advanced Placement tests.

COSTS AND FINANCIAL AID

Annual tuition $30,462. Room and board $9,280. Required fees $390. Average book expense $820. **Required Forms and Deadlines:** FAFSA, Institution's own financial aid form, State aid form. **Notification of Awards:** Applicants will be notified of awards on a rolling basis beginning 3/2. **Types of Aid:** *Need-based scholarships/grants:* Federal Pell, SEOG, state scholarships/grants, the school's own gift aid. *Loans:* Subsidized Stafford, Unsubsidized Stafford, PLUS, Federal Perkins, college/university loans from institutional funds. *Student Employment:* Highest amount earned per year from on-campus jobs $3,144. Off-campus job opportunities are good. **Financial Aid Statistics:** 97% freshmen, 94% undergrads receive need-based scholarship or grant aid. 21% freshmen, 25% undergrads receive non-need-based scholarship or grant aid. 97% freshmen, 94% undergrads receive need-based self-help aid. 9% freshmen, 3% undergrads receive athletic scholarships. 90% freshmen, 80% undergrads receive any aid. 59% undergrads borrow to pay for school. Average cumulative indebtedness $19,600. **Criteria for awarding institutional aid:** *Non-need-based:* academics, art, leadership, state/district residency.

WARTBURG COLLEGE

100 Wartburg Blvd., Waverly, IA 50677-0903
Phone: 319-352-8264 · **Financial Aid Phone:** 319-352-8262
E-mail: admissions@wartburg.edu · **CEEB Code:** 6926
Fax: 319-352-8579 · **Website:** www.wartburg.edu · **ACT Code:** 1364

This private school, affiliated with the Lutheran Church, was founded in 1852. It has a 118-acre campus.

RATINGS

Admissions Selectivity Rating: 84   Fire Safety Rating: 73

STUDENTS AND FACULTY

Enrollment: 1,755. **Student Body:** 52% female, 48% male, 25% out-of-state, 5% international (38 countries represented). Asian 2%, African American 5%, Caucasian 82%, Hispanic 1%, Native American <1%
Retention and Graduation: 82% freshmen return for sophomore year. 61% freshmen graduate within 4 years. 64% freshmen graduate within 6 years. 23% grads go on to further study within 1 year. 11% grads pursue arts and sciences degrees. 1% grads pursue law degrees. 2% grads pursue business degrees. 6% grads pursue medical degrees. **Faculty:** 109 full-time faculty, 84% hold PhDs, 48% are are members of minority groups, 5% are women. 0% of classes are taught by teaching assistants.

ACADEMICS

Degrees: bachelor's. **Classes:** Most classes have 20-29 students. Most lab/discussion sessions have 20-29 students. **Majors with Highest Enrollment:** Business, Management, Marketing, and Related Support Services; Biology/Biological Sciences; Speech Communication and Rhetoric. **Special Study Options:** Accelerated program, double major, dual enrollment, honors program, independent study, internships, student-designed major, study abroad, teacher certification program. **Honors programs:** Scholars Program—features small seminar classes, distinguished speaker series, sophomore-year program of lectures, concerts, and performances, student involvement in designing courses and activities, variety of social and travel opportunities, student-designed senior project **Combined degree programs:** 2-2 nursing, 3-1 occup. therapy, 3-2

phys therapy. **Disability Services:** Special programs offered to physically disabled students include note-taking services, reader services, tutors. **Career services:** Alumni network.

FACILITIES

Housing: Coed dorms, men's dorms, women's dorms, apartments for single students, Theme HousingSuite-style living. 85% of campus accessible to physically disabled. **Special Academic Facilities/Equipment:** Art gallery, fine arts center, institute for leadership education, planetarium, prairie preserve, state-of-the-art library, center for community engagement, wellness center. **Computers:** 30% of classrooms, 10% of dorms, 100% of libraries, 100% of dining areas, 100% of student union, 10% of common outdoor areas have wireless network access. Students can register for classes online. Administrative functions (other than registration) can be performed online.

CAMPUS LIFE

Environment: Village. **Activities:** Choral groups, concert band, dance, drama/theater, jazz band, literary magazine, music ensembles, musical theater, opera, pep band, radio station, student government, student newspaper, student-run film society, symphony orchestra, television station, yearbook, Campus Ministries, International Student Organization. 90 registered organizations, 12 honor societies, 9 religious organizations. **Athletics (Intercollegiate):** *Men:* baseball, basketball, cross-country, football, golf, soccer, tennis, track/field (outdoor), track/field (indoor), wrestling. *Women:* basketball, cross-country, golf, soccer, softball, tennis, track/field (outdoor), track/field (indoor), volleyball. **On-Campus Highlights:** Konditorei Coffee Shop/Vogel Library, Sports and Wellness Center (new 2007), Saemann Student Center (renovated 2004), Walston-Hoover Stadium (new 2001), Old Main (on National Historic Registry), $31 million Sports and Wellness Center. **Environmental Initiatives:** LEED requirements for new Sports and Wellness Center; Partnership with Waverly Light and Power on wind generation to offset-carbon-based energy in new Sports and Wellness Center; Trayless dining; use of front load washers to reduce water and energy use.

ADMISSIONS

Freshman Academic Profile: Average high school GPA 3.48. 28% in top 10% of high school class, 56% in top 25% of high school class, 84% in top 50% of high school class. SAT Math middle 50% range 470-610. SAT Critical Reading middle 50% range 420-600. SAT Writing middle 50% range 410-570. ACT middle 50% range 21-27. Minimum internet-based TOEFL 55. Minimum paper TOEFL 480. **Basis for Candidate Selection:** *Very important factors considered include:* Class rank, academic GPA, recommendation(s), rigor of secondary school record, standardized test scores. *Important factors considered include:* character/personal qualities, interview. *Other factors considered include:* application essay, extracurricular activities, level of applicant's interest, racial/ethnic status, talent/ability, volunteer work, work experience. **Freshman Admission Requirements:** High school diploma is required and GED is accepted. **Freshman Admission Statistics:** 2,278 applied, 73% admitted, 29% enrolled. **Transfer Admission Requirements:** High school transcript, college transcript(s), standardized test scores, statement of good standing from prior institution(s). Minimum college GPA of 2.0 required. Lowest grade transferable C-. **General Admission Information:** Notification on a rolling basis, beginning on or about 7/1. Nonfall registration accepted. Admission may be deferred for a maximum of 1 year. Credit and/or placement offered for CEEB Advanced Placement tests.

COSTS AND FINANCIAL AID

Required Forms and Deadlines: FAFSA. **Notification of Awards:** Applicants will be notified of awards on a rolling basis beginning 3/21. **Types of Aid:** *Need-based scholarships/grants:* Federal Pell, SEOG, state scholarships/grants, private scholarships, the school's own gift aid. *Loans:* Subsidized Stafford, Unsubsidized Stafford, PLUS, Federal Perkins, Alternative. *Student Employment:* Federal Work-Study Program available. Institutional employment available. Highest amount earned per year from on-campus jobs $8,435. Off-campus job opportunities are good. **Financial Aid Statistics:** 100% freshmen, 100% undergrads receive need-based scholarship or grant aid. 19% freshmen, 15% undergrads receive non-need-based scholarship or grant aid. 79% freshmen, 84% undergrads receive need-based self-help aid. 0% freshmen, 0% undergrads receive athletic scholarships. 99% freshmen, 98% undergrads receive any aid. 81% undergrads borrow to pay for school. Average cumulative indebtedness $15,500. **Criteria for awarding institutional aid:** *Non-need-based:* academics, alumni affiliation, leadership, music/drama, religious affiliation.

WASHBURN UNIVERSITY

1700 SW College Ave, Topeka, KS 66621
Phone: 785-670-1030
E-mail: admissions@washburn.edu
Fax: 785-670-1113 • **Website:** www.washburn.edu

This is a public school.

RATINGS

Admissions Selectivity Rating: 72   **Fire Safety Rating:** 60*

STUDENTS AND FACULTY

Enrollment: 5,031. **Student Body:** 59% female, 41% male, 9% out-of-state. **Retention and Graduation:** 66% freshmen return for sophomore year. 13% freshmen graduate within 4 years. 35% freshmen graduate within 6 years. **Faculty:** 278 full-time faculty, 87% hold PhDs, 54% are are members of minority groups, 14% are women.

ACADEMICS

Degrees: associate, bachelor's, certificate, first professional, first professional certificate, master's, post-bachelor's certificate. **Classes:** Most classes have 20-29 students. Most lab/discussion sessions have 10-19 students. **Special Study Options:** cooperative education program, cross-registration, distance learning, double major, dual enrollment, English as a Second Language (ESL), honors program, independent study, internships, liberal arts/career combination, student-designed major, study abroad, teacher certification program, Transformational Experience.

FACILITIES

Housing: Coed dorms, fraternity/sorority housing, apartments for single students, Wellness Housing, Special interest housing.

CAMPUS LIFE

Activities: Choral groups, concert band, dance, drama/theater, jazz band, literary magazine, marching band, music ensembles, musical theater, pep band, student government, student newspaper, student-run film society, symphony orchestra, television station, yearbook, Campus Ministries, International Student Organization, Model UN.

ADMISSIONS

Freshman Academic Profile: Average high school GPA 3.41. 13% in top 10% of high school class, 35% in top 25% of high school class, 67% in top 50% of high school class. 96% from public high schools. ACT middle 50% range 19-25. Minimum paper TOEFL 450. **Basis for Candidate Selection:** *Very important factors considered include:* academic GPA, rigor of secondary school record, standardized test scores. **Freshman Admission Requirements:** High school diploma is required and GED is accepted. **Freshman Admission Statistics:** 1,416 applied, 98% admitted, 58% enrolled. **Transfer Admission Requirements:** college transcript(s), statement of good standing from prior institution(s). Minimum college GPA of 2.0 required. Lowest grade transferable 1. **General Admission Information:** Application Fee $20. Regular application deadline 8/1. Notification on a rolling basis, beginning on or about 9/1. Nonfall registration accepted. Credit and/or placement offered for CEEB Advanced Placement tests.

COSTS AND FINANCIAL AID

Annual in-state tuition $5,952. Annual out-of-state tuition $13,440. Room and board $6,541. Required fees $86. Average book expense $1,000. **Required Forms and Deadlines:** FAFSA. **Notification of Awards:** Applicants will be notified of awards on a rolling basis beginning 3/15. **Types of Aid:** *Need-based scholarships/grants:* Federal Pell, SEOG, state scholarships/grants, private scholarships, the school's own gift aid. *Loans:* Direct Subsidized Stafford, Direct Unsubsidized Stafford, Direct PLUS, Federal Perkins, college/university loans from institutional funds, Alternative Loans. **Financial Aid Statistics:** 65% freshmen, 64% undergrads receive need-based scholarship or grant aid. 65% freshmen, 48% undergrads receive non-need-based scholarship or grant aid. 71% freshmen, 75% undergrads receive need-based self-help aid. 4% freshmen, 4% undergrads receive athletic scholarships. 70% undergrads borrow to pay for school. Average cumulative indebtedness $26,872. **Criteria for awarding institutional aid:** *Non-need-based:* academics, alumni affiliation, art, athletics, job skills, leadership, minority status, music/drama, religious affiliation, state/district residency.

WASHINGTON & JEFFERSON COLLEGE

60 South Lincoln Street, Washington, PA 15301
Phone: 724-223-6025 • **Financial Aid Phone:** 724-223-6019
E-mail: admission@washjeff.edu • **CEEB Code:** 2967
Fax: 724-223-6534 • **Website:** www.washjeff.edu • **ACT Code:** 3746

This private school was founded in 1781. It has a 60-acre campus.

RATINGS

Admissions Selectivity Rating: 89   **Fire Safety Rating:** 92

STUDENTS AND FACULTY

Enrollment: 1,323. **Student Body:** 49% female, 51% male, 23% out-of-state, 2% international (22 countries represented). Asian 2%, African American 3%, Caucasian 83%, Hispanic 3%, Native American <1%. **Retention and Graduation:** 72% freshmen graduate within 4 years. 39% grads go on to further study within 1 year. 25% grads pursue arts and sciences degrees. 11% grads pursue law degrees. 1% grads pursue business degrees. 9% grads pursue medical degrees. **Faculty:** 109 full-time faculty, 94% hold PhDs, 48% are members of minority groups, 14% are women. 0% of classes are taught by teaching assistants.

ACADEMICS

Degrees: bachelor's. **Classes:** Most classes have 10-19 students. Most lab/discussion sessions have 10-19 students. **Majors with Highest Enrollment:** Psychology; Business/Commerce; Accounting. **Special Study Options:** Accelerated program, double major, dual enrollment, honors program, independent study, internships, student-designed major, study abroad, teacher certification program, Advanced placement credit. **Combined degree programs:** BA/MD, BA/JD, BA/MEng, 3/3 law, 3/4 podiatry, 3/4 optometry. **Disability Services:** Special programs offered to physically disabled students include tutors. **Career services:** Alumni network, alumni services, career/job search classes, career assessment, internships, regional alumni. Career services highlights include the support of the alumni of the college, particularly with hosting interns. Many of these experiences result in full time employment.

FACILITIES

Housing: Coed dorms, special housing for disabled students, men's dorms, women's dorms, fraternity/sorority housing, apartments for single students, Wellness Housing, Theme Housing, On-campus suites. 48% of campus accessible to physically disabled. **Special Academic Facilities/Equipment:** Microplate Reader, Cell Culture Labs, Isolator Lab, X-Ray Diffraction Unit, Neuropsychology Lab, Atomic Absorption Unit, Nuclear Magnetic Resonance (NMR) Lab, Refrigerated Centrifuge, Global Learning Unit, Language Lab, Spectrometers, Laser Scanning Confocal Microscope Facility, Abernathy Field Station. **Computers:** 100% of classrooms, 100% of dorms, 100% of libraries, 100% of dining areas, 100% of student union, 95% of common outdoor areas have wireless network access. Students can register for classes online. Administrative functions (other than registration) can be performed online.

CAMPUS LIFE

Environment: Village. **Activities:** Choral groups, concert band, dance, drama/theater, jazz band, literary magazine, music ensembles, musical theater, pep band, radio station, student government, student newspaper, student-run film society, symphony orchestra, yearbook, Campus Ministries, International Student Organization, Model UN. 94 registered organizations, 21 honor societies, 4 religious organizations. 6 fraternities, 4 sororities. **Athletics (Intercollegiate):** *Men:* baseball, basketball, cheerleading, cross-country, diving, football, golf, lacrosse, soccer, swimming, tennis, track/field (outdoor), track/field (indoor), water polo, wrestling. *Women:* basketball, cheerleading, cross-country, diving, field hockey, golf, lacrosse, soccer, softball, swimming, tennis, track/field (outdoor), track/field (indoor), volleyball, water polo. **On-Campus Highlights:** The Hub (Student Center), Swanson Wellness Center, Monticellos Coffee House, Burnett (for meetings/studying), Ski Lodge/Barista in the Commons. **Environmental Initiatives:** Signed the ACUPCC, created the Sustainability Committee and a Climate Action Plan, which outlines many past accomplishments and current initiatives. In January 2010 we opened our first Leadership in Energy and Environmental Design (LEED) building, the Swanson Science Center, whose gold-level LEED certification was awarded in spring 2012. We promote the use of renewable energy in two ways: 1) In 2008 we began purchasing annual wind-power offsets for 15% of our electricity purchases. We increased the offset to 20% in 2010 and to 50% in 2011 and 2) Created the Swanson Solar Laboratory (https://enlighten.enphaseenergy.com/public/systems/JNwx96265) which is an array of 18 solar panels that students and faculty are using to test the ecological and economical cost benefits of small scale solar power in southwestern Pennsylvania.

ADMISSIONS

Freshman Academic Profile: Average high school GPA 3.35. 31% in top 10% of high school class, 63% in top 25% of high school class, 91% in top 50% of high school class. 86% from public high schools. SAT Math middle 50% range 520-620. SAT Critical Reading middle 50% range 520-610. ACT middle 50% range 22-28. Minimum internet-based TOEFL 85. Minimum paper TOEFL 563. **Basis for Candidate Selection:** *Very important factors considered include:* Class rank, application essay, academic GPA, recommendation(s), rigor of secondary school record, character/personal qualities, interview. *Important factors considered include:* standardized test scores, extracurricular activities. *Other factors considered include:* alumni/ae relation, geographical residence, level of applicant's interest, racial/ethnic status, state residency, talent/ability, volunteer work, work experience. **Freshman Admission Requirements:** High school diploma is required and GED is accepted. **Academic units required:** 3 English, 3 mathematics, 2 foreign language, 1 history, 6 Six or more academic courses from English, Mathematics, Foreign Language, History (Social or Natural. **Freshman Admission Statistics:** 7,094 applied, 42% admitted, 14% enrolled. **Transfer Admission Requirements:** High school transcript, college transcript(s), essay or personal statement, standardized test scores, statement of good standing from prior institution(s). Minimum college GPA of 2.50 required. Lowest grade transferable C. **General Admission Information:** Application Fee $25. Early decision application deadline 12/1. Regular application deadline 3/1. Notification on a rolling basis, beginning on or about 10/1. Nonfall registration accepted. Admission may be deferred for a maximum of 1 Year. Credit and/or placement offered for CEEB Advanced Placement tests.

COSTS AND FINANCIAL AID

Annual tuition $40,722. Room and board $10,884. Required fees $560. Average book expense $800. **Required Forms and Deadlines:** FAFSA. **Notification of Awards:** Applicants will be notified of awards on a rolling basis beginning 3/1. **Types of Aid:** *Need-based scholarships/grants:* Federal Pell, SEOG, state scholarships/grants, private scholarships, the school's own gift aid, ACG and SMART Grants. *Loans:* Subsidized Stafford, Unsubsidized Stafford, PLUS, Federal Perkins, college/university loans from institutional funds. *Student Employment:* Federal Work-Study Program available. Institutional employment available. Highest amount earned per year from on-campus jobs $3,440. Off-campus job opportunities are good. **Financial Aid Statistics:** 89% freshmen, 87% undergrads receive need-based scholarship or grant aid. 98% freshmen, 90% undergrads receive non-need-based scholarship or grant aid. 89% freshmen, 87% undergrads receive need-based self-help aid, 0% freshmen, 0% undergrads receive athletic scholarships. 100% freshmen, 99% undergrads receive any aid. 83% undergrads borrow to pay for school. Average cumulative indebtedness $26,100. **Criteria for awarding institutional aid:** *Non-need-based:* academics, alumni affiliation.

WASHINGTON ADVENTIST UNIVERSITY

7600 Flower Avenue, Takoma Park, MD 20912
Phone: 301-891-4080 · **Financial Aid Phone:** 301-891-4005
E-mail: enroll@wau.edu · **CEEB Code:** 5890
Fax: 301-891-4230 · **ACT Code:** 1687

This private school, affiliated with the Seventh Day Adventist Church, was founded in 1904. It has a 19-acre campus.

RATINGS

Admissions Selectivity Rating: 60*   Fire Safety Rating: 60*

STUDENTS AND FACULTY

Enrollment: 986. **Student Body:** 65% female, 35% male, 57% out-of-state, (47 countries represented). Asian 6%, African American 52%, Caucasian 11%, Hispanic 11%, Native American <1%
Retention and Graduation: 13% freshmen graduate within 4 years. **Faculty:** 41 full-time faculty, 51% hold PhDs, 51% are are members of minority groups, 44% are women. 0% of classes are taught by teaching assistants.

ACADEMICS

Degrees: associate, bachelor's, master's. **Classes:** Most classes have fewer than 10 students. **Majors with Highest Enrollment:** Communication and Media Studies; Registered Nursing/Registered Nurse; Business/Commerce. **Special Study Options:** Accelerated program, cooperative education program, cross-registration, distance learning, double major, dual enrollment, English as a Second Language (ESL), external degree program, honors program, independent study, internships, student-designed major, study abroad, teacher certification program, Co-Op Programs: Business, Biochemistry, Communication/Journalism, Computer Science, English. Other Special Programs: Adult education and

external degree programs. **Honors programs:** The Honors Program at CUC strives to provide academically talented students the opportunity to engage and explore subject material in greater depth. This does not mean more work, it means a different kind of work, with more individual attention. The honors classes are different in design as each class explores the topic from an interdisciplinary perspective, where areas of study are combined into one course. **Combined degree programs:** Liberal Studies—Combination of bachelors programs designed by students. **Disability Services:** Special programs offered to physically disabled students include reader services, tutors. **Career services:** career assessment, internships. Career services highlights include Internships on Capitol Hill, NASA Cooperative Learning Experiences, White House Internships, NOAA Internships.

FACILITIES

Housing: men's dorms, women's dorms, apartments for married students, apartments for single students. 30% of campus accessible to physically disabled. **Special Academic Facilities/Equipment:** Hospital adjacent to campus for students in health fields, performing arts at adfacent large church auditorium, learning center, radio station, playing fields and gymnasium. **Computers:** 100% of classrooms, 100% of dorms, 100% of libraries, 100% of dining areas, 100% of student union, 100% of common outdoor areas have wireless network access. Students can register for classes online. Administrative functions (other than registration) can be performed online.

CAMPUS LIFE

Environment: Metropolis. **Activities:** Choral groups, concert band, literary magazine, music ensembles, musical theater, radio station, student government, student newspaper, symphony orchestra, yearbook, Campus Ministries, International Student Organization 6 honor societies. **Athletics (Intercollegiate):** *Men:* baseball, basketball, cross-country, soccer, track/field (outdoor). *Women:* basketball, cross-country, soccer, softball, track/field (outdoor).

ADMISSIONS

Freshman Academic Profile: 53% from public high schools. Minimum paper TOEFL 550. **Basis for Candidate Selection:** *Very important factors considered include:* academic GPA, rigor of secondary school record, standardized test scores. *Important factors considered include:* recommendation(s), character/personal qualities, religious affiliation/commitment, talent/ability. *Other factors considered include:* application essay, extracurricular activities, volunteer work, work experience. **Freshman Admission Requirements:** High school diploma is required and GED is accepted. **Academic units required:** 4 English, 2 mathematics, 2 science, (2 science labs), 2 history, 4 academic electives. **Transfer Admission Requirements:** college transcript(s), Minimum college GPA of 2.0 required. Lowest grade transferable C. **General Admission Information:** Application Fee $25. Regular application deadline 8/1. Nonfall registration accepted. Admission may be deferred for a maximum of 1 year. Credit and/or placement offered for CEEB Advanced Placement tests.

COSTS AND FINANCIAL AID

Average book expense $1,200. **Required Forms and Deadlines:** FAFSA, State aid form. **Notification of Awards:** Applicants will be notified of awards on a rolling basis beginning 5/1. **Types of Aid:** *Need-based scholarships/grants:* Federal Pell, SEOG, state scholarships/grants, private scholarships. *Loans:* Direct Subsidized Stafford, Direct Unsubsidized Stafford, Direct PLUS, Subsidized Stafford, PLUS, Federal Perkins. *Student Employment:* Federal Work-Study Program available. Institutional employment available. Off-campus job opportunities are excellent. **Criteria for awarding institutional aid:** *Non-need-based:* academics, athletics, music/drama.

WASHINGTON AND LEE UNIVERSITY

204 W. Washington Street, Lexington, VA 24450-0303
Phone: 540-458-8710
E-mail: admissions@wlu.edu · **CEEB Code:** 5887
Fax: 540-458-8062 · **Website:** www.wlu.edu · **ACT Code:** 4430

This private school was founded in 1749. It has a 322-acre campus.

RATINGS

Admissions Selectivity Rating: 97   Fire Safety Rating: 60*

STUDENTS AND FACULTY

Enrollment: 1,834. **Student Body:** 49% female, 51% male, 86% out-of-state, 4% international (47 countries represented). Asian 3%, African American 3%, Caucasian 83%, Hispanic 3%, Native American <1%
Retention and Graduation: 88% freshmen graduate within 4 years. 90% freshmen graduate within 6 years. 24% grads go on to further study within 1 year. 6% grads pursue arts and sciences degrees. 9% grads pursue law degrees. 1% grads pursue business degrees. 5% grads pursue medical degrees. **Faculty:**

242 full-time faculty, 95% hold PhDs, 37% are are members of minority groups, 10% are women. 0% of classes are taught by teaching assistants.

ACADEMICS

Degrees: bachelor's, first professional, master's. **Classes:** Most classes have 10-19 students. Most lab/discussion sessions have fewer than 10 students. **Majors with Highest Enrollment:** Economics; Business/Commerce; History. **Special Study Options:** double major, exchange student program (domestic), honors program, independent study, internships, liberal arts/career combination, student-designed major, study abroad, teacher certification program. **Honors programs:** University Scholars, Bonner Scholars **Combined degree programs:** BA/JD, 3-3 JD with Washington and Lee School of Law. **Career services:** Alumni network, career/job search classes, career assessment, internships, regional alumni.

FACILITIES

Housing: Coed dorms, special housing for international students, fraternity/sorority housing, apartments for single students, Outing Club House, Spanish House, Chavis House. 80% of campus accessible to physically disabled. **Special Academic Facilities/Equipment:** History and porcelain museums performing arts center communications labs nuclear science lab scanning electron microscope **Computers:** Students can register for classes online. Administrative functions (other than registration) can be performed online.

CAMPUS LIFE

Environment: Village. **Activities:** Choral groups, dance, drama/theater, jazz band, literary magazine, music ensembles, radio station, student government, student newspaper, student-run film society, symphony orchestra, television station, yearbook. 90 registered organizations, 5 honor societies, 11 religious organizations. 14 fraternities, 5 sororities. **Athletics (Intercollegiate):** *Men:* baseball, basketball, cross-country, equestrian sports, football, golf, lacrosse, soccer, swimming, tennis, track/field (outdoor), track/field (indoor), wrestling. *Women:* basketball, cheerleading, cross-country, equestrian sports, field hockey, lacrosse, soccer, swimming, tennis, track/field (outdoor), track/field (indoor), volleyball. **On-Campus Highlights:** Lee Chapel, Elrod University Commons, Lenfest Center for the Arts, Doremus Fitness Center, Reeves Center and Watson Pavillion.

ADMISSIONS

Freshman Academic Profile: 80% in top 10% of high school class, 98% in top 25% of high school class, 100% in top 50% of high school class. SAT Math middle 50% range 650-740. SAT Critical Reading middle 50% range 650-740. SAT Writing middle 50% range 640-730. ACT middle 50% range 29-32. **Basis for Candidate Selection:** *Very important factors considered include:* Class rank, rigor of secondary school record, standardized test scores, character/personal qualities, extracurricular activities. *Important factors considered include:* recommendation(s), interview. *Other factors considered include:* application essay, alumni/ae relation, geographical residence, racial/ethnic status, state residency, talent/ability, volunteer work, work experience. **Freshman Admission Requirements:** High school diploma or equivalent is not required. **Academic units required:** 4 English, 3 mathematics, 1 science, (1 science labs), 3 foreign language, 1 social studies, 1 history, 4 academic electives. **Freshman Admission Statistics:** 5,972 applied, 19% admitted, 41% enrolled. **Transfer Admission Requirements:** High school transcript, college transcript(s), essay or personal statement, standardized test scores, statement of good standing from prior institution(s). Minimum college GPA of 2.0 required. Lowest grade transferable C. **General Admission Information:** Application Fee $50. Early decision application deadline 11/15. Regular application deadline 1/15. Regular notification 4/1. Nonfall registration not accepted. Admission may be deferred for a maximum of 1 year. Credit and/or placement offered for CEEB Advanced Placement tests.

COSTS AND FINANCIAL AID

Annual tuition $42,425. Room and board $9,450. Required fees $937. Average book expense $1,800. **Required Forms and Deadlines:** FAFSA, CSS/Financial Aid PROFILE, Noncustodial PROFILE. **Notification of Awards:** Applicants will be notified of awards on or about 4/6. **Types of Aid:** *Need-based scholarships/grants:* Federal Pell, SEOG, state scholarships/grants, private scholarships, the school's own gift aid. *Loans:* Subsidized Stafford, Unsubsidized Stafford, PLUS, Federal Perkins, college/university loans from institutional funds. *Student Employment:* Federal Work-Study Program available. Institutional employment available. Off-campus job opportunities are fair. **Financial Aid Statistics:** 100% freshmen, 100% undergrads receive need-based scholarship or grant aid. 25% freshmen, 34% undergrads receive non-need-based scholarship or grant aid. 71% freshmen, 61% undergrads receive need-based self-help aid. 0% freshmen, 0% undergrads receive athletic scholarships. 31% undergrads borrow to pay for school. Average cumulative indebtedness $17,996. **Criteria for awarding institutional aid:** *Non-need-based:* academics.

WASHINGTON BIBLE COLLEGE

6511 Princess Garden Parkway, Lanham, MD 20706-3599
Phone: 301-552-1400
E-mail: admissions@bible.edu
Fax: 301-552-2775 • **Website:** www.bible.edu • **ACT Code:** 1462

This private school was founded in 1938. It has a 63-acre campus.

RATINGS

Admissions Selectivity Rating: 67   **Fire Safety Rating:** 60*

STUDENTS AND FACULTY

Enrollment: 352. **Student Body:** 42% female, 58% male.
Retention and Graduation: 10% freshmen graduate within 4 years. 60% freshmen graduate within 6 years. **Faculty:** 70% of classes are taught by teaching assistants.

ACADEMICS

Degrees: associate, bachelor's, certificate. **Special Study Options:** English as a Second Language (ESL), independent study, internships. **Career services:** alumni services.

FACILITIES

Housing: men's dorms, women's dorms, apartments for married students. 60% of campus accessible to physically disabled.

CAMPUS LIFE

Environment: Village. **Activities:** Choral groups, music ensembles, student government, yearbook 1 honor society. **Athletics (Intercollegiate):** *Men:* basketball, soccer. *Women:* basketball, cheerleading, volleyball.

ADMISSIONS

Freshman Academic Profile: Minimum paper TOEFL 550. **Basis for Candidate Selection:** *Very important factors considered include:* application essay, recommendation(s), religious affiliation/commitment. *Important factors considered include:* Class rank, rigor of secondary school record, standardized test scores, character/personal qualities. *Other factors considered include:* alumni/ae relation, extracurricular activities, interview, talent/ability, volunteer work. **Freshman Admission Requirements:** High school diploma is required and GED is accepted. **Freshman Admission Statistics:** 56 applied, 29% admitted, 263% enrolled. **Transfer Admission Requirements:** college transcript(s), essay or personal statement, statement of good standing from prior institution(s). Minimum college GPA of 2.0 required. Lowest grade transferable C. **General Admission Information:** Application Fee $25. Regular application deadline 8/4. Nonfall registration accepted. Admission may be deferred for a maximum of 36.

COSTS AND FINANCIAL AID

Annual tuition $10,140. Room and board $4,180. Required fees $100. Average book expense $300. **Required Forms and Deadlines:** FAFSA, Institution's own financial aid form. **Notification of Awards:** Applicants will be notified of awards on a rolling basis beginning 1/30. **Types of Aid:** *Need-based scholarships/grants:* Federal Pell, SEOG, state scholarships/grants, private scholarships, the school's own gift aid. *Loans:* Subsidized Stafford, Unsubsidized Stafford, PLUS. *Student Employment:* Federal Work-Study Program available. Institutional employment available. Highest amount earned per year from on-campus jobs $3,000. Off-campus job opportunities are excellent. **Financial Aid Statistics:** 38% freshmen, 17% undergrads receive need-based scholarship or grant aid. 15% freshmen, 5% undergrads receive non-need-based scholarship or grant aid. 62% freshmen, 83% undergrads receive need-based self-help aid. 0% freshmen, 0% undergrads receive athletic scholarships. 20% undergrads borrow to pay for school. **Criteria for awarding institutional aid:** *Non-need-based:* academics, leadership, minority status, music/drama.

WASHINGTON COLLEGE

300 Washington Avenue, Chestertown, MD 21620
Phone: 410-778-7700 · **Financial Aid Phone:** 410-778-7214
E-mail: adm.off@washcoll.edu · **CEEB Code:** 5888
Fax: 410-778-7287 · **Website:** www.washcoll.edu · **ACT Code:** 1754

This private school was founded in 1782. It has a 144-acre campus.

RATINGS

Admissions Selectivity Rating: 89   **Fire Safety Rating:** 95

STUDENTS AND FACULTY

Enrollment: 1,404. **Student Body:** 57% female, 43% male, 55% out-of-state, 8% international (30 countries represented). Asian 2%, African American 4%, Caucasian 76%, Hispanic 4%, Native American <1% **Retention and Graduation:** 70% freshmen graduate within 4 years. 50% grads go on to further study within 1 year. 12% grads pursue arts and sciences degrees. 4% grads pursue law degrees. 8% grads pursue business degrees. 3% grads pursue medical degrees. **Faculty:** 101 full-time faculty, 95% hold PhDs, 43% are are members of minority groups, 13% are women. 0% of classes are taught by teaching assistants.

ACADEMICS

Degrees: bachelor's, master's. **Classes:** Most classes have 10-19 students. Most lab/discussion sessions have fewer than 10 students. **Majors with Highest Enrollment:** Psychology; Business Administration and Management; Biology/Biological Sciences. **Special Study Options:** cross-registration, double major, dual enrollment, exchange student program (domestic), honors program, independent study, internships, liberal arts/career combination, student-designed major, study abroad, teacher certification program. **Honors programs:** The Douglass Cater Society of Junior Fellows is the College's flagship academic enrichment program—one that rewards creativity, initiative and intellectual curiosity with competitive grants to support self-directed undergraduate research and scholarship anywhere in the world. The intent is to bring together the best and brightest in what founder Douglass Cater called "a companionship of learning." **Combined degree programs:** 3+2 nursing. **Career services:** Alumni network, alumni services, career assessment, internships, regional alumni. The Washington Center has over 35,000 alumni, many of whom are leaders in numerous professions and nations around the world. Based in the nation's capitol it offers exceptional experiential learning opportunities in various government and public service sectors.

FACILITIES

Housing: Coed dorms, special housing for disabled students, men's dorms, special housing for international students, women's dorms, fraternity/sorority housing, Wellness Housing, Theme Housing. 90% of campus accessible to physically disabled. **Special Academic Facilities/Equipment:** Language lab, computer classroom, C.V. Starr Center for the Study of the American Experience, The Center for the Environment and Society, O'Neil Literary House. **Computers:** Administrative functions (other than registration) can be performed online.

CAMPUS LIFE

Environment: Rural. **Activities:** Choral groups, concert band, dance, drama/theater, jazz band, literary magazine, music ensembles, radio station, student government, student newspaper, yearbook, Campus Ministries, International Student Organization, Model UN. 50 registered organizations, 13 honor societies, 4 religious organizations. 4 fraternities, 3 sororities. **Athletics (Intercollegiate):** *Men:* baseball, basketball, crew/rowing, lacrosse, sailing, soccer, swimming, tennis. *Women:* basketball, crew/rowing, field hockey, lacrosse, sailing, soccer, softball, swimming, tennis, volleyball. **On-Campus Highlights:** Miller Library, Johnson Lifetime Fitness Center, Gibson Center for the Arts, O'Neill Literary House, Hodson Commons Student Center, Hynson Pavillion and Washington College Boathouse providing water access and kayaks, sail boats, pantoons, canoes, motor boats, wakeboarding boats, etc. **Environmental Initiatives:** George Goes Green (G3) is Washington College's initiative for stewardship and sustainability. Situated on Maryland's Eastern Shore, the College is surrounded by the coastal and inland waters of the Chesapeake Bay, which informs our sense of history, our sense of self, and our sense of place. Our benefactor George Washington promoted sustainable economic cycles by advocating compost as a method to amend damaged soils. Today, Washington College is nationally renowned for promoting sustainability. Green at a Glance: Chesapeake Semester composting recycling environmentally-friendly products local foods native plant landscaping green facilities Recycling is now available in every building on campus. On campus, we recycle plastic and glass bottles, aluminum and tin cans, cardboard, and most types of paper. In the academic buildings, bottles and cans can be recycled in the blue bins, while paper can be recycled in the tall green bins or the locked blue paper bins where they are available. Student Environmental Alliance: The Washington College Student Environmental Alliance (SEA) is a student-run organization on campus. It promotes sustainability on campus and within the community, and works with various outside organizations to help promote sustainable practices. SEA welcomes all majors and disciplines to join at weekly meetings and events. SEA primarily focuses on: Promoting awareness of local, national, and international environmental issues and concerns Environmental education Keeping a record of accomplishments to provide for future SEA generations Providing a group that fosters personal environmental well-being Positively impacting the Washington College, Chestertown, and outside communities through its environmental initiatives.

ADMISSIONS

Freshman Academic Profile: Average high school GPA 3.56. 34% in top 10% of high school class, 62% in top 25% of high school class, 88% in top 50% of high school class. 68% from public high schools. SAT Math middle 50% range 520-640. SAT Critical Reading middle 50% range 520-630. SAT Writing middle 50% range 510-620. ACT middle 50% range 25-29. **Basis for Candidate Selection:** *Very important factors considered include:* academic GPA, rigor of secondary school record, interview. *Important factors considered include:* Class rank, standardized test scores, level of applicant's interest, work experience. *Other factors considered include:* application essay, recommendation(s), alumni/ae relation, character/personal qualities, extracurricular activities, first generation, geographical residence, racial/ethnic status, state residency, talent/ability, volunteer work. **Freshman Admission Requirements:** High school diploma is required and GED is accepted. **Academic units required:** 4 English, 3 mathematics, 3 science, (2 science labs), 2 foreign language, 2 social studies, 2 history. **Freshman Admission Statistics:** 5,318 applied, 56% admitted, 13% enrolled. **Transfer Admission Requirements:** High school transcript, college transcript(s), essay or personal statement, statement of good standing from prior institution(s). **General Admission Information:** Application Fee $55. Early decision application deadline 11/1. Regular application deadline 3/1. Notification on a rolling basis, beginning on or about 10/15. Nonfall registration accepted. Admission may be deferred for a maximum of 1 year. Credit and/or placement offered for CEEB Advanced Placement tests.

COSTS AND FINANCIAL AID

Annual tuition $41,596. Room and board $10,010. Required fees $996. Average book expense $1,250. **Required Forms and Deadlines:** FAFSA. **Notification of Awards:** Applicants will be notified of awards on a rolling basis beginning 2/15. **Types of Aid:** *Need-based scholarships/grants:* Federal Pell, SEOG, state scholarships/grants, private scholarships, the school's own gift aid. *Loans:* Subsidized Stafford, Unsubsidized Stafford, PLUS, Federal Perkins. *Student Employment:* Federal Work-Study Program available. Institutional employment available. Highest amount earned per year from on-campus jobs $2,000. Off-campus job opportunities are good. **Financial Aid Statistics:** 100% freshmen, 99% undergrads receive need-based scholarship or grant aid. 13% freshmen, 11% undergrads receive non-need-based scholarship or grant aid. 100% freshmen, 88% undergrads receive need-based self-help aid. 0% freshmen, 0% undergrads receive athletic scholarships. 95% freshmen, 93% undergrads receive any aid. 73% undergrads borrow to pay for school. Average cumulative indebtedness $25,113. **Criteria for awarding institutional aid:** *Non-need-based:* academics.

See page 1206.

WASHINGTON STATE UNIVERSITY

PO Box 641067, Pullman, WA 99164-1067
Phone: 509-335-5586 · **Financial Aid Phone:** 509-335-9711
E-mail: admissions@wsu.edu · **CEEB Code:** 3800
Fax: 509-335-4902 · **Website:** www.wsu.edu · **ACT Code:** 4482

This public school was founded in 1890. It has a 1745-acre campus.

RATINGS

Admissions Selectivity Rating: 81   **Fire Safety Rating:** 87

STUDENTS AND FACULTY

Enrollment: 22,825. **Student Body:** 51% female, 49% male, 8% out-of-state, 4% international (96 countries represented). Asian 5%, African American 3%, Caucasian 66%, Hispanic 11%, Native American 1%
Retention and Graduation: 80% freshmen return for sophomore year. 40% freshmen graduate within 4 years. 65% freshmen graduate within 6 years. 22% grads go on to further study within 1 year. **Faculty:** 1,242 full-time faculty, 88% hold PhDs, 39% are are members of minority groups, 13% are women. 8% of classes are taught by teaching assistants.

ACADEMICS

Degrees: bachelor's, certificate, master's, post-bachelor's certificate, post-master's certificate. **Classes:** Most classes have 20-29 students. **Majors with Highest Enrollment:** Business Administration and Management; Social Sciences; Registered Nursing/Registered Nurse. **Special Study Options:** Accelerated program, cooperative education program, cross-registration, distance learning, double major, dual enrollment, English as a Second Language (ESL), exchange student program (domestic), external degree program, honors program, independent study, internships, liberal arts/career combination, student-designed major, study abroad, teacher certification program. **Honors programs:** Now in its fiftieth year, the Honors College is one of the oldest and most highly regarded public university honors colleges in the country. It attracts top students in all majors from throughout the United States and around the world. The Honors College curriculum emphasizes global awareness and international impact. It immerses students in the study of international issues, builds their proficiency in a second language, and encourages them to study abroad. Instead of lecturing, professors teach courses interactively, inspiring discussions among students. Honors students conduct research as undergraduates, exploring an academic question of importance to them, documenting their analysis and conclusions, and orally presenting their work to faculty. The Honors College deepens students' intellectual curiosity and builds a lifelong love of learning, as well as skills in critical thinking, writing, public presentation, and information literacy. Graduates emerge with the tools required to become leaders in their fields. **Disability Services:** Special programs offered to physically disabled students include note-taking services, reader services, tape recorders, tutors. **Career services:** Alumni network, alumni services, career/job search classes, career assessment, internships. Career services highlights include Experiential Learning opportunities and Internships. The Internship Program at The Center for Advising and Career Development provides comprehensive career counseling and services to help students integrate educational experiences with internships in the government, business, industry and non-profit sectors. The program is free for participants. The program is also a resource to WSU faculty, staff and employers. It provides faculty/staff assistance regarding internship concerns and issues. The program assists employers with creating internship programs, recruiting for interns, and connecting with faculty/staff and students. On average, 1600 students participate in internships per academic year.

FACILITIES

Housing: Coed dorms, special housing for disabled students, men's dorms, special housing for international students, women's dorms, fraternity/sorority housing, apartments for married students, apartments for single students, Wellness Housing, Theme Housing, freshman focus-living/learning communities. 90% of campus accessible to physically disabled. **Special Academic Facilities/Equipment:** Anthropology museum; arboretum; art museum; audio labs; bear research center; beef center; behavioral lab; cadaver anatomy laboratory; child development laboratory; composite materials and engineering center; creamery; culinary lab and teaching kitchen; dairy center; ecological reserve; electronic piano/music computer lab; electronic trading room; engineering and teaching research laboratory; feed preparation laboratory; food sensory evaluation laboratory; geological collections; greenhouses; historic textiles and costume collection; horticultural orchard and organic farm; entomological collection; natural history museum; observatory; oil and gas processing laboratory; planetarium; herbarium and mycological herbarium; soil monolith collection; veterinary anatomy teaching museum; laboratory for atmospheric research; laboratory for biotechnology and bioanalysis; electron microscopy center; environmental research center; geoanalytical laboratory; music listening library; music recording studio; nuclear radiation center; planetarium; public and student-run television stations; student-run radio stations; social and economic sciences research center; state of Washington water research center; center for spectroscopy; speech and hearing clinic; center for teaching, learning and technology; TV production studios and editing suites; vet teaching hospital; vertebrate zoology museum. **Computers:** 100% of classrooms, 100% of dorms, 100% of libraries, 100% of dining areas, 100% of student union, 25% of common outdoor areas have wireless network access. Students can register for classes online. Administrative functions (other than registration) can be performed online.

CAMPUS LIFE

Environment: Town. **Activities:** Choral groups, concert band, dance, drama/theater, jazz band, literary magazine, marching band, music ensembles, musical theater, opera, pep band, radio station, student government, student newspaper, student-run film society, symphony orchestra, television station, yearbook, Campus Ministries, International Student Organization, Model UN. 300 registered

organizations, 36 honor societies, 19 religious organizations. 26 fraternities, 13 sororities. **Athletics (Intercollegiate):** *Men:* baseball, basketball, cross-country, football, golf, track/field (outdoor). *Women:* basketball, crew/rowing, cross-country, golf, soccer, swimming, tennis, track/field (outdoor), volleyball. **On-Campus Highlights:** Compton Union Building (CUB), Terrell Friendship Mall, Student Recreation Center, Beasley Performing Arts Coliseum, Martin Stadium, The newly renovated CUB stands at the heart of student leadership, engagement, and culture on campus. It is home to offices for student government and many student services. The building houses a selection of food vendors, the campus bookstore, banks, and a post office. Both wired and wireless Internet services serve students and faculty. Ballrooms, meeting rooms, and a surround-sound auditorium host a variety of events. A passage through the CUB gives students 24-hour access to the library. The whole student body comes together on Glenn Terrell Friendship Mall. Located at the heart of campus, the Mall is where culture, ideas, and lively dialogue are exchanged daily. It is the site of many outdoor events, including frequent live performances by student musicians. Students gather here as they walk to and from the library, the Compton Union Building (student union), and academic buildings, often staking out favorite spots to talk, relax, study, or catch a bite to eat. The 160,000-square-foot Student Recreation Center features the largest student weight and cardio center in the country, basketball and volleyball courts, indoor soccer, a four-lane indoor track, racquetball and squash courts, roller hockey, badminton, and much more. Swimmers enjoy the five-lane lap pool, leisure pool, and 53-person spa. Big crowds pack Beasley Performing Arts Coliseum for Pac-10 Cougar men's and women's basketball games and for big name entertainment for Dad's and Mom's Weekends. WSU students turn out for entertainment ranging from pop music concerts to ballet to wresting. Located in the center of campus, Martin Stadium is home to the Pac-10 Cougars. 2008 stadium renovations include a north-side concourse, additional concession and restroom areas, and a state-of-the-art scoreboard. Still to come are the addition of more seats and premium seating, slated for completion by fall of 2012. **Environmental Initiatives:** Sustainability & Environment Committee, established by the President of WSU, meets monthly and has campus-wide representation; Greenhouse Gas Inventory for the Pullman campus; Ongoing Environmental Management System Implementation.

ADMISSIONS

Freshman Academic Profile: Average high school GPA 3.29. 30% in top 10% of high school class, 52% in top 25% of high school class, 83% in top 50% of high school class. 99% from public high schools. SAT Math middle 50% range 460-580. SAT Critical Reading middle 50% range 450-570. SAT Writing middle 50% range 440-550. ACT middle 50% range 19-25. Minimum internet-based TOEFL 68. Minimum paper TOEFL 520. **Basis for Candidate Selection:** *Very important factors considered include:* academic GPA, standardized test scores. *Important factors considered include:* Class rank, application essay, rigor of secondary school record. *Other factors considered include:* recommendation(s), character/personal qualities, extracurricular activities, talent/ability, volunteer work, work experience. **Freshman Admission Requirements:** High school diploma is required and GED is accepted. **Academic units required:** 4 English, 3 mathematics, 2 science, (3 science labs), 1 One unit of fine, visual, or performing arts, or one additional unit of academic elective. **Freshman Admission Statistics:** 14,887 applied, 82% admitted, 34% enrolled. **Transfer Admission Requirements:** college transcript(s), Minimum college GPA of 2.5 required. Lowest grade transferable D. **General Admission Information:** Application Fee $50. Notification on a rolling basis, beginning on or about 11/1. Nonfall registration accepted. Credit offered for CEEB Advanced Placement tests.

COSTS AND FINANCIAL AID

Required Forms and Deadlines: FAFSA. **Notification of Awards:** Applicants will be notified of awards on a rolling basis beginning 4/15. **Types of Aid:** *Need-based scholarships/grants:* Federal Pell, SEOG, state scholarships/grants, private scholarships, the school's own gift aid, United Negro College Fund, Federal Nursing Scholarships. *Loans:* Subsidized Stafford, Unsubsidized Stafford, PLUS, Federal Perkins, Federal Nursing. *Student Employment:* Federal Work-Study Program available. Institutional employment available. Highest amount earned per year from on-campus jobs $8,517. Off-campus job opportunities are good. **Financial Aid Statistics:** 75% freshmen, 72% undergrads receive need-based scholarship or grant aid. 37% freshmen, 29% undergrads receive non-need-based scholarship or grant aid. 58% freshmen, 69% undergrads receive need-based self-help aid. 2% freshmen, 2% undergrads receive athletic scholarships. 72% freshmen, 68% undergrads receive any aid. 59% undergrads borrow to pay for school. Average cumulative indebtedness $21,781. **Criteria for awarding institutional aid:** *Non-need-based:* academics, alumni affiliation, art, athletics, job skills, leadership, minority status, music/drama, religious affiliation, state/district residency.

WASHINGTON UNIVERSITY IN ST. LOUIS

Campus Box 1089, St. Louis, MO 63130-4899
Phone: 314-935-6000 · **Financial Aid Phone:** 888-547-6670
E-mail: admissions@wustl.edu · **CEEB Code:** 6929
Fax: 314-935-4290 · **Website:** wustl.edu · **ACT Code:** 2386

This private school was founded in 1853. It has a 169-acre campus.

RATINGS
Admissions Selectivity Rating: 99   **Fire Safety Rating:** 95

STUDENTS AND FACULTY
Enrollment: 6,913. **Student Body:** 51% female, 49% male, 93% out-of-state, 8% international (84 countries represented). Asian 18%, African American 5%, Caucasian 55%, Hispanic 6%, Native American <1%
Retention and Graduation: 97% freshmen return for sophomore year. 90% freshmen graduate within 4 years. 95% freshmen graduate within 6 years. 33% grads go on to further study within 1 year. **Faculty:** 893 full-time faculty, 94% hold PhDs, 38% are are members of minority groups.

ACADEMICS
Degrees: bachelor's, certificate, doctoral, master's, post-bachelor's certificate, post-master's certificate. **Classes:** Most classes have fewer than 10 students. Most lab/discussion sessions have 10-19 students. **Majors with Highest Enrollment:** Biology/Biological Sciences; Engineering; Business Administration and Management. **Special Study Options:** Accelerated program, cooperative education program, cross-registration, double major, dual enrollment, English as a Second Language (ESL), exchange student program (domestic), independent study, internships, liberal arts/career combination, student-designed major, study abroad, teacher certification program, The University Scholars Program at Washington University gives selected students the opportunity to be admitted to undergraduate study and a graduate program at the same time. **Combined degree programs:** BA/MA, BA/MEng, 5 year BA/BFA 3/2 AB/MSOT. **Disability Services:** Special programs offered to physically disabled students include note-taking services, reader services, tape recorders, tutors. **Career services:** Alumni network, alumni services, career/job search classes, career assessment, internships, regional alumni. Career services highlights include Opportunities for cooperative education programs in Engineering. Internships are available in most areas including business, communications, social service, and many others. Internships and study abroad are available in numerous foreign countries.

FACILITIES
Housing: Coed dorms, fraternity/sorority housing, apartments for married students, cooperative housing, apartments for single students, Wellness Housing-special interest suites, upper-class housing, single sex floors in coed buildings, on-campus transfer-specific housing, and small-group housing for students who share common interests and goals. 95% of campus accessible to physically disabled. **Special Academic Facilities/Equipment:** Art gallery, business/economics experimental lab, botanical garden, NASA planetary imaging facility, TAP reactor system, triple monochromator, Computer Automated Radioactive Particle Tracking and gamma ray Computed Tomography, Observatory, EADS learning center, Student Enterprise Zone, Edison Theatre, lab science building, outdoor Tyson Research Center. **Computers:** Students can register for classes online. Administrative functions (other than registration) can be performed online.

CAMPUS LIFE
Environment: City. **Activities:** Choral groups, concert band, dance, drama/theater, jazz band, literary magazine, music ensembles, musical theater, opera, pep band, radio station, student government, student newspaper, student-run film society, symphony orchestra, television station, Campus Ministries, International Student Organization, Model UN. 200 registered organizations, 18 honor societies, 19 religious organizations. 12 fraternities, 6 sororities. **Athletics (Intercollegiate):** *Men:* baseball, basketball, cross-country, diving, football, soccer, swimming, tennis, track/field (outdoor), track/field (indoor). *Women:* basketball, cross-country, diving, golf, soccer, softball, swimming, tennis, track/field (outdoor), track/field (indoor), volleyball. **On-Campus Highlights:** Gallery of Art, Edison Theatre, Ursa's Café, Francis Gymnasium and Francis Field, Residence Halls.

ADMISSIONS
Freshman Academic Profile: 92% in top 10% of high school class, 99% in top 25% of high school class, 100% in top 50% of high school class. 56% from public high schools. SAT Math middle 50% range 720-800. SAT Critical Reading middle 50% range 700-770. SAT Writing middle 50% range 700-

770. ACT middle 50% range 32-34. **Basis for Candidate Selection:** *Very important factors considered include:* Class rank, application essay, academic GPA, recommendation(s), rigor of secondary school record, standardized test scores, character/personal qualities, extracurricular activities, talent/ability, volunteer work, work experience. *Other factors considered include:* alumni/ae relation, first generation, interview, level of applicant's interest, racial/ethnic status. **Freshman Admission Requirements:** High school diploma is required and GED is accepted. **Freshman Admission Statistics:** 29,211 applied, 17% admitted, 35% enrolled. **Transfer Admission Requirements:** college transcript(s), essay or personal statement, statement of good standing from prior institution(s). Lowest grade transferable C. **General Admission Information:** Application Fee $55. Early decision application deadline 11/15. Regular application deadline 1/15. Regular notification 4/1. Nonfall registration not accepted. Admission may be deferred for a maximum of 24 months. Credit and/or placement offered for CEEB Advanced Placement tests.

COSTS AND FINANCIAL AID
Annual tuition $47,300. Room and board $15,280. Required fees $793. Average book expense $977. **Required Forms and Deadlines:** FAFSA, Institution's own financial aid form, CSS/Financial Aid PROFILE, Noncustodial PROFILE. **Notification of Awards:** Applicants will be notified of awards on or about 4/1. **Types of Aid:** *Need-based scholarships/grants:* Federal Pell, SEOG, state scholarships/grants, private scholarships, the school's own gift aid, United Negro College Fund, Federal Academic Competitive Grant, Federal SMART Grant. *Loans:* Direct Subsidized Stafford, Direct Unsubsidized Stafford, Direct PLUS, Subsidized Stafford, Unsubsidized Stafford, PLUS, Federal Perkins, state loans, college/university loans from institutional funds. *Student Employment:* Federal Work-Study Program available. Institutional employment available. Highest amount earned per year from on-campus jobs $2,000. Off-campus job opportunities are excellent. **Financial Aid Statistics:** 93% freshmen, 96% undergrads receive need-based scholarship or grant aid. 9% freshmen, 6% undergrads receive non-need-based scholarship or grant aid. 72% freshmen, 64% undergrads receive need-based self-help aid. 0% freshmen, 0% undergrads receive athletic scholarships. 53% freshmen, 53% undergrads receive any aid. 30% undergrads borrow to pay for school. Average cumulative indebtedness $20,895. **Criteria for awarding institutional aid:** *Non-need-based:* academics.

WATKINS COLLEGE OF ART, DESIGN & FILM

2298 Rosa L Parks Blvd, Nashville, TN 37228
Phone: 615-277-7418 · **Financial Aid Phone:** 615-277-7421
E-mail: admissions@watkins.edu · **CEEB Code:**
Fax: 615-383-4849 · **Website:** www.watkins.edu · **ACT Code:** 4027

This private school was founded in 1895. It has a 13-acre campus.

RATINGS
Admissions Selectivity Rating: 71   **Fire Safety Rating:** 92

STUDENTS AND FACULTY
Enrollment: 396. **Student Body:** 30% out-of-state, (4 countries represented). **Retention and Graduation:** 67% freshmen graduate within 6 years. 10% grads go on to further study within 1 year. 10% grads pursue arts and sciences degrees. **Faculty:** 20 full-time faculty, 60% hold PhDs, 50% are are members of minority groups, 0% are women. 0% of classes are taught by teaching assistants.

ACADEMICS
Degrees: bachelor's, post-bachelor's certificate. **Classes:** Most classes have 10-19 students. **Majors with Highest Enrollment:** Film/Cinema/Video Studies; Graphic Design; Fine/Studio Arts. **Special Study Options:** dual enrollment, independent study, internships, study abroad. **Disability Services:** Special programs offered to physically disabled students include note-taking services, reader services, tape recorders, tutors. **Career services:** Alumni network, alumni services, career/job search classes, career assessment, internships. Career services highlights include internships available in all majors.

FACILITIES
Housing: Coed dorms, special housing for disabled students, women's dorms, apartments for single students. 100% of campus accessible to physically disabled. **Special Academic Facilities/Equipment:** Brownlee O. Currey Gallery. **Computers:** 100% of classrooms, 100% of dorms, 100% of libraries, 100% of dining areas, 100% of student union, 50% of common outdoor areas have wireless network access. Administrative functions (other than registration) can be performed online.

CAMPUS LIFE
Environment: Metropolis. **Activities:** student newspaper, student-run film society. **Environmental Initiatives:** Recycling Program; Filtered Water Bottle filling stations; Sustainability classes in certain majors.

ADMISSIONS

Freshman Academic Profile: 60% from public high schools. ACT middle 50% range 20-25. Minimum internet-based TOEFL 60. Minimum paper TOEFL 340. **Freshman Admission Statistics:** 113 applied, 83% admitted, 61% enrolled. **Transfer Admission Requirements:** college transcript(s), essay or personal statement, Minimum college GPA of 3.0 required. Lowest grade transferable C.

COSTS AND FINANCIAL AID

Average book expense $1,500. **Required Forms and Deadlines:** FAFSA, Institution's own financial aid form. *Student Employment:* Federal Work-Study Program available. Institutional employment available. Off-campus job opportunities are excellent. **Financial Aid Statistics:** 68% freshmen, 83% undergrads receive need-based scholarship or grant aid. 37% freshmen, 10% undergrads receive non-need-based scholarship or grant aid. 100% freshmen, 83% undergrads receive need-based self-help aid. 0% freshmen, 0% undergrads receive athletic scholarships. 50% freshmen, 40% undergrads receive any aid. 50% undergrads borrow to pay for school. Average cumulative indebtedness $18,000.

WAYLAND BAPTIST UNIVERSITY

1900 West 7th Street, Plainview, TX 79072
Phone: 806-291-3500 · **Financial Aid Phone:** 806-291-3520
E-mail: admityou@wbu.edu
Fax: 806-291-1963 · **ACT Code:** 4246

This private school, affiliated with the Southern Baptist Church, was founded in 1908. It has a 80-acre campus.

RATINGS

Admissions Selectivity Rating: 71   **Fire Safety Rating:** 80

STUDENTS AND FACULTY

Enrollment: 3,715. **Student Body:** 48% female, 52% male, 31% out-of-state, 1% international (20 countries represented). Asian 2%, African American 16%, Caucasian 43%, Hispanic 28%, Native American 1%
Retention and Graduation: 11% freshmen graduate within 4 years. 32% freshmen graduate within 6 years. **Faculty:** 174 full-time faculty, 78% hold PhDs, 34% are are members of minority groups, 14% are women. 0% of classes are taught by teaching assistants.

ACADEMICS

Degrees: associate, bachelor's, master's, transfer associate. **Classes:** Most classes have 10-19 students. **Majors with Highest Enrollment:** Business Administration and Management; Liberal Arts and Sciences Studies and Humanities; Criminal Justice/Law Enforcement Administration. **Special Study Options:** Accelerated program, distance learning, double major, dual enrollment, external degree program, honors program, internships, study abroad, teacher certification program. **Honors programs:** The Honors Program offered by Wayland is designed to challenge the academically superior student to develop initiative and abilities beyond what is expected in a normal course of study. Electing an Honors program offers breadth and depth of content through independent study and research, aiding the student in preparation for entering a career upon graduation or attending graduate school in a field of choice. Honors work represents the highest level of academic work available at Wayland on the undergraduate level. **Disability Services:** Special programs offered to physically disabled students include note-taking services, reader services, tutors. **Career services:** career assessment.

FACILITIES

Housing: men's dorms, women's dorms, apartments for married students. 100% of campus accessible to physically disabled. **Special Academic Facilities/Equipment:** Llano Estacado Museum. **Computers:** 80% of classrooms, 80% of dorms, 100% of libraries, 100% of dining areas, have wireless network access. Students can register for classes online. Administrative functions (other than registration) can be performed online.

CAMPUS LIFE

Environment: Town. **Activities:** Choral groups, concert band, drama/theater, marching band, music ensembles, musical theater, pep band, radio station, student government, student newspaper, television station, yearbook, Campus Ministries. 34 registered organizations, 4 honor societies, 7 religious organizations. **Athletics (Intercollegiate):** *Men:* baseball, basketball, cheerleading, cross-country, golf, soccer, track/field (outdoor), track/field (indoor). *Women:* basketball, cheerleading, cross-country, golf, soccer, track/field (outdoor), track/field (indoor), volleyball. **On-Campus Highlights:** McClung University Center, Mabee Learning Resource Center, Gates Hall, Hutcherson Gymnasium, Harral Auditorium, Pete and Nelda Laney Activities Center. **Environmental**

Initiatives: Installed energy efficient lighting campuswide. Have utilized a portion of estate holdings to establish renewable energy wind farm. Taking steps to be have more efficient mechanical energy systems.

ADMISSIONS

Freshman Academic Profile: Average high school GPA 3.34. 9% in top 10% of high school class, 29% in top 25% of high school class, 60% in top 50% of high school class. 86% from public high schools. SAT Math middle 50% range 420-530. SAT Critical Reading middle 50% range 390-520. SAT Writing middle 50% range 380-490. ACT middle 50% range 17.5-23. Minimum internet-based TOEFL 61. Minimum paper TOEFL 500. **Basis for Candidate Selection:** *Very important factors considered include:* Class rank, standardized test scores. *Important factors considered include:* rigor of secondary school record. **Freshman Admission Requirements:** High school diploma is required and GED is accepted. **Academic units required:** 3 English, 2 mathematics, 2 science, 2 history. **Freshman Admission Statistics:** 548 applied, 97% admitted, 59% enrolled. **Transfer Admission Requirements:** college transcript(s), statement of good standing from prior institution(s). Minimum college GPA of 2.0 required. Lowest grade transferable D. **General Admission Information:** Application Fee $35. Notification on a rolling basis, beginning on or about 3/1. Nonfall registration accepted. Credit offered for CEEB Advanced Placement tests.

COSTS AND FINANCIAL AID

Annual tuition $14,850. Room and board $6,072. Required fees $1,080. Average book expense $1,650. **Required Forms and Deadlines:** FAFSA, Institution's own financial aid form, State aid form. **Notification of Awards:** Applicants will be notified of awards on a rolling basis beginning 2/15. **Types of Aid:** *Need-based scholarships/grants:* Federal Pell, SEOG, state scholarships/grants, private scholarships, the school's own gift aid. *Loans:* Subsidized Stafford, Unsubsidized Stafford, PLUS, Federal Perkins, state loans. *Student Employment:* Federal Work-Study Program available. Institutional employment available. Off-campus job opportunities are fair. **Financial Aid Statistics:** 99% freshmen, 97% undergrads receive need-based scholarship or grant aid. 11% freshmen, 9% undergrads receive non-need-based scholarship or grant aid. 68% freshmen, 77% undergrads receive need-based self-help aid. 13% freshmen, 8% undergrads receive athletic scholarships. 66% freshmen, 65% undergrads receive any aid. 71% undergrads borrow to pay for school. Average cumulative indebtedness $25,725. **Criteria for awarding institutional aid:** *Non-need-based:* academics, alumni affiliation, art, athletics, music/drama, religious affiliation.

WAYNE STATE COLLEGE

1111 Main Street, Wayne, NE 68787
Phone: 402-375-7234 · **Financial Aid Phone:** 402-375-7230
E-mail: admit1@wsc.edu · **CEEB Code:** 6469
Fax: 402-375-7204 · **Website:** www.wsc.edu · **ACT Code:** 2472

This public school was founded in 1909. It has a 128-acre campus.

RATINGS

Admissions Selectivity Rating: 70   **Fire Safety Rating:** 60*

STUDENTS AND FACULTY

Enrollment: 2,869. **Student Body:** 57% female, 43% male, 12% out-of-state, 0% international (21 countries represented). Asian 1%, African American 3%, Caucasian 81%, Hispanic 7%, Native American 1%
Retention and Graduation: 68% freshmen return for sophomore year. **Faculty:** 126 full-time faculty, 82% hold PhDs, 45% are are members of minority groups, 5% are women.

ACADEMICS

Degrees: bachelor's, master's, post-master's certificate. **Classes:** Most classes have 20-29 students. Most lab/discussion sessions have 30-39 students. **Special Study Options:** cooperative education program, distance learning, double major, dual enrollment, honors program, independent study, internships, student-designed major, study abroad, teacher certification program, Learning Communities; First-Year Experience; Service Learning. **Disability Services:** Special programs offered to physically disabled students include note-taking services, reader services, tape recorders, tutors. **Career services:** Alumni network, alumni services, career/job search classes, career assessment, internships.

FACILITIES

Housing: Coed dorms. **Special Academic Facilities/Equipment:** Art gallery, fine arts center, planetarium, recreation center, telecommunications network. **Computers:** 100% of classrooms, 100% of dorms, 100% of libraries, 100% of dining areas, 100% of student union, 40% of common outdoor areas have wireless network access. Students can register for classes online. Administrative functions (other than registration) can be performed online.

CAMPUS LIFE

Environment: Rural. **Activities:** Choral groups, concert band, dance, drama/theater, jazz band, literary magazine, marching band, music ensembles, musical theater, pep band, radio station, student government, student newspaper, television station, Campus Ministries, International Student Organization. 96 registered organizations, 18 honor societies, 7 religious organizations. 2 fraternities, 3 sororities. **Athletics (Intercollegiate): Men:** baseball, basketball, cross-country, football, golf, track/field (outdoor), track/field (indoor). **Women:** basketball, cross-country, golf, soccer, softball, track/field (outdoor), track/field (indoor), volleyball.

ADMISSIONS

Freshman Academic Profile: Average high school GPA 3.24. 10% in top 10% of high school class, 29% in top 25% of high school class, 60% in top 50% of high school class. ACT middle 50% range 18-24. Minimum paper TOEFL 550. **Freshman Admission Requirements:** High school diploma is required and GED is accepted. **Freshman Admission Statistics:** 2,060 applied, 100% admitted, 33% enrolled. **Transfer Admission Requirements:** college transcript(s), Minimum college GPA of 2.0 required. Lowest grade transferable C-. **General Admission Information:** Application Fee $30. Regular application deadline 8/24. Notification on a rolling basis, beginning on or about 9/15. Nonfall registration accepted. Admission may be deferred for a maximum of 1 semester. Credit and/or placement offered for CEEB Advanced Placement tests.

COSTS AND FINANCIAL AID

Required Forms and Deadlines: FAFSA. **Notification of Awards:** Applicants will be notified of awards on a rolling basis beginning 3/1. **Types of Aid:** Need-based scholarships/grants: Federal Pell, SEOG, state scholarships/grants, private scholarships, the school's own gift aid. Loans: Subsidized Stafford, Unsubsidized Stafford, PLUS, Federal Perkins. Student Employment: Federal Work-Study Program available. Institutional employment available. Off-campus job opportunities are fair. **Financial Aid Statistics:** 77% freshmen, 68% undergrads receive need-based scholarship or grant aid. 68% freshmen, 58% undergrads receive non-need-based scholarship or grant aid. 66% freshmen, 66% undergrads receive need-based self-help aid. 9% freshmen, 7% undergrads receive athletic scholarships. **Criteria for awarding institutional aid:** Non-need-based: academics, art, athletics, leadership, minority status, music/drama, religious affiliation, state/district residency.

WAYNE STATE UNIVERSITY

42 West Warren, Detroit, MI 48202
Phone: 313-577-2100 · **Financial Aid Phone:** 313-577-2100
E-mail: admissions@wayne.edu · **CEEB Code:** 1898
Website: www.wayne.edu · **ACT Code:** 2064

This public school was founded in 1868. It has a 219-acre campus.

RATINGS

Admissions Selectivity Rating: 79   **Fire Safety Rating:** 74

STUDENTS AND FACULTY

Enrollment: 17,242. **Student Body:** 55% female, 45% male, 1% out-of-state, 2% international (60 countries represented). Asian 8%, African American 21%, Caucasian 55%, Hispanic 3%, Native American <1%
Retention and Graduation: 76% freshmen return for sophomore year. 11% freshmen graduate within 4 years. 34% freshmen graduate within 6 years. **Faculty:** 1,038 full-time faculty, 45% are are members of minority groups, 29% are women.

ACADEMICS

Degrees: bachelor's, first professional, master's, post-bachelor's certificate, post-master's certificate. **Majors with Highest Enrollment:** Psychology; Biology/Biological Sciences; Criminal Justice/Safety Studies. **Special Study Options:** Accelerated program, cooperative education program, cross-registration, distance learning, double major, dual enrollment, English as a Second Language (ESL), external degree program, honors program, independent study, internships, liberal arts/career combination, study abroad, teacher certification program, weekend college. **Disability Services:** Special programs offered to physically disabled students include note-taking services, reader services, tape recorders, tutors. **Career services:** career/job search classes, career assessment, internships.

FACILITIES

Housing: Coed dorms, special housing for disabled students, fraternity/sorority housing, apartments for married students, apartments for single students. 100% of campus accessible to physically disabled. **Special Academic Facilities/Equipment:** Detroit Institute of Arts; Detroit Historical Museum; Detroit

Science Museum; Charles H Wright Museum of African American History. **Computers:** Students can register for classes online. Administrative functions (other than registration) can be performed online.

CAMPUS LIFE

Environment: Metropolis. **Activities:** Choral groups, concert band, dance, drama/theater, jazz band, literary magazine, music ensembles, musical theater, opera, pep band, student government, student newspaper, student-run film society, symphony orchestra, yearbook. 166 registered organizations, 4 honor societies, 12 religious organizations. 7 fraternities, 8 sororities. **Athletics (Intercollegiate): Men:** baseball, basketball, cross-country, diving, fencing, football, golf, ice hockey, swimming, tennis. **Women:** basketball, cross-country, diving, fencing, ice hockey, softball, swimming, tennis, volleyball. **On-Campus Highlights:** Recreation and Fitness Center, Student Center Building, Subway, Starbucks, Residence Halls. **Environmental Initiatives:** Past and ongoing LEED certified buildings being constructed. Energy audits leading to permanent change that are energy efficient. Lighting retrofits & building envelope audit.

ADMISSIONS

Freshman Academic Profile: Average high school GPA 3.28. 21% in top 10% of high school class, 48% in top 25% of high school class, 79% in top 50% of high school class. ACT middle 50% range 20-26. Minimum internet-based TOEFL 79. Minimum paper TOEFL 550. **Basis for Candidate Selection:** *Very important factors considered include:* rigor of secondary school record, standardized test scores. *Other factors considered include:* Class rank, extracurricular activities. **Freshman Admission Requirements:** High school diploma is required and GED is accepted. **Freshman Admission Statistics:** 12,199 applied, 77% admitted, 23% enrolled. **Transfer Admission Requirements:** college transcript(s), Minimum college GPA of 2.0 required. Lowest grade transferable C. **General Admission Information:** Application Fee $30. Regular application deadline 8/1. Nonfall registration accepted. Admission may be deferred for a maximum of One Year. Credit and/or placement offered for CEEB Advanced Placement tests.

COSTS AND FINANCIAL AID

Annual in-state tuition $10,094. Annual out-of-state tuition $23,117. Room and board $9,713. Required fees $1,355. Average book expense $1,196. **Required Forms and Deadlines:** FAFSA. **Notification of Awards:** Applicants will be notified of awards on a rolling basis beginning 4/1. **Types of Aid:** Need-based scholarships/grants: Federal Pell, SEOG, state scholarships/grants, private scholarships, the school's own gift aid. Loans: Subsidized Stafford, Unsubsidized Stafford, PLUS, Federal Perkins, Federal Nursing, state loans, college/university loans from institutional funds. Student Employment: Institutional employment available. Off-campus job opportunities are fair. **Financial Aid Statistics:** 76% freshmen, 78% undergrads receive need-based scholarship or grant aid. 47% freshmen, 37% undergrads receive non-need-based scholarship or grant aid. 62% freshmen, 74% undergrads receive need-based self-help aid. 1% freshmen, 1% undergrads receive athletic scholarships. 89% freshmen, 82% undergrads receive any aid. 60% undergrads borrow to pay for school. Average cumulative indebtedness $22,032. **Criteria for awarding institutional aid:** Non-need-based: academics, art, athletics, leadership, music/drama.

WAYNESBURG UNIVERSITY

51 West College Street, Waynesburg, PA 15370
Phone: 724-852-3248 · **Financial Aid Phone:** 724-852-3208
E-mail: admissions@waynesburg.edu · **CEEB Code:** 2969
Fax: 724-627-8124 · **ACT Code:** 3748

This private school, affiliated with the Presbyterian Church, was founded in 1849. It has a 30-acre campus.

RATINGS

Admissions Selectivity Rating: 78   **Fire Safety Rating:** 93

STUDENTS AND FACULTY

Enrollment: 1,553. **Student Body:** 61% female, 39% male, 20% out-of-state, 0% international (4 countries represented). Asian 1%, African American 3%, Caucasian 88%, Hispanic 1%, Native American <1%
Retention and Graduation: 82% freshmen return for sophomore year. 45% freshmen graduate within 4 years. 54% freshmen graduate within 6 years. **Faculty:** 78 full-time faculty, 65% hold PhDs, 46% are are members of minority groups, 8% are women. 0% of classes are taught by teaching assistants.

ACADEMICS

Degrees: associate, bachelor's, master's. **Classes:** Most classes have 10-19 students. Most lab/discussion sessions have 10-19 students. **Majors with Highest Enrollment:** Business, Management, Marketing, and Related Support Services; Registered Nursing/Registered Nurse; Criminal Justice/Law Enforcement Administration. **Special Study Options:** Accelerated program, distance learning, double major, dual enrollment, English as a Second Language (ESL), honors program, independent study, internships, liberal arts/career combination, study abroad, teacher certification program, 3-2 program in engineering with Penn State University in State College, PA and Washington University in Saint Louis, MO, 3-1 program in marine bioloy with Florida Institute of Technology; 3-3 law program with Duquesne University. **Combined degree programs:** BA/JD, 3/2 Pre-Law -Waynesburg and Duquense. **Disability Services:** Special programs offered to physically disabled students include tutors. **Career services:** Alumni network, alumni services, career/job search classes, career assessment, internships, regional alumni. Career services highlights include a Professional Development course for second semester juniors and seniors.

FACILITIES

Housing: Coed dorms, men's dorms, women's dorms. 90% of campus accessible to physically disabled. **Special Academic Facilities/Equipment:** Geology, biology, archaeology, and ceramics museum, arboretum, 174-acre farm, Center for Research and Economic Development. **Computers:** 95% of classrooms, 95% of libraries, 100% of dining areas, 100% of student union, 20% of common outdoor areas have wireless network access. Students can register for classes online. Administrative functions (other than registration) can be performed online.

CAMPUS LIFE

Environment: Village. **Activities:** Choral groups, concert band, dance, drama/theater, literary magazine, marching band, music ensembles, musical theater, pep band, radio station, student government, student newspaper, television station, yearbook. 40 registered organizations, 16 honor societies, 7 religious organizations. **Athletics (Intercollegiate):** *Men:* baseball, basketball, cross-country, football, golf, soccer, tennis, track/field (outdoor), wrestling. *Women:* basketball, cross-country, golf, lacrosse, soccer, softball, tennis, track/field (outdoor), volleyball. **On-Campus Highlights:** Communication Department, Stover Campus Center, Museum, Alumni Hall/Chapel, New Residence Halls.

ADMISSIONS

Freshman Academic Profile: Average high school GPA 3.57. 18% in top 10% of high school class, 47% in top 25% of high school class, 85% in top 50% of high school class. SAT Math middle 50% range 450-560. SAT Critical Reading middle 50% range 440-550. ACT middle 50% range 20-25. Minimum internet-based TOEFL 83. Minimum paper TOEFL 557. **Basis for Candidate Selection:** *Very important factors considered include:* Class rank, academic GPA, rigor of secondary school record, standardized test scores, interview. *Important factors considered include:* extracurricular activities. *Other factors considered include:* application essay, recommendation(s), alumni/ae relation, character/personal qualities, level of applicant's interest, volunteer work, work experience. **Freshman Admission Requirements:** High school diploma is required and GED is accepted. **Academic units required:** 4 English, 3 mathematics, 2 science, 2 social studies, 5 academic electives. **Freshman Admission Statistics:** 1,681 applied, 83% admitted, 29% enrolled. **Transfer Admission Requirements:** High school transcript, college transcript(s), statement of good standing from prior institution(s). Minimum college GPA of 2.5 required. Lowest grade transferable C. **General Admission Information:** Application Fee $20. Non-fall registration accepted. Credit offered for CEEB Advanced Placement tests.

COSTS AND FINANCIAL AID

Required Forms and Deadlines: FAFSA. **Notification of Awards:** Applicants will be notified of awards on a rolling basis beginning 2/15. **Types of Aid:** *Need-based scholarships/grants:* Federal Pell, SEOG, state scholarships/grants, private scholarships, the school's own gift aid. *Loans:* Subsidized Stafford, Unsubsidized Stafford, PLUS, Federal Perkins, Federal Nursing, Private Alternative Loans. *Student Employment:* Federal Work-Study Program available. Institutional employment available. Highest amount earned per year from on-campus jobs $3,000. Off-campus job opportunities are good. **Financial Aid Statistics:** 100% freshmen, 94% undergrads receive need-based scholarship or grant aid. 12% freshmen, 9% undergrads receive non-need-based scholarship or grant aid. 82% freshmen, 84% undergrads receive need-based self-help aid. 0% freshmen, 0% undergrads receive athletic scholarships. 94% freshmen, 88% undergrads receive any aid. 69% undergrads borrow to pay for school. Average cumulative indebtedness $13,166. **Criteria for awarding institutional aid:** *Non-need-based:* academics, alumni affiliation, art, job skills, leadership, minority status, music/drama, religious affiliation, state/district residency.

WEBB INSTITUTE

298 Crescent Beach Road, Glen Cove, NY 11542
Phone: 516-671-8355 • **Financial Aid Phone:** 516-671-8355
E-mail: admissions@webb.edu • **CEEB Code:** 2970
Fax: 516-674-9838 • **Website:** www.webb.edu • **ACT Code:** 2987

This private school was founded in 1889. It has a 26-acre campus.

RATINGS

Admissions Selectivity Rating: 94   **Fire Safety Rating:** 80

STUDENTS AND FACULTY

Enrollment: 90. **Student Body:** 13% female, 87% male, 72% out-of-state, 1% international (3 countries represented). Asian 9%, African American 0%, Caucasian 84%, Hispanic 0%, Native American <1%
Retention and Graduation: 85% freshmen return for sophomore year. 86% freshmen graduate within 4 years. 91% freshmen graduate within 6 years. 25% grads go on to further study within 1 year. **Faculty:** 10 full-time faculty, 60% hold PhDs, 10% are are members of minority groups, 0% are women. 0% of classes are taught by teaching assistants.

ACADEMICS

Degrees: bachelor's. **Classes:** Most classes have 20-29 students. **Special Study Options:** double major, independent study, internships. **Career services:** Alumni network, career/job search classes, internships, regional alumni. Career services highlights include the Winter Work program. All students are required to work in the industry for 2 months of each academic year. Freshmen work in shipyards; Sophomore work onboard ships; Juniors and Seniors work in engineering design offices.

FACILITIES

Housing: Coed dorms, men's dorms, women's dorms. 70% of campus accessible to physically disabled. **Special Academic Facilities/Equipment:** Towing tank for model testing, marine engineering lab. **Computers:** 100% of classrooms, 100% of dorms, 100% of libraries, 100% of dining areas, 100% of student union, 100% of common outdoor areas have wireless network access.

CAMPUS LIFE

Environment: Village. **Activities:** Choral groups, drama/theater, music ensembles, student government, yearbook. 2 registered organizations. **Athletics (Intercollegiate):** *Men:* basketball, cross-country, sailing, soccer, tennis, volleyball. *Women:* basketball, cross-country, sailing, soccer, tennis, volleyball. **On-Campus Highlights:** Stevenson Taylor Hall, Brockett Pub, Waterfront Facility.

ADMISSIONS

Freshman Academic Profile: Average high school GPA 4.1. 71% in top 10% of high school class, 21% in top 25% of high school class, 8% in top 50% of high school class. 92% from public high schools. SAT Math middle 50% range 680-790. SAT Critical Reading middle 50% range 640-730. SAT Writing middle 50% range 620-710. ACT middle 50% range 31-33. **Basis for Candidate Selection:** *Very important factors considered include:* Class rank, academic GPA, rigor of secondary school record, standardized test scores, character/personal qualities, interview, level of applicant's interest. *Important factors considered include:* recommendation(s), extracurricular activities. *Other factors considered include:* talent/ability, volunteer work, work experience. **Freshman Admission Requirements:** High school diploma is required and GED is not accepted. **Academic units required:** 4 English, 4 mathematics, 2 science, (2 science labs), 0 foreign language, 2 social studies, 0 history, 4 academic electives. **Freshman Admission Statistics:** 97 applied, 33% admitted, 75% enrolled. **Transfer Admission Requirements:** High school transcript, college transcript(s), interview, standardized test scores, Minimum college GPA of 3.5 required. **General Admission Information:** Application Fee $25. Early decision application deadline 10/15. Regular application deadline 2/15. Notification on a rolling basis, beginning on or about 4/15. Nonfall registration not accepted. Neither credit nor placement offered for CEEB Advanced Placement tests.

COSTS AND FINANCIAL AID

Annual tuition $44,000. Room and board $14,050. Required fees $0. Average book expense $1,080. **Required Forms and Deadlines:** FAFSA, Institution's own financial aid form, Business/Farm Supplement. **Notification of Awards:** Applicants will be notified of awards on or about 8/1. **Types of Aid:** *Need-based scholarships/grants:* Federal Pell, state scholarships/grants, private scholarships, the school's own gift aid. *Loans:* Subsidized Stafford, Unsubsidized Stafford, PLUS. *Student Employment:* Off-campus job opportunities are fair. **Financial Aid Statistics:** 50% freshmen, 176% undergrads receive need-based scholarship or grant aid. 0% freshmen, 0% undergrads receive non-need-based scholarship or grant aid. 0% freshmen, 0% undergrads receive need-based self-help aid. 0% freshmen, 0% undergrads receive athletic scholarships. 23% freshmen, 18% undergrads receive any aid. 33% undergrads borrow to pay for school. Average cumulative indebtedness $4,500. **Criteria for awarding institutional aid:** *Non-need-based:* academics.

WEBBER INTERNATIONAL UNIVERSITY

PO Box 96, Babson Park, FL 33827
Phone: 863-628-2910 · **Financial Aid Phone:** 863-638-2930
E-mail: admissions@webber.edu · **CEEB Code:** 5893
Fax: 863-638-1591 · **Website:** www.webber.edu · **ACT Code:** 773

This private school was founded in 1927. It has a 110-acre campus.

RATINGS

Admissions Selectivity Rating: 91   Fire Safety Rating: 86

STUDENTS AND FACULTY

Enrollment: 681. **Student Body:** 31% female, 69% male, 13% out-of-state, 24% international (45 countries represented). Asian 1%, African American 22%, Caucasian 39%, Hispanic 11%, Native American <1%
Retention and Graduation: 22% freshmen graduate within 4 years. 28% freshmen graduate within 6 years. 7% grads go on to further study within 1 year. 2% grads pursue law degrees. 5% grads pursue business degrees. **Faculty:** 21 full-time faculty, 71% hold PhDs, 33% are are members of minority groups, 10% are women. 0% of classes are taught by teaching assistants.

ACADEMICS

Degrees: associate, bachelor's, master's. **Classes:** Most classes have 20-29 students. **Majors with Highest Enrollment:** Parks, Recreation and Leisure Facilities Management; Business/Commerce; Business Administration and Management. **Special Study Options:** cooperative education program, cross-registration, distance learning, double major, dual enrollment, English as a Second Language (ESL), exchange student program (domestic), external degree program, independent study, internships, study abroad, weekend college. **Career services:** career/job search classes, career assessment, internships. Career services highlights include experiential learning in the classroom in classes like Career Development where we engage the learner at a more personal level by addressing the needs of the individual. In career development each student is treated as an individual and the learning process is individual not necessarily as a group. Students are given individual personality assessments and must demonstrate goal setting abilities while observing different occupations, in hands on setting and finally presenting the occupation they have chosen as a career. I am also very proud of our internship program which gives students a valuable learning tooland hands-on opportunity in the field they are most intersted in.

FACILITIES

Housing: men's dorms, women's dorms. 70% of campus accessible to physically disabled. **Computers:** Administrative functions (other than registration) can be performed online.

CAMPUS LIFE

Environment: Rural. **Activities:** marching band, pep band, student government, student newspaper, International Student Organization. 6 registered organizations. **Athletics (Intercollegiate):** *Men:* baseball, basketball, bowling, cheerleading, cross-country, football, golf, soccer, tennis, track/field (outdoor). *Women:* basketball, bowling, cheerleading, cross-country, golf, soccer, softball, tennis, track/field (outdoor), volleyball. **On-Campus Highlights:** Student Union, Fitness Center, Computer Lab, Career Center.

ADMISSIONS

Freshman Academic Profile: Average high school GPA 3.14. 72% in top 10% of high school class, 100% in top 25% of high school class, 0% in top 50% of high school class. 75% from public high schools. SAT Math middle 50% range 430-530. SAT Critical Reading middle 50% range 430-510. ACT middle 50% range 17-23. Minimum paper TOEFL 500. **Basis for Candidate Selection:** *Very important factors considered include:* academic GPA, standardized test scores. *Important factors considered include:* rigor of secondary school record. *Other factors considered include:* Class rank, application essay, recommendation(s), alumni/ae relation, character/personal qualities, interview. **Freshman Admission Requirements:** High school diploma is required and GED is accepted. **Academic units required:** 4 English, 2 mathematics, 1 science, 2 social studies, 2. **Freshman Admission Statistics:** 710 applied, 51% admitted, 42% enrolled. **Transfer Admission Requirements:** college transcript(s), statement of good standing from prior institution(s). Minimum college GPA of 2.0 required. Lowest grade transferable C. **General Admis-**

sion Information: Application Fee $35. Regular application deadline 8/1. Notification on a rolling basis, beginning on or about 12/1. Nonfall registration accepted. Admission may be deferred for a maximum of 1 semester. Credit offered for CEEB Advanced Placement tests.

COSTS AND FINANCIAL AID

Annual tuition $21,686. Room and board $8,462. Average book expense $1,148. **Required Forms and Deadlines:** FAFSA, Institution's own financial aid form. **Notification of Awards:** Applicants will be notified of awards on a rolling basis beginning 4/1. **Types of Aid:** *Need-based scholarships/grants:* Federal Pell, SEOG, state scholarships/grants, private scholarships, the school's own gift aid. *Loans:* Subsidized Stafford, Unsubsidized Stafford, PLUS, Federal Perkins. *Student Employment:* Federal Work-Study Program available. Institutional employment available. Highest amount earned per year from on-campus jobs $1,950. Off-campus job opportunities are good. **Financial Aid Statistics:** 98% freshmen, 97% undergrads receive need-based scholarship or grant aid. 5% freshmen, 6% undergrads receive non-need-based scholarship or grant aid. 82% freshmen, 80% undergrads receive need-based self-help aid. 10% freshmen, 16% undergrads receive athletic scholarships; 97% freshmen, 96% undergrads receive any aid. 47% undergrads borrow to pay for school. Average cumulative indebtedness $23,825. **Criteria for awarding institutional aid:** *Non-need-based:* academics, alumni affiliation, athletics, leadership, state/district residency.

WEBER STATE UNIVERSITY

1137 University Circle, Ogden, UT 84408-1137
Phone: 801-626-6743 · **Financial Aid Phone:** 801-626-7569
E-mail: admissions@weber.edu · **CEEB Code:** 4941
Fax: 801-626-6747 · **Website:** weber.edu/ · **ACT Code:** 4282

This public school was founded in 1889. It has a 526-acre campus.

RATINGS

Admissions Selectivity Rating: 68   Fire Safety Rating: 79

STUDENTS AND FACULTY

Enrollment: 17,795. **Student Body:** 53% female, 47% male, 10% out-of-state, 2% international (49 countries represented). Asian 2%, African American 2%, Caucasian 69%, Hispanic 10%, Native American 1%
Retention and Graduation: 72% freshmen return for sophomore year. 12% freshmen graduate within 4 years. 35% freshmen graduate within 6 years. **Faculty:** 487 full-time faculty, 84% hold PhDs, 47% are are members of minority groups, 13% are women. 0% of classes are taught by teaching assistants.

ACADEMICS

Degrees: associate, bachelor's, certificate, master's, post-bachelor's certificate, terminal associate, transfer associate. **Classes:** Most classes have 10-19 students. Most lab/discussion sessions have 10-19 students. **Majors with Highest Enrollment:** Registered Nursing/Registered Nurse; Business Administration and Management; Computer Science. **Special Study Options:** Accelerated program, cooperative education program, distance learning, double major, dual enrollment, English as a Second Language (ESL), exchange student program (domestic), external degree program, honors program, independent study, internships, student-designed major, study abroad, teacher certification program, First Year Experience. **Disability Services:** Special programs offered to physically disabled students include note-taking services, reader services, tape recorders, tutors. **Career services:** Alumni network, alumni services, career/job search classes, career assessment, internships, regional alumni.

FACILITIES

Housing: special housing for disabled students, men's dorms, women's dorms, apartments for married students, apartments for single students. 99% of campus accessible to physically disabled. **Special Academic Facilities/Equipment:** Art gallery, language lab, TV studio, communication arts/technologies facilities, natural science museum, herbarium, planetarium, aerospace technology equipment for developing satellite projects, dental hygiene clinic. **Computers:** 50% of classrooms, 50% of dorms, 100% of libraries, 100% of dining areas, 100% of student union, 100% of common outdoor areas have wireless network access. Students can register for classes online. Administrative functions (other than registration) can be performed online.

CAMPUS LIFE

Environment: Town. **Activities:** Choral groups, concert band, dance, drama/theater, jazz band, literary magazine, marching band, music ensembles, musical theater, opera, pep band, radio station, student government, student newspaper, student-run film society, symphony orchestra, television station. 100 registered organizations, 1 honor society, 4 religious organizations. 2 fraternities, 3 sororities. **Athletics (Intercollegiate): Men:** basketball, cheerleading, cross-country, football, golf, tennis, track/field (outdoor), track/field (indoor). *Women:* basketball, cheerleading, cross-country, golf, soccer, tennis, track/field (outdoor), track/field (indoor), volleyball. **On-Campus Highlights:** Health and Physical Education Center, Bowling Alley and Arcade, Student Union Building, Kimball Visual Arts Building, Val A. Browning Center, Student Union Building is under renovation, West side is completed, the East side will be completed summer 2008. Pool tables and games have been moved to Promontory Tower for the time being. Bowling has been contracted out to a local alley. **Environmental Initiatives:** Weber State University is in the process of upgrading all interior and exterior campus lighting to high-efficiency flourescents, CLFs and LEDs in some applications. This project began last year and will continue for another 3 years. Weber State University is in the process of upgrading its vast system of steam tunnel pipes to make them more energy and water efficient. Expansion joints and steam traps will be replaced, isolation valves will be added, and the entire network of pipes will be re-insulated with aerogel. Aerogel is a high performance thermal insulator that has been used by NASA to insulate the Mars Rover and spacesuits. All new construction at Weber State University must meet LEED silver standards. Our two newest buildings, Elizabeth Hall and the Hurst Center, have both been LEED silver certified.

ADMISSIONS
Freshman Academic Profile: Average high school GPA 3.25. 99% from public high schools. ACT middle 50% range 18-24. **Basis for Candidate Selection:** *Important factors considered include:* rigor of secondary school record, standardized test scores. *Other factors considered include:* character/personal qualities, extracurricular activities, interview. **Freshman Admission Requirements:** High school diploma is required and GED is accepted. **Freshman Admission Statistics:** 5,188 applied, 100% admitted, 45% enrolled. **Transfer Admission Requirements:** college transcript(s), Minimum college GPA of 2.0 required. Lowest grade transferable C. **General Admission Information:** Application Fee $45. Regular application deadline 8/22. Nonfall registration accepted. Admission may be deferred for a maximum of 1 year. Placement offered for CEEB Advanced Placement tests.

COSTS AND FINANCIAL AID
Annual in-state tuition $4,326. Annual out-of-state tuition $12,980. Room and board $7,536. Required fees $858. Average book expense $1,200. **Required Forms and Deadlines:** FAFSA, Institution's own financial aid form. **Notification of Awards:** Applicants will be notified of awards on a rolling basis beginning 3/15. **Types of Aid:** *Need-based scholarships/grants:* Federal Pell, SEOG, state scholarships/grants, private scholarships, the school's own gift aid. *Loans:* Subsidized Stafford, Unsubsidized Stafford, PLUS, Federal Perkins, Short-term Tuition Loan. *Student Employment:* Federal Work-Study Program available. Institutional employment available. Off-campus job opportunities are good. **Financial Aid Statistics:** 66% freshmen, 72% undergrads receive need-based scholarship or grant aid. 14% freshmen, 21% undergrads receive non-need-based scholarship or grant aid. 48% freshmen, 55% undergrads receive need-based self-help aid. 0% freshmen, 0% undergrads receive athletic scholarships. 82% freshmen, 63% undergrads receive any aid. **Criteria for awarding institutional aid:** *Non-need-based:* academics, alumni affiliation, art, athletics, job skills, leadership, minority status, music/drama, state/district residency.

WEBSTER UNIVERSITY

470 East Lockwood Avenue, Saint Louis, MO 63119-3194
Phone: 314-968-6991 · **Financial Aid Phone:** 314-968-6992
E-mail: admit@webster.edu · **CEEB Code:** 6933
Fax: 314-968-7115 · **Website:** www.webster.edu · **ACT Code:** 2388

This private school was founded in 1915. It has a 47-acre campus.

RATINGS
Admissions Selectivity Rating: 87   **Fire Safety Rating:** 93

STUDENTS AND FACULTY
Enrollment: 3,249. **Student Body:** 57% female, 43% male, 21% out-of-state, 2% international (48 countries represented). Asian 2%, African American 11%, Caucasian 69%, Hispanic 3%, Native American <1%
Retention and Graduation: 51% freshmen graduate within 4 years. 65% freshmen graduate within 6 years. 21% grads go on to further study within 1 year. **Faculty:** 184 full-time faculty, 80% hold PhDs, 47% are are members of minority groups, 10% are women. 0% of classes are taught by teaching assistants.

ACADEMICS
Degrees: bachelor's, certificate, master's, post-bachelor's certificate, post-master's certificate. **Classes:** Most classes have 10-19 students. **Majors with Highest Enrollment:** Business Administration and Management; Psychol-

ogy; International Relations and Affairs. **Special Study Options:** Accelerated program, cooperative education program, cross-registration, distance learning, double major, dual enrollment, English as a Second Language (ESL), exchange student program (domestic), independent study, internships, liberal arts/career combination, student-designed major, study abroad, teacher certification program, Certificate Programs, Combination bachelor's/master's degree in many subject areas, Independent study, Student Leadership Development Program. In addition to the programs offered at its four St. Louis area campuses, Webster University offers undergraduate degree completion programs at the following extended campus locations in the United States: Charleston, SC; Columbia, SC; Greenville, SC; Kansas City, MO; Orlando, FL; Irvine, CA; San Diego, CA. Undergraduate students may also study at Webster's international campuses, where they may complete their entire degree at the following locations: Geneva, Switzerland website: www.webster.ch Leiden, The Netherlands website: www. webster.nl London, UK, at Webster at Regent's College website: www.bacl. ac.uk Vienna, Austria website: www.webster.ac.at Cha-am, Thailand website: www.webster.ac.th. **Combined degree programs:** BA/MA, 3/4 BA-BFA/MS w/ Washington Univ. in Architecture. **Disability Services:** Special programs offered to physically disabled students include note-taking services, reader services, tape recorders, tutors. **Career services:** Alumni network, alumni services, career assessment, internships.

FACILITIES
Housing: Coed dorms, special housing for international students, women's dorms, apartments for married students, apartments for single students. 85% of campus accessible to physically disabled. **Special Academic Facilities/Equipment:** Loretto-Hilton Center for Performing Arts (Houses St. Louis Repertory company, Opera Theatre of St. Louis, and Webster Symphony); Community Music School of Webster University. **Computers:** 10% of classrooms, 12% of dorms, 50% of libraries, 100% of dining areas, 100% of student union, 60% of common outdoor areas have wireless network access. Students can register for classes online. Administrative functions (other than registration) can be performed online.

CAMPUS LIFE
Environment: Metropolis. **Activities:** Choral groups, dance, drama/theater, jazz band, literary magazine, music ensembles, musical theater, opera, radio station, student government, student newspaper, student-run film society, symphony orchestra, television station, yearbook, Campus Ministries. 62 registered organizations, 1 honor society, 1 religous organization. 1 fraternity. **Athletics (Intercollegiate): Men:** baseball, basketball, cross-country, golf, soccer, tennis, track/field (outdoor). *Women:* basketball, cross-country, soccer, softball, tennis, track/field (outdoor), volleyball. **On-Campus Highlights:** University Center, The Quadrangle, Emerson Library, Fitness Center, Marletto's Marketplace (dining hall). **Environmental Initiatives:** Recycling program .

ADMISSIONS
Freshman Academic Profile: Average high school GPA 3.45. 24% in top 10% of high school class, 55% in top 25% of high school class, 83% in top 50% of high school class. 77% from public high schools. SAT Math middle 50% range 460-630. SAT Critical Reading middle 50% range 520-650. ACT middle 50% range 21-28. Minimum paper TOEFL 550. **Basis for Candidate Selection:** *Very important factors considered include:* academic GPA, standardized test scores, talent/ability. *Important factors considered include:* Class rank, application essay, recommendation(s), rigor of secondary school record, level of applicant's interest. *Other factors considered include:* extracurricular activities, geographical residence, interview, racial/ethnic status, volunteer work. **Freshman Admission Requirements:** High school diploma is required and GED is accepted. **Freshman Admission Statistics:** 1,584 applied, 52% admitted, 60% enrolled. **Transfer Admission Requirements:** college transcript(s), essay or personal statement, Minimum college GPA of 2.5 required. Lowest grade transferable C. **General Admission Information:** Application Fee $35. Regular application deadline 6/1. Notification on a rolling basis, beginning on or about 9/1. Nonfall registration accepted. Admission may be deferred for a maximum of 12 months. Credit offered for CEEB Advanced Placement tests.

COSTS AND FINANCIAL AID
Required fees $0. **Required Forms and Deadlines:** FAFSA, Institution's own financial aid form. **Notification of Awards:** Applicants will be notified of awards on a rolling basis beginning 2/1. **Types of Aid:** *Need-based scholarships/grants:* Federal Pell, SEOG, state scholarships/grants, private scholarships, the school's own gift aid. *Loans:* Subsidized Stafford, Unsubsidized Stafford, PLUS, Federal Perkins. *Student Employment:* Federal Work-Study Program available. Institutional employment available. Off-campus job opportunities are good. **Financial Aid Statistics:** 87% freshmen, 83% undergrads receive need-based scholarship or grant aid. 84% freshmen, 73% undergrads receive non-need-based scholarship or grant aid. 93% freshmen, 93% undergrads receive need-based self-help aid. 0% freshmen, 0% undergrads receive athletic scholarships. 95% freshmen, 68% undergrads receive any aid. 53% undergrads borrow to pay for school. Average cumulative indebtedness $22,809. **Criteria for awarding institutional aid:** *Non-need-based:* academics, art, music/drama, state/district residency.

WELLESLEY COLLEGE

Board of Admission, Wellesley, MA 02481-8203
Phone: 781-283-2270 · **Financial Aid Phone:** 781-283-2360
E-mail: admission@wellesley.edu · **CEEB Code:** 3957
Fax: 781-283-3678 · **Website:** www.wellesley.edu · **ACT Code:** 1926

This private school was founded in 1870. It has a 500-acre campus.

RATINGS

Admissions Selectivity Rating: 96   **Fire Safety Rating:** 97

STUDENTS AND FACULTY

Enrollment: 2,172. **Student Body:** 100% female, 0% male, 84% out-of-state, 11% international (93 countries represented). Asian 24%, African American 6%, Caucasian 41%, Hispanic 9%, Native American <1%
Retention and Graduation: 94% freshmen return for sophomore year. 82% freshmen graduate within 4 years. 91% freshmen graduate within 6 years. 34% grads go on to further study within 1 year. 31% grads pursue arts and sciences degrees. 5% grads pursue law degrees. 1% grads pursue business degrees. 9% grads pursue medical degrees. **Faculty:** 296 full-time faculty, 96% hold PhDs, 58% are are members of minority groups, 26% are women. 0% of classes are taught by teaching assistants.

ACADEMICS

Degrees: bachelor's. **Classes:** Most classes have 10-19 students. Most lab/discussion sessions have 10-19 students. **Majors with Highest Enrollment:** Economics; Psychology; Political Science and Government. **Special Study Options:** cross-registration, double major, dual enrollment, exchange student program (domestic), honors program, independent study, internships, student-designed major, study abroad, teacher certification program. **Combined degree programs:** BA/MA, Brandeis MA ief (International Economics and Finance). **Disability Services:** Special programs offered to physically disabled students include note-taking services, reader services, tape recorders, tutors. **Career services:** Alumni network, alumni services, career/job search classes, career assessment, internships, regional alumni. Career services highlights include at least one internship funded by the college for more than half the class of 2009. This included grants of up $3,500 for what otherwise would have been unpaid internships over the summer.

FACILITIES

Housing: women's dorms, cooperative housing, apartments for single students, Wellness Housing, Theme Housing. 85% of campus accessible to physically disabled. **Special Academic Facilities/Equipment:** Clapp Library Davis Museum and Cultural Center; Harambee House; Houghton Memorial Chapel; Hunnewell Arboretum, Alexandra Botanic Gardens, and Ferguson Greenhouses; Jewett Art Museum; Keohane Sports Center; Knapp Media and Technology Center; Knapp Social Science Center; Lake Waban Pforzheimer Learning and Teaching Center; Ruth Nagel Jones Theatre; Science Center, including NMR Spectrometers; Slater International Center; Wang Campus Center; Wellesley Centers for Women; Whitin Observatory, including 3 telescopes. **Computers:** 100% of classrooms, 100% of dorms, 100% of libraries, 100% of dining areas, 100% of student union, 5% of common outdoor areas have wireless network access. Students can register for classes online. Administrative functions (other than registration) can be performed online.

CAMPUS LIFE

Environment: Town. **Activities:** Choral groups, dance, drama/theater, jazz band, literary magazine, music ensembles, radio station, student government, student newspaper, student-run film society, symphony orchestra, yearbook, Campus Ministries, International Student Organization. 160 registered organizations, 7 honor societies, 30 religious organizations. **Athletics (Intercollegiate):** *Women:* basketball, crew/rowing, cross-country, diving, fencing, field hockey, golf, lacrosse, soccer, softball, squash, swimming, tennis, track/field (outdoor), track/field (indoor), volleyball. **On-Campus Highlights:** Wang Campus Center, Davis Museum and Cultural Center, Clapp Library and Knapp Media Center, Science Center, Lake Waban.

ADMISSIONS

Freshman Academic Profile: 78% in top 10% of high school class, 97% in top 25% of high school class, 100% in top 50% of high school class. 59% from public high schools. SAT Math middle 50% range 640-740. SAT Critical Reading middle 50% range -740. SAT Writing middle 50% range 670-750. ACT middle 50% range 30-33. **Basis for Candidate Selection:** *Very important factors*

considered include: application essay, academic GPA, recommendation(s), rigor of secondary school record, standardized test scores, character/personal qualities. *Important factors considered include:* Class rank, extracurricular activities. *Other factors considered include:* alumni/ae relation, first generation, geographical residence, interview, level of applicant's interest, racial/ethnic status, state residency, talent/ability, volunteer work, work experience. **Freshman Admission Requirements:** High school diploma or equivalent is not required. High school diploma is required and GED is not accepted. **Freshman Admission Statistics:** 4,667 applied, 30% admitted, 42% enrolled. **Transfer Admission Requirements:** High school transcript, college transcript(s), essay or personal statement, interview, standardized test scores, statement of good standing from prior institution(s). Lowest grade transferable C. **General Admission Information:** Application Fee $50. Early decision application deadline 11/1. Regular application deadline 1/15. Regular notification 4/1. Nonfall registration not accepted. Admission may be deferred for a maximum of 1 year. Credit and/or placement offered for CEEB Advanced Placement tests.

COSTS AND FINANCIAL AID

Annual tuition $44,802. Room and board $13,960. Required fees $276. Average book expense $800. **Required Forms and Deadlines:** FAFSA, CSS/Financial Aid PROFILE, Noncustodial PROFILE. **Notification of Awards:** Applicants will be notified of awards on or about 4/1. **Types of Aid:** *Need-based scholarships/grants:* Federal Pell, SEOG, state scholarships/grants, private scholarships, the school's own gift aid, ACG Grant and SMART Grant. *Loans:* Direct Subsidized Stafford, Direct Unsubsidized Stafford, Direct PLUS, Federal Perkins, state loans, college/university loans from institutional funds. *Student Employment:* Federal Work-Study Program available. Institutional employment available. Off-campus job opportunities are excellent. **Financial Aid Statistics:** 96% freshmen, 97% undergrads receive need-based scholarship or grant aid. 0% freshmen, 0% undergrads receive non-need-based scholarship or grant aid. 91% freshmen, 90% undergrads receive need-based self-help aid. 0% freshmen, 0% undergrads receive athletic scholarships. 61% freshmen, 61% undergrads receive any aid. 52% undergrads borrow to pay for school. Average cumulative indebtedness $10,081.

WELLS COLLEGE

Best 380

Route 90, Aurora, NY 13026
Phone: 315-364-3264 · **Financial Aid Phone:** 315-364-3289
E-mail: admissions@wells.edu · **CEEB Code:** 2971
Fax: 315-364-3227 · **Website:** www.wells.edu · **ACT Code:** 2971

This private school was founded in 1868. It has a 365-acre campus.

RATINGS

Admissions Selectivity Rating: 86   **Fire Safety Rating:** 84

STUDENTS AND FACULTY

Enrollment: 552. **Student Body:** 71% female, 29% male, 32% out-of-state, 2% international (13 countries represented). Asian 2%, African American 6%, Caucasian 67%, Hispanic 4%, Native American 1%
Retention and Graduation: 53% freshmen graduate within 4 years. 51% freshmen graduate within 6 years. 25% grads go on to further study within 1 year. 18% grads pursue arts and sciences degrees. 4% grads pursue law degrees. 1% grads pursue business degrees. 2% grads pursue medical degrees. **Faculty:** 39 full-time faculty, 95% hold PhDs, 54% are are members of minority groups, 18% are women. 0% of classes are taught by teaching assistants.

ACADEMICS

Degrees: bachelor's. **Classes:** Most classes have 10-19 students. **Majors with Highest Enrollment:** English Language and Literature; Psychology; Molecular Biology. **Special Study Options:** Accelerated program, cross-registration, double major, English as a Second Language (ESL), independent study, internships, student-designed major, study abroad, teacher certification program, Cross registration with Cornell University, Ithaca College, and Cayuga Community College. **Combined degree programs:** BA/MBA, BA/MPH, BA/DVM, BA/M.Ed. **Disability Services:** Special programs offered to physically disabled students include tutors. **Career services:** Alumni network, alumni services, career assessment, internships, regional alumni. Career services highlights include Wells College's ability to connect our students to the real world, through the use of internships, study abroad and experiential learning makes us unlike any other.

FACILITIES

Housing: Coed dorms, women's dorms, Off campus college affiliated housing as well as an Environmental Science theme house. 58% of campus accessible to physically disabled. **Special Academic Facilities/Equipment:** Two greenhouses, environmentally regulated animal room, the college theatre (Phillips Auditorium), recital hall, electronic music studio, 15 pianos, a Dowd harpsichord, an early instrument collection, a sculpture and ceramics studio, dark rooms, painting and drawing studio, a Book Arts Center, lithography presses, an extensive art library, art gallery, general and specialized clusters for the social sciences, foreign languages, and natural and mathematical sciences. **Computers:** 10% of classrooms, 90% of dorms, 100% of libraries, 100% of student union, have wireless network access. Students can register for classes online. Administrative functions (other than registration) can be performed online.

CAMPUS LIFE

Environment: Rural. **Activities:** Choral groups, dance, drama/theater, literary magazine, music ensembles, student government, student newspaper, yearbook, Model UN. 35 registered organizations, 2 honor societies, 2 religious organizations. **Athletics (Intercollegiate):** *Men:* basketball, cross-country, golf, lacrosse, soccer, swimming. *Women:* basketball, cross-country, field hockey, golf, lacrosse, soccer, softball, swimming, tennis. **On-Campus Highlights:** Sommer Center, Boat House, Schwartz Student Union, Macmillan Hall, Main Building.

ADMISSIONS

Freshman Academic Profile: Average high school GPA 3.5. 31% in top 10% of high school class, 65% in top 25% of high school class, 91% in top 50% of high school class. 88% from public high schools. SAT Math middle 50% range 480-600. SAT Critical Reading middle 50% range 500-630. SAT Writing middle 50% range 480-590. ACT middle 50% range 22-27. Minimum paper TOEFL 550. **Basis for Candidate Selection:** *Very important factors considered include:* academic GPA, recommendation(s), rigor of secondary school record, standardized test scores, extracurricular activities. *Important factors considered include:* application essay, interview. *Other factors considered include:* Class rank, alumni/ae relation, character/personal qualities, level of applicant's interest, talent/ability, volunteer work, work experience. **Freshman Admission Requirements:** High school diploma is required and GED is accepted. **Academic units required:** 4 English, 3 mathematics, 2 science, (2 science labs), 0 foreign language, 1 social studies, 3 history, 2 academic electives. **Freshman Admission Statistics:** 1,673 applied, 71% admitted, 12% enrolled. **Transfer Admission Requirements:** High school transcript, college transcript(s), essay or personal statement, standardized test scores, statement of good standing from prior institution(s). Minimum college GPA of 2.0 required. Lowest grade transferable C-. **General Admission Information:** Application Fee $40. Early decision application deadline 12/15. Regular application deadline 3/1. Regular notification 4/1. Nonfall registration accepted. Admission may be deferred for a maximum of 12 months. Credit and/or placement offered for CEEB Advanced Placement tests.

COSTS AND FINANCIAL AID

Annual tuition $33,200. Room and board $11,900. Required fees $1,500. Average book expense $800. **Required Forms and Deadlines:** FAFSA. **Notification of Awards:** Applicants will be notified of awards on a rolling basis beginning 3/1. **Types of Aid:** *Need-based scholarships/grants:* Federal Pell, SEOG, state scholarships/grants, private scholarships, the school's own gift aid. *Loans:* Subsidized Stafford, Unsubsidized Stafford, PLUS, Federal Perkins. *Student Employment:* Federal Work-Study Program available. Institutional employment available. Highest amount earned per year from on-campus jobs $1,600. Off-campus job opportunities are poor. **Financial Aid Statistics:** 93% freshmen, 93% undergrads receive need-based scholarship or grant aid. 13% freshmen, 15% undergrads receive non-need-based scholarship or grant aid. 75% freshmen, 69% undergrads receive need-based self-help aid. 0% freshmen, 0% undergrads receive athletic scholarships. 96% freshmen, 95% undergrads receive any aid. 90% undergrads borrow to pay for school. Average cumulative indebtedness $20,523. **Criteria for awarding institutional aid:** *Non-need-based:* academics, alumni affiliation, leadership.

See page 1208.

WENTWORTH INSTITUTE OF TECHNOLOGY

550 Huntington Avenue, Boston, MA 02115-5998
Phone: 617-989-4000 · **Financial Aid Phone:** 617-989-4174
E-mail: admissions@wit.edu · **CEEB Code:** 3958
Fax: 617-989-4010 · **Website:** www.wit.edu

This private school was founded in 1904. It has a 35-acre campus.

STUDENTS AND FACULTY

Enrollment: 4,287. **Student Body:** 19% female, 81% male, 36% out-of-state, 6% international (53 countries represented). Asian 7%, African American 5%, Caucasian 61%, Hispanic 3%, Native American <1%
Retention and Graduation: 85% freshmen return for sophomore year. 50% freshmen graduate within 4 years. 17% grads go on to further study within 1 year. 11% grads pursue arts and sciences degrees. 2% grads pursue business degrees. **Faculty:** 152 full-time faculty, 56% hold PhDs, 31% are are members of minority groups, 15% are women. 0% of classes are taught by teaching assistants.

ACADEMICS

Degrees: associate, bachelor's, master's, terminal associate. **Classes:** Most classes have 20-29 students. Most lab/discussion sessions have 10-19 students. **Majors with Highest Enrollment:** Construction Management; Mechanical Engineering; Architecture. **Special Study Options:** cooperative education program, cross-registration, distance learning, study abroad, Cross registration available through the Colleges of the Fenway Consortium with member colleges: Simmons College, Emmanuel College, Wheelock College, Massachusetts College of Pharmacy and Health Sciences, Massachusetts College of Art, and Wentworth Institute of Technology. **Disability Services:** Special programs offered to physically disabled students include note-taking services, reader services, tape recorders, tutors. **Career services:** Alumni network, career/job search classes, internships. Career services highlights include WIT's co-op program, which has been active for over 30 years, and is one of the largest and most comprehensive cooperative education programs of its kind in the nation. Co-op is a requirement for all majors. 100% of WIT's co-op placements are directly related to the student's field of study.

FACILITIES

Housing: Coed dorms. 75% of campus accessible to physically disabled. **Computers:** 100% of classrooms, 100% of dorms, 100% of libraries, 100% of dining areas, have wireless network access. Students can register for classes online. Administrative functions (other than registration) can be performed online.

CAMPUS LIFE

Environment: Metropolis. **Activities:** Choral groups, dance, drama/theater, music ensembles, musical theater, radio station, student government, student newspaper, student-run film society, yearbook, International Student Organization. 50 registered organizations, 3 honor societies, 1 religous organization. **Athletics (Intercollegiate):** *Men:* baseball, basketball, golf, ice hockey, lacrosse, riflery, soccer, tennis, volleyball. *Women:* basketball, golf, riflery, soccer, softball, tennis, volleyball. **On-Campus Highlights:** 550 Huntington Ave (newest residence hall), Beatty Hall (Café, library, student activities), Computer Info Systems Networking Lab (, Tansey Gymnasium, Annex (architecture and design studios), Daily tours and info sessions, fall Open Houses, spring Special Events, see website www.wit.edu (under Prospective Students) for details. **Environmental Initiatives:** Cogeneration System; High Efficient Boilers; Lighting Upgrade.

ADMISSIONS

Freshman Academic Profile: Average high school GPA 3.05. N/A% from public high schools. SAT Math middle 50% range 530-630. SAT Critical Reading middle 50% range 480-590. SAT Writing middle 50% range 470-570. ACT middle 50% range 22-27. Minimum internet-based TOEFL 79. Minimum paper TOEFL 550. **Basis for Candidate Selection:** *Important factors considered include:* application essay, recommendation(s), rigor of secondary school record, standardized test scores. *Other factors considered include:* academic GPA, alumni/ae relation, character/personal qualities, extracurricular activities, first generation, geographical residence, level of applicant's interest, talent/ability, volunteer work, work experience. **Freshman Admission Requirements:** High school diploma is required and GED is accepted. **Academic units required:** 4 English, 3 mathematics, 2 science, (1 science labs), 0 foreign language, 1 social studies, 0 history, 0 visual/performing arts, 0 computer science, 0 academic electives, 0 3 college-preparatory math, 1 physics recommended for many programs & 4 years of mathmematics for some. **Freshman Admission Statistics:** 5,316 applied, 83% admitted, 24% enrolled. **Transfer Admission Requirements:** High school transcript, college transcript(s), essay or personal statement, Lowest grade transferable C. **General Admission Information:** Application Fee $50. Notification on a rolling basis, beginning on or about 10/30. Nonfall registration accepted. Admission may be deferred for a maximum of 12 months. Credit offered for CEEB Advanced Placement tests.

COSTS AND FINANCIAL AID

Annual tuition $29,320. Room and board $12,840. Average book expense $1,500. **Required Forms and Deadlines:** FAFSA. **Notification of Awards:** Applicants will be notified of awards on a rolling basis beginning 3/15. **Types of Aid:** *Need-based scholarships/grants:* Federal Pell, SEOG, state scholarships/grants, private scholarships, the school's own gift aid. *Loans:* Subsidized Stafford, Unsubsidized Stafford, PLUS, Federal Perkins, state loans. *Student Employment:* Federal Work-Study Program available. Institutional employment

RATINGS

Admissions Selectivity Rating: 73   **Fire Safety Rating:** 83

available. Highest amount earned per year from on-campus jobs $875. Off-campus job opportunities are good. **Financial Aid Statistics:** 86% freshmen, 79% undergrads receive need-based scholarship or grant aid. 99% freshmen, 94% undergrads receive non-need-based scholarship or grant aid. 90% freshmen, 91% undergrads receive need-based self-help aid. 0% freshmen, 0% undergrads receive athletic scholarships. 100% freshmen, 96% undergrads receive any aid. 82% undergrads borrow to pay for school. Average cumulative indebtedness $28,693. **Criteria for awarding institutional aid:** *Non-need-based:* academics, leadership, state/district residency.

See page 1210.

WESLEY COLLEGE (DE)

120 North State Street, Dover, DE 19901-3875
Phone: 302-736-2400
E-mail: admissions@wesley.edu • **CEEB Code:** 1433
Fax: 302-736-2382 • **Website:** www.wesley.eud • **ACT Code:** 636

This private school, affiliated with the Methodist Church, was founded in 1873. It has a 40-acre campus.

RATINGS

Admissions Selectivity Rating: 81   **Fire Safety Rating:** 69

STUDENTS AND FACULTY

Enrollment: 1,605. **Student Body:** 52% female, 48% male, 63% out-of-state, 1% international. Asian 2%, African American 22%, Caucasian 72%, Hispanic 3%, Native American 1%
Retention and Graduation: 82% freshmen return for sophomore year. 34% freshmen graduate within 4 years. 50% freshmen graduate within 6 years. 30% grads go on to further study within 1 year. 2% grads pursue arts and sciences degrees. 1% grads pursue law degrees. 10% grads pursue business degrees. **Faculty:** 66 full-time faculty, 79% hold PhDs, 50% are are members of minority groups, 11% are women. 0% of classes are taught by teaching assistants.

ACADEMICS

Degrees: associate, bachelor's, certificate, master's, post-bachelor's certificate. **Classes:** Most classes have 20-29 students. Most lab/discussion sessions have fewer than 10 students. **Majors with Highest Enrollment:** Psychology; Business/Commerce; Elementary Education and Teaching. **Special Study Options:** double major, honors program, independent study, internships, liberal arts/career combination, teacher certification program. **Disability Services:** Special programs offered to physically disabled students include tape recorders, tutors. **Career services:** internships.

FACILITIES

Housing: Coed dorms, men's dorms, women's dorms, apartments for single students. 80% of campus accessible to physically disabled. **Computers:** Students can register for classes online. Administrative functions (other than registration) can be performed online.

CAMPUS LIFE

Environment: Town. **Activities:** Choral groups, drama/theater, literary magazine, music ensembles, radio station, student government, student newspaper, yearbook .30 registered organizations, 2 honor societies, 2 religious organizations. 3 fraternities, 3 sororities. **Athletics (Intercollegiate):** *Men:* baseball, basketball, cheerleading, cross-country, football, golf, lacrosse, soccer, tennis. *Women:* baseball, basketball, cheerleading, cross-country, field hockey, golf, lacrosse, soccer, softball, tennis.

ADMISSIONS

Freshman Academic Profile: Average high school GPA 2.98. 24% in top 10% of high school class, 56% in top 25% of high school class, 78% in top 50% of high school class. 80% from public high schools. SAT Math middle 50% range 400-500. SAT Critical Reading middle 50% range 499-490. SAT Writing middle 50% range 390-490. Minimum paper TOEFL 550. **Basis for Candidate Selection:** *Very important factors considered include:* academic GPA. *Important factors considered include:* Class rank, rigor of secondary school record, standardized test scores. *Other factors considered include:* application essay, recommendation(s), alumni/ae relation, character/personal qualities, extracurricular activities, interview, level of applicant's interest, talent/ability, volunteer work, work experience. **Freshman Admission Requirements:** High school diploma is required and GED is accepted. **Academic units required:** 0 English, 0 mathematics, 0 science, (0 science labs), 0 foreign language, 0 social studies, 0 history, 0 academic electives. **Freshman Admission Statistics:** 2,633 applied, 76% admitted, 25% enrolled. **Transfer Admission Requirements:** High school transcript, college transcript(s), Minimum college GPA of

2.0 required. Lowest grade transferable C. **General Admission Information:** Application Fee $25. Nonfall registration accepted. Admission may be deferred for a maximum of 2 sems (1 yr). Credit and/or placement offered for CEEB Advanced Placement tests.

COSTS AND FINANCIAL AID

Annual tuition $16,750. Room and board $7,800. Required fees $829. Average book expense $1,000. **Required Forms and Deadlines:** FAFSA, Institution's own financial aid form. **Notification of Awards:** Applicants will be notified of awards on a rolling basis beginning 1/1. **Types of Aid:** *Need-based scholarships/grants:* Federal Pell, SEOG, state scholarships/grants, private scholarships. *Loans:* Direct PLUS, Subsidized Stafford, Unsubsidized Stafford, PLUS, Federal Perkins. *Student Employment:* Highest amount earned per year from on-campus jobs $2,550. **Financial Aid Statistics:** 78% freshmen, 87% undergrads receive need-based scholarship or grant aid. 46% freshmen, 50% undergrads receive non-need-based scholarship or grant aid. 100% freshmen, 100% undergrads receive need-based self-help aid. 0% freshmen, 0% undergrads receive athletic scholarships. 95% freshmen, 95% undergrads receive any aid. 93% undergrads borrow to pay for school. Average cumulative indebtedness $28,368. **Criteria for awarding institutional aid:** *Non-need-based:* academics, alumni affiliation, religious affiliation.

WESLEYAN COLLEGE

Best 380

4760 Forsyth Road, Macon, GA 31210-4462
Phone: 478-477-1110 • **Financial Aid Phone:** 478-757-5205
E-mail: admissions@wesleyancollege.edu • **CEEB Code:** 5895
Fax: 478-757-4030 • **Website:** www.wesleyancollege.edu • **ACT Code:** 876

This private school, affiliated with the Methodist Church, was founded in 1836. It has a 200-acre campus.

RATINGS

Admissions Selectivity Rating: 81   **Fire Safety Rating:** 87

STUDENTS AND FACULTY

Enrollment: 648. **Student Body:** 100% female, 0% male, 82% out-of-state, 1% international (25 countries represented). Asian 1%, African American 29%, Caucasian 41%, Hispanic 4%, Native American <1%
Retention and Graduation: 67% freshmen return for sophomore year. 46% freshmen graduate within 4 years. 48% freshmen graduate within 6 years. 32% grads go on to further study within 1 year. 6% grads pursue arts and sciences degrees. 1% grads pursue law degrees. 20% grads pursue business degrees. 4% grads pursue medical degrees. **Faculty:** 51 full-time faculty, 92% hold PhDs, 55% are are members of minority groups, 14% are women. 0% of classes are taught by teaching assistants.

ACADEMICS

Degrees: bachelor's, master's. **Classes:** Most classes have 10-19 students. **Majors with Highest Enrollment:** Business Administration, Management and Operations; International Business/Trade/Commerce; Registered Nursing/Registered Nurse. **Special Study Options:** Accelerated program, cross-registration, double major, dual enrollment, exchange student program (domestic), honors program, independent study, internships, liberal arts/career combination, student-designed major, study abroad, teacher certification program, weekend college, Dual degree engineering(3/2) with Georgia Tech, Auburn University and Mercer University. **Honors programs:** Honors Program **Combined degree programs:** 3-2 eng. prg. w/ Auburn U, Georgia Tech, Mercer. **Disability Services:** Special programs offered to physically disabled students include note-taking services, tutors. **Career services:** Alumni network, career/job search classes, career assessment, internships. Career services highlights include internships that are required for all graduating seniors.

FACILITIES

Housing: special housing for disabled students, women's dorms, apartments for single studentsStudents required to live on campus unless married or living with family in the local area. 70% of campus accessible to physically disabled. **Special Academic Facilities/Equipment:** Art and history museums, special collection of Georgiana and Americana, on-campus equestrian center. **Computers:** 80% of classrooms, 100% of libraries, 100% of dining areas, 100% of student union, 50% of common outdoor areas have wireless network access. Students can register for classes online. Administrative functions (other than registration) can be performed online.

CAMPUS LIFE

Environment: City. **Activities:** Choral groups, dance, drama/theater, literary magazine, music ensembles, student government, student newspaper, yearbook, Campus Ministries, International Student Organization, Model UN. 40 registered organizations, 10 honor societies, 5 religious organizations. **Athletics (Intercollegiate):** *Women:* basketball, cross-country, equestrian sports, soccer, softball, tennis, volleyball. **On-Campus Highlights:** Historic quad of buildings Georgian brick design, Equestrian and Fitness Centers, Lake, Residence Halls, Art Galleries. **Environmental Initiatives:** We are currently renovating one of our main teaching buildings to achieve LEED Silver Certification. We have established an Energy Star purchasing policy in accordance with the President's Climate Commitment. We have begun a campus-wide recycling program.

ADMISSIONS

Freshman Academic Profile: 0% in top 10% of high school class, 0% in top 25% of high school class, 0% in top 50% of high school class. 81% from public high schools. SAT Math middle 50% range 425-550. SAT Critical Reading middle 50% range 445-560. SAT Writing middle 50% range 440-515. ACT middle 50% range 18-23. Minimum internet-based TOEFL 80. Minimum paper TOEFL 550. **Basis for Candidate Selection:** *Very important factors considered include:* rigor of secondary school record. *Important factors considered include:* Class rank, academic GPA, recommendation(s), standardized test scores, extracurricular activities, interview, talent/ability. *Other factors considered include:* application essay, alumni/ae relation, level of applicant's interest, volunteer work, work experience. **Freshman Admission Requirements:** High school diploma is required and GED is accepted. **Academic units required:** 4 English, 3 mathematics, 3 science, (2 science labs), 2 foreign language, 3 social studies. **Freshman Admission Statistics:** 829 applied, 45% admitted, 29% enrolled. **Transfer Admission Requirements:** college transcript(s), essay or personal statement, statement of good standing from prior institution(s). Minimum college GPA of 2.5 required. Lowest grade transferable C. **General Admission Information:** Application Fee $30. Early decision application deadline 11/15. Regular application deadline 6/1. Notification on a rolling basis, beginning on or about 10/1. Nonfall registration accepted. Admission may be deferred for a maximum of 1 year. Credit and/or placement offered for CEEB Advanced Placement tests.

COSTS AND FINANCIAL AID

Annual tuition $19,750. Room and board $8,800. Required fees $150. Average book expense $2,000. **Required Forms and Deadlines:** FAFSA, Institution's own financial aid form, State aid form. **Notification of Awards:** Applicants will be notified of awards on a rolling basis beginning 3/1. **Types of Aid:** *Need-based scholarships/grants:* Federal Pell, SEOG, state scholarships/grants, private scholarships, the school's own gift aid. *Loans:* Subsidized Stafford, Unsubsidized Stafford, PLUS, Federal Perkins, state loans, college/university loans from institutional funds, CitiAssist, Wells FARGO, Collegiate Loans, Key Alternative Loans. *Student Employment:* Federal Work-Study Program available. Highest amount earned per year from on-campus jobs $1,500. Off-campus job opportunities are good. **Financial Aid Statistics:** 76% freshmen, 98% undergrads receive need-based scholarship or grant aid. 10% freshmen, 8% undergrads receive non-need-based scholarship or grant aid. 76% freshmen, 80% undergrads receive need-based self-help aid. 0% freshmen, 0% undergrads receive athletic scholarships. 100% freshmen, 95% undergrads receive any aid. 52% undergrads borrow to pay for school. Average cumulative indebtedness $30,940. **Criteria for awarding institutional aid:** *Non-need-based:* academics, alumni affiliation, art, job skills, leadership, minority status, music/drama, religious affiliation, state/district residency.

WESLEYAN UNIVERSITY

70 Wyllys Avenue, Middletown, CT 6459
Phone: 860-685-3000 · **Financial Aid Phone:** 860-685-2800
E-mail: admissions@wesleyan.edu · **CEEB Code:** 3959
Fax: 860-685-3001 · **Website:** www.wesleyan.edu · **ACT Code:** 614

This private school was founded in 1831. It has a 240-acre campus.

RATINGS

Admissions Selectivity Rating: 97	**Fire Safety Rating:** 88

STUDENTS AND FACULTY

Enrollment: 2,888. **Student Body:** 52% female, 48% male, 92% out-of-state, 8% international (46 countries represented). Asian 8%, African American 7%, Caucasian 53%, Hispanic 10%, Native American <1%

Retention and Graduation: 95% freshmen return for sophomore year. 86% freshmen graduate within 4 years. **Faculty:** 338 full-time faculty, 95% hold PhDs, 47% are are members of minority groups, 16% are women. 0% of classes are taught by teaching assistants.

ACADEMICS

Degrees: bachelor's, master's, post-master's certificate. **Classes:** Most classes have 10-19 students. Most lab/discussion sessions have 20-29 students. **Majors with Highest Enrollment:** Psychology; Economics. **Special Study Options:** cross-registration, double major, dual enrollment, exchange student program (domestic), honors program, independent study, student-designed major, study abroad. **Combined degree programs:** BA/MA. **Disability Services:** Special programs offered to physically disabled students include note-taking services, reader services, tape recorders, tutors.

FACILITIES

Housing: Coed dorms, special housing for disabled students, fraternity/sorority housing, apartments for married students, apartments for single students, Wellness Housing, Theme Housing, 14 Residence halls, 32 program houses, 139 woodframe houses. **Special Academic Facilities/Equipment:** Art center, art galleries, Center for Afro-American studies, East Asian Studies Center, Cinema Archives, concert hall, public affairs center, language lab, electron microscope, observatory, nuclear magnetic resonance spectrometers. **Computers:** 90% of classrooms, 100% of dorms, 90% of libraries, 90% of dining areas, 100% of student union, 90% of common outdoor areas have wireless network access. Students can register for classes online. Administrative functions (other than registration) can be performed online.

CAMPUS LIFE

Environment: Town. **Activities:** Choral groups, concert band, dance, drama/theater, jazz band, literary magazine, music ensembles, musical theater, pep band, radio station, student government, student newspaper, student-run film society, symphony orchestra, yearbook, Campus Ministries. 220 registered organizations, 2 honor societies, 10 religious organizations. 9 fraternities, 4 sororities. **Athletics (Intercollegiate):** *Men:* baseball, basketball, crew/rowing, cross-country, diving, football, golf, ice hockey, lacrosse, soccer, squash, swimming, tennis, track/field (outdoor), track/field (indoor), wrestling. *Women:* basketball, crew/rowing, cross-country, diving, field hockey, ice hockey, lacrosse, soccer, softball, squash, swimming, tennis, track/field (outdoor), track/field (indoor), volleyball. **On-Campus Highlights:** Center for the Arts, Freeman Athletic Center, Center for Film Studies, Olin Memorial Library, Van Vleck Observatory, Freeman East Asian Studies Center. **Environmental Initiatives:** Energy conservation activities resulting in a 28% reduction of energy consumption campus wide and the construction of 3 PV solar system with a combined output of 215 kW. Education of campus community on Wesleyan's Carbon footprint and the steps required to meet the 2020 and 2050 goals towards carbon neutrality. Campus community commitment to climate change and education of personal impact on global climate change starting with your home and office.

ADMISSIONS

Freshman Academic Profile: Average high school GPA 3.76. 67% in top 10% of high school class, 91% in top 25% of high school class, 99% in top 50% of high school class. 52% from public high schools. SAT Math middle 50% range 660-750. SAT Critical Reading middle 50% range 650-740. SAT Writing middle 50% range 660-750. ACT middle 50% range 30-33. Minimum internet-based TOEFL 100. Minimum paper TOEFL 600. **Basis for Candidate Selection:** *Very important factors considered include:* rigor of secondary school record. *Important factors considered include:* Class rank, application essay, academic GPA, recommendation(s), standardized test scores, character/personal qualities, first generation, racial/ethnic status, talent/ability. *Other factors considered include:* alumni/ae relation, extracurricular activities, geographical residence, interview, volunteer work, work experience. **Freshman Admission Requirements:** High school diploma is required and GED is accepted. **Freshman Admission Statistics:** 10,690 applied, 20% admitted, 34% enrolled. **Transfer Admission Requirements:** High school transcript, college transcript(s), essay or personal statement, standardized test scores, statement of good standing from prior institution(s). Lowest grade transferable C-. **General Admission Information:** Application Fee $55. Early decision application deadline 11/15. Regular application deadline 1/1. Regular notification 4/1. Nonfall registration not accepted. Admission may be deferred for a maximum of 1 year. Credit and/or placement offered for CEEB Advanced Placement tests.

COSTS AND FINANCIAL AID

Annual tuition $47,702. Room and board $13,226. Required fees $570. Average book expense $1,300. **Required Forms and Deadlines:** FAFSA, CSS/Financial Aid PROFILE, Noncustodial PROFILE. **Notification of Awards:** Applicants will be notified of awards on or about 4/1. **Types of Aid:** *Need-based scholarships/grants:* Federal Pell, SEOG, state scholarships/grants, private scholarships, the school's own gift aid. *Loans:* Direct Subsidized Stafford, Direct Unsubsidized Stafford, Direct PLUS, Federal Perkins, college/university loans from institutional funds. *Student Employment:* Federal Work-Study Program

The Princeton Review's Complete Book of Colleges

available. Institutional employment available. Off-campus job opportunities are good. **Financial Aid Statistics:** 93% freshmen, 94% undergrads receive need-based scholarship or grant aid. 0% freshmen, 0% undergrads receive non-need-based scholarship or grant aid. 96% freshmen, 97% undergrads receive need-based self-help aid. 0% freshmen, 0% undergrads receive athletic scholarships. 47% freshmen, 48% undergrads receive any aid. 44% undergrads borrow to pay for school. Average cumulative indebtedness $17,808. **Criteria for awarding institutional aid:** *Non-need-based:* academics.

WEST CHESTER UNIVERSITY
OF PENNSYLVANIA

Messikomer Hall, West Chester, PA 19383
Phone: 610-436-3411 · **Financial Aid Phone:** 610-436-2627
E-mail: ugadmiss@wcupa.edu · **CEEB Code:** 3328
Fax: 610-436-2907 · **Website:** www.wcupa.edu · **ACT Code:** 3750

This public school was founded in 1871. It has a 403.4-acre campus.

RATINGS

Admissions Selectivity Rating: 85   **Fire Safety Rating:** 97

STUDENTS AND FACULTY

Enrollment: 13,610. **Student Body:** 60% female, 40% male, 12% out-of-state, 0% international (82 countries represented). Asian 2%, African American 10%, Caucasian 80%, Hispanic 5%, Native American <1%
Retention and Graduation: 44% freshmen graduate within 4 years. **Faculty:** 655 full-time faculty, 85% hold PhDs, 54% are are members of minority groups, 14% are women. 0% of classes are taught by teaching assistants.

ACADEMICS

Degrees: bachelor's, master's, post-bachelor's certificate, post-master's certificate. **Classes:** Most classes have 20-29 students. **Majors with Highest Enrollment:** Liberal Arts and Sciences/Liberal Studies; Psychology; Rhetoric and Composition. **Special Study Options:** cooperative education program, cross-registration, distance learning, double major, dual enrollment, English as a Second Language (ESL), exchange student program (domestic), honors program, independent study, internships, liberal arts/career combination, student-designed major, study abroad, teacher certification program. **Honors programs:** See the Honors College section of the WCU website: http://www. wcupa.edu/honors/. **Disability Services:** Special programs offered to physically disabled students include note-taking services, reader services, tape recorders, tutors. **Career services:** Alumni network, alumni services, career/job search classes, career assessment, internships, regional alumni. Career services highlights include Student Teaching.

FACILITIES

Housing: Coed dorms, special housing for disabled students, men's dorms, special housing for international students, women's dorms, fraternity/sorority housing, apartments for single students, Wellness Housing. 95% of campus accessible to physically disabled. **Special Academic Facilities/Equipment:** McKinney Gallery, Long Gallery, Emile K. Asplundh Concert Hall, Swope Auditorium, EO Bull Main Stage, Sykes Theater, Frances Harvey Green Library, Presser Music Library, Darlington Herbarium, Geology Museum, Speech and Hearing Clinic, Philips Autograph Library, Farrell Stadium, Hollinger Fieldhouse, Schmucker Science Center, The Center for Advanced Scientific Imaging and the Materials Research Center, WCU Planetarium, WCU Observatory, Robert B. Gordon Natural Area for Environmental Studies, The Children's Center, Southeastern PA Autism Resource Center, Geography and Planning Geographic Informatino Systems Lab, Philips Auditorium, Main Hall Auditorium, Schmucker Auditorium, Boucher Lecture Hall, Center for Government and Community Affairs, The Poetry Center. **Computers:** 100% of classrooms, 20% of dorms, 100% of libraries, 100% of dining areas, 100% of student union, 100% of common outdoor areas have wireless network access. Students can register for classes online. Administrative functions (other than registration) can be performed online.

CAMPUS LIFE

Environment: Village. **Activities:** Choral groups, concert band, dance, drama/theater, jazz band, literary magazine, marching band, music ensembles, musical theater, opera, pep band, radio station, student government, student newspaper, symphony orchestra, television station, yearbook, Campus Ministries, International Student Organization. 233 registered organizations, 26 honor societies, 12 religious organizations. 12 fraternities, 13 sororities. **Athletics (Intercollegiate):** *Men:* baseball, basketball, cross-country, diving, football, golf, soccer, swimming, tennis, track/field (outdoor). *Women:* basketball, cheerleading, cross-country, diving, field hockey, golf, gymnastics, lacrosse, rugby, soccer, softball, swimming, tennis, track/field (outdoor), volleyball. **On-Campus Highlights:**

Emilie K. Asplundh Concert Hall, E.O. Bull Main Stage, Farrell Stadium, Sykes Student Union Building, Educational Center for Earth Observation Systems, Please see our website for a campus events calendar: http://www.wcupa.edu/_INFORMATION/events/. **Environmental Initiatives:** Geothermal heating and cooling is used for new residence halls and other new buildings. Also all buildings undergoing lifecycle renovations and some old existing buildings are having their HVAC systems changed out to geothermal systems. Construction of new buildings and the renovation of existing buildings are done so that they could meet LEED Silver if the necessary paper work was filed and fees paid. Sustainability is one of five themes in the University's new strategic plan.

ADMISSIONS

Freshman Academic Profile: Average high school GPA 3.51. 13% in top 10% of high school class, 39% in top 25% of high school class, 80% in top 50% of high school class. 82% from public high schools. SAT Math middle 50% range 500-580. SAT Critical Reading middle 50% range 490-570. SAT Writing middle 50% range 480-570. ACT middle 50% range 22-25. Minimum internet-based TOEFL 80. Minimum paper TOEFL 550. **Basis for Candidate Selection:** *Very important factors considered include:* Class rank, academic GPA, rigor of secondary school record. *Important factors considered include:* standardized test scores. *Other factors considered include:* application essay, character/personal qualities, extracurricular activities, racial/ethnic status, talent/ability, volunteer work, work experience. **Freshman Admission Requirements:** High school diploma is required and GED is accepted. **Academic units required:** 4 English, 3 mathematics, 2 science, (1 science labs), 2 social studies, 2 history, 1 academic elective. **Freshman Admission Statistics:** 13,291 applied, 53% admitted, 33% enrolled. **Transfer Admission Requirements:** college transcript(s), essay or personal statement, Minimum college GPA of 2.0 required. Lowest grade transferable C. **General Admission Information:** Application Fee $35. Notification on a rolling basis, beginning on or about 10/1. Nonfall registration accepted. Admission may be deferred for a maximum of Varies. Credit and/or placement offered for CEEB Advanced Placement tests.

COSTS AND FINANCIAL AID

Annual in-state tuition $6,820. Annual out-of-state tuition $17,050. Room and board $8,042. Required fees $2,324. Average book expense $1,200. **Required Forms and Deadlines:** FAFSA. **Notification of Awards:** Applicants will be notified of awards on or about 4/1. **Types of Aid:** *Need-based scholarships/grants:* Federal Pell, SEOG, state scholarships/grants, the school's own gift aid. *Loans:* Subsidized Stafford, Unsubsidized Stafford, PLUS, Federal Perkins, Federal Nursing. *Student Employment:* Federal Work-Study Program available. Institutional employment available. Off-campus job opportunities are good. **Financial Aid Statistics:** 47% freshmen, 53% undergrads receive need-based scholarship or grant aid. 22% freshmen, 14% undergrads receive non-need-based scholarship or grant aid. 86% freshmen, 88% undergrads receive need-based self-help aid. 1% freshmen, 1% undergrads receive athletic scholarships. 80% freshmen, 74% undergrads receive any aid. 74% undergrads borrow to pay for school. Average cumulative indebtedness $23,964.

WEST LIBERTY STATE COLLEGE

PO Box 295, West Liberty, WV 26074
Phone: 304-336-8076 · **Financial Aid Phone:** 304-336-8016
E-mail: wladmsn1@wlsc.edu · **CEEB Code:** 5901
Fax: 304-336-8403 · **Website:** www.wlsc.edu · **ACT Code:** 4534

This public school was founded in 1837. It has a 290-acre campus.

RATINGS

Admissions Selectivity Rating: 70   **Fire Safety Rating:** 60*

STUDENTS AND FACULTY

Enrollment: 2,305. **Student Body:** 55% female, 45% male, 28% out-of-state, 1% international. Asian 0%, African American 3%, Caucasian 95%, Hispanic 1%, Native American <1%
Retention and Graduation: 43% grads go on to further study within 1 year. 6% grads pursue arts and sciences degrees. 1% grads pursue law degrees. 1% grads pursue business degrees. 1% grads pursue medical degrees. **Faculty:** 98 full-time faculty, 45% hold PhDs, 40% are are members of minority groups, 5% are women. 0% of classes are taught by teaching assistants.

ACADEMICS

Degrees: associate, bachelor's. **Classes:** Most classes have 10-19 students. Most lab/discussion sessions have 10-19 students. **Majors with Highest Enrollment:** Elementary Education and Teaching; Criminal Justice/Safety Studies; Business/Commerce. **Special Study Options:** Accelerated program, double major, external degree program, honors program, independent study, internships, student-designed major, teacher certification program. **Honors**

programs: The goal of the Honors Program is to foster excellence through personal endeavors. These are original challenging studies, experiments, or other creative accomplishments which students wish to pursue in order to enhance their intellectual development. **Disability Services:** Special programs offered to physically disabled students include note-taking services, reader services, tape recorders, tutors.

FACILITIES
Housing: Coed dorms, men's dorms, women's dorms, apartments for married students, Honors Dorm. 90% of campus accessible to physically disabled. **Special Academic Facilities/Equipment:** Book museums, language lab, clinical lab sciences and dental hygiene labs. clinical lab sciences and dental hygiene labs.

CAMPUS LIFE
Environment: Rural. **Activities:** Choral groups, concert band, drama/theater, jazz band, literary magazine, marching band, music ensembles, musical theater, pep band, radio station, student government, student newspaper, television station. 50 registered organizations, 10 honor societies, 4 religious organizations. 5 fraternities, 4 sororities. **Athletics (Intercollegiate):** *Men:* baseball, basketball, cheerleading, cross-country, football, golf, swimming, tennis, track/field (outdoor), wrestling. *Women:* basketball, cheerleading, cross-country, golf, softball, swimming, tennis, track/field (outdoor), volleyball.

ADMISSIONS
Freshman Academic Profile: Average high school GPA 3.05. 5% in top 10% of high school class, 32% in top 25% of high school class, 58% in top 50% of high school class. 88% from public high schools. SAT Math middle 50% range 390-490. SAT Critical Reading middle 50% range 400-500. ACT middle 50% range 17-22. Minimum paper TOEFL 500. **Basis for Candidate Selection:** *Very important factors considered include:* rigor of secondary school record, standardized test scores. **Freshman Admission Requirements:** High school diploma is required and GED is accepted. **Academic units required:** 4 English, 2 mathematics, 2 science, (2 science labs), 2 social studies, 1 history. **Freshman Admission Statistics:** 1,202 applied, 98% admitted, 38% enrolled. **Transfer Admission Requirements:** college transcript(s), Minimum college GPA of 2.0 required. Lowest grade transferable D. **General Admission Information:** Notification on a rolling basis, beginning on or about 10/1. Nonfall registration accepted. Credit offered for CEEB Advanced Placement tests.

COSTS AND FINANCIAL AID
Annual in-state tuition $3,138. Annual out-of-state tuition $7,790. Room and board $4,730. Average book expense $800. **Required Forms and Deadlines:** FAFSA. **Notification of Awards:** Applicants will be notified of awards on a rolling basis beginning 2/15. **Types of Aid:** *Need-based scholarships/grants:* Federal Pell, SEOG, state scholarships/grants, private scholarships, the school's own gift aid. *Loans:* Direct Subsidized Stafford, Direct Unsubsidized Stafford, Direct PLUS, Federal Perkins, Federal Nursing. *Student Employment:* Off-campus job opportunities are good. **Financial Aid Statistics:** 78% freshmen, 63% undergrads receive need-based scholarship or grant aid. 75% freshmen, 31% undergrads receive non-need-based scholarship or grant aid. 69% freshmen, 85% undergrads receive need-based self-help aid. 0% freshmen, 0% undergrads receive athletic scholarships. 64% undergrads borrow to pay for school. **Criteria for awarding institutional aid:** *Non-need-based:* state/district residency.

WEST SUBURBAN COLLEGE OF NURSING

3 Erie Court, Oak Park, IL 60302
Phone: 708-763-6530 · **Financial Aid Phone:** 708-763-1426
E-mail: admission@wscn.edu
Fax: 708-763-1531 · **Website:** www.wscn.edu

This private school, affiliated with the Roman Catholic Church, was founded in 1914.

RATINGS
Admissions Selectivity Rating: 60*   **Fire Safety Rating:** 60*

STUDENTS AND FACULTY
Enrollment: 236. **Student Body:** 86% female, 14% male, 0% international. Asian 24%, African American 10%, Caucasian 40%, Hispanic 13%, Native American <1%
Faculty: 23 full-time faculty, 17% hold PhDs, 100% are are members of minority groups, 17% are women. 0% of classes are taught by teaching assistants.

ACADEMICS
Degrees: bachelor's, master's. **Classes:** Most classes have 10-19 students. Most lab/discussion sessions have fewer than 10 students. **Special Study Options:**

Accelerated program, WSCN offers an Evening & Weekend program. There is also a Master of Science in Nursing program, which offers four separate majors. **Career services:** alumni services, career assessment.

FACILITIES
Computers: 100% of classrooms, 100% of libraries, 100% of dining areas, have wireless network access. Students can register for classes online. Administrative functions (other than registration) can be performed online. Undergraduates are required to own a computer.

CAMPUS LIFE
Environment: Metropolis. **Activities:** student government. 2 registered organizations.

ADMISSIONS
Freshman Admission Requirements: High school diploma is required and GED is accepted. **Transfer Admission Requirements:** college transcript(s), essay or personal statement, standardized test scores, Minimum college GPA of 2.75 required. Lowest grade transferable C. **General Admission Information:** Application Fee $30. Regular application deadline 4/1. Admission may be deferred for a maximum of 1 semester.

COSTS AND FINANCIAL AID
Types of Aid: *Need-based scholarships/grants:* Federal Pell, SEOG, state scholarships/grants, private scholarships, the school's own gift aid, Federal Nursing Scholarships. *Loans:* Subsidized Stafford, Unsubsidized Stafford, PLUS, college/university loans from institutional funds. *Student Employment:* Federal Work-Study Program available. Institutional employment available. Highest amount earned per year from on-campus jobs $5,353. Off-campus job opportunities are good. **Financial Aid Statistics:** 100% undergrads receive need-based scholarship or grant aid. 18% undergrads receive non-need-based scholarship or grant aid. 79% undergrads receive need-based self-help aid. 0% undergrads receive athletic scholarships. 86% undergrads receive any aid. 86% undergrads borrow to pay for school. **Criteria for awarding institutional aid:** *Non-need-based:* academics.

WEST TEXAS A&M UNIVERSITY

PO Box 60907, Canyon, TX 79016-0001
Phone: 806-651-2020 · **Financial Aid Phone:** 806-651-2055
E-mail: admissions@mail.wtamu.edu · **CEEB Code:** 3665
Fax: 806-651-5268 · **Website:** www.wtamu.edu · **ACT Code:** 4250

This public school was founded in 1910. It has a 135-acre campus.

RATINGS
Admissions Selectivity Rating: 77   **Fire Safety Rating:** 85

STUDENTS AND FACULTY
Enrollment: 7,123. **Student Body:** 54% female, 46% male, 12% out-of-state, 2% international (37 countries represented). Asian 1%, African American 6%, Caucasian 62%, Hispanic 25%, Native American 1%
Retention and Graduation: 23% freshmen graduate within 4 years. 40% freshmen graduate within 6 years. 22% grads go on to further study within 1 year. **Faculty:** 322 full-time faculty, 67% hold PhDs, 44% are are members of minority groups, 12% are women. 4% of classes are taught by teaching assistants.

ACADEMICS
Degrees: bachelor's, diploma, master's. **Classes:** Most classes have 20-29 students. Most lab/discussion sessions have 20-29 students. **Majors with Highest Enrollment:** Multi-/Interdisciplinary Studies; Business/Commerce; Registered Nursing/Registered Nurse. **Special Study Options:** cooperative education program, distance learning, double major, English as a Second Language (ESL), honors program, independent study, internships, liberal arts/career combination, study abroad, teacher certification program. **Honors programs:** The Honors Program at West Texas AandM University is committed to providing exceptional students with challenging academic studies, innovative approaches to instruction; increased opportunities for improving skills in critical thinking, research, developing creative works and writing; expanded cultural knowledge; and the opportunity to interact closely with faculty and similarly motivated students. **Combined degree programs:** BBA/MPA. **Disability Services:** Special programs offered to physically disabled students include note-taking services, reader services, tape recorders, tutors. **Career services:** Alumni network, alumni services, career/job search classes, career assessment, internships, regional alumni.

The Princeton Review's Complete Book of Colleges

FACILITIES

Housing: Coed dorms, special housing for disabled students, men's dorms, women's dorms, fraternity/sorority housing, Honors Program. 100% of campus accessible to physically disabled. **Special Academic Facilities/Equipment:** Regional History Museum, Research Center, Panhandle Plains Historical Museum, Killgore Research Center. **Computers:** Students can register for classes online. Administrative functions (other than registration) can be performed online.

CAMPUS LIFE

Environment: Village. **Activities:** Choral groups, concert band, dance, drama/theater, jazz band, literary magazine, marching band, music ensembles, musical theater, opera, radio station, student government, student newspaper, symphony orchestra, Campus Ministries, International Student Organization. 110 registered organizations, 15 honor societies, 13 religious organizations. 5 fraternities, 5 sororities. **Athletics (Intercollegiate): Men:** baseball, basketball, cross-country, football, golf, soccer. *Women:* basketball, cheerleading, cross-country, equestrian sports, golf, soccer, softball, volleyball. **On-Campus Highlights:** Panhandle-Plains Historical Museum, Jack B. Kelley Student Center, Virgil Henson Activities Center, Old Main (first building built on campus), WTAMU Horse Center, Panhandle-Plains Historical Museum is the largest historical museum in the State of Texas.

ADMISSIONS

Freshman Academic Profile: 15% in top 10% of high school class, 39% in top 25% of high school class, 75% in top 50% of high school class. 97% from public high schools. SAT Math middle 50% range 440-550. SAT Critical Reading middle 50% range 420-530. ACT middle 50% range 18-23. Minimum internet-based TOEFL 190. Minimum paper TOEFL 520. **Basis for Candidate Selection:** *Very important factors considered include:* Class rank, academic GPA, standardized test scores. *Important factors considered include:* rigor of secondary school record. *Other factors considered include:* recommendation(s). **Freshman Admission Requirements:** High school diploma is required and GED is accepted. **Academic units required:** 4 English, 3 mathematics, 3 science. **Freshman Admission Statistics:** 5,234 applied, 67% admitted, 38% enrolled. **Transfer Admission Requirements:** college transcript(s), Minimum college GPA of 2.0 required. Lowest grade transferable C. **General Admission Information:** Application Fee $25. Notification on a rolling basis, beginning on or about 9/1. Nonfall registration accepted. Admission may be deferred for a maximum of 1 term. Credit offered for CEEB Advanced Placement tests.

COSTS AND FINANCIAL AID

Annual in-state tuition $5,022. Annual out-of-state tuition $6,533. Room and board $7,196. Required fees $1,242. Average book expense $1,000. **Required Forms and Deadlines:** FAFSA. **Notification of Awards:** Applicants will be notified of awards on a rolling basis beginning 2/1. **Types of Aid:** *Need-based scholarships/grants:* Federal Pell, SEOG, state scholarships/grants, private scholarships, the school's own gift aid. *Loans:* Subsidized Stafford, Unsubsidized Stafford, PLUS, Federal Perkins, state loans. *Student Employment:* Highest amount earned per year from on-campus jobs $5,850. **Financial Aid Statistics:** 80% freshmen, 76% undergrads receive need-based scholarship or grant aid. 49% freshmen, 36% undergrads receive non-need-based scholarship or grant aid. 90% freshmen, 92% undergrads receive need-based self-help aid. 7% freshmen, 6% undergrads receive athletic scholarships. 52% freshmen, 53% undergrads receive any aid. 86% undergrads borrow to pay for school. Average cumulative indebtedness $21,787. **Criteria for awarding institutional aid:** *Non-need-based:* academics, art, athletics, leadership, music/drama, state/district residency.

WEST VIRGINIA STATE UNIVERSITY

106 Ferrell Hall, Institute, WV 25112
Phone: 304-766-3033 · **Financial Aid Phone:** 304-766-3131
E-mail: admissions@wvstateu.edu · **CEEB Code:** 5903
Fax: 304-766-5182 · **Website:** www.wvstateu.edu · **ACT Code:** 4538

This public school was founded in 1891. It has a 95-acre campus.

RATINGS

Admissions Selectivity Rating: 60*   **Fire Safety Rating:** 60*

STUDENTS AND FACULTY

Enrollment: 3,455. **Student Body:** 59% female, 41% male, 8% out-of-state, 0% international (8 countries represented). Asian 1%, African American 15%, Caucasian 81%, Hispanic 1%, Native American <1%
Retention and Graduation: 6% grads go on to further study within 1 year. 3% grads pursue arts and sciences degrees. 1% grads pursue law degrees. 1% grads pursue business degrees. 1% grads pursue medical degrees.

ACADEMICS

Degrees: bachelor's, master's. **Majors with Highest Enrollment:** Elementary Education and Teaching; General Studies; Business Administration and Management. **Special Study Options:** cooperative education program, off-campus study: Washington, DC. **Disability Services:** Special programs offered to physically disabled students include tutors.

FACILITIES

Housing: Coed dorms, men's dorms, women's dorms, apartments for married students. **Special Academic Facilities/Equipment:** On-campus day-care center, art gallery, ROTC Hall of Fame, Sports Hall of Fame.

CAMPUS LIFE

Environment: Village. **Activities:** Choral groups, concert band, jazz band, literary magazine, marching band, music ensembles, radio station, student government, student newspaper, television station, yearbook 4 honor societies, 2 religious organizations. 6 fraternities, 3 sororities. **Athletics (Intercollegiate):** *Men:* baseball, basketball, cross-country, football, softball, tennis, track/field (outdoor), volleyball. *Women:* basketball, cross-country, softball, tennis, track/field (outdoor), volleyball.

ADMISSIONS

Freshman Academic Profile: 99% from public high schools. **Freshman Admission Requirements:** High school diploma is required and GED is accepted. High school diploma is required and GED is not accepted. **Academic units required:** 4 English, 2 mathematics, 2 science, 2 foreign language, 3 social studies, 1 history. **Transfer Admission Requirements:** college transcript(s), Minimum college GPA of 2.0 required. Lowest grade transferable D. **General Admission Information:** Regular application deadline 8/22. Nonfall registration accepted. Credit and/or placement offered for CEEB Advanced Placement tests.

COSTS AND FINANCIAL AID

Average book expense $500. **Required Forms and Deadlines:** FAFSA, Institution's own financial aid form. **Types of Aid:** *Loans:* Subsidized Stafford, PLUS. *Student Employment:* Highest amount earned per year from on-campus jobs $1,300. **Financial Aid Statistics:**

WEST VIRGINIA UNIVERSITY

Best 380

Admissions Office, Morgantown, WV 26506-6009
Phone: 304-293-2121 · **Financial Aid Phone:** 304-293-5242
E-mail: go2wvu@mail.wvu.edu · **CEEB Code:** 5904
Fax: 304-293-3080 · **Website:** www.wvu.edu · **ACT Code:** 4540

This public school was founded in 1867.

RATINGS

Admissions Selectivity Rating: 79   **Fire Safety Rating:** 98

STUDENTS AND FACULTY

Enrollment: 21,945. **Student Body:** 45% female, 55% male, 48% out-of-state, 5% international (83 countries represented). Asian 2%, African American 5%, Caucasian 81%, Hispanic 4%, Native American <1%
Retention and Graduation: 77% freshmen return for sophomore year. 33% freshmen graduate within 4 years. 57% freshmen graduate within 6 years. **Faculty:** 1,078 full-time faculty, 85% hold PhDs, 42% are are members of minority groups, 17% are women.

ACADEMICS

Degrees: bachelor's, master's. **Classes:** Most classes have 20-29 students. Most lab/discussion sessions have 20-29 students. **Majors with Highest Enrollment:** Engineering; Health Professions and Related Clinical Sciences; Business Administration, Management and Operations. **Special Study Options:** Accelerated program, cooperative education program, distance learning, double major, English as a Second Language (ESL), exchange student program (domestic), external degree program, honors program, independent study, internships, student-designed major, study abroad, teacher certification program, weekend college. **Honors programs:** Honors Leadership Academy **Combined degree programs:** BA/MA, BA/MA in Ed., BSBAd/BA Lang, BA/MOT, BA/MPT, MPA/BSW. **Disability Services:** Special programs offered to physically disabled students include note-taking services, reader services, tape recorders, tutors. **Career services:** Alumni network, alumni services, career/job search classes, career assessment, internships.

FACILITIES

Housing: Coed dorms, special housing for disabled students, men's dorms, special housing for international students, women's dorms, fraternity/sorority housing, apartments for married students, cooperative housing, apartments for single students, (Special interest "floors" available, Operation Jump Start places faculty residence hall leaders adjacent to residence halls allowing frequent opportunities for faculty-student interaction outside classroom. This program mandatory for freshmen). 90% of campus accessible to physically disabled. **Special Academic Facilities/Equipment:** Art galleries, creative arts center, arboretum, herbarium, planetarium, concurrent engineering research center, discovery lab (for inventors), Appalachian hardwood center, small business development center, pharmacy museum, coal and energy museum, center for economic research, fluidization center, center for software development. **Computers:** 80% of classrooms, 75% of dorms, 100% of libraries, 40% of dining areas, 100% of student union, 10% of common outdoor areas have wireless network access. Students can register for classes online. Administrative functions (other than registration) can be performed online.

CAMPUS LIFE

Environment: Town. **Activities:** Choral groups, concert band, dance, drama/theater, jazz band, literary magazine, marching band, music ensembles, musical theater, pep band, radio station, student government, student newspaper, symphony orchestra, television station, yearbook, Campus Ministries, International Student Organization. 370 registered organizations, 31 honor societies, 28 religious organizations. 14 fraternities, 9 sororities. **Athletics (Intercollegiate):** *Men:* baseball, basketball, diving, football, riflery, soccer, swimming, wrestling. *Women:* basketball, crew/rowing, cross-country, diving, gymnastics, riflery, soccer, swimming, tennis, track/field (outdoor), track/field (indoor), volleyball. **On-Campus Highlights:** New State of the Art Student Recreation Center, Mountainlair (Student Union), Personal Rapid Transit (PRT), Mountaineer Field, Historic Woodburn Circle, Core Arboretum. **Environmental Initiatives:** 1. Energy performance management and emissions reduction through a performance contract (approx. $30 million) between WVU and Siemens Inc. 2. Dining: Trayless dining in four dining halls, cage free shell eggs served in all dining halls, and food donations to local charities. 3. Alt. Transportation offerings such as car-sharing (Zipcar), carpool (Zimride), Vanpool (VSNI), occasional parking program, Mountain Line Bus, and PRT.

ADMISSIONS

Freshman Academic Profile: Average high school GPA 3.42. 19% in top 10% of high school class, 44% in top 25% of high school class, 79% in top 50% of high school class. SAT Math middle 50% range 480-580. SAT Critical Reading middle 50% range 460-560. ACT middle 50% range 21-26. Minimum internet-based TOEFL 61. Minimum paper TOEFL 550. **Basis for Candidate Selection:** *Very important factors considered include:* academic GPA, standardized test scores. *Important factors considered:* rigor of secondary school record, level of applicant's interest, state residency. *Other factors considered include:* recommendation(s), extracurricular activities, talent/ability, volunteer work. **Freshman Admission Requirements:** High school diploma is required and GED is accepted. **Academic units required:** 4 English, 4 mathematics, 3 science, (3 science labs), 2 foreign language, 3 social studies, 1 visual/performing arts. **Freshman Admission Statistics:** 15,604 applied, 86% admitted, 36% enrolled. **Transfer Admission Requirements:** college transcript(s), Minimum college GPA of 2.0 required. Lowest grade transferable D. **General Admission Information:** Application Fee $25. Regular application deadline 8/1. Notification on a rolling basis, beginning on or about 10/1. Nonfall registration accepted. Admission may be deferred for a maximum of 1 year. Credit and/or placement offered for CEEB Advanced Placement tests.

COSTS AND FINANCIAL AID

Annual in-state tuition $6,960. Annual out-of-state tuition $20,424. Room and board $9,582. Average book expense $1,100. **Required Forms and Deadlines:** FAFSA, State aid form. **Notification of Awards:** Applicants will be notified of awards on a rolling basis beginning 3/15. **Types of Aid:** *Need-based scholarships/grants:* Federal Pell, SEOG, state scholarships/grants, private scholarships, the school's own gift aid. *Loans:* Direct Subsidized Stafford, Direct Unsubsidized Stafford, Direct PLUS, Federal Perkins, college/university loans from institutional funds. *Student Employment:* Federal Work-Study Program available. Institutional employment available. Highest amount earned per year from on-campus jobs $2,500. Off-campus job opportunities are good. **Financial Aid Statistics:** 53% freshmen, 99% undergrads receive need-based scholarship or grant aid. 74% freshmen, 78% undergrads receive non-need-based scholarship or grant aid. 53% freshmen, 75% undergrads receive need-based self-help aid. 1% freshmen, 1% undergrads receive athletic scholarships. 72% freshmen, 75% undergrads receive any aid. 47% undergrads borrow to pay for school. Average cumulative indebtedness $22,139. **Criteria for awarding institutional aid:** *Non-need-based:* academics, alumni affiliation, art, athletics, job skills, leadership, minority status, music/drama, state/district residency.

WEST VIRGINIA UNIVERSITY INSTITUTE OF TECHNOLOGY

Box 10 Old Main, Montgomery, WV 25136
Phone: 304-442-3167
E-mail: admissions@wvutech.edu
Fax: 304-442-3097 • **Website:** www.wvutech.edu

This is a public school.

RATINGS

Admissions Selectivity Rating: 74   **Fire Safety Rating:** 60*

STUDENTS AND FACULTY

Enrollment: 2,001. **Student Body:** 39% female, 61% male, 6% out-of-state, 4% international. Asian 1%, African American 8%, Caucasian 87%, Hispanic 1%, Native American <1%
Retention and Graduation: 62% freshmen return for sophomore year. **Faculty:** 119 full-time faculty, 47% hold PhDs, 28% are are members of minority groups, 18% are women.

ACADEMICS

Degrees: associate, bachelor's, certificate, master's. **Classes:** Most classes have 10-19 students. Most lab/discussion sessions have 20-29 students. **Special Study Options:** cooperative education program, distance learning, double major, dual enrollment, internships, student-designed major.

FACILITIES

Housing: Coed dorms, men's dorms, women's dorms, fraternity/sorority housing.

CAMPUS LIFE

Activities: Choral groups, concert band, drama/theater, jazz band, marching band, music ensembles, pep band, student government, student newspaper.

ADMISSIONS

Freshman Academic Profile: Average high school GPA 3.16. 20% in top 10% of high school class, 21% in top 25% of high school class, 43% in top 50% of high school class. 88% from public high schools. SAT Math middle 50% range 400-580. SAT Critical Reading middle 50% range 380-530. ACT middle 50% range 17-23. Minimum paper TOEFL 500. **Basis for Candidate Selection:** *Very important factors considered include:* rigor of secondary school record, standardized test scores. *Other factors considered include:* Class rank, recommendation(s), alumni/ae relation, character/personal qualities, extracurricular activities, interview, state residency, talent/ability, volunteer work. **Freshman Admission Requirements:** High school diploma is required and GED is accepted. **Academic units required:** 4 English, 2 mathematics, 2 science, (2 science labs), 3 social studies. **Freshman Admission Statistics:** 1,191 applied, 74% admitted, 47% enrolled. **Transfer Admission Requirements:** college transcript(s), Minimum college GPA of 1.7 required. Lowest grade transferable D. **General Admission Information:** Notification on a rolling basis, beginning on or about 9/30. Nonfall registration accepted. Admission may be deferred for a maximum of 1 semester. Credit offered for CEEB Advanced Placement tests.

COSTS AND FINANCIAL AID

Annual in-state tuition $3,200. Annual out-of-state tuition $8,400. Room and board $4,896. Required fees $0. Average book expense $800. **Required Forms and Deadlines:** FAFSA, Institution's own financial aid form. **Notification of Awards:** Applicants will be notified of awards on a rolling basis beginning 3/3. **Types of Aid:** *Need-based scholarships/grants:* Federal Pell, SEOG, state scholarships/grants, private scholarships, the school's own gift aid. *Loans:* Direct Subsidized Stafford, Direct Unsubsidized Stafford, Direct PLUS, Subsidized Stafford, Unsubsidized Stafford, PLUS, Federal Perkins. **Financial Aid Statistics:** 78% freshmen, 78% undergrads receive need-based scholarship or grant aid. 70% freshmen, 48% undergrads receive non-need-based scholarship or grant aid. 59% freshmen, 69% undergrads receive need-based self-help aid. 2% freshmen, 6% undergrads receive athletic scholarships. 47% undergrads borrow to pay for school. Average cumulative indebtedness $14,057. **Criteria for awarding institutional aid:** *Non-need-based:* academics, alumni affiliation, art, athletics, music/drama.

WEST VIRGINIA WESLEYAN COLLEGE

59 College Avenue, Buckhannon, WV 26201
Phone: 304-473-8510 · **Financial Aid Phone:** 304-473-8080
E-mail: admission@wwc.edu · **CEEB Code:** 5905
Fax: 304-473-8108 · **Website:** www.wwc.edu · **ACT Code:** 4544

This private school, affiliated with the Methodist Church, was founded in 1890. It has a 120-acre campus.

RATINGS

Admissions Selectivity Rating: 83   **Fire Safety Rating:** 60*

STUDENTS AND FACULTY

Enrollment: 1,375. **Student Body:** 54% female, 46% male, 38% out-of-state, 5% international (13 countries represented). Asian 0%, African American 9%, Caucasian 80%, Hispanic 2%, Native American <1%
Retention and Graduation: 73% freshmen return for sophomore year. 44% freshmen graduate within 4 years. 35% grads go on to further study within 1 year. 57% grads pursue arts and sciences degrees. 11% grads pursue law degrees. 16% grads pursue business degrees. 6% grads pursue medical degrees. **Faculty:** 89 full-time faculty, 72% hold PhDs, 61% are are members of minority groups, 6% are women. 0% of classes are taught by teaching assistants.

ACADEMICS

Degrees: bachelor's, master's. **Classes:** Most classes have 10-19 students. Most lab/discussion sessions have 10-19 students. **Majors with Highest Enrollment:** Biology/Biological Sciences; Elementary Education and Teaching; Business Administration and Management. **Special Study Options:** double major, English as a Second Language (ESL), exchange student program (domestic), honors program, independent study, internships, liberal arts/career combination, student-designed major, study abroad, teacher certification program. **Honors programs:** The Honors Program is offered to recognize and challenge the College's most academically talented students. Participation is voluntary for all qualified students. **Combined degree programs:** BA/MA. **Disability Services:** Special programs offered to physically disabled students include note-taking services, reader services, tape recorders, tutors. **Career services:** Alumni network, alumni services, career/job search classes, internships.

FACILITIES

Housing: Coed dorms, special housing for disabled students, men's dorms, women's dorms, fraternity/sorority housing. **Computers:** Students can register for classes online. Undergraduates are required to own a computer.

CAMPUS LIFE

Environment: Village. **Activities:** Choral groups, dance, drama/theater, jazz band, literary magazine, music ensembles, musical theater, opera, radio station, student government, student newspaper, yearbook, Campus Ministries, International Student Organization. 75 registered organizations, 31 honor societies, 6 religious organizations. 6 fraternities, 5 sororities. **Athletics (Intercollegiate):** *Men:* baseball, basketball, cross-country, football, golf, soccer, softball, swimming, tennis, track/field (outdoor), track/field (indoor). *Women:* basketball, cross-country, golf, lacrosse, soccer, swimming, tennis, track/field (outdoor), track/field (indoor), volleyball. **On-Campus Highlights:** Cat's Claw (alternate dining facility), Sunny Bucks (Convenience Store), Wesley Chapel, Sleeth Art Gallery, Atkinson Theatre.

ADMISSIONS

Freshman Academic Profile: Average high school GPA 3.49. 27% in top 10% of high school class, 56% in top 25% of high school class, 85% in top 50% of high school class. 88% from public high schools. SAT Math middle 50% range 430-533. SAT Critical Reading middle 50% range 430-530. SAT Writing middle 50% range 418-520. ACT middle 50% range 19-25. Minimum paper TOEFL 500. **Basis for Candidate Selection:** *Very important factors considered include:* rigor of secondary school record. *Important factors considered include:* Class rank, academic GPA, standardized test scores, alumni/ae relation, character/personal qualities, extracurricular activities, first generation, interview, level of applicant's interest, talent/ability, volunteer work. *Other factors considered include:* application essay, recommendation(s), geographical residence, religious affiliation/commitment, state residency, work experience. **Freshman Admission Requirements:** High school diploma is required and GED is accepted. **Freshman Admission Statistics:** 1,789 applied, 78% admitted, 30% enrolled. **Transfer Admission Requirements:** High school transcript, college transcript(s), statement of good standing from prior institution(s). Minimum college GPA of 2.50 required. Lowest grade transferable C-. **General Admission Information:** Application Fee $35. Notification on a rolling basis, beginning on or about 9/15. Nonfall registration accepted. Admission may be deferred for a maximum of 1 year. Credit offered for CEEB Advanced Placement tests.

COSTS AND FINANCIAL AID

Annual tuition $27,614. Room and board $8,066. Required fees $1,378. Average book expense $2,500. **Required Forms and Deadlines:** FAFSA. **Types of Aid:** *Need-based scholarships/grants:* ACG and SMART Grants. *Student Employment:* Federal Work-Study Program available. Institutional employment available. Highest amount earned per year from on-campus jobs $1,000. Off-campus job opportunities are fair. **Financial Aid Statistics:** 70% freshmen, 70% undergrads receive need-based scholarship or grant aid. 19% freshmen, 21% undergrads receive non-need-based scholarship or grant aid. 71% freshmen, 81% undergrads receive need-based self-help aid. 4% freshmen, 8% undergrads receive athletic scholarships. 99% freshmen, 98% undergrads receive any aid. 71% undergrads borrow to pay for school. Average cumulative indebtedness $26,713.

See page 1212.

WESTERN CAROLINA UNIVERSITY

102 Camp Building, Cullowhee, NC 28723
Phone: 828-227-7317 · **Financial Aid Phone:** 828-227-7290
E-mail: admiss@email.wcu.edu · **CEEB Code:** 5897
Fax: 828-227-7319 · **Website:** www.wcu.edu · **ACT Code:** 3172

This public school was founded in 1889. It has a 682-acre campus.

RATINGS

Admissions Selectivity Rating: 86   **Fire Safety Rating:** 90

STUDENTS AND FACULTY

Enrollment: 7,796. **Student Body:** 53% female, 47% male, 7% out-of-state, 1% international (28 countries represented). Asian 1%, African American 7%, Caucasian 83%, Hispanic 3%, Native American 1%
Retention and Graduation: 28% freshmen graduate within 4 years. **Faculty:** 478 full-time faculty, 75% hold PhDs, 47% are are members of minority groups, 5% are women. 1.3% of classes are taught by teaching assistants.

ACADEMICS

Degrees: bachelor's, master's, post-bachelor's certificate, post-master's certificate. **Classes:** Most classes have 20-29 students. Most lab/discussion sessions have 10-19 students. **Majors with Highest Enrollment:** Registered Nursing/Registered Nurse; Criminal Justice/Safety Studies; Junior High/Intermediate/Middle School Education and Teaching. **Special Study Options:** cooperative education program, distance learning, double major, dual enrollment, English as a Second Language (ESL), exchange student program (domestic), honors program, independent study, internships, student-designed major, study abroad, teacher certification program. **Honors programs:** Western has a residential Honors College designed to enhance the academic and social university experience for high-achieving students. The college consists of honors courses throughout liberal studies with an emphasis on special projects and undergraduate research in the major. Also, special housing, academic, leadership and social programs are available for honors students. **Disability Services:** Special programs offered to physically disabled students include note-taking services, reader services, tape recorders, tutors. **Career services:** Alumni network, alumni services, career assessment, internships. Career services highlights include Co-op and internship experiences that are very common among WCU students. Some departments require them for degree completion. Intern and co-op opportunities are available domestically and internationally.

FACILITIES

Housing: Coed dorms, special housing for disabled students, men's dorms, women's dorms, fraternity/sorority housing, apartments for married students, Wellness Housing, Theme Housing. 89% of campus accessible to physically disabled. **Special Academic Facilities/Equipment:** Fine Arts Gallery, Mountain Heritage Center, Reading Center, North Carolina Center for the Advancement of Teaching, Speech/Hearing Center, Center for Applied Technology, CATA Lab (high technology computer lab), Fine and Performing Arts Center, Institute for the Economy and the Future, Public Policy Institute. **Computers:** 90% of classrooms, 10% of dorms, 100% of libraries, 70% of dining areas, 100% of student union, 50% of common outdoor areas have wireless network access. Students can register for classes online. Administrative functions (other than registration) can be performed online. Undergraduates are required to own a computer.

CAMPUS LIFE

Environment: Rural. **Activities:** Choral groups, concert band, dance, drama/theater, jazz band, literary magazine, marching band, music ensembles, musical theater, pep band, radio station, student government, student newspaper, student-run film society, television station, Campus Ministries, International Student Organization, Model UN. 103 registered organizations, 7 honor societies, 12 religious organizations. 11 fraternities, 8 sororities. **Athletics (Intercollegiate):** *Men:* baseball, basketball, cheerleading, cross-country, football, golf, track/field (outdoor), track/field (indoor). *Women:* basketball, cheerleading, cross-country, golf, soccer, softball, tennis, track/field (outdoor), track/field (indoor), volleyball. **On-Campus Highlights:** University Center, Campus Recreation Center, Hunter Library, Fine & Performing Arts Center, Ramsey Regional Activity Center, Courtyard Dining Hall is a new facility that opened in summer 2009. It provides students with the following options: All-you-can-eat, foodcourt with 4 restaurants, McAlisters Deli, Starbucks, and a C-store. **Environmental Initiatives:** Currently have two buildings under construction that will be LEED certified and completed in 2012. Continuing the development of our Carbon Paw Print program. Our largest efforts this year are Sustainability Council, Recyclmania 2012, Campus Conservation Nationals Energy Competition 2012, Earth and Wellness Celebration and the Wild and Scenic Film Festival. In 2010-11 we achieved a 32% btu/sq ft. reduction in energy consumption using 2002-03 as the baseline year.

ADMISSIONS

Freshman Academic Profile: Average high school GPA 3.63. 12.7% in top 10% of high school class, 38.8% in top 25% of high school class, 78.1% in top 50% of high school class. SAT Math middle 50% range 480-570. SAT Critical Reading middle 50% range 460-560. SAT Writing middle 50% range 440-530. ACT middle 50% range 20-24. Minimum internet-based TOEFL 79. Minimum paper TOEFL 550. **Basis for Candidate Selection:** *Very important factors considered include:* academic GPA, rigor of secondary school record, standardized test scores, level of applicant's interest, talent/ability. *Important factors considered include:* Class rank, application essay, recommendation(s), character/personal qualities, extracurricular activities, volunteer work, work experience. *Other factors considered include:* alumni/ae relation, first generation, geographical residence, interview, state residency. **Freshman Admission Requirements:** High school diploma is required and GED is accepted. **Academic units required:** 4 English, 4 mathematics, 3 science, (3 science labs), 2 foreign language, 2 social studies, 1 history, 4 academic electives. **Freshman Admission Statistics:** 15,234 applied, 38% admitted, 27% enrolled. **Transfer Admission Requirements:** college transcript(s), statement of good standing from prior institution(s). Minimum college GPA of 2.0 required. Lowest grade transferable C. **General Admission Information:** Application Fee $45. Regular application deadline 3/1. Notification on a rolling basis, beginning on or about 1/15. Nonfall registration accepted. Credit and/or placement offered for CEEB Advanced Placement tests.

COSTS AND FINANCIAL AID

Annual in-state tuition $3,397. Annual out-of-state tuition $12,994. Room and board $6,932. Required fees $2,528. Average book expense $758. **Required Forms and Deadlines:** FAFSA, Institution's own financial aid form. **Notification of Awards:** Applicants will be notified of awards on a rolling basis beginning 4/1. **Types of Aid:** *Need-based scholarships/grants:* Federal Pell, SEOG, state scholarships/grants, private scholarships, the school's own gift aid. *Loans:* Direct Subsidized Stafford, Direct Unsubsidized Stafford, Direct PLUS, Subsidized Stafford, Unsubsidized Stafford, PLUS, Federal Perkins. *Student Employment:* Federal Work-Study Program available. Institutional employment available. Off-campus job opportunities are fair. **Financial Aid Statistics:** 97% freshmen, 95% undergrads receive need-based scholarship or grant aid. 3% freshmen, 3% undergrads receive non-need-based scholarship or grant aid. 72% freshmen, 76% undergrads receive need-based self-help aid. 5% freshmen, 4% undergrads receive athletic scholarships. **Criteria for awarding institutional aid:** *Non-need-based:* academics, art, athletics, leadership, music/drama, state/district residency.

WESTERN CONNECTICUT STATE UNIVERSITY

Undergraduate Admissions Office, Danbury, CT 06810-6855
Phone: 203-837-9000 · **Financial Aid Phone:** 203-837-8588
E-mail: admissions@wcsu.edu · **CEEB Code:** 3350
Fax: 203-837-8338 · **Website:** www.wcsu.edu · **ACT Code:** 558

This public school was founded in 1903. It has a 364-acre campus.

RATINGS

Admissions Selectivity Rating: 75   **Fire Safety Rating:** 86

STUDENTS AND FACULTY

Enrollment: 5,467. **Student Body:** 55% female, 45% male, 8% out-of-state, 0% international (7 countries represented). Asian 3%, African American 8%, Caucasian 73%, Hispanic 12%, Native American <1%.
Retention and Graduation: 72% freshmen return for sophomore year. 16% freshmen graduate within 4 years. 23% grads go on to further study within 1

year. 10% grads pursue arts and sciences degrees. 2% grads pursue law degrees. 3% grads pursue business degrees. 1% grads pursue medical degrees. **Faculty:** 226 full-time faculty, 84% hold PhDs, 51% are are members of minority groups, 13% are women. 0% of classes are taught by teaching assistants.

ACADEMICS

Degrees: associate, bachelor's, certificate, master's. **Classes:** Most classes have 20-29 students. Most lab/discussion sessions have 20-29 students. **Majors with Highest Enrollment:** Elementary Education and Teaching; Criminal Justice/Police Science; Registered Nursing/Registered Nurse. **Special Study Options:** cooperative education program, cross-registration, distance learning, double major, dual enrollment, English as a Second Language (ESL), honors program, independent study, internships, student-designed major, study abroad, teacher certification program. **Honors programs:** University Scholars Program. **Disability Services:** Special programs offered to physically disabled students include note-taking services, reader services, tape recorders, tutors. **Career services:** career/job search classes, career assessment, internships. Career services highlights include Career assessment that utilizes career software, "SIG13", which assesses career interests; maintains an extensive career library which offers a large collection of literature on career fields, job search, company profiles, and graduate/professional school information; and hosts a major Career Fair each year.

FACILITIES

Housing: Coed dorms, women's dorms, apartments for single students, On campus housing assigned on a first-come, first-served basis. 100% of campus accessible to physically disabled. **Special Academic Facilities/Equipment:** Language lab, observatory, electron microscope, nature preserve, computer-enhanced classrooms, business library, Jane Goodall Institute. **Computers:** 50% of classrooms, 80% of dorms, 100% of libraries, 100% of dining areas, 100% of student union, have wireless network access. Students can register for classes online. Administrative functions (other than registration) can be performed online.

CAMPUS LIFE

Environment: City. **Activities:** Choral groups, concert band, dance, drama/theater, jazz band, literary magazine, music ensembles, musical theater, opera, pep band, radio station, student government, student newspaper, symphony orchestra, yearbook, Campus Ministries, International Student Organization. 40 registered organizations, 8 honor societies, 3 religious organizations. 3 fraternities, 4 sororities. **Athletics (Intercollegiate):** *Men:* baseball, basketball, football, lacrosse, soccer, tennis. *Women:* basketball, field hockey, lacrosse, soccer, softball, swimming, tennis, volleyball. **On-Campus Highlights:** Student Centers (Midtown and Westside), O'Neill Center, Science Building, White Hall, Ancell Classroom Building. **Environmental Initiatives:** Think Green: Go Blue recycling efforts (with distribution campus wide of an instruction brochure); Building Automation; Controls monitoring.

ADMISSIONS

Freshman Academic Profile: Average high school GPA 2.79. 5% in top 10% of high school class, 20% in top 25% of high school class, 61% in top 50% of high school class. 91% from public high schools. SAT Math middle 50% range 450-540. SAT Critical Reading middle 50% range 450-540. Minimum internet-based TOEFL 79. Minimum paper TOEFL 550. **Basis for Candidate Selection:** *Very important factors considered include:* rigor of secondary school record, standardized test scores, talent/ability. *Important factors considered include:* Class rank, extracurricular activities. *Other factors considered include:* application essay, recommendation(s), alumni/ae relation, character/personal qualities, interview, racial/ethnic status, state residency, volunteer work, work experience. **Freshman Admission Requirements:** High school diploma is required and GED is accepted. **Academic units required:** 4 English, 3 mathematics, 2 science, (2 science labs), 2 foreign language, 1 social studies, 1 history. **Freshman Admission Statistics:** 4,157 applied, 62% admitted, 34% enrolled. **Transfer Admission Requirements:** college transcript(s), Minimum college GPA of 2.0 required. Lowest grade transferable C-. **General Admission Information:** Application Fee $50. Notification on a rolling basis, beginning on or about 12/1. Nonfall registration accepted. Admission may be deferred for a maximum of 1 year. Credit offered for CEEB Advanced Placement tests.

COSTS AND FINANCIAL AID

Required Forms and Deadlines: FAFSA, Institution's own financial aid form. **Notification of Awards:** Applicants will be notified of awards on a rolling basis beginning 4/15. **Types of Aid:** *Need-based scholarships/grants:* Federal Pell, SEOG, state scholarships/grants, private scholarships, the school's own gift aid. *Loans:* Direct Subsidized Stafford, Direct Unsubsidized Stafford, Direct PLUS, Subsidized Stafford, Unsubsidized Stafford, PLUS, Federal Perkins. *Student Employment:* Highest amount earned per year from on-campus jobs $1,500. Off-campus job opportunities are excellent. **Financial Aid Statistics:** 87% freshmen, 86% undergrads receive need-based scholarship or grant aid. 19% freshmen, 14% undergrads receive non-need-based scholarship or grant aid. 82% freshmen, 84% undergrads receive need-based self-help aid. 0% freshmen, 0% undergrads receive athletic scholarships. 63% freshmen, 61%

undergrads receive any aid. 66% undergrads borrow to pay for school. Average cumulative indebtedness $20,984. **Criteria for awarding institutional aid:** *Non-need-based:* academics.

WESTERN ILLINOIS UNIVERSITY

1 University Circle, Macomb, IL 61455-1390
Phone: 309-298-3157 · **Financial Aid Phone:** 309-298-2446
E-mail: admissions@wiu.edu · **CEEB Code:** 1900
Fax: 309-298-3111 · **Website:** http://www.wiu.edu · **ACT Code:** 1158

This public school was founded in 1899. It has a 1050-acre campus.

RATINGS

Admissions Selectivity Rating: 74   **Fire Safety Rating:** 82

STUDENTS AND FACULTY

Enrollment: 9,645. **Student Body:** 49% female, 51% male, 12% out-of-state, 2% international (57 countries represented). Asian 1%, African American 19%, Caucasian 63%, Hispanic 9%, Native American <1%
Retention and Graduation: 30% freshmen graduate within 4 years. 19% grads go on to further study within 1 year. 12% grads pursue arts and sciences degrees. 1% grads pursue law degrees. 6% grads pursue business degrees. 1% grads pursue medical degrees. **Faculty:** 633 full-time faculty, 72% hold PhDs, 45% are are members of minority groups, 17% are women. 5% of classes are taught by teaching assistants.

ACADEMICS

Degrees: bachelor's, doctoral, master's, post-bachelor's certificate. **Classes:** Most classes have 20-29 students. Most lab/discussion sessions have 10-19 students. **Majors with Highest Enrollment:** Criminal Justice/Law Enforcement Administration; Biology/Biological Sciences; Psychology. **Special Study Options:** distance learning, double major, dual enrollment, English as a Second Language (ESL), external degree program, honors program, independent study, internships, student-designed major, study abroad, teacher certification program, weekend college. **Honors programs:** Illinois Centennial Honors College. **Disability Services:** Special programs offered to physically disabled students include note-taking services, reader services, tape recorders, tutors.

FACILITIES

Housing: Coed dorms, men's dorms, special housing for international students, women's dorms, fraternity/sorority housing, apartments for married students, Wellness Housing. 95% of campus accessible to physically disabled. **Special Academic Facilities/Equipment:** Art gallery, electron microscope **Computers:** 100% of classrooms, 100% of dorms, 100% of libraries, 100% of dining areas, 100% of student union, 100% of common outdoor areas have wireless network access. Students can register for classes online. Administrative functions (other than registration) can be performed online.

CAMPUS LIFE

Environment: Village. **Activities:** Choral groups, concert band, dance, drama/theater, jazz band, marching band, music ensembles, musical theater, pep band, radio station, student government, student newspaper, symphony orchestra, television station, yearbook, Campus Ministries, International Student Organization. 200 registered organizations, 25 honor societies, 12 religious organizations. 14 fraternities, 11 sororities. **Athletics (Intercollegiate):** *Men:* baseball, basketball, cross-country, diving, football, golf, soccer, swimming, tennis, track/field (outdoor), track/field (indoor). *Women:* basketball, cheerleading, cross-country, diving, golf, soccer, softball, swimming, tennis, track/field (outdoor), track/field (indoor), volleyball. **On-Campus Highlights:** University Union, Student Recreation Center, Leslie Malpass Library. **Environmental Initiatives:** n the last year Western has received two Illinois Clean Energy Community Foundation grants for energy efficient lighting upgrades. The most recent award of $59,262 is for an energy-efficient lighting upgrade in Morgan Hall consisting of retrofitting existing fluorescent lighting fixtures with high efficiency electronic ballasts and lamps that use 35 percent less energy than the original 35-year-old equipment. The University recently completed work from a previous Clean Energy Foundation grant to upgrade the lighting in Stipes Hall. The $83,680 project grant is projected to save nearly $15,000 a year in energy costs due to more efficient lighting Western students have been involved in campus beautification through the Litter Patrol, the Adopt-a-Street Program and the We Care Program to keep the campus and community clean and attractive.

ADMISSIONS

Freshman Academic Profile: Average high school GPA 3.15. 9% in top 10% of high school class, 28% in top 25% of high school class, 63% in top 50% of high school class. 90% from public high schools. ACT middle 50% range 18-23. Minimum internet-based TOEFL 79. Minimum paper TOEFL 550. **Basis**

for Candidate Selection: *Very important factors considered include:* Class rank, academic GPA, rigor of secondary school record, standardized test scores. **Freshman Admission Requirements:** High school diploma is required and GED is accepted. **Freshman Admission Statistics:** 10,671 applied, 70% admitted, 21% enrolled. **Transfer Admission Requirements:** college transcript(s), Minimum college GPA of 2.0 required. Lowest grade transferable D. **General Admission Information:** Application Fee $30. Regular application deadline 5/15. Nonfall registration accepted. Admission may be deferred for a maximum of none. Credit offered for CEEB Advanced Placement tests.

COSTS AND FINANCIAL AID

Annual in-state tuition $8,812. Annual out-of-state tuition $12,018. Room and board $8,820. Required fees $2,431. Average book expense $1,200. **Required Forms and Deadlines:** FAFSA. **Notification of Awards:** Applicants will be notified of awards on a rolling basis beginning 1/15. **Types of Aid:** *Need-based scholarships/grants:* Federal Pell, SEOG, state scholarships/grants, private scholarships, the school's own gift aid. *Loans:* Subsidized Stafford, Unsubsidized Stafford, PLUS, Federal Perkins, college/university loans from institutional funds. *Student Employment:* Federal Work-Study Program available. Institutional employment available. Highest amount earned per year from on-campus jobs $6,500. Off-campus job opportunities are fair. **Financial Aid Statistics:** 89% freshmen, 80% undergrads receive need-based scholarship or grant aid. 0% freshmen, 0% undergrads receive non-need-based scholarship or grant aid. 92% freshmen, 92% undergrads receive need-based self-help aid. 3% freshmen, 4% undergrads receive athletic scholarships. 92% freshmen, 87% undergrads receive any aid. 80% undergrads borrow to pay for school. Average cumulative indebtedness $24,363. **Criteria for awarding institutional aid:** *Non-need-based:* academics, alumni affiliation, art, athletics, leadership, minority status, music/drama.

WESTERN KENTUCKY UNIVERSITY

Potter Hall 117, Bowling Green, KY 42101-1020
Phone: 270-745-2551 · **Financial Aid Phone:** 270-745-2755
E-mail: admission@wku.edu · **CEEB Code:** 1901
Fax: 270-745-6133 · **Website:** www.wku.edu · **ACT Code:** 1562

This public school was founded in 1906. It has a 235-acre campus.

RATINGS

Admissions Selectivity Rating: 76   **Fire Safety Rating:** 98

STUDENTS AND FACULTY

Enrollment: 15,388. **Student Body:** 56% female, 44% male, 18% out-of-state, 6% international (79 countries represented). Asian 1%, African American 10%, Caucasian 76%, Hispanic 3%, Native American <1%
Retention and Graduation: 27% freshmen graduate within 4 years. 50% freshmen graduate within 6 years. **Faculty:** 776 full-time faculty, 75% hold PhDs, 51% are are members of minority groups, 18% are women. 0.56% of classes are taught by teaching assistants.

ACADEMICS

Degrees: associate, bachelor's, certificate, master's, post-bachelor's certificate, post-master's certificate. **Classes:** Most classes have 20-29 students. Most lab/discussion sessions have 10-19 students. **Majors with Highest Enrollment:** Registered Nursing/Registered Nurse; Elementary Education and Teaching; Biology/Biological Sciences. **Special Study Options:** cooperative education program, distance learning, double major, dual enrollment, English as a Second Language (ESL), exchange student program (domestic), honors program, independent study, internships, study abroad, teacher certification program, Gatton Academy of Math and Science, Learning Communities/Block Scheduling, Honors College, American Democracy Project. **Honors programs:** University Honors College Gatton Academy of Mathematics and Science. **Disability Services:** Special programs offered to physically disabled students include note-taking services, reader services, tape recorders, tutors. **Career services:** Alumni network, alumni services, career/job search classes, career assessment, internships.

FACILITIES

Housing: Coed dorms, men's dorms, special housing for international students, women's dorms, fraternity/sorority housing, Theme Housing, Gatton Academy, Learning Communities, Themed Living options—Fit,Honors, Mosiac Communities. **Special Academic Facilities/Equipment:** Kentucky Museum, University Farm, Hardin Planetarium, Media and Technology Hall **Computers:** 100% of classrooms, 68% of dorms, 100% of libraries, 100% of dining areas, 100% of student union, have wireless network access. Students can register for classes online. Administrative functions (other than registration) can be performed online.

CAMPUS LIFE

Environment: Town. **Activities:** Choral groups, concert band, dance, drama/ theater, jazz band, literary magazine, marching band, music ensembles, musical theater, opera, pep band, radio station, student government, student newspaper, student-run film society, symphony orchestra, television station, yearbook, Campus Ministries, International Student Organization. 360 registered organizations, 28 honor societies, 23 religious organizations. 18 fraternities, 13 sororities. **Athletics (Intercollegiate): Men:** baseball, basketball, cross-country, diving, football, golf, riflery, swimming, tennis, track/field (outdoor), track/field (indoor). **Women:** basketball, cross-country, diving, golf, riflery, soccer, swimming, tennis, track/field (outdoor), track/field (indoor), volleyball. **On-Campus Highlights:** Downing University Center, Preston Health and Activities Center, E.A. Diddle Arena and L.T. Smith Stadium, Mass Media and Technology Hall, Guthrie Tower, Please visit www.wku.edu/tour.html for further information and an interactive tour of the university. **Environmental Initiatives:** Sustainability-oriented staff positions and Sustainability Committee, Education for Sustainability resolution adopted 2010, Sustainability in operations, services, and academics included in 2010-2012 University Strategic Plan. Creation of comprehensive Energy Policy that guides purchasing, building operation, building design and construction, transportation, and personal energy use more responsibly. Commitment to LEED guidelines for all new building and renovation.

ADMISSIONS

Freshman Academic Profile: Average high school GPA 3.26. 24.7% in top 10% of high school class, 48% in top 25% of high school class, 75.4% in top 50% of high school class. SAT Math middle 50% range 440-570. SAT Critical Reading middle 50% range 440-560. ACT middle 50% range 19-26. Minimum internet-based TOEFL 71. Minimum paper TOEFL 525. **Basis for Candidate Selection:** *Very important factors considered include:* academic GPA, standardized test scores. **Freshman Admission Requirements:** High school diploma is required and GED is accepted. **Academic units required:** 4 English, 3 mathematics, 3 science, (1 science labs), 2 foreign language, 3 social studies, 1 1/2 credits each: Health and PE, History, Performing Arts. **Freshman Admission Statistics:** 8,462 applied, 93% admitted, 40% enrolled. **Transfer Admission Requirements:** college transcript(s), statement of good standing from prior institution(s). Minimum college GPA of 2.0 required. Lowest grade transferable D°. **General Admission Information:** Application Fee $40. Regular application deadline 8/1. Nonfall registration accepted. Admission may be deferred for a maximum of N/A. Credit and/or placement offered for CEEB Advanced Placement tests.

COSTS AND FINANCIAL AID

Annual in-state tuition $9,140. Annual out-of-state tuition $23,352. Room and board $7,171. Average book expense $1,000. **Required Forms and Deadlines:** FAFSA. **Notification of Awards:** Applicants will be notified of awards on a rolling basis beginning 3/1. **Types of Aid:** *Need-based scholarships/grants:* Federal Pell, SEOG, state scholarships/grants, private scholarships, the school's own gift aid, United Negro College Fund. *Loans:* Subsidized Stafford, Unsubsidized Stafford, PLUS, Federal Perkins, Alternative private loans, Federal Parent Plus *Student Employment:* Federal Work-Study Program available. Institutional employment available. Off-campus job opportunities are good. **Financial Aid Statistics:** 63% freshmen, 67% undergrads receive need-based scholarship or grant aid. 86% freshmen, 63% undergrads receive non-need-based scholarship or grant aid. 67% freshmen, 74% undergrads receive need-based self-help aid. 3% freshmen, 3% undergrads receive athletic scholarships. 91% freshmen, 87% undergrads receive any aid. 62% undergrads borrow to pay for school. Average cumulative indebtedness $25,580. **Criteria for awarding institutional aid:** *Non-need-based:* academics, alumni affiliation, art, athletics, job skills, leadership, minority status, music/drama, religious affiliation, state/ district residency.

WESTERN MICHIGAN UNIVERSITY

1903 W. Michigan Avenue, Kalamazoo, MI 49008-5211
Phone: 269-387-2000 · **Financial Aid Phone:** 269-387-6000
E-mail: ask-wmu@wmich.edu · **CEEB Code:** 1902
Fax: 269-387-2096 · **Website:** http://www.wmich.edu · **ACT Code:** 2066

This public school was founded in 1903. It has a 1200-acre campus.

RATINGS

Admissions Selectivity Rating: 74   Fire Safety Rating: 79

STUDENTS AND FACULTY

Enrollment: 18,450. **Student Body:** 50% female, 50% male, 7% out-of-state, 3% international (57 countries represented). Asian 2%, African American 12%, Caucasian 73%, Hispanic 5%, Native American <1%

Retention and Graduation: 23% freshmen graduate within 4 years. **Faculty:** 934 full-time faculty, 79% hold PhDs, 43% are are members of minority groups, 16% are women. 12.5% of classes are taught by teaching assistants.

ACADEMICS

Degrees: bachelor's, master's, post-bachelor's certificate, post-master's certificate. **Classes:** Most classes have 20-29 students. Most lab/discussion sessions have 20-29 students. **Majors with Highest Enrollment:** Multi-/Interdisciplinary Studies; Health and Medical Administrative Services; Business Administration and Management. **Special Study Options:** Accelerated program, cross-registration, distance learning, double major, dual enrollment, English as a Second Language (ESL), exchange student program (domestic), honors program, independent study, internships, student-designed major, study abroad, teacher certification program. **Honors programs:** The Lee Honors College The mission of the Carl and Winifred Lee Honors College is to provide a lively, rigorous undergraduate program for bright, highly motivated, and active students. **Combined degree programs:** BA/MA, BA/MEng, Computer; Music. **Disability Services:** Special programs offered to physically disabled students include note-taking services, reader services, tape recorders, tutors. **Career services:** Alumni network, alumni services, career/job search classes, career assessment, internships, regional alumni.

FACILITIES

Housing: Coed dorms, special housing for disabled students, men's dorms, special housing for international students, women's dorms, fraternity/sorority housing, apartments for married students, apartments for single students, Wellness Housing, Theme HousingEach hall has a special thematic concept that is developed through programming and student involvment. Examples are: Community Service, Honors, Arts and Athletics, First Year Initiative, Upper Class Students, Diversity. 85% of campus accessible to physically disabled. **Special Academic Facilities/Equipment:** Pilot plant for manufacturing and printing of paper and for fiber recovery, behavior research and development center, nuclear accelerator, center for electron microscopy, particle accelerator lab, Library Department of Special Collections: Cistercian and Monastic Studies Collections, Medieval Studies Collections , Carol Ann Haenicke American Women's Poetry Collection, Nineteenth and Twentieth Century Literature and History Collection, Book Arts Collections: Paper and Fine Printing; Aviation **Computers:** 100% of classrooms, 25% of dorms, 100% of libraries, 100% of dining areas, 100% of student union, 100% of common outdoor areas have wireless network access. Students can register for classes online. Administrative functions (other than registration) can be performed online.

CAMPUS LIFE

Environment: City. **Activities:** Choral groups, concert band, dance, drama/ theater, jazz band, literary magazine, marching band, music ensembles, musical theater, opera, pep band, radio station, student government, student newspaper, student-run film society, symphony orchestra, Campus Ministries, International Student Organization. 300 registered organizations, 7 honor societies, 21 religious organizations. 16 fraternities, 11 sororities. **Athletics (Intercollegiate): Men:** baseball, basketball, football, ice hockey, soccer, tennis. **Women:** basketball, cross-country, golf, gymnastics, soccer, softball, tennis, track/field (outdoor), track/field (indoor), volleyball. **On-Campus Highlights:** Bernhard Center, Waldo Library, University Recreation Center, Miller Auditorium, Gilmore Theatre Complex, Lawson Ice Arena and Gabel Natatorium provide swimming and skating facilities including lessons and family activities. **Environmental Initiatives:** Strategic Planning for Sustainability Climate Action Plan (2012); University Strategic Plan Implementation utilizing the Sustainability Tracking, Assessment, and Rating System program as an overarching framework for evaluation; Sustainability Across Research & Teaching Survey, Luncheon Series, and Faculty Learning Community; Humanities Center Climate Change Study Group and lecture series; creation of a 7000 square foot Office for Sustainability building hosting several 2012 events; Office for Sustainability website upgrade (www.wmich.edu/sustainability and http://www.youtube.com/user/ WMUSustainability); Student Engagement—$75,000 Student Sustainability Grants Program funded by a Student Sustainability Fee (decisions made totally by students); a Sustainability Intern Program with 20-30 interns/yr.; the Campus Beet (student run café initiative), a bike co-op initiative, and a student farm initiative among many other student-led initiatives and research projects; 2012 National Campus Sustainability event coinciding with Annual Sustainability Speaker Series speaker, the Planetwalker, Dr. John Francis; hosted Sustainabili-BASH, an annual end of year celebration of campus and community sustainability efforts. Sustainable Operations—WMU has the most extensive electric vehicle infrastructure on campuses nationwide, including five battery electric work vans, a 50kW photovoltaic array and 21 EV charging stations; a deep green building programming study; numerous other initiatives involve GHG reduction, green cleaning, water reduction, comprehensive storm water management (no net discharge), xeriscaping, waste reduction, green building, waste oil to mowers, and purchasing.

ADMISSIONS

Freshman Academic Profile: Average high school GPA 3.35. 12% in top 10% of high school class, 33% in top 25% of high school class, 72% in top 50% of high school class. ACT middle 50% range 19-25. Minimum internet-based TOEFL 80. Minimum paper TOEFL 550. **Basis for Candidate Selection:** *Very important factors considered include:* academic GPA. *Important factors considered include:* rigor of secondary school record, standardized test scores. *Other factors considered include:* application essay, recommendation(s). **Freshman Admission Requirements:** High school diploma is required and GED is accepted. **Academic units required:** 4 English, 3 mathematics, 2 science, (1 science labs), 0 foreign language, 2 social studies, 1 history, 2 academic electives. **Freshman Admission Statistics:** 14,008 applied, 84% admitted, 26% enrolled. **Transfer Admission Requirements:** college transcript(s), Minimum college GPA of 2.0 required. Lowest grade transferable C. **General Admission Information:** Application Fee $35. Regular application deadline 8/1. Notification on a rolling basis, beginning on or about 7/1. Nonfall registration accepted. Admission may be deferred for a maximum of 1 semester. Credit and/or placement offered for CEEB Advanced Placement tests.

COSTS AND FINANCIAL AID

Annual out-of-state tuition $24,026. Room and board $8,943. Required fees $1,191. Average book expense $918. **Required Forms and Deadlines:** FAFSA. **Notification of Awards:** Applicants will be notified of awards on a rolling basis beginning 3/15. **Types of Aid:** *Need-based scholarships/grants:* Federal Pell, SEOG, state scholarships/grants, private scholarships, the school's own gift aid. *Loans:* Direct Subsidized Stafford, Direct Unsubsidized Stafford, Direct PLUS, Federal Perkins, Alternative Loans. *Student Employment:* Federal Work-Study Program available. Institutional employment available. Highest amount earned per year from on-campus jobs $5,000. Off-campus job opportunities are excellent. **Financial Aid Statistics:** 69% freshmen, 69% undergrads receive need-based scholarship or grant aid. 62% freshmen, 37% undergrads receive non-need-based scholarship or grant aid. 98% freshmen, 93% undergrads receive need-based self-help aid. 2% freshmen, 2% undergrads receive athletic scholarships. 83% freshmen, 84% undergrads receive any aid. 64% undergrads borrow to pay for school. Average cumulative indebtedness $26,916. **Criteria for awarding institutional aid:** *Non-need-based:* academics, alumni affiliation, art, athletics, minority status, music/drama, state/district residency.

WESTERN NEW ENGLAND UNIVERSITY

Admissions Office, Springfield, MA 1119
Phone: 413-782-1321 • **Financial Aid Phone:** 413-796-2080
E-mail: learn@wne.edu • **CEEB Code:** 3962
Fax: 413-782-1777 • **ACT Code:** 1930

This private school was founded in 1919. It has a 215-acre campus.

RATINGS

Admissions Selectivity Rating: 81   **Fire Safety Rating:** 66

STUDENTS AND FACULTY

Enrollment: 2,648. **Student Body:** 39% female, 61% male, 53% out-of-state, 2% international (22 countries represented). Asian 3%, African American 5%, Caucasian 77%, Hispanic 8%, Native American <1%
Retention and Graduation: 74% freshmen return for sophomore year. 52% freshmen graduate within 4 years. 59% freshmen graduate within 6 years. **Faculty:** 221 full-time faculty, 90% hold PhDs, 42% are are members of minority groups, 12% are women. 0% of classes are taught by teaching assistants.

ACADEMICS

Degrees: bachelor's, certificate, master's, terminal associate. **Classes:** Most classes have 20-29 students. Most lab/discussion sessions have 10-19 students. **Majors with Highest Enrollment:** Mechanical Engineering; Accounting; Psychology. **Special Study Options:** Accelerated program, cross-registration, distance learning, double major, dual enrollment, exchange student program (domestic), honors program, independent study, internships, liberal arts/career combination, student-designed major, study abroad, teacher certification program, 3+3 law program with Western New England College School of Law. Washington Semester Program. 5 Yr BSBS/MBA and Engr/MBA. 6 Yr BSBE/Law and 6 Yr BiomedEngr/Law. 5 yr BSEM/MSEM. **Honors programs:** The Honors Program at Western New England College gives academically qualified and motivated students the opportunity to join a community of like students and participate in challenging courses taught by some of the College's best faculty. Honors students generally take one honors course per semester for their first three years and work on a senior honors project during their final year. **Combined degree programs:** BA/JD. **Disability Services:** Special programs offered to physically disabled students include note-taking services, reader

services, tape recorders, tutors. **Career services:** Alumni network, career assessment, internships.

FACILITIES

Housing: Coed dorms, special housing for disabled students, apartments for single students. 90% of campus accessible to physically disabled. **Special Academic Facilities/Equipment:** Art Gallery; Math, Writing, Science Centers. **Computers:** Students can register for classes online. Administrative functions (other than registration) can be performed online.

CAMPUS LIFE

Environment: City. **Activities:** Choral groups, concert band, dance, drama/theater, jazz band, literary magazine, music ensembles, pep band, radio station, student government, student newspaper, yearbook, Campus Ministries, International Student Organization. 60 registered organizations, 8 honor societies. **Athletics (Intercollegiate):** *Men:* baseball, basketball, cross-country, football, golf, ice hockey, lacrosse, soccer, tennis, wrestling. *Women:* basketball, cross-country, field hockey, lacrosse, soccer, softball, swimming, tennis, volleyball. **On-Campus Highlights:** Alumni Healthful Living Center, St Germain Campus Center, D'Amour Library, Computer Labs, Rock Café.

ADMISSIONS

Freshman Academic Profile: Average high school GPA 3.32. 17% in top 10% of high school class, 44% in top 25% of high school class, 74% in top 50% of high school class. SAT Math middle 50% range 490-610. SAT Critical Reading middle 50% range 470-570. ACT middle 50% range 22-26. Minimum internet-based TOEFL 79. Minimum paper TOEFL 550. **Basis for Candidate Selection:** *Very important factors considered include:* academic GPA, recommendation(s), standardized test scores. *Other factors considered include:* Class rank, application essay, rigor of secondary school record, alumni/ae relation, character/personal qualities, extracurricular activities, interview, level of applicant's interest, racial/ethnic status, talent/ability, volunteer work, work experience. **Freshman Admission Requirements:** High school diploma is required and GED is accepted. **Academic units required:** 4 English, 2 mathematics, 1 science, (1 science labs), 0 foreign language, 1 social studies, 1 history. **Freshman Admission Statistics:** 5,988 applied, 82% admitted, 14% enrolled. **Transfer Admission Requirements:** High school transcript, college transcript(s), Minimum college GPA of 2.3 required. Lowest grade transferable C-. **General Admission Information:** Application Fee $50. Notification on a rolling basis, beginning on or about 12/1. Nonfall registration accepted. Admission may be deferred for a maximum of 12 months. Credit and/or placement offered for CEEB Advanced Placement tests.

COSTS AND FINANCIAL AID

Annual tuition $30,780. Room and board $12,570. Required fees $2,240. Average book expense $1,240. **Required Forms and Deadlines:** FAFSA. **Notification of Awards:** Applicants will be notified of awards on a rolling basis beginning 3/15. **Types of Aid:** *Need-based scholarships/grants:* Federal Pell, SEOG, state scholarships/grants, private scholarships, the school's own gift aid, ACG, Smart Grants. *Loans:* Direct Subsidized Stafford, Direct Unsubsidized Stafford, Direct PLUS, PLUS, Federal Perkins, state loans, Private loan programs. *Student Employment:* Federal Work-Study Program available. Institutional employment available. Off-campus job opportunities are good. **Financial Aid Statistics:** 100% freshmen, 100% undergrads receive need-based scholarship or grant aid. 7% freshmen, 6% undergrads receive non-need-based scholarship or grant aid. 88% freshmen, 90% undergrads receive need-based self-help aid. 0% freshmen, 0% undergrads receive athletic scholarships. 97% freshmen, 93% undergrads receive any aid. **Criteria for awarding institutional aid:** *Non-need-based:* academics.

WESTERN OREGON UNIVERSITY

345 N Monmouth Avenue, Monmouth, OR 97361
Phone: 503-838-8211 • **Financial Aid Phone:** 877-877-1593
E-mail: wolfgram@wou.edu • **CEEB Code:** 4585
Fax: 503-838-8067 • **Website:** www.wou.edu • **ACT Code:** 3480

This public school was founded in 1856. It has a 157-acre campus.

RATINGS

Admissions Selectivity Rating: 70   **Fire Safety Rating:** 91

STUDENTS AND FACULTY

Enrollment: 4,820. **Student Body:** 58% female, 42% male, 21% out-of-state, 6% international (19 countries represented). Asian 4%, African American 4%, Caucasian 67%, Hispanic 8%, Native American 2%
Retention and Graduation: 70% freshmen return for sophomore year. 22% freshmen graduate within 4 years. **Faculty:** 296 full-time faculty, 61% hold

PhDs, 52% are are members of minority groups. 0% of classes are taught by teaching assistants.

ACADEMICS
Degrees: associate, bachelor's, master's, post-bachelor's certificate. **Classes:** Most classes have 10-19 students. Most lab/discussion sessions have 20-29 students. **Majors with Highest Enrollment:** Teacher Education, Multiple Levels; Social Sciences; Business/Commerce. **Special Study Options:** distance learning, double major, dual enrollment, English as a Second Language (ESL), honors program, independent study, internships, study abroad, teacher certification program. **Honors programs:** WOU Honors Program. **Disability Services:** Special programs offered to physically disabled students include note-taking services, reader services, tape recorders, tutors. **Career services:** career/job search classes, internships.

FACILITIES
Housing: Coed dorms, special housing for disabled students, apartments for married students, apartments for single students. 95% of campus accessible to physically disabled. **Special Academic Facilities/Equipment:** Jensen Arctic Museum **Computers:** 70% of classrooms, 90% of dorms, 100% of libraries, 90% of dining areas, 90% of student union, 20% of common outdoor areas have wireless network access. Students can register for classes online. Administrative functions (other than registration) can be performed online.

CAMPUS LIFE
Environment: Village. **Activities:** Choral groups, concert band, dance, drama/theater, jazz band, literary magazine, music ensembles, musical theater, student government, student newspaper, symphony orchestra, Campus Ministries, International Student Organization. 50 registered organizations, 4 honor societies, 6 religious organizations. **Athletics (Intercollegiate):** *Men:* baseball, basketball, cheerleading, cross-country, football, track/field (outdoor). *Women:* basketball, cheerleading, cross-country, soccer, softball, track/field (outdoor), volleyball. **On-Campus Highlights:** Wayne and Lynn Hamersly Library, Neal Werner University Center, Paul Jensen Arctic Museum, Campbell Hall Art Gallery, Arbor Park Apartments. **Environmental Initiatives:** paper recyling.

ADMISSIONS
Freshman Academic Profile: Average high school GPA 3.2. 0% in top 10% of high school class, 5% in top 25% of high school class, 29% in top 50% of high school class. 95% from public high schools. SAT Math middle 50% range 430-580. SAT Critical Reading middle 50% range 430-600. SAT Writing middle 50% range 420-560. Minimum paper TOEFL 500. **Basis for Candidate Selection:** *Very important factors considered include:* academic GPA, rigor of secondary school record, standardized test scores. *Important factors considered include:* Class rank. *Other factors considered include:* recommendation(s), alumni/ae relation, racial/ethnic status, talent/ability. **Freshman Admission Requirements:** High school diploma is required and GED is accepted. **Academic units required:** 4 English, 3 mathematics, 2 science, 2 foreign language, 2 social studies, 1 history. **Freshman Admission Statistics:** 2,887 applied, 89% admitted, 34% enrolled. **Transfer Admission Requirements:** college transcript(s), Minimum college GPA of 2.0 required. Lowest grade transferable D-. **General Admission Information:** Application Fee $50. Notification on a rolling basis, beginning on or about 1/1. Nonfall registration accepted. Admission may be deferred for a maximum of 0. Credit and/or placement offered for CEEB Advanced Placement tests.

COSTS AND FINANCIAL AID
Annual in-state tuition $8,723. Annual out-of-state tuition $22,257. Room and board $8,816. Average book expense $1,650. **Required Forms and Deadlines:** FAFSA. **Notification of Awards:** Applicants will be notified of awards on a rolling basis beginning 2/28. **Types of Aid:** *Need-based scholarships/grants:* Federal Pell, SEOG, state scholarships/grants, private scholarships, the school's own gift aid. *Loans:* Direct Subsidized Stafford, Direct Unsubsidized Stafford, Direct PLUS, Federal Perkins, college/university loans from institutional funds. *Student Employment:* Federal Work-Study Program available. Highest amount earned per year from on-campus jobs $5,000. Off-campus job opportunities are good. **Financial Aid Statistics:** 52% freshmen, 78% undergrads receive need-based scholarship or grant aid. 5% freshmen, 2% undergrads receive non-need-based scholarship or grant aid. 78% freshmen, 80% undergrads receive need-based self-help aid. 2% freshmen, 2% undergrads receive athletic scholarships. 65% freshmen, 58% undergrads receive any aid. 68% undergrads borrow to pay for school. Average cumulative indebtedness $26,817. **Criteria for awarding institutional aid:** *Non-need-based:* academics, alumni affiliation, art, athletics, leadership, music/drama.

WESTERN STATE COLORADO UNIVERSITY

600 N. Adams, Gunnison, CO 81231
Phone: 970-943-2119 • **Financial Aid Phone:** 970-943-3085
E-mail: admissions@western.edu • **CEEB Code:** 4946
Fax: 970-943-2363 • **Website:** www.western.edu • **ACT Code:** 536

This public school was founded in 1911. It has a 228-acre campus.

RATINGS
Admissions Selectivity Rating: 69   **Fire Safety Rating:** 84

STUDENTS AND FACULTY
Enrollment: 1,938. **Student Body:** 40% female, 60% male, 1% international (7 countries represented). Asian 1%, African American 3%, Caucasian 75%, Hispanic 9%, Native American <1%
Retention and Graduation: 19% freshmen graduate within 4 years. 37% freshmen graduate within 6 years. 15% grads go on to further study within 1 year. **Faculty:** 115 full-time faculty, 80% hold PhDs, 41% are are members of minority groups, 8% are women. 0% of classes are taught by teaching assistants.

ACADEMICS
Degrees: bachelor's. **Classes:** Most classes have 10-19 students. **Majors with Highest Enrollment:** Parks, Recreation and Leisure Studies; Business Administration and Management; Biology/Biological Sciences. **Special Study Options:** distance learning, double major, dual enrollment, honors program, independent study, internships, liberal arts/career combination, study abroad, teacher certification program. **Honors programs:** Honors Program—based on the National Collegiate Honors Council-modeled City of Text explores urban environments, while the Partners in the Parks: Black Canyon of the Gunnison course immerses students in the ecosystems of one of America's most amazing national parks. **Disability Services:** Special programs offered to physically disabled students include note-taking services, reader services, tape recorders, tutors. **Career services:** Alumni network, alumni services, career/job search classes, career assessment, internships, regional alumni.

FACILITIES
Housing: Coed dorms, men's dorms, women's dorms, apartments for married students, apartments for single students, Theme Housing. 80% of campus accessible to physically disabled. **Computers:** 100% of classrooms, 50% of dorms, 100% of libraries, 100% of dining areas, 100% of student union, have wireless network access. Students can register for classes online. Administrative functions (other than registration) can be performed online.

CAMPUS LIFE
Environment: Rural. **Activities:** Choral groups, concert band, dance, drama/theater, jazz band, literary magazine, music ensembles, pep band, radio station, student government, student newspaper, student-run film society, symphony orchestra, television station, Campus Ministries, International Student Organization. 60 registered organizations, 8 honor societies, 5 religious organizations. **Athletics (Intercollegiate):** *Men:* basketball, cross-country, football, track/field (outdoor), track/field (indoor), wrestling. *Women:* basketball, cross-country, track/field (outdoor), track/field (indoor), volleyball. **On-Campus Highlights:** College Center—new student center, Hurst Hall—renovated science building, Kelley Hall—renovated social sciences, Gym—Highest Elevation NCAA basketball Court, Borick Business—new business building, College Center, Borick, Business Building and Kelley Hall are either LEED certified or seeking LEED certification. Kelley also features solar panels for energy efficiency. The new College Center features campus dining and a first-run movie theatre. **Environmental Initiatives:** President's Climate Committment—which is a significant challenge for one of the coldest locations in the nation and the isolated nature of Gunnison Bio Mass boiler system and LEED certified buildings. 4th construction project seeking will be underway in spring 2010 with biomass bioler which has received a competitive NEED grant food purchasing, pulping and composting.

ADMISSIONS
Freshman Academic Profile: Average high school GPA 3.13. 0% in top 10% of high school class, 0% in top 25% of high school class, 0% in top 50% of high school class. SAT Math middle 50% range 340-507. SAT Critical Reading middle 50% range 440-550. ACT middle 50% range 19-24. Minimum paper TOEFL 550. **Basis for Candidate Selection:** *Very important factors considered include:* Class rank, rigor of secondary school record, standardized test scores. *Other factors considered include:* application essay, recommendation(s), alumni/ae relation, character/personal qualities, extracurricular activities, first generation, interview, talent/ability, volunteer work. **Freshman Admission Requirements:** High school diploma is required and GED is accepted. **Academic units required:** 4 English, 4 mathematics, 3 science, (2 science labs), 1 foreign language, 2 social studies, 2 history, 3 academic electives. **Freshman**

Admission Statistics: 1,199 applied, 97% admitted, 39% enrolled. **Transfer Admission Requirements:** college transcript(s), Minimum college GPA of 2.0 required. Lowest grade transferable C. **General Admission Information:** Application Fee $40. Regular application deadline 8/1. Notification on a rolling basis, beginning on or about 11/1. Nonfall registration accepted. Admission may be deferred for a maximum of 1 year. Credit and/or placement offered for CEEB Advanced Placement tests.

COSTS AND FINANCIAL AID

Required Forms and Deadlines: FAFSA. **Notification of Awards:** Applicants will be notified of awards on a rolling basis beginning 4/1. **Types of Aid:** *Need-based scholarships/grants:* Federal Pell, SEOG, state scholarships/grants, the school's own gift aid. *Loans:* Direct Subsidized Stafford, Direct Unsubsidized Stafford, Direct PLUS, Federal Perkins. *Student Employment:* Federal Work-Study Program available. Institutional employment available. Highest amount earned per year from on-campus jobs $1,500. Off-campus job opportunities are good. **Financial Aid Statistics:** 94% freshmen, 91% undergrads receive need-based scholarship or grant aid. 0% freshmen, 0% undergrads receive non-need-based scholarship or grant aid. 87% freshmen, 90% undergrads receive need-based self-help aid. 8% freshmen, 6% undergrads receive athletic scholarships. 85% freshmen, 75% undergrads receive any aid. 60% undergrads borrow to pay for school. Average cumulative indebtedness $20,339. **Criteria for awarding institutional aid:** *Non-need-based:* academics, art, athletics, leadership, music/drama.

WESTERN UNIVERSITY

Western Student Services Bldg., RM 3140, London, ON N6A 3K7
Phone: 519-661-2100 · **Financial Aid Phone:** 519-661-2100
E-mail: reg-admissions@uwo.ca · **CEEB Code:**
Fax: 519-661-3710 · **Website:** www.westernu.ca

This public school was founded in 1878. It has a 1178-acre campus.

RATINGS

Admissions Selectivity Rating: 60*   Fire Safety Rating: 73

STUDENTS AND FACULTY

Enrollment: 31,903. **Student Body:** (114 countries represented). **Retention and Graduation:** 50% freshmen graduate within 4 years. 78% freshmen graduate within 6 years. **Faculty:** 1,410 full-time faculty, 34% are are members of minority groups.

ACADEMICS

Degrees: bachelor's, certificate, diploma, doctoral, master's. **Majors with Highest Enrollment:** Health Services/Allied Health/Health Sciences; Business Administration and Management; Biology/Biological Sciences. **Special Study Options:** Accelerated program, cooperative education program, cross-registration, distance learning, double major, dual enrollment, English as a Second Language (ESL), exchange student program (domestic), honors program, independent study, internships, liberal arts/career combination, student-designed major, study abroad, teacher certification program. **Honors programs:** Scholar's Electives **Combined degree programs:** BESc/MD, BESc/LLB, LLB/MBA, BSc/LLB, HBA/BMSc. **Disability Services:** Special programs offered to physically disabled students include note-taking services, reader services, tape recorders. **Career services:** Alumni network, alumni services, career/job search classes, career assessment, internships, regional alumni. Career services highlights include Western's Internship Program (www.career.uwo.ca/wip), Backpack2briefcase (http://www.alumni.uwo.ca/b2b/), Interview Stream—Online mock interview tool, Career Week/Job Fairs.

FACILITIES

Housing: Coed dorms, special housing for disabled students, men's dorms, special housing for international students, women's dorms, apartments for married students, apartments for single students. 92% of campus accessible to physically disabled. **Special Academic Facilities/Equipment:** McIntosh Gallery, Hume Cronyn Memorial Observatory, Student Recreation Centre. **Computers:** 100% of libraries, 100% of student union, have wireless network access. Students can register for classes online. Administrative functions (other than registration) can be performed online.

CAMPUS LIFE

Environment: City. **Activities:** Choral groups, concert band, dance, drama/theater, jazz band, marching band, music ensembles, musical theater, opera, pep band, radio station, student government, student newspaper, student-run film society, symphony orchestra, television station, Campus Ministries, International Student Organization, Model UN. 189 registered organizations, 14 fraternities, 5 sororities. **Athletics (Intercollegiate):** *Men:* badminton, baseball, basketball, crew/rowing, cross-country, curling, fencing, football, golf,

ice hockey, rugby, soccer, squash, swimming, tennis, track/field (outdoor), track/field (indoor), volleyball, water polo, wrestling. *Women:* badminton, basketball, crew/rowing, cross-country, curling, fencing, field hockey, golf, ice hockey, lacrosse, rugby, soccer, squash, swimming, tennis, track/field (outdoor), track/field (indoor), volleyball, wrestling. **On-Campus Highlights:** University Community Centre, Student Recreation Centre, TD Waterhouse Stadium, Von Kuster Hall, McIntosh Gallery, McIntosh Gallery—Oldest university art gallery in Canada. **Environmental Initiatives:** Hiring an employee dedicated to sustainability initiatives on campus. Meters installed in all buildings which allow for real-time monitoring of electricity. The implementation of a President's Advisory Committee on Environmental Sustainability (http://sustainability.uwo.ca/about_us/paces.html).

ADMISSIONS

Freshman Academic Profile: Average high school GPA 89.3. Minimum internet-based TOEFL 83. Minimum paper TOEFL 550. **Basis for Candidate Selection:** *Very important factors considered include:* academic GPA, standardized test scores. *Important factors considered include:* rigor of secondary school record. *Other factors considered include:* Class rank, application essay, recommendation(s), alumni/ae relation, character/personal qualities, extracurricular activities, talent/ability, volunteer work, work experience. **Freshman Admission Requirements:** High school diploma is required and GED is accepted. **Academic units required:** 4 English, 3 mathematics, 3 science, 2 foreign language, 3 social studies. **Transfer Admission Requirements:** High school transcript, college transcript(s), Lowest grade transferable C. **General Admission Information:** Application Fee $50. Notification on a rolling basis, beginning on or about 11/1. Nonfall registration accepted. Admission may be deferred for a maximum of 1 year.

COSTS AND FINANCIAL AID

Average book expense $1,500. **Required Forms and Deadlines:** FAFSA, Institution's own financial aid form, State aid form.

WESTERN WASHINGTON UNIVERSITY

Mail Stop 9009, Bellingham, WA 98225-9009
Phone: 360-650-3440 · **Financial Aid Phone:** 360-650-3470
E-mail: admit@cc.wwu.edu · **CEEB Code:** 4947
Fax: 360-650-7369 · **Website:** http://www.wwu.edu/ · **ACT Code:** 4490

This public school was founded in 1893. It has a 300-acre campus.

RATINGS

Admissions Selectivity Rating: 79   Fire Safety Rating: 85

STUDENTS AND FACULTY

Enrollment: 14,152. **Student Body:** 55% female, 45% male, 9% out-of-state, 1% international (30 countries represented). Asian 7%, African American 2%, Caucasian 74%, Hispanic 7%, Native American <1%
Retention and Graduation: 40% freshmen graduate within 4 years. 72% freshmen graduate within 6 years. 14% grads go on to further study within 1 year. **Faculty:** 570 full-time faculty, 89% hold PhDs, 46% are are members of minority groups, 11% are women. 2% of classes are taught by teaching assistants.

ACADEMICS

Degrees: bachelor's, certificate, master's, post-bachelor's certificate, post-master's certificate. **Classes:** Most classes have 20-29 students. Most lab/discussion sessions have 10-19 students. **Majors with Highest Enrollment:** Business Administration, Management and Operations; Social Sciences; English Language and Literature. **Special Study Options:** distance learning, double major, English as a Second Language (ESL), exchange student program (domestic), honors program, independent study, internships, student-designed major, study abroad, teacher certification program. **Honors programs:** Honors Program features small classes and interaction between students and faculty. It is an exciting opportunity for accomplished students who would like a more intimate college experience within the setting of a larger institution. Honors students are welcome to pursue any academic major, and all students complete a self-designed capstone senior project. **Disability Services:** Special programs offered to physically disabled students include note-taking services, reader services, tape recorders, tutors. **Career services:** Alumni network, career/job search classes, career assessment, internships, regional alumni.

FACILITIES

Housing: Coed dorms, special housing for disabled students, apartments for married students, apartments for single students, Theme HousingWellness floors, multicultural floors available. 100% of campus accessible to physically disabled. **Special Academic Facilities/Equipment:** Outdoor art museum, planetarium, electronic music studio, air pollution lab, motor vehicle research lab, marine lab, wind tunnel, electron microscope, neutron generator lab. **Computers:** 100% of classrooms, 100% of dorms, 100% of libraries, 100% of dining areas, 100% of student union, 100% of common outdoor areas have wireless network access. Students can register for classes online. Administrative functions (other than registration) can be performed online.

CAMPUS LIFE

Environment: City. **Activities:** concert band, dance, drama/theater, jazz band, literary magazine, marching band, music ensembles, musical theater, opera, pep band, radio station, student government, student newspaper, symphony orchestra, television station, Campus Ministries, International Student Organization. 200 registered organizations, 4 honor societies, 18 religious organizations. **Athletics (Intercollegiate):** *Men:* basketball, cheerleading, crew/rowing, cross-country, golf, soccer, track/field (outdoor), track/field (indoor). *Women:* basketball, cheerleading, crew/rowing, cross-country, golf, soccer, softball, track/field (outdoor), track/field (indoor), volleyball. **On-Campus Highlights:** Viking Union Student Center, Red Square, Performing Arts Center, Sehome Arboretum, Student Recreation Center. **Environmental Initiatives:** WWU Green Energy Fee—The GEF pays for purchase of Renewable Energy Credits to offset 100% of WWU's CO_2 emissions from electrical energy consumption, and pays for approximately $260,000 per year of on-campus sustainability projects. Due to our purchase of Renewable Energy Credits, WWU is ranked 17th by the EPA for largest higher ed. purchase of renewable energy in the US. This year's projects include a $167,000 solar array, high-speed hand driers, conversion of parking lot lights to high-efficiency LEDs, a paper towel composting system, and water bottle refilling stations. 10x12 Program The 10x12 Program is a partnership between Facilities Management and the OS aimed at goal of a 10% reduction in utility consumption in academic buildings by the end of 2012. This program includes changes in building operations (set points, building operating hours), energy conservation retrofits electricity, NG, and water), a departmental behavior change campaign (via Departmental Conservation Coordinators), and reinvestment of utility savings. Total savings of all current projects is estimated at 3 to 3.5 million dollars in savings over twelve years as well as a 5% drop in carbon emissions. Sustainability in the Curriculum Approximately 30 faulty are currently and actively invested in the Faculty Sustainability Academy, organizing Westerns sustainability programs and developing methods for furthering sustainability education. A series of surveys distributed between 2008 and 2011 indicate approximately 120 additional faculty members either teach sustainability curriculum in their classes or have professional interest in sustainability education. Between 2009 and 2011 SII, the Academy, and students successfully launched a three-part General Education course sequence titled Sustainability Literacy and drafted curriculum concepts for several minors and majors in Sustainability. Survey data shows that over 900 WWU classes contain some sustainability information, while 20-25 classes are sustainability focused. WWU offers six environmentally-themed majors and one minor. The College of Business and Economics has been recognized for its efforts to integrate sustainability into the MBA program by ranking 74th globally within the 2010 Beyond Grey Pinstripes list of green business schools from the Aspen Institute.

ADMISSIONS

Freshman Academic Profile: Average high school GPA 3.43. 19% in top 10% of high school class, 51% in top 25% of high school class, 85% in top 50% of high school class. 90% from public high schools. SAT Math middle 50% range 500-600. SAT Critical Reading middle 50% range 500-610. SAT Writing middle 50% range 470-580. ACT middle 50% range 22-27. Minimum internet-based TOEFL 80. Minimum paper TOEFL 550. **Basis for Candidate Selection:** *Very important factors considered include:* rigor of secondary school record. *Important factors considered include:* application essay, academic GPA, standardized test scores, level of applicant's interest. *Other factors considered include:* Class rank, recommendation(s), character/personal qualities, extracurricular activities, first generation, geographical residence, state residency, talent/ability, volunteer work, work experience. **Freshman Admission Requirements:** High school diploma is required and GED is accepted. **Academic units required:** 4 English, 3 mathematics, 2 science, (1 science labs), 2 foreign language, 3 social studies. **Freshman Admission Statistics:** 9,283 applied, 85% admitted, 35% enrolled. **Transfer Admission Requirements:** college transcript(s), statement of good standing from prior institution(s). Minimum college GPA of 2.0 required. Lowest grade transferable D-. **General Admission Information:** Application Fee $50. Regular application deadline 3/1. Notification on a rolling basis, beginning on or about 11/1. Nonfall registration accepted. Admission may be deferred for a maximum of 1 year. Credit and/or placement offered for CEEB Advanced Placement tests.

COSTS AND FINANCIAL AID

Required Forms and Deadlines: FAFSA. **Notification of Awards:** Applicants will be notified of awards on a rolling basis beginning 3/20. **Types of Aid:** *Need-based scholarships/grants:* Federal Pell, SEOG, state scholarships/grants, private scholarships, the school's own gift aid. *Loans:* Direct Subsidized Stafford, Direct Unsubsidized Stafford, Direct PLUS, Federal Perkins, state loans, Private *Student Employment:* Institutional employment available. Highest amount earned per year from on-campus jobs $2,690. Off-campus job opportunities are good. **Financial Aid Statistics:** 85% freshmen, 76% undergrads

receive need-based scholarship or grant aid. 7% freshmen, 3% undergrads receive non-need-based scholarship or grant aid. 79% freshmen, 82% undergrads receive need-based self-help aid. 0% freshmen, 1% undergrads receive athletic scholarships. 54% freshmen, 49% undergrads receive any aid. 57% undergrads borrow to pay for school. Average cumulative indebtedness $20,199. **Criteria for awarding institutional aid:** *Non-need-based:* academics, alumni affiliation, art, athletics, job skills, leadership, minority status, music/drama, state/district residency.

WESTFIELD STATE UNIVERSITY

Westfield State University, Westfield, MA 1086
Phone: 413-572-5218 · **Financial Aid Phone:** 413-572-5218
E-mail: admissions@westfield.ma.edu · **CEEB Code:** 3523
Fax: 413-572-0520 · **Website:** www.westfield.ma.edu · **ACT Code:** 1912

This public school was founded in 1838. It has a 227-acre campus.

RATINGS

Admissions Selectivity Rating: 72   **Fire Safety Rating:** 79

STUDENTS AND FACULTY

Enrollment: 5,429. **Student Body:** 53% female, 47% male, 8% out-of-state, 0% international (10 countries represented). Asian 1%, African American 4%, Caucasian 78%, Hispanic 8%, Native American <1%
Retention and Graduation: 48% freshmen graduate within 4 years. **Faculty:** 233 full-time faculty, 83% hold PhDs, 48% are are members of minority groups, 16% are women. 0% of classes are taught by teaching assistants.

ACADEMICS

Degrees: bachelor's, master's, post-bachelor's certificate, post-master's certificate. **Classes:** Most classes have 20-29 students. Most lab/discussion sessions have 10-19 students. **Majors with Highest Enrollment:** Elementary Education and Teaching; Criminal Justice/Safety Studies; Business/Commerce. **Special Study Options:** cooperative education program, cross-registration, distance learning, double major, dual enrollment, exchange student program (domestic), honors program, independent study, internships, student-designed major, study abroad, teacher certification program. **Disability Services:** Special programs offered to physically disabled students include note-taking services, reader services, tape recorders, tutors. **Career services:** career/job search classes, career assessment.

FACILITIES

Housing: Coed dorms, special housing for disabled students, apartments for single students, Living/Learning Unit (Honors/Academic Intensive) Quiet Living Section All Women Section Designated smoking Section(other housing smoke free) Movement Science Student Section. **Special Academic Facilities/Equipment:** Art gallery, language lab, electron microscope.

CAMPUS LIFE

Environment: Village. **Activities:** Choral groups, concert band, drama/theater, jazz band, literary magazine, music ensembles, musical theater, pep band, radio station, student government, student newspaper, television station, yearbook. **Athletics (Intercollegiate):** *Men:* baseball, basketball, cross-country, football, golf, soccer, track/field (outdoor). *Women:* basketball, cheerleading, cross-country, field hockey, soccer, softball, swimming, volleyball. **Environmental Initiatives:** RecycleMania: placed 1st in the targeted paper competition in 2012 Environmental Science program; Solar panels (http://www.westfield.ma.edu/news/solar-panels-a-sea-of-green/).

ADMISSIONS

Freshman Academic Profile: Average high school GPA 3.1. SAT Math middle 50% range 460-550. SAT Critical Reading middle 50% range 450-540. SAT Writing middle 50% range 440-540. ACT middle 50% range 18-23. Minimum internet-based TOEFL 79. Minimum paper TOEFL 550. **Basis for Candidate Selection:** *Very important factors considered include:* rigor of secondary school record, standardized test scores. *Important factors considered include:* extracurricular activities, talent/ability. *Other factors considered include:* application essay, recommendation(s), character/personal qualities, racial/ethnic status, volunteer work, work experience. **Freshman Admission Requirements:** High school diploma is required and GED is accepted. **Academic units required:** 4 English, 3 mathematics, 3 science, (2 science labs), 2 foreign language, 1 social studies, 1 history, 2 academic electives. **Freshman Admission Statistics:** 5,163 applied, 75% admitted, 32% enrolled. **Transfer Admission Requirements:** college transcript(s), Minimum college GPA of 2.0 required. Lowest grade transferable C-. **General Admission Information:** Application Fee $25. Regular application deadline 3/1. Nonfall registration accepted. Admission may be deferred for a maximum of 1 semester. Credit and/or placement offered for CEEB Advanced Placement tests.

COSTS AND FINANCIAL AID

Annual in-state tuition $970. Annual out-of-state tuition $7,050. Room and board $9,615. Required fees $7,712. Average book expense $1,200. **Required Forms and Deadlines:** FAFSA. **Notification of Awards:** Applicants will be notified of awards on or about 4/15. **Types of Aid:** *Need-based scholarships/grants:* Federal Pell, SEOG, state scholarships/grants, private scholarships, the school's own gift aid. *Loans:* Subsidized Stafford, Unsubsidized Stafford, PLUS, Federal Perkins, state loans. *Student Employment:* Federal Work-Study Program available. Highest amount earned per year from on-campus jobs $1,000. Off-campus job opportunities are good. **Financial Aid Statistics:** 73% freshmen, 71% undergrads receive need-based scholarship or grant aid. 36% freshmen, 22% undergrads receive non-need-based scholarship or grant aid. 88% freshmen, 97% undergrads receive need-based self-help aid. 0% freshmen, 0% undergrads receive athletic scholarships. 66% freshmen, 67% undergrads receive any aid. 79% undergrads borrow to pay for school. Average cumulative indebtedness $23,743.

WESTMINSTER CHOIR COLLEGE OF RIDER UNIVERSITY

101 Walnut Lane, Princeton, NJ 08540-3899
Phone: 800-962-4647 • **CEEB Code:** 2758
Fax: 609-921-8829 • **Website:** www.rider.edu • **ACT Code:** 2590

This private school was founded in 1926. It has a 23-acre campus.

RATINGS

Admissions Selectivity Rating: 73   **Fire Safety Rating:** 60*

STUDENTS AND FACULTY

Enrollment: 328. **Student Body:** 64% female, 36% male, 56% out-of-state, 4% international. Asian 2%, African American 7%, Caucasian 75%, Hispanic 4%, Native American 1%
Retention and Graduation: 79% freshmen return for sophomore year.

ACADEMICS

Degrees: bachelor's, master's. **Majors with Highest Enrollment:** Accounting; Business Administration, Management and Operations; Elementary Education and Teaching.

FACILITIES

Housing: Coed dorms.

CAMPUS LIFE

Environment: Town. **Activities:** Choral groups, concert band, dance, jazz band, music ensembles, opera. 8 registered organizations, 4 honor societies.

ADMISSIONS

Freshman Academic Profile: Average high school GPA 3.41. SAT Math middle 50% range 490-610. SAT Critical Reading middle 50% range 490-620. Minimum paper TOEFL 563. **Basis for Candidate Selection:** *Very important factors considered include:* application essay, academic GPA, recommendation(s), rigor of secondary school record, standardized test scores. *Important factors considered include:* level of applicant's interest. *Other factors considered include:* Class rank, alumni/ae relation, character/personal qualities, extracurricular activities, geographical residence, interview, state residency, talent/ability, volunteer work, work experience. **Freshman Admission Requirements:** High school diploma is required and GED is accepted. **Academic units required:** 4 English, 3 mathematics. **Freshman Admission Statistics:** 206 applied, 76% admitted, 56% enrolled. **General Admission Information:** Application Fee $45.

COSTS AND FINANCIAL AID

Average book expense $1,000.

WESTMINSTER COLLEGE (MO)

Champ Auditorium, Westminster College, Fulton, MO 65251
Phone: 573-592-5251 • **Financial Aid Phone:** 800-475-3361
E-mail: admissions@westminster-mo.edu • **CEEB Code:** 6937
Fax: 573-592-5255 • **Website:** http://www.westminster-mo.edu/ • **ACT Code:** 2392

This private school, affiliated with the Presbyterian Church, was founded in 1851. It has a 86-acre campus.

RATINGS

Admissions Selectivity Rating: 85   **Fire Safety Rating:** 79

STUDENTS AND FACULTY

Enrollment: 935. **Student Body:** 42% female, 58% male, 20% out-of-state, 16% international (75 countries represented). Asian 1%, African American 8%, Caucasian 65%, Hispanic 4%, Native American 2%
Retention and Graduation: 78% freshmen return for sophomore year. 51% freshmen graduate within 4 years. 30% grads go on to further study within 1 year. 10% grads pursue arts and sciences degrees. 4% grads pursue law degrees. 6% grads pursue business degrees. 3% grads pursue medical degrees. **Faculty:** 58 full-time faculty, 91% hold PhDs, 43% are are members of minority groups, 12% are women. 0% of classes are taught by teaching assistants.

ACADEMICS

Degrees: bachelor's. **Classes:** Most classes have 10-19 students. **Majors with Highest Enrollment:** Biology/Biological Sciences; Political Science and Government; Business/Commerce. **Special Study Options:** cooperative education program, cross-registration, double major, dual enrollment, exchange student program (domestic), honors program, independent study, internships, liberal arts/career combination, student-designed major, study abroad, teacher certification program, Urban Studies Program (Chicago). Other off-campus study opportunities supported through Office of International Programs. Coursework and certification are also available through the Center of Leadership and the Remley Women's Center. **Combined degree programs:** BA/MEng, BA/MEng—University of Missouri-Columbia. **Disability Services:** Special programs offered to physically disabled students include note-taking services, reader services, tape recorders, tutors. **Career services:** career/job search classes, career assessment, internships, regional alumni.

FACILITIES

Housing: Coed dorms, special housing for disabled students, men's dorms, women's dorms, fraternity/sorority housing, apartments for single students, Theme Housing. 70% of campus accessible to physically disabled. **Special Academic Facilities/Equipment:** Winston Churchill Memorial Museum, Coulter Science Center, language lab, NMR spectrometer, laser equipment. **Computers:** 100% of classrooms, 100% of libraries, 100% of dining areas, 100% of student union, 40% of common outdoor areas have wireless network access. Students can register for classes online. Administrative functions (other than registration) can be performed online.

CAMPUS LIFE

Environment: Village. **Activities:** Choral groups, dance, drama/theater, literary magazine, music ensembles, pep band, student government, student newspaper, yearbook, Campus Ministries, International Student Organization, Model UN. 49 registered organizations, 15 honor societies, 2 religious organizations. 6 fraternities, 3 sororities. **Athletics (Intercollegiate):** *Men:* baseball, basketball, cheerleading, cross-country, football, golf, soccer, tennis, track/field (outdoor). *Women:* basketball, cheerleading, cross-country, golf, soccer, softball, tennis, track/field (outdoor), volleyball. **On-Campus Highlights:** Coulter Science Center, Johnson College Inn (student center), Hunter Activity Center, Library, Wetterau Athletic Facility.

ADMISSIONS

Freshman Academic Profile: Average high school GPA 3.47. 27% in top 10% of high school class, 48% in top 25% of high school class, 74% in top 50% of high school class. 70% from public high schools. SAT Math middle 50% range 415-613. SAT Critical Reading middle 50% range 435-580. ACT middle 50% range 22-27. Minimum paper TOEFL 550. **Basis for Candidate Selection:** *Very important factors considered include:* rigor of secondary school record, standardized test scores, character/personal qualities. *Important factors considered include:* Class rank, academic GPA, recommendation(s), extracurricular activities, volunteer work. *Other factors considered include:* application essay, alumni/ae relation, interview, talent/ability, work experience. **Freshman Admission Requirements:** High school diploma is required and GED is accepted. **Academic units required:** 4 English, 3 mathematics, 2 science, (2 science labs). **Freshman Admission Statistics:** 1,356 applied, 67% admitted, 24% enrolled. **Transfer Admission Requirements:** college transcript(s), Lowest grade transferable C. **General Admission Information:** Notification on a rolling basis, beginning on or about 10/1. Nonfall registration accepted. Admission may be deferred for a maximum of 12 months. Credit and/or placement offered for CEEB Advanced Placement tests.

COSTS AND FINANCIAL AID

Annual tuition $21,360. Room and board $9,160. Required fees $1,200. Average book expense $1,100. **Required Forms and Deadlines:** FAFSA. **Notification of Awards:** Applicants will be notified of awards on a rolling basis beginning 3/15. **Types of Aid:** *Need-based scholarships/grants:* Federal Pell, SEOG, state scholarships/grants, private scholarships, the school's own gift aid. *Loans:* Subsidized Stafford, Unsubsidized Stafford, PLUS, Federal Perkins. *Student Employment:* Federal Work-Study Program available. Institutional employment available. Highest amount earned per year from on-campus jobs $2,500. Off-campus job opportunities are good. **Financial Aid Statistics:** 100% freshmen, 100% undergrads receive need-based scholarship or grant aid. 0% freshmen, 0% undergrads receive non-need-based scholarship or grant aid. 88% freshmen, 88% undergrads receive need-based self-help aid. 0% freshmen, 0% undergrads receive athletic scholarships. 100% freshmen, 98% undergrads receive any aid. 61% undergrads borrow to pay for school. Average cumulative indebtedness $26,248. **Criteria for awarding institutional aid:** *Non-need-based:* academics, alumni affiliation, leadership, minority status, music/drama, religious affiliation.

WESTMINSTER COLLEGE (PA)

319 South Market Street, New Wilmington, PA 16172
Phone: 724-946-7100
E-mail: admis@westminster.edu • **CEEB Code:** 2975
Fax: 724-946-7171 • **Website:** www.westminster.edu • **ACT Code:** 2975

This private school, affiliated with the Presbyterian Church, was founded in 1852. It has a 350-acre campus.

RATINGS

Admissions Selectivity Rating: 76   **Fire Safety Rating:** 96

STUDENTS AND FACULTY

Enrollment: 1,387. **Student Body:** 64% female, 36% male, 22% out-of-state, 0% international (2 countries represented). Asian 0%, African American 3%, Caucasian 80%, Hispanic 1%, Native American <1%
Retention and Graduation: 83% freshmen return for sophomore year. 65% freshmen graduate within 4 years. 76% freshmen graduate within 6 years. 21% grads go on to further study within 1 year. 3% grads pursue law degrees. 2% grads pursue business degrees. 3% grads pursue medical degrees. **Faculty:** 98 full-time faculty, 93% hold PhDs, 48% are are members of minority groups, 6% are women. 0% of classes are taught by teaching assistants.

ACADEMICS

Degrees: bachelor's, master's. **Classes:** Most classes have 10-19 students. Most lab/discussion sessions have 10-19 students. **Majors with Highest Enrollment:** Education; Biology/Biological Sciences; Business/Commerce. **Special Study Options:** double major, exchange student program (domestic), honors program, independent study, internships, liberal arts/career combination, student-designed major, study abroad, teacher certification program. **Combined degree programs:** BA/JD, BA/MA. **Disability Services:** Special programs offered to physically disabled students include tutors.

FACILITIES

Housing: special housing for disabled students, men's dorms, women's dorms, fraternity/sorority housing, We offer townhouses for upperclass men and women. 90% of campus accessible to physically disabled. **Special Academic Facilities/Equipment:** On-campus preschool, Moeller pipe organs, planetarium, observatory, electron microscopes, X-ray diffractor, spectrometer. **Computers:** Administrative functions (other than registration) can be performed online.

CAMPUS LIFE

Environment: Village. **Activities:** Choral groups, concert band, dance, drama/theater, jazz band, literary magazine, marching band, music ensembles, musical theater, pep band, radio station, student government, student newspaper, television station, yearbook. 60 registered organizations, 21 honor societies, 3 religious organizations. 5 fraternities, 5 sororities. **Athletics (Intercollegiate):** *Men:* baseball, basketball, cheerleading, cross-country, football, golf, soccer, swimming, tennis, track/field (outdoor), track/field (indoor). *Women:* basketball, cheerleading, cross-country, golf, soccer, softball, swimming, tennis, track/field (outdoor), track/field (indoor), volleyball.

ADMISSIONS

Freshman Academic Profile: Average high school GPA 3.5. 17% in top 10% of high school class, 50% in top 25% of high school class, 85% in top 50% of high school class. 90% from public high schools. SAT Math middle 50% range 460-590. SAT Critical Reading middle 50% range 480-570. SAT

Writing middle 50% range 450-540. ACT middle 50% range 19-27. Minimum paper TOEFL 550. **Basis for Candidate Selection:** *Very important factors considered include:* rigor of secondary school record, standardized test scores, interview. *Important factors considered include:* Class rank, application essay, recommendation(s), character/personal qualities. *Other factors considered include:* alumni/ae relation, extracurricular activities, racial/ethnic status, talent/ability, volunteer work, work experience. **Freshman Admission Requirements:** High school diploma is required and GED is accepted. **Academic units required:** 4 English, 3 mathematics, 2 science, (2 science labs), 2 foreign language, 2 social studies, 1 history, 3 academic electives. **Freshman Admission Statistics:** 2,082 applied, 94% admitted, 15% enrolled. **Transfer Admission Requirements:** High school transcript, college transcript(s), essay or personal statement, interview, standardized test scores, Minimum college GPA of 2.5 required. Lowest grade transferable C. **General Admission Information:** Application Fee $35. Regular application deadline 4/15. Notification on a rolling basis, beginning on or about 9/1. Nonfall registration not accepted. Admission may be deferred for a maximum of 1 year. Credit and/or placement offered for CEEB Advanced Placement tests.

COSTS AND FINANCIAL AID

Annual tuition $32,170. Room and board $10,160. Required fees $1,240. Average book expense $2,250. **Required Forms and Deadlines:** FAFSA, Institution's own financial aid form. **Notification of Awards:** Applicants will be notified of awards on a rolling basis beginning 11/1. **Types of Aid:** *Need-based scholarships/grants:* Federal Pell, SEOG, state scholarships/grants, private scholarships, the school's own gift aid. *Loans:* Subsidized Stafford, Unsubsidized Stafford, PLUS, Federal Perkins, Resource *Student Employment:* Highest amount earned per year from on-campus jobs $1,300. **Financial Aid Statistics:** 100% freshmen, 99% undergrads receive need-based scholarship or grant aid. 99% freshmen, 97% undergrads receive non-need-based scholarship or grant aid. 79% freshmen, 81% undergrads receive need-based self-help aid. 0% freshmen, 0% undergrads receive athletic scholarships. 83% undergrads borrow to pay for school. Average cumulative indebtedness $25,304. **Criteria for awarding institutional aid:** *Non-need-based:* academics, alumni affiliation, leadership, minority status, music/drama.

WESTMINSTER COLLEGE OF SALT LAKE CITY

1840 South 1300 East, Salt Lake City, UT 84105
Phone: 801-832-2200 • **Financial Aid Phone:** 801-832-2502
E-mail: admission@westminstercollege.edu • **CEEB Code:** 4948
Fax: 801-832-3101 • **Website:** www.westminstercollege.edu • **ACT Code:** 4284

This private school was founded in 1875. It has a 27-acre campus.

RATINGS

Admissions Selectivity Rating: 80   **Fire Safety Rating:** 91

STUDENTS AND FACULTY

Enrollment: 2,188. **Student Body:** 54% female, 46% male, 38% out-of-state, 5% international (23 countries represented). Asian 2%, African American 1%, Caucasian 71%, Hispanic 10%, Native American <1%
Retention and Graduation: 72% freshmen return for sophomore year. 49% freshmen graduate within 4 years. 61% freshmen graduate within 6 years. 13% grads go on to further study within 1 year. 3% grads pursue arts and sciences degrees. 1% grads pursue law degrees. 2% grads pursue business degrees. 1% grads pursue medical degrees. **Faculty:** 161 full-time faculty, 82% hold PhDs, 50% are are members of minority groups, 11% are women. 0% of classes are taught by teaching assistants.

ACADEMICS

Degrees: bachelor's, master's, post-bachelor's certificate. **Classes:** Most classes have 10-19 students. Most lab/discussion sessions have 10-19 students. **Majors with Highest Enrollment:** Business/Commerce; Health Services/Allied Health/Health Sciences; Psychology. **Special Study Options:** Accelerated program, cooperative education program, distance learning, double major, dual enrollment, English as a Second Language (ESL), honors program, independent study, internships, liberal arts/career combination, student-designed major, study abroad, teacher certification program, weekend college. **Honors programs:** http://www.westminstercollege.edu/honors/. **Disability Services:** Special programs offered to physically disabled students include note-taking services, reader services, tape recorders, tutors. **Career services:** alumni services, career/job search classes, career assessment, internships. Career services highlights include our Internship Program.

FACILITIES
Housing: Coed dorms, men's dorms, women's dorms, apartments for single students. 98% of campus accessible to physically disabled. **Special Academic Facilities/Equipment:** Emma Eccles Jones Conservatory, Gore school of Business, Giovale Library, Dick Science Building, Climbing Wall, Converse Hall, Dolores Dore Eccles Health, Wellness, and Athletic Center. **Computers:** 100% of classrooms, 100% of dorms, 100% of libraries, 100% of dining areas, 100% of student union, 25% of common outdoor areas have wireless network access. Students can register for classes online. Administrative functions (other than registration) can be performed online.

CAMPUS LIFE
Environment: Metropolis. **Activities:** Choral groups, dance, drama/theater, jazz band, literary magazine, music ensembles, musical theater, student government, student newspaper, student-run film society, symphony orchestra, Campus Ministries, International Student Organization. 55 registered organizations, 4 honor societies, 4 religious organizations. **Athletics (Intercollegiate):** *Men:* basketball, cross-country, golf, lacrosse, skiing (downhill/alpine), snowboarding, soccer, track/field (outdoor), track/field (indoor). *Women:* basketball, cross-country, golf, lacrosse, skiing (downhill/alpine), snowboarding, soccer, track/field (outdoor), track/field (indoor), volleyball. **On-Campus Highlights:** Shaw Student Center, Giovale Library, Emma Eccles Jones Conservatory, Dolores Dore Eccles Health, Wellness, and Athletic, Residential Village. **Environmental Initiatives:** With guidance from the Environmental Center, students completed the STARS assessment in 2010, achieving a Silver rating. Westminster scored particularly well in co-curricular and curricular sustainability efforts. Campus as a Sustainability Teaching Tool: New LEED Platinum Meldrum Science Center was completed in 2010. Demonstration gardens, organic vegetable garden, and residence hall energy monitoring also all contribute to transforming campus itself into a sustainability demonstration and laboratory. American College & University Presidents' Climate Commitment charter signatory with a target climate neutrality date of 2030.

ADMISSIONS
Freshman Academic Profile: Average high school GPA 3.53. 23% in top 10% of high school class, 55% in top 25% of high school class, 87% in top 50% of high school class. 80% from public high schools. SAT Math middle 50% range 500-620. SAT Critical Reading middle 50% range 495-620. ACT middle 50% range 22-27. Minimum internet-based TOEFL 79. Minimum paper TOEFL 550. **Basis for Candidate Selection:** *Very important factors considered include:* academic GPA, rigor of secondary school record. *Important factors considered include:* Class rank, application essay, standardized test scores, interview. *Other factors considered include:* recommendation(s), alumni/ae relation, character/personal qualities, extracurricular activities, geographical residence, talent/ability. **Freshman Admission Requirements:** High school diploma is required and GED is accepted. **Academic units required:** 4 English, 2 mathematics, 3 science, 2 foreign language, 2 social studies, 1 history, 2 academic electives. **Freshman Admission Statistics:** 1,784 applied, 97% admitted, 28% enrolled. **Transfer Admission Requirements:** High school transcript, college transcript(s), essay or personal statement, Minimum college GPA of 2.5 required. Lowest grade transferable C-. **General Admission Information:** Application Fee $40. Notification on a rolling basis, beginning on or about 9/1. Nonfall registration accepted. Admission may be deferred for a maximum of 1 year. Credit and/or placement offered for CEEB Advanced Placement tests.

COSTS AND FINANCIAL AID
Annual tuition $29,856. Room and board $8,456. Required fees $508. Average book expense $1,000. **Required Forms and Deadlines:** FAFSA. **Notification of Awards:** Applicants will be notified of awards on a rolling basis beginning 3/1. **Types of Aid:** *Need-based scholarships/grants:* Federal Pell, SEOG, state scholarships/grants, private scholarships, the school's own gift aid. *Loans:* Subsidized Stafford, Unsubsidized Stafford, PLUS, Federal Perkins. *Student Employment:* Federal Work-Study Program available. Institutional employment available. Highest amount earned per year from on-campus jobs $6,934. Off-campus job opportunities are excellent. **Financial Aid Statistics:** 100% freshmen, 98% undergrads receive need-based scholarship or grant aid. 24% freshmen, 21% undergrads receive non-need-based scholarship or grant aid. 80% freshmen, 85% undergrads receive need-based self-help aid. 4% freshmen, 3% undergrads receive athletic scholarships. 98% freshmen, 91% undergrads receive any aid. 60% undergrads borrow to pay for school. Average cumulative indebtedness $24,445. **Criteria for awarding institutional aid:** *Non-need-based:* academics, alumni affiliation, art, athletics, leadership, minority status, music/drama, religious affiliation.

WESTMONT COLLEGE

955 La Paz Road, Santa Barbara, CA 93108
Phone: 805-565-6200 · **Financial Aid Phone:** 888-963-4624
E-mail: admissions@westmont.edu · **CEEB Code:** 4950
Fax: 805-565-6234 · **Website:** www.westmont.edu · **ACT Code:** 478

This private school, affiliated with the Christian (Nondenominational) Church, was founded in 1937. It has a 133-acre campus.

RATINGS
Admissions Selectivity Rating: 87   **Fire Safety Rating:** 60*

STUDENTS AND FACULTY
Enrollment: 1,289. **Student Body:** 61% female, 39% male, 25% out-of-state, 1% international (8 countries represented). Asian 5%, African American 1%, Caucasian 51%, Hispanic 9%, Native American <1%
Retention and Graduation: 85% freshmen return for sophomore year. 72% freshmen graduate within 4 years. **Faculty:** 96 full-time faculty, 90% hold PhDs, 39% are are members of minority groups, 13% are women. 0% of classes are taught by teaching assistants.

ACADEMICS
Degrees: bachelor's, post-bachelor's certificate. **Classes:** Most classes have 10-19 students. Most lab/discussion sessions have 10-19 students. **Majors with Highest Enrollment:** English/Language Arts Teacher Education; Cell/Cellular and Molecular Biology. **Special Study Options:** Accelerated program, double major, exchange student program (domestic), honors program, independent study, internships, student-designed major, study abroad, teacher certification program. **Honors programs:** Some general education courses are designated as honors courses. **Combined degree programs:** 3/2 Engineering Program. **Disability Services:** Special programs offered to physically disabled students include note-taking services, reader services, tape recorders, tutors. **Career services:** career/job search classes, career assessment, internships.

FACILITIES
Housing: Coed dorms, apartments for single students, The Coed dorms are segregated by floors and/or suites. Men and women do not share hallways and bathrooms. There are selected visiting hours for members of the opposite sex. 65% of campus accessible to physically disabled. **Special Academic Facilities/Equipment:** Reynolds Art Gallery features the gallery, art studios and classrooms; Carroll Observatory houses a 24-inch reflector telescope; Mericos Whittier Science facility includes state of the art technical equipment such as ultracentrifuge, Fouriertransform NMR spectrometer, etc., as well as the pre-med center; Voskuyl Library holds over 150,000 bound volumes; the physics department is developing advanced experiments for the lab; Ellen Porter Hall of Fine Arts showcases ten to twenty live musical and theatrical performances each year; Physiology Lab and Fithess Center for Kinesiology studies. **Computers:** Administrative functions (other than registration) can be performed online.

CAMPUS LIFE
Environment: City. **Activities:** Choral groups, dance, drama/theater, jazz band, literary magazine, music ensembles, musical theater, radio station, student government, student newspaper, student-run film society, symphony orchestra, yearbook, Campus Ministries. 50 registered organizations, 7 honor societies, 40 religious organizations. **Athletics (Intercollegiate):** *Men:* baseball, basketball, cross-country, soccer, tennis, track/field (outdoor). *Women:* basketball, cross-country, soccer, tennis, track/field (outdoor), volleyball.

ADMISSIONS
Freshman Academic Profile: Average high school GPA 3.84. 29% in top 10% of high school class, 66% in top 25% of high school class, 94% in top 50% of high school class. 70% from public high schools. SAT Math middle 50% range 540-660. SAT Critical Reading middle 50% range 520-650. SAT Writing middle 50% range -650. ACT middle 50% range 24-29. Minimum paper TOEFL 560. **Basis for Candidate Selection:** *Very important factors considered include:* academic GPA, standardized test scores, character/personal qualities, religious affiliation/commitment. *Important factors considered include:* application essay, recommendation(s), rigor of secondary school record, extracurricular activities, interview, racial/ethnic status, talent/ability. *Other factors considered include:* Class rank, alumni/ae relation, first generation, geographical residence, level of applicant's interest, state residency, volunteer work, work experience. **Freshman Admission Requirements:** High school diploma is required and GED is accepted. **Academic units required:** 4 English, 3 mathematics, 3 science, (2 science labs), 2 foreign language, 2 social studies, 0 history, 4 academic electives. **Freshman Admission Statistics:** 2,145 applied, 70% admitted, 20% enrolled. **Transfer Admission Requirements:** High school transcript, college transcript(s), essay or personal statement, statement of good standing from prior institution(s). Lowest grade transferable C-. **General Admission Informa-**

tion: Application Fee $50. Notification on a rolling basis, beginning on or about 4/1. Nonfall registration accepted. Credit and/or placement offered for CEEB Advanced Placement tests.

COSTS AND FINANCIAL AID

Annual tuition $38,960. Room and board $12,580. Required fees $1,030. Average book expense $1,600. **Required Forms and Deadlines:** FAFSA, Institution's own financial aid form. **Notification of Awards:** Applicants will be notified of awards on a rolling basis beginning 4/1. *Types of Aid: Need-based scholarships/grants:* Federal Pell, SEOG, state scholarships/grants, private scholarships, the school's own gift aid. *Loans:* Subsidized Stafford, Unsubsidized Stafford, PLUS, Federal Perkins, college/university loans from institutional funds, Work-Study. *Student Employment:* Federal Work-Study Program available. Institutional employment available. **Financial Aid Statistics:** 99% freshmen, 99% undergrads receive need-based scholarship or grant aid. 11% freshmen, 12% undergrads receive non-need-based scholarship or grant aid. 97% freshmen, 87% undergrads receive need-based self-help aid. 85% undergrads receive any aid. 69% undergrads borrow to pay for school. Average cumulative indebtedness $21,196. **Criteria for awarding institutional aid:** *Non-need-based:* academics, art, athletics, leadership, minority status, music/drama.

WHEATON COLLEGE (IL)

501 College Avenue, Wheaton, IL 60187
Phone: 630-752-5011 · **Financial Aid Phone:** 630-752-5021
E-mail: admissions@wheaton.edu · **CEEB Code:** 1905
Fax: 630-752-5285 · **Website:** www.wheaton.edu · **ACT Code:** 1160

This private school was founded in 1860. It has a 80-acre campus.

RATINGS

Admissions Selectivity Rating: 91   **Fire Safety Rating:** 89

STUDENTS AND FACULTY

Enrollment: 2,402. **Student Body:** 52% female, 48% male, 74% out-of-state, 3% international (39 countries represented). Asian 9%, African American 2%, Caucasian 76%, Hispanic 5%, Native American <1%
Retention and Graduation: 80% freshmen graduate within 4 years. 32% grads go on to further study within 1 year. 19% grads pursue arts and sciences degrees. 1% grads pursue law degrees. 8% grads pursue medical degrees. **Faculty:** 203 full-time faculty, 97% hold PhDs, 36% are are members of minority groups, 13% are women. 0% of classes are taught by teaching assistants.

ACADEMICS

Degrees: bachelor's, master's, post-bachelor's certificate. **Classes:** Most classes have 10-19 students. Most lab/discussion sessions have 10-19 students. **Majors with Highest Enrollment:** English Language and Literature; Business/Managerial Economics; Health Services/Allied Health/Health Sciences. **Special Study Options:** cross-registration, double major, exchange student program (domestic), independent study, internships, liberal arts/career combination, student-designed major, study abroad, teacher certification program. **Honors programs:** Some departments offer qualified students to submit an honors project. **Combined degree programs:** Liberal Arts/Engineering; Liberal Arts/N. **Disability Services:** Special programs offered to physically disabled students include note-taking services, reader services, tape recorders, tutors. **Career services:** Alumni network, alumni services, career/job search classes, career assessment, internships, regional alumni.

FACILITIES

Housing: Coed dorms, men's dorms, women's dorms, apartments for married students, cooperative housing, apartments for single students, Housing for disabled provided as needed. 97% of campus accessible to physically disabled. **Special Academic Facilities/Equipment:** World evangelism museum, language lab, observatory, Collection of works/papers of seven British authors, Billy Graham Center Museum **Computers:** 10% of classrooms, 100% of dorms, 100% of libraries, 100% of dining areas, 100% of student union, 75% of common outdoor areas have wireless network access. Students can register for classes online. Administrative functions (other than registration) can be performed online.

CAMPUS LIFE

Environment: Town. **Activities:** Choral groups, concert band, dance, drama/theater, jazz band, literary magazine, music ensembles, musical theater, opera,

pep band, radio station, student government, student newspaper, student-run film society, symphony orchestra, television station, yearbook, Campus Ministries, International Student Organization, Model UN. 85 registered organizations, 13 honor societies, 12 religious organizations. **Athletics (Intercollegiate):** *Men:* baseball, basketball, cross-country, football, golf, soccer, swimming, tennis, track/field (outdoor), track/field (indoor), wrestling. *Women:* basketball, cross-country, golf, soccer, softball, swimming, tennis, track/field (outdoor), track/field (indoor), volleyball, water polo. **On-Campus Highlights:** Billy Graham Center—archive, museum, Wade Center—collection of English auth, New Science Building opens Fall 2010, Todd M. Beamer Student Center, J. Dennis Hastert Center. **Environmental Initiatives:** Environmental Science Major; LEED Certifications; Recycling.

ADMISSIONS

Freshman Academic Profile: Average high school GPA 3.68. 52% in top 10% of high school class, 75% in top 25% of high school class, 93% in top 50% of high school class. 49% from public high schools. SAT Math middle 50% range 590-700. SAT Critical Reading middle 50% range 600-710. SAT Writing middle 50% range 600-700. ACT middle 50% range 27-32. Minimum internet-based TOEFL 95. Minimum paper TOEFL 587. **Basis for Candidate Selection:** *Very important factors considered include:* application essay, academic GPA, recommendation(s), rigor of secondary school record, standardized test scores, character/personal qualities, interview, religious affiliation/commitment. *Important factors considered include:* extracurricular activities, talent/ability, volunteer work, work experience. *Other factors considered include:* Class rank, alumni/ae relation, first generation, geographical residence, level of applicant's interest, racial/ethnic status, state residency. **Freshman Admission Requirements:** High school diploma is required and GED is accepted. **Freshman Admission Statistics:** 2,010 applied, 69% admitted, 44% enrolled. **Transfer Admission Requirements:** High school transcript, college transcript(s), essay or personal statement, Minimum college GPA of 3.0 required. Lowest grade transferable C-. **General Admission Information:** Application Fee $50. Regular application deadline 1/10. Regular notification 4/1. Nonfall registration not accepted. Admission may be deferred for a maximum of 1 year. Credit and/or placement offered for CEEB Advanced Placement tests.

COSTS AND FINANCIAL AID

Average book expense $1,120. **Required Forms and Deadlines:** FAFSA, Institution's own financial aid form. **Notification of Awards:** Applicants will be notified of awards on a rolling basis beginning 3/1. **Types of Aid:** *Need-based scholarships/grants:* Federal Pell, SEOG, state scholarships/grants, the school's own gift aid. *Loans:* Subsidized Stafford, Unsubsidized Stafford, PLUS, Federal Perkins. *Student Employment:* Federal Work-Study Program available. Institutional employment available. Off-campus job opportunities are excellent. **Financial Aid Statistics:** 100% freshmen, 99% undergrads receive need-based scholarship or grant aid. 9% freshmen, 9% undergrads receive non-need-based scholarship or grant aid. 79% freshmen, 79% undergrads receive need-based self-help aid. 0% freshmen, 0% undergrads receive athletic scholarships. 73% freshmen, 74% undergrads receive any aid. 57% undergrads borrow to pay for school. Average cumulative indebtedness $22,482. **Criteria for awarding institutional aid:** *Non-need-based:* academics, alumni affiliation, art, minority status, music/drama.

WHEATON COLLEGE (MA)

26 E Main Street, Norton, MA 2766
Phone: 508-286-8251 · **Financial Aid Phone:** 508-286-8232
E-mail: admission@wheatoncollege.edu · **CEEB Code:** 3963
Fax: 508-286-8271 · **Website:** www.wheatoncollege.edu · **ACT Code:** 1932

This private school was founded in 1834. It has a 400-acre campus.

RATINGS

Admissions Selectivity Rating: 88   **Fire Safety Rating:** 75

STUDENTS AND FACULTY

Enrollment: 1,575. **Student Body:** 64% female, 36% male, 66% out-of-state, 10% international (42 countries represented). Asian 4%, African American 6%, Caucasian 69%, Hispanic 7%, Native American <1%
Retention and Graduation: 83% freshmen return for sophomore year. 75% freshmen graduate within 4 years. 77% freshmen graduate within 6 years. 21% grads go on to further study within 1 year. **Faculty:** 132 full-time faculty, 89%

hold PhDs, 51% are are members of minority groups, 17% are women. 0% of classes are taught by teaching assistants.

ACADEMICS
Degrees: bachelor's. **Classes:** Most classes have 10-19 students. Most lab/discussion sessions have 10-19 students. **Majors with Highest Enrollment:** Economics; Psychology; Neuroscience. **Special Study Options:** Accelerated program, cross-registration, double major, dual enrollment, exchange student program (domestic), honors program, independent study, internships, liberal arts/career combination, student-designed major, study abroad, teacher certification program. **Combined degree programs:** BA/MA, BA/MEng, BA/MBA; BA/BFA;BA/BS;BA/Doctor of Optometry. **Disability Services:** Special programs offered to physically disabled students include note-taking services, reader services, tape recorders, tutors. **Career services:** Alumni network, alumni services, career/job search classes, career assessment, internships, regional alumni. Career services highlights include stipends ranging from $3,000 to $6,000 for at least 60% of our students to partcipate in unpaid internships, research opportunities and other out of classroom learning opportunities.

FACILITIES
Housing: Coed dorms, special housing for disabled students, men's dorms, special housing for international students, women's dorms, Wellness Housing, Theme Housing, Quiet house. 50% of campus accessible to physically disabled. **Special Academic Facilities/Equipment:** Art gallery,language lab, photography darkrooms,dance studio,on-campus nursery school, media center, observatory. **Computers:** 100% of classrooms, 100% of dorms, 100% of libraries, 100% of dining areas, 100% of student union, have wireless network access. Students can register for classes online. Administrative functions (other than registration) can be performed online.

CAMPUS LIFE
Environment: Village. **Activities:** Choral groups, dance, drama/theater, jazz band, literary magazine, music ensembles, musical theater, pep band, radio station, student government, student newspaper, student-run film society, symphony orchestra, yearbook, International Student Organization, Model UN. 60 registered organizations, 8 honor societies, 4 religious organizations. **Athletics (Intercollegiate):** *Men:* baseball, basketball, cross-country, diving, lacrosse, soccer, swimming, tennis, track/field (outdoor), track/field (indoor). *Women:* basketball, cross-country, diving, field hockey, lacrosse, soccer, softball, swimming, synchronized swimming, tennis, track/field (outdoor), track/field (indoor), volleyball. **On-Campus Highlights:** Mars Arts and Humanities:a$20 million arts facility, Haas Athletic Center, Lyon's Den—coffee house, Mary Lyon Hall—college's oldest building, Balfour-Hood Student Center. **Environmental Initiatives:** Modeling Sustainability: The opening of the new Mars Science Center. Along with the opening of the Mars Science Center, Wheaton's unique curriculum of "cross-disciplinary" and "connected" courses engage students in academic areas other than their chosen course of study. In addition, the Wheaton curriculum now offers an Environmental Science Major, Environmental Studies Minor,an Environmental List-serve to expand discussion of environmental issues, and a growing list of Environmental Science Internship opportunities offering students field experience in addition to summer research opportunities for students to conduct research in the field of environmental Science by working with faculty in the summer. The Wheaton College Farmers' market initiative, which embodies the mission of the Real Food Challenge.

ADMISSIONS
Freshman Academic Profile: Average high school GPA 3.33. 34% in top 10% of high school class, 69% in top 25% of high school class, 91% in top 50% of high school class. 64% from public high schools. SAT Math middle 50% range 560-670. SAT Critical Reading middle 50% range 560-680. SAT Writing middle 50% range 550-650. ACT middle 50% range 25-28. Minimum internet-based TOEFL 90. **Basis for Candidate Selection:** *Very important factors considered include:* application essay, academic GPA, rigor of secondary school record, character/personal qualities, extracurricular activities, first generation, talent/ability. *Important factors considered include:* Class rank, recommendation(s), alumni/ae relation, interview, volunteer work, work experience. *Other factors considered include:* geographical residence, level of applicant's interest, racial/ethnic status, state residency. **Freshman Admission Requirements:** High school diploma is required and GED is accepted. **Freshman Admission Statistics:** 4,047 applied, 70% admitted, 15% enrolled. **Transfer Admission Requirements:** High school transcript, college transcript(s), essay or personal statement, statement of good standing from prior institution(s). Minimum college GPA of 3.0 required. Lowest grade transferable C. **General Admission Information:** Application Fee $55. Early decision application deadline 11/15. Regular application deadline 1/15. Regular notification 4/1. Nonfall registration accepted. Admission may be deferred for a maximum of 1 year. Credit and/or placement offered for CEEB Advanced Placement tests.

COSTS AND FINANCIAL AID
Annual tuition $46,120. Room and board $11,840. Required fees $303. Average book expense $940. **Required Forms and Deadlines:** FAFSA, CSS/

Financial Aid PROFILE, Noncustodial PROFILE, Business/Farm Supplement. **Notification of Awards:** Applicants will be notified of awards on or about 4/1. **Types of Aid:** *Need-based scholarships/grants:* Federal Pell, SEOG, state scholarships/grants, private scholarships, the school's own gift aid. *Loans:* Subsidized Stafford, Unsubsidized Stafford, PLUS, Federal Perkins. *Student Employment:* Federal Work-Study Program available. Institutional employment available. Highest amount earned per year from on-campus jobs $2,528. Off-campus job opportunities are good. **Financial Aid Statistics:** 99% freshmen, 99% undergrads receive need-based scholarship or grant aid. 15% freshmen, 9% undergrads receive non-need-based scholarship or grant aid. 94% freshmen, 96% undergrads receive need-based self-help aid. 0% freshmen, 0% undergrads receive athletic scholarships. 92% freshmen, 85% undergrads receive any aid. 63% undergrads borrow to pay for school. Average cumulative indebtedness $24,229. **Criteria for awarding institutional aid:** *Non-need-based:* academics.

WHEELING JESUIT UNIVERSITY

316 Washington Avenue, Wheeling, WV 26003
Phone: 304-243-2359 · **Financial Aid Phone:** 304-243–2304
E-mail: admiss@wju.edu · **CEEB Code:** 5906
Fax: 304-243-2397 · **Website:** www.wju.edu · **ACT Code:** 4546

This private school, affiliated with the Roman Catholic Church, was founded in 1954. It has a 70-acre campus.

RATINGS
Admissions Selectivity Rating: 83   **Fire Safety Rating:** 98

STUDENTS AND FACULTY
Enrollment: 1,131. **Student Body:** 52% female, 48% male, 63% out-of-state, 3% international (23 countries represented). Asian 1%, African American 3%, Caucasian 61%, Hispanic 2%, Native American <1%
Retention and Graduation: 74% freshmen return for sophomore year. 54% freshmen graduate within 4 years. 26% grads go on to further study within 1 year. 10% grads pursue arts and sciences degrees. 4% grads pursue law degrees. 8% grads pursue business degrees. 4% grads pursue medical degrees. **Faculty:** 81 full-time faculty, 53% hold PhDs, 59% are are members of minority groups, 5% are women. 0% of classes are taught by teaching assistants.

ACADEMICS
Degrees: bachelor's, master's. **Classes:** Most classes have 10-19 students. Most lab/discussion sessions have 10-19 students. **Majors with Highest Enrollment:** Registered Nursing/Registered Nurse; Business Administration and Management; Psychology. **Special Study Options:** distance learning, double major, English as a Second Language (ESL), honors program, independent study, internships, liberal arts/career combination, student-designed major, study abroad, teacher certification program, Off-campus study: Washington, DC. **Honors programs:** The Laut Honors program which is designed to introduces students to aspects of the arts and sciences that are not available in the regular curriculum in order to inspire and awaken curiosity through a variety of enriching experiences offered. **Combined degree programs:** 3-2 engineering program with Case Western Reserve. **Disability Services:** Special programs offered to physically disabled students include note-taking services, reader services, tutors. **Career services:** Alumni network, alumni services, career/job search classes, career assessment, internships, regional alumni.

FACILITIES
Housing: Coed dorms, special housing for disabled students, men's dorms, special housing for international students, women's dorms, apartments for married students. 85% of campus accessible to physically disabled. **Special Academic Facilities/Equipment:** Center for Educational Technologies (NASA). **Computers:** 10% of classrooms, 100% of libraries, 100% of dining areas, 100% of student union, 10% of common outdoor areas have wireless network access. Students can register for classes online. Administrative functions (other than registration) can be performed online.

CAMPUS LIFE
Environment: Town. **Activities:** Choral groups, dance, drama/theater, literary magazine, musical theater, pep band, radio station, student government, student newspaper, television station, yearbook, Campus Ministries, International Student Organization. 30 registered organizations, 9 honor societies, 6 religious organizations. **Athletics (Intercollegiate):** *Men:* baseball, basketball, cross-country, golf, lacrosse, soccer, swimming, track/field (outdoor), track/field (indoor). *Women:* basketball, cross-country, golf, soccer, softball, swimming, track/field (outdoor), track/field (indoor), volleyball. **On-Campus Highlights:** Coffee Shop- located in Swint Hall, McDonough Fitness Center, Creek Bank

surrounding campus, Rathskeller-Pub on campus, McDonough indoor swimming pool and racquetball court. **Environmental Initiatives:** Faculty/student research related to environmental topics. Sustainability major with student-led projects. Appalachian Institute's collaborative programs with Appalachian communities, including education/research/advocacy related to environmental issues.

ADMISSIONS

Freshman Academic Profile: Average high school GPA 3.38. 16% in top 10% of high school class, 38% in top 25% of high school class, 71% in top 50% of high school class. 78% from public high schools. SAT Math middle 50% range 460-560. SAT Critical Reading middle 50% range 430-540. SAT Writing middle 50% range 410-510. ACT middle 50% range 20-25. Minimum internet-based TOEFL 80. Minimum paper TOEFL 550. **Basis for Candidate Selection:** *Very important factors considered include:* academic GPA, standardized test scores. *Important factors considered include:* application essay, rigor of secondary school record, interview. *Other factors considered include:* recommendation(s), character/personal qualities, extracurricular activities, level of applicant's interest, talent/ability, volunteer work, work experience. **Freshman Admission Requirements:** High school diploma is required and GED is accepted. **Academic units required:** 4 English, 2 mathematics, 1 science, (1 science labs), 2 social studies, 2 history, 6 academic electives. **Freshman Admission Statistics:** 1,445 applied, 63% admitted, 28% enrolled. **Transfer Admission Requirements:** college transcript(s), Minimum college GPA of 2.3 required. Lowest grade transferable C. **General Admission Information:** Application Fee $25. Regular notification 8/15. Notification on a rolling basis, beginning on or about 9/1. Nonfall registration accepted. Admission may be deferred for a maximum of 1 semester. Credit and/or placement offered for CEEB Advanced Placement tests.

COSTS AND FINANCIAL AID

Annual tuition $27,000. Room and board $5,470. Required fees $1,030. Average book expense $1,300. **Required Forms and Deadlines:** FAFSA. **Notification of Awards:** Applicants will be notified of awards on a rolling basis beginning 3/15. **Types of Aid:** *Need-based scholarships/grants:* Federal Pell, SEOG, state scholarships/grants, private scholarships, the school's own gift aid. *Loans:* Direct Subsidized Stafford, Direct Unsubsidized Stafford, Direct PLUS, Subsidized Stafford, Unsubsidized Stafford, PLUS, Federal Perkins, Federal Nursing, Private Alternative Loans. *Student Employment:* Federal Work-Study Program available. Institutional employment available. Highest amount earned per year from on-campus jobs $2,200. Off-campus job opportunities are good. **Financial Aid Statistics:** 65% freshmen, 62% undergrads receive need-based scholarship or grant aid. 95% freshmen, 90% undergrads receive non-need-based scholarship or grant aid. 68% freshmen, 70% undergrads receive need-based self-help aid. 31% freshmen, 28% undergrads receive athletic scholarships. 99% freshmen, 99% undergrads receive any aid. 78% undergrads borrow to pay for school. Average cumulative indebtedness $26,405. **Criteria for awarding institutional aid:** *Non-need-based:* academics, alumni affiliation, athletics, leadership, music/drama.

WHEELOCK COLLEGE

200 The Riverway, Boston, MA 2215
Phone: 617-879-2206 · **Financial Aid Phone:** 617-879-2443
E-mail: undergrad@wheelock.edu · **CEEB Code:** 3964
Fax: 617-879-2449 · **Website:** www.wheelock.edu · **ACT Code:** 1934

This private school was founded in 1888. It has a 6-acre campus.

RATINGS

Admissions Selectivity Rating: 74   **Fire Safety Rating:** 88

STUDENTS AND FACULTY

Enrollment: 867. **Student Body:** 88% female, 12% male, 39% out-of-state, 2% international (20 countries represented). Asian 3%, African American 11%, Caucasian 60%, Hispanic 12%, Native American <1%
Retention and Graduation: 76% freshmen return for sophomore year. 44% freshmen graduate within 4 years. 55% freshmen graduate within 6 years. 19% grads go on to further study within 1 year. 1% grads pursue arts and sciences degrees. 1% grads pursue medical degrees. **Faculty:** 69 full-time faculty, 83% hold PhDs, 74% are are members of minority groups, 26% are women. 0% of classes are taught by teaching assistants.

ACADEMICS

Degrees: bachelor's, master's, post-bachelor's certificate, post-master's certificate. **Classes:** Most classes have 10-19 students. **Majors with Highest Enrollment:** Social Work; Early Childhood Education and Teaching; Elemen-

tary Education and Teaching. **Special Study Options:** cross-registration, double major, honors program, independent study, internships, liberal arts/career combination, study abroad, teacher certification program. **Combined degree programs:** BA/MA. **Disability Services:** Special programs offered to physically disabled students include note-taking services, reader services, tape recorders, tutors. **Career services:** Alumni network, career/job search classes, career assessment, internships.

FACILITIES

Housing: Coed dorms, men's dorms, women's dorms, Wellness Floor, First Year Floors. 67% of campus accessible to physically disabled. **Special Academic Facilities/Equipment:** Art studio, resource center with fully equipped workshop for creating and developing original curriculum tools.

CAMPUS LIFE

Environment: Metropolis. **Activities:** Choral groups, dance, drama/theater, music ensembles, musical theater, student government, symphony orchestra 20 registered organizations, 1 honor society, 1 religous organization. **Athletics (Intercollegiate):** *Men:* basketball, tennis. *Women:* basketball, diving, field hockey, soccer, softball, swimming. **On-Campus Highlights:** The Wheelock Family Theater, The Student Center, The Library, Brookline Campus—Hawes Street, The Resource Center.

ADMISSIONS

Freshman Academic Profile: Average high school GPA 3.11. 8% in top 10% of high school class, 35% in top 25% of high school class, 63% in top 50% of high school class. 85% from public high schools. SAT Math middle 50% range 420-530. SAT Critical Reading middle 50% range 430-550. SAT Writing middle 50% range 430-550. ACT middle 50% range 15-24. Minimum internet-based TOEFL 80. Minimum paper TOEFL 550. **Basis for Candidate Selection:** *Very important factors considered include:* application essay, academic GPA, rigor of secondary school record. *Important factors considered include:* Class rank, recommendation(s), character/personal qualities, extracurricular activities, volunteer work. *Other factors considered include:* standardized test scores, alumni/ae relation, interview, talent/ability, work experience. **Freshman Admission Requirements:** High school diploma is required and GED is accepted. **Academic units required:** 4 English, 3 mathematics, 2 science, (1 science labs), 0 foreign language, 2 social studies, 0 history, 0 academic electives, 0 Child Development Classes. **Freshman Admission Statistics:** 1,458 applied, 88% admitted, 21% enrolled. **Transfer Admission Requirements:** High school transcript, college transcript(s), essay or personal statement, Minimum college GPA of 2.0 required. Lowest grade transferable C. **General Admission Information:** Application Fee $35. Regular application deadline 3/1. Notification on a rolling basis, beginning on or about 1/1. Nonfall registration accepted. Admission may be deferred for a maximum of 1 year. Credit offered for CEEB Advanced Placement tests.

COSTS AND FINANCIAL AID

Annual tuition $29,860. Room and board $12,800. Required fees $1,095. Average book expense $880. **Required Forms and Deadlines:** FAFSA. **Notification of Awards:** Applicants will be notified of awards on a rolling basis beginning 3/5. **Types of Aid:** *Need-based scholarships/grants:* Federal Pell, SEOG, state scholarships/grants, the school's own gift aid, Merit scholarships are available for all freshmen applicants with a 3.0 G.P.A.(or higher) and SAT scores of 1050(or higher). Scholarhips range from $3000 to $12,000. *Loans:* Subsidized Stafford, Unsubsidized Stafford, PLUS, Federal Perkins, college/university loans from institutional funds. *Student Employment:* Federal Work-Study Program available. Institutional employment available. Highest amount earned per year from on-campus jobs $2,000. Off-campus job opportunities are good. **Financial Aid Statistics:** 100% freshmen, 100% undergrads receive need-based scholarship or grant aid. 11% freshmen, 10% undergrads receive non-need-based scholarship or grant aid. 87% freshmen, 87% undergrads receive need-based self-help aid. 0% freshmen, 0% undergrads receive athletic scholarships. 85% freshmen, 83% undergrads receive any aid. 85% undergrads borrow to pay for school. Average cumulative indebtedness $28,971. **Criteria for awarding institutional aid:** *Non-need-based:* academics, leadership.

WHITMAN COLLEGE

Best 380

345 Boyer Ave, Walla Walla, WA 99362
Phone: 509-527-5176 • **Financial Aid Phone:** 509-527-5178
E-mail: admission@whitman.edu • **CEEB Code:** 4951
Fax: 509-527-4967 • **Website:** www.whitman.edu • **ACT Code:** 4492

This private school was founded in 1883. It has a 117-acre campus.

RATINGS

Admissions Selectivity Rating: 94   **Fire Safety Rating:** 73

STUDENTS AND FACULTY

Enrollment: 1,480. **Student Body:** 56% female, 44% male, 65% out-of-state, 4% international (28 countries represented). Asian 5%, African American 1%, Caucasian 73%, Hispanic 8%, Native American <1%
Retention and Graduation: 94% freshmen return for sophomore year. 82% freshmen graduate within 4 years. 87% freshmen graduate within 6 years. **Faculty:** 154 full-time faculty, 91% hold PhDs, 47% are are members of minority groups, 7% are women. 0% of classes are taught by teaching assistants.

ACADEMICS

Degrees: bachelor's. **Classes:** Most classes have 10-19 students. Most lab/discussion sessions have 20-29 students. **Majors with Highest Enrollment:** Biology/Biological Sciences; Psychology; English Language and Literature. **Special Study Options:** Accelerated program, cooperative education program, cross-registration, double major, dual enrollment, exchange student program (domestic), honors program, independent study, liberal arts/career combination, student-designed major, study abroad, Undergraduate research conference. **Combined degree programs:** BA/JD, BA/MA, 3-2 Forest./Duke; 3-2 Ocean./Bio. or Geo. **Disability Services:** Special programs offered to physically disabled students include note-taking services, reader services, tape recorders, tutors. **Career services:** Alumni network, alumni services, career assessment.

FACILITIES

Housing: Coed dorms, special housing for international students, women's dorms, fraternity/sorority housing, apartments for single students, Theme HousingInterest houses. 85% of campus accessible to physically disabled. **Special Academic Facilities/Equipment:** Art gallery, Asian art collection, anthropology museum, planetarium, outdoor observatory, two electron microscopes, outdoor sculpture walk, technology/video-conferencing center, indoor and outdoor rock-climbing walls, organic garden. **Computers:** 100% of classrooms, 100% of dorms, 100% of libraries, 100% of dining areas, 100% of student union, 40% of common outdoor areas have wireless network access. Students can register for classes online. Administrative functions (other than registration) can be performed online.

CAMPUS LIFE

Environment: Town. **Activities:** Choral groups, concert band, dance, drama/theater, jazz band, literary magazine, music ensembles, musical theater, radio station, student government, student newspaper, student-run film society, symphony orchestra, Campus Ministries, International Student Organization, Model UN. 80 registered organizations, 3 honor societies, 7 religious organizations. 4 fraternities, 3 sororities. **Athletics (Intercollegiate):** *Men:* baseball, basketball, cross-country, golf, soccer, swimming, tennis. *Women:* basketball, cross-country, golf, soccer, swimming, tennis, volleyball. **On-Campus Highlights:** Reid Campus Center, Penrose Library, Baker Fergueson Fitness Center, Sheehan Art Gallery, Olin Hall, Harper Joy Theatre. **Environmental Initiatives:** Installed 21kW Solar Panels on roof of Bratton Tennis Center. Co-sponsored the inaugural 2014 Washington State Higher Education Sustainability Conference along with other schools in Washington State. Creation of a Sustainability Revolving Loan Fund, a $50,000 line of credit that is designated for campus improvements that significantly benefit Whitman's sustainability efforts by conserving resources and improving efficiency.

ADMISSIONS

Freshman Academic Profile: Average high school GPA 3.79. 53% in top 10% of high school class, 88.3% in top 25% of high school class, 98.7% in top 50% of high school class. 71% from public high schools. SAT Math middle 50% range 600-710. SAT Critical Reading middle 50% range 600-720. SAT Writing middle 50% range 600-710. ACT middle 50% range 28-32. Minimum internet-based TOEFL 85. Minimum paper TOEFL 560. **Basis for Candidate Selection:** *Very important factors considered include:* application essay, academic GPA, rigor of secondary school record, character/personal qualities. *Important factors*

considered include: recommendation(s), standardized test scores, extracurricular activities, racial/ethnic status, talent/ability. *Other factors considered include:* Class rank, alumni/ae relation, first generation, geographical residence, interview, level of applicant's interest, state residency, volunteer work, work experience. **Freshman Admission Requirements:** High school diploma is required and GED is accepted. **Freshman Admission Statistics:** 3,653 applied, 41% admitted, 26% enrolled. **Transfer Admission Requirements:** High school transcript, college transcript(s), essay or personal statement, statement of good standing from prior institution(s). Lowest grade transferable C-. **General Admission Information:** Application Fee $50. Early decision application deadline 11/15. Regular application deadline 1/15. Regular notification 4/1. Nonfall registration accepted. Admission may be deferred for a maximum of 1 year. Credit and/or placement offered for CEEB Advanced Placement tests.

COSTS AND FINANCIAL AID

Annual tuition $44,440. Room and board $11,228. Required fees $360. Average book expense $1,400. **Required Forms and Deadlines:** FAFSA, CSS/Financial Aid PROFILE, Noncustodial PROFILE. **Notification of Awards:** Applicants will be notified of awards on a rolling basis beginning 12/20. **Types of Aid:** *Need-based scholarships/grants:* Federal Pell, SEOG, state scholarships/grants, private scholarships, the school's own gift aid. *Loans:* Subsidized Stafford, Unsubsidized Stafford, PLUS, Federal Perkins, state loans, Alternative Loans. Student *Student Employment:* Federal Work-Study Program available. Institutional employment available. Highest amount earned per year from on-campus jobs $2,463. Off-campus job opportunities are good. **Financial Aid Statistics:** 100% freshmen, 100% undergrads receive need-based scholarship or grant aid. 0% freshmen, 0% undergrads receive non-need-based scholarship or grant aid. 69% freshmen, 68% undergrads receive need-based self-help aid. 0% freshmen, 0% undergrads receive athletic scholarships. 73% freshmen, 77% undergrads receive any aid. 49% undergrads borrow to pay for school. Average cumulative indebtedness $17,395. **Criteria for awarding institutional aid:** *Non-need-based:* academics, art, leadership, minority status, music/drama.

WHITTIER COLLEGE

Best 380

13406 Philadelphia Street, Whittier, CA 90608
Phone: 562-907-4238 • **Financial Aid Phone:** 562-907-4285
E-mail: admission@whittier.edu • **CEEB Code:** 4952
Fax: 562-907-4870 • **Website:** www.whittier.edu • **ACT Code:** 480

This private school was founded in 1887. It has a 75-acre campus.

RATINGS

Admissions Selectivity Rating: 84   **Fire Safety Rating:** 90

STUDENTS AND FACULTY

Enrollment: 1,361. **Student Body:** 53% female, 47% male, 27% out-of-state, 2% international (24 countries represented). Asian 9%, African American 6%, Caucasian 41%, Hispanic 30%, Native American 1%
Retention and Graduation: 55% freshmen graduate within 4 years. 61% freshmen graduate within 6 years. 18% grads go on to further study within 1 year. 7% grads pursue arts and sciences degrees. 2% grads pursue law degrees. 3% grads pursue business degrees. 1% grads pursue medical degrees. **Faculty:** 96 full-time faculty, 99% hold PhDs, 47% are are members of minority groups, 27% are women. 0% of classes are taught by teaching assistants.

ACADEMICS

Degrees: bachelor's, master's. **Classes:** Most classes have 10-19 students. Most lab/discussion sessions have 20-29 students. **Majors with Highest Enrollment:** Biology/Biological Sciences; Criminal Justice/Safety Studies; Business Administration and Management. **Special Study Options:** double major, independent study, internships, liberal arts/career combination, student-designed major, study abroad, teacher certification program. **Combined degree programs:** BA/JD, 3-2 engineering programs. **Disability Services:** Special programs offered to physically disabled students include note-taking services, reader services, tape recorders. **Career services:** Alumni network, alumni services, career/job search classes, career assessment, internships, regional alumni. Career services highlights include Backpack to Briefcase: The Office of Career Services and the Office of Alumni Relations have teamed up to present a series of workshops throughout the school year to enable students to learn and develop practical career skills and explore diverse career paths, and at the same time showcase Whittier College alumni professionals, who serve as volunteer mentors and workshop leaders.

FACILITIES

Housing: Coed dorms, special housing for international students, living and learning community; special interest housing. 60% of campus accessible to physically disabled. **Special Academic Facilities/Equipment:** Performing arts center, on-campus pre-school/ elementary school, image processing lab, state-of-the-art nightclub, on-air radio studio and production room, video production room **Computers:** 100% of classrooms, 100% of dorms, 100% of libraries, 100% of dining areas, 100% of student union, have wireless network access. Students can register for classes online. Administrative functions (other than registration) can be performed online.

CAMPUS LIFE

Environment: City. **Activities:** Choral groups, dance, drama/theater, jazz band, literary magazine, music ensembles, musical theater, radio station, student government, student newspaper, student-run film society, yearbook, Campus Ministries, International Student Organization, Model UN. 60 registered organizations, 17 honor societies, 6 religious organizations. 4 fraternities, 5 sororities. **Athletics (Intercollegiate):** *Men:* baseball, basketball, cross-country, diving, football, golf, lacrosse, soccer, swimming, tennis, track/ field (outdoor), water polo. *Women:* basketball, cross-country, diving, lacrosse, soccer, softball, swimming, tennis, track/field (outdoor), volleyball, water polo. **On-Campus Highlights:** The Campus Center, Bonnie Bell Wardman Library, Donald Graham Athletics Center, Ruth B. Shannon Center for the Performing Arts, the Rock (campus icon), The recently renovated Campus Center houses the student services division, campus dining, The Spot (campus Café),student organization offices, KPOET radio, student newspaper Quaker Campus, and an outdoor amphitheatre. **Environmental Initiatives:** Climate Commitment signatory; EnergyStar purchasing policy; Waste minimization program.

ADMISSIONS

Freshman Academic Profile: Average high school GPA 3.37. 28% in top 10% of high school class, 44% in top 25% of high school class, 92% in top 50% of high school class. SAT Math middle 50% range 480-590. SAT Critical Reading middle 50% range 460-580. SAT Writing middle 50% range 470-580. ACT middle 50% range 20-25. Minimum paper TOEFL 550. **Basis for Candidate Selection:** *Very important factors considered include:* application essay, rigor of secondary school record. *Important factors considered include:* academic GPA, recommendation(s), standardized test scores, character/personal qualities, extracurricular activities, interview, talent/ability, volunteer work. *Other factors considered include:* Class rank, alumni/ae relation, first generation, geographical residence, racial/ethnic status, state residency, work experience. **Freshman Admission Requirements:** High school diploma is required and GED is accepted. **Academic units required:** 3 English, 2 mathematics, 1 science, (1 science labs), 2 foreign language, 1 social studies. **Freshman Admission Statistics:** 4,123 applied, 64% admitted, 16% enrolled. **Transfer Admission Requirements:** High school transcript, college transcript(s), essay or personal statement, Lowest grade transferable C-. **General Admission Information:** Application Fee $50. Notification on a rolling basis, beginning on or about 12/30. Nonfall registration accepted. Admission may be deferred for a maximum of 1 year. Credit and/or placement offered for CEEB Advanced Placement tests.

COSTS AND FINANCIAL AID

Annual tuition $39,736. Room and board $11,494. Required fees $560. Average book expense $650. **Required Forms and Deadlines:** FAFSA. **Notification of Awards:** Applicants will be notified of awards on a rolling basis beginning 2/15. **Types of Aid:** *Need-based scholarships/grants:* Federal Pell, SEOG, state scholarships/grants, private scholarships, the school's own gift aid. *Loans:* Direct PLUS, Subsidized Stafford, Unsubsidized Stafford, PLUS, Federal Perkins, Alternative Financing *Student Employment:* Federal Work-Study Program available. Highest amount earned per year from on-campus jobs $1,250. Off-campus job opportunities are good. **Financial Aid Statistics:** 91% freshmen, 92% undergrads receive need-based scholarship or grant aid. 8% freshmen, 8% undergrads receive non-need-based scholarship or grant aid. 85% freshmen, 87% undergrads receive need-based self-help aid. 0% freshmen, 0% undergrads receive athletic scholarships. 92% freshmen, 89% undergrads receive any aid. 74% undergrads borrow to pay for school. Average cumulative indebtedness $26,199. **Criteria for awarding institutional aid:** *Non-need-based:* academics, alumni affiliation, art, music/drama.

WHITWORTH UNIVERSITY

300 West Hawthorne Road, Spokane, WA 99251
Phone: 509-777-4786 · **Financial Aid Phone:** 509-777-4306
E-mail: admissions@whitworth.edu · **CEEB Code:** 4953
Fax: 509-777-3758 · **ACT Code:** 4494

This private school, affiliated with the Presbyterian Church, was founded in 1890. It has a 200-acre campus.

RATINGS

Admissions Selectivity Rating: 87   **Fire Safety Rating:** 70

STUDENTS AND FACULTY

Enrollment: 2,340. **Student Body:** 59% female, 41% male, 36% out-of-state, 2% international (15 countries represented). Asian 4%, African American 2%, Caucasian 76%, Hispanic 9%, Native American 1%
Retention and Graduation: 65% freshmen graduate within 4 years. 75% freshmen graduate within 6 years. 20% grads go on to further study within 1 year. **Faculty:** 178 full-time faculty, 79% hold PhDs, 43% are are members of minority groups, 9% are women. 0% of classes are taught by teaching assistants.

ACADEMICS

Degrees: bachelor's, master's. **Classes:** Most classes have 10-19 students. Most lab/discussion sessions have 10-19 students. **Majors with Highest Enrollment:** Psychology; Health Services/Allied Health/Health Sciences; Biology/ Biological Sciences. **Special Study Options:** cooperative education program, cross-registration, double major, dual enrollment, English as a Second Language (ESL), exchange student program (domestic), honors program, independent study, internships, liberal arts/career combination, student-designed major, study abroad, teacher certification program. **Disability Services:** Special programs offered to physically disabled students include note-taking services, reader services, tape recorders.

FACILITIES

Housing: Coed dorms, men's dorms, women's dorms, Theme houses within walking distance to the campus. 80% of campus accessible to physically disabled. **Special Academic Facilities/Equipment:** Language laboratory, art gallery, computer labs **Computers:** Students can register for classes online. Administrative functions (other than registration) can be performed online.

CAMPUS LIFE

Environment: City. **Activities:** Choral groups, concert band, dance, drama/ theater, jazz band, music ensembles, musical theater, pep band, radio station, student government, student newspaper, symphony orchestra, yearbook. 50 registered organizations, 5 honor societies. **Athletics (Intercollegiate):** *Men:* baseball, basketball, cheerleading, cross-country, football, golf, soccer, swimming, tennis, track/field (outdoor). *Women:* basketball, cheerleading, cross-country, golf, soccer, softball, swimming, tennis, track/field (outdoor), volleyball. **On-Campus Highlights:** Hixon Union Building (Student Union)—Café, Weyerhauser Hall (Teaching Theatre), Boppell Hall—new dormitory for upperclassman, Athletic Complex, Library.

ADMISSIONS

Freshman Academic Profile: Average high school GPA 3.76. 83% from public high schools. SAT Math middle 50% range 530-640. SAT Critical Reading middle 50% range 520-640. SAT Writing middle 50% range 510-620. ACT middle 50% range 24-29. Minimum paper TOEFL 550. **Basis for Candidate Selection:** *Very important factors considered include:* Class rank, application essay, recommendation(s), rigor of secondary school record, standardized test scores. *Important factors considered include:* alumni/ae relation, character/ personal qualities, extracurricular activities, geographical residence, interview, talent/ability. *Other factors considered include:* racial/ethnic status, religious affiliation/commitment, volunteer work. **Freshman Admission Requirements:** High school diploma is required and GED is accepted. **Freshman Admission Statistics:** 3,208 applied, 99% admitted, 19% enrolled. **Transfer Admission Requirements:** High school transcript, college transcript(s), essay or personal statement, standardized test scores, statement of good standing from prior institution(s). Minimum college GPA of 2.5 required. Lowest grade transferable C-. **General Admission Information:** Regular application deadline 3/1. Notification on a rolling basis, beginning on or about 12/20. Nonfall registration accepted. Admission may be deferred for a maximum of 12 months. Credit offered for CEEB Advanced Placement tests.

COSTS AND FINANCIAL AID

Annual tuition $35,320. Room and board $9,814. Required fees $692. Average book expense $687. **Required Forms and Deadlines:** FAFSA. **Notification of Awards:** Applicants will be notified of awards on a rolling basis beginning 4/1. **Types of Aid:** *Need-based scholarships/grants:* Federal Pell, SEOG, state scholarships/grants, private scholarships, the school's own gift aid. *Loans:* Direct

Subsidized Stafford, Direct Unsubsidized Stafford, Direct PLUS, Federal Perkins, college/university loans from institutional funds. *Student Employment:* Highest amount earned per year from on-campus jobs $2,500. **Financial Aid Statistics:** 99% freshmen, 99% undergrads receive need-based scholarship or grant aid. 11% freshmen, 9% undergrads receive non-need-based scholarship or grant aid. 84% freshmen, 83% undergrads receive need-based self-help aid. 0% freshmen, 0% undergrads receive athletic scholarships. 97% freshmen, 90% undergrads receive any aid. 69% undergrads borrow to pay for school. Average cumulative indebtedness $23,521. **Criteria for awarding institutional aid:** *Non-need-based:* academics, alumni affiliation, art, music/drama, religious affiliation.

WICHITA STATE UNIVERSITY

1845 Fairmount, Wichita, KS 67260
Phone: 316-978-3085 · **Financial Aid Phone:** 1-855-978-1787
E-mail: admissions@wichita.edu · **CEEB Code:** 6884
Fax: 316-978-3174 · **Website:** www.wichita.edu · **ACT Code:** 1472

This public school was founded in 1895. It has a 330-acre campus.

RATINGS
Admissions Selectivity Rating: 77   **Fire Safety Rating:** 72

STUDENTS AND FACULTY
Enrollment: 11,299. **Student Body:** 52% female, 48% male, 6% out-of-state, 6% international (72 countries represented). Asian 7%, African American 6%, Caucasian 63%, Hispanic 10%, Native American 1%
Retention and Graduation: 70% freshmen return for sophomore year. 19% freshmen graduate within 4 years. 44% freshmen graduate within 6 years. **Faculty:** 527 full-time faculty, 72% hold PhDs, 44% are are members of minority groups, 15% are women. 20% of classes are taught by teaching assistants.

ACADEMICS
Degrees: associate, bachelor's, certificate, diploma, doctoral, master's, post-bachelor's certificate, post-master's certificate, terminal associate, transfer associate. **Classes:** Most classes have 10-19 students. Most lab/discussion sessions have 20-29 students. **Majors with Highest Enrollment:** Aerospace, Aeronautical and Astronautical/Space Engineering; Business Administration and Management; Registered Nursing/Registered Nurse. **Special Study Options:** Accelerated program, cooperative education program, cross-registration, distance learning, double major, dual enrollment, English as a Second Language (ESL), exchange student program (domestic), honors program, independent study, internships, study abroad, teacher certification program. **Honors programs:** Emory Lindquist Honors Program. The Honors Program offers freshman/sophomore seminars, lower division regular classes, honors colloquia, and honors upper division sections of regular classes. Students can also choose to do independent study projects. The Honors Program also offers a Senior Project, which is an opportunity for students to earn special honors recognition in a student's academic major. **Disability Services:** Special programs offered to physically disabled students include note-taking services, reader services, tape recorders, tutors. **Career services:** Alumni network, alumni services, career/job search classes, career assessment, internships, regional alumni. Career services highlights include our mission to empower our clients (students, alumni, faculty, staff and community members) with the skills, knowledge and resources necessary for effective career development, and to build partnerships with employers to expand client career opportunities.

FACILITIES
Housing: Coed dorms, fraternity/sorority housing, apartments for married students, apartments for single students. Some dorm floors are reserved for students majoring in Fine Arts, Health Professions, and for students in the Emory Lindquist Honors Program. 98% of campus accessible to physically disabled. **Special Academic Facilities/Equipment:** Art museum, performance hall, media resource center, observatory, national institute of aviation research, supersonic wind tunnels, 24-hour study room in library, outdoor sculpture collection. **Computers:** Students can register for classes online. Administrative functions (other than registration) can be performed online.

CAMPUS LIFE
Environment: Metropolis. **Activities:** Choral groups, concert band, dance, drama/theater, jazz band, literary magazine, music ensembles, musical theater, opera, pep band, radio station, student government, student newspaper, student-run film society, symphony orchestra, television station, Campus Ministries, International Student Organization, Model UN. 140 registered organizations, 11 honor societies, 10 religious organizations. 11 fraternities, 10 sororities. **Athletics (Intercollegiate):** *Men:* baseball, basketball, bowling, cheerleading,

cross-country, golf, rugby, swimming, tennis, track/field (outdoor). *Women:* basketball, bowling, cheerleading, cross-country, golf, softball, swimming, tennis, track/field (outdoor), volleyball. **On-Campus Highlights:** Rhatigan Student Center, Ulrich Museum of Art, Heskett Center, outdoor sculpture collection, Charles Koch arena, Wichita State University, founded in 1895 as a Congregational institution, is distinguished from other state supported schools in Kansas by its urban setting. Wichita State's location in the largest city in Kansas enhances the traditional classroom experience by providing students greater opportunities in resources, contacts with business and government leaders, employment, and internships. **Environmental Initiatives:** Recycle Program.

ADMISSIONS
Freshman Academic Profile: Average high school GPA 3.45. 21.4% in top 10% of high school class, 48.3% in top 25% of high school class, 79.6% in top 50% of high school class. SAT Math middle 50% range 510-610. SAT Critical Reading middle 50% range 480-620. ACT middle 50% range 21-26. Minimum internet-based TOEFL 72. Minimum paper TOEFL 530. **Basis for Candidate Selection:** *Very important factors considered include:* Class rank, academic GPA, rigor of secondary school record, standardized test scores. **Freshman Admission Requirements:** High school diploma is required and GED is accepted. **Academic units required:** 4 English, 4 mathematics, 3 science, 3 social studies, 1 computer proficiency. **Freshman Admission Statistics:** 4,517 applied, 96% admitted, 37% enrolled. **Transfer Admission Requirements:** college transcript(s), Minimum college GPA of 2.0 required. Lowest grade transferable C. **General Admission Information:** Application Fee $30. Non-fall registration accepted. Admission may be deferred for a maximum of 2 years. Credit and/or placement offered for CEEB Advanced Placement tests.

COSTS AND FINANCIAL AID
Annual in-state tuition $5,869. Annual out-of-state tuition $13,903. Room and board $8,373. Required fees $1,396. Average book expense $975. **Required Forms and Deadlines:** FAFSA. **Notification of Awards:** Applicants will be notified of awards on a rolling basis beginning 3/15. **Types of Aid:** *Need-based scholarships/grants:* Federal Pell, SEOG, state scholarships/grants, private scholarships, the school's own gift aid, Bureau of Indian Affairs. *Loans:* Subsidized Stafford, Unsubsidized Stafford, PLUS, Federal Perkins. *Student Employment:* Federal Work-Study Program available. Institutional employment available. Highest amount earned per year from on-campus jobs $14,224. Off-campus job opportunities are excellent. **Financial Aid Statistics:** 73% freshmen, 64% undergrads receive need-based scholarship or grant aid. 60% freshmen, 30% undergrads receive non-need-based scholarship or grant aid. 62% freshmen, 77% undergrads receive need-based self-help aid. 4% freshmen, 4% undergrads receive athletic scholarships. 58% freshmen, 85% undergrads receive any aid. 68% undergrads borrow to pay for school. Average cumulative indebtedness $22,863. **Criteria for awarding institutional aid:** *Non-need-based:* academics, alumni affiliation, art, athletics, leadership, music/drama.

WIDENER UNIVERSITY

One University Place, Chester, PA 19013
Phone: 610-499-4126 · **Financial Aid Phone:** 610-499-4152
E-mail: admissions.office@widener.edu · **CEEB Code:** 2642
Fax: 610-499-4676 · **Website:** www.widener.edu · **ACT Code:** 3652

This private school was founded in 1821. It has a 110-acre campus.

RATINGS
Admissions Selectivity Rating: 82   **Fire Safety Rating:** 60*

STUDENTS AND FACULTY
Enrollment: 3,218. **Student Body:** 55% female, 45% male, 40% out-of-state, 4% international (38 countries represented). Asian 4%, African American 13%, Caucasian 70%, Hispanic 5%, Native American <1%
Retention and Graduation: 76% freshmen return for sophomore year. 37% freshmen graduate within 4 years. 53% freshmen graduate within 6 years. 20% grads go on to further study within 1 year. **Faculty:** 286 full-time faculty, 90% hold PhDs, 55% are are members of minority groups, 17% are women. 0% of classes are taught by teaching assistants.

ACADEMICS
Degrees: associate, bachelor's, certificate, master's. **Classes:** Most classes have 10-19 students. Most lab/discussion sessions have fewer than 10 students. **Majors with Highest Enrollment:** Registered Nursing/Registered Nurse; Business/Commerce; Psychology. **Special Study Options:** Accelerated program, cooperative education program, distance learning, double major, English as a Second Language (ESL), honors program, independent study, internships, liberal arts/career combination, student-designed major, study abroad, teacher

certification program, weekend college. **Honors programs:** Honors Program in General Education. **Combined degree programs:** BA/MD, BA/MA, BA/MEng. **Disability Services:** Special programs offered to physically disabled students include note-taking services, reader services, tape recorders, tutors. **Career services:** Alumni network, alumni services, career/job search classes, career assessment, regional alumni.

FACILITIES

Housing: Coed dorms, men's dorms, women's dorms, fraternity/sorority housing, cooperative housing, apartments for single students, Wellness Housing, Theme Housing. **Special Academic Facilities/Equipment:** Art gallery, restaurant lab, child development center education lab, recording studio, commercial graphics lab, physical therapy lab, science labs, engineering labs, nursing labs, multimedia classrooms, Media Center. **Computers:** Students can register for classes online. Administrative functions (other than registration) can be performed online.

CAMPUS LIFE

Environment: Town. **Activities:** Choral groups, concert band, dance, drama/theater, jazz band, literary magazine, music ensembles, pep band, radio station, student government, student newspaper, student-run film society, television station, yearbook, Campus Ministries, International Student Organization. 80 registered organizations, 29 honor societies, 3 religious organizations. 7 fraternities, 3 sororities. **Athletics (Intercollegiate):** *Men:* baseball, basketball, cross-country, football, golf, lacrosse, soccer, swimming, tennis, track/field (outdoor), track/field (indoor). *Women:* basketball, cheerleading, cross-country, field hockey, lacrosse, soccer, softball, swimming, tennis, track/field (outdoor), track/field (indoor), volleyball. **On-Campus Highlights:** University Center, Java City and Residential Restaurant, Schwartz Athletic Center, Greek Row, Art Gallery, PMC Museum, Media Center, Observatory.

ADMISSIONS

Freshman Academic Profile: Average high school GPA 3.46. 12% in top 10% of high school class, 36% in top 25% of high school class, 73% in top 50% of high school class. 55% from public high schools. SAT Math middle 50% range 470-580. SAT Critical Reading middle 50% range 450-550. ACT middle 50% range 19-24. Minimum paper TOEFL 500. **Basis for Candidate Selection:** *Very important factors considered include:* Class rank, academic GPA, rigor of secondary school record, standardized test scores. *Other factors considered include:* application essay, recommendation(s), alumni/ae relation, character/personal qualities, extracurricular activities, interview, level of applicant's interest, talent/ability, volunteer work. **Freshman Admission Requirements:** High school diploma is required and GED is accepted. **Academic units required:** 4 English, 3 mathematics, 3 science, (0 science labs), 2 foreign language, 3 social studies, 3 academic electives. **Freshman Admission Statistics:** 5,501 applied, 65% admitted, 21% enrolled. **Transfer Admission Requirements:** college transcript(s), Minimum college GPA of 2.0 required. Lowest grade transferable C. **General Admission Information:** Application Fee $35. Notification on a rolling basis, beginning on or about 10/1. Nonfall registration accepted. Admission may be deferred for a maximum of 1 academic year. Credit offered for CEEB Advanced Placement tests.

COSTS AND FINANCIAL AID

Annual tuition $39,052. Room and board $12,588. Required fees $778. Average book expense $1,300. **Required Forms and Deadlines:** FAFSA. **Notification of Awards:** Applicants will be notified of awards on a rolling basis beginning 3/15. **Types of Aid:** *Need-based scholarships/grants:* Federal Pell, SEOG, state scholarships/grants, private scholarships, the school's own gift aid, Federal Nursing Scholarships. *Loans:* Subsidized Stafford, Unsubsidized Stafford, PLUS, Federal Perkins. *Student Employment:* Federal Work-Study Program available. Institutional employment available. Off-campus job opportunities are good. **Financial Aid Statistics:** 97% freshmen, 97% undergrads receive need-based scholarship or grant aid. 96% freshmen, 89% undergrads receive non-need-based scholarship or grant aid. 77% freshmen, 93% undergrads receive need-based self-help aid. 0% freshmen, 0% undergrads receive athletic scholarships. 99% freshmen, 90% undergrads receive any aid. **Criteria for awarding institutional aid:** *Non-need-based:* academics, leadership, music/drama.

WILBERFORCE UNIVERSITY

1055 N. Bickett Road, Wilberforce, OH 45384
Phone: 800-367-8568
E-mail: kchristm@shorter.wilberforce · **CEEB Code:** 1906
Fax: 937-376-4751 · **Website:** www.wilberforce.edu · **ACT Code:** 3360

This private school was founded in 1856. It has a 125-acre campus.

RATINGS

Admissions Selectivity Rating: 70   **Fire Safety Rating:** 60*

STUDENTS AND FACULTY

Enrollment: 1,180. **Student Body:** 60% female, 40% male, 39% out-of-state, 0% international (2 countries represented). Asian 0%, African American 90%, Caucasian 5%, Hispanic 1%, Native American <1%
Faculty: 49 full-time faculty, 45% are are members of minority groups, 67% are women.

ACADEMICS

Degrees: bachelor's. **Special Study Options:** Accelerated program, cooperative education program, cross-registration, distance learning, double major, external degree program, honors program, independent study, internships, liberal arts/career combination, student-designed major, study abroad. **Career services:** career/job search classes, career assessment, internships.

FACILITIES

Housing: Coed dorms, men's dorms, women's dorms, apartments for married students. **Special Academic Facilities/Equipment:** African Methodist Church archives.

CAMPUS LIFE

Activities: Choral groups, concert band, dance, jazz band, literary magazine, music ensembles, radio station, student government, student newspaper, yearbook 4 religious organizations. 4 fraternities, 4 sororities.

ADMISSIONS

Freshman Academic Profile: Minimum paper TOEFL 500. **Freshman Admission Requirements:** High school diploma is required and GED is accepted. **Academic units required:** 4 English, 2 mathematics, 2 science, 2 social studies, 5 academic electives. **Freshman Admission Statistics:** 2,405 applied, 22% admitted, 36% enrolled. **Transfer Admission Requirements:** college transcript(s), Minimum college GPA of 2.0 required. Lowest grade transferable C. **General Admission Information:** Application Fee $20. Regular application deadline 6/1. Nonfall registration accepted. Credit and/or placement offered for CEEB Advanced Placement tests.

COSTS AND FINANCIAL AID

Required fees $1,060. Average book expense $1,000. **Required Forms and Deadlines:** FAFSA, Institution's own financial aid form, State aid form. **Types of Aid:** *Need-based scholarships/grants:* United Negro College Fund. *Loans:* Subsidized Stafford, PLUS. *Student Employment:* Federal Work-Study Program available. Highest amount earned per year from on-campus jobs $2,000. Off-campus job opportunities are good.

WILKES UNIVERSITY

84 W South St, Wilkes-Barre, PA 18766
Phone: 570-408-4400 · **Financial Aid Phone:** 570-408-2000
E-mail: admissions@wilkes.edu · **CEEB Code:** 2977
Fax: 570-408-4904 · **Website:** www.wilkes.edu · **ACT Code:** 3756

This private school was founded in 1933. It has a 27-acre campus.

RATINGS

Admissions Selectivity Rating: 79   **Fire Safety Rating:** 78

STUDENTS AND FACULTY

Enrollment: 2,316. **Student Body:** 47% female, 53% male, 16% out-of-state, 9% international (21 countries represented). Asian 2%, African American 3%, Caucasian 74%, Hispanic 6%, Native American <1%
Retention and Graduation: 79% freshmen return for sophomore year. 45% freshmen graduate within 4 years. 56% freshmen graduate within 6 years. **Faculty:** 172 full-time faculty, 90% hold PhDs, 47% are are members of minority groups, 11% are women. 0% of classes are taught by teaching assistants.

ACADEMICS

Degrees: bachelor's, doctoral, master's. **Classes:** Most classes have 10-19 students. Most lab/discussion sessions have 10-19 students. **Majors with Highest Enrollment:** Business Administration and Management; Registered Nursing/Registered Nurse; Psychology. **Special Study Options:** cooperative education program, cross-registration, distance learning, double major, dual enrollment, English as a Second Language (ESL), external degree program, honors program, independent study, internships, student-designed major, study abroad, teacher certification program, weekend college. **Disability Services:** Special programs offered to physically disabled students include note-taking services, reader services, tape recorders, tutors. **Career services:** Alumni network, alumni services, career/job search classes, career assessment, internships, regional alumni.

FACILITIES

Housing: Coed dorms, men's dorms, women's dorms, apartments for single students. **Special Academic Facilities/Equipment:** Art gallery, performing arts center, electron microscope, television studio. **Computers:** Students can register for classes online. Administrative functions (other than registration) can be performed online.

CAMPUS LIFE

Environment: City. **Activities:** Choral groups, dance, drama/theater, jazz band, literary magazine, music ensembles, musical theater, pep band, radio station, student government, student newspaper, television station, yearbook, Campus Ministries, International Student Organization. 65 registered organizations, 19 honor societies. **Athletics (Intercollegiate):** *Men:* baseball, basketball, cross-country, football, golf, soccer, tennis, wrestling. *Women:* basketball, cross-country, field hockey, lacrosse, soccer, softball, tennis, volleyball.

ADMISSIONS

Freshman Academic Profile: 25% in top 10% of high school class, 53% in top 25% of high school class, 82% in top 50% of high school class. SAT Math middle 50% range 470-590. SAT Critical Reading middle 50% range 460-570. SAT Writing middle 50% range 440-560. Minimum internet-based TOEFL 61. Minimum paper TOEFL 500. **Basis for Candidate Selection:** *Very important factors considered include:* Class rank, rigor of secondary school record. *Important factors considered include:* academic GPA, standardized test scores, character/personal qualities, extracurricular activities. *Other factors considered include:* recommendation(s), alumni/ae relation, interview, talent/ability, volunteer work, work experience. **Freshman Admission Requirements:** High school diploma is required and GED is accepted. **Freshman Admission Statistics:** 2,812 applied, 79% admitted, 25% enrolled. **Transfer Admission Requirements:** college transcript(s), statement of good standing from prior institution(s). Minimum college GPA of 2.0 required. Lowest grade transferable C. **General Admission Information:** Application Fee $40. Notification on a rolling basis, beginning on or about 9/1. Nonfall registration accepted. Admission may be deferred for a maximum of 12 months. Credit and/or placement offered for CEEB Advanced Placement tests.

COSTS AND FINANCIAL AID

Annual tuition $29,750. Room and board $12,808. Required fees $1,512. Average book expense $1,500. **Required Forms and Deadlines:** FAFSA. **Notification of Awards:** Applicants will be notified of awards on a rolling basis beginning 3/1. **Types of Aid:** *Need-based scholarships/grants:* Federal Pell, SEOG, state scholarships/grants, private scholarships, the school's own gift aid. *Loans:* Subsidized Stafford, Unsubsidized Stafford, PLUS, Federal Perkins, Federal Nursing, state loans, college/university loans from institutional funds. *Student Employment:* Federal Work-Study Program available. Institutional employment available. Off-campus job opportunities are good. **Financial Aid Statistics:** 99% freshmen, 97% undergrads receive need-based scholarship or grant aid. 83% freshmen, 81% undergrads receive non-need-based scholarship or grant aid. 91% freshmen, 90% undergrads receive need-based self-help aid. 0% freshmen, 0% undergrads receive athletic scholarships. 96% freshmen, 89% undergrads receive any aid. 86% undergrads borrow to pay for school. Average cumulative indebtedness $26,033. **Criteria for awarding institutional aid:** *Non-need-based:* academics, leadership, minority status, music/drama.

WILLAMETTE UNIVERSITY

900 State Street, Salem, OR 97301
Phone: 503-370-6303 · **Financial Aid Phone:** 503-370-6273
E-mail: libarts@willamette.edu · **CEEB Code:** 4954
Fax: 503-375-5363 · **Website:** www.willamette.edu · **ACT Code:** 3504

This private school, affiliated with the Methodist Church, was founded in 1842. It has a 72-acre campus.

RATINGS

Admissions Selectivity Rating: 88   **Fire Safety Rating:** 98

STUDENTS AND FACULTY

Enrollment: 2,009. **Student Body:** 57% female, 43% male, 73% out-of-state, 2% international (41 countries represented). Asian 8%, African American 2%, Caucasian 62%, Hispanic 11%, Native American 1%
Retention and Graduation: 70% freshmen graduate within 4 years. 20% grads go on to further study within 1 year. 5% grads pursue arts and sciences degrees. 3% grads pursue law degrees. 4% grads pursue business degrees. 2% grads pursue medical degrees. **Faculty:** 214 full-time faculty, 98% hold PhDs, 46% are are members of minority groups, 18% are women. 0% of classes are taught by teaching assistants.

ACADEMICS

Degrees: bachelor's, first professional, first professional certificate, master's. **Classes:** Most classes have 10-19 students. **Majors with Highest Enrollment:** Biology/Biological Sciences; Economics; Psychology. **Special Study Options:** Accelerated program, cross-registration, double major, dual enrollment, exchange student program (domestic), independent study, internships, student-designed major, study abroad, teacher certification program. **Honors programs:** Our challenging curriculum includes a variety of opportunities for individualized honors study, for example: Presidential Scholars (senior year), Carson Undergraduate Research Program, Science Collaborative Research Program, various departmental honors programs. **Combined degree programs:** BA/JD, 5 year (BA/MBA);4-2 program in eng(BA/MS). **Disability Services:** Special programs offered to physically disabled students include note-taking services, reader services, tape recorders, tutors. **Career services:** Alumni network, career/job search classes, career assessment, internships. Career services highlights include a long tradition of academic internships. Three internship programs are in place: to explore career choices (Insight Internship), to gain deeper knowledge of a chosen field (Major Program Internship), or a program which places an emphasis on bridging the gap between liberal arts study and professional responsibilities (Professional Internship). Generally these internships offer one course credit as part of the student's regular academic load though some one-half and two credit internships are available. Internships are an effective means to selecting an interesting, sustaining career; helping students assign meaning and context to their course work; and smoothing the transition from college to work or graduate study. Interns are regularly placed with agencies of the Oregon state government, the Salem city government and the Oregon State Legislature. Other facilities include the Oregon School for the Blind, the Oregon State Hospital and the Salem public schools. Majors in economics, politics, sociology and psychology frequently undertake internships at such sites. Rhetoric and media studies majors may intern with local radio and television stations; English majors intern with the local newspaper or with art organizations; exercise science majors with parks and recreation programs; and others in a variety of settings. Students seeking an internship opportunity will find it at Willamette! Sites in the Salem area which have hosted Willamette interns: Legislative internships are available with many senators and representatives at the Oregon State Capitol—located across the street from campus; Historic Deepwood Estate offers a variety of projects geared toward students majoring in the humanities; the gardens and nature trails provide opportunities for biology and environmental science majors as well; Auburn Elementary School in Salem offers an internship focusing on issues facing children and how they are addressed in the school system; Marion County Children's Mental Health Services offers internships in counseling; SAIF Corporation offers internships in industrial psychology; Silver Falls Soccer Club offers internships in coaching; The District Attorney's office offers internships in victim's assistance. Internships are available at distant sites as well. These programs often occur during the summer, in which case the academic credit is completed on campus with the assistance of the on-campus supervisor. Some of the organizations which have recently served as internship sites are: Oregon Public Broadcasting in Portland, OR—summer internship for students studying journalism and telecommunications; Albany Police Department, Albany, OR—experience in the criminal justice system; Conari Press in Berkeley, CA—editing; Hart Crowser, environmental consulting firm in Lake Oswego, OR—site assessment and remedial technologies; Olympic National Forest in Olympia, WA—watershed restoration and geology; Corporate Realty Advisors/CRESA in Portland, OR—summer research and marketing internship in commercial real estate; The Taylor Family Foundation in Lafayette, CA—corporate fundraising; TCI Media Services in Seattle, WA—advertising and communication For further information please refer to http://www.willamette.edu/cla/intern/index.html.

FACILITIES

Housing: Coed dorms, fraternity/sorority housing, apartments for single students, Substance-free Residence, Environmental Residence (Terra House), Intensive Study (24 hour quiet study) Residence. 95% of campus accessible to physically disabled. **Special Academic Facilities/Equipment:** Student Art purchased annually,and displayed in all public access buildings, Hallie Ford Museum of Art,Collections and papers of Congressional leaders from Oregon,Electron Microscope Lab (scanning and transmission), Herbarium, Japanese and Botanical Gardens, Carnegie Library (fully restored). **Computers:** 100% of classrooms, 100% of dorms, 100% of libraries, 100% of dining areas, 100% of student union, 50% of common outdoor areas have wireless network access. Students can register for classes online. Administrative functions (other than registration) can be performed online.

CAMPUS LIFE

Environment: City. **Activities:** Choral groups, concert band, dance, drama/theater, jazz band, literary magazine, music ensembles, musical theater, opera, student government, student newspaper, student-run film society, symphony orchestra, yearbook, Campus Ministries, International Student Organization, Model UN. 107 registered organizations, 7 honor societies, 5 religious organizations. 4 fraternities, 3 sororities. **Athletics (Intercollegiate):** *Men:* baseball, basketball, crew/rowing, cross-country, football, golf, soccer, swimming, tennis, track/field (outdoor), track/field (indoor). *Women:* basketball, crew/rowing, cross-country, golf, soccer, softball, swimming, tennis, track/field (outdoor), track/field (indoor), volleyball. **On-Campus Highlights:** Hallie Ford Museum of Art, Montag Student Center, Sparks Sports and Recreation Center, Willamette Bistro, Mill Stream on campus. **Environmental Initiatives:** Kaneko Commons Residential Hall Ford Hall-Academic Building Purchased Zena Forest-nearby 308 Acre Sustainable forest for research and teaching New Construction Achieved LEED Gold status in 2007. Photo Voltaic panels, solar hot water heating, rainwater reclamation for flushing toilets, FSC wood products, Indoor Air Quality measures, low/no VOC materials and products, sustainability educational signage, high recycled content materials, energy efficient boilers, lighting control system, Energy Management System controls, 50% reduction in irrigation, low flow plumbing fixtures, use of plate to plate heat exchangers, sun shades, 95% recycle of construction waste, reflective roof coatings, use of local materials & labor, FSC cert furnishings, Fat Spaniel PV panel monitoring, electrical use monitoring, FLEX CAR program initiated, purchase of Green Power, energy star appliances, and more. Development and approval of a sustainability law certificate program in the University Law School (2007), and planning for a sustainable MBA tract in the MBA program and sustainability concentration in the undergraduate curriculum (2008). Active work groups integrated with curriculum in Law, MBA and undergraduate that research and seek solutions to campus sustainaibility objectives. 2009-2010 projects include Efficacy of purchasing Carbon Offsets (Law), efficacy of Solar Panels on Campus(MBA, Wind Generation (CLA) Solutions for green and post consumer Waste (MBA). President M. Lee Pelton has done much to institutionalize sustainability in both our infrastructure and our educational mission. He created the university wide Sustainability Council in November of 2004, with representation throughout the university, including staff, students, faculty, and administrators. The Sustainability Council is charged with promoting sustainability and environmental literacy, advancing strategic initiatives and best practices on campus (including all new construction and renovations), and enhancing sustainability beyond the campus. Please see http://www.willamette.edu/about/sustainability/ for more details. In 2007, President Pelton created the Willamette Center for Sustainable Communities (CSC). The CSC is charged with advancing the faculty research and teaching in the area of sustainability, developing meaningful research and learning opportunities for students, and encouraging the adoption of sustainability both on campus and beyond. For more information, see http://www.willamette.edu/centers/csc/.

ADMISSIONS

Freshman Academic Profile: Average high school GPA 3.75. 40% in top 10% of high school class, 72% in top 25% of high school class, 96% in top 50% of high school class. 76% from public high schools. SAT Math middle 50% range 540-650. SAT Critical Reading middle 50% range 540-670. SAT Writing middle 50% range 540-650. ACT middle 50% range 24-30. Minimum paper TOEFL 550. **Basis for Candidate Selection:** *Very important factors considered include:* Class rank, application essay, academic GPA, rigor of secondary school record, standardized test scores. *Important factors considered include:*

recommendation(s), interview. *Other factors considered include:* alumni/ae relation, character/personal qualities, extracurricular activities, first generation, geographical residence, racial/ethnic status, talent/ability. Freshman Admission Requirements. **Academic units required:** 4 English, 4 mathematics, 3 science, (3 science labs), 1 foreign language, 2 social studies. **Freshman Admission Statistics:** 5,729 applied, 81% admitted, 12% enrolled. **Transfer Admission Requirements:** High school transcript, college transcript(s), essay or personal statement, statement of good standing from prior institution(s). Lowest grade transferable C. **General Admission Information:** Application Fee $50. Notification on a rolling basis, beginning on or about 10/1. Nonfall registration accepted. Admission may be deferred for a maximum of 1 year. Credit and/or placement offered for CEEB Advanced Placement tests.

COSTS AND FINANCIAL AID

Annual tuition $43,760. Room and board $10,820. Required fees $316. Average book expense $950. **Required Forms and Deadlines:** FAFSA. **Notification of Awards:** Applicants will be notified of awards on a rolling basis beginning 4/1. **Types of Aid:** *Need-based scholarships/grants:* Federal Pell, SEOG, state scholarships/grants, private scholarships, the school's own gift aid. *Loans:* Subsidized Stafford, Unsubsidized Stafford, PLUS, Federal Perkins. *Student Employment:* Federal Work-Study Program available. Institutional employment available. Highest amount earned per year from on-campus jobs $2,000. Off-campus job opportunities are excellent. **Financial Aid Statistics:** 97% freshmen, 99% undergrads receive need-based scholarship or grant aid. 27% freshmen, 16% undergrads receive non-need-based scholarship or grant aid. 78% freshmen, 82% undergrads receive need-based self-help aid. 0% freshmen, 0% undergrads receive athletic scholarships. 67% freshmen, 62% undergrads receive any aid. 66% undergrads borrow to pay for school. Average cumulative indebtedness $23,730. **Criteria for awarding institutional aid:** *Non-need-based:* academics, alumni affiliation, leadership, minority status, music/drama, religious affiliation,

WILLIAM JEWELL COLLEGE

500 College Hill, Liberty, MO 64068
Phone: 816-415-7511 · **Financial Aid Phone:** 816-415-5975
E-mail: admission@william.jewell.edu · **CEEB Code:** 6941
Fax: 816-415-5040 · **Website:** www.jewell.edu · **ACT Code:** 2394

This private school was founded in 1849. It has a 200-acre campus.

RATINGS

Admissions Selectivity Rating: 88   **Fire Safety Rating:** 80

STUDENTS AND FACULTY

Enrollment: 1,060. **Student Body:** 59% female, 41% male, 34% out-of-state, 3% international (12 countries represented). Asian 2%, African American 4%, Caucasian 82%, Hispanic 4%, Native American 1%
Retention and Graduation: 75% freshmen return for sophomore year. 58% freshmen graduate within 4 years. 63% freshmen graduate within 6 years. 27% grads go on to further study within 1 year. 5% grads pursue arts and sciences degrees. 2% grads pursue law degrees. 2% grads pursue business degrees. 3% grads pursue medical degrees. **Faculty:** 82 full-time faculty, 79% hold PhDs, 52% are are members of minority groups, 2% are women. 0% of classes are taught by teaching assistants.

ACADEMICS

Degrees: bachelor's, certificate. **Classes:** Most classes have fewer than 10 students. Most lab/discussion sessions have 30-39 students. **Majors with Highest Enrollment:** Elementary Education and Teaching; Secondary Education and Teaching; Biology/Biological Sciences. **Special Study Options:** Accelerated program, double major, dual enrollment, honors program, independent study, internships, liberal arts/career combination, student-designed major, study abroad, teacher certification program, Pryor Leadership Studies. **Honors programs:** The Oxbridge Honors Program combines British tutorial methods of instruction with opportunities for a year of study in Oxford or Cambridge. **Career services:** Alumni network, alumni services, career/job search classes, career assessment, internships, regional alumni. Career services highlights include The Pryor Leadership Program, which requires 2 internships—one in service; one career-related. Over 50% of Jewell students participate in some form of internship or similar experiential learning opportunity.

FACILITIES

Housing: Coed dorms, men's dorms, women's dorms, fraternity/sorority housing, Off-campus housing utilized like residence halls. ADA compliant housing available for disabled students. 80% of campus accessible to physically disabled. **Special Academic Facilities/Equipment:** Radio station, art gallery, observatory, language and computer labs, high-ropes course, Teleconferencing center. **Computers:** 80% of classrooms, 20% of dorms, 25% of libraries, 80% of dining areas, 90% of student union, have wireless network access. Students can register for classes online. Administrative functions (other than registration) can be performed online.

CAMPUS LIFE

Environment: Town. **Activities:** Choral groups, concert band, dance, drama/theater, jazz band, literary magazine, music ensembles, pep band, radio station, student government, student newspaper, symphony orchestra, Campus Ministries. 70 registered organizations, 13 honor societies, 7 religious organizations. 4 fraternities, 4 sororities. **Athletics (Intercollegiate):** *Men:* baseball, basketball, cheerleading, cross-country, football, golf, soccer, tennis, track/field (outdoor), track/field (indoor). *Women:* basketball, cheerleading, cross-country, golf, soccer, softball, tennis, track/field (outdoor), track/field (indoor), volleyball. **On-Campus Highlights:** The Perch—campus coffee shop, Mabee Center—athletic facility, The Quad—central campus quadrangle, Yates College Union—student union buil, Ely Triangle—first-year residence hall, Fitness Center. **Environmental Initiatives:** Campus recycling program; Food composting; Community garden.

ADMISSIONS

Freshman Academic Profile: Average high school GPA 3.69. 25% in top 10% of high school class, 59% in top 25% of high school class, 91% in top 50% of high school class. 90% from public high schools. SAT Math middle 50% range 520-620. SAT Critical Reading middle 50% range 490-640. ACT middle 50% range 23-28. Minimum internet-based TOEFL 80. Minimum paper TOEFL 550. **Basis for Candidate Selection:** *Very important factors considered include:* rigor of secondary school record. *Important factors considered include:* Class rank, academic GPA, recommendation(s), standardized test scores. *Other factors considered include:* application essay, alumni/ae relation, character/personal qualities, extracurricular activities, first generation, interview, talent/ability, volunteer work, work experience. **Freshman Admission Requirements:** High school diploma is required and GED is accepted. **Academic units required:** 4 English, 3 mathematics, 3 science, (1 science labs), 2 foreign language, 3 social studies. **Freshman Admission Statistics:** 3,333 applied, 54% admitted, 15% enrolled. **Transfer Admission Requirements:** college transcript(s), statement of good standing from prior institution(s). Minimum college GPA of 2.5 required. Lowest grade transferable C-. **General Admission Information:** Application Fee $25. Regular application deadline 8/15. Notification on a rolling basis, beginning on or about 9/15. Nonfall registration accepted. Admission may be deferred for a maximum of 1 year, w/ a. Credit and/or placement offered for CEEB Advanced Placement tests.

COSTS AND FINANCIAL AID

Annual tuition $30,200. Room and board $7,790. Average book expense $1,200. **Required Forms and Deadlines:** FAFSA. **Notification of Awards:** Applicants will be notified of awards on a rolling basis beginning 2/15. **Types of Aid:** *Need-based scholarships/grants:* Federal Pell, SEOG, state scholarships/grants, the school's own gift aid. *Loans:* Subsidized Stafford, Unsubsidized Stafford, PLUS/Federal Perkins, Federal Nursing, Non-Federal Private *Student Employment:* Federal Work-Study Program available. Institutional employment available. Highest amount earned per year from on-campus jobs $1,300. Off-campus job opportunities are excellent. **Financial Aid Statistics:** 100% freshmen, 95% undergrads receive need-based scholarship or grant aid. 100% freshmen, 95% undergrads receive non-need-based scholarship or grant aid. 72% freshmen, 77% undergrads receive need-based self-help aid. 15% freshmen, 13% undergrads receive athletic scholarships. 99% freshmen, 96% undergrads receive any aid. 64% undergrads borrow to pay for school. Average cumulative indebtedness $26,790. **Criteria for awarding institutional aid:** *Non-need-based:* academics, alumni affiliation, art, athletics, music/drama.

WILLIAM PATERSON UNIVERSITY

Admissions Hall, Wayne, NJ 7470
Phone: 973-720-2125 · **Financial Aid Phone:** 973-720-2202
E-mail: admissions@wpunj.edu · **CEEB Code:** 2518
Fax: 973-720-2910 · **Website:** ww2.wpunj.edu · **ACT Code:** 2584

This public school was founded in 1855. It has a 370-acre campus.

RATINGS

Admissions Selectivity Rating: 76   Fire Safety Rating: 98

STUDENTS AND FACULTY

Enrollment: 9,921. **Student Body:** 55% female, 45% male, 2% out-of-state, 1% international (38 countries represented). Asian 7%, African American 14%, Caucasian 50%, Hispanic 22%, Native American <1%
Retention and Graduation: 76% freshmen return for sophomore year. 19% freshmen graduate within 4 years. 47% freshmen graduate within 6 years. 14% grads go on to further study within 1 year. 33% grads pursue arts and sciences degrees. 3% grads pursue law degrees. 12% grads pursue business degrees.
Faculty: 389 full-time faculty, 92% hold PhDs, 51% are are members of minority groups, 33% are women. 0% of classes are taught by teaching assistants.

ACADEMICS

Degrees: bachelor's, master's, post-bachelor's certificate, post-master's certificate. **Classes:** Most classes have 10-19 students. **Majors with Highest Enrollment:** Psychology; Business/Commerce; Speech Communication and Rhetoric. **Special Study Options:** Accelerated program, cross-registration, distance learning, double major, dual enrollment, English as a Second Language (ESL), exchange student program (domestic), honors program, independent study, internships, study abroad, teacher certification program, Cluster courses (a program that provides opportunities for students and faculty to study and learn together in courses grouped in interdisciplinary clusters of three. Three faculty members teach these courses that meet together once every week to help students see the interdisciplinary connections). University Honors Program (Honors major tracks are available, and "honors" general education courses are offered.) International exchange program. **Honors programs:** University Honors Program offers honors major tracks as well as honors general education courses. For more information please visit our Honors College Homepage at: http://www.wpunj.edu/icip/honors/default.htm. **Disability Services:** Special programs offered to physically disabled students include note-taking services, reader services, tape recorders, tutors. **Career services:** alumni services, career/job search classes, career assessment. Career services highlights include Career Counseling and job search assistance, a unique combination of career services for all students as well as advisement services for undeclared and transfer students.

FACILITIES

Housing: Coed dorms, special housing for disabled students, apartments for single students, a floor for women is available in one of the residence halls. Apartment style housing is available in groups of single students who are 21 or older or are 20 with 58 or more credits. Academic interest housing is available; High Mountain East is freshmen scholars and High Mountain West houses upperclass students who maintain a 2.5 GPA or better. One residence hall is reserved for students who are 21 or older. 88% of campus accessible to physically disabled. **Special Academic Facilities/Equipment:** Art galleries; Collection of NJ State Documents; Collection of William Paterson's private papers; Interactive television classroom; Neurobiology facility;E-Trading Campus Network with ATM technology; Center for Computer Art and Animation; State-of-the-art electron microscopy facility; Teleconference Center with uplink and downlink capabilities; 44,000 square foot, state-of-the-art studio art facility; Center for Electro-Acoustic Music (CEM); E-Trade Financial Learning Center, a real-time simulated trading and financial educational facility; Russ Berrie Institute for Professional Sales including real-time Sales Laboratory. **Computers:** Students can register for classes online. Administrative functions (other than registration) can be performed online.

CAMPUS LIFE

Environment: Metropolis. **Activities:** Choral groups, concert band, dance, drama/theater, jazz band, literary magazine, music ensembles, student government, student newspaper, student-run film society, television station, yearbook, Campus Ministries, International Student Organization, Model UN. 61 registered organizations, 21 honor societies, 4 religious organizations. 11 fraternities, 10 sororities. **Athletics (Intercollegiate):** *Men:* baseball, basketball, football, soccer, swimming. *Women:* basketball, cheerleading, field hockey, soccer, softball, swimming, volleyball. **On-Campus Highlights:** Student Center: Coffee Café (Starbucks), College of Business E-Trading Center, Power Art Gallery, Atrium Lobby, Library, New Student Center Facility, New Center for Student Services. **Environmental Initiatives:** ACUPCC NJHEPS challenge; LEED Standard adoption.

ADMISSIONS

Freshman Academic Profile: 11% in top 10% of high school class, 31% in top 25% of high school class, 64% in top 50% of high school class. 86% from public high schools. SAT Math middle 50% range 460-550. SAT Critical Reading middle 50% range 440-550. Minimum internet-based TOEFL 79. Minimum paper TOEFL 550. **Basis for Candidate Selection:** *Very important factors considered include:* Class rank, rigor of secondary school record, standardized test scores. *Important factors considered include:* academic GPA, level of applicant's interest. *Other factors considered include:* application essay, recommendation(s), alumni/ae relation, character/personal qualities, extracurricular activities, geographical residence, interview, talent/ability, volunteer work. **Freshman Admission Requirements:** High school diploma is required and GED is accepted. **Academic units required:** 4 English, 3 mathematics, 2 science, (2 science labs), 2 social studies, 5 5 Additional college preparatory courses (in Advanced Math, Literature, Foreign Language and Social Science) are also required. **Freshman Admission Statistics:** 10,059 applied, 71% admitted, 20% enrolled. **Transfer Admission Requirements:** college transcript(s), Minimum college GPA of 2.00 required. Lowest grade transferable C. **General Admission Information:** Application Fee $50. Regular application deadline 5/1. Notification on a rolling basis, beginning on or about 10/1. Nonfall registration accepted. Admission may be deferred for a maximum of 1 semester. Credit and/or placement offered for CEEB Advanced Placement tests.

COSTS AND FINANCIAL AID
Annual out-of-state tuition $14,131. Room and board $9,540. Required fees $8,832. Average book expense $1,600. **Required Forms and Deadlines:** FAFSA. **Notification of Awards:** Applicants will be notified of awards on a rolling basis beginning 3/15. **Types of Aid:** *Need-based scholarships/grants:* Federal Pell, SEOG, state scholarships/grants, the school's own gift aid. *Loans:* Subsidized Stafford, Unsubsidized Stafford, PLUS, Federal Perkins, state loans. *Student Employment:* Federal Work-Study Program available. Institutional employment available. Highest amount earned per year from on-campus jobs $3,200. Off-campus job opportunities are good. **Financial Aid Statistics:** 60% freshmen, 63% undergrads receive need-based scholarship or grant aid. 27% freshmen, 17% undergrads receive non-need-based scholarship or grant aid. 84% freshmen, 86% undergrads receive need-based self-help aid. 0% freshmen, 0% undergrads receive athletic scholarships. 89% freshmen, 78% undergrads receive any aid. 70% undergrads borrow to pay for school. Average cumulative indebtedness $21,673. **Criteria for awarding institutional aid:** *Non-need-based:* academics, music/drama.

WILLIAM PEACE UNIVERSITY

15 East Peace Street, Raleigh, NC 27604
Phone: 919-508-2214 • **Financial Aid Phone:** 919-508-2214
E-mail: admissions@peace.edu • **CEEB Code:** 005533
Fax: 919-508-2306 • **Website:** www.peace.edu • **ACT Code:** 3136

This private school, affiliated with the Presbyterian Churrch, was founded in 1857. It as a 21-acre campus.

RATINGS
Admissions Selectivity Rating: 60*   **Fire Safety Rating:** 60*

STUDENTS AND FACULTY
Enrollment: 1,076. **Student Body:** 72% female, 28% male. Asian 2%, African American 34%, Caucasian 43%, Hispanic 4%, Native American 1% **Retention and Graduation:** 63% freshman return for sophomore year. 28% freshmen graduate within 4 years. 41% freshmen graduate within 6 years. **Faculty:** Student/faculty ratio 15:1. 24 full-time faculty, 79% hold PhDs, 4% are are members of minority groups, 58% are women.

CAMPUS LIFE
Environment: Metropolis

ADMISSIONS
Freshman Academic Profile: Average high school GPA 3.14. 6% in top 10% of high school class, 26% in top 25% of high school class, 57% in top 50% of high school class. SAT Math middle 50% range 400-510. SAT Critical Reading middle 50% range 410-520. ACT middle 50% range 16-21. Minimum internet-based TOEFL 80. Minimum paper TOEFL 550. *Freshman Admission Requirements:* High school diploma is required and GED is accepted. *Academic units required:* 4 English, 3 mathematics, 3 science, (2 science labs),2 Social Studies. *Academic units recommended:* 4 mathematics, 2 foreign language. **Freshman Admission Statistics:** 1,083 applied, 91% admitted, 33% enrolled.

COSTS AND FINANCIAL AID
Annual Tuition $24,450. Room and board $9,450. Required fees $200. **Required Forms and Deadlines:** Rolling. **Notification of Awards:** Rolling starting on 3/15. **Types of Aid:** *Need-based scholarships/grants:* Federal pell, SEOG, State scholoarships/grants, private scholarships, college/university's own gift aid. *Loans:* Direct subsidized Stafford loans, direct unsubsidized Stafford loans, direct PLUS loans. **Financial Aid Statistics:** 84% freshmen, 85% undergrads receive need-based scholarship or grant aid. 72% freshmen, 78% undergrads receive non-need-based scholarship or grant aid. 89% freshmen, 89% undergrads receive need-based self-help aid. 91% freshmen, 91% undergrads receive any aid. 86% undergrads borrow to pay for school. Average cumulative indebtedness $34,765.

See page 1214.

WILLIAM PENN UNIVERSITY

201 Trueblood Avenue, Oskaloosa, IA 52577
Phone: 641-673-1012
E-mail: admissions@wmpenn.edu • **CEEB Code:** 6943
Fax: 641-673-2113 • **Website:** www.wmpenn.edu • **ACT Code:** 1372

This private school, affiliated with the Quaker Church, was founded in 1873. It has a 53-acre campus.

RATINGS
Admissions Selectivity Rating: 65   **Fire Safety Rating:** 60*

STUDENTS AND FACULTY
Enrollment: 1,586. **Student Body:** 48% female, 52% male, 28% out-of-state, 2% international. Asian 1%, African American 14%, Caucasian 64%, Hispanic 6%, Native American 1% **Faculty:** 35 full-time faculty, 49% hold PhDs, 29% are are members of minority groups, 3% are women. 0% of classes are taught by teaching assistants.

ACADEMICS
Degrees: associate, bachelor's, transfer associate. **Classes:** Most classes have fewer than 10 students. **Majors with Highest Enrollment:** Education; Business/Commerce; Psychology. **Special Study Options:** cooperative education program, double major, English as a Second Language (ESL), independent study, internships, study abroad, teacher certification program, College for Working Adults. **Disability Services:** Special programs offered to physically disabled students include tape recorders, tutors. **Career services:** alumni services, career/job search classes, internships.

FACILITIES
Housing: Coed dorms, women's dorms, apartments for married students, apartments for single students. 75% of campus accessible to physically disabled. **Special Academic Facilities/Equipment:** Foyer Gallery, Mid-East art and artifact collection.

CAMPUS LIFE
Environment: Rural. **Activities:** Choral groups, drama/theater, jazz band, literary magazine, music ensembles, musical theater, radio station, student government, student newspaper, yearbook. 34 registered organizations, 3 honor societies, 4 religious organizations. 3 fraternities, 3 sororities. **Athletics (Intercollegiate):** *Men:* baseball, basketball, cheerleading, cross-country, football, golf, soccer, track/field (outdoor), wrestling. *Women:* basketball, cheerleading, cross-country, soccer, softball, track/field (outdoor), volleyball.

ADMISSIONS
Freshman Academic Profile: 14% in top 25% of high school class, 47% in top 50% of high school class. 97% from public high schools. Minimum internet-based TOEFL 61. Minimum paper TOEFL 500. **Basis for Candidate Selection:** *Very important factors considered include:* rigor of secondary school record. *Important factors considered include:* Class rank, standardized test scores, character/personal qualities. *Other factors considered include:* application essay, recommendation(s), alumni/ae relation, extracurricular activities, interview, talent/ability, volunteer work, work experience. **Freshman Admission Requirements:** High school diploma is required and GED is accepted. **Freshman Admission Statistics:** 841 applied, 54% admitted, 53% enrolled. **Transfer Admission Requirements:** college transcript(s), Minimum college GPA of 2.0 required. Lowest grade transferable D. **General Admission Information:** Application Fee $20. Notification on a rolling basis, beginning on or about 10/1. Nonfall registration accepted. Credit offered for CEEB Advanced Placement tests.

COSTS AND FINANCIAL AID
Annual tuition $22,840. Room and board $5,472. Required fees $370. Average book expense $1,150. **Required Forms and Deadlines:** FAFSA. **Notification of Awards:** Applicants will be notified of awards on a rolling basis beginning 1/1. **Types of Aid:** *Need-based scholarships/grants:* Federal Pell, SEOG, state scholarships/grants, private scholarships, the school's own gift aid. *Loans:* Subsidized Stafford, Unsubsidized Stafford, PLUS, Federal Perkins. *Student Employment:* Federal Work-Study Program available. Institutional employment available. Off-campus job opportunities are excellent. **Financial Aid Statistics:** 74% undergrads borrow to pay for school. **Criteria for awarding institutional aid:** *Non-need-based:* academics, alumni affiliation, athletics, leadership, music/drama, religious

WILLIAM TYNDALE COLLEGE

35700 W. Twelve Mile Road, Farmington Hills, MI 48331-3147
Phone: 800-483-0707
E-mail: admissions@williamtyndale.edu · **CEEB Code:** 1167
Fax: 248-553-5963 · **Website:** www.williamtyndale.edu · **ACT Code:** 2252

This private school was founded in 1945. It has a 28-acre campus.

RATINGS

Admissions Selectivity Rating: 85   **Fire Safety Rating:** 60*

STUDENTS AND FACULTY

Enrollment: 278. **Student Body:** 45% female, 55% male, 7% out-of-state, 3% international (6 countries represented). Asian 1%, African American 31%, Caucasian 63%, Hispanic 0%, Native American 1%
Retention and Graduation: 66% freshmen return for sophomore year. 21% freshmen graduate within 4 years. **Faculty:** 4 full-time faculty, 50% hold PhDs, 50% are are members of minority groups, 0% are women. 0% of classes are taught by teaching assistants.

ACADEMICS

Degrees: associate, bachelor's, certificate. **Classes:** Most classes have fewer than 10 students. **Majors with Highest Enrollment:** Religion/Religious Studies Business/Commerce. **Special Study Options:** Accelerated program, distance learning, double major, dual enrollment, independent study, internships. **Disability Services:** Special programs offered to physically disabled students include note-taking services, tutors.

FACILITIES

Housing: Coed dorms. 100% of campus accessible to physically disabled.

CAMPUS LIFE

Environment: Village. **Activities:** Choral groups, drama/theater, music ensembles, student government, student newspaper. 2 registered organizations, 2 honor societies. **On-Campus Highlights:** Billy T's Café.

ADMISSIONS

Freshman Academic Profile: Average high school GPA 3.3. 20% in top 10% of high school class, 60% in top 25% of high school class, 40% in top 50% of high school class. 76% from public high schools. ACT middle 50% range 23-24. Minimum paper TOEFL 500. **Basis for Candidate Selection:** *Very important factors considered include:* rigor of secondary school record, standardized test scores. *Other factors considered include:* application essay, recommendation(s), character/personal qualities, interview, religious affiliation/commitment. **Freshman Admission Requirements:** High school diploma is required and GED is accepted. **Freshman Admission Statistics:** 40 applied, 50% admitted, 80% enrolled. **Transfer Admission Requirements:** High school transcript, college transcript(s), statement of good standing from prior institution(s). Minimum college GPA of 2.0 required. Lowest grade transferable C. **General Admission Information:** Nonfall registration accepted. Admission may be deferred for a maximum of 12 months. Credit and/or placement offered for CEEB Advanced Placement tests.

COSTS AND FINANCIAL AID

Annual tuition $8,550. Room and board $3,520. Required fees $100. Average book expense $1,328. *Student Employment:* Federal Work-Study Program available. Institutional employment available. Highest amount earned per year from on-campus jobs $1,500. Off-campus job opportunities are good. **Financial Aid Statistics:** 60% freshmen, 60% undergrads receive any aid.

WILLIAM WOODS UNIVERSITY

One University Avenue, Fulton, MO 65251
Phone: 573-592-4221 · **Financial Aid Phone:** 573-592-4236
E-mail: admissions@williamwoods.edu
Fax: 573-592-1146 · **Website:** www.williamwoods.edu · **ACT Code:** 2396

This private school, affiliated with the Disciples of Christ Church, was founded in 1870. It has a 170-acre campus.

RATINGS

Admissions Selectivity Rating: 80   **Fire Safety Rating:** 78

STUDENTS AND FACULTY

Enrollment: 1,118. **Student Body:** 75% female, 25% male, 19% out-of-state, 4% international. Asian 0%, African American 3%, Caucasian 87%, Hispanic 2%, Native American 1%

Retention and Graduation: 76% freshmen return for sophomore year. 39% freshmen graduate within 4 years. 48% freshmen graduate within 6 years. **Faculty:** 50 full-time faculty, 52% are are members of minority groups, 4% are women. 0% of classes are taught by teaching assistants.

ACADEMICS

Degrees: associate, bachelor's, master's, post-master's certificate. **Classes:** Most classes have fewer than 10 students. Most lab/discussion sessions have fewer than 10 students. **Majors with Highest Enrollment:** Animal Sciences; Education; Business/Commerce. **Special Study Options:** Accelerated program, cross-registration, double major, dual enrollment, honors program, independent study, internships, liberal arts/career combination, student-designed major, study abroad, teacher certification program, Hollywood semester. **Disability Services:** Special programs offered to physically disabled students include note-taking services, reader services, tape recorders, tutors. **Career services:** career/job search classes, career assessment.

FACILITIES

Housing: Coed dorms, special housing for disabled students, men's dorms, special housing for international students, women's dorms, fraternity/sorority housing, apartments for single students. 80% of campus accessible to physically disabled. **Special Academic Facilities/Equipment:** Weitzman Court Room; Mildred Cox Gallery; Gladys Woods Kemper Center for the Arts; ASL Interpreting Lab; Equestrian Facilities. **Computers:** Administrative functions (other than registration) can be performed online.

CAMPUS LIFE

Environment: Village. **Activities:** Choral groups, dance, drama/theater, literary magazine, musical theater, radio station, student government, student newspaper. 42 registered organizations, 3 honor societies, 1 religous organization. 2 fraternities, 4 sororities. **Athletics (Intercollegiate):** *Men:* baseball, golf, soccer. *Women:* basketball, golf, soccer, softball, volleyball. **On-Campus Highlights:** Center for Human Performance, McNutt Student Center.

ADMISSIONS

Freshman Academic Profile: Average high school GPA 3.3. 15% in top 10% of high school class, 40% in top 25% of high school class, 77% in top 50% of high school class. SAT Math middle 50% range 420-570. SAT Critical Reading middle 50% range 455-575. ACT middle 50% range 19-25. Minimum paper TOEFL 550. **Basis for Candidate Selection:** *Very important factors considered include:* Class rank, academic GPA, rigor of secondary school record. *Important factors considered include:* recommendation(s), standardized test scores, extracurricular activities. *Other factors considered include:* character/personal qualities, interview. **Freshman Admission Requirements:** High school diploma is required and GED is accepted. **Academic units required:** 3 English, 3 mathematics. **Freshman Admission Statistics:** 792 applied, 68% admitted, 43% enrolled. **Transfer Admission Requirements:** college transcript(s), statement of good standing from prior institution(s). Minimum college GPA of 2.5 required. Lowest grade transferable C. **General Admission Information:** Application Fee $25. Notification on a rolling basis, beginning on or about 9/1. Nonfall registration accepted. Admission may be deferred for a maximum of 1. Credit and/or placement offered for CEEB Advanced Placement tests.

COSTS AND FINANCIAL AID

Annual tuition $14,700. Room and board $5,900. Required fees $420. Average book expense $1,000. **Required Forms and Deadlines:** FAFSA, Institution's own financial aid form. **Notification of Awards:** Applicants will be notified of awards on a rolling basis beginning 3/15. **Types of Aid:** *Need-based scholarships/grants:* Federal Pell, SEOG, state scholarships/grants, private scholarships, the school's own gift aid. *Loans:* Subsidized Stafford, Unsubsidized Stafford, PLUS, Federal Perkins, college/university loans from institutional funds. *Student Employment:* Federal Work-Study Program available. Institutional employment available. Highest amount earned per year from on-campus jobs $800. Off-campus job opportunities are good. **Financial Aid Statistics:** 100% freshmen, 95% undergrads receive need-based scholarship or grant aid. 23% freshmen, 18% undergrads receive non-need-based scholarship or grant aid. 75% freshmen, 77% undergrads receive need-based self-help aid. 2% freshmen, 3% undergrads receive athletic scholarships. 100% freshmen, 95% undergrads receive any aid. 85% undergrads borrow to pay for school. **Criteria for awarding institutional aid:** *Non-need-based:* academics, alumni affiliation, art, athletics, leadership, music/drama, religious affiliation, state/district residency. affiliation.

WILLIAMS COLLEGE

Best 380

PO Box 487, Williamstown, MA 1267
Phone: 413-597-2211 · **Financial Aid Phone:** 413-597-4181
E-mail: admission@williams.edu · **CEEB Code:** 3965
Fax: 413-597-4052 · **Website:** www.williams.edu · **ACT Code:** 1936

This private school was founded in 1793. It has a 450-acre campus.

RATINGS
Admissions Selectivity Rating: 98   **Fire Safety Rating:** 60*

STUDENTS AND FACULTY
Enrollment: 2,014. **Student Body:** 51% female, 49% male, 86% out-of-state, 7% international (54 countries represented). Asian 11%, African American 7%, Caucasian 56%, Hispanic 12%, Native American <1%
Retention and Graduation: 98% freshmen return for sophomore year. 88% freshmen graduate within 4 years. 95% freshmen graduate within 6 years. **Faculty:** 276 full-time faculty, 97% hold PhDs, 43% are are members of minority groups, 20% are women. 0% of classes are taught by teaching assistants.

ACADEMICS
Degrees: bachelor's, master's. **Classes:** Most classes have fewer than 10 students. Most lab/discussion sessions have 10-19 students. **Majors with Highest Enrollment:** Economics; English Language and Literature; History. **Special Study Options:** cross-registration, double major, independent study, internships, student-designed major, study abroad. **Combined degree programs:** Combined program in liberal arts and eng. **Disability Services:** Special programs offered to physically disabled students include note-taking services, reader services, tape recorders, tutors. **Career services:** Alumni network, alumni services, career/job search classes, internships, regional alumni.

FACILITIES
Housing: Coed dorms, cooperative housing. **Special Academic Facilities/ Equipment:** Hopkins Observatory; Williams College Museum of Art; Adams Memorial Theatre; Chapin Rare Books. Library; Spencer Studio Art Building, '62 Center for Theatre and Dance, Hopkins Experimental Forest **Computers:** 100% of classrooms, 100% of dorms, 100% of libraries, 100% of dining areas, 100% of student union, 100% of common outdoor areas have wireless network access. Students can register for classes online. Administrative functions (other than registration) can be performed online.

CAMPUS LIFE
Environment: Village. **Activities:** Choral groups, dance, drama/theater, literary magazine, music ensembles, radio station, student government, student newspaper, student-run film society, symphony orchestra, yearbook, International Student Organization. 110 registered organizations, 3 honor societies, 8 religious organizations. **Athletics (Intercollegiate):** *Men:* baseball, basketball, crew/rowing, cross-country, diving, football, golf, ice hockey, lacrosse, skiing (downhill/alpine), skiing (nordic/cross-country), soccer, squash, swimming, tennis, track/field (outdoor), track/field (indoor), wrestling. *Women:* basketball, crew/rowing, cross-country, diving, field hockey, golf, ice hockey, lacrosse, skiing (downhill/alpine), skiing (nordic/cross-country), soccer, softball, squash, swimming, tennis, track/field (outdoor), track/field (indoor), volleyball. **On-Campus Highlights:** Paresky Student Center, Schow Science Library, Williams College Museum of Art, '62 Center for Theatre and Dance, Chandler Gymnasium.

ADMISSIONS
Freshman Academic Profile: 95% in top 10% of high school class, 99% in top 25% of high school class, 100% in top 50% of high school class. SAT Math middle 50% range 670-770. SAT Critical Reading middle 50% range 680-790. SAT Writing middle 50% range 690-780. ACT middle 50% range 31-34. **Basis for Candidate Selection:** *Very important factors considered include:* application essay, academic GPA, recommendation(s), rigor of secondary school record, standardized test scores. *Important factors considered include:* Class rank, extracurricular activities, talent/ability. *Other factors considered include:* alumni/ae relation, character/personal qualities, first generation, geographical residence, racial/ethnic status, volunteer work, work experience. **Freshman Admission Requirements:** High school diploma or equivalent is not required. **Freshman Admission Statistics:** 6,511 applied, 19% admitted, 45% enrolled. **Transfer Admission Requirements:** High school transcript, college transcript(s), essay or personal statement, standardized test scores, statement of good standing from prior institution(s). Minimum college GPA of 3.5 required. Lowest grade transferable C-. **General Admission Information:** Application Fee $60. Early decision application deadline 11/10. Regular application deadline 1/1. Regular notification 4/1. Nonfall registration not accepted. Admission may be deferred

for a maximum of negotiable. Placement offered for CEEB Advanced Placement tests.

COSTS AND FINANCIAL AID
Annual tuition $48,030. Room and board $12,760. Required fees $280. Average book expense $800. **Required Forms and Deadlines:** FAFSA, CSS/ Financial Aid PROFILE, Noncustodial PROFILE. **Notification of Awards:** Applicants will be notified of awards on or about 4/1. **Types of Aid:** *Need-based scholarships/grants:* Federal Pell, SEOG, state scholarships/grants, private scholarships, the school's own gift aid. *Loans:* Direct Subsidized Stafford, Direct Unsubsidized Stafford, Direct PLUS, Federal Perkins, college/university loans from institutional funds. *Student Employment:* Federal Work-Study Program available. Institutional employment available. **Financial Aid Statistics:** 100% freshmen, 100% undergrads receive need-based scholarship or grant aid. 0% freshmen, 0% undergrads receive non-need-based scholarship or grant aid. 100% freshmen, 100% undergrads receive need-based self-help aid. 0% freshmen, 0% undergrads receive athletic scholarships. 48% freshmen, 50% undergrads receive any aid. 34% undergrads borrow to pay for school. Average cumulative indebtedness $13,472.

WILLISTON STATE COLLEGE

PO Box 1326, Williston, ND 58802-1326
Phone: 701-774-4210
E-mail: Lacey.Madison@wsc.nodak.edu
Fax: 701-774-4211 · **Website:** www.wsc.nodak.edu

This public school was founded in 1961. It has a 80-acre campus.

RATINGS
Admissions Selectivity Rating: 69   **Fire Safety Rating:** 60*

STUDENTS AND FACULTY
Enrollment: 937. **Student Body:** 71% female, 29% male, 19% out-of-state, 2% international (2 countries represented). Asian 0%, African American 1%, Caucasian 91%, Hispanic 1%, Native American 4%
Faculty: 38 full-time faculty, 39% are are members of minority groups. 0% of classes are taught by teaching assistants.

ACADEMICS
Degrees: associate, certificate, diploma, terminal associate, transfer associate. **Special Study Options:** cooperative education program, distance learning, dual enrollment, external degree program, independent study, internships, liberal arts/career combination. **Disability Services:** Special programs offered to physically disabled students include note-taking services, reader services, tape recorders, tutors.

FACILITIES
Housing: Coed dorms, special housing for disabled students, men's dorms, women's dorms, Athletic Housing units Married/Family Housing units. 90% of campus accessible to physically disabled.

CAMPUS LIFE
Environment: Rural. **Activities:** Choral groups, drama/theater, literary magazine, pep band, student government. 18 registered organizations, 1 honor society, 1 religous organization. **Athletics (Intercollegiate):** *Men:* baseball, basketball, golf. *Women:* basketball, golf, volleyball.

ADMISSIONS
Freshman Academic Profile: Average high school GPA 2.83. 12% in top 10% of high school class, 22% in top 25% of high school class, 71% in top 50% of high school class. ACT middle 50% range 16-22. Minimum paper TOEFL 330. **Freshman Admission Requirements:** High school diploma is required and GED is accepted. **Transfer Admission Requirements:** college transcript(s), statement of good standing from prior institution(s). Lowest grade transferable D. **General Admission Information:** Application Fee $35. Notification on a rolling basis, beginning on or about 1/1. Nonfall registration accepted. Credit and/or placement offered for CEEB Advanced Placement tests.

COSTS AND FINANCIAL AID
Required Forms and Deadlines: FAFSA. **Notification of Awards:** Applicants will be notified of awards on a rolling basis beginning 5/15. **Types of Aid:** *Need-based scholarships/grants:* Federal Pell, SEOG, state scholarships/grants, private scholarships, the school's own gift aid. *Loans:* Subsidized Stafford, Unsubsidized Stafford, PLUS, Federal Perkins. *Student Employment:* Federal Work-Study Program available. Institutional employment available. Off-campus job opportunities are good. **Criteria for awarding institutional aid:** *Non-need-based:* academics, athletics, minority status.

WILMINGTON COLLEGE (DE)

320 Dupont Highway, New Castle, DE 19720
Phone: 302-328-9401
E-mail: mlee@wilmcoll.edu • **CEEB Code:** 5925
Fax: 302-328-5902 • **Website:** www.wilmcoll.edu • **ACT Code:** 635

This private school was founded in 1967. It has a 15-acre campus.

RATINGS

Admissions Selectivity Rating: 60*   **Fire Safety Rating:** 60*

STUDENTS AND FACULTY

Enrollment: 4,399. **Student Body:** 53% female, 47% male, 3% out-of-state, 0% international. Asian 1%, African American 14%, Caucasian 64%, Hispanic 2%, Native American <1%
Retention and Graduation: 87% freshmen return for sophomore year. 50% grads go on to further study within 1 year. 9% grads pursue arts and sciences degrees. 10% grads pursue law degrees. 80% grads pursue business degrees. 1% grads pursue medical degrees. **Faculty:** 0% of classes are taught by teaching assistants.

ACADEMICS

Degrees: associate, bachelor's, certificate, master's, post-master's certificate. **Majors with Highest Enrollment:** Education; Business/Commerce. **Special Study Options:** Accelerated program, cooperative education program, distance learning, double major, independent study, internships, teacher certification program, weekend college. **Disability Services:** Special programs offered to physically disabled students include tutors. **Career services:** alumni services, career/job search classes, career assessment, internships.

FACILITIES

Housing: All housing is off campus.

CAMPUS LIFE

Environment: Village. **Activities:** student government 1 honor society. **Athletics (Intercollegiate):** *Men:* baseball, basketball, cross-country, soccer. *Women:* basketball, softball.

ADMISSIONS

Freshman Academic Profile: Minimum paper TOEFL 500. **Basis for Candidate Selection:** *Important factors considered include:* recommendation(s), rigor of secondary school record. **Freshman Admission Requirements:** High school diploma is required and GED is accepted.High school diploma is required and GED is not accepted. **Transfer Admission Requirements:** college transcript(s), Minimum college GPA of 2.0 required. Lowest grade transferable C. **General Admission Information:** Application Fee $25. Nonfall registration accepted. Admission may be deferred for a maximum of 12 months. Credit offered for CEEB Advanced Placement tests.

COSTS AND FINANCIAL AID

Annual tuition $6,060. Average book expense $500. **Required Forms and Deadlines:** FAFSA. *Student Employment:* Federal Work-Study Program available. Highest amount earned per year from on-campus jobs $1,000. Off-campus job opportunities are excellent.

WILMINGTON COLLEGE (OH)

1870 Quaker Way, Wilmington, OH 45177
Phone: 937-382-6661 • **CEEB Code:** 1909
Website: www.wilmington.edu • **ACT Code:** 3362

This private school, affiliated with the Quaker Church, was founded in 1870. It has a 65-acre campus.

RATINGS

Admissions Selectivity Rating: 86   **Fire Safety Rating:** 60*

STUDENTS AND FACULTY

Enrollment: 1,274. **Student Body:** 56% female, 44% male, 6% out-of-state, 1% international. Asian 0%, African American 11%, Caucasian 73%, Hispanic 1%, Native American 1%
Retention and Graduation: 67% freshmen return for sophomore year. 46% freshmen graduate within 4 years. **Faculty:** 66 full-time faculty. 0% of classes are taught by teaching assistants.

ACADEMICS

Degrees: bachelor's, master's. **Classes:** Most classes have 10-19 students. **Special Study Options:** cross-registration, double major, dual enrollment, honors program, independent study, internships, liberal arts/career combination, student-designed major, study abroad, teacher certification program, weekend college. **Disability Services:** Special programs offered to physically disabled students include note-taking services, reader services, tape recorders, tutors. **Career services:** alumni services, internships.

FACILITIES

Housing: Coed dorms, women's dorms, fraternity/sorority housing, apartments for single students. 100% of campus accessible to physically disabled. **Special Academic Facilities/Equipment:** Hiroshima-Nagasaki memorial collection and peace resource center, education lab, language lab, three farms, observatory, electron microscope.

CAMPUS LIFE

Environment: Rural. **Activities:** Choral groups, drama/theater, literary magazine, music ensembles, musical theater, student government, student newspaper, yearbook, Campus Ministries, International Student Organization. 48 registered organizations, 3 honor societies, 3 religious organizations. 6 fraternities, 5 sororities. **Athletics (Intercollegiate):** *Men:* baseball, basketball, cheerleading, cross-country, football, golf, soccer, swimming, tennis, track/field (outdoor), wrestling. *Women:* basketball, cheerleading, cross-country, golf, soccer, softball, swimming, tennis, track/field (outdoor), volleyball. **On-Campus Highlights:** Residence Hall room, Athletic Center, Student Center/Dining Hall, Computer labs, Class room.

ADMISSIONS

Freshman Academic Profile: Average high school GPA 3.2. 11% in top 10% of high school class, 36% in top 25% of high school class, 70% in top 50% of high school class. SAT Math middle 50% range 420-550. SAT Critical Reading middle 50% range 440-560. ACT middle 50% range 18-23. Minimum paper TOEFL 500. **Basis for Candidate Selection:** *Very important factors considered include:* academic GPA. *Important factors considered include:* Class rank, rigor of secondary school record, standardized test scores, alumni/ae relation, character/personal qualities, talent/ability. *Other factors considered include:* recommendation(s), extracurricular activities, interview, level of applicant's interest, volunteer work. **Freshman Admission Requirements:** High school diploma is required and GED is accepted. **Academic units required:** 4 English, 2 mathematics, 2 science, (2 science labs). **Freshman Admission Statistics:** 1,651 applied, 28% admitted, 45% enrolled. **Transfer Admission Requirements:** college transcript(s), statement of good standing from prior institution(s). Minimum college GPA of 2.0 required. Lowest grade transferable C-. **General Admission Information:** Application Fee $25. Regular application deadline 8/1. Notification on a rolling basis, beginning on or about 12/1. Nonfall registration accepted. Admission may be deferred for a maximum of 1 year. Credit and/or placement offered for CEEB Advanced Placement tests.

COSTS AND FINANCIAL AID

Annual tuition $25,214. Room and board $8,520. Required fees $500. *Student Employment:* Federal Work-Study Program available. Institutional employment available. Off-campus job opportunities are excellent.

WILSON COLLEGE

1015 Philadelphia Avenue, Chambersburg, PA 17201
Phone: 717-262-2002 • **Financial Aid Phone:** 717-262-2016
E-mail: admissions@wilson.edu • **CEEB Code:** 2979
Fax: 717-262-2546 • **ACT Code:** 3758

This private school, affiliated with the Presbyterian Church, was founded in 1869. It has a 300-acre campus.

RATINGS

Admissions Selectivity Rating: 86   **Fire Safety Rating:** 79

STUDENTS AND FACULTY

Enrollment: 515. **Student Body:** 92% female, 8% male, 24% out-of-state, 4% international (10 countries represented). Asian 0%, African American 5%, Caucasian 76%, Hispanic 3%, Native American <1%
Retention and Graduation: 57% freshmen return for sophomore year. 43% freshmen graduate within 4 years. 56% freshmen graduate within 6 years. 30% grads go on to further study within 1 year. 6% grads pursue arts and sciences degrees. 9% grads pursue law degrees. 8% grads pursue business degrees. 8% grads pursue medical degrees. **Faculty:** 45 full-time faculty, 82% hold PhDs, 56% are are members of minority groups, 7% are women. 0% of classes are taught by teaching assistants.

ACADEMICS

Degrees: associate, bachelor's, master's. **Classes:** Most classes have 10-19 students. Most lab/discussion sessions have 10-19 students. **Majors with Highest Enrollment:** Veterinary/Animal Health Technology/Technician and Veterinary Assistant; Elementary Education and Teaching; Equestrian/Equine Studies. **Special Study Options:** cooperative education program, cross-registration, double major, English as a Second Language (ESL), honors program, independent study, internships, liberal arts/career combination, student-designed major, study abroad, teacher certification program. **Honors programs:** Wilson Scholars Program. **Disability Services:** Special programs offered to physically disabled students include note-taking services, reader services, tape recorders, tutors. **Career services:** Alumni network, alumni services, career/job search classes, career assessment, internships. Career services highlights include an increased number and variety of services offered. An alum commented recently on how much more we offer in the Career Development Center.

FACILITIES

Housing: women's dorms, Students of junior standing or above are guaranteed single residence hall room. We also offer women with children housing, maximum of 2 children. 70% of campus accessible to physically disabled. **Special Academic Facilities/Equipment:** Archives, Bogigian Art gallery, Dance Studio, Helen M. Beach '24 Veterinary Medical Center, Penn Hall Equestrian Center, Natural History Museum, electron microscope, NMR spectrometer. **Computers:** 50% of classrooms, 100% of dining areas, 100% of student union, 15% of common outdoor areas have wireless network access. Students can register for classes online. Administrative functions (other than registration) can be performed online.

CAMPUS LIFE

Environment: Village. **Activities:** Choral groups, dance, drama/theater, literary magazine, music ensembles, radio station, student government, student newspaper, yearbook, Campus Ministries, International Student Organization. 35 registered organizations, 1 honor society, 4 religious organizations. **Athletics (Intercollegiate):** *Women:* basketball, field hockey, gymnastics, lacrosse, soccer, softball, tennis. **On-Campus Highlights:** Penn Hall Equestrian Center, Helen M. Beach '24 Veterinary Medical Center, Complex for Science, Math & Technology, Prentis Hall Women with Children Residence, Lenfest Commons with Fitness Center and Coffee House. **Environmental Initiatives:** Organic farm; Alternative Energy Production; Environmental Sustainability mission statement of college.

ADMISSIONS

Freshman Academic Profile: Average high school GPA 3.43. 22% in top 10% of high school class, 50% in top 25% of high school class, 82% in top 50% of high school class. 84% from public high schools. SAT Math middle 50% range 430-550. SAT Critical Reading middle 50% range 450-570. SAT Writing middle 50% range 430-550. ACT middle 50% range 21-23. Minimum internet-based TOEFL 61. Minimum paper TOEFL 500. **Basis for Candidate Selection:** *Very important factors considered include:* rigor of secondary school record. *Important factors considered include:* Class rank, academic GPA, recommendation(s). *Other factors considered include:* application essay, standardized test scores, alumni/ae relation, character/personal qualities, extracurricular activities, interview, talent/ability, volunteer work, work experience. **Freshman Admission Requirements:** High school diploma is required and GED is accepted. **Academic units required:** 4 English, 3 mathematics, 2 science, (2 science labs), 2 foreign language, 4 social studies. **Freshman Admission Statistics:** 563 applied, 50% admitted, 33% enrolled. **Transfer Admission Requirements:** High school transcript, college transcript(s), essay or personal statement, Minimum college GPA of 2.0 required. Lowest grade transferable C. **General Admission Information:** Application Fee $35. Notification on a rolling basis, beginning on or about 9/15. Nonfall registration accepted. Admission may be deferred for a maximum of 12 Months. Credit and/or placement offered for CEEB Advanced Placement tests.

COSTS AND FINANCIAL AID

Annual tuition $28,745. Room and board $9,710. Required fees $595. Average book expense $1,000. **Required Forms and Deadlines:** FAFSA, Institution's own financial aid form, State aid form. **Notification of Awards:** Applicants will be notified of awards on a rolling basis beginning 2/15. **Types of Aid:** *Need-based scholarships/grants:* Federal Pell, SEOG, state scholarships/grants, private scholarships, the school's own gift aid. *Loans:* Subsidized Stafford, Unsubsidized Stafford, PLUS, Federal Perkins, college/university loans from institutional funds. *Student Employment:* Federal Work-Study Program available. Institutional employment available. Highest amount earned per year from on-campus jobs $1,500. Off-campus job opportunities are fair. **Financial Aid Statistics:** 100% freshmen, 99% undergrads receive need-based scholarship or grant aid. 11% freshmen, 9% undergrads receive non-need-based scholarship or grant aid. 83% freshmen, 81% undergrads receive need-based self-help aid. 0% freshmen, 0% undergrads receive athletic scholarships. 99% freshmen, 97% undergrads receive any aid. 81% undergrads borrow to pay for school. Average cumulative indebtedness $29,570. **Criteria for awarding institutional aid:** *Non-need-based:* academics, alumni affiliation, religious affiliation, state/district residency.

WINGATE UNIVERSITY

Campus Box 3059, Wingate, NC 28174
Phone: 704-233-8200 • **Financial Aid Phone:** 704-233-8209
E-mail: admit@wingate.edu • **CEEB Code:** 5908
Fax: 704-233-8110 • **Website:** www.wingate.edu • **ACT Code:** 3176

This private school, affiliated with the Baptist Church, was founded in 1896. It has a 390-acre campus.

RATINGS

Admissions Selectivity Rating: 79   **Fire Safety Rating:** 79

STUDENTS AND FACULTY

Enrollment: 2,001. **Student Body:** 59% female, 41% male, 17% out-of-state, 4% international (21 countries represented). Asian 2%, African American 15%, Caucasian 64%, Hispanic 2%, Native American 1%
Retention and Graduation: 75% freshmen return for sophomore year. 43% freshmen graduate within 4 years. 53% freshmen graduate within 6 years. 20% grads go on to further study within 1 year. 9% grads pursue arts and sciences degrees. 2% grads pursue law degrees. 8% grads pursue business degrees. 1% grads pursue medical degrees. **Faculty:** 145 full-time faculty, 94% hold PhDs, 54% are are members of minority groups, 8% are women. 0% of classes are taught by teaching assistants.

ACADEMICS

Degrees: bachelor's, first professional, master's. **Classes:** Most classes have 20-29 students. Most lab/discussion sessions have 10-19 students. **Majors with Highest Enrollment:** Biology/Biological Sciences; Business Administration and Management; Psychology. **Special Study Options:** cross-registration, double major, dual enrollment, honors program, independent study, internships, study abroad, teacher certification program, A Bachelor in Liberal Arts is offered to non-traditional students looking to complete a degree. This programs is offered at the Wingate Metro Center in Matthews, NC. **Honors programs:** Our University Honors program offers students 18 hours of honors courses covering a spectrum of disciplines. Students may travel to New York City as part of the program. **Disability Services:** Special programs offered to physically disabled students include note-taking services, tape recorders, tutors.

FACILITIES

Housing: men's dorms, women's dorms, apartments for single students. 95% of campus accessible to physically disabled. **Special Academic Facilities/Equipment:** Douglas Helms Art Gallery, outdoor recreation lab, Batte Fine Arts Center. **Computers:** Administrative functions (other than registration) can be performed online.

CAMPUS LIFE

Environment: Village. **Activities:** Choral groups, drama/theater, jazz band, literary magazine, music ensembles, musical theater, student government, student newspaper, television station, yearbook. 45 registered organizations, 10 honor societies, 8 religious organizations. 4 fraternities, 4 sororities. **Athletics (Intercollegiate):** *Men:* baseball, basketball, cheerleading, cross-country, football, golf, lacrosse, soccer, swimming, tennis. *Women:* basketball, cheerleading, cross-country, golf, soccer, softball, swimming, tennis, volleyball. **On-Campus Highlights:** George A. Batte Jr. Fine Arts Center, Kondike Grill, Irwin Belk Football Stadium, Ehtel's Café (in the Ethel K. Smith Library), Jefferson Clubhouse, Batte Fine Arts Center—a 44,000 sq. foot facility provides a venue foe musicians, singers, actors, and artists. The center features a 554 theatre, among other facilities. Ethel's Café provides a quiet environment to study while enjoying coffee, pastries, and other refreshments. Jefferson Clubhouse, houses a convinience store, gym, swinmming pool, Health Services, and the offices of Greek Life.

ADMISSIONS

Freshman Academic Profile: Average high school GPA 3.34. 18% in top 10% of high school class, 49.5% in top 25% of high school class, 84.9% in top 50% of high school class. 85% from public high schools. SAT Math middle 50% range 470-570. SAT Critical Reading middle 50% range 440-550. SAT Writing middle 50% range 430-530. ACT middle 50% range 19-24. Minimum paper TOEFL 550. **Basis for Candidate Selection:** *Very important factors considered include:* Class rank, rigor of secondary school record. *Important factors considered include:* academic GPA, recommendation(s), standardized test scores. *Other factors considered include:* character/personal qualities, extracurricular activities, talent/ability. **Freshman Admission Requirements:** High school diploma is required and GED is accepted. **Freshman Admission Statistics:** 5,323 applied, 79% admitted, 15% enrolled. **Transfer Admission Requirements:** High school transcript, college transcript(s), statement of good standing from prior institution(s). Minimum college GPA of 2.0 required. Lowest grade transferable C. **General Admission Information:** Application Fee $30.

Notification on a rolling basis, beginning on or about 9/15. Nonfall registration accepted. Admission may be deferred for a maximum of 1 year. Credit and/or placement offered for CEEB Advanced Placement tests.

COSTS AND FINANCIAL AID

Annual tuition $24,750. Room and board $10,400. Required fees $1,550. Average book expense $1,100. **Required Forms and Deadlines:** FAFSA, State aid form. **Notification of Awards:** Applicants will be notified of awards on a rolling basis beginning 3/1. **Types of Aid:** *Need-based scholarships/grants:* Federal Pell, SEOG, state scholarships/grants, private scholarships, the school's own gift aid. *Loans:* Direct Subsidized Stafford, Direct Unsubsidized Stafford, Direct PLUS, Subsidized Stafford, Unsubsidized Stafford, PLUS. *Student Employment:* Federal Work-Study Program available. Institutional employment available. Highest amount earned per year from on-campus jobs $1,200. Off-campus job opportunities are good. **Financial Aid Statistics:** 100% freshmen, 99% undergrads receive need-based scholarship or grant aid. 17% freshmen, 16% undergrads receive non-need-based scholarship or grant aid. 82% freshmen, 84% undergrads receive need-based self-help aid. 11% freshmen, 11% undergrads receive athletic scholarships. 97% freshmen, 96% undergrads receive any aid. 53% undergrads borrow to pay for school. Average cumulative indebtedness $26,432. **Criteria for awarding institutional aid:** *Non-need-based:* academics, alumni affiliation, art, athletics, leadership, music/drama, religious affiliation, state/district residency.

WINONA STATE UNIVERSITY

175 Mark Street, Winona, MN 55987
Phone: 507-457-5100 · **Financial Aid Phone:** 507-457-5090
E-mail: admissions@winona.edu · **CEEB Code:** 6680
Fax: 507-457-5620 · **Website:** www.winona.edu · **ACT Code:** 2162

This public school was founded in 1858. It has a 40-acre campus.

RATINGS

Admissions Selectivity Rating: 81   **Fire Safety Rating:** 87

STUDENTS AND FACULTY

Enrollment: 8,077. **Student Body:** 61% female, 39% male, 31% out-of-state, 2% international (46 countries represented). Asian 2%, African American 2%, Caucasian 88%, Hispanic 3%, Native American <1%
Retention and Graduation: 78% freshmen return for sophomore year. 30% freshmen graduate within 4 years. 15% grads go on to further study within 1 year. 10% grads pursue arts and sciences degrees. 1% grads pursue law degrees. 6% grads pursue business degrees. 1% grads pursue medical degrees. **Faculty:** 307 full-time faculty, 60% hold PhDs, 61% are are members of minority groups, 10% are women. 0% of classes are taught by teaching assistants.

ACADEMICS

Degrees: associate, bachelor's, master's, post-bachelor's certificate, post-master's certificate. **Classes:** Most classes have 20-29 students. Most lab/discussion sessions have 20-29 students. **Majors with Highest Enrollment:** Elementary Education and Teaching; Registered Nursing/Registered Nurse; Biology/Biological Sciences. **Special Study Options:** Accelerated program, cross-registration, distance learning, double major, dual enrollment, English as a Second Language (ESL), external degree program, independent study, internships, student-designed major, study abroad, teacher certification program. **Disability Services:** Special programs offered to physically disabled students include note-taking services, reader services, tape recorders. **Career services:** alumni services, career assessment, internships. Career services highlights include nearly 150 workshops and presentations annually reaching an average of 5000 students; we also have podcasts on a variety of topics available online 24/7.

FACILITIES

Housing: Coed dorms, special housing for disabled students, men's dorms, women's dorms, apartments for single students, Residential College-Residence halls with classrooms and faculty offices. 100% of campus accessible to physically disabled. **Special Academic Facilities/Equipment:** Paul Watkins Art Gallery. **Computers:** 100% of classrooms, 50% of dorms, 100% of libraries, 100% of dining areas, 100% of student union, 85% of common outdoor areas have wireless network access. Students can register for classes online. Administrative functions (other than registration) can be performed online. Undergraduates are required to own a computer.

CAMPUS LIFE

Environment: Town. **Activities:** Choral groups, concert band, dance, drama/theater, jazz band, literary magazine, music ensembles, musical theater, pep band, radio station, student government, student newspaper, student-run film society, symphony orchestra, television station, Campus Ministries, Interna-

tional Student Organization, Model UN. 208 registered organizations, 14 honor societies, 10 religious organizations. 2 fraternities, 3 sororities. **Athletics (Intercollegiate):** *Men:* baseball, basketball, cross-country, football, golf. *Women:* basketball, cross-country, golf, gymnastics, soccer, softball, tennis, track/field (outdoor), track/field (indoor), volleyball. **On-Campus Highlights:** The Library, Lourdes Hall—Residential College, Central Courtyard and Clock Tower, The Smaug—Kryzsko Commons, Wabasha Hall Fitness Center. **Environmental Initiatives:** Recycling/Post Consumer Waste Reduction; Community Education on Sustainability and Local Food; Energy Conservation.

ADMISSIONS

Freshman Academic Profile: Average high school GPA 3.31. 8% in top 10% of high school class, 31% in top 25% of high school class, 72% in top 50% of high school class. ACT middle 50% range 21-25. Minimum internet-based TOEFL 68. Minimum paper TOEFL 520. **Basis for Candidate Selection:** *Very important factors considered include:* Class rank, rigor of secondary school record, standardized test scores. *Important factors considered include:* academic GPA. *Other factors considered include:* recommendation(s). **Freshman Admission Requirements:** High school diploma is required and GED is accepted. **Academic units required:** 4 English, 3 mathematics, 3 science, (3 science labs), 2 foreign language, 2 social studies, 1 history, 1 academic elective. **Freshman Admission Statistics:** 7,212 applied, 61% admitted, 38% enrolled. **Transfer Admission Requirements:** college transcript(s), Minimum college GPA of 2.4 required. Lowest grade transferable D. **General Admission Information:** Application Fee $20. Regular application deadline 3/1. Notification on a rolling basis, beginning on or about 9/1. Nonfall registration accepted. Admission may be deferred for a maximum of 12 months. Credit and/or placement offered for CEEB Advanced Placement tests.

COSTS AND FINANCIAL AID

Annual in-state tuition $6,860. Annual out-of-state tuition $12,360. Room and board $7,890. Required fees $1,890. Average book expense $1,200. **Required Forms and Deadlines:** FAFSA. **Notification of Awards:** Applicants will be notified of awards on a rolling basis beginning 3/1. **Types of Aid:** *Need-based scholarships/grants:* Federal Pell, SEOG, state scholarships/grants, private scholarships, the school's own gift aid. *Loans:* Subsidized Stafford, Unsubsidized Stafford, PLUS, Federal Perkins, state loans, college/university loans from institutional funds. *Student Employment:* Federal Work-Study Program available. Institutional employment available. Highest amount earned per year from on-campus jobs $2,200. Off-campus job opportunities are fair. **Financial Aid Statistics:** 72% freshmen, 68% undergrads receive need-based scholarship or grant aid. 16% freshmen, 9% undergrads receive non-need-based scholarship or grant aid. 86% freshmen, 88% undergrads receive need-based self-help aid. 28% freshmen, 16% undergrads receive athletic scholarships. 61% freshmen, 60% undergrads receive any aid. 76% undergrads borrow to pay for school. **Criteria for awarding institutional aid:** *Non-need-based:* academics, alumni affiliation, art, athletics, minority status, music/drama, state/district residency.

WINSTON-SALEM STATE UNIVERSITY

601 MLK, Jr. Drive, Winston-Salem, NC 27110
Phone: 336-750-2070
E-mail: admissions@wssu1.adp.wssu.edu · **CEEB Code:** 5909
Fax: 336-750-2079 · **Website:** www.wssu.edu · **ACT Code:** 3178

This public school was founded in 1892. It has a 94-acre campus.

RATINGS

Admissions Selectivity Rating: 61   **Fire Safety Rating:** 60*

STUDENTS AND FACULTY

Enrollment: 5,254. **Student Body:** 70% female, 30% male, 6% out-of-state, 0% international. Asian 1%, African American 84%, Caucasian 12%, Hispanic 1%, Native American <1%
Retention and Graduation: 72% freshmen return for sophomore year. 14% freshmen graduate within 6 years. **Faculty:** 275 full-time faculty, 63% hold PhDs, 62% are are members of minority groups.

ACADEMICS

Degrees: bachelor's, master's, post-bachelor's certificate, post-master's certificate. **Classes:** Most classes have fewer than 10 students. **Special Study Options:** cooperative education program, double major, dual enrollment, exchange student program (domestic), honors program, independent study, internships, liberal arts/career combination, study abroad, teacher certification program. **Disability Services:** Special programs offered to physically disabled students include tutors. **Career services:** alumni services, internships.

FACILITIES

Housing: Coed dorms, men's dorms, women's dorms. **Special Academic Facilities/Equipment:** Art gallery.

CAMPUS LIFE

Activities: Choral groups, jazz band, marching band, music ensembles, radio station, student government, student newspaper, yearbook. **On-Campus Highlights:** CLEON Thompson Student Center, Fitness Center, O'Kelly Library.

ADMISSIONS

Basis for Candidate Selection: *Very important factors considered include:* Class rank, rigor of secondary school record, standardized test scores. *Other factors considered include:* alumni/ae relation, character/personal qualities, extracurricular activities, interview, talent/ability. **Freshman Admission Statistics:** 1,353 applied, 80% admitted, 46% enrolled. **Transfer Admission Requirements:** college transcript(s), Lowest grade transferable C. **General Admission Information:** Application Fee $20. Nonfall registration accepted.

COSTS AND FINANCIAL AID

Annual out-of-state tuition $8,049. Room and board $3,403. Required fees $863. **Required Forms and Deadlines:** FAFSA. **Notification of Awards:** Applicants will be notified of awards on or about 5/15. **Types of Aid:** *Need-based scholarships/grants:* Federal Pell, SEOG, state scholarships/grants, private scholarships, the school's own gift aid, Federal Nursing Scholarships. *Loans:* Subsidized Stafford, Unsubsidized Stafford, PLUS, Federal Perkins, state loans, college/university loans from institutional funds. *Student Employment:* Federal Work-Study Program available. Institutional employment available. Highest amount earned per year from on-campus jobs $800. Off-campus job opportunities are good. **Financial Aid Statistics:** 83% freshmen, 92% undergrads receive need-based scholarship or grant aid. 11% freshmen, 7% undergrads receive non-need-based scholarship or grant aid. 78% freshmen, 88% undergrads receive need-based self-help aid. 7% freshmen, 5% undergrads receive athletic scholarships.

WINTHROP UNIVERSITY

Admissions, Winthrop University, Rock Hill, SC 29733
Phone: 803-323-2191 · **Financial Aid Phone:** 803-323-2189
E-mail: admissions@winthrop.edu · **CEEB Code:** 5910
Fax: 803-323-2137 · **Website:** www.winthrop.edu · **ACT Code:** 3884

This public school was founded in 1886. It has a 418-acre campus.

RATINGS

Admissions Selectivity Rating: 74   **Fire Safety Rating:** 86

STUDENTS AND FACULTY

Enrollment: 4,653. **Student Body:** 67% female, 33% male, 7% out-of-state, 3% international (37 countries represented). Asian 1%, African American 30%, Caucasian 58%, Hispanic 4%, Native American <1%
Retention and Graduation: 35% freshmen graduate within 4 years. 52% freshmen graduate within 6 years. 11% grads go on to further study within 1 year. 20% grads pursue arts and sciences degrees. 3% grads pursue law degrees. 25% grads pursue business degrees. 5% grads pursue medical degrees. **Faculty:** 287 full-time faculty, 88% hold PhDs, 52% are are members of minority groups, 13% are women. 0% of classes are taught by teaching assistants.

ACADEMICS

Degrees: bachelor's, master's, post-bachelor's certificate. **Classes:** Most classes have 20-29 students. Most lab/discussion sessions have 20-29 students. **Majors with Highest Enrollment:** Business/Commerce; Design and Visual Communications; Biology/Biological Sciences. **Special Study Options:** cooperative education program, cross-registration, distance learning, double major, exchange student program (domestic), honors program, independent study, internships, study abroad, teacher certification program. **Disability Services:** Special programs offered to physically disabled students include note-taking services, reader services, tape recorders. **Career services:** Alumni network, alumni services, career assessment, internships, regional alumni.

FACILITIES

Housing: Coed dorms, men's dorms, women's dorms, fraternity/sorority housing, apartments for married students, apartments for single students. 85% of campus accessible to physically disabled. **Special Academic Facilities/Equipment:** Art gallery, on-campus nursery and kindergarten. **Computers:** 25% of classrooms, 10% of dorms, 100% of libraries, 100% of dining areas, 100% of student union, 10% of common outdoor areas have wireless network access. Students can register for classes online. Administrative functions (other than registration) can be performed online.

CAMPUS LIFE

Environment: Town. **Activities:** Choral groups, concert band, dance, drama/theater, jazz band, literary magazine, music ensembles, musical theater, opera, pep band, radio station, student government, student newspaper, yearbook, Campus Ministries, International Student Organization, Model UN. 184 registered organizations, 23 honor societies, 10 religious organizations. 8 fraternities, 9 sororities. **Athletics (Intercollegiate):** *Men:* baseball, basketball, cross-country, golf, soccer, tennis, track/field (outdoor). *Women:* basketball, cross-country, golf, soccer, softball, tennis, track/field (outdoor), volleyball. **On-Campus Highlights:** Java City, Winthrop Coliseum, Frisbee-Golf Course **Environmental Initiatives:** Very strong recycling program. Commitment to have all new buildings be green certified or green features. Outstanding record of reducing energy use by upgrading historic buildings (electrical, windows, etc.)

ADMISSIONS

Freshman Academic Profile: Average high school GPA 3.91. SAT Math middle 50% range 470-580. SAT Critical Reading middle 50% range 470-590. ACT middle 50% range 19-26. Minimum internet-based TOEFL 68. Minimum paper TOEFL 520. **Basis for Candidate Selection:** *Very important factors considered include:* rigor of secondary school record. *Important factors considered include:* Class rank, academic GPA, standardized test scores. *Other factors considered include:* application essay, recommendation(s), extracurricular activities, interview, talent/ability, volunteer work. **Freshman Admission Requirements:** High school diploma is required and GED is accepted. **Academic units required:** 4 English, 3 mathematics, 3 science, (3 science labs), 2 foreign language, 2 social studies, 1 history, 4 academic electives, 1 P.E. or ROTC. **Freshman Admission Statistics:** 4,538 applied, 71% admitted, 32% enrolled. **Transfer Admission Requirements:** college transcript(s), statement of good standing from prior institution(s). Minimum college GPA of 2.0 required. Lowest grade transferable C. **General Admission Information:** Application Fee $40. Regular application deadline 5/1. Notification on a rolling basis, beginning on or about 12/1. Nonfall registration accepted. Admission may be deferred for a maximum of 1 semester. Credit offered for CEEB Advanced Placement tests.

COSTS AND FINANCIAL AID

Annual in-state tuition $13,812. Annual out-of-state tuition $26,738. Room and board $8,182. Required fees $0. Average book expense $1,000. **Required Forms and Deadlines:** FAFSA. **Notification of Awards:** Applicants will be notified of awards on a rolling basis beginning 3/15. **Types of Aid:** *Need-based scholarships/grants:* Federal Pell, SEOG, state scholarships/grants, private scholarships, the school's own gift aid. *Loans:* Direct Subsidized Stafford, Direct Unsubsidized Stafford, PLUS, Federal Perkins. *Student Employment:* Federal Work-Study Program available. Institutional employment available. Highest amount earned per year from on-campus jobs $1,750. Off-campus job opportunities are fair. **Financial Aid Statistics:** 99% freshmen, 89% undergrads receive need-based scholarship or grant aid. 16% freshmen, 11% undergrads receive non-need-based scholarship or grant aid. 77% freshmen, 82% undergrads receive need-based self-help aid. 2% freshmen, 3% undergrads receive athletic scholarships. 70% freshmen, 83% undergrads receive any aid. 78% undergrads borrow to pay for school. Average cumulative indebtedness $28,695. **Criteria for awarding institutional aid:** *Non-need-based:* academics, art, athletics, job skills, music/drama.

WISCONSIN LUTHERAN COLLEGE

8800 West Bluemound Road, Milwaukee, WI 53226
Phone: 414-443-8811 · **Financial Aid Phone:** 414-443-8856
E-mail: admissions@wlc.edu · **CEEB Code:** 1513
Fax: 414-443-8514 · **Website:** www.wlc.edu · **ACT Code:** 4699

This private school, affiliated with the Lutheran Church, was founded in 1973. It has a 21-acre campus.

RATINGS

Admissions Selectivity Rating: 80   **Fire Safety Rating:** 69

STUDENTS AND FACULTY

Enrollment: 707. **Student Body:** 56% female, 44% male, 23% out-of-state, 2% international (9 countries represented). Asian 2%, African American 4%, Caucasian 89%, Hispanic 2%, Native American <1%
Retention and Graduation: 76% freshmen return for sophomore year. 51% freshmen graduate within 4 years. 66% freshmen graduate within 6 years. **Faculty:** 60 full-time faculty, 67% hold PhDs, 33% are are members of minority groups. 0% of classes are taught by teaching assistants.

ACADEMICS

Degrees: bachelor's. **Classes:** Most classes have 10-19 students. Most lab/discussion sessions have fewer than 10 students. **Majors with Highest Enroll-**

ment: Speech Communication and Rhetoric; Psychology; Biology/Biological Sciences. **Special Study Options:** double major, dual enrollment, English as a Second Language (ESL), independent study, internships, student-designed major, study abroad, teacher certification program. **Disability Services:** Special programs offered to physically disabled students include note-taking services, reader services, tape recorders, tutors. **Career services:** Alumni network, career assessment, internships.

FACILITIES

Housing: men's dorms, women's dorms, apartments for single students. 90% of campus accessible to physically disabled. **Special Academic Facilities/Equipment:** Center for Arts and Performance, Science Hall **Computers:** Students can register for classes online.

CAMPUS LIFE

Environment: Metropolis. **Activities:** Choral groups, concert band, dance, jazz band, music ensembles, pep band, student government, student newspaper, Campus Ministries, International Student Organization. 31 registered organizations. **Athletics (Intercollegiate):** *Men:* baseball, basketball, cross-country, football, golf, soccer, tennis, track/field (outdoor), track/field (indoor). *Women:* basketball, cross-country, golf, soccer, softball, tennis, track/field (outdoor), track/field (indoor), volleyball. **On-Campus Highlights:** Residence Halls, Center for Arts and Performance, Chapel, The Warrior Underground, The Recreation Complex, Science Hall, Warrior Fields.

ADMISSIONS

Freshman Academic Profile: Average high school GPA 3.34. 17.7% in top 10% of high school class, 43.1% in top 25% of high school class, 77% in top 50% of high school class. ACT middle 50% range 21-26. Minimum paper TOEFL 550. **Basis for Candidate Selection:** *Important factors considered include:* academic GPA, recommendation(s), rigor of secondary school record, standardized test scores, character/personal qualities, level of applicant's interest, religious affiliation/commitment. *Other factors considered include:* Class rank, application essay, alumni/ae relation, extracurricular activities, first generation, interview, racial/ethnic status, talent/ability, volunteer work, work experience. **Freshman Admission Requirements:** High school diploma is required and GED is accepted. **Academic units required:** 4 English, 3 mathematics, 2 science, (1 science labs), 2 foreign language, 2 history, 3 academic electives. **Freshman Admission Statistics:** 646 applied, 76% admitted, 46% enrolled. **Transfer Admission Requirements:** college transcript(s), statement of good standing from prior institution(s). Minimum college GPA of 2.5 required. Lowest grade transferable CD. **General Admission Information:** Application Fee $20. Notification on a rolling basis, beginning on or about 9/1. Nonfall registration accepted. Admission may be deferred for a maximum of 1 semester. Credit and/or placement offered for CEEB Advanced Placement tests.

COSTS AND FINANCIAL AID

Annual tuition $21,040. Room and board $7,700. Required fees $140. Average book expense $700. **Required Forms and Deadlines:** FAFSA, Institution's own financial aid form, Business/Farm Supplement. **Notification of Awards:** Applicants will be notified of awards on a rolling basis beginning 3/15. **Types of Aid:** *Need-based scholarships/grants:* Federal Pell, SEOG, state scholarships/grants, private scholarships, the school's own gift aid. *Loans:* Subsidized Stafford, Unsubsidized Stafford, PLUS, state loans, Private Educational *Student Employment:* Federal Work-Study Program available. Institutional employment available. Highest amount earned per year from on-campus jobs $2,800. Off-campus job opportunities are excellent. **Financial Aid Statistics:** 100% freshmen, 99% undergrads receive need-based scholarship or grant aid. 11% freshmen, 10% undergrads receive non-need-based scholarship or grant aid. 91% freshmen, 91% undergrads receive need-based self-help aid. 0% freshmen, 0% undergrads receive athletic scholarships. 100% freshmen, 98% undergrads receive any aid. 71% undergrads borrow to pay for school. Average cumulative indebtedness $15,194. **Criteria for awarding institutional aid:** *Non-need-based:* academics, art, leadership, music/drama.

WITTENBERG UNIVERSITY

Best 380

PO Box 720, Springfield, OH 45501
Phone: 937-327-6314 · **Financial Aid Phone:** 937-327-7321
E-mail: admission@wittenberg.edu · **CEEB Code:** 1922
Fax: 937-327-6379 · **Website:** www.wittenberg.edu · **ACT Code:** 3364

This private school, affiliated with the Lutheran Church, was founded in 1845. It has a 71-acre campus.

RATINGS

Admissions Selectivity Rating: 79   **Fire Safety Rating:** 97

STUDENTS AND FACULTY

Enrollment: 1,780. **Student Body:** 56% female, 44% male, 28% out-of-state, 2% international (25 countries represented). Asian 1%, African American 7%, Caucasian 86%, Hispanic 3%, Native American <1%
Retention and Graduation: 80% freshmen return for sophomore year. 65% freshmen graduate within 4 years. 69% freshmen graduate within 6 years. **Faculty:** 127 full-time faculty, 97% hold PhDs, 43% are members of minority groups, 10% are women. 0% of classes are taught by teaching assistants.

ACADEMICS

Degrees: bachelor's, master's. **Classes:** Most classes have 10-19 students. Most lab/discussion sessions have 10-19 students. **Majors with Highest Enrollment:** Biology/Biological Sciences; Business/Commerce; Economics. **Special Study Options:** cross-registration, double major, dual enrollment, honors program, independent study, internships, liberal arts/career combination, student-designed major, study abroad, teacher certification program. **Honors programs:** Honors Program, 3-2 Engineering Program, Pre-Health Programs. **Disability Services:** Special programs offered to physically disabled students include note-taking services, reader services, tape recorders, tutors. **Career services:** Alumni network, alumni services, career/job search classes, career assessment, internships, regional alumni. Career services highlights include Lutheran College Washington Semester.

FACILITIES

Housing: Coed dorms, special housing for international students, women's dorms, fraternity/sorority housing, apartments for married students, apartments for single students, University owned houses around campus. 81% of campus accessible to physically disabled. **Special Academic Facilities/Equipment:** Language lab, electron microscope, observatory. **Computers:** 50% of classrooms, 100% of libraries, 100% of dining areas, 100% of student union, 100% of common outdoor areas have wireless network access. Students can register for classes online. Administrative functions (other than registration) can be performed online.

CAMPUS LIFE

Environment: Town. **Activities:** Choral groups, concert band, dance, drama/theater, jazz band, literary magazine, music ensembles, musical theater, opera, pep band, radio station, student government, student newspaper, student-run film society, symphony orchestra, yearbook, Campus Ministries, International Student Organization. 126 registered organizations, 24 honor societies, 10 religious organizations. 6 fraternities, 5 sororities. **Athletics (Intercollegiate):** *Men:* baseball, basketball, cross-country, diving, football, golf, lacrosse, soccer, swimming, tennis, track/field (outdoor), track/field (indoor). *Women:* basketball, cheerleading, cross-country, diving, field hockey, golf, lacrosse, soccer, softball, swimming, tennis, track/field (outdoor), track/field (indoor), volleyball. **On-Campus Highlights:** HPERC Athletic Center, Benham Prince Student Center, Chakers Theatre, Weaver Observatory, Thomas Library.

ADMISSIONS

Freshman Academic Profile: Average high school GPA 3.42. 22% in top 10% of high school class, 46% in top 25% of high school class, 77% in top 50% of high school class. 79% from public high schools. SAT Math middle 50% range 490-620. SAT Critical Reading middle 50% range 510-630. SAT Writing middle 50% range 470-600. ACT middle 50% range 22-28. Minimum paper TOEFL 550. **Basis for Candidate Selection:** *Very important factors considered include:* Class rank, academic GPA, rigor of secondary school record. *Important factors considered include:* application essay, recommendation(s), character/personal qualities, extracurricular activities, talent/ability, volunteer work. *Other factors considered include:* standardized test scores, alumni/ae relation, first generation, interview, work experience. **Freshman Admission Requirements:** High school diploma is required and GED is accepted. **Academic**

units required: 4 English, 3 mathematics, 3 science, (2 science labs), 2 foreign language, 0 social studies, 2 history. **Freshman Admission Statistics:** 4,850 applied, 91% admitted, 12% enrolled. **Transfer Admission Requirements:** college transcript(s), Minimum college GPA of 2.0 required. Lowest grade transferable C. **General Admission Information:** Application Fee $40. Early decision application deadline 11/15. Notification on a rolling basis, beginning on or about 1/1. Nonfall registration accepted. Admission may be deferred for a maximum of 12 months. Credit and/or placement offered for CEEB Advanced Placement tests.

COSTS AND FINANCIAL AID

Annual tuition $37,230. Room and board $10,028. Required fees $800. Average book expense $1,000. **Required Forms and Deadlines:** FAFSA. **Notification of Awards:** Applicants will be notified of awards on a rolling basis beginning 3/1. **Types of Aid:** *Need-based scholarships/grants:* Federal Pell, SEOG, state scholarships/grants, private scholarships, the school's own gift aid. *Loans:* Subsidized Stafford, Unsubsidized Stafford, PLUS, Federal Perkins, college/university loans from institutional funds, Private "alternative" Loans. *Student Employment:* Federal Work-Study Program available. Institutional employment available. Off-campus job opportunities are excellent. **Financial Aid Statistics:** 100% freshmen, 100% undergrads receive need-based scholarship or grant aid. 0% freshmen, 0% undergrads receive non-need-based scholarship or grant aid. 100% freshmen, 94% undergrads receive need-based self-help aid. 0% freshmen, 0% undergrads receive athletic scholarships. 100% freshmen, 95% undergrads receive any aid. 74% undergrads borrow to pay for school. Average cumulative indebtedness $25,540. **Criteria for awarding institutional aid:** *Non-need-based:* academics, alumni affiliation, art, leadership, minority status, music/drama, religious affiliation, state/district residency.

See page 1216.

WOFFORD COLLEGE

429 North Church Street, Spartanburg, SC 29303-3663
Phone: 864-597-4130 • **Financial Aid Phone:** 864-597-4160
E-mail: admission@wofford.edu • **CEEB Code:** 5912
Fax: 864-597-4147 • **Website:** www.wofford.edu • **ACT Code:** 3886

This private school, affiliated with the Methodist Church, was founded in 1854. It has a 170-acre campus.

RATINGS

Admissions Selectivity Rating: 60*   **Fire Safety Rating:** 60*

STUDENTS AND FACULTY

Enrollment: 1,597. **Student Body:** 51% female, 49% male, 44% out-of-state, 2% international (15 countries represented). Asian 2%, African American 8%, Caucasian 80%, Hispanic 3%, Native American <1%
Retention and Graduation: 71% freshmen graduate within 4 years. 78% freshmen graduate within 6 years. **Faculty:** 131 full-time faculty, 90% hold PhDs, 40% are are members of minority groups, 10% are women. 0% of classes are taught by teaching assistants.

ACADEMICS

Degrees: bachelor's. **Classes:** Most classes have 10-19 students. Most lab/discussion sessions have 20-29 students. **Majors with Highest Enrollment:** Biology/Biological Sciences; Finance; Business/Managerial Economics. **Special Study Options:** Accelerated program, cross-registration, double major, dual enrollment, independent study, internships, student-designed major, study abroad, teacher certification program, Presidential International Scholar program; "Success Initiative, " Bonner Scholars, Community of Scholars, Learning Communities and Creative Writing Concentration. **Combined degree programs:** BA/MEng. **Disability Services:** Special programs offered to physically disabled students include note-taking services, reader services, tape recorders, tutors. **Career services:** Alumni network, alumni services, career/job search classes, career assessment, internships, regional alumni. Career services highlights include the Institute for Professional Development.

FACILITIES

Housing: Coed dorms, apartments for single students, Wellness Housing. 85% of campus accessible to physically disabled. **Special Academic Facilities/Equipment:** Campus is an Arboretum, Art galleries, Franklin W. Olin Building (teaching technology center), Milliken Science Center. **Computers:** 100% of classrooms, 10% of dorms, 100% of libraries, 100% of dining areas, 100% of student union, 40% of common outdoor areas have wireless network access. Students can register for classes online. Administrative functions (other than registration) can be performed online.

CAMPUS LIFE

Environment: City. **Activities:** Choral groups, concert band, dance, drama/theater, literary magazine, music ensembles, pep band, student government, student newspaper, yearbook, Campus Ministries. 105 registered organizations, 10 honor societies, 8 religious organizations. 8 fraternities, 4 sororities. **Athletics (Intercollegiate):** *Men:* baseball, basketball, cross-country, football, golf, riflery, soccer, tennis, track/field (outdoor), track/field (indoor). *Women:* basketball, cross-country, golf, riflery, soccer, tennis, track/field (outdoor), track/field (indoor), volleyball. **On-Campus Highlights:** The Roger Milliken Arboretum, Roger Milliken Science Center/Great Oaks, Main Building/Leonard Auditorium, Franklin W. Olin Building, Village Student Housing, Gibbs Stadium, Richardson Physical Activities Building, Russell C. King Field and Switzer Stadium, Joe E. Taylor Athletic Center. **Environmental Initiatives:** Establishment of an innovative and inter-disciplinary Environmental Studies program (a BS/BA major are offered through this program). Wofford "houses its Environmental Studies field studies, research, and community outreach programs in the state-of-the-art, LEED Platinum, historically significant Goodall Environmental Studies Center, situated eight miles from campus. The facility substantiates Wofford's commitment to real life, engaged learning. Wofford students, faculty, and staff, as well as area K-12 educators and community members all benefit from the Center's status as a living-learning laboratory for sustainability and environmental literacy." The college has a director for the environmental studies program. Santee Cooper Lecture Series on Sustainability & Energy. This endowed two-year series is designed to introduce the campus and Spartanburg community to preeminent experts from the field of sustainability. For more information, go to http://www.wofford.edu/newsroom/story.aspx?id=60490. As of 2011-2012, the Wofford College Board of Trustees has formed a formal Committee on Conservation and Sustainability.

ADMISSIONS

Freshman Academic Profile: Average high school GPA 3.54. 46% in top 10% of high school class, 77% in top 25% of high school class, 96% in top 50% of high school class. 68% from public high schools. SAT Math middle 50% range 530-640. SAT Critical Reading middle 50% range 530-630. SAT Writing middle 50% range 520-620. ACT middle 50% range 24-30. Minimum internet-based TOEFL 80. Minimum paper TOEFL 550. **Basis for Candidate Selection:** *Very important factors considered include:* academic GPA, rigor of secondary school record. *Important factors considered include:* Class rank, application essay, standardized test scores, character/personal qualities, extracurricular activities, talent/ability, volunteer work. *Other factors considered include:* recommendation(s), alumni/ae relation, first generation, geographical residence, interview, racial/ethnic status, work experience. **Freshman Admission Requirements:** High school diploma is required and GED is accepted. **Freshman Admission Statistics:** 2,556 applied, 77% admitted, 25% enrolled. **Transfer Admission Requirements:** High school transcript, college transcript(s), essay or personal statement, standardized test scores, statement of good standing from prior institution(s). Minimum college GPA of 2.5 required. Lowest grade transferable C. **General Admission Information:** Application Fee $35. Early decision application deadline 11/15. Regular application deadline 2/1. Regular notification 3/15. Nonfall registration accepted. Admission may be deferred for a maximum of 1 year. Credit and/or placement offered for CEEB Advanced Placement tests.

COSTS AND FINANCIAL AID

Annual tuition $37,120. Room and board $10,730. Average book expense $1,200. **Required Forms and Deadlines:** FAFSA. **Notification of Awards:** Applicants will be notified of awards on or about 3/31. **Types of Aid:** *Need-based scholarships/grants:* Federal Pell, SEOG, state scholarships/grants, the school's own gift aid. *Loans:* Subsidized Stafford, Unsubsidized Stafford, PLUS, Federal Perkins. *Student Employment:* Federal Work-Study Program available. Institutional employment available. Highest amount earned per year from on-campus jobs $1,940. Off-campus job opportunities are good. **Financial Aid Statistics:** 100% freshmen, 100% undergrads receive need-based scholarship or grant aid. 27% freshmen, 28% undergrads receive non-need-based scholarship or grant aid. 55% freshmen, 56% undergrads receive need-based self-help aid. 8% freshmen, 10% undergrads receive athletic scholarships. 96% freshmen, 94% undergrads receive any aid. 45% undergrads borrow to pay for school. Average cumulative indebtedness $21,489. **Criteria for awarding institutional aid:** *Non-need-based:* academics, athletics, leadership, music/drama, religious affiliation, state/district residency.

WOODBURY UNIVERSITY

7500 Glenoaks Boulevard, Burbank, CA 91510-7846
Phone: 818-767-0888 · **Financial Aid Phone:** 818-767-0888
E-mail: admissions@woodbury.edu · **CEEB Code:** 4955
Fax: 818-767-7520 · **ACT Code:** 481

This private school was founded in 1884. It has a 22-acre campus.

RATINGS

Admissions Selectivity Rating: 82   **Fire Safety Rating:** 62

STUDENTS AND FACULTY

Enrollment: 1,269. **Student Body:** 53% female, 47% male, 10% international (41 countries represented). Asian 10%, African American 5%, Caucasian 41%, Hispanic 33%, Native American <1%
Retention and Graduation: 80% freshmen return for sophomore year. **Faculty:** 59 full-time faculty, 83% hold PhDs, 56% are are members of minority groups, 12% are women. 0% of classes are taught by teaching assistants.

ACADEMICS

Degrees: bachelor's, master's. **Classes:** Most classes have 10-19 students. **Majors with Highest Enrollment:** Business Administration and Management Fashion/Apparel Design. **Special Study Options:** Accelerated program, double major, dual enrollment, English as a Second Language (ESL), exchange student program (domestic), independent study, internships, liberal arts/career combination, student-designed major, study abroad, weekend college. **Disability Services:** Special programs offered to physically disabled students include note-taking services, tape recorders, tutors. **Career services:** alumni services, career assessment, internships.

FACILITIES

Housing: Coed dorms, off-campus overflow apartments. 90% of campus accessible to physically disabled. **Special Academic Facilities/Equipment:** Art Gallery; Architecture Gallery; **Computers:** 100% of classrooms, 100% of libraries, 100% of dining areas, have wireless network access. Students can register for classes online. Administrative functions (other than registration) can be performed online. Undergraduates are required to own a computer.

CAMPUS LIFE

Environment: City. **Activities:** student government. 20 registered organizations, 3 honor societies, 2 fraternities, 2 sororities.

ADMISSIONS

Freshman Academic Profile: SAT Math middle 50% range 400-530. SAT Critical Reading middle 50% range 390-520. ACT middle 50% range 16-23. Minimum paper TOEFL 500. **Basis for Candidate Selection:** *Very important factors considered include:* academic GPA, rigor of secondary school record, standardized test scores. *Other factors considered include:* Class rank, application essay, recommendation(s), alumni/ae relation, extracurricular activities, first generation, interview, level of applicant's interest, volunteer work, work experience. **Freshman Admission Requirements:** High school diploma is required and GED is accepted. **Freshman Admission Statistics:** 514 applied, 41% admitted, 61% enrolled. **Transfer Admission Requirements:** college transcript(s), Minimum college GPA of 2.5 required. Lowest grade transferable C. **General Admission Information:** Application Fee $50. Notification on a rolling basis, beginning on or about 11/1. Nonfall registration accepted. Admission may be deferred for a maximum of 2 years. Credit offered for CEEB Advanced Placement tests.

COSTS AND FINANCIAL AID

Annual tuition $28,465. Room and board $9,293. Required fees $390. Average book expense $1,700. **Required Forms and Deadlines:** FAFSA, Institution's own financial aid form. **Notification of Awards:** Applicants will be notified of awards on a rolling basis beginning 3/15. **Types of Aid:** *Need-based scholarships/grants:* Federal Pell, SEOG, state scholarships/grants, private scholarships, the school's own gift aid. *Loans:* Subsidized Stafford, Unsubsidized Stafford, PLUS, Federal Perkins. *Student Employment:* Federal Work-Study Program available. Institutional employment available. Off-campus job opportunities are good. **Financial Aid Statistics:** 98% freshmen, 96% undergrads receive need-based scholarship or grant aid. 4% freshmen, 3% undergrads receive non-need-based scholarship or grant aid. 91% freshmen, 93% undergrads receive need-based self-help aid. 0% freshmen, 0% undergrads receive athletic scholarships. 79% freshmen, 86% undergrads receive any aid. 91% undergrads borrow to pay for school. Average cumulative indebtedness $28,696. **Criteria for awarding institutional aid:** *Non-need-based:* academics.

WORCESTER POLYTECHNIC INSTITUTE

Best 380

Admissions Office, Bartlett Center, Worcester, MA 1609
Phone: 508-831-5286 · **Financial Aid Phone:** 508-831-5469
E-mail: admissions@wpi.edu · **CEEB Code:** 3969
Fax: 508-831-5875 · **Website:** http://www.wpi.edu · **ACT Code:** 1942

This private school was founded in 1865. It has a 80-acre campus.

RATINGS

Admissions Selectivity Rating: 95   **Fire Safety Rating:** 85

STUDENTS AND FACULTY

Enrollment: 4,123. **Student Body:** 32% female, 68% male, 58% out-of-state, 13% international (81 countries represented). Asian 5%, African American 2%, Caucasian 62%, Hispanic 8%, Native American <1%
Retention and Graduation: 97% freshmen return for sophomore year. 74% freshmen graduate within 4 years. 85% freshmen graduate within 6 years. 27% grads go on to further study within 1 year. 2% grads pursue law degrees. 2% grads pursue business degrees. 2% grads pursue medical degrees. **Faculty:** 336 full-time faculty, 93% hold PhDs, 27% are are members of minority groups, 16% are women. 0% of classes are taught by teaching assistants.

ACADEMICS

Degrees: bachelor's, master's, post-bachelor's certificate, post-master's certificate. **Classes:** Most classes have fewer than 10 students. Most lab/discussion sessions have 20-29 students. **Majors with Highest Enrollment:** Computer Science; Electrical and Electronics Engineering; Mechanical Engineering. **Special Study Options:** Accelerated program, cooperative education program, cross-registration, distance learning, double major, dual enrollment, English as a Second Language (ESL), honors program, independent study, liberal arts/career combination, student-designed major, study abroad, teacher certification program, Completion of degree-required projects at off-campus locations (international and domestic) supervised by WPI faculty. This program requires the students to reside at the site for 2 months after having prepared for the experience for two months while on campus. **Honors programs:** Chemistry and Biochemistry Scholars Program: Students selected for this highly competitive program will be given the opportunity to participate in faculty research within these departments beginning in the freshman year. In addition to the scholars program, each CBSP Scholar receives an academic merit scholarship. Scholarship amounts will vary, but typically range between $12,500 and $25,000, and are renewable for four years. **Combined degree programs:** BS/MS, BS/MBA, BS/MEng. **Disability Services:** Special programs offered to physically disabled students include note-taking services, reader services, tape recorders, tutors. **Career services:** Alumni network, alumni services, career/job search classes, career assessment, internships, regional alumni. Career services highlights include two hands-on, professional-level projects that are the equivalent of three courses each are a requirement in our curriculum. They provide students with the opportunity to apply theory to practice through real-world problems and to find solutions that can be implemented by the project sponsors. As an example, one company implemented eight of nine student recommendations and saved $35,000 a day.

FACILITIES

Housing: Coed dorms, special housing for disabled students, special housing for international students, fraternity/sorority housing, apartments for single students, 4 co-ed residential houses/special interest housing. 90% of campus accessible to physically disabled. **Special Academic Facilities/Equipment:** Several off-campus project centers, TV studio, robotics lab, CAD-CAM lab, laser labs, electron microscopes, wind tunnel, manufacturing engineering applications center, VLSI design lab, nuclear reactor. **Computers:** 100% of classrooms, 100% of dorms, 100% of libraries, 100% of dining areas, 100% of student union, 100% of common outdoor areas have wireless network access. Students can register for classes online. Administrative functions (other than registration) can be performed online.

CAMPUS LIFE

Environment: City. **Activities:** Choral groups, concert band, dance, drama/theater, jazz band, literary magazine, marching band, music ensembles, musical theater, pep band, radio station, student government, student newspaper, student-run film society, symphony orchestra, yearbook, International Student Organization. 200 registered organizations, 20 honor societies, 4 religious organizations. 13 fraternities, 3 sororities. **Athletics (Intercollegiate):** *Men:* baseball, basketball, crew/rowing, cross-country, diving, football, soccer, swimming, track/field (outdoor), track/field (indoor), wrestling. *Women:* basketball, crew/rowing, cross-country, diving, field hockey, soccer, softball, swimming, track/field (outdoor), track/field (indoor), volleyball. **On-Campus Highlights:** Student invented fountain, Campus Center, Robotics Lab, Wind Tunnels, Fire Protection Engineering Lab, new biomedical and life sciences research center at Gateway Park, New pub-style restaurant on-campus, New apartment-style residence hall opened in summer 2008, New Sports and Recreation Center opened in 2012. **Environmental Initiatives:** Creation of the President's Task Force on Sustainability, the creation of a Sustainability Coordinator position, and the creation of a Student Sustainability Coordination position. In 2007, WPI's Board of Trustees adopted a policy for all future buildings to be designed to meet LEED certification. And the newly formed Institute for Energy and Sustainability, collaboration between WPI and other institutions and businesses, funded by a grant from the Massachusetts Clean Energy Center is working to develop jobs in the clean energy sector.

ADMISSIONS

Freshman Academic Profile: Average high school GPA 3.8. 68% in top 10% of high school class, 92% in top 25% of high school class, 100% in top 50% of high school class. 66% from public high schools. SAT Math middle 50% range 640-740. SAT Critical Reading middle 50% range 570-670. SAT Writing middle 50% range 570-670. ACT middle 50% range 28-32. Minimum internet-based TOEFL 79. Minimum paper TOEFL 550. **Basis for Candidate Selection:** *Very important factors considered include:* academic GPA, rigor of secondary school record. *Important factors considered include:* Class rank, application essay, recommendation(s), standardized test scores, character/personal qualities, extracurricular activities. *Other factors considered include:* alumni/ae relation, first generation, geographical residence, interview, level of applicant's interest, talent/ability, volunteer work, work experience. **Freshman Admission Requirements:** High school diploma is required and GED is accepted. **Academic units required:** 4 English, 4 mathematics, 2 science, (2 science labs). **Freshman Admission Statistics:** 10,233 applied, 44% admitted, 24% enrolled. **Transfer Admission Requirements:** college transcript(s), essay or personal statement, statement of good standing from prior institution(s). Minimum college GPA of 3.0 required. Lowest grade transferable C. **General Admission Information:** Application Fee $60. Regular application deadline 2/1. Regular notification 4/1. Nonfall registration accepted. Admission may be deferred for a maximum of 1 year. Credit and/or placement offered for CEEB Advanced Placement tests.

COSTS AND FINANCIAL AID

Annual tuition $43,612. Room and board $13,082. Required fees $810. Average book expense $1,000. **Required Forms and Deadlines:** FAFSA, CSS/Financial Aid PROFILE, Noncustodial PROFILE. **Notification of Awards:** Applicants will be notified of awards on or about 4/1. **Types of Aid:** *Need-based scholarships/grants:* Federal Pell, SEOG, state scholarships/grants, private scholarships, the school's own gift aid. *Loans:* Subsidized Stafford, Unsubsidized Stafford, PLUS, Federal Perkins, state loans, college/university loans from institutional funds. *Student Employment:* Federal Work-Study Program available. Institutional employment available. Off-campus job opportunities are good. **Financial Aid Statistics:** 100% freshmen, 95% undergrads receive need-based scholarship or grant aid. 46% freshmen, 35% undergrads receive non-need-based scholarship or grant aid. 56% freshmen, 57% undergrads receive need-based self-help aid. 0% freshmen, 0% undergrads receive athletic scholarships. 98% freshmen, 95% undergrads receive any aid. Average cumulative indebtedness $26,143. **Criteria for awarding institutional aid:** *Non-need-based:* academics, leadership, minority status.

See page 1218.

WORCESTER STATE UNIVERSITY

486 Chandler Street, Worcester, MA 01602-2597
Phone: 508-929-8040 · **Financial Aid Phone:** 508-929-8058
E-mail: admissions@worcester.edu · **CEEB Code:** 3524
Fax: 508-929-8183 · **Website:** www.worcester.edu · **ACT Code:** 1914

This public school was founded in 1874. It has a 58-acre campus.

RATINGS

Admissions Selectivity Rating: 76   Fire Safety Rating: 98

STUDENTS AND FACULTY

Enrollment: 5,063. **Student Body:** 60% female, 40% male, 3% out-of-state, 1% international (27 countries represented). Asian 4%, African American 7%, Caucasian 72%, Hispanic 9%, Native American 1%
Retention and Graduation: 31% freshmen graduate within 4 years. 53% freshmen graduate within 6 years. **Faculty:** 206 full-time faculty, 82% hold PhDs, 57% are are members of minority groups, 14% are women. 0% of classes are taught by teaching assistants.

ACADEMICS

Degrees: bachelor's, certificate, master's, post-bachelor's certificate, post-master's certificate. **Classes:** Most classes have 20-29 students. Most lab/discussion sessions have 10-19 students. **Majors with Highest Enrollment:** Business Administration and Management; Psychology; Criminal Justice/Safety Studies. **Special Study Options:** cross-registration, distance learning, double major, English as a Second Language (ESL), exchange student program (domestic), honors program, independent study, internships, liberal arts/career combination, study abroad, teacher certification program, Foreign Exchange Student Program. **Honors programs:** Commonwealth Honors Program: The mission of the honors program at Worcester State College is to offer all qualified students an outstanding undergraduate experience through courses that emphasize innovative pedagogy and the values of liberal learning. Honors classes are small (often fewer than 20 students) and are designed to encourage active and lifelong learning. Small classes and extracurricular programs provide honors students with greater interaction between their peers and a select core of dedicated faculty members. In addition to stimulating classes, honors students also enjoy campus speakers, field trips to cultural centers, occasional luncheons with faculty members, and an annual dinner with the college president. Founded in 1996, the program currently enrolls 150 students and recently earned accreditation as a Commonwealth Honors Program from the Massachusetts Board of Higher Education. **Combined degree programs:** BA/MA, Occupational Therapy. **Disability Services:** Special programs offered to physically disabled students include note-taking services, reader services, tape recorders, tutors. **Career services:** Alumni network, alumni services, career/job search classes, career assessment, internships, regional alumni. Career services highlights include Sustainability Fair, Green Work.

FACILITIES

Housing: Coed dorms, special housing for disabled students, men's dorms, women's dorms. 100% of campus accessible to physically disabled. **Special Academic Facilities/Equipment:** Art Studio. **Computers:** 100% of classrooms, 100% of dorms, 100% of libraries, 100% of dining areas, 100% of student union, 100% of common outdoor areas have wireless network access. Students can register for classes online. Administrative functions (other than registration) can be performed online. Undergraduates are required to own a computer.

CAMPUS LIFE

Environment: City. **Activities:** Choral groups, concert band, dance, drama/theater, jazz band, music ensembles, radio station, student government, student newspaper, television station, yearbook, Campus Ministries, International Student Organization. 39 registered organizations, 17 honor societies, 1 religous organization. **Athletics (Intercollegiate):** *Men:* baseball, basketball, cheerleading, cross-country, football, golf, ice hockey, soccer, track/field (outdoor), track/field (indoor). *Women:* basketball, cheerleading, cross-country, field hockey, lacrosse, soccer, softball, tennis, track/field (outdoor), track/field (indoor), volleyball. **On-Campus Highlights:** Wasylean Hall, Student Center Living Room, Science and Technology Building, Food Court, Campus Bookstore. **Environmental Initiatives:** 2013 saw us break ground on 2 new LEED Gold Buildings—one is a new residence hall with dining hall and the other is a new athletic center to replace the 1950s gym we are knocking down. This is in addition to the two LEED Gold Buildings already on campus. In the Summer of 2012, WSU entered into a 20 year agreement to purchase all net metering credits from a 2.5 MW solar PV array located in Orange, MA. By entering into this agreement, we enabled this project to go online and for Massachusetts to gain another 2.5 MW of PV as part of the 400 MW "Solar Carve-Out Project" (see link). One of the reasons we have entered into this agreement is to support our sister agency—Mass DOER and their renewable energy initiatives for the State of Massachusetts (http://www.mass.gov/eea/energy-utilities-clean-tech/renewable-energy/solar/rps-solar-carve-out/about-the-rps-solar-carve-out-program.html). Many smaller projects include: switching to LED lighting; composting food waste; recycling education program; new sustainability coordinator; move out donation drive to divert move out waste; annual sustainability fair; new hydration stations.

ADMISSIONS

Freshman Academic Profile: Average high school GPA 3.19. 91% from public high schools. SAT Math middle 50% range 450-560. SAT Critical Reading middle 50% range 440-540. SAT Writing middle 50% range 440-530. ACT middle 50% range 19-25. Minimum internet-based TOEFL 79. Minimum paper TOEFL 550. **Basis for Candidate Selection:** *Very important factors considered include:* academic GPA, rigor of secondary school record, standardized test scores. *Important factors considered include:* Class rank, character/personal qualities. *Other factors considered include:* application essay, recommendation(s), alumni/ae relation, extracurricular activities, first generation, geographical residence, racial/ethnic status, state residency, talent/ability, volunteer work, work experience. **Freshman Admission Requirements:** High school diploma is required and GED is accepted. **Academic units required:** 4 English, 3 mathematics, 3 science, (1 science labs), 2 foreign language, 1 social studies, 1 history, 2 academic electives. **Freshman Admission Statistics:** 4,158 applied, 61% admitted, 31% enrolled. **Transfer Admission Requirements:** High school transcript, college transcript(s), statement of good standing from prior institution(s). Minimum college GPA of 2.5 required. Lowest grade transferable C-. **General Admission Information:** Application Fee $40. Regular application deadline 5/1. Notification on a rolling basis, beginning on or about 12/1. Nonfall registration accepted. Admission may be deferred for a maximum of 1 year. Credit and/or placement offered for CEEB Advanced Placement tests.

COSTS AND FINANCIAL AID

Annual in-state tuition $970. Annual out-of-state tuition $7,050. Room and board $11,255. Required fees $7,587. Average book expense $984. **Required Forms and Deadlines:** FAFSA. **Notification of Awards:** Applicants will be notified of awards on a rolling basis beginning 3/1. **Types of Aid:** *Need-based scholarships/grants:* Federal Pell, SEOG, state scholarships/grants, private scholarships, the school's own gift aid. *Loans:* Subsidized Stafford, Unsubsidized Stafford, PLUS, Federal Perkins, state loans. *Student Employment:* Federal Work-Study Program available. Institutional employment available. Highest amount earned per year from on-campus jobs $17,184. Off-campus job opportunities are good. **Financial Aid Statistics:** 86% freshmen, 79% undergrads receive need-based scholarship or grant aid. 45% freshmen, 33% undergrads receive non-need-based scholarship or grant aid. 93% freshmen, 92% undergrads receive need-based self-help aid. 0% freshmen, 0% undergrads receive athletic scholarships. 65% freshmen, 61% undergrads receive any aid. 80% undergrads borrow to pay for school. Average cumulative indebtedness $20,622. **Criteria for awarding institutional aid:** *Non-need-based:* academics.

WRIGHT STATE UNIVERSITY

3640 Colonel Glenn Highway, Dayton, OH 45435
Phone: 937-775-5700 · **Financial Aid Phone:** 937-775-4000
E-mail: admissions@wright.edu · **CEEB Code:** 1179
Fax: 937-775-4410 · **Website:** www.wright.edu · **ACT Code:** 3295

This public school was founded in 1964. It has a 557-acre campus.

RATINGS

Admissions Selectivity Rating: 73   **Fire Safety Rating:** 89

STUDENTS AND FACULTY

Enrollment: 12,090. **Student Body:** 51% female, 49% male, 3% out-of-state, 6% international (69 countries represented). Asian 2%, African American 13%, Caucasian 72%, Hispanic 3%, Native American <1%
Retention and Graduation: 66% freshmen return for sophomore year. 21% freshmen graduate within 4 years. 39% freshmen graduate within 6 years. **Faculty:** 658 full-time faculty, 45% are are members of minority groups, 16% are women. 0.8% of classes are taught by teaching assistants.

ACADEMICS

Degrees: associate, bachelor's, certificate, doctoral, master's, post-master's certificate, terminal associate, transfer associate. **Classes:** Most classes have 20-29 students. Most lab/discussion sessions have fewer than 10 students. **Special Study Options:** cooperative education program, cross-registration, distance learning, double major, dual enrollment, English as a Second Language (ESL), honors program, independent study, internships, student-designed major, study abroad, teacher certification program, weekend college. **Honors programs:** Honors Program. **Disability Services:** Special programs offered to physically disabled students include note-taking services, reader services, tape recorders, tutors. **Career services:** Alumni network, alumni services, career/job search classes, career assessment, internships. Career services highlights include a very flexible set of programs that meet the needs of our students.

FACILITIES

Housing: Coed dorms, special housing for disabled students, apartments for married students, apartments for single students, Honors Dorm. 100% of campus accessible to physically disabled. **Special Academic Facilities/Equipment:** Art gallery located in the Creative Arts Center **Computers:** 100% of classrooms, 100% of dorms, 100% of libraries, 100% of dining areas, 100% of student union, have wireless network access. Students can register for classes online. Administrative functions (other than registration) can be performed online.

CAMPUS LIFE

Environment: City. **Activities:** Choral groups, concert band, dance, drama/theater, jazz band, literary magazine, music ensembles, musical theater, opera, pep band, radio station, student government, student newspaper, symphony orchestra, television station, Campus Ministries, Model UN. 145 registered organizations, 22 honor societies, 9 religious organizations. 8 fraternities, 8 sororities. **Athletics (Intercollegiate):** *Men:* baseball, basketball, cheerlead-

ing, cross-country, diving, golf, soccer, swimming, tennis. *Women:* basketball, cheerleading, cross-country, diving, soccer, softball, swimming, tennis, track/field (outdoor), volleyball. **On-Campus Highlights:** Student Union, Garden of the Senses, Rec Center, Fitness Center, Nutter Center. **Environmental Initiatives:** Matthew O. Diggs III Laboratory for Life Sciences Research achieved LEED Gold status, the first laboratory in Ohio to achieve LEED-NC Gold status. Recycling (86 tons collected for RecycleMania competition in 2012)—has increased every year; Energy Efficiency (20% savings by 2014).

ADMISSIONS

Freshman Academic Profile: Average high school GPA 3.2. 15% in top 10% of high school class, 36% in top 25% of high school class, 67% in top 50% of high school class. 90% from public high schools. SAT Math middle 50% range 450-570. SAT Critical Reading middle 50% range 450-590. SAT Writing middle 50% range 430-550. ACT middle 50% range 18-25. Minimum internet-based TOEFL 61. **Basis for Candidate Selection:** *Very important factors considered include:* academic GPA, rigor of secondary school record, standardized test scores. *Important factors considered include:* Class rank. *Other factors considered include:* recommendation(s), state residency. **Freshman Admission Requirements:** High school diploma is required and GED is accepted. **Academic units required:** 4 English, 3 mathematics, 3 science, (3 science labs), 2 foreign language, 3 social studies, 1 visual/performing arts. **Freshman Admission Statistics:** 5,237 applied, 97% admitted, 45% enrolled. **Transfer Admission Requirements:** college transcript(s), Minimum college GPA of 2.0 required. Lowest grade transferable D. **General Admission Information:** Application Fee $30. Notification on a rolling basis, beginning on or about 10/1. Nonfall registration accepted. Admission may be deferred for a maximum of Four Quarters. Credit offered for CEEB Advanced Placement tests.

COSTS AND FINANCIAL AID

Annual in-state tuition $8,730. Annual out-of-state tuition $16,910. Room and board $9,108. Average book expense $1,008. **Required Forms and Deadlines:** FAFSA. **Notification of Awards:** Applicants will be notified of awards on a rolling basis beginning 3/15. **Types of Aid:** *Need-based scholarships/grants:* Federal Pell, SEOG, state scholarships/grants, private scholarships, the school's own gift aid, United Negro College Fund, Federal Nursing Scholarships, Choose Ohio First Scholarships. *Loans:* Subsidized Stafford, Unsubsidized Stafford, PLUS, Federal Perkins, Federal Nursing, state loans, college/university loans from institutional funds, Private Loans. *Student Employment:* Federal Work-Study Program available. Institutional employment available. Off-campus job opportunities are good. **Financial Aid Statistics:** 87% freshmen, 79% undergrads receive need-based scholarship or grant aid. 9% freshmen, 6% undergrads receive non-need-based scholarship or grant aid. 89% freshmen, 92% undergrads receive need-based self-help aid. 2% freshmen, 2% undergrads receive athletic scholarships. 87% freshmen, 75% undergrads receive any aid. 71% undergrads borrow to pay for school. Average cumulative indebtedness $27,757. **Criteria for awarding institutional aid:** *Non-need-based:* academics, alumni affiliation, art, athletics, leadership, minority status, music/drama.

XAVIER UNIVERSITY OF LOUISIANA

Best 380

1 Drexel Drive, New Orleans, LA 70125
Phone: 504-520-7388 · **Financial Aid Phone:** 504-520-7835
E-mail: apply@xula.edu · **CEEB Code:** 6975
Fax: 504-520-7941 · **Website:** www.xula.edu · **ACT Code:** 1618

This private school, affiliated with the Roman Catholic Church, was founded in 1915. It has a 29-acre campus.

RATINGS

Admissions Selectivity Rating: 86   **Fire Safety Rating:** 87

STUDENTS AND FACULTY

Enrollment: 2,317. **Student Body:** 73% female, 27% male, 49% out-of-state, 2% international (8 countries represented). Asian 10%, African American 77%, Caucasian 4%, Hispanic 3%, Native American <1%
Retention and Graduation: 71% freshmen return for sophomore year. 28% freshmen graduate within 4 years. 31% grads go on to further study within 1 year. **Faculty:** 218 full-time faculty, 95% hold PhDs, 48% are are members of minority groups, 41% are women. 0% of classes are taught by teaching assistants.

ACADEMICS

Degrees: bachelor's, master's, post-master's certificate. **Classes:** Most classes have 10-19 students. Most lab/discussion sessions have 20-29 students. **Majors with Highest Enrollment:** Psychology; Pre-Medicine/Pre-Medical Studies; Pre-Pharmacy Studies. **Special Study Options:** Accelerated program, cooperative education program, cross-registration, double major, dual enrollment, exchange student program (domestic), honors program, independent study, internships, study abroad, African American Studies Minor; Women Studies. **Disability Services:** Special programs offered to physically disabled students include note-taking services, reader services, tape recorders, tutors. **Career services:** career/job search classes, career assessment, internships.

FACILITIES

Housing: Coed dorms, special housing for disabled students, men's dorms, women's dorms. 99% of campus accessible to physically disabled. **Computers:** 100% of classrooms, 100% of dorms, 100% of libraries, 100% of dining areas, 100% of student union, 100% of common outdoor areas have wireless network access. Students can register for classes online. Administrative functions (other than registration) can be performed online.

CAMPUS LIFE

Environment: Metropolis. **Activities:** Choral groups, concert band, dance, drama/theater, jazz band, literary magazine, music ensembles, opera, student government, student newspaper, symphony orchestra, television station, yearbook, Campus Ministries, International Student Organization. 88 registered organizations, 8 honor societies, 1 religous organization. 4 fraternities, 4 sororities. **Athletics (Intercollegiate):** *Men:* basketball, cross-country, tennis, track/field (outdoor), track/field (indoor). *Women:* basketball, cross-country, tennis, track/field (outdoor), track/field (indoor), volleyball. **On-Campus Highlights:** New University Center, Gymnasium (The Barn), Library, University Quadrangle, Historic Administration Building.

ADMISSIONS

Freshman Academic Profile: Average high school GPA 3.41. 36% in top 10% of high school class, 58% in top 25% of high school class, 83% in top 50% of high school class. SAT Math middle 50% range 460-550. SAT Critical Reading middle 50% range 450-550. SAT Writing middle 50% range 440-520. ACT middle 50% range 20-25. Minimum paper TOEFL 550. **Basis for Candidate Selection:** *Very important factors considered include:* academic GPA, recommendation(s), rigor of secondary school record, standardized test scores. *Important factors considered include:* Class rank, application essay. *Other factors considered include:* alumni/ae relation, character/personal qualities, extracurricular activities, interview, talent/ability, volunteer work, work experience. **Freshman Admission Requirements:** High school diploma is required and GED is accepted. **Academic units required:** 4 English, 2 mathematics, 1 science, 1 social studies, 8 academic electives. **Freshman Admission Statistics:** 3,963 applied, 66% admitted, 22% enrolled. **Transfer Admission Requirements:** college transcript(s), Minimum college GPA of 2.00 required. Lowest grade transferable C. **General Admission Information:** Application Fee $25. Regular application deadline 7/1. Regular notification 10/15. Nonfall registration accepted. Credit and/or placement offered for CEEB Advanced Placement tests.

COSTS AND FINANCIAL AID

Annual tuition $18,500. Room and board $7,800. Required fees $2,060. Average book expense $1,200. **Required Forms and Deadlines:** FAFSA. **Notification of Awards:** Applicants will be notified of awards on a rolling basis beginning 4/1. **Types of Aid:** *Need-based scholarships/grants:* Federal Pell, SEOG, state scholarships/grants, private scholarships, the school's own gift aid, United Negro College Fund. *Loans:* Direct Subsidized Stafford, Direct Unsubsidized Stafford, Direct PLUS, Subsidized Stafford, Unsubsidized Stafford, PLUS, Federal Perkins. *Student Employment:* Federal Work-Study Program available. Institutional employment available. Highest amount earned per year from on-campus jobs $1,000. Off-campus job opportunities are good. **Financial Aid Statistics:** 65% freshmen, 65% undergrads receive need-based scholarship or grant aid. 91% freshmen, 79% undergrads receive non-need-based scholarship or grant aid. 93% freshmen, 95% undergrads receive need-based self-help aid. 3% freshmen, 4% undergrads receive athletic scholarships. 94% freshmen, 24% undergrads receive any aid. 87% undergrads borrow to pay for school. Average cumulative indebtedness $22,367. **Criteria for awarding institutional aid:** *Non-need-based:* music/drama.

XAVIER UNIVERSITY (OH)

3800 Victory Parkway, Cincinnati, OH 45207-5311
Phone: 513-745-3301 · **Financial Aid Phone:** 513-745-3142
E-mail: xuadmit@xavier.edu · **CEEB Code:** 1965
Fax: 513-745-4319 · **Website:** www.xavier.edu · **ACT Code:** 3366

This private school, affiliated with the Roman Catholic-Jesuit Church, was founded in 1831. It has a 146-acre campus.

RATINGS

Admissions Selectivity Rating: 84   **Fire Safety Rating:** 80

STUDENTS AND FACULTY

Enrollment: 4,464. **Student Body:** 54% female, 46% male, 49% out-of-state, 2% international (47 countries represented). Asian 2%, African American 10%, Caucasian 72%, Hispanic 5%, Native American <1%
Retention and Graduation: 85% freshmen return for sophomore year. 63% freshmen graduate within 4 years. 31% grads go on to further study within 1 year. 4% grads pursue arts and sciences degrees. 2% grads pursue law degrees. 2% grads pursue business degrees. 3% grads pursue medical degrees. **Faculty:** 352 full-time faculty, 78% hold PhDs, 50% are are members of minority groups, 15% are women. 0% of classes are taught by teaching assistants.

ACADEMICS

Degrees: associate, bachelor's, certificate, master's, terminal associate. **Classes:** Most classes have 20-29 students. Most lab/discussion sessions have 20-29 students. **Majors with Highest Enrollment:** Liberal Arts and Sciences/ Liberal Studies; Registered Nursing/Registered Nurse; Marketing/Marketing Management. **Special Study Options:** cooperative education program, cross-registration, double major, dual enrollment, English as a Second Language (ESL), honors program, independent study, internships, study abroad, teacher certification program, weekend college, Service Learning Semester. **Honors programs:** University Scholars Progam Philosophy, Politics and the Public Honors AB **Combined degree programs:** BSBA/MBA in Accounting. **Disability Services:** Special programs offered to physically disabled students include note-taking services, reader services, tape recorders, tutors. **Career services:** Alumni network, alumni services, career/job search classes, career assessment, internships, regional alumni. Career services highlights include our Executive Mentor Program in which students are matched with a business executive in their sophomore year to guide, advise and serve as a sounding board on career, academic and life issues. Additionally our Business Profession Program, an intentional four-year career development program for business undergraduates has received national attention.

FACILITIES

Housing: Coed dorms, special housing for disabled students, apartments for single students, Theme Housing. 95% of campus accessible to physically disabled. **Special Academic Facilities/Equipment:** Student-run art gallery, Montessori lab school. **Computers:** 100% of classrooms, 100% of dorms, 100% of libraries, 100% of dining areas, 100% of student union, 100% of common outdoor areas have wireless network access. Students can register for classes online. Administrative functions (other than registration) can be performed online.

CAMPUS LIFE

Environment: Metropolis. **Activities:** Choral groups, concert band, dance, drama/theater, jazz band, literary magazine, music ensembles, musical theater, opera, pep band, radio station, student government, student newspaper, student-run film society, symphony orchestra, television station, Campus Ministries, International Student Organization. 124 registered organizations, 10 honor societies, 11 religious organizations. **Athletics (Intercollegiate):** *Men:* baseball, basketball, cheerleading, cross-country, golf, soccer, swimming, tennis, track/field (outdoor), track/field (indoor). *Women:* basketball, cheerleading, cross-country, golf, soccer, swimming, tennis, track/field (outdoor), track/field (indoor), volleyball. **On-Campus Highlights:** Cintas Center basketball arena and conce, McDonald Library, The Gallagher Student Center, O'Conner Sports Center, Bellarmine Chapel. **Environmental Initiatives:** Three new undergraduate and one new masters (Urban Sustainability) launched during 2012-2014 plus multi-departmental co-curricular emphasis on experiential learning and evaluation. Active student management of all waste streams and diversion of food scraps, demolition, and recycling of the waste stream throughout the year. Investment in large central plant hot-cold water high-efficiency equipment to provide heating and cooling for the majority of the building on campus, and in high-performance buildings for new construction resulting in lower carbon generation and lower expenses.

ADMISSIONS

Freshman Academic Profile: Average high school GPA 3.52. 20% in top 10% of high school class, 48% in top 25% of high school class, 84% in top 50% of high school class. 52% from public high schools. SAT Math middle 50% range 490-600. SAT Critical Reading middle 50% range 490-600. SAT Writing middle 50% range 480-590. ACT middle 50% range 22-27. Minimum internet-based TOEFL 79. Minimum paper TOEFL 550. **Basis for Candidate Selection:** *Very important factors considered include:* rigor of secondary school record. *Important factors considered include:* Class rank, application essay, academic GPA, recommendation(s), standardized test scores, character/personal qualities. *Other factors considered include:* alumni/ae relation, extracurricular activities, first generation, level of applicant's interest, talent/ability, volunteer work, work experience. **Freshman Admission Requirements:** High school diploma is required and GED is accepted. **Freshman Admission Statistics:** 11,605 applied, 73% admitted, 14% enrolled. **Transfer Admission Requirements:** High school transcript, college transcript(s), statement of good standing from prior institution(s). Minimum college GPA of 2.0 required. Lowest grade transferable C-. **General Admission Information:** Application Fee $35. Regular application deadline 2/1. Notification on a rolling basis, beginning on or about 10/15. Nonfall registration accepted. Admission may be deferred for a maximum of 1 year. Credit and/or placement offered for CEEB Advanced Placement tests.

COSTS AND FINANCIAL AID

Average book expense $1,000. **Required Forms and Deadlines:** FAFSA. **Notification of Awards:** Applicants will be notified of awards on a rolling basis beginning 2/15. **Types of Aid:** *Need-based scholarships/grants:* Federal Pell, SEOG, state scholarships/grants, private scholarships, the school's own gift aid. *Loans:* Subsidized Stafford, Unsubsidized Stafford, PLUS, Federal Perkins. *Student Employment:* Federal Work-Study Program available. Institutional employment available. Highest amount earned per year from on-campus jobs $4,900. Off-campus job opportunities are excellent. **Financial Aid Statistics:** 97% freshmen, 96% undergrads receive need-based scholarship or grant aid. 17% freshmen, 14% undergrads receive non-need-based scholarship or grant aid. 75% freshmen, 77% undergrads receive need-based self-help aid. 3% freshmen, 3% undergrads receive athletic scholarships. 100% freshmen, 90% undergrads receive any aid. 67% undergrads borrow to pay for school. Average cumulative indebtedness $24,957. **Criteria for awarding institutional aid:** *Non-need-based:* academics, alumni affiliation, art, athletics, leadership, music/drama, religious affiliation.

YALE UNIVERSITY

PO Box 208234, New Haven, CT 06521-8234
Phone: 203-432-9300 · **Financial Aid Phone:** 203-432-2700
E-mail: student.questions@yale.edu · **CEEB Code:** 3987
Fax: 203-432-9392 · **Website:** www.yale.edu · **ACT Code:** 618

This private school was founded in 1701. It has a 320-acre campus.

RATINGS

Admissions Selectivity Rating: 99   **Fire Safety Rating:** 62

STUDENTS AND FACULTY

Enrollment: 5,422. **Student Body:** 49% female, 51% male, 94% out-of-state, 11% international (118 countries represented). Asian 16%, African American 7%, Caucasian 47%, Hispanic 10%, Native American 1%
Retention and Graduation: 99% freshmen return for sophomore year. 90% freshmen graduate within 4 years. 98% freshmen graduate within 6 years. 21% grads go on to further study within 1 year. 7% grads pursue arts and sciences degrees. 4% grads pursue law degrees. 4% grads pursue medical degrees. **Faculty:** 1,176 full-time faculty, 93% hold PhDs, 36% are are members of minority groups, 28% are women.

ACADEMICS

Degrees: bachelor's, master's, post-master's certificate. **Classes:** Most classes have 10-19 students. **Majors with Highest Enrollment:** Economics; Political Science and Government; History. **Special Study Options:** Accelerated program, distance learning, double major, English as a Second Language (ESL), honors program, independent study, internships, liberal arts/career combination, student-designed major, study abroad, teacher certification program. **Combined degree programs:** BA/MA, BA/MM in Music, BA/MA, BS/MS.

Disability Services: Special programs offered to physically disabled students include note-taking services, reader services, tape recorders, tutors. **Career services:** Alumni network, alumni services, career/job search classes, internships, regional alumni. In coordination with the Yale Undergraduate Career Services department, the university helps place hundreds of students in internships across the country and around the world every year. UCS utilizes a vast array of resources, including alumni, private firms and research fellowships to place students in a wide variety of internships.

FACILITIES

Housing: Coed dorms, special housing for disabled students, Students are randomly assigned to 1 of 12 residential colleges where they live,eat,socialize,and pursue various academic and extracurricular activities. All undergraduate housing is provided through residential college system. **Special Academic Facilities/Equipment:** Art and history museums, observatory, electron microscopes, nuclear accelerators, center for international and areas studies, child study center, marsh botanical gardens, center for parallel supercomputing. **Computers:** 100% of classrooms, 100% of dorms, 100% of libraries, 100% of dining areas, 100% of student union, 100% of common outdoor areas have wireless network access. Students can register for classes online. Administrative functions (other than registration) can be performed online.

CAMPUS LIFE

Environment: City. **Activities:** Choral groups, concert band, dance, drama/theater, jazz band, literary magazine, marching band, music ensembles, musical theater, opera, pep band, radio station, student government, student newspaper, student-run film society, symphony orchestra, television station, yearbook, Campus Ministries, International Student Organization, Model UN. 350 registered organizations. **Athletics (Intercollegiate):** *Men:* baseball, basketball, crew/rowing, cross-country, diving, fencing, football, golf, ice hockey, lacrosse, sailing, soccer, squash, swimming, tennis, track/field (outdoor), track/field (indoor). *Women:* basketball, crew/rowing, cross-country, diving, fencing, field hockey, golf, gymnastics, ice hockey, lacrosse, sailing, soccer, softball, squash, swimming, tennis, track/field (outdoor), track/field (indoor), volleyball. **On-Campus Highlights:** Old Campus, Sterling Memorial Library, Yale British Art Center, Beinecke Rare Book and Manuscript Library, Payne-Whitney Gymnasium, (http://www.yale.edu/admit/visit/index.html). **Environmental Initiatives:** Greenhouse gas commitment of 43% below 2005 levels by 2020; 40% of food served in the dining halls is local/organic; LEED Silver for all new construction.

ADMISSIONS

Freshman Academic Profile: 95% in top 10% of high school class, 99% in top 25% of high school class, 100% in top 50% of high school class. 57% from public high schools. SAT Math middle 50% range 710-790. SAT Critical Reading middle 50% range 710-800. SAT Writing middle 50% range 720-800. ACT middle 50% range 31-35. Minimum internet-based TOEFL 100. Minimum paper TOEFL 600. **Basis for Candidate Selection:** *Very important factors considered include:* Class rank, application essay, academic GPA, recommendation(s), rigor of secondary school record, standardized test scores, character/personal qualities, extracurricular activities, talent/ability. *Other factors considered include:* alumni/ae relation, first generation, geographical residence, interview, level of applicant's interest, racial/ethnic status, state residency, volunteer work, work experience. **Freshman Admission Requirements:** High school diploma or equivalent is not required. **Freshman Admission Statistics:** 29,610 applied, 7% admitted, 67% enrolled. **Transfer Admission Requirements:** High school transcript, college transcript(s), essay or personal statement, standardized test scores, statement of good standing from prior institution(s). Lowest grade transferable C. **General Admission Information:** Application Fee $75. Regular application deadline 12/31. Regular notification 4/1. Nonfall registration not accepted. Admission may be deferred for a maximum of one year. Placement offered for CEEB Advanced Placement tests.

COSTS AND FINANCIAL AID

Annual tuition $44,000. Room and board $13,500. Required fees $0. Average book expense $1,200. **Required Forms and Deadlines:** FAFSA, CSS/Financial Aid PROFILE, Noncustodial PROFILE. **Notification of Awards:** Applicants will be notified of awards on or about 4/1. **Types of Aid:** *Need-based scholarships/grants:* Federal Pell, SEOG, state scholarships/grants, private scholarships, the school's own gift aid, United Negro College Fund. *Loans:* Subsidized Stafford, Unsubsidized Stafford, PLUS, Federal Perkins, state loans, college/university loans from institutional funds. *Student Employment:* Institutional employment available. **Financial Aid Statistics:** 100% freshmen, 100% undergrads receive need-based scholarship or grant aid. 0% freshmen, 0% undergrads receive non-need-based scholarship or grant aid. 74% freshmen, 87% undergrads receive need-based self-help aid. 0% freshmen, 0% undergrads receive athletic scholarships. 51% freshmen, 52% undergrads receive any aid. 16% undergrads borrow to pay for school. Average cumulative indebtedness $12,729.

YESHIVA UNIVERSITY

500 West 185th Street, New York, NY 10033-3299
Phone: 212-960-5277
E-mail: yuadmit@yu.edu • **CEEB Code:** 2990
Fax: 212-960-0086 • **Website:** www.yu.edu • **ACT Code:** 2992

This private school was founded in 1886. It has a 12-acre campus.

RATINGS

Admissions Selectivity Rating: 89   **Fire Safety Rating:** 60*

STUDENTS AND FACULTY

Enrollment: 2,866. **Student Body:** 46% female, 54% male, 35% out-of-state, 12% international (53 countries represented). Asian 0%, African American 0%, Caucasian 83%, Hispanic 2%, Native American <1%
Retention and Graduation: 90% freshmen return for sophomore year. 49% freshmen graduate within 4 years. **Faculty:** 0% of classes are taught by teaching assistants.

ACADEMICS

Degrees: bachelor's, master's. **Classes:** Most classes have 10-19 students. Most lab/discussion sessions have 10-19 students. **Majors with Highest Enrollment:** Political Science and Government; Psychology; Jewish/Judaic Studies. **Special Study Options:** double major, honors program, independent study, internships, student-designed major, study abroad, teacher certification program. **Combined degree programs:** BA/MA, 3-2 and 4-2 engineering programs with Columbia U. **Career services:** career/job search classes, career assessment, internships.

FACILITIES

Housing: men's dorms, women's dorms, apartments for married students, apartments for single students **Special Academic Facilities/Equipment:** Archives and rare book collection, museum of Jewish art, architecture, history, and culture.

CAMPUS LIFE

Activities: Choral groups, concert band, drama/theater, jazz band, literary magazine, music ensembles, musical theater, radio station, student government, student newspaper, yearbook. **Athletics (Intercollegiate):** *Men:* basketball, tennis, volleyball. *Women:* basketball, tennis.

ADMISSIONS

Freshman Academic Profile: Average high school GPA 3.46. 48% in top 10% of high school class, 77% in top 25% of high school class, 95% in top 50% of high school class. SAT Math middle 50% range 550-680. SAT Critical Reading middle 50% range 550-690. ACT middle 50% range 22-28. Minimum paper TOEFL 500. **Basis for Candidate Selection:** *Important factors considered include:* application essay, academic GPA, rigor of secondary school record, standardized test scores, extracurricular activities, interview, talent/ability. *Other factors considered include:* volunteer work, work experience. **Freshman Admission Requirements:** High school diploma is required and GED is accepted. **Freshman Admission Statistics:** 2,027 applied, 63% admitted, 65% enrolled. **Transfer Admission Requirements:** High school transcript, college transcript(s), essay or personal statement, interview, standardized test scores, Lowest grade transferable 75. **General Admission Information:** Application Fee $40. Regular application deadline 2/15. Regular notification 4/1. Nonfall registration accepted. Credit and/or placement offered for CEEB Advanced Placement tests.

COSTS AND FINANCIAL AID

Average book expense $1,224. **Required Forms and Deadlines:** FAFSA, Institution's own financial aid form, CSS/Financial Aid PROFILE, State aid form, Noncustodial PROFILE, Business/Farm Supplement. **Types of Aid:** *Need-based scholarships/grants:* Federal Pell, SEOG, state scholarships/grants, private scholarships, the school's own gift aid. *Loans:* Subsidized Stafford, Unsubsidized Stafford, PLUS, Federal Perkins, college/university loans from institutional funds. *Student Employment:* Federal Work-Study Program available. Institutional employment available. Highest amount earned per year from on-campus jobs $500. Off-campus job opportunities are good. **Financial Aid Statistics:** 89% freshmen, 85% undergrads receive need-based scholarship or grant aid. 13% freshmen, 9% undergrads receive non-need-based scholarship or grant aid. 75% freshmen, 68% undergrads receive need-based self-help aid. 0% freshmen, 0% undergrads receive athletic scholarships. **Criteria for awarding institutional aid:** *Non-need-based:* academics.

YORK COLLEGE

1125 E. 8th Street, York, NE 68467
Phone: 402-363-5627 • **Financial Aid Phone:** 402-363-5625
E-mail: enroll@york.edu
Fax: 402-363-5623 • **Website:** www.york.edu • **ACT Code:** 2484

This private school, affiliated with the Church of Christ Church, was founded in 1890. It has a 200-acre campus.

RATINGS

Admissions Selectivity Rating: 82   **Fire Safety Rating:** 94

STUDENTS AND FACULTY

Enrollment: 385. **Student Body:** 51% female, 49% male, 69% out-of-state, 1% international (6 countries represented). Asian 2%, African American 5%, Caucasian 72%, Hispanic 4%, Native American <1%
Retention and Graduation: 55% freshmen return for sophomore year. **Faculty:** 33 full-time faculty, 36% hold PhDs, 27% are are members of minority groups, 3% are women. 0% of classes are taught by teaching assistants.

ACADEMICS

Degrees: associate, bachelor's, transfer associate. **Classes:** Most classes have fewer than 10 students. **Majors with Highest Enrollment:** Education; Psychology; Business Administration and Management. **Special Study Options:** double major, dual enrollment, internships, student-designed major, teacher certification program. **Career services:** Alumni network, career assessment, Career services highlights include a requirement for most degrees for students to serve in some type of internship before graduation.

FACILITIES

Housing: special housing for disabled students, men's dorms, women's dorms, apartments for married students. 60% of campus accessible to physically disabled. **Computers:** 100% of libraries, 100% of student union, have wireless network access.

CAMPUS LIFE

Environment: Village. **Activities:** Choral groups, drama/theater, literary magazine, music ensembles, musical theater, student government, student newspaper, yearbook, Campus Ministries. 12 registered organizations, 2 honor societies, 1 religous organization. 4 fraternities, 4 sororities. **Athletics (Intercollegiate):** *Men:* baseball, basketball, soccer, wrestling. *Women:* basketball, soccer, softball, volleyball. **On-Campus Highlights:** Mackey Center, Prayer Chapel, Spiritual Life Center/Coffee Shop, Gurganus Hall, Freeman Center.

ADMISSIONS

Freshman Academic Profile: Average high school GPA 3.41. 13% in top 10% of high school class, 25% in top 25% of high school class, 60% in top 50% of high school class. SAT Math middle 50% range 440-560. SAT Critical Reading middle 50% range 450-590. ACT middle 50% range 18-26. Minimum paper TOEFL 500. **Basis for Candidate Selection:** *Very important factors considered include:* Class rank, academic GPA, rigor of secondary school record, standardized test scores. *Other factors considered include:* application essay, recommendation(s), alumni/ae relation, character/personal qualities, extracurricular activities, first generation, level of applicant's interest, religious affiliation/commitment, talent/ability, volunteer work. **Freshman Admission Requirements:** High school diploma is required and GED is accepted. **Academic units required:** 3 English, 2 mathematics, 2 science, 1 social studies, 1 history. **Freshman Admission Statistics:** 531 applied, 57% admitted, 30% enrolled. **Transfer Admission Requirements:** High school transcript, college transcript(s), Minimum college GPA of 2.0 required. Lowest grade transferable 1.0. **General Admission Information:** Application Fee $20. Regular application deadline 8/31. Nonfall registration accepted.

COSTS AND FINANCIAL AID

Annual tuition $12,500. Room and board $4,500. Required fees $1,500. Average book expense $1,500. **Required Forms and Deadlines:** FAFSA. **Notification of Awards:** Applicants will be notified of awards on a rolling basis beginning 3/1. **Types of Aid:** *Need-based scholarships/grants:* Federal Pell, SEOG, state scholarships/grants, private scholarships, the school's own gift aid. *Loans:* Direct Subsidized Stafford, Direct Unsubsidized Stafford, Direct PLUS, Subsidized Stafford, Unsubsidized Stafford, PLUS, Federal Perkins, Federal Nursing, college/university loans from institutional funds. *Student Employment:* Federal Work-Study Program available. Off-campus job opportunities are good. **Financial Aid Statistics:** 0% freshmen, 0% undergrads receive athletic scholarships. 89% freshmen, 89% undergrads receive any aid. 89% undergrads borrow to pay for school. Average cumulative indebtedness $19,223. **Criteria for awarding institutional aid:** *Non-need-based:* academics, athletics, leadership, music/drama.

YORK COLLEGE OF PENNSYLVANIA

441 Country Club Road, York, PA 17403-3651
Phone: 717-849-1600 • **Financial Aid Phone:** 717-849-1682
E-mail: admissions@ycp.edu • **CEEB Code:** 2991
Fax: 717-849-1607 • **Website:** www.ycp.edu • **ACT Code:** 3762

This private school was founded in 1787. It has a 190-acre campus.

RATINGS

Admissions Selectivity Rating: 81   **Fire Safety Rating:** 94

STUDENTS AND FACULTY

Enrollment: 4,847. **Student Body:** 55% female, 45% male, 42% out-of-state, 0% international (32 countries represented). Asian 1%, African American 5%, Caucasian 83%, Hispanic 5%, Native American <1%
Retention and Graduation: 75% freshmen return for sophomore year. 37% freshmen graduate within 4 years. 58% freshmen graduate within 6 years. **Faculty:** 189 full-time faculty, 81% hold PhDs, 43% are are members of minority groups, 4% are women. 0% of classes are taught by teaching assistants.

ACADEMICS

Degrees: associate, bachelor's, master's. **Classes:** Most classes have 20-29 students. Most lab/discussion sessions have 10-19 students. **Majors with Highest Enrollment:** Biology/Biological Sciences; Business Administration and Management; Registered Nursing/Registered Nurse. **Special Study Options:** Accelerated program, cooperative education program, double major, dual enrollment, honors program, independent study, internships, liberal arts/career combination, student-designed major, study abroad, teacher certification program. **Honors programs:** Honors Program includes coursework, special academic and career advising and extracurricular enrichment activities. **Combined degree programs:** BS/MBA. **Disability Services:** Special programs offered to physically disabled students include tape recorders, tutors. **Career services:** Alumni network, alumni services, career/job search classes, career assessment, internships, regional alumni. Career services highlights include the experiential education opportunities that all of our students enjoy. Credit-based experiential learning is available in all academic programs and provides reflective learning and practical application of skills. Experiential education offerings vary based upon the academic program, and include internships, independent research, service-learning, course based projects, practica, student teaching, clinical rotations, and many other special learning opportunities. Co-ops are exclusive to our three engineering programs, and students are required to participate in 3 before graduating as well as a number of other hands-on experiences and projects.

FACILITIES

Housing: Coed dorms, men's dorms, women's dorms, fraternity/sorority housing, apartments for single students, Wellness Housing, Theme Housing. 98% of campus accessible to physically disabled. **Special Academic Facilities/Equipment:** Museum, telecommunications center, science and foreign language labs. All of campus is wired to the computer network. **Computers:** 50% of classrooms, 35% of dorms, 100% of libraries, 100% of dining areas, 80% of student union, 65% of common outdoor areas have wireless network access. Students can register for classes online. Administrative functions (other than registration) can be performed online.

CAMPUS LIFE

Environment: City. **Activities:** Choral groups, concert band, drama/theater, jazz band, literary magazine, music ensembles, musical theater, radio station, student government, student newspaper, symphony orchestra, television station, Campus Ministries, International Student Organization, Model UN. 80 registered organizations, 7 honor societies, 4 religious organizations. 9 fraternities, 7 sororities. **Athletics (Intercollegiate):** *Men:* baseball, basketball, cheerleading, cross-country, golf, lacrosse, soccer, swimming, tennis, track/field (outdoor), wrestling. *Women:* basketball, cheerleading, cross-country, field hockey, lacrosse, soccer, softball, swimming, tennis, track/field (outdoor), volleyball. **On-Campus Highlights:** Student Union Spart's Den, TV and Radio Studios, Bookstore, York College Art Galleries, Tyler Run Walking Path.

ADMISSIONS

Freshman Academic Profile: Average high school GPA 3.54. 12% in top 10% of high school class, 40% in top 25% of high school class, 77% in top 50% of high school class. SAT Math middle 50% range 480-578. SAT Critical Reading middle 50% range 470-560. SAT Writing middle 50% range 450-550. ACT middle 50% range 20-25. Minimum internet-based TOEFL 72. Minimum paper TOEFL 530. **Basis for Candidate Selection:** *Very important factors considered include:* academic GPA, rigor of secondary school record. *Important factors considered include:* Class rank, standardized test scores, character/personal qualities. *Other factors considered include:* application essay, recommendation(s), alumni/ae relation, extracurricular activities, interview,

level of applicant's interest, talent/ability, volunteer work, work experience. **Freshman Admission Requirements:** High school diploma is required and GED is accepted. **Academic units required:** 4 English, 3 mathematics, 3 science, 2 foreign language, 3 social studies. **Freshman Admission Statistics:** 9,934 applied, 74% admitted, 15% enrolled. **Transfer Admission Requirements:** college transcript(s), Minimum college GPA of 2.0 required. Lowest grade transferable C. **General Admission Information:** Application Fee $30. Notification on a rolling basis, beginning on or about 10/1. Nonfall registration accepted. Admission may be deferred for a maximum of 12 months. Credit and/ or placement offered for CEEB Advanced Placement tests.

COSTS AND FINANCIAL AID

Annual tuition $15,350. Room and board $9,580. Required fees $1,660. Average book expense $1,200. **Required Forms and Deadlines:** FAFSA. **Notification of Awards:** Applicants will be notified of awards on a rolling basis beginning 3/1. **Types of Aid:** *Need-based scholarships/grants:* Federal Pell, SEOG, state scholarships/grants, private scholarships, the school's own gift aid. *Loans:* Direct Subsidized Stafford, Direct Unsubsidized Stafford, Direct PLUS, Subsidized Stafford, Unsubsidized Stafford, PLUS, Federal Perkins, Federal Nursing, college/university loans from institutional funds. *Student Employment:* Federal Work-Study Program available. Institutional employment available. Highest amount earned per year from on-campus jobs $12,022. Off-campus job opportunities are good. **Financial Aid Statistics:** 61% freshmen, 67% undergrads receive need-based scholarship or grant aid. 99% freshmen, 78% undergrads receive non-need-based scholarship or grant aid. 85% freshmen, 88% undergrads receive need-based self-help aid. 0% freshmen, 0% undergrads receive athletic scholarships. 99% freshmen, 89% undergrads receive any aid. 82% undergrads borrow to pay for school. Average cumulative indebtedness $25,140. **Criteria for awarding institutional aid:** *Non-need-based:* academics, alumni affiliation, music/drama.

YORK UNIVERSITY

Bennett Centre for Student Services, Toronto, ON M3J 1P3
Phone: 416-736-5000 • **Financial Aid Phone:** 416-872-9675
E-mail: intlenq@yorku.ca • **CEEB Code:** 894
Fax: 416-736-5536 • **Website:** www.yorku.ca

This public school was founded in 1959. It has a 550-acre campus.

RATINGS

Admissions Selectivity Rating: 60*   **Fire Safety Rating:** 62

STUDENTS AND FACULTY

Enrollment: 48,631. **Student Body:** 59% female, 41% male, 0% international (170 countries represented). Asian 0%, African American 0%, Caucasian 0%, Hispanic 0%, Native American <1%
Faculty: 1,480 full-time faculty, 46% are are members of minority groups.

ACADEMICS

Degrees: bachelor's, certificate, diploma, doctoral, master's, post-bachelor's certificate. **Majors with Highest Enrollment:** Psychology. **Special Study Options:** Accelerated program, distance learning, double major, English as a Second Language (ESL), exchange student program (domestic), honors program, independent study, internships, student-designed major, study abroad, teacher certification program. **Combined degree programs:** MBA/LLB, BA/BEd, BSc/BEd, BFA/BEd, MES/LLB, MBA/MFA. **Disability Services:** Special programs offered to physically disabled students include note-taking services, reader services, tape recorders, tutors. **Career services:** career/job search classes, career assessment, internships. Career services highlights include The York University International Internship Program (YIIP), which provides both York undergraduate and graduate students a non-credit opportunity to apply their academic knowledge to an international work environment and enhance their job-related skills in an international and intercultural setting.

FACILITIES

Housing: Coed dorms, special housing for disabled students, men's dorms, special housing for international students, women's dorms, apartments for married students, apartments for single students, Theme Housing. **Special Academic Facilities/Equipment:** 5 museums with more than 4.4 million items. Observatory with 2 telescopes. Robotics laboratory. 2 professionally staffed art galleries. 6 student-run art exhibition spaces. 3 theatres. 2 cinemas. 1 screening room. Wide-variety professional standard film and video production facilities. **Computers:** Students can register for classes online. Administrative functions (other than registration) can be performed online.

CAMPUS LIFE

Environment: Metropolis. **Activities:** Choral groups, concert band, dance, drama/theater, jazz band, music ensembles, pep band, radio station, student government, student newspaper, symphony orchestra, yearbook, International Student Organization, Model UN. 259 registered organizations, 35 religious organizations. **Athletics (Intercollegiate):** *Men:* badminton, basketball, cross-country, fencing, football, ice hockey, soccer, swimming, tennis, track/field (outdoor), volleyball, water polo. *Women:* badminton, basketball, cross-country, fencing, field hockey, ice hockey, rugby, soccer, swimming, tennis, track/field (outdoor), volleyball, water polo. **On-Campus Highlights:** York Lanes: on-campus mall, Tait McKenzie Centre: sports complex, Student Centre: food court/lounge/club, Accolade East: theatre, art gallery, Central Square: Scott library, food court.

ADMISSIONS

Freshman Academic Profile: Minimum internet-based TOEFL 83. Minimum paper TOEFL 560. **Basis for Candidate Selection:** *Very important factors considered include:* academic GPA, rigor of secondary school record. *Important factors considered include:* standardized test scores. *Other factors considered include:* Class rank, interview. **Freshman Admission Requirements:** High school diploma is required and GED is not accepted. **Transfer Admission Requirements:** college transcript(s), Minimum college GPA of 2.5 required. Lowest grade transferable C. **General Admission Information:** Application Fee $90. Regular application deadline 2/1. Notification on a rolling basis, beginning on or about 1/1. Nonfall registration accepted. Admission may be deferred for a maximum of 1 year. Credit offered for CEEB Advanced Placement tests.

COSTS AND FINANCIAL AID

Annual in-state tuition $6,712. Annual out-of-state tuition $6,712. Room and board $7,702. Average book expense $1,000. **Required Forms and Deadlines:** FAFSA. **Types of Aid:** Need-based scholarships/grants. *Loans:* Subsidized Stafford, Unsubsidized Stafford, PLUS, Federal Perkins, Institutionally administered bursaries and international work study positions available on a limited basis. Canadian Student Loans and Provincial Student Loans (for Canadian citizens only). *Student Employment:* Institutional employment available. Off-campus job opportunities are good. **Financial Aid Statistics:** 0% undergrads receive athletic scholarships. **Criteria for awarding institutional aid:** *Non-need-based:* academics, art, music/drama.

SCHOOL SAYS . . .

In this section you'll find hundreds of colleges with extended listings describing admissions, curriculum, internships, and much more. This is your chance to get in-depth information on colleges that interest you. The Princeton Review charges each school a small fee to be listed, and the editorial responsibility is solely that of the college.

ALVERNIA UNIVERSITY

AT A GLANCE

Located in Berks County, Pennsylvania, Alvernia University offers all the best features of an outstanding university—specialized professional programs, experiential learning, internships, and a variety of leadership opportunities—in the personal setting of a college environment. A private Franciscan institution rooted in the Catholic and liberal arts tradition, the core institutional values—service, humility, peacemaking, contemplation, and collegiality—are as relevant today as they were in 1958 when the school was founded. Students appreciate the small class sizes and breadth of academic programs offered, all taught by faculty who are experts in their fields and equally committed to their students' success. Graduates are prepared to achieve their personal dreams and professional success, and to be engaged citizens and lifelong learners. Alvernia has been honored by the Templeton Foundation as one of the top 100 character-building colleges in the nation and a model of excellence in education. Alvernia was also named a Military Friendly School for 2014 by G.I. Jobs magazine. In addition, the University is regularly named to the President's Higher Education Community Service Honor Roll for its commitment to and achievement in community service.

The University's 3,000 total students (1,500 traditional undergraduates) can choose from more than 600 courses and 50 majors and minors in the college of Arts and Sciences and College of Professional Programs. Programs are geared toward real-world learning and preparing students for a rewarding career. Study abroad, internships, and international service trips make learning come alive and allow students to develop practical, valuable skills.

Master's degrees are awarded in occupational therapy, business administration, nursing, community counseling, education, organizational leadership and liberal studies. A Ph.D. program in leadership and Doctor of Physical Therapy program (currently a candidate for accreditation status) are also available.

LOCATION AND ENVIRONMENT

Situated on a scenic 121-acre suburban campus, Alvernia is bordered by a park that features hiking trails, a picnic grove, and a nine-hole disk-golf course. When students want to explore big city life, Philadelphia (60 miles), New York, Baltimore, and Washington, D.C. are all just a short drive away.

OFF-CAMPUS OPPORTUNITIES

The Washington Center experience is a popular way for students to expand their education beyond the classroom. Earning college credit while spending a semester in Washington D.C., students serve as interns in a congressional office, government agency, major corporation, newspaper, news network, or nonprofit groups, or an agency devoted to legal affairs, international relations, or business and economics.

Study abroad has become increasingly popular. A new program allows Alvernia students to study in Austria, Belgium, China, Ecuador, England, Germany, Greece, India, Ireland, Mexico, New Zealand, Palestine and Spain!

MAJORS AND DEGREES OFFERED

Alvernia offers a breadth of academic programs with a boundary-free learning approach. Bachelor's degrees are awarded in the following majors: accounting, athletic training, behavioral health, biochemistry, biology, biology–medical laboratory science, chemistry, communication, criminal justice administration, education (concentrations in early childhood and early childhood and special), English, environmental biochemistry, finance, forensic science, general science, healthcare science, history, human resource management, marketing, management, mathematics, nursing, occupational therapy, philosophy, political science, psychology, social work, sport management, theatre, and theology.

Pre-professional programs are available in dentistry, law, medicine, pharmacology, and veterinary studies. Alvernia also offers minors and certificate programs.

Since 1967, the Middle States Association of Colleges and Schools has granted Alvernia accreditation. The education program curriculum is approved by the Pennsylvania State Department of Education. The occupational therapy program is fully accredited by the American Occupational Therapy Association. The Bachelor of Science in Nursing has approval by the Pennsylvania State Board of Nursing and is accredited by the Commission on Collegiate Nursing Education. The athletic training program is accredited by the Commission on Accreditation of Athletic Training Education. The social work program is accredited by the Council on Social Work Education. The behavioral health program is certified by the Pennsylvania Certification Board. The business department is accredited by the Accreditation Council for Business Schools and Programs.

ACADEMIC PROGRAMS

Alvernia offers a range of academic programs with a learning approach grounded in the real world. With a foundation in the liberal arts tradition, the curriculum and instruction is designed to help students develop critical thinking skills and explore their own ideas. This approach produces well-rounded individuals who are ready to succeed no matter what path they choose.

Qualified students may participate in the Honors Program, which assists students of outstanding intellectual promise and high motivation that seek a more challenging program and are interested in pursuing future graduate or professional studies. The program encourages students to achieve, often letting them work at their own pace. It facilitates a stimulating exchange of ideas and information between students' varied interests and different disciplines.

In order to earn a bachelor's degree from Alvernia, students must complete a minimum of 123 credits, with 54 credits in the liberal arts. Additional requirements vary by major.

CAMPUS FACILITIES AND EQUIPMENT

Alvernia has recently invested in several additions to campus including a laser laboratory to support science programs, state-of-the-art learning suites developed for our criminal justice and counseling programs, a theater and recital hall, with an art gallery, music studios and rehearsal spaces, an educational technology center and media suite, a healthcare science wing with multiple labs, an expanded library learning commons and a physical therapy center to support the Doctor of Physical Therapy program. On-campus housing includes traditional residence halls, apartments, suites, and town houses. All residential facilities are clean, spacious and equipped with laundry, cable TV, and phones with voicemail.

The Campus Commons houses a fitness center; dance/aerobics studio; and a campus "living room," complete with a fireplace, for leisure activities, study, and programs.

Alvernia's campus is fully networked. Students have access to the academic information network and the Internet from their residence hall rooms, as well as from other campus locations including classrooms, the library, and labs. All students may connect personal computers through the University's secure system. Network access and Alvernia email accounts are available to all students.

TUITION, ROOM, BOARD AND FEES

For the 2015–16 academic year, tuition is $30,500 and room and board is $10,820 (an approximate cost based on Veronica Hall residence and an all-you-can-eat meal plan).

FINANCIAL AID

Ninety-eight percent of students receive some form of financial aid. Financial aid is offered to students whose personal and family resources are insufficient to meet the full cost of an education. Aid usually comes in the form of scholarships, grants, loans, and work-study arrangements. Depending upon their academic record, incoming first-year students may be eligible for one of three merit-based scholarships: the Presidential Scholarship ($17,500), the Trustee's Scholarship ($15,500), and the Veronica Founder's Scholarship ($15,000). Applicants interested in financial aid should submit the FAFSA as soon as possible after January 1.

STUDENT ORGANIZATIONS AND ACTIVITIES

Alvernia encourages students to take advantage of learning opportunities outside the classroom by participating in any of the more than fifty-five groups including intramural and intercollegiate sports, academic clubs, honor societies, student government, and faith-based environmental and service clubs. Campus organizations offer opportunities to suit the interests of all students, to meet new people, to learn various skills, and to develop leadership abilities.

Athletics are a proud and integral part of the educational mission. Students may participate in intercollegiate, intramural, and club-level programs. Intercollegiate teams compete at the NCAA Division III level. Alvernia is part of the highly competitive Middle Atlantic States Athletic Conference (MAC), and is also a member of the Eastern Collegiate Athletic Conference.

The Office of Student Activities works with the many student organizations to provide a calendar of social, cultural, and other co-curricular activities. The Student Government Association provides an opportunity for leadership through the exercise of personal and group responsibility. All students complete approved community service hours as part of Alvernia's commitment to peace, justice, and the dignity of life. This helps foster devotion to service of others, especially the materially and spiritually disadvantaged of the local and global community.

ADMISSIONS PROCESS

Admission requirements normally include a high school diploma with 16 Carnegie units in the following subjects: English, 4 units; mathematics, 2 units; science, 2 units; social studies, 2 units; and modern languages, 2 units. The remaining units may be made up of academic electives. The University is willing to consider good students whose preparation does not include all of these subjects. Nursing students must fulfill the admission requirements established by the Pennsylvania State Board of Nurse Examiners. The State High School Equivalency Diploma is generally recognized as fulfilling the minimum entrance requirements. Applicants are required to take the SAT; the ACT is also acceptable. Outstanding candidates are considered for entrance to Alvernia at the end of their junior year of high school on the basis of requests made by the candidate and the school. With the approval of their school officials, students may also be admitted to certain courses during their senior year, simultaneously earning credit toward their high school diploma and a college degree.

APPLICATION AND INFORMATION

Many factors are considered for admission, including academic performance, standardized test scores, extracurricular activities, and community involvement. Application and admission notification is on a rolling basis; however, applicants are encouraged to submit the admission application as early as possible. In addition to their transcripts and SAT or ACT scores, nursing applicants must also submit two letters of recommendation.

Alvernia accepts and/or offers special programs for accelerated high school students, nontraditional students (older than 24), transfer students, students with disabilities, veterans, and international students.

Applicants should submit an application for admission and enclose a nonrefundable $25 processing fee. The application form may be obtained from the Office of Admissions or the University's website at www.alvernia.edu/admissions/undergraduate/apply.html. Applicants should have an official copy of their high school record sent to the Office of Admissions, along with the official results of the SAT or ACT.

Because Alvernia has a rolling admission policy, the Director of Admissions notifies an applicant of acceptance shortly after the necessary credentials are on file and have been reviewed, generally within one month. To reserve a place in the freshman class, all students must make a $300 deposit by May 1. This deposit is credited to the student's account for the first semester but is not refunded if the student fails to attend. Transfer students should have a grade point average of 2.0 or higher on a 4.0 scale and should be aware that only grades of C or better are eligible for credit transfer. Alvernia accepts a maximum of 75 transfer credits; at least 45 credits that are required for graduation must be earned at Alvernia and must satisfy all graduation requirements. A detailed analysis of credits to be transferred is done only after the University has accepted students.

The best way to get to know Alvernia is through a campus visit and tour. Applicants and those considering the school are strongly encouraged to come for an individual campus visit, which will be personalized to match each student's unique interests. Alvernia also hosts information sessions and open houses throughout the year that allow prospective freshmen or transfers to meet current students, talk to admissions and financial aid counselors, and meet faculty and coaches. Overnight and shadow visits are also available.

For more information or to schedule a visit, students should contact:

Director of Admissions

Alvernia University

400 Saint Bernardine Street

Reading, Pennsylvania 19607

Phone: 888-ALVERNIA (258-3764, toll-free)

Fax: 610-790-2873

E-mail: admissions@alvernia.edu

Website: http://www.alvernia.edu

Featured Video: https://www.youtube.com/watch?v=PO3CNuGrRdc

Facebook: http://on.fb.me/Alvernia_University

Twitter: http://twitter.com/alverniauniv

YouTube: https://www.youtube.com/user/AlverniaU

ASSUMPTION COLLEGE

AT A GLANCE

Established in 1904 by the Augustinians of the Assumption, Assumption College is a coeducational institution known for its classic liberal arts curriculum and strong academic programs in business and professional studies. Our 2,000+ undergraduates choose among 42 majors and 48 minors, gaining the depth and breadth of knowledge that is the foundation of lifelong success and personal fulfillment.

The educational experience is grounded in the rich Catholic intellectual tradition, which cultivates both the intellect and personal values students need to meet the demands of a constantly changing world. Undergraduates and graduate students closely interact with faculty members and staff in a thriving community that forms graduates known for critical intelligence, thoughtful citizenship and compassionate service.

The academic atmosphere is marked by individual attention and the quest for personal excellence. With a student/faculty ratio of just 12:1, Assumption's professors serve as mentors who challenge students to ask questions, find their own answers, and grow—intellectually, socially and spiritually. Students are encouraged to gain professional experience at internships and to participate in individual research projects. Ninety-six percent of Assumption's 2014 graduates were employed or in graduate school within six months of graduation.

Located on 185 acres, the Assumption campus is situated in a beautiful, residential neighborhood just minutes from downtown Worcester, Massachusetts. The college also has its own campus in the heart of Rome, Italy, nationally ranked as a top ten study abroad program. At Assumption, 90 percent of the undergraduates live on campus and housing is guaranteed for all four years. The campus is lively seven days a week with academic programming, activities sponsored by student clubs and organizations, community service opportunities, campus ministry programs and intercollegiate, intramural and club sports. The college's state-of-the-art recreation center supports the well-being of all students.

LOCATION AND ENVIRONMENT

Worcester, the second-largest city in New England, is a college town that is home to more than 30,000 students. Assumption has established an array of internship opportunities in virtually every field, and a great network for career placements. Students enjoy a variety of local restaurants, cultural venues and programs, retail and entertainment options, and professional sports teams. In addition, Boston and Providence are only an hour's drive away, and there is regular commuter rail service to Boston.

The Rome campus is close to the metro and walking distance to Vatican City. The newly renovated facility accommodates up to 25 students a semester.

OFF-CAMPUS OPPORTUNITIES

Assumption encourages students to expand their horizons. In addition to the Rome campus, undergraduates can spend a semester or a year studying abroad — from France and England, to Japan, the Czech Republic and Australia, to name a few locations. Many students also augment their education and hone professional skills through local, regional, national and international internships. Assumption students have worked at diverse organizations around the globe, from the Department of Commerce, Central America Bureau and the Department of State (NAFTA Agreement), to Smith Barney, Fidelity, Morgan Stanley, ABC News, and the Alliance Francaise in Paris.

As a member of the colleges of Worcester Consortium, an association of 12 higher education institutions in the Worcester region, Assumption students can register for courses at the other colleges and participate in their social and cultural events.

MAJORS AND DEGREES OFFERED

The College offers 42 different majors. Some of the most popular academic programs include English (concentrations in literature or writing and mass communications), history, political science, psychology and the natural sciences—biology, biotechnology and molecular biology, neuroscience, chemistry and environmental science. Other popular academic programs include education, human services and sport management, and business—accounting, international business, management, marketing and organizational communication. Minors are offered in 48 areas.

Pre-professional preparation is available for dentistry, medicine, and law. Assumption has partnered with prestigious colleges and universities to provide students an array of academic options. Eligible students can attend Assumption for three years and then go on to law school at Duquesne, Vermont or Western New England Law Schools. There is guaranteed admission to specific graduate programs in the health and natural sciences for eligible students. There is also a 3 + 2 engineering degree with University of Notre Dame. In addition, Assumption College offers graduate degrees in business, special education, school counseling, counseling psychology and rehabilitation counseling.

ACADEMIC PROGRAMS

The College's classic liberal arts curriculum promotes the lively discussion of the books, ideas, people and events that have shaped civilization. Faculty and students explore the rich Catholic intellectual tradition as they seek "truth" and the nature of the world. In all areas of academic study, students learn not only how to ask questions, but also how to find the answers. That is why so many classes at Assumption are discussions, not lectures, and why the faculty assign cooperative projects and frequent writing and hands-on assignments. The curriculum is designed to teach the student how to think, not simply memorize.

Assumption also offers academic programs and courses that help students achieve their full potential. Honors Program and the Fortin and Gonthier Foundations of Western Civilization Program encourage students to challenge themselves intellectually. Students broaden their world view and their practical experiences through study abroad and internships. Cross-registration through the colleges of Worcester Consortium enables Assumption students to take classes at Clark University, Worcester Polytechnic Institute and the college of the Holy Cross, among others. Air Force and Army ROTC are also available.

Assumption College follows a traditional two-semester calendar, from late August to mid-May, as well as an optional January intersession. The college offers two separate undergraduate summer sessions to Assumption and local students. Graduate Studies programs and the Center for Continuing and Career Education also offer two summer sessions for students.

In order to earn their degrees, undergraduates must have 120 credit hours, and a minimum of 38 courses. Assumption liberal arts core curriculum requires all students complete courses in English, philosophy, theology, humanities, history, social sciences, and some select courses in art, music or theater, mathematics, laboratory science, and/or foreign language.

CAMPUS FACILITIES AND EQUIPMENT

Assumption offers first-rate facilities for learning and living and the campus is wireless. Key facilities include:

The Information Technology Center has computer labs, and classrooms used for collaborative projects, multimedia presentations, foreign language work and leading-edge software and computer systems.

The Richard and Janet Testa Science Center houses the Department of Natural Sciences and features multi-use classrooms with state-of-the-art technology; 10 teaching laboratories, seven laboratories dedicated for faculty and student research; a working greenhouse, conference rooms and student lounge areas.

The Emmanuel d'Alzon Library is an ideal location to study, research and relax. The professional library staff, collection of 200,000 volumes, 1,125 journal subscriptions and extensive access to local, regional and national library networks and databases are vital resources for students and faculty.

Assumption's Multi-Sport Stadium, a lighted, synthetic turf field with seating for 1,200 is the home of Assumption's intercollegiate field hockey, football, men's and women's lacrosse and men's and women's soccer teams and the college's extensive outdoor intramural programs. The Plourde Recreation Center features a swimming pool, exercise and wellness classes, courts, and a fitness facility that is accessible to all students, faculty and staff.

A variety of housing options are available to accommodate the 90 percent of under-graduates who live on campus. Traditional residence halls, the living/learning center, suites and apartments with full kitchens provide housing options for all four years. All resident students have individual hard-wired and wireless high speed Internet access in their rooms, as well as in the computer labs.

TUITION, ROOM, BOARD AND FEES

For 2015–2016, tuition is $35,510; room and board is $11,264 and student fees are $650. The board plan is required for all first-year residential students.

When you choose Assumption College, you gain the ability to develop a reliable financial plan for the next four years, with the assurance that tuition rates will not increase. The class entering in fall 2015 will pay the 2014–2015 tuition rate for their four years at Assumption. The program is evaluated each year and an announcement is made in May regarding the status of the program for the next entering class.

FINANCIAL AID

This past year, Assumption awarded more than $33 million in financial assistance to students. The college offers need-based financial aid, as well as merit-based assistance. All students who apply for admission are considered for merit scholar-ships ranging from $2,500–$22,000 annually and recipients are chosen based on their academic excellence and demonstrated student leadership. To qualify for need-based financial aid, students must submit the Free Application for Federal Student Aid (FAFSA) by February 1.

STUDENT ORGANIZATIONS AND ACTIVITIES

The 2,000+ undergraduates at Assumption come from 25 states and 36 countries. Ninety percent of the students reside on campus and housing is guaranteed for all four years. Numerous social, athletic, recreational and cultural activities are offered on- and off-campus and make Assumption a dynamic place to live.

Assumption College has 60+ clubs and organizations that seek to complement the educational process and offer opportunities for students to develop their interests and talents. Students can participate in academic/professional clubs, arts and entertainment groups, student publications, politics and student government, service projects, special interest groups, or spiritual activities. These groups also give students opportunities to develop their leadership and team-building skills.

The various student clubs and organizations plan a wide range of events. This includes many large-scale programs, such as Family Weekend, Siblings Weekend, Welcome Week, Midnight Madness and the Spring Concert. Other more frequent events include comedians, coffeehouses, films, lectures, off-campus trips and many special events.

Assumption offers 23 intercollegiate teams, as well as 8 club and 21 intramural sports. The college is a charter member of the Northeast-10 Conference and competes as an NCAA Division II institution. The intercollegiate sports for men include: baseball, basketball, cross country, football, golf, hockey, lacrosse, soccer, tennis and track & field (indoor and outdoor). Women's sports include: basketball, cross country, field hockey, lacrosse, rowing, soccer, softball, swimming, tennis, track & field (indoor and outdoor) and volleyball.

ADMISSIONS PROCESS

Assumption College admits students who demonstrate an active intellect and self-motivation and who have compiled a solid academic record and completed all prescribed high school requirements.

The College encourages prospective students to schedule a campus visit prior to applying for admission. During the summer months, high school students are en-couraged to attend group information sessions, tours and interviews Monday-Friday. In the fall semester, prospective students may attend group information sessions, including some Saturdays, or schedule a campus visit during the week.

To apply, students are required to submit the Common Application, a $50 application fee, official high school transcripts, and a letter of recommendation. Assumption is test-score optional, so SAT or ACT scores are not required. Applications, including all supporting documents and recommendations, must be received in the Office of Admissions by February 15. Students who want to be considered for Early Action must apply by November 1 and for Early Action II by December 15.

For more information, please contact:

Assumption College

Office of Admissions

500 Salisbury Street

Worcester, MA 01609

Telephone: 866-477-7776 (toll free) or 508-767-7285

Web: www.assumption.edu

E-mail: admiss@assumption.edu

BABSON COLLEGE

AT A GLANCE

Babson College is the educator, convener, and thought leader for Entrepreneurship of All Kinds™. As the only school to teach Entrepreneurial Thought and Action®, Babson shapes the leaders our world needs most: those with strong functional knowledge and the skills and vision to navigate change, accommodate ambiguity, surmount complexity, and motivate teams in a common purpose.

LOCATION AND ENVIRONMENT

This 370-acre suburban campus is located in Wellesley, Massachusetts. This is the ideal charming New England town, a classic setting for a college environment. A mere 14 miles outside of Boston, students here are sure to experience the best of both worlds: the quaintness of small town life bordering the cultural and social excitement of the big city. Although Boston is accessible by means of public transportation and a shuttle service, approximately half of all students have cars. 85% of students live on campus all four years they are at Babson.

MAJORS AND DEGREES OFFERED

At Babson College, all graduates earn a Bachelor of Science degree. Concentrations are an optional way for you to organize your advanced studies, and certify that your focus of study is on your final transcript. Students may choose to plan their course of study around one of twenty-seven concentrations in both business and liberal arts disciplines.

ACADEMIC PROGRAMS

Our academic program, with an emphasis on hands-on experiential learning, is uniquely designed for students who want to study business and learn about the world around them. In the first year at Babson, the groundwork is laid for future courses—and a career. It all starts with the Foundations of Management and Entrepreneurship course, a yearlong immersion into the business world where students start their own business with a team of fellow students. Students also take liberal arts courses, breaking down artificial barriers between disciplines with an integrated learning approach, and understanding how these skills play into businesses of all types and sizes. A weekly First-Year Seminar addresses the transition to college life by learning key resources on campus, discussing challenges that come up with roommates, and improving time management and study skills in their new environment. Members of the Babson community—including alumni, faculty, staff, and peer mentors—give students personal and professional support throughout the four years.

In your second year, students take an integrated series of courses in finance, microeconomics, marketing, information technology, management accounting, and operations management, giving the broad perspective of a CEO. Students look at actual business problems via case studies and gain real-world experience by studying, touring, and interacting with and presenting to local companies.

Throughout the third and fourth years at the college, students reflect on your career options and pursue courses that align with their personal and professional goals; various concentrations can guide their focus. Students gain field experience with internships or consulting programs, and also may opt to take their education abroad.

Babson has a partnership with Wellesley College and the Franklin W. Olin College of Engineering to provide extraordinary opportunities in all aspects of the student experience, including joint academic and research programming, student life programming, and lecture series.

Because of Babson's close-knit community, students are able to form close relationships with the faculty. Faculty members are accomplished entrepreneurs, executives, scholars, authors, researchers, poets, and artists who bring an intellectual diversity that adds depth to Babson's educational programs and offers students a rich, challenging experience. Faculty members teach 100 percent of the courses at Babson.

Beginning in the first year and building throughout their four years at Babson, students are supported through the career development process. Babson's Undergraduate Center for Career Development (CCD) offers a comprehensive, integrated career development program that is closely linked to academic and co-curricular experiences. Students take advantage of one-on-one career advising with CCD advisors who specialize in particular sectors—something only a small college can provide. Babson's reputation and long-standing relationships with employers, alumni, and faculty allow students make the connections necessary to find the right experiences and internships, and ultimately the right career.

CAMPUS FACILITIES AND EQUIPMENT

Babson's contemporary facilities provide students with access to dynamic academic and social resources. Students frequent the Donald W. Reynolds Campus Center, the Richard W. Sorenson Family Visual Arts Center, the Richard W. Sorenson Center for the Arts, the Webster Athletic Center, and the Glavin Family Chapel.

Horn Library houses an extensive business collection of print, media, and computerized information resources. Students have campus-wide access to library resources.

Babson also boasts several robust academic centers whose aim—in addition to spearheading groundbreaking research—is to provide students with ways to put their education into practice.

Stephen D. Cutler Center For Investments And Finance

The Cutler Center is home to the Babson College Fund, a student-managed equity fund that is part of the College's endowment.

Center For Women's Entrepreneurial Leadership (Cwel)

The CWEL Scholars program inspires undergraduate women to pursue their entrepreneurial potential through exclusive events and hands-on coaching.

Arthur M. Blank Center For Entrepreneurship

The Blank Center hosts the John E. And Alice L. Butler Venture Accelerator, which serves all students seeking to start or advance an entrepreneurial venture.

Lewis Institute For Social Innovation

Through programs like the Babson Social Innovation Lab, the Lewis Institute serves as a bridge connecting students, faculty, and outside organizations looking to create sustainable value in the world.

Wireless access is available everywhere on campus. Every incoming Babson undergraduate student receives a leased laptop computer. After their sophomore year, Babson students return their laptops and receive brand new ones, which are then returned at the end of their senior year. When students graduate, they have the option to purchase a new laptop at Babson's discounted rate.

FINANCIAL AID

Babson is committed to educating students from diverse backgrounds, and we will do all we can to make it financially possible for any student to attend Babson. In 2013-2014, Babson is awarded $30 million from its own funds to undergraduate students. Federal and state grants, loans, and work-study are awarded based on financial need. Students who wish to apply for financial aid should submit the CSS/Financial Aid PROFILE and FAFSA.

STUDENT ORGANIZATIONS AND ACTIVITIES

Babson offers students an extensive variety of student activities. These extracurriculars include 22 NCAA Division III (11 men's and 11 women's) intercollegiate athletic teams. Intramural sports are also popular student activities. More than 115 student-run clubs, organizations, and publishing opportunities are available across every interest spectrum. Some of these activities include: dance groups, theater, literary magazine, cultural groups, music ensembles, radio station, student government, and more, . New student organizations are created each year. The school also has three fraternities and three sororities. Approximately 15 percent of students are involved in Greek life.

ADMISSIONS PROCESS

Babson College bases its acceptance of students on both academic and nonacademic factors. The academic factors include high school record, recommendations, standardized test scores, and essays. The nonacademic factors include extracurricular activities, shown leadership, character/personal qualities, volunteer work, work experience, creativity and enthusiasm, and a willingness to contribute to the Babson community in meaningful ways. Graduation from secondary school is required for admission. The most competitive students have taken approximately 5 solid academic courses per year at the highest available level (Honors, Advanced Placement or International Baccalaureate). The SAT or ACT with writing is required for admission. The TOEFL or IELTS is required for students who are nonnative English speakers.

Babson offers several application programs. Students may apply Early Decision (binding process), Early Action, or Regular Decision. The deadline for Early Decision and Early Action is November 1. The Regular Decision Deadline is January 4. Transfer students may apply for September entrance by April 1 and for January entrance by November 1.

BARNARD COLLEGE

AT A GLANCE

Founded in 1889, Barnard College was among the first colleges to offer young women the chance to earn a college degree. Today, Barnard College remains committed to the education of more than 2,400 undergraduate women from over 50 countries and nearly 50 states. Partnered with Columbia University since 1900, under an agreement unique in the world of higher education, Barnard is an independent college for women, maintaining its own Board of Trustees, campus, curriculum, faculty, staff, and admissions process. Barnard also operates from its own endowment, while Columbia University confers degrees to Barnard students. The fully residential campus features countless, independent resources and facilities; students at Barnard also have academic and extra-curricular access to the Columbia campus across the street, including cross-registration for courses, and benefit from both an all women and a coeducational experience. Additionally, Barnard women complete alongside Columbia students on 16 NCAA Division I athletic teams as part of the Ivy League conference. The small, personal, and close-knit character of Barnard is augmented by the resources of a large research university.

LOCATION AND ENVIRONMENT

Barnard is located in New York City and offers students endless cultural, academic, and professional opportunities. New York is an extension of our classrooms and students make use of its resources for both study and exploration. Barnard's Office of Career Development lists over 2,500 student internships throughout New York City each year and classes often incorporate visits to museums, tours of historic neighborhoods, or participation in civic engagement projects. Barnard's location in the neighborhood of Morningside Heights offers a retreat from the fast pace of Mid-town Manhattan and is often referred to as an educational Mecca with students, staff and faculty from a number of institutions of higher education all calling the Heights "home." Institutions neighboring the Barnard campus, in addition to Columbia University, include the Manhattan School of Music, Teachers College, Bank Street College of Education, Union Theological Seminary, and the Jewish Theological Seminary. New York City is the ultimate college town, drawing more than 500,000 college students each year.

OFF-CAMPUS OPPORTUNITIES

There are numerous opportunities for Barnard students to explore academics beyond the Barnard gates. Barnard students have full access to Columbia resources including more than 30 libraries and collections, research facilities, and courses which complement the Barnard curriculum, even at a graduate or professional level. The Jewish Theological Seminary allows Barnard students to enroll in courses for credit and the Juilliard School and the Manhattan School of Music allow highly qualified Barnard musicians to enroll in a selective lesson exchange program.

Barnard students also explore academics beyond both New York and the United States through over 150 study-abroad programs in more than 50 countries including, but not limited to: Argentina, Australia, China, Costa Rica, Czech Republic, Egypt, France, Greece, Ireland, Israel, Kenya, Panama, Peru, Russia, Scotland, and Tibet. Programs focus on cultural immersion, advanced or independent study, and field-based or experiential learning and may include a single semester or a full year of study. Other Barnard students enroll in a variety of programs offered through other universities, liberal arts college consortiums and international organizations. Atlanta's Spelman College and Washington, D.C.'s Howard University offer domestic exchange programs with Barnard.

MAJORS AND DEGREES OFFERED

Barnard offers the bachelor of arts (BA) degree, and students choose from more than 50 majors, including Africana studies, American studies, ancient studies, anthropology, architecture, art history (including visual arts), Asian and Middle Eastern cultures, biochemistry, biological studies, chemistry, classics (Greek and Latin), comparative literature, computer science, dance, economics, education, English (including creative writing), environmental science and policy, European studies, film studies, French, German, history, human rights studies, Italian, Jewish studies, mathematics, Medieval and Renaissance studies, music, neuroscience and behavior, philosophy, physics and astronomy, political science (including international politics), psychology, religion, Slavic studies, sociology, Spanish and Latin American cultures, statistics, theatre, urban studies, and women's, sexuality and gender studies. With this foundation in the liberal arts and sciences, Barnard women succeed in a variety of career fields, including business, communications, health and public service, and are well prepared for global and diverse settings.

Opportunities for double and joint degrees are also available at Barnard in conjunction with other schools within Columbia University. One option is the five-year AB/MIA or AB/MPA program where Barnard students also earn their masters from Columbia's School of International and Public Affairs. Barnard may also nominate juniors with outstanding records for early admission to Columbia Law School under the Accelerated Program in Interdisciplinary Legal Education and may recommend candidates for an accelerated degree with Columbia's School of Oral and Dental Surgery. Students interested in both the liberal arts and engineering may earn the AB/BS degrees in a five-year (3-2) program with Columbia's Fu Foundation School of Engineering and Applied Science. Advanced music students can apply and audition for the Juilliard School's five-year (3-2) program, earning their AB from Barnard and the MM degree from Julliard. Finally, students may earn an AB from Barnard and a BA from the nearby Jewish Theological Seminary's List College, if admitted to the double degree program.

ACADEMIC PROGRAMS

A Barnard education seeks to provide women with the tools and techniques necessary to think critically and act effectively in the world today. Barnard requires students to complete 122 points of course work (including First-Year English, First-Year Seminar, and two semesters of physical education) in addition to a major for the Bachelor of Arts (AB) degree. Barnard believes that a successful liberal arts education revolves around central "ways of knowing" the world. This philosophy forms the basis of the general education requirements within Nine Ways of Knowing, organized in the following categories: ethics and value, social analysis, cultures in comparison, language, laboratory science, historical studies, literature, visual and performing arts, and quantitative reasoning. To allow for flexibility within this framework, a student chooses among the designated courses, typically 40-100 choices in each area, that fulfill the nine requirements. Thus, each student will shape her own academic program by electing a combination of wide-ranging introductory courses and more specialized upper level courses.

The College has a long-standing commitment to prepare students sufficiently in a subject so that they may undertake a semester- or year-long thesis or project, usually during the senior year, on a topic related to their major. Students are encouraged to explore internships in their field, thereby acquiring information and experience that complement what is learned through formal study. A student may major in two fields by satisfying all the major requirements prescribed by each department.

CAMPUS FACILITIES AND EQUIPMENT

Barnard's Campus covers four acres of prime New York real estate stretching from 116th to 120th Street along Broadway with 15 buildings comprising Barnard's cozy campus. Milbank Hall, a nationally registered historic landmark, contains offices, classrooms, a cutting-edge greenhouse, and the Minor Latham Playhouse. 14-story Altschul Hall houses state-of-the-art science research facilities and equipment, along with classrooms, offices, and laboratories. A full gymnasium is located on the first floor of Barnard Hall, facing the college's main entrance. Barnard Hall is also the home of the Barnard Center for Research on Women in addition to the Athena Center for Leadership Studies. Brooks, Reid, and Sulzberger Halls along with Hewitt, make up the Quad, the residence life complex serving first-year students situated at the southern end of campus. Campus housing is guaranteed to continuously enrolled first-years for four years and housing options include opportunities for coeducational living. The heart of student life is our Diana Center, the student center which opened January of 2010, where students have access to many amenities which augment academic life, including an art gallery, black box theatre, event and dining spaces, art and architecture studios, music practice rooms, and more. Finally, Wollman Library offers three floors of study space and along with Columbia's libraries, with more than 10 million volumes, over 100,000 current journals and serials, and an extensive collection of electronic resources, manuscripts, rare books, microforms, and other non-print formats, provides access to one of the top five academic library systems in the nation.

TUITION, ROOM, BOARD AND FEES

Tuition and fees for 2014–15 are $46,040. Room and board is an additional $14,660.

FINANCIAL AID

Financial aid at Barnard is strictly need-based. A student's need is determined using criteria established by both the federal government and Barnard's institutional analysis. The financial aid awarded by Barnard supplements a family's own financial resources, while Barnard meets 100 percent of the remaining demonstrated need. Financial aid awards typically consist of grants, work study jobs, and student loans. Students who are awarded Barnard College grants should expect grants throughout their four years at Barnard, providing the students' families maintain their level of need and the students maintain their academic standing. Fifty-five percent of first-year students received some form of financial aid during the 2014–2015 school year and the average total grant (including state and federal funds) was $41,722. Need plays no role in the Barnard admissions process for US citizens and permanent residents; admission for these first-year students is need-blind, and admissibility is evaluated solely on merit. For international citizens and transfer students, Barnard is need aware in the admissions evaluation.

STUDENT ORGANIZATIONS AND ACTIVITIES

The Barnard College community offers numerous activities and opportunities to an active student body. The Office of Student Life engages each student and promotes active and involved citizenship through leadership development, multicultural education, and a foundation in social justice. More than 80 Barnard student-run organizations are available to Barnard students, a sampling include: Asian American Alliance, Barnard Bulletin, Gospel Choir, Community Impact, Late Nite Theatre, Model United Nations, Mujeres, McIntosh Activities Council, Orchesis Dance Troupe, Russian Cultural Association, Students Against Silence, and Women's International Business Council. Barnard and Columbia students take part in organizations and activities on both campuses; and Barnard women take leadership roles in many of nearly 500 additional Columbia-sponsored clubs. Women's intercollegiate, intramural and club athletics are also popular. Barnard's varsity athletes compete at the NCAA Division I level alongside their Columbia peers as part of the Ivy League conference through the Barnard/Columbia Athletic Consortium. The 16 intercollegiate teams include archery, basketball, crew, cross-country, fencing, field hockey, golf, indoor and outdoor track and field, lacrosse, soccer, softball, squash, swimming and diving, tennis, and volleyball. Intramural and club sports include cycling, equestrian, ice hockey, martial arts, rugby, and sailing.

ADMISSIONS PROCESS

High school transcripts, letters of recommendation, standardized test scores, personal attributes and achievements all play a role in Barnard's highly selective and holistic admissions process. The college seeks women with strong academic records who exhibit the capacity and desire to grow intellectually and personally. While there is not a set group of criteria that an applicant must match, the successful applicant will have completed a rigorous college preparatory program or its equivalent, with a recommended 4 years of English, 3 or more years of math, 3 or more years of a foreign language, 3 or more years of laboratory science, and 3 or more years of history at minimum. The most successful applicants have succeeded in the most challenging curriculum available to them. Every applicant is evaluated on both the qualities that she personally espouses and her potential for success at Barnard. Applicants must submit the following test scores: either the ACT with writing, or the SAT Reasoning Test and two SAT Subject Tests. Students for whom English is not their primary language of instruction or who have been in the United States for less than 5 years must submit results from the TOEFL or IELTS exams. Interviews, available only for first-year applicants, are optional.

BELMONT UNIVERSITY

AT A GLANCE

Belmont University sits on 75 historic acres in the heart of Nashville, Tennessee, a thriving metropolis known worldwide as Music City USA. Belmont University is among the fastest growing Christian universities in the nation with approximately 7,300 students hailing from every state and 25 countries. Belmont University is accredited by the Commission on Colleges of the Southern Association of Colleges and Schools to award baccalaureate, master's, and doctoral degrees. Belmont offers over 80 areas of undergraduate study, 22 master's programs and five doctoral degrees through its ten colleges: Jack C. Massey College of Business, Liberal Arts & Social Sciences, Mike Curb College of Entertainment and Music Business, Gordon E. Inman College of Health Sciences & Nursing, Law, Pharmacy, Theology & Christian Ministry, Science & Mathematics, University College, and Visual & Performing Arts.

ACADEMICS

Intent on being a leader among teaching universities, Belmont brings together the best of liberal arts and professional education in a Christian community of learning and service. Belmont was ranked fifth on the U.S. News & World Report listing of "Best Universities" in the South for the 2015 edition of America's Best Colleges, making Belmont the highest ranked university in Tennessee in this category. In addition, Belmont was lauded for the seventh year in a row as a top "Up-and-Comer," a high honor that indicates the strength of the university's reputation and innovations. Both Rolling Stone and Time magazines have hailed Belmont's Mike Curb College of Entertainment & Music Business as one of the best music business programs in the country. The Jack C. Massey Graduate School of Business has been named the best MBA program in the region, while Belmont's business administration and accounting programs have been accredited by AACSB International, the premier accrediting agency in that arena. Moreover, for the forth year in a row, Belmont University's undergraduate School of Business achieved a Top 100 national ranking in BusinessWeek's annual report on "The Best Undergrad B-Schools" in the U.S. Belmont's Entrepreneurship major was even named National Model Undergraduate Program of the Year by the United States Association of Small Business and Entrepreneurship. Belmont's Enactus team has won multiple national championships and a recent World Cup.

Located in the heart of Music City USA, one of Belmont's consistent success stories is its world-renowned music and music business programs, including songwriting. Several big names in the music industry started their careers at Belmont including "American Idol" finalist Melinda Doolittle, Christian recording artists Ginny Owens and Steven Curtis Chapman, and country stars Trisha Yearwood, Lee Ann Womack, Brad Paisley, Josh Turner and Florida Georgia Line. The annual "Christmas at Belmont" concert showcases performing ensembles from many different genres and has been broadcast nationwide on PBS for several years.

Students who have passions outside of the music industry also have a home at Belmont. From international business and accounting to education, sport administration, nursing, journalism and the humanities, Belmont provides avenues of learning for almost any interest. Recent program additions include an undergraduate degree in motion pictures and publishing, in addition to, a four-year dual PharmD/MBA degree and Doctor of Nursing Practice program. Belmont's also received attention for its innovative, year-long programming around the university's hosting of the 2008 Town Hall Presidential Debate. And this year a variety of speaker series, visual and performing arts programs, and special events occurred on campus, all around the central theme "Living in a Global Community."

Belmont faculty members display a consistent commitment to excellence as well. Multiple professors have been awarded Fulbright awards, including a nursing professor who spent a year recently in Uganda as a guest lecturer while conducting research on how standards of nursing are adapted to austere conditions. Also, five Belmont professors from four different schools—Finance, Psychology, Spanish, Philosophy and Mathematics—have been chosen as Tennessee Professor of the Year by CASE/Carnegie Foundation since 2000.

Belmont's boundaries extend beyond the Nashville campus through its Cool Springs campus and organized programs such as the Washington Center program and Belmont West in Los Angeles and Belmont East in New York City. Study-abroad programs place students in China, Costa Rica, Great Britain, France, Germany, Italy, Russia, South Africa and Spain, among other foreign nations.

CAMPUS GROWTH

As Belmont's academic program offerings grow, so too does the physical campus. Additions in the last several years include the opening of an entertainment and student life complex which houses the Curb Event Center arena, the Beaman Student Life Center and the Maddox Grand Atrium. The Gordon E. Inman Center opened in 2006, a facility that houses Belmont's nursing, social work, occupational therapy and physical therapy programs. The School of Nursing was recognized by Laerdal Medical Corporation as a Center of Educational Excellence in part due to the advanced training the school's multiple simulation models offer to its students.

More recent additions to the campus include the Baskin Center, home to Belmont's College of Law; McWhorter Hall (the 90,000 square foot, state-of-the-art academic building that houses the University's College of Pharmacy, Physical Therapy program, and Department of Psychological Science); and the wonderful McAfee Concert Hall, a large concert venue suitable for acoustic performances. Multiple new residence halls for freshmen through seniors have opened since 2010. Also the Wedgewood Academic Center a new home to the liberal arts, social sciences, mathematics, natural sciences, and religion opened in 2014 (the largest construction project to date at Belmont). And a new dining services center and home to the Mike Curb College of Entertainment and Music Business will open in fall 2015.

ATHLETICS

In addition to celebrating academic excellence and phenomenal growth, Belmont boasts 17 intercollegiate sports teams. The Belmont Bruins men's basketball team won the Ohio Valley Conference regular season championship in 2013, 2014 and 2015 and made its seventh appearance in the NCAA National Tournament in 2015 and the NIT in 2014. Baseball, both cross country teams, and the volleyball team have earned recent conference titles. Belmont student-athletes excel in the classroom, too, as Belmont has won the conference's All-Academic Trophy multiple times. The award is given annually to the conference school with the greatest percentage of student-athletes who earned a GPA of 3.0 or higher.

A CHRISTIAN COMMUNITY OF LEARNING AND SERVICE

Belmont is a student-focused, Christian community of learning and service where students hear from their first visit to campus until the day they graduate that they are created for a purpose in life. The Belmont faculty and staff dedicate themselves to preparing and empowering students to find their passion and use it to change the world. The university seeks to show every student how the love of Christ can compel them to lead lives of disciplined intelligence, compassion, courage and faith.

In fact, Belmont students, faculty and staff are consistently challenged to look at the hardest circumstances and ask, "What can we do?" Students are encouraged to engage and transform the world, locally and globally, by participation in disaster relief trips to everywhere from the tsunami-stricken areas of Southeast Asia to the Gulf Coast after Hurricane Katrina. Students serve locally at various relief and community organizations in Nashville throughout the year, and student-athletes take part annually in sports evangelism mission trips to South Africa, Ukraine and Brazil. Others have taken advantage of what they're learning at Belmont, incorporating their major studies into various service projects around the world, including working with orphans in India and assisting with physical therapy needs in Guatemala.

TUITION, ROOM, BOARD AND FEES

The total cost of attending Belmont is only 80 percent of the national average for a private college. For a full-time undergraduate student living on campus, the total cost for the 2015–16 academic year is approximately $40,970 which includes tuition, fees, room, and board.

FINANCIAL AID

The financial aid program at Belmont combines merit-based assistance with need-based assistance to make the university education affordable. Institutional merit awards range from full-tuition Presidential Scholarships to various levels of partial merit awards. Athletic and artistic scholarships are also available. Belmont also administers traditional state and federal financial aid programs. Campus employment is available. Parents may arrange monthly tuition payments through an outside vendor. To apply for need-based financial assistance, the student must complete the Free Application for Federal Student Aid (FAFSA). FAFSA Code: 003479

ADMISSIONS PROCESS

Belmont's Admissions Committee considers applications based on the total picture that a student's credentials present. High school students will be considered competitive for admission if they present a rigorous course of college-preparatory, academic studies. Students should have an above-average academic and cumulative grade point average and rank in the top half of their graduating class. Any college-level work is also expected to be at the above-average level. A strong correlation between high school grades and entrance examination scores is expected. The personal supplemental information, résumé of activities, and recommendations are also strongly considered as indicators of success at Belmont. Additional requirements such as portfolios or auditions are considered in conjunction with the academic credentials for those programs that require them. Each application is considered on an individual basis. No two applicants will present the same credentials or the same "fit" with the university. Our desire is to work with each student to determine the likelihood of that student to enroll in, graduate from, and use the benefits of the Belmont educational experience.

For more information, contact:

Office of Admissions

Belmont University

1900 Belmont Boulevard

Nashville, TN 37212

615-460-6785

800-56ENROLL

Fax: 615-460-5434

admissions@belmont.edu

www.belmont.edu

CEEB Code: 1058

ACT Code: 3946

BELOIT COLLEGE

AT A GLANCE

Beloit College is a four-year, independent, national college of liberal arts and sciences in Southern Wisconsin. It is a college where great teaching and mentoring prepare students to lead lives of consequence and where students work on their transcripts and their résumés at the same time. Beloit's campus engages students in an uncommonly diverse residential community. The flexible curriculum crosses traditional academic boundaries, emphasizes the importance of putting theory into practice, and teaches students to develop global perspectives on wide-ranging issues. Beloit's 1,250 students come from nearly every state and more than 30 countries. With an incredible breadth of opportunities, a historic campus with modern facilities, a nationally recognized faculty, and creative, motivated students, Beloit is truly a college that changes lives. Beloit is also Wisconsin's first college, founded in 1846 on the Midwestern frontier.

LOCATION AND ENVIRONMENT

Beloit's 40-acre campus is located on the Wisconsin-Illinois state line, 90 miles northwest of Chicago, 50 miles south of Madison, and 70 miles southwest of Milwaukee in a small city that noted cultural anthropologist Margaret Mead called "American society in a microcosm." Beloit's academic buildings are clustered around lawns dotted with trees and ancient North American Indian mounds. Student residences are within easy walking distance of classroom, lab, studio locations, and the college's athletic facilities. Nearly all students reside on campus (95 percent) in a tight-knit, active community. Beloit's downtown is just two blocks from campus, with banks, restaurants, and shops, and a vibrant schedule of events, including the region's most popular farmers market on Saturdays from spring through late fall.

OFF-CAMPUS OPPORTUNITIES

On average, more than half of any Beloit College class has studied off campus, in either international or domestic programs. Study abroad is transformative at Beloit, with courses that prepare students before they leave, Cities in Transitions courses that engage students in studying urban change (in select locations) while in their locations abroad, and courses and creative projects that help students integrate what they've learned once they return from their host sites. Beloit students study worldwide through a combination of college programs, offerings by other institutions and partners, and direct enrollment in universities. Off-campus study programs in North America are also robust and include semesters in Chicago focused on the arts, entrepreneurship, teaching, and urban studies; American University Programs in Washington, D.C.; and environmental science at the Marine Biological Laboratory in Woods Hole, Mass. Beloit's Liberal Arts in Practice Center connects community needs with students interested in pursuing internships, field terms, and special projects. Beloit makes as much as $500,000 available to fund student projects annually.

MAJORS AND DEGREES OFFERED

Beloit offers undergraduate degree programs exclusively and confers bachelor of arts and bachelor of science degrees. There are more than 50 fields of study in 19 departments. Majors include: anthropology, art history, art (studio), biochemistry, biology (ecology, evolution, and behavioral; environmental; molecular, cellular, and integrative), business economics, chemistry (applied, biological, environmental), Chinese language and culture, classics, comparative literature, computer science, critical identity studies, dance, economics, education and youth studies, English (creative writing and literary studies), environmental studies, French, geology (environmental), German, health and society, history, interdisciplinary studies (self-designed), international relations, international political economy, Japanese language and culture, mathematics, media studies, modern languages and literatures, music, philosophy, physics, political science, psychology, religious studies, Russian, science for elementary teaching, sociology, Spanish, and theatre (performance, production).

Education certification (BA, BS): Children & schools (grades 1-8), Adolescents & schools (grades 9-12). Minors: African studies, American studies, ancient Mediterranean studies, anthropology, art & art history, Asian studies, biology, chemistry, computer science, critical identity studies, English, environmental studies, European studies, geology, health & society, history, interdisciplinary studies, journalism,

Latin American & Caribbean studies, legal studies, mathematics, medieval studies, modern languages (Chinese, French, German, Japanese, Russian, Spanish), museum studies, music, performing arts, philosophy, physics, political science, religious studies, Russian studies.

Pre-professional programs: 3-2 engineering program; forestry and environmental management program; pre-law; and health professions programs.

ACADEMIC PROGRAMS

Beloit offers a variety of programs that supplement and complement its curriculum. The Initiatives program inspires and supports students through their first four semesters of college and includes New Student Days, a first-year interdisciplinary seminar, and optional courses designed to link each student with a peer group and an experienced professor/advisor who leads them toward their choice of major. Through the Initiatives program, Venture Grants are available the summer after students' second academic year, allowing them to pursue intellectually challenging activities that are self-testing or will benefit others and the campus community.

Advising Practicum, a full-day series of workshops and discussions held every semester before advising week, is designed to help students reflect on Beloit's educational opportunities and develop an academic plan tailored to individual interests and goals. The Upton Programs expose both economics majors and non-majors alike to the work of leading economic thinkers and then brings those economists to campus for an annual residency. The Weissberg Program in Human Rights prepares students to engage with issues surrounding human rights as well as promoting and defending these rights responsibly. Through the Weissberg Program, students have access to a network of alumni and experts and may apply for grants, scholarships, and a fellows program.

In summer, the Center for Language Studies offers intensive summer language instruction in Arabic, Chinese, Japanese, and Russian. The anthropology field training program has taken students to excavation sites from Colorado to Chile, and geology field expeditions include trips to Iceland, New Zealand, and Scotland. Each spring, students present their research at a conference-style Student Symposium event, and in the fall, International Symposium Day is a forum set aside for students to present research and projects they have conducted abroad. Beloit students serve on the editorial board of the Beloit Fiction Journal. The Lois and Willard Mackey Chair in Creative Writing brings well-known writers to campus to conduct writing workshops in residency. The Center for Entrepreneurship in Liberal Education at Beloit (CELEB) serves as an incubator for student ventures in a variety of fields, with special emphasis on entrepreneurship in the fine arts.

CAMPUS FACILITIES AND EQUIPMENT

Beloit's academic buildings are both historic and cutting edge and are located toward the southern half of campus as well as in nearby downtown Beloit. The Hendricks Center for the Arts, a beautifully renovated historic building in Beloit's nearby downtown, opened in 2010, offering students studio space for music, dance, theatre, a state-of-the-art film classroom, and set design and staging labs. A 25-acre athletic field and Strong Stadium, featuring a new turf field and track, are located just a few blocks east of the main campus. Plans are underway to convert a decommissioned powerhouse next to campus into a recreation center and student union. This one-of-a-kind reimagining of an industrial building will feature student life spaces, fitness and training facilities, a 200-meter training track and indoor turf field house, a competition pool, and a wellness center, all along the Rock River shoreline. The Powerhouse is planned to open for the 2018–19 school year.

Students may live in traditional settings, quiet or substance-free floors, in one of three fraternity houses or three sorority houses, or in special-interest houses. Two town-house complexes offer roomy, apartment-style living. Meals, served in two campus locations by premier food service provider Bon Appetit, include fresh, locally sourced, organic, vegetarian, and vegan meal options, often featuring student-grown produce. More than half of Beloit's students participate in some form of athletics—club, intramural, or varsity.

Beloit's sports and recreation facilities reflect the high rate of student participation in athletics. The Sports Center includes the Flood Arena, with three collegiate basketball/volleyball courts; the Marvin Field House, with indoor facilities for soccer, tennis, track, golf, baseball, and softball; a fitness center; and a six-lane swimming pool. The 25-acre field complex offers the 3,500-seat Strong Stadium for football and soccer, fields for softball, lacrosse, and baseball, and six all-weather surface tennis courts.

Beloit is noteworthy for having two teaching museums on campus. The Logan Museum of Anthropology holds more than 300,000 archaeological and 15,000 ethnographic objects from 126 countries and nearly 500 cultural groups. The Wright Museum of Art holds a permanent collection of 5,000 works of art, including significant works of American impressionism, modernist paintings, 19th century plaster casts, German expressionism, and Japanese modern prints. Both offer students opportunities to do the work of the museums in collaboration with faculty and staff.

The Laura Aldrich Neese Performing Arts theatre complex features a large thrust stage theater built to Equity standards, a black box theater with flexible staging, a scenic design studio, costume shop, make-up rooms, dressing rooms, and a greenroom.

Off-campus facilities include Chamberlin Springs, 50 acres of oak and hickory woods and wildlife northwest of the city; the Smith Limnology Lab, a small boat launch and aquatic station on the Rock River; and the Newark Road Prairie, a 32.5 acre virgin prairie with more than 300 species of flowering plants.

Beloit's Center for the Sciences, a platinum LEED-certified green building, opened in 2008. Besides its spectacular four-story open foyer, roof garden, and rain garden, it features student offices and space for studio format and inquiry-based courses that integrate class, laboratory, and collaborative group work. Special facilities include a visualization lab, a 1,900 square-foot greenhouse with three climate zones, a herbarium, and a rooftop small-telescope astronomy area. Major scientific equipment includes a scanning electron microscope with EDS elemental analysis system, a nuclear magnetic resonance spectrometer, and more.

TUITION, ROOM, BOARD AND FEES

Costs for the 2015–16 academic year are as follows:

Tuition and fees: $45,050

Room: $4,490

Board: $3,400

Total: $ 52,940

FINANCIAL AID

Beloit College is committed to making the Beloit experience affordable to all qualified students. The financial aid program recognizes two criteria—scholastic ability and financial need. During the 2014–15 academic year, 97 percent of enrolling first-year students received Beloit gift aid. The average need-based grant for first-year students was $26,034.

STUDENT ORGANIZATIONS AND ACTIVITIES

Beloit students are eclectic, defy definition, and place a premium on individual expression. Students serve on college governance and search committees, establish their own organizations, orchestrate events such as the annual Folk 'n' Blues music festival, and host their own radio and cable TV shows. The college has more than 60 active student clubs ranging in focus from ballroom dance to Ultimate Frisbee to yoga. As an NCAA Division III school, Beloit offers numerous varsity and club sports. Men's varsity sports include baseball, basketball, cross country, football, lacrosse, soccer, swimming, and track. Women's varsity sports include basketball, cross country, lacrosse, soccer, softball, swimming, tennis, track, and volleyball.

ADMISSIONS PROCESS

Beloit offers a binding early decision plan with a deadline of November 1 and notification on or before November 30. In addition, there are two non-binding early action plans with deadlines of either November 1 or December 1; notification is December 15 and January 15 respectively. The regular decision priority application deadline is January 15, with notification beginning in March. Applications received after January 15 will be given full consideration as space remains available. Admitted students have until May 1 to reply to Beloit.

Review of transfer applications for the fall term begins March 15 and continues through the spring; the deadline for the spring term is October 15. Notification for transfer applications is rolling.

BENTLEY UNIVERSITY

AT A GLANCE

At Bentley University, we believe your education should prepare you for whatever the world sends your way. That's why our one-of-a-kind curriculum starts with a core business foundation, infused with the kind of critical thinking and cultural understanding that comes from the study of the arts and sciences. As a result, Bentley students are highly sought after by today's leading organizations because of their professionalism, exposure to state-of-the-art research tools, and diverse, real-world experience.

Located on a classic New England campus minutes from Boston, Bentley offers a wide variety of majors and minors, as well as optional liberal studies and business studies majors designed to create a modern intersection of the arts and sciences and business that's unique in higher education. Bentley students are highly sought after by today's leading organizations because of their professionalism, exposure to state-of-the-art research tools, and diverse, real-world experience.

Our career services office was recently ranked No. 4 in the country by the Princeton Review. The Miller Center for Career Services offers resources including an on-campus recruiting program involving 1,000 national and international companies; an online job and internship database; career fairs; workshops on topics such as interviewing and networking; and a newly developed Career Development Seminar (CDI 1901) for first-year students.

In addition, students can develop a customized four-year development plan, which contributes to the university's outstanding placement rates. In 2014, more than 95 percent of students found employment or enrolled in graduate school within six months of graduation. Their median annual salary was $52,000.

LOCATION AND ENVIRONMENT

Bentley's location in Waltham, Massachusetts—just minutes west of Boston—puts the city within easy reach. As the country's ultimate university town, Boston's options range from theater to art exhibits, dance clubs to concerts, and championship sports to world-class shopping. Bentley's free shuttle makes regular trips to Harvard Square in Cambridge, just a subway ride from Boston. Boston also offers many opportunities for internships and jobs after graduation.

OFF-CAMPUS OPPORTUNITIES

Hands-on experience is emphasized across the curriculum. Internships, study abroad, service-learning, and other opportunities allow students to apply classroom theory in the community.

Each year, more than 90 percent of students complete at least one internship, building valuable work experience and networking connections. Some of the top internship employers include Fidelity Investments, the TJX Companies, Liberty Mutual, Bain & Company, and all of the Big Four accounting firms.

Bentley students can gain insight into different cultures by studying abroad. Programs take place in more than 25 countries and vary in length from one week to a full academic year.

Through Bentley's Service-Learning Center, students build skills in business, communication, and teamwork while assisting nonprofit and community-based organizations both locally and internationally.

MAJORS AND DEGREES OFFERED

The Bentley curriculum is a groundbreaking integration of business and the arts and sciences that has been featured in the Wall Street Journal. "It's not about pitting lifelong learning skills against professional skills," President Gloria Larson told the paper. "A college degree should reflect both."

To that end, Bachelor of Science (B.S.) degree programs enable our students to gain in-depth knowledge and skills in specific business disciplines: accountancy, actuarial science, computer information systems, corporate finance and accounting, creative industries, economics–finance, finance, information design and corporate communication, information systems audit and control, management, managerial economics, marketing, mathematical sciences and professional sales.

Bentley also offers Bachelor of Arts (B.A.) degree programs with majors in global studies, health studies, history, liberal arts, media and culture, philosophy, public policy, Spanish studies, and sustainable science. All Bachelor of Arts students gain business experience through either the Business Studies Major (BSM) or minor. All students can also choose from minors such as entrepreneurial studies, law, and sports management.

The Liberal Studies Major (LSM), an optional double major, can be combined with any business program. It provides students with a competitive edge by building meaningful connections across and within disciplines. To complete the LSM, students do not need to take any extra courses beyond those normally required. It allows students to add another credential to their degree, helping them stand out to employers. LSM concentrations include American studies; diversity and society; earth, environment, and global sustainability; ethics and social responsibility; global perspectives; health and industry; media arts and society; and quantitative perspectives.

ACADEMIC PROGRAMS

The Bentley curriculum is a unique fusion of business and the liberal arts. The university's 4,200 undergraduates benefit from a breadth of programs and the ability to combine subjects to best fit their interests.

A Bentley education also focuses on gaining hands-on experience in the classroom. Students benefit from classes where they partner with outside companies to solve current business problems and present their solutions directly to company executives. Bentley also offers top applicants a chance to enroll in the Honors Program. Participants select honors-level courses each semester that offer extra intellectual challenge in a seminar atmosphere.

The Master's Candidate program enables students to earn a Bachelor of Business Administration degree and either an Emerging Leaders M.B.A. or Master of Science (M.S.) degree.

CAMPUS FACILITIES AND EQUIPMENT

Concepts taught in the classroom are put to use in several high-tech learning laboratories.

Bentley's financial Trading Room combines state-of-the-art technology and real-time data to offer first-hand exposure to financial concepts in simulated trading sessions. Resources include Bloomberg, Capital IQ, Datastream, FactSet, Thomson One Analytics, Portfolio Analysis, MATLAB, S&P Compustat, and Worldscope.

The Center for Marketing Technology plays an integral role in marketing programs. Students gain a full grasp of software options, familiarity with research tools and techniques, and knowledge of new digital marketing frameworks.

The Accounting Center for Electronic Learning and Business Management (ACELAB) introduces cutting-edge technologies that are reshaping the accounting profession. Students have access to auditing and tax preparation software as well as other professional applications from industry leaders such as SAP and Oracle.

The Center for Languages and International Collaboration (CLIC) is a key resource for language courses, international studies majors, and students with an interest in global issues. The center promotes collaboration among Bentley students and their counterparts overseas.

The Media and Culture Labs and Studio feature resources for video production and editing as well as digital photography. The lab provides students with industry-standard software programs for screenwriting, sound mixing, graphic design, and DVD authoring.

The User Experience Center (UXC) features labs ideal for usability testing. Students use the applications employed by technical communicators, Web developers, user-interface designers, and usability specialists.

The brand-new CIS Learning and Technology Sandbox is a collaborative space for learning new technologies. Its resources include Google TVs, Xbox 360 with Kinect, study spaces, large-screen TVs, a smart board, specialized networking equipment, and tools such as Windows 8, Linux, and android development software.

The Bentley Library is outfitted with computer workstations, group study rooms, and wireless network access. It also has an exceptional number of online database resources. In 2010, Bentley was ranked 14th on the Princeton Review's list of best college libraries.

FINANCIAL AID

Bentley's financial aid program includes both scholarships based on academic achievement, which are awarded through the admission process, as well as grants based on financial need. Bentley administered over $95 million in aid to undergraduate students last year. Well over half of that amount came in the form of grants and scholarships directly from Bentley. Significant institutional resources are committed each year so that all academically qualified students have access to a Bentley education regardless of their financial resources. Currently, more than 70 percent of undergraduates receive some type of financial assistance—including grants, scholarships, loans and/or work study.

STUDENT ORGANIZATIONS AND ACTIVITIES

Approximately 98 percent of freshmen live on campus. Twenty-three residence halls provide a range of housing options: dorms, suites, and apartments. Housing is provided for all four years; all residence halls are air-conditioned and typically include study lounges, exercise facilities, TV lounges, and game rooms.

Students live and learn in a multicultural environment that prepares them to thrive in today's diverse world. International students representing nearly 100 countries make up a large percentage of the student body and bring valuable perspectives to the Bentley community.

Supporting Bentley's commitment to diversity are offices such as the Multicultural Center, Spiritual Life Center, Center for International Students and Scholars, Equity Center, Center for Women in Business, and the Women's Center.

The Student Center is the hub of campus activity and is home to Seasons Dining Room and more than 100 student organizations. These groups represent academics, the arts, media, fraternity and sorority life, and cultural interests.

Athletic programs are a Bentley hallmark and include intramurals, recreational sports, and more than 20 varsity teams in NCAA Divisions I and II. The Dana Athletic Center houses a weight and fitness complex, food court, locker rooms, a gym, a basketball court, volleyball and racquetball courts, a competition-size pool with a diving tank, and saunas. Outdoor facilities include soccer and baseball fields, a track, and tennis courts.

ADMISSIONS PROCESS

Bentley University accepts the Common Application. Candidates for the fall semester are notified by April 1; spring semester candidates are notified on a rolling basis.

Prospective students can visit bentley.edu/undergraduate/applying for application information and deadlines.

For more information, students should contact:

Office of Undergraduate Admission

Bentley University

175 Forest Street

Waltham, Massachusetts 02452-4705

Phone: 781.891.2244

800.523.2354 (toll-free)

Fax: 781.891.3414

E-mail: ugadmission@bentley.edu

Website: bentley.edu/undergraduate

facebook.com/bentleyadmission

twitter.com/bentleyu

BETHANY COLLEGE (WV)

AT A GLANCE

Bethany, a small college of national distinction, was founded March 2, 1840. For 175 years, Bethany College has been a highly contemporary institution based in the tradition of the liberal arts.

The college's program of classical liberal arts education prepares students for a lifetime of work and a life of significance. Teaching and learning form the mission of Bethany College. Central to this broad purpose is providing a liberal arts education for students, including the preparation of professionals, in an atmosphere of study, work, and service.

Bethany College is an academic community founded on the close interaction between students and faculty in the educational process. Bethany College values intellectual rigor and freedom, diversity of thought and lifestyle, personal growth within a community context, and responsible engagement with public issues.

All students pursuing a bachelor's degree must complete The Bethany Plan—a detailed academic and co-curricular program, focused on building skills employers seek, and grounded in the liberal arts. Bethany has achieved national distinction as one of the few institutions requiring a Senior Capstone Project and written and oral Senior Comprehensive Exams. For more information on the Bethany Plan, visit www.bethanywv.edu/bethany-plan.

Founded by Alexander Campbell, who provided the land and funds for the first building and served as the first president, Bethany has been a four-year private liberal arts college affiliated with the Christian Church (Disciples of Christ) since its inception. This religious body, of which Campbell was one of the principal founders, continues to support and encourage the college, but exercises no sectarian control. Students from virtually every religious community attend Bethany.

LOCATION AND ENVIRONMENT

Bethany's 1,300-acre campus is located only 39 miles from America's Most Livable City, Pittsburgh, and is a 40-minute drive from the Pittsburgh International Airport. Situated in the beautiful foothills of the Allegheny Mountains in the northern panhandle of West Virginia, Wheeling, West Virginia and Washington, Pennsylvania, are less than a half-hour away.

MAJORS AND DEGREES OFFERED

The college offers a wide array of studies, awarding Bachelor of Science, Bachelor of Arts, and Master of Arts in Teaching degrees. Students may choose from more than 25 departmental and 6 interdisciplinary majors, many with options for emphasis. Students also have the option of including one or more of 35 optional minors as part of their programs.

ACADEMIC PROGRAMS

Accounting

Biology

(with options for emphasis on Biology, Biochemistry, and Biology Education Grades 9-12)

Chemistry

(with options for emphasis on Professional Chemistry, Forensic Chemistry, Biochemistry, and Chemistry Education Grades 9-12)

Communications and Media Arts

(with options for emphasis on Digital Media and Production, Graphics, Integrated Media and Marketing, and Sports Communication)

Computer Science

Computer Science and Accounting (Dual Major)

Economics

(with options for emphasis on Managerial Economics and International Economics)

Economics and Mathematics (Dual Major)

Education

(Elementary Education; Middle Childhood Education through individual department programs in the areas of General Science, Language Arts, Mathematics, Physical Education, Social Studies, and Spanish; Secondary Education through individual department programs in the areas of Art, Biology, Chemistry, English, Mathematics, Physical Education, Psychology, Social Science, and Spanish; Education in a Non-School Setting)

English

(with options for emphasis on Creative Writing, Education, Literature, and Writing and Language)

Environmental Science (Interdisciplinary)

Equine Studies

(with options for Equine Management and Pre-Veterinary Medicine)

Finance

History

International Economics with study abroad (Interdisciplinary)

International Relations (Interdisciplinary)

Mathematics

(with options for emphasis on Mathematics, Mathematics-Economics, Mathematics-Physics, Mathematics-Computer Science, Mathematics-Actuarial Science, and Mathematics Education)

Music

Physical Education and Sports Studies

(with options for emphasis on Sports Management, Recreational and Athletic Programming, and Teaching Physical Education)

Pre-Engineering/Physical Science

Political Science

Psychology

(with options for emphasis on Scientific Psychology, Human Services, Pre-Physical Therapy, and Pre-Occupational Therapy)

Psychology and Education (Interdisciplinary)

Psychology and Social Work (Dual Major)

Religious Studies

Social Studies (Interdisciplinary)

Social Work

Spanish

Theatre

(with options for emphasis on Performance and Technical Theatre)

Visual Art

Pre-Professional Studies

Pre-Dentistry

Pre-Engineering

Pre-Law

Pre-Medical

Pre-Ministry

Pre-Physical Therapy

Pre-Veterinary

CAMPUS FACILITIES AND EQUIPMENT

The campus features rolling wooded hills and a lush, green academic mall. Facilities include beautiful historic landmarks, modern well-equipped classrooms, spacious sports/recreational areas, indoor and outdoor theaters, art galleries, an equestrian center, a teaching greenhouse and more. The college operates the Mountainside Conference Center, which includes Gresham Inn, and also the Campbell Mansion and Museum.

The 31,140 square-foot Mary Cutlip Center for Library and Information Services contains computers, collaborative learning spaces, and a multi-media area. Its holdings include more than 200,000 bound volumes, 50,000 electronic books, 2,000 periodical subscriptions, and nearly 100,000 microforms along with numerous online information resources. The library also contains two extensive special collections. The college is a partner in the Bowen Central Library of Appalachia, a widely acclaimed research library collaborative of the 36 Appalachian College Association institutions. Bethany is also one of seven colleges in three states participating in the Independent College Enterprise, a state-of-the-art collaborative addressing academic computing.

The Thomas Phillips Johnson Health and Recreation Center includes Hummel Fieldhouse (Nutting Gymnasium), three-court multi-use gymnasium (Sandwen Arena), Knight Natatorium (Olympic-size pool), two racquetball courts, a free-weight exercise fitness center with cardiovascular equipment, and an indoor jogging track. The Cummins Community Center is a state-of-the-art, 24-hour fitness center.

Outdoor Facilities: A multi-purpose stadium (Bison Stadium) with artificial turf and lights that primarily serves football, lacrosse, women's field hockey, and track and field, Hoag Soccer Field, John Cunningham Soccer Complex, equestrian center, 6 tennis courts, baseball and softball fields, football practice fields, and additional playing fields for intramural and club sports. The equestrian team trains at the Oglebay Stables.

More than 90 percent of students live in spacious on-campus apartments, residential halls or fraternity/sorority houses, which include Internet, cable TV and voice-mail access. Computer labs with Internet and library access, e-mail, digital media labs, rehearsal halls, research and language labs, The McCann Learning Center for academic support, and other amenities are provided.

TUITION, ROOM, BOARD AND FEES

The 2014–15 costs for resident students enrolled in the Fall 2014 semester were:

Tuition	$24,836
Fees	$900
Room and Board	$9,436 to $9,836 (depending on option)
Books and Supplies (est)	$1,200
Personal/Transportation (est)	$2,000
Total°	$38,372 (approximate)

° Total cost may vary depending on housing option.

FINANCIAL AID

Bethany College is committed to making a financial commitment to our students. If your desire is to receive a Bethany education, our financial aid office will do everything we can to make it affordable for you and your family.

The college awards scholarships based on academic performance, leadership capability and other academic factors.

Additionally, need-based aid is awarded to all eligible students in accordance with FAFSA results. Financial aid packages generally consist of loans, grants, scholarships and student employment.

STUDENT ORGANIZATIONS AND ACTIVITIES

Bethany's 22 varsity athletic teams (11 women's and 11 men's) compete in the NCAA Division III Presidents Athletic Conference (PAC) and the Eastern College Athletic Association (ECAC).

Bethany also offers more than 50 student organizations: scholastic and honorary, government, special interest and departmental.

The Stampede, Bethany College's Marching Band, made its debut during the 2013 fall semester.

Greek organizations include Phi Kappa Tau, Delta Tau Delta, Phi Mu, Alpha Xi Delta, Alpha Sigma Phi, Zeta Tau Alpha, Beta Theta Pi and Sigma Nu.

Student Clubs and Service/Philanthropic Organizations include:

Alpha Phi Omega, American Chemical Society (ACS), Amnesty International, Baseball Club, Bethanians for Life, Circle K, Collegiate Middle Level Association (CMLA), Drama Club, Economics and Business Club, Environmental Science Club, Equestrian Club, Film Club, Fire and Rescue Club, French Club, Gay Straight Alliance (GSA), German Club, International Relations Club, International Students Association (ISA), Japanese Club, Math and Computer Science Club (MCSC), Men's Lacrosse, National Broadcasting Society (NBS) (Alpha Epsilon Rho), Outdoors Club, Photography Club, Physical Education Club, Political Awareness Society, Psychology Club, Public Relations Student Society of America (PRSSA), Soccer Club, Social Awareness, Society of Physics Students (SPS), Society of Collegiate Journalists (SCJ), Softball Club, Spanish Club, Special Education Club, Student Activities Council (SAC), Student Art Guild, Student Athletic Advisory Committee (SAAC), Student Literacy Association, Student National Education Association (SNEA), Tri Beta, Writers Club

Campus Media include: Bethany Political Journal, Bethanian Yearbook, Folio Magazine, Harbinger, Tower Online, WTVX TV-3, WVBC Online

ADMISSIONS PROCESS

Bethany College specializes in a personalized admission process for each student. As a small college, our enrollment counselors evaluate each applicant individually—because of this, we are not limited by designated "cut-offs."

Enrollment Fast Facts

- Application Deadline: Rolling
- Interview Required: No, but strongly recommended
- SAT average: 1060
- ACT average: 23.2
- Average GPA: 3.30
- Enrollment Toll Free Number: (800) 922-7611
- Enrollment E-mail: enrollment@bethanywv.edu

BOSTON UNIVERSITY

AT A GLANCE

Is Boston University the right place for you? At BU, you'll be taught by Pulitzer Prize winners, Nobel Laureates, Fulbright Scholars, or a MacArthur Fellow. With an average class size of 27 students and a faculty-to-student ratio of 13:1, your professors will want to hear what you have to say. They're looking for students who embrace academic challenges. If hands-on research is what interests you, the Undergraduate Research Opportunities Program (UROP) offers hundreds of research opportunities across all areas of study. And if you're not sure what your academic interests are yet, BU offers more than 250 programs of study to choose from, and you don't have to declare a major until the end of your sophomore year. So you can take classes in subjects as varied as biology, broadcast journalism, business, computer engineering, elementary education, film, international relations, physical therapy, psychology, and theatre, just to name a few. Offering thousands of extracurricular activities and social opportunities, and surrounded by the exciting city of Boston, you'll never experience a dull moment as a student.

LOCATION AND ENVIRONMENT

No other city in the world can compete with Boston's remarkable concentration of history, higher education institutions, and culture. The city provides many opportunities for internship and research positions as well. The Undergraduate Research Opportunities Program (UROP) helps students locate research positions both within and beyond the university; BU's Center for Career Development works to provide students with the resources they need to get internships or part-time jobs in any number of fields. Boston is a world-class center for attractions including museums, libraries, baseball at Fenway Park, the Boston Symphony Orchestra, and a thriving theater district. In fact, students make up 20 percent of Boston's population during the academic year.

OFF-CAMPUS OPPORTUNITIES

Boston University has one of the world's most extensive study abroad programs. Among the University's 100+ programs are language and liberal arts programs; programs that combine studies with internships; fieldwork programs for students wishing to pursue academic or scientific research; and summer programs. Programs are available in Argentina, Australia, Belgium, China, Denmark, Ecuador, England, France, Germany, Guatemala, Ireland, Israel, Italy, Japan, Lebanon, Morocco, New Zealand, Peru, Singapore, South Korea, Spain, Switzerland, and Turkey. There are also programs available in Washington, D.C. And Los Angeles.

MAJORS AND DEGREES OFFERED

The university awards the BA, BS, BSBA, BLS, MusB, and BFA undergraduate degrees. Ten of Boston University's 17 colleges and schools have undergraduate programs. The listing below shows the wide variety of study options available to undergraduates.

College of Arts & Sciences students may pursue degrees in American studies; Ancient Greek; Ancient Greek and Latin; anthropology; anthropology and religion; archaeology; architectural studies; astronomy; astronomy and physics; biochemistry and molecular biology; biology; biology with a specialization in behavioral biology; biology with a specialization in cell biology, molecular biology, and genetics; biology with a specialization in ecology and conservation; biology with a specialization in neurobiology; biology with a specialization in quantitative biology; chemistry; chemistry: biochemistry; chemistry: teaching; Chinese language and literature; cinema and media studies (also offered in the college of Communication); classical civilization; classics and philosophy; classics and religion; comparative literature; computer science; earth sciences; economics; economics and mathematics; English; environmental analysis and policy; environmental science; French and linguistics; French studies; geography with specialization in human geography; geography with specialization in physical geography; geophysics and planetary sciences; German language and literature; Hispanic language and literatures; history; history of art and architecture; Italian and linguistics; Italian studies; Japanese and linguistics; Japanese language and literature; Latin; linguistics; linguistics and philosophy; marine science; mathematics (includes statistics); mathematics and computer science; mathematics and mathematics education; mathematics and philosophy; music (nonperformance); neuroscience; philosophy; philosophy and physics; philosophy and political science; philosophy and psychology; philosophy and religion; physics;

political science; psychology; religion; Russian language and literature; sociology; and Spanish and linguistics. Special curricula are also available, including the Boston University Dual Degree program (allowing you to earn two degrees), seven-year Accelerated Medical and Accelerated Dental programs, the Modular Medical Integrated Curriculum (MMEDIC), and a variety of combined BA/MA degree programs. Pre-medical, pre-veterinary, and pre-dental studies are supported through the college of Arts & Sciences with nearly any major.

Through the college of Communication, students can pursue majors in cinema and media studies (also offered in the college of Arts & Sciences); communication (includes advertising, public relations and communication), film and television (includes production, writing and management), and journalism (includes news-editorial, broadcast, magazine, online, and photojournalism).

At the college of Engineering, students may choose from programs in biomedical, computer, electrical, mechanical, mechanical with specialization in aerospace, and mechanical with specialization in manufacturing engineering. Cutting-edge minors in nano-technology, energy technologies, and technology innovation are also offered.

At the college of Fine Arts, students may pursue studies in the School of Music (composition theory, music education, musicology, and performance), the School of Theatre (conservatory-style acting, theatre arts, design, stage management, production), and the School of Visual Arts (art education, graphic design, painting, printmaking and sculpture). There is also a five-year, BFA/BA Double Degree program which allows students to earn degrees simultaneously in the college of Fine Arts and the college of Arts & Sciences.

The College of General Studies offers a two-year, general education program centered on an interdisciplinary curriculum. The program is designed for students to continue their studies in one of the university's degree-granting schools and colleges in their junior year. CGS also offers the January Boston-London Program, which offers students an interdisciplinary and global curriculum for their freshman year beginning in the spring semester and ending with a summer term abroad in London.

At the college of Health & Rehabilitation Sciences: Sargent College, students may pursue concentrations in athletic training; behavior and health; health science; human physiology; nutrition; and speech, language, and hearing sciences. Also available are six-year combined programs in physical therapy (BS/DPT) and athletic training/physical therapy (AD/DPT) (not open to transfer students).

The Frederick S. Pardee School of Global Studies is dedicated to education, research, and initiatives that aim to produce global leaders. Consisting of two divisions—international studies and regional studies—the School offers programs in Asian studies, European studies, international relations, Latin American studies, and Middle East and North Africa studies.

The School of Education allows students to pursue deaf studies, early childhood education, elementary education, English education, mathematics education, modern foreign languages education, science education, social studies education, and special education. There is also a five-year Double Degree Program which allows students to earn degrees simultaneously in the School of Education and the college of Arts & Sciences.

The School of Hospitality Administration's intense curriculum trains students in the business management of hotels, restaurants, food and beverage service, travel and tourism, and entertainment.

The Questrom School of Business allows students to pursue concentrations in accounting, entrepreneurship, finance, general management, international management, business law, management information systems, marketing, operations and technology management, and organizational behavior.

ACADEMIC PROGRAMS

Boston University is committed to providing outstanding instruction, combining a strong liberal arts program with superior preparation for the professional job market. The Kilachand Honors College provides exceptional students with an innovative interdisciplinary curriculum. Outstanding sophomores in the School of Management are invited to apply to participate in an honors program that offers specialized colloquia and seminars.

CAMPUS FACILITIES AND EQUIPMENT

Boston University's academic and athletic facilities are some of the best in the country. The Engineering Product Innovation Center (EPIC) is home to teaching space, a full carpentry and machine shop, a metals foundry, and laboratories; while the Photonics Center houses state-of-the-art laboratories devoted to developing new light-based technologies. The Student Village provides first-rate recreation, athletics, high-rise apartments, and dining. The Village includes the Fitness and Recreation Center and Agganis Arena, offering space for University sporting events as well as concerts and family shows. The University also offers the Yawkey Center for Student Services, which houses the Center for Career Development, Educational Resource Center, Pre-Professional Advising Offices, and Marciano Commons, a two-story dining hall.

TUITION, ROOM, BOARD AND FEES

Tuition for the 2014–2015 academic year is $45,686; standard room and board is $14,030. Additional mandatory fees are $978. Allowances for the cost of books, supplies, travel, and other incidental expenses brings the total cost of attendance for a student to $63,644.

FINANCIAL AID

Boston University Financial Assistance offers a wide variety of financial assistance programs and provides resources to help inform students and their families about payment strategies and financing options. Merit and scholarship awards, need-based scholarships, loans, student employment, and a payment plan are all offered.

Because Boston University believes scholars should be encouraged and recognized for their efforts, the University is committed to offering a variety of scholarships to selected freshmen. University need-based scholarships are offered based on several factors, including calculated financial eligibility, academic achievement, and the availability of funds for a student's program of study. While every effort is made to assist students with limited resources, the university does not have sufficient funds to offer a grant award to every admitted student who has calculated financial eligibility. Those who present the strongest academic credentials are most likely to be offered grant or scholarship aid.

STUDENT ORGANIZATIONS AND ACTIVITIES

Boston University students are extremely engaged, participating in academic clubs, cultural or religious organizations, and community service groups. There are more than 450 student organizations and more than 50 intramural and club sports that students can participate in. You can get involved with organizations such as Alianza Latina, Holistic Yoga Society, BU Habitat for Humanity, the Debate Society, or the Alpine Ski Team. A separate student government exists at each school and college to manage student affairs, and the Student Union includes members who represent all schools and colleges within the university.

ADMISSIONS PROCESS

The Board of Admissions evaluates each prospective student individually. The Board's main focus centers on the merits of a student's high school record, but required standardized test scores (SAT and ACT Plus Writing), personal qualities and integrity, interests, teacher and counselor references, and other relevant attributes are also considered carefully. All candidates must have graduated from high school or earned an equivalency diploma to be considered. For admission to the college of Fine Arts, students must either audition or submit a portfolio (some programs also require pre-screening). A few select programs require interviews.

Students should visit www.bu.edu/admissions for additional information. Boston University also considers students with transferable credit from other institutions for admission. Boston University considers applicants for September or January admission, depending on the program of interest.

Boston University offers early decision (which is a binding agreement) and regular decision programs. All applications for early decision must be submitted by November 1 and applications for regular decision must be submitted by January 1. Accelerated program applications must be submitted by November 15. Nominations and/or applications for admission to qualify for the Presidential or Trustee Scholarships must be submitted by December 1.

Transfer students seeking January admission must submit their application forms by November 1. Those seeking September admission must submit their application forms by March 1.

Transfer students cannot be admitted to the Accelerated Liberal Arts Medical or Dental Programs; or the six-year, combined AT/DPT and DPT programs in the college of Health & Rehabilitation Sciences: Sargent College. Transfer students may not apply for January admission to the School of Theatre in the college of Fine Arts. They also cannot apply as "undeclared" to any school or college.

Boston University accepts qualified applicants regardless of age, color, disability, national origin, race, religion, sexual orientation, or gender to all of its activities and programs.

BRYANT UNIVERSITY

AT A GLANCE

Bryant delivers an exceptional education for success in an age of unlimited global opportunity. The undergraduate curriculum is nationally recognized for innovation.

From the very first semester, you'll find that Bryant's interdisciplinary studies and engaged learning are designed with your success in mind.

Bryant faculty are "good at teaching, but even better at providing real working knowledge," according to the Princeton Review.

Our world-class professors integrate theoretical and applied concepts in a broad range of majors from accounting to sociology, all complemented by rich co-curricular opportunities.

A Bryant education speaks for itself—98% of our students are employed or enrolled in graduate school within six months of Commencement.

ACADEMICS & MAJORS

Bryant's student-centered learning community will inspire you to discover your passion and create your own path as you develop the knowledge, skills, credentials, and qualities of character to become an active contributor who thinks in a global context.

Uniquely dedicated to the integration of business and the liberal arts, and committed to an educational experience that blends knowledge and practice, Bryant students choose from nearly 100 courses of study.

STUDENT BODY

Who is a Bryant student? He/she is hard working, motivated, and driven to succeed. Willing to go the extra mile, Bryant students apply what they learn in the classroom to real-world situations through internships, practicums, and service-learning projects. Hailing from 63 countries and 32 states, the diverse student body enhances Bryant's international focus.

From attending a Bulldogs football game to practicing for a business competition, Bryant students participate in more than 100 organizations and clubs. Eighty-one percent of Bryant undergraduates reside on campus to take advantage of the 24/7 experiential learning opportunities.

CAMPUS/FACILITIES

Our stunning, 435-acre campus in Smithfield, Rhode Island, is just 15 minutes from downtown Providence, an hour from Boston, and three hours from New York City.

Our strategic location provides students with exciting internship and employment opportunities within driving distance, including the headquarters of multinational corporations, such as CVS and Hasbro, small businesses, and tech startups.

Bryant has invested $244 million in its facilities since 1996. This winter, Bryant unveiled the brand new School of Health Sciences and the debut of the physician assistant program, which marks Bryant's strategic and significant entry into healthcare education and training. Building on the University's nationally recognized programs in business, these initiatives are expected to include healthcare management and healthcare policy, in addition to clinical programs.

TUITION AND AID

- Tuition, 2015–2016: $39,421

*Includes a new laptop

- Room and board: $14,163

- Student activity fee: $387

The value of a Bryant education is measured in the academic, professional, cultural, and personal growth opportunities available to help you create your path, expand your world, and achieve success.

However, we understand that financing your education is a vital part of the decision about which college you will attend. To help ease that financial burden, Bryant University awarded more than $13.9 million in grants and merit scholarships to incoming students in 2014–2015.

VISITING AND CONTACT INFORMATION

Visit Bryant to experience what it is like to live and learn in our close-knit, friendly community. You might even run into our mascot, Tupper the Bulldog, who often appears at football games and visits with students during class breaks in the main lobby.

According to Barron's Best Buys in College Education, "At Bryant University, 12 miles outside Providence, Rhode Island, seeing is believing...."

Contact:

Bryant University

(800) 622-7002

admission@bryant.edu

www.admission.bryant.edu

BUCKNELL UNIVERSITY

At Bucknell, you will connect with your professors who are mentors and innovators in their fields, engage critically with diverse perspectives, learn to write well, present your ideas and apply what you learn. We offer more than 50 majors and 65 minors in the arts, engineering, humanities, management, sciences and social sciences. Each department will ask you to be part of our thriving intellectual community that uses knowledge, ideas and skills from a liberal arts perspective to help you take the lead in a successful future.

AT A GLANCE

Established in 1846, Bucknell is highly selective, private, nonsectarian, coeducational (since 1883), residential and undergraduate, with a small graduate program.

- 93% of first-year students return as sophomores

- 89% of our students graduate within four years—a rate well above the national average

- All of our classes are taught by faculty

- Our student-faculty ratio is 9:1

LOCATION AND ENVIRONMENT

With its green spaces, red brick buildings and striking vistas, Bucknell's 450-acre campus is a quintessential college environment in the heart of scenic central Pennsylvania. The shops of historic downtown Lewisburg—including Barnes & Noble at Bucknell University and the historic Campus Theatre—lie within walking distance of campus. The University is located within three to four hours by car of New York City, Baltimore, Washington, D.C., Philadelphia and Pittsburgh. For more information about Bucknell's location, see bucknell.edu/visit.

OFF-CAMPUS OPPORTUNITIES

Bucknell is a residential university, so most students live on campus, but learning, service, research and recreation extend off campus. You will have the opportunity to volunteer as close as the local nursing home, community center and sustainable farm and as far away as New Orleans and Uganda. Every year, students also travel off campus to conduct research with faculty mentors. Destinations have included Alaska, Suriname, Australia and the Sudan.

More than 45 percent of students spend a summer, semester, or year abroad through one of the university's own "in" programs or 160 other approved programs in Africa, Asia, Australia, the Caribbean, Europe and South America.

At Bucknell, you'll take advantage of career services such as advising, networking, mock interviews, internship support and employer fairs. You can explore your career options and network with alumni through summer internships with corporations, government organizations and non-profits locally, nationally and internationally. An externship program provides job-shadowing opportunities for sophomores. And all that work will pay off. The career placement rate for recent Bucknell graduates is consistently high: 97% of the Class of 2014 was employed, in graduate school, both employed and in graduate school, volunteering or engaged in another activity within nine months of graduation.

MAJORS AND DEGREES OFFERED

You can choose from more than 50 majors and 65 minors at Bucknell. Students build robots, write and perform in their own plays and debate solutions to global issues. Engineers can make art, artists can analyze DNA and philosophers can make music. You will choose your own pathway, but what unites everyone is a shared enthusiasm for learning and a desire to achieve deeper levels of understanding about life and the world.

The College of Arts & Sciences offers bachelor's degrees in science, arts, music and education. Master's degrees are available in select disciplines.

The School of Management, accredited by the Association to Advance Collegiate Schools of Business (AACSB), offers bachelor of science degrees in business administration with four majors: accounting and financial management; global management; managing for sustainability; and markets, innovation and design.

The College of Engineering offers a bachelor of science degree in eight majors, a five-year dual degree in engineering and management, a five-year dual degree in engineering and the liberal arts, and a five-year combined bachelor's and master's degree. As one of a select group of private colleges and universities admitted to the Kern Entrepreneurship Education Network, Bucknell offers its engineers even more resources to build entrepreneurial spirit and become technical leaders.

For details about any academic program, see bucknell.edu/catalog.

ACADEMIC PROGRAMS

Your Bucknell professors will inspire you with their passion for the material and their depth of knowledge. Our student-faculty ratio is 9:1, which means you will find that they take the time to get to know you personally and provide help and advice—and not just in class. These accomplished scholars will involve you in their research and creative projects. All you need to do is seek the opportunity.

In addition to our faculty, you will be able to experience hearing from visiting scholars and speakers regularly. Recent visitors include astrophysicist Neil deGrasse Tyson; U.S. Poet Laureate and Pulitzer Prize winner Rita Dove; founder of the Harvard Stem Cell Institute, Dr. David Scadden; and author Neil Gaiman.

Distinctive programs that complement the curriculum include, but are not limited to:

- Residential Colleges—bucknell.edu/ResColleges

  o Theme-based living and learning environments that combine classroom learning with the residential experience

  o Themes: Arts, Discovery, Environmental, Global, Humanities, Languages and Cultures, Social Justice, Society and Technology

  o Participating first-year students take a class together and join in programs and social activities that complement their classroom learning

- Bucknell University Center for Sustainability and the Environment—bucknell. edu/EnvironmentalCenter

  o Faculty, staff, and students collaborate on environmental and nature-related learning, teaching, scholarship and service

  o Initiatives: Place Studies, Sustainable Design, Marcellus Shale, Watershed Sciences and Engineering

- Civic Engagement—bucknell.edu/CivicEngagement

  o Educational experiences link academic course work with efforts to meet a community need

  o Opportunities include Bucknell Brigade to Nicaragua, Katrina Recovery Trips, Alternative Spring Break trips, tutoring in local schools and international service

- Institute for Leadership in Technology and Management—bucknell.edu/ILTM

  o This two-summer program bridges the disciplines of engineering and management for select students in engineering, management and the liberal arts

CAMPUS FACILITIES AND EQUIPMENT

Bucknell's 450-acre tree-lined campus contains state-of-the-art facilities for performing arts, poetry, science, engineering, athletics and more, all accessible to undergraduates.

Bertrand Library holds nearly 860,000 volumes, providing you access to books, maps, journals (both electronic and print) and nearly 300 databases and offers a video editing lab, thousands of audiovisual materials and multimedia equipment. Computer labs are available across campus, and there are more than 900 wireless access points spread out across campus to ensure almost complete wireless coverage no matter where you go. There are more than 900 classroom and lab computers on campus and all student residences are connected to the residential network, which features a high-speed data connection and digital television programming for each student. Science and engineering programs offer sophisticated instrumentation available for student use, including a structural testing lab, an atomic force microscope and a nuclear magnetic resonance spectrometer.

TUITION, ROOM, BOARD, AND FEES

For the 2015–16 academic year, tuition and fees are set at:

Tuition and fees: $50,152

Room and Board: $12,216

FINANCIAL AID

Bucknell's Office of Financial Aid is here to help you—through advice and through financial aid if you qualify. We offer a range of financial aid options, including need-based grants and scholarships, limited academic and arts merit scholarships, loans and student employment. We consider each family's financial circumstances on an individual basis and if your circumstances remain relatively constant from year to year, you apply by the deadline, and you maintain satisfactory academic progress, we will award you need-based aid at about the same level each year.

• About 50 percent of students receive financial aid from Bucknell, and 62 percent receive financial aid of some form.

• The average financial aid award for first-year students with financial need in the fall of 2013 was about $30,000, including scholarships, loans and work-study.

• The average loan total upon graduation is about $22,500.

• With its unique combination of professional programs and the liberal arts, Bucknell offers an education that provides lifelong personal and career benefits. Consider it an investment worth making.

Important Note: If you are applying for Bucknell University financial aid, you must submit your CSS PROFILE by November 15 for Early Decision I and January 15 for Early Decision II and Regular Decision applications. To apply for federal financial aid, complete the Free Application for Federal Student Aid (FAFSA).

STUDENT ORGANIZATIONS AND ACTIVITIES

Bucknell's social environment will inspire you and expand your learning. You'll join with active students whose voices are valued in student government and in shaping the University community. Take advantage of speaker series, arts performances and scholarly lectures on campus. Become a member or leader of a student-run organization. From participating in the arts, honor societies, cultural, political or religious organizations, to exploring the outdoors, you'll find your niche. You can compete in and support Division I athletics as well as intramural and club sports and be active in our state-of-the-art fitness center. More than half of sophomores, juniors and seniors participate in fraternity and sorority life, and students frequently volunteer in the local community or on one of our many national and international service trip opportunities.

ADMISSIONS PROCESS

Bucknell is looking for you to have high academic achievement and leadership or creative skills, a sense of commitment to your community and a desire to achieve broad learning throughout your life. Grades, test scores and recommendations are extremely important, but we also look for students who are daring, who show us they'll cultivate their interests outside the classroom and contribute to the world in thoughtful, bold and compassionate ways.

We hope you'll be able to visit campus to determine whether Bucknell is a good fit. View visit options at bucknell.edu/visit. Get in touch with us at admissions@bucknell.edu if you have any questions.

To apply for admission, fill out and submit the Common Application at commonapp.org. Early Decision students should also complete an Early Decision Form.

DEADLINES

• For students seeking to begin college in the fall, Regular Decision applications should be filed before January 15 for notification by April 1.

• SAT and/or ACT results must be submitted before March 1.

• Early Decision candidates may apply for Early Decision I consideration by November 15 or Early Decision II consideration by January 15.

• Transfer student information is available on our website at bucknell.edu/admissions/transfer-admissions. Applications for transfer students should be submitted by March 15 for studies beginning the following fall and by November 1 for the spring semester.

To request application information by mail, please call 570-577-3000.

For detailed information about admissions at Bucknell, go to bucknell.edu/admissions.

CALIFORNIA COLLEGE OF THE ARTS

AT A GLANCE

California College of the Arts. Empowering students to make art that matters.

California College of the Arts (CCA), founded in 1907, offers studies in 22 undergraduate and 14 graduate majors in the areas of fine arts, architecture, design, and writing. The college has world-class facilities at its two campuses in San Francisco and Oakland. Nearly 500 highly regarded artists and scholars instruct a population of approximately 1,500 undergraduate and 450 graduate students. The average class size is 14.

Students at CCA discover cross-disciplinary opportunities, innovative courses with real-world applications, and outstanding faculty. Wherever their art takes them— producing an experimental film, painting outside the canvas, designing sustainable products, or working in the community—CCA offers an ideal environment to make it happen. Students develop competencies that will serve them well, both while they are in school and long after they graduate. Our alumni have been successful in all kinds of creative endeavors, and students have intimate access to this valuable network while they are at CCA and after graduation.

CCA prepares students to build a successful creative life. Our faculty, visiting artists, and industry partners guide students through critiquing and mentoring, and our Office of Career Development provides many career-building opportunities. We are proud to report that 78 percent of our alumni are actively working in fields related to art, architecture, design, or writing, and 76 percent of our graduates were employed full time six months after graduation.

LOCATION AND ENVIRONMENT

CCA is located in the San Francisco Bay Area, near Silicon Valley and tech giants such as Google, Yahoo, Facebook, and Twitter. The region is known for creative and technological innovation, environmental leadership, and thriving art and design communities. It is home to first-rate museums and alternative gallery spaces as well as active scenes in theater, music, dance, film, and literature. Close by are beaches, hiking and biking trails, the Napa Valley, Mendocino, Monterey, Lake Tahoe, the Sierra Nevada mountains, and Yosemite National Park.

CCA's Oakland campus occupies four acres in the residential Rockridge neighborhood, three miles from UC Berkeley. The San Francisco campus spans a city block in Potrero Hill, near Mission Bay and the design district. Both campuses are easily accessible via bus and train. CCA also operates a free shuttle between its campuses.

OPPORTUNITIES

Artist talks, lectures, and other special events take place on both campuses almost every day.

Internships (required by some programs, and encouraged by all) allow students to gain practical experience and make professional connections while they earn academic credit.

CCA's Center for Art and Public Life organizes a wide range of programs that put students into direct contact with the diverse communities of the Bay Area and beyond.

Sponsored studio courses, offered throughout the year, enable students to work directly with professional practitioners from globally distinguished firms such as Gensler, Intel, and IDEO.

Through the International Exchange Program, students may spend a semester at one of more than 30 colleges of art and design around the globe. CCA also offers summer study-abroad courses.

Qualified upper-division students may spend a semester at one of 32 other art schools throughout the United States through the Association of Independent Colleges of Art and Design (AICAD). Students may cross-register at Mills College or Holy Names University, both in Oakland.

The CCA Wattis Institute for Contemporary Arts, housed near the San Francisco campus, presents several exhibitions every year featuring internationally prominent contemporary artists.

MAJORS AND DEGREES OFFERED

CCA offers the bachelor of fine arts (BFA) degree in Animation, Ceramics, Community Arts, Fashion Design, Film, Furniture, Glass, Graphic Design, Illustration, Industrial Design, Interaction Design, Interior Design, Jewelry / Metal Arts, Painting/Drawing, Photography, Printmaking, Sculpture, and Textiles. The college offers the bachelor of arts (BA) degree in Writing and Literature and in Visual Studies. In addition, CCA offers a bachelor of architecture (BArch) degree, a five-year program. Students may also formulate an Individualized Major (BFA) in collaboration with an advisor.

CCA offers the master of architecture (MArch) and the master of advanced architectural design (MAAD) degrees; the master of business administration (MBA) in Design Strategy, Civic Innovation, and Strategic Foresight; the master of fine arts (MFA) in Comics, Design, Film, Fine Arts, and Writing; the master of design (MDes) in Interaction Design; and the master of arts (MA) in Social Practice, Curatorial Practice, and Visual and Critical Studies. There are also several dual-degree options for graduate students.

ACADEMIC PROGRAMS

CCA's curriculum emphasizes interdisciplinarity, community engagement, and professional practice. Undergraduates begin with a core curriculum that introduces a variety of artistic media, principles, and processes as well as humanities courses in writing, literature, art history, and critical theory.

The college runs on a two-semester academic calendar with a six-week summer session. Summer programs include the Pre-College Program for high school students (participants earn college credit). Various summer art and design programs that emphasize English skills are available to international students entering in the fall. Extension courses are offered throughout the year.

FACILITIES AND EQUIPMENT

CCA offers outstanding facilities for making art, with over 20 instructional computer, classroom, and large-format color output labs. The labs have Mac computers and a complete range of software to support the creative arts, design, and architecture. Each campus is equipped with wireless access and media centers with equipment for checkout by students.

OAKLAND CAMPUS

The Oakland campus is home to the First Year Program and the programs in Animation, Ceramics, Community Arts, Glass, Jewelry / Metal Arts, Photography, Printmaking, Sculpture, Textiles, Visual Studies, and Writing and Literature. (Painting/Drawing courses are held on both campuses.)

Animation students have dedicated studios and equipment for digital video, film, and sound production. Ceramics facilities include numerous gas and electric kilns. Sculpture facilities include a bronze foundry, a wax-working area, a plaster and mold-making room, a metal fabrication studio, and a woodworking shop. Textiles facilities include a weaving studio with a digital Jacquard TC-1 loom, print studio, dye lab, fiber sculpture studio, and computer lab. For printmaking there are lithography presses, a 40 x 60 American French Tool etching press, a silkscreening and papermaking complex, and a letterpress lab with Vandercook presses and a polymer plate maker. The photography center supports both analog and digital processes.

SAN FRANCISCO CAMPUS

The San Francisco campus houses the programs in Architecture, Fashion Design, Film, Furniture, Graphic Design, Illustration, Industrial Design, Interaction Design, Interior Design, and Painting/Drawing as well as all of the graduate programs.

To support these programs, the San Francisco campus provides a diverse range of making spaces across design, craft, and technology. These areas include rapid prototyping, 3D printing, laser cutting and CNC studios; model-making and alternative material studios; woodworking studios; welding and metalworking studios; casting, spray painting, and airbrush studios; plaster, cement, and work studios, and a Hybrid lab that explores high-tech, robotics, physical computing, and programming in design. There is also a full digital production facility and stage and several large painting/drawing studios. The MFA Program in Writing has its own building.

LIBRARIES

CCA libraries—one on each campus and a Materials Library on the San Francisco campus—specialize in art and design. The collections include 90,000 volumes representing 65,000 titles, more than 200 print periodical subscriptions, nearly 2,000 full-text online periodicals, more than 3,000 audiovisual titles, and nearly 25,000 digital resources in VAULT (CCA's institutional repository). Special collections include the Small Press Traffic collection, Capp Street Project archives, Sinel collection, Hamaguchi print collection, an artist's book collection, and the CCA/C archives. The Materials Library contains over 600 circulating material samples and is one of very few such libraries at an educational institution.

GALLERIES

The college has several dedicated on-campus spaces for exhibitions of student work, and individual departments and courses frequently present off-campus shows of student work. Many of these exhibitions are organized by the students themselves, giving them valuable hands-on gallery experience. Student exhibitions on both campuses change weekly.

TUITION, ROOM, BOARD, AND FEES

Tuition for the 2015–16 academic year is $43,248 for full-time undergraduate students and $1,802 per unit for part-time students. Tuition is the same for California and out-of-state residents. Campus housing costs an additional $9,050. Total costs for 2015–16 are approximately $60,558 per year, which includes $43,708 in tuition and fees, $11,900 for room and board, $1,500 for books and supplies, and $3,450 for miscellaneous expenses.

FINANCIAL AID

In 2013–14, 73 percent of CCA students received financial aid from some source. Approximately 70 percent of CCA students received CCA scholarship assistance. The college offers financial aid in the form of scholarships, grants, loans, and work-study programs. There are both need-based and merit-based awards. For an estimate of your scholarship and financial aid, see the net price calculator at cca.edu/calculator.

Students applying for merit scholarships must complete their admission application by February 1. Students applying for financial assistance should submit the Free Application for Federal Student Aid (FAFSA) by March 1. CCA will continue to award aid to applicants after March 1 as funding permits. Students can apply for Federal Pell Grants and Federal Direct Loans throughout the year. CCA is approved for veterans who wish to attend under the Veterans Administration Educational Benefits Program. In addition to financial aid awards, CCA offers an interest-free payment plan.

STUDENT ORGANIZATIONS AND ACTIVITIES

At CCA, education takes place both inside and outside the classroom. About 80 percent of first-year students live on campus. Throughout the year, the residential-life staff hosts social and educational programs ranging from movie nights and barbecues to museum trips and professional lectures.

Students are encouraged to join existing clubs and organizations or to form new ones. Clubs and activities range in focus from community building to politics to physical fitness. Students may also become involved in student government. The Student Council sponsors a variety of activities throughout the year, including dinners, films, and shuttles to San Francisco galleries.

Our students are active in many pre-professional groups that are affiliated with corresponding Bay Area professional chapters: American Institute of Architecture Students (AIAS), American Institute of Graphic Arts (AIGA), Industrial Designers Society of America (IDSA), and International Interior Design Association (IIDA).

Student services include counseling, tutoring, advising, career development, health and wellness, disability and access services, fitness classes, stress relief, and safety workshops. There are many services specifically for international students, including dedicated staff, special workshops, social events, and exhibitions.

ADMISSIONS PROCESS

Applications are reviewed on an individualized basis, taking into account academic achievements, creative abilities, individual achievements and activities, a personal essay, recommendations, and a portfolio. Undergraduate applicants must have a high school diploma or the equivalent. First-year applicants should follow a college preparatory program in high school, including courses in studio art and art history whenever possible. CCA does not have specific transfer course requirements, but to learn how to maximize your number of transferable units visit cca.edu/transfer-credit.

Undergraduates interested in applying for merit scholarships should submit their applications by February 1. The priority deadline for all other undergraduate applicants is March 1. The priority deadline for spring undergraduate applicants is October 1. Students who meet the priority deadlines receive first consideration for housing, financial aid, and course selection. Admissions decisions are made on a rolling basis; this means that applications are reviewed in the order they are received. The nonrefundable application fee is $60. It is possible to register for courses as a non-degree student (on a space-available basis).

Schedule a campus visit, request information, and apply online at cca.edu/admissions. For additional information please contact:

Office of Enrollment Services

California College of the Arts

1111 Eighth Street

San Francisco CA 94107-2247

800.447.1ART

cca.edu

enroll@cca.edu

CENTRAL CONNECTICUT STATE UNIVERSITY

AT A GLANCE

Central Connecticut State University (CCSU) is a comprehensive public university dedicated to learning in the liberal arts and sciences and to education for the professions. Comprising five schools—Carol Ammon College of Liberal Arts & Social Sciences; Business; Education & Professional Studies; Engineering, Science & Technology; and Graduate Studies—CCSU offers full- and part-time undergraduate programs in more than 100 areas of study.

Conveniently located in New Britain, CCSU's innovative undergraduate curriculum inspires student learning in a wide range of fields, while extensive internship and co-op opportunities help students prepare for rewarding careers. The University's Division I athletics teams provide exciting opportunities to play or watch.

LOCATION AND ENVIRONMENT

CCSU is located in suburban New Britain, conveniently located in the center of Connecticut, approximately 2 hours from Boston or New York. The campus has been recently renovated. The University is surrounded by a pleasant neighborhood, with shopping and dining facilities nearby.

OFF-CAMPUS OPPORTUNITIES

CCSU's Center for Advising and Career Exploration coordinates a comprehensive Co-op Education Program as well as internships at local and area corporations, agencies, and government offices. Annual career fairs bring some 200 area and regional businesses to campus. CCSU Co-op students annually earn $4 million, and more than 65% are offered full-time career starting jobs with their Co-op employers.

The School of Education has many connections to area schools, including several Professional Development Schools, which provide CCSU students nearly unique opportunities to perfect their teaching skills in a full range of elementary and secondary classrooms.

The School of Engineering, Science & Technology offers a wide array of internship opportunities in engineering, construction, manufacturing, and technology businesses.

The Center for International Education, nationally recognized for the quality of its Study Abroad programs, offers students a rich variety of study-abroad opportunities at more than 40 locations throughout the world and provides academic and cultural programs that promote a better understanding of peoples and cultures.

And the University and the New Britain Museum of American Art (an internationally acclaimed museum) have a partnership allowing students and faculty to visit the museum for free.

MAJORS AND DEGREES OFFERED

CCSU is accredited by the New England Association of Schools and Colleges (NEASC). The University operates on a two-semester calendar and offers four summer sessions plus one winter session. Undergraduate programs include: Accounting; Anthropology; Art (Art History); Athletic Training; Biochemistry; Biology (Ecology; Biodiversity; Evolutionary; Environmental Science; General); Biomolecular Sciences; Chemistry; Civil Engineering; Civil Engineering Technology; Communication (Broadcast Journalism; Media Studies; Organizational Communications; Promotion/Public Relations); Computer Engineering Technology; Computer Science; Construction Management; Criminology; Design (Graphic/Information); Digital Printing Graphics Technology; Earth Sciences; Economics (General; Operations Research); Education (Elementary; K-12; Secondary; Special Education); Electronics Technology; Engineering &Technology Education; Engineering Technology; English; Entrepreneurship; Exercise Science; Finance; French; Geography (Environmental; General Regional; Planning; Geographic Information Science; Tourism); German; History; Hospitality & Tourism; Industrial Technology; Interdisciplinary Science (Environmental Interpretation; Physical Sciences); International Business; International Studies; Italian; Journalism; Management (Entrepreneurship; Human Resource); Management Information Systems; Manufacturing Engineering Technology; Marketing; Mathematics (Actuarial; Statistics); Mechanical Engineering; Mechanical Engineering Technology; Music; Nursing (BSN & RN to BSN); Philosophy; Physical Education (Exercise Science & Health Promotion); Physics; Political Science (General; Public Administration); Psychologal Science; Robotics & Mechatronics Engineering Technology; Social Sciences; Social Work; Sociology; Spanish; Theatre.

Degrees: BA, BFA (Theatre); BS; BSN; BS-RN, Teacher Certification (elementary; secondary; k-12)

ACADEMIC PROGRAMS

CCSU also offers a number of interdisciplinary programs as well as independently designed majors. The Honors Program, a challenging interdisciplinary program of study for academically qualified students, offers half- and full-tuition merit scholarships and a variety of other benefits and resources, including a new Honors Lab.

CAMPUS FACILITIES AND EQUIPMENT

CCSU offers an attractive campus with new and renovated buildings adding to the classic collegiate style of its architecture. The academic buildings feature technologically state-of-the-art "smart classrooms" and seminar rooms, and the entire campus offers wireless access. The Student Center provides lounges, dining services, conference and game rooms, information services, and a range of other support services. Three theatres offer space for plays, concerts, and guest lectures. The S.T. Chen Art Gallery hosts shows by student, faculty, and visiting artists. The Student Technology Center features 250 computers plus printers and scanners for student use. Campus-based TV and radio stations provide exciting entertainment as well as opportunities to learn about the professions. The Elihu Burritt Library provides access to over 2 million books through an online catalog, a wide array of electronic databases and online resources, and special collections ranging from the unparalleled collection of Polish American materials to the Equity Archive. The University also offers many new athletic facilities, including an Olympic-sized swimming pool, modern exercise equipment, a state-of-the-art fitness center, a weight-training room, and an athletic training center. In the Kaiser Annex students can walk, jog, and play tennis or a pickup basketball game. CCSU recently opened new football, soccer, softball, and baseball fields to complement its basketball and volleyball arena. The residence halls and classrooms are fully networked. Approximately 20% of the students live on campus in nine residence halls.

TUITION, ROOM, BOARD AND FEES

Expenses for the 2014–15 academic year include tuition (in-state: $9,300; out-of-state: $21,570), room and board ($11,138 [approx.]); expenses for books, transportation, fees, and other expenses range from $5000 (in residence) to $6000 (off-campus residence).

FINANCIAL AID

Approximately 75% of CCSU full-time students receive some form of financial aid. CCSU's office of Financial Aid works with students to help them meet educational expenses from their first year until graduation. To apply for financial aid students must complete the FAFSA form. For more information, call 860-832-2200, e-mail FinancialAid3@ccsu.edu, or on the Web at www.ccsu.edu/finaid.

STUDENT ORGANIZATIONS AND ACTIVITIES

There are 130 student clubs and organizations, which cover a broad range of interests: academic—such as the Anthropology or the Investment clubs; athletic—such as the crew or flying clubs; cultural—for example, the art club, the jazz band, and other musical organizations; ethnic—such as the Black Student Union, Latin American Students Organization, and the Muslim Student Association; religious—such as Hillel and the Newman Club; and such honors organizations as Delta Mu Delta, Lambda Delta, and Kappa Delta Pi. On-campus entertainment is wide and varied, including, most recently, "Devils Den@ 10" student-run entertainment on Thursday evenings.

ADMISSIONS PROCESS

CCSU is a learning community of students with a broad range of abilities, interests, and backgrounds. We value excellence and achievement in academic scholarship, community involvement, and extracurricular activities. Our admissions process evaluates the readiness of applicants to succeed based on past demonstrations of academic and personal successes.

CCSU has a "rolling" admissions policy, not a set admissions deadline, which gives students greater flexibility in applying. The University urges prospective students to apply as early as possible in their senior year. The University begins accepting students for the fall semester in mid-October and will continue to review applications until the class is filled.

First-year applicants are considered on the basis of performance in college preparatory classes, rank in class, SAT or ACT test scores, recommendations, and community and extracurricular involvement and leadership. A personal essay is required. For some applicants an interview with a representative of the Office of Recruitment & Admissions may be necessary. If the applicant ranks in the top 20% of his/her class, is an A-B student, and has SAT scores of 1100 or higher, the student should consider finding out about CCSU's Honors Program by calling 860-832-2938 for details. CCSU accepts most Advanced Placement (AP) courses for college credit, provided the minimum CCSU required score is achieved. Check with Admissions for the required scores.

Admission criteria include graduation from a regionally accredited secondary school. High school work should include college preparatory courses in: English (four years); Mathematics (covering algebra I, geometry, and algebra II); Science (two years including one-year lab science); Social sciences (two to three years including U.S. history). Coursework in foreign language is recommended (at least three consecutive years of the same foreign language up through the third level will satisfy the foreign language proficiency required of all CCSU-enrolled students). Students whose preparation does not follow this pattern may still qualify for admission if, in the judgment of the Director of Recruitment and Admissions, there is strong evidence that they have the potential to complete a degree program or if they meet other established criteria as authorized by the University President under authority delegated by the Board of Regents of the Connecticut State College & University System. Applicants who are not graduates of a secondary school should submit their secondary school transcript up to the time of withdrawal and a copy of their high school equivalency diploma and scores.

The most important thing for the applicant to remember is to provide as much information as possible—achievements, awards, and examples of leadership—when applying.

HOW TO APPLY

Students are encouraged to apply online at www.ccsu.edu/apply. For paper applications, please provide the Office of Recruitment & Admissions with 1) completed application for undergraduate admission 2) official high school transcript, SAT or ACT test scores, recommendations, and essay and 3) a non-refundable application fee of $50. All correspondence should be sent to the Office of Recruitment and Admissions, CCSU, P.O. Box 4010, 1615 Stanley Street, New Britain, CT 06050-4010.

Tours and information sessions may be arranged by calling 860-832-2289 or via e-mail at: admissions@ccsu.edu.

CHAPMAN UNIVERSITY

AT A GLANCE

During its 154-year history, Chapman University has evolved from a small, traditional liberal arts college into a comprehensive university distinguished for its extraordinary blend of liberal arts, science, and professional programs. Film and television production, business and economics, theatre, dance, music, education, and the natural and applied sciences — Chapman boasts a breadth of fields usually only found at larger institutions. Chapman University's mission is to develop global citizen-leaders who are distinctively prepared to improve their community and their world.

With beautiful grounds and stately buildings, Chapman is one of the oldest schools on the West Coast, yet its park-like campus is also one of the most modern. More than a dozen buildings have been built or renovated in just the last two decades, with several more currently under construction or in the approval process. Architecturally impressive residence halls and apartment buildings offer students exciting lifestyle amenities within a vibrant Southern California setting.

With its central Orange County, California, location and just under 8,000 undergraduate, graduate, and professional school students, the University environment is alive with activity. In addition to the temperate climate, Chapman students enjoy a dynamic, eclectic, and outdoor-oriented lifestyle, both on campus and off. Students come from all walks of life; from across the country and from all over the world, each student brings his or her own unique view of what makes a true global citizen. In recent years, Chapman students have been named Fulbright Scholars, Soros Scholars, Truman Scholars, Coro Fellows, USA Today All-USA College Academic Team members, NCAA All-Americans, and NCAA Academic All-Americans.

Chapman's academic preparation and wide breadth of excellence is evidenced by the University's accomplished alumni, some of whom include the Hon. Loretta Sanchez ('88), member of Congress; the Hon. David Bonior ('85), former member of Congress and house minority whip; the Hon. Jose Gomez ('75) member of the Panamanian National Assembly; television and film producers John Copeland ('73), Jon Garcia ('90), and John David Currey ('98); cinematographer Gene Jackson ('70); fashion designer and founder of Ambiguous Clothing, Frank Delgadillo ('96); St. John's University men's basketball coach Steve Lavin ('88); Tony Award nominee and Broadway star of Showboat Michel Bell ('68); Indy car racing star Jacques Lazier ('93); Major League Baseball umpire, the late Emmitt Ashford ('36); former major league baseball stars Tim Flannery ('80), Marty Castillo ('80), Gary Lucas ('76), and Randy Jones ('72); and the Hon. George L. Argyros ('65), developer, philanthropist and former U.S. Ambassador to Spain.

LOCATION AND ENVIRONMENT

Orange County, California, has been rated by Places Rated Almanac as "the #1 place to live in North America," citing superior climate and cultural, recreational, educational, and career-entree opportunities. Orange County's central location between two major cities means there is never a lack of entertainment choices. It is, in fact, home to the happiest place on Earth—Disneyland is literally minutes from campus.

The Orange County Performing Arts Center, Major League Baseball's Los Angeles Angels of Anaheim, and the National Hockey League's Anaheim Ducks are all within a few miles of Chapman's campus in Old Towne Orange. Pristine West Coast beaches are less than 15 miles from the campus, and seasonal snow skiing is 35 miles away. The average year-round temperature on campus is 71°F, and the daily sea breeze from nearby Pacific Ocean keeps the air cool, clean, and smog free.

On campus, Chapman students take part in the dynamic student activities program. There are over 120 student run clubs, including community service organizations, 16 national fraternities and sororities, 20 NCAA D-III intercollegiate athletic programs, an active intramural sports program, music, art, and theatre productions.

OFF-CAMPUS OPPORTUNITIES

Chapman's Career Development Center provides a variety of services to students, graduates, and former students. These include internship opportunities, an on-campus recruiting program, full-time job postings and computer-networked job listings, individual career counseling and career assessment, a career resource library, job search and resume writing skills development, interview coaching, and an alumni mentor program. The center will assist teachers in establishing a self-managed educational placement file.

Chapman students are encouraged to participate in study abroad programs in many academic fields in almost every part of the world. Students studying abroad through Chapman-approved programs are enrolled in a full course of study at the host institution, but receive academic credit from Chapman. The study abroad program directly supports Chapman's emphasis on encouraging students to recognize and develop their roles as global citizens in an increasingly interdependent world.

MAJORS AND BACHELORS DEGREES OFFERED

Chapman University confers degrees in the following fields of study:

Accounting, Art, Art History, Biochemistry and Molecular Biology, Biological Sciences, Business Administration, Chemistry, Communication Studies, Computer Information Systems, Computer Science, Creative Producing, Creative Writing, Dance, Dance Performance, Digital Arts, Economics, English, Environmental Science and Policy, Film Production, Film Studies, French, Graphic Design, Health Sciences, History, Integrated Educational Studies (teaching), Kinesiology, Mathematics, Mathematics and Civil Engineering, Music, Music Composition, Music Education, Music Performance , News and Documentary, Peace Studies, Philosophy, Physics and Computational Science, Political Science, Pre-Law, Pre-Medicine, Pre-Pharmacy, Psychology, Public Relations and Advertising, Religious Studies, Screen Acting, Screenwriting, Sociology, Software Engineering, Spanish, Strategic and Corporate Communication, Television Writing and Production, Theatre, Theatre Performance , Integrated (Bachelors and Advanced) Degree Programs, Pharmacy Freshman Early Assurance Program (2+3 Pharm.D.), Integrated MBA (4+1), Integrated MS Computational Science (4+1), Bridge Program to Doctorate of Physical Therapy (DPT), Integrated MS Health Communication (4+1), Integrated MS Food Science (4+1), Integrated MS Economic System Design (4+1)

ACADEMIC PROGRAMS

Chapman University strives to provide every student with a comprehensive, liberal arts-based course of study, with the goal of producing an engaging, articulate, and communicative world citizen with specific expertise and skills to offer. Chapman University's academic structure includes the AACSB International—accredited Argyros School of Business and Economics; the CTC-approved College of Educational Studies; the Crean College of Health and Behavioral Sciences; the college of Performing Arts which includes the NASD-accredited Department of Dance, the NASM-accredited Hall-Musco Conservatory of Music, and the NAST-accredited Department of Theater; the ABA-accredited Fowler School of Law; the Dodge College of Film and Media Arts; the Schmid College of Science and Technology; the School of Pharmacy; and the Wilkinson College of Humanities and Social Sciences.

CAMPUS FACILITIES AND EQUIPMENT

Chapman's stunning campus continues to grow by leaps and bounds. Major additions to the campus over the past few years include the Dodge College of Film and Media Arts which features 76,000 square feet of professional sound stages, digital editing bays, the 500-seat Folino Theatre, and a state-of-the-art digital arts center. The 100,000-square-foot Leatherby Libraries complex, housing eight discipline-specific individual libraries, a cyber courtyard, and a 24-hour study commons and coffee bar. The Oliphant Hall addition to the Conservatory of Music is a 24,000-square-foot space featuring fourteen teaching studios, a 60-seat lecture hall, music therapy laboratory, and orchestra hall. In addition to the Conservatory of Music's Bertea and Oliphant Halls, the college of Performing Arts facilities include the Moulton Fine Arts Complex featuring the 250-seat repertory-style Waltmar Theatre, a black box theater, the Guggenheim Art Gallery, and the Partridge Dance Center. The Fish Interfaith Center features the 12,500-square-foot Wallace All-Faiths Chapel, recognized by Architectural Digest for innovation in design. The 200,000-square-foot Sandhu Residence and Conference center houses the primary on-campus dining facility for resident students, as well as a conference center and residence hall. The 90,000-square-foot Argyros Forum includes the newly expanded student union with additional campus dining options, as well as conference and classroom facilities. The 800-seat Memorial Auditorium is the primary performance and assembly venue on campus and is listed on the National Register of Historic Places. Athletic and fitness facilities include the 2,500-seat Hutton Sports Center; the 2,700-seat Ernie Chapman Stadium for football, lacrosse, and soccer; the 500-seat Allred Aquatics Center swim stadium/Olympic pool; and the Julia Argyros Fitness Center complex.

Beckman Hall is the center for business and information technology and includes the newly opened Janes Financial Center with its eleven Bloomberg terminals. The Hashinger Science Center features laboratories for nuclear science, radiation, crystallography, genetics, food science, physics, and computational sciences. The new 200,000 square foot Rinker Health Science Campus in Irvine, California is home to Chapman's professional schools of Pharmacy and Physical Therapy, as well as the graduate Athletic Training program. Adjacent to the main campus in Orange, Chapman's ABA-accredited Fowler School of Law is housed in an architecturally stunning facility that includes state-of-the-art classrooms, two courtrooms, and a 3-story law library. In addition to Chapman's athletic facilities, the residence hall area features an indoor climbing wall, a resort-style pool and deck, an outdoor basketball court and sand volleyball court.

TUITION, ROOM, BOARD AND FEES

Undergraduate tuition (annual, 12-18 semester credits), room, board, and fees for the 2014–2015 academic are as follows:

Annual tuition: $44,710

Accident/Sickness plan: optional

Associated students fee: $140

Wellness Center fee: $244

Total tuition/fees: $45,094

Room/board cost for academic year 2014–2015:

Room & Board: $14,700

Parking fee: $350

Total room/board $15,050 with on-campus parking

FINANCIAL AID

More than 85 percent of Chapman students benefit from some form of need based aid, merit, or talent scholarship. Awards are made through a combination of grants, scholarships, loans, and work-study programs. Awards may be renewed throughout a student's term of study. A student's financial needs are usually met through a combination of internal assets and federal and state funding. Chapman awards merit scholarships, regardless of financial need, to all eligible admitted new students using a standardized test score/entering grade point average-driven formula. Chapman also offers talent scholarships in areas such as art, music, dance, theatre, writing, film and television, and science awarded regardless of financial need. Audition, submission of portfolio, or supplemental application materials will be required to be considered for talent awards.

STUDENT ORGANIZATIONS AND ACTIVITIES

More than 120 clubs and organizations are recognized on campus, many with commitments to a wide range of community service efforts. Chapman's Greek system includes eight nationally chartered fraternities for men and eight nationally chartered sororities for women. Intramural sports, on-campus intercollegiate athletic events, as well as music, art, and theater productions provide students with plenty to do outside of class.

Chapman's long and distinguished heritage in intercollegiate athletics includes five NCAA national championships in baseball, tennis, and softball. The Panthers compete in the NCAA Division III Southern California Intercollegiate Athletic Conference (SCIAC) and field intercollegiate or club-level teams in baseball, basketball, crew, cross-country, football, golf, ice hockey, lacrosse, soccer, softball, swimming, tennis, track and field, volleyball, and water polo. Approximately 25 percent of Chapman's student body participates in intercollegiate varsity or club-level athletics. In 2014–15 Chapman won the SCIAC championship in football, and were co-champions in men's basketball.

ADMISSIONS PROCESS

Admission to Chapman is selective. In 2015, admission was offered to 43% of the applicant pool. The University is interested in admitting students whose prior records indicate that they will be successful in a competitive collegiate environment. Freshman applicants are considered for admission based primarily on the nature and sequence of their high school course work, grade point average achieved, their results on either the SAT or ACT examination, co-curricular involvements, and personal characteristics. Transfer candidates are considered for admission on the basis of their course work and cumulative grade point average earned at other regionally accredited postsecondary institutions, their co-curricular involvements, and personal characteristics.

Chapman University exclusively uses The Common Application (http://www.commonapp.org), as well as Chapman-specific questions to The Common Application and departmental applications via the Art Supplement for those applying to Art, Dance, any Dodge College major, Music, or Theater. Candidates are strongly encouraged to visit and tour the campus and participate in an information session led by an admission officer. Arrangements for a group information session and campus tour can be made through the Office of Admission.

Students may request more information by contacting:

Office of Admission

Chapman University

One University Drive

Orange, CA 92866

Telephone: (714) 997-6711 888-CUAPPLY (toll free)

Fax: 714-997-6713

E-mail: admit@chapman.edu

www.chapman.edu

CHESTNUT HILL COLLEGE

AT A GLANCE

A college of distinction, Chestnut Hill College is a four-year Catholic, coed, liberal arts college located in Philadelphia, Pennsylvania. Founded in 1924 by the Sisters of St. Joseph, it is situated on a 75-acre campus overlooking the Wissahickon Creek. Since opportunities for leadership and self-expression are frequent, the Chestnut Hill College graduate can enter a competitive world well prepared for success. Students come from 28 states, 31 countries, and every imaginable background. In addition to its undergraduate degrees, Chestnut Hill College awards the M.Ed., M.A., and M.S. in four fields, including Education, Clinical and Counseling Psychology, Administration of Human Services, and Instructional Technology.

When it comes to student activities, students enthusiastically engage in the many clubs and organizations available. The college is NCAA Division II and competes in softball, baseball, MW golf, W volleyball, MW cross country, MW soccer, MW lacrosse, MW tennis, MW track and field, and MW basketball. A swimming pool, gymnasium, soccer/lacrosse field, softball field, fitness center, outdoor volleyball and basketball courts and six tennis courts provide excellent athletic facilities for Chestnut Hill College students.

LOCATION AND ENVIRONMENT

Located in an historic area of Philadelphia, Chestnut Hill College's beautiful campus is bordered by Fairmount Park, yet is a quick train or car ride away from bustling downtown Philadelphia. One of the mid-Atlantic's premiere cities, Philadelphia offers a wide variety of restaurants, sports, and cultural and recreational activities. In particular, Philadelphia is home to a number of world-class museums, including the Philadelphia Museum of Art, the Rodin Museum, and the Franklin Institute. A historic city, the atmosphere and architecture around Independence Hall, Society Hill, and Penn's Landing are gems of colonial architecture and atmosphere. In addition to the city's cultural resources, Philadelphia is home to over 25 colleges and universities, creating a vibrant collegiate environment for study and social life.

While students at Chestnut Hill College have access to cosmopolitan Philadelphia, the college is set in a lovely suburban neighborhood in the northwest corner of the city. The charming colonial area of Chestnut Hill is just a mile from campus. Well known in and beyond Philadelphia, Chestnut Hill gives students easy access to shopping and cultural events, as well as convenient transportation downtown.

MAJORS AND DEGREES OFFERED

The Bachelor of Arts and Bachelor of Science degrees are offered with majors in: Accounting; Biochemistry; Biology; Business Administration; Chemistry; Communications; Communications and Technology; Computer and Information Sciences; Computer and Information Technology; Criminal Justice; Education—Early Education (Pre-K–4), Elementary/Middle Education (4–8), Secondary Education (7–12); English Literature; English Literature and Communications; Environmental Sciences; Forensic Biology; Forensic Chemistry; French; Global Affairs; History; Human Services; International Business, Language and Culture; Management; Marketing; Mathematical and Computer Sciences; Mathematics; Molecular Biology; Music; Music Education; Political Science; Psychology; Sociology; Spanish.

ACADEMIC PROGRAMS

Chestnut Hill College's core curriculum is designed to provide students with a meaningful education that is rooted in college's mission. Steeped in the liberal arts, the curriculum recognizes the impact of the information-age revolution and addresses career demands of the twenty-first century, while at the same time providing an unparalleled holistic education to all of the college's students. The core curriculum consists of fundamental requirements, Ways of Knowing perspectives, proficiencies, and free electives. In addition, students fulfill all of the requirements specified in a major program of study.

Focused on six perspectives (Historical, Literary, Artistic, Scientific, Behavioral, and Problem-Solving and Analysis), the Ways of Knowing component of the Core Curriculum is designed to introduce students to different learning methodologies and strategies for interpreting and understanding the world in which we live.

Students may be approved to pursue a degree simultaneously within two major disciplines. Students who wish to double major must discuss their proposed course of study with the chair of each department and submit a proposal to the Dean of the college. To earn a dual degree, students must satisfy the individual requirements of both department programs.

Select students have the opportunity to participate in the challenging Interdisciplinary Honors Program (IDHP). The courses in the IDHP consist of seminars co-taught by two faculty members from different disciplines. In these reading- and writing-intensive seminars, learning is achieved through active discussion involving students and professors alike. Each is interdisciplinary to promote the integration of knowledge. An atmosphere of cooperation replaces competition for grades, fostering in students their own unique potential and enthusiasm for learning.

Chestnut Hill College's faculty is accomplished in research, publication, and travel, but are teachers first and foremost. The undergraduate college faculty consists of 170 faculty members, 65 of whom are full-time. Over 75 percent of faculty members hold doctoral or terminal degrees in their subject area. Chestnut Hill College instructors take teaching seriously, and with an excellent student/faculty ratio of 11:1, students have ample opportunity to work individually with professors. Chestnut Hill's distinguished instructors have earned degrees from such premiere institutions as the University of Oxford in England, the University of Paris, the University of Budapest, Catholic University of America, Middlebury College, Bryn Mawr College, Columbia University, the University of Notre Dame, the University of Pennsylvania, Duke University, New York University, the New School for Social Research, Purdue University, Temple University, and the University of Minnesota.

STUDENT ORGANIZATIONS AND ACTIVITIES

The Student Activities Office organizes and hosts weekly campus events, off campus trips, and late night programming on every Friday night. The office also coordinates large campus wide events such as Griffin Days, Orientation, and Family Weekend. Events hosted by clubs and organizations receive the support of the Activities Office in order to achieve success throughout the year. Student Activities also offers leadership development programs such as workshops, conferences, and more.

Each student at Chestnut Hill College is part of the most influential organization on campus, the Student Government Association (SGA). SGA commits itself to actively representing the student body while striving to serve the school community with leadership, equality, dedication, loyalty, and responsibility. Moreover, by preserving the traditions of the college, SGA encourages an appreciation and awareness of the college and the world at-large.

Student Activities serves as the home for many academic interest groups, drama and music groups, cultural organizations, yearbook and newspaper staffs, and community action groups. While not comprehensive, this list includes:

- African American Awareness Society
- APA (Association for Performing Arts)
- Archery Club
- Brazilian Jiu Jitsu
- Business Club
- Chamber Ensemble
- CHAT (Chestnut Hill College Activities Team)
- Chemistry Club
- Commuter Club
- Council for Exceptional Children
- Crown the King Chess Club
- Earth Club
- FADD (Fighting Against Dangerous Decisions)
- Feel Good
- Flute Ensemble
- Griffins for Paws
- Hill Singers
- History Club
- International Society
- Japanese Culture Club
- Jazz Ensemble
- La Voz Latina
- Mask & Foil
- Orienteering Club
- Poetry Club
- String Ensemble
- Student Political Science Association
- The Computer Club
- The Grackle
- The Griffin Newspaper

CAMPUS FACILITIES AND EQUIPMENT

CHC's Logue Library affords students wireless internet connectivity, access to 130,000 books, 450 periodicals, subscriptions to scholarly research databases, a rare book room that contains first editions and special editions, the Gruber Theater, the fine Curriculum Library for elementary education, and an Irish literature collection. Well-equipped science laboratories, a math center, a multimedia technology center, a writing enrichment center, individual practice rooms for music students, a spacious art studio, a planetarium, and an observatory are among the many other outstanding facilities on campus. Opened in the fall of 2000, Martino Hall houses a performance center, gymnasium, and convocation center. The second and third floors house cutting-edge, "smart" classrooms. Fitzsimmons Hall opened in fall 2006 and houses 150 students in suite style living. The college recently acquired the neighboring 35-acre Sugarloaf Mansion estate and has renovated the existing buildings. This new facility offers additional resident housing, classrooms, a second student dining facility, and office areas, along with conference and meeting facilities.

OFF-CAMPUS OPPORTUNITIES

Chestnut Hill College participates in a consortium arrangement with eight colleges throughout the nation, founded by the Sisters of St. Joseph. As participants, students can study at any other member institution for a semester or a year, while maintaining status as a full-time Chestnut Hill student. Chestnut Hill College is also a member of SEPCHE (Southeastern Pennsylvania Consortium for Higher Education); the collaboration allows Chestnut Hill College the ability to learn best practices surrounding student life, academics, and technology. SEPCHE membership also allows students to share various resources at other member institutions.

An average of B or above and approval of the academic dean allow an upper class student to pursue organized study in another country. The major department must approve the course of study. In recent years, Chestnut Hill College students have enrolled in institutions in London, Rome, Madrid, Vienna, Salzburg, and other European centers.

The Office of Career Development at Chestnut Hill College provides information and guidance on careers, professions, employment, and graduate school opportunities for current and prospective students as well as alumni. Additionally, the Office of Career Development coordinates the college's experiential education program. In today's competitive job market, there is a growing need for students to acquire on-the-job experience while still in college. Through credit-bearing experiential education opportunities like internships and co-ops, students are able to link the world of learning with the world of work, synthesizing academic theory with practice.

TUITION, ROOM, BOARD AND FEES

Over 75 percent of students at Chestnut Hill College receive financial aid. Chestnut Hill College offers financial aid in the form of scholarships, loans, work-study, federal grants, and Chestnut Hill College grants. Each package is tailored to suit a student's needs and abilities. All prospective students applying for aid must file the Free Application for Federal Student Aid (FAFSA). In addition to need-based awards, Chestnut Hill awards merit-based scholarships; the average merit-based award is $11,500. Tuition for 2015–2016 is $33,535.00 plus additional estimated room and board cost of $10,200.00.

ADMISSIONS PROCESS

CHC seeks accomplished students prepared to benefit from a challenging undergraduate curriculum. Admissions counselors review all applications and evaluate students on their intellectual ability and academic achievement. To be considered for admission, students must submit an application, a nonrefundable application fee, an official high school transcript, and scores from the SAT or ACT. A personal statement and letters of recommendation are strongly encouraged. Though usually not required, a personal interview is recommended.

Prospective transfer students are required to submit an official transcript of all college or university work. International students may be required to submit additional materials to support English proficiency.

Admissions decisions are made on a rolling basis. To set up an interview or request more information about academics or admissions, students may contact:

Office of Undergraduate Admissions

Chestnut Hill College

9601 Germantown Avenue

Philadelphia, PA 19118

Telephone: 215-248-7001

800-248-0052 (toll free)

E-mail: admissions@chc.edu

Website: www.chc.edu

CITY UNIVERSITY OF NEW YORK—CITY COLLEGE

COME EXPLORE THE CITY EXPERIENCE.

City College is ranked among the nation's best colleges and provides an outstanding education by an award-winning faculty in the heart of the world's most exciting city. Founded in 1847, City College is the flagship of the City University of New York and offers undergraduate and graduate degrees in liberal arts, science, interdisciplinary studies, education, architecture, engineering, and biomedical education.

GET TO KNOW CITY COLLEGE

At City College, 13,000 undergraduates and 3,000 graduate students pursue a world-class education at tuition rates that are designed to be affordable. Undergraduate majors and minors provide a full spectrum of choices, from biomedical engineering to economics and business to theatre, computer science, advertising/PR, environmental earth system science, electronic design and multimedia, and journalism.

Research opportunities and mentoring are hallmarks of a City College undergraduate education, and City College students in all disciplines frequently achieve prestigious national recognition. Access to excellence is the mission.

VISIT US IN NEW YORK CITY

Prospective students are encouraged to tour City College's large, leafy campus in Harlem, one of New York's most historic and dynamic neighborhoods. Discover the abundant resources and facilities, the diversity of the college community, and the advantages of studying at one of New York's most celebrated public institutions. To tour City College, reserving in advance is requested. Please visit the City College website and Admissions office pages for further information and to make quick and simple online reservations.

CLEMSON UNIVERSITY

AT A GLANCE

One of the country's most selective public research universities, Clemson was founded in 1889 with a mission to be a "high seminary of learning" dedicated to teaching, research, and service. Today, these three concepts remain at the heart of the University and provide the framework for an exceptional educational experience.

At Clemson University, professors take the time to get to know students and explore innovative ways of teaching. Exceptional teaching is one reason Clemson's retention and graduation rates rank among the highest in the country for public universities.

Exceptional teaching is also why Clemson continues to attract an increasingly talented student body. In 2014, more than half of the entering freshmen were ranked in the top 10 percent of their high school classes, and the freshman class averaged 1253 on the critical reading and math sections of the SAT.

Clemson is committed to world-class research. Research expenditures in 2013 totaled nearly $101 million.

The University is also invested in the success of its students. For the fall 2012 class, Clemson's student retention rate was 92 percent. Much of this is due to the Academic Success Center (ASC), established in 2001 and recognized nationally and internationally for its programs in tutoring, supplemental instruction, and collegiate learning. The ASC moved into a new facility in 2012 where it offers free one-on-one tutoring services for more than 80 courses as well as for additional courses as the need arises. Supplemental instruction, academic skills workshops, and academic counseling are also available—free to all Clemson students. It is estimated that more than 50 percent of freshmen use ASC services during their first semester.

Clemson has also received national recognition for its innovative Communication Across the Curriculum (CAC) program, ranking ninth on the U.S.News & World Report list of public colleges and universities identified as making writing across all curriculums a priority. At Clemson, CAC has become a standard teaching method used in nearly every department to provide real-life challenges that require students to think and communicate effectively.

From cheering the Tigers at a football game to socializing at the Hendrix Student Center, Clemson students can participate in a wide variety of activities outside the classroom. The more than 400 campus clubs and organizations include fraternities and sororities, as well as honorary, international, military, performing arts, political, professional, religious, service, social interest, special interest, sports and fitness, and student media.

With 19 intercollegiate sports, Clemson offers exciting spectator sports year-round. Clemson is a charter member of the Atlantic Coast Conference and is an NCAA Division I school. Admission to regular-season home events is included in University fees for full-time students.

LOCATION AND ENVIRONMENT

Clemson University is located in Clemson, S.C., a town of about 14,000 located in the middle of the I-85 corridor between Atlanta, Ga., and Charlotte, N.C. The 1,400-acre campus borders the shores of Hartwell Lake and the foothills of the Blue Ridge Mountains.

OFF-CAMPUS OPPORTUNITIES
Study Abroad

Clemson students are strongly encouraged to incorporate a study-abroad experience in their overall Clemson journey. Programs are available on six continents for all disciplines and interests. These include faculty-led programs, exchange programs, and programs available through Clemson's partnerships with study-abroad providers and institutions. Students in a variety of majors also have opportunities at Clemson campuses in South Carolina and around the world, including the Archbold Center in Dominica; the Daniel Center in Genoa, Italy; and the Brussels Center in Belgium.

Cooperative Education

The Cooperative Education program provides an opportunity for students to alternate periods of academic study with semesters of paid, career-related, engaged-learning experiences to bridge the gap between academic study and its application in professional practice. Clemson's career center pairs about 2,200 students annually with companies seeking interns or co-op students. Internships are also available on campus where students can work part- or full-time, with many in full-time positions having the option of earning credit. The Princeton Review ranks Clemson's career services program as the No. 5 career office in the nation.

Community Service

An important aspect of Clemson is its dedication to improving the world through public service. In a typical year, more than 6,000 Clemson students contribute about 105,000 service hours, earning the University national recognition on the President's Higher Education Community Service Honor Roll. Opportunities to make a difference are available through student service organizations, ongoing service projects, and one-time service events—on campus, in the community, across the nation, or around the world. The National Survey on Student Engagement reports that 43 percent of first-year Clemson students and 58 percent of seniors said "at least some" of their courses included a community-based service-learning project.

ACADEMIC PROGRAMS
Majors and Degrees

Students can select from more than 80 undergraduate and 119 graduate degree programs offered by five colleges and the Eugene T. Moore School of Education: Agriculture, Forestry and Life Sciences; Architecture, Arts and Humanities; Business and Behavioral Science; Engineering and Science; and Health, Education and Human Development. To find out what majors are available go to: clemson.edu/majors.

Clemson University is accredited by the Commission on Colleges of the Southern Association of Colleges and Schools to award bachelor's, master's, specialist, and doctoral degrees. Questions about the accreditation of Clemson University can be directed to the Commission on Colleges at 1866 Southern Lane, Decatur, Georgia 30033-4097; phone: 404-679-4500.

Honors College

Calhoun Honors College is a University-wide program that combines the strengths of a public, land-grant university with those of a highly selective small college. Calhoun Scholars may choose to pursue departmental honors within their specific academic discipline. In addition, EUREKA! (Experiences in Undergraduate Research, Exploration, and Knowledge Advancement) is a unique and exciting program that enables honors students to pursue research and scholarly activities with faculty members across all disciplines. The advantages of membership in the Honors College include priority registration, extended library loan privileges, honors research grants, and a special living-learning community.

The National Scholars Program is a highly selective program for exceptional students who strive to meet their highest intellectual potential. One of its goals is to develop the interests and talents students need to compete for Rhodes, Marshall, and Truman scholarships; Fulbright Grants; National Science Foundation Graduate Fellowships; and other prestigious international fellowships. In 2013, 11 Clemson students received National Science Foundation Graduate Fellowships. Three recent Clemson graduates received Fulbright grants to conduct research or teach abroad, and three students were named Goldwater Scholars.

Undergraduate Research

Clemson's Creative Inquiry (CI) program allows undergraduate students to engage in research about problems that spring from their own curiosity, from a professor's challenge or from the pressing needs of the world around them. Team-based investigations are led by a faculty mentor and typically span two to four semesters. Students take ownership of their projects and take the risks necessary to solve problems and get answers. This invaluable experience produces exceptional graduates, capable of thinking critically, solving problems as a team, and communicating and presenting their ideas to others. In 2013–14, 3,439 students participated in 519 CI teams.

Programs for Educational Enrichment and Retention

Clemson's nationally recognized Programs for Educational Enrichment and Retention (PEER) is committed to improving the academic performance of underrepresented students in engineering and science. According to a 2012 survey by the magazine Diverse: Issues In Higher Education, Clemson ranks 15th among the nation's universities in graduating African-American students in engineering.

Living-Learning Communities

Living-learning communities offer the chance for students to live and work with others who have similar interests and goals. There are living options for students interested in business, engineering and science, civics and service, honors courses, professional golf management, and much more. Recognized as a national model, the communities are designed to help students be more successful by offering on-site advising and academic support, common course assignments, guest speakers, service opportunities and a variety of social activities.

CAMPUS FACILITIES
Information Technology

The University's wireless networking capability lets students communicate with professors and classmates, read online course materials, check e-mail and conduct research—all from their own laptops. Students are required to complete an electronic portfolio prior to graduation, allowing them the opportunity to present themselves through a creative venue to prospective employers and graduate schools.

Housing

Located within a 10- to 15-minute walk to class, Clemson's 22 residence halls and five apartment complexes offer a vast selection of living arrangements.

Fike Recreation Center

Fike is a 200,000-square-foot recreation center that features a fitness atrium complete with a suspended running track that overlooks the indoor courts. It's also equipped with indoor swimming facilities, fitness studios, racquetball courts, state-of-the-art cardio equipment, weights, locker rooms and a climbing wall.

Hendrix Student Center

The Hendrix Center is the hub of campus activity and is located a step away from most housing. Here you can find people taking a yoga class or enjoying a meal at the food court. It's home to the University Bookstore and offers plenty of quiet places to stop and study. It has a movie theater, ice cream parlor and much more.

Health Center

Redfern Health Center provides medical services, counseling and psychological services, and health-related programs like alcohol and drug education. It's one of the nation's few on-campus accredited health centers.

COSTS
Tuition, Room, Board, and Fees

2012-13 Academic Year

S.C Resident Full Time

Tuition and Fees°	$13,054
Room and Board (approximate)	$8,142
Books and Supplies (approximate)	$1,112
Total	$22,308

Nonresident Full Time

Tuition and Fees°	$30,488
Room and Board (approximate)	$8,142
Books and Supplies (approximate)	$1,112
Total	$39,742

Other Expenses

Estimated Personal and Transportation Expenses	$3,520
One-time computer cost°°	$1,900

°Assumes health and other mandatory fees (required for all full-time students) and average lab and loan fees.

°°All students are required to own a laptop computer. For details, go to clemson.edu/laptop.

FINANCIAL AID

Each year Clemson awards $226 million in financial aid in the form of grants, scholarships, loans and part-time employment to more than 15,000 students. Eighty-eight percent of first-time students receive scholarships ranging from $500 to all-inclusive cost coverage. All financial aid is awarded annually, and FAFSA applications for the next year are available in January. Entering freshmen are evaluated on a competitive basis for scholarships using the admission application.

ADMISSION REQUIREMENTS

In 2014, the University received about 20,756 applications for a fall freshman class of more than 3,400. Transfer applications were received from 2,477 students, 1,147 of whom enrolled.

For freshman applicants, the following factors are considered: class standing, standardized test scores (SAT or ACT), high school curriculum, grades and choice of major. All entering freshmen must have completed 4 credits of English, 3 credits of mathematics, 3 credits of laboratory science, 3 credits of a foreign language (in the same language), 3 credits of social sciences, 1 credit of U.S. history, 1 credit of physical education or ROTC, and 1 credit of fine arts.

To be considered for transfer admission, candidates must have completed a full year of college study (a minimum of 30 semester hours or 45 quarter hours of transferable work), earned a cumulative GPA of at least 2.5 on a 4.0 scale (3.0 preferred), and completed freshman-level courses in English, science and mathematics for their intended major at Clemson.

Application deadlines for freshman admission are December 1 (priority date for fall semester), May 1 (fall semester), and December 15 (spring semester). For transfer admissions, the application deadlines are July 1 (fall semester) and December 15 (spring semester).

Admissions:

864-656-2287

clemson.edu/admissions/undergraduate

Campus Tours:

864-656-4789

clemson.edu/visitors

THE COLLEGE OF NEW JERSEY

AT A GLANCE

The College of New Jersey (TCNJ) has created a culture of constant questioning. In small classes, students and faculty members collaborate in a rewarding process. They seek to understand fundamental principles, apply key concepts, reveal new problems and pursue lines of inquiry to gain a fluency of thought in their disciplines. This transformative process is at the core of the educational experience at The College.

Many students extend their classroom work by participating in research with faculty members or studying abroad. Often, professors and students co-author papers published in academic journals. The mentor relationship helps students discuss career options and land pertinent fellowships, internships, and summer research positions.

TCNJ admits a diverse class each year full of ambitious students, eager to build on their educational foundations and plunge into new topics. These students will ultimately find a home away from home on campus, and ninety-five percent of first year students will return for their second year. The most successful admits are prepared to steer their own academic pursuits toward post-graduation goals of graduate school, professional training, or satisfying careers.

Prestigious graduate schools, including the University of Pennsylvania, Georgetown Law School, Maxwell School at Syracuse University, NYU Law School, and Harvard, Yale, and Northwestern Universities, routinely welcome TCNJ alumni into their ranks. Eighty-four percent of TCNJ students who apply to medical school and other professional programs are accepted.

Many top corporations recruit TCNJ graduates, providing avenues into rewarding jobs directly after graduation. Other barometers of student success include the 100 percent pass rate of education majors taking the state teacher preparation test and the 85 percent three-year pass rate for nursing students going for their license. The numerous learning opportunities at The College prepare students to prosper in any arena after the conclusion of their undergraduate career.

LOCATION AND ENVIRONMENT

Neoclassical Georgian Colonial architecture, meticulous landscaping and intentional design merge to meet the evolving needs of TCNJ students. Students enjoy a campus with 289 acres of trees, lakes, and open spaces within the suburban setting of Ewing Township, New Jersey. Two out of three undergraduate students take part in the on-campus residence hall experience. The residence halls vary in configuration from the freshman towers to suites and townhouse arrangements for upper class students. An on-campus 600-bed apartment complex is the most recent addition. The college ensures that on-campus housing is available to all students in their first two years, with out-of-state students receiving housing for all four years of study.

Nearby cities, such as Princeton, Trenton, Philadelphia, and New York, allow for abundant entertainment, employment, and social options. Many courses incorporate field trips to New York City or Washington DC.

In the summer of 2015, TCNJ is scheduled to open Campus Town, a commercial and residential "Main Street" that will feature restaurants, a new fitness center, shops and a Barnes and Noble bookstore. One, two and four-bedroom apartments will be available on the floors above each commercial establishment.

OFF-CAMPUS OPPORTUNITIES

TCNJ fosters global engagement through an extensive international study program, featuring exchange programs in locations as diverse as Johannesburg, London and the University of Santiago. Some students choose to attend one of the 131 available institutions in the U.S., while others venture to one of the 33 countries offering full-year or semester-long programs.

Mentored internships, both on and off campus, expose students to career options as they gain professional skills. With the college's location in the East Coast's center of corporate activity, providing easy access to New York and Philadelphia, many internships are available—some with pay and some for credit.

Faculty members lend their advice and help students locate and procure appropriate opportunities including fellowships, research positions and internships. Students may also use resources at the Career Center to find positions in New York, Philadelphia, or any of the corporations, government agencies, or research organizations closer to campus.

MAJORS AND DEGREES OFFERED

The College of New Jersey hosts seven schools: Arts and Communication; Business; Humanities and Social Sciences; Education; Engineering; Nursing, Health & Exercise Science; and Science. The college offers programs leading to the Bachelor of Arts, Bachelor of Fine Arts, Bachelor of Music, Bachelor of Science, and Bachelor of Science in Nursing degrees.

TCNJ grants degrees in the following majors: Accountancy, Art Teacher Preparation (K-12), Art History, Biomedical Engineering, Biology°, Business Administration (specializations in Finance, Interdisciplinary Business, Management, and Marketing), Chemistry°, Civil Engineering, Communication Studies, Computer Engineering, Computer Science, Criminology, Early Childhood Education, Education of the Deaf and Hard of Hearing, Economics°, Electrical Engineering, Elementary Education, Engineering Science (specializations in Engineering Management and Policy and Society), English°, Global Business, Health and Exercise Science, Health and Physical Education (Teacher Preparation K-12), History°, Interactive Multimedia, International Studies, i-STEM (Integrative Science, Technology, Engineering, and Mathematics), Mathematics°, Mechanical Engineering, Music (options in Performance and K-12 Teacher Preparation), Nursing, Philosophy, Physics°, Political Science, Psychology, Sociology and Anthropology, Special Education, Spanish°, Technology Education/Pre-Engineering (K-12), Urban Education, Visual Arts (options in Fine Arts, Graphic Design, and Lens-Based Art), and Women and Gender Studies.

(° Programs in which students may prepare for teacher certification)

The College also offers a unique Self-Designed major option, catering to students who wish to forge their own academic path.

In addition to full degree programs, students may also choose to complete a minor, in one of the previously mentioned fields or another subject area, such as African American Studies, Classical Studies, Comparative Literature, Religion, Public Administration, Communication Disorders and Public Health.

Joint degrees are also available at TCNJ. In conjunction with NJMS, students can pursue a seven-year combined BS/MD degree. A seven-year combined BS/OD degree program is also available through the State University of New York College of Optometry. Students can study for five years to receive their Master of Arts in teaching (along with a certification in Elementary Education at the bachelor's level) in the following areas: Education of the Deaf and Hard of Hearing, Special Education, and Urban Education.

ACADEMIC PROGRAMS

A Liberal Learning Curriculum ensures that all students are grounded in the values of civic responsibility, intellectual and scholarly growth, and that they receive a well-rounded education in the liberal arts.

In 2004, the college completed a transformation of its curriculum requiring fewer, more in-depth courses. All courses have been transformed and contain a significant out-of-class requirement that provides for even more student and faculty interaction.

These small classes enable dialog between students and with TCNJ's accomplished teaching staff. This staff is composed of professors with terminal degrees in exclusivity; no courses are taught by graduate students or Teacher's Assistants. The college shapes its curricula and educational experiences around the concept of personalized, collaborative, and rigorous intellectual development.

The required First-Year Seminar, the cornerstone of the Liberal Learning program, introduces students to the habits of mind and the methodologies of research; it's seminar format of no more than 15 students reinforces the message that students are not to be passive recipients of knowledge but rather active contributors to their own learning. Requirements are grouped as diversity and community engagement goals that can be self-designed or designated as interdisciplinary concentrations.

Top students may enroll in TCNJ's honors program, designed to provide a core curriculum with additional challenges and opportunities for individualized work. Most honors classes take an interdisciplinary approach and encourage collaboration between faculty and students from multiple academic departments and disciplines. Independent study arrangements fall easily within the parameters of the honors program, as well.

CAMPUS FACILITIES AND EQUIPMENT

Learning, like everything else, is contextual. The surroundings in which students learn and the tools they use influence their experience. Not surprisingly, the college supports its educational aspirations with careful attention to the quality of its facilities. In the first decade of the 21st century, more than $250 million in ongoing and new facilities construction is ensuring that TCNJ students continue to thrive in an environment that not only meets their academic, athletic, social and living needs, but extends their reach resulting in higher scholarship, better health and fitness, closer community, and greater comfort.

TUITION, ROOM, BOARD AND FEES

Because TCNJ is a public institution, costs are lower than most equivalent private institutions. The tuition and fees for undergraduates in the 2014–2015 academic year are as follow:

In-state tuition and fees: $16,526

Out-of-state tuition and fees: $27,138

Room and board (all students): $11,677

FINANCIAL AID

Close to 50 percent of full-time undergraduates benefit from financial aid, whether from merit-based scholarships, work-study programs, loans, or government/institutional grants. All students seeking financial aid at the state or federal level must submit the Free Application for Federal Student Aid (FAFSA) form or renewal FAFSA to apply. The Title IV FAFSA Code for The College is 002642.

TCNJ also offers institutional need-based scholarships. Students interested in seeking institutional need-based aid must submit the CSS / Financial Aid Profile.

Students may compete for the college's merit scholarships. These awards are offered to those applicants with top SAT/ACT scores and class rankings. Over the last six years, TCNJ has given scholarships totaling more than $30 million.

STUDENT ORGANIZATIONS AND ACTIVITIES

Classroom learning at TCNJ is complemented by an extensive and acclaimed Leadership Development Program. Life outside the classroom is not something our students do on the side. It's an extension of the learning experience. At every turn from the first year on, students blur the boundary between living and learning, closing the gap between "scholar" and "citizen."

More than 200 student organizations flourish at The College. Anyone can find an intramural sports team, Greek organization, cultural club, or academic group to suit his or her interests. Many students build friendships and optimize their leisure time participating in these groups. In addition, the college Union Board—administered by TCNJ students—organizes events, including concerts, performances, and comedy nights.

The College's highly successful Division III athletic programs also provide an opportunity to socialize and cheer on fellow classmates. TCNJ fields ten sports for men and ten for women. With 40 national titles, The College holds the record for championship and runner-up titles since Division III was implemented in 1979. For those looking for something a little less competitive, intramural and club sports, including flag football, volleyball, softball, floor hockey, and basketball, have thriving coed leagues of their own. Intramural and club teams play in state, regional, and national tournaments.

ADMISSIONS PROCESS

The admissions committee at TCNJ accepts a class of motivated, ambitious, and highly talented students. Most successful applicants have taken 16 college-preparatory units in high school. They also show impressive class ranks and SAT/ACT scores. Most students admitted fall within the top 10 percent of their graduating class. The committee also considers extracurricular involvement, individual pursuits, and community participation. Standardized test scores are not required for students applying into the art, music or interactive multimedia disciplines.

Those applying for Fall enrollment must have their applications submitted by February 1st. TCNJ offers an early-decision program to those who know The College is their top choice school: applications received by November 1st for this program will receive a response by December 1st. Students may also apply as Early Decision candidates by January 1st and receive their decision by February 1st. A small number of students begin classes in January, and those students must apply by November 1st for Spring Enrollment. For further information, please contact:

Office of Admissions

The College of New Jersey

PO Box 7718

Ewing, NJ 08628-0718

Telephone: 609-771-2132

E-mail: tcnjinfo@tcnj.edu

Visit us at: tomorrow@tcnj

COLUMBIA COLLEGE (MO)

AT A GLANCE

Focused on hands-on learning and student-driven discussions, Columbia College opens doors for its students with numerous majors to choose from and a career center prepared to help them from day one through graduation. Rigorous academics are grounded in the liberal arts and sciences and offered in a learning environment characterized by civility and respect. Students feel at home on the beautiful campus, located in Columbia, Mo., thanks to the private college's close-knit community where opportunities to get involved are plentiful.

Each year, nearly 1,000 students attend the traditional Day Campus and represent 17 states and 23 countries. At Columbia College, students choose from 40 outstanding majors and pre-professional programs. Undergraduate and graduate degrees are offered at the home campus in Columbia, Mo., as well as at 36 locations across the nation and online. Alumni total 84,000 worldwide and often help students find internships and jobs after graduation through a variety of networking opportunities.

An interest in the student as an individual has been a hallmark of the institution since it was founded in 1851—traditions that can be seen and felt with a student-faculty ratio of 11-to-1 and meaningful relationships with professors and classmates. More than 80 percent of faculty have earned the highest academic degrees possible in their fields.

Whether you're an athlete or a fan, you'll appreciate Cougar Athletics with award-winning NAIA varsity sports in men's and women's basketball, soccer, golf, track and cross country, as well as men's baseball (2016), and women's volleyball and softball.

Though maintaining a covenant with the Christian Church (Disciples of Christ), Columbia College welcomes students of all religious affiliations. The covenant dates back to our founding as Christian Female College, the first women's college west of the Mississippi River to be chartered by a state legislature. In 1970, the college opened its doors to both women and men and changed its name to Columbia College.

LOCATION AND ENVIRONMENT

At Columbia College, you'll live on a campus of 30 beautiful acres, where you'll bump into friends and faculty everywhere you go. Columbia, Mo. Is often called Collegetown U.S.A. And Columbia College shares this beautiful city with both Stephens College and the University of Missouri, leading to a town of more than 30,000 college students along with roughly 100,000 full-time residents. Located between the large, urban areas of Kansas City and St. Louis, Columbia is perfectly situated for a mix of both city and suburban living. Plus, the city has consistently been ranked among the best places to live in the nation by national publications and offers a surprisingly affordable cost of living. Downtown (known as The District) boasts some of the best pizza, ice cream and cafes around, and the city has an independent movie theater and a thriving art scene. There are also a host of outdoor adventures waiting at the Devil's Ice Box, Rock Bridge State Park, MKT Trail and the city is home to a variety of cultural events such as the True/False Film Festival, Roots & Blues Festival and more.

OFF-CAMPUS OPPORTUNITIES

Many of our students can list one or more real-world professional experiences on their résumés by the time they graduate thanks to our alumni network and the Grossnickle Career Services Center. Our students have presented cutting-edge research to prestigious professional gatherings, landed internships with the FBI and at Walt Disney World, volunteered at local elementary schools and traveled to New York, Ireland and China as members of the Jane Froman Singers. Our students also have the opportunity to explore new cultures through study abroad programs to countries like England, Japan, Australia, New Zealand, Italy and France, just to name a few.

MAJORS AND DEGREES OFFERED

Columbia College awards the Associate in Arts, Associate in General Studies, Associate in Science, Bachelor of Science, Bachelor of Arts, Bachelor of Arts in General Studies, Bachelor of Fine Arts, Master of Business Administration, Master of Art in Teaching, Master of Education, Master of Human Services, Master of Science in Criminal Justice and Master of Arts in Military Studies.

Students can major in accounting, American studies, art, biology, business administration, ceramics, chemistry, communication studies, computer information systems, computer science, creative writing, criminal justice administration, education certification, English, entrepreneurship, environmental science, finance, forensic science, graphic design, healthcare management, history, human resource management, human services, international business, international relations, literature, management, management information systems, marketing, mathematics, music, philosophy, printing and drawing, photography, political science, printmaking, psychology, public administration, public relations and advertising, sociology, speech communication and sports management.

Pre-professional tracks are available to students who wish to attend law, medical or veterinary school or study engineering after graduation. Students work with their academic advisor to choose courses that will prepare them for further study. The college also offers an outstanding teacher education program, including the DAYSTAR program, and exemplary nursing program boasting a 100% pass rate for 2014 nursing exams.

ACADEMIC PROGRAMS

If you are a first-time freshman confident in the major you have chosen, the college will commit to offering you all the classes you require to graduate in four years through the Four-Year Graduation Plan.

Columbia College also offers a unique program for teachers. Students can earn a Bachelor of Arts, Master of Arts in Teaching and teacher certification in a little more than four years through the DAYSTAR teacher education program. Graduates are eligible to be certified to teach at the elementary, middle or secondary school level anywhere in the state of Missouri.

CAMPUS FACILITIES AND EQUIPMENT

The campus is a wonderful mix of historic and contemporary buildings situated on 30 park-like acres, yet all the buildings are within a five-minute walk no matter where you are on campus. Great pride is taken in preserving the campus's historic buildings, many of which are 100-150 years old. However, new buildings, such as the Atkins-Holman Student Commons and the Southwell Athletic Complex, are designed to tastefully blend in with the existing historic structures. The most recent addition to campus is the state-of-the-art Brouder Science Center, home to nursing and science majors and housing numerous lecture halls and labs. Columbia College is also pleased to host the Sidney Larson Art Gallery featuring artwork from students and professionals year-round.

There are three residence halls; Banks, Hughes and Miller, along with upperclassmen apartments known as Cougar Village. Each residence hall features extra-spacious rooms; individually controlled heating and air conditioning; e-mail and Internet services; cable television hook-ups; computer labs with printers; study lounges; free laundry facilities; and access to a kitchenette with a microwave station. Banks Hall also includes a Wellness Floor exclusively reserved for students committed to a substance-free lifestyle.

TUITION, ROOM, BOARD AND FEES

At Columbia College you should be able to plan your finances with confidence. That's why, while some colleges introduce unexpected tuition changes, Columbia College offers you a fixed rate tuition program. From the fall of 2013, the tuition rate charged for your first academic year at the college will remain fixed for five consecutive years. For the 2015-2016 academic year, tuition is $20,936; and room and board is $6,440. The room & board rates are based on a double-room rate and a standard 20-meal plan.

FINANCIAL AID

In addition to maintaining competitive tuition costs, Columbia College also awards upwards of $4 million in financial aid and scholarships every year. Around 90 percent of students receive financial aid in one form or another. Both need-based and merit scholarships are awarded.

STUDENT ORGANIZATIONS AND ACTIVITIES

As a Columbia College student, you'll quickly discover that your initiative and involvement are key to your own success. Maybe that's why nearly all of our Day Campus students are involved in at least one of the 50+ student clubs and organizations on campus.

At Columbia College, you'll have the opportunity to become a respected voice on the Student Government Association, an admired actor in the Elysium Players, a responsible resident assistant, or an inspiring leader from the Emerging Leaders Institute. Other student interest groups include mock trial, international club, honor societies, academic clubs along with many social or service clubs. It's also easy to start your own club or organization with assistance from Campus Life.

Columbia College also offers competitive athletic programs with 8 NAIA sports which are men's and women's basketball, men and women's soccer, men and women's golf, men and women's track and cross country, men's baseball (starting 2016) and women's volleyball and softball. In the past 10 years, almost all of our athletic programs have produced All-Americans and All-America Scholar-Athletes. Our women's volleyball team has brought home the NAIA national championship title three times. In 2013-2014, the men's basketball team was ranked 1st in the NAIA and finished their season 32-3. And for eight of the past 10 years two or more Columbia College coaches have been recognized as conference or regional coach of the year. In 2012, head men's basketball coach Bob Burchard was inducted into the NAIA Hall of Fame and in 2013 was named NAIA/NABC National Coach of the Year.

ADMISSIONS PROCESS

While Columbia College is selective about admission, students with a minimum high school cumulative GPA of 2.5 who rank in the top half of their graduating class, or score at 21 or above on the ACT, SAT I or GED generally can expect to be admitted to the college. Transfer students who have maintained a minimum cumulative grade point average of 2.0 are welcome and Columbia College accepts previous college credits from accredited college-level coursework, as well as from programs like CLEP, Advanced Placement, International Baccalaureate, dual credit, proficiency exams and DANTES.

With more than 3,000 colleges and universities in the country, it can be a challenge to find the school that best fits you. There's no better way to make a final decision than to visit the colleges on your short list and get a feel for each one. Columbia College offers private tours as well as hosts Cougar Days and Scholarship Days, the latter hosts a competition for 10 full ride scholarships each year. To set up a tour or find out more about Cougar or Scholarship days, contact the Admissions Office at (800) 231-2391, ext. 7352. Columbia College accepts applications throughout the year and the non-refundable application fee is $35. The fee is waived for applications received by Jan. 1 for the following fall semester. Plan a visit today and learn about the wealth of opportunities that await you at Columbia College.

COLUMBIA UNIVERSITY SCHOOL OF GENERAL STUDIES

AT A GLANCE

The School of General Studies (GS) of Columbia University is one of the finest liberal arts colleges in the United States created specifically for returning and nontraditional students seeking a rigorous, traditional, Ivy League undergraduate degree full or part time. Most students at GS have, for personal or professional reasons, interrupted their education, never attended college, or are only able to attend part time. GS is unique among colleges of its type, because its students are fully integrated into the Columbia undergraduate curriculum: they take the same courses with the same faculty members and earn the same degree as all other Columbia undergraduates.

GS students come from varied backgrounds and all walks of life. Many students work full time while pursuing a degree, and many have family responsibilities; others attend classes full time and experience Columbia's more traditional college life. In the classroom, the diversity and varied personal experience of the student body promote discussion and debate, fostering an environment of academic rigor and intellectual development. GS has approximately 1,800 undergraduate degree candidates and more than 450 Postbaccalaureate Premedical students. The average age of a GS student is 28. More than 70 percent of GS students attend classes full time.

In addition to its bachelor's degree program, GS offers combined undergraduate/graduate degree programs with Columbia's Schools of Engineering and Applied Science, Social Work, International and Public Affairs, Law, Business, Dental Medicine, Teachers College, Public Health, and the college of Physicians and Surgeons. More than 70 percent of the students go on to earn advanced degrees after graduation.

LOCATION AND ENVIRONMENT

Columbia University is located in Morningside Heights, on the Upper West Side of Manhattan. The University's neighbors include the Union Theological Seminary, the Jewish Theological Seminary, the Manhattan School of Music, St. Luke's Hospital, Women's Hospital, Riverside Church, and the Cathedral of St. John the Divine. The diversity of intellectual and social activities offered by these institutions is one of Columbia's great assets as a university; another is its location in New York City, which offers students at Columbia a rich and almost boundless variety of social, cultural, and recreational opportunities that are themselves an education.

OFF-CAMPUS OPPORTUNITIES

Columbia students may enhance their academic experiences through various study-abroad programs around the world. For example, students may spend a term at the Reid Hall Program in the Montparnasse district of Paris, the Berlin Consortium for German Studies, Kyoto Consortium for Japanese Studies, or the Language Program in Beijing, China. Additionally, students may apply to participate in one of the Columbia approved study abroad programs located in countries all over the world.

MAJORS AND DEGREES OFFERED

The School of General Studies grants a B.A. degree and offers more than eighty majors and concentrations, which include: African studies; African American studies; American studies; ancient studies; anthropology; applied mathematics; archaeology; architecture; architecture, history and theory; art history; art history–visual arts; astronomy; astrophysics; biochemistry; biology; biophysics; business management; chemical physics; chemistry; classics; comparative literature and society; computer science; computer science–mathematics; computer science-statistics; creative writing; dance; drama and theater arts; earth and environmental science; East Asian studies; ecology, evolution, and environmental Biology; economics; economics–mathematics; economics–philosophy; economics–political science; economics–statistics; education; English; environmental biology; environmental chemistry; environmental science; ethnicity and race studies; evolutionary biology of the human species; film and media studies; financial economics; French; French and Francophone studies; German literature and cultural history; Hispanic studies; history; human rights; information science, Italian cultural studies; Italian language and literature; jazz studies; Jewish studies; Latin American and Caribbean studies; Latin American and Iberian culture; linguistics; mathematics; mathematics–statistics; medieval and renaissance studies; Middle Eastern, South Asian, and African studies; modern Greek studies; music; neuroscience and behavior; philosophy; physics; political science; political science–statistics; Portuguese studies; premedical sciences; psychology; regional studies; religion; Russian language and culture; Russian literature and culture; Slavic language and culture; sociology; statistics; sustainable development; urban studies; visual arts; women's and gender studies; and Yiddish studies.

GS is home to the oldest and largest Postbaccalaureate Premedical Program in the United States, as well as dual-degree programs with the French university Sciences Po, Hong Kong's City University, and the Jewish Theological Seminary. Students enrolled in these interdisciplinary programs can earn two bachelor's degrees from two schools over four years.

The Dual BA Program is an intensive, transatlantic course of study in which undergraduate students earn bachelor's degrees from both Sciences Po and Columbia University in four years. Students will spend two years at one of three Sciences Po campuses, each of which is devoted to a particular region of the world and offers a heavy linguistic and cultural focus. After completing Sciences Po's interdisciplinary social-sciences curriculum, Dual BA students matriculate at GS to complete the requirements for a major, as well as fulfill core distribution requirements in a variety of disciplines, including literature, art, music, science, and the humanities. Upon graduation, Dual BA Program students are eligible for guaranteed admission to a graduate program at Sciences Po. Admission to the program is highly competitive, and high school seniors are eligible to apply.

The Joint Bachelor's Degree Program between City University of Hong Kong and Columbia University offers students an international undergraduate educational experience a program spanning two continents, in cosmopolitan cities that allow students to engage directly with the world around them. Joint Bachelor's Degree Program students will earn two bachelors degrees—one from City University of Hong Kong and one from Columbia University. Students who wish to be considered for admission to the Joint Bachelor's Degree Program must first apply and be accepted to the City University of Hong Kong, at which time they will be eligible for consideration for the Program.

ACADEMIC PROGRAMS

The School of General Studies offers a traditional liberal arts education designed to provide students with the broad knowledge and intellectual skills that foster continued education and growth in the years after college, as well as providing a sound foundation for positions of responsibility in the professional world. Requirements for the bachelor's degree comprise three elements: (1) core requirements, intended to develop in students the ability to write and communicate clearly; to understand the modes of thought that characterize the humanities, social sciences, and sciences; to gain familiarity with central cultural ideas through literature, fine arts, and music; and to acquire a working proficiency in a foreign language; (2) major requirements, designed to give students sustained and coherent exposure to a particular discipline in an area of strong intellectual interest; and (3) elective courses, in which students pursue particular interests and skills for their own personal growth or for their

lationship to future professional or personal objectives. Students are required
complete a minimum of 124 points for the bachelor's degree; 60 of these may
e in transfer credit, but at least 64 points (including the last 30 points) must be
ompleted at Columbia. In addition to the usual graduation honors (cum laude,
agna cum laude, and summa cum laude), honors programs for superior students
re available in a majority of the University's departments.

CADEMIC FACILITIES

he Columbia University Libraries constitute the nation's fifth-largest academic
brary system, with a collection of more than 12 million volumes, over 160,000
urnals and serials, and an extensive array electronic resources, manuscripts, rare
ooks, microforms, maps, and graphic and audio-visual materials. Of the twenty-two
braries in the system, five are designated Distinctive Collections because of their
nusual depth and nationally recognized excellence. The University's Computer
enter is one of the largest and most powerful university installations in the world
nd has remote units and terminals in several parts of the campus to enhance its
ccessibility. The Fairchild Life Science Building houses research facilities, labora-
ries, electron microscopes, and a vast amount of biochemical equipment used for
aching and research. The University's physics building has been the scene of many
nportant developments in the recent history of physics, including the invention of
e laser and the first U.S. demonstration of nuclear fission.

UITION, ROOM, BOARD AND FEES

or the 2014–15 academic year, tuition was $1,570 per point, and annual living (room
nd board) and personal expenses (books, local commuting costs, and miscellaneous
xpenses) were $22,685.

INANCIAL AID

he School of General Studies awards financial aid based upon need and academic
bility. Approximately 70 percent of General Studies degree candidates receive some
orm of financial aid, including Federal Pell Grants, New York State TAP Grants,
ederal Stafford and unsubsidized Stafford Loans, Federal Perkins Loans, General
tudies Scholarships, and Federal Work-Study Program awards. Priority application
eadlines for new students are March 1 (early action) and June 1 (regular decision)
or the fall semester and October 1 (early action) and November 1 (regular deci-
on) for the spring semester. The average scholarship award ranges from $8,000
$10,000 for first-year students.

TUDENT ORGANIZATIONS AND ACTIVITIES

ne student represents GS students in the University Senate, a decision-making
ody comprising students, faculty, and administrative staff members from each
ivision of the University. In addition, two GS students sit as voting members on
e Committee on Instruction, which oversees the curriculum of the School. The
eneral Studies Student Council elects officers each year and sponsors activities
or students. The Observer, the School's student-run magazine, is published several
mes each year. The Premedical Association (PMA) sponsors events related to the
edical school admissions process. Additionally, students are eligible to participate
any of the more than 500 student organizations on campus.

DMISSIONS PROCESS

he GS admission policy is geared to the maturity and varied backgrounds of its
udents. Aptitude and motivation are considered along with past academic perfor-
ance, standardized test scores, and employment history. The School's admission
ecisions are based on a careful review of each application and reflect the Admissions
ommittee's considered judgment of the applicant's maturity, academic potential,
nd present ability to undertake course work at Columbia.

dmission requirements include a completed application form; a 1,500- to 2,000-
ord autobiographical statement describing the applicant's past educational history
nd work experience, present situation, and future plans; two letters of recommen-
ation from academic or professional evaluators; an official high school transcript;
fficial transcripts from all colleges and universities attended; official SAT or ACT
cores (applicants may take the General Studies Admissions Examination); and a
onrefundable application fee of $80.

Students from outside the United States may apply to the School of General Studies
to start or complete a baccalaureate degree. In addition to the materials described
above, international applicants must submit official TOEFL scores or take the
Columbia University American Language Program Essay Exam.

APPLICATION AND INFORMATION

Fall Admission

Early Action

Fall Early Action applications completed by January 15 will receive a March 1 decision; applications completed by March 1 will receive a decision by May 1.

Regular Decision

Regular Decision applicants are notified of their admission decisions approximately
6–8 weeks after their applications are complete.

Spring Admission

Early Action

Spring Early Action applications completed by September 1 will receive an October 1 decision; applications completed by October 1 will receive a decision by
November 15.

Regular Decision

Regular Decision applicants are notified of their admission decisions approximately
6–8 weeks after their applications are completed.

For more information, please contact:

Curtis M. Rodgers, Vice Dean

Office of Admissions and Financial Aid

School of General Studies

408 Lewisohn Hall

2970 Broadway

Columbia University, Mail Code 4101

New York, New York 10027

Phone: 212-854-2772

E-mail: gsdegree@columbia.edu

Website: http://gs.columbia.edu

http://facebook.com/ColumbiaGS

http://twitter.com/ColumbiaGS

http://youtube.com/GSColumbia

http://vimeo.com/Columbiags

CONNECTICUT COLLEGE

One of the nation's premiere liberal arts colleges, Connecticut College is a small, highly selective, residential, private institution that recruits nationally and internationally.

AT A GLANCE

Chartered in 1911, Connecticut College was founded in the spirit of political and social equality, self-determination, and shared governance. The college actively seeks out students who are not only smart and intellectually curious, but who also bring a wide range of life experiences and perspectives that enable this spirit to endure within the college community. The college's near century-old Honor Code defines campus life. Intellectually and academically, the Honor Code inspires students to challenge themselves and their peers to see the world from diverse perspectives, to remain receptive to new ideas and experiences, and, by instilling a sense of mutual respect, to consider how their actions and education may ultimately better the common good. The college offers 42 majors and participates in the NCAA Division III New England Small College Athletic Conference (NESCAC). The college is nationally known for its career program, offering all students the opportunity for a College-funded summer internship. The college has been called a "college with a conscience," for its record of sending students to Teach for America and the Peace Corps. Enrollment at the college is approximately 1,900. In the past three years, 20 Connecticut College students have been awarded Fulbright Scholarships.

LOCATION AND ENVIRONMENT

Connecticut College's beautiful 750-acre arboretum campus is located in the historic New England seaport community of New London. Just a two-hour drive from Boston and New York, the region is dotted with beaches, concert venues and theaters, shopping districts and great restaurants and there are plenty of opportunities for local internships. At the heart of the campus, Tempel Green sweeps down to offer commanding views of Long Island Sound. The college's athletic and fitness center is located along the Thames River.

OFF-CAMPUS OPPORTUNITIES

The college is conveniently located near shopping and the New London transportation center, which features train, bus, and ferry service to points along the eastern seaboard. New London is a diverse community home to numerous restaurants and cafes, galleries, and historic sites. The city also serves as the region's legal, medical, and social service center. The college operates a shuttle service for students to area locations and provides three ZipCars for students. Sophomores, juniors and seniors are permitted to have cars on campus. The college's career and volunteer offices work closely with students to arrange for service learning or internship opportunities. Each year, more than 500 students intern, work or volunteer for local businesses and organizations or in local schools or afterschool programs.

MAJORS AND DEGREES OFFERED

Connecticut College offers 42 majors and, with faculty approval, students can design their own major. Courses lead toward a Bachelor of Arts degree. Students complete General Education Requirements that ensure broad engagement with a range of disciplines across the liberal arts. Connecticut College students explore interests across subject areas and geographic boundaries and consider the campus and course catalogue open to them in this pursuit. The college offers free music lessons to all students. Students in a variety of majors may pursue certification in elementary, secondary, or private school education or receive a certificate demonstrating experience in museum studies. The most popular majors are economics, psychology, biological sciences, government, international relations, English, history, environmental studies, American studies and art. The college's dance program is internationally reputed, as is its theater program, which offers students the opportunity to study at the Eugene O'Neill Theater Center in Waterford, Connecticut, and the Eugene O'Neill Moscow Art Theater in Russia.

ACADEMIC PROGRAMS

Students benefit from small classes that foster discussion and lead to personalize relationships with professors who serve as teacher-scholars. Professors frequent spark interests that inspire students for a lifetime. The student to faculty ratio is to 1. Average class size is 19. Each first-year student takes a seminar course with maximum enrollment of 16. Ninety-two percent of full-time faculty members hav a PhD or other terminal degree.

More than half of all students study away in a variety of domestic or internationa programs. Study away complements and informs Connecticut College's liberal ar curriculum (students who choose to study away do so primarily through the co lege's affiliation with institutions in over 40 countries.) The college also maintair domestic affiliations, including those with the Williams-Mystic Seaport Progran the Maritime Biological Laboratory Ecosystems Center at Woods Hole, and th Twelve College Exchange. In addition, students study away through Connectic College's Study Away-Teach Away (SATA) program, in which a group of 10 to 1 students and one or two professors travel overseas for a semester and affiliate wit a foreign university. SATA programs have been conducted in the Czech Republi Cuba, China, Peru, Egypt, Ghana, Greece, India, Italy, Mexico, Morocco, Sout Africa, Spain, Tanzania, and Vietnam.

To ensure that students consider the practical application of their study, the colleg provides each student with $3,000 to fund an internship or research project betwee their junior and senior year. About 80 percent of all students attend the series o seminars and complete the work required to become eligible for the funding. On in five students conducts an internship overseas. Recent internships have bee conducted with such organizations as The Field Museum of Chicago, Google, J. Morgan, Azafady in Madagascar, Vera Wang, New Line Cinema, and, CBS Sport

The college operates five centers for interdisciplinary scholarship that prepar students to understand and address complex issues across multiple areas of stud The Centers are certificate-granting programs within the college that serve as a intellectual commons to bring together professors, students, and outside expert There are five Centers, each with their own focus: The Toor Cummings Center fc International Studies and the Liberal Arts; The Ammerman Center for Arts an Technology; The Holleran Center for Community Action and Public Policy; Th Goodwin-Niering Center for the Environment; and, the Center for the Comparativ Study of Race and Ethnicity. Students combine their coursework with an integrate project and a paid overseas or domestic internship organized through the Cente to receive a certificate.

CAMPUS FACILITIES AND EQUIPMENT

Connecticut College occupies 750 acres (all of which are included in the Connecticu College Arboretum) on a hill overlooking the Thames River and Long Island Sounc The Arboretum's diverse acreage includes the landscaped grounds of the campu as well as the surrounding plant collections and natural areas. The resources of th Arboretum support the college's mission of preparing the next generation of citize leaders to craft a sustainable relationship with the natural world. The symbios of the Environmental Studies major and the Goodwin-Niering Center provide an outstanding model of an ethically and environmentally sound community an places the college in a singular environment, which offers a quality of life uniqu among liberal arts institutions.

The Charles E. Shain Library was completely renovated in 2015. The newly renovated library serves as a center for academic, social and cultural life on campus, with enhanced spaces for collaboration, modern technology services, and a café that serves as a 24-hour study space. Shain offers more than 616,000 books and bound periodicals, 151,000 media and computing materials, and 5,599 subscriptions to periodicals. The collection is augmented through a consortium with Trinity College and Wesleyan University that provides fast access to more than 2.2 million items.

The library is also home to the college's Academic Resource Center, which helps all students reach their full academic potential through academic and career advising, student support services, peer-to-peer learning, and skill-development training.

Other key buildings, include: the state-of-the art science center at New London Hall; Hale Laboratory; the Frank Loomis Palmer Auditorium; the F.W. Olin Science Center; Dayton Arena; the college Athletic Center; the Lee and Ann Higdon Fitness Center, the Lyn and David Silfen Track and Field; and, Cummings Arts Center, which includes the Greer Music Library.

TUITION, ROOM, BOARD, AND FEES

The comprehensive fee for 2014–15 is $60,895. This covers tuition; room and board; lab fees; studio fees; special programs, such as our funded internship; some course-related travel; study away and even music lessons. Ninety-nine percent of students live on campus.

FINANCIAL AID

Connecticut College offers need-based financial aid and meets 100 percent of a student's financial aid eligibility. Forty-nine percent of students received some form of institutional aid. The average aid award is $37,300 and 88 percent of all aid awarded is scholarships and grants that do not need to be repaid.

STUDENT ORGANIZATIONS AND ACTIVITIES

As a small, residential liberal arts college, Connecticut College encourages students to pursue many interests outside the classroom, with the Crozier-Williams Student Center serving as the main hub for extracurricular activity as the site of club offices, WCNI-FM radio station, the weekly College Voice newspaper, and forums for live music, debate, dance, and poetry. Galleries, student run cafes, and performance spaces are found throughout campus. The Tansill Theater, a blackbox theater, is frequently home to student written productions. Students participate in dozens of clubs and organizations, including the Pegotty Investment Club, the Connecticut College Asian/Asian-American Student Association, Hillel, and Habitat for Humanity. Students compete in a range of varsity, club, and intramural sports. The campus LGBTQ Center and Women's Center host events focused on issues of sexuality, equity, and gender, while Unity House is the campus multicultural center and works with the Director of Unity House to host events focused on issues of race.

ADMISSIONS PROCESS

Connecticut College is one of the nation's most highly selective colleges. In 2014, 37.6 percent of applicants were offered a place in the class of 2018. The college requires the Common Application and Member Page. An interview is recommended but not required. The submission of standardized tests (SAT Reasoning, SAT II, or ACT) is optional, although students whose primary language is not English are required to submit TOEFL scores or an equivalent. The college expects applicants will have taken the most appropriately rigorous courses available.

Application deadlines: Early Decision I, Nov. 15 for all ED1 application materials; Early Decision II and Regular Decision, Jan. 1 for all application materials. Financial Aid application dates: ED I, Nov. 15; ED II, Jan. 15; Regular Decision, Feb. 1.

CURRY COLLEGE

AT A GLANCE

Curry College is a private, four-year, liberal arts-based institution located on a wooded 131-acre campus in Milton, MA just seven miles from downtown Boston. At Curry, we educate and graduate students prepared to engage in successful careers and active citizenship with a global perspective. We are an inclusive community of diverse learners and educators, and we mentor and empower our students, building meaningful relationships that inspire them to achieve their ambitions. Our relevant, career-directed programs and co-and extracurricular activities allow students to gain hands-on, practical field experiences, early and often in their college experience, both on campus and off campus.

LOCATION AND ENVIRONMENT

The wooded, 131-acre Milton campus is one of the most attractive small college campuses in New England. Unlike other isolated suburban or rural campuses, Curry College is just seven miles from downtown Boston, one of the most exciting cities in the world. The college's location offers students an exceptional advantage, and opportunities for internships and entertainment in this New England capital is a significant part of the Curry experience.

Curry's location has yet another advantage: it is less than two miles from the scenic Blue Hills, a natural reservation which offers skiing, hiking, horseback riding, and a range of resources for environmental education and recreation.

Back on campus, students also enjoy the comfort of Curry's tight-knit, friendly community and the security services provided by the Department of Public Safety. Students have a wealth of resources on campus to help them excel academically, socially, and physically and find endless sources of entertainment, action, and challenge.

Curry College is home to a caring and committed community where visitors are always welcome. We invite you to visit our interactive campus map online to learn about our campus facilities and to consider visiting Curry in person. We hope to see you on campus soon!

Major and Degrees Offered

Curry College provides rigorous and relevant academic programs to undergraduate and graduate students, and our rich blend of liberal arts and career-directed programs is enhanced by practical field experiences and co-curricular activities. Learning at Curry extends beyond the classroom and is embedded in all that we do.

At Curry, we recognize the potential in all of our students. We take a personalized approach to education that allows students to build on their dreams while they simultaneously explore new ideas and uncover talents, strengths, and abilities they never thought they had. Students find challenge through our honors programs or support through the Program for Advancement of Learning.

Students can select from 22 majors and 65-plus minors and concentrations ranging from biology to theatre. Academic majors at Curry College include:

- Biochemistry
- Biology
- Business Management
- Communication
- Community Health and Wellness
- Criminal Justice
- Education:
  o Child Youth & Community
  o Early Childhood Education (Licensure)
  o Elementary Education (Licensure)
  o Special Education (Licensure)
- English and Writing
- Environmental Science
- Graphic Design
- Individually Initiated Major
- Information Technology
- Integrated Liberal Studies
- Mobile Application Development
- Nursing
- Philosophy
- Politics and History
- Psychology
- Sociology
- Visual Arts

OFF-CAMPUS OPPORTUNITIES

Curry College's proximity to Boston gives students access to a wide variety of internships at leading companies and clinical placements at world-class hospitals. Curry students may earn up to 30 credit hours for field internships. In consultation with faculty members, students develop learning contracts that articulate their educational and personal goals and establish criteria for the evaluation of their field experience. Students may also arrange to study abroad or at another institution within the United States while enrolled at Curry.

FACILITIES AND EQUIPMENT

Curry College opened its newest residence hall, Alexander Graham Bell Hall, in 2014. The 46,000 square-foot building has 168 beds, along with a classroom and other multi-functional areas where students can study and socialize in a true living and learning environment.

In total, there are 19 residential buildings on campus, offering a variety of living options ranging from traditional residence halls of over 150 students to smaller houses for under 20 residents. Four new residence halls were constructed between 1999 and 2005 as the college achieved an ambitious campus expansion plan. The college has also invested significant resources in modernizing well-established residential buildings that have classic architecture and a great history on campus. The expansion and enhancement of our residence halls has had a positive impact on the learning and living environment and experience of Curry College students.

Curry College's Student Center is an 84,000 square foot facility full of state-of-the-art areas for dinning, studying, athletics, student activities, or simply lounging around. The Student Center has become a place to study between classes, to meet up with friends for dinner, work out or take on a roommate in a game of billiards or foosball.

The Gertrude M. Webb Learning Center is a unique, Tudor-style building with several thousand square feet of space dedicated to students with learning differences receiving support through our Program of Advancement of Learning (PAL).

The Kennedy Academic Center, located on South Campus, houses many of Curry's classrooms as well as nursing and computer labs (PC and Mac).

The John S. Hafer Academic Building, located on the academic quad on North Campus houses many of Curry's classrooms. The Hafer Building is also a popular location on campus for hosting cultural activities and guest speakers. The building features our state-of-the art television studio, the Hirsh Communication Center, a full-service HD studio that utilizes advanced virtual set technology to create dozens of set options at a click of a mouse, in addition to physical sets in a 20 x 40 television studio.

The studio also includes classroom space and digital editing facilities, which include, AVID, Final Cut Pro HD, Premiere Pro, and After Effects. We are an affiliate for CNN Newsource and our TV Practicum class produces content for our college TV station, CC8, ranging from a regularly scheduled newscast to live sports productions including basketball, baseball, hockey, football, soccer and more. Students also produce and script creative content like comedy shorts and documentary reports.

The College also houses an award-winning, non-commercial radio station on campus. Licensed by the Federal Communications Commission on April 1, 1975, WMLN-FM operates on an assigned frequency of 91.5 MHz with a power of 172 watts. WMLN serves a potential audience of 250,000 within a 40-mile radius on Boston's South Shore. Most programs are produced by radio station students who earn credits for their participation. WMLN-FM is affiliated with the following professional organizations: NBC/CNN, Associated Press, Intercollegiate Broadcasters Association, Massachusetts Broadcasters Association, National Association of Broadcasters, and the New England Broadcasters Association

The Academic and Performance Center is a three-story, 30,000 square-foot building with eight classrooms, including an amphitheatre-style lecture hall and a stock trading classroom, faculty office suites, a student lounge, conference and breakout meeting rooms, and a two-story atrium with a smart-café offering quick and healthy eating options. The building includes a 229-seat multi-purpose auditorium, which also serves as a performance space for Curry College students.

TUITION, ROOM AND BOARD, AND FEES

Annual Tuition and Fees 2015–2016

   Tuition: $34,730

   Fees: $2,035

   Room/Board: $13,900

   Total (exclusive of PAL)

   Resident: $53,850 °°

   Commuter: $42,572

   PAL Fee

   (if applicable): $6,940

°°The total cost for resident students is based on 14 meals per week and a multiple occupancy room. The plan including 17 meals per week would increase the cost by $590. The 10 meals per week plan would decrease the total cost by $1,330. A single occupancy room would increase the total cost by $1,960. Additional fees may apply.

FINANCIAL AID

Recognizing that meeting the total cost of a higher education today can be challenging for students and families, Curry College provides a variety of financing options and participates in federal and state financial aid programs.

The Student Financial Services staff is committed to helping students create a financial plan that will allow them to reach their enrollment goals. In order to be considered for need-based financial aid, students must complete a FAFSA annually. You can fill out a FAFSA online at www.fafsa.ed.gov or use the paper application. If you would like us to mail you a paper FAFSA application, please contact our office and we would be happy to mail one to you. FAFSA forms are also available at any high school. Financial aid comes in three forms: grants and scholarships; loans; and student employment. Curry College provides students with millions of dollars in financial aid each year. The college uses its own endowment funds, gifts from friends, foundations and corporations, alumni, parents, and other donors to be able to provide this funding to our students. We believe in the potential of every Curry College student and realize that financing a student's education can be a difficult task for a family. Curry also receives substantial funding from the various state and federal financial aid programs.

STUDENT ORGANIZATIONS AND ACTIVITIES

At Curry College, you'll instantly become part of a unique, upbeat community with all the resources to help you excel academically, socially, and physically. The college serves approximately 2,100 traditional students from more than 31 states and 7 countries; more than 1,500 of its students reside on the Curry campus. Whether you're a resident student or commuter student, we'll help you find your niche.

You can choose from a wide array of extracurricular activities ranging from 14 NCAA Division III athletic teams—seven men's team and seven women's teams—to an outstanding theatre program. The Curry College experience is as unique as you are and the opportunities are endless.

Right on campus you'll find countless sources of entertainment, action, and challenge. You can unwind in the Student Center over a game of pool, meet friends at a movie night, take a turn behind the mic, or just listen, at a coffeehouse or comedy night. Work out in the weight room or exercise your voice in the Currier Times newspaper or campus chorale. Join one of the many student clubs and organizations or volunteer for community service projects.

The staff in the offices of Student Affairs—Student Activities, Residence Life, Public Safety, Health and Counseling, and the Chaplaincy—are all committed to helping you develop your personal goals and establish relationships within the Curry College community. We encourage your involvement and leadership in all aspects of college life.

ADMISSIONS PROCESSES AND REQUIREMENTS

As you explore enrollment at Curry College, the Office of Admission encourages you to visit the campus and meet with an Admission Counselor. To be considered for admission to Curry College, we require you to submit the following:

• A completed application with a nonrefundable fee of $50

• An official high school transcript

• Results of the SAT or ACT

• A letter of recommendation from a guidance counselor or high school teacher

• A college essay

DAEMEN COLLEGE

AT A GLANCE

Located just outside of Buffalo, New York, Daemen College is a private college offering strong liberal arts majors, exceptional professional degrees, and widely acclaimed graduate programs. Daemen is distinguished by a low student/faculty ratio and consistently small class sizes, which encourage students to interact with professors and grow as individuals. Daemen has approximately 2,000 undergraduate and 1,000 graduate students. Daemen students have their education enriched by challenging opportunities that engage them in learning experiences through international education programs, collaborative research with faculty, clinical and field experiences, internships for credit, and service learning positions. Daemen students embrace an academically challenging atmosphere where they are encouraged to develop a strong repertoire of knowledge and skills. Daemen College meets the individual goals and needs of each student, preparing them for leadership and professional life in a global economy.

LOCATION AND ENVIRONMENT

Daemen's beautiful 39-acre campus is located in Amherst, New York, a peaceful suburb of Buffalo. Due to its proximity to Buffalo, Daemen's campus is close to many major rail, plane, and motor routes. While the campus setting is tranquil and residential, Buffalo is a vibrant cultural city, bustling with world-class entertainment, such as the Philharmonic Orchestra, the Albright-Knox Art Gallery, and Shea's Theater. The greater Buffalo area is rich with sports and recreational activities all year round, whether it be skiing and swimming, or watching our professional sports teams. Niagara Falls is only 30 minutes away and Toronto is just two hours by car. On campus, the numerous trees and open green spaces create a lovely environment to work and study.

OFF-CAMPUS OPPORTUNITIES: CAREER SERVICES, GLOBAL PROGRAMS, AND SERVICE LEARNING

Daemen's Career Service Office provides students and graduates with a wide variety of services specially geared to the vocational and self-development needs of the college community before and after graduation. Career Services also helps students create a personalized strategy through the iCAP—individual career action plan. In addition, Career Services helps students find an internship so that they can gain real-world experience in their area of interest. Students often express how prepared they feel to have had the chance to experience what careers in their fields are really like. An added bonus, internship employers sometimes offer Daemen interns full-time positions after graduation. The opportunities are local, national, or international—including excellent opportunities with the Washington Internship Institute. Each year they bring employers on campus for career and internship fairs.

Daemen's Global Programs office coordinates distinctive study abroad opportunities designed to facilitate students' professional aspirations. In today's global economy, it makes sense to learn all you can about different cultures, political systems, and histories. International study is a staple of the Daemen experience. There are several options when looking at the amount of time students want to study abroad—whether it's a week, semester, or even a year! Students have studied in Australia, China, Costa Rica, England, France, Greece, Italy, Mexico, and many other countries.

Daemen believes in "learning through service." Each academic year, nearly 500 Daemen students contribute over 30,000 volunteer hours to make a difference in the lives of youth, families and communities. In the process, students serve, learn, and gain the leadership, cross-cultural, and communication skills necessary to become civic-minded individuals prepared to participate in a democratic society. Students can choose from a variety of service-learning courses and site placements in settings that include Boys & Girls Clubs, community centers, soup kitchens, housing rehabilitation and refugee resettlement agencies, shelters for the homeless, nursing homes, and many other health and human service agencies.

MAJORS AND DEGREES OFFERED

Daemen College offers BA, BFA, BS, MS, DNP and DPT programs.

Majors offered at Daemen include: Accounting BS/MS, Animation, Art; Applied Theater, Drawing, Graphic Design, Illustration, Painting, Sculpture, Visual Arts Education K-12, Arts Administration BS/MS, Athletic Training BS/MS, Biology; Adolescence Education 7-12, Environmental Studies, Biology/Cytotechnology BS/MS, Biochemistry; Pre-Professional, Business Administration; Human Resource Management, International Business, Marketing, Sport Management, Education; Childhood Education 1-6, Childhood Education/ Special Education1-6, Early Childhood Education/Special Education B-12, English; Adolescence Education 7-12, Communications/Public Relations, French; Adolescence Education 7-12, Health Care Studies; Community Health, Complementary and Alternative Health Care Practices, Health and Fitness Training, History, History and Political Science; Adolescence Education 7-12, Environmental Studies, Mathematics; Adolescence Education 7-12, Natural Sciences; Environmental Studies, Forensic Science, Health Science, Individualized Studies, Nursing, Paralegal, Physical Therapy BS,NS/DPT, Physician Assistant BS/MS, Political Science, Psychology, Religious Studies, Social Work, Spanish; Adolescence Education 7-12, Sustainability (Global and Local) Interdisciplinary studies; Environmental Studies, Health Care Studies, Individualized Study, and Pre-Professional Programs; Pre-Dentistry, Pre-Law, Pre-Medicine, and Pre-Veterinary.

Graduate MS programs include Accounting; Professional Accountancy, Athletic Training, Arts Administration, Special Education 1-6, Executive Leadership and Change, Global Business, Nursing; Adult-Gerontology Primary Care Nurse Practitioner, Nursing Education, Nursing Executive Leadership, Physician Assistant, Social Work and Public Health.

Doctorate programs include Doctor of Nursing Practice and Direct Entry Doctor of Physical Therapy. In addition Physical Therapy offers an Orthopedic Manual Physical Therapy Fellowship Program/ MS in OMPT.

ACADEMIC PROGRAMS

Daemen College is committed to complimenting the depth of study in a major field with a well-rounded academic understanding in the liberal arts. The college's core curriculum ensures that every student graduates with the following seven core competencies: critical thinking and creative problem solving; communication skills; information and literacy; civic responsibility; contextual competency; affective awareness; and moral and ethical discernment. This innovative core curriculum competes with those of Ivy League Institutions and prepares the student in a holistic manner which not only makes them more marketable upon graduation, but instructs them in alternative ways of approaching education and learning.

Daemen provides students with small classes and a caring and committed faculty, allowing for a personalized educational experience. Academics at Daemen will challenge you to test your knowledge, raise your expectations, and think critically and creatively. Daemen's core competencies, honors program, academic exchanges, global programs, and undergraduate research are just a few examples of what makes the college challenging and distinctive.

Daemen students are well-prepared for professional success. The vast majority of them obtain a position of choice or admission to graduate study in less than a year after graduation. They are leaders in their communities, with a strong dedication to the improvement of the communities in which they live.

CAMPUS FACILITIES AND EQUIPMENT

Modern apartment-style residence halls provide separate housing for male and female students, in addition to our existing five-story residence hall. All residence halls have kitchens, laundry facilities, lounges, and in-room phone/Internet connections.

Full-service meals are served in the main dining hall, with an a la carte selection in the snack bar. The recreation room and Cyber Cafe are popular spots for socializing and relaxing during the day or evening.

The Research and Information Commons is a technological showcase that has become the hub of academic research, as well as the academic and social heart of the campus.

The new Center for Visual and Performing Arts is equipped with an interactive performance/lecture space with seating for 50, featuring high-resolution projection and state-of-the-art smart board technology. The Center features flexible studio space allowing for studio instruction and theatrical space, with moveable walls making it possible to transform one large studio into three smaller ones. A second floor, dedicated to Graphic Design, houses a large, open production space as well as computer labs and faculty offices.

TUITION, ROOM, BOARD AND FEES

Tuition for the 2014–2015 academic year is $24,480, with additional room and board fees of $11,430. (Cost varies according to meal plan and residence facility.)

FINANCIAL AID

Learning to navigate the financial aid system can be a daunting task. That's why Daemen has trained professionals on hand to assist you every step of the way. The Admissions staff and Financial Aid counselors will assist you and your family with the process, and will ensure you understand the necessary paperwork and deadlines required in order for you to receive the best financial aid package available.

Daemen strives to create individualized financial aid packages for you and your family that will meet your needs and enable you to get the most out of your college education. Daemen offers merit-based and need-based financial assistance, as well as aid based on a combination of financial need and academic achievement. More than 94% of current students receive some form of financial assistance. In addition to the college's own scholarships, Daemen participates in all federal and state programs.

STUDENT ORGANIZATIONS AND ACTIVITIES

Student activities provide for the development of the whole person outside of the classroom. The Director of Student Activities on campus helps students participate in recognized organizations, form new ones, and plan events. With over 50 student organizations the possibilities for involvement at Daemen are limitless. Whether your interests are in art or skiing, there is bound to be something that grabs your interest and introduces you to students who share similar passions. Daemen believes that now is the time to discover exactly who you are; cultivating your hidden talents, taking new risks and challenging yourself to grow are all part of the Daemen experience. Daemen encourages all students to become actively engaged in the campus community.

Athletics

The Wildcats are a member of the United States Collegiate Athletic Association (US-CAA) and have entered the Provisional Year of the NCAA Division II membership process. Daemen offers men's and women's basketball, cross-country, soccer, tennis, and track and field (indoor/outdoor), as well as men's golf and women's volleyball.

ADMISSIONS PROCESS

The average student enrolled has a 91 GPA and 1060 SAT. Daemen has a test-optional policy which provides students with a choice regarding the submission of standardized test scores. Daemen has a rolling admissions policy. However, due to program and residence-hall capacity limits, we highly encourage you to send your deposit as soon as you have made your decision.

The admissions staff helps guide students through the process from start to finish. Students can create a personalized Daemen Connection web page at http://daemen.edu/admissions.

Prospective students can apply for free online at daemen.edu/apply or commonapp.org.

The best way to get to know Daemen is in person. On your visit, we'll take you on a campus tour, arrange for you to meet professors and current students, and plan a one-on-one meeting with an Admissions counselor.

To schedule your appointment, contact the Office of Admissions at 800-462-7652 or 716-839-8225. You may make an individual visit Mon-Sat, attend our Fall and Spring Open Houses, or join us for many of our other special admissions events. We hope to see you on campus soon! If you have any questions you can email admissions@daemen.edu.

DESALES UNIVERSITY

DeSales University is a medium-sized, Catholic liberal arts university for men and women administered by the Oblates of St. Francis de Sales.

AT A GLANCE

Founded in 1964, DeSales University is a Catholic liberal arts university that offers courses in a wide range of disciplines. DeSales provides personal attention, small class size, and a feeling of community. The University uses a holistic approach to help students develop a "sense of self," enabling every student to reach their personal and academic potential. This student-centered philosophy is conveyed by an enthusiastic, accessible faculty.

LOCATION AND ENVIRONMENT

DeSales University's suburban campus is located 15 minutes south of Bethlehem and Allentown, Pa., and only 1 hour from Philadelphia, 90 minutes from Scranton and Wilkes-Barre, Pa., less than 2 hours from New York City, and 3 hours from Baltimore. The campus is 500 acres with more than 16 major buildings.

OFF-CAMPUS OPPORTUNITIES

Allentown and Bethlehem are a short 15-minute drive from campus and offer many dining, shopping, and outdoor activities, including the Promenade Shops at Saucon Valley, just minutes from campus. The Lehigh Valley, aka "College Valley," boasts beautiful hiking and biking trails, historic sites, museums, cultural festivals, and Dorney Park and Wildwater Kingdom. Skiing at nearby Blue Mountain and other Pocono resorts is just a short drive away. The Poconos also offer white water rafting trips down the Lehigh and Delaware Rivers.

MAJORS AND DEGREES OFFERED

DeSales University offers more than 30 bachelor's degrees including 8 pre-professional programs, and 8 graduate programs through the divisions of business, liberal arts and social sciences, performing arts, and science and health care. Our more popular majors include criminal justice, theatre, medical studies, and business administration.

ACADEMIC PROGRAMS

DeSales University defines "global competence" as using an open, inquisitive mind to understand the norms and expectations of other cultures, and using this acquired knowledge to communicate and to work effectively outside of one's usual environment in the promotion of human solidarity. DeSales University presents opportunities for students to enlarge their world view, from activities and concerts to short- and long-term study abroad programs.

Study abroad programs through DeSales present the opportunity for our students to live and work in this vibrantly interdependent world and range from semester long study to short stay travel of 10 days. Our students can spend semesters in England, Greece, Italy, Ireland, Switzerland, France, and Monte Carlo. More importantly, DeSales uses a model of intense hands-on engagement through short-stay co-curricular trips of students, faculty, and staff. Trips to Ireland, Germany, Istanbul, South Africa, and Austria for short stay intensive travel have been combined with academic courses, the activities of student organizations, or out of season competition for our athletic teams.

Freshman students are asked to participate in the Character U program, a self assessment program based on the Golden Counsels of St. Francis de Sales. Each month, University programming addresses one of these Golden Counsels or traits including patience, trust and cooperation, and perseverance. The DeSales Experience offers opportunities to learn and lead outside the classroom.

The University's Academic Resource Center can offer assistance in reading comprehension, study skills, time management and effective writing techniques. Additionally they can help find a tutor if you need it or provide you with the opportunity to become a peer tutor.

CAMPUS FACILITIES AND EQUIPMENT

Trexler Library has a collection of more than 500,000 items and there are electronic databases of newspapers, journal articles, and the Oxford Dictionary of National Biography. There are computer and multimedia labs and a staff who will help with any research topic. Trexler Library has wireless access both with personal laptops or laptops that can be borrowed to use in the building. The Library's resources can be accessed from anywhere on campus. There is online access to databases and full text journal articles. Students can also instant message a librarian with a question.

The DeSales University Center features many menu choices—especially for healthy eaters—in a food court setting. The University Center also has wireless laptop capability so you can eat and surf, as well as see panoramic views of campus.

The Priscilla Payne Hurd Science Center, a 37,500 square foot facility, is equipped with up-to-date computers, labs, and medical equipment. The Hurd Science Center also features a sterile molecular/cell biology suite, complete with a freezer room, bench room, support room, dark room, and instrument room. An ecology/environmental lab with a growing chamber, an analytical/physical chemistry/inorganic laboratory, and a bioinformatics/physics lab also inhabit the two-story building.

The Gambet Center for Business and Health Care Education is a 77,000 square foot academic building that houses the school's business division and health care majors. It features a simulated trading room for business and finance majors, standardized patient areas, and a gross anatomy lab.

TUITION, ROOM, BOARD, AND FEES

Tuition and Fees (2014–15): $31,000

Room and Board: $11,762

Student & Technology Fee: $1,350

Total: $44,112

FINANCIAL AID

Nine out of ten DeSales University students receive financial aid in the form of grants, scholarships, work study, and loans. About 85 percent of the students receive grants directly from DeSales University, and funds are also available from federal and state programs to those who qualify. The amount of aid received and the composition of an aid package will depend on financial need and on academic achievement and potential.

Academic scholarships are also available through DeSales University. All applicants for admission are automatically considered for each of the scholarships offered by the University.

STUDENT ORGANIZATIONS AND ACTIVITIES

DeSales University has more than 30 campus organizations, including the Student Activities crew, which helps plan student events, bus trips, and on-campus performances. The McShea Student Union includes a student activities lounge open to students for entertainment and socializing and a café that offers another dining option. The McShea Student Union has been renovated to accommodate increased special events such as independent movie nights, comedians, music acts, and expanded space for programs sponsored by various student organizations.

DeSales University has 16 intercollegiate varsity sports teams and all are members of the NCAA Division III, Middle Atlantic States Collegiate Athletic Corporation (MAC) Freedom Conference, and the Eastern College Athletic Conference (ECAC).

The University's men's sports are baseball, basketball, cross-country, golf, lacrosse, soccer, and indoor and outdoor track and field. Women's sports are basketball, cross-country, field hockey, soccer, softball, indoor and outdoor track & field, and volleyball. The University also has seven club sports: cheerleading, cycling, disc golf, equestrian, ice hockey, tennis, and men's volleyball.

There are intramural sports for all seasons, or student can visit the Billera Hall fitness center, which offers aerobic, Nautilus, and free-weight training.

ADMISSIONS PROCESS

To Apply for Admission you need to:

Complete a DeSales University application and submit it to our Admissions Office.

Have your high school guidance department send your official high school transcript to our Admissions Office.

Have your standardized test scores (SAT or ACT) sent to our Admissions Office. Our code number for SAT scores is 2021.

Have a guidance counselor and teacher complete the recommendation forms and send to our Admissions Office.

DRAKE UNIVERSITY

AT A GLANCE

Drake University provides a thriving intellectual environment offering more than 70 majors, covering subjects from the liberal arts to professional and pre-professional programs. The University employs professors who demonstrate a dedication to students along with academic prowess. Students benefit from the low 12:1 student-faculty ratio, and they never take classes from graduate students or teaching assistants. Drake enrolls a heterogeneous group of nearly 5,600 students, from 49 states and more than 50 foreign countries. Drake prides itself on alumni success, noting that 98.3% percent of 2014 Drake graduates embarked on careers or started graduate programs during their first six months out of school.

Drake grants master's degrees in: accounting, athletic training (starting in 2017), business administration, communication leadership, education, financial management, jurisprudence, and public administration. Students may also pursue their Doctor of Pharmacy, Doctor of Occupational Therapy, Doctor of Jurisprudence, and Doctor of Education degrees. Joint degrees are also available in MBA/JD, MPA/JD, MBA/PharmD, MPA/PharmD, and PharmD/JD.

LOCATION AND ENVIRONMENT

Students take advantage of Drake's location in Des Moines, Iowa, the state capital and a thriving business center. Internships are available in fields such as government, banking, insurance, publishing, nonprofit organizations, and health care, and nearly 80 percent of students participate in at least one internship during their four years at the University.

OFF-CAMPUS OPPORTUNITIES

Many students take advantage of overseas studies options offered through January Term options or the Center for International Programs and Services. Through the Center's work with international institutions and consortia, semester- and yearlong programs are offered in more than 60 countries.

MAJORS AND DEGREES OFFERED

Those studying in the college of Arts and Sciences receive a classic liberal arts education, preparing them for futures in science, mathematics, politics, and the arts, among many other areas. Students may earn their Bachelor of Arts and Bachelor of Science degrees in the following areas: anthropology and sociology; astronomy; biochemistry, cell and molecular biology; biology; chemistry; computer science; data analytics; English; environmental policy; environmental science; history; international relations; kinesiology, law, politics, and society; mathematics; mathematics education (secondary); neuroscience; philosophy; physics; politics; psychology; religion; rhetoric and communication studies; sociology; study of culture and society; and writing. Some students design their own majors, while others opt for open enrollment and do not immediately declare a major. The University also administers pre-professional study in dentistry, engineering, law, medicine and veterinary medicine. Concentrations are available in anthropology, geography, Latin American studies, animal behavior, , women and gender studies, and most fields that offer majors.

Students who attend the School of Fine Arts pursue their Bachelor of Arts, Bachelor of Fine Arts, Bachelor of Music, and Bachelor of Music Education degrees. The available fields include art, music, and theatre arts with a dual focus on teaching excellence and artistic creativity. Holding accreditation from by the National Association of Schools of Art and Design, Drake's Department of Art and Design offers instruction in art history, graphic design, and studio art (drawing, painting, printmaking, and sculpture). Students in the Department of Music select from degrees in applied music (instrumental, piano or vocal music performance) and music education. Other alternatives exist, such as a Bachelor of Arts degree with a music major, a Bachelor of Music degree with elective studies in business, and a Bachelor of Music with a jazz studies concentration. Those who wish to study theatre, acting, directing, theatre design, musical theatre, and theatre education enroll in the Department of Theatre Arts.

Students enrolled in the Drake University College of Business and Public Administration complete their undergraduate degree of Bachelor of Science in Business Administration in four years. Available majors include accounting, actuarial science, data analytics, economics, entrepreneurial management, finance, general business, information systems, international business, management, and marketing. Concentrations in insurance and law and business are also available. The college allows interdisciplinary majors, combinations of majors, and open business (undeclared) status. The college is a member of AACSB International—The International Association to Advance Collegiate Schools of Business.

First-year students admitted directly to the PharmD program in the college of Pharmacy and Health Sciences complete a two-year pre-pharmacy program then are guaranteed consideration for admission into a four-year PharmD program. A health sciences major with two tracks—clinical and applied sciences and health services management—is also available. In 2016, the college of Pharmacy and Health Sciences in launching a pre-OT/Doctor of Occupational Therapy six-year program. In 2017, the college is launching a 3+2 health sciences/master's in athletic training program. The college is accredited by the Accreditation Council for Pharmacy Education and belongs to the American Association of Colleges of Pharmacy.

Students who wish to pursue Bachelor of Arts majors in advertising, digital media production, news journalism, magazines, strategic political communication, public relations study in the School of Journalism and Mass Communication. The School allows an open enrolled (undeclared) option and holds accreditation from the Accrediting Council on Education in Journalism and Mass Communication.

Interdisciplinary concentrations are offered in behavior analysis of developmental disabilities, global public health and comparative studies and human resources management.

In addition, the college of Arts and Sciences, the college of Business and Public Administration, the college of Pharmacy and Health Sciences, and the School of Journalism offer combined 3+3 programs with the Drake University Law School. Students in this program can obtain their undergraduate degrees in three years in one of the aforementioned colleges or schools, then pursue a law degree for the next three years at the Law School.

Programs at the School of Education lead to degrees in elementary or secondary education. Students may earn a Bachelor of Science or Bachelor of Arts degree that is tailored to prepare graduates for employment in elementary or secondary schools. Other options include adding middle school and coaching endorsements to teaching credentials. Drake University has belonged to the American Association of Colleges for Teacher Education since the association's founding.

ACADEMIC PROGRAMS

From their first classes on the Drake campus, students have the chance to learn in an individualized, challenging, and supportive environment. Research opportunities abound; students work closely with their professors and often publish their findings. With more than 160 student-run organizations on campus, there is an outlet for students to investigate career paths and network with professionals in their field.

Students benefit from a combination of liberal arts training and professional preparation. Through the Drake Curriculum, all students take interactive classes that develop their critical thinking and expressive skills. Students also receive personalized academic advising. At the end of their four years, students undertake the Senior Capstone, which is a research project, thesis, or other major work that shows the concepts and skills the student has acquired at Drake. Drake's Honors Program is open to top students who wish to undertake a rigorous, interdisciplinary course of study.

CAMPUS FACILITIES AND EQUIPMENT

Students have access to the Cowles Library and its more than more than 600,000 books and journals, 100,000 federal and state government documents, 777,000 microform records, 118 electronic databases, and approximately 22,000 scholarly online journals. The collections also include DVDs and music CDs, as well as a digital repository of scholarship and historical material unique to Drake. In addition, many classes utilize the resources in specialized collections in the Law School, College of Pharmacy and Health Sciences, Center for Teacher Education, and School of Fine Arts. Between the Dwight D. Opperman Hall and Law Library, there are 330,000 volumes, along with computer labs and study facilities. The Studio Theater, the Monroe Recital Hall, and the Hall of the Performing Arts are housed in the Harmon Fine Arts Center. Another performance hall, Sheslow Auditorium with a capacity of 755 seats, is located in Old Main. The Bell Center offers a gym, pool, aerobic dance room, fitness room, basketball, volleyball, and badminton courts. A student-only fitness facility is also located in the student union. Additional athletic facilities are available in the Knapp Center, such as racquetball, volleyball and basketball courts, a jogging track, and a weight room. More than 7,000 people can congregate in Knapp for major events. Basketball courts and a track are available at the Fieldhouse, while the Tennis Center provides six indoor and six outdoor tennis courts. In 2015, Drake University is breaking ground on a $65 million dollar STEM complex.

TUITION, ROOM, BOARD AND FEES

20115–16 tuition, room and board costs, and student fees total $43,292.

FINANCIAL AID

More than 98 percent of full-time students at Drake have their education financed to some degree with the help of financial aid. In the 2014–15 school year, students enrolling directly from high school received on average $16,610 in grants and scholarships from Drake University; $17,980 from all sources. More than 5,000 awards, worth $48 million, are given annually, in the form of need- or merit-based grants and scholarships.

STUDENT ORGANIZATIONS AND ACTIVITIES

With more than 160 organizations operating on campus, students can always find activities that suit their interests. Elected student representatives run the Student Senate. Students also hold seats on some committees in the Faculty Senate. The Student Activities Board is charged with putting on special events, including cultural celebrations, social functions, guest speakers, and concerts. Drake also maintains the Residence Hall Association, composed of students who manage the logistics and activities surrounding residential life.

ADMISSIONS PROCESS

While admission is selective, Drake University considers the full record of each candidate for admission. Since the University prefers students with varied talents and interests, there is no single and inflexible set of admission standards applied to all candidates for admission. The admission process involves a comprehensive review of a student s academic background (courses and grades), standardized test scores (ACT or SAT), personal essay, recommendations, and activities both in high school and the community. Drake University does not discriminate on the basis of age, sex, sexual orientation, race, religion, color, national or ethnic origin, or disability.

A completed application for first-year admission contains the following items: a completed application form, the $25 nonrefundable application fee (the fee is waived for those who apply online), the High School Report and Counselor Recommendation Form, an official high school transcript, and ACT or SAT scores and a personal essay. Students applying to transfer to Drake are required to submit official transcripts for all previous college-level coursework.

Application for admission to undergraduate degree programs, except pre-pharmacy, may be made for any fall, spring, or summer term. Beginning October 15, students are notified of the admission decision within four to six weeks of the date that all materials are received. March 1 is the priority deadline for consideration for admission and merit- and need-based financial aid. Freshman applicants to the pre-pharmacy program in the college of Pharmacy and Health Sciences must submit a completed application by the December 1 deadline. Transfer students are only admitted to the professional PharmD program.

Candidates should contact:

Drake University

Office of Admission

2507 University Avenue

Des Moines, IA 50311

800-44-DRAKE, x3181 or 1-800-443-7253 x 3181

515-271-3181 (locally and outside the U.S)

Fax: 515-271-2831

www.drake.edu

admission@drake.edu

ELMHURST COLLEGE

AT A GLANCE

A private college in the heart of the Chicago metropolitan area, Elmhurst is among the top colleges and best values in the Midwest, according to college guides like U.S. News and Money magazine. And we make college affordable by awarding financial aid to 98 percent of our students.

Elmhurst is known for its seamless blend of liberal learning with professional preparation. More than 80 percent of undergraduates gain on-the-job experience through internships or service work, and 93 percent of our students find full-time employment or enter graduate school within a year of graduation.

With a student-faculty ratio of only 13:1, Elmhurst takes a personal approach where every student counts. All classes at Elmhurst are taught by professors, not teaching assistants, and about 80 percent of the college's full-time faculty hold the highest degree in their field.

The College's gorgeous campus is a green oasis in the heart of a safe, quiet suburb—but it's also just a half-hour train ride from downtown Chicago, one of the world's great cities, giving students unlimited access to world-class cultural and professional opportunities.

ACADEMICS

Elmhurst offers 59 majors, ranging from art and music to business, education and nursing. No matter which major you choose, you'll be the faculty's first priority. Our student-to-faculty ratio is only 13:1, and a faculty member (not a teaching assistant) teaches every course. Your professors will get to know you as an individual, and help you succeed.

The Elmhurst Experience is not only rigorously intellectual; it's also intensely practical. You'll master cutting-edge theory and technology, and gain hands-on experience through internships and many other professional opportunities. Students regularly work with prestigious area medical institutions, schools, corporations and not-for-profits; often, internships and other professional experiences lead to full-time job offers.

Elmhurst offers international education experiences in 44 countries, including Spain, the Netherlands, Poland, Germany, Bulgaria and Australia. Students can go abroad for a term, a year or a month during the college's distinctive January Term.

TUITION & AID

Elmhurst offers a comprehensive range of need- and merit-based financial aid programs, including scholarships, grants, loans and student employment. Nearly 99 percent of full-time students receive some form of financial aid, much of which comes in the form of grants and scholarships that don't need to be repaid.

Admission decisions at Elmhurst are made independently from any consideration of financial need.

STUDENT BODY

Students come to Elmhurst from many states and countries, and from nearly every religious, racial and ethnic background. The most recent incoming class of first-year students included individuals from 24 states, and students of color make up 37 percent of the class. The student body comprises 2,900 undergraduates and 400 graduate students.

CAMPUS LIFE

The Elmhurst College campus combines the charm of a classic college campus with the high-tech necessities of a modern education. Just minutes from campus, you'll find an eight-screen movie house, lots of great restaurants, a bowling alley and a lot more.

On campus, students get involved in more than 100 activities, from theatre to intramurals to the Mock Trial Team. The student newspaper wins awards; the radio station has been on the air since 1947. The campus regularly hosts performances, art exhibits and an outstanding array of guest speakers.

Elmhurst's 20 varsity sports teams compete in the CCIW, one of the top conferences in NCAA Division III athletics. We're big enough to offer a wide choice of sports, but small enough that you can make a real contribution to your team's success. Bluejay teams have won conference championships in a variety of sports. And they compete in first-rate facilities.

The College is a short train ride from downtown Chicago, where students enjoy unlimited access to world-class cultural and professional opportunities—from internships to sporting events to concerts of all kinds. The Chicago region is the Midwest's capital of industry, finance, arts and culture, and scientific discovery. From WGN and Morgan Stanley to the Shedd Aquarium and House of Blues, the Chicago area offers plenty of opportunities for internships and fun.

ELMIRA COLLEGE

AT A GLANCE

Founded in 1855, Elmira College is a private, coeducational, liberal arts college. Elmira, a city of 35,000, is located in the beautiful Finger Lakes Region of Upstate New York.

Campus: 55 historic acres which include 7 classroom buildings, 12 dormitories, 2 administrative office buildings, library, health center, campus center, President's Home and Mark Twain Study. A major athletic facility completes the total campus. Eight college buildings are listed on the National Register of Historic Places.

Academic calendar: Two twelve-week terms followed in April and May by a unique six-week Term III devoted to travel, field experience, research, independent study, and innovative courses.

Enrollment: 1,200 students, thirteen percent of whom are valedictorians or salutatorians of their high schools or prep schools, from 35 states and 31 foreign countries.

Faculty: All have earned the Ph.D. or the highest degree in their field required for undergraduate instruction; 11:1 student faculty ratio. No classes are taught by teaching assistants.

Average Class Size: 16 students per class; 90% of all offerings have 25 or fewer students; 35% have fewer than 12 students. Elmira ranks in the Top Five colleges in the eleven Northern states for small class size.

Athletics: NCAA Division III in men's and women's intercollegiate sports. Member of the Eastern College Athletic Conference, the United Volleyball Conference, and the Empire 8 Conference.

LOCATION AND ENVIRONMENT

Elmira, a city of 35,000, is located in the beautiful Finger Lakes Region of Upstate New York. Nestled in the lush, rolling hills of the southern Finger Lakes region, Elmira is a thriving, forward-thinking American community, with fresh air and wide-open spaces in harmony with the modern amenities of a larger city. Nearby, you can attend superb, live entertainment; soar back into American aviation's lofty past; tour historic neighborhoods; investigate Mark Twain's imagination or visit the beautiful lakes that give this region its name.

Within a ten-block radius of the Elmira College campus, there are many restaurants, a performing arts center, a fine arts museum, and shopping. There are about 60 churches, serving most denominations, within walking distance of campus.

Elmira is the place that many scholars say Samuel Clemens (Mark Twain) did his best work, penning the American literary classic The Adventures of Huckleberry Finn and many other works in his study. In 1870, Clemens married Elmira College alumna Olivia Langdon of the Class of 1864. In 1983, the Langdon family gave the study and the historic Quarry Farm to Elmira College. Now Quarry Farm is used as a residence for visiting Twain scholars from all over the world. The Center for Mark Twain Studies at Quarry Farm offers year-round educational programs.

OFF-CAMPUS OPPORTUNITIES

Elmira College offers a wide range of exciting Off-Campus Opportunities. During the Spring Term, for instance, Elmira College students have traveled with faculty to San Salvador in the Bahamas, Spain, France, Russia, England, Italy, Germany, China, Scotland, Japan, Peru, Egypt, Belgium, Greece, Mexico, Australia, the American West, Alaska, and Hawaii.

The highly selective and competitive Junior Year Abroad (JYA) program facilitates the study of foreign language and cultures. Generally, financial aid applies to the JYA program; however, tuition exchange programs do not apply. Interested students apply in the Fall Term of their sophomore year for an experience during their junior year.

All Elmira College students participate in a community service activity for a minimum of 60 hours. This service is an academic course required for graduation. New students register for Community Service before beginning their second term at Elmira, with the expectation that they will complete the requirement by the end of their second year. Many find the experience so rewarding that they continue volunteering to help others all four years.

MAJORS AND DEGREES OFFERED

Elmira College offers majors in more than 35 academic areas, but our range of program options is even greater. In ten of these subjects you may pursue either a Bachelor of Science or a Bachelor of Arts degree. While the B.S. degree encourages specialization in a specific area, the B.A. degree offers a broader education in the liberal arts and sciences. EC offers signature programs in Education, Business Administration, the Sciences, and Nursing.

Students must earn a stipulated number of credits in the major—with a passing grade—as well as complete the General Degree Requirements.

Academic Majors Include:

Accounting

American Studies

Anthropology and Sociology

Art

Biology

Biology - Chemistry

Business Administration

Chemistry

Classical Studies

Criminal Justice

Economics

Education

Educational Studies

English Literature

Environmental Studies

Foreign Languages

History

Human Services

Individualized Studies

International Studies

Mathematics

Medical Technology

Music

Nursing

Philosophy & Religion

Political Science

Pre-Medical

Psychology

Public Affairs

Social Studies

Sociology and Anthropology

Speech & Hearing

Speech and Language Disabilities

Theatre

ACADEMIC PROGRAMS

With a faculty-student ratio of 11:1, you will have the chance to express your ideas in class. Debate the nature of the universe with fellow students and professors. And learn from each other: well over half our students are from beyond New York State, representing 35 states, six Canadian provinces and 31 foreign countries. You will end up discussing your future one-on-one with people, who are committed to your success.

The requirements for baccalaureate degrees granted by Elmira College have been established by members of the faculty so that each graduate receives a broad general education, explores different fields of knowledge, examines one or more of those fields intensively, and applies the knowledge acquired in the classroom to realistic and appropriate work experiences.

Special Academic Programs:

Interested in becoming a doctor or lawyer? Elmira College offers a variety of academic programs that will prepare students for a range of career choices. Special Academic Programs include: Chemical Engineering, Army & Air Force ROTC, Pre-Law, Pre-Professional Programs, English as a Second Language, a 4+1 MBA Program, and Athletic Coaching Certificate.

Our Distinctive Academic Programs make the Elmira College experience unique. Required community service and internships allow students to grow and gain practical experience in a workplace dynamic. Encore, the college's performing arts appreciation requirement, and Off-Campus Opportunities, such as, the Junior Year Abroad program expose students to a diversity of experiences not always found in a traditional classroom. The six-week Term III provides students with an exceptional opportunity to immerse themselves into one or two subjects intensely. Additionally (as you probably know by now), Elmira College is one of the best places in the world to study the work and life of Mark Twain.

TUITION, ROOM, BOARD AND FEES

2013-2014 Full-time Student Charges

Dorm Students°

Tuition: $36,600

Room & Board: $11,800

Required Fees: $1,500

Elmira College is a residential campus. All Undergraduate students, except those who live with parents locally, are required to live on campus.

Town Students

Tuition: $36,600

Required Fees: $1,700

FINANCIAL AID

Elmira College Financial Aid is based on need and merit. Free Application for Federal Student Aid (FAFSA) is required and Financial Aid PROFILE is accepted. Grants and distinctive Honor Scholarships are awarded to students based on academic achievement, leadership activity, and financial need. Awards start at $13,000 per year and range up to full tuition for Valedictorians and Salutatorians of their high school classes. Students may also be eligible for federal and state grants, loans, and work on campus.

No student has ever paid the full cost of an Elmira College education since its founding in 1855.

Elmira College awards more than $14 million each year in academic scholarships and awards.

100% of students demonstrating need receive financial assistance.

Elmira College administers more than $40 million each year in scholarships and awards, grants, loans and work study programs.

STUDENT ORGANIZATIONS AND ACTIVITIES

Students are welcome to join one of more than 100 clubs or organizations any time during the academic year. During Summer Registration, new students can browse our Club and Organization Guide and sign up to receive more information from club officers. Two Activities Fairs, one during Fall Orientation and another in mid-September, offer the opportunity to meet current club members, ask questions, and see photos of past events and projects.

Some of our clubs and organizations include: Classics Society, Equestrian Club, French Club, Political Science Club, Silent Voices, Spanish Club, College Republicans, Circle K, College Democrats, EC Ambassadors, Orientation Leaders, Red Cross Club, Work for a Cure, Relay for Life, Christian Fellowship, Hillel - Jewish Student Association, and the Ski Club.

National Honor Societies include: Phi Beta Kappa, Psi Chi, Kappa Delta Pi, Phi Eta Sigma, Phi Alpha Theta, Alpha Phi Sigma, Omicron Delta Kappa, Beta Beta Beta, Sigma Beta Delta, Lambda Iota Tau, National Residence Hall Honorary, Pi Sigma Alpha, Sigma Theta Tau, Lambda Alpha, Pi Gamma Mu, and Alpha Sigma Lambda.

Elmira is an NCAA Division III college, as well as a member of the Eastern College Athletic Conference, United Volleyball Conference, and the Empire 8 Conference. We field varsity teams in men's and women's basketball, cheerleading, field hockey, men's and women's golf, men's and women's ice hockey, men's and women's lacrosse, men's and women's soccer, softball, men's and women's tennis, and men's and women's volleyball. National rankings and post-season tournaments have become annual traditions for the Soaring Eagles. Baseball and Women's Cross Country will be added beginning in the Fall of 2014.

Elmira College offers its students the chance to compete in collegiate athletics at many levels. The goal of the Junior Varsity and Intramural program is to offer students a chance to participate in athletics without the focus on skill level. Intramural sports range anywhere from flag football to ultimate frisbee. The success of our intramural program can be seen every Term III as our students softball teams compete daily.

ADMISSIONS PROCESS

We offer two admissions plans for freshmen applicants. Early Decision and Regular Admission.

International students may apply only under the Regular Admission program.

Regular Admission

If you are applying to several colleges, here is what you do for Elmira College:

1. Submit a completed application to Elmira College. You can fill out an application online, or print an application that you can send in. We also accept the Common Application.

2. Have your college counselor send your official transcript, including senior year courses and grades to date. Have your official SAT I or ACT scores sent to Elmira College.

3. Have at least one letter of recommendation sent to the college.

4. Write a great and memorable essay.

5. While not required, we strongly suggest you sit down with an Elmira College admissions counselor for an interview. You can schedule your interview by calling the Office of Admissions at 800-935-6472.

Early Decision

If Elmira College is your first choice college, Early Decision is the program for you. We'll make a decision on your application as soon as it is complete, but you do have to meet the deadlines. There are two Early Decision programs; the first deadline is November 15, and the second is January 15. We promise to notify you of our decision by December 15 for Early Decision I applicants and by January 31 for Early Decision II applicants.

EMERSON COLLEGE

AT A GLANCE

Emerson College is the only college in America dedicated exclusively to communication and the arts in a liberal arts context. Established in 1880 as a small regional school of oratory, Emerson has evolved into a diverse, coeducational, and multifaceted institution that educates students to assume positions of leadership in communication and the arts. Emerson is forward thinking, grounded in academic excellence, and committed to advancing the scholarship and creative work that brings innovation, depth, and diversity to those disciplines. Emerson has always been at the forefront of instruction in communications and the arts. Students are taking classes taught by industry professionals while engaging in hands-on projects to put what they learn in the classroom into practice.

LOCATION AND ENVIRONMENT

Emerson's campus is located across from historic Boston Common in the heart of the city's thriving Theatre District, and offers multiple theaters, television and film studios, and cutting-edge technical facilities for students. Emerson's connection with Boston's media, theater, and arts industries, as well as government, hospitals, and businesses, provides many opportunities for student internships and professional growth.

Emerson is home to 14 varsity sport teams, and over 80 student organizations including performance groups, student publications, and honor societies. More than half of the students are housed on-campus, some in learning communities such as the Writers' Block, Film Immersion Community, and Digital Culture Floor.

OFF-CAMPUS OPPORTUNITIES

Internships are popular with Emerson students and hundreds of opportunities exist throughout Boston and in major cities across the country, including exclusive placements at in Los Angeles, home to Emerson's residential study and internship program.

Emerson's relationship with Los Angeles is long-standing, but Emerson Los Angeles (ELA) is a brand new, state-of-the-art facility that houses classrooms, residential space, faculty offices, an auditorium, screening room, event spaces, studios and more. It solidifies Emerson's commitment to their Los Angeles program and to creating opportunities for students and alumni on the west coast. The internship program enrolls approximately 200 students, mostly seniors, during the fall and spring semesters. Emerson students who participate in the ELA program gain the knowledge, skills, and confidence to pursue their chosen fields before launching their post-graduate lives on the west coast.

In addition to ELA, Emerson owns a restored 14th-century medieval castle, Kasteel Well, which is home to their semester abroad program in The Netherlands. The castle is a national historical monument that provides living accommodations, classrooms, a resource center, and related facilities. Emerson also sponsors a semester in Washington, D.C. And, Beijing (at Communication University of China University), along with summer programs in Prague, Salzburg, and Greece.

ACADEMICS AND MAJORS

Emerson offers a wide range of undergraduate, graduate, and professional studies programs in communications and the arts. All undergraduate students take part in a robust curriculum including general education and liberal arts courses with advanced, specialized classes that are specific to individual departments and academic programs. Internships for academic credit are available to juniors and seniors, and the college's Institute for Liberal Arts and Interdisciplinary Studies offers first year seminars, independent study options, and innovative courses that cut across academic disciplines. In addition, students can cross-register for courses with the six-member ProArts Consortium (Berklee College of Music, Boston Architectural College, Boston Conservatory, Emerson, Massachusetts College of Art, and the School of the Museum of Fine Arts).

Undergraduate students can earn a Bachelor of Arts, Bachelor of Science, or Bachelor of Fine Arts degree, depending on which major they select. More than a dozen majors are available throughout the departments of Communication Studies, Communication Sciences & Disorders, Journalism, Marketing Communication, Performing Arts, Visual & Media Arts, and Writing, Literature & Publishing. Students can also minor in several areas, including comedy, dance, entrepreneurship, fiction, hearing and deafness, history, literature, management, music appreciation, philosophy, photography, poetry, political science, psychology, publishing, sociology, and women's and gender studies.

Emerson is accredited by the New England Association of Schools and Colleges and operates on a two-semester calendar.

CAMPUS FACILITIES AND EQUIPMENT

Emerson has the highest quality equipment, including sound-treated television studios, digital editing labs, audio post-production suites, industry standard software, a professional marketing research suite, and an integrated digital newsroom for aspiring journalists. Additionally, an 11-story performance and production center houses a theatre design/technology center, makeup lab, and costume shop. The college's Paramount Center opened in 2010 and includes a 560-seat theater, black box, scene shop, film screening room, and sound stage. Emerson is also home to the Robbins Speech, Language and Hearing Center, which provides evaluation and treatment for children and adults with communication challenges and serves as the primary clinical training facility for the Department of Communication Sciences and Disorders.

TUITION, ROOM, BOARD AND FEES

Basic expenses related to attending Emerson for the 2015–2016 academic year are $40,320 (tuition), $15,700 (double room and board), and $732 (Student Service Fee).

FINANCIAL AID

Emerson is committed to offering its students an excellent education at an affordable price. They have consistently set their tuition below their nearest competitors and are seen as a superb value in higher education. Students have all of the benefits of living in a world-class city, working with state-of-the-art equipment and in beautiful facilities, and learning from faculty who are top in their fields.

The Office of Financial Aid will makes every effort to help students finance the cost of their education. Emerson offers several types of financial assistance programs: need-based grants, employment, low-interest loans, merit scholarships, and alternative payment plans to help make an Emerson education possible. Each year, approximately two-thirds of the students receive some form of financial assistance. The college makes every effort to help students finance their education and provides need-based support packaged in awards that typically combine grant and scholarship, loan, and college work-study aid.

To apply for financial aid, students must complete the Free Application for Federal Student Assistance (FAFSA) and CSS PROFILE forms. More information can be found online at http://www.emerson.edu/financial_services or by contacting the Office of Student Financial Services at 617-824-8655 or finaid@emerson.edu.

STUDENT ORGANIZATIONS AND ACTIVITIES

In addition to the myriad of activities and events in Boston, student life at Emerson revolves around the more than 80 student-run organizations. These include radio stations, TV networks, publications, performance groups, service clubs, spiritual and cultural organizations, non-residential fraternities and sororities, professional societies, and intercollegiate and recreational athletics. Information about the specific organizations on campus can be found at http://www.emerson.edu/student-life/activities-organizations.

ADMISSIONS PROCESS

Emerson College accepts the Common Application or Universal Application and requires an application supplement. Admission is competitive. The college looks for students who present academic promise in their secondary school record, recommendations, and writing competency, as well as personal qualities as seen in extracurricular activities, community involvement, and demonstrated leadership.

Successful candidates typically have four years of English and three years each of mathematics, science, social science, and three years of a single foreign language. The application deadline for September admission is January 15 (Early Action, November 1), and for January admission it is November 1. Transfer applicants should apply by March 15 for September admission, or by November 1 for January admission.

Prospective students are encouraged to visit campus. Tours and information sessions may be scheduled online at www.emerson.edu/ugvisit or by contacting the Admission Office at 617-824-8600 or admission@emerson.edu.

FASHION INSTITUTE OF TECHNOLOGY

The Fashion Institute of Technology (FIT), a leader in career-oriented education, is a college of art and design, business and technology of the State University of New York (SUNY).

AT A GLANCE

FIT has been a leader in career education in art, design, business, and technology for nearly 70 years. With a curriculum that provides its 10,000 students with a singular blend of hands-on, practical experience, classroom study, and a firm grounding in the liberal arts, FIT offers a wide range of outstanding programs that are affordable and relevant to today's rapidly changing industries. The college grants AAS, BFA, BS, MA, MFA, and MPS degrees, and offers more than 45 majors in fields ranging from marketing and textiles to toy design and entrepreneurship, preparing students for professional success and leadership in the global marketplace.

FIT's special brand of education reflects the college's close ties to industry. Top executives serve as curriculum advisors, faculty, and mentors to students; industry members and leading companies provide scholarships, internships, and support for critical FIT initiatives. Relationships with industry enable the college to offer students experiences that mirror the marketplace and give them a competitive edge.

LOCATION AND ENVIRONMENT

Occupying an entire tree-lined block in Manhattan's dynamic Chelsea neighborhood, FIT's campus places students at the heart of the fashion, advertising, visual arts, design, business, and communications industries. Approximately 2,300 students live on campus, in accommodations ranging from traditional dorm-style rooms with meal plans to apartment-style suites with kitchens, and from single to quad occupancy.

OFF-CAMPUS OPPORTUNITIES

FIT draws on its New York City location to provide a vibrant, creative environment for our college community. Students enjoy a wealth of opportunities to learn, to play, and to explore the city's abundant resources. A wide range of cultural and entertainment options—from museums to dining to theater—are available within walking distance of the campus, which also offers convenient access to subway and bus lines and major rail and bus transportation hubs. One of New York's most dynamic neighborhoods, Chelsea boasts a lively gallery scene, exotic restaurants, a wide variety of retail outlets, and historic landmarks.

MAJORS AND DEGREES OFFERED

FIT offers programs leading to the AAS, BFA, BS, MFA, MA, and MPS degrees. Undergraduates choose from among 40 majors and 16 liberal arts minors. The School of Graduate Studies offers seven master's degree programs.

SCHOOL OF ART AND DESIGN

Accessories Design, Advertising Design, Communication Design Foundation, Computer Animation and Interactive Media, Fabric Styling, Fashion Design, Fine Arts, Graphic Design, Illustration, Interior Design, Jewelry Design, Menswear, Packaging Design, Photography, Textile/Surface Design, Toy Design, and Visual Presentation and Exhibition Design

JAY AND PATTY BAKER SCHOOL OF BUSINESS AND TECHNOLOGY

Advertising and Marketing Communications, Cosmetics and Fragrance Marketing, Direct and Interactive Marketing, Entrepreneurship for the Fashion and Design Industries, Fashion Merchandising Management, Home Products Development, International Trade and Marketing for the Fashion Industries, Production Management: Fashion and Related Industries, Technical Design, and Textile Development and Marketing

SCHOOL OF LIBERAL ARTS

Art History and Museum Professions, Film and Media, and liberal arts minors (subject-based and interdisciplinary minors are offered)

SCHOOL OF GRADUATE STUDIES

Art Market: Principles and Practices; Cosmetics and Fragrance Marketing and Management; Exhibition Design; Fashion and Textile Studies: History, Theory, Museum Practice; Global Fashion Management; Illustration; and Sustainable Interior Environments

ACADEMIC PROGRAMS

FIT's programs offer a vibrant learning environment, combining the practical and the theoretical. Each provides hands-on instruction, each is supported by a focused liberal arts curriculum, and each draws on a faculty of dedicated working professionals who are influential in their fields. The School of Liberal Arts offers the opportunity to minor in a variety of liberal arts areas in two forms: subject-based minors and interdisciplinary minors unique to the FIT liberal arts curriculum. Minors include economics, Latin American studies, and sustainability.

The Presidential Scholars honors program, open to academically exceptional students in all disciplines, offers special liberal arts courses, projects, colloquiums, and cultural and community service activities designed to broaden horizons and stimulate discourse.

Internships are an essential part of many majors. The college's extensive internship program provides students with vital experience in their field. The Career and Internship Center helps students with career planning and offers lifetime placement services to graduates.

The study-abroad experience allows students to immerse themselves in diverse cultures and prepares them to live and work in a global community. FIT offers programs in Italy—in Florence and Milan—where students study fashion design or fashion merchandising management gain firsthand experience in the dynamics of European fashion. Australia, China, England, France, and Mexico are a few of the other countries where FIT offers semester-long programs. Students can also study abroad during the winter or summer sessions.

The School of Continuing Education and Professional Studies provides noncredit classes to students and working professionals who want to pursue a certificate or just gain skills and knowledge. FIT also offers a wide range of classes for high school students on weekends and in the summer.

Online courses are offered on a wide variety of subjects. An AAS degree in Fashion Merchandising Management and a BS in International Trade and Marketing are available fully online.

CAMPUS FACILITIES AND EQUIPMENT

Students have access to state-of-the-art technology and equipment in FIT's studios and labs. Facilities include art, printmaking, display design, and photography studios, a model-making workshop, a graphics printing service bureau, a toy design lab, and a textile testing lab. A computer-aided design and communications facility allows students to explore the latest advancements in technology and their integration in design, photography, and computer graphics and animation. The Annette Green Fragrance Foundation Studio, a professionally equipped fragrance development lab, is the only one of its kind on a U.S. college campus. Cutting and sewing labs offer the most advanced apparel production machinery among educational facilities in the nation. Other facilities include a lighting laboratory, broadcast studio, knitting and weaving labs, and a multimedia foreign language lab.

The Museum at FIT is New York City's only museum dedicated to fashion. Students, designers, and historians use the museum for research and inspiration. The museum, which is accredited by the American Alliance of Museums, operates year-round, and its exhibitions are free and open to the public. The Gladys Marcus Library provides more than 300,000 volumes of print, non-print, and electronic materials. The newspaper and periodicals collection includes 500 current subscriptions. On-line resources include more than 90 searchable databases. The library also offers specialized resources, such as clipping files, fashion and trend forecasting services, and sketch collections.

Also on campus are three multimedia venues—the Katie Murphy Amphitheatre, the Morris W. And Fannie B. Haft Auditorium, and the John E. Reeves Great Hall—used for fashion shows, exhibitions, student presentations, industry panels, conferences, and special events.

Tuition, Room, Board, and Fees

For 2014–15, the associate-level tuition per semester was $2,250 for in-state residents and $6,750 for nonresidents. Baccalaureate-level tuition per semester was $3,085 for in-state residents and $8,905 for nonresidents. Housing costs ranged from $6,300 to $6,700 per semester for traditional residence hall accommodations with mandatory meal plan and from $6,300 to $6,900 for apartment-style accommodations. Meal plans varied from $1,750 to $2,240 per semester. Textbook costs and other nominal fees, such as locker rental or laboratory use, vary per program. Costs are subject to change.

FINANCIAL AID

FIT attempts to remove financial barriers to college entrance by providing scholarships, grants, loans, and part-time employment based on available funds for students with financial need. The Free Application for Federal Student Aid (FAFSA) is the core application for all financial aid programs.

STUDENT ORGANIZATIONS AND ACTIVITIES

The college is home to more than 70 student organizations, including merit societies, athletic teams, major-related organizations, and clubs based on areas of interest. Concerts, dances, field trips, films, flea markets, and other events are regularly scheduled. Student-run publications include a campus newspaper, a literary and art magazine, and the FIT yearbook.

FIT has intercollegiate teams in cross-country, half marathon, track and field, dance, table tennis, tennis, soccer, swimming and diving, and volleyball. Athletics and Recreation offers students group fitness classes at no extra cost. Open gym activities allow students to participate in team and individual sports.

The David Dubinsky Student Center houses lounges, a game room, a dining hall, a student radio station, a student-run boutique, student government and club offices, health services, gyms, a dance studio, a fitness center, a counseling center, studios, and laboratories.

ADMISSIONS PROCESS

For applicants to undergraduate programs, the admissions committee considers academic accomplishments that predict success on the college level, as well as students' demonstrated talent. For transfer applicants, overall grade point average and performance in liberal arts courses are also considered. All applicants, whether to a full-time day program or evening/weekend program, must meet the same admissions standards.

All applicants are required to submit a personal essay indicating why they selected their major, and highlighting all activities and accomplishments. FIT believes that creative and leadership abilities are revealed through activities in various fields, such as a governing organization, student clubs, or the visual or performing arts.

Applicants to the School of Art and Design must submit a portfolio that demonstrates their artistic and creative ability. Fashion Design applicants should be versed in both art and garment construction. Applicants to the School of Business and Technology programs must demonstrate the ability to work with others, leadership, and sound mathematical skills.

First-year students must apply for the two-year Associate in Applied Science Degree. Upon completing the AAS degree, students may enter a bachelor's program. Transfer applicants may qualify for a one-year AAS or bachelor's degree program depending on their previous college coursework and intended major.

In evaluating candidates, the School of Graduate Studies considers factors such as academic preparation, communication skills, professional experience, maturity, passion for knowledge, and potential for growth, as well as the degree to which the candidate's and the program's goals coincide.

All prospective students are invited to attend an information session with an admissions counselor and take a student-led campus tour. For more information and to make a reservation for a campus visit, please go to fitnyc.edu/visitfit.

Admission Dates and Deadlines for Undergraduate Study

Fall semester	Spring semester
Application deadline: January 1	Application deadline: October 1
Notification date: April 1	Notification date: November 1
Tuition deposit due: May 1	Tuition deposit due: December 1

Please visit fitnyc.edu for information on the admissions process and deadlines for applicants to FIT's graduate programs.

FLORIDA ATLANTIC UNIVERSITY

AT A GLANCE

Florida Atlantic University offers students the best of everything—a world-class education in a beautiful sub-tropical setting. Life as an FAU Owl has never been better! From a football team playing in the on-campus stadium to clubs that serve every academic and leisure-time interest, there's something for everyone at FAU! Best of all is the University's outstanding faculty of more than 1,000 accomplished scholars and researchers who are known for their excellence in teaching and mentoring. The student to faculty ratio is 25:1 an advantage normally offered by small, private colleges. If you're looking for a top-notch educational experience in one of the world's most beautiful places, FAU is the university for you! The University serves more than 30,000 freshmen, transfers and graduate students. People from all 50 states and more than 180 countries have studied, lived and worked at FAU. With 49 percent of its student body classified as minority or international students, FAU ranks as the most racially, ethnically and culturally diverse institution in Florida's State University System. FAU housing is home to 4,200 in-state and out-of-state students, along with students from many different countries. FAU is a comprehensive public university that is fully accredited by the Southern Association of Colleges and Schools. FAU is classified as a High Research Activity institution by the Carnegie Foundation for the Advancement of Teaching. Undergraduate research takes place in every discipline – not only the life sciences and physical sciences but also the humanities, social sciences, and creative and performing arts.

Take a virtual tour at http://www.fau.edu/admissions/campusvirtualtour.php.

ACADEMICS

Ten distinguished colleges offer more than 180 degree programs in fields that span the arts and humanities, the sciences, medicine, nursing, psychology, economics, music, accounting, business, education, public administration, social work, architecture, engineering, computer science and more.

For a complete list of degree programs visit http://www.fau.edu/explore/degrees.php.

HONORS PROGRAMS:

The Harriet L. Wilkes Honors College provides a unique living/learning environment for students who are highly motivated and want the challenge of an all honors program. The Harriet L. Wilkes Honors College is located in Jupiter, FL (40 miles north of the Boca Raton campus). The University Honors Program is designed to provide freshmen and sophomores exceptional and rewarding learning opportunities through special honors seminars. This program is located on the Boca Raton campus. We invite you to explore both of these special opportunities at www.fau.edu/admissions and click on "Honors Programs."

ADMISSIONS

Freshman requirements:

Admission to the University is limited to applicants who have graduated from a regionally accredited high school or who hold a General Equivalency Degree (GED). The admissions application is available online at www.fau.edu/admissions. A non-refundable $30.00 application fee, official high school transcripts and official SAT or ACT test scores must be submitted. All scores must be reported by either the SAT College Board (FAU code: 5229) or the ACT Program (FAU Code: 0729). For more information visit http://www.fau.edu/admissions/freshmanreq.php.

FAU Stats Fall 2014

Entering Freshmen Class Mid-Range Test Scores:

ACT: 22-26 SAT (all 3 sections): 1520–1730

Entering Freshmen Class Mid-Range GPA: 3.44–4.19

FAU Stats Summer 2014

ACT: 20-23 SAT (all 3 sections): 1410–1580

Entering Freshmen Class Mid-Range GPA: 3.28–3.92

Transfer student requirements with less than 60 credit hours: Applicants should present a cumulative GPA of 2.5 or higher on all attempted college work and must be in good academic standing at their last attended institution. Applicants must also meet all freshman admissions requirements as stated in freshman admissions section.

In addition to the requirements above, transfer students with greater than 60 credit hours must have completed eight to ten credit hours of sequential foreign language or its equivalent in quarter hours prior to enrollment at Florida Atlantic University. This requirement may be satisfied by presenting proof that two units of a sequential foreign language were completed in high school or by passing a CLEP or other designated examination of proficiency. If the foreign language admission requirement is not met at the time of transfer, then it becomes a graduation requirement.

Transferring with an Associate in Arts Degree from a Florida College System or State University System institution: Guaranteed admission is applicable only if transferring directly to Florida Atlantic University after receiving your Associate in Arts Degree from a Florida College System or State University System institution. Admission to the School of Architecture, Honors College, and Nursing is limited access. All applicants must meet the specific course and grade point average requirements for direct admission to those colleges. College of Business, College of Engineering & Computer Science, School of Communication and Multimedia Studies, and Music majors are selective and have additional requirements.

FAU currently hosts over 1,000 students from 80 foreign countries. For information on international student admissions requirements visit http://fau.edu/admissions/international.php.

Please note that meeting the minimum admission requirements does not guarantee admission into the university.

DEADLINES:

Freshmen Application Deadlines: The priority deadline for the fall semester is February 15. The deadline for the fall semester is May 1. The deadline for the summer semester is February 15. The deadline for International students is April 1 for the fall semester, October 1 for the spring semester and February 15 for the summer semester.

Transfer Application Deadlines: The deadline for the fall semester is July 1. The deadline for the spring semester is November 15. The deadline for the summer semester is April 15.

Visit www.fau.edu/admissions for more information.

CAMPUS LIFE

Join one of FAU's 300 student clubs and organizations. Students can participate in Academic Organizations, Honor Societies, Spiritual/Religious Organizations, Personal Interest Clubs, Diversity Association Organizations, Service Organizations, Sports Clubs, and Greek Life.

Work out or relax in FAU's Recreation & Fitness Center. The 77,000-sq.-ft., state-of-the-art facility includes a workout area, three indoor basketball and volleyball courts, badminton courts, an outdoor leisure and lap pool, health-club-style lockers and a mind-body studio.

Unite with fellow FAU students to cheer for a home team victory at the on-campus stadium. FAU's 500 student-athletes participate in 19 varsity teams plus cheer and dance. FAU is a proud member of Conference USA.

Study Abroad with FAU's Office of International Programs. Conduct international research, attend classes, and receive specialized training while living within a diverse culture.

Catch a movie at the all-digital theater complex on campus which includes four 49-seat theaters.

Record an album at FAU's record label, Hoot/Wisdom Recordings. 19 albums have been produced by students.

LOCATION AND ENVIRONMENT

Located in Boca Raton, FL and less than a mile off I-95, Florida Atlantic University is within 20 miles of Fort Lauderdale, 20 miles of West Palm Beach and 45 miles of Miami. The beautiful beaches of the Atlantic Ocean are less than 3 miles away, and the sunny, warm South Florida weather is perfect for many outdoor activities: biking, swimming, surfing, marathons, ocean kayaking, diving, tennis, golf, etc. We have the convenience of being in close proximity to two airports; the West Palm Beach Airport to the north and the Fort Lauderdale/Hollywood Airport to the south. Both airports are within 30 miles of FAU. FAU offers classes for upper division students throughout its six-county service region in southeast Florida.

TUITION, ROOM, BOARD AND FEES

Undergraduate tuition is $201.29 per semester credit for Florida residents. Florida resident tuition for 24 credits is $4,830.96. Undergraduate tuition is $719.84 per semester credit for non-Florida residents. Non-Florida resident tuition for 24 credits is $17,276.16. 24 credits are based on 12 credits per semester for 2 semesters (Fall/Spring). Graduate tuition is $369.82 per semester credit for Florida residents and $1,024.81 for non-Florida residents. In addition, the estimated nine-month budget for room and board on campus is $11,556; books and supplies cost approximately $1,220. Costs and tuition prices are subject to change.

FINANCIAL AID

Financial Aid is available to FAU degree-seeking students and includes grants, loans, scholarships and employment opportunities. The Student Financial Aid Office provides full service to students from application to award. Learn more about financial aid by visiting www.fau.edu/finaid. FAU is proud to offer numerous scholarships to incoming freshman students. Merit scholarships are competitive, do not require an application and are awarded on a rolling basis early in the admission cycle. Meeting minimum scholarship requirements does not guarantee an award. Need-based scholarships are also offered and require an application and submission of the FAFSA. The deadline to submit a scholarship application is January 15. For maximum consideration, submit your application early in your senior year. For additional information, visit www.fau.edu/admissions/scholarships-all.php.

Florida Atlantic University

Office of Undergraduate Admissions

777 Glades Road Boca Raton, FL 33431

Telephone: 561-297-3040

Fax: 561-297-2758

www.fau.edu/admissions

GONZAGA UNIVERSITY

AT A GLANCE

Gonzaga University, founded in 1887, is an independent, comprehensive university with a distinguished background in the Catholic, Jesuit, and humanistic tradition. Gonzaga emphasizes the moral and ethical implications of learning, living, and working in today's global society. Through the University Core Curriculum, each student develops a strong liberal arts foundation, which many alumni cite as a most valuable asset. In addition, students specialize in any of more than 75 academic programs and majors. Gonzaga enrolls approximately 4,800 undergraduates and 2,500 graduate and law students.

Gonzaga's 131-acre campus combines the old and new: College Hall, the original administration building, and DeSmet Residence Hall with the modern architectural structures of the John J. Hemmingson Center, Foley Library, Hughes Life Sciences Building, Jundt Art Center and Museum, and the PACCAR Center for Applied Science. The campus is characterized by sprawling green lawns and majestic evergreen trees. Towering above the campus are the stately spires of St. Aloysius Church, the well-recognized landmark featured in the University logo.

Gonzaga encompasses five undergraduate schools: Arts and Sciences, Business Administration, Education, Engineering and Applied Science, and Nursing and Human Physiology. The University offers the BA, BBA, BEd, BS, BSCE, BSCpE, BSCS, BSEE, BSEM, BSME, and BSN degrees.

Gonzaga offers several unique options for students. The Honors Program provides a rigorous liberal arts curriculum for intellectually curious students who thrive in a competitive academic environment. Business leaders mentor the Hogan Entrepreneurial Leadership Program students, and internships are an integral part of the program. The award-winning Gonzaga Alumni Mentor Program (GAMP) connects current students and recent graduates with alumni in their professional areas of interest. Students in the Comprehensive Leadership Program take a leadership certificate curriculum that may be combined with any major, and they participate in valuable, interactive leadership experiences. The Army ROTC unit prepares select women and men as leaders in service for their communities and their country. Gonzaga's nationally ranked debate team includes all skill levels. The Mock Trial Team competes nationally and involves students majoring in many different areas of study. Internships, research with faculty, and community service learning enhance class time while providing students first-hand experience.

LOCATION AND ENVIRONMENT

As the hub of the Inland Northwest, Spokane plays a vital role in shaping the University's character. While offering urban advantages such as museum exhibits, shopping, symphony, Broadway and ballet performances, Spokane still maintains an intimate, friendly, and community atmosphere. Used for running and cycling, part of the 37-mile Centennial Trail, runs through campus and to Coeur d' Alene, Idaho. Within a short distance of campus, students snow and water ski, hike, cycle, rock climb, swim, camp, and golf. With an average rainfall of only 16.7 inches per year, outdoor activities are easily accessible.

The 24 residence halls and apartments on campus, both single-sex and coed, house 40 to 360 students each. Freshmen and sophomores are required to live on campus. The Zagweb network provides students round-the-clock electronic access to email, Internet, campus intranet, and library holdings, all directly from residence hall rooms. Additionally, the whole campus is wireless. Resident Directors and Assistants, along with a Resident Chaplain, provide a fun, secure, and nurturing environment.

OFF-CAMPUS OPPORTUNITIES

Recognizing the importance of an international perspective for learning, Gonzaga offers study abroad programs in over 35 countries, including Argentina, Australia, Austria, Belgium, Benin, China, Costa Rica, El Salvador, England, Finland, France, Ireland, Italy, Japan, Jordan, Mexico, the Netherlands, Northern Ireland, Panama, Scotland (Honors Program students), South Africa, Spain, Taiwan, Tanzania, Thailand, Turkey, Turks and Caicos, and Zambia. Gonzaga's campus in Florence, Italy is the most popular option.

MAJORS AND DEGREES OFFERED

Gonzaga offers the following areas of study in the five undergraduate schools. The college of Arts and Sciences offers art, biochemistry, biology (research), broadcast studies, chemistry, classical civilizations, communication studies, computer science and computational thinking, criminal justice, economics, English (writing concentration), environmental studies, French, history, international studies (including international relations and Asian, European, and Latin American studies), Italian studies, journalism, mathematics, mathematics/computer science, music (including emphases in composition, general studies, and performance), music education, philosophy (Kossel concentration option), physics, political science, psychology, public relations, religious studies (Christian theology and religious pluralism concentrations), sociology, Spanish, and theatre arts (performance and technical concentrations). Additionally, the School offers minors in Catholic studies, conducting, dance, German, Italian, jazz performance, Native American studies, solidarity and social justice, women's & gender studies, and writing. Students interested in the following areas take tracks of classes respectively in pre-dentistry, pre-law, pre-medicine, pre-physical therapy, and pre-veterinary studies. The School of Business Administration offers majors in accounting or business administration (with concentrations in economics, entrepreneurship and innovation, finance, human resource management, individualized study, international business, law and public policy, management information systems, marketing, and operations and supply chain management). As well as granting teacher certification on both the elementary and secondary levels, the School of Education offers degrees in physical education, special education, and sport management. The School of Engineering and Applied Science offers computer science and civil, computer, electrical, and mechanical engineering degrees, as well as an engineering management degree and a 5-year BSEM/MBA option. Also, The School of Nursing and Human Physiology offers human physiology and nursing degrees at the undergraduate level. Advanced degrees in accounting, business, communication and leadership, education, engineering, law, leadership studies, nursing, organizational leadership, philosophy, teaching English as a second language, and theology and leadership are also offered.

ACADEMIC PROGRAMS

The core curriculum (a basic set of courses in thought and expression, philosophy, religious studies, mathematics, and English literature) is at the foundation of every student's academic experience at Gonzaga. Various schools in the University add courses that complement the core such as modern/classical language requirements, history and science classes, additional math courses, etc. Often, classes at Gonzaga require oral presentations or use of the written and discussion-based communication skills emphasized in the core curriculum.

CAMPUS FACILITIES AND EQUIPMENT

The Foley Library contains more than 800,000 volumes and microform titles, with two special collections of material especially rich in the areas of philosophy and classical civilization, as well as the nation's most extensive collection of works concerning the famous Jesuit poet Gerard Manley Hopkins. The historic College Hall houses the recently-renovated Harry & Colleen Magnuson Theatre, a 24-hour computer lab, a Florentine-style University Chapel, and numerous classrooms and faculty offices.

Students are able to produce sophisticated multimedia presentations and research hundreds of libraries across the country from their own residence hall rooms, by accessing campus-wide wireless, or from one of the 10 labs on campus. The Communications Building offers an arts lab for the Bulletin (the weekly student-published newspaper), KAGU, the University's radio station, and GUTV, a state-of-the-art TV production station where students learn all aspects of broadcast studies. The Herak Center for Engineering offers state-of-the-art CAD/CAM, electronic, digital, microwave, and calibration labs, and the PACCAR Center for Applied Science, which received a "Gold" certification rating from the Leadership in Energy and Environmental Design (LEED), adds more classroom space, a robotics lab, a computer science lab with a high-speed cluster computer array, and the rapidly growing Electric Utility Transmission & Distribution program.

The Martin Athletic Centre boasts a 13,000 sq. ft. state-of-the-art fitness center, and next door, the 6000-seat McCarthey Athletic Center houses the men's and women's basketball games as well as concerts and events throughout the year. Washington Trust Field at Patterson Baseball Complex hosts the Gonzaga baseball program.

Gonzaga has committed that any new buildings on campus (including the recent addition of the 167,726 square-foot John J. Hemmingson Center) will seek at least "Silver" LEED certification (and Hemmingson is seeking "Gold"). Additionally, as a signatory of the Presidents' Climate Commitment, Gonzaga has created a Climate Action Plan to reduce its carbon footprint by 20% by 2020 and 50% by 2035 (from 2009 levels).

TUITION, ROOM, BOARD AND FEES

Tuition for the 2015–2016 academic year is $37,480; room and board is estimated at $10,835. Including tuition, room and board, books, fees, transportation, and living expenses, Gonzaga estimates $53,316 as the total cost of attendance for the 2015–2016 year.

FINANCIAL AID

99% percent of students receive financial aid. The average package for 2014–2015 was $25,189 awarded in the form of grants, scholarships, loans, and campus employment. A number of merit-based, merit/need-based, athletic, music, debate, and other program scholarships are awarded to students each year. Students should file the Free Application for Federal Student Aid (FAFSA) by the priority date of February 1 and check the website for scholarship information and applications. Gonzaga is committed to working with students and families to finance their investment in a quality education.

STUDENT ORGANIZATIONS AND ACTIVITIES

GU students enjoy a wide variety of activities on and off campus. The Gonzaga Student Body Association (GSBA) oversees over one hundred academic, social, and cultural clubs and provides the structure of student government. Some of the most popular clubs include the Outdoors Club, THIRST (a non-denominational worship group), GUTS (an improvisational comedy team), and the Hawaii Pacific Islanders Club. GSBA organizes service and conservation projects, dances, and countless other activities to channel and challenge the talents and passions of motivated men and women who seek to make a difference.

As the leading provider of service hours in the entire city of Spokane, Gonzaga University encourages students to volunteer their services at any of the area nonprofit organizations. University Ministry, the Gonzaga Student Body Association, Unity Multicultural Education Center, and the Center for Community Action and Service Learning (CCASL) provide organized projects through which students become involved in the greater Spokane community and other cities.

Division I, West Coast Conference sports include baseball (men), basketball, crew, cross-country/track, golf, soccer, tennis, and volleyball (women). Approximately 60% of students participate in intramural and club sports such as ultimate frisbee and rugby. The Harry & Colleen Magnuson Theatre hosts main-stage plays (including musicals), dance recitals, GUTS, sketch comedy, numerous one-acts and student directed scenes. Gonzaga's musical groups include a nationally recognized University Choir, a Chorale, the GU Symphony, the Jazz Ensemble, the Gonzaga Bulldog Band, The Big Bing Theory—an a cappella group, the Boone Street Band, and numerous other ensembles. GU's students also host programs on Gonzaga's TV and radio stations. Additionally, many students participate in University Ministry events, such as retreats, the annual Pilgrimage hike, THIRST, Masses, Christian Life Communities, and interdenominational and/or interfaith services.

ADMISSIONS PROCESS

The University seeks diligent, inquisitive applicants with diverse backgrounds who will benefit from the rigorous Jesuit instruction at Gonzaga as well as enhance the University environment. A Common Application (www.commonapp.org) and the Gonzaga member page, SAT I (Writing Section not used universally) or ACT scores (Writing Section not required), a transcript, a teacher recommendation, a school report, an activities list or resume, and an essay are required. Transfer students and students with any college credit must submit official transcripts from all colleges. Transfer students must also complete the Common Application for Transfers, including the College Official's Report. International students must also submit official transcripts from all colleges attended. Additionally, international students must submit official results of their TOEFL examination. The Non-binding Early Action application deadline for freshmen is November 15th. The main advantages of the Early Action Program are early communication of admission and potential scholarship notice (by January 15th). The Regular Decision application date for freshmen is February 1. Students applying Regular Decision by this date will receive an admission decision by the beginning of April. After February 1, applications will be accepted only if space is available.

GRACELAND UNIVERSITY

Founded in 1895 and sponsored by Community of Christ, Graceland University is more than a school. Graceland is a community of passionate, caring and dedicated individuals who make up a worldwide community network that reaches far beyond the two campuses, located in Lamoni, Iowa, and Independence, Missouri.

AT A GLANCE

Graceland University creates and maintains high academic standards of excellence by prioritizing a close student/faculty learning environment, providing nurturing communities that foster intellectual engagement and curiosity, and embracing the philosophy that learning is not confined to the classroom. Graceland integrates a strong tradition in the liberal arts with targeted professional learning.

LOCATION AND ENVIRONMENT

Situated on 170 acres of rolling hills, our main campus in Lamoni, Iowa, is home to about 1,000 students. It's a short, one-hour drive to Des Moines, Iowa, or two hours to Kansas City, MO. Graceland offers a beautiful, safe residential campus where diversity of thought and culture are celebrated.

Graceland University integrates learning inside and outside of the classroom and provides limitless opportunities for involvement in educational service, leadership and entertainment activities. The Independence Campus offers online learning opportunities—both graduate and undergraduate—in nursing, religion, education and more.

Life at Graceland includes forums and guest speakers on the current issues of the day; community service projects; poetry readings at a downtown coffee house; world-class entertainment with the Visual Performing Arts Series; new opportunities in an active Sustainability group or 50 other club organizations, as well as quiet time in a relaxed, countryside setting.

OFF-CAMPUS OPPORTUNITIES

Lamoni is a small, friendly town with a big heart. There's an old-fashioned pizza place, a bustling coffee house, and a university-owned movie theatre, called the Coliseum, all just a five-minute walk from campus. It's easy to venture into the Lamoni community. Hike around a beautiful nearby lake or use new, city bike trails by checking out one of the GU Sustainability bicycles available. Popular lakes at Slip Bluff County Park and Nine Eagles State Park offer swimming, boating, fishing and camping, and both are only a few miles away. There are close bonds between Graceland and the small, but vibrant town of Lamoni, home to 2,500 residents.

MAJORS AND DEGREES OFFERED

Bachelor's Degrees

Accounting

Agricultural Business

Art: Studio°

Art: Visual Communication

Athletic Training

Basic Science°

Biology°

Business Administration

Chemistry°

Communications°

Computer Science and Information Technology

Corrective Exercise and Performance Enhancement

Criminal Justice

Criminal Justice Administration

Economics

Elementary Education

English°

Health°

Health Care Management

History°

Human Services

International Studies

Liberal Studies

Mathematics°

Music°

Nursing

Organizational Leadership

Physical Education°

Psychology

Publication Writing and Design

Recreation

Religion and Philosophy

Social Media Marketing

Spanish

Sport Management

Theatre°

Theatre and Film°

Web Design

°Secondary teacher education program offered.

Pre-Professional Programs

Pre-Chiropractic

Pre-Dentistry

Pre-Forensic Science

Pre-Law

Pre-Medicine

Pre-Optometry

Pre-Pharmacy

Pre-Physical Therapy

Pre-Veterinary Medicine

Masters Programs

Master of Arts in Religion

Master of Education

Master of Science in Nursing

Doctorate Program

Doctor of Nursing Practice

ACADEMIC PROGRAMS

Students learn in an individualized, challenging, yet supportive environment, with a 15:1 student/faculty ratio. "First Year Experience" classes assist students with university life and expectations. The university offers over 50 academic majors and programs. Students will work closely with professors who are both teachers and scholars. Most of GU's professors hold a doctorate or the highest degree in their field. The Honors Program, highly acclaimed by participants, is designed for motivated students who want to expand their learning beyond the regular curriculum. The program takes annual cultural trips to Chicago and Minneapolis and gives students the opportunity to present at regional Honors conferences.

The GU Enactus team participates in national and international service efforts. The team has won regional championships 11 times of the last 12 years. Our 80-strong Enactus team placed first in the U.S. And second in the world (at the competition in Paris) in 2006.

The Graceland Experience combines a personalized education and an ongoing adventure. Graceland graduates go on to stellar careers in the sciences, the arts, nursing, education, business, athletics and human services. The GU alumni network is worldwide and alumni state that the Graceland Experience helped focus their passions and shape their futures.

In addition to traditional programs, Graceland offers many options for distance learners. Programs offered online by our renowned School of Nursing include the Bachelor in Healthcare Management, R.N.-B.S.N., R.N.-M.S.N. And M.S.N. programs. The M.S.N. program has two tracks: family nurse practitioner and nurse educator. The nationally ranked School of Education offers a Master of Education with six different emphases. The Master of Education program is offered in Cedar Rapids, Des Moines, and Lamoni, Iowa; Independence, Missouri; and online. The Community of Christ Seminary at Graceland offers a Master of Arts in Religion in a blended delivery system.

CAMPUS FACILITIES AND EQUIPMENT

In 2012, Graceland finished construction of the $1.6 million Fitzgerald Fitness Center, a new student wellness center with a group exercise area and a variety of weight and cardio equipment.

Graceland also re-introduced the Shaw Center in the fall of 2012 after the $16 million expansion and renovation project. The new Shaw Center features JR Theatre, a state-of-the-art black box facility; Carol Hall, an acoustically perfect recital hall; the Shaw Family Auditorium, with over 500 seating capacity; the outdoor Amphitheatre for spring jazz concerts and more. The new Shaw Center is one of the most remarkable performing arts venues in southern Iowa.

The Resch Science and Technology Hall was dedicated in 2009. It provides state-of-the-art-sciences and math facilities. Nearly everything, including the computer science equipment, is new and industry-standard in Resch Hall. The Helene Center for the Visual Arts (2004) includes 29,000 square feet of classrooms, studios and exhibit space and a large Mac lab with industry standard programs. It is regarded by artists as "the perfect place to be creative."

Campus computer facilities include three microcomputer labs and industry-standard equipment for desktop publishing and graphic design. Graceland's Enter.Net.C@fe provides 24-hour computer and printing access in a cozy atmosphere.

Our Closson Athletic Center boasts an indoor track and field facility, a beautiful hardwood basketball and volleyball court, and an indoor pool. We have a new FieldTurf, an artificial turf football field, a wonderful outdoor track facility, and a top soccer complex, home to our perennial conference champion men's and women's teams.

The Frederick Madison Smith Library uses the latest technologies to provide information services to accommodate student needs. Fully networked computer workstations offer access to the Internet and many research databases, including seven reference databases and more than 45 periodical databases, many providing access to full-text articles. Access to LIBBIE, the library's online catalog, and to the online reference sources, is available to all patrons. Articles and books may be ordered from a worldwide network of research libraries.

Tuition, Room, Board, and Fees

Graceland University has been named a "Best College in the Midwest" by The Princeton Review. We are committed to managing our costs, now and in the future, while maintaining the quality of education we provide every student. Costs for traditional students for the 2015–2016 academic year are listed below. Online program costs vary.

	Annual	Semester
Tuition	$25,420	$12,710
Room	$3,230	$1,615
Board	$4,870	$2,435
Activity Fee	$470	$235
Total Direct Costs	$33,990	$16,9905

FINANCIAL AID

Student Financial Aid is available for those students who qualify. All aid is based upon financial need, academic achievement, and/or meritorious performance. Financial aid is viewed as a supplement to the effort of the family to finance their student's college education. In order to receive federal or state financial aid, students must file a Free Application for Federal Student Aid (FAFSA) each year (add Graceland's code: 001866), and maintain satisfactory academic progress. Institutional Scholarships and Grants may be awarded to full-time students for academics, athletics, performing arts, and for Community of Christ students. When Graceland University receives all documents needed to complete a Financial Aid Package, an award notice will be sent to the student for review. More than 98 percent of Graceland students receive some form of financial aid.

STUDENT ORGANIZATIONS AND ACTIVITIES

Graceland sponsors more than 50 student clubs and organizations. GU boasts 22 varsity and numerous junior varsity teams and a variety of performing arts groups. Anyone who wants to play or perform at Graceland has ample opportunities to do so.

The basic residential and social unit of student life is known as a "House." The house system at GU is a unique program that started in the 1960s and is based on the principle of inclusion. The importance of each student is recognized. Unlike fraternities and sororities, every student is involved in the House system. Members of each House elect a leadership council that plans social events and represents students in Student Government. By cooperative effort, the House organizes its own social, religious and intramural programs. Each student determines the extent of his/her participation in all House activities. GU students love this community approach to residential life.

Students hail from more than 44 states and 32 countries. Graceland's International Club is a hub of constant activity. GU is committed to providing an environment that is free of alcohol and tobacco. Graceland cares about spiritual life as well. Whatever faith tradition, GU student's spiritual lives will be nurtured as much as desired while at Graceland.

ADMISSIONS PROCESS

To be considered for acceptance at Graceland, students must meet two of the three following criteria: rank in the upper 50 percent of high school class, have a 2.5 grade point average (based on a 4.0 system) and a minimum composite ACT score of 21, or a minimum combined SAT score of 960. International students also need to score at or above 550 on TOEFL and prove ability to cover expenses while enrolled. Transfer students need a minimum 2.0 GPA on previous college coursework.

HAVERFORD COLLEGE

AT A GLANCE

Haverford College, founded in 1833, is a small liberal arts college located on an idyllic campus in the Philadelphia suburb of Haverford. Haverford provides a rigorous and intensely personal undergraduate education inspired by intellectual depth, integrity, collaboration, and dedication to improving the human condition. There is no place where students are more trusted, are more directly engaged with their educations, and have more opportunities to shape their own paths.

This community has 1,200 students from 45 different states and nearly 40 countries. More than 80% of the classes at Haverford have fewer than 20 students, and 36% have fewer than 10 students. It's a truly residential college with 99% of students and 61% of faculty members living on campus.

Haverford's academic program focuses on individual growth, intellectual exploration, and pushing the boundaries of each discipline. Most classes are taught seminar style with an emphasis on discussion and debate. Special emphasis is placed on collaborative work and research. Professors work side-by-side with students to do high-level research while also developing analytical thinking and pushing the boundaries of each discipline. Haverford is one of the very few institutions where all students produce a senior thesis or final project.

Founded on Quaker values, Haverford has one of the oldest student-run Honor Codes in the country. The Honor Code—a philosophy of trust, concern, and respect—is written and governed solely by students. Reflections of the Honor Code include the absence of RAs in dorms, 24-hour lab access, and unproctored exams. Since its inception in 1897, the cherished Honor Code has become the purest expression of the college's values and an intrinsic part of a Haverford education. Students are expected to maintain a strong sense of individual responsibility as well as intellectual integrity, honesty, and genuine concern for others.

Students are entrusted with an unprecedented amount of freedom and responsibility and have a strong voice in the college's operations. Students play a major role in hiring decisions, sit on administrative committees, manage budgets, and head events and organizations.

Haverford's three academic centers—the Center for Peace and Global Citizenship, the John B. Hurford '60 Center for the Arts and Humanities, and the Marian E. Koshland Integrated Natural Sciences Center—support student and faculty engagement beyond the boundaries of the traditional classroom.

Extensive cooperation with nearby colleges adds an important dimension to the resources available at Haverford. Our unique four-college exchange program with Bryn Mawr, Swarthmore and the University of Pennsylvania allows us to retain the strengths of the small college, while offering the expanded resources and opportunities usually found at a larger university. Haverford students can take a staggering array of classes at any of these Quaker Consortium schools.

Haverford College offers an atmosphere of intellectual and personal challenge, excitement, and growth in a close-knit community that is dedicated to encouraging humane values during the undergraduate years and for a lifetime.

LOCATION AND ENVIRONMENT

Haverford's serene campus, located just outside Philadelphia, is a beautiful and stimulating environment. One of the oldest planned college landscapes in the country; the park-like, 204-acre campus includes more than 400 species of trees and shrubs, a nature walk, and a duck pond. The varied architectural styles of campus buildings, representing more than 150 years of architectural evolution, give the campus a unique character and charm. Frequent train service to and from downtown Philadelphia adds to campus resources and enhances student opportunities.

OFF-CAMPUS OPPORTUNITIES

In addition to course offerings at Swarthmore, Bryn Mawr and the University of Pennsylvania, there are numerous opportunities for internships and volunteer service in the surrounding communities and in Philadelphia. If students want to go farther afield they may participate in one of over 50 study abroad programs supported by Haverford. Domestic study away programs include exchanges with Claremont McKenna, Spellman, and Fiske Colleges.

MAJORS AND DEGREES OFFERED

Haverford College offers the Bachelor of Arts Degree in the following areas:

In the Natural Sciences: astronomy, astrophysics, biology, chemistry, computer science, geology, mathematics, physics.

In the Social Sciences: anthropology, archaeology, East Asian studies, economics, growth and structure of cities, history, political science, psychology, sociology.

In the Humanities: Chinese, classics, comparative literature, English, fine arts, French, German, history of art, Italian, Japanese, linguistics, music, philosophy, religion, Russian, Spanish.

Science majors have the option of choosing a Bachelor of Science.

ACADEMIC PROGRAMS

Haverford offers the following academic programs, in addition to the majors and minors named above, as Concentrations: Africana and African studies; biochemistry and biophysics; creative writing; dance; education; environmental studies; gender and sexuality studies; health studies; Hebrew and Judaic studies; Hispanic and Hispanic American studies; international economic relations; Latin American, Iberian, and Latino studies; mathematical economics; Middle East and Islamic studies; neuroscience; peace, justice, and human rights; romance languages; scientific computing; and theater. Students may pursue pre-medical, pre-law or pre-business intentions through any major; special advising is offered in these areas.

Haverford College has forged innovative partnerships with some of the world's top academic institutions to offer students additional opportunities for graduate study. Our partnership programs allow students to pursue an accelerated course of study in a Master's degree in engineering, bioethics, or city and regional planning at The University of Pennsylvania. There is a five-year joint degree program partnership with Georgetown University, and students can apply for a one-year Master's in Finance at the Claremont McKenna College.

CAMPUS FACILITIES AND EQUIPMENT

Some highlights of Haverford's facilities include the Koshland Integrated Natural Sciences Center, which houses state of the art laboratories, computer workrooms, faculty offices and classrooms. The Gardner Integrated Athletic Center, a 100,000 square foot athletic complex serving the entire College community. New residence halls, Kim Hall and Tritton Hall, feature an interior courtyard, skylights, two common rooms (each with a kitchenette and wall-mounted TV) and a study room on each floor.

Please visit Haverford's website at www.haverford.edu for a campus tour and to learn more about the college's facilities.

TUITION, ROOM, BOARD AND FEES

For the 2015–2016 school year, tuition for Haverford College is as follows: For tuition, the cost is $48,656, for room and board $14,888. In addition, there is an activity fee of $442. There is a one-time orientation fee of $230 for first-year students.

FINANCIAL AID

Haverford College meets 100% of the demonstrated need of all admitted students and seeks to minimize or eliminate debt for our graduates. Students with family income below $60,000 will not have any loans included in their financial aid package; students with family income above this level will have loans ranging from $1,500 to $3,000 per year. And our need-blind admission policy means that an application for financial aid has no bearing on the admission decision for U.S. citizens and eligible non-citizens.

Financial aid decisions are made solely according to a need-based allocation formula developed by the college. In other words, Haverford does not offer any financial aid on the basis of academic, musical, athletic, or other evaluation of merit.

Applicants are required to submit the FAFSA and the PROFILE application if they want to be considered for financial aid. Regular Decision candidates must register for the PROFILE by January 1 of the senior year of high school and submit by February 1. The FAFSA should be mailed to the federal government with Haverford's Federal Code (003274) by February 1. Early Decision candidates are held to different deadlines; please visit www.haverford.edu/financialaid/dates.php for further details.

STUDENT ORGANIZATIONS AND ACTIVITIES

There are more than 145 student organizations on campus. Musicians, athletes, writers, actors, rock climbers, gourmet cooks, feminists, political activists . . . everyone finds ways to pursue their extracurricular passions at Haverford. There are 11 varsity sports for women and 12 for men, including the only varsity cricket team in the nation. In addition, the students support a host of club sports and intramural teams.

ADMISSION PROCESS

The admission process at Haverford is conducted as a comprehensive review, treating each application personally and individually and with extraordinary care and attention to detail. We aim to provide you with the opportunity to convey the broadest sense possible of who you are, what you have achieved during your secondary school experience, and how you will both contribute to and grow from a Haverford education.

Our primary consideration in the evaluation process is academic excellence. Haverford is interested in students who demonstrate ability and interest in achieving at the highest levels of scholarship and service; who will engage deeply and substantively with the community; and who are intent on growing deeply both intellectually and personally. To this end, we consider:

- Secondary school transcript

- Standardized tests

- Teacher and counselor recommendations

- Quality of writing as demonstrated in your essays, testing, and recommendations

- Potential for contribution to the campus community

- Interview

Students may begin their studies in the fall semester only. The college uses the Common Application, along with a Supplement, both of which can be obtained and submitted on-line via www.commonapp.org. Decisions are announced before April 1. Students are required to submit all forms and supporting documents included in the application. In addition, they must also have their official standardized test scores (either the SAT Critical Reasoning Test with the essay section and any two SAT Subject Tests; or the ACT with the optional writing test) sent to Haverford.

HILLSDALE COLLEGE

Convinced that it is the best preparation for meeting the challenges of modern life, Hillsdale offers the traditional, classically based, liberal arts with teaching faculty and a strong core curriculum.

AT A GLANCE

Hillsdale College is a private, independent, nonsectarian institution of higher learning founded in 1844 by men and women who described themselves as "grateful to God for the inestimable blessings" resulting from civil and religious liberty and as "believing that the diffusion of learning is essential to the perpetuity of those blessings." The College has maintained institutional independence since its founding by refusing to accept aid from or control by federal authorities. Far-reaching private support from a national constituency has enabled Hillsdale to continue its trusteeship of the intellectual and spiritual inheritance derived from the Judeo-Christian faith and Greco-Roman culture.

The undergraduate enrollment for fall 2014 was 1,437, of whom 48 percent were men. The college draws students from forty-nine states and nine other countries. Approximately 34 percent of students are from Michigan. The entering freshman class in 2014 had an average high school grade-point average of 3.81 and mean ACT (29) and SAT (1933) scores well above national averages. Hillsdale students are housed in dormitories, fraternity and sorority houses, and various off-campus dwellings. Single and double rooms are available on campus; there are no coed dormitories. Each College-owned residence hall is supervised by a resident director and resident advisers. All freshmen (except commuters) are required to live on campus; upperclass students seeking to live off campus must apply to the dean of men or dean of women for this privilege.

Special student services provided by the college include career planning and placement counseling, academic advising and tutoring, and a health service staffed by a physician and a resident nurse.

LOCATION AND ENVIRONMENT

Hillsdale College is located amidst the hills, dales, and lakes of south-central Michigan. The Indiana and Ohio turnpikes are each 30 minutes away, and the college is within close reach of such metropolitan areas as Detroit, Chicago, Cleveland, Toledo, Ft. Wayne, and Indianapolis. The town of Hillsdale is a county seat with a population of 10,000. Stores, churches, restaurants, and movie theaters are all within walking distance of the campus.

OFF-CAMPUS OPPORTUNITIES

For forty years, the Washington Hillsdale Internship Program (WHIP) has provided students the opportunity to participate in full-time, academically intensive internships in the nation's capital. The program has been significantly bolstered with the 2008 establishment of the Hillsdale College Allan P. Kirby, Jr. Center for Constitutional Studies and Citizenship in Washington, D.C. Past interns and fellows have been placed in locations as challenging and rewarding as the U.S. House of Representatives, the U.S. Senate, the White House, various think tanks including the Heritage Foundation, news and media outlets, national security agencies, lobbying firms, international trade and relations organizations, and private sector companies.

Through the college's affiliations with the Center for Medieval and Renaissance Studies and the Oxford Study Abroad Program, Hillsdale students are able to study abroad for a summer or a year at one of the more than thirty colleges of Oxford University. Hillsdale offers a summer business program in cooperation with Regent's College in London, England, and the opportunity to study at the University of St. Andrews in St. Andrews, Scotland. Science students benefit from Hillsdale's 685-acre field research laboratory in northern Michigan, as well as from a marine biology program in the Florida Keys, and internship opportunities with the Omaha Zoo. Foreign language students frequently study abroad in Argentina, France, Germany, and Spain. Qualified individual students who wish to study in another country for a semester or a year are assisted by their faculty adviser and the registrar in planning a program that enables them to gain academic credit as well as take full advantage of their experience.

MAJORS AND DEGREES OFFERED

Hillsdale awards Bachelor of Arts and Bachelor of Science degrees in accounting, art, biochemistry, biology, chemistry, classics, computational mathematics, economics, education, English, exercise science, financial management, French, German, Greek, history, Latin, marketing/management, mathematics, music, music education, philosophy, physical education, physics, politics, psychology, religion, Spanish, speech, sport management, sport psychology, and theater. Interdisciplinary majors in American studies, Christian studies, comparative literature, European studies, international studies in business and foreign language, political economy, and sociology and social thought are also available. Pre-professional programs are offered in allied health services (including optometry, pharmacy, physical therapy, nursing, and medical technology), dentistry, engineering, environmental sciences, forestry, law, medicine, osteopathy, theology, and veterinary medicine.

ACADEMIC PROGRAMS

Hillsdale operates on a two-semester schedule, with the fall term beginning in late August and ending in mid-December and the spring term beginning in mid-January and ending in mid-May. Two 3-week summer sessions are also offered.

The College believes that a sound classical liberal arts education includes study in the humanities, natural sciences, and social sciences, and each student is required to complete a structured core of courses in these areas. All students declare a major by the end of the sophomore year. To graduate, students must complete a minimum 124 hours of course work and fulfill the requirements of at least one major field. The B.A. program includes a foreign language proficiency requirement. The B.S. program requires additional studies in mathematics and the natural sciences.

The honors program enables exceptionally talented students interested in an interdisciplinary community of learning to develop their intellectual potential through an accelerated college core and honors seminars in the junior and senior years. Discussions, guest lectures, and travel opportunities contribute to the social cohesiveness of the group. All honors students complete a senior thesis on an interdisciplinary topic of their choosing.

The Center for Constructive Alternatives conducts four weeklong symposia during the academic year and is one of the largest college lecture series in America. These programs, with themes ranging from historical to political, business, science, and the arts, bring to the campus distinguished scholars and public figures of national and international renown. All students are required to enroll in one seminar for credit.

CAMPUS FACILITIES AND EQUIPMENT

The Hillsdale College Mossey Library is a three-floor facility with a collection of more than 1,000,000 volumes. In addition to the main study and research collections, the Library also contains a number of rare and special holdings, including the Ludwig von Mises, Russell Kirk, Richardson Heritage, and Richard Weaver collections. Connected to other Michigan libraries through MelCat, and with college libraries nationwide via interlibrary loan, students have access to most any material necessary for on-campus research. Numerous individual study areas and group study rooms are available for students, as well as computer research terminals.

Lane and Kendall Halls at the front of campus serve as the primary academic facilities in the humanities and contain classroom space and faculty offices, as well as a special laboratory for experimental psychology. The Strosacker Science Center houses the departments of biology, chemistry, and physics. The Joseph H. Moss Family Laboratory Wing, completed in 2008, is a 17,000-square-foot addition that includes a microbiology/cell biology lab, anatomy/physiology lab with human cadaver access, conservation genetics lab, water lab, greenhouse, and organic/general chemistry labs. The 32,000-square-foot Herbert Henry Dow Science Building provides additional classrooms, research laboratories, animal rooms, and a computer lab. The Mary Randall Preschool is a circular laboratory school in which nursery school children are taught by students specializing in early childhood education and psychology. Experts in the field have called this building "a model for the nation." The Hillsdale Academy, a K–12 private model school, provides additional opportunities for classroom observation.

The Roche Sports Complex is a facility available to varsity athletes and the general student body alike. The building houses the 60,000-square-foot Dawn Tibbetts Potter Arena, which features a student fitness center and basketball/volleyball courts. The building also houses the John "Jack" McAvoy Natatorium for swimming and diving, an exercise physiology and sports medicine facility, four racquetball courts, extensive locker room space, and a weight/fitness room. Adjacent is the 7,000-seat capacity Frank "Muddy" Waters Stadium, which features an artificial surface football field; all-weather, Olympic-quality eight-lane running track; outdoor tennis courts; and fields for soccer, baseball, and women's softball. The new Margot V. Biermann Athletic Center houses a six-lane track and four tennis courts.

The Sage Center for the Arts is home to the departments of art, theatre, and speech. This 47,000-square-foot facility contains studios, classroom space, an exhibition gallery, a prop- and scene-construction shop, a sound studio, graphics lab, black box theatre, and the Markel Auditorium, a 353-seat performance hall (with orchestra pit). Completed in 2003, the 32,809-square-foot Howard Music Hall houses office, studio, classroom, rehearsal, and performance space for the John E. N. and Dede Howard Department of Music. Notable features include the McNamara Rehearsal Hall, Conrad Recital Hall, and studio space for percussion and jazz studies. Lower-level practice rooms are available to students during business hours without reservation.

Dedicated in January 2008, the 53,000-square-foot Grewcock Student Union is the center of student life. The two-story structure houses the cafeteria, bookstore, student mail center, offices for student activities and publications, a lounge with a 100-inch flat screen television, a formal lounge and conference room, AJ's Café, and a game area. The entire building is wireless, and any Hillsdale student can check out a laptop at the main desk.

TUITION, ROOM, BOARD, AND FEES

Annual tuition for the 2014–15 academic year was $22,920, room was $4,570, board was $4,680, and mandatory fees were $696. Books, supplies, and personal expenses (including travel, recreation, and clothing) are estimated at $3,000 per year.

FINANCIAL AID

Financial aid at Hillsdale is available in many forms. Academic scholarships are awarded on a competitive basis, regardless of financial need, to students who rank in the top 10 percent of their high school class and have standardized test scores in the top 10 percent according to national test norms. The priority deadline for academic scholarship consideration is January 1. The application for admission also serves as the Hillsdale application for merit-based aid. Athletic scholarships are available on a competitive basis in men's baseball and football; men's and women's basketball, track, and cross-country; and women's swimming and volleyball. The departments of art and music also award a select number of scholarships based on strength of portfolio/audition. To apply for aid on the basis of financial need, students are required to file Hillsdale's Confidential Family Financial Statement (CFFS) in January or February of the year of prospective enrollment at Hillsdale. Grants and loans are available from the college.

STUDENT ORGANIZATIONS AND ACTIVITIES

Hillsdale's Charger athletes compete in 14 intercollegiate NCAA Division II varsity sports as part of the Great Lakes Intercollegiate Athletic Conference (GLIAC). Since 1998, the college has produced 118 athletic All-Americans and 28 conference champions, and Hillsdale teams have qualified for national tournaments 21 times. Thirty-four athletes have earned national academic honors in their respective sports as well. An active intramural program is also available. Four national fraternities, three national sororities, and more than 100 other social, academic, spiritual, and service organizations provide Hillsdale students with a diverse array of co-curricular opportunities. A resident drama troupe and dance company, a concert choir and chamber chorale, a jazz program with big band and combos, instrumental chamber ensembles from string quartets to percussion ensemble, and a symphony orchestra and band constitute the college's performing arts organizations.

ADMISSIONS PROCESS

Admission is a privilege extended to students who will benefit from, and contribute to, the academic, social, and spiritual environments of the college. Important determinants for admission are intellectual curiosity, ambition, leadership, and volunteerism. Accordingly, grade-point average, test scores, class rank, strength of curriculum, extracurricular activities, interviews, self-evaluations, writing samples in the form of two essays, and recommendations are all reviewed carefully and are important in the evaluation process. An admissions interview is strongly encouraged. Although some factors are necessarily more important than others, seldom is any single criterion, however important, decisive.

Transfer students must submit the standard application, including the high school record, SAT or ACT scores, transcripts from all colleges previously attended, and a transfer form from the dean of students of the most recent college attended. Applications by transfers are evaluated similarly to non-transfers.

Candidates for admission from other countries follow the regular entrance procedures. Students who come from a non-English-speaking country must demonstrate proficiency in English by satisfactory performance on the Test of English as a Foreign Language (TOEFL) or the Michigan Test of English Proficiency or at an ESL Center.

Students may apply to Hillsdale College any time after the completion of the junior year of high school. A formal application includes a completed application form accompanied by a nonrefundable fee of $35 (free if submitted online) and all required credentials. Application plans include early decision (November 1), and regular decision (April 1). Hillsdale College has been distinguished since its founding in 1844 by voluntarily adhering to a nondiscriminatory policy regarding race, religion, sex, and national or ethnic origin—long before the government began regulating such matters.

HOFSTRA UNIVERSITY

AT A GLANCE

At Hofstra University, students live, work and study on a beautiful, state-of-the-art campus that's only 25 miles east of Manhattan. Our 240-acre campus is lush, green and spacious, with ivy-covered buildings and outstanding facilities, just minutes from all the adventure and opportunity the New York metropolitan region has to offer.

BEST OF BOTH WORLDS

With the top-notch resources and wide-ranging programs of a large university, and the sense of community and personal attention of small college, Hofstra is a great place for students who are looking for a traditional campus experience without sacrificing the networking opportunities, internship experiences, and cultural offerings of a bustling metropolis.

Hofstra students have endless opportunities for experiential learning, on and off-campus. Opportunities are available to conduct research with a distinguished professor; intern with top-tier companies in finance or media, in the state Legislature or Congress; work in our cutting-edge facilities such as the Martin B. Greenberg Trading Room or WRHU-88.7 FM, Radio Hofstra University which was named the top college radio station in the country by The Princeton Review (2014).

As a Hofstra student, you can chose to live and learn in one of our 35 residence halls, each with a unique flair, community and life of its own. We also offer eight living/learning communities, which give students the opportunity to live with many of the same students they are in classes with, and well as students who share the same passion for leadership, health sciences, or the visual or performing arts.

A PROGRAM MEANT FOR YOU

Hofstra offers six undergraduate degrees with 145 undergraduate program options in the liberal arts and sciences, business, communications, education, engineering and applied science, and health sciences and human services. More than 100 dual degree program options are also offered, giving students the opportunity to earn both a graduate and undergraduate degree in less time than if each degree was pursued separately.

Hofstra's faculty members are knowledgeable and insightful thinkers, dedicated to providing the foundation and tools students need to succeed. With an average undergraduate class size of 21 and a student-faculty ratio of 14-to-1, students are challenged and encouraged to debate, question, do research, discuss and think critically in an open, collaborative learning environment. and, 92 percent of our full-time faculty hold the highest degree in their respective fields.

MUCH MORE THAN ACADEMICS

Hofstra hosts hundreds of social, academic and cultural events each year, drawing together scholars, business leaders, authors, celebrities, health care professionals, politicians, and journalists from across the nation and around the world. These events help foster that connection between in-classroom work and extracurricular interests we know you're looking for. In addition, Hofstra offers 17 intercollegiate athletic programs that compete at the NCAA Division I level and more than 200 academic, fraternal/sororal, media, multicultural, performance, pre-professional, religious, social, social/political, and sports clubs and organizations.

The David S. Mack Sports and Exhibition Complex, a 93,000-square-foot facility, is home to the Hofstra Pride men's and women's basketball teams and wrestling, and is also the site for events such as commencements, exhibitions, trade shows, televised political events, and concerts. Other recreational and athletic facilities include an indoor, Olympic-sized swimming pool, and various athletic fields.

PRIDE & PURPOSE

Our students roll up their sleeves, and make things happen. You will be encouraged to grow academically, as well as personally, through community service, leadership development, cultural and social exploration, study abroad and internships on Long Island and in New York City.

Since its founding in 1935, Hofstra has evolved into an internationally renowned university that continues to achieve recognition as an institution of academic excellence. Hofstra is consistently recognized on the Best College lists of U.S. News & World Report, The Princeton Review, Fiske, Washington Monthly, and Forbes.

Hofstra was named to the President's Higher Education Community Service Honor Roll four consecutive years, and more than 1,000 of our students served as volunteers when Hofstra hosted presidential debates in 2008 and 2012.

At Hofstra, Pride & Purpose means celebrating our history and traditions, and challenging ourselves, individually and collectively, to use our talents to make our campus, our community and our world a better place.

APPLYING TO HOFSTRA

Hofstra University seeks to enroll talented first-year and transfer students from diverse backgrounds and locations, with varied interests. Applications are accepted for fall and spring admission. The Admission Committee reviews each application individually to assess academic achievement, curricular rigor, leadership potential, depth of extracurricular activities, standardized test scores and overall interest in attending Hofstra University. The application process provides an opportunity for the applicant to share information that may not be apparent on a transcript or through a test score. For more information about the admission process, go to hofstra.edu/admission or go to hofstra.edu/visit and schedule a campus visit, today!

JOHNS HOPKINS UNIVERSITY

The Johns Hopkins undergraduate experience is all about exploration and discovery, for all students in every major.

AT A GLANCE

Johns Hopkins University is a place where ambitious, talented, and creative students thrive. Here, students in all majors embrace a spirit of learning through exploration and discovery. We offer students the freedom to pursue their intellectual passions, the opportunity to learn from academic leaders, and the chance to make an impact right away. With no core curriculum, students are able—and encouraged—to build the academic path that is right for them, with guidance from staff and administrators to help them find their way. Our students can combine their interests—academic and otherwise—in ways that are meaningful to them, and often discover new passions while they're here. Double majoring and majoring or taking classes across disciplines are common practices; in addition, over 97% of students have at least one career-related experience as undergraduates. Studying abroad is also a common option. Outside of the classroom, students are active and engaged on a lively campus, involved in activities from dance or singing groups to international service organizations. The admissions committee approaches applications from a holistic perspective, evaluating the "whole student." In addition to looking at a student's academic achievement and intellectual curiosity, we seek to admit students who are excited about learning and living at Johns Hopkins. We look for students who will bring something to the campus community while taking advantage of all Johns Hopkins has to offer.

ACADEMICS

At Johns Hopkins, research is engrained in our culture. Academic boundaries are not. From traditional labs and libraries to museums or field work, research here is not about a single project. It's about encouraging our students to think of new and exciting ways to delve into the subjects that matter most to them. They'll find a supportive network of professors and administrators dedicated to helping them get their projects started, including several generous research funding opportunities, such as the Provost's Undergraduate Research Awards and the Woodrow Wilson Undergraduate Research Fellowships. Because there's no core curriculum here, students can take advantage of fluid academic boundaries to take classes that are interesting and engaging. Allowing students to explore their academic interests results in a more stimulating learning environment, one that is enriched by students who truly enjoy learning and sharing their unique perspectives. Classes are small here, and the resources are big. That means as an undergraduate, you get to know your professors and classmates the way you would at a small liberal arts college, but you have all of the opportunities of a global research institution, right at your fingertips. Many students complete independent projects with professors, mentors, and teams. Lots more take advantage of study abroad, internships, semesters in Washington, D.C., and advanced graduate study. Johns Hopkins has schools, centers, and affiliates all over the Baltimore area—and they are often linked by free shuttle bus—in Washington, D.C., across the country, and around the world. Cross registration, independent projects, and internships are all encouraged options. Instead of a rigid core of compulsory courses, Johns Hopkins leaves you free to concentrate on what you love, or to explore more broadly. Academic and faculty advisers, career advisers, and pre-professional advisers help you chart the waters.

ADMISSIONS

The University looks for students who will take advantage of the resources and support a Johns Hopkins education offers, and who are eager to contribute to the campus community. A student's intellectual interests and accomplishments are of primary importance, and the admissions committee carefully examines each applicant's academic record, standardized test results, essays, extracurricular involvement, and recommendations from secondary school officials. However, the student's character, intellectual curiosity, and seriousness of purpose play the most significant role in application review. Each year we review more than 20,000 applications, from which we select a freshman class of around 1,300. Also each year, we welcome transfer students from other colleges and universities. Transfer students apply for entrance during their sophomore or junior years. Each application we receive represents an individual, and the admissions committee considers each one individually during a holistic review process. High school students should complete and submit applications by January 1 (by November 1 for Early Decision). We accept both the Common Application and the Universal College Application; both require a supplement, including a supplemental essay. To apply, complete either application and the Johns Hopkins supplement and submit them as soon as possible, but no later than the deadline, with your $70 nonrefundable application fee. Essays and two teacher recommendations are also required parts of the application. Visit http://apply.jhu.edu/apply/ for detailed information about the application process.

STANDARDIZED TEST REQUIREMENTS

Applicants must submit scores from all SAT tests, including Subject Tests, or ACT tests taken. For freshmen, the SAT Reasoning Test or the ACT with Writing Test are required. For those submitting SAT scores, Johns Hopkins strongly encourages submitting SAT Subject Test scores, and if submitted, requests results from three tests. For transfer students, SAT Reasoning Test scores are optional; SAT Subject Tests are not required. For international students, the TOEFL is required of applicants who do not speak English at home AND have not attended an English-language school for five years or longer. All other international applicants are not required to submit TOEFL scores but may do so to supplement their application.

Applicants should score a minimum of 600 (written test) or 250 (computer test). Applicants taking the Internet-based TOEFL (iBT) should have minimum sub-scores of 26 (Reading), 26 (Listening), 22 (Writing), and 25 (Speaking). A Critical Reading SAT score of 670 or higher waives for the TOEFL requirement for all students.

CAMPUS FACILITIES AND EQUIPMENT

Hopkins students dive into their lives outside of the classroom with the same enthusiasm and energy with which they approach their academic pursuits. Student life is centered around the 140 acres of the Homewood campus. A park-like setting within the city of Baltimore, our campus has had many renovations in recent years and continues to grow with exciting additions for our students. Most recently, we've unveiled the Undergraduate Teaching Labs (UTL). The UTL, housed in a beautiful glass building, includes lab teaching space that facilitates cross-disciplinary collaboration. Another recent addition, the Brody Learning Commons, is an exciting addition to Homewood that has already been embraced by the student community as a place to gather, study, and collaborate. The building connects to the Milton S. Eisenhower Library and contains the latest learning technology, including TeamSpot, interactive projectors that allow student to write on walls, Lifecam cameras, and video teleconferencing capabilities, all to support collaborative work. The building, constructed with current student input, features ample natural light and has achieved LEED Silver certification. Another campus highlight is the Mattin Center, which offers space for student groups and artistic endeavors. The center features a theater, café, art studios, darkrooms, music practice rooms, dance studios, the Digital Media Center, multipurpose rooms, and meeting spaces. The Ralph S. O'Connor Recreation Center, open for use by all students, houses basketball and volleyball courts, a rock-climbing wall, a weight room, and fitness training and aerobics areas, as well as access to the Athletic Center's swimming facilities. Popular fitness classes include yoga, Pilates, kickboxing, step aerobics, spinning, West African dance, and sports conditioning. Charles Commons, a two-building residential complex, features suites with single rooms, kitchenettes, and in many cases, living rooms. The complex is also home to a number of student amenities and common areas. The renovated Gilman Hall, located in the heart of campus, is home to the humanities departments and also features the Hutzler Reading Room, or "the Hut," a popular spot for quiet study or group projects; a glass-ceilinged atrium; the Johns Hopkins Archaeological Museum, and a coffee bar. Our campus is also home to many academic resources, including the Baltimore Museum of Art, the Homewood Museum, a world-class archaeological collection, and the six-story Milton S. Eisenhower Library.

Surrounding the campus is Baltimore's vibrant Charles Village community, home to many shops, restaurants, some student housing, and the Barnes and Noble bookstore. Students can often be found here, grabbing lunch or coffee at sub shops or local spots; using services like banks and dry cleaners; and grocery shopping.

CAMPUS LIFE

Homewood is an active, engaged campus where students are rounding out their academic pursuits with all kinds of activities, interests, and events. There are over 300 student groups and organizations on campus. All Johns Hopkins student groups are governed and managed by students, and there is something for everybody, from theater and performing arts groups, to political, special interest, and cultural groups, to publications, student government, and religious groups. Published since 1896, the News-Letter is one of the oldest student papers in the country. In 124 years of competition, the men's lacrosse team has won 44 national championships, including the 2005 and 2007 NCAA Division I National Championship, and twice represented the United States in the Olympic Games. For the past 10 years, the women's lacrosse team has also competed in Division I. Outside of lacrosse, one out of six Johns Hopkins students participates in one of our twenty Division III teams or club athletics, and more than half participate in the popular intramural program. Campus life extends to the city of Baltimore, our hometown, where students can explore concert venues large and small; a number of art galleries, theaters, and museums; and countless dining options. Many students come to adopt Baltimore as their hometown.

TUITION AND FEES

Tuition: $45,470

Room and Board: $13,832°

°University room and board charges are based on type of room selected, location, and meal plan. Shown above is an estimate for a typical double room and an anytime dining plan.

Johns Hopkins is dedicated to enrolling the strongest students each year, and it's our goal to help students able to make their college decision without being limited by their family financial circumstances. We are committed to meeting 100% of demonstrated financial need for our students for all four years of undergraduate study. We award more than $70 million in need-based Johns Hopkins grants to undergraduates each year, with an average freshman grant of more than $35,000. Both Kiplinger's Personal Finance and Princeton Review have named Hopkins a "best value" college among private universities. Johns Hopkins values every single student, and we support all aspects of their academic careers. In addition to an academic adviser, each student—even those who did not apply for aid—is given a financial aid adviser to explain financing options. Whether families need a better understanding of their student's aid package, would like to investigate the monthly payment plan, or want to talk through the pros and cons of the different loans, the Office of Student Financial Services is available to help all families understand and explore their options.

KETTERING UNIVERSITY

AT A GLANCE

Kettering University is a national leader in experiential STEM education, integrating an intense academic curriculum in science, technology, engineering, mathematics and business with applied professional and cooperative learning experiences. Through this proven approach, Kettering University inspires students to realize their potential and advance their ideas.

During study terms, students learn in small classes taught by professors, not teaching assistants. During work terms, they gain professional experience at corporations related to their studies. Students in all degree programs alternate between study terms and work terms.

Kettering students graduate with up to 2.5 years of real world experience and envyworthy resumes. Our students have done everything from testing ballistic systems and re-engineering crowd management to designing biomedical tools.

All of this experience pays off. Research shows that students who participate in co-op and experiential learning programs are more mature, better problem solvers, and more technically knowledgeable. Employers know that Kettering students are the cream of the crop—98% of Kettering University students graduate with job offers within their fields or are attending graduate school within six months of graduating. The average yearly starting salary of a Kettering student is $58,698. Kettering ranks among the top 1% of private institutions in the U.S. to offer $1 million plus return on investment to its graduates according to Affordable Colleges Online.

LOCATION AND ENVIRONMENT

Kettering University is located in Flint, MI, roughly 60 miles north of Detroit and a short drive from Lake Huron. Flint has approximately 100,000 residents. The Flint Cultural Center—located just one-and-a-half miles from campus – houses the Sloan Museum, Whiting Auditorium, Longway Planetarium, the Flint Institute of Music, and the Flint Institute of Arts. The nearby DTE Energy Music Center is one of the nation's top-ranked amphitheater venues and hosts more than 70 events each summer. While a sizable city, Flint also has 11,000 acres of woods, water and trails to offer – all part of Michigan's largest country park system. Students can enjoy golfing, hiking, kayaking, hunting, skiing and snowmobiling, and more. All freshmen live on campus while 34% percent of students live on campus the remainder of their college experience.

CO-OP AND EXPERIENTIAL LEARNING

More than half of a Kettering student's time is spent off campus, fulfilling professional co-op and experiential work requirements at a corporation that relates to their degree or interests. On average, students spend 11 academic semesters working for their employer and nine academic semesters in the classroom. Students work at one of Kettering's more than 500 employer partners located throughout North America and the globe. On average, students earn between $40,000 and $65,000 over their entire college career.

MAJORS AND DEGREES OFFERED

Kettering University's four and a half year cooperative and experiential learning program allows students to earn designated Bachelor of Science degrees in:

Applied Biology

Applied Mathematics

Applied Physics

Biochemistry

Bioinformatics

Business Administration

Chemical Engineering

Chemistry

Computer Engineering

Computer Science

Electrical Engineering

Engineering Physics

Industrial Engineering

Mechanical Engineering

Kettering also offers more than 50 minors, concentrations, specialties, courses of study and dual degrees, in areas such as Applied Optics, Pre-Law, Computer Gaming, System and Data Security, and Pre-Med. Additionally, the school offers 12 Master's Degrees, including an accredited MBA program. Please visit kettering.edu for more information.

ACADEMIC PROGRAMS

The unique structure of Kettering's program allows students to fulfill the academic requirements of 160 credit hours throughout a four and a half year period. This is completed over nine academic semesters and up to 11 co-op work semesters. Students also complete a culminating undergraduate experience during their senior year for credit toward the 160 required hours. These capstone experiences come in the form of a thesis project on behalf of their co-op employer, a research thesis project, a professional practice thesis project or an entrepreneurship thesis project. The academic year consists of two 11-week academic terms on-campus in Flint and two 12-week co-op terms working for the corporate employer; students alternate their time between Flint and the employer's site.

CAMPUS FACILITIES AND EQUIPMENT

Kettering University's state-of-the-art Mechanical Engineering & Chemistry Center is loaded with hands-on learning laboratories such as automotive labs with several unique test cells and the most advanced chemistry labs around! Engineering and chemistry facilities of this caliber are usually found only in graduate-level programs.

The Academic Building houses more classrooms, advanced laboratories (including our brand new, fully-equipped Applied Biology labs, which opened in 2014), and department offices. More than 100,000 square feet of this facility is dedicated to labs, which are stocked with equipment to demonstrate and experiment with methods in the engineering industry, from basic machining to emerging technologies. The entire campus—including residence hall rooms, campus apartments, and labs—is networked, providing each student with 24-hour access to computer resources and the Internet.

The library contains more than 118,000 volumes, more than 390 periodicals, and various online services. Special facilities include a microfilm area, database search services, record and tape listening- and videotape viewing-facilities, and a special collection of SAE, SME, and ASME technical papers.

TUITION, ROOM, BOARD, AND FEES*

Tuition for the 2014–2015 academic year is $18,490 per term. Kettering is proud to offer students a Fixed Tuition Guarantee. Students making normal progress towards their degree will pay the same tuition rates for their entire college career. Kettering has also eliminated all academically-related fees in its all-inclusive tuition package.

Room and Board for the 2014–2015 academic year is $3,620 per term.

*Please remember that tuition and fees are subject to change at any time.

FINANCIAL AID

Kettering University offers traditional need- and merit-based financial aid, including a generous merit scholarship program. In fact, more than 92% of Kettering students receive some level of financial assistance. Factor in co-op earnings—the average hourly wage of a Kettering student is $14.20 for freshmen and $18.44 for seniors—and our fixed-rate tuition guarantee, and students are looking at one of the best values in education today. Aid is given as grants, scholarships, loans, and work-study awards. Students should fill out the Free Application for Federal Student Aid (FAFSA) and request a copy of the analysis be sent to Kettering University. The University works to create a financial package based on those results.

STUDENT ORGANIZATIONS AND ACTIVITIES

College life should offer students more than just learning opportunities. To this end, Kettering offers more than 50 student organizations, such as SAE, DECA and Engineers without Borders, and numerous social activities and intramural sports. Approximately a third of Kettering students join the 13 national fraternities and six sororities that are represented on campus. The school's active student government produces programs to develop peers' leadership skills, self-confidence, interpersonal relations, and organizational operations.

Students come from approximately 48 states and 18 countries, so they also benefit from learning and sharing with this diverse community.

ADMISSIONS PROCESS

Admission to Kettering University is competitive and based on scholastic achievement and extracurricular interests, activities, and achievements. Applicants are required to have completed the following courses (one credit represents two semesters or one year of study): Two credits algebra, one credit geometry, a half credit trigonometry, two credits laboratory science (one of these credits must be from physics or chemistry, and both are strongly recommended), and three credits English. Applicants must submit SAT or ACT scores. Most Kettering University students rank at or near the top 10 percent of their high school class.

Kettering University also accepts transfer students. A minimum of 14 credits is required, but 16-20 credits are strongly encouraged. Admission decisions for transfer applicants are based on college records for those who have completed at least 30 credits.

Although applications are accepted all year long, prospective students are encouraged to file their application early in their senior year. Early application significantly improves students' chances for early co-op employment. Interested students can apply online at http://www.kettering.edu/apply.

KNOX COLLEGE

We're not simply an education; we're an experience. And when you take that experience out into the so-called real world, you discover that it works for you.

AT A GLANCE

Veritas, meaning "truth," is the motto of Knox College—a top ranked, private liberal arts college in Galesburg, Illinois. Established in 1837 by social reformers from upstate New York, Knox has stayed true to its Mission of Access: that those truly wanting a liberal arts education should be free to achieve it—regardless of race, gender, cultural background, or economic standing.

In this spirit, Abraham Lincoln chose Knox's Old Main as his platform to advocate for unity, equality, and freedom during the historic Lincoln-Douglas debates.

Today, Knox's egalitarian spirit lives on in our commitment to give every student a voice and an education that enables lifelong learning and the Freedom to Flourish. A student-established Honor Code guides academic and intellectual integrity.

Knox also celebrates one of the most culturally diverse campuses in the U.S. with 1,392 students from 48 states and 46 countries, including 21% U.S. students of color and 7% international students.

As independent thinkers, Knox students actively plan their own program of study. More than 80% complete hands-on work through research, independent study, internships, creative projects, and off-campus study. Knox devotes much of its resources toward developing and supporting experiential learning opportunities.

Knox follows a 3-3 calendar—3 terms with 3 classes per term. Popular programs include: Biology, Business, Chemistry, Computer Science, Creative Writing, Economics, English, International Relations, Mathematics, Neuroscience, Physics, Political Science, Pre-Law, Pre-Med, and Psychology—as well as internships and study abroad.

Classes are taught by distinguished scholar-teachers, 96% of whom have a Ph.D. or the highest degree in their field—more than 60% have been published or publicly honored in the past 3 years. A 12:1 student-faculty ratio and small classes averaging 17 students allow for one-on-one student-professor interaction.

Knox students embrace extracurricular activities for fun, athletics, and social causes—the college has more than 100 clubs and organizations. Our radio station, WVKC, has been ranked as one of the top 10 nationwide. And our internationally acclaimed Catch is the country's oldest collegiate literary magazine.

Knox athletic programs include 21 NCAA Division III teams, and 11 club and intramural sports teams. The Prairie Fire is the official moniker of Knox's sports teams.

Named one of the colleges That Change Lives by former New York Times education editor Loren Pope, Knox is consistently ranked as one of the best values among U.S. liberal arts colleges.

LOCATION AND ENVIRONMENT

Under the open skies of west-central Illinois sits the 82-acre Knox campus. Built on prairieland, its broad lawns and big trees offer plenty of prime spots to study, play or simply relax and enjoy. Days are generally clear and sunny, with warm springs and colorful falls. Knox's nearby Green Oaks Biological Field Station offers an additional 700 acres of restored prairie, woods, and waterways to explore.

Campus buildings are a blend of histories, old and new. The stone hewn, wood-paneled Seymour Library is a favorite study spot. Old Main, with its working bell, well-worn marble steps, and grand Alumni Room (featuring Lincoln's chair) is Knox's oldest building. Students, faculty, and staff also "hang out" at Seymour Union—in the Gizmo café, on the boardwalk patio, or in the new student lounge, with its game room and stage.

Life at Knox encompasses a deeply woven sense of community, where professors and students can freely meet and share ideas. Most faculty live nearby and nearly all seniors have been to their professor's home.

More than 95% of Knox students live on campus in a unique array of historic houses, apartments, suites and traditional residence halls. Fraternity houses and theme houses such as International House, Casa Latina, ABLE Center for Black Culture, Jazz House, and Eco House are fixtures.

Joining the Knox community means meeting everyone—before your first day of class. That's when Knox holds its Pumphandle tradition. Students, faculty, and staff gather at Old Main to meet one another, eventually forming a meandering line on the lawn (and through buildings) as everyone shakes hands with everyone else.

OFF-CAMPUS OPPORTUNITIES

Galesburg was established by the founders of Knox in 1837, and shares the college's roots of diversity and freedom—it was a key center for the Underground Railroad in Illinois. In town you'll find the same Midwest generosity that gives the Knox campus such an easy-going atmosphere.

The city's many historic charms include brick streets and an abundance of Victorian and Craftsman architecture. Within walking distance from campus, downtown Galesburg offers shops, restaurants, and many venues for live entertainment. Its historic Seminary Street district features quaint cafés and boutiques—and the train station with daily Amtrak service to and from Chicago.

The arts and culture scene has always thrived in Galesburg, and includes the award-winning Knox-Galesburg Symphony, Prairie Players Civic Theatre, Discovery Depot Children's Museum, Civic Art Center, and restored Orpheum Theatre. The city's daily newspaper, The Register Mail, is near campus.

Knox students also work closely with the community in volunteer and internship capacities for schools, hospitals, and neighborhood agencies.

About 45 minutes in either direction are the urban centers of Peoria and Moline, with access to airports, shopping, museums, galleries—and attractions on the Illinois and Mississippi rivers.

MAJORS AND DEGREES OFFERED

The Knox bachelor's program provides a balanced curriculum in the arts, humanities, sciences, and social sciences. Knox's 3-3 academic calendar—3 terms (fall, winter, and spring), 3 courses per term—allows students to fully explore course subject matter and fulfill research expectations.

Knox offers 38 majors, 49 minors, 10 cooperative degree programs, and 30-plus off-campus and study abroad programs—in addition to grant-sponsored hands-on research and internship opportunities. Self-designed majors are also popular.

Knox graduates enjoy one of the highest acceptance rates to post-graduate and professional school programs. The college is in the top 4% of institutions producing successful Ph.D. candidates, and ranks 11th for post-graduate math and science degree candidates.

ACADEMIC PROGRAMS

Experiential learning is a cornerstone of Knox's curriculum and the college offers many hands-on opportunities.

Research, Honors, & Independent Study: Knox provides more than $250,000 in grants and funding for graduate-style research, Honors research, and creative projects. Over 85% of Knox students complete independent study courses or projects, where they're encouraged to explore interests, generate ideas, and pursue a well-planned course of study under the guidance of a faculty member.

Immersion Experiences: Knox's unique and exciting immersion terms allow students to fully explore specific subjects in real world style. Clinical Psychology Term involves courses and fieldwork as a clinical psychology intern. During the interdisciplinary Green Oaks Term, students live at Green Oaks Biological Field Station, conducting scientific and historical research, and working on creative projects. Japan Term students fully explore Japanese language, history, and philosophy, followed by a two-week trip to Japan. Open Studio Term allows students to work independently as full-time artists and concludes in a Senior Show. Repertory Theatre Term teaches students how to run a repertory theatre and culminates in the staging of two major theatrical productions.

Off-Campus & Study Abroad: More than 30 off-campus study and study abroad programs are available in the U.S. And 20 different countries through the Center for Global Studies.

Public Service: Knox is the first college or university in the country to offer an official Peace Corps Program. Knox also provides opportunities for community, national, and international internships, and volunteer work.

CAMPUS FACILITIES AND EQUIPMENT

Knox College provides about $250,000 annually to support independent study, creative projects, and Honors projects, as well as student access to superior research resources and equipment.

Libraries: Knox College maintains three libraries: Seymour Library, the Science-Mathematics Library, and the Ford Center for Fine Arts music library. Seymour, the main library, houses more than 350,000 volumes, and the Special Collections and Archives—which contains primary source materials used by students, faculty, and researchers from around the world.

Arts: Ford Center for the Fine Arts—a comprehensive facility for the visual arts, theatre, dance, and music—features the 600-seat Harbach theatre with its rotating stage and the 325-seat Kresge Recital Hall. Other resources include the Studio Theatre, the 360-degree Art Gallery and Round Room, and numerous art and music studios.

Science: Major grants from the National Science Foundation, National Institutes of Health, and Howard Hughes Medical Institute, help Knox continue to expand an equipment roster that includes electron microscopes, NMR, ESR, GC-MS, other spectrometers and chromatographs, X-ray, laser labs, experimental psychology labs, four computer labs, and a greenhouse.

Green Oaks Biological Field Station, near the Spoon River about 20 miles east of Knox, encompasses 700 acres of forest, aquatic habitat, and North America's second-oldest restored tall-grass prairie.

Athletics: The 50,000 sq. ft. Fleming Fieldhouse provides an indoor six-lane 200-meter track, and court space for numerous activities. Andrew Fitness Center offers separate cardio/weight machine, and free-weight floors. Knosher Bowl, a true bowl stadium, features artificial turf and one of the best playing surfaces in Division III football. Blodgett Field, a pro-level baseball diamond, features its own sprinkler system and special soil composition. Knox also maintains a main gym and basketball court, a 6-lane outdoor track, softball and soccer fields, tennis courts, a wrestling complex, and natatorium. Golf is played at a nearby private 18-hole course.

TUITION, ROOM, BOARD, AND FEES

Expenses per academic year:

Tuition: $39,765

Room: $4,368

Board: $4,356

Fees: $366

Total: $48,855

Average cost for books and supplies: $900

FINANCIAL AID

Knox is committed to ensuring that cost is not a barrier to a high-caliber college education. The college offers a wide variety of merit-based scholarships and need-based financial aid to help cover expenses. Writer's, Visual and Performing Arts, Social Concerns, and Regional scholarships are also available.

For more information on scholarships or financial aid, visit www.knox.edu, or contact us at 800-678-KNOX.

STUDENT ORGANIZATIONS AND ACTIVITIES

Student Clubs and Organizations: The more than 100 student-run organizations on campus provide an outlet for everything from academics, such as chemistry or physics, to the arts—13 music and dance ensembles—to social and community concerns to national fraternities and sororities. Clubs such as Common Ground, Model United Nations, Alliance for Peaceful Action, Asian Student Association, and Intervarsity Christian Fellowship, focus on identity, culture, and politics.

Prairie Fire Athletics: The Athletic Program at Knox has been building a winning tradition for more than a century. Knox is a member of the NCAA Division III and the Midwest Conference (MWC), one of the oldest conferences in the nation. Competition in the conference is intense and spirited, including the local rivalry between Knox and Monmouth College—the sixth-oldest athletic rivalry in the country. As a Knox student-athlete, you'll train in some of the best athletic facilities, and your coaches will challenge you to grow and achieve at even higher levels than you might have expected.

Club and Intramural Sports: Intramural sports are organized in student-directed leagues. Regular offerings include volleyball, basketball, indoor soccer, dodgeball, and softball. Our competitive club sports include co-ed and women's water polo; equestrian; women's lacrosse; fencing; and co-ed, men's, and women's Ultimate Frisbee.

Student Governance: Getting involved is a key principle of a Knox liberal arts education. Knox prides itself on an active and self-governing student body—students sit on all committees. The Honor Code, initiated by students in 1951, continues to anchor the sense of responsibility and self-direction that is central to intellectual life at Knox.

ADMISSIONS PROCESS

Visiting Knox is the best way to get to know us. Visits include a student-guided tour of campus and an opportunity to meet with your admission counselor, professors, and coaches, and to sit in on classes. We also offer open houses throughout the year for prospective students and their families.

Knox uses the Common Application. Deadlines for first-year admission are November 1 for Early Action I, December 1 for Early Action II, and February 1 for Regular Decision. We also accept transfer applications for Fall, Winter, and Spring terms.

For more information please visit admission online or contact us directly.

Office of Admission

Knox College

2 East South Street

Galesburg, Illinois 61401-4999

United States

Phone: 800-678-KNOX or 309-341-7100

Fax: 309-341-7070

E-mail: admission@knox.edu

Web: www.knox.edu

LA ROCHE COLLEGE

AT A GLANCE

Students at La Roche College find a combination of innovation education and hands-on instruction.

This small, residential college provides a supportive and intimate learning environment for more than 1,400 men and women, including 1,065 full-time undergraduates. With a 13:1 student-faculty ratio, La Roche's small class sizes allow faculty to provide personalized attention for students to reach their academic and career goals. Through a practice-based liberal arts curriculum and real-world training, the college provides students with the skills and knowledge that they need to succeed in a competitive workforce.

Founded by the Congregation of the Sisters of Divine Providence in 1963, La Roche fosters global citizenship and creates a community of scholars from around the region, the nation and the world. It embraces its Catholic heritage while welcoming people of all religions and socioeconomic backgrounds, including students from 20 states and territories and 35 countries. With a legacy of social justice and a commitment to international exchange, La Roche educates students to be lifelong learners and achievers in an increasingly diverse and global society. La Roche promotes global awareness and provides opportunities for students to explore other cultures and traditions.

LOCATION AND ENVIRONMENT

Located in the North Hills of Pittsburgh, La Roche's residential campus offers just the right blend of suburban and metropolitan life. Just 15 minutes north of downtown Pittsburgh, this convenient location puts students at the doorstep of a major metropolitan area and a variety of cultural, recreational and career opportunities.

The second-largest city in Pennsylvania, Pittsburgh is the headquarters of several multinational corporations. Forbes has ranked Pittsburgh as the nation's most livable city more than once, and The Economist named Pittsburgh a top U.S. city in its list of the world's most livable cities in 2011 and again in 2014.

Situated on more than 40 acres, the college itself is home to a dynamic environment that draws students from across the country and around the world. An education at La Roche offers a cross-cultural experience rarely found at a small, private college. This safe and diverse environment allows students to actively participate in a variety of sports, on-campus events and community-based activities.

MAJORS AND DEGREES OFFERED

La Roche College's 50-plus undergraduate majors include the high-demand fields of business, education, and health and medical sciences, as well as the creative disciplines of interior design, graphic design, dance, and film and media:

- Biochemistry
- Biology
- Biology/Forensic Science

BUSINESS

- Accounting
- Finance
- Information Technology
- International Management
- Management
- Management Information Systems
- Marketing
- Chemistry
- Chemistry/Environmental Science and Management (3:2)°
- Chemistry/Forensic Science
- Child and Family Studies
- Communication, Media and Technology
- Computer Science
- Criminal Justice

EDUCATION

- PreK-4 Special Education
- Middle Level Education – English/Language Arts and Reading
- Middle Level Education – Mathematics

- Middle Level Education – Science
- Middle Level Education – Social Studies
- Middle Level Education – Social Studies and History
- Middle Level Education – Social Studies and Political Science
- Secondary Education – English

ENGINEERING

- Bioengineering (3:2)°
- Chemical Engineering (3:2)°
- Computer Engineering (3:2)°
- Electrical Engineering (3:2)°
- Engineering Science
- (Nanotechnology: Chemistry/Bioengineering) (3:2)°
- Industrial Engineering (3:2)°
- Software Engineering (3:2)°
- English Studies: Journalism and Professional Writing
- English Studies: Language and Literature
- Film, Video and Media°
- Graphic Design

HEALTH-RELATED

- Athletic Training (2:2)°
- Dentistry (3:4 and 4:4)°
- Health Science
- Nursing – Associate of Science
- Nursing – RN to BSN Completion Degree
- Occupational Therapy (2:3)°
- Osteopathic Medicine (3:4 and 4:4)°
- Pharmacy (3+ and 4+ track)°
- Physical Therapy (3:3)°
- Physician Assistant (2:3)°
- Radiologic Technology – Associate of Science°
- Speech and Language Pathology (2:3)°
- History
- Interior Design
- International Affairs
- International Management
- Liberal Studies
- Mathematics
- National Security Studies
- Performing Arts – Dance
- Political Science
- Psychology
- Religious Studies
- Self-Designed
- Sociology
- Undeclared

°This program involves taking courses at a partner institution to obtain a degree. Not all programs are available to transfer students.

MORE DISTINCTIONS

Most recently La Roche was named a Best Regional College by U.S. News & World Report in its 2015 edition of the Best Colleges guidebook. For the past eight consecutive years, The Princeton Review has ranked La Roche as one of the Best Northeastern Colleges. La Roche has been named a Military Friendly College for six consecutive years. In 2013 the Institute of International Education listed La Roche as one of the top 25 baccalaureate colleges hosting international students. In 2010 La Roche was one of three colleges in the country to receive the Senator Paul Simon Spotlight Award for Innovation in International Higher Education.

GREAT TEACHING

As a private liberal arts institution, La Roche places an emphasis on the higher-level skills sought by today's employers, such as writing, analyzing, collaboration and problem solving allowing graduates to segue into a variety of careers in an ever-changing global economy. A practice-based curriculum and personalized instruction provides students with the knowledge and self-confidence that they need to become leaders in the workforce.

The College's signature program is The La Roche Experience (LRX). This four-credit course sequence introduces students to the rich heritage of a La Roche education, which is grounded in promoting peace and justice in a global society. Through eye-opening simulation exercises, LRX students learn to think critically about social justice issues.

Another unique feature is the Study Abroad+Study USA program, which offers the value-added component of studying abroad or domestically at little or no cost. After completing 60 La Roche credits and meeting all eligibility requirements, students may apply for a Study Abroad+Study USA travel course. Students only are responsible for passport costs, visas, some meals and spending money.

Students have the opportunity to strive for even greater academic achievement through the La Roche College Honors Institute. Designed to recognize and promote academic excellence, the Institute combines classroom learning with distinctive co-curricular activities, allowing students to engage in group discussion and independent inquiry research.

La Roche faculty members are an acclaimed group of scholars who work closely with students to challenge and encourage them. Full-time faculty members are experts in their fields of study; a large percentage hold terminal degrees. These highly trained and experienced professionals engage in research and spend time in classrooms, laboratories and studios.

CAMPUS FACILITIES AND EQUIPMENT

La Roche offers a unique combination of 21st-century education and advanced technology in an intimate setting.

The College offers special services to help students meet their academic, personal and career goals. The Student Academic Support Services Office provides individualized and group tutoring sessions, career development resources, mentoring services and one-on-one appointments with an academic counselor. Students also may visit The Writers' Center on campus, where consultants offer advice for writing and reading assignments.

The John J. Wright Library is a state-of-the-art facility on campus, with a collection of more than 70,000 volumes, 80,000 electronic books, 44 electronic databases, 500 periodical subscriptions and access to 30,000 government documents through a United States Government Depository Library. As a member of the Pennsylvania Academic Library Consortium, Inc., the library also offers Interlibrary Loan and EZ-Borrow services. Housed within the building is the Providence World Café, where students enjoy the comfortable setting of a local coffee house.

TUITION, ROOM, BOARD AND FEES

Full-time tuition for the 2014–2015 academic year is $25,514. Room and board costs are $10,324. Student support and development has a $400 annual fee, and the curricular learning support tech fee is $350.

La Roche's residence halls offer students all of the comforts of home. The college's spacious residence rooms include a refrigerator, microwave, private bathroom, Internet and cable television access, and free laundry facilities. Apartment-style suites are available for upper classmen. All residence halls include lounges that are perfect for studying or informal gatherings. Free parking is available to commuter students, and resident students with cars on campus pay a nominal fee annually to park.

To maintain a safe atmosphere, La Roche public safety staff patrol the campus 24 hours a day. Access to the residence halls is restricted to only those students and staff who possess an electronic ID card. Forty-eight percent of the student body resides on campus.

FINANCIAL AID

La Roche provides quality education at an affordable cost by awarding grants, scholarships, loans, several repayment plans and work-study employment. Nearly 95 percent of students receive financial aid, and the average financial aid package is approximately $25,820 per student.

All students who intend to apply for financial aid must submit the Free Application for Federal Student Aid (FAFSA) after Jan. 1 of their senior year in high school. Students who live outside of Pennsylvania should submit their own state grant form, if applicable.

La Roche encourages all students to submit the proper forms as soon as possible after Jan. 1 so that they are processed prior to the college's May 1 priority deadline.

STUDENT ORGANIZATIONS AND ACTIVITIES

The suburban campus provides a safe and encouraging environment for students to actively participate in a variety of sports, on–campus events and community-based activities. Student life is vibrant and exciting, with more than 30 clubs and organizations, intramurals, as well as 12 NCAA Div. III athletic teams and service-learning programs. The college's outdoor athletic complex recently underwent a $2.7 million renovation and now features state-of-the-art amenities including an artificial turf field. Student activities tailor many interests and include:

• Academic organizations for individual majors

• Professional and honor societies that provide students with distinction in their fields of study

• Special interest clubs that encourage students to explore new hobbies and meet classmates who share similar interests

• Multicultural clubs and organizations to promote and represent the unique cultures on campus. One example is G.L.O.B.E.; a popular event is the annual G.L.O.B.E. International Fashion Show.

In addition, the Office of Mission and Ministry offers valuable opportunities for students to develop service and leadership skills while giving back to the community. Service projects acknowledge at-risk children, the elderly, the homeless, and other special needs populations. Every year student volunteers travel to a select location for Alternative Spring Break. Previous projects have included recovery efforts following Hurricanes Sandy and Katrina.

ADMISSIONS PROCESS

La Roche College, which is selective in its admission process, seeks students who have a clear commitment to personal growth and achievement and demonstrate a strong desire to fulfill their academic potential.

The admission committee reviews each applicant individually, assessing personal and academic strengths in light of a student's background. Committee members carefully examine high school records, including course work, grade point average and SAT or ACT scores. SAT and ACT scores should be sent directly to the Office of Admissions at La Roche. (La Roche's code numbers are SAT: 2379 and ACT: 3607). We offer numerous academic scholarships, including merit-based scholarships ranging from $1,000 to $15,000 annually.

For more information regarding the La Roche College admission process, prospective students should contact:

Office of Freshman Admissions
La Roche College
9000 Babcock Boulevard
Pittsburgh, Pennsylvania 15237
United States
Phone: 412-536-1272
800-838-4572 (toll-free)
Fax: 412-847-1820
Email: admissions@laroche.edu
Web site: www.laroche.edu

LAKE FOREST COLLEGE

AT A GLANCE

The beautiful 107-acre campus is ideally located on Chicago's North Shore near Lake Michigan. Lake Forest College gives every student direct access to superb faculty and a powerful network of alumni who help graduates begin careers. This access provides every student with a valuable edge on a bright future.

The flexible curriculum supports double majors and minors, and students are also offered unparalleled internships in Chicago, great lab research experiences, championship athletics, and study-abroad opportunities. Students learn in a rigorous academic environment in small class settings where professors do all of the teaching and advising. Career-building internships are plentiful in the Chicago area, and students can pursue up to three for credit. Study abroad is encouraged, and students can also spend a semester living and interning in Chicago.

The student body is comprised of students from nearly every state and eighty-one countries around the world and together they form a diverse learning community that prepares them to succeed in today's global society.

Developing career goals—and a plan of action to achieve them—is a fundamental goal of the Career Advancement Center and the college community as a whole. Students have access to programs, resources, career advisors, and a powerful network of alumni throughout their four years.

The outcomes are hard to match: More than 90 percent of graduates had jobs, graduate school, or other opportunities secured within six months of graduation, well above the national average.

LOCATION AND ENVIRONMENT

Just an hour's train ride to Chicago, the college is located in the town of Lake Forest, Illinois, 30 miles north of the city. The 107-acre residential campus is a safe academic home in a beautiful wooded suburban setting within walking distance to the train to downtown Chicago, historic Lake Forest, and the beaches of Lake Michigan.

The College is only 25 miles from O'Hare International Airport and is also served by Midway Airport and Mitchell International Airport in Milwaukee.

The campus is surrounded by lush wooded neighborhoods, ravines, natural prairies, the beautiful beaches along Lake Michigan, and an extensive network of bike and running trails. Nearby Chicago boasts nearly 70 world-class museums, more than 200 theaters, seven major league sports teams, and one of the nation's top opera companies. Chicago is known for its cleanliness, abundant green space, good transportation system, and friendly people.

OFF-CAMPUS OPPORTUNITIES

Lake Forest encourages students to take advantage of study, internship, and research opportunities in Chicago, around the United States, and abroad. Internship opportunities are plentiful in the Chicago area and students have interned at places such as the Art Institute of Chicago, Chicago Blackhawks, Chicago Board of Trade, Chicago Council on Global Affairs, Edelman Public Relations Worldwide, Morgan Stanley, NBC Chicago, Second City, and the John G. Shedd Aquarium, among others.

In addition to a well-established internship program, Lake Forest College provides students with a wide variety of opportunities for off-campus study. Semester-long options in the United States include the "Lake Forest College In The Loop" Chicago Semester Program, Chicago Arts Program, Oak Ridge Science Semester, Chicago Urban Studies Program, Chicago Program in Business and Society, Newberry Library Program in the Humanities, and the Washington Semester Program at American University.

There are many options for international study, such as Lake Forest's own international internship programs in Paris, France; Granada, Spain; and Beijing, China; the Ancient Civilizations Program in Greece, which uses historical and archaeological sites and museums to study the ancient Aegean world; the Border Studies Program in Mexico and the U.S.; as well as a semester-long program in New Zealand. As a member of the Associated Colleges of the Midwest, Lake Forest also offers programs in Botswana, Costa Rica, England, India, Italy, Japan, Jordan, and Tanzania. The off-campus program director works with students to facilitate participation in many other approved off-campus study programs.

MAJORS AND DEGREES OFFERED

Lake Forest College has a long tradition of academic excellence and is known for its innovative curriculum. In addition to majors in the humanities, social sciences, and natural sciences, the college features programs of study in pre-law, pre-medicine, communication, business, finance, computer science, and still other practical areas.

There are no teaching assistants at the college. Courses are taught in small classroom settings by professors who are experts in their fields and who also serve students as one-on-one advisors. In addition to classroom studies, students are encouraged to complete an internship, conduct original research, and study abroad for a semester.

Lake Forest awards the Bachelor of Arts (BA) degree in both traditional academic departments and interdisciplinary programs. Majors and minors include: African American studies, American studies, anthropology, area studies, art (studio art and art history), Asian studies, biology, border studies, business, chemistry, cinema studies, classical studies, communication, computer science, digital media design, economics, education (elementary, secondary, and educational studies), engineering (dual degree), English (literature and writing), entrepreneurship and innovation, environmental studies, finance, gender, sexuality, and women's studies, history history, independent scholar, international relations, Islamic world studies, Latin American studies, legal studies, mathematics, medieval and renaissance studies, modern languages and literatures (Arabic, Chinese, French, German, Italian, Japanese, and Spanish), music, music education, neuroscience, philosophy, physics, politics, print and digital publishing, psychology, religion, rhetoric, social justice, sociology, theater, urban studies. Lake Forest also offers pre-professional programs in law, medicine, dentistry, and veterinary medicine.

Accelerated and dual-degree programs are offered. Three-year degree programs are available in communication and philosophy. Dual-degree programs are available in law, international studies, pharmacy, and engineering. Lake Forest is affiliated with several competitive law schools that allow students to complete a bachelor's degree and a law degree in a total of six years, rather than the usual seven. Qualified Lake Forest College students may be admitted to the Monterey Institute of International Studies with accelerated status, and can complete their master's degrees with 48 credits as opposed to the 60 normally required. A dual-degree program in partnership with Rosalind Franklin University of Medicine and Science allows students to complete a bachelor of arts degree in biology and a doctor of pharmacy. The engineering program is in cooperation with the Sever Institute of Technology at Washington University (St. Louis). Lake Forest's affiliation with Rush University School of Nursing and DePaul University School of Nursing allows students to complete a bachelor's degree and then pursue a master's in nursing

ACADEMIC PROGRAMS

The First-Year Studies Program (FIYS)

First-year studies classes are small in size to encourage interaction and discussion. The FIYS professors also serve as the students' primary academic advisors and help them navigate the college's academic offerings during their first year. With many topics to choose from, first-year studies courses cover a wide range of academic interests from music, art, and politics to neuroscience, terrorism, and religion, many with a focus on Chicago or directly utilizing the resources available there. Chicago plays an integral role in the FIYS program. Students travel to the city with their class during orientation week, providing a first-hand introduction to how the educational, cultural, and social resources of Chicago will influence their coursework and experiences during their four years at Lake Forest.

Honors Fellow Program

As part of the first-year student admission application process, select students are invited to apply to the Honors Fellow Program.

The Richter Apprentice Scholars Program

This program provides students, early in their academic careers, with the opportunity to conduct independent, individual research with Lake Forest faculty. In the summer after their first year, each student in the Richter Program is employed for a ten-week period and does independent research one-on-one with a faculty member.

The Independent Scholar Program

This program allows students to develop an academic major of their own, working closely with a faculty advisor, culminating in a thesis or a creative project.

CAMPUS FACILITIES AND EQUIPMENT

A new 230-bed residence hall opened in August 2013 and features doubles, suites, and super suites with living rooms, lounges, kitchen, and a multipurpose room for group events.

A new recreation, sports, and fitness facility opened in April 2010 and includes three new multipurpose courts, a suspended running track, an aerobic and dance studio, a swimming pool, a batting/golf cage, strength, cardio, and fitness spaces, among other amenities.

New Johnson Science Center to open fall 2017: Envisioning that future discoveries will be increasingly interdisciplinary in nature, the new Science Center will accommodate the multi-disciplinary needs of the biology, chemistry, physics, and psychology departments, as well as the environmental studies and neuroscience programs. The $40 million renovation and addition project will result in a 130,000-square-foot state-of-the-art research and teaching facility.

The Mohr Student Center is a student-centered social space that is the hub of social activity on campus. It features pool tables and other games, stage and performance space, large-screen TVs, lounges, deli/snack bar, and an outdoor terrace with seating.

Center for Chicago Programs

Chicago provides a hands-on resource for student learning through research, internships, study, and fun. At the Center for Chicago Programs on campus, students can plan visits to the city and professors can get help incorporating Chicago resources into their classrooms. The Center also brings well-known Chicagoans to the college for lectures and performances.

TUITION, ROOM, BOARD AND FEES

2014–2015

Tuition: $40,448.00

Room: $4,480.00

Board: $5,000.00

Fees: $724.00

FINANCIAL AID

Lake Forest College provides an affordable, high-quality education through maintaining a strong commitment to supporting each student's demonstrated financial need.

The College offers up to $20,000 in combined scholarships. Academic scholarships are awarded up to $12,000 and talent scholarships up to $8,000 for recognized dedication in the fine arts, foreign languages, leadership, music, sciences (including math and computers), theater, or writing.

STUDENT ORGANIZATIONS AND ACTIVITIES

With the diversity of the student body there is an eclectic mix of activities and opportunities outside the classroom.

Student organizations include student government, international interest groups, Greek Life, academic honor societies, community service, publications and media, music and performance, spiritual and religious groups, and many others.

Students have a voice in how the college is run and are actively involved in governance committees such as the college Council and have representation on the Board of Trustees. Academic honor societies enjoy active student participation, as do the community service groups and many special-interest clubs. The college provides and maintains a comprehensive intramural and intercollegiate athletic program. There are two national fraternities and five national sororities, all housed within the residence halls.

Lake Forest College competes in the NCAA Division III fielding nine women's and eight men's intercollegiate varsity teams. Women's teams include basketball, cross-country, golf, handball, ice hockey, soccer, softball, swimming and diving, tennis, and volleyball. Men's teams include basketball, cross-country, football, golf, handball, ice hockey, soccer, swimming and diving, and tennis. The college also offers an extensive roster of intramural and club sports.

The College's Center for Chicago Programs facilitates engagement with the resources of Chicago, which often complements programs for student organizations as well as provides students with information on cultural and social activities happening downtown. The train to Chicago is a short walk from campus and students enjoy traveling to the city for fun and entertainment. The college shuttle provides service seven days a week to popular shopping areas and destinations around campus.

ADMISSIONS PROCESS

The criteria used for selection include assessment of a student's program of study, academic achievement, aptitude, intellectual curiosity, qualities of character and personality, and activities.

Standardized test scores (ACT/SAT) are optional, except for international or home-schooled candidates, and those applying for some academic scholarships. A personal interview is highly recommended.

LAWRENCE TECHNOLOGICAL UNIVERSITY

AT A GLANCE

Lawrence Technological University is a private, personally focused university providing students a rigorous, high-quality education—an education that pays off. According to the latest PayScale.com survey, the earning power of a Lawrence Tech bachelor's degree ranks in the top 100 of all U.S. universities. Some 80 percent of students are employed by the date of their graduation, nearly double the national average.

The University, including its graduate programs, is accredited by the Higher Learning Commission and is a member of the North Central Association of Colleges and Schools. In addition to its ranking by the Princeton Review LTU placed in the top tier of Best University-Masters-Midwest in the U.S. News and World Report's 2015 America's Best Colleges rankings. Other distinctions include the designation as a Military Friendly School by G.I. Jobs.

Lawrence Tech's honors program is available for highly motivated and qualified students, as well as Quest, which encourages students to go above and beyond their studies and explore their interests on a deeper level. A scholars program is also available, designed to ease the transition from high school to college by providing support services. LTU's unique Leadership Program, integrated into all bachelor's degrees, helps students gain critical thinking, teamwork, and communication skills.

LTU's student-faculty ratio is 11:1. Most undergraduate classes have 19 or fewer students, and less than 1 percent of the classes enroll more than 50. More than 600 students live in University Housing. Women make up 24 percent of the student body, and 28 states and 43 nations are represented on campus.

LOCATION AND ENVIRONMENT

The University is situated in Southfield, a dynamic suburb in Oakland County, Michigan. Hundreds of Fortune 500 and international companies are located nearby, and the region has one of the largest concentrations of engineering, architecture, and technological jobs in the world. Southeastern Michigan also offers a rich variety of recreational and cultural activities, with public transportation making most areas accessible to students. Hundreds of major research, manufacturing, scientific, and business enterprises are located nearby, aiding students who work full- or part-time while attending classes, as well as those in co-ops and internships, and participating in professional societies. The campus is close to major freeways and about a 30-minute drive north of downtown Detroit and Detroit Metro Airport.

OFF-CAMPUS OPPORTUNITIES

Students can participate in applied research partnerships that offer remarkable hands-on experience. Professional organizations provide additional opportunities to network with industry leaders.

Lawrence Tech's Detroit design programs are housed under one roof at the new Detroit Center for Design + Technology, allowing students to explore community-based architectural, urban design, and community development projects. Architecture students regularly build homes for Habitat for Humanity.

The Global Engineering Program arranges for engineering students to work and study abroad. The Study-Abroad Program is open to all students.

The University also maintains relationships with universities in China, India, Canada, Brazil, Mexico, Europe, and the Middle East.

MAJORS AND DEGREES OFFERED

LTU is a 4,500-student university offering over 100 undergraduate, master's, and doctoral programs in Colleges of Architecture and Design, Arts and Sciences, Engineering, and Management. Most programs are available days or evenings; many are offered on weekends and online. Dual majors and customized degree programs combining either associate and bachelor's programs or bachelor's and master's programs also are available. Pre-professional preparation includes pre-dental, pre-law, and pre-medical programs, as well as a post-baccalaureate certificate in premedical studies.

LTU's College of Architecture and Design offers bachelor's degrees in architecture, game art, graphic design, industrial design, interaction design, interior architecture, and transportation design. Lawrence Tech enrolls more architectural students than any other school in Michigan, and is one of the top 10 largest architecture schools in the nation.

Lawrence Tech's College of Arts and Sciences offers bachelor's degrees in chemical biology, chemistry, computer science (business software development, game software development, network software development, scientific software development, and software engineering), English and communication arts, environmental chemistry, humanities, mathematical sciences, mathematics and computer science, media communication, molecular and cell biology, physics, physics and computer science, and psychology (clinical psychology, general and applied, industrial/organizational psychology, and pre-med/biobehavioral psychology).

Bachelor's degrees offered by LTU's College of Engineering are architectural engineering (combined bachelor's and master's program), audio engineering technology, biomedical engineering, civil engineering, computer engineering, construction engineering technology and management, electrical engineering (electrical energy systems and electronics engineering), embedded software engineering, industrial operations engineering, mechanical engineering (alternative energy, automotive, manufacturing, nanoscience and nanotechnology, solid mechanics, and thermal fluids), and robotics engineering.

The College of Management offers undergraduate degrees in business administration (accounting, finance, general business, information technology, and marketing) and a minor in business.

Minors include aeronautical engineering, biology, business, chemistry, computer science, economics, energy engineering, English, general sciences, history, mathematics, media communication, military sciences and leadership (ROTC), nanoscience and nanotechnology, philosophy, physics, psychology, Spanish, and technical and professional communication.

Associate degrees are offered in chemical technology, construction engineering technology, general studies, manufacturing engineering technology, and radio and television broadcasting.

Undergraduate certificates can be earned in building information modeling and computer visualization, computer science, electrical power systems, embedded systems, entrepreneurial skills, industrial/organizational psychology, technical and professional communication, and television and video production.

THEORY AND PRACTICE

LTU provides students the tools they need to compete and succeed within their chosen profession. Whether inside or outside of the classroom, the University's theory and practice approach to learning gives opportunities to combine practical knowledge with real-world applications.

Lawrence Tech is the recipient of numerous grants and awards for the development and implementation of innovative materials and practices that are expected to double the lifespan of concrete bridges, highways, and new armor protection for soldiers.

Student engineering teams design, build, and race hybrid, Supermileage, Baja, and Formula-style vehicles. Students also compete in bridge building and assembling, designing zero energy homes, and in airplane design, robotics, and concrete canoe competitions.

CAMPUS FACILITIES AND EQUIPMENT

Lawrence Tech's modern 102-acre campus includes a variety of academic, recreational, and housing facilities. Students use advanced, leading-edge facilities, including the acclaimed Center for Innovative Materials Research; the region's only environmental scanning microscope; architectural and design studios; a structural testing lab; a wind tunnel; wood, metal, and model shops; a 4 x 4 chassis dynamometer; and labs for alternative energy, robotics, biomedical research, graphics, and much more. LTU's $55 million Taubman Engineering, Life Sciences, and Architecture Complex will open in 2016.

High-end personal laptops, tablets, or devices, customized with all the professional software students need, are provided through the LTuZone program. This unique benefit, valued up to $15,000, is the only one of its kind in the nation. Lawrence Tech is Michigan's first wireless laptop computer campus and is ranked among the nation's top 50 "unwired" universities.

The University's third residence hall opens in 2015. The modern buildings feature one- and two-bedroom apartment-style suites that accommodate two to four students. Single rooms also are available. All utilities, wireless Internet access, basic cable TV, and individual telephone lines and voicemail are included.

LTU's library offers a wide selection of print and electronic materials, including numerous online databases, visual resources, digital images, and full-text periodical titles accessible on and off campus. Librarians provide research guidance and instruction. As a key part of the research community in Michigan, the library participates in the reciprocal borrowing and sharing of resources with many other institutions.

The A. Alfred Taubman Student Services Center consolidates all student support services—from admissions through career services—into a convenient one-stop center. This innovative 42,000-square-foot building, which utilizes many energy-efficient and environmentally friendly features and technologies, serves as a "living laboratory" and is part of a regional storm water management effort. LTU's Center for Innovative Materials Research (CIMR) is a state-of-the-art laboratory for the research, development, and testing of materials for defense and infrastructure applications. Students participate in related research projects as part of their academic programs.

The Automotive Engineering Institute provides students opportunities to conduct sponsored research on a unique 4 x 4 vehicle chassis dynamometer, which measures many areas of vehicle performance.

TUITION, ROOM, BOARD, AND FEES

Tuition for all undergrads includes a laptop, tablet or device with all required software. The 2014–15 tuition for students majoring in arts and sciences was $800 per credit hour for basic studies courses and $930 for other arts and sciences and management courses. Sophomores in arts and sciences and management paid $985 per credit hour, while the tuition for juniors and seniors in the two majors was $1025 per credit hour. In architecture and design and engineering, tuition for freshmen, sophomores, juniors, and seniors was $1025 per credit hour.

A normal course load is 12–17 credit hours per semester. The undergraduate registration fee is $135 each semester. International students on temporary visas must have sufficient funds to pay for an entire year of tuition, room and board, and books at the time of first registration. Additional fees for specific labs and studio courses vary.

Room costs vary, but average $6,600 per year. Average board is $2,400, with a variety of meal plans available.

FINANCIAL AID

Approximately 71 percent of students receive financial assistance and the University awards more than $40 million in scholarships, grants, loans, and work-study funds each academic year. The average annual, need-based financial aid package is $22,095. Many privately funded scholarships are awarded to qualified students, based on need and/or scholastic performance. Part-time employment is available at the University on a first-come, first-served basis for full-time students. Student loans are also available from a variety of sources—state, federal, and private. Prospective students are urged to contact the Office of Financial Aid for information on deadlines and requirements for eligibility (ltu.edu/financial_aid).

STUDENT ORGANIZATIONS AND ACTIVITIES

More than 60 student clubs and organizations, including fraternities, sororities, honor societies, and student chapters of professional groups are active on campus and sponsor a variety of activities during the year. The Student Government sponsors and supports a variety of campus activities.

LTU features NAIA, ACHA, MCLA, NWLL and USBC athletics in men's and women's basketball, soccer, cross-country, lacrosse, bowling, golf, and tennis; as well as women's volleyball and men's ACHA hockey; baseball and softball teams are coming in 2016. Students can also show their Blue Devil spirit on LTU's pep band and dance team. Intramural leagues and tournaments are active in 14 sports. Club sports include lacrosse, mixed martial arts, and biking. LTU's Don Ridler Field House is open to all students and features a fitness track, gymnasium, racquetball courts, game room, saunas, and weight and conditioning room.

ADMISSIONS PROCESS

Admissions decisions are based on a student's recalculated GPA, ACT/SAT scores, essay, and letters of recommendation. Strong emphasis is placed on grade trends as well as the strength of the curriculum and rigor of a student's senior schedule. A portfolio is required for transportation design, industrial design, and game art majors.

Lawrence Tech's ACT code is 2020 and SAT is 1399. Required high school courses vary with the curriculum, and LTU offers a number of basic studies courses designed to augment incoming students' backgrounds if deficiencies exist.

Programs start in August and January. An optional summer semester begins in May. Entry in the fall semester is advised but not required. Students must submit transcripts from all schools attended, along with a nonrefundable $30 application fee. Students may also fill out a brief survey and apply free at ltu.edu/applyfree. See our campus video at www.ltu.edu/svv. To learn more, visit www.ltu.edu or contact:

Lawrence Technological University
Office of Admissions
21000 West Ten Mile Road
Southfield, MI 48075-1058
800.225.5588 or 248.204.3160
admissions@ltu.edu
www.ltu.edu

LE MOYNE COLLEGE

Le Moyne College is a four-year, coeducational Jesuit college of approximately 2,500 full-time undergraduate students that uniquely balances a comprehensive liberal arts education with preparation for specific career paths or graduate study.

AT A GLANCE

Founded by the Society of Jesus in 1946, Le Moyne is the second youngest of the twenty-eight Jesuit colleges and universities in the United States. Its emphasis is on the education of the whole person and on the search for meaning and value as integral parts of an intellectual life. Learning, leadership and service are the hallmarks of a Le Moyne College education. Those values are evident in the College's undergraduate majors in more than 30 areas of study, as well as in its pre-professional studies and graduate programs in business administration, education, nursing, occupational therapy, information systems and physician assistant studies.

Le Moyne's personal approach to education is reflected in the quality of contact between students and faculty members. With approximately 150 full-time faculty members, Le Moyne has a student-faculty ratio of 13:1 and an average class size of 22.

LOCATION AND ENVIRONMENT

Le Moyne's 160-plus acre, tree-lined campus is located in a residential setting 10 minutes from downtown Syracuse, the heart of New York state, whose metropolitan population is about 700,000. Just a few miles outside the city are the rolling hills, picturesque lakes, and miles of open country for which central New York is renowned.

OFF CAMPUS OPPORTUNITIES

Syracuse is convenient to most major cities throughout the Northeast, New England, and Canada and offers a wide array of shopping centers and restaurants, many near Le Moyne. Syracuse offers year-round entertainment in the form of rock concerts at the Landmark Theatre, professional baseball and hockey, the Bristol Omni-theatre, the Syracuse Stage, the Everson Museum of Art, and the Armory Square district downtown, which offers one-of-a-kind eateries, pubs, and coffeehouses in addition to a wide variety of social and cultural events. Central New York is home to an extensive network of state and county parks, recreational areas, and other facilities that offer an abundance of recreational opportunities, including swimming, boating, hiking, downhill and cross-country skiing, snowboarding, and golf.

MAJORS AND DEGREES

Le Moyne College awards the Bachelor of Arts degree in biological sciences, communication (advertising, filmmaking, journalism, media studies, music and culture, music industry, music journalism, public relations, television/radio), computer science, criminology (human services, international affairs, law enforcement, research), economics, English (creative writing, literature), French, history, mathematics (actuarial science, pure mathematics, statistics), peace and global studies, philosophy, physics, political science, psychology, religious studies, sociology (anthropology, criminology, human services, research and theory), software application and system development, Spanish, and theatre arts. The Bachelor of Science degree is awarded in biochemistry, biological sciences (health professions, molecular biology, neurobiology), chemistry, economics, environmental science systems, environmental studies, general science, physics, and psychology. The Bachelor of Science in business is awarded in accounting, business analytics, finance, human resource management, information systems, management and leadership, and marketing. A Bachelor of Science in nursing is also offered.

Students may minor in arts administration, Catholic studies, classical humanities, film, gender and women's studies, health information systems, Irish literature, Italian, Latin, legal studies, medieval studies, music, urban and regional studies, or visual arts as well as most of the major fields of study offered. Pre-professional programs are offered in dentistry, law, medicine, optometry, physical therapy, direct entry physician assistant studies, podiatry, and veterinary science. Students may prepare for teaching careers through certification programs in adolescent education, dual adolescent/special education, dual childhood/special education, and TESOL.

Le Moyne College and the L. C. Smith College of Engineering and Computer Science at Syracuse University have a dual-degree program in which students may earn a bachelor's degree from Le Moyne and a master's degree in engineering from Syracuse University in as few as five years. Concentrations include aerospace, chemical, electrical, and mechanical engineering, as well as computer science and other fields of engineering.

Formal accelerated 3-4 programs are offered in dentistry, optometry, and podiatry in cooperation with the State University of New York at Buffalo School of Dental Medicine, Pennsylvania College of Optometry at Salus University, and the New York College of Podiatric Medicine. Pre-dental students may also participate in an early assurance program with the State University of New York at Buffalo School of Dental Medicine. Cooperative 3-2 dual-degree programs in engineering are available with Clarkson University, Manhattan College, and University of Detroit Mercy.

SUNY Upstate Medical University in Syracuse offers students pursuing careers in the health-related professions an accelerated 3-3 doctoral-level transfer program in physical therapy as well as two-year cooperative transfer programs in medical technology and respiratory care. Pre-medical students at Le Moyne are also offered the opportunity to participate in a medical school early assurance program. An early assurance program for premedical students is also available through the State University of New York at Buffalo School of Medicine. Formal agreements also exist with Fordham's School of Law and Syracuse University School of Law.

ACADEMIC PROGRAMS

While each major department has its own sequence requirements for the minimum 120 credit hours needed for the Le Moyne degree, the College is convinced that there is a fundamental intellectual discipline that should characterize the graduate of a superior liberal arts college. Le Moyne's interdisciplinary core curriculum provides the foundation by including studies of English language and literature, mathematics, philosophy, history, theology and religion, natural science, and social science to reflect international trends within a liberal arts education.

For exceptional students, Le Moyne offers an integral honors program that includes an interdisciplinary humanities sequence as well as departmental honors courses.

The study-abroad program allows qualified students to spend a semester or year in numerous countries around the world. Le Moyne College has study-abroad programs or affiliations in Czech Republic, Dominican Republic, England, Germany, Ireland, Scotland, and Spain. Students can also use partner programs to study in locations such as Australia, Costa Rica, Egypt, France, Italy, Japan, and South Africa. Le Moyne is a participant in the sixty-member New York State Visiting Student Program.

As part of the mission of preparing future leaders, Le Moyne College places a strong emphasis on career preparation through internships and other forms of experiential education. Academic departments and the Office of Career Advising and Development both provide programs and services for students interested in interning part time and full time, both locally and in major cities such as New York and Washington, D.C. The Offices of Service Learning and the Academic Deans are also involved in experiential education to promote learning outside the classroom. In the sciences, students take part in campus research with faculty mentors. Others receive assistance in pursuing outstanding opportunities off campus in leading research laboratories and health-care settings. Through the College's long-standing relationship with The Washington Center for Internships and Academic Seminars, students from all majors complete full-time semester-long internships in Washington, D.C., with government, business, or major nonprofit organizations. Faculty members in the Department of Political Science assist students interested in opportunities in Albany, N.Y., the state's seat of government, with either the State Senate or Assembly. Finally, the education programs at Le Moyne put students into school classrooms starting immediately as freshmen and continuing each year until graduation.

Le Moyne students may enroll in Army and Air Force ROTC programs in conjunction with Syracuse University.

CAMPUS FACILITIES AND EQUIPMENT

Le Moyne students benefit from an ongoing commitment to technological excellence. The College's 42 buildings are equipped with accounting, biological sciences, chemistry, computer science, physics, psychology, and statistics laboratories. The W. Carroll Coyne Center for the Performing Arts houses generous production, performance, and classroom space; the latest light and sound technology; scene and costume shops; an aerobics and dance studio; and rehearsal rooms for instrumental and choral music. Academic facilities also include an extensively renovated color television studio; a radio/recording studio; a receiver-antenna satellite dish; transmission and scanning electron microscopes; a nuclear magnetic resonance spectrometer; a gas chromatograph/mass spectrophotometer; a 240,000-volume, open-stack library; and extensive on-site computer facilities. A wireless network allows students easy access to the campus network and Internet. All classrooms are smart classrooms, with multimedia capabilities that expand and enrich the learning process. Le Moyne students have access to other libraries through the Central New York Library Resources Council, and the campus Academic Support Center is available to students for instructional support. In addition, Le Moyne recently opened a 48,000 square foot addition to its existing science complex and this past fall, welcomed students to the new Madden School of Business featuring a state-of-the-art live trading floor and analytics lab. Athletic facilities include a new soccer and lacrosse turf field, a new softball field; baseball field, tennis, basketball, and racquetball courts; a weight-training and fitness center; practice fields; and two gymnasiums. A recreation center houses an Olympic-size indoor swimming pool, jogging track, indoor tennis and volleyball courts, and additional basketball, racquetball, and fitness areas. The College also has a plaza, which houses its bookstore, a café, and a pizzeria. The new Dolphin Den, which features a food court and a convenience store, is a popular space for students to meet, have a bite to eat, or just spend a quiet moment relaxing by the fireplace.

TUITION, ROOM, BOARD AND FEES

For 2014–15, Le Moyne's tuition is $30,350. Room and board charges are $12,130. Additional fees amount to approximately $990, and books and supplies cost approximately $700.

FINANCIAL AID

Financial aid is offered to a large percentage of Le Moyne's students through scholarships, grants, loans, and work-study assignments. Le Moyne offers a generous program of merit-based academic and athletic scholarships as well as financial aid based on a student's need and academic promise. Federal funds are available through the Federal Pell Grant, Federal Work-Study, Federal Supplemental Educational Opportunity Grant, and Federal Perkins Loan programs. A student's eligibility for need-based financial aid is determined from both the Free Application for Federal Student Aid (FAFSA) and the Le Moyne Financial Aid Application Form. It is recommended that these forms be mailed by February 1.

STUDENT ORGANIZATIONS AND ACTIVITIES

A wide range of student-directed activities, athletics, clubs, and service organizations complement the academic experience. Intramural sports are very popular with Le Moyne students; nearly 85 percent of the students participate. Le Moyne also has twenty-one NCAA intercollegiate teams (ten for men and eleven for women). Between 80 and 85 percent of students live in residence halls, apartments, and town houses on campus. The Residence Hall Councils and the Le Moyne Student Programming Board organize a variety of campus activities, including concerts, dances, a weekly film series, student talent programs, and special lectures as well as off-campus trips and skiing excursions.

The College encourages student leadership in all activities with positions open to students in all class years. Students are represented by a Student Government Association and have formal representation through the senate on most College-wide committees involved in decision making and policy formation.

ADMISSIONS PROCESS

Le Moyne seeks qualified students who are well prepared for serious academic study. Secondary school preparation must have included at least 17 college-preparatory high school units, 4 of which must be in English, 4 in social studies, 3–4 in mathematics, 3–4 in foreign language, and 3–4 in science. It is also recommended that prospective science and mathematics majors complete 4 units of mathematics and science. The SAT or ACT is required and should be taken no later than December or January of the senior year in high school. Campus visits are strongly recommended, as the admission process is a personal one. As bases for selection, academic achievement and secondary school recommendations are of primary importance. SAT or ACT scores are important as they relate to the record of achievement and to recommendations. Out-of-state students are encouraged to apply.

Le Moyne offers students the opportunity to apply in two ways: early action or regular admission. The early action program is nonbinding and provides high school students the opportunity to receive an admission decision by December 15 of their senior year. The early action application deadline is November 15. Regular admission applications are reviewed and admission decisions are made on a rolling basis beginning January 1. The priority deadline for applications is February 1; all students who wish to be considered for academic merit scholarships should have a completed application on file in the Office of Admission before this date. Transfer students are encouraged to apply before June 1 for the fall semester and December 1 for the spring semester. Orientation programs for incoming freshmen take place in June and early July. Transfer student orientation programs are offered throughout the summer.

LEWIS & CLARK COLLEGE

AT A GLANCE

On a stunning campus in one of the most exciting and progressive cities anywhere, the next generation of global thinkers gathers to discard conventional thinking, civic complacency, and outmoded preconceptions. Leaders, visionaries, and problem-solvers, we come together to explore new ways of knowing through classic liberal learning and innovative collaboration.

At Lewis & Clark College in Portland, Oregon, we welcome all who are alive to inquiry, open to diversity, and eager to shape the new global century. Through our undergraduate programs in the arts, humanities, and sciences, and through our graduate and professional studies in education, counseling, and law, we undertake original research, interdisciplinary studies, and community service. We push beyond what is known in order to discover something new every day.

Reflecting the College's national and global reach, approximately 79 percent of Lewis & Clark's 2,179 undergraduate students come from outside Oregon, representing forty-seven states plus the District of Columbia and 76 countries.

LOCATION AND ENVIRONMENT

Founded in 1867, Lewis & Clark College moved to its present location in Portland's southwest hills in 1942. The 137-acre campus sits on a wooded hilltop just six miles from Portland's dynamic downtown, offering stunning views of snow-covered Mount Hood.

Portland is a very livable city with an excellent public transportation system that includes buses, light-rail, and the Portland Streetcar. In addition, a free Lewis & Clark shuttle runs frequently into the heart of the city and back to campus. The scenic Willamette River bisects Metropolitan Portland, which is home to approximately 2 million people. There are endless things to do in Portland: 10,477 acres of parks; diverse galleries, museums, music groups, and theater and dance companies; and a nationally recognized food scene. The city also offers professional hockey, soccer, and the NBA's Portland Trailblazers. Our students take advantage of the many internship and service opportunities available in the Portland metro area.

Just 50 miles east of campus rises Mount Hood with its 10-month-a-year skiing and snow-boarding. The rugged Oregon coastline is just 90 miles to the west. Throughout the state lie innumerable hiking, climbing, and backpacking opportunities.

OFF-CAMPUS OPPORTUNITIES

Overseas and off-campus study programs have been a big part of Lewis & Clark for more than 50 years. Each year, about 300 students participate in approximately 30 programs abroad and in selected areas of the United States. During the next few years, programs will be offered in the Arizona borderlands, Australia, Chile, China, Cuba, Dominican Republic, East Africa, Ecuador, England, France, Germany, Ghana, Greece, India, Ireland, Italy, Japan, Morocco, New York, New Zealand, Russia, Scotland, Senegal, Spain, Swaziland, Vietnam and Washington, D.C.

Whether their off-campus study is domestic or abroad, students earn credit (equivalent to a full semester or year) for their academic work. Depending on the specific program content, it is possible to earn General Education and/or major credit during these programs. Typically, over 50% of students participate in one of these programs prior to graduating from Lewis & Clark. Students can use Lewis & Clark's financial aid and scholarships for assistance in these programs.

MAJORS AND DEGREES OFFERED

Lewis & Clark offers one degree: the Bachelor of Arts. Students have a wide selection of majors from which to choose: art (studio), art history, biochemistry and molecular biology, biology, chemistry, classics, computer science, computer science and mathematics, East Asian studies, economics (international, public policy, and theory), English, environmental studies, foreign languages, French, German, Hispanic studies, history, international affairs, mathematics, music, philosophy, physics, political science, psychology, religious studies, rhetoric and media studies, sociology/anthropology, and theater. Students may also design their own major, pursue a double major, or select from 26 minors. Pre-professional preparation is available in the fields of law, business, education, entrepreneurship, and medicine. Dual degree (3-2 or 4-2) programs in engineering are offered in cooperation with Columbia University, Washington University in St. Louis, and the University of Southern California. A dual degree, 4-2 B.A/M.B.A. program is available in conjunction with the Simon Graduate School of Business at the University of Rochester. A dual degree, 4-1 B.A/M.A.T program is offered through Lewis & Clark's Graduate School of Education and Counseling. In addition, there is a guaranteed admission agreement with Lewis & Clark's Law School for students meeting certain criteria.

ACADEMIC PROGRAMS

A liberal arts education at Lewis & Clark connects classical learning with fresh inquiry and exciting research that pushes the frontiers of knowledge. Lewis & Clark considers the following elements essential to a liberal arts education:

1. Mastery of the fundamental techniques of intellectual inquiry: effective writing and speaking, active reading, and critical and imaginative thinking.

2. Exposure to the major assumptions, knowledge, and approaches in the fine arts, humanities, natural sciences and social sciences.

3. Critical understanding of important contemporary and historical issues.

4. Awareness of international and cross-cultural issues and gender relations.

5. Application of theory and knowledge to the search for informed, thoughtful and responsible solutions to important human problems.

The curriculum combines structure and freedom. Depth and breadth of subject matter are highly valued, but equally important are creativity and critical thinking. There are many opportunities for students to take their learning to a higher level, such as honors projects within academic departments, independent research, and internships. And our fast-growing Center for Entrepreneurship offers academic and cocurricular opportunities to translate knowledge and experiences into skills for success beyond college.

Two 15-week semesters make up the academic year, and each semester students normally take four 4-semester-hour courses, and one or more activity courses. The average student course load is 16 credits per semester. The requirement for graduation is 128 semester hours - approximately eight classes each year.

CAMPUS FACILITIES AND EQUIPMENT

Located on Palatine Hill on a former estate, Lewis & Clark offers students a campus of unmatched physical beauty, along with academic and residential buildings designed to support a rigorous academic environment and strong sense of community.

The academic buildings include: the Aubrey R. Watzek library, which is open 24 hours on weekdays during the school year and houses over 740,000 items including books, documents, audiovisual materials, microforms, and periodicals. Through the Summit catalog, access to approximately 28 million items from 37 member institutions in the Pacific Northwest. Watzek library also houses the most extensive collection of printed materials known to exist on the Lewis and Clark Expedition. Evans Music Center, which includes a 410-seat recital hall equipped with an orchestra pit and stage elevator, 22 practice rooms, 43 pianos, two harpsichords, four pipe organs including an 85-rank Casavant pipe organ, a Baroque organ, Javanese gamelan, and an electronic music studio with CD production capability; Fir Acres Theatre, which houses a 225-seat Main Stage performance/teaching theatre and a black-box experimental theatre (also used as dance studio) along with a scene shop, costume room, green room and design lab; the Olin Center (physics and chemistry), the Biology-Psychology building, and BoDine (mathematical sciences), which all house well-equipped classrooms and extensive laboratory spaces for our natural sciences. Among our notable science facilities are a scanning electron microscope, a molecular modeling lab, a gas chromatograph/mass spectrometer, a high-pressure liquid chromatograph, 300 MHz FTNRM spectrometer, inert spectrophotometers, infrared spectrometers, observatory with Newtonian and solar telescopes, computer-enhanced optical microscope, a solid-state physics lab with variable temperature cryostat and superconducting magnet, a lab for studying the biomechanics of animal locomotion, an astrophysics lab and a lab for studying parallel computing. Nearby Tryon Creek State Park and the Columbia River Gorge are frequently used as laboratories for field courses in biology and geology.

Among other academic buildings are the Fields Center, which includes studio facilities for drawing, painting, sculpture, ceramics, computer graphics, graphic design, and photography; the Miller Center and Howard Hall are home to the humanities and social sciences with state-of-the-art classrooms, small auditoriums, and the Keck Interactive Language Lab.

Computer facilities include several public computer labs around campus available for student use. These labs house more than 130 Macintosh and Microsoft Windows computers, along with peripherals such as scanners, color and black & white laser printer, and digital video editing equipment. Other equipment including digital still and video cameras, digital audio recorders and more are available for checkout. All residence halls have wireless capability. The institution has an 800 Mbps (Megabits per second) connection to the internet.

TUITION, ROOM, BOARD AND FEES

2015-16 tuition and fees are $45,104, and room and board are $11,218.

FINANCIAL AID

During the 2013-14 academic year approximately 86 percent of Lewis & Clark students received some form of financial assistance. Individual aid packages ranged from $1000 to $57,000. Institutional, state, and federal resources including grants, loans and work-study may be part of an aid package. Eligibility for need-based funds is based primarily on an analysis of the income and asset information submitted on the Free Application for Federal Student Aid (FAFSA) and the College Board's CSS/Financial Aid PROFILE. Household size and the number of students in college (excluding parents) are also considered in the analysis. Students must submit the FAFSA and PROFILE by February 15 in order to be considered for funding from all sources.

STUDENT ORGANIZATIONS AND ACTIVITIES

With over 50 student organizations, there's never a lack of things to do at Lewis & Clark. Cultural events include lectures, symposia, art exhibits, plays, musical events, and dance performances. Athletics play an important role on campus, where 19 varsity teams, 14 club teams, and numerous intramural sports keep students physically active. Nature-lovers will enjoy the College Outdoors program, which offers activities such as hiking, backpacking, rafting, skiing, and kayaking in the wilderness of the Pacific Northwest. There are also plenty of opportunities for volunteering in and around the Portland area.

Lewis & Clark is committed to residential education, to creating a community dedicated to the exploration of ideas, values, beliefs and backgrounds, to the discovery of lifelong friendships; and to collaboration, both formal and informal, with peers, faculty, and staff. There is no Greek system at Lewis & Clark.

About 65 percent of undergraduates live on campus in residence halls; most of our residential space is co-ed. Along with personal living space (usually shared by two to four students) are several community venues within the residence halls, including coffee houses, convenience stores, art centers, outdoor basketball courts, recreation and fitness centers, lounges, and game rooms. A variety of themed communities within the residence halls are also available (visual and performing arts, multicultural engagement, outdoor pursuits, environmental action, holistic wellness, global village).

ADMISSIONS PROCESS

Commitment to academic excellence and personal and intellectual growth is imperative for successful Lewis & Clark applicants. Lewis & Clark is very selective, and every part of the application matters: academic records, essays, involvement in activities at school and in the community, leadership, and the strength of recommendations. Students are encouraged to visit our campus. Interviews are available but not required. The best-prepared applicants will have had four years of English, four years of mathematics, three to four years of history or social sciences, three years of laboratory sciences, two to three years of a foreign language, and one year of fine arts. Required credentials include: an essay; an official transcript including senior grades from first semester; a counselor recommendation; and one academic teacher recommendation. Lewis & Clark requires the SAT or ACT, except if the student is applying via the Test-Optional Portfolio Path (see www.lclark.edu for details). Students apply using the on-line Common Application. There is no application fee. Keep in mind these deadlines: First-year applicants – November 1 for binding Early Decision (notification, December 15), November 1 for non-binding Early Action (notification, January 1) and January 15 for Regular Decision (notification, April 1). Transfer applicants are reviewed on a rolling basis.

LIM COLLEGE

AT A GLANCE

Situated in the center of the fashion capital of the world, LIM College has been a major force in fashion and business education for over 75 years. Its graduates can be found throughout all areas of the fashion industry, and its high quality of education has earned LIM College accreditation from the Middle States Association of Colleges and Schools. The college's MBA, BBA, BPS, and associate degrees are also accredited by the Accreditation Council of Business Schools and Programs (ACBSP).

LIM College offers a highly personal environment where students learn about the business of fashion, with an emphasis on academic and professional study. Lifelong friends are made at LIM College, as well as lifelong careers. Although most students come to the college directly from high school or transfer from other colleges, there are also those of nontraditional college age who enroll. Students come to LIM College from many parts of the country and the world. The current undergraduate enrollment is approximately 1,550.

The Department of Experiential Education & Career Management is one of LIM College's chief assets. Each student receives extensive career advising throughout their time at the college, beginning in the first semester. This helps direct students to career opportunities within their field of study. The relationship is one intended to strengthen over the post-graduation years as the department is able to assist with employment for life. This relationship is one intended to strengthen during the college years into post-graduation, as the department offers lifetime services.

The unique nature of LIM College's curriculum provides students with a foundation of core courses in liberal arts and business while offering diverse and intensive hands-on preparation in the fashion industry. This affords graduates the opportunity to accept executive training, merchandising, management, marketing, visual, and communications positions in a wide variety of areas within the fashion and business worlds.

Support services are important at LIM College. In addition to academic and career advising, personal counseling is available. Because of the college's small size and the close relationships between students and staff members, any faculty member or administrator is readily accessible to help and advise all students.

Student life at LIM College is very dynamic. Active clubs include the Fashion Show Production Club, Student Life Activities Board, Student Leadership Council, Dance Team, and many more. There are also student publications including the LIMLIGHT yearbook and *The Lexington Line* magazine.

LIM College proudly opened a new residence hall in 2008. Located at 1760 Third Avenue, this state-of-the-art facility boasts a plethora of modern amenities. All rooms have private bathrooms, complementary wireless Internet access, phone service, and over 100 cable channels. Rooms are also equipped with full refrigerators and 25-inch flat-screen televisions. In addition, the facility contains a private gym, game room, computer lab, and a state-of-the-art kitchen.

LIM College's Open House program offers students and their families the opportunity to tour the school's campus and learn not only about LIM College's unique academic programs, but also the vast array of careers found in the fashion industry. The day also includes special presentations on financial aid, study abroad, student activities, and much more. Current LIM College students assist in hosting the event and are available to answer questions. LIM College also offers many other opportunities to visit including weekly information sessions, Transfer Services Days, mock classes for accepted students, and other periodically scheduled special events.

LOCATION AND ENVIRONMENT

LIM College is situated in three buildings—on East 53rd Street, East 45th Street, and on Fifth Avenue, one of the most fashionable locales in the world. A whole world of fashion is at the college's doorstep and includes such famous stores as Saks Fifth Avenue, Henri Bendel, Armani, and Ralph Lauren. New York City is the headquarters for the garment, cosmetics, advertising, publishing, and textile industries, all of which are essential to the fashion industry and are visited regularly by LIM College students. The college incorporates all of these resources into the curriculum. For example, the Fashion Magazines course may include trips to photography studios, modeling agencies, or tours of magazine offices and advertising firms. New York City offers LIM College students an unparalleled learning experience.

ACADEMICS

LIM College offers a combination of classroom education and supervised internships that have been designed to prepare students for executive training programs and other entry-level executive positions in various areas of the fashion industry.

Experiential learning is an integral part of the LIM College curriculum. The internship program helps students become truly prepared for successful careers within fashion and fashion-related industries. All students are required to take three internships in order to earn their bachelor's degree at LIM College. Each internship has a prerequisite seminar attached to it that includes activities such as field trips, guest speakers, and portfolio-building that help students network with industry professionals and develop into dynamic business leaders.

Courses are sequential, each built upon the knowledge and experience a student gains through the process of learning. The experiential education program at LIM College commences with a course designed to increase a student's knowledge of the industry, hence building a foundation upon which to build a career in fashion. The program culminates with a nearly full-time co-op internship intended to be a real working experience while the student works closely with instructors and advisers.

To graduate, students must complete 127 credits for the Bachelor of Science degree and 124 credits for the Bachelor of Business Administration and the Bachelor of Professional Studies degrees. Associate degree candidates must earn 67 credits. All students must have at least a GPA of 2.00 and satisfactory completion of all coursework and other curriculum requirements.

LIM College accepts qualified students as transfers throughout the four years. The maximum number of credits that LIM will accept is 65. Transfer students must complete the last consecutive 46 credits at LIM College, including the Senior Co-op semester.

The College calendar runs on a traditional semester format, offering both fall and spring start dates. Also offered are summer and Saturday Fashion Lab programs for high school students. The specially selected courses, such as Fashion Buying and Fashion Magazines, blend academics with hands-on experience and are a great way to explore the fashion industry.

LIM College offers four-year programs in Fashion Merchandising, Management, Marketing, and Visual Merchandising, leading to the Bachelor of Business Administration (BBA) degree and International Business leading to the Bachelor of Science (BS) degree. Also offered is a four-year Bachelor of Professional Studies (BPS) program in Fashion Merchandising as well as two-year programs in Fashion Merchandising leading to the Associate in Applied Sciences (AAS) and the Associate in Occupational Studies (AOS) degrees. The Fashion Merchandising program has tracks in either home fashions or Retail Buying & Planning. LIM College also offers four graduate programs: the Master of Professional Studies (MPS) in Fashion Merchandising and Retail Management; the Master of Professional Studies (MPS) in Fashion Marketing, the Master of Professional Studies (MPS) in Global Fashion Supply Chain Management, and the Master of Professional Studies (MPS) in Visual Merchandising. The college also offers a broad variety of concentrations, such as Fashion Publishing and Event Planning, which allow students to pursue a focused area of study that complements their major.

CAMPUS FACILITIES AND EQUIPMENT

Facilities include the 5,000-square-foot Adrian G. Marcuse Library, with over 14,583 books, 1,081 librarian-selected e-books, 203 scholarly journals and print magazines, 799 bound volumes of magazine back issues, 1,135 DVDs, an archive of historic materials, and a large collection of fashion, business, and marketing books to assist students in their research. The library also has forty-two CAD-enabled computers, copiers, and printers, both black and white and color. The 44 subscription databases located on the library-run website are available 24/7, on- or off-campus, and can be accessed by computer, tablet, smart phone, or any other Internet-ready device. The Math Center and Writing Center also offer one-on-one tutoring for all students.

LIM College's facility on Fifth Avenue is equipped with two fashion merchandising studios. There are also two 1,100-square-foot visual merchandising studios, as well as a state-of-the-art Color and Materials Lab.

TUITION, ROOM, BOARD AND FEES

Tuition for the 2014–15 school year is $23,650 with additional mandatory fees of $575. Housing charges for the 2014–15 year are $15,850. Books and supplies expenses average around $900 per academic year and students living on campus may spend up to $4,000 a year on meal expenses. Students who commute spend from $1,200 to $2,000 for transportation, depending on distance. Personal expenses for the academic year are estimated to be $1,500 dollars.

FINANCIAL AID

LIM College believes that lack of funds should not keep students from attaining a degree, thus, admissions decisions and financial aid are totally separate, and a request for aid has no effect on admissions. About 80 percent of LIM College's students received some form of financial aid during the 2013–14 school year. Institutional scholarships, Federal Pell Grants, Federal Supplemental Educational Opportunity Grants, and New York State TAP grants are all available for eligible students. In addition, the college participates in the Federal Stafford Loan program for students and Federal PLUS Loan program for parents. The college also works with several private lenders to offer alternative education loans for students to supplement their federal loans. International students are eligible to apply for alternative loans with a credit-worthy U.S.-based co-signer. The Free Application for Federal Student Aid (FAFSA) should be filed by all applicants by March 1 for priority consideration. Aid is granted on the basis of financial need and scholarships are merit based, although some awards take need into consideration. Details of the financial aid programs are available on the LIM College website or are available directly from the Office of Student Financial Services.

LIM College features a Merit Scholarship Program for incoming freshmen and transfer students. These scholarship monies are awarded for academic achievement in high school or college. Students can remain eligible for their scholarship throughout their stay at the college by maintaining a GPA of 3.0 or above.

STUDENT ORGANIZATIONS AND ACTIVITIES

The Office of Student Life is the center of student activities and clubs at LIM College. This department supports student government, approves student organizations, and establishes operating budgets. One of LIM College's more popular clubs is the Fashion Show Production Club, which plans an annual fashion show attended by more than 1,000 people. Another popular activity is the student-run The Lexington Line magazine. LIM College's Office of Student Life plans many other activities including diversity programming, philanthropic service, and new student orientation.

STUDY ABROAD OPPORTUNITIES

From two-week immersion programs to semester-long study abroad experiences, LIM College offers students the opportunity to see the world and experience fashion on an international stage. With programs in Australia, China, England, France, Spain, and Italy, students are given a global education for a global industry..

ADMISSIONS

LIM College's Admissions Committee recognizes that many intangibles go into the making of a successful student, and it evaluates each applicant individually and holistically. The college uses a rolling admission policy. Applicants are informed of the admission decision within approximately four to six weeks after all admission requirements have been fulfilled. An application may be obtained from the LIM College website or by contacting the Admissions Office.

All undergraduate applicants are required to submit high school transcripts, SAT or ACT scores, two letters of recommendation, an essay, and the completed application with the application fee. Transfer students must also submit all college transcripts. Undergraduate Admissions will waive the standardized test requirement if the student has satisfactorily earned 15 credit hours (21 on a quarter or trimester system) at the time of application. International students should review the LIM College website and contact the Office of Admissions for specific requirements. It is also strongly suggested that all applicants create an activity sheet or resume highlighting their experience, with emphasis on business and fashion activities.

LOYOLA UNIVERSITY

Committed to preparing people to lead extraordinary lives, Loyola University Chicago is one of the largest Jesuit Catholic universities in the U.S., with 15,902 students. Loyola has three campuses in the Chicago area, and one in Rome, Italy.

AT A GLANCE

Consistently ranked a "Top National University" by U.S. News & World Report, Loyola University Chicago continues to advance the 450-year-old Jesuit tradition of rigorous academic study firmly grounded in the liberal arts.

Loyola is the largest Jesuit Catholic university in the United States, enrolling 15,902 students. Incoming freshmen come from 43 states and 33 countries. Loyola offers more than 80 undergraduate majors and more than 140 graduate, professional, and graduate-level certificate programs as well as three professional programs in law, medicine, and nursing.

Loyola helps students prepare for meaningful careers with top academic programs in business, the sciences, and numerous other disciplines, along with opportunities for internships throughout the city of Chicago and beyond. Loyola's well-rounded, transformative education will help students develop as a whole person—intellectually, socially, physically, and spiritually.

LOCATION AND ENVIRONMENT

Loyola gives students the best of campus and city life with diverse living and learning opportunities in the world-class city of Chicago. Located off North Michigan Avenue, Chicago's Magnificent Mile, Loyola's dynamic Water Tower Campus is home to the Quinlan School of Business as well as the Schools of Communication, Continuing and Professional Studies, Education, Law, and Social Work and connects students to myriad internship, job, and service opportunities. Loyola's Lake Shore Campus, home to the college of Arts and Sciences, the Graduate School, and the Marcella Niehoff School of Nursing, is located on the picturesque shore of Lake Michigan and offers students the comforts of a traditional residential campus. The Stritch School of Medicine is housed at the Medical Sciences Campus in west suburban Maywood, Illinois.

Exposure to Loyola's three Chicago campuses gives students three diverse experiences: a vibrant urban environment, the comfort of a more traditional collegiate setting, and the bustle of a professional medical environment. At each campus, students have access to computers, study areas, and dining halls, as well as a network of student groups and activities. A free intercampus shuttle is available between the Lake Shore and Water Tower Campuses, and an intracampus shuttle is available at the Medical Sciences Campus.

Students may also study abroad at Loyola's fourth campus, the John Felice Rome Center in Italy; or they may attend The Beijing Center for Chinese Studies or choose from one of 100 other study abroad programs in 60 countries.

MAJORS AND DEGREES OFFERED

Loyola students may choose from more than 80 majors and 70 minors. Undergraduate degrees offered include the Bachelor of Arts (BA), BA Classics, Bachelor of Science (BS), Bachelor of Business Administration (BBA), Bachelor of Science in Education (BSEd), Bachelor of Science in Nursing (BSN), and the Bachelor of Social Work (BSW) degrees.

Learn more at LUC.edu/majors.

The College of Arts and Sciences offers undergraduate majors in African Studies and the African Diaspora, anthropology, art history, biochemistry, bioinformatics, biology, biophysics, chemistry, classical civilization, communications networks and security, computer science, criminal justice and criminology, dance, economics, engineering science, English, forensic science, French, Greek (ancient), history, human services, information technology, international studies, Italian, Latin, mathematics, mathematics and computer science, music, philosophy, physics, physics and computer science, physics and engineering, political science, psychology, religious studies, sociology, sociology and anthropology, software engineering, Spanish, statistics, studio art, theater, theology, theoretical physics and applied mathematics, visual communication, and women's studies and gender studies (as a second major only).

The Institute of Environmental Sustainability offers majors in Environmental Policy, Environmental Science, and Environmental Studies.

The Quinlan School of Business offers majors in accounting, economics, entrepreneurship, finance, human resource management, information systems, international business, management, marketing, operations management, and sport management.

The School of Communication offers majors in advertising and public relations, communication studies, film and digital media, and journalism.

The School of Education offers majors in bilingual/bicultural education, early childhood/special education, elementary education, middle grade education, secondary education and foreign language, and special education.

The Marcella Niehoff School of Nursing offers the Bachelor of Science in Nursing, a Bachelor of Science in Health Systems Management, a Bachelor of Science in Exercise Science, an RN to BSN, and an Accelerated BSN program, which is available to students who have already completed a baccalaureate degree.

The School of Social Work offers an undergraduate major in social work and a combined bachelor's and master's degree in social work, which can be completed in five years.

ACADEMIC PROGRAMS

The Core Curriculum is the foundation of Loyola's liberal arts education. Core courses are aimed at increasing students' understanding of themselves and the world while they explore diverse subjects and cultivate new interests. Courses provide a strong base of knowledge, skills, and values that will help students achieve academic, professional, and personal success throughout their lives.

Exceptionally well-qualified students may apply to the Interdisciplinary Honors Program.

Other special academic opportunities include pre-professional programs for law and health professions; 27 five-year (bachelor's/master's) degree programs; 19 interdisciplinary programs; a six-year, early admission to Loyola's School of Law; early assurance to Loyola's Stritch School of Medicine; and the Loyola/Midwestern University Dual-Acceptance Pharmacy Program.

CAMPUS FACILITIES

The recently completed, 100,000+ sq. ft. Damen Student Center is a LEED Silver certified building. Named after the founder of Loyola University Chicago, the Arnold J. Damen, S.J. Student Center provides students a dedicated space to build community and encourage co-curricular engagement. Damen is the place to relax, study, play pool, watch TV, grab a snack, or hang out with friends.

Not only is the recently completed Cuneo Hall a state-of-the-art building with a cutting-edge academic center—but it also uses sustainable technologies to reduce its ecological footprint. Cuneo is LEED Gold certified and will use approximately 60% less energy than comparable academic buildings.

The renovated Mundelein Center offers new options for fine arts programming. For plays and theatre are the new Newhart Family Theatre and the Underground Laboratory Theatre. Mundelein Music Hall has been completely renovated as well. These new spaces give students an opportunity to hone their craft in contemporary surroundings.

The School of Communication is in the heart of Chicago's creative and business communities. Located at the Water Tower Campus, the building features generously equipped computer labs, state-of-the-art classrooms and offices, and on-site production facilities, including street-side lab with a TV studio and radio interview sets.

The Information Commons is a four-story lakeside research facility that provides individual and group study space for students, as well as state-of-the-art technology with more than 200 computers, wireless internet connections, and a lakefront café.

Loyola's Michael R. And Marilyn C. Quinlan Life Sciences Education and Research Center provides numerous opportunities for undergraduates to engage in the latest scientific research alongside their professors in modern labs for biology, bioinformatics, chemistry, ecology, and other life sciences.

The Loyola University Museum of Art (LUMA) showcases permanent and rotating exhibitions of professional and student work. The Sullivan Center for Student Services consolidates a dozen student services offices into one convenient location.

For more information about campus facilities, visit http://www.luc.edu/campus_community.shtml.

TUITION, ROOM, BOARD AND FEES

Tuition for 2014–2015 entering students (per year): $37,270

Room and board (per year): Room and board cost is dependent on students' selection of residence hall and meal plan (average is $13,620).

Tuition part-time (per credit hour): $705

FINANCIAL AID

At Loyola, we're committed to making a high-quality education affordable. Our Financial Aid Office works with students and families to address each student's specific situation and needs. Our expert staff evaluates financial aid eligibility for resources such as grants, scholarships, and loans to help make a Loyola education a possibility for students.

Approximately 96% of Loyola freshmen receive some form of financial aid. Students are encouraged to file the Free Application for Federal Student Aid (FAFSA) by February 15 in order to meet Loyola's March 1 priority processing date.

In addition to the many scholarships awarded with admission, students may also explore more than 75 types of additional scholarships. For more information, visit LUC.edu/scholarships.

STUDENT ORGANIZATIONS AND ACTIVITIES

Loyola offers students the chance to develop leadership and social skills by participating in any of its more than 200 academic, athletic, cultural, hobby, media, political, social, and spiritual student-run organizations.

ADMISSION PROCESS

Students seeking admission to Loyola are evaluated on their overall academic record, including ACT or SAT scores. The freshman class entering in Fall 2014 had middle 50% ACT score ranges between 25 and 29, middle 50% range on the SAT Verbal between 520 and 630, middle 50% range on the SAT Math between 530 and 630, and an average GPA of 3.80. Most Loyola students rank in the upper quarter of their graduating class, but consideration is given to students in the upper half.

Transfer students with 20 credit hours or more are evaluated on the basis of their college work only. The minimum acceptable GPA varies from 2.0 to 2.5, depending upon academic interest. Candidates must also be in good standing at the last college attended.

Loyola notifies applicants four to six weeks after the application, supporting credentials, and secondary school counselor or teacher recommendation are received. The application is only available online and there is no application fee at LUC.edu/applyluc.

Prospective students are encouraged to visit campus by arranging individual appointments and campus tours up to two weeks in advance. Arrange a visit at LUC.edu/visit.

To obtain an application, get more information, or arrange a visit, contact:

Undergraduate Admission Office

Loyola University Chicago

820 North Michigan Avenue

Chicago, IL 60611

Telephone: 312.915.6500 or 800.262.2373 (toll-free)

E-mail: admission@luc.edu

Web site: LUC.edu/undergrad

MANHATTAN COLLEGE

AT A GLANCE

Manhattan College is a Lasallian Catholic educational institution founded in 1853 by the De La Salle Christian Brothers, a Catholic teaching order established by Saint John Baptist De La Salle.

Today, these same ideals ring true at Manhattan College, where students embody the core Lasallian principles of an inclusive community, concern for the poor and social justice, respect for all people, all while obtaining a quality education.

There are some 40 major fields of study within five undergraduate schools, guided by an internationally recognized faculty, sought-after leaders and real-world consultants in their fields, 93 percent of whom hold doctoral degrees. Students have opportunities to study abroad in more than 30 countries.

Manhattan College participates in Division I sports as part of the MAAC, there are 18 teams. Every year brings excitement to the courts, fields and track as the Jaspers compete. The college is known for its student-athletes, having many ranking among the MAAC All Academic teams.

LOCATION AND ENVIRONMENT

The College's campus is in Riverdale, a quiet neighborhood in the Bronx, is located 10 miles from the bustling streets of midtown Manhattan. Students enjoy the best of both worlds—a traditional college campus that's just a short subway ride from the endless opportunities available in the country's biggest and brightest city. Manhattan's professors often use NYC as a classroom with field trips to Wall Street, museums and other world-famous locations.

The student body of 3,675 hails from 32 states and 37 countries. With a four-year guarantee of resident housing, 82 percent of freshmen choose to live on campus. Throughout the academic year, there are many activities offered at the college, which creates a family atmosphere for the entire student body.

OFF-CAMPUS OPPORTUNITIES

Manhattan College students actively define their commitment toward community around the city, country and world.

Each year, Campus Ministry and Social Action (CMSA) runs its L.O.V.E. program (Lasallian Outreach Volunteer Experience), which gives students the chance to participate in service experiences allowing them to travel to areas such as New Orleans, Kenya, Ecuador, the Dominican Republic and West Virginia, and volunteer with people of very different socio-economic backgrounds.

Many students also participate in local community service projects. These include Habitat for Humanity, work with the elderly in nearby nursing homes, volunteering in soup kitchens, tutoring at the local schools , the Annual Toy Drive, blood drives, the American Cancer Society's Relay for Life and more. New projects are regularly developed in response to students' interests.

Each year more than 300 students find internships in their field of study. Students participate in internships throughout the metropolitan area, gaining experience in the fields they are studying. With so many college alumni living in the tri-state area, networking opportunities are in every profession.

MAJORS AND DEGREES OFFERED

Manhattan College offers more than 40 major fields of study in the programs of arts, business, education and health, engineering and science, and graduate degrees are also offered in education, engineering and business. The college's professional schools are externally accredited by the following accrediting organizations: school of business, Association to Advance Collegiate Schools of Business (AACSB); school of education, Teacher Education Accrediting Council (TEAC); and individual school of engineering programs are accredited by the Engineering Accreditation Commission (EAC) of ABET, Inc. Within these programs, Manhattan College is able to provide students with the knowledge they need to succeed in the classroom and in the workforce.

The Arts students may major in: Art History, Communication, Economics, English, French, Government, History, International Studies, Labor Studies, Peace Studies, Philosophy, Psychology, Religious Studies, Sociology, Spanish, Urban Affairs and General Studies.

The Business students may choose from: Accounting, Computer Information Systems, Economics, Finance, Global Business Studies, Management and Marketing.

In addition, Manhattan College also offers the following graduate programs: the Bachelor of Science in Professional Accounting / Master of Business Administration Program and the Bachelor of Science in Business / Master of Business Administration Program, which offers students an option to complete a five-year multiple award program.

The Education program offers three options for undergraduate students interested in earning a bachelor's degree in teaching including: Early Childhood Education, Childhood Education, Dual: Childhood/Special Education and Adolescent Education. In addition, the program features two undergraduate majors in the department of Physical Education and Human Performance in Physical Education Teaching (grades K-12) or Exercise Science.

Another option is the Five-Year Childhood/Special Education Program, which combines baccalaureate and graduate work, allowing the student to receive a bachelor's and master's degree with eligibility to pursue certification for grades 1-6 in regular and special education. The school of education also offers master's degrees and professional diplomas in school counseling, mental health counseling, special education and school building leadership.

The Radiological and Health Professions Program is also part of the school of education and health and is available to students pursuing a Bachelor of Science with three major selections: Nuclear Medicine Technology, Radiation Therapy Technology, Radiologic Technology (X-ray) or Allied Health.

The Engineering program offers programs leading to the baccalaureate degree in five disciplines: Chemical Engineering, Civil Engineering, Computer Engineering, Electrical Engineering and Mechanical Engineering. Graduate study at the master's level is also available in: Chemical Engineering, Civil Engineering, Computer Engineering, Electrical Engineering, Environmental Engineering and Mechanical Engineering.

Graduate Certificate programs currently available to engineering students are: Engineering Management, Environmental Management, Engineering Law, Engineering Mathematics, Biochemical Engineering, Manufacturing/Systems, HVAC (Heating, Ventilation and Air Conditioning), Construction Management, Electrical Power Engineering, Computer Engineering and Energy Management.

The Science program offers students the chance to major in the following areas: Biology, Biochemistry, Chemistry, Computer Science, Mathematics and Physics.

ACADEMIC PROGRAMS

Manhattan College is one of the few American colleges to have chapters of all five of these distinguished national honor societies: Beta Gamma Sigma, Kappa Delta Pi, Phi Beta Kappa, Sigma Xi and Tau Beta Pi.

Manhattan College is one of 276 institutions in the United States with a chapter of Phi Beta Kappa, the nation's oldest and most widely known academic honor society, which celebrates and advocates excellence in the liberal arts and sciences.

Other programs at Manhattan College:

1. The National Model United Nations offers a unique opportunity for students to better understand the inner workings of the United Nations and other international organizations while building skills in diplomacy and compromise.

2. The Branigan Fellowships program promotes undergraduate research in the humanities by awarding several grants per year in excess of $3,000 each for student-initiated projects.

3. The Fellowships Committee works with students and alumni to encourage graduate study and help work through sometimes challenging application processes.

4. The Pre-Law Advisory Committee works with students interested in pursuing law.

5. There are several study abroad options open to students. Students can choose to study abroad for a semester, an academic year, a month-long summer program or a seven-week summer program.

6. Manhattan's Mentorship program provides opportunities for students to gain insight into their intended careers by being paired with professionals, generally Manhattan alumni in those careers.

. The College's Internship program allows students to complete at the minimum
f one internship within their four years of study.

. Manhattan's Finance and Economics club organizes student preparation and
articipation in the Volunteer Income Tax Assistance Program (VITA) and other
ervice activities.

CAMPUS FACILITIES AND EQUIPMENT

O'Malley Library is home to a number of new features and services, including more
han 100 computer workstations, a round-the-clock Internet Café, a media center
quipped with teleconferencing capabilities, and many group study rooms scattered
hroughout the five-story layout.

Both commuters and residents can take advantage of the Fitness Center and newly
enovated cafeterias. There are a variety of dining options, as well as spaces to relax
nd enjoy a snack while watching large screen televisions. The Commuter Lounge
erves as a crossroads for students between classes while on campus.

The Raymond W. Kelly ('63) Student Commons is scheduled to open in fall 2014.
he 70,000-square-foot building will significantly enhance the college's ability to
ntegrate academics and student life, and will provide space for fitness and well-
ess programming, cultural and community events, dining, student activities, and
tudent collaboration.

TUITION, ROOM, BOARD, AND FEES

Undergraduate Tuition and Fees 2014–2015

A. Full Time Students, 2014–15

Full time students register for 12 or more credits per semester.

Tuition Charges per Semester

New Students entering 2014–15	$17,150
Continuing students	$17,150

Program Fees per Semester

Arts, Education	$645
Business	$765
Science	$825
Engineering	$1,290

Over credit Charges° per credit hour

B. Part Time Students, 2012–2013

Part time students in day, evening or special (January and Summer) sessions register
or less than 12 credits per semester.

C. Room and Board Fee, per Semester, 2014–15

Room and Board Standard Room Occupancy with the following plans:

Room/Board- °standard meal plan, $13,740

Mandatory plan for all incoming freshman.

D. One-Time Fees

Application	$60

Student Acceptance Deposit (Credited toward Matriculation)

Commuter	$500
Resident	$900

Resident deposit includes:

Damage Deposit (Refundable upon $300
ompletion of contract and absence of damage to dormitory facilities)

Orientation (new students)	$285

Graduation (Charged upon achieving Senior status—90 credits)

Matriculation	$310

E. Other Fees

Non-matriculation— per semester	$165
English as a Second Language	$725
Returned Check	$75
Student Activity—per semester	$480
Health Services Fee- per year	$140

FINANCIAL AID

Manhattan College provides the maximum financial aid available to qualified students to make their attendance at Manhattan financially possible.

New Students: Students admitted to the college and demonstrating financial need
will receive a financial aid assistance offer in the form of a financial aid award letter
from the Office of Admissions and Financial Aid, which is based on an assessment
of your financial need.

Continuing Eligibility: All financial aid is renewable on a yearly basis provided the
student remains eligible.

Manhattan College Programs:

Presidential Scholarships: Non-need based scholarships awarded to extraordinary
applicants. Eligibility is based on exceptional SAT or ACT scores, secondary school
grade point average, and rank in class.

Dean's Award: Dean's Awards are offered to academically gifted students who fall
slightly below Presidential Scholarship requirements.

Manhattan College Grant-in-Aid: Manhattan College awards grants-in-aid to accepted students who demonstrate financial need.

Manhattan College Campus Employment Program: Manhattan offers its own
campus work program to students who need employment to meet college expenses
but are not eligible for Federal Work Study

Athletic Grants: The Manhattan College Athletics department may fund athletic
grants to students who, by the possession of certain athletic skills, can add to the
community spirit and morale of the campus.

Resident Assistant Grants: These grants are awarded to students selected to serve
as Resident Assistants in the dormitories.

Dollars for Scholars: As a collegiate partner, Manhattan College matches Scholarship
of America awards up to $500 a year.

Other programs: Veterans Administration Educational Benefits, Post-9/11 GI Bill
Participant, Tuition Remission, Tuition Exchange Scholarship

The school also awards endowed and special category scholarships as part of the
existing financial aid package.

ADMISSIONS PROCESS

1) Course Selection and Performance: Most emphasis is placed upon student course
selection on the secondary level and grades earned in those subjects.

2) SAT and/or ACT Scores

3) Recommendations

4) Personal Statement

5) General Equivalency Diploma (G.E.D.)

Students who are transferring without an associate degree or with an A.A.S. degree
must submit:

1) A high school transcript

2) Official college transcripts

3) A list of courses presently being taken

4) College catalogs from all institutions previously attended

5) Financial aid transcripts from all collegiate institutions previously attended (even
if you only took one or two courses while in high school)

MARLBORO COLLEGE

AT A GLANCE

Marlboro College is an intentionally small, intellectually demanding liberal arts school located in southern Vermont. Home to 300 students, Marlboro empowers students with the freedom and responsibility to create an individualized course of study in collaboration with faculty members and to participate in a self-governing community. Instead of traditional majors, students pursue a self-designed Plan of Concentration based on their academic interests, culminating in a major work of scholarship. Students graduate having completed a profound intellectual journey, and go out into the world with greater self-reliance and the skills needed to forge their own career path or pursue graduate-level study.

LOCATION AND ENVIRONMENT

Marlboro College's setting in rural southern Vermont provides students with space for quiet contemplation as well as myriad opportunities for outdoor recreation. With 17 miles of trails on or near our 450-acre campus, and the Green Mountain National Forest nearby, students have easy access to hiking, mountain biking, skiing, caving, climbing, and kayaking (among other activities). Each season includes Marlboro traditions such as Apple Days in the fall and the broomball tournament in winter.

Tucked on its own Potash Hill, the college is an integral part of the town of Marlboro, a community of less than 1,000 where many staff, faculty, and students are active citizens. Some of the many benefits shared by both the college and the town include a volunteer fire company, a community newsletter called the Marlboro Mixer, cross-country ski trails, the Marlboro Historical Society, the Southern Vermont Natural History Museum, the Marlboro Community Fair, and the January Book Swap. Marlboro is also the site of the world famous Marlboro Music Festival, which occupies the campus during the summer.

OFF-CAMPUS OPPORTUNITIES

With the vibrant town of Brattleboro just 10 miles away, Marlboro students have easy access to many resources and activities. Brattleboro is an eclectic community located in the Connecticut River Valley and a regional center for art, commerce, and technology. It was listed as one of the "20 Best Small Towns in America" by Smithsonian magazine, one of the "10 Best Small Towns in America" by Fodor's, and in the top 10 in the book The 100 Best Art Towns in America, with many galleries, music venues, bookstores, and performance spaces to experience. Among the blocks of historic red-brick buildings you can find cozy cafes and four-star restaurants featuring local fare and international cuisines, including Thai, Korean, Greek, and Italian. Mother Earth News named Brattleboro one of "Eight Great Places You've Never Heard Of", and it's college-town feel was recently highlighted on Vermont Public Radio. Vans run from the college into Brattleboro multiple times a day and trips to Northeastern cities such as Northampton, Boston, New York and Montreal occur several weekends each semester.

MAJORS AND DEGREES OFFERED

Marlboro College empowers undergraduate students to create an individualized course of study in collaboration with faculty members. Based on their personal academic interests and goals, students study broadly across disciplines before embarking on a self-designed Plan of Concentration that culminates in a major work of scholarship. This approach allows students to take ownership of and responsibility for the scope and structure of their intellectual exploration. Degrees offered include Bachelor of Arts, Bachelor of Science and, through the World Studies Program, Bachelor of Arts or Science in International Studies. Our degree fields are:

American Studies
Anthropology
Art History
Asian Studies
Astronomy
Biochemistry
Biology
Ceramics
Chemistry
Classics
Computer Science
Cultural History
Dance
Economics
Environmental Studies
Film/Video Studies
Gender Studies
History
Languages
Liberal Studies
Literature
Mathematics
Music
Painting, Drawing, and Mixed Media
Philosophy
Photography
Physics
Politics
Psychology
Religion
Sculpture
Sociology
Theater
Visual Arts
World Studies
Writing

ACADEMIC PROGRAMS

Rather than follow a prescribed academic program, Marlboro students work closely with faculty advisors to map out an individualized course of study based on their intellectual interests. This approach allows students to study broadly and creatively across disciplines before embarking on their self-designed Plan of Concentration, an in-depth examination of a focused academic area that culminates in a major work of scholarship. By taking ownership of and responsibility for the scope and topography of their intellectual exploration, Marlboro students learn how to define a set of goals, develop a comprehensive plan to meet them, and work through the obstacles that inevitably arise along the way. They employ initiative and grit throughout the process and emerge at the end with a joyful sense of accomplishment, heightened confidence, and invaluable experience.

Marlboro's faculty members bring an extraordinary degree of commitment, passion, and academic mentoring to their teaching endeavors. Beyond the traditional classroom setting, faculty members interact with students through one-on-one tutorials, Plan advising sessions, service-learning trips, and collaborative projects ranging from scholarly papers to films. Whether participating in Town Meeting or composing original music for a promotional video, faculty members make significant contributions to the vitality and spirit of Marlboro's learning community on a regular basis.

Whether their academic interests lean toward Russian literature or contemporary dance, students write prodigiously over the course of their time at Marlboro. Within their first three semesters, students must fulfill the Clear Writing Requirement, which involves submitting a portfolio of clear, concise, and grammatically correct writing samples for approval by the faculty. Marlboro's focus on helping students develop their command of the written word speaks to the college's underlying focus on clear thinking, which is both a product and reflection of clear writing. Whatever career paths Marlboro students forge, they all benefit from the ability to process complex information and effectively communicate their ideas to others.

CAMPUS FACILITIES AND EQUIPMENT

The core of campus buildings is made up of historic farmhouses and barns, renovated into classrooms and dorms by the first students who attended Marlboro. These include Dalrymple Hall, which is the main classroom building; the dining hall; the admissions building; and Mather, the administrative building. Over many years the college has added more buildings, including residence halls, student cabins and cottages, Persons Auditorium/gym, Whittemore Theater, Rice-Aron Library, Campus Center and Total Health Center, and Serkin Center for Performing Arts. The new Snyder Visual Arts Center, scheduled for completion in 2015, will add exciting new gallery, studio, and classroom space for the integration of visual arts with other disciplines. Other facilities include an integrated science lab, a DNA lab, a computer lab, and a digital media lab.

TUITION, ROOM, BOARD, AND FEES

For the 2015–2016 academic year, the fees are as follows:

Tuition: $38,320

Fees: $910

Room: $5,830

Board: $4,760

Total: $49,840

FINANCIAL AID

As a very small, private liberal arts college, Marlboro makes a conscious and continuous effort to keep tuition and fees as affordable as possible. In recent years, we've increased the amount of need-based grant aid provided to students and increased other awards for financial aid. Today more than 90 percent of full-time Marlboro students receive some form of financial assistance. We are also proud to report that in recent years the Marlboro average student debt has been more than $5,000 below the national average. Applicants should contact the Financial Aid Office directly to request a financial aid packet, which includes step-by-step instructions. The deadline for completing the Free Application for Federal Student Aid (FAFSA) is March 1. After that date, the college cannot promise a full financial aid package. The financial aid office can be reached at 802-258-9312 or finaid@marlboro.edu.

STUDENT ORGANIZATIONS AND ACTIVITIES

Marlboro College operates based on a model of community governance. Students, faculty, and staff play an integral role in shaping campus life through their participation in Town Meeting, a monthly assembly during which college-wide issues are discussed and brought to vote. Students also serve on committees in areas ranging from curriculum development and faculty hiring to public art and food services.

Campus life at Marlboro College correlates directly with student interests. Extracurricular groups and activities evolve yearly with each incoming class. Through this ongoing collective creation of community, Marlboro students develop valuable skills in teamwork and community organizing as well as a strong sense of civic investment.

One of the most popular resources for student activities is the Outdoor Program, OP for short. The OP offers a variety of activities from week-long orientation trips for new students to weekend mini trips, to winter- and spring-break trips in tropical climates. Some of the popular activities have been rock climbing, hiking, rafting, kayaking, camping, yoga, intramural soccer, broomball, and Ultimate Frisbee. The college also has an indoor climbing wall and regular intramural activities.

For a small campus, students enjoy a wide range of social, artistic, and cultural activities. A sampling of student activities in one semester would include performances by rock, folk, jazz, and ethnic bands; dances; lectures; poetry readings; recitals; plays; and concerts. Annual events that are considered traditions include midnight breakfast, Wendell-Judd Cup cross country ski event, Work Day, President's Fall Ball, Trails Day, broomball tournament, community and international dinners, Gender Bender Ball, and Apple Days.

ADMISSIONS PROCESS

If you are looking for an intentionally small, intellectually demanding liberal arts school where students are seen, heard, known, and valued, Marlboro College would be a great college choice for you. Marlboro assesses student potential in the unique context of each applicant's experience, without the confines of GPAs or standardized test scores. There is no formula for what makes a student a "good fit" for Marlboro, but applicants are reviewed with an eye towards intellectual promise, self-motivation, self-discipline, and ability to positively contribute to our community.

Students may apply to Marlboro under three different application plans.

Early Decision: Deadline-November 15; Notification-December 1

Early Action: Deadline-January 15; Notification-February 1

Regular Admission: Rolling

Please note that if you are applying for financial aid it is important to file the FAFSA by March 1.

In order to be considered for admission, please submit the following: a completed Common Application and Marlboro College Supplement with the "Why Marlboro?" personal statement (or the optional Marlboro College Application, if you are not already filling out the Common Application), the $50 nonrefundable application fee, all high school and college transcript(s), an expository writing sample, and two letters of recommendation (teacher and general). An interview is required for all students. Submission of SAT or ACT scores is optional.

MERCER UNIVERSITY—MACON

AT A GLANCE

Mercer University is one of America's oldest and most distinctive universities, offering rigorous programs that span the undergraduate liberal arts to doctoral-level programs. With more than 8,500 students enrolled in 12 schools and colleges across three campuses in Georgia—Macon, Atlanta and Savannah—Mercer's reputation for exceptional academics in an engaged learning environment attracts students from across the United States and around the world.

Founded in 1833, Mercer holds the distinction of being the only university in the South to offer liberal arts, engineering, law, medicine and pharmacy at the same institution. Mercer also offers degree programs in business, teacher education, music, professional studies, theology, nursing and health professions. Mercer successfully combines the "best of both worlds," boasting a wide breadth of academic programs and resources of a large research university while maintaining an intimate, student-focused culture more characteristic of smaller liberal arts colleges.

The Mercer experience is defined by the integration of student leadership, academic research and service to others, and Mercer students rank among the most engaged in the nation. The University's hallmark initiative, Mercer On Mission, takes students out of the classroom and into foreign countries where they use academic knowledge and research to solve significant real-world problems, transforming the lives of those they serve around the world.

The Mercer Bears are longtime members of NCAA Division I athletics. During a remarkable 2013-2014 season, the return of football after a 72-year hiatus broke the NCAA all-time record for victories by a start-up program, and the men's basketball team, men's golf team, and men's lacrosse team were all crowned conference champions. Mercer recently joined the Southern Conference—the nation's fifth-oldest NCAA Division I athletic association—and the Bears compete in men's baseball, basketball, cross country, football, golf, lacrosse, soccer and tennis, and women's basketball, cross country, golf, lacrosse, sand volleyball, soccer, softball, tennis, track & field and volleyball.

ACADEMIC PROGRAMS

Mercer offers distinctive academic and experiential opportunities during the undergraduate years that prepare students to excel in graduate and professional school as well as to successfully enter the workforce immediately after graduation.

With an average class size of 21 and a 13:1 student/faculty ratio, Mercer's courses are characterized by spirited interchange among talented students and acclaimed faculty. No classes are taught by teaching assistants; instead, they are led by faculty members who hold Ph.D.s (or the equivalent terminal degrees in their fields) from some of the most prestigious institutions in the world. Mercer's professors excel in both scholarly research and teaching abilities, and they mentor and challenge their students to think critically, communicate clearly, act ethically and care passionately.

Mercer students and alumni continue to garner prestigious national awards and accolades, and last year alone, a sophomore was awarded a Goldwater Scholarship; two student-athletes were named First Team Academic All-American; three Mercerians were selected to receive Fulbright U.S. Student Awards to teach abroad; and a graduating senior was awarded a Woodrow Wilson Ohio Teaching Fellowship.

Mercer's core curriculum features two options for students: the Integrative Program combines traditional disciplinary course requirements with several signature multidisciplinary courses, and the Great Books Program engages students through thoughtful conversation sparked by some of the most significant works of literature throughout history, including books by Homer, Plato, Chaucer and Shakespeare.

Many Mercer students choose to pursue undergraduate research—regardless of major—working independently or alongside a faculty member on projects ranging from the forefront of medical advances to cutting-edge econometrics.

For students seeking an intensely transformative challenge, the Mercer University Honors Program engages exceptional students in an exclusive and enriching academic experience that integrates undergraduate research with interdisciplinary seminars, service-learning courses, cultural and social events, and study abroad opportunities. Students invited to the program select from five academic tracks: business, engineering, international, research and service.

Mercer Abroad provides holistic and experiential learning opportunities for student to earn academic credit while seeing the world. Mercer's partnerships with schoo across the globe allow students to choose from a variety of study abroad programs— ranging from trips lasting a few weeks to a full year abroad.

The University's innovative Center for Collaborative Journalism has been calle "one of the nation's boldest journalism experiments" by The New York Times fo taking the "teaching hospital" model to the newsroom. In collaboration with medi partners The (Macon) Telegraph and Georgia Public Broadcasting, journalism an media studies students are placed alongside industry professionals to learn, engag with the community and build an unrivaled portfolio of published work.

MAJORS AND DEGREES OFFERED

Students may choose from more than 60 undergraduate majors across the Colleg of Liberal Arts, School of Engineering, Stetson School of Business and Economics Tift College of Education, Townsend School of Music, Georgia Baptist College o Nursing and the College of Health Professions to find the degree program that fit their interests and goals.

Mercer offers a variety of pre-professional tracks that prepare students for graduate or professional school: pre-anesthesiologist assistant, pre-dentistry, pre-law, pre medicine, pre-occupational therapy, pre-optometry, pre-podiatry, pre-pharmacy pre-physical therapy, pre-physician assistant, pre-theology and pre-veterinar medicine. Students are paired with a pre-professional advisor who guides them through the undergraduate class selection process as well as the graduate/profes sional school application process.

Graduate and/or professional degree programs are offered on one or more campuse through the School of Engineering, Stetson School of Business and Economics Tift College of Education, Townsend School of Music, Georgia Baptist College o Nursing, Walter F. George School of Law, School of Medicine, College of Pharmacy McAfee School of Theology, College of Health Professions and Penfield College Qualified undergraduate students have the unique opportunity to pursue guarantee admission to the University's nationally recognized and highly competitive gradu ate and professional programs in medicine, pharmacy, business, physical therapy law and nursing.

Mercer students also have the option to earn both their bachelor's and master's de grees in just five years through combined degree programs in accounting, busines and engineering. The University's accelerated law degree program offers qualifie students the opportunity to complete a bachelor's degree and law degree in six years instead of seven. Mercer's dual-degree graduate programs help students diversif their skill set by earning two complementary degrees—such as a law degree (J.D. along with a master of business administration (M.B.A.)—that prepare graduate more comprehensively for their chosen profession.

STUDENT ORGANIZATIONS AND ACTIVITIES

Mercer students have rewritten the definition of the word "involved," and the activ undergraduate campus in Macon is home to 140 student organizations, includin the Student Government Association, national honor societies, academic and career oriented clubs, national fraternities and sororities, intramural and club sports, servic organizations and diverse special-interest groups.

CAMPUS AND FACILITIES

Macon has served as Mercer's home since 1871, when the institution moved from its original campus in Penfield, Georgia. The beautiful Macon campus is home to the University's traditional undergraduate program and houses the College o Liberal Arts, School of Medicine, School of Engineering, Stetson School of Busi ness and Economics, Tift College of Education and Townsend School of Music Mercer's Walter F. George School of Law is located one mile away on Colema Hill overlooking downtown Macon. This charming city serves as the educational medical, cultural and commercial hub of Central Georgia, boasting a rich arts and musical heritage and offering easy access to the Georgia coast, Florida beaches and the Blue Ridge Mountains.

The Macon campus is a blend of tradition and innovation. Breathtaking, historical landmarks like the Godsey Administration Building with its iconic spires are complemented by newer, modern structures, such as the 230,000-square-foot University Center and the new Moye Football and Lacrosse Complex. On the edge of campus, students and the local community converge in Mercer Village, the vibrant, thriving go-to destination for food, coffee, shopping and fun.

Living on campus is a significant part of the Mercer experience, and undergraduates may choose from a range of on-campus housing options, including traditional residence halls, modern apartments, and fraternity and sorority houses.

Located on 200 heavily wooded acres inside the Atlanta Perimeter, Mercer's Cecil B. Day Graduate and Professional Campus is home to the College of Pharmacy, College of Health Professions, McAfee School of Theology, Georgia Baptist College of Nursing and Penfield College, along with programs of the Stetson School of Business and Economics and the Tift College of Education.

Savannah is home to a four-year M.D. program of the School of Medicine, located on the campus of Memorial University Medical Center.

TUITION, ROOM, BOARD AND FEES

Estimated costs for the 2015–2016 academic year are $34,450 for tuition and fees and $10,898 for room and board. Estimated student expenses may include $1,200 for books and supplies, $1,200 for transportation or travel, and $1,645 for personal expenses.

FINANCIAL AID

More than 90 percent of Mercer students receive merit-based scholarships for academic achievement, exceptional talent, community service and leadership. Mercer's most prestigious and competitive scholarships are awarded to the top 10 percent of applicants, including awards ranging up to full tuition and a select few beyond. Georgia residents may also be eligible for the Zell Miller Scholarship, the HOPE Scholarship or the Georgia Tuition Equalization Grant. Students will be notified of scholarship eligibility and opportunities upon acceptance to the University.

Mercer also offers need-based, University-funded financial assistance to qualified undergraduate students, and many students are eligible for additional federal and state aid through grants, loans and work-study. All students seeking financial aid should submit the Free Application for Federal Student Aid (FAFSA) or the Georgia Scholarship/Grant Application (GSFAPPS) prior to March 1 for priority consideration.

ADMISSIONS PROCESS

Students seeking first-year admission to Mercer University's traditional undergraduate program should submit an application for admission (either the University's application at apply.mercer.edu or The Common Application at commonapp.org); an official high school transcript (accepted students intending to enroll also must submit a final transcript following completion of high school to finalize their admission); an official standardized test score report (SAT and/or ACT), a letter of recommendation and a non-refundable $50 application fee.

Applications are evaluated on the following six factors: academic rigor of high school curriculum, performance and grade point average in high school coursework, standardized SAT or ACT scores, extracurricular activities—with emphasis on leadership and service, quality of written expression as reflected in application essay and letter of recommendation from teacher or high school guidance counselor.

Students seeking enrollment for fall semester should submit applications by the appropriate deadline during their senior year of high school. To be considered for the University's most prestigious scholarship opportunities, students should submit their application and all supporting materials by the November 1 priority deadline. Mercer's regular decision deadline to be considered for University-funded scholarships and financial aid is February 1. Mercer processes admission decisions on a rolling basis.

For more information, visit undergrad.mercer.edu.

MICHIGAN TECHNOLOGICAL UNIVERSITY

Michigan Technological University (www.mtu.edu) is a leading public research university developing new technologies and preparing students to create the future for a prosperous and sustainable world.

AT A GLANCE

Michigan Tech began in 1885 as a school for mining engineers, to support the copper mines that flourished here. As the mines closed and the economy changed, Michigan Tech changed too, developing recognized expertise in automotive, civil, environmental and chemical engineering, as well as more recently, biomedical engineering and environmental science.

Michigan Tech stresses hands-on learning. Undergraduate participation in research is the norm. In our Enterprise Program and other special opportunities, students can try their hand at solving real-world problems, using the skills they've learned in class. They invest real money in the stock market; build satellites, snowboards, and video games; and journey to foreign nations to help the less-fortunate improve their access to clean water, sanitation, schools and other societal needs.

LOCATION AND ENVIRONMENT

Our rural setting on the Upper Peninsula of Michigan enables us to provide an excellent education in a spectacular location. Recreational opportunities abound, including our own ski hill, golf course, and 600 acres of on-campus recreational forest and trails for cross country running, skiing, hiking, and biking.

The 925-acre campus is on the banks of the Keweenaw Waterway and just a few miles from Lake Superior. The air and water are clean and the North Woods that surround us, pristine.

Ford Forest, in nearby Alberta, Michigan, is a 4,000-acre research forest managed by our School of Forest Resources and Environmental Science

OFF-CAMPUS OPPORTUNITIES

The entire local area is great for outdoor enthusiasts, with easy access to rivers, lakes, woods, downhill and cross-country skiing and hiking/biking trails. There is an extensive system of snowmobile and ATV trails. Downtown Houghton and its sister city, Hancock (combined population 14,000) offer coffee shops, theaters, stores and restaurants, as well as many kinds of specialty shops. Major retailers are a short drive or bus ride from campus. There is local bus service. Theatre, concerts, plays, ballet and other performances provide cultural experiences. Houghton and Hancock are safe communities with little traffic. It's said that in Houghton and Hancock "rush hours" are "rush minutes." All in all, it's a great combination: a world-class education in a beautiful location.

MAJORS AND DEGREES OFFERED

Michigan Tech offers more than 130 undergraduate and graduate degree programs in engineering; forest resources; computing; technology; business; economics; natural, physical and environmental sciences; arts; humanities; and social sciences.

Our graduates are among the most highly paid in the nation, with a typical starting salary of $61,000. Our Physics Department awards one of the highest percentages nationally of PhDs to women. Our scientific and technical communication program is among the nation's largest, and our Peace Corps Master's International program has more students serving overseas than any other university.

Our newest academic programs include the BS in Engineering Management, a BS in Bioinformatics and an MS in Accounting.

ACADEMIC PROGRAMS

The Enterprise Program involves more than 1,000 students on 37 teams from all across campus, working to solve real problems for industry. Currently, students are working on projects related to biofuels, the environment, better bicycles, video games, and homeland security, to name just a few.

The new Pavlis Honors College drew together students and faculty from several honors programs throughout the university and broadened its reach to embrace any student with a sincere desire to become a scholar and a leader..

The Applied Portfolio Management Program has won a NASDAQ national investment competition two years in a row. They control the investment of $1 million in actual money. They also have their own "stock exchange," the LSGI Trading Room.

Dedicated to prosperity by design, the D80 Center focuses on helping the most vulnerable 80 percent of humanity meet their most basic needs. D80 programs include Engineers Without Borders, Aqua Terra Tech Enterprise, International Sustainable Development Engineering Certificate and Research Experiences, International Senior Design, the Peace Corps Master's International Program, and Global City.

The Senior Design Program connects students and industry. Students gain the skills and experience that can launch them into successful careers, while industry partners gain access to tomorrow's engineers—today. Senior Design students say it's not their last class; it is their first job.

More than 500 companies recruit students on campus at two Career Fairs annually, and within six months of graduation, 95 percent of those reporting got jobs, entered graduate school, or joined the armed forces.

CAMPUS FACILITIES AND EQUIPMENT

State-of-the-art laboratories and classrooms are found across the campus, and wireless networking is everywhere. On the waterfront, our new Great Lakes Research Center is advancing knowledge in environmental studies, particularly winter-related studies, aided by our proximity to Lake Superior.

More than twenty research centers and institutes allow Michigan Tech faculty, staff, and students to focus on a broad range of inquiry, from climate change to transportation, from power and energy to computational science. The newest research center looks at precollege outreach innovations. Its goal is to motivate young people to study and pursue careers in science and engineering, Michigan Tech strengths.

Tech recently upgraded Sherman Field, our football and soccer stadium, with a state-of-the-art playing surface. The MacInnes Student Ice Arena features skyboxes, a new ice plant, and a high-tech video scoreboard.

Tuition, Room, Board, and Fees

Annual Tuition

Undergraduate (in-state)	$13,740 per academic year (2 semesters)
Room and Board	$9,516 per academic year (2 semesters)
Graduate Tuition	$820.50/credit hour

*Tuition is based on 12-18 credit hours per semester. Out-of-state students pay $29,220 tuition per academic year (2 semesters).

FINANCIAL AID

Scholarships are the most familiar and sought-after type of financial aid. All admitted students are automatically considered for most merit-based scholarships; a special application form is not required, except for the Michigan Tech Leading Scholars Award and career-interest scholarships.

Grants are aid based on financial need and are available to US citizens and permanent residents. Accepted students are automatically considered for grants if their FAFSA results are released to Michigan Tech. Students must apply for grant renewal each year.

Loans consist of borrowed funds that must be repaid. They are available to most US citizens and permanent residents. Each loan program has certain maximum limits for borrowing; however, students may not borrow more than the cost of attendance, less any other financial aid received. Accepted students are automatically considered for loans if their FAFSA results are released to Michigan Tech and they have indicated on the FAFSA an interest in receiving loans. Students must apply for loan renewal each year and make progress in obtaining their degree according to the Satisfactory Progress Policy.

Part-time employment on campus is available through government-funded and University-funded programs. Students who complete the FAFSA and indicate they would like to work on campus are automatically considered for work-study employment.

Federal Work-Study Program

These programs provide funds to employ students who are US citizens or permanent residents and who have financial need. Students must reapply for work-study each year and meet the Satisfactory Progress Policy requirements.

Specific departmental work-study assignments are made by the Financial Aid Office. Students normally work eight to ten hours per week. The hourly rate paid is equivalent to at least minimum wage.

University-Funded Student Employment

University-funded, on-campus employment is available to students regardless of need. Students may apply directly to the desired departments. On average, 2,000 to 2,500 students are employed on campus each year. Nearly every department employs students.

STUDENT ORGANIZATIONS AND ACTIVITIES

More than 180 student organizations offer leadership opportunities in many categories: Academic/Honors, Arts and Culture, Club Sports, Governance, Greeks, Programming/Social, Religious, and Service.

Our traditions include Winter Carnival featuring massive snow statues and broomball; Parade of Nations, celebrating more than 60 nations with students here; K-Day on Lake Superior's shore; and Spring Fling on campus.

ADMISSIONS PROCESS

Applying to college doesn't have to be stressful. In fact, Michigan Tech makes it pretty easy. You don't need to get teacher recommendations or even apply for scholarships with a separate form. Just submit your application for admission, official high school and/or college transcripts, and official ACT or SAT test scores.

Additional application materials are required for students applying for admission into the following degree programs: Audio Production and Technology, Sound Design, Theatre and Electronic Media Performance, and Theatre and Entertainment Technology.

Apply by January 15 of the year you plan to enroll for priority consideration for admission, financial aid, and scholarships.

We'll review your high school transcript (including your freshman year) and evaluate the courses you took in high school and the grades you received. The cumulative GPA provided by your high school is used in the admissions process. We do not recalculate your GPA.

MOLLOY COLLEGE

AT A GLANCE

At Molloy College, students gain that "I will" attitude they need to make a difference in our fast-paced, ever changing world.

Located in Rockville Centre, NY, Molloy offers students a rich and multidimensional educational experience. Our faculty is accomplished, yet approachable, leading small classes where students are encouraged to think critically and explore creatively.

Through our International Education program, students study abroad, traveling to such exotic and enriching destinations as India, Thailand, Spain, Italy, Belgium, and even Australia.

Molloy's campus provides for abundant opportunities to explore new interests, pursue career goals, and enrich our community.

Molloy opened its first residence hall in September 2011, and added a second one 2014. A new student center also opened in 2011, providing numerous opportunities for students to study and interact with their peers. The student center also includes a new performing arts center, which attracts artists from around the world.

Whether it's participating in a music ensemble, writing for a campus publication, or serving as a student government representative, with more than 50 clubs and honor societies, Molloy has something for each and every student. and with the addition of residence halls to the campus, Molloy has expanded its Student Life program to include a wide variety of social and service activities and events.

New academic programs provide additional opportunities for Molloy students to learn and grow. Recent additions include a New Media major, a four-year degree in Nuclear Medicine Technology, a Theatre Arts degree linked to a leading New York City musical theatre conservatory, a Master's in Clinical Mental Health Counseling and a Healthcare MBA, among others.

Athletics and academics go hand-in-hand at Molloy, where students are known for both their athletic and academic success. Molloy has a winning tradition in a wide variety of NCAA Division II sports, and in 2013 and 2010 the women's softball team became one of only eight teams in the country to qualify for the college World Series.

Students have exciting opportunities to "fast track" their careers. With dual bachelor's/master's degree program offerings in Accounting, Business Management, Criminal Justice, Music Therapy and Education, Molloy students can complete a dual degree in five years.

Students are encouraged to make a difference in local communities and many become involved in Molloy-sponsored service projects such as BoxTown, a simulation program that educates students about homelessness. There are also numerous service trips as well, enabling Molloy students to help the less fortunate both in the United States and abroad.

The College also provides forums welcoming regional, national, and international leaders such as Secretary of State Gen. Colin Powell, best-selling author Malcolm Gladwell, and New York Times columnist andrew Ross Sorkin.

Molloy College has built a rich, dynamic, and diverse educational environment over the past 50+ years. It is within this welcoming yet challenging environment that Molloy College students develop that all-important confidence, that strong, "I will" attitude that enables them to succeed in their careers, and more importantly, to make a difference in our world.

LOCATION AND ENVIRONMENT

Molloy College is located on the South Shore of Long Island in Rockville Centre. Our proximity to New York City allows for our students to benefit from the cultural and social opportunities that Manhattan has to offer - and it's just a short train ride away from our 30-acre campus.

Molloy College also offers off campus locations for study at the Suffolk Center in East Farmingdale, just off of the Rt. 110 corridor. In addition, the college offers courses at area hospitals and schools - all designed to provide convenience for our graduate and continuing education students.

OFF-CAMPUS OPPORTUNITIES

You can stay local—but still go far—with the International Education program available at Molloy College. At Molloy you can study what you want, where you want, for as long as you want.

Molloy College also offers students the opportunity to combine job experience and classroom exposure through its internship program. At Molloy, students are encouraged to participate in internships so that they can gain first-hand knowledge and experience in their future career path.

MAJORS AND DEGREES OFFERED

Molloy College offers the AA degree in liberal arts; the AAS degree in cardiovascular technology and respiratory care; and the BA or BS degree in accounting, art, biology, business management, communications, computer science, computer information systems, criminal justice, education, English, earth and environmental studies, finance, history, interdisciplinary studies, marketing, mathematics, modern languages, music, music therapy, new media, nuclear medicine technology, nursing, philosophy, political science, psychology, sociology, speech language pathology/audiology, theatre arts and theology; the BSW degree in Social Work; and the BFA in art, music and theatre arts. Teacher certification programs are available in childhood (1-6), adolescence (7-12), special education and birth—grade 2 childhood special education.

On the graduate level, Molloy offers a Master of Science degree as well as postmaster's certification in nursing and education. M.B.A. programs are available in business, accounting, healthcare and personal financial planning; a master's program in clinical mental health counseling was recently launched as well. A master's in social work is offered through Molloy's partnership with Fordham University. Molloy also offers graduate degrees in criminal justice , music therapy, and speech therapy. The college offers two doctoral programs, a Ph.D. in nursing and a Doctor of Nursing Practice (D.N.P.); other doctoral programs are in the planning stages.

Students interested in pre-dental, pre-law, pre-medical, or pre-veterinary programs are offered special advisement.

ACADEMIC PROGRAMS

A minimum of 128 credit hours is required for a baccalaureate degree; these courses include a strong liberal arts general education curriculum for every major field of study. Students may choose a double major, and many minors are available. Molloy has a 4-1-4 academic calendar.

Students may earn CLEP and CPE credit, and advanced placement credit is granted for a score of 3 or better on the AP exam. Qualified full-time students may participate in the Army ROTC program at Hofstra University or St. John's University on a cross enrolled basis. Molloy students may also elect Air Force ROTC on a cross enrolled basis with New York Institute of Technology.

CAMPUS FACILITIES AND EQUIPMENT

Molloy is a wireless campus and our computer labs house more than 325 PCs. Also, many departments have their own computer labs with state-of-the-art equipment.

The James E. Tobin Library is the center of academic research on the Molloy College campus. The library houses 110,000 volumes, as well as 685 journals and periodicals in its collection. On-line access to information is very important. The library subscribes to over 40 subscription databases, including but not limited to EBSCO's Academic Search Premier, ProQuest Direct and Sage's Nursing and Health Sciences database giving students and faculty access to thousands of full-text resources. Also in the library is a "smart" classroom used by the librarians for library instruction classes.

The media center houses an extensive collection of DVD's and videos as well as state of the art digital equipment. There is a Faculty Development / Instructional Technology Lab in the Media Center. The library is a wireless facility.

The Wilbur Arts Center features numerous art and music studios, a cable television studio, and the Lucille B. Hays Theatre. The school also has six science labs, a language lab, the education resource center, two nursing labs, and a behavioral sciences research facility.

TUITION, ROOM, BOARD AND FEES

For 2014–15, tuition was $25,800 and required fees were approximately $1,050. Students can expect to spend about $1,400 on books and supplies and approximately $2,400 in miscellaneous expenses

FINANCIAL AID

Financial aid, which is based on academic achievement and financial need, is awarded to more than 85 percent of the student body. Aid is awarded in the form of scholarships, grants, loans, and Federal Work-Study Program employment. Non-need scholarships and grants are also available. Students are required to complete the FAFSA application every year. Students who graduate from high school with a 95 percent average and a minimum combined score of 1280 on the SAT I critical reading and math sections are considered for the Molloy Scholars' Program, which awards full tuition scholarships. Partial scholarships are available through the following: Dominican Scholarships, Fine and Performing Arts Scholarships, Community Service Awards, and other funded scholarships. The Transfer Scholarship Program awards partial tuition scholarships to students transferring into Molloy College with at least a 3.0 cumulative GPA. Nursing transfers are required to have a 3.3 GPA to be eligible for a transfer scholarship. Athletic grants (Division II only) are awarded to full-time students who show superior athletic ability in baseball, basketball, cross-country, equestrian, lacrosse, soccer, softball, tennis, or volleyball.

STUDENT ORGANIZATIONS AND ACTIVITIES

Molloy students are involved in a highly active life outside the classroom, something that the college administration supports and encourages. Whether you are an athlete, an aspiring journalist, someone with a strong opinion, or just someone with a desire to expand your horizons, you will find a group to join here. Such organizations provide students with the opportunity to interact with fellow students as leaders, as part of a team, or in a social environment.

Student-run publications include the yearbook, a literary magazine, and the school newspaper. Molloy College sponsors a number of varsity sports, including baseball, men's and women's basketball, men's and women's cross country, men's and women's lacrosse, men's and women's soccer, softball, women's tennis and women's volleyball. Recently, women's basketball participated in the NCAA tournament, and the women's softball team was one of eight schools in the country to qualify for the NCAA College World Series. The college is a member of the East Coast Conference (ECC) in NCAA Division II. In addition, Molloy sponsors a club dance team and a co-ed club equestrian team. The equestrian team is part of the Intercollegiate Horse Show Association.

The student government is elected from the Molloy Student Association, made up of every member of the student body. Members of the Molloy Student Government provide their classmates with a leadership that keeps extracurricular activities alive, productive, and practical.

ADMISSIONS PROCESS

Molloy College's admissions committee recommends that applicants meet the following admission qualifications: graduation from a four-year public or private high school or equivalent (GED test) with a minimum of 20.5 units, including 4 in English, 4 in social studies, 3 in a foreign language, 3 in mathematics, and 3 in science. Nursing applicants must have completed biology and chemistry courses. Mathematics applicants must have taken 4 units of math and 2 of science (including chemistry or physics). Biology applicants must have credits in biology, chemistry, and physics and 4 units in math. Art applicants must submit a portfolio; music students must audition. The committee selects candidates based on the following: high school record, SAT I or ACT scores, class rank, and the school's recommendation. Personality and character are considered in admissions decisions, as are talent or ability in a non-curricular field, as well as alumni relationships.

A select group of freshmen are invited to participate in the Molloy College Honors Program. This program offers challenging coursework and encourages reflection and personal growth. Honors students are provided with several special participation incentives such as a laptop computer, and priority registration.

The HEOP and the Albertus Magnus programs may be options for students not normally eligible for admission.

Early admission is available. Molloy admits students on a rolling basis and students are advised of the admission decision within a few weeks of completion of the application filing process.

Prospective students should submit the following to the admissions office to be considered for enrollment: a completed application for admission (the Common Application is accepted), a nonrefundable $40 application fee, an official high school transcript or GED score report, official SAT I or ACT score, and official college transcripts (transfer students only).

MOUNT ALOYSIUS COLLEGE

AT A GLANCE

Mount Aloysius College is a private and affordable Catholic liberal arts college sponsored by the Sisters of Mercy. The college welcomes people of all faith traditions. Established in 1853, Mount Aloysius College offers undergraduate and graduate education. Today, there are nearly 15,500 alumni world-wide. The college provides small class sizes, and students benefit from accessible faculty and staff. Mount Aloysius students come mostly from throughout Pennsylvania and the mid-Atlantic Region. There are over 2,500 students enrolled (unduplicated headcount).

Mount Aloysius College is one of 18 Mercy-sponsored colleges and universities in the United Sates and is a member of the Conference for Mercy Higher Education. Students are encouraged to synthesize faith with learning, to develop competence with compassion, to apply their talents and gifts to the service of others, and to assume leadership in their community.

Student activities play a distinctive role in personal growth. At Mount Aloysius College, there are approximately 100 organized clubs, groups, honor societies, and an intramural sports program. Activities include a student newspaper, residence hall associations, student government, cheerleading, dance team, scholarship-funded theater and choir programs, and a student activities planning board. Mount Aloysius fun includes social events, intramural sports, athletic events, comedians, live music, theater, educational events, campus forums, and awesome guest lectures.

Mount Aloysius College is a member of NCAA Division III. Athletic programs involve both women and men and include basketball, cross-country, golf, soccer, and tennis. Men's baseball and women's bowling, softball and volleyball are also offered. Athletes benefit from the Ray S. And Louise S. Walker Athletic Field Complex, which includes a softball field, one of the finest soccer fields in the area, and the Calandra-Smith baseball complex. Recently the Mountie Stables were opened to the college and to the community. The Stables add dugouts, lockers, showers, storage, and concession facilities to the school's athletic infrastructure.

In autumn 2014, the Athletic Convocation and Wellness Center, a spectacular 84,700-foot multi-purpose facility, opened on the western edge of the beautiful and expansive 193-acre campus. This facility takes Mount Aloysius athletics to a new level and adds a welcomed special events venue to the southern Allegheny Mountains.

Located within the Athletic Convocation and Wellness Center (ACWC) is a main gymnasium and events venue with seating for over 2500. Athletic offices, Intuitional Advancement, Student Affairs and Business faculty offices are located within the building. The ACWC also contains home and visitor lockers and trainer facilities. On the ground floor, a new state-of-the-art Wellness Center offers both cardio and resistance training in a spacious and modern environment.

The main campus building is a picturesque structure dating to 1897; it houses the admissions, financial aid, security, health, and academic offices, along with the Office of the President, classrooms, the Region's premiere nursing simulation center, and the Wolf-Kuhn Art Gallery. Cosgrave Center is the hub of campus life. The building contains the dining hall, snack bar, bookstore, child-care center (part of the elementary education/early childhood program at the college), lounges, recreational rooms, student affairs offices, and meeting rooms. The Sr. Virginia Bertschi Center and Technology Commons just opened in Spring 2015. A multi-purpose facility with student-centered space where commuter and residential students can relax, socialize, study, conduct meetings, enjoy games and manage the business of over 100 student clubs, teams and organizations on campus. The Digital Grotto—the video and social media hub—is also located in this building. Ihmsen Halls are key housing facilities for residential students. Misciagna Residence is a state-of-the-art residence hall, providing 25 suites and private bathrooms. McAuley Hall features both double and single rooms and a large multipurpose room and study lounges on all three floors. Alumni Hall is a historic, multipurpose facility used for College drama, musicals, lectures, and performing arts events. The college operates 12 months per year and opens its facilities to the Southern Allegheny community.

The College is 100 percent wireless, and smart classrooms are located throughout the campus.

Mount Aloysius is fully accredited by the Middle States Association of Colleges and Schools and approved by the Pennsylvania Department of Education. All nursing and health studies programs are fully accredited by their professional accrediting bodies, including the National League for Nursing Accrediting Commission, the Commission on Accreditation for Programs of Diagnostic Medical Sonography, the Commission on Accreditation in Physical Therapy Education, the American Association of Medical Assistants, and the Joint Commission on Accreditation for Programs of Surgical Technology.

In addition to its undergraduate programs, Mount Aloysius offers master's degrees in business administration, behavioral specialist consulting, community counseling, and psychology.

LOCATION

The College is located in the scenic Southern Allegheny Mountains of west-central Pennsylvania, in the town of Cresson. Convenient and accessible from U.S. Route 22, the college's setting is rural but mere minutes from State College, Altoona, and Johnstown, Pennsylvania. The area has warm, beautiful summers; brisk, breathtaking autumns; invigorating winters; and cool, blooming springs. Well maintained facilities are close and available for biking, golfing, swimming, horseback riding, waterskiing, boating, hiking, spelunking, cross-country and down-hill skiing, picnicking, and amusement and water parks. A well-kept system of State Parks is convenient to the college as are shopping malls, golf courses, and numerous historical sites.

MAJORS AND DEGREES

Mount Aloysius College awards bachelor's and associate degrees in the arts, sciences, and health studies fields in both career-oriented and traditional liberal arts programs. Baccalaureate degrees are available in accounting, behavioral and social science, biology and general science, business administration, which includes a fifth-year M.B.A. option, computer science, criminology, elementary/early childhood education and secondary education (with certifications), English, general science, history/political science, humanities, information technology, math/science, medical imaging, nursing (RN-B.S.N. program), nursing (2+2), occupational therapy (3-2), physical therapy (4-3), physician assistant studies (3-2),dental medicine (4-4), osteopathic medicine (3-4), pharmacy (3-3), prelaw, psychology, sign language/interpreter education, and undecided/exploratory. Associate degrees are offered in applied technology, business administration, criminology, early childhood studies, general studies, legal studies, liberal arts, medical assistant studies, nursing, nursing (LPN to RN), physical therapist assistant studies, pre-nursing, radiography/medical imaging, American sign language/English interpreting, and surgical technology.

ACADEMIC PROGRAMS

Whether preparing students for careers upon graduation or for graduate school, Mount Aloysius recognizes the importance of a broad and liberal education. Thus, in addition to receiving solid preparation for a chosen career, every student at the college receives a foundation in the arts, sciences, and humanities through an outstanding core curriculum. Strong emphasis is placed on the specialized courses within each program of study, and many academic programs combine classroom experience with internships and related training at area clinical sites, agencies, and institutions. In addition to its regular academic programs, Mount Aloysius offers independent and directed study with a commitment to service, a central component to a Mercy education. The college has an excellent honors program and academic services area. The academic calendar has two traditional semesters and optional summer sessions.

OFF-CAMPUS PROGRAMS

An important feature of many academic programs is off-campus training. The majority of the college's programs of study require credit-yielding practicums at partnering hospitals, public and private schools, or health or human service agencies. Students in all health programs benefit from required clinical training during their time at the college.

ACADEMIC FACILITIES

In 1995, Mount Aloysius College opened both a new Library and a new era, signifying greater access to information for the college community. This state-of-the-art Library is the campus hub for technology and study. With a Buhl Electronic Classroom and more than 80,000 print and non-print titles, the Library is an impressive, 1,000-square-foot facility with ample seating space, four group-study rooms, a reading lounge, a law library and classroom, an unparalleled 18,000-volume Ecumenical Collection donated by Pastor Gerald Myers, and ample room for expansion. This facility is completely automated, with an online catalog and access to remote libraries and the Internet through the more than 30 workstations. The Library also houses the Information Technology Center, home to 15 multimedia workstations and the latest educational software.

Pierce Hall serves as the campus science center. A state-of-the-art, 31,000-square-foot facility, it was completed in 1997. Pierce Hall houses all science labs, health science centers, and the offices of science faculty. Academic Hall is home to the college Honors Program. It houses classrooms, labs, seminar rooms, faculty offices, and electronic classrooms. The college is proud of its bridge to the past and its progress in providing twenty-first century learning facilities.

COSTS

Annual tuition, fees and room and board for the 2014–15 academic year for full-time students are $29,970. Up-to-date cost information is available online at http://www.mtaloy.edu/tuition-fees/.

FINANCIAL AID

Mount Aloysius prides itself on affordability. Many MAC students hail from proud families of modest means and many are first-generation students. The college understands the expense involved in acquiring a quality education and encourages all students to apply for all available aid. Through the Office of Financial Aid, the college assists students in applying for state and federal grants, loans, work-study awards, merit scholar-ships and more. The college awards academic monies based on GPA and SAT or ACT scores. These awards are renewable over a four-year period and range from $2000 to $12,000 per year. Mount Aloysius College participates in all federal and state programs; fully 94 percent of Mount Aloysius College students receive some form of financial aid. U.S. News & World Report has ranked Mount Aloysius College as one of the best-priced private liberal arts colleges in the United States.

FACULTY

The Mount Aloysius faculty consists of approximately 175 members, whose primary responsibility is teaching and advising students. Many faculty members hold advanced or terminal degrees and are expected to maintain close instructional ties with students. Many professors hold national professional certificates in such disciplines as criminology, education, law, and nursing. The Mount Aloysius student-faculty ratio of 13:1 allows close contact between students and faculty members, providing personal attention in a highly structured environment—a key ingredient in the college's academic philosophy.

STUDENT GOVERNMENT

The Student Government Association (SGA) represents students on all issues that concern the college. The SGA appoints student representatives to all student-oriented College committees. The college encourages active student participation in the general governance structure and in other matters concerning the development and implementation of policies on residential student life.

ADMISSION REQUIREMENTS

The College enrolls a freshman class of approximately 350 students. The total class of 550 includes transfer students. Admission is selective and based on academic promise, as indicated by a student's secondary school performance and activities, standardized test scores, and special experience and talents. Applicants are required to have, or expect to earn, a diploma from an approved secondary school or a GED diploma. Submission of official transcripts and SAT or ACT scores is required. In addition to the general admission requirements, specific admission requirements exist for the health programs.

For further information, students should visit the college's Web site at http://www.mtaloy.edu. Prospective students are encouraged to visit the scenic 193-acre campus. The college is open Monday to Friday from 8:30 to 5 and on select Saturdays.

To apply for admission to Mount Aloysius College, candidates are encouraged to submit their application and $30 application fee to the Office of Undergraduate and Graduate Admissions. In addition, students may apply online.

For further information, students should contact:

Office of Undergraduate and Graduate Admissions

Mount Aloysius College

7373 Admiral Peary Highway

Cresson, Pennsylvania 16630

Phone: 814-886-6383

888-823-2220 (toll-free)

Fax: 814-886-6441

E-mail: admissions@mtaloy.edu

Web site: http://www.mtaloy.edu

Mount Aloysius College, located on a beautiful 193-acre campus in Cresson, Pennsylvania provides a safe, vibrant learning community. Nestled in the southern Allegheny Mountains, Mount Aloysius College is one of 18 Mercy-sponsored colleges and universities in the United Sates and is a member of the Conference for Mercy Higher Education. Mount Aloysius offers year-round recreational and cultural opportunities. Students enjoy both the security of the campus and the proximity to State College to the east and Pittsburgh to the west. Mount Aloysius College is minutes away from all the amenities of Altoona and Johnstown, Pennsylvania. Interstate highways, the Pennsylvania Turnpike, AMTRAK train service, bus service, and several airports make Mount Aloysius College convenient from anywhere.

NAZARETH COLLEGE

AT A GLANCE

Nazareth College's academic strengths cross an unusually broad spectrum of 60 majors, including education, health and human services, management, the fine arts, music, theater, math and science, foreign languages, and the liberal arts. The coeducational, religiously independent, classic campus in a charming suburb of Rochester, N.Y., challenges and supports 2,000 undergrads and 800 graduate students. Nazareth is recognized nationally for its Fulbright global student scholars and commitment to civic engagement. Rigorous programs, an uncommon core, experiential learning, career skills, and a global focus prepare graduates for not just one job, but for their life's work. For more: go.naz.edu/about

LOCATION AND ENVIRONMENT

Nazareth has a cozy setting, situated on more than 150 acres of expansive lawns, shady woodland groves, and landscaped gardens. Climate-controlled tunnels make it easy to get around in the winter. Cultural opportunities abound on campus. Students get free tickets to world-class theatre, music, dance, and international entertainment at the Nazareth College Arts Center. Cross-cultural events on campus include gourmet cooking classes and Italian meals in our Casa Italiana, frequent foreign films, Black History Month celebrations, foreign language conversation clubs, professional conferences, and talks by visiting overseas scholars.

Nazareth College is in the charming town of Pittsford, a short walk from specialty shops and restaurants in the village center as well as bike trails and boat rides along the Erie Canal. The campus is seven miles from Rochester, New York state's third-largest city, known for its universities, important inventions, and innovations in consumer products. Rochester is rich in culture and entertainment, including the internationally renowned George Eastman House/International Museum of Photography and Film and Strong National Museum of Play. Ski and snowboarding resorts are within an hour's drive. For more: naz.edu/campus-life

ACADEMICS

Through rigorous academic programs, global and cross-cultural experiences, and hands-on career experience, Nazareth College prepares students not just for one job, but for their life's work.

Liberal arts courses comprise about a third of a college student's investment in time and money, and Nazareth's approach is to make that part as valuable and rewarding as the classes in a student's major. The college's uncommon core curriculum gives students the tools, experience, guidance, and support to be the architect of their education, career, and future. Nazareth's core curriculum is also ideal for students who are still exploring which major they'll select, providing a foundation of engaging classes and experiential learning while students also get help from professors, academic advisors, and tools such as assessments to find their path.

All students choose courses across a liberal arts menu to build knowledge, pursue interests, and develop the skills most sought by employers — problem solving, critical thinking, and exceptional communication. Along the way, students learn how to analyze deep questions in different disciplines and then explore a question of their choosing through three courses they select. Nazareth's general education curriculum requires experiential learning in the form of credit-based internships, co-curricular service, fieldwork, research, leadership roles, and more. These hands-on experiences directly challenge and reinforce coursework, connect students with career contacts and employers, and/or help students better understand themselves, the broader world, and current issues.

Nazareth's Center for Civic Engagement, Center for Entrepreneurship and Innovation, Center for International Education, and Center for Spirituality support students in this work. Nazareth College was named one of just five Presidential Awardees in the 2013 President's Higher Education Community Service Honor Roll and was a finalist for the 2014 award. The distinction is the highest honor a college or university can receive for its commitment to volunteering, service learning, and civic engagement.

Professors help students integrate the full experience, so that you leave college with the knowledge, adaptable skills, and comfort with complexity that you'll need to be successful in today's constantly changing world. More about the core: naz.edu/core

Majors and Minors

Nazareth offers Bachelor of Arts, Bachelor of Fine Arts, Bachelor of Music, and Bachelor of Science degrees in the following areas: accounting, acting, American studies, anthropology, art (studio), art education (B.S./M.S.), art history, biochemistry, biology, biomedical sciences, business management, chemistry, Chinese, clinical laboratory sciences, communication and media, communication science and disorders (speech pathology), community youth development, dance studies, economics, education (adolescence, inclusive childhood), English, environmental science and sustainability, finance, French, German, history, international business, international studies, Italian, law (3+3 with Syracuse University), legal studies, marketing, mathematics, modern foreign languages, music, music/business, music education, music performance, music therapy, musical theatre, nursing, occupational therapy (5-year master's), peace and justice, philosophy, physical therapy (6-year D.P.T. program), political science, psychology, public health, religious studies, social science, social work, sociology, Spanish, technical production, theatre arts, toxicology, visual communication design, and women and gender studies.

Nazareth offers pre-professional programs in audiology, dentistry, law, medicine, and veterinary science. Students may combine education certification with their declared major to earn certification in secondary education (grades 7-12) or double major in inclusive education (elementary and special education with a liberal arts major). Nazareth offers certification in art (5-year B.S./M.S.), music, and speech and hearing (birth-grade 12).

Most majors are also available as academic minors. Other minors include African American Studies; bioethics; digital marketing and design; entertainment and recording industry; entrepreneurship; environmental science; environmental studies; ethics; foreign language for business; gerontology; graphic design; horticultural therapy; information technology; interfaith studies; Islamic studies; jazz; middle eastern studies; multicultural studies; music history (concentration for B.A. music); music theory (concentration for B.A. music); pre-audiology; pre-dental; pre-law; pre-medical; pre-veterinary; religious studies: Christian studies; religious studies: religion in contemporary culture; religious studies: sacred texts; social research; Spanish; and sport management.

Graduate degrees include Master of Science in the following areas: American studies, art education, arts therapy, educational technology specialist, higher education, student affairs administration, human resource development, human resource management, inclusive education (early childhood, childhood, adolescence), integrated marketing and communications, law (3+3 program with Syracuse University), literacy specialist, management, music education, music therapy, social work, speech-language pathology, TESOL, TESOL for international educators; and a doctoral program in physical therapy. Details about each program: naz.edu/academics

EXPERIENTIAL LEARNING FOR CAREER PREPAREDNESS

A Nazareth College education includes abundant opportunity for experiential learning, allowing students to build perspective, skills, confidence, and proficiency while broadening career horizons. 74 percent of the class of 2014 gained career experience by participating in internships, field placements, research, student teaching, clinical experience, and practicum. These learning experiences reinforce classroom learning with the career skills and experience employers seek.

Most new alumni report being employed or enrolled in graduate school 12 months after graduating. Of the Class of 2013, 66 percent were employed while 19 percent continued their education at Nazareth, pursuing fields that require advanced degrees such as physical therapy (D.P.T.), social work (M.S.W.), and education (M.S.Ed.), and the remaining 15 percent pursued graduate studies with other colleges and universities. More information about the outcomes of a Nazareth education: naz.edu/outcomes

CAMPUS FACILITIES

The newest campus improvement is Nazareth's completely renovated Wellness and Rehabilitation Institute, reopening in 2015, which will double the clinic and collaboration space for health and human services and bring all of those fields under one roof. The building's design promotes interdisciplinary work among nursing, speech-language pathology, occupational therapy, physical therapy, art and music therapy, speech and hearing services, and social work. The proximity and new meeting spaces will facilitate important student-faculty research to improve health outcomes and clinical practice. For more: naz.edu/health-and-human-services/clinics

The college's Integrated Center for Math and Science in Peckham Hall, built in 2012, features state-of-the-art labs for instruction and research as well as classrooms and space for student-faculty collaboration. For more: naz.edu/icms

A $10.5 million renovation to the Nazareth College Arts Center provided state-of-the-art sound, lighting, and other upgrades for our 1,000-seat theater with a proscenium-thrust stage and modified fly system. In addition to student theatre productions, the Arts Center presents internationally renowned performers—and Nazareth students receive a free ticket to each production. For more: artscenter.naz.edu

Three foreign-language houses on campus attract students who want to be immersed in French, Spanish, or Italian language and customs; Nazareth also has a German Cultural Center.

ATHLETICS

One in four students participates in organized athletics in addition to focusing on academics. Nazareth's NCAA Division III teams include men's and women's basketball, cross-country, equestrian, golf, lacrosse, soccer, swimming and diving, tennis, volleyball, track and field; as well as women's field hockey and softball and men's ice hockey. For more: athletics.naz.edu

ADMISSIONS, COSTS, AND FINANCIAL AID

Nazareth seeks students who are ready for academic rigor and excited by the chance to learn, grow, and make their mark on the world. That's why the college recommends that applicants complete a rigorous college-preparatory curriculum in high school that includes English, mathematics, social studies, science, and foreign language. Admissions decisions are primarily based on academic achievement. In addition, there are audition requirements for the music and theatre programs and portfolio requirements for art majors. Co-curricular activities are also considered. A campus tour and interview are highly recommended but not required. Information sessions and campus tours are available Mondays through Saturdays.

Nazareth is a test optional college. Approximately 75 percent of Nazareth applicants submit test scores, but there is no disadvantage for those who do not. The scores are helpful, but the college also realizes there are inequities in students' resources and high school offerings to prepare for the exams. Full admissions details: naz.edu/admissions, or email admissions@naz.edu, or call 585-389-2860 or toll-free 800-462-3944.

The college offers merit-based awards for excellence in academics, art, music, and drama, as well as need-based aid. Students seeking aid complete the Free Application for Federal Student Aid (FAFSA). Full cost and financial aid details: go.naz.edu/tuition-aid

STUDENT ORGANIZATION AND ACTIVITIES

All campus clubs are initiated and led by students. Current campus clubs and organizations include Amnesty International; Art Club; Art Therapy Club; Association of Social Work Students; Campus Activities Board; Center for Spirituality Council; Chinese Club; Communications, Sciences and Disorders Association; Club Italianissimo; Colleges Against Cancer; Dare2Dance; Diversity Council; Finance Society; French Club; German Club; Gerontology Club; Golden Gazette; Habitat for Humanity, Inc.; Inter-Ethnic Nazareth Coalition; International Club; Jazz Club; Lambda Association; LASMA-Spanish Club; Math Club; Music Business Club; Music Therapy Club; National Association for Music Education; Nazareth Commuter Association; Nazareth Dance Organization; Naz Ultimate; Nursing Club; Philosophy Club; Physical Therapy Club; Pre-Health Professionals Club; Psychology; Quidditch Club; Residence Hall Council; Science Club; Ski and Snowboard Club; Student Athlete Mentors; Student Occupational Therapy Association; Take Note; Theatre League; Wishing Well; and WNAZ- Campus Radio Station. The Undergraduate Association provides student advocacy. For more: naz.edu/student-activities

NEW YORK UNIVERSITY

New York University is unlike any other institution of higher education in the world. Whether your home campus is in New York, Abu Dhabi, or Shanghai, you'll challenge yourself beyond the classroom and around the world—becoming a global-minded, academically confident, and truly independent thinker who stands apart from your peers.

AT A GLANCE

NYU is the largest independent research university in the United States, yet it also retains a close-knit community that combines the intellectual atmosphere of a small- to medium-sized college with the myriad cultural offerings and research opportunities. The energy and resources of New York City, Abu Dhabi, and Shanghai serve as extensions of our campuses, providing unique opportunities for research, internships, and job placement. A faculty of world-famous scholars, researchers, and artists teach both undergraduate and graduate courses and foster NYU's intellectual climate. NYU's more than 20,000 undergraduates come from all 50 states and over 130 countries. They choose from thousands of courses in over 230 areas of study.

ACADEMICS

At NYU in New York City, students enroll into one of the University's undergraduate schools, colleges, or programs: The College of Arts and Science; the Core Program in Liberal Studies; the Global Liberal Studies Program; the Leonard N. Stern School of Business; the Steinhardt School of Culture, Education, and Human Development; the Tisch School of the Arts; the Gallatin School of Individualized Study; the Silver School of Social Work; the college of Nursing; the School of Professional Studies; and the NYU Polytechnic School of Engineering.

NYU Abu Dhabi is NYU's second degree-granting campus and a major research center. Located in the United Arab Emirates, it draws students from around the world, preparing them for the challenges and opportunities of our interconnected world. It offers degrees in the liberal arts and sciences as well as engineering, and is the first comprehensive liberal arts college in the Middle East to be operated by and integrated into an American private research university.

NYU Shanghai, NYU's third and newest degree-granting campus in China, welcomed its inaugural class in fall 2013. NYU Shanghai offers students an immensely cross-cultural, close-knit learning community, along with a strong foundation in the liberal arts and sciences with emphasis in science, technology, engineering, and mathematics, as well as Chinese language and culture. It supports world-class academic research and graduate and professional education.

NYU faculty are among the world's leading scholars, and have received Nobel, Crafoord, and Pulitzer Prizes; MacArthur, Guggenheim, and Fulbright Fellowships; and Oscar and Emmy Awards. Faculty members teach undergraduate and graduate courses, allowing undergraduate students to become directly involved in research projects with internationally renowned professors and experts in their fields.

ADMISSIONS

When choosing a new entering class, the Admissions Committee reviews each application holistically, carefully considering many significant factors, including a comprehensive review of the applicant's academic background, standardized test scores, extracurricular activities, an essay, personal statements, and recommendation letters. Several programs also require the applicant to audition or submit creative materials. Applicants who have successfully completed a broad range of challenging course work throughout high school are the most desirable candidates. Also considered are your unique talents, personal attributes, and future goals.

Applicants are expected to demonstrate their talents and mastery of subject matter to support their applications and to make their best case for admission. As a result, NYU accepts a wide range of national examinations in addition to the SAT, ACT, SAT Subject Tests, AP exams, and IB scores. International students may be required to submit TOEFL, iELTS, or PTE Academic results as proof of English language proficiency. More information about NYU's complete standardized testing requirements can be found online at admissions.nyu.edu.

NYU accepts applications in three separate rounds: Early Decision I, Early Decision II, and Regular Decision.

Certain programs at NYU conduct interviews, which are by invitation only. Prospective students are strongly encouraged to visit campus and attend an information session. The admissions staff also visits high schools and hosts receptions worldwide. For dates and times, and for reserving a space at our information sessions and campus tours, go to admissions.nyu.edu/visit.

CAMPUS FACILITIES AND EQUIPMENT

NYU offers an exceptional range of facilities and student services, including a range of residence halls, meal plans, and dining locations on each campus. Academic facilities include nine libraries and institutes renowned for their research in applied mathematics, physics, neural science, and fine arts. Foreign language and cultural centers offer lectures, films, and concerts. Students may also access NYU's Wasserman Center for Career Development, and student support offices addressing almost every student need, from health and wellness to academic support and enrichment. The Kimmel Center for Student Life houses dining facilities, student lounges, computers, club spaces, and the Skirball Center for the Performing Arts, lower Manhattan's largest performance space.

CAMPUS LIFE

With 21 varsity sports teams that compete at the NCAA Division III level, as well as intramural sports, club athletics, over 400 student clubs, and numerous volunteer activities, NYU students are actively involved both on and off campus.

Student-run clubs are as varied as the student body. Whether their interests lie in world languages, politics, ballroom dancing, writing for the Washington Square News or working at NYU's radio station, students will find something (or more likely, a dozen things!) they love to do.

Hundreds of students annually serve communities across the city, country and world through the Office of Student Activities' C-Team, Alternative Breaks Program, student OutReach Program, fraternities and sororities, and student grassroots organizations. Students deliver meals to the needy and homebound, tutor children, paint public schools, clean up parks, rebuild areas devastated by natural disasters, provide healthcare services in underdeveloped areas, and more.

LOCATION AND ENVIRONMENT

At NYU, great cities around the world are the integral backdrop to the undergraduate experience. NYU's Washington Square campus is located in the heart of Greenwich Village, a historic neighborhood that has attracted generations of writers, musicians, artists, and intellectuals. The campus surrounds beautiful Washington Square Park, where students gather to study, enjoy musical performances and events, and spend time with friends. Rather than building walls to separate the campus from the community, NYU embraces the city as an essential element of academic life. New York is a world center of finance, media, and art, offering internships, part-time jobs and research experiences that pair course work with practical experience. The city offers the best in theatre, dance, music, film, museums, and galleries. Undergraduates can be found presenting academic papers at annual conferences; winning prizes at film festivals; working on innovative technology in Brooklyn's "Tech Triangle"; interning on Wall Street; and completing field work in some of the world's best hospitals and schools.

In this same tradition, NYU's Abu Dhabi and Shanghai campuses both put students in the center of entrepreneurial hubs of ideas, talent, and commerce. Abu Dhabi has developed a progressive agenda in health care, the arts, economic and environmental sustainability, and educational human development; Shanghai is the fast-growing, bustling financial and commercial capital of China.

TUITION AND FEES

On average, tuition and fees are approximately $47,750 for two semesters; room and board cost approximately $17,580 per year. Most NYU students receive one or more forms of financial aid to support contributions made by them and their families. (Financial aid information is subject to change; please visit admissions. nyu.edu for the most up-to-date information.)

MAJORS AND DEGREES

NYU students begin their studies at one of NYU's three dynamic urban locations: in New York City; in Abu Dhabi, UAE; or in Shanghai, China. No matter where their home campus is, all students graduate with an NYU degree, and may travel throughout the NYU global network as they complete their majors.

In New York, students enroll directly into one of the aforementioned undergraduate schools, colleges, or programs, all of which have earned national recognition in their respective fields.

Among the more than 230 areas of study offered by NYU's three campuses are: Anthropology, Arab Crossroads Studies, Biochemistry, Economics, Dance, Education, Engineering, Environmental Science, Film and Television, Finance, Global Public Health, Hospitality and Tourism Management, Individualized Study, Integrated Digital Media, Marketing, Metropolitan Studies, Nursing, Real Estate, Social Work, Theatre, and Recorded Music.

OFF-CAMPUS OPPORTUNITIES

Students have access to NYU's extensive global network, within which they can pursue their studies and explore new cultures and perspectives while remaining connected to all of the University's academic resources. They may choose from 11 global academic centers—in Accra, Ghana; Berlin, Germany; Buenos Aires, Argentina; Florence, Italy; London, England; Madrid, Spain; Paris, France; Prague, Czech Republic; Sydney, Australia; Tel Aviv, Israel; and Washington, DC—or in one of many exchange programs NYU has with outstanding research universities around the world. Each location provides a rich curriculum in which students—whose financial aid will travel with them—can complete some of their general degree requirements and, in many fields, take courses in their major. In fact, a number of NYU's schools, colleges, and programs (like the Global Liberal Studies program and the major in Business and Political Economy) offer specific curricula and majors with an international focus. With all of these opportunities, it's no surprise that NYU is #1 for the number of students who study abroad (per the most recent IIE Open Doors report).

TUITION AND AID

The vast majority of financial aid awarded at NYU is need-based. Low-interest education loans are available for both students and parents. NYU also offers or participates in a variety of payment plans, ranging from interest-free prepayment plans to extensive loan programs that allow families to finance the cost of a college education over many years. A financial aid package might include any combination of scholarships, loans, or work-study programs. The average scholarship/grant for incoming freshmen is nearly $26,000.

Students wishing to be considered for financial aid must submit the Free Application for Federal Student Aid (FAFSA)° and the CSS/Financial Aid PROFILE (and CSS Noncustodial Parent PROFILE, if applicable), administered by the college Board.

Financial aid information is subject to change; visit admissions.nyu.edu for the latest deadlines and more specific details pertaining to financial aid for each NYU campus.

°NYU Abu Dhabi applicants, and any non-US citizens or US permanent residents are not required to complete the FAFSA.

STUDENT ORGANIZATIONS AND ACTIVITIES

NYU is anything but cookie-cutter—that's one of the best things about being a part of a larger, global university. The culture of openness, opportunity, and inclusion that is cultivated here allows NYU students to thrive. There are so many choices here about what to do that no two students make the same selection.

Students at NYU find their niche by doing what they love. With more than 400 student organizations, there are many ways to get involved at NYU—including a dynamic student government, a variety of sports teams, myriad community service opportunities, and much more. You can determine your future as you contribute to university life, and learn to become a leader in the process.

NIAGARA UNIVERSITY

AT A GLANCE

Founded by the Vincentian community in 1856, Niagara University is a comprehensive institution, blending the best of a liberal arts and professional education, grounded in a values-based Catholic tradition. The suburban 160-acre campus combines the old and new; both ivy-covered buildings and modern architectural structures line its picturesque landscape. The university is easily accessible from every major city in the eastern and midwestern United States via the New York State Thruway, Buffalo-Niagara International Airport, and rail and bus service.

There are approximately 3,200 undergraduate and 825 graduate students enrolled at Niagara. A large percentage of these students take advantage of the more than 100 extracurricular and co-curricular activities offered. Volunteer work in the community is popular among the students and enhances community relations. Students work with numerous organizations, including the United Way, Habitat for Humanity, Roswell Park Cancer Institute, Community Missions and the Heart, Love and Soul food pantry.

University athletics teams compete on the Division I level and are members of the NCAA, the Metro Atlantic Athletic Conference and Atlantic Hockey Association. Intercollegiate sports for men include baseball, basketball, cross-country, golf, ice hockey, soccer, swimming and diving, and tennis. Intercollegiate sports for women include basketball, cross-country, golf, lacrosse, outdoor track & field, soccer, softball, swimming and diving, tennis, and volleyball. An extensive club and intramural sports program includes cheerleading, danceline, hockey, rugby and lacrosse, just to name a few. The Kiernan Center offers a variety of sports and recreational facilities, including a multipurpose gymnasium, a swimming and diving pool, an indoor track, racquetball courts, free-weight and Nautilus rooms, and aerobics rooms. There are several outdoor athletic fields as well as basketball and tennis courts.

Additional student services include the Health Center, which provides inpatient and outpatient care during the day; the Learning Center, which provides free tutoring services; and the Career Services Office, which offers professional and career counseling. Other services include counseling, orientation, academic planning, and job placement.

Niagara University's housing accommodations include five residence halls, a grouping of five small cottages, and a student apartment complex.

The university offers graduate studies in business, counseling, criminal justice, education, finance, healthcare administration, interdisciplinary studies, and sport management, as well as a Ph.D. program in leadership and policy.

LOCATION AND ENVIRONMENT

Niagara University's picturesque, suburban campus is located in the town of Lewiston, New York, two minutes off of the I-190 on Route 104. The campus is situated on Monteagle Ridge overlooking the lower Niagara River, which connects the two Great Lakes of Erie and Ontario. The university's convenient campus setting is just a few miles from the world-famous Niagara Falls, 20 minutes from Buffalo, which offers a variety of cultural events, sports and entertainment opportunities, and just 90 minutes from Rochester and Toronto, Canada's largest metropolitan area. In addition, the university is minutes away from the quaint village of Lewiston, New York, and the city of Niagara Falls, New York.

MAJORS AND DEGREES OFFERED

The College of Arts and Sciences offers the bachelor of arts degree in art history with museum studies, chemistry, communication studies, English, French, gerontology, history, international studies, liberal arts, life sciences, mathematics, philosophy, political science, psychology, religious studies, social sciences, sociology, and Spanish. The bachelor of science degree is awarded in biochemistry (with a concentration in bioinformatics), biology (with concentrations in bioinformatics and biotechnology), chemistry (with a concentration in computational chemistry), computer and information sciences, criminal justice and criminology, mathematics, nursing, and social work. This division also offers the bachelor of fine arts degree in theatre studies (with concentrations in design technology, general theatre, and performance). Preprofessional programs are offered in dentistry, law, medicine, pharmacy, veterinary medicine, and Army-ROTC. An associate of arts degree is available in general studies. In addition, Niagara offers a coordinate major in envi-

ronmental studies concentration to supplement a degree in biology, chemistry, or political science. Combined master's programs include a five-year program in criminal justice administration and a six-year program is clinical mental health counseling. The university also offers an accelerated nursing program for registered nurses seeking a baccalaureate degree and enrichment courses in fine arts and languages.

In addition to the programs listed above, NU offers a number of pre-professional partnerships. These include a 3+4 partnership in pharmacy with the State University of New York at Buffalo (SUNY), a 2+3 partnership in pharmacy with Lake Erie College of Osteopathic Medicine (LECOM), a 3+4 partnership in medicine with LECOM, and a 3+4 partnership in dentistry with SUNY at Buffalo. Qualified premedical Niagara students are eligible to apply for the early assurance program sponsored by the SUNY at Buffalo.

Niagara University's College of Business Administration is accredited by AACSB International—The Association to Advance Collegiate Schools of Business and offers a B.B.A. And a combination B.B.A./M.B.A. degree (five-year program) in accounting as well as an M.S. in finance. This division offers B.S. degrees in economics, finance, management (with concentrations in human resources, international business, and supply chain management), and marketing. In addition, an A.A.S. degree can be earned in business.

Business students can gain real-world learning experiences through internships, study abroad, cooperative education programs and research conducted in several business-focused campus centers. These centers include the Family Business Center, the Center for Supply Chain Management, the Technology Transfer Center, and the Center for International Accounting and Research.

Holding the highest accreditations possible in both the United States and Canada—the Council for the Accreditation of Educator Preparation (formerly NCATE) and Canada's Ontario College of Teachers—Niagara University's College of Education provides students with an option of earning dual certification to teach in both countries. The College of Education offers bachelor's degree programs leading to New York state initial certification in early childhood (birth–grade 6), childhood (grades 1–6), childhood and middle childhood (grades 1–9), middle childhood and adolescence (grades 5–12), adolescence (grades 7–12), certification for teaching students with disabilities (grades 1–6 childhood and grades 7–12 adolescence), and in Teaching English to Speakers of Other Languages (TESOL). All education majors pursue an academic concentration to establish expertise in one of the following subject areas: biology, business, chemistry, English, French, liberal arts, mathematics, social studies, and Spanish. Business education is offered only at grades 5–12. The academic concentration in liberal arts can only be pursued in the early childhood and childhood (birth–grade 6), and special education and childhood (grades 1–6). Most other states, and Puerto Rico, have reciprocity agreements with New York, meaning that an NU education would qualify education majors to teach in those states as well. In addition, the Canadian province of Ontario recognizes Niagara graduates as qualified for the Letter of Eligibility to teach in that province. Committed to working with individuals with special needs, NU offers bachelor's degree programs in developmental disabilities and early childhood development and cognition. These programs prepare students for work in human service fields where opportunities are far-reaching.

The College of Hospitality and Tourism Management provides a career-oriented curriculum leading to a B.S. degree in three specific areas: hotel and restaurant management (with concentrations in food and beverage management; luxury hospitality operations; and hotel planning, development, and operations), sport management (with concentrations in sport operations and revenue management), and tourism and recreation management (with concentrations in event and meeting management and tourism destination management). The College of Hospitality and Tourism Management offered the world's first bachelor's degree in tourism. Meanwhile, NU's hotel and restaurant program, the second-oldest in New York, has the distinction of being the seventh program nationally to be accredited by the Accreditation Commission for Programs in Hospitality Administration by the Council of Hotel, Restaurant, and Institutional Education. The college introduces students to a comprehensive body of knowledge about the hotel, restaurant, tourism, and recreational areas and applies this knowledge to current industry challenges. The college requires that its students accumulate 800 hours of industry-related experience. These and other practical experiences offer NU students the knowledge necessary to advance in the field. Students work with industry leaders in classroom projects, join academic clubs and professional organizations, and participate in special trips to trade shows and conventions and specially designed study-abroad experiences, making NU a national leader in the area.

For students who are undecided about which major to choose, Niagara University offers an award-winning Academic Exploration Program (AEP). AEP provides a structured opportunity for students to participate in a thorough, organized process of selecting a major that meets their academic talents and career goals, while meeting the requirements to graduate on time.

ACADEMIC PROGRAMS

Niagara University's curricula enable students to pursue their academic preferences and to complete courses that lead to proficiency in other academic areas. Courses that have been considered upper-division courses are available to all students. This provides students with the opportunity to avoid introductory and survey courses and permits motivated students to take advantage of more challenging courses early in their collegiate career. The honors program provides special academic opportunities that stimulate, encourage and challenge participants. In addition, an accelerated three-year degree program is offered to qualified students.

Students pursuing a bachelor's degree must complete a total of 40 or 42 course units (120 or 126 credit hours) to meet graduation requirements. Niagara grants credit for successful scores on the Advanced Placement and the College-Level Examination Program and the International Baccalaureate tests.

Internships, research, independent study, study abroad and cooperative education are available in many academic programs. An Army-ROTC program is also offered.

NU is fully accredited by the Middle States Association of Colleges and Schools. Its programs in the respective areas are accredited by the National Council for Accreditation of Teacher Education, AACSB International–The Association to Advance Collegiate Schools of Business, and the Council on Social Work Education, and the chemistry department has the approval of the American Chemical Society. The travel, hotel and restaurant administration program is accredited by the Commission for Programs in Hospitality Administration.

OFF-CAMPUS OPPORTUNITIES

For those students who wish to study abroad, the university offers semester and summer programs in Chile, China, England, France, Ireland, Mexico, Spain Thailand, and many other countries. In fact, students may choose from more than 200 available programs in more than 30 countries through the university's membership in the American Institute for Foreign Studies, Center for Cross Cultural Studies, College Consortium for International Studies, Global Learning Semesters and Semester at Sea.

CAMPUS FACILITIES

The university's open-stack library exceeds 300,000 books and has more than 30,000 periodical titles as well as reference databases accessible through the Web. The library is housed in a modern facility that features seating for 500 people, including individual study carrels. The library is affiliated with the Online Computer Library Center (OCLC) network.

The B. Thomas Golisano Center for Integrated Sciences is a state-of-the-art facility, featuring more than 50,000-square-feet of interactive learning space. The Academic Complex, home to the College of Education and the College of Business Administration (Bisgrove Hall), is a cutting-edge learning facility. Dunleavy Hall, outstanding both educationally and architecturally, includes a computerized lecture hall and TV production rooms. The university's facilities also include the Gallagher Center (gymnasium and student union); the Computer Center; DePaul Hall; St. Vincent's Hall; the Kiernan Center, NU's athletic and recreation center; the Elizabeth Ann Clune Center for Theatre; the Castellani Art Museum; and Dwyer Arena, a dual-rink ice hockey complex.

TUITION

Tuition for 2014–15 was $27,700. Room and board (with a choice of meal plans) is an additional $11,950 per year. Fees were estimated at $1,360 per year. Niagara estimates that an additional $2,500 to $3,050 per year is adequate for books, laundry and other essentials, such as travel to and from home.

FINANCIAL AID

Ninety-eight percent of entering freshmen and transfers receive financial aid. This aid may come in the form of merit scholarships, loans, grants, or campus employment. Students seeking financial assistance should file the Free Application for Federal Student Aid (FAFSA). New York State residents should also file a Tuition Assistance Program (TAP) application.

FACULTY

Niagara University has a dedicated, accessible faculty who genuinely cares about the academic and personal growth of their students. Their commitment to teaching is their primary concern. A student-faculty ratio of 12:1 and an average class size of approximately 20 allow personal attention and classroom interaction.

STUDENT GOVERNMENT

The student government represents all parts of the student body equally. It coordinates and legislates all student activities, serving as both liaison to and a participating member of the university. In addition, students serve on all major departmental committees and on the University Senate, which is the major advisory committee to the president and Board of Trustees.

ADMISSIONS PROCESS

The university welcomes men and women who have demonstrated aptitude and academic achievement at the high school level. Either SAT or ACT test scores are required. International students are required to submit the results of their TOEFL examination and, if transcripts are not in English, all transcripts must be sent to Niagara University via World Education Services (WES) for the "Course by Course Report" evaluation. Interviews are recommended. Transfer students are accepted during any semester. (Transfer credit is evaluated individually by the dean of each division.) Students who complete high school in less than four years are eligible for early admission. Students may also apply under an early action program. Economically and educationally disadvantaged students from New York state are eligible to apply for admission through the Higher Educational Opportunity Program (HEOP).

APPLICATION AND INFORMATION

For all majors except nursing, Niagara operates on a rolling admission basis and adheres to the college Board Candidates Reply Date. Nursing applicants must apply by mid-December of their senior year. A visit to the campus is encouraged and overnight accommodations in a residence hall are available through the Niagara Nights program.

Information on all aspects of the university can be obtained by contacting the Office of Admissions or through www.niagara.edu.

Mark Wojnowski
Director of Admissions
Niagara University
Niagara University, New York 14109-2011
United States
Phone: 716-286-8700
800-462-2111 (toll-free)
Fax: 716-286-8710
Email: admissions@niagara.edu
Website: http://www.niagara.edu
Facebook: http://www.facebook.com/niagarau
Twitter: http://twitter.com/niagarauniv
Instagram: http://instagram.com/niagarauniversity
YouTube: http://www.youtube.com/NiagaraUniversity
LinkedIn: https://www.linkedin.com/edu/school?id=18997

NORTHEASTERN UNIVERSITY

AT A GLANCE

There's a certain energy about Northeastern University. It comes from the bright, ambitious students, exhibiting a strong sense of purpose in the classroom and while working or studying abroad. In the city of Boston—the ultimate college town—and across the globe, Northeastern students challenge themselves intellectually, investigate career options, participate in community service, and graduate both personally and professionally prepared for their future careers and graduate school.

Founded in 1898, Northeastern is a leader in interdisciplinary research, urban engagement, and the seamless integration of classroom learning with real-world experiences. The academic curriculum is enhanced by experiential learning through research, professional, global, and service experiences. Anchored by the world's largest, most innovative cooperative education program, Northeastern prepares students for a lifetime of achievement. And allows them to make an impact on the world before they graduate.

The current undergraduate enrollment of 17,506 is made up of students of all backgrounds and interests, giving Northeastern its distinctive culture. Students can participate in any of Northeastern's 340 student organizations, join a cultural club, participate in cutting-edge research with faculty from various disciplines, or perform with an award-winning a capella group. They can travel to nearby New Hampshire for a ski club trip, play varsity or club basketball, tutor local children, and more. Students have countless opportunities to make lifelong friendships, to try something brand new—a class, a sport, or a career path—to hone their leadership skills, and have fun. Quiet corners of the campus feel far from city streets and give students a secluded haven to read, write, or relax. The 73-acre campus is dynamic and welcoming, a beautiful stretch of leafy green in the heart of Boston.

LOCATION AND ENVIRONMENT

Northeastern's residential campus is located in the heart of Boston, where the distinctive neighborhoods of the Back Bay, the South End, the Fenway, and Roxbury meet. Over half of the student body lives on campus and many of the residence halls have amazing views of the Boston skyline.

The Back Bay area, known for its many cultural and educational institutions, is just steps away from Symphony Hall, the New England Conservatory of Music, the Museum of Fine Arts, and the Isabella Stewart Gardner Museum. The South End is home to elegant Victorian row houses, a vibrant arts scene, hidden gardens, and some of the finest dining in Boston. The Fenway area, with its beautiful rose garden, bicycle and jogging paths, and Fenway Park (home of the Boston Red Sox) is also just a few blocks away.

MAJORS AND DEGREES OFFERED

Northeastern's academic programs are divided among eight colleges:

The College of Arts, Media and Design awards undergraduate degrees in architecture, art, communication studies, digital art, graphic design, landscape architecture, and journalism; combined majors in cinema studies, game design, and interactive media; as well as music (concentrations in music history and analysis, music industry, and music technology), studio art (in collaboration with the School of the Museum of Fine Arts), and theater (including concentrations in performance and production).

The D'Amore-McKim School of Business offers two degree options: the Bachelor of Science in Business Administration (B.S.B.A.) and the Bachelor of Science in International Business (B.S.I.B.). The B.S.I.B. program includes language instruction and international study and work. The college offers concentrations in accounting, entrepreneurship and innovation, finance and insurance, management, management information systems, marketing, and supply chain management.

The College of Computer and Information Science awards degrees in computer science and information science and also offers combined majors that pair computer science with business, cognitive psychology, game design, mathematics, physics, biology, multimedia arts, music technology, or digital art.

The College of Engineering offers degrees in chemical, civil, computer, electrical, industrial, and mechanical engineering.

The Bouvé College of Health Sciences awards degrees in health sciences, nursing, pharmacy, and speech-language pathology and audiology. The college also offers a six-year Doctor of Pharmacy degree and a six-year program leading to a Doctor of Physical Therapy.

The College of Science awards undergraduate degrees in applied physics, behavioral neuroscience, biochemistry, biology, biomedical physics, chemistry, environmental science, environmental studies, linguistics, mathematics, physics, and psychology.

The College of Social Sciences and Humanities awards undergraduate degrees in African American studies, American Sign Language, Asian studies, criminal justice, cultural anthropology, economics, English, history, human services, international affairs, Jewish studies (combined major only), philosophy, political science, religious studies, sociology, and Spanish.

The Program for Undeclared students offers a wide array of academic opportunities designed to help students who feel strongly about exploring their options before making a commitment to a major. The program provides the support and guidance students need to explore and eventually choose one of Northeastern's undergraduate programs.

ACADEMIC PROGRAMS

At the heart of a Northeastern education are award-winning faculty mentors, a rigorous and innovative curriculum, and undergraduate research and global experiences that challenge and transform. Northeastern's innovative programs encompass a wide range of majors, concentrations, and interdisciplinary studies along with honors, pre-professional, and study-abroad programs.

Northeastern's approach to educating its students integrates a challenging academic curriculum with a variety of experiential learning opportunities including research, global experiences, service learning, and the university's signature cooperative education program (co-op), enabling students to make deep connections between their field of study and the world around them.

After completing their freshman year, Northeastern students integrate classroom learning with six-month periods of full-time, immersive professional work, global study, or research experiences related to their major or interests. Northeastern's flexibility enables students to choose a four- or five-year path with up to eighteen months of experience, strengthening their professional network and giving them confidence—and a significant edge in the job market. Students learn what career is a good fit for them—and what careers are not—all before graduating. In addition, over half of the students are offered full-time jobs from co-op employers.

Northeastern partners with over 2,900 co-op employers around the globe, including some of the world's largest and most reputable companies: Pfizer, John Hancock, Yahoo, Fidelity Investments, IBM, General Electric, Massachusetts General Hospital, Microsoft, and the Boston Globe, just to name a few.

Experiential learning opportunities—including U.S. And international professional co-op, service learning, research, and study abroad—are currently available in 128 countries around the world.

The University Honors Program allows students to participate in enriched educational experiences and offers opportunities that include honors sections of required academic courses, honors seminars, independent research, and specialized study abroad. With broad access to the resources of the university, the University Scholars Program, Northeastern's most prestigious scholarship program, provides Scholars with the opportunity to design a tailored program that potentially spans colleges, departments, and global partner institutions to address each Scholar's unique academic goals and career aspirations, and advance their entrepreneurial ideas.

The university has more than 1,500 full- and part-time faculty members with a wide variety of research and teaching interests and specialties. Academic counselors in each college work closely with students to assist them in developing programs suited to their interests and abilities. Co-op advisers assist students in resumé-building, honing interview skills and tactics, and in developing contacts with businesses and employers to support networking and professional opportunities.

CAMPUS FACILITIES AND EQUIPMENT

Northeastern is home to forty-three research centers and undergraduates have ample opportunities to work alongside their professors to aid and conduct research on a variety of topics.

The university library system is comprised of Snell Library, a 240,000-square-foot central library on the Boston campus, the School of Law Library, and a small supplemental collection at the Nahant Marine Science Center. Snell Library houses almost 900,000 print volumes, 399,488 e-books, 1,332,128 microfilms, and access to 60,270 licensed electronic journals, as well as 23,437 audio, video, and computer software items, and 5,712 linear feet of archival material as of June 2012.

Northeastern University provides a broad range of academic and administrative computer resources to students, faculty, and staff members. Many computing resources are available, including an extensive wireless network, internet connections for all offices and university-owned residence halls, technology-assisted classrooms, computer labs, and the myNEU portal, which allows students to access many administrative and academic functions online.

TUITION, ROOM AND BOARD, AND FEES

For 2014–15, tuition was $42,534, and room and board fees were $14,050. Regardless of time to degree, tuition is charged only while students are earning course credits.

FINANCIAL AID

The university operates a substantial aid program designed to make attendance feasible for all qualified students. By coordinating the resources of the university and various public and private scholarship programs, the Office of Student Financial Services was able to provide more than $204 million in grant and scholarship assistance. About 78 percent of students receive some form of financial aid. Northeastern participates in all federal aid programs. Financial aid is based on need and academic merit and may consist of grants, loans, work-study employment, or any combination of the three. To apply, students must file the Free Application for Federal Student Aid (FAFSA) and a CSS PROFILE form with the college Scholarship Service by the priority filing date of February 15.

ADMISSION REQUIREMENTS

Students may enter the university with advanced credit on the basis of test scores on Advanced Placement (AP) examinations, the International Baccalaureate (I.B.) examinations, or with successful completion of accredited college-level courses. In addition to the application for admission, prospective freshmen must submit official high school transcript(s) (or official GED score reports); official transcripts for any college-level course work taken while a secondary-school student; written recommendations from their secondary school counselor and a teacher; and scores on the SAT (Northeastern's College Board code is 3667) or ACT, including the writing section. Please visit the university's website for additional admission details for specific student populations and transfer admissions requirements (northeastern.edu/admissions).

APPLICATION AND INFORMATION

Admission to Northeastern is selective and competitive. For the freshman class entering in Fall 2015, the university received more than 50,500 applications for 2,800 seats in the freshman class. Students are reviewed in the context of their environment, with attention paid to their academic course selections and rigor, academic achievement, extracurricular involvement and impact, and their potential fit with Northeastern, including the demonstration of personal traits like leadership, adaptability, a global perspective, or an entrepreneurial spirit.

November 1 is the deadline for the early action admission program. For first-year students applying for Fall 2015, Northeastern will also offer a binding early decision program for which the deadline will be November 1. Students who have carefully explored their college options and have decided that Northeastern is where they want to enroll may choose to apply under the early decision program. Also beginning for students entering college in Fall 2015, the deadline for the regular admission program is January 1. Admitted students are required to pay a deposit by May 1 to secure a place in the class. For transfer students, the admissions deadlines are April 1 for fall and October 1 for spring admission. Fall transfer and spring admission decisions are made on a space-available, rolling basis.

Northeastern offers a variety of visit options including information sessions and campus tours. For more information, or to register, visit northeastern.edu/admissions/visitcampus.

For more information, students should contact:

Office of Undergraduate Admissions

240 West Village F

Northeastern University

360 Huntington Avenue

Boston, Massachusetts 02115

Phone: 617-373-2200

E-mail: admissions@neu.edu

Website: http://www.northeastern.edu/admissions

NOTRE DAME COLLEGE

AT A GLANCE

Notre Dame College offers stimulating academics, personalized attention, small class sizes, NCAA Division II intercollegiate athletics and vibrant student life.

Founded in 1922 by the Sisters of Notre Dame, the college has grown strategically to keep pace with the rapidly changing needs of students and the dramatic changes in higher education. But it has never lost sight of its emphasis on teaching students not only how to make a good living but also how to live a good life.

Notre Dame College has rapidly become one of the finest small, Catholic, residential, liberal arts colleges in the Great Lakes region. Founded as an all-women's school, the college became coeducational in 2001. Since 2003, total enrollment has since grown from 875 to 2,029.

A snapshot of the fall 2014 traditional NDC student population shows: 44% female, 56% male; 55% Catholic; 31% minority; 55% student-athletes; and 53% live on campus. The mosaic of NDC students represents 40 states and 23 foreign countries.

Notre Dame offers high quality academic programs in over 30 disciplines with majors housed in five academic divisions: arts and humanities, business, education, nursing and science and math.

MISSION

A Catholic institution in the tradition of the Sisters of Notre Dame, the college educates a diverse population in the liberal arts for personal, professional and global responsibility. The college believes that truly progressive education selectively blends traditional values with new ideas that represent real growth. Within the scope of a career-oriented liberal arts education, students can grow to meet the challenges of the present and the future.

LOCATION

Located in South Euclid, Ohio, the 48-acre campus is in a residential neighborhood just 25 minutes from downtown Cleveland and all the excitement and cultural wealth of the city, such as the Rock and Roll Hall of Fame and Museum, the Cleveland Metroparks, University Circle, several professional sports teams, and one of the richest cultural, theatrical, entertainment, healthcare, and employment regions in the nation. Only five minutes from Legacy Village and Beachwood Place, Cleveland's lifestyle retail centers, the area combines all the opportunities of a major urban and educational center with the relaxed atmosphere of a suburban setting.

The beautiful campus provides the perfect setting for the Clara Fritzsche Library; the historic Administration Building which houses classrooms, labs and offices; Regina Hall and Regina Auditorium; Connelly Center, the dining hall and student center; Keller Center, the recreational and fitness facility; Falcon Café; and five residence halls that accommodate 650 students. Other students commute or reside in nearby off-campus housing.

CAMPUS LIFE

A variety of clubs and activities enrich the overall experience of the 2,000+ students. Campus Ministry promotes the spiritual growth of the college community and facilitates community service, and the award-winning FalconCorps service program provides students opportunities to serve at local charities and national programs such as Habitat for Humanity.

Most on-campus events are free, and students often may purchase tickets at reduced rates for off-campus programs such as performances of the world-famous Cleveland Orchestra, the Cleveland Opera, and road shows of Broadway productions at the Cleveland Play House, the Palace Theatre, the State Theatre, and the Ohio Theatre at Playhouse Square.

ATHLETICS

Notre Dame is an NCAA Division II institution and an associate member of the Mountain East Conference with 22 intercollegiate sports for men and women.

ACADEMICS

The College awards bachelor's degrees in arts and humanities (communication, criminal justice, English, graphic design, history, intelligence studies, political science, public relations, studio art and theology); business (accounting, business administration, finance, human resources, information systems, international business, management, marketing and sports management); education (adolescent, early childhood, middle childhood, mild/moderate intervention specialist and visual arts); nursing (direct entry program) and science and math (biology, chemistry, environmental science and mathematics).

Notre Dame College also offers a Bachelor of Science in Nursing program and an online RN to B.S.N. completion program.

A Master of Education degree is offered with concentrations available in special education, reading, and critical and creative thinking. The college has an online Master of Arts in Security Policy Studies and an online Master's of Science in Nursing.

Teacher licensure is available in early childhood education, middle childhood education, adolescent/young adult education, and multiage for mild/moderate intervention specialist studies. The college is accredited by both the North Central Association of Colleges and Schools and NCATE and is registered for the awarding of State Teachers' Licenses by the State of Ohio Department of Education.

Minors include biblical studies, coaching, computer programming, entrepreneurship, economics, fine arts, health education, performing arts, sociology, Spanish, theater and more.

Concentrations are available in gaming design (graphic design), exercise science (biology), pre-law (English and history), engineering-binary program (math and chemistry), comprehensive biology (biology), biochemistry (chemistry).

A student can also design his or her own major that leads to a bachelor's degree by combining two or three academic areas, such as graphic design, human resource management, and public relations.

The Finn Center for Adult, Graduate, Online and Professional Programs unifies all aspects of adult education at NDC, providing convenient, flexible programs for educational advancement on days, nights, weekends and the Web. Housing the Office of Adult and Graduate Admissions and the Office of Professional Development, the Finn Center offers professional development classes, associate's degrees, bachelor's degrees, post-baccalaureate programs and master's degrees.

For the bachelor's degree, students must earn 128 semester hours of credit, with a minimum cumulative grade point average of 2.0. From 36 to 68 semester hours of credit are required in the major field of study.

Through a cooperative education program, students can earn up to six credit hours for paid or volunteer work experience related to their academic field of study.

Advanced Placement credit is awarded to students who have demonstrated the ability to pursue coursework beyond the level of entering freshmen, as indicated by their scores on the Advanced Placement (AP) or College-Level Examination Program (CLEP) tests of the college Board. College credit is given on the basis of a decision made jointly by the academic dean and the department involved.

FACULTY

The College has 59 full-time faculty members, augmented by highly qualified instructors. Faculty members hold advanced degrees from more than 30 universities in the United States, Canada and Europe.

CAMPUS FACILITIES AND EQUIPMENT

Students with documented learning differences, such as Attention Deficit Disorder (ADD), Attention Deficit Hyperactivity Disorder (ADHD), dyslexia, Asperger's Syndrome and Specific Learning Disabilities (SLD) can enroll in our Academic Support Center to receive comprehensive support services. These include tutoring, academic advising and access to a large array of adaptive equipment. In order to be accepted into the Learning Differences Program, students must first meet the admission requirements of Notre Dame College. To participate in the Academic Support Center, students must submit documentation of a learning disability.

The Career Services Center coordinates cooperative education and internships for students and interacts with faculty to create meaningful programs that link academics to the workplace. It further offers graduate school advising, résumé preparation assistance, interviewing and job search coaching, posting of positions available and a resource library. On-campus recruiting opportunities attract employers to the college to meet with students firsthand.

The Clara Fritzsche Library has a capacity for 100,000 volumes. As a member of OhioLINK, the college also has online access to members throughout the state, with access to more than 31 million library items and more than 90 research databases.

The Dwyer Success Center consists of an electronic classroom, a student computer lab, a writing lab, a test proctoring room and a tutoring room. The writing lab is staffed by English faculty who provide professional writing assistance to students free of charge. The tutoring room is staffed with graduate assistants and upper-class peer tutors for one-on-one study skills and subject specific assistance.

TUITION, ROOM, BOARD AND FEES

For the 2015–16 academic year tuition and fee charges are $27,520. Room and board costs are $9,180 for double occupancy.

FINANCIAL AID

Notre Dame believes that all qualified students should have the opportunity to attend college, and provides need, merit and athletic-based aid to our students. A comprehensive financial assistance program of more than $25 million assists approximately 95 percent of all full-time students. Students applying for aid must submit the Free Application for Federal Student Aid (FAFSA).

ADMISSIONS PROCESS

Notre Dame College admits students who demonstrate potential for success in rigorous academic work. In fulfilling its mission, the college seeks to attract students of diverse religious, racial and economic backgrounds. Candidates for admission as first-time, full-time freshmen are reviewed on an individual basis, and decisions are based on a broad range of criteria. The most important consideration is the candidate's high school performance, as demonstrated by her/his overall grade average, class rank, grade trends and level of courses completed. Aptitude for verbal and mathematical reasoning, as measured by performance on standardized tests, is also considered. In addition, counselor and teacher recommendations are reviewed.

Notre Dame College recommends that students complete at least 16 units of high school credit in academic subjects as a prerequisite for matriculation in the college. The distribution of these subject areas and the units are as follows: English, 4; mathematics, 3 (to include algebra I, geometry and algebra II); science, 3 (with laboratory experience); social studies, 3; foreign language, 2 (from the same language); and fine arts, 1. Applicants should generally rank in the upper half of their high school graduating class and have a minimum average of C+. Either ACT or SAT scores are accepted.

The College has a fair and generous policy on the transfer of academic credit earned within the preceding five years at a regionally accredited college or university. Students wishing to transfer from other regionally accredited colleges and universities are admitted to advanced standing upon presentation of satisfactory evidence of scholarship and character.

Special consideration may be granted to an applicant whose academic preparation is not consistent with the requirements stated above.

Notre Dame College strongly recommends that prospective students schedule an appointment to visit the campus and talk with an admissions counselor.

A free application is available online at NotreDameCollege.edu. The college maintains a rolling admission policy. To apply, students should submit the completed application for undergraduate admission, an official transcript of their high school record and results of the ACT or SAT to:

Office of Admissions

Notre Dame College

4545 College Road

South Euclid, Ohio 44121

Telephone: 877-NDC-OHIO ext. 5355

Fax: 216-373-5278

E-mail: admissions@ndc.edu

Web: NotreDameCollege.edu

PRINCETON UNIVERSITY

AT A GLANCE

Princeton combines the strengths of a major research university with the qualities of an outstanding liberal arts college. The University prepares its 5,200 undergraduates for lives of leadership and service.

Chartered in 1746, Princeton is the fourth-oldest college in the nation. It is a private, non-sectarian university.

LOCATION AND ENVIRONMENT

Princeton is a residential campus set on 500 park-like acres located in the town of Princeton (pop: 30,000) in central New Jersey. Known for its beauty and architectural variety, including the famed "Collegiate Gothic" style of architecture, the campus is home to historic landmarks such as Nassau Hall, which was built in 1756 and played an important role during the American Revolution.

Princeton students enjoy convenient transportation options to New York City and Philadelphia, both only about an hour away by car. Other nearby attractions include numerous parks, cultural venues, and commercial hubs. For arts lovers, the McCarter Theatre is a campus treasure within easy walking distance.

ACADEMICS

Princeton undergraduates pursue either the bachelor of arts (A.B.) or the bachelor of science in engineering (B.S.E.) degree. Students in the A.B. degree program choose a concentration (major) in one of 34 departments in the arts, humanities, social sciences, and natural sciences, including undergraduate programs in the Woodrow Wilson School of Public and International Affairs and the School of Architecture. The B.S.E. degree is granted by the School of Engineering and Applied Science, which has six engineering departments.

Princeton offers doctoral programs in a range of subjects in the humanities, natural sciences, social sciences, School of Architecture, School of Engineering and Applied Science, and within the Woodrow Wilson School of Public and International Affairs.

In addition to their major course of study, students are encouraged to enroll in one or more of the University's 47 interdisciplinary certificate programs, which offer diverse fields of study. For example, a student may wish to concentrate in ecology and evolutionary biology while pursuing a certificate in musical performance.

Undergraduates benefit from small class sizes, a 6-to-1 student-to-faculty ratio, and one-on-one advising with faculty, particularly while working on independent projects such as the junior paper and senior thesis. The university's 1,148 faculty members are leaders in their disciplines, and it is not uncommon for students to receive classroom instruction from a Nobel laureate, Pulitzer Prize winner, or MacArthur fellow. During their freshman year, students are introduced to many of Princeton's notable faculty through the freshman seminars program, which offers small discussion-focused classes on a variety of topics. One such freshman seminar may cover the art and science of motorcycle design; another may explore the qualities that make a poem endure.

Students are encouraged to bring a multidisciplinary approach to their studies, synthesizing what they discover in different classes and through their own research. This approach may be informal, based on a student's particular avenue of study, or it may be more formally structured, such as with the integrated science curriculum that combines the study of physics, mathematics, computer science, and molecular biology.

A global perspective is emphasized across the curriculum, with special opportunities such as the Study Abroad Program and the Princeton Institute for International and Regional Studies. Global summer internships are available through the International Internship Program and the Princeton Environmental Institute Summer Internship Program. A relatively recent initiative, the Bridge Year Program, allows selected students to delay the start of their freshman year to engage in nine months of University-sponsored service abroad.

FACILITIES AND EQUIPMENT

Academic support services include academic advising centered in each of the six residential colleges (for A.B. students) and in the engineering school (for B.S.E. students); the McGraw Center, which offers workshops and individual consultations with students as they evolve as scholars; and the Writing Program, which strengthens students' writing skills through a required seminar. Ongoing tutoring sessions also are available at the program's Writing Center.

Throughout their undergraduate careers, Princeton students are supported by a range of first-rate academic resources, including libraries, laboratories, and one of the leading university art museums in the country. The largest library on campus, Firestone Library, contains more than 70 miles of shelving and a vast range of electronic resources. The Peter B. Lewis Library, designed by renowned architect Frank Gehry, offers impressive print and digital collections in the sciences. In the past several years, new initiatives in African American studies and neuroscience have resulted in expanded activities.

A new state-of-art and environmentally sustainable science facility houses the chemistry department and provides laboratory space for research and teaching. A new neuroscience and psychology building recently opened, and the new andlinger Center for Energy and the Environment is scheduled to open in 2015.

Numerous venues for the arts as well as a range of athletic facilities also are available.

TUITION AND FEES

Estimated cost of attendance for 2013–14

Tuition: $41,820

Room charge: $7,570

Board rate: $6,050

Estimated miscellaneous expenses (books, supplies, laundry, telephone, recreation, etc.): $3,525

Total: $58,965

FINANCIAL AID

Princeton offers one of the strongest need-based financial aid programs in the country, ensuring that all qualified students, regardless of financial need, can afford to attend. There is no income cutoff on Princeton's aid application; any family who feels the need for financial assistance is welcome to apply for aid.

Since 2001, when Princeton initiated its landmark no-loan financial aid program, the university has been a leader in changing the face of financial aid policy. Central to the program is Princeton's groundbreaking "no-loan" policy; the university offers every aid recipient a financial aid package that replaces loans with grant aid that students do not pay back.

If admitted, applicants can be confident that their financial need, as determined by Princeton's aid office, will be met. Today, about 60 percent of undergraduates receive aid, compared with 38 percent more than a decade ago. As a result, Princeton has been able to enroll growing numbers of students from low- and middle-income backgrounds. About 75 percent of students graduate without debt, and those who choose to borrow for additional expenses, such as a laptop computer, graduate with an average debt of $5,500. The average aid package for the Class of 2018 was $44,700, which exceeds the cost of tuition.

CAMPUS LIFE

Princeton is a residential campus that provides a close-knit living environment for its undergraduates. Through its six residential colleges, students pursue a host of recreational and academic activities. The residential colleges also serve as home base for academic advising for students, who learn about all that the university has to offer from faculty and staff advisers, peer mentors, and fellow students.

With more than 300 student organizations, as well as an extensive calendar of cultural and athletic events, students find it easy to pursue their interests or explore new ones. The Frist Campus Center serves as the hub of campus life, and is home to the Women's Center, the Davis International Center, the LGBT Center, the Pace Center for Civic Engagement, and the Undergraduate Student Government, as well as many other student clubs and organizations.

For many students, social life at Princeton includes becoming a member of an eating club. The 10 historic eating clubs are open to juniors and seniors and are run independently of the university. Fraternities and sororities are not recognized as official student organizations on campus.

Princeton is an NCAA Division I school. The university offers 38 varsity sports and 36 club teams. Each year more than 1,000 students participate in intercollegiate varsity and junior varsity sports. In any given year, more than half of Princeton's varsity athletic teams compete in national championships. In recent years, Princeton teams have won national titles in lacrosse, rowing, fencing, track and field, and squash. The women's basketball team finished its 2014–15 regular season with an unprecedented 30-0 record.

ADMISSIONS

Princeton's admission process goes beyond simply looking for academically accomplished students. For each freshman class, Princeton brings together a varied mix of high-achieving, intellectually gifted students from diverse backgrounds to create an exceptional learning community. American minorities comprise about 41 percent of the undergraduate student body, and students from nearly 100 countries are represented.

Princeton cares about what students have accomplished in and out of the classroom. The admission process is highly selective. In 2014, the university offered admission to 7.4 percent of applicants for the class of 2018.

Students applying to Princeton are asked to describe their talents, academic accomplishments, and personal achievements. A transcript and recommendations also are required. To be considered for admission to Princeton, students must submit the results of the SAT Reasoning Test or ACT (with Writing, where offered). In addition, all applicants must submit the results of two different SAT Subject Tests. The university accepts both online and paper applications. Princeton does not accept transfer students.

Under Princeton's admission policy, need for financial aid is not in any way a disadvantage. Princeton welcomes applications from talented students of diverse economic backgrounds.

QUINNIPIAC UNIVERSITY

AT A GLANCE

Quinnipiac, founded in 1929, is a private, co-educational, non-sectarian university located in a uniquely attractive New England setting in Hamden, CT and nearby North Haven. Quinnipiac's mission is to provide a supportive and stimulating environment for the intellectual and personal growth of its 6500 undergraduate and 2300 graduate, law and medical students.

The university offers broadly based undergraduate programs together with graduate programs in selected professional fields. At the undergraduate level, through integrated liberal arts and professional curricula, programs in the Schools of Business and Engineering, Communications, Health Sciences, Nursing, and the college of Arts and Sciences prepare students for career entry or advanced studies. Graduate programs are designed to provide professional qualifications for success in business, education, health sciences, nursing, communications, social work, medicine and law. Several are offered online.

An education at Quinnipiac embodies the university's commitment to three important values: excellence in education, a student-centered campus, and a spirit of community. The entire university shares a service orientation toward students and their needs. Its collegial atmosphere fosters a strong sense of community, identity and purpose among faculty, staff and students.

LOCATION AND ENVIRONMENT

Hamden, Connecticut: 8 miles north of New Haven, midway between Boston and New York City. Quinnipiac is a suburban campus with 600 acres on three sites. The Mount Carmel Campus is adjacent to Sleeping Giant State Park, with 1,700 acres of trails for hiking and walking. A campus shuttle system provides easy access to theaters, shopping, museums, sports, recreation and a variety of dining and entertainment options in Hamden and New Haven. The nearby York Hill Campus is home to the TD Bank Sports Center with twin arenas for basketball and ice hockey, "Rocky Top" a lodge-like student/recreation center, plus suite-style residence halls with single and double rooms, kitchens and common living areas, which accommodate 1500 students. The North Haven Campus, 100 acres, just 4 miles away, provides upper-level and graduate students programs in Health Sciences, Nursing, Education, Social Work, Medicine, and Law.

Students from 30 states and 30 countries study at Quinnipiac. Ninety-five percent of the incoming 1800 freshmen choose to live on campus. Housing options include traditional residence halls, suites, and suites with kitchens. Freshmen and sophomores generally live on the Mt. Carmel campus; juniors and seniors live on the York Hill campus and in university-owned houses and an apartment complex.

Driving time to Quinnipiac from Boston or New York City is about two hours. Metro-North and Amtrak provide train service to New Haven's Union Station, which is 15 minutes from campus.

All programs at Quinnipiac offer an excellent combination of classroom learning with internships or clinical experiences. Students in business, engineering, communications, and liberal arts and sciences intern at nearby corporations, health care agencies, or media outlets. Students in health sciences and nursing are placed in clinical affiliations as part of their course work.

Career Services in each School provides assistance with résumé writing, interview skills and job placement. A survey of recent graduates indicated that close to 90 percent were either employed or in graduate school within six months of graduation. Each year about half of students in internships are offered permanent jobs as a result of their work.

Students can take advantage of study abroad opportunities during the academic year or summer months (3.0 cumulative GPA required.) Program sites include: Ireland, Australia, Austria, Czech Republic, England, France, Spain, Italy, Netherlands, Russia, South Africa, and Spain, to name a few, and through affiliates such as AIFS, API, and Semester at Sea. Study abroad is an experience of a lifetime allowing you to live in a different country for a period of time while earning credits at your home institution.

OFF-CAMPUS OPPORTUNITIES

Quinnipiac is a suburban campus with easy access to nearby shopping, restaurant and activities offered in Hamden, New Haven and North Haven. Students, facult and staff are involved in community service through the "Big Event" held eac April. Local community service opportunities also include Habitat for Humanit and tutoring in the elementary schools.

MAJORS AND DEGREES OFFERED

Undergraduate students can choose from more than 58 majors through the School of Business and Engineering, Communications, Health Sciences, Nursing, Edu cation and the college of Arts and Sciences. About 35% of all entering freshme remain at Quinnipiac through their graduate degree program.

Graduate students specialize in law, business, organizational leadership, healt management, computer information systems, journalism, interactive media, sport journalism, public relations, education, social work, and health science programs fo physician assistant, pathologists' assistant, occupational therapy, physical therap medical and laboratory sciences, molecular and cell biology, radiologist assistan and nursing. Several are offered online.

ACADEMIC PROGRAMS

The School of Business and Engineering majors include: accounting, biomedica marketing, computer information systems, entrepreneurship, finance, internationa business, management, marketing as well as civil, mechanical, industrial and softwar engineering. The Lender School of Business Center has case method classroom a high-tech Financial Technology Center 'trading room' and team study rooms fo project work. An innovative 4 year BS/MBA invites academically strong student to complete two degrees in four years. (AACSB accredited)

The Schools of Health Sciences and Nursing majors include: athletic training, bio medical science, diagnostic medical sonography, radiologic science, health scienc studies, microbiology/immunology, nursing, occupational therapy (5 1/2 -year fresh men entry-level BS/MOT Master's program), physician assistant (6-year freshme entry-level BS/MHS Master's program), physical therapy (6- or 7-year freshme entry-level BS/DPT Doctorate). The North Haven facility offers cutting-edge lab including a diagnostic imaging suite, orthopedics lab, model adaptive apartmen clinical skills labs, intensive care unit, pediatric/neonatal lab, gross anatomy lab clinical simulation labs and biomechanics lab.

The College of Arts and Sciences majors include: behavioral neuroscience, biolog biochemistry, chemistry, economics, English, computer science, criminal justic game design and development, gerontology, history, legal studies, mathematics, ph losophy, political science, psychology, social services, sociology, Spanish and theate

The School of Communications majors include: film, television and interactive art interactive digital design, advertising, journalism, communications/media studie and public relations. The Ed McMahon Center for Mass Communications provide a high-tech facility with a digital high-definition television production studio, new technology center, audio production studio, and editing suites. Students also ma study for a semester in Los Angeles, combining classes with an internship.

For those interested in teaching, completion of an undergraduate major in liberal arts or natural sciences, combined with junior and senior year courses in the School of Education, ending with a fifth year full-time graduate study, culminates in the Master of Arts in Teaching degree.

A pre-med program is designed to provide the undergraduate student interested in a career as a health professional the appropriate background necessary to meet the entrance requirements of a variety of medical schools. Quinnipiac's own Frank H. Netter MD School of Medicine emphasizes family practice, global health and rehabilitative medicine.

CAMPUS FACILITIES AND EQUIPMENT
Quinnipiac offers the latest campus and academic technology, which is reflected in its facilities, services and programs. The entire campus and residential areas offer a security-enhanced wireless network. All incoming students must bring or purchase a university-recommended laptop computer for use in the classroom and residence halls. Service is provided through technology centers on each campus.

Academic life focuses on the Bernhard Library, open 24 x 7 during the fall and spring semesters. Automated library systems, wireless technology, 60 public computers and 600 power/data connections are located throughout the library, along with individual study carrels and team study rooms.

The Learning Commons offers free academic tutoring as well as sessions to improve study techniques, writing skills and research methods. Quinnipiac's Writing Across the Curriculum program is designed to help students develop strong critical thinking and communication skills through writing. Essential Learning Outcomes (ELOs) have been identified that broaden students' knowledge and engage them in the educational process.

The University Honors Program fosters the needs and interests of our most academically talented and committed students. Service Learning courses integrate meaningful community service with instruction and reflection to enrich the learning experience, teach civic responsibility and strengthen communities.

TUITION, ROOM, BOARD, AND FEES
Costs for 2015–16: Tuition & fees $42,270, Room & Board $14,820.

FINANCIAL AID
The Quinnipiac University Office of Financial Aid works with all applicants to assure that they receive the maximum state and federal aid for which they are eligible. Families are encouraged to file the FAFSA for federal student aid (code: 001402) and the CSS Profile for Quinnipiac grant aid (code: 3712). The University also offers merit-based scholarships to incoming freshmen (fall semester). No additional application is necessary for scholarship consideration; recipients are notified by the admissions office. If you have any questions, please contact the Office of Financial Aid at (203) 582-8750 or (800) 462-1944, or e-mail: finaid@quinnipiac.edu.

STUDENT ORGANIZATIONS AND ACTIVITIES
Quinnipiac University has more than 120 student clubs and organizations including student government, newspaper, yearbook, radio station, service organizations, community activities, religious fellowships, diversity awareness (Black Student Union, Latino Cultural Society, Asian and Pacific Islander Association), dance and drama productions, and Greek life, along with numerous recreation activities, providing a balanced college experience. An active Intramural program has team competition in more than 30 sports and activities.

Quinnipiac Bobcats:

www.quinnipiacbobcats.com

The Division I athletic program in 21 sports includes Men: basketball, baseball, cross country, lacrosse, ice hockey, tennis, and soccer. Women: acrobatics & tumbling, basketball, softball, cross country and track (indoor and outdoor), field hockey, golf, ice hockey, lacrosse, rugby, soccer, tennis and volleyball. Quinnipiac competes in the MAAC (Metro Atlantic Athletic Conference) in most sports and the ECAC in men's and women's ice hockey.

Athletic facilities include a multi-purpose gymnasium, two fully-equipped fitness centers, dance/yoga studios, tennis courts, a 24,000-square-foot recreation center with an indoor track, and a sports center with twin 3500-seat arenas for ice hockey and basketball.

ADMISSIONS PROCESS
High school students should begin applying for admissions early in their senior year. Visit www.quinnipiac.edu/apply for application information. Quinnipiac is a member of the Common Application. A completed application consists of the application form, official high school transcript, SAT I test scores (QU SAT code: 3712) or ACT scores (QU ACT code: 0582) senior year, first-quarter grades, essay, and one letter of recommendation. Students are asked to supply official SAT and/or ACT test scores. The University will select the highest (critical reading plus math or ACT composite) scores for admission or merit aid.

Quinnipiac reviews applications on a 'rolling admissions' basis but also offers an Early Decision option for freshmen applicants. Early Decision students must file their application by November 1. The admissions office begins reviewing applications as soon as they are complete, and begins notifying students of admission decisions in early December. Students applying for the physical therapy, nursing and physician assistant programs should apply by November 15. For all other applicants, February 1 is the recommended deadline.

All programs subscribe to the nationally recognized candidate reply date of May 1. Waitlisted students who indicate an interest in being considered if spaces become available will be notified as soon after May 1 as possible. In general, Quinnipiac admits between 55–60% of its applicants.

Transfer students who have or will receive an associate's degree prior to entrance are not required to provide high school transcripts and SAT results. We must receive transcripts of all courses taken at other colleges. The physician assistant and physical therapy programs are not available to transfer students.

To schedule an interview, tour, group information session or register for an open house, go to http://www.quinnipiac.edu/visit/. For questions, email admissions@quinnipiac.edu or call 800-462-1944 or 203-582-8600. www.quinnipiac.edu.

RAMAPO COLLEGE OF NEW JERSEY

AT A GLANCE

Ramapo College of New Jersey is a comprehensive institution of higher education dedicated to the promotion of teaching and learning within a strong liberal arts based curriculum, thus earning the designation "New Jersey's Public Liberal Arts College." Its curricular emphases include the liberal arts and sciences, social sciences, fine and performing arts, and professional programs such as business, nursing, and teacher certification, within a residential and sustainable living and learning environment.

Ramapo College provides academic excellence through its interdisciplinary curriculum, international education, intercultural understanding and experiential learning opportunities. These four pillars, supported by global partnerships established in Europe, Africa, Asia, South America, the Caribbean, and several Native American tribal communities, have become central themes in Ramapo College's excellence in the teaching and learning continuum.

Ramapo College provides students with individual academic attention and social support within a caring, sensitive and intellectually vigorous community. The college provides service and leadership opportunities for students and faculty through a combination of internships, field placements, community service, study abroad, and cooperative education. These opportunities allow students, faculty and staff to encounter the world beyond the campus.

Ramapo College is committed to maintaining strength and opportunity through diversity of age, race, gender, sexual orientation, ethnicity, and economic background among faculty, staff, and students. Ramapo College is a selective institution committed to providing equal access to under-represented populations. Barrier-free, the college maintains a continuing commitment to persons with disabilities.

Ramapo College provides a rich living and learning environment through over one hundred student organizations, intramural sports, and intercollegiate athletics. The college maintains a strong positive and economic impact on the surrounding communities by partnering with area communities, corporations, schools, service organizations, and governmental entities, while sharing its intellectual and cultural resources and its facilities. Ramapo College of New Jersey is committed to providing service and ethical leadership through international understanding and the creation of 21st century partnerships.

LOCATION AND ENVIRONMENT

Set on approximately 300 wooded acres with a stunning mountain backdrop, the Ramapo College campus is one of the most picturesque suburban environments in American higher education. Enhancing these tranquil surroundings is the knowledge that the campus is approximately 30 miles from the nation's cultural Mecca, New York City.

A magnificent turn-of-the-century mansion sits among state-of-the-art academic buildings, residence halls, and other facilities. The campus is centrally located near county and state parks, skiing and recreation areas, as well as activities such as riding, hiking and camping. Major highways bring you right to Ramapo's doorstep.

Once on campus, Ramapo's barrier-free facilities make accessibility to all buildings, classrooms, residence halls, dining and recreation areas easy.

OFF-CAMPUS OPPORTUNITIES

As a progressive college with a vigilant eye to the future, Ramapo combines a comprehensive curriculum with opportunities for working partnerships in business and industry. It is these factors which help graduates develop the solid foundation of knowledge and skills, abilities and values required to be productive members of tomorrow's society.

Ramapo College's internships and cooperative education program has consistently provided a distinct advantage to Ramapo graduate school applicants and job-seekers. The percentage of Ramapo graduates who obtain entrance to graduate and professional schools has been lauded as comparable to the nation's most elite colleges. Many of these graduates point to the experiential aspect of their college preparation as a principal factor in their admission to highly ranked, prestigious graduate programs. Employers such as American Home Products, Becton Dickinson, Google, IBM, MTV, Withum Smith+Brown, Sanyo, Sharp, and Sony, among thousands of others, seek Ramapo graduates because they know a Ramapo degree represents completion of work experience in the field as well as a rigorous academic curriculum.

MAJORS AND DEGREES OFFERED

The College offers the following degrees: Bachelor of Arts, Bachelor of Science, Bachelor of Social Work, Bachelor of Science in Nursing, Bachelor of Science in Clinical Laboratory Science, Bachelor of Science in Biology/Doctor of Physical Therapy, Bachelor of Science in Biology/Master of Science in Physician Assistant (joint degree programs with Rutgers Biomedical and Health Sciences), Bachelor of Science/Doctor of Chiropractic (joint degree program with New York Chiropractic College); Bachelor of Science/Doctor of Optometry (join degree program with SUNY College of Optometry), Master of Arts in Liberal Studies, Master of Science in Educational Technology, Master of Arts in Sustainability Studies, Master of Arts in Special Education, Master of Arts in Educational Leadership, Masters in Business Administration, Master of Science in Nursing (Nursing Education) and a Master of Social Work.

ACADEMIC PROGRAMS

At Ramapo, a "liberating" education means student's gain the means to acquire the knowledge, skills, abilities, and values to seek both general and expert knowledge and expand their views of humanity in a multicultural setting.

Ramapo's curriculum provides a balance between practical and theoretical knowledge. The curriculum and support programs foster the acquisition of knowledge and skills related to individual programs of study and, ultimately, to future careers.

To strengthen the college background before concentrating on major courses for a degree, students are required to complete an all-college general education program consisting of courses in English, mathematics, the humanities, social sciences, and natural sciences.

All students are assigned an academic advisor during their first semester, allowing the choice of major to be made by the end of the sophomore year (with the exception of Nursing and Biology). There is ample time to explore several fields of interest before selecting a major.

CAMPUS FACILITIES AND EQUIPMENT

The campus features new and upgraded facilities that enhance all areas of campus life, including a library with electronic research facilities; a student life building with FM radio station, student offices, cafeteria, and entertainment and meeting rooms; housing for over 3,000 students; and modern academic buildings with 24-hour computer labs and a real-time Global Financial Market Trading Laboratory. The Angelica and Russ Berrie Center for Performing and Visual Arts offers Shakespearean and Broadway theatres, fine arts studios, art galleries, photography suite, and new music recording studio. The Bill Bradley Sports and Recreation Center features a 1,500-seat arena, fitness center, 25-meter pool, climbing wall, jogging track, and locker room facilities. Other key campus facilities include the Salameno Spirituality Center, established in 2009; the Marge Roukema Center for International Education and Entrepreneurship, and the Sharp Sustainability Center. Set for completion in the fall 2015 semester the Adler Center for Nursing Excellence will add new, technologically advanced microbiology labs, classrooms, a student lounge and study areas.

TUITION, ROOM, BOARD AND FEES

Undergraduate tuition and tuition related fees are calculated on a flat rate for full-time (12 or more credits) students. Full-time charges are calculated on a flat rate between 12-18 credits. The flat rate amount is based on 16 credits. If a full-time student takes more than 18 credits, the charges are calculated on the flat rate plus the per credit rate. The rates as follows are for the 2014–2015 academic year:

Per Credit Rate/Semester Flat Rate (In-State): $418.35/$6,694.00

Per Credit Rate/Semester Flat Rate (Out-of-State): $688.65/$11,019.00

Per Credit Rate/Semester Flat Rate (Qualified Rockland County College Graduates): $554.00/$8,864.00

FINANCIAL AID

About 40 percent of Ramapo's students receive more than $15 million in aid. This aid includes grants - funds which the students are awarded but don't have to pay back - and loans, which must be repaid. Students also can receive a work-study job to earn money to help pay for school.

Applying for Financial Aid:

To apply for aid at Ramapo, students should complete the Free Application for Federal Student Aid (FAFSA) and mail it by March 1. No other application forms are required. By complying with this priority deadline, students will be notified by April 1 about their expected aid package. The FAFSA is usually available from any high school after January 1, or may be found on-line at www.fafsa.ed.gov. Applicants should use Ramapo's school code (009344) when filing.

Transfer students must initiate a school code change on the Student Aid Report (SAR) to ensure that their account will be appropriately credited. Students should begin this process at the time of application. Contact Ramapo's Financial Aid Office at (201) 684-7549.

STUDENT ORGANIZATIONS AND ACTIVITIES

Arriving on campus amid a scenic summer landscape, students quickly realize that life at Ramapo includes a warm environment blending a diverse campus community that serves as a catalyst for study, friendship and discovery.

There is a firm belief that learning occurs both inside and outside the classroom. Both commuting and residential students have a wide variety of activities, organizations, and experiences from which to choose.

Participation enables students to become more involved with the inner workings of the campus community. Serving together with administrators, faculty members and staff, students play direct roles in planning and implementing a variety of college activities. Whatever the interest, Ramapo has an outlet to match it.

ADMISSIONS PROCESS

Each year Ramapo College welcomes about 900 freshmen and 700 transfer students, primarily from the Mid-Atlantic and Northeast regions and from many foreign countries. You may apply online at www.ramapo.edu/admissions/apply.html. Ramapo College is a member of the Common Application and also has its own web based application.

Ramapo College practices a holistic review process. Each application is evaluated individually with emphasis placed on academic achievement in high school and standardized test scores.

Ramapo College offers binding Early Decision for students who know Ramapo College is their number one choice. Early Decision applicants must apply by November 1st and will receive their decision by December 15th.

Students who are applying to the Nursing or Biology program must apply by December 15th. The priority deadline for merit scholarship consideration for all majors is also December 15th. The supporting documents and credential deadline (date by which Ramapo College must be receipt of your documents, including transcript, test scores, recommendation letters, and EOF questionnaire, if applicable) is January 15th.

Students wishing to apply for all other majors not for priority admission may apply by March 1st. All supporting documents must be received by March 15th. All decisions for completed applications will be sent by April 1st.

Scholarships

Ramapo College of New Jersey offers a variety of merit based scholarships for students who have excelled academically. Scholarship awards include the Academic Achievement Award ($12,000), the Deans Award ($24,000), Provost's Award ($40,000) and Presidential Scholarship ($72,000) and are disbursed over the duration of four years.

Please note all applications received by December 15th are automatically reviewed for our prestigious academic scholarships. As such, all high school seniors are encouraged to apply early.

Applications

A completed application for freshmen admission includes: high school transcript, SAT or ACT scores, at least one letter of recommendation, application, essay, and $60 application fee. Transfer students are encouraged to review our website for application information specific to the amount of credits they hold and program of interest.

If you have a General Equivalency Diploma (GED), you must submit an official copy of your test scores. Prospective full-time students with a GED are still required to take the SAT. The Test of English as a Foreign Language (TOEFL) is required of all international students and is recommended for all students who have resided in the United States fewer than four years.

Ramapo College seeks the very best students for its Educational Opportunity Fund (EOF) Program. If you qualify, you will join a community of achievers who are supported by a partnership between the college and EOF that is outstanding not only in financial assistance to cover your college cost, but also in personal and academic counseling, career planning, and leadership training. Your admission to the Ramapo College EOF program depends upon meeting our financial eligibility requirements and academic standards.

Application Deadlines:

Early Decision: November 1st

December 15th: Biology, Nursing, Lab Sciences, Merit Scholarships°

March 1st: All other programs

If you have any questions, please e-mail us at admissions@ramapo.edu.

REED COLLEGE

AT A GLANCE

Intellectual. Free-thinking. Laid back. Classical. Iconoclastic. Paradoxical. Liberal. College guides grapple to define the Reed College experience, but they tend to agree that Reed is one of the most distinctive colleges in the nation. Reed attracts serious students; always engaged and often engrossed in a demanding, exhilarating educational adventure, "Reedies" thrive on a mix of classical study, critical analysis, and guided inquiry that rewards creativity, independence, and reflection. Classes are small, faculty are highly accessible, and students adhere to an honor principle both inside and outside the classroom.

Reed recruits nationally, with strong representation from California, the Pacific Northwest, and the East Coast. The student body is also composed of 8 percent international students. Reed ranks second among U.S. liberal arts colleges in percentage of graduates going on to earn doctoral degrees and fourth among all institutions of higher education. The breadth, depth, and rigor of the curriculum provide great preparation for nearly any career. Many Reed alumni found or lead companies and organizations, earn medical or law degrees, write books or create works of art, and work to make life on the planet better for all.

LOCATION AND ENVIRONMENT

Talk about the best of both worlds! Located in a quiet residential neighborhood is a 116-acre campus of verdant lawns, winding paths, statuesque trees, a wooded natural wetland preserve, and a spring-fed lake frequented by migratory birds and other wildlife. Reed is a short bicycle, bus, and soon light rail ride, from the energy and excitement of downtown Portland, which is widely cited as the nation's most livable urban center. Portland boasts a wealth of diverse cultural, entertainment, shopping, and dining opportunities in an environment characterized by a combination of youthful exuberance and Pacific Northwest nonchalance. The Oregon Coast is 90 minutes to the west and Mt. Hood 90 minutes to the east where Reed has its own ski cabin.

On the campus itself, century-old brick Tudor gothic buildings are interspersed with newer traditionally designed and remodeled facilities. The library, classrooms, and laboratories resonate with the history of decades of inquiry and discovery, supported with modern technology. Extensive facility expansion and renovation financed by a $112 million development campaign increased the overall square footage of Reed's buildings by almost 30 percent and added seven acres of contiguous property to the northwest corner of the campus. For those who want it, housing on campus in one of the 23 residence halls is all but guaranteed for all four years, because a healthy percentage of Reed students enjoy living in Portland neighborhoods near campus.

OFF-CAMPUS OPPORTUNITIES

Reed undergraduates may participate in a number of domestic exchange and study abroad opportunities. Domestic programs include: Howard University in Washington, D.C.; Sarah Lawrence College in New York; and Sea Education Association in Massachusetts. In addition, Reed provides study-abroad opportunities for students in Australia, Argentina, China, Costa Rica, Cuba, Ecuador, Egypt, France, Germany, Greece, Hungary, Ireland, Israel, Italy, Morocco, Kenya, Lebanon, Palestine, Russia, South Africa, Spain, Turks and Caicos, and the United Kingdom. Students may also arrange independent study plans in consultation with appropriate faculty members.

MAJORS AND DEGREES OFFERED

Reed confers the bachelor of arts degree in 35 traditional academic departments and interdisciplinary combinations across a wide selection of fields. Approval of an interdisciplinary program (linking two or more disciplines) is reviewed by the student's adviser and the departments concerned.

Reed offers a number of 3-2 (dual degree) programs; these allow undergraduates to earn a three-year bachelor's degree from Reed, then earn a professional degree in engineering, computer science, or forestry from a cooperating institution (Cal Tech, Columbia, Duke, RPI, the University of Washington) in two additional years.

ACADEMIC PROGRAMS

The curriculum at Reed is both demanding and wide-ranging. Through required studies, Reed students receive a solid grounding in the liberal arts and sciences.

All freshmen must complete Humanities 110, a survey of Greek, Roman, and other Mediterranean scholars from Homer to Petronius. Distribution requirements set a substantial portion of a student's curriculum for the first two years at Reed. Freshmen and sophomores must complete two courses in each of the four major divisions of the college. Beyond Humanities 110, no specific courses are required; students are free to pursue their interests within the boundaries of the requirements.

Reed juniors take a comprehensive qualifying exam in their major, to allow faculty members the chance to evaluate and assist in the student's readiness for his or her senior thesis project. The required senior thesis is the capstone experience of a Reed education. Every senior produces an original independent research project over the course of the final year.

Reed strongly believes that learning should be undertaken for its own sake, not for the sake of letter grades. Accordingly, students do not receive grade reports unless they wish to. A student's transcript does include letter grades for all courses taken, but students can better gauge their progress through professors' written evaluations of their work and one-on-one meetings with faculty. Most prefer this system, which greatly reduces competition among students and allows them to focus on the content of their academic work.

FACILITIES AND EQUIPMENT

The Reed College campus was established on a tract of land known in 1910 as Crystal Springs Farm. The social center of the college is the Gray Campus Center. It includes a commons building, student union, kitchen, dining room, private meeting rooms, student activities offices, bookstore, and mail services. In a park-like setting near the heart of the city, the rolling lawns and open spaces of Reed's 116-acre campus include some of the largest and finest specimen trees in the Portland area.

At the physical center of campus is the canyon, a beautiful wooded upland surrounding a spring-fed lake and emergent marsh. A walking trail around the lake provides numerous opportunities to observe migratory birds and other woodland wildlife. The college recently built a fish passageway that creates a link from the upper Reed Lake area to the Crystal Springs stream below.

In fall 2013, Reed opened a new $28-million Performing Arts Building, representing a major step forward in the college's commitment to the important role the arts have played throughout Reed's first 100 years. For the first time in Reed's history, the departments of music, dance, and theatre are housed in one building that includes rehearsal and performance space, offices, scene and costume studios, collaborative spaces, and a multimedia lab.

Housing at Reed includes traditional residence halls, as well as theme dorms, co-ops, and language houses.

TUITION, ROOM & BOARD, AND FEES

Tuition for the 2014–2015 academic year is $47,500. A $260 student body fee is added. Room and board is an additional $12,200, bringing the yearly total cost to $59,960.

FINANCIAL AID

Reed College funds 100% of the demonstrated need for its incoming students and continuing students who maintain good academic standing and who meet all other requirements of the aid process (such as application deadlines). The college maintains a need-based assistance program that allows students of all economic backgrounds to attend the college. For the 2013-14 academic year, the average financial aid package – including grants, loans, and work opportunities—was approximately $35,365. Reed students' average graduating loan debt for all four years is $19,407, well below the national average. The college is the primary source of grant money for its students. Reed also administers federal grants and a number of other awards. Students may take Perkins Loans and other federally subsidized loans; campus employment and work-study programs also figure into many aid packages. Roughly 50% of Reed undergraduates receive financial aid.

STUDENT ORGANIZATIONS AND ACTIVITIES

Reed maintains inclusivity in all organizations and activities, so the college has no fraternities or sororities and no NCAA or NAIA athletic teams (more about sports below). All campus organizations are student-created and student-run. Student organizations must lobby the Student Senate for funding annually, after which the Senate oversees a vote in which the entire student body decides what organizations should be funded. Thus, the number and nature of campus organizations at Reed changes every year to meet current student interests. Instead of NCAA or NAIA competition, students participate in sports on an informal basis. Intramural sports and club sports proliferate in basketball, fencing, rugby, sailing, soccer, squash and ultimate Frisbee. A three-semester physical education requirement underscores the importance of physical fitness and the balance of healthy mind and body.

ADMISSION PROCESSES AND REQUIREMENTS

Reed seeks students who demonstrate a commitment to learning and to the ideals embodied by a rigorous and stimulating liberal arts education. Freshman and transfer applications are welcome. The ideal incoming class is diverse in its range of talents, interests, ethnic and socioeconomic backgrounds, and perspectives, and comprised of students who share a common passion for academic inquiry. The admission committee places most emphasis on an applicant's record of previous academic accomplishment. Successful applicants have pursued a rigorous secondary school curriculum that includes honors and advanced courses and typically includes 4 years of English, at least 3 years of a foreign or classical language, 3 to 4 years of mathematics, 3 to 4 years of science, and 3 to 4 years of history or social studies. Because secondary school curricula vary widely in quality and content, Reed sets no fixed requirements in this area.

With rare exceptions, incoming students have obtained a secondary school diploma prior to enrollment. The admissions committee sets no "cutoff points" for high school grades, college grades (for transfer students), or standardized test scores. Reed seeks candidates who demonstrate excellence of character, motivation, intellectual curiosity, individual responsibility, and social consciousness. The admission committee recognizes the importance of creating a diverse community in which individual differences contribute to the vitality of the campus. Reed strongly recommends a personal interview, especially for Early Decision candidates, but an interview is not required. Early Decision applications should arrive at Reed by November 15 (Option 1) or December 20 (Option 2). Early Decision at Reed is binding: students who are accepted under Early Decision are expected to matriculate. The deadline for regular freshman admission applications is January 15. Transfer candidates should apply no later than March 1.

REGIS COLLEGE

Regis College is a multifaceted, Catholic university in Greater Boston with 2,000 undergraduate, graduate and doctoral students in the arts, sciences and health professions devoted to engagement, service and advancement in a global community.

AT A GLANCE

We believe that learning happens best in a setting that values the individual—a place where dedicated professors, experiential learning, academic support, and opportunities for leadership and service enable a student to thrive on campus, in the greater community, and in the world. It's a philosophy that dates back to the college's founding by the Sisters of St. Joseph of Boston in 1927.

LOCATION AND ENVIRONMENT

From the moment you turn onto the tree-lined driveway, you will sense that Regis is a special place where you can experience the best of both worlds—a closely knit, small-college community with easy access to big city life. Our beautiful, 132-acre campus is located in Weston, Mass., one of the state's safest suburbs, and is just 12 miles from downtown Boston, America's ultimate college town.

Off-Campus Opportunities Located just 12 miles from Boston, Regis offers a countless number of opportunities for students to take advantage of in the city. Home to over 250,000 college students, Boston boasts a wide array of cultural attractions, world renowned historic sites, diverse communities, championship sporting events, and some of the finest research and medical facilities in the nation. With the Regis Shuttle running regularly, students are able to get to neighboring colleges and to the MBTA rapid-transit system with ease.

MAJORS AND DEGREES OFFERED

The School of Liberal Arts, Education and Social Sciences at Regis offers both baccalaureate and master's level programs. Undergraduate majors include communication, criminal justice studies, education, English, global business management, liberal studies, mathematics education, psychology, and social work and are designed to combine academic knowledge with practical experience.

The School of Nursing, Science, and Health Professions is the academic home for numerous undergraduate and graduate health professions programs. We welcome you to biochemistry, biology, exercise science, nuclear medicine, nursing, nutrition, public health and sports management.

ACADEMIC PROGRAMS

Our rigorous curriculum is designed to reflect the realities of today's world as we challenge students to examine theories, explore concepts, and pursue practical applications from a global perspective.

Career-Focused Education

Against the backdrop of a strong liberal arts foundation, your Regis education will be career-focused. From the day you step onto campus, you will participate in career workshops and seminars, and work closely with faculty advisors and counselors to plan and pursue a path of study tailored to your interests and professional goals.

Experience the Regis Difference

While many schools offer experiential learning, Regis infuses it across the curriculum—in every major. From internships, service-learning projects, undergraduate research and performance, clinical placements, summer programs, and more, students choose from a variety of active learning styles which extend education beyond the classroom and into the real world. Our relationships with companies and organizations in and around Boston provide a wide array of opportunities, and Regis' Center for Internships and Career Placement offers strong student support.

Expand Your Educational Horizons

Regis offers you the opportunity to create an educational experience that is broad, deep and as individual as you are.

• Student Exchange Programs

Regis is part of the Sisters of St. Joseph College Consortium, where students can attend member colleges located across the United States.

• Cross Registration

In addition to your coursework at Regis, you may also cross-register for classes at Babson College, Bentley University, or Boston College.

• Globally Connected

Affiliated institutions where Regis students pursue studies overseas include Regents University London, University College Cork in Ireland, Assumption College Rome, and Kyoto Notre Dame University in Japan. Students also have several opportunities to travel the world through programs including our renowned Erat Scholars Program – a semester-long religious studies and philosophy seminar that has taken participants to China, France, Italy, Jerusalem, Kenya and Switzerland – as well as Alternative Spring Break trips and overseas class excursions.

Honors Program

The Regis Honors Program provides stimulating, challenging learning experiences and a supportive network for our most academically accomplished students. In addition to taking honors-level courses, students participate in a variety of service-learning projects.

Fast Track to a Master's Degree

Regis students can earn combined bachelor's and master's degrees in as little as five years. Because students are able to take up to three courses for graduate credit while completing their bachelor's degree, the transition to graduate school is essentially seamless.

CAMPUS FACILITIES AND EQUIPMENT

Our campus, situated on 132 landscaped acres of a former estate, is beautiful, historic, and updated. We are conveniently located near Route 128, I-95, and the Massachusetts Turnpike (I-90), and with the MBTA "D" green line just minutes away, undergraduate students can easily complete internships, clinicals, and practicum off campus.

Along with the great laboratories and classrooms, the Fine Arts Center offers an exhilarating mix of performing and visual arts. Opened in 1993, the Center provides cultural enrichment to the Greater Boston community while promoting the educational mission of Regis. Three state-of-the-art venues as well as classrooms, workshops, and lecture spaces allow the Center to present offerings that engage, challenge and offer students valuable experience as designers, stage technicians, scriptwriters, guest curators, actors, musicians, choreographers, and vocalists.

Athletic activities get a special boost from our excellent facilities, including the gym, pool, and state-of-the-art fitness center. Among our newest facilities are synthetic turf playing fields, an eight-lane track, tennis courts, and softball complex.

Tuition, Room, Board, and Fees

Estimated costs for the school year include:

	Resident	Commuter
Tuition	$37,540	$37,540
Room & Board	$14,380	n/a

FINANCIAL AID

Regis offers many types of financial aid. Students may be awarded Regis' own scholarship funds, or one of the many federal and state programs in which the college participates. Students' financial aid packages will be made up of one or several of the following sources depending on their calculated financial need, academic standing, state residency, enrollment status, and timely application.

• Merit Scholarships for academic excellence, such as the S. Therese Higgins CSJ Merit Scholarship, S. Jeanne d'Arc O'Hare Merit Scholarship, Tower Scholarship, and Anniversary Award

• Need-based scholarships—from Regis and other sources

• State and federal education grants

• State and federal loan program—low interest and deferred payment

• Work-study programs

To be considered for any type of financial aid, students must be accepted into a degree program.

STUDENT ORGANIZATIONS AND ACTIVITIES

Here is our best advice to students seeking a great college experience: get involved, stay involved. With more than 30 student clubs and organizations, there really is no better way to stay active, meet new people, and try new things. Whether it's a musical or comedy performance, a multicultural celebration, a sporting event, or monthly "Pizza with the President," Regis has something for everyone. And, on the off-chance we don't have the club or activity you're most passionate about—you can start one of your own!

Regis Clubs & Organizations

Asian-American Association

Black Student Association

Campus Ministry

Cape Verdean Student Association

Dance Company

DYNASTY Step Squad

Education Club

Gay-Straight Alliance

Glee Club

Hemetera

International Club

Latin-American Student Organization

Mentor Program

Minutes for Memories

Mount Regis (Yearbook)

Orientation Leaders

Politics and Global Events

Pride Photo

Regis College Science Association

Student Athletic Advisory Committee

Student Government Association

Student Nursing Association

WRGS Radio Station

NCAA Division III Athletics

Teams, Intramurals and Classes

Women's Teams

Basketball

Cross Country

Field Hockey

Lacrosse

Soccer

Softball

Swimming and Diving

Tennis

Track and Field

Volleyball

Men's Teams

Basketball

Cross Country

Lacrosse

Soccer

Swimming and Diving

Tennis

Track and Field

Volleyball

Intramural Sports

Basketball

Dodgeball

Flag Football

Indoor Soccer

Volleyball

Health and Fitness Classes

Barre Blast

Cardio Kickboxing

Dance

Golf

Individual Fitness

Introduction to Martial Arts

Pilates

Self-Defense

Strength Training

Swim for Fitness

Yoga

Zumba

ADMISSIONS PROCESS

Complete and submit an online application for undergraduate admission.

- The Common Application for Spring/Fall 2016 (online)

In addition to the application, first-year applicants are required to submit:

- Application fee of $50 payable to Regis College

- Essay

- Official high school transcript or official GED score report

- First-quarter senior grades

- One signed letter of recommendation on official letterhead: one from a secondary school counselor or from a teacher

- Optional submission of Official test results from either SAT or ACT; TOEFL if your native language is not English

RIPON COLLEGE

AT A GLANCE

Ripon College's intentionally small residential campus enrolls some 1,000 bright, high-achieving young men and women from nearly every state and from countries around the world. Because of our small size and the fact we are 100 percent dedicated to undergraduate education our students benefit from a high degree of personalized attention. With seventy percent of classes averaging less than 20 students, our students receive quality time with faculty at a rate of 11:1. Ninety-five percent of our students indicate they are satisfied or more than satisfied with the amount of attention they receive from faculty, who also provide direct academic, career and club advising, and collaborate on serious research pursuits. Graduates of the college go on to serve in a variety of roles and have achieved notoriety at the highest levels of national and international government, politics, medicine, finance, the arts, business and in a host of other professional fields. An incredible 96 percent of graduates are employed or in professional school six months after graduation, and the five-year acceptance rate to medical school is 82 percent—more than twice the national average.

LOCATION AND ENVIRONMENT

Ripon College is a private undergraduate liberal arts and sciences college located in the historic city of Ripon, Wisconsin. Nestled in the heart of the Green Lake region of Wisconsin—a premier year-round destination for outdoor enthusiasts—the college's 250-acre tree-lined campus is centrally located within an hour to hour-and-a-half drive of each of the state's three largest cities: Milwaukee, Madison and Green Bay. The nearest airport is located 45 minutes away in Appleton, Wisconsin.

Ripon's buildings are a striking combination of historic (10 campus structures listed on the national register of historic buildings) and modern architecture. Constant improvements, like a new apartment-style residence hall, a multimillion dollar renovation of one of our main classroom buildings, upgrades to the library, student union, the campus bookstore, our dining facilities, and numerous student activity spaces ensure you have the spaces and amenities you need to be successful.

Through collaborative learning, group living, teamwork, and networking experiences, you'll tap into the power of a community where we all take a vested interest in ensuring your success as a student at Ripon and throughout life.

OFF-CAMPUS OPPORTUNITIES

U.S. or abroad? Two semesters, one semester, three weeks or one week? Ripon offers more than fifty different off-campus programs of varying lengths to choose from, each one officially sanctioned by and affiliated with Ripon. Although most programs are connected with a major or minor program, all are open to every Ripon student, regardless of major.

U.S. programs include Chicago Arts, Entrepreneurship and Urban Studies; Chicago Urban Education; Teach Chicago!; Chicago Newberry Seminar in the Humanities; Fisk University–Ripon Exchange Program; Tennessee Oak Ridge Science; Kentucky ROTC Leader's Training Course; American Indian Reservation Student Teaching Program; Washington, D.C.; Laboratory at Sea; and, Woods Hole Marine Biology.

International programs include: Cordoba, Argentina; Bostswana; Brazil; Costa Rica; London & Florence; Montpellier, France; Paris, France; Bonn, Germany; Budapest, Hungary; Pune, India; Coldigioco, Italy; Florence, Italy; Tokyo, Japan; Amman, Jordan; St. Petersburg, Russia; St. Andrews, Scotland; Alicante, Spain; Madrid, Spain; Seville, Spain; Toledo, Spain; Tanzania; Bangor, Wales; and Swansea, Wales.

The College also offers a number of three-week Liberal Arts InFocus courses (domestic and international) immediately after the spring term.

In addition, several short-term servant leadership programs are offered during fall, winter and spring breaks.

MAJORS AND DEGREES OFFERED

Majors include anthropology, art history, biology, business management, chemistry, chemistry–biology, communication, computer science, economics, education, English, environmental studies, exercise science, French, German, global studies, history, journalism, Latin American and Caribbean studies, mathematics, military science, music, philosophy, physics, politics and government, pre-engineering, pre-law, pre-med and health sciences, psychobiology, psychology, religion, sociology, Spanish, studio art, and theatre.

Programs are also available in class studies, communication and civic advocacy, dramatic literature, early childhood education, entrepreneurship, environmental biology, health, Latin, law and society, military leadership, museum studies, national security studies, nonprofit management, socially responsible leadership, sports medicine/athletic training, theatre production, and women's and gender studies.

Pre-professional programs include chiropractic medicine, dentistry, engineering, journalism, law and government, library and information science, medicine, ministry, optometry, physical therapy, and veterinary medicine.

Dual-degree programs include allied health sciences/medical technology, engineering, forestry, and social welfare.

Certification programs include education certification, early childhood, elementary, elementary/middle school, secondary, secondary/middle, music K–12, and physical education K–12.

ACADEMIC PROGRAMS

The rigorous liberal arts curriculum and active residential campus prepares students of diverse interests for lives of productive, socially responsible citizenship. Coursework challenges students to examine questions in-depth, identify patterns of logic and reasoning, think critically, consider multiple contexts, and pursue independent research and present findings publicly—regardless of major.

Ripon's liberal arts and sciences curriculum is designed to introduce students to a wide variety of disciplines. More than 50 percent of our students complete double or triple majors, and graduate in four years. Over the years, several students have also pursued special self-designed majors in a variety of fields such as film studies, journalism, criminal justice and more.

In addition, the innovative Center for Social Responsibility provides a strong foundation for leadership skills. An Army ROTC program is also available.

A Ripon education will take you anywhere! You could study psychology and play basketball at Ripon, and then become a five-time Grammy winner like jazz singer Al Jarreau (1962). You could guide the space shuttle into orbit like Jeff Bantle (1980), a chief flight director with NASA, or become an international opera star like Gail Dobish (1976). Perhaps you'll set records in medical science like neonatologist Dr. John Muraskas (1978), who is on record for saving the world's smallest premature baby. Or perhaps you'll end up studying at Oxford University as a Rhodes Scholar like Zach Morris '02, who also found time to play touch football with former President Bill Clinton and spend an evening at Buckingham Palace with the Queen.

CAMPUS FACILITIES AND EQUIPMENT

Ripon has a long tradition of excellence in facilitating transformational interdisciplinary learning within its beautiful century-old buildings and green spaces, and in communities near and far.

Technology services include high-speed Internet and e-mail, telephone and video communication. Intranet and Internet services are accessible from systems located throughout the college. Our campus-wide network provides access from every room, and several wireless "hot-spots."

Our science labs contain a variety of high-tech instruments, including a 300-Mhz FTNMR Spectrometer, spectrophotometers, an X-ray diffraction instrument, chromatographs, a spectrofluorimeter, modern electroanalytical instrumentation, a HeliumCadmium Laser Lab, transmission and scanning electron microscopes, a super-speed refrigerated centrifuge, a Zeiss universal microscope with digitizing tablet and two Nikon diaphot inverted microscopes. Ripon also has a small planetarium classroom and is home to the Ceresco Prairie Conservancy—a 130-acre area natural prairie ecosystem where students can study science and become involved in service learning through prairie restoration.

The campus grows its own herbs and vegetables in a hoop house, harvests its own honey from student-run honey bee hives, grows herbs in a hydroponic garden and composts its own solid waste.

The library staff provides friendly, efficient circulation, reference, instruction, and interlibrary loan services that aid in research. The library also houses the college archives, a computer lab, and more than a dozen online databases. The library provides access to multiple reading rooms for group and silent study, more than 180,000 volumes and a variety of electronic databases supporting the research needs of the college. Our electronic library resources are accessible from anywhere with an internet connection.

The C.J. Rodman Center for the Arts is home to a theater with a state-of-the-art computerized lighting system, a recital hall with one of only 50 existing Bedient organs, an art gallery, a sculpture garden and resource library.

The J.M. Storzer Center includes an Olympic-size pool, a first-class gymnasium, tennis and racquetball courts, a dance studio, training facilities, and a weight room. Our outdoor playing fields and courts are the best in their class. In addition, a large, modern exercise facility was recently added in the main student residence area.

TUITION, ROOM, BOARD AND FEES

Education is an investment, but you don't want to mortgage your future. Ripon has been consistently recognized as a best value by all of the national ranking organizations. Nighty-eight percent of Ripon students receive some form of merit-based scholarship and/or need-based grants and loans.

Tuition is $36,214, room and board is $8,177, and fees are $300, for a total cost of $44,691.

FINANCIAL AID

Ripon College is committed to offering a uniquely personalized experience that is within reach of most families and takes pride in providing students a significant return on their investment. Ripon is more affordable than many similar private colleges, and in some cases, large public universities. The total out-of-pocket cost to attend Ripon varies for each student based on individual academic and performance-based achievement and demonstrated financial need. One-hundred percent of our incoming first-year students receive aid awards. That funding comes from many sources: merit-based scholarships, need-based grants, loans, work study, and scholarships from outside organizations to help meet costs. We recognize and reward your success in high school with Ripon's institutionally funded scholarships, based not only on academic merit, but also on special achievements in other areas such as the creative arts. Our scholarships range from $1,000 to full tuition. Ripon participates in all federal and state need-based financial aid programs. Our financial aid counselors will work individually with you and your family to investigate every possible financial resource for which you are eligible.

STUDENT ORGANIZATIONS AND ACTIVITIES

Opportunities are available to join a number of Ripon's more than 50 student-led clubs and organizations, including academic, political, environmental, pre-professional, athletic, cultural and social groups. The list of student clubs and organizations is ever-changing, reflecting our students' ever-changing interests. A recent addition is FUERZA Alliance, designed to educate students about Latino cultures and to provide services to the Spanish-speaking community of Ripon. Student initiated and sponsored club sports include Equestrian, Lacrosse, Rugby and Women's Boxing. These competitive teams travel throughout the Midwest.

Every day at Ripon is packed with a host of activities that include: we have eight vocal and instrumental groups that perform regularly on campus, as well as many individual student and faculty recitals. The Caestecker Fine Arts Series and the Chamber Music at Ripon Series annually bring international artists and performers to campus. The Theatre Department sponsors three major productions annually, plus a series of student-directed one-acts.

Ripon is host to 21 NCAA Division III varsity athletic teams as part of the Midwest Conference, with 35 percent of the student body participating:

Men's varsity sports: baseball, basketball, cross-country, cycling, football, soccer, swimming and diving, tennis, indoor track and field, and outdoor track and field.

Women's varsity sports: basketball, cross-country, cycling, dance, soccer, softball, swimming and diving, tennis, indoor track and field, outdoor track and field, volleyball.

ADMISSIONS PROCESS

Ripon enrolls students who will contribute to and benefit from the academic and residential programs we provide. Ripon does not discriminate on the basis of gender, sexual orientation, race, color, age, religion, national and ethnic origin, or disability in the administration of its educational policies, admission practices, scholarship and loan programs, athletic, and other college-administered programs.

The faculty committee on academic standards establishes the criteria for admission. The school considers a variety of factors, including secondary school record, standardized test scores (SAT or ACT), recommendations, a written essay, and extracurricular or community service activities. Ripon's admission process reflects the personal attention students can expect to receive during their college careers, and applicants are encouraged to provide any additional information that they consider helpful.

For more information contact:

Admission Office
Ripon College
300 Seward Street
PO Box 248
Ripon, WI 54971
Telephone: 800-947-4766
E-mail: adminfo@ripon.edu

ROBERT MORRIS UNIVERSITY

AT A GLANCE

A private university in Pittsburgh's suburban hills, Robert Morris University (RMU) is set on a 230-acre former estate that is a short drive from the cultural and commercial opportunities of a major city. Founded in 1921, RMU offers more than sixty undergraduate programs and twenty graduate programs, including many online options, providing more than 5,400 students academic excellence with a professional focus.

The University built its reputation in the business fields of accounting, finance, marketing, and management. It has grown to include programs in communications, information systems, engineering, mathematics, science, education, social sciences, and nursing. RMU uses a Student Engagement Transcript to document internships, service-learning activities, study abroad, leadership roles, and other learning outside the classroom. This focus on engaged learning contributes to the 92 percent placement rate of graduates within a year of graduation.

RMU is a teaching-centered institution featuring small classes taught by professors and a student-faculty ratio of 15:1. The campus is growing, with new buildings for both the School of Business and the School of Communications and Information Systems, and a new nursing simulation center due to open in 2015. New residence halls accommodate a growing student population. More than 85 percent of freshmen live in campus housing.

Visiting international scholars and a variety of opportunities to study abroad—for a semester or just a few weeks—enrich students' global perspectives. Students can participate in any of nearly 100 clubs and organizations. The Student Life Office organizes dances, parties, movie screenings, comedy acts, health and wellness fairs, educational programs, and day trips. Business organizations, professional clubs, and honor societies provide students with career preparation opportunities.

The University's competitive athletics program fields sixteen NCAA Division I teams, and the Colonials have won numerous titles and championships. The men's basketball team famously upset the reigning NCAA champion Kentucky Wildcats in the Charles Sewall Center in the first round of the 2013 NIT. Coach John Banaszak, former Pittsburgh Steeler and three-time Super Bowl winner, leads the football team at Joe Walton Stadium. Nationally ranked Division I men's and women's ice hockey teams play at the RMU Island Sports Center, a 32-acre sports and recreation complex with two ice rinks, two multipurpose rinks, an indoor golf driving range, a miniature golf course, a pro shop, and a restaurant and banquet facility. Students can also participate in a number of club and intramural sports on campus.

For more information, visit www.rmu.edu.

LOCATION AND ENVIRONMENT

Robert Morris University's main campus is on 230 scenic acres of rolling hills in suburban Moon Township, Pa. The campus is continuously growing and changing to meet the needs of its students. In recent years RMU has added new apartment-style residence halls as well as new buildings for the School of Business, the School of Communications and Information Systems, and the School of Nursing and Health Sciences.

OFF-CAMPUS OPPORTUNITIES

Pittsburgh is regularly named by major publications as one of the country's most livable cities. The city is compact, cultured, safe, neighborly, historic, and very affordable. Besides big-city offerings like professional spectator sports, concerts, museums, amusement parks, and a thriving and varied nightlife, the region is rich with outdoor activities, including skiing, hiking, sailing, whitewater rafting and a 300-mile bike trail that stretches to Washington, D.C.

MAJORS AND DEGREES OFFERED

Robert Morris University offers more than sixty undergraduate programs of study: accounting, actuarial science, advertising, biology, biomedical engineering, business, communication, competitive intelligence systems, computer information systems, corporate communication, cyber forensics and information security, economics, education (specializing in grades pre-K-4, 4–8, or 7–12), engineering, English, environmental science, finance, graphic design, health services administration, history, hospitality and tourism management, industrial engineering, information sciences, intelligence systems, journalism, management, manufacturing engineering, marketing, mathematics, mechanical engineering, media arts, nuclear medicine technology, nursing, organizational leadership, photography, political science, pre-medicine, professional communications/information systems, psychology, public relations, social science, sociology, software development, software engineering, special education, sport management, sport psychology, theater, TV/video production, web design, and writing.

Fully online bachelor's degree programs are available in business, cyber forensics and information security, English, health services administration, hospitality and tourism management, organizational leadership, psychology, and RN–M.S.N.

The University offers five-year integrated bachelor's/master's degree programs, medical school affiliation, cooperative education programs, an integrated 3+3 J.D. program with Duquesne University School of Law, and an honors program.

ACADEMIC PROGRAMS

Other programs open to qualified undergraduate students include: the University Honors Program, in which students follow an advanced curriculum including an honors seminar and thesis project, and Study Abroad, which offers opportunities for international study in such places as Australia, China, France, Ireland, Italy, Japan, Mexico, Switzerland, Turkey, and the United Kingdom.

CAMPUS FACILITIES AND EQUIPMENT

RMU emphasizes technology, whether you're an aspiring engineer, designer, nurse, or news anchor. Our state-of-the-art facilities include science and nursing laboratories, an industry-grade engineering laboratory, a cutting-edge design studio, and the region's second-largest television studio.

TUITION, ROOM, BOARD AND FEES

Robert Morris University has one of the lowest tuition rates of any private university in Pennsylvania. The annual tuition for undergraduates in 2014–15 was $25,380, based on a 24- to 36-credit, two-semester schedule. Additional tuition charges apply for certain majors. Room and board fees were $10,250 annually, based on standard residence hall double occupancy and the Patriot meal plan.

FINANCIAL AID

Eighty-nine percent of full-time undergraduate students receive some sort of financial aid, including grants, loans, scholarships and work-study jobs. Veterans qualifying under the Post-9/11 GI Bill attend RMU tuition-free.

STUDENT ORGANIZATIONS AND ACTIVITIES

A wide range of activities and experiences is available at RMU, and students are encouraged to get involved in existing activities or establish new ones. Student organizations include academic/professional organizations, student government, honor societies, service and philanthropic organizations, fraternities and sororities, and special interest groups and activities. RMU has several intramural sports leagues, 17 club sports, and 16 NCAA Division I intercollegiate athletics teams: basketball (M/W), cross country (W), football (M), golf (M), ice hockey (M/W), lacrosse (M/W), rowing (W), soccer (M/W), softball (W), indoor and outdoor track & field (W), and volleyball (W).

ADMISSIONS PROCESS

Robert Morris University has a rolling admissions process. Students are considered for acceptance as soon as their application materials are received and evaluated. Applications, official transcripts, official test scores and letters of recommendation should be sent directly to: Office of Admissions, Robert Morris University, 6001 University Boulevard, Moon Township, PA 15108. Apply for free on the RMU website at www.rmu.edu.

ROCHESTER INSTITUTE OF TECHNOLOGY

As one of the world's leading career-oriented, technological universities, RIT's goal is to prepare students for 21st century career success.

AT A GLANCE

RIT is a place where brilliant minds assemble and collaborate, where they pool together their individual talents across disciplines in service of big projects and big ideas. It is a vibrant community teeming with students collaborating with experts and specialists; a hub of innovation and creativity. As one of the nation's largest private universities, RIT has an unmatched array of specialized, career-oriented academic programs that attracts designers, artists, photographers, journalists, and filmmakers on the one hand, and scientists, engineers, computing scientists, social scientists, and entrepreneurs on the other. It is a launching pad for a brilliant career, and a highly unique state of mind. It is a perfect environment in which to pursue your passion. Here, the future is envisioned each day. And remade each day after.

ACADEMICS

RIT is one of the world's leading career-oriented, technological universities. At RIT, some of the world's most talented, ambitious, and creative students find a remarkable array of academic programs; diverse, talented and accessible faculty; sophisticated facilities; an unusual emphasis on experiential learning; and a vibrant, connected community that is home to students from more than 100 countries. RIT's nine colleges offer more than 90 undergraduate programs in areas such as engineering, computing, information technology, engineering technology, business, hospitality, art, design, science, psychology, public policy, game design, photography, film and animation, health sciences, and biomedical sciences. Excelling in teaching and research, RIT's faculty are passionate about their role in the classroom and in their field. RIT's faculty are diverse, innovative and resourceful, and engage students in the process of personal and professional discovery. To complement their specialized field of study, students select from more than 80 minors available at RIT. Students can also complete a master's degree in five years through one of the university's accelerated BS/MS or 4+1 MBA programs. Since 1912, the hallmark of an RIT has been experiential education. RIT was among the first universities in the world to offer cooperative education, and its co-op program is now one of the largest in the world. Last year more than 4,100 co-op students alternated periods of study on campus with paid employment in nearly 2,100 firms across the United States and overseas. Experiential learning also includes internships, study abroad, and undergraduate research. Regardless of background or academic interest, students find that RIT offers a stimulating environment for intellectual and personal growth.

ADMISSIONS

RIT seeks a diverse and multicultural student body. Entering students come from a variety of geographic, social, cultural, economic, and ethnic backgrounds. Admission to RIT is competitive, but the admission process is a personal one. The university is interested in learning about students' interests, abilities, and goals in order to provide the best information and guidance as they select the college that is right for them. Students applying for freshman admission for the fall semester (September) may apply through an Early Decision Plan or Regular Decision Plan. The Early Decision Plan is designed for students who consider RIT their first-choice college and wish to make an early commitment regarding admission. Early Decision requires that candidates file their applications and supporting documents by December 1 in order to receive admission notification by January 15. Freshmen who choose not to apply for Early Decision are considered under our Regular Decision Plan. Regular Decision applicants who have provided all required application materials by February 1 will receive admission notification by March 15. Applications received after February 1 will be reviewed on a space-available basis, with notification letters mailed four to six weeks after the application is complete. Students interested in being considered for merit-based (academic and extracurricular) scholarships or the RIT Honors program must apply by February 1. For best consideration for admission and scholarships, it is recommended that applicants for transfer admission file their materials on or before March 15 for fall or summer admission and November 15 for spring admission. Factors considered in our admission decisions include, but are not limited to, past high school and/or college performance (particularly in required academic subjects), admission test scores, competitiveness of high school or previous college, and academic program selected. Recommendations from those familiar with your academic performance and interviews with admissions counselors are often influential. Most students applying to RIT choose a specific academic program as part of the admission process. This is important because there are a variety of academic programs, and admission requirements may differ from one program to another. For example, a student applying for admission to our computer science program would present a strong academic record with particular strength in mathematics, while a student applying for a fine art or design major would need to show artistic talent through a required portfolio. For incoming freshmen who wish to explore their options before declaring a major, RIT offers the following undeclared options: University Studies (for students wishing to explore programs in two or more colleges); Undeclared Art & Design: Business Exploration; Computing Exploration; Undeclared Crafts; Engineering Exploration; Undeclared Engineering Technology; Liberal Arts Exploration; Undeclared Photography, and General Science Exploration.

CAMPUS FACILITIES AND EQUIPMENT

The campus is filled with the latest equipment, software, laboratories, and conveniences to give students the tools they need to excel. RIT offers academic facilities that are rarely matched on other university campuses, and students use the latest technology to solve problems creatively. RIT plays leadership role in academic computing and gives students maximum access to research and information resources via two OC3 connections to the Internet, 20,000 network connections, and an eight-million-foot fiber-optic backbone. RIT is one of a select group of universities with access to the Internet 2 research network.

CAMPUS LIFE

Students take their academic pursuits seriously, but they'll be the first to tell you that they are passionate about life outside of the lectures, labs and studios. RIT is alive with energy and excitement—24/7. It won't take long for you to find your niche in this community because there are so many ways to be involved. The backgrounds and interests of RIT students contribute in many ways to the quality of campus life. With students from all 50 states and more than 100 countries, RIT is a living-learning environment rich in diversity in classrooms, residence halls, and everywhere else on campus. A number of campus organizations and student services focus on the unique needs and interests of minority, deaf, and international students at RIT. You'll have plenty of opportunity to interact with a mind-expanding mix of people. More than 7,100 full-time students live on campus in residence halls or apartments, and our self-contained, suburban location creates a safe and secure atmosphere. Clubs and organizations exist to bring students of similar interest together and provide them with opportunities to become effective leaders. These groups enhance the quality of student life by fostering social interaction, leadership development, school spirit and an affinity to RIT. Clubs and Organizations promote activities, diversity, service and learning outside of the classroom. Currently there are approximately 200 active clubs, 10 Major Student Organizations, and 30 Greek Organizations on campus. Last year, clubs and organizations held nearly 1,300 events on campus.

RIT's intercollegiate teams have a history of excellence, recording many impressive seasons and capturing a number of conference and national championships. The men's and women's hockey teams are Division I. The remainder of the intercollegiate teams competes at Division III. RIT teams are members of the National Collegiate Athletic Association (NCAA), the Eastern College Athletic Conference (ECAC), the Atlantic Hockey Association, the college Hockey America, the Liberty League, and the New York State Women's Collegiate Athletic Association.

LOCATION AND ENVIRONMENT

RIT's 1,300-acre campus is located in the suburbs, about six miles from downtown Rochester, NY. More than 7,100 diverse, creative, ambitious students live on campus in residence halls or apartments, and the self-contained, suburban location gives the campus a safe, residential atmosphere. RIT also maintains campuses in Croatia, Dubai, and Kosovo.

MAJORS AND DEGREES

Few universities provide RIT's variety of career-oriented programs. RIT's nine colleges offer more than 90 undergraduate programs in areas such as engineering, computing, information technology, engineering technology, business, hospitality, art, design, science, psychology, public policy, game design, photography, film and animation, health sciences, and biomedical sciences.

OFF-CAMPUS OPPORTUNITIES

Rochester provides a perfect setting—it's large enough to provide the dining, shopping, and night life opportunities found in a bigger city, yet small and friendly enough to be inviting and accessible. In fact, Rochester was ranked 10th best among large cities in the Northeast in a recent Money magazine Best Places to Live in America survey. The greater Rochester area is home to more than 1 million people, making it the third-largest metropolitan area in New York State. Rochester's reputation as an active and inventive community is supported by extensive cultural and intellectual opportunities.

TUITION AND FEES

For 2014–15, tuition and fees cost $35,768; room and board averaged $11,568; and books, transportation, and other expenses averaged $2,025.

FINANCIAL AID

RIT's Office of Financial Aid and Scholarships assists students and their families in identifying sources of financial aid to help meet the cost of a quality education. Currently, more than 12,000 RIT undergraduate and graduate students receive over $291 million dollars in financial assistance from federal, state, and institutional resources, in the form of scholarships, grants, loans, and part-time employment.

SAINT ANSELM COLLEGE

AT A GLANCE

Saint Anselm College prepares students for life. With a liberal arts education, they're ready for real career experience, for the challenges that lie ahead. They take their Saint Anselm experience with them to think critically, communicate effectively, and solve problems creatively.

Saint Anselm graduates are CEOs, doctors, engineers, teachers, marketers, and researchers. They are humanitarians, healers, and philanthropists. They graduate Saint Anselm with the drive to achieve, empowered to make the world a better place.

In fact, 97% of the class of 2014 was employed, in graduate school, or engaged in service within 6 months of graduation.

The Princeton Review ranks Saint Anselm as one of the country's best institutions for an undergraduate education and number 10 out of 3,000 national colleges for its food. See all Saint Anselm College's rankings.

ACADEMICS

At Saint Anselm College, a comprehensive liberal arts education gives students the essential skills to be successful in the career of their choice. It's an education that challenges them to stretch their minds and encourages a lifelong pursuit of truth to enrich their lives.

The core curriculum focuses on humanities, college writing, and learning outcomes. It is a balance between common courses that foster academic community and elective courses that allow for individual choice.

At Saint Anselm College's New Hampshire Institute of Politics & Political Library, students hear major policy speeches and meet today's most prominent political policy thinkers, journalists, scientists, industry executives, and global leaders. The Institute, nationally known to political scholars and strategists, is an essential campaign stop for presidential candidates offering unparalleled opportunities for students to be in the front row of the democratic process. In fact, every United States president in the last 50 years has visited Saint Anselm College.

ADMISSIONS

In reviewing applicants for the first-year class, admission considers each prospective student carefully. Counselors assess each applicant's secondary school performance, SAT I or ACT scores (optional for non-nursing majors, nursing major must submit scores), recommendation letters, extracurricular involvement, and the written essay. Of highest priority is the applicant's secondary school transcript, with a specific focus on both the rigor of course study and the marks received. Saint Anselm invites transfer and international students to apply.

Saint Anselm College has the following admission deadlines:

Early Action, November 15

Nursing Majors, November 15

Regular Decision, February 1

Saint Anselm College invites students and families to visit campus for a tour, information session and/or interview.

For more information, students should contact:

Office of Admission

Saint Anselm College

100 Saint Anselm Drive

Manchester, NH 03102-1310

Telephone: 603-641-7500 or 888-426-7356 (toll-free)

Fax: 603-641-7550

Email: admission@anselm.edu

website: www.anselm.edu

MAJORS AND DEGREES OFFERED

At Saint Anselm College, students may pursue the Bachelor of Arts degree in the following academic programs and majors: accounting, American studies, biochemistry, biology, business, chemistry, classics, classical archaeology, communication, computer science, computer science with business, computer science with mathematics, criminal justice, economics, education (secondary and elementary), engineering physics (3-2 program), English, environmental studies, environmental science, finance, fine arts, forensic science, French, German studies, history, international business, international relations, integrated studies, mathematics, mathematics with economics, natural science, peace and justice studies, philosophy, physics (applied), physics, politics, psychology, sociology, Spanish, and theology. The college also offers a Bachelor of Science in Nursing (BSN) through a traditional, undergraduate nursing program and a hybrid RN to BSN Program.

Saint Anselm students may pursue pre-professional programs in dentistry, law, medicine, theology, and veterinary medicine.

The engineering physics (3-2 program) partners with the University of Notre Dame, University of Massachusetts-Lowell, Catholic University of America, and Manhattan College. Learn more at www.anselm.edu/engineering.

CAMPUS FACILITIES AND EQUIPMENT

Saint Anselm College is located on 380 acres in Manchester, N.H. with more than 60 campus buildings. There's much to see and do on campus from open skate nights at Sullivan Arena to spring concerts on the quad. Academic buildings including the Goulet Science Center and Gadbois Hall house innovative labs where remarkable research happens every day. There are cell culture labs, climate controlled environmental chambers, a green house, a sleep lab, SimMan labs in Nursing, and more. In the library students have access to a range of workspaces for individuals and groups in addition to technological advances.

Recreational facilities include the Carr Center with basketball courts and the recently renovated 9,000-square-foot, three-level fitness center. Saint Anselm College boasts some of the top athletic facilities in the Northeast-10 Conference. The college's 20 intercollegiate athletic teams play all of their home contests on campus (with the exception of the golf and alpine ski teams) whether at Grappone Stadium, Sullivan Arena, or Melucci Field.

Ninety-two percent of Saint Anselm students live on campus in traditional residence halls, suites, townhouses, or apartments. A new 47,000-square-foot, 150-bed residence hall will be completed in August 2014 offering students an innovative, living-learning community. Whether students live on campus or commute, every one has access to Saint Anselm College's amazing food, named 10th in the nation by the Princeton Review.

Finally, Saint Anselm is home to the New Hampshire Institute of Politics & Political Library (NHIOP), which offers unparalleled opportunities for students to be in the front row of the democratic process. It's auditorium, West Wing, TV-studio, and classrooms are where students meet today's most prominent political policy thinkers and researchers, journalists and authors, scientists, industry executives, global leaders and presidential candidates. Have we mentioned all the U.S. presidents in the last 50 years have visited Saint Anselm?

CAMPUS LIFE

With more than 65 clubs and organizations, 20 varsity athletic teams, a performing arts center, and an art gallery, Saint Anselm students have plenty of activities to explore. From the soccer club to the mock trial team to the Muslim Student Association, there is a club for every interest, cultural to academic.

Students interested in service will be right at home volunteering through the Meelia Center for Community Engagement or through Campus Ministry. Saint Anselm students volunteered more than 50,926 hours last year doing everything from teaching English to new Americans to working the crisis hotline at the YWCA. Every winter and spring break, Saint Anselm students travel to organizations around the country to volunteer at service sites through Service & Solidarity Mission Trips.

Saint Anselm College is part of the Division II Northeast-10 and ECAC Conferences with 20 varsity teams: men's intercollegiate sports in baseball, basketball, cross-country, football, golf, ice hockey, lacrosse, skiing, soccer, and tennis and women's sports in basketball, cross-country, field hockey, ice hockey, lacrosse, skiing, soccer, softball, tennis, and volleyball. For students interested in club or intramurals, Saint Anselm has a variety of club, recreational, and intramural sports teams.

COLLEGE BASICS

At Saint Anselm College, students find their direction. Through the college's distinctive liberal arts education, students gain insight into how the world works and how they can make it better.

The core curriculum challenges them and stretches their minds. They gain the essential skills employers are looking for through their courses and experiential learning opportunities. And they become part of a special community, a 120-year tradition of excellence. They become Anselmians.

Founded in 1889, Saint Anselm is the third-oldest Catholic college in New England. It is an hour drive from Boston, the seacoast, and the White Mountains and enrolls 1,954 students.

Saint Anselm has 42 majors and 40 minors in the liberal arts, business, nursing and the sciences. With an average class size of 18, students receive individual attention in small classes. And with 198 professors and no teaching assistants, Saint Anselm faculty are committed to the success of their students.

LOCATION AND ENVIRONMENT

Saint Anselm College is located on 380 acres in Manchester, N.H., the largest city in the state. Just minutes from downtown Manchester, students can find great restaurants and coffee shops and all the venues a small city has to offer, a theatre, museum, minor league baseball and hockey teams, and the Verizon Arena to name a few. The Manchester-Boston Regional Airport is also just minutes from campus. The college is an hour drive from Boston, the seacoast, and the White Mountains.

OFF-CAMPUS OPPORTUNITIES

At Saint Anselm College, a liberal arts education gives students a solid foundation for any career but opportunities out-of-the-classroom give students a competitive edge and real job experience.

Students find all kinds of experiential learning opportunities at Saint Anselm College including internships, research, study abroad, and volunteering. Students of all majors and interests can find opportunities for internships through the Office Career Services, which also brings employers to campus and advises students throughout their job search.

Internships are offered in Boston, MA., New York City, NY, Washington, D.C. And Manchester, NH. Recent internships opportunities include: The Boston Bruins, United States Secret Service, Fidelity Investments, The United States Senate, Fox

News, and the American Cancer Society.

Many students work closely on research projects with faculty on campus to gain valuable lab skills but there are also opportunities at local hospitals and businesses.

Students interested in study abroad can travel the world visiting such places as Thailand, Morocco, and South Africa. In recent years, students have studied marine biology on Australia's Great Barrier Reef, art history in the museums of Florence, finance in London, language in Spain and France, the culture of peace in Peru, and political history in Ireland.

And if studying abroad for an entire semester seems too long, Saint Anselm students have traveled with faculty members on week-long trips to places such as China, Panama, Vietnam, and Belize.

In addition, every winter and spring break, Saint Anselm students travel to organizations around the country to volunteer at service sites through Service & Solidarity Mission Trips. These service trips challenge students, giving them valuable perspectives and changing their views on the world.

TUITION AND FEES

The 2015–2016 school year tuition is $36,724 and room and board costs are $13,334. Total cost is $51,028.

FINANCIAL AID

Saint Anselm provides students with financial aid opportunities through both private and federal aid programs. The college provides financial aid to offset the reasonable monetary investment that the student and family are expected to contribute.

Ninety-seven percent of the college's undergraduates receive some degree of financial aid. Saint Anselm's financial aid opportunities include grants, loans, scholarships, and employment positions.

Merit awards are awarded to outstanding students. Two forms are required in applying for institutional need-based aid; the student must submit the CSS/Financial Aid PROFILE and the Free Application for Federal Student Aid (FAFSA) by March 15.

SAINT FRANCIS UNIVERSITY (PA)

AT A GLANCE

Saint Francis is a private, Catholic, co-educational liberal arts university. Established in 1847, the University is among America's first Franciscan institutions and is the nation's 12th-oldest Catholic institution of higher education. Saint Francis operates under the conventions of the Franciscan Friars of the Third Order Regular. The University is dedicated to providing each student with top-rated academics, a vibrant student life, opportunities for leadership, and unflagging attention from a distinguished faculty. For the past century and a half, Saint Francis University's commitment to academics and student life has embodied two important values: high-quality education and respecting students as individuals.

LOCATION AND ENVIRONMENT

Saint Francis University is located on a 600-acre mountaintop campus in the town of Loretto, Pennsylvania. Just 80 miles east of Pittsburgh and 60 miles west of State College, the campus has its own lake, nature trails, ski tubing park and championship golf course. Near to campus are three state parks, four biking/walking trails and four ski resorts. The beautiful campus has an impressive suite of academic and research facilities as well as 19 residence halls to offer students a comprehensive experience.

OFF-CAMPUS OPPORTUNITIES

Saint Francis University's Office for Study Abroad offers a truly unique semester abroad program in the beautiful village of Ambialet, in southern France. Students can experience the adventure, beauty, and history of Europe in the halls of a centuries-old Franciscan monastery. Travel and research abroad are components of many academic programs at Saint Francis University.

MAJORS AND DEGREES OFFERED

Integrating distinct learning communities within the University, Saint Francis University has four schools: School of Business; School of Health Science; School of Art & Letters; and School of Sciences. Students may pursue bachelor degrees, master and doctoral offerings at the institution. All students benefit from the liberal art core of courses. These courses, coupled with high-demand academic major offerings make Saint Francis University graduates highly sought after in the marketplace.

Highlighted Majors

Accounting, Aquarium & Zoo Science, Computer Science, Criminal Justice Education, Environmental Engineering, Management, Physical Therapy, Physician Assistant Science, Petroleum & Natural Gas Engineering, Pre-Professional Studies (Pre-Medicine, etc), Public Health and Strategic Communications.

Graduate Programs

Business Administration, Education, Educational Leadership, Human Resource Management, Medical Science, Occupational Therapy, Physician Assistant Science, and Physical Therapy, as well as various online programs. Post-Bachelorette certificates are also available in Paralegal Studies.

ACADEMIC PROGRAMS

Bachelor degrees are typically earned within eight semesters. To graduate, each student is required to complete a course of study that meets with approval from the University Provost. The University operates on a two-semester academic calendar, with three sessions in the summer. The University offers students over forty academic programs of study and a wide variety of minors and concentrations to choose. Among the most competitive academic offerings are 2 entry-level Masters health science majors (Occupational Therapy and Physician Assistant Science) and an entry-level Doctoral program in Physical Therapy. The institution is well known for the cooperative student-faculty research that occurs within the School of Science. Petroleum & Natural Gas Engineering and Environmental Engineering are among the most recent program additions to the School of Science. In the School of Arts & Letters Early Childhood Education students may complete dual certification in Special Education in four years. Saint Francis University also has an extensive list of minors and concentrations available for students to complement their academic program of study.

CAMPUS FACILITIES AND EQUIPMENT

Saint Francis offers a totally wireless campus, computer labs, a Macintosh-based computer lab, and numerous Smart Classrooms. The cost of attendance at Saint Francis includes a laptop computer as well as technical support. Other facilities that complement student learning include well-equipped science labs, on-campus radio and television stations, and the Southern Alleghenies Museum of Art.

A recently completed state-of-the-art Science Center sits at the center of campus. The facility houses highly competitive science, technology, engineering and mathematics programs. The DiSepio Institute for Rural Health and Wellness education and research center features the DiSepio Center for Rehabilitation, Student Health Services, Fitness Center, Spiritual Wellness Center, Human Performance Laboratory, and Ernest J. Scharpf Family Conference Center. A complete renovation of Schwab Hall is currently underway and will serve as a home for the highly competitive accredited School of Business.

TUITION, ROOM, BOARD AND FEES

2015-2016 Tuition and Fees:

Tuition $31,078

Technology Fee $1,100

Room/Board $11,190

FINANCIAL AID

Saint Francis University awards financial aid to greater than 90 percent of its student body. Aside from offering aid through federal and state programs, the University's ample grant and scholarship programs provide awards ranging from $1,000 to $16,500 scholarships to students who have demonstrated their academic potential through strong high-school grade point averages and impressive ACT or SAT I (math and critical reading) scores. As a member of the NCAA Division I, scholarships may be granted to athletes in all 22 sports. Students can also receive schorarship money in all sports, Pep Band, Marching Band, Cheerleading, and Dance.

STUDENT ORGANIZATIONS AND ACTIVITIES

The University provides students many opportunities to exercise their interests and talents. For instance, 60-plus on-campus clubs and organizations are active. These range from departmental clubs to volunteer organizations, and include social and service sororities and social, service, and business fraternities. Student-run activities on campus include the Bell Tower yearbook, Red Radio, theatre, SFU singers, and the Troubadour newspaper. Each year, the Student Activities Organization brings a lively docket of comedians, concerts, films, and lectures to campus. The University is a NCAA Division I member institution and maintains a comprehensive program that consists of men's and women's teams. Extensive club sports teams and intramurals provide students varied recreational outlets. Students may also participate in cheerleading, pep band, and marching band.

ADMISSIONS PROCESS

Admission to Saint Francis University is granted on rolling basis. All applicants must submit a completed admissions application including essay, an official high-school transcript, ACT or SAT I (critical reading and math) scores, and a minimum of one recommendation letter. A December 1 priority application deadlines applies to the physician assistant program, physical therapy and occupational therapy programs. To learn more about Saint Francis University, students and families are encouraged to call the Office of Admissions at

1-866-DIAL-SFU (toll free).

ST. JOSEPH'S COLLEGE

AT A GLANCE

Founded in 1916, St. Joseph's College (SJC) is an independent, coeducational college with campuses in Brooklyn and Long Island, NY. With a history of national recognition for affordability and value, we are dedicated to putting a top-quality private education within your reach. We offer one of the lowest tuition rates of any private college in the Northeast, delivering a personal, practice-oriented education rooted in the liberal arts. As a student at St. Joseph's, you'll learn and grow, becoming prepared for numerous and diverse careers, ready to give the world your best.

At St. Joseph's College, our faculty members are renowned scholars and dedicated professionals who bring a wealth of experience to the classroom. They provide individual attention, interactive instruction and thoughtful advising. You will be prepared for career success through work experience opportunities, field studies, hands-on projects, internships and—if you choose—study abroad. Our core curriculum is exciting and relevant, and offers you a depth of knowledge with valuable, hands-on professional preparation and career-building experiences. Here, you will become well-prepared to meet, and exceed, evolving market needs.

Service is at the heart of a St. Joseph's education. In 2014, our students embraced a service-based alternative spring break, where we helped rebuild communities in Colorado that were devastated by flooding. In 2015, our students traveled to Breezy Point, NJ, to assist Habitat for Humanity in rebuilding houses that were destroyed by Superstorm Sandy. SJC also sponsors Liberation Theology in Nicaragua, a service-learning experience that allows students to work with community stakeholders in the Central American nation.

A liberal arts education is becoming increasingly important to employers locally and nationally. Through numerous internship opportunities, you will be placed on a fast track into the field. Recently, our students gained invaluable experience interning at the offices of local politicians, as well as top businesses such as Viacom (MTV), Major League Baseball, the Brooklyn Navy Yard and several accounting firms, including Grant Thornton LLP. Some of our accounting internships have led to full-time positions upon completion.

ADMISSIONS

St. Joseph's College is a selective institution. Applicants are evaluated on an individual basis. The college enrolls students who are academically talented and diverse. Successful admissions candidates typically have:

• A high school diploma or its equivalent or your postsecondary transcripts

• A personal statement of essay of recommendation

• Standardized test scores that demonstrate the promise of success in college-level courses

Recommended to also submit: two letters of recommendation and a personal essay

St. Joseph's College offers generous scholarships and financial aid packages to students who qualify. For a listing of our scholarships, please visit our website at sjcny.edu/admissions/financial-aid.

Students can obtain a copy of our application or also apply online, by visiting sjcny.edu/applynow.

When should I apply? When is the application deadline?

St. Joseph's College admits students on a rolling basis, but there are scholarship priority dates. For the fall semester, the scholarship priority date is March 15 for freshmen and August 1 for transfer students. For the spring semester, the priority date is January 1 for both freshmen and transfer students.

What do I need to submit as a transfer student?

Applications can be submitted by mail or online. Transfer students should request that official transcripts from all former colleges, and a listing of courses in progress be sent to our Office of Admissions. You are not required to submit a high school transcript if you have an A.A. degree or have successfully completed 24 or more credits from an accredited college. You may transfer a maximum of 64 credits if you have an A.A. degree; certain A.A.S. degrees are also transferable.

ACADEMICS

Majors

Accounting

Biology

Business Administration

• Finance

• Sports Management

Chemistry

Computer Information Technology

Criminal Justice

• Community Correctional Alternatives

• Criminal Justice and Technology

• Juvenile Justice

• Law and Justice

• Mental Health

Economics

Education

• Adolescence Education

(Secondary Education)

- Biology, Chemistry, English,

History, Mathematics, Spanish

• Child Study/Special Education

English

History

Human Relations

Hospitality and Tourism Management

• Health Care Hospitality

• Hotel Management

• Tourism

Journalism and New Media Studies

Marketing

Mathematics

Mathematics/Computer Science

Medical Technology

Nursing

Political Science

Psychology

Recreation

• Leisure Services Management

• Therapeutic Recreation

Religious Studies and Philosophy

Social Sciences

• Economics

Sociology

Spanish

Speech (Communication Studies)

Five-year Dual-Degree Programs

B.S./M.B.A. in Accounting

B.S. in Adolescence Education in Chemistry/M.A. in Childhood or Adolescence Special Education

B.A. in Adolescence Education in English/M.A. in Childhood or Adolescence Special Education

B.A. in Adolescence Education in History/M.A. in Childhood or Adolescence Special Education

B.A. or B.S. in Adolescence Education in Mathematics/M.A. in Childhood or Adolescence Special Education

B.A. in Adolescence Education in Spanish/M.A. in Childhood or Adolescence Special Education

Pre-Professional Programs

Accounting

Business Administration

Pre-Dental

Pre-Law

Pre-Medical

Pre-Veterinarian

Recreation

Teacher Education

Special Programs

Anthropology

CISCO Certification

Dance

Drama and Theatre

Physics

Speech Pathology

Certificate Programs

In addition to our undergraduate programs, St. Joseph's College offers credit-bearing certificates that part-time students can complete in less than a year. These certificates may be earned by themselves or as part of an undergraduate degree. Certificate programs enable you to delve deeper into your specific interests, help you focus on your career goals and give you a head start when entering the work world.

We offer certificate programs in:

• Alcoholism and Addictions Counseling
• Care Management
• Counseling
• Criminology/Criminal Justice
• Gerontology
• Health Care Management
• Home Care Administration
• Hospice
• Human Resources (also online)
• Information Technology Applications
• Leadership and Supervision (also online)
• Management
• Marketing, Advertising, and Public Relations
• Training and Staff Development

Affiliated Programs

If you're studying at our Brooklyn Campus, you can participate in a fast track to an advanced degree through:

St. Joseph's College Accounting Program (B.S. plus M.B.A., a five-year program)

Podiatric Medicine: St. Joseph's College/New York College of Podiatric Medicine (leads to a Doctor of Podiatric Medicine, D.P.M.)

A Service Members Opportunity College

As a member of SOC (Service Members Opportunity College), a consortium of more than 1,800 institutions pledged to work with Service Members, their families and veterans, St. Joseph's College is committed to the transfer of relevant course credits, flexible academic residence requirements and credit learning from appropriate military training and work experience. St. Joseph's College is a Post-9/11 GI Bill Yellow Ribbon Program participant. For more information and to apply for the Post-9/11 GI Bill benefits, visit gibill.va.gov.

TUITION AND AID

St. Joseph's College is committed to providing quality education while maintaining the lowest private college tuition rates in New York. To supplement the cost of education, scholarships, loans, and work-study programs are some of the financial aid options available to you. Currently, more than 80 percent of our students receive some form of financial aid.

STUDENT BODY

As a St. Joseph's student, you will have a plethora of extracurricular opportunities within reach through our Office of Co-Curricular Programs where you can join clubs, athletics, organizations and committees that emphasize leadership, community service and effective communication. We also arrange for student's health insurance. To learn more about the Office of Student Life, visit sjcny.edu.

CAMPUS LIFE
Brooklyn Campus

Architecturally stunning halls in the historic Clinton Hill neighborhood. Advanced technology. An outdoor theater. The Hill Center. And the nationally recognized Dillon Child Study Center. These combine to help make SJC's Brooklyn Campus a unique community. Dillon, as it is commonly referred to as, offers toddler, pre-school and kindergarten programs based on the child development approach to the education of young children. The recently opened Hill Center is home to our NCAA Division III sports, offering a regulation-size gymnasium and many multi-purpose areas. Situated in the Clinton Hill section of Brooklyn, which is home to several prestigious schools, and is a hub of cultural and intellectual activity. Career opportunities and extensive cultural attractions in Manhattan are within reach via public transportation.

Long Island Campus

The Long Island Campus features the Business Technology Center, the John A. Danzi Athletic Center, the Clare Rose Playhouse, the Callahan Library and a state-of-the-art outdoor athletic field complex for soccer, lacrosse, baseball, softball and tennis.

Located in the Village of Patchogue on the Great South Bay, our 27-acre Long Island Campus is approximately 50 miles from Manhattan and 60 miles from Montauk Point in Suffolk County. Patchogue offers fine marinas, shops, restaurants, athletic fields and tennis courts right in the Village.

SAINT LOUIS UNIVERSITY

AT A GLANCE

Founded in 1818, Saint Louis University (SLU) is a premier Catholic, Jesuit research university offering a broad range of nationally ranked undergraduate, graduate and professional programs. The second-oldest Catholic university in the nation, SLU has been a pioneer in higher education for nearly 200 years, and today continues its strong tradition of serving a higher purpose by contributing to the greater good.

With campuses in St. Louis, Missouri, and Madrid, Spain, SLU fosters the intellectual, moral and spiritual development of more than 13,000 students from all 50 U.S. states and nearly 80 foreign countries. SLU students—who rank the near the top 10 percent of all college students in the country—come to the University to pursue a top-notch education in a broad range of disciplines. They also take advantage of SLU's highly ranked programs in business, law and engineering; special opportunities such as direct-entry nursing and health sciences programs, and early admission to the University's medical and law schools; and extensive study-abroad program options.

IN THE CLASSROOM AND BEYOND

SLU offers students something rare in higher education: The opportunity to study at a place where academic achievement and scientific advancement unite with a commitment to community and Jesuit values.

Here, 99 percent of tenured and tenure-track faculty members hold a Ph.D. or the highest degree in their field. And with SLU's low student-faculty ratio (12-1), students receive personalized attention from the top scholars in their fields. As one of only nine Catholic universities with a high or very high research activity designation, SLU also offers students the chance to collaborate with innovative researchers on groundbreaking work that is changing lives.

This emphasis on making a difference takes SLU students beyond the classroom, and the University is consistently recognized on the national level for its dedication to educating the whole person. SLU was named to the President's Higher Education Community Service Honor Roll for the seventh consecutive year in 2014, and it has been designated as a "character-building college" by the Templeton Foundation. Each year, SLU students, faculty and staff members collectively complete more than 1 million hours of community service.

Around the world, Saint Louis University students put their education into practice. Six months after graduation, 96 percent of SLU graduates report that they are satisfied in their postgraduate activities, including pursuing careers and graduate studies. SLU alumni have directed Hollywood blockbusters, become mayors of major cities, helped put men on the moon and worked side-by-side with Mother Theresa. Alumni are also highly successful doctors, lawyers, physical therapists, engineers and social workers, among countless other careers.

Learn more about SLU at slu.edu and beabilliken.com.

LOCATION AND ENVIRONMENT

At Saint Louis University, students are in the center of everything. SLU's beautiful urban campus in Midtown St. Louis stretches across more than 230 acres of lush greenery, flowers and fountains. Students and visitors alike appreciate the unique vibe of a close-knit community nestled in the middle of a bustling city. Get a taste of campus and schedule your own visit at visit.slu.edu.

The St. Louis metro region boasts nearly 3 million people, with approximately 320,000 residents in the city itself. The city's mix of Midwestern friendliness and large-city amenities has helped St. Louis garner its ranking as one of the best cities for young professionals. In 2015, St. Louis grabbed the No. 1 spot on Popular Mechanics' "Best Startup Cities in America" list. The city is home to the famous Gateway Arch and a variety of cultural, historical and sporting attractions.

Midtown St. Louis serves as a starting point to explore the city's vibrant downtown and the dozens of unique neighborhoods nearby. Just steps away from SLU's urban campus is Grand Center, the region's premier arts district, rich with theater and music. Students can also hop onto a light rail train or bus and sample international delicacies in one of the many popular restaurants; stroll through Forest Park, home to the city's free zoo, art museum, science center and history museum; or catch the country's hottest bands or up-and-coming indie acts at the Pageant.

With three professional sports teams and a number of independent sports teams, St. Louis is always high on any sports fan's list of must-see cities. Students also love cheering on the Saint Louis University Billikens as the only NCAA Division I school in St. Louis. SLU fields teams in 18 different sports, and the Billikens have earned many accolades, including 10 NCAA men's soccer championships, more than any other team in the United States. The Billiken basketball teams play in the 10,600-seat Chaifetz Arena, and the men's team recently made three straight NCAA Tournament appearances.

But that's not all SLU has to offer. The University expanded internationally in 1969 by establishing a campus in Madrid, Spain, becoming one of the first American institutions of higher education to open a campus abroad. SLU-Madrid has been recognized by Spain's higher education authority as an official foreign university, the first U.S. institution ever so recognized. Each semester, more than 650 students pursue their studies at the Madrid campus.

ACADEMIC PROGRAMS

At Saint Louis University, students can be confident they're getting a world-class education. SLU is highly ranked by the Princeton Review's "Top 379 Colleges" and by U.S. News & World Report, with 13 graduate and professional programs ranked in the top 100 in their fields. Students also have lots of options. SLU offers nearly 100 undergraduate programs of study and nearly 80 graduate and professional programs.

UNDERGRADUATE PROGRAMS

Business

Offered by the John Cook School of Business

Accounting	International Business
Economics (B.S.)	Leadership and Change Management
Entrepreneurship	Marketing
Finance	Sports Business
Information Technology Management	

Engineering and Aviation

Offered by the Parks College of Engineering, Aviation and Technology

Aerospace Engineering	Engineering Physics
Aviation Management	Flight Science ^
Biomedical Engineering	Interdisciplinary Engineering
Civil Engineering	Mechanical Engineering
Computer Engineering	Physics
Electrical Engineering	

Health Care

Offered by the Doisy College of Health Sciences

Athletic Training °	Medical Laboratory Science
Cytotechnology	Nuclear Medicine Technology
Health Information Management	Nutrition and Dietetics
Health Sciences	Occupational Science and Occupational Therapy °
Investigative and Medical Sciences	Physical Therapy °
Magnetic Resonance Imaging	Radiation Therapy

Offered by the School of Nursing

Nursing

Offered by the college for Public Health and Social Justice

Biostatistics	Health Management
Emergency Management	Public Health

Liberal Arts

Offered by the college of Arts and Sciences

African American Studies	Italian Studies
American Studies	Latin American Studies
Anthropology	Medieval Studies
Art History	Music
Classical Humanities	Philosophy
Communication	Political Science
Economics (B.A.)	Russian Studies
English	Sociology
French	Spanish
German Studies	Studio Art
Greek and Latin Languages and Literature	Theater
History	Theological Studies
International Studies	Women's and Gender Studies

Sciences

Offered by the college of Arts and Sciences

Biochemistry	Geology
Biology	Geophysics
Chemistry	Mathematics
Communication Sciences and Disorders	Meteorology
Computer Science	Neuroscience
Environmental Science	Physics
Environmental Studies	Psychology
Forensic Science	

Education and Service

Offered by the college of Education and Public Service

Early Childhood Education	Middle School Education
Early Childhood Special Education	Secondary Education
Elementary Education	Education (without certification)
Elementary Education with Special Education	
for Mild/Moderate Disabilities	

Offered by the college for Public Health and Social Justice

Criminology and Criminal Justice	Social Work

Professional Studies

Offered by the School for Professional Studies

Criminal Justice and Security Management	Computer Information Systems
Education/Teacher Certification Programs	Nursing
General Studies	Organizational Leadership
Organizational Studies	Social Work
Aviation Management Concentration	Contract Degree Option

Key

° A five-year, direct-entry master's degree program.

^ Students are strongly encouraged to apply by Dec. 1 for the Flight Science program.

° Physical Therapy is a direct-entry doctoral program. Students must apply by Dec. 1 for consideration.

For the most up-to-date selection of majors and programs offered, visit admission. slu.edu.

CAMPUS FACILITIES AND EQUIPMENT

Over the past three decades, Saint Louis University improvements and expansions have totaled approximately $850 million. During the past few years, Saint Louis University unveiled the two most significant building projects in its history. The $82 million Edward A. Doisy Research Center offers SLU's world-class researchers a world-class facility. The $81 million Chaifetz Arena is not only the home for Billiken men's and women's basketball and Billiken volleyball, but also regularly hosts other sporting events, concerts, family shows, trade shows and more. SLU also recently moved its law school to a newly renovated 12-story building in downtown St. Louis, in the heart of the city's legal community.

In the fall of 2014, SLU announced a campus housing master plan that calls for new residence halls and extensive renovations to existing facilities. Construction has already begun on a new $43.8 million residence hall with the eight-story, 153,000-square-foot facility scheduled for completion in July 2016. The project is the first in what will be a series of potential projects designed to enhance the on-campus student experience.

Other recent campus enhancements include a major renovation of Pius XII Memorial Library and the addition of a new Center for Global Citizenship and the Everest Education Union at the University's Medical Center. The SLU Laclede Park Recreational Complex includes three lakes, walking paths, a picnic area, softball field and recreation fields. The campus is also home to the historic Cupples House, a fully restored mansion built in 1890, as well as several unique art galleries and St. Francis Xavier College Church.

TUITION, ROOM, BOARD AND FEES

Annual tuition for full-time undergraduate students is $37,350. Room and board amounts to approximately $10,088 per student (depending on specific residence hall and board plan). Fees average $616 per year.

FINANCIAL AID

Saint Louis University remains committed to keeping its one-of-a-kind education affordable and understands the sacrifices students and families make for quality education. SLU is dedicated to serving others, in part, by providing financial access to an unparalleled and life-changing educational experience.

For the fiscal year 2014, 97 percent of SLU's first-time freshmen received some sort of scholarship or financial assistance, as did 87 percent of all SLU students. The financial aid package for first-time freshmen entering in 2013-14 averaged $26,891.

Scholarships are awarded based on academic merit, talents, service, leadership and financial need. In addition to SLU's financial aid programs, the state of Missouri and the federal government also provide assistance.

Contact SLU's office of student financial services at 314-977-2350, 800-SLU-FOR-U or finaid@slu.edu.

STUDENT ORGANIZATIONS AND ACTIVITIES

Students support nearly 200 clubs, honor societies and service organizations; 18 NCAA Division I teams; intramural sports; and community service efforts that see more than 80 percent of SLU students volunteering at least once during the academic year.

Talent and commitment matter at SLU, and high levels of energy and dedication exist in everything Saint Louis University students pursue: academic societies, athletics, performing arts and media groups, student government, cultural and political organizations, and fraternities and sororities. Students come out in force to support Billiken athletics, and the Simon Recreation Center is popular with both serious and more casual athletes. Co-curricular life extends throughout the campus with numerous lectures, workshops, films, festivals, concerts and plays.

ADMISSION PROCESS

For information about the admission process at Saint Louis University or to schedule a campus visit, call the office of admission at 800-SLU-FOR-U, email admission@ slu.edu, or check out visit.slu.edu.

SAINT MICHAEL'S COLLEGE

AT A GLANCE

At Saint Michael's College, we believe that a college education should prepare students not only for a meaningful career, but for a meaningful life.

That's why our students start by building a strong liberal studies foundation, then dive deep into their majors. By the time they graduate, they've developed essential skills and knowledge that will help ensure success in any field. And in the meantime, they've also been engaged in service (through our popular MOVE program), in the great outdoors (with our pioneering Wilderness Program and Smuggs' Ski Pass), and with the close campus community in meaningful ways that educate the body, mind and spirit.

And happiness matters. At Saint Michael's, you'll find bright, engaged, friendly, happy students and faculty. Our formula for happiness is our close campus community, our perspective-changing exploration of the liberal arts with experiential learning, our legacy of faith and service, and our stunning Vermont location.

All this happiness and engagement underscores Saint Michael's successes: We are among only ten percent of colleges and universities nationwide that host a prestigious Phi Beta Kappa chapter on campus. Our recent graduates are Rhodes Scholars, Pickering Fellows, medical students, law students, dental students, researchers, pharmacists, new media specialists, sports writers, entrepreneurs, and more. Alumni include a United States Senator, one of the founders of MTV, published authors, acclaimed scientists, investment bankers, psychologists, teachers, professors and scholars. No matter what career paths they choose, our alumni take with them a solid liberal arts foundation, a strong sense of self and a desire to give back to their communities.

Students at Saint Michael's are seriously involved with life on campus, taking on leadership roles, rallying support for worthy causes and generally making things happen. Because everyone lives on campus (student housing is guaranteed for all four years), there's a profound sense of community, and you'll always find someone ready for whatever adventures you have in mind, from taking on a research project to rock climbing. Over one third of St. Mike's students study abroad for a semester, an academic year or a summer.

LOCATION

Saint Michael's beautiful, safe 440-acre campus is just three miles from Burlington, which Travel + Leisure ranks number 13 in America's best college towns. Burlington is Vermont's biggest city, and home to 14,000 students who attend five local colleges and universities. Downtown Burlington is a thriving city center of businesses that offer great opportunities for hands-on learning through internships. There are tons of shops, restaurants, and cafés, the Church Street Marketplace and a lively local music scene as well as numerous places to ski, skate, kayak and bike. Our Smuggs' Pass gives students access to some of the best skiing in the East, and our renowned Wilderness Program offers dozens of outdoor adventure opportunities. Our Cultural Pass provides students with significantly reduced ticket prices to fine arts performances at Burlington's famous Flynn Center.

The Burlington International Airport, Amtrak station, Megabus stop, and the Greyhound bus station are all only a 10-minute drive from campus.

MAJORS AND DEGREES

Saint Michael's College offers bachelor's degrees with a liberal arts foundation. Students choose from 36 majors in the following areas: accounting, American studies, art, art education, biochemistry, biology, business administration, chemistry, classics, computer science, economics, elementary education, engineering (3+2), English, environmental science, environmental studies, French, gender studies, history, information systems, international relations, mathematics, media studies, digital arts & journalism, music, neuroscience, philosophy, physics, political science, pre-pharmacy, psychology, religious studies, secondary education, sociology and anthropology, Spanish, and theater. In addition, advising programs for pre-medicine, prelaw, pre-dentistry, pre-physical therapy, and pre-veterinary studies are available. 37 minors are also available, including interdisciplinary studies.

Dual degree programs are available in engineering through the University of Vermont (Burlington, Vermont) and Clarkson University (Potsdam, New York); pharmacy through Albany College of Pharmacy's Burlington campus as well as graduate degree partnerships with other colleges and universities.

ACADEMIC PROGRAMS

Saint Michael's prepares its students for life after college with a dynamic liberal arts curriculum designed to foster intellectual curiosity and exploration, including a highly competitive honors program and many opportunities for self-directed study. Our curriculum emphasizes a solid understanding of building blocks of a meaningful life as a well-rounded, thoughtful person: humanities, social sciences, religious studies, philosophy, natural sciences, mathematics and fine arts. Our students develop excellent communication skills through writing intensive courses, and foreign language requirements. And our curriculum pays serious attention to questions of ethics and responsible citizenship.

Saint Michael's operates on a two-semester system with an optional accelerated summer session. The college's focus is on undergraduate instruction, and our small classes support this primary emphasis. Saint Michael's emphasizes faculty-student research and offers competitive opportunities for research for academic credit during the academic year and over the summer.

Saint Michael's mission is most evident in our service-learning and experiential-learning opportunities. These are credit-bearing, educational experiences where students in an academic course participate in a thoughtfully organized service activity to meet identified community needs. Students reflect on this hands-on learning in ways that develop further understanding of course content, a broader appreciation of the discipline and an enhanced sense of civic responsibility.

OFF-CAMPUS PROGRAMS

At Saint Michael's, you can gain hands-on experience in an internship related to your career goals and major. Internships are available both locally and in other selected areas around the U.S. and abroad. Sites include scientific research laboratories, brokerage houses, hospitals, schools, media outlets and accounting firms.

More than a third of our students study abroad for a semester or an academic year. Unique Saint Michael's programs include study-abroad experiences at University of the Americas, Mexico; College of Ripon and York St. John, England; Kansai Gaidai University, Japan; and a Washington, D.C., semester program. In recent years, many students have studied abroad in locations such as Botswana, China, France, Ghana, Ireland, Italy, Nepal, Samoa, and Spain.

Through the Association of Vermont Independent Colleges, Saint Michael's students can take a semester at another private college in Vermont including Middlebury, Bennington, Marlboro, Sterling, and Green Mountain College.

ACADEMIC FACILITIES

Saint Michael's has a Main Campus and a North Campus. Main Campus is home to almost all academic and administrative buildings. Durick Library provides students with state-of-the-art technology for research and a perfect environment for study. Collections include over 430,000 books and e-books, 120,000 online journals, and 5,000 DVDs. Students can log in to library research databases from on or off campus, even when studying abroad. The library building seats over 500 for individual or group study and is open until 1:00 a.m. daily.

Students have access to approximately 500 computers connected to the college's campus-wide information technology network. All campus areas have wireless internet access.

Cheray Science Center includes up-to-date laboratories, classrooms and other facilities for the study of biochemistry, biology, chemistry, environmental studies, and physics.

Saint Edmund's Hall, an impressive academic complex, includes media labs, psychology labs, computer facilities, and language labs, in addition to traditional classroom and lecture hall space.

COSTS

Tuition and residence fees for the 2015–2016 academic year are $51,175. The residence fee includes housing and meals and is based on a standard double room and a standard meal plan. One hundred percent of students live on campus, and on-campus housing for all four years is both guaranteed and required. Housing options include traditional residence halls, apartment-style housing, theme housing, and suites.

FINANCIAL AID

Approximately 90 percent of admitted students receive financial aid in the form of loans, grants and scholarships, and work-study dollars. Students must file the FAFSA by February 1 for fall-semester enrollment.

FACULTY

Saint Michael's faculty are known not only for being experts in their fields but for sharing that expertise effectively with their students. Their doors are always open, too—it's not unusual to join professors for coffee or lunch, or to be invited to their homes for dinner. You'll find them at fundraisers and on the sidelines of athletic games. And chances are excellent that they'll know your name by the end of your first week of class. Saint Michael's professors include 152 full-time faculty members, 88 percent whom have the doctoral or terminal degree in their field. Many have been recipients of grants, awards, and honors in recent years. While undergraduate instruction is the focus of the college, faculty members remain active in their field through research and publication.

STUDENT GOVERNMENT

The Student Association (SA), an active and important part of campus life, is an elected body of students that authorizes and funds most other student activities and organizations. Representatives from the SA sit on many campus-wide committees, including the Curriculum Committee and various committees of the Board of Trustees.

ADMISSION REQUIREMENTS

Successful applicants to Saint Michael's typically rank in the top 25 percent of their high school class and have a strong college-preparatory background. Students should have completed 16 units of courses in English, foreign language, mathematics, science, and social science. The average SAT score last year for accepted students ranged between 1600 and 1900, and the average ACT score ranged between 25 and 26. SAT or ACT scores are optional for admission purposes, but applicants wishing to be considered for merit-based aid are strongly advised to submit test scores if they fall within those ranges. In addition, students should submit a counselor recommendation and any teacher recommendations they choose. Transfer applicants must submit their final high school transcript and transcripts of all college work.

APPLICATION AND INFORMATION

Saint Michael's offers an Early Action admission program deadline (non-binding) of either November 1 or December 1, as well as a Regular Action deadline of February 1. Students should consult the website for application deadlines and information. Candidates for the fall semester are notified of their admission decision no later than April 1. A limited number of students may be admitted to the spring semester and should have their applications in by November 1. The college adheres to the Candidates Reply Date of May 1 for the fall semester.

For further information, students should contact:

Office of Admission

Saint Michael's College

One Winooski Park, Box 7

Colchester, Vermont 05439

United States

Phone: 800-762-8000

Fax: 802-654-2906

E-mail: admission@smcvt.edu

Website: www.smcvt.edu

SAINT XAVIER UNIVERSITY

AT A GLANCE

Saint Xavier is a private, four-year Catholic university where time-honored achievements meet cutting-edge programs. At Saint Xavier, our focus is on providing a meaningful education while preparing students for successful, 21st century careers. Small class sizes and engaging professors offer a unique, small-school experience, while 43 undergraduate and 25 graduate programs offer endless opportunities.

Founded by the Sisters of Mercy in 1846, Saint Xavier was the first Mercy institution of higher learning in the United States. As one of 17 colleges and universities sponsored by the Sisters of Mercy, Saint Xavier is part of a vibrant network that links nearly 43,000 students nationwide and a global community of educators.

As a Mercy university, our mission is to educate men and women to search for truth, to think critically, to communicate effectively and to serve wisely and compassionately in support of human dignity and the common good. The University is committed to service and we challenge our community members to teach, learn, research and act not only for themselves but also for others.

LOCATION AND ENVIRONMENT

Saint Xavier University has a small campus size with a total enrollment of over 4,000 students and is located in Chicago, Illinois.

This fall, the University will open its doors to an 87,000-square-foot satellite location in the downtown Heritage District of Gilbert, Arizona. Saint Xavier University's brand new, four-story building will provide students premier access to state-of-the-art technology, smart classrooms, nursing labs and student lounges, as well as gathering and study space.

OFF-CAMPUS OPPORTUNITIES

Saint Xavier University's lush 74-acre main campus is located in Chicago's southwest side. Students enjoy the quaint charm of the historic Mount Greenwood neighborhood while being conveniently located only 30 minutes from downtown Chicago, with all of the sights, attractions, and culture the city has to offer. Student life centers around academic enrichment, exciting social events and award-winning athletics that bring the entire campus together as a community.

Through the "Discover Chicago" program, SXU makes it easy for you to take advantage of the city's one-of-a-kind entertainment and cultural resources. The program offers access, including transportation, to a wide range of attractions and events—from visits to the Chicago Art Institute to Chicago Bulls home games—all for free or at a low cost to Saint Xavier University students.

MAJORS AND DEGREES OFFERED

Bachelor's degrees, post baccalaureate certificates, and master's degrees are offered.

ACADEMIC PROGRAMS

Saint Xavier University is accredited at the institutional level by the Higher Learning Commission. With four academic divisions and 43 undergraduate programs, the possibilities are endless. Saint Xavier provides programs in arts and sciences, management, education, and nursing.

CAMPUS FACILITIES AND EQUIPMENT

Shannon Center—The main arena in this 85,000-square-foot facility seats up to 3,200 for athletic events, graduation ceremonies, concerts and other special events. Athletic resources in the center include a state-of-the-art fitness center; two recreation gyms; indoor running track; racquetball courts; and athletic training rooms.

Dining Services—With six locations to choose from, there are a variety of dining options on campus that allow students to sample international cuisine or grab a quick sandwich between classes. The SXU Diner menus are constructed around our "Profiles in Good Taste" concepts, featuring a combination of freshly prepared, made-to-order entrees, salads and sandwiches developed by our campus executive chef.

Health Center—The Health Center is staffed by two family practice nurse practitioners who provide comprehensive medical care for students, staff and the surrounding community. Other services include immunizations and limited laboratory services.

Counseling Center—The mission of the Counseling Center is to guide students toward personal wellness, balance and growth. Licensed counselors facilitate this through personal counseling and the Alcohol and Other Drug and Education Program/Committee (AODEP).

Public Safety Department—Saint Xavier University provides a professional Public Safety Department to serve its students, faculty and staff. The Department of Public Safety is committed to the highest quality of protective services in order to maintain and improve our unique educational environment and quality of life.

Residence Halls—The Chicago campus includes six residence halls that house approximately 800 students. Housing includes halls built with Leadership in Energy & Environmental Design technology. The University housing staff also includes Resident Directors and Resident Assistants to help students adjust to life on campus.

TUITION, ROOM, BOARD, AND FEES

Record numbers of our students are taking advantage of the University's residential facilities. Students interested in living on campus need to submit a $150 housing deposit and the housing contract. Room and board costs are approximately $10,000 per year. Most residents receive additional financial aid just by choosing to live on campus. Tuition at Saint Xavier University is $30,020 per year for undergraduate students and $915 per semester hour for graduate students.

FINANCIAL AID

Ninety-nine percent of new full-time undergraduates in 2014–2015 received an academic scholarship, a grant or both from Saint Xavier. Saint Xavier University is committed to serving the educational needs of students from all backgrounds, including those with significant financial need. Some of the scholarships provided by SXU include art, music, athletic, academic, and merit-based scholarships.

UDENT ORGANIZATIONS AND ACTIVITIES

ant to get involved on campus? On-campus activities and events help to keep sidents and commuter students connected and involved. There are 47 SXU clubs d organizations related to academic, cultural, spiritual, social, political, club sports, udent media, government, and leadership groups.

int Xavier also provides international education opportunities. Studying abroad can one of the most memorable experiences of your life. It allows you the opportunity learn about the world and other cultures through first-hand experiences. Stunts can participate in a semester abroad through program providers with college dents from across the United States. Our students have interned, volunteered d studied in such wide-ranging destinations as Australia, Jordan, Korea and Peru.

hletics are another aspect of the Saint Xavier experience. Saint Xavier University mpetes in the National Association of Intercollegiate Athletics (NAIA). Since 05, 10 of Saint Xavier's 17 varsity teams have qualified for the NAIA national ampionships including football, baseball, softball, women's volleyball, and men's d women's soccer, cross country and basketball.

ADMISSIONS PROCESS

A Saint Xavier University education opens the door to a broad array of opportunities—for professional development, personal fulfillment and much more. Here you'll discover rigorous, values-based education in a dynamic and supportive learning community. Saint Xavier prepares you to use your talents and education as a foundation for professional achievement and a successful life.

If you're ready to apply for admission, follow these steps to complete the process:

1. Apply online (no fee);

2. Request an °official high school transcript or GED score report;

3. Request your official ACT or SAT score(s), unless included on high school transcript.

°Options for official transcript submission:

•Paper transcripts can be accepted as official provided they are either mailed or personally delivered to the Office of Admission in the original, sealed envelope from the school.

•Electronic transcripts can be accepted as official provided they are emailed directly from the school or are submitted via an electronic transcript service to admission@sxu.edu.

SEATTLE UNIVERSITY

Students who are adventurous, forward-thinking, creative and have an interest in social justice are drawn to Seattle University, located in the heart of a city with unparalleled access to innovation and culture.

AT A GLANCE

Seattle has produced some of the world's most prestigious and influential companies such as Microsoft, Starbucks, Amazon and Costco. This urban setting is where all walks converge to find a better way forward. Seattle University is a school of action with an ever-growing impact on the city, the community and throughout the world.

The greatest successes at Seattle University are the result of people coming together and standing united to bring about great change. A good example: The Seattle University Youth Initiative, the university's largest-ever community engagement project, which continues to grow as it transforms academic achievement at the city's most underperforming public elementary school. The lure of the Youth Initiative is compelling—so much so that an increasing number of incoming students say it's the top reason they choose to come to SU. Worldwide, other universities—20 and counting—see the Youth Initiative as a successful prototype. The White House took notice, too, and honored the Youth Initiative with several awards for community service in each of the last three years.

In a state like Washington, where dozens of different languages are spoken and every race, religion and perspective is represented, Seattle University's 4,500 undergraduate students from 53 states and 89 nations fit right in.

A transformation happens when you're a student here. A Seattle University education instills in you a lifelong capacity to create a more just and humane world.

LOCATION AND ENVIRONMENT

You have discovered a lively and lush 50-acre campus at the center of an exceptional city. Seattle University's campus is pesticide-free and continues to win top awards for its commitment to environmental leadership, energy conservation, recycling and composting programs. Add to that, the university's Center for Environmental Justice and Sustainability is housed in the greenest commercial building in the world.

International Education Week presents a host of cultural events and lectures on campus each winter. There's also an annual luau.

If music is your thing, don't miss the biggest student-supported event of the year, Quadstock, an annual all-day music and arts festival in the spring. In winter quarter, there's Battle of the Bands where student bands compete for prizes and bragging rights.

Keeping students healthy and happy gets a boost when the anxiety of final exams hits. That's when the university hosts "De-Stress with Dogs," an invitation to put down the books for a bit and spend some time with energetic furry friends.

OFF-CAMPUS ADVENTURES

As the Pacific Northwest's largest city, Seattle is a cultural center known for first-run entertainment.

The Seattle International Film Festival is the largest and most highly attended its kind in the United States. With more than 250 feature and 150 short films fro 70-plus countries, this 25-day festival takes place here every spring.

You can catch a professional sporting event such as Sounders FC soccer or Marine baseball. And what about those Seattle Seahawks? You, too, can become part of t 12th Man crowd and cheer them on with the loudest fans in the NFL.

Just a quick walk from Seattle University, you'll find music, coffee houses a restaurants galore in the Capitol Hill neighborhood. People watch at a café, expe ence an author reading in a quirky bookstore or browse through one of the are many thrift shops. Feeling hungry? Consider a night out at one of the city's ethn eateries and restaurants nearby.

Take in the breathtaking skyline at the top of the iconic Space Needle or on t Seattle Great Wheel, a 175-foot Ferris wheel on Seattle's waterfront alongside Pug Sound. Catch a sightseeing ferry ride across Puget Sound or wander through Pi Place Market, the Olympic Sculpture Park or the Museum of History and Indust all a short distance from campus.

Even in the city, you're not far from wooded hiking trails and challenging s slopes. Experience mountain views of the Cascades to the East and the Olympi to the West.

Numerous lakes, the largest of which are Lake Washington and Lake Union, al are part of the territory. With the blast of a cannon and a parade of boats, Seatt rings in Opening Day of boating season. There's also Seafair featuring a flig demonstration by the Blue Angels.

In the summer, there's the famous Fremont Solstice Parade and Festival. Nort west Folklife and Bumbershoot are a pair of music festivals that take place ov Memorial Day and Labor Day weekends that draw national acts to Seattle Cent under the Space Needle.

There's plenty more to grab your attention in this dynamic and diverse city. Seatt Center also hosts more than 20 ethnic festivals that range from the Seattle Cher Blossom and Japanese Cultural Festival to French Fest, from a Vietnamese Lun New Year celebration to an Irish Festival around St. Patrick's Day.

MAJORS AND DEGREES OFFERED

The university offers 64 majors and 31 minors in five colleges and schools: Albe School of Business and Economics, College of Arts and Sciences, College of Nur ing, College of Science and Engineering and Matteo Ricci College. Undergradua degrees include Bachelor of Arts, of Science, of Science in Nursing, of Social Wor of Criminal Justice and of Arts in Business Administration. For specifics on majo and minors, visit the Seattle University website at www.seattleu.edu.

ACADEMIC PROGRAMS

Central to the academic excellence of SU is the Core curriculum, which enriches academic rigor and engages new students quickly, deeply and thoughtfully. The Core offers a glimpse at how SU inspires insightful and creative thinkers and serves as an important foundation for studies in the various majors and minors.

Designed to help students develop intellectual abilities, there's a strong liberal arts focus with broad exposure to the humanities, social sciences, natural sciences and arts. Instead of broad survey courses, Core courses focus on specific questions. The study of those questions gives students a closer look at a discipline and how knowledge is pursued. Theology and philosophy play critical roles. There's also a focus on global engagement so students can examine their roles in local, regional, national and transnational cultures and communities.

Seattle University continues its long-term relationship with the University of Central America in Nicaragua for exchange programs. In addition, students are in educational service programs abroad in more than 40 countries. Among them, the senior economics major who spent a quarter in Chiang Mai, Thailand, at a sanctuary that's home to more than 30 rescued elephants, and the junior political science major in a yearlong study in Santiago, Chile, where he wrote for the Santiago Times.

CAMPUS FACILITIES AND EQUIPMENT

The university is cradled between the First Hill and Capitol Hill neighborhoods in the center of Seattle. The campus has 28 buildings enhanced by $200 million in additions, renovations or new construction in the past 15 years.

A major expansion of the campus library, now the Lemieux Library and McGoldrick Learning Commons, provides state-of-the-art digital learning opportunities. The library's media production center features a recording studio, control room, audio/video editing facilities and a theater-style screening room.

The College of Nursing's 20,000-square-foot Clinical Performance Lab is among the most technically advanced in the nation, with two clinical practice rooms and a suite of laboratories.

The state-of-the-art William F. Eisiminger Fitness Center, tennis courts, track and both natural and synthetic turf playing fields draw students in their off hours. School spirit gets a big boost from Division I athletics.

TUITION, ROOM, BOARD AND FEES

For the 2015–16 academic year, full-time tuition is $38,970; room and meals are $11,120. The estimate for books, supplies, fees and personal expenses is an additional $6,390. Travel costs vary. Costs are subject to change. Seattle University operates on a quarter calendar with fall term beginning in late September. Students are required to live on campus for their first two years, and six on-campus residence halls house more than 2,000 students.

FINANCIAL AID

More than 94 percent of new freshmen in 2013-14 received financial aid; the average award was $24,699 per year. These awards usually include scholarships, grants, loans and Federal Work-Study. Last year, Seattle University awarded more than $102.4 million in aid to undergraduates. Nearly $72 million of that came from the university's own funds. Students are required to apply for financial aid by Feb. 1, as awards are made early each spring for the following fall quarter. Applications that are received after this deadline will be evaluated in the order received for any remaining aid. Students must submit the Free Application for Federal Student Aid (FAFSA) and be accepted for admission to be considered for financial assistance. A number of freshman scholarships are awarded on the basis of academic achievement, extracurricular involvement and community service. Transfer scholarships also are available.

STUDENT ORGANIZATIONS AND ACTIVITIES

Student Government of Seattle University promotes opportunities for student leadership and involvement and assists in the development of a cohesive undergraduate community. You also can take your pick from more than 130 extracurricular clubs and organizations.

ADMISSIONS

Seattle University is committed to qualitative decision making based on evaluations of students as a whole. Decisions are based primarily on individual course selection, performance and trends. The expected academic program comprises 16 units of coursework, including four years of English, three years of social studies or history, two years of a foreign language, three years of college-preparatory mathematics and two units of lab science (three are preferred). Laboratory physics and chemistry, as well as four units of college-preparatory mathematics are required for engineering; the university also requires laboratory chemistry and biology for admission to the nursing program. Also required for all programs are official scores from either the ACT or the SAT I. The middle 50 percent of enrolling freshmen have secondary school averages of 3.4–3.9 (on a 4.0 scale).

Essays or personal statements are required for admission and are carefully considered during application review. College credit is awarded to those who have successfully earned minimum scores on Advanced Placement or International Baccalaureate examinations.

Applications and information can be obtained by contacting the Admissions Office. Secondary school students who have completed at least six semesters are encouraged to complete the application process no later than Jan. 15 of their senior year, the deadline for regular admission. For those who wish to apply via Early Action, the deadline is Nov. 15. Transfer students must submit official transcripts from all post-secondary institutions attended, regardless of whether course work was completed. The recommended financial aid/admission deadline for transfers is March 1, however transfer applications are welcomed until Aug. 15.

Campus visits are scheduled Monday through Friday and many Saturdays. Guests can attend a class, meet with faculty, participate in a campus tour and speak individually with representatives from admissions. Students can apply directly or online at www.seattleu.edu. Seattle University is a member of The Common Application.

SETON HALL UNIVERSITY

AT A GLANCE

As one of the nation's leading Catholic universities, Seton Hall provides over 90 rigorous academic programs that are highly ranked by The Princeton Review, U.S.News & World Report and Bloomberg Businessweek. We offer all the advantages of a large research university—national reputation; challenging academic programs; notable alumni; state-of-the-art facilities; renowned faculty; and extensive opportunities for internships, research and scholarship—with all the benefits of a small, supportive and nurturing environment. Our 14:1 student-to-faculty ratio and average class size of 21 students means faculty know more than just your name.

Our accomplished faculty include Fulbright Scholars, prominent researchers, authors, artists, filmmakers, former school superintendents and principals, leaders in nursing, former ambassadors, analysts and lawmakers—all of whom are dedicated to their fields and their students. They have graduated from some of the nation's leading institutions, including Seton Hall, Harvard, Columbia, Yale, Princeton and Dartmouth. Each day, our faculty members shine in the lecture halls and on the national stage. They meet regularly with students outside the classroom and help them learn to think critically.

Seton Hall offers more than 15,000 internship opportunities, and over 80 percent of our students have an internship—or two—on their resume before graduation, this is just one of the reasons our students have an employment rate of 86 percent—almost 20 percent higher than the national average. In fact, Seton Hall was recently ranked top 5 in the nation for providing internship opportunities. Our national reputation and stellar academic programs draw over 550 employers to campus each year just to recruit our graduates.

Seton Hall is a Catholic university with almost a 160-year tradition of educational excellence. A welcoming community, Seton Hall embraces students of all faiths and inspires students to become servant leaders who make a difference in the world. That's why our community performs over 40,000 hours of community service annually. You'll feel at home on our campus, where it's easy to make friends and get involved.

LOCATION AND ENVIRONMENT

Nestled in the suburban village of South Orange, New Jersey, Seton Hall provides small-town charm combined with big-city opportunities. The University's suburban, 58-acre park-like campus sits proudly within this picturesque town with tree-lined streets; historic, gracious homes; and quaint shops just 14 miles from New York City—close to all the action, yet not engulfed by it.

Just a five-minute walk from campus lands you in the middle of a bustling town center where you'll find diners and pizzerias, banks, pharmacies, Starbucks, Cold Stone Creamery, a gourmet marketplace, South Orange Performing Arts Center, a movie Theatre, and so much more. You might not ever want to leave this quiet suburbia, but if you do, the train station, right in the center of town, is your direct link to NYC's Penn Station—just 30 minutes away.

We take full advantage of all the Big Apple has to offer—where the worlds of entertainment, art, publishing, global finance, international diplomacy and fashion collide. NYC is also one of the world's largest job markets, brimming with internship and job placement opportunities in a variety of companies. Over 80% of Seton Hall students have an internship or two on their resume before graduation at leading companies like Goldman Sacs, American Express, CNN, the Secret Service, the United Nations, The New York Times, NBC, Sony Music, JP Morgan Chase and more.

And if all the advantage and opportunity of the Big Apple aren't enough, New Jersey's got you covered. One of the wealthiest states in the nation, New Jersey is brimming with opportunity. Seton Hall's backyard boasts a powerhouse corporate corridor of more than 50 Fortune 500 companies, pharmaceutical giants and major corporations. For you this means networking, internships and career opportunities.

MAJORS AND DEGREES OFFERED

Seton Hall is a place where leaders learn. This is evident in the nearly two dozen student and alumni national scholars and fellows, including nearly 20 prestigious Fulbright Scholars since 2009, as well as Rhodes, Udall, Pickering, Marshall, Critical Language and Truman Scholars and more than 100,000 alumni who are now successful as CEOS, judges, doctors, principals, CFOs, journalists, nurses,

diplomats and more. About 1,000 Seton Hall graduates have served in executive positions like Presidents, CEOs, CFOs, and Executive Vice Presidents at places like Oppenheim, the Visiting Nurse Service of New York, American Express and Merrill Lynch. They have served our nation as elected officials—in Washington, in Trenton and in hundreds of town halls throughout the country. In fact, in New Jersey alone almost 20% of our state's legislature holds a Seton Hall degree.

Seton Hall's commitment to academic excellence is evident in the more than 90 stellar academic programs offered through our six undergraduate schools and colleges. In addition the University has recently announced plans to form a medical school in partnership with Hackensack University Medical Center. The first medical school class is schedule to begin in the fall of 2017. A joint degree program for direct admission as a freshman applicant is also planned.

Majors and Programs

Accounting•, Accounting (5-year B.S./M.S. dual-degree∞), Africana Studies•, American Humanics√, Ancient Greek†, Anthropology•, Applied Scientific Mathematics†, Arabic†, Archaeology†, Art (Art History•, Fine Arts•, Graphic Interactive and Advertising Design•), Asian Studies•, Athletic Training (5-year B.S./M.S. B.A./M.S. dual-degree)∞, Biochemistry, Biology (B.A. or B.S.), Broadcasting, Visual and Interactive Media•, Business Administration•‡, Catholic Studies•‡, Catholic Theology•, Chemistry•, Classical Culture†, Classical Languages†, Classical Studies•, Communication Studies•, Computer Graphics√, Computer Science•, Creative Writing, Criminal Justice•, Data Visualization and Analysis√, Digital Media and Video√, Digital Media Production for the Web√, Diplomacy and International Relations•, Early Childhood (integrated with elementary and special education), Elementary Education (integrated with early childhood and special education), Education with Speech Language Pathology (6-year B.S.E./M.S. dual- degree)∞, Economics (B.A. or B.S.), Engineering (Biomedical, Chemical, Civil,, Computer, Electrical, Industrial, Mechanical)§, English•, Entrepreneurial Studies√, Environmental Sciences†, Environmental Studies•, Ethics and Applied Ethics†, Finance, French•, Gerontology√, History•, Information Technologies√, Information Technology Management‡, International Business†, Italian•, Italian Studies†, Journalism and Public Relations•, Latin†, Latin America and Latino/Latina Studies•, Law (dual admission program with Seton Hall Law)∞, Legal Studies in Business, Liberal Studies, Management, Marketing, Mathematical Finance , Mathematics•, M.B.A. (5-year B.S./M.B.A. or B.A./ M.B.A. dual-degree)∞, Modern Languages, Music (Comprehensive Music/Music Education, Music Performance•), Music Theatre†, Nonprofit Studies†, Nursing, Occupational Therapy (6-year B.A./M.S. dual-degree)∞, Online Course Development and Management√, Philosophic Theology√, Philosophy•, Physical Therapy (7-year B.S./D.P.T. dual-degree)∞, Physician Assistant (6-year B.S./M.S. dual-degree)∞, Physics (B.A. or B.S.)•, Political Science•, Pre-Dental°, Pre-Law°, Pre-Medical°, Pre-Optometry°, Pre-Veterinary° Psychology (B.A. or B.S.)•, Religion•, Russian†, Russian and East European Studies†√, Secondary Education (optional integration with special education), Social and Behavioral Sciences, Social Work•, Sociology•, Spanish•, Special Education (integrated with early childhood, elementary, and secondary education), Speech Language Pathology (6-year B.S.E./M.S. dual- degree)∞, Sport Management•, Supply Chain Management√, Theatre and Performance•, Web Design√, Women and Gender Studies†, Writing†, Undecided

• Minor also available

† Minor only

√ Certificate program only

‡ Certificate program also available

§ Dual-degree Program with NJIT

∞ Seton Hall dual-degree program

(please contact the Office of

Admissions for details)

° Pre-professional programs (you must also select a major)

CAMPUS FACILITIES AND EQUIPMENT

Seton Hall places a strong emphasis on the use of state-of-the-art technology, facilities and support services to aid in its students' development. Many investments have been made to the campus infrastructure, including the recent construction of a new academic classroom building, new residence hall space, a new parking deck, a Dunkin Donuts and a new state of the art recreation and fitness center. In addition the campus boasts a state-of-the-art research library complete with a computerized catalog and 200 computer terminals. The Science and Technology Center, is home to state-of-the-future biology and chemistry labs, an atrium and auditorium, as well as an observatory and greenhouse.

The campus also offers man unique learning labs like our Mock Trading Room, Patient Simulation Laboratory, Market Research Center, student-run radio station, Sport Polling Center. Plus all incoming students are provided new, fully loaded laptop.

TUITION, ROOM, BOARD AND FEES

Seton Hall offers a flat-tuition rate for students taking between 12–18 credit hours. The 2014–15 tuition and fees are $37,226. Room and Board fees range depending on meal plans; however, an average cost is $12,254.

FINANCIAL AID

Paying for college is a major investment. Seton Hall University is committed to providing students with the resources needed to make your dreams a reality. The University gives over $75 million in aid each year and 98 percent of our students receive some form of financial aid with 97 percent receiving scholarships or grants directly from the University. Seton Hall University has been rated as one of the best schools in the nation for a return on your investment. Most scholarships are automatically awarded upon admission and do not require a separate applications. However there are also several special scholarships for which students can apply learn more at www.shu.edu/go/scholarships. Seton Hall also provides need-based aid to eligible students who complete the Free Application for Federal Student Aid (FAFSA) form by March 1.

STUDENT ORGANIZATIONS AND ACTIVITIES

On campus, Seton Hall leaders learn to put their ideas into action; discover something new; become part of a community; and build trust, spirit and lasting friendships. Here, you'll find activities galore, over 130 clubs and organizations and 22 Greek societies. You can audition for one of the nearly dozen theatre performances cast each year or broadcast at our award-winning, student-run radio station, WSOU-FM, which attracts more than 120,000 listeners a week from the NYC area. Join the Brownson Speech and Debate Team, ranked in the Top 20 college and university forensic teams for years or write for one of our three student newspapers. You'll not only make lots of new friends and have fun, you'll also learn about your leadership style. More than two-thirds of our students participate in clubs and organizations.

You don't have to be a superstar athlete to be part of the game at Seton Hall. Our athletic programs include competition on varsity, intramural and club levels. In fact, almost 50 percent of our students participate in club or intramural sports. Even if you don't know a handball from a handoff, you'll be decked out in blue and cheering your heart out when you attend any one of Seton Hall's 14 NCAA division I Big East athletic events. So grab your friends and catch some Pirate fever!

ADMISSIONS PROCESS

At Seton Hall, we take a holistic approach to reviewing your application. When we receive your application, we start by considering your academic performance in high school, your grades and the rigor of your curriculum, as well as your standardized SAT and/or ACT scores. These are essential indicators of your ability to succeed at Seton Hall. We also will consider your personal essay, recommendations and extracurricular activities.

The typical student who enter Seton hall last year had an average GPA of 3.4 (B+) and an average SAT score of 1130 on the Critical Reading and Math sections (24 on the ACT).

Visit

The best way to experience Seton Hall is to visit in person. We offer tours Mon-Fri at 10 am and 2 pm and on Saturdays at 10 am, noon and 2 pm. Open Houses are offered in mid-October, mid-November mid-February and late April. To schedule a visit or sign up for Open House visit www.shu.edu/visiting

For more information, contact the Office of Undergraduate Admission:

Website: admissions.shu.edu

Telephone: 1-800-THE-HALL (843-4255)

E-mail: thehall@shu.edu

#halladmissions

SIMMONS COLLEGE

AT A GLANCE

For more than a century, Simmons College has offered a pioneering liberals arts education integrated with professional work experience. Founded in 1899, Simmons was the first college in the United States to offer women a liberal arts education integrated with career preparation. At Simmons, we ignore arguments about whether leaders are born or made. Because here, leaders make themselves. Students work, discover and evolve, eventually becoming a leader for themselves, their community and the world.

Located in the heart of Boston, Simmons is best known for its small classes, access to faculty, and internship and research opportunities. Students say that Simmons's location offers the best of both worlds—an intimate college experience in the heart of a vibrant and bustling city. Simmons's nearly 2,000 undergraduates love the fact that they can easily access the city's rich social and cultural resources but also come home to a safe, friendly campus.

ACADEMICS AND MAJORS

Simmons offers more than 50 majors and programs. Popular majors include psychology, nursing, business, political science, and communications. Advisors help each student create a plan that fulfills requirements and satisfies her personal and professional goals. A number of integrated degrees and accelerated programs allow students to go directly from undergraduate study to earning a graduate degree in less time than traditional programs. Students can accelerate to graduate degrees in areas such as business, education, health care, liberal arts, physical therapy, social work, and library science. Simmons also offers individually designed pre-professional programs for dentistry, law, medicine, and veterinary medicine. Simmons students typically declare a major by the end of their sophomore year, and nearly a third choose to double major.

The hallmark of a Simmons education is the independent learning requirement, which students fulfill through internships, fieldwork, and research projects. Science students co-publish research with faculty in nationally recognized academic journals as undergraduate students. Most students take advantage of the abundance of competitive internship opportunities available in Boston. In addition, Simmons's Longwood Medical Area partnerships provide outstanding clinical opportunities at Boston's world-renowned hospitals. On campus, students conduct research using state-of-the-art equipment in areas such as materials science, gene splicing, and computer modeling. Yet the most important aspect of Simmons's approach to hands-on learning is that professors frequently invite undergraduates to collaborate on professional research projects, articles, and presentations, as early as their freshman year.

ADMISSION

Admission to Simmons College is highly selective. The admission committee looks for students who have shown academic excellence both in and out of the classroom, and evaluates high school performance, SAT or ACT scores, recommendations, and the application essay. If English is not the applicant's first language, the TOEFL, IELTS, or a comparable exam score is required. Typical high school preparation for entrance includes 4 years of English, 4 years of math, 3-4 years of social science, 3-4 years of lab sciences, and 3-4 years of a foreign language. Although not required, an interview and campus visit is strongly recommended.

Simmons welcomes applications from prospective freshmen, transfer students, international students, and students who are beyond the traditional college age.

Students may apply online, using the Common Application or the Simmons College online application, along with the $55 fee and all supporting credentials. The early action deadline I (nonbinding) is November 1, the Early Action II (nonbinding) is December 1. The regular freshman application deadline is February 1. Transfer students are evaluated on a continual basis; the preferred filing date for applications for the fall semester is April 1. All students applying for the spring should submit their application by November 1.

STUDENT BODY

Simmons fosters a student-centered environment and encourages each individual to actively participate in the college community in a way that is right for her. Simmons has more than fifty student organizations, clubs, and academic liaisons, including honor societies, cultural organizations, volunteer programs, a literary magazine, a campus newspaper, and ten NCAA Division III varsity teams. In addition, every academic department has a student liaison that participates in department evaluations and helps promote educational and social activities for students and faculty and staff members.

CAMPUS LIFE AND FACILITIES

Simmons's historic, tree-lined campus is located in Boston's eclectic Fenway neighborhood, which is alive with music and fine arts, medical care and research, action and activism, and the resounding cheers of baseball fans at legendary Fenway Park. Considered by many to be the best college town in the nation, Boston has more than 50 colleges and universities, and approximately 300,000 students. Compact, historic, charming, and clean, the city is easy to get around on foot or via the T, Boston's public transportation system.

SPECIAL NEEDS

Simmons College is committed to the full participation of all students in its programs and activities. Although Simmons has no academic program specifically designed for students with disabilities who are otherwise qualified for admission, Simmons is committed to providing support service and reasonable accommodations when requested by students who qualify for them.

The Disability Services staff assist students, both undergraduate and graduate, who have a disability, by reviewing documentation supplied by licensed professionals and by completing Student Accommodation Letters. The Disability Services staff will make referrals for diagnostic services (at student expense), provide advice and personal contact for students with disabilities, and assist with locating needed resources. The Disability Services staff is also available to faculty and staff who have questions regarding a student's accommodation and other issues pertaining to a disability.

Tuition & Aid

Tuition and fees for the 2014–2015 academic year are as follows:

Undergraduate tuition and fees: $37,380

Room and board: $14,040

Total: $51,420

Graduate tuition costs vary by program.

FINANCIAL AID

More than 95 percent of Simmons first-year students receive some form of financial aid. Scholarships, grants, loans, and federal work-study are determined by the Free Application for Federal Student Aid (FAFSA). Simmons also awards academic merit scholarships, ranging from $2000 to full tuition awards, renewable for four years.

For further information, contact:

Office of Undergraduate Admission

Simmons College

300 The Fenway

Boston, MA 02115

Telephone: 617-521-2051

Fax: 617-521-3190

E-mail: ugadm@simmons.edu

Website: www.simmons.edu/undergraduate

Ellen Johnson

Director of Undergraduate Admission

SKIDMORE COLLEGE

AT A GLANCE

Founded in 1903 and located in Saratoga Springs, N.Y., Skidmore is an independent, coeducational liberal arts college that prides itself on its creative approaches to just about everything. Hence, the college's core belief that creative thought matters. With a diverse student body of 2,400 from 45 states and 60 countries and a faculty of 250 dedicated teacher-scholars, Skidmore offers more than 40 majors in the humanities, sciences, and social sciences, as well as in career-specific fields such as business, education, exercise science, and social work.

Skidmore is known for its interdisciplinary approach to learning, faculty-student collaborative research, off-campus study (60% of students study abroad), and the prominence of the performing and visual arts, enhanced by the unique Tang Teaching Museum and Art Gallery and award-winning Arthur Zankel Music Center. The college's rigorous academic program begins with the foundational First-Year Experience, which integrates the curricular and cocurricular aspects of a student's first year, and gets them connected and involved in the life of the community from day one. Students enjoy close relationships with talented faculty members who have earned recognition through Guggenheim, Pulitzer, and Emmy awards, and fellowships and grants from Fulbright, MacArthur, and the National Science Foundation, among others. At least half of students carry two majors or add a related minor to their major. More than half of Skidmore students pursue advanced degrees within five years of graduation.

ADMISSIONS JOURNAL

Searching for a college experience that will challenge you? Give you virtually unlimited opportunities to create and explore? Then consider Skidmore. Creativity is embodied in all that is Skidmore: academics, co-curricular life, campus setting, and the nature of Saratoga Springs itself. We are a diverse world of thinkers and doers—academics, performing artists, community volunteers, and athletes who come together in the shared belief and commitment that creative thought matters. If you share that belief, consider visiting and applying to Skidmore.

LOCATION AND ENVIRONMENT

Saratoga Springs, 30 miles north of Albany, New York State's capital, is perennially short-listed as one of the most interesting and vibrant small cities in the U.S. Famed for "health, history, and horses"—its mineral waters, Revolutionary War battlefield, and the nation's oldest thoroughbred racetrack—Saratoga is equally renowned as an arts and cultural destination. The Saratoga Performing Arts Center is summer home to the New York City Ballet, Philadelphia Orchestra, and Lake George Opera, and is a performing venue for top rock and jazz musicians. The city's downtown—a 10-minute walk from Skidmore—is brimming with galleries, clubs, museums, shops, coffeehouses, bistros, and restaurants. No wonder Travel & Leisure magazine named it the sixth-best college town in the nation and the dailymeal.com rated it as the seventh-best college food town in America. The city's location near the foothills of the Adirondack Mountains puts an abundance of outdoor recreational opportunities within an hour's drive, including great downhill and Nordic skiing. Boston, New York City, and Montreal are each approximately 180 miles from the campus.

OFF-CAMPUS OPPORTUNITIES

About sixty percent of Skidmore's students spend a semester or year off campus. In addition to Skidmore programs in England, France, and Spain, students can access more than 130 international programs through the college's Approved Programs structure, including programs in Africa, Asia, Europe, Latin America, and Australia. All academic majors and minors can be accommodated, and transfer credits are guaranteed for students studying on an approved program. Financial aid is transferable to approved off-campus study programs. Students can also participate in a select group of U.S.-based off-campus programs, including an exchange with Spelman College, the Washington Semester (internship in conjunction with American University) and a semester at the Marine Biological Lab in Woods Hole, Mass. Arrangements for student internships (for academic credit, many funded) are made through Skidmore's academic departments or Career Development. More than 50% of Skidmore students are involved in volunteer work, much of it in the local community. There are also as many as 70 courses each semester with service-learning components.

MAJORS AND DEGREES OFFERED

Skidmore College grants a Bachelor of Arts degree in American studies, anthropology, Asian studies, biology, chemistry, classics, computer science, economics, English, environmental studies, foreign languages and literatures (French, German, and Spanish), gender studies, geosciences, government, history, history of art, international affairs, mathematics, music, neuroscience, philosophy, physics, psychology, religious studies, and sociology. The Bachelor of Science degree is granted in the following pre-professional areas: business, dance, education studies, exercise science, social work, studio art, and theater. There is also a self-determined major and 11 interdepartmental offerings. Most majors have corresponding minors. Minors are also available in arts administration, Chinese, intergroup relations, Italian, Japanese, Latin American studies, and media and film studies.

Skidmore offers dual-degree engineering programs with Clarkson, Dartmouth, and RPI; 4+1 M.B.A. programs with Clarkson, Rochester Institute of Technology, and Union Graduate College; the Whitman MBA Advantage program with Syracuse; 4+1 M.S.A. And M.S.F. programs with Syracuse; a 4+1 dual degree program in nursing with New York University's School of Nursing, and dual degree programs in occupational therapy and physical therapy at the Sage College Graduate School; M.S. in accountancy (Wake Forest University).

The college also offers a nonresidential program leading to a master of arts in liberal studies (MALS). An external degree program, MALS offers multidisciplinary graduate study to adult learners.

ACADEMIC PROGRAMS

The Skidmore academic journey begins with the First-Year Experience, which introduces students to the college's rigorous academic program and overall approach to learning and connects them with a faculty advisor/mentor. Talented but economically disadvantaged students who have been accepted into the Opportunity Program (Higher Education Opportunity Program and Academic Opportunity Program) participate in a month-long summer program. A small percentage of students also apply for entry into Periclean Honors Forum, Skidmore's own honors program, on the basis of academic achievement, leadership qualities, and civic commitment. Generally, students choose a major by the end of sophomore year. They are also expected to take one or two courses in both quantitative reasoning and expository writing, and at least one course in each of the following: lab science, social science, arts, and humanities. There is plenty of academic support through Student Academic Services. In addition, there are advising programs for pre-law and pre-med students. In their junior and senior years, most students (more than 80%) add value to their courses of study through faculty-student collaborative research, internships, volunteerism, service-learning, and off-campus study.

CAMPUS FACILITIES AND EQUIPMENT

Skidmore's 1,000-acre-plus campus offers buildings that are designed and arranged to blend with the natural surroundings and to foster intellectual and social interaction. The newest academic building, the Arthur Zankel Music Center, features a spectacular 600-seat recital hall and a state-of-the-art recording studio. The beautifully renovated Murray-Aikins Dining Hall boasts a variety of food stations and intimate seating arrangements. On the residential side, the Sussman Village apartment project was completed in late 2013, meaning 90% of Skidmore's student body resides on campus. And field hockey, lacrosse, soccer, and softball venues have all been recently outfitted with the latest turf fields.

In 2014, Skidmore installed a solar array that meets 12% of Skidmore's electricity needs. Also in 2014, Skidmore began receiving 18% of its electricity needs through a micro-hydro facility. Forty-percent of Skidmore's heating and cooling needs come through geothermal energy.

Skidmore's visual and performing arts space includes the Saisselin Art Building, the Schick Art Gallery, and Bernhard Theater. The Tang Museum, designed by renowned architect Antoine Predock, provides a focal point for cross-disciplinary study through the visual arts and serves as a major cultural resource for Saratoga Springs and the region, attracting nearly 40,000 visitors a year. Dana Science Center offers high-quality teaching and research space, including a greenhouse, specialized labs, and a science machine shop. Dana links the college's science departments to the Department of Mathematics and Computer Science in neighboring Harder Hall, which features a Linux lab of 24 workstations for advanced computer science projects.

TUITION, ROOM, BOARD, AND FEES

Costs 2014–2015: $47,324 tuition and fees, $7,466 room, and $5,162 board

FINANCIAL AID

More than half of Skidmore's students receive some form of financial assistance. Aid is awarded on the basis of demonstrated financial need and is provided in the form of a student-aid "package" that usually includes a grant, campus job, and loan.

We encourage any student interested in applying for admission to do so regardless of his/her intention to seek financial aid. The Free Application for Federal Student Aid (FAFSA), a copy of the federal income tax form, and the CSS Profile must be filed each year. The application date is February 1 for entering freshmen. The college hosts an annual Filene Music Scholarship Competition to award four $48,000 ($12,000 per year) scholarships on the basis of musical ability without regard to financial need. Five $15,000 scholarships in math and science are also awarded annually ($60,000 over four years). Detailed information concerning scholarships, grants, loans, and/or work awards can be obtained through the Office of Financial Aid.

STUDENT ORGANIZATIONS AND ACTIVITIES

The college's nearly 100 student clubs and organizations run the gamut, including five a capella groups; SkidTV and WSPN Radio; Model European Union; sports and recreation activities; and academic, cultural awareness, and religious groups. Skidmore's 19 intercollegiate teams compete at the NCAA Division III level. Students are active in the intramural sports program and enjoy abundant opportunities for personal fitness and recreation, both on campus and in the nearby Adirondack Mountains.

Skidmore students participate in all aspects of academic and social life on campus. They play a major role in governing the college through the Student Government Association (SGA) and numerous major college committees. Elected faculty members and students serve on three panels: the Academic Integrity Board, the All-College Council, and the Social Integrity Board.

ADMISSIONS PROCESS

Those seeking admission to Skidmore's first-year class should complete a secondary school curriculum that includes at least 16 credits in college-preparatory courses. The Admissions Committee is also pleased to consider applications from qualified high school juniors who plan to accelerate and enter college early. Applicants typically have completed four years of English, four years of a foreign language, four years of mathematics, four years of social studies, and three to four years of laboratory science. Applicants must provide a secondary school transcript, standardized test scores (SAT I with writing or ACT with writing), letters of recommendation from two teachers of academic subjects, and a report from their guidance counselor. Skidmore recommends that applicants submit scores for three SAT II Subject Tests. The school also strongly recommends a campus visit and interview.

Through its participation in the Higher Education Opportunity Program (HEOP), Skidmore enrolls capable, energetic, and ambitious New Yorkers who, because of their academic and financial situations, would not otherwise gain admission to the college under traditional requirements. Skidmore's Academic Opportunity Program (AOP) enrolls similar students who reside out of state and/or whose family income slightly exceeds HEOP guidelines.

An applicant for admission registers by completing the Common Application and submitting it with a $65 fee. All information should be postmarked by January 15. Applications from early decision candidates should be submitted by November 15 for the Round I early decision plan or by January 15 for the Round II early decision plan.

International students are given special attention throughout the admissions process. Applicants whose first language is not English are encouraged to submit the results of the Test of English as a Foreign Language (TOEFL). There are a limited number of need-based financial-aid awards available for outstanding international students.

Transfer applicants should apply online at www.commonapp.org and return the application (with the $65 application fee or request for a fee waiver from your advisor) by November 15 for admission in January, or by April 1 for admission in September. In addition to a high school transcript and standardized test scores, we require by the appropriate deadlines an official transcript of all college-level work completed, recommendations from two professors, and a statement regarding personal and academic standing from the dean of students at the current college.

ST. LAWRENCE UNIVERSITY

AT A GLANCE

St. Lawrence University is a private, independent, non-denominational, university that seeks to provide a stimulating and rigorous liberal arts education to undergraduate students chosen for their intellectual potential and seriousness of purpose. Chartered in 1856, it is New York State's oldest continuously coeducational college or university. St. Lawrence's 2,400 students arrive from 42 states and 50 countries. The school is situated in Canton, New York, midway between the Adirondacks Mountains and Ottawa, Canada's national capital. The University provides unmatched access to social and cultural opportunities, international government, and outdoor recreation.

LOCATION AND ENVIRONMENT

St. Lawrence University provides a distinctive learning environment, offering 36 majors, 37 minors, and 3 graduate programs in education. Its First-Year Program is nationally recognized. St. Lawrence offers international study programs on six continents; it also belongs to the International Student Exchange Program. The University offers four off-campus programs within the United States, including a semester program in the Adirondack wilderness and a program in New York City. St. Lawrence is currently undergoing an educational renaissance; bold academic initiatives are underway to maximize the learning potential of each and every student. A major facilities upgrade has been completed to provide expanded resources to undergraduates. A new residence hall opened in Fall, 2014.

OFF-CAMPUS OPPORTUNITIES

St. Lawrence University offers international programs in 17 countries: Australia, Austria, Canada, China, Costa Rica, Czech Republic, Denmark, England, France, India, Italy, Japan, Kenya, New Zealand, Spain, Thailand and Trinidad and Tobago; students can also direct-enroll in foreign universities in countries through the International Student Exchange Program (ISEP).

The University also offers four off-campus study programs within the United States. These are located at: American University, Washington, D.C.; Fisk University, Nashville, Tennessee; New York City and the Adirondack Semester, near Tupper Lake, New York.

MAJORS AND DEGREES OFFERED

Students have the following major/minors to choose from:

African Studies, African-American Studies, Anthropology, Art & Art History, Asian Studies, Biochemistry, Biology, Biology-Physics, Business in the Liberal Arts, Canadian Studies, Caribbean and Latin American Studies, Chemistry, Communications, Computer Science, Conservation Biology, Creative Writing, Dance, Economics, Economics-Mathematics, Education, English, Environmental Studies, Estudios Hispanicos (Spanish), European Studies, Exercise Science, Film and Representation Studies, Foreign Languages, Francophone Studies (French), Gender and Sexuality Studies, Geology, Geology-Physics, German Studies, Global Studies, Government, History, International Economics, International Studies, Japanese Studies, Journalism, Languages, Latin American Studies, Mathematics, Modern Languages & Literatures, Multifield (self-designed), Music, Native American Studies, Neuroscience, Outdoor Studies, Peace Studies, Performance and Communication Arts, Philosophy, Physics, Political Science, Psychology, Religious Studies, Sociology, Spanish, Sports Studies and Exercise Science, Statistics, Studio Art, Theatre, Visual Art, and Writing.

ACADEMIC PROGRAMS

The University confers the Bachelor of Arts and Bachelor of Science degrees; it also awards graduate degrees in education.

Thirty-six majors are available, as is the option to declare a double major (see Major and Degrees Offered.)

The University offers 37 optional minors (see Majors and Degrees Offered.)

Qualified students may pursue five-year programs in business administration (this program leads to the MBA) and engineering, combining coursework at St. Lawrence with work at other institutions.

Specialized advising is available for postgraduate work in dentistry, law, medicine and veterinary medicine.

The St. Lawrence distribution requirements involve coursework in six areas.

All students are expected to demonstrate writing competence before graduating.

The University provides extensive opportunities for honors projects and independent work.

CAMPUS FACILITIES AND EQUIPMENT

The University's two libraries, the Owen D. Young Library and Launders Science Library, contain more than half a million volumes, electronic resources, and ample space for reading and research.

Students also enjoy an arts center with recital hall, two theaters, and an art gallery as well as a 7,000-piece art collection. The Peterson-Kermani Performance Hall, a 19,000 square-foot space for the performing arts, is part of the campus dedicated to the arts.

St. Lawrence's science complex—including the Gold LEED-certified Johnson Hall of Science—is connected to the science library and computing center.

A 15,000-square-foot Sullivan Student Center is available for student meetings, studying, staff offices and one of the dining areas available on campus.

Recreational facilities include cross-country ski, mountain bike, and running trails; a 133-station fitness center; a three-story climbing wall; indoor and outdoor tennis courts; and two gymnasium/fieldhouse complexes, one with a 9-lane/400-meter track and five tennis/basketball courts and the other with a 200-meter track, three tennis courts, and ten squash courts. Facilities also include a pool, ice arena, equestrian center, golf course, indoor golf facility, boathouse, AstroTurf field, baseball, soccer and softball fields.

TUITION, ROOM, BOARD AND FEES

For the 2014–2015 academic year, the comprehensive fee (including tuition, fees and typical room and board) is $59,982.

Typically, annual personal costs and book expenditures cost an additional $1,650.

FINANCIAL AID

St. Lawrence University offers merit scholarships as well as need-based financial assistance.

The school grants aid in some form to more than 93 percent of its students. Aid packages typically consist of grants, student loans, and campus jobs.

Aid applicants must submit the Free Application for Federal Student Aid (FAFSA) between January 1 and February 1, and request that results be sent to St. Lawrence. Applicants may also submit the CSS PROFILE form.

STUDENT ORGANIZATIONS AND ACTIVITIES

Undergraduates commence their studies with the First-Year Program, which places approximately 30 first-year students in communities that live and learn together.

Once they achieve upper-class status, students may choose to live in traditional residence halls, interest-based theme suites, theme cottages, Greek houses, or senior townhouses.

St. Lawrence provides a full range of services to students, including comprehensive career planning as well as graduate and professional school guidance

Students seeking co-curricular activities can choose from over 100 organizations, including everything from student government to interest groups to arts and culture.

St. Lawrence boasts 32 intercollegiate teams including NCAA Division I teams in men's and women's ice hockey. All other teams compete in the NCAA's Division III. Club sports are also available, as is participation in a broad range of popular intramural sports.

The University is home to numerous recreational facilities, including: a 133-station fitness center; a three-story climbing wall; cross-country ski and running trails; and indoor and outdoor tennis courts. Students enjoy access to two gymnasium/fieldhouse complexes; one has a 9-lane/400-meter track as well as five basketball/tennis courts, while the other has a 200-meter track, ten squash courts, and three tennis courts. Other facilities include an AstroTurf field; baseball, softball, and soccer fields; an equestrian center; a golf course; an indoor golf facility; an ice arena; a boathouse; and a pool.

ADMISSIONS PROCESS

St. Lawrence seeks undergraduates with the capacity to manage a demanding academic regimen successfully. In addition, the ideal student contributes substantially to the quality of community life. The University strives to enroll students who represent the broadest possible range of economic, ethnic, geographic, and social backgrounds. The admissions committee values academic achievement, but ability in athletics, community service, leadership, or the creative arts is also considered a strong indicator of a student's capacity to benefit from her or his time at St. Lawrence. The University is test optional for all domestic students; students may choose whether they would like the results of their SAT and/or ACT used during the evaluation process. Students are strongly encouraged to plan a campus visit; interviews may be scheduled to occur on campus. In certain areas, off-campus interviews are also an option.

The University makes no requirement of applicants' high school curricula; however, successful applicants generally demonstrate extensive preparation in the humanities, mathematics, the natural sciences, and the social sciences. Advanced Placement, IB and honors work are looked upon favorably, as they demonstrate the applicants intellectual curiosity and maturity. These are qualities that are highly sought by the admission committee.

St. Lawrence uses the Common Application exclusively and students are free to use any version of the Common Application. An application supplement is required and is available on-line. The application processing fee is $60. Applicants pursuing regular decision should submit all materials by February 1; they will be notified in March of their decision. Students whose first choice is St. Lawrence may apply for Early Decision: the priority deadline for Early Decision applications begins on November 1. Applicants for transfer to St. Lawrence should submit all application materials by November 1 for the spring semester or March 1 for the fall semester.

To request an application or for more information, students should contact:

Office of Admissions and Financial Aid

St. Lawrence University

Canton, NY 13617

Telephone: 315-229-5261

800-285-1856 (toll free)

admissions@stlawu.edu

www.stlawu.edu

ST. MARY'S COLLEGE OF MARYLAND

AT A GLANCE

St. Mary's College of Maryland is designated the Honors College of the State of Maryland in recognition of the quality of our students, faculty and curriculum. St. Mary's offers an undergraduate, liberal arts education and small-college experience like those found at exceptional private colleges. Home to approximately 2,000 students, the campus is located on the St. Mary's River in the heart of the Chesapeake region, about 70 miles outside of Washington, D.C.

The school shares the hallmarks of private institutions: an outstanding faculty, talented students, high academic standards, a challenging curriculum, small classes, a sense of community, and a spirit of intellectual inquiry. By combining the virtues of public and private education, St. Mary's provides a unique alternative for students and their families. The special identity underpins the college's success and its reputation for excellence.

In 1992, the Maryland legislature designated this public, coeducational institution the state's honors college. Over 98% of the faculty holds the Ph.D. or other terminal degree and 11 of the current faculty have received Fulbright Awards. Although professors are exceptionally active in research and writing, the faculty's primary interest and central concern is teaching. The college is home to the Zeta Chapter of Phi Beta Kappa.

Small classes, dedicated teachers, and an informal atmosphere encourage faculty and students to share in the intellectual life of the college, both in and out of the classroom. Professors serve as academic advisors, work with students in extracurricular programs, involve students in research, and mentor them in individualized projects.

More than 50% of St. Mary's graduates continue on to graduate school. St. Mary's alumni have distinguished themselves in every academic field and creative pursuit. When the State of Maryland surveys graduates of its public colleges and universities, St. Mary's alumni consistently report higher levels of satisfaction with their education than do alumni of other institutions.

ACADEMICS

St. Mary's offers a wide and diverse variety of majors and minors and a Master of Arts in Teaching (M.A.T.) for certification in early childhood, elementary and secondary education. English, biology, psychology, political science, and economics typically enroll the largest numbers of majors.

The cornerstone of a St. Mary's education is the First Year Seminar. These small, discussion-focused classes are taught by professors from every discipline at the college, and introduce students to the richness and complexity of intellectual inquiry in a setting of active learning. Students may choose from dozens of topics — ranging from "A Softer Energy Footprint" to "Math, Music, and the Mind" — in order to cultivate an area of particular interest while building the critical thinking, researching, writing, and speaking skills they will use throughout their time at St. Mary's. The First Year Seminar also has a co-curricular component, which through flexibly structured attendance at campus events helps to integrate first year students into college life. St. Mary's also provides students the opportunity to explore cross-disciplinary studies in African and African Diaspora Studies, Asian Studies, Environmental Studies, Museum Studies, Neurosciences, and Women, Gender and Sexuality Studies. Cross-disciplinary studies can increase intellectual community across disciplines, encourage cohesion in the choice of electives, and promote combinations of methods and materials that challenge the boundaries of knowledge.

Many St. Mary's students consider careers in professional fields such as medicine, la and business. Our pre-professional programs work with interested students throug out their four years by providing academic advice, career exploration, and he applying to professional programs. These include pre-dentistry, pre-engineerin pre-law, pre-medicine, pre-optometry, pre-pharmacy, and pre-veterinary scienc

The Paul H. Nitze Scholars Program is designed for highly motivated students wi exceptional academic potential and a proven record of leadership and service. a small cohort of peers, Nitze Scholars meet some of the components of the co curriculum through a series of thematically organized interdisciplinary cours with special components such as a study-tour abroad and collaborative activiti on campus.

The DeSousa-Brent Scholars program builds leadership skills and provides ment ship for students from traditionally underserved populations. The mission of t program is to further cultivate the academic and professional leadership potential students who are the first in their families to attend college, are from rural and urb communities, are ethnic minorities, are students with disabilities, or are econon cally disadvantaged. These students bring unique experiences and knowledge to Mary's, and the college is committed to ensuring that they shine as campus leade

In compliance with St. Mary's College's position as Maryland's public honors colleg the St. Mary's Project (SMP) is the senior capstone experience at the college. T project is an eight-credit, independent, sustained endeavor of research or creati expression that is supervised by a faculty mentor and presented in a public foru

St. Mary's College of Maryland offers semester and year-long international exchan programs, study tours, and internship opportunities. Approximately 45% of studer who start college at St. Mary's study abroad at some point before they gradua From semester and year-long programs, study tours, and international internship there are many options for students to choose from. Some of the more popul study-abroad sites include the Centre for Medieval and Renaissance Studies Oxford University (England), the University of The Gambia, the Institute for Cent American Development Studies (Costa Rica), and Fudan University (China). A ditional international programs and study tours provide opportunities to study in t Gambia, Argentina, Thailand, Ireland, India, Belize, Germany, Greece, and Japa

St. Mary's operates on a two-semester academic calendar. Students customari complete four courses, or 16 credits, each semester and must complete 128 cre its for graduation. Students do not need to declare a major until the end of the sophomore year.

ADMISSIONS

St. Mary's College is a selective institution. We admit students with records high academic achievements, personal abilities, and accomplishments of superi quality. High school or college grades, the quality of course selection, standar ized test scores, and letters of recommendation provide evidence of academ accomplishment and potential. These measures are supplemented by the require application essay and resume of co-curricular activities. Individual involveme outside the classroom and in the community also is given attention. Activities th have resulted in honors and awards, or other recognition of special talents, shou be listed on the application.

At St. Mary's, we are proud to be a public honors college and are looking for students who are ready to be challenged. We are a member of the Common Application (www.commonapp.org), and we accept applications from first-year and transfer students for the fall and spring semesters. Our Early Decision Deadlines are November 1 and January 1. When students apply under the Early Decision option, they are indicating to us that St. Mary's is their top choice and will attend if admitted. Notification of an admissions decision is approximately six weeks past the Early Decision deadline. Regular Decision applicants must apply by January 1 and notification will be no later than April 1. Fall transfer applicants must apply February 1 and spring transfer students must apply by November 1. For details, visit www.smcm.edu/admissions.

Prospective students are strongly encouraged to come to campus for a student-led tour and an information session or interview with an admissions counselor. These visits should be scheduled in advance by calling 800-492-7181.

CAMPUS FACILITIES AND EQUIPMENT

At the crossroads of the campus, the Campus Center offers a wide range of activities and services including dining, meeting rooms and lounges, a café, the campus store, student activity offices, and a movie theater. The library, overlooking St. John's Pond, houses state-of-the-art media and computer centers that serve the needs of students as well as faculty and staff. Academic buildings feature computerized classrooms, modern laboratories, and specialized instructional spaces. To ensure that development preserves the natural beauty and Tidewater charm of the St. Mary's campus, the college has adopted a campus master plan calling for courtyards, walkways, and gardens that enrich the landscape. In addition, the environmental fragility of its waterfront combined with its historic location inspires the college to approach campus development with special sensitivity to the ecology of the Chesapeake Bay watershed and the archaeology of Maryland's 17th-century capital.

Campus Life

Almost 85% of our students live on campus all four years, contributing a wonderful and safe learning and living environment. Our students enjoy the options of residence halls, suites, apartments and townhouses, and find living on campus an essential part of their college experience.

When our students are not in the classroom, they are busy doing independent research, traveling abroad, interning, and volunteering in the community. They unwind by enjoying the waterfront recreation, watching movies in Cole Cinema, partaking in our 90 clubs and organizations, and competing in intramural and varsity athletics.

LOCATION AND ENVIRONMENT

A unique aspect of St. Mary's culture is the influence of the river. Our campus is located on 361 acres and sits on a horseshoe bend of the St. Mary's River just upstream from the confluence of the Potomac River and Chesapeake Bay. It is no wonder we have earned 14 national sailing championships. You don't have to be an expert; the waterfront is open to recreational and novice sailors alike. With our unique location, students also swim, kayak, windsurf, row and are drawn to environmental research. Once you see the campus you'll know you have arrived at a college like no other.

TUITION AND FEES

Basic educational fees for 2013-2014:

$14,865 per year (Maryland Resident)

$28,665 per year (Non-Maryland Resident)

Room: $6,575

Board: $5,060

MAJORS AND DEGREES

Anthropology
Art and Art History
Asian Studies
Biochemistry
Biology
Chemistry
Computer Science
Economics
English
History
International Languages and Cultures (Chinese, French, German, Latin American
Studies, Spanish, Courses in Translation)
Mathematics
Music
Natural Science
Philosophy
Physics
Political Science
Psychology
Public Policy Studies
Religious Studies
Sociology
Student Designed Major
Theater, Film and Media Studies

OFF-CAMPUS OPPORTUNITIES

Located about 20 minutes from the college is Solomons Island, a quiet waterfront fishing village offering museums and attractions, shopping, waterfront dining, sailing and other water sports. Historic Leonardtown, located 20 minutes from St. Mary's, boasts one of the state's few preserved town squares. Maryland's state capital, Annapolis, is located 70 miles from the college. The Nation's Capital, Washington, D.C., is 70 miles from the college and the harbor city of Baltimore is approximately 100 miles from campus.

TUITION AND AID

St. Mary's College believes that qualified students should have an opportunity for a college education. The primary responsibility for paying for the cost of education is the family's. However, as a public institution, St. Mary's College recognizes that students and their families are not always able to fund the full cost of a college education. For this, the school offers a variety of programs designed to assist in meeting college expenses. These programs include scholarships, grants, loans, work opportunities, and a tuition payment plan. In the end, the goal is to ensure that qualified applicants have the opportunity to obtain a liberal arts education at St. Mary's.

To be considered for need-based aid, including federal, state and college grants, loan, and employment programs, students must fill out the Free Application for Federal Student Aid (FAFSA); St. Mary's College's FAFSA filing deadline for fall semester applicants is February 28. In order to be considered for merit-based aid from St. Mary's, students should submit their admissions application by our priority scholarship deadline of November 15. Applicants are automatically reviewed by the Scholarship Review Committee with consideration in the areas of academic record, standardized test scores, strength of curriculum, essay, recommendations, and co-curricular involvement.

ST. NORBERT COLLEGE

AT A GLANCE

With a liberal arts foundation that teaches critical-thinking, problem-solving, communication and leadership skills, St. Norbert College offers academic excellence, individual attention and faculty members focused on student success.

St. Norbert is a private, coeducational institution with more than 40 fields of study, including several pre-professional programs, all of which can be enhanced by our honors program, student-faculty collaborative research (as early as your first year), professional internships and our study-abroad program. With a four-year graduation guarantee, St. Norbert offers students a true value when considering the personal attention that we offer, and the high graduate school and career placement that our graduates achieve.

Founded in 1898, St. Norbert has become one of the top 10 Catholic liberal arts colleges in the nation. St. Norbert is open to students of all faiths and committed to a well-rounded education fueled by the Norbertine tradition of communio (a deep-rooted, heartfelt sense of community). At St. Norbert, our goal is to help you connect your passions with the needs of the world.

ACADEMICS AND MAJORS

Experiential learning is the norm at St. Norbert. Research fellowships, as early as freshman year, give students hands-on opportunities to experience graduate-level research from Day One. Those opportunities for collaborating with St. Norbert faculty continue throughout their four years, and students often have the opportunity to present their work at local, regional or national conferences.

Students are also privileged to experience one of the more prolific study-abroad programs in the country, offering six continents, 29 countries and more than 75 program sites for St. Norbert students to experience a global perspective. In fact, an average of 30 percent of St. Norbert students study abroad each year—well above the national average.

That international perspective is part of the fabric at St. Norbert. Our Center for International Education on campus encourages a diverse student body, with more than 100 students, representing more than 20 countries, typically on campus. An additional 50+ students are in our English as a Second Language (ESL) program; many stay to complete their bachelor's degree.

All students are assigned an adviser, who helps them chart their academic career and ensure they can graduate in four years. Students have the option of designing a personal major to help them achieve their academic objectives.

For high-achieving students, a challenging honors program provides plenty of opportunity for academic engagement. Honors students have been particularly fond of participating in the living-learning community of intellectually curious and creative students.

The metropolitan Green Bay area offers students nearly unlimited opportunities for internships. More than just cheese and the Green Bay Packers, the region boasts Fortune 500 companies, hospitals, schools and service organizations that play host to many student internships. Of course, students also regularly intern for the 13-time world champion Packers, who hold their summer training camp on campus.

For those students more interested in volunteering, the Norbertine philosophy of self-emptying service is a perfect fit. Local, national and international service opportunities are one of the hallmarks of a St. Norbert education.

MAJORS AND DEGREES OFFERED

We offer Bachelor of Arts (BA), Bachelor of Science (BS), Bachelor of Music (BM) and Bachelor of Business Administration (BBA) undergraduate degrees.

Undergraduate Programs

- Accounting
- American Studies
- Art – fine arts and graphic design
- Biology – biomedical and organismal
- Business Administration
- Chemistry and Biochemistry
- Classical Studies
- Communication and Media Studies
- Computer Science – business information systems and graphic design & implementation
- Economics
- Education
- English and Creative Writing
- Environmental Science
- French
- Geography
- Geology
- German
- History
- Human Services (Social Work)
- International Business and Language Area Studies
- International Studies
- Japanese
- Leadership Studies
- Mathematics
- Military Science/ROTC
- Modern Languages and Literatures
- Music
- Natural Sciences
- Peace and Justice
- Philosophy
- Physics
- Political Science
- Pre-Dental
- Pre-Engineering
- Pre-Law
- Pre-Medical
- Pre-Nursing
- Pre-Veterinary
- Psychology
- Theology and Religious Studies
- Sociology
- Spanish
- Teacher Education
- Theatre Studies
- Women's and Gender Studies

ADMISSION

Students can apply using either the St. Norbert College online application or the Common Application.

Because St. Norbert reviews applications on a rolling basis and gives housing preference to students according to the date of admission and enrollment deposit, it benefits students to apply as early as possible during their senior year.

Notification of the admission decision is made on a rolling basis beginning in late September. After St. Norbert receives all of the required admission information, students receive notification via mail of their admission status within 2-4 weeks. A nonrefundable $350 deposit is required to confirm enrollment.

U.S. applications require a $10.00 online application fee. International applications require a $50.00 application fee.

First-year domestic student important dates:

- September 15 – admission office begins reviewing applications

- October 1 – admission office begins notifying students of their application status

- January 1 – apply for financial aid at www.fafsa.ed.gov; St. Norbert's FAFSA school code is 003892

- March 1 – financial aid priority deadline

- May 1 – priority date for enrollment deposit

- June – summer orientation

For more information, prospective students are encouraged to contact:

St. Norbert College

Office of Admission

100 Grant Street

De Pere, WI 54115-2099

Phone: 920-403-3005 or 800-236-4878

Fax: 920-403-4072

Email: admit@snc.edu

Web: www.snc.edu

STUDENT BODY

Students quickly adjust to campus with a welcoming community of faculty, students and staff. First Year Experience (FYE) programming helps students acclimate to campus and to college life in general. The Norbertine principle of radical hospitality is immediately evident when arriving on campus.

Students at St. Norbert tend to be very involved. Because it's a residential campus, activities and opportunities are close at hand. The college offers more than 70 student organizations and clubs that provide a rich co-curricular campus environment. Students can find opportunities in academic, diversity, ethnic and cultural, Greek, social, special interest, governing, programming and media, recreation, and service and faith organizations. And if students are looking for a particular interest that hasn't found its place on campus yet, they can create a new student organization.

A Division III school, we offer 10 men's and 10 women's varsity sports, and our athletes have been named Academic All-Americans more times than any other school in the Midwest Conference. Additionally, our men's and women's hockey teams compete in the Northern Collegiate Hockey Association. The Green Knights are frequent conference champions—averaging about four per year. Nearly one quarter of our students are involved in varsity sports, with many others participating in intramurals.

CAMPUS LIFE AND FACILITIES

Located on the banks of the Fox River in De Pere (a residential community 23,000) in northeastern Wisconsin, the St. Norbert campus comprises 40+ buildings on 108 beautifully landscaped acres. Students also have easy access to the neighboring all-American city of Green Bay and its suburbs, with a metropolitan population of about 300,000. With a safe, supportive atmosphere on campus and a thriving corporate, cultural and entertainment industry close at hand, St. Norbert is a place that students love so much that they often refer to it as "home."

St. Norbert continues to experience great momentum with record high enrollment in recent years, as well as increasingly high-achieving students. And as the students come, so do the facilities to support them. New in 2015 is St. Norbert's $40 million Gehl-Mulva Science Center, also home to the Medical College of Wisconsin's northeast Wisconsin campus. Integrated facilities for hands-on learning, collaborative research and interdisciplinary study abound in this LEED-certified, state-of-the-art science center.

The past several years have also seen the opening of the Cassandra Voss Center, for women's and gender studies, and Dudley Birder Hall, a performing-arts space, both in renovated, historic buildings. In 2011, a remodeled welcome center, and a $7.7 million completely renovated student dining facility—Michels Commons—were added to the campus.

Built in 2010, an outdoor athletics complex serves as the practice and competition venue for Green Knights football, soccer, and track and field. The Miriam B. And James J Mulva library was dedicated in 2009, and in 2013 its lower level became home to a high-tech collaborative workspace for students.

Among other facilities, a campus center and marina located on the Fox River offer students a relaxing environment to grab a bite to eat, sit out on the deck or in the gazebo, work out in the fitness center or gym, or gather for a concert or movie. The campus coffee shop—Ed's—is another favorite student hangout.

Only a five-minute drive from campus, Green Bay and all its restaurants, shopping malls, museums and performing arts opportunities can be easily accessed by students when they've exhausted the shops and boutiques of charming De Pere. Metro bus services offer free transportation throughout the metropolitan area with a student ID.

TUITION AND AID

Full-time undergraduate students (3 or more full courses/12-18 credits):

$33,622 2014–15 academic year tuition

$615 Fees

$8,793 Average room and board

More than 97 percent of St. Norbert students receive some form of financial aid, with the average award being more than $24,500. To achieve our goal of helping students obtain an affordable and quality college education, St. Norbert allocates funds each year for distribution to students whose families lack necessary funds. More than $50 million in financial aid is available annually at St. Norbert College in the form of scholarships, grants, student employment and loans. We encourage students to submit the Free Application for Federal Student Aid (FAFSA) as early as possible, and preferably by March 1. The St. Norbert FAFSA code is 003892. Financial aid awards typically go out in mid-March.

INSTITUTE OF TECHNOLOGY

...ken, NJ on the Hudson River overlooking the Manhat-
... energy, highly engaged campus community. Our location
... of Stevens' tech-oriented students: they are driven to explore,
... ake advantage of opportunities both in the classroom and in their
... ular activities.

...vens, students and faculty collaborate in an interdisciplinary, student-centric,
...trepreneurial environment. Exceptional opportunities for internships, undergraduate research and cooperative education give students the experience and
connections to engage in high level intellectual and practical pursuits that prepare
students for their futures.

Students choose from 34 undergraduate majors in Business, Humanities, Arts,
Computer Science, Engineering and the Sciences; many students double major
or choose to pursue both bachelor's and master's degrees. Graduates are highly
skilled in creating solutions at the intersections of disciplines and can lead in today's
complex, cross-functional and highly technical environments, and have always fared
exceptionally well in career and graduate school placement. Stevens is consistently
ranked among the nation's elite for total return on investment and mid-career
salaries of graduates—#3 and #12 in the nation respectively, according to reports
by PayScale. Our graduates are recruited into highly competitive positions and
accepted into top graduate programs: 95% of the Class of 2014 secured outcomes
within six months of graduation.

Stevens' 2,892 undergraduate students come from more than 45 states and 68 countries, creating a diverse, dynamic environment. Stevens also boasts an outstanding
campus life—students will find more than 75 student clubs and organizations and
26 NCAA Division III athletics teams.

LOCATION AND ENVIRONMENT

Stevens is located in one of the most exciting, cosmopolitan towns in the United
States. Hoboken, New Jersey, is a quaint one-mile-square city with old Victorian
brownstones and tree-lined streets dotted with great restaurants and trendy shops.
Located on the Hudson River, the 55-acre campus is home to stretches of green
lawns, majestic trees, and historic classroom buildings that have been updated with
the most current teaching and learning technologies. With the heart of NYC a mere
10-minute commute away, Stevens students take advantage of being close to top
companies with exciting internships and career placements as well as unlimited
cultural experiences and events throughout the year.

In addition to the robust on-campus student life, Stevens' location provides for
exciting off-campus activities. Dining, entertainment, and major attractions offer
numerous artistic, cultural, athletic and recreational opportunities.

Stevens students enjoy a safe and dynamic living environment. Eighty-eight percent
of Stevens undergraduate students live on campus, and housing is guaranteed for
undergraduates. There are seven on-campus residence halls in addition to various
on- and off-campus apartments for upperclassmen. Sixteen fraternities and sororities have chapters on campus and most maintain houses where members may live.
Stevens also features "affinity housing" for students interested in community service
and civic engagement, as well as a women's center. The dining program features late
night hours to meet students' busy schedules, and many establishments in Hoboken
also accept Stevens' Duck Bills, reloadable on student ID cards.

OFF-CAMPUS OPPORTUNITIES

Stevens cultivates the value of being a world citizen, giving back to the community
and building bridges across cultures. In addition to the popular internship, research,
and cooperative education opportunities offered at Stevens, students take their
educational experience across the globe through study abroad, service-oriented
organizations, and department-sponsored trips.

Community service has a prominent place in campus life. From tutoring local school
children to assisting the elderly and participating in neighborhood community
projects, Stevens students are very much a part of our hometown. This service
orientation extends beyond Hoboken to the global community, with opportunities
to bring the benefits of Stevens innovation to countries and areas of need.

MAJORS AND DEGREES OFFERED

Stevens students are committed to exploring the frontiers of engineering, computer
science, sciences, business, the humanities and arts. Undergraduate degrees awarded
include the Bachelor of Engineering (BE), Bachelor of Science (BS), and Bachelor
of Art (BA) degrees.

Business Majors: Business and Technology; Economics; Finance; Information
Systems; Management; Marketing; Quantitative Finance.

Humanities & Arts Majors: History; Literature; Music and Technology; Philosophy;
Science Communication; Science, Technology and Society; Social Sciences; Visual
Arts and Technology.

Computer Science Majors: Computer Science; Cybersecurity.

Engineering Majors: Biomedical Engineering; Chemical Engineering; Civil En-
gineering; Computer Engineering; Electrical Engineering; Engineering Management; Environmental Engineering; Mechanical Engineering; Naval Engineering;
Software Engineering.

Science Majors: Biology; Chemical Biology; Chemistry; Computational Science;
Engineering Physics; Mathematics; Physics.

Many students pursue dual degree options or opt to complete requirements for
both bachelor's and master's degrees during their four or five years on campus.

Stevens offers a 6-year Accelerated Law program (Bachelor's/J.D.) and a 7-year
Accelerated Medicine (B.S./M.D.) program with partner universities; a 5-year
Master's program; a competitive Scholars program; and the unique Innovation and
Entrepreneurship Summer Research Program.

ACADEMIC PROGRAMS

Stevens offers unique and challenging educational opportunities that foster innovation and lead students to success. Research projects and summer internships are
available for all major fields of study. Stevens blends humanities and technology
subjects, and is distinctive in the encouragement of students to bridge disciplines
and interests. Our technology orientation, combined with humanities and business
offerings, are an optimal blend for developing leadership qualities. Considering these
fields together helps students gain perspective not only about the ways in which
things work, but also why they matter, what the societal impact might be, and how
we can influence progress. Students in different majors collaborate on high-impact
projects, like the U.S. Department of Energy's Solar Decathlon competition.

The Cooperative Education (co-op) program is also distinctive. Co-op students
alternate semesters of on-campus study with semesters of paid, professional work
experience. Co-op students graduate with a competitive edge in the job market,
having gained a higher level of confidence through development of significant
workplace skills. Our co-op program is one of the reasons Stevens ranks 3rd in the
nation for career placement (Princeton Review's Colleges That Pay You Back, 2015).

The Stevens Scholars Program allows exceptional students to participate in honor
seminars and summer research. Many take advantage of the option to accelerate
their course work and graduate with a bachelor's and master's degree in four years
at no additional cost.

The Annual Stevens Innovation Expo is one of many programs aimed at promoting
entrepreneurial thinking at Stevens. In addition to the design project showcase, student inventors present their technologies in a fast-paced and exciting venture-style
pitch competition, where students propose business ideas for their new technologies
to a panel of five experts, who evaluate and award the most viable projects with the
greatest potential for market realization.

Stevens Technical Enrichment Program (STEP) helps broaden the access of minority and economically disadvantaged students to careers in engineering, science,
and technology through pre-college and in-college programs and support services.

CAMPUS FACILITIES AND EQUIPMENT

Stevens operates within a technology-centric environment to meet the needs of a technologically fluent campus, offering a variety of centralized, departmental, and individual resources. Facilities include "smart" classrooms, computer-aided design and manufacturing labs, graphics labs, robotic sites, a media arts center, green screen, sound synthesis lab, a computer-aided education lab, a new motion capture lab, and a financial systems center with a Wall Street trading room. Stevens offers its community an extensive wireless networking system. Two pioneering projects underway, the Unified Communications and Collaboration Environment and the Virtual Learning Environment, will have transformative impact on our graphic- and computing-intensive technology applications for learning.

Our research enterprise focuses on key areas that address major interdisciplinary topics of national significance: healthcare and medicine, sustainable energy, financial systems, security, coastal sustainability, and STEM education. Supporting these areas are many specialized laboratory facilities on campus used for academic and research functions, applied research, and educational programs in systems integration that meet and support the needs of government and industry. The Office of Innovation and Entrepreneurship fosters an entrepreneurial culture across the university, advances the outcomes of the research, and engages in the technology transfer that brings new ideas to the marketplace.

TUITION, ROOM, BOARD, AND FEES

Stevens tuition and fees for 2015–2016 are $47,366. Room and board total $15,200 (typical on-campus, double occupancy/typical meal plan; other plans vary). Student fees consist of a student activity fee, health service fee and technology fee.

FINANCIAL AID

Stevens is committed to assisting, investing in, and ensuring the highest quality of service to its students. The university offers a wide range of institutional need- and merit-based scholarships and grants, and government grants, loan, and work opportunity programs. Stevens encourages students to file the College Scholarship Service (CSS) Profile for consideration for all institutional grant and scholarships and file the Free Application for Federal Student Aid (FAFSA) for consideration for all Federal and State Grant and Loan Programs. The requested deadline to submit both the FAFSA and CSS Profile is February 15 (Early Decision I and II applicants submit the CSS Profile by December 1 or January 15 respectively if they would like an estimated Financial Aid package.)

STUDENT ORGANIZATIONS AND ACTIVITIES

The energy at Stevens extends well beyond the classroom activities and career orientation of our students into a robust student life. Nearly 100 student organizations and twenty-six NCAA Division III athletics teams add to an enriching student experience and prepare students for a healthy and energizing balance of hard work and fun.

Clubs and organizations include sororities and fraternities, performing arts and athletic groups, student government, ethnic organizations, professional societies, and more. The Alpha Phi Omega service fraternity, Engineers Without Borders, and Habitat for Humanity are service-oriented groups with active student engagement. Campus traditions like Boken and TechFest (campus-wide festivals), the Unity Show, and Midnight Breakfast during finals study periods are among students' favorites.

The Schaefer Athletic and Recreation Center features a NCAA competition-size pool with Jacuzzi, four-court basketball gymnasium, racquetball courts, and a fitness center. DeBaun Field has been surfaced in a state-of the-art, durable, year-round playing surface for varsity and intramural competition. Walker Gym has an elevated indoor track plus a weightlifting facility and dance studios. There are also six outdoor tennis courts with spectacular Manhattan skyline views and a sand volleyball court. In 2013, Stevens was the recipient of the ECAC/Jostens "Institution of the Year" award, from among more than 320 Division I, II, and III schools, for excellence in academics and athletics—one of only three schools to have received this honor more than once.

Stevens competes in NCAA Division III sports. For men: baseball, basketball, cross-country, fencing, golf, indoor/outdoor track and field, lacrosse, soccer, swimming, tennis, volleyball and wrestling. For women: basketball, cross-country, equestrian, fencing, field hockey, indoor/outdoor track and field, lacrosse, soccer, swimming, tennis, softball and volleyball. Students may also join a club team or play intramural sports, take health and wellness or fitness classes, or participate in outdoor adventure trips.

ADMISSIONS

Stevens is highly competitive. Undergraduate applicants must submit:

An application for admission; official high school transcript which includes four years of English, four years of mathematics, and a minimum of three years of science; two letters of recommendation; personal statement or essay; standardized test scores as described below.

SAT I or ACT scores are required for all domestic applicants. International applicants can satisfy testing requirements by submitting TOEFL or IELTS scores as well as one of the following options:

• Two (2) SAT II Tests – Math and either Chemistry or Physics

• Two (2) AP Exams – Calculus and either Chemistry or Physics

• International Baccalaureate Degree with two higher level exams scores in math or science.

International students may also submit SAT I or ACT scores in lieu of the previous recommendation.

Admissions interviews, while not required, are strongly recommended. Interviews are required for Accelerated Law and Accelerated Medical programs. Additionally, SAT II scores are required for those applying to the Accelerated Medical (at least two SAT II exams, math level I or II and biology or chemistry).

Stevens typically accepts 44% percent of its applicants and enrolls more than 700 students each fall; SAT scores range from 1260–1410 (middle 50%) and the average high school GPA is 3.83. The application deadline for the fall semester is February 1 (Early Decision I and II deadlines are November 15 and January 15, respectively).

SWARTHMORE COLLEGE

Swarthmore College, a forward-thinking institution of liberal arts and engineering, celebrates a life of creativity and purpose. With a global outlook and 8:1 student/faculty ratio, Swarthmore unlocks its students' potential to become leaders of industries and agents of change. It exudes innovation, but it also knows where it came from. Whether it's meeting the financial need of all admitted students, modeling sustainable practices, or cultivating an environment of equality, the college honors its 150-year history and Quaker roots. Swarthmore harnesses the wisdom of the past to drive the future. And at Swarthmore, the future isn't a fuzzy or faraway concept. It starts now.

AT A GLANCE

When you step onto the Swarthmore campus, you engage the world. A world of intellect and action, collaboration and connection. Where lush gardens and woods trace your journey to a class on plasma physics or international cinema. Think intellectual exploration with no limits, whether it's sharing perspectives with a classmate from another continent or listening to a Rhodes Scholar. Nights that stretch into mornings critiquing educational policy; or integrating music and art into a new performance piece; or building, with classmates, a robot that can navigate rough terrain. This is a community fueled by the free exchange of ideas. Professors will flip your viewpoint with a question, or travel with you to assess environmental damage, or help you to discover a forgotten language. The collaborative Honors program crackles with intellectual exploration, and an innovative externship program matches students with alumni from Capitol Hill to Silicon Valley. When you become a Swarthmore student, in fact, you forge connections with alumni around the world—cutting-edge professionals as invested in the success of their alma mater and its graduates as they are in making a difference. The college community pushes students out of their comfort zones, urging open-mindedness and boldness. Whether it's designing their own major or starting a new club or bringing a national thought leader to campus, students forge paths they could not have imagined. At Swarthmore, exceptions are the norm.

LOCATION AND ENVIRONMENT

Swarthmore's awe-inspiring campus marks your adventure, offering opportunities for self-reflection and solace. Located 11 miles southwest of Philadelphia, the idyllic, 425-acre campus is an arboretum, replete with rolling lawns, a creek, hiking trails, and wooded hills. The reverence for nature extends to physical spaces, as well. From the solar energy labs of the Science Center to the newest residence halls with loft-style living and environmentally friendly green roofs, Swarthmore's buildings and architecture stand as a national model for entwining sustainability into the student life experience.

OFF-CAMPUS OPPORTUNITIES

Swarthmore belongs to the Tri-College consortium, linking it to Bryn Mawr and Haverford Colleges both academically and socially. Students can also take courses at the University of Pennsylvania. The college offers shuttles to the other Tri-Co schools, community service sites, local café's and shops, and more. There's also a train station adjacent to campus, inviting students to the rich cultural tapestry of center city Philadelphia (just 20 minutes away). Opportunities for enrichment and collaboration overflow.

MAJORS AND DEGREES OFFERED

Swarthmore College awards two degrees, the Bachelor of Arts and the Bachelor of Science. The college offers the following courses of study:

Art and Art History

Asian Studies

Astronomy

Biology

Black Studies

Chemistry and Biochemistry

Classics

Cognitive Science

Comparative Literature

Computer Science

Dance

Design Your Own Major

Economics

Educational Studies

Engineering

English Literature

Environmental Studies

Film and Media Studies

Gender and Sexuality Studies

History

Interpretation Theory

Islamic Studies

Latin American Studies

Linguistics

Mathematics and Statistics

Medieval Studies

Modern Languages and Literatures (including Arabic, Chinese, French, German, Japanese, Russian, and Spanish)

Music

Peace and Conflict Studies

Philosophy

Physics

Political Science

Psychology

Religion

Sociology and Anthropology

Theater

ACADEMIC PROGRAMS

The College offers more than 600 courses a year; an exceptional Honors Program; individual special majors; a program in education that leads to Pennsylvania secondary school certification; and undergraduate research opportunities in the sciences, social sciences, humanities, and engineering.

Swarthmore's Honors Program is unparalleled in the United States. It features small groups of dedicated and accomplished students working closely with faculty, with an emphasis on independent learning, and affirms the community's reputation as a place where everyone encourages one another's success. External examiners who shine in their fields, such as World Bank economists and Google software engineers, evaluate senior Honors Program students through written and oral examinations.

CAMPUS FACILITIES AND EQUIPMENT

Swarthmore has a dynamic array of arts spaces to enjoy—or stage—a performance. Avenues of exploration abound, whether it's immersing yourself in Language Resource Center technology to learn a new dialect, getting lost in the stars in the observatory, or studying or sharing samosas with friends in the Kohlberg coffee bar. The forthcoming biology, engineering, psychology (BEP) building will open new doors of discovery for students. The gleaming Matchbox facility offers a multifaceted, modern approach to wellness, recreation, and the performing arts, imbuing creativity and community.

TUITION, ROOM, BOARD, AND FEES

For 2015–2016, the college charges, including tuition, room, board, and student activity fee, amount to $61,400. The activity fee covers not only the usual student services—health, library, laboratory fees, for example—but admission to all social, cultural, and athletic events on campus. In addition, the college's Quaker roots manifest themselves in a cash-free campus, as the annual activity fee covers everything from digital printing and laundry to sporting events, campus movie screenings, and dance performances.

FINANCIAL AID

Swarthmore's robust financial aid program provides all capable students access to the college. This year, Swarthmore will award over $31 million in scholarships. The average aid award for the Class of 2018 was $43,250. Swarthmore makes its admissions and financial aid decisions separately for U.S. citizens and permanent residents. That means that its doors are open to all, regardless of financial need, and without students taking on loans. Swarthmore carefully considers many factors to assess a family's ability to pay tuition and then covers the rest, up to 100 percent, as it did for half of its students in 2014–15. It also provides assistance to some international students. This comprehensive program reflects Swarthmore's commitment to maximizing access.

STUDENT ORGANIZATIONS AND ACTIVITIES

With more than 100 student clubs and organizations on campus, dozens of community service groups, 22 Division III varsity athletic teams, free lectures and performances occurring daily on campus, and full course loads, Swarthmore students are in perpetual motion. Action and inclusiveness are the core value here.

ADMISSIONS PROCESS

Striving for a diverse, well-rounded class, the admissions staff carefully considers a number of criteria without a rigid emphasis on any one factor. Applicants are evaluated holistically, based on the following criteria:

- High school record (as well as strength of curriculum)
- Rank in class (if high school ranks)
- Standardized tests (SAT with 2 SAT Subject Tests or ACT with Writing)
- Extracurricular commitments
- Essays (included in application)
- Recommendations (two from academic teachers, one from counselor)
- Interview (highly recommended but not required)

TEMPLE UNIVERSITY

AT A GLANCE

Temple University attracts some of the most diverse, driven and motivated minds from across the nation and around the world. These students and faculty bring the university to life and fuel its palpable momentum in academics, athletics, research and the arts. Powering Temple's ascent are innovative approaches in admissions and affordability; a campus transformation; plentiful creative and research opportunities at both the undergraduate and graduate levels; rigorous academic programs; an indelible bond with the city of Philadelphia; and groundbreaking work in science, research and technology.

Temple is home to 38,000 students, is the fifth-largest provider of professional education in the U.S., and offers more than 400 academic programs in 17 schools and colleges on nine campuses, including locations in Japan and Italy.

More than 3,500 distinguished faculty; top art, business, dental, law and medical schools; five professional schools; and dozens of renowned programs make Temple an academic powerhouse. Students enjoy the advantages and atmosphere of a large urban, public research university with the individualized attention that is a result of its 14:1 student-to-faculty ratio.

The majority of freshman students live on campus, where they are steps away from class; dozens of computer labs; the library; fitness and recreation facilities; dining options from cafés and dining halls to food trucks; and the many arts, cultural, sports and scholarly events that happen daily universitywide.

One of Temple's newest living and learning residences is 27-story Morgan Hall, which offers unparalleled views of the Philadelphia skyline. Because Temple is in the midst of a transformation, Morgan Hall is only one of several state-of-the-art facilities rising on the university's Main Campus. The new 250,000-square-foot Science Education and Research Center boosts student and faculty opportunities for discovery and innovation. Plans are also under way for a state-of-the-art, 21st-century library and the university's largest-ever quad.

Temple's influence also extends around the globe, with longstanding campuses in Tokyo and Rome; programs in London, Beijing and other locations; 150 partnerships with international universities; and nearly 300,000 living alumni. In addition, students on Main Campus hail from more than 100 countries.

No matter their backgrounds, Temple students—called Owls—are drawn to the university's vibrant location in the heart of Philadelphia. The professional world is right outside their doors, where thousands of possibilities exist for hands-on learning and internships in business, healthcare, education, the arts and more.

By living and learning in an urban environment, Temple students are well prepared for the real world. Employers consistently laud Owls for their tenacity, teamwork and talent. In addition to job readiness, students are equipped with access to an immense Temple alumni network for mentoring, guidance, connections and opportunities.

LOCATION AND ENVIRONMENT

Temple students enjoy an eclectic, electric campus in one of the country's liveliest urban centers. Among the most walkable cities in the nation, Philadelphia is home to history, arts and culture, government, technology and innovation, healthcare, and myriad other fields and interests. Opportunities for learning, whether through a class, an internship or a research project, abound.

More than 13,000 students now live on or near main campus. They take tree-canopied walks to class, relax on the grass outside the library, get lunch at one of the many food trucks, and work out at several different fitness facilities.

Temple's main campus features seven residence halls, and students can choose a living and learning community tailored to their major or interest.

OFF-CAMPUS OPPORTUNITIES

Temple's main campus is located 1.5 miles from the center of Philadelphia. And the city blends seamlessly with the studies of Temple students. Those studying stormwater management work hands-on with the water department; art students restore fading historical signs on older buildings; and political science majors learn from civic leaders.

As much as the city is a classroom, it's also a place of adventure. Students may explore nearly 200 museums, a thriving restaurant scene, numerous sports teams and the largest landscaped, urban park in the nation.

Owls interested in experiencing different languages and cultures by studying abroad face dozens of options. They may study at Temple campuses in Tokyo or Rome or join summer programs in Brazil, South Africa, Spain and beyond. Many of the programs tie in to areas of study, such as business students studying real markets in Paris and Mumbai, or art and architecture students studying among classical masterpieces in Rome.

MAJORS AND DEGREES OFFERED

Temple University offers 129 undergraduate majors through 17 schools and colleges: a variety that translates into paths for every interest. Students who need time to decide on a major work with advisors and professors to discover their strengths and options.

ACADEMIC PROGRAMS

Temple has a long tradition of self-made success. It started in 1884 as a night school, so students who worked during the day could keep their jobs. Though a lot has changed, Temple's heritage still drives the work ethic of its students. Owls turn opportunities into accomplishments. World-class laboratories are proving grounds for world-changing ideas. A classroom doubles as a tech startup's boardroom. Professors mentor students through graduate school and beyond. And it's all because of the uncommon drive Temple students and faculty share.

Students have numerous ways to customize their college life: living and learning communities, an immersive honors program, interdisciplinary majors, creative and research grants, internships, and career preparation and placement.

Temple encourages the spirit of entrepreneurship universitywide, so Owls know how to thrive no matter their course in life. To help foster such skills, annual innovation and business-idea competitions are open to the entire Temple community, and all students have access to mentors, resources and guidance to develop business ideas and plans.

Temple also propels students into top graduate programs through challenging academic work, research opportunities and close partnerships with professors.

CAMPUS FACILITIES AND EQUIPMENT

Whether in the glass-blowing studio or the virtual balance lab, Temple students are immersed in extraordinary facilities. The Science Education and Research Center is one of the university's newest buildings and home to 68 research and teaching labs and leading-edge technologies such as clean rooms, powerful supercomputers and a scanning tunneling microscope that allows scientists to study matter at nanoscale.

In the TECH Center—one of the largest student computing labs in the country—students can collaborate in breakout rooms, edit video in specialized labs, get assistance from the 24-hour help desk or work on one of 700 computers. There are also more than 100 other computer labs on campus, 3,600 student workstations and 450 technology-enabled classrooms.

Temple's libraries host intrepid, curious students and scholars. With the equivalent of more than 4 million bound volumes and an extensive special collection of rare books and archives, Temple's libraries rank among the top research libraries in North America.

TUITION, ROOM, BOARD AND FEES

Tuition and fees for the 2014–2015 academic year were approximately $14,696 for Pennsylvania residents and $24,722 for out-of-state residents (tuition rates vary by degree program). Room and board for the same period was about $10,700.

FINANCIAL AID

Temple is known for its innovation in student-loan debt reduction and college affordability. A variety of scholarships, grants, loans and work-study programs are available. Seventy percent of first-year students receive need-based financial aid, and 42 percent receive academic scholarships. Four-year academic merit scholarships for freshmen range from $3,000 to full tuition, and several include summer stipends for research, internships and study abroad. Students need only apply for admission to be eligible.

Applicants for need-based aid must file the Free Application for Federal Student Aid, also called FAFSA. Transfer students must file a financial aid transcript, even if they have received no aid from their previous school.

In fall 2014, 88 percent of incoming freshman signed up for Temple's Fly in 4 program, which helps students limit their debt by ensuring they graduate in four years. As a part of Fly in 4, Temple awards four-year grants to 500 eligible students to reduce their need to work for pay. Temple also helps Owls take charge of their finances through courses, workshops and a money-management website.

STUDENT ORGANIZATIONS AND ACTIVITIES

No matter their interests, likes or passions, students find a place at Temple, thanks to hundreds of student organizations, clubs, events and activities. From political and cultural groups to scientific and scholarly pursuits, there is no shortage of ways to express one's individuality.

All over campus, students can attend music and dance performances, theater productions, academic talks and panels, films, art exhibits, and sports and cultural events.

There are several large venues for concerts and shows, including the historic Temple Performing Arts Center and the university's 10,200-seat entertainment complex, which also hosts its NCAA Division I basketball games.

To keep students healthy and strong, Temple offers multiple indoor and outdoor sports, recreation and fitness facilities, including an outdoor volleyball court, a rock-climbing wall, running tracks, pools and several locations for weightlifting and classes.

ADMISSIONS PROCESS

The Temple Option is a new admissions path for talented students who may not perform well on standardized tests. If students choose the Temple Option, they answer brief essay questions instead of submitting SAT or ACT scores. The Temple Option reflects the university's commitment to provide students of all backgrounds opportunities for high-quality college experiences.

For freshman admissions, high-school grades, standardized test scores or the Temple Option responses, and other factors (such as a required essay, recommendations, extracurricular activities, work or leadership experience and other personal circumstances) are considered.

Temple has rolling admissions and early-action plans for the fall semester. The early-action deadline is November 1, with notifications scheduled for mid-January (or before). The rolling admissions deadline is March 1.

Temple's admissions process is holistic: Every aspect of a student's academic history is considered. Typically, students with B+ averages or better in strong, college-preparatory curricula in grades 9 through 12 and in the top 30 percent of their graduating classes are accepted. For students submitting SAT scores, all three sections are considered, and admitted students average scores of 500–600 on each section. If students opt to take the ACT, they must also complete the writing section.

Students who apply as freshmen are automatically considered for merit-based scholarships and honors.

The application fee is $55, and most students apply online through Temple or the Common Application.

Temple University welcomes transfer applicants who make up more than half of each entering class. Applicants are considered transfer students if they have attempted 15 or more college-level credits after high school.

Apply to Temple at admissions.temple.edu/apply or via the Common Application. If you have questions, visit admissions.temple.edu, email askanowl@temple.edu or find Temple Admissions on Twitter: @admissionsTU. To see what it's like to be a Temple Owl, visit nextstop.temple.edu.

TRANSYLVANIA UNIVERSITY

AT A GLANCE

Transylvania, a private co-ed liberal arts college of approximately 1,100 students, is consistently ranked among the best colleges in the nation. With a rich history dating back to its founding in 1780, Transylvania holds the distinction of being the sixteenth oldest college in the United States and the first college founded west of the Allegheny Mountains. Meaning "across the woods" in Latin, Transylvania established the first schools of medicine and law in what was then the West and educated the doctors, lawyers, ministers, political leaders, and others who helped shape the young nation. Transylvania also founded the first college literary magazine in the West, The Transylvanian, still published by students today.

Transylvania continues as a pioneer in higher education, preparing future leaders in business, government, education, the sciences, and the arts. On campus, professors work side by side with students in small classes. None of Transylvania's classes have more than 35 students, and 37 percent of classes have 10 or fewer students. The student-faculty ratio is 11:1, and 98 percent of tenured and tenure-track faculty members hold a doctorate or the highest degree in their fields. Many faculty members are recognized for their scholarship and professional activities, but their central concern is teaching and advising. Due in large part to these small classes and close collaborations with faculty, a high percentage of graduates attend selective medical, law, and other graduate and professional programs.

Transylvania students are an active and involved group, who take advantage of the vibrant and dynamic campus community. Students benefit from tremendous opportunities for learning outside the classroom and off-campus, often choosing to participate in campus and community organizations. Many students reach out to the Lexington community by pursuing research projects, internships, and volunteer activities that allow them to grow and learn in a broader context. Also, nearly 70 percent of students embrace the global community through study abroad programs at Transylvania.

LOCATION AND ENVIRONMENT

Transylvania is located in Lexington, Kentucky, a city of 310,000 and a growing center of commerce, culture, research, and education. Known as the "horse capital of the world," rolling green pastures of the famous Bluegrass region of central Kentucky surround the city. The area is also home to over 30,000 college students. Transylvania's park-like campus is situated in lively downtown, with easy access to restaurants, shops, and entertainment. The downtown location is also an advantage for students who want convenient part-time jobs and internship opportunities in law offices, financial firms, hospitals, non-profits, and other organizations.

OFF-CAMPUS OPPORTUNITIES

Experiencing diverse cultures through international study is a vital part of a Transylvania liberal arts education. Students are encouraged to study abroad during May Term, for a summer, or a semester. In recent years, Transylvania students have studied in 62 foreign countries. Scholarships are available for both semester-long and summer study abroad programs. Summer study programs, including those in Austria, Chile, China, Costa Rica, Cuba, Denmark, Ecuador, Greece, France, Germany, Italy, Japan, Mexico, Spain, and Tanzania are available through Transylvania's affiliation with the Kentucky Institute for International Studies (KIIS). Transylvania also cooperates with the Kentucky branch of the English-Speaking Union to offer advanced students scholarships for summer study at Cambridge and Oxford Universities. Internships with congressional offices, Kentucky state government, city government, and local firms are easily arranged.

MAJORS AND DEGREES OFFERED

The Bachelor of Arts degree is awarded in the following majors: accounting, anthropology, art history, art studio, biology, business administration (concentrations in finance, hospitality management, management, and marketing), chemistry (concentrations in chemistry and in biochemistry), classics, computer science, drama, economics, education, educational studies, English, exercise science, French, German, history, international affairs, mathematics, music, music technology, neuroscience, PPE (philosophy, politics, and economics), philosophy, physics, political science, psychology, religion, sociology, sociology/anthropology, Spanish, and writing, rhetoric, and communication. Individually designed majors also may be arranged, and students have the option to double major. Minors are available in most majors and in Asian studies, classical studies, communication, creative writing, environmental studies, hospitality management, interdisciplinary business, Latin American and Caribbean studies, and women's studies. Advising and undergraduate preparation are provided for pre-professional programs in engineering, law, ministry, medicine, dentistry, pharmacy, physical therapy, optometry, physician's assistant and veterinary medicine. Transylvania also offers a pre-engineering partnership with the University of Kentucky, providing students with a seamless transition to engineering graduate programs of their choosing.

ACADEMIC PROGRAMS

The academic year is based on a 4-4-1 academic calendar, with two 14-week terms (fall and winter) and a one-month May term. During May term, students participate in a variety of programs on and off campus. Students normally take four courses in each of the fall and winter terms and one course in May term. Thirty-six courses are required to graduate. Freshmen participate in a unique first-year academic experience beginning with August Term. August Term is an innovative three-week course designed to prepare students for academic success and personal growth. Students learn their way around campus, explore the city of Lexington, and earn a full-course credit in the First Engagements seminar. August Term is followed by a two-semester First Year Seminar program, which features small-group discussions with a faculty leader; lectures, films, concerts, and other presentations; and a tutorial program in critical reading, critical thinking, and research skills. Students must complete requirements designed to ensure broad familiarity with the major areas of learning and human endeavor in the humanities and fine arts, social sciences, natural sciences and mathematics, logic, and languages.

CAMPUS FACILITIES

Transylvania University's academic facilities pay homage to its rich historical design while keeping up-to-date with current technology. In all of the academic buildings, students have access to wireless internet. Two Georgian-style buildings combine elegance with high-tech facilities to offer the latest advances in teaching and learning. The Cowgill Center for Business, Economics, and Education includes a multimedia classroom where professors from any discipline can use a large display screen to show the entire class information from one of the twenty-five networked student computers. A specialized area for education majors includes a laboratory classroom for teacher training. The Lucille C. Little Theater, used for faculty- and student-directed productions and drama classes, is a technically innovative facility that includes computerized lighting and sound, flexible staging options, and movable seating. The Frances Carrick Thomas/J. Douglas Gay, Jr. Library offers sophisticated computerized databases, which are invaluable for research and can be accessed from any computer connected to Transylvania's server. The Mitchell Fine Arts Center provides music program facilities, including practice rooms, a recital hall, and an auditorium. It also houses the Career Development Center, which helps students research career options, improve job search skills, arrange internships and part-time jobs, and apply to graduate schools and to professional positions. Mitchell is also home to a state-of-the-art Fine Arts Technology Lab. The Charles L. Shearer Art Building is dedicated to instructional space, student and faculty studios, and a student gallery. Other modern facilities include the newly renovated L. A. Brown Science Center, the Haupt Humanities Building, and the Clive M. Beck Athletic and Recreation Center, which includes a state-of-the-art fitness center.

Seventy-five percent of students, and 93 percent of first-year students, live on campus in six residence facilities. These include traditional-style accommodations, apartment-style living for upper-class students, and suite-style rooms. In the summer of 2015, Transylvania will open a new suite-style facility dedicated to combining living and learning spaces, with two new additional halls to open in the summer of 2016. Thomson Hall, opened in fall 2008, was only the second residence hall in the southeast to earn the EPA's Energy Star certification. All rooms are air-conditioned and completely furnished, with access to Transylvania's cable television and computer networks. Each residence hall has ample lounge and study space and easy access to computer labs and recreational facilities. Dining options include a cafeteria, two grills, and a coffee shop. The William T. Young Campus Center offers a competition-size indoor pool, a gymnasium, and other meeting and recreation facilities.

TUITION, ROOM, BOARD AND FEES

Transylvania charges an annual tuition that covers fall, winter, and May terms for a normal full-time schedule of courses. For 2015–2016, tuition and fees are $34,370 and room and board (double occupancy) are $9,560.

FINANCIAL AID

Transylvania is committed to providing financial aid to students and their families and four types of financial assistance. Scholarships are awarded based on academic performance and leadership. Grants, loans, and work-study are based on financial need. Over 98 percent of Transylvania students receive some form of financial assistance, and many receive more than one type of aid. Outstanding entering freshmen may qualify for the William T. Young Scholarship, worth more than $137,000 over four years. Submission of Transylvania's Application for Admission and Scholarships or the Common Application is necessary to be considered for academic scholarships at Transylvania. Students who are interested in need-based aid must file the Free Application for Federal Student Aid (FAFSA).

STUDENT ORGANIZATIONS AND ACTIVITIES

Transylvania offers more than seventy co-curricular organizations covering a range of student interests. The athletics program, in NCAA Division III, includes 12 varsity sports for men, 14 for women, and more than a dozen intramural sports. Transylvania also has four national sororities and four national fraternities.

ADMISSIONS PROCESS

In the fall of 2015, Transylvania will introduce a test-optional admissions policy. Regardless of their application track, applicants are considered individually on the basis of academic performance, activities, interests, essays, and recommendations. Admission is also offered to transfer students, international students and nontraditional students.

Transylvania enrolls approximately 310 new students each academic year. The middle 50 percent composite ACT score for the freshman class is 25 to 30. Over 50 percent are in the top 10 percent of their high school graduating class.

The early action deadline is December 1 for applicants who wish to learn of their admission by January 15 and who want to be considered for all Transylvania scholarships. February 1 is the regular admission and scholarships deadline for applicants who wish to be considered for all Transylvania scholarships except the William T. Young, Trustee, and Kenan Scholarships. Applicants who apply after February 1 are considered on a space-available basis. The deadline for applications for the winter term, which begins in January, is December 1.

Students considering Transylvania are urged to visit the campus, and high school seniors are encouraged to stay overnight in a residence hall with a student ambassador. Weekday visits may include a customized campus tour; the opportunity to attend classes; meetings with professors, coaches, students, and admissions and financial aid counselors; and a meal on campus. Visits should be arranged with the Office of Admissions, preferably one to two weeks in advance. Preview Days are held in the fall, spring, and summer.

To request application materials and additional information, contact:

Office of Admissions

Transylvania University

300 North Broadway

Lexington, KY 40508-1797

Telephone: (859) 233-8242 or (800) 872-6798

E-mail: admissions@transy.edu

Web site: www.transy.edu / www.beapioneer.org (admissions specific)

Twitter: @beapioneer

Transylvania University – Social Media

- Transylvania University Twitter https://twitter.com/transy
- Transylvania Admissions Twitter https://twitter.com/beapioneer
- Transylvania University Facebook https://www.facebook.com/transylvaniauniversity
- Transylvania Admissions Facebook https://www.facebook.com/beapioneer?fref=ts
- Transylvania University Instagram https://instagram.com/transylvaniauniversity/
- Transylvania Admissions Instagram https://instagram.com/pioneerguides
- Transylvania Admissions Blog https://beapioneer.wordpress.com/
- Transylvania University YouTube https://www.youtube.com/user/TransylvaniaUniv
- Transylvania Admissions YouTube https://www.youtube.com/user/beapioneer

TRINITY COLLEGE (CT)

AT A GLANCE

Trinity College is an independent, nonsectarian liberal arts college located in the historic capital city of Hartford, Connecticut. Founded in 1823, Trinity is one of the oldest colleges in the country and is consistently ranked among the best. It brings the great tradition of the liberal arts into the 21st century with a dynamic living and learning community where education doesn't stop at the classroom door.

Our approximately 2,200 students work closely with faculty and extend their education through campus activities and organizations. They engage with the city of Hartford through internships and community learning and service and explore the wider world through study abroad and international initiatives on campus. With a 10-to-1 student-faculty ratio, each student is challenged and encouraged by Trinity's outstanding faculty. Students are offered a rigorous curriculum that is firmly grounded in the traditional liberal arts and also incorporates newer fields, an interdisciplinary approach, and urban engagement.

With 39 majors and approximately 900 courses from which to choose, students are immersed in a community of learning that is facilitated by a stimulating academic environment, small classes, and exceptional facilities, including fully networked classrooms and residence halls. Opportunities to explore the arts abound on campus, and students can nurture and hone artistic skills. More than 40 percent of our students play varsity and club sports, and many more participate in intramurals and fitness activities.

As a student at Trinity College, you will explore new worlds, thoughts, and ideas, becoming prepared for a successful, fulfilling life.

LOCATION AND ENVIRONMENT

Trinity is situated on a beautiful, 100-acre campus in Hartford, midway between Boston and New York. Hartford has a rich history that offers many opportunities for urban engagement. Mark Twain lived here, as did Harriet Beecher Stowe. Dentist Horace Wells discovered anesthesia here. It is the home of the oldest continuously published newspaper in America and the oldest public art museum, the Wadsworth Atheneum. Trinity effectively uses the city as a classroom, with access to assets and resources that is matched by few liberal arts colleges of our size.

Anyone who visits the college sees the beauty of the campus, with our hilltop location, mix of historic and contemporary buildings, and abundant trees and lawns. Trinity is one of the earliest examples of "Collegiate Gothic;" many of the original buildings are modeled after the architecture of Oxford and Cambridge and symbolize Trinity's roots in the classical liberal arts. A major campus and community revitalization initiative created the state-of-the-art Raether Library and Information Technology Center on campus and the neighboring innovative Learning Corridor of magnet schools and academic resources, which now also includes the Hartford Magnet Trinity College Academy. Also, in 2006, the award-winning Koeppel Community Sports Center opened its doors as a multiuse athletic facility on the southern edge of campus.

As a Trinity student, you have numerous opportunities to engage in internships, research with faculty, community learning projects, and volunteer work. Many courses–from art history to political science and from economics to neuroscience–incorporate aspects of city life. And whatever your tastes, there are cultural and entertainment events throughout the city and a shuttle service provided by the college.

OFF-CAMPUS OPPORTUNITIES

Trinity students have a wide variety of opportunities to take advantage of the college special relationship with the city of Hartford. The Community Learning Initiati comprises courses that weave direct contact with local residents and institutio into the learning process. Such urban engagement builds on Trinity's liberal a foundation, and for some students, has led to independent studies or collaborati research papers published in scholarly journals.

Trinity offers more than 200 internships in the Hartford area, which represe excellent preparation for life after college. Students can explore career interests a wide variety of fields, including law, banking, journalism, communications, heal care, engineering, computer science, government, and nonprofit organizations. T college's Legislative Internship Program offers students the opportunity to work f a member of the Connecticut General Assembly. Trinity challenges its students make a difference in the real world–starting with their Hartford community. Studer can choose from a wide range of community service activities, from child-mentori programs to the Boys and Girls Club at Trinity to Habitat for Humanity.

Trinity's study-abroad programs provide unforgettable learning experienc that broaden perspectives and deepen understanding. Among the rich menu study-abroad choices are Trinity's own campus in Rome and our seven additio international program sites, as well as more than 90 approved international a domestic programs. Equally valuable are many study-away programs in the Unit States, including the Trinity/La Mama Performing Arts Semester in New York Ci research and internships in Washington D.C., and theater courses at the O'Ne National Theater Institute. Students can also take advantage of the Twelve-Colle Exchange Program.

Trinity also created the Center for Urban and Global Studies to integrate the colleg well-established tradition of urban engagement with our strong global progran The center, the first of its kind at a liberal arts college in the United States, tak advantage of Trinity's location and strengthens the long-standing mutually benefic relationship between the college and Hartford. Playing off Trinity's global reac the center is expanding new learning and research opportunities in world cities.

MAJORS AND DEGREES OFFERED

Undergraduates completing the necessary requirements receive bachelor of arts bachelor of science degrees from Trinity College.

Trinity offers approximately 900 courses in 39 majors. At Trinity, your educatio is student-centered, and our array of curricular options will provide you with th tools to help you to meet your goals.

Trinity offers majors in: American studies, anthropology, art history, biochemistr biology, chemistry, classical studies, computer science, economics, educational stu ies, engineering, English, environmental science, French studies, German studie Hispanic studies, history, interdisciplinary computing, international studies, Itali studies, Jewish studies, language and culture studies (Arabic, Chinese, Hebre Japanese), mathematics, music, neuroscience, philosophy, physics, political scienc psychology, public policy and law, religion, Russian, sociology, student-designed i terdisciplinary major, studio arts, theater and dance, urban studies, women, gende and sexuality, and world literature and culture studies

ACADEMIC PROGRAMS

At Trinity, the curriculum features the First-Year Seminars, where a small group of students and a faculty member explore a topic through critical reading and discussion, analysis, and writing. It's a shared introduction to intellectual life at Trinity and an important way to meet other students and make friends. All first-year students are housed in first-year residence halls and are supported by a student mentor who participates in your seminar.

There are many special curricular options, including the Guided Studies, Interdisciplinary Science, InterArts, and Cities programs, as well as the Trinity/La MaMa Performing Arts Semester in New York. Trinity is also home to the first undergraduate Human Rights Program in the United States and the unique Center for Urban and Global Studies.

The key words here are variety and flexibility–if you don't see exactly what you want, that doesn't mean we don't have it. Independent study? Study abroad? Engineering? Neuroscience? Law courses? How about an academic leave of absence to work on a political campaign or hike the Appalachian Trail? Many Trinity students pursue these and other existing opportunities. And it is very easy to work with faculty to create your own opportunities. Your motivation and imagination are your only limits.

CAMPUS FACILITIES AND EQUIPMENT

The campus is fully wired, with every student room connected to the campus network and the Internet. The newly expanded Raether Library and Information Technology Center combines the resources of one of the leading small-college library facilities in the nation with an array of electronic resources, including digital media labs and video-conferencing capabilities. The library houses more than 1.2 million books, bound collections, and electronic books, as well as approximately 90,000 periodical titles. It also houses the Watkinson Library rare-book collections.

The science labs offer our undergraduates an opportunity to work hands-on with sophisticated equipment, including a research nuclear magnetic resonance spectrometer, a scanning electron microscope, incubators, and climatically controlled growth chambers.

Focal points for the visual arts are the Widener Gallery in the Austin Arts Center and the Broad Street Gallery. In addition to a proscenium theater and a more intimate black box performance space, each art medium has its own studio.

The Ferris Athletic Center houses a fully equipped fitness center, an Olympic-size pool, premier international-size squash courts, crew tanks, an indoor track, a field house, and basketball and tennis courts. Outdoor features include an all-weather track, soccer fields, softball and baseball diamonds, the Paul D. Assaiante Tennis Center, an artificial turf field hockey field, and an artificial turf playing surface for football and lacrosse. In addition, the Koeppel Community Sports Center serves as home ice for Trinity men's and women's ice hockey teams and a place for community academic and athletic mentoring programs.

TUITION, ROOM AND BOARD, AND FEES

Estimated college costs for 2015–16 are as follows:

Tuition: $48,446

Room and Board: $13,144

Fees: $2,380

FINANCIAL AID

Through the generosity of alumni and friends, the college has an endowment sufficient to give our students an education that's worth considerably more than the actual tuition charged. If you decide that Trinity is the right college for you, we are determined not to let money stand in your way. We are committed to making a Trinity education accessible to promising students who are unable to meet the full educational costs. More than 40 percent of our students receive need-based financial aid from Trinity, federal, or state funds. If you have any questions about financial aid at Trinity during any point in your college search, you should not hesitate to contact the Financial Aid Office at (860) 297-2046 or financial-aid@trincoll.edu.

STUDENT ORGANIZATIONS AND ACTIVITIES

With more than 100 student organizations on campus, the opportunities for active involvement are wide open– whether continuing something in which you've already been involved or something that is completely new to you. Student organizations include community service organizations, cultural organizations, media groups (such as the college newspaper and radio station), academic clubs, fraternities/sororities, and club sports. And if you have an interest that isn't covered by an existing organization, start one! It will probably be impossible for you not to find at least one activity that appeals to you, whether on campus or in the city. Academics are the most important part of your education, but they aren't the only part. We encourage you to get involved beyond the classroom. The opportunities are right at hand.

ADMISSIONS PROCESS

Selecting candidates for admission to Trinity is a complex but personalized process. The components of your evaluation include your academic credentials. Your grades are very important, but so is the strength of the academic programs in which you participated. We require one form of standardized test: either the SAT I, ACT, or any two SAT II subject tests. Non-native speakers of English must also submit the TOEFL or IELTS.

In addition, two teachers' evaluations and one college counselor evaluation are required. Teachers give us insight into your scholarship, work habits, and classroom contributions. Personal qualities are considered, as well. What talents, skills, or qualities can you bring to the life of the campus? What contributions have you made to your school and community? We aren't as concerned with the number of your activities as we are with the quality and depth of them.

If we may be of assistance, please don't hesitate to call upon us in the Office of Admissions at (860) 297-2180 or e-mail admissions.office@trincoll.edu.

TRUMAN STATE UNIVERSITY

AT A GLANCE

Truman State University is Missouri's premier liberal arts and sciences university and the only highly selective public institution in the state. As one of the very few publicly funded liberal arts schools in the nation, Truman successfully combines affordability with the type of education and personal attention typically only offered at a private institution.

Truman has established an impeccable reputation in the Midwest and throughout the nation for the high-quality undergraduate programs offered. In fact, for the eighteenth consecutive year, U.S. News & World Report has ranked Truman State University as the number one master's level public institution in the Midwest. A commitment to student achievement and learning is the focus of the University.

LOCATION AND ENVIRONMENT

The Truman campus is beautifully situated on 180 acres in Kirksville, a town of approximately 17,000 located in the northeast corner of Missouri. The historic downtown area is within walking distance of the Truman campus and provides a connection to the Kirksville community with local restaurants, shops, and entertainment.

MAJORS AND DEGREES

Undergraduate degrees offered by Truman include the Bachelor of Arts (B.A.), Bachelor of Science (B.S.), Bachelor of Music (B.M.), Bachelor of Fine Arts (B.F.A.), and Bachelor of Science in Nursing (B.S.N.). Truman offers more than forty areas of study in the following disciplines: Accounting, Agricultural Science, Art, Art History, Athletic Training, Biology, Business Administration, Chemistry, Classics, Communication, Communication Disorders, Computer Science, Creative Writing, Economics, English, Exercise Science, French, German, Health Science, History, Interdisciplinary Studies, Justice Systems, Linguistics, Mathematics, Music, Nursing, Philosophy and Religion, Physics, Political Science, Psychology, Romance Languages, Russian, Sociology/Anthropology, Spanish, and Theatre.

Professional paths include but are not limited to dentistry, engineering, law, medicine, optometry, pharmacy, physical therapy, occupational therapy and veterinary medicine.

The teaching degree at Truman is the Master of Arts in Education. Students wishing to pursue a teaching career first complete a bachelor's degree in an academic discipline and then apply for admission into professional study at the master's level. Master's programs in special education, elementary education, middle school education, and secondary education are available.

Truman also offers Master's level degrees in Accountancy (MAc), Biology (MS), Communication Disorders (MA), Counseling (MA), English (MA), Leadership (MA) and Music (MA).

ACADEMICS

The Liberal Studies Program is the heart of Truman's curriculum and is intended to serve as a foundation for all major programs of study. The philosophy behind the Liberal Studies Program is based upon a commitment that Truman has made to provide students with essential skills needed for lifelong learning, breadth across the traditional liberal arts and sciences through exposure to various discipline-based modes of inquiry, and interconnecting perspectives that stress interdisciplinary thinking and integration as well as linkage to other cultures and experiences.

Students at Truman complete a "capstone," or culminating experience their senior year. This experience prompts seniors to reflect on the knowledge they have gained throughout their learning experience and to integrate the knowledge, skills, and attitudes of liberal learning with an in-depth understanding of the major.

Truman also offers a challenging Honors Scholar Program. Students have the opportunity to select the most rigorous honors courses to satisfy the liberal arts component of their respective programs. Those who successfully complete this program benefit from an even richer academic experience at Truman and receive special recognition at graduation. Departmental honors are also available in several disciplines.

OFF-CAMPUS OPPORTUNITIES

Students at Truman are active both inside and outside of the classroom. More than 400 Truman students participate in enriching and life-changing study abroad experiences each year. Students can participate in programs ranging from a couple weeks to a year in duration, and can choose from numerous destinations worldwide. In 2015, Truman ranked 9th among Master's Institutions for the number of Fulbright grants awarded. This federal grant provides funds for studying or working abroad after graduation.

Truman offers a wide variety of experiential internships, a required component of some academic programs. The "Truman in Washington" program provides work-experience opportunities in the nation's capitol in such areas as foreign affairs, diplomacy, government affairs, criminal justice, international relations, health and human services, and communications as well as other areas. Truman also offers internship opportunities with the Missouri State Legislature. In recent years, students have completed internships with United States senators, the United States Supreme Court, the governor of Missouri, business and industry managers, advertising agencies, physical therapists, and artists.

CAMPUS LIFE

With approximately 250 student organizations to choose from, encompassing service, Greek, honorary, professional, religious, social, political and recreational influences, Truman students have tremendous opportunities to become involved on campus and in the Kirksville community. Truman student organizations sponsor a number of events throughout the year, such as Truman Live, International Idol, guest speakers, poetry slams, musical performances, dance recitals, volunteering events, and ever-popular food nights.

The Kohlenberg Lyceum Series also provides a variety of cultural programs that interest students throughout the year. Past programs have included brilliant performances by the Peking Acrobats, American Shakespeare Center, Preservation Hall Jazz Band, and the Russian Festival Ballet. Truman's Student Activity Board sponsors a variety of entertainment events. Recent SAB concerts include Phillip Phillips, Lee Brice, and B.o.B.. Comedic acts like Vanessa Bayer and Judah Friedlander have also come to Truman's campus in recent years.

FACILITIES AND EQUIPMENT

Students take advantage of numerous academic resources and facilities available to them. Improvements to campus facilities have included the renovation and expansion of Truman's Science facility, Magruder Hall, which was completed for the spring 2006 semester. Renovations to Barnett Hall include a new Student Media Center encompassing facilities for the student-produced newspaper, Midwest travel magazine, radio station, and TV studio. Students also enjoy dining, socializing, and relaxing in the newly renovated Student Union Building.

Opened for the 2011 fall semester is the Health Sciences Building which houses a speech and hearing clinic for Communication Disorders students, an independent learning center for Nursing students, a Human Performance lab, and the Fontaine C. Piper Movement Analysis lab. Additional facilities include a biofeedback laboratory, an organic chemistry lab, an observatory, a 400-acre university farm, a multicultural affairs center, student health center, and a career center. Athletic facilities include a 5,000-seat football stadium, a 3,000-seat arena with three basketball courts, an Olympic-size swimming pool, soccer and rugby fields, baseball and softball fields, tennis courts, a dance studio, and a Student Recreation Center.

Residence halls also provide comfortable and enriching living environments for students. Most of the halls have been renovated within the last five years. All residence halls offer lounges, kitchenettes, laundry facilities, high-speed internet (including wireless), cable TV, and many other amenities. Students can eat in dining halls or in the food court style dining in the Student Union Building.

TUITION, ROOM, BOARD, AND FEES

Tuition for Missouri residents for the 2014–15 academic year is $7,096; out-of-state tuition is $13,160. The average room and board rate for both Missouri residents and nonresidents is $8,480. Additional fees include a one-time $315 freshman orientation fee, and annual fees including an $84 activities fee, a $100 athletic fee, a $54 Student Health Center fee, a $115 parking fee for those with a vehicle, and costs of books and personal expenses.

FINANCIAL AID

Truman offers automatic scholarships ranging from $500 to $5,000. Competitive scholarship awards vary from $500 up to full tuition, room and board, plus a $4,000 study-abroad stipend. The application for admission also serves as the application for the automatic and competitive scholarship programs, and it is free to apply.

A limited number of scholarships are awarded to students for excellence in fine arts, debate or foreign language. These scholarships are available for instrumental or vocal music; acting or dramatic production; studio art or art history; speech or debate; and foreign languages offered at Truman. Of special interest to piano students is the Truman Piano Fellowship Competition, a February competition offering scholarships to top pianists.

Truman, a National Collegiate Athletic Association Division II member, offers 20 men's and women's sports. The NCAA and the University authorize a limited number of grants to outstanding athletes. The value of this aid may vary with each individual recipient.

ADMISSIONS

Truman accepts the Free Application for Federal Student Aid (FASFA) and participates in all Federal Title IV financial aid programs. Financial aid estimates are available upon request.

Each applicant is evaluated for admission based upon academic and co-curricular record, ACT or SAT results, and the admission essay. Truman requires the following high school core: 4 units of English, 3 units of mathematics (4 recommended), 3 units of social studies/history, 3 units of natural science, 1 unit of fine arts and 2 units of the same foreign language.

Students interested in being considered for all scholarships are encouraged to apply by December 1 of their senior year. The recommended final deadline to apply for the fall semester is March 1. There is no application fee. Students may apply online at the website listed below. For further information or to schedule a campus visit, students should contact:

Office of Admission

Truman State University

100 East Normal

Kirksville, Missouri 63501

Telephone: 660.785.4114 or 800.892.7792

Fax: 660.785.7456

E-mail: admissions@truman.edu

http://admissions.truman.edu

UNION COLLEGE (NY)

AT A GLANCE

Union College, chartered by the state of New York in 1795, is one of the nation's oldest and most distinguished liberal arts colleges. Union is a leader in educating students to be engaged, innovative and ethical contributors to a diverse, global and technologically complex society. The Union curriculum emphasizes collaboration with students and faculty through small classes and undergraduate research, international study and service learning. The approximately 2,200 full-time undergraduates come from 41 U.S. states and territories and 35 other countries. Some 19 percent of students identify themselves as members of a multicultural group.

LOCATION AND ENVIRONMENT

The first planned campus in America, Union was designed by noted French architect Joseph Ramée and includes the 16-sided Nott Memorial, a historic landmark, and Jackson's Garden, a certified natural wildlife habitat. Union is located on 130 acres in the revitalized city of Schenectady, part of Upstate New York's Capital Region. Along with Albany and Troy, Schenectady is among "The 20 Best Small Cities for College Students" (as reported by The Huffington Post). Steps from campus, the city has a mix of shops, restaurants, the Sunday greenmarket, movies, professional theater and more. The region's rich cultural heritage and thriving high-tech industry offer opportunities for student/faculty research, internships and jobs. A 20-minute drive from Albany International Airport, Union is within easy reach of New York City and Boston (three hours), Montreal (four hours), and rural and wilderness areas, including the Adirondack Mountains (one-to-two hours).

OFF-CAMPUS OPPORTUNITIES

Union offers more than 50 terms abroad and mini-term programs in 40 countries. Sixty percent of Union students go on terms abroad, one of the highest percentages among colleges and universities. Most programs are led by Union faculty. Students also may design their own program of study abroad, and participate in non-Union and exchange programs. Three-week mini-terms are offered during winter and summer breaks in various U.S. cities and countries.

MAJORS AND DEGREES OFFERED

Union offers more than 40 majors and 55 minors. Students may choose double majors; combine majors and minors; pursue interdepartmental and multidisciplinary concentrations; or opt for area, ethnic and cultural studies. Many students design their own Organizing Theme major. Most students take three courses in each of the three 10-week terms that comprise Union's academic calendar. The average introductory class has 22 students; the average upper level class, 14.

Union offers Bachelor of Arts (B.A.) and Bachelor of Science (B.S.) degrees. Union also offers a five-year Business/Management program with Union Graduate College (B.A. or B.S. And M.B.A.); five-year Education program with Union Graduate College (B.A. or B.S. And M.A.T.); six-year Law and Public Policy program with Albany Law School (B.A. And J.D.); and an eight-year Leadership in Medicine program with Albany Medical College and Union Graduate College (B.S., M.S. or M.B.A., and M.D.).

ACADEMIC PROGRAMS

Union's interdisciplinary approach to the liberal arts combines the humanities and social sciences with science and engineering, emphasizing the practical application of ideas through experience. Students gain deep knowledge within their majors and also experience the cross-pollination of ideas and insights from multiple disciplines.

Students must complete a minimum of 36 courses (up to 40 for engineering degrees) and satisfy departmental and Common Curriculum requirements, including the First-Year Preceptorial and Sophomore Research Seminar, which promote reading, writing, research and critical thinking skills. Distribution requirements in the humanities, literature, social sciences, linguistic and cultural competency, quantitative mathematical reasoning and the sciences promote a breadth of knowledge about the social and natural world, and key skills in analysis, literacy and numeracy.

Union encourages student research in all disciplines. Three-quarters of students actively engage in research. They work one-on-one with professors in top-notch facilities and have access to sophisticated instrumentation often reserved for graduate students at large universities. At Steinmetz Symposium each spring, some 450 students present their research, scholarship and creative work. Approximately 140 students participate in summer research. Many students co-author publications with faculty and present at major conferences. Union consistently ranks among the top of its peer institutions in National Science Foundation awards.

Academic advisers help students select the right coursework, develop research topics, and pursue internships and service. Union's innovative custom advising tool, Notice-Choose-Tell, embraces a process of self-reflection and communication. This encourages students to make meaningful, informed academic decisions consistent with their goals and aspirations, and it helps them build a strong résumé.

Students participate in businesses, health care, government and social service internships. The Michael Rapaport '59 Ethics Across the Curriculum initiative provides training in everyday ethics. Writing Across the Curriculum requires students to take five designated courses from at least two divisions and one Senior Writing Experience.

CAMPUS FACILITIES AND EQUIPMENT

The Nott Memorial is used for study, exhibits and special events. The Peter Irving Wold Center is an interdisciplinary hub, with leading-edge programs in biochemistry, environmental studies, electrical engineering and music research. The F.W. Olin Center houses high-tech classrooms and laboratories. The Science and Engineering Center, home to the Center for Bioengineering and Computational Biology, contains specialized research tools available for student use, including a nuclear magnetic resonance spectrometer, Pelletron accelerator and scanning electron microscope. The Center for Neuroscience in Butterfield Hall brings together computer and research labs, classrooms, offices and collaborative spaces. The Peschel Computer Center houses the IBM High-Performance Computing Cluster, offering some of the most advanced computing capabilities among undergraduate liberal arts schools.

Schaffer Library has over 637,000 volumes, some 800 periodicals (paper) and more than 11,000 total subscriptions. Three hundred databases provide access to a quarter million printed books, documents and musical scores. The college Archives, Language Lab, Special Collections and Writing Center are also housed here, as is the Learning Commons, a high-tech, student-focused area supporting independent and collaborative research. Karp Hall houses the departments of English, and Modern Languages and Literature. Lippman Hall is home to the Social Sciences, including the departments of Economics, History, Political Science and Sociology. Lamont House is home to the departments of Anthropology, Classics and Philosophy, and the Religious Studies program.

Arts facilities include the Mandeville Gallery and Wikoff Student Gallery; the all-Steinway Taylor Music Center, which features Emerson Auditorium, a music technology studio and the World Musics Room. The Visual Arts Building includes painting, drawing and sculpture studios, Art History classrooms, darkrooms and the Burns Art Atrium gallery. The Yulman Theater is home to Mountebanks, the country's oldest student performing group. The Henle Dance Pavilion, overlooking Jackson's Garden, features classrooms, rehearsal and performance studios, and a costume shop. The Kelly Adirondack Center in nearby Niskayuna houses one of the largest research collections on the Adirondack region.

Residential options for students include traditional dorms, apartment-style housing, theme houses, Minerva Houses, Greek houses and College Park Hall. Reamer Campus Center includes dining facilities, the bookstore and various student activities. Among the athletic facilities are Alumni Gymnasium, which features the Breazzano Fitness Center, a swimming/diving pool, and dance, aerobics, spinning and yoga studios. Other recreational and sports facilities include the 3,000-seat Messa Rink at Achilles Center, home of Union's Div. I hockey teams; the Viniar Athletic Center for basketball and volleyball; and the Travis J. Clark '00 Strength Training Facility for varsity athletes. The men's and women's crew teams train at the college's boathouse on the Mohawk River. The Wicker Wellness Center offers health, wellness and counseling services and is the home of Jenna the therapy dog.

The Becker Career Center offers a range of career planning programs and services, from résumé writing and internship searches to career fairs. It works with employers and alumni to guide students in competing effectively in today's job market. Students can connect with alumni in all fields through the Union Career Advisory Network (UCAN). HireU, the center's internship and job database, contains opportunities from alumni and employers who are looking specifically for Union students.

STUDENT ORGANIZATIONS AND ACTIVITIES

Union has more than 100 campus clubs, including performance and arts clubs; cultural groups; the student newspaper, Concordiensis, and radio station, WRUC; sports clubs; 10 residential Greek organizations; 13 theme houses (from cooking to sustainability to technology); academic societies; and service and political interest groups. Cultural events include concerts, theater, dance, film and exhibits. Union's comprehensive athletics program offers 26 varsity intercollegiate sports, organized intramurals, club sports, and recreational and fitness activities. Union is a member of the NCAA, Liberty League and ECAC Hockey. Men's and women's ice hockey compete in NCAA Division I programs; other teams are Division III. Union triumphed in the Frozen Four to capture the national hockey title in 2014.

The Minerva House system is a vibrant community and launch pad for an array of college experiences. All students and faculty members belong to one of seven on-campus houses, where they contribute in distinct ways to Union's social, cultural, academic and intellectual life. Student-run Minerva programs range from book clubs and barbecues to film series, theater outings, and cooking dinner with professors. The Kenney Community Center connects students with Big Brothers Big Sisters, Habitat for Humanity, tutoring programs and many civic projects. Some 1,200 students each year are involved more than 30 service programs and other opportunities for service and leadership.

TUITION, ROOM, BOARD AND FEES

Union's comprehensive fee, which includes tuition, room, board, and mandatory fees, is $62,274 for the 2015–16 academic year. The estimated cost for books and personal expenses is approximately $2,000.

FINANCIAL AID

Union is committed to admitting an economically diverse student body and to meeting the full demonstrated need of all admitted students. The college offers $40 million annually in aid. The average Union need-based scholarship is $32,000; the average merit scholarship is $10,000. Families who are unable to pay full tuition and fees are typically covered by a financial aid package consisting of a grant, loan and work opportunity. About half of all applicants apply for financial aid; more than 60 percent of students receive assistance from the college. Scholarship awards are based on academic performance and financial need. Candidates for aid should complete the Free Application for Federal Student Aid (FAFSA) and the college Scholarship Service's PROFILE form and mail them directly to the appropriate agencies by Feb. 1.

ADMISSION PROCESS

More than 5,000 applicants typically seek first-year class positions; roughly 70 percent are in the top 10 percent of their secondary school class. Admissions counselors look at grades, rigor of courses taken, class rank, teacher recommendations and extracurricular involvement. Typically, 16 units of secondary school preparation are required for admission. These should include credits in such fundamental subjects as English, foreign language, mathematics, social studies and science. It is strongly recommended that students visit Union for an interview and student-guided tour. Alumni interviews may be requested online. A student can choose not to submit his or her SAT or ACT scores for review, except for accelerated programs, which require applicants to submit the SAT and two SAT Subject Tests.

Early decision (ED) candidates have two options. The application deadline (including all supporting credentials) for Option I is Nov. 15, with notification by Dec. 15. Option II has a Jan. 15 deadline (including all supporting credentials) and Feb. 15 notification. Applications for regular decision (RD) admission must be filed by Jan.15; decisions are mailed by April 1. Applications to the Leadership in Medicine program are due no later than Dec. 15, and for Law and Public Policy, by Jan. 1. Those deferred under ED and all regular applicants are given a final decision by April 1. Accepted students have until May 1 to commit.

UNITED STATES MILITARY ACADEMY AT WEST POINT

The United States Military Academy at West Point, world-renowned for its leadership training, is the only college in the U.S. that exists solely to prepare its students for professional service as regular Army officers.

AT A GLANCE

The United States Military Academy at West Point (USMA), the nation's first engineering school and original service academy, has been an educational leader in the United States for more than 200 years. The Academy is a four-year educational institution located on the banks of the Hudson River, just 50 miles north of New York City. Founded in 1802, USMA's mission is "to educate, train, and inspire the Corps of Cadets so that each graduate is a commissioned leader of character committed to the values of Duty, Honor, Country and prepared for a career of professional excellence and service to the Nation as an officer in the United States Army." West Point provides a 47-month leader development program steeped in academic rigor, military discipline, and physical challenges, all built upon a moral-ethical foundation.

Graduates of the United States Military Academy have included US presidents, governors, members of Congress, foreign heads of state, astronauts, educators, and national and international leaders of business and industry.

Consistently ranked among the best colleges in the nation, West Point was recognized by "Forbes" as the No. 1 Public College in the country, No. 1 Best Value, No. 3 Liberal Arts College, and No. 7 Overall College in the country. Similarly, "US News and World Report" rated it as No. 2 Public Liberal Arts College and No. 3 Best Undergrad Engineering Program.

Admission to West Point is competitive. More than 10,000 students apply each year for about 1,200 positions. Women represent about 15 percent of each class.

When students enter USMA, they begin the journey of a lifetime serving in a time-honored profession.

LOCATION AND ENVIRONMENT

USMA is located on 16,000 scenic and historic acres on the banks of the Hudson River, about 50 miles north of New York City. Framed by the majestic Hudson Highlands and poised above the Hudson River, the massive Gothic structures of the campus blend with the rugged beauty of the surrounding hills.

OFF-CAMPUS OPPORTUNITIES

New York City is about an hour away from campus.

MAJORS AND DEGREES OFFERED

USMA offers Bachelor of Science degrees in more than 35 majors offered within the general areas of engineering, sciences, and liberal arts. Academic departments include: Civil and Mechanical Engineering, Electrical Engineering and Computer Science, Geography and Environmental Engineering, Physics and Nuclear Engineering, Systems Engineering, Chemistry and Life Science, Mathematical Sciences, Behavioral Sciences and Leadership, English and Philosophy, Foreign Languages, History, Law, and Social Sciences.

Class size is small, averaging 12 to 18 cadets per class, so instructors know each of their cadets by name. There are no teaching assistants; each class is taught by a fully qualified faculty member who is available regularly to provide any extra assistance.

ACADEMIC PROGRAMS

West Point has established Centers of Excellence that enhance the quality of the academic program. These centers make full use of professional expertise and technical resources to enrich cadet education. The centers help enhance cadet academic performance, improve faculty teaching, promote faculty and cadet research and provide outreach and support to the U.S. Army. Cadets and faculty conduct research in conjunction with the academic departments through such centers as the Center for Environmental and Geographic Sciences, the Operations Research Center, the Photonics Research Center, the Office of Artificial Intelligence Analysis and Evaluation, and the Information Technology Center, as well as others.

CAMPUS FACILITIES AND EQUIPMENT

The United States Military Academy Library, located in Jefferson Hall, a new, state-of-the-art learning center in the academic area, provides up-to-date, fully networked library service to the cadets, faculty and remote users. Supplementing a collection of more than 600,000 volumes, the library offers numerous full-text databases providing access to the contents of thousands of scholarly journals. Open more than 100 hours per week during the academic year, the library also offers a highly skilled staff, group study rooms, and an extensive microfilm collection. The institutional records of the Academy are maintained as part of the library's collections, and these provide invaluable primary source material for research.

West Point's modern academic facilities are matched by its athletic facilities. Michie Stadium, home of Army Football, attracts crowds in excess of 40,000 during picturesque football weekends in the fall.

The Kimsey Athletic Center, the Hoffman Press Box, Randall Hall, the Lichtenberg Tennis Center, the Lou Gross Center and the anderson Rugby Center are new facilities that provide first-class resources for football, basketball, hockey, tennis, lacrosse, gymnastics and rugby programs. The Foley Athletic Center houses a state-of-the-art, climate-controlled indoor playing field. Holleder Athletic Center, adjacent to the stadium, is a multi-sport complex housing a hockey rink with seating for 2,700 and a basketball arena with a 5,000-seat capacity.

The 500,000-square-foot Arvin Cadet Physical Development Center is a state-of-the-art physical fitness facility that includes two gymnasiums, two multipurpose rooms, two swimming pools, six racquetball courts, five wrestling rooms, a rock-climbing wall, two fitness rooms, and a sports medicine facility.

Five separate chapels provide a variety of religious services: Christian, Jewish, Muslim, and Buddhist services are available, as are a number of interdenominational prayer groups, clubs, and events. The cadet activities center, Eisenhower Hall, contains a 4,500-seat auditorium, a 1,000-seat restaurant, a large ballroom overlooking the Hudson River, a games area, an art gallery, and a spacious reception foyer for cadets and guests. Grant Hall offers additional cadet snack and lounge facilities.

TUITION, ROOM, BOARD, AND FEES

Tuition is covered by the U.S. Government for all students who attend West Point. All students are on Active Duty status as members of the U.S. Army and receive an annual salary. The only cost for students is a one-time deposit upon admission to defray the initial costs of uniforms, books, supplies, equipment and fees. A portion of the cadet pay is deposited into a "Cadet Account" to help pay for uniforms, books, laptop, and other incidentals.

STUDENT ORGANIZATIONS AND ACTIVITIES

Guided by the dictum "Every cadet an athlete, every athlete challenged," USMA's physical fitness program is an integral part of the training needed to succeed. Every cadet is required to participate in a competitive athletic activity. USMA offers many choices, including 25 NCAA Division I sports, 21 intercollegiate club teams and a wide variety of intramural sports. Available sports include everything form team sports like football, soccer, basketball, softball, volleyball, lacrosse and crew, to more-individual competitive sports like tennis, track, boxing, fencing, judo and equestrian.

USMA has about 100 cadet clubs that cover every interest from academic activities, such as Model United Nations and debate to National Society of Black Engineers; to hobby clubs like snowboard and paintball; and support clubs like Glee Club, Mule Riders and Theater Arts Guild.

ADMISSIONS PROCESS

Candidates for admission to USMA must be at least 17 but not older than 22 on July 1 of the year they enter West Point; not be married; not be pregnant; and not be legally responsible for support of any children.

Candidates must also be in good physical and mental health, and pass a medical exam.

Candidates should also have above average strength, agility, and endurance and perform well on the West Point Candidate Fitness Assessment.

Candidates must also obtain a nomination to compete for admission. They should apply for all nominations for which they are eligible during the spring of their junior year. At a minimum, candidates are eligible for a congressional nomination from their representative in Congress, their two U.S. senators, and the vice president of the United States.

USMA also conducts a Summer Leaders Experience each June for high school juniors going into their senior year. This fast-faced program of academic classes, military training, physical fitness training and intramural athletics gives high school juniors a taste of life at West Point. USMA cadets serve as squad leaders for all aspects of the week-long seminar. Approximately 1,000 high school juniors are selected to attend the seminar each year.

UNIVERSITY OF CENTRAL FLORIDA

AT A GLANCE

The University of Central Florida is a comprehensive research university with approximately 60,000 students. As one of the nation's fastest growing universities and the 2nd largest in the nation, UCF enrolls a diverse student body representing all 50 states and over 120 countries. The University offers educational and research programs that complement the economy, with strong components in aerospace engineering, business, education, film, health, nursing, social sciences, and hospitality management. UCF's programs in communication and the fine arts help to meet the cultural and recreational needs of a growing metropolitan area. The University also offers many graduate programs leading to masters and doctoral degrees.

UCF has established extensive partnerships with businesses and industry in the central Florida area that provide students with exceptional research and learning experiences. These partnerships bring practical learning environments to UCF students through co-op and internship programs. Joint curriculum development strategies are used throughout the university.

The on-campus and campus-affiliated housing facilities include traditional residence halls, apartment-style options, and Greek housing that accommodates approximately 11,500 students. Several thousand students live in apartments located within walking distance of the campus.

LOCATION AND ENVIRONMENT

The University of Central Florida: Competitive Advantages

A Focus on Undergraduate Education: We're committed to teaching and providing advising and academic support services for all students. Our undergraduates have access to state-of-the-art wireless buildings, high-tech classrooms and research labs, Web-based classes and an undergraduate Research and Mentoring program.

A Talented Student Body: As one of the fastest growing universities in the southeast, total enrollment has reached over 60,000; 50,000 are undergraduates. Our emphasis on excellence in undergraduate education has produced many rewarding results: a Goldwater Scholarship awardee, a Rhodes Scholarship finalist, a Clarion awardee in Radio/Television, a Zonta International Amelia Earhart fellowship awardee, and a nationally ranked Computer Science programming team.

Career Opportunities: Our Career Services professionals help students gain practical experiences at NASA, schools, hospitals, high-tech companies, local municipalities, and the entertainment industry. UCF faculty sit on boards and planning committees, and our graduates make their mark in engineering, business, computer science, education, health care, science, tourism, film and public service.

An International Presence: With an international focus to our curricula and research programs, we currently enroll international students from over 120 nations. Our study abroad programs and other study and research opportunities include agreements with 98 institutions and 36 countries, including Australia, France, Germany, Holland, Italy, Russia, South Africa, Spain and Wales.

A Spacious, Modern Campus, plus Orlando: UCF's 1,415-acre campus provides a safe and serene setting for learning, with natural lakes and woodlands. The university provides housing for approximately 11,500 students on campus and through affiliated housing. The bustle of Orlando lies a short distance away: the Orlando Magic, the Orlando Predators, the Kennedy Space Center, major film studios, Walt Disney World, Universal Orlando, Sea World, and sandy beaches are all nearby.

OFF-CAMPUS OPPORTUNITIES

Career Services and Experiential Learning offers programs in which student's alternate semesters of classroom study with equal periods of paid employment in government, industry, or business. The Department of Modern Languages offers summer study-abroad programs. Courses are available in the subject areas of language (all levels), art, and civilization. UCF is also a participant in the National Student Exchange Consortium.

MAJORS AND DEGREES OFFERED

The University offers the degrees of Bachelor of Applied Science, Bachelor of Arts, Bachelor of Arts in Business Administration, Bachelor of Design, Bachelor or Engineering Technology, Bachelor of Fine Arts, Bachelor of Music, Bachelor of Music Education, Bachelor of Science, Bachelor of Science in Business Administration, Bachelor of Science in Education, Bachelor of Science in Engineering, Bachelor of Science in Nursing, Bachelor of Social Work, and Bachelor of Science in Social Sciences.

These degrees are available in the colleges listed below, with majors or areas of specialization as indicated.

The College of Arts and Humanities offers degrees in art, Architecture, digital media, English, film, , French, history, humanities and cultural studies, Latin American Studies, music, philosophy, Photography, Religion and Cultural Studies, Spanish, Theatre Studies, and Writing and Rhetoric.

The College of Business Administration offers degrees in accounting, Business Economics, economics, finance, general business, management, real estate and marketing.

The College of Education offers degrees in art education, early childhood development and education, elementary education, English language arts education, world languages education, mathematics education, science education, sport and exercise science, social science education, and technical education and industry training.

The College of Engineering and Computer Science offers degrees in aerospace engineering, civil engineering, computer engineering, computer science, construction engineering, electrical engineering, environmental engineering, industrial engineering, Information Technology and mechanical engineering.

The College of Health and Public Affairs offers degrees in athletic training, Communication Sciences and Disorders, criminal justice, Health Informatics and information management, health services administration, health sciences, legal studies, public administration, and social work.

The College of Nursing offers degrees in nursing.

The College of Optics and Photonics offers degrees in Photonic Science and Engineering.

The College of Sciences offers degrees in advertising/public relations, anthropology, biology, chemistry, forensic science, International and Global Studies, Human Communication, journalism, mathematics, physics, political science, psychology, radio/television, social sciences, sociology, and statistics.

The Rosen College of Hospitality Management offers degrees in Hospitality Management, Event Management, and in Restaurant and Foodservice Management.

The College of Medicine and the Burnett School of Biomedical Sciences offers degrees in Biotechnology, Medical Laboratory Sciences, and biomedical sciences. Pre-professional programs are offered in chiropractic, medicine, optometry, osteopathy, pharmacy, physical therapy, physical assistant, podiatry, dentistry and veterinary medicine.

Degrees in Interdisciplinary Studies are available through the Office of Undergraduate Studies.

CAMPUS FACILITIES AND EQUIPMENT

In addition to the academic programs offered on the Orlando campus, upper division students can work toward a degree at 10 locations around the central Florida area. These regional campuses work cooperatively with local state colleges to provide all four years of course work in many academic areas. The library houses over 2.4 million volumes and subscribes to more than 43,000 periodicals and journals (40,500 in electronic format). Students have access to an online computer catalog that provides information on the collections of the State University System libraries. An extensive online network of more than 600 computer terminals (both PC and Mac) cover the campus. The Institute for Simulation and Training gives students the opportunity to pursue undergraduate research. The School of Optics allows faculty members and students to work directly with industrial personnel in conducting basic and applied research at the regional and national level. The Central Florida Research Park, located next to the UCF campus, houses more than ninety high-technology firms and agencies. This proximity fosters relationships between industry and the University, which strengthens the academic programs at UCF.

TUITION, ROOM, BOARD AND FEES

Approximate Tuition, Health Fee, Room and Board Annual Rates 2014–15:

	Florida Resident	Non-Florida Resident
Tuition and Fees	$6,368	$22,466
Room and Board	$9,570	$9,570
Books (estimate)	$800	$800
Approximate Total	$16,738	$32,836
Annual Cost		

Based on 15 credit hours per semester, double room and meal plan.

FINANCIAL AID

Financial aid is awarded according to each student's demonstrated need in relation to college costs and may include grants, loans, scholarships and part-time employment. Programs based on need include the Federal Perkins Loan, Federal Pell Grant, Florida Student Assistance Grant, Federal Work-Study, Florida College Career Work-Study Program, and Federal Stafford Student Loan. To qualify for these programs, students must complete the Free Application for Federal Student Aid. The priority application deadline is March 1. Approximately 76 percent of UCF students receive some form of financial aid.

STUDENT ORGANIZATIONS AND ACTIVITIES

Students participate in approximately 600 organizations, including special interest clubs, multicultural associations, fraternities and sororities, honor societies, and academic and pre-professional organizations. The Office of Student Involvement schedules a wide array of extracurricular programs, including concerts, movies, and guest speakers. The innovative LEAD Scholars Academy fosters leadership and service commitment through a comprehensive student development program for freshman. The Major Exploration Program (MEP) helps entering freshmen define their career goals and develop an academic strategy to reach their goals. UCF offers Air Force and Army ROTC programs.

The University of Central Florida is a member of the NCAA and the American Athletic Conference. All teams compete on the NCAA Division 1 Level. UCF's men's teams compete in intercollegiate baseball, basketball, football, golf, soccer, and tennis. Women's teams compete in basketball, cross-country, golf, rowing, soccer, softball, tennis, track and field, and volleyball. Intercollegiate coed club activities include championship cheerleading, crew, and waterskiing teams. The university offers an extensive intramural sports program.

ADMISSIONS PROCESS

A freshman applicant is a student with fewer than 12 hours of college coursework after high school graduation. The most important criteria in the admission decision for these applicants is the high school academic record, rigor of course work, grade point average, grade trends, and SAT I or ACT Plus Writing test scores. UCF operates on a rolling admission basis. Students are generally notified of their initial admission decision within two to three weeks after receipt of the application and all supporting documents. If the number of qualified applicants exceeds the number that the university is permitted to enroll, a waiting list will be established.

All applicants must have earned a minimum of 18 high school academic units (yearlong courses that are not remedial in nature). These include 4 units of English (3 must include substantial writing), 4 units of mathematics at or above algebra I, 3 units of natural science (2 must include a laboratory), 3 units of social science, 2 units of one world language, and 2 units of academic electives. Grades in honors courses, International Baccalaureate, Advanced Placement, AICE and dual enrollment courses are given additional weight in the GPA computation. Students must meet the Department of Education minimum eligibility to be considered for admission. Applicants should understand that the satisfaction of minimum requirements does not automatically guarantee admission to UCF.

Transfer applicants with fewer than 60 semester hours of college course work must submit official high school transcripts, SAT I or ACT Plus Writing test scores, and all official college transcripts. Transfer students with more than 60 semester hours or who have earned an Associate in Arts degree or a state-wide articulated Associate in Science degree from a Florida public community or state college need only submit all official college transcripts. A transfer credit summary evaluation is provided to students once they are offered admission to UCF.

Students are encouraged to apply several months in advance and can apply online at www.admissions.ucf.edu. It is recommended that freshman students apply early during the fall semester of their senior year. Applications are accepted up to one year prior to the start of the term for which entry is desired. Priority application deadlines are May 1 for the fall term (July 1 for transfers), November 1 for the spring term, and March 1 for the summer term.

THE UNIVERSITY OF CHICAGO

AT A GLANCE

The University of Chicago encourages a close-knit, collaborative learning environment on their campus in Hyde Park. Drawn to theoretical inquiry and open discussion, UChicago's 5,300 undergraduates enjoy small classes and spirited give-and-take discussions where they are free to break down disciplinary barriers and frequently explore research and coursework outside their selected field. The school promotes this close collaboration outside of the classroom as well. UChicago's eleven residence halls are distinct communities comprised of the college Houses. Each House is made up of undergraduate students as well as Resident Heads, who are advanced graduate students or faculty members. These communities become a home away from home and are a focal point for campus life.

Chartered as a private university in 1890, UChicago quickly became a world leader in research. Additionally, UChicago's coherent program of general education for undergraduates, the Core, became a model for American general education. The Core is the University of Chicago student's introduction to the tools of inquiry used in every discipline—science, mathematics, humanities, and social sciences. The goal is not just to transfer knowledge, but to raise fundamental questions and become familiar with the powerful ideas that shape our society.

This atmosphere of free and open inquiry—shaped by the Core, the college Houses, and an emphasis on interdisciplinary collaboration—attracts exceptional students and faculty from around the globe, including at total of 89 Nobel laureates. The intellectual environment on campus has also led to the development of academic disciplines in fields ranging from literary criticism and urban sociology to ecology and the study of religions, as well as world-renowned programs in anthropology, sociology, physics, and economics.

LOCATION AND ENVIRONMENT

UChicago is located in Hyde Park: a vibrant, yet relaxed, residential neighborhood in Chicago, seven miles south of the Loop—the main business center of the city. More than 60% of the faculty and their families call Hyde Park home. The neighborhood is filled with restaurants, cafes, shops, and a new movie theater. The University's 215-acre campus is distinguished by its Collegiate Gothic architecture and its designation as a botanic garden. With its stimulating diversity Hyde Park boasts a thriving cultural scene ranging from the Checkerboard Blues Lounge and the Museum of Science and Industry to The Point, a park on a promontory extending into Lake Michigan and a site for sunbathing and barbeques. Hyde Park is home to a community whose common bond is a shared passion for the type of invigorating discussion bred by such close proximity to UChicago's many educational resources.

ACADEMIC PROGRAMS

Bachelor of Arts or Bachelor of Science degrees are awarded in the following programs:

Akkadian, Near Eastern Languages and Civilizations
American Sign Language, Linguistics
Ancient Anatolian Languages, Near Eastern Languages and Civilizations
Anthropology
Applied Mathematics
Arabic, Near Eastern Languages and Civilizations
Aramaic, Near Eastern Languages and Civilizations
Armenian, Near Eastern Languages and Civilizations
Art History
Asian Languages and Civilizations
Art History
Astronomy and Astrophysics°
Bangla (Bengali), South Asian Languages and Civilizations
Big Problems°
Biological Chemistry
Biological Sciences
Bosnian/Croatian/Serbian, Slavic Languages and Literature
Cancer Biology, Biological Sciences
Catalan, Romance Languages and Literature
Cellular and Molecular Biology, Biological Sciences
Chemistry

Chicago Studies°
Chinese, East Asian Languages and Civilizations
Cinema and Media Studies
Classical Studies
Comparative Human Development
Comparative Literature
Comparative Race and Ethnic Studies
Computer Science
Computational Neuroscience°
Early Christian Literature
East Asian Languages and Civilizations
East European, Slavic Languages and Literatures
Ecology and Evolution, Biological Sciences
Economics
Education°
Egyptian, Near Eastern Languages and Civilizations
Endocrinology, Biological Sciences
Engineering, Molecular
English and Creative Writing°
English Language and Literature
Environmental Science
Environmental Studies
French, Romance Languages and Literatures
Fundamentals: Issues and Texts
Ge'ez, Near Eastern Languages and Civilizations
Gender and Sexuality Studies
General Slavic, Slavic Languages and Literatures
Genetics, Biological Sciences
Geographical Studies
Geophysical Sciences
Germanic Studies
Greek and Roman Cultures, Classical Studies
Hebrew, Near Eastern Languages and Civilizations
History
History, Philosophy, and Social Sciences (HIPS)
Human Rights (minor only)°
Immunology, Biological Sciences
Interdisciplinary Studies in the Humanities
International Studies
Italian, Romance Languages and Literatures
Japanese, East Asian Languages and Civilizations
Jewish Studies
Kazakh, Near Eastern Languages and Civilizations
Korean, East Asian Languages and Civilizations
Language and Literature, Classical Studies
Language Intensive, Classical Studies
Languages in Linguistics, Linguistics
Latin American Studies
Law, Letters, and Society
Linguistics
Malayalam, South Asian Languages and Civilizations
Marathi, South Asian Languages and Civilizations
Mathematics
Mathematics with a Specialization in Economics, Mathematics
Medieval Studies
Microbiology, Biological Sciences
Music
Near Eastern Art and Archaeology, Near Eastern Languages and Civilizations
Near Eastern History and Civilization, Near Eastern Languages and Civilizations
Neuroscience, Biological Sciences
Norwegian Studies (minor only)
Pali, South Asian Languages and Civilizations
Persian, Near Eastern Languages and Civilizations
Philosophy

Philosophy and Allied Fields
Physics
Polish, Slavic Languages and Literatures
Political Science
Portuguese, Romance Languages and Literatures
Psychology
Public Policy Studies
Religion and the Humanities
Religious Studies
Romance Languages and Literatures
Russian Studies
Russian, Slavic Languages and Literatures
Sanskrit, South Asian Languages and Civilizations
Slavic Languages and Literatures
Sociology
South Asian Languages and Civilizations
South Slavic, Slavic Languages and Literatures
Spanish, Romance Languages and Literatures
Statistics
Sumerian, Near Eastern Languages and Civilizations
Swahili, Linguistics
Tamil, South Asian Languages and Civilizations
Telugu, South Asian Languages and Civilizations
Theatre and Performance Studies
Tibetan, South Asian Languages and Civilizations
Turkish, Near Eastern Languages and Civilizations
Tutorial Studies
Ugaritic, Near Eastern Languages and Civilizations
Urdu, Near Eastern Languages and Civilizations
Uzbek, Near Eastern Languages and Civilizations
Visual Arts

°Interdisciplinary option

CAMPUS FACILITIES AND EQUIPMENT

Campus facilities offer a broad array of academic, cultural, and other resources. The University of Chicago is first and foremost known as a major research institution—there are over 170 research centers and institutes that are on UChicago's campus or run by the University. UChicago oversees two Department of Energy labs: Fermi Lab and Argon National Lab. The University also recently became affiliated with the Marine Biological Laboratory in Woods Hole, MA. The Institute of Politics (IOP) is a non-partisan initiative on campus to bringing political officials, policymakers, journalists, and others to UChicago and to provide programming, internships, and guidance for students who are interested in going into public service. The inaugural director of the IOP is David Axelrod, an alum of the college and former Senior Advisor to President Obama. The University is currently finishing construction on a lab building to house their new Institute for Molecular Engineering (IME). The IME will lead engineering research and education in new directions—their mission is to translate advances in basic physics, chemistry, biology, and computation into new tools to address important societal problems.

The University of Chicago also houses numerous other facilities and resources on its campus, including the Logan Arts Center; the Oriental Institute Museum; the David and Alfred Smart Museum of Art; Court Theatre; the University of Chicago Hospitals; the Ryerson Astronomical Observatory; and the Department of Ecology and Evolution's rooftop greenhouse. The Biological Sciences Learning Center is the most up-to-date biology teaching and medical facility of its kind in the nation.

TUITION, ROOM, BOARD, AND FEES

For freshmen living on campus, the cost of attending the University of Chicago for the 2013-2014 academic year is $63,860. Of that, tuition amounts to $45,324, and room and board and fees total $13,653. Personal expenses and books are estimated to cost $3,821, and a student life fee of $1,062 supports student programming and campus-wide activities. The University of Chicago is need-blind when reading applications for US citizens and permanent residents, and citizens of Canada. They are need-sensitive when reading international student applications. For all admitted students, the University guarantees to meet 100 percent of demonstrated need through grants and no loans as part of the No Barriers initiative. UChicago offers primarily need-based financial aid, although it does offer some merit scholarships as well. Families who apply for financial aid do not have to pay a college application fee to UChicago.

STUDENT ORGANIZATIONS AND ACTIVITIES

More than 400 student organizations flourish at UChicago. These range from Off-Off Campus, an improvisational comedy group in the tradition of Chicago's own Second City (which originated at the University of Chicago), to the largest club, University Theater—a student-run theater company that, together with Off-Off Campus, puts on 30 shows a year. Some groups—like Model United Nations, the national champion Debate Society, and the winningest college quiz bowl team in the world—have long traditions of awards in regional and national competition. Students organize and run fourteen fraternities and seven sororities, clubs devoted to such varied interests as political economy and modern dance, and volunteer groups such as Alpha Phi Omega and Habitat for Humanity. Others spring up wherever student interests come together, such as JELLY (Jugglers Enriching Lives Like Yours) or Luigi, a club devoted to studying, developing, and designing video games.

An annual scavenger hunt and the winter festival Kuviasungnerk (from an Icelandic word roughly translated as "happy times") are among the traditional "UChicago" events on campus. With one of the most extensive intramural and club sports programs in the country, UChicago students take athletics seriously, and more than 70 percent participate in intramurals. Varsity athletics attract 14 percent of the undergraduate student population, where competition at the NCAA Division III level has resulted in numerous Academic All-American awards; team league championships in women's cross-country, soccer, softball and tennis, and men's basketball, wrestling, and cross country; and national champions in track and field and women's tennis.

ADMISSIONS PROCESS

The Office of College Admissions reviews each application on a holistic basis. The admissions committee considers a candidate's entire application—academic and extracurricular records, essays, letters of recommendation, and SAT or ACT scores in order to gain a comprehensive understanding of a student's qualifications and potential. No formula exists for the successful Chicago applicant; all have displayed the capacity to inquire, to contribute to their schools and communities, and to succeed at the tasks before them. Among the 1426 students in the Class of 2017 (high school graduation year 2013), approximately 98% graduated in the top 10 percent of their high school classes. The middle 50 percent of admitted students had a combined score of between 1450 and 1550 on the SAT (out of 1600) or between 32 and 35 on the ACT.

To apply for admission or to obtain more information about the University of Chicago, please email the Office of College Admissions at collegeadmissions@uchicago.edu or call 773-702-8650. Information can also be obtained on their website: collegeadmissions.uchicago.edu.

UNIVERSITY OF THE CUMBERLANDS

AT A GLANCE

Chartered in 1888, University of the Cumberlands is committed to providing a superior education in an exceptional Christian atmosphere. The University emphasizes the growth of the individual student and strives to instill in students the desire to be agents of change in the world and to use knowledge for the benefit of others, as well as themselves.

University of the Cumberlands is a four-year, coed liberal arts university offering a broad curriculum with more than 40 programs of study from which to choose. UC serves a diverse body of 1,800 undergraduate students from 42 states and 32 countries. Primarily a residential campus, about 75% of students live in University housing in one of the University's eleven residence halls. A director assisted by student staff members supervises each hall.

Students benefit from such special services as the Career Services Center, Center for Leadership Studies, Academic Resource Center, and free tutorial assistance.

LOCATION AND ENVIRONMENT

University of the Cumberlands is located in Williamsburg, Kentucky, one of the older cities of the state. Located in the southern part of the mountains of Eastern Kentucky, Williamsburg is about two hundred miles south of Cincinnati, about an equal distance from Louisville, about 80 miles north of Knoxville, and about 100 miles south of Lexington.

UC offers a well-kept historical campus which is Antebellum in structure, blending stately old buildings with new ones and has a panoramic view of the Cumberland River Valley. Nestled in the foothills of the Appalachian mountain range, the main campus is situated on three hills which divide it into three distinct parts and afford a magnificent view of the surrounding area. The University's buildings, which are situated on these hills and a viaduct, spanning the south and middle hills, provide an easy and pleasant passageway to each part of the campus.

Within a few miles of campus are Laurel Lake, Cumberland Falls State Park, Cumberland Gap National Park, and the Daniel Boone National Forest.

OFF-CAMPUS OPPORTUNITIES

Study Abroad

Ministry Opportunities

Internships

MAJORS AND DEGREES OFFERED

Major fields of study include accounting, art°, biological science°, biology, business administration, chemistry, church music, Christian ministries, Christian studies, communication arts, communication and theatre arts°, criminal justice, early elementary education°, English°, exercise and sport science°, fitness and sport management, health, health education°, history, history and political science, human services, journalism and public relations, management information systems, mathematics°, middle school education°, missions and ministry, music°, physical science°, physician assistant studies, physics, political science, psychology, public health, social studies°, Spanish°, special education°, and theatre arts. Minor fields of study include biblical languages, and French°. Pre-professional and special curricula are offered in military science, pre-dentistry, pre-engineering, pre-law, pre-medicine, pre-optometry, pre-pharmacy, pre-physical therapy, pre-physician assistant studies, pre-veterinary medicine, and religious vocations.

°Denotes teacher certification available

University of the Cumberlands is accredited by the Commission of Colleges of the Southern Association of Colleges and Schools to award baccalaureate, master's, and doctoral degrees. Inquiries concerning the accreditation status of the University may be directed to the Commission on Colleges at 1866 Southern Lane, Decatur, Georgia 30033-4097or by calling 404-679-4500. The University's Teacher Education and Certification programs are also approved by the Kentucky State Department of Education

ACADEMIC PROGRAMS

The University remains keenly aware of the importance of a traditional liberal arts education and seeks to provide academic specialization within this broad framework. Providing the foundation for a deeper understanding of advanced studies regardless of the chosen major, 37 semester hours of general studies from the areas of Christian faith and values, cultural and aesthetic values, the English language, humanities, leadership and community service, natural and mathematical sciences, physical education, and social sciences are required. Students must earn 128 semester hours to graduate with a bachelor's degree.

Professors work diligently to arrange internships for students within the community, larger cities around the country, and through study abroad options. Listed as a "Top Tier" institution by US News and World Report, our graduates enjoy a high acceptance rate to graduate and professional schools, particularly in science, business, and education.

University of the Cumberlands is one of the few institutions where all students complete a leadership program, which helps fulfill our mission to prepare students for lives of ethical and responsible leadership. Students gain practical hands-on experience working with established service organizations and designing and implementing community service projects.

The academic year begins in late-August, with the first semester ending in mid-December. The second semester runs from early January to early May. Two online undergraduate and graduate summer sessions are also offered. Orientation, pre-registration, and academic advising by faculty members begin in the summer preceding entrance.

students may receive credit for passing the college Board Advanced Placement (AP exams), the college-Level Examination Programs (CLEP), and special departmental tests. Highly qualified students have the opportunity to undertake advanced independent study through Presidential Research options.

CAMPUS FACILITIES AND EQUIPMENT

UC's campus contains 36 buildings in the architectural style of the early 1900s. Recent additions to campus include the state-of-the-art Hutton School of Business, a 27,000 square foot addition to the science building, featuring well-equipped labs providing graduate-level research opportunities, a women's residence hall and a baseball complex. The McGaw Music Building contains individual rehearsal and studio areas as well as a recital hall. The Norma Perkins Hagan Memorial Library houses thousands of book titles, current serial subscriptions, and microform titles. Sophisticated computer equipment provides access to millions of items from many of the nation's outstanding libraries. The instructional media center includes a children's library, a computerized language lab, and a listening library.

Other special academic features include a computer center, an art gallery, a word processing center for English composition, a theatre, the Career Services Center, a 600-seat chapel, four large lecture halls, and the Distance Learning laboratory.

TUITION, ROOM, BOARD AND FEES

For 2015–2016, the basic academic year expenses are $22,000 for tuition and fees and $8,500 for room and board. The average cost for books and supplies is approximately $1,000 per academic year. There are no additional fees for out of state students.

FINANCIAL AID

University of the Cumberlands sponsors a large financial aid program that coordinates money from federal, state, private, and University sources. Last year, 95 percent of UC students shared more than $34 million in aid. Academic, athletic and other scholarships are available.

STUDENT ORGANIZATIONS AND ACTIVITIES

Our students bring with them fresh perspectives and diverse experiences. UC students quickly become integral parts of the campus family and are involved with all aspects of campus life from ministry programs, student government and athletics to stimulating academic programs, internships and research opportunities. Whether your interest lies in athletics, creative expression, student government, academic enrichment, community service, spiritual development, or in any combination of these areas, you'll find an outlet here for your energy.

Many academic departments sponsor clubs and academic honor societies for students with a particular interest in the discipline, so be sure to visit the departments that interest you or contact a faculty member in that department for more information.

Each year, University of the Cumberlands hosts numerous guest performers and speakers and celebrates the talents of its students and faculty through a variety of lectures, concerts, art exhibitions, and theatrical productions. Many of these events are free of charge, and most are open to the public.

UC is proud of its competitive athletic program which fields 26 varsity sports for men and women. Competing in the Mid-South Conference, UC is a member of the NAIA and is Division I. Core values of respect, responsibility, integrity, servant leadership and sportsmanship are enhanced by our participation in the Champions of Character program, a national initiative through the NAIA.

The Student Government Association is dedicated to giving students a voice through elected representatives. In addition to promoting student concerns and working as a liaison between students and college administrators, the SGA provides a number of important services, and sponsors a number of student-centered events throughout the year.

ADMISSIONS PROCESS

The purpose of the admission process is to identify applicants who are likely to succeed academically at University of the Cumberlands and at the same time contribute positively to the campus community. The process considers such factors as high school records (including courses taken, grade trends, and rank in class), scores on the American College Test (ACT), or on the Scholastic Aptitude Test (SAT), application essay (not required of all applicants), extracurricular activities and honors, and personal contact.

UNIVERSITY OF DELAWARE

AT A GLANCE

At the center of the East Coast is a classic college campus rich in history and academic offerings. Both public and private, the University of Delaware is a unique institution with students from all 50 states and 100+ countries. Our alumni—including U.S. Vice President Joe Biden, NJ Governor Chris Christie, and Super Bowl winning quarterback Joe Flacco—are leaders in their fields. Students choose Delaware for our Study Abroad Program (1st in the U.S.), 145+ majors, and discovery learning experiences that ensure they will graduate with impressive resumés and meaningful degrees.

LOCATION AND ENVIRONMENT

The University of Delaware looks and feels the way many dream a college campus should. With a central green mall flanked by Georgian brick buildings, our medium-sized campus is walkable and historic. UD's Northeast location is enviable—located minutes from I-95, we are a safe, green campus less than two hours between New York City and Washington, D.C., a short drive to Philadelphia International Airport, and steps away from our very own Main Street, a charming strip of shops and restaurants at the center of campus.

OFF-CAMPUS OPPORTUNITIES

At the University of Delaware, students not only learn in classrooms, but also gain practical experience through service learning, internships and research opportunities. Employers recognize that our graduates are well prepared to enter their profession. The University's Career Services Center reports that over 96 percent of Delaware grads go on to graduate schools or full-time jobs within twelve months of leaving the University. Fifteen major career fairs are hosted on campus each year with over 600 employers in attendance. In addition, more than 300 corporations and non-profits participate in the Campus Interview Program and contribute to the 20,000 employment possibilities listed at the Career Services Center.

MAJORS AND DEGREES OFFERED

Students at the University of Delaware can choose from over 145 majors and 100 minors, from accounting to wildlife conservation to engineering,. In fact, close to one-third of Delaware students choose to do more, pursuing double majors and multiple minors. Academic programs of study are found in our seven colleges: Arts & Sciences; Agriculture & Natural Resources; Lerner College of Business & Economics; Earth, Ocean, & Environment; Education and Human Development; Engineering; and Health Sciences. Students can explore the many options with our major finder at http://www.udel.edu/majorfinder/

ACADEMIC PROGRAMS

Delaware's wealth of academic programs draws students who have more than one academic interest. UD undergrads make the most of their college investment by pursuing multiple majors, minors, and interdisciplinary studies. and they tackle UD's discovery learning requirement through participation in one of more of the following:

University Honors Program

At the intellectual heart of the University is the University of Delaware Honors Program (UDHP). Entrance into the Program is highly selective, with about 450 new freshmen enrolled each year. Advantages of the Honors Program include smaller classes, private music instruction, academic scholarships, superb teaching, special housing options, personal attention, interdisciplinary colloquia, tutorials, lectures, and student-run activities and field trips.

Service-Learning

Service-Learning at UD allows students to participate in an organized service experience that heightens their academic experience. As part of their course work, students will provide a service to a community - From Newark to Wilmington to Costa Rica to Vietnam—and then reflect on these real-world experiences in light of the academic theories and information being taught in the course.

Study Abroad

UD founded the first Study Abroad program in 1923 and continues to lead in overseas opportunities. More than one-third of our student body chooses to study abroad at least once. The reasons are compelling: UD credits applicable toward any major; UD faculty; UD's reasonable tuition rate; special study abroad scholarships; & exotic destinations.

Undergraduate Research

The University of Delaware is recognized as a national leader in fostering undergraduate research by offering research apprenticeships with faculty mentors in a variety of disciplines. Over 1,000 faculty take students (including freshmen) on each year to work alongside them in the frontiers of knowledge.

CAMPUS FACILITIES AND EQUIPMENT

Although the University traces its roots to 1743, it remains firmly planted in the 21st century with continuing construction and enhancements to campus facilities. Within the past 20 years, Delaware students have benefitted from hundreds of millions of dollars worth of improvements and additions to campus including: a state-of-the-art learning laboratory designed to replicate the trading floors on Wall Street; newly constructed athletic complex, the Interdisciplinary Science & Engineering Laboratory (ISE Lab), and recently expanded Science, Technology and Advanced Research (STAR) campus, home to UD's College of Health Sciences and collaborative partners. UD's Hugh R. Sharp Campus in coastal Lewes, Del., is home to marine biosciences and oceanography facilities and UD's 146-foot research vessel, the Hugh R. Sharp. A 2-megawatt wind turbine helps power the Hugh R. Sharp Campus in Lewes, Del., and serves as a wind energy research platform for faculty, students and industry partners.

Extensive facilities and resources exist to meet the needs of UD students. Over 7,000 students live on campus in one of 65 residence halls and dine in any of more than 16 eateries. Morris Library, a six-acre structure, houses millions of books, journals, and items on microtext, with additional access to over 75 networked databases. Students can plug in their own computers or log on at one of 28 microcomputing sites on campus. Socializing, performing, and engaging in a variety of entertainment options takes place at Perkins Student Center, Trabant University Center, the Roselle Center for the Arts, on the Green, in the residence halls, or at one of the smaller theatres on campus. Athletic facilities abound at the University, including the 23,000-seat Delaware Stadium; 5,000-seat Bob Carpenter Sports/Convocation Center; Rust & Gold Ice Skating Arenas (home of the Ice Skating Development Center and training ground for Olympic skaters); outdoor hockey rink; track, softball, and practice fields; indoor and outdoor swimming pools; Outdoor Recreation Resource Center; and indoor climbing wall, fitness centers, and weight rooms.

TUITION, ROOM, BOARD AND FEES

*New rates are released every July. See www.udel.edu/rates for the most up-to-date cost.

Residents

Tuition $10,900

Room $7,014

Board $4,544

Health Service Fee $454

Comprehensive Student Fee $750

Student Center Fee $238

TOTAL $23,900

Non-Residents

Tuition $29,250

Room $7,014

Board $4,544

Health Service Fee $454

Comprehensive Student Fee $750

Student Center Fee $238

TOTAL $42,250

Cost Per Credit Hour $1,183

FINANCIAL AID

The University of Delaware awards more than $201 million annually in aid. We strive to provide a quality education at a reasonable cost. We accomplish this through a variety of scholarships (including scholarships for merit, athletics, music, art, and more), need-based grants, federal and state financial aid programs, outside resources, and financing plans.

Additional information can be found online at http://www.udel.edu/finance

STUDENT ORGANIZATIONS AND ACTIVITIES

The Fightin' Blue Hens are a spirited community with the mix of academics, campus activities, and athletics that fit the profile of a national university. UD supports 21 varsity sports, all NCAA Division I members of the Colonial Athletic Association, except women's rowing, which is independent. You could say that athletics are a big part of the UD culture, since over 80% of the undergraduate body participates in intramurals, varsity, club, band, cheerleading, or other sports.

In addition to athletics, the University is home to over 400 campus organizations covering a spectrum of interests and communities. Visit the Web at www.udel.edu/RSO/ for a complete list. The UD undergraduate experience begins with New Student Orientation and New Student Convocation. Annual events on The Green, at the Bob Carpenter Center, in theatres across campus, and in the Trabant University or Perkins Student Centers keep students entertained and active. Delaware students fill their free time with movie nights; Mallstock; and concerts and performances such as Elton John, Jon Stewart, Common, O.A.R., Margaret Cho, and Dane Cook. In addition, there are 38 Greek letter organizations, including 17 NIC fraternities, 11 NPC sororities, and 5 National PanHellenic Council chapters (traditionally African-American membership).

ADMISSIONS PROCESS

The complete admissions process and requirements can be found on the UD website at www.udel.edu/apply.

THE UNIVERSITY OF FINDLAY

AT A GLANCE

Students thrive at The University of Findlay because of the hands-on learning environment and dedication to mentorship and student success that is evident throughout all facets of life at Findlay. As a private university built on a liberal arts foundation, the University is ranked in the top tier of U.S. News & World Report's "America's Best Colleges" and has been named a "Best Midwestern College" by the Princeton Review. Findlay offers nearly 60 majors, 13 graduate degrees and NCAA Division II athletics. The University also has a robust campus life that includes 1,400 students living on campus, 100+ student-run clubs, visual and performing arts opportunities and an active intramural sport program.

ACADEMICS

The University of Findlay is known for exceptional academic programs including the health professions, animal science/pre-veterinary medicine, equestrian studies, environmental, safety and occupational health management, business and education. From the college of Health Professions whose graduates have a 99 percent employment rate, to the Pre-Veterinary Medicine Program students who have a vet school acceptance rate of more than two times the national average, the quality of our academic programs is clear in our outcomes.

Faculty and staff are focused on students, with personal attention, individual academic advising and a caring environment cited by students and alumni as hallmarks of their education at Findlay. Classes are taught by professors, not graduate assistants. Most faculty have worked in their chosen professions, bringing a wealth of experience to the classroom, where their true love is teaching.

Findlay's undergraduate and graduate students showcase their best work during the University's annual Symposium for Scholarship and Creativity. Each year more than 300 students share their research, creativity and professional learning experiences with the University and the community. Many students also present their research at professional forums regionally, nationally and internationally.

LOCATION AND ENVIRONMENT

Located in Findlay, Ohio, UF benefits from the city's progressive business growth and exceptional community atmosphere. The city of Findlay has been rated as the number one micropolitan community in the nation by Site Selection magazine and has been designated as a "dreamtown" by Bizjournals.com. It is the only municipality in Ohio to be selected four times as one of the 100 Best Communities for Young People by America's Promise.

The campus has a great location—just 45 minutes from Toledo, Ohio, two hours from Cleveland and Columbus, Ohio, and five hours from Chicago.

OFF-CAMPUS OPPORTUNITIES

The University offers career planning and placement services that assist students in determining career goals, developing job search skills, locating internship, cooperative education and degree-related work experience, in finding paid employment in their fields, and in selecting and applying to graduate programs.

MAJORS AND DEGREES OFFERED

College of Business

Accounting
Business Management
Economics
Entrepreneurship
Finance
Hospitality Management
Human Resource Management
International Business
Marketing
Operations & Logistics
Sport & Event Management
Master of Business Administration

College of Education

Adolescent/Young Adult
Early Childhood
Intervention Specialist Education/Mild to Moderate Disabilities
Middle Childhood
Multi-Age
Master of Arts in Education
Doctor of Education (Ed.D.)
Post-Baccalaureate licensure and endorsements

College of Health Professions

Diagnostic Medical Sonography
Health and Physical Education
Health Science
Pre-Occupational Therapy
Pre-Physical Therapy
Health Care Management
Medical Laboratory Science
Nuclear Medicine Technology
Positron Emission Tomography/Computed Tomography
Nursing
Social Work
Strength & Conditioning
Master of Athletic Training
Master of Occupational Therapy
Master of Physician Assitant
Doctor of Physical Therapy

College of Pharmacy

Doctor of Pharmacy (Pharm.D.)

College of Liberal Arts

Art
Art Management
Children's Book Illustration
Criminal Justice
Criminal Justice
-White-Collar Crime and Fraud Investigation
English
English as an International Language
Forensic Science
Graphic Design
History
Japanese
Journalism
Law and the Liberal Arts (Pre-Law)
Philosophy/Applied Philosophy
Political Science
Psychology
Public Relations
Religious Studies
Sociology
Spanish
Teaching English to Speakers of Other Languages (TESOL)
Theatre
Master of Arts in Teaching English to Speakers of Other Languages (TESOL)
Master of Rhetoric and Writing.

College of Sciences

Animal Science
Animal Science
Pre-Veterinary Medicine
Science
Biology
Chemistry

Computer Science
Environmental, Safety and Occupational Health Management
Equestrian Studies
English Riding/Training
Western Riding/Training
Equine Business Management
Mathematics
Master of Science in Environmental, Safety and Health Management

CAMPUS FACILITIES AND EQUIPMENT

The University of Findlay has more than 80 acres at the main campus on North Main Street, which includes major academic, administrative and athletic buildings; residence halls, townhouses, apartment-style cottages and special interest houses; and a number of facilities housing faculty and staff offices and academic units.

In addition, the University operates a 32-acre facility on the east side of Findlay, containing the English equestrian studies program and University Equine Veterinary Services Inc. The University's 152-acre Animal Sciences Center is located eight miles south of campus and houses the western riding and animal science/pre-veterinary medicine programs. A five-acre site on State Route 12 east of Findlay provides hands-on training simulations for the All Hazards Training Center.

In 2009, the University opened a 31,000-square-foot animal science building that combines a working barn with first-rate academic facilities for pre-veterinary medicine.

During 2010, a new Student Recreation Center was installed in the Koehler Fitness and Recreation Complex, featuring basketball, volleyball and tennis courts, a three-lane running/jogging track, a rock climbing wall, racquetball/wallyball court, varsity weight room, golf simulator, game room, student lounge, and juice bar. The second floor already housed a cardio center with treadmills, weight machines, exercise bikes, stair-steppers, and other fitness equipment.

In 2012, UF open a 42,000-square-foot addition to its newest academic building, providing high-technology classrooms and lecture halls, eight cutting-edge science laboratories and faculty offices.

STUDENT ORGANIZATIONS AND ACTIVITIES

Extracurricular Activities

Students may participate in any of more than 100 organizations, including special interest clubs, student media, student government, music and theatre groups, service clubs, and academic honorary organizations.

The fine arts flourish on campus with a variety of theatre productions, art exhibits and vocal and instrumental music concerts that offer creative outlets and training for students and serve as a source of cultural enrichment for the community.

Findlay participates in 24 intercollegiate sports and is a member of the National Collegiate Athletic Association (NCAA), Division II, and the Great Lakes Intercollegiate Athletic Conference (GLIAC). Its equestrian teams compete in the Intercollegiate Horse Show Association (IHSA). Women's lacrosse will be added as an NCAA sport for the 2012-13 academic year.

NCAA Sports at The University of Findlay:

Baseball (M)
Basketball (M)
Basketball (W)
Cross country (M)
Cross country (W)
Football
Golf (M)
Golf (W)
Lacrosse (W)
Soccer (M)
Soccer (W)
Softball (W)
Swimming (M)
Swimming (W)

Indoor track (M)
Indoor track (W)
Outdoor track (M)
Outdoor track (W)
Tennis (M)
Tennis (W)
Volleyball (W)
Wrestling (M)
English equestrian (IHSA)
Western equestrian (IHSA)

ADMISSIONS PROCESS

Admission as a first-time, full-time undergraduate student to The University of Findlay requires an earned diploma from an accredited high school in a college preparatory course of study or a GED certificate. Candidates for admission should successfully complete the following requirements: four units of English, three units of mathematics, two units of science, two units of social science and two units of foreign language.

Students who intend to major in equestrian studies, equine business management, animal science-pre-veterinary medicine option or pharmacy are encouraged to complete the application as early as possible, due to limited space available in these programs.

APPLICATION INSTRUCTIONS

Students should complete the Application for Undergraduate Admission after they've finished their junior year course work. Students can apply online at www.findlay.edu or request a paper application from the Office of Undergraduate Admissions. No application fee is required.

Applicants should send an official high school transcript that includes class rank, attendance information, a calculated GPA, and proficiency tests results. Post-secondary option participants should submit transcripts of all college-level work.

Applicants may send the results of the ACT and/or SAT tests directly to The University of Findlay by listing the following codes during test registration: ACT-3272, SAT-1223.

To enroll, all candidates must submit their final transcript after graduation.

Tuition, Room, Board and Fees (2015–16)

Tuition: $15,282/semester

Room and Board: $4,721/semester

Student Fees: $472/semester (includes Activity Fee and General Service Fee)

FINANCIAL AID

To apply for financial aid, the student must complete the Free Application for Federal Student Aid (FAFSA). Ninety-nine percent of students attending The University of Findlay receive some form of financial assistance. Students received $33 million in financial aid in 20014-15 through scholarships, work-study grants, and/or government loans.

Scholarships:

Findlay offers a robust scholarship package based on academic merit and need. The average net price to attend Findlay is $21,500. The University of Findlay's college investment plan is a partnership between the University and our students. Our goal is to guide students to graduation with the least amount of debt possible. The student's part is to work hard to build the knowledge based needed to become a successful alum. Students can find out what the total cost of their degree at Findlay can be by filling out our Total Degree Cost Calculator at Findlay.edu/totalcostcalculator. The calculator considers the same factors a traditional net price calculator does, including scholarships and financial aid, but shows a comprehensive cost estimate over the length of the student's chosen academic program.

UNIVERSITY OF HARTFORD

The University of Hartford offers an environment where students will be both challenged and supported to tap into their full potential and become the successful leaders of our community.

AT A GLANCE

The University of Hartford, a fully accredited, independent, nonsectarian institution, is composed of the college of Arts and Sciences; the college of Engineering, Technology and Architecture; the college of Education, Nursing, and Health Professions; Hillyer College; the Barney School of Business; the Hartford Art School; and The Hartt School.

Our full-time undergraduate enrollment of approximately 4,600 men and women includes students from nearly all 50 states and 44 countries. With an average class size of about 20—25 students, each student benefits from more personalized attention from faculty members. Students can expect to get to know not only their classroom professors well, but also all faculty members in their department. Faculty members focus on helping students apply what they learn in the classroom to real-world scenarios and provide the mentorship necessary to push students past perceived limits. Students participate in about 100 organized student groups, including clubs devoted to special interests or political, professional, religious, or civic activities. Athletics include intercollegiate (NCAA Division I) and intramural sports. These activities, as well as the recreational and fitness needs of the university, are served by a 130,000-square-foot Sports Center. Students are also involved in school publications and AM and FM radio stations, and the Hartt School, the Hartford Art School, and the University Players present a variety of concerts, exhibitions, and theatrical productions each year.

The university's Career Services Center provides career counseling and information on occupations, employers, testing, and graduate schools; serves as a reference and credential source; and provides graduating students with an on-campus recruiting program. Courses, programs, and educational counseling are provided by the Office of Graduate and Adult Academic Services for part-time adult students.

LOCATION AND ENVIRONMENT

The university is located in the peaceful residential suburb of West Hartford, which was named one of the best cities for the next decade by Kiplinger's magazine. The West Hartford area offers hundreds of shops and restaurants along with many opportunities for students to discover new cultural and intellectual experiences. With museums, theaters, libraries, the XL Center, a symphony orchestra, shopping, great restaurants, an international airport, and local and intercity transportation systems, the opportunities are plentiful.

OFF-CAMPUS OPPORTUNITIES

Through the Hartford Consortium for Higher Education, Hartford students have the opportunity to register for select courses at Saint Joseph College and Trinity College. Opportunities are available to education and health profession majors for field and/or clinical experiences where applicable. The Career Services Center and cooperative education office is available to custom-tailor work experiences within many of the University's programs. Our study abroad office works with students to arrange an international learning experience that promotes cultural exploration and lifelong memories. The University of Hartford has garnered affiliations with schools in more than 60 different countries, making study abroad a vast and popular option on campus.

ACADEMICS

The University of Hartford is known nationally for the breadth and depth of i programs. Hartford's seven schools and colleges offer over 100 fields of study. T university encourages students to sample a variety of academic areas and enroll courses in any of the colleges in campus. Students interested in interdisciplina majors can combine courses from the different schools within the university. Studen are assigned academic advisors who help guide them in curriculum choices, care exploration, and the transition to university life. The All-University curriculu was developed in order to help students learn more about how different academ disciplines approach related topics and issues. Courses in different fields of experti are team taught, and topics are examined from the perspective of several academ disciplines. Students who are undecided on their majors are assisted by a speci program at the university. Individual students will also find help in the areas writing proficiency, reading comprehension, and research and test-taking ski at the reading and writing center, which is available to the entire student bod The Math Tutoring Lab, which is staffed by full-time faculty members and ma majors, offers further help for students in math. Selected students are encourage to participate in the Honors Program. Honors students have the opportunity graduate with an Honors degree.

MAJORS AND DEGREES OFFERED

About 25% of students apply undecided which, at the University of Hartford, is a opportunity to explore many academic interests among our more than 100 areas study. Students receive support from offices like Career Services, the Student Su cess Center and a Dialogue course which allows them to meet with and learn fro other undecided students. The college of Arts and Sciences offers majors in biolog chemistry, chemistry-biology, cinema, communication, computer science, crimin justice, economics, English, history, international studies, Judaic studies, mathema ics, philosophy, physics, politics and government, psychology, and sociology.

Within the college of Education, Nursing, and Health Professions, there are majo in early childhood education, elementary education, integrated special educatio elementary education, secondary education with a concentration in English or mat ematics, health sciences, nursing (for registered nurses only), radiologic technolog respiratory therapy, a combined B.S. in health science, and doctorate in physic therapy (B.S./D.P.T.) program, as well as a combined B.S. in health science and Master of Science in Prosthetics and Orthotics (B.S./M.S.P.O.) program.

The Hartford Art School offers Bachelor of Fine Arts degrees in ceramics, desig drawing, illustration, media arts, painting, photography, printmaking, sculpture, an visual communication as well as a Bachelor of Arts in Art History.

At the Hartt School, students can major in actor training, applied music (guita orchestral instrument, organ, piano, pre–cantorial studies, and voice), compositio dance (ballet pedagogy or performance emphases), jazz studies, music, music ed cation, music history, music management, music production and technology, musi theater, music theory, and performing arts management (interdisciplinary progra offered in conjunction with the Barney School of Business). There are also five-yea double majors offered within the Hartt School.

Majors for the Bachelor of Science in Business Administration (B.S.B.A.) degre in the Barney School of Business are accounting, economics and finance, entrepre neurial studies, insurance and finance, management, and marketing. The Barne School of Business also offers a minor in actuarial science.

Additional B.S. programs, offered by the college of Engineering, Technology, and Architecture include ABET-EAC engineering accredited programs in electrical, mechanical, civil, computer, biomedical, and Acoustical Engineering & Music. The newest offering in the mechanical engineering department is a concentration in energy engineering and sustainable design. The most popular B.S.E. options are acoustical engineering and music (interdisciplinary program in conjunction with the Hartt School) and biomedical engineering. Additionally, the college offers interdisciplinary B.S.E. options. Technology programs include the Bachelor of Science in architectural engineering technology, audio engineering technology, computer engineering technology, electronic engineering technology, mechanical engineering technology as well as the Associate in Applied Science in electronic engineering technology (A.S.) and the Associate in Applied Science in computer engineering technology (A.S.). New to the technology majors this year is a BS in Electromechanical Engineering Technology. The programs in Architecture, Electronics and Mechanical are ABET-ETAC accredited.

Hillyer College offers the Associate of Arts and provides the general education course work required to complete most of the University's baccalaureate programs. Particular emphasis is placed on the development of academic skills through small classes and close faculty-student interaction.

University Studies offers the Bachelor of University Studies, a B.A. degree program created for the part-time adult student who typically has previous college experience and seeks to complete a baccalaureate degree. Also offered is a B.A. degree program in multimedia website design and development for full-time undergraduates. Created for students who want to learn how to use and develop multimedia technologies that fit into today's wired world, this program combines courses across several disciplines where students create and use technology with user interaction in mind.

CAMPUS FACILITIES AND EQUIPMENT

Our suburban West Hartford campus houses the buildings and facilities of our seven colleges and schools.

The newest additions to the campus are the Shaw Center at Hillyer College a 10,000-square-foot addition to Hillyer Hall that provides faculty offices, state-of-the-art classrooms, a dedicated seminar classroom, a conference room, and a large common area; the Handel Center for Performing Arts for students in theater and dance; the Integrated Science, Engineering and Technology Complex, which houses 37,000 square feet of new state-of-the-art classrooms and laboratories as well as a complete renovation of the existing science and engineering facilities; and the Renee Samuels Center which provides state-of-the art digital equipment and studios specifically designed for Media Arts and Photography.

The Harry Jack Gray Center is the home of the Mildred P. Allen Memorial Library; the William H. Mortensen Library; the Museum of American Political Life; the Harry J. Gray Conference Center; the Joseloff Gallery; the newly renovated Campus Store; the School of Communication; and studios for art, radio, and television. The library has approximately 600,000 items, including books, musical scores, recordings, periodicals, journals, and microfilm units. The Hartford Consortium for Higher Education, the Hartford Library, and the Interlibrary-Loan systems also offer extensive resources.

The University of Hartford has installed fiber optic cabling, wiring, and telecommunications equipment to all of the student residences on the main campus. All students have their own high speed Ethernet connection to the Campus Network and the Internet. Our network is designed to work with both Windows and Macintosh computers.

The University completed the installation of a wireless network system in the main-campus residence halls, all academic buildings and some surrounding outside areas. It is our hope that students find the wireless system convenient, and find ways to use it to enhance your learning experience at the University.

Computer labs are available in academic buildings throughout the campus as well in the University Libraries. Students have access to a wide range of online resources, software, collaboration systems, scanners and printers.

TUITION, ROOM, BOARD, AND FEES:

Costs for 2014–2015

Tuition $32,758

Double Room (Complexes) $7,548

Freshman Meal Plan $3,970

Fees $2,686

Total $46,962

Ninety-three percent of University of Hartford students receive a scholarship or grant from the university. For most students, the cost of a University of Hartford education is significantly reduced by financial assistance.

The average "out of pocket" expense for new students this year was $17,999.

FINANCIAL AID

The university's financial aid program, which administers over $90 million annually including student loans, consists of scholarships, grants, loans, and work-study opportunities provided through the federal government, private agencies, interested individuals, and the University. Factors contributing to disbursal of university funds are the college or school in which the student is enrolled, availability of funds, applicant pool, and competition for funds. About 92 percent of all full-time undergraduate students receive assistance; the average amount is $27,857 per year. Students who have demonstrated outstanding academic achievement are eligible for full and partial-tuition scholarships.

STUDENT BODY

The Student Government Association (SGA) represents all full-time students at the University. SGA gives students and faculty a platform to work together to develop and coordinate the co-curriculars of the university. In addition, students are represented on all major administrative committees, including the Board of Regents.

ADMISSIONS

The admissions decision is based on a combination of the following: quality of the secondary school curriculum, course selection, academic performance in secondary school, recommendations of the secondary school principal or guidance counselor, ACT or SAT scores, evidence of a desire to succeed, and leadership qualities shown by academic and extracurricular activities. Music and art applicants are required to audition, show portfolios, and take other tests depending upon the program to which they are applying.

The University has a rolling admission policy.

For more information, students should contact:

Richard A. Zeiser

Dean of Admission

University of Hartford

West Hartford, CT 06117-0395

Phone: 860-768-4296

Toll free: 800-947-4303

Fax: 860-768-4961

E-mail: admission@hartford.edu

Website: http://admission.hartford.edu

UNIVERSITY OF ILLINOIS AT URBANA-CHAMPAIGN

Fostering a diverse community of creative minds, the University of Illinois at Urbana-Champaign is a leading public institution emphasizing innovative thinking, research opportunities, and collaborative work with renowned faculty.

AT A GLANCE

Established as a land-grant university in 1867, the University of Illinois has a rich, committed history to teaching, research, and public engagement. Illinois offers unlimited opportunities with 150+ majors, 1,000+ student organizations, and 400+ study abroad options, along with countless research and leadership experiences. Students also enjoy Big Ten, Division I sports and impressive recreation facilities.

LOCATION AND ENVIRONMENT

Centrally located among Chicago, Indianapolis, and St. Louis, the University of Illinois is a large, public research institution with 32,000+ undergraduate and 11,000+ graduate students. It's one of the most diverse public universities in the Big Ten, and in-state students comprise about 58% of the undergraduate student body.

At Illinois, you'll find a traditional college environment where a majority of students live on campus and life is centered around the Quad. Campustown offers a large assortment of restaurants, shops, cafés, and nightlife venues. The wide variety of cultural opportunities enhances campus life by providing an inclusive and educational atmosphere.

Because of the university's stature and size, you'll be able to attend so many diverse and exciting events: top performances by nationally touring bands for student-friendly prices at the State Farm Center and The Canopy Club, renowned theatre and dance shows at Krannert Center for the Performing Arts, and hot-topic talks and lectures from award-winning speakers.

OFF-CAMPUS OPPORTUNITIES

Champaign-Urbana is the ideal setting for your college education. As an active micro-urban community, C-U maintains an intimate small-town feel while offering big-city advantages. This means that you get a wide variety of delicious culinary options, a diverse live music scene that continually brings in national and independent acts, and an active visual and performing arts community. Exciting C-U events include:

Ebertfest—An annual weekend-long festival of movie screenings, actor visits, and panel discussions, established by Roger Ebert (American film critic, screenwriter, and Illinois alumnus).

Illinois Marathon—Ending on the 50-yard line of the university's own Memorial Stadium, one of the best new marathons around.

Pygmalion Music Festival—An annual showcase of live music held in multiple locations throughout the downtowns of Champaign, Urbana, and campustown.

Market at the Square—Located in downtown Urbana, one of the largest and most diverse farmers' markets in Illinois.

Boneyard Arts Festival—A community-wide festival featuring over 100 different venues and offering an incredibly diverse range of spoken, performing, and visual art.

For more info about C-U, check out www.visitchampaigncounty.org, www.40north.org, and www.smilepolitely.com.

MAJORS AND DEGREES OFFERED

The University of Illinois offers Bachelor's, Master's, and Doctoral degrees. Undergraduates can choose from 150+ majors, many of which are highly ranked, within 10 academic communities:

- Colleges of Agricultural, Consumer, and Environmental Sciences
- College of Applied Health Sciences
- College of Business
- College of Education
- College of Engineering
- College of Fine and Applied Arts
- College of Liberal Arts and Sciences
- College of Media
- Division of General Studies (for those who are "undeclared")
- School of Social Work

ACADEMIC PROGRAMS

Illinois provides a 148-year tradition of academic excellence and success. By learning from faculty members who are among the best in their fields, participating in undergraduate research, and gaining invaluable hands-on experience, Illinois students receive an education that's second to none.

Study Abroad—Over 30% of the Illinois student body studies abroad. All students are encouraged to do so, and there's a program for you no matter your major or interests. With 400+ programs in 60+ countries, you can study in a different country over an academic break, throughout a semester, or even for an entire year. From learning about business in Hong Kong to studying cinema in London, the opportunities are endless.

Honors Programs—For high-achieving students, Illinois offers interconnected and cooperating honors programs at the campus, college, and departmental levels. Students can participate in more than one program over the course of an undergraduate career. Additionally, the National and International Scholarships Program assists high-achieving students in applying for various nationally competitive awards, such as the Rhodes and Fulbright scholarships.

Career Services—One of the most important resources on campus is The Career Center, which acts as an umbrella for both college and departmental career centers across campus. Having a network of centers will greatly benefit you as an Illinois student—not only will you be able to utilize the larger center, but you'll also have access to a center that specializes in your specific major. The Career Center provides invaluable services like career counseling, pre-health advising, résumé and cover letter reviews, mock interviews, and workshops on salary negotiations and professional etiquette.

Leadership Center—The Leadership Center's professionals are committed to helping you develop and enhance your executive skills through active participation in leadership consulting programs, leadership retreats, and a certificate program that involves extended leadership involvement through activities, classes, and employment.

The Princeton Review's Complete Book of Colleges

CAMPUS FACILITIES AND EQUIPMENT

You'll find everything from traditional campus classrooms to state-of-the-art research facilities at Illinois. Some of our highlights include:

Illini Union—As the central hub of campus, thousands of students pass through the Illini Union each day for its restaurants, shops, rec centers, lecture rooms, galleries, offices, and more. Year-round, you can study in its lounges, watch performances in the Courtyard Café, attend lectures from nationally touring speakers, or enjoy the Friday Illinites.

Student Dining and Residential Programs (SDRP)—Opened in 2010, SDRP is a dining facility and common area for students to learn and gather. It's been recognized with silver Leadership in Energy and Environmental Design (LEED) certification. The main hall seats over 1,200 students and offers delicious and diverse options for each meal, including vegetarian, vegan, and dietary-specific menus. You'll also find a residential library, study rooms, a fitness area, and a new state-of-the-art residence hall for students with physical disabilities.

Cultural Centers and Houses—From La Casa Cultural Latina to the Japan House, Illinois cultural centers and houses help to host and encourage an inclusive, educational atmosphere on campus through celebrations of art, history, discourse, and community.

Krannert Center for the Performing Arts—At this world-renowned center, students and professionals showcase their talents in music, theatre, and dance. In fact, Krannert hosts 4,000 audience members on any given night and 300+ performances each year.

Libraries—Illinois is proud to have the 2nd-largest university library in the U.S. with 13,158,748 volumes. The Undergraduate and Main libraries, the foundation of 25+ departmental libraries and special collections, are even connected underground by a tunnel!

Business Instructional Facility (BIF)—Opened in 2009, BIF has earned the world's highest honor for sustainable, environmentally friendly construction and design with platinum Leadership in Energy and Environmental Design (LEED) certification. It's the first such building at any public university business school in the world and boasts state-of-the-art classrooms, a trading floor, career development and academic counseling centers, student program offices, a recruitment suite, and a 300-seat auditorium.

Electrical and Computer Engineering (ECE) Building—Opened in 2014, the new ECE Building is groundbreaking in both its design and use. The facility is striving to be net-zero energy capable and boasts 230,000 square feet of classrooms, labs, and offices, all platinum Leadership in Energy and Environmental Design (LEED) certified.

Beckman Institute for Advanced Science and Technology—This interdisciplinary institute is devoted to cutting-edge research in the physical sciences, computation, engineering, biology, behavior, cognition, and neuroscience. More than 1,500 researchers work in Beckman.

Rec Centers—Campus Rec boasts two main centers, the Activities and Recreation Center (ARC) and Campus Recreation Center East (CRCE), which offer abundant options for staying physically active. In fact, at 340,000 square feet, the ARC is one of the largest on-campus recreation centers in the country. You'll have access to a climbing wall, saunas, swimming pools, running tracks, courts, an instructional kitchen, fitness classes, a wellness center, and so much more. Campus Rec also provides an ice arena, many additional gyms and pools, and outdoor recreational spaces.

Sports Facilities—Illinois has a booming Big Ten spirit, and our major sports facilities are physical testaments to this. Both the State Farm Center and Memorial Stadium, home to our basketball and football teams, have undergone renovations as part of the ongoing Illinois Renaissance project to create a state-of-the-art Illini home advantage.

TUITION, ROOM, BOARD, AND FEES

Undergraduate students at Illinois are guaranteed the same tuition rate for 4 continuous academic years. The estimated summary of expenses for 2015–2016 is as follows:

	Residents	Non-Residents	International
Tuition and fees	$15,636-20,640°	$30,796-35,800°	$31,626-$38,764°
Books and supplies	$1,200	$1,200	$1,200
Room and board (10 meals/week)	$11,010	$11,010	$11,010
Other expenses	$2,500	$2,500	$2,500
Total	$30,346-35,350°	$45,506-50,510°	$46,336-$53,474°

°The low end of the tuition range indicates the base rate. Students enrolled in certain programs may have a higher tuition rate up to the high end of the range shown. For tuition details for specific programs, visit www.osfa.illinois.edu/cost.

FINANCIAL AID

The Office of Student Financial Aid (OSFA) assists students by awarding financial aid to help pay for educational expenses. Financial aid is available from federal, state, university, and private resources. There are 3 primary types of financial aid at Illinois: scholarships and grants, loans, and employment. Last year, over $812 million in financial aid funds were administered, and 72% of students received financial aid.

STUDENT ORGANIZATIONS AND ACTIVITIES

A great advantage of going to Illinois is that you can pick and choose how you'd like to get involved. You can continue to stay involved in something important to you, or you can try something new.

Illinois has 1,000+ student clubs to choose from, running the gamut from academic to philanthropic to athletic to just for fun! Even if you can't find one that fits your interests, you can easily create your own.

As a Big Ten university, Illinois also has 21 Division I sports teams. Cheer with other fans as a member of the student cheering group, Illini Pride, at the historic Memorial Stadium or State Farm Center. Or join a team yourself—there are 43 traveling club sports teams, and Campus Recreation organizes 10 to 15 intramural sports for students each semester.

Finally, Illinois offers one of the largest Greek communities in the nation. About 23% of undergraduates participate through 97 fraternities and sororities, of which over 30% are culturally based.

ADMISSIONS PROCESS

Admission is selective. Illinois performs a holistic review of your application in order to form a complete picture of you and how you can benefit from being a part of campus. In an admission decision, Illinois considers coursework, academic performance, class rank, ACT/SAT scores, application essays, extracurricular activities, volunteer work, work experience, and awards and honors.

Check the University of Illinois Admissions website, admissions.illinois.edu, for the most up-to-date information regarding dates and deadlines, as they are subject to change.

Freshmen—In 2014–2015, our application filing period was September 1 to December 1, with admission decisions announced in mid-February. Students applying to performing arts majors (dance, music, or theatre) received their decisions by mid-March.

Transfers—In 2014–2015, the deadline for fall applicants was February 1, with admission decisions announced by mid-April.

THE UNIVERSITY OF MAINE ORONO

UMAINE: BEYOND YOUR EXPECTATIONS

The University of Maine offers the major research, close-knit community and lauded academics that go beyond your expectations. As Maine's flagship public university, UMaine offers offers the state's most comprehensive academic experience with more than 90 undergraduate majors and academic programs, 75 master's programs and 30 doctoral programs. Top students are invited to join UMaine's Honors College—one of the country's oldest and most prestigious.

Ranked in the National Science Foundation's top 105 research universities, UMaine is also included in the top 8 percent of colleges and universities nationwide to be classified by the Carnegie Foundation for the Advancement of Teaching as a "Research University–High Research Activity" institution. The Laboratory for Surface Science and Technology is a hub for cutting-edge sensor and nanotechnology research, and our Advanced Structures and Composites Center is a global leader in deepwater offshore wind energy development.

UMaine students have extraordinary opportunities to garner real-world, immersive experience. SPIFFY, the student investment club, manages a $2.3 million, real-money portfolio. Wildlife ecology majors learn about bear behavior by going out and tagging cubs. Engineering majors secure co-ops and internships that often lead to employment after graduation. Education majors take advantage of urban, rural and international student-teaching opportunities. Marine science undergrads can spend a semester by the sea at our internationally renowned Darling Marine Center.

THE BEST LOCATION

There's no place like Maine, and UMaine students explore the great outdoors whenever they can. There are 15 miles of walking, biking and cross-country skiing trails on campus. Some of the best skiing in the East is located within easy driving distance of campus, as are Bar Harbor, Acadia National Park and Baxter State Park, the northern terminus of the Appalachian Trail.

The Maine Bound adventure center on campus offers a comprehensive outdoor experience for all skill levels. By combining recreation and education, our programs offer adventure opportunities for every lifestyle, instilling safety and survival training. Students can kayak, ski, snowshoe, canoe, hike and even learn about wilderness first aid.

Orono is a classic college town, bounded by the Stillwater and Penobscot rivers, located in the heart of Maine. The University of Maine is 10 minutes from the state's third-largest city, Bangor, and its international airport.

UMaine's 660-acre campus was designed by legendary landscape architect Frederick Law Olmsted, who also designed Central Park in New York City and the U.S. Capitol grounds in Washington, D.C. It is a traditional New England campus, with ivy-covered brick buildings, towering pines and incredible fall foliage.

THE UMAINE ACADEMIC DIFFERENCE

At UMaine, we provide a comprehensive academic and student experience, yielding graduates who are well-educated, well-adjusted and well-prepared to assume leadership roles in our society. We foster excellence and innovation through inspired, dedicated teaching and the discovery of new knowledge.

UMaine's more than 90 majors and programs are offered by five colleges—the college of Education and Human Development; the college of Engineering; the college of Liberal Arts and Sciences; the college of Natural Sciences, Forestry, and Agriculture; the Honors College—and the Maine Business School. In addition, the Explorations program is designed to help undecided students identify a major from across UMaine's colleges while making progress toward their degree. The Division of Lifelong Learning offers online classes and distance-learning opportunities for students who need a flexible class schedule.

UMaine's Honors College, one of the country's oldest and most prestigious, provides an in-depth, academically challenging curriculum for qualified students in any major. Honors students take advantage of unique research, academic and cultural opportunities, as well as exclusive housing.

All students at the University of Maine benefit from a solid liberal arts foundation. Here, students develop and refine the qualities they need to more fully engage with the world around them—critical thinking, curiosity, a sense of discovery, a broader perspective—no matter what discipline they choose.

Fogler Library, the state's largest library, houses approximately 1 million volumes, subscribes to more than 4,000 periodicals and serial titles and serves as a depository for more than 2.2 million government documents. In addition, Fogler provides access to countless online documents.

UNDERGRADUATE RESEARCH OPPORTUNITIES

At the University of Maine, undergraduate research is a priority and point of pride. The University provides rich and varied opportunities for undergraduates to participate in research. Our students publish, travel and work alongside UMaine's world-class scholars and scientists.

The Center for Undergraduate Research connects students with faculty projects that suit their interests. For many, research provides an opportunity for a mentor-mentee relationship different from—and often richer than—that of teacher-student. Skills developed through research and scholarship make students more competitive in the workplace and in graduate school.

ACCESSIBLE PROFESSORS

There's a common misconception that if students choose a university rather than a small college, they'll get lost in the shuffle. They'll never see a professor—only teaching assistants—until they're in grad school. But at the University of Maine, the majority of undergraduate classes are taught by professors—and many of those faculty members go on to become friends and mentors to their students. Here, professors are known for having an open-door policy. Our students have opportunities to work alongside some of the most renowned scholars and scientists in the world—whether they're talking civil engineering over pies at Pat's Pizza or traversing an Antarctic ice sheet with researchers from UMaine's Climate Change Institute.

SO MUCH TO DO

In addition to state-of-the art research and classroom facilities, the University of Maine is also a cultural hub. It is home to the region's premier performing arts center, the Collins Center for the Arts, as well as several museums and galleries. Student Entertainment brings in national acts, such as Janelle Monae, Boys Like Girls and All American Rejects. The New Balance Student Recreation Center is a campus hot spot, and is ranked 7th in Best College Reviews' 25 Most Amazing Campus Student Recreation Centers.

Students can get involved in more than 200 clubs and organizations—academic and social—including 18 fraternities or 9 sororities, Student Government, community service-oriented groups, intramural sports and much, much more. Student Government is an active student led organization that funds and supports student organizations, acts as a liaison between the students, administration and faculty and appoints over 200 student representatives to various university committees.

When UMaine students travel, they can easily explore Maine, New England and the east coast or go global, through study abroad, international volunteerism and the worldwide undergraduate research opportunities In recent semesters, UMaine students have traveled to China to learn more about the country's emerging financial markets, to Italy to explore Renaissance art history at the source, to Turkey to study film and to Brazil to learn about a sensitive and diverse ecosystem.

ADMISSIONS AND FINANCIAL AID INFORMATION

Admission to the University of Maine is a selective process. Successful applicants are those whose scholastic achievement, intellectual curiosity and established study habits promise success in a comprehensive university environment. Space availability in certain programs may also be considered when selecting candidates for admission. Applicants may apply using the University of Maine System application, or the Common Application.

The University of Maine has an Early Action deadline of December 15. Students whose complete applications are postmarked by December 15 are reviewed by the end of January. Early Action candidates are given first consideration for the Honors College and merit scholarships awarded by the Admissions Office.

All other applicants are encouraged to submit their applications and all supporting documents by February 1, and are notified by rolling admission. An admission decision is typically be made within six weeks from the receipt of the application and all supporting documents.

Students should submit their Free Application for Federal Student Aid (FAFSA) by March 1st to be considered for the maximum possible financial aid eligibility. UMaine's School Code for the FAFSA is 002053.

UNIVERSITY OF MARYLAND, BALTIMORE COUNTY (UMBC)

An Honors University with the teaching and student support traditions of a small liberal arts college, UMBC is also among the most rapidly developing and diverse research universities in the nation.

AT A GLANCE

UMBC attracts creative and motivated students and rewards them with the resources and attention they need to succeed. A selective, medium-sized public research university, UMBC provides students with opportunities for hands-on research and liberal arts experience working with professors at the top of their fields. This fall, U.S. News & World Report again ranked UMBC number one among "Up and Coming" national universities, "schools everyone should be watching." UMBC also is tied with Yale on a list of the top national universities "where the faculty has an unusual commitment to undergraduate teaching."

UMBC President Freeman A. Hrabowski, III, has been named "one of the 10 best college presidents" and "one of the 100 most influential people in the world" by Time Magazine. Theatre students rank 3rd nationally in invitations to perform at the Kennedy Center American College Theatre Festival. The Carnegie Foundation ranks UMBC in the category of Research Universities with high research activity. UMBC is a two-time winner of the U.S. Presidential Award for Excellence in Science, Mathematics and Engineering Mentoring.

The University's academic reputation and industry partnerships help place students in promising careers and leading graduate programs. One-third of UMBC students immediately go on to leading graduate or professional schools such as Harvard, Johns Hopkins, Stanford, and Yale. Three UMBC graduates have received one of the world's most selective academic awards, the Gates Cambridge Fellowship.

Undergraduates have access to the latest technology in areas from geography to art history to chemistry.

A new Performing Arts and Humanities building opened in 2012, providing state-of-the-art facilities for several arts and humanities departments and programs. The Goddard Earth Science and Technology Center brings NASA scientists, UMBC professors, and students together to study the earth. Students in UMBC's Imaging Research Center (IRC) gain professional experience with companies such as the Discovery Channel, CNN, and PBS. UMBC also has a Howard Hughes Medical Institute laboratory, a privately sponsored research facility dedicated to the study of the structural building blocks of the AIDS virus.

The UMBC climate is friendly and energetic; 10,953 undergraduates have enough ideas and interests to support more than 250 groups, including Greek organizations, recreational sports clubs, community outreach efforts, and campus events. Students enthusiastically follow UMBC NCAA Division I athletic teams and attend games in the UMBC Stadium and Retriever Activities Center. The new book, Higher Education? How Colleges Are Wasting Our Money and Failing Our Kids—and What We Can Do About It, features UMBC as a school where students can receive a first-class undergraduate education at a reasonable price. Approximately 75% of freshman students live on campus, with 14% from out of state. The undergraduate student population is 45% female, 24% Asian American, 12% African American, 4% Hispanic American and Native American. UMBC houses nearly 3,900 students, 1,600 live in UMBC's three new residence suites and apartment communities. Residential communities feature nine living-learning programs, including the Center for Women in Technology; Intercultural Living Exchange; Shriver Living Learning Center.

LOCATION AND ENVIRONMENT

Located a few miles south of Baltimore, UMBC is 15 minutes from downtown Baltimore and 30 minutes from Washington, D.C. The Baltimore-Washington area is known for its music, sports, museums, restaurants, and historical traditions. UMBC's 530-acre campus includes more than 40 buildings accessed by a two-mile elliptical drive, with housing and dining facilities on one side and core facilities (classroom/lab buildings, performing arts center, a library, galleries, a student union, a bookstore, a gymnasium, an Olympic-size pool, and tennis courts) surrounding a central walkway. bwtech@UMBC Research and Technology Park, adjacent to the campus, attracts firms in the high-technology fields, including engineering, information technology, and the life sciences.

OFF-CAMPUS OPPORTUNITIES

Surrounded by business, government, and metropolitan centers, UMBC places students in over 1,200 co-ops and internships in more than 500 organizations each year in the Baltimore-Washington area. UMBC matches students with such employers as the federal Centers for Medicare and Medicaid, Bank of America, Silicon Graphics, MBNA, the Smithsonian Institution, NASA, and the National Aquarium. The university encourages students to participate in study abroad experiences during the semester or travel-study opportunities during winter and summer breaks. The Shriver Center links the resources of the campus to urgent social problems, places students in co-ops and internships at hundreds of businesses and organizations, organizes and manages community service projects that bring the resources of the university to people in need, and connects students to a wide range of social service projects.

ACADEMICS

UMBC's academic calendar consists of fall and spring semesters, a four-week mini session in January, and summer sessions from six to eight weeks. To receive a UMBC degree, students complete 120 to 128 credits plus two physical education courses. In addition to the requirements for the chosen major, the general education program (GEP), provides a solid basis for a lifetime of learning. GEP courses encompass humanities and fine arts, mathematics and natural sciences, social sciences, and languages and culture. The Honors College at UMBC is a special option for students seeking a community of like-minded people for whom the quest for knowledge is its own reward. All Honors College students must take at least one honors course per semester. Students choose from honors versions of core courses, special honors seminars, and plenty of other honors courses.

MPUS FACILITIES AND EQUIPMENT

MBC's landmark building, the Albin O. Kuhn Library and Gallery, contains over
million books and bound volumes of journals, an extensive reference collection,
,00 journal and database subscriptions, more than 200 computers , wireless and
ed connections for laptops, and more than 3 million other items, including slides,
otographs, maps, musical scores, recordings, and microforms. The Commons,
MBC's state-of-the-art student center, the hub of campus life includes a food court,
eral lounges, the University bookstore, meeting spaces, a student recreation
ter, a full-service bank, student organization offices, retail-type spaces, wireless
mputer connectivity, and Web-accessible kiosks. UMBC students have access to
earch opportunities and equipment such as conducting AIDS research on one of
world's largest nuclear magnetic resonance spectrometers in the only Howard
ughes Medical Institute lab at a public university in Maryland. Newer facilities
lude a Public Policy Building and a state-of-the-art Information Technology/
gineering Building. UMBC's a new Performing Arts and Humanities Building
uses seven departments and new performance space that showcase the University's
ong arts and humanities programs and creates a regional and national appreciation
UMBC as a cultural attraction.

MPUS LIFE

e campus climate is friendly and energetic. UMBC's more than 10,973 under-
duates have enough ideas and interests to support more than 250 student groups,
luding Greek organizations and recreational sports clubs, such as fencing and
ling; community outreach efforts, such as Habitat for Humanity; and campus
nts, including lectures, films, concerts, and plays. Students enthusiastically follow
MBC NCAA Division I athletic teams, such as basketball, lacrosse, and soccer
d attend games in the UMBC Stadium and Retriever Activities Center, which
ludes a multipurpose gym, auxiliary gym, weight room, and classrooms. Elections
held each year for officers in UMBC's Student Government Association (SGA).
e SGA represents the student body on a number of administrative committees,
luding the Undergraduate Council, the Library Committee, and the Student
alth Advisory Committee.

AJORS AND DEGREES

ograms leading to Bachelor of Arts, Bachelor of Fine Arts, and Bachelor of Science
grees: acting, Africana studies, American studies, aging services, ancient studies,
ian studies, biochemistry and molecular biology, bioinformatics and computational
logy, biological sciences, business technology administration, chemical engineer-
, chemistry and biochemistry, chemistry education, computer engineering and
mputer science, cultural anthropology, dance, economics and financial econom-
, emergency health services, English, environmental science and environmental
dies, gender and women's studies, geography, health administration and policy,
story, information systems, innovation and entrepreneurship, interdisciplinary
dies, mathematics and statistics, mechanical engineering, media and communica-
n studies, modern languages, linguistics and intercultural communication, music,
ilosophy, physics education, physics, political science, psychology, social work,
ciology, theater, and visual arts. New programs include computer gaming, media
d communication studies, Asian studies, global studies and physics education.
interdisciplinary studies program allows students to design their own course of
dy according to their specific educational and career goals. UMBC offers pre-
ofessional studies programs, including two-and four-year advisement programs
prepare students for clinical training in dental hygiene, medical and research
hnology, medicine, nursing, pharmacy, physical therapy, and veterinary medicine.
inors include Africana studies, American studies, ancient studies, anthropology,
plied politics, art history and theory, astronomy, biological sciences, chemistry,
mputer science, dance, East Asian history, economics, emergency health ser-
es, environmental geography, gender and women's studies, geography, history,
ternational affairs, international economics, Judaic studies, legal policy, literature,
athematics, modern languages and linguistics, music, philosophy, physics, political
ience, political thought, psychology, public administration, religious studies, social
lfare, sociology, statistics, theater, writing, and media and communication studies.

FINANCIAL AID

More than 45% of undergraduates receive some financial aid. UMBC uses the Free Application for Federal Student Aid (FAFSA) to help determine a student's financial need. Aid is awarded to qualified applicants on a first-come, first-served basis. Since aid is awarded only to admitted students, early application for admission is also important. Well-qualified freshmen are automatically considered for general merit scholarships once they are admitted to the University. The Scholars Programs at UMBC provide special opportunities for outstanding entering freshmen who want to focus their education through intense study in their major. Scholars participate in a wide range of academic and cultural enrichment activities, extracurricular travel, or summer study. The selection process for specialty scholarships includes application, an interview, and, in some cases, nomination from a high school official.

TUITION AND FEES

Tuition and fees for 2011–2012 are $9,764 for Maryland residents and $20,825 for out-of-state students. Room and board averaged $10,214. Miscellaneous expenses, books, and transportation cost about $1,500 per year.

ADMISSIONS

In fall 2012, the average incoming freshman had a 3.71 cumulative GPA, 52% ranked in the top quarter of his or her senior class, and had a combined SAT I score of 1206. Approximately 65% of freshman applicants are admitted each year. Academic performance and curriculum strength play an important part in the decision. An essay is required, and a letter of recommendation is strongly encouraged. Transfer students with at least 30 semester hours of college-level work are admitted based on the strength of college success. A minimum 2.5 GPA is recommended for full consideration. Prospective freshmen are encouraged to submit applications by the early action deadline of November 1. The final deadline is February 1 for full consideration for admission, campus housing, financial aid, and scholarships. The priority deadline for transfer students is March 15 for fall admission and November 1 for spring admission for students seeking admission to special programs or wish-ing to be considered for campus housing, financial aid, or scholarships. The final deadline for applications is May 31 for fall and December 15 for spring. For further information, students or parents may contact:

Dale Bittinger

Director of Undergraduate Admissions and Orientation

Office of Undergraduate Admissions and Orientation

UMBC

1000 Hilltop Circle

Baltimore, Maryland 21250

Telephone: 410-455-2291 or 800-UMBC-4U2

Fax: 410-455-1094

Web: www.umbc.edu

UNIVERSITY OF MASSACHUSETTS LOWELL

The University of Massachusetts Lowell is a nationally recognized doctoral-level research university whose graduates are ready for work, for life and for all that the world has to offer.

AT A GLANCE

The University of Massachusetts Lowell (UMass Lowell) is a research university ranked in the top tier of U.S. News & World Report's national universities. Founded in 1894, the university is built on a tradition of innovation and entrepreneurship. Extensive partnerships with industry and community advance research, provide public service, and enrich the student experience. UMass Lowell graduates are ready to contribute meaningfully in the workplace, build lives around the principles and passions they develop in college, and make a difference in the world.

The university is part of the University of Massachusetts system and comprises: the Francis College of Engineering; the College of Fine Arts, Humanities and Social Sciences (includes the School of Criminology and Justice Studies); the College of Health Sciences (includes the School of Nursing); the College of Sciences; the Graduate School of Education; the Manning School of Business; and the Honors College. Together, the colleges offer more than 100 bachelor's, 39 master's, 33 doctoral degrees, and dozens of certificate programs. All programs are accredited at the highest levels and incorporate vigorous hands-on learning and personalized attention. Students in all undergraduate disciplines who participate in the Honors College and complete its program requirements graduate with a Commonwealth Honors designation on their degrees.

UMass Lowell maintains a student-faculty ratio of 18:1 and focuses on putting the lessons of the classroom into practice in real-world settings through co-ops, internships, service learning, and research. A growing number of interdisciplinary programs, such as the biomedical engineering and technology minor offered jointly by the colleges of Engineering, Sciences, and Health Sciences, reflect emerging fields in the global economy. Dozens of accelerated bachelor's-to-master's programs allow students to earn two degrees in as few as five years.

Approximately 50 percent of undergraduate classes have fewer than 20 students. All first-year students belong to academic learning communities. Optional Living-Learning Communities in the residence halls include: honors, art, music, women in science and engineering, pre-med, business innovation, health professions, DifferenceMakers, criminal justice, creative arts and veterans. The Centers for Learning offers tutoring and academic support programs. The Career Services and Cooperative Education Center helps students prepare for the transition to the working world. The DifferenceMaker program encourages student teams to address real-world problems through entrepreneurial action and sponsors the annual $25,000 Idea Challenge pitch contest.

The campus community is ethnically, culturally, and economically diverse. Students come from 30 states and 50 countries. Twenty-nine percent of undergraduates identify as students of color. The majority of freshmen choose to live in university housing, which includes traditional residence halls, apartments, suites, and a former downtown hotel. Housing is guaranteed for freshmen and available to most returning and transfer students who want it. More than 200 active student organizations include gaming group, dance and sport clubs, leadership societies and a student-run FM radio station. The campus features over a dozen eateries, including Sal's Pizza, Starbucks, Subway, Red Mango, and traditional dining halls. The vibrant campus life includes supporting eighteen Division I athletics teams, which compete in the America East and Hockey East Conferences. The Campus Recreation Center runs intramural sports, fitness classes, and an outdoor adventure program. The 7,800-seat Tsongas Center at UMass Lowell is a popular venue for national acts and hosts the university's men's hockey team.

LOCATION AND ENVIRONMENT

The university sits along the Merrimack River in Lowell, a city of 110,000 that ha gained national attention by successfully leveraging its history, ethnic diversity, an entrepreneurial spirit to create a vital urban center. The site of a unique, urba National Historical Park, Lowell is also home to an acclaimed professional theate company, literary and folk festivals, and numerous restaurants and museums. Lowe is located 25 miles from Boston and Cambridge and within the region's major busi ness corridors, which provide internship and co-op opportunities for students. It i also within easy reach of major outdoor recreational areas via major highways an regional train and bus service.

OFF-CAMPUS OPPORTUNITIES

Extensive opportunities for study abroad with credit include faculty-led course affiliate programs, exchanges, and more than 120 partnerships with prestigiou institutions in 40 countries. Recent faculty-led courses include seminars on healt care in Peru; business in China; crime, law, and asset protection in Hong Kon and Macau; and innovation and entrepreneurship in India. Professional co-op internships, and service-learning also take place off campus.

MAJORS AND DEGREES OFFERED

Dual majors are permitted. Dual BA/BS degrees and bachelor's-to-master's degre programs (indicated with an asterisk in the lists below) are available in all field Pre-medical, pre-law and other pre-professional advising is available to intereste students in all majors. Many of the majors offered have additional program option available, as noted in parentheses below.

The College of Fine Arts, Humanities, and Social Sciences offers baccalaureat programs in: American studies; criminal justice and criminology° (correction homeland security, information technology, police, violence), economics°, Englis (creative writing, journalism and professional writing, literature, theatre arts), fin arts (animation, painting, printmaking, sculpture, photography, graphic desig web design, interactive media), history, legal studies, liberal arts (art history, Asia studies, comparative arts, cultural studies, economics, education, English/literatur environmental studies, gender studies, history, languages, legal studies, musi philosophy, political science, psychology, sociology, theatre arts, writing), mode languages (French, Spanish, French/Spanish, Italian/Spanish), music business, mus performance (instrumental, vocal), music studies (instrumental, vocal), peace an conflict studies°, philosophy (communication and critical thinking), political scienc psychology°, sociology, and sound recording technology°.

The College of Sciences offers baccalaureate programs in: biology° (bioinformatic biotechnology, ecology), chemistry (cheminformatics, forensics), computer scienc (bioinformatics/cheminformatics), environmental science (atmospheric scienc [meteorology], environmental studies, geoscience), mathematics° (applied comput tational mathematics, bioinformatics, business applications, computer science, prob ability and statistics, teaching), and physics° (general, optics, radiological health)

The James B. Francis College of Engineering offers baccalaureate programs i chemical engineering° (biological engineering, computer-aided process design an controls, engineered materials, nanomaterials engineering, nuclear engineerin paper engineering), civil and environmental engineering°, electrical and comput engineering°, mechanical engineering°, and plastics engineering°. Engineerin programs are accredited by the Accreditation Board for Engineering and Techn ogy, Inc.

...e College of Health Sciences and School of Nursing offer baccalaureate pro-
...ams in: clinical laboratory and nutritional sciences (clinical laboratory sciences,
...nical science, medical laboratory science, nutritional science), community health
...d sustainability (community health, environmental health), exercise physiology,
...rsing, and public health (community health/health promotion, environmental/
...cupational health). A BS degree-completion program for RNs is offered through
...e Division of Online and Continuing Education. Accreditation is by the National
...crediting Agency for Clinical Laboratory Sciences and the National League for
...ursing Accrediting Commission.

...e Manning School of Business offers baccalaureate programs in: business ad-
...inistration° (accounting, corporate finance, entrepreneurship, financial markets,
...neral finance, international business, management, management information
...stems, marketing, and supply chain/operations management). A one-year MBA
...available as a bachelor's-to-master's program. All programs are accredited by the
...ssociation to Advance Collegiate Schools of Business International.

...e university's Graduate School of Education offers widely respected master's and
...octoral programs as well as a range of initial certification courses. Undergradu-
...es in STEM majors who are considering teaching can get classroom experience
...d a teaching minor through UTeach, a national teacher-training program whose
...ly Northeast chapter is at UMass Lowell. Bachelor's-to-master's programs with
...itial Massachusetts teacher licensure are also available through the Fast Track to
...aching program.

...e Division of Online and Continuing Education offers a wide range of programs
...at are delivered online and on campus.

...tercollegiate programs in aerospace studies, robotics, and joint military studies
...e also available.

...CADEMIC PROGRAMS

...e university calendar includes two semesters, a three-week intersession in Janu-
...y, and a summer term with two sessions. Full-time undergraduates generally take
...e courses each semester. A minimum of 120 credits is required for baccalaure-
...e degrees; the minimum credits required for professional degree programs are
...nerally higher. A general education requirement is imposed for all baccalaureate
...ograms. Majors require 30–60 credits. Elective course options vary widely by
...ajor. Professional degree program options and requirements follow specific ac-
...editation guidelines. Qualified students in all majors are invited to join the Honors
...ollege. The academic climate is serious, competitive and requires self-motivation.

...AMPUS FACILITIES AND EQUIPMENT

...e campus is in the midst of a bold expansion. Ten new facilities have opened in
...e last five years, including the Mark and Elisia Saab Emerging Technologies and
...novation Center, the Health and Social Sciences Building (criminal justice and
...iminology, psychology and nursing), two suite-style residence halls, and two parking
...rages. A new writing center, a television studio, and a 14,500-square-foot anatomy
...d physiology lab opened in January 2014. University Crossing, the hub of student
...rvices and activities, opened in summer 2014 and connects the university's three
...mpuses to the downtown business and cultural district. Construction is underway
...r a new building to house the Manning School of Business. Both libraries feature
...w learning commons with areas for quiet and group study as well as Starbucks
...fés. Other academic facilities include six sound recording technology studios.

...ITION, ROOM, BOARD, AND FEES

...otal Tuition and fees 2014-2015

...-State Residents: $12,447

...ut-of-State Residents: $27,400

...ew England Regional Program: $21,014

...otal Room and Board $11,278

...e university offers a wide range of merit-based scholarships in addition to
...nancial aid.

FINANCIAL AID

The university is committed to making higher education accessible to all qualified
students. The university participates in federal and state programs, assisting students
through grants-in-aid, loans, employment opportunities, and scholarships. The
amount of a financial aid awarded is determined by need, as indicated by the Free
Application for Federal Student Aid (FAFSA), which should be filed by March 1.
The university awards a growing number of merit-based scholarships. More than
$160 million in financial aid was awarded to students in the 2012-2013 academic
year, meeting approximately 90 percent of need.

STUDENT ORGANIZATIONS AND ACTIVITIES

The majority of freshmen choose to live in university housing, which includes traditional residence halls, apartments, suites, and a former downtown hotel. Housing
is guaranteed for freshmen.

More than 200 active student organizations include a marching band, a weekly
newspaper, and an FM radio station. The campus features over a dozen eateries,
including Crossroads Café, Sal's Pizza, Starbucks, Subway, Red Mango, and traditional dining halls. The vibrant campus life includes supporting eighteen Division
I athletics teams, which compete in the America East and Hockey East Conferences. The Campus Recreation Center runs intramural sports, fitness classes, and
an outdoor adventure program. The 7,800-seat Tsongas Center is a popular venue
for national acts.

Leadership opportunities are provided through the Student Government Association, the Residence Hall Association and a variety of other student-run organizations. Students also participate in the disciplinary system and in most university
committees.

ADMISSIONS PROCESS

All undergraduate day applicants must have a high school or a general equivalency
diploma and satisfactory SAT scores. Admissions standards vary by program. Last
year's incoming freshmen had an average GPA of 3.44 and SAT scores of 1150
(reading and math).

Transfer students are considered for fall or spring semester admissions. Transcripts
of completed work must be on file prior to acceptance. Depending on the number of
transfer credits and college GPA, transfer students who seek admission as matricu-
lating day students may be asked to provide a high school record and SAT scores.

Special-entrance programs that provide nontraditional admissions pathways for
international students are available.

The university admits students through early action, regular admission, and transfer
admission. Entering freshmen are admitted for the fall or spring semester. The
early action deadline for freshmen is November 1; the regular admission deadline
is February 1. Applicants to the School of Nursing are encouraged to apply by the
early action deadline. The preferred deadline for transfer applications is August 15
for the fall and January 7 for the spring. The Common Application or the UMass
Lowell application is accepted; both require an essay and a letter of recommendation and are available online at www.uml.edu/apply.

For application forms and further information, please contact:

Office of Undergraduate Admissions

University of Massachusetts Lowell

University Crossing, Suite 420

200 Pawtucket St.

Lowell, Massachusetts 01854-5104

Phone: 978-934-3931

Website: http://www.uml.edu

http://www.facebook.com/umlowell

http://www.twitter.com/umasslowell

http://www.youtube.com/user/umasslowell

http://instagram.com/umasslowell

UNIVERSITY OF NEW ENGLAND

AT A GLANCE

The University of New England is an innovative health sciences university grounded in the liberal arts, with two distinctive coastal Maine campuses and unique study abroad opportunities. UNE has internationally recognized scholars in the sciences, health, medicine and humanities; offers more than 40 undergraduate, graduate and professional degree programs; and is home to Maine's only medical school and the only college of dental medicine in Northern New England. UNE is one of a handful of private universities with a comprehensive health education mission including medicine, pharmacy, dental medicine, nursing and an array of allied health professions. Academic programs ensure that students have plenty of opportunities for extensive fieldwork, clinical experiences, research, internships and global experiences at both the undergraduate and graduate levels.

UNE's 6,429 students are enrolled in a wide variety of academic programs at the undergraduate, graduate, and professional levels in six colleges: the College of Arts and Sciences, the College of Dental Medicine, the College of Osteopathic Medicine, the College of Pharmacy, the Westbrook College of Health Professions, and the online College of Graduate and Professional Studies. At the undergraduate level, UNE has approximately 2,749 students enrolled from 35 different states and several foreign countries in more than 40 undergraduate degree programs.

UNE traces its history to 1831 with the founding of Westbrook College, one of Maine's oldest institutions of learning. Today's University represents the joining of three unique higher education institutions through the combining of St. Francis College and the New England College of Osteopathic Medicine in 1978, and Westbrook College in 1996.

LOCATION AND ENVIRONMENT

The University of New England has two campuses located in picturesque southern Maine communities and a third campus in Tangier, Morocco.

UNE's Biddeford Campus is located on a beautiful site in Biddeford, Maine, where the Saco River meets the Atlantic Ocean. With more than 4,000 feet of water frontage, enjoying the ocean comes naturally to students. The campus is home to the College of Arts and Sciences and the College of Osteopathic Medicine, which offers the doctor of osteopathic medicine (D.O.) degree. With more than 540 acres, the Biddeford Campus is also home to the Harold Alfond Center for Health Sciences, a modern 80,000-square-foot science education facility, the Marine Science Center and the Harold Alfond Forum.

UNE's quintessential historic New England campus in suburban Portland is home to the College of Dental Medicine, the College of Pharmacy, and the Westbrook College of Health Professions, which offers undergraduate programs in Dental Hygiene and Nursing and graduate programs in Nurse Anesthesia, Occupational Therapy, Physical Therapy, Physician Assistant, and Social Work. The College of Dental Medicine, which opened in the fall of 2013, is the only one of its kind in Northern New England and is housed in the state-of-the-art Oral Health Center. The 41-acre Portland Campus is also home to the Center for Global Humanities, the Art Gallery and the Maine Women Writers Collection.

UNE's third campus is in Tangier, Morocco, and offers students the opportunity to spend a semester or academic year abroad, taking English-language classes in their regular courses of study while discovering the culture of Morocco and the city of Tangier at no additional cost. UNE's campus location offers easy access to downtown, the main beach, and the major cultural activities the city has to offer.

OFF-CAMPUS OPPORTUNITIES

UNE is committed to supplementing the traditional learning process with practical applications. All students are encouraged to participate in cooperative education programs, field placements, and practicums. These experiences are required for graduation by most majors and provide valuable learning situations that increase student's exposure to job-related opportunities. Students also have the opportunity for vibrant study-abroad experiences. For the same cost as a semester or academic year on campus in Maine, students can study at UNE's Tangier, Morocco campus or in Seville, Spain and take courses in Spanish and intercultural communication as well as a variety of courses in the sciences, humanities, social sciences, business and the arts taught in English by the host university. Faculty-led short-term travel courses offer other exciting opportunities to study abroad. Students and faculty meet throughout the term to prepare for travel academically and practically through readings, lectures and coursework.

MAJORS AND DEGREES OFFERED

UNE offers highly competitive undergraduate and graduate programs in a variety of areas.

Bachelor degrees are offered in animal behavior, applied exercise science, applied mathematics, applied social and cultural studies, aquaculture and aquarium science, art and design media, art education, athletic training, biochemistry, biological sciences, business, chemistry, communications, dental hygiene, elementary education, English, environmental science, environmental studies, health, wellness and occupational studies, history, laboratory science, liberal studies, marine science, medical biology (pre-dental, pre-medicine, pre-optometry, pre–physician assistant studies, and pre–veterinary science), neuroscience, nursing, ocean studies and marine affairs, political science (including pre-law), pre-pharmacy, pre–physical therapy, psychology, public health, secondary education, sociology, and sport and recreation management.

Master's degrees are offered in biological sciences, education, marine sciences, medical education leadership, nurse anesthesia studies, occupational therapy, physician assistant studies, public health, and social work.

Doctoral degrees offered include dental medicine (D.M.D.), education leadership (Ed.D.), osteopathic medicine (D.O.), pharmacy (Pharm.D.), and physical therapy (D.P.T.).

ACADEMIC PROGRAMS

UNE's academic programs ensure that students have plenty of opportunities for extensive fieldwork, clinical experiences, research, internships and global experiences at both the undergraduate and graduate levels. All undergraduate programs at UNE have a core curriculum as a common thread. Designed to provide a foundation in the liberal arts, the core reflects the values of the University and is designed to prepare students for living informed, thoughtful, and active lives in a complex and changing society.

UNE's Student Academic Success Center provides a wide range of services to assist students with health, academic support, educational and career planning and equal opportunities during their academic experience. The Office of Career Services provides academic and career exploration assistance, assistance in applying to graduate schools, self-assessment and personal interest exploration, resume help and information and access to job listings and job fairs.

CAMPUS FACILITIES AND EQUIPMENT

Both the Biddeford and Portland Campuses feature buildings with a variety of uses to support the needs of the University community. On the Biddeford Campus, classroom and office spaces are housed in several facilities across campus. Several research facilities are on campus, including the Marine Science Center; the Harold Alfond Center for Health Sciences, with biology and chemistry labs as well as lecture halls, classrooms, a gross anatomy lab, and UNE's medical school facilities; the Pickus Center for Biomedical Research, and the Peter and Cécile Morgane Hall, a science center providing additional classrooms and an undergraduate teaching laboratory. The Department of Creative and Fine Arts offers a dedicated building that provides faculty offices and studio space for drawing, painting, printmaking, sculpting and photography.

On the Portland Campus, Ludcke Auditorium is used for a variety of academic programs. Coleman Dental Hygiene Building houses classroom, clinic and faculty space. The Blewett Science Center, home to UNE's nursing program, consists of science labs and classrooms, and the Clinical Simulation Program (CSP), which provides customized training and education for students and health professionals. Proctor Hall is also a classroom building and is home to the Proctor Learning and Career Center. The Josephine S. Abplanalp Library houses study space and computer labs, as well as the Maine Women Writers Collection. The College of Pharmacy is a LEED-certified academic and research facility with teaching and research laboratories and a lecture hall. The College of Dental Medicine has its administration offices in historical Goddard Hall, and the Oral Health Center is a teaching clinic and simulation facility.

Both campuses also provide a variety of facilities in support of community life. The 55,000 square-foot Campus Center on the Biddeford Campus houses both a sports complex and student union. The student union provides multipurpose rooms, snack bar, the University bookstore, and offices. The sports complex includes a gymnasium with indoor track, collegiate swimming pool, fully equipped fitness center, racquetball courts and athletic training room. The Harold Alfond Forum, a 106,000 square-foot facility on the Biddeford Campus, features an ice hockey rink, a basketball court, classroom and lab space, a fitness center, and multipurpose rooms and administrative offices. UNE's Big Blue Turf Field (one of only a few at colleges in the country) is home to UNE's field hockey and lacrosse teams. The Finley Recreation Center on the Portland Campus also provides a variety of fitness, health, wellness, and recreational programs and includes a gymnasium, fitness center, and multi-purpose rooms.

TUITION, ROOM, BOARD AND FEES

For 2014–2015, full-time (12 to 18 credits) undergraduate comprehensive annual costs are $46,750. This includes:

Full-time tuition $32,880

Room and Board $12,670 (traditional double occupancy)

General Services Fee $1,200

FINANCIAL AID

Approximately 98% of full-time undergraduate students received some form of financial assistance. The average package was $26,000, including scholarships, grants, loans and employment. The University of New England has an extensive academic scholarship program with awards ranging from $3,000 to $18,000 per year. The Office of Financial Services uses the Free Application for Federal Student Aid (FAFSA) as its primary application for institutional, federal, and state aid programs.

STUDENT ORGANIZATIONS AND ACTIVITIES

UNE's campuses offer a variety of cultural and social events and students are encouraged to become involved in activities, clubs and sports. Popular interests include scuba diving, skiing, hiking, biking, swimming, surfing, music, theater, photography, community service, and student leadership development programs.

UNE's Department of Athletics operates an NCAA Division III varsity athletics program. Varsity sports for men are basketball, cross country, golf, ice hockey, lacrosse and soccer. Varsity sports for women are basketball, cross country, field hockey, ice hockey, lacrosse, soccer, softball, swimming and volleyball.

ADMISSIONS PROCESS

Students applying for undergraduate admission should submit a completed application, a $40 nonrefundable application fee, transcripts of all academic work (high school and college), and scores on either the ACT or SAT. Students who do not use English as their primary language must submit TOEFL scores. Students applying for admission should have completed a curriculum that includes English, mathematics, science, and social sciences. International students must also complete an International Student Supplemental Application.

The undergraduate freshman admission application deadline is February 15. Applications received after this date are reviewed on a space-available basis. There is a nonbinding December 1 early action application deadline with a December 31 notification date. Applications for the spring term are accepted through December 1.

All prospective students are strongly encouraged to visit the campuses of the University of New England for an information session and tour. Tours are held daily Monday through Friday, and Saturday tours are also available. For more information about visiting UNE, visit www.une.edu/admissions.

UNIVERSITY OF PITTSBURGH AT BRADFORD

AT A GLANCE

The University of Pittsburgh at Bradford takes students beyond: beyond the classroom by offering internships and research opportunities; beyond the degree by providing a robust Career Services Office and an informal alumni network; beyond 9 to 5 by offering an active student life, a friendly residence life environment, excellent athletic and cultural facilities, and a wide range of recreational opportunities; beyond place by providing a liberal arts education that exposes students to the world and offering students many study-abroad opportunities; and beyond students' expectations by giving them a college experience that will transform them.

Students at Pitt-Bradford live and learn on a safe, intimate campus, where they receive individual and personalized attention from committed professors who work side by side with them. And, they earn a degree from the University of Pittsburgh, which commands respect around the world.

LOCATION AND ENVIRONMENT

Pitt-Bradford is nestled in the foothills of the Allegheny Mountains and only steps away from the Allegheny National Forest.

Pitt-Bradford also is a short drive from larger cities such as Buffalo, N.Y., 80 miles to the north; Pittsburgh, 160 miles to the southeast; and Erie, PA, 90 miles to the west. Pitt-Bradford can also be reach easily by car and plane.

OFF-CAMPUS OPPORTUNITIES

Pitt-Bradford students have many opportunities to participate in co-curricular opportunities in the region, including cross-country and downhill skiing, snowboarding, snowshoeing, ice skating, biking, fishing, hiking, and hunting.

MAJORS AND DEGREES OFFERED

Students at Pitt-Bradford may pursue four-year degrees in Accounting, Applied Mathematics, Athletic Training, Biology, Biology Education 7–12, Broadcast Communications, Business Computer and Information Technology Education K-12, Business Management, Chemistry, Chemistry Education 7–12, Computer Information Systems and Technology, Criminal Justice, Early Level Education Pre-K–4, Economics, Energy Science and Technology, English, English Education 7–12, Environmental Studies, Exercise Science, General Studies, Health and Physical Education, History/Political Science, Hospitality Management, Human Relations, Interdisciplinary Arts, Mathematics Education 7–12, Nursing, Physical Sciences, Psychology, Public Relations, Radiological Science, Social Sciences, Social Studies Education 7–12, Sociology, Sport and Recreation Management and Writing.

Students may pursue associate degrees in information systems, engineering science, nursing (RN), liberal studies, information systems, and petroleum technology.

Students may study engineering for up to two years at Pitt-Bradford then complete a program at the Oakland campus in bioengineering, chemical and petroleum engineering, civil and environmental engineering, electrical and computer engineering, industrial engineering, materials science and engineering, or mechanical engineering.

Students may pursue programs offered in conjunction with the University of Pittsburgh School of Dental Medicine and the Pennsylvania College of Optometry. Undergraduates begin their studies at Pitt-Bradford and, after three years, transfer to the appropriate graduate school to complete four more years of study.

Pitt-Bradford also offers the first two years of study leading to the doctorate in pharmacy. Students must complete the program at the Oakland campus, where admission is competitive. The Pittsburgh School of Pharmacy pre-admits some qualified high school seniors, pending completion of the first two years of the pre-professional program at Pitt-Bradford.

ACADEMIC PROGRAMS

The academic programs stress critical-thinking skills and communication and encourage hands-on learning through field experience, internships, and faculty-student collaboration on research. A Pitt-Bradford bachelor's degree requires 120–128 credit hours (requirements differ slightly among programs). Students must complete between 60 and 70 credit hours to earn an associate's degree.

The biology program prepares students for careers in health-related professions; education; research; field work; with companies that produce food, pharmaceuticals chemicals, and biotechnology; and technical positions with governmental agencies. Most students interested in medicine, dentistry, optometry, pharmacy, osteopathy, optometry, physical therapy, occupational therapy, podiatry, chiropractic medicine, veterinary medicine, pre-clinical dietetics and nutrition, and a variety of careers in health and rehabilitation sciences, are biology majors.

Students in the broadcast communications, English, public relations, and writing programs work on the student newspaper, The Source; broadcast over the college radio station, WDRQ; and publish original works in the student literary magazine, Baily's Beads. Students also have access to a state-of-the-art electronic newsroom, radio studio, television studio, and video editing room with analog and digital technology.

Students who choose to major in computer information systems and technology will get a broad IT background and gain hands-on lab experiences. Students will learn programming applications, network development, systems design and analysis, web technologies, multimedia applications, database development, and systems administration.

The criminal justice program provides opportunities for hands-on learning through the university's Crime Scene Investigation House, where students can solve mock crime scenes using many of the same tools as professional law enforcement agents; and internships with local and regional police departments, county courts and probation offices, and a federal prison.

The Early Level Education Pre K–4 and secondary education majors prepare students for careers as teachers in a world of rapid political, economic, scientific and cultural change. The Education Department seeks to graduate students who have general knowledge and specific content knowledge, as well as sound theory and practice.

The nursing program at Pitt-Bradford offers an associate of science degree that can be completed in two years, and the bachelor of science in nursing that requires two more years. Students may commence this program on completion of the ASN. The University also offers a School Nurse Certification program for registered nurses who wish to work in the school system.

In psychology, students gain knowledge in the scientific and theoretical aspects of psychology as well as the application of this knowledge. The major prepares students for graduate work in psychology and related disciplines and for employment in social service agencies, mental health centers, industries, and not-for-profit and governmental agencies.

Students may relocate to another university campus to complete academic programs not offered at Pitt-Bradford. They may earn no more than 70 credits before transferring. All students in the arts and sciences may relocate provided they are students in good standing. Engineering students may relocate if they maintain quality point average of at least 2.5.

CAMPUS FACILITIES AND EQUIPMENT

Students who want to work out in a state-of-the-art fitness center or swim in the six-lane swimming pool do so in the Richard E. And Ruth McDowell Sport and Fitness Center. The building also houses facilities for intercollegiate and intramural athletic events. Pitt-Bradford competes in Division III of the NCAA and fields seven men's (baseball, basketball, cross country, golf, soccer, swimming and tennis) and eight women's teams (basketball, bowling cross country, soccer, softball, swimming, tennis, and volleyball).

The Frame-Westerberg Commons building gives students a place to eat, gather and participate in campus life. The building houses the dining hall, where students can help themselves to a wide assortment of meals; a bookstore, which features an after-hours convenience store; offices for many student clubs and organizations; and areas for students to read or relax.

Blaisdell Hall, the university's fine arts and communication arts building, houses the communication arts, theater and music programs and features state-of-the-art equipment. The building also houses a multi-purpose theater, where students can participate in dramatic and musical performances. The building also serves as the cultural center for the region by housing plays, concerts, lectures and other arts-related events.

TUITION, ROOM, BOARD AND FEES

We know the impact a Pitt-Bradford education can have on your future. That's why we work so hard to make that education affordable. Our tuition and housing fees are competitive compared to other area institutions, and we offer a wide variety of merit- and need-based scholarships to qualified students. Therefore, Pitt-Bradford's 1,500 students earn their degree at a cost that is roughly 10 percent of what their peers at a private college pay. More than 90 percent of our students receive some form of financial aid through grants, loans, work study, or scholarships. In fact, for the 2014–15 academic year, the average award will be $18,529 for Pennsylvania students and $19,542 for out-of-state students.

Full-time tuition for the two-term academic year in 2014–15 is $12,452 for Pennsylvania residents and $23,268 for out-of-state students. Tuition for students in the nursing program is $15,952 for Pennsylvania residents and $29,672 for nonresidents.

A double-occupancy room for the year is $5,160. A full meal plan per year is $3,620. Students must also pay yearly fees: $200 activity fee, $350 computer fee, $100 health fee, and a $140 recreation fee. On average, students spend about $500 per term on books and supplies.

FINANCIAL AID

Pitt-Bradford believes that the cost of a college education should not be a deterrent to any student regardless of family financial circumstances. A variety of grants, scholarships, loans, and work-study opportunities are administered through the Financial Aid Office. All aid applicants must submit the Free Application for Federal Student Aid (FAFSA) by March 1 to receive priority consideration. Pennsylvania residents who complete the FAFSA by March 1 are also eligible for Pennsylvania Higher Education Assistance Agency (PHEAA) grants. Students who live outside of Pennsylvania should contact their state agency to learn more about the prerequisites for grants.

The university awards merit-based scholarships upon entry to those who demonstrate exceptional academic achievement. The university ROTC program is another possible source of financial aid. The university encourages veterans to contact the VA about educational benefits.

Contact the Financial Aid Office or visit the Pitt-Bradford's financial aid website to learn more about financial assistance.

STUDENT ORGANIZATIONS AND ACTIVITIES

There are more than 60 clubs and organizations, ranging from the campus radio station and newspaper to academic clubs, honor societies, fraternities and sororities.

Because Pitt-Bradford is a personalized campus, opportunities for leadership abound. Many students become campus leaders as early as their sophomore year. Regardless of your background or interests, you will find many places to become involved as a student at Pitt-Bradford.

The Student Activities Council schedules comedy performances, lectures, art exhibits, movies, and trips to such places as Toronto, Canada; Niagara Falls, N.Y.; Cooperstown, N.Y.; and New York City.

ADMISSIONS PROCESS

The Admissions committee primarily looks at three factors in evaluating applicants: the applicant's record of high school achievement; standardized test results (SAT I or ACT), and letters of recommendation from teachers and/or a counselor at their high school. Class rank, extracurricular activities, personal qualifications, and potential role in the school community are also considered.

Pitt-Bradford accepts applicants on a rolling basis. Applications are welcome at any time. The Admissions committee notifies candidates as soon as a decision has been made on their application.

Applicants must complete and submit the application form and a non-refundable $45 fee. An official high school transcript and an official standardized test score report (SAT I or ACT) are also required. Transfer applicants must also submit official copies of all college transcripts, which must reflect a GPA of at least 2.0. Students and their families are welcome to visit our campus. The Office of Admissions schedules interviews and tours Monday through Friday, 9 A.M. to 4 P.M. all year long, as well as on selected Saturdays during the school year. Contact the Office of Admissions to arrange a visit.

Students seeking more information should contact:

The Office of Admissions

The University of Pittsburgh at Bradford

300 Campus Drive

Bradford, PA 16701-2898

Telephone: 814-362-7555

800-872-1787 (toll free)

Fax: 814-362-5150

www.upb.pitt.edu

Email: admissions@www.upb.pitt.edu

UNIVERSITY OF SAINT JOSEPH

At University of Saint Joseph, students thrive in a supportive, inspiring environment that focuses on their ultimate success. USJ graduates are leaders in their careers and communities.

AT A GLANCE

The University of Saint Joseph (USJ) offers career-focused undergraduate, graduate, and certificate programs. Enhanced by the intellectual tradition and values of its founding Sisters of Mercy, the university allows students to thrive in a culture of achievement and collaboration.

As a private, liberal arts institution, USJ is nationally recognized for the quality of its academic programs. It consists of five schools and 25 undergraduate and graduate programs, along with pre-professional and certificate programs. USJ serves a diverse, intergenerational student body enrolled in: the undergraduate Women's College; the Program for Adult Learners (serving women and men earning their bachelor's degrees); and the coeducational Graduate and Professional Studies program.

Founded in 1932, USJ offers students opportunities to excel intellectually, socially, and ethically. They choose from a variety of rigorous academic programs and are mentored by faculty who help them fulfill their potential. Students often work alongside faculty on research, as well as participate in internships throughout the region—all of which leads to applicable skills, professional networking, and career success.

The core values of compassionate service, Catholic identity, and commitment to women through academic excellence are evident in the curriculum and daily life on campus. Students from a multitude of faith traditions are empowered for success. USJ is a diverse community of 987 undergraduate and 1,578 graduate students. It is a caring environment that encourages strong ethical values, personal integrity, and a sense of responsibility to the needs of society.

LOCATION AND ENVIRONMENT

The university is located on 90 acres in suburban West Hartford, four miles from Hartford, the capital city, and its thriving corporate, arts and entertainment districts—ideal for internships. West Hartford Center offers an array of coffee bars, boutiques, restaurants, and entertainment.

The campus has seven residence halls, two with apartment-style living. Approximately 75 percent of first-year students live on campus and have access to special services including a free weekend shuttle to off campus shops and restaurants. Amenities in each residence hall include spacious rooms, study/lounge space, internet access, cable television, and free laundry facilities.

Two laboratory schools are located on or adjacent to campus. The Gengras Center, a state approved, private special education school serves students with autism, intellectual and developmental disabilities. The School for Young Children serves pre-school students with a science-based curriculum. Both serve as lab schools for teacher training.

OFF-CAMPUS OPPORTUNITIES

Located near Hartford and within easy access to Boston and New York, USJ's students are actively engaged in the local and global communities. Central Connecticut is a thriving corridor for industry, innovation, and arts. Students participate in a wide array of internships and experiential learning opportunities that provide them with real-world opportunities and professional connections. They can cross-register at other colleges in the local area through the Hartford Consortium for Higher Education. No additional tuition is charged, credits are transferable, and free transportation is provided.

Community service is a core aspect of the USJ experience. Students gain practical work experience and develop leadership skills through volunteer opportunities at the Wellness Center in Hartford and other local health and social service agencies. USJ has been named to the Presidential Honor Roll for Community Service consistently since 2009. In 2015, USJ hosted three alternate spring break community service trips to Ireland, Guyana, and New Jersey.

USJ students also make a global impact through study abroad programs and international exchanges. USJ has formal partnership agreements with universities in Japan, The Netherlands, and Israel. It has a specialized program in Guyana through a sister hospital. Students can work with the Director of International Studies to plan for an international study experience anywhere in the world. They can also travel domestically and work on community service projects through alternative breaks.

MAJORS AND DEGREES OFFERED

USJ is known for its high-quality programs in the natural sciences, social sciences, and liberal arts. It has a strong academic reputation based on a combination of liberal arts and career-focused, professional majors. Its programs emphasize quality instruction, challenging course work, and close connections between students and faculty in the spirit of collaboration and mentorship. The university offers bachelor's, master's, and doctoral degrees, along with certificates. It has more than 25 academic majors and six pre-professional programs, plus accelerated bachelor's- to-master's degrees.

Bachelor degrees are offered in: accounting, art history, biochemistry, biology, chemistry, child study, English, family studies, history, international studies, management, mathematics, nursing, nutrition and dietetics, philosophy, psychology, public health, public policy and advocacy, religious studies, social work, Spanish, special education, and women's studies. The Education program offers teaching certification in elementary education, secondary education, and special education.

Pre-professional programs are available in: pre-dental, pre-law, pre-medical, pre-pharmacy, pre-physical therapy and pre-veterinary programs.

Graduate programs include master and doctoral degrees. Master's are offered in: autism and applied behavior analysis (the only program in Connecticut), biochemistry, biology, chemistry, clinical mental health counseling, early childhood education/special education, education, management, marriage and family therapy, nursing, nutrition, school counseling, social work, special education, and teacher licensure—four of which are offered online (biology, biochemistry, chemistry, and nutrition). Graduate certificate programs are offered in applied behavior analysis, autism spectrum disorders, dietetic internship, emerging diseases, healthcare systems management, homeland security management, gerontology, and Latino community practice. Doctorates are available in: Pharmacy and Nursing Practice.

Research, clinical, and work placements are factored into all majors as important components of each student's program. The university is known as a leader in the field of Autism and is home to the Institute for Autism and Behavioral Studies. It offers the only master's degree program in Applied Behavior Analysis in of Connecticut. In 2015, USJ opened its Center for Applied Research and Education, an expansion to its Gengras Center School. This is a leading institute for special education that addresses the growing need for autism professionals.

ACADEMIC PROGRAMS

USJ provides students the opportunity to pursue a rigorous academic major while achieving their ultimate professional goals. Average class size is 14 with a student-faculty ratio of 10:1, which promotes faculty mentorship. Classes are taught by faculty members—not teaching assistants—so students study and work with professors throughout their four years of study. The curriculum successfully combines professional preparation with broad humanistic studies, incorporating themes like: the social/historical contexts of science and technology; global awareness; women's studies; ethical analysis. All majors combine practical experience with professional opportunity as part of the curriculum. Students are provided internships, mentorship, study abroad programs, and professional networking opportunities.

The Honors Program offers enhanced learning opportunities and a motivated community of learners who excel as they combine academics with intensive practical experiences. Many Honors students present research at conferences, publish in periodicals, and work alongside faculty on professional research.

Students are given every opportunity to succeed on campus. The Center for Academic Excellence manages the university's Writing Portfolio Program, which enhances students writing skills. It also provides tutoring and other academic support services. Students can design their own major or develop an interdisciplinary major around a particular theme or area related to their talents, interests, or career goals.

The university's faculty consists of 108 full-time faculty members, six of whom are Fulbright Scholars. Of the full-time faculty, 85% percent hold the highest possible degrees in their fields. The faculty and all members of the university community promote the welfare students and help them attain the objectives set forth by the college's mission.

CAMPUS FACILITIES AND EQUIPMENT

The University of Saint Joseph has two campuses—the main campus is located at 1678 Asylum Avenue, West Hartford; the downtown Hartford campus, which houses the School of Pharmacy, is at 229 Trumbull Street.

The main campus is easily accessible and offers ample parking, seven residence halls, dining facilities, student lounge, and bookstore. McDonough Hall features several state-of-the-art laboratories including a Clinical Nursing Lab equipped with a Meti-man simulation mannequin. The Pope Pius XII Library has a collection of approximately 134,000 volumes, computer databases, periodicals, microforms, audiovisuals, and OCLC interlibrary loans.

The O'Connell Athletic Center features a fitness center, swimming pool, suspended indoor track, dance studio, and gym. The Athletic Complex features an outdoor track, soccer/lacrosse field, softball field and six tennis courts. Division III athletics teams include basketball, cross-country, lacrosse, soccer, softball, swimming and diving, tennis, and volleyball.

The Carol Autorino Center for the Arts and Humanities is the cultural center of campus and features the Bruyette Athenaeum, the 365-seat Hoffman Auditorium, and the University of Saint Joseph Art Gallery. Professional performers, speakers, comedians and musicians engage the community in various events held on campus in this facility.

The university's primary technology center is located in McDonough Hall; internet access is available throughout both campuses including many WiFi hotspots.

The School of Pharmacy is adjacent to the XL Center in Hartford. Graduate Pharmacy students often live and study in the downtown area. Undergraduate students are transported to the Hartford campus for research and other related opportunities. The School of Pharmacy is a 53,000 square foot state-of-the-art facility with the latest laboratory and learning technology.

Tuition, Room, Board, and Fees

Tuition and fees for full-time freshmen: $36,140. Room and board: approximately $12,610 (15-meal plan, double room).

FINANCIAL AID

The goal of the Financial Aid Program is to place a high-quality, private education within the reach of as many qualified students as possible. This is achieved by offering need- and merit-based financial aid that includes a combination of grants, loans and on-campus employment opportunities. 99% of USJ students receive USJ grants/scholarships. Our average financial aid package is $30,578 (including federal loans). Merit scholarships up to $21,000 and are available to all eligible first-year, transfer and international students. Students are considered for merit-based scholarship awards upon admission and for additional financial aid after completion of the FAFSA form. Financial Aid counselors are available to assist families with the process at any time.

STUDENT ORGANIZATIONS AND ACTIVITIES

USJ is a tight-knit community where faculty and students know one another by name. It is primarily a residential community and therefore offers many opportunities on campus for students to become involved. On-campus activities, including concerts, performances, multicultural events, dances, service projects and NCAA Division III sports, draw guests from the surrounding area. Free shuttle transportation to and from campus to West Hartford Center and the West Farms Mall offers students the opportunity to enjoy time in local restaurants and shops. Students visit Hartford's arts and entertainment district, which features galleries, coffee bars, theaters, concert venues and professional sports teams. Bus trips to nearby Boston and New York City, as well as Six Flags and the Big E are very popular.

USJ has more than 30 student clubs and organizations, which reflect the diverse interests of the student body. Examples include the Students Programming and Events Council (SPEC), the Green Team, Honor societies, the Queenes Compayne (drama club), Voices of Praise Gospel Choir, the USJ Dance Ensemble, and more. Through clubs students engage in leadership roles on campus. Opportunities for students empower and encourage them to become involved in every aspect of their college experience.

ADMISSIONS PROCESS

The University of Saint Joseph offers rolling admissions and a free, online application. USJ is selective, with an acceptance rate of 78.4%. For information, please visit our website: www.usj.edu/admissions.

You can reach the Office of Admissions at: 860.231.5216, admissions@usj.edu, or:

Office of Admissions

University of Saint Joseph

1678 Asylum Avenue

West Hartford, CT 06117

UNIVERSITY OF SAN FRANCISCO

AT A GLANCE

When the Jesuits founded the University of San Francisco in 1855, it was a one-room schoolhouse. Now, it is one of the West Coast's largest Catholic universities. Some things haven't changed: class size is still small, and student/faculty ratio is still low. USF has been dedicated to helping students learn the skills they need to improve their world for over 150 years. USF's Jesuit education is committed to providing all students with individual attention. Both love of learning and the willingness to face the challenge of serving society are fostered in programs in the arts, the sciences, business, education, nursing, and law.

San Francisco itself is a laboratory for students. The city and its university have interconnected histories, and today, this vibrant partnership gives students the wonderful opportunity to bring classroom theory into real, twenty-first-century life. There are 5,937 undergraduates on the 55-acre residential campus, and these students come from all 50 states and 80 countries. All new undergraduate students admitted with 40 or fewer transfer credits must live on campus for their first two semesters of enrollment, unless they have permanent residence within forty miles of the university. Students have access to facilities including libraries, a health and recreation center with an Olympic-size swimming pool, a coffeehouse, and several dining areas. Right outside is the city of San Francisco, and it has "facilities" of its own: the ballet, opera, museum exhibits, concerts, theater, and sports events. In addition, students have the opportunity to live with their peers in a cozy, laid-back environment within the residence halls. There are traditional residence halls and also University apartment-style facilities on campus. There are laundry facilities, study/computer rooms, and television lounges in every residence hall. Most floors in each dormitory also contain a community kitchen.

There are six dining facilities on campus that are convenient to the residence halls and classrooms. The Market has a dining environment similar to a food court with options for vegans, vegetarians and those who only consume organic or gluten-free foods. Other selections include a student-run coffeehouse, and a convenience store/cafe.

There are over 100 student-run associations for undergraduates at USF, including culturally-focused clubs, leadership and community service organizations, honors and professional societies, and club sports and intramural programs. These associations include the oldest continuously performing theater group west of the Mississippi River: The College Players, a weekly newspaper, and a literary magazine. The Career Services Center is one of the most active offices, aiding students in choosing a career path and learning about employment and internship opportunities. The exciting Koret Health and Recreation Center offers facilities for exercise, racquetball, swimming, court games, and socializing.

There are graduate programs in the arts and sciences, business, education, law, and nursing.

LOCATION AND ENVIRONMENT

The beautiful University of San Francisco campus is 55 acres, and is located in a residential neighborhood. Downtown San Francisco and the Pacific Ocean are just minutes away, and the 1,000-acre Golden Gate Park is only a few blocks away. There are many benefits of an urban campus, and San Francisco's diversity and compact geography allow students to discover research facilities, community involvement options, and work opportunities found in few other cities.

OFF-CAMPUS OPPORTUNITIES

USF students have many opportunities for university-sponsored study abroad programs, such as ones to Sophia University (Tokyo) and Oxford (England) through USF's St. Ignatius Institute, as well as a program at Universidad Iberoamericana in Mexico City. USF is connected to Gonzaga University's study abroad program in Florence (Italy) and to Loyola University of Chicago's program in Rome. The Institute of European and Asian Studies, of which USF is an associate member, offers programs in Durham and London, England; Paris, Dijon, and Nantes, France; Berlin and Freiburg, Germany; Vienna, Austria; Madrid and Salamanca, Spain; Milan, Italy; Tokyo and Nagoya, Japan; Moscow, Russia; Adelaide and Canberra, Australia; Beijing, China; and Singapore. There are many other study abroad opportunities as well. Students receive assistance from USF in all aspects of the program: choosing a location, completing applications, arranging financial matters, registering for academic credit, obtaining a passport and visa, and organizing travel plans.

MAJORS AND DEGREES OFFERED

BA and BS degrees are available through USF. The college of Arts and Sciences offers majors in Advertising, Architecture and Community Design, Arts History, Arts Management, Asian Studies, Biology, Chemistry, Communication Studies, Comparative Literature and Culture, Computer Science, Design, Economics, English, Environmental Science, Environmental Studies, Fine Arts, French, History, International Studies, Kinesiology, Latin American Studies, Mathematics, Media Studies, Performing Arts and Social Justice, Philosophy, Physics, Politics, Psychology, Sociology, Spanish, Theology and Religious Studies, Undeclared Arts, Science. The McLaren School of Management offers degrees in Accounting, Business Administration, Entrepreneurship and Innovation, Finance, Hospitality Industry Management, International Business, and Marketing. Qualified high school graduates and second-baccalaureate candidates can pursue a four-year baccalaureate program through the School of Nursing and Health Professions. Students can receive teacher certification at the elementary or secondary level by completing a fifth year of study in the Dual Degree in Teacher Preparation program.

he Pre-Professional Health Committee at USF advises and recommends students medical, dental, pharmacy, veterinary, podiatry, and optometry professional ealth schools. The pre-medical or other pre-health science requirements can be ken as part of, or in addition to, the requirements of an academic major. The re-Professional Health Committee helps students with the application process, eates a professional file for each student, gathers and sends recommendations to rofessional schools, gives interviews in preparation for application, and endorses pproved candidates through a committee letter of recommendation that is sent to l professional schools the student selects. The University currently has, on average, 70% acceptance rate to medical school.

CADEMIC PROGRAMS

is hoped that students leave USF with a well-rounded education and with a focus d awareness of social justice. A curriculum of 128 credits is required for the degree. ore Curriculum requirements from six particular categories of knowledge make p 44 credits of the curriculum, including a nine-credit block of basic skills courses d 88 credits divided between major requirements and electives. Superior students ay be selected for an honors program that provides a high academic challenge.

SF urges qualified high school students to study subjects traditionally reserved for lleges as early as possible. To this end, advanced placement courses, as certified y the college Board's Advanced Placement Program tests, are honored. USF also ooperates with the college-Level Examination Program (CLEP). Students inter-sted in obtaining this credit are required to take the CLEP tests before registering r their freshman courses.

special program is available through the St. Ignatius Institute. The Institute offers distinguished Great Books curriculum – a historical sequence of courses based classical works of literature, theology, and philosophy, from ancient Greece to e contemporary world.

rmy ROTC is also available at USF, and qualified applicants and continuing students ave access to ROTC scholarships.

vo semesters make up the academic year, and there are also summer sessions d a January intersession.

AMPUS FACILITIES AND EQUIPMENT

SF students enjoy access to the more than 700,000 volumes at Gleeson Library d access to the Computer Center, the Applied Math Laboratory, the Institute of hemical Biology, and the Physics Research Laboratories, all in the Harney Science enter. The Instructional Media Center is located in Cowell Hall, along with the ome base of nursing classes and the Nursing Skills Laboratory. The headquarters for e School of Management is Malloy Hall, which also holds an additional computer boratory and special seminar rooms.

TUITION, ROOM, BOARD AND FEES

Estimated cost of tuition for the 2013–2014 school year is $39,840. Room and board are $12,990 for the academic year. An additional $5,454 per year is generally required for books, fees, travel, and other expenses.

FINANCIAL AID

Many scholarships, grants, loans, and work-study programs are available for USF students, and all students must submit the Free Application for Federal Student Aid (FAFSA). Approximately 65% of all University students receive some form of financial assistance. Students have access to many jobs both on and off campus.

New freshman applicants with a minimum cumulative grade point average of 3.8 and a combined SAT I score of 1320 (Critical Reading + Math sections only) or an ACT composite score of 30 can participate in the University Scholars Program. University Scholars receive a non-need-based scholarship that covers a large portion of tuition costs for four years of undergraduate work. Scholars must maintain a GPA of 3.25 to remain eligible. Students eligible for University Scholars are identified during the admission process, and interested students must apply for admission by the January 15 priority application deadline.

The President's Merit Award, the Provost's Merit Award and the Dean's Merit Award, also for new freshmen, are non-need-based awards of $10,000, 8,000 and $6,000 respectively. Awardees are also identified during the admission process, and students must apply by the January 15 priority application deadline to be considered.

STUDENT ORGANIZATIONS AND ACTIVITIES

Every undergraduate student is a member of the Associated Students of the Univer-sity of San Francisco (ASUSF). There are three purposes to the ASUSF: to represent the official student viewpoint, to recommend policies, and to fund activities and services. There are three branches: the executive branch, the Student Senate, and the Student Court. The main representative body of the undergraduate day students is the Senate, and it monitors the expenditures of the $200,000-plus student budget.

USF offers over 100 different clubs and organizations. They give students opportu-nities to be involved in leadership and professional organizations, honor societies, culturally focused clubs, fraternities and sororities, club sports and intramurals.

ADMISSIONS PROCESS

Admission is selective, and each application receives an individual review. USF desires a high-quality and diverse student body, and thus encourages applications from men and women of all races, nationalities, and religious beliefs. Prospective students are evaluated on many criteria, including high school grade point average, the application essay, a personal recommendation, extracurricular involvement, and satisfactory test scores. All applicants must take the SAT I or the ACT, and interna-tional applicants must take the TOEFL or IELTS. A completed application file is made up of the application form, an essay, all academic transcripts, test scores, and one letter of recommendation. For the fall semester, November 15 is the deadline for early action and January 15 is the deadline for regular action.

For additional information, please contact:

Office of Admission

University of San Francisco

2130 Fulton Street

San Francisco, CA 94117-1046

Telephone: 415-422-6563

800-CALL-USF (toll free outside California)

Fax: 415-422-2217

E-mail: admissions@usfca.edu

World Wide Web: www.usfca.edu

THE UNIVERSITY OF TAMPA

AT A GLANCE

The University of Tampa is a private, medium-sized, comprehensive university in the heart of Tampa. The university offers exciting learning experiences in over 200 areas of study. All programs offer students a combination of challenging coursework and real world experience. Situated on a beautiful 105 acre campus, the University is adjacent to the Hillsborough River and downtown Tampa. Students enjoy a traditional self-contained campus, only steps away from the excitement and opportunities of the bustling city. At the center of campus lies Plant Hall, once a luxurious hotel for the rich and famous. This historical landmark is complemented by modern surroundings and excellent facilities including a student union, art studios and gallery, theatres, computer resource center, complete athletic facilities, science labs, and new residence halls. Over 7,700 students (6,300 full-time undergraduates) are enrolled at the university. UT students represent 50 states and 137 countries. Students choose from more than 200 different clubs and organizations including honors societies, social clubs, Greek Life, community service and others. The University of Tampa has one of the top NCAA Division II sports programs in the nation, winning fourteen national championships including recent championships in Baseball (2006, 2007 & 2013), Women's Volleyball (2006 & 2014), and Women's Soccer (2007).

LOCATION AND ENVIRONMENT

Located on the west central coast of Florida, Tampa has far more to offer than just beautiful beaches and a pleasant climate. Tampa Bay is one of the fastest growing areas in the United States. The city is a leading center for the arts, international business, law, education, media, and health and scientific research. Forbes magazine and Newsweek magazine consistently pick Tampa Bay as one of the best places to live in the United States.

OFF-CAMPUS OPPORTUNITIES

Across the river in downtown Tampa is the Museum of Art, Tampa Bay Center for the Performing Arts, the Florida Aquarium, Amalie Arena, and an outstanding public library. Busch Gardens is only several miles from campus and Walt Disney World and Universal Studios are only 90 minutes away. Tampa International Airport is five miles from campus

MAJOR AND DEGREES OFFERED

The University of Tampa offers bachelor's degrees in accounting, advertising public relations, allied health, applied dance, art, athletic training & sports me cine, biochemistry, biology, chemistry, communication, criminology, cybersecuri digital arts, economics, education (elementary and secondary certification), Englis entrepreneurship, environmental science, exercise science & sport studies, fil & media arts, finance, financial enterprise systems, forensic science, governme and world affairs, graphic design, history, human performance, internatio business, international & cultural studies, journalism, liberal studies, manag ment, management information systems, marine science (biology and chemistr marketing, mathematical programming, mathematics, music, music educatio music performance, new media production, nursing, painting, performing ar philosophy, physics, psychology, public health, social sciences, sociology, Spanis sport management, theatre, and writing. Minors and concentrations are offer in adult fitness, advertising, aerospace studies, art history, arts administration management, Asian studies, biology/business, biology/molecular, biology/organ mal & evolutionary, business administration, French, humanities, interdisciplina studies, international studies, law & justice, leadership studies, military scienc physical education, physics, recreation, speech/theatre, urban studies, wome studies, and world affairs. Pre-professional programs offered include pre-dentist pre-law, pre-medicine, pre-veterinary science, allied health, art therapy, and che istry. Certificate programs include early childhood education, European studi French, German, gerontology, Italian, Latin American studies, and Spanish. undergraduate School of Continuing Studies offers 23 degree programs design for adults who want to study part-time. Four summer sessions also offer excelle learning and professional advancement opportunities. At the graduate level, t business school offers the Master of Business Administration degree, a 4+1 M program and Master of Science degrees in accounting, finance, and marketing. Master of Science in Nursing, Master of Science in Exercise Science & Nutritio Master of Fine Arts in Creative Writing, Master of Arts in Teaching, and Master Science in Instructional Design & Technology degrees are also offered to studen

ACADEMIC PROGRAMS

The University of Tampa's undergraduate curriculum is designed to give student broad academic and cultural background as well as a concentrated study in a maj Students complete a comprehensive core curriculum known as the Baccalaurea Experience, which is highlighted by the unique and innovative first year progra known as Gateways. Gateways is an extensive orientation program which enco ages student development via exploration of global issues, career possibilities, a development of critical thinking and communication skills. International experien has always been a major focus at The University of Tampa. Students are essentia educated and prepared to live and work internationally. Academic opportunities this area are available to students immediately and in 2015 there are over 20 facu led study abroad opportunities available to students. For qualifying students, t university has a rigorous and rewarding Honors Program of expanded instructi student research, and University of Oxford semester.

CAMPUS FACILITIES AND EQUIPMENT

$400 million has been invested in new academic facilities, technology, and residence halls since 2000, making this national historic landmark the model of a modern university. 93% of all residence halls are new within the past 14 years and most of the others have been renovated recently. The Vaughn Student Center and residence hall complex serves as the hub of student life. Here students find food courts, a two-story cyber cafe, recreational areas, the Reeves Theatre, student office space, Barnes & Noble campus store and a 9th floor conference center with incredible views of downtown Tampa. The Frank and Carol Morsani Hall opened in Fall 2007 with state-of-the-art amenities and eight separate dining venues. Other outstanding facilities and resources include the Sykes College of Business, a waterfront Marine Science Field Station and research vessels, the Ferman Music Center, Reeves Theatre, 1,000-seat Falk Theatre, the R.K. Bailey Art Studio, and Sykes Chapel & Center for Faith and Values. The newly renovated Martinez Sports Complex, Naimoli Family Softball Complex, and Naimoli Family Lacrosse Stadium represent some of the best athletic facilities in the country.

TUITION, ROOM, BOARD, AND FEES

The cost for the 2014–2015 academic year is $26,330 for tuition & fees and $9,624 for room & board. The average financial aid award for students at The University of Tampa in 2014 was $18,296 with 92% of students receiving financial assistance.

FINANCIAL AID

A high-quality, private education at The University of Tampa presents students with exceptional value and is not as difficult to finance as some students may think. Each family's situation is evaluated individually for need-based assistance. Academic achievements, leadership potential, athletic skills, and other special talents are also recognized, regardless of need. Academic scholarships are awarded to most entering first year students with a 3.0 unweighted grade point average or above. Transfer, leadership, departmental, Phi Theta Kappa, International Baccalaureate and ROTC scholarships are also available.

STUDENT ORGANIZATIONS AND ACTIVITIES

Students choose from more than 200 student clubs and organizations including honors societies, social clubs, and community service groups amongst many others. Visit The University of Tampa website at www.ut.edu to learn more about student organizations and activities.

ADMISSIONS PROCESS

The University of Tampa is an academically competitive institution that offers several non-binding early action admission dates. Check The University of Tampa website at www.ut.edu for specific admission details.

THE UNIVERSITY OF TEXAS AT DALLAS

AT A GLANCE

Founded in 1969, UT Dallas has evolved into one of the top research institutions in Texas, and its programs in engineering and the biomedical sciences have gained national attention. With an enrollment of 21,193, The University of Texas at Dallas offers students the close-knit community of a small university with excellent student-faculty ratios of 22:1. However, UT Dallas is also backed by the powerful UT System and is aligned strategically with other institutions to offer advanced research opportunities traditionally found at larger institutions.

As a young, agile and rapidly growing university, The University of Texas at Dallas attracts a unique combination of student and faculty resources to the vibrant, dynamic and globally connected Dallas-Fort Worth area. UT Dallas is ranked in the top 100 by Kiplinger's and in the top 75 by The Princeton Review as a best value among public universities, and Times Higher Education ranks UT Dallas as #1 in Texas and #15 in the world among the top 100 universities under 50 years of age.

UT Dallas consistently draws a high caliber of student. The average entering freshman SAT for Fall 2013 was 1261. Nearly 38% of freshmen ranked in the top 10% of their high school class, with 71% in the top 25%. UT Dallas is ranked among the top 100 American universities in the number of National Merit Scholars enrolled, and the University confers a higher percentage of science, engineering and business degrees -(86%) than all other Texas public doctoral-granting institutions combined (59%).

About 64% of our pre-med students are admitted to medical schools, compared to an average national admission rate of 45%. In addition, 89% of students advised through our Pre-Law Advising and Resource Center were admitted to one or more law schools.

LOCATION AND ENVIRONMENT

UT Dallas is located in suburban Richardson, Texas, a prime location that places the University in the second largest state and the fourth largest metropolitan area in the nation. Because of the two local airports, Dallas Love Field and Dallas/Fort Worth International Airport, the Dallas area is an international destination. Richardson, known as The Telecom Corridor, is home to diverse global technology-based companies.

OFF-CAMPUS OPPORTUNITIES

The Dallas-Fort Worth Metroplex is one of the nation's largest urban areas, with shopping, entertainment venues, five major sports teams, museums and art galleries, and places for outdoor running, biking, hiking and skating. Area attractions include the Fort Worth Stockyards, the Dallas and Fort Worth zoos, Fair Park, the Dallas World Aquarium, the Perot Museum of Nature and Science, the Kimbell and Amon Carter museums and the Dallas Arts District. Major sports teams include the Dallas Cowboys and their $1.2 billion stadium, the Dallas Mavericks, the Dallas Stars, the Texas Rangers and the soccer team FC Dallas. Dallas' vibrant music scene covers the spectrum—rock, jazz, blues, country, classical and more.

To get to all these venues, we offer free DART (Dallas Area Rapid Transit) gold passes to all students, giving unlimited access to buses, light rail and the University's own Comet Cruiser line that runs to local businesses and grocery stores near campus.

ACADEMIC PROGRAMS

The University of Texas at Dallas offers more than 130 academic programs across its seven schools. Undergraduate degrees include:

- Accounting
- Actuarial Science
- American Studies
- Art and Performance
- Arts and Technology
- Biochemistry
- Biology
- Biomedical Engineering
- Business Administration
- Chemistry
- Child Learning and Development
- Cognitive Science
- Computer Engineering
- Computer Science
- Criminology
- Economics
- Electrical Engineering
- Emerging Media and Communication
- Finance
- Geosciences
- Geospatial Information Sciences
- Global Business
- Healthcare Studies
- Historical Studies
- Interdisciplinary Studies
- International Political Economy
- Literary Studies
- Management Information Systems
- Marketing
- Mathematics
- Mechanical Engineering
- Molecular Biology
- Neuroscience
- Physics
- Political Science
- Psychology
- Public Affairs
- Sociology
- Software Engineering
- Speech-Language Pathology and Audiology
- Supply Chain Management
- Telecommunications Engineering

FRESHMAN YEAR EXPERIENCE

To help students with the transition to college life, UT Dallas offers two-day orientation programs that include the option to stay overnight in the Freshman Residence Hall. New students are advised on mastering their courses, meeting new friends and learning about advisors. Freshman Convocation, held the day before fall classes begin, provides an official welcome ceremony for all incoming students.

HONORS PROGRAMS

The University offers a four-year comprehensive program for outstanding students known as Collegium V. Collegium V includes special seminar-style classes offered by selected University professors as well as a program of extracurricular activities designed to encourage and reward exceptional academic achievement. Each of the University's seven schools also offers qualified students the opportunity to participate in an honors program within their discipline.

STUDY ABROAD

As a research-focused university, we help students seeking study abroad opportunities. Faculty and staff actively help students identify and apply for competitive programs with prestigious international universities. Students secure opportunities as varied as their interests. They have worked with an international research team in Ireland studying Lou Gehrig's disease, conducted a study on cognition and depression in Scotland, and collected public policy data in Zimbabwe. Faculty also lead travel study experiences, using the world as their classroom.

CAMPUS FACILITIES AND EQUIPMENT
ATEC

The Edith O'Donnell Arts and Technology Building is a 155,000-square-foot facility which houses programs in arts and technology, visual arts and emerging media and communication, as well as a 1,200-seat lecture hall.

NSERL

The Natural Science and Engineering Research Laboratory (NSERL) includes a nanoelectronics materials laboratory. The four-story, 192,000-square-foot, $8 million state-of-the-art facility draws faculty, graduate students and post-doctoral researchers from all disciplines around the world.

Activity Center

Students are able to work out on the latest equipment and participate in athletics and recreational sports. The university's Activity Center features a gym; racquetball, squash and basketball courts; a rock climbing wall; and a 25-yard indoor swimming pool.

Career Center

The Career Center offers a variety of services for students during all stages of their job search. Licensed professional career counselors provide career assessments and mock interview training. A full-time resume editor helps prepare resumes and cover letters, business communications and personal statements. The center also has career workshops and an online job-search database, and helps students find internships for the summer or school year. Because DFW is one of the nation's busiest and fastest growing business regions, UT Dallas graduates are highly recruited by leading local and national companies and receive prestigious graduate fellowships, scholarships and advanced research opportunities. Nearly all of the Fortune 500 companies headquartered in the DFW area recruit UT Dallas students. More than 84% of a recent UT Dallas graduating class reported employment or continuing education upon graduation. Recent graduates have received job offers from corporations that included Amazon, Citigroup, Exxon Mobil, Hewlett Packard, Merrill Lynch, Microsoft, Texas Instruments and Xerox.

Student Success Center

The Student Success Center is part of the Office of Undergraduate Education and is a portal to educational enhancement and success. Our student success team members make every attempt to help students achieve their academic goals, whether it is through individualized tutoring, peer-led team learning, supplemental instruction or coordinated group study. Services include a math lab, writing center, and testing center. Success coaches help with time management, navigating the University and personalized plans for studying.

TUITION, ROOM, BOARD, AND FEES

Estimated Cost of Attendance 2013-2014°

Per Year	Texas Resident	Out of State
Tuition & Fees	$11,806	$30,378
Books & Supplies	$1,200	$1,200
Room & Board	$9,240	$9,240
Total	$22,246	$40,818

Note: For the most up-to-date numbers, visit utdallas.edu/tuition. For residents of Oklahoma, tuition is the Texas resident rate shown plus $30 per semester credit hour.

FINANCIAL AID

The Financial Aid Office awards scholarships to undergraduate and graduate students based on financial need, residency status and other criteria specific to the scholarship program. UT Dallas participates in all federal and state need-based financial aid programs, including grants, loans and work study.

All first-time college freshman undergraduates are considered for an Academic Excellence Scholarship Award, which range from $3,000 per semester up to complete coverage of tuition and fees.

The Guaranteed Tuition Plan is designed to help new students and their families better plan for the cost of a college education. It gives students a four-year, locked-in rate on up to 15 credit hours per semester.

The Tuition Promise dedicates resources to cover the tuition and mandatory fees for newly enrolling students whose families earn $25,000 or less annually and who meet other specific qualifications.

Transfer students are considered for scholarship awards based on incoming transfer GPA and membership in organizations such as Phi Theta Kappa.

Scholarships offered through private sources are available throughout the academic year. Students apply for these types of scholarships through either a University scholarship committee or the specific donor.

McDermott Scholars, selected from top students across the country, have educational expenses—including tuition and fees, and stipends for living expenses, books, travel and post-graduation preparation—covered for four years. They also participate in a wide variety of cultural and educational enrichment experiences in the Dallas area and beyond.

Terry Scholars are Texas students nominated for their leadership potential and academic ability. The scholarships cover a broad range of student expenses over four years of study, including tuition and fees, housing, books and living expenses. Terry Scholars also have access to a broad range of academic, service, cultural, social and leadership opportunities intended to enhance their undergraduate experience.

STUDENT ORGANIZATIONS AND ACTIVITIES

Student organizations sponsor a variety of activities for the campus including service projects and community outreach. With more than 200 registered student organizations at UT Dallas, it is easy for students to get connected. UT Dallas is also home to 20 national Greek-letter fraternities and sororities, 13 competitive athletic teams, and 25 club sports. The School of Arts and Humanities presents an average of 50 artistic, musical and theatrical events a year. The UT Dallas chess team has won state, national and international titles and regularly represents the University in the Final Four of Chess.

Our students' ideas and visions for the University have become reality. From writing the alma mater and the fight song to founding the Greek System, the cheerleading squad, the Power Dancers and the student radio station, to helping design the freshman residence hall and campus dining facility, our students are making a difference.

ADMISSIONS PROCESS

To apply to UT Dallas, all students should submit an application for admission, which is available at https://www.applytexas.org. Applicants are required to submit official copies of all past academic transcripts, test scores and other degree specific documentation by the appropriate application deadlines to be considered for admission to The University of Texas at Dallas.

Official transcripts in envelopes sealed by the issuing institution may be delivered to the Office of Admission and Enrollment Services, or may be mailed directly from the educational institution. All materials submitted in the process of making application become the property of the University and will not be returned to the applicant.

Students in good standing from an accredited high school who have an SAT of 1200 (combined math and critical reading) or higher, a composite ACT score of 26 or greater or are in the top 15% of their high school class will be admitted to UT Dallas.

APPLICATION FEES AND DEADLINES

All fees are non-refundable.

• The application fee is $50 if your application is submitted on or before the regular application deadline.

• If you submit your application after the application deadline but prior to the Completed Application Deadline (application and all required documents) the application fee is $125 in order to process your application for decision in time to register for classes.

• Applicants with international academic documents will be assessed an additional foreign credential evaluation fee of $50.

• All supporting documents and transcripts, with the exception of courses in progress, must be postmarked by the Completed Application Deadline (see Deadlines for U.S. Citizens and Residents chart below).

• A new application must be completed and submitted for consideration for any subsequent semester for all incomplete applications after the Documentation Questions related to undergraduate admissions should be addressed to:

Office of Admission and Enrollment Services – ROC11
The University of Texas at Dallas
800 West Campbell Road
Richardson, Texas 75080-3021
Telephone (972) 883-2270
Fax (972) 883-2599
Email: interest@utdallas.edu
Website: utdallas.edu

School Says . . .

THE UNIVERSITY OF TULSA

AT A GLANCE

The University of Tulsa (TU) is a private, comprehensive doctoral-degree-granting university that provides education of the highest quality in the arts, humanities, sciences, engineering, business, education, applied health sciences, and law. TU features four undergraduate colleges: the Henry Kendall College of Arts and Sciences, the Collins College of Business, the college of Engineering and Natural Sciences, and the college of Health Sciences, as well as the college of Law and Graduate School.

TU's 11:1 student/faculty ratio, average class size of 20, and emphasis on individual attention anchor an educational culture where students are rigorously challenged and comprehensively supported.

The university is fully accredited by the North Central Association of Colleges and Universities, and is an NCAA Division IA participant in the American Athletic Conference. TU maintains a covenant relationship with the Presbyterian Church (USA).

Extracurricular opportunities include intramural sports, special-interest clubs, pre-professional organizations, national fraternities and sororities, community service organizations, an active student government, departmental honorary organizations, and campus ministry groups.

Total fall 2014 enrollment was 4,682, with 3,473 undergraduates and 1,209 graduate and law students. The ratio of men to women is 57:43 and 18% are multicultural students. Over half the students are from out of state and international students make up about 20 percent of the student population, with 81 countries represented. U.S. News & World Report's 2015 Best Colleges ranks TU among the top 100 doctoral/research national universities.

LOCATION AND ENVIRONMENT

TU's 216-acre residential campus is in Tulsa, Oklahoma (961,561 MSA). The city's prominent industries include energy, telecommunications, high technology, manufacturing, health care, aerospace, and education which present opportunities for internships and employment after graduation. Tulsans enjoy Broadway shows in the Performing Arts Center and pop concerts in the BOK Center (arena) as well as acclaimed ballet and opera companies, symphony, Philbrook Museum, Gilcrease Museum, Brady Arts District, and cultural festivals. Local professional sports include minor league baseball, hockey, WNBA basketball, and arena football. The popular River Parks features jogging and bicycling trails, while Guthrie Green is a popular arts, music, and food truck destination.

OFF-CAMPUS OPPORTUNITIES

The university strongly supports studying abroad, and the Center for Global Education helps students locate the perfect program, whether it is for TU credit or as an intern/volunteer. Students have hundreds of options through direct exchange with an international university, through an affiliate-sponsored program, or as part of a faculty-led course.

Many students take advantage of the of internship opportunities afforded by the city of Tulsa's business and industry community, as well as in the arts, social services and government agencies.

MAJORS AND DEGREES OFFERED

The Kendall College of Arts and Sciences grants the Bachelor of Arts or Bachelor of Science degree in anthropology, art, art history, arts management, Chinese studies, communication, deaf education, economics, elementary education, English, environmental policy, film studies, French, German, history, music, musical theatre, organizational studies, philosophy, political science, psychology, religion, Russian studies, sociology, Spanish, theatre, women's and gender studies, and a self-designed major. Minors include most disciplines as well as advertising, classics, creative writing, dance, early childhood intervention, film scoring, Greek, Latin, and Russian. Secondary teacher certification is available in designated disciplines. Interdisciplinary certificate programs offer a way for students to focus their interests in advertising, African American studies, classics, creative writing, international studies, journalism studies, Judaic studies, legal thought, museum studies, and political philosophy.

The Collins College of Business awards the Bachelor of Science in Business Administration degree in accounting, economics, energy management, finance, management, management information systems, and marketing and a Bachelor of Science in international business and language. Minors are available in most disciplines plus business administration (for non-majors), coaching, healthcare informatics, and international business. Certificate programs are available in accounting, finance, MIS, not-for-profit administration, and sport administration. Management majors may choose specializations in business law, entrepreneurship and family business management, or human resource management. The college is home to several specialized centers, including the Family Owned Business Institute, the Genave King Rogers Center for Business Law, the Williams Risk Management Center, and Studio Blue.

The College of Engineering and Natural Sciences offers the Bachelor of Science degree in applied mathematics, biochemistry, biogeosciences, biological science (options in Pre-Medicine, Pre-Dentistry, and Pre-Veterinary), chemical engineering, chemistry, computer science, computer simulation and gaming, earth and environmental science, electrical engineering, electrical and computer engineering, engineering physics, geology, geophysics, information technology, mathematics, mechanical engineering, petroleum engineering and physics. Minors are available in the science and computational science disciplines. The college features state-of-the-art research facilities, including the Center for Information Security and the Williams Communications Fiber Optic Networking Laboratory. Since 1995, more than 50 TU engineering students were named recipients of the prestigious Barry M. Goldwater Scholarship, the nation's premier award for undergraduate students studying engineering, math, or science.

The College of Health Sciences, TU's newest college, offers the Bachelor of Science degree in athletic training, exercise and sports science, nursing and speech-language pathology. The college, which includes a physician assistant program and houses TU's faculty of Community Medicine, will advance the university's strong partnership with the Laureate Institute for Brain Research.

Master of Arts, Master of Science, Master of Business Administration and Ph.D. degrees are offered in each college through the Graduate School. The college of Law awards the J.D. And L.L.M degrees.

ACADEMIC PROGRAMS

The Tulsa Curriculum links a broad, humanities-based core and writing for all students across all disciplines. TU students can receive a personalized education that is well-rounded. Candidates for graduation must complete at least 124 semester hours of course work.

The Honors Program engages students in a critical examination of the major epochs and ideas of Western thought and culture through careful study of primary texts. A separate application is required. The Tulsa Undergraduate Research Challenge (TURC) program combines advanced research, scholarship, and community service.

TU's Global Scholars Program engages students in global issues from the perspective of their particular major. Students take a set of classes that explore the big questions affecting the world today and participate in monthly programming on campus and an international study, research, or intern experience.

The TU Center for Information Security is developing defenses against cyberterrorist attacks and information warfare. The center supports TU's National Security Agency (NSA)-accredited certificate program in information assurance and a curriculum that integrates information security with computer law and policy issues. TU has been designated a Center of Excellence in Information Assurance by the NSA and is one of six pioneer institutions selected by the National Science Foundation for the Federal Cyber Service Initiative (Cyber Corps).

Air Force ROTC is available through a satellite program.

Students may receive credit through Advanced Placement testing. Depending on their test scores, students who complete the International Baccalaureate diploma can receive up to 30 college credits.

The University of Tulsa operates on a semester calendar. The fall term begins in late August, the spring term in mid January, and the summer session in late May.

CAMPUS FACILITIES AND EQUIPMENT

Since 2002, The University of Tulsa has added one million square feet of building space and a stunning entrance.

The Lorton Performance Center, which houses the School of Music and the Department of Film Studies, features a 700-seat concert hall, specialized rehearsal and practice rooms and a film production suite with post-production editing and scoring capabilities.

In 2012, the college of Engineering & Natural Sciences added J. Newton Rayzor Hall, which features 24 integrated classroom and state-of-the-art teaching/research laboratories. Razor houses the Tandy School of Computer Science and the Department of Electrical and Computer Engineering, while Stephenson Hall is home for the McDougall School of Petroleum Engineering and the Department of Mechanical Engineering. Additional research facilities are located at TU's North Campus where government and industry-funded research consortia foster student learning while exploring innovations and solving petroleum industry problems.

The historic McFarlin Library and the Mabee Legal Information Center house more than 3.6 million items. McFarlin holdings include 920,000 volumes, 40,000 electronic journals, 1,000 print journals, 120,000 electronic books, and more than 1,000 collections of electronic reference sources and databases as well as print resources. McFarlin's Department of Special Collections and University Archives' rare book holdings are internationally recognized, particularly in Native American history and law. The department includes one of the five largest collections in the world on James Joyce, the life archive of Nobel Laureate Sir V.S. Naipaul, and holdings in nineteenth and twentieth century Irish, British, and American Literature. The library's Academic Technology Center annex includes computer labs, a coffee shop, and reading rooms.

Helmerich Hall, which houses the Collins College of Business, was renovated to include innovative learning spaces such as the Williams Student Services Center and Studio Blue. Academic centers include the Schools of Accounting and MIS; Energy Economics, Policy and Commerce and Finance, Operations Management and International Business; as well as the Departments of Economics and Management and Marketing.

The Mary K. Chapman Center for Communicative Disorders, part of the university's new College of Health Sciences, serves the community in its clinical facility and is the learning center for the Department of Communication Disorders. The department has the latest equipment for research, diagnostic, and therapy activities.

Kendall Hall is home to the Departments of Theatre and Musical Theatre and features two fully equipped theatres, a scene shop, costume shop and computer design lab.

Renovated in summer 2014, the Allen Chapman Student Union incudes a food court with nine eateries and a convenience store. It also houses an ATM, offices for student organizations, lecture and meeting rooms, the Faculty Club, post office and the sports grill.

The Donald W. Reynolds Center is TU's arena and convocation center. This facility, home for the intercollegiate basketball and volleyball programs, has cutting-edge facilities for video editing and training.

The Case Athletic Complex is home to the Golden Hurricane football program and adjoins the H.A. Chapman Stadium.

The university's sports and recreation complex features the Collins Fitness Center, Michael Case Tennis Center, track, intramural and NCAA-grade soccer fields, and softball fields.

In partnership with the city of Tulsa, the university manages Gilcrease Museum as well as the Zarrow Center for Art and Education, which provides gallery space, classes and studio space in the city's Brady Arts District.

TU students have the option of hundreds of attractive and convenient on-campus apartments and residence halls.

TUITION, ROOM, BOARD AND FEES

In 2015–16, the typical cost for students living on campus is $50,201 including $38,556 for tuition, $10,630 for room and board, and $1,015 fees. Expenses for books average about $1,200 per year.

FINANCIAL AID

In 2014, 91 percent of entering students received some form of financial aid (including grants, scholarships, work-study, and loans). TU offers a limited number of highly competitive Presidential Scholarships that cover full tuition, room, and board. All applicants may be considered for a range of university scholarships based on academic merit. Performance scholarships are available in music and theater by audition. The University of Tulsa participates in National Merit and National Achievement Scholarship Corporation's Finalist program, and the National Hispanic Scholar Program. Applicants for aid should submit the Free Application for Federal Student Aid (FAFSA) by March 1 for priority consideration.

ADMISSION PROCESS

The University of Tulsa seeks students whose academic background indicates potential for success in the university's rigorous academic environment. Performance in high school college-preparatory subjects and scores on the SAT or ACT are key factors in the admission evaluation, but each applicant is reviewed holistically. The counselor recommendation, extracurricular activities, and indicators of leadership, creativity, and focus are all taken into consideration. Campus visits and interviews are highly recommended.

TU has a non-binding, Early Action freshman admission plan with an application deadline of November 1. Decisions are mailed within five weeks. Applications received after November 1 are reviewed under a Rolling Admission process with notifications made on an ongoing basis after January 1.

An application with a $50 application fee, official high school transcript, ACT or SAT score results, and a guidance counselor recommendation are required of freshman applicants. TU accepts the Common Application or TU's application online, or paper application form. TU adheres to the national Candidate's Reply Date of May 1.

For additional information, students should contact:

The University of Tulsa

Office of Admission

800 South Tucker Drive

Tulsa, Oklahoma 74104-3189

Telephone: 918-631-2307 (in Tulsa), 800-331-3050 (toll-free)

Fax: 918-631-5008

E-mail: admission@utulsa.edu

Web: www.utulsa.edu/admission

VANDERBILT UNIVERSITY

AT A GLANCE

In 1873, on the heels of the Civil War, "Commodore" Cornelius Vanderbilt gave $1 million to the university that now bears his name, with the hope that it would "contribute to strengthening the ties which should exist between all sections of our common country." Since then, Vanderbilt has consistently enrolled America's most talented students and challenged them daily to expand their intellectual horizons in an inclusive environment based on open inquiry and respect. Vanderbilt's comprehensive interdisciplinary approach to education allows students to pursue a wide array of academic and curricular interests outside of their main focus of study, and the university's Opportunity Vanderbilt financial aid program ensures that it is often cited among the country's best values in national universities.

Consistently ranked among the top 20 universities in the country by U.S. News & World Report, Vanderbilt is a private research university that features four undergraduate schools and six graduate and professional schools. Each year, 1,600 first-year students join the university, bringing the total undergraduate population to approximately 6,800 students, many of whom collaborate with professors on cutting-edge research projects and present their findings at professional conferences. The university's 8:1 student-faculty ratio gives students access to faculty members of prominence in every area of academic study. Faculty members provide a challenging, comprehensive education that encourages broad perspectives and critical thinking.

ACADEMICS

Students apply directly to one of Vanderbilt's four undergraduate schools: the college of Arts and Science, School of Engineering, Peabody College of Education and Human Development, or Blair School of Music. In all four schools, honors programs and opportunities for research, independent study, and internships are available. Roughly a third of undergraduate students pursue double majors within and across all four undergraduate schools. This leads to some diverse combinations, such as pre-med students who study Spanish, engineers who study violin, elementary education majors who study communication, and chemistry majors who study art history.

The College of Arts and Science provides many opportunities to experience a wide range of academic disciplines and subjects. Within the requirements of the AXLE (Achieving eXcellence in Liberal Education) curriculum, students refine their skills in writing, mathematics, foreign language, the humanities, natural sciences, social sciences, history, and culture.

The Blair School of Music offers the Bachelor of Music degree in composition, musical arts, musical arts/teacher education, and performance. Instruction is available in every instrument of the orchestra as well as piano, organ, euphonium, multiple woodwinds, saxophone, classical guitar, and voice. Unlike many schools of music, Blair has no graduate students. The curriculum combines intensive musical training with liberal arts studies. The Blair School also offers music minors and a wide variety of courses, private instruction, and performing organizations for non-majors.

For more than 125 years, the School of Engineering has educated engineers for careers in industry, government, consulting, teaching, and research. In addition to technical courses, each student's program includes a complement of course work in the humanities and social sciences, resulting in a balanced foundation for future achievement. All programs leading to a Bachelor of Engineering degree are ABET-accredited, and students can earn the Bachelor of Science degree while majoring in Computer Science or Engineering Science.

Ranked one of the top three graduate school of education (according to U.S. News & World Report) for eight consecutive years, Peabody College offers degree programs leading to teacher certification and to careers in other areas of education and human development, including child development, child studies, cognitive studies, and human and organizational development. The degree reflects a strong liberal arts foundation combined with a solid program of pre-professional courses and a multitude of internship and practicum opportunities. All undergraduates must complete requirements in communications, the humanities, mathematics, the natural sciences, and the social sciences. Students have an abundance of field experiences throughout their four years.

ADMISSIONS

Vanderbilt seeks students with high standards of scholarship and character. Admission is based on a holistic review of academic and personal credentials. The typical applicant will have completed 20 or more units in a challenging high school curriculum, including at least two years of a foreign language. School of Engineering applicants should complete at least four units of mathematics; calculus and physics are strongly recommended.

Generally, applicants who are admitted to Vanderbilt have exceptional academic credentials and are highly engaged in their communities, often serving in leadership roles. Admissions decisions are based on strength of high school transcript, standardized test results (either the SAT Reasoning Test or ACT with Writing), personal essays, official recommendations, and extracurricular activities. SAT Subject Tests are not required. In addition to completing standard application materials, candidates for the Blair School of Music must submit a Blair DecisionDesk Application, which includes a prescreening video. Selected applicants will be invited to audition in person.

Campus visits are recommended, although a student's demonstrated interest in Vanderbilt is not considered in admissions decisions. Students should visit admissions.vanderbilt.edu/visit to learn about group information sessions, campus tours, half- and full-day visit programs, and opportunities to attend classes and to "shadow" a current Vanderbilt student. To visit Vanderbilt without traveling, take the virtual tour at admissions.vanderbilt.edu/tour. Vanderbilt does not conduct on-campus interviews, but optional alumni interviews are available to first-year applicants in many locations.

Students whose first choice is Vanderbilt may apply under one of Vanderbilt's early decision plans. The application deadline is November 1 for Early Decision I and January 1 for Early Decision II; admissions decisions are available by December 15 for Early Decision I and by February 15 for Early Decision II. Regular Decision applications are due January 1 and admissions decisions are available by April 1. To apply, applicants must submit official standardized test scores and all required parts of the Common Application or the Universal College Application, including the School Report (counselor recommendation and official high school transcript), two academic teacher recommendations, and a $50 application fee.

CAMPUS FACILITIES AND EQUIPMENT

Vanderbilt University sits 1.5 miles southwest of downtown Nashville on a 330-acre, park-like campus that was designated a national arboretum in 1988. The university comprises over 200 buildings, including a world-class medical center and the Jean and Alexander Heard Library, home to over 8 million items. Recent additions to campus include The Martha Rivers Ingram Commons, a group of 10 new or newly renovated residence houses designed specifically for first-year students. Seven of these buildings have received the gold LEED (Leadership in Energy and Environmental Design) certification. Additionally, Warren and Moore residential colleges opened in August 2014. Each college houses approximately 330 upperclass students and is led by a faculty director and two graduate fellows in residence.

CAMPUS LIFE

Vanderbilt is recognized for an active campus life, where students balance their academic lives with enriching experiences outside the classroom. Students can select from among 530+ student-run organizations, including pre-professional, cultural, religious, political, recreational, and social clubs. Elected representatives of Vanderbilt Student Government work in conjunction with other student leaders and faculty to bring noted speakers, events, and musicians to campus. Vanderbilt also has a thriving college athletics program. A founding member of the SEC, Vanderbilt sponsors 16 Division I teams. Since 2000, Vanderbilt has claimed 24 individual and team SEC championships, and in 2014, the Vanderbilt baseball team won the College World Series.

LOCATION AND ENVIRONMENT

Vanderbilt is located in the heart of Nashville, home to a diverse population of 1.7 million and marked by its unique blend of cosmopolitan flair and small-town charm. A thriving center of entertainment, publishing, health care, and technology, Nashville is consistently ranked as one of America's friendliest cities and was honored as "The South's Red-Hot Town" by Time in 2014. Nashville sits at the intersection of three major interstates, and the international airport is served by all major airlines.

MAJORS AND DEGREES

College of Arts & Science: African American and Diaspora Studies; American Studies; Anthropology; Art; Asian Studies; Biological Sciences; Chemistry; Cinema and Media Arts; Classical Civilization; Classical Languages; Classics; Communication of Science and Technology; Communication Studies; Earth and Environmental Sciences; Ecology, Evolution, and Organismal Biology; Economics; Economics and History; English; European Studies; French; French and European Studies; German; German and European Studies; History; History of Art; Italian and European Studies; Jewish Studies; Latin American Studies; Latino and Latina Studies; Mathematics; Medicine, Health, and Society; Molecular and Cellular Biology; Neuroscience; Philosophy; Physics; Political Science; Psychology; Public Policy Studies; Religious Studies; Russian; Russian and European Studies; Sociology; Spanish; Spanish and European Studies; Spanish and Portuguese; Spanish, Portuguese, and European Studies; Theater; Women's and Gender Studies; and individually-designed, unique interdisciplinary majors.

Blair School of Music: Composition; Musical Arts; Musical Arts/Teacher Education; and Performance

School of Engineering: Biomedical Engineering; Chemical Engineering; Civil Engineering; Computer Engineering; Computer Science; Electrical Engineering; Engineering Science; and Mechanical Engineering

Peabody College of Education and Human Development: Child Development; Child Studies; Cognitive Studies; Early Childhood Education; Elementary Education; Human and Organizational Development; Secondary Education; and Special Education

Graduate/Professional Schools: Divinity School; The Graduate School; Law School; Owen Graduate School of Management; School of Medicine; and School of Nursing

Pre-professional advising is available for students interested in pursuing graduate degrees in architecture, business, law, and medicine.

OFF-CAMPUS OPPORTUNITIES

Study abroad programs allow students to immerse themselves in languages and cultures around the world. More than 125 programs are offered in Argentina, Australia, Austria, Chile, China, Costa Rica, the Czech Republic, Denmark, the Dominican Republic, Egypt, England, France, Germany, Israel, Italy, Japan, Russia, Singapore, South Africa, and Spain, among others. Students receive direct credit for courses, and the cost of tuition is usually the same as for study on campus in Nashville. In addition, any scholarships, grants, or loans a student has been awarded apply to Vanderbilt study abroad programs. Students may also participate in programs sponsored by other universities by working with an adviser.

Students also take advantage of internships in many industries located in Nashville, including entertainment, business, health care, government, publishing, and education.

FINANCIAL AID

Through Opportunity Vanderbilt, the university makes three important commitments to ensure that students from many different economic circumstances can enroll as undergraduates at Vanderbilt: the admissions process is need-blind for all U.S. citizens and eligible non-citizens; Vanderbilt meets 100 percent of demonstrated need for all admitted students; and Vanderbilt's financial aid packages do not include loans. These three commitments combined place Vanderbilt among a small number of universities to adopt such progressive policies.

In the 2014–2015 school year, 65 percent of the University's undergraduate students received some type of financial assistance. Need-based aid is awarded according to the evaluation of the FAFSA and the CSS/Financial Aid PROFILE.

Vanderbilt also awards merit-based scholarships to select first-year applicants who demonstrate exceptional accomplishment and intellectual promise. Three signature scholarship programs comprise the majority of these merit scholarships: the Ingram Scholarship Program (for students who plan to combine a professional or business career with an exceptional commitment to community service), the Cornelius Vanderbilt Scholarship Program (for students who combine outstanding academic achievements with strong leadership and contributions outside the classroom), and the Chancellor's Scholarship Program (for students who have worked to build strong high school communities by bridging gaps among economically, culturally, and racially diverse groups). All three programs require a separate application in addition to the application for admission.

TUITION AND FEES

The estimated costs for 2015–2016 include: tuition, $43,620; housing, $9,580; meals, $5,090; books and supplies, $1,370; student activities and recreation fee, $1,092; personal expenses allowance, $2,780; travel allowance varies; first-year experience fee, $718; new student transcript fee, $30; engineering lab fee°, $650; and engineering laptop allowance°, $1,500 °The engineering laptop allowance and laboratory fee are for engineering students only. First-year engineering students are required to provide their own computer that meets published requirements.

VAUGHN COLLEGE OF AERONAUTICS AND TECHNOLOGY

AT A GLANCE

Located in New York City, Vaughn College of Aeronautics and Technology is a private, four-year college committed to providing its students with the excellent education and skills needed to achieve professional success in engineering, technology, management and aviation. Founded in 1932, the college, adjacent to LaGuardia Airport, is a small, high-quality institution where students can experience personal attention as they progress through academic course work. The college offer master's, bachelor's and associate degree programs in engineering, technology, management and aviation and fosters a culture of excellence in rigorous degree, professional, technical, and certification programs. These programs incorporate the latest technology and meet the universal needs of the industries they serve. The result is well-educated graduates who are successful in their fields. The college's student body of more than 1,700 and its low, 15:1 student-faculty ratio ensure a highly personalized learning environment. More than 92 percent of Vaughn College graduates are employed or continue their educations within one year of obtaining their degrees, and they work in twenty countries and all fifty states. Vaughn College is also committed to making education affordable for students. Vaughn's reasonable tuition can be an important consideration in your decision-making process.

In recent years, opportunities generated by technology have crossed all segments of American industry. There is a high demand for jobs in electronics, engineering firms, computer software companies, fiber-optics communication corporations, local, state and federal government, defense and airport authorities as well as major transportation companies. Recent graduates have pursued advanced degrees at such institutions as Columbia, Stony Brook and Texas A&M, or landed positions at well-known organizations such as Lockheed Martin, The Port Authority of New York and New Jersey, United Technologies, Consolidated Edison, Embraer and JetBlue Airways. Vaughn's master's degree in airport management is uniquely targeted to an industry that contributes significantly to the regional economy.

ACADEMICS

All students in associate and baccalaureate degree programs complete a core curriculum as part of their degree requirements. The core curriculum is derived from the mission of the college and reflects what the institution believes is important and elementary to students' education and development. In general, the core instills in students critical-thinking skills, values appropriate to an educated person and the ability to communicate. It also provides context for advanced learning. The baccalaureate core consists of three components: academic seminars (2 credits, the freshman year workshop), the liberal arts (21 credits, including a year of world and American literature), and math and science (16 credits).

For the fifth year in a row, Vaughn's curriculum, faculty and overall academic reputation earned it a place in U.S. News and World Report's survey of the best regional colleges in the North. The college was also ranked fifth in the same category in the publication's inaugural Best Colleges for Veterans rankings.

ADMISSIONS

Vaughn College offers equal educational opportunity to all students without regard to age, citizenship status, color, disability, marital status, national origin, race, religion, creed, veteran status, gender or sexual orientation. High school graduates must submit a completed application (available online at www.vaughn.edu); the $40 application fee; SAT or ACT scores; an official copy of the high school transcript and any college transcripts (if applicable); a copy of the high school diploma (or GED), complete with scores; and immunization records. Some students may need to take a placement exam, while flight operations applicants must pass the FAA Class III physical examination. An interview with an admissions counselor and a financial aid counselor is required for all flight operations applicants and recommended for all others.

Students who have lived in the United States for less than three years and for whom English is a second language, or international applicants from countries where English is not an official language, can substitute results of the TOEFL exam. Students who have completed 24 or more college credits are exempt from the SAT/ACT requirement.

The admissions counseling staff is available to advise applicants and their parents and to provide up-to-date advisement material to high school guidance offices. The admissions office reviews applications on a rolling basis. All applicants are encouraged to file by March 1 for the fall semester and November 15 for the spring semester to best take advantage of scholarship opportunities. For more information, contact the office of admissions at 1.866.6VAUGHN, ext. 118.

CAMPUS FACILITIES AND EQUIPMENT

Each laboratory provides the work/study environment suited to the requirements of each program. This practical, hands-on experience helps qualify students for immediate employment upon graduation. From the new mechatronics laboratory to the CATIA/NASTRAN computer center, the college is committed to providing students with the knowledge and tools they are likely to find in today's businesses. The college's $1-million flight simulator center features Frasca 142 and 241 simulators, a Canadair regional jet trainer, and two Redbird simulators. The addition of a new air traffic control laboratory with radar and tower components complements the $1 million flight simulator laboratory to support students in their pursuit of a career in flight or air traffic control. Our partnership with Heritage Flight Academy enables students to pursue Federal Aviation Administration (FAA) flight certifications and ratings on Long Island, NY.

The College has substantially upgraded its technology environment over the past few years. Students have access to more than 200 computers in classrooms and labs, providing software applications for desktop publishing, word processing, spreadsheets, databases, and shared printing services. These computers also afford students the opportunity to interact with industry-leading applications used within their academic programs, including CATIA, SolidWorks, Nastran and Patran. The college's recently created student portal provides online access to tools that enhance and support academic efforts. All of Vaughn's classrooms have updated instructional technologies, including projection, and Internet connectivity to classrooms and labs. Wireless access exists across campus, including within the residential facilities, and each student is provided a vaughn.edu e-mail address. Identification cards provide students with access to secured facilities, laundry payment, dining services, library access, vending and purchasing options, and more.

The College's library offers extensive general, technical, resource, and periodical material totaling more than 125,000 volumes. The real and virtual resources include books, periodicals, videos, and research databases. The video collection consists of subject videos to support the college's curriculum, general-interest videos, and movies. The library houses VHS tapes and DVDs and its research databases contain more than 8,000 full-text periodicals and newspapers. Ten personal computers are available for student use in the reference area.

Vaughn's new library and teaching and learning center opened in fall 2014. The new library provides students and faculty with a one-stop location for research materials, academic support services and technology support. Its construction was part of a nearly $40 million campus renovation investment.

CAMPUS LIFE

Vaughn recognizes that the college experience also takes place outside the classroom. The college's residence hall features panoramic views of Manhattan and a staff eager to help students take advantage of all that New York City has to offer. An array of clubs and organizations exist, including the Robotics Club, American Association of Airport Executives–Student Chapter and Women in Aviation-International. Vaughn also offers competes in the Hudson Valley Intercollegiate Athletic Conference (HVIAC). And, as of the 2014–2015 fiscal year, Vaughn College became a member of the United States Collegiate Athletic Association, which allows athletics teams to compete on a national level. The eight intercollegiate sports programs are men's and women's basketball, men's soccer, men's and women's cross country, and men's and women's tennis and men's baseball.

LOCATION AND ENVIRONMENT

Located in New York City, the college offers numerous internship opportunities with an array of technology, manufacturing, and aviation companies. The cultural, spiritual, and physical needs of the students are met by the outstanding facilities of New York City. Restaurants are easily accessible, and hospitals and other medical facilities are among the best in the world. New York City's legendary museums focus on arts, natural history, science, and world civilization.

MAJORS AND DEGREES

The College awards the Associate of Applied Science (A.A.S.) degree in aeronautical engineering technology, airport management, aviation maintenance, animation and digital technologies, electronic engineering technology—avionics, and flight.

The Bachelor of Science (B.S.) degree is available in general management, airline management, airport management, aeronautical sciences, aviation maintenance, aviation maintenance management, electronic engineering technology–avionics, electronic engineering technology–general electronics, flight, mechatronics engineering, mechanical engineering, mechanical engineering technology–aeronautical option, and mechanical engineering technology—computer-aided design option. A nondegree course of study in air traffic control, is also available. There is also an aircraft dispatch program offered.

OFF-CAMPUS OPPORTUNITIES

Internships are an important part of a student's learning experience at Vaughn College, and they have led to job offers upon graduation. The department of career services and faculty chairs arrange for internships with top U.S. corporations. As a federally designated Hispanic-serving institution, the college participates with the Hispanic Association of Colleges and Universities (HACU) to place students in internships with various federal agencies year-round. Other active internships and cooperatives include the Boeing Company, Federal Aviation Administration (FAA), Federal Express, Global Air Dispatch, HACU, JetBlue, Lockheed Martin, the Metropolitan Transportation Authority (MTA), the National Broadcasting Company, the Northrop Grumman Corporation, Northwest Airlines, ORBIS, the Port Authority of New York and New Jersey, and Teterboro Airport.

STUDENT ORGANIZATIONS AND ACTIVITIES

Vaughn College supports a variety of student organizations. Activities are moderated by members of the faculty and staff. The Student Government Association (SGA) is primarily concerned with the quality of student life on campus. SGA carries the concerns of its constituency, the student body, to the administration and is the voice of the student body. Serving students as the liaison to the administration, SGA coordinates social programming and provides a system for cocurricular involvement through many clubs and organizations. SGA meets on a regular basis and encourages all students to attend meetings and become involved.

TUITION, ROOM, BOARD AND FEES

The 2014–15, full-time tuition (12 to 18 credits per semester) was $10,420. Students taking 12-18 credits or fewer paid $700 per credit. The semester fee, which covers the cost of orientation courses, Internet and computer usage, and student-support services, activities, and leadership programs, was $200.

For the 2014–15 academic year, rooms in Vaughn's four-year-old residence hall cost $4,982 for a double room and $5,712 for a single room, per semester. A $250 housing deposit is required. Residents live in either a two-person or a four-person suite with a semi-private bath. The residence hall has laundry, study, and kitchen facilities in a common area within the building. Residence hall rooms are supplied with a bed, dresser, closet, desk, chair, and wastebasket for each student. Each room is also equipped with phone and cable TV hookup and computer port.

FINANCIAL AID

Vaughn College offers federal, state, and institutional funds to help students pay for their education. Ninety percent of students are eligible for some type of financial aid. The first step is to file the Free Application for Federal Student Aid (FAFSA) and, if appropriate, the New York State Tuition Assistance Program (TAP) application. Applications for the fall semester should be filed by March 1. The college recognizes academic excellence by awarding scholarships to high-achieving students pursuing Bachelor of Science degree programs. Applicants must file the FAFSA to be eligible.

Awards for new students include Founders' Scholarships, which are merit-based and range from $500 to $15,000 per year, and the need-based Vaughn College financial grants, which range from $250 to $2,200.

Financial aid is determined by a variety of factors, including income, assets, family size and other family information. Each applicant has unique circumstances and the financial aid office is committed to helping students and their parents through the process. It is strongly recommended that students file for financial assistance as early in the year prior to enrollment as possible.

Financial aid eligibility requires that the student maintain satisfactory academic progress and program pursuit after enrolling.

WASHINGTON COLLEGE

AT A GLANCE

The first college chartered in the new nation, Washington College was founded in 1782 to cultivate responsible, educated citizen-leaders who could nurture the new democracy. Today, the ideals of that founding purpose hold true. The college's rich history helps distinguish it among the nation's selective liberal arts colleges: General George Washington lent his name, donated 50 guineas to our founding, and served on our first Board of Visitors and Governors. His examples of citizenship and leadership continue to shape our traditions and our high expectations for our students.

We believe that a broad, general education in the liberal arts—one shaped by personal relationships with professors and classmates in a supportive residential community—is not only mentally liberating but also the most effective way to prepare for a successful career and a meaningful life. In your first two years on campus, we will encourage you to explore many interests, examine different perspectives, and challenge old ways of thinking. We also will invite you to pursue creative endeavors, athletic competition, recreational activities, and leadership roles.

LOCATION AND ENVIRONMENT

Located in Chestertown, Md., our 120-acre campus breathes history, natural beauty, and rural charm, yet it's only 75 miles from the urban hubs of Washington, D.C., Baltimore, and Philadelphia. This proximity brings our students a wealth of distinguished speakers, intern opportunities, institutional partnerships, and other occasions for academic and cultural enrichment. That said, we also take full advantage of our setting in a historic river town close by the Chesapeake Bay. The Eastern Shore becomes an extension of the campus—a learning laboratory for intellectual, social, and personal growth.

Historic Chestertown is rooted in a strong sense of self and a diverse and creative local character. You'll experience this through events like First Fridays, when downtown reverts once a month to one big street party; the Farmers' Market on Saturdays, loaded with goods showcasing the region's rich agrarian culture; and at venues like the Garfield Center for the Arts in the beautifully restored Prince Theatre.

The Chester River meets the town at the foot of High Street. At its riverfront facility, just blocks from the main campus, the college maintains a variety of vessels that support coursework in underwater archaeology, marine and estuarine biology, environmental chemistry, and environmental studies. The college also supports nationally ranked programs in rowing and sailing.

ACADEMIC ENRICHMENT

With a student body of 1,500 undergraduates, the college's deliberately small size celebrates the interaction between student and professor. The average class size is 17 students; only one class in seven will have more than 25 students enrolled. Faculty members challenge and nurture a student's maturing intellect and creativity with collaborative research, independent and self-directed study, and a rigorous senior "capstone" project.

Washington College is recognized for its rich literary arts environment. The Rose O'Neill Literary House hosts a steady stream of significant writers and editors supported by the Sophie Kerr Program, and each year, one graduating senior is awarded the Sophie Kerr Prize, the largest undergraduate literary award in the world (the 2013 winner took home $61,000). The college is committed to helping all students become stronger writers. Writing-intensive courses across disciplines and majors help students cultivate proficiency in the language arts.

Two centers of special research and programming, The C.V. Starr Center for the Study of the American Experience and the Center for Environment & Society, take advantage of the region's history, rural and maritime cultures, and natural resources. The Chesapeake Semester, offered through the Center for Environment & Society, uses the nation's largest estuary as a classroom and then connects those studies globally with a trip to Peru. Based on the Chesapeake Semester's successful model, the CES in 2014 initiated the Puget Sound Summer Program.

The Douglass Cater Society of Junior Fellows is our flagship academic enrichment program, rewarding initiative and intellectual curiosity with competitive grants to support self-directed undergraduate research, internships, and scholarship anywhere in the world. Another important academic opportunity, the Presidential Fellows program, puts high-achieving freshmen on the fast track to academic distinction, including the chance to work with full Cater Fellows as an apprentice.

Washington College offers a growing array of internships and field experiences, as we believe that hands-on education outside of the classroom best prepares students for their careers. Among them are: The Comegys Bight Fellowships, which place students in paid summer internships at prestigious institutions including the Library of Congress, National Constitution Center, and the Smithsonian American Art Museum; the Alex. Brown Fund, which enables students to manage an equities portfolio of $500,000; the Washington to Wall Street Program, which uses the college's strong alumni network to offer internships to students pursuing careers in business or the financial sector (100 percent of those who participated in 2013's inaugural program are in graduate school or employed in the field); the John S. Toll Science Fellows and Hodson Science Fellows programs, which enable students to conduct in-depth research with faculty while earning a stipend and a housing allowance; the Summer Archaeology Field School, in which students conduct digs at area sites, bringing artifacts back to the school's Archaeology Lab for further study; the celebrated Kiplin Hall Program offered through the English department, which takes students to England, Ireland, and Scotland to study Romantic poets and writers while hiking and traveling through the world that inspired them; and the biology department's Maine Summer Program, in which students spend two weeks earning four credits while studying the diverse ecology of Acadia National Park in Mt. Desert Island, Maine.

Washington College also offers an extensive study abroad program. With 28 partner institutions for semester and academic-year study abroad, and up to ten short-term programs led by College faculty, the programs traverse 24 countries, including South Africa, Australia, Ecuador, and the United Kingdom.

MAJORS AND DEGREES OFFERED

We believe that a liberal arts education gives students the strongest set of lifelong skills to never stop exploring the world. More than 40 areas of study allow you to investigate a wide variety of possibilities and combinations that will lead to a bachelor of arts or a bachelor of science. You will choose a major (or two) at the end of sophomore year.

American Studies
Anthropology
    Archaeology
Art and Art History
Biology
    Biochemistry
Black Studies
Business Management
    Accounting and Finance
Chemistry
Chesapeake Regional Studies
Creative Writing
Dance
Drama
Earth and Planetary Science
Economics
Engineering
English
Environmental Science and Studies
Gender Studies
History
Human Development
    Secondary Education Studies
    Teacher Certification
Information Systems
International Literature and Culture
International Studies
    African Studies
    Asian Studies
    European Studies
    Latin American Studies
    Near Eastern Studies

Global Business Studies
 Peace and Conflict Studies
Justice, Law and Society
Mathematics and Computer Science
Modern Languages
 French Studies
 German Studies
 Hispanic Studies
 Other Courses/Languages
Music
Nursing
Pharmacy
Philosophy and Religion
Physics
Political Science
Pre-Law
Premedical
 Pre-veterinary
 Pre-dentistry
 Pre-optometry
 Pre-podiatry
 Osteopathy
Psychology
 Clinical Counseling
 Behavioral Neuroscience
Sociology

CAMPUS FACILITIES

Our beautiful campus is a collection of historic redbrick, Georgian-style structures, large shade trees, and brick walkways, seamlessly combined with new and renovated buildings featuring expanses of glass that create modern spaces flooded with light. The oldest buildings, the Hill Dorms, were built in the mid-nineteenth century; the newest, the $2.1 million Johnson Fitness Center, opened in 2013.

The Gibson Center for the Arts, opened in August 2009, is a glittering showcase where students can learn, rehearse, practice, perform, and exhibit their work. The $24 million facility encompasses a main stage, an experimental theater, a music recital hall, and an art gallery, as well as all the latest tools and technology to support professional theater, concerts, and exhibitions.

Opened in fall 2009, Hodson Hall Commons includes the main dining hall, a student lounge, an intimate space for meetings and performances, and several specialty eateries.

The Chester and Sassafras residence halls, completed in Summer 2008, were the first buildings on campus to incorporate geothermal heating and cooling. A major renovation of the campus library in 2012 included a geothermal system along with a new coffee shop and popular group-study rooms.

According to Lacrosse Magazine, our Roy Kirby, Jr. Stadium is among the top ten venues for collegiate lacrosse in the nation. The stadium, completed in 2008, is the only Division III venue to make the cut. In 2009, Athey Park, the college's baseball park, was built to mirror Kirby Stadium.

Advances in technology are incorporated throughout the curriculum, from sequencing DNA in the lab to accessing primary sources for a Shakespeare project via the library's Early English Books Online database. Other examples include the new mass spectrometry lab, used for environmental chemistry, geology, and biology research; side-scan sonar, sub-bottom profilers, remotely operated vehicles (ROVs), and marine magnetometers to explore below the surface of the Chester River; and eye-scanning and brain-mapping technology the psychology department uses to test cognitive function.

TUITION, ROOM, BOARD AND FEES

Basic educational fees for 2015–2016

Tuition (full-time)	$42,844
Student Service Fee	$756
Student Health Fee	$250
Campus Housing	$5,390
Meal Plans per year	
19/week	$5,222

FINANCIAL AID

Washington College is committed to providing educational excellence and equity for all students; 85% of our students receive need-based financial aid and/or merit-based scholarships. We develop financial packages that include tuition scholarships, tuition grants, work/study, and low-interest loans, in addition to federal, state, and independent aid programs for eligible students. With the investment of funds for scholarships and grants from donors and benefactors, the college provides more than $20 million annually in scholarships and grants to help make it possible for students to get an education here. More than 50% of all Washington College students qualify for merit-based tuition scholarships averaging from $11,000 to $21,000 per year.

STUDENT ORGANIZATIONS AND ACTIVITIES

We cherish our residential tradition because it brings constant opportunities for academic, social, and personal growth. We may be a small campus, but Washington College supports more than 80 clubs, from the nationally recognized Habitat for Humanity Club to wakeboarding, sailing, and entrepreneurial activism through Enactus.

A Division III member of the NCAA, the college fields 17 intercollegiate teams that compete in the Centennial Conference. About 25% of students are varsity athletes, while 60% of students participate in sports including clubs and intramurals. The Student Events Board creates a variety of activities that everyone on campus can enjoy, from festivals and quiz nights to the semi-formal George Washington's Birthday Ball. While students reap the benefits of living in one of the best small college towns on the East Coast and the relaxed informality characteristic of the Chesapeake Bay region, they also take advantage of the campus's proximity to Washington, D.C, Baltimore, and Philadelphia.

ADMISSIONS PROCESS

Washington College is a selective institution. In order to assess an applicant's "fit" with the college, the Admission Committee requires the submission of all relevant academic records and test scores, an activity profile, an essay/personal statement, and a letter of recommendation. In some cases, an on-campus interview may also be required.

Prospective applicants are strongly encouraged to come to campus for an information session and tour. These visits should be scheduled in advance by calling 410-778-7700 or visiting washcoll.edu/admissions.

Prospective students may apply online using the Common Application or via washcoll.edu/apply. Application deadlines are: November 15 for early decision; December 1 for early action; February 15 for regular decision.

Admitted applicants must pay a $700.00 enrollment deposit by May 1. For details, visit www.washcoll.edu/admissions.

WELLS COLLEGE

AT A GLANCE

Wells College is a coeducational, private, liberal arts college enrolling 551 students from across the United States and throughout the world. Today, true to its heritage, Wells maintains a national reputation for academic excellence. The college prides itself on offering one of the most collaborative learning environments in higher education today. The top five reasons to consider Wells: (1) Wells offers students a personal role in shaping their education: the average class size is 13 and professors know students by name; (2) 85% of Wells faculty members have doctoral degrees and all classes are taught by professors—not teaching assistants; (3) Wells students prepare for careers and entrance into top graduate and professional schools through experiential learning: internships, research with faculty members, and community service; (4) Wells offers an extensive study abroad program with affiliated programs in 17 different countries; (5) All students at Wells benefit from an academic experience similar to honors programs available only to a small number of students at other institutions. Throughout their four years, they work toward a senior thesis that is comparable to graduate-level study. Wells prides itself on offering one of the most collaborative learning environments in higher education.

ACADEMICS

The Wells experience is deeply personal and intensely focused on superior academic achievement. Wells offers more than 20 majors and nearly 50 minors. With one professor for every ten students, professors really get to know each student. The average class size has thirteen students and is taught seminar-style, with discussions taking precedence over lectures. Fundamental to the Wells curriculum is an interdisciplinary approach to the liberal arts with the opportunity to experience hands-on work and innovative teaching methods. Through the Wells experiential learning program, students have opportunities to participate in quality internships, off campus study programs around the world, and academic research projects tailored to individual interests and goals. Experiential learning in the curriculum enables students to apply principles learned in the classroom to real-life situations in professional organizations.

ADMISSIONS

Wells students are intellectually curious, open-minded, and creative. They are comfortable expressing themselves, listening to others and sharing ideas. They are caring citizens of the world, eager to travel beyond the campus. Wells students love to learn. If you love learning, you will love the Wells experience.

Candidates for admission are expected to complete a solid college preparatory program throughout their four years in secondary school. The college recommends a program which provides the best background for study at Wells, including four years of English grammar, composition, and literature; four years of history; three years of mathematics; two years of laboratory science; and coursework in a foreign language. Student records are enhanced by the addition of courses such as computer science, art, and music, when appropriate curricular choices are offered. To apply for admission to Wells College candidates must submit completed application forms to the Admissions Office by March 1 of the year of entrance.

In addition, the following credentials are required: a transcript of all secondary school work, including the recommendation of the high school principal or school counselor; scores from either the college Entrance Examination Board Scholastic Aptitude Test (SAT I) or the American College Testing Program (ACT); two letters of recommendation from teachers in academic subject areas. A personal interview is recommended.

ADMISSIONS DEADLINE OPTIONS:

Early Decision. December 15: Students whose first choice is Wells College are encouraged to apply under the early decision option. This is a binding admissions option; if admitted; early decision applicants agree to accept Wells offer of admission and agree to withdraw their applications from all other colleges.

Early Action. December 15: Students who would like to receive an early review of their application files are encouraged to apply under the early action option. This is a non-binding admissions option.

Regular Admission. March 1: All other applications to the college should be received by the regular admission deadline. Applications are reviewed after this date and decisions are mailed by April 1.

CAMPUS LIFE

Wells students enjoy all of the advantages of living in a closely-knit community. A well-respected Honor Code shapes the educational and social atmosphere of the campus. Wells supports more than 30 clubs and organizations including a literary journal and social issues magazine, music and drama groups, and political and cultural organizations, in addition to student-sponsored events, lectures, and performances. Wells is also a member of Division III NCAA. Wells women compete in eight intercollegiate sports: cross country, field hockey, tennis, lacrosse, soccer, basketball, volleyball and swimming. Wells men compete in six intercollegiate sports: basketball, cross country, lacrosse, soccer, volleyball and swimming. Wells campus also has a nine-hole golf course and canoes, kayaks and sailboats available for seasonal student use.

LOCATION AND ENVIRONMENT

The beautiful 300-acre lakeside campus is situated in the heart of the Finger Lakes Region of New York State, located in the historical village of Aurora on Cayuga Lake. Students enjoy phenomenal views and access to our campus boathouse. The campus is 30 minutes from Ithaca, one hour from Syracuse and Rochester, and approximately five hours from New York City.

MAJORS AND DEGREES

Wells College offers the Bachelor of Arts degree with majors in the following areas (concentrations within the majors appear in parentheses): Biochemistry and Molecular Biology; Biology; Chemistry; Computer Science; Economics and Management (Economics, Management); English (Creative Writing, Literature); Environmental Science; Film and Media Studies; History; International Studies; Mathematics; Philosophy; Physics; Political Science; Psychology; Sociology and Anthropology; Spanish; Theatre and Dance; Visual Arts (Art History, Book Arts, Studio Art); and Women's and Gender Studies. In consultation with the dean and faculty, students may also design their own concentrations and majors. In addition, Wells offers programs that lead to provisional certification in elementary and secondary education.

TUITION AND FEES

For the 2015–2016 year: Tuition: $37,500; Room and board: $13,000; Fees: $1,500

WENTWORTH INSTITUTE OF TECHNOLOGY

AT A GLANCE

Founded in 1904, Wentworth Institute of Technology is an independent, co-educational, nationally-ranked institution offering career-focused education through 19 bachelor's degree programs in areas such as applied mathematics, architecture, business management, computer science and networking, construction management, design, engineering, and engineering technology. The Institute also offers master's degrees in architecture, construction management, and facility management.

A leader in engineering, technology, design and management education, Wentworth's unique three-part experiential learning model combines class work, laboratory/studio work, and cooperative education (co-op) experience to provide students with a hands-on approach to learning. The co-op program, one of the largest and most comprehensive of its kind in the nation, has been active for more than 35 years and provides Wentworth students the ability to gain the professional work experience needed to succeed in their field. Wentworth is well-known for its academic excellence, community service, and support for the economic growth of the region. For more information, please visit www.wit.edu.

Additionally, Wentworth is a member of one of Boston's largest academic collaborations, the colleges of the Fenway consortium, which is an association of six Fenway area institutions including Emmanuel College, Massachusetts College of Art and Design, Massachusetts College of Pharmacy and Health Sciences University, Simmons College, Wentworth Institute of Technology, and Wheelock College.

LOCATION AND ENVIRONMENT

Small school benefits, big city resources.

This private, coeducational college is located on 31 acres in the heart of Boston. With over students, it provides the friendliness of a small school, alongside the resources and excitement of the ultimate college town.

When it comes to college towns, there is no place more exciting or full of more opportunities than Boston. The original center of higher education in the U.S., it hosts 50 colleges and universities and draws a quarter of a million students every year, with nearly 20,000 of those students coming from outside the country. Boston is a city with exceptional character. In addition to its rich history, it's also a hub for technology, business and medicine - giving Wentworth students access to educational and career opportunities they would not find elsewhere.

OFF-CAMPUS OPPORTUNITIES

At Wentworth, building professional, paid work experience into the academic program is a priority. Co-op has been a fundamental part of our curriculum for over 35 years, and ours is one of the largest and most comprehensive programs of its kind in the nation. All full-time day bachelor's degree candidates must complete two semesters of co-op, beginning after the first two years of study.

Wentworth's Office of Career Services assists students every step of the way, as they take advantage of opportunities in Boston, in other areas of the US, and abroad.

MAJORS AND DEGREES OFFERED

-Applied Mathematics (three-year program with a four-year option)

- Architecture

-Business Management

-Biomedical Engineering

-Civil Engineering

-Computer Engineering

-Computer Engineering Technology

-Computer Information Systems

-Computer Networking

-Computer Science

-Construction Management

-Electrical Engineering

-Electromechanical Engineering (five-year program)

-Electronic Engineering

-Engineering

-Facility Planning & Management

-Industrial Design

-Interior Design

-Mechanical Engineering

ACADEMIC PROGRAMS

A leader in technology education for over a century, Wentworth offers bachelor's degrees in 19 practical, career-oriented majors. All programs center on Wentworth's distinctive three part experiential learning model, which incorporates classes, labs and studios, and co-op.

As Wentworth is a member of the colleges of the Fenway, students can cross-register for one course each semester at the participating colleges (Emmanuel, Simmons, and Wheelock Colleges, the Massachusetts College of Art and Design, and the Massachusetts College of Pharmacy and Health Sciences University).

CAMPUS FACILITIES AND EQUIPMENT

The Wentworth campus is well-appointed to deliver the top-notch education and living conditions demanded by today's students. Our modernized laboratories are at the vanguard of technology; the equipment mirrors that found in the leading employers in industry. The Institute has spent millions of dollars to upgrade its information technology infrastructure. And the facilities for sleeping are just as impressive as the ones for studying. The Institute operates six residence halls—Evans Way/Tudbury Hall, Edwards/Rodgers Hall, Baker Hall, Louis Prang Apartments, 610 Huntington Avenue, and 555 Huntington Avenue. The Apartments at 525 Huntington Avenue, a brand new residence hall will open Fall 2014.

Whether you're looking for state-of-the-art computing resources, healthcare you can rely on, or one of any of a number of other services that make campus life better, you can rest assured that Wentworth is working hard to meet your needs.

The Flanagan Campus Center is the hub of student life at Wentworth. The campus center is home to the bookstore, the cafeteria, the Schuman Fitness Center. The Intercultural Center, Wentworth Internet Radio Experience (WIRE), a recreation room, study areas, and the Office of Campus Life.

The Learning Center and The Writing Center provide students with academic support services such as peer and faculty tutoring, computer-based tutorials, and subject study groups. We are dedicated to preparing students for academic success.

Wentworth is committed to helping you make the best use of computers. We offer a range of computing resources including: a wireless campus; labs equipped with the latest hardware and software; and a full-time Office of Information Technology. The result is a highly connected academic and social community where advanced computing is accessible and convenient.

Wentworth subscribes to the policies set forth in the Americans with Disabilities Act and in Section 504 of the Federal Rehabilitation Act of 1973, which mandate equal opportunity in educational programs and activities for students with disabilities.

At Wentworth, we work hard to provide the very best health services. In addition to expert primary medical care, we also offer specialized services including counseling, disability services and comprehensive health education.

In order to make the transition for international students as smooth as possible, Wentworth employs a full-time international student advisor who has extensive experience with international students, and assists them in their personal, social and academic adjustment to Wentworth and the U.S..

Conveniently located at the center of campus, the Wentworth Alumni Library is a valuable resource. The online catalogue includes the holdings of nine other libraries – all available for use by Wentworth students. And, membership in the 14-institution Fenway Library Consortium provides access to more than 2,900,000 volumes and 13,000 periodical titles. Various services are also available through the Alumni Library.

TUITION, ROOM, BOARD AND FEES

Tuition for full-time students (12-20 credits) for 2014–2015 is $29,320per year. Tuition includes the cost of a laptop computer. Laptops are provided to each student along with the specific software required for their major.

The per credit charge (less than 12 and over 20) is $915 per credit.

Room and Board is approximately $12,840 per year.

Health Insurance, required by Commonwealth of Massachusetts is approximately $1,250 per year (can be waived if student is covered by parent's health insurance). (TBD, 2013–2014 amount was $1,250)

FINANCIAL AID

We are dedicated to helping you to create a financial plan that allows you and your family to afford a Wentworth education. In cooperation with financial aid specialists, financial services specialists can help discern how best to combine a student's financial aid package with alternative parent or student loans, as well as with Wentworth's monthly payment plan.

More than 80 percent of our students receive financial aid. For the fall of 2013, the average financial aid package for a first-time full time student was $16,190A typical package is made up of a combination of grants, loans, and work-study earnings. To be considered for financial aid you must complete the Free Application for Federal Student Aid (FAFSA) as early as possible after January 1. You do not have to be an applicant for admission to complete the FAFSA. However, you must be accepted to Wentworth to receive notification of your actual financial aid award.

Student Organizations and Activities. Wentworth participates in 15 NCAA-sponsored varsity sports. More than twenty professional organizations operate on campus, offering unbeatable networking opportunities to students in every field. In addition, there are more than a forty clubs and organizations to help students make productive and fun use of their hours outside the classroom. And if students can't find what they're looking for on the Wentworth campus, they simply visit one of the five neighboring Colleges of the Fenway institutions with which the Institute is affiliated. In addition to Wentworth, the colleges of the Fenway consist of the Massachusetts College of Art and Design, Massachusetts College of Pharmacy and Health Science University, and Emmanuel, Simmons, and Wheelock Colleges.

ADMISSIONS PROCESS

At Wentworth, we look for students who are qualified and motivated to succeed in engineering, technology, design, and management programs. We make our admissions decisions based on:

- Academic achievement, measured by official transcripts

- Performance on standardized tests (SAT I or ACT)

- Personal qualities, such as leadership or creativity, indicated by information in the completed application form

At Wentworth, it's our goal to assist students and their parents as much as possible as they move through the admissions process. In fact, every applicant has a regional admissions counselor they can contact directly with questions.

To apply to Wentworth, you must submit the following materials:

- A completed Wentworth application ($50 application fee)
- Official high school transcripts
- SAT I or ACT scores
- A written personal statement
- At least one letter of recommendation from a guidance counselor or teacher
- TOEFL score, if your native language is not English

Wentworth practices rolling admissions, which means we review each completed application as soon as we receive it—so you can apply early and get a decision early.

WEST VIRGINIA WESLEYAN COLLEGE

AT A GLANCE

West Virginia Wesleyan is a private four-year co-educational residential college that is affiliated with The United Methodist Church. West Virginia Wesleyan creates a unique learning environment enabling our students to develop the skills, values, relationships, and perspective needed for them to obtain employment, enhance their careers, and demonstrate leadership throughout their lives. Wesleyan graduates are well prepared to be successful and respected citizens in a rapidly changing world.

Over 80 percent of Wesleyan's faculty hold the highest degree in their respective teaching field and the student faculty ratio is 14:1. The curriculum foundation begins with a general studies liberal arts program where students complete one-third of their course of study. The college offers over 40 majors and over 40 minors of study, and several additional Master's programs spanning Athletic Training, Business Administration, Education, English (Creative Writing), and Nursing.

West Virginia Wesleyan is accredited by the Commission on Institutions of Higher Education of the North Central Association of Colleges and Schools, and approved by the University Senate of The United Methodist Church. It is a member of the National Association of Schools of Music and is approved by the West Virginia Department of Education and the National Council for the Accreditation of Teacher Education. The college participates in the Interstate Certification Project whereby a number of states certify teachers graduating from Wesleyan's Department of Education. The athletic training program is accredited by the Commission on Accreditation of Allied Health Education Programs. Degree programs offered in business and economics, including the Master of Business Administration program, are accredited by the International Assembly for Collegiate Business Education.

All academic programs either require or strongly encourage the completion of an internship experience. Wesleyan's academic calendar is 4-4-1 that includes an optional May Term in which over 50 students pursue study abroad courses or intensive study curricular offerings. The Advising and Career Center assists students with course scheduling, academic advising, internships and study abroad, resume writing, job searches, and graduate and professional school placement. The Learning Center provides tutoring services as well as comprehensive services for students with diagnosed learning disabilities.

Of the more than 1,480 undergraduate students, 53 percent are from West Virginia, while the other 47 percent originate from 39 states and 19 countries. 16 percent of Wesleyan's American students are minority students. Over 90 percent of Wesleyan's students live on-campus and the college guarantees four years of on-campus housing for all undergraduate students. Housing options include double and single rooms, suites, and apartments. Campus dining is provided and prepared by a contracted professional catering service.

LOCATION AND ENVIRONMENT

Situated in the foothills of the Allegheny Mountains, Wesleyan's beautiful 100-acre campus is located in the quaint, residential town of Buckhannon, West Virginia. Buckhannon has been included in Norman Crampton's book, The Top 100 Best Small Towns in America, a Random House Publication. Many students are drawn to this personal and picturesque setting and the numerous outdoor opportunities located in close proximity to campus. The local community offers movie theatres, coffee houses, department stores, and a wide selection of local and chain restaurants. Wesleyan is a short two-hour drive from Pittsburgh, Pennsylvania, and 90 minutes from Charleston, West Virginia, the state capital.

ACADEMIC PROGRAMS

Wesleyan's liberal arts curriculum begins with a broad base view in a variety of core courses designed to enrich the student's whole view. The classes range from the humanities to contemporary issues and can be intermingled with the courses in the individual's major throughout the four-year program.

Wesleyan's Honors Program is offered for superior students who meet the specific requirements and demonstrate a high quality of academic excellence. Challenging, yet rewarding, classes, along with culturally enriching outings, offer Honors students a diverse and unique educational experience.

MAJORS AND DEGREES OFFERED

West Virginia Wesleyan offers four undergraduate degrees: the Bachelor of Arts; the Bachelor of Music Education; the Bachelor of Science; and the Bachelor of Science in Nursing. The most popular programs of study are in the sciences (biology, physics / engineering, pre-professional studies, etc.); education; business; athletic training; and nursing. Wesleyan also offers a number of master's degree programs.

STUDENT ORGANIZATIONS AND ACTIVITIES

Wesleyan has a balanced and diverse student life program that includes more than 70 campus organizations. Included among these are a campus radio station, newspaper, student government, departmental clubs, national fraternities and sororities, and religious organizations. Over 87 percent of Wesleyan students participate in community service activities that include the complete administration of a youth basketball program to Special Olympics, to tutoring, mentoring, and educational activities to senior citizens programs to more global programs such as hurricane relief and international service trips.

Wesleyan features 19 varsity programs in NCAA Division II. Wesleyan competes in the West Virginia Intercollegiate Athletic Conference. Together the 19 programs have combined to win an unprecedented 163 conference championships.

While Wesleyan is affiliated with The United Methodist Church, students of all faiths are welcome and active. The college holds an optional weekly ecumenical worship service every Tuesday morning and a Catholic Mass each Saturday evening.

OFF-CAMPUS OPPORTUNITIES

Wesleyan encourages all students to expand their education beyond the traditional classroom. Many students have studied abroad in such places as England, Ireland, Wales, Germany, Spain, Kenya, Scotland, and Australia. Professional internships are available in the Buckhannon area, Charleston, WV, Washington, D.C.; New York, NY; Pittsburgh, PA; and other states and countries.

CAMPUS FACILITIES AND EQUIPMENT

Wesleyan's 23 buildings include 10 modern residence hall units, including one brand new residence hall and another completely renovated suite-style residence hall. Located in the center of campus is Wesley Chapel, which chapel serves as a focal point of campus and houses many campus events, both religious and cultural. The hub of the campus, Benedum Campus and Community Center, houses a convenience store, bookstore, swimming pool, campus radio station, student development offices, study lounges, and a cabaret-style restaurant, The Cat's Claw. The Rockefeller Physical Education Center includes a main arena that seats 3,700 spectators, an intramural gymnasium, training rooms, and an indoor astro-turf training area. The multimillion dollar Reemsnyder Research Center was opened in 2009 and boasts state of the art laboratory space for the sciences. Other vital buildings on campus include Christopher Hall of Science; Middleton Hall, which houses Admission as well as the Nursing Department; and the Lynch-Raine Administration Building. In addition, the multimillion dollar Virginia Thomas Law Center for the Performing Arts, opened in 2009, offers the most advanced performing arts facility of its kind in the region. Most recently, a brand new student wellness center was opened in 2012.

Wesleyan's Annie Merner Pfeiffer Library is committed to providing high quality resources and services that empower students for advanced learning. Currently, the number of print and electronic books is nearly equal at 150,000 each, and the nearly 20,000 electronic journal titles far exceed the 300 received in print. In addition to its collections and research services, the Library offers media viewing facilities, areas for group study, and a quiet place for reading and reflection.

The entire campus has been outfitted with a ubiquitous campus-wide wireless network ensuring access to all students, faculty, and staff from all major campus buildings and every residence hall room.

TUITION, ROOM, BOARD AND FEES

The 2012–2013 total direct costs at Wesleyan are $24,780 for tuition, $7,510 for standard room and board, and $1,024 for student fees, which includes a student activity fee, facilities fee, and a technology fee. These costs do not include books, travel, clothing, the laptop computer, medical insurance, or other personal expenses. Wesleyan offers an interest-free monthly payment plan during the academic year.

FINANCIAL AID

The College offers financial aid on the basis of a variety of criteria: scholastic achievements, special talents and abilities, and financial need. A number of scholarships are available including awards for academics, athletics, performing arts, leadership, community service, and visual arts. Student employment is available in most areas of the college community, financed through a blend of institutional and federal funds. Students may apply for low-cost federal loans. Students should file the Free Application for Federal Student Aid by March 1. Currently, more than 95 percent of all students receive grants or scholarships from Wesleyan.

ADMISSION PROCESS

Students are selected by the Office of Admission on the basis of ability, interests, academic preparation, character, and promise, as indicated by their own statements on the application, as well as by high school or college records, recommendations, and standardized test results. Open without discrimination to all qualified students, the college reserves the right to refuse to admit any applicant who, because of low scholarship or citizenship record, is deemed by the Admission and Academic Standing Council to be unlikely to succeed within the standards the college seeks to maintain.

Persons wishing to be admitted directly from high school should present an application for admission with $35 fee (waived for online applications); a transcript of record from an accredited high school; and a record of either SAT or ACT scores. Applicants from non-accredited high schools or completing General Educational Development may be considered for admission if satisfactory ability and achievement are demonstrated.

Persons seeking to transfer from another accredited college or university may be admitted to advanced standing upon presentation of an application for admission with $35 fee (waived for on-line applications); an official transcript showing all credits attempted at all post-secondary institutions previously attended; a high school transcript certifying graduation and showing courses pursued and grades earned and, if the cumulative grade point average is less than 2.5, either SAT I or ACT scores.

Wesleyan will accept transfer credit courses compatible with its academic program. Grades and hours so earned shall count toward graduation. The college accepts no more than 60 semester hours of credit from a junior or community college.

Students who transfer to Wesleyan with an associate degree from a regionally accredited community or junior college may be admitted with the degree credited as fulfilling Wesleyan's general studies requirements when the total educational background, including high school record, shows compatibility with Wesleyan's general studies requirements. Deficiencies in general studies requirements, as determined by the Admission and Academic Standing Council, must be satisfied after enrollment at Wesleyan.

Wesleyan participates in the Advanced Placement Program of the college Entrance Examination Board and the International Baccalaureate Diploma Program. Students who have successfully completed AP or IB programs should contact the Office of Admission for credit transfer policies.

WILLIAM PEACE UNIVERSITY

William Peace University located in downtown Raleigh, offers innovative academic programs rooted in the liberal arts tradition as well as countless clubs and activities.

AT A GLANCE

The University is ranked No.1 in the nation for student internships (according to a 2013 study by U.S. News & World Report), and is ranked in the top 10 percent nationally for student engagement (according to the 2013 National Survey for Student Engagement).

The school's mission is to prepare its students for careers in the organizations of tomorrow, emphasizing a skill-based curriculum rooted in the liberal arts. Because of that mission, the University consistently boasts a high job/graduate school placement rate. In fact, 97 percent of William Peace University's 2013 graduates found jobs or were enrolled in graduate school within a year of graduation (according to 2014 University data). The school believes in quality over quantity, employing industry professionals and professors who are hands-on with their small classes (student to faculty ratio—15:1).

LOCATION AND ENVIRONMENT

William Peace University offers the comfort of a small school with the back drop of a big city. Surrounded by beautiful oak trees and a large front lawn, the historic campus has carved its own niche in downtown Raleigh, the capital of North Carolina. The University is just a short distance from the state capitol, museums, music halls, restaurants, theaters, and nightlife—all accessible by foot and the R-Line, a free bus service that circulates the capital city.

OFF-CAMPUS OPPORTUNITIES

Raleigh is consistently regarded as one of the nation's best places to live for its economic, cultural and professional opportunities. In addition to being named the No. 1 ranking in BusinessWeek's list of America's 50 Best Cities, Raleigh was ranked one of the top five Hottest Job Markets for Young Adults, a Top 10 Technology Town and a Top 10 City for Singles.

Malls, retail areas and shopping centers complete a lively shopping scene in Raleigh. From the major department stores of Triangle Town Center and Crabtree Valley Mall to the exclusive shops and boutiques of Cameron Village, one can enjoy exceptional shopping in any part of the city.

Raleigh is also home to North Carolina's museums of art, history and natural sciences and every inch of Raleigh is easily accessible from William Peace University. The R-Line, a free downtown bus service with stops on campus, connects you to restaurants, retail and entertainment venues, museums and hotels. The Amtrak train station is less than two miles from campus and RDU International Airport is an easy 20-minute drive.

Whether you are in the mood for a round of golf or edge-of-your-seat football, professional baseball or NHL hockey, the greater Raleigh area has a game for everyone. With several surrounding colleges and universities along Tobacco Road, there is great football and basketball action.

There are also several thriving cities and towns just outside Raleigh, including Chapel Hill, Durham and Cary, and the Research Triangle Park offers a flourishing business landscape for career opportunities before and after graduation.

MAJORS AND DEGREES OFFERED

William Peace University offers dozens of majors and concentrations, including biology, business administration communication, criminal justice, education, English, environmental studies, global studies, liberal studies, political science, pre-law, pre-med, psychology, simulation and game design, sport management, theatre, and writing.

A Bachelor of Fine Arts degree in musical theatre is also offered.

A new core curriculum focuses on ethical decision making and emphasizes basic knowledge needed beyond graduation. In addition, there are mandatory courses in personal financial management, media literacy, and four years of writing courses within the English department. Students are also required to take a series of three classes focusing on career and professional development.

William Peace University also offers evening, online, and/or Saturday classes through its School of Professional Studies. Students can earn a Bachelor of Arts degree in education, liberal studies, or psychology or a Bachelor of Science degree in business administration—all without virtually ever having to step foot on campus.

Courses are taught by experienced faculty members in seven-week accelerated formats and include many opportunities for individualized academic advising. Classes are geared toward the unique needs of nontraditional students and working professionals.

An academic internship related to any major is a requirement with a goal of combining educational theory with job experience. Students are required to complete internships within their field of study during their junior or senior years (100 percent of students graduate with an internship). Recent student internship sites include Duke University Medical Center, Mothers Against Drunk Driving, The Governor's Office, and the North Carolina General Assembly. On average, more than 60 percent of WPU graduates report that their internship experience resulted in a job offer.

ACADEMIC PROGRAMS

Eligible students have the ability to join several national honors' societies such as Sigma Tau Delta, Alpha Chi, Psi Chi and TriBeta at William Peace University.

Additionally, students can also join the University's Honor Program that includes academic challenges, enriching experiences outside of the classroom and opportunities to work on undergraduate research. The program is one of the most exciting and prestigious on campus providing academically talented and motivated students to study, conduct research and exchange ideas in a challenging and supportive academic environment. It brings outstanding students and dynamic faculty together in courses that arouse curiosity and promote intellectual discovery and development.

Program members are encouraged to choose from a variety of courses that fulfill liberal education requirements that include psychology, biology, cultural and physical anthropology, literature and public speaking.

Students also have lifetime access to the Career Services Office, which provides career counseling, listings of internship options, workshops, mock interviews, and a resource library.

International study programs are offered in several parts of the world, including Costa Rica, Italy, Mexico, Qatar, and Spain. Other opportunities are available annually in a variety of other locations for short-term work or internships, or for a semester abroad.

CAMPUS FACILITIES AND EQUIPMENT

William Peace University is a wireless campus. Students have access to courses and library facilities and online databases of other Raleigh colleges and universities through the Cooperating Raleigh Colleges (CRC) consortium.

Computer laboratories, the library, and the student publications area are equipped with state-of-the-art computer hardware and software. There are specialized computer laboratories in the biology, business, media, physics, simulation and game design, theatre, and visual communication departments. Student laboratories in the chemistry, general biology, and molecular and cellular biology departments are also available.

A recital hall, the Leggett Theatre and a studio are available for students in the fine arts department.

The Hermann Athletic Center on campus was recently upgraded in 2012 and includes a state-of-the art fitness center, training room, weight rooms, home and visiting locker rooms, a field house for spring training and intramural space.

The University also offers an expanded student union center (upgraded in 2014), a renovated dining hall (2013) and student bookstore/Student Services building (2014).

Residential living at William Peace University is an extended classroom where students have the unique opportunity to learn about different people and new cultures and to experience life on their own in a supportive community.

There are seven residence halls on campus equipped with free wireless Internet and cable services, lounges, study rooms, kitchens, living areas and bedrooms. There are no cost laundry machines that notify students [via a text message] when their laundry is finished.

TUITION, ROOM, BOARD, AND FEES

The 2015–2016 cost of attending William Peace University is:

Tuition & Fees	$25,850
Room & Board	$9,900

The charges are the same for in-state and out-of-state.

FINANCIAL AID

William Peace University strongly believes that everyone should have access to a college education; therefore, the University is committed to making it as affordable as possible. At a time where colleges across the country raised prices, WPU actually lowered its costs.

Every accepted student is automatically considered for merit- and need-based aid (with a submitted FAFSA), and 100% of students receive financial aid. In fact, more than $22 million was awarded in financial aid in the 2014–15 academic year. Academic awards are available for the performing arts, community service, leadership, extracurricular activities, and more. Through a combination of financial aid packaging, pursuit of scholarship and grant opportunities, and on-campus work-study groups, WPU works to make its educational program available to all qualified students, regardless of financial need.

Information about payment options and the necessary forms are available online. Prospective students may call 919.508.2214 or email finaid@peace.edu for more information on how to pay for college.

STUDENT ORGANIZATIONS AND ACTIVITIES

There are more than 30 student clubs and organizations, including publications, performance groups and academic honor societies at William Peace University. Some of them include:

(Selected Clubs Listed)

— Anthropology Club

— Cheer/Drill Collaboration

— Campus Activities Board (CAB)

— Commuter Student Association

— Helping Hands

— MOSAIC (Multicultural Association)

— Peace Times (student newspaper)

— Student Government Association (SGA)

— Student Recreation Association

— Society for Human Resource Management

— Spectrum (LGBTQ)

— Student Athlete Advisory Committee

— William Peace University Singers

ADMISSIONS PROCESS

William Peace University seeks to enroll individuals who will benefit from the academic programs and who will contribute to university life—a community upheld by the honor system, which requires students to maintain academic and personal integrity.

The University encourages individuals with varied talents and interests representative of all social, economic, ethnic, and racial backgrounds to apply. Admission decisions are made on a rolling basis. The University does not discriminate in its recruitment and admission of students, regardless of gender, race, creed, color, religion, age, national and ethnic origin, sexual orientation, disability, or veteran status.

Admission requirements/procedures for students are defined by five categories: traditional first-year student (high school senior or graduate), high school student applying as a junior for early entrance, transfer student, international student, or former student (readmission).

Applications are reviewed individually and decisions are based on the following credentials: GPA in academic courses, SAT (verbal and math only) or ACT scores, course selection, rank in class, and an interview with an admissions representative, if requested. Further consideration will be given to an applicant's personal qualifications, co-curricular activities, community involvement, and overall potential for success. Consideration of a students' acceptance will also be granted upon the discretion of the Vice President for Enrollment and Marketing.

Admissions decisions are made on a rolling basis. The Admissions Committee begins reviewing applications in July for the following fall. Applications received after April 1 for the fall semester and after November 1 for the spring semester are reviewed on a space-available basis.

The University requires each first-year applicant to submit an application, a non-refundable $35 fee, SAT or ACT scores (senior-year scores are preferred), and an official transcript of all courses taken in high school. Transfer applicants must also submit official transcripts from all colleges and/or universities attended.

Inquiry cards and application forms may be completed online at www.peace.edu. Application forms and additional information may be obtained by contacting:

Office of Admissions

William Peace University

15 East Peace Street

Raleigh, North Carolina 27604

Phone: 919-508-2214

Fax: 919-508-2306

Website: http://www.peace.edu

William Peace University takes a different approach to higher education, going beyond lecture-based instruction and involving students more directly in their learning. William Peace students don't graduate college looking for any job; they graduate ready to enter the fields they went to college for in the first place.

WITTENBERG UNIVERSITY

AT A GLANCE

Wittenberg University offers a highly personal, active and engaged academic experience in a supportive environment that facilitates close interaction with award-winning faculty. Wittenberg enrolls approximately 1,900 full-time students, representing more than 40 states and 26 countries around the world. With most students living on or near campus, Wittenberg's campus is alive with activity.

Founded in 1845 in Springfield, Ohio, Wittenberg is a private, coeducational, liberal arts and sciences college affiliated with the Evangelical Lutheran Church in America. In keeping with its mission, Wittenberg provides an education dedicated to intellectual inquiry and wholeness of person within a diverse residential community. Reflecting its Lutheran heritage, Wittenberg also challenges students to become responsible global citizens, to discover their callings, and to lead personal, professional, and civic lives of creativity, service, compassion, and integrity.

Wittenberg's strong arts and sciences programs, coupled with internships and community service, make its graduates attractive to prominent medical, law, and graduate programs. More than 20 percent of students begin graduate programs immediately after graduation, and 70 percent pursue an advanced degree at some point in their careers. Graduates have enjoyed successful careers in education, business, science, fine and performing arts, politics, medicine, ministry, dentistry, and law.

Wittenberg competes in the nationally renowned Division III North Coast Athletic Conference (NCAC), which consists of 10 academically selective colleges and universities in Ohio, Pennsylvania, and Indiana. The NCAC features championship competition in 23 sports—11 for men and 12 for women, while Wittenberg offers intercollegiate athletics opportunities in 24 sports—12 for men and 12 for women. Intramurals are also very popular among students, and club sports, including ice hockey, rugby, sailing, soccer, volleyball and basketball, are available.

Wittenberg is accredited by the Higher Education Commission of the North Central Association of Colleges and Schools, the American Association of University Women, the American Chemical Society, the National Council for the Accreditation of Teacher Education, and the National Association of Schools of Music.

LOCATION AND ENVIRONMENT

Located in Springfield, Ohio, Wittenberg's campus, ranked as one of the nation's most beautiful, rests on 114 wooded, rolling acres in a residential neighborhood. With a population of just over 60,000, Springfield offers cultural events and internship opportunities found in larger urban areas, as well as the friendliness and sense of community typical of small towns.

The university's Hagen Center for Civic & Urban Engagement celebrates Wittenberg's distinct urban environment and promotes scholarship, service, and collaboration between the university and the greater Springfield area, creating a more vibrant, cohesive community.

Recreational opportunities include an extensive bike trail system and recently constructed kayaking structures on Buck Creek, both of which border the Wittenberg campus. Students also enjoy the nearby Frank Lloyd Wright Westcott House; the Heritage Center, a museum showcasing Springfield's vibrant history; skating at the indoor Chiller ice skating arena downtown, beautiful state parks; and the Springfield Museum of Art, located adjacent to campus.

Springfield's proximity to Dayton (25 miles), Columbus (45 miles), and Cincinnati (75 miles) gives students convenient access to airports and additional social and recreational opportunities, such as concerts, shopping, parks, museums, and sporting events.

OFF-CAMPUS OPPORTUNITIES

Every day Wittenberg students engage in the world around them—and apply what they have learned in the classroom to real-world situations—through community service, internships, and part-time jobs. One of a select few universities requiring community service of all its students, Wittenberg believes students learn more of themselves when they give of themselves, and students annually contribute thousands of hours to the local community.

Off-campus academic opportunities include an extensive student-teaching program, a marine biology/freshwater ecology program in the Bahamas, the Local Government Management Program, the Africana Studies/community service program in Lesotho, the Wittenberg in Wittenberg, Germany, program, and the Lutheran College Washington, D.C. Semester Program. Students also have interned with business and non-profits across the country, including the U.S. Library of Congress, ABC Primetime Live, The Children's Museum of Indianapolis, and the National Institutes of Health.

The Office of International Education assists students with selecting study-abroad programs and counsels them on integrating international study with their academic and career goals. Through memberships in several consortia, more than 20 percent of Wittenberg students participate in study-abroad programs at 40 sites in more than 20 countries in Europe, Asia, Africa, and Latin America.

MAJORS AND DEGREES OFFERED

Wittenberg offers four undergraduate degrees: Bachelor of Arts (BA), Bachelor of Science (BS), Bachelor of Music Education (BME), and Bachelor of Fine Arts (BFA). Wittenberg also offers a Master of Arts in Education.

More than 30 majors are offered: accounting, American studies, art, biochemistry & molecular biology, biology, chemistry, communication, dance, earth science, East Asian studies, economics, education, English, entrepreneurship, finance, financial economics, French, geology, German, history, international studies, management, marketing, mathematics, music, nursing, philosophy, physics, political science, psychology, religion, Russian and Central Eurasian studies, sociology, Spanish, sport management and theatre.

In addition to the above, Wittenberg offers minors in African and Diaspora Studies, archaeology, business, Chinese, computational science, computer science, creative writing, environmental studies, health science, journalism, marine science, neuroscience, pre-modern and ancient world studies, Russian, statistics, urban studies, and women's studies.

ACADEMIC PROGRAMS

A Wittenberg education consists of three parts: a broad base in the liberal arts, an intensive course of study in a major, and an enhanced course of study that makes up a minor or electives. Wittenberg also places considerable emphasis on strong speaking, writing, critical thinking and research skills to ensure that its students are competitive graduate school applicants, outstanding future employees, and global leaders. At the same time, a Wittenberg education provides an in-depth investigation of human behavior and diversity.

Wittenberg students engage in experiential learning, pursue independent studies and honors theses, and collaborate with award-winning faculty on research projects. The Honors Program, which offers special seminars, honors theses or projects, and a variety of academic and cultural activities, is available to outstanding students who want to challenge themselves and enhance their academic program.

The WittEntrepreneurs Program, for both business and non-business majors, combines cutting-edge classes with opportunities for students to launch, operate and manage an enterprise on campus. Popular summer programs include the Screenwriters' Institute, in which award-winning alumni in television and theatre share their professional expertise with students, and the Journalism Institute, during which students create an original magazine.

For students interested in the health professions, more than 45 internships are available each semester through the Clinical Internship Program, which pairs them with area physicians and medical health professionals in ways that offer unprecedented access and hands-on learning opportunities.

Cooperative education programs with other leading research institutions, including Case Western Reserve, Columbia University, Duke University, Clark State and Washington University in St. Louis, are available to help students complete their majors. These special programs include engineering, marine/aquatic biology, nursing, and occupational therapy.

Pre-professional programs include engineering, law, theology, and the pre-health fields of pre-medicine, pre-dentistry, pre-veterinary, physical therapy and pre-optometry. With approval, students may plan interdepartmental majors composed of courses selected from several departments that reflect a unified purpose or theme.

CAMPUS FACILITIES AND EQUIPMENT

Wittenberg's campus consists of 26 major buildings, including nine academic buildings designed to enhance learning and encourage interaction and collaboration among faculty and students. The state-of-the-art Barbara Deer Kuss Science Center contains modern technology and equipment, including new cell and microbiology labs, organic chemistry labs, and neurobiology and physiology labs that, along with the Math Workshop, provide hands-on learning experiences for all students, regardless of major.

Home to the humanities and the Wittenberg Center for Applied Management (WittCAM), through which students serve as consultants to help area businesses and non-profit organizations succeed, Hollenbeck Hall houses a 24-hour computer lab, the Writing Center, and the Foreign Language Learning Center.

The recently renovated Blair Hall, home to the university's nationally recognized education program, earned LEED Gold certification for its green-focused building strategies. The Springfield Center for the Arts at Wittenberg University is the new home for the visual and performing arts and features a blackbox theatre for theatre and dance performances and an art gallery. Students interested in music have access to the John M. Chowning Laboratory for Music and Technology, practice rooms and recital space. Thomas Library, open extensive hours, offers an abundance of both digital and print resources and houses the Oral Communication Center and Research Help Center.

Wittenberg's 24 men's and women's Division III athletics teams compete using outstanding facilities and fields. Athletics facilities include basketball, volleyball, and racquetball courts; a football field and outdoor track; access to nearby baseball fields; a tennis complex; a softball field; a natatorium; a state-of-the-art fitness center; and a weight room.

Seven residence halls offer a variety of living arrangements for freshmen and sophomores in both historic and new buildings, all equipped with computer labs and lounges. Upperclass students can choose to live in the residence halls or on-campus apartments, the Campus Ministries House, or sorority and fraternity houses.

TUITION, ROOM, BOARD AND FEES

Basic costs for full-time undergraduates for the 2015–2016 academic year are:

Tuition: $37,230

Room: $5,158

Board: $4,870

Activity fee: $300

Technology fee: $500

Total: $48,058

FINANCIAL AID

Wittenberg is aggressive in offering different ways to finance an outstanding, affordable education, including both need-based and merit-based assistance. Need-based assistance includes grants, loans, and work-study programs. Approximately 85 percent of Wittenberg students qualify for need-based aid, and the average scholarship and grant financial assistance award is $27,517 per year. To be considered, applicants must file the Free Application for Federal Student Aid (FAFSA) by March 1.

All accepted students are automatically considered for academic scholarships, and special interest awards. To be given priority consideration, students should submit a complete application for admission by December 1.

Accepted students may compete for special interest awards that recognize commitment to community service, superior student leadership experience, entrepreneurship, environmental science, or a passion for East Asian business and culture. Fine arts scholarships reward students for talent in art, dance, music, and theatre. Each of these scholarships requires a separate audition/application process.

STUDENT ORGANIZATIONS AND ACTIVITIES

With more than 125 organizations and clubs, students can easily pursue their passions while at the same time develop management and leadership skills. Student groups are formed on topics ranging from cultural and social awareness to recreational to religious involvement and communication. For aspiring leaders, Wittenberg offers the Emerging Leaders program for first-year students.

Approximately 30 percent of the students are involved in Greek life. Many academic departments have major-specific honor societies and clubs. Weekend activities include lectures, art exhibits, concerts, dances, movies, coffeehouses, and comedians. New organizations and activities are created regularly to meet the changing interests of students.

ADMISSIONS PROCESS

Admission to Wittenberg is selective and based on the following information: high school record, including the strength of the high school and its curriculum, and trends in the student's academic work; SAT or ACT scores; co-curricular activities and community participation; recommendations; and an essay. Wittenberg is a test optional school. International students, transfer students and International Baccalaureate diploma holders are encouraged to apply. An on-campus interview is not required but is highly recommended. Students may apply using the free online application at www.wittenberg.edu/apply or the Common Application.

The deadlines for applying are as follows for incoming freshmen:

Early Decision: November 15

Early Action I: December 1

Early Action II: January 15

Regular Action: March 15

Students must apply by December 1 to receive full consideration for merit-based scholarships. Transfer application deadlines are December 1 for spring semester and July 15 for fall semester. The international student application deadline is March 15.

WORCESTER POLYTECHNIC INSTITUTE

AT A GLANCE

You want to be on the first Mars mission, find alternative energy sources, or cure cancer. WPI wants to help you make an impact. Our students do much more than study science and technology. They delve into the arts and humanities. They complete projects on campus and around the globe, connecting what they've learned in the classroom with pressing real-life challenges—from health to the environment to global competitiveness. Students grow - personally, professionally, and intellectually - as they discover how to apply their talents and turn ideas into tangible solutions.

WPI's aim is to educate students broadly, so they achieve greatly. Though WPI has been around for more than 145 years, our approach to education, like our students, is innovative and practical. Small classes, a flexible curriculum, and one-on-one interaction with professors at the top of their fields make learning at WPI an experience unlike any other.

WPI has been widely recognized for its quality. It was the only technological university out of 16 national Leadership Institutions selected by the Association of American Colleges and Universities to serve as models of outstanding practices in liberal education. WPI consistently ranks among the top national universities by U.S. News & World Report and was recently ranked in the top 20 in the nation for Best Career Services, Most Popular Study Abroad, and for Happiest Students by the Princeton Review.

LOCATION AND ENVIRONMENT

With its beautiful architecture, grassy quad, and ivy-covered walls, WPI has a traditional New England campus. Students stop and chat with friends and professors on tree-lined paths. They play pool or get a coffee between classes at the Campus Center. They study by the fountain in Reunion Plaza, get a group together an on-campus movie night, stop and smell the roses in the formal English garden behind Higgins House, or see a student play at the Little Theatre.

Home to 12 other colleges and universities and over 35,000 college students, greater Worcester is a great college town. WPI is a member of the colleges of Worcester Consortium, through which WPI students may register for courses at other colleges and take advantage of a wide range of cultural programming offered by consortium members. A shuttle provides free transportation between campuses.

Late-night diners, clubs, museums, concert venues, and theaters are right down the hill from WPI in Worcester's vibrant downtown. Boston is less than an hour away by commuter rail if you want to catch Red Sox fever. There's great skiing and boarding at nearby Wachusett Mountain. If you want to go a bit farther, Worcester is centrally located with easy access to Providence, New York City, the Berkshire and White Mountains, and Cape Cod.

OFF-CAMPUS OPPORTUNITIES

In Worcester you'll find:

35,000+ college students at 13 colleges and universities

14,800 seats at the DCU Center for arena concerts and sporting events

5,000 years of art and 36 galleries at the Worcester Art Museum

53 parks including the largest urban nature sanctuary in New England and the Olmstead-designed Elm Park

20 ski trails at nearby Wachusett Mountain

1 Gompei the goat (WPI mascot)

MAJORS AND DEGREES OFFERED

WPI offers over 36 areas of study in engineering, science, management, and the liberal arts leading to the Bachelor of Science (B.S.) or Bachelor of Arts (B.A.) degree. Exciting new interdisciplinary programs, driven by real-world demand, include interactive media and game development, environmental engineering, architectural engineering, and the nation's first undergraduate program in robotics engineering.

We offer pre-professional programs (law, medicine, dentistry, and veterinary) and a five-year BS/MS program. You can even create your own major or minor program. Not surprisingly, over 40 percent of students change their major at least once. A comprehensive academic advising program and a wide array of academic support services help students make the right choices and reach their goals.

WPI students have received some of the nation's highest academic honors. Over just the last decade, two students have received the prestigious Marshall Scholarship, 14 have been awarded Goldwater scholarships, five have received the Rotary Ambassadorial Scholarship, three have won National Science Foundation Fellowships, two have been named to the USA Today All-USA College Academic Team, and one has been named an NIH-Oxford/Cambridge Biomedical Research Scholar.

ACADEMIC PROGRAMS

At WPI, learning is about more than just theories and ideas. Students put what they learn into practice through a unique project-enriched curriculum. Each undergraduate complete two projects: one directly related to their major and one in which they work with a team of students to solve a problem at the intersection of society and technology. Students gain valuable professional skills, a talent for teamwork, and the confidence to dive right in—no matter what the challenge.

WPI's academic program is built to be flexible. Students take the equivalent of three courses (as courses or project work) during each of four 7-week terms (two in the fall and two in the spring). It is also designed to encourage collaboration, not competition. Students work closely on projects and in project-oriented classes. Learning to work in teams prepares students to get results and become leaders, no matter what path they take in life.

WPI's award-winning Global Perspective Program, with more than 30 project centers on five continents, is one of the most comprehensive and highly regarded global studies programs in the nation. Most WPI students complete projects off campus; over half complete project work outside the United States in places like Thailand, Namibia, New Zealand, Costa Rica, and Italy. Global project experiences not only give students the chance to work in teams to solve meaningful real-life problems for people around the world, they immerse students in other cultures and give them a powerful sense of self-confidence.

Top-tier employers seek out WPI graduates for their real-world experience and ability to work collaboratively. With a placement rate of over 90 percent, students are recruited by leading organizations such as Pfizer, General Electric, Fidelity Investments, IBM and Google. Not surprisingly, WPI graduates' starting salaries are higher than those of many other college graduates, according to the National Association of Colleges and Employers. Each year, WPI graduates are accepted at many prestigious graduate schools, including MIT, Yale University, Princeton University, Johns Hopkins University and Tufts University Medical School.

CAMPUS FACILITIES AND EQUIPMENT

With all of the amazing things WPI students and faculty do, our outstanding research facilities should come as no surprise.

Our 125,000-square-foot WPI Life Sciences and Bioengineering Center at Gateway Park is a state-of-the-art research center housing faculty from four departments. Our two atomic force microscopes let you see individual atoms on a material's surface. The Fire Science Laboratory enables students and faculty to evaluate fire safety measures in actual fire simulations. Laser holography labs, computer music labs, medical imaging labs, a bioprocess lab - they're all here, and lots more.

Recent additions to WPI's undergraduate teaching facilities include a newly constructed chemistry laboratory center that facilitates team-based work a new $11 million Undergraduate Life Sciences Laboratory Center that is the focal point for undergraduate teaching and research in biology and biotechnology, biomedical engineering, chemistry and biochemistry, and chemical engineering.

The Princeton Review's Complete Book of Colleges

WPI also opened a brand new $53 million Sports and Recreation Center in 2012 including a four-court gymnasium, indoor jogging track, 14,000 sq. ft. of fitness space, racquetball and squash courts, competition pool, workout studios, and rowing tanks.

TUITION, ROOM, BOARD AND FEES

(2013–2014)

Tuition: $42,178.00

Social Fee: $260.00

Health Fee: $340.00

Total: $42,778.00

Typical Room: $7,466.00

Typical Board Plan: $5,616.00

Books and Supplies: $1,000.00

Personal Expenses: $1,200.00

Total: $58,060.00

FINANCIAL AID

It's no secret. A great education costs a lot of money, but think about the return on your investment. College graduates in general earn over the course of their careers at least $1 million more than those without a degree. For WPI graduates, starting salaries frequently exceed the national averages and graduates are able to move quickly up the ranks to positions of influence as a result of their excellent preparation. In fact, WPI was recently ranked No. 4 for the highest average starting salaries among all national universities.

APPLYING FOR FINANCIAL AID

Students should file the FAFSA and CSS Profile on or near their admissions application deadline. WPI should receive all financial aid materials by February 1. Applications after this date will be reviewed subject to funds available.

Most applicants (including early applicants) will receive a financial aid package within two weeks of their acceptance. We'll inform you of the Financial Aid Committee's decision no later than April 15 for regular decision admissions, and you'll have until the Candidates Common Reply Date (May 1) to either accept or decline the offer.

Academic Scholarships

WPI offers academic scholarships to freshman applicants based upon academic performance, standardized test scores, leadership, extracurricular involvement and community service. All admitted applicants are considered and there is no separate application required.

Scholarships vary in amounts, but typically range between $10,000 and $25,000, and are renewable for four years. Valedictorians and Salutatorians are guaranteed a minimum scholarship of $20,000. National Merit, National Achievement, and National Hispanic Recognition Finalists are guaranteed a minimum of $20,000.

STUDENT ORGANIZATIONS AND ACTIVITIES

WPI has 20 varsity (NCAA Division III) athletics teams and 34 club and intramural athletics. WPI won the "Worcester Cup" for the sixth time in seven years, recognizing it as the top collegiate program in Worcester County. WPI has 14 fraternities and five sororities, 20 music and performing arts group, dozens of academic clubs, international organizations, religious groups and other organizations. Overall, there are more than 200 student clubs and activities.

ADMISSIONS PROCESS

WPI Admissions offers a variety of application options. Students can apply using the Common Application (paper or on-line). A $65 application fee is required for all applicants. (WPI endorses the fee waiver policy of the college Board, as well as accepts fee waivers from guidance or college counselors.)

Academic Requirements

four years of math (including pre-calculus)

four years of English

two years of lab science

Other requirements include:

High school transcript

Science or math recommendation

Guidance counselor's recommendation

Personal essay

SAT I or ACT scores or alternate materials through WPI's "Flex Path"

TOEFL, IELTS, or Pearson Exam scores for international students whose first language is not English

Interviews

While interviews are optional, this is your chance to meet one-on-one with an Admissions staff member or a trained Admissions intern. We'll have the chance to learn more about you, and can answer specific questions you may have. Seniors in high school should interview before December 15th of their senior year if they are interested in an interview.

Deadlines

Early Action (Round 1)— Nov. 1

Early Action (Round 2)— Jan. 1

Regular Decision— Feb. 1

January Admission—Transfer Students Only - Nov. 15 (Rolling notification)

Fall Admission—Transfer Students - Apr. 15° (Rolling notification)

INDEXES

ALPHABETICAL INDEX

N

INDEX BY LOCATION

INTERNATIONAL

CANADA

EGYPT

IRELAND

PUERTO RICO

VIRGIN ISLANDS

INDEX BY SIZE

2,000-5,000 STUDENTS

The Princeton Review's Complete Book of Colleges

5,000–10,000 STUDENTS

INDEX BY TUITION

University of California-Irvine	779	Chowan University	153	Pacific Northwest College of Art	565

University of California-Irvine 779
University of California, Los Angeles 780
University of California, Riverside 780
University of California, Santa Cruz 783
University of the Cumberlands 792, 1172
University of Delaware 795, 1174
University of Illinois at Chicago 808
University of Illinois
   at Urbana-Champaign 809, 1180
University of Massachusetts Amherst 826
University of Minnesota, Crookston 832
University of New Hampshire 846
University of New Hampshire
   at Manchester 847
University of Pittsburgh
   at Bradford 865, 1190
University of Pittsburgh—Greensburg 865
University of Rhode Island 871
University of Science & Arts of Oklahoma 878
University of South Carolina—Columbia 881
University of the Southwest 887
University of Tennessee, Knoxville 891
The University of Texas at Dallas 894, 1198
The University of Vermont 900
University of Virginia 901
University of West Alabama 904
Warner Southern College 937
Washington Bible College 942
Wayland Baptist University 946
Wayne State University 947
William Paterson University 979
William Woods University 981
Winthrop University 986
York College 994

$15,001-$20,000

The Art Institute Of Pittsburgh 43
Asbury College 44
Auburn University at Montgomery 47
Aurora University 51
Bethel College (IN) 78
Belhaven University 66
Belmont Abbey College 67
Berkeley College 75
Bethany College (KS) 76
Bloomsburg University of Pennsylvania 84
Brescia University 96
Bryn Athyn College of the New Church 104
Campbell University 127
Capitol College 130
Centenary College 141

Chowan University 153
Christendom College 154
Clark Atlanta University 167
Clearwater Christian College 171
Cogswell College 175
College of Notre Dame of Maryland 184
College of St. Joseph in Vermont 187
Colorado Christian University 191
Columbia College (MO) 195, 1034
Cornerstone University 212
Curry College 216, 1040
Dakota Wesleyan University 218
DeVry University (Decatur, GA) 231
East Carolina University 248
Eastern Kentucky University 252
Eastern University 255
Eureka College 270
Felician College 277
Fisk University 278
Flagler College 279
Gallaudet University 298
Geneva College 300
Georgia Southwestern State University 307
Hampton University 329
Harding University 331
Hilbert College 341
Husson University 355
Keene State College 384
Kentucky State University 387
LaGrange College 396
Lambuth University 400
Lancaster Bible College 400
Lincoln Memorial University 415
Lock Haven University of Pennsylvania 420
Lourdes University 424
MacMurray College 434
Marian University 442
McKendree College 457
McPherson College 458
Mercy College 463
Midway College 472
Mississippi State University 482
Montana State University 489
Montana Tech of the University
   of Montana 491
Newberry College 520
New Mexico Institute of Mining
   and Technology 516
New York Institute of Technology 518
Northeastern Illinois University 528
North Dakota State University 527
Notre Dame College 541, 1108
Oakland City University 543
Oklahoma Christian University 554
Olivet College 557
Olivet Nazarene University 558

Pacific Northwest College of Art 565
Pennsylvania State University—
   University Park 578
Point University 586
Pontifical College Josephinum 589
Regent University 604
Salem College 643
Shorter University 664
Simpson College (IA) 666
Simpson University 667
Sonoma State University 670
Southern Adventist University 675
Southern Connecticut State University 676
Southern Illinois University-Edwardsville 677
Southern Wesleyan University 683
Southwest Baptist University 683
Southwestern College (KS) 684
St. Joseph's College 696
St. Joseph's College, New York
   (Patchogue) 697, 1130
State University of New York
   at Cobleskill 709
State University of New York—
   Purchase College 721
Sterling College 723
Thomas College 744
Thomas More College 745
Trinity Christian College 752
Trinity (Washington) University 756
Tuskegee University 760
Union College 761
University of Advancing Technology
   (UAT) 768
University of Alaska Fairbanks 772
University of Charleston 787
University of Great Falls 802
University of Hawaii-West Oahu 805
University of Illinois Springfield 809
University of Jamestown 812
University of Kentucky 814
University of Maine at Machias 820
University of Nebraska at Omaha 842
University of North Dakota 854
University of Pikevile 864
University of Pittsburgh—
   Pittsburgh Campus 867
University of South Alabama 880
University of South Carolina Aiken 880
University of Southern Mississippi 887
Utah State University 918
Virginia Intermont College 927
Viterbo University 931
Wesleyan College 953
Wesley College (DE) 953
Xavier University of Louisiana 991
York College of Pennsylvania 995

INDEX BY SELECTIVITY

NOTES

NOTES

NOTES

NOTES

NOTES

NOTES

NOTES